Directory of Special Libraries and Information Centers

The **Directory of Special Libraries and Information Centers** is Published in Three Volumes:

> Volume 1—**Directory of Special Libraries and Information Centers**
>
> Volume 2—**Geographic and Personnel Indexes**
>
> Volume 3—**New Special Libraries** (a periodic supplement to Volume 1)

The **Subject Directory of Special Libraries and Information Centers,** a Subject Classified Edition of Material Taken From Volume 1 of the Basic Directory, is Published in Five Volumes:

> Volume 1—**Business and Law Libraries**
>
> Volume 2—**Education and Information Science Libraries**
>
> Volume 3—**Health Science Libraries**
>
> Volume 4—**Social Sciences and Humanities Libraries**
>
> Volume 5—**Science and Technology Libraries**

Directory of Special Libraries and Information Centers

9th Edition

A Guide to Special Libraries, Research Libraries, Information Centers, Archives, and Data Centers Maintained by Government Agencies, Business, Industry, Newspapers, Educational Institutions, Nonprofit Organizations, and Societies in the Fields of Science and Technology, Medicine, Law, Art, Religion, the Social Sciences, and Humanistic Studies.

BRIGITTE T. DARNAY
Editor

JOHN NIMCHUK
Associate Editor

VOLUME 2

Geographic and Personnel Indexes

GALE RESEARCH COMPANY • BOOK TOWER • DETROIT, MICHIGAN 48226

Brigitte T. Darnay, *Editor*

John Nimchuk, *Associate Editor*

Virginia K. Bergman, Dianne E. Boardman, Holly M.G. Leighton, Mary J. Motzko,
Carol Southward, Susan M. Winslow, *Assistant Editors*

Henrietta Krohn, *Editorial Assistant*

Carol Blanchard, *Production Director*
Dorothy Kalleberg, *External Production Associate*
Arthur Chartow, *Art Director*

Laura Bryant, *Internal Production Supervisor*
Louise Gagné, *Internal Production Associate*
Sandy Rock, *Senior Internal Production Assistant*

Lois Lenroot-Ernt, *Contributing Editor*

Frederick G. Ruffner, *Publisher*
James M. Ethridge, *Executive Vice President/Editorial*
Dedria Bryfonski, *Editorial Director*
John Schmittroth, Jr., *Director, Directories Division*
Robert C. Thomas, *Senior Editor, Special Editorial Projects*

Computerized photocomposition by
Computer Composition Corporation,
Madison Heights, Michigan

ISBN 0-8103-1889-X
Library of Congress Catalog Card Number 84-640165 (set)
ISSN 0731-633X

Printed in the United States

Contents

Introduction

The "Geographic and Personnel Indexes" volume consists of selected parts of the entries which are arranged by library name in Volume 1, *Directory of Special Libraries and Information Centers.*

As the title of the volume indicates, the selected data have been rearranged in geographic sequence, with respect to libraries, and in alphabetical sequence, with respect to the personal names of professional staff. This volume makes it possible:

1) to find libraries according to their geographical locations;

2) to determine which and/or how many libraries are located in a specific city;

3) to learn where a librarian is employed when only her/his name is known.

The entries in Volume 2 are brief and include only a library's name, address, head librarian, and phone number. However, Volume 1 may be consulted to find additional details concerning founding date, staff size, subject specialty, number of holdings, publications, and other features.

This volume is arranged in two sections, as follows:

GEOGRAPHIC INDEX—Libraries included in Volume 1 are reported in this section in geographic order by state or province and city in the following manner: first, the United States; next U.S. territories and possessions; last, Canada. Entries within each city are arranged alphabetically according to the name of the parent institution housing the special library.

PERSONNEL INDEX—This section, beginning on page 491, lists alphabetically by surname the professional staff of the special libraries and information centers listed in the Geographic Index and in Volume 1.

The editors invite comments and suggestions for improvements of this directory from the users of this volume.

Abbreviations and Symbols

(State, Province and Territory)

UNITED STATES

AL	Alabama	MT	Montana
AK	Alaska	NE	Nebraska
AZ	Arizona	NV	Nevada
AR	Arkansas	NH	Hew Hampshire
CA	California	NJ	New Jersey
CO	Colorado	NM	New Mexico
CT	Connecticut	NY	New York
DE	Delaware	NC	North Carolina
DC	District of Columbia	ND	North Dakota
FL	Florida	OH	Ohio
GA	Georgia	OK	Oklahoma
HI	Hawaii	OR	Oregon
ID	Idaho	PA	Pennsylvania
IL	Illinois	RI	Rhode Island
IN	Indiana	SC	South Carolina
IA	Iowa	SD	South Dakota
KS	Kansas	TN	Tennessee
KY	Kentucky	TX	Texas
LA	Louisiana	UT	Utah
ME	Maine	VT	Vermont
MD	Maryland	VA	Virginia
MA	Massachusetts	WA	Washington
MI	Michigan	WV	West Virginia
MN	Minnesota	WI	Wisconsin
MS	Mississippi	WY	Wyoming
MO	Missouri		

U.S. TERRITORIES

AS	American Samoa	PR	Puerto Rico
GU	Guam	VI	Virgin Islands

CANADA

AB	Alberta	NS	Nova Scotia
BC	British Columbia	ON	Ontario
MB	Manitoba	PE	Prince Edward Island
NB	New Brunswick	PQ	Quebec
NF	Newfoundland	SK	Saskatchewan
NT	Northwest Territories	YT	Yukon Territory

An asterisk (*) after the library's name indicates a library that did not answer the four requests for updated information, but that it is one the editors are reasonably certain exists.

A dagger (†) after the library's name denotes a library which did not reply but whose existence was verified in current secondary sources.

Section 1
GEOGRAPHIC INDEX

GEOGRAPHIC INDEX

The following is a geographical listing of U.S. and Canadian libraries by state/province and city. Within each city facilities are arranged in alphabetical sequence. Listings of libraries in the U.S. and U.S. Territories are followed by Canadian facilities.

United States

ALABAMA

NORTHEAST ALABAMA REGIONAL MEDICAL CENTER - MEDICAL LIBRARY
400 East Tenth St.
Box 2208   Phone: (205) 235-5877
Anniston, AL 36202   Priscilla Lloyd, Med.Libn.

PARKER MEMORIAL BAPTIST CHURCH - LIBRARY †
1205 Quintard Ave.   Phone: (205) 236-5628
Anniston, AL 36201   Mrs. Gale Main, Libn.

AUBURN UNIVERSITY - ARCHITECTURE AND FINE ARTS LIBRARY
Dudley Hall   Phone: (205) 826-4510
Auburn, AL 36830

AUBURN UNIVERSITY - ARCHIVES
Ralph B. Draughon Library   Phone: (205) 826-4465
Auburn, AL 36849   Dr. Allen W. Jones, Archv.

AUBURN UNIVERSITY - DEPARTMENT OF SPECIAL COLLECTIONS
University Libraries   Phone: (205) 826-4500
Auburn, AL 36830   Gene Geiger, Spec.Coll.Libn.

AUBURN UNIVERSITY - LEARNING RESOURCES CENTER
Haley Center   Phone: (205) 826-4420
Auburn, AL 36830   Dr. C.D. Wright, Dir.

AUBURN UNIVERSITY - OFFICE OF PUBLIC SERVICE & RESEARCH -
   RESOURCE CENTER
2232 Haley Center   Phone: (205) 826-4781
Auburn, AL 36849   Joanne S. Patton, Res.Assoc.

U.S.D.A. - AGRICULTURAL RESEARCH SERVICE - NATL. TILLAGE
   MACHINERY LABORATORY LIBRARY
Box 792   Phone: (205) 887-8596
Auburn, AL 36830   Robert L. Schafer, Dir.

AUBURN UNIVERSITY - INTERNATIONAL CENTER FOR AQUACULTURE -
   LIBRARY
Swingle Hall   Phone: (205) 826-4786
Auburn University, AL 36849   Dr. E.W. Shell, Dir.

AUBURN UNIVERSITY - VETERINARY MEDICAL LIBRARY
Veterinary Medical Complex   Phone: (205) 826-4780
Auburn University, AL 36849   Robert J. Veenstra, Libn.

AUBURN UNIVERSITY - WATER RESOURCES RESEARCH INSTITUTE -
   INFORMATION CENTER
202 Hargis Hall   Phone: (205) 826-5075
Auburn University, AL 36849   James C. Warman, Dir.

ALABAMA POWER COMPANY - LIBRARY
600 N. 18th St.
Box 2641   Phone: (205) 250-2180
Birmingham, AL 35291   Carol J. Davis, Libn.

AMERICAN CAST IRON PIPE COMPANY - TECHNICAL LIBRARY
2930 N. 16th St.
Box 2727   Phone: (205) 325-7886
Birmingham, AL 35202   Lela Turner, Tech.Libn.

AMERICAN TRUCK HISTORICAL SOCIETY - LIBRARY
201 Office Park Dr.   Phone: (205) 879-2131
Birmingham, AL 35223   Zoe S. James, Exec.Dir.

BALCH, BINGHAM, BAKER, WARD, SMITH, BOWMAN & THAGARD -
   LIBRARY
600 N. 18th St.
Box 306   Phone: (205) 251-8100
Birmingham, AL 35201   Erin Kellen, Libn.

BAPTIST MEDICAL CENTER - MEDICAL LIBRARY
701 Princeton Ave., S.W.   Phone: (205) 783-3078
Birmingham, AL 35211   Romilda F. Cook, Med.Libn.

BAPTIST MEDICAL CENTERS-SAMFORD UNIVERSITY - IDA V. MOFFETT
   SCHOOL OF NURSING - L.R. JORDAN LIBRARY †
820 Montclair Rd.   Phone: (205) 591-2371
Birmingham, AL 35213   Jewell Alexander Carter, Lib.Dir.

1

BIRMINGHAM BOTANICAL GARDENS - HORACE HAMMOND MEMORIAL
  LIBRARY
2612 Lane Park Rd.   Phone: (205) 879-1227
Birmingham, AL 35223   Gary G. Gerlach, Dir.

BIRMINGHAM MUSEUM OF ART - REFERENCE LIBRARY
2000 Eighth Ave., N.   Phone: (205) 254-2565
Birmingham, AL 35203-2278   Marie Lichtman, Libn.

BIRMINGHAM NEWS - REFERENCE LIBRARY
2200 Fourth Ave., N.   Phone: (205) 325-2409
Birmingham, AL 35203   Laurie Orr Dean, Hd., Ref.Lib.

BIRMINGHAM PUBLIC AND JEFFERSON COUNTY FREE LIBRARY - ART AND
  MUSIC DEPARTMENT
2100 Park Place   Phone: (205) 254-2538
Birmingham, AL 35203   Jane F. Greene, Dept.Hd.

BIRMINGHAM PUBLIC AND JEFFERSON COUNTY FREE LIBRARY - COLLINS
  COLLECTION OF THE DANCE
2100 Park Place   Phone: (205) 254-2538
Birmingham, AL 35203   Lois A. Eady, Cur.

BIRMINGHAM PUBLIC AND JEFFERSON COUNTY FREE LIBRARY -
  GOVERNMENT DOCUMENTS DEPARTMENT
2020 Park Place   Phone: (205) 254-2555
Birmingham, AL 35203   Rebecca Scarborough, Hd., Govt.Doc.Dept.

BIRMINGHAM PUBLIC AND JEFFERSON COUNTY FREE LIBRARY - MEDIA
  SERVICES
2020 Park Place
Birmingham, AL 35203   Betty D. Clark, Hd. of Media Serv.

BIRMINGHAM PUBLIC AND JEFFERSON COUNTY FREE LIBRARY - SCIENCE,
  TECHNOLOGY & BUSINESS DEPT. - SPECIAL COLLECTIONS
2020 Park Place   Phone: (205) 254-2533
Birmingham, AL 35203   Deborah C. Dahlin, Dept.Hd.

BIRMINGHAM PUBLIC AND JEFFERSON COUNTY FREE LIBRARY -
  SOUTHERN WOMEN'S ARCHIVES
2020 Park Place   Phone: (205) 254-2822
Birmingham, AL 35203   Teresa A. Ceravolo, Archv.

BIRMINGHAM-SOUTHERN COLLEGE - CHARLES ANDREW RUSH LEARNING
  CENTER/LIBRARY - SPECIAL COLLECTIONS *
800 8th Ave., W.   Phone: (205) 328-5250
Birmingham, AL 35254   Barbara G. Scott, Dir.

CARRAWAY METHODIST MEDICAL CENTER - MEDICAL LIBRARY
1600 N. 26th St.   Phone: (205) 226-6265
Birmingham, AL 35234   Mrs. Bobby H. Powell, Med.Libn.

EYE FOUNDATION HOSPITAL - JOHN E. MEYER EYE FOUNDATION LIBRARY
  †
1720 8th Ave., S.   Phone: (205) 325-8505
Birmingham, AL 35233   Hugh Thomas, Med.Libn.

JEFFERSON COUNTY LAW LIBRARY
900 Jefferson County Court House   Phone: (205) 325-5628
Birmingham, AL 35263   Linda M. Hand, Libn.

LAMBDA, INC. - BARNES LIBRARY
Box 73062   Phone: (205) 251-0682
Birmingham, AL 35253   R. Joullian, Dir.

LANGE, SIMPSON, ROBINSON & SOMERVILLE - LIBRARY †
1700 First Alabama Bank Bldg.   Phone: (205) 252-7000
Birmingham, AL 35203   Angela J. Wier, Libn.

LINN-HENLEY LIBRARY FOR SOUTHERN HISTORICAL RESEARCH -
  DEPARTMENT OF ARCHIVES AND MANUSCRIPTS
2020 Park Place   Phone: (205) 254-2698
Birmingham, AL 35203   Marvin Y. Whiting, Archv./Cur., Mss.

LINN-HENLEY LIBRARY FOR SOUTHERN HISTORICAL RESEARCH - J.
  HUBERT SCRUGGS, JR. COLLECTION OF PHILATELY
2020 Park Place   Phone: (205) 254-2698
Birmingham, AL 35203   Marvin Y. Whiting, Cur.

LINN-HENLEY LIBRARY FOR SOUTHERN HISTORICAL RESEARCH - RUCKER
  AGEE CARTOGRAPHICAL COLLECTION
2020 Park Place   Phone: (205) 254-2534
Birmingham, AL 35203

LINN-HENLEY LIBRARY FOR SOUTHERN HISTORICAL RESEARCH -
  TUTWILER COLLECTION OF SOUTHERN HISTORY AND LITERATURE
2020 Park Place   Phone: (205) 254-2534
Birmingham, AL 35203   Virginia Scott, Hd.Libn.

LINN-HENLEY LIBRARY FOR SOUTHERN HISTORICAL RESEARCH - YOUTH
  DEPARTMENT
2020 Park Place   Phone: (205) 254-2530
Birmingham, AL 35203   Marvin Y. Whiting, Cur.

PROFESSIONAL CONVENTION MANAGEMENT ASSOCIATION - LIBRARY
Commerce Ctr., Suite 1007
2027 First Ave. N.   Phone: (205) 251-1717
Birmingham, AL 35203   Roy B. Evans, Exec. V.P.

RUST INTERNATIONAL CORPORATION - LIBRARY
1130 S. 22nd St.
Box 101   Phone: (205) 254-4400
Birmingham, AL 35201   Calberta O. Atkinson, Libn.

ST. VINCENT'S HOSPITAL - CUNNINGHAM WILSON LIBRARY
Box 915   Phone: (205) 320-7830
Birmingham, AL 35201   Joyce Sims, Libn.

SAMFORD UNIVERSITY - BAPTIST HISTORICAL COLLECTION
Harwell G. Davis Library
800 Lakeshore Dr.   Phone: (205) 870-2749
Birmingham, AL 35209   F. Wilbur Helmbold, Cur.

SAMFORD UNIVERSITY - CUMBERLAND SCHOOL OF LAW - CORDELL HULL
  LAW LIBRARY
800 Lakeshore Dr.   Phone: (205) 870-2714
Birmingham, AL 35209   Laurel R. Clapp, Law Libn.

SAMFORD UNIVERSITY - HARWELL GOODWIN DAVIS LIBRARY - SPECIAL
  COLLECTION
800 Lakeshore Dr.   Phone: (205) 870-2749
Birmingham, AL 35229   Elizabeth C. Wells, Spec.Coll.Libn.

SIROTE, PERMUTT, FRIEND, FRIEDMAN, HELD & APOLINSKY, P.C. - LAW
  LIBRARY
2222 Arlington Ave., S.   Phone: (205) 933-7111
Birmingham, AL 35205   Patricia L. Mennicke, Libn.

SONAT INC. - CORPORATE LIBRARY
Box 2563   Phone: (205) 325-7409
Birmingham, AL 35202   Gina Hinkle, Corp.Libn.

SOUTH CENTRAL BELL TELEPHONE COMPANY - RESOURCE CENTER
600 N. 19th St., 12th Fl.
Box 771   Phone: (205) 321-2064
Birmingham, AL 35201   Bonnie B. Browning, Asst. Staff Supv.

SOUTH HIGHLANDS HOSPITAL - MEDICAL LIBRARY *
1127 S. 12th St.   Phone: (205) 250-7703
Birmingham, AL 35205   Dena Metts, Libn.

SOUTHEASTERN BIBLE COLLEGE - ROWE MEMORIAL LIBRARY
2901 Pawnee Ave., S.   Phone: (205) 251-2311
Birmingham, AL 35256   Edith Taff, Libn.

SOUTHERN RESEARCH INSTITUTE - THOMAS W. MARTIN MEMORIAL
  LIBRARY
2000 Ninth Ave., S.
Box 55305   Phone: (205) 323-6592
Birmingham, AL 35255-5305   Mary L. Pullen, Lib.Mgr.

TEMPLE EMANU-EL - WILLIAM P. ENGEL LIBRARY
2100 Highland Ave.   Phone: (205) 933-8037
Birmingham, AL 35255   Adele Cohn, Libn.

U.S. DEPT. OF COMMERCE - INTERNATIONAL TRADE ADMINISTRATION -
  BIRMINGHAM DISTRICT OFFICE LIBRARY *
908 S. 20th St., Suites 200-201   Phone: (205) 254-1331
Birmingham, AL 35205   Gayle C. Shelton, Jr., Dir.

U.S. VETERANS ADMINISTRATION (AL-Birmingham) - HOSPITAL MEDICAL
   LIBRARY
700 S. 19th St.   Phone: (205) 933-8101
Birmingham, AL 35233   Mary Ann Knotts, Chf., Lib.Serv.

UNIVERSITY OF ALABAMA IN BIRMINGHAM - LISTER HILL LIBRARY OF
   THE HEALTH SCIENCES
University Sta.   Phone: (205) 934-5460
Birmingham, AL 35294   Richard B. Fredericksen, Dir.

UNIVERSITY OF ALABAMA IN BIRMINGHAM - SCHOOL OF MEDICINE -
   ANESTHESIOLOGY LIBRARY
Kracke - 5
Dept. of Anesthesiology
University Sta.   Phone: (205) 934-6500
Birmingham, AL 35294   A.J. Wright, Clinical Libn.

U.S. NATL. PARK SERVICE - RUSSELL CAVE NATL. MONUMENT - LIBRARY
Rte. 1, Box 175   Phone: (205) 495-2672
Bridgeport, AL 35740   Dorothy Marsh, Unit Mgr.

ALABAMA STATE DEPARTMENT OF CONSERVATION & NATURAL
   RESOURCES - ALABAMA MARINE RESOURCES LAB. - LIBRARY
Box 189
Dauphin Island, AL 36528

MARINE ENVIRONMENTAL SCIENCES CONSORTIUM - LIBRARY
Dauphin Island Sea Lab
Box 386   Phone: (205) 861-2141
Dauphin Island, AL 36528   Judy Stout, Libn.

U.S. FOOD & DRUG ADMINISTRATION - FISHERY RESEARCH BRANCH -
   LIBRARY
Box 158   Phone: (205) 861-2962
Dauphin Island, AL 36528   Patsy C. Purvis

MONSANTO FIBERS & INTERMEDIATES COMPANY - TECHNICAL CENTER
   LIBRARY
Box 2204   Phone: (205) 355-5798
Decatur, AL 35602   Betty H. Patterson, Tech.Libn.

NORTH CENTRAL ALABAMA REGIONAL COUNCIL OF GOVERNMENTS -
   LIBRARY *
City Hall Tower, 5th Fl.
Box C   Phone: (205) 355-4515
Decatur, AL 35602

SOUTHEAST ALABAMA MEDICAL CENTER - MEDICAL LIBRARY
Box 6987   Phone: (205) 793-8111
Dothan, AL 36302   Ruth Baxter, Med.Lib.Dir.

NOLAND (Lloyd) HOSPITAL - DAVID KNOX MC KAMY MEDICAL LIBRARY *
701 Ridgeway Rd.   Phone: (205) 783-5121
Fairfield, AL 35064   Elisabeth Burton, Libn.

FLORENCE CITY SCHOOLS - CENTRAL RESOURCE CENTER *
541 Riverview Dr.   Phone: (205) 766-3234
Florence, AL 35630   Lois E. Henderson, Lib.Supv.

U.S. ARMY CHEMICAL SCHOOL - FISHER LIBRARY
Bldg. 2281   Phone: (205) 238-4414
Fort McClellan, AL 36205   Carla J. Pomager, Libn.

U.S. ARMY HOSPITALS - NOBLE ARMY HOSPITAL - MEDICAL LIBRARY
                                               Phone: (205) 238-2411
Ft. McClellan, AL 36205   Pauline Mayhall, Lib.Mgr.

U.S. ARMY MILITARY POLICE SCHOOL - LIBRARY
Bldg. 3181, Rm. 10   Phone: (205) 238-3737
Ft. McClellan, AL 36201   Sybil P. Parker, Supv.Libn.

U.S. ARMY - AEROMEDICAL RESEARCH LABORATORY - SCIENTIFIC
   INFORMATION CENTER
Box 577   Phone: (205) 255-6907
Ft. Rucker, AL 36362   Sybil H. Bullock, Libn.

U.S. ARMY - AVIATION MUSEUM - LIBRARY
Bldg. 6007   Phone: (205) 255-4507
Fort Rucker, AL 36362   Harford Edwards, Jr., Hist.

U.S. ARMY AVIATION TRAINING LIBRARY
Bldgs. 5906 & 5907
Drawer O   Phone: (205) 255-5014
Ft. Rucker, AL 36362   Anne P. Foreman, Chf.Libn.

U.S. ARMY HOSPITALS - LYSTER ARMY COMMUNITY HOSPITAL - MEDICAL
   LIBRARY
Bldg. 301
U.S. Army Aeromedical Center   Phone: (205) 255-4504
Ft. Rucker, AL 36362   Jeanette A. Chambers, Lib.Techn.

BAPTIST MEMORIAL HOSPITAL - MEDICAL LIBRARY
1007 Goodyear Ave.   Phone: (205) 543-4128
Gadsden, AL 35903   Rebecca S. Buckner, Med.Libn.

FIRST PRESBYTERIAN CHURCH OF GADSDEN - LIBRARY
530 Chestnut St.
Box 676   Phone: (201) 547-5747
Gadsden, AL 35902   Mrs. Tom Smith, Libn.

HOLY NAME OF JESUS HOSPITAL - LIBRARY
Box 268   Phone: (205) 547-4911
Gadsden, AL 35902   Jean F. Bonds, Supv.

U.S. AIR FORCE BASE - GUNTER BASE LIBRARY
FL 3370   Phone: (205) 279-3179
Gunter AFS, AL 36114   Alta N. Hunt, Libn.

INTERNATIONAL ASSOCIATION OF EDUCATORS FOR WORLD PEACE -
   IAEWP CENTER OF INTERCULTURAL INFORMATION
Blue Springs Sta.
Box 3282   Phone: (205) 539-7205
Huntsville, AL 35810   Dr. Charles Mercieca, Exec. V.P.

MADISON COUNTY - ELBERT H. PARSONS PUBLIC LAW LIBRARY
205 East Side Sq.   Phone: (205) 536-5911
Huntsville, AL 35801   Cleo S. Cason, Law Libn.

NATIONAL SPELEOLOGICAL SOCIETY - NSS LIBRARY
1 Cave Ave.   Phone: (205) 852-1300
Huntsville, AL 35810   William W. Torode, Libn.

TELEDYNE BROWN ENGINEERING - TECHNICAL LIBRARY *
Cummings Research Pk.
300 Sparkman Dr. N.W.   Phone: (205) 532-1433
Huntsville, AL 35807   Peggy Shelton, Chf.Libn.

UNIVERSITY OF ALABAMA AT HUNTSVILLE - ARCHIVES AND SPECIAL
   COLLECTIONS
The Library
Box 1247   Phone: (205) 895-6540
Huntsville, AL 35807

U.S. NASA - MSFC LIBRARY
Code AS24L   Phone: (205) 453-1880
Marshall Space Flight Ctr., AL 35812   Annette K. Tingle, Lib.Mgr.

U.S. AIR FORCE - AIR UNIVERSITY - LIBRARY
                                               Phone: (205) 293-2606
Maxwell AFB, AL 36112   Robert B. Lane, Dir.

U.S. AIR FORCE - HISTORICAL RESEARCH CENTER
                                               Phone: (205) 293-5958
Maxwell AFB, AL 36112   Lloyd H. Cornett, Jr., Dir.

FINE ARTS MUSEUM OF THE SOUTH AT MOBILE - FAMOS LIBRARY
Museum Dr., Langan Park
Box 8426   Phone: (205) 343-2667
Mobile, AL 36608   Iras F. Smith, Educ.Coord.

HISTORIC MOBILE PRESERVATION SOCIETY - MITCHELL ARCHIVES
350 Oakleigh Pl.   Phone: (205) 432-6161
Mobile, AL 36604

INTERNATIONAL PAPER COMPANY - ERLING RIIS RESEARCH LABORATORY
   - INFORMATION SERVICES
Box 2787   Phone: (205) 457-8911
Mobile, AL 36652   Janice T. Pope, Supv.

INTERNATIONAL PAPER COMPANY - LAND & TIMBER GROUP - FOREST
     PRODUCTIVITY & RESEARCH - FOREST RESEARCH LIBRARY †
Paper Mill Rd.   Phone: (205) 470-4000
Mobile, AL 36601   LaMerle C. Green, Act.Libn.

MERCHANTS NATIONAL BANK OF MOBILE - EMPLOYEES LIBRARY *
58 St. Francis St.
Box 2527   Phone: (205) 690-1139
Mobile, AL 36622   Pat Looney, Libn.

MOBILE COUNTY PUBLIC LAW LIBRARY
County Court House   Phone: (205) 690-8436
Mobile, AL 36602   May Lowe, Libn.

MOBILE PUBLIC LIBRARY - SPECIAL COLLECTIONS DIVISION
704 Government St.   Phone: (205) 438-7094
Mobile, AL 36602   Robert J. Zietz, Hd.

MUSEUMS OF THE CITY OF MOBILE - MUSEUM REFERENCE LIBRARY
355 Government St.   Phone: (205) 438-7569
Mobile, AL 36602   Caldwell Delaney, Musm.Dir.

PROVIDENCE HOSPITAL & SCHOOL OF NURSING - PROVIDENCE HEALTH
     SCIENCE LIBRARY
Box 208   Phone: (205) 438-7869
Mobile, AL 36601   Mary Ann Donnell, Libn.

UNITED STATES SPORTS ACADEMY - LIBRARY
124 University Blvd.
Box 8650   Phone: (205) 343-7700
Mobile, AL 36605   Judy Burnham, Act.Libn.

UNIVERSITY OF SOUTH ALABAMA - COLLEGE OF MEDICINE - BIOMEDICAL
     LIBRARY
Library 312   Phone: (205) 460-7043
Mobile, AL 36688   Robert Donnell, Hd.

UNIVERSITY OF SOUTH ALABAMA - LIBRARY - SPECIAL COLLECTIONS
                                        Phone: (205) 460-7028
Mobile, AL 36688

ALABAMA LEAGUE OF MUNICIPALITIES - LIBRARY
Box 1270   Phone: (205) 262-2566
Montgomery, AL 36102   John F. Watkins, Exec.Dir.

ALABAMA PUBLIC LIBRARY SERVICE - INFORMATION SERVICE
6030 Monticello Dr.   Phone: (205) 277-7330
Montgomery, AL 36130   Anthony W. Miele, Dir.

ALABAMA REGIONAL LIBRARY FOR THE BLIND AND PHYSICALLY
     HANDICAPPED
Alabama Public Library Service
6030 Monticello Dr.   Phone: (205) 277-7330
Montgomery, AL 36130   Hulen E. Bivins, Hd.

ALABAMA STATE DEPARTMENT OF ARCHIVES AND HISTORY - REFERENCE
     ROOM
624 Washington Ave.   Phone: (205) 261-4361
Montgomery, AL 36130   Miriam C. Jones, Hd., Pub.Serv.Div.

ALABAMA STATE DEPARTMENT OF ECONOMIC & COMMUNITY AFFAIRS -
     PLANNING & FLOOD HAZARD MITIGATION INFORMATION CENTER
State Capitol   Phone: (205) 832-6400
Montgomery, AL 36130   John P. Worsham, Jr., Adm.

ALABAMA STATE DEPARTMENT OF PUBLIC HEALTH - REFERENCE LIBRARY
206 State Office Bldg.   Phone: (205) 832-3194
Montgomery, AL 36130   Fran Edwards, Lib.Techn.

ALABAMA (State) SUPREME COURT - SUPREME COURT AND STATE LAW
     LIBRARY
Judicial Bldg., 445 Dexter Ave.   Phone: (205) 832-6410
Montgomery, AL 36130   William C. Younger, Dir.

ALABAMA STATE UNIVERSITY - UNIVERSITY LIBRARY & LEARNING
     RESOURCES - SPECIAL COLLECTIONS
915 S. Jackson St.   Phone: (205) 293-4112
Montgomery, AL 36195-0301   Bertha P. Williams, Spec.Coll.Libn.

BAPTIST MEDICAL CENTER - MEDICAL LIBRARY
2105 East South Blvd.   Phone: (205) 288-2100
Montgomery, AL 36198   Anne Rhodes, Libn.

ENVIRONMENTAL PROTECTION AGENCY - EASTERN ENVIRONMENTAL
     RADIATION LAB - LIBRARY
Box 3009   Phone: (205) 272-3402
Montgomery, AL 36193   Charles M. Petko, Supv., Spec.Serv.

HUNTINGDON COLLEGE - HOUGHTON MEMORIAL LIBRARY - DEPOSITORY
     OF ARCHIVAL AND HISTORICAL MATERIALS
1500 E. Fairview Ave.   Phone: (205) 263-1611
Montgomery, AL 36106   R.G. Massengale, Conference Archv./Hist.

JACKSON HOSPITAL & CLINIC, INC. - MEDICAL LIBRARY
1235 Forest Ave.   Phone: (205) 832-4000
Montgomery, AL 36106   Fran Smith, Med.Libn.

MONTGOMERY ADVERTISER AND ALABAMA JOURNAL - LIBRARY *
200 Washington Ave.   Phone: (205) 262-1611
Montgomery, AL 36104   Peggy Ross, Libn.

MONTGOMERY COUNTY LAW LIBRARY *
Box 1667   Phone: (205) 832-4950
Montgomery, AL 36192   Jean M. Bowar, Law Libn.

MONTGOMERY MUSEUM OF FINE ARTS - LIBRARY
440 S. McDonough St.   Phone: (205) 832-2976
Montgomery, AL 36104   Suzanne W. Black, Libn.

SOUTHERN POVERTY LAW CENTER - KLANWATCH - LIBRARY
1001 S. Hull St.   Phone: (205) 264-0286
Montgomery, AL 36104   Randall Williams, Dir.

U.S. AIR FORCE HOSPITAL - MEDICAL LIBRARY (AL-Montgomery)
Maxwell AFB   Phone: (205) 293-5852
Montgomery, AL 36112   Patricia A. Kuther, Med.Lib.Techn.

U.S. VETERANS ADMINISTRATION (AL-Montgomery) - MEDICAL CENTER
     LIBRARY (142D)
215 Perry Hill Rd.   Phone: (205) 272-4670
Montgomery, AL 36193   M. Johnette Cummins, Chf., Lib.Serv.

UNIVERSITY OF ALABAMA - JONES LAW INSTITUTE - LIBRARY *
1500 East Fairview Ave.   Phone: (205) 832-5588
Montgomery, AL 36106   John R. Huthnance, Dir.

NORTHWEST ALABAMA COUNCIL OF LOCAL GOVERNMENTS - LIBRARY
Box 2603   Phone: (205) 383-3861
Muscle Shoals, AL 35660   Bill Howard, Exec.Dir.

TENNESSEE VALLEY AUTHORITY - TECHNICAL LIBRARY
National Fertilizer Development Ctr.   Phone: (205) 386-2871
Muscle Shoals, AL 35660   Shirley G. Nichols, Supv.Libn.

ALABAMA A & M UNIVERSITY - J. F. DRAKE MEMORIAL LEARNING
     RESOURCES CENTER
Box 489   Phone: (205) 859-7309
Normal, AL 35762   Dr. Birdie O. Weir, Dir.

PRICHARD (Cleveland) MEMORIAL LIBRARY
4559 Old Citronelle Hwy.   Phone: (205) 457-5242
Prichard, AL 36613   Johnnie Andrews, Jr., Dir.

U.S. ARMY - MISSILE COMMAND & MARSHALL SPACE FLIGHT CENTER -
     REDSTONE SCIENTIFIC INFORMATION CENTER
                                        Phone: (205) 876-3251
Redstone Arsenal, AL 35898   James P. Clark, Dir.

U.S. ARMY MISSILE & MUNITIONS CENTER & SCHOOL - MMCS TECHNICAL
     LIBRARY
Bldg. 3323   Phone: (205) 876-7425
Redstone Arsenal, AL 35897-6280   Eva M. Cathey, Adm.Libn.

DALLAS COUNTY CIRCUIT COURT - LIBRARY
Dallas County Courthouse
Box 1158   Phone: (205) 872-3461
Selma, AL 36701   Martha Lee Chisholm, Libn.

REYNOLDS METALS COMPANY - REDUCTION LABORATORY LIBRARY
E. Second St.
Box 1200   Phone: (205) 386-9536
Sheffield, AL 35660   Beth B. Stanford, Libn.

FIRST BAPTIST CHURCH - LIBRARY
Drawer I   Phone: (205) 886-2200
Slocomb, AL 36375   Helen Trampe, Libn.

ALABAMA INSTITUTE FOR THE DEAF AND BLIND - LIBRARY FOR THE
    BLIND AND PHYSICALLY HANDICAPPED
525 North Court St.   Phone: (205) 362-1050
Talladega, AL 35160   Gloria S. Lemaster, Libn.

TALLADEGA COLLEGE - HISTORICAL COLLECTIONS
                                                  Phone: (205) 362-0206
Talladega, AL 35160   Leon P. Spencer, Archv.

TALLADEGA COUNTY LAW LIBRARY *
Judicial Bldg.   Phone: (205) 362-2050
Talladega, AL 35160   Jeffrey A. Willis, Hd.Libn.

TROY STATE UNIVERSITY - LIBRARY - SPECIAL COLLECTIONS
University Ave.   Phone: (205) 566-3000
Troy, AL 36082   Kenneth Croslin, Dir.

U.S. VETERANS ADMINISTRATION (AL-Tuscaloosa) - HOSPITAL MEDICAL
    LIBRARY
                                                  Phone: (205) 553-3760
Tuscaloosa, AL 35404   Olivia S. Maniece, Chf.Libn.

U.S. VETERANS ADMINISTRATION (AL-Tuskegee) - MEDICAL CENTER
    LIBRARY
                                                  Phone: (205) 727-0550
Tuskegee, AL 36083   Artemisia J. Junier, Chf., Lib.Serv.

TUSKEGEE INSTITUTE - DEPARTMENT OF ARCHITECTURE LIBRARY
                                                  Phone: (205) 727-8351
Tuskegee Institute, AL 36088   Luester Williams, Lib.Asst.

TUSKEGEE INSTITUTE - DIVISION OF BEHAVIORAL SCIENCE RESEARCH -
    RURAL DEVELOPMENT RESOURCE CENTER
Carnegie Hall, 4th Fl.   Phone: (205) 727-8575
Tuskegee Institute, AL 36088   Dr. Paul L. Wall, Dir.

TUSKEGEE INSTITUTE - HOLLIS BURKE FRISSELL LIBRARY-ARCHIVES
                                                  Phone: (205) 727-8888
Tuskegee Institute, AL 36088   Daniel T. Williams, Archv.

TUSKEGEE INSTITUTE - SCHOOL OF ENGINEERING LIBRARY
                                                  Phone: (205) 727-8901
Tuskegee Institute, AL 36088   Frances F. Davis, Libn.

TUSKEGEE INSTITUTE - VETERINARY MEDICINE LIBRARY †
                                                  Phone: (205) 727-8307
Tuskegee Institute, AL 36088   Carolyn Ford, Libn.

AMERICAN COLLEGE OF HERALDRY - LIBRARY
Drawer CG
University, AL 35486   Dr. David P. Johnson

GEOLOGICAL SURVEY OF ALABAMA - LIBRARY
Drawer O   Phone: (205) 349-2852
University, AL 35486   Dorothy L. Brady, Libn.

U.S. BUREAU OF MINES - TUSCALOOSA RESEARCH CENTER - REFERENCE
    LIBRARY
Box L   Phone: (205) 758-0491
University, AL 35486   Susan D. Markham, Lib.Techn.

UNIVERSITY OF ALABAMA - BUSINESS LIBRARY
Box S   Phone: (205) 348-6096
University, AL 35486   Dorothy Eady Brown, Sr.Libn.

UNIVERSITY OF ALABAMA - COLLEGE OF COMMUNITY HEALTH SCIENCES -
    HEALTH SCIENCES LIBRARY
Box 6331   Phone: (205) 348-4950
University, AL 35486   Lisa Rains, Chf.Med.Libn.

UNIVERSITY OF ALABAMA - ENGINEERING LIBRARY
Box S   Phone: (205) 348-6551
University, AL 35486   Aydan Kalyoncu, Sr.Libn.

UNIVERSITY OF ALABAMA - MC LURE EDUCATION LIBRARY
Box S   Phone: (205) 348-6055
University, AL 35486   Sharon Lee Stewart, Act.Sr.Libn.

UNIVERSITY OF ALABAMA - SCHOOL OF LAW - ALABAMA LAW REVIEW -
    LIBRARY
Box 1976   Phone: (205) 348-7191
University, AL 35486   Deborah Fisher, Res.Ed.

UNIVERSITY OF ALABAMA - SCHOOL OF LAW LIBRARY
Box 6205   Phone: (205) 348-5925
University, AL 35486-6205   Cherry L. Thomas, Act. Law Libn.

UNIVERSITY OF ALABAMA - SCIENCE LIBRARY
Box S   Phone: (205) 348-5959
University, AL 35486   John S. Langen, Sr.Libn.

UNIVERSITY OF ALABAMA - WILLIAM STANLEY HOOLE SPECIAL
    COLLECTIONS LIBRARY
Box S   Phone: (205) 348-5512
University, AL 35486   Joyce H. Lamont, Cur.

WESTPOINT PEPPERELL - RESEARCH CENTER - INFORMATION SERVICES
    LIBRARY
3300 23rd Dr.
Box 398   Phone: (205) 756-7111
Valley, AL 36876   Philip D. Lawrence, Jr., Supv., Info.Serv.

ALASKA

ALASKA AIR NATIONAL GUARD - 176TH TACTICAL CLINIC MEDICAL
    LIBRARY
Kulis Air Natl. Guard Base
6000 Air Guard Rd.   Phone: (907) 266-1276
Anchorage, AK 99502-1998   Patricia A. Plesko, Med.Libn.

ALASKA PUBLIC UTILITIES COMMISSION - LIBRARY
420 L St., Suite 100   Phone: (907) 279-0583
Anchorage, AK 99501   Eric Hansen, Res.Anl.

ALASKA (State) COURT SYSTEM - ALASKA COURT LIBRARIES
303 K St.   Phone: (907) 264-0585
Anchorage, AK 99501   Aimee Ruzicka, State Law Libn.

ANCHORAGE HISTORICAL AND FINE ARTS MUSEUM - ARCHIVES
121 W. Seventh Ave.   Phone: (907) 264-4326
Anchorage, AK 99501   M. Diane Brenner, Musm.Archv.

NATIONAL BANK OF ALASKA - HERITAGE LIBRARY AND MUSEUM
Box 600   Phone: (907) 276-1132
Anchorage, AK 99510   Vanny Davenport, Libn. & Cur.

SOHIO ALASKA PETROLEUM COMPANY - INFORMATION RESOURCE
    CENTER
3111 C St., Pouch 6-612   Phone: (907) 267-4574
Anchorage, AK 99502   Lorraine M. Culbert, Libn.

U.S. DEPT. OF COMMERCE - INTERNATIONAL TRADE ADMINISTRATION -
    ANCHORAGE DISTRICT OFFICE LIBRARY
701 C St.
Box 32   Phone: (907) 271-5041
Anchorage, AK 99513   Richard M. Lenahan, Act.Dir.

U.S. DEPT. OF THE INTERIOR - ALASKA RESOURCES LIBRARY
701 C St.
Box 36   Phone: (907) 271-5025
Anchorage, AK 99513   Martha L. Shepard, Libn.

U.S. DEPT. OF THE INTERIOR - MINERALS MANAGEMENT SERVICE -
    ALASKA OUTER CONTINENTAL SHELF REGIONAL LIBRARY
Box 101159   Phone: (907) 261-2409
Anchorage, AK 99510   Christine R. Huffaker, Rec.Mgr.

U.S. DISTRICT COURT - LAW LIBRARY
701 C St.
Box 4   Phone: (907) 271-5655
Anchorage, AK 99513   Laura Bunnell, Libn.

U.S. FISH & WILDLIFE SERVICE - LIBRARY
1011 E. Tudor Rd.   Phone: (907) 786-3358
Anchorage, AK 99503   Sharon Palmisano, Libn.

UNIVERSITY OF ALASKA, ANCHORAGE - ALASKA HEALTH SCIENCES
   LIBRARY
3211 Providence Dr.   Phone: (907) 786-1870
Anchorage, AK 99508   Stanley Truelson, Dir.

UNIVERSITY OF ALASKA, ANCHORAGE - ANCHORAGE URBAN
   OBSERVATORY - LIBRARY
3210 Providence Dr.   Phone: (907) 786-1760
Anchorage, AK 99508   Susan Gorski

UNIVERSITY OF ALASKA, ANCHORAGE - ARCTIC ENVIRONMENTAL
   INFORMATION AND DATA CENTER
707 A St.   Phone: (907) 279-4523
Anchorage, AK 99501   Barbara J. Sokolov, Supv., Info.Sci. Group

UNIVERSITY OF ALASKA, ANCHORAGE - LIBRARY - ARCHIVES &
   MANUSCRIPTS DEPARTMENT
3211 Providence Dr.   Phone: (907) 786-1849
Anchorage, AK 99508   Dennis F. Walle, Archv./Mss.Cur.

UNIVERSITY OF ALASKA, ANCHORAGE - LIBRARY - GOVERNMENT
   DOCUMENTS
3211 Providence Dr.   Phone: (907) 786-1874
Anchorage, AK 99508   Alden Rollins, Gov.Docs.Libn.

UNIVERSITY OF ALASKA, ANCHORAGE - LIBRARY - SPECIAL COLLECTIONS
3211 Providence Dr.   Phone: (907) 786-1873
Anchorage, AK 99508   John Summerhill, Supv., Spec.Coll.

U.S. NATL. MARINE FISHERIES SERVICE - AUKE BAY FISHERIES
   LABORATORY - FISHERIES RESEARCH LIBRARY
Box 210155   Phone: (907) 789-7231
Auke Bay, AK 99821   Paula Johnson, Libn.

CORDOVA HISTORICAL SOCIETY, INC. - ARCHIVES
Box 391   Phone: (907) 424-7443
Cordova, AK 99574

U.S. AIR FORCE BASE - EIELSON BASE LIBRARY *
FL 5004, 5010 CSG/SSL   Phone: (907) 372-4184
Eielson AFB, AK 99702   Stella E. Ludwikowski, Adm.Libn.

U.S. AIR FORCE HOSPITAL - MEDICAL LIBRARY (AK-Elmendorf AFB)
             Phone: (907) 552-5325
Elmendorf AFB, AK 99506   Jeraldine J. Van den Top, Libn.

FAIRBANKS ENVIRONMENTAL CENTER - LIBRARY *
218 Driveway   Phone: (907) 452-5021
Fairbanks, AK 99701   Brian Allen, Dir.

PHILOSOPHICAL HERITAGE INSTITUTE - LIBRARY OF ESOTERIC STUDIES
Box 929   Phone: (907) 452-2424
Fairbanks, AK 99707   LaVedi Lafferty, Libn.

U.S. FOREST SERVICE - INSTITUTE OF NORTHERN FORESTRY - LIBRARY
308 Tanana Dr.   Phone: (907) 474-7443
Fairbanks, AK 99701

UNIVERSITY OF ALASKA - ALASKA NATIVE LANGUAGE CENTER -
   RESEARCH LIBRARY
302 Chapman Bldg.   Phone: (907) 474-7874
Fairbanks, AK 99701

UNIVERSITY OF ALASKA - ALASKA AND POLAR REGIONS DEPARTMENT
Elmer E. Rasmuson Library   Phone: (907) 479-7261
Fairbanks, AK 99701   Paul H. McCarthy, Archv./Hd.

UNIVERSITY OF ALASKA - BIO-MEDICAL LIBRARY
             Phone: (907) 479-7442
Fairbanks, AK 99701   Dwight Ittner, Libn.

UNIVERSITY OF ALASKA - COLLEGE OF HUMAN & RURAL DEVELOPMENT -
   RESOURCE CENTER
Gruening Bldg., Rm. 50A   Phone: (907) 474-6634
Fairbanks, AK 99701   Jim Stricks, Coord.

UNIVERSITY OF ALASKA - GEOPHYSICAL INSTITUTE LIBRARY †
             Phone: (907) 479-7503
Fairbanks, AK 99701   Julia H. Tryslehorn, Libn.

UNIVERSITY OF ALASKA - INSTITUTE OF MARINE SCIENCE - LIBRARY
             Phone: (907) 474-7740
Fairbanks, AK 99701   Robert C. Williams, Libn.

UNIVERSITY OF ALASKA - WILDLIFE LIBRARY
Division of Life Sciences   Phone: (907) 474-7672
Fairbanks, AK 99701   Dr. Frederick C. Dean, Supv.

U.S. ARMY POST - FORT RICHARDSON - LIBRARY
Bldg. 636   Phone: (907) 862-9188
Ft. Richardson, AK 99505   Virginia Chaney, Lib.Dir.

U.S. ARMY HOSPITALS - BASSETT ARMY HOSPITAL - MEDICAL LIBRARY
             Phone: (907) 353-5194
Ft. Wainwright, AK 99703   Mary Heidel, Lib.Techn.

U.S. ARMY POST - FORT WAINWRIGHT - LIBRARY
Bldg. 3717   Phone: (907) 353-6114
Ft. Wainwright, AK 99703   Isabelle Mudd, Adm.Libn.

CHILKAT VALLEY HISTORICAL SOCIETY - THE SHELDON MUSEUM &
   CULTURAL CENTER
Box 236   Phone: (907) 766-2366
Haines, AK 99829

U.S. FOOD & DRUG ADMINISTRATION - NATIONAL CENTER FOR
   TOXICOLOGICAL RESEARCH - LIBRARY
Jefferson, AK 72079   Susan Laney-Sheehan, Supv.Libn.

ALASKA STATE DEPARTMENT OF ADMINISTRATION - STATE ARCHIVES
Pouch C   Phone: (907) 465-2275
Juneau, AK 99811   John M. Kinney, State Archv.

ALASKA STATE DEPARTMENT OF FISH AND GAME - LIBRARY
Box 3-2000   Phone: (907) 465-4119
Juneau, AK 99802   Sondra Stanway, Libn.

ALASKA STATE DEPARTMENT OF LAW - ATTORNEY GENERAL'S LIBRARY
Pouch K, State Capitol Bldg.   Phone: (907) 465-3600
Juneau, AK 99811   Beverly Haywood, Legal Adm.

ALASKA STATE DEPARTMENT OF TRANSPORTATION & PUBLIC FACILITIES
   - TECHNICAL LIBRARY ***
Box 1467   Phone: (907) 465-2461
Juneau, AK 99802   Carol Ottesen, Libn.

ALASKA STATE DIVISION OF STATE LIBRARIES & MUSEUMS - HISTORICAL
   LIBRARY
Pouch G   Phone: (907) 465-2925
Juneau, AK 99811-0571   Phyllis J. DeMuth, Libn.

ALASKA STATE DIVISION OF STATE LIBRARIES & MUSEUMS - STATE
   LIBRARY
Pouch G, State Office Bldg.   Phone: (907) 465-2910
Juneau, AK 99811   Richard B. Engen, Dir., Lib. & Musm.Div.

ALASKA STATE LEGISLATURE/LEGISLATIVE AFFAIRS AGENCY -
   REFERENCE LIBRARY
Pouch Y, State Capitol   Phone: (907) 465-3808
Juneau, AK 99811

U.S. BUREAU OF MINES - ALASKA FIELD OPERATIONS CENTER LIBRARY
Box 550   Phone: (907) 364-2111
Juneau, AK 99802   Helen Jacobson, Lib.Techn.

U.S. COURT OF APPEALS, 9TH CIRCUIT - LIBRARY
709 W. 9th St.
Box 3-4000   Phone: (907) 586-7458
Juneau, AK 99802

U.S. DEPT. OF ENERGY - ALASKA POWER ADMINISTRATION - LIBRARY
Box 50   Phone: (907) 586-7405
Juneau, AK 99802   Linda F. Peele, Plan.Div.Asst.

U.S. FOREST SERVICE - PACIFIC NORTHWEST FOREST & RANGE
    EXPERIMENT STATION - FORESTRY SCI. LAB. LIB.
653 Federal Bldg.
Box 909   Phone: (907) 586-7301
Juneau, AK 99802   Carol A. Ayer, Libn.

ALASKA STATE COURT SYSTEM - KETCHIKAN LAW LIBRARY
State Office Bldg.
415 Main St., Rm. 403   Phone: (907) 225-3196
Ketchikan, AK 99901   Berniece Cleveland, Act.Libn.

ALASKA STATE DEPARTMENT OF NATURAL RESOURCES - DIVISION OF
    GEOLOGICAL SURVEY - INFORMATION CENTER *
415 Main St.
Box 7438   Phone: (907) 225-4181
Ketchikan, AK 99901   Geraldine Zartman, Mining Info.Spec.

TONGASS HISTORICAL SOCIETY, INC. - ROBBIE BARTHOLOMEW
    MEMORIAL LIBRARY
629 Dock St.   Phone: (907) 225-5600
Ketchikan, AK 99901   Virginia McGillvray, Dir.

ST. HERMAN'S ORTHODOX THEOLOGICAL SEMINARY - LIBRARY *
414 Mission Rd.
Box 728   Phone: (907) 486-3524
Kodiak, AK 99615   Rev.Fr. Joseph P. Kreta, Dean

U.S. NATL. MARINE FISHERIES SERVICE - W.F. THOMPSON MEMORIAL
    LIBRARY
Box 1638   Phone: (907) 486-3298
Kodiak, AK 99615   Patricia Branson, Libn.

U.S. NATL. PARK SERVICE - DENALI NATL. PARK - LIBRARY
Box 9   Phone: (907) 683-2294
McKinley Park, AK 99755   Doug Cuillard, Chf. Naturalist

NOME LIBRARY/KEGOAYAH KOZGA LIBRARY *
Box 1168   Phone: (907) 443-5133
Nome, AK 99762   Dee McKenna, Libn.

UNIVERSITY OF ALASKA - ALASKA AGRICULTURAL EXPERIMENT STATION
    - LIBRARY
Box AE   Phone: (907) 745-3257
Palmer, AK 99645   Dr. Winston M. Laughlin, Soil Sci.

UNIVERSITY OF ALASKA - INSTITUTE OF MARINE SCIENCE - SEWARD
    MARINE STATION LIBRARY
Box 617   Phone: (907) 224-5261
Seward, AK 99664   Robert C. Williams, Inst.Libn.

U.S. NATL. PARK SERVICE - SITKA NATL. HISTORICAL PARK - LIBRARY
Box 738   Phone: (907) 747-6281
Sitka, AK 99835   Gary Candelaria, Chf. Park Ranger

U.S. PUBLIC HEALTH SERVICE - ALASKA NATIVE HEALTH SERVICE -
    HEALTH SCIENCES LIBRARY
Mt. Edgecumbe Hospital
Box 4577   Phone: (907) 966-2411
Sitka, AK 99835   Frank Sutton, Adm.Off.

ALASKA STATE COURT SYSTEM - VALDEZ LAW LIBRARY *
Box 127   Phone: (907) 835-2266
Valdez, AK 99686   Aimee Ruzicka

VALDEZ HISTORICAL SOCIETY, INC. N-P - VALDEZ HERITAGE ARCHIVES
    ALIVE
Royal Center Egan Drive
Box 6   Phone: (907) 835-4367
Valdez, AK 99686   Dorothy I. Clifton, Dir.

ARIZONA

U.S. NATL. PARK SERVICE - ORGAN PIPE CACTUS NATL. MONUMENT -
    LIBRARY
Rte. 1, Box 100
Ajo, AZ 85321   Caroline Wilson, Interp.

COCHISE COUNTY LAW LIBRARY
Drawer P   Phone: (602) 432-5703
Bisbee, AZ 85603   Herlinda Tafoya, Law Libn.

CASA GRANDE VALLEY HISTORICAL SOCIETY - MUSEUM LIBRARY
110 W. Florence Blvd.   Phone: (602) 836-2223
Casa Grande, AZ 85222   Kay Benedict, Cur.

INTEL CORPORATION - TECHNICAL INFORMATION CENTER
5000 W. Williams Field Rd.   Phone: (602) 961-8015
Chandler, AZ 85224   John McGorray, Tech.Info.Spec.

ARIZONA STATE DEPARTMENT OF ECONOMIC SECURITY - ARIZONA
    TRAINING PROGRAM AT COOLIDGE - STAFF LIBRARY
Box 1467   Phone: (602) 723-4151
Coolidge, AZ 85228-1467   Fredrick Mobley, Training Dir.

AMERIND FOUNDATION, INC. - FULTON-HAYDEN MEMORIAL LIBRARY
                                               Phone: (602) 586-3003
Dragoon, AZ 85609   Mario N. Klimiades, Libn.

COCONINO COUNTY LAW LIBRARY
County Court House   Phone: (602) 774-5011
Flagstaff, AZ 86001   Rebecca H. Ruiz, Law Libn.

LOWELL OBSERVATORY - LIBRARY
Box 1269   Phone: (602) 774-3358
Flagstaff, AZ 86002   Dorothy Brumbaugh

MUSEUM OF NORTHERN ARIZONA - HAROLD S. COLTON MEMORIAL
    LIBRARY †
Rte. 4, Box 720   Phone: (602) 774-5211
Flagstaff, AZ 86001   Dorothy A. House, Libn.

NORTH AMERICAN RADIO ARCHIVES (NARA) - TAPE AND PRINTED
    MATERIALS LIBRARIES
Northern Arizona Univ.
Box 15300
Flagstaff, AZ 86011   Hal Widdison, Tape Libn.

NORTHERN ARIZONA UNIVERSITY - LIBRARIES †
Box 6022   Phone: (602) 523-2951
Flagstaff, AZ 86011   Robert E. Kemper, Dir.

NORTHERN ARIZONA UNIVERSITY - SPECIAL COLLECTIONS LIBRARY
CU Box 6022   Phone: (602) 523-4730
Flagstaff, AZ 86011   Peter M. Whiteley, Spec.Coll.Coord./Archv.

U.S. GEOLOGICAL SURVEY - FLAGSTAFF FIELD CENTER - BRANCH LIBRARY
2255 N. Gemini Dr.   Phone: (602) 779-3311
Flagstaff, AZ 86001   James R. Nation, Libn.

U.S. NATL. PARK SERVICE - WALNUT CANYON NATL. MONUMENT -
    LIBRARY
Rte. 1, Box 25   Phone: (602) 526-3367
Flagstaff, AZ 86001

U.S. NATL. PARK SERVICE - WUPATKI-SUNSET CRATER LIBRARY
HC 33, Box 444A   Phone: (602) 527-7040
Flagstaff, AZ 86001   Jan S. Ryan, Park Techn./Libn.

PINAL COUNTY HISTORICAL SOCIETY, INC. - LIBRARY
2201 S. Main St.
Box 851   Phone: (602) 868-4382
Florence, AZ 85232   Mary A. Faul, Libn.

U.S. ARMY HOSPITALS - BLISS ARMY HOSPITAL - MEDICAL LIBRARY
                                               Phone: (602) 538-5668
Ft. Huachuca, AZ 85613   Thomasa J. Martin, Lib.Off.

U.S. ARMY INTELLIGENCE CENTER & SCHOOL - ACADEMIC LIBRARY
Alvarado Hall
Ft. Huachuca, AZ 85613
Phone: (602) 538-5930
Sylvia J. Webber, Chf.

U.S. ARMY POST - FORT HUACHUCA LIBRARY DIVISION - TECHNICAL
LIBRARY
Greely Hall, Rm. 2102
Fort Huachuca, AZ 85613
Phone: (602) 538-6304
Dorothy C. Tompkins, Chf.Libn.

AMERICAN GRADUATE SCHOOL OF INTERNATIONAL MANAGEMENT -
LIBRARY †
Thunderbird Campus
Glendale, AZ 85306
Phone: (602) 938-7620
Lora Jeanne Wheeler, Libn.

GILA COUNTY LAW LIBRARY
1400 E. Ash
Globe, AZ 85501
Phone: (602) 425-3231
Dave Crossett, Libn.

U.S. NATL. PARK SERVICE - GRAND CANYON RESEARCH LIBRARY †
Grand Canyon Natl. Park
Grand Canyon, AZ 86023
Phone: (602) 638-2411
Louise M. Hinchliffe, Lib.Techn.

CORONADO NATIONAL MEMORIAL - ARCHIVES
R.R. 1, Box 126
Hereford, AZ 85615
Phone: (602) 366-5515

MOHAVE MUSEUM OF HISTORY AND ARTS - LIBRARY
400 W. Beale St.
Kingman, AZ 86401
Phone: (602) 753-3195
Norma Hughes, Dir.

U.S. AIR FORCE BASE - LUKE BASE LIBRARY †
FL 4887
Luke AFB, AZ 85309
Phone: (602) 856-6301
Betty L. Horn, Base Libn.

AMERICAN COLLEGE OF NATURAL THERAPEUTICS & ARIZONA COLLEGE OF
NATUROPATHIC MEDICINE - LIBRARY *
Box 1406
Mesa, AZ 85201
Phone: (602) 969-5293
Zona P. Dial, Libn.

CHURCH OF JESUS CHRIST OF LATTER-DAY SAINTS - MESA BRANCH
GENEALOGICAL LIBRARY
464 E. First Ave.
Mesa, AZ 85204
Phone: (602) 964-1200
Benner A. Hall, Pres.

MESA LUTHERAN HOSPITAL - MEDICAL LIBRARY
525 W. Brown Rd.
Mesa, AZ 85201
Phone: (602) 834-1211
Susan Moreth, Med.Libn.

PIMERIA ALTA HISTORICAL SOCIETY - MUSEUM/ARCHIVES
223 Grand Ave.
Box 2281
Nogales, AZ 85621
Phone: (602) 287-5402

POWELL (John Wesley) MEMORIAL MUSEUM - LIBRARY
6 N. 7th Ave.
Box 747
Page, AZ 86040
Phone: (602) 645-2741

U.S. NATL. PARK SERVICE - PETRIFIED FOREST NATL. PARK - LIBRARY
Phone: (602) 524-6228
Petrified Forest Natl. Park, AZ 86028
Terry E. Maze, Interp.Spec.

AMERICAN EXPRESS COMPANY - CARD DIVISION - WESTERN REGION
OPERATIONS CENTER - SYSTEMS LIBRARY *
2423 E. Lincoln Dr.
Phoenix, AZ 85016
Phone: (602) 248-3914
Judith Kettner, Sys.Libn.

AMERICAN INDIAN BIBLE COLLEGE - DOROTHY CUMMINGS MEMORIAL
LIBRARY
10020 N. 15th Ave.
Phoenix, AZ 85021
Phone: (602) 944-3335
Robert W. Moore, Sr.Libn.

ARIZONA PHOTOGRAPHIC ASSOCIATES, INC. - LIBRARY
2344 W. Holly
Phoenix, AZ 85009
Phone: (602) 258-6551
Dorothy McLaughlin, Dir.

ARIZONA STATE DEPARTMENT OF ECONOMIC SECURITY - AUTHORITY
LIBRARY
1717 W. Jefferson
Phoenix, AZ 85007
Phone: (602) 255-4777

ARIZONA STATE DEPARTMENT OF EDUCATION - EDUCATIONAL
INFORMATION CENTER
1535 W. Jefferson
Phoenix, AZ 85007
Phone: (602) 255-5391
Dr. Beverly Wheeler, Dir.

ARIZONA STATE DEPARTMENT OF HEALTH SERVICES - PUBLIC HEALTH
LIBRARY
1740 W. Adams
Phoenix, AZ 85007
Phone: (602) 255-1013
Charles L. Nelson, Sr.Libn.

ARIZONA STATE DEPARTMENT OF LIBRARY, ARCHIVES & PUBLIC
RECORDS
State Capitol
1700 W. Washington
Phoenix, AZ 85007
Phone: (602) 255-5240
Sharon Turgeon, Dir.

ARIZONA STATE DEPARTMENT OF MINERAL RESOURCES - LIBRARY
State Fairgrounds
Phoenix, AZ 85007
Phone: (602) 255-3791
John H. Jett, Dir.

ARIZONA STATE ENERGY INFORMATION CENTER
1700 W. Washington, 5th Fl.
Phoenix, AZ 85007
Phone: (602) 255-3303
Debbie Moore, Info.Spec.

ARIZONA STATE HOSPITAL - MEDICAL LIBRARY
2500 E. Van Buren
Phoenix, AZ 85008
Phone: (602) 244-1331
Marguerite Cooper, Med.Libn.

ARIZONA STATE OFFICE OF ECONOMIC PLANNING AND DEVELOPMENT -
RESEARCH LIBRARY
1700 W. Washington, Rm. 400
Phoenix, AZ 85007
Phone: (602) 255-5725
Anna M. Alonzo, Libr◆

ARIZONA STATE REGIONAL LIBRARY FOR THE BLIND AND PHYSICALLY
HANDICAPPED
1030 N. 32nd St.
Phoenix, AZ 85008
Phone: (602) 255-5578
Richard C. Peel, Adm.Libn.

AT & T TECHNOLOGIES, INC. - LIBRARY
505 N. 51st Ave.
Box 13369
Phoenix, AZ 85002
Phone: (602) 233-5268
Helen M. Corrales, Employee Serv.

BROWN & BAIN, P.A. - LIBRARY
222 N. Central
Box 400
Phoenix, AZ 85001
Phone: (602) 257-8777
Alison Ewing, Libn.

CENTRAL ARIZONA MUSEUM - LIBRARY & ARCHIVES
1242 N. Central Ave.
Phoenix, AZ 85004
Phone: (602) 255-4470
Janet Michaelieu, Libn.

DESERT BOTANICAL GARDEN - RICHTER LIBRARY
Papago Pk.
1201 N. Galvin Pkwy.
Phoenix, AZ 85008
Phone: (602) 941-1217
Jane B. Cole, Libn.

ERICKSON (Milton) FOUNDATION, INC. - ARCHIVES
3606 N. 24th St.
Phoenix, AZ 85016
Phone: (602) 956-6196
Barbara B. LaRaia, Archv.

EVANS, KITCHEL & JENCKES, P.C. - LIBRARY
2600 N. Central Ave., Suite 1900
Phoenix, AZ 85004-3099
Phone: (602) 234-2600
Patricia A. Wood, Libn.

GARRETT CORPORATION - GARRETT TURBINE ENGINE COMPANY -
ENGINEERING LIBRARY
111 S. 34th St.
Box 5217
Phoenix, AZ 85010
Phone: (602) 231-2062
Dr. Nelson W. Hope, Tech.Res.Libn.

GOOD SAMARITAN MEDICAL CENTER - HEALTH SCIENCE LIBRARY
1111 E. McDowell St.
Box 2989
Phoenix, AZ 85062
Phone: (602) 257-4353
Jacqueline D. Doyle, Dir.

GREYHOUND CORPORATION - LAW DEPARTMENT LIBRARY *
Greyhound Tower
111 W. Clarendon Ave.
Phoenix, AZ 85077
Phone: (602) 248-4000
Ms. E. Feltz, Law Dept.Adm.

GTE NETWORK SYSTEMS - TECHNICAL LIBRARY
2500 W. Utopia Rd.   Phone: (602) 582-7268
Phoenix, AZ 85027   Suzanne Lennon, Tech.Libn.

HALL OF FLAME - RICHARD S. FOWLER MEMORIAL LIBRARY
6101 E. Van Buren   Phone: (602) 275-3473
Phoenix, AZ 85008   George F. Getz, Jr., Pres.

HEARD MUSEUM - LIBRARY
22 E. Monte Vista Rd.   Phone: (602) 252-8840
Phoenix, AZ 85004   Mary E. Graham, Libn.

HONEYWELL, INC. - HONEYWELL INFORMATION SYSTEMS - TECHNICAL
    INFORMATION CENTER
Box 8000   Phone: (602) 862-4115
Phoenix, AZ 85005   Vera Minkel, Mgr., Lib.Serv.

INTEL CORPORATION - TECHNICAL INFORMATION CENTER
MS DVI-106
2402 W. Beardsley Rd.   Phone: (602) 869-4333
Phoenix, AZ 85027   Diane Karr, Tech.Libn.

LEWIS & ROCA - LIBRARY
100 W. Washington St.   Phone: (602) 262-5303
Phoenix, AZ 85003   Walter E. Doherty, Law Libn.

MARICOPA COUNTY LAW LIBRARY
East Court Bldg., 2nd Fl.
101 W. Jefferson St.   Phone: (602) 262-3461
Phoenix, AZ 85003   Kelley Schneider, Dir.

MARICOPA MEDICAL CENTER - MEDICAL LIBRARY
2601 E. Roosevelt St.
Box 5099   Phone: (602) 267-5197
Phoenix, AZ 85010   Fernande Hebert, Med.Libn.

MARICOPA MEDICAL SOCIETY - LIBRARY *
2025 N. Central Ave.   Phone: (602) 258-6461
Phoenix, AZ 85004

MARICOPA TECHNICAL COMMUNITY COLLEGE - LIBRARY RESOURCE
    CENTER
108 N. 40th St.   Phone: (602) 257-8500
Phoenix, AZ 85034   Peg Smith, Dir.

MOTOROLA, INC. - BIPOLAR INTEGRATED CIRCUITS DIVISION -
    TECHNICAL LIBRARY
Box 20906   Phone: (602) 962-2157
Phoenix, AZ 85036   C. Denise Ashford, Sr.Libn. & Mgr.

MOTOROLA, INC. - SEMICONDUCTOR PRODUCTS SECTOR - TECHNICAL
    LIBRARY
Box 2953   Phone: (602) 244-6065
Phoenix, AZ 85062   C. Denise Ashford, Sr.Libn. & Mgr.

O'CONNOR, CAVANAGH, ANDERSON, WESTOVER, KILLINGSWORTH,
    BESHEARS - LAW LIBRARY
3003 N. Central Ave., Suite 1800   Phone: (602) 263-3811
Phoenix, AZ 85012   Sharron L. Pettengill, Hd. Law Libn.

PHOENIX ART MUSEUM - LIBRARY
1625 N. Central Ave.   Phone: (602) 257-1222
Phoenix, AZ 85004   Clayton C. Kirking, Libn.

PHOENIX DAY SCHOOL FOR THE DEAF - LIBRARY/MEDIA CENTER
1935 W. Hayward Ave.   Phone: (602) 255-3448
Phoenix, AZ 85021   Donna L. Farman, Libn.

PHOENIX ELEMENTARY SCHOOLS - DISTRICT NO. 1 - CURRICULUM MEDIA
    CENTER
125 E. Lincoln St.   Phone: (602) 257-3774
Phoenix, AZ 85004   Mary Cook, Coord., Instr.Sup.Serv.

PHOENIX GENERAL HOSPITAL - MEDICAL LIBRARY *
Box 21331   Phone: (602) 279-4411
Phoenix, AZ 85036   Myrtle Idland, Libn.

PHOENIX INDIAN MEDICAL CENTER - LIBRARY
4212 N. 16th St.   Phone: (602) 263-1200
Phoenix, AZ 85016   Rebekah G. Hinton, Adm.Libn.

PHOENIX NEWSPAPERS, INC. - LIBRARY
Box 1950   Phone: (602) 271-8555
Phoenix, AZ 85001   Marcy Bagley, Hd.Libn.

PHOENIX PLANNING DEPARTMENT - LONG RANGE PLANNING DIVISION -
    LIBRARY
Municipal Bldg., 6th Fl.
251 W. Washington St.   Phone: (602) 262-6881
Phoenix, AZ 85003   Catherine N. Donovan, Sec.

PUEBLO GRANDE MUSEUM - RESEARCH LIBRARY *
4619 E. Washington St.   Phone: (602) 275-3452
Phoenix, AZ 85034   Chad T. Phinney, Musm.Asst.

ST. JOSEPH'S HOSPITAL - MEDICAL LIBRARY
350 W. Thomas Rd.
Box 2071   Phone: (602) 285-3299
Phoenix, AZ 85001   Evelyn S. Gorman, Dir., Lib.Serv.

ST. LUKE'S MEDICAL CENTER - ROSENZWEIG HEALTH SCIENCES LIBRARY
1800 E. Van Buren   Phone: (602) 251-8100
Phoenix, AZ 85006   Kay E. Wellik, Dir.

SALT RIVER PROJECT - LIBRARY
Box 1980   Phone: (602) 273-5304
Phoenix, AZ 85001   Bonnie M. Klassen, Libn.

SEMANTODONTICS, INC. - LIBRARY
Box 15668   Phone: (602) 955-5662
Phoenix, AZ 85060   Jim Rhode, Pres.

SERGENT, HAUSKINS & BECKWITH, CONSULTING GEOTECHNICAL
    ENGINEERS - LIBRARY
3940 W. Clarendon Ave.   Phone: (602) 272-6848
Phoenix, AZ 85019   John A. Cassidy, Libn.

SNELL & WILMER - LAW LIBRARY
3100 Valley Bank Center   Phone: (602) 257-7316
Phoenix, AZ 85073   Mary Grace Oakes, Libn.

SPERRY FLIGHT SYSTEMS - ENGINEERING LIBRARY
Box 21111   Phone: (602) 869-2278
Phoenix, AZ 85036   Pat DeVillier, Libn.

TEMPLE BETH ISRAEL - LIBRARY *
3310 N. 10th Ave.   Phone: (602) 264-4428
Phoenix, AZ 85013   Mrs. Elliot Tempkin, Libn.

U-HAUL INTERNATIONAL, INC. - CORPORATE LIBRARY
2727 N. Central Ave.   Phone: (602) 263-6606
Phoenix, AZ 85036   Tom Schutter, Corp.Libn.

UFO INFORMATION RETRIEVAL CENTER, INC.
Points West No. 158
3131 W. Cochise Dr.   Phone: (602) 997-1523
Phoenix, AZ 85021   Thomas M. Olsen, Pres.

UNIDYNAMICS/PHOENIX, INC. - LIBRARY
Box 2990
Phoenix, AZ 85062

U.S. COURT OF APPEALS, 9TH CIRCUIT - LIBRARY
U.S. Courthouse, Rm. 6434
230 N. First Ave.   Phone: (602) 261-3879
Phoenix, AZ 85025-0074   Delores E. Daniels, Libn.

U.S.D.A. - AGRICULTURAL RESEARCH SERVICE - WATER CONSERVATION
    LABORATORY LIBRARY †
4331 E. Broadway Rd.   Phone: (602) 261-4356
Phoenix, AZ 85040   Frieda Bell, Libn.

U.S. DEPT. OF COMMERCE - INTERNATIONAL TRADE ADMINISTRATION -
    PHOENIX DISTRICT OFFICE LIBRARY
Valley Bank Center
201 N. Central Ave., Suite 2750   Phone: (602) 261-3285
Phoenix, AZ 85073   Donald W. Fry, Dir.

U.S. VETERANS ADMINISTRATION (AZ-Phoenix) - HOSPITAL LIBRARY
Seventh St. & Indian School Rd.   Phone: (602) 277-5551
Phoenix, AZ 85012   Diane Wiesenthal, Chf., Lib.Serv.

VALLEY NATIONAL BANK - LIBRARY/INFORMATION CENTER
Box 71, A-315   Phone: (602) 261-2456
Phoenix, AZ 85001   J.F. Gorman, Mgr.

SHARLOT HALL/PRESCOTT HISTORICAL SOCIETIES - LIBRARY/ARCHIVES
415 W. Gurley St.   Phone: (602) 445-3122
Prescott, AZ 86301   Sue Abbey, Archv.

U.S. VETERANS ADMINISTRATION (AZ-Prescott) - HEALTH SCIENCES
    LIBRARY
                                         Phone: (602) 445-4860
Prescott, AZ 86313   Carol Mills, Chf., Lib.Serv.

YAVAPAI COUNTY LAW LIBRARY †
County Courthouse, Fl. 4   Phone: (602) 445-7450
Prescott, AZ 86301   Richard Corson, Law Libn.

CHURCH OF JESUS CHRIST OF LATTER-DAY SAINTS - SAFFORD-
    THATCHER STAKES - GENEALOGICAL LIBRARY
Box 1218   Phone: (602) 428-3194
Safford, AZ 85548   Ervin Cluff, Libn.

ARMOUR RESEARCH CENTER - LIBRARY
15101 N. Scottsdale Rd.   Phone: (602) 998-6120
Scottsdale, AZ 85260   Lorraine Nesvig, Libn.

FOUNDATION FOR BLIND CHILDREN - LIBRARY
1201 North 85th Pl.   Phone: (602) 947-3744
Scottsdale, AZ 85257   Bess D. Kaplan, Materials Coord.

GREYHOUND CORPORATION - PATENT LAW DEPARTMENT LIBRARY
Armour Research Center
15101 N. Scottsdale Rd.   Phone: (602) 998-6365
Scottsdale, AZ 85260   Frank T. Barber, Chf., Patent Counsel

MOTOROLA, INC. - GOVERNMENT ELECTRONICS GROUP - TECHNICAL
    LIBRARY
8201 E. McDowell Rd.   Phone: (602) 949-3471
Scottsdale, AZ 85252   Judith E. Stewart, Mgr., Tech.Info.Ctr.

SCOTTSDALE MEMORIAL HOSPITAL - DR. ROBERT C. FOREMAN HEALTH
    SCIENCES LIBRARY
7400 E. Osborn Rd.   Phone: (602) 994-9616
Scottsdale, AZ 85251   Marihelen O'Connor, Med.Libn.

SINGLE DAD'S LIFESTYLE MAGAZINE - LIBRARY
Box 4842   Phone: (602) 998-0980
Scottsdale, AZ 85258   Robert A. Hirschfeld, Ed./Publ.

U.S. FOREST SERVICE - APACHE-SITGREAVES NATL. FOREST - ARCHIVES
Box 640   Phone: (602) 333-4301
Springerville, AZ 85938

AMERICAN FEDERATION OF ASTROLOGERS, INC. - LIBRARY
6535 S. Rural Rd.
Box 22040   Phone: (602) 838-1751
Tempe, AZ 85282   Robert W. Cooper, Exec.Sec.

ARIZONA HISTORICAL FOUNDATION - HAYDEN LIBRARY
Arizona State University   Phone: (602) 966-8331
Tempe, AZ 85287   Dean E. Smith, Exec. V.P.

ARIZONA STATE UNIVERSITY - ARIZONA COLLECTIONS †
Hayden Library   Phone: (602) 965-3145
Tempe, AZ 85287   Dr. Geoffrey P. Mawn, Cur.

ARIZONA STATE UNIVERSITY - CENTER FOR METEORITE STUDIES -
    LIBRARY
                                         Phone: (602) 965-6511
Tempe, AZ 85281   Carleton B. Moore, Dir.

ARIZONA STATE UNIVERSITY - CHICANO STUDIES COLLECTION †
Hayden Library   Phone: (602) 965-2594
Tempe, AZ 85287   Christine N. Marin, Chicano Bibliog.

ARIZONA STATE UNIVERSITY - COLLEGE OF LAW - LIBRARY
Armstrong Hall   Phone: (602) 966-6141
Tempe, AZ 85282   Richard L. Brown, Dir.

ARIZONA STATE UNIVERSITY - DANIEL E. NOBLE SCIENCE AND
    ENGINEERING LIBRARY
                                         Phone: (602) 965-7607
Tempe, AZ 85287   Vladimir T. Borovansky, Hd.

ARIZONA STATE UNIVERSITY - DANIEL E. NOBLE SCIENCE AND
    ENGINEERING LIBRARY - MAP COLLECTION
                                         Phone: (602) 965-3582
Tempe, AZ 85287   Rosanna Miller, Hd.

ARIZONA STATE UNIVERSITY - EAST ASIAN LANGUAGE COLLECTION
University Library   Phone: (602) 965-3354
Tempe, AZ 85287   Ai-Hwa Wu, Subject Spec./Cat.Libn.

ARIZONA STATE UNIVERSITY - HOWE ARCHITECTURE LIBRARY
College of Architecture   Phone: (602) 965-6400
Tempe, AZ 85287   Donald Koozer, Hd.

ARIZONA STATE UNIVERSITY - LLOYD BIMSON MEMORIAL LIBRARY
College of Business Administration   Phone: (602) 965-6138
Tempe, AZ 85287   Virginia Steel, Bus.Ref.Libn.

ARIZONA STATE UNIVERSITY - MUSIC LIBRARY
                                         Phone: (602) 965-3513
Tempe, AZ 85287   Arlys L. McDonald, Hd., Music Lib.

ARIZONA STATE UNIVERSITY - SPACE PHOTOGRAPHY LABORATORY
Department of Geology   Phone: (602) 965-7029
Tempe, AZ 85281   Ronald Greeley, Professor

ARIZONA STATE UNIVERSITY - SPECIAL COLLECTIONS
University Library   Phone: (602) 965-6519
Tempe, AZ 85287   Marilyn Wurzburger, Hd., Spec.Coll.

ARIZONA STATE UNIVERSITY - UNIVERSITY ARCHIVES *
University Archives Bldg.   Phone: (602) 965-7645
Tempe, AZ 85287   Alfred Thomas, Jr., Univ.Archv.

AERIAL PHENOMENA RESEARCH ORGANIZATION, INC. - LIBRARY
    INFORMATION SERVICES
3910 E. Kleindale Rd.   Phone: (602) 323-1825
Tucson, AZ 85712   Carol Lorenzen, Libn.

ARABIAN HORSE OWNERS FOUNDATION - W.R. BROWN MEMORIAL
    LIBRARY
4633 E. Broadway, Suite 121   Phone: (602) 326-1515
Tucson, AZ 85711   Priscilla Maynard, Exec.Sec.

ARIZONA DAILY STAR - LIBRARY
4850 S. Park Ave.
Box 26807   Phone: (602) 294-4433
Tucson, AZ 85726   Elaine Y. Raines, Chf.Libn.

ARIZONA HISTORICAL SOCIETY - LIBRARY *
949 E. Second St.   Phone: (602) 882-5774
Tucson, AZ 85719   Margaret S. Bret-Harte, Hd.Libn.

ARIZONA-SONORA DESERT MUSEUM - LIBRARY *
Rte. 9, Box 900   Phone: (602) 883-1380
Tucson, AZ 85743   Janice Hunter, Lib.Supv.

ATLANTIC-RICHFIELD COMPANY - ANACONDA MINERALS COMPANY -
    TECHNICAL INFORMATION CENTER
Interstate 10 E. and Kolb Rd.
Box 27007   Phone: (602) 573-7948
Tucson, AZ 85726   Evelyn K. McLenna, Supv.

BURR-BROWN RESEARCH CORPORATION - LIBRARY
Box 11400   Phone: (602) 294-0559
Tucson, AZ 85734   David B. Buus, Libn.

DIOCESE OF TUCSON - REGINA CLERI RESOURCE LIBRARY *
8800 E. 22nd St.   Phone: (602) 886-5201
Tucson, AZ 85710   Sr. Bibiane Roy, O.P., Coord.

FIRST SOUTHERN BAPTIST CHURCH - LIBRARY
445 E. Speedway   Phone: (602) 623-5858
Tucson, AZ 85705   Eleanor Potts, Dir.

KINO COMMUNITY HOSPITAL - LIBRARY *
2800 E. Ajo Way   Phone: (602) 294-4471
Tucson, AZ 85713   Connie Skinner, Libn.

KITT PEAK NATIONAL OBSERVATORY - LIBRARY
Box 26732   Phone: (602) 327-5511
Tucson, AZ 85726   Cathaleen Van Atta, Libn.

L-5 SOCIETY - LIBRARY
1060 E. Elm   Phone: (602) 622-6351
Tucson, AZ 85719   Philip Chapman, Pres.

MOLLOY, JONES, DONAHUE, TRACHTA, CHILDERS & MALLAMO - LIBRARY †
Arizona Bank Plaza
Box 2268   Phone: (602) 622-3531
Tucson, AZ 85702   Paula H. Nordin, Libn.

NATIONAL RUNNING DATA CENTER - LIBRARY
Box 42888   Phone: (602) 326-6416
Tucson, AZ 85733

PALO VERDE HOSPITAL - MEDICAL LIBRARY †
801 S. Prudence
Tucson, AZ 85710

PENNZOIL COMPANY - DUVAL RESEARCH & DEVELOPMENT LIBRARY
4715 E. Ft. Lowell Rd.   Phone: (602) 323-5632
Tucson, AZ 85712   Candy L. Gadke, Libn.

PIMA COUNCIL ON AGING - LIBRARY
100 E. Alameda, Suite 406   Phone: (602) 624-4419
Tucson, AZ 85701   Mary C. Guilbert, Libn.

PIMA COUNTY JUVENILE COURT CENTER - LIBRARY
2225 E. Ajo Way   Phone: (602) 882-2082
Tucson, AZ 85713   Gwen Reid, Ct.Libn.

PIMA COUNTY LAW LIBRARY
111 W. Congress   Phone: (602) 792-8456
Tucson, AZ 85701   Cecilia Torres Zawada, Law Libn.

PIMA COUNTY PLANNING DEPARTMENT - LIBRARY
131 W. Congress St.   Phone: (602) 792-8361
Tucson, AZ 85701   Paul Matty, Libn.

ST. JOSEPH'S HOSPITAL - BRUCE COLE MEMORIAL LIBRARY
350 N. Wilmot   Phone: (602) 296-3211
Tucson, AZ 85732   Polin Lei, Med.Libn.

ST. MARK'S PRESBYTERIAN CHURCH - LIBRARY *
3809 E. 3rd St.   Phone: (602) 325-1519
Tucson, AZ 85716

ST. MARY'S HOSPITAL & HEALTH CENTER - RALPH FULLER MEDICAL
   LIBRARY
1601 W. St. Mary's Rd.
Box 5386   Phone: (602) 622-5833
Tucson, AZ 85703   Jeffrey W. St. Clair, Med.Libn.

ST. THOMAS MORE CENTER - TIMOTHY PARKMAN MEMORIAL LIBRARY
1615 E. Second St.   Phone: (602) 327-6662
Tucson, AZ 85719   Thomas DeMan, O.P., Dir.

SOUTHWESTERN UNIVERSITY - A.J. GERUNTINO LIBRARY
2525 North Country Club Rd.   Phone: (602) 327-3156
Tucson, AZ 85716   Dr. Geruntino

TUCSON CITIZEN - LIBRARY
Box 26767   Phone: (602) 573-4570
Tucson, AZ 85726   Charlotte Kenan, Libn.

TUCSON CITY PLANNING DEPARTMENT - LIBRARY
Box 27210   Phone: (602) 791-4234
Tucson, AZ 85726   Olya T. Tymciurak, Libn.

TUCSON MEDICAL CENTER - MEDICAL LIBRARY
Box 42195   Phone: (602) 327-5461
Tucson, AZ 85733   Christee King, Mgr., Lib.Serv.

TUCSON MUSEUM OF ART - LIBRARY
140 N. Main   Phone: (602) 623-4881
Tucson, AZ 85705   Dorcas Worsley, Libn.

TUCSON PUBLIC LIBRARY - STEINHEIMER COLLECTION OF
   SOUTHWESTERN CHILDREN'S LITERATURE
200 S. 6th Ave.   Phone: (602) 791-4391
Tucson, AZ 85701   Karen Brown, Children's Libn.

TUCSON PUBLIC LIBRARY - TUCSON GOVERNMENTAL REFERENCE
   LIBRARY
City Hall, Local Government Info.Ctr.
Box 27210   Phone: (602) 791-4041
Tucson, AZ 85726   Ann T. Strickland, Libn.

U.S.D.A. - AGRICULTURAL RESEARCH SERVICE - SOUTHWEST RANGELAND
   WATERSHED RESEARCH CENTER
442 E. 7th St.   Phone: (602) 792-6381
Tucson, AZ 85705-8599   E. Sue Anderson, Libn.

U.S. NATL. PARK SERVICE - WESTERN ARCHEOLOGICAL AND
   CONSERVATION CENTER - LIBRARY
1415 N. 6th Ave.
Box 41058   Phone: (602) 629-6995
Tucson, AZ 85717   W. Richard Horn, Libn.

U.S. VETERANS ADMINISTRATION (AZ-Tucson) - MEDICAL CENTER
   LIBRARY
S. 6th Ave.   Phone: (602) 792-1450
Tucson, AZ 85723   Mark Peterson, Chf., Lib.Serv.

UNIVERSITY OF ARIZONA - ARID LANDS INFORMATION CENTER
845 N. Park Ave.   Phone: (602) 621-7897
Tucson, AZ 85719   Deirdre Campbell, Libn.

UNIVERSITY OF ARIZONA - ARIZONA BUREAU OF GEOLOGY & MINERAL
   TECHNOLOGY LIBRARY
845 N. Park Ave.   Phone: (602) 621-7906
Tucson, AZ 85719   Thomas G. McGarvin, Res.Asst.

UNIVERSITY OF ARIZONA - ARIZONA COOPERATIVE WILDLIFE RESEARCH
   UNIT - RESEARCH COLLECTION
218 Biological Sciences Bldg.   Phone: (602) 621-7297
Tucson, AZ 85721   Valery Catt, Unit Sec.

UNIVERSITY OF ARIZONA - ARIZONA HEALTH SCIENCES CENTER LIBRARY
1501 N. Campbell Ave.   Phone: (602) 626-6121
Tucson, AZ 85724   Thomas D. Higdon, Libn.

UNIVERSITY OF ARIZONA - ARIZONA STATE MUSEUM LIBRARY
                              Phone: (602) 626-4695
Tucson, AZ 85721   Hans Bart, Musm.Libn.

UNIVERSITY OF ARIZONA - CENTER FOR CREATIVE PHOTOGRAPHY
843 E. University Blvd.   Phone: (602) 626-4636
Tucson, AZ 85719   Terence Pitts, Cur., Photo Archv.

UNIVERSITY OF ARIZONA - COLLEGE OF ARCHITECTURE LIBRARY
                              Phone: (602) 626-2498
Tucson, AZ 85721   Kathryn Wayne, Libn.

UNIVERSITY OF ARIZONA - COLLEGE OF LAW LIBRARY †
                              Phone: (602) 626-1413
Tucson, AZ 85721   Ronald L. Cherry, Dir.

UNIVERSITY OF ARIZONA - DIVISION OF ECONOMIC AND BUSINESS
   RESEARCH - LIBRARY
College of Business
& Public Administration   Phone: (602) 621-2109
Tucson, AZ 85721   Holly A. Penix, Lib.Asst.

UNIVERSITY OF ARIZONA - DIVISION OF MEDIA & INSTRUCTIONAL
   SERVICES - FILM LIBRARY
Audiovisual Bldg.   Phone: (602) 621-3282
Tucson, AZ 85721   Katherine Holsinger, Mgr.

UNIVERSITY OF ARIZONA ENVIRONMENTAL PSYCHOLOGY PROGRAM -
   LIBRARY
Dept. of Psychology   Phone: (602) 626-2921
Tucson, AZ 85721   Robert B. Bechtel, Dir., Env.Psych.

UNIVERSITY OF ARIZONA - ENVIRONMENTAL RESEARCH LABORATORY -
   LIBRARY
Tucson International Airport   Phone: (602) 621-7962
Tucson, AZ 85706   Susan Morales, Info.Spec.

UNIVERSITY OF ARIZONA - GOVERNMENT DOCUMENTS DEPARTMENT
University Library   Phone: (602) 621-4871
Tucson, AZ 85721   Cynthia E. Bower, Hd.Doc.Libn.

UNIVERSITY OF ARIZONA - INSTITUTE OF ATMOSPHERIC PHYSICS
   LIBRARY
PAS Bldg., Rm. 542
Tucson, AZ 85721   Christine Hanrahan, Libn.

UNIVERSITY OF ARIZONA - LIBRARY SCIENCE COLLECTION
Graduate Library School
1515 E. First   Phone: (602) 621-3383
Tucson, AZ 85721   Cecil W. Wellborn, Hd.Libn.

UNIVERSITY OF ARIZONA - MAP COLLECTION
University Library   Phone: (602) 621-2596
Tucson, AZ 85721   James Minton, Hd. Map Libn.

UNIVERSITY OF ARIZONA - MEDIA CENTER
Library   Phone: (602) 621-3441
Tucson, AZ 85721   Bonnie L. Woollet, Hd. Media Libn.

UNIVERSITY OF ARIZONA - MUSIC COLLECTION
                                                Phone: (602) 626-2140
Tucson, AZ 85721   Dorman H. Smith, Hd. Music Libn.

UNIVERSITY OF ARIZONA - OFFICE OF ARID LANDS STUDIES -
   BIORESOURCES RESEARCH LIBRARY
250 E. Valencia   Phone: (602) 621-7928
Tucson, AZ 85706   Pamela Portwood, Lib.Asst.

UNIVERSITY OF ARIZONA - OPTICAL SCIENCES CENTER - READING ROOM
   †
                                                Phone: (602) 626-3143
Tucson, AZ 85721   Dr. Hyatt Gibbs, Supv.

UNIVERSITY OF ARIZONA - ORIENTAL STUDIES COLLECTION
University Library   Phone: (602) 621-6380
Tucson, AZ 85721   Mary J. McWhorter, Act.Hd.Libn.

UNIVERSITY OF ARIZONA - POETRY CENTER
1086 N. Highland Ave.   Phone: (602) 621-2462
Tucson, AZ 85719   Lois Shelton, Dir.

UNIVERSITY OF ARIZONA - SCIENCE-ENGINEERING LIBRARY
                                                Phone: (602) 621-6394
Tucson, AZ 85721   Shelley E. Phipps, Hd.Libn.

UNIVERSITY OF ARIZONA - SPACE IMAGERY CENTER
Lunar & Planetary Laboratory   Phone: (602) 621-4861
Tucson, AZ 85721   Gail S. Georgenson, Res.Libn.

UNIVERSITY OF ARIZONA - SPECIAL COLLECTIONS DEPARTMENT †
University Library   Phone: (602) 621-6423
Tucson, AZ 85721   Louis A. Hieb, Hd.Libn.

WESTERNERS INTERNATIONAL, A FOUNDATION - LIBRARY
College Sta., Box 3485
Tucson, AZ 85722   Carolyn Nelson, Libn.

WORLD UNIVERSITY ROUNDTABLE - WORLD UNIVERSITY LIBRARY
711 E. Blacklidge Dr.
Sun Sta., Box 40638   Phone: (602) 622-2170
Tucson, AZ 85719   Howard John Zitko, Act.Libn.

NAVAJO NATION LIBRARY
Box K   Phone: (602) 871-4941
Window Rock, AZ 86515   Barbara F. Baun, Libn.

U.S. ARMY - YUMA PROVING GROUND - FOREIGN INTELLIGENCE,
   SCIENTIFIC & TECHNICAL INFO.DIV. - TECHNICAL LIB.
Attn: STEYP-FIO-TL   Phone: (602) 328-2527
Yuma, AZ 85364   Jean McCall, Chf.

YUMA COUNTY LAW LIBRARY
219 W. 2nd St., Court House   Phone: (602) 782-4534
Yuma, AZ 85364   Anna Margaret Sibley, Libn.

ARKANSAS

JOINT EDUCATIONAL CONSORTIUM - ARCHIVES
Box 499   Phone: (501) 246-9283
Arkadelphia, AR 71923   Dolphus Whitten, Jr., Exec.Dir.

OUACHITA BAPTIST UNIVERSITY - RILEY LIBRARY
                                                Phone: (501) 246-4531
Arkadelphia, AR 71923   Ray Granade, Libn.

BENTON SERVICES CENTER - MEDICAL LIBRARY
                                                Phone: (501) 778-1111
Benton, AR 72015   Wilma Umberson, Lib.Techn.

U.S. AIR FORCE BASE - BLYTHEVILLE BASE LIBRARY
FL 4634, Bldg. 555
Blytheville AFB, AR 72315   Bethey J. Johnson, Libn.

AMERICAN HEMEROCALLIS SOCIETY - ARCHIVES
c/o Joan D. Senior
Rt.2, Box 360   Phone: (501) 642-3778
DeQueen, AR 71832   Ned Irish, Chm., Pubn.Comm.

MURPHY OIL USA, INC. - LAW DEPARTMENT LIBRARY
200 Peach St.   Phone: (501) 862-6411
El Dorado, AR 71730   Ann Ripley, Asst.

MURPHY OIL USA, INC. - LIBRARY
200 Peach St.   Phone: (501) 862-6411
El Dorado, AR 71730   Peggy H. Makepeace, Libn.

MURPHY OIL USA, INC. - TAX LIBRARY
200 Peach St.   Phone: (501) 862-6411
El Dorado, AR 71730   Harry Bain, Tax Mgr.

OZARK INSTITUTE - RURAL MEDIA CENTER LIBRARY
99 Spring St.
Box 549
Eureka Springs, AR 72632

ANTAEUS RESEARCH INSTITUTE - LIBRARY
2470 Gregg Ave.   Phone: (501) 443-3050
Fayetteville, AR 72701   Larry Horn, Libn.

U.S. VETERANS ADMINISTRATION (AR-Fayetteville) - MEDICAL CENTER
   LIBRARY
1100 N. College   Phone: (501) 443-4301
Fayetteville, AR 72701   Jeanine Brown, Chf., Lib.Serv.

UNIVERSITY OF ARKANSAS, FAYETTEVILLE - CHEMISTRY LIBRARY
Chemistry Bldg.   Phone: (501) 575-4601
Fayetteville, AR 72701   Carolyn DeLille, Libn.

UNIVERSITY OF ARKANSAS, FAYETTEVILLE - FINE ARTS LIBRARY
                                                Phone: (501) 575-4708
Fayetteville, AR 72701   Joyce M. Clinkscales, Libn.

UNIVERSITY OF ARKANSAS, FAYETTEVILLE - LAW LIBRARY
                                                Phone: (501) 575-5604
Fayetteville, AR 72701   George E. Skinner, Dir.

UNIVERSITY OF ARKANSAS, FAYETTEVILLE - SPECIAL COLLECTIONS
   DIVISION
                                                Phone: (501) 575-4101
Fayetteville, AR 72701   Michael J. Dabrishus, Cur.

UNIVERSITY OF ARKANSAS FOR MEDICAL SCIENCES - NORTHWEST
    ARKANSAS HEALTH EDUCATION CENTER - LIBRARY
1125 N. College   Phone: (501) 521-7615
Fayetteville, AR 72701   Connie M. Wilson, Libn.

SEBASTIAN COUNTY LAW LIBRARY †
503 Stephens Bldg.   Phone: (501) 783-4730
Fort Smith, AR 72901   Frances F. Newhouse, Libn.

SPARKS REGIONAL MEDICAL CENTER - REGIONAL HEALTH SCIENCES
    LIBRARY *
1311 S. Eye St.   Phone: (501) 441-4221
Fort Smith, AR 72901   Grace Anderson, Libn.

GARLAND COUNTY HISTORICAL SOCIETY - ARCHIVES
914 Summer   Phone: (501) 623-5875
Hot Springs, AR 71913   Inez E. Cline, City/County Hist./Dir.

WEYERHAEUSER COMPANY - SFRD TECHNICAL INFORMATION CENTER
Box 1060   Phone: (501) 624-8536
Hot Springs, AR 71901   Memory R. Froncek, Info.Spec.

CROWLEY RIDGE REGIONAL LIBRARY - LOCAL HISTORY COLLECTION
315 W. Oak   Phone: (501) 935-5133
Jonesboro, AR 72401

ARKANSAS ARTS CENTER - ELIZABETH PREWITT TAYLOR MEMORIAL
    LIBRARY
MacArthur Park, Box 2137   Phone: (501) 372-4000
Little Rock, AR 72203   Evelyn McCoy, Libn.

ARKANSAS GAZETTE - NEWS LIBRARY
Box 1821   Phone: (501) 371-3740
Little Rock, AR 72203   Alfred M. Thomas, Hd.Libn.

ARKANSAS REHABILITATION INSTITUTE - LIBRARY
12th & Marshall   Phone: (501) 227-3235
Little Rock, AR 72202   Mrs. Theo H. Storey, Libn.

ARKANSAS STATE DEPARTMENT OF POLLUTION CONTROL - BUSINESS
    LIBRARY
8001 National Dr.   Phone: (501) 562-7444
Little Rock, AR 72219   Rebecca Hooten, Doc. Examiner

ARKANSAS STATE ENERGY OFFICE LIBRARY
One Capitol Mall   Phone: (501) 371-1370
Little Rock, AR 72201   Nancy C. Lewis, Libn.

ARKANSAS (State) HISTORY COMMISSION - ARCHIVES
One Capitol Mall   Phone: (501) 371-2141
Little Rock, AR 72201   Dr. John L. Ferguson, State Hist.

ARKANSAS STATE HOSPITAL - MEDICAL LIBRARY
4313 W. Markham St.   Phone: (501) 664-4500
Little Rock, AR 72205   Bernadine Zerr, Asst.Med.Libn.

ARKANSAS STATE LIBRARY †
One Capitol Mall   Phone: (501) 371-1524
Little Rock, AR 72201   Frances Nix, Assoc.Dir.

ARKANSAS STATE SUPREME COURT LIBRARY
Justice Bldg.   Phone: (501) 374-2512
Little Rock, AR 72201

ARKANSAS TERRITORIAL RESTORATION - LIBRARY
Third & Scott   Phone: (501) 371-2348
Little Rock, AR 72201   Lynda Langford, Musm.Prog.Spec.

AT & T BELL LABORATORIES & TECHNOLOGIES - TELETYPE LIBRARY
8000 Interstate 30   Phone: (501) 562-5856
Little Rock, AR 72209   Diane Reed, Libn.

BAPTIST MEDICAL CENTER SYSTEM - MARGARET CLARK GILBREATH
    MEMORIAL LIBRARY
9601 Interstate 630   Phone: (501) 227-2671
Little Rock, AR 72205   Auburn Steward, Libn.

METROPLAN - INFORMATION CENTER
Wallace Bldg.
105 Main St.   Phone: (501) 372-3300
Little Rock, AR 72201   Katherine Stanick, Libn.

REYNOLDS METALS COMPANY - ALUMINA DIVISION - TECHNICAL
    INFORMATION CENTER †
One Union National Plaza, Suite 975   Phone: (501) 376-4037
Little Rock, AR 72201   Sherry Townsend, Tech.Libn.

ST. VINCENT INFIRMARY - MEDICAL LIBRARY †
Markham & University   Phone: (501) 661-3991
Little Rock, AR 72201   Sr. Jean B. Roberts, S.C.N., Med.Libn.

U.S. COURT OF APPEALS, 8TH CIRCUIT - BRANCH LIBRARY
Post Office and Courthouse
600 W. Capitol, Rm. 220   Phone: (501) 378-5039
Little Rock, AR 72201   Allison Pitcock, Libn.

U.S. VETERANS ADMINISTRATION (AR-Little Rock) - HOSPITAL LIBRARIES
300 E. Roosevelt Rd.   Phone: (501) 372-8361
Little Rock, AR 72206   George M. Zumwalt, Chf., Lib.Serv.

UNIVERSITY OF ARKANSAS, FAYETTEVILLE - TECHNOLOGY CAMPUS
    LIBRARY
1201 McAlmont St.
Box 3017   Phone: (501) 373-2754
Little Rock, AR 72203   Brent A. Nelson, Libn.

UNIVERSITY OF ARKANSAS AT LITTLE ROCK - CENTER FOR LIBRARY &
    INFORMATION SCIENCE EDUCATION & RES. (CLISER)
Library Suite 507
33rd & University   Phone: (501) 569-3421
Little Rock, AR 72204   Donald D. Foos, Dir.

UNIVERSITY OF ARKANSAS AT LITTLE ROCK - PULASKI COUNTY LAW
    LIBRARY
400 W. Markham   Phone: (501) 371-1071
Little Rock, AR 72201   Ruth H. Brunson, Dir.

UNIVERSITY OF ARKANSAS FOR MEDICAL SCIENCES - MEDICAL SCIENCES
    LIBRARY
4301 W. Markham   Phone: (501) 661-5980
Little Rock, AR 72205   Rose Hogan, Dir.

U.S. AIR FORCE BASE - LITTLE ROCK BASE LIBRARY
FL 4460, Bldg. 976   Phone: (501) 988-6979
Little Rock AFB, AR 72076   James Lee Clark, Base Libn.

DREW COUNTY HISTORICAL SOCIETY - MUSEUM AND ARCHIVES
404 S. Main St.   Phone: (501) 367-7446
Monticello, AR 71655   Mrs. Clyde Rogers, Hostess

UNIVERSITY OF ARKANSAS, MONTICELLO - LIBRARY - SPECIAL
    COLLECTIONS
Box 3599   Phone: (501) 367-6811
Monticello, AR 71655   William F. Droessler, Libn.

WINROCK INTERNATIONAL - LIBRARY †
Petit Jean Mountain, Rte. 3   Phone: (501) 727-5435
Morrilton, AR 72110   Joan Newton, Libn.

OZARK FOLK CENTER - LIBRARY
                                                 Phone: (501) 269-3851
Mt. View, AR 72560   W.K. McNeil, Folklorist

FIRST ASSEMBLY OF GOD - CHURCH LIBRARY
22nd & Franklin Sts.   Phone: (501) 758-8553
North Little Rock, AR 72114   Joye Murry, Dir.

U.S. NATL. PARK SERVICE - PEA RIDGE NATL. MILITARY PARK - LIBRARY
                                                 Phone: (501) 451-8122
Pea Ridge, AR 72751   Billy D. Stout, Hist.

UNIVERSITY OF ARKANSAS, PINE BLUFF - JOHN BROWN WATSON
    MEMORIAL LIBRARY †
N. Cedar St.
U.S. Hwy. 79   Phone: (501) 541-6825
Pine Bluff, AR 71601   E.J. Fontenette, Libn.

ARKANSAS TECH UNIVERSITY - TOMLINSON LIBRARY - SPECIAL
   COLLECTIONS
                                         Phone: (501) 968-0304
Russellville, AR 72801   W.A. Vaughn, Lib.Dir.

BENTON COUNTY HISTORICAL SOCIETY - MUSEUM & LIBRARY/ARCHIVES
Box 355   Phone: (501) 524-3217
Siloam Springs, AR 72761   Bernice Freeze, Pres.

ARKANSAS STATE UNIVERSITY - DEAN B. ELLIS LIBRARY - SPECIAL
   COLLECTIONS
Box 2040   Phone: (501) 972-3078
State University, AR 72467   William Hansard, Lib.Dir.

ARKANSAS STATE UNIVERSITY MUSEUM - HISTORICAL LIBRARY
Box 490   Phone: (501) 972-2074
State University, AR 72467   Mary Coles, Musm. Registrar

U.S. FISH & WILDLIFE SERVICE - FISH FARMING EXPERIMENTAL STATION
   - LIBRARY
Box 860   Phone: (501) 673-8761
Stuttgart, AR 72160   Harry K. Dupree, Dir.

SOUTHWEST ARKANSAS REGIONAL ARCHIVES (SARA)
Box 134   Phone: (501) 983-2633
Washington, AR 71862   Mary Medearis, Dir.

CALIFORNIA

THE LATHAM FOUNDATION - HUMAN/ANIMAL BOND RESOURCE LIBRARY
Latham Plaza Bldg.
Clement and Schiller   Phone: (415) 521-0920
Alameda, CA 94501   Hugh H. Tebault, Pres.

U.S. NAVY - NAVAL AIR STATION (CA-Alameda) - LIBRARY
Bldg. 2, Wing 3   Phone: (415) 869-2519
Alameda, CA 94501   Barbara A. Arnott, Adm.Libn.

BRAUN (C.F.) COMPANY - REFERENCE LIBRARY
1000 S. Fremont Ave.   Phone: (213) 570-2233
Alhambra, CA 91802   Beverly Muller, Lib.Mgr.

FIRST UNITED METHODIST CHURCH OF ALHAMBRA - LIBRARY
9 N. Almansor   Phone: (213) 289-4258
Alhambra, CA 91801   Dorothy L. Hooper, Chm., Lib.Comm.

THEOSOPHICAL UNIVERSITY - LIBRARY
2416 N. Lake Ave.   Phone: (818) 798-8020
Altadena, CA 91001   John P. Van Mater, Libn.

ANAHEIM MEMORIAL HOSPITAL - MEDICAL LIBRARY
1111 W. LaPalma Ave.   Phone: (714) 999-6020
Anaheim, CA 92801   Hilary J. Brover, Med.Libn.

AUTOMATIC SPRINKLER COMPANY - INTERSTATE ELECTRONICS
   DIVISION - LIBRARY
1001 E. Ball Rd., Dept. 2540
Box 3117   Phone: (714) 635-7210
Anaheim, CA 92803   Frances P. Zuehlsdorf, Libn.

GOOD SAMARITAN HOSPITAL OF ORANGE COUNTY, INC. - MEDICAL
   LIBRARY *
1025 S. Anaheim Blvd.   Phone: (714) 533-6220
Anaheim, CA 92805   Evelyn Simpson, Med.Libn.

NORTHROP CORPORATION - ELECTRO-MECHANICAL DIVISION -
   TECHNICAL INFORMATION CENTER
500 E. Orangethorpe Ave.   Phone: (714) 871-5000
Anaheim, CA 92801   B.J. Duba, Mgr.

PSYNETICS FOUNDATION - LIBRARY
1212 E. Lincoln Ave.   Phone: (714) 533-2311
Anaheim, CA 92805   Marilyn Livingston, Off.Mgr.

ROCKWELL INTERNATIONAL - TECHNICAL INFORMATION CENTER
3370 Miraloma Ave.   Phone: (714) 632-2089
Anaheim, CA 92803   Carol Glover, Mgr.

UNITED STATES BORAX RESEARCH CORPORATION - RESEARCH LIBRARY
412 Crescent Way   Phone: (714) 774-2670
Anaheim, CA 92801   Betty J. Robson, Res.Libn.

PACIFIC UNION COLLEGE - PITCAIRN ISLANDS STUDY CENTER - LIBRARY
                                         Phone: (707) 965-6241
Angwin, CA 94508   Gary Shearer, Cur.

CALIFORNIA THOROUGHBRED BREEDERS ASSOCIATION - CARLETON F.
   BURKE MEMORIAL LIBRARY
201 Colorado Pl.
Box 750   Phone: (818) 445-7800
Arcadia, CA 91006-9986

ENGINEERING-SCIENCE, INC. - TECHNICAL LIBRARY
125 W. Huntington Dr.
Arcadia, CA 91006

LOS ANGELES COUNTY DEPARTMENT OF ARBORETA AND BOTANIC
   GARDENS - PLANT SCIENCE LIBRARY
301 N. Baldwin Ave.   Phone: (818) 446-8251
Arcadia, CA 91006-2697   Joan DeFato, Plant Sci.Libn.

ATASCADERO HISTORICAL SOCIETY - MUSEUM
6500 Palma Ave.
Box 1047
Atascadero, CA 93422   W.H. Lewis

ATASCADERO STATE HOSPITAL - PROFESSIONAL LIBRARY
Box A   Phone: (805) 461-2491
Atascadero, CA 93423   Marie V. Logan, Sr.Libn.

CEDAR SPRINGS FOUNDATION - LIBRARY
42421 Auberry Rd.   Phone: (209) 855-2438
Auberry, CA 93602   William H. Young, Libn.

PLACER COUNTY LAW LIBRARY
350 Nevada St.   Phone: (916) 823-4391
Auburn, CA 95603   Tanemi Klahn, Law Libn.

UNIVERSITY OF SOUTHERN CALIFORNIA - CATALINA MARINE SCIENCE
   CENTER - LIBRARY
Big Fisherman Cove
Box 398   Phone: (213) 743-6792
Avalon, CA 90704   Dr. Ann M. Muscat, Asst.Dir.

AZUSA PACIFIC UNIVERSITY - SPECIAL COLLECTIONS
Citrus & Alosta Aves.   Phone: (213) 969-3434
Azusa, CA 91702

CALIFORNIA STATE COLLEGE, BAKERSFIELD - CALIFORNIA WELL SAMPLE
   REPOSITORY
9001 Stockdale Hwy.   Phone: (805) 833-2324
Bakersfield, CA 93311-1099   Jack Tucker, Cur.

KERN COUNTY LAW LIBRARY
Courts & Administration Bldg., Rm. 301   Phone: (805) 861-2379
Bakersfield, CA 93301   Marian N. Smrekar, Law Libn.

KERN COUNTY LIBRARY SYSTEM - BEALE MEMORIAL LIBRARY
1315 Truxtun Ave.   Phone: (805) 861-2136
Bakersfield, CA 93301   Louann Nickerson, Ref.Coord.

KERN COUNTY MUSEUM - LIBRARY
3801 Chester Ave.   Phone: (805) 861-2132
Bakersfield, CA 93301   Diana L. Seider, Asst.Dir.

KERN COUNTY SUPERINTENDENT OF SCHOOLS OFFICE - INSTRUCTIONAL
   RESOURCES CENTER
5801 Sundale   Phone: (805) 861-2446
Bakersfield, CA 93309   Karl R. Hardin, Libn.

KERN MEDICAL CENTER - KERN HEALTH SCIENCES LIBRARY
1830 Flower St.   Phone: (805) 326-2227
Bakersfield, CA 93305-4197   L.L. Rizzo, Health Sci.Libn.

MERCY HOSPITAL - MEDICAL LIBRARY
2215 Truxtun Ave.   Phone: (805) 327-3371
Bakersfield, CA 93301   Kathy Coble, Med.Libn.

OCCIDENTAL EXPLORATION & PRODUCTION COMPANY - LIBRARY
5000 Stockdale Hwy.   Phone: (805) 395-8565
Bakersfield, CA 93309   Barbara Rogers, Libn.

MALKI MUSEUM, INC. - ARCHIVES
11-795 Fields Rd.
Morongo Indian Reservation   Phone: (714) 849-7289
Banning, CA 92220

SAN GORGONIO PASS MEMORIAL HOSPITAL - MEDICAL LIBRARY
600 N. Highland Springs Ave.   Phone: (714) 845-1121
Banning, CA 92220   Elaine Burns, Libn.

U.S. AIR FORCE BASE - BEALE BASE LIBRARY
FL 4686   Phone: (916) 634-2706
Beale AFB, CA 95903   Sylvia J. Sefcik, Base Libn.

CALIFORNIA MISSIONARY BAPTIST INSTITUTE & SEMINARY - SCHOOL
    LIBRARY
9246 Rosser St.
Box 848   Phone: (213) 925-4082
Bellflower, CA 90706   Maxine Cross, Libn.

SOUTHERN CALIFORNIA PERMANENTE MEDICAL CENTER - HEALTH
    SCIENCES LIBRARY/MEDIA CENTER
9400 E. Rosecrans Ave.   Phone: (213) 920-4247
Bellflower, CA 90706   Geraldine N. Graves, Dir., Lib.Serv.

TEXTRON, INC. - BELL AEROSPACE TEXTRON - DALMO VICTOR
    OPERATIONS - TECHNICAL LIBRARY
1515 Industrial Way   Phone: (415) 595-1414
Belmont, CA 94002

ALTA BATES HOSPITAL - STUART MEMORIAL LIBRARY
3001 Colby at Ashby   Phone: (415) 845-7110
Berkeley, CA 94705   Kay Kammerer, Health Sci.Libn.

ARMSTRONG COLLEGE - LIBRARY
2222 Harold Way   Phone: (415) 848-2500
Berkeley, CA 94704   Carroll R. Phillips, Coll.Libn.

BERKELEY PUBLIC LIBRARY - ART AND MUSIC DEPARTMENT
2090 Kittredge St.   Phone: (415) 644-6785
Berkeley, CA 94704   Diane Davenport, Supv.Prog.Libn.

CALIFORNIA SCHOOL OF PROFESSIONAL PSYCHOLOGY - BERKELEY
    LIBRARY
1900 Addison   Phone: (415) 548-5415
Berkeley, CA 94704   Karen Hildebrand, Libn.

CALIFORNIA STATE DEPARTMENT OF HEALTH SERVICES - VECTOR
    BIOLOGY AND CONTROL SECTION - LIBRARY
2151 Berkeley Way   Phone: (415) 843-7900
Berkeley, CA 94704   Edna Hernandez, Libn.

CENTER FOR THE STUDY, EDUCATION & ADVANCEMENT OF WOMEN -
    CSEAW LIBRARY
CSEAW Bldg. T-9
University of California   Phone: (415) 642-4786
Berkeley, CA 94720   Jane Scantlebury, Libn.

CLINICAL PHARMACOLOGY RESEARCH INSTITUTE - LIBRARY
2006 Dwight Way, No. 208
Berkeley, CA 94704

CUTTER LABORATORIES - LIBRARY
4th & Parker Sts.
Box 1986   Phone: (415) 420-5188
Berkeley, CA 94710   Hwei Wen Ng, Libn.

ECOLOGY CENTER - LIBRARY
1403 Addison St.   Phone: (415) 548-2221
Berkeley, CA 94702   Karen Pickett, Coord.

GRADUATE THEOLOGICAL UNION - LIBRARY
2400 Ridge Rd.   Phone: (415) 841-8222
Berkeley, CA 94709   John. D. Baker-Batsel, Dir.

HERRICK HOSPITAL AND HEALTH CENTER - PSYCHIATRIC LIBRARY
2001 Dwight Way   Phone: (415) 540-4517
Berkeley, CA 94704   Marlene Rozofsky, Libn.

INFO/SEARCH - LIBRARY
2608 Ninth St.   Phone: (415) 644-2111
Berkeley, CA 94710   Larry M. Marks, Dir.

INSTITUTE OF BUDDHIST STUDIES - LIBRARY *
2717 Haste St.   Phone: (415) 849-2383
Berkeley, CA 94704   Haruyoshi Kusada, Dir.

INTERNATIONAL BIRD RESCUE RESEARCH CENTER - LIBRARY
Aquatic Pk.   Phone: (415) 841-9086
Berkeley, CA 94710   Alice Berkner, Dir.

LAWRENCE BERKELEY LABORATORY - LIBRARY
University of California
Bldg. 50B, Rm. 4206   Phone: (415) 486-4626
Berkeley, CA 94720   Gloria Haire, Hd.Libn.

MAGNES (Judah L.) MEMORIAL MUSEUM - MORRIS GOLDSTEIN LIBRARY
2911 Russell St.   Phone: (415) 849-2710
Berkeley, CA 94705   Jane Levy, Libn./Archv.

MAGNES (Judah L.) MEMORIAL MUSEUM - WESTERN JEWISH HISTORY
    CENTER
2911 Russell St.   Phone: (415) 849-2710
Berkeley, CA 94705   Ruth K. Rafael, Archv./Libn.

MEIKLEJOHN CIVIL LIBERTIES INSTITUTE - LIBRARY
1715 Francisco St.   Phone: (415) 848-0599
Berkeley, CA 94703   Ann Fagan Ginger, Pres.

NATIONAL HOUSING LAW PROJECT/NATIONAL ECONOMIC DEVELOPMENT
    AND LAW CENTER - LIBRARY
1950 Addison St.   Phone: (415) 548-9400
Berkeley, CA 94704   Katherine Parkes, Libn.

SOUTHEAST ASIA RESOURCE CENTER
Box 4000-D   Phone: (415) 548-2546
Berkeley, CA 94704   Joel Rocamora, Dir.

SYNERGY POWER INSTITUTE - LIBRARY
Box 9096   Phone: (415) 549-0839
Berkeley, CA 94709   James H. Craig, Dir.

U.S.D.A. - AGRICULTURAL RESEARCH SERVICE - WESTERN REGIONAL
    RESEARCH CENTER LIBRARY
                                                       Phone: (415) 486-3351
Berkeley, CA 94710   Rena Schonbrun, Libn.

U.S. FOREST SERV. - PACIFIC SOUTHWEST FOREST & RANGE EXPERIMENT
    STA. - WESTFORNET-BERKELEY SERV.CTR.
1960 Addision St.
Box 245   Phone: (415) 486-3686
Berkeley, CA 94701   Theodor B. Yerke, WESTFORNET Prog.Mgr.

UNIVERSITY OF CALIFORNIA, BERKELEY - ANTHROPOLOGY LIBRARY
230 Kroeber Hall   Phone: (415) 642-2400
Berkeley, CA 94720   Dorothy A. Koenig, Libn.

UNIVERSITY OF CALIFORNIA, BERKELEY - ASIAN AMERICAN STUDIES
    LIBRARY
3407 Dwinelle Hall   Phone: (415) 642-2218
Berkeley, CA 94720   Mrs. Wei Chi Poon, Hd.Libn.

UNIVERSITY OF CALIFORNIA, BERKELEY - ASTRONOMY-MATHEMATICS-
    STATISTICS-COMPUTER SCIENCES LIBRARY
100 Evans Hall   Phone: (415) 642-3381
Berkeley, CA 94720   Kimiyo T. Hom, Libn.

UNIVERSITY OF CALIFORNIA, BERKELEY - BANCROFT LIBRARY
                                                       Phone: (415) 642-3781
Berkeley, CA 94720   James D. Hart, Dir.

UNIVERSITY OF CALIFORNIA, BERKELEY - BIOCHEMISTRY LIBRARY
430 Biochemistry Bldg.   Phone: (415) 642-5112
Berkeley, CA 94720   Rebecca Martin, Hd.Libn.

UNIVERSITY OF CALIFORNIA, BERKELEY - BIOLOGY LIBRARY
3503 Life Sciences Bldg.   Phone: (415) 642-2531
Berkeley, CA 94720   Rebecca Martin, Hd.Libn.

UNIVERSITY OF CALIFORNIA, BERKELEY - BOTANICAL GARDEN - LIBRARY
Centennial Dr.   Phone: (415) 642-3343
Berkeley, CA 94720   Dr. James Affolter, Cur.

UNIVERSITY OF CALIFORNIA, BERKELEY - CENTER FOR CHINESE STUDIES
    - LIBRARY
12 Barrows Hall, Rm. 64   Phone: (415) 642-6510
Berkeley, CA 94720   Chi-Ping Chen, Libn.

UNIVERSITY OF CALIFORNIA, BERKELEY - CHEMISTRY LIBRARY
100 Hildebrand Hall   Phone: (415) 642-3753
Berkeley, CA 94720   George Vdovin, Libn.

UNIVERSITY OF CALIFORNIA, BERKELEY - CHICANO STUDIES LIBRARY †
110 Wheeler Hall   Phone: (415) 642-3859
Berkeley, CA 94720   Francisco Garcia-Ayvens, Coord.

UNIVERSITY OF CALIFORNIA, BERKELEY - EARTH SCIENCES LIBRARY
230 Earth Sciences Bldg.   Phone: (415) 642-2997
Berkeley, CA 94720   Julie Rinaldi, Act.Hd.

UNIVERSITY OF CALIFORNIA, BERKELEY - EAST ASIATIC LIBRARY
208 Durant Hall   Phone: (415) 642-2556
Berkeley, CA 94720   Donald H. Shively, Hd.

UNIVERSITY OF CALIFORNIA, BERKELEY - EDUCATION/PSYCHOLOGY
    LIBRARY
2600 Tolman Hall   Phone: (415) 642-4208
Berkeley, CA 94720   Barbara Kornstein, Hd., Lib.

UNIVERSITY OF CALIFORNIA, BERKELEY - ENERGY AND RESOURCES
    PROGRAM - ENERGY INFORMATION CENTER †
Rm. 100, Bldg. T-4   Phone: (415) 642-1004
Berkeley, CA 94720   Mari Wilson, Assoc.Libn.

UNIVERSITY OF CALIFORNIA, BERKELEY - ENTOMOLOGY LIBRARY
Wellman Hall, Rm. 210   Phone: (415) 642-2030
Berkeley, CA 94720   Nancy Axelrod, Unit Hd.

UNIVERSITY OF CALIFORNIA, BERKELEY - ENVIRONMENTAL DESIGN
    LIBRARY
210 Wurster Hall   Phone: (415) 642-4818
Berkeley, CA 94720   James R. Burch, Act.Hd.

UNIVERSITY OF CALIFORNIA, BERKELEY - EXTENSION MEDIA CENTER
2223 Fulton St.   Phone: (415) 642-0460
Berkeley, CA 94720   Olga Knight, Dir.

UNIVERSITY OF CALIFORNIA, BERKELEY - FORESTRY LIBRARY
260 Mulford Hall   Phone: (415) 642-2936
Berkeley, CA 94720   Esther Johnson, Libn.

UNIVERSITY OF CALIFORNIA, BERKELEY - GIANNINI FOUNDATION OF
    AGRICULTURAL ECONOMICS - RESEARCH LIBRARY
248 Giannini Hall   Phone: (415) 642-7121
Berkeley, CA 94720   Grace Dote, Libn.

UNIVERSITY OF CALIFORNIA, BERKELEY - GOVERNMENT DOCUMENTS
    DEPARTMENT
General Library   Phone: (415) 642-3287
Berkeley, CA 94720   Elizabeth Myers, Hd.

UNIVERSITY OF CALIFORNIA, BERKELEY - GRADUATE SCHOOL OF
    JOURNALISM - LIBRARY †
140 North Gate Hall   Phone: (415) 642-0415
Berkeley, CA 94720   David W. Brown, Libn.

UNIVERSITY OF CALIFORNIA, BERKELEY - INSTITUTE OF GOVERNMENTAL
    STUDIES - LIBRARY
Moses Hall, Rm. 109   Phone: (415) 642-5659
Berkeley, CA 94720   Jack Leister, Hd.Libn.

UNIVERSITY OF CALIFORNIA, BERKELEY - INST. OF INDUSTRIAL
    RELATIONS - LABOR OCCUPATIONAL HEALTH PROGRAM LIB.
2521 Channing Way   Phone: (415) 642-5507
Berkeley, CA 94720   Susan Salisbury, Staff Libn.

UNIVERSITY OF CALIFORNIA, BERKELEY - INSTITUTE OF INDUSTRIAL
    RELATIONS LIBRARY
2521 Channing Way, Rm. 110   Phone: (415) 642-1705
Berkeley, CA 94720   Nanette O. Sand, Libn.

UNIVERSITY OF CALIFORNIA, BERKELEY - INSTITUTE OF INTERNATIONAL
    STUDIES LIBRARY
340 Stephens Hall   Phone: (415) 642-3633
Berkeley, CA 94720   Colette G. Myles, Hd.

UNIVERSITY OF CALIFORNIA, BERKELEY - INSTITUTE OF
    TRANSPORTATION STUDIES LIBRARY
412 McLaughlin Hall   Phone: (415) 642-3604
Berkeley, CA 94720   Michael C. Kleiber, Hd.Libn.

UNIVERSITY OF CALIFORNIA, BERKELEY - LAW LIBRARY
230 Law Bldg.   Phone: (415) 642-4044
Berkeley, CA 94720   Robert Berring, Law Libn.

UNIVERSITY OF CALIFORNIA, BERKELEY - LIBRARY SCHOOL LIBRARY
2 South Hall   Phone: (415) 642-2253
Berkeley, CA 94720   Virginia Pratt, Libn.

UNIVERSITY OF CALIFORNIA, BERKELEY - MAP ROOM
137 General Library   Phone: (415) 642-4940
Berkeley, CA 94720   Philip Hoehn, Map Libn.

UNIVERSITY OF CALIFORNIA, BERKELEY - MUSIC LIBRARY
240 Morrison Hall   Phone: (415) 642-2623
Berkeley, CA 94720   Michael A. Keller, Hd.

UNIVERSITY OF CALIFORNIA, BERKELEY - NATIVE AMERICAN STUDIES
    LIBRARY
3415 Dwinelle Hall   Phone: (415) 642-2793
Berkeley, CA 94720   Rosalie McKay, Libn.

UNIVERSITY OF CALIFORNIA, BERKELEY - NATURAL RESOURCES LIBRARY
40 Giannini Hall   Phone: (415) 642-4493
Berkeley, CA 94720   Norma Kobzina, Hd.

UNIVERSITY OF CALIFORNIA, BERKELEY - OPTOMETRY LIBRARY
490 Minor Hall   Phone: (415) 642-1020
Berkeley, CA 94720   Alison Howard, Hd.

UNIVERSITY OF CALIFORNIA, BERKELEY - PHYSICS LIBRARY
                                                      Phone: (415) 642-3122
Berkeley, CA 94720   Camille Wanat, Hd.

UNIVERSITY OF CALIFORNIA, BERKELEY - PUBLIC HEALTH LIBRARY
42 Earl Warren Hall   Phone: (415) 642-2511
Berkeley, CA 94720   Thomas J. Alexander, Hd.

UNIVERSITY OF CALIFORNIA, BERKELEY - SCIENCE & MATHEMATICS
    EDUCATION LIBRARY
Lawrence Hall of Science
Centennial Dr.   Phone: (415) 642-1334
Berkeley, CA 94720   Ann M. Jensen, Libn.

UNIVERSITY OF CALIFORNIA, BERKELEY - SEBASTIAN S. KRESGE
    ENGINEERING LIBRARY
Stephen D. Bechtel Engineering Center   Phone: (415) 642-3339
Berkeley, CA 94720   Patricia Davitt Maughan, Libn.

UNIVERSITY OF CALIFORNIA, BERKELEY - SOCIAL SCIENCE LIBRARY
30 Stephens Hall   Phone: (415) 642-0370
Berkeley, CA 94720   Geraldine Scalzo, Hd.

UNIVERSITY OF CALIFORNIA, BERKELEY - SOCIAL WELFARE LIBRARY
216 Haviland Hall   Phone: (415) 642-4432
Berkeley, CA 94720   Geraldine Scalzo, Hd.

UNIVERSITY OF CALIFORNIA, BERKELEY - SOUTH/SOUTHEAST ASIA
    LIBRARY SERVICE
438 General Library   Phone: (415) 642-3095
Berkeley, CA 94720   Peter Ananda, Hd.

UNIVERSITY OF CALIFORNIA, BERKELEY - STATE DATA PROGRAM
    LIBRARY
Survey Research Center
2538 Channing Way   Phone: (415) 642-6571
Berkeley, CA 94720   Ilona Einowski, Archv.

UNIVERSITY OF CALIFORNIA, BERKELEY - UNIVERSITY EXTENSION -
CONTINUING EDUCATION OF THE BAR - LIBRARY
2300 Shattuck Ave.   Phone: (415) 642-5343
Berkeley, CA 94704   Virginia Polak, Libn.

UNIVERSITY OF CALIFORNIA, BERKELEY - UNIVERSITY HERBARIUM -
LIBRARY
Department of Botany   Phone: (415) 642-2465
Berkeley, CA 94720

UNIVERSITY OF CALIFORNIA, BERKELEY - WATER RESOURCES CENTER
ARCHIVES
410 O'Brien Hall   Phone: (415) 642-2666
Berkeley, CA 94720   Gerald J. Giefer, Libn.

WOMEN'S HISTORY RESEARCH CENTER, INC. - NATIONAL
CLEARINGHOUSE ON MARITAL RAPE
2325 Oak St.   Phone: (415) 548-1770
Berkeley, CA 94708   Laura X, Exec.Dir.

WOMEN'S HISTORY RESEARCH CENTER, INC. - WOMEN'S HISTORY
LIBRARY
2325 Oak St.   Phone: (415) 548-1770
Berkeley, CA 94708   Laura X, Dir.

WRIGHT INSTITUTE - GRADUATE DIVISION LIBRARY
2728 Durant Ave.   Phone: (415) 841-9230
Berkeley, CA 94704   Lorraine D. Kos, Libn.

ACADEMY OF MOTION PICTURE ARTS AND SCIENCES - MARGARET
HERRICK LIBRARY
8949 Wilshire Blvd.   Phone: (213) 278-4313
Beverly Hills, CA 90211   Linda Harris Mehr, Lib.Adm.

BEVERLY HILLS PUBLIC LIBRARY - FINE ARTS DIVISION
444 N. Rexford Dr.   Phone: (213) 550-4720
Beverly Hills, CA 90210   Nick Cellini, Libn.

INSTITUTE FOR CANCER AND BLOOD RESEARCH - LIBRARY
140 N. Robertson Blvd.   Phone: (213) 655-4706
Beverly Hills, CA 90211   Belle Gould

LESSER (Robert Charles) AND COMPANY - RESOURCE DEPARTMENT
8383 Wilshire Blvd., Suite 240   Phone: (213) 658-7600
Beverly Hills, CA 90211   Barry A. Stulberg, Info.Serv.Anl.

LITTON INDUSTRIES - LAW LIBRARY
360 N. Crescent Dr.   Phone: (213) 859-5102
Beverly Hills, CA 90210   Judith Runyon Leyva, Law Libn.

SOUTHERN CALIFORNIA PSYCHOANALYTIC INSTITUTE - FRANZ
ALEXANDER LIBRARY
9024 Olympic Blvd.   Phone: (213) 276-2455
Beverly Hills, CA 90211   Lena Pincus, Libn.

TWENTIETH CENTURY FOX FILM CORPORATION - RESEARCH LIBRARY
10201 W. Pico Blvd.
Box 900   Phone: (213) 203-2782
Beverly Hills, CA 90213   Kenneth Kenyon, Hd. of Res.Dept.

U.S. FOREST SERVICE - INYO NATL. FOREST - INFORMATION CENTER
873 N. Main St.   Phone: (714) 873-5841
Bishop, CA 93514   Ray Schaaf, Pub.Aff.Off.

COMMONWEAL - RESEARCH INSTITUTE LIBRARY
Box 316
Bolinas, CA 94924

BRANDEIS-BARDIN INSTITUTE - HOUSE OF THE BOOK
                                            Phone: (818) 348-7201
Brandeis, CA 93064   Hannah R. Kuhn, Spec.Libn.

AIRCRAFT TECHNICAL PUBLISHERS - RESOURCE CENTER
101 South Hill Dr.   Phone: (415) 468-1705
Brisbane, CA 94005   Elizabeth A. Donini, Rsrc.Ctr.Mgr.

NUTRILITE PRODUCTS, INC. - RESEARCH LIBRARY
5600 Beach Blvd.   Phone: (714) 521-3900
Buena Park, CA 90620   Jacqueline M. Painter, Libn.

AMERICAN LIBRARY OF RAILWAY AND TRACTION HISTORY
455-A Riverside Dr.   Phone: (818) 846-6098
Burbank, CA 91506   Brian C. Smith, Dir.

BURBANK COMMUNITY HOSPITAL - MEDICAL LIBRARY
466 E. Olive Ave.   Phone: (818) 953-6516
Burbank, CA 91501   Narciso M. Garganta, Dir., Med.Lib.

BURBANK PUBLIC LIBRARY - WARNER RESEARCH COLLECTION
110 N. Glenoaks Blvd.   Phone: (818) 847-9743
Burbank, CA 91501   Mary Ann Grasso, Lib.Coord.

CALIFORNIA FAMILY STUDY CENTER - LEARNING RESOURCE CENTER
4400 Riverside Dr.   Phone: (818) 843-0711
Burbank, CA 91505   Margaret Pappas, Dir.

CRANE COMPANY - HYDRO-AIRE DIVISION - TECHNICAL LIBRARY
3000 Winona Ave.   Phone: (818) 842-6121
Burbank, CA 91510   Douglas Longyear, Engr.Dir.

DISNEY (Walt) PRODUCTIONS - ARCHIVES
500 S. Buena Vista St.   Phone: (818) 840-5424
Burbank, CA 91521   David R. Smith, Archv.

DISNEY (Walt) PRODUCTIONS - LIBRARY
500 S. Buena Vista St.   Phone: (818) 840-5326
Burbank, CA 91521   Mary Jo Terry, Libn.

LOCKHEED-CALIFORNIA COMPANY - TECHNICAL INFORMATION CENTER
Dept. 82-40, Bldg. U-51, Plant B-1
Box 551   Phone: (818) 847-5646
Burbank, CA 91520   Stanley A. Elman, Mgr.

LOCKHEED CORPORATION - INTERNATIONAL MARKETING LIBRARY 07-50
Bldg. 61
Box 551   Phone: (818) 847-6527
Burbank, CA 91520   Betty Scanlon, Libn.

ST. JOSEPH MEDICAL CENTER - HEALTH SCIENCE LIBRARY
Buena Vista & Alameda Sts.   Phone: (818) 843-5111
Burbank, CA 91505   Sr. Naomi Hurd, S.P., Libn.

COEN COMPANY, INC. - TECHNICAL LIBRARY †
1510 Rollins Rd.   Phone: (415) 697-0440
Burlingame, CA 94010   Clark Hutchason, Supv.

PENINSULA COMMUNITY FOUNDATION - COMMUNITY RESOURCE LIBRARY
1204 Burlingame Ave.
Box 627   Phone: (415) 342-2505
Burlingame, CA 94011-0627   Cathy Somerton, Libn.

PENINSULA HOSPITAL AND MEDICAL CENTER - MEDICAL STAFF LIBRARY
†
1783 El Camino Real   Phone: (415) 697-4061
Burlingame, CA 94010   Prudence Harvey Hamilton, Chf.Libn.

YOUTH RESOURCES, INC. - LIBRARY
14580 Mission St.
Box DD   Phone: (714) 327-2639
Cabazon, CA 92230   Paul J. Marks, Pres.

WOODVIEW-CALABASAS PSYCHIATRIC HOSPITAL - LIBRARY
25100 Calabasas Rd.   Phone: (818) 888-7500
Calabasas, CA 91302   Ching-Fen Wu Tsiang, Libn.

CAMARILLO STATE HOSPITAL - PROFESSIONAL LIBRARY
1878 S. Lewis Rd.
Box A   Phone: (805) 484-3661
Camarillo, CA 93011   Kaye Schmitt, Act.Libn.

ENVIRONMENTAL EDUCATION GROUP - LIBRARY
5762 Firebird Ct.
Camarillo, CA 93010   Alan Arthur Tratner, Exec.Dir.

GEOTHERMAL WORLD CORPORATION - INFORMATION CENTER
5762 Firebird Ct.   Phone: (805) 482-6288
Camarillo, CA 93010   Alan A. Tratner, Dir.

ST. JOHN'S SEMINARY - EDWARD LAURENCE DOHENY MEMORIAL LIBRARY
5012 E. Seminary Rd.   Phone: (805) 482-2755
Camarillo, CA 93010   Rev. N.C. Eberhardt, Dir., Lib.Serv.

U.S. MARINE CORPS - CAMP PENDLETON LIBRARY SYSTEM
Marine Corps Base
1122 E St.   Phone: (619) 725-5104
Camp Pendleton, CA 92055   Patrick J. Carney, Lib.Dir.

U.S. NAVY - NAVAL HOSPITAL (CA-Camp Pendleton) - MEDICAL LIBRARY
                                              Phone: (714) 725-1322
Camp Pendleton, CA 92055   Deborah G. Batey, Med.Libn.

QUADREX CORPORATION - LIBRARY
1700 Dell Ave.   Phone: (408) 866-4510
Campbell, CA 95008   Margaret C. Ma, Libn.

HUGHES AIRCRAFT COMPANY - CANOGA PARK LIBRARY
Bldg. CP-2, Mail Sta. T-10
8433 Fallbrook Ave.   Phone: (818) 833-2400
Canoga Park, CA 91304   Donald C. Paul, Libn.

ROCKWELL INTERNATIONAL - ENERGY SYSTEMS GROUP - LIBRARY
8900 De Soto Ave., NA00   Phone: (818) 700-4406
Canoga Park, CA 91304   Ms. Y.O. Fackler, Mgr.

ROCKWELL INTERNATIONAL - ROCKETDYNE DIVISION - TECHNICAL
    INFORMATION CENTER
6633 Canoga Ave.   Phone: (818) 710-2575
Canoga Park, CA 91304   Laura J. Rainey, Mgr.

CARLSBAD CITY LIBRARY - SPECIAL COLLECTIONS DEPARTMENT
1250 Elm Ave.   Phone: (619) 438-5614
Carlsbad, CA 92008   Clifford E. Lange, Lib.Dir.

HUMAN RESOURCES RESEARCH ORGANIZATION - CALIFORNIA LIBRARY
27857 Berwick Dr.
Carmel, CA 93923

ESKATON AMERICAN RIVER HOSPITAL - ERLE M. BLUNDEN, M.D.
    MEMORIAL LIBRARY
4747 Engle Rd.   Phone: (916) 486-2128
Carmichael, CA 95608   Carolyn Kopper, Med.Libn.

NISSAN MOTOR CORPORATION - CORPORATE LIBRARY †
18501 S. Figueroa St.
Box 191   Phone: (213) 532-3111
Carson, CA 90247   Moon H. Kim, Libn.

PUREX CORPORATION - TECHNICAL LIBRARY
24600 S. Main St.
Box 6200   Phone: (213) 775-2111
Carson, CA 90749   Louise Y. Sakamoto, Libn.

REILLY TRANSLATIONS - LIBRARY
Box 4346   Phone: (213) 515-6839
Carson, CA 90749-4346   Michael M. Reilly, Dir.

U.S. AIR FORCE BASE - CASTLE BASE - BAKER LIBRARY †
FL 4672, Bldg. 422   Phone: (209) 726-2630
Castle AFB, CA 95342   Enid L. Wilford, Base Libn.

LAUREL GROVE HOSPITAL - MEDICAL & DENTAL STAFF LIBRARY
19933 Lake Chabot Rd.   Phone: (415) 538-6464
Castro Valley, CA 94546   Marie Culwell, Med.Rec.Mgr.

CHATSWORTH HISTORICAL SOCIETY - HISTORICAL COLLECTION
Box 102   Phone: (818) 341-3053
Chatsworth, CA 91311

EDWARD-DEAN MUSEUM ART REFERENCE LIBRARY
9401 Oak Glen Rd.   Phone: (714) 845-2626
Cherry Valley, CA 92223   Jan Holmlund, Dir.

CALIFORNIA STATE UNIVERSITY, CHICO - MERIAM LIBRARY - SPECIAL
    COLLECTIONS
First & Hazel Sts.   Phone: (916) 895-6342
Chico, CA 95929   William A. Jones, Spec.Coll.Libn.

U.S. NAVY - NAVAL WEAPONS CENTER - LIBRARY DIVISION
Mail Code 3433   Phone: (619) 939-2507
China Lake, CA 93555   Joseph M. Burge, Hd., Lib.Div.

AMERICAN THEATRE ORGAN SOCIETY - ARCHIVES/LIBRARY
1393 Don Carlos Ct.   Phone: (619) 421-9629
Chula Vista, CA 92010   Vernon P. Bickel, Cur.

ROHR INDUSTRIES - CORPORATE LIBRARY
Box 1516   Phone: (619) 691-3010
Chula Vista, CA 92012   James C. Fuscoe, Chf.Libn.

SAN DIEGO COUNTY LAW LIBRARY - SOUTH BAY BRANCH
500 Third Ave.   Phone: (619) 575-4929
Chula Vista, CA 92010   O. James Werner, Dir.

CITY OF INDUSTRY - RALPH W. MILLER GOLF LIBRARY
One Industry Hills Pkwy.
Box 3287   Phone: (213) 965-0861
City of Industry, CA 91744   Jean Bryant, Lib.Dir.

CALIFORNIA INSTITUTE OF PUBLIC AFFAIRS - LIBRARY
226 W. Foothill Blvd.
Box 10   Phone: (714) 624-5212
Claremont, CA 91711   T.C. Trzyna, Pres.

CENTER FOR PROCESS STUDIES - LIBRARY
1325 N. College Ave.   Phone: (714) 626-3521
Claremont, CA 91711   Philip Ricards, Libn.

THE CLAREMONT COLLEGES - ELLA STRONG DENISON LIBRARY
Scripps College   Phone: (714) 621-8000
Claremont, CA 91711   Judy Harvey Sahak, Libn.

THE CLAREMONT COLLEGES - LIBRARY
800 Dartmouth   Phone: (714) 621-8000
Claremont, CA 91711   Patrick Barkey, Dir.

THE CLAREMONT COLLEGES - NORMAN F. SPRAGUE MEMORIAL LIBRARY
Harvey Mudd College   Phone: (714) 621-8000
Claremont, CA 91711   David Kuhner, Libn.

THE CLAREMONT COLLEGES - SEELEY G. MUDD SCIENCE LIBRARY
Pomona College   Phone: (714) 621-8000
Claremont, CA 91711   David Kuhner, Libn.

CLAREMONT GRADUATE SCHOOL - EDUCATIONAL RESOURCE &
    INFORMATION CENTER
131 E. Tenth St.   Phone: (714) 621-8000
Claremont, CA 91711   Julie L. Robinson, Mng.Libn.

CLAREMONT GRADUATE SCHOOL - GEORGE G. STONE CENTER FOR
    CHILDREN'S BOOKS
131 E. Tenth St.   Phone: (714) 621-8000
Claremont, CA 91711   Julie L. Robinson, Mng.Libn.

FRANCIS BACON FOUNDATION, INC. - FRANCIS BACON LIBRARY
655 N. Dartmouth Ave.   Phone: (714) 624-6305
Claremont, CA 91711   Elizabeth S. Wrigley, Dir.-Libn.

RANCHO SANTA ANA BOTANIC GARDEN - LIBRARY
1500 N. College Ave.   Phone: (714) 626-3922
Claremont, CA 91711   Beatrice M. Beck, Libn.

SCHOOL OF THEOLOGY AT CLAREMONT - THEOLOGY LIBRARY
1325 N. College Ave.   Phone: (714) 626-3521
Claremont, CA 91711   Dr. Caroline Becker Whipple, Dir.

ARCHDIOCESE OF SAN FRANCISCO - CHANCERY ARCHIVES
Box 1799   Phone: (415) 994-5211
Colma, CA 94014   Dr. Jeffrey M. Burns, Archv.

WORLD LIFE RESEARCH INSTITUTE - LIBRARY
23000 Grand Terrace Rd.   Phone: (714) 825-4773
Colton, CA 92324   Bruce W. Halstead, Lib.Dir.

CITY OF COMMERCE PUBLIC LIBRARY
5655 Jillson St.   Phone: (213) 722-6660
Commerce, CA 90040   Catherine J. Penprase, Dir.

CONTRA COSTA COUNTY OFFICE OF EDUCATION - ACCESS INFORMATION
   CENTER & PROFESSIONAL LIBRARY
2371 Stanwell Dr.   Phone: (415) 671-4318
Concord, CA 94520   Marilyn Matosian, Sr.Res.

MOUNT DIABLO UNIFIED SCHOOL DISTRICT - TEACHERS' PROFESSIONAL
   LIBRARY *
Willow Creek Center
1026 Mohr Lane
Concord, CA 94518

U.S. NAVY - FLEET ANALYSIS CENTER (FLTAC) - LIBRARY *
Naval Weapons Sta.
Seal Beach
Corona Annex   Phone: (714) 736-4467
Corona, CA 91720   Daysi Hollingsworth, Libn.

SHERMAN RESEARCH LIBRARY
614 Dahlia Ave.   Phone: (714) 673-1880
Corona Del Mar, CA 92625   Dr. William O. Hendricks, Dir.

BRUNSWICK CORPORATION - DEFENSE DIVISION - TECHNICAL LIBRARY *
3333 Harbor Blvd.   Phone: (714) 546-8030
Costa Mesa, CA 92626   Clay Zlomke, Dir. of Engr.

FAIRVIEW STATE HOSPITAL - STAFF LIBRARY
2501 Harbor Blvd.   Phone: (714) 957-5394
Costa Mesa, CA 92626   Barbara Rycroft, Sr.Libn.

NEWPORT AERONAUTICAL SALES (NAS) - LIBRARY †
1011 Brioso St., Rm. 111   Phone: (714) 631-8250
Costa Mesa, CA 92627   George M. Posey, III, V.P., Res.

RUTAN AND TUCKER - LIBRARY
611 Anton, Suite 1400   Phone: (714) 641-3460
Costa Mesa, CA 92626   Hazel Bader, Libn.

PROCUREMENT ASSOCIATES - LIBRARY †
733 N. Dodsworth Ave.   Phone: (213) 966-4576
Covina, CA 91724   Marie McDonald, Libn.

DEL NORTE COUNTY HISTORICAL SOCIETY - LIBRARY
577 H St.   Phone: (707) 464-3922
Crescent City, CA 95531   Judy Knitter, Pres.

DEL NORTE COUNTY LAW LIBRARY
Courthouse   Phone: (707) 464-4139
Crescent City, CA 95531   Patricia Lamb, Law Libn.

HUGHES HELICOPTERS - LIBRARY
Centinela & Teale Sts.
Mail Code 6/A69   Phone: (213) 305-3723
Culver City, CA 90230   Dorothy K. Goss, Chf.Libn.

METRO-GOLDWYN-MAYER, INC. - PICTURE RESEARCH LIBRARY
10202 W. Washington Blvd.   Phone: (213) 558-5518
Culver City, CA 90230   Bonnie Rothbart, Mgr.

UNIVERSITY OF WEST LOS ANGELES - LAW LIBRARY *
10811 W. Washington Blvd.   Phone: (213) 204-4603
Culver City, CA 90230   Dinah Granifei, Hd.Libn.

APPLE COMPUTER INC. - LIBRARY AND INFORMATION RESOURCES
20525 Mariani Ave., 18AJ   Phone: (408) 973-2400
Cupertino, CA 95014   Monica Ertel, Mgr., Info.Rsrcs.

FOUR-PHASE SYSTEMS - CORPORATE LIBRARY
10700 N. De Anza Blvd.   Phone: (408) 255-0900
Cupertino, CA 95014   Dorothy Grevera, Mgr., Lib.Serv.

HEWLETT-PACKARD COMPANY - CUPERTINO LIBRARY *
11000 Wolfe Rd.   Phone: (408) 257-7000
Cupertino, CA 95014   Catherine Biggs, Libn.

TANDEM COMPUTERS, INC. - CORPORATE INFORMATION CENTER
19333 Vallco Pkwy.   Phone: (408) 725-6000
Cupertino, CA 95014   Selma Zinker, Mgr., Lib.Serv.

TYMSHARE, INC. - TECHNICAL LIBRARY
20705 Valley Green Dr.   Phone: (408) 446-6229
Cupertino, CA 95014   Dorothy Sands, Libn.

SETON MEDICAL CENTER - LIBRARY
1900 Sullivan Ave.   Phone: (415) 992-4000
Daly City, CA 94015   Marie Grace Abbruzzese, Libn.

GEOTHERMAL RESOURCES COUNCIL - LIBRARY
Box 1350   Phone: (916) 758-2360
Davis, CA 95617   David N. Anderson, Exec.Dir.

MEALS FOR MILLIONS/FREEDOM FROM HUNGER FOUNDATION - LIBRARY
1644 Da Vinci Court   Phone: (213) 829-5337
Davis, CA 95616   Patricia Butzer Larson, Dir., Resource Ctr.

U.S. ARMY - CORPS OF ENGINEERS - HYDROLOGIC ENGINEERING CENTER
   - LIBRARY
609 2nd St.   Phone: (916) 756-1104
Davis, CA 95616   Lynne L. Stevenson, Libn.

UNIVERSITY OF CALIFORNIA, DAVIS - AGRICULTURAL ECONOMICS
   BRANCH LIBRARY
Voorhies Hall   Phone: (916) 752-1540
Davis, CA 95616   Susan Casement, Libn.

UNIVERSITY OF CALIFORNIA, DAVIS - ENVIRONMENTAL TOXICOLOGY
   LIBRARY
                                             Phone: (916) 752-2562
Davis, CA 95616   Dr. Ming-Yu Li, Doc.Spec.

UNIVERSITY OF CALIFORNIA, DAVIS - HEALTH SCIENCES LIBRARY
                                             Phone: (916) 752-1214
Davis, CA 95616   Marjan Merala, Libn.

UNIVERSITY OF CALIFORNIA, DAVIS - INSTITUTE OF GOVERNMENTAL
   AFFAIRS - LIBRARY
                                             Phone: (916) 752-2045
Davis, CA 95616   Katherine Bruce Bostock, Hd.Libn.

UNIVERSITY OF CALIFORNIA, DAVIS - MICHAEL AND MARGARET B.
   HARRISON WESTERN RESEARCH CENTER
Department of Special Collections
Shields Library   Phone: (916) 752-1621
Davis, CA 95616   Michael Harrison, Dir.

UNIVERSITY OF CALIFORNIA, DAVIS - PHYSICAL SCIENCES LIBRARY
University Library   Phone: (916) 752-1627
Davis, CA 95616   Marlene Tebo, Hd.Libn.

UNIVERSITY OF CALIFORNIA, DAVIS - SCHOOL OF LAW - LAW LIBRARY
                                             Phone: (916) 752-3322
Davis, CA 95616   Mortimer D. Schwartz, Law Libn.

UNIVERSITY OF CALIFORNIA, DAVIS - UNIVERSITY LIBRARIES - SPECIAL
   COLLECTIONS
                                             Phone: (916) 752-2110
Davis, CA 95616   Donald Kunitz, Hd., Spec.Coll.

UNIVERSITY OF CALIFORNIA, DAVIS - WOMEN'S RESOURCES & RESEARCH
   CENTER - LIBRARY
Women's Center   Phone: (916) 752-3372
Davis, CA 95616   Joy Fergoda, Lib.Coord.

U.S. NATL. PARK SERVICE - DEATH VALLEY NATL. MONUMENT -
   REFERENCE AND RESEARCH LIBRARY
                                             Phone: (714) 786-2331
Death Valley, CA 92328   Shirley A. Harding, Cur./Libn.

LANDMARK CONSERVATORS - CABOTS OLD INDIAN PUEBLO MUSEUM
   LIBRARY
67-616 E. Desert View Ave.   Phone: (714) 329-7610
Desert Hot Springs, CA 92240   Colbert H. Eyraud, Pres./Cur.

DOWNEY COMMUNITY HOSPITAL - HEALTH SCIENCES LIBRARY
11500 Brookshire Ave.   Phone: (213) 869-3061
Downey, CA 90241   Marguerite Bladen, Med.Lib.Cons.

DOWNEY HISTORICAL SOCIETY MUSEUM - LIBRARY
12458 Rives Ave.
Box 554   Phone: (213) 862-2777
Downey, CA 90241   Barbara Callarman, Dir.

LOS ANGELES COUNTY - DEPARTMENT OF DATA PROCESSING -
  TECHNICAL LIBRARY
9150 E. Imperial Hwy., Rm. R-118   Phone: (213) 771-5421
Downey, CA 90242   Millie Jones, Tech.Libn.

LOS ANGELES COUNTY SUPERINTENDENT OF SCHOOLS - PROFESSIONAL
  REFERENCE CENTER †
9300 E. Imperial Hwy.   Phone: (213) 922-6350
Downey, CA 90241   Margaret Marquette, Coord.

LOS ANGELES COUNTY SUPERINTENDENT OF SCHOOLS - SOUTHERN
  CALIFORNIA CENTER FOR EDUCATIONAL IMPROVEMENT
9300 E. Imperial Hwy.   Phone: (213) 922-6170
Downey, CA 90242   Dr. Murray Via, Cons./Prog.Mgr.

RANCHO LOS AMIGOS HOSPITAL - MEDICAL LIBRARY
7601 E. Imperial Hwy.   Phone: (213) 922-7696
Downey, CA 90242   Janet Judson, Med.Libn.

ROCKWELL INTERNATIONAL - SPACE BUSINESSES - TECHNICAL
  INFORMATION CENTER
12214 Lakewood Blvd.   Phone: (213) 922-4648
Downey, CA 90241   Nan H. Paik, Supv.

SIERRA COUNTY LAW LIBRARY
Courthouse   Phone: (916) 289-3269
Downieville, CA 95936

CITY OF HOPE NATIONAL MEDICAL CENTER - GRAFF MEDICAL AND
  SCIENTIFIC LIBRARY
                                         Phone: (213) 359-8111
Duarte, CA 91010   Anne Dillibe, Dir.

STEREO CLUB OF SOUTHERN CALIFORNIA - LIBRARY
Box 35   Phone: (818) 357-8345
Duarte, CA 91010   David Starkman, Tech.Dir.

TRAVENOL LABORATORIES, INC. - HYLAND DIVISION - RESEARCH
  LIBRARY
1710 Flower Ave.   Phone: (213) 303-2491
Duarte, CA 91010   Monica Hermesch, Chf.Libn.

MC KESSON - R & D CENTER LIBRARY
Box 2277   Phone: (415) 828-1440
Dublin, CA 94568   Joan La Manna, Libn.

U.S. NASA - AMES RESEARCH CENTER - DRYDEN FLIGHT RESEARCH
  FACILITY - LIBRARY
Box 273   Phone: (805) 258-3311
Edwards, CA 93523

U.S. AIR FORCE BASE - EDWARDS BASE LIBRARY †
6510th ABG/SSL STOP 115
FL 2805
Bldg. 2665   Phone: (805) 277-2375
Edwards AFB, CA 93523   Orin M. Moyer, Libn.

U.S. AIR FORCE - FLIGHT TEST CENTER - TECHNICAL LIBRARY
6520 Test Group/Stop 238   Phone: (805) 277-3606
Edwards AFB, CA 93523   Carol Maples, Chf., Tech.Lib.

INSTITUTE FOR CREATION RESEARCH - LIBRARY
2100 Greenfield Dr.
Box 2666   Phone: (619) 440-2443
El Cajon, CA 92021   Arnold D. Ehlert, Dir., Lib.

SAN DIEGO COUNTY LAW LIBRARY - EAST COUNTY BRANCH
250 E. Main   Phone: (619) 579-3525
El Cajon, CA 92020   O. James Werner, Dir.

IMPERIAL COUNTY LAW LIBRARY †
Court House
939 Main St.   Phone: (619) 339-4374
El Centro, CA 92243   Mary Ann Azzarello, Law Libn.

ESPERANTO LEAGUE FOR NORTH AMERICA - ESPERANTO INFORMATION
  SERVICE
Box 1129   Phone: (415) 653-0998
El Cerrito, CA 94530   Gregory V. Wasson, Dir.

JAPANESE-AMERICAN SOCIETY FOR PHILATELY - LIBRARY
Box 1049
El Cerrito, CA 94530   George M. Baka, Libn.

EL MONTE HISTORICAL SOCIETY - MUSEUM LIBRARY *
3100 Tyler Ave.   Phone: (213) 444-3813
El Monte, CA 91733   Lillian Wiggins, Dir.-Cur.

GOULD, INC. - NAVCOM SYSTEMS DIVISION - TECHNICAL LIBRARY †
Hoffman Electronic Pk.
4323 N. Arden Dr.   Phone: (213) 442-0123
El Monte, CA 91731

PROSPEROS - LIBRARY
Box 5505   Phone: (818) 350-3293
El Monte, CA 91734   Barbara Hill, Dir./Trustee

AGBABIAN ASSOCIATES - LIBRARY †
250 N. Nash St.   Phone: (213) 640-0576
El Segundo, CA 90245   Elizabeth Tucker, Info.Dir.

COMPUTER SCIENCES CORPORATION - TECHNICAL LIBRARY
650 N. Sepulveda Blvd.   Phone: (213) 615-0311
El Segundo, CA 90245   Jeannette H. Nelson, Mgr.

HUGHES AIRCRAFT COMPANY - ELECTRO-OPTICAL & DATA SYSTEMS
  GROUP - COMPANY TECHNICAL DOCUMENT CENTER
2000 E. El Segundo Blvd.
Bldg. E1, Mail Sta. E110
Box 902   Phone: (213) 616-0414
El Segundo, CA 90245   Billy W. Campbell, Supv.

HUGHES AIRCRAFT COMPANY - ELECTRO-OPTICAL & DATA SYSTEMS
  GROUP - INFORMATION RESOURCES SECTION
2000 E. El Segundo Blvd.
Bldg. E1, Mail Sta. J145
Box 902   Phone: (213) 616-8178
El Segundo, CA 90245   Clinton E. Merritt, Hd.

HUGHES AIRCRAFT COMPANY - ELECTRO-OPTICAL & DATA SYSTEMS
  GROUP - TECHNICAL LIBRARY
2000 E. El Segundo Blvd.,
Bldg. E1, Mail Sta. E117
Box 902   Phone: (213) 616-3333
El Segundo, CA 90245   Mr. Masse Bloomfield, Supv.

WYLE LABORATORIES - TECHNICAL INFORMATION LIBRARY
128 Maryland St.   Phone: (213) 322-1763
El Segundo, CA 90245   Linda Rogers, Res.Libn.

XEROX CORPORATION - EL SEGUNDO TECHNICAL LIBRARY
701 S. Aviation Blvd., A3-25   Phone: (213) 536-5222
El Segundo, CA 90245   Marilyn Durkin, Tech.Libn.

SONOMA STATE HOSPITAL AND DEVELOPMENTAL CENTER - STAFF
  LIBRARY
Box 1400   Phone: (707) 938-6561
Eldridge, CA 95431   Barbara Fetesoff, Sr.Libn.

CETUS CORPORATION - RESEARCH LIBRARY
1400 53rd St.   Phone: (415) 420-3300
Emeryville, CA 94608   Judy Labovitz, Mgr.

JHK & ASSOCIATES - TECHNICAL LIBRARY - WEST
5801 Christie Ave., No. 220   Phone: (415) 428-2550
Emeryville, CA 94608   Richard Presby, Dir. of Libs.

MEDI-PHYSICS, INC. - SCIENTIFIC LIBRARY
5801 Christie Ave.
Box 8684   Phone: (415) 652-7650
Emeryville, CA 94608   Selma Graham, Sci.Libn.

JOHNSON (Donald) ARCHIVE
16401 Otsego St.   Phone: (818) 788-5355
Encino, CA 91436   Richard Burroughs, Libn.

LOS ENCINOS DOCENT ASSOCIATION - LOS ENCINOS STATE HISTORIC
    PARK - LIBRARY
16756 Moorpark St.
Encino, CA 91436

CHURCH OF JESUS CHRIST OF LATTER-DAY SAINTS - EUREKA,
    CALIFORNIA STAKE BRANCH GENEALOGICAL LIBRARY
2734 Dolbeer St.   Phone: (707) 443-7411
Eureka, CA 95501   Ruth Allen, Libn.

HUMBOLDT COUNTY LAW LIBRARY †
Court House, 825 Fifth St.   Phone: (707) 445-7201
Eureka, CA 95501   Nancy A. Guy, Law Libn.

REDWOOD COMMUNITY ACTION AGENCY - ENERGY DEMONSTRATION
    CENTER - APPROPRIATE TECHNOLOGY LIBRARY
539 T St.   Phone: (707) 444-3831
Eureka, CA 95501   T. Michael Mills, Energy Educ.Coord.

SOLANO COUNTY LAW LIBRARY
Hall of Justice
600 Union Ave.   Phone: (707) 429-6655
Fairfield, CA 94533   Hon. Richard M. Harris, Pres., Lib. Trustees

KAISER FOUNDATION HOSPITAL - MEDICAL LIBRARY
9961 Sierra Ave.   Phone: (714) 829-5085
Fontana, CA 92335   Sue D. Layvas, Chf.Med.Libn.

U.S. ARMY COMBAT DEVELOPMENTS EXPERIMENTATION COMMAND -
    TECHNICAL INFORMATION CENTER †
HQ USACDEC
Bldg. 2925   Phone: (408) 242-3757
Ft. Ord, CA 93941   Carolyn I. Alexander, Chf.Libn.

CALIFORNIA SCHOOL FOR THE BLIND - LIBRARY MEDIA CENTER
500 Walnut Ave.   Phone: (415) 794-3854
Fremont, CA 94536   Vernalee Nullmeyer, Lib.Techn.

CALIFORNIA STATE DEPARTMENT OF EDUCATION - SCHOOL FOR THE
    DEAF LIBRARY
39350 Gallaudet Dr.   Phone: (415) 794-3666
Fremont, CA 94538   Elsa C. Kleinman, Libn.

NORTH AMERICAN RADIO ARCHIVES (NARA) - LIBRARY
4418 Irvington Ave.   Phone: (415) 656-6436
Fremont, CA 94538   Steven K. Ham, Pres.

XEROX CORPORATION - DIABLO SYSTEMS, INC. - TECHNICAL LIBRARY
Box 5030, MS 319   Phone: (415) 498-7921
Fremont, CA 94537   Sally Turk, Tech.Info.Spec.

CALIFORNIA SCHOOL OF PROFESSIONAL PSYCHOLOGY - FRESNO LIBRARY
1350 M St.   Phone: (209) 486-8424
Fresno, CA 93721   Inge Kauffman, Dir.

CALIFORNIA STATE - COURT OF APPEAL, 5TH APPELLATE DISTRICT -
    LAW LIBRARY
5002 State Bldg.   Phone: (209) 445-5686
Fresno, CA 93721   Kathleen Pearce, Libn.

CALIFORNIA STATE UNIVERSITY, FRESNO - HENRY MADDEN LIBRARY -
    DEPARTMENT OF SPECIAL COLLECTIONS
                                                    Phone: (209) 294-2595
Fresno, CA 93740   Ronald J. Mahoney, Hd.

FRESNO CITY AND COUNTY HISTORICAL SOCIETY - ARCHIVES
7160 W. Kearney Blvd.   Phone: (209) 441-0862
Fresno, CA 93706   Maria Ortiz, Archv.

FRESNO COMMUNITY HOSPITAL - MEDICAL LIBRARY
Box 1232   Phone: (209) 442-3968
Fresno, CA 93715   Ann Robertson, Med.Libn.

FRESNO COUNTY FREE LIBRARY - SPECIAL COLLECTIONS
2420 Mariposa St.   Phone: (209) 488-3196
Fresno, CA 93721   Linda J. Goff, Local Hist.Libn.

FRESNO COUNTY LAW LIBRARY †
Fresno County Courthouse, Rm. 600
1100 Van Ness Ave.   Phone: (209) 237-2227
Fresno, CA 93721   Dorothy G. Morris, Libn.

FRESNO COUNTY OFFICE OF EDUCATION - IMC-LIBRARY
2314 Mariposa St.   Phone: (209) 488-3272
Fresno, CA 93721-2286   Beverly Braun, IMC Dir.

FRESNO DIOCESAN LIBRARY *
Box 1668   Phone: (209) 237-5125
Fresno, CA 93717   Fr. Walter Minhoto, Libn.

FRESNO GENEALOGICAL SOCIETY - LIBRARY
Box 1429
Fresno, CA 93716   Patricia Logsden, Libn.

MENNONITE BRETHREN BIBLICAL SEMINARY - HIEBERT LIBRARY
1717 S. Chestnut Ave.   Phone: (209) 251-7194
Fresno, CA 93702   Steven Brandt, Dir.

SAN JOAQUIN COLLEGE OF LAW - LIBRARY †
3385 E. Shields Ave.   Phone: (209) 225-4953
Fresno, CA 93726   Mary Ann Parker, Law Libn.

THOMAS, SNELL, JAMISON, RUSSELL, WILLIAMSON AND ASPERGER -
    LIBRARY
Fresno's Towne House, 10th Fl.
Box 1641   Phone: (209) 442-0600
Fresno, CA 93716   Susan Herzog, Libn.

U.S.D.A. - AGRICULTURAL RESEARCH SERVICE - HORTICULTURAL CROPS
    RESEARCH LABORATORY - LIBRARY
5578 E. Air Terminal Dr.   Phone: (209) 487-5310
Fresno, CA 93727   J. Steven Tebbets, Biol.Techn./Libn.

U.S. VETERANS ADMINISTRATION (CA-Fresno) - HOSPITAL MEDICAL
    LIBRARY
2615 E. Clinton Ave.   Phone: (209) 225-6100
Fresno, CA 93703   Cynthia K. Meyer, Chf., Lib.Serv.

VALLEY MEDICAL CENTER OF FRESNO - MEDICAL LIBRARY
445 S. Cedar Ave.   Phone: (209) 453-5030
Fresno, CA 93702   Vicky Christianson, Med.Libn.

THE VINEYARD - REAL ESTATE, SHOPPING CENTER & URBAN
    DEVELOPMENT INFORMATION CENTER
50 W. Shaw Ave.   Phone: (209) 222-0182
Fresno, CA 93704   Richard Erganian, Info.Dir.

WEST COAST BIBLE COLLEGE - MC BRAYER LIBRARY - HUGHES MEMORIAL
    RESEARCH PENTECOSTAL CENTER
6901 N. Maple Ave.   Phone: (209) 299-7201
Fresno, CA 93710   Edward E. Call, Hd.Libn.

BECKMAN INSTRUMENTS, INC. - RESEARCH LIBRARY
2500 Harbor Blvd.   Phone: (714) 773-8906
Fullerton, CA 92634   Jean R. Miller, Chf.Libn.

CALIFORNIA STATE UNIVERSITY, FULLERTON - COLLECTION FOR THE
    HISTORY OF CARTOGRAPHY †
The Library, Rm. L444-B
800 N. State College Blvd.
Box 4150   Phone: (714) 773-3444
Fullerton, CA 92634   Linda E. Herman, Spec.Coll.Libn.

CALIFORNIA STATE UNIVERSITY, FULLERTON - LIBRARY - FREEDOM
    CENTER †
Box 4150   Phone: (714) 773-3186
Fullerton, CA 92634   Lynn M. Coppel, Coord.

FULLERTON COLLEGE - WILLIAM T. BOYCE LIBRARY - ARCHIVES
321 E. Chapman Ave.   Phone: (714) 871-8000
Fullerton, CA 92634   Anne Riley, Lib.Asst.

HUGHES AIRCRAFT COMPANY - GROUND SYSTEMS GROUP - TECHNICAL
   LIBRARY
Bldg. 600, M.S. C-222   Phone: (714) 732-3506
Fullerton, CA 92633   Don H. Matsumiya, Libn.

HUNT-WESSON FOODS - INFORMATION CENTER
1645 W. Valencia Dr.   Phone: (714) 680-2158
Fullerton, CA 92634   Joy Hastings, Mgr.

PACIFIC CHRISTIAN COLLEGE - HURST MEMORIAL LIBRARY
2500 E. Nutwood Ave.   Phone: (714) 879-3901
Fullerton, CA 92631   Jeffrey L. Wilson, Dir.

ST. JUDE HOSPITAL & REHABILITATION CENTER - MEDICAL LIBRARY
101 E. Valencia Mesa Dr.   Phone: (714) 871-3280
Fullerton, CA 92635   Barbara Garside, Med.Libn.

SOUTHERN CALIFORNIA COLLEGE OF OPTOMETRY - M.B. KETCHUM
   MEMORIAL LIBRARY
2001 Associated Rd.   Phone: (714) 870-7226
Fullerton, CA 92631   Mrs. Pat Carlson, Hd.Libn.

WESTERN STATE UNIVERSITY - COLLEGE OF LAW - LIBRARY †
1111 N. State College Blvd.   Phone: (714) 738-1000
Fullerton, CA 92631   Frank Phillips, Univ.Libn.

GARDEN GROVE HISTORICAL SOCIETY - E.G. WARE LIBRARY
12174 Euclid Ave.   Phone: (714) 530-8871
Garden Grove, CA 92640   Fred Coles, Pres.

ORANGE COUNTY TRANSIT DISTRICT - RESOURCE CENTER
11222 Acacia Pkwy.
Box 3005   Phone: (714) 971-6375
Garden Grove, CA 92642   Robin J. Masters, Rsrc.Spec.

HITCO - TECHNICAL LIBRARY
1600 W. 135th St.   Phone: (213) 516-5799
Gardena, CA 90249   Anita Hicks, Tech.Libn.

U.S. AIR FORCE BASE - GEORGE BASE LIBRARY †
FL 4812   Phone: (714) 269-3228
George AFB, CA 92392   Mrs. Frances Haysley, Base Libn.

JACK LONDON RESEARCH CENTER AND LIBRARY
14300 Arnold Dr.
Box 337   Phone: (707) 996-2888
Glen Ellen, CA 95442   Winifred Kingman, Libn.

GLENDALE ADVENTIST MEDICAL CENTER - LIBRARY
1509 Wilson Terrace   Phone: (818) 240-8000
Glendale, CA 91206   Eugenie Prime, Lib.Dir.

GLENDALE CITY - PLANNING DIVISION - TECHNICAL LIBRARY
633 E. Broadway   Phone: (818) 956-2144
Glendale, CA 91205   Gerald J. Jamriska, Dir. of Plan.

GLENDALE PUBLIC LIBRARY - BRAND LIBRARY
1601 W. Mountain St.   Phone: (818) 956-2051
Glendale, CA 91201   Jane Hagan, Lib.Serv.Supv.

GLENDALE PUBLIC LIBRARY - SPECIAL COLLECTIONS
222 E. Harvard St.   Phone: (818) 956-2037
Glendale, CA 91205   Barbara J. Boyd, Spec.Coll.Libn.

GLENDALE UNIVERSITY - COLLEGE OF LAW LIBRARY
220 N. Glendale Ave.   Phone: (818) 247-0770
Glendale, CA 91206   Timothy Sheehy, Libn.

REPUBLICAN ASSOCIATES OF LOS ANGELES COUNTY - RESEARCH LIBRARY
1153 N. Brand Blvd.   Phone: (818) 240-9100
Glendale, CA 91202   Mark S. Harmsen, Res.Dir.

SINGER COMPANY - LIBRASCOPE DIVISION - TECHNICAL INFORMATION
   CENTER
833 Sonora Ave.   Phone: (818) 244-6541
Glendale, CA 91201   Nathan J. Sands, Mgr.

SONS OF THE REVOLUTION IN THE STATE OF CALIFORNIA SOCIETY -
   LIBRARY
600 S. Central Ave.   Phone: (818) 240-1775
Glendale, CA 91204   Richard E. Coe, Lib.Dir.

WED ENTERPRISES - RESEARCH LIBRARY
1401 Flower St.   Phone: (818) 956-7263
Glendale, CA 91201   Joen B. Kommer, Mgr., Lib.Serv.

WOLFE (Harvey G.) LIBRARY
Box 3514   Phone: (818) 241-7284
Glendale, CA 91201   Douglas L. Evans, Libn.

EG&G, INC. - SANTA BARBARA DIVISION - LIBRARY
130 Robin Hill Rd.
Box 98   Phone: (805) 967-0456
Goleta, CA 93117   Kathy Barnett, Libn.

GENERAL MOTORS CORPORATION - DELCO SYSTEMS OPERATIONS -
   TECHNICAL LIBRARY
6767 Hollister Ave.   Phone: (805) 961-5080
Goleta, CA 93017   Kenneth C. Crombie, Tech.Libn.

HUGHES AIRCRAFT COMPANY - SANTA BARBARA RESEARCH CENTER -
   TECHNICAL LIBRARY
75 Coromar Dr.   Phone: (805) 968-3511
Goleta, CA 93117   Susan K. Gentry, Tech.Libn.

HUMAN FACTORS RESEARCH, INC. - TECHNICAL LIBRARY *
5775 Dawson Ave.   Phone: (805) 964-0591
Goleta, CA 93117   Paulette Moggia, Libn.

OCEANOGRAPHIC SERVICES, INC. - TECHNICAL LIBRARY
25 Castilian Dr.   Phone: (805) 685-4521
Goleta, CA 93117

RAYTHEON COMPANY - ELECTROMAGNETIC SYSTEMS DIVISION -
   ENGINEERING LIBRARY
6380 Hollister Ave.   Phone: (805) 967-5511
Goleta, CA 93117   S. Anderson, Libn.

SANTA BARBARA COUNTY GENEALOGICAL SOCIETY - LIBRARY
Box 1174
Goleta, CA 93116   Ruth B. Scollin, Libn.

SUNRAE LEARNING RESOURCES CENTER *
5679 Hollister Ave.   Phone: (805) 964-4483
Goleta, CA 93017   Kate Christensen, Libn.

BLOCH (Ernest) SOCIETY - ARCHIVES
34844 Old Stage Rd.   Phone: (707) 884-3473
Gualala, CA 95445   Lucienne Bloch Dimitroff, Supv.

KINGS COUNTY LAW LIBRARY
County Government Ctr.
Hanford, CA 93230   Jean H. Borraccino, Law Libn.

BAY HARBOR HOSPITAL - MEDICAL LIBRARY
1437 W. Lomita Blvd.   Phone: (213) 325-1221
Harbor City, CA 90710   Lily Yang, Med.Libn.

NORTHROP CORPORATION - AIRCRAFT DIVISION - LIBRARY SERVICES
One Northrop Ave.   Phone: (213) 970-4136
Hawthorne, CA 90250   John E. Reynolds, Lib.Mgr.

ALAMEDA COUNTY LAW LIBRARY
South County Branch
224 W. Winton Ave.   Phone: (415) 881-6380
Hayward, CA 94544   Cossette T. Sun, Law Lib.Dir.

ALAMEDA COUNTY PLANNING DEPARTMENT - STAFF LIBRARY *
399 Elmhurst St.   Phone: (415) 881-6401
Hayward, CA 94544

ALAMEDA COUNTY SUPERINTENDENT OF SCHOOLS - TEACHERS'
   PROFESSIONAL AND CURRICULUM LIBRARY
313 W. Winton Ave.   Phone: (415) 881-6372
Hayward, CA 94544-1198   Dr. Loretta M. Chin, Lib./Media Spec.

AQUATIC RESEARCH INSTITUTE - AQUATIC SCIENCES & TECHNOLOGY
  ARCHIVE
2242 Davis Court   Phone: (415) 785-2216
Hayward, CA 94545   V. Parker, Archv.

KAISER-PERMANENTE MEDICAL CENTER - HEALTH EDUCATION CENTER
27400 Hesprian Blvd.
Hayward, CA 94545   Lorinda Sheets, Health Educ.Coord.

KAISER-PERMANENTE MEDICAL CENTER - HEALTH SCIENCES LIBRARY †
27400 Hesperian Blvd.   Phone: (415) 784-5298
Hayward, CA 94545   Alice Pipes, Med.Libn.

HEMET VALLEY HOSPITAL DISTRICT - DR. LESLIE J. CLARK MEMORIAL
  LIBRARY
1116 E. Latham Ave.   Phone: (714) 652-2811
Hemet, CA 92343   Dixie Cirocco, Dir.

AMERICAN HARP SOCIETY REPOSITORY
6331 Quebec Dr.
Hollywood, CA 90068   Lucile H. Jennings, Proj.Dir.

DE FOREST RESEARCH, INC. - LIBRARY
5555 Melrose   Phone: (213) 469-2271
Hollywood, CA 90038   Kellam de Forest, Dir.

HOLLYWOOD COMMUNITY HOSPITAL - MEDICAL STAFF LIBRARY
6245 DeLongpre Ave.   Phone: (213) 462-2271
Hollywood, CA 90028   Beverly E. Carlton, Med.Libn.

HOLLYWOOD FILM ARCHIVE - LIBRARY
8344 Melrose Ave.   Phone: (213) 933-3345
Hollywood, CA 90069   D. Richard Baer, Dir.

HOMOSEXUAL INFORMATION CENTER - TANGENT GROUP
6758 Hollywood Blvd., No. 208   Phone: (213) 464-8431
Hollywood, CA 90028   Leslie Colfax, Libn.

MAX FACTOR & COMPANY - R & D LIBRARY
1655 N. McCadden Pl.   Phone: (213) 856-6648
Hollywood, CA 90028   Dawn A. Wingate, Libn.

TEMPLE ISRAEL OF HOLLYWOOD - JOSEPH H. CORWIN MEMORIAL
  LIBRARY *
7300 Hollywood Blvd.   Phone: (213) 876-8330
Hollywood, CA 90046

MC DONNELL DOUGLAS CORPORATION - MC DONNELL DOUGLAS
  ASTRONAUTICS COMPANY - TECHNICAL LIBRARY SERVICES
5301 Bolsa Ave.   Phone: (714) 896-2317
Huntington Beach, CA 92647   Sandra L. Killian, Supv., Lib.Serv.

TRICO-KOBE, INC. - ENGINEERING LIBRARY
3040 E. Slauson Ave.   Phone: (213) 588-1271
Huntington Park, CA 90255   Zenny Mamdani, Engr.Adm.Asst.

NAPA STATE HOSPITAL - WRENSHALL A. OLIVER PROFESSIONAL LIBRARY
Box A   Phone: (707) 253-5477
Imola, CA 94558   Malcolm Reynolds, Sr.Libn.

INYO COUNTY LAW LIBRARY
168 N. Edwards
Drawer K   Phone: (619) 878-2411
Independence, CA 93526

INDIO COMMUNITY HOSPITAL - MEDICAL LIBRARY
47-111 Monroe St.   Phone: (619) 347-6191
Indio, CA 92201   Dan Dickinson, Med.Libn.

RIVERSIDE COUNTY LAW LIBRARY - INDIO LAW LIBRARY
46-209 Oasis St.
Indio, CA 92201   Marilyn Stafford, Sr.Lib.Ck.

SPECTROL ELECTRONICS CORPORATION - LIBRARY *
17070 E. Gale Ave.
Box 1220   Phone: (213) 964-6565
Industry, CA 91749   James Roehrich, Engr. Standards Supv.

CENTINELA HOSPITAL MEDICAL CENTER - EDWIN W. DEAN MEMORIAL
  LIBRARY
555 E. Hardy St.
Box 720   Phone: (213) 673-4660
Inglewood, CA 90307   Jeanne Spala, Dir.

NORTHROP UNIVERSITY - ALUMNI LIBRARY - SPECIAL COLLECTIONS †
1155 W. Arbor Vitae St.   Phone: (213) 776-5466
Inglewood, CA 90306   Chere Negaard, Dir., Lib.Serv.

PANEL DISPLAYS, INC. - TECHNICAL LIBRARY
211 S. Hindry Ave.   Phone: (213) 641-6661
Inglewood, CA 90301   K.O. Fugate, Pres. & Libn.

ALLERGAN PHARMACEUTICALS, INC. - MEDICAL & SCIENCE
  INFORMATION
2525 Dupont Dr.   Phone: (714) 752-4500
Irvine, CA 92713   Carolyn Henderson, Mgr.

OCCIDENTAL RESEARCH CORPORATION - TECHNICAL INFORMATION
  CENTER †
2100 S.E. Main
Box 19601   Phone: (714) 957-7450
Irvine, CA 92713   Patricia M. Petring, Mgr., Tech.Info.Serv.

UNIVERSITY OF CALIFORNIA, IRVINE - BIOLOGICAL SCIENCES LIBRARY
                                              Phone: (714) 856-6730
Irvine, CA 92717   Margaret Aguirre, Lib.Asst.

UNIVERSITY OF CALIFORNIA, IRVINE - BIOMEDICAL LIBRARY
Box 19556   Phone: (714) 856-6652
Irvine, CA 92713   F. Raymond Long, Asst.Univ.Libn.

UNIVERSITY OF CALIFORNIA, IRVINE - INSTITUTE OF TRANSPORTATION
  STUDIES - RESOURCE CENTER
Rm. 150 SST   Phone: (714) 856-6564
Irvine, CA 92717   Lyn Wong, Libn.

AMADOR COUNTY LAW LIBRARY
108 Court St.   Phone: (209) 223-3230
Jackson, CA 95642   Catherine J. Montgomery, Law Lib.Ck.

UNITED FARM WORKERS OF AMERICA, AFL-CIO - I.C. LIBRARY
La Paz   Phone: (805) 822-5571
Keene, CA 93531   Garland Taylor, Dir.

CHEVRON OIL FIELD RESEARCH COMPANY - TECHNICAL INFORMATION
  SERVICES
Box 446   Phone: (213) 694-7500
La Habra, CA 90631   Ann S. Coppin, Supv.

AMERICAN HOECHST CORPORATION - BEHRING DIAGNOSTICS - LIBRARY
10933 N. Torrey Pines Rd.   Phone: (619) 450-5645
La Jolla, CA 92037   Aznive Sabonjian, Libn.

COPLEY PRESS, INC. - THE JAMES S. COPLEY LIBRARY
Box 1530   Phone: (619) 454-0411
La Jolla, CA 92038   Richard Reilly, Cur.

LA JOLLA MUSEUM OF CONTEMPORARY ART - HELEN PALMER GEISEL
  LIBRARY
700 Prospect St.   Phone: (619) 454-3541
La Jolla, CA 92037   Gail Richardson, Libn.

LIBRARY ASSOCIATION OF LA JOLLA - ATHENAEUM MUSIC AND ARTS
  LIBRARY
1008 Wall St.   Phone: (619) 454-5872
La Jolla, CA 92037   Evelyn Neumann, Lib.Adm.

S-CUBED - TECHNICAL LIBRARY
Box 1620   Phone: (619) 453-0060
La Jolla, CA 92038-1620   LaDonna L. Rowe, Libn.

SCRIPPS CLINIC & RESEARCH FOUNDATION - KRESGE MEDICAL LIBRARY
10666 N. Torrey Pines Rd.   Phone: (619) 455-8705
La Jolla, CA 92037   Jesse G. Neely, Med.Libn.

U.S. NATL. MARINE FISHERIES SERVICE - SOUTHWEST FISHERIES
  CENTER - LIBRARY
Box 271   Phone: (619) 453-2820
La Jolla, CA 92038   Dan Gittings, Libn.

UNIVERSITY OF CALIFORNIA, SAN DIEGO - BIOMEDICAL LIBRARY
                                     Phone: (619) 452-3253
La Jolla, CA 92093   Mary Horres, Libn.

UNIVERSITY OF CALIFORNIA, SAN DIEGO - SCIENCE & ENGINEERING
  LIBRARY
C-075E   Phone: (619) 452-3257
La Jolla, CA 92093   Beverlee French, Libn.

UNIVERSITY OF CALIFORNIA, SAN DIEGO - SCRIPPS INSTITUTION OF
  OCEANOGRAPHY LIBRARY
                                     Phone: (619) 452-3274
La Jolla, CA 92093   William J. Goff, Libn.

UNIVERSITY OF CALIFORNIA, SAN DIEGO - UNIVERSITY LIBRARIES
                                     Phone: (619) 452-3336
La Jolla, CA 92093   Millicent D. Abell, Univ.Libn.

BIOLA UNIVERSITY - LIBRARY *
13800 Biola Ave.   Phone: (213) 944-0351
La Mirada, CA 90639   Gerald L. Gooden, Dir.

DENNY'S INC. - COMPUTER SERVICES LIBRARY *
14256 E. Firestone Blvd.   Phone: (714) 739-8100
La Mirada, CA 90637   Penny Shubnell, Tech.Libn.

UNIVERSITY OF LA VERNE - COLLEGE OF LAW - LIBRARY
1950 3rd St.   Phone: (714) 593-7184
La Verne, CA 91750   Suzanne Miller, Law Libn.

SOYFOODS CENTER LIBRARY
Box 234   Phone: (415) 283-2991
Lafayette, CA 94549   William R. Shurtleff, Dir.

U.S. NATL. ARCHIVES & RECORDS SERVICE - FEDERAL ARCHIVES AND
  RECORDS CENTER, REGION 9
24000 Avila Rd.   Phone: (714) 831-4220
Laguna Niguel, CA 92677   Kenneth F. Rossman, Dir.

LAKE COUNTY HISTORICAL SOCIETY - MUSEUM LIBRARY
175 3rd St.
Box 1011   Phone: (707) 263-4555
Lakeport, CA 95453

U.S. ARMY - SPECIAL SERVICES DIVISION - SHARPE ARMY DEPOT -
  LIBRARY
                                     Phone: (209) 982-2404
Lathrop, CA 95331   Donna Eaton, Lib.Techn.

U.S. NAVY - NAVAL AIR STATION (CA-Lemoore) - LIBRARY
Bldg. 821   Phone: (209) 998-3144
Lemoore, CA 93245   Lois C. Gruntorad, Libn.

LAWRENCE LIVERMORE NATIONAL LABORATORY - TECHNICAL
  INFORMATION DEPARTMENT LIBRARY
Box 808   Phone: (415) 422-5277
Livermore, CA 94550   John B. Verity, Lib.Mgr.

SANDIA NATIONAL LABORATORIES - TECHNICAL LIBRARY †
Box 969   Phone: (415) 422-2525
Livermore, CA 94550   M.A. Pound, Supv.

U.S. VETERANS ADMINISTRATION (CA-Livermore) - MEDICAL LIBRARY
Arroyo Rd.   Phone: (415) 447-2560
Livermore, CA 94550   Jane H. Levie, Chf.Libn.

SAN JOAQUIN COUNTY HISTORICAL MUSEUM
Micke Grove Pk.
Box 21   Phone: (209) 368-9154
Lodi, CA 95240   Michael W. Bennett, Musm.Dir.

LOMA LINDA UNIVERSITY - DEL E. WEBB MEMORIAL LIBRARY
                                     Phone: (714) 824-4550
Loma Linda, CA 92350   H. Maynard Lowry, Dir.

LOMA LINDA UNIVERSITY - NIELS BJORN JORGENSEN MEMORIAL LIBRARY
  †
School of Dentistry   Phone: (714) 796-0141
Loma Linda, CA 92350   Carol Richardson, Libn.

U.S. VETERANS ADMINISTRATION (CA-Loma Linda) - HOSPITAL LIBRARY
  SERVICE
11201 Benton St.   Phone: (714) 825-7084
Loma Linda, CA 92357   Kathleen M. Puffer, Chf.

LA PURISIMA MISSION - ARCHIVES
La Purisima Mission State Historic Pk.
R.F.D. Box 102   Phone: (805) 733-3713
Lompoc, CA 93436   Ronald J. Dupuy, Interpretive Ranger

LOMPOC MUSEUM - LIBRARY *
200 South H St.   Phone: (805) 736-3888
Lompoc, CA 93436   Lucille Christie, Dir.

U.S. AIR FORCE BASE - VANDENBERG BASE LIBRARY
Vandenberg AFB, Bldg. 10317   Phone: (805) 866-6414
Lompoc, CA 93437   Joseph L. Buelna, Base Libn.

CALIFORNIA STATE UNIVERSITY, LONG BEACH - MUSIC-FINE ARTS
  DEPARTMENT - LIBRARY
5400 Bellflower Blvd.   Phone: (213) 498-4023
Long Beach, CA 90840

ERTEC WESTERN, INC. - LIBRARY †
3777 Long Beach Blvd.   Phone: (213) 595-6611
Long Beach, CA 90807   Fia Vitar, Libn.

FIRST BAPTIST CHURCH OF LAKEWOOD - CHURCH LIBRARY *
5336 Arbor Rd.   Phone: (213) 420-1471
Long Beach, CA 90808   Judy L. Hughes, Libn.

HISTORICAL SOCIETY OF LONG BEACH - ARCHIVES
1150 E. 4th St.
Box 1869   Phone: (213) 435-7511
Long Beach, CA 90801   Zona Gale Forbes, Archv./Libn.

LONG BEACH CITY COLLEGE - PACIFIC COAST CAMPUS LIBRARY
1305 E. Pacific Coast Hwy.   Phone: (213) 420-4548
Long Beach, CA 90806   John L. Ayala, Lib.Dir./Assoc.Prof.

LONG BEACH COMMUNITY HOSPITAL - MEDICAL LIBRARY
1720 Termino Ave.   Phone: (213) 597-6655
Long Beach, CA 90801   Lois O. Clark, Med.Libn.

LONG BEACH MUSEUM OF ART - LIBRARY
2300 E. Ocean Blvd.   Phone: (213) 439-2119
Long Beach, CA 90803   Kent Smith, Cur.

LONG BEACH PRESS-TELEGRAM - LIBRARY
604 Pine Ave.   Phone: (213) 435-1161
Long Beach, CA 90844   Violet R. Phillips, Hd.Libn.

LONG BEACH PUBLIC LIBRARY - CALIFORNIA PETROLEUM INDUSTRY
  COLLECTION
101 Pacific Ave.   Phone: (213) 437-2949
Long Beach, CA 90802   James Jackson, Dept.Libn.

LONG BEACH PUBLIC LIBRARY - LITERATURE AND HISTORY DEPARTMENT
101 Pacific Ave.   Phone: (213) 437-2949
Long Beach, CA 90802   Harriet Friis, Dept.Hd.

LONG BEACH PUBLIC LIBRARY - PERFORMING ARTS DEPARTMENT
101 Pacific Ave.   Phone: (213) 437-2949
Long Beach, CA 90802   Barbara Davis, Dept.Hd.

LONG BEACH PUBLIC LIBRARY - RANCHO LOS CERRITOS MUSEUM -
  LIBRARY
4600 Virginia Rd.   Phone: (213) 424-9423
Long Beach, CA 90807   Ellen Calomiris, Hist.Cur.

LONG BEACH UNIFIED SCHOOL DISTRICT - PROFESSIONAL LIBRARY
701 Locust Ave.
Long Beach, CA 90813

LOS ANGELES COUNTY/LONG BEACH GENERAL HOSPITAL - MEDICAL
   LIBRARY *
2597 Redondo Ave.   Phone: (213) 636-0784
Long Beach, CA 90806   Thomas P. Dengler, Med.Libn.

MC DONNELL DOUGLAS CORPORATION - DOUGLAS AIRCRAFT COMPANY -
   TECHNICAL LIBRARY
3855 Lakewood Blvd.   Phone: (213) 593-9541
Long Beach, CA 90846   Pat M. Ackerman, Sect.Mgr.

MEMORIAL HOSPITAL MEDICAL CENTER OF LONG BEACH - MEDICAL
   LIBRARY †
2801 Atlantic Ave.
Box 1428   Phone: (213) 595-3841
Long Beach, CA 90801   Frances Lyon, Dir. of Lib.Serv.

PACIFIC HOSPITAL OF LONG BEACH - MEDICAL STAFF LIBRARY †
2776 Pacific Ave.
Box 1268   Phone: (213) 595-1911
Long Beach, CA 90801   Lois E. Harris, Dir., Lib. & AV Serv.

ST. MARY MEDICAL CENTER - BELLIS MEDICAL LIBRARY
1050 Linden Ave.
Box 887   Phone: (213) 435-4441
Long Beach, CA 90801-0887   Emily L. Giustino, Dir.

U.S. NAVY - NAVAL SHIPYARD (CA-Long Beach) - TECHNICAL LIBRARY
Code 202.4, Bldg. 300, Rm. 358   Phone: (213) 547-6515
Long Beach, CA 90822   Mari S. Zeoli, Libn.

U.S. VETERANS ADMINISTRATION (CA-Long Beach) - MEDICAL CENTER
   LIBRARY
5901 E. Seventh St.   Phone: (213) 498-1313
Long Beach, CA 90822   Betty F. Connolly, Chf., Lib.Serv.

WRATHER PORT PROPERTIES, LTD. - ARCHIVES AND RESOURCE CENTER
RMS Queen Mary
Box 8   Phone: (213) 435-4747
Long Beach, CA 90801   Richard Gano, Dir., Exhibits

SOUTHWEST REGIONAL LABORATORY FOR EDUCATIONAL RESEARCH AND
   DEVELOPMENT - LIBRARY *
4665 Lampson Ave.   Phone: (213) 598-7661
Los Alamitos, CA 90720   Louise D. Riedel, Libn.

CONGREGATION BETH AM - LIBRARY †
26790 Arastradero Rd.   Phone: (415) 493-4661
Los Altos Hills, CA 94022   Ken Fehl, Chm., Lib.Comm.

PERHAM FOUNDATION - FOOTHILL ELECTRONICS MUSEUM - DE FOREST
   MEMORIAL ARCHIVES
12345 El Monte Rd.   Phone: (415) 948-8590
Los Altos Hills, CA 94022   Len Lansdowne, Cur.

ADAMS, DUQUE & HAZELTINE - LIBRARY
523 W. 6th St.   Phone: (213) 620-1240
Los Angeles, CA 90014   Randall J. Gray, Dir. of Info.Serv.

AEROSPACE CORPORATION - CHARLES C. LAURITSEN LIBRARY
Box 92957, Sta. M1-199   Phone: (213) 648-6738
Los Angeles, CA 90009   Edythe Moore, Mgr., Lib.Serv.

AMERICAN FILM INSTITUTE - LOUIS B. MAYER LIBRARY
2021 N. Western Ave.
Box 27999   Phone: (213) 856-7655
Los Angeles, CA 90027   Anne G. Schlosser, Lib.Dir.

AMERICAN SOCIETY OF MILITARY HISTORY - LIBRARY
1816 S. Figueroa St.   Phone: (213) 746-1776
Los Angeles, CA 90015   Donald Michelson, Exec.Dir.

AMERICAN UNIVERSITY OF ORIENTAL STUDIES - LIBRARY
2835 W. Olympic Blvd.   Phone: (213) 487-1235
Los Angeles, CA 90006   Edward Krafchow, Libn.

ARCHDIOCESE OF LOS ANGELES - CHANCERY ARCHIVES
1531 W. Ninth St.   Phone: (213) 388-8108
Los Angeles, CA 90015   Msgr. Francis J. Weber, Archv.

ARNOLD SCHOENBERG INSTITUTE - ARCHIVES
University of Southern California
University Park - MC 1101   Phone: (213) 743-5393
Los Angeles, CA 90089-1101   Jerry McBride, Act.Archv.

ASOCIACION NACIONAL PRO PERSONAS MAYORES - LIBRARY
1730 W. Olympic Blvd., Suite 401   Phone: (213) 487-1922
Los Angeles, CA 90015   Carmela G. Lacayo, Natl.Exec.Dir.

ATLANTIC RICHFIELD COMPANY - CORPORATE ARCHIVES
515 S. Flower St., WIB 800   Phone: (213) 486-1962
Los Angeles, CA 90071   Roxanne Burg, Archv.

ATLANTIC-RICHFIELD COMPANY - GOVERNMENT RESOURCE CENTER †
515 S. Flower St., Rm. 4010   Phone: (213) 486-0777
Los Angeles, CA 90071   Esther Eastman, Coord.

ATLANTIC-RICHFIELD COMPANY - INFORMATION RESEARCH CENTER
Box 2679, Terminal Annex   Phone: (213) 486-2400
Los Angeles, CA 90051   Meryl H. Swanigan, Mgr.

ATLANTIC-RICHFIELD COMPANY - PHOTOGRAPHY COLLECTION
515 S. Flower St., Suite 300   Phone: (213) 486-3386
Los Angeles, CA 90071   Mildred Simpson, Libn.

AUTOMOBILE CLUB OF SOUTHERN CALIFORNIA - TECHNICAL
   INFORMATION CENTER
Term. Annex, Box 2890   Phone: (213) 741-4490
Los Angeles, CA 90051   Donnalee L. Simmons, Libn./Info.Spec.

BANK OF AMERICA - SOUTHERN CALIFORNIA HEADQUARTERS - LAW
   LIBRARY NO. 4017
555 S. Flower St.   Phone: (213) 228-3101
Los Angeles, CA 90071   Kathleen G. Slattery, Law Libn.

BARLOW HOSPITAL - ELKS LIBRARY
2000 Stadium Way   Phone: (213) 628-4165
Los Angeles, CA 90026   Rose Thompson, Libn.

BATEMAN EICHLER, HILL RICHARDS, INC. - RESEARCH LIBRARY
700 S. Flower St.   Phone: (213) 625-3545
Los Angeles, CA 90013   Paula DeMaria, Libn.

BECHTEL POWER CORPORATION - LIBRARY
12440 E. Imperial Hwy.
Box 60860, Terminal Annex   Phone: (213) 807-3545
Los Angeles, CA 90060   Jean Gregory, Chf.Libn.

BRAILLE INSTITUTE OF AMERICA - LIBRARY
741 N. Vermont Ave.   Phone: (213) 660-3880
Los Angeles, CA 90029   Phyllis Cairns, Lib.Dir.

BROWNSTEIN (Richard A.) LAW OFFICES - LIBRARY
520 S. Virgil, Suite 300   Phone: (213) 739-9320
Los Angeles, CA 90020

CALIFORNIA FEDERAL SAVINGS AND LOAN ASSOCIATION - MANAGEMENT
   LIBRARY
5670 Wilshire Blvd.   Phone: (213) 932-4655
Los Angeles, CA 90036   Pamela J. Taranto, Libn.

CALIFORNIA HISTORICAL SOCIETY - HISTORY CENTER LIBRARY
6300 Wilshire Blvd.   Phone: (213) 651-5655
Los Angeles, CA 90048   Louise Braunschweiger, Dir.

CALIFORNIA HOSPITAL MEDICAL CENTER - MEDICAL STAFF LIBRARY
1414 South Hope St.   Phone: (213) 748-2411
Los Angeles, CA 90015   Cheryl Duran, Ph.D., Dir.

CALIFORNIA SCHOOL OF PROFESSIONAL PSYCHOLOGY - LOS ANGELES
   LIBRARY
2235 Beverly Blvd.   Phone: (213) 483-7034
Los Angeles, CA 90057   Tobeylynn Birch, Hd.Libn.

CALIFORNIA STATE - COLORADO RIVER BOARD OF CALIFORNIA - LIBRARY
107 S. Broadway, Rm. 8103   Phone: (213) 620-4480
Los Angeles, CA 90012   Loretta E. Austin, Tech.Lib.Asst.

CALIFORNIA STATE - COURT OF APPEAL, 2ND APPELLATE DISTRICT -
 LAW LIBRARY
3580 Wilshire Blvd., Rm. 448   Phone: (213) 736-2661
Los Angeles, CA 90010   Cheryl Stanwood, Law Libn.

CALIFORNIA STATE DEPARTMENT OF CORPORATIONS - LAW LIBRARY
600 S. Commonwealth, 16th Fl.   Phone: (213) 736-3632
Los Angeles, CA 90005   Sharon Akey, Sr.Libn.

CALIFORNIA STATE DEPARTMENT OF JUSTICE - ATTORNEY GENERAL'S
 OFFICE - LAW LIBRARY
3580 Wilshire Blvd., Rm. 701   Phone: (213) 736-2196
Los Angeles, CA 90010   Janet T. Whitney, Supv.Libn.

CALIFORNIA STATE DEPARTMENT OF TRANSPORTATION - DISTRICT 7
 LIBRARY
120 N. Spring St.   Phone: (213) 620-5500
Los Angeles, CA 90012   Alyce L. Davis, Sr.Libn.

CALIFORNIA STATE UNIVERSITY, LOS ANGELES - SCIENCE AND
 TECHNOLOGY REFERENCE ROOM †
John F. Kennedy Memorial Library
5151 State University Dr.   Phone: (213) 224-2232
Los Angeles, CA 90032   Cornelia O. Balogh, Act.Hd.

CAPITAL RESEARCH COMPANY - RESEARCH LIBRARY
333 S. Hope St., 51st Fl.   Phone: (213) 486-9261
Los Angeles, CA 90071   S. Kathleen Reilly, Mgr., Lib.Serv.

CARNATION COMPANY - LIBRARY †
5045 Wilshire Blvd.   Phone: (213) 932-6558
Los Angeles, CA 90036   Vicki C. Giella, Info.Ctr.Coord.

CEDARS-SINAI MEDICAL CENTER - HEALTH SCIENCES INFORMATION
 CENTER
8700 Beverly Blvd.
Box 48956   Phone: (213) 855-3751
Los Angeles, CA 90048   Ellen Wilson Green, Dir. of Libs.

CENTER FOR COMPUTER/LAW - LIBRARY
Box 54308 T.A.   Phone: (312) 372-0198
Los Angeles, CA 90054   Michael D. Scott, Exec.Dir.

CENTER FOR EARLY EDUCATION - LAURA M. ELLIS MEMORIAL LIBRARY
563 N. Alfred St.   Phone: (213) 655-4878
Los Angeles, CA 90048   Janice M. Eastman, Libn.

CENTER FOR ULCER RESEARCH AND EDUCATION FOUNDATION (CURE) -
 LIBRARY
VA Wadsworth Hospital Center
Bldg. 115, Rm. 217   Phone: (217) 206-6603
Los Angeles, CA 90073   Leona Green, Exec.Sec.

CHILDREN'S HOSPITAL OF LOS ANGELES - MEDICAL LIBRARY *
4650 Sunset Blvd.   Phone: (213) 663-3341
Los Angeles, CA 90027

CHURCH OF JESUS CHRIST OF LATTER-DAY SAINTS - SOUTHERN
 CALIFORNIA AREA GENEALOGICAL LIBRARY
10741 Santa Monica Blvd.   Phone: (213) 474-9990
Los Angeles, CA 90025   Fred E. Klingman, Pres.

CITIZENS' RESEARCH FOUNDATION - LIBRARY
Research Annex, 3716 S. Hope St.
University of Southern California   Phone: (213) 743-5440
Los Angeles, CA 90007   Herbert E. Alexander, Dir.

COOPERS & LYBRAND - LIBRARY
1000 W. 6th St.   Phone: (213) 481-1000
Los Angeles, CA 90017   Joan Schlimgen, Libn.

CRAFT AND FOLK ART MUSEUM - LIBRARY/MEDIA RESOURCE CENTER
5814 Wilshire Blvd.   Phone: (213) 937-5544
Los Angeles, CA 90036   Joan M. Benedetti, Musm.Libn.

DAMES & MOORE - LIBRARY
445 S. Figueroa St.   Phone: (213) 683-1560
Los Angeles, CA 90071-1665   Alice M. Ohst, Libn.

DANIEL FREEMAN MEMORIAL HOSPITAL - MEDICAL LIBRARY & RESOURCE
 CENTER
333 N. Prairie Ave.   Phone: (213) 674-7050
Los Angeles, CA 90301   Gillian Olechno, Dir.

DANIEL, MANN, JOHNSON AND MENDENHALL - LIBRARY
3250 Wilshire Blvd.   Phone: (213) 381-3663
Los Angeles, CA 90010   Marlene Barkley, Mgr., Info.Serv.

DOCUMENTATION ASSOCIATES
Box 84005   Phone: (213) 477-5081
Los Angeles, CA 90073   Skye Atman, Pres.

DOHENY (Estelle) EYE FOUNDATION - KENNETH T. NORRIS, JR. VISUAL
 SCIENCE LIBRARY
1355 San Pablo St.   Phone: (213) 224-7744
Los Angeles, CA 90033   David Morse, Libn.

DOYLE DANE BERNBACH/WEST - RESEARCH LIBRARY
5900 Wilshire Blvd.   Phone: (213) 937-5100
Los Angeles, CA 90036   Lois S. Steinmann, Mgr., Info.Serv.

ECOLOGY CENTER OF SOUTHERN CALIFORNIA
P.O. Box 35473   Phone: (213) 559-9160
Los Angeles, CA 90035   Nancy Pearlman, Exec.Dir.

ECONOMICS RESEARCH ASSOCIATES - LIBRARY
10960 Wilshire Blvd.   Phone: (213) 477-9585
Los Angeles, CA 90024   Barbara J. Thompson, Libn.

ELYSIUM ARCHIVES
5436 Fernwood Ave.   Phone: (213) 465-7121
Los Angeles, CA 90027   R. Gerowitz, Res.

ERIC CLEARINGHOUSE FOR JUNIOR COLLEGES
University of California, Los Angeles
8118 Math Sciences Bldg.   Phone: (213) 825-3931
Los Angeles, CA 90024   Arthur M. Cohen, Dir.

ERNST & WHINNEY - LIBRARY
515 S. Flower St.   Phone: (213) 621-1666
Los Angeles, CA 90071   Jeffrey M. Lambert, Libn.

FARMERS INSURANCE GROUP, INC. - LIBRARY
4680 Wilshire Blvd.   Phone: (213) 932-3615
Los Angeles, CA 90010   Debra Rogenmoser, Libn.

FASHION INSTITUTE OF DESIGN & MERCHANDISING - RESOURCE AND
 RESEARCH CENTER †
818 W. 7th St.   Phone: (213) 624-1200
Los Angeles, CA 90017   Kaycee Hale, Dir.

FIRST INTERSTATE BANK ATHLETIC FOUNDATION - LIBRARY
2141 W. Adams Blvd.   Phone: (213) 614-2995
Los Angeles, CA 90018   W.R. Bill Schroeder, Mng.Dir.

FIRST INTERSTATE BANK OF CALIFORNIA - LIBRARY
Terminal Annex
Box 3666   Phone: (213) 614-4097
Los Angeles, CA 90051   Peggy Wilson, Info.Off./Chf.Libn.

GATEWAYS HOSPITAL AND COMMUNITY MENTAL HEALTH CENTER -
 PROFESSIONAL LIBRARY
1891 Effie St.   Phone: (213) 666-0171
Los Angeles, CA 90026   Celia A. Palant, Libn.

GETTY OIL COMPANY, INC. - CORPORATE LIBRARY †
Box 54050   Phone: (213) 739-2275
Los Angeles, CA 90054   Mary Krupp, Adm., Corp.Lib.

GIBSON, DUNN & CRUTCHER - LAW LIBRARY
333 S. Grand Ave.   Phone: (213) 229-7216
Los Angeles, CA 90071   Irwin G. Manley, Adm., Info.Serv.

GREATER LOS ANGELES ZOO ASSOCIATION - LIBRARY
Andrew Norman Education Ctr.
5333 Zoo Dr.   Phone: (213) 664-1100
Los Angeles, CA 90027   Ruth Anne Barton, Chm., Lib.Commn.

GREENBERG, GLUSKER, FIELDS CLAMAN & MACHTINGER - LIBRARY
1900 Avenue of the Stars
Los Angeles, CA 90067   Lisa Winslow, Law Libn.

GRIFFITH OBSERVATORY - LIBRARY
2800 E. Observatory Rd.   Phone: (213) 664-1181
Los Angeles, CA 90027   Dr. E.C. Krupp, Dir.

HANCOCK (Allan) FOUNDATION - HANCOCK LIBRARY OF BIOLOGY & OCEANOGRAPHY
University Park
University of Southern California   Phone: (213) 743-6005
Los Angeles, CA 90089-0371   Kimberly Douglas, Dir.

HEBREW UNION COLLEGE - JEWISH INSTITUTE OF RELIGION - FRANCES-HENRY LIBRARY
3077 University Ave.   Phone: (213) 749-3424
Los Angeles, CA 90007   Harvey P. Horowitz, Libn.

HILL, FARRER & BURRILL - LAW LIBRARY *
445 S. Figueroa St.
Union Bank Bldg., 34th Fl.   Phone: (213) 620-0460
Los Angeles, CA 90071   Fleur C. Osmanson, Libn.

HOLLYWOOD PRESBYTERIAN MEDICAL CENTER - HEALTH SCIENCES LIBRARY
1300 N. Vermont Ave.   Phone: (213) 660-3530
Los Angeles, CA 90027   Erika M. Hansen, Med.Libn.

HOSPITAL OF THE GOOD SAMARITAN - MEDICAL LIBRARY
616 S. Witmer St.   Phone: (213) 977-2326
Los Angeles, CA 90017   Elizabeth Sherson, Med.Libn.

HOUSE EAR INSTITUTE - GEORGE KELEMEN LIBRARY
256 S. Lake St.   Phone: (213) 483-4431
Los Angeles, CA 90057   Ron Charbonneau, Res.Libn.

HOUSE EAR INSTITUTE - PARENT RESOURCE LIBRARY
256 S. Lake St.   Phone: (213) 483-4431
Los Angeles, CA 90057   Sr. Mark Szczepanik, Coord., Rsrc.Ctr.

HUGHES AIRCRAFT COMPANY - EL SEGUNDO LIBRARY
S-12, Mail Sta. V311
Box 92919   Phone: (213) 648-4192
Los Angeles, CA 90009   Susan G. Clifford, Lib.Supv.

IMODCO - BUSINESS LIBRARY
10960 Wilshire Blvd., Suite 1100   Phone: (213) 477-1441
Los Angeles, CA 91405   Laura Frakes, Libn.

INNER CITY CULTURAL CENTER - LANGSTON HUGHES MEMORIAL LIBRARY †
1308 S. New Hampshire Ave.   Phone: (213) 387-1161
Los Angeles, CA 90006   Fred Beauford, Lib.Cons.

INSTITUTE OF THE AMERICAN MUSICAL, INC. - LIBRARY
121 N. Detroit St.   Phone: (213) 934-1221
Los Angeles, CA 90036   Miles M. Kreuger, Cur.

INSTITUTE FOR STUDIES OF DESTRUCTIVE BEHAVIORS AND THE SUICIDE PREVENTION CENTER - HAROLD M. HILDRETH MEMORIAL LIB.
1041 S. Menlo Ave.
Los Angeles, CA 90006

INSURANCE EDUCATIONAL ASSOCIATION - THE INSURANCE LIBRARY OF LOS ANGELES
1541 Wilshire Blvd., Suite 106   Phone: (213) 738-9973
Los Angeles, CA 90017   Kathryn Lee, Libn.

IRELL & MANELLA - LIBRARY
1800 Ave. of the Stars, Suite 900   Phone: (213) 277-1010
Los Angeles, CA 90067   Louise Laughlin Lieb, Lib.Adm.

JEWISH FEDERATION COUNCIL OF GREATER LOS ANGELES - PETER M. KAHN JEWISH COMMUNITY LIBRARY
6505 Wilshire Blvd.   Phone: (213) 852-1234
Los Angeles, CA 90048   Mrs. Hava Ben-Zvi, Libn.

JONES, DAY, REAVIS & POGUE - LIBRARY
2029 Century Park E., 36th Fl.   Phone: (213) 553-3939
Los Angeles, CA 90067   I. Jean Stevens, Libn.

JUNG (C.G.) INSTITUTE OF LOS ANGELES, INC. - MAX AND LORE ZELLER LIBRARY
10349 West Pico Blvd.   Phone: (213) 556-1193
Los Angeles, CA 90064   Claire Oksner, Dir.

KADISON, PFAELZER, WOODARD, QUINN & ROSSI - LAW LIBRARY
707 Wilshire Blvd., 40th Fl.   Phone: (213) 688-9000
Los Angeles, CA 90017   Diane G. Sapienza, Law Libn.

KAISER FOUNDATION HOSPITAL - MANAGEMENT EFFECTIVENESS LIBRARY
4747 Sunset Blvd.   Phone: (213) 667-5460
Los Angeles, CA 90027   Marilyn Crawford, Libn.

KAISER-PERMANENTE MEDICAL CENTER - KAISER FOUNDATION HOSPITAL MEDICAL LIBRARY
4867 Sunset Blvd.   Phone: (213) 667-8568
Los Angeles, CA 90027   Judith A. Dowd, Dept.Hd.

KAISER-PERMANENTE MENTAL HEALTH CENTER - LIBRARY
765 College St.   Phone: (213) 378-3522
Los Angeles, CA 90012   L.G. Hirschfeld, Libn.

KINDEL & ANDERSON - LIBRARY †
555 S. Flower St., 26th Fl.   Phone: (213) 680-2222
Los Angeles, CA 90071   Marie Wallace, Law Libn.

KOREAN CULTURAL SERVICE - LIBRARY
5505 Wilshire Blvd.   Phone: (213) 936-7141
Los Angeles, CA 90036   Kyung Eun Aum, Libn.

LATHAM & WATKINS - LAW LIBRARY
555 S. Flower St.   Phone: (213) 485-1234
Los Angeles, CA 90071   Marie G. Wallace, Law Libn.

LAWLER, FELIX & HALL - LAW LIBRARY
700 S. Flower St.   Phone: (213) 629-9513
Los Angeles, CA 90017   C.M. Palmer, Libn.

LAWRY'S FOODS, INC. - LIBRARY
570 West Ave. 26   Phone: (213) 225-2491
Los Angeles, CA 90065   Susan Newcomer, Corp.Libn.

LEVENTHAL (Kenneth) & COMPANY - LIBRARY
2049 Century Park E., 17th Fl.   Phone: (213) 277-0880
Los Angeles, CA 90067   Linda Nauman, Natl.Libn.

LILLICK MC HOSE & CHARLES, ATTORNEYS AT LAW - LAW LIBRARY
707 Wilshire Blvd., Suite 4500   Phone: (213) 620-9000
Los Angeles, CA 90017   Mary Lou Straub, Law Libn.

LOCARE MOTION PICTURE RESEARCH GROUP - LIBRARY
1615 N. Laurel Ave.   Phone: (213) 656-4420
Los Angeles, CA 90046   Bebe Bergsten, Libn.

LOEB AND LOEB - LAW LIBRARY
One Wilshire Bldg., Suite 1600   Phone: (213) 629-0200
Los Angeles, CA 90017   Nella L. Jarett, Libn.

LOO MERIDETH & MC MILLAN - LAW LIBRARY
1800 Century Park East, Suite 200   Phone: (213) 277-0300
Los Angeles, CA 90067   Susan A. Lichten, Libn.

LOS ANGELES CENTER FOR PHOTOGRAPHIC STUDIES - RESOURCE CENTER
814 S. Spring St., 3rd Fl.   Phone: (213) 623-9410
Los Angeles, CA 90014   Howard Spector, Exec.Dir.

LOS ANGELES CHAMBER OF COMMERCE - ECONOMIC INFORMATION & RESEARCH DEPARTMENT LIBRARY
404 S. Bixel
Box 3696   Phone: (213) 629-0711
Los Angeles, CA 90051   Jack Kyser, Chamber Econ.

LOS ANGELES CITY ATTORNEY - LAW LIBRARY †
200 N. Main, Rm. 1700
Los Angeles, CA 90012
Phone: (213) 485-5400
Sandee Mirell, Libn.

LOS ANGELES CITY CLERK'S OFFICE - LOS ANGELES CITY ARCHIVES
Piper Technical Ctr.
555 Ramirez St., Space 320
Los Angeles, CA 90012
Phone: (213) 485-3512
Hynda L. Rudd, Archv.

LOS ANGELES COUNTY DEPT. OF HEALTH SERVICES-PREVENTIVE PUBLIC
HEALTH - HEALTH ADMINISTRATION/MANAGEMENT LIBRARY
313 N. Figueroa St., Rm. Mz1
Los Angeles, CA 90012
Phone: (213) 974-7780
Sharon Pruhs, Med.Libn.

LOS ANGELES COUNTY - DEPARTMENT OF MENTAL HEALTH - LIBRARY
2415 W. Sixth St.
Los Angeles, CA 90057
Phone: (213) 738-4730
Edward E. Asawa, Libn.

LOS ANGELES COUNTY/KING/DREW MEDICAL CENTER - HEALTH
SCIENCES LIBRARY
12021 S. Wilmington Ave., Rm. 1070
Los Angeles, CA 90059
Phone: (213) 603-4068
Ms. M. Moss Humphrey, Sr.Med.Libn.

LOS ANGELES COUNTY LAW LIBRARY
301 W. First St.
Los Angeles, CA 90012
Phone: (213) 629-3531
Richard T. Iamele, Lib.Dir.

LOS ANGELES COUNTY MEDICAL ASSOCIATION - LIBRARY †
634 S. Westlake Ave.
Los Angeles, CA 90057
Phone: (213) 483-4555
Elizabeth S. Crahan, Dir., Lib.Serv.

LOS ANGELES COUNTY MUSEUM OF ART - RESEARCH LIBRARY
5905 Wilshire Blvd.
Los Angeles, CA 90036
Phone: (213) 857-6118
Eleanor C. Hartman, Musm.Libn.

LOS ANGELES COUNTY MUSEUM OF NATURAL HISTORY - RESEARCH
LIBRARY
900 Exposition Blvd.
Los Angeles, CA 90007
Phone: (213) 744-3387
Katharine E. Donahue, Musm.Libn.

LOS ANGELES COUNTY/UNIVERSITY OF SOUTHERN CALIFORNIA MEDICAL
CENTER - MEDICAL LIBRARIES
1200 N. State St.
Los Angeles, CA 90033
Phone: (213) 226-7006
Alice Reinhardt, Chf., Lib.Serv.

LOS ANGELES COUNTY/UNIVERSITY OF SOUTHERN CALIFORNIA MEDICAL
CENTER - PEDIATRICS LIBRARY
1129 N. State St.
Los Angeles, CA 90033

LOS ANGELES - DEPARTMENT OF WATER AND POWER - LEGAL DIVISION -
LAW LIBRARY *
1520 General Office Bldg.
111 N. Hope St.
Los Angeles, CA 90012
Phone: (213) 481-6309
Ethel Hardy

LOS ANGELES HERALD-EXAMINER - NEWSPAPER LIBRARY
1111 S. Broadway
Los Angeles, CA 90015
Phone: (213) 744-8420
Ann E. Sausedo, Lib.Dir.

LOS ANGELES INSTITUTE OF CONTEMPORARY ART - LIBRARY
2020 S. Robertson Blvd.
Los Angeles, CA 90034
Phone: (213) 559-5033
Dan Wasil, Cur.

LOS ANGELES PSYCHOANALYTIC SOCIETY AND INSTITUTE - SIMMEL-
FENICHEL LIBRARY
2014 Sawtelle Blvd.
Los Angeles, CA 90025
Phone: (213) 478-6851

LOS ANGELES PUBLIC LIBRARY - ART, MUSIC & RECREATION
DEPARTMENT
630 W. Fifth St.
Los Angeles, CA 90071
Phone: (213) 626-7461
Melvin H. Rosenberg, Prin.Libn.

LOS ANGELES PUBLIC LIBRARY - AUDIO-VISUAL DEPARTMENT
630 W. Fifth St.
Los Angeles, CA 90071
Phone: (213) 626-7461
Richard V. Partlow, Dept.Mgr.

LOS ANGELES PUBLIC LIBRARY - BUSINESS & ECONOMICS DEPARTMENT
630 W. Fifth St.
Los Angeles, CA 90071
Phone: (213) 626-7461
Virginia Walter, Dept.Mgr.

LOS ANGELES PUBLIC LIBRARY - CHILDREN'S LITERATURE DEPARTMENT
630 W. Fifth St.
Los Angeles, CA 90071
Phone: (213) 626-7461
Serenna Day, Sr.Libn.

LOS ANGELES PUBLIC LIBRARY, CHINATOWN BRANCH - CHINESE
COLLECTION
536 W. College St.
Los Angeles, CA 90012
Phone: (213) 620-0925
Juliana Cheng, Sr.Libn.

LOS ANGELES PUBLIC LIBRARY - FICTION DEPARTMENT
630 W. Fifth St.
Los Angeles, CA 90071
Phone: (213) 626-7461
Helene G. Mochedlover, Dept.Mgr.

LOS ANGELES PUBLIC LIBRARY - FOREIGN LANGUAGES DEPARTMENT
630 W. Fifth St.
Los Angeles, CA 90071
Phone: (213) 626-7461
Sylva N. Manoogian, Prin.Libn.

LOS ANGELES PUBLIC LIBRARY - HISTORY DEPARTMENT
630 W. Fifth St.
Los Angeles, CA 90071
Phone: (213) 626-7461
Mary S. Pratt, Dept.Mgr.

LOS ANGELES PUBLIC LIBRARY - JAMES ALLAN DOHERTY MUNICIPAL
REFERENCE LIBRARY
530 City Hall E.
200 N. Main St.
Los Angeles, CA 90012
Phone: (213) 485-3791

LOS ANGELES PUBLIC LIBRARY - LITERATURE & PHILOLOGY DEPARTMENT
630 W. Fifth St.
Los Angeles, CA 90071
Phone: (213) 626-7461
Helene G. Mochedlover, Dept.Mgr.

LOS ANGELES PUBLIC LIBRARY - MUNICIPAL REFERENCE DEPARTMENT -
PLANNING DIVISION
City Hall, Rm. 618
200 N. Spring St.
Los Angeles, CA 90012
Phone: (213) 485-5077
Sarah D. Wolf, Libn.

LOS ANGELES PUBLIC LIBRARY - MUNICIPAL REFERENCE DEPARTMENT -
WATER & POWER LIBRARY
Rm. 518 GOB
Box 111
Los Angeles, CA 90051
Phone: (213) 481-4610
Donald F. Hinrichs, Sr.Libn.

LOS ANGELES PUBLIC LIBRARY - NEWSPAPER ROOM
630 W. Fifth St.
Los Angeles, CA 90071
Phone: (213) 646-7461
Dan Strehl, Libn.

LOS ANGELES PUBLIC LIBRARY - PHILOSOPHY & RELIGION DEPARTMENT
630 W. Fifth St.
Los Angeles, CA 90071
Phone: (213) 626-7461
Marilyn C. Wherley, Dept.Hd.

LOS ANGELES PUBLIC LIBRARY - SCIENCE & TECHNOLOGY DEPARTMENT
630 W. Fifth St.
Los Angeles, CA 90071
Phone: (213) 626-7461
Billie M. Connor, Dept.Mgr.

LOS ANGELES PUBLIC LIBRARY - SOCIAL SCIENCES DEPARTMENT
630 W. Fifth St.
Los Angeles, CA 90071
Phone: (213) 626-7461
Marilyn C. Wherley, Dept.Hd.

LOS ANGELES TIMES - EDITORIAL LIBRARY
Times-Mirror Square
Los Angeles, CA 90053
Phone: (213) 972-7181
Cecily J. Surace, Lib.Dir.

LOS ANGELES TRADE-TECHNICAL COLLEGE - LIBRARY
400 W. Washington Blvd.
Los Angeles, CA 90015
Phone: (213) 746-0800
Jean McTyre, Asst. Dean, LRC

LOYOLA LAW SCHOOL - LIBRARY
1440 W. 9th St.
Los Angeles, CA 90015-1295
Phone: (213) 736-1120
Frederica M. Sedgwick, Dir.

MC CUTCHEN, BLACK, VERLEGER AND SHEA - LAW LIBRARY
600 Wilshire Blvd.
Los Angeles, CA 90017
Phone: (213) 624-2400
Stewart Annand, Libn.

MC KINSEY & COMPANY, INC. - INFORMATION CENTER
611 W. Sixth St.   Phone: (213) 624-1414
Los Angeles, CA 90017   Doreen A. Welborn, Mgr., Info.Serv.

MANATT PHELPS ROTHENBERG & TUNNEY - LEGAL INFORMATION CENTER
11355 W. Olympic Blvd.   Phone: (213) 312-4283
Los Angeles, CA 90064   Laura M. Strain, Lib.Dir.

MARTIN (Albert C.) & ASSOCIATES - INFORMATION RESEARCH CENTER
445 S. Figueroa St.   Phone: (213) 683-1900
Los Angeles, CA 90071   Millie Nicholson, Libn.

MOLYCORP, INC. - LIBRARY
Box 54945   Phone: (213) 977-6932
Los Angeles, CA 90054   Jean K. Martin, Lib.Mgr.

MORRISON & FOERSTER - LIBRARY
601 W. 5th St., 5th Fl.   Phone: (213) 626-3800
Los Angeles, CA 90017   Robert Creamer, Libn.

MOUNT ST. MARY'S COLLEGE - NEWMAN SEMINAR
Coe Memorial Library
12001 Chalon Rd.   Phone: (213) 476-2237
Los Angeles, CA 90049   Erika Condon, Lib.Dir.

MUNGER, TOLLES & RICKERSHAUSER - LIBRARY
612 S. Flower St., 5th Fl.   Phone: (213) 683-9100
Los Angeles, CA 90017   Helen Kim, Libn.

MUSIC CENTER OPERATING COMPANY - ARCHIVES
135 N. Grand Ave.   Phone: (213) 972-7499
Los Angeles, CA 90012   Joel M. Pritkin, Cur.

NATIONAL CENTER FOR COMPUTER CRIME DATA
John F. Kennedy Memorial Library
California State University, Los Angeles
5151 State College Dr.   Phone: (213) 874-8233
Los Angeles, CA 90032   Jay J. BloomBecker, Dir.

NATIONAL ECONOMIC RESEARCH ASSOCIATES, INC. - LIBRARY
555 S. Flower St., Suite 4100   Phone: (213) 628-0131
Los Angeles, CA 90071   Annie S. Lam, Libn.

NATIONAL JEWISH INFORMATION SERVICE FOR THE PROPAGATION OF
   JUDAISM - RESEARCH LIBRARY AND ARCHIVES
5174 W. 8th St.   Phone: (213) 936-6033
Los Angeles, CA 90036   Rachel D. Maggal, P.R. Dir.

NEUROPSYCHIATRIC INSTITUTE - MENTAL HEALTH INFORMATION
   SERVICE
University of California, Los Angeles
Center for the Health Sciences
760 Westwood Plaza   Phone: (213) 825-0597
Los Angeles, CA 90024   Sherry Terzian, Dir.

NORTHROP CORPORATION - CORPORATE LIBRARY
1800 Century Park E.   Phone: (213) 553-6262
Los Angeles, CA 90067   Janice Chang, Mgr.

OCCIDENTAL COLLEGE - MARY NORTON CLAPP LIBRARY
1600 Campus Rd.   Phone: (213) 259-2852
Los Angeles, CA 90041   Michael C. Sutherland, Spec.Coll.Libn.

O'MELVENY AND MYERS - INFORMATION SERVICES
400 S. Hope St.   Phone: (213) 669-6000
Los Angeles, CA 90071-2899   Stanley Pearce, Dir., Info.Serv.

ONE, INC. - BLANCHE M. BAKER MEMORIAL LIBRARY
3340 Country Club Dr.   Phone: (213) 735-5252
Los Angeles, CA 90019   David G. Moore, Libn.

ORTHOPAEDIC HOSPITAL - RUBEL MEMORIAL LIBRARY
2400 S. Flower St.
Box 60132, Terminal Annex   Phone: (213) 742-1530
Los Angeles, CA 90060   Veena N. Vyas, Dir., Med.Lib.

PACIFIC LIGHTING CORPORATION - LAW LIBRARY
810 S. Flower St.   Phone: (213) 689-3352
Los Angeles, CA 90017   Terence Pragnell, Law Libn.

PACIFIC LIGHTING GAS SUPPLY COMPANY - REFERENCE CENTER
720 W. 8th St. - ML 10MW   Phone: (213) 689-3930
Los Angeles, CA 90017   Janice Moisant, Res. & Info.Supv.

PACIFIC-SIERRA RESEARCH CORPORATION - LIBRARY
12340 Santa Monica Blvd.   Phone: (213) 820-2200
Los Angeles, CA 90025   Letitia A. McIntosh, Res.Libn.

PACIFICA RADIO NETWORK - PACIFICA RADIO ARCHIVE
5316 Venice Blvd.   Phone: (213) 931-1625
Los Angeles, CA 90019   Janice Woo, Libn.

PARSONS SCHOOL OF DESIGN - OTIS ART INSTITUTE - LIBRARY
2307 W. 6th St.   Phone: (213) 387-5288
Los Angeles, CA 90057   Justine V. Clancy, Dir.

PAUL, HASTINGS, JANOFSKY AND WALKER - LAW LIBRARY †
555 S. Flower, 22nd Floor   Phone: (213) 489-4000
Los Angeles, CA 90071   Bobbie Johnson, Hd.Libn.

PEAT, MARWICK, MITCHELL & CO. - CENTRAL LIBRARY †
555 S. Flower St.   Phone: (213) 972-4000
Los Angeles, CA 90071   Vickie Taylor, Hd.Libn.

PHILOSOPHICAL RESEARCH SOCIETY - RESEARCH LIBRARY
3910 Los Feliz Blvd.   Phone: (213) 663-2167
Los Angeles, CA 90027   Pearl M. Thomas, Libn.

POLISH AMERICAN CONGRESS - SOUTHERN CALIFORNIA-ARIZONA
   DIVISION - POLAND'S MILLENIUM LIBRARY
3424 W. Adams Blvd.   Phone: (213) 664-0662
Los Angeles, CA 90018   Danuta M. Zawadzki, V.P.

PRICE WATERHOUSE - LIBRARY
400 S. Hope St.   Phone: (213) 625-4583
Los Angeles, CA 90071-2889   Mignon Veasley, Hd.Libn.

REISS-DAVIS CHILD STUDY CENTER - RESEARCH LIBRARY
3200 Motor Ave.   Phone: (213) 204-1666
Los Angeles, CA 90034   Leonore Freehling, Libn.

RIFKIND CENTER FOR GERMAN EXPRESSIONIST STUDIES - ART LIBRARY
   AND GRAPHICS COLLECTION
Los Angeles County Museum of Art
5905 Wilshire Blvd.   Phone: (213) 278-0970
Los Angeles, CA 90036   Susan Trauger, Art Libn.

RIGHT TO LIFE LEAGUE OF SOUTHERN CALIFORNIA - LIBRARY
1616 W. 9th St., Suite 220   Phone: (213) 380-8750
Los Angeles, CA 90015   Karen Bodziak, Dir. of Educ.

ROCKWELL INTERNATIONAL - NORTH AMERICAN AIRCRAFT OPERATIONS
   - TECHNICAL INFORMATION CENTER
Box 92098   Phone: (213) 647-2961
Los Angeles, CA 90009   Linda R. Roberts, Supv.

ROUNCE AND COFFIN CLUB, LOS ANGELES - LIBRARY
Occidental College Library
1600 Campus Rd.   Phone: (213) 259-2852
Los Angeles, CA 90041   Michael C. Sutherland, Spec.Coll.Libn.

ST. VINCENT MEDICAL CENTER - HEALTH SCIENCES LIBRARY *
2131 W. Third St.   Phone: (213) 484-5530
Los Angeles, CA 90057   Doreen B. Keough, Libn.

SECURITY PACIFIC NATIONAL BANK - ECONOMICS AND BUSINESS
   LIBRARY
333 S. Hope St.   Phone: (213) 613-8623
Los Angeles, CA 90071   Ann E. Wiedel, Res.Off.

SEYFARTH, SHAW, FAIRWEATHER & GERALDSON - LIBRARY
2029 Century Park East, Suite 3300   Phone: (213) 277-7200
Los Angeles, CA 90067   Beth Bernstein, Libn.

SHAKESPEARE SOCIETY OF AMERICA - NEW PLACE RARE BOOK LIBRARY
1107 N. Kings Rd.   Phone: (213) 654-5623
Los Angeles, CA 90069   Thad Taylor, Pres.

SHEPPARD, MULLIN, RICHTER & HAMPTON - LAW LIBRARY †
333 S. Hope St., 47th Fl.   Phone: (213) 620-1780
Los Angeles, CA 90071   Debra K. Hogan, Libn.

SISTERS OF SOCIAL SERVICE - ARCHIVES
1120 Westchester Pl.
Los Angeles, CA 90019

SOUTHERN CALIFORNIA ASSOCIATION OF GOVERNMENTS -
  INFORMATION RESOURCE CENTER
600 S. Commonwealth Ave.   Phone: (213) 385-1000
Los Angeles, CA 90005   Shelli Snyder, Libn.

SOUTHERN CALIFORNIA GAS COMPANY - ENGINEERING INFORMATION
  CENTER
Box 3249, Terminal Annex, ML730D   Phone: (818) 307-2872
Los Angeles, CA 90051   Gordon L. Sandviken, Info.Ctr.Spec.

SOUTHERN CALIFORNIA LIBRARY FOR SOCIAL STUDIES AND RESEARCH
6120 S. Vermont Ave.   Phone: (213) 759-6063
Los Angeles, CA 90044   Sarah Cooper, Dir.

SOUTHERN CALIFORNIA RAPID TRANSIT DISTRICT - INFORMATION
  CENTER LIBRARY
425 S. Main St.   Phone: (213) 972-6467
Los Angeles, CA 90013   Nola Wolf, Libn.

SOUTHWEST MUSEUM - RESEARCH LIBRARY †
Highland Park Sta., Box 42128   Phone: (213) 221-2163
Los Angeles, CA 90042   Ruth M. Christensen, Libn.

SOUTHWESTERN UNIVERSITY - SCHOOL OF LAW LIBRARY
675 S. Westmoreland Ave.   Phone: (213) 738-6725
Los Angeles, CA 90005   Linda Whisman, Dir.

THOMPSON (J. Walter) COMPANY - RESEARCH LIBRARY
10100 Santa Monica Blvd.   Phone: (213) 553-8383
Los Angeles, CA 90067   Suzanne Rampton, Assoc.Dir. of Res.

TOUCHE ROSS AND COMPANY - LIBRARY
3700 Wilshire Blvd.   Phone: (213) 381-3251
Los Angeles, CA 90010   Kathy Tice, Libn.

TRANSAMERICA OCCIDENTAL LIFE INSURANCE COMPANY - LAW LIBRARY
1150 S. Olive St., Suite T-2500   Phone: (213) 741-5083
Los Angeles, CA 90015   Susan Cuellar, Adm.Asst.

TYRE, KAMINS, KATZ & GRANOF - LIBRARY
1800 Century Park E., Suite 1000   Phone: (213) 553-6822
Los Angeles, CA 90067   Becky C. Davis, Libn.

UNCAP INTERNATIONAL, INC. - PROJECT COLLECTORS RESEARCH
  LIBRARY
2613 Huron St.   Phone: (213) 222-2012
Los Angeles, CA 90065   James J. O'Connell, III, Cur.

UNION BANK - LIBRARY
714 W. Olympic Blvd.   Phone: (213) 236-6642
Los Angeles, CA 90015   John D. Shea, Hd.Libn.

UNION OIL COMPANY OF CALIFORNIA - INTERNATIONAL EXPLORATION
  LIBRARY
461 S. Boylston St.   Phone: (213) 977-6381
Los Angeles, CA 90017   Ardis Weiss, Lib.Mgr.

UNITED CHURCH OF RELIGIOUS SCIENCE - ERNEST HOLMES COLLEGE
  LIBRARY
3251 W. Sixth St.
Box 75127   Phone: (213) 388-2181
Los Angeles, CA 90075   Albert T. Wickham, Hd.Libn.

U.S. BUREAU OF THE CENSUS - INFORMATION SERVICES PROGRAM - LOS
  ANGELES REGIONAL OFFICE - LIBRARY
11777 San Vincente Blvd., 8th Fl.   Phone: (213) 209-6612
Los Angeles, CA 90049

U.S. COURT OF APPEALS, 9TH CIRCUIT - LIBRARY
1702 U.S. Courthouse   Phone: (213) 688-3636
Los Angeles, CA 90012   Joanne Mazza, Libn.

U.S. DEFENSE TECHNICAL INFORMATION CENTER - DTIC ON-LINE
  SERVICE FACILITY
11099 S. LaCienega Blvd.   Phone: (213) 643-1108
Los Angeles, CA 90045   Carol D. Finney, Mgr.

U.S. DEPT. OF JUSTICE - UNITED STATES ATTORNEY, CENTRAL DISTRICT
  OF CALIFORNIA - LIBRARY *
1214 U.S. Court House
312 N. Spring St.   Phone: (213) 688-2419
Los Angeles, CA 90012

U.S. VETERANS ADMINISTRATION (CA-Los Angeles) - MEDICAL RESEARCH
  LIBRARY
Wilshire & Sawtelle Blvds.   Phone: (213) 478-3711
Los Angeles, CA 90073   Christine Anderson, Chf., Med.Res.Lib.

U.S. VETERANS ADMINISTRATION (CA-Los Angeles) - WADSWORTH
  MEDICAL LIBRARY 691W/142D
Wilshire & Sawtelle Blvds.   Phone: (213) 824-3102
Los Angeles, CA 90073   Christa Buswell, Chf., Lib.Serv.

UNITED WAY, INC., LOS ANGELES - LIBRARY
621 S. Virgil Ave.   Phone: (213) 736-1300
Los Angeles, CA 90005   Jim Pursley, Coord., Proj.Oper.

UNIVERSITY OF CALIFORNIA, LOS ANGELES - ACADEMY OF TELEVISION
  ARTS & SCIENCES - TELEVISION ARCHIVES
Theater Arts Dept.
1438 Melnitz Hall   Phone: (213) 206-8013
Los Angeles, CA 90024   Dan Einstein, Archv.

UNIVERSITY OF CALIFORNIA, LOS ANGELES - AFRICAN STUDIES CENTER -
  LIBRARY
10367 Bunche Hall   Phone: (213) 825-2944
Los Angeles, CA 90024   Dr. Michael Lofchie, Dir.

UNIVERSITY OF CALIFORNIA, LOS ANGELES - AMERICAN INDIAN STUDIES
  CENTER - LIBRARY
3220 Campbell Hall   Phone: (213) 825-4591
Los Angeles, CA 90024   Velma S. Salabiye, Libn.

UNIVERSITY OF CALIFORNIA, LOS ANGELES - ARCHITECTURE & URBAN
  PLANNING LIBRARY
1302 Architecture Bldg.   Phone: (213) 825-2747
Los Angeles, CA 90024   Jon S. Greene, Libn.

UNIVERSITY OF CALIFORNIA, LOS ANGELES - ART DEPARTMENT - VISUAL
  RESOURCE COLLECTION & SERVICES
3239 Dickson Art Center
405 Hilgard Ave.   Phone: (213) 825-3725
Los Angeles, CA 90024   Sandra Ducoff Garber, Slide Cur.

UNIVERSITY OF CALIFORNIA, LOS ANGELES - ART LIBRARY
2250 Dickson Art Center   Phone: (213) 825-3817
Los Angeles, CA 90024   Joyce P. Ludmer, Art Libn.

UNIVERSITY OF CALIFORNIA, LOS ANGELES - ART LIBRARY - ELMER BELT
  LIBRARY OF VINCIANA
Dickson Art Center   Phone: (213) 825-3817
Los Angeles, CA 90024   Joyce Ludmer, Art Libn./Dir.

UNIVERSITY OF CALIFORNIA, LOS ANGELES - ASIAN AMERICAN STUDIES
  CENTER READING ROOM
2230 Campbell Hall   Phone: (213) 825-5043
Los Angeles, CA 90024   Marjorie Lee, Coord.

UNIVERSITY OF CALIFORNIA, LOS ANGELES - BIOMEDICAL LIBRARY
Center for Health Sciences   Phone: (213) 825-5781
Los Angeles, CA 90024   Alison Bunting, Act.Hd.Libn.

UNIVERSITY OF CALIFORNIA, LOS ANGELES - BRAIN INFORMATION
  SERVICE
Center for Health Sciences   Phone: (213) 825-6011
Los Angeles, CA 90024   Michael H. Chase, Dir.

UNIVERSITY OF CALIFORNIA, LOS ANGELES - CHEMISTRY LIBRARY
4238 Young Hall   Phone: (213) 825-3342
Los Angeles, CA 90024   Marion C. Peters, Libn.

UNIVERSITY OF CALIFORNIA, LOS ANGELES - CHICANO STUDIES
   RESEARCH LIBRARY
3121 Campbell Hall
405 Hilgard Ave.   Phone: (213) 206-6052
Los Angeles, CA 90024   Richard Chabran, Assoc.Libn./Coord.

UNIVERSITY OF CALIFORNIA, LOS ANGELES - COMPUTER SCIENCE
   DEPARTMENT - ARCHIVES
3440 Boelter Hall   Phone: (213) 825-4317
Los Angeles, CA 90024   Doris Sublette, Libn.

UNIVERSITY OF CALIFORNIA, LOS ANGELES - DEPARTMENT OF SPECIAL
   COLLECTIONS
University Research Library, Fl. A   Phone: (213) 825-4988
Los Angeles, CA 90024   David Zeidberg, Hd.

UNIVERSITY OF CALIFORNIA, LOS ANGELES - EDUCATION & PSYCHOLOGY
   LIBRARY
390 Powell Library Bldg.   Phone: (213) 825-4081
Los Angeles, CA 90024   Barbara Duke, Hd.

UNIVERSITY OF CALIFORNIA, LOS ANGELES - ENGINEERING &
   MATHEMATICAL SCIENCES LIBRARY
8270 Boelter Hall   Phone: (213) 825-3982
Los Angeles, CA 90024   Karen L. Andrews, Hd.Libn.

UNIVERSITY OF CALIFORNIA, LOS ANGELES - ENGLISH READING ROOM
1120 Rolfe Hall   Phone: (213) 825-4511
Los Angeles, CA 90024   Tim Strawn, Hd.

UNIVERSITY OF CALIFORNIA, LOS ANGELES - ENVIRONMENTAL SCIENCE
   AND ENGINEERING - LIBRARY
2066 Engineering I Bldg.   Phone: (213) 825-7332
Los Angeles, CA 90024

UNIVERSITY OF CALIFORNIA, LOS ANGELES - GEOLOGY-GEOPHYSICS
   LIBRARY
Geology Bldg., Rm. 4697   Phone: (213) 825-1055
Los Angeles, CA 90024   Sarah E. How, Hd.

UNIVERSITY OF CALIFORNIA, LOS ANGELES - HOUSING, REAL ESTATE &
   URBAN LAND STUDIES PROGRAM COLLECTION
405 Hilgard
Graduate School of Management 4274   Phone: (213) 825-3977
Los Angeles, CA 90024   Frank G. Mittelbach, Dir./Prof.

UNIVERSITY OF CALIFORNIA, LOS ANGELES - INSTITUTE FOR SOCIAL
   SCIENCE RESEARCH - SOCIAL SCIENCE DATA ARCHIVE
405 Hilgard Ave.   Phone: (213) 825-0711
Los Angeles, CA 90024   Elizabeth Stephenson, Data Archv.

UNIVERSITY OF CALIFORNIA, LOS ANGELES - LABORATORY OF
   BIOMEDICAL AND ENVIRONMENTAL SCIENCES - LIBRARY
900 Veteran Ave.   Phone: (213) 825-8741
Los Angeles, CA 90024

UNIVERSITY OF CALIFORNIA, LOS ANGELES - LAW LIBRARY
School of Law Bldg.
405 Hilgard Ave.   Phone: (213) 825-7826
Los Angeles, CA 90024   Frederick E. Smith, Law Libn.

UNIVERSITY OF CALIFORNIA, LOS ANGELES - MANAGEMENT LIBRARY
Graduate School of Management   Phone: (213) 825-3138
Los Angeles, CA 90024   Robert Bellanti, Hd.

UNIVERSITY OF CALIFORNIA, LOS ANGELES - MAP LIBRARY
Bunche Hall, Rm. A-253   Phone: (213) 825-3526
Los Angeles, CA 90024   Carlos B. Hagen, Hd.

UNIVERSITY OF CALIFORNIA, LOS ANGELES - MATHEMATICS READING
   ROOM
Mathematics Science Bldg., Rm. 5379   Phone: (213) 825-4930
Los Angeles, CA 90024   Sharon Marcus, Libn.

UNIVERSITY OF CALIFORNIA, LOS ANGELES - MUSIC LIBRARY
1102 Schoenberg Hall
405 Hilgard Ave.   Phone: (213) 825-4881
Los Angeles, CA 90024   Stephen M. Fry, Music Libn.

UNIVERSITY OF CALIFORNIA, LOS ANGELES - ORAL HISTORY PROGRAM
   LIBRARY
136 Powell Library   Phone: (213) 825-4932
Los Angeles, CA 90024   Dale Treleven, Dir.

UNIVERSITY OF CALIFORNIA, LOS ANGELES - ORIENTAL LIBRARY
21617 University Research Library   Phone: (213) 825-4836
Los Angeles, CA 90024   Mr. Ik-Sam Kim, Hd.

UNIVERSITY OF CALIFORNIA, LOS ANGELES - PHYSICAL SCIENCES &
   TECHNOLOGY LIBRARIES
8251 Boelter Hall   Phone: (213) 825-6515
Los Angeles, CA 90024   Alan R. Benenfeld, Coord.

UNIVERSITY OF CALIFORNIA, LOS ANGELES - PHYSICS LIBRARY
213 Kinsey Hall   Phone: (213) 825-4792
Los Angeles, CA 90024   J. Wally Pegram, Libn.

UNIVERSITY OF CALIFORNIA, LOS ANGELES - PUBLIC AFFAIRS SERVICE
405 Hilgard   Phone: (213) 825-3135
Los Angeles, CA 90024   Eugenia Eaton, Hd.

UNIVERSITY OF CALIFORNIA, LOS ANGELES - THEATER ARTS LIBRARY
22478 University Research Library   Phone: (213) 825-4880
Los Angeles, CA 90024   Mrs. Audree Malkin, Libn.

UNIVERSITY OF CALIFORNIA, LOS ANGELES - UCLA FILM ARCHIVES
Department of Theater Arts   Phone: (213) 206-8013
Los Angeles, CA 90024   Charles Hopkins, Film Archv.

UNIVERSITY OF CALIFORNIA, LOS ANGELES - UCLA RADIO ARCHIVES
Department of Theater Arts   Phone: (213) 206-8013
Los Angeles, CA 90024   Ronald Staley, Radio Archv.

UNIVERSITY OF CALIFORNIA, LOS ANGELES - UNIVERSITY ELEMENTARY
   SCHOOL LIBRARY
405 Hilgard Ave.   Phone: (213) 825-4928
Los Angeles, CA 90024   Judith Kantor, Hd.Libn.

UNIVERSITY OF CALIFORNIA, LOS ANGELES - WATER RESOURCES CENTER
   ARCHIVES
2081 Engineering I   Phone: (213) 825-7734
Los Angeles, CA 90024   Beth R. Willard, Assoc.Libn.

UNIVERSITY OF CALIFORNIA, LOS ANGELES - WAYLAND D. HAND LIBRARY
   OF FOLKLORE AND MYTHOLOGY
                             Phone: (213) 825-4242
Los Angeles, CA 90024   Inkeri Rank, Libn.

UNIVERSITY OF CALIFORNIA, LOS ANGELES - WILLIAM ANDREWS CLARK
   MEMORIAL LIBRARY
2520 Cimarron St.   Phone: (213) 731-8529
Los Angeles, CA 90018-2098   Norman J.W. Thrower, Dir.

UNIVERSITY OF SOUTHERN CALIFORNIA - ARCHITECTURE & FINE ARTS
   LIBRARY
University Park - MC 0182   Phone: (213) 743-2798
Los Angeles, CA 90089-0182   Alson Clark, Libn.

UNIVERSITY OF SOUTHERN CALIFORNIA - CROCKER BUSINESS LIBRARY
University Park - MC 1421   Phone: (213) 743-7348
Los Angeles, CA 90089-1421   Judith A. Truelson, Dir.

UNIVERSITY OF SOUTHERN CALIFORNIA - EDUCATION & INFORMATION
   STUDIES LIBRARY
University Park - MC 0182   Phone: (213) 743-6249
Los Angeles, CA 90089-0182 Mae L. Furbeyre, Interim Hd.Libn.

UNIVERSITY OF SOUTHERN CALIFORNIA - ETHEL PERCY ANDRUS
   GERONTOLOGY CENTER - GERONTOLOGICAL INFO. CENTER
3715 McClintock Ave.   Phone: (213) 743-5990
Los Angeles, CA 90007   Jean E. Mueller, Libn.

UNIVERSITY OF SOUTHERN CALIFORNIA - HEALTH SCIENCES CAMPUS -
   DENTISTRY LIBRARY
Norris Medical Library
2025 Zonal Ave.   Phone: (213) 224-7231
Los Angeles, CA 90033   Frank O. Mason, Libn.

UNIVERSITY OF SOUTHERN CALIFORNIA - HEALTH SCIENCES CAMPUS -
  NORRIS MEDICAL LIBRARY
2025 Zonal Ave.   Phone: (213) 224-7231
Los Angeles, CA 90033   Nelson J. Gilman, Libn./Dir.

UNIVERSITY OF SOUTHERN CALIFORNIA - INSTITUTE OF SAFETY &
  SYSTEMS MANAGEMENT - LIBRARY
University Park - MC 0021   Phone: (213) 743-6253
Los Angeles, CA 90089-0021   Monir Ziaian, Hd.Libn.

UNIVERSITY OF SOUTHERN CALIFORNIA - LAW LIBRARY
University Park - MC 0072   Phone: (213) 743-6487
Los Angeles, CA 90089-0072   Albert Brecht, Dir.

UNIVERSITY OF SOUTHERN CALIFORNIA - LIBRARY - CINEMA LIBRARY
University Park - MC 0182   Phone: (213) 743-6058
Los Angeles, CA 90089-0182   Robert Knutson, Hd., Dept.Spec.Coll.

UNIVERSITY OF SOUTHERN CALIFORNIA - LIBRARY - DEPARTMENT OF
  SPECIAL COLLECTIONS
University Park - MC 0182   Phone: (213) 743-6058
Los Angeles, CA 90089-0182   Robert Knutson, Hd.

UNIVERSITY OF SOUTHERN CALIFORNIA - LIBRARY - DEPARTMENT OF
  SPECIAL COLLECTIONS - AMERICAN LITERATURE COLLECTION
University Park - MC 0182   Phone: (213) 743-6058
Los Angeles, CA 90089-0182   William Jankos, Cur.

UNIVERSITY OF SOUTHERN CALIFORNIA - MUSIC LIBRARY
University Park - MC 0182   Phone: (213) 743-2525
Los Angeles, CA 90089-0182   Rodney D. Rolfs, Music Libn.

UNIVERSITY OF SOUTHERN CALIFORNIA - NASA INDUSTRIAL
  APPLICATION CENTER (NIAC)
Denney Research Bldg., 3rd Fl.
University Park   Phone: (213) 743-6132
Los Angeles, CA 90007   Radford G. King, Dir.

UNIVERSITY OF SOUTHERN CALIFORNIA - PHILOSOPHY LIBRARY
University Park - MC 0182   Phone: (213) 743-2634
Los Angeles, CA 90089-0182   Bridget Molloy, Libn.

UNIVERSITY OF SOUTHERN CALIFORNIA - POPULATION RESEARCH
  LABORATORY - LIBRARY
University Pk., Research Annex 385   Phone: (213) 743-2950
Los Angeles, CA 90007   Prof. David M. Heer, Assoc.Dir.

UNIVERSITY OF SOUTHERN CALIFORNIA - SCIENCE & ENGINEERING
  LIBRARY
University Park - MC 0481   Phone: (213) 743-2118
Los Angeles, CA 90089-0481   A. Albert Baker, Hd.

UNIVERSITY OF SOUTHERN CALIFORNIA - SOCIAL WORK LIBRARY
University Park - MC 0411   Phone: (213) 743-7932
Los Angeles, CA 90089-0411   Ruth Britton, Libn.

UNIVERSITY OF SOUTHERN CALIFORNIA - VON KLEINSMID LIBRARY
University Park - MC 0182   Phone: (213) 743-7347
Los Angeles, CA 90089-0182   Mr. Lynn Sipe, Libn.

UNIVERSITY OF SOUTHERN CALIFORNIA - VON KLEINSMID LIBRARY -
  ORIENTALIA COLLECTION
University Park - MC 0182   Phone: (213) 743-7347
Los Angeles, CA 90089-0182   Ken Kline, Libn.

UPDATA PUBLICATIONS, INC. - LIBRARY
1746 Westwood Blvd.   Phone: (213) 474-5900
Los Angeles, CA 90024   Judy Harrington, Libn.

VISUAL COMMUNICATIONS - ASIAN PACIFIC AMERICAN PHOTOGRAPHIC
  ARCHIVES
244 S. San Pedro St., Rm. 309   Phone: (213) 608-4462
Los Angeles, CA 90012   Nancy Araki, Exec.Dir.

WEINSTEIN (Robert) MARITIME HISTORICAL COLLECTION
1253 S. Stanley Ave.   Phone: (213) 936-0558
Los Angeles, CA 90019   R. Weinstein, Owner

WEST COAST UNIVERSITY - ELCONIN CENTER LIBRARY
440 Shatto Pl.   Phone: (213) 487-4433
Los Angeles, CA 90020   Nancy K. Dennis, Dir. of Lib.

WESTERN CENTER ON LAW AND POVERTY, INC. - LIBRARY
3535 W. 6th St.   Phone: (213) 487-7211
Los Angeles, CA 90020   Michelle Epstein, Coord. of Lib.Serv.

WESTERN COSTUME COMPANY - RESEARCH LIBRARY
5335 Melrose Ave.   Phone: (213) 469-1451
Los Angeles, CA 90038   Nancy S. Kinney, Dir. of Res.

WHITE MEMORIAL MEDICAL CENTER - COURVILLE-ABBOTT MEMORIAL
  LIBRARY
1720 Brooklyn Ave.   Phone: (213) 268-5000
Los Angeles, CA 90033   Joyce Marson, Dir.

WHITTIER COLLEGE - SCHOOL OF LAW - LIBRARY
5353 W. 3d St.   Phone: (213) 938-3621
Los Angeles, CA 90020   J. Denny Haythorn, Dir./Assoc.Prof.

WILLIAM M. MERCER, INC. - LIBRARY INFORMATION CENTER
3303 Wilshire Blvd.   Phone: (213) 386-7840
Los Angeles, CA 90010   Robert C. Costello

WILSHIRE BOULEVARD TEMPLE - SIGMUND HECHT LIBRARY †
3663 Wilshire Blvd.   Phone: (213) 388-2401
Los Angeles, CA 90010   Mitzi Weinstein, Libn.

WOODBURY UNIVERSITY - LIBRARY
1027 Wilshire Blvd.   Phone: (213) 482-8491
Los Angeles, CA 90017   Dr. Everett L. Moore, Dir., Lib.Serv.

ZEITLIN PERIODICALS COMPANY, INC. - LIBRARY
817 S. La Brea Ave.   Phone: (213) 933-7175
Los Angeles, CA 90036   Stanley Zeitlin, Pres.

ZEITLIN & VER BRUGGE, BOOKSELLERS - LIBRARY †
815 N. La Cienega Blvd.   Phone: (213) 655-7581
Los Angeles, CA 90069   Jacob Israel Zeitlin, Pres.

CALIFORNIA PROVINCE OF THE SOCIETY OF JESUS - JESUIT CENTER
  LIBRARY *
300 College Ave.
Box 128   Phone: (408) 354-9240
Los Gatos, CA 95031   Rev. Edward T. Burke, S.J., Libn.

ST. FRANCIS MEDICAL CENTER - MOTHER MACARIA HEALTH SCIENCE
  LIBRARY
3630 E. Imperial Hwy.   Phone: (213) 603-6045
Lynwood, CA 90262   Eva Kratz, Dir. of Lib.Serv.

U.S. AIR FORCE BASE - MC CLELLAN BASE LIBRARY
2852 ABG/SSL   Phone: (916) 643-4640
McClellan AFB, CA 95652   Weldon B. Champreys, Libn.

MADERA COUNTY HISTORICAL SOCIETY - MUSEUM/LIBRARY
210 W. Yosemite Ave.
Box 478   Phone: (209) 673-0291
Madera, CA 93637   Rintha Robbins, Libn.

HUGHES AIRCRAFT COMPANY - HUGHES RESEARCH LABORATORIES
  LIBRARY
3011 Malibu Canyon Rd.   Phone: (213) 456-6411
Malibu, CA 90265   Tobyann Mandel, Libn.

MEDICAL PLANNING ASSOCIATES - LIBRARY
1601 Rambla Pacifico   Phone: (213) 456-2084
Malibu, CA 90265   David C. Lennartz, Ph.D., Res.Anl.

PEPPERDINE UNIVERSITY - LAW LIBRARY
24255 Pacific Coast Hwy.   Phone: (213) 456-4647
Malibu, CA 90265   Nancy J. Kitchen, Dir.

PEPPERDINE UNIVERSITY - LIBRARY - SPECIAL COLLECTIONS
24255 Pacific Coast Hwy.   Phone: (213) 456-4243
Malibu, CA 90265   Dr. Harold Holland, Dir.

U.S. AIR FORCE BASE - MARCH BASE LIBRARY
FL 4664   Phone: (714) 655-2203
March AFB, CA 92518   Marian M. Hamilton, Base Libn.

DANIEL FREEMAN MARINA HOSPITAL MEDICAL LIBRARY & RESOURCE
    CENTER
4650 Lincoln Blvd.   Phone: (213) 823-8911
Marina del Rey, CA 90292   Jill Olechno, Lib.Dir.

R & D ASSOCIATES - TECHNICAL INFORMATION SERVICES
4640 Admiralty Way
Box 9695   Phone: (213) 822-1715
Marina Del Rey, CA 90295   Margaret R. Anderson, Mgr.

UNIVERSITY OF SOUTHERN CALIFORNIA - INFORMATION SCIENCES
    INSTITUTE - LIBRARY
4676 Admiralty Way   Phone: (213) 822-1511
Marina Del Rey, CA 90292   Alicia Sabatine Drake, Tech.Libn.

EARTHMIND - LIBRARY
4844 Hirsch Rd.
Mariposa, CA 95338   Michael A. Hackleman, Res.Dir.

ALPINE COUNTY LAW LIBRARY
Box 158   Phone: (916) 694-2281
Markleeville, CA 96120   Karen Keebaugh, Alpine County Ck.

CONTRA COSTA COUNTY LAW LIBRARY
Court House   Phone: (415) 372-2783
Martinez, CA 94553-1276   Jean Steffensen, Law Libn.

U.S. VETERANS ADMINISTRATION (CA-Martinez) - HOSPITAL LIBRARY
150 Muir Rd.   Phone: (415) 228-6800
Martinez, CA 94553   Dorothea E. Bennett, Chf., Lib.Serv.

U.S. AIR FORCE BASE - MATHER BASE LIBRARY †
FL 3067   Phone: (916) 364-4759
Mather AFB, CA 95655   Mary Kay Briggs, Libn.

U.S. AIR FORCE HOSPITAL - MEDICAL LIBRARY (CA-Mather AFB)
                                          Phone: (916) 364-3180
Mather AFB, CA 95655   Carl Lord, Lib.Off.

MENDOCINO ART CENTER - ART LIBRARY
Box 765   Phone: (707) 937-5818
Mendocino, CA 95460   Joan Burleigh, Libn.

ADDISON-WESLEY PUBLISHING COMPANY - LIBRARY
2725 Sand Hill Rd.   Phone: (415) 854-0300
Menlo Park, CA 94025   Elede Toppy Hall, Libn.

BOSTON CONSULTING GROUP - WEST COAST INFORMATION CENTER
2180 Sand Hill Rd.   Phone: (415) 854-5515
Menlo Park, CA 94020   Gary L. Lance, Info.Serv.Mgr.

MENLO PARK PUBLIC LIBRARY - LOCAL HISTORY COLLECTION
Civic Center
Alma and Ravenswood Aves.   Phone: (415) 858-3460
Menlo Park, CA 94025

RAYCHEM CORPORATION - CORPORATE LIBRARY †
300 Constitution Dr.   Phone: (415) 329-3282
Menlo Park, CA 94025   Phyllis Oda, Mgr.

SAGA CORPORATION - MARKETING LIBRARY
One Saga Ln.   Phone: (415) 854-5150
Menlo Park, CA 94025   Caroline S. Peters, Libn.

ST. PATRICK'S SEMINARY - MC KEON MEMORIAL LIBRARY
320 Middlefield Rd.   Phone: (415) 322-2224
Menlo Park, CA 94025   John F. Mattingly, Dir.

SRI INTERNATIONAL - BUSINESS INTELLIGENCE PROGRAM -
    INFORMATION CENTER †
333 Ravenswood Ave.   Phone: (415) 859-2400
Menlo Park, CA 94025   Edward F. Christie, Mgr., Inquiry Serv.

SRI INTERNATIONAL - LIBRARY AND RESEARCH INFORMATION SERVICES
    DEPARTMENT
333 Ravenswood Ave.   Phone: (415) 326-6200
Menlo Park, CA 94025   Elizabeth D. Gill, Dir.

U.S. GEOLOGICAL SURVEY - LIBRARY
345 Middlefield Rd., MS955   Phone: (415) 323-8111
Menlo Park, CA 94025   Eleanore E. Wilkins, Libn.

U.S. GEOLOGICAL SURVEY - NATL. CARTOGRAPHIC INFORMATION CENTER
    (NCIC) - WESTERN BRANCH
345 Middlefield Rd., M.S. 32   Phone: (415) 323-8111
Menlo Park, CA 94025   William J. Johnson, Chf., NCIC - W.

MERCED COMMUNITY MEDICAL CENTER - MEDICAL LIBRARY
301 E. 13th St.
Box 231   Phone: (209) 385-7058
Merced, CA 95340   Betty Maddalena, Med.Libn.

MERCED COUNTY LAW LIBRARY
County Courts Bldg.
670 W. 22nd St.   Phone: (209) 723-3101
Merced, CA 95340-3798   Margaret W. Lawrance, Law Libn.

GOLDEN GATE BAPTIST THEOLOGICAL SEMINARY - LIBRARY
Strawberry Point   Phone: (415) 388-8080
Mill Valley, CA 94941   Cecil R. White, Libn.

U.S. NATL. PARK SERVICE - MUIR WOODS NATL. MONUMENT - LIBRARY ★
Mill Valley, CA 94941

HOLY CROSS HOSPITAL - HEALTH SCIENCES LIBRARY
15031 Rinaldi St.   Phone: (818) 898-4545
Mission Hills, CA 91345   Lucille R. Moss, Mgr., Health Sci.Lib.

HOLY FAMILY COLLEGE - MOTHER DOLORES MEMORIAL LIBRARY
159 Washington Blvd.
Box 3426   Phone: (415) 651-1639
Mission San Jose, CA 94539   Sr. Patricia Wittman, Libn.

BURROUGHS CORPORATION - TECHNICAL INFORMATION CENTER
25725 Jeronimo Rd.   Phone: (714) 768-2685
Mission Viejo, CA 92691   M. Patricia Feeney, Tech.Libn.Sr.

JACK G. RAUB COMPANY - LIBRARY
24741 Chrisanta Dr.   Phone: (714) 859-4948
Mission Viejo, CA 92691   Gretchen W. Gabbert, Libn.

DOCTORS' MEDICAL CENTER - PROFESSIONAL LIBRARY
1441 Florida Ave.
Box 4138   Phone: (209) 578-1211
Modesto, CA 95352   Margaret F. Luebke, Med.Libn.

GALLO (E. & J.) WINERY - LIBRARY
Box 1130   Phone: (209) 521-3230
Modesto, CA 95353   Jill Elliott, Libn.

MC HENRY MUSEUM - LIBRARY
1402 I St.   Phone: (209) 577-5366
Modesto, CA 95354   Heidi L. Warner, Cur.

MEMORIAL HOSPITALS ASSOCIATION - MEDICAL LIBRARY
Box 942   Phone: (209) 526-4500
Modesto, CA 95353   S.A. Hammett, Med.Libn.

MODESTO BEE - EDITORIAL LIBRARY
Box 3928   Phone: (209) 578-2101
Modesto, CA 95352   Lillian Wendt, Libn.

SCENIC GENERAL HOSPITAL - STANISLAUS COUNTY MEDICAL LIBRARY
830 Scenic Dr.
Box 3271   Phone: (209) 571-6132
Modesto, CA 95353   Margie A. Felt, Med.Lib.Asst.

SHELL DEVELOPMENT COMPANY - BIOLOGICAL SCIENCES RESEARCH
    CENTER - LIBRARY
Box 4248   Phone: (209) 545-8224
Modesto, CA 95352   Patt Snyder, Supv.

STANISLAUS COUNTY LAW LIBRARY
Rm. 223, Courthouse   Phone: (209) 571-6967
Modesto, CA 95354   Mindi E. Conley, Hd. Law Libn.

STANISLAUS COUNTY SCHOOLS - TEACHERS' PROFESSIONAL LIBRARY
801 County Center No. 3 Ct.   Phone: (209) 526-6593
Modesto, CA 95355   V. Ruth Smith, Hd.

WORLD VISION INTERNATIONAL - INFORMATION RESOURCE CENTER
919 W. Huntington Dr.   Phone: (213) 574-9017
Monrovia, CA 91016   Mary H. Janss, Res.Assoc.

COLTON HALL MUSEUM - LIBRARY
Civic Ctr.   Phone: (408) 646-3851
Monterey, CA 93940   Donna Penwell, Musm.Mgr.

COMMUNITY HOSPITAL OF THE MONTEREY PENINSULA - MEDICAL STAFF
    LIBRARY
Box HH   Phone: (408) 624-5311
Monterey, CA 93942   Ruthanne Lowe, Med. Libn.

CTB/MC GRAW-HILL - LIBRARY
Del Monte Research Park   Phone: (408) 649-7919
Monterey, CA 93940   Phyllis H. O'Donovan, Libn.

MARITIME MUSEUM (Allen Knight) - LIBRARY
550 Calle Principal
Box 805   Phone: (408) 375-2553
Monterey, CA 93940   G. Robert Giet, Libn.

MONTEREY HISTORY & ART ASSOCIATION - MAYO HAYES O'DONNELL
    LIBRARY
155 Van Buren St.
Box 805
Monterey, CA 93940   Elizabeth Fielder, Lib.Chm.

MONTEREY INSTITUTE OF INTERNATIONAL STUDIES - LIBRARY
425 Van Buren St.
Box 1978   Phone: (408) 649-3113
Monterey, CA 93940   Dr. Glynn Wood, Dir.

MONTEREY INSTITUTE FOR RESEARCH IN ASTRONOMY - PRISCILLA
    FAIRFIELD BOK LIBRARY
900 Major Sherman Ln.   Phone: (408) 375-3220
Monterey, CA 93940   Cynthia E. Irvine, Pres./Adm.

MONTEREY PUBLIC LIBRARY - RAE COLLECTION ON ARCHITECTURE
625 Pacific St.   Phone: (408) 646-3930
Monterey, CA 93940

U.S. ARMY MUSEUM, PRESIDIO OF MONTEREY - LIBRARY
Ewing Rd., Bldg. 113
AFZW - POM - Museum   Phone: (408) 242-8414
Monterey, CA 93944   Margaret B. Adams, Cur.

U.S. DEPT. OF DEFENSE - LANGUAGE INSTITUTE - ACADEMIC LIBRARY *
Presidio, Bldg. 618   Phone: (408) 242-8206
Monterey, CA 93940   Gary D. Walter, Libn.

U.S. NAVY - NAVAL ENVIRONMENTAL PREDICTION RESEARCH FACILITY -
    TECHNICAL LIBRARY
Naval Postgraduate School
Annex Bldg. 22   Phone: (408) 646-2813
Monterey, CA 93943   Joanne M. May, Libn.

U.S. NAVY - NAVAL POSTGRADUATE SCHOOL - DUDLEY KNOX LIBRARY
                                             Phone: (408) 646-2341
Monterey, CA 93943   Paul Spinks, Dir. of Libs.

MEXICAN-AMERICAN OPPORTUNITY FOUNDATION - INFORMATION AND
    REFERRAL SERVICE - RESOURCE CENTER
670 Monterey Pass Rd.   Phone: (213) 289-0286
Monterey Park, CA 91754   Gloria Cortez, Info. & Referral Coord.

MORAGA HISTORICAL SOCIETY - ARCHIVES
Moraga Public Library
1500 St. Mary's Rd.   Phone: (415) 376-6852
Moraga, CA 94556   Bro. L. Dennis Goodman, F.S.C., Archv.

CALIFORNIA STATE UNIVERSITY AND COLLEGES - MOSS LANDING
    MARINE LABORATORIES - LIBRARY
Box 223   Phone: (408) 633-3304
Moss Landing, CA 95039   Sheila Baldridge, Libn.

ACUREX CORPORATION - CORPORATE LIBRARY
555 Clyde Ave. MS 2-0212   Phone: (415) 964-3200
Mountain View, CA 94039   Charlotte Thunen, Chf.Libn.

BNR INC. - INFORMATION RESOURCE CENTER †
685A E. Middlefield Rd.   Phone: (415) 940-2182
Mountain View, CA 94043   Ms. L.S. Menashian, Mgr.

GTE PRODUCTS CORPORATION - SYLVANIA SYSTEMS GROUP - WESTERN
    DIVISION - TECHNICAL LIBRARY
MC2201
Box F188   Phone: (415) 966-3082
Mountain View, CA 94039   Julie B. del Fierro, Lib.Serv.Supv.

NIELSEN ENGINEERING & RESEARCH, INC. - NEAR TECHNICAL LIBRARY
510 Clyde Ave.   Phone: (415) 968-9457
Mountain View, CA 94043   Judy Faltz, Libn.

PACIFIC STUDIES CENTER - LIBRARY
222B View St.   Phone: (415) 969-1545
Mountain View, CA 94041   Leonard M. Siegel, Dir.

STAUFFER CHEMICAL COMPANY - MOUNTAIN VIEW RESEARCH CENTER
    LIBRARY
Box 760   Phone: (408) 739-0511
Mountain View, CA 94042   Martha L. Manion, Libn.

U.S. NASA - AMES RESEARCH CENTER - LIBRARY
Moffett Field, Mail Stop 202-3   Phone: (415) 965-5157
Mountain View, CA 94035   Sarah C. Dueker, Chf., Lib.Br.

NAPA COUNTY HISTORICAL SOCIETY - LIBRARY
Goodman Library Bldg.
1219 First St.   Phone: (707) 224-1739
Napa, CA 94559   Jess Doud, Exec.Dir./Archv.

RAINBOW CHILD CARE COUNCIL - TOY AND RESOURCE LIBRARY
703 Jefferson St.   Phone: (707) 253-0366
Napa, CA 94559   Katherine Todd, Resource Libn.

PARADISE VALLEY HOSPITAL - MEDICAL LIBRARY
2400 E. Fourth St.   Phone: (714) 470-6311
National City, CA 92050   Norma A. Reyes, Libn.

RMI, INC. - TECHNICAL LIBRARY
225 W. 30th St.   Phone: (619) 474-1076
National City, CA 92050   John M. Truesdell, Mgr., Adm.

NEVADA COUNTY HISTORICAL SOCIETY - SEARLS HISTORICAL LIBRARY
214 Church St.
Nevada City, CA 95959   Edwin L. Tyson, Libn.

NEVADA COUNTY LAW LIBRARY
Courthouse Annex   Phone: (916) 265-1475
Nevada City, CA 95959

NEW ALMADEN MERCURY MINING MUSEUM - LIBRARY
21570 Almaden Rd.
Box 1   Phone: (408) 268-7869
New Almaden, CA 95042   Constance B. Perham, Owner-Dir.

ENVIRONMENTAL RESEARCH & TECHNOLOGY, INC. - WESTERN REGIONAL
    OFFICE - LIBRARY
975 Business Center Dr.   Phone: (805) 499-6582
Newbury Park, CA 91320   Marcia Henry, Libn.

NORTHROP CORPORATION - VENTURA DIVISION - TECHNICAL
    INFORMATION CENTER
1515 Rancho Conejo Blvd.   Phone: (805) 373-2037
Newbury Park, CA 91320   Sarah Anderson, Libn.

LOS ANGELES BAPTIST COLLEGE - ROBERT L. POWELL MEMORIAL LIBRARY
21726 W. Placerita Canyon Rd.
Box 878   Phone: (805) 259-3540
Newhall, CA 91322   Agnes M. Holt, Libn.

FORD AEROSPACE & COMMUNICATIONS CORP. - AERONUTRONIC
DIVISION - TECHNICAL INFORMATION SERVICES
Ford Rd. Phone: (714) 720-4667
Newport Beach, CA 92660 L.H. Linder, Mgr., Tech.Info.Serv.

HOAG MEMORIAL HOSPITAL-PRESBYTERIAN - MEDICAL LIBRARY
301 Newport Blvd.
Box Y Phone: (714) 760-2308
Newport Beach, CA 92663 Mrs. Ute Simons, Med.Libn.

HUGHES AIRCRAFT COMPANY - ENGINEERING LIBRARY
500 Superior Ave. Phone: (714) 759-2492
Newport Beach, CA 92663 Barbara Squyres, Engr.Libn.

NEWPORT HARBOR ART MUSEUM - LIBRARY
850 San Clemente Dr. Phone: (714) 759-1122
Newport Beach, CA 92660 Ruth E. Roe, Libn.

ROCKWELL INTERNATIONAL - NEWPORT BEACH INFORMATION CENTER
4311 Jamboree Blvd., (501-345) Phone: (714) 833-4389
Newport Beach, CA 92660 K.H. Preston, Mgr.

CALIFORNIA STATE REHABILITATION CENTER - RESIDENT LIBRARY †
Box 841 Phone: (714) 737-2683
Norco, CA 91760 Gerald O. Nelson, Libn.

WILDERNESS LEADERSHIP INTERNATIONAL - OUTDOOR LIVING LIBRARY
Wilderness Leadership Center
Box 770
North Fork, CA 93643

AMERICAN INSTITUTE OF FAMILY RELATIONS - ROSWELL H. JOHNSON
RESEARCH LIBRARY
4942 Vineland Ave. Phone: (213) 763-7285
North Hollywood, CA 91601 Dr. Edward Peacock, Exec.Dir.

CALIFORNIA STATE UNIVERSITY, NORTHRIDGE - INSTRUCTIONAL
MATERIALS LABORATORY
South Library
18111 Nordhoff St. Phone: (818) 885-2501
Northridge, CA 91330 Karin Duran, Dir.

CALIFORNIA STATE UNIVERSITY, NORTHRIDGE - LIBRARY - HEALTH
SCIENCE COLLECTION
18111 Nordhoff St. Phone: (818) 885-3012
Northridge, CA 91330 Snowdy Dodson, Sci.Ref.Libn.

CALIFORNIA STATE UNIVERSITY, NORTHRIDGE - MAP LIBRARY
18111 Nordhoff St. Phone: (818) 885-3465
Northridge, CA 91330

CALIFORNIA STATE UNIVERSITY, NORTHRIDGE - OVIATT LIBRARY -
SPECIAL COLLECTIONS DEPARTMENT
18111 Nordhoff St. Phone: (818) 885-2832
Northridge, CA 91330 Donald L. Read, Spec.Coll.Libn.

CALIFORNIA STATE UNIVERSITY, NORTHRIDGE - WOMEN'S CENTER *
18111 Nordhoff Phone: (818) 885-2780
Northridge, CA 91330 Deborah Kae Walker, Dir.

NORTHRIDGE HOSPITAL MEDICAL CENTER - ATCHERLEY MEDICAL
LIBRARY
18300 Roscoe Blvd. Phone: (818) 885-8500
Northridge, CA 91328 Kati Kreie, Libn.

TELEDYNE SYSTEMS COMPANY - TECHNICAL LIBRARY
19601 Nordhoff St. Phone: (818) 886-2211
Northridge, CA 91324 Linda Zazueta, Tech.Libn.

U.S. AIR FORCE BASE - NORTON BASE LIBRARY
FL 4448 Phone: (714) 382-7119
Norton AFB, CA 92409 Robert R. DeBaun, Base Libn.

U.S. DEFENSE AUDIOVISUAL AGENCY - DEPOSITORY ACCESSIONS BRANCH
(DAVA-N-OAA)
Norton Activity Phone: (714) 382-6315
Norton AFB, CA 92409 John Faibisy, Br.Chf.

METROPOLITAN STATE HOSPITAL - STAFF LIBRARY
11400 Norwalk Blvd. Phone: (213) 863-7011
Norwalk, CA 90650 G. Calvin Tooker, Libn.

FIREMAN'S FUND INSURANCE COMPANIES - INSURANCE INFORMATION
CENTER
777 San Marin Dr.
Box 777 Phone: (415) 899-2871
Novato, CA 94998

MARIN MUSEUM OF THE AMERICAN INDIAN - LIBRARY
Box 864 Phone: (415) 897-4064
Novato, CA 94948 Helen Stoll, Adm.Asst.

NOVATO UNIFIED SCHOOL DISTRICT - INSTRUCTIONAL MATERIALS
CENTER *
1015 7th St. Phone: (415) 897-4247
Novato, CA 94947 Annette Conklin, Rsrcs.Libn.

SAN RAFAEL INDEPENDENT JOURNAL - NEWSPAPER LIBRARY
7100 Alameda del Prado Phone: (415) 883-8600
Novato, CA 94947 Virginia McKeever, Libn.

ALAMEDA-CONTRA COSTA MEDICAL ASSOCIATION - LIBRARY
1411 E. 31st St. Phone: (415) 534-8055
Oakland, CA 94602 Julia T. Duboczy, Med.Libn.

ALAMEDA COUNTY LAW LIBRARY
1225 Fallon St. Phone: (415) 874-5823
Oakland, CA 94612 Cossette T. Sun, Law Lib.Dir.

ALAMEDA COUNTY LIBRARY - BUSINESS & GOVERNMENT LIBRARY
2201 Broadway Phone: (415) 874-5178
Oakland, CA 94612-3044 David Lewallen, Mgr.

ARCHIVES OF CALIFORNIA ART
Oakland Museum
1000 Oak St. Phone: (415) 273-3005
Oakland, CA 94607 Christine Doran, Libn.

CALIFORNIA COLLEGE OF ARTS AND CRAFTS - MEYER LIBRARY
Broadway at College Phone: (415) 653-8118
Oakland, CA 94618 Robert L. Harper, Hd.Libn.

CALIFORNIA STATE REGIONAL WATER QUALITY CONTROL BOARD, SAN
FRANCISCO BAY REGION - LIBRARY
1111 Jackson St., Rm. 6040 Phone: (415) 464-1255
Oakland, CA 94618 Lawrence P. Kolb, Hd.

CHILDREN'S HOSPITAL MEDICAL CENTER OF NORTHERN CALIFORNIA -
MEDICAL LIBRARY
51st & Grove Sts. Phone: (415) 428-3000
Oakland, CA 94609 Barbara Davenport, Med.Libn.

CROSBY, HEAFEY, ROACH & MAY - LAW LIBRARY
1939 Harrison St. Phone: (415) 834-4820
Oakland, CA 94612 Patrick O'Leary, Libn.

FITZGERALD, ABBOTT AND BEARDSLEY - LAW LIBRARY
1330 Broadway
Oakland, CA 94612-2557 Kathleen Rosso Gage, Legal Asst.Adm.

GLADMAN (Everett A.) MEMORIAL HOSPITAL - MEDICAL LIBRARY
2633 E. 27th St. Phone: (415) 536-8111
Oakland, CA 94601 Elizabeth Edelstein, Libn.

INSTITUTE FOR RESEARCH IN SOCIAL BEHAVIOR - LIBRARY
456 22nd St. Phone: (415) 465-2791
Oakland, CA 94612 Patricia Chun-Spielberg, Libn.

INVESTIGATIVE RESOURCE CENTER - DATA CENTER
464 19th St. Phone: (415) 835-4692
Oakland, CA 94612 Fred Goff, Exec.Dir.

ISI CORPORATION - RESEARCH LIBRARY *
Box 23330 Phone: (415) 832-1400
Oakland, CA 94623 Lynn Krekemeyer, Libn.

KAISER ALUMINUM & CHEMICAL CORPORATION - BUSINESS LIBRARY
300 Lakeside Dr.   Phone: (415) 271-3995
Oakland, CA 94643   Gertrude I. Rooshan, Info.Spec./lib.Mgr.

KAISER-PERMANENTE MEDICAL CENTER - HEALTH LIBRARY
280 W. MacArthur Blvd.   Phone: (415) 428-5000
Oakland, CA 94611   Eileen McAdam, Libn.

KAISER-PERMANENTE MEDICAL CENTER - MEDICAL LIBRARY
280 W. MacArthur Blvd.   Phone: (415) 428-5033
Oakland, CA 94611   Helen C. Sheward, Libn.

KAISER-PERMANENTE MEDICAL CENTERS, NORTHERN CALIFORNIA
    REGION - REGIONAL HEALTH LIBRARY SERVICES
3451 Piedmont Ave.   Phone: (415) 428-7176
Oakland, CA 94611   Caren K. Quay, Regional Cons.

MERRITT (Samuel) HOSPITAL - MEDICAL LIBRARY
Hawthorne & Webster Sts.   Phone: (415) 655-4000
Oakland, CA 94609   Linda Charlmyra Thomas, Med.Libn.

METROPOLITAN TRANSPORTATION COMMISSION - ASSOCIATION OF BAY
    AREA GOVERNMENTS (ABAG) - LIBRARY
101 8th St.   Phone: (415) 849-3223
Oakland, CA 94607   Dian Gillmar, Info.Coord.

MILLS COLLEGE - ARCHIVES
Library   Phone: (415) 632-2700
Oakland, CA 94613

MILLS COLLEGE - MARGARET PRALL MUSIC LIBRARY
5000 MacArthur Blvd.
Oakland, CA 94613   Hedy Wong, Coord.

OAKLAND CITY PLANNING DEPARTMENT - LIBRARY *
City Hall, 6th Fl.
Oakland, CA 94612

OAKLAND PUBLIC LIBRARY - AMERICAN INDIAN LIBRARY PROJECT
Dimond Branch Library
3536 Fruitvale Ave.   Phone: (415) 273-3511
Oakland, CA 94602   Marian Nichols, Supv.

OAKLAND PUBLIC LIBRARY - ART, MUSIC, RECREATION
125 14th St.   Phone: (415) 273-3178
Oakland, CA 94612   Richard Colvig, Sr.Libn.

OAKLAND PUBLIC LIBRARY - ASIAN LIBRARY
449 9th St.   Phone: (415) 273-3400
Oakland, CA 94607   Suzanne Lo, Hd.Libn.

OAKLAND PUBLIC LIBRARY - CITYLINE INFORMATION SERVICE
Oakland City Hall
1 City Hall Plaza   Phone: (415) 444-2489
Oakland, CA 94612   MaryLou T. Martin, Libn.

OAKLAND PUBLIC LIBRARY - HANDICAPPED SERVICES
125 14th St.   Phone: (415) 273-3133
Oakland, CA 94612   Jean Paeth, Supv.Libn.

OAKLAND PUBLIC LIBRARY - HISTORY/LITERATURE DIVISION
125 14th St.   Phone: (415) 273-3136
Oakland, CA 94612   Marilyn G. Rowan, Sr.Libn.

OAKLAND PUBLIC LIBRARY - LATIN AMERICAN LIBRARY
1900 Fruitvale Ave., Suite 1-A   Phone: (415) 532-7882
Oakland, CA 94601   Patrick Haggarty, Libn.

OAKLAND PUBLIC LIBRARY - SCIENCE/SOCIOLOGY DIVISION
125 14th St.   Phone: (415) 273-3138
Oakland, CA 94612   Richard Ragsdale, Sr.Libn.

THE (Oakland) TRIBUNE - LIBRARY
Box 24424   Phone: (415) 645-2745
Oakland, CA 94623   Yae Shinomiya, Libn.

RAYMOND KAISER ENGINEERS, INC. - ENGINEERING LIBRARY
300 Lakeside Dr.
Box 23210   Phone: (415) 271-4375
Oakland, CA 94623   Elaine Zacher, Tech.Libn.

SAFEWAY STORES, INC. - LIBRARY
201 Fourth St.   Phone: (415) 891-3175
Oakland, CA 94660   Virginia A. Veit, Lib.Mgr.

SOCIETY OF MAYFLOWER DESCENDANTS IN THE STATE OF CALIFORNIA -
    LIBRARY
Terrace Level
405 14th St.   Phone: (415) 451-9599
Oakland, CA 94612   Oliver S. Hayward, Libn.

TRANS-PACIFIC GEOTHERMAL, INC. - LIBRARY
1419 Broadway, Suite 415   Phone: (415) 763-7812
Oakland, CA 94612   Katherine Bertolucci, Libn.

U.S. NAVY - NAVAL HOSPITAL (CA-Oakland) - MEDICAL LIBRARY
8750 Mountain Blvd.   Phone: (415) 639-2031
Oakland, CA 94627   Jane C. O'Sullivan, Adm.Libn.

UNIVERSITY OF CALIFORNIA, BERKELEY - NAVAL BIOSCIENCES
    LABORATORY - LIBRARY
Bldg. 844, Naval Supply Ctr.   Phone: (415) 832-5217
Oakland, CA 94625   Theresa Dundon, Libn.

WEST COAST LESBIAN COLLECTIONS, INC.
Box 23753   Phone: (415) 465-8080
Oakland, CA 94623

WHALE CENTER - EXTINCT SPECIES MEMORIAL FUND - LIBRARY
3929 Piedmont Ave.   Phone: (415) 654-6621
Oakland, CA 94611   Kathy Bertolucci, Hd.Libn.

WILSON, IHRIG & ASSOCIATES - LIBRARY
5776 Broadway   Phone: (415) 658-6719
Oakland, CA 94618   Thomas Mugglestone, Libn.

ROSICRUCIAN FELLOWSHIP - LIBRARY
2220 Mission Ave.   Phone: (619) 757-6601
Oceanside, CA 92054   N.D. Willoughby, Libn.

WITCO CHEMICAL CORPORATION - GOLDEN BEAR DIVISION - QC/R & D
    LIBRARY
Ferguson & Manor Rds.
Box 5446   Phone: (805) 393-7110
Oildale, CA 93388   Euthene Snell, Libn.

KROTONA INSTITUTE OF THEOSOPHY - KROTONA LIBRARY - BETTY
    WARRINGTON MEMORIAL †
Krotona 2   Phone: (805) 646-2653
Ojai, CA 93023   Erna Achenbach, Hd.Libn.

THEOSOPHICAL BOOK ASSOCIATION FOR THE BLIND, INC.
Krotona 54   Phone: (805) 646-2121
Ojai, CA 93023   Dennis Gottschalk, Pres.

SUNKIST GROWERS, INC. - RESEARCH LIBRARY
760 E. Sunkist St.   Phone: (714) 983-9811
Ontario, CA 91761   Martha C. Nemeth, Tech.Libn.

GREENLEAF (Simon) SCHOOL OF LAW - LIBRARY †
2530 Shadow Ridge Ln.   Phone: (714) 998-2888
Orange, CA 92667   Dr. John Warwick Montgomery, Esq., Dir.

HOLMES & NARVER, INC. - TECHNICAL LIBRARY *
999 Town & Country Rd.   Phone: (714) 973-1100
Orange, CA 92668   Connie Rickerson, Libn.

LOYOLA MARYMOUNT UNIVERSITY - ORANGE CAMPUS LIBRARY
480 S. Batavia St.   Phone: (714) 633-8121
Orange, CA 92668-3998   Sr. Therese Zickgraf, C.S.J., Libn.

ST. JOSEPH HOSPITAL - BURLEW MEDICAL LIBRARY
1100 Stewart Dr.   Phone: (714) 771-8291
Orange, CA 92668   Julie Smith, Dir., Lib.Serv.

SANTA FE DRILLING COMPANY - LIBRARY
505 S. Main St.   Phone: (714) 567-8818
Orange, CA 92668-0401   Helen Kramer, Libn.

UNIVERSITY OF CALIFORNIA, IRVINE - MEDICAL CENTER LIBRARY
101 City Dr., S.   Phone: (714) 634-5798
Orange, CA 92668   Susan Russell, Hd.Libn.

BUTTE COUNTY LAW LIBRARY
Courthouse, One Court St.   Phone: (916) 534-4611
Oroville, CA 95965   Evlyn L. Turner, Law Libn.

BUTTE COUNTY SUPERINTENDENT OF SCHOOLS - NORTHERN CALIFORNIA
    CENTER FOR EDUCATIONAL IMPROVEMENT
5A County Center Dr.   Phone: (916) 534-4267
Oroville, CA 95965   Mary Lee Six, Dir.

OROVILLE HOSPITAL AND MEDICAL CENTER - EDWARD P. GODDARD, M.D.,
    MEMORIAL LIBRARY
2767 Olive Hwy.   Phone: (916) 533-8500
Oroville, CA 95965   Gertrude N. Bartley, Libn.

ST. JOHN'S MEDICAL CENTER - HEALTH SCIENCE LIBRARY †
333 N. F St.   Phone: (805) 487-7861
Oxnard, CA 93030   Joanne Kennedy, Libn.

PACIFIC GROVE MUSEUM OF NATURAL HISTORY - LIBRARY
165 Forest Ave.
Pacific Grove, CA 93950   Vernal L. Yadon, Musm.Dir.

PACIFIC GROVE PUBLIC LIBRARY - ALVIN SEALE SOUTH SEAS
    COLLECTION
550 Central Ave.   Phone: (408) 373-0603
Pacific Grove, CA 93950   Margaret McBride, Lib.Dir.

STANFORD UNIVERSITY - HOPKINS MARINE STATION - LIBRARY
Cabrillo Point   Phone: (408) 373-0460
Pacific Grove, CA 93950   Alan Baldridge, Hd.Libn.

AMERICAN LAWN BOWLS ASSOCIATION - LIBRARY
445 Surfview Dr.   Phone: (213) 454-2775
Pacific Palisades, CA 90272   Harold L. Esch, Hist.

LIVING DESERT RESERVE - HAYNES MEMORIAL LIBRARY
Box 1775   Phone: (619) 346-5694
Palm Desert, CA 92261

UNIVERSITY OF CALIFORNIA, RIVERSIDE - DEEP CANYON DESERT
    RESEARCH CENTER - LIBRARY
Box 1738   Phone: (619) 341-3655
Palm Desert, CA 92261   Allan Muth, Ph.D., Resident Dir.

ALZA CORPORATION - RESEARCH LIBRARY
950 Page Mill Rd.   Phone: (415) 494-5215
Palo Alto, CA 94304   Mary Susan Laird, Mgr., Lib.Serv.

AMERICAN INSTITUTES FOR RESEARCH - LIBRARY
1791 Arastradero Rd.
Box 1113   Phone: (415) 493-3550
Palo Alto, CA 94302   Nancy Hull, Libn.

AMERICAN INSTITUTES FOR RESEARCH - PROJECT TALENT DATA BANK *
Box 1113   Phone: (415) 493-3550
Palo Alto, CA 94302   Lauri Steel, Dir., Data Bank

BECKMAN INSTRUMENTS, INC. - SPINCO DIVISION - TECHNICAL LIBRARY
1050 Page Mill Rd.   Phone: (415) 859-1734
Palo Alto, CA 94304   Yvonne Boxerman, Libn.

COLLAGEN CORPORATION - LIBRARY
2500 Faber Pl.   Phone: (415) 856-0200
Palo Alto, CA 94303   Hunter McCleary, Lit.Sci.

DIALOG INFORMATION SERVICES, INC.
3460 Hillview Ave.   Phone: (415) 858-3785
Palo Alto, CA 94304   Dr. Roger K. Summit, Pres.

DNAX RESEARCH INSTITUTE - LIBRARY
1450 Page Mill Rd.   Phone: (415) 856-8444
Palo Alto, CA 94304   Katherine Little, Info.Coord.

DYNAPOL - LIBRARY †
445 Cambridge Ave.   Phone: (415) 321-1032
Palo Alto, CA 94304   Sharon R. Hamrick, Libn.

ELECTRIC POWER RESEARCH INSTITUTE - TECHNICAL LIBRARY
3412 Hillview Ave.   Phone: (415) 855-2354
Palo Alto, CA 94304   Stephen B. Parker, Libn.

FAIRCHILD CAMERA AND INSTRUMENT CORPORATION - RESEARCH
    CENTER LIBRARY
4001 Miranda Ave.   Phone: (415) 858-4298
Palo Alto, CA 94304   Betty L. Whitney, Asst.Libn.

FIRST CONGREGATIONAL CHURCH - LIBRARY *
1985 Louis Rd.   Phone: (415) 856-6662
Palo Alto, CA 94303

FORD AEROSPACE & COMMUNICATIONS CORP. - WESTERN DEVELOPMENT
    LABORATORIES (WDL) - TECHNICAL LIBRARY
3939 Fabian Way   Phone: (415) 852-6993
Palo Alto, CA 94303   Lee F. Perkins, Chf.Libn.

HEWLETT-PACKARD COMPANY - CORPORATE LIBRARY
1501 Page Mill Rd.   Phone: (415) 857-3091
Palo Alto, CA 94304   William C. Petru, Mgr. of Libs.

HEWLETT-PACKARD COMPANY - HP LABORATORIES - DEER CREEK
    LIBRARY
Box 10350   Phone: (415) 857-5205
Palo Alto, CA 94303-0867   Nancy E. Lem, Libn.

LOCKHEED MISSILES & SPACE COMPANY, INC. - TECHNICAL
    INFORMATION CENTER
3251 Hanover St.   Phone: (415) 424-2802
Palo Alto, CA 94304   Ralph W. Lewis, Mgr.

OCEANROUTES, INC. - TECHNICAL LIBRARY
3260 Hillview Ave.   Phone: (415) 493-3600
Palo Alto, CA 94304   Mari Wilson, Tech.Libn.

PALO ALTO MEDICAL FOUNDATION - BARNETT-HALL LIBRARY
860 Bryant St.   Phone: (415) 321-4121
Palo Alto, CA 94301   Eileen E. Cassidy, Hd.Libn.

PALO ALTO UNIFIED SCHOOL DISTRICT - INSTRUCTIONAL MATERIALS
    CENTER
Greendell School, Rm. 9
4120 Middlefield Rd.   Phone: (415) 855-8355
Palo Alto, CA 94306   Jack Gibbany, Prog.Coord.

PENINSULA CONSERVATION FOUNDATION - LIBRARY OF THE
    ENVIRONMENT
2253 Park Blvd.   Phone: (415) 328-5313
Palo Alto, CA 94306   Nancy S. Olson, Libn.

PENINSULA TIMES TRIBUNE - LIBRARY
245 Lytton Ave.
Box 300   Phone: (415) 853-5244
Palo Alto, CA 94302   Elizabeth R. Miller, Hd.Libn.

R & E RESEARCH ASSOCIATES - LIBRARY
936 Industrial
Palo Alto, CA 94303

SYNTEX, U.S.A. - CORPORATE LIBRARY/INFORMATION SERVICES
3401 Hillview Ave.   Phone: (415) 855-5431
Palo Alto, CA 94304   Gerry Seward, Mgr.

SYSTEMS CONTROL GROUP - TECHNICAL LIBRARY
1801 Page Mill Rd.
Box 10025   Phone: (408) 494-1165
Palo Alto, CA 94303   Martha Liles, Libn.

SYVA COMPANY - LIBRARY/INFORMATION CENTER
900 Arastradero Rd.   Phone: (415) 493-2200
Palo Alto, CA 94304   Louise Lohr, Mgr.

U.S. VETERANS ADMINISTRATION (CA-Palo Alto) - MEDICAL CENTER -
  MEDICAL LIBRARIES
3801 Miranda Ave.   Phone: (415) 493-5000
Palo Alto, CA 94304   C.R. Gallimore, Chf., Lib.Serv.

VARIAN ASSOCIATES - TECHNICAL LIBRARY
611 Hansen Way   Phone: (415) 493-4000
Palo Alto, CA 94303   Joan Murphy, Mgr., Lib.Serv.

XEROX CORPORATION - PALO ALTO RESEARCH CENTER - TECHNICAL
  INFORMATION CENTER
3333 Coyote Hill Rd.   Phone: (415) 494-4042
Palo Alto, CA 94304   Giuliana A. Lavendel, Mgr.

ZOECON CORPORATION - LIBRARY
975 California Ave.
Box 10975   Phone: (415) 857-1130
Palo Alto, CA 94303   Carolyn A. Erickson, Libn.

NORTHROP CORPORATION - RESEARCH AND TECHNOLOGY CENTER -
  LIBRARY SERVICES
One Research Park   Phone: (213) 377-4811
Palos Verdes Peninsula, CA 90274

KAISER-PERMANENTE MEDICAL CENTER - PANORAMA CITY HEALTH
  SCIENCE LIBRARY †
13652 Cantara St.   Phone: (213) 781-2361
Panorama City, CA 91402   Winnie Yu, Hd.Libn.

UNIVERSITY OF CALIFORNIA - KEARNEY AGRICULTURAL CENTER
9240 S. Riverbend Ave.   Phone: (209) 646-2794
Parlier, CA 93648   Fred H. Swanson, Act.Dir.

ART CENTER COLLEGE OF DESIGN - JAMES LEMONT FOGG MEMORIAL
  LIBRARY
1700 Lida St.   Phone: (818) 577-1700
Pasadena, CA 91103   Elizabeth Galloway, Lib.Dir.

AVERY INTERNATIONAL CORPORATION - RESEARCH CENTER LIBRARY *
325 N. Altadena Dr.   Phone: (818) 799-0881
Pasadena, CA 91107   Joanne McKinney, Info.Spec.

BELL & HOWELL COMPANY - DATATAPE DIVISION - LIBRARY/TECHNICAL
  INFORMATION SERVICES †
360 Sierra Madre Villa   Phone: (818) 796-9381
Pasadena, CA 91109   Beverly V. Busenbark, Mgr., Lib.Serv.

BURROUGHS CORPORATION - COMPUTER SYSTEMS GROUP - TECHNICAL
  INFORMATION RESOURCES CENTER
460 Sierra Madre Villa   Phone: (818) 351-6551
Pasadena, CA 91109   Jean Robbins, Mgr.

CALIFORNIA INSTITUTE OF TECHNOLOGY - AERONAUTICS LIBRARY
1201 E. California Blvd.   Phone: (818) 356-4521
Pasadena, CA 91125   Virginia N. Anderson, Libn.

CALIFORNIA INSTITUTE OF TECHNOLOGY - APPLIED PHYSICS/
  ELECTRICAL ENGINEERING LIBRARY
116-81 Steele Labs., Rm. 114   Phone: (818) 356-4851
Pasadena, CA 91125   Paula C. Samazan, Sr.Lib.Asst.

CALIFORNIA INSTITUTE OF TECHNOLOGY - ASTROPHYSICS LIBRARY
1201 E. California Blvd.   Phone: (818) 356-4008
Pasadena, CA 91125   Helen Z. Knudsen, Libn.

CALIFORNIA INSTITUTE OF TECHNOLOGY - CHEMICAL ENGINEERING
  LIBRARY
202 Spaulding Lab.   Phone: (818) 356-4188
Pasadena, CA 91125   April Olson, Lib.Asst.

CALIFORNIA INSTITUTE OF TECHNOLOGY - COMPUTER SCIENCE LIBRARY
1201 E. California Blvd.   Phone: (818) 356-6704
Pasadena, CA 91125   Patricia Gladson, Lib.Asst.

CALIFORNIA INSTITUTE OF TECHNOLOGY - EARTHQUAKE ENGINEERING
  RESEARCH LIBRARY
201 Thomas Lab.   Phone: (818) 356-4227
Pasadena, CA 91125   Donna Covarrubias, Lib.Asst.

CALIFORNIA INSTITUTE OF TECHNOLOGY - ENVIRONMENTAL
  ENGINEERING LIBRARY
136 W.M. Keck Laboratory (138-78)   Phone: (818) 356-4381
Pasadena, CA 91125   Rayma Harrison, Assoc.Libn.

CALIFORNIA INSTITUTE OF TECHNOLOGY - GEOLOGY LIBRARY
201 North Mudd Bldg.   Phone: (818) 356-6699
Pasadena, CA 91125   Daphne Plane, Geology Libn.

CALIFORNIA INSTITUTE OF TECHNOLOGY - INDUSTRIAL RELATIONS
  CENTER - MANAGEMENT LIBRARY
383 S. Hill (1-90)   Phone: (818) 356-4048
Pasadena, CA 91125   Dennis Petticoffer, Libn.

CALIFORNIA INSTITUTE OF TECHNOLOGY - JET PROPULSION
  LABORATORY - LIBRARY
4800 Oak Grove Dr.   Phone: (818) 354-4200
Pasadena, CA 91109   D. Adel Wilder, Mgr., Lib.

CALIFORNIA INSTITUTE OF TECHNOLOGY - MILLIKAN LIBRARY
1201 E. California Blvd.   Phone: (818) 356-6405
Pasadena, CA 91125   Glenn L. Brudvig, Dir. of Libs.

CALIFORNIA INSTITUTE OF TECHNOLOGY - MUNGER AFRICANA LIBRARY
115 Baxter Hall   Phone: (818) 795-6811
Pasadena, CA 91125   Dr. Edwin S. Munger, Dir.

CARNEGIE INSTITUTION OF WASHINGTON - MOUNT WILSON & LAS
  CAMPANAS OBSERVATORIES - LIBRARY
813 Santa Barbara St.   Phone: (818) 577-1122
Pasadena, CA 91101   Joan Gantz, Libn.

CONVERSE CONSULTANTS - CORPORATE LIBRARY *
126 W. Del Mar Blvd.   Phone: (818) 795-0461
Pasadena, CA 91105   Andrea B. Berman, Corp.Libn.

FULLER THEOLOGICAL SEMINARY - MC ALISTER LIBRARY †
135 N. Oakland Ave.   Phone: (818) 449-1745
Pasadena, CA 91101   Christine C. Jewett, Libn.

GREENE AND GREENE LIBRARY
David B. Gamble House
4 Westmoreland Pl.   Phone: (818) 793-3334
Pasadena, CA 91103   Mary Alice Waugh, Lib.Comm.Chm.

HUNTINGTON MEMORIAL HOSPITAL - HEALTH SCIENCES LIBRARY
100 Congress St.   Phone: (818) 258-7869
Pasadena, CA 91105   Samir Zeind, Dir.

INTERNATIONAL INSTITUTE OF MUNICIPAL CLERKS - MANAGEMENT
  INFORMATION CENTER
160 N. Altadena Dr.   Phone: (818) 795-6153
Pasadena, CA 91107   John J. Hunnewell, Exec.Dir.

JEFFERSON (Thomas) RESEARCH CENTER - LIBRARY
1143 N. Lake Ave.   Phone: (818) 798-0791
Pasadena, CA 91104   Frank G. Goble, Pres.

MONTGOMERY (James M.), CONSULTING ENGINEERS - LIBRARY
250 N. Madison Ave.   Phone: (818) 796-9141
Pasadena, CA 91101   Marjorie M. Ford, Libn.

NORTON SIMON MUSEUM OF ART AT PASADENA - LIBRARY AND ARCHIVES
411 W. Colorado Blvd.   Phone: (818) 449-6840
Pasadena, CA 91105

PARSONS (Ralph M.) COMPANY - CENTRAL LIBRARY
100 W. Walnut St.   Phone: (818) 440-3999
Pasadena, CA 91124   Jennifer Stein, Libn.

PASADENA COLLEGE OF CHIROPRACTIC - LIBRARY
1505 N. Marengo   Phone: (818) 798-1141
Pasadena, CA 91103   Mary Beth Hayes, Libn.

PASADENA HISTORICAL SOCIETY - LIBRARY
470 W. Walnut St.   Phone: (818) 577-1660
Pasadena, CA 91103   Sue F. Schechter, Exec.Dir.

PASADENA PUBLIC LIBRARY - ALICE COLEMAN BATCHELDER MUSIC
LIBRARY
285 E. Walnut St.   Phone: (818) 577-4049
Pasadena, CA 91101   Anne Cain, Prin.Libn./Ref.Serv.

PASADENA PUBLIC LIBRARY - BUSINESS-TECHNOLOGY DIVISION
285 E. Walnut St.   Phone: (818) 577-4052
Pasadena, CA 91101   Anne Cain, Prin.Libn./Ref.Serv.

PASADENA PUBLIC LIBRARY - FINE ARTS DIVISION
285 E. Walnut St.   Phone: (818) 577-4049
Pasadena, CA 91101   Anne Cain, Prin.Libn./Ref.Serv.

PASADENA PUBLIC LIBRARY - REFERENCE DIVISION
285 E. Walnut St.   Phone: (818) 577-4054
Pasadena, CA 91101   Anne Cain, Prin.Libn./Ref.Serv.

ST. LUKE HOSPITAL - MEDICAL LIBRARY
2632 E. Washington Blvd.
Box 7021   Phone: (818) 797-1141
Pasadena, CA 91109-7021   Jacquelin Erwin, Libn.

TETRA TECH, INC. - LIBRARY †
630 N. Rosemead Blvd.   Phone: (818) 449-6400
Pasadena, CA 91107   Ella J. Jackson, Libn.

XEROX SPECIAL INFORMATION SYSTEMS - TECHNICAL LIBRARY
250 N. Halstead St., M/S 1369   Phone: (818) 351-2351
Pasadena, CA 91109   Frances A. Piatt, Libn.

PATTON STATE HOSPITAL - STAFF LIBRARY
3102 E. Highland Ave.   Phone: (714) 862-8121
Patton, CA 92369   Mary Sue Stumberg, Libn.

CONTRA COSTA CHILDREN'S COUNCIL - EAST BRANCH LIBRARY
2075-A Railroad Ave.   Phone: (415) 427-5437
Pittsburg, CA 94565   JoAnne Aiello, Mgr.

DOW CHEMICAL U.S.A. - WESTERN DIVISION - LIBRARY
Box 1398   Phone: (415) 432-5199
Pittsburg, CA 94565   Mary Ellen Christensen, Libn.

UNION OIL COMPANY OF CALIFORNIA - TECHNICAL INFORMATION
CENTER
376 S. Valencia Ave.
Box 76   Phone: (714) 528-7201
Placentia, CA 92621   Barbara J. Orosz, Hd.Libn.

EL DORADO COUNTY LAW LIBRARY †
495 Main St.   Phone: (916) 626-2416
Placerville, CA 95667   James Blackford, Lib.Adm.

CONTRA COSTA COUNTY - CENTRAL LIBRARY - LOCAL HISTORY
COLLECTION
1750 Oak Park Blvd.   Phone: (415) 944-3434
Pleasant Hill, CA 94523   Ruth Russell, Hd., Ctrl.Lib.

CLOROX COMPANY - TECHNICAL CENTER LIBRARY
7200 Johnson Dr.
Box 493   Phone: (415) 847-6343
Pleasanton, CA 94566   Mary Anne Hoopes, Libn.

KAISER ALUMINUM & CHEMICAL CORPORATION - TECHNICAL
INFORMATION CENTER
Center for Technology
6177 Sunol Blvd.
Box 877   Phone: (415) 462-1122
Pleasanton, CA 94566   Gary Gerard, Mgr.

U.S. NAVY - NAVAL AIR STATION - TECHNICAL LIBRARY †
Code 6860   Phone: (805) 982-8156
Point Mugu, CA 93042   I.K. Burtnett, Hd.Libn.

U.S. NATL. PARK SERVICE - POINT REYES NATL. SEASHORE - LIBRARY
                                     Phone: (415) 663-1092
Point Reyes, CA 94956

ATMANIKETAN ASHRAM - LIBRARY
1291 Weber St.   Phone: (714) 629-8255
Pomona, CA 91768   Michael Zucker, Libn.

CALIFORNIA STATE POLYTECHNIC UNIVERSITY, POMONA - LIBRARY -
SPECIAL COLLECTIONS
3801 W. Temple Ave.   Phone: (714) 598-4671
Pomona, CA 91768   Mary Lee DeVilbiss, Spec.Coll.Libn.

GENERAL DYNAMICS CORPORATION - POMONA DIVISION - DIVISION
LIBRARY MZ 4-20
Box 2507   Phone: (714) 620-7511
Pomona, CA 91769   J.G. Boyajian, Chf.Libn.

LANTERMAN (Frank D.) STATE HOSPITAL AND DEVELOPMENT CENTER -
STAFF LIBRARY
3530 W. Pomona Blvd.
Box 100   Phone: (714) 595-1221
Pomona, CA 91769   Laurie Piccolotti, Libn.

POMONA PUBLIC LIBRARY - SPECIAL COLLECTIONS DEPARTMENT
625 S. Garey Ave.
Box 2271   Phone: (714) 620-2033
Pomona, CA 91766   David Streeter, Spec.Coll.Libn.

POMONA VALLEY COMMUNITY HOSPITAL - MEDICAL LIBRARY
1798 N. Garey Ave.   Phone: (714) 623-8715
Pomona, CA 91767   Shirley Chervin, Libn.

U.S. NAVY - NAVAL CONSTRUCTION BATTALION CENTER - LIBRARY
Code 31L   Phone: (805) 982-4411
Port Hueneme, CA 93043   Betty M. Smith, Libn.

U.S. NAVY - NAVAL FACILITIES ENGINEERING COMMAND - HISTORICAL
INFORMATION OFFICE
Naval Construction Batalion Ctr.   Phone: (805) 982-5563
Port Hueneme, CA 93043

U.S. NAVY - NAVAL SCHOOL - CIVIL ENGINEER CORPS OFFICERS -
MOREELL LIBRARY
                                     Phone: (805) 982-3241
Port Hueneme, CA 93043   Dianne G. Thompson, Lib.Dir.

PORTERVILLE STATE HOSPITAL - MEDICAL LIBRARY
Box 2000   Phone: (209) 784-2000
Porterville, CA 93257   Mary Jane Berry, Libn.

SIERRA VIEW DISTRICT HOSPITAL - MEDICAL LIBRARY
465 W. Putnam Ave.   Phone: (209) 784-1110
Porterville, CA 93257   Marilyn R. Pankey, Dir., Med.Rec.

U.S. ARMY HOSPITALS - LETTERMAN ARMY MEDICAL CENTER - MEDICAL
LIBRARY
Bldg. 1100, Rm. 338   Phone: (415) 561-2465
Presidio of San Francisco, CA 94123   William Koch, Adm.Libn.

U.S. ARMY POST - PRESIDIO OF SAN FRANCISCO - POST LIBRARY SYSTEM
Bldg. 386   Phone: (415) 561-3448
Presidio of San Francisco, CA 94129   Juanita Taylor, Chf.Libn.

PLUMAS COUNTY LAW LIBRARY
Court House
Box 686   Phone: (916) 283-2365
Quincy, CA 95971   Thomas H. Davis, Libn.

EISENHOWER MEDICAL CENTER - DEL E. WEBB MEMORIAL MEDICAL
INFORMATION CENTER
39000 Bob Hope Dr.   Phone: (714) 340-3911
Rancho Mirage, CA 92270   Jean Atkinson, Chf.Med.Libn.

SALVATION ARMY SCHOOL FOR OFFICERS TRAINING - ELFTMAN
MEMORIAL LIBRARY
30840 Hawthorne Blvd.   Phone: (213) 377-0481
Rancho Palos Verdes, CA 90274   Lavonne D. Robertson, Hd.Libn.

TEHAMA COUNTY LAW LIBRARY
Court House, Rm. 20
Red Bluff, CA 96080   Jill Miller, Lib.Ck.

CH2M HILL, INC. - INFORMATION CENTER
1525 Court St.
Box 2088   Phone: (916) 243-5831
Redding, CA 96001   Virginia Merryman, Libn.

SHASTA COUNTY LAW LIBRARY
Court House
Redding, CA 96001   Joan Odell, Law Libn.

LINCOLN MEMORIAL SHRINE - LIBRARY
120 4th St.
Box 751   Phone: (714) 793-6622
Redlands, CA 92373   Dr. Larry E. Burgess, Cur.

SAN BERNARDINO COUNTY MUSEUM - WILSON C. HANNA LIBRARY/
   RESEARCH LIBRARY †
2024 Orange Tree Lane   Phone: (714) 792-1334
Redlands, CA 92373   Dr. Gerald A. Smith, Dir.

TRW, INC. - OPERATIONS & SUPPORT GROUP - ELECTRONICS & DEFENSE
   SECTOR - TECH. INFORMATION CENTER
One Space Park, Bldg. S., Rm. 1930   Phone: (213) 536-2631
Redondo Beach, CA 90278   Donna M. Mendenhall, Mgr.

AMPEX CORPORATION - TECHNICAL INFORMATION SERVICES
401 Broadway   Phone: (415) 367-3368
Redwood City, CA 94063   Marjorie Pettit Wilbur, Mgr.Tech.Info.Serv.

CANADA COLLEGE - RUSSELL L. STIMSON OPHTHALMIC REFERENCE
   LIBRARY
4200 Farm Hill Blvd.   Phone: (415) 364-1212
Redwood City, CA 94061   Irwin Vogel, Coord.

FLUOR ENGINEERS, INC. - MINING & METALS DIVISION - TECHNICAL
   LIBRARY
10 Twin Dolphin Dr., B308   Phone: (415) 595-6177
Redwood City, CA 94065   Sue Polzoni, Lib.Mgr.

MOBIL LAND DEVELOPMENT CORPORATION - LIBRARY
3 Twin Dolphin Dr., Suite 200   Phone: (415) 594-4200
Redwood City, CA 94065   Barbara Bernhart, Libn.

SAN MATEO COUNTY EDUCATIONAL RESOURCES CENTER
333 Main St.   Phone: (415) 363-5470
Redwood City, CA 94063   Dr. Curtis May, Adm., Media & Lib.Serv.

SAN MATEO COUNTY LAW LIBRARY *
Hall of Justice & Records   Phone: (415) 363-4160
Redwood City, CA 94063   Robert D. Harrington, Dir.

WILLIAMS-KUEBELBECK & ASSOCIATES, INC. - LIBRARY
611 Veterans Blvd., Suite 205   Phone: (415) 365-7202
Redwood City, CA 94063   Nancy Jane Myers, Libn.

CHEVRON ENVIRONMENTAL HEALTH CENTER, INC. - TECHNICAL
   INFORMATION CENTER †
576 Standard Ave.   Phone: (415) 620-3716
Richmond, CA 94802   J. Thomas Kerns, Supv., Tech.Info.Serv.

CHEVRON RESEARCH COMPANY - TECHNICAL INFORMATION CENTER
576 Standard Ave.   Phone: (415) 620-2105
Richmond, CA 94802   J.M. Hubert, Mgr., Tech.Info.Ctr.

EUREKA (The California Career Information System)
5625 Sutter Ave.   Phone: (415) 524-4976
Richmond, CA 94804   Marilyn Maze, Dir.

STAUFFER CHEMICAL COMPANY - DE GUIGNE TECHNICAL CENTER -
   RESEARCH LIBRARY
1200 S. 47th St.   Phone: (415) 231-1018
Richmond, CA 94804   Linda Saylor, Lib.Supv.

UNIVERSITY OF CALIFORNIA, BERKELEY - EARTHQUAKE ENGINEERING
   RESEARCH CENTER LIBRARY
1301 S. 46th St.   Phone: (415) 231-9403
Richmond, CA 94804   S. Joy Svihra, Hd.

UNIVERSITY OF CALIFORNIA, BERKELEY - FOREST PRODUCTS LIBRARY
47th & Hoffman Blvd.   Phone: (415) 231-9549
Richmond, CA 94804   Peter A. Evans, Libn.

GOLD PARACHUTE LIBRARY, ARCHIVES & TECHNICAL INFORMATION
   CENTER
741 W. Haloid Ave.
Ridgecrest, CA 93555   David Gold, Dir. & Archv.

CANCER FEDERATION - LIBRARY
10932 Magnolia Ave.   Phone: (714) 359-3794
Riverside, CA 92505   John Steinbacher, Exec.Dir.

MOORE (Julie) & ASSOCIATES - LIBRARY
6130 Camino Real, No. 225
Box 5156   Phone: (714) 684-0441
Riverside, CA 92517-5156   Julie L. Moore, Bibliog.

RIVERSIDE COUNTY LAW LIBRARY
3535 Tenth St., Suite 100   Phone: (714) 787-2460
Riverside, CA 92501   Gayle Edelman, Law Libn.

RIVERSIDE GENERAL HOSPITAL - MEDICAL LIBRARY
9851 Magnolia Ave.   Phone: (714) 351-7066
Riverside, CA 92503   Richard M. Butler, Dir., Medical Rec.

RIVERSIDE MUNICIPAL MUSEUM - LIBRARY
3720 Orange St.   Phone: (714) 787-7273
Riverside, CA 92501

RIVERSIDE PRESS-ENTERPRISE COMPANY - EDITORIAL LIBRARY
3512 14th St.   Phone: (714) 684-1200
Riverside, CA 92502   Joan Minesinger, Chf.Libn.

UNIVERSITY OF CALIFORNIA, RIVERSIDE - BIO-AGRICULTURAL LIBRARY
                                    Phone: (714) 787-3238
Riverside, CA 92521   Barbara Montanary, Hd.Libn.

UNIVERSITY OF CALIFORNIA, RIVERSIDE - CALIFORNIA MUSEUM OF
   PHOTOGRAPHY
                                    Phone: (714) 787-4787
Riverside, CA 92521   Charles Desmarais, Dir.

UNIVERSITY OF CALIFORNIA, RIVERSIDE - DEPARTMENT OF
   ENTOMOLOGY - LIBRARY
                                    Phone: (714) 787-4315
Riverside, CA 92521   Saul I. Frommer, Sr.Musm.Sci.

UNIVERSITY OF CALIFORNIA, RIVERSIDE - EDUCATION SERVICES
   LIBRARY
Box 5900   Phone: (714) 787-3715
Riverside, CA 92517   Marie Genung, Hd., Educ.Serv.

UNIVERSITY OF CALIFORNIA, RIVERSIDE - ENGLISH DEPARTMENT
   LIBRARY
Humanities Bldg.   Phone: (714) 787-5301
Riverside, CA 92521   Elizabeth Lang, Hd.

UNIVERSITY OF CALIFORNIA, RIVERSIDE - GOVERNMENT PUBLICATIONS
   DEPARTMENT - LIBRARY
Box 5900   Phone: (714) 787-3226
Riverside, CA 92517   James Rothenberger, Dept.Hd.

UNIVERSITY OF CALIFORNIA, RIVERSIDE - MAP SECTION - LIBRARY
Box 5900   Phone: (714) 787-3226
Riverside, CA 92517   James Rothenberger, Dept.Hd.

UNIVERSITY OF CALIFORNIA, RIVERSIDE - MUSIC LIBRARY
                                    Phone: (714) 787-3137
Riverside, CA 92521   John W. Tanno, Assoc.Univ.Libn.

UNIVERSITY OF CALIFORNIA, RIVERSIDE - OFFICE OF TECHNICAL INFO. -
   STATEWIDE AIR POLLUTION RESEARCH CTR.
Riverside, CA 92521

UNIVERSITY OF CALIFORNIA, RIVERSIDE - PHYSICAL SCIENCES LIBRARY
                                    Phone: (714) 787-3511
Riverside, CA 92517   Richard W. Vierich, Hd.Libn.

UNIVERSITY OF CALIFORNIA, RIVERSIDE - SPECIAL COLLECTIONS
Box 5900   Phone: (714) 787-3233
Riverside, CA 92517   Clifford R. Wurfel, Hd., Spec.Coll.

HOUZE, SHOURDS & MONTGOMERY, INC. - RESEARCH LIBRARY
27520 Hawthorne Blvd., Suite 190   Phone: (213) 377-6400
Rolling Hills Estates, CA 90274   Evan Shanea

ASSOCIATION OF BALLOON & AIRSHIP CONSTRUCTORS - TECHNICAL
    LIBRARY
Box 7
Rosemead, CA 91770   George E. Wright, Jr., Pres.

DON BOSCO TECHNICAL INSTITUTE - LEE LIBRARY †
1151 N. San Gabriel Blvd.   Phone: (213) 280-0451
Rosemead, CA 91770   Phyllis Swistock, Hd.Libn.

SOUTHERN CALIFORNIA EDISON COMPANY - LIBRARY
2244 Walnut Grove Ave.
Box 800   Phone: (213) 572-2096
Rosemead, CA 91770   Mary L. Parker, Corp.Libn.

FIREARMS RESEARCH AND IDENTIFICATION ASSOCIATION - LIBRARY
18638 Alderbury Dr.   Phone: (818) 964-7885
Rowland Heights, CA 91748   John Armand Caudron, Pres.

RIVERSIDE COUNTY HISTORICAL COMMISSION - LIBRARY
4600 Crestmore Rd.
Box 3507   Phone: (714) 787-2551
Rubidoux, CA 92509   Stephen Becker, Dir.

AEROJET-CHEMICAL CORPORATION - AEROJET SOLID PROPULSION
    COMPANY - TECHNICAL INFORMATION CENTER †
Box 13400   Phone: (916) 355-4076
Sacramento, CA 95813   Rimma Mironenko, Tech.Libn.

AMERICAN INTERNATIONAL DATASEARCH
2326 Fair Oaks Blvd., Suite C   Phone: (800) 223-2437
Sacramento, CA 95825   Joseph Hustein, Pres.

AMERICAN JUSTICE INSTITUTE - LIBRARY
725 University Ave.   Phone: (916) 924-3700
Sacramento, CA 95825-6793   Deborah Scowcroft, Adm.Asst.

CALIFORNIA AIR RESOURCES BOARD - LIBRARY
1131 S St.
Box 2815   Phone: (916) 323-8377
Sacramento, CA 95812   Mark T. Edwards, Libn.

CALIFORNIA - STATE ARCHIVES
Archives Bldg., Rm. 130
1020 O St.   Phone: (916) 445-4293
Sacramento, CA 95814   John F. Burns, Chf. of Archv.

CALIFORNIA STATE BOARD OF EQUALIZATION - LAW LIBRARY
1020 North St., Rm. 289   Phone: (916) 445-7356
Sacramento, CA 95808   Barbara Griffith Elbrecht, Sr.Libn.

CALIFORNIA STATE DEPARTMENT OF ALCOHOL AND DRUG PROGRAMS -
    INFORMATION CLEARINGHOUSE
111 Capitol Mall   Phone: (916) 323-1873
Sacramento, CA 95814   Thomas D. Peck, Educ.Cons.

CALIFORNIA STATE DEPARTMENT OF TRANSPORTATION - LABORATORY
    LIBRARY
5900 Folsom Blvd.   Phone: (916) 739-2152
Sacramento, CA 95819   Christine Portillo, Sr.Libn.

CALIFORNIA STATE DEPARTMENT OF TRANSPORTATION - LAW LIBRARY
1120 N St., Rm. 1315   Phone: (916) 445-2291
Sacramento, CA 95807   Lorna J. Flesher, Supv.Libn.

CALIFORNIA STATE DEPARTMENT OF TRANSPORTATION -
    TRANSPORTATION LIBRARY
1120 N St.   Phone: (916) 445-3230
Sacramento, CA 95807   Edith Darknell, Supv.Libn.

CALIFORNIA STATE DEPARTMENT OF WATER RESOURCES - LAW LIBRARY
1416 Ninth St., Rm. 1118-13   Phone: (916) 445-2839
Sacramento, CA 95814   Frances Pearson, Libn.

CALIFORNIA STATE ENERGY COMMISSION - LIBRARY
1516 Ninth St.   Phone: (916) 324-3006
Sacramento, CA 95814   Diana Fay Watkins, Sr.Libn.

CALIFORNIA STATE HEALTH AND WELFARE AGENCY DATA CENTER -
    TECHNICAL LIBRARY UNIT *
112 J St.   Phone: (916) 323-7739
Sacramento, CA 95814   Geraldine I. Fontes, Staff Serv.Anl.

CALIFORNIA STATE LIBRARY
Library & Courts Bldg.
914 Capitol Mall
Box 2037   Phone: (916) 445-2585
Sacramento, CA 95809   Gary E. Strong, State Libn.

CALIFORNIA STATE OFFICE OF LEGISLATIVE COUNSEL - LIBRARY
3021 State Capitol   Phone: (916) 445-2609
Sacramento, CA 95814   Virginia Castro, Lib.Tech.Asst.

CALIFORNIA STATE OFFICE OF THE STATE ARCHITECT - ARCHITECTURE/
    ENGINEERING LIBRARY
1500 5th St.   Phone: (916) 445-8661
Sacramento, CA 95814   Rose A. Granados, Tech.Libn.

CALIFORNIA STATE POSTSECONDARY EDUCATION COMMISSION -
    LIBRARY
1020 Twelfth St.   Phone: (916) 322-8031
Sacramento, CA 95814   Elizabeth Testa, Sr.Libn.

CALIFORNIA STATE RAILROAD MUSEUM - LIBRARY
111 I St.   Phone: (916) 323-8073
Sacramento, CA 95814   Stephen E. Drew, Cur.

CALIFORNIA STATE RESOURCES AGENCY - LIBRARY
1416 Ninth St., Rm. 117   Phone: (916) 445-7752
Sacramento, CA 95814   Madeleine A. Darcy, Sr.Libn.

CALIFORNIA STATE UNIVERSITY, SACRAMENTO - LIBRARY - MEDIA
    SERVICES CENTER
2000 Jed Smith Dr.   Phone: (916) 454-6466
Sacramento, CA 95819   Sheila J. Marsh, Media Libn.

CALIFORNIA STATE UNIVERSITY, SACRAMENTO - LIBRARY - SCIENCE &
    TECHNOLOGY REFERENCE DEPARTMENT
2000 Jed Smith Dr.   Phone: (916) 454-6373
Sacramento, CA 95819   Barbara A. Charlton, Sci./Tech.Ref.Libn.

CH2M HILL, INC. - LIBRARY
555 Capitol Mall, Suite 1290   Phone: (916) 441-3955
Sacramento, CA 95814   Joy Steveson, Libn.

CROCKER ART MUSEUM - RESEARCH LIBRARY
216 O St.   Phone: (916) 446-4677
Sacramento, CA 95814   Gordon P. Martin, Dir., Res.Lib.

KAISER-PERMANENTE MEDICAL CENTER - HEALTH SCIENCES LIBRARY
2025 Morse Ave.
Box 254999   Phone: (916) 486-5813
Sacramento, CA 95825   Michael W. Bennett, Health Sci.Libn.

MC GEORGE SCHOOL OF LAW - LAW LIBRARY
3282 Fifth Ave.
University of the Pacific
Sacramento, CA 95817   Alice J. Murray, Dir.

MEN'S RIGHTS, INC. - READING CENTER
Box 163180   Phone: (916) 482-1622
Sacramento, CA 95816   Fredric Hayward, Dir.

SACRAMENTO AREA COUNCIL OF GOVERNMENTS - LIBRARY *
800 H St.   Phone: (916) 441-5930
Sacramento, CA 95814   Rhonda R. Egan, Libn.

SACRAMENTO BEE - REFERENCE LIBRARY
21st & Q Sts.
Sacramento, CA 95814
Anna M. Michael, Libn.

SACRAMENTO COUNCIL FOR DELAYED PRESCHOOLERS - DAISY TOY
LENDING LIBRARY
890 Morse Ave.
Phone: (916) 485-7494
Sacramento, CA 95825
Tammy Guensler, Dir.

SACRAMENTO COUNTY LAW LIBRARY
Sacramento County Courthouse
720 9th St.
Phone: (916) 444-5910
Sacramento, CA 95814
Shirley H. David, County Law Libn.

SACRAMENTO-EL DORADO MEDICAL SOCIETY - PAUL H. GUTTMAN
LIBRARY
5380 Elvas Ave.
Phone: (916) 452-2671
Sacramento, CA 95819
Kathleen D. Proffit, Libn.

SACRAMENTO - MUSEUM AND HISTORY DIVISION - LIBRARY
1930 J St.
Phone: (916) 447-2958
Sacramento, CA 95814
James E. Henley, Exec.Dir.

SACRAMENTO PUBLIC LIBRARY - BUSINESS & MUNICIPAL DEPARTMENT †
828 I St.
Phone: (916) 449-5203
Sacramento, CA 95814
Dorothy Harvey, Dept.Hd.

SACRAMENTO UNION - EDITORIAL LIBRARY
301 Capitol Mall
Phone: (916) 442-7811
Sacramento, CA 95812
Robin E. Reidy, Libn.

SEARCH GROUP, INC. - LIBRARY
925 Secret River Dr.
Phone: (916) 392-2550
Sacramento, CA 95831
Thomas F. Wilson, Dir., Info. & Pubns.

U.S. ARMY - CORPS OF ENGINEERS - SACRAMENTO DISTRICT -
TECHNICAL INFORMATION CENTER
650 Capitol Mall
Phone: (916) 440-3404
Sacramento, CA 95814
Deborah A. Newton, District Libn.

U.S. BUREAU OF LAND MANAGEMENT - CALIFORNIA STATE OFFICE -
LIBRARY
2800 Cottage Way
Phone: (916) 484-4253
Sacramento, CA 95825
Louise Tichy, Mgt.Asst.

U.S. BUREAU OF RECLAMATION - LIBRARY
2800 Cottage Way
Phone: (916) 484-4404
Sacramento, CA 95825
Margaret Elder, Lib.Techn.

UNIVERSITY OF CALIFORNIA, DAVIS - MEDICAL CENTER LIBRARY
4301 X St.
Phone: (916) 453-3529
Sacramento, CA 95817
Terri L. Malmgren, Libn.

NAPA VALLEY WINE LIBRARY ASSOCIATION - LIBRARY
Box 328
Phone: (707) 963-5244
St. Helena, CA 94574
Mrs. Clayla Davis, Lib.Dir.

SILVERADO MUSEUM
1490 Library Lane
Box 409
Phone: (707) 963-3757
St. Helena, CA 94574
Ellen Shaffer, Cur.

MONTEREY COUNTY LAW LIBRARY
Courthouse
Salinas, CA 93901
Rebecca Serdehely, Libn.

MONTEREY COUNTY OFFICE OF EDUCATION - TEACHERS' RESOURCE
CENTER
Box 80851
Phone: (408) 373-2955
Salinas, CA 93912
Ron Eastwood, Supv.

SALINAS PUBLIC LIBRARY - JOHN STEINBECK LIBRARY
110 W. San Luis St.
Phone: (408) 758-7311
Salinas, CA 93901
John Gross, Dir.

CALAVERAS COUNTY LAW LIBRARY
Government Center
Phone: (209) 754-4252
San Andreas, CA 95249
Jeffrey Tuttle, County Couns.

CALAVERAS COUNTY MUSEUM AND ARCHIVES
Government Center
30 N. Main St.
Phone: (209) 754-4203
San Andreas, CA 95249
Judith Cunningham, Dir./Cur.

YOUNG WOMEN'S CHRISTIAN ASSOCIATION OF MARIN - RESOURCE
CENTER
1000 Sir Francis Drake Blvd.
San Anselmo, CA 94960
Bonnie Rose Hough, Coord.

CALIFORNIA STATE - COURT OF APPEAL, 4TH APPELLATE DISTRICT,
DIVISION TWO - LAW LIBRARY
303 W. Third St.
Phone: (914) 383-4441
San Bernardino, CA 92401
Clint Rees, Libn.

INTERNATIONAL CHRISTIAN GRADUATE UNIVERSITY - LIBRARY
Arrowhead Springs
Phone: (714) 886-7876
San Bernardino, CA 92414
George A. Mindeman, Dir.

ST. BERNARDINE HOSPITAL - NORMAN F. FELDHEYM LIBRARY
2101 North Waterman Ave.
Phone: (714) 883-8711
San Bernardino, CA 92404
Marilyn L. Popik, Med.Libn.

SAN BERNARDINO COMMUNITY HOSPITAL - MEDICAL LIBRARY
1500 W. 17th St.
Phone: (714) 887-6333
San Bernardino, CA 92411
Marlene Goodwin, Med.Libn.

SAN BERNARDINO COUNTY - ENVIRONMENTAL PUBLIC WORKS AGENCY -
RESOURCE CENTER
385 N. Arrowhead
Phone: (714) 383-3438
San Bernardino, CA 92415
Jane Young Bellamy, Libn.

SAN BERNARDINO COUNTY HISTORICAL ARCHIVES
104 W. Fourth St.
Phone: (714) 383-3374
San Bernardino, CA 92415
Jeanette Bernthaler, Act.Archv.

SAN BERNARDINO COUNTY LAW LIBRARY
Court House Annex, Ground Fl.
351 N. Arrowhead Ave.
Phone: (714) 383-1957
San Bernardino, CA 92415-0015
Duncan C. Webb, Dir.

SAN BERNARDINO COUNTY MEDICAL CENTER - MEDICAL LIBRARY
780 E. Gilbert St.
Phone: (714) 383-3367
San Bernardino, CA 92404
Jacqueline M. Wakefield, Med.Libn.

SAN BERNARDINO SUN-TELEGRAM - LIBRARY
399 North D St.
Phone: (714) 889-9666
San Bernardino, CA 92401
Blanche A. Lewis, Libn.

U.S. NATL. ARCHIVES & RECORDS SERVICE - FEDERAL ARCHIVES AND
RECORDS CENTER, REGION 9
1000 Commodore Dr.
Phone: (415) 876-9009
San Bruno, CA 94066
Michael Anderson, Chf., Archv.Br.

WESTERN HIGHWAY INSTITUTE - RESEARCH LIBRARY
1200 Bayhill Dr., Suite 112
San Bruno, CA 94066
Mae Frances Moore, Libn.

CROATIAN-SLOVENIAN-SERBIAN GENEALOGICAL SOCIETY - LIBRARY
2527 San Carlos Ave.
Phone: (415) 592-1190
San Carlos, CA 94070
Adam S. Eterovich, Dir.

LITTON INDUSTRIES - ELECTRON TUBE DIVISION - LIBRARY *
960 Industrial Rd.
Phone: (415) 591-8411
San Carlos, CA 94070
Anne Vaughan, Libn.

VARIAN ASSOCIATES - EIMAC DIVISION - TECHNICAL LIBRARY †
301 Industrial Way
Phone: (415) 592-1221
San Carlos, CA 94070
Merald Shrader, Hd., Engr.

SAN CLEMENTE PRESBYTERIAN CHURCH - SUTHERLAND MEMORIAL
LIBRARY
119 Estrella Ave.
Phone: (714) 492-6158
San Clemente, CA 92672
Ethel Wolleson, Libn.

ARINC RESEARCH CORPORATION - TECHNICAL LIBRARY
4055 Hancock St.
Phone: (619) 222-7447
San Diego, CA 92138
Jill Miller, Libn.

BURROUGHS CORPORATION - RANCHO BERNARDO TECHNICAL
 INFORMATION CENTER
10850 Via Frontera
Box 28810
San Diego, CA 92128
Phone: (619) 451-4438
Marianna M. Seeley, Tech.Libn.

CALIFORNIA SCHOOL OF PROFESSIONAL PSYCHOLOGY - SAN DIEGO
 LIBRARY
3974 Sorrento Valley Blvd.
San Diego, CA 92121
Phone: (619) 453-6880
Richard Sanborn, Libn.

CALIFORNIA STATE - COURT OF APPEAL, 4TH APPELLATE DISTRICT,
 DIVISION ONE - LAW LIBRARY
1350 Front St., Rm. 6010
San Diego, CA 92103
Phone: (619) 237-6023
Kathryn Wagnild Fuller, Sr.Libn.

CALIFORNIA STATE DEPARTMENT OF JUSTICE - ATTORNEY GENERAL'S
 OFFICE - LAW LIBRARY
110 West A St., Suite 600
San Diego, CA 92101
Phone: (619) 237-7642
Fay Henexson, Libn.

CALIFORNIA STATE DEPARTMENT OF TRANSPORTATION - DISTRICT 11
 LIBRARY
2829 Juan St.
San Diego, CA 92110
Phone: (619) 237-6644
Peggy A. Veeder, Libn.

CALIFORNIA WESTERN SCHOOL OF LAW - LIBRARY
350 Cedar St.
San Diego, CA 92101
Phone: (619) 239-0391
Chin Kim, Lib.Dir.

CENTER FOR WOMEN'S STUDIES AND SERVICES - CWSS LIBRARY
908 E St.
San Diego, CA 92101

CHILDHOOD SENSUALITY CIRCLE - LIBRARY
Box 5164
San Diego, CA 92105
Valida Davila, Libn.

CHURCH OF JESUS CHRIST OF LATTER-DAY SAINTS - SAN DIEGO BRANCH
 GENEALOGICAL LIBRARY
3705 Tenth Ave.
San Diego, CA 92103
Phone: (619) 295-9808

CREATION-SCIENCE RESEARCH CENTER - INFORMATION CENTER
5466 Complex St.
San Diego, CA 92123
Phone: (619) 569-8673

CUBIC CORPORATION - TECHNICAL LIBRARY
Box 85587
San Diego, CA 92138-5587
Phone: (619) 277-6780
Maxine Moser, Mgr.

FIRST PRESBYTERIAN CHURCH - CHRISTIAN EDUCATION DEPARTMENT -
 LIBRARY
320 Date St.
San Diego, CA 92101
Phone: (619) 232-7513
Peggy Sparks, Libn.

G.A. TECHNOLOGIES INC. - LIBRARY †
10955 John Jay Hopkins Dr.
Box 85608
San Diego, CA 92138
Phone: (619) 455-3322
Richard J. Tommey, Libn.

GENERAL DYNAMICS CORPORATION - CONVAIR DIVISION - RESEARCH
 LIBRARY
Box 85386
San Diego, CA 92138-5386
Phone: (619) 277-8900
Urban J. Sweeney, Chf.Libn.

GENERAL DYNAMICS CORPORATION - DATAGRAPHIX, INC. -
 ENGINEERING LIBRARY
Box 82449
San Diego, CA 92138
Phone: (619) 291-9960
Ms. M.A. Johnson, Engr.Libn.

GRAY, CARY, AMES & FRYE - LAW LIBRARY
525 B St., Suite 2100
San Diego, CA 92101
Phone: (619) 699-2770
June F. Mac Leod, Law Libn.

HEWLETT-PACKARD COMPANY - SAN DIEGO DIVISION - TECHNICAL
 LIBRARY
16399 W. Bernardo Drive
San Diego, CA 92127
Phone: (619) 487-4100
Cherlyn A. Williams, Lib.Supv.

HIGGS, FLETCHER & MACK - LAW LIBRARY
Box 568
San Diego, CA 92112
Phone: (619) 236-1551
Micki Hallmark, Libn.

IMED CORPORATION - LIBRARY
9925 Carroll Canyon Rd.
San Diego, CA 92131
Phone: (619) 566-9000
Sue R. Albright, Lib.Supv.

JEWISH COMMUNITY CENTER - SAMUEL & REBECCA ASTOR JUDAICA
 LIBRARY
4079 54th St.
San Diego, CA 92105
Phone: (619) 583-3300
Mollie S. Harris, Hd.Libn.

KAISER-PERMANENTE MEDICAL CENTER - HEALTH SCIENCES LIBRARY
4647 Zion Ave.
San Diego, CA 92120
Phone: (619) 563-2190
Sheila E. Latus, Med.Libn.

LOGICON, INC. - TACTICAL & TRAINING SYSTEMS DIVISION LIBRARY
Box 80158
San Diego, CA 92138
Phone: (619) 455-1330
Paula Oquita, Libn.

LUCE, FORWARD, HAMILTON & SCRIPPS - LIBRARY †
110 West A St.
San Diego, CA 92101
Phone: (619) 236-1414
June B. Williams, Libn.

MARKETING INFORMATION INSTITUTE - SELECTED INFORMATION
 LIBRARY CENTER *
861 Sixth Ave., Suite 510
San Diego, CA 92101
Phone: (619) 231-8939
Angela M. Nossal, Libn.

MERCK & COMPANY, INC. - KELCO DIVISION - LITERATURE AND
 INFORMATION SERVICES
8355 Aero Dr.
San Diego, CA 92123
Phone: (619) 292-4900
Ann A. Jenkins, Mgr.

MERCY HOSPITAL AND MEDICAL CENTER - JEAN FARB MEMORIAL
 MEDICAL LIBRARY
4077 Fifth Ave.
San Diego, CA 92103
Phone: (619) 260-7024
Anna M. Habetler, Lib.Dir.

NATIONAL COUNCIL ON YEAR-ROUND EDUCATION - LIBRARY
6401 Linda Vista Rd.
San Diego, CA 92111
Phone: (619) 292-3679
Lucille Guido, Pres.

NATIONAL UNIVERSITY - LAW LIBRARY
3580 Aero Ct.
San Diego, CA 92123
Phone: (619) 563-7318
Lynne Potter

NCR CORPORATION - E&M DIVISION LIBRARY
16550 W. Bernardo Dr.
San Diego, CA 92127
Phone: (619) 485-3291
Doris M. Leeds, Adm./Libn.

NCR CORPORATION - SE/SR LIBRARY
9900 Old Grove Rd.
San Diego, CA 92131
Phone: (619) 963-5473
Deanna Black, Libn.

NESTE, BRUDIN & STONE, INC. - CORPORATE LIBRARY
Box 28100
San Diego, CA 92128
Phone: (619) 485-1500
Patti Perez

PHOTOPHILE - LIBRARY
2311 Kettner Blvd.
San Diego, CA 92101
Phone: (619) 234-4431
Linda L. Rill, Dir.

POINT LOMA NAZARENE COLLEGE - RYAN LIBRARY
3900 Lomaland Dr.
San Diego, CA 92106
Phone: (619) 222-6474
James D. Newburg, Act.Dir.

PRICE-POTTENGER NUTRITION FOUNDATION - LIBRARY
5871 El Cajon Blvd.
San Diego, CA 92115
Phone: (619) 582-4168
Patricia Connolly, Cur.

REES-STEALY MEDICAL GROUP - LIBRARY
2001 Fourth Ave.
San Diego, CA 92101
Phone: (619) 234-6261
Margaret M. O'Rourke, Libn.

SALK INSTITUTE FOR BIOLOGICAL STUDIES - LIBRARY
Box 85800
San Diego, CA 92138
Phone: (619) 453-4100
June A. Gittings, Lib.Coord.

SAN DIEGO AERO-SPACE MUSEUM - N. PAUL WHITTIER HISTORICAL
  AVIATION LIBRARY
2001 Pan America Plaza, Balboa Park   Phone: (619) 234-8291
San Diego, CA 92101   Brewster C. Reynolds, Archv.

SAN DIEGO COUNTY - DEPARTMENT OF PLANNING AND LAND USE -
  LIBRARY
5201 Ruffin Rd., Suite B-2   Phone: (619) 565-3043
San Diego, CA 92123   Sonya Heiserman, Libn.

SAN DIEGO COUNTY LAW LIBRARY
1105 Front St.   Phone: (619) 236-2231
San Diego, CA 92101   O. James Werner, Dir.

SAN DIEGO COUNTY LIBRARY - GOVERNMENTAL REFERENCE LIBRARY
602 County Administration Center
1600 Pacific Hwy.   Phone: (619) 236-2760
San Diego, CA 92101   Ann Terrell, Govt.Ref.Libn.

SAN DIEGO COUNTY OFFICE OF EDUCATION - PROFESSIONAL
  INFORMATION AND RESOURCE CENTER
6401 Linda Vista Rd.   Phone: (619) 292-3669
San Diego, CA 92111   P. Marvin Barbula, Dir.

SAN DIEGO ECOLOGY CENTER - LIBRARY
430 Olive St.   Phone: (619) 294-2926
San Diego, CA 92103   Gaye M. Dingeman, Libn.

SAN DIEGO GAS AND ELECTRIC COMPANY - LIBRARY
Box 1831   Phone: (619) 232-4252
San Diego, CA 92112   Marie A. Peelman, Hd.Libn.

SAN DIEGO HALL OF SCIENCE - BERNICE HARDING LIBRARY
Box 33303   Phone: (619) 238-1233
San Diego, CA 92103   Annajean Naylor, Exec.Sec.

SAN DIEGO HISTORICAL SOCIETY - RESEARCH ARCHIVES
1649 El Prado, Balboa Pk.   Phone: (619) 232-6203
San Diego, CA 92101   Sylvia Arden, Hd.Libn./Archv.

SAN DIEGO HISTORICAL SOCIETY - RESEARCH ARCHIVES - PHOTOGRAPH
  COLLECTION
Box 81825   Phone: (619) 297-3258
San Diego, CA 92138   Larry Booth, Cur.

SAN DIEGO MUSEUM OF ART - REFERENCE LIBRARY
Balboa Park
Box 2107   Phone: (619) 232-7931
San Diego, CA 92112   Nancy J. Andrews, Libn.

SAN DIEGO MUSEUM OF MAN - SCIENTIFIC LIBRARY
1350 El Prado, Balboa Pk.   Phone: (619) 239-2001
San Diego, CA 92101   Jane Bentley, Libn.

SAN DIEGO PUBLIC LIBRARY - ART, MUSIC & RECREATION SECTION
820 E St.   Phone: (619) 236-5810
San Diego, CA 92101   Barbara Tuthill, Supv.Libn.

SAN DIEGO PUBLIC LIBRARY - CALIFORNIA ROOM
820 E St.   Phone: (619) 236-5834
San Diego, CA 92101   Rhoda E. Kruse, Sr.Libn.

SAN DIEGO PUBLIC LIBRARY - GENEALOGY ROOM
820 E St.
San Diego, CA 92101   Rhoda E. Kruse, Sr.Libn.

SAN DIEGO PUBLIC LIBRARY - HISTORY & WORLD AFFAIRS SECTION
820 E St.   Phone: (619) 236-5820
San Diego, CA 92101   Jean Hughes, Sr.Libn.

SAN DIEGO PUBLIC LIBRARY - INFORMATION/DIRECTORY SERVICE
  SECTION
820 E St.   Phone: (619) 236-5800
San Diego, CA 92101   Jean Hughes, Sr.Libn.

SAN DIEGO PUBLIC LIBRARY - LITERATURE & LANGUAGES SECTION
820 E St.   Phone: (619) 236-5816
San Diego, CA 92101   Alyce Archuleta, Sr.Libn.

SAN DIEGO PUBLIC LIBRARY - SCIENCE & INDUSTRY SECTION
820 E St.   Phone: (619) 236-5813
San Diego, CA 92101   Joanne Anderson, Sr.Libn.

SAN DIEGO PUBLIC LIBRARY - SOCIAL SCIENCES SECTION
820 E St.   Phone: (619) 236-5564
San Diego, CA 92101   Margaret E. Queen, Supv.Libn.

SAN DIEGO PUBLIC LIBRARY - WANGENHEIM ROOM
820 E St.   Phone: (619) 236-5807
San Diego, CA 92101   Eileen Boyle, Libn.

SAN DIEGO SOCIETY OF NATURAL HISTORY - NATURAL HISTORY MUSEUM
  LIBRARY
Box 1390   Phone: (619) 232-3821
San Diego, CA 92112   Judith C. Dyer, Libn.

SAN DIEGO STATE UNIVERSITY - BUREAU OF BUSINESS & ECONOMIC
  RESEARCH LIBRARY *
College of Business Administration   Phone: (619) 265-6873
San Diego, CA 92182   Robert P. Hungate, Act.Dir.

SAN DIEGO STATE UNIVERSITY - CENTER FOR PUBLIC ECONOMICS
  LIBRARY *
                                             Phone: (619) 286-6707
San Diego, CA 92182-0511   Dr. George Babilot, Dir.

SAN DIEGO STATE UNIVERSITY - EUROPEAN STUDIES CENTER - LIBRARY
                                             Phone: (619) 265-5928
San Diego, CA 92182-0511   Dr. Leon Rosenstein, Dir.

SAN DIEGO STATE UNIVERSITY - GOVERNMENT PUBLICATIONS
  DEPARTMENT †
                                             Phone: (619) 265-5832
San Diego, CA 92182-0511   Charles Dintrone, Doc.Libn.

SAN DIEGO STATE UNIVERSITY - MALCOLM A. LOVE LIBRARY - SPECIAL
  COLLECTIONS †
                                             Phone: (619) 265-6014
San Diego, CA 92182-0511   Don L. Bosseau, Univ.Libn.

SAN DIEGO STATE UNIVERSITY - MEDIA & CURRICULUM CENTER †
                                             Phone: (619) 265-6757
San Diego, CA 92182-0511   Carole F. Wilson, Chm.

SAN DIEGO STATE UNIVERSITY - PUBLIC ADMINISTRATION RESEARCH
  CENTER LIBRARY
                                             Phone: (619) 286-6084
San Diego, CA 92182-0511   Elaine Wonsowicz, Mgr.

SAN DIEGO STATE UNIVERSITY - SAN DIEGO HISTORY RESEARCH CENTER
  †
University Library   Phone: (619) 265-5751
San Diego, CA 92182-0511   Stephen A. Colston, Dir.

SAN DIEGO STATE UNIVERSITY - SCIENCE DEPARTMENT †
University Library   Phone: (619) 265-6715
San Diego, CA 92182-0511   Lillian Chan, Sci.Libn.

SAN DIEGO STATE UNIVERSITY - SOCIAL SCIENCE RESEARCH
  LABORATORY - LIBRARY *
                                             Phone: (619) 265-5845
San Diego, CA 92182-0511   Paul J. Strand, Dir.

SAN DIEGO UNION-TRIBUNE PUBLISHING COMPANY - LIBRARY
350 Camino De La Reina   Phone: (619) 299-3131
San Diego, CA 92108   Sharon Stewart Reeves, Dir., Lib.Serv.

SCOTTISH RITE BODIES, SAN DIEGO - SCOTTISH RITE MASONIC LIBRARY
1895 Camino Del Rio   Phone: (619) 297-0395
San Diego, CA 92108   Alfred D. Sawyer, Chm., Lib.Comm.

SEA WORLD, INC. - LIBRARY
1720 S. Shores Rd.   Phone: (619) 222-6363
San Diego, CA 92109   Carlo A. Mosca, Corp.Dir., Educ.

SHARP MEMORIAL HOSPITAL - HEALTH SCIENCE LIBRARY
7901 Frost St.   Phone: (619) 292-2538
San Diego, CA 92123   Estelle Davis, Dir. of Lib.Serv.

SOLAR TURBINES INCORPORATED - LIBRARY
Box 80966   Phone: (619) 238-5992
San Diego, CA 92138   George Hall, Libn.

TELEDYNE RYAN AERONAUTICAL - TECHNICAL INFORMATION SERVICES
2701 N. Harbor Dr.   Phone: (619) 291-7311
San Diego, CA 92101   William E. Ebner, Chf.

UNITED STATES LIFESAVING ASSOCIATION - LIBRARY & INFORMATION
   CENTER
3650 5th Ave.   Phone: (619) 291-2620
San Diego, CA 92103   Byron Wear, Natl.Exec.Dir.

U.S. NATL. PARK SERVICE - CABRILLO NATL. MONUMENT - LIBRARY &
   INFORMATION CENTER †
Box 6670   Phone: (619) 293-5450
San Diego, CA 92106

U.S. NAVY - FLEET COMBAT DIRECTION SYSTEMS SUPPORT ACTIVITY,
   SAN DIEGO - TECHNICAL INFO. SERVICES OFFICE
200 Catalina Blvd.   Phone: **(619) 225-2950**
San Diego, CA 92147   Marilyn Soldwisch, Tech.Info.Serv.Spec.

U.S. NAVY - NAVAL AIR STATION (CA-North Island) - LIBRARY
Bldg. 650   Phone: (619) 437-7041
San Diego, CA 92135   Sharon Nelson, Adm.Libn.

U.S. NAVY - NAVAL AMPHIBIOUS BASE (CA-Coronado) - LIBRARY
                                             Phone: (619) 437-2473
San Diego, CA 92155   Nadine Bangsberg, Adm. Libn.

U.S. NAVY - NAVAL ELECTRONICS SYSTEMS ENGINEERING CENTER - SAN
   DIEGO LIBRARY
4297 Pacific Hwy.
Box 80337   Phone: (619) 260-2482
San Diego, CA 92138

U.S. NAVY - NAVAL HEALTH RESEARCH CENTER - WALTER L. WILKINS
   BIO-MEDICAL LIBRARY
Box 85122   Phone: (619) 225-6640
San Diego, CA 92138   Mary Aldous, Libn.

U.S. NAVY - NAVAL HOSPITAL (CA-San Diego) - THOMPSON MEDICAL
   LIBRARY
                                             Phone: (619) 233-2367
San Diego, CA 92134

U.S. NAVY - NAVAL OCEAN SYSTEMS CENTER - TECHNICAL LIBRARY
                                             Phone: (619) 225-6171
San Diego, CA 92152   Joan Ingersoll, Hd.

U.S. NAVY - NAVAL STATION LIBRARY (CA-San Diego)
Naval Station, Box 15   Phone: (619) 235-1403
San Diego, CA 92136   Christine E. Larsen, Dir./Adm.Libn.

U.S. NAVY - NAVAL SUPERVISOR OF SHIPBUILDING, CONVERSION AND
   REPAIR - TECHNICAL LIBRARY
U.S. Naval Station, Code 253
Box 119   Phone: (619) 235-2455
San Diego, CA 92136   Pat Merritt, Libn.

U.S. NAVY - NAVAL SUPPLY CENTER - TECHNICAL DIVISION - TECHNICAL
   LIBRARY
937 North Harbor Dr.   Phone: (619) 235-3237
San Diego, CA 92132   Ivy Seaberry, Lib.Techn.

U.S. NAVY - NAVY PERSONNEL RESEARCH & DEVELOPMENT CENTER -
   TECHNICAL LIBRARY
Code P22L   Phone: (619) 225-7971
San Diego, CA 92152   Marie D. McDowell, Libn.

U.S. VETERANS ADMINISTRATION (CA-San Diego) - MEDICAL CENTER
   LIBRARY
3350 La Jolla Village Dr.   Phone: (619) 453-7500
San Diego, CA 92161   Connie Baker, Chf.Libn.

UNIVERSITY OF CALIFORNIA, SAN DIEGO - MEDICAL CENTER LIBRARY
225 Dickinson St.   Phone: (619) 294-6520
San Diego, CA 92103   Sue Ann M. Johnson, Hd.Libn.

UNIVERSITY OF SAN DIEGO - MARVIN & LILLIAN KRATTER LAW LIBRARY
Alcala Pk.   Phone: (619) 293-4541
San Diego, CA 92110   Joseph S. Ciesielski, Dir.

WESTERN STATE UNIVERSITY - COLLEGE OF LAW - LIBRARY
2121 San Diego Ave.   Phone: (619) 297-9700
San Diego, CA 92110   Karla M. Randich, Asst.Prof./Libn.

ZOOLOGICAL SOCIETY OF SAN DIEGO - ERNST SCHWARZ LIBRARY
San Diego Zoo
Box 551   Phone: (619) 231-1515
San Diego, CA 92112   Michaele M. Robinson, Libn.

ALAN WOFSY FINE ARTS - REFERENCE LIBRARY
401 China Basin St.   Phone: (415) 986-3030
San Francisco, CA 94107   Adios Butler, Libn.

AMERICAN ACADEMY OF ASIAN STUDIES - LIBRARY *
2842 Buchanan
San Francisco, CA 94110

AMERICAN HYPNOTISTS' ASSOCIATION - HYPNOSIS TECHNICAL CENTER
Glanworth Bldg., Suite 6
1159 Green St.   Phone: (415) 775-6130
San Francisco, CA 94109   Dr. Angela Bertuccelli, Libn.

AMERICAN INDIAN HISTORICAL SOCIETY - LIBRARY
1451 Masonic Ave.   Phone: (415) 626-5235
San Francisco, CA 94117   Dr. Jeanette Henry Costo, Exec.Sec.

ANSHEN & ALLEN, ARCHITECTS - LIBRARY
461 Bush St.   Phone: (415) 391-7100
San Francisco, CA 94108

ARTHUR ANDERSEN & CO. - LIBRARY
Box 3938   Phone: (415) 546-8485
San Francisco, CA 94119   Mary Lou Pierce, Libn.

ASIAN ART MUSEUM OF SAN FRANCISCO - LIBRARY
Golden Gate Pk.   Phone: (415) 558-2993
San Francisco, CA 94118   Fred A. Cline, Jr., Libn.

ATHEARN, CHANDLER AND HOFFMAN - LIBRARY *
111 Sutter St.   Phone: (415) 421-5484
San Francisco, CA 94104

BA INVESTMENT MANAGEMENT CORPORATION - LIBRARY
555 California St.   Phone: (415) 622-6883
San Francisco, CA 94104   Lee Stocks, Lib.Serv.Mgr.

BAKER & MC KENZIE - LIBRARY
Box 7258   Phone: (415) 433-7600
San Francisco, CA 94131   Manuel J. Koff

BANCROFT, AVERY AND MC ALISTER - LAW LIBRARY
601 Montgomery St., Suite 900   Phone: (415) 788-8855
San Francisco, CA 94111   Catherine Finnegan, Dir., Lib.Serv.

BANCROFT-WHITNEY COMPANY - EDITORIAL LIBRARY
301 Brannan St.   Phone: (415) 986-4410
San Francisco, CA 94107   Phyllis M. Ross, Libn.

BANK OF AMERICA, NT & SA - LAW LIBRARY
Dept. 3220
Box 37000   Phone: (415) 622-6040
San Francisco, CA 94137   Sharon K. French, Libn.

BANK OF AMERICA, NT & SA - REFERENCE LIBRARY
555 California St.
Box 37000   Phone: (415) 622-2068
San Francisco, CA 94137   Marydee Ojala, Lib.Mgr.

BANK OF AMERICA - TECHNOLOGY LIBRARY - 3099 B
150 Spear St.   Phone: (415) 624-3950
San Francisco, CA 94105   Jeannette E. Glynn, Mgr.

BAY AREA COUNCIL ON SOVIET JEWRY - ARCHIVES *
106 Baden St.   Phone: (415) 585-1400
San Francisco, CA 94131   Natasha Kats, Exec.Sec.

BECHTEL - AUDIO-VISUAL LIBRARY
Box 3965   Phone: (415) 768-5799
San Francisco, CA 94119   Dorothy Judd, Supv.

BECHTEL - CENTRAL LIBRARY
50 Beale St.   Phone: (415) 768-5306
San Francisco, CA 94119   Betty Jo Hardison, Chf.Libn.

BECHTEL CIVIL & MINERALS, INC. - MINING & METALS BUSINESS
   DEVELOPMENT LIBRARY
Box 3965   Phone: (415) 768-7294
San Francisco, CA 94119   O. Paul Oraha, Libn.

BECHTEL - DATA PROCESSING LIBRARY
Box 3965   Phone: (415) 768-9015
San Francisco, CA 94119   Sherry Cook, Libn.

BECHTEL - FINANCE LIBRARY
Box 3965   Phone: (415) 768-5100
San Francisco, CA 94119   Kathleen A. McLaughlin, Finance Libn.

BECHTEL - GEOLOGY LIBRARY
Box 3965   Phone: (415) 786-5353
San Francisco, CA 94119   Gail Sorrough, Libn.

BECHTEL PETROLEUM INC. - LIBRARY
Box 3965   Phone: (415) 768-5306
San Francisco, CA 94119   Gary Cohn, Libn.

BECHTEL POWER CORPORATION - LEGAL DEPARTMENT LIBRARY
Box 3965   Phone: (415) 768-7635
San Francisco, CA 94119   Patricia Boyd, Law Libn.

BECHTEL POWER CORPORATION - SFPD LIBRARY
Box 3965   Phone: (415) 768-1152
San Francisco, CA 94119   Fran Brunet, Hd.Libn.

BERTRAND RUSSELL SOCIETY, INC. - LIBRARY
4461 23rd St.   Phone: (415) 648-3826
San Francisco, CA 94114   Jack Ragsdale, Libn.

BOOK CLUB OF CALIFORNIA - LIBRARY
312 Sutter St.   Phone: (415) 781-7532
San Francisco, CA 94108

BRITISH CONSULATE-GENERAL - LIBRARY
120 Montgomery St., Suite 900   Phone: (415) 981-3030
San Francisco, CA 94104

BROBECK, PHLEGER & HARRISON - LIBRARY
1 Market Plaza
Spear St. Tower   Phone: (415) 442-1054
San Francisco, CA 94105   Alice McKenzie, Libn.

BUREAU OF JEWISH EDUCATION - JEWISH COMMUNITY LIBRARY
601 14th Ave.   Phone: (415) 751-6983
San Francisco, CA 94118   Nanette Stahl, Hd.Libn.

CALIFORNIA ACADEMY OF SCIENCES - J.W. MAILLIARD, JR. LIBRARY
Golden Gate Park   Phone: (415) 221-5100
San Francisco, CA 94118   Ray Brian, Libn.

CALIFORNIA COLLEGE OF PODIATRIC MEDICINE - SCHMIDT MEDICAL
   LIBRARY
Rincon Annex, Box 7855   Phone: (415) 563-3444
San Francisco, CA 94120   Leonard P. Shapiro, Dir.

CALIFORNIA HISTORICAL SOCIETY - SCHUBERT HALL LIBRARY
2099 Pacific Ave.   Phone: (415) 567-1848
San Francisco, CA 94109   Bruce L. Johnson, Lib.Dir.

CALIFORNIA INSTITUTE OF INTEGRAL STUDIES - LIBRARY
3494 21st St.   Phone: (415) 648-1489
San Francisco, CA 94110   Vern Haddick, Lib.Dir.

CALIFORNIA MEDICAL ASSOCIATION - LIBRARY
44 Gough St.   Phone: (415) 863-5522
San Francisco, CA 94103   Clare J. Potter, Res.Libn.

CALIFORNIA STATE AUTOMOBILE ASSOCIATION - LIBRARY †
150 Van Ness Ave., B2-3F   Phone: (415) 565-2300
San Francisco, CA 94101   Pauline Jones Tighe, Libn.

CALIFORNIA STATE BANKING DEPARTMENT - LIBRARY
235 Montgomery St., Suite 750
San Francisco, CA 94104

CALIFORNIA STATE - COURT OF APPEAL, 1ST APPELLATE DISTRICT - LAW
   LIBRARY
350 McAllister St.   Phone: (415) 557-0859
San Francisco, CA 94102   Jane W. Evans, Libn.

CALIFORNIA STATE DEPARTMENT OF INDUSTRIAL RELATIONS - DIVISION
   OF LABOR STATISTICS AND RESEARCH LIBRARY
Box 603   Phone: (415) 557-2184
San Francisco, CA 94101   Ruth Mark, Res.Anl.

CALIFORNIA STATE DEPARTMENT OF JUSTICE - ATTORNEY GENERAL'S
   LIBRARY
6248 State Bldg.
350 McAllister St.   Phone: (415) 557-2177
San Francisco, CA 94102   Dorothy M. Graham, Sr.Libn.

CALIFORNIA STATE DEPARTMENT OF TRANSPORTATION - DISTRICT 4
   LIBRARY
150 Oak St., Rm. 56
Box 7310   Phone: (415) 557-0567
San Francisco, CA 94120   Alice Y. Whitten, Lib.Tech.Asst.

CALIFORNIA STATE DIVISION OF MINES AND GEOLOGY - LIBRARY
Ferry Bldg., Rm. 2022   Phone: (415) 557-0308
San Francisco, CA 94111-4266   Angela Brunton, Libn.

CALIFORNIA STATE LIBRARY - SUTRO LIBRARY
480 Winston Dr.   Phone: (415) 557-4477
San Francisco, CA 94132   Eleanor Capelle, Sr.Libn.

CALIFORNIA STATE SUPREME COURT LIBRARY
4241 State Bldg. Annex
455 Golden Gate Ave.   Phone: (415) 557-1922
San Francisco, CA 94102   John A. Sigel

CASTLE & COOKE, INC. - LAW & GOVERNMENT DEPARTMENT
   INFORMATION CENTER
50 California St., 18th Fl.   Phone: (415) 986-3000
San Francisco, CA 94111   Betty Hardin, Libn./Info.Spec.

CENTER FOR INVESTIGATIVE REPORTING - LIBRARY
54 Mint St., 4th Fl.   Phone: (415) 543-1200
San Francisco, CA 94103   Dan Noyes, Mng.Ed.

CHILDREN'S HOSPITAL OF SAN FRANCISCO - EMGE MEDICAL LIBRARY
Box 3805   Phone: (415) 387-8700
San Francisco, CA 94119   Angie Durso, Dir.

CHINESE HISTORICAL SOCIETY OF AMERICA - ARCHIVES
17 Adler Place   Phone: (415) 391-1188
San Francisco, CA 94133

CITY COLLEGE OF SAN FRANCISCO - HOTEL AND RESTAURANT
   DEPARTMENT - ALICE STATLER LIBRARY
50 Phelan Ave.   Phone: (415) 239-3460
San Francisco, CA 94112   Mary B. Smyth, Lib.Mgr.

COGSWELL COLLEGE - LIBRARY
600 Stockton St.   Phone: (415) 433-5550
San Francisco, CA 94108   Judith Carson-Croes, Dir., Lib. & Lrng.Serv.

COLLEGE OF THE SAN FRANCISCO ART INSTITUTE - ANNE BREMER
   MEMORIAL LIBRARY
800 Chestnut St.   Phone: (415) 771-7020
San Francisco, CA 94133   Jeff Gunderson, Lib.Dir.

COOLEY, GODWARD, CASTRO, HUDDLESON & TATUM - LIBRARY
1 Maritime Plaza, 20th Fl.   Phone: (415) 981-5252
San Francisco, CA 94111   Nancy J. Lewis, Libn.

COOPERS & LYBRAND - LIBRARY
333 Market St.   Phone: (415) 957-3172
San Francisco, CA 94105   Karen E. Ivy, Libn.

CROCKER NATIONAL BANK - LIBRARY
Box 38000   Phone: (415) 983-2111
San Francisco, CA 94138   Inga Govaars, Libn.

CROWN ZELLERBACH CORPORATION - CORPORATE INFORMATION
   CENTER
One Bush St.   Phone: (415) 823-5403
San Francisco, CA 94104   Gloria Capel, Adm.

DAMES & MOORE - LIBRARY SERVICES
500 Sansome St.   Phone: (415) 433-0700
San Francisco, CA 94111   Ilene Storace, Ref.Libn./Info.Spec.

DAVIES (Ralph K.) MEDICAL CENTER - FRANKLIN HOSPITAL MEDICAL
   LIBRARY
Castro & Duboce St.   Phone: (415) 565-6352
San Francisco, CA 94114   Anne Shew, Med.Libn.

DEGENKOLB (H.J.) ASSOCIATES, ENGINEERS - LIBRARY
350 Sansome St., Suite 500   Phone: (415) 392-6952
San Francisco, CA 94104   Wess-John Murdough, Libn.

DELOITTE HASKINS & SELLS - AUDIT/MAS & TAX LIBRARY
44 Montgomery St.   Phone: (415) 393-4300
San Francisco, CA 94104   Eunice J. Azzani, Libn.

DESIGN PROFESSIONALS FINANCIAL CORPORATION - LIBRARY †
500 Sansome St., Suite 401   Phone: (415) 433-1676
San Francisco, CA 94111   Annette C. Gaskin, Libn.

DORR, COOPER & HAYS - LAW LIBRARY
50 Francisco St., Suite 210   Phone: (415) 398-2800
San Francisco, CA 94133   Mark J. Newman, Libn.

ENVIRONMENTAL IMPACT PLANNING CORPORATION - LIBRARY
319 Eleventh St.   Phone: (415) 864-2311
San Francisco, CA 94103   Cathleen Galloway Brown, Libn.

ENVIRONMENTAL PROTECTION AGENCY - REGION IX LIBRARY/
   INFORMATION CENTER
215 Fremont St.   Phone: (415) 974-8076
San Francisco, CA 94105   Jean Circiello, Chf., Info.Sys.Sect.

ESHERICK HOMSEY DODGE AND DAVIS - LIBRARY
2789 25th St.   Phone: (415) 285-9193
San Francisco, CA 94110   Elizabeth Walton, Libn.

FAR WEST LABORATORY FOR EDUCATIONAL RESEARCH AND
   DEVELOPMENT - LIBRARY AND ARCHIVES †
1855 Folsom St.   Phone: (415) 565-3065
San Francisco, CA 94103   Lillian Chinn, Libn.

FASHION INSTITUTE OF DESIGN & MERCHANDISING - LIBRARY
790 Market St.   Phone: (415) 433-6691
San Francisco, CA 94102   F. Samuel Douglas, Libn.

FEDERAL HOME LOAN BANK OF SAN FRANCISCO - LIBRARY
Box 7948   Phone: (415) 393-1215
San Francisco, CA 94120   Molly M. Skeen, Libn.

FEDERAL RESERVE BANK OF SAN FRANCISCO - RESEARCH LIBRARY
101 Market St.
Box 7702   Phone: (415) 974-3216
San Francisco, CA 94120   Miriam Ciochon, Lib.Mgr.

FINE ARTS MUSEUMS OF SAN FRANCISCO - LIBRARY
M.H. De Young Memorial Museum
Golden Gate Pk.   Phone: (415) 558-2887
San Francisco, CA 94118   Jane Gray Nelson, Musm.Libn.

FOUNDATION CENTER - SAN FRANCISCO OFFICE - LIBRARY
312 Sutter St., 3rd Fl.   Phone: (415) 397-0902
San Francisco, CA 94108   Roberta Steiner, Dir.

GARBELL RESEARCH FOUNDATION - LIBRARY
1714 Lake St.   Phone: (415) 752-0871
San Francisco, CA 94121

GENSTAR CORP. - LIBRARY *
4 Embarcadero Center, Suite 3700
San Francisco, CA 94111   Jana Selph, Libn.

GEORGE (Henry) SCHOOL OF SOCIAL SCIENCE - RESEARCH LIBRARY
3410 19th St.   Phone: (415) 362-7944
San Francisco, CA 94110   Robert Scrofani, Exec. V.P.

GOETHE INSTITUTE - LIBRARY
530 Bush St.   Phone: (415) 391-0370
San Francisco, CA 94108   Ursula Maisch, Libn.

GOLDEN GATE UNIVERSITY - LIBRARIES
536 Mission St.   Phone: (415) 442-7242
San Francisco, CA 94105   Harold E. Korf, Dir.

GOLDEN GATE UNIVERSITY - SCHOOL OF LAW LIBRARY
536 Mission St.   Phone: (415) 442-7260
San Francisco, CA 94105   Nancy Carol Carter, Dir.

GRAND LODGE OF FREE AND ACCEPTED MASONS OF CALIFORNIA -
   LIBRARY AND MUSEUM
1111 California St.   Phone: (415) 776-7000
San Francisco, CA 94108   Robert A. Klinger, Grand Libn.

GUEDEL MEMORIAL ANESTHESIA CENTER - LIBRARY
2395 Sacramento St.
Box 7999
San Francisco, CA 94120   Harold R. Gibson, Libn.

HALL OF JUSTICE LIBRARY †
850 Bryant St., Rm. 305   Phone: (415) 553-1763
San Francisco, CA 94103   Robert R. Schmidt, Libn.

HASSARD, BONNINGTON, ROGERS & HUBER - LIBRARY
44 Montgomery St., Suite 3500   Phone: (415) 781-8787
San Francisco, CA 94104   Linda Conley, Libn.

HELLER, EHRMAN, WHITE & MC AULIFFE - LIBRARY †
44 Montgomery St., Suite 3000   Phone: (415) 772-6105
San Francisco, CA 94104   Loretta Mak, Libn.

HELLMUTH, OBATA & KASSABAUM, INC. - LIBRARY/ARCHIVES
1 Lombard St.   Phone: (415) 986-4275
San Francisco, CA 94111   Mary Kingshill, Libn.

HOLOCAUST LIBRARY AND RESEARCH CENTER OF SAN FRANCISCO
601 14th Ave.   Phone: (415) 751-6040
San Francisco, CA 94118   Joel Neuberg, Exec.Dir.

HOWARD RICE NEMEROVSKI CANADY ROBERTSON & FALK - LIBRARY
Three Embarcadero Center, Suite 700   Phone: (415) 399-3043
San Francisco, CA 94111   Margaret Shediac, Libn.

INDUSTRIAL INDEMNITY COMPANY - LIBRARY
255 California St.   Phone: (415) 986-3535
San Francisco, CA 94111   Louise R. Murata, Libn.

INSTITUTE FOR ADVANCED STUDY OF HUMAN SEXUALITY - RESEARCH
   LIBRARY
1523 Franklin St.   Phone: (415) 928-1133
San Francisco, CA 94109   Dr. Erwin J. Haeberle, Dir.

INSTITUTE FOR CHILDHOOD RESOURCES - LIBRARY
1169 Howard St.   Phone: (415) 864-1169
San Francisco, CA 94103   Stevanne Auerbach, Ph.D., Dir.

INSTITUTE FOR THE STUDY OF LABOR AND ECONOMIC CRISIS - LIBRARY
   AND DATABANK
2701 Folsom St.   Phone: (415) 550-1703
San Francisco, CA 94110   Nancy P. Kelly, Libn.

INSTITUTE FOR THE STUDY OF SEXUAL ASSAULT - INFORMATION CENTER
403 Ashbury St.   Phone: (415) 861-2048
San Francisco, CA 94117   Judith L. Musick, Ph.D., Res.Dir.

INTERNATIONAL ENGINEERING COMPANY, INC. - LIBRARY
180 Howard St.   Phone: (415) 442-7300
San Francisco, CA 94105   Louis I. Pigott, Jr., Libn.

INTERNATIONAL LONGSHOREMEN'S AND WAREHOUSEMEN'S UNION -
   ANNE RAND RESEARCH LIBRARY
1188 Franklin St.   Phone: (415) 775-0533
San Francisco, CA 94109   Carol Schwartz, Libn.

JANUS FOUNDATION - LIBRARY
2420 Sutter St.   Phone: (415) 563-0344
San Francisco, CA 94115   Janet L. Bergman, Libn.

JANUS INFORMATION FACILITY
1952 Union St.   Phone: (415) 567-0162
San Francisco, CA 94123   Paul A. Walker, Dir.

KAISER-PERMANENTE MEDICAL CENTER - HEALTH SCIENCES LIBRARY
2425 Geary Blvd.   Phone: (415) 929-4101
San Francisco, CA 94115   Vincent Lagano, Med.Libn.

KAPLAN/MC LAUGHLIN/DIAZ ARCHITECTS & PLANNERS - LIBRARY
222 Vallejo   Phone: (415) 398-5191
San Francisco, CA 94111   Janice Vargo, Libn.

KENNEDY/JENKS ENGINEERS, INC. - LIBRARY
657 Howard St.   Phone: (415) 362-6065
San Francisco, CA 94105   Jean C. Sansobrino, Libn.

KENNEDY (John F.) UNIVERSITY - CENTER FOR MUSEUM STUDIES -
   LIBRARY
1717 17th St.   Phone: (415) 626-1787
San Francisco, CA 94103   Colette Tanaka, Supv., Lib.Serv.

KMG/MAIN HURDMAN - LIBRARY
Two Embarcadero, 25th Fl.   Phone: (415) 981-7720
San Francisco, CA 94111   Anne Larson, Libn.

LANDELS, RIPLEY & DIAMOND - LIBRARY
450 Pacific Ave.   Phone: (415) 788-5000
San Francisco, CA 94133   Jeanette S. Lizotte, Libn.

LANGLEY PORTER PSYCHIATRIC INSTITUTE - PROFESSIONAL LIBRARY
University of California
401 Parnassus Ave.
Box 13-B/C   Phone: (415) 681-8080
San Francisco, CA 94143   Lisa M. Dunkel, Libn.

LAUTZE & LAUTZE ACCOUNTANCY CORPORATION - RESOURCES
   DEVELOPMENT CENTER
100 Pine St.   Phone: (415) 362-1970
San Francisco, CA 94111

LEEDSHILL-HERKENHOFF, INC.- LIBRARY
1275 Market St., Suite 1500   Phone: (415) 626-2070
San Francisco, CA 94103   Gregory B. Sedgwick, Tech.Libn.

LEVI STRAUSS & COMPANY - CORPORATE LAW LIBRARY
1155 Battery St.   Phone: (415) 544-7676
San Francisco, CA 94106   Yvonne B. Marty, Legal Info.Sys.Adm.

LEVI STRAUSS & COMPANY - CORPORATE MARKETING INFORMATION
   CENTER †
1155 Battery St.
Box 7215
San Francisco, CA 94120-6935   Catherine Rock, Adm.

LINCOLN UNIVERSITY - LAW LIBRARY †
281 Masonic Ave.   Phone: (415) 221-1212
San Francisco, CA 94118   Andrea Segall, Law Libn.

LUDLOW MEMORIAL LIBRARY
Box 99346
San Francisco, CA 94109

LUTHERAN CHURCH - MISSOURI SYNOD - CALIFORNIA, NEVADA AND
   HAWAII DISTRICT ARCHIVES
465 Woolsey St.   Phone: (415) 468-2336
San Francisco, CA 94134   Rev. Karl H. Wyneken, Archv.

MC CUTCHEN, DOYLE, BROWN & ENERSEN - LAW LIBRARY
3 Embarcadero Ctr.   Phone: (415) 393-2198
San Francisco, CA 94111   Elizabeth S. Nicholson, Libn.

MC KINSEY & COMPANY, INC. - LIBRARY
555 California St., Suite 4800   Phone: (415) 981-0250
San Francisco, CA 94104   Linda L. Kraemer, Mgr., Info.Serv.

MANALYTICS, INC. - LIBRARY
625 Third St.   Phone: (415) 788-4143
San Francisco, CA 94107   Seyem Deus Petrites, Libn.

MECHANICS' INSTITUTE LIBRARY
57 Post St.   Phone: (415) 421-1750
San Francisco, CA 94104   Kathleen T. Pabst, Lib.Dir.

MEXICAN AMERICAN LEGAL DEFENSE AND EDUCATIONAL FUND - LIBRARY
28 Geary St., 6th Fl.   Phone: (415) 981-5800
San Francisco, CA 94108   R. Margarita Recino, Libn.

MORRISON & FOERSTER - LAW LIBRARY
One Market Plaza
Spear St. Tower   Phone: (415) 777-6000
San Francisco, CA 94105   Carl Whitaker, Chf.Libn.

MOUNT ZION HOSPITAL AND MEDICAL CENTER - HARRIS M. FISHBON
   MEMORIAL LIBRARY
Box 7921   Phone: (415) 567-6600
San Francisco, CA 94120   Angela Green Wesling, Lib.Dir.

MUSIC AND ARTS INSTITUTE OF SAN FRANCISCO - COLLEGE LIBRARY
2622 Jackson St.   Phone: (415) 567-1445
San Francisco, CA 94115   Ross McKee, Dir.

NATIONAL MARITIME MUSEUM - J. PORTER SHAW LIBRARY
Bldg. E, 3rd Fl.
Fort Mason   Phone: (415) 556-9870
San Francisco, CA 94123   David Hull, Prin.Libn.

OLD ST. MARY'S CHURCH - PAULIST LIBRARY
614 Grant Ave.   Phone: (415) 362-0959
San Francisco, CA 94108   Walter Anthony, C.S.P., Dir.

ORRICK, HERRINGTON, ROWLEY & SUTCLIFFE - LIBRARY
600 Montgomery St.   Phone: (415) 392-1122
San Francisco, CA 94111   Cynthia Papermaster, Law Libn.

PACIFIC GAS AND ELECTRIC COMPANY - CORPORATE LIBRARY
77 Beale St., Rm. 1220   Phone: (415) 781-4211
San Francisco, CA 94106   Patricia A. Lawrence, Dir.

PACIFIC GAS AND ELECTRIC COMPANY - LAW LIBRARY
Box 7442   Phone: (415) 781-4211
San Francisco, CA 94120   Gary L. Stromme, Law Libn.

PACIFIC MEDICAL CENTER & UNIVERSITY OF THE PACIFIC SCHOOL OF
   DENTISTRY - HEALTH SCIENCES LIBRARY
2395 Sacramento St.
Box 7999   Phone: (415) 563-4321
San Francisco, CA 94120   Harold R. Gibson, Libn.

PACIFIC-UNION CLUB - LIBRARY
1000 California St.   Phone: (415) 775-1234
San Francisco, CA 94108   Barbara Borden, Libn.

PEAT, MARWICK, MITCHELL & CO. - LIBRARY
San Francisco Intl. Airport
Box 8007   Phone: (415) 347-9521
San Francisco, CA 94128   Karen A. Mayers, Libn.

PETTIT & MARTIN - LIBRARY
101 California, 35th Fl.   Phone: (415) 434-4000
San Francisco, CA 94111   Lynn Brazil, Hd.Libn.

PILLSBURY, MADISON AND SUTRO - LIBRARY
Box 7880   Phone: (415) 983-1130
San Francisco, CA 94120   Lynn A. Green, Dir., Lib. & Info.Serv.

PRESS CLUB OF SAN FRANCISCO - WILL AUBREY MEMORIAL LIBRARY
555 Post St.   Phone: (415) 775-7800
San Francisco, CA 94102   Harry R. Illman, Libn.

PROGRAM PLANETREE - HEALTH RESOURCE CENTER
2040 Webster St.   Phone: (415) 346-4636
San Francisco, CA 94115   Rochelle Perrine Schmalz, Med.Libn.

RAND INFORMATION SYSTEMS, INC. - LIBRARY
98 Battery St., 4th Fl.   Phone: (415) 392-2500
San Francisco, CA 94111   Diane Huijgen, Libn.

REDWOOD EMPIRE ASSOCIATION - LIBRARY
One Market Plaza
Spear St. Tower, Suite 1001   Phone: (415) 543-8334
San Francisco, CA 94105   Stuart Nixon, Gen.Mgr.

ROSENBERG CAPITAL MANAGEMENT - LIBRARY
Four Embarcadero Center, Suite 2900   Phone: (415) 954-5474
San Francisco, CA 94111   Maggie O'Brien, Res.Libn.

ST. FRANCIS MEMORIAL HOSPITAL - WALTER F. SCHALLER MEMORIAL
   LIBRARY
Box 7726   Phone: (415) 775-4321
San Francisco, CA 94120   Maryann Zaremska, Dir., Lib.Serv.

ST. LUKE'S HOSPITAL - MEDICAL LIBRARY
3555 Army St.   Phone: (415) 647-8600
San Francisco, CA 94110   Corazon O'S. Ismarin, Libn.

ST. MARY'S HOSPITAL AND MEDICAL CENTER - MEDICAL LIBRARY
450 Stanyan St.   Phone: (415) 750-5784
San Francisco, CA 94117   Eleanor Benelisha, Dir., Lib.Serv.

SAN FRANCISCO ACADEMY OF COMIC ART - LIBRARY †
2850 Ulloa   Phone: (415) 681-1737
San Francisco, CA 94116   Bill Blackbeard, Dir.

SAN FRANCISCO CHRONICLE - LIBRARY
5th & Mission Sts.   Phone: (415) 777-1111
San Francisco, CA 94103   Suzanne Caster, Hd.Libn.

SAN FRANCISCO - CITY ATTORNEY'S OFFICE - LIBRARY
206 City Hall   Phone: (415) 558-4993
San Francisco, CA 94102   Ruth Stevenson, Law Libn.

SAN FRANCISCO COLLEGE OF MORTUARY SCIENCE - LIBRARY
1450 Post St.   Phone: (415) 567-0674
San Francisco, CA 94109   Dale W. Sly, Pres.

SAN FRANCISCO CONSERVATORY OF MUSIC - LIBRARY
1201 Ortega St.   Phone: (415) 564-8086
San Francisco, CA 94122   Lucretia Wolfe, Libn.

SAN FRANCISCO EXAMINER - LIBRARY
110 Fifth St.   Phone: (415) 777-7845
San Francisco, CA 94103   Judy Gerritts Canter, Chf.Libn.

SAN FRANCISCO GENERAL HOSPITAL MEDICAL CENTER - BARNETT-
   BRIGGS LIBRARY
1001 Potrero Ave.   Phone: (415) 821-8553
San Francisco, CA 94110   Miriam Hirsch, Med.Libn.

SAN FRANCISCO LAW LIBRARY
436 City Hall
400 Van Ness Ave.   Phone: (415) 558-4627
San Francisco, CA 94102-4672   John H. Hauff, Libn.

SAN FRANCISCO LIGHTHOUSE CENTER FOR THE BLIND - LIBRARY
745 Buchanan St.   Phone: (415) 431-1481
San Francisco, CA 94102   Daniel Forer, Coord.

SAN FRANCISCO MUNICIPAL RAILWAY - LIBRARY
949 Presidio Ave., Rm. 204   Phone: (415) 673-6864
San Francisco, CA 94115   Dr. Marc Hofstadter, Libn.

SAN FRANCISCO MUSEUM OF MODERN ART - LOUISE S. ACKERMAN FINE
   ARTS LIBRARY
McAllister at Van Ness   Phone: (415) 863-8800
San Francisco, CA 94102   Eugenie Candau, Libn.

SAN FRANCISCO PSYCHOANALYTIC INSTITUTE - LIBRARY
2420 Sutter St.   Phone: (415) 563-4477
San Francisco, CA 94115   Anne L. Regner, Libn.

SAN FRANCISCO PUBLIC LIBRARY - BUSINESS LIBRARY
530 Kearny St.   Phone: (415) 558-3946
San Francisco, CA 94108   Gilbert McNamee, Prin.Libn.

SAN FRANCISCO PUBLIC LIBRARY - SAN FRANCISCO ROOM AND
   ARCHIVES
Civic Ctr.   Phone: (415) 558-3949
San Francisco, CA 94102   Gladys Hansen, City Archv.

SAN FRANCISCO PUBLIC LIBRARY - SPECIAL COLLECTIONS DEPARTMENT
Civic Ctr.   Phone: (415) 558-3940
San Francisco, CA 94102   Johanna Goldschmid, Spec.Coll.Libn.

SAN FRANCISCO STATE UNIVERSITY - FRANK V. DE BELLIS COLLECTION
1630 Holloway Ave.   Phone: (415) 469-1649
San Francisco, CA 94132   Serena De Bellis, Cur.

SAN FRANCISCO STATE UNIVERSITY - J. PAUL LEONARD LIBRARY -
   SPECIAL COLLECTIONS/ARCHIVES
1630 Holloway Ave.   Phone: (415) 469-1856
San Francisco, CA 94132   Helene Whitson, Coord.

SAN FRANCISCO THEOSOPHICAL SOCIETY - LIBRARY
809 Mason St.   Phone: (415) 771-8777
San Francisco, CA 94108   Richard Power, Libn.

SAN FRANCISCO UNIFIED SCHOOL DISTRICT - TEACHERS PROFESSIONAL
   LIBRARY
135 Van Ness Ave.   Phone: (415) 565-9272
San Francisco, CA 94102   Helen M. Boutin, Lib.Techn.

SEDGWICK, DETERT, MORAN & ARNOLD - LIBRARY AND INFORMATION
   CENTER
111 Pine St.   Phone: (415) 982-0303
San Francisco, CA 94111   Francis Gates, Libn.

SIERRA CLUB - WILLIAM E. COLBY MEMORIAL LIBRARY
530 Bush St.   Phone: (415) 981-8634
San Francisco, CA 94108   Barbara Lekisch, Rsrcs.Libn.

SOCIETY OF CALIFORNIA PIONEERS - JOSEPH A. MOORE LIBRARY
456 McAllister St.   Phone: (415) 861-5278
San Francisco, CA 94102   Grace E. Baker, Libn.

SOHIO PETROLEUM COMPANY - CENTRAL LIBRARY AND INFORMATION
   SERVICES
50 Fremont St.   Phone: (415) 445-9511
San Francisco, CA 94105   Aileen M. Donovan, Mgr.

SPIRIT OF THE FUTURE CREATIVE INSTITUTE - CENTRAL LIBRARY
   ARCHIVES
3027 22nd St., Suite 3
Box 40296   Phone: (415) 821-7800
San Francisco, CA 94110   Gary Marchi, Creative Dir.

STANDARD OIL COMPANY OF CALIFORNIA - CORPORATE LIBRARY
225 Bush St.   Phone: (415) 894-2945
San Francisco, CA 94104   Margaret J. Linden, Mgr.

STONE, MARRACCINI & PATTERSON - RESEARCH & DEVELOPMENT
   LIBRARY
455 Beach St.   Phone: (415) 775-7300
San Francisco, CA 94133   Ronnie Cadam, Libn.

STRYBING ARBORETUM SOCIETY - HELEN CROCKER RUSSELL LIBRARY †
Golden Gate Pk.
9th Ave. & Lincoln Way   Phone: (415) 661-1316
San Francisco, CA 94122   M. Jane Gates, Hd.Libn.

THELEN, MARRIN, JOHNSON & BRIDGES - LAW LIBRARY
Two Embarcadero Center   Phone: (415) 392-6320
San Francisco, CA 94111   Marlene Weicht, Law Libn.

TUTTLE (Lyle) TATTOOING - TATTOO ART MUSEUM - LIBRARY
30 Seventh St.   Phone: (415) 864-9798
San Francisco, CA 94103   Lyle Tuttle, Dir.

UNITED AIR LINES, INC. - ENGINEERING DEPARTMENT - LIBRARY
San Francisco International Airport   Phone: (415) 876-3730
San Francisco, CA 94128   Josephine J. Whitney, Tech.Libn.

U.S. ARMY - CORPS OF ENGINEERS - SOUTH PACIFIC DIVISION - LIBRARY
630 Sansome St., Rm. 1216   Phone: (415) 556-9727
San Francisco, CA 94111   Mary G. Anderson, Div.Libn.

U.S. COURT OF APPEALS, 9TH CIRCUIT - LIBRARY
Box 5731   Phone: (415) 556-6129
San Francisco, CA 94101   Edward Chichura, Chf.Libn.

U.S. DEPT. OF HOUSING AND URBAN DEVELOPMENT - REGION IX -
   LIBRARY
450 Golden Gate Ave.
Box 36003   Phone: (415) 556-6484
San Francisco, CA 94102   Joanne Lee, Libn.

U.S. DISTRICT COURT - NORTHERN CALIFORNIA DISTRICT - LOUIS E.
   GOODMAN MEMORIAL LIBRARY
450 Golden Gate Ave.
Box 36060   Phone: (415) 556-7979
San Francisco, CA 94102   Lynn Lundstrom, Libn.

U.S. FOREST SERVICE - RECREATION RESOURCE MGT. - CULTURAL
   RESOURCE MGT. - RES. & ARCHV. CTR.
630 Sansome St.   Phone: (415) 556-4175
San Francisco, CA 94111

U.S. GENERAL ACCOUNTING OFFICE - SAN FRANCISCO REGIONAL OFFICE
   - LIBRARY
1275 Market St.   Phone: (415) 556-6200
San Francisco, CA 94103   Linda F. Sharp, Tech.Info.Spec.

U.S. NATL. PARK SERVICE - WESTERN REGIONAL OFFICE - REGIONAL
   RESOURCES LIBRARY
450 Golden Gate Ave., Rm. 14009
Box 36063   Phone: (415) 556-4165
San Francisco, CA 94102   Gordon Chappell, Regional Hist.

U.S. NAVY - NAVAL HOSPITAL (Guam) - MEDICAL LIBRARY
Box 7747   Phone: (671) 344-9250
FPO San Francisco, CA 96630

U.S. NAVY - NAVAL STATION LIBRARY (Guam)
Box 174
FPO San Francisco, CA 96630   Beverly J. Endsley, Lib.Techn.

U.S. VETERANS ADMINISTRATION (CA-San Francisco) - MEDICAL CENTER
   LIBRARY
42nd Ave. & Clement St.   Phone: (415) 221-4810
San Francisco, CA 94121   Cynthia A. Avallone, Chf.Libn.

UNIVERSITY OF CALIFORNIA, SAN FRANCISCO - HASTINGS COLLEGE OF
   THE LAW - LEGAL INFORMATION CENTER
200 McAllister St.   Phone: (415) 557-1354
San Francisco, CA 94102-4978   Dan F. Henke, Dir.

UNIVERSITY OF CALIFORNIA, SAN FRANCISCO - LIBRARY
Parnassus Ave., 257-S   Phone: (415) 666-2334
San Francisco, CA 94143   David Bishop, Univ.Libn.

UNIVERSITY OF SAN FRANCISCO - SCHOOL OF LAW LIBRARY
Kendrick Hall   Phone: (415) 666-6679
San Francisco, CA 94117   Virginia Kelsh, Law Libn./Assoc.Prof.

UNIVERSITY OF SAN FRANCISCO - SPECIAL COLLECTIONS DEPARTMENT/
   DONOHUE RARE BOOK ROOM
Richard A. Gleeson Library
2130 Fulton St.   Phone: (415) 666-6718
San Francisco, CA 94117   D. Steven Corey, Spec.Coll.Libn.

UTAH INTERNATIONAL, INC. - INFORMATION SERVICES/LIBRARY
550 California St.   Phone: (415) 981-1515
San Francisco, CA 94104   Jerry McWilliams, Mgr.

VIDEO FREE AMERICA - LIBRARY
442 Shotwell St.   Phone: (415) 648-9040
San Francisco, CA 94110   Joanne Kelly, Co-Dir.

WELLS FARGO BANK - HISTORY DEPARTMENT 921
475 Sansome St.   Phone: (415) 396-4157
San Francisco, CA 94111   Grace A. Evans, Hist.Spec.

WELLS FARGO BANK - LIBRARY 888
475 Sansome St.   Phone: (415) 396-3744
San Francisco, CA 94163   Alice E. Hunsucker, Asst.V.P./Mgr.

WINE INSTITUTE - LIBRARY
165 Post St.   Phone: (415) 986-0878
San Francisco, CA 94108   Joan V. Ingalls, Libn.

WORLD AFFAIRS COUNCIL OF NORTHERN CALIFORNIA - LIBRARY
312 Sutter St., Suite 200   Phone: (415) 982-2541
San Francisco, CA 94108   Lone C. Beeson, Hd.Libn.

BIBLIOGRAPHIC RESEARCH LIBRARY
964 Chapel Hill Way   Phone: (408) 247-2810
San Jose, CA 95122   Robert B. Harmon, Res.Bibliog.

CALIFORNIA STATE DEPARTMENT OF DEVELOPMENTAL SERVICES - STAFF
   LIBRARY
Agnews Residential Facility   Phone: (408) 262-2100
San Jose, CA 95134

FMC CORPORATION - ORDNANCE DIVISION - OD TECHNICAL LIBRARY
1105 Coleman Ave.
Box 1201   Phone: (408) 289-3490
San Jose, CA 95108   Sheila Smokey, Supv., Tech.Lib.

GENERAL ELECTRIC COMPANY - NUCLEAR ENERGY GROUP - LIBRARY
175 Curtner Ave., M/C 528   Phone: (408) 925-3522
San Jose, CA 95125   Mrs. Scotty A. McEwen, Tech.Libn.

IBM CORPORATION - GENERAL PRODUCTS DIVISION - STL LIBRARY
Dept. J17/Bldg. K15
555 Bailey Ave.   Phone: (408) 463-4050
San Jose, CA 95150   Ruth Winik, Mgr.

IBM CORPORATION - GENERAL PRODUCTS DIVISION - TECHNICAL
   INFORMATION CENTER
275/141
5600 Cottle Rd.   Phone: (408) 256-2908
San Jose, CA 95193   P. Grincewich, Mgr., Tech.Info.Ctr.

IBM CORPORATION - RESEARCH LIBRARY
Dept. K 74, Bldg. 281
5600 Cottle Rd.   Phone: (408) 256-2562
San Jose, CA 95193   William T. Gallagher, Mgr.

INDIAN CENTER OF SAN JOSE, INC. - LIBRARY *
3485 East Hills Dr.
San Jose, CA 95127

NATIONAL LIBRARY OF SPORTS
San Jose Public Library
180 W. San Carlos St.   Phone: (408) 287-0993
San Jose, CA 95113   Wes Mathis, Lib.Dir.

ROSICRUCIAN ORDER, AMORC - ROSICRUCIAN RESEARCH LIBRARY
Rosicrucian Park
Park & Naglee Aves.   Phone: (408) 287-9171
San Jose, CA 95191   Clara Campbell, Libn.

SAN JOSE BIBLE COLLEGE - MEMORIAL LIBRARY
790 S. 12th St.
Box 1090   Phone: (408) 295-1307
San Jose, CA 95108-1090   Minnie Mick, Libn.

SAN JOSE HEALTH CENTER - HEALTH SCIENCE LIBRARY *
675 E. Santa Clara St.   Phone: (408) 998-3212
San Jose, CA 95114   Susan L. Russell, Mgr.

SAN JOSE HISTORICAL MUSEUM - ARCHIVES
635 Phelan Ave.   Phone: (408) 287-2290
San Jose, CA 95112   Mignon Gibson, Musm.Dir.

SAN JOSE MEDICAL CLINIC - STAFF LIBRARY
45 S. 17th St.
San Jose, CA 95112

SAN JOSE MERCURY NEWS - LIBRARY
750 Ridder Park Dr.   Phone: (408) 920-5345
San Jose, CA 95190   Richard Geiger, Lib.Mgr.

SAN JOSE MUSEUM OF ART - LIBRARY
110 S. Market St.   Phone: (408) 294-2787
San Jose, CA 95113   Martha Manson, Cur.

SAN JOSE STATE UNIVERSITY - JOHN STEINBECK RESEARCH CENTER
Wahlquist Library
One Washington Square   Phone: (408) 277-3377
San Jose, CA 95192-0028   Robert DeMott, Res.Ctr.Dir.

SAN JOSE STATE UNIVERSITY - WAHLQUIST LIBRARY - CHICANO LIBRARY
   RESOURCE CENTER
1 Washington Sq.   Phone: (408) 277-3346
San Jose, CA 95192   Jeff Paul,, Coord.

SANTA CLARA COUNTY HEALTH DEPARTMENT - LIBRARY *
2220 Moorpark Ave.   Phone: (408) 279-6021
San Jose, CA 95128

SANTA CLARA COUNTY HEALTH SYSTEMS AGENCY - LIBRARY
830 N. First St., 2nd Fl.   Phone: (408) 292-9572
San Jose, CA 95112   Scarlett Sato, Health Planner

SANTA CLARA COUNTY LAW LIBRARY
191 N. First St.   Phone: (408) 299-3567
San Jose, CA 95113   Susan B. Kuklin, County Law Libn.

SANTA CLARA COUNTY OFFICE OF EDUCATION - CENTRAL CALIFORNIA
   CENTER FOR EDUCATIONAL IMPROVEMENT - LIBRARY
100 Skyport Dr., Mail Code 223   Phone: (408) 947-6808
San Jose, CA 95115   Dale Winslow Dana, Proj.Coord.

SANTA CLARA COUNTY PLANNING AND DEVELOPMENT DEPARTMENT -
   LIBRARY
County Government Center, East Wing
70 W. Hedding St.   Phone: (408) 299-2521
San Jose, CA 95110   W. Eric Carruthers, Prin. Planner

SANTA CLARA VALLEY MEDICAL CENTER - MILTON J. CHATTON MEDICAL
   LIBRARY
751 S. Bascom Ave.   Phone: (408) 279-5650
San Jose, CA 95128   Barbara A. Wilson, Med.Libn.

UNITED TECHNOLOGIES CORPORATION - CHEMICAL SYSTEMS DIVISION -
   LIBRARY
Box 50015   Phone: (408) 778-4784
San Jose, CA 95150-0015   Harold E. Wilcox, Supv.

PHYSICS INTERNATIONAL COMPANY - LIBRARY
2700 Merced St.
Box 1538   Phone: (415) 577-7278
San Leandro, CA 94577   Emil Kovtun, Libn.

U.P.E.C. CULTURAL CENTER - J.A. FREITAS LIBRARY
1120-24 E. 14th St.   Phone: (408) 483-7676
San Leandro, CA 94577   Carlos Almeida, Dir.

LIFE CHIROPRACTIC COLLEGE-WEST - LIBRARY
2005 Via Barrett   Phone: (415) 276-9345
San Lorenzo, CA 94580   Marda Woodbury, Lib.Dir.

CALIFORNIA POLYTECHNIC STATE UNIVERSITY - ROBERT E. KENNEDY
   LIBRARY
                                                  Phone: (805) 546-2344
San Luis Obispo, CA 93407   Dr. David B. Walch, Dir.

SAN LUIS OBISPO COUNTY LAW LIBRARY
Courthouse Annex, Rm. 236   Phone: (805) 549-5855
San Luis Obispo, CA 93408   Barbara S. Butler, Libn.

SAN LUIS OBISPO COUNTY PLANNING DEPARTMENT - TECHNICAL
   INFORMATION LIBRARY
County Government Center   Phone: (805) 549-5600
San Luis Obispo, CA 93408   Paul C. Crawford, Plan.Dir.

INVISIBLE MINISTRY - LIBRARY
Box 37   Phone: (714) 746-9430
San Marcos, CA 92069   A. Stuart Otto, Dir.

PALOMAR COMMUNITY COLLEGE - LIBRARY - SPECIAL COLLECTIONS
1140 Mission Rd.   Phone: (714) 744-1150
San Marcos, CA 92069   Bonnie L. Rogers, Dean, Instr.Rsrcs.

HUNTINGTON (Henry E.) LIBRARY, ART GALLERY AND BOTANICAL
   GARDENS
1151 Oxford Rd.   Phone: (213) 792-6141
San Marino, CA 91108   Robert Middlekauff, Dir.

ALUMAX INC. - RESEARCH LIBRARY
400 S. El Camino Real   Phone: (415) 348-3400
San Mateo, CA 94402   Ann Lindahl, Info.Spec.

CALIFORNIA JOCKEY CLUB AT BAY MEADOWS - WILLIAM P. KYNE
   MEMORIAL LIBRARY
Box 5050   Phone: (415) 574-7223
San Mateo, CA 94402   Gretchen G. Kramer, Libn.

COYOTE POINT MUSEUM - RESOURCE CENTER
Coyote Point Dr.   Phone: (415) 342-7755
San Mateo, CA 94401   Lori Mann, Educ.Dir.

GNOSTIC CONCEPTS, INC. - TECHNICAL LIBRARY
951 Mariner's Island Blvd., Suite 300   Phone: (415) 345-7400
San Mateo, CA 94404   A. Jeannine Caudill, Mgr., Lib.Serv.

PENINSULA TEMPLE BETH EL - LIBRARY *
1700 Alameda de Las Pulgas   Phone: (415) 341-7701
San Mateo, CA 94403   Ann Levin, Libn.

SAN MATEO COUNTY DEPARTMENT OF HEALTH SERVICES - LIBRARY
225 37th Ave.   Phone: (415) 573-2520
San Mateo, CA 94403   Mark Quinn Constantz, Med.Libn.

SAN MATEO COUNTY HISTORICAL ASSOCIATION - LIBRARY
1700 W. Hillsdale Blvd.
College of San Mateo Campus   Phone: (415) 574-6441
San Mateo, CA 94402   Marion C. Holmes, Archv.

SAN MATEO PUBLIC LIBRARY - BUSINESS SECTION
55 W. Third Ave.   Phone: (415) 574-6955
San Mateo, CA 94402   Cheryl H. Silverblatt, Bus.Ref.Libn.

BROOKSIDE HOSPITAL - MEDICAL STAFF LIBRARY
2000 Vale Rd.   Phone: (415) 235-7000
San Pablo, CA 94806   Barbara Dorham, Libn.

AMERICAN CETACEAN SOCIETY - NATIONAL LIBRARY
Box 4416   Phone: (213) 548-6279
San Pedro, CA 90731   Virginia C. Callahan, Libn.

LOGICON, INC. - INFORMATION CENTER
255 W. 5th St.
Box 471   Phone: (213) 831-0611
San Pedro, CA 90733   Constance B. Davenport, Info.Ctr.Supv.

LOS ANGELES - DEPARTMENT OF RECREATION AND PARKS - CABRILLO
   MARINE MUSEUM - LIBRARY *
3720 Stephen White Dr.   Phone: (213) 548-7562
San Pedro, CA 90731   Dr. Susanne Lawrenz-Miller, Assoc.Dir.

SAN PEDRO PENINSULA HOSPITAL - MEDICAL LIBRARY
1300 W. 7th St.   Phone: (213) 832-3311
San Pedro, CA 90732   James H. Harlan, Libn.

AMERICAN MUSIC RESEARCH CENTER - LIBRARY
Dominican College   Phone: (415) 457-4440
San Rafael, CA 94901   Sr. Mary Dominic Ray, Founder-Dir.

BRADWELL (David) & ASSOCIATES, INC. - LIBRARY
880 Las Gallinas Ave.   Phone: (415) 479-4980
San Rafael, CA 94903   David Bradwell, Pres.

DOMINICAN SISTERS - CONGREGATION OF THE HOLY NAME - ARCHIVES
1520 Grand Ave.   Phone: (415) 454-9221
San Rafael, CA 94901   Sr. Justin Barry, O.P., Archv.

MARIN COUNTY HISTORICAL SOCIETY - LIBRARY
1125 B St.   Phone: (415) 454-8538
San Rafael, CA 94901   Dorothy C. Morgan, Dir.

MARIN COUNTY LAW LIBRARY
Hall of Justice, C-33   Phone: (415) 499-6355
San Rafael, CA 94903   Meyer W. Halpern, Hd. Law Libn.

MARIN GENERAL HOSPITAL - LIBRARY
Box 2129   Phone: (415) 461-0100
San Rafael, CA 94912   Katherine Renick, Hd.Med.Libn.

MARIN WILDLIFE CENTER - LIBRARY
76 Albert Park Lane
Box 957   Phone: (415) 454-6961
San Rafael, CA 94915   Alice C. Katzung, Libn.

SPIRITUAL COMMUNITY PUBLICATIONS - INFORMATION CENTER
Box 1080
San Rafael, CA 94902

BEHRING EDUCATIONAL INSTITUTE - BLACKHAWK CLASSIC AUTO
   COLLECTION - LIBRARY OF VEHICLES
1975 San Ramon Valley Blvd.
San Ramon, CA 94583

MC KEE (Davy) CORPORATION - LIBRARY CENTER
2303 Camino Ramon   Phone: (415) 831-0389
San Ramon, CA 94583   Bill Repp, Tech.Libn.

AMERICAN AVIATION HISTORICAL SOCIETY - AAHS REFERENCE LIBRARY
2333 Otis   Phone: (714) 549-4818
Santa Ana, CA 92704   Jacqueline M. Sweaza, Off.Mgr.

AMERICAN MC GAW - TECHNICAL INFORMATION CENTER
Box 11887   Phone: (714) 660-2066
Santa Ana, CA 92711   Carol DeLape, Sr.Sci.Info.Coord.

BOWERS MEMORIAL MUSEUM - LIBRARY AND ARCHIVES
2002 N. Main St.
Santa Ana, CA 92706

GLOBAL ENGINEERING DOCUMENTS - LIBRARY
2625 S. Hickory St.   Phone: (714) 540-9870
Santa Ana, CA 92707   Oliver Thurman, Chf.Oper.Off.

ORANGE COUNTY DEPARTMENT OF EDUCATION - LIBRARY *
1300 S. Grand Ave., Bldg. B
Box 15029   Phone: (714) 953-3980
Santa Ana, CA 92705   Faith M. Herbert, Lib.Techn.

ORANGE COUNTY ENVIRONMENTAL MANAGEMENT AGENCY - EMA
   LIBRARY
400 Civic Center Dr., W.
Box 4048   Phone: (714) 834-6395
Santa Ana, CA 92702   Janet Hilford, Libn.

ORANGE COUNTY LAW LIBRARY
515 N. Flower St.   Phone: (714) 834-3397
Santa Ana, CA 92703   Bethany J. Ochal, Dir.

ORANGE COUNTY SHERIFF/CORONER - FORENSIC SCIENCE SERVICES
   LIBRARY
550 N. Flower St.
Box 449   Phone: (714) 834-3073
Santa Ana, CA 92702   Mr. J.L. Ragle, Lab.Dir.

TRINITY UNITED PRESBYTERIAN CHURCH - LIBRARY
13922 Prospect Ave.   Phone: (714) 544-7850
Santa Ana, CA 92705   Patricia A. Veeh, Hd.Libn.

U.S. MARINE CORPS - EL TORO AIR STATION LIBRARY
Bldg. 280   Phone: (714) 651-3474
Santa Ana, CA 92709-5007   Marianna Clark, Hd.Libn.

WESTERN MEDICAL CENTER - MEDICAL LIBRARY
1001 N. Tustin Ave.   Phone: (714) 835-3555
Santa Ana, CA 92705   Evelyn Simpson, Dir., Med.Lib.

WOODWARD-CLYDE CONSULTANTS - LIBRARY/INFORMATION CENTER
203 N. Golden Circle Dr.   Phone: (714) 835-6886
Santa Ana, CA 92705   Ute Hertel, Rec.Mgr./Libn.

ABC-CLIO INFORMATION SERVICES - THE INGE BOEHM LIBRARY
2040 Alameda Padre Serra   Phone: (805) 963-4221
Santa Barbara, CA 93103   Hope Smith, Libn.

BROOKS INSTITUTE OF PHOTOGRAPHY - LIBRARY
2020 Alameda Padre Serra   Phone: (805) 969-2291
Santa Barbara, CA 93103   James B. Maher, Libn.

COMMUNITY ENVIRONMENTAL COUNCIL, INC. - ECOLOGY CENTER -
   LENDING LIBRARY
924 Anacapa St., Suite B-4   Phone: (805) 962-2210
Santa Barbara, CA 93101   Lutie Fitzgerald, Ctr.Coord.

CONFLUENT EDUCATION DEVELOPMENT AND RESEARCH CENTER -
   CEDARC INFORMATION CENTER
833 Via Granada   Phone: (805) 569-1754
Santa Barbara, CA 93103   Aaron W. Hillman, Ph.D., Sec.

COTTAGE HOSPITAL - DAVID L. REEVES MEDICAL LIBRARY
Box 689   Phone: (805) 682-7393
Santa Barbara, CA 93102   Evelyn Fay, Lib.Supv.

FIRST UNITED METHODIST CHURCH - MEMORIAL LIBRARY
305 E. Anapamu St.   Phone: (805) 963-3579
Santa Barbara, CA 93101   Homer W. Freeman, Church Libn.

GENERAL RESEARCH CORPORATION - LIBRARY
Box 6770   Phone: (805) 964-7724
Santa Barbara, CA 93111   Kathryn Tammen, Supv., Acq.

INFORMATION CONNECTION
Box 6061   Phone: (805) 967-0922
Santa Barbara, CA 93160   Linda R. Phillips, Ph.D., Info.Dir.

INTERNATIONAL ACADEMY AT SANTA BARBARA - LIBRARY
2074 Alameda Padre Serra   Phone: (805) 965-5010
Santa Barbara, CA 93103   Helen K. Rocky, Sec./Treas.

KAMAN-TEMPO - METAL MATRIX COMPOSITES INFORMATION ANALYSIS
   CENTER
816 State St.
P.O. Drawer QQ   Phone: (805) 963-6455
Santa Barbara, CA 93102   Louis Gonzalez, Dir.

KAMAN-TEMPO - TECHNICAL INFORMATION CENTER
Drawer QQ   Phone: (805) 965-0551
Santa Barbara, CA 93102   Sara B. Ellinwood, Libn.

MISSION RESEARCH CORPORATION - INFORMATION CENTER
735 State St.
P.O. Drawer 719   Phone: (805) 963-8761
Santa Barbara, CA 93102   Elaine Messier, Libn.

OGLE PETROLEUM INC. - LIBRARY
4213 State St.   Phone: (805) 964-9911
Santa Barbara, CA 93110   Joyce Foresman, Libn.

OUR LADY OF LIGHT LIBRARY *
1500 Chapala   Phone: (805) 962-9708
Santa Barbara, CA 93101   Lucile Chinnici, Pres.

ST. FRANCIS HOSPITAL - MEDICAL LIBRARY
601 E. Micheltorena
Santa Barbara, CA 93103
Phone: (805) 962-7661
Marilyn Shearer, Dir.

SANTA BARBARA BOTANIC GARDEN - LIBRARY
1212 Mission Canyon Rd.
Santa Barbara, CA 93105
Phone: (805) 682-4726
Nancy Hawver, Libn.

SANTA BARBARA COUNTY LAW LIBRARY
Court House
Santa Barbara, CA 93101
Phone: (805) 966-1611
Kathy Jordan, Law Libn.

SANTA BARBARA HISTORICAL SOCIETY - GLEDHILL LIBRARY
136 E. De La Guerra St.
Box 578
Santa Barbara, CA 93102
Phone: (805) 966-1601
Michael Redmon, Hd.Libn.

SANTA BARBARA MISSION ARCHIVE-LIBRARY
Old Mission, Upper Laguna St.
Santa Barbara, CA 93105
Phone: (805) 682-4713
Rev. Francis F. Guest, O.F.M., Archv.-Hist.

SANTA BARBARA MUSEUM OF ART - MUSEUM LIBRARY AND ARCHIVES
1130 State St.
Santa Barbara, CA 93101
Phone: (805) 963-4364
Ron Crozier, Libn.

SANTA BARBARA MUSEUM OF NATURAL HISTORY - LIBRARY
2559 Puesta del Sol Rd.
Santa Barbara, CA 93105
Phone: (805) 682-4711
Clifton F. Smith, Libn.

SANTA BARBARA NEWS PRESS - LIBRARY
De la Guerra Plaza
Drawer N-N
Santa Barbara, CA 93102
Phone: (805) 966-3911
Carol J. Hardy, Libn.

STONEHENGE STUDY GROUP - STONEHENGE VIEWPOINT LIBRARY
2821 De La Vina St.
Santa Barbara, CA 93105
Phone: (805) 687-9350
Joan L. Cyr, Libn.

TRINITY EPISCOPAL CHURCH - LIBRARY *
1500 State St.
Santa Barbara, CA 93101
Phone: (805) 965-7419
Edith P. Stickney, Libn.

UNIVERSITY OF CALIFORNIA, SANTA BARBARA - ARTS LIBRARY
Phone: (805) 961-3613
Santa Barbara, CA 93106
William R. Treese, Hd./Art Libn.

UNIVERSITY OF CALIFORNIA, SANTA BARBARA - BLACK STUDIES LIBRARY
UNIT
Phone: (805) 961-2922
Santa Barbara, CA 93106
Sylvia Y. Curtis, Act.Libn.

UNIVERSITY OF CALIFORNIA, SANTA BARBARA - DEPARTMENT OF
SPECIAL COLLECTIONS
University Library
Santa Barbara, CA 93106
Phone: (805) 961-3420
Christian Brun, Dept.Hd.

UNIVERSITY OF CALIFORNIA, SANTA BARBARA - GOVERNMENT
PUBLICATIONS DEPARTMENT
University Library
Santa Barbara, CA 93106
Phone: (805) 961-2863
Herbert Linville, Hd.

UNIVERSITY OF CALIFORNIA, SANTA BARBARA - LIBRARY - CHICANO
STUDIES COLLECTION
University Library
Santa Barbara, CA 93106
Phone: (805) 961-2756
Sal Guerena, Assoc.Libn./Unit Hd.

UNIVERSITY OF CALIFORNIA, SANTA BARBARA - MAP AND IMAGERY
LABORATORY - LIBRARY
Phone: (805) 961-2779
Santa Barbara, CA 93106
Larry Carver, Dept.Hd.

UNIVERSITY OF CALIFORNIA, SANTA BARBARA - ORIENTAL COLLECTION
University Library
Santa Barbara, CA 93106
Phone: (805) 961-2365
Henry H. Tai, Oriental Libn.

UNIVERSITY OF CALIFORNIA, SANTA BARBARA - SCIENCES-ENGINEERING
LIBRARY
Phone: (805) 961-2765
Santa Barbara, CA 93106
Alfred J. Hodina, Hd.

AMERICAN MICROSYSTEMS, INC. - CORPORATE INFORMATION CENTER
3800 Homestead Rd., Bldg. 800
Santa Clara, CA 95051
Phone: (408) 246-0330
Nancy Kay Walton, Info./Rec.Ctr.Mgr.

AVANTEK, INC. - TECHNICAL INFORMATION SERVICE
3175 Bowers Ave.
Santa Clara, CA 95051
Phone: (408) 727-0700
Sarah P. Morrison, Corp.Libn.

FMC CORPORATION - CENTRAL ENGINEERING LABORATORIES - LIBRARY
1185 Coleman Ave.
Box 580
Santa Clara, CA 95052
Phone: (408) 289-2529
Keye L. Luke, Libn.

HEALD COLLEGE TECHNICAL DIVISION - TECHNICAL LIBRARY
890 Pepper Tree Ln.
Santa Clara, CA 95051
Phone: (408) 244-9666
Marilyn May Kanemura, Libn.

HEWLETT-PACKARD COMPANY - SANTA CLARA DIVISION LIBRARY †
5301 Stevens Creek Blvd.
Santa Clara, CA 95050
Phone: (408) 246-4300
Diana Robba, Lib.Spec.

HYDRO RESEARCH SCIENCE - LIBRARY †
3334 Victor Ct.
Santa Clara, CA 95050
Phone: (408) 988-1027
Judith C. Lee, Info.Rsrcs.Mgr.

INTEL CORPORATION - TECHNICAL INFORMATION CENTER
2625 Walsh Ave. 4-106
Santa Clara, CA 95051
Phone: (408) 987-6014
Marge Boyd, Mgr.

INTEL CORPORATION - TECHNICAL INFORMATION CENTER
3200 Lakeside Dr., SC6-106
Santa Clara, CA 95051
Phone: (408) 987-5578
Vivienne Virani, Supv.

MEMOREX CORPORATION - TECHNICAL INFORMATION CENTER
San Tomas at Central Expy., M/S14-05
Santa Clara, CA 95052
Phone: (408) 987-3599
Lynn Szabo, Mgr.

TECHNICON DATA SYSTEMS - TECHNICAL LIBRARY
3255-1 Scott Blvd.
Santa Clara, CA 95051
Phone: (408) 727-9400
Margaret Yesso Watson, Libn.

TRITON MUSEUM OF ART - LIBRARY
1505 Warburton Ave.
Santa Clara, CA 95050
Phone: (408) 248-4585
Jo Farb Hernandez, Dir.

UNIVERSITY OF SANTA CLARA - ARCHIVES
Santa Clara, CA 95053
Gerald McKevitt, S.J., Dir.

UNIVERSITY OF SANTA CLARA - EDWIN A. HEAFEY LAW LIBRARY †
University of Santa Clara Law School
Santa Clara, CA 95053
Phone: (408) 984-4451
Mary B. Emery, Libn.

VERSATEC - TECHNICAL INFORMATION CENTER
2805 Bowers Ave.
Santa Clara, CA 95051
Phone: (408) 988-2801
Sharon Tyler, Tech.Info.Spec.

DOMINICAN SANTA CRUZ HOSPITAL - HEALTH INFORMATION LIBRARY
1555 Soquel Dr.
Santa Cruz, CA 95065
Phone: (408) 476-0220
Mrs. Merle W. Ochs, Med.Libn.

SANTA CRUZ COUNTY LAW LIBRARY
701 Ocean St., Courts Bldg.
Santa Cruz, CA 95060
Phone: (408) 425-2211
Patricia J. Pfremmer, Law Libn.

SANTA CRUZ HISTORICAL SOCIETY, INC. - ARCHIVES
Box 246
Santa Cruz, CA 95061
Phone: (408) 426-9035

UNIVERSITY OF CALIFORNIA, SANTA CRUZ - DEAN E. MC HENRY LIBRARY
Phone: (408) 429-2801
Santa Cruz, CA 95064
Allan J. Dyson, Univ.Libn.

UNIVERSITY OF CALIFORNIA, SANTA CRUZ - MAP COLLECTION
McHenry Library Bldg.
Santa Cruz, CA 95064
Phone: (408) 429-2364
Stanley D. Stevens, Map Libn.

UNIVERSITY OF CALIFORNIA, SANTA CRUZ - REGIONAL HISTORY
PROJECT
Dean E. McHenry Library
Santa Cruz, CA 95064
Phone: (408) 429-2847
Randall Jarrell, Dir.

UNIVERSITY OF CALIFORNIA, SANTA CRUZ - SCIENCE LIBRARY
Phone: (408) 429-2050
Santa Cruz, CA 95064   Carolyn Miller, Sci.Libn.

REPUBLIC GEOTHERMAL, INC. - INFORMATION RESOURCES CENTER
11823 E. Slauson Ave.   Phone: (213) 945-3661
Santa Fe Springs, CA 90670   Gloria Barnett, Info.Spec.

BUSHMAN (Ted) LAW OFFICES - LIBRARY
Bushman Bldg., Box 1261   Phone: (805) 773-4200
Santa Maria, CA 93456   Ted Bushman, Libn.

CITICORP/TRANSACTION TECHNOLOGY INC. - TECHNICAL INFORMATION
RESEARCH CENTER
3100 Ocean Park Blvd., Zone No. 26   Phone: (213) 450-9111
Santa Monica, CA 90405   Zorana Ercegovac, Info.Mgr.

GEMOLOGICAL INSTITUTE OF AMERICA - RESEARCH LIBRARY
1660 Stewart St.   Phone: (213) 829-2991
Santa Monica, CA 90404   Dona Mary Dirlam, Libn.

GENERAL TELEPHONE OF CALIFORNIA - FILM LIBRARY
100 Wilshire Blvd.
RC 3120 BC 102   Phone: (213) 390-9064
Santa Monica, CA 90401   Pegi Matsuda, Community Rel.Rep.

GETTY (J. Paul) CENTER FOR THE HISTORY OF ART AND THE HUMANITIES
- LIBRARY
401 Wilshire Blvd., Suite 400   Phone: (213) 458-9811
Santa Monica, CA 90401   Anne-Mieke Halbrook, Libn.

LEAR SIEGLER, INC. - ASTRONICS DIVISION - TECHNICAL LIBRARY
3400 Airport Ave.   Phone: (213) 452-6000
Santa Monica, CA 90406   Felicia Bagby, Tech.Libn.

RAND CORPORATION - LIBRARY †
1700 Main St.   Phone: (213) 393-0411
Santa Monica, CA 90406   Vivian J. Arterbery, Lib.Dir.

ST. JOHN'S HOSPITAL AND HEALTH CENTER - HOSPITAL LIBRARY
1328 22nd St.   Phone: (213) 829-8494
Santa Monica, CA 90404   Cathey L. Pinckney, Libn.

SANTA MONICA HOSPITAL MEDICAL CENTER - LIBRARY
1225 15th St.   Phone: (213) 451-1511
Santa Monica, CA 90404   Lenore F. Orfirer, Librarian

SANTA MONICA PUBLIC LIBRARY - CALIFORNIA SPECIAL COLLECTION
1343 Sixth St.   Phone: (213) 451-5751
Santa Monica, CA 90401   Nancy O'Neill, Hd., Rd.Serv.

SOUTHERN CALIFORNIA INSTITUTE OF ARCHITECTURE - ARCHITECTURE
AND URBAN PLANNING LIBRARY
1800 Berkeley St.   Phone: (213) 829-3482
Santa Monica, CA 90404   Rose Marie Rabin, Libn.

SYSTEM DEVELOPMENT CORPORATION - LIBRARY
2500 Colorado Ave.   Phone: (213) 820-4111
Santa Monica, CA 90406   Ellen Sol, Supv., Lib.Oper.

VIVITAR CORPORATION - TECHNICAL LIBRARY
1630 Stewart St.
Santa Monica, CA 90406

ANATEC LABORATORIES, INC. - LIBRARY
435 Tesconi Circle, No. 14   Phone: (707) 526-7200
Santa Rosa, CA 95401   Dalene Ried, Lib.Mgr.

COMMUNITY HOSPITAL - MEDICAL LIBRARY
3325 Chanate Rd.   Phone: (707) 544-3340
Santa Rosa, CA 95404   Joan Chilton, Med.Libn.

SANTA ROSA PRESS DEMOCRAT - EDITORIAL LIBRARY
427 Mendocino Ave.
Box 569   Phone: (707) 546-2020
Santa Rosa, CA 95402   Elaine Cant, Libn.

SOCIETY OF WIRELESS PIONEERS, INC. - BRENIMAN NAUTICAL-
WIRELESS LIBRARY & MUSEUM OF COMMUNICATIONS
Box 530   Phone: (707) 542-0898
Santa Rosa, CA 95402   Elmer Burgman, Dir.

SONOMA COUNTY LAW LIBRARY
Hall of Justice, Rm. 213-J
600 Administration Dr.   Phone: (707) 527-2668
Santa Rosa, CA 95401   Charlotte S. von Gunten, Law Libn.

SONOMA COUNTY PLANNING DEPARTMENT - LIBRARY
575 Administration Dr.   Phone: (707) 527-2931
Santa Rosa, CA 95401   Ruth Lund, Supv.Ck.

SANTA YNEZ VALLEY HISTORICAL SOCIETY - ELLEN GLEASON LIBRARY
Box 181   Phone: (805) 688-7889
Santa Ynez, CA 93460   Phil Lockwood, Cur.

GOLDEN GATE ENERGY CENTER - LIBRARY
Bldg. 1055, Fort Cronkhite   Phone: (415) 332-8200
Sausalito, CA 94965   Shirley Cooperrider, Rsrcs.Coord.

INSTITUTE OF NOETIC SCIENCES - LIBRARY
475 Gate Five Rd., Suite 300   Phone: (415) 331-5650
Sausalito, CA 94965   Tom Hurley

BETHANY BIBLE COLLEGE - LIBRARY
800 Bethany Dr.   Phone: (408) 438-3800
Scotts Valley, CA 95066   Arnold McLellan, Hd.Libn.

SAN FERNANDO VALLEY COLLEGE OF LAW - LAW LIBRARY †
8353 Sepulveda Blvd.   Phone: (818) 894-5711
Sepulveda, CA 91343   James G. Sherman, Lib.Dir.

U.S. VETERANS ADMINISTRATION (CA-Sepulveda) - BIOMEDICAL
ENGINEERING & COMPUTING CENTER - LIBRARY
V.A. Hospital   Phone: (213) 891-7711
Sepulveda, CA 91343   William R. West, Chf., Lib.Serv.

IMA INCORPORATED - LIBRARY †
15233 Ventura Blvd., Suite 500   Phone: (213) 783-4461
Sherman Oaks, CA 91403   Susan F. Sudduth, Libn.

SUNKIST GROWERS, INC. - CORPORATE LIBRARY
14130 Riverside Dr.   Phone: (818) 986-4800
Sherman Oaks, CA 91423   Claire H. Burday, Corp.Libn.

SIMI VALLEY HISTORICAL SOCIETY - ARCHIVES
R.P. Strathearn Historical Park
137 Strathearn Place
Box 351   Phone: (805) 526-6453
Simi Valley, CA 93065

WHITTAKER CORPORATION - TASKER SYSTEMS DIVISION - TECHNICAL
LIBRARY
1785 Voyager Ave.
Box 8000   Phone: (818) 341-3010
Simi Valley, CA 93063   Orlean A. Hinds, Libn.

GEOSCIENCE, LTD. - LIBRARY
410 S. Cedros Ave.   Phone: (714) 755-9396
Solana Beach, CA 92075

TUOLUMNE COUNTY LAW LIBRARY
Court House
2 S. Green St.   Phone: (209) 533-5675
Sonora, CA 95370   Rose Engler, Law Libn.

LEE PHARMACEUTICALS - LIBRARY
1444 Santa Anita Ave.
South El Monte, CA 91733

KAISER-PERMANENTE MEDICAL CENTER - SOUTH SAN FRANCISCO
HEALTH SCIENCES LIBRARY †
1200 El Camino Real   Phone: (415) 876-0408
South San Francisco, CA 94080   Ysabel R. Bertolucci, Health Sci.Libn.

CARNEGIE INSTITUTION OF WASHINGTON - DEPARTMENT OF PLANT
  BIOLOGY - LIBRARY
290 Panama
Stanford, CA 94305

CENTER FOR ADVANCED STUDY IN THE BEHAVIORAL SCIENCES - LIBRARY
202 Junipero Serra Blvd.   Phone: (415) 321-2052
Stanford, CA 94305   Margaret Amara, Libn.

STANFORD ENVIRONMENTAL LAW SOCIETY - LIBRARY
Stanford University Law School   Phone: (415) 497-4421
Stanford, CA 94305   Jack Haugrud, Pres.

STANFORD LINEAR ACCELERATOR CENTER - LIBRARY
Box 4349   Phone: (415) 854-3300
Stanford, CA 94305   Robert C. Gex, Chf.Libn.

STANFORD UNIVERSITY - ART AND ARCHITECTURE LIBRARY
Nathan Cummings Art Bldg.   Phone: (415) 497-3408
Stanford, CA 94305   Alexander D. Ross, Hd.Libn.

STANFORD UNIVERSITY - BRANNER EARTH SCIENCES LIBRARY
School of Earth Sciences   Phone: (415) 497-2746
Stanford, CA 94305   Charlotte R.M. Derksen, Libn./Bibliog.

STANFORD UNIVERSITY - CENTRAL MAP COLLECTION
Cecil H. Green Library   Phone: (415) 497-1811
Stanford, CA 94305   Karyl Tonge, Map Libn.

STANFORD UNIVERSITY - CUBBERLEY EDUCATION LIBRARY
                                            Phone: (415) 497-2121
Stanford, CA 94305   Barbara Celone, Hd.Libn.

STANFORD UNIVERSITY - DEPARTMENT OF SPECIAL COLLECTIONS
Cecil H. Green Library   Phone: (415) 497-4054
Stanford, CA 94305   Michael Ryan, Chf.

STANFORD UNIVERSITY - ENGINEERING LIBRARY
                                            Phone: (415) 497-1513
Stanford, CA 94305   Michael V. Sullivan, Hd.

STANFORD UNIVERSITY - FALCONER BIOLOGY LIBRARY
                                            Phone: (415) 497-1528
Stanford, CA 94305   Beth Weil, Hd.Libn.

STANFORD UNIVERSITY - FOOD RESEARCH INSTITUTE - LIBRARY
                                            Phone: (415) 497-3943
Stanford, CA 94305   Charles C. Milford, Libn.

STANFORD UNIVERSITY - HOOVER INSTITUTION ON WAR, REVOLUTION
  AND PEACE - LIBRARY
                                            Phone: (415) 497-2058
Stanford, CA 94305   Dr. John B. Dunlop, Assoc.Dir., Lib./Archv.

STANFORD UNIVERSITY - INSTITUTE FOR ENERGY STUDIES - ENERGY
  INFORMATION CENTER
Bldg. 500, Rm. 500C   Phone: (415) 497-3237
Stanford, CA 94305   Marian J. Rees, Dir.

STANFORD UNIVERSITY - J. HUGH JACKSON LIBRARY
Graduate School of Business   Phone: (415) 497-2161
Stanford, CA 94305   Bela Gallo, Dir.

STANFORD UNIVERSITY - LANE MEDICAL LIBRARY
Stanford University Medical Center   Phone: (415) 497-6831
Stanford, CA 94305   Peter Stangl, Dir.

STANFORD UNIVERSITY - LAW LIBRARY
                                            Phone: (415) 497-2721
Stanford, CA 94305   Prof. J. Myron Jacobstein, Law Libn.

STANFORD UNIVERSITY - MATHEMATICAL AND COMPUTER SCIENCES
  LIBRARY
Bldg. 380, Sloan Mathematics Center   Phone: (415) 497-4672
Stanford, CA 94305   Harry P. Llull, Hd.Libn./Bibliog.

STANFORD UNIVERSITY - MUSIC LIBRARY
Braun Music Center   Phone: (415) 497-1211
Stanford, CA 94305   Jerry Persons, Hd.Libn.

STANFORD UNIVERSITY - PHYSICS LIBRARY
                                            Phone: (415) 497-4342
Stanford, CA 94305   Virginia M. Kosanovic, Hd.Libn.

STANFORD UNIVERSITY - SWAIN LIBRARY OF CHEMISTRY AND CHEMICAL
  ENGINEERING
                                            Phone: (415) 497-9237
Stanford, CA 94305

STANFORD UNIVERSITY - TANNER MEMORIAL PHILOSOPHY LIBRARY
Department of Philosophy   Phone: (415) 497-1539
Stanford, CA 94303

STANFORD UNIVERSITY - UNIVERSITY ARCHIVES
Cecil H. Green Library   Phone: (415) 497-4055
Stanford, CA 94305   Roxanne-Louise Nilan, Univ.Archv.

THE HAGGIN MUSEUM - ALMEDA MAY CASTLE PETZINGER LIBRARY
1201 N. Pershing Ave.   Phone: (209) 462-4116
Stockton, CA 95203   Diane Freggiaro, Libn./Archv.

ST. JOSEPH'S HOSPITAL - MEDICAL LIBRARY *
1800 N. California St.   Phone: (209) 943-2000
Stockton, CA 95204   Dr. Bernard

SAN JOAQUIN COUNTY LAW LIBRARY
County Court House, Rm. 300   Phone: (209) 944-2207
Stockton, CA 95202   Gertrudes J. Ladion, Law Libn.

SAN JOAQUIN LOCAL HEALTH DISTRICT - LIBRARY
1601 E. Hazelton Ave.
Box 2009   Phone: (209) 466-6781
Stockton, CA 95201   Doris Beckwith, Libn.

STOCKTON NEWSPAPERS INC. - STOCKTON RECORD LIBRARY
530 Market St.   Phone: (209) 943-6397
Stockton, CA 95201   Dorothy M. Frankhouse, Libn.

STOCKTON-SAN JOAQUIN COUNTY PUBLIC LIBRARY - CALIFORNIA ROOM
603 N. El Dorado   Phone: (209) 944-8415
Stockton, CA 95202   Isabel Benson, Libn.

STOCKTON STATE HOSPITAL - PROFESSIONAL LIBRARY
510 El Magnolia   Phone: (209) 948-7181
Stockton, CA 95202   Walter Greening, Sr.Libn.

UNITED METHODIST CHURCH - NORTHERN CALIFORNIA-NEVADA
  CONFERENCE - J.A.B. FRY RESEARCH LIBRARY
University of the Pacific   Phone: (209) 946-2269
Stockton, CA 95211   Rev. William Bowler Jefferies, Dir. of Archv.

UNIVERSITY OF THE PACIFIC - SCIENCE LIBRARY †
751 Brookside Rd.   Phone: (209) 946-2568
Stockton, CA 95207   Judith K. Andrews, Sci.Libn.

UNIVERSITY OF THE PACIFIC - STUART LIBRARY OF WESTERN
  AMERICANA
                                            Phone: (209) 946-2404
Stockton, CA 95211   John Porter Bloom, Dir.

PACIFIC INFORMATION INC. - INFORMATION SERVICES
11684 Ventura Blvd., Suite 295   Phone: (818) 797-7654
Studio City, CA 91604

CALIFORNIA RAILWAY MUSEUM - LIBRARY
Star Rte. 283, Box 150   Phone: (415) 534-0071
Suisun City, CA 94585   Vernon J. Sappers, Cur.

ADVANCED MICRO DEVICES, INC. - TECHNICAL LIBRARY
901 Thompson Pl., M/S 1
Box 3453   Phone: (408) 749-2260
Sunnyvale, CA 94088   Pamela McCoy, Tech.Libn.

AMDAHL CORPORATION - CORPORATE LIBRARY
1250 E. Arques Ave.   Phone: (408) 746-6376
Sunnyvale, CA 94086   Lourdes (Ludy) Dorilag, Mgr.

ARGOSYSTEMS - INC. - TECHNICAL LIBRARY †
884 Hermosa Court   Phone: (408) 737-2000
Sunnyvale, CA 94086   Randy J. Galloway, Info.Rsrcs.Mgr.

ATARI INC. - CORPORATE LIBRARY/INFORMATION CENTER
1399 Moffett Park Blvd.   Phone: (408) 745-4634
Sunnyvale, CA 94086   Anne Porter-Roth, Mgr.

CONTROL DATA CORPORATION - SUNNYVALE OPERATIONS LIBRARY
Box 3492   Phone: (408) 744-5798
Sunnyvale, CA 94088-3492   Jaxon K. Matthews, Libn.

ESL/SUBSIDIARY OF TRW - RESEARCH LIBRARY
495 Java Dr.
Box 3510   Phone: (408) 738-2888
Sunnyvale, CA 94088-3510   Verna Van Velzer, Chf.Libn.

FRIENDS OF THE WESTERN PHILATELIC LIBRARY
Box 2219   Phone: (408) 245-9171
Sunnyvale, CA 94087   Richard E. Clever, Pres.

GENERAL ELECTRIC COMPANY - ADVANCED REACTOR SYSTEMS DEPT. -
    LIBRARY
310 DeGuigne Drive
Box 3508   Phone: (408) 738-7177
Sunnyvale, CA 94088   Dorothy Hutson, Mgr., Tech.Serv.

LITTON APPLIED TECHNOLOGY - LIBRARY
645 Almanor Ave.   Phone: (408) 773-7059
Sunnyvale, CA 94088-3478   Doron A. Dula, Tech.Libn.

LITTON MELLONICS - TECHNICAL LIBRARY
1001 W. Maude Ave.   Phone: (408) 245-0795
Sunnyvale, CA 94086   James L. Wood, Mgr.

PALMER COLLEGE OF CHIROPRACTIC - WEST - LIBRARY
1095 Dunford Way   Phone: (408) 244-8907
Sunnyvale, CA 94087   Phyllis Hazekamp, Libn.

SIGNETICS CORPORATION - LIBRARY
811 E. Arques Ave.   Phone: (408) 739-7700
Sunnyvale, CA 94086   Stephanie Jang, Libn.

SINGER COMPANY - LINK DIVISION - TECHNICAL LIBRARY
1077 E. Arques Ave.   Phone: (408) 720-5719
Sunnyvale, CA 94088-3484   Shu-nan T. Chiang, Tech.Libn.

SUNNYVALE PATENT INFORMATION CLEARINGHOUSE
1500 Partridge Ave., Bldg. 7   Phone: (408) 738-5588
Sunnyvale, CA 94087   H. Maria Patermann, Dir. of Libs.

CALIFORNIA LUTHERAN COLLEGE - LIBRARY - SPECIAL COLLECTIONS †
                                               Phone: (805) 492-2411
Thousand Oaks, CA 91360   Kenneth E. Pflueger, Dir., Lib.Serv.

ROCKWELL INTERNATIONAL - SCIENCE CENTER LIBRARY
1049 Camino Dos Rios
Box 1085   Phone: (805) 498-4545
Thousand Oaks, CA 91360   Helen M. Coogan, Supv., Lib.

SOUTHERN CALIFORNIA SOCIETY FOR PSYCHICAL RESEARCH, INC. -
    LIBRARY
Box 3901   Phone: (213) 936-0904
Thousand Oaks, CA 91359   Andrew T. Shields, Lib.Coord.

H.M.S. BOUNTY SOCIETY, INTERNATIONAL - RESEARCH LIBRARY AND
    DEPOSITORY
174 Trinidad Dr.   Phone: (415) 435-9749
Tiburon, CA 94920   A. Munro Christian, Dir.

U.S. NATL. MARINE FISHERIES SERVICE - TIBURON LABORATORY LIBRARY
3150 Paradise Dr.   Phone: (415) 435-3149
Tiburon, CA 94920   Maureen Woods, Libn.

FEMINIST HISTORY RESEARCH PROJECT - LIBRARY
19988 Observation Dr.
Box 1156   Phone: (213) 455-1283
Topanga, CA 90290

GARRETT CORPORATION - AIRESEARCH MANUFACTURING COMPANY -
    TECHNICAL LIBRARY
Dept. 93-45/T-40
2525 W. 190th St.   Phone: (213) 512-3667
Torrance, CA 90509   Joanna M. Sutton, Hd.Libn.

LOS ANGELES COUNTY HARBOR-UCLA MEDICAL CENTER - A.F. PARLOW
    LIBRARY OF THE HEALTH SCIENCES
1000 W. Carson St.
Box 18   Phone: (213) 533-2373
Torrance, CA 90509   Mary Ann Berliner, Dir., Lib.Serv.

MAGNAVOX GOVERNMENT & INDUSTRIAL ELECTRONICS COMPANY -
    ADVANCED PRODUCTS DIVISION - LIBRARY
2829 Maricopa Ave.   Phone: (213) 328-0770
Torrance, CA 90503   Cecilia Foutana, Libn.

TORRANCE MEMORIAL HOSPITAL MEDICAL CENTER - HEALTH SCIENCES
    LIBRARY
3330 W. Lomita Blvd.   Phone: (213) 325-9110
Torrance, CA 90509   Anita N. Klecker, Dir. of Lib.Serv.

U.S. AIR FORCE BASE - TRAVIS BASE LIBRARY
Mitchell Memorial Library
60 ABGp/SSL   Phone: (707) 438-5254
Travis AFB, CA 94535   Nina Jacobs, Libn.

U.S. AIR FORCE HOSPITAL - DAVID GRANT MEDICAL CENTER - MEDICAL
    LIBRARY
                                               Phone: (707) 438-3257
Travis AFB, CA 94535   A. Peri Worthington, Med.Libn./Dir.

GEORGE (Henry) SCHOOL OF LOS ANGELES - RESEARCH LIBRARY
10242 Mahogany Trail
Box 655   Phone: (818) 352-4141
Tujunga, CA 91042   Mrs. G.E. Pollard, Libn.

TULARE PUBLIC LIBRARY - INEZ L. HYDE MEMORIAL COLLECTION
113 North F. St.
Tulare, CA 93274   Louise Longan, Libn.

U.S. NATL. PARK SERVICE - LAVA BEDS NATL. MONUMENT - LIBRARY
                                               Phone: (916) 667-2282
Tulelake, CA 96134   Gary Hathaway, Chf., Div. of Interp.

CALIFORNIA STATE COLLEGE, STANISLAUS - LIBRARY - SPECIAL
    COLLECTIONS
                                               Phone: (209) 667-3232
Turlock, CA 95380   J. Carlyle Parker, Act.Dir.

EMANUEL MEDICAL CENTER - MEDICAL LIBRARY
Box 2120   Phone: (209) 634-9151
Turlock, CA 95381-2120   Donna Cardoza, Lib.Ck.

MEDIC ALERT FOUNDATION INTERNATIONAL - CENTRAL REFERENCE FILE
    OF MEMBERSHIP
2323 Colorado Ave.
Box 1009   Phone: (209) 668-3333
Turlock, CA 95381   Alfred A. Hodder, Pres.

AEROJET ORDNANCE COMPANY - TECHNICAL LIBRARY
2521 Michelle Dr.   Phone: (714) 730-6004
Tustin, CA 92680   Norman J. Storrer, Sr.Tech.Libn.

HELD-POAGE MEMORIAL HOME & RESEARCH LIBRARY
603 W. Perkins St.   Phone: (707) 462-6969
Ukiah, CA 95482   Lila J. Lee, Libn.

MENDOCINO COUNTY LAW LIBRARY
Courthouse, Rm. 207   Phone: (707) 468-4481
Ukiah, CA 95482   Ginny Holmen, Law Libn.

UNIVERSAL CITY STUDIOS - RESEARCH DEPARTMENT LIBRARY
100 Universal City Plaza   Phone: (213) 985-4321
Universal City, CA 91608   Robert A. Lee, Hd., Res.Dept.

FIRST PRESBYTERIAN CHURCH - LIBRARY †
869 N. Euclid Ave.   Phone: (714) 982-8811
Upland, CA 91786   Courtney Brunworth, Libn.

SAN ANTONIO COMMUNITY HOSPITAL - WEBER MEMORIAL LIBRARY
999 San Bernardino Rd.
Phone: (714) 985-2811
Upland, CA 91786
Francena Johnston, Med.Libn.

CALIFORNIA STATE MEDICAL FACILITY - STAFF LIBRARY *
1600 California Dr.
Phone: (707) 448-6841
Vacaville, CA 95696
Roberta Carson, Med.Rec.Libn.

CALIFORNIA INSTITUTE OF THE ARTS - LIBRARY
24700 McBean Pkwy.
Phone: (805) 255-1050
Valencia, CA 91355
James Elrod, Lib.Dir.

CALIFORNIA MARITIME ACADEMY LIBRARY
Box 1392
Phone: (707) 644-5601
Vallejo, CA 94590
Paul W. O'Bannon, Sr.Libn.

U.S. NAVY - NAVAL SHIPYARD (CA-Mare Island) - TECHNICAL LIBRARY
Code 202.13, Stop T-4
Phone: (707) 646-4306
Vallejo, CA 94592-5100
Layne Huseth, Hd., Shipyard Tech.Lib.

VALLEJO NAVAL AND HISTORICAL MUSEUM - LIBRARY
734 Marin St.
Phone: (707) 643-0022
Vallejo, CA 94590
Dorothy E. Marsden, Libn.

AMERICAN BIO-SCIENCE LABORATORIES - LIBRARY
7600 Tyrone Ave.
Phone: (818) 989-2520
Van Nuys, CA 91405

BLUE CROSS OF CALIFORNIA - LIBRARY
Box 70,000
Phone: (818) 703-3162
Van Nuys, CA 91470
Frances Baur Linke, Hd.Libn.

CARNATION RESEARCH LABORATORIES - LIBRARY
8015 Van Nuys Blvd.
Phone: (818) 787-7820
Van Nuys, CA 91412
Kathryn A. Stewart, Libn.

INTERNATIONAL STAMP COLLECTORS SOCIETY - LIBRARY
Box 854
Phone: (818) 997-6496
Van Nuys, CA 91408
Israel Bick, Exec.Dir.

ITT CORPORATION - GILFILLAN ENGINEERING LIBRARY †
7821 Orion Ave.
Box 7713
Phone: (818) 988-2600
Van Nuys, CA 91409
Dawn N. Villere, Sr.Tech.Libn.

LITTON INDUSTRIES - DATA SYSTEMS DIVISION - ENGINEERING LIBRARY
†
8000 Woodley Ave.
Phone: (818) 781-8211
Van Nuys, CA 91409
Joe Ann Clifton, Mgr., Tech.Libs.

LOS ANGELES COUNTY/OLIVE VIEW MEDICAL CENTER - HEALTH
SCIENCES LIBRARY
7533 Van Nuys Blvd.
Rm. 303, South Tower
Phone: (818) 901-3040
Van Nuys, CA 91405
Miriam Kafka, Act.Libn.

LOS ANGELES DAILY NEWS - EDITORIAL LIBRARY
14539 Sylvan St.
Phone: (818) 997-4162
Van Nuys, CA 91411
Andrew Merrill, Chf.Libn.

NATIONAL INVESTIGATIONS COMMITTEE ON UFOS - NEW AGE CENTER
14617 Victory Blvd., Suite 4
Phone: (818) 781-7704
Van Nuys, CA 91411
Madeleine Udin, Mgr.

VALLEY PRESBYTERIAN HOSPITAL - LIBRARY FOR MEDICAL AND HEALTH
SCIENCES
15107 Vanowen St.
Phone: (818) 902-2973
Van Nuys, CA 91405
Francine Kubrin, Libn.

U.S. AIR FORCE - WESTERN SPACE AND MISSILE CENTER - WSMC/PMET
TECHNICAL LIBRARY
Western Space and Missile Center
Phone: (805) 866-9745
Vandenberg AFB, CA 93437
Paula Turley, Chf.Libn.

BEYOND BAROQUE FOUNDATION - LIBRARY
Old Venice City Hall
681 Venice Blvd.
Phone: (213) 822-3006
Venice, CA 90291
Jocelyn Fisher, Dir.

PACIFIC BIO-MARINE LABORATORIES, INC. - RESEARCH LIBRARY †
4134 Del Rey Ave.
Box 536
Phone: (213) 822-5757
Venice, CA 90291
Michael J. Fishman, Libn.

CHURCH OF JESUS CHRIST OF LATTER-DAY SAINTS - VENTURA BRANCH
GENEALOGICAL LIBRARY
3501 Loma Vista Rd.
Box 3517
Phone: (805) 643-5607
Ventura, CA 93003
Louise W. La Count, Chf.Libn.

UNION OIL COMPANY OF CALIFORNIA - LIBRARY-FILE ROOM
2323 Knoll Dr.
Box 6176
Phone: (805) 656-7600
Ventura, CA 93006
Jeanne Gallagher, Libn.

VENTURA COUNTY HISTORICAL SOCIETY - LIBRARY & ARCHIVES
100 E. Main St.
Phone: (805) 653-0323
Ventura, CA 93001
Patricia Sales, Res.Libn.

VENTURA COUNTY LAW LIBRARY
800 S. Victoria Ave.
Phone: (805) 654-2695
Ventura, CA 93009
Naydean L. Baker, Law Libn.

VENTURA COUNTY RESOURCE MANAGEMENT AGENCY - TECHNICAL
LIBRARY
800 S. Victoria Ave.
Phone: (805) 654-2480
Ventura, CA 93009
Evelyn Adams, Tech.Libn.

VENTURA COUNTY STAR-FREE PRESS - LIBRARY
Box 6711
Phone: (805) 656-4111
Ventura, CA 93006
Sara J. Riley, Libn.

VETCO OFFSHORE, INC. - TECHNICAL LIBRARY
250 W. Stanley Ave.
Box 1688
Phone: (805) 653-2500
Ventura, CA 93001
Larry Markworth, Tech.Libn.

TULARE COUNTY FREE LIBRARY - CALIFORNIA HISTORICAL RESEARCH
COLLECTION - ANNIE R. MITCHELL ROOM
200 W. Oak St.
Phone: (209) 733-8440
Visalia, CA 93277
Mary Anne Terstegge, Hist.Libn.

TULARE COUNTY LAW LIBRARY
County Civic Center, Rm. 1
Phone: (209) 733-6395
Visalia, CA 93291
Sharon Borbon, Law Lib.Coord.

SAN DIEGO COUNTY LAW LIBRARY - VISTA BRANCH
325 S. Melrose
Phone: (619) 758-6247
Vista, CA 92083
O. James Werner, Dir.

BROWN & CALDWELL - LIBRARY
Box 8045
Phone: (415) 937-9010
Walnut Creek, CA 94596-1220
Bruce Hubbard, Libn.

CONTRA COSTA TIMES - LIBRARY
2640 Shadelands Dr.
Box 5088
Phone: (415) 935-2525
Walnut Creek, CA 94596
Elyse A. Eisner, Libn.

DOW CHEMICAL U.S.A. - WESTERN DIVISION RESEARCH LABORATORIES -
LIBRARY
Box 9002
Phone: (415) 944-2064
Walnut Creek, CA 94598
Mary Lao, Libn.

JOHN MUIR MEMORIAL HOSPITAL - HEALTH SCIENCES LIBRARY
1601 Ygnacio Valley Rd.
Phone: (415) 939-3000
Walnut Creek, CA 94598
Helen M. Reyes, Libn.

WALNUT CREEK HISTORICAL SOCIETY - SHADELANDS RANCH
HISTORICAL MUSEUM - HISTORY ROOM
2660 Ygnacio Valley Rd.
Phone: (415) 935-7871
Walnut Creek, CA 94598
Beverly C. Clemson, Musm.Dir.

WOODWARD-CLYDE CONSULTANTS - ENVIRONMENTAL SYSTEMS
DIVISION - INFORMATION CENTER †
One Walnut Creek Center
100 Pringle Ave.
Phone: (415) 945-3000
Walnut Creek, CA 94596
Harriet Annino, Libn.

WOODWARD-CLYDE CONSULTANTS, WESTERN REGION - INFORMATION
  CENTER †
One Walnut Creek Center
100 Pringle Ave.   Phone: (415) 945-3000
Walnut Creek, CA 94596   Anne T. Harrigan, Libn.

PAJARO VALLEY HISTORICAL ASSOCIATION - WILLIAM H. VOLCK MUSEUM
  - ARCHIVES
261 E. Beach St.   Phone: (408) 722-0305
Watsonville, CA 95076   Alzora Snyder, Archv.

TRINITY COUNTY LAW LIBRARY *
Box R   Phone: (916) 623-4000
Weaverville, CA 96093   Carol Rose, Sec.

HONEYWELL, INC. - DEFENSE & MARINE SYSTEMS GROUP, TRAINING AND
  CONTROL SYSTEMS OPERATION - TECHNICAL LIBRARY
1200 E. San Bernardino Rd.
West Covina, CA 91790

ALLIED CORPORATION - BUNKER-RAMO ELECTRONIC SYSTEMS DIVISION
  - MAIN LIBRARY
Mail Code MS 1
31717 La Tienda Dr.   Phone: (818) 889-2211
Westlake, CA 91359   Donald A. Larson, Rec.Mgr.

LOS ANGELES COLLEGE OF CHIROPRACTIC - HENRY G. HIGHLY LIBRARY
16200 E. Amber Valley Dr.   Phone: (213) 947-8755
Whittier, CA 90604   Robin L. Lober, Dir.

LOS ANGELES COUNTY - SANITATION DISTRICTS TECHNICAL LIBRARY
1955 Workman Mill Rd.   Phone: (213) 699-7411
Whittier, CA 90601   Beverly Yoshida, Libn.

WHITTIER COLLEGE - DEPARTMENT OF GEOLOGY - FAIRCHILD AERIAL
  PHOTOGRAPH COLLECTION †
                                          Phone: (213) 693-0771
Whittier, CA 90608   Dallas D. Rhodes, Dir.

LOS ANGELES HARBOR COLLEGE - LIBRARY - ARCHIVES
1111 Figueroa Place   Phone: (213) 835-0161
Wilmington, CA 90744   Sylvia Lamont

ATLANTIC-RICHFIELD COMPANY - ARCO SOLAR INC. - RESEARCH
  LIBRARY
21011 Warner Center Ln.   Phone: (818) 700-7186
Woodland Hills, CA 91365   Aggi Raeder, Lib.Mgr.

LITTON INDUSTRIES - GUIDANCE AND CONTROL SYSTEMS - LIBRARY
5500 Canoga Ave.   Phone: (818) 887-3867
Woodland Hills, CA 91364   Joe Ann Clifton, Mgr., Info.Serv.

LOS ANGELES UNIFIED SCHOOL DISTRICTS - WEST VALLEY
  OCCUPATIONAL CENTER - LEARNING CENTER *
6200 Winnetka Ave.
Woodland Hills, CA 91364

MARISKA ALDRICH MEMORIAL FOUNDATION, INC. - ALDRICH LIBRARY OF
  MUSIC
8451-8491 Swarthout Canyon Rd.
Box 369   Phone: (619) 249-6751
Wrightwood, CA 92397-0369   Dr. Ric Anderson, Chm./Chf.Exec.Off.

U.S. NATL. PARK SERVICE - YOSEMITE NATL. PARK - RESEARCH LIBRARY
Box 577   Phone: (209) 372-4461
Yosemite National Park, CA 95389   Mary Vocelka, Lib.Techn.

VETERANS HOME OF CALIFORNIA - LINCOLN MEMORIAL LIBRARY
                                          Phone: (707) 944-4279
Yountville, CA 94599

SISKIYOU COUNTY HISTORICAL SOCIETY - LIBRARY
910 S. Main St.   Phone: (916) 842-3836
Yreka, CA 96097   Eleanor Brown, Musm.Cur.

SISKIYOU COUNTY LAW LIBRARY
311 Fourth St., Courthouse   Phone: (916) 842-3531
Yreka, CA 96097   Patricia Howard, Libn.

SUTTER COUNTY LAW LIBRARY
Court House   Phone: (916) 673-6544
Yuba City, CA 95991   Lillian R. Boss, Law Libn.

COLORADO

U.S.D.A. - AGRICULTURAL RESEARCH SERVICE - CENTRAL GREAT PLAINS
  RESEARCH STATION - LIBRARY
Box K   Phone: (303) 345-2259
Akron, CO 80720   Dr. D.E. Smika, Location Leader

ADAMS STATE COLLEGE - LIBRARY - SPECIAL COLLECTIONS
                                          Phone: (303) 589-7781
Alamosa, CO 81102   Nellie N. Hasfjord, Dir.

CLASSIC AMX CLUB, INTERNATIONAL - AMX LIBRARY
7963 Depew St.
Arvada, CO 80003   Larry G. Mitchell, Cur.

ASPEN HISTORICAL SOCIETY - LIBRARY
620 W. Bleeker St.   Phone: (303) 925-3721
Aspen, CO 81611   Vera Haberman, Archv.

ASPEN INSTITUTE FOR HUMANISTIC STUDIES - DAVID MAYER LIBRARY
1000 N. 3rd St.
Aspen, CO 81611

ROARING FORK ENERGY CENTER - LIBRARY
Box 9950   Phone: (303) 925-8885
Aspen, CO 81612

AURORA PUBLIC SCHOOLS - PROFESSIONAL LIBRARY
Peoria Center
875 Peoria St.   Phone: (303) 344-8060
Aurora, CO 80011   Bill Murray, Dir.

LUTHERAN CHURCH - MISSOURI SYNOD - COLORADO DISTRICT ARCHIVES
1591 Fulton St.
Box 488   Phone: (303) 364-9148
Aurora, CO 80010   Lyle Schaefer, District Archv.

NATIONAL WRITERS CLUB - LIBRARY
1450 S. Havana, Suite 620   Phone: (303) 751-7844
Aurora, CO 80012   Donald E. Bower, Dir.

U.S. ARMY HOSPITALS - FITZSIMONS ARMY MEDICAL CENTER - MEDICAL-
  TECHNICAL LIBRARY
                                          Phone: (303) 361-3378
Aurora, CO 80045-5000   Sharon Johnson, Adm.Libn.

GEM VILLAGE MUSEUM - GREEN MEMORIAL LIBRARY
39671 Highway 160   Phone: (303) 884-2811
Bayfield, CO 81122   Elizabeth X. Gilbert, Sec.-Treas.

ASSOCIATION FOR EXPERIENTIAL EDUCATION - LIBRARY
Box 249-CU   Phone: (303) 492-1547
Boulder, CO 80309   Stephanie Takis, Exec.Off.

BALL AEROSPACE SYSTEMS DIVISION - TECHNICAL LIBRARY
Boulder Industrial Park
Box 1062   Phone: (303) 441-4436
Boulder, CO 80306   Judy Dayhoff, Supv., Info.Serv.

BOULDER HISTORICAL SOCIETY AND MUSEUM - DOCUMENTARY
  COLLECTIONS DEPARTMENT
1019 Spruce St.   Phone: (303) 449-3464
Boulder, CO 80302   Phyllis Plehaty, Cur.

BOULDER PUBLIC LIBRARY - CARNEGIE BRANCH LIBRARY FOR LOCAL
  HISTORY
1125 Pine St.
Drawer H   Phone: (303) 441-3110
Boulder, CO 80306   Lois Anderton, Libn./Archv.

BOULDER PUBLIC LIBRARY - MUNICIPAL GOVERNMENT REFERENCE
  CENTER
1000 Canyon Blvd.
P.O. Drawer H   Phone: (303) 441-3100
Boulder, CO 80306   Virginia Braddock, Hd., MGRC

BOULDER VALLEY MEDICAL LIBRARY
Boulder Community Hospital
1100 Balsam Ave.   Phone: (303) 442-8190
Boulder, CO 80302   Carol M. Boyer, Med.Libn.

BOULDER VALLEY PUBLIC SCHOOLS, REGION 2 - PROFESSIONAL LIBRARY
6500 E. Arapahoe Ave.   Phone: (303) 447-1010
Boulder, CO 80302   Carol Newman, Libn.

CAUSE - LIBRARY
737 29th St.   Phone: (303) 449-4430
Boulder, CO 80303   Charles R. Thomas, Exec.Dir.

ERIC CLEARINGHOUSE FOR SOCIAL STUDIES/SOCIAL SCIENCE
    EDUCATION - RESOURCE & DEMONSTRATION CENTER
Social Science Education Consortium
855 Broadway   Phone: (303) 492-8434
Boulder, CO 80302   Sydney J. Meredith, Asst.Dir., ERIC Oper.

IBM CORPORATION - BOULDER LIBRARY
Dept. 419, Box 1900   Phone: (303) 447-5064
Boulder, CO 80302

NAROPA INSTITUTE - LIBRARY
2130 Arapahoe   Phone: (303) 444-0202
Boulder, CO 80302   Gail Schuler, Lib.Dir.

NATIONAL CENTER FOR ATMOSPHERIC RESEARCH - HIGH ALTITUDE
    OBSERVATORY LIBRARY
Box 3000   Phone: (303) 494-5151
Boulder, CO 80307   Kathryn Strand, Libn.

NATIONAL CENTER FOR ATMOSPHERIC RESEARCH - MESA LIBRARY
Box 3000   Phone: (303) 494-5151
Boulder, CO 80307   Charles B. Wenger, Chf.Libn.

NATIVE AMERICAN RIGHTS FUND - NATIONAL INDIAN LAW LIBRARY
1506 Broadway   Phone: (303) 447-8760
Boulder, CO 80302   Diana Lim Garry, Libn.

U.S. DEPT. OF JUSTICE - NATIONAL INSTITUTE OF CORRECTIONS - NIC
    INFORMATION CENTER
1790 30th St., Suite 130   Phone: (303) 444-1101
Boulder, CO 80301   Coralie Whitmore, Dir.

U.S. NATL. OCEANIC & ATMOSPHERIC ADMINISTRATION - MOUNTAIN
    ADMINISTRATIVE SUPPORT CTR. - LIBRARY
325 Broadway, RAS/MC5   Phone: (303) 497-3271
Boulder, CO 80303   Joan Maier McKean, Chf., Lib.Serv.

UNIVERSITY OF COLORADO, BOULDER - ACADEMIC MEDIA SERVICES
Stadium Bldg., Rm. 361
Campus Box 455   Phone: (303) 492-7341
Boulder, CO 80309   Dr. Elwood E. Miller, Dir.

UNIVERSITY OF COLORADO, BOULDER - ART AND ARCHITECTURE
    LIBRARY
Norlin Library
Campus Box 184   Phone: (303) 492-7955
Boulder, CO 80309   Liesel Nolan, Libn.

UNIVERSITY OF COLORADO, BOULDER - AUDIOVISUAL/MICROFORMS
    DEPARTMENT
Norlin Library
Campus Box 184   Phone: (303) 492-6930
Boulder, CO 80309   Sharon Gause, Libn.

UNIVERSITY OF COLORADO, BOULDER - BUSINESS RESEARCH DIVISION -
    BUSINESS & ECONOMIC COLLECTION
Campus Box 420   Phone: (303) 492-8227
Boulder, CO 80309   C.R. Goeldner, Dir.

UNIVERSITY OF COLORADO, BOULDER - BUSINESS RESEARCH DIVISION -
    TRAVEL REFERENCE CENTER
Campus Box 420   Phone: (303) 492-8227
Boulder, CO 80309   C.R. Goeldner, Dir.

UNIVERSITY OF COLORADO, BOULDER - CENTER FOR ECONOMIC
    ANALYSIS - LIBRARY
Economics Bldg. 208
Campus Box 257   Phone: (303) 492-7413
Boulder, CO 80309   Michael Greenwood

UNIVERSITY OF COLORADO, BOULDER - EARTH SCIENCES LIBRARY
Campus Box 184   Phone: (303) 492-6133
Boulder, CO 80309   Terrie O'Neal, Lib.Techn.

UNIVERSITY OF COLORADO, BOULDER - ENGINEERING LIBRARY
Campus Box 184   Phone: (303) 492-5396
Boulder, CO 80309   Jean D. Messimer, Libn.

UNIVERSITY OF COLORADO, BOULDER - GOVERNMENT PUBLICATIONS
    DIVISION
Norlin Library
Campus Box 184   Phone: (303) 492-8834
Boulder, CO 80309   Catharine J. Reynolds, Hd., Govt.Pubn.

UNIVERSITY OF COLORADO, BOULDER - INSTITUTE OF ARCTIC & ALPINE
    RESEARCH - READING ROOM
Rose M. Litman Research Lab.
Campus Box 450   Phone: (303) 492-6387
Boulder, CO 80309   Martha Andrews, Prof.Res.Asst.

UNIVERSITY OF COLORADO, BOULDER - INSTITUTE OF BEHAVIORAL
    SCIENCE - IBS RESEARCH LIBRARY
IBS Bldg. 1
Campus Box 483   Phone: (303) 492-8340
Boulder, CO 80309   Diana Oldsen, Lib.Techn.

UNIVERSITY OF COLORADO, BOULDER - JOINT INSTITUTE FOR
    LABORATORY ASTROPHYSICS - DATA CENTER
Campus Box 440   Phone: (303) 492-7801
Boulder, CO 80309   J.W. Gallagher, Mgr.

UNIVERSITY OF COLORADO, BOULDER - LAW LIBRARY
Fleming Law Bldg.   Phone: (303) 492-7534
Boulder, CO 80309   Oscar J. Miller, Law Libn.

UNIVERSITY OF COLORADO, BOULDER - MAP LIBRARY
Norlin Library
Campus Box 184   Phone: (303) 492-7578
Boulder, CO 80309

UNIVERSITY OF COLORADO, BOULDER - MATHEMATICS & PHYSICS
    LIBRARY
Duane Physical Laboratories G140
Campus Box 184   Phone: (303) 492-8231
Boulder, CO 80309   Allen Wynne, Dept.Hd.

UNIVERSITY OF COLORADO, BOULDER - MUSIC LIBRARY
N-290 Warner Imig Music Bldg.
Campus Box 184   Phone: (303) 492-8093
Boulder, CO 80309   Karl Kroeger, Music Libn.

UNIVERSITY OF COLORADO, BOULDER - SCIENCE LIBRARY
Norlin Library
Campus Box 184   Phone: (303) 492-5136
Boulder, CO 80309   David Fagerstrom, Libn.

UNIVERSITY OF COLORADO, BOULDER - SPECIAL COLLECTIONS
    DEPARTMENT
Norlin Library
Campus Box 184   Phone: (303) 492-6144
Boulder, CO 80309   Nora Quinlan, Hd.

UNIVERSITY OF COLORADO, BOULDER - WESTERN HISTORICAL
    COLLECTION & UNIVERSITY ARCHIVES
Norlin Library
Campus Box 184   Phone: (303) 492-7242
Boulder, CO 80309   Dr. John A. Brennan, Cur.

UNIVERSITY OF COLORADO, BOULDER - WILLIAM M. WHITE BUSINESS
    LIBRARY
Business Bldg.
Campus Box 184   Phone: (303) 492-8367
Boulder, CO 80309   Carol Krismann, Bus.Libn.

WESTERN INTERSTATE COMMISSION FOR HIGHER EDUCATION - LIBRARY
Drawer P   Phone: (303) 497-0284
Boulder, CO 80302   Karon M. Kelly, Dir.

WORLD DATA CENTER A - GLACIOLOGY INFORMATION CENTER
CIRES, Campus Box 449
University of Colorado   Phone: (303) 492-5171
Boulder, CO 80309   Ann M. Brennan, Info.Spec.

WORLD DATA CENTER A - SOLAR-TERRESTRIAL PHYSICS
Natl. Oceanic and Atmospheric Adm.
E/GC2
325 Broadway   Phone: (303) 497-6323
Boulder, CO 80303   Joe H. Allen, Dir.

DENVER THEOLOGICAL SEMINARY/BIBLE INSTITUTE - SAMUEL JAMES
    BRADFORD MEMORIAL LIBRARY
1200 Miramonte St.
Broomfield, CO 80020   Anita R. Meyer, Act.Libn.

ROCKY MOUNTAIN ENERGY - LIBRARY
10 Longs Peak Dr.
Box 2000   Phone: (303) 469-8844
Broomfield, CO 80020   Sunny Adair, Libn.

ST. THOMAS MORE HOSPITAL - MEDICAL LIBRARY *
1019 Sheridan St.   Phone: (303) 275-3381
Canon City, CO 81212   Mrs. James G. Bruner, Libn.

ORPHAN VOYAGE - MUSEUM OF ORPHANHOOD - LIBRARY
2141 Road 2300   Phone: (303) 856-3937
Cedaredge, CO 81413   Jean Paton

AMAX, INC. - CLIMAX MOLYBDENUM COMPANY - TECHNICAL LIBRARY
                                                Phone: (303) 486-2150
Climax, CO 80429   Howard Hallman, Jr., Indus.Engr.

AMERICAN NUMISMATIC ASSOCIATION - LIBRARY
818 N. Cascade   Phone: (303) 632-2646
Colorado Springs, CO 80903   Nancy Green, Libn.

ARJUNA LIBRARY
1025 Garner St.
Box 18   Phone: (303) 632-1934
Colorado Springs, CO 80905   Joseph A. Uphoff, Jr., Dir.

CHEYENNE MOUNTAIN ZOOLOGICAL PARK - LIBRARY
Box 158   Phone: (303) 633-0917
Colorado Springs, CO 80901   Bill Aragon, Cur.

COLORADO COLLEGE - CHARLES LEAMING TUTT LIBRARY
                                                Phone: (303) 473-2233
Colorado Springs, CO 80903   John Sheridan, Hd.Libn.

COLORADO COLLEGE - CHARLES LEAMING TUTT LIBRARY - SPECIAL
    COLLECTIONS
Cascade & San Rafael   Phone: (303) 473-2233
Colorado Springs, CO 80903   Barbara L. Neilon, Spec.Coll.Libn.

COLORADO SCHOOL FOR THE DEAF AND THE BLIND - MEDIA CENTER
Kiowa at Institute   Phone: (303) 636-5186
Colorado Springs, CO 80903   Janet L. Fleharty, Media Spec.

COLORADO SPRINGS FINE ARTS CENTER - REFERENCE LIBRARY AND
    TAYLOR MUSEUM LIBRARY
30 W. Dale St.   Phone: (303) 634-5581
Colorado Springs, CO 80903   Roderick Dew, Libn.

COLORADO SPRINGS GAZETTE TELEGRAPH - LIBRARY
30 S. Prospect
Box 1779   Phone: (303) 632-5511
Colorado Springs, CO 80903   Elizabeth Burns, Hd.Libn.

COLORADO SPRINGS PUBLIC SCHOOLS - DISTRICT NO. 11 - TEACHERS'
    PROFESSIONAL LIBRARY *
1036 N. Franklin St.   Phone: (303) 635-6275
Colorado Springs, CO 80903   Sandy Patton, Media Supv.

EL PASO COUNTY LAW LIBRARY
104 Judicial Bldg.
20 E. Vermijo   Phone: (303) 630-2880
Colorado Springs, CO 80903   Margaret B. Walker, Law Libn.

FIRST PRESBYTERIAN CHURCH - JOHN C. GARDNER MEMORIAL LIBRARY
219 E. Bijou   Phone: (303) 634-4301
Colorado Springs, CO 80903   Elouise Young, Libn.

HEWLETT-PACKARD COMPANY - COLORADO SPRINGS DIVISION -
    ENGINEERING RESOURCE CENTER
Box 2197   Phone: (303) 598-1900
Colorado Springs, CO 80901-2197   Jacquelyn Nichols, Libn.

HORTICULTURAL ART SOCIETY OF COLORADO SPRINGS, INC. - LIBRARY
White House Ranch
3202 Chambers Way   Phone: (303) 578-6916
Colorado Springs, CO 80907   Ernestine H. Fagen, Volunteer Libn.

KAMAN SCIENCES CORPORATION - LIBRARY
1500 Garden of the Gods Rd.
Box 7463   Phone: (303) 599-1777
Colorado Springs, CO 80933   Barbara A. Kinslow, Libn.

MEMORIAL HOSPITAL - MEDICAL-NURSING LIBRARY
1400 E. Boulder   Phone: (303) 475-5182
Colorado Springs, CO 80901   Frances Meese, Dir. of Libs.

NAZARENE BIBLE COLLEGE - TRIMBLE LIBRARY
Box 15749   Phone: (303) 596-5110
Colorado Springs, CO 80935   Roger M. Williams, Libn./Archv.

PENROSE HOSPITAL - WEBB MEMORIAL LIBRARY
2215 N. Cascade Ave.
Box 7021   Phone: (303) 630-5288
Colorado Springs, CO 80933   Elana Heiberger, Med.Libn.

PIKES PEAK LIBRARY DISTRICT - LOCAL HISTORY COLLECTION
20 N. Cascade
Box 1579   Phone: (303) 473-2080
Colorado Springs, CO 80901

PIONEERS' MUSEUM - LIBRARY AND ARCHIVES
215 S. Tejon St.   Phone: (303) 578-6786
Colorado Springs, CO 80903   Rosemary Hetzler, Hist.-Libn.

ST. FRANCIS HOSPITAL - DOCTORS' LIBRARY
East Pikes Peak Ave. & Prospect   Phone: (303) 636-8800
Colorado Springs, CO 80903   Sr. Mary Louis Wenzl, Lib.Ck.

SHEPARD'S/MC GRAW-HILL - LIBRARY
420 N. Cascade Ave.
Box 1235   Phone: (303) 475-7230
Colorado Springs, CO 80901   Gregory P. Harris, Libn.

U.S. AIR FORCE ACADEMY - LAW LIBRARY
                                                Phone: (303) 472-3680
Colorado Springs, CO 80840   Col. M.E. Kinevan, Prof. of Law

U.S. AIR FORCE ACADEMY - LIBRARY
                                                Phone: (303) 472-2590
Colorado Springs, CO 80840   Lt.Col. Reiner H. Schaeffer, Dir. of Libs.

U.S. AIR FORCE ACADEMY - MEDICAL LIBRARY
                                                Phone: (303) 472-5107
Colorado Springs, CO 80840   Jeanne Entze, Libn.

U.S. OLYMPIC COMMITTEE - SPORTS MEDICINE INFORMATION CENTER
Sports Medicine Div.
Dept. of Education Services
1750 E. Boulder St.   Phone: (303) 632-5551
Colorado Springs, CO 80909   Mary Margaret Newsom, Coord. of Educ.Serv.

U.S. TEAM HANDBALL FEDERATION - ADMINISTRATIVE OFFICE LIBRARY
1750 E. Boulder   Phone: (303) 632-5551
Colorado Springs, CO 80909   Dr. Peter Buehning, Pres.

WESTERN MUSEUM OF MINING & INDUSTRY - LIBRARY
1025 Northgate Rd.   Phone: (303) 598-8850
Colorado Springs, CO 80908   Bob Lincoln, Cur. of Educ.

CORTEZ PUBLIC LIBRARY - SOUTHWEST COLLECTION
802 E. Montezuma   Phone: (303) 565-8117
Cortez, CO 81321   Maryellen Brubaker, Lib.Dir.

AMERICAN INSTITUTE OF ISLAMIC STUDIES - MUSLIM BIBLIOGRAPHIC
    CENTER
Box 10398   Phone: (303) 936-0108
Denver, CO 80210   C.L. Geddes, Dir.

AMERICAN NATIONAL BUILDING - JOINT VENTURE LAW LIBRARY *
818 17th St., Suite 730
Denver, CO 80202   Frances Ellis

AMERICAN WATER WORKS ASSOCIATION - INFORMATION SERVICES
    DEPARTMENT
6666 W. Quincy   Phone: (303) 794-7711
Denver, CO 80235   Kurt M. Keeley, Dir., Info.Serv.

ARABIAN HORSE TRUST - LIBRARY
8751 E. Hampden, Suite B-8   Phone: (303) 750-5689
Denver, CO 80231   William M. Riley, Jr., Exec.Dir.

ASSOCIATION OF OPERATING ROOM NURSES - LIBRARY
10170 E. Mississippi Ave.   Phone: (303) 755-6300
Denver, CO 80231   Sara Katsh, Libn.

AT & T - TECHNICAL LIBRARY
11900 Pecos St.   Phone: (303) 538-4275
Denver, CO 80234   James H. Varner, Lib. Group Supv.

ATLANTIC-RICHFIELD COMPANY - ANACONDA MINERALS COMPANY -
    INFORMATION CENTER
555 17th St.
Anaconda Tower   Phone: (303) 293-4629
Denver, CO 80202   Gretchen Platt, Supv.

AUGUSTANA LUTHERAN CHURCH - LIBRARY *
5000 E. Alameda Ave.   Phone: (303) 388-4678
Denver, CO 80222   Ellen Swanson, Chm., Lib.Comm.

BETH ISRAEL HOSPITAL & GERIATRIC CENTER - HEALTH SCIENCE
    LIBRARY †
1601 Lowell Blvd.   Phone: (303) 825-2190
Denver, CO 80204   Bunny Braunger, Health Sci.Libn.

BETHESDA HOSPITAL - PROFESSIONAL LIBRARY
4400 E. Iliff Ave.   Phone: (303) 758-1514
Denver, CO 80222   Dolores Leone, Educ.Dir.

BIBLIOGRAPHICAL CENTER FOR RESEARCH - ROCKY MOUNTAIN REGION,
    INC.
1777 S. Bellaire, G-150   Phone: (303) 388-9261
Denver, CO 80222   JoAn S. Segal, Exec.Dir.

CHEVRON USA INC. - CENTRAL REGION - TECHNICAL LIBRARY
700 S. Colorado Blvd., Rm. 845   Phone: (303) 691-7347
Denver, CO 80222   Elaine Naranjo, Libn.

CHILDREN'S HOSPITAL - FORBES MEDICAL LIBRARY
1056 E. 19th Ave.   Phone: (303) 861-6400
Denver, CO 80218   Melanie R. Birnbach, Med.Libn.

CHRIST CENTERED MINISTRIES - COLLEGE OF THE ROCKIES - LIBRARY
750 Clarkson   Phone: (303) 832-1547
Denver, CO 80218

CH2M HILL, INC. - ROCKY MOUNTAIN REGIONAL OFFICE - LIBRARY
Box 22508   Phone: (303) 771-0900
Denver, CO 80222   LaRue Fontenot, Libn.

COLORADO HISTORICAL SOCIETY - STEPHEN H. HART LIBRARY
Colorado Heritage Ctr.
1300 Broadway   Phone: (303) 866-2305
Denver, CO 80203   Katherine Kane, Hd., Pub.Serv. & Access

COLORADO MINING ASSOCIATION - LIBRARY
1515 Cleveland Place, Suite 410   Phone: (303) 534-1181
Denver, CO 80202

COLORADO STATE BANK BUILDING - LAW LIBRARY
1600 Broadway, Suite 1510   Phone: (303) 861-1720
Denver, CO 80202

COLORADO STATE DEPARTMENT OF EDUCATION - INSTRUCTIONAL
    MATERIALS CENTER FOR THE VISUALLY HANDICAPPED
1362 Lincoln St.   Phone: (303) 866-2181
Denver, CO 80203   W. Buck Schrotberger, Sr.Cons.

COLORADO STATE DEPARTMENT OF NATURAL RESOURCES - COLORADO
    GEOLOGICAL SURVEY LIBRARY
1313 Sherman, Rm. 715   Phone: (303) 866-2611
Denver, CO 80203   Louise M. Slade, Staff Asst.

COLORADO STATE DEPARTMENT OF SOCIAL SERVICE - LIBRARY
1575 Sherman St.   Phone: (303) 866-2253
Denver, CO 80203   Margaret Long Humphrey, Libn.

COLORADO STATE DIVISION OF EMPLOYMENT & TRAINING - LABOR
    MARKET INFORMATION LIBRARY
251 E. 12th Ave.   Phone: (303) 839-5833
Denver, CO 80203   Marvin H. Wojahn, Economist

COLORADO STATE DIVISION OF HIGHWAYS - TECHNICAL LIBRARY
4340 E. Louisiana Ave., Rm. L201   Phone: (303) 757-9220
Denver, CO 80222   Beth Moore, Lib.Asst.

COLORADO STATE DIVISION OF LOCAL GOVERNMENT - LIBRARY
1313 Sherman St., Rm. 520
Denver, CO 80203

COLORADO (State) DIVISION OF STATE ARCHIVES AND PUBLIC RECORDS
Dept. of Administration
1313 Sherman St., Rm. 1B20   Phone: (303) 866-2055
Denver, CO 80203   George E. Warren, State Archv.

COLORADO (State) DIVISION OF WILDLIFE - LIBRARY
6060 Broadway
Denver, CO 80216   Rita C. Green, Libn.

COLORADO STATE LIBRARY
1362 Lincoln
Denver, CO 80203

COLORADO STATE SUPREME COURT LIBRARY
B 112 State Judicial Bldg.
2 E. 14th Ave.   Phone: (303) 861-1111
Denver, CO 80203   Frances D. Campbell, Libn.

COLORADO STATE WATER CONSERVATION BOARD - LIBRARY
1313 Sherman St.
Denver, CO 80203

CONOCO, INC. - MINERALS LIBRARY †
555 17th St.   Phone: (303) 575-6025
Denver, CO 80202   Sharon P. Brown, Libn.

DAVIS, GRAHAM & STUBBS/COLORADO NATIONAL BUILDING - CNB LAW
    LIBRARY
2500 Colorado National Bldg.
950 17th St.   Phone: (303) 892-9400
Denver, CO 80202   Pamela K. Lewis, Law Libn.

DENVER ART MUSEUM - FREDERIC H. DOUGLAS LIBRARY OF
    ANTHROPOLOGY AND ART
100 W. 14th Ave. Pkwy.   Phone: (303) 575-2256
Denver, CO 80204   Margaret Goodrich, Libn.

DENVER BOTANIC GARDENS - HELEN FOWLER LIBRARY
909 York St.   Phone: (303) 575-2548
Denver, CO 80206   Solange G. Gignac, Libn.

DENVER CONSERVATIVE BAPTIST SEMINARY - CAREY S. THOMAS
    LIBRARY
Univ.Pk.Sta.
Box 10,000   Phone: (303) 781-8691
Denver, CO 80210   Sarah Lyons, Libn.

DENVER DISTRICT COURT, 2ND JUDICIAL DISTRICT - LAW LIBRARY
389 City & County Bldg.   Phone: (303) 575-2233
Denver, CO 80202   Janine Bujak, Law Libn.

DENVER MEDICAL LIBRARY
1601 E. 19th Ave.   Phone: (303) 839-6670
Denver, CO 80218   Mary De Mund, Lib.Dir.

DENVER MUSEUM OF NATURAL HISTORY - LIBRARY
City Park   Phone: (303) 575-3610
Denver, CO 80205   Stephanie H. Stowe, Libn.

DENVER POST - LIBRARY
650 15th St.   Phone: (303) 820-1691
Denver, CO 80202   Judi Acre, Act.Libn.

DENVER PUBLIC LIBRARY - ARCHERY COLLECTION
1357 Broadway   Phone: (303) 571-2000
Denver, CO 80203   JoAnne McBride, Info.Serv.Supv.

DENVER PUBLIC LIBRARY - BUSINESS, SCIENCE & TECHNOLOGY DIVISION
1357 Broadway   Phone: (303) 571-2122
Denver, CO 80203   Rich Patton, Info.Serv.Supv.

DENVER PUBLIC LIBRARY - CONSERVATION LIBRARY
1357 Broadway
Denver, CO 80203

DENVER PUBLIC LIBRARY - DENVER GENERAL HOSPITAL LIBRARY
W. 8th & Cherokee Sts.   Phone: (303) 893-7422
Denver, CO 80204   Anita F. Westwood, Med.Subj.Spec.

DENVER PUBLIC LIBRARY - FOLK MUSIC COLLECTION, FRIENDS OF MUSIC
1357 Broadway   Phone: (303) 571-2000
Denver, CO 80203   JoAnne McBride, Info.Serv.Supv.

DENVER PUBLIC LIBRARY - FOUNDATION CENTER COLLECTION
1357 Broadway   Phone: (303) 571-2190
Denver, CO 80203   Kathy Lawrence, Info.Serv.Supv.

DENVER PUBLIC LIBRARY - GENEALOGY DIVISION
1357 Broadway   Phone: (303) 571-2077
Denver, CO 80203   Joanne E. Classen, Coll.Spec.

DENVER PUBLIC LIBRARY - MAP COLLECTION
1357 Broadway   Phone: (303) 571-2130
Denver, CO 80203   Donna Koepp, Map Spec.

DENVER PUBLIC LIBRARY - SPECIAL COLLECTIONS ROOM
1357 Broadway   Phone: (303) 571-2010
Denver, CO 80203   Eleanor M. Gehres, Mgr., Western Hist.Dept.

DENVER PUBLIC LIBRARY - WESTERN HISTORY DEPARTMENT
1357 Broadway   Phone: (303) 571-2009
Denver, CO 80203   Eleanor M. Gehres, Mgr.

DENVER PUBLIC SCHOOL DISTRICT 1 - PROFESSIONAL LIBRARY
3800 York St., Bldg.1, Unit B   Phone: (303) 837-1000
Denver, CO 80205   Phyllis Dodd, Supv.

DENVER ZOOLOGICAL GARDEN - LIBRARY
23rd & Steele   Phone: (303) 575-2432
Denver, CO 80205   Paul Linger, Asst.Dir.

EMMAUS LUTHERAN CHURCH - LIBRARY
3120 Irving St.   Phone: (303) 477-5358
Denver, CO 80211   Herbert Harms, Libn.

ENVIRONMENTAL PROTECTION AGENCY - NATIONAL ENFORCEMENT
   INVESTIGATIONS - LIBRARY
Denver Federal Ctr., Bldg. 53
Box 25227   Phone: (303) 234-5765
Denver, CO 80225   Mary Quinlivan, Libn.

ENVIRONMENTAL PROTECTION AGENCY - REGION VIII LIBRARY
1860 Lincoln St., Suite 103   Phone: (303) 837-2560
Denver, CO 80295-0699   Dolores D. Eddy, Regional Libn.

FORT LOGAN MENTAL HEALTH CENTER - MEDICAL LIBRARY
3520 Oxford Ave., W.   Phone: (303) 761-0220
Denver, CO 80236   Kate Elder, Supv.Libn.

GATES CORPORATION - TECHNICAL INFORMATION CENTER
900 S. Broadway
Box 5887   Phone: (303) 744-4150
Denver, CO 80217   Kathleen Rainwater, Res.Libn.

GREAT-WEST LIFE ASSURANCE COMPANY - CORPORATE LIBRARY
1675 Broadway   Phone: (303) 892-3098
Denver, CO 80202   Geetha Gangadharan, Libn.

GULF OIL CORPORATION - PITTSBURGH & MIDWAY COAL MINING CO. -
   INFORMATION RESOURCE CENTER
1720 S. Bellaire St.   Phone: (303) 759-6974
Denver, CO 80222   Marriott W. Smart, Libn.

HEBREW EDUCATIONAL ALLIANCE - LIBRARY
1555 Stuart St.   Phone: (303) 629-0410
Denver, CO 80204   William David Ellis, Libn.

HOLLAND & HART - LIBRARY
Box 8749   Phone: (303) 295-8069
Denver, CO 80201   Connie M. Pirosko, Libn.

HOLME ROBERTS & OWEN - LIBRARY
1700 Broadway, Suite 1800   Phone: (303) 861-7000
Denver, CO 80290   Mark E. Estes, Libn.

ILIFF SCHOOL OF THEOLOGY - IRA J. TAYLOR LIBRARY
2201 S. University Blvd.   Phone: (303) 744-1287
Denver, CO 80210-4796   Milton J. Coalter, Jr., Act.Dir.

INTERNATIONAL FEDERATION OF PETROLEUM AND CHEMICAL WORKERS
   - LIBRARY
Box 6603   Phone: (303) 388-9237
Denver, CO 80206   Curtis J. Hogan, Gen.Sec.

MANVILLE SERVICE CORPORATION - HEALTH, SAFETY & ENVIRONMENT
   LIBRARY
Box 5108   Phone: (303) 978-2580
Denver, CO 80217   Connee Wethey, Libn.

MANVILLE SERVICE CORPORATION - RESEARCH AND DEVELOPMENT
   INFORMATION CENTER
Box 5108   Phone: (303) 978-5477
Denver, CO 80217   Judy Gerber, Chf.Libn., R & D

MARTIN MARIETTA AEROSPACE - DENVER RESEARCH LIBRARY
Box 179   Phone: (303) 977-5512
Denver, CO 80201   Jay R. McKee, Chf.Libn.

MEDICAL GROUP MANAGEMENT ASSOCIATION - INFORMATION SERVICE
1355 S. Colorado Blvd., Suite 900   Phone: (303) 753-1111
Denver, CO 80222   Barbara U. Hamilton, Dir.

MERCY MEDICAL CENTER - LIBRARY AND MEDIA RESOURCES
   DEPARTMENT
1619 Milwaukee St.   Phone: (303) 393-3296
Denver, CO 80206   Rosalind Dudden, Dir. of Lib.Serv.

MOBIL OIL CORPORATION - E & P DIVISION LIBRARY
Box 5444   Phone: (303) 572-2287
Denver, CO 80217   C.J. Smith, Coord.

MOUNTAIN BELL TELEPHONE COMPANY - LIBRARY
1005 17th St., Rm. 180   Phone: (303) 896-4607
Denver, CO 80202   Jody L. Georgeson, Libn.

MOUNTAIN STATES EMPLOYERS COUNCIL - INFORMATION CENTER
1790 Logan St.   Phone: (303) 839-5177
Denver, CO 80203   Mariwayne Scully, Info.Ctr.Mgr.

NATIONAL CABLE TELEVISION INSTITUTE - LIBRARY
Box 27277   Phone: (303) 761-8554
Denver, CO 80227   Roland D. Hieb, Exec.Dir.

NATIONAL JEWISH HOSPITAL & RESEARCH CTR./NATIONAL ASTHMA
CTR. - GERALD TUCKER MEMORIAL MEDICAL LIBRARY
3800 E. Colfax Ave.   Phone: (303) 388-4461
Denver, CO 80206   Helen-Ann Brown, Med.Libn.

PORTER MEMORIAL HOSPITAL - HARLEY E. RICE MEMORIAL LIBRARY
2525 S. Downing St.   Phone: (303) 778-5656
Denver, CO 80210   Karla Britain, Dir.

PRESBYTERIAN DENVER HOSPITAL - BRADFORD MEMORIAL LIBRARY
1719 E. 19th Ave.   Phone: (303) 839-6440
Denver, CO 80218   Jody Helmer, Libn.

PUBLIC SERVICE COMPANY OF COLORADO - LIBRARY
550 15th St.
Box 840   Phone: (303) 571-7084
Denver, CO 80201   Mary Ann Hamm, Libn.

REGIONAL TRANSPORTATION DISTRICT (Metropolitan Denver Area) -
RESEARCH & RECORDS SERVICES
1600 Blake St.   Phone: (303) 628-9000
Denver, CO 80202   Rodene Harwood, Supv.

ROATH & BREGA, P.C. - LAW LIBRARY
1873 S. Bellaire, Suite 1700
Box 5560, Terminal Annex   Phone: (303) 691-5400
Denver, CO 80217   Dorothy Norbie, Law Libn.

ROCKY MOUNTAIN HOSPITAL - C. LLOYD PETERSON MEMORIAL LIBRARY
4701 E. Ninth Ave.   Phone: (303) 388-5588
Denver, CO 80220   Patricia Perry, Libn.

ROCKY MOUNTAIN JEWISH HISTORICAL SOCIETY - IRA M. BECK
MEMORIAL LIBRARY
Center for Judaic Studies
University of Denver   Phone: (303) 753-3178
Denver, CO 80208   Jeanne Abrams, Archv.

ROCKY MOUNTAIN NEWS - LIBRARY
400 W. Colfax Ave.   Phone: (303) 892-5000
Denver, CO 80204   Paula Shonkwiler, Hd.Libn.

ROSE MEDICAL CENTER - LIBRARY
4567 E. 9th Ave.   Phone: (303) 320-2160
Denver, CO 80220   Nancy Simon, Med.Libn.

ST. ANTHONY HOSPITAL SYSTEMS - MEMORIAL MEDICAL LIBRARY
4231 W. 16th Ave.   Phone: (303) 629-3790
Denver, CO 80204   Christine Yolanda Crespin, Supv.Libn.

ST. JOSEPH HOSPITAL - HEALTH SCIENCES LIBRARY
1835 Franklin St.   Phone: (303) 837-7188
Denver, CO 80218   Margaret Bandy, Libn.

ST. LUKE'S HOSPITAL - HEALTH SCIENCES LIBRARY
601 E. 19th Ave.   Phone: (303) 869-2395
Denver, CO 80203   Karen Guth, Dir.

ST. THOMAS SEMINARY - LIBRARY
1300 S. Steele   Phone: (303) 722-4687
Denver, CO 80210   Marguerite W. Travis, Libn.

SKIDMORE, OWINGS & MERRILL - LIBRARY
1675 Broadway   Phone: (303) 825-3100
Denver, CO 80202   Jay Schafer, Libn.

SOUTHEAST METROPOLITAN BOARD OF COOPERATIVE SERVICES -
PROFESSIONAL INFORMATION CENTER
3301 S. Monaco   Phone: (303) 757-6201
Denver, CO 80222   Lynda Welborn, Mgr./Info.Spec.

STAGECOACH LIBRARY FOR GENEALOGICAL RESEARCH
1840 S. Wolcott Ct.   Phone: (303) 922-8856
Denver, CO 80219   Donna J. Porter, Owner

STEARNS-ROGER ENGINEERING CORPORATION - TECHNICAL LIBRARY
4500 Cherry Creek, S.
Box 5888   Phone: (303) 692-2658
Denver, CO 80217   J.C. Hoover, Libn.

STONE AND WEBSTER ENGINEERING CORPORATION - TECHNICAL
INFORMATION CENTER
Box 5406   Phone: (303) 770-7700
Denver, CO 80217   Susan Newhams, Libn.

SYMES BUILDING LAW LIBRARY
820-16th St., Suite 800
Denver, CO 80202

UNITED BANK OF DENVER, N.A. - INFORMATION CENTER LIBRARY
1700 Broadway
Box 5247   Phone: (303) 861-8811
Denver, CO 80274   Nancy Ransier, Mktg.Res.Anl.

UNITED BANK OF DENVER, N.A. - UNITED BANK CENTER - LAW LIBRARY
1700 Broadway
Tower Bldg., Suite 1215   Phone: (303) 861-4304
Denver, CO 80290   Breta M. Krodshen, Law Libn.

U.S. AIR FORCE - ACCOUNTING AND FINANCE CENTER - TECHNICAL
LIBRARY
AFAFC/FL7040   Phone: (303) 370-7566
Denver, CO 80279   Alreeta Viehdorfer, Chf.Adm.Libn.

U.S. BUREAU OF THE CENSUS - INFORMATION SERVICES PROGRAM -
DENVER REG. OFFICE - CENSUS PUBLICATION CENTER
7655 W. Mississippi Ave.
Box 26750   Phone: (303) 234-5825
Denver, CO 80226   Gerald O'Donnell, Info.Serv.

U.S. BUREAU OF LAND MANAGEMENT - DENVER LIBRARY
Denver Federal Ctr.
Bldg. 50 - D245   Phone: (303) 234-4578
Denver, CO 80225   Ora Wagoner, Libn.

U.S. BUREAU OF MINES - CHARLES W. HENDERSON MEMORIAL LIBRARY
Denver Federal Center, Bldg. 20   Phone: (303) 234-2817
Denver, CO 80225   Ann Elizabeth Chapel, Libn.

U.S. BUREAU OF RECLAMATION - LIBRARY †
Engineering & Research Center
Denver Federal Center
Box 25007   Phone: (303) 234-3019
Denver, CO 80225   Paul F. Mulloney, Chf., Lib.Br.

U.S. COURT OF APPEALS, 10TH CIRCUIT - LIBRARY
U.S. Court House, Rm. C 411   Phone: (303) 837-3591
Denver, CO 80294   J. Terry Hemming, Chf.Libn.

U.S. DEPT. OF THE INTERIOR - OFFICE OF REGIONAL SOLICITOR - LAW
LIBRARY *
Bldg. 67, Rm. 1400
Denver Federal Center   Phone: (303) 234-3175
Denver, CO 80225   Sally Raines, Libn.

U.S. DEPT. OF LABOR - EMPLOYMENT & TRAINING ADMINISTRATION -
REGION VIII TECHNICAL RESOURCE LIBRARY *
1617 Federal Office Bldg.
1961 Stout St.   Phone: (303) 837-4571
Denver, CO 80294   Larry Wieland, Libn.

U.S. DEPT. OF LABOR - MINE SAFETY & HEALTH ADMINISTRATION -
INFORMATIONAL SERVICES LIBRARY
Box 25367   Phone: (303) 234-4961
Denver, CO 80225   James A. Greenhalgh, Libn.

U.S. FISH & WILDLIFE SERVICE - WILDLIFE RESEARCH CENTER LIBRARY
Federal Center, Bldg. 16   Phone: (303) 234-4919
Denver, CO 80225   Diana L. Dwyer, Libn.

U.S. GEOLOGICAL SURVEY - DENVER LIBRARY
Denver Federal Ctr.
Stop 914, Box 25046   Phone: (303) 236-1000
Denver, CO 80225   Robert A. Bier, Jr., Chf.Libn.

U.S. GEOLOGICAL SURVEY - NATL. CARTOGRAPHIC INFORMATION CENTER
(NCIC)
Federal Ctr., Stop 511
Box 25046   Phone: (303) 234-4388
Denver, CO 80225   Rudolph Hildebrandt, Cartographer

U.S. GEOLOGICAL SURVEY - WATER RESOURCES DIVISION - COLORADO
    DISTRICT LIBRARY
Federal Center
Box 25046, Stop 415   Phone: (303) 234-3487
Denver, CO 80225   Barbara J. Condron, Libn.

U.S. NATL. ARCHIVES & RECORDS SERVICE - FEDERAL ARCHIVES AND
    RECORDS CENTER, REGION 8
Denver Federal Center, Bldg. 48   Phone: (303) 234-3187
Denver, CO 80225

U.S. NATL. PARK SERVICE - LIBRARY
655 Parfet St.
Box 25287   Phone: (303) 234-4443
Denver, CO 80225   Ruth A. Larison, Libn.

U.S. VETERANS ADMINISTRATION (CO-Denver) - HOSPITAL LIBRARY
1055 Clermont St.
Denver, CO 80220   Ruth E. Gilbert, Chf., Lib.Serv.

UNIVERSITY OF COLORADO HEALTH SCIENCES CENTER - DENISON
    MEMORIAL LIBRARY †
4200 E. 9th Ave.   Phone: (303) 394-7469
Denver, CO 80262   Charles Bandy, Dir.

UNIVERSITY OF COLORADO HEALTH SCIENCES CENTER - RENE A. SPITZ
    PSYCHIATRIC LIBRARY
4200 E. 9th Ave., C-249   Phone: (303) 394-7039
Denver, CO 80262   Irwin Berry, Libn.

UNIVERSITY OF DENVER - COLLEGE OF LAW - WESTMINSTER LAW
    LIBRARY
1900 Olive St. - LTLB   Phone: (303) 753-3406
Denver, CO 80220   Alfred J. Coco, Libn.

UNIVERSITY OF DENVER AND DENVER RESEARCH INSTITUTE -
    INDUSTRIAL ECONOMICS AND MANAGEMENT DIVISION LIBRARY
2455 E. Asbury   Phone: (303) 753-3206
Denver, CO 80208   Judith Farris, Info.Spec.

UNIVERSITY OF DENVER AND DENVER RESEARCH INSTITUTE -
    LABORATORY FOR APPLIED MECHANICS - LIBRARY
2360 S. Gaylord   Phone: (303) 753-3623
Denver, CO 80208

UNIVERSITY OF DENVER AND DENVER RESEARCH INSTITUTE - SOCIAL
    SYSTEMS RESEARCH AND EVALUATION LIBRARY
2135 E. Wesley   Phone: (303) 871-3381
Denver, CO 80208   Bonnie Moul, Info.Spec.

UNIVERSITY OF DENVER - PENROSE LIBRARY - SPECIAL COLLECTIONS
2150 E. Evans Ave.   Phone: (303) 871-3428
Denver, CO 80208   Steven Fisher, Spec.Coll.Libn.

WELBORN, DUFFORD, BROWN & TOOLEY - LAW LIBRARY
1700 Broadway   Phone: (303) 861-8013
Denver, CO 80290-1199   Cori Arsenault, Firm Libn.

COLORADO STATE DISTRICT COURT, 6TH JUDICIAL DISTRICT - LAW
    LIBRARY
Box 3340   Phone: (303) 247-1301
Durango, CO 81301   Al H. Haas, Chf. Judge

FORT LEWIS COLLEGE - CENTER OF SOUTHWEST STUDIES
Fort Lewis College Library   Phone: (303) 247-7456
Durango, CO 81301   Dr. Robert W. Delaney, Dir.

STANDARD & POOR'S COMPUSTAT SERVICES, INC. - DATA RESOURCE
    CENTER
7400 S. Alton Court   Phone: (303) 771-6510
Englewood, CO 80112   Nancy Bundren, Oper. Control Supv.

ENGINEERING DYNAMICS, INC. - LIBRARY †
3925 S. Kalamath   Phone: (303) 761-4367
Englewood, CO 80110   Howard McGregor, Pres.

FRYE-SILLS, INC. - LIBRARY *
5500 S. Syracuse Circle   Phone: (303) 773-3900
Englewood, CO 80111   Libbie Gottschalk, Libn.

INFORMATION HANDLING SERVICES - LIBRARY
15 Inverness Way E.   Phone: (303) 779-0600
Englewood, CO 80150   Terrie O'Rourke, Info.Spec.

MORRIS ANIMAL FOUNDATION - LIBRARY
45 Inverness Dr., E.   Phone: (303) 779-8867
Englewood, CO 80123   Dorothy Biggs, Libn.

PAUL DE HAEN INTERNATIONAL, INC. - DRUG INFORMATION SYSTEMS
    AND SERVICES
2750 S. Shoshone St.   Phone: (303) 781-6683
Englewood, CO 80110   Paul E. Groth, Pres.

PRYOR, CARNEY AND JOHNSON - LIBRARY
6200 S. Syracuse, Suite 400   Phone: (303) 771-6200
Englewood, CO 80111   Lavonne Axford, Libn.

SCIENCE APPLICATIONS, INC. - FOREIGN SYSTEMS RESEARCH CENTER -
    LIBRARY
40 DTC W.
7935 E. Prentice Ave.   Phone: (303) 773-6900
Englewood, CO 80111   Jennifer Doran, Libn.

SWEDISH MEDICAL CENTER - LIBRARY
501 E. Hampden Ave.   Phone: (303) 786-6616
Englewood, CO 80110   Sandra Parker, Dir., Lib.Serv.

UKRAINIAN RESEARCH FOUNDATION - LIBRARY
6931 S. Yosemite   Phone: (303) 770-1220
Englewood, CO 80112   Bohdan Wynar, Pres.

U.S. NATL. PARK SERVICE - ROCKY MOUNTAIN NATIONAL PARK - LIBRARY
                                        Phone: (303) 586-2371
Estes Park, CO 80517   Helen M. Burgener, Libn.

U.S. NATL. PARK SERVICE - FLORISSANT FOSSIL BEDS NATIONAL
    MONUMENT - LIBRARY
Box 185   Phone: (303) 748-3253
Florissant, CO 80816   Walt Saenger, Chf., Visitor Serv.

U.S. ARMY HOSPITALS - FORT CARSON ARMY HOSPITAL - MEDICAL
    LIBRARY
Bldg. 6235   Phone: (303) 579-3209
Ft. Carson, CO 80913   Alfreda H. Hanna, Med.Libn.

U.S. ARMY POST - FORT CARSON - LIBRARY
                                        Phone: (303) 579-2350
Ft. Carson, CO 80913   Roger M. Miller, Lib.Dir.

AMERICAN SOCIETY OF SUGAR BEET TECHNOLOGISTS - LIBRARY
Box 1546   Phone: (303) 482-8250
Fort Collins, CO 80522   James H. Fischer, Sec.-Treas.

COLORADO (State) DIVISION OF WILDLIFE - RESEARCH CENTER LIBRARY
317 W. Prospect   Phone: (303) 484-2836
Fort Collins, CO 80526   Marian Hershcopf, Libn.

COLORADO STATE UNIVERSITY - ENGINEERING SCIENCES BRANCH
    LIBRARY
                                        Phone: (303) 491-8694
Fort Collins, CO 80523   Marjorie Rhoades, Asst.Engr.Sci.Libn.

COLORADO STATE UNIVERSITY - GERMANS FROM RUSSIA PROJECT
    LIBRARY
History Department   Phone: (303) 491-6854
Fort Collins, CO 80523   John Newman, Proj.Archv.

COLORADO STATE UNIVERSITY - VIETNAM WAR LITERATURE
    COLLECTION
Colorado State University Libraries   Phone: (303) 491-5911
Fort Collins, CO 80523   John Newman, Spec.Coll.Libn.

COLORADO STATE UNIVERSITY - WILLIAM E. MORGAN LIBRARY
                                        Phone: (303) 491-5911
Fort Collins, CO 80523   LeMoyne W. Anderson, Dir. of Lib.

ENVIRONMENTAL RESEARCH & TECHNOLOGY, INC. - ENVIRONMENTAL
    CONTRACTING CENTER LIBRARY
Box 2105   Phone: (303) 493-8878
Fort Collins, CO 80522   Sally Ramsey, Adm.

FORT COLLINS PUBLIC LIBRARY - ORAL HISTORY COLLECTION
201 Peterson   Phone: (303) 493-4422
Fort Collins, CO 80524   Charlene Tresner, Local Hist.Coord.

HEWLETT-PACKARD COMPANY - FORT COLLINS FACILITY LIBRARY
3404 E. Harmony Rd.   Phone: (303) 226-3800
Fort Collins, CO 80525   Jane Fiasconaro, Libn.

IDEAL BASIC INDUSTRIES - CEMENT DIVISION - RESEARCH DEPARTMENT
   - LIBRARY
Box 1667   Phone: (303) 482-5600
Fort Collins, CO 80522   F.M. Miller, Res.Dir.

PLATTE RIVER POWER AUTHORITY - LIBRARY
Timberline & Horsetooth Rds.   Phone: (303) 226-4000
Fort Collins, CO 80525   Rosalie Feldman, Libn.

POUDRE VALLEY HOSPITAL - MEDIA RESOURCES LIBRARY †
1024 Lemay Ave.   Phone: (303) 482-4111
Fort Collins, CO 80524   Carole Trask, Libn.

U.S. FOREST SERVICE - ROCKY MOUNTAIN FOREST & RANGE EXPERIMENT
   STATION - LIBRARY
240 W. Prospect St.   Phone: (303) 221-4390
Fort Collins, CO 80526   Frances J. Barney, Libn.

AMAX EXPLORATION, INC. - SCIENCE LIBRARY
1707 Cole Blvd.   Phone: (303) 231-0647
Golden, CO 80401   Laura A. Christensen, Mgr., Info.Serv.

AMAX EXTRACTIVE RESEARCH & DEVELOPMENT, INC. - TECHNICAL
   INFORMATION CENTER
5950 McIntyre St.   Phone: (303) 279-7636
Golden, CO 80401   Jane Riggs, Libn.

AMAX, INC. - LAW LIBRARY
1707 Cole Blvd.   Phone: (303) 231-0258
Golden, CO 80401   Gary Alexander, Law Libn.

AT & T INFORMATION SYSTEMS - SERVICES DIVISION EDUCATION
   CENTER
13952 Denver West Pkwy., Bldg. 53   Phone: (303) 273-2165
Golden, CO 80407   Kathy L. Weimer, Serv.Mgr.-Educ.

BUFFALO BILL MEMORIAL MUSEUM - INFORMATION CENTER
Rte. 5, Box 950   Phone: (303) 526-0747
Golden, CO 80401   Stanley W. Zamonski, Cur.

COLORADO RAILROAD HISTORICAL FOUNDATION - LIBRARY
17155 W. 44th Ave.
Box 10   Phone: (303) 279-4591
Golden, CO 80402   Robert W. Richardson, Exec.Dir.

COLORADO SCHOOL OF MINES - ARTHUR LAKES LIBRARY
14th & Illinois St.   Phone: (303) 273-3690
Golden, CO 80401   Hartley K. Phinney, Jr., Dir.

COORS (Adolph) COMPANY - TECHNICAL LIBRARY
Mail 105   Phone: (303) 279-6565
Golden, CO 80401   Mary Bond, Libn.

DAMES & MOORE - ENGINEERING LIBRARY †
1626 Cole Blvd.   Phone: (303) 232-6262
Golden, CO 80401   Ellie Reiter, Libn.

ROCKWELL INTERNATIONAL - ENERGY SYSTEMS GROUP - ROCKY FLATS
   PLANT - TECHNICAL LIBRARY †
Box 938   Phone: (303) 497-2863
Golden, CO 80401   Mary Ann Paliani, Lib.Mgr.

SOLAR ENERGY RESEARCH INSTITUTE - SERI TECHNICAL LIBRARY
1617 Cole Blvd.   Phone: (303) 231-1415
Golden, CO 80401   Jerome T. Maddock, Br.Chf.

BENDIX FIELD ENGINEERING CORPORATION - GRAND JUNCTION OFFICE -
   TECHNICAL LIBRARY
Box 1569   Phone: (303) 242-8621
Grand Junction, CO 81502-1569   Sara L. Murphy, Sr.Libn.

MESA COUNTY VALLEY SCHOOL DISTRICT 51 - DEPARTMENT OF
   RESOURCES, RESEARCH AND DEVELOPMENT
410 Hill Ave.   Phone: (303) 245-1788
Grand Junction, CO 81501   Tedd S. Brumbaugh, Dir.

MUNRO (Dr. E.H.) MEDICAL LIBRARY
St. Mary's Hospital & Medical Ctr.   Phone: (303) 244-2171
Grand Junction, CO 84102   Cynthia M. Tharaud, Dir.

MUSEUM OF WESTERN COLORADO - ARCHIVES
4th & Ute Sts.   Phone: (303) 242-0971
Grand Junction, CO 81501   Larry Bowles, Interim Dir.

NATL. ASSN. OF PRIVATE, NONTRADITIONAL SCHOOLS & COLLEGES -
   ACCREDITING COMMN. ON POSTSECONDARY EDUC. - LIB.
182 Thompson Rd.   Phone: (303) 243-5441
Grand Junction, CO 81503   Dolly Heusser, Exec.Sec./Treas.

U.S. GEOLOGICAL SURVEY - WATER RESOURCES LIBRARY
Aspinall Federal Bldg., Rm. 223
Box 2027   Phone: (303) 245-5257
Grand Junction, CO 81502   D.L. Collins, Subdistrict Chf.

U.S. VETERANS ADMINISTRATION (CO-Grand Junction) - MEDICAL CENTER
   MEDICAL LIBRARY
2121 North Ave.   Phone: (303) 242-0731
Grand Junction, CO 81501   Lynn L. Bragdon, Chf., Lib.Serv.

GREELEY MUNICIPAL MUSEUM - LIBRARY *
Civic Ctr. Complex, 919 7th St.   Phone: (303) 353-6123
Greeley, CO 80631   Peggy A. Ford, Musm.Coord.

GREELEY PUBLIC LIBRARY - SPECIAL COLLECTIONS
City Complex Bldg.   Phone: (303) 353-6123
Greeley, CO 80631   Esther Fromm, Archv./Dir., GPL

NORTH COLORADO MEDICAL CENTER - MEDICAL LIBRARY
1801 16th St.
Greeley, CO 80631   Meta Shore, Libn.

UNIVERSITY OF NORTHERN COLORADO - UNIVERSITY ARCHIVES
James A. Michener Library   Phone: (303) 351-2632
Greeley, CO 80639   Dr. Robert P. Markham, Coord. of Archv.

WELD COUNTY DISTRICT COURT - LAW LIBRARY †
Weld County Court House   Phone: (303) 356-4000
Greeley, CO 80631   Joy W. Ahlborn, Libn.

AMC CANCER RESEARCH CENTER AND HOSPITAL - GRACE & PHILIP
   LICHTENSTEIN SCIENTIFIC LIBRARY
6401 W. Colfax Ave.   Phone: (303) 233-6501
Lakewood, CO 80214   Eleanor Krakauer, Libn.

BROOKS MINERALS, INC. - LIBRARY
8700 W. 14th Ave.   Phone: (303) 232-5955
Lakewood, CO 80215   Lois J. Brooks, Libn.

JEFFERSON COUNTY PUBLIC SCHOOLS R1 - PROFESSIONAL LIBRARY
   MEDIA CENTER
1209 Quail St.   Phone: (303) 231-2309
Lakewood, CO 80215   Roberta Ponis, Rsrc.Spec.

TENNECO MINERALS COMPANY - LIBRARY
300 Union Blvd., Suite 300
Box 27F   Phone: (303) 692-6200
Lakewood, CO 80210   Sara E. Martin, Hd.Libn.

PROWERS COUNTY HISTORICAL SOCIETY - BIG TIMBERS MUSEUM -
   LIBRARY
North Santa Fe Trail
Box 362   Phone: (303) 336-2472
Lamar, CO 81052   Edith Birchler, Cur.

LAKE COUNTY PUBLIC LIBRARY - SPECIAL COLLECTIONS
1115 Harrison Ave.   Phone: (303) 486-0569
Leadville, CO 80461   David R. Parry, Dir.

TABOR OPERA HOUSE - LIBRARY
308 Harrison Ave.
Leadville, CO 80461

LITTLETON AREA HISTORICAL MUSEUM - LIBRARY
6028 S. Gallup   Phone: (303) 795-3850
Littleton, CO 80120   Robert J. McQuarie, Dir.

MARATHON OIL COMPANY - RESEARCH TECHNICAL INFORMATION
   CENTER
Box 269   Phone: (303) 794-2601
Littleton, CO 80160   Clarence A. Sturdivant, Supv.

RADIO HISTORICAL ASSOCIATION OF COLORADO, INC. - RENTAL TAPE
   LIBRARY
7213 W. Roxbury Pl.   Phone: (303) 979-0755
Littleton, CO 30123   John Migrala, Treas.-Libn.

COLORADO STATE DEPARTMENT OF EDUCATION - COLORADO CAREER
   INFORMATION SYSTEM
830 S. Lincoln   Phone: (303) 772-3136
Longmont, CO 80501   Donald Rea, Dir.

GREAT WESTERN SUGAR COMPANY - AGRICULTURAL RESEARCH CENTER -
   RESEARCH LIBRARY
11939 Sugarmill Rd.   Phone: (303) 776-1802
Longmont, CO 80501   James F. Gonyou, Dir., Agri.Res.

HEWLETT-PACKARD COMPANY - LOVELAND FACILITY LIBRARY
Box 301   Phone: (303) 667-5000
Loveland, CO 80537   Marsha Haugen, Libn.

U.S. AIR FORCE BASE - LOWRY BASE LIBRARY †
Lowry Technical Training Ctr.
FL 3059, ABG/SSL   Phone: (303) 394-3093
Lowry AFB, CO 80230   Helen C. McClaughry, Base Libn.

U.S. NATL. PARK SERVICE - MESA VERDE NATL. PARK - MUSEUM LIBRARY
Box 38   Phone: (303) 529-4475
Mesa Verde Natl. Park, CO 81330   Wanda L. Padilla, Park Lib.Techn.

COLORADO STATE HOSPITAL - PROFESSIONAL LIBRARY
1600 W. 24th St.   Phone: (303) 543-1170
Pueblo, CO 81003   Helen Wack, Libn.

PARKVIEW EPISCOPAL MEDICAL CENTER - MEDICAL LIBRARY
400 W. 16th St.   Phone: (303) 584-4582
Pueblo, CO 81003   Ms. Lyn Smith Hammond, Med.Libn.

PUEBLO CHIEFTAIN AND STAR-JOURNAL PUBLISHING CORPORATION -
   LIBRARY
825 W. 6th St.   Phone: (303) 544-3520
Pueblo, CO 81003   Betty M. Carnes, Libn.

PUEBLO REGIONAL PLANNING COMMISSION - LIBRARY
Box 1427   Phone: (303) 543-6006
Pueblo, CO 81002   Donald R. Vest, Res.Libn.

ST. MARY-CORWIN HOSPITAL - FINNEY MEMORIAL LIBRARY
1008 Minnequa Ave.   Phone: (303) 560-5598
Pueblo, CO 81004   Shirley Harper, Med.Libn.

SOUTHERN COLORADO ECONOMIC DEVELOPMENT DISTRICT - REGIONAL
   PLANNING & DEVELOPMENT CENTER - DATA FILE
3418 N. Elizabeth   Phone: (303) 543-6006
Pueblo, CO 81008   Don Vest, Libn.

U.S. DEPT. OF TRANSPORTATION - TRANSPORTATION TEST CENTER -
   TECHNICAL LIBRARY
Box 11130   Phone: (303) 545-5660
Pueblo, CO 81001   Georgeann Guagliardo, Sec./Libn.

UNIVERSITY OF SOUTHERN COLORADO - LIBRARY - SPECIAL
   COLLECTIONS
2200 Bonforte Blvd.   Phone: (303) 549-2361
Pueblo, CO 81001   Beverly A. Moore, Dir.

SAN JUAN COUNTY HISTORICAL SOCIETY - ARCHIVE
1111 Reese St.   Phone: (303) 387-5770
Silverton, CO 81433   Allen Nossaman, Dir.

TREAD OF PIONEERS MUSEUM - ROUTT COUNTY COLLECTION
Box 772829   Phone: (303) 879-0240
Steamboat Springs, CO 80477   Diane Duquette, Chf.Libn.

CAMP DRESSER & MC KEE, INC. - CDM ENVIRONMENTAL LIBRARY
11455 W. 48th Ave.
Wheat Ridge, CO 80033

LUTHERAN MEDICAL CENTER - MEDICAL LIBRARY
8300 W. 38th Ave.   Phone: (303) 425-8662
Wheat Ridge, CO 80033   Susan B. Higginbotham, Med.Libn.

WHEAT RIDGE REGIONAL CENTER - EMPLOYEE'S LIBRARY
10285 Ridge Rd.   Phone: (303) 424-7791
Wheat Ridge, CO 80033   Clara Ann Glover, Dir.

EASTMAN KODAK COMPANY - COLORADO DIVISION - ENGINEERING AND
   INFORMATION SERVICES LIBRARY *
Bldg. CS02A   Phone: (303) 686-7611
Windsor, CO 80551   Audrey Hoover, Libn.

CONNECTICUT

ABBEY OF REGINA LAUDIS, ORDER OF ST. BENEDICT - LIBRARY
                                        Phone: (203) 266-7727
Bethlehem, CT 06751   Mother Agnes, O.S.B., Libn.

ANDERSEN LABORATORIES, INC. - LIBRARY
1280 Blue Hills Ave.   Phone: (203) 242-0761
Bloomfield, CT 06002   Fran Feldman, Libn.

MONSANTO CORPORATION - FABRICATED PRODUCTS DIVISION -
   TECHNICAL INFORMATION CENTER
101 Granby St.   Phone: (203) 242-6221
Bloomfield, CT 06002   Nicole Marenbach, Adm.Mgr.

NORTH CENTRAL REGIONAL CENTER - TREES LIBRARY
120 Mountain Ave.   Phone: (203) 243-9517
Bloomfield, CT 06002   Paula A. Szabo

ST. THOMAS SEMINARY LIBRARY - ALUMNI COLLECTION
467 Bloomfield Ave.   Phone: (201) 242-5573
Bloomfield, CT 06002   Rev. Charles B. Johnson, Dir.

BRIDGEPORT CITY ARCHIVES, RECORDS AND INFORMATION SERVICES
   DEPARTMENT
City Hall, Rm. 14
45 Lyon Terrace   Phone: (203) 576-8192
Bridgeport, CT 06604   David W. Palmquist, City Archv.

BRIDGEPORT HOSPITAL - REEVES MEMORIAL LIBRARY †
267 Grant St.
Box 5000   Phone: (203) 384-3254
Bridgeport, CT 06610   Violet Rigia, Dir. of Lib.Serv.

BRIDGEPORT PUBLIC LIBRARY - HISTORICAL COLLECTIONS
925 Broad St.   Phone: (203) 576-7417
Bridgeport, CT 06604   David W. Palmquist, Hd., Hist.Coll.

BRIDGEPORT PUBLIC LIBRARY - TECHNOLOGY AND BUSINESS
   DEPARTMENT
925 Broad St.   Phone: (203) 576-7406
Bridgeport, CT 06604   Michael A. Golrick, Hd.

CONNECTICUT STATE LIBRARY - LAW LIBRARY AT BRIDGEPORT
1061 Main St., 7th Fl.
New Court House   Phone: (203) 579-6237
Bridgeport, CT 06604   Robert Nathan Plotnick, Libn.

GENERAL ELECTRIC COMPANY - CORPORATE INFORMATION SYSTEMS
   LIBRARY
Bldg. 30ES
1285 Boston Ave.   Phone: (203) 382-3921
Bridgeport, CT 06602   Mary Kay Frost, Info.Spec.

PARK CITY HOSPITAL - CARLSON FOUNDATION MEMORIAL LIBRARY
695 Park Ave.   Phone: (203) 579-5097
Bridgeport, CT 06604   Suzanne Porter-Zadera, Dir.

SACRED HEART UNIVERSITY - LIBRARY
5229 Park Ave.   Phone: (203) 371-7700
Bridgeport, CT 06606   Roch-Josef di Lisio, Act.Dir.

ST. VINCENT'S MEDICAL CENTER - DANIEL T. BANKS HEALTH SCIENCE
    LIBRARY
2800 Main St.   Phone: (203) 576-5336
Bridgeport, CT 06606   Janet Goerig, Dir., Lib.Serv.

UNIVERSITY OF BRIDGEPORT - MAGNUS WAHLSTROM LIBRARY - SPECIAL
    COLLECTIONS
126 Park Ave.   Phone: (203) 576-4740
Bridgeport, CT 06601   Judith Lin Hunt, Univ.Libn.

UNIVERSITY OF BRIDGEPORT - SCHOOL OF LAW - LAW LIBRARY
126 Park Ave.   Phone: (203) 576-4056
Bridgeport, CT 06601   Madeleine J. Wilken, Prof./Dir.,Law Info.Serv.

AMERICAN CLOCK AND WATCH MUSEUM - EDWARD INGRAHAM LIBRARY
100 Maple St.   Phone: (203) 583-6070
Bristol, CT 06010   Mr. Chris H. Bailey, Mng.Dir.

ASSOCIATED SPRING BARNES GROUP, INC. - CORPORATE LIBRARY
18 Main St.   Phone: (203) 583-1331
Bristol, CT 06010   Jackie A. Ives, Libn.

CRANDALL (Prudence) MEMORIAL MUSEUM - LIBRARY
Box 12   Phone: (203) 546-9916
Canterbury, CT 06331   Margaret W. Nareff, Cur.Assoc.

FIRST CONGREGATIONAL CHURCH OF CHESHIRE - LIBRARY
111 Church Dr.   Phone: (203) 272-5323
Cheshire, CT 06410

CLINTON HISTORICAL SOCIETY - LIBRARY
Andrews Memorial Town Hall
Box 174
Clinton, CT 06413   Ernest Burnham, Pres.

COLEBROOK HISTORICAL SOCIETY - LIBRARY AND ARCHIVES
                                          Phone: (203) 379-3509
Colebrook, CT 06021

CANTON HISTORICAL SOCIETY - LIBRARY
11 Front St.   Phone: (203) 693-2793
Collinsville, CT 06022   Jane L. Goedecke, Libn.

HISTORICAL SOCIETY OF THE TOWN OF GREENWICH, INC. - LIBRARY
Bush-Holley House
39 Strickland Rd.   Phone: (203) 622-9686
Cos Cob, CT 06807   Marion Nicholson, V.P.-Lib.

HOLY APOSTLES COLLEGE - LIBRARY
33 Prospect Hill Rd.
Cromwell, CT 06416   Rev. Francis C. O'Hara, Dir., Lib.Serv.

DANBURY HOSPITAL - HEALTH SCIENCES LIBRARY †
24 Hospital Ave.   Phone: (203) 797-7279
Danbury, CT 06810   Maryanne Witters, Dir.

DANBURY SCOTT-FANTON MUSEUM AND HISTORICAL SOCIETY - LIBRARY
43 Main St.   Phone: (203) 743-5200
Danbury, CT 06810   Julie B. Barrows, Dir.

GENERAL DATACOMM INDUSTRIES, INC. - CORPORATE LIBRARY
One Kennedy Ave.   Phone: (203) 797-0711
Danbury, CT 06810   Catherine Greene, Libn.

GROLIER INCORPORATED - LIBRARY
Sherman Tpk.   Phone: (203) 797-3500
Danbury, CT 06816   Chun Chuan Chang, Chf.Libn.

UNION CARBIDE CORPORATION - CORPORATE LIBRARY
Section N2, Old Ridgebury Rd.   Phone: (203) 794-5314
Danbury, CT 06817   L. Arless Leve, Mgr.

UNION CARBIDE CORPORATION - LAW DEPARTMENT LIBRARY
Section N2, Old Ridgebury Rd.   Phone: (203) 794-6396
Danbury, CT 06817   Carolyn A. Lebl, Hd. Law Libn.

UNION CARBIDE CORPORATION - LINDE DIVISION - COMMUNICATIONS
    LIBRARY
Old Ridgebury Rd.   Phone: (203) 794-2000
Danbury, CT 06817   Marie Montgomery, Hd.Libn.

WESTERN CONNECTICUT STATE UNIVERSITY - RUTH A. HAAS LIBRARY -
    SPECIAL COLLECTIONS
181 White St.   Phone: (203) 797-4052
Danbury, CT 06810   Katherine J. Sholtz, Dir. of Lib.Serv.

DARIEN HISTORICAL SOCIETY - LIBRARY
45 Old Kings Hwy., N.   Phone: (203) 655-9233
Darien, CT 06829   Mrs. John McKitterick

DUNLAP AND ASSOCIATES EAST, INC. - LIBRARY
One Parkland Dr.   Phone: (203) 655-3971
Darien, CT 06820   Joan M. Edwards, Dir.

PATIENT CARE COMMUNICATIONS, INC. - LIBRARY
16 Thorndal Circle   Phone: (203) 655-8951
Darien, CT 06820   Sylvia Boyd, Libn.

TWENTIETH CENTURY TRENDS INSTITUTE, INC. - SOURCE LIBRARY
c/o Darien High School
Nutmeg Ln.   Phone: (203) 655-3981
Darien, CT 06820   Norma Bellis, Libn.

COMPUTER PROCESSING INSTITUTE - INFORMATION CENTER †
111 Ash St.   Phone: (203) 528-9211
East Hartford, CT 06108   Noreen M. Quinn, Dir., Info.Serv.

TRC ENVIRONMENTAL CONSULTANTS, INC. - LIBRARY
800 Connecticut Blvd.   Phone: (203) 289-8631
East Hartford, CT 06108   Judith A. Douville, Info.Sci. & Mgr.

UNITED TECHNOLOGIES CORPORATION - LIBRARY
United Technologies Research Center   Phone: (203) 727-7120
East Hartford, CT 06108   Irving H. Neufeld, Chf., UTC Lib.Sys.

VANDERBILT (R.T.) COMPANY, INC. - LIBRARY
33 Winfield St.   Phone: (203) 853-1400
East Norwalk, CT 06855   Jane Wilson, Libn.

CONNECTICUT ELECTRIC RAILWAY ASSOCIATION, INC. - LIBRARY
    DEPARTMENT
Box 360   Phone: (203) 623-7417
East Windsor, CT 06088   W.E. Wood, Libn.

ST. BERNARD'S PARISH - HAZARDVILLE CATHOLIC LIBRARY
426 Hazard Ave.
Enfield, CT 06082   Rose Hartman, Libn.

CONNECTICUT AUDUBON CENTER - LIBRARY
2325 Burr St.   Phone: (203) 259-6305
Fairfield, CT 06430   John Reiger, Exec.Dir.

FAIRFIELD HISTORICAL SOCIETY - REFERENCE AND RESEARCH LIBRARY
636 Old Post Rd.   Phone: (203) 259-1598
Fairfield, CT 06430   Irene K. Miller, Libn.

VOLTARC TUBES INC. - LIBRARY
74 Linwood Ave.   Phone: (202) 255-2633
Fairfield, CT 06430   Evlyn Perkins, Libn.

CENTER FOR FARM AND FOOD RESEARCH, INC. - LIBRARY *
Box 88   Phone: (203) 824-5945
Falls Village, CT 06031   Lucille Sadwith, Dir.

AMERICAN NUCLEAR INSURERS - INFORMATION RECORDS CENTER
The Exchange, Bldg. 3
245 Farmington Ave.   Phone: (203) 677-7305
Farmington, CT 06032   Dottie Sherman, Dir., Lib./Info.Ctr.

STAUFFER CHEMICAL COMPANY - TECHNICAL INFORMATION CENTER
400 Farmington Ave.   Phone: (203) 674-6312
Farmington, CT 06032   Joanna W. Eickenhorst, Tech.Info.Spec.

UNIVERSITY OF CONNECTICUT - HEALTH CENTER - LYMAN MAYNARD
  STOWE LIBRARY
                                        Phone: (203) 674-2547
Farmington, CT 06032-9984   Ralph Arcari, Dir. of Lib.

YALE UNIVERSITY - LEWIS WALPOLE LIBRARY
154 Main St.   Phone: (203) 677-2140
Farmington, CT 06032   Catherine Jestin, Libn.

FUTURES GROUP, INC. - LIBRARY
76 Eastern Blvd.   Phone: (203) 633-3501
Glastonbury, CT 06033   Katherine H. Willson, Mgr., Info.Serv.

GOSHEN HISTORICAL SOCIETY - LIBRARY
Old Middle Rd.
RD 1   Phone: (203) 491-2665
Goshen, CT 06756   Mrs. John Tuttle, Cur.

SALMON BROOK HISTORICAL SOCIETY - REFERENCE AND EDUCATIONAL
  CENTER
208 Salmon Brook St.   Phone: (203) 653-3965
Granby, CT 06035   Carol Laun, Asst.Cur.

SOUTH CONGREGATIONAL CHURCH - ETHEL L. AUSTIN LIBRARY
242 Salmon Brook St.
Box 779   Phone: (203) 653-7289
Granby, CT 06035   Joan Griswold, Libn.

AMAX, INC. - CLIMAX MOLYBDENUM COMPANY - TECHNICAL
  INFORMATION DEPARTMENT †
1 Greenwich Plaza   Phone: (203) 622-3587
Greenwich, CT 06830   Ellen Jones, Supv., Info.Serv.

AMAX, INC. - LAW LIBRARY
AMAX Center   Phone: (203) 622-3021
Greenwich, CT 06830   Virginia S. Grayson, Libn.

AMAX, INC. - LIBRARY
AMAX Center   Phone: (203) 629-6022
Greenwich, CT 06836   Virginia S. Grayson, Libn.

AMERICAN CAN COMPANY - BUSINESS INFORMATION CENTER
American Ln. - 2B8   Phone: (203) 552-3137
Greenwich, CT 06830   Estelle C. Adler, Mgr.

COPPER DEVELOPMENT ASSOCIATION, INC. - COPPER DATA CENTER
Greenwich Off., Pk. 2
Box 1840   Phone: (203) 625-8210
Greenwich, CT 06836-1840   Janice L. Valuskas, Libn., Tech.Info.Ctr.

DMS, INC. - TECHNICAL LIBRARY
100 Northfield St.   Phone: (203) 661-7800
Greenwich, CT 06830   James Appleyard, Dir.

GREENWICH HOSPITAL ASSOCIATION - GRAY CARTER LIBRARY
                                        Phone: (203) 869-7000
Greenwich, CT 06830   Carmel Fedors, Lib.Mgr.

GREENWICH LIBRARY - ORAL HISTORY PROJECT
101 W. Putnam Ave.   Phone: (203) 622-7900
Greenwich CT 06830   Louise Gudelis, Local Hist.Ref.Libn.

REDDY COMMUNICATIONS, INC. - INFORMATION/RESEARCH SERVICES
537 Steamboat Rd.   Phone: (203) 661-4800
Greenwich, CT 06830   Elizabeth A. Muskus, Mgr., Info./Res.Serv.

GENERAL DYNAMICS CORPORATION - ELECTRIC BOAT DIVISION -
  DIVISION LIBRARY
Eastern Point Rd.   Phone: (203) 446-3481
Groton, CT 06340   Charles E. Giles, Chf.Libn.

PFIZER, INC. - CENTRAL RESEARCH TECHNICAL INFORMATION SERVICES
Eastern Point Rd.   Phone: (203) 445-5611
Groton, CT 06340   Dr. Jay S. Buckley, Jr., Dir., Tech.Info.

U.S. COAST GUARD - RESEARCH AND DEVELOPMENT CENTER - TECHNICAL
  INFORMATION CENTER *
Avery Point   Phone: (203) 445-8501
Groton, CT 06340   Dorothy E. Siegfried, Tech.Info.Spec.

U.S. NAVY - NAVAL SUBMARINE MEDICAL RESEARCH LABORATORY -
  MEDICAL LIBRARY
Naval Submarine Base New London
Box 900   Phone: (203) 449-3629
Groton, CT 06340   Elaine M. Gaucher, Libn.

U.S. NAVY - SUBMARINE BASE - SUBMARINE FORCE LIBRARY AND
  MUSEUM
Code 340, Box 16   Phone: (203) 449-3174
Groton, CT 06349   Robert J. Zollars, Dir.

GUILFORD KEEPING SOCIETY, INC. - LIBRARY *
171 Boston St.
Box 363   Phone: (203) 453-3176
Guilford, CT 06437   Joel Helander, Lib.Comm.Chm.

WIRE ASSOCIATION INTERNATIONAL - TECHNICAL INFORMATION
  CENTER
1570 Boston Post Rd.
Box H   Phone: (203) 453-2777
Guilford, CT 06437   Deborah Rutter, Tech.Info.Mgr.

CONGREGATION MISHKAN ISRAEL - ADULT LIBRARY
785 Ridge Rd.   Phone: (203) 288-3877
Hamden, CT 06517   Jay M. Brown

PAIER COLLEGE OF ART, INC. - LIBRARY
6 Prospect Court
Hamden, CT 06511   Christine de Vallet, Libn.

AETNA LIFE & CASUALTY COMPANY - CORPORATE INFORMATION CENTER
151 Farmington Ave.   Phone: (203) 727-4310
Hartford, CT 06156   Kathryn W. Porter, Adm.

AETNA LIFE & CASUALTY COMPANY - ENGINEERING LIBRARY
151 Farmington Ave.   Phone: (203) 683-3648
Hartford, CT 06156   Melissa Pierce, Libn.

AETNA LIFE & CASUALTY COMPANY - FINANCIAL LIBRARY
Bond Investment Dept.
Financial Division
City Place   Phone: (203) 275-2697
Hartford, CT 06156   Elaine Z. Jennerich, Info.Spec.

AETNA LIFE & CASUALTY COMPANY - LAW LIBRARY
151 Farmington Ave.   Phone: (203) 273-8183
Hartford, CT 06156   Patricia Sechrist, Law Libn.

ARCHDIOCESE OF HARTFORD - CATHOLIC LIBRARY & INFORMATION
  CENTER *
125 Market St.   Phone: (203) 522-0602
Hartford, CT 06103   Rev. Edward J. McLean, Exec.Dir.

ARTHUR ANDERSEN & CO. - LIBRARY
One Financial Plaza   Phone: (203) 522-2600
Hartford, CT 06103   Cornelia A. Toohey, Libn.

CONNECTICUT GENERAL LIFE INSURANCE COMPANY - CORPORATE
  LIBRARY †
                                        Phone: (203) 726-4327
Hartford, CT 06152   Brenda H. Claflin, Corp.Libn.

CONNECTICUT HISTORICAL SOCIETY - LIBRARY
1 Elizabeth St.   Phone: (203) 236-5621
Hartford, CT 06105   Elizabeth Abbe, Libn.

CONNECTICUT MUTUAL LIFE INSURANCE COMPANY - BUSINESS
  INFORMATION SERVICES †
140 Garden St.   Phone: (203) 727-6500
Hartford, CT 06115   Ellen Cartledge, Libn.

CONNECTICUT STATE DEPARTMENT ON AGING - LIBRARY
80 Washington St.   Phone: (203) 566-7728
Hartford, CT 06106   Alice Gilbert, Libn.

CONNECTICUT STATE DEPARTMENT OF CHILDREN & YOUTH SERVICES -
    STAFF LIBRARY
170 Sigourney St.   Phone: (203) 566-2941
Hartford, CT 06105-9962   Gerald Seagrave, Staff Libn.

CONNECTICUT STATE DEPARTMENT OF HEALTH SERVICES - STANLEY H.
    OSBORN MEDICAL LIBRARY
150 Washington St.   Phone: (203) 566-2198
Hartford, CT 06106   Margery A. Cohen, Libn.

CONNECTICUT STATE LIBRARY
231 Capitol Ave.   Phone: (203) 566-4777
Hartford, CT 06115   Clarence R. Walters, State Libn.

CONNECTICUT STATE LIBRARY - HARTFORD LAW BRANCH
95 Washington St.   Phone: (203) 566-3900
Hartford, CT 06106   Evangeline Luddy, Libn.

CONNECTICUT STATE LIBRARY - LIBRARY FOR THE BLIND AND
    PHYSICALLY HANDICAPPED
90 Washington St.   Phone: (203) 563-7561
Hartford, CT 06106   Dale Wierzbicki, Dir.

CONNECTICUT STATE OFFICE OF POLICY AND MANAGEMENT - LIBRARY *
80 Washington St.
Hartford, CT 06115

HARTFORD - CITY PLAN LIBRARY *
550 Main St.   Phone: (203) 722-6630
Hartford, CT 06103   Patricia Williams, Planning Dir.

HARTFORD COURANT - NEWS LIBRARY
285 Broad St.   Phone: (203) 241-6470
Hartford, CT 06115   Kathleen McKula, News Libn.

HARTFORD HOSPITAL - HEALTH SCIENCE LIBRARIES
80 Seymour St.   Phone: (203) 524-2971
Hartford, CT 06115   Gertrude Lamb, Ph.D., Dir.

HARTFORD INSURANCE GROUP - CORPORATE LIBRARY
Hartford Plaza   Phone: (203) 547-5516
Hartford, CT 06115   Bonnie Jean Woodworth, Corp.Libn.

HARTFORD INSURANCE GROUP - LOSS CONTROL DEPARTMENT LIBRARY
Hartford Plaza   Phone: (203) 547-5000
Hartford, CT 06115   Laurice Klemarczyk, Libn.

HARTFORD MEDICAL SOCIETY - WALTER STEINER MEMORIAL LIBRARY
230 Scarborough St.   Phone: (203) 236-5613
Hartford, CT 06035   H. David Crombie, M.D., Libn.

HARTFORD PUBLIC LIBRARY - ART, MUSIC AND RECREATION
    DEPARTMENT
500 Main St.   Phone: (203) 525-9121
Hartford, CT 06103   Vernon Martin, Hd.

HARTFORD PUBLIC LIBRARY - BUSINESS, SCIENCE & TECHNOLOGY
    DEPARTMENT
500 Main St.   Phone: (203) 525-9121
Hartford, CT 06103   Charles S. Griffen, Hd.

HARTFORD PUBLIC LIBRARY - REFERENCE AND GENERAL READING
    DEPARTMENT
500 Main St.   Phone: (203) 525-9121
Hartford, CT 06103   Martha D. Nolan, Hd.

HARTFORD SEMINARY LIBRARY
77 Sherman St.   Phone: (203) 232-4451
Hartford, CT 06105   Dr. Richard B. Eberhart, Adm.

HARTFORD STATE TECHNICAL COLLEGE - GROM HAYES LIBRARY
401 Flatbush Ave.   Phone: (203) 527-4111
Hartford, CT 06106   Dr. Larry W. Yother, Lib.Dir.

HARTFORD WOMEN'S CENTER - HARTFORD FEMINIST LIBRARY
350 Farmington Ave.   Phone: (203) 232-7393
Hartford, CT 06105   Irene Scheibner, Founder

INDUSTRIAL RISK INSURERS - LIBRARY
85 Woodland St.   Phone: (203) 525-2601
Hartford, CT 06102   Patricia Sasso, Libn.

INSTITUTE OF LIVING - MEDICAL LIBRARY
400 Washington St.   Phone: (203) 241-6824
Hartford, CT 06106   Helen R. Lansberg, Dir.

LIFE INSURANCE MARKETING AND RESEARCH ASSOCIATION - LIBRARY
Box 208   Phone: (203) 677-0033
Hartford, CT 06141   William J. Mortimer, Mgr., Lib./Ref.Serv.

MARK TWAIN MEMORIAL - LIBRARY
351 Farmington Ave.   Phone: (203) 247-0998
Hartford, CT 06105   Mr. Wynn Lee, Dir.

MORSE SCHOOL OF BUSINESS - LIBRARY
275 Asylum St.   Phone: (203) 522-2261
Hartford, CT 06103   Sylvia B. Taub, Libn.

MOUNT SINAI HOSPITAL - HEALTH SCIENCES LIBRARY †
500 Blue Hills Ave.   Phone: (203) 242-4431
Hartford, CT 06112   Nancy B. Cohen, Dir.

NORTHEAST UTILITIES SERVICE COMPANY - LIBRARY
Box 270   Phone: (203) 665-5141
Hartford, CT 06141   Joan N. Terry, Libn.

PHOENIX MUTUAL LIFE INSURANCE COMPANY - LIBRARY
One American Row   Phone: (203) 278-1212
Hartford, CT 06115   Margaret Colton, Libn.

PROTESTANT EPISCOPAL CHURCH - EPISCOPAL DIOCESE OF
    CONNECTICUT - DIOCESAN LIBRARY AND ARCHIVES
1335 Asylum Ave.   Phone: (203) 233-4481
Hartford, CT 06105   Rev. Kenneth W. Cameron, Archv./Histographer

ST. FRANCIS HOSPITAL AND MEDICAL CENTER - SCHOOL OF NURSING
    LIBRARY
338 Asylum St.   Phone: (203) 247-4411
Hartford, CT 06103   Ruth P. Carroll, Dir.

ST. FRANCIS HOSPITAL AND MEDICAL CENTER - WILSON C. JAINSEN
    LIBRARY
114 Woodland St.   Phone: (203) 548-4746
Hartford, CT 06105   Ruth Carroll, Dir. of Libs.

STOWE-DAY FOUNDATION - LIBRARY
77 Forest St.   Phone: (203) 522-9258
Hartford, CT 06105   Joseph S. Van Why, Dir.

TRAVELERS INSURANCE COMPANIES - CORPORATE LIBRARY
One Tower Square   Phone: (203) 277-5048
Hartford, CT 06115   Margaret Q. Orloske, Corp.Libn. & Hist.

TRINITY COLLEGE - WATKINSON LIBRARY
300 Summit St.   Phone: (203) 527-3151
Hartford, CT 06106   Dr. Jeffrey H. Kaimowitz, Cur.

UNITED CHURCH OF CHRIST - CONNECTICUT CONFERENCE - ARCHIVES
125 Sherman St.   Phone: (203) 233-5564
Hartford, CT 06105   Rev. Wesley C. Ewert, Archv.

U.S. DEPT. OF COMMERCE - INTERNATIONAL TRADE ADMINISTRATION -
    HARTFORD DISTRICT OFFICE LIBRARY *
Federal Office Bldg., Rm. 610-B
450 Main St.   Phone: (203) 244-3530
Hartford, CT 06103   Richard C. Kilbourn, Dir.

UNIVERSITY OF CONNECTICUT - LAW SCHOOL LIBRARY
120 Sherman St.   Phone: (203) 523-4841
Hartford, CT 06105-2289   Dennis J. Stone, Law Libn.

UNIVERSITY OF CONNECTICUT - SCHOOL OF BUSINESS ADMINISTRATION
    LIBRARY
39 Woodland St.   Phone: (203) 241-4905
Hartford, CT 06105   Patricia A. Slevinsky, Libn.

WADSWORTH ATHENEUM - AUERBACH ART LIBRARY
600 Main St.   Phone: (203) 278-2670
Hartford, CT 06103   John W. Teahan, Libn.

YOUNG MEN'S CHRISTIAN ASSOCIATION OF METROPOLITAN HARTFORD,
     INC. - CAREER COUNSELING CENTER LIBRARY
160 Jewell St.   Phone: (203) 522-4183
Hartford, CT 06103   Dr. William N. Goodwin, Dir.

KENT HISTORICAL SOCIETY - LIBRARY
R.D. 1
Box 417   Phone: (203) 927-3055
Kent, CT 06757   Mrs. J. Floyd Barton, Libn.

CONNECTICUT STATE LIBRARY - LAW LIBRARY AT LITCHFIELD
Court House, West St.   Phone: (203) 567-0598
Litchfield, CT 06759   Evelina E. Lemelin, Libn.

LITCHFIELD HISTORICAL SOCIETY - INGRAHAM LIBRARY
Box 385   Phone: (203) 567-5862
Litchfield, CT 06759   Robert G. Carroon, Dir.

MADISON HISTORICAL SOCIETY, INC. - LIBRARY
853 Boston Post Rd.
Box 17   Phone: (203) 245-4567
Madison, CT 06443   William T. Mills, Pres.

MANCHESTER MEMORIAL HOSPITAL - LIBRARY †
71 Haynes St.   Phone: (203) 646-1222
Manchester, CT 06040   Anna B. Salo

ALTOBELLO (Henry D.) CHILDREN AND YOUTH CENTER - PROFESSIONAL
     LIBRARY
Box 902   Phone: (203) 238-6097
Meriden, CT 06450   Ann Juknis, Libn.

CONNECTICUT POLICE ACADEMY - RESOURCE CENTER
285 Preston Ave.   Phone: (203) 238-6531
Meriden, CT 06450   Theresa A. Wyser, Libn.

INTERNATIONAL SILVER COMPANY - HISTORICAL LIBRARY †
550 Research Pkwy.   Phone: (203) 238-8058
Meriden, CT 06450   Ed P. Hogan, Hist.

MERIDEN-WALLINGFORD HOSPITAL - HEALTH SCIENCES LIBRARY
181 Cook Ave.   Phone: (203) 238-0771
Meriden, CT 06450   Patricia C. Westbrook, Libn.

TIMEX GROUP, LTD. - LEGAL & CORPORATE LIBRARY
Park Road Ext.   Phone: (203) 573-5268
Middlebury, CT 06762   Beth Abend, Libn.

UNIROYAL, INC. - CORPORATE LIBRARY
World Headquarters   Phone: (203) 573-2000
Middlebury, CT 06749

CONNECTICUT STATE LIBRARY - FILM SERVICE
Middletown Library Service Ctr.
786 S. Main St.   Phone: (203) 344-2645
Middletown, CT 06457   Ilene Tobey, AV Cons.

CONNECTICUT VALLEY HOSPITAL - HALLOCK MEDICAL LIBRARY
Box 351   Phone: (203) 344-2304
Middletown, CT 06457   Mildred Asbell, Med.Libn.

GODFREY MEMORIAL LIBRARY
134 Newfield St.   Phone: (203) 346-4375
Middletown, CT 06457   Doris Post, Dir.

MIDDLESEX COUNTY HISTORICAL SOCIETY - LIBRARY
151 Main St.   Phone: (203) 346-0746
Middletown, CT 06457   Lisa Broberg, Dir.

MIDDLESEX MEMORIAL HOSPITAL - HEALTH SCIENCES LIBRARY
28 Crescent St.   Phone: (203) 347-9471
Middletown, CT 06457   Evelyn M. Breck, Dir.

UNITED TECHNOLOGIES CORPORATION - PRATT & WHITNEY AIRCRAFT
     GROUP - MATERIALS ENGINEERING RESEARCH LIB.
Aircraft Rd.   Phone: (203) 344-5138
Middletown, CT 06457   Noreen O. Steele, Libn.

WESLEYAN UNIVERSITY - ART LIBRARY
Davison Art Center
301 High St.   Phone: (203) 347-9411
Middletown, CT 06457   Richard H. Wood, Libn.

WESLEYAN UNIVERSITY - LIBRARY - SPECIAL COLLECTIONS
        Phone: (203) 347-9411
Middletown, CT 06457   Elizabeth A. Swaim, Spec.Coll.Libn./Archv.

WESLEYAN UNIVERSITY - LIBRARY - WORLD MUSIC ARCHIVES
        Phone: (203) 347-9411
Middletown, CT 06457   Chris Montgomery, Music Libn.

WESLEYAN UNIVERSITY - PSYCHOLOGY DEPARTMENT LIBRARY
Judd Hall   Phone: (203) 347-9411
Middletown, CT 06457   Shirley Schmottlach, Lib.Asst.

WESLEYAN UNIVERSITY - SCIENCE LIBRARY
        Phone: (203) 347-9411
Middletown, CT 06457   William Calhoon, Sci.Libn.

WESLEYAN WOMEN'S CENTER - LIBRARY
287 High St.
Wesleyan Station, Box WW   Phone: (203) 347-9411
Middletown, CT 06457   R. Rosenthal, Libn.

XEROX CORPORATION - XEROX EDUCATION PUBLICATIONS - LIBRARY
245 Long Hill Rd.   Phone: (203) 347-7251
Middletown, CT 06457   Harriet S. Osburn, Hd.Libn.

U.S. NATL. MARINE FISHERIES SERVICE - MILFORD LABORATORY LIBRARY
212 Rogers Ave.   Phone: (203) 783-4234
Milford, CT 06460

MYSTIC SEAPORT, INC. - G.W. BLUNT WHITE LIBRARY
        Phone: (203) 572-0711
Mystic, CT 06355   Gerald E. Morris, Libn.

UNIROYAL, INC. - UNIROYAL CHEMICAL DIVISION - MANAGEMENT &
     TECHNICAL INFORMATION SERVICES/LIBRARY
Elm St.   Phone: (203) 723-3252
Naugatuck, CT 06770   Patricia Ann Harmon, Libn.

CAPITOL REGION EDUCATION COUNCIL - ED SEARCH
Elihu Burritt Library, Rm. 401
Central Connecticut State University   Phone: (203) 827-7649
New Britain CT 06050   John Allen Shearer, Jr., Hd.

CENTRAL CONNECTICUT STATE UNIVERSITY - ELIHU BURRITT LIBRARY
Wells St.   Phone: (203) 827-7530
New Britain, CT 06050   Dr. William Aguilar, Dir.

HERALD PUBLISHING COMPANY - HERALD LIBRARY
One Herald Square   Phone: (203) 225-4601
New Britain, CT 06050   Linda Senkus, Libn.

NEW BRITAIN GENERAL HOSPITAL - HEALTH SCIENCE LIBRARY
100 Grand St.   Phone: (203) 224-5011
New Britain, CT 06050   Debora K. Mortensen, Libn./Dir.

NEW BRITAIN MUSEUM OF AMERICAN ART - LIBRARY
56 Lexington St.   Phone: (203) 229-0257
New Britain, CT 06052   Lois L. Blomstrann, Asst. to Dir.

NEW CANAAN HISTORICAL SOCIETY - LIBRARY
13 Oenoke Ridge   Phone: (203) 966-1776
New Canaan, CT 06840   Mary C. Durbrow, Libn.

SILVERMINE SCHOOL OF THE ARTS - LIBRARY
1037 Silvermine Rd.
New Canaan, CT 06840

CONNECTICUT AGRICULTURAL EXPERIMENT STATION - OSBORNE
    LIBRARY
123 Huntington St.
Box 1106   Phone: (203) 789-7265
New Haven, CT 06504   Paul Gough, Libn.

CONNECTICUT STATE LIBRARY - LAW LIBRARY AT NEW HAVEN
County Courthouse
235 Church St.   Phone: (203) 789-7889
New Haven, CT 06510   Martha J. Sullivan, Lib.Adm.

GESELL INSTITUTE OF HUMAN DEVELOPMENT - LIBRARY
310 Prospect St.   Phone: (203) 777-3481
New Haven, CT 06511   Louise Bates Ames, Ph.D.

HASKINS LABORATORIES - LIBRARY
270 Crown St.   Phone: (203) 436-1774
New Haven, CT 06510   Nancy O'Brien, Libn.

HOSPITAL OF ST. RAPHAEL - HEALTH SCIENCES LIBRARY
1450 Chapel St.   Phone: (203) 789-3330
New Haven, CT 06511   Patricia L. Wales, Dir., Lib.Serv.

HUMAN RELATIONS AREA FILES, INC.
755 Prospect St.   Phone: (203) 777-2334
New Haven, CT 06511   Timothy J. O'Leary, Dir., File Res.

NEW HAVEN COLONY HISTORICAL SOCIETY - WHITNEY LIBRARY
114 Whitney Ave.   Phone: (203) 562-4183
New Haven, CT 06510   Ottilia Koel, Libn. & Cur. of Mss.

OLIN CORPORATION - METALS RESEARCH LABORATORIES - METALS
    INFORMATION CENTER †
91 Shelton Ave.   Phone: (203) 789-6000
New Haven, CT 06511   Marcella C. Tammard, Libn.

OLIN CORPORATION - RESEARCH CENTER/INFORMATION CENTER
Box 30-275   Phone: (203) 789-6038
New Haven, CT 06511   R.P. Peraza, Mgr.

SOUTHERN CONNECTICUT STATE UNIVERSITY - H.C. BULEY LIBRARY -
    SPECIAL COLLECTIONS
501 Crescent St.   Phone: (203) 397-4505
New Haven, CT 06515   Claire Bennett, Spec.Coll.Libn.

UNITED ILLUMINATING COMPANY - LIBRARY
80 Temple St.   Phone: (203) 787-7690
New Haven, CT 06506   Marie S. Richardson, Libn.

WIGGIN AND DANA - LIBRARY *
195 Church St.   Phone: (203) 789-1511
New Haven, CT 06508   Kathleen A. Ingraham, Libn.

YALE UNIVERSITY - AMERICAN ORIENTAL SOCIETY LIBRARY
Sterling Memorial Library, Rm. 329   Phone: (203) 436-1040
New Haven, CT 06520   Mary Ann T. Itoga, Libn.

YALE UNIVERSITY - ANTHROPOLOGY LIBRARY
Kline Science Library
Box 6666   Phone: (203) 436-0874
New Haven, CT 06511   Richard J. Dionne, Libn.

YALE UNIVERSITY - ART AND ARCHITECTURE LIBRARY
Art & Architecture Bldg.
Yale Sta., Box 1605A   Phone: (203) 436-2055
New Haven, CT 06520   Nancy S. Lambert, Libn.

YALE UNIVERSITY - ARTS OF THE BOOK COLLECTION
Sterling Memorial Library   Phone: (203) 436-2200
New Haven, CT 06520   Gay Walker, Cur.

YALE UNIVERSITY - BABYLONIAN COLLECTION
Sterling Memorial Library
120 High St.   Phone: (203) 432-4725
New Haven, CT 06520   William W. Hallo, Cur.

YALE UNIVERSITY - BEINECKE RARE BOOK AND MANUSCRIPT LIBRARY
Wall & High Sts.   Phone: (203) 436-8438
New Haven, CT 06520   Ralph Franklin, Dir.

YALE UNIVERSITY - BENJAMIN FRANKLIN COLLECTION
Sterling Memorial Library, Rm. 230
Yale Sta., Box 1603A   Phone: (203) 436-8646
New Haven, CT 06520   Dorothy W. Bridgwater, Asst.Libn.

YALE UNIVERSITY - CLASSICS LIBRARY
Phelps Hall, 344 College St.   Phone: (203) 436-1130
New Haven, CT 06520   Carla M. Lukas, Libn.

YALE UNIVERSITY - COLLECTION OF THE LITERATURE OF THE AMERICAN
    MUSICAL THEATRE
Sterling Memorial Library, Rm. 226   Phone: (203) 436-1822
New Haven, CT 06520   Richard Warren, Jr., Cur.

YALE UNIVERSITY - COLLECTION OF MUSICAL INSTRUMENTS - LIBRARY
15 Hillhouse Ave.
Box 2117   Phone: (203) 436-4935
New Haven, CT 06520   Richard Rephann, Dir.

YALE UNIVERSITY - COWLES FOUNDATION FOR RESEARCH IN
    ECONOMICS - LIBRARY
30 Hillhouse Ave.   Phone: (203) 436-0249
New Haven, CT 06520   Karlee Gifford, Libn.

YALE UNIVERSITY - DIVINITY SCHOOL LIBRARY
409 Prospect St.   Phone: (203) 436-8440
New Haven, CT 06510   Stephen L. Peterson, Divinity Libn.

YALE UNIVERSITY - EAST ASIAN COLLECTION
Sterling Memorial Library   Phone: (203) 436-4810
New Haven, CT 06520   Hideo Kaneko, Cur.

YALE UNIVERSITY - ECONOMIC GROWTH CENTER COLLECTION
140 Prospect St.   Phone: (203) 436-3412
New Haven, CT 06520   Billie I. Salter, Libn. for Social Sci.

YALE UNIVERSITY - ELIZABETHAN CLUB COLLECTION
459 College St.   Phone: (203) 436-8535
New Haven, CT 06511   Stephen R. Parks, Libn.

YALE UNIVERSITY - ENGINEERING AND APPLIED SCIENCE LIBRARY
Becton Ctr., 15 Prospect St.   Phone: (203) 432-4539
New Haven, CT 06520   Elizabeth Hayes, Hd.

YALE UNIVERSITY - FORESTRY LIBRARY †
205 Prospect St.
22 Sage Hall   Phone: (203) 436-0577
New Haven, CT 06511   Joseph A. Miller, Libn.

YALE UNIVERSITY - GEOLOGY LIBRARY
Box 6666   Phone: (203) 436-2480
New Haven, CT 06511   Harry D. Scammell, Libn.

YALE UNIVERSITY - INDOLOGICAL AND LINGUISTIC SEMINAR - LIBRARY
302 Hall of Graduate Studies
320 York St.   Phone: (203) 436-1862
New Haven, CT 06520   Prof. Stanley Insler, Chm.

YALE UNIVERSITY - JOHN HERRICK JACKSON MUSIC LIBRARY
98 Wall St.   Phone: (203) 436-8240
New Haven, CT 06520   Harold E. Samuel, Libn.

YALE UNIVERSITY - KLINE SCIENCE LIBRARY
Kline Biology Tower, Rm. C-8   Phone: (203) 436-3710
New Haven, CT 06520   Richard J. Dionne, Sci.Libn.

YALE UNIVERSITY - LAW LIBRARY
127 Wall St.   Phone: (203) 436-2215
New Haven, CT 06520   Morris L. Cohen, Libn.

YALE UNIVERSITY - MANUSCRIPTS AND ARCHIVES
Sterling Memorial Library   Phone: (203) 432-4695
New Haven, CT 06520   Katharine Morton, Hd.Libn.

YALE UNIVERSITY - MAP COLLECTION
Sterling Memorial Library, Map Rm.   Phone: (203) 436-8638
New Haven, CT 06520   Barbara B. McCorkle, Cur. of Maps

YALE UNIVERSITY - MATHEMATICS LIBRARY
12 Hillhouse Ave.
Yale Sta., Box 2155   Phone: (203) 436-0725
New Haven, CT 06520   Paul J. Lukasiewicz, Mathematics Libn.

YALE UNIVERSITY - MEDICAL LIBRARY
333 Cedar St.   Phone: (203) 785-5354
New Haven, CT 06510   Bella Z. Berson, Act.Med.Libn.

YALE UNIVERSITY - OBSERVATORY LIBRARY
260 Whitney Ave., J.W. Gibbs Laboratory
Box 6666   Phone: (203) 436-3460
New Haven, CT 06511   Ann Dallavalle, Lib.Serv.Asst.

YALE UNIVERSITY - ORNITHOLOGY LIBRARY
310 Bingham Lab., Peabody Museum
170 Whitney Ave.
Box 6666   Phone: (203) 436-8547
New Haven, CT 06511   Eleanor H. Stickney, Sr.Musm.Asst.

YALE UNIVERSITY - SCHOOL OF DRAMA LIBRARY
222 York St.
Yale Sta., Box 1903A   Phone: (203) 436-2213
New Haven, CT 06520   Pamela C. Jordan, Libn.

YALE UNIVERSITY - SEMITIC REFERENCE LIBRARY †
314 Sterling Memorial Library
Yale University Library
New Haven, CT 06520   Edward A. Jajko, Near East Bibliog.

YALE UNIVERSITY - SLAVIC & EAST EUROPEAN COLLECTIONS
Sterling Memorial Library   Phone: (203) 436-0230
New Haven, CT 06520   Tatiana Rannit, Cur.

YALE UNIVERSITY - SOCIAL SCIENCE LIBRARY
140 Prospect St.
Yale Sta., Box 1958   Phone: (203) 436-3412
New Haven, CT 06520   Billie I. Salter, Libn. for Social Sci.

YALE UNIVERSITY - SOUTHEAST ASIA COLLECTION
Sterling Memorial Library   Phone: (203) 436-1092
New Haven, CT 06520   Charles R. Bryant, Cur.

YALE UNIVERSITY - STERLING CHEMISTRY LIBRARY
225 Prospect St.   Phone: (203) 436-3397
New Haven, CT 06520   Deborah Paolillo, Hd.

YALE UNIVERSITY - YALE CENTER FOR BRITISH ART - PHOTO ARCHIVE
2120 Yale Sta.   Phone: (203) 432-4097
New Haven, CT 06520   Dr. Anne-Marie Logan, Libn./Photo Archv.

YALE UNIVERSITY - YALE CENTER FOR BRITISH ART - RARE BOOK
     COLLECTION
2120 Yale Sta.   Phone: (203) 432-4099
New Haven, CT 06520   Joan M. Friedman, Cur. of Rare Bks.

YALE UNIVERSITY - YALE CENTER FOR BRITISH ART - REFERENCE
     LIBRARY
1080 Chapel St.
Yale Sta., Box 2120   Phone: (203) 432-4097
New Haven, CT 06520   Dr. Anne-Marie Logan, Libn./Photo Archv.

YALE UNIVERSITY - YALE COLLECTION OF HISTORICAL SOUND
     RECORDINGS
Sterling Memorial Library   Phone: (203) 436-1822
New Haven, CT 06520   Richard Warren, Jr., Cur.

CONNECTICUT COLLEGE - GREER MUSIC LIBRARY
                                       Phone: (203) 447-7535
New London, CT 06320   Philip Youngholm, Music Libn.

CONNECTICUT COLLEGE - LIBRARY - SPECIAL COLLECTIONS
Mohegan Ave.   Phone: (203) 442-1630
New London, CT 06320   Brian D. Rogers, Coll.Libn.

EUGENE O'NEILL MEMORIAL THEATER CENTER, INC. - MONTE CRISTO
     COTTAGE LIBRARY
325 Pequot Ave.   Phone: (203) 443-0051
New London, CT 06320   Sally Thomas Pavetti, Cur.

LYMAN ALLYN MUSEUM - LIBRARY
625 Williams St.   Phone: (203) 443-2345
New London, CT 06320   Marianne S. Dinsmore, Libn.

NEW LONDON COUNTY HISTORICAL SOCIETY - LIBRARY
11 Blinman St.   Phone: (203) 443-1209
New London, CT 06320   Elizabeth B. Knox, Sec./Libn./Cur.

U.S. COAST GUARD ACADEMY - LIBRARY
                                       Phone: (203) 444-8510
New London, CT 06320   Paul H. Johnson, Hd.Libn.

U.S. NAVY - NAVAL UNDERWATER SYSTEMS CENTER - NEW LONDON
     TECHNICAL LIBRARY †
Bldg. 80   Phone: (203) 447-4276
New London, CT 06320   David L. Hanna, Hd.Libn.

WOMEN'S CENTER OF SOUTHEASTERN CONNECTICUT - LIBRARY *
120 Broad St.
Box 572   Phone: (203) 447-0366
New London, CT 06320   Jessica S. Owaroff, Libn.

NEW MILFORD HOSPITAL - HEALTH SCIENCES LIBRARY
21 Elm St.   Phone: (203) 355-2611
New Milford, CT 06776   Susan E. Hays, Health Sci.Libn.

WESTRECO, INC. - TECHNICAL LIBRARY
Boardman Rd.   Phone: (203) 355-0911
New Milford, CT 06776   Jean Trapani, Mgr., Info.Serv.

CEDARCREST REGIONAL HOSPITAL - MEDICAL LIBRARY
525 Russell Rd.   Phone: (203) 666-4613
Newington, CT 06111   Mary L. Conlon, Libn.

LOCTITE CORPORATION - RESEARCH AND DEVELOPMENT LIBRARY
705 N. Mountain Rd.   Phone: (203) 278-1280
Newington, CT 06111   Daniel L. Weinstein, Corp.Libn.

NEWINGTON CHILDREN'S HOSPITAL - PROFESSIONAL LIBRARY
181 E. Cedar St.   Phone: (203) 667-5380
Newington, CT 06111   Jean Long, Dir., Prof.Lib.

U.S. VETERANS ADMINISTRATION (CT-Newington) - HOSPITAL HEALTH
     SCIENCES LIBRARY
555 Willard Ave.   Phone: (203) 666-6951
Newington, CT 06111   Julie A. Lueders, Chf., Lib.Serv.

FAIRFIELD HILLS HOSPITAL - HEALTH SCIENCES LIBRARY
Box W   Phone: (203) 426-2531
Newtown, CT 06470   Pauline A. Kruk, Libn.

WHITNEY (Eli) MUSEUM - LIBRARY
Route 139   Phone: (203) 488-2157
North Branford, CT 06471   Merrill K. Lindsay, Pres.

AREA COOPERATIVE EDUCATIONAL SERVICES - TEACHER LIBRARY
295 Mill Rd.   Phone: (203) 234-0130
North Haven, CT 06473   Virginia Evitts, Libn.

UPJOHN COMPANY - D.S. GILMORE RESEARCH LABORATORIES - LIBRARY †
410 Sackett Point Rd.   Phone: (203) 281-2782
North Haven, CT 06473   A. Munim Nashu, EPA Coord./Libn.

EASTCONN - PROJECT CONNECT - LIBRARY
Rt. 203, Box 245   Phone: (203) 456-3254
North Windham, CT 06256   Linda Welchman

BURNDY LIBRARY
Electra Sq.   Phone: (203) 852-6294
Norwalk, CT 06856   Dr. Bern Dibner, Dir.

HOFFREL INSTRUMENTS, INC. - LIBRARY *
345 Wilson Ave.
Box 825   Phone: (203) 866-9205
Norwalk, CT 06856   Donald P. Relyes, Hd.

NEW ENGLAND INSTITUTE - LIBRARY *
90 Grove St.
Box 308   Phone: (203) 762-7369
Norwalk, CT 06877   M. Vaccaro, Asst.Libn.

NORDEN SYSTEMS, INC. - TECHNICAL LIBRARY
Norden Pl.   Phone: (203) 852-4724
Norwalk, CT 06856   Bernice Astheimer, Br.Libn.

NORWALK HOSPITAL - R. GLEN WIGGANS MEMORIAL LIBRARY
Maple St.   Phone: (203) 852-2793
Norwalk, CT 06856   Joan Sjostrom, Dir.

NORWALK STATE TECHNICAL COLLEGE - LIBRARY
181 Richards Ave.   Phone: (203) 838-0601
Norwalk, CT 06854   Rita Schara, Libn.

PERKIN-ELMER CORPORATION - CORPORATE LIBRARY
Main Ave.   Phone: (203) 834-4798
Norwalk, CT 06856   Margaret D. Wood, Mgr.

PURDUE FREDERICK COMPANY - RESEARCH LIBRARY
100 Connecticut Ave.   Phone: (203) 853-0123
Norwalk, CT 06856   Kathryn Walsh, Libn.

BACKUS (William W.) HOSPITAL - MEDICAL/NURSING LIBRARY *
326 Washington St.   Phone: (203) 889-8331
Norwich, CT 06360   Florence Lamoureux, Med.Libn.

BETH JACOB SYNAGOGUE - LIBRARY
400 New London Tpke.   Phone: (203) 886-2459
Norwich, CT 06360

NORWICH HOSPITAL - HEALTH SCIENCES LIBRARY
Box 508   Phone: (203) 889-7361
Norwich, CT 06360   Julia M. Smith, Libn.

SOCIETY OF THE FOUNDERS OF NORWICH, CONNECTICUT - LEFFINGWELL
    INN LIBRARY
348 Washington St.
Norwich, CT 06360   Linda Kate Edgerton, Libn.

WATERTOWN HISTORICAL SOCIETY INC. - LIBRARY
22 DeForest St.
Oakville, CT 06779   Florence Crowell, Cur.

LYME HISTORICAL SOCIETY, INC. - ARCHIVES
Lyme St.   Phone: (203) 434-5542
Old Lyme, CT 06371   Jeffrey W. Andersen, Dir.

INDIAN AND COLONIAL RESEARCH CENTER, INC. - EVA BUTLER LIBRARY
Route 27   Phone: (203) 536-9771
Old Mystic, CT 06372   Kathleen Greenhalgh, Libn.

TEMPLE EMANUEL - LIBRARY
150 Derby Ave.   Phone: (203) 397-3000
Orange, CT 06477   Michael S. Chosak, Chm., Lib.Comm.

YARDNEY ELECTRIC CORPORATION - TECHNICAL INFORMATION CENTER
    †
82 Mechanic St.   Phone: (203) 559-1100
Pawcatuck, CT 06379   Pamela J. Lochner, Libn.

ELMCREST PSYCHIATRIC INSTITUTE - PROFESSIONAL LIBRARY
25 Marlborough St.   Phone: (203) 342-0480
Portland, CT 06480   David Cimino, Media Techn.

BELDING HEMINWAY COMPANY - BELDING CORTICELLI RESEARCH
    CENTER - LIBRARY
                                             Phone: (203) 928-2784
Putnam, CT 06260   E.J. Page, Chf. Chemist

CONNECTICUT STATE LIBRARY - LAW LIBRARY AT PUTNAM
155 Church St.   Phone: (203) 928-3716
Putnam, CT 06260   Donna R. Izbicki, Libn.

BOEHRINGER INGELHEIM LTD. - SCIENTIFIC INFORMATION SERVICES
90 E. Ridge   Phone: (203) 748-4200
Ridgefield, CT 06877   Margaret Norman, Mgr., Sci.Info.Serv.

SCHLUMBERGER-DOLL - RESEARCH LIBRARY
Old Quarry Rd.
Box 307   Phone: (203) 431-5600
Ridgefield, CT 06877   Henry Edmundson, Mgr., Info.

CONNECTICUT STATE LIBRARY - LAW LIBRARY AT ROCKVILLE
Box 510   Phone: (203) 875-6294
Rockville, CT 06066   Virginia Scanlon, Libn.

ROCKVILLE GENERAL HOSPITAL - MEDICAL LIBRARY/RESOURCE ROOM †
31 Union St.   Phone: (203) 872-0501
Rockville, CT 06066   Dorothea M. Zabilansky, Med.Libn.

FRENCH-CANADIAN GENEALOGICAL SOCIETY OF CONNECTICUT, INC. -
    LIBRARY
Box 262   Phone: (203) 529-9040
Rocky Hill, CT 06067   Roderick A. Wilscam, Pres.

ROCKY HILL HISTORICAL SOCIETY - ACADEMY HALL MUSEUM - LIBRARY
785 Old Main St.
Box 185   Phone: (203) 563-8710
Rocky Hill, CT 06067   Mrs. Dudley S. Cooke, Libn.

ROGERS CORPORATION - LURIE LIBRARY
                                             Phone: (203) 774-9605
Rogers, CT 06263   Myrna D. Riquier, Corp.Libn.

SHARON HOSPITAL - HEALTH SCIENCES LIBRARY
W. Main St.   Phone: (203) 364-5511
Sharon, CT 06069

ITT ADVANCED TECHNOLOGY CENTER - LIBRARY
1 Research Dr.   Phone: (203) 929-7341
Shelton, CT 06484   Monica Denman, Tech.Libn.

RICHARDSON-VICKS, INC. - VICKS RESEARCH CENTER - LIBRARY
One Far Mill Crossing   Phone: (203) 929-2500
Shelton, CT 06484   Susanne Silverman, Libn.

SIMSBURY HISTORICAL SOCIETY - SIMSBURY RESEARCH LIBRARY
800 Hopmeadow St.   Phone: (203) 658-2500
Simsbury, CT 06070   Robert A. Hawley, Dir.

SOMERS HISTORICAL SOCIETY - ARCHIVES
574 Main St.   Phone: (203) 749-7273
Somers, CT 06071   Jeanne K. DeBell, Cur.

AMERICAN CYANAMID COMPANY - TECHNICAL INFORMATION SERVICES
1937 W. Main St.
Box 60   Phone: (203) 348-7331
Stamford, CT 06904   Martha Reiter, Mgr.

AMF, INC. - TECHNICAL INFORMATION CENTER
689 Hope St.   Phone: (203) 325-2211
Stamford, CT 06907   Maria B. Jacobson, Tech.Libn.

BARNES ENGINEERING COMPANY - LIBRARY
44 Commerce Rd.
Box 53   Phone: (203) 348-5381
Stamford, CT 06904   Belle B. Shipe, Libn.

BRAKELEY, JOHN PRICE JONES, INC. - LIBRARY
1600 Summer St.   Phone: (203) 348-8100
Stamford, CT 06905   Rose M. Price, Libn.

BUSINESS COMMUNICATIONS CO., INC. - LIBRARY
Box 2070C   Phone: (203) 325-2208
Stamford, CT 06906   Mehrnoz Rubin, Dir. of Oper.

CBS INC. - CBS TECHNOLOGY CENTER †
227 High Ridge Rd.   Phone: (203) 327-2000
Stamford, CT 06905   Rita Reade, Chf.Libn.

CHAMPION INTERNATIONAL - CORPORATE INFORMATION CENTER †
1 Champion Plaza   Phone: (203) 358-7390
Stamford, CT 06921   Phyllis Prince, Mgr.

CLAIROL, INC. - RESEARCH LIBRARY
2 Blachley Rd.   Phone: (203) 357-5001
Stamford, CT 06922   Theodora J. Reardon, Libn.

CONNECTICUT NEWSPAPERS INC. - ADVOCATE & GREENWICH TIME
    LIBRARY
75 Tresser Blvd.   Phone: (203) 964-2297
Stamford, CT 06904-9307   Anne McRae, Libn.

CONNECTICUT STATE BOARD OF EDUCATION - J.M. WRIGHT TECHNICAL
  SCHOOL - LIBRARY
Box 1416   Phone: (203) 324-7363
Stamford, CT 06904   Robert J. Dolan, Lib./Media Spec.

CONNECTICUT STATE LIBRARY - LAW LIBRARY AT STAMFORD
Court House, 123 Hoyt St.   Phone: (203) 359-1114
Stamford, CT 06905   Jonathan C. Stock, Libn.

CONTINENTAL GROUP, INC. - INFORMATION RESOURCE CENTER
One Harbor Plaza   Phone: (203) 964-6593
Stamford, CT 06904-2129   Debra Kaufman, Supv.

CRAWFORD AND RUSSELL, INC.-JOHN BROWN - TECHNICAL LIBRARY
17 Amelia Pl.
Box 1432   Phone: (203) 327-1450
Stamford, CT 06904   Bonnie Russ, Tech.Libn.

DORR-OLIVER INC. - CENTRAL TECHNOLOGY LIBRARY †
77 Havemeyer Lane   Phone: (203) 358-3770
Stamford, CT 06904   William D. Kallaway, Tech.Libn.

EASTER SEAL REHABILITATION CENTER OF SOUTHWESTERN
  CONNECTICUT - FRANCIS M. HARRISON MEMORIAL LIBRARY †
26 Palmer's Hill Rd.   Phone: (203) 325-1544
Stamford, CT 06902   Ruth C. Adams, Libn.

FERGUSON LIBRARY - BUSINESS-TECHNOLOGY DEPARTMENT
96 Broad St.   Phone: (203) 964-1000
Stamford, CT 06901   Doris Goodlett, Hd., Adult Serv.

FINANCIAL ACCOUNTING STANDARDS BOARD (FASB) - LIBRARY
High Ridge Pk.   Phone: (203) 329-8401
Stamford, CT 06905   Judith T. Rosum, Libn.

OLIN CORPORATION - BUSINESS INFORMATION CENTER
120 Long Ridge Rd.   Phone: (203) 356-2498
Stamford, CT 06904   L.A. Magistrate, Mgr., Bus.Onfo.

PITNEY BOWES - TECHNICAL INFORMATION CENTER †
Walter Wheeler Dr.   Phone: (203) 853-0727
Stamford, CT 06904   Mary Lynn Ainsworth, Mgr., Tech.Info.Ctr.

PROGRESSIVE GROCER - RESEARCH LIBRARY
1351 Washington Blvd.
Stamford, CT 06902   Shirley Palmer, Res.Libn.

ST. JOSEPH HOSPITAL - HEALTH SCIENCES LIBRARY
128 Strawberry Hill Ave.   Phone: (203) 327-3500
Stamford, CT 06904-1222   Lucille Lieberman, Dir.

STAMFORD CATHOLIC LIBRARY, INC. †
195 Glenbrook Rd.   Phone: (203) 348-4422
Stamford, CT 06902   Mary C. Cash, Libn.

STAMFORD HISTORICAL SOCIETY - LIBRARY
713 Bedford St.   Phone: (203) 323-1975
Stamford, CT 06901   Ann M. Hermann, Dir.

STAMFORD HOSPITAL - HEALTH SCIENCES LIBRARY
Shelburne Rd.
Box 9317   Phone: (203) 325-7522
Stamford, CT 06904-9317   Joanna Faraday, Dir.

TEXASGULF, INC. - RESEARCH LIBRARY †
High Ridge Park   Phone: (203) 358-5135
Stamford, CT 06904   Patricia R. O'Shea, Corp.Libn.

XEROX CORPORATION - LAW LIBRARY
                                          Phone: (203) 329-8700
Stamford, CT 06904   Geraldine McColgan Brown, Hd.Libn.

YORK RESEARCH CORPORATION - LIBRARY †
One Research Dr.   Phone: (203) 325-1371
Stamford, CT 06906   Barbara A. Goodhouse, Libn.

STONINGTON HISTORICAL SOCIETY - WHITEHALL LIBRARY
Box 2D2
Stonington, CT 06378   Capt. Robert J. Ramsbotham, Pres.

MANSFIELD HISTORICAL SOCIETY - EDITH MASON LIBRARY
954 Storrs Rd.
Box 145
Storrs, CT 06268   Richard Schimmelpfeng, Libn.

MOLESWORTH INSTITUTE - LIBRARY AND ARCHIVES
143 Hanks Hill Rd.   Phone: (203) 486-2220
Storrs, CT 06268   Cecily Cardew, Lib.Dir. & Archv.

UNIVERSITY OF CONNECTICUT - CENTER FOR REAL ESTATE & URBAN
  ECONOMIC STUDIES - REFERENCE & DOCUMENTS ROOM
U-41-RE   Phone: (203) 486-3227
Storrs, CT 06268   Judith B. Paesani, Asst.Dir.

UNIVERSITY OF CONNECTICUT - HOMER BABBIDGE LIBRARY - SPECIAL
  COLLECTIONS
                                          Phone: (203) 486-2524
Storrs, CT 06268   Richard H. Schimmelpfeng, Dir., Spec.Coll.

UNIVERSITY OF CONNECTICUT - INSTITUTE OF MATERIALS SCIENCE -
  READING ROOM
                                          Phone: (203) 486-3637
Storrs, CT 06268   Mary Roche, Adm.Asst.

UNIVERSITY OF CONNECTICUT - INSTITUTE FOR SOCIAL INQUIRY
Box U-164   Phone: (203) 486-4440
Storrs, CT 06268   Everett C. Ladd, Jr., Exec.Dir.

UNIVERSITY OF CONNECTICUT - INSTITUTE OF URBAN RESEARCH -
  LIBRARY
                                          Phone: (203) 486-4518
Storrs, CT 06268   Jean W. Gosselin, Educ.Asst.

UNIVERSITY OF CONNECTICUT - LABOR EDUCATION CENTER -
  INFORMATION CENTER
Bishop Bldg., Rm. 213   Phone: (203) 486-3417
Storrs, CT 06268   George E. O'Connell, Dir.

UNIVERSITY OF CONNECTICUT - LEARNING RESOURCES DIVISION -
  CENTER FOR INSTRUCTIONAL MEDIA & TECHNOLOGY
249 Glenbrook Rd., Rm. 3
Box U-1   Phone: (203) 486-2530
Storrs, CT 06268

UNIVERSITY OF CONNECTICUT - MAP LIBRARY
                                          Phone: (203) 486-4589
Storrs, CT 06268   Thornton P. McGlamery, Map Libn.

UNIVERSITY OF CONNECTICUT - MUSIC LIBRARY
U-12   Phone: (203) 486-2502
Storrs, CT 06268   Dorothy McAdoo Bognar, Hd.

UNIVERSITY OF CONNECTICUT - PHARMACY LIBRARY AND LEARNING
  CENTER
Box U-92   Phone: (203) 486-2218
Storrs, CT 06268   Georgia Scura, Dir.

UNIVERSITY OF CONNECTICUT - PUERTO RICAN CENTER - ROBERTO
  CLEMENTE LIBRARY
Univ. Box 188   Phone: (203) 486-2204
Storrs, CT 06268   Ino Rios, Dir.

UNIVERSITY OF CONNECTICUT - ROPER CENTER
Box U-164R   Phone: (203) 486-4440
Storrs, CT 06268   Everett C. Ladd, Exec.Dir.

UNIVERSITY OF CONNECTICUT - SCHOOL OF EDUCATION - I.N. THUT
  WORLD EDUCATION CENTER
Box U-32   Phone: (203) 486-3321
Storrs, CT 06268   Dr. Frank A. Stone, Dir.

AVCO - LYCOMING DIVISION - LIBRARY & TECHNICAL INFORMATION
  CENTER
550 S. Main St.   Phone: (202) 385-2547
Stratford, CT 06497   Lee G. Russell, Hd.Libn.

REMINGTON ARMS COMPANY, INC. - RESEARCH LIBRARY
Broadbridge Ave.   Phone: (203) 333-1112
Stratford, CT 06497

STRATFORD HISTORICAL SOCIETY - LIBRARY
967 Academy Hill
Box 382   Phone: (203) 378-0630
Stratford, CT 06497   Mrs. Einar M. Larson, Libn.

UNITED TECHNOLOGIES CORPORATION - SIKORSKY AIRCRAFT DIVISION
    - DIVISION LIBRARY
N. Main St.   Phone: (203) 386-4713
Stratford, CT 06601   Robert M. Knapik, Lib.Supv.

KENT MEMORIAL LIBRARY - HISTORICAL ROOM
50 N. Main St.   Phone: (203) 668-2325
Suffield, CT 06078   Anne W. Borg, Asst.Dir.

TORRINGTON HISTORICAL SOCIETY - LIBRARY
192 Main St.   Phone: (203) 482-8260
Torrington, CT 06790   Catherine Calhoun, Exec.Dir.

CHESEBROUGH-POND'S, INC. - RESEARCH LIBRARY
Trumbull Industrial Pk.   Phone: (203) 377-7100
Trumbull, CT 06611   Carol Gannon, Libn.

GAYLORD HOSPITAL - MEDICAL LIBRARY
Box 400   Phone: (203) 269-3344
Wallingford, CT 06492   Kathleen Byrne, Med.Libn.

WALLINGFORD HISTORICAL SOCIETY, INC. - LIBRARY
Box 73   Phone: (203) 269-6257
Wallingford, CT 06492   Peter P. Hale, Pres.

AMERICAN INDIAN ARCHAEOLOGICAL INSTITUTE, INC. - LIBRARY
Box 260   Phone: (203) 868-0518
Washington, CT 06793   Dr. Roger Moeller, Dir. of Res.

BRONSON (Silas) LIBRARY - BUSINESS, INDUSTRY, AND TECHNOLOGY
    DEPARTMENT †
267 Grand St.   Phone: (203) 574-8233
Waterbury, CT 06702   Blanche T. Clark, Dept.Hd.

CONDIESEL MOBILE EQUIPMENT - ENGINEERING LIBRARY
84 Progress Ln.   Phone: (203) 575-8840
Waterbury, CT 06705   Denise M. Mellott, Tech.Libn.

CONNECTICUT STATE LIBRARY - LAW LIBRARY AT WATERBURY †
Court House, 300 Grand St.   Phone: (203) 754-2644
Waterbury, CT 06702   Lucy L. Cyr, Libn.

COUNCIL OF GOVERNMENTS OF THE CENTRAL NAUGATUCK VALLEY -
    LIBRARY
20 E. Main St.   Phone: (203) 757-0535
Waterbury, CT 06702   Duncan M. Graham, Exec.Dir.

ST. MARY'S HOSPITAL - FINKELSTEIN LIBRARY
56 Franklin St.   Phone: (203) 574-6408
Waterbury, CT 06702   Jean Fuller, Libn.

UNIROYAL, INC. - TECHNICAL LIBRARY
Box 117   Phone: (203) 573-4509
Waterbury, CT 06720   D.H. Winslow, Mgr.

UNITED CEREBRAL PALSY ASSOCIATION OF THE GREATER WATERBURY
    AREA - PROFESSIONAL RESOURCE CENTER
61 Bidwell St.   Phone: (203) 756-7843
Waterbury, CT 06770   Thomas R. Briggs, Ph.D., Principal

WATERBURY AMERICAN-REPUBLICAN - LIBRARY
389 Meadow St.   Phone: (203) 574-3636
Waterbury, CT 06722   Mary B. Fuller, Libn.

WATERBURY HOSPITAL HEALTH CENTER - HEALTH CENTER LIBRARY
64 Robbins St.   Phone: (203) 573-6136
Waterbury, CT 06720   Mrs. M.F. Carmichael, Lib.Dir.

WATERBURY STATE TECHNICAL COLLEGE - HELEN HAHLO LIBRARY
1460 W. Main St.   Phone: (203) 575-8106
Waterbury, CT 06708   John Kiernan, Jr., Hd.Libn.

OPTIKON RESEARCH LABORATORIES - LIBRARY †
Box 947   Phone: (203) 672-6614
West Cornwall, CT 06796   William Covington, Libn.

CHANDLER EVANS, INC. - COMPANY LIBRARY †
One Charter Oak Blvd.   Phone: (203) 236-0651
West Hartford, CT 06101   Christina Jablonowski, Libn.

FIRST CHURCH OF CHRIST CONGREGATIONAL - JOHN P. WEBSTER
    LIBRARY
12 S. Main St.   Phone: (203) 233-9605
West Hartford, CT 06107   Rev. Lee K. Ellenwood, Lib.Dir.

UNIVERSITY OF CONNECTICUT - SCHOOL OF SOCIAL WORK - HARLEIGH B.
    TRECKER LIBRARY
Greater Hartford Campus   Phone: (203) 241-4722
West Hartford, CT 06117

UNIVERSITY OF HARTFORD - ANNE BUNCE CHENEY LIBRARY
200 Bloomfield Ave.   Phone: (203) 243-4397
West Hartford, CT 06117   Jean J. Miller, Libn.

UNIVERSITY OF HARTFORD - DANA SCIENCE & ENGINEERING LIBRARY
200 Bloomfield Ave., Dana Bldg.   Phone: (203) 243-4404
West Hartford, CT 06117   Frances T. Libbey, Sci./Engr.Libn.

UNIVERSITY OF HARTFORD - HARTT SCHOOL OF MUSIC - ALLEN
    MEMORIAL LIBRARY
200 Bloomfield Ave.   Phone: (203) 243-4491
West Hartford, CT 06117   Ethel Bacon, Libn.

WEBSTER (Noah) FOUNDATION & HISTORICAL SOCIETY OF WEST
    HARTFORD - LIBRARY
227 S. Main St.   Phone: (203) 521-5362
West Hartford, CT 06107   Elliott W. Hoffman, Dir.

MILES LABORATORIES, INC. - DELBAY PHARMACEUTICALS - RESEARCH
    LIBRARY
400 Morgan Lane   Phone: (203) 934-9221
West Haven, CT 06516   M.W. Jackson, Sr.Libn.

U.S. VETERANS ADMINISTRATION (CT-West Haven) - MEDICAL CENTER
    LIBRARY
West Spring St.   Phone: (203) 932-5711
West Haven, CT 06516   William J. Preston, Chf., Lib.Serv.

GREENWOOD PRESS - LIBRARY
88 Post Rd., W.
Box 5007   Phone: (203) 226-3571
Westport, CT 06881   Mary Kalb, Urban Doc.Prog.

HALL-BROOKE HOSPITAL - PROFESSIONAL LIBRARY
47 Long Lots Rd.   Phone: (203) 227-1251
Westport, CT 06881   Janet B. Pankiewicz, Libn.

HUMAN LACTATION CENTER, LTD. - LIBRARY
666 Sturges Hwy.   Phone: (203) 259-5995
Westport, CT 06880   Dana Raphael, Dir.

LIFWYNN FOUNDATION, INC. - LIBRARY
30 Turkey Hill Rd., S.   Phone: (203) 227-4139
Westport, CT 06880   Alfreda S. Galt, Sec.

NATURE CENTER FOR ENVIRONMENTAL ACTIVITIES - REFERENCE
    LIBRARY
10 Woodside Ln.   Phone: (203) 227-7253
Westport, CT 06880   Mary Lou Amirault, Libn.

SAVE THE CHILDREN FOUNDATION, INC. - LIBRARY
54 Wilton Rd.   Phone: (203) 226-7271
Westport, CT 06880   Nancy N. Faesy, Libn.

STAUFFER CHEMICAL COMPANY - CORPORATE LIBRARY
Nyala Farm Rd.   Phone: (203) 222-4371
Westport, CT 06881   Jose G. Escarilla, Jr., Corp.Libn.

WETHERSFIELD HISTORICAL SOCIETY - OLD ACADEMY MUSEUM LIBRARY
150 Main St.   Phone: (203) 529-7656
Wethersfield, CT 06109   C. Douglas Alves, Jr., Dir.

EASTERN CONNECTICUT STATE UNIVERSITY - CENTER FOR
    CONNECTICUT STUDIES
J. Eugene Smith Library   Phone: (203) 456-2231
Willimantic, CT 06226   Dr. David M. Roth, Dir.

CRAFT CENTER MUSEUM - CRAFT CENTER LIBRARY
78 Danbury Rd.
Box 488
Wilton, CT 06897   Miss E. Gilbaine, Libn.

NABISCO BRANDS, INC. - TECHNICAL INFORMATION CENTER
15 River Rd.   Phone: (203) 762-2500
Wilton, CT 06987   Lois A. Samuels, Libn.

NOVO LABORATORIES INC. - LIBRARY
59 Danbury Rd.   Phone: (203) 762-2401
Wilton, CT 06897-0608   James W. Fleagle, Mgr., Info.Serv.

RICHARDSON-VICKS, INC. - MARKETING INFORMATION CENTER
10 Westport Rd.   Phone: (203) 834-5000
Wilton, CT 06897   Mary Lou Wells, Mgr.

WILTON HISTORICAL SOCIETY, INC. - LIBRARY
249 Danbury Rd.   Phone: (203) 762-7257
Wilton, CT 06897

COMBUSTION ENGINEERING, INC. - POWER SYSTEMS GROUP LIBRARY
    SERVICES †
Dept. 6435-405   Phone: (203) 688-1911
Windsor, CT 06095   Zena C. Grot-Zakrzewski, Mgr.

EMHART INDUSTRIES, INC. - HARTFORD DIVISION LIBRARY
123 Day Hill Rd.
Box 700
Windsor, CT 06095

WINDSOR HISTORICAL SOCIETY, INC. - LIBRARY
96 Palisado Ave.   Phone: (203) 688-3813
Windsor, CT 06095   Robert T. Silliman, Dir.

CONNECTICUT AERONAUTICAL HISTORICAL ASSOCIATION - NEW
    ENGLAND AIR MUSEUM REFERENCE LIBRARY
Bradley International Airport   Phone: (203) 623-3305
Windsor Locks, CT 06096   John W. Ramsay, Dir., Hist. & Info.

DEXTER CORPORATION - C.H. DEXTER DIVISION - TECHNICAL LIBRARY
Two Elm St.   Phone: (203) 623-9801
Windsor Locks, CT 06096   Fred N. Masters, Jr., Mgr.Tech.Info.Rsrcs.

NORTHWESTERN CONNECTICUT COMMUNITY COLLEGE - LIBRARY
Park Place   Phone: (203) 379-8543
Winsted, CT 06098   Arthur Pethybridge, Dir. of Lib.Serv.

WINCHESTER HISTORICAL SOCIETY - ARCHIVE
225 Prospect St.
Box 206   Phone: (203) 379-8433
Winsted, CT 06098   Pauline Fancher, Cur.

DELAWARE

GETTY REFINING AND MARKETING COMPANY - TECHNICAL LIBRARY
                    Phone: (302) 834-6247
Delaware City, DE 19706   K.C. Jordan, Libn.

GOVERNOR BACON HEALTH CENTER - MEDICAL LIBRARY
                    Phone: (302) 834-9201
Delaware City, DE 19706   Ivonne K. Go, Libn.

DELAWARE STATE DEPARTMENT OF COMMUNITY AFFAIRS - DIVISION OF
    LIBRARIES
43 S. Dupont Hwy.
Box 639   Phone: (302) 736-4748
Dover, DE 19903   Sylvia Short, State Libn.

DELAWARE STATE DEPARTMENT OF PUBLIC INSTRUCTION - LIBRARY
    INFORMATION CENTER
Townsend Bldg.
Box 1402   Phone: (302) 736-4692
Dover, DE 19903   Richard L. Krueger, Lib.Spec.

DELAWARE STATE DEPARTMENT OF TRANSPORTATION - LIBRARY
Rte. 113, Administrative Bldg.   Phone: (302) 678-4157
Dover, DE 19901   Juliana Cheng, Libn.

DELAWARE STATE DEVELOPMENT OFFICE - TECHNICAL LIBRARY
99 Kings Hwy.   Phone: (302) 736-4271
Dover, DE 19903   Cora Bonniwell

DELAWARE STATE DIV. OF HISTORICAL & CULTURAL AFFAIRS - BUR. OF
    MUSEUMS & HISTORIC SITES - E.R. JOHNSON MEM. COLL.
Delaware State Museum
316 S. Governors Ave.   Phone: (302) 736-3262
Dover, DE 19901

DELAWARE STATE DIVISION OF HISTORICAL & CULTURAL AFFAIRS -
    DELAWARE STATE ARCHIVES
Hall of Records   Phone: (302) 736-5318
Dover, DE 19901   Roy H. Tryon, Chf./Archv. & Rec.Mgt.Bur

DELAWARE STATE GENERAL ASSEMBLY - LEGISLATIVE LIBRARY
Box 1401   Phone: (302) 736-5808
Dover, DE 19901   Ruth Ann Melson, Libn.

DELAWARE STATE LAW LIBRARY IN KENT COUNTY
Kent County Courthouse   Phone: (302) 736-5467
Dover, DE 19901   Carol N. Russell, Law Libn.

DELAWARE STATE TRAVEL SERVICE
99 Kings Hwy.
Box 1401   Phone: (302) 678-4254
Dover, DE 19903   Janice C. Geddes, Dir. of Tourism

U.S. AIR FORCE BASE - DOVER BASE LIBRARY †
FL 4497   Phone: (302) 678-6246
Dover AFB, DE 19901   Linda Yorde, Lib.Techn.

DELAWARE MUSEUM OF NATURAL HISTORY - LIBRARY
Kennett Pike, Rte. 52
Box 3937   Phone: (302) 658-9111
Greenville, DE 19807   Robert L. Dimit, Dir.

UNIVERSITY OF DELAWARE, NEWARK - COLLEGE OF MARINE STUDIES -
    MARINE STUDIES COMPLEX LIBRARY
Harry L. Cannon Marine Studies Laboratory   Phone: (302) 645-4290
Lewes, DE 19958   Dorothy Allen, Marine Stud.Lib.Supv.

DELAWARE STATE HOSPITAL - MEDICAL LIBRARY
Rte. 13   Phone: (302) 421-6368
New Castle, DE 19720   Ruth A. Irwin, Libn.

DELAWARE STATE GEOLOGICAL SURVEY - LIBRARY
101 Penny Hall
University of Delaware   Phone: (302) 451-2833
Newark, DE 19716   Robert R. Jordan, State Geologist

DU PONT DE NEMOURS (E.I.) & COMPANY, INC. - HASKELL LABORATORY
    FOR TOXICOLOGY & INDUSTRIAL MEDICINE - LIBRARY
Elkton Rd.
Box 50   Phone: (302) 366-5225
Newark, DE 19714   Nancy S. Selzer, Libn.

DU PONT DE NEMOURS (E.I.) & COMPANY, INC. - STINE LABORATORY
    LIBRARY †
Elkton Rd.
Box 30   Phone: (302) 366-5354
Newark, DE 19711   Virginia Bredemeier, Libn.

INTERNATIONAL READING ASSOCIATION - RALPH C. STAIGER LIBRARY
800 Barksdale Rd.
Box 8139   Phone: (302) 731-1600
Newark, DE 19714-8139   Wendy Wei, Libn.

PIAGET (Jean) SOCIETY - LIBRARY
College of Education
University of Delaware   Phone: (609) 921-9000
Newark, DE 19716   George Forman, Pres.

PRODUCE MARKETING ASSOCIATION - PMA INFORMATION CENTER
700 Barksdale Plaza
Phone: (302) 738-7100
Newark, DE 19711   J.S. Raybourn, Staff V.P., Commun.

UNIVERSITY OF DELAWARE, NEWARK - AGRICULTURE LIBRARY
002 Agricultural Hall
Phone: (302) 451-2530
Newark, DE 19711   Frederick B. Getze, Assoc.Libn.

UNIVERSITY OF DELAWARE, NEWARK - ARCHIVES
78 E. Delaware Ave.
Phone: (302) 451-2750
Newark, DE 19711   John M. Clayton, Jr., Archv./Dir., Rec.Mgt

UNIVERSITY OF DELAWARE, NEWARK - CENTER FOR COMPOSITE
   MATERIALS - COMPOSITE MATERIALS REFERENCE ROOM
201 Spencer Laboratory   Phone: (302) 738-8149
Newark, DE 19716

UNIVERSITY OF DELAWARE, NEWARK - CHEMISTRY/CHEMICAL
   ENGINEERING LIBRARY
202 Brown Laboratory   Phone: (302) 451-2993
Newark, DE 19711   Grace Vattilano, Chem.Lib.Supv.

UNIVERSITY OF DELAWARE, NEWARK - COLLEGE OF EDUCATION -
   COMPUTER BASED EDUCATION RESEARCH LIBRARY
Willard Hall Education Bldg., Rm. 105   Phone: (302) 451-2927
Newark, DE 19711   Gary A. Feurer, Coord.

UNIVERSITY OF DELAWARE, NEWARK - COLLEGE OF URBAN AFFAIRS -
   LIBRARY *
Willard Hall Bldg.   Phone: (302) 451-2394
Newark, DE 19711   Mary Helen Callahan, Accounts Adm.

UNIVERSITY OF DELAWARE, NEWARK - DISASTER RESEARCH CENTER -
   LIBRARY
                                                Phone: (302) 451-2581
Newark, DE 19716

UNIVERSITY OF DELAWARE, NEWARK - EDUCATION RESOURCE CENTER
013 Willard Hall Education Bldg.   Phone: (302) 451-2335
Newark, DE 19716   Janet Hill Dove, Dir.

UNIVERSITY OF DELAWARE, NEWARK - HUGH M. MORRIS LIBRARY -
   PHYSICS BRANCH LIBRARY
221 Sharp Laboratory   Phone: (302) 451-2323
Newark, DE 19711   Joseph W. Bradley, Physics Lib.Supv.

BISSELL (Emily P.) HOSPITAL - MEDICAL LIBRARY
3000 Newport Gap Pike   Phone: (302) 995-8435
Wilmington, DE 19808   Margaret A. Lacy, Med.Serv.Sec.

COLUMBIA GAS SYSTEM SERVICE CORPORATION - LAW LIBRARY
20 Montchanin Rd.   Phone: (302) 429-5320
Wilmington, DE 19807   Kathryn C. Bossler, Law Libn.

DELAWARE ACADEMY OF MEDICINE - LIBRARY
1925 Lovering Ave.   Phone: (302) 656-1629
Wilmington, DE 19806   Gail P. Gill, Libn.

DELAWARE ART MUSEUM - LIBRARY
2301 Kentmere Pkwy.   Phone: (302) 571-9590
Wilmington, DE 19806   Anne Marie Haslam, Libn.

DELAWARE LAW SCHOOL OF WIDENER UNIVERSITY - LAW LIBRARY
Concord Pike, Box 7475   Phone: (302) 478-5280
Wilmington, DE 19803   Richard H. Humphreys, Libn.

DIOCESE OF WILMINGTON - OFFICE OF TOTAL EDUCATION - RESOURCE
   CENTER
1626 N. Union St.   Phone: (302) 655-8555
Wilmington, DE 19806   Kathleen Triboletti, Resource Coord.

DU PONT (Alfred I.) INSTITUTE OF THE NEMOURS FOUNDATION LIBRARY
Box 269   Phone: (302) 651-5820
Wilmington, DE 19899   Joan Fierberg, Dir. of Lib.Serv./Libn.

DU PONT DE NEMOURS (E.I.) & COMPANY, INC. - LAVOISIER LIBRARY
Central Research & Development Dept.
Experimental Sta.   Phone: (302) 772-2086
Wilmington, DE 19898   Frances E. Parsons, Lib.Supv.

DU PONT DE NEMOURS (E.I.) & COMPANY, INC. - LEGAL DEPARTMENT
   LIBRARY
6067 Du Pont Bldg.   Phone: (302) 774-3307
Wilmington, DE 19898   M. Jane DiCecco, Law Libn.

DU PONT DE NEMOURS (E.I.) & COMPANY, INC. - LIBRARY NETWORK
Montchanin G-3   Phone: (302) 774-7232
Wilmington, DE 19898   Helen S. Strolle, Lib. Network Mgr.

GOLDEY BEACOM COLLEGE - J. WILBUR HIRONS LIBRARY
4701 Limestone Rd.   Phone: (302) 998-8814
Wilmington, DE 19808   R.M. Beach, Dir.

HAGLEY MUSEUM AND LIBRARY
Greenville
Box 3630   Phone: (302) 658-2400
Wilmington, DE 19807   Dr. Richmond D. Williams, Dp.Dir. for Lib.Adm.

HERCULES, INC. - LAW DEPARTMENT LIBRARY †
1313 Market St.   Phone: (302) 594-5000
Wilmington, DE 19894   Brenda S. Burris, Law Libn.

HERCULES, INC. - LIBRARY
Hercules Plaza, 4160NW   Phone: (302) 594-5401
Wilmington, DE 19894   Barbara Beaman, Supv.

HERCULES, INC. - RESEARCH CENTER - TECHNICAL INFORMATION
   DIVISION
                                                Phone: (302) 995-3484
Wilmington, DE 19899   Dr. H.H. Espy, Mgr.

HISTORICAL SOCIETY OF DELAWARE - LIBRARY
505 Market Street Mall   Phone: (302) 655-7161
Wilmington, DE 19801   Dr. Barbara E. Benson, Dir. of Lib.

HOLY TRINITY (Old Swedes) CHURCH FOUNDATION, INC. - HENDRICKSON
   HOUSE LIBRARY
606 Church St.   Phone: (302) 652-5629
Wilmington, DE 19801   Ann Lee S. Bugbee, Cur.

ICI AMERICAS INC. - ATLAS LIBRARY
Concord Pike & New Murphy Rd.   Phone: (302) 575-8231
Wilmington, DE 19897   Velga B. Rukuts, Libn.

LOMBARDY HALL FOUNDATION - LIBRARY
1611 Concord Pike
Box 7036   Phone: (302) 772-4286
Wilmington, DE 19803   Harold J. Littleton, Pres./Cur.

MOUNT CUBA ASTRONOMICAL OBSERVATORY - LAMBERT L. JACKSON
   MEMORIAL LIBRARY
Greenville, Box 3915   Phone: (302) 654-6407
Wilmington, DE 19807   Leo G. Glasser, Dir.

NEW CASTLE COUNTY LAW LIBRARY
Public Bldg./Courthouse   Phone: (302) 571-2437
Wilmington, DE 19801   Rene Yucht, Hd.Libn.

RICHARDS, LAYTON & FINGER - LAW LIBRARY
One Rodney Square, 10th Fl.   Phone: (302) 658-6541
Wilmington, DE 19899   Crystal K. Rambo, Law Libn.

RIVERSIDE HOSPITAL - MEDICAL LIBRARY
700 Lea Blvd.   Phone: (302) 764-6120
Wilmington, DE 19802   Ruth Irwin, Cons.

ST. FRANCIS HOSPITAL, INC. - MEDICAL LIBRARY
7th & Clayton Sts.   Phone: (302) 421-4123
Wilmington, DE 19805   Sr. Joan Ignatius McCleary, O.S.F., Libn.

U.S. VETERANS ADMINISTRATION (DE-Wilmington) - CENTER MEDICAL
   LIBRARY
1601 Kirkwood Hwy.   Phone: (302) 994-2511
Wilmington, DE 19805   Donald A. Passidomo, Chf.Libn.

WILMINGTON MEDICAL CENTER (Delaware Division) - MEDICAL STAFF
   LIBRARY
501 W. 14th St.
Box 1668   Phone: (302) 428-2201
Wilmington, DE 19899   Helen St. Clair, Med.Libn.

WILMINGTON NEWS-JOURNAL COMPANY - LIBRARY
831 Orange St.   Phone: (302) 573-2038
Wilmington, DE 19899   Charlotte Walker, Chf.Libn.

YOUNG, CONAWAY, STARGATT & TAYLOR - LIBRARY
Rodney Sq. N., 11th Fl.
Box 391   Phone: (302) 571-6680
Wilmington, DE 19899-0391   Grace L. Simmons, Libn./Rec.Mgr.

DU PONT (Henry Francis) WINTERTHUR MUSEUM - LIBRARY
                                            Phone: (302) 656-8591
Winterthur, DE 19735   Dr. Frank H. Sommer, III, Hd. of Lib.

DISTRICT OF COLUMBIA

U.S. AIR FORCE - OFFICE OF SCIENTIFIC RESEARCH - LIBRARY
Bldg. 410   Phone: (202) 767-4910
Bolling AFB, DC 20332   Anthony G. Bialecki, Libn.

ACACIA MUTUAL LIFE INSURANCE COMPANY - LIBRARY
51 Louisiana Ave., N.W.   Phone: (202) 628-4506
Washington, DC 20001   Bonnie Bell, Mgr., Off.Serv.

ADMINISTRATIVE CONFERENCE OF THE UNITED STATES (ACUS) -
    LIBRARY
2120 L St., N.W., Suite 500   Phone: (202) 254-7065
Washington, DC 20037   Sue Judith Boley, Libn./Info.Off.

AEROSPACE CORPORATION - WASHINGTON LIBRARY
955 L'Enfant Plaza, S.W., Suite 4000   Phone: (202) 488-6154
Washington, DC 20024   Patricia W. Green, Libn.

AEROSPACE INDUSTRIES ASSOCIATION OF AMERICA - LIBRARY
1725 DeSales St., N.W.   Phone: (203) 429-4653
Washington, DC 20036   Mrs. Billie Ann Perry, Libn.

AFRICAN-AMERICAN LABOR CENTER (AALC) - LIBRARY *
1125 Fifteenth St., N.W.
Washington, DC 20005   John T. Sarr, Pubn.Off.

AHMADIYYA MOVEMENT IN ISLAM - MUSLIM LIBRARY *
2141 Leroy Place, N.W.   Phone: (202) 232-3737
Washington, DC 20008   Ata Ullah Kaleem, Info.Dir.

AIR FORCE ASSOCIATION - RESEARCH LIBRARY
1750 Pennsylvania Ave., N.W.   Phone: (202) 637-3300
Washington, DC 20006   Pearlie M. Draughn, Res.Libn.

AIR TRANSPORT ASSOCIATION OF AMERICA - LIBRARY
1709 New York Ave., N.W.   Phone: (202) 626-4184
Washington, DC 20006   Mrs. Marion Mistrik, Libn.

AIRPORT OPERATORS COUNCIL INTERNATIONAL - LIBRARY
1700 K St., N.W.   Phone: (202) 296-3270
Washington, DC 20006   Deborah E. Lunn, V.P., Pub.Rel.

ALEXANDER GRAHAM BELL ASSOCIATION FOR THE DEAF - VOLTA BUREAU
    LIBRARY
3417 Volta Place, N.W.   Phone: (202) 337-5220
Washington, DC 20007   Suzanne Pickering Neel, Dir., Prof.Prog./Serv.

ALLIANCE TO SAVE ENERGY - LIBRARY
1925 K St., N.W., Suite 507   Phone: (202) 857-0668
Washington, DC 20006   Robin Miller, Res.Assoc.

ALUMINUM ASSOCIATION - INFORMATION CENTER
818 Connecticut Ave., N.W.   Phone: (202) 862-5100
Washington, DC 20006   Robert J. Skarr, Mgr., Info.Ctr.

AMERICAN ACADEMY OF OPTOMETRY - LIBRARY
5530 Wisconsin Ave., N.W., Suite 950
Washington, DC 20815   Dr. Frank Brazelton, Sec.-Tres.

AMERICAN ASSOCIATION FOR THE ADVANCEMENT OF SCIENCE - LIBRARY
1515 Massachusetts Ave., N.W.   Phone: (202) 467-4428
Washington, DC 20005   Janet Kegg, Libn.

AMERICAN ASSOCIATION OF HIGHER EDUCATION - THE CENTER FOR
    LEARNING AND TELECOMMUNICATIONS
One Dupont Circle, Suite 600   Phone: (202) 293-6440
Washington, DC 20036   Marilyn Kressel, Dir.

AMERICAN ASSOCIATION OF MUSEUMS - MUSEUM RESOURCES AND
    INFORMATION SERVICE
1055 Thomas Jefferson St., N.W.
Washington, DC 20007   Sybil Walker, Ed.Asst.

AMERICAN ASSOCIATION OF RETIRED PERSONS - NATIONAL
    GERONTOLOGY RESOURCE CENTER †
1909 K St., N.W.   Phone: (202) 728-4700
Washington, DC 20049   Paula M. Lovas, Hd.

AMERICAN ASSOCIATION OF UNIVERSITY WOMEN - EDUCATIONAL
    FOUNDATION LIBRARY AND ARCHIVES
2401 Virginia Ave., N.W.   Phone: (202) 785-7763
Washington, DC 20037   Nancy L. Floyd, Lib.Info.Asst.

AMERICAN BANKERS ASSOCIATION - LIBRARY & INFORMATION SERVICES
1120 Connecticut Ave., N.W.   Phone: (202) 467-4180
Washington, DC 20036   Joan Gervino, Dir.

AMERICAN BAR ASSOCIATION - WASHINGTON OFFICE - INFORMATION
    SERVICES
1800 M St., N.W., 2nd Fl.   Phone: (202) 331-2207
Washington, DC 20036   Peggy A. Richter, Staff Dir.

AMERICAN CHEMICAL SOCIETY, INC. - LIBRARY
1155 16th St., N.W.   Phone: (202) 872-4509
Washington, DC 20036   Barbara A. Gallagher, Hd., Lib.Serv.

AMERICAN COLLEGE OF OBSTETRICIANS AND GYNECOLOGISTS -
    RESOURCE CENTER
600 Maryland Ave., S.W., Suite 300   Phone: (202) 638-5577
Washington, DC 20024   Pamela Van Hine, Libn.

AMERICAN COUNCIL ON EDUCATION - LIBRARY AND INFORMATION
    SERVICES
One Dupont Circle, Suite 640   Phone: (202) 833-4690
Washington, DC 20036   Judith A. Pfeiffer, Dir.

AMERICAN COUNCIL OF LIFE INSURANCE - LIBRARY
1850 K St., N.W.   Phone: (202) 862-4050
Washington, DC 20006   Kim Lowry, Supv., Lib.Serv.

AMERICAN ENTERPRISE INSTITUTE FOR PUBLIC POLICY RESEARCH -
    LIBRARY
1150 17th St., N.W.   Phone: (202) 862-5831
Washington, DC 20036   Evelyn B. Caldwell, Libn.

AMERICAN FEDERATION OF LABOR AND CONGRESS OF INDUSTRIAL
    ORGANIZATIONS - LIBRARY
815 16th St., N.W.   Phone: (202) 637-5297
Washington, DC 20006

AMERICAN FEDERATION OF STATE, COUNTY AND MUNICIPAL
    EMPLOYEES, AFL-CIO (AFSCME) - INFORMATION CENTER
1625 L St., N.W.   Phone: (202) 452-4882
Washington, DC 20036   William Wilkinson, Libn.

AMERICAN FILM INSTITUTE - RESOURCE CENTER
JFK Center for the Performing Arts   Phone: (202) 828-4088
Washington, DC 20566   Catherine Yelloz, Coord.

AMERICAN FORESTRY ASSOCIATION - LIBRARY
1319 18th St., N.W.   Phone: (202) 467-5810
Washington, DC 20036

AMERICAN HOME ECONOMICS ASSOCIATION - LIBRARY
2010 Massachusetts Ave., N.W.
Washington, DC 20036

AMERICAN INSTITUTE OF ARCHITECTS - LIBRARY
1735 New York Ave., N.W.   Phone: (202) 626-7493
Washington, DC 20006   Stephanie C. Byrnes, Libn.

AMERICAN INSTITUTES FOR RESEARCH - LIBRARY
1055 Thomas Jefferson St., N.W.   Phone: (202) 342-5000
Washington, DC 20007   Robert F. Archer, Libn.

AMERICAN LIBRARY ASSOCIATION - WASHINGTON OFFICE
110 Maryland Ave., N.E.
Box 54   Phone: (202) 547-4440
Washington, DC 20002   Eileen D. Cooke, Dir.

AMERICAN MEDICAL ASSOCIATION - WASHINGTON OFFICE LIBRARY
1101 Vermont Ave., N.W.   Phone: (202) 857-1338
Washington, DC 20005   James H. Jackson, Libn.

AMERICAN MINING CONGRESS - AMC LIBRARY
1920 N St., N.W., Suite 300   Phone: (202) 861-2813
Washington, DC 20036   Shirley Kessel, Libn.

AMERICAN PETROLEUM INSTITUTE - LIBRARY
1220 L St., N.W.   Phone: (202) 457-7269
Washington, DC 20005   Gladys E. Siegel, Libn.

AMERICAN PHARMACEUTICAL ASSOCIATION - FOUNDATION LIBRARY
2215 Constitution Ave., N.W.   Phone: (202) 429-7523
Washington, DC 20037   Colleen Pritchard, Libn.

AMERICAN PODIATRY ASSOCIATION - WILLIAM J. STICKEL MEMORIAL
  LIBRARY
20 Chevy Chase Circle, N.W.   Phone: (202) 537-4900
Washington, DC 20015   Roberta McVeigh, Libn.

AMERICAN PSYCHIATRIC ASSOCIATION - LIBRARY AND ARCHIVES
1400 K St., N.W.   Phone: (202) 682-6080
Washington, DC 20005   Zing Jung, Dir.

AMERICAN PSYCHOLOGICAL ASSOCIATION - PSYCHOLOGY TODAY
  LIBRARY
1200 17th St., N.W.   Phone: (202) 955-7800
Washington, DC 20036   Joshua Fischman, Res.

AMERICAN PUBLIC HEALTH ASSOCIATION - INTERNATIONAL HEALTH
  PROGRAMS - RESOURCE CENTER
1015 15th St., N.W.   Phone: (202) 789-5600
Washington, DC 20005   Gayle Gibbons, Info.Spec.

AMERICAN PUBLIC POWER ASSOCIATION - LIBRARY
2301 M St., N.W.   Phone: (202) 342-7200
Washington, DC 20037   Deborah Nuttall, Libn.

AMERICAN PUBLIC TRANSIT ASSOCIATION - APTA INFORMATION
  CENTER
1225 Connecticut Ave., N.W., Suite 200   Phone: (202) 828-2843
Washington, DC 20036   Tandy L. Stevens, Mgr.

AMERICAN PUBLIC WELFARE ASSOCIATION - RESOURCE CENTER
1125 15th St., N.W., Suite 300.   Phone: (202) 293-7550
Washington, DC 20005   Richard J. McKinney, Resource Ctr.Mgr.

AMERICAN RED CROSS - NATIONAL HEADQUARTERS LIBRARY
17th & D Sts., N.W.   Phone: (202) 737-8300
Washington, DC 20006   Roberta F. Biles, Lib.Dir.

AMERICAN SEED TRADE ASSOCIATION - LIBRARY
Suite 964 Executive Bldg.
1030 15th St., N.W.
Washington, DC 20005

AMERICAN SHORT LINE RAILROAD ASSOCIATION - LIBRARY
2000 Massachusetts Ave., N.W.   Phone: (202) 785-2250
Washington, DC 20036   P.H. Croft, Pres.

AMERICAN SOCIETY OF APPRAISERS - INTERNATIONAL VALUATION
  SCIENCES CENTRE LIBRARY
Box 17265   Phone: (703) 620-3838
Washington, DC 20041   Nancy Porciello, Hd.Libn.

AMERICAN SOCIETY OF ASSOCIATION EXECUTIVES - INFORMATION
  CENTRAL
1575 Eye St., N.W., 12th Fl.   Phone: (202) 626-2723
Washington, DC 20005   Elissa Matulis Myers, Dir., Member Serv.

AMERICAN SOCIETY FOR INFORMATION SCIENCE - INFORMATION
  CENTER
1010 Sixteenth St., N.W.   Phone: (202) 659-3644
Washington, DC 20036

AMERICAN SOCIETY OF INTERNATIONAL LAW - LIBRARY
2223 Massachusetts Ave., N.W.   Phone: (202) 265-4313
Washington, DC 20008   Helen S. Philos, Libn.

AMERICAN SOCIETY OF NOTARIES - LIBRARY
810 18th St., N.W.   Phone: (202) 347-7303
Washington, DC 20006   Eugene E. Hines, Exec.Dir.

AMERICAN SOCIETY OF TRAVEL AGENTS - LIBRARY
4400 MacArthur Blvd., N.W.   Phone: (202) 965-7520
Washington, DC 20007   Arthur Schiff, Staff V.P.

AMERICAN SYMPHONY ORCHESTRA LEAGUE - LIBRARY
633 E St., N.W.   Phone: (202) 628-0099
Washington, DC 20004

AMERICAN TEXTILE MANUFACTURERS INSTITUTE (ATMI) - LIBRARY
1101 Connecticut Ave., N.W., No. 300   Phone: (202) 862-0500
Washington, DC 20036   Mabry R. McCloud, Libn.

AMERICAN UNIVERSITY - FOREIGN AREA STUDIES LIBRARY
5010 Wisconsin Ave., N.W.   Phone: (202) 686-2740
Washington, DC 20016   Gilda Nimer, Libn.

AMERICAN UNIVERSITY - WASHINGTON COLLEGE OF LAW - LIBRARY
4400 Massachusetts Ave., N.W.   Phone: (202) 686-2625
Washington, DC 20016   Patrick E. Kehoe, Dir.

ANTIOCH SCHOOL OF LAW - LIBRARY *
1624 Crescent Place, N.W.   Phone: (202) 265-9500
Washington, DC 20009   William P. Statsky, Libn.

APPALACHIAN REGIONAL COMMISSION - LIBRARY
1666 Connecticut Ave., N.W.   Phone: (202) 673-7845
Washington, DC 20235   Della Smith, Libn.

ARENT, FOX, KINTNER, PLOTKIN & KAHN - LIBRARY †
1815 H St., N.W.   Phone: (202) 857-6296
Washington, DC 20006   Mark P. Shaw, Libn.

ARMENIAN ASSEMBLY CHARITABLE TRUST - LIBRARY AND INFORMATION
  CENTER
1420 N St., N.W.   Phone: (202) 332-3434
Washington, DC 20005   Ross Vartian, Adm.Dir.

ARMY AND NAVY CLUB - LIBRARY
Farragut Sq. & I St., N.W.
Washington, DC 20006

ARNOLD AND PORTER - LIBRARY
1200 New Hampshire Ave., N.W.   Phone: (202) 872-3994
Washington, DC 20036   James W. Shelar, Libn.

ASSOCIATED GENERAL CONTRACTORS OF AMERICA - JAMES L. ALLHANDS
  MEMORIAL LIBRARY
1957 E St., N.W.   Phone: (202) 393-2040
Washington, DC 20006   John C. Ellis, Dir.

ASSOCIATION OF AMERICAN MEDICAL COLLEGES - ARCHIVES
One DuPont Circle, N.W.   Phone: (202) 828-0400
Washington, DC 20008   Mary H. Littlemeyer, Archv.

ASSOCIATION OF AMERICAN RAILROADS - ECONOMICS AND FINANCE
  DEPARTMENT - RAIL INFORMATION CENTER
American Railroads Bldg., Rm. 523
1920 L St., N.W.   Phone: (202) 835-9387
Washington, DC 20036   Helen M. Rowland, Supv., Lib.Serv.

ASSOCIATION FOR GERONTOLOGY IN HIGHER EDUCATION - RESOURCE
  LIBRARY
600 Maryland Ave., S.W., West Wing 204   Phone: (202) 484-7505
Washington, DC 20024   Elizabeth Douglass, Exec.Dir.

ASSOCIATION OF GOVERNING BOARDS OF UNIVERSITIES AND COLLEGES -
    TRUSTEE INFORMATION CENTER
One Dupont Circle, Suite 400   Phone: (202) 296-8400
Washington, DC 20036   Linda E. Henderson, Info.Ctr.Coord.

ASSOCIATION OF STUDENT INTERNATIONAL LAW SOCIETIES -
    INFORMATION CENTER
2223 Massachusetts Ave., N.W.   Phone: (202) 387-8467
Washington, DC 20008   Elizabeth L. Rodgers, Exec.Sec.

ASSOCIATION FOR THE STUDY OF AFRO-AMERICAN LIFE AND HISTORY,
    INC. - CARTER G. WOODSON LIBRARY
1401 14th St., N.W.
Washington, DC 20005

ASSOCIATION OF TRIAL LAWYERS OF AMERICA - ATLA LIBRARY
1050 31st St., N.W.   Phone: (202) 965-3500
Washington, DC 20007   Keith A. Searls, Libn.

AT & T - GOVERNMENT COMMUNICATIONS LIBRARY
1120 20th St., N.W., 5th Fl.   Phone: (202) 457-3028
Washington, DC 20036   Mary B. Freeman, Staff Supv.-Lib.

ATLANTIC COUNCIL OF THE UNITED STATES, INC. - LIBRARY
1616 H St., N.W.   Phone: (202) 347-9353
Washington, DC 20006   June Haley, Libn.

AUSTRALIAN EMBASSY - LIBRARY
1601 Massachusetts Ave., N.W.   Phone: (202) 797-3126
Washington, DC 20036   Patricia Kay, Libn.

BAR ASSOCIATION OF THE DISTRICT OF COLUMBIA - LIBRARY †
3518 U.S. Court House Bldg.   Phone: (202) 535-3573
Washington, DC 22101   Elizabeth K. Van Horn, Libn.

BARBER (Richard J.) ASSOCIATES, INC. - LIBRARY
1828 L St., N.W., Suite 406   Phone: (202) 785-0597
Washington, DC 20036   Verna Wolfe, Chf.Libn.

BIO-ENERGY COUNCIL - LIBRARY
1625 Eye St., N.W.   Phone: (202) 833-5656
Washington, DC 20006   Dr. Paul F. Bente, Jr., Exec.Dir.

BRAZILIAN-AMERICAN CULTURAL INSTITUTE, INC. - HAROLD E.
    WIBBERLEY, JR. LIBRARY
4201 Connecticut Ave., N.W., Suite 211   Phone: (202) 362-8334
Washington, DC 20008   Paulo Costa, Libn.

BROADCAST PIONEERS LIBRARY
1771 N St., N.W.   Phone: (202) 223-0088
Washington, DC 20036   Catharine Heinz, Dir.

BROOKINGS INSTITUTION - LIBRARY
1775 Massachusetts Ave., N.W.   Phone: (202) 797-6240
Washington, DC 20036   Laura Walker, Libn.

BUREAU OF NATIONAL AFFAIRS, INC. - LIBRARY AND INFORMATION
    CENTER
1231 25th St., N.W.   Phone: (202) 452-4466
Washington, DC 20037   Mildred Mason, Dir.

BUREAU OF SOCIAL SCIENCE RESEARCH - LIBRARY
1990 M St., N.W.   Phone: (202) 223-4300
Washington, DC 20036

BUSINESS AND PROFESSIONAL WOMEN'S FOUNDATION - MARGUERITE
    RAWALT RESOURCE CENTER
2012 Massachusetts Ave., N.W.   Phone: (202) 293-1200
Washington, DC 20036   Cheryl A. Sloan, Libn.

CAHILL GORDON & REINDEL - LIBRARY
1990 K St., N.W., Suite 950   Phone: (202) 862-8960
Washington, DC 20006   Mary J. Becker, Law Libn.

CANADIAN EMBASSY - LIBRARY
1771 N St., N.W.   Phone: (202) 785-1400
Washington, DC 20036   Ms. Merle G. Fabian, Libn.

CAPITOL HILL HOSPITAL - WILLIAM MERCER SPRIGG MEMORIAL LIBRARY
700 Constitution Ave., N.E.   Phone: (202) 269-8729
Washington, DC 20002   Mrs. Penny Martin, Med.Libn.

CAPLIN & DRYSDALE - LIBRARY †
1101 17th St., N.W., Suite 1100   Phone: (202) 862-5073
Washington, DC 20036   Karen M. Meyer, Law Libn.

CARMELITANA COLLECTION
1600 Webster St., N.E.   Phone: (202) 526-1221
Washington, DC 20017   Calvin Alderson, O.C., Dir.

CARNEGIE INSTITUTION OF WASHINGTON - GEOPHYSICAL LABORATORY
    LIBRARY
2801 Upton St., N.W.   Phone: (202) 966-0334
Washington, DC 20008   Dolores M. Petry, Libn.

CARNEGIE INSTITUTION OF WASHINGTON - LIBRARY †
1530 P St., N.W.   Phone: (202) 387-6411
Washington, DC 20005   Pat Parratt, Libn.

CARNEGIE INSTITUTION OF WASHINGTON - TERRESTRIAL MAGNETISM
    DEPARTMENT LIBRARY
5241 Broad Branch Rd., N.W.   Phone: (202) 966-0863
Washington, DC 20015   Dorothy B. Dillin, Libn.

CATHOLIC UNIVERSITY OF AMERICA - CHEMISTRY LIBRARY
301 Maloney Bldg.   Phone: (202) 635-5389
Washington, DC 20064   N.L. Powell, Coord., Campus Libs.

CATHOLIC UNIVERSITY OF AMERICA - CLEMENTINE LIBRARY
Mullen Library, Rm. 400-401   Phone: (202) 635-5091
Washington, DC 20064   Carolyn T. Lee, Cur.

CATHOLIC UNIVERSITY OF AMERICA - DEPARTMENT OF ARCHIVES AND
    MANUSCRIPTS
Mullen Library, Rm. 4   Phone: (202) 635-5065
Washington, DC 20064   Dr. Anthony Zito, Univ.Archv.

CATHOLIC UNIVERSITY OF AMERICA - ENGINEERING/ARCHITECTURE/
    MATHEMATICS LIBRARY
200 Pangborn Bldg.   Phone: (202) 635-5167
Washington, DC 20064   Robert Kimberlin, Act.Hd.

CATHOLIC UNIVERSITY OF AMERICA - LIBRARY SCIENCE LIBRARY
Marist Bldg.
620 Michigan Ave., N.E.   Phone: (202) 635-5092
Washington, DC 20064   Vivian Templin, Act.Hd.

CATHOLIC UNIVERSITY OF AMERICA - MUSIC LIBRARY
Ward Music Bldg.   Phone: (202) 635-5424
Washington, DC 20064   Elizabeth M. Libbey, Music Libn.

CATHOLIC UNIVERSITY OF AMERICA - NURSING/BIOLOGY LIBRARY
                                             Phone: (202) 635-5411
Washington, DC 20064   N.L. Powell, Libn.

CATHOLIC UNIVERSITY OF AMERICA - OLIVEIRA LIMA LIBRARY
                                             Phone: (202) 635-5059
Washington, DC 20064   Manoel Cardozo, Cur.

CATHOLIC UNIVERSITY OF AMERICA - PHYSICS LIBRARY
208 Keane Bldg.   Phone: (202) 635-5320
Washington, DC 20064   N.L. Powell, Coord., Campus Libs.

CATHOLIC UNIVERSITY OF AMERICA - RELIGIOUS STUDIES/
    PHILOSOPHY/HUMANITIES DIVISION LIBRARY
Mullen Library, Rm. 300   Phone: (202) 635-5088
Washington, DC 20064   Bruce Miller, Coord.

CATHOLIC UNIVERSITY OF AMERICA - SCHOOL OF LAW - ROBERT J.
    WHITE LAW LIBRARY
Michigan Ave.   Phone: (202) 635-5000
Washington, DC 20064   Prof. John R. Valeri, Dir.

CATHOLIC UNIVERSITY OF AMERICA - SEMITICS - INSTITUTE OF
    CHRISTIAN ORIENTAL RESEARCH (ICOR) LIBRARY
Mullen Library, Rm. 18   Phone: (202) 635-5091
Washington, DC 20064   Carolyn T. Lee, Cur.

CENTER FOR APPLIED RESEARCH IN THE APOSTOLATE - ARCHIVES AND
RESEARCH LIBRARY
3700 Oakview Terrace, N.E.   Phone: (202) 832-2300
Washington, DC 20017   Dolores Liptak, R.S.M., Spec.Libn./Archv.

CENTER OF CONCERN - INFORMATION CENTER
3700 13th St., N.E.   Phone: (202) 635-2757
Washington, DC 20017   Mary Jo Zenk, Ed.

CENTER FOR NATIONAL SECURITY STUDIES - CNSS LIBRARY
122 Maryland Ave., N.E.   Phone: (202) 544-5380
Washington, DC 20002

CENTER FOR WOMEN POLICY STUDIES - FAMILY VIOLENCE PROJECT
LIBRARY
2000 P St., N.W., Suite 508   Phone: (202) 872-1770
Washington, DC 20036   Elinor Tucker, Supv.

CHAMBER OF COMMERCE OF THE UNITED STATES OF AMERICA -
NATIONAL CHAMBER FOUNDATION LIBRARY
1615 H St., N.W.   Phone: (202) 463-5448
Washington, DC 20062   Rose Racine, Libn.

CHEMICAL MANUFACTURERS ASSOCIATION - LIBRARY
2501 M St., N.W.   Phone: (202) 328-4229
Washington, DC 20037

CHEVY CHASE BAPTIST CHURCH - SEBRING MEMORIAL LIBRARY
5671 Western Ave., N.W.
Washington, DC 20015   May Kardell, Libn.

CHICAGO TRIBUNE PRESS SERVICE - WASHINGTON BUREAU - LIBRARY
1707 H St., N.W., 9th Fl.   Phone: (202) 785-9430
Washington, DC 20006   Carolyn J. Hardnett, Chf.Libn.

CHILDREN'S HOSPITAL/NATIONAL MEDICAL CENTER - HOSPITAL LIBRARY
†
111 Michigan Ave., N.W.   Phone: (202) 745-3195
Washington, DC 20010   Deborah D. Gilbert, Chf.Hosp.Libn.

CHRONICLE OF HIGHER EDUCATION - LIBRARY
1333 New Hampshire Ave., N.W.   Phone: (202) 828-3525
Washington, DC 20036   Edith Uunila, Sr.Ed.

CITIZENS' ENERGY PROJECT, INC. - LIBRARY
1110 Sixth St., N.W., Suite 300   Phone: (202) 289-4999
Washington, DC 20001   Ken Bossong, Coord.

CITIZENS' ENERGY PROJECT, INC. - PASSIVE SOLAR FOUNDATION -
LIBRARY
1110 Sixth St., N.W., Suite 300   Phone: (202) 289-4999
Washington, DC 20001   Ken Bossong, Coord.

CLEARINGHOUSE ON CHILD ABUSE AND NEGLECT INFORMATION
Box 1182   Phone: (703) 558-8222
Washington, DC 20013   Joseph G. Wechsler, Dir.

CLUB MANAGERS ASSOCIATION OF AMERICA - INFORMATION, RESEARCH
& STATISTICS DEPARTMENT
7615 Winterberry Place
Box 34482   Phone: (301) 229-3600
Washington, DC 20817   Julie A. DeBardeleben, Dir./Info., Res., Pubn.

COHEN AND URETZ - LAW LIBRARY
1775 K St., N.W.   Phone: (202) 293-4740
Washington, DC 20006   Kathleen S. Martin, Libn.

COLLEGE OF PREACHERS - LIBRARY
3510 Woodley Rd., N.W.
Washington, DC 20016   Mildred Coleman, Libn.

COLUMBIA HISTORICAL SOCIETY - LIBRARY
1307 New Hampshire Ave., N.W.   Phone: (202) 785-2068
Washington, DC 20036   Perry G. Fisher, Exec.Dir./Libn.

COLUMBIA HOSPITAL FOR WOMEN - MEDICAL LIBRARY
2425 L St., N.W.   Phone: (202) 293-6560
Washington, DC 20037   Elizabeth M. Haggart, Libn.

COMMODITY FUTURES TRADING COMMISSION - LIBRARY
2033 K St., N.W., Rm. 540   Phone: (202) 254-5901
Washington, DC 20581   John Fragale, Adm.Libn.

COMMUNICATIONS SATELLITE CORPORATION - CENTRAL LIBRARY †
950 L'Enfant Plaza, S.W.   Phone: (202) 863-6834
Washington, DC 20024   Rita A. Carter, Libn.

COMMUNICATIONS WORKERS OF AMERICA - CWA INFORMATION
LIBRARY
1925 K St., N.W.   Phone: (202) 728-2549
Washington, DC 20006   Frances Snider, Libn.

CONAC - LIBRARY
Binational Ctr. for Education
2717 Ontario Rd., N.W., Suite 200   Phone: (202) 223-1174
Washington, DC 20009   Cecelia Bustamante-Barron, Libn.

CONFERENCE ON ECONOMIC PROGRESS - LIBRARY
2610 Upton St., N.W.   Phone: (202) 363-6222
Washington, DC 20008   Leon H. Keyserling, Pres./Dir. of Staff

CONGRESSIONAL BUDGET OFFICE - LIBRARY
House Office Bldg., Annex 2
2nd & D Sts., S.W.   Phone: (202) 225-4525
Washington, DC 20515   Jane T. Sessa, Libn.

CONGRESSIONAL CLEARINGHOUSE ON THE FUTURE
H2-555 House Annex 2   Phone: (202) 225-3153
Washington, DC 20515   Elaine Wicker, Ed.

CONGRESSIONAL QUARTERLY, INC. - EDITORIAL REPORTS LIBRARY
1414 22nd St., N.W.   Phone: (202) 887-8569
Washington, DC 20037   Martha Bomgardner, Lib.Dir.

CONSERVATION FOUNDATION - LIBRARY
1717 Massachusetts Ave., N.W.   Phone: (202) 797-4300
Washington, DC 20036   Barbara K. Rodes, Libn.

CONSUMER PRODUCT SAFETY COMMISSION - LIBRARY
5401 Westbard Ave.   Phone: (301) 492-6544
Washington, DC 20207   Elizabeth D. Goldberg, Adm.Libn.

COOPERS & LYBRAND - LIBRARY
1800 M St., N.W.   Phone: (202) 822-4000
Washington, DC 20036   Mary Lou James, Libn.

CORCORAN GALLERY OF ART - CORCORAN ARCHIVES
17th & New York Ave., N.W.   Phone: (202) 638-3211
Washington, DC 20006   Katherine Maras Kovacs, Archv.

CORCORAN MUSEUM AND SCHOOL OF ART - LIBRARY
17th St. & New York Ave., N.W.   Phone: (202) 638-3211
Washington, DC 20006   Ann Maginnis, Lib.Dir.

CORN REFINERS ASSOCIATION, INC. - CORN INDUSTRIES RESEARCH
FOUNDATION - LIBRARY
1001 Connecticut Ave., N.W.   Phone: (202) 331-1634
Washington, DC 20036

COUNCIL FOR ADVANCEMENT AND SUPPORT OF EDUCATION - REFERENCE
CENTER
Eleven Dupont Circle, N.W., Suite 400   Phone: (202) 328-5900
Washington, DC 20036   Cynthia Snyder, Dir.

COVINGTON AND BURLING - LIBRARY
1201 Pennsylvania Ave., N.W.   Phone: (202) 662-6152
Washington, DC 20004   Ellen P. Mahar, Libn.

CROWELL & MORING - LIBRARY
1100 Connecticut Ave., N.W.   Phone: (202) 452-5857
Washington, DC 20036   Joan L. Axelroth, Libn.

DELOITTE HASKINS & SELLS - LIBRARY
1101 15th St., N.W., 9th Fl.   Phone: (202) 862-3548
Washington, DC 20005   June B. Williams, Libn.

DEMOCRATIC NATIONAL COMMITTEE - RESEARCH LIBRARY †
1625 Massachusetts Ave., N.W.   Phone: (202) 797-5900
Washington, DC 20036   John Francis Bierlein, Dir., Res.Dev.

DISTILLED SPIRITS COUNCIL OF THE U.S., INC. - LIBRARY
1250 Eye St., N.W., 8th Fl.   Phone: (202) 628-3544
Washington, DC 20005   Matthew J. Vellucci, Libn.

DISTRICT OF COLUMBIA - CORPORATION COUNSEL LAW LIBRARY
Rm. 302, District Bldg.
14th & E Sts., N.W.   Phone: (202) 727-6274
Washington, DC 20004   Deborah M. Murray, Law Libn.

**DISTRICT OF COLUMBIA DEPARTMENT OF HOUSING AND COMMUNITY
DEVELOPMENT LIBRARY**
1133 North Capitol St., Rm. 203   Phone: (202) 535-1004
Washington, DC 20002   Anne L. Meglis, Libn.

DISTRICT OF COLUMBIA GENERAL HOSPITAL - MEDICAL LIBRARY
19th St. & Massachusetts Ave., S.E.   Phone: (202) 675-5348
Washington, DC 20003   Ms. Dale Eliasson, Chf.Libn.

DISTRICT OF COLUMBIA PUBLIC LIBRARY - ART DIVISION
Martin Luther King Memorial Library
901 G St., N.W.   Phone: (202) 727-1291
Washington, DC 20001   Lois Kent Stiles, Chf.

DISTRICT OF COLUMBIA PUBLIC LIBRARY - AUDIOVISUAL DIVISION
Martin Luther King Memorial Library
901 G St., N.W.   Phone: (202) 727-1265
Washington, DC 20001   Marcia Zalbowitz, Chf.

DISTRICT OF COLUMBIA PUBLIC LIBRARY - BIOGRAPHY DIVISION
Martin Luther King Memorial Library
901 G St., N.W.   Phone: (202) 727-2079
Washington, DC 20001   Helen Bergan, Chf.

DISTRICT OF COLUMBIA PUBLIC LIBRARY - BLACK STUDIES DIVISION
Martin Luther King Memorial Library
901 G St., N.W.   Phone: (202) 727-1211
Washington, DC 20001   Alice B. Robinson, Chf.

**DISTRICT OF COLUMBIA PUBLIC LIBRARY - BUSINESS, ECONOMICS &
VOCATIONS DIVISION**
Martin Luther King Memorial Library
901 G St., N.W.   Phone: (202) 727-1171
Washington, DC 20001   Wayne D. Kryszak, Chf.

DISTRICT OF COLUMBIA PUBLIC LIBRARY - CHILDREN'S DIVISION
Martin Luther King Memorial Library
901 G St., N.W.   Phone: (202) 727-1248
Washington, DC 20001   Barbara F. Geyger, Chf.

**DISTRICT OF COLUMBIA PUBLIC LIBRARY - HISTORY, TRAVEL AND
GEOGRAPHY DIVISION**
Martin Luther King Memorial Library
901 G St., N.W.   Phone: (202) 727-1161
Washington, DC 20001   Eleanor A. Bartlett, Chf.

**DISTRICT OF COLUMBIA PUBLIC LIBRARY - LANGUAGE, LITERATURE &
FOREIGN LANGUAGE DIVISION**
Martin Luther King Memorial Library
901 G St., N.W.   Phone: (202) 727-1281
Washington, DC 20001   Octave S. Stevenson, Chf.

**DISTRICT OF COLUMBIA PUBLIC LIBRARY - LIBRARY FOR THE BLIND AND
PHYSICALLY HANDICAPPED**
Martin Luther King Memorial Library
901 G St., N.W.   Phone: (202) 727-2142
Washington, DC 20001   Grace Lyons, Chf.

**DISTRICT OF COLUMBIA PUBLIC LIBRARY - MUSIC & RECREATION
DIVISION**
Martin Luther King Memorial Library
901 G St., N.W.   Phone: (202) 727-1285
Washington, DC 20001   Mary Elliott, Chf.

**DISTRICT OF COLUMBIA PUBLIC LIBRARY - PHILOSOPHY, PSYCHOLOGY
AND RELIGION DIVISION**
Martin Luther King Memorial Library
901 G St., N.W.   Phone: (202) 727-1251
Washington, DC 20001   Vicky Rogers, Chf.

DISTRICT OF COLUMBIA PUBLIC LIBRARY - POPULAR LIBRARY
Martin Luther King Memorial Library
901 G St., N.W.   Phone: (202) 727-1295
Washington, DC 20001   Mildred R. Greene, Chf.

**DISTRICT OF COLUMBIA PUBLIC LIBRARY - SOCIOLOGY, GOVERNMENT &
EDUCATION DIVISION**
Martin Luther King Memorial Library
901 G St., N.W.   Phone: (202) 727-1261
Washington, DC 20001   Ann K. Ross, Chf.

**DISTRICT OF COLUMBIA PUBLIC LIBRARY - TECHNOLOGY AND SCIENCE
DIVISION**
Martin Luther King Memorial Library
901 G St., N.W.   Phone: (202) 727-1175
Washington, DC 20001   Barbara Lundquist, Chf.

DISTRICT OF COLUMBIA PUBLIC LIBRARY - WASHINGTONIANA DIVISION
Martin Luther King Memorial Library
901 G St., N.W.   Phone: (202) 727-1213
Washington, DC 20001   Roxanne Deane, Chf.

**DISTRICT OF COLUMBIA PUBLIC SCHOOLS - DIVISION OF QUALITY
ASSURANCE - RESEARCH INFORMATION CENTER**
415 12th St., N.W.   Phone: (202) 724-4249
Washington, DC 20004   Erika Robinson, Coord.

DISTRICT OF COLUMBIA SUPERIOR COURT - LIBRARY
500 Indiana Ave., N.W.   Phone: (202) 727-1435
Washington, DC 20001   Harriet Rotter, Libn.

DOMINICAN COLLEGE LIBRARY
487 Michigan Ave., N.E.   Phone: (202) 529-5300
Washington, DC 20017-1584   Rev. J. Raymond Vandegrift, O.P., Libn.

DOW, LOHNES & ALBERTSON - LAW LIBRARY
1225 Connecticut Ave., Suite 500   Phone: (202) 862-8021
Washington, DC 20036   Susanne D. Thevenet, Law Libn.

EDISON ELECTRIC INSTITUTE - LIBRARY
1111 19th St., N.W., 8th Fl.   Phone: (202) 828-7520
Washington, DC 20036   Ethel Tiberg, Mgr., Lib.Serv.

EMBASSY OF ZIMBABWE - LIBRARY ★
2852 McGill Terrace, N.W.   Phone: (202) 332-7100
Washington, DC 20008

EMPLOYEE BENEFIT RESEARCH INSTITUTE - LIBRARY
1920 M St., N.W., Suite 520
Washington, DC 20036   Margaret B. Riordan, Libn.

**ENGLISH-SPEAKING UNION OF THE U.S.A. - WASHINGTON D.C. BRANCH
LIBRARY**
2131 S St., N.W.   Phone: (202) 234-4602
Washington, DC 20008   Dirk Zylstra, Exec.Dir.

ENVIRONMENTAL LAW INSTITUTE - LIBRARY
1346 Connecticut Ave., N.W., Suite 620   Phone: (202) 452-9600
Washington, DC 20036   Iva M. Futrell, Libn.

ENVIRONMENTAL PROTECTION AGENCY - HEADQUARTERS LIBRARY †
401 M St., S.W., Rm. 2404   Phone: (202) 755-0308
Washington, DC 20460   Sami Klein, Chf.

ERIC CLEARINGHOUSE ON HIGHER EDUCATION
George Washington University
One Dupont Circle, Suite 630   Phone: (202) 296-2597
Washington, DC 20036   Dr. Jonathan D. Fife, Dir.

ERIC CLEARINGHOUSE ON LANGUAGES AND LINGUISTICS
3520 Prospect St., N.W.   Phone: (202) 298-9292
Washington, DC 20007   John L.D. Clark, Dir.

ERIC CLEARINGHOUSE ON TEACHER EDUCATION
American Assn. of Colleges
For Teacher Education
One Dupont Circle, N.W., Suite 610   Phone: (202) 293-2450
Washington, DC 20036   Francie Gilman, User Serv.Coord.

ESPERANTIC STUDIES FOUNDATION - LIBRARY
6451 Barnaby St., N.W.   Phone: (202) 362-3963
Washington, DC 20015   E. James Lieberman, Dir.

EUROPEAN COMMUNITY INFORMATION SERVICE - LIBRARY
2100 M St., N.W., Suite 707   Phone: (202) 862-9500
Washington, DC 20037   Barbara Sloan, Hd., Pub. Inquiries

EXPORT-IMPORT BANK OF THE UNITED STATES - LIBRARY
811 Vermont Ave., N.W.   Phone: (202) 566-8897
Washington, DC 20571   Theodora McGill, Libn.

FEDERAL ELECTION COMMISSION - NATIONAL CLEARINGHOUSE ON
ELECTION ADMINISTRATION - DOCUMENT CENTER
1325 K St., N.W.   Phone: (800) 424-9530
Washington, DC 20463   Gwenn Hofmann, Asst. to Dir.

FEDERAL ENERGY REGULATORY COMMISSION - LIBRARY
825 N. Capitol St., N.E., Rm. 8502   Phone: (202) 357-5479
Washington, DC 20426   Robert F. Kimberlin, III, Chf.

FEDERAL RESERVE SYSTEM - BOARD OF GOVERNORS - LAW LIBRARY
20th & Constitution Ave., N.W.   Phone: (202) 452-3284
Washington, DC 20551   Judith M. Weiss, Law Libn.

FEDERAL RESERVE SYSTEM - BOARD OF GOVERNORS - RESEARCH
LIBRARY
20th & Constitution Ave., N.W.   Phone: (202) 452-3332
Washington, DC 20551   Ann Roane Clary, Chf.Libn.

FERTILIZER INSTITUTE
1015 18th St., N.W.   Phone: (202) 466-2700
Washington, DC 20036   Donald N. Collins, V.P., Commun.

FOLGER SHAKESPEARE LIBRARY
201 E. Capitol St.   Phone: (202) 544-4600
Washington, DC 20003   Dr. Philip A. Knachel, Act.Dir.

FOOD MARKETING INSTITUTE - INFORMATION SERVICE
1750 K St., N.W.   Phone: (202) 452-8444
Washington, DC 20006   Barbara L. McBride, Mgr., Info.Serv.

FOREIGN CLAIMS SETTLEMENT COMMISSION OF THE UNITED STATES -
LIBRARY
1111 20th St., N.W., Rm. 401   Phone: (202) 653-5883
Washington, DC 20579   David H. Rogers, Gen.Couns.

FOREIGN SERVICES RESEARCH INSTITUTE - WHITEFORD MEMORIAL
LIBRARY
Box 6317   Phone: (202) 362-1588
Washington, DC 20015-0317   Ellspath Lawrence, Libn.

FOSTER ASSOCIATES, INC. - LIBRARY
1101 17th St., N.W.   Phone: (202) 296-2380
Washington, DC 20036   Ann Blandamer, Libn.

FOUNDATION CENTER - WASHINGTON BRANCH LIBRARY
1001 Connecticut Ave., N.W., Suite 938   Phone: (202) 331-1400
Washington, DC 20036   Margot Brinkley, Dir.

FOUNDATION OF THE FEDERAL BAR ASSOCIATION - FEDERAL BAR
FOUNDATION LIBRARY
1815 H St., N.W.   Phone: (202) 638-1956
Washington, DC 20006   Richard M. Flynn, Libn.

FOUNDATION FOR PUBLIC AFFAIRS - RESOURCE CENTER
1220 16th St., N.W.   Phone: (202) 872-1750
Washington, DC 20036   John F. Mancini, Exec.Dir.

FOUNDATION OF THE WALL & CEILING INDUSTRY - JOHN H. HAMPSHIRE
REFERENCE & RESEARCH LIBRARY
25 K St., N.E.   Phone: (202) 783-2924
Washington, DC 20002   Betty Jacobson, Libn.

FRANCISCAN FRIARS OF THE ATONEMENT - ATONEMENT SEMINARY
LIBRARY
145 Taylor St., N.E.   Phone: (202) 529-1114
Washington, DC 20017   Bro. Edward Rankey, S.A., Libn.

FRANCISCAN MONASTERY LIBRARY
1400 Quincy St., N.E.   Phone: (202) 526-6800
Washington, DC 20017   Bro. Eugene Kleczewski, Dir.

FRIED FRANK HARRIS SHRIVER & KAMPELMAN - LIBRARY
600 New Hampshire Ave., N.W.   Phone: (202) 342-3681
Washington, DC 20037   G. Diane Sandford, Hd.Libn.

FRIENDS COMMITTEE ON NATIONAL LEGISLATION - LEGISLATIVE
LIBRARY
245 2nd St., N.E.   Phone: (202) 547-6000
Washington, DC 20002

FUND FOR PEACE - CENTER FOR DEFENSE INFORMATION - LIBRARY
303 Capital Gallery West
600 Maryland Ave., S.W.   Phone: (202) 484-9490
Washington, DC 20024   Thomas R. Greenberg, Res.Libn.

FUND FOR PEACE - CENTER FOR INTERNATIONAL POLICY
120 Maryland Ave., N.E.   Phone: (202) 544-4666
Washington, DC 20002   Virginia Adams, Off.Mgr., Pubn.

GALLAUDET COLLEGE LIBRARY - SPECIAL COLLECTIONS †
800 Florida Ave., N.E.   Phone: (202) 651-5566
Washington, DC 20002   Fern Edwards, College Libn.

GALLAUDET COLLEGE - NATIONAL INFORMATION CENTER ON DEAFNESS
800 Florida Ave., N.E.   Phone: (202) 651-5109
Washington, DC 20002   Loraine DiPietro, Dir.

GEORGE WASHINGTON UNIVERSITY - MEDICAL CENTER - PAUL
HIMMELFARB HEALTH SCIENCES LIBRARY
2300 Eye St., N.W.   Phone: (202) 676-3528
Washington, DC 20037   Shelley A. Bader, Dir.

GEORGE WASHINGTON UNIVERSITY - MELVIN GELMAN LIBRARY - SINO-
SOVIET INFORMATION CENTER
2130 H St., N.W.   Phone: (202) 676-7105
Washington, DC 20052   Lisa Deyo, Lib.Asst.

GEORGE WASHINGTON UNIVERSITY - NATIONAL LAW CENTER - JACOB
BURNS LAW LIBRARY
716 20th St., N.W.   Phone: (202) 676-6646
Washington, DC 20052   Anita K. Head, Prof. of Law/Law Libn.

GEORGE WASHINGTON UNIVERSITY - TELECOMMUNICATIONS
INFORMATION CENTER
Melvin Gelman Library
2130 H St., N.W., Rm. 610   Phone: (202) 676-5740
Washington, DC 20052   Cathy Haworth, Libn.

GEORGETOWN UNIVERSITY - BLOMMER SCIENCE LIBRARY
Reiss Science Bldg., 3rd Fl.
Box 37445   Phone: (202) 625-4733
Washington, DC 20013   Peg O'Rourke

GEORGETOWN UNIVERSITY - CENTER FOR POPULATION RESEARCH -
LIBRARY
37th & O Sts., N.W.   Phone: (202) 625-4333
Washington, DC 20057   Joan Helde, Libn.

GEORGETOWN UNIVERSITY - FRED O. DENNIS LAW LIBRARY
600 New Jersey Ave., N.W.   Phone: (202) 624-8033
Washington, DC 20001   Robert L. Oakly, Law Libn.

GEORGETOWN UNIVERSITY - KENNEDY INSTITUTE OF ETHICS - CENTER
FOR BIOETHICS LIBRARY
3520 Prospect St., N.W.   Phone: (202) 625-2383
Washington, DC 20057   Doris Goldstein, Dir., Lib. & Info.Serv.

GEORGETOWN UNIVERSITY - MEDICAL CENTER - DAHLGREN MEMORIAL
LIBRARY
3900 Reservoir Rd.   Phone: (202) 625-7673
Washington, DC 20007   Naomi C. Broering, Libn.

GEORGETOWN UNIVERSITY - SPECIAL COLLECTIONS DIVISION -
   LAUINGER MEMORIAL LIBRARY
37th and O Sts., N.W.   Phone: (202) 635-3230
Washington, DC 20057   George M. Barringer, Spec.Coll.Libn.

GINSBURG, FELDMAN, & BRESS - LAW LIBRARY
1700 Pennsylvania Ave., N.W.   Phone: (202) 637-9108
Washington, DC 20006   Kathleen S. Martin, Libn.

GOLEMBE ASSOCIATES - LIBRARY
1800 M St., N.W., Suite 900 North   Phone: (202) 296-5305
Washington, DC 20036   Jane Gallup, Libn.

GRANGE-FARM FILM FOUNDATION - LIBRARY
1616 H St., N.W.   Phone: (202) 628-3507
Washington, DC 20006   Judy T. Massabny, Exec.Dir.

GREATER SOUTHEAST COMMUNITY HOSPITAL - LURA HEALTH SCIENCES
   LIBRARY †
1310 Southern Ave., S.E.   Phone: (202) 574-6793
Washington, DC 20032   Brenda Lewis, Chf.Libn.

GROUP HEALTH ASSOCIATION OF AMERICA, INC. - GERTRUDE STURGES
   MEMORIAL LIBRARY
624 9th St., N.W.   Phone: (202) 737-4311
Washington, DC 20001   Nina M. Lane, Lib.Dir.

HARVARD UNIVERSITY - CENTER FOR HELLENIC STUDIES - LIBRARY
3100 Whitehaven St., N.W.   Phone: (202) 234-3738
Washington, DC 20008   Jeno Platthy, Ph.D., Libn.

HARVARD UNIVERSITY - DUMBARTON OAKS CENTER FOR PRE-
   COLUMBIAN STUDIES - LIBRARY
1703 32nd St., N.W.   Phone: (202) 342-3265
Washington, DC 20007   Dr. Elizabeth Boone, Dir. of Stud.

HARVARD UNIVERSITY - DUMBARTON OAKS GARDEN LIBRARY OF THE
   CENTER FOR STUDIES IN LANDSCAPE ARCHITECTURE
1703 32nd St., N.W.   Phone: (202) 342-3280
Washington, DC 20007   Laura Byers, Libn.

HARVARD UNIVERSITY - DUMBARTON OAKS RESEARCH LIBRARY AND
   COLLECTION
1703 32nd St., N.W.   Phone: (202) 342-3240
Washington, DC 20007   Dr. Irene Vaslef, Libn.

HIGHWAY USERS FEDERATION - LIBRARY †
1776 Massachusetts Ave., N.W.
Washington, DC 20036

HJK&A ADVERTISING & PUBLIC RELATIONS - INFORMATION CENTER *
2233 Wisconsin Ave., N.W.   Phone: (202) 333-0700
Washington, DC 20007   Jennifer White, Info.Spec.

HOGAN & HARTSON - LIBRARY
815 Connecticut Ave., N.W.   Phone: (202) 331-5799
Washington, DC 20006   R. Austin Doherty, Libn.

HOTEL SALES AND MARKETING ASSOCIATION INTERNATIONAL - SALES
   RESEARCH LIBRARY †
1400 K St., N.W., Suite 810   Phone: (202) 789-0089
Washington, DC 20005   Frank W. Berkman, Exec.Dir.

HOWARD UNIVERSITY - ARCHITECTURE & PLANNING LIBRARY
6th St. & Howard Pl., N.W.   Phone: (202) 636-7773
Washington, DC 20059   Margaret Dorsey, Act.Libn.

HOWARD UNIVERSITY - BERNARD B. FALL COLLECTION
Founders Library, Room 300A   Phone: (202) 636-7261
Washington, DC 20059   Steven I. Yoon, Cur.

HOWARD UNIVERSITY - CHANNING POLLOCK THEATRE COLLECTION
University Library   Phone: (202) 636-7259
Washington, DC 20059   Marilyn E. Mahanand, Cur.

HOWARD UNIVERSITY - HEALTH SCIENCES LIBRARY
600 W St., N.W.   Phone: (202) 636-6433
Washington, DC 20059   Joseph Forrest, Assoc.Dir.

HOWARD UNIVERSITY - HEALTH SCIENCES LIBRARY - ANNEX (Pharmacy)
2300 4th St.   Phone: (202) 636-6545
Washington, DC 20059   Mr. Jei Whan Kim, Libn.

HOWARD UNIVERSITY - MOORLAND-SPINGARN RESEARCH CENTER -
   LIBRARY DIVISION
500 Howard Pl., N.W.   Phone: (202) 636-7260
Washington, DC 20059   James P. Johnson, Chf.Libn.

HOWARD UNIVERSITY - MOORLAND-SPINGARN RESEARCH CENTER -
   MANUSCRIPT DIVISION
500 Howard Pl., N.W.   Phone: (202) 636-7480
Washington, DC 20059   Clifford L. Muse, Jr., Act.Dir. of Ctr.

HOWARD UNIVERSITY - SCHOOL OF BUSINESS AND PUBLIC
   ADMINISTRATION - LIBRARY
2345 Sherman Ave., N.W.   Phone: (202) 636-5683
Washington, DC 20059   Lucille B. Smiley, Libn.

HOWARD UNIVERSITY - SCHOOL OF DIVINITY LIBRARY
1240 Randolph St. N.E.   Phone: (202) 636-7282
Washington, DC 20017   Irene Owens, Libn.

HOWARD UNIVERSITY - SCHOOL OF LAW - ALLEN MERCER DANIEL LAW
   LIBRARY
2900 Van Ness St., N.W.   Phone: (202) 686-6684
Washington, DC 20008   Judy Dimes-Smith, Dir.

HOWARD UNIVERSITY - SOCIAL WORK LIBRARY
6th St. & Howard Pl., N.W.   Phone: (202) 636-7316
Washington, DC 20059   Brenda J. Cox, Libn.

HUMAN RIGHTS INTERNET - LIBRARY
1338 G St., S.E.   Phone: (202) 462-4320
Washington, DC 20003   William T. Owens-Smith, Dir.

ICF INC. - LIBRARY
1850 K St., N.W., Suite 950   Phone: (202) 862-1100
Washington, DC 20006   Kathy Stinger, Libn.

INDEPENDENT PETROLEUM ASSOCIATION OF AMERICA -
   COMMUNICATIONS DEPARTMENT
1101 16th St., N.W.   Phone: (202) 857-4770
Washington, DC 20036

INDIA - EMBASSY OF INDIA - LIBRARY OF THE INFORMATION SERVICE OF
   INDIA *
2107 Massachusetts Ave., N.W.   Phone: (202) 265-5050
Washington, DC 20008   Baburaj Stephen, Libn.

INFORMATION/DOCUMENTATION
Box 17109   Phone: (703) 979-5363
Washington, DC 20041   Michael S. Saboe, Dir.

INSTITUTE FOR BEHAVIORAL RESEARCH - LIBRARY
3201 New Mexico Ave., N.W., Suite 250   Phone: (202) 362-5172
Washington, DC 20016   Ken Williams, Libn.

INSTITUTE FOR LOCAL SELF-RELIANCE - LIBRARY
2425 18th St., N.W.   Phone: (202) 232-4108
Washington, DC 20009   Neil Seldman, Dir.

INSTITUTE OF NAVIGATION - LIBRARY
815 15th St., N.W., Suite 832   Phone: (202) 783-4121
Washington, DC 20005   Frank B. Brady, Exec.Dir.

INSTITUTE OF TRANSPORTATION ENGINEERS - LIBRARY
525 School St., S.W., Suite 410   Phone: (202) 554-8050
Washington, DC 20024   Thomas W. Brahms, Exec.Dir.

INSURANCE INSTITUTE FOR HIGHWAY SAFETY - LIBRARY
600 New Hampshire Ave., Suite 300   Phone: (202) 333-0770
Washington, DC 20037   Christine A. Pruzin, Libn.

INTER-AMERICAN DEFENSE COLLEGE - LIBRARY
Fort McNair   Phone: (202) 693-8154
Washington, DC 20319   Mercedes M. Bailey, Chf.Libn.

INTER-AMERICAN DEVELOPMENT BANK - TECHNICAL INFORMATION
CENTER
808 17th St., N.W.   Phone: (202) 634-8385
Washington, DC 20577   Ana I. Conde, Hd.

INTERFAITH FORUM ON RELIGION, ART AND ARCHITECTURE - LIBRARY
1777 Church St., N.W.
Washington, DC 20036

INTERNATIONAL ASSOCIATION OF INDEPENDENT PRODUCERS - LIBRARY
Box 2801   Phone: (202) 638-5595
Washington, DC 20013   Dr. Edward Von Rothkirch, Dir.

INTERNATIONAL BROTHERHOOD OF TEAMSTERS, CHAUFFEURS,
WAREHOUSEMEN AND HELPERS OF AMERICA - INFO. CTR. LIBRARY
25 Louisiana Ave., N.W.   Phone: (202) 624-6978
Washington, DC 20001   Susan J. Strehl, Libn.

INTERNATIONAL CENTER FOR RESEARCH ON WOMEN - RESOURCE
CENTER
1717 Massachusetts Ave., N.W., Suite 501   Phone: (202) 797-0007
Washington, DC 20036   Karen White, Staff Libn.

INTERNATIONAL CITY MANAGEMENT ASSOCIATION - LIBRARY
1120 G St., N.W.   Phone: (202) 626-4600
Washington, DC 20005   Mary Od'Neal, Libn.

INTERNATIONAL FOOD POLICY RESEARCH INSTITUTE - LIBRARY
1776 Massachusetts Ave., N.W.   Phone: (202) 862-5614
Washington, DC 20036   Patricia W. Klosky, Libn.

INTERNATIONAL FRANCHISE ASSOCIATION - LIBRARY
1025 Connecticut Ave., N.W.   Phone: (202) 659-0790
Washington, DC 20036   Peter Fisher, Info.Spec.

INTERNATIONAL HUMAN RIGHTS LAW GROUP - LIBRARY
1346 Connecticut Ave., N.W., Suite 502   Phone: (202) 659-5023
Washington, DC 20036   Kathleen Yancey, Adm.Asst.

INTERNATIONAL LABOR OFFICE - WASHINGTON BRANCH LIBRARY
1750 New York Ave., N.W.   Phone: (202) 376-2315
Washington, DC 20006   Karen J. Mark, Tech.Info.Off.

INTERNATIONAL MILITARY ARCHIVES
Government Box 30051
Washington, DC 20014   Helga K. Knoeppel, Libn.

INTERNATIONAL MONETARY FUND - LAW LIBRARY
700 19th St., N.W.   Phone: (202) 477-6148
Washington, DC 20431   Eliana D. Prebisch, Libn.

INTERNATIONAL MONETARY FUND/WORLD BANK - JOINT BANK-FUND
LIBRARY
700 19th St., N.W.   Phone: (202) 473-7054
Washington, DC 20431   Maureen M. Moore, Libn.

INTERNATIONAL NUMISMATIC SOCIETY - LIBRARY
1100 17th St. N.W.
Box 19386   Phone: (202) 223-4496
Washington, DC 20036   Charles R. Hoskins, Info.Dir.

INTERNATIONAL VISITORS INFORMATION SERVICE
801 19th St., N.W.   Phone: (202) 872-8747
Washington, DC 20006   Marianne H. Cruze, Exec.Dir.

INVESTMENT COMPANY INSTITUTE - LIBRARY
1775 K St., N.W.   Phone: (202) 293-7700
Washington, DC 20006   Cut Parker, Libn.

JAPAN ECONOMIC INSTITUTE OF AMERICA - LIBRARY
1000 Connecticut Ave., N.W.   Phone: (202) 296-5633
Washington, DC 20036   Phyllis A. Genther, Res.

JEFFERSON FOUNDATION - LIBRARY
Box 33108, Farragut Sta.   Phone: (202) 466-2311
Washington, DC 20033   Alice O'Connor, Dir.

JOHNS HOPKINS UNIVERSITY - SCHOOL OF ADVANCED INTERNATIONAL
STUDIES - SYDNEY R. & ELSA W. MASON LIBRARY
1740 Massachusetts Ave., N.W.   Phone: (202) 785-6296
Washington, DC 20036   Peter J. Promen, Libn.

JOHNSON (Lawrence) & ASSOCIATES, INC. - LIBRARY
4545 42nd St., N.W.   Phone: (202) 537-6900
Washington, DC 20016   Mrs. Tish Nearon, Hd., Adm.Serv.

JOINT CENTER FOR POLITICAL STUDIES, INC. - OFFICE OF INFORMATION
RESOURCES
1301 Pennsylvania Ave., N.W., Suite 400   Phone: (202) 626-3530
Washington, DC 20004   Auriel J. Pilgrim, Dir., Info.Rsrcs.

KIRKLAND & ELLIS - LIBRARY
1776 K St., N.W.   Phone: (202) 857-5109
Washington, DC 20006   George B. Kirlin, Libn.

LEAGUE FOR INTERNATIONAL FOOD EDUCATION - LIBRARY
915 15th St., N.W., Suite 915   Phone: (202) 331-1658
Washington, DC 20005   Rae Gallaway, Dir. of Res.

LIBRARY OF CONGRESS - AFRICAN & MIDDLE EASTERN DIVISION
John Adams Bldg., Rm. 1015   Phone: (202) 287-7937
Washington, DC 20540   Dr. Julian W. Witherell, Chf.

LIBRARY OF CONGRESS - AMERICAN FOLKLIFE CENTER
Thomas Jefferson Bldg. - G104D   Phone: (202) 287-6590
Washington, DC 20540   Alan Jabbour, Dir.

LIBRARY OF CONGRESS - AMERICAN FOLKLIFE CENTER - ARCHIVE OF
FOLK CULTURE
Thomas Jefferson Bldg. - G152   Phone: (202) 287-5505
Washington, DC 20540   Joseph C. Hickerson, Hd.

LIBRARY OF CONGRESS - ASIAN DIVISION
John Adams Bldg., Rm. 1024   Phone: (202) 287-5420
Washington, DC 20540   Dr. J. Thomas Rimer, Chf.

LIBRARY OF CONGRESS - CHILDREN'S LITERATURE CENTER
Thomas Jefferson Bldg., Rm. 140H   Phone: (202) 287-5535
Washington, DC 20540   Sybille Jagusch, Chf.

LIBRARY OF CONGRESS - CONGRESSIONAL RESEARCH SERVICE
James Madison Memorial Bldg., LM213   Phone: (202) 287-5735
Washington, DC 20540   Gilbert Gude, Dir.

LIBRARY OF CONGRESS - COPYRIGHT PUBLIC INFORMATION OFFICE
James Madison Memorial Bldg., LM-401
101 Independence Ave., S.E.   Phone: (202) 287-8700
Washington, DC 20559   Victor Marton, Supv., Info. Unit

LIBRARY OF CONGRESS - EUROPEAN DIVISION
John Adams Bldg., Rm. 5244   Phone: (202) 287-5414
Washington, DC 20540   David H. Kraus, Act.Chf.

LIBRARY OF CONGRESS - GEN. READING ROOMS DIV.
Thomas Jefferson Bldg. - GRR B144   Phone: (202) 287-5530
Washington, DC 20540   Ellen Hahn, Chf.

LIBRARY OF CONGRESS - GEN. READING ROOMS DIV. - LOCAL HISTORY &
GENEALOGY READING ROOM SECTION
Thomas Jefferson Bldg., Rm. LJ244   Phone: (202) 287-5537
Washington, DC 20540   Judith P. Austin, Hd.

LIBRARY OF CONGRESS - GEN. READING ROOMS DIV. - MICROFORM
READING ROOM SECTION
Thomas Jefferson Bldg. - GRR 140B   Phone: (202) 287-5471
Washington, DC 20540   Alan C. Solomon, Hd.

LIBRARY OF CONGRESS - GEOGRAPHY & MAP DIVISION
James Madison Memorial Bldg., LMB01   Phone: (202) 287-6277
Washington, DC 20540   Dr. John A. Wolter, Chf.

LIBRARY OF CONGRESS - HISPANIC DIVISION
Thomas Jefferson Bldg., Rm. 239E   Phone: (202) 287-5400
Washington, DC 20540   John R. Hebert, Act.Chf.

LIBRARY OF CONGRESS - JOHN F. KENNEDY CENTER FOR THE
PERFORMING ARTS - THE PERFORMING ARTS LIB.
John F. Kennedy Ctr.   Phone: (202) 287-6245
Washington, DC 20566   Peter J. Fay, Hd.Libn.

LIBRARY OF CONGRESS - LAW LIBRARY
James Madison Memorial Bldg., Rm. 240   Phone: (202) 287-5065
Washington, DC 20540   Carleton W. Kenyon, Law Libn.

LIBRARY OF CONGRESS - LAW LIBRARY - AMERICAN-BRITISH LAW
DIVISION
James Madison Memorial Bldg., Rm. 235   Phone: (202) 287-5077
Washington, DC 20540   Marlene C. McGuirl, Chf.

LIBRARY OF CONGRESS - LAW LIBRARY - EUROPEAN LAW DIVISION
James Madison Memorial Bldg., Rm. 240   Phone: (202) 287-5088
Washington, DC 20540   Ivan Sipkov, Chf.

LIBRARY OF CONGRESS - LAW LIBRARY - FAR EASTERN LAW DIVISION
James Madison Memorial Bldg., Rm. 235   Phone: (202) 287-5085
Washington, DC 20540   Tao-Tai Hsia, Chf.

LIBRARY OF CONGRESS - LAW LIBRARY - HISPANIC LAW DIVISION
James Madison Memorial Bldg., Rm. 235   Phone: (202) 287-5070
Washington, DC 20540   Rubens Medina, Chf.

LIBRARY OF CONGRESS - LAW LIBRARY - NEAR EASTERN AND AFRICAN
LAW DIVISION
James Madison Memorial Bldg., Rm. 240   Phone: (202) 287-5073
Washington, DC 20540   Zuhair E. Jwaideh, Chf.

LIBRARY OF CONGRESS - LOAN DIVISION
Thomas Jefferson Bldg. - G151   Phone: (202) 287-5441
Washington, DC 20540   Olive C. James, Chf.

LIBRARY OF CONGRESS - MANUSCRIPT DIVISION
James Madison Memorial Bldg., Rms. 101-102 Phone: (202) 287-5383
Washington, DC 20540   James H. Hutson, Chf.

LIBRARY OF CONGRESS - MOTION PICTURE, BROADCASTING & RECORDED
SOUND DIVISION
James Madison Memorial Bldg., Rm. 338   Phone: (202) 287-5840
Washington, DC 20540   Robert Saudek, Chf.

LIBRARY OF CONGRESS - MUSIC DIVISION
Thomas Jefferson Bldg., Rm. G144   Phone: (202) 287-5507
Washington, DC 20540   Donald L. Leavitt, Chf.

LIBRARY OF CONGRESS - NATIONAL LIBRARY SERVICE FOR THE BLIND
AND PHYSICALLY HANDICAPPED
1291 Taylor St., N.W.   Phone: (202) 287-5100
Washington, DC 20542   Frank Kurt Cylke, Dir.

LIBRARY OF CONGRESS - NATIONAL REFERRAL CENTER
John Adams Bldg., Rm. 5228   Phone: (202) 287-5670
Washington, DC 20540   Edward N. MacConomy, Chf.

LIBRARY OF CONGRESS - PRESERVATION OFFICE
James Madison Memorial Bldg., Rm. G-21   Phone: (202) 287-5213
Washington, DC 20540   Peter G. Sparks, Dir. for Preservation

LIBRARY OF CONGRESS - PRINTS & PHOTOGRAPHS DIVISION
James Madison Memorial Bldg., Rm. LM 339   Phone: (202) 287-5836
Washington, DC 20540   Stephen Edward Ostrow, Chf.

LIBRARY OF CONGRESS - RARE BOOK & SPECIAL COLLECTIONS DIVISION
Thomas Jefferson Bldg., Rm. 256   Phone: (202) 287-5434
Washington, DC 20540   William Matheson, Chf.

LIBRARY OF CONGRESS - SCIENCE & TECHNOLOGY DIVISION
John Adams Bldg., Rm. 5104   Phone: (202) 287-5639
Washington, DC 20540   Joseph W. Price, Chf.

LIBRARY OF CONGRESS - SERIAL AND GOVERNMENT PUBLICATIONS
DIVISION
James Madison Memorial Bldg., Rm. LM-133   Phone: (202) 287-5690
Washington, DC 20540   Donald F. Wisdom, Chf.

LOGISTICS MANAGEMENT INSTITUTE - LIBRARY
4701 Sangamore Rd.
Box 9489   Phone: (301) 229-1000
Washington, DC 20016

MC KINSEY & COMPANY, INC. - LIBRARY
1700 Pennsylvania Ave., N.W.   Phone: (202) 393-6820
Washington, DC 20006   Ann Robertson, Mgr., Info. & Anl.Serv.

MARIST COLLEGE - LIBRARY
220 Taylor St., N.E.   Phone: (202) 529-2821
Washington, DC 20017   Paul M. Cabrita, Hd.Libn.

METROPOLITAN WASHINGTON COUNCIL OF GOVERNMENTS - LIBRARY †
1875 Eye St., N.W.   Phone: (202) 223-6800
Washington, DC 20006

MIDDLE EAST INSTITUTE - GEORGE CAMP KEISER LIBRARY
1761 N St., N.W.   Phone: (202) 785-1141
Washington, DC 20036   Ruth K. Baacke, Libn.

MORGAN, LEWIS & BOCKIUS - LIBRARY
1800 M St., N.W.   Phone: (202) 872-7691
Washington, DC 20036   Victoria M. Ward, Law Libn.

MORRISON & FOERSTER - BRANCH LAW LIBRARY
1920 N St., N.W., Suite 800   Phone: (202) 887-1500
Washington, DC 20036   Jane Amon, Libn.

MORTGAGE BANKERS ASSOCIATION OF AMERICA - LIBRARY
1125 15th St., N.W.   Phone: (202) 861-6580
Washington, DC 20005   Cassie Kupstas, Libn.

MOTT RESEARCH GROUP - LIBRARY
3220 Rittenhouse St., N.W.   Phone: (202) 363-3809
Washington, DC 20015   Dorothy Williams Mott, Libn./Cur.

MOUNT VERNON PLACE UNITED METHODIST CHURCH - DESSIE M.
HALLETT LIBRARY †
900 Massachusetts Ave., N.W.   Phone: (202) 347-9620
Washington, DC 20001   Dessie M. Hallett, Libn.

MPR ASSOCIATES, INC. - TECHNICAL LIBRARY
1050 Connecticut Ave., N.W., Suite 400   Phone: (202) 659-2320
Washington, DC 20036   Alice P. McNamara, Libn.

MUNICIPAL FINANCE OFFICERS ASSOCIATION OF THE U.S. AND CANADA -
GOVERNMENT FINANCE RESEARCH CENTER LIB.
1750 K St., Suite 200   Phone: (202) 466-2014
Washington, DC 20006   Barbara Weiss, Asst.Dir.

NARCOTICS EDUCATION, INC. - SCHARFFENBERG MEMORIAL LIBRARY
6830 Laurel St., N.W.
Box 4390   Phone: (202) 722-6739
Washington, DC 20012   James Ford, Libn.

NATHAN (Robert R.) ASSOCIATES, INC. - LIBRARY
1301 Pennsylvania Ave., N.W.   Phone: (202) 393-2700
Washington, DC 20004   Joan Bow, Libn.

NATIONAL ACADEMY OF SCIENCES - NATIONAL ACADEMY OF
ENGINEERING - LIBRARY
2101 Constitution Ave., N.W.   Phone: (202) 334-2125
Washington, DC 20418   James L. Olsen, Jr., Libn.

NATIONAL ACADEMY OF SCIENCES - NATIONAL RESEARCH COUNCIL -
HIGHWAY RESEARCH INFORMATION SERVICE
Transportation Research Bd.
2101 Constitution Ave., N.W.   Phone: (202) 334-3250
Washington, DC 20418   Arthur B. Mobley, HRIS Mgr.

NATIONAL ACADEMY OF SCIENCES - NATIONAL RESEARCH COUNCIL -
TRANSPORTATION RESEARCH BOARD LIBRARY
2101 Constitution Ave., N.W.   Phone: (202) 334-2989
Washington, DC 20418   Lisbeth L. Luke, Libn.

NATIONAL AERONAUTIC ASSOCIATION - LIBRARY
821 15th St., N.W.   Phone: (202) 347-2808
Washington, DC 20005   Milton M. Brown, Sec.

NATIONAL ASSOCIATION OF BROADCASTERS - LIBRARY
1771 N St., N.W.   Phone: (202) 293-3578
Washington, DC 20036   Susan M. Hill, Dir.

NATIONAL ASSOCIATION OF HOME BUILDERS - NATIONAL HOUSING
   CENTER LIBRARY
15th & M Sts., N.W.   Phone: (202) 822-0203
Washington, DC 20005   Margery M. Clark, Chf.Libn.

NATIONAL BIOMEDICAL RESEARCH FOUNDATION - LIBRARY
Georgetown University Medical Ctr.
3900 Reservoir Rd., N.W.   Phone: (202) 625-2121
Washington, DC 20007   Doris K. Mela, Libn.

NATIONAL COMMISSION ON WORKING WOMEN - RESOURCE CENTER
2000 P St., N.W., Suite 508   Phone: (202) 872-1782
Washington, DC 20036   Sally Steenland, Dp.Dir.

THE NATIONAL COUNCIL ON THE AGING, INC. - LIBRARY
600 Maryland Ave., S.W., West Wing 100   Phone: (202) 223-6250
Washington, DC 20024

NATIONAL COUNCIL OF SAVINGS INSTITUTIONS - LIBRARY
1101 15th St., N.W.   Phone: (202) 331-0270
Washington, DC 20005   Arlene Samowitz, Libn.

NATIONAL COUNCIL OF SENIOR CITIZENS, INC. - LIBRARY
925 15th St., N.W.   Phone: (202) 347-8800
Washington, DC 20005   Teman Treadway, Lib.Serv.Coord.

NATIONAL COUNCIL FOR U.S.-CHINA TRADE - LIBRARY
1050 17th St., N.W., Suite 350   Phone: (202) 429-0340
Washington, DC 20036   Marianna Graham, Libn.

NATIONAL ECONOMIC RESEARCH ASSOCIATES, INC. - LIBRARY
1800 M St., N.W.   Phone: (202) 466-3510
Washington, DC 20036   Jane Platt-Brown, Libn.

NATIONAL ECUMENICAL COALITION, INC. - LIBRARY *
Georgetown Sta., Box 3554   Phone: (202) 833-2616
Washington, DC 20007   Bro. Scott Desmond, F.O.C., Libn.

NATIONAL EDUCATION ASSOCIATION - RESEARCH INFORMATION
   SECTION
1201 16th St., N.W.   Phone: (202) 822-7404
Washington, DC 20036   Donald Walker, Mgr., Info.Serv.

NATIONAL ENDOWMENT FOR THE ARTS - ARTS LIBRARY/INFORMATION
   CENTER
1200 Pennsylvania Ave., N.W.   Phone: (202) 634-7640
Washington, DC 20004   M. Christine Morrison, Hd.

NATIONAL ENDOWMENT FOR THE ARTS - LAW LIBRARY
Office of the General Counsel
1100 Pennsylvania Ave., N.W.
Washington, DC 20004

NATIONAL ENDOWMENT FOR THE HUMANITIES - LIBRARY
Old Post Office
1100 Pennsylvania Ave., N.W.   Phone: (202) 724-0360
Washington, DC 20004   Jeannette D. Coletti, Libn.

NATIONAL FEDERATION OF LOCAL CABLE PROGRAMMERS - LIBRARY
906 Pennsylvania Ave., S.E.   Phone: (202) 544-7272
Washington, DC 20003   Joan Gudgel, Dir., Info.Serv.

NATIONAL FOREST PRODUCTS ASSOCIATION - INFORMATION CENTER
1619 Massachusetts Ave., N.W.   Phone: (202) 797-5836
Washington, DC 20036

NATIONAL GALLERY OF ART - DEPARTMENT OF EXTENSION PROGRAMS
Sixth and Constitution Ave., N.W.   Phone: (202) 842-6273
Washington, DC 20565   Ruth R. Perlin, Cur.-in-Charge

NATIONAL GALLERY OF ART - EDUCATION DIVISION SLIDE LIBRARY
Sixth and Constitution Ave., N.W.   Phone: (202) 842-6100
Washington, DC 20565   Anne von Rebhan, Chf. Slide Libn.

NATIONAL GALLERY OF ART - INDEX OF AMERICAN DESIGN
Sixth and Constitution Ave., N.W.   Phone: (202) 842-6604
Washington, DC 20565   Laurie Weitzenkorn, Asst.Cur.

NATIONAL GALLERY OF ART - LIBRARY
Sixth and Constitution Ave., N.W.   Phone: (202) 842-6511
Washington, DC 20565   J.M. Edelstein, Chf.Libn.

NATIONAL GALLERY OF ART - PHOTOGRAPHIC ARCHIVES
Sixth and Constitution Ave., N.W.   Phone: (202) 842-6026
Washington, DC 20565   Ruth R. Philbrick, Cur.

NATIONAL GENEALOGICAL SOCIETY - LIBRARY
1921 Sunderland Pl., N.W.   Phone: (202) 785-2123
Washington, DC 20036   Joyce Page, Libn.

NATIONAL GEOGRAPHIC SOCIETY - AUDIOVISUAL LIBRARY
17th and M Sts., N.W.   Phone: (202) 857-7691
Washington, DC 20036   Betty Kotcher, AV Libn.

NATIONAL GEOGRAPHIC SOCIETY - ILLUSTRATIONS LIBRARY
17th & M Sts., N.W.   Phone: (202) 857-7492
Washington, DC 20036   Fern Shrewsberry Dame, Illus.Libn.

NATIONAL GEOGRAPHIC SOCIETY - LIBRARY
1146 16th St., N.W.   Phone: (202) 857-7787
Washington, DC 20036   Susan M. Fifer Canby, Dir.

NATIONAL GUARD ASSOCIATION OF THE UNITED STATES - LIBRARY
One Massachusetts Ave., N.W.
Washington, DC 20001   Capt. Thomas M. Weaver, Res.Asst./Libn.

NATIONAL HEALTH INFORMATION CLEARINGHOUSE
Box 1133   Phone: (800) 336-4797
Washington, DC 20013   Joanne Angle, Proj.Dir.

NATIONAL HOME STUDY COUNCIL - LIBRARY
1601 18th St., N.W.   Phone: (202) 234-5100
Washington, DC 20009   Michael P. Lambert, Asst.Dir.

NATIONAL INJURY INFORMATION CLEARINGHOUSE
5401 Westbard Ave.
Westwood Towers Bldg., Rm. 625   Phone: (301) 492-6424
Washington, DC 20207   Nancy S. Johnston, Dir.

NATIONAL INSTITUTE OF EDUCATION - EDUCATIONAL RESEARCH
   LIBRARY
1200 19th St., N.W., 2nd Fl.   Phone: (202) 254-5060
Washington, DC 20208   Charles D. Missar, Supv.Libn.

NATIONAL INSTITUTE OF MUNICIPAL LAW OFFICES - LIBRARY
1000 Connecticut Ave., N.W., Suite 800
Washington, DC 20036   Charles S. Rhyne, Gen.Couns.

NATIONAL JOURNAL LIBRARY
1730 M St., N.W.   Phone: (202) 857-1400
Washington, DC 20036   Jennifer Belton, Dir., Info.Serv.

NATIONAL LEAGUE OF CITIES - MUNICIPAL REFERENCE SERVICE
1301 Pennsylvania Ave., N.W.   Phone: (202) 626-3210
Washington, DC 20004   Olivia Kredel, Mgr.

NATIONAL LEGAL AID AND DEFENDER ASSOCIATION - LIBRARY
1625 K St., N.W.
Washington, DC 20006

NATIONAL ORGANIZATION FOR WOMEN (NOW) - ACTION CENTER
   LIBRARY
425 13th St., N.W., No. 1048   Phone: (202) 347-2279
Washington, DC 20004   Jenny Tipton, Libn.

NATIONAL PARKS AND CONSERVATION ASSOCIATION - LIBRARY
1701 18th St., N.W.
Washington, DC 20009

NATIONAL PRESBYTERIAN CHURCH - WILLIAM S. CULBERTSON LIBRARY
4101 Nebraska Ave., N.W.   Phone: (202) 537-0800
Washington, DC 20016   Roma P. Samuel, Libn.

NATIONAL PUBLIC RADIO - BROADCAST LIBRARY
2025 M St., N.W.　　　　　　　　　Phone: (202) 822-2064
Washington, DC 20036

NATIONAL REHABILITATION INFORMATION CENTER
4407 8th St., N.E.
Catholic University of America　　　　Phone: (202) 635-5826
Washington, DC 20017　　　　　　　　Eleanor Biscoe, Dir.

NATIONAL RESOURCE CENTER FOR CONSUMERS OF LEGAL SERVICES -
　　CLEARINGHOUSE
3254 Jones Court, N.W.　　　　　　Phone: (202) 338-0714
Washington, DC 20007　　　　　Shelley Benson, Clghse.Dept.

NATIONAL RESTAURANT ASSOCIATION - INFORMATION SERVICE AND
　　LIBRARY
311 First St., N.W.　　　　　　　　Phone: (202) 638-6100
Washington, DC 20001　　　　　　Joan E. Campbell, Mgr.

NATIONAL RIFLE ASSOCIATION - TECHNICAL LIBRARY
1600 Rhode Island Ave., N.W.　　　　Phone: (202) 828-6227
Washington, DC 20036　　　　　　　　Joe Roberts, Ed.

NATIONAL RURAL ELECTRIC COOPERATIVE ASSOCIATION - NORRIS
　　MEMORIAL LIBRARY
1800 Massachusetts Ave., N.W.　　　Phone: (202) 857-9788
Washington, DC 20036　　　　　Chuck Rice, Lib.Serv.Spec.

NATIONAL SCHOOL BOARDS ASSOCIATION - RESOURCE CENTER
1055 Thomas Jefferson St., N.W.　　Phone: (202) 337-7666
Washington, DC 20007　　　　Eve Shepard, Mgr., Info.Serv.

NATIONAL SCIENCE FOUNDATION - LIBRARY
1800 G St., N.W.　　　　　　　　　Phone: (202) 357-7811
Washington, DC 20550　　　　　　Marie Savoy, Adm.Mgr.

NATIONAL SCIENCE TEACHERS ASSOCIATION - GLENN O. BLOUGH
　　LIBRARY
1742 Connecticut Ave., N.W.　　　　Phone: (202) 328-5800
Washington, DC 20009　　　　Phyllis Marcuccio, Chf.Libn.

NATIONAL SHERIFFS' ASSOCIATION - EDUCATION AND RESOURCE
　　CENTER
1250 Connecticut Ave., N.W., Suite 320
Washington, DC 20036

NATIONAL SOCIETY FOR CHILDREN AND ADULTS WITH AUTISM -
　　INFORMATION & REFERRAL SERVICE
1234 Massachusetts Ave., N.W., Suite 1017　　Phone: (202) 783-0125
Washington, DC 20005　　　　　Frank Warren, Exec.Dir.

NATIONAL SOCIETY, DAUGHTERS OF THE AMERICAN REVOLUTION -
　　LIBRARY
1776 D St., N.W.　　　　　　　　　Phone: (202) 628-1776
Washington, DC 20006-5392　　Eric G. Grundset, Staff Libn.

NATIONAL SOCIETY FOR MEDICAL RESEARCH - NSMR DATA BANK
1029 Vermont Ave., N.W.　　　　　Phone: (202) 347-9565
Washington, DC 20005　　　　William M. Samuels, Exec.Dir.

NATIONAL SOCIETY OF PROFESSIONAL ENGINEERS - INFORMATION
　　CENTER
2029 K St., N.W.　　　　　　　　　Phone: (202) 463-2300
Washington, DC 20006　　　　　Donald G. Weinert, Exec.Dir.

NATIONAL TAX EQUALITY ASSOCIATION - LIBRARY
1000 Connecticut Ave. Bldg.　　　　Phone: (202) 296-5424
Washington, DC 20036　　　　　　Ray M. Stroupe, Pres.

NATIONAL TRUST FOR HISTORIC PRESERVATION - INFORMATION
　　SERVICES
1785 Massachusetts Ave., N.W.　　　Phone: (202) 673-4000
Washington, DC 20036　　　Susan Shearer, Info.Serv.Coord.

NATIONAL WILDLIFE FEDERATION - FRAZIER MEMORIAL LIBRARY
1412 16th St., N.W.　　　　　　　Phone: (202) 797-6828
Washington, DC 20036　　　　　　　Sharon Levy, Libn.

NATIONAL WOMAN'S PARTY - FLORENCE BAYARD HILLES LIBRARY
144 Constitution Ave., N.E.　　　　Phone: (202) 546-1210
Washington, DC 20002　　　　Elizabeth L. Chittick, Dir.

NATIONAL YOUTH WORK ALLIANCE, INC. - CLEARINGHOUSE/LIBRARY
1346 Connecticut Ave., N.W.　　　　Phone: (202) 785-0764
Washington, DC 20036　　　　Thomas R. McCarthy, Dir.

NETHERLANDS EMBASSY - REFERENCE ROOM LIBRARY
4200 Linnean Ave., N.W.　　　　　Phone: (202) 244-5300
Washington, DC 20008

NEW TRANSCENTURY FOUNDATION - DOCUMENTATION CENTER
1724 Kalorama Rd., N.W.　　　　　Phone: (202) 328-4400
Washington, DC 20009　　　　　　Marilyn Richards

NEW ZEALAND EMBASSY - LIBRARY
37 Observatory Circle, N.W.　　　　Phone: (202) 328-4800
Washington, DC 20008　　　　　Robert Hole, Second Sec.

NEWSPAPER GUILD - HEYWOOD BROUN LIBRARY
1125 15th St., N.W.　　　　　　　Phone: (202) 296-2990
Washington, DC 20005　　David J. Eisen, Dir. of Res. & Info.

NEWSWEEK, INC. - WASHINGTON BUREAU LIBRARY
1750 Pennsylvania Ave., N.W.
Suite 1220　　　　　　　　　　Phone: (202) 626-2040
Washington, DC 20006　　　　Nancy Ganahl, Bureau Libn.

OBLATES THEOLOGY LIBRARY
391 Michigan Ave., N.E.　　　　　Phone: (202) 529-5244
Washington, DC 20017　　　　Ward E. Gongoll, Hd.Libn.

ORGANIZATION OF AMERICAN STATES - COLUMBUS MEMORIAL LIBRARY
17th St. & Constitution Ave., N.W.　　Phone: (202) 789-6040
Washington, DC 20006　　　　　Thomas L. Welch, Dir.

ORGANIZATION FOR ECONOMIC COOPERATION AND DEVELOPMENT -
　　PUBLICATIONS AND INFORMATION CENTER
1750 Pennsylvania Ave., N.W, Suite 1207　　Phone: (202) 724-1857
Washington, DC 20006-4582　　Hendrikus D. DeVroom, Hd.

OVERSEAS DEVELOPMENT COUNCIL - LIBRARY
1717 Massachusetts Ave., N.W.　　　Phone: (202) 234-8701
Washington, DC 20036　　　　　James E. Boyle, Libn.

OVERSEAS PRIVATE INVESTMENT CORPORATION - LIBRARY
1129 20th St., N.W., Rm. 711　　　Phone: (202) 632-0146
Washington, DC 20527　　　　　　Myra Norton, Libn.

PAN AMERICAN HEALTH ORGANIZATION - BIBLIOGRAPHIC INFORMATION
　　OFFICE †
525 23rd St., N.W.　　　　　　　Phone: (202) 861-3300
Washington, DC 20037　　　Dr. Carlos A. Gamboa, Chf.

PATTON BOGGS AND BLOW - LAW LIBRARY
2550 M St., N.W.　　　　　　　　Phone: (202) 223-4040
Washington, DC 20037　　　　　　Kevin McCall, Libn.

PEAT, MARWICK, MITCHELL & CO. - LIBRARY
1990 K St., N.W.　　　　　　　　Phone: (202) 223-9525
Washington, DC 20006　　　　Nancy J. Holland, Hd.Libn.

PENSION BENEFIT GUARANTY CORPORATION - OFFICE OF THE GENERAL
　　COUNSEL - LIBRARY
2020 K St., N.W., Suite 7200　　　Phone: (202) 254-4889
Washington, DC 20006　　　　　Anita J. Newman, Libn.

PHARMACEUTICAL MANUFACTURERS ASSOCIATION - LIBRARY
1100 15th St., N.W.　　　　　　　Phone: (202) 463-2000
Washington, DC 20005　　　Lucy G. Gritzmacher, Libn.

THE PHILLIPS COLLECTION - LIBRARY
1600 21st St., N.W.　　　　　　　Phone: (202) 387-2151
Washington, DC 20009　　　　Karen Schneider, Libn.

PIERSON, BALL & DOWD - LAW LIBRARY
1200 18th St., N.W.　　　　　　　Phone: (202) 331-8566
Washington, DC 20036　　　　　Sandra Parrish, Libn.

POPULATION CRISIS COMMITTEE/DRAPER FUND - LIBRARY
1120 19th St., N.W., Suite 550   Phone: (202) 659-1833
Washington, DC 20036   Linda N. Jenks, Sr.Libn./Info.Mgr.

POPULATION REFERENCE BUREAU, INC. - LIBRARY/INFORMATION
   SERVICE
2213 M St., N.W.   Phone: (202) 785-4664
Washington, DC 20037   Janice Beattie, Tech.Info.Spec.

POTOMAC ELECTRIC POWER COMPANY - LIBRARY
1900 Pennsylvania Ave., N.W.   Phone: (202) 872-2361
Washington, DC 20068   Helen C. Jessup, Libn.

PRISON FELLOWSHIP - RESOURCE CENTER
Justice Fellowship Resource Center
Box 17181   Phone: (703) 759-4521
Washington, DC 20041   Elizabeth Leahy, Coord.

PROVIDENCE HOSPITAL - HEALTH SCIENCES LIBRARY
1150 Varnum St., N.E.   Phone: (202) 269-7141
Washington, DC 20017   Sr. Frances Healy, Dir.

PUBLIC BROADCASTING SERVICE - PTV ARCHIVES
475 L'Enfant Plaza, S.W.   Phone: (202) 488-5227
Washington, DC 20036   Salomea A. Swaim, Archv.Libn.

PUBLIC CITIZEN - CONGRESS WATCH - LIBRARY
215 Pennsylvania Ave., S.E.   Phone: (202) 546-4996
Washington, DC 20003   Martha Oesch, Libn.

PUBLIC LAW EDUCATION INSTITUTE - LIBRARY
1346 Connecticut Ave. N.W., Suite 610   Phone: (202) 296-7590
Washington, DC 20036   William J. Straub, Circ.Mgr.

RAND CORPORATION - LIBRARY
2100 M St., N.W.   Phone: (202) 296-5000
Washington, DC 20037   Casey Kane, Libn.

REDMOND (J.W.) COMPANY - LIBRARY
1750 Pennsylvania Ave., N.W.
Washington, DC 20006   June Johnson, Libn.

REPUBLICAN NATIONAL COMMITTEE - LIBRARY
310 First St., S.E.   Phone: (202) 484-6626
Washington, DC 20003   Joanna Evans, Libn.

ROGERS & WELLS - LIBRARY
1737 H St., N.W.   Phone: (202) 331-7760
Washington, DC 20006   Bart Woodke, Libn.

ST. ELIZABETHS HOSPITAL - HEALTH SCIENCES LIBRARY
Administration Bldg.
2700 Martin Luther King Jr. Ave., S.E.   Phone: (202) 574-7274
Washington, DC 20032   Toby G. Port, Adm.Libn.

ST. JOSEPH'S SEMINARY - LIBRARY *
1200 Varnum St., N.E.   Phone: (202) 526-4231
Washington, DC 20017   Laurence A. Schmitt, Libn.

ST. PAUL'S COLLEGE - LIBRARY
3015 Fourth St., N.E.   Phone: (202) 832-6262
Washington, DC 20017   Lawrence E. Boadt, C.S.P., Libn.

SCIENCE SERVICE, INC. - LIBRARY
1719 N St., N.W.   Phone: (202) 785-2255
Washington, DC 20036   Jane M. Livermore, Libn.

SCIENCE TRENDS - LIBRARY
National Press Bldg., Suite 233   Phone: (202) 393-0031
Washington, DC 20045   Arthur Kranish, Hd.

SCOTTISH RITE SUPREME COUNCIL - LIBRARY
1733 Sixteenth St. N.W.   Phone: (202) 232-3579
Washington, DC 20009   Inge Baum, Libn.

SEVENTH-DAY ADVENTISTS - GENERAL CONFERENCE - OFFICE OF
   ARCHIVES AND STATISTICS
6840 Eastern Ave. N.W.   Phone: (202) 723-0800
Washington, DC 20012   Dr. F. Donald Yost, Archv.

SHAW, PITTMAN, POTTS & TROWBRIDGE - LIBRARY
1800 M St., N.W.   Phone: (202) 822-1317
Washington, DC 20036   Carolyn P. Ahearn, Libn.

SHEA & GARDNER - LIBRARY
1800 Massachusetts Ave., N.W.   Phone: (202) 828-2069
Washington, DC 20036   Susan Perrine, Libn.

SIBLEY MEMORIAL HOSPITAL - MEDICAL LIBRARY
5255 Loughboro Rd., N.W.   Phone: (202) 537-4110
Washington, DC 20016   Annie B. Footman, Libn.

SILVER INSTITUTE - LIBRARY
1001 Connecticut Ave., N.W., Suite 1138   Phone: (202) 331-1485
Washington, DC 20036   Richard L. Davies, Exec.Dir.

SKIDMORE, OWINGS & MERRILL - LIBRARY
1201 Pennsylvania Ave., N.W.   Phone: (202) 393-1400
Washington, DC 20004   Gail Markowitz, Libn.

SMITHSONIAN INSTITUTION - ARCHIVES
Arts and Industries Bldg., Rm. 2135   Phone: (202) 381-4075
Washington, DC 20560

SMITHSONIAN INSTITUTION - FREER GALLERY OF ART - LIBRARY
Twelfth & Jefferson Dr., S.W.   Phone: (202) 357-2091
Washington, DC 20560   Ellen A. Nollman, Hd.Libn.

SMITHSONIAN INSTITUTION - HIRSHHORN MUSEUM AND SCULPTURE
   GARDEN - LIBRARY
Independence Ave. & 8th St., S.W.   Phone: (202) 357-3223
Washington, DC 20560   Anna Brooke, Libn.

SMITHSONIAN INSTITUTION LIBRARIES
National Museum of Natural History
10th & Constitution Ave., N.W.   Phone: (202) 357-2240
Washington, DC 20560   Robert Maloy, Dir.

SMITHSONIAN INSTITUTION LIBRARIES - CENTRAL REFERENCE
   SERVICES †
Central Library
10th & Constitution Ave., N.W.   Phone: (202) 357-2139
Washington, DC 20560   Mary Clare Gray, Chf.

SMITHSONIAN INSTITUTION LIBRARIES - MUSEUM REFERENCE CENTER
Arts & Industries Bldg., Rm. 2235
900 Jefferson Dr., S.W.   Phone: (202) 357-3101
Washington, DC 20560   Catherine D. Scott, Libn.

SMITHSONIAN INSTITUTION LIBRARIES - MUSEUM SUPPORT CENTER
   LIBRARY
Museum of American History, AB-070   Phone: (202) 357-2444
Washington, DC 20560   Karen Preslock, Chf.Libn.

SMITHSONIAN INSTITUTION LIBRARIES - NATIONAL AIR AND SPACE
   MUSEUM - LIBRARY
National Air & Space Museum, Rm. 3100
Independence Ave. & Seventh St., S.W.   Phone: (202) 357-3133
Washington, DC 20560   Frank A. Pietropaoli, Libn.

SMITHSONIAN INSTITUTION LIBRARIES - NATIONAL MUSEUM OF
   AFRICAN ART - BRANCH LIBRARY
318 A St., N.E.   Phone: (202) 287-3490
Washington, DC 20002   Janet L. Stanley, Chf.Libn.

SMITHSONIAN INSTITUTION LIBRARIES - NATIONAL MUSEUM OF
   AFRICAN ART - ELIOT ELISOFON ARCHIVES
318 A St., N.E.   Phone: (202) 287-3490
Washington, DC 20002   Edward Lifschitz, Archv.

SMITHSONIAN INSTITUTION LIBRARIES - NATIONAL MUSEUM OF
   AMERICAN HISTORY - ARCHIVES CENTER
3rd Fl., NMAH
14th St. & Constitution Ave., N.W.   Phone: (202) 357-3270
Washington, DC 20560   John A. Fleckner, Archv.

SMITHSONIAN INSTITUTION LIBRARIES - NATIONAL MUSEUM OF
   AMERICAN HISTORY - LIBRARY
Museum of American History   Phone: (202) 357-2414
Washington, DC 20560   Rhoda Ratner, Chf.Libn.

SMITHSONIAN INSTITUTION LIBRARIES - NATIONAL MUSEUM OF
   NATURAL HISTORY - ANTHROPOLOGY BRANCH LIBRARY
Natural History Bldg., Rm. 330/331   Phone: (202) 357-1819
Washington, DC 20560   Angeline Smith, Libn.

SMITHSONIAN INSTITUTION LIBRARIES - NATIONAL MUSEUM OF
   NATURAL HISTORY - BOTANY BRANCH LIBRARY
Natural History Bldg.
10th & Constitution Ave.   Phone: (202) 357-2715
Washington, DC 20560   Ruth Schallert, Libn.

SMITHSONIAN INSTITUTION LIBRARIES - NATIONAL MUSEUM OF
   NATURAL HISTORY - ENTOMOLOGY BRANCH LIBRARY
Natural History Bldg.   Phone: (202) 357-2354
Washington, DC 20560   Ruth Schallert, Libn.

SMITHSONIAN INSTITUTION LIBRARIES - NATIONAL MUSEUM OF
   NATURAL HISTORY - LIBRARY
Natural History Bldg.
10th & Constitution Ave.   Phone: (202) 357-1496
Washington, DC 20560   Ruth Schallert, Act.Nat.Hist.Libn.

SMITHSONIAN INSTITUTION LIBRARIES - NATIONAL ZOOLOGICAL PARK -
   LIBRARY
3001 Connecticut Ave., N.W.   Phone: (202) 673-4771
Washington, DC 20008   Kay A. Kenyon, Chf.Libn.

SMITHSONIAN INSTITUTION LIBRARIES - SPECIAL COLLECTIONS BRANCH
MAH 5016   Phone: (202) 357-1568
Washington, DC 20560   Ellen B. Wells, Chf.

SMITHSONIAN INSTITUTION - NATIONAL ANTHROPOLOGICAL ARCHIVES
Natl. Museum of
Natural History Bldg., Rm. 60-A, MRC 152
10th & Constitution Ave., N.W.   Phone: (202) 357-1976
Washington, DC 20560   Dr. Herman J. Viola, Dir.

SMITHSONIAN INSTITUTION - NATL. MUSEUM OF AMERICAN ART -
   INVENTORY OF AMERICAN PAINTINGS EXECUTED BEFORE 1914
8th and G Sts., N.W.   Phone: (202) 357-2941
Washington, DC 20560   Martha Shipman Andrews, Coord.

SMITHSONIAN INSTITUTION - NATIONAL MUSEUM OF AMERICAN ART/
   NATIONAL PORTRAIT GALLERY - LIBRARY
8th & F Sts., N.W.   Phone: (202) 357-1886
Washington, DC 20560   Cecilia Chin, Chf.Libn.

SMITHSONIAN INSTITUTION - NATIONAL MUSEUM OF AMERICAN ART -
   OFFICE OF VISUAL RSRCS. - SLIDE/PHOTOGRAPH ARCHIVE
8th & G Sts., N.W.   Phone: (202) 357-1626
Washington, DC 20560   Eleanor E. Fink, Chf.

SOCIETY OF THE CINCINNATI - ANDERSON HOUSE LIBRARY AND MUSEUM
2118 Massachusetts Ave., N.W.   Phone: (202) 785-2040
Washington, DC 20008   John D. Kilbourne, Dir.

SOCIETY OF FRIENDS - FRIENDS MEETING OF WASHINGTON - LIBRARY *
2111 Florida Ave., N.W.   Phone: (202) 483-3310
Washington, DC 20008   Stephen McNeil, Ck.

STEPTOE AND JOHNSON - LIBRARY
1330 Connecticut Ave., N.W.   Phone: (202) 429-3000
Washington, DC 20036   Stephen G. Margeton, Libn.

STRAYER COLLEGE - WILKES LIBRARY
1100 Vermont Ave., N.W.   Phone: (202) 861-5241
Washington, DC 20005   H. Barbara Krell, Dir. of Libs.

SUGAR ASSOCIATION, INC. - LIBRARY
1511 K St., N.W.   Phone: (202) 628-0189
Washington, DC 20005   Margaret E. Simon, Libn.

SULLIVAN & CROMWELL - WASHINGTON D.C. LIBRARY
1775 Pennsylvania Ave., N.W.   Phone: (202) 857-1038
Washington, DC 20006   Stephannie K. Newton, Libn.

SULPHUR INSTITUTE - LIBRARY
1725 K St., N.W.   Phone: (202) 331-9660
Washington, DC 20006   J.S. Platou, Dir. of Info.

SUTHERLAND, ASBILL & BRENNAN - LIBRARY
1666 K St., N.W., Suite 800   Phone: (202) 887-3495
Washington, DC 20006   Nalini Rajguru, Libn.

SWEDISH EMBASSY - LIBRARY-INFORMATION CENTER *
Watergate 600, Suite 1200
600 New Hampshire Ave., N.W.   Phone: (202) 298-3500
Washington, DC 20037   Larilyn Reitnauer, Libn.

TAX FOUNDATION - LIBRARY
One Thomas Circle, N.W., Suite 500   Phone: (202) 328-4500
Washington, DC 20005   Marion Marshall, Libn.

TEACHERS OF ENGLISH TO SPEAKERS OF OTHER LANGUAGES - TESOL
   LENDING LIBRARY
201 D.C. Transit Bldg.
Georgetown University   Phone: (202) 625-4569
Washington, DC 20057   Ahmad Fassihian, Resource Spec.

TEMPLE SINAI - LIBRARY
3100 Military Rd., N.W.   Phone: (202) 363-6394
Washington, DC 20015   Ellen Rosenberg Murphy, Libn.

TEXTILE MUSEUM - ARTHUR D. JENKINS LIBRARY
2320 S St., N.W.   Phone: (202) 667-0442
Washington, DC 20008   Katherine T. Freshley, Libn.

TOBACCO INSTITUTE - INFORMATION CENTER
1875 Eye St., N.W., Suite 800   Phone: (202) 457-4800
Washington, DC 20006   Brenda B. Clark, Mgr., Info.Ctr.

TRADE RELATIONS COUNCIL OF THE UNITED STATES - LIBRARY
1001 Connecticut Ave., N.W.
Washington, DC 20036   Eugene L. Stewart, Exec.Sec.

TRINITY COLLEGE - ARCHIVES
      Phone: (202) 269-2220
Washington, DC 20017   Sr. Columba Mullaly, Ph.D., Archv.

UNITED FOOD AND COMMERCIAL WORKERS INTERNATIONAL UNION -
   LIBRARY †
1775 K St., N.W.   Phone: (202) 223-3111
Washington, DC 20006   Ellen Newton, Libn.

UNITED METHODIST CHURCH - WESLEY THEOLOGICAL SEMINARY -
   LIBRARY
4500 Massachusetts Ave., N.W.   Phone: (202) 363-0922
Washington, DC 20016   Roland E. Kircher, Dir.

U.S. ADVISORY COMMISSION ON INTERGOVERNMENTAL RELATIONS -
   LIBRARY
1111 20th St., N.W.   Phone: (202) 653-5034
Washington, DC 20575   Patricia A. Koch, Libn.

U.S. AGENCY FOR INTERNATIONAL DEVELOPMENT - DEVELOPMENT
   INFORMATION CENTER
320 21st St., N.W., Rm. 105, SA-18   Phone: (703) 235-1000
Washington, DC 20523   Joanne M. Paskar, Hd.

U.S. AIR FORCE - AIR FORCE SYSTEMS COMMAND - LIBRARY DIVISION
AFSC/MPSL, Andrews Air Force Base   Phone: (301) 981-2598
Washington, DC 20334   Frances M. Quinn, Dir., Command Libs.

U.S. AIR FORCE - AIR FORCE SYSTEMS COMMAND - TECHNICAL
   INFORMATION CENTER
Andrews AFB, MPSLT   Phone: (301) 981-3551
Washington, DC 20334   Yvonne A. Kinkaid, Chf.

U.S. AIR FORCE BASE - ANDREWS BASE LIBRARY
FL 4425, Andrews AFB   Phone: (301) 981-6454
Washington, DC 20331

U.S. AIR FORCE BASE - BOLLING BASE LIBRARY
Bolling AFB   Phone: (202) 767-4251
Washington, DC 20332   Gloria Guffey, Libn.

U.S. AIR FORCE HOSPITAL - MALCOLM GROW MEDICAL CENTER - LIBRARY
Andrews AFB   Phone: (202) 981-2354
Washington, DC 20331   Mary Alice Zelinka, Med.Libn.

U.S. AIR FORCE - OFFICE OF JUDGE ADVOCATE GENERAL - LEGAL REFERENCE LIBRARY
1900 Half St., S.W., Rm. 5113
Washington, DC 20324
Phone: (202) 693-5638
William J. Zschunke, Libn.

U.S. ARCHITECTURAL AND TRANSPORTATION BARRIERS COMPLIANCE BOARD (ATBCB) - TECHNICAL RESOURCES LIBRARY
330 C St., S.W.
Washington, DC 20202
Phone: (202) 472-2700
Judy Newton, Mgt.Anl.

U.S. ARMED FORCES INSTITUTE OF PATHOLOGY - ASH LIBRARY †
Walter Reed Army Medical Ctr., Rm. 407
Stop 215
Washington, DC 20306
Phone: (202) 576-2983
Sally G. Allinson, Libn.

U.S. ARMS CONTROL AND DISARMAMENT AGENCY - LIBRARY
Dept. of State Bldg., Rm. 5851
21st & C St., N.W.
Washington, DC 20541
Phone: (202) 632-1592
Diane A. Ferguson, Libn.

U.S. ARMY - ARMED FORCES PEST MANAGEMENT BOARD - DEFENSE PEST MANAGEMENT INFORMATION ANALYSIS CENTER
Walter Reed Army Medical Center
Forest Glen Section
Washington, DC 20307
Phone: (202) 427-5365
Cdr. Fred J. Santana, MSC, Hd.

U.S. ARMY HOSPITALS - WALTER REED ARMY MEDICAL CENTER - MEDICAL LIBRARY
Bldg. 2, Rm. 2G
Washington, DC 20307
Phone: (202) 576-1238
Beth E. Smith, Chf.Libn.

U.S. ARMY - OFFICE OF THE CHIEF OF ENGINEERS - LIBRARY
20 Massachusetts Ave., N.W.
Washington, DC 20314
Phone: (202) 272-0455
Sarah A. Mikel, Chf., Tech.Info.Div.

U.S. ARMY - PENTAGON LIBRARY
The Pentagon, Rm. 1 A 518
Washington, DC 20310
Phone: (202) 695-5346
Dorothy A. Cross, Dir.

U.S. ARMY/U.S. AIR FORCE - OFFICES OF THE SURGEONS GENERAL - JOINT MEDICAL LIBRARY
The Pentagon, Rm. 1B - 473
Washington, DC 20310
Phone: (202) 695-5752
Donna K. Griffitts, Adm.Libn.

U.S. ARMY - WALTER REED ARMY INSTITUTE OF RESEARCH - LIBRARY
Walter Reed Army Medical Center
Washington, DC 20307
Phone: (202) 576-3314
V. Lynn Gera, Adm.Libn.

U.S. BUREAU OF ALCOHOL, TOBACCO AND FIREARMS - REFERENCE LIBRARY
1200 Pennsylvania Ave., N.W.
Washington, DC 20226
Phone: (202) 566-7602
Vicki R. Herrmann, Libn.

U.S. BUREAU OF THE CENSUS - LIBRARY & INFORMATION SERVICES BRANCH
Federal Bldg. No. 3
Washington, DC 20233
Phone: (301) 763-5040
Betty Baxtresser, Chf.

U.S. BUREAU OF MINES - BRANCH OF OPERATIONS & SUPPORT - LIBRARY
2401 E St., N.W.
Washington, DC 20241
Phone: (202) 634-1116
Judy C. Jordan, Lib.Techn.

U.S. CIVIL AERONAUTICS BOARD - LIBRARY
Universal Bldg., Rm. 912
Connecticut & Florida Aves., N.W.
Washington, DC 20428
Phone: (202) 673-5101
Mary Louise Ransom, Supv.libn.

U.S. COMMISSION ON CIVIL RIGHTS - NATL. CLEARINGHOUSE LIBRARY
1121 Vermont Ave., N.W.
Washington, DC 20425
Phone: (202) 254-6636
Lenora W. McMillan, Chf.Libn.

U.S. COMPTROLLER OF THE CURRENCY - LIBRARY
490 L'Enfant Plaza, S.W., 5th Fl.
Washington, DC 20219
Phone: (202) 447-1843
Audrey L. Ruge, Libn.

U.S. COURT OF APPEALS, DISTRICT OF COLUMBIA CIRCUIT - LIBRARY
5518 U.S. Court House
3rd & Constitution Ave., N.W.
Washington, DC 20001
Phone: (202) 535-3401
Nancy Lazar, Circuit Libn.

U.S. COURT OF APPEALS FOR THE FEDERAL CIRCUIT - NATIONAL COURTS' LIBRARY
717 Madison Pl., N.W., Rm. 218
Washington, DC 20439
Phone: (202) 633-5871
Patricia M. McDermott, Libn.

U.S. COURT OF MILITARY APPEALS - LIBRARY
450 E St., N.W.
Washington, DC 20442
Phone: (202) 693-7573
Mary S. Kuck, Libn.

U.S. CUSTOMS SERVICE - LIBRARY AND INFORMATION CENTER
1301 Constitution Ave., N.W., Rm. 3340
Washington, DC 20229
Phone: (202) 566-5642
Patricia M. Dobrosky, Dir.

U.S. DEFENSE AUDIOVISUAL AGENCY - STILL PICTURE LIBRARY
Bldg. 168, NDW
Washington, DC 20374
Phone: (202) 433-2166
Roy K. Heitman

U.S. DEFENSE COMMUNICATIONS AGENCY - TECHNICAL AND MANAGEMENT INFORMATION CENTER
Headquarters, DCA, Code H308C
Washington, DC 20305
Phone: (202) 692-2468
Donald A. Guerriero, Lib.Dir.

U.S. DEFENSE INTELLIGENCE AGENCY - LIBRARY RTS-2A
Washington, DC 20301
Phone: (202) 692-5311
H. Holzbauer, Chief Libn.

U.S. DEFENSE MAPPING AGENCY - HYDROGRAPHIC/TOPOGRAPHIC CENTER- SUPPORT DIVISION - SCIENTIFIC DATA DEPARTMENT
6500 Brookes Lane
Washington, DC 20315
Phone: (301) 227-2080
Frank Lozupone, Chf., Sup.Div.

U.S. DEFENSE NUCLEAR AGENCY - TECHNICAL LIBRARY
Washington, DC 20305
Phone: (202) 325-7780
Betty L. Fox, Info. Programs Mgr.

U.S.D.A. - ECONOMIC RESEARCH SERVICE - ERS REFERENCE CENTER
500 12th St., S.W., Rm. 147
Washington, DC 20250
Phone: (202) 447-4382
Cynthia Kenyon, Dir.

U.S.D.A. - OFFICE OF GENERAL COUNSEL - LAW LIBRARY
Independence Ave. at 12th St., S.W.
Rm. 1406, S Bldg.
Washington, DC 20250
Phone: (202) 447-7751
Edward S. Billings, Law Libn.

U.S.D.A. - PHOTOGRAPHY DIVISION - PHOTOGRAPH LIBRARY
14th & Independence Ave., S.W.
Washington, DC 20250
Phone: (202) 447-6633

U.S. DEPT. OF COMMERCE - COMMERCE PRODUCTIVITY CENTER
14th St. & Constitution Ave., N.W., Rm. 7413
Washington, DC 20230
Phone: (202) 377-0940
States Clawson, Mgr.

U.S. DEPT. OF COMMERCE - LAW LIBRARY
14th & Pennsylvania Ave., N.W., Rm. 1894
Washington, DC 20230
Phone: (202) 377-5517
Thomas B. Fleming, Chf. Law Libn.

U.S. DEPT. OF COMMERCE - LIBRARY
14th & Constitution Ave., N.W.
Washington, DC 20230
Phone: (202) 377-3611
Stanley J. Bougas, Dir.

U.S. DEPT. OF ENERGY - ENERGY INFORMATION ADMINISTRATION - NATIONAL ENERGY INFORMATION CENTER
Forrestal Bldg., Rm. 1F-048
Washington, DC 20585
Phone: (202) 252-8800
John E. Daniels, Dir.

U.S. DEPT. OF ENERGY - ENERGY LIBRARY
MA 232
Washington, DC 20585
Phone: (202) 252-5955
Ronald R. Turner, Act.Chf.

U.S. DEPT. OF ENERGY - OFFICE OF GENERAL COUNSEL LAW LIBRARY
1000 Independence Ave., S.W., Rm. 6A 156
Washington, DC 20585
Phone: (202) 252-4848
Oscar E. Strothers, Chf. Law Libn.

U.S. DEPT. OF HEALTH AND HUMAN SERVICES - DEPARTMENT LIBRARY †
330 Independence Ave., S.W., Rm 1436 N.
Washington, DC 20201
Phone: (202) 245-6791
Charles F. Gately, Dir.

U.S. DEPT. OF HEALTH AND HUMAN SERVICES - EVALUATION
   DOCUMENTATION CENTER (EDC)
200 Independence Ave., S.W.   Phone: (202) 245-6833
Washington, DC 20201   Carolyn G. Solomon, Tech.Info.Spec.

U.S. DEPT. OF HOUSING AND URBAN DEVELOPMENT - LIBRARY
451 Seventh St., S.W., Rm. 8141   Phone: (202) 755-6376
Washington, DC 20410   Carol A. Johnson, Proj.Mgr.

U.S. DEPT. OF HOUSING & URBAN DEVELOPMENT - PHOTOGRAPHY
   LIBRARY
451 7th St., S.W., Rm. B-120   Phone: (202) 755-7305
Washington, DC 20410   David A. Murdock, Visual Info.Spec.

U.S. DEPT. OF THE INTERIOR - DIVISION OF INFORMATION AND LIBRARY
   SERVICES - LAW BRANCH
18th & C Sts., N.W., Rm. 7100W   Phone: (202) 343-4571
Washington, DC 20240   Carl Kessler, Chf.

U.S. DEPT. OF THE INTERIOR - INDIAN ARTS AND CRAFTS BOARD
Rm. 4004, 18th & C Sts., N.W.   Phone: (202) 343-2773
Washington, DC 20240   Robert G. Hart, Gen.Mgr.

U.S. DEPT. OF THE INTERIOR - NATURAL RESOURCES LIBRARY
18th & C Sts., N.W.   Phone: (202) 343-5815
Washington, DC 20240   Phillip M. Haymond, Chf., Info./Lib.Serv.Dir.

U.S. DEPT. OF JUSTICE - ANTITRUST DIVISION LIBRARY
10th & Pennsylvania Ave., N.W., Rm. 3310   Phone: (202) 633-2431
Washington, DC 20530   Roger N. Karr, Libn.

U.S. DEPT. OF JUSTICE - CIVIL DIVISION LIBRARY
10th & Pennsylvania Ave., N.W., Rm. 3344   Phone: (202) 633-3523
Washington, DC 20530   Evangeline Mastriani, Libn.

U.S. DEPT. OF JUSTICE - CIVIL RIGHTS DIVISION - LIBRARY
10th & Pennsylvania Ave., N.W., Rm. 7618   Phone: (202) 633-4098
Washington, DC 20530   Kathleen T. Larson, Libn.

U.S. DEPT. OF JUSTICE - CRIMINAL DIVISION - LIBRARY
10th & Pennsylvania Ave., N.W., Rm. 2420   Phone: (202) 633-2383
Washington, DC 20530   Winifred M. Hart, Libn.

U.S. DEPT. OF JUSTICE - FEDERAL PRISON SYSTEM - LIBRARY
320 First St., N.W.   Phone: (202) 724-3029
Washington, DC 20534   Lloyd W. Hooker, Libn.

U.S. DEPT. OF JUSTICE - LAND AND NATURAL RESOURCES DIVISION
   LIBRARY
10th & Pennsylvania Ave., N.W., Rm. 2333   Phone: (202) 633-2768
Washington, DC 20530   Adelaide Loretta Brown, Libn.

U.S. DEPT. OF JUSTICE - MAIN LIBRARY
10th & Pennsylvania Ave., N.W., Rm. 5400   Phone: (202) 633-3775
Washington, DC 20530   Dee Sampson, Chf., Rd.Serv.

U.S. DEPT. OF JUSTICE - NATIONAL INSTITUTE OF JUSTICE - LIBRARY
633 Indiana Ave., N.W., Rm. 900   Phone: (202) 724-5884
Washington, DC 20531   Kyle Kramer, Libn.

U.S. DEPT. OF JUSTICE - TAX DIVISION LIBRARY
10th & Pennsylvania Ave., N.W., Rm. 4335   Phone: (202) 633-2819
Washington, DC 20530   Michael Rahill, Libn.

U.S. DEPT. OF LABOR - LIBRARY †
200 Constitution Ave., N.W.   Phone: (202) 523-6988
Washington, DC 20210

U.S. DEPT. OF LABOR - LIBRARY - LAW LIBRARY DIVISION
200 Constitution Ave., N.W., Rm. N-2439   Phone: (202) 523-7991
Washington, DC 20210   Donald L. Martin, Law Libn.

U.S. DEPT. OF LABOR - OSHA - TECHNICAL DATA CENTER
200 Constitution Ave., N.W.
Rm. N-2439 Rear   Phone: (202) 523-9700
Washington, DC 20210   Thomas A. Towers, Dir.

U.S. DEPT. OF STATE - LIBRARY
         Phone: (202) 632-0372
Washington, DC 20520   Conrad P. Eaton, Libn.

U.S. DEPT. OF STATE - OFFICE OF THE LEGAL ADVISER - LAW LIBRARY
Rm. 6422, Dept. of State   Phone: (202) 632-4130
Washington, DC 20520   Helena P. von Pfeil, Law Libn.

U.S. DEPT. OF TRANSPORTATION - LIBRARY AND DISTRIBUTION
   SERVICES DIVISION
400 7th St., S.W.   Phone: (202) 426-1792
Washington, DC 20590   Lawrence E. Leonard, Lib.Dir.

U.S. DEPT. OF TRANSPORTATION - URBAN MASS TRANSPORTATION ADM.
   - TRANSPORTATION RESEARCH INFO. CENTER (TRIC)
400 7th St., S.W.   Phone: (202) 426-9157
Washington, DC 20590   Ronald J. Fisher, Chf., Info.Serv.Div.

U.S. DEPT. OF THE TREASURY - INFORMATION SERVICES DIVISION -
   TREASURY DEPT. LIBRARY
Main Treasury Bldg., Rm. 5030   Phone: (202) 566-2777
Washington, DC 20220   Elisabeth S. Knauff, Mgr., Info.Serv.Div.

U.S. DRUG ENFORCEMENT ADMINISTRATION - LIBRARY
1405 Eye St., N.W.   Phone: (202) 633-1369
Washington, DC 20537   Morton S. Goren, Libn.

U.S. EQUAL EMPLOYMENT OPPORTUNITY COMMISSION - LIBRARY
2401 E St., N.W.   Phone: (202) 634-6990
Washington, DC 20507   Susan D. Taylor, Lib.Dir.

U.S. EXECUTIVE OFFICE OF THE PRESIDENT - LIBRARY
726 Jackson Place, N.W., Rm. G-102   Phone: (202) 395-3654
Washington, DC 20503   Adrienne Kosciusko, Dir., Lib. & Info.Serv.

U.S. FEDERAL AVIATION ADMINISTRATION - LAW LIBRARY
800 Independence Ave., S.W.   Phone: (202) 426-3604
Washington, DC 20591   Jane Braucher, Libn.

U.S. FEDERAL COMMUNICATIONS COMMISSION - LIBRARY †
1919 M St., N.W.   Phone: (202) 632-7100
Washington, DC 20554   Sheryl A. Segal, Lib.Dir.

U.S. FEDERAL DEPOSIT INSURANCE CORPORATION - LIBRARY
550 Seventeenth St., N.W.   Phone: (202) 389-4314
Washington, DC 20429   Carole Cleland, Chf.Libn.

U.S. FEDERAL HIGHWAY ADMINISTRATION - OFFICE OF THE CHIEF
   COUNSEL - LEGISLATIVE/REFERENCE LIBRARY
400 Seventh St., S.W., Rm. 4205   Phone: (202) 426-0754
Washington, DC 20590   Sherie A. Abbasi, Law Libn.

U.S. FEDERAL HOME LOAN BANK BOARD - LAW LIBRARY
1700 G St., N.W.   Phone: (202) 377-6470
Washington, DC 20552   Joyce A. Potter, Libn.

U.S. FEDERAL HOME LOAN BANK BOARD - RESEARCH LIBRARY
1700 G St., N.W.   Phone: (202) 377-6296
Washington, DC 20552   Janet B. Smith, Libn.

U.S. FEDERAL JUDICIAL CENTER - INFORMATION SERVICE †
1520 H St., N.W.   Phone: (202) 633-6365
Washington, DC 20005   Jane M. Gafvert, Info.Spec.

U.S. FEDERAL MARITIME COMMISSION - LIBRARY
1100 L St., N.W.   Phone: (202) 523-5762
Washington, DC 20573   Mary Ellen Daffron, Libn.

U.S. FEDERAL TRADE COMMISSION - LIBRARY
6th St. & Pennsylvania Ave., N.W.   Phone: (202) 523-3871
Washington, DC 20580   Susanne B. Hendsey, Lib.Dir.

U.S. FISH & WILDLIFE SERVICE - OFFICE OF AUDIO-VISUAL - LIBRARY
Dept. of the Interior, Rm. 8070   Phone: (202) 343-8770
Washington, DC 20240   Craig A. Koppie, Visual Info.Spec.

U.S. FOOD & DRUG ADMINISTRATION - CENTER FOR FOOD SAFETY &
   APPLIED NUTRITION - LIBRARY
200 C St., S.W., Rm. 3321, HFF-37   Phone: (202) 245-1235
Washington, DC 20204   Robert F. Clarke, Ph.D., Dir.

U.S. FOREST SERVICE - PERMANENT PHOTOGRAPHIC COLLECTION
Box 2417, Rm. 51-RPE
Phone: (703) 235-8215
Washington, DC 20013   William G. Hauser, Visual Info.Off.

U.S. GENERAL ACCOUNTING OFFICE - OFFICE OF LIBRARY SERVICES
441 G St., N.W.
Phone: (202) 275-5180
Washington, DC 20548   Phyllis Christenson, Dir.

U.S. GENERAL SERVICES ADMINISTRATION - CONSUMER INFORMATION
  CENTER
18th & F St., N.W.
Phone: (202) 566-1794
Washington, DC 20405   Teresa Nasif, Director

U.S. GENERAL SERVICES ADMINISTRATION - GSA LIBRARY
General Services Bldg., Rm. 1033
18th & F Sts., N.W.
Phone: (202) 535-7788
Washington, DC 20405   Gail L. Kohlhorst, Chf.

U.S. HOUSE OF REPRESENTATIVES - LIBRARY
B-18 Cannon Bldg.
Phone: (202) 225-0462
Washington, DC 20515   E. Raymond Lewis, Libn.

U.S. INFORMATION AGENCY - LIBRARY †
400 C St., S.W.
Phone: (202) 655-4000
Washington, DC 20024   Jeanne R. Zeydel, Agency Libn.

U.S. INFORMATION AGENCY - LIBRARY PROGRAM DIVISION
301 4th St., S.W., Rm. 324
Phone: (202) 485-2932
Washington, DC 20547   Robert Murphy, Dir.

U.S. INTERNAL REVENUE SERVICE - LAW LIBRARY †
Internal Revenue Service Bldg., Rm. 4324
1111 Constitution Ave., N.W.
Phone: (202) 566-6342
Washington, DC 20224   Anne B. Scheer, Libn.

U.S. INTERNATIONAL TRADE COMMISSION - LIBRARY
701 E St., N.W.
Phone: (202) 523-0013
Washington, DC 20436   Barbara J. Pruett, Chf., Lib.Div.

U.S. INTERSTATE COMMERCE COMMISSION - LIBRARY †
Twelfth & Constitution Ave., N.W., Rm. 3392   Phone: (202) 275-7328
Washington, DC 20423   Doris E. Watts, Libn.

U.S. LEAGUE OF SAVINGS INSTITUTIONS - LIBRARY
1709 New York Ave., N.W.
Phone: (202) 637-8920
Washington, DC 20006   Katherine Harahan, Libn.

U.S. MARINE CORPS - HISTORICAL CENTER LIBRARY †
Washington Navy Yard, Bldg. 58
Phone: (202) 433-4253
Washington, DC 20374   Lt.Col. P.A. Forbes, Hd.Sup.Br.

U.S. MARINE CORPS - MARINE BAND LIBRARY
Marine Barracks
Eighth & Eye Sts., S.E.
Phone: (202) 433-4298
Washington, DC 20390   Frank P. Byrne, Jr., Chf.Libn.

U.S. NASA - HEADQUARTERS LIBRARY
600 Independence Ave., S.W.
Code NHS-4, Rm. A39
Phone: (202) 453-8545
Washington, DC 20546   Mary Elizabeth Anderson, Libn.

U.S. NATL. ARBORETUM - LIBRARY
3501 New York Ave., N.E.
Phone: (202) 475-4815
Washington, DC 20002

U.S. NATL. ARCHIVES & RECORDS SERVICE - LIBRARY AND PRINTED
  ARCHIVES BRANCH
Eighth & Pennsylvania Ave., N.W.
Phone: (202) 523-3049
Washington, DC 20408   Nancy V. Menan, Chf.

U.S. NATL. ARCHIVES & RECORDS SERVICE - NATL. ARCHIVES
Eighth & Constitution Ave., N.W.
Phone: (202) 523-3218
Washington, DC 20408   Dr. Robert M. Warner, U.S. Archv.

U.S. NATL. ARCHIVES & RECORDS SERVICE - NATL. ARCHIVES -
  CARTOGRAPHIC & ARCHITECTURAL BRANCH
8th & Pennsylvania Ave., N.W.
Phone: (703) 756-6700
Washington, DC 20408   William H. Cunliffe, Chf.

U.S. NATL. ARCHIVES & RECORDS SERVICE - NATL. ARCHIVES - MOTION
  PICTURE, SOUND, & VIDEO BRANCH
7th St. & Pennsylvania Ave., N.W.
Phone: (202) 523-3063
Washington, DC 20408   William Murphy, Br.Chf.

U.S. NATL. ARCHIVES & RECORDS SERVICE - NATL. AUDIOVISUAL CENTER
  - INFORMATION SERVICES SECTION
Phone: (301) 763-1896
Washington, DC 20409   John McLean, Dir.

U.S. NATL. ARCHIVES & RECORDS SERVICE - STILL PICTURE BRANCH
Pennsylvania Ave. at 8th St., N.W.
Phone: (202) 523-3236
Washington, DC 20408   Joe D. Thomas, Chf.

U.S. NATL. BUREAU OF STANDARDS - ALLOY PHASE DIAGRAM DATA
  CENTER
Bldg. 223, Rm. B-150
Phone: (301) 921-2917
Washington, DC 20234   K.J. Bhansali, Dir.

U.S. NATL. BUREAU OF STANDARDS - ATOMIC ENERGY LEVELS DATA
  CENTER
Physics Bldg., Rm. A155
Phone: (301) 921-2011
Washington, DC 20234   Dr. William C. Martin, Physicist

U.S. NATL. BUREAU OF STANDARDS - CHEMICAL THERMODYNAMICS DATA
  CENTER
Chemistry Bldg., Rm. A158
Washington, DC 20234   David Garvin, Mgr.

U.S. NATL. BUREAU OF STANDARDS - DATA CENTER ON ATOMIC LINE
  SHAPES AND SHIFTS
Bldg. 221, Rm. A267
Washington, DC 20234

U.S. NATL. BUREAU OF STANDARDS - DATA CENTER ON ATOMIC
  TRANSITION PROBABILITIES
A267 Physics Bldg.
Phone: (301) 921-2071
Washington, DC 20234   Dr. W.L. Wiese, Dir.

U.S. NATL. BUREAU OF STANDARDS - FIRE RESEARCH INFORMATION
  SERVICES
Bldg. 224, Rm. A252
Natl. Bureau of Standards
Phone: (301) 921-3249
Washington, DC 20234   Nora H. Jason, Project Ldr.

U.S. NATL. BUREAU OF STANDARDS - FUNDAMENTAL CONSTANTS DATA
  CENTER
Bldg. 220, Rm. B258
Phone: (301) 921-2701
Washington, DC 20234   Dr. Barry N. Taylor, Chf.

U.S. NATL. BUREAU OF STANDARDS - ION KINETICS AND ENERGETICS
  DATA CENTER
A265 - Chemistry
Phone: (301) 921-2783
Washington, DC 20234   Dr. Sharon G. Lias, Dir.

U.S. NATL. BUREAU OF STANDARDS - LIBRARY
E106 Administration Bldg.
Phone: (301) 921-3451
Washington, DC 20234   Patricia W. Berger, Chf.Info.Rsrcs./Serv.Dir.

U.S. NATL. BUREAU OF STANDARDS - METALLURGY DIVISION - DIFFUSION
  IN METALS DATA CENTER
Bldg. 223, Rm. A153
Phone: (301) 921-3356
Washington, DC 20234   John R. Manning, Task Leader

U.S. NATL. BUREAU OF STANDARDS - NATIONAL CENTER FOR STANDARDS
  AND CERTIFICATION INFORMATION
Rm. 617, Administration
Phone: (301) 921-2587
Washington, DC 20234   Sophie J. Chumas, NCSCI Supv.

U.S. NATL. BUREAU OF STANDARDS - OFFICE OF STANDARD REFERENCE
  DATA - REFERENCE CENTER
A-320 Physics Bldg.
Phone: (301) 921-2228
Washington, DC 20234   Cynthia A. Goldman, Libn.

U.S. NATL. BUREAU OF STANDARDS - PHASE DIAGRAMS FOR CERAMISTS -
  DATA CENTER
Phone: (301) 921-2844
Washington, DC 20234   Lawrence P. Cook, Dir.

U.S. NATL. DEFENSE UNIVERSITY - DEPARTMENT OF DEFENSE COMPUTER
INSTITUTE - DODCI TECHNICAL LIBRARY
Bldg. 175, Rm. 37
Washington Navy Yard   Phone: (202) 433-3653
Washington, DC 20374   Penelope F. Moore, Lib.Techn.

U.S. NATL. DEFENSE UNIVERSITY - LIBRARY
Fort Lesley J. McNair
4th & P Sts., S.W.   Phone: (202) 693-8437
Washington, DC 20319   J. Thomas Russell, Lib.Dir.

U.S. NATL. HIGHWAY TRAFFIC SAFETY ADMINISTRATION - TECHNICAL
REFERENCE DIVISION
400 7th St., S.W., Rm. 5108   Phone: (202) 426-2768
Washington, DC 20590   Jerome A. Holiber, Chf.

U.S. NATL. LABOR RELATIONS BOARD - LAW LIBRARY
1717 Pennsylvania Ave., N.W., Rm. 900   Phone: (202) 254-9055
Washington, DC 20570   Barbara W. Hazelett, Adm.Libn.

U.S. NATL. OCEANIC & ATMOSPHERIC ADMINISTRATION - GEORGETOWN
CENTER
3300 Whitehaven   Phone: (202) 634-7346
Washington, DC 20235   Ida Lewis

U.S. NATL. OCEANIC & ATMOSPHERIC ADMINISTRATION - NATIONAL
OCEANOGRAPHIC DATA CENTER
                                        Phone: (202) 634-7500
Washington, DC 20235   Edward L. Ridley, Dir.

U.S. NATL. PARK SERVICE - FREDERICK DOUGLASS HOME AND VISITOR
CENTER - LIBRARY
1411 W St., S.E.   Phone: (202) 426-5962
Washington, DC 20020   Tyra Walker

U.S. NATL. PARK SERVICE - NATL. CAPITAL REGION - ROCK CREEK
NATURE CENTER LIBRARY
5200 Glover Rd., N.W.   Phone: (202) 426-6829
Washington, DC 20015   Lurrie V. Pope, Supv. Park Ranger

U.S. NAVY - DEPARTMENT LIBRARY
Bldg. 44
Washington Navy Yard   Phone: (202) 433-2386
Washington, DC 20374   Stanley Kalkus, Dir.

U.S. NAVY - NAVAL AIR SYSTEMS COMMAND - TECHNICAL LIBRARY AIR-
7226
                                        Phone: (202) 692-9006
Washington, DC 20361   Pat Stone, Hd.Libn.

U.S. NAVY - NAVAL HISTORICAL CENTER - OPERATIONAL ARCHIVES
Bldg. 210, Washington Navy Yard   Phone: (202) 433-3170
Washington, DC 20374   Dr. Dean C. Allard, Dir.

U.S. NAVY - NAVAL HISTORICAL CENTER - PHOTOGRAPHIC SECTION
Washington Navy Yard   Phone: (202) 433-2765
Washington, DC 20374

U.S. NAVY - NAVAL INTELLIGENCE SUPPORT CENTER - INFORMATION
SERVICES DIVISION
4301 Suitland Rd.
Code 63   Phone: (202) 763-1606
Washington, DC 20390   Alice T. Cranor, Hd., Info.Serv.Div.

U.S. NAVY - NAVAL MILITARY PERSONNEL COMMAND - TECHNICAL
LIBRARY
Arlington Annex, Rm. 1403   Phone: (202) 694-2073
Washington, DC 20370   Joyce A. Lane, Libn.

U.S. NAVY - NAVAL OBSERVATORY - MATTHEW FONTAINE MAURY
MEMORIAL LIBRARY
34th and Massachusetts Ave., N.W.   Phone: (202) 653-1499
Washington, DC 20390   Brenda G. Corbin, Libn.

U.S. NAVY - NAVAL RESEARCH LABORATORY - RUTH H. HOOKER
TECHNICAL LIBRARY
Code 2620   Phone: (202) 767-2357
Washington, DC 20375   Peter H. Imhof, Libn.

U.S. NAVY - NAVAL RESEARCH LABORATORY - SHOCK AND VIBRATION
INFORMATION CENTER
Code 5804   Phone: (202) 767-3306
Washington, DC 20375   J. Gordan Showalter, Hd.

U.S. NAVY - NAVAL SEA SYSTEMS COMMAND - LIBRARY DOCUMENTATION
BRANCH (SEA 09B31)
Rm. 1S28, National Center, Bldg. 3   Phone: (202) 692-3349
Washington, DC 20362   Alan M. Lewis, Hd., Lib.Doc.Br.

U.S. NAVY - NAVAL SUPPLY SYSTEMS COMMAND - LIBRARY
Rm. 509, Bldg. 3, Crystal Mall   Phone: (202) 695-4704
Washington, DC 20376   James Crouch, Libn.

U.S. NAVY - OFFICE OF THE GENERAL COUNSEL - LAW LIBRARY
Crystal Plaza 5, Rm. 450   Phone: (202) 692-7378
Washington, DC 20360   Mary E. Williams, Hd.Libn.

U.S. NAVY - REGIONAL DATA AUTOMATION CENTER - TECHNICAL
LIBRARY
Bldg. 143, Washington Navy Yard   Phone: (202) 433-5700
Washington, DC 20374   William H. Hagen, Libn.

U.S. NAVY - STRATEGIC SYSTEMS PROJECT OFFICE - TECHNICAL
LIBRARY
                                        Phone: (202) 697-2852
Washington, DC 20376   June R. Gable, Tech.Lib.Br.Hd.

U.S. NEWS & WORLD REPORT - LIBRARY
2400 N St., N.W.   Phone: (202) 955-2350
Washington, DC 20037   Kathleen Trimble, Lib.Dir.

U.S. NUCLEAR REGULATORY COMMISSION - LAW LIBRARY
STOP 555   Phone: (301) 492-7584
Washington, DC 20555   Charlotte David, Chf., Legal Info.Serv.

U.S. OFFICE OF PERSONNEL MANAGEMENT - LIBRARY
1900 E St., N.W.   Phone: (202) 632-4432
Washington, DC 20415   Betty B. Guerin, Supv.Libn.

U.S. OFFICE OF TECHNOLOGY ASSESSMENT - INFORMATION CENTER
Congress of the United States   Phone: (202) 226-2160
Washington, DC 20510   Martha M. Dexter, Mgr., Info.Serv.

U.S. PEACE CORPS - INFORMATION SERVICES DIVISION
806 Connecticut Ave., N.W., Rm. M-407   Phone: (202) 254-3307
Washington, DC 20526   Rita C. Warpeha, Chf.Libn.

U.S. POSTAL SERVICE - LIBRARY
475 L'Enfant Plaza, S.W.   Phone: (202) 245-4021
Washington, DC 20260   Jane F. Kennedy, Gen.Mgr.

UNITED STATES RAILWAY ASSOCIATION - USRA DOCUMENT CENTER
955 L'Enfant Plaza North, S.W.   Phone: (202) 488-8777
Washington, DC 20595   James R. Gasser, Mgr., Doc.Ctr.

U.S. SECURITIES AND EXCHANGE COMMISSION - LIBRARY
450 5th St., N.W.   Phone: (202) 272-2618
Washington, DC 20549   Charlene C. Derge, Libn.

U.S. SENATE - LIBRARY
Capitol Bldg., Suite S-332   Phone: (202) 224-7106
Washington, DC 20510   Roger K. Haley, Senate Libn.

U.S. SMALL BUSINESS ADMINISTRATION - REFERENCE LIBRARY
1441 L St., N.W.   Phone: (202) 653-6914
Washington, DC 20416   Margaret Hickey, Libn.

U.S. SOCIAL SECURITY ADMINISTRATION - BRANCH LIBRARY
Universal N. Bldg., Rm. 320-0
1875 Connecticut Ave. N.W.   Phone: (202) 673-5624
Washington, DC 20009   Octavio Alvarez, Libn.

U.S. SOCIAL SECURITY ADMINISTRATION - COMPARATIVE STUDIES
STAFF REFERENCE ROOM
1875 Connecticut Ave., N.W.
Universal North Bldg., Rm. 940   Phone: (202) 673-5713
Washington, DC 20009   Ilene Zeitzer, Tech.Info.Spec.

U.S. SOIL CONSERVATION SERVICE - NATIONAL PHOTOGRAPHIC LIBRARY
Box 2890   Phone: (202) 447-7547
Washington, DC 20013   E. Joseph Larson, Chf., AV Br.

UNITED STATES STUDENT ASSOCIATION - INFORMATION SERVICES
One Dupont Circle, Suite 300   Phone: (202) 775-8943
Washington, DC 20036   Gregory Moore, Pres.

U.S. SUPREME COURT - LIBRARY
One First St., N.E.   Phone: (202) 252-3000
Washington, DC 20543   Roger F. Jacobs, Libn.

U.S. TAX COURT - LIBRARY
400 Second St., N.W.   Phone: (202) 376-2707
Washington, DC 20217   Jeanne R. Bonynge, Libn.

U.S. TRAVEL DATA CENTER - LIBRARY
1899 L St., N.W.   Phone: (202) 293-1040
Washington, DC 20036   Dr. Douglas Frechtling, Dir.

U.S. VETERANS ADMINISTRATION (DC-Washington) - GENERAL COUNSEL'S
   LAW LIBRARY (026H)
810 Vermont Ave., N.W., Rm. 1039   Phone: (202) 389-2159
Washington, DC 20420   Nina Kahn, Law Libn.

U.S. VETERANS ADMINISTRATION (DC-Washington) - HEADQUARTERS
   CENTRAL OFFICE LIBRARY (142D1)
Veterans Administration
810 Vermont Ave., N.W.   Phone: (202) 389-2430
Washington, DC 20420   Karen Renninger, Chf., Lib.Div.

U.S. VETERANS ADMINISTRATION (DC-Washington) - HEADQUARTERS
   LIBRARY DIVISION (142D)
Veterans Administration Bldg.
810 Vermont Ave., N.W.   Phone: (202) 389-2781
Washington, DC 20420   Karen Renninger, Chf., Lib.Div.

U.S. VETERANS ADMINISTRATION (DC-Washington) - MEDICAL CENTER
   LIBRARY
50 Irving St., N.W.   Phone: (202) 745-8262
Washington, DC 20422   Mary Netzow, Chf.Libn.

UNIVERSAL SERIALS & BOOK EXCHANGE, INC. - DUPLICATE EXCHANGE
   CLEARINGHOUSE & INFORMATION CENTER
3335 V St., N.E.   Phone: (202) 636-8723
Washington, DC 20018   Mary W. Ghikas, Exec.Dir.

UNIVERSITY OF THE DISTRICT OF COLUMBIA - HARVARD STREET
   LIBRARY †
1100 Harvard St., N.W.   Phone: (202) 673-7018
Washington, DC 20009   Lottie Wright, Supv.

UNIVERSITY OF THE DISTRICT OF COLUMBIA - LEARNING RESOURCES
   DIVISION †
4200 Connecticut Ave., N.W.   Phone: (202) 282-7536
Washington, DC 20008   Albert J. Casciero, Dir.

URBAN INSTITUTE - LIBRARY
2100 M St., N.W.   Phone: (202) 223-1950
Washington, DC 20037   Camille A. Motta, Dir. of Lib./Archv.

URBAN LAND INSTITUTE - LIBRARY †
1090 Vermont Ave., N.W., Suite 300   Phone: (202) 289-8500
Washington, DC 20005   Elizabeth Baker, Libn.

VERNER, LIIPFERT, BERNHARD & MC PHERSON - LIBRARY †
1660 L St., N.W., Suite 1000   Phone: (202) 452-7495
Washington, DC 20036   May Haruye Yoneyama, Law Libn.

WASHINGTON AREA WOMEN'S CENTER - WAWC FEMINIST LIBRARY &
   ARCHIVES
1638 R St., No. 2
Washington, DC 20009

WASHINGTON CATHEDRAL FOUNDATION - CATHEDRAL RARE BOOK
   LIBRARY
Mount St. Alban, N.W.
Washington, DC 20016   Irwin H. Wensink, Chm., Lib.Comm.

WASHINGTON HOSPITAL CENTER - MEDICAL LIBRARY
110 Irving St., N.W., Rm. 2A-21   Phone: (202) 541-6221
Washington, DC 20010   Marilyn Cook, Dir.

WASHINGTON METROPOLITAN AREA TRANSIT AUTHORITY - OFFICE OF
   PUBLIC AFFAIRS - LIBRARY
600 Fifth St., N.W., Rm. 2G-02   Phone: (202) 637-1052
Washington, DC 20001   Michaela M. Cohan, Libn.

WASHINGTON POST - LIBRARY
1150 15th St., N.W.   Phone: (202) 334-7341
Washington, DC 20071   William Hifner, Libn.

WASHINGTON PSYCHOANALYTIC SOCIETY - ERNEST E. HADLEY
   MEMORIAL LIBRARY
4925 MacArthur Blvd., N.W.   Phone: (202) 338-5453
Washington, DC 20007   Mary W. Allen, Libn.

WATER POLLUTION CONTROL FEDERATION - LIBRARY
2626 Pennsylvania Ave., N.W.   Phone: (202) 337-2500
Washington, DC 20037   Berinda J. Ross, Asst.Mgr., Tech.Serv.

WHALE PROTECTION FUND - ENVIRONMENTAL EDUCATION RESOURCE
   LIBRARY
624 Ninth St., N.W.   Phone: (202) 737-3600
Washington, DC 20001   Twig C. George, Educ.Coord.

WILDLIFE MANAGEMENT INSTITUTE - LIBRARY
1101 Fourteenth St., N.W., Suite 725   Phone: (202) 347-1774
Washington, DC 20005   Richard E. McCabe, Dir.Pubns.

WILMER, CUTLER & PICKERING - LAW LIBRARY
1666 K St., N.W.   Phone: (202) 872-6183
Washington, DC 20006   Elaine Mitchell, Dir. of Info.Serv.

WILSON (Woodrow) INTERNATIONAL CENTER FOR SCHOLARS - LIBRARY
Smithsonian Institution Bldg.   Phone: (202) 357-2567
Washington, DC 20560   Zdenek V. David, Libn.

WOMEN'S EQUITY ACTION LEAGUE - NATIONAL INFORMATION CENTER
   ON WOMEN AND THE MILITARY
805 15th St., N.W., Suite 822   Phone: (202) 638-1961
Washington, DC 20005   Carolyn Becraft, Proj.Dir.

WOODSTOCK THEOLOGICAL CENTER - LIBRARY
Georgetown University
Box 37445   Phone: (202) 625-3120
Washington, DC 20013   Thomas A. Marshall, S.J., Libn.

WORLD BANK LAW LIBRARY
1818 H St., N.W. (E-743)   Phone: (202) 477-2128
Washington, DC 20433   Linda L. Thompson, Law Libn.

WORLD DATA CENTER A - OCEANOGRAPHY
Natl. Oceanic and Atmospheric Adm.   Phone: (202) 634-7249
Washington, DC 20235   James Churgin, Dir.

WORLD HUNGER EDUCATION SERVICE - LIBRARY
1317 G St., N.W.   Phone: (202) 223-2995
Washington, DC 20005   Dr. Patricia L. Kutzner, Exec.Dir.

WORLD PEACE THROUGH LAW CENTER - ARCHIVES
1000 Connecticut Ave., N.W., Suite 800   Phone: (202) 466-5428
Washington, DC 20036

WORLD PEACE THROUGH LAW CENTER - INFORMATION CENTER
1000 Connecticut Ave., N.W., Suite 800
Washington, DC 20036

FLORIDA

INSTITUTE OF INTERNAL AUDITORS, INC. - LIBRARY
International Headquarters
249 Maitland Ave.   Phone: (305) 830-7600
Altamonte Springs, FL 32701   Betty J. Adler, Off.Mgr.

WALKER MEMORIAL HOSPITAL - LIBRARY
Box 1200   Phone: (813) 453-7511
Avon Park, FL 33825-1200   Monica Lescay, Dir., Med.Rec./Libn.

FLORIDA INSTITUTE OF PHOSPHATE RESEARCH - LIBRARY AND
   INFORMATION CLEARINGHOUSE
1855 W. Main St.   Phone: (813) 533-0983
Bartow, FL 33830   Betty Faye Stidham, Libn.

POLK COUNTY HISTORICAL AND GENEALOGICAL LIBRARY
495 N. Hendry Ave.
Box 1719   Phone: (813) 533-5146
Bartow, FL 33830   LaCona Raines Padgett, Hd.Libn.

POLK COUNTY LAW LIBRARY
Courthouse, Rm. 307   Phone: (813) 533-0411
Bartow, FL 33830   Nancy H. Tabler, Libn.

U.S. VETERANS ADMINISTRATION (FL-Bay Pines) - CENTER LIBRARY
                                  Phone: (813) 391-9644
Bay Pines, FL 33504   Ann A. Conlan, Chf., Lib.Serv.

UNIVERSITY OF FLORIDA - AGRICULTURAL RESEARCH & EDUCATION
   CENTER - BELLE GLADE LIBRARY
Inst. of Food & Agricultural Sciences
Drawer A   Phone: (305) 996-3062
Belle Glade, FL 33430   Dr. Myers, Lib.Comm.Chm.

BOCA RATON COMMUNITY HOSPITAL - HEALTH SCIENCES LIBRARY
800 Meadows Rd.   Phone: (305) 395-7100
Boca Raton, FL 33432   Carolyn F. Hill, Med.Libn.

CHURCH OF JESUS CHRIST OF LATTER-DAY SAINTS - WEST PALM BEACH
   FLORIDA STAKE BRANCH GENEALOGICAL LIBRARY
1530 W. Camino Real
Box 2350   Phone: (305) 395-6644
Boca Raton, FL 33427-2350   Phyllis M. Heiss, Br.Libn.

CRC PRESS, INC. - LIBRARY †
2000 Corporate Blvd., N.W.   Phone: (305) 994-0555
Boca Raton, FL 33431   Janelle Sparks, Ed.

BETHESDA MEMORIAL HOSPITAL - MEDICAL LIBRARY †
2815 S. Seacrest Blvd.   Phone: (305) 737-7733
Boynton Beach, FL 33435   Carol S. Ploch, Med.Libn.

REL INCORPORATED - CORPORATE LIBRARY
3800 S. Congress Ave.   Phone: (305) 732-0300
Boynton Beach, FL 33435   Linda L. Wyman, Libn.

ST. VINCENT DE PAUL REGIONAL SEMINARY - LIBRARY
10701 Military Trail
Box 460   Phone: (305) 732-4424
Boynton Beach, FL 33425   Bro. Frank J. Mazsick, C.F.X., Lib.Dir.

MANATEE COUNTY BAR ASSOCIATION - LAW LIBRARY
County Court House
Box 1000   Phone: (813) 748-4501
Bradenton, FL 33506   L. Marie Ingram, Law Libn.

MANATEE COUNTY PLANNING AND DEVELOPMENT DEPARTMENT -
   TECHNICAL REFERENCE LIBRARY
212 6th Ave., E.   Phone: (813) 748-4501
Bradenton, FL 33508   Carol B. Clarke

MANATEE MEMORIAL HOSPITAL - WENTZEL MEDICAL LIBRARY
206 2nd St., E.   Phone: (813) 746-5111
Bradenton, FL 33508   Jeanette Mosher, Med.Libn.

U.S. NATL. PARK SERVICE - DE SOTO NATL. MEMORIAL - LIBRARY
75th St., N.W.   Phone: (813) 792-0458
Bradenton, FL 33529   Guy L. LaChine, Supv. Park Ranger

UNIVERSITY OF FLORIDA - GULF COAST RESEARCH & EDUCATION CENTER
   - BRADENTON LIBRARY
Inst. of Food & Agricultural Sciences
5007 60th St., E.   Phone: (813) 755-1568
Bradenton, FL 34203

FLORIDA STATE - SOUTHWEST FLORIDA MANAGEMENT DISTRICT -
   LIBRARY
2379 Broad St.   Phone: (904) 796-7201
Brooksville, FL 33512-9712   Charles Tornabene, Jr., Libn.

COMMUNITY HOSPITAL OF BUNNELL - MEDICAL LIBRARY
Box 98   Phone: (904) 437-2211
Bunnell, FL 32010   Laine Bridges, Libn.

FLORIDA SOLAR ENERGY CENTER - LIBRARY
300 State Rd. 401   Phone: (305) 783-0300
Cape Canaveral, FL 32920   Iraida B. Rickling, Libn.

FLORIDA STATE HOSPITAL - HEALTH SCIENCE LIBRARY
                                  Phone: (904) 663-7205
Chattahoochee, FL 32324   Ada C. Ethridge, Med.Libn.

FLORIDA STATE HOSPITAL - PATIENT/STAFF LIBRARY
                                  Phone: (904) 663-7453
Chattahoochee, FL 32324   Linda Gail Brown, Dir. of Lib.Serv.

PINELLAS COUNTY LAW LIBRARY - CLEARWATER BRANCH
315 Court St.   Phone: (813) 448-2411
Clearwater, FL 33516

SPERRY - SPERRY ELECTRONIC SYSTEMS - TECHNICAL INFORMATION
   CENTER
Box 4648   Phone: (813) 577-1900
Clearwater, FL 33518   Margaret M. Cort, Hd.Libn.

TODAY NEWSPAPER - LIBRARY †
308 Forrest Ave.
Box 1330   Phone: (305) 632-8700
Cocoa, FL 32922   Pamela P. Fortman, Lib.Dir.

FELLOWSHIP OF RELIGIOUS HUMANISTS - BRANCH LIBRARY
1044 Samar Rd.   Phone: (305) 783-8359
Cocoa Beach, FL 32931   Rev. Edwin H. Wilson, Hist.

BEHAVIORAL SCIENCE RESEARCH CORPORATION - INFORMATION
   CENTER
1000 Ponce de Leon Blvd.   Phone: (305) 448-7622
Coral Gables, FL 33134   Robert Ladner, Sr.Res.Assoc.

TEMPLE JUDEA - MEL HARRISON MEMORIAL LIBRARY
5500 Granada Blvd.
Coral Gables, FL 33146   Zelda Harrison, Libn.

U.S. NATL. OCEANIC & ATMOSPHERIC ADMINISTRATION - CORAL GABLES
   LIBRARY
Gables 1 Tower, 6th Fl.   Phone: (305) 666-0413
Coral Gables, FL 33146   Robert Ting, Chf.Libn.

UNIVERSITY OF MIAMI - LOWE ART MUSEUM LIBRARY
1301 Stanford Dr.   Phone: (305) 284-3535
Coral Gables, FL 33146   Ms. Zan Gay, Libn.

UNIVERSITY OF MIAMI - MORTON COLLECTANEA
Box 8204   Phone: (305) 284-3741
Coral Gables, FL 33124   Dr. Julia F. Morton, Dir.

UNIVERSITY OF MIAMI - RICHTER LIBRARY - ARCHIVES DIVISION
                                  Phone: (305) 284-3247
Coral Gables, FL 33124

UNIVERSITY OF MIAMI - SCHOOL OF LAW LIBRARY
Box 248087   Phone: (305) 284-2250
Coral Gables, FL 33124   Westwell R. Daniels, Law Libn.

UNIVERSITY OF MIAMI - SCHOOL OF MUSIC - ALBERT PICK MUSIC
   LIBRARY
                                  Phone: (305) 284-2429
Coral Gables, FL 33124   Nancy Kobialka, Music Libn.

KLEIN (B.) PUBLICATIONS - RESEARCH LIBRARY
Box 8503   Phone: (305) 752-1708
Coral Springs, FL 33065   B. Stecher, Libn.

NOVA UNIVERSITY - OCEANOGRAPHIC CENTER LIBRARY
8000 N. Ocean Dr.   Phone: (305) 475-7487
Dania, FL 33004   Stephen Lessner

BROWARD COUNTY PUBLIC SCHOOLS - LEARNING RESOURCES -
   PROFESSIONAL LIBRARY
6650 Griffin Rd.   Phone: (305) 765-6153
Davie, FL 33314   Jane P. Klasing, Educ.Spec., Media

EMBRY RIDDLE AERONAUTICAL UNIVERSITY - LEARNING RESOURCES
   CENTER
Regional Airport   Phone: (904) 252-5561
Daytona Beach, FL 32014   M. Judy Luther, Dir., Lrng.Rsrcs.

FLORIDA STATE DIVISION OF BLIND SERVICES - FLORIDA REGIONAL LIB.
   FOR THE BLIND & PHYSICALLY HANDICAPPED
Box 2299   Phone: (904) 252-4722
Daytona Beach, FL 32015   Donald John Weber, Dir.

HALIFAX HISTORICAL SOCIETY, INC. - LIBRARY
Box 2686   Phone: (904) 255-6976
Daytona Beach, FL 32015   Susan Lofaro, Pres.

HALIFAX HOSPITAL MEDICAL CENTER - MEDICAL LIBRARY
Clyde Morris Blvd.   Phone: (904) 254-4051
Daytona Beach, FL 32014   Ken Mead, Dir., Med.Lib.

MUSEUM OF ARTS AND SCIENCES - BRUCE EVERETT BATES MEMORIAL
   LIBRARY
1040 Museum Blvd.   Phone: (904) 255-0285
Daytona Beach, FL 32014   Marjorie L. Sigerson, Libn.

PATRIOTIC EDUCATION, INC. - LIBRARY
Box 2121   Phone: (904) 252-3414
Daytona Beach, FL 32015   Sedgley Thornbury, Pres.

VOLUSIA COUNTY LAW LIBRARY *
Courthouse Annex, Rm. 207
125 S. Orange Ave.   Phone: (904) 258-7000
Daytona Beach, FL 32014   Rae Mastropierro, Law Libn.

VOLUSIA COUNTY SCHOOL BOARD - RESOURCE LIBRARY
729 Loomis Ave.
Box 1910   Phone: (904) 255-6475
Daytona Beach, FL 32015   Loretta O. Wright, Rsrc. Media Spec.

FIRST PRESBYTERIAN CHURCH - LIBRARY
724 N. Woodland Blvd.   Phone: (904) 734-6212
De Land, FL 32720   Dorthea Beiler, Libn.

FISH MEMORIAL HOSPITAL - MEDICAL LIBRARY *
245 E. New York Ave.   Phone: (904) 734-2323
De Land, FL 32720   Paula Greenwood, Circuit Libn.

STETSON UNIVERSITY - CHEMISTRY LIBRARY †
Box 1271   Phone: (904) 734-4121
De Land, FL 32720   James H. DeLap, Chem. Professor

STETSON UNIVERSITY - FLORIDA BAPTIST HISTORICAL COLLECTION
Box 1353   Phone: (904) 734-2559
De Land, FL 32720   E. Earl Joiner, Cur.

STETSON UNIVERSITY - SCHOOL OF MUSIC LIBRARY
Woodland Blvd.   Phone: (904) 734-4121
De Land, FL 32720   Janice Jenkins, Music Libn.

WEST VOLUSIA MEMORIAL HOSPITAL - MEDICAL LIBRARY
Box 509   Phone: (904) 734-3320
De Land, FL 32721   Marjorie E. Cook, Med.Libn.

STETSON UNIVERSITY - ARCHIVES
Box 1418   Phone: (904) 734-4121
DeLand, FL 32720   Joe I. Myers, Archv.

MORIKAMI MUSEUM OF JAPANESE CULTURE - DONALD B. GORDON
   MEMORIAL LIBRARY
4000 Morikami Park Rd.   Phone: (305) 495-0233
Delray Beach, FL 33446   Larry Rosensweig, Cur.

U.S. AIR FORCE - ARMAMENT DIVISION, AIR FORCE ARMAMENT
   LABORATORY - TECHNICAL LIBRARY
                                                Phone: (904) 882-3212
Eglin AFB, FL 32542   June C. Stercho, Chf.

U.S. AIR FORCE BASE - EGLIN BASE LIBRARY
FL 2823   Phone: (904) 882-5088
Eglin AFB, FL 32542   F.P. Morgan, Chf., Lib.Br.

BENDIX CORPORATION - BENDIX AVIONICS DIVISION - LIBRARY
2100 N.W. 62nd St.
Box 9414   Phone: (305) 928-3316
Fort Lauderdale, FL 33310   Patricia Ferguson, Libn.

BROWARD COUNTY HISTORICAL COMMISSION - LIBRARY & ARCHIVES
100-B S. New River Dr., E.   Phone: (305) 765-5872
Fort Lauderdale, FL 33301   Midge Turpen, Adm.Sec.

BROWARD COUNTY LAW LIBRARY
444 County Courthouse   Phone: (305) 765-4096
Fort Lauderdale, FL 33301   Jeanne Underhill, Dir.

DUNHILL - BUSINESS RESEARCH LIBRARY
2430 W. Oakland Park Blvd.   Phone: (305) 484-8300
Fort Lauderdale, FL 33311   Ruth Balaban, Libn.

ENGLISH, MC CAUGHAN AND O'BRYAN - LAW LIBRARY
Box 14098   Phone: (305) 462-3301
Fort Lauderdale, FL 33302   Angela R. Stramiello, Libn.

FORT LAUDERDALE HISTORICAL SOCIETY - LIBRARY & ARCHIVES
219 Southwest 2nd Ave.   Phone: (305) 463-4431
Fort Lauderdale, FL 33301   Daniel T. Hobby, Exec.Dir.

GOULD, INC. - COMPUTER SYSTEMS DIVISION - TECHNICAL
   INFORMATION CENTER
6901 W. Sunrise Blvd.   Phone: (305) 587-2900
Fort Lauderdale, FL 33313   L. Susan Hayes, Info.Spec.

INTERNATIONAL GAME FISH ASSOCIATION - INTERNATIONAL LIBRARY
   OF FISHES
3000 E. Las Olas Blvd.   Phone: (305) 467-0161
Fort Lauderdale, FL 33316   M.B. McCracken, Libn.

INTERNATIONAL SWIMMING HALL OF FAME - MUSEUM & LIBRARY
One Hall of Fame Dr.   Phone: (305) 462-6536
Fort Lauderdale, FL 33316   Marion Washburn, Libn.

MOTOROLA, INC. - PORTABLE PRODUCTS DIVISION - TECHNICAL LIBRARY
8000 W. Sunrise Blvd.   Phone: (305) 475-5049
Fort Lauderdale, FL 33322   Mary Anne Foley, Tech.Libn.

NOVA UNIVERSITY - LAW LIBRARY
3100 S.W. 9th Ave.   Phone: (305) 522-2300
Fort Lauderdale, FL 33315   Carole Roehrenbeck, Dir.

UNIVERSITY OF FLORIDA - AGRICULTURAL RESEARCH & EDUCATION
   CENTER - FORT LAUDERDALE LIBRARY
Inst. of Food & Agricultural Sciences
3205 S.W. 70th Ave.   Phone: (305) 475-8990
Fort Lauderdale, FL 33314   Dr. William B. Ennis, Jr., Ctr.Dir.

EDISON WINTER HOME AND MUSEUM
2350 MacGregor Blvd.   Phone: (813) 334-3614
Ft. Myers, FL 33901

LEE COUNTY LAW LIBRARY
Courthouse   Phone: (813) 335-2230
Fort Myers, FL 33901   Owen Grant, Libn.

HARBOR BRANCH FOUNDATION, INC. - LIBRARY
R.R.1, Box 196   Phone: (305) 465-2400
Fort Pierce, FL 33450   Kristen L. Metzger, Libn.

ST. LUCIE COUNTY HISTORICAL MUSEUM - LIBRARY
414 Seaway Dr.   Phone: (305) 464-6635
Fort Pierce, FL 33450   Edward T. McCarron, Dir.

ST. LUCIE COUNTY - LAW LIBRARY
County Courthouse, 3rd Fl.   Phone: (305) 464-8904
Fort Pierce, FL 33450   Annie M. Fain, Libn.

CH2M HILL, INC. - SOUTHEAST REGIONAL OFFICE - INFORMATION
   CENTER
7201 N.W. 11th Place
Box 1647   Phone: (904) 377-2442
Gainesville, FL 32602   Bobbi Sean Walton, Libn.

FIRST BAPTIST CHURCH - MEDIA CENTER
425 W. University Ave.   Phone: (904) 376-2131
Gainesville, FL 32601   Dorothy S. Hammond, Dir. of Lib.Serv.

FLORIDA STATE DEPT. OF AGRICULTURE AND CONSUMER SERVICES -
   DIVISION OF PLANT INDUSTRY - LIBRARY
Box 1269   Phone: (904) 372-3505
Gainesville, FL 32602   June B. Jacobson, Libn.

GAINESVILLE SUN - LIBRARY
Drawer A   Phone: (904) 378-1411
Gainesville, FL 32602   Robert Ivey, Libn.

NORTH CENTRAL BAPTIST CHURCH - MEDIA LIBRARY *
1404 N.W. 14th Ave.   Phone: (904) 373-3341
Gainesville, FL 32601   Lena M. Bush, Media Lib.Dir.

SUNLAND CENTER AT GAINESVILLE - LIBRARY
Box 1150   Phone: (904) 395-1650
Gainesville, FL 32602   Susan L. Stephan, Libn.

TREE OF LIFE PRESS - LIBRARY AND ARCHIVES
420 N.E. Blvd.
Gainesville, FL 32601   Reva Pachefsky, Libn.

U.S. VETERANS ADMINISTRATION (FL-Gainesville) - HOSPITAL LIBRARY
                                                   Phone: (904) 376-1611
Gainesville, FL 32602   Marylyn E. Gresser, Chf., Lib.Serv.

UNIVERSITY OF FLORIDA - AQUATIC WEED PROGRAM - INFORMATION
   AND RETRIEVAL CENTER
2183 McCarty Hall   Phone: (904) 392-1799
Gainesville, FL 32611   Victor Ramey, Info.Spec.

UNIVERSITY OF FLORIDA - ARCHITECTURE & FINE ARTS LIBRARY
201 FAA   Phone: (904) 392-0222
Gainesville, FL 32611   Edward H. Teague, AFA Libn.

UNIVERSITY OF FLORIDA - BALDWIN LIBRARY
308 Library East
Gainesville, FL 32611   Dr. Ruth Baldwin

UNIVERSITY OF FLORIDA - BELKNAP COLLECTION FOR THE PERFORMING
   ARTS
512 Library W.   Phone: (904) 392-0322
Gainesville, FL 32611   Sidney Ives, Libn.

UNIVERSITY OF FLORIDA - CENTER FOR CLIMACTERIC STUDIES - ROBERT
   B. GREENBLATT LIBRARY
901 N.W. 8th Ave., Suite B1   Phone: (904) 392-3184
Gainesville, FL 32601   Morris Note Lovitz, M.D., Dir.

UNIVERSITY OF FLORIDA - CENTER FOR WETLANDS REFERENCE LIBRARY
Phelps Laboratory   Phone: (904) 392-2424
Gainesville, FL 32611   G. Ronnie Best, Assoc.Dir.

UNIVERSITY OF FLORIDA - CHEMISTRY LIBRARY
216 Leigh Hall   Phone: (904) 392-0573
Gainesville, FL 32611   Carol Drum, Univ.Libn.

UNIVERSITY OF FLORIDA - COASTAL & OCEANOGRAPHIC ENGINEERING
   DEPARTMENT - COASTAL ENGINEERING ARCHIVES
433 Weil Hall   Phone: (904) 392-2710
Gainesville, FL 32611   Lucile Lehmann, Archv.

UNIVERSITY OF FLORIDA - DOCUMENTS LIBRARY
254 Library West   Phone: (904) 392-0367
Gainesville, FL 32611   Sally Cravens, Libn.

UNIVERSITY OF FLORIDA - EDUCATION LIBRARY
1500 Norman Hall   Phone: (904) 392-0707
Gainesville, FL 32611   Myra Suzanne Brown, Act.Chm./Assoc.Libn.

UNIVERSITY OF FLORIDA - ENGINEERING & PHYSICS LIBRARY
410 Weil Hall   Phone: (904) 392-0987
Gainesville, FL 32611   Roger V. Krumm, Libn.

UNIVERSITY OF FLORIDA - FLORIDA STATE MUSEUM LIBRARY
Museum Rd.   Phone: (904) 392-1721
Gainesville, FL 32611   F. Wayne King, Dir.

UNIVERSITY OF FLORIDA - HUME LIBRARY
Inst. of Food & Agricultural Sciences
McCarty Hall   Phone: (904) 392-1934
Gainesville, FL 32611   Albert C. Strickland, Libn.

UNIVERSITY OF FLORIDA - ISSER AND RAE PRICE LIBRARY OF JUDAICA
18 Library East   Phone: (904) 392-0308
Gainesville, FL 32611   Robert Singerman, Hd. & Assoc.Libn.

UNIVERSITY OF FLORIDA - J. HILLIS MILLER HEALTH CENTER LIBRARY
Box J-206   Phone: (904) 392-4016
Gainesville, FL 32611   Ted F. Srygley, Dir.

UNIVERSITY OF FLORIDA - LATIN AMERICAN COLLECTION
4th Fl., Library East   Phone: (904) 392-0360
Gainesville, FL 32611   Dr. Rosa Q. Mesa, Dir.

UNIVERSITY OF FLORIDA - LAW LIBRARY
                                                   Phone: (904) 392-0418
Gainesville, FL 32611   Betty W. Taylor, Dir.

UNIVERSITY OF FLORIDA - MAP LIBRARY
Library East   Phone: (904) 392-0803
Gainesville, FL 32611   Dr. HelenJane Armstrong, Map Libn.

UNIVERSITY OF FLORIDA - MUSIC LIBRARY
231 Music Bldg.   Phone: (904) 392-6678
Gainesville, FL 32611   Robena Eng Cornwell, Asst.Univ.Libn.

UNIVERSITY OF FLORIDA - MUSIC LIBRARY - THE AMERICAN LISZT
   SOCIETY, INC. - ARCHIVES
                                                   Phone: (904) 392-6674
Gainesville, FL 32611

UNIVERSITY OF FLORIDA - P.K. YONGE LABORATORY SCHOOL - MEAD
   LIBRARY
1080 S.W. 11th Ave.   Phone: (904) 392-1506
Gainesville, FL 32611   Thelma B. Larche, Hd.Libn.

UNIVERSITY OF FLORIDA - P.K. YONGE LIBRARY OF FLORIDA HISTORY
4th Fl., Library West   Phone: (904) 392-0319
Gainesville, FL 32611   Elizabeth Alexander, Libn.

UNIVERSITY OF FLORIDA - PHYSICS AND ASTRONOMY READING ROOM
261 Williamson Hall   Phone: (904) 392-6686
Gainesville, FL 32611   Dorothy Patterson Lisca, Supv./Lib.Tech.Asst.

UNIVERSITY OF FLORIDA - RARE BOOKS & MANUSCRIPTS
531 Library West   Phone: (904) 392-0321
Gainesville, FL 32611   Sidney Ives, Libn.

UNIVERSITY OF FLORIDA - TRANSPORTATION RESEARCH CENTER
Civil Engineering Dept.
245 Weil Hall   Phone: (904) 392-6656
Gainesville, FL 32611   Deborah Reaves, Asst. in Engr.

UNIVERSITY OF FLORIDA - UNIVERSITY ARCHIVES AND UNIVERSITY
   COLLECTION
303 Library East   Phone: (904) 392-6547
Gainesville, FL 32611   Carla Kemp, Univ.Archv.

UNIVERSITY OF FLORIDA - URBAN AND REGIONAL PLANNING DOCUMENTS
   COLLECTION
Library West   Phone: (904) 392-0317
Gainesville, FL 32611   Margaret S. LeSourd, Assoc.Univ.Libn.

BAPTIST BIBLE INSTITUTE - IDA J. MC MILLAN LIBRARY
1306 College Dr.   Phone: (904) 263-3261
Graceville, FL 32440   Prof. William D, Jones, Libn.

ENVIRONMENTAL PROTECTION AGENCY - ENVIRONMENTAL RESEARCH
   LABORATORY, GULF BREEZE - LIBRARY
Sabine Island, 6   Phone: (904) 932-5311
Gulf Breeze, FL 32561   Andree Lowry, Libn.

UNIVERSITY OF FLORIDA - AGRICULTURAL RESEARCH CENTER - LIBRARY
   *
Box 728   Phone: (904) 692-1792
Hastings, FL 32045   R.B. Workman, Assoc. Professor

HIALEAH HOSPITAL - HEALTH SCIENCE LIBRARY
651 East 25th St.   Phone: (305) 835-4635
Hialeah, FL 33013   Yvonne Barkman, Health Sci.Libn.

HOBE SOUND BIBLE COLLEGE - LIBRARY
Box 1065   Phone: (305) 546-5534
Hobe Sound, FL 33455   Estaline Allison, Dir.

SOUTH FLORIDA REGIONAL PLANNING COUNCIL - LIBRARY
3440 Hollywood Blvd., Suite 140   Phone: (305) 961-2999
Hollywood, FL 33021   M. Keegan, Info.Spec.

SOUTH FLORIDA STATE HOSPITAL - MEDICAL AND PROFESSIONAL
   LIBRARY †
1000 S.W. 84th Ave.   Phone: (305) 983-4321
Hollywood, FL 33025   Mabel E. Harvey, Med.Libn.

TEMPLE BETH EL - BILLIE DAVIS RODENBERG MEMORIAL LIBRARY
1351 S. 14th Ave.   Phone: (305) 920-8225
Hollywood, FL 33020   Roslyn Kurland, Libn.

U.S. NATL. PARK SERVICE - EVERGLADES NATL. PARK - REFERENCE
   LIBRARY †
Box 279   Phone: (305) 245-5266
Homestead, FL 33030

UNIVERSITY OF FLORIDA - TROPICAL RESEARCH & EDUCATION CENTER -
   HOMESTEAD LIBRARY
Inst. of Food & Agricultural Sciences
18905 S.W. 280th St.   Phone: (305) 247-4624
Homestead, FL 33031   R.T. McSorley, Act.Dir.

U.S. AIR FORCE BASE - HOMESTEAD BASE LIBRARY †
FL 4829, 31 CSG/SSL   Phone: (305) 257-8184
Homestead AFB, FL 33039   Bettylou Rosen, Libn.

EASTMINSTER PRESBYTERIAN CHURCH - LIBRARY †
106 N. Riverside Dr.   Phone: (305) 723-8371
Indialantic, FL 32903   Gratia Richman, Libn.

BLUE CROSS AND BLUE SHIELD OF FLORIDA - CORPORATE RESEARCH
   LIBRARY
532 Riverside Ave.   Phone: (904) 791-6937
Jacksonville, FL 32231   William J. Condon, Lib.Mgr.

CHURCH OF JESUS CHRIST OF LATTER-DAY SAINTS - JACKSONVILLE,
   FLORIDA BRANCH GENEALOGICAL LIBRARY
4087 Hendricks Ave.   Phone: (904) 398-3487
Jacksonville, FL 32207   Vela M. Milton, Br. Genealogy Libn.

CUMMER GALLERY OF ART - LIBRARY
829 Riverside Ave.   Phone: (904) 356-6857
Jacksonville, FL 32204   Laura R. Joost, Chm., Lib.Comm.

DUVAL COUNTY LAW LIBRARY
220 Court House   Phone: (904) 633-4756
Jacksonville, FL 32202   Jack T. Sheng, Law Libn.

FLORIDA PUBLISHING CO. - EDITORIAL LIBRARY
1 Riverside Ave.   Phone: (904) 359-4237
Jacksonville, FL 32202   Maryann P. Sterzel, Dir.

JACKSONVILLE ART MUSEUM - LIBRARY *
4160 Boulevard Center Dr.
Jacksonville, FL 32207

JACKSONVILLE HEALTH EDUCATION PROGRAMS, INC. - BORLAND HEALTH
   SCIENCES LIBRARY
580 W. 8th St.   Phone: (904) 359-6516
Jacksonville, FL 32209   Robert P. Hinz, Dir.

JACKSONVILLE PUBLIC LIBRARY - FLORIDA COLLECTION
122 N. Ocean St.   Phone: (904) 633-3305
Jacksonville, FL 32202   Mr. Carol Harris, Cur.

LUTHER RICE SEMINARY - BERTHA SMITH LIBRARY
1050 Hendricks Ave.   Phone: (904) 396-2316
Jacksonville, FL 32207   David Rhew, Libn.

PRUDENTIAL INSURANCE COMPANY OF AMERICA - EMPLOYEES' BUSINESS
   & RECREATIONAL LIBRARY
Prudential Dr.   Phone: (904) 399-2002
Jacksonville, FL 32207   Barbara K. Williams, Libn.

REYNOLDS, SMITH & HILLS - LIBRARY
4019 Blvd. Center Dr.   Phone: (904) 396-2011
Jacksonville, FL 32201   R.C. Frost, Libn.

RIVERSIDE PRESBYTERIAN CHURCH - JEAN MILLER LIBRARY
849 Park St.   Phone: (904) 355-4585
Jacksonville, FL 32204   Evelyn Parker, Libn.

ST. LUKE'S HOSPITAL ASSOCIATION - MEDICAL, NURSING AND ALLIED
   HELP LIBRARY *
1900 Boulevard   Phone: (904) 356-1992
Jacksonville, FL 32206   Margarette Wally, Libn.

SCM CORPORATION - ORGANIC CHEMICALS DIVISION - TECHNICAL
   LIBRARY
Box 389   Phone: (904) 764-1711
Jacksonville, FL 32201   Marian M. Derfer, Mgr., Info.Serv.

SEABOARD COAST LINE RAILROAD COMPANY - LAW LIBRARY *
500 Water St., Rm. 1523   Phone: (904) 353-2011
Jacksonville, FL 32202

U.S. ARMY - CORPS OF ENGINEERS - JACKSONVILLE DISTRICT -
   TECHNICAL LIBRARY
400 W. Bay St.
Box 4970   Phone: (904) 791-3643
Jacksonville, FL 32232   Oriana Brown West, District Libn.

U.S. NAVY - NAVAL AIR STATION (FL-Jacksonville) - LIBRARY
Bldg. 930, Box 52   Phone: (904) 772-3415
Jacksonville, FL 32212   Patricia C. Doyle, Adm.Libn.

U.S. NAVY - NAVAL HOSPITAL (FL-Jacksonville) - MEDICAL LIBRARY
                                                  Phone: (904) 772-3439
Jacksonville, FL 32214   Bettye W. Stilley, Med.Libn.

WESTINGHOUSE ELECTRIC CORPORATION - OFFSHORE POWER SYSTEMS
   LIBRARY †
7960 Arlington Expy.
Box 8000   Phone: (904) 724-7700
Jacksonville, FL 32211   Minnie G. Thurston, Supv., Lib.Serv.

FLORIDA INSTITUTE OF TECHNOLOGY - COLLEGE OF APPLIED
   TECHNOLOGY - LIBRARY
1707 N.E. Indian River Dr.   Phone: (305) 334-4200
Jensen Beach, FL 33457   Eleanor S. Harris, Br.Libn.

U.S. NASA - JOHN F. KENNEDY SPACE CENTER - LIBRARY
SAN 302 - 9905   Phone: (305) 867-3600
Kennedy Space Center, FL 32899   M. Konjevich, Lib.Mgr.

U.S. NAVY - NAVAL AIR STATION (FL-Key West) - LIBRARY *
Bldg. 623A   Phone: (305) 296-3561
Key West, FL 33040   LCDR M. Gore, Lib.Off.

UNIVERSITY OF FLORIDA - AGRICULTURAL RESEARCH & EDUCATION
   CENTER - LAKE ALFRED LIBRARY
Inst. of Food & Agricultural Sciences
700 Experiment Station Rd.   Phone: (813) 956-1151
Lake Alfred, FL 33850   Pamela K. Russ, Assoc.Univ.Libn.

U.S. VETERANS ADMINISTRATION (FL-Lake City) - MEDICAL CENTER - LEARNING RESOURCE CENTER
Baya & Marion Sts.
Phone: (904) 752-1400
Lake City, FL 32055
Shirley Mabry, Chf., Lib.Serv.

ARCHBOLD BIOLOGICAL STATION - LIBRARY
Rte. 2, Box 180
Phone: (813) 465-2571
Lake Placid, FL 33852
Fred E. Lohrer, Libn.

FLORIDA BAPTIST SCHOOLS, INC. - COPELAND MEMORIAL LIBRARY
1030 W. Olive St.
Box 1641
Lakeland, FL 33801
Joy E. Williams, Libn.

FLORIDA STATE COURT OF APPEAL - 2ND DISTRICT - LAW LIBRARY
1005 E. Memorial Blvd.
Box 327
Phone: (813) 686-8171
Lakeland, FL 33802
Herboth S. Ryder, Judge

LAKELAND GENERAL HOSPITAL - MEDICAL LIBRARY
Lakeland Hills Blvd.
Drawer 448
Phone: (813) 683-0411
Lakeland, FL 33802
Cheryl R. Dee, Med.Libn.

POLK PUBLIC MUSEUM - MEMORIAL LIBRARY
800 E. Palmetto
Phone: (813) 688-7743
Lakeland, FL 33801
Ken Rollins, Dir.

WATSON CLINIC - MEDICAL LIBRARY
Box 1429
Phone: (813) 687-4000
Lakeland, FL 33802
Cheryl Dee, Med.Libn.

HOLLEY (A.G.) STATE HOSPITAL - BENJAMIN L. BROCK MEDICAL LIBRARY
Box 3084
Phone: (305) 582-5666
Lantana, FL 33462
Andree Sweek, Med.Rec.Libn.

NATIONAL ENQUIRER - RESEARCH DEPARTMENT LIBRARY
600 Southeast Coast Ave.
Phone: (305) 586-1111
Lantana, FL 33464
Martha Moffett, Res.Libn.

AMERICAN EXPRESS COMPANY - SYSTEMS LIBRARY *
4780 N. State Rd. 7
Phone: (305) 474-6084
Lauderhill, FL 33319
Marva Blair, Asst.Libn.

UNIVERSITY OF FLORIDA - AGRICULTURAL RESEARCH CENTER - LIBRARY
Inst. of Food & Agricultural Sciences
Box 388
Phone: (904) 787-3423
Leesburg, FL 32748
Dr. Gary W. Elmstrom, Ctr.Dir.

STROMBERG-CARLSON - TECHNICAL LIBRARY
1291 Hwy. 17-92
Box 700
Phone: (305) 339-1600
Longwood, FL 32750
Dolores Rosenbloom, Libn.

U.S. AIR FORCE BASE - MAC DILL BASE LIBRARY
FL 4814
Phone: (813) 830-3607
MacDill AFB, FL 33608
Jacob Phillips, Base Libn.

FLORIDA AUDUBON SOCIETY - INFORMATION CENTER
1101 Audubon Way
Maitland, FL 32751

MAITLAND PUBLIC LIBRARY - ANDRE SMITH COLLECTION
501 S. Maitland Ave.
Phone: (305) 647-7700
Maitland, FL 32751
Marilyn M. Seymour, Dir.

U.S. NAVY - NAVAL STATION LIBRARY (FL-Mayport)
Box 235
Phone: (904) 246-5393
Mayport, FL 32228
Ron Argentati, Libn.

FLORIDA INSTITUTE OF TECHNOLOGY - LIBRARY
Box 1150
Phone: (305) 723-3701
Melbourne, FL 32901
Llewellyn L. Henson, Dir.

AMERICAN DADE - AMERICAN HOSPITAL SUPPLY CORPORATION - LIBRARY
1851 Delaware Pkwy.
Box 520672
Phone: (305) 633-6461
Miami, FL 33152
Regina L. Knight, Info.Res.Spec.

AMERICAN INDIAN REFUGEES - NATIVE LIBRARY
Box 015368
Miami, FL 33143
Alonzo M. Barker, Pres.

AMERIFIRST FEDERAL SAVINGS & LOAN - LIBRARY
One S.E. Third Ave.
Phone: (305) 577-6397
Miami, FL 33131
Emerita M. Cuesta, Res.Libn.

BAPTIST HOSPITAL OF MIAMI - HEALTH SCIENCES LIBRARY
8900 S.W. 88th St.
Phone: (305) 596-1960
Miami, FL 33176
Diane F. Ream, Dir.,Health Sci.Lib.Serv.

BETH DAVID CONGREGATION - HARRY SIMONS LIBRARY †
2625 S.W. Third Ave.
Box 561718
Phone: (305) 854-3911
Miami, FL 33156

BLACKWELL, WALKER, GRAY, POWERS, FLICK & HOEHL - LAW LIBRARY
2400 Amerifirst Bldg.
One S.E. Third Ave.
Phone: (305) 358-8880
Miami, FL 33131
Dr. Cesar J. Armstrong, Res.Libn.

CEDARS MEDICAL CENTER - MEDICAL LIBRARY
1400 N.W. 12th Ave.
Phone: (305) 325-5737
Miami, FL 33136
Irene Bohlmann, Hd.

CENTRAL AGENCY FOR JEWISH EDUCATION - EDUCATIONAL RESOURCE CENTER/LIBRARY †
4200 Biscayne Blvd.
Phone: (305) 576-3030
Miami, FL 33137
Shirley Wolfe, Dir.

CORDIS CORPORATION - LIBRARY
Box 025700
Phone: (305) 551-2380
Miami, FL 33102-5700
Sharon Ladner, Adm., Lib.Serv.

DADE COUNTY LAW LIBRARY
321A County Court House
Phone: (305) 579-5422
Miami, FL 33130
Robert B. Wallace, Libn.

DOCTORS' HOSPITAL - MEDICAL LIBRARY
5000 University Dr.
Phone: (305) 666-2111
Miami, FL 33143
Lyn O'Brien, Med.Libn.

FAIRCHILD TROPICAL GARDEN - MONTGOMERY LIBRARY
10901 Old Cutler Rd.
Phone: (305) 667-1651
Miami, FL 33156
John Popenoe, Dir.

FLORIDA POWER & LIGHT COMPANY - CORPORATE LIBRARY
9250 W. Flagler St.
Box 029100
Phone: (305) 552-3210
Miami, FL 33102
Caryl Congleton, Libn.

FLORIDA STATE COMPREHENSIVE CANCER CENTER - CANCER INFORMATION SERVICE FOR THE STATES OF FLORIDA AND GEORGIA
Box 016960 (D8-4)
Phone: (305) 545-7707
Miami, FL 33101
Lari Wenzel, Dir.

FLORIDA STATE COURT OF APPEAL - 3RD DISTRICT - LAW LIBRARY
2001 S.W. 117th Ave.
Box 650307
Phone: (305) 554-2900
Miami, FL 33165
Rosemary E. Helsabeck, Libn.

GORGAS ARMY HOSPITAL - SAMUEL TAYLOR DARLING MEMORIAL LIBRARY
USA MEDDAC Panama
APO Miami, FL 34004
Mary E. Stark, Chf.Libn.

GORGAS MEMORIAL LABORATORY OF TROPICAL AND PREVENTIVE MEDICINE, INC. - BIO-MEDICAL RESEARCH LIBRARY
Box 935
APO Miami, FL 34002
Prof. Manuel Victor De Las Casas, Dir. & Med.Libn.

GORGAS MEMORIAL LABORATORY OF TROPICAL AND PREVENTIVE MEDICINE, INC. - VIROLOGY UNIT LIBRARY
Box 935
APO Miami, FL 34002
Prof. Manuel Victor De Las Casas, Dir. & Med.Libn.

HISTORICAL ASSOCIATION OF SOUTHERN FLORIDA - CHARLTON W. TEBEAU LIBRARY OF FLORIDA HISTORY
101 W. Flagler St.
Phone: (305) 372-7747
Miami, FL 33130
Rebecca A. Smith, Cur., Res.Mtls.

JACKSON MEMORIAL HOSPITAL - SCHOOL OF NURSING LIBRARY
1611 N.W. 12th Ave.   Phone: (305) 325-6833
Miami, FL 33136   Lynn Towers, Libn.

MERCY HOSPITAL - MEDICAL LIBRARY
3663 S. Miami Ave.   Phone: (305) 854-4400
Miami, FL 33133   David Archer, Libn.

MERSHON, SAWYER, JOHNSTON, DUNWODY & COLE - LIBRARY
100 S. Biscayne Blvd., Suite 1600   Phone: (305) 358-5100
Miami, FL 33131   Jean Snyder, Libn.

METROPOLITAN DADE COUNTY PLANNING DEPARTMENT - LIBRARY/
   INFORMATION CENTER
909 S.E. 1st Ave., Suite 900   Phone: (305) 579-2869
Miami, FL 33131   Morton Gutterman, Info.Off.

MIAMI-DADE PUBLIC LIBRARY - ART AND MUSIC DIVISION
1 Biscayne Blvd.   Phone: (305) 579-5001
Miami, FL 33132   Barbara Young, Hd.

MIAMI-DADE PUBLIC LIBRARY - AUDIO/VISUAL DEPARTMENT
1 Biscayne Blvd.   Phone: (305) 579-5001
Miami, FL 33132   Donald E. Chauncey, Film Libn.

MIAMI-DADE PUBLIC LIBRARY - BUSINESS, SCIENCE AND TECHNOLOGY
   DEPARTMENT
1 Biscayne Blvd.   Phone: (305) 579-5001
Miami, FL 33132   Edward Oswald, Bus.Libn.

MIAMI-DADE PUBLIC LIBRARY - FEDERAL DOCUMENTS DIVISION
1 Biscayne Blvd.   Phone: (305) 579-4141
Miami, FL 33132   Eva Conrad, Fed.Doc.Libn.

MIAMI-DADE PUBLIC LIBRARY - FLORIDA COLLECTION
1 Biscayne Blvd.   Phone: (305) 579-5189
Miami, FL 33132   Sam J. Boldrick, Libn.

MIAMI-DADE PUBLIC LIBRARY - FOREIGN LANGUAGES DIVISION
1 Biscayne Blvd.   Phone: (305) 579-5001
Miami, FL 33132   Alicia Godoy, Libn. II

MIAMI-DADE PUBLIC LIBRARY - GENEALOGY ROOM
1 Biscayne Blvd.   Phone: (305) 579-5015
Miami, FL 33132   Lucretia D. Warren, Libn.

MIAMI-DADE PUBLIC LIBRARY - URBAN AFFAIRS LIBRARY
1 Biscayne Blvd.   Phone: (305) 579-5487
Miami, FL 33132   Richard G. Frow, Libn.

MIAMI HERALD - LIBRARY
One Herald Plaza   Phone: (305) 350-2418
Miami, FL 33101   Nora Paul, Lib.Dir.

MIAMI NEWS - LIBRARY
One Herald Plaza   Phone: (305) 350-2189
Miami, FL 33101   Joseph F. Wright, Hd.Libn.

NORTH SHORE MEDICAL CENTER - MEDICAL LIBRARY *
1100 N.W. 95th St.   Phone: (305) 835-6000
Miami, FL 33150   Linda Day, Libn.

PANAMA CANAL COMMISSION - LIBRARY
APO Miami, FL 34011   Beverly C. Williams, Libn.

PAPANICOLAOU CANCER RESEARCH INSTITUTE AT MIAMI - RESEARCH
   LIBRARY
1155 N.W. 14th St.
Box 016188
Miami, FL 33101   Phone: (305) 324-5572

PRICE WATERHOUSE - INFORMATION CENTER
3500 One Biscayne Tower   Phone: (305) 358-3682
Miami, FL 33131   Susan Waters, Info.Spec.

RACAL-MILGO, INC. - INFORMATION RESOURCES †
8600 N.W. 41st St.   Phone: (305) 591-5186
Miami, FL 33166   Jan Stern

RYDER SYSTEM, INC. - INFORMATION CENTRAL
Box 520816   Phone: (305) 593-3456
Miami, FL 33152   Jamie Townsend, Sec., Corp.Plan.

ST. JOHN VIANNEY COLLEGE SEMINARY - MARY LOUISE MAYTAG
   MEMORIAL LIBRARY
2900 S.W. 87th Ave.   Phone: (305) 223-4561
Miami, FL 33165   Sr. Mary Julia O'Donnell, Hd.Libn.

SMATHERS & THOMPSON - LAW LIBRARY
1301 Alfred I. duPont Bldg.   Phone: (305) 379-6523
Miami, FL 33131   Sid Kaskey, Libn.

TEMPLE ISRAEL OF GREATER MIAMI - LIBRARY
137 N.E. 19th St.   Phone: (305) 573-5900
Miami, FL 33132   Beatrice T. Muskat, Libn.

THEOSOPHICAL SOCIETY IN MIAMI - LIBRARY
119 N.E. 62nd St.   Phone: (305) 754-4331
Miami, FL 33138   Louise S. Ward, Libn.

U.S. AIR FORCE BASE - HOWARD BASE LIBRARY
FL 4810
Howard AFB
APO Miami, FL 34001   S.K. Murdoch, Base Libn.

U.S. ARMY POST - FORT CLAYTON - MORALE SUPPORT ACTIVITIES -
   LIBRARY
P.O. Drawer 933
APO Miami, FL 34004   Pamela A. Shelton, Post Libn.

U.S. ARMY SCHOOL OF THE AMERICAS - LIBRARY/LEARNING CENTER
Bldg. 400, MOLASC-SS
APO Miami, FL 34008   Rafael E. Coulson, Lib.Dir.

U.S. ARMY - TROPIC TEST CENTER - TECHNICAL INFORMATION CENTER
Fort Clayton
Drawer 942
APO Miami, FL 34004   Ann B. Guerriers, Tech.Info.Spec.

U.S. DEPT. OF COMMERCE - INTERNATIONAL TRADE ADMINISTRATION -
   MIAMI DISTRICT OFFICE LIBRARY
Federal Bldg., Rm. 224
51 S.W. First Ave.   Phone: (305) 350-5267
Miami, FL 33130   Ivan A. Cosimi, Dir.

U.S. NATL. MARINE FISHERIES SERVICE - SOUTHEAST FISHERIES CENTER
   - MIAMI LAB. LIBRARY
75 Virginia Beach Dr.   Phone: (305) 361-4229
Miami, FL 33149   Julianne Josiek, Hd.Libn.

U.S. NATL. OCEANIC & ATMOSPHERIC ADMINISTRATION - MIAMI
   LIBRARY
4301 Rickenbacker Causeway   Phone: (305) 361-4428
Miami, FL 33149   Robert N. Ting, Chf.Libn.

U.S. VETERANS ADMINISTRATION (FL-Miami) - MEDICAL CENTER LIBRARY
1201 N.W. 16th St.   Phone: (305) 324-3187
Miami, FL 33125   Raissa Maurin, Chf.Libn.

UNIVERSITY OF MIAMI - DOROTHY & LEWIS ROSENSTIEL SCHOOL OF
   MARINE & ATMOSPHERIC SCIENCES - LIBRARY
4600 Rickenbacker Causeway   Phone: (305) 361-4007
Miami, FL 33149   Kay K. Hale, Libn.

UNIVERSITY OF MIAMI - SCHOOL OF MEDICINE - BASCOM PALMER EYE
   INSTITUTE - LIBRARY
Ann Bates Leach Eye Hospital
900 N.W. 17th St.
Box 016880   Phone: (305) 326-6078
Miami, FL 33101   Reva Hurtes, Libn.

UNIVERSITY OF MIAMI - SCHOOL OF MEDICINE - LOUIS CALDER
   MEMORIAL LIBRARY
Box 016950   Phone: (305) 547-6441
Miami, FL 33101   Henry L. Lemkau, Jr., Dir.

UP FRONT, INC. - LIBRARY
Coconut Grove Sta.
Box 330589   Phone: (305) 446-3585
Miami, FL 33233-0589   James N. Hall, Dir.

VIZCAYA GUIDES LIBRARY
3251 S. Miami Ave.   Phone: (305) 579-2808
Miami, FL 33129   Joy Mason, Lib.Chm.

WALTON LANTAFF SCHROEDER & CARSON - LAW LIBRARY
900 Alfred I. DuPont Bldg.   Phone: (305) 379-6411
Miami, FL 33131   Daniel Linehan, Libn.

FLORIDA STATE SUPREME COURT - 11TH JUDICIAL CIRCUIT - DADE
    COUNTY AUXILIARY LAW LIBRARY
420 Lincoln Rd., Suite 245   Phone: (305) 538-0314
Miami Beach, FL 33139   Johanna Porpiglia, Br.Libn.

MIAMI HEART INSTITUTE HOSPITAL - MEDICAL LIBRARY
4701 N. Meridian Ave.   Phone: (305) 672-1111
Miami Beach, FL 33140   Bronia Barbash, Libn.

MOUNT SINAI MEDICAL CENTER OF GREATER MIAMI - MEDICAL LIBRARY
4300 Alton Rd.   Phone: (305) 674-2840
Miami Beach, FL 33139   Isabel Ezquerra, Chf.Med.Libn.

NATIONAL NETWORK OF YOUTH ADVISORY BOARDS, INC. - TECHNICAL
    ASSISTANCE LIBRARY
Ocean View Branch
Box 402036   Phone: (305) 532-2607
Miami Beach, FL 33140   Stuart Alan Rado, Exec.Dir.

ST. FRANCIS HOSPITAL - MEDICAL LIBRARY
250 W. 63rd St.   Phone: (305) 868-5000
Miami Beach, FL 33141   Wilma S. Grover, Libn.

TEMPLE BETH SHOLOM - LIBRARY
4144 Chase Ave.   Phone: (305) 538-7231
Miami Beach, FL 33140   Celia R. Huber, Libn.

TEMPLE EMANU-EL - LIBRARY
1701 Washington Ave.   Phone: (305) 538-2503
Miami Beach, FL 33139   Ruth M. Abelow, Libn.

AMERICAN CYANAMID COMPANY - SANTA ROSA PLANT - LIBRARY
1801 Cyanamid Rd.   Phone: (904) 994-5311
Milton, FL 32570   Dee Rogers, Libn.

THE CONSERVANCY, INC. - CONSERVANCY NATURE CENTER LIBRARY
1450 Merrihue Dr.   Phone: (813) 262-0304
Naples, FL 33942   Gary W. Schmelz, Ph.D., Educ.Dir.

ISOTTA FRASCHINI OWNERS ASSOCIATION - RESEARCH LIBRARY
35 Ligonier Dr., N.E.
North Fort Meyers, FL 33903   H.B. Willis, Dir.

AMERICAN FEDERATION OF POLICE RESEARCH CENTER AND LIBRARY
1100 N.E. 125th St.   Phone: (305) 891-1700
North Miami, FL 33161   Gerald Arenberg, Exec.Dir.

SOUTHEASTERN COLLEGE OF OSTEOPATHIC MEDICINE - MEDICAL
    LIBRARY
1750 N.E. 168th St.   Phone: (305) 947-6130
North Miami Beach, FL 33162   Naomi E. Prussiano, Hd.Med.Libn.

MARION COUNTY SCHOOL BOARD - TEACHERS' PROFESSIONAL LIBRARY
406 S.E. Alvarez Ave.   Phone: (904) 732-8041
Ocala, FL 32670   Mary Tillman, Lib. Media Supv.

WITHLACOOCHEE REGIONAL PLANNING COUNCIL - LIBRARY
1241 S.W. 10th St.   Phone: (904) 732-3307
Ocala, FL 32674-2798   Vivian A. Whittier, Res.Asst.

VOLTAIRE SOCIETY - LIBRARY *
1837 N. Azalea St., Basswood
Okeechobee, FL 33472   R.L. Marchfield, Pres.

AKERMAN, SENTERFITT, & EIDSON - LAW LIBRARY
255 S. Orange Ave.
Box 231   Phone: (305) 843-7860
Orlando, FL 32802   Mary Bourget, Libn.

FLORIDA HOSPITAL - MEDICAL LIBRARY
601 E. Rollins St.   Phone: (305) 896-6611
Orlando, FL 32803   Barbara Beckner, Libn.

LOCH HAVEN ART CENTER, INC. - LIBRARY
2416 North Mills Ave.   Phone: (305) 896-4231
Orlando, FL 32803   Marena Grant, Exec.Dir.

MAGUIRE, VOORHIS & WELLS - LIBRARY
2 S. Orange Plaza
Box 633
Orlando, FL 32802   John D. Vanston, Law Libn.

MARTIN MARIETTA CORPORATION - ORLANDO AEROSPACE DIVISION -
    INFORMATION CENTER
Box 5837 MP-30   Phone: (305) 352-2051
Orlando, FL 32855   Morton Meltzer, Mgr.

ORANGE COUNTY HISTORICAL COMMISSION - MUSEUM LIBRARY
812 E. Rollins St.
Loch Haven Park
Orlando, FL 32803   Frank Mendola, Libn.

ORANGE COUNTY LAW LIBRARY †
County Court House, Rm. 558   Phone: (305) 420-3240
Orlando, FL 32801   Sarilou A. Barrow, Libn.

ORANGE COUNTY LIBRARY DISTRICT - GENEALOGY DEPARTMENT
10 N. Rosalind Ave.   Phone: (305) 425-4694
Orlando, FL 32801   Eileen B. Willis, Dept.Hd.

ORLANDO MUNICIPAL REFERENCE LIBRARY
City Hall, 400 S. Orange Ave.   Phone: (305) 849-2249
Orlando, FL 32801   Nancy Ahlin, Libn.

ORLANDO REGIONAL MEDICAL CENTER - MEDICAL LIBRARY
1414 S. Kuhl Ave.   Phone: (305) 855-8771
Orlando, FL 32806   Mary C. Garmany, Dir.

ORLANDO SENTINEL NEWSPAPER - LIBRARY
633 N. Orange Ave.
Box 2833   Phone: (305) 420-5510
Orlando, FL 32802   Judy L. Grimsley, Info.Rsrcs.Supv.

SOUTHERN COLLEGE - LIBRARY *
5600 Lake Underhill Rd.   Phone: (305) 273-1000
Orlando, FL 32807   Mary Love Hammond, Libn.

U.S.D.A. - AGRICULTURAL RESEARCH SERVICE - HORTICULTURAL
    RESEARCH LABORATORY LIBRARY
2120 Camden Rd.   Phone: (305) 898-6791
Orlando, FL 32803   Joyce S. Darr, Libn.

U.S. NAVY - NAVAL HOSPITAL (FL-Orlando) - MEDICAL LIBRARY †
                                    Phone: (305) 646-4959
Orlando, FL 32813   Alice Crownfield, Med.Libn.

U.S. NAVY - NAVAL RESEARCH LABORATORY - UNDERWATER SOUND
    REFERENCE DETACHMENT - TECHNICAL LIBRARY
755 Gatlin Ave.
Box 8337   Phone: (305) 859-5120
Orlando, FL 32856   Marge Tarnowski, Libn.

U.S. NAVY - NAVAL TRAINING EQUIPMENT CENTER - TECHNICAL
    INFORMATION CENTER
TIC, Bldg. 2068   Phone: (305) 646-4797
Orlando, FL 32813   Marcia Davidoff, Chf.Libn.

WESTINGHOUSE ELECTRIC CORPORATION - STEAM TURBINE GENERATOR
    DIVISION - LIBRARY
The Quadrangle   Phone: (305) 281-2171
Orlando, FL 32817   Tena Crenshaw, Libn.

BRILEY, WILD AND ASSOCIATES, INC. - LIBRARY
1042 U.S. Highway 1 North
Box 607   Phone: (904) 672-5660
Ormond Beach, FL 32074   John W. Casey, Libn.

HISTORICAL SOCIETY OF PALM BEACH COUNTY - LIBRARY, ARCHIVES
    AND MUSEUM †
Henry Morrison Flagler Museum
One Whitehall Way
Box 1147   Phone: (305) 655-1492
Palm Beach, FL 33480   Maxine Wisner Banash, Dir.

SOCIETY OF THE FOUR ARTS - LIBRARY
Four Arts Plaza   Phone: (305) 655-7226
Palm Beach, FL 33480   Winnifred Romoser, Libn.

PROFESSIONAL GOLFERS' ASSOCIATION OF AMERICA - LIBRARY *
100 Ave. of the Champions
Box 12458
Palm Beach Gardens, FL 33410

U.S. NATL. MARINE FISHERIES SERVICE - SOUTHEAST FISHERIES CENTER
    - PANAMA CITY LAB. - LIBRARY
3500 Delwood Beach Rd.   Phone: (904) 234-6541
Panama City, FL 32407   Rosalie Vaught, Libn.

U.S. NAVY - NAVAL COASTAL SYSTEMS CENTER - TECHNICAL
    INFORMATION SERVICES BRANCH †
                                                   Phone: (904) 234-4381
Panama City, FL 32407   Myrtle J. Rhodes, Supv.Libn.

U.S. AIR FORCE BASE - PATRICK BASE LIBRARY †
FL 2829   Phone: (305) 494-6881
Patrick AFB, FL 32925   Marie D. Jennings, Adm.Libn.

U.S. AIR FORCE HOSPITAL - MEDICAL LIBRARY (FL-Patrick AFB)
                                                   Phone: (305) 494-5501
Patrick AFB, FL 32925   Douglas M. Jackson, Libn.

BAPTIST HOSPITAL - MEDICAL LIBRARY
1000 W. Moreno   Phone: (904) 434-4877
Pensacola, FL 32501   Ellen Richbourg, Libn.

ESCAMBIA COUNTY HEALTH DEPARTMENT - LIBRARY *
Box 12604   Phone: (904) 438-8571
Pensacola, FL 32574-2604   Barbara McCullough, Health Educ.

HISTORIC PENSACOLA PRESERVATION BOARD - LIBRARY
205 E. Zaragoza St.   Phone: (904) 434-1042
Pensacola, FL 32501   Linda V. Ellsworth, Hist.

MONSANTO FIBERS & INTERMEDIATES COMPANY - TECHNICAL LIBRARY
Box 12830   Phone: (904) 968-8248
Pensacola, FL 32575   Farrell J. Allen, Supv., Lib.Sys.

PENSACOLA HISTORICAL SOCIETY - LELIA ABERCROMBIE HISTORICAL
    LIBRARY
405 S. Adams St.   Phone: (904) 433-1559
Pensacola, FL 32501   Gordon N. Simons, Cur.

PENSACOLA MUSEUM OF ART - HARRY THORNTON MEMORIAL LIBRARY
407 S. Jefferson St.   Phone: (904) 432-6247
Pensacola, FL 32501

REICHHOLD CHEMICALS, INC. - RESEARCH LIBRARY
Box 1433   Phone: (904) 433-7621
Pensacola, FL 32596   Rosemary Milner Kiefer, Info.Rsrcs.Mgr.

SACRED HEART HOSPITAL - MEDICAL LIBRARY
5151 N. 9th Ave.   Phone: (904) 476-7851
Pensacola, FL 32504   Florence V. Ruby, Hosp.Libn.

STILL WATERS FOUNDATION, INC. - STILL WATERS CENTRE LIBRARY
615 Stafford Ln.
Pensacola, FL 32506   Dana Faye Cobb

U.S. NAVY - NAVAL AEROSPACE MEDICAL INSTITUTE - LIBRARY
Bldg. 1953, Code 012   Phone: (904) 452-2256
Pensacola, FL 32508   Ruth T. Rogers, Adm.Libn.

U.S. NAVY - NAVAL AIR STATION (FL-Pensacola) - LIBRARY
Bldg. 633   Phone: (904) 452-4362
Pensacola, FL 32508   C. R. Moreland, Hd.Libn.

U.S. NAVY - NAVAL HOSPITAL (FL-Pensacola) - MEDICAL LIBRARY
                                                   Phone: (904) 453-6635
Pensacola, FL 32512   Juan E. Terry, Med.Libn.

UNIVERSITY HOSPITAL AND CLINIC - HERBERT L. BRYANS MEMORIAL
    LIBRARY
1200 West Leonard St.   Phone: (904) 436-9187
Pensacola, FL 32501   Ms. Sammie Campbell, Libn.

UNIVERSITY OF WEST FLORIDA - JOHN C. PACE LIBRARY - CURRICULUM
    MATERIALS LIBRARY
                                                   Phone: (904) 474-2439
Pensacola, FL 32504   Ron Toifel, Dir.

UNIVERSITY OF WEST FLORIDA - JOHN C. PACE LIBRARY - SPECIAL
    COLLECTIONS
                                                   Phone: (904) 474-2213
Pensacola, FL 32504   Dean DeBolt, Spec.Coll.Libn.

WENTWORTH (T.T., Jr.) MUSEUM - LIBRARY
8382 Palafox Hwy.
Box 806   Phone: (904) 438-3638
Pensacola, FL 32594   T.T. Wentworth, Jr., Pres.

COCA-COLA COMPANY - FOODS DIVISION - CITRUS RESEARCH &
    DEVELOPMENT TECHNICAL LIBRARY *
Orange St.
Box 550   Phone: (305) 886-1568
Plymouth, FL 32768   Mary Ivey-Clark, Libn.

UNIVERSITY OF FLORIDA - AGRICULTURAL RESEARCH & EDUCATION
    CENTER - QUINCY LIBRARY
Rte. 3, Box 638
Quincy, FL 32351

MERYMAN ENVIRONMENTAL ENTERPRISES, INC. - MERYMAN LIBRARY OF
    AQUATIC RESEARCH
10408 Bloomingdale Ave.   Phone: (813) 626-9551
Riverview, FL 33569   Dr. Charles Dale Meryman, Pres.

WUESTHOFF MEMORIAL HOSPITAL - MEDICAL LIBRARY
110 Longwood Ave.
Box 6   Phone: (305) 636-2211
Rockledge, FL 32955   Nancy A. Hanson, Med.Libn.

FLAGLER HOSPITAL - MEDICAL LIBRARY *
Marine St.
St. Augustine, FL 32084

FLORIDA SCHOOL FOR THE DEAF AND BLIND - LIBRARY FOR THE DEAF
Box 1209   Phone: (904) 824-1654
St. Augustine, FL 32084   Joan Embry, Hd.Libn.

HISTORIC ST. AUGUSTINE PRESERVATION BOARD - HISPANIC RESEARCH
    LIBRARY
Box 1987   Phone: (904) 824-3355
St. Augustine, FL 32084   Dr. Amy Turner Bushnell, Hist.

MARINELAND, INC. - RESEARCH LABORATORY
Route 1, Box 122
St. Augustine, FL 32084

ST. AUGUSTINE HISTORICAL SOCIETY - LIBRARY
271 Charlotte St.   Phone: (904) 829-5514
St. Augustine, FL 32084   Jacqueline K. Fretwell, Lib.Dir.

SOCIETY OF PHILATICIANS - LIBRARY
154 Laguna Ct.
St. Augustine, FL 32086   Gustav Detjen, Jr., Libn.

U.S. NATL. PARK SERVICE - CASTILLO DE SAN MARCOS NATL. MONUMENT
    & FORT MATANZAS NATL. MONUMENT - LIBRARY
1 Castillo Dr.   Phone: (904) 829-6506
St. Augustine, FL 32084

BAYFRONT MEDICAL CENTER, INC. - HEALTH SCIENCES LIBRARY
701 6th St.,S.   Phone: (813) 823-1234
St. Petersburg, FL 33701   Barbara Hijek, Health Sci.Libn.

E-SYSTEMS, INC. - ECI DIVISION - TECHNICAL INFORMATION CENTER
1501 72nd St., N.
Box 12248
St. Petersburg, FL 33733   Susan Weiss, Tech.Info. Data Spec.

FLORIDA POWER CORPORATION - CORPORATE LIBRARY
3201 34th St., S.   Phone: (813) 866-5304
St. Petersburg, FL 33711   Douglas Cornwell, Corp.Libn.

FLORIDA STATE DEPT. OF NATURAL RESOURCES - BUREAU OF MARINE
    RESEARCH - LIBRARY
100 Eighth Ave., S.E.   Phone: (813) 896-8626
St. Petersburg, FL 33701   Keir Gray, Libn.Asst.

GENERAL ELECTRIC COMPANY - TECHNICAL INFORMATION CENTER
Box 11508   Phone: (813) 541-8300
St. Petersburg, FL 33733   Shirley L. Taylor, Mgr.

INTERNATIONAL FESTIVALS ASSOCIATION - LIBRARY
Bayfront Concourse Hotel
333 First St. S.   Phone: (813) 898-3656
St. Petersburg, FL 33701   Herbert C. Melleney, Exec.V.P./Mng.Dir.

JIM WALTER RESEARCH CORPORATION - LIBRARY
10301 9th St., N.   Phone: (813) 576-4171
St. Petersburg, FL 33702   Judith Dolce, Info.Spec.

MUSEUM OF FINE ARTS - ART REFERENCE LIBRARY
255 Beach Dr., N.   Phone: (813) 896-2667
St. Petersburg, FL 33701   Muriel S. Kirk, Coord. for Lib.

PASADENA PRESBYTERIAN CHURCH - LIBRARY
100 Pasadena Ave., N.   Phone: (813) 345-0148
St. Petersburg, FL 33710   Elizabeth Howe, Libn.

PINELLAS COUNTY JUVENILE WELFARE BOARD - MAILANDE W. HOLLAND
    LIBRARY
4140 49th St., N.   Phone: (813) 521-1853
St. Petersburg, FL 33709   Molly Gill, Libn.

PINELLAS COUNTY LAW LIBRARY - ST. PETERSBURG BRANCH
Judicial Bldg., Rm. 500
545 1st Ave., N.   Phone: (813) 825-1875
St. Petersburg, FL 33701   Martha F. Otting, Libn.

PINELLAS COUNTY SCHOOL BOARD - MIRROR LAKE/TOMLINSON
    EDUCATION CENTER - LIBRARY/MEDIA CENTER
709 Mirror Lake Dr.   Phone: (813) 821-4593
St. Petersburg, FL 33701   Helen G. Campbell, Media Spec.

ST. ANTHONY'S HOSPITAL, INC. - MEDICAL LIBRARY †
718 12th St., N.
Box 12588   Phone: (813) 825-1100
St. Petersburg, FL 33705   Linda Jo Rowe, Libn.

ST. PETERSBURG HISTORICAL SOCIETY - LIBRARY AND ARCHIVES
335 Second Ave., N.E.   Phone: (813) 894-1052
St. Petersburg, FL 33701   John Warren, Pres.

ST. PETERSBURG TIMES AND EVENING INDEPENDENT - LIBRARY
490 First Ave., S.
Box 1121   Phone: (813) 893-8111
St. Petersburg, FL 33731   James S. Scofield, Chf.Libn.

STETSON UNIVERSITY - COLLEGE OF LAW - CHARLES A. DANA LAW
    LIBRARY
1401 61st St., S.   Phone: (813) 345-1335
St. Petersburg, FL 33707   J. Lamar Woodard, Libn./Professor of Law

TAMPA BAY REGIONAL PLANNING COUNCIL - RESEARCH & INFORMATION
    LIBRARY
9455 Koger Blvd.   Phone: (813) 577-5151
St. Petersburg, FL 33702   Gertrude M. Bechtel, Asst.Libn.

MEMORIAL HOSPITAL - MEDICAL LIBRARY
1901 Arlington St.   Phone: (813) 953-1238
Sarasota, FL 33579   Doris Marose, Dir., Med.Lib.

MOTE MARINE LABORATORY - DAVIS LIBRARY
1600 City Island Pk.   Phone: (813) 388-4441
Sarasota, FL 33577   Mary A. Parks, Libn.

RINGLING (John and Mable) MUSEUM OF ART - ART RESEARCH LIBRARY
Box 1838   Phone: (813) 355-5101
Sarasota, FL 33578   Lynell A. Morr, Art Libn.

RINGLING SCHOOL OF ART AND DESIGN - LIBRARY
1191 27th St.   Phone: (813) 355-1232
Sarasota, FL 33580   Yvonne Morse, Dir.

FLORIDA A&M UNIVERSITY - ARCH/TECH LIBRARY
B.B. Tech Center A-301
Box 164   Phone: (904) 599-3050
Tallahassee, FL 32307   Margaret F. Wilson, Assoc.Univ.Libn.

FLORIDA A&M UNIVERSITY - PHARMACY LIBRARY
Box 367   Phone: (904) 599-3304
Tallahassee, FL 32307   Pauline Hicks, Assoc.Univ.Libn.

FLORIDA A&M UNIVERSITY - SCHOOL OF BUSINESS & INDUSTRY LIBRARY
Box 309   Phone: (904) 599-3457
Tallahassee, FL 32307   Elizabeth N. Carr, Libn.

FLORIDA A & M UNIVERSITY - SCHOOL OF JOURNALISM, MEDIA &
    GRAPHIC ARTS - JOURNALISM RESOURCE CENTER
                                        Phone: (904) 599-3718
Tallahassee, FL 32307   Gloria T. Woody, Dir./Libn.

FLORIDA A&M UNIVERSITY - SCHOOL OF NURSING LIBRARY
Box 136   Phone: (904) 599-3048
Tallahassee, FL 32307   Marva L. Carter, Lib.Tech.Asst.Supv.

FLORIDA STATE BOARD OF REGENTS - RECORDS AND ARCHIVES
107 W. Gaines St.   Phone: (904) 488-6826
Tallahassee, FL 32304   Carol Wade, Rec.Adm.

FLORIDA STATE DEPT. OF COMMERCE - RESEARCH LIBRARY
Fletcher Bldg., Rm. 408   Phone: (904) 487-2971
Tallahassee, FL 32301   Dennis Hitchens, Libn.

FLORIDA STATE DEPT. OF ENVIRONMENTAL REGULATION - LIBRARY
2600 Blair Stone Rd.   Phone: (904) 488-0870
Tallahassee, FL 32301   Jacqueline W. McGorty, Libn.

FLORIDA STATE DEPT. OF INSURANCE AND STATE TREASURER - DEPT. OF
    INSURANCE - LAW LIBRARY
Rm. 413-B Larson Bldg.
200 E. Gaines St.   Phone: (904) 488-4540
Tallahassee, FL 32301   Cindy McKenzie, Libn.

FLORIDA STATE DEPT. OF LAW ENFORCEMENT - LAW LIBRARY
208 W. Carolina St.
Box 1489   Phone: (904) 488-8323
Tallahassee, FL 32302   Clarice S. Wilks, Staff Asst. I

FLORIDA STATE DEPT. OF LEGAL AFFAIRS - ATTORNEY GENERAL'S
    LIBRARY
Capitol Bldg.   Phone: (904) 488-6040
Tallahassee, FL 32304   Ann C. Kaklamanos, Libn.

FLORIDA STATE DEPT. OF NATURAL RESOURCES - BUREAU OF GEOLOGY
    LIBRARY
903 W. Tennessee St.   Phone: (904) 488-9380
Tallahassee, FL 32304   Alison M. Lewis, Libn.

FLORIDA STATE DEPT. OF NATURAL RESOURCES - DIV. OF STATE LANDS -
    BUREAU OF STATE LAND MANAGEMENT - TITLE SECTION *
3900 Commonwealth Blvd.   Phone: (904) 488-8123
Tallahassee, FL 32303   F.R. Williams, Adm., Land Records

FLORIDA STATE DEPT. OF TRANSPORTATION - CENTRAL REFERENCE
    LIBRARY
Burns Bldg.   Phone: (904) 488-8572
Tallahassee, FL 32301   Robert Morse, Libn.

FLORIDA STATE DIVISION OF ARCHIVES, HISTORY & RECORDS
     MANAGEMENT - FLORIDA PHOTOGRAPHIC COLLECTION
Florida State Archives
R.A. Gray Bldg., Rm. 107   Phone: (904) 487-2073
Tallahassee, FL 32301   Joan L. Morris, Archv.Supv.

FLORIDA STATE DIVISION OF ARCHIVES, HISTORY & RECORDS
     MANAGEMENT - FLORIDA STATE ARCHIVES *
R.A. Gray Bldg.
500 S. Bronough   Phone: (904) 487-2073
Tallahassee, FL 32301   Ed Tribble, State Archv.

FLORIDA STATE LEGISLATURE - DIVISION OF LEGISLATIVE LIBRARY
     SERVICES
701, The Capitol   Phone: (904) 488-2812
Tallahassee, FL 32301   B. Gene Baker, Dir.

FLORIDA STATE OFFICE OF THE COMPTROLLER - DEPARTMENT OF
     BANKING & FINANCE - LEGAL LIBRARY
The Capitol, Suite 1302   Phone: (904) 488-9896
Tallahassee, FL 32301   Linda Blackwell, Sec. IV/Hd.Libn.

FLORIDA STATE SUPREME COURT LIBRARY
Supreme Court Bldg.   Phone: (904) 488-8919
Tallahassee, FL 32301   Brian S. Polley, Libn.

FLORIDA STATE UNIVERSITY - CTR. FOR STUDIES IN VOCATIONAL EDUC.
     - FLORIDA EDUCATIONAL INFO. SERV.
2003 Apalachee Pkwy.   Phone: (904) 644-2440
Tallahassee, FL 32301   Margaret Winkler, Coord.

FLORIDA STATE UNIVERSITY - COMMUNICATION RESEARCH CENTER -
     LIBRARY
College of Communication
401A Diffenbaugh Bldg.   Phone: (904) 644-5034
Tallahassee, FL 32306   Dr. Barry S. Sapolsky, Dir.

FLORIDA STATE UNIVERSITY - INSTITUTE OF SOCIAL RESEARCH -
     CENTER FOR THE STUDY OF POPULATION
659 Bellamy   Phone: (904) 644-1762
Tallahassee, FL 32306   Dr. David Sly, Dir.

FLORIDA STATE UNIVERSITY - INSTRUCTIONAL SUPPORT CENTER - FILM
     LIBRARY
                                           Phone: (904) 644-2820
Tallahassee, FL 32306   Dr. John W. McLanahan, Dir.

FLORIDA STATE UNIVERSITY - LAW LIBRARY
                                           Phone: (904) 644-1004
Tallahassee, FL 32306   Edwin M. Schroeder, Dir.

FLORIDA STATE UNIVERSITY - LIBRARY SCIENCE LIBRARY †
Robert Manning Strozier Library   Phone: (904) 644-1803
Tallahassee, FL 32306   Adeline W. Wilkes, Univ.Libn.

FLORIDA STATE UNIVERSITY - SCHOOL OF NURSING - LEARNING
     RESOURCE CENTER
310 School of Nursing   Phone: (904) 644-1291
Tallahassee, FL 32306   Leonard N. Barnes, Sr., AV Libn.

FLORIDA STATE UNIVERSITY - SCIENCE-TECHNOLOGY DIVISION
Robert Manning Strozier Library   Phone: (904) 644-3079
Tallahassee, FL 32306   James C. Myers, Hd.

FLORIDA STATE UNIVERSITY - SPECIAL COLLECTIONS
Robert Manning Strozier Library   Phone: (904) 644-3271
Tallahassee, FL 32306   Opal M. Free, Hd.

FLORIDA STATE UNIVERSITY - WARREN D. ALLEN MUSIC LIBRARY
                                           Phone: (904) 644-5028
Tallahassee, FL 32306   Dale L. Hudson, Music Libn.

GRAPHIC COMMUNICATIONS WORLD/TECHNICAL INFORMATION, INC. -
     LIBRARY
Box 9500   Phone: (904) 878-0322
Tallahassee, FL 32315   A.E. Gardner, Libn.

NAIAD PRESS, INC. - LESBIAN AND GAY ARCHIVES
Box 10543   Phone: (904) 539-9322
Tallahassee, FL 32302   Donna J. McBride, Hd.Libn.

STATE LIBRARY OF FLORIDA
R.A. Gray Bldg.   Phone: (904) 487-2651
Tallahassee, FL 32301   Barratt Wilkins, State Libn.

TALL TIMBERS RESEARCH STATION - LIBRARY
Rte. 1, Box 160   Phone: (904) 893-4153
Tallahassee, FL 32312   Sharri Moroshok, Libn.

U.S. FOREST SERVICE - NATL. FORESTS IN FLORIDA - LIBRARY
227 N. Brorough St., Suite 4061   Phone: (904) 681-7266
Tallahassee, FL 32301

CARLTON, FIELDS, WARD, EMMANUEL, SMITH & CUTLER, P.A. - LIBRARY
610 N. Florida Ave., 20th Fl.
Exchange Bldg.   Phone: (813) 223-5366
Tampa, FL 33602   Donald G. Ziegenfuss, Law Libn.

CHURCH OF JESUS CHRIST OF LATTER-DAY SAINTS - TAMPA BRANCH
     GENEALOGICAL LIBRARY
4106 E. Fletcher Ave.   Phone: (813) 971-2869
Tampa, FL 33617   Barbara M. Dalby, Hd.Libn.

FLORIDA HISTORICAL SOCIETY - LIBRARY †
Univ. of South Florida Library   Phone: (813) 974-2732
Tampa, FL 33620   Paul Eugen Camp, Exec.Sec.

HILLSBOROUGH COUNTY HISTORICAL COMMISSION - LIBRARY
County Court House   Phone: (813) 272-5919
Tampa, FL 33602   Anthony P. Pizzo, Chm.

HILLSBOROUGH COUNTY LAW LIBRARY
County Court House
Tampa, FL 33602   William M. Bailey, Libn.

HONEYWELL, INC. - ENGINEERING LIBRARY
10901 Malcolm McKinley Dr.
Box 17500   Phone: (813) 977-8511
Tampa, FL 33682   Betsy King, Libn.

JOHNSON & JOHNSON-CRITIKON, INC. - R & D INFORMATION SERVICES
4110 George Rd.   Phone: (813) 887-2558
Tampa, FL 33614   Dennis J. Vecsey, Supv., Info.Serv.

LAMALIE ASSOCIATES, INC. - RESEARCH DEPARTMENT
13920 N. Dale Mabry   Phone: (813) 961-7494
Tampa, FL 33618   Nancy M. Clausen, Dir. of Res.

LUTHERAN CHURCH IN AMERICA - FLORIDA SYNOD - MULTI-MEDIA
     LIBRARY
3838 W. Cypress St.   Phone: (813) 876-7660
Tampa, FL 33607   Grace Little, Libn.

REFLECTONE, INC. - ENGINEERING LIBRARY
5125 Tampa West Blvd.   Phone: (813) 885-7481
Tampa, FL 33614   Sue Kaczor, Tech.Libn.

ST. JOSEPH'S HOSPITAL - MEDICAL LIBRARY
3000 W. Buffalo Ave.
Box 4227   Phone: (813) 870-4658
Tampa, FL 33677   Adelia P. Seglin, Dir., Med.Lib.

TAMPA ELECTRIC COMPANY - TECHNICAL REFERENCE CENTER
702 N. Franklin St.   Phone: (813) 228-4547
Tampa, FL 33602   Patricia W. Boody, Tech.Libn.

TAMPA GENERAL HOSPITAL - MEDICAL LIBRARY
Davis Islands   Phone: (813) 251-7328
Tampa, FL 33606   Loretta Holliday, Dir.

TAMPA TRIBUNE & TAMPA TIMES - LIBRARY
202 S. Parker St.   Phone: (813) 272-7665
Tampa, FL 33601   Louise N. LeGette, Chf.Libn.

U.S. VETERANS ADMINISTRATION (FL-Tampa) - MEDICAL LIBRARY
James A. Haley Veterans Hospital
13000 N. 30th St.   Phone: (813) 971-4500
Tampa, FL 33612   Iris A. Renner, Chf., Lib.Serv.

UNIVERSITY COMMUNITY HOSPITAL - MEDICAL LIBRARY
3100 E. Fletcher Ave.   Phone: (813) 971-6000
Tampa, FL 33612   Gwen E. Walters, Lib.Mgr.

UNIVERSITY OF SOUTH FLORIDA - DIVISION OF EDUCATIONAL
   RESOURCES - FILM LIBRARY
4202 Fowler Ave.   Phone: (813) 974-2874
Tampa, FL 33620   Delma Rodriguez, AV Media Dir.

UNIVERSITY OF SOUTH FLORIDA - LIBRARY - SPECIAL COLLECTIONS
   DEPARTMENT
                                          Phone: (813) 974-2732
Tampa, FL 33620   Mr. J.B. Dobkin, Spec.Coll.Libn.

UNIVERSITY OF SOUTH FLORIDA - MEDICAL CENTER LIBRARY
Box 31   Phone: (813) 974-2399
Tampa, FL 33612   Maxyne M. Grimes, Act.Dir.

ANCLOTE PSYCHIATRIC CENTER - MEDICAL LIBRARY
Box 1224   Phone: (813) 937-4211
Tarpon Springs, FL 33589   Carol Lynn, Med.Libn.

LAKE COUNTY HISTORICAL SOCIETY - LIBRARY
115 N. New Hampshire Ave.
Tavares, FL 32778   Mrs. M. Brownberger, Sec./Libn.

LAKE COUNTY LAW LIBRARY
315 W. Main St.
Lake County Courthouse   Phone: (904) 343-9730
Tavares, FL 32278   Pamela L. Woodworth, Libn.

BREVARD COUNTY - A. MAX BREWER MEMORIAL LAW LIBRARY
County Courthouse, Fl. 4
400 South St.   Phone: (305) 269-8197
Titusville, FL 32780   Mrs. George McFarland, Law Libn.

U.S. AIR FORCE ENGINEERING AND SERVICES CENTER - TECHNICAL
   LIBRARY
                                          Phone: (904) 283-6449
Tyndall AFB, FL 32403   Andrew D. Poulis, Chf.Tech.Libn.

HISTORICAL SOCIETY OF OKALOOSA & WALTON COUNTIES, INC. -
   MUSEUM LIBRARY
115 Westview Ave.   Phone: (904) 678-2615
Valparaiso, FL 32580   Christian LaRoche, Musm.Dir.

FLORIDA STATE MEDICAL ENTOMOLOGY LABORATORY LIBRARY
IFAS, University of Florida
Box 520   Phone: (305) 562-5435
Vero Beach, FL 32960   Carolee Zimmerman, Sec. II-Libn.

INDIAN RIVER MEMORIAL HOSPITAL - PROFESSIONAL LIBRARY
1000 36th St.   Phone: (305) 567-4311
Vero Beach, FL 32960   Josephine Kirkpatrick, Chm.

AMERICAN PSYCHOTHERAPY ASSOCIATION - LIBRARY
Box 2436
West Palm Beach, FL 33402

FLORIDA STATE - SOUTH FLORIDA WATER MANAGEMENT DISTRICT -
   REFERENCE CENTER
Box V   Phone: (305) 686-8800
West Palm Beach, FL 33402-4238 Cynthia H. Plockelman, Ref.Libn.

GEE & JENSON ENGINEERS, ARCHITECTS, PLANNERS, INC. - LIBRARY
2090 Palm Beach Lakes Blvd.
Drawer 4600   Phone: (305) 683-3301
West Palm Beach, FL 33402   Helen M. Foster, Lib.Mgr.

GOOD SAMARITAN HOSPITAL - RICHARD S. BEINECKE MEDICAL LIBRARY
Box 3166   Phone: (305) 655-5511
West Palm Beach, FL 33402   Elizabeth H. Day, Med.Libn.

NORTON GALLERY AND SCHOOL OF ART - LIBRARY
1451 S. Olive Ave.   Phone: (305) 832-5194
West Palm Beach, FL 33401   Hilda Scott, Libn.

PALM BEACH COUNTY - LAW LIBRARY
339 Courthouse   Phone: (305) 837-2928
West Palm Beach, FL 33401   Marguerite H. Johnson, Law Libn.

ST. MARY'S HOSPITAL - HEALTH SCIENCES LIBRARY
901 45th St.   Phone: (305) 844-6300
West Palm Beach, FL 33407   Jennie Glock, Libn.

TEMPLE ISRAEL - LIBRARY
1901 N. Flagler Dr.   Phone: (305) 833-8421
West Palm Beach, FL 33407   Elsie Leviton, Chm., Lib.Comm.

TREVES (Ralph) WORKSHOP FEATURES - WORKSHOP PHOTOS
311 Lake Evelyn Dr.   Phone: (305) 683-5167
West Palm Beach, FL 33411   Ralph Treves, Owner

FLORIDA STATE DIVISION OF ARCHIVES, HISTORY & REC. MANAGEMENT
   - BUREAU OF FLORIDA FOLKLIFE PROGRAMS - ARCHIVES
Box 265   Phone: (904) 397-2192
White Springs, FL 32096   Barbara Beauchamp, Archv.Asst.

GESSLER CLINIC - MEDICAL LIBRARY *
635 First St., North
Winter Haven, FL 33880

WINTER HAVEN HOSPITAL - J.G. CONVERSE MEMORIAL MEDICAL LIBRARY
200 Ave. F., N.E.   Phone: (813) 293-1121
Winter Haven, FL 33881   Henry Hasse, Lrng.Rsrcs.Spec.

FLORIDA CONSERVATION FOUNDATION, INC. - ENVIRONMENTAL
   INFORMATION CENTER
1203 Orange Ave.   Phone: (305) 644-5377
Winter Park, FL 32789   William M. Partington, Jr., Dir.

ROLLINS COLLEGE - BEAL-MALTBIE SHELL MUSEUM - LIBRARY
Box 2753
Winter Park, FL 32789   Linda L. Mojer, Cur.

WINTER PARK MEMORIAL HOSPITAL - MEDICAL STAFF LIBRARY †
200 N. Lakemont Ave.   Phone: (305) 646-7049
Winter Park, FL 32792   Patricia N. Cole, Med.Libn.

GEORGIA

U.S. MARINE CORPS - LOGISTICS BASE, ALBANY, GA - TECHNICAL
   LIBRARY
                                          Phone: (912) 439-6470
Albany, GA 31704   John Larry Nesmith, Libn.

ENVIRONMENTAL PROTECTION AGENCY - ENVIRONMENTAL RESEARCH
   LABORATORY, ATHENS - LIBRARY
College Station Rd.   Phone: (404) 546-3324
Athens, GA 30613   Charlotte C. Folk, Libn.

U.S.D.A. - AGRICULTURAL RESEARCH SERVICE - SOUTH ATLANTIC AREA -
   RICHARD B. RUSSELL AGRI. RESEARCH CTR. LIB.
College Station Rd., Box 5677   Phone: (404) 546-3314
Athens, GA 30613   Benna Brodsky Thompson, Libn.

UNIVERSITY OF GEORGIA - DEPARTMENT OF RECORDS MANAGEMENT &
   UNIVERSITY ARCHIVES
4th Fl., Old Section
Ilah Dunlap Little Memorial Library   Phone: (404) 542-8151
Athens, GA 30602   Dr. John Carver Edwards, Rec.Off./Archv.

UNIVERSITY OF GEORGIA - GOVERNMENT DOCUMENTS DEPARTMENT
University of Georgia Libraries   Phone: (404) 542-8949
Athens, GA 30602   Susan C. Field, Docs.Libn.

UNIVERSITY OF GEORGIA - LAW LIBRARY
                                          Phone: (404) 542-8480
Athens, GA 30602   Erwin C. Surrency, Prof./Libn.

UNIVERSITY OF GEORGIA - MANUSCRIPTS COLLECTION
University of Georgia Libraries   Phone: (404) 542-2972
Athens, GA 30602   Larry Gulley, Mss.Libn.

UNIVERSITY OF GEORGIA - RARE BOOKS DEPARTMENT
                                                   Phone: (404) 542-2972
Athens, GA 30602   Robert M. Willingham, Rare Bks.Cur.

UNIVERSITY OF GEORGIA - RICHARD B. RUSSELL MEMORIAL LIBRARY
University of Georgia Libraries   Phone: (404) 542-5788
Athens, GA 30602   Sheryl Vogt, Hd.

UNIVERSITY OF GEORGIA - SCIENCE LIBRARY
                                                   Phone: (404) 542-4535
Athens, GA 30602   Arlene E. Luchsinger, Hd.

UNIVERSITY OF GEORGIA - SCIENCE LIBRARY - MAP COLLECTION
University of Georgia Libraries   Phone: (404) 542-4535
Athens, GA 30602   John Sutherland, Map Cur.

ALSTON & BIRD - LIBRARY
35 Broad St., Suite 1200   Phone: (404) 586-1508
Atlanta, GA 30335   Anne H. Butler, Libn.

AMERICAN ASSOCIATION OF OCCUPATIONAL HEALTH NURSES - LIBRARY
3500 Piedmont Rd., N.E.   Phone: (404) 262-1162
Atlanta, GA 30305   Ricki Herrling, Libn.

ATLANTA BUREAU OF PLANNING - LIBRARY
10 Pryor St., S.W., Suite 200   Phone: (404) 658-6400
Atlanta, GA 30303   John Wright Heath, Dir./Lib. & Info.Serv.

ATLANTA COLLEGE OF ART - LIBRARY
1280 Peachtree St.   Phone: (404) 892-3600
Atlanta, GA 30309   Jo Anne Paschall, Hd.Libn.

ATLANTA FULTON PUBLIC LIBRARY - IVAN ALLEN, JR. DEPARTMENT OF
  SCIENCE, INDUSTRY AND GOVERNMENT
1 Margaret Mitchell Sq.   Phone: (404) 688-4636
Atlanta, GA 30303   William Munro, Hd.

ATLANTA FULTON PUBLIC LIBRARY - IVAN ALLEN, JR. DEPT. OF SCIENCE,
  INDUSTRY & GOVERNMENT - FOUNDATION COLL.
1 Margaret Mitchell Sq.   Phone: (404) 688-4636
Atlanta, GA 30303   Nancy Powers, Hd.

ATLANTA FULTON PUBLIC LIBRARY - SPECIAL COLLECTIONS
  DEPARTMENT
1 Margaret Mitchell Sq.   Phone: (404) 688-4636
Atlanta, GA 30303   Janice White Sikes, Cur.

ATLANTA HISTORICAL SOCIETY - ARCHIVES
3101 Andrews Dr., N.W.   Phone: (404) 261-1837
Atlanta, GA 30305   Nancy J. Bryant, Dir., Lib. & Archv.

ATLANTA LAW SCHOOL - LIBRARY
56 Tenth St., N.E.   Phone: (404) 872-0990
Atlanta, GA 30309   Michael Bray, Law Libn.

ATLANTA LESBIAN FEMINIST ALLIANCE - SOUTHEASTERN LESBIAN
  ARCHIVES
Box 5502   Phone: (404) 523-7786
Atlanta, GA 30307   Alea Feall, Libn.

ATLANTA NEWSPAPERS - REFERENCE LIBRARY
72 Marietta St., N.W.   Phone: (404) 526-5420
Atlanta, GA 30303   Diane C. Hunter, Mgr., Lib.Serv.

ATLANTA UNIVERSITY CENTER - ROBERT W. WOODRUFF LIBRARY
111 Chestnut St., S.W.   Phone: (404) 223-5378
Atlanta, GA 30314   Minnie H. Clayton, Div.Hd./Archv.

ATLANTA UNIVERSITY CENTER - ROBERT W. WOODRUFF LIBRARY -
  INTERDENOMINATIONAL THEOLOGICAL CENTER ARCHIVES
111 Chestnut St., S.W.   Phone: (404) 522-8980
Atlanta, GA 30314

ATLANTA UNIVERSITY - SCHOOL OF LIBRARY & INFORMATION STUDIES -
  LIBRARY
223 Chestnut St., S.W.   Phone: (404) 681-0251
Atlanta, GA 30314   Chih Wang, Libn.

CARVER BIBLE COLLEGE - LIBRARY
437 Nelson St., S.W.
Atlanta, GA 30302   Ruth A. Wedel, Libn.

CLARK COLLEGE - SOUTHERN CENTER FOR STUDIES IN PUBLIC POLICY -
  RESEARCH LIBRARY
240 Chestnut St., S.W.   Phone: (404) 752-6422
Atlanta, GA 30314   Mrs. Ollye G. Davis, Res.Libn.

COCA-COLA COMPANY - COCA COLA USA - MARKETING INFORMATION
  CENTER
P.O. Drawer 1734   Phone: (404) 676-3314
Atlanta, GA 30301   Judy A. Cassell, Libn.

THE COCA-COLA COMPANY - LAW LIBRARY
P.O. Drawer 1734   Phone: (404) 676-2096
Atlanta, GA 30301   H. Christine Johnson, Mgr., Law Lib. & Rec.Ctr.

COCA-COLA COMPANY - TECHNICAL INFORMATION SERVICES
P.O. Drawer 1734   Phone: (404) 676-2008
Atlanta, GA 30301   Bernard Prudhomme, Mgr.

CONFEDERATION LIFE INSURANCE COMPANY - LIBRARY
280 Interstate North Pkwy.
Box 105103   Phone: (404) 953-5249
Atlanta, GA 30348   Michael Aiken, Libn.

CRAWFORD W. LONG MEMORIAL HOSPITAL - MEDICAL LIBRARY
35 Linden Ave., N.E.   Phone: (404) 892-4411
Atlanta, GA 30365   Mrs. Girija Vijay, Dir., Med.Lib.

DAMES & MOORE - LIBRARY
445 East Paces Ferry Rd., N.E., Suite 200   Phone: (404) 262-2915
Atlanta, GA 30363   Becky Kear, Libn.

EMORY UNIVERSITY - DIVISION OF LIBRARY AND INFORMATION
  MANAGEMENT LIBRARY
420 Candler Library Bldg.   Phone: (404) 329-6846
Atlanta, GA 30322   Ann W. Morton, Libn.

EMORY UNIVERSITY - DOCUMENTS DEPARTMENT
Woodruff Library   Phone: (404) 329-6880
Atlanta, GA 30322   Elizabeth A. McBride, Hd., Doc.Dept.

EMORY UNIVERSITY - JAMES SAMUEL GUY LIBRARY
440 Chemistry Bldg.   Phone: (404) 329-6618
Atlanta, GA 30322   Pamela E. Pickens, Chem.Libn.

EMORY UNIVERSITY - PITTS THEOLOGY LIBRARY
Theology Bldg.   Phone: (404) 329-4166
Atlanta, GA 30322   Channing R. Jeschke, Libn.

EMORY UNIVERSITY - REHABILITATION RESEARCH AND TRAINING
  LIBRARY
Center for Rehabilitation Medicine
1441 Clifton Rd., N.E.   Phone: (404) 329-5583
Atlanta, GA 30322   John Banja, Dir. of Training

EMORY UNIVERSITY - SCHOOL OF LAW LIBRARY
Gambrell Hall   Phone: (404) 329-6823
Atlanta, GA 30322   Robin K. Mills, Law Libn.

EMORY UNIVERSITY - SCHOOL OF MEDICINE - A.W. CALHOUN MEDICAL
  LIBRARY
                                                   Phone: (404) 329-5820
Atlanta, GA 30322   Carol A. Burns, Dir.

EMORY UNIVERSITY - SCIENCE LIBRARY †
Woodruff Library   Phone: (404) 329-6885
Atlanta, GA 30322   Irene K. Mallison, Hd., Sci.Dept.

EMORY UNIVERSITY - SPECIAL COLLECTIONS DEPARTMENT
Woodruff Library   Phone: (404) 329-6887
Atlanta, GA 30322   Linda M. Matthews, Hd.

EMORY UNIVERSITY - YERKES REGIONAL PRIMATE CENTER - LIBRARY
Phone: (404) 329-7764
Atlanta, GA 30322   Nellie Johns, Libn.

ENVIRONMENTAL PROTECTION AGENCY - REGION IV LIBRARY
345 Courtland St.   Phone: (404) 881-4216
Atlanta, GA 30308   Carolyn W. Mitchell, Hd.Libn.

EQUIFAX, INC. - CORPORATE INFORMATION RESOURCES
Box 4081   Phone: (404) 885-8320
Atlanta, GA 30302   Michael McDavid, Mgr.

FEDERAL RESERVE BANK OF ATLANTA - RESEARCH LIBRARY
Box 1731   Phone: (404) 521-8829
Atlanta, GA 30301   Leigh Watson Healy, Libn.

FERNBANK SCIENCE CENTER - LIBRARY
156 Heaton Park Dr., N.E.   Phone: (404) 378-4311
Atlanta, GA 30307   Mary Larsen, Libn.

FULTON COUNTY LAW LIBRARY
709 Courthouse
136 Pryor St., S.W.   Phone: (404) 572-2330
Atlanta, GA 30303   Sandra Howell, Law Libn.

GENEALOGICAL CENTER - LIBRARY
2815 Clearview Pl.   Phone: (404) 457-7801
Atlanta, GA 30340   Diane Dieterle, Dir.

GEORGIA BAPTIST MEDICAL CENTER - MEDICAL LIBRARY
300 Boulevard, N.E.   Phone: (404) 653-4603
Atlanta, GA 30312   Fay E. Boyer, Med.Libn.

GEORGIA CONSERVANCY, INC. - LIBRARY
3110 Maple Dr., Suite 407   Phone: (404) 262-1967
Atlanta, GA 30305

GEORGIA INSTITUTE OF TECHNOLOGY - PRICE GILBERT MEMORIAL
LIBRARY
Campus Dr.   Phone: (404) 894-4510
Atlanta, GA 30332   Dr. Edward Graham Roberts, Dir.

GEORGIA INSTITUTE OF TECHNOLOGY - PRICE GILBERT MEMORIAL
LIBRARY - ARCHITECTURE LIBRARY
Phone: (404) 894-4877
Atlanta, GA 30332   Kathryn S. Brackney, Arch.Libn.

GEORGIA INSTITUTE OF TECHNOLOGY - SYSTEMS ENGINEERING
LABORATORY - TECHNICAL INFORMATION CENTER
347 Ferst Dr.   Phone: (404) 894-3587
Atlanta, GA 30318   Deborah W. Thomas, Res.Assoc.

GEORGIA MUNICIPAL ASSOCIATION - LIBRARY
34 Peachtree St., Suite 2300   Phone: (404) 688-0472
Atlanta, GA 30303   Lahna Young, Libn.

GEORGIA POWER COMPANY - LIBRARY SERVICES
333 Piedmont Ave.
Box 4545   Phone: (404) 526-6857
Atlanta, GA 30302   Beth Ansley, Lib.Serv.Supv.

GEORGIA STATE DEPARTMENT OF ARCHIVES AND HISTORY - CENTRAL
RESEARCH LIBRARY †
330 Capitol Ave., S.E.   Phone: (404) 656-2350
Atlanta, GA 30334   Ruth L. Corry, Hd., Ctrl.Res.

GEORGIA STATE DEPARTMENT OF EDUCATION - DIVISION OF PUBLIC
LIBRARY SERVICES
156 Trinity Ave., S.W.   Phone: (404) 656-2461
Atlanta, GA 30303   Joe B. Forsee, Dir.

GEORGIA STATE DEPARTMENT OF EDUCATION - LIBRARY FOR THE BLIND
& PHYSICALLY HANDICAPPED
1050 Murphy Ave., S.W.   Phone: (404) 656-2465
Atlanta, GA 30310   Jim DeJarnatt, Dir.

GEORGIA STATE DEPARTMENT OF HUMAN RESOURCES - GEORGIA
MENTAL HEALTH INSTITUTE - ADDISON M. DUVAL LIBRARY †
1256 Briarcliff Rd., N.E.   Phone: (404) 894-5663
Atlanta, GA 30306   Brenda Scott, Dir. of Libs.

GEORGIA STATE DEPARTMENT OF HUMAN RESOURCES - LIBRARY
47 Trinity Ave., S.W.   Phone: (404) 656-4969
Atlanta, GA 30334-1202   Miriam Boland, Lib.Dir.

GEORGIA STATE DEPARTMENT OF NATURAL RESOURCES - PARKS AND
HISTORICAL SITES DIV. - HISTORIC PRESERVATION SECTION
270 Washington St., S.W., Rm. 704   Phone: (404) 656-2840
Atlanta, GA 30334   Kenneth H. Thomas, Jr., Hist.

GEORGIA STATE DEPARTMENT OF OFFENDER REHABILITATION -
REFERENCE/RESOURCE CENTER
2 Martin Luther King Dr., S.E.   Phone: (404) 894-5383
Atlanta, GA 30334   Karen Dornseif, Libn.

GEORGIA STATE DEPARTMENT OF TRANSPORTATION - RESEARCH
LIBRARY
15 Kennedy Dr.   Phone: (404) 363-7567
Atlanta, GA 30050   Alfredia A. Scott, Libn.

GEORGIA STATE LIBRARY
301 Judicial Bldg.
40 Capitol Sq., S.W.   Phone: (404) 656-3468
Atlanta, GA 30334   Carroll T. Parker, State Libn.

GEORGIA STATE OFFICE OF PLANNING AND BUDGET - STATE DATA
CENTER
270 Washington St., S.W., Rm. 608   Phone: (404) 656-2191
Atlanta, GA 30334   Thomas M. Wagner, Prog.Mgr.

GEORGIA STATE SUPREME COURT LIBRARY
Judicial Bldg., 5th Fl.
40 Capitol Sq., S.W.   Phone: (404) 656-4212
Atlanta, GA 30334   Curtis M. French, Libn.

GEORGIA STATE SURVEYOR GENERAL DEPARTMENT - LIBRARY
330 Capitol Ave.
Archives & Records Bldg.   Phone: (404) 656-2367
Atlanta, GA 30334   Mr. Marion R. Hemperley, Dp. Surveyor Gen.

GEORGIA STATE UNIVERSITY - COLLEGE OF LAW LIBRARY
University Plaza   Phone: (404) 658-2479
Atlanta, GA 30303   Orrin Walker, Law Libn.

GEORGIA STATE UNIVERSITY - SMALL BUSINESS DEVELOPMENT CENTER
Box 874, University Plaza   Phone: (404) 658-3550
Atlanta, GA 30303   Peggy Triplett

GEORGIA STATE UNIVERSITY - SPECIAL COLLECTIONS DEPARTMENT
University Library   Phone: (404) 658-2476
Atlanta, GA 30303   Leslie S. Hough, Dir.

GOETHE INSTITUTE ATLANTA - GERMAN CULTURAL CENTER - LIBRARY
400 Colony Sq.   Phone: (404) 892-2226
Atlanta, GA 30361   Margit Rostock, Libn.

HANSELL & POST - LIBRARY
3300 First National Bank Tower   Phone: (404) 581-8000
Atlanta, GA 30383   Fran Pughslen, Libn.

KILPATRICK & CODY - LIBRARY
3100 Equitable Bldg.
100 Peachtree St.   Phone: (404) 572-6397
Atlanta, GA 30303   Peggy Martin, Libn.

KING (Martin Luther, Jr.) CENTER FOR SOCIAL CHANGE - KING LIBRARY
AND ARCHIVES
449 Auburn Ave.   Phone: (404) 524-1956
Atlanta, GA 30312   D. Louise Cook, Dir.

KING & SPALDING - LAW LIBRARY †
2500 Trust Company Tower   Phone: (404) 572-4808
Atlanta, GA 30303   Mary Anne C. Fry, Libn.

KUTAK ROCK & HUIE, ATTORNEYS AT LAW - LAW LIBRARY
1200 Anchor Savings Bank Bldg.   Phone: (404) 522-8700
Atlanta, GA 30303   Jane G. Miller, Libn.

LIFE OFFICE MANAGEMENT ASSOCIATION - INFORMATION CENTER
100 Colony Sq.   Phone: (404) 892-7272
Atlanta, GA 30361   Patricia A. Toups, Libn.

LONG & ALDRIDGE - LAW LIBRARY
1900 Rhodes-Haverty Bldg.
134 Peachtree St.   Phone: (404) 681-3000
Atlanta, GA 30043   Cindy Adams, Libn.

MAC FARLANE & COMPANY, INC. - FRY CONSULTANTS INCORPORATED -
    MANAGEMENT CENTRE, INC.
One Park Place, Suite 450   Phone: (404) 352-2293
Atlanta, GA 30318   Beth Clark, Mgr.

MERCER UNIVERSITY - SOUTHERN COLLEGE OF PHARMACY - H. CUSTER
    NAYLOR LIBRARY
345 Boulevard, N.E.   Phone: (404) 688-6291
Atlanta, GA 30312   Elizabeth Christian Jackson, Lib.Dir.

METROPOLITAN ATLANTA RAPID TRANSIT AUTHORITY - LIBRARY
2200 Peachtree Summit
401 W. Peachtree St., N.E.
Atlanta, GA 30365   Bruce B. Emory, Dp.Asst.Gen.Mgr.

MOREHOUSE SCHOOL OF MEDICINE - MULTI-MEDIA CENTER
720 Westview Dr., S.W.   Phone: (404) 752-1047
Atlanta, GA 30310   Beverly E. Allen, Dir.

NATIONAL PARENTS' RESOURCE INSTITUTE FOR DRUG EDUCATION, INC.
100 Edgewood Ave., Suite 1216
Atlanta, GA 30303

NORTHSIDE HOSPITAL - WOODRUFF HEALTH SCIENCE LIBRARY
1000 Johnson Ferry Rd., N.E.   Phone: (404) 256-8744
Atlanta, GA 30042   Sharon Cann, Libn.

OGLETHORPE UNIVERSITY - LIBRARY - ARCHIVES
4484 Peachtree Rd., N.E.   Phone: (404) 261-1441
Atlanta, GA 30319

PIEDMONT HOSPITAL - SAULS MEMORIAL LIBRARY
1968 Peachtree Rd., N.W.   Phone: (404) 350-2222
Atlanta, GA 30309   Alice DeVierno, Med.Libn.

PORTMAN (John) & ASSOCIATES - LIBRARY
225 Peachtree St.   Phone: (404) 522-8811
Atlanta, GA 30303   Nancy Williams, Libn.

POWELL, GOLDSTEIN, FRAZER & MURPHY - LIBRARY
1100 C & S National Bank Bldg.   Phone: (404) 572-6600
Atlanta, GA 30335   Margarette M. Dye, Libn.

ROLLS-ROYCE INC. - LIBRARY
1895 Phoenix Blvd.   Phone: (404) 996-8400
Atlanta, GA 30349   Karen L. Bell, Info.Off.

ST. JOSEPH'S HOSPITAL - RUSSELL BELLMAN MEDICAL LIBRARY †
5665 Peachtree Dunwoody Rd., N.E.   Phone: (404) 256-7040
Atlanta, GA 30342   Gail Waverchak, Med.Libn.

SCIENTIFIC-ATLANTA, INC. - LIBRARY
3845 Pleasantdale Rd.   Phone: (404) 449-2000
Atlanta, GA 30340   Peggy A. Price, Libn.

SMITH, CURRIE & HANCOCK - LAW LIBRARY
233 Peachtree St., N.E.
2600 Peachtree Ctr., Harris Tower   Phone: (404) 521-3800
Atlanta, GA 30303   Elisa F. Kadish, Libn.

SOUTHERN BELL TELEPHONE AND TELEGRAPH COMPANY - LAW LIBRARY
4300 Southern Bell Ctr.   Phone: (404) 529-7937
Atlanta, GA 30375   Cheryl L. McKenzie, Libn.

SOUTHERN REGIONAL COUNCIL, INC. - REFERENCE LIBRARY
75 Marietta St., N.W.   Phone: (404) 522-8764
Atlanta, GA 30303   Stephen T. Suitts, Exec.Dir.

SOUTHERN REGIONAL EDUCATION BOARD - LIBRARY
1340 Spring St., N.W.   Phone: (404) 875-9211
Atlanta, GA 30345   Ann Hadley Carter, Res.Asst./Libn.

SOUTHERN STATES ENERGY BOARD (SSEB) - SOUTHERN ENERGY/
    ENVIRONMENTAL INFORMATION CENTER (SEEIC)
One Exchange Place, Suite 1230
2300 Peachford Rd.   Phone: (404) 455-8841
Atlanta, GA 30338   Jane F. Clark, Dir.

TECHNICAL ASSOCIATION OF THE PULP AND PAPER INDUSTRY - LIBRARY
Box 105113   Phone: (404) 394-6130
Atlanta, GA 30348   Elizabeth A. Bibby, Info.Rsrc.Adm.

THORNDIKE, DORAN, PAINE AND LEWIS INC. - RESEARCH LIBRARY
233 Peachtree St., N.E., Suite 700   Phone: (404) 688-2782
Atlanta, GA 30303   Linda Swann Austin, Libn.

U.S. ARMY - CORPS OF ENGINEERS - SOUTH ATLANTIC DIVISION -
    LIBRARY & INFORMATION CENTER
510 Title Bldg.
30 Pryor St., S.W.   Phone: (404) 221-6620
Atlanta, GA 30303   James D. Chestnut, Div.Libn.

U.S. BUREAU OF THE CENSUS - INFORMATION SERVICES PROGRAM -
    ATLANTA REGIONAL OFFICE
1365 Peachtree St., N.E., Rm. 523   Phone: (404) 881-3312
Atlanta, GA 30309   Joseph T. Reilly, Data User Serv.Off.

U.S. CENTERS FOR DISEASE CONTROL - CDC LIBRARY
1600 Clifton Rd., N.E.   Phone: (404) 329-3396
Atlanta, GA 30333   Mary Alice Mills, Dir.

U.S. CENTERS FOR DISEASE CONTROL - CHAMBLEE FACILITY LIBRARY
1600 Clifton Rd., N.E., 30/35   Phone: (404) 452-4167
Atlanta, GA 30333

U.S. COURT OF APPEALS, 11TH CIRCUIT - LIBRARY
56 Forsyth St., N.W.   Phone: (404) 221-2510
Atlanta, GA 30303   Elaine P. Fenton, Circuit Libn.

U.S. DEPT. OF COMMERCE - INTERNATIONAL TRADE ADMINISTRATION -
    ATLANTA DISTRICT OFFICE LIBRARY *
1365 Peachtree St., N.E., Suite 600   Phone: (404) 881-4873
Atlanta, GA 30032   Christine B. Brown, Trade Ref.Asst.

U.S. DEPT. OF HOUSING AND URBAN DEVELOPMENT - REGION IV -
    LIBRARY *
Richard B. Russell Fed. Bldg., Rm. 722
75 Spring St., S.W.   Phone: (404) 221-3367
Atlanta, GA 30303   Mrs. Davide B. Williams, Regional Libn.

U.S. DEPT. OF LABOR - EMPLOYMENT & TRAINING ADMINISTRATION -
    REGION IV RESOURCE CENTER *
1371 Peachtree St., N.E., Suite 434   Phone: (404) 881-3534
Atlanta, GA 30367   Toussaint Hayes, Training Dir.

U.S. NATL. PARK SERVICE - INFORMATION CLEARINGHOUSE *
75 Spring St., S.W., Suite 1092   Phone: (404) 221-3889
Atlanta, GA 30303   Linda Hall, Libn.

U.S. PRESIDENTIAL LIBRARIES - CARTER PRESIDENTIAL MATERIALS
    PROJECT
77 Forsyth St., S.W.   Phone: (404) 221-3942
Atlanta, GA 30303   Dr. Donald B. Schewe, Dir.

AUGUSTA CHRONICLE-HERALD NEWS - LIBRARY *
Box 1928(13)   Phone: (404) 724-0851
Augusta, GA 30913   P. Craig Morris, Libn.

MEDICAL COLLEGE OF GEORGIA - LIBRARY
1120 15th St.   Phone: (404) 828-3441
Augusta, GA 30912   Thomas G. Basler, Dir. of Libs.

ST. PAUL'S CHURCH - ARCHIVES
605 Reynolds St.   Phone: (404) 724-2485
Augusta, GA 30902

U.S. VETERANS ADMINISTRATION (GA-Augusta) - HOSPITAL LIBRARY
Phone: (404) 724-5116
Augusta, GA 30910   Dorothy K. Jones, Chf., Lib.Serv.

UNIVERSITY HOSPITAL - HEALTH SCIENCES LIBRARY
1350 Walton Way   Phone: (404) 722-9011
Augusta, GA 30910   Jane B. Wells, Libn.

GEORGIA STATE DEPARTMENT OF NATURAL RESOURCES - COASTAL
RESOURCES DIVISION - ANDERSON LIBRARY
1200 Glynn Ave.   Phone: (912) 264-7330
Brunswick, GA 31523   Eleanor Y. Waters, Libn.

SOUTHWIRE COMPANY - R & D TECHNICAL LIBRARY
Fertilla St.   Phone: (404) 832-5080
Carrollton, GA 30119   Linda League, Libn.

WEST GEORGIA COLLEGE - IRVINE SULLIVAN INGRAM LIBRARY - ANNIE
BELLE WEAVER SPECIAL COLLECTIONS
Phone: (404) 834-1370
Carrollton, GA 30118   Myron W. House, Spec.Coll.Libn.

COLUMBUS LEDGER-ENQUIRER - LIBRARY
17 W. 12th St.   Phone: (404) 324-5526
Columbus, GA 31902   Patricia F. Hardy, Libn.

COLUMBUS MUSEUM OF ARTS AND SCIENCES - RESEARCH LIBRARY
1251 Wynnton Rd.   Phone: (404) 323-3617
Columbus, GA 31906   William E. Scheele, Dir.

MEDICAL CENTER - SIMON SCHWOB MEDICAL LIBRARY
710 Center St.   Phone: (404) 324-4711
Columbus, GA 31902   Opal Bartlett, Libn.

WEST CENTRAL GEORGIA REGIONAL HOSPITAL - THE LIBRARY
3000 Schatulga Rd.
Box 12435   Phone: (404) 568-5236
Columbus, GA 31995-7499   Linda A. Sears, Libn., Sr.

COLUMBIA THEOLOGICAL SEMINARY - JOHN BULOW CAMPBELL LIBRARY
701 Columbia Dr.   Phone: (404) 378-8821
Decatur, GA 30031-0520   Dr. James A. Overbeck, Lib.Dir.

DE KALB GENERAL HOSPITAL - MEDICAL LIBRARY
2701 N. Decatur Rd.   Phone: (404) 292-4444
Decatur, GA 30033   Marilyn Gibbs Barry, Med.Libn.

FUTURE AVIATION PROFESSIONALS OF AMERICA (FAPA) - INFORMATION
CENTER
4291-J Memorial Dr.   Phone: (404) 294-0226
Decatur, GA 30032   W. Louis Smith, Pres.

U.S. VETERANS ADMINISTRATION (GA-Atlanta) - HOSPITAL MEDICAL
LIBRARY
1670 Clairmont Rd.   Phone: (404) 321-6111
Decatur, GA 30033   Eugenia H. Abbey, Chf.Libn.

U.S. VETERANS ADMINISTRATION (GA-Dublin) - CENTER LIBRARY
Phone: (912) 272-1210
Dublin, GA 31021   Mrs. Kodell M. Thomas, Chf., Lib.Serv.

U.S. FEDERAL AVIATION ADMINISTRATION - SOUTHERN REGION LIBRARY
†
3400 Norman Berry Dr.   Phone: (404) 763-7276
East Point, GA 30344   Doris P. Little, Libn.

U.S. NATL. ARCHIVES & RECORDS SERVICE - FEDERAL ARCHIVES AND
RECORDS CENTER, REGION 4
1557 St. Joseph Ave.   Phone: (404) 763-7474
East Point, GA 30344   Thomas G. Hudson, Dir.

UNIVERSITY OF GEORGIA - GEORGIA AGRICULTURAL EXPERIMENT
STATION LIBRARY
Phone: (404) 228-7238
Experiment, GA 30212   Carole L. Ledford, Libn.

U.S. ARMY HOSPITALS - MARTIN ARMY COMMUNITY HOSPITAL - MEDICAL
LIBRARY
Phone: (404) 544-1341
Ft. Benning, GA 31905   E.A. Tate, Med.Libn.

U.S. ARMY INFANTRY SCHOOL - DONOVAN TECHNICAL LIBRARY
Infantry Hall, Bldg. 4   Phone: (404) 544-4053
Ft. Benning, GA 31905   Vivian S. Dodson, Chf., Lrng.Rsrcs.Div.

U.S. ARMY POST - FORT BENNING - RECREATION SERVICES LIBRARY
BRANCH †
Bldg. 93   Phone: (404) 544-4911
Ft. Benning, GA 31905   Gwendolyn I. Lewis, Supv.Libn.

U.S. ARMY HOSPITALS - D.D. EISENHOWER ARMY MEDICAL CENTER -
MEDICAL LIBRARY †
Phone: (404) 791-6765
Ft. Gordon, GA 30905   Judy M. Krivanek, Med.Libn.

U.S. ARMY SIGNAL CENTER & FORT GORDON - CONRAD TECHNICAL
LIBRARY
Bldg. 29807   Phone: (404) 791-3922
Ft. Gordon, GA 30905   Margaret H. Novinger, Adm.Libn.

U.S. ARMY POST - FORT MC PHERSON - LIBRARY SYSTEM
Bldg. T-44   Phone: (404) 752-3218
Ft. McPherson, GA 30330   Terri Kiss, Chf.Libn.

U.S. ARMY POST - FORT STEWART/HUNTER AAF LIBRARY SYSTEM
Box 3179   Phone: (912) 767-2828
Ft. Stewart, GA 31314   Richard D. Boyce, Morale Sup.Lib.Coord.

AMERICAN CAMELLIA SOCIETY - LIBRARY
Box 1217   Phone: (912) 967-2358
Fort Valley, GA 31030   Milton H. Brown, Exec.Sec.

FORT VALLEY STATE COLLEGE - HENRY ALEXANDER HUNT MEMORIAL
LEARNING RESOURCES CENTER
State College Dr.   Phone: (912) 825-6342
Fort Valley, GA 31030   Elizabeth Brinson, Act.Dir.

NORTHEAST GEORGIA MEDICAL CENTER AND HALL SCHOOL OF NURSING/
BRENAU COLLEGE - LIBRARY
741 Spring St.   Phone: (404) 536-1114
Gainesville, GA 30505   Caroline Alday, Libn.

GEORGIA REGIONAL HOSPITAL AT AUGUSTA - HOSPITAL LIBRARY
3405 Old Savannah Rd.
Box 327   Phone: (404) 790-2699
Gracewood, GA 30812   Joyce Fears, Libn.

GRACEWOOD STATE SCHOOL AND HOSPITAL - LIBRARY †
Phone: (404) 790-2183
Gracewood, GA 30812-1299   Alice K. Garren, Libn.

CHEROKEE REGIONAL LIBRARY - GEORGIA HISTORY & GENEALOGICAL
ROOM †
305 S. Duke St.
Box 707   Phone: (404) 638-2992
LaFayette, GA 30728   Diana Ray Tope, Dir.

CALLAWAY EDUCATIONAL ASSOCIATION - COLEMAN LIBRARY
Lincoln St.   Phone: (404) 882-0946
LaGrange, GA 30240   M. Christopher Boner, Dir.

LA GRANGE COLLEGE - WILLIAM AND EVELYN BANKS LIBRARY - SPECIAL
COLLECTIONS
Phone: (404) 882-2911
LaGrange, GA 30240   Frank Lewis, Libn.

BIBB COUNTY LAW LIBRARY *
Bibb County Court House
New Annex, Rm. A500   Phone: (912) 745-6871
Macon, GA 31207   Lucille Waldron, Libn.

GEORGIA BAPTIST HISTORICAL SOCIETY - LIBRARY
Stetson Memorial Library   Phone: (912) 744-2700
Macon, GA 31207   Mary E. Overby, Cur., Spec.Coll.

GEORGIA STATE FORESTRY COMMISSION - LIBRARY
Box 819   Phone: (912) 744-3231
Macon, GA 31298-4599   F. Brown, Act.Libn.

MACON TELEGRAPH AND NEWS - LIBRARY
Broadway & Riverside Dr.   Phone: (912) 744-4328
Macon, GA 31208   Harriet Comer, Libn.

MERCER UNIVERSITY - LAW SCHOOL - FURMAN SMITH LAW LIBRARY
                                                 Phone: (912) 744-2612
Macon, GA 31207   Leah F. Chanin, Dir., Law Lib.

MERCER UNIVERSITY - MEDICAL SCHOOL LIBRARY
                                                 Phone: (912) 744-2519
Macon, GA 31207   Jocelyn Rankin, Dir., Med.Lib.

MIDDLE GEORGIA REGIONAL LIBRARY - WASHINGTON MEMORIAL
   LIBRARY - GENEALOGICAL & HISTORICAL ROOM
1180 Washington Ave.   Phone: (912) 744-0821
Macon, GA 31201   Willard L. Rocker, Chf. of Genealogy

LOCKHEED-GEORGIA COMPANY - TECHNICAL INFORMATION
   DEPARTMENT
86 S. Cobb Dr.   Phone: (404) 424-2928
Marietta, GA 30063   C. David Rife, Mgr.

SOUTHERN TECHNICAL INSTITUTE - LIBRARY
Clay St.   Phone: (404) 424-7275
Marietta, GA 30060   John W. Pattillo, Dir.

U.S. NATL. PARK SERVICE - KENNESAW MOUNTAIN NATL. BATTLEFIELD
   PARK - LIBRARY
Box 1167   Phone: (404) 427-4686
Marietta, GA 30061   Emmet A. Nichols, Chf. Interpreter

CENTRAL STATE HOSPITAL - MEDICAL LIBRARY
                                                 Phone: (912) 453-4153
Milledgeville, GA 31062   Aurelia S. Spence, Lib.Dir.

CENTRAL STATE HOSPITAL - MENTAL HEALTH LIBRARY
                                                 Phone: (912) 453-4371
Milledgeville, GA 31062   Kathy Ridley, Libn.

GEORGIA COLLEGE - INA DILLARD RUSSELL LIBRARY - SPECIAL
   COLLECTIONS
231 W. Hancock   Phone: (912) 453-4047
Milledgeville, GA 31061   Janice C. Fennell, Lib.Dir.

GEORGIA COLLEGE - MEDIA SERVICES
Box 689   Phone: (912) 453-4714
Milledgeville, GA 31061   Dr. Kathy Davis, Coord.

U.S. AIR FORCE BASE - MOODY BASE LIBRARY
                                                 Phone: (912) 333-3539
Moody AFB, GA 31699   Madeleine A. Peyton, Libn.

COWETA COUNTY GENEALOGICAL SOCIETY - LIBRARY
Box 1014
Newnan, GA 30264   Norma Gunby, Owner

AT & T BELL LABORATORIES & TECHNOLOGIES - LIBRARY
2000 Northeast Expy.   Phone: (404) 447-2803
Norcross, GA 30071   John T. Shaw, Lib. Group Supv.

CONTEL LABORATORIES - TECHNICAL LIBRARY
270 Scientific Dr., Suite 10
Technology Park/Atlanta   Phone: (404) 448-2206
Norcross, GA 30092   Virginia Lawrence, Sr.Tech.Sec.

INSTITUTE OF INDUSTRIAL ENGINEERS, INC. - FILM LIBRARY
25 Technology Park/Atlanta   Phone: (404) 449-0460
Norcross, GA 30092   Rosemarie Perrin, Film Lib.Mgr.

INSTITUTE OF INDUSTRIAL ENGINEERS, INC. - FRANK & LILIAN GILBRETH
   MEMORIAL LIBRARY
25 Technology Park/Atlanta   Phone: (404) 449-0460
Norcross, GA 30092   Rosemarie Perrin, Lib.Mgr.

NUCLEAR ASSURANCE CORPORATION - INFORMATION CENTER
5720 Peachtree Pkwy.   Phone: (404) 447-1144
Norcross, GA 30092   Glenda Casper, Mgr., Info.Ctr.

THE FOXFIRE FUND, INC. - ARCHIVES
                                                 Phone: (404) 746-2561
Rabun Gap, GA 30568

U.S. AIR FORCE BASE - ROBINS BASE LIBRARY
2853 ABG/SSL   Phone: (912) 926-5411
Robins AFB, GA 31098   Carolyn M. Covington, Chf., Lib.Br.

FLOYD MEDICAL CENTER - LIBRARY †
Turner McCall Blvd.   Phone: (404) 295-5500
Rome, GA 30161   Mark W. Lashley, Med.Libn.

HIGHTOWER (Sara) REGIONAL LIBRARY - BUSINESS LIBRARY †
606 W. First St.
Box 277   Phone: (404) 291-9360
Rome, GA 30161   Jim L. Doyle, Bus.Libn.

HIGHTOWER (Sara) REGIONAL LIBRARY - HENDERSON ROOM
606 W. First St.   Phone: (404) 291-9360
Rome, GA 30161   Beatrice Millican, Spec.Coll.Libn.

NORTHWEST GEORGIA REGIONAL HOSPITAL AT ROME - MEDICAL
   LIBRARY †
Redmond Rd.   Phone: (404) 295-6060
Rome, GA 30161   James R. Fletcher, Lib.Ck.

SHORTER COLLEGE - MEMORABILIA ROOM
                                                 Phone: (404) 291-2121
Rome, GA 30161   Robert Gardner, College Historian

KIMBERLY-CLARK CORPORATION - TECHNICAL LIBRARY
1400 Holcomb Bridge Rd.   Phone: (404) 587-8479
Roswell, GA 30076   Byrnice R. Hurt, Tech.Libn.

THIELE KAOLIN COMPANY - RESEARCH & DEVELOPMENT LIBRARY
Box 1056   Phone: (912) 552-3951
Sandersville, GA 31082   Barbara W. Goodman, Tech.Sec.-Libn.

CANDLER GENERAL HOSPITAL - MEDICAL LIBRARY
5353 Reynolds St.   Phone: (912) 356-6011
Savannah, GA 31412   Mary V. Fielder, Libn.

DIOCESE OF SAVANNAH - CHANCERY ARCHIVES & DIOCESAN ARCHIVES
302 E. Liberty St.
Box 8789   Phone: (912) 232-6479
Savannah, GA 31402   Priscilla B. Bravo, Archv.

GEORGIA HISTORICAL SOCIETY - LIBRARY
W.B. Hodgson Hall
501 Whitaker St.   Phone: (912) 944-2128
Savannah, GA 31499   Anthony R. Dees, Dir.

GIRL SCOUTS OF THE USA - JULIETTE GORDON LOW GIRL SCOUT
   NATIONAL CENTER
142 Bull St.   Phone: (912) 233-4501
Savannah, GA 31401   Katherine Keena, Prog.Spec.

HERTY FOUNDATION - LIBRARY
Brampton Rd.
Box 1963   Phone: (912) 964-5541
Savannah, GA 31402   J. Robert Hart, Dir.

ST. JOSEPH'S HOSPITAL - MEDICAL LIBRARY *
11705 Mercy Blvd.   Phone: (912) 925-4100
Savannah, GA 31406   Judy G. Henry, Libn.

SAVANNAH (City) - MUNICIPAL RESEARCH LIBRARY †
City Hall, Rm. 402
Box 1027   Phone: (912) 233-9321
Savannah, GA 31402   Glenda E. Anderson, Res.Libn.

SAVANNAH (City) - POLICE DEPARTMENT - LIBRARY †
323 Oglethorpe Ave.
Box 1027   Phone: (912) 233-9321
Savannah, GA 31402   Glenda E. Anderson, Res.Libn.

SAVANNAH SCIENCE MUSEUM - ENERGY LIBRARY *
4405 Paulsen St.   Phone: (912) 355-6705
Savannah, GA 31405

U.S. ARMY - CORPS OF ENGINEERS - SAVANNAH DISTRICT - TECHNICAL
   LIBRARY
Box 889   Phone: (912) 944-5461
Savannah, GA 31402   James C. Dorsey, Chf., Tech.Lib.

U.S.D.A. - AGRICULTURAL RESEARCH SERVICE - STORED-PRODUCT
   INSECTS RESEARCH & DEVELOPMENT LAB. - LIB.
Box 22909   Phone: (912) 233-7981
Savannah, GA 31403   Charlene F. Davis, Lib.Techn.

U.S. DEPT. OF COMMERCE - INTERNATIONAL TRADE ADMINISTRATION -
   SAVANNAH DISTRICT OFFICE LIBRARY
222 U.S. Courthouse & P.O. Bldg.
125-29 Bull St.
Box 9746   Phone: (912) 944-4204
Savannah, GA 31412   James W. McIntire, Dir.

UNIVERSITY OF GEORGIA - SKIDAWAY INSTITUTE OF OCEANOGRAPHY -
   LIBRARY
Box 13687   Phone: (912) 356-2474
Savannah, GA 31406-0687   Teri Lynn Herbert, Libn.

GEORGIA SOUTHERN COLLEGE - ARCHIVES/SPECIAL COLLECTIONS †
College Library
Landrum Box 8074   Phone: (912) 681-5645
Statesboro, GA 30460   Andrew Penson, Asst.Ref.Libn.

ARCHBOLD (John D.) MEMORIAL HOSPITAL - RALPH PERKINS MEMORIAL
   LIBRARY
Gordon Ave. & Mimosa Dr.
Box 1018   Phone: (912) 226-4121
Thomasville, GA 31792   Susan Danner, Med.Libn.

ABRAHAM BALDWIN AGRICULTURAL COLLEGE - LIBRARY
ABAC Station   Phone: (912) 386-3223
Tifton, GA 31794   Mary Emma S. Henderson, Libn.

UNIVERSITY OF GEORGIA - GEORGIA COASTAL PLAIN EXPERIMENT
   STATION LIBRARY
                                           Phone: (912) 386-3447
Tifton, GA 31793   Emory Cheek, Lib.Assoc.

TOCCOA FALLS COLLEGE - SEBY JONES LIBRARY
Box 38   Phone: (404) 886-6831
Toccoa Falls, GA 30598   Ruth Good, Hd.Libn.

U.S. NATL. PARK SERVICE - FORT PULASKI NATL. MONUMENT - LIBRARY
Box 98   Phone: (912) 786-5787
Tybee Island, GA 31328   Talley Kirkland, Hist.

LOWNDES COUNTY HISTORICAL SOCIETY - ARCHIVES
305 W. Central Ave.
Box 434   Phone: (912) 242-8962
Valdosta, GA 31601

SOUTH GEORGIA MEDICAL CENTER - MEDICAL LIBRARY
Box 1727   Phone: (912) 333-1160
Valdosta, GA 31603-1727   Susan T. Danner, Med.Libn.

LITTLE WHITE HOUSE HISTORIC SITE - ARCHIVES
Drawer 68   Phone: (404) 655-3511
Warm Springs, GA 31830   Norman Edwards, Supt.

HAWAII

HAWAIIAN SUGAR PLANTERS' ASSOCIATION EXPERIMENT STATION -
   LIBRARY
99-193 Aiea Heights Dr.
Box 1057   Phone: (808) 487-5561
Aiea, HI 96701   Ann L. Marsteller, Libn.

U.S. NATL. PARK SERVICE - HAWAII VOLCANOES NATL. PARK - LIBRARY
                                           Phone: (808) 967-7311
Hawaii National Park, HI 96718

U.S. AIR FORCE BASE - HICKAM BASE LIBRARY
FL 5260   Phone: (808) 449-2831
Hickam AFB, HI 96744   Stella K. Watanabe, Chf.Libn.

CARLSMITH, CARLSMITH, WICHMAN & CASE - LIBRARY *
121 Waianuenue Ave.
Box 686   Phone: (808) 935-6644
Hilo, HI 96720   Raymond K. Hasegawa, Att.

HAWAII STATE CIRCUIT COURT - 3RD CIRCUIT - LAW LIBRARY
Federal Bldg., 75 Aupini St.
Box 1007   Phone: (808) 961-7226
Hilo, HI 96720

HILO HOSPITAL - FRED IRWIN MEDICAL LIBRARY
1190 Waianuenue Ave.   Phone: (808) 961-4288
Hilo, HI 96720   Claire Hamasu

LYMAN HOUSE MEMORIAL MUSEUM - KATHRYN E. LYLE MEMORIAL
   LIBRARY
276 Haili St.   Phone: (808) 935-5021
Hilo, HI 96720   Christina R.N. Lothian, Archv./Libn.

UNIVERSITY OF HAWAII - INSTITUTE FOR ASTRONOMY - MAUNA KEA
   OBSERVATORY - LIBRARY
177 Makaala   Phone: (808) 935-3371
Hilo, HI 96720   Sara Thompson, Libn.

U.S. NATL. PARK SERVICE - PU'UHONUA O HONAUNAU NATL. HISTORICAL
   PARK - LIBRARY
Box 129   Phone: (808) 328-2326
Honaunau, HI 96726   Blossom Sapp, Libn.

AMERICAN CANCER SOCIETY - HAWAII DIVISION - LIBRARY
200 N. Vineyard Blvd.   Phone: (808) 531-1662
Honolulu, HI 96817   Donna Farr, Dir., Field Serv. & Prog.

AMERICAN LUNG ASSOCIATION OF HAWAII - LEARNING CENTER FOR
   LUNG HEALTH *
245 N. Kukui St.   Phone: (808) 537-5966
Honolulu, HI 96817   Catherine C. Tamura, Learning Ctr.Coord.

BANK OF HAWAII - INFORMATION CENTER
Financial Plaza Tower Bldg., 20th Fl.
Box 2900   Phone: (808) 537-8375
Honolulu, HI 96846   Sally Campbell, Info.Mgr.

BISHOP (Bernice P.) MUSEUM - LIBRARY
1525 Bernice St.
Box 19000-A   Phone: (808) 847-3511
Honolulu, HI 96817   Cynthia Timberlake, Hd.Libn.

THE CELTIC EVANGELICAL CHURCH - COMMUNITY OF ST. COLUMBA -
   LIBRARY
1666 St. Louis Dr.
Honolulu, HI 96816   Rev. Wayne W. Gau, Abbot

CHAMBER OF COMMERCE OF HAWAII - INFORMATION OFFICE
Dillingham Bldg., 735 Bishop St.   Phone: (808) 531-4111
Honolulu, HI 96813   Miss Tatsuko Honjo, Dir. of Info.

DALY (Leo A.) COMPANY - YEE DIVISION - LIBRARY
1441 Kapiolani Blvd., Suite 810   Phone: (808) 946-3161
Honolulu, HI 96814   Phyllis Kanekuni, Tech. Writer/Libn.

EAST-WEST CENTER - EAPI/PI/RSI RESEARCH MATERIALS COLLECTION
1777 East-West Rd.   Phone: (808) 944-7451
Honolulu, HI 96848   Alice D. Harris, Res.Info.Spec.

FIRST HAWAIIAN BANK - RESEARCH DIVISION LIBRARY †
165 S. King St.
Box 3200   Phone: (808) 525-7000
Honolulu, HI 96847   Mary I. Kuramoto, Res.Libn.

HAWAII CHINESE HISTORY CENTER - LIBRARY
111 N. King St., No. 410   Phone: (808) 521-5948
Honolulu, HI 96817   Violet L. Lai, Hd.Libn.

HAWAII EMPLOYERS COUNCIL - LIBRARY *
2682 Waiwai Loop
Honolulu, HI 96819   Phone: (808) 836-1511

HAWAII INSTITUTE OF GEOPHYSICS - LIBRARY
2525 Correa Rd.
University of Hawaii   Phone: (808) 948-7040
Honolulu, HI 96822   Patricia E. Price, Libn.

HAWAII MEDICAL LIBRARY, INC.
1221 Punchbowl St.   Phone: (808) 536-9302
Honolulu, HI 96813   John A. Breinich, Dir.

HAWAII NEWSPAPER AGENCY - LIBRARY
News Bldg., 605 Kapiolani Blvd.   Phone: (808) 525-7669
Honolulu, HI 96813   Beatrice S. Kaya, Chf.Libn.

HAWAII STATE DEPARTMENT OF ACCOUNTING AND GENERAL SERVICES -
   PUBLIC ARCHIVES *
Iolani Palace Grounds   Phone: (808) 548-2357
Honolulu, HI 96813

HAWAII STATE DEPARTMENT OF EDUCATION - AUDIOVISUAL SERVICES
641 18th Ave.   Phone: (808) 732-2824
Honolulu, HI 96816   Franklin S. Tamaribuchi, TAC Spec.

HAWAII STATE DEPARTMENT OF HEALTH - HASTINGS H. WALKER
   MEDICAL LIBRARY
Leahi Hospital
3675 Kilauea Ave.   Phone: (808) 734-0221
Honolulu, HI 96816   Verne Waite, Med.Dir.

HAWAII STATE DEPARTMENT OF PLANNING & ECONOMIC DEVELOPMENT
   - LIBRARY
Box 2359   Phone: (808) 548-3059
Honolulu, HI 96804   Anthony M. Oliver, Libn.

HAWAII STATE - LEGISLATIVE REFERENCE BUREAU LIBRARY
State Capitol   Phone: (808) 548-7853
Honolulu, HI 96813   Hanako Kobayashi, Res.Libn.

HAWAII STATE LIBRARY - BUSINESS, SCIENCE, TECHNOLOGY UNIT
478 S. King St.
Honolulu, HI 96813   Hanako S. Nakamura, Hd.

HAWAII STATE LIBRARY - EDNA ALLYN ROOM
478 S. King St.   Phone: (808) 548-2341
Honolulu, HI 96813   Shirley S. Naito, Oahu Ch.Coord.

HAWAII STATE LIBRARY - FEDERAL DOCUMENTS SECTION
478 S. King St.   Phone: (808) 548-2386
Honolulu, HI 96813   Norma T. Herkes, Hd.

HAWAII STATE LIBRARY - FINE ARTS AND AUDIOVISUAL SECTION
478 S. King St.   Phone: (808) 548-2340
Honolulu, HI 96813   Eloise Van Niel, Hd./Perf. Arts Spec.

HAWAII STATE LIBRARY - HAWAII AND PACIFIC SECTION I
478 S. King St.   Phone: (808) 548-2346
Honolulu, HI 96813   Proserfina A. Strona, Act.Hd.

HAWAII STATE LIBRARY - LANGUAGE, LITERATURE AND HISTORY
   SECTION
478 S. King St.   Phone: (808) 548-4165
Honolulu, HI 96813   Sandra Kolloge, Act.Hd.

HAWAII STATE LIBRARY - SERIALS SECTION
478 S. King St.   Phone: (808) 548-2389
Honolulu, HI 96813   Vincent Van Brocklin, Ser. Unit Hd.

HAWAII STATE LIBRARY - SOCIAL SCIENCE AND PHILOSOPHY SECTION
478 S. King St.   Phone: (808) 548-2340
Honolulu, HI 96813   Judith Middlebrook Prakash, Section Hd.

HAWAII STATE LIBRARY - STATE LIBRARY FOR THE BLIND AND
   PHYSICALLY HANDICAPPED
402 Kapahulu Ave.   Phone: (808) 732-7767
Honolulu, HI 96815   Lydia S. Ranger, Hd.Libn.

HAWAII STATE LIBRARY - YOUNG ADULT SECTION
478 S. King St.   Phone: (808) 548-2337
Honolulu, HI 96813   Sylvia C. Mitchell, Young Adult Libn.

HAWAII STATE SUPREME COURT - LAW LIBRARY
Box 779   Phone: (808) 548-7432
Honolulu, HI 96808   Momoe Tanaka, State Law Libn.

HAWAIIAN ELECTRIC CO., INC. - CORPORATE LIBRARY
Box 2750   Phone: (808) 548-7915
Honolulu, HI 96840   Deborah Knowlton, Corp.Libn.

HAWAIIAN ELECTRIC CO., INC. - ENGINEERING LIBRARY
820 Ward Ave.
Box 2750   Phone: (808) 548-7915
Honolulu, HI 96840   Deborah Knowlton, Corp.Libn.

HAWAIIAN HISTORICAL SOCIETY - MISSION-HISTORICAL LIBRARY
560 Kawaiahao St.   Phone: (808) 537-6271
Honolulu, HI 96813   Barbara E. Dunn, Libn.

HAWAIIAN MISSION CHILDREN'S SOCIETY - LIBRARY
553 S. King St.   Phone: (808) 531-0481
Honolulu, HI 96813   Mary Jane Knight, Libn.

HAWAIIAN TELEPHONE COMPANY - LIBRARY *
1177 Bishop St.
Box 2200   Phone: (808) 546-2600
Honolulu, HI 96841   Michelle A. Pommer, Libn.

HONOLULU ACADEMY OF ARTS - ROBERT ALLERTON LIBRARY
900 S. Beretania St.   Phone: (808) 538-3693
Honolulu, HI 96814   Anne T. Seaman, Libn.

HONOLULU ACADEMY OF ARTS - SLIDE COLLECTION
900 S. Beretania St.   Phone: (808) 538-3693
Honolulu, HI 96814   Doris Lutzky, Kpr.

HONOLULU (City and County) - MUNICIPAL REFERENCE AND RECORDS
   CENTER
558 S. King St.   Phone: (808) 523-4577
Honolulu, HI 96813   Marsha C. Petersen, Dir.

INSTITUTE OF CULTURE AND COMMUNICATION - CCPC - RESOURCE
   MATERIALS COLLECTION
University of Hawaii
John A. Burns Hall, Rm. 4063   Phone: (808) 944-7345
Honolulu, HI 96848   Sumiye Konoshima, Res.Info.Spec.

INSTITUTE OF CULTURE AND COMMUNICATION - EPR - RESOURCE
   MATERIALS COLLECTION
University of Hawaii
John A. Burns Hall, 2nd Fl.
Honolulu, HI 96848

INTERNATIONAL TSUNAMI INFORMATION CENTER
Box 50027   Phone: (808) 546-2847
Honolulu, HI 96850   Dr. George Pararas-Carayannis, Dir.

KAISER MEDICAL CENTER - MEDICAL LIBRARY *
1697 Ala Moana Blvd.   Phone: (808) 944-6149
Honolulu, HI 96815   Janice Varner Nakagawara, Med.Libn.

KAPIOLANI-CHILDREN'S MEDICAL CENTER - KCMC MEDICAL LIBRARY *
1319 Punahou St.   Phone: (808) 947-8573
Honolulu, HI 96826   Ikuko Uesato, Libn.

LEEWARD COMMUNITY COLLEGE LIBRARY - SPECIAL COLLECTIONS
96-045 Ala Ike   Phone: (808) 455-0210
Honolulu, HI 96782

LEGAL AID SOCIETY OF HAWAII - LIBRARY †
1164 Bishop St., Suite 1100   Phone: (808) 536-4302
Honolulu, HI 96813   Thomas P. Churma, Libn.

NATIONAL SOCIETY, DAUGHTERS OF THE AMERICAN REVOLUTION -
   ALOHA CHAPTER - MEMORIAL LIBRARY
1914 Makiki Heights Dr.
Honolulu, HI 96822   Florine H. Greenwood, Libn.

PACIFIC AND ASIAN AFFAIRS COUNCIL - PACIFIC HOUSE LIBRARY *
2004 University Ave.   Phone: (808) 941-5355
Honolulu, HI 96822

ST. FRANCIS HOSPITAL - MEDICAL LIBRARY
2230 Liliha St.   Phone: (808) 547-6481
Honolulu, HI 96817   Julie J. Sirois, Libn.

STRAUB CLINIC & HOSPITAL, INC. - ARNOLD LIBRARY
888 S. King St.   Phone: (808) 544-0317
Honolulu, HI 96813   Frances P. Smith, Libn.

U.S. ARMY MUSEUM OF HAWAII - REFERENCE LIBRARY
Box 8064   Phone: (808) 543-2639
Honolulu, HI 96830   Thomas M. Fairfull, Musm.Dir.

U.S. DISTRICT COURT - LIBRARY *
U.S. Court House
Box 50128   Phone: (808) 546-3163
Honolulu, HI 96850   Isabel T. Anduha, Court Libn.

U.S. MARINE CORPS - CAMP H.M. SMITH LIBRARY
Bldg. 27   Phone: (808) 477-6348
Honolulu, HI 96861   Evelyn Mau, Libn.

U.S. NATL. MARINE FISHERIES SERVICE - HONOLULU LABORATORY -
    LIBRARY *
2750 Dole St.
Box 3830   Phone: (808) 946-2181
Honolulu, HI 98612   Hazel S. Nishimura, Libn.

UNIVERSITY OF HAWAII - ASIA COLLECTION
Hamilton Library, 2550 The Mall   Phone: (808) 948-8116
Honolulu, HI 96822   Joyce Wright, Hd., Asia Coll.

UNIVERSITY OF HAWAII - CENTER FOR KOREAN STUDIES - LIBRARY
1881 East-West Rd.   Phone: (808) 948-7041
Honolulu, HI 96822   Charlotte Oser, Adm.Off.

UNIVERSITY OF HAWAII - DEPARTMENT OF HISTORY - PACIFIC
    REGIONAL ORAL HISTORY PROGRAM - LIBRARY
2530 Dole St.   Phone: (808) 948-8486
Honolulu, HI 96822   Edward Beechert, Dir.

UNIVERSITY OF HAWAII - PACIFIC BIO-MEDICAL RESEARCH CENTER -
    LIBRARY
41 Ahui St.   Phone: (808) 531-3538
Honolulu, HI 96813   Dr. Barbara H. Gibbons, Res.

UNIVERSITY OF HAWAII - PUBLIC SERVICES - GOVERNMENT
    DOCUMENTS, MAPS & MICROFORMS
Hamilton Library, 2550 The Mall   Phone: (808) 948-8230
Honolulu, HI 96822   Janet Morrison, Hd.

UNIVERSITY OF HAWAII - SCHOOL OF PUBLIC HEALTH - LIBRARY
1960 East-West Rd.
Court D., Rm. 207   Phone: (808) 948-8666
Honolulu, HI 96822   Carol W. Arnold, Hd.Libn.

UNIVERSITY OF HAWAII - SOCIAL SCIENCE RESEARCH INSTITUTE
Porteus Hall 704, Maile Way   Phone: (808) 948-8930
Honolulu, HI 96822   Donald M. Topping, Dir.

UNIVERSITY OF HAWAII - SPECIAL COLLECTIONS - ARCHIVES
Sinclair Library, 2425 Campus Rd.   Phone: (808) 948-6673
Honolulu, HI 96822   David Kittelson, Assoc.Lib.Spec.

UNIVERSITY OF HAWAII - SPECIAL COLLECTIONS - HAWAIIAN
    COLLECTION
Hamilton Library, 2550 The Mall   Phone: (808) 948-8264
Honolulu, HI 96822   Dr. Chieko Tachihata, Asst.Lib.Spec.

UNIVERSITY OFHAWAII - SPECIAL COLLECTIONS - JEAN CHARLOT
    COLLECTION
Hamilton Library, Rm. 501
2550 The Mall   Phone: (808) 948-8473
Honolulu, HI 96822   Eleanor Au, Hd., Spec.Coll.

UNIVERSITY OF HAWAII - SPECIAL COLLECTIONS - PACIFIC COLLECTION
Hamilton Library, 2550 The Mall   Phone: (808) 948-8264
Honolulu, HI 96822   Renee Heyum, Cur.

UNIVERSITY OF HAWAII - SPECIAL COLLECTIONS - RARE BOOKS
Hamilton Library, 2550 The Mall   Phone: (808) 948-8230
Honolulu, HI 96822   Eleanor C. Au, Hd., Spec.Coll.

UNIVERSITY OF HAWAII - WAIKIKI AQUARIUM - LIBRARY
2777 Kalakaua Ave.   Phone: (808) 923-9741
Honolulu, HI 96815   Denise M. Davies, Libn.

WESTERN CURRICULUM COORDINATION CENTER (WCCC) - RESOURCE
    CENTER
1776 University Ave., Wist 216   Phone: (808) 948-6496
Honolulu, HI 96822   Gail M. Urago, Libn.

ST. CHRISTOPHER'S CHURCH - LIBRARY *
Box 456   Phone: (808) 262-8176
Kailua, HI 96734

HAWAII STATE HOSPITAL - MEDICAL LIBRARY
45-710 Keaahala Rd.   Phone: (808) 247-2191
Kaneohe, HI 96744   Diana C. Stephens, Med.Libn.

U.S. MARINE CORPS - KANEOHE AIR STATION LIBRARY
Bldg. 219   Phone: (808) 257-3583
Kaneohe Bay, HI 96863   Murray R. Visser, Supv.Libn.

BRIGHAM YOUNG UNIVERSITY, HAWAII CAMPUS - JOSEPH F. SMITH
    LIBRARY AND MEDIA CENTER - SPECIAL COLLECTION *
55-220 Kulanui St.   Phone: (808) 293-3850
Laie, HI 96762   Richard C. Pearson, Dir.

CHURCH OF JESUS CHRIST OF LATTER-DAY SAINTS - LAIE, HAWAII
    STAKE BRANCH GENEALOGICAL LIBRARY
c/o BYU, Box 1907   Phone: (808) 293-3880
Laie, HI 96762   Cassandra K. Johnson, Libn.

WILCOX (G.N.) MEMORIAL HOSPITAL & HEALTH CENTER - MEDICAL
    LIBRARY *
3420 Kuhio Hwy.   Phone: (808) 245-4811
Lihue, HI 96766

U.S. NATL. PARK SERVICE - HALEAKALA NATL. PARK - LIBRARY
Box 369   Phone: (808) 572-9306
Makawao, HI 96768   Carol Beadle, Pk.Techn., Interp.

NITROGEN FIXATION BY TROPICAL AGRICULTURAL LEGUMES - NIFTAL
    INFORMATION CENTER
Box O   Phone: (808) 579-9568
Paia, HI 96779   James W. King, Info.Spec.

U.S. NAVY - NAVAL SHIPYARD (HI-Pearl Harbor) - TECHNICAL LIBRARY
Code 250.4, Box 400   Phone: (808) 471-3408
Pearl Harbor, HI 96860   Lincoln H.S. Yu, Libn.

U.S. ARMY HOSPITALS - TRIPLER ARMY MEDICAL CENTER - MEDICAL
    LIBRARY
Tripler AMC, HI 96859   Linda Requena, Chf., Med.Lib.

HAWAII STATE CIRCUIT COURT - 2ND CIRCUIT - LAW LIBRARY †
Box 969   Phone: (808) 244-5227
Wailuku, HI 96793   Sandra Wada, Libn.

MAUI HISTORICAL SOCIETY - RESEARCH LIBRARY
2375 A Main St.
Box 1018   Phone: (808) 244-3326
Wailuku, HI 96793

OCEANIC INSTITUTE - WORKING LIBRARY
Makapuu Point   Phone: (808) 259-7951
Waimanalo, HI 96795   Ellen Antill, Adm.Asst.

U.S. AIR FORCE BASE - WHEELER BASE LIBRARY †
FL 5296, 15 Air Base Squadron (SSL)   Phone: (808) 655-1867
Wheeler AFB, HI 96854   Deborah A. Thompson, Base Libn.

IDAHO

BINGHAM MEMORIAL HOSPITAL - MEDICAL LIBRARY
98 Poplar St.   Phone: (208) 785-4100
Blackfoot, ID 83221   Gerry Harrah, Med.Libn.

BOISE BIBLE COLLEGE - LIBRARY
8695 Marigold   Phone: (208) 376-7731
Boise, ID 83714   Carl A. Douthit, Libn.

BOISE CASCADE CORPORATION - CORPORATE LIBRARY SERVICES
One Jefferson Square   Phone: (208) 384-6694
Boise, ID 83728   Patricia Metcalf, Libn.

BOISE GALLERY OF ART - LIBRARY
670 S. Julia Davis Dr.   Phone: (208) 345-8330
Boise, ID 83701   Sandy Harthorn, Cur./Registrar

HEWLETT PACKARD COMPANY - BOISE SITE SCIENCE/TECHNICAL
  LIBRARY
11413 Chinden Blvd.   Phone: (208) 376-6000
Boise, ID 83702   Gail Prescott, Libn.

IDAHO STATE HISTORICAL SOCIETY - GENEALOGICAL LIBRARY
610 N. Julia Davis Dr.   Phone: (208) 334-2305
Boise, ID 83706   Frieda O. March, Libn.

IDAHO STATE HISTORICAL SOCIETY - LIBRARY AND ARCHIVES
610 N. Julia Davis Dr.   Phone: (208) 334-3356
Boise, ID 83702   Elizabeth P. Jacox, Libn.

IDAHO STATE LAW LIBRARY
Supreme Court Bldg.
451 W. State St.   Phone: (208) 334-3316
Boise, ID 83720   Laura M. Pershing, Law Libn.

IDAHO STATE LIBRARY
325 W. State St.   Phone: (208) 334-2150
Boise, ID 83702   Charles Bolles, State Libn.

IDAHO STATE LIBRARY - REGIONAL LIBRARY FOR THE BLIND AND
  PHYSICALLY HANDICAPPED
325 W. State St.   Phone: (208) 334-2150
Boise, ID 83702   Evva L. Larson, Asst.State Libn.

IDAHO STATESMAN - LIBRARY
1200 N. Curtis Rd.
Box 40   Phone: (208) 377-6435
Boise, ID 83707   Nancy Van Dinter, Chf.Libn.

MORRISON-KNUDSEN CO., INC. - INFORMATION RESEARCH CENTER
Box 7808   Phone: (206) 386-7039
Boise, ID 83729   John Tribby, Supv.

ST. ALPHONSUS REGIONAL MEDICAL CENTER - HEALTH SCIENCES
  LIBRARY
1055 N. Curtis Rd.   Phone: (208) 378-2271
Boise, ID 83706   Martha R. Stolz, Libn.

ST. LUKE'S REGIONAL MEDICAL CENTER - MEDICAL LIBRARY
190 E. Bannock   Phone: (208) 386-2277
Boise, ID 83712   Christine K. Vogelheim, Dir.

U.S. DEPT. OF LABOR - OSHA - IDAHO AREA OFFICE - LIBRARY
550 W. Fort St., Rm. 324   Phone: (208) 334-1867
Boise, ID 83703   David M. Bernard, Area Dir.

U.S. VETERANS ADMINISTRATION (ID-Boise) - MEDICAL CENTER LIBRARY
  (142D)
500 W. Fort St.   Phone: (208) 338-7206
Boise, ID 83702-4598   Gordon Carlson, Chf.Libn.

CALDWELL MEMORIAL HOSPITAL - G.M. MEDICAL LIBRARY
1717 Arlington   Phone: (208) 459-4641
Caldwell, ID 83605   Jan Walters, Med.Libn.

COLLEGE OF IDAHO - REGIONAL STUDIES CENTER - LIBRARY
Boone Science Hall, Rm. 257   Phone: (208) 459-5214
Caldwell, ID 83605   Donna Parsons, Dir.

MUSEUM OF NORTH IDAHO, INC. - ARCHIVES
Box 812   Phone: (208) 664-3448
Coeur d'Alene, ID 83814   Dorothy Dahlgren, Cur.

ARGONNE NATIONAL LABORATORY - ARGONNE-WEST TECHNICAL
  LIBRARY
Box 2528   Phone: (208) 526-7237
Idaho Falls, ID 83403   Barbara J. Swanson, Libn.

EG&G, INC. - IDAHO NATIONAL ENGINEERING LABORATORY - INEL
  TECHNICAL LIBRARY
Box 1625   Phone: (208) 526-1195
Idaho Falls, ID 83415   Brent N. Jacobsen, Lib.Adm.

ENERGY, INC. - TECHNICAL INFORMATION SERVICES
Box 736   Phone: (208) 529-1000
Idaho Falls, ID 83402   Jacqueline Loop, Libn.

IDAHO FALLS CONSOLIDATED HOSPITALS - HEALTH SCIENCES LIBRARY
2525 S. Boulevard   Phone: (208) 529-7128
Idaho Falls, ID 83401   Coleen C. Winward, Med.Libn.

WESTINGHOUSE ELECTRIC CORPORATION - NAVAL REACTOR FACILITY
  LIBRARY
Box 2068
Idaho Falls, ID 83401   Coy E. Stewart, Libn.

U.S.D.A. - AGRICULTURAL RESEARCH SERVICE - SNAKE RIVER
  CONSERVATION RESEARCH CENTER - LIBRARY
Route 1, Box 186   Phone: (208) 423-5582
Kimberly, ID 83341   A. Smith, Libn.

LEWISTON TRIBUNE LIBRARY
505 C St.   Phone: (208) 743-9411
Lewiston, ID 83501   Lynn King, Libn.

NEZ PERCE COUNTY LAW LIBRARY *
Court House
Box 896   Phone: (208) 799-3040
Lewiston, ID 83501   Judge John Maynard, Sr. District Judge

POTLATCH CORPORATION - WESTERN WOOD PRODUCTS DIV.
  ENGINEERING & TECHNICAL SERV. DEPT. - INFORMATION CTR.
Box 1016   Phone: (208) 799-0123
Lewiston, ID 83501   J.B. Snodgrass, Mgr.

LATAH COUNTY HISTORICAL SOCIETY - LIBRARY
110 S. Adams   Phone: (208) 882-1004
Moscow, ID 83843   Mary E. Reed, Dir.

UNIVERSITY OF IDAHO - ARCHIVE OF PACIFIC NORTHWEST
  ARCHAEOLOGY
Dept. of Sociology/Anthropology   Phone: (208) 885-6123
Moscow, ID 83843   Roderick Sprague, Dir.

UNIVERSITY OF IDAHO - THE BOYD AND GRACE MARTIN INSTITUTE OF
  HUMAN BEHAVIOR - LIBRARY
                                                       Phone: (208) 885-6527
Moscow, ID 83843   Boyd A. Martin, Dir.

UNIVERSITY OF IDAHO - BUREAU OF PUBLIC AFFAIRS RESEARCH -
  LIBRARY
                                                       Phone: (208) 885-6563
Moscow, ID 83843   Sid Duncombe, Dir.

UNIVERSITY OF IDAHO - HUMANITIES LIBRARY
                                                       Phone: (208) 885-6584
Moscow, ID 83843   Margaret Snyder, Libn.

UNIVERSITY OF IDAHO - IDAHO WATER RESOURCES RESEARCH
  INSTITUTE - TECHNICAL INFO. CENTER & READING ROOM
                                                       Phone: (208) 885-6429
Moscow, ID 83843   John R. Busch

UNIVERSITY OF IDAHO - LAW LIBRARY
College of Law   Phone: (208) 885-6521
Moscow, ID 83843   James Heller, Libn.

UNIVERSITY OF IDAHO - SCIENCE AND TECHNOLOGY LIBRARY
                                            Phone: (208) 885-6235
Moscow, ID 83843   Donna Hanson, Libn.

UNIVERSITY OF IDAHO - SOCIAL SCIENCE LIBRARY
                                            Phone: (208) 885-6344
Moscow, ID 83843   Dennis Baird, Libn.

UNIVERSITY OF IDAHO - SPECIAL COLLECTIONS LIBRARY
                                            Phone: (208) 885-7951
Moscow, ID 83843   Stanley A. Shepard, Libn.

OWYHEE COUNTY HISTORICAL COMPLEX MUSEUM - LIBRARY
                                            Phone: (208) 495-2319
Murphy, ID 83650   Linda Morton, Dir.

IDAHO STATE UNIVERSITY - COLLEGE OF EDUCATION - INSTRUCTIONAL
   MATERIALS CENTER
                                            Phone: (208) 236-2652
Pocatello, ID 83209   Art Cullen, Asst.Prof.

IDAHO STATE UNIVERSITY - IDAHO MUSEUM OF NATURAL HISTORY -
   LIBRARY
Campus Box 8096   Phone: (208) 232-3168
Pocatello, ID 83209   Lucille Harten, Pubn.Ed.

CHURCH OF JESUS CHRIST OF LATTER-DAY SAINTS - UPPER SNAKE RIVER
   BRANCH GENEALOGICAL LIBRARY
Ricks College Library   Phone: (208) 356-2351
Rexburg, ID 83440   Neal S. Southwick, Libn.

UPPER SNAKE RIVER VALLEY HISTORICAL SOCIETY - LIBRARY
49 North Center
Box 244
Rexburg, ID 83440   Jerry Glenn, Libn.

BONNER COUNTY HISTORICAL SOCIETY, INC. - RESEARCH LIBRARY
Lakeside Pk.
Box 1063   Phone: (208) 263-2344
Sandpoint, ID 83864   Colleen E. Atmore

U.S. NATL. PARK SERVICE - NEZ PERCE NATL. HISTORICAL PARK -
   LIBRARY
Box 93   Phone: (208) 843-2261
Spalding, ID 83551   Fahy C. Whitaker, Supt.

MORITZ COMMUNITY HOSPITAL - DEAN PIEROSE MEMORIAL HEALTH
   SCIENCES LIBRARY
Box 86
Sun Valley, ID 83353

ASGROW SEED COMPANY - RESEARCH CENTER
Box 1235   Phone: (208) 326-4321
Twin Falls, ID 83301   Leland R. Schweitzer, Mgr. of Res.Lab.

ILLINOIS

ALTON MEMORIAL HOSPITAL - HEALTH SCIENCES LIBRARY
One Memorial Dr.   Phone: (618) 463-7343
Alton, IL 62002   Betty Jameson, Libn.

ALTON MENTAL HEALTH CENTER - PROFESSIONAL LIBRARY
4500 College Ave.   Phone: (618) 465-5593
Alton, IL 62002   Thomas M. McConahey, Dir. of Training

ALTON TELEGRAPH PRINTING COMPANY - LIBRARY
111 E. Broadway   Phone: (618) 463-2573
Alton, IL 62002   Julie Stuckey, Libn.

ST. ANTHONY'S HOSPITAL - LIBRARY
Saint Anthony's Way   Phone: (618) 465-2571
Alton, IL 62002   Dorothy Kulenkamp, Lib.Asst.

ST. JOSEPH HOSPITAL - INFORMATION SERVICES
915 E. 5th St.   Phone: (618) 463-5284
Alton, IL 62002   Judith Messerle, Dir.Educ.Rsrcs.

CPC INTERNATIONAL - MOFFETT TECHNICAL LIBRARY
Box 345   Phone: (312) 458-2000
Argo, IL 60501   Joy Louise Caruso, Mgr., Info.Serv.

ARGONNE NATIONAL LABORATORY - NATIONAL ENERGY SOFTWARE
   CENTER
9700 S. Cass Ave.   Phone: (312) 972-7250
Argonne, IL 60439   Margaret K. Butler, Dir.

ARGONNE NATIONAL LABORATORY - TECHNICAL INFORMATION SERVICES
   DEPARTMENT †
9700 S. Cass Ave., Bldg. 203-C110   Phone: (312) 972-4221
Argonne, IL 60439   Hillis L. Griffin, Dir.

AMERICAN FISHING TACKLE MANUFACTURERS ASSOCIATION - RESOURCE
   & RESEARCH LIBRARY
2625 Clearbrook Dr.   Phone: (312) 364-4666
Arlington Heights, IL 60005   Judy Haynes, Educ.Spec.

ATLANTIC-RICHFIELD COMPANY - ARCO METALS COMPANY - TECHNICAL
   INFORMATION CENTER †
3205 N. Frontage Rd.
Box 3010   Phone: (312) 577-5527
Arlington Heights, IL 60006   Donna M. Mendenhall, Supv., Tech.Info.

HONEYWELL, INC. - COMMERCIAL DIVISION - LIBRARY
1500 W. Dundee   Phone: (312) 394-4000
Arlington Heights, IL 60004   Paul M. Klekner, Libn.

INFOTEK CONSULTANTS - LIBRARY
2411 E. Lillian Ln.   Phone: (312) 577-5390
Arlington Heights, IL 60004   Bernice C. Kao, Pres.

NORTHWEST COMMUNITY HOSPITAL - MEDICAL LIBRARY
800 West Central Rd.   Phone: (312) 259-1000
Arlington Heights, IL 60005   Sharon Glinski, Med.Libn.

NORTHWEST EDUCATIONAL COOPERATIVE - LIBRARY
500 S. Dwyer Ave.   Phone: (312) 870-4113
Arlington Heights, IL 60005   Richard H. Peiser, Cat./Libn.

AURORA COLLEGE - JENKS MEMORIAL COLLECTION OF ADVENTUAL
   MATERIALS
347 S. Gladstone   Phone: (312) 892-6431
Aurora, IL 60507   Moses C. Crouse, Cur.

AURORA HISTORICAL SOCIETY - MUSEUM LIBRARY
305 Cedar St.   Phone: (312) 897-9029
Aurora, IL 60506   John R. Jaros, Cur.

MERCY CENTER FOR HEALTH CARE SERVICES - MEDICAL LIBRARY
1325 N. Highland Ave.   Phone: (312) 859-2222
Aurora, IL 60506   Mary P. Murray, Libn.

AMERICAN CAN COMPANY - BARRINGTON TECHNICAL CENTER -
   TECHNICAL INFORMATION CENTER
433 N. Northwest Hwy.   Phone: (312) 381-1900
Barrington, IL 60010   Mary T. Gormley, Supv.

CAI - TECHNICAL LIBRARY *
550 W. Northwest Hwy.   Phone: (312) 381-2400
Barrington, IL 60010   Steven Kormanak, Tech.Libn.

QUAKER OATS COMPANY - JOHN STUART RESEARCH LABORATORIES -
   RESEARCH LIBRARY
617 W. Main St.   Phone: (312) 381-1980
Barrington, IL 60010   Geraldine R. Horton, Mgr., Lib.

WIGHT CONSULTING ENGINEERS, INC. - TECHNICAL LIBRARY †
127 S. Northwest Hwy.   Phone: (312) 381-1800
Barrington, IL 60010   Sally M. Trainer, Sec.

FERMI NATIONAL ACCELERATOR LABORATORY - LIBRARY
Box 500   Phone: (312) 840-3401
Batavia, IL 60510   Roger S. Thompson, Libn.

LUTHERAN CHURCH - MISSOURI SYNOD - SOUTHERN ILLINOIS DISTRICT
  ARCHIVES
2408 Lebanon Ave.   Phone: (618) 234-4767
Belleville, IL 62221   Rev. Elvin R. Harms, Exec.Asst.

MEMORIAL HOSPITAL - LIBRARY
4501 N. Park Dr.   Phone: (618) 233-7750
Belleville, IL 62223   Barbara Grout, Dir.

ST. ELIZABETH'S HOSPITAL - HEALTH SCIENCE LIBRARY
211 S. Third St.   Phone: (618) 234-2120
Belleville, IL 62221   Michael A. Campese, Lib.Dir.

AMERICAN SOKOL EDUCATION AND PHYSICAL CULTURE ORGANIZATION -
  LIBRARY
6424 W. Cermak Rd.   Phone: (312) 795-6671
Berwyn, IL 60402

CZECHOSLOVAK HERITAGE MUSEUM - LIBRARY AND ARCHIVES
2701 S. Harlem Ave.   Phone: (312) 795-5800
Berwyn, IL 60153   Lillian K. Chorvat, Libn./Musm.Cur.

MAC NEAL HOSPITAL - HEALTH SCIENCES RESOURCE CENTER
3249 S. Oak Park Ave.   Phone: (312) 797-3089
Berwyn, IL 60402   Rya Ben-Shir, Mgr.

ORDER OF SERVANTS OF MARY - EASTERN PROVINCE LIBRARY - MORINI
  MEMORIAL COLLECTION
3401 S. Home Ave.   Phone: (312) 484-0063
Berwyn, IL 60402   Rev. Conrad M. Borntrager, O.S.M., Archv.

BLOOMINGTON-NORMAL DAILY PANTAGRAPH - NEWSPAPER LIBRARY
301 W. Washington St.
Box 2907   Phone: (309) 829-9411
Bloomington, IL 61701   Diane Miller, Lib.Dir.

ILLINOIS AGRICULTURAL ASSOCIATION - IAA AND AFFILIATED
  COMPANIES LIBRARY
1701 Towanda Ave.
Box 2901   Phone: (309) 557-2550
Bloomington, IL 61701   Rue E. Olson, Libn.

ILLINOIS WESLEYAN UNIVERSITY - THORPE MUSIC LIBRARY
                                                    Phone: (309) 556-3003
Bloomington, IL 61701   Robert C. Delvin, Fine Arts Libn.

INSTITUTE FOR THEOLOGICAL & PHILOSOPHICAL STUDIES - LIBRARY
Box 3563
Bloomington, IL 61701   Dr. James Kurtz, Dir.

MC LEAN COUNTY HISTORICAL SOCIETY - MUSEUM AND LIBRARY
201 E. Grove St.   Phone: (309) 827-0428
Bloomington, IL 61701   Barbara Dunbar, Dir.

MENNONITE HOSPITAL AND COLLEGE OF NURSING - HEALTH SCIENCES
  LIBRARY
807 N. Main St.   Phone: (309) 827-4321
Bloomington, IL 61701   Sue Stroyan, Dir.

SECOND PRESBYTERIAN CHURCH - CAPEN MEMORIAL LIBRARY
313 N. East St.   Phone: (309) 828-6297
Bloomington, IL 61701

STATE FARM MUTUAL AUTOMOBILE INSURANCE COMPANY - LAW
  LIBRARY
One State Farm Plaza   Phone: (309) 766-5224
Bloomington, IL 61701   Laura Garrett, Libn.

UNITED METHODIST CHURCH - CENTRAL ILLINOIS CONFERENCE -
  CONFERENCE HISTORICAL SOCIETY LIBRARY
1211 N. Park
Box 2050
Bloomington, IL 61702-2050

CHICAGO ZOOLOGICAL PARK - BROOKFIELD ZOO - LIBRARY
8400 W. 31st St.   Phone: (312) 485-0263
Brookfield, IL 60513   Mary Rabb, Libn.

ST. LOUIS UNIVERSITY - PARKS COLLEGE OF AERONAUTICAL
  TECHNOLOGY - LIBRARY †
                                                    Phone: (618) 337-7500
Cahokia, IL 62206   Nancy Nobbe, Libn.

FULTON COUNTY HISTORICAL AND GENEALOGICAL SOCIETY - RESEARCH
  ROOM *
Parlin-Ingersoll Library
205 W. Chestnut   Phone: (309) 647-0328
Canton, IL 61520   Beverly Stewart, Hd.Libn.

GRAHAM HOSPITAL ASSOCIATION - MEDICAL STAFF LIBRARY
210 W. Walnut St.   Phone: (309) 647-5240
Canton, IL 61520   Mrs. Moneta Bedwell, Libn.

GRAHAM HOSPITAL ASSOCIATION - SCHOOL OF NURSING LIBRARY
210 W. Walnut St.   Phone: (309) 647-5240
Canton, IL 61520   Mrs. Moneta Bedwell, Libn.

GREATER EGYPT REGIONAL PLANNING AND DEVELOPMENT COMMISSION -
  LIBRARY-RESEARCH CENTER
Box 3160   Phone: (618) 549-3306
Carbondale, IL 62901   Kay Clary, Res.Anl.

SHAWNEE SOLAR PROJECT, INC. - ENERGY CONSERVATION & SOLAR
  RETROFIT DEMONSTRATION CENTER
808 S. Forest   Phone: (618) 457-8172
Carbondale, IL 62901   Yolande Tullar, Dir.

SOUTHERN ILLINOIS UNIVERSITY, CARBONDALE - EDUCATION AND
  PSYCHOLOGY DIVISION LIBRARY
Morris Library   Phone: (618) 453-2274
Carbondale, IL 62901   Dr. Ruth Bauner, Educ. & Psych.Libn.

SOUTHERN ILLINOIS UNIVERSITY, CARBONDALE - HUMANITIES DIVISION
  LIBRARY
Morris Library   Phone: (618) 536-3391
Carbondale, IL 62901   Alan M. Cohn, Hum.Libn.

SOUTHERN ILLINOIS UNIVERSITY, CARBONDALE - SCHOOL OF LAW
  LIBRARY
                                                    Phone: (618) 536-7711
Carbondale, IL 62901   Elizabeth Slusser Kelly, Law Lib.Dir.

SOUTHERN ILLINOIS UNIVERSITY, CARBONDALE - SCIENCE DIVISION
  LIBRARY
Morris Library   Phone: (618) 453-2700
Carbondale, IL 62901   George W. Black, Sci.Libn.

SOUTHERN ILLINOIS UNIVERSITY, CARBONDALE - SOCIAL STUDIES
  DIVISION LIBRARY
Morris Library   Phone: (618) 453-2708
Carbondale, IL 62901   James Fox, Soc.Stud.Libn.

SOUTHERN ILLINOIS UNIVERSITY, CARBONDALE - SPECIAL COLLECTIONS
Morris Library   Phone: (618) 453-2516
Carbondale, IL 62901   David V. Koch, Cur./Archv.

SOUTHERN ILLINOIS UNIVERSITY, CARBONDALE - UNDERGRADUATE
  LIBRARY
Morris Library   Phone: (618) 453-2818
Carbondale, IL 62901   Dr. Judith Ann Harwood, Libn.

MURRAY (Warren G.) DEVELOPMENTAL CENTER - LIBRARY
1717 W. Broadway   Phone: (618) 532-1811
Centralia, IL 62801   Edith Jacke, Libn.

BURNHAM HOSPITAL - LIBRARY
407 S. Fourth St.   Phone: (217) 337-2591
Champaign, IL 61820   Teresa M. Manthey, Libn.

CHAMPAIGN COUNTY HISTORICAL MUSEUM - LIBRARY *
709 W. University Ave.   Phone: (217) 356-1010
Champaign, IL 61820   Michael Cahall, Dir.

CHAMPAIGN NEWS-GAZETTE - LIBRARY
48 Main St.   Phone: (217) 351-5228
Champaign, IL 61820   Carolyn J. Vance, Chf.Libn.

ERIC CLEARINGHOUSE ON ELEMENTARY AND EARLY CHILDHOOD
   EDUCATION
805 W. Pennsylvania Ave.
University of Illinois   Phone: (217) 333-1386
Champaign, IL 61820   Lilian G. Katz, Ph.D., Dir.

ILLINOIS STATE GEOLOGICAL SURVEY - LIBRARY
615 E. Peabody   Phone: (217) 344-1481
Champaign, IL 61820   Mary Krick, Libn.

ILLINOIS STATE WATER SURVEY - LIBRARY
605 E. Springfield
Sta. A
Box 5050   Phone: (217) 333-4956
Champaign, IL 61820   Marcia E. Nelson, Hd.Libn.

PARKLAND COLLEGE - LEARNING RESOURCE CENTER
2400 W. Bradley Ave.   Phone: (217) 351-2241
Champaign, IL 61820   David L. Johnson, Dir.

U.S. ARMY - CONSTRUCTION ENGINEERING RESEARCH LABORATORY -
   H.B. ZACKRISON MEMORIAL LIBRARY
Interstate Research Pk.
Box 4005   Phone: (217) 373-7217
Champaign, IL 61820   Martha A. Blake, Libn.

UNIVERSITY OF ILLINOIS - COMMUNITY RESEARCH CENTER -
   INFORMATION RESOURCE CENTER
505 E. Green St., Suite 210   Phone: (217) 333-0443
Champaign, IL 61820   James W. Brown, Dir.

UNIVERSITY OF ILLINOIS - ILLINOIS STATE NATURAL HISTORY SURVEY -
   LIBRARY
196 Natural Resources Bldg.
607 E. Peabody   Phone: (217) 333-6892
Champaign, IL 61820   Carla G Heister, Libn.

UNIVERSITY OF ILLINOIS - INSTITUTE OF LABOR AND INDUSTRIAL
   RELATIONS LIBRARY
504 E. Armory   Phone: (217) 333-2380
Champaign, IL 61820   Margaret A. Chaplan, Libn.

UNIVERSITY OF ILLINOIS - LAW LIBRARY
104 Law Bldg.
504 E. Pennsylvania Ave.   Phone: (217) 333-2914
Champaign, IL 61820   Richard Surles, Dir.

U.S. AIR FORCE BASE - CHANUTE BASE LIBRARY †
FL 3018, Bldg. 95   Phone: (217) 495-3191
Chanute AFB, IL 61868

U.S. AIR FORCE BASE - CHANUTE BASE TECHNICAL BRANCH LIBRARY †
Bldg. 95   Phone: (217) 495-3191
Chanute AFB, IL 61868   Annette Gohlke, Libn.

COLES COUNTY HISTORICAL SOCIETY - GREENWOOD SCHOOL MUSEUM -
   LIBRARY
800 Hayes Ave.   Phone: (217) 581-3310
Charleston, IL 61920   Dr. E. Duane Elbert, Musm.Cur.

A.G. BECKER PARIBAS, INC. - LIBRARY
One First National Plaza   Phone: (312) 630-5000
Chicago, IL 60603   Barbara P. Allamian, Supv.

ADAMS ADVERTISING AGENCY, INC. - LIBRARY
111 N. Canal St.   Phone: (312) 922-0856
Chicago, IL 60606   George Lewis, Libn.

ADLER (Alfred) INSTITUTE - SOL AND ELAINE MOSAK LIBRARY
159 N. Dearborn St.   Phone: (312) 346-3458
Chicago, IL 60601   Eugene McClory, Pres.

ADLER PLANETARIUM - LIBRARY
1300 S. Lake Shore Dr.   Phone: (312) 322-0304
Chicago, IL 60605   James Seevers, Astronomer

AMERICAN BAR FOUNDATION - THE CROMWELL LIBRARY
750 N. Lake Shore Dr.
Chicago, IL 60611   Olavi Maru, Libn.

AMERICAN COLLEGE OF HOSPITAL ADMINISTRATORS - RAY E. BROWN
   MANAGEMENT COLLECTION
840 N. Lakeshore Dr.   Phone: (312) 943-0544
Chicago, IL 60611   Diana L. Brown, Res.Assoc./Coord.

AMERICAN COLLEGE OF SURGEONS - LIBRARY †
55 E. Erie St.   Phone: (312) 664-4050
Chicago, IL 60611   Mrs. Jeri A. Ryan, Libn.

AMERICAN CONSERVATORY OF MUSIC - LIBRARY
116 S. Michigan Ave.   Phone: (312) 263-4161
Chicago, IL 60603   Lauren Dennhardt, Hd.Libn.

AMERICAN DENTAL ASSOCIATION - BUREAU OF LIBRARY SERVICES
211 E. Chicago Ave.   Phone: (312) 440-2653
Chicago, IL 60611   Aletha A. Kowitz, Dir.

AMERICAN DIETETIC ASSOCIATION - LULU G. GRAVES MEMORIAL
   LIBRARY
430 N. Michigan Ave.
Chicago, IL 60611

AMERICAN DRY MILK INSTITUTE - LIBRARY
130 N. Franklin St.   Phone: (312) 782-4888
Chicago, IL 60606   Warren S. Clark, Jr., Exec.Dir.

AMERICAN FEDERATION OF SMALL BUSINESS - INFORMATION CENTER
407 S. Dearborn St., Rm. 980   Phone: (312) 427-0206
Chicago, IL 60605   Ira H. Latimer, Exec. V.P.

AMERICAN FLORAL ART SCHOOL - FLORAL LIBRARY
3347 North Clark St., 3rd Fl.   Phone: (312) 922-9328
Chicago, IL 60657   James Moretz, Dir.

AMERICAN HOSPITAL ASSOCIATION - ASA S. BACON MEMORIAL LIBRARY
840 N. Lake Shore Dr.   Phone: (312) 280-6263
Chicago, IL 60611   Eloise C. Foster, Dir.

AMERICAN HOSPITAL ASSOCIATION - CLEARINGHOUSE FOR HOSPITAL
   MANAGEMENT & SYSTEMS
840 N. Lake Shore Dr.   Phone: (312) 280-6023
Chicago, IL 60611   Richard P. Covert, Dir.

AMERICAN JUDICATURE SOCIETY - RESEARCH LIBRARY
25 E. Washington St., 16th Fl.   Phone: (312) 558-6900
Chicago, IL 60602   Kathleen M. Sampson, Libn.

AMERICAN LIBRARY ASSOCIATION - HEADQUARTERS LIBRARY
50 E. Huron St.   Phone: (312) 944-6780
Chicago, IL 60611   Joel M. Lee, Libn.

AMERICAN MARKETING ASSOCIATION - INFORMATION CENTER
250 S. Wacker Dr.   Phone: (312) 648-0536
Chicago, IL 60606   Lorraine V. Caliendo, Dir.

AMERICAN MEDICAL ASSOCIATION - DIVISION OF LIBRARY AND
   ARCHIVAL SERVICES
535 N. Dearborn St.   Phone: (312) 645-4818
Chicago, IL 60610-4377   Arthur W. Hafner, Ph.D., Dir.

AMERICAN MEDICAL RECORD ASSOCIATION - FORE RESOURCE CENTER
875 N. Michigan Ave., Suite 1850 Phone: (312) 787-2672
Chicago, IL 60611   Mary Kay Siebert, Libn.

AMERICAN OSTEOPATHIC ASSOCIATION - ANDREW TAYLOR STILL
   MEMORIAL LIBRARY
212 E. Ohio St.   Phone: (312) 944-2713
Chicago, IL 60611   Barbara Wendorf, Exec.Ed.

AMERICAN PUBLIC WORKS ASSOCIATION - INFORMATION SERVICE
1313 E. 60th St.   Phone: (312) 667-2200
Chicago, IL 60637   Mary K. Simon, Dir. of Info.

AMERICAN RAILWAY CAR INSTITUTE - LIBRARY
303 E. Wacker Dr.
Chicago, IL 60601   Elwyn T. Ahnquist, Pres.

AMERICAN SOCIETY OF BAKERY ENGINEERS - INFORMATION SERVICE
   AND LIBRARY
2 N. Riverside Plaza, Rm. 1921   Phone: (312) 332-2246
Chicago, IL 60606   Robert A. Fischer, Sec.-Treas.

AMERICANS UNITED FOR LIFE - AUL LEGAL DEFENSE FUND -
   INFORMATION CENTER
230 N. Michigan Ave., Suite 915   Phone: (312) 263-5029
Chicago, IL 60601   Steven Baer, Dir. of Educ.

ART INSTITUTE OF CHICAGO - RYERSON AND BURNHAM LIBRARIES
Michigan Ave. at Adams St.   Phone: (312) 443-3666
Chicago, IL 60603   Daphne C. Roloff, Dir.

ART INSTITUTE OF CHICAGO - SCHOOL OF THE ART INSTITUTE OF
   CHICAGO - LIBRARY
280 S. Columbus Dr.
Chicago, IL 60603   Nadene Byrne, Dir.

ARTHUR ANDERSEN & CO. - GENERAL LIBRARY
33 W. Monroe St.   Phone: (312) 580-0033
Chicago, IL 60603   Marilyn R. Murray, Libn.

ARTHUR ANDERSEN & CO. - TAX LIBRARY
33 W. Monroe   Phone: (312) 580-0033
Chicago, IL 60603   Caroline Basciani, Tax Libn.

ARTHUR YOUNG & COMPANY - LIBRARY
One IBM Plaza
Chicago, IL 60611   Martha Jameson, Libn.

AUGUSTANA HOSPITAL AND HEALTH CARE CENTER - CARL A. HEDBERG
   HEALTH SCIENCE LIBRARY
2035 N. Lincoln   Phone: (312) 975-5109
Chicago, IL 60614   Laura Mueller, Chf.Libn.

AVERY, HODES, COSTELLO & BURMAN - LIBRARY
180 N. LaSalle St., Suite 3800   Phone: (312) 855-7929
Chicago, IL 60601   Linda Lockwood, Libn.

BAKER & MC KENZIE - LIBRARY
2800 Prudential Plaza   Phone: (312) 861-2915
Chicago, IL 60601   Frank Lukes, Law Libn.

BALZEKAS MUSEUM OF LITHUANIAN CULTURE - RESEARCH LIBRARY
4012 Archer Ave.   Phone: (312) 847-2441
Chicago, IL 60632   Jurgis Kasakaitis, Hd.Libn.

BANK MARKETING ASSOCIATION - INFORMATION CENTER
309 W. Washington St.   Phone: (312) 782-1442
Chicago, IL 60606   Lois A. Remeikis, Dir.

BANKERS LIFE & CASUALTY COMPANY - MARKETING INFORMATION
   DEPARTMENT - LIBRARY
4444 W. Lawrence Ave.   Phone: (312) 777-7000
Chicago, IL 60630   William B. Grow, Marketing Anl.

BATTEN, BARTON, DURSTINE & OSBORN (BBDO) - CHICAGO INFORMATION
   CENTER
410 N. Michigan Ave.   Phone: (312) 337-7860
Chicago, IL 60611   Patricia Fujimoto, Info.Ctr.Dir.

BEATRICE FOODS CO. - RESEARCH LIBRARY
1526 South State St.   Phone: (312) 791-8292
Chicago, IL 60605   Muriel McKune, Asst.Libn.

BELL & HOWELL EDUCATION GROUP - DE VRY INSTITUTE OF TECHNOLOGY
   - LEARNING RESOURCE CENTER †
3300 N. Campbell Ave.   Phone: (312) 929-8500
Chicago, IL 60618   Gary A. Meszaros, Libn.

BILLINGTON, FOX & ELLIS - RESEARCH DEPARTMENT - LIBRARY
20 N. Wacker Drive   Phone: (312) 236-5000
Chicago, IL 60606   Mary Ann Bock, Res.Assoc.

BLUE CROSS AND BLUE SHIELD ASSOCIATION - LIBRARY
676 N. St. Clair   Phone: (312) 440-6147
Chicago, IL 60611   Mary T. Drazba, Libn.

BODINE ELECTRIC COMPANY - LIBRARY *
2500 W. Bradley Pl.   Phone: (312) 478-3515
Chicago, IL 60618

BOOZ, ALLEN & HAMILTON, INC. - LIBRARY
Three First National Plaza   Phone: (312) 346-1900
Chicago, IL 60602   Carla W. Owens, Mgr.

BOZELL & JACOBS, INC. - CORPORATE INFORMATION CENTER
360 N. Michigan Ave.   Phone: (312) 580-4600
Chicago, IL 60601   Laura M. Johnson, Mgr.

BURNETT (Leo) COMPANY, INC. - INFORMATION CENTER
Prudential Plaza, 4th Fl.   Phone: (312) 565-5959
Chicago, IL 60601   Deborah Morrow, Hd.

CAMPBELL-MITHUN, INC. - RESEARCH INFORMATION CENTER
111 E. Wacker Dr.   Phone: (312) 565-3800
Chicago, IL 60601   Steve Heffernan, Libn.

CANADIAN CONSULATE GENERAL - INFORMATION CENTER †
310 S. Michigan Ave., Suite 1200   Phone: (312) 427-1031
Chicago, IL 60604   Carol A. Summers, Info.Mgr.

CATHOLIC THEOLOGICAL UNION AT CHICAGO - LIBRARY
5401 S. Cornell Ave.   Phone: (312) 324-8000
Chicago, IL 60615   Rev. Kenneth O'Malley, C.P., Lib.Dir.

CENTER FOR RESEARCH LIBRARIES
6050 S. Kenwood Ave.   Phone: (312) 955-4545
Chicago, IL 60637   Donald B. Simpson, Dir.

CENTER FOR THE STUDY OF ETHICS IN THE PROFESSIONS - LIBRARY *
IIT Center
Illinois Institute of Technology   Phone: (312) 567-3017
Chicago, IL 60616   David T. Thackery, Libn.

CENTER FOR STUDY OF MULTIPLE BIRTH - RESOURCE LIBRARY
333 E. Superior St., Suite 463-5
Chicago, IL 60611   Donald Keith, Exec.Dir.

CENTRAL STATES INSTITUTE OF ADDICTIONS - ADDICTION MATERIAL
   CENTER
120 W. Huron St.   Phone: (312) 266-6100
Chicago, IL 60610   Mrs. Vi Springenberg, Libn.

CHADWELL & KAYSER, LTD. - LAW LIBRARY
233 S. Wacker Dr.
8500 Sears Tower   Phone: (312) 876-2209
Chicago, IL 60606-6592   Betty Roizman, Libn.

CHAPMAN AND CUTLER - LAW LIBRARY
111 W. Monroe St.   Phone: (312) 845-3749
Chicago, IL 60603   Denis S. Kowalewski, Libn.

CHICAGO ACADEMY OF SCIENCES - MATTHEW LAUGHLIN MEMORIAL
   LIBRARY
2001 N. Clark St.   Phone: (312) 549-0606
Chicago, IL 60614   Louise Lunak, Libn.

CHICAGO BAR ASSOCIATION - LIBRARY
29 S. LaSalle St.   Phone: (312) 782-7348
Chicago, IL 60603   Stephen F. Czike, Exec.Libn.

CHICAGO BOARD OF EDUCATION - LIBRARY
1819 W. Pershing Rd., 4C N   Phone: (312) 890-8990
Chicago, IL 60601   Mary Ann Ross, Ref.Libn.

CHICAGO BOARD OF TRADE - LIBRARY †
141 W. Jackson Blvd.   Phone: (312) 435-3552
Chicago, IL 60604   Laura J. Miracle, Libn.

CHICAGO COLLEGE OF OSTEOPATHIC MEDICINE - ALUMNI MEMORIAL
   LIBRARY
5200 S. Ellis Ave.   Phone: (312) 947-4380
Chicago, IL 60615   Sandra A. Worley, Dir. of Lib.Serv.

CHICAGO DEPARTMENT OF HUMAN SERVICES - LIBRARY *
640 N. LaSalle St.   Phone: (312) 744-6653
Chicago, IL 60610   Janice Bradshaw, Supv.

CHICAGO HISTORICAL SOCIETY - RESEARCH COLLECTIONS
Clark St. at North Ave.   Phone: (312) 642-4600
Chicago, IL 60614

CHICAGO INSTITUTE FOR PSYCHOANALYSIS - MC LEAN LIBRARY
180 N. Michigan Ave.   Phone: (312) 726-6300
Chicago, IL 60601   Glenn E. Miller, Libn.

CHICAGO MERCANTILE EXCHANGE - LIBRARY
30 S. Wacker Dr.   Phone: (312) 930-8239
Chicago, IL 60606   Catherine J. Carter, Libn.

CHICAGO MUNICIPAL REFERENCE LIBRARY
City Hall, Rm. 1004   Phone: (312) 744-4992
Chicago, IL 60602   Joyce Malden, Libn.

CHICAGO PUBLIC LIBRARY CENTRAL LIBRARY - BUSINESS/SCIENCE/
  TECHNOLOGY DIVISION
425 N. Michigan Ave.   Phone: (312) 269-2814
Chicago, IL 60611   Emelie Shroder, Division Chief

CHICAGO PUBLIC LIBRARY CENTRAL LIBRARY - GENERAL INFORMATION
  SERVICES DIVISION-BIBLIOGRAPHIC & ILL CENTER
425 N. Michigan Ave.   Phone: (312) 269-2958
Chicago, IL 60611   Kathleen C. O'Meara, Hd.

CHICAGO PUBLIC LIBRARY CENTRAL LIBRARY - GENERAL INFORMATION
  SERVICES DIVISION - INFORMATION CENTER
425 N. Michigan Ave.   Phone: (312) 269-2800
Chicago, IL 60611   Bronwyn Parhad, Hd.

CHICAGO PUBLIC LIBRARY CENTRAL LIBRARY - GENERAL INFORMATION
  SERVICES DIV. - NEWSPAPERS & GEN. PERIODICALS CTR.
425 N. Michigan Ave.   Phone: (312) 269-2913
Chicago, IL 60611   Jerry Delaney, Hd.

CHICAGO PUBLIC LIBRARY CENTRAL LIBRARY - GOVERNMENT
  PUBLICATIONS DEPARTMENT
425 N. Michigan Ave.   Phone: (312) 269-3002
Chicago, IL 60611   Robert Baumruk, Dept.Hd.

CHICAGO PUBLIC LIBRARY CENTRAL LIBRARY - PROFESSIONAL LIBRARY
425 N. Michigan Ave.   Phone: (312) 269-2965
Chicago, IL 60611   Mildred Vannorsdall, Prof.Lib.Libn.

CHICAGO PUBLIC LIBRARY CENTRAL LIBRARY - SOCIAL SCIENCES &
  HISTORY DIVISION
425 N. Michigan Ave.   Phone: (312) 269-2830
Chicago, IL 60611   Diane Purtill, Div.Chf.

CHICAGO PUBLIC LIBRARY CULTURAL CENTER - AUDIOVISUAL CENTER
78 E. Washington St.   Phone: (312) 269-2910
Chicago, IL 60602   Barbara L. Flynn, Hd., AV Center

CHICAGO PUBLIC LIBRARY CULTURAL CENTER - FINE ARTS DIVISION -
  ART SECTION
78 E. Washington St.   Phone: (312) 269-2858
Chicago, IL 60602   Rosalinda Hack, Div.Chf.

CHICAGO PUBLIC LIBRARY CULTURAL CENTER - FINE ARTS DIVISION -
  MUSIC SECTION
78 E. Washington St.   Phone: (312) 269-2886
Chicago, IL 60602   Rosalinda Hack, Div.Chf.

CHICAGO PUBLIC LIBRARY CULTURAL CENTER - LITERATURE AND
  LANGUAGE DIVISION
78 E. Washington St.   Phone: (312) 269-2880
Chicago, IL 60602   David T. Bosca, Div.Chf.

CHICAGO PUBLIC LIBRARY CULTURAL CENTER - SPECIAL COLLECTIONS
  DIVISION
78 E. Washington St.   Phone: (312) 269-2926
Chicago, IL 60602   Laura Linard, Cur.

CHICAGO PUBLIC LIBRARY CULTURAL CENTER - THOMAS HUGHES
  CHILDREN'S LIBRARY
78 E. Washington St.   Phone: (312) 269-2835
Chicago, IL 60602   Lillian R. New, Hd.

CHICAGO PUBLIC LIBRARY CULTURAL CENTER - VIVIAN G. HARSH
  COLLECTION OF AFRO-AMERICAN HISTORY & LIT. †
9525 S. Halsted St.   Phone: (312) 881-6910
Chicago, IL 60628   Hattie Power, Dir.

CHICAGO-READ MENTAL HEALTH CENTER - PROFESSIONAL LIBRARY †
4200 N. Oak Park Ave.   Phone: (312) 794-3746
Chicago, IL 60634   Ruth Greenberg, Libn.

CHICAGO REGIONAL TRANSPORTATION AUTHORITY - LIBRARY
300 N. State St.   Phone: (312) 836-4091
Chicago, IL 60610   Connie Tinner, Supv., Rec.Mgt.

CHICAGO SINAI CONGREGATION - EMIL G. HIRSCH LIBRARY
5350 S. Shore Dr.   Phone: (312) 288-1600
Chicago, IL 60615   Howard A. Berman, Rabbi

CHICAGO STATE UNIVERSITY - DOUGLAS LIBRARY - SPECIAL
  COLLECTIONS †
E. 95th St. & King Dr.   Phone: (312) 995-2254
Chicago, IL 60628   Dr. W. Patrick Leonard, Dean

CHICAGO SUN-TIMES - EDITORIAL LIBRARY
401 N. Wabash Ave.   Phone: (312) 321-2593
Chicago, IL 60611   Ernest Perez, Chf.Libn.

CHICAGO THEOLOGICAL SEMINARY - HAMMOND LIBRARY
5757 S. University Ave.   Phone: (312) 752-5757
Chicago, IL 60637   Rev. Neil W. Gerdes, Libn.

CHICAGO TRANSIT AUTHORITY - HAROLD S. ANTHON MEMORIAL LIBRARY
Merchandise Mart Plaza
Box 3555   Phone: (312) 664-7200
Chicago, IL 60654   Joseph Benson, Dir., Info.Serv.

CHICAGO TRIBUNE - EDITORIAL INFORMATION CENTER
435 N. Michigan Ave.   Phone: (312) 222-3871
Chicago, IL 60611   Barbara T. Newcombe, Mgr.

CHICAGO TRIBUNE - RESEARCH LIBRARY
435 N. Michigan, 11th Fl.   Phone: (312) 222-3188
Chicago, IL 60610   Bernadette Szczech, Res.Libn.

CHICAGO URBAN SKILLS INSTITUTE - DAWSON SKILL CENTER LIBRARY
3901 S. State St.   Phone: (312) 624-7300
Chicago, IL 60609   Barbara G. Washington, LRC Mgr.

CHILDREN'S MEMORIAL HOSPITAL - JOSEPH BRENNEMANN LIBRARY
2300 Children's Plaza   Phone: (312) 880-4505
Chicago, IL 60614   Leslie Goodale, Dir.

CHRISTMAS SEAL AND CHARITY STAMP SOCIETY - LIBRARY
5825 Dorchester Ave.   Phone: (312) 493-4208
Chicago, IL 60637   Dr. H. Denny Donnell, Jr., Hist./Libn.

CNA LIBRARY
CNA Plaza, Van Buren and Wabash   Phone: (312) 822-7630
Chicago, IL 60685   Sandra Masson, Libn.

COFFIELD UNGARETTI HARRIS & SLAVIN - LIBRARY
3500 Three First National Plaza   Phone: (312) 977-4499
Chicago, IL 60602   Patricia Anne Felch, Libn.

COLLECTORS CLUB OF CHICAGO - LIBRARY
1029 N. Dearborn St.   Phone: (312) 642-7981
Chicago, IL 60610   Lester E. Winick, Lib.Comm.

COLUMBUS-CUNEO-CABRINI MEDICAL CENTER - COLUMBUS HOSPITAL
  MEDICAL LIBRARY
2520 N. Lakeview Ave.   Phone: (312) 883-7341
Chicago, IL 60614   James L. Finnerty, Ph.D., Dir., Lib.

COMMONWEALTH EDISON COMPANY - LIBRARY
Box 767   Phone: (312) 294-3064
Chicago, IL 60690   Barbara R. Kelly, Libn.

COMPREHENSIVE HEALTH COUNCIL OF METROPOLITAN CHICAGO -
    ALCOHOLISM CENTER - LIBRARY
108 N. State St., Suite 1201   Phone: (312) 263-1000
Chicago, IL 60601   April W. Filis, Info. & Referral Coord.

CONGREGATION KINS OF WEST ROGERS PARK - JORDAN E. FEUER
    LIBRARY
2800 W. North Shore   Phone: (312) 761-4000
Chicago, IL 60645   Mrs. Milton Greenstein, Libn.

CONGREGATION RODFEI ZEDEK - J.S. HOFFMAN MEMORIAL LIBRARY *
5200 Hyde Park Blvd.   Phone: (312) 752-4489
Chicago, IL 60615   Henrietta Schultz, Libn.

CONTINENTAL CHEMISTE CORPORATION - LIBRARY
2256 W. Ogden Ave.   Phone: (312) 226-2134
Chicago, IL 60612   Kenneth J. Kass, Pres.

CONTINENTAL ILLINOIS NATIONAL BANK AND TRUST COMPANY OF
    CHICAGO - INFORMATION SERVICES DIVISION
231 S. La Salle St.   Phone: (312) 923-6920
Chicago, IL 60697   Susan J. Montgomery, Mgr.

COOK COUNTY HOSPITAL - HEALTH SCIENCE LIBRARY AND ARCHIVES
1900 W. Polk St.
Chicago, IL 60612   Grace Auer, Coord., Lib. & Archv.

COOK COUNTY HOSPITAL - TICE MEMORIAL LIBRARY
720 S. Wolcott St.   Phone: (312) 633-6724
Chicago, IL 60612   Grace Auer, Hd.Med.Libn.

COOK COUNTY LAW LIBRARY
2900 Richard J. Daley Ctr.   Phone: (312) 443-5423
Chicago, IL 60602   William J. Powers, Jr., Exec. Law Libn.

COOK COUNTY LAW LIBRARY - CRIMINAL COURT BRANCH
2650 S. California Ave., Rm. 4D00   Phone: (312) 890-7396
Chicago, IL 60608   Bennie E. Martin, Chf.Libn.

COOK COUNTY STATE'S ATTORNEY'S OFFICE LIBRARY
500 Richard J. Daley Center   Phone: (312) 443-5665
Chicago, IL 60602   Valerie K. Kruk, Libn.

COOPERS & LYBRAND - AUDIT LIBRARY
222 S. Riverside Plaza   Phone: (312) 559-5684
Chicago, IL 60606   Mallory Otten, Audit Libn.

CRAIN COMMUNICATIONS, INC. - INFORMATION CENTER
740 N. Rush St.   Phone: (312) 649-5476
Chicago, IL 60611   Carol A. David, Hd.Libn.

DARTNELL CORPORATION - PUBLISHING-RESEARCH LIBRARY
4660 N. Ravenswood Ave.   Phone: (312) 561-4000
Chicago, IL 60640   Juanita Roberts, Libn.

DATAQUE INTERNATIONAL INC. - TECHNICAL INFORMATION CENTER
Lake Point Tower 5509
505 N. Lakeshore   Phone: (312) 329-0322
Chicago, IL 60611   Sophia D. Beene, Pres.

DE LEUW, CATHER AND COMPANY - LIBRARY
165 W. Wacker Dr.
Chicago, IL 60601

DE PAUL UNIVERSITY - LAW SCHOOL LIBRARY
25 E. Jackson Blvd.   Phone: (312) 321-7710
Chicago, IL 60604   Judith G. Gecas, Dir.

DE PAUL UNIVERSITY, LINCOLN PARK CAMPUS LIBRARY - SPECIAL
    COLLECTIONS DEPARTMENT
2323 N. Seminary   Phone: (312) 321-7940
Chicago, IL 60614   Kathryn DeGraff, Spec.Coll.Libn.

DEFENSE RESEARCH INSTITUTE, INC. - BRIEF BANK
750 N. Lakeshore Dr., Suite 5000   Phone: (312) 944-0575
Chicago, IL 60611   Fred L. Bardenwerper, Asst.Res.Dir.

DICK (A.B.) COMPANY - LIBRARY †
5700 W. Touhy Ave.   Phone: (312) 763-1900
Chicago, IL 60648   Jo Ann Miller, Assoc.Libn.

DONORS FORUM OF CHICAGO - LIBRARY
208 S. LaSalle St., Rm. 600   Phone: (312) 726-4882
Chicago, IL 60604   Susan M. Levy, Libn.

DU SABLE MUSEUM OF AFRICAN AMERICAN HISTORY - LIBRARY
740 E. 56th Pl.   Phone: (312) 947-0600
Chicago, IL 60637   Dr. Margaret Burroughs, Dir.

DUFF AND PHELPS, INC. - RESEARCH LIBRARY
55 E. Monroe St., Suite 4000   Phone: (312) 263-2610
Chicago, IL 60603   Sheila A. Collins, Libn./Info.Spec.

EDGEWATER HOSPITAL - MEDICAL LIBRARY
5700 N. Ashland Ave.   Phone: (312) 878-6000
Chicago, IL 60660   Laura Wimmer, Dir., Lib.Serv.

ELRICK AND LAVIDGE, INC. - LIBRARY *
10 S. Riverside Plaza   Phone: (312) 726-0666
Chicago, IL 60606   G. Birch Ripley, Libn.

ENCYCLOPAEDIA BRITANNICA, INC. - EDITORIAL LIBRARY
310 S. Michigan Ave.   Phone: (312) 347-7000
Chicago, IL 60604   Terry Miller, Hd.Libn.

ENVIRONMENTAL PROTECTION AGENCY - REGION V LIBRARY
230 S. Dearborn St., Rm. 1420   Phone: (312) 353-2022
Chicago, IL 60604   Ms. Lou W. Tilley, Regional Libn.

ERIKSON INSTITUTE - LIBRARY
233 N. Michigan Ave., Suite 2200   Phone: (312) 565-2970
Chicago, IL 60601   Maija B. May, Libn.

EVANGELICAL COVENANT CHURCH OF AMERICA - COVENANT ARCHIVES
    AND HISTORICAL LIBRARY
5125 N. Spaulding Ave.   Phone: (312) 583-2700
Chicago, IL 60625   Sigurd F. Westberg, Archv.

FAMILY INSTITUTE OF CHICAGO - CROWLEY MEMORIAL LIBRARY
666 Lake Shore Dr., Suite 1530   Phone: (312) 649-7854
Chicago, IL 60611   Susan L. Fine, Libn.

FEDERAL RESERVE BANK OF CHICAGO - LIBRARY
164 W. Jackson
Box 834   Phone: (312) 322-5824
Chicago, IL 60690   Dorothy Phillips, Adm.

FIELD MUSEUM OF NATURAL HISTORY - LIBRARY
Roosevelt Rd. & Lake Shore Dr.   Phone: (312) 922-9410
Chicago, IL 60605   W. Peyton Fawcett, Hd.Libn.

FIRST NATIONAL BANK OF CHICAGO - INFORMATION TECHNOLOGY
    LIBRARY
1 First National Plaza, D-13, Suite 0187   Phone: (312) 732-4760
Chicago, IL 60670   Naomi Adler, Lib.Supv.

FIRST NATIONAL BANK OF CHICAGO - LIBRARY *
One First National Plaza, Suite 0477   Phone: (312) 732-3590
Chicago, IL 60670   Martha Whaley, Libn.

FLUOR ENGINEERING INC. - FLUOR POWER SERVICES, INC. - LIBRARY †
200 W. Monroe   Phone: (312) 368-3719
Chicago, IL 60606   Eileen J. Seaberg, Hd.Libn.

FMC CORPORATION - CORPORATE LIBRARY
200 E. Randolph   Phone: (312) 861-5705
Chicago, IL 60601   Judith E. Purcell, Corp.Libn.

FOOTE CONE & BELDING - INFORMATION CENTER
401 N. Michigan Ave.   Phone: (312) 467-9200
Chicago, IL 60611   John Kok, Dir.

FRANKEL & COMPANY - RESEARCH LIBRARY
111 E. Wacker Dr.   Phone: (312) 938-1900
Chicago, IL 60601   Nancy R. Kovitz, Res.Libn.

FRIEDMAN & KOVEN - LAW LIBRARY
208 S. LaSalle St.   Phone: (312) 346-8500
Chicago, IL 60604   Cynthia Lowe Rynning, Hd. Law Libn.

GAS RESEARCH INSTITUTE - LIBRARY SERVICES
8600 W. Bryn Mawr Ave.   Phone: (312) 399-8354
Chicago, IL 60631   Ann B. Michael, Mgr., Lib.Serv.

GOETHE INSTITUT CHICAGO - GERMAN CULTURAL CENTER - LIBRARY
401 N. Michigan Ave.   Phone: (312) 329-0915
Chicago, IL 60611   Christiane Schmidt, Libn.

GRANT (Alexander) & COMPANY - CHICAGO OFFICE LIBRARY
600 Prudential Plaza   Phone: (312) 856-0200
Chicago, IL 60601   Linda Scott, Hd.Libn.

GRANT HOSPITAL OF CHICAGO - LINDON SEED LIBRARY
550 W. Webster Ave.   Phone: (312) 883-5380
Chicago, IL 60614   Dalia S. Kleinmuntz, Lib.Dir.

GREELEY AND HANSEN - LIBRARY †
222 S. Riverside Plaza   Phone: (312) 648-1155
Chicago, IL 60606   Elizabeth L. Ell, Libn.

HARRINGTON INSTITUTE OF INTERIOR DESIGN - DESIGN LIBRARY
410 S. Michigan, Rm. 541   Phone: (312) 939-4975
Chicago, IL 60605   Adeline Schuster, Hd.Libn.

HARRIS TRUST AND SAVINGS BANK - RESEARCH LIBRARY
111 W. Monroe St.   Phone: (312) 461-7625
Chicago, IL 60690   Claudette S. Warner, Info.Serv.Off.

HAYES/HILL INCORPORATED - LIBRARY
312 W. Randolph, Suite 300   Phone: (312) 984-5250
Chicago, IL 60606   Sandra K. Rollheiser, Res.Mgr.

HEIDRICK & STRUGGLES, INC. - LIBRARY RESEARCH CENTER
125 S. Wacker Dr., Suite 2800   Phone: (312) 372-8811
Chicago, IL 60606   Margaret E. Mason, Corp.Libn.

HELENE CURTIS INDUSTRIES, INC. - CORPORATE INFORMATION CENTER
4401 W. North Ave.   Phone: (312) 661-0222
Chicago, IL 60639   Jacquelyn B. Becker, Mgr.

HENROTIN HOSPITAL - MEDICAL LIBRARY
111 West Oak St.   Phone: (312) 440-7759
Chicago, IL 60610   Diana P. Thomas, Med.Libn.

HISTORICAL PICTURES SERVICE, INC.
601 W. Randolph St.   Phone: (312) 346-0599
Chicago, IL 60606   Jeane M. Williams, Archv.

HOLY CROSS HOSPITAL - HEALTH SCIENCE LIBRARY
2701 W. 68th St.   Phone: (312) 471-5643
Chicago, IL 60629   Olivija Fistrovic, Med.Libn.

IIT RESEARCH INSTITUTE - COMPUTER SEARCH CENTER †
10 W. 35th St.   Phone: (312) 567-4802
Chicago, IL 60616   Gerald J. Yucuis, Mgr.

IIT RESEARCH INSTITUTE - GUIDANCE AND CONTROL INFORMATION
   ANALYSIS CENTER (GACIAC)
10 W. 35th St.   Phone: (312) 567-4345
Chicago, IL 60616   Charles Smoots, Dir.

IIT RESEARCH INSTITUTE - LIBRARY & INFORMATION CENTER
10 W. 35th St.   Phone: (312) 567-4802
Chicago, IL 60616   Jeanette Harlow, Tech.Libn.

ILLINOIS BELL TELEPHONE COMPANY - LIBRARY
225 W. Randolph St., HQ 20-D   Phone: (312) 727-2668
Chicago, IL 60606   Marguerite J. Krynicki, Hd.Libn.

ILLINOIS COLLEGE OF OPTOMETRY - CARL F. SHEPARD MEMORIAL
   LIBRARY
3241 S. Michigan Ave.   Phone: (312) 225-1700
Chicago, IL 60616   Kevin Wah, Dir. of Lib./Instr.Serv.

ILLINOIS INSTITUTE OF TECHNOLOGY - CHICAGO KENT LAW SCHOOL -
   LIBRARY †
77 S. Wacker Dr.   Phone: (312) 567-5014
Chicago, IL 60606   Georgia Strohm, Assoc.Libn.

ILLINOIS INSTITUTE OF TECHNOLOGY - INFORMATION AND LIBRARY
   RESOURCES CENTER †
3300 S. Federal St.   Phone: (312) 567-6846
Chicago, IL 60616   David R. Dowell, Dir.

ILLINOIS MASONIC MEDICAL CENTER - NOAH VAN CLEEF MEDICAL
   MEMORIAL LIBRARY
836 W. Wellington Ave., Rm. 7501   Phone: (312) 975-1600
Chicago IL 60657   Karen Primov, Dir., Med.Lib.Serv.

ILLINOIS MASONIC MEDICAL CENTER - SCHOOL OF NURSING - DR.
   JOSEPH DEUTSCH MEMORIAL LIBRARY
836 W. Nelson   Phone: (312) 975-1600
Chicago, IL 60657   Ann Markham, Lrng.Rsrc.Coord.

ILLINOIS STATE BUREAU OF EMPLOYMENT SECURITY - LABOR MARKET
   INFORMATION CENTER †
910 S. Michigan Ave., Rm. 1255   Phone: (312) 793-5277
Chicago, IL 60605   Eunice Choi, Libn.

ILLINOIS STATE DEPARTMENT OF ENERGY AND NATURAL RESOURCES -
   CHICAGO ENERGY OPERATIONS LIBRARY
400 W. Madison, Rm. 241   Phone: (312) 793-7695
Chicago, IL 60606   Alice I. Lane, Lib.Assoc.

ILLINOIS STATE PSYCHIATRIC INSTITUTE - JACK WEINBERG LIBRARY
1601 W. Taylor St.   Phone: (312) 996-1320
Chicago, IL 60612   Margo McClelland, Libn.

INDUSTRIAL WORKERS OF THE WORLD - LIBRARY
3435 N. Sheffield, Suite 202   Phone: (312) 549-5045
Chicago, IL 60657

INLAND STEEL COMPANY - INDUSTRIAL RELATIONS LIBRARY
30 W. Monroe   Phone: (312) 346-0300
Chicago, IL 60603   Barbara G. Morton, Libn.

INSTITUTE OF GAS TECHNOLOGY - TECHNICAL INFORMATION CENTER
3424 S. State St.   Phone: (312) 567-3870
Chicago, IL 60616   H.L. Mensch, Assoc.Dir.

INSTITUTE FOR JUVENILE RESEARCH - PROFESSIONAL LIBRARY
907 S. Wolcott   Phone: (312) 996-1874
Chicago, IL 60612

INTERNATIONAL ASSOCIATION OF ASSESSING OFFICERS - RESEARCH
   AND TECHNICAL SERVICES DEPT. - LIBRARY
1313 E. 60th St.   Phone: (312) 947-2050
Chicago, IL 60637-9990   Stuart W. Miller, Libn.

INTERNATIONAL COLLEGE OF SURGEONS HALL OF FAME - DR. JOSEPH
   MONTAGUE PROCTOLOGIC LIBRARY
1524 N. Lake Shore Dr.   Phone: (312) 642-3555
Chicago, IL 60610   Dolores Leber, Asst. to Cur.

INTERNATIONAL FOODSERVICE MANUFACTURERS ASSOCIATION -
   INFORMATION SERVICE
875 N. Michigan, Suite 3460   Phone: (312) 944-3838
Chicago, IL 60611   Michael Hoffman, Dir. of Marketing

INTERNATIONAL HARVESTER COMPANY - CORPORATE ARCHIVES
401 N. Michigan, 15th Fl.   Phone: (312) 836-2149
Chicago, IL 60611   Gregory Lennes, Archv.

IRISH-AMERICAN CULTURAL ASSOCIATION - LIBRARY
10415 S. Western   Phone: (312) 239-6760
Chicago, IL 60643   Cynthia L. Buescher, Libn.

ISHAM, LINCOLN & BEALE - LIBRARY
3 First National Plaza   Phone: (312) 558-7488
Chicago, IL 60602   Terezia Rabai, Libn.

JACKSON PARK HOSPITAL - MEDICAL LIBRARY †
7531 South Stony Island Ave.   Phone: (312) 947-7653
Chicago, IL 60649   Syed A. Maghrabi, Med.Ref.Libn.

JESUIT SCHOOL OF THEOLOGY IN CHICAGO - LIBRARY †
1100 E. 55th St.   Phone: (312) 667-3500
Chicago, IL 60615   Dr. W. Earle Hilgert, Act.Libn.

JEWISH VOCATIONAL SERVICE - LIBRARY
1 S. Franklin   Phone: (312) 346-6700
Chicago, IL 60606

JOHN MARSHALL LAW SCHOOL - LIBRARY
315 S. Plymouth Ct.   Phone: (312) 427-2737
Chicago, IL 60604   Randall T. Peterson, Dir.

JOHNSON PUBLISHING COMPANY, INC. - LIBRARY
820 S. Michigan Ave.   Phone: (312) 322-9320
Chicago, IL 60605   Pamela J. Cash, Libn.

KATTEN, MUCHIN, ZAVIS, PEARL & GALLER - LIBRARY
55 E. Monroe, Suite 4100   Phone: (312) 558-3675
Chicago, IL 60603   Susan P. Spector, Libn.

KEARNEY (A.T.), INC. - INFORMATION CENTER
222 S. Riverside Plaza   Phone: (312) 648-0111
Chicago, IL 60606   Linda Larsen, Mgr., Info.Ctr.

KENNEDY-KING COLLEGE - LIBRARY †
6800 S. Wentworth Ave.   Phone: (312) 962-3200
Chicago, IL 60621   Mrs. Noel R. Grego, Hd.

KIRKLAND & ELLIS - LIBRARY
200 E. Randolph Dr.   Phone: (312) 861-3202
Chicago, IL 60601   Charles E. Kregel, Jr., Info.Serv.Mgr.

KNIGHT (Lester B.) & ASSOCIATES, INC. - MANAGEMENT CONSULTING
  LIBRARY †
549 W. Randolph St.   Phone: (312) 346-2100
Chicago, IL 60606   Clarita M. Generao, Libn.

KORN/FERRY INTERNATIONAL - RESEARCH LIBRARY
120 S. Riverside Plaza, Suite 918   Phone: (312) 726-1841
Chicago, IL 60606   Victoria Cheshire, Dir. of Res.

LA RABIDA CHILDREN'S HOSPITAL AND RESEARCH CENTER - LAWRENCE
  MERCER PICK MEMORIAL LIBRARY *
E. 65th St. at Lake Michigan   Phone: (312) 363-6700
Chicago, IL 60649   Dr. Burton J. Grossman, Chf. of Med. Staff

LAKE MICHIGAN FEDERATION - ENVIRONMENTAL LIBRARY
53 W. Jackson, No. 1710   Phone: (312) 427-5121
Chicago, IL 60604   Judy Kiriazis, Exec.Dir.

LEGAL ASSISTANCE FOUNDATION OF CHICAGO - LIBRARY
343 S. Dearborn   Phone: (312) 341-1070
Chicago, IL 60604   John Ryden, Libn.

LIBRARY OF INTERNATIONAL RELATIONS
77 S. Wacker Dr.   Phone: (312) 567-6803
Chicago, IL 60606   Eloise ReQua, Dir.

LINCOLN PARK ZOOLOGICAL GARDENS - LIBRARY
2200 N. Cannon Dr.   Phone: (312) 294-4640
Chicago, IL 60614   Joyce M. Shaw, Libn.

LIQUID CARBONIC CORPORATION - LIBRARY
3740 W. 74th St.   Phone: (312) 855-2500
Chicago, IL 60629   M.A. Armstrong, Libn.

LITHUANIAN AMERICAN COMMUNITY OF THE U.S.A. - LITHUANIAN
  WORLD ARCHIVES
5620 S. Claremont
Chicago, IL 60636   Ceslovas V. Grincevicius, Dir.

LORD, BISSELL AND BROOK - LAW LIBRARY
115 S. LaSalle St.   Phone: (312) 443-0647
Chicago, IL 60603   Jane L. Gaddis, Libn.

LORETTO HOSPITAL - HEALTH SCIENCES LIBRARY
645 S. Central Ave.   Phone: (312) 626-4300
Chicago, IL 60644   Ina Ostertag, Dir.

LOYOLA UNIVERSITY OF CHICAGO - CUDAHY MEMORIAL LIBRARY -
  UNIVERSITY ARCHIVES
6525 Sheridan Rd.   Phone: (312) 274-3000
Chicago, IL 60626   Michael J. Grace, S.J., Univ.Archv.

LOYOLA UNIVERSITY OF CHICAGO - JULIA DEAL LEWIS LIBRARY
820 N. Michigan Ave.   Phone: (312) 670-2875
Chicago, IL 60611   Genevieve Delana, Hd.Libn.

LOYOLA UNIVERSITY OF CHICAGO - LAW LIBRARY
1 E. Pearson St.   Phone: (312) 670-2952
Chicago, IL 60611   Francis R. Doyle, Law Libn.

LUTHERAN CHURCH IN AMERICA - ARCHIVES
Lutheran School of Theology at Chicago
1100 E. 55th St.   Phone: (312) 753-0766
Chicago, IL 60615-5199   Elisabeth Wittman, Asst.Archv.

LUTHERAN SCHOOL OF THEOLOGY AT CHICAGO - KRAUSS LIBRARY †
1100 E. 55th St.   Phone: (312) 667-3500
Chicago, IL 60615   Rev. Lowell Albee, Jr., Libn.

MC BRIDE, BAKER, WIENKE - LAW LIBRARY †
Three First National Plaza, Suite 3800   Phone: (312) 346-6191
Chicago, IL 60602   Mary Ann Alfonsi-Gini, Libn.

MC CORMICK THEOLOGICAL SEMINARY - LIBRARY †
1100 E. 55th St.   Phone: (312) 667-3500
Chicago, IL 60615   Elvire R. Hilgert, Libn.

MC CRONE (Walter C.) ASSOCIATES - LIBRARY
2820 S. Michigan   Phone: (312) 842-7100
Chicago, IL 60616   Juliet Robinson, Libn.

MC DERMOTT, WILL & EMERY - LIBRARY
111 W. Monroe St.   Phone: (312) 372-2000
Chicago, IL 60603   Louis J. Covotsos, Hd.Libn.

MC KINSEY & COMPANY, INC. - LIBRARY
Two First National Plaza   Phone: (312) 368-0600
Chicago, IL 60603   Loramae Smith, Mgr., Info.Serv.

MARQUIS WHO'S WHO, INC. - RESEARCH DEPARTMENT LIBRARY
200 E. Ohio St.   Phone: (312) 787-2008
Chicago, IL 60611   Adele Hast, Editor-in-Chief

MARSTELLER, INC. - INFORMATION SERVICES †
One E. Wacker Dr.   Phone: (312) 329-1100
Chicago, IL 60601   Ellen Steininger, Mgr., Info.Serv.

MAYER, BROWN & PLATT - LIBRARY †
231 S. LaSalle St.   Phone: (312) 782-0600
Chicago, IL 60604   Janice B. Bentley, Libn.

MEADVILLE/LOMBARD THEOLOGICAL SCHOOL - LIBRARY
5701 S. Woodlawn Ave.   Phone: (312) 753-3196
Chicago, IL 60637   Rev. Neil W. Gerdes, Libn.

MERCY HOSPITAL & MEDICAL CENTER - MEDICAL LIBRARY
2510 S. King Dr.   Phone: (312) 567-2364
Chicago, IL 60616   Timothy T. Oh, Dir. of Lib.

MERRIAM CENTER LIBRARY
Charles E. Merriam Center
for Public Administration
1313 E. 60th St.   Phone: (312) 947-2162
Chicago, IL 60637   Patricia Coatsworth, Hd.Libn.

METROPOLITAN SANITARY DISTRICT OF GREATER CHICAGO -
  TECHNICAL LIBRARY
100 E. Erie St.   Phone: (312) 751-5782
Chicago, IL 60611   Rudolph C. Ellsworth, Libn.

MICHAEL REESE HOSPITAL & MEDICAL CENTER - DEPARTMENT OF
  LIBRARY & MEDIA RESOURCES
2908 S. Ellis Ave.   Phone: (312) 791-2474
Chicago, IL 60616   Dr. George Mozes, Dir.

MIDWEST STOCK EXCHANGE, INC. - LISTINGS DEPARTMENT
120 S. LaSalle St., Rm. 1200
Chicago, IL 60603

MONTGOMERY WARD AND CO. - INFORMATION SERVICES †
One Montgomery Ward Plaza   Phone: (312) 467-2334
Chicago, IL 60671   Barbara J. Burnett, Mgr.

MOODY BIBLE INSTITUTE - LIBRARY
820 N. LaSalle St.   Phone: (312) 329-4139
Chicago, IL 60610   Richard G. Schock, Dir.

MOODY BIBLE INSTITUTE - MOODYANA COLLECTION
820 N. LaSalle St.   Phone: (312) 329-4140
Chicago, IL 60610   Richard G. Schock, Dir.

MORTON THIOKOL INC. - CORPORATE LIBRARY
110 N. Wacker Dr.   Phone: (312) 621-5305
Chicago, IL 60606   Mary Beth Van Cura, Supv., Lib.Serv.

MOUNT SINAI HOSPITAL MEDICAL CENTER - LEWISOHN MEMORIAL
  LIBRARY *
California Ave. at 15th St.   Phone: (312) 542-2056
Chicago, IL 60608   Emily Sobkowiak, Med.Libn.

MUSEUM OF CONTEMPORARY ART - LIBRARY
237 E. Ontario St.   Phone: (312) 943-7755
Chicago, IL 60611   Alice Piron, Libn.

MUSEUM OF SCIENCE & INDUSTRY - KRESGE LIBRARY
57th St. & Lake Shore Dr.   Phone: (312) 684-1414
Chicago, IL 60637   Carla Hayden, Lib.Serv.Coord.

NAES COLLEGE - LIBRARY AND RESOURCE CENTER
2838 W. Peterson   Phone: (312) 728-1662
Chicago, IL 60659   Armin Beck, Dean

NATIONAL ANTI-VIVISECTION SOCIETY - LIBRARY
100 E. Ohio St.   Phone: (312) 787-4486
Chicago, IL 60611

NATIONAL ASSOCIATION OF BOARDS OF PHARMACY - LIBRARY
One E. Wacker Dr., Suite 2210   Phone: (312) 467-6220
Chicago, IL 60601   Fred T. Mahaffey, Exec.Dir.

NATIONAL ASSOCIATION OF QUICK PRINTERS - INTERNATIONAL QUICK
  PRINTING FOUNDATION LIBRARY
111 E. Wacker Dr., Suite 600   Phone: (312) 644-6610
Chicago, IL 60601   Barbara Chalik, Exec.Dir.

NATIONAL ASSOCIATION OF REALTORS - LIBRARY
430 N. Michigan Ave.   Phone: (312) 329-8292
Chicago, IL 60611-4087   Karen J. Switt, Chf.Libn.

NATIONAL ASSOCIATION OF SUGGESTION SYSTEMS - LIBRARY
230 N. Michigan Ave., Suite 1200   Phone: (312) 372-1770
Chicago, IL 60601

NATIONAL CLEARINGHOUSE FOR LEGAL SERVICES - LIBRARY
407 S. Dearborn, Suite 400   Phone: (312) 939-3830
Chicago, IL 60605   Katherine Stevenson, Libn.

NATIONAL COLLEGE OF EDUCATION - URBAN CAMPUS LEARNING
  RESOURCE CENTER
18 S. Michigan Ave.   Phone: (312) 621-9676
Chicago, IL 60603   Benjamin Hall Schapiro, Coord.

NATIONAL LIVESTOCK AND MEAT BOARD - MEAT INDUSTRY
  INFORMATION CENTER
444 N. Michigan Ave.   Phone: (312) 467-5520
Chicago, IL 60611   William D. Siarny, Jr., Dir.

NATIONAL MARINE MANUFACTURERS ASSOCIATION - INFORMATION
  CENTER
401 N. Michigan Ave.
Chicago, IL 60611

NATIONAL PARENT TEACHER ASSOCIATION - INFORMATION RESOURCE
  CENTER
700 N. Rush St.
Chicago, IL 60611   Wilma E. Benjamin, Rec.Coord.

NATIONAL SAFETY COUNCIL - LIBRARY
444 N. Michigan Ave.   Phone: (312) 527-4800
Chicago, IL 60611   Ruth K. Hammersmith, Dir.

NATIONAL SISTERS VOCATION CONFERENCE - LIBRARY
1307 S. Wabash Ave.   Phone: (312) 939-6180
Chicago, IL 60605   Sr. Sarah M. Sherman, RSM, Exec.Dir.

NEEDHAM, HARPER & STEERS ADVERTISING, INC. - INFORMATION
  SERVICES
303 E. Wacker Dr.   Phone: (312) 861-0200
Chicago, IL 60601   Belle Mest, Mgr., Info.Serv.

NEWBERRY LIBRARY
60 W. Walton St.   Phone: (312) 943-9090
Chicago, IL 60610   Lawrence W. Towner, Pres./Libn.

NORTH PARK COLLEGE AND THEOLOGICAL SEMINARY - MELLANDER
  LIBRARY
5125 N. Spaulding Ave.   Phone: (312) 583-2700
Chicago, IL 60625   Norma S. Goertzen, Dir.

NORTHEASTERN ILLINOIS PLANNING COMMISSION - LIBRARY †
400 W. Madison St.   Phone: (312) 454-0400
Chicago, IL 60606

NORTHEASTERN ILLINOIS UNIVERSITY - LIBRARY
5500 N. St. Louis Ave.   Phone: (312) 583-4050
Chicago, IL 60625   Melvin R. George, Dir.

NORTHERN TRUST COMPANY - LIBRARY †
50 S. LaSalle St.   Phone: (312) 630-6000
Chicago, IL 60675   Marianne S. Lee, Hd.Libn.

NORTHWEST HOSPITAL - MEDICAL LIBRARY
5645 W. Addison St.   Phone: (312) 282-7000
Chicago, IL 60634   Therese Wiedenfeld, Libn.

NORTHWESTERN UNIVERSITY - DENTAL SCHOOL LIBRARY
311 E. Chicago Ave.   Phone: (312) 649-8332
Chicago, IL 60611   Minnie Orfanos, Hd.Libn.

NORTHWESTERN UNIVERSITY - HEALTH SCIENCES LIBRARY †
303 E. Chicago Ave.   Phone: (312) 649-8133
Chicago, IL 60611   Cecile E. Kramer, Dir.

NORTHWESTERN UNIVERSITY - LAW SCHOOL LIBRARY
357 E. Chicago Ave.   Phone: (312) 649-8450
Chicago, IL 60611   George S. Grossman, Libn.

NORWEGIAN-AMERICAN HOSPITAL, INC. - SEUFERT MEMORIAL LIBRARY
  †
1044 N. Francisco Ave.   Phone: (312) 278-8800
Chicago, IL 60622   Estrella P. de la Cruz, Libn.

OGILVY & MATHER, INC. - INFORMATION SERVICES DEPARTMENT
200 E. Randolph Dr., 69th Fl.   Phone: (312) 861-1166
Chicago, IL 60601   Grace A. Villamora, Mgr.

OPEN LANDS PROJECT - LIBRARY
53 W. Jackson Blvd., Rm. 850   Phone: (312) 427-4256
Chicago, IL 60604   Judith M. Stockdale, Exec.Dir.

OUR LADY OF SORROWS BASILICA - ARCHIVES
3121 W. Jackson Blvd.   Phone: (312) 638-5800
Chicago, IL 60612   Rev. Conrad M. Borntrager, O.S.M., Archv.

PACIFIC/ASIAN AMERICAN MENTAL HEALTH RESEARCH CENTER -
  DOCUMENTATION CENTER
Publications Division
1001 W. Van Buren   Phone: (312) 226-0117
Chicago, IL 60607   Dr. Indu Vohra-Sahu, Dir., Doc.Ctr.

PANNELL KERR FORSTER - MANAGEMENT ADVISORY SERVICES - LIBRARY
122 S. Michigan Ave.   Phone: (312) 427-7955
Chicago, IL 60603   Carole A. Ditchie, Res.Asst./Libn.

PEAT, MARWICK, MITCHELL & CO. - AUDIT/MCD LIBRARY
Peat Marwick Plaza
303 E. Wacker Dr.   Phone: (312) 938-1000
Chicago, IL 60601   Mary LaRue Groft, Supv., Info.Serv.

PEOPLES GAS LIGHT AND COKE COMPANY - LIBRARY
122 S. Michigan Ave., Rm. 727   Phone: (312) 431-4677
Chicago, IL 60603   Anne C. Roess, Chf.Libn.

PERKINS AND WILL ARCHITECTS, INC. - RESOURCE CENTER
2 N. LaSalle   Phone: (312) 977-1100
Chicago, IL 60602   Baron Whateley, Specifier

PLAYBOY ENTERPRISES, INC. - PHOTO LIBRARY †
919 N. Michigan Ave.   Phone: (312) 751-8000
Chicago, IL 60611   Clydia Jones, Pict.Libn.

POLISH MUSEUM OF AMERICA - ARCHIVES & LIBRARY
984 Milwaukee Ave.   Phone: (312) 384-3352
Chicago, IL 60622   Rev. Donald Bilinski, O.F.M., Dir./Libn.

POPE, BALLARD, SHEPARD AND FOWLE - LIBRARY †
69 W. Washington St.   Phone: (312) 630-4283
Chicago, IL 60602   Ronald E. Feret

PPG INDUSTRIES, INC. - SPECIALTY PRODUCTS UNIT - LIBRARY
12555 W. Higgins Rd.
Box 66251   Phone: (312) 694-2700
Chicago, IL 60666   Pamela R. Fritz, Info.Spec.

PRC CONSOER, TOWNSEND, INC. - LIBRARY AND INFORMATION CENTER
3 Illinois Center
303 E. Wacker Dr., Suite 600   Phone: (312) 938-0300
Chicago, IL 60601   Mary T. Schramm, Libn./Mgr., Info.Ctr.

PRICE WATERHOUSE - LIBRARY †
200 E. Randolph Dr., Rm. 6200   Phone: (312) 565-1500
Chicago, IL 60601   E. Ann Raup, Libn.

PUERTO RICAN CONGRESS OF MUSIC & ART - LIBRARY
2315 W. North Ave.   Phone: (312) 772-4223
Chicago, IL 60647   Carlos C. Ruiz, Exec.Dir.

RAVENSWOOD HOSPITAL MEDICAL CENTER - MEDICAL-NURSING LIBRARY
  *
4550 N. Winchester at Wilson   Phone: (312) 878-4300
Chicago, IL 60640   Mr. Zia Solomon Gilliana, Med.Libn.

REAL ESTATE RESEARCH CORPORATION - LIBRARY
72 W. Adams St.   Phone: (312) 346-5885
Chicago, IL 60603   Mary Oleksy, Libn.

RED CROSS OF CONSTANTINE - UNITED GRAND IMPERIAL COUNCIL -
  EDWARD A. GLAD MEMORIAL LIBRARY
14 E. Jackson Blvd., Suite 1700   Phone: (312) 427-5670
Chicago, IL 60604   Paul C. Rodenhauser, Grand Recorder

REHABILITATION INSTITUTE OF CHICAGO - LEARNING RESOURCES
  CENTER
345 E. Superior, Rm. 1671   Phone: (312) 649-2859
Chicago, IL 60611   Carol Ann Lauer, Coord.

RESURRECTION HOSPITAL - MEDICAL LIBRARY & ALLIED HEALTH
  SCIENCES
7435 W. Talcott Rd.   Phone: (312) 774-8000
Chicago, IL 60631   Klara B. Goodrich, Med.Libn.

REYNOLDS (Russell) ASSOCIATES, INC. - LIBRARY
200 S. Wacker Dr., Suite 3600   Phone: (312) 782-9862
Chicago, IL 60606-4958   Gerri Hilt, Dir. of Res.

ROCKWELL INTERNATIONAL - GRAPHIC SYSTEMS - TECHNICAL
  INFORMATION CENTER
3100 S. Central Ave.   Phone: (312) 656-8600
Chicago, IL 60650   Joyce Tykol, Libn.

ROOKS, PITTS, FULLAGAR & POUST - LIBRARY
55 W. Monroe, Suite 1500   Phone: (312) 372-5600
Chicago, IL 60603   Nancy J. Henry, Hd.Libn.

ROOSEVELT UNIVERSITY - ARCHIVES
430 S. Michigan Ave.   Phone: (312) 341-3643
Chicago, IL 60605   Wendy Moorhead, Ref.Libn.

ROOSEVELT UNIVERSITY - MUSIC LIBRARY
430 S. Michigan Ave.   Phone: (312) 341-3651
Chicago, IL 60605   Donald Draganski, Libn.

ROOSEVELT UNIVERSITY - ORAL HISTORY PROJECT IN LABOR HISTORY
430 S. Michigan Ave.   Phone: (219) 931-9791
Chicago, IL 60605   Elizabeth Balanoff, Dir.

ROSELAND COMMUNITY HOSPITAL - HEALTH SCIENCE LIBRARY
45 W. 111th St.   Phone: (312) 995-3191
Chicago, IL 60628   Mary T. Hanlon, Libn.

ROSS & HARDIES - LAW LIBRARY
150 N. Michigan Ave., Suite 2500   Phone: (312) 558-1000
Chicago, IL 60601   Janet Collins, Libn.

RUSH-PRESBYTERIAN-ST. LUKE'S MEDICAL CENTER - LIBRARY OF RUSH
  UNIVERSITY
600 S. Paulina St.   Phone: (312) 942-5950
Chicago, IL 60612   Doris Bolef, Dir.

ST. ANNE'S HOSPITAL - PRESIDENTS HEALTH SCIENCES LIBRARY
4950 W. Thomas St.   Phone: (312) 378-7100
Chicago, IL 60651   Christina Rudawski, Lib.Dir.

ST. ANTHONY HOSPITAL - SPRAFKA MEMORIAL HEALTH SCIENCE LIBRARY
  *
2875 W. 19th St.   Phone: (312) 521-1710
Chicago, IL 60623   Karen Ambrose, Lib.Cons.

ST. ELIZABETH'S HOSPITAL - LUKEN HEALTH SCIENCES LIBRARY
1431 N. Claremont Ave.   Phone: (312) 278-2000
Chicago, IL 60622   Christina Rudawski, Lib.Dir.

ST. JOSEPH HOSPITAL - LIBRARY
2900 N. Lake Shore   Phone: (312) 975-3038
Chicago, IL 60657   Katherine Wimmer, Dir., Lib.Serv.

ST. MARY OF NAZARETH HOSPITAL CENTER - SCHOOL OF NURSING
  LIBRARY
1127 N. Oakley Blvd.   Phone: (312) 384-5360
Chicago, IL 60622   Phebe Tinker, Libn.

ST. MARY OF NAZARETH HOSPITAL - SISTER STELLA LOUISE HEALTH
  SCIENCE LIBRARY †
2233 W. Division St.   Phone: (312) 770-2219
Chicago, IL 60622   Janet S. Klieman, Med.Libn.

SARGENT & LUNDY ENGINEERS - COMPUTER SOFTWARE LIBRARY
55 E. Monroe   Phone: (312) 269-3658
Chicago, IL 60603   William J. Kakish, Chf.Libn.

SARGENT & LUNDY ENGINEERS - TECHNICAL LIBRARY
55 E. Monroe St., Rm. 16P41   Phone: (312) 269-3524
Chicago, IL 60603   Helen P. Heisler, Libn.

SCHOLL (Dr. William M.) COLLEGE OF PODIATRIC MEDICINE - LIBRARY
1001 N. Dearborn St.   Phone: (312) 280-2891
Chicago, IL 60610   Richard S. Klein, Dir., Lib.Serv.

SEARS, ROEBUCK AND CO. - ARCHIVES, BUSINESS HISTORY AND
     INFORMATION CENTER
Sears Tower, Dept. 703   Phone: (312) 875-8321
Chicago, IL 60684   Lenore Swoiskin, Dir. of Archv.

SEARS, ROEBUCK AND CO. - MERCHANDISE DEVELOPMENT AND TESTING
     LABORATORY - LIBRARY, DEPARTMENT 817
Sears Tower, 23rd Fl.   Phone: (312) 875-5991
Chicago, IL 60684   Mary M. McCarron, Libn.

SEYFARTH, SHAW, FAIRWEATHER & GERALDSON - LIBRARY
55 E. Monroe St.   Phone: (312) 346-8000
Chicago, IL 60603   Kenneth C. Halicki, Libn.

SHEDD (John G.) AQUARIUM - LIBRARY
1200 S. Lake Shore Dr.   Phone: (312) 939-2426
Chicago, IL 60605   Janet E. Powers, Libn.

SIDLEY AND AUSTIN - LIBRARY
One First National Plaza, Suite 4800   Phone: (312) 853-7475
Chicago, IL 60603   Allyson D. Withers, Hd. Law Libn.

SKIDMORE, OWINGS & MERRILL - LIBRARY
33 W. Monroe St.   Phone: (312) 641-5959
Chicago, IL 60603   Mary K. Woolever, Libn.

SOCIETY OF REAL ESTATE APPRAISERS - LIBRARY
645 N. Michigan Ave.   Phone: (312) 346-7422
Chicago, IL 60611

SONNENSCHEIN CARLIN NATH & ROSENTHAL - LIBRARY
8000 Sears Tower
233 S. Wacker Dr.   Phone: (312) 876-7906
Chicago, IL 60606   Colleen L. McCarroll, Libn.

SOUTH CHICAGO COMMUNITY HOSPITAL - DEPARTMENT OF LIBRARY
     SERVICES
2320 E. 93rd St.   Phone: (312) 978-2000
Chicago, IL 60617   Bruce Ardis, Dir.

SOUTH SHORE HOSPITAL - MEDICAL STAFF LIBRARY *
8015 S. Luella Ave.   Phone: (312) 768-0810
Chicago, IL 60617   Maline Mars, Sec./Libn.

SPERTUS COLLEGE OF JUDAICA - NORMAN AND HELEN ASHER LIBRARY
618 S. Michigan Ave.   Phone: (312) 922-9012
Chicago, IL 60605   Richard W. Marcus, Dir.

STANDARD EDUCATIONAL CORPORATION - EDITORIAL LIBRARY
200 W. Monroe St.   Phone: (312) 346-7440
Chicago, IL 60606   David E. King, Libn.

STANDARD OIL COMPANY OF INDIANA - LIBRARY/INFORMATION CENTER
200 E. Randolph St.   Phone: (312) 856-5961
Chicago, IL 60601   Vicky A. Perlman, Mgr.

STEIN ROE AND FARNHAM - LIBRARY
150 S. Wacker Dr.   Phone: (312) 368-7840
Chicago, IL 60606   Nancy Marano, Libn.

SWEDISH COVENANT HOSPITAL - JOSEPH G. STROMBERG LIBRARY OF
     THE HEALTH SCIENCES
5145 North California Ave.   Phone: (312) 878-8200
Chicago, IL 60625   Jan Zibrat, Health Sci.Libn.

SWEDISH PIONEER HISTORICAL SOCIETY - SWEDISH-AMERICAN
     ARCHIVES OF GREATER CHICAGO
5125 N. Spaulding Ave.   Phone: (312) 583-5722
Chicago, IL 60625   Nancy Kahlich, Archv.

TECHNOMIC INFORMATION SERVICES
One N. Wacker Dr.   Phone: (312) 346-5900
Chicago, IL 60606   Robert W. Depke, II, Mgr., Info.Serv.

TELEMEDIA, INC. - INFORMATION CENTER
310 S. Michigan Ave.   Phone: (312) 987-4068
Chicago, IL 60604   Jane Gibson, Hd.

THEATRE HISTORICAL SOCIETY COLLECTION
2215 W. North Ave.   Phone: (312) 252-7200
Chicago, IL 60647   William Benedict

THOMPSON (J. Walter) COMPANY - INFORMATION CENTER
875 N. Michigan Ave.   Phone: (312) 951-4000
Chicago, IL 60611   Edward G. Strable, V.P., Dir., Info.Serv.

UKRAINIAN MEDICAL ASSOCIATION OF NORTH AMERICA - UKRAINIAN
     MEDICAL ARCHIVES AND LIBRARY
2320 W. Chicago Ave.   Phone: (312) 235-8883
Chicago, IL 60622   Paul Pundy, M.D., Dir.

UNION CARBIDE CORPORATION - FILMS-PACKAGING DIVISION -
     TECHNICAL LIBRARY
6733 W. 65th St.   Phone: (312) 496-4286
Chicago, IL 60638   Mrs. Nijole K. Pupius, Tech.Libn.

UNITED CHARITIES OF CHICAGO - LIBRARY
14 E. Jackson Blvd.   Phone: (312) 461-0800
Chicago, IL 60604   Marie T. Burns, Libn./Rec.Mgr.

U.S. BUREAU OF THE CENSUS - INFORMATION SERVICES PROGRAM -
     CHICAGO REGIONAL OFFICE - REFERENCE CENTER
55 E. Jackson Blvd., Rm. 1306   Phone: (312) 353-0980
Chicago, IL 60604   Stanley D. Moore, Reg.Dir.

U.S. DEPT. OF COMMERCE - INTERNATIONAL TRADE ADMINISTRATION -
     CHICAGO DISTRICT OFFICE LIBRARY
Mid-Continental Plaza Bldg., Rm. 1406
55 E. Monroe   Phone: (312) 353-4450
Chicago, IL 60603   Bernadine C. Roberson, Libn.

U.S. DEPT. OF JUSTICE - UNITED STATES ATTORNEY, NORTHERN
     DISTRICT OF ILLINOIS - LIBRARY
1500 Dirksen Federal Bldg.
219 S. Dearborn St.   Phone: (312) 353-5338
Chicago, IL 60604   Mary Alice Stack, Libn.

U.S. DEPT. OF LABOR - BUREAU OF LABOR STATISTICS - NORTH CENTRAL
     REGIONAL OFFICE REFERENCE LIBRARY
230 S. Dearborn St., 9th Fl.   Phone: (312) 353-1880
Chicago, IL 60604   Ronald M. Guzicki, Supv. Economist

UNITED STATES GYPSUM COMPANY - CORPORATE LIBRARY
101 S. Wacker Dr.   Phone: (312) 321-5810
Chicago, IL 60606   Patricia A. Julien, Libn.

U.S. NATL. ARCHIVES & RECORDS SERVICE - FEDERAL ARCHIVES AND
     RECORDS CENTER, REGION 5
7358 S. Pulaski Rd.   Phone: (312) 581-7816
Chicago, IL 60629   Peter W. Bunce, Chf., Archv.Br.

U.S. RAILROAD RETIREMENT BOARD - LIBRARY
844 Rush St.   Phone: (312) 751-4928
Chicago, IL 60611   Kay Collins, Libn.

U.S. SECURITIES AND EXCHANGE COMMISSION - PUBLIC REFERENCE
     LIBRARY
219 S. Dearborn, Rm. 1242   Phone: (312) 353-7433
Chicago, IL 60604   Donald J. Evers, Chf.Ref.Libn.

U.S. VETERANS ADMINISTRATION (IL-Chicago) - LAKESIDE HOSPITAL
     MEDICAL LIBRARY
333 E. Huron St.   Phone: (312) 943-6600
Chicago, IL 60611   Lydia Tkaczuk, Chf., Lib.Serv.

U.S. VETERANS ADMINISTRATION (IL-Chicago) - WESTSIDE HOSPITAL
     LIBRARY
820 S. Damen Ave.   Phone: (312) 666-6500
Chicago, IL 60612   Lynne D. Morris, Chf., Lib.Serv.

UNITED WAY OF CHICAGO - LIBRARY
125 S. Clark St.   Phone: (312) 580-2697
Chicago, IL 60603-4012   Sally J. Barnum, Mgr.

UNIVERSITY OF CHICAGO - ART LIBRARY
Joseph Regenstein Library
1100 E. 57th St.   Phone: (312) 962-8439
Chicago, IL 60637   Hans Lenneberg, Art Libn.

UNIVERSITY OF CHICAGO - BUSINESS/ECONOMICS LIBRARY
Joseph Regenstein Library
1100 E. 57th St.   Phone: (312) 753-3428
Chicago, IL 60637   Jennette S. Rader, Bus./Econ.Libn.

UNIVERSITY OF CHICAGO - DEPARTMENT OF ART - MAX EPSTEIN
   ARCHIVE
Regenstein Library, Rm. 420
1100 E. 57th St.   Phone: (312) 962-7080
Chicago, IL 60637

UNIVERSITY OF CHICAGO - FAR EASTERN LIBRARY
Joseph Regenstein Library
1100 E. 57th St.   Phone: (312) 962-8436
Chicago, IL 60637   James K.M. Cheng, Cur.

UNIVERSITY OF CHICAGO HOSPITALS & CLINICS - PHARMACEUTICAL
   SERVICES - DRUG INFORMATION CENTER
5841 S. Maryland Ave.   Phone: (312) 947-6046
Chicago, IL 60637   Jeannell M. Mansur, Pharm.D., Dir.

UNIVERSITY OF CHICAGO - JOHN CRERAR LIBRARY
5730 S. Ellis   Phone: (312) 962-7715
Chicago, IL 60637   Patricia K. Swanson, Asst.Dir. for Sci.Libs.

UNIVERSITY OF CHICAGO - LAW SCHOOL LIBRARY
1121 E. 60th St.   Phone: (312) 753-3425
Chicago, IL 60637   Judith M. Wright, Law Libn.

UNIVERSITY OF CHICAGO - MAP COLLECTION
Joseph Regenstein Library
1100 E. 57th St.   Phone: (312) 962-8761
Chicago, IL 60637

UNIVERSITY OF CHICAGO - MUSIC COLLECTION
Joseph Regenstein Library
1100 E. 57th St.   Phone: (312) 962-8451
Chicago, IL 60637   Hans Lenneberg, Music Libn.

UNIVERSITY OF CHICAGO - NATIONAL OPINION RESEARCH CENTER -
   LIBRARY AND DATA ARCHIVES
6030 S. Ellis Ave.   Phone: (312) 962-1213
Chicago, IL 60637   Patrick Bova, Libn.

UNIVERSITY OF CHICAGO - ORIENTAL INSTITUTE - ARCHIVES
1155 E. 58th St.   Phone: (312) 962-9520
Chicago, IL 60637-1569   John A. Larson, Archv.

UNIVERSITY OF CHICAGO - ORIENTAL INSTITUTE - DIRECTOR'S LIBRARY
1155 E. 58th St.   Phone: (312) 962-9537
Chicago, IL 60637   Charles E. Jones, Res.Archv.

UNIVERSITY OF CHICAGO - SOCIAL SERVICES ADMINISTRATION LIBRARY
969 E. 60th St.   Phone: (312) 753-3426
Chicago, IL 60637   Eileen Libby, Libn.

UNIVERSITY OF CHICAGO - SOUTH ASIA COLLECTION
1100 E. 57th St.   Phone: (312) 962-8430
Chicago, IL 60637   Maureen L.P. Patterson, Bibliog./Hd.

UNIVERSITY OF CHICAGO - SPECIAL COLLECTIONS
Joseph Regenstein Library
1100 E. 57th St.   Phone: (312) 962-8705
Chicago, IL 60637   Robert Rosenthal, Cur.

UNIVERSITY OF ILLINOIS AT CHICAGO - ENERGY RESOURCES CENTER -
   DOCUMENTS CENTER
412 S. Peoria St.
Box 4348   Phone: (312) 996-4490
Chicago, IL 60680   Donald R. Bless, Res.Libn.

UNIVERSITY OF ILLINOIS AT CHICAGO - HEALTH SCIENCES CENTER -
   LIBRARY OF THE HEALTH SCIENCES
1750 W. Polk St.   Phone: (312) 996-8974
Chicago, IL 60612   Irwin H. Pizer, Univ.Libn.

UNIVERSITY OF ILLINOIS AT CHICAGO - SCIENCE LIBRARY
Science & Engineering South Bldg.
Box 7565   Phone: (312) 996-5396
Chicago, IL 60680   Cynthia A. Steinke, Sci.Libn.

UNIVERSITY OF ILLINOIS AT CHICAGO - UNIVERSITY LIBRARY - MAP
   SECTION
Box 8198   Phone: (312) 996-5277
Chicago, IL 60680   Marsha L. Selmer, Map Libn.

URBAN INVESTMENT AND DEVELOPMENT COMPANY - INFORMATION
   CENTER
333 N. Wacker Dr.   Phone: (312) 845-3596
Chicago, IL 60606   Charles LaGrutta, Info./Rec.Mgr..

VANDERCOOK COLLEGE OF MUSIC - HARRY RUPPEL MEMORIAL LIBRARY
3209 S. Michigan Ave.   Phone: (312) 225-6288
Chicago, IL 60616   Peter L. Eisenberg, Libn.

VELSICOL CHEMICAL CORPORATION - RESEARCH AND DEVELOPMENT
   DEPARTMENT - LIBRARY
341 E. Ohio St., 3rd Fl.   Phone: (312) 670-4771
Chicago, IL 60611   June M. Snyder, Libn.

VISITING NURSE ASSOCIATION OF CHICAGO - LIBRARY
310 S. Michigan Ave.   Phone: (312) 663-1810
Chicago, IL 60604   Sarah Redinger, Libn.

WEIR (Paul) COMPANY - LIBRARY
20 N. Wacker Dr., Suite 2828   Phone: (312) 346-0275
Chicago, IL 60606   Mary A. Vacula, Libn./Info.Spec.

WEISS (Louis A.) MEMORIAL HOSPITAL - L. LEWIS COHEN MEMORIAL
   MEDICAL LIBRARY
4646 N. Marine Dr.   Phone: (312) 878-8700
Chicago, IL 60640   Iris Sachs, Med.Libn.

WINSTON & STRAWN - LIBRARY
One 1st National Plaza   Phone: (312) 558-5740
Chicago, IL 60603   Donna M. Tuke, Chf.Libn.

WORLD ASSOCIATION OF DOCUMENT EXAMINERS - WADE LIBRARY
111 N. Canal St.   Phone: (312) 930-9446
Chicago, IL 60606   Lee Arnold, Libn.

WORLD BOOK INC.- RESEARCH LIBRARY
Merchandise Mart Plaza   Phone: (312) 341-8777
Chicago, IL 60654   Mary Kayaian, Hd., Lib.Serv.

WORLD WITHOUT WAR COUNCIL - MIDWEST LIBRARY
421 S. Wabash   Phone: (312) 236-7459
Chicago, IL 60605   Robert Woito, Pubn.Dir.

WRIGLEY (Wm., Jr.) COMPANY - CORPORATE LIBRARY
410 N. Michigan Ave.   Phone: (312) 644-2121
Chicago, IL 60611   Linda Hanrath, Corp.Libn.

WRIGLEY (Wm., Jr.) COMPANY - QUALITY ASSURANCE BRANCH LIBRARY
3535 S. Ashland Ave.   Phone: (312) 523-4040
Chicago, IL 60609   Elizabeth R. Cibulskis, Tech.Libn.

WRIGLEY (Wm., Jr.) COMPANY - RESEARCH & DEVELOPMENT LIBRARY
3535 S. Ashland Ave.   Phone: (312) 523-4040
Chicago, IL 60609   Elizabeth R. Cibulskis, Tech.Libn.

YOUNG MEN'S CHRISTIAN ASSOCIATIONS OF THE UNITED STATES OF
   AMERICA - YMCA HISTORICAL LIBRARY
101 N. Wacker Dr.   Phone: (312) 977-0031
Chicago, IL 60606   Ellen Sowchek, Libn.

YOUTH NETWORK COUNCIL, INC. - CLEARINGHOUSE
104 N. Halsted St.   Phone: (312) 226-1200
Chicago, IL 60606   Denis Murstein, Adm.Dir.

ST. JAMES HOSPITAL - HUGO LONG LIBRARY
1423 Chicago Rd.   Phone: (312) 756-1000
Chicago Heights, IL 60411   Margaret A. Lindstrand, Libn.

ST. JOHN UNITED CHURCH OF CHRIST - LIBRARY
307 W. Clay St.   Phone: (618) 344-2526
Collinsville, IL 62234   Norma L. Fischer, Libn.

SOUTHWESTERN ILLINOIS METROPOLITAN AND REGIONAL PLANNING
   COMMISSION - TECHNICAL LIBRARY
203 W. Main St.   Phone: (618) 344-4250
Collinsville, IL 62234   Bonnie C. Moore, Info.Mgr.

LAKEVIEW MEDICAL CENTER - LEARNING RESOURCE CENTER
812 N. Logan Ave.   Phone: (217) 443-5270
Danville, IL 61832   Donna Judd, Libn./Dir.

ST. ELIZABETH HOSPITAL - MEDICAL LIBRARY
600 Sager   Phone: (217) 442-6300
Danville, IL 61832   Rosemary M. Flanagan, Med.Libn.

U.S. VETERANS ADMINISTRATION (IL-Danville) - MEDICAL CENTER
   LIBRARY
                                         Phone: (217) 442-8000
Danville, IL 61832   Betsy Taylor, Chf., Lib.Serv.

ARCHER DANIELS MIDLAND COMPANY - LIBRARY
4666 Faries Pkwy.   Phone: (217) 424-5397
Decatur, IL 62526   Richard E. Wallace, Mgr., Info.Serv.

DECATUR DEPARTMENT OF COMMUNITY DEVELOPMENT - PLANNING
   LIBRARY
One Civic Center Plaza   Phone: (217) 424-2778
Decatur, IL 62523   Robert Menzies, Plan.Coord.

DECATUR HERALD AND REVIEW - LIBRARY
601 E. William St.
Box 311   Phone: (217) 429-5151
Decatur, IL 62523   Gerry Hearn, Lib.Supv.

DECATUR MEMORIAL HOSPITAL - HEALTH SCIENCE LIBRARY
2300 N. Edward St.   Phone: (217) 877-8121
Decatur, IL 62526   John W. Law, Libn.

MACON COUNTY LAW LIBRARY
County Bldg.   Phone: (217) 424-1434
Decatur, IL 62523   Norman C. Higgs, Libn.

MILLIKIN UNIVERSITY - STALEY LIBRARY - SPECIAL COLLECTIONS
1184 W. Main St.   Phone: (217) 424-6214
Decatur, IL 62522   Dr. Charles E. Hale, Lib.Dir.

ST. MARY'S HOSPITAL - HEALTH SCIENCE LIBRARY
1800 E. Lake Shore Dr.   Phone: (217) 429-2966
Decatur, IL 62525   Laura L. Brosamer, Libn.

STALEY (A.E.) MANUFACTURING COMPANY - TECHNICAL INFORMATION
   CENTER
2200 E. Eldorado St.   Phone: (217) 423-4411
Decatur, IL 62525   Ann M. Seidman, Mgr.

BAXTER TRAVENOL LABORATORIES, INC. - BUSINESS AND LAW
   INFORMATION RESOURCE CENTER
2-2W, One Baxter Pkwy.   Phone: (312) 948-3881
Deerfield, IL 60015   Frank J. Locker, Supv.

JENSEN (Rolf) & ASSOCIATES - LIBRARY
104 Wilmot Rd., Suite 201   Phone: (312) 948-0700
Deerfield, IL 60015-5169   Andrea Kiene, Libn.

TRINITY EVANGELICAL DIVINITY SCHOOL - ROLFING MEMORIAL LIBRARY
2065 Half Day Rd.   Phone: (312) 945-8800
Deerfield, IL 60015   Dr. Brewster Porcella, Libn.

CLEARINGHOUSE FOR SOCIOLOGICAL LITERATURE
Dept. of Sociology
Northern Illinois Univ.   Phone: (815) 753-0303
Dekalb, IL 60115   Hugo O. Engelmann, Ed.

DE KALB-PFIZER GENETICS - RESEARCH LIBRARY
Sycamore Rd.   Phone: (815) 758-3461
DeKalb, IL 60115   Dr. Charles F. Krull, V.P., Corn Res.

NORTHERN ILLINOIS UNIVERSITY - FARADAY LIBRARY
Faraday Hall, Rm. 212   Phone: (815) 753-1257
DeKalb, IL 60115   Nestor L. Osorio, Sci.Libn.

NORTHERN ILLINOIS UNIVERSITY - FILM LIBRARY
Altgeld 114   Phone: (815) 753-0171
DeKalb, IL 60115   Gilbert Silverstein, Film Lib.Dir.

NORTHERN ILLINOIS UNIVERSITY - MUSIC LIBRARY
175 Music Bldg.   Phone: (815) 753-1426
DeKalb, IL 60115   Gordon S. Rowley, Music Libn.

NORTHERN ILLINOIS UNIVERSITY - PROGRAM FOR BIOSOCIAL RESEARCH
   - LIBRARY
                                         Phone: (815) 753-0431
DeKalb, IL 60115   Thomas C. Wiegele, Dir.

NORTHERN ILLINOIS UNIVERSITY - REGIONAL HISTORY CENTER
268 Swen Parson Hall   Phone: (815) 753-1779
DeKalb, IL 60115   Glen A. Gildemeister, Dir.

NORTHERN ILLINOIS UNIVERSITY - SOUTHEAST ASIA COLLECTION
Founders Memorial Library   Phone: (815) 753-1819
DeKalb, IL 60115   Lee Dutton, Cur.

NORTHERN ILLINOIS UNIVERSITY - UNIVERSITY ARCHIVES
                                         Phone: (815) 753-1779
DeKalb, IL 60115   Glen A. Gildemeister, Archv.

AMERICAN FOUNDRYMEN'S SOCIETY - TECHNICAL INFORMATION
   CENTER
Golf & Wolf Rds.   Phone: (312) 824-0181
Des Plaines, IL 60016   Ann V. Duggan, Mgr., Lib.Serv.

BORG-WARNER CORPORATION - ROY C. INGERSOLL RESEARCH CENTER -
   TECHNICAL INFORMATION SERVICES
Wolf & Algonquin Sts.   Phone: (312) 827-3131
Des Plaines, IL 60018   Roberta B. Seefeldt, Mgr., Info.Serv.

DE SOTO, INC. - INFORMATION CENTER
1700 S. Mt. Prospect Rd.   Phone: (312) 391-9556
Des Plaines, IL 60018   Cathy Collins Kozelka, Mgr.

DES PLAINES HISTORICAL SOCIETY - JOHN BYRNE MEMORIAL LIBRARY
789 Pearson St.   Phone: (312) 391-5399
Des Plaines, IL 60016   James R. Williams, Musm.Dir.

DOALL COMPANY - LIBRARY
245 N. Laurel Ave.   Phone: (312) 824-1122
Des Plaines, IL 60016

FOREST INSTITUTE OF PROFESSIONAL PSYCHOLOGY - LIBRARY
1717 Rand Rd.   Phone: (312) 635-4333
Des Plaines, IL 60090   Donna E. Bush, Dir., Lib.Serv.

HOLY FAMILY HOSPITAL - HEALTH SCIENCES LIBRARY
100 N. River Rd.   Phone: (312) 297-1800
Des Plaines, IL 60016   Elizabeth Klein, Libn.

MILLION DOLLAR ROUND TABLE - INFORMATION SERVICES
2340 River Rd.   Phone: (312) 298-1120
Des Plaines, IL 60018   John P. Bell, Dir., Info.Serv.

REFRIGERATION SERVICE ENGINEERS SOCIETY - LIBRARY
1666 Rand Rd.   Phone: (312) 297-6464
Des Plaines, IL 60016   Mr. Nari Sethna, Exec.Mgr.

SIEMENS GAMMASONICS, INC. - NUCLEAR MEDICAL DIVISION -
   RESEARCH LIBRARY
2000 Nuclear Dr.   Phone: (312) 635-3643
Des Plaines, IL 60018   Arlene M. Lowden, Libn.

SIGNAL UOP RESEARCH CENTER - TECHNICAL INFORMATION CENTER
50 UOP Plaza
Algonquin & Mt. Prospect Rds.   Phone: (312) 391-3361
Des Plaines, IL 60016-6187   Leonore Rogalski, Mgr.

ZEIGLER COAL COMPANY - BUSINESS LIBRARY
2700 River Rd., Suite 400
Des Plaines, IL 60018

DIXON DEVELOPMENTAL CENTER - PROFESSIONAL LIBRARY
2600 N. Brinton Ave.   Phone: (815) 288-5561
Dixon, IL 61021   Charles Padgett, Libn.

BIBLIOGRAPHIC SERVICE *
4912 Wallbank Ave.
Downers Grove, IL 60515

MITTELHAUSER CORPORATION - LIBRARY
5120 Belmont Rd., Suite G
Downers Grove, IL 60515

OLIN CORPORATION - BRASS GROUP LIBRARY †
                                                 Phone: (618) 258-3198
East Alton, IL 62024   Barbara A. Allen, Libn.

TRI-COUNTY REGIONAL PLANNING COMMISSION - LIBRARY
Box 2200   Phone: (309) 694-4391
East Peoria, IL 61611   Robert L. Pinkerton, Exec.Dir.

MADISON COUNTY HISTORICAL SOCIETY - MUSEUM LIBRARY
715 N. Main St.   Phone: (618) 656-7562
Edwardsville, IL 62025   Josephine Motz, Libn.

SOUTHERN ILLINOIS UNIVERSITY, EDWARDSVILLE - DOCUMENTS
   COLLECTION
Lovejoy Library   Phone: (618) 692-2606
Edwardsville, IL 62026-1001   Robert J. Fortado, Doc.Libn.

SOUTHERN ILLINOIS UNIVERSITY, EDWARDSVILLE - EDUCATION LIBRARY
   †
Lovejoy Library   Phone: (618) 692-2906
Edwardsville, IL 62026-1001   Don Smith, Educ.Libn.

SOUTHERN ILLINOIS UNIVERSITY, EDWARDSVILLE - HUMAN SERVICES
   LIBRARY
SIU Box 24   Phone: (618) 692-2881
Edwardsville, IL 62026   Nancy Bramhall, Sec.

SOUTHERN ILLINOIS UNIVERSITY, EDWARDSVILLE - HUMANITIES & FINE
   ARTS LIBRARY
Lovejoy Library   Phone: (618) 692-2670
Edwardsville, IL 62026-1001

SOUTHERN ILLINOIS UNIVERSITY, EDWARDSVILLE - RESEARCH &
   PROJECTS OFFICE LIBRARY
Graduate School   Phone: (618) 692-3162
Edwardsville, IL 62026-1001   Kate Chappell, Rsrcs.Anl.

SOUTHERN ILLINOIS UNIVERSITY, EDWARDSVILLE - SCIENCE LIBRARY
Lovejoy Library   Phone: (618) 692-3828
Edwardsville, IL 62026-1001   Charlotte Johnson, Sci.Libn.

SOUTHERN ILLINOIS UNIVERSITY, EDWARDSVILLE - SOCIAL SCIENCE/
   BUSINESS/MAP LIBRARY †
Lovejoy Library   Phone: (618) 692-2422
Edwardsville, IL 62026-1001   Marvin Soloman, Soc.Sci./Map Libn.

ST. ANTHONY'S MEMORIAL HOSPITAL - HEALTH SCIENCE LIBRARY
503 N. Maple St.   Phone: (217) 342-2121
Effingham, IL 62401   Sr. M. Angelus Gardiner, Libn.

AEROPHILATELIC FEDERATION OF THE AMERICAS - LIBRARY
Box 1239   Phone: (312) 742-3328
Elgin, IL 60121   Harry Collier, Libn.

CHURCH OF THE BRETHREN GENERAL BOARD - BRETHREN HISTORICAL
   LIBRARY AND ARCHIVES
1451 Dundee Ave.   Phone: (312) 742-5100
Elgin, IL 60120   James R. Lynch, Archv.

ELGIN MENTAL HEALTH CENTER - ANTON BOISEN PROFESSIONAL LIBRARY
750 S. State St.   Phone: (312) 742-1040
Elgin, IL 60120   Jennifer Ford, Libn.

ALEXIAN BROTHERS MEDICAL CENTER - MEDICAL LIBRARY †
800 W. Biesterfield Rd.   Phone: (312) 437-5500
Elk Grove Village, IL 60007   Jocelyn A. Bernholdt, Med.Libn.

CONGREGATION OF THE ALEXIAN BROTHERS - PROVINCIAL ARCHIVES
600 Alexian Way
Elk Grove Village, IL 60007   Bro. Roy Godwin, C.F.A., Prov.Archv.

ELMHURST HISTORICAL MUSEUM - LIBRARY
120 E. Park Ave.   Phone: (312) 833-1457
Elmhurst, IL 60126   Virginia Stewart, Dir.

ELMHURST MEMORIAL HOSPITAL - MARQUARDT MEMORIAL LIBRARY
200 Berteau Ave.   Phone: (312) 833-1400
Elmhurst, IL 60126   Pauline Ng, Dir.

LIZZADRO MUSEUM OF LAPIDARY ART - LIBRARY
220 Cottage Hill Ave.   Phone: (312) 833-1616
Elmhurst, IL 60126   Judith Greene, Exec.Sec.

MASONIC HISTORICAL LIBRARY COLLECTION
1924 N. 74th Ct.   Phone: (312) 456-3260
Elmwood Park, IL 60635   Edmund R. Sadowski, Libn.

AMERICAN ACADEMY OF PEDIATRICS - LIBRARY
1801 Hinman Ave.
Box 1034   Phone: (312) 869-4255
Evanston, IL 60204

AMERICAN HOSPITAL SUPPLY CORPORATION - CORPORATE
   INFORMATION CENTER
One American Plaza   Phone: (312) 866-4586
Evanston, IL 60201   Sharon I. Meyer, Mgr.

BETH EMET, THE FREE SYNAGOGUE - BRUCE GORDON MEMORIAL LIBRARY
1224 Dempster   Phone: (312) 869-4230
Evanston, IL 60202   Myrtle Gordon, Libn.

EVANSTON HISTORICAL SOCIETY - CHARLES GATES DAWES HOME -
   LIBRARY
225 Greenwood St.   Phone: (312) 475-3410
Evanston, IL 60201   Margaret Nicholsen, Libn.

EVANSTON HOSPITAL - WEBSTER MEDICAL LIBRARY
2650 Ridge Ave.   Phone: (312) 492-4585
Evanston, IL 60201   Rose Slowinski, Dir.

FIRST PRESBYTERIAN CHURCH - THOMAS E. BOSWELL MEMORIAL
   LIBRARY
1427 Chicago Ave.   Phone: (312) 864-1472
Evanston, IL 60201   Ruth Powers, Libn.

GARRETT-EVANGELICAL AND SEABURY-WESTERN THEOLOGICAL
   SEMINARIES - UNITED LIBRARY
2021 Sheridan Rd.   Phone: (312) 866-3900
Evanston, IL 60201

LEKOTEK TOY LIBRARY
613 Dempster St.   Phone: (312) 328-0001
Evanston, IL 60201   Sarah deVincentis, Exec.Dir.

LEVERE MEMORIAL FOUNDATION - LIBRARY
1856 Sheridan Rd.   Phone: (312) 475-1856
Evanston, IL 60201   Kenneth D. Tracey, Exec.Dir.

NATIONAL COLLEGE OF EDUCATION - LEARNING RESOURCE CENTERS
2840 Sheridan Rd.   Phone: (312) 256-5150
Evanston, IL 60201   Marilyn A. Lester, Dir. of Lrng.Rsrcs.

NATIONAL FOUNDATION OF FUNERAL SERVICE - BERYL L. BOYER LIBRARY
1600-1612 Central St.   Phone: (312) 328-6545
Evanston, IL 60201   Joe A. Adams, Ph.D., Dir.

NATIONAL WOMAN'S CHRISTIAN TEMPERANCE UNION - FRANCES E.
   WILLARD MEMORIAL LIBRARY
1730 Chicago Ave.   Phone: (312) 864-1396
Evanston, IL 60201   Rosalita J. Leonard, Libn.

NORTHWESTERN UNIVERSITY - ARCHIVES
University Library   Phone: (312) 492-3354
Evanston, IL 60201   Patrick M. Quinn, Univ.Archv.

NORTHWESTERN UNIVERSITY - GEOLOGY LIBRARY
Locy Hall, Rm. 101
Phone: (312) 492-5525
Evanston, IL 60201
Janet Ayers, Geology Libn.

NORTHWESTERN UNIVERSITY - MAP COLLECTION
University Library
Phone: (312) 492-7603
Evanston, IL 60201
Mary Fortney, Map Libn.

NORTHWESTERN UNIVERSITY - MATHEMATICS LIBRARY
Lunt Bldg., Rm. 111
Phone: (312) 492-7627
Evanston, IL 60201
Zita Hayward, Lib.Asst.

NORTHWESTERN UNIVERSITY - MELVILLE J. HERSKOVITS LIBRARY OF
  AFRICAN STUDIES
University Library
Phone: (312) 492-7684
Evanston, IL 60201
Hans E. Panofsky, Cur. of Africana

NORTHWESTERN UNIVERSITY - MUSIC LIBRARY
Phone: (312) 492-3434
Evanston, IL 60201
Don L. Roberts, Hd.

NORTHWESTERN UNIVERSITY - SEELEY G. MUDD LIBRARY FOR SCIENCE
  AND ENGINEERING
2233 Sheridan Rd.
Phone: (312) 492-3362
Evanston, IL 60201
Robert Michaelson, Hd.Libn.

NORTHWESTERN UNIVERSITY - SPECIAL COLLECTIONS DEPARTMENT -
  WOMEN'S COLLECTION
University Library
1935 Sheridan Rd.
Evanston, IL 60201
Sarah Sherman, Women's Coll.Libn.

NORTHWESTERN UNIVERSITY - TRANSPORTATION LIBRARY
Phone: (312) 492-5273
Evanston, IL 60201
Mary Roy, Hd.Libn.

RUST-OLEUM CORPORATION - R & D LIBRARY
2301 Oakton St.
Phone: (312) 864-8200
Evanston, IL 60204
Shari Capra, Supv.

ST. FRANCIS HOSPITAL - SCHOOL OF NURSING LIBRARY
319 Ridge Ave.
Phone: (312) 492-6268
Evanston, IL 60202
Patricia Gibson, Libn.

SHAND, MORAHAN & COMPANY, INC. - LIBRARY
One American Plaza
Phone: (312) 866-2800
Evanston, IL 60201
Deborah A. Schaffer, Libn.

WASHINGTON NATIONAL INSURANCE COMPANY - INFORMATION
  RESOURCES CENTER
1630 Chicago Ave.
Phone: (312) 866-3651
Evanston, IL 60201
Joy M. Blackburn, Libn.

MOTOROLA, INC. - SYSTEMS DIVISION - TECHNICAL LIBRARY
2553 N. Edgington St.
Phone: (312) 451-1000
Franklin Park, IL 60131
Rose Marie Bowsher, Libn.

HONEYWELL, INC. - MICRO SWITCH RESOURCE CENTER
11 Spring St.
Phone: (815) 235-5609
Freeport, IL 61032
Mary Schneider, Libn.

GALESBURG COTTAGE HOSPITAL - HEALTH SERVICES LIBRARY
695 N. Kellogg St.
Phone: (309) 343-8131
Galesburg, IL 61401
Barbara Olson-Bullis, Med.Libn.

GALESBURG PUBLIC LIBRARY - SPECIAL COLLECTIONS
40 E. Simmons St.
Phone: (309) 343-6118
Galesburg, IL 61401
Jane M. Willenborg, Spec.Coll.Libn.

DU PAGE LIBRARY SYSTEM - SYSTEM CENTER
127 S. First St.
Box 268
Phone: (312) 232-8457
Geneva, IL 60134
Alice E. McKinley, Exec.Dir.

CHICAGO MOUNTAINEERING CLUB - JOHN SPECK MEMORIAL LIBRARY
739 Forest Ave.
Phone: (312) 469-3443
Glen Ellyn, IL 60137
George Pokorny, Libn.

FIRST UNITED METHODIST CHURCH - LIBRARY
424 Forest Ave.
Phone: (312) 469-3510
Glen Ellyn, IL 60137
Kathryn Collord, Libn.

CHICAGO BOTANIC GARDEN - LIBRARY
Box 400
Phone: (312) 835-5440
Glencoe, IL 60022
Virginia Henrichs, Libn.

NORTH SHORE CONGREGATION ISRAEL - ROMANEK LIBRARY *
1185 Sheridan Rd.
Phone: (312) 835-0724
Glencoe, IL 60022
Matalie Cohen, Libn.

GLENVIEW AREA HISTORICAL SOCIETY - LIBRARY
1121 Waukegan Rd.
Phone: (312) 724-2235
Glenview, IL 60025
Richard L. Hibbard, Dir.

KRAFT, INC. - BUSINESS RESEARCH CENTER
Kraft Ct.
Phone: (312) 998-2951
Glenview, IL 60025
Dorothy Schmidt, Coord.

KRAFT, INC. - RESEARCH & DEVELOPMENT LIBRARY
801 Waukegan Rd.
Phone: (312) 998-3707
Glenview, IL 60025
Helen Pettway, Libn.

NATIONAL INVESTIGATIONS COMMITTEE ON AERIAL PHENOMENA -
  INFORMATION CENTER
2926 Applegate Rd.
Glenview, IL 60025
Sherman J. Larsen, Pres.

SCOTT, FORESMAN & COMPANY, INC. - EDITORIAL LIBRARY
1900 E. Lake Ave.
Phone: (312) 729-3000
Glenview, IL 60025
S. Donald Robertson, Hd.Libn.

ZENITH ELECTRONICS CORPORATION - TECHNICAL LIBRARY
1000 N. Milwaukee Ave.
Phone: (312) 391-8452
Glenview, IL 60025
Ruby Chu, Hd.Libn.

U.S. NAVY - NAVAL DENTAL RESEARCH INSTITUTE - LIBRARY
Naval Base, Bldg. 1-H
Phone: (312) 688-5647
Great Lakes, IL 60088
Myra J. Rouse, Libn.

U.S. NAVY - NAVAL HOSPITAL (IL-Great Lakes) - MEDICAL LIBRARY
Bldg. 200-H
Phone: (312) 688-4601
Great Lakes, IL 60088
Phyllis A. Gibbs, Med.Libn.

INGALLS MEMORIAL HOSPITAL - MEDICAL LIBRARY
One Ingalls Dr.
Phone: (312) 333-2300
Harvey, IL 60426
Carol Ross, Libn.

CONGREGATION SOLEL - LIBRARY
1301 Clavey Rd.
Box 838
Phone: (312) 433-3555
Highland Park, IL 60035

HIGHLAND PARK HISTORICAL SOCIETY - LIBRARY
326 Central Ave.
Box 56
Phone: (312) 432-7090
Highland Park, IL 60035
Betty M. Mills, Exec.Dir.

NATIONAL ASSOCIATION OF ANOREXIA NERVOSA AND ASSOCIATED
  DISORDERS, INC. (ANAD) - LIBRARY
Box 271
Phone: (312) 831-3438
Highland Park, IL 60035
Vivian Meehan, Adm.Dir.

NORTH SUBURBAN SYNAGOGUE BETH EL - MAXWELL ABBELL LIBRARY
1175 Sheridan Rd.
Phone: (312) 432-8900
Highland Park, IL 60035
Edie Salzman, Libn.

MADDEN (John J.) MENTAL HEALTH CENTER - PROFESSIONAL LIBRARY
1200 S. 1st Ave.
Phone: (312) 345-9870
Hines, IL 60141
Dr. Thomas Lombardo, Dir., Staff Dev.

U.S. VETERANS ADMINISTRATION (IL-Hines) - LIBRARY SERVICES (142D)
Edward Hines, Jr. Medical Center
Phone: (312) 343-7200
Hines, IL 60141
Bill Leavens, Chf.Libn.

HERMAN SMITH (Herman) ASSOCIATES - LIBRARY
120 E. Ogden Ave.
Phone: (312) 323-3510
Hinsdale, IL 60521
Kim M. Garber, Libn.

HINSDALE SANITARIUM AND HOSPITAL - A.C. LARSON LIBRARY
120 N. Oak St.   Phone: (312) 887-2868
Hinsdale, IL 60521   Richard L. Cook, Hosp.Libn.

ILLINOIS SCHOOL FOR THE DEAF - SCHOOL MEDIA CENTER
125 Webster   Phone: (217) 245-5141
Jacksonville, IL 62650   Bill Stark, Dir.

ILLINOIS SCHOOL FOR THE VISUALLY IMPAIRED - LIBRARY
658 E. State St.   Phone: (217) 245-4101
Jacksonville, IL 62650   Helen L. Curtis, Libn.

JACKSONVILLE MENTAL HEALTH AND DEVELOPMENTAL CENTER - LIBRARY
1201 S. Main St.   Phone: (217) 245-2111
Jacksonville, IL 62650

PASSAVANT MEMORIAL AREA HOSPITAL ASSOCIATION - SIBERT LIBRARY
1600 W. Walnut St.   Phone: (217) 245-9541
Jacksonville, IL 62650   Dorothy H. Knight, Libn.

ST. JOSEPH HOSPITAL - HEALTH SCIENCE LIBRARY *
333 N. Madison St.   Phone: (815) 725-7133
Joliet, IL 60435   Catherine Siron, Coord., Lib.Serv.

SILVER CROSS HOSPITAL - MEDICAL LIBRARY
1200 Maple Rd.   Phone: (815) 740-1100
Joliet, IL 60432   Mary Ingmire, Libn.

ARMOUR PHARMACEUTICAL COMPANY - LIBRARY *
Rte. 50 N., Box 511   Phone: (815) 932-6771
Kankakee, IL 60901   Shirley Wells, Libn.

KANKAKEE COUNTY HISTORICAL SOCIETY - LIBRARY
Eighth & Water St.   Phone: (815) 932-5279
Kankakee, IL 60901   Don Des Lauriers, Cur.

KANKAKEE DAILY JOURNAL - LIBRARY
8 Dearborn Sq.   Phone: (815) 937-3378
Kankakee, IL 60901   Glory Klasey, Hd.Libn.

RIVERSIDE MEDICAL CENTER - MEDICAL LIBRARY †
350 N. Wall St.   Phone: (815) 933-1671
Kankakee, IL 60901

SHAPIRO (Samuel H.) DEVELOPMENTAL CENTER - PROFESSIONAL LIBRARY
100 E. Jeffery St.   Phone: (815) 939-8419
Kankakee, IL 60901   Juanita Licht, Resident Staff Libn.

KENILWORTH HISTORICAL SOCIETY - KILNER LIBRARY
415 Kenilworth Ave.   Phone: (312) 251-2565
Kenilworth, IL 60043   George A. Veeder, Pres.

COMMUNITY MEMORIAL GENERAL HOSPITAL - MEDICAL LIBRARY
5101 Willow Springs Rd.   Phone: (312) 579-4040
La Grange, IL 60525   Patricia J. Grundke, Libn.

GENERAL MOTORS CORPORATION - ELECTRO-MOTIVE DIVISION -
    ENGINEERING LIBRARY
9301 55th St.   Phone: (312) 387-6706
La Grange, IL 60525   Eleanor Spolarich, Libn.

AMERICAN NUCLEAR SOCIETY - LIBRARY
555 N. Kensington Ave.   Phone: (312) 352-6611
La Grange Park, IL 60525   Lois S. Webster, Mgr., Info.Rsrcs.

NORTH SUBURBAN LIBRARY SYSTEM & SUBURBAN LIBRARY SYSTEM -
    SUBURBAN AV SERVICE
920 Barnsdale Rd.   Phone: (312) 352-7671
La Grange Park, IL 60525   Leon L. Drolet, Jr., Dir.

LAKE FOREST COLLEGE - DONNELLEY LIBRARY - SPECIAL COLLECTIONS
College & Sheridan Rds.   Phone: (312) 234-3100
Lake Forest, IL 60045   Arthur H. Miller, Jr., Coll.Libn.

LAKE FOREST COLLEGE - THOMAS OSCAR FREEMAN MEMORIAL LIBRARY
                                          Phone: (312) 234-3100
Lake Forest, IL 60045   Arthur H. Miller, Jr., Coll.Libn.

LAKE FOREST HOSPITAL - MEDICAL STAFF LIBRARY
660 N. Westmoreland Rd.   Phone: (312) 234-5600
Lake Forest, IL 60045   Bettylou Cummings, Med. Staff Coord.

GRACE (W.R.) AND COMPANY - DEARBORN CHEMICAL (U.S.) LIBRARY
300 Genesee St.   Phone: (312) 483-8241
Lake Zurich, IL 60047   Martha M. Mitchell, Libn.

CONDELL MEMORIAL HOSPITAL - FOHRMAN LIBRARY *
900 S. Garfield Ave.   Phone: (312) 362-2900
Libertyville, IL 60048   Emily Bergmann, Libn.

FIRST PRESBYTERIAN CHURCH - LIBRARY *
225 W. Maple Ave.   Phone: (312) 362-2174
Libertyville, IL 60048

HOLLISTER INCORPORATED - CORPORATE LIBRARY
2000 Hollister Dr.   Phone: (312) 680-1000
Libertyville, IL 60090   Elizabeth A. Cunningham, Corp.Libn.

LAKE COUNTY FOREST PRESERVE DISTRICT - RYERSON NATURE LIBRARY
2000 N. Milwaukee Ave.   Phone: (312) 948-7750
Libertyville, IL 60048   Steven E. Meyer, Supv. of Educ.

UNITED STATES GYPSUM COMPANY - GRAHAM J. MORGAN RESEARCH
    LIBRARY
700 N. Hwy. 45   Phone: (312) 362-9797
Libertyville, IL 60048   Marie Ehrmann, Res.Libn.

LINCOLN CHRISTIAN COLLEGE & SEMINARY - JESSIE C. EURY LIBRARY †
Keokuk & Limit Sts.
Box 178   Phone: (217) 732-3168
Lincoln, IL 62656   Thomas M. Tanner, Libn.

HEWITT ASSOCIATES - LIBRARY
100 Half Day   Phone: (312) 295-5000
Lincolnshire, IL 60015   Loralie Van Sluys, Libn.

DAWE'S LABORATORIES, LTD. - TECHNICAL AND AGRICULTURAL
    LIBRARIES *
7100 N. Tripp Ave.   Phone: (312) 982-9540
Lincolnwood, IL 60646   Cameron Gillingham

AT & T BELL LABORATORIES & TECHNOLOGIES - INFORMATION RESOURCE
    CENTER
2600 Warrenville Rd.   Phone: (312) 260-4342
Lisle, IL 60532   Patti Ruocco, Libn.

BELL COMMUNICATIONS TECHNICAL EDUCATION CENTER - LEARNING
    RESOURCE CENTER
6200 Rt. 53   Phone: (312) 960-6377
Lisle, IL 60532   Garnet Hicks, Assoc.Mgr.

ILLINOIS BENEDICTINE COLLEGE - THEODORE LOWNIK LIBRARY
5700 College Rd.   Phone: (312) 960-1500
Lisle, IL 60532   Bert A. Thompson, Dir., Lib.Serv.

MORTON ARBORETUM - STERLING MORTON LIBRARY
                                          Phone: (312) 968-0074
Lisle, IL 60532   Ian MacPhail, Libn.

WATER QUALITY ASSOCIATION - RESEARCH COUNCIL LIBRARY
4151 Naperville Rd.   Phone: (312) 369-1600
Lisle, IL 60532   Douglas R. Oberhamer, Exec.Dir.

WILL COUNTY HISTORICAL SOCIETY - ARCHIVES
803 S. State St.   Phone: (815) 838-5080
Lockport, IL 60441   Rose Bucciferro, Cur.

MIDWEST COLLEGE OF ENGINEERING - JOSEPH M. HARRER LIBRARY
440 S. Finley Rd.
Box 127   Phone: (312) 627-6850
Lombard, IL 60148   Margot Fruehe, Dir.

NATIONAL COLLEGE OF CHIROPRACTIC - LEARNING RESOURCE CENTER
200 E. Roosevelt Rd.   Phone: (312) 629-2000
Lombard, IL 60148   Joyce Whitehead, Dir.

KEMPER GROUP - LIBRARY
Library, F-5   Phone: (312) 540-2229
Long Grove, IL 60049   Evelyn Giannini, Libn.

AKZO CHEMIE AMERICA - RESEARCH LIBRARY
8401 W. 47th St.   Phone: (312) 442-7100
McCook, IL 60525   Robyn Petry, Hd.Libn.

AMERICAN CRITICAL CARE - INFORMATION CENTER
1600 Waukegan Rd.   Phone: (312) 473-3000
McGaw Park, IL 60085   Marlene Galante Kozak, Mgr., Info.Serv.

WESTERN ILLINOIS UNIVERSITY - CENTER FOR WEST CENTRAL ILLINOIS
    REGIONAL STUDIES
                                                Phone: (309) 298-2411
Macomb, IL 61455   Dr. John Hallwas, Dir.

WESTERN ILLINOIS UNIVERSITY - GEOGRAPHY & MAP LIBRARY
                                                Phone: (309) 298-1171
Macomb, IL 61455   John V. Bergen, Map Libn.

WESTERN ILLINOIS UNIVERSITY - LIBRARIES
                                                Phone: (309) 298-2411
Macomb, IL 61455   Patricia A. Gogeen, Dir.

WESTERN ILLINOIS UNIVERSITY - MUSIC LIBRARY
204 Browne Hall   Phone: (309) 298-1105
Macomb, IL 61455   Allie Wise Goudy, Music Libn.

OLIN CORPORATION - SOLID PROPELLANT ORGANIZATION - RESEARCH
    LIBRARY †
Drawer G   Phone: (618) 985-8211
Marion, IL 62959

U.S. VETERANS ADMINISTRATION (IL- Marion) - HOSPITAL LIBRARY
W. Main St.   Phone: (618) 997-5311
Marion, IL 62959   Joy E. Zuger, Chf., Lib.Serv.

MARISSA HISTORICAL & GENEALOGICAL SOCIETY - LIBRARY
Box 27
Marissa, IL 62257

LOYOLA UNIVERSITY OF CHICAGO - MEDICAL CENTER LIBRARY
2160 S. First Ave.   Phone: (312) 531-3192
Maywood, IL 60153   James C. Cox, Chf.Libn.

ALBERTO-CULVER COMPANY - RESEARCH LIBRARY
2525 Armitage Ave.
Melrose Park, IL 60160

WESTLAKE COMMUNITY HOSPITAL - LIBRARY
1225 Superior St.   Phone: (312) 681-3000
Melrose Park, IL 60160   Carol D. Strauss, Libn.

WITCO CHEMICAL CORPORATION - RICHARDSON GROUP - LIBRARY *
2701 W. Lake St.   Phone: (312) 344-4300
Melrose Park, IL 60160   Candi Strecker, Libn.

FORT MASSAC HISTORIC SITE - LIBRARY
Box 708   Phone: (618) 524-9321
Metropolis, IL 62960   Paul E. Fellows, Site Supt.

BLACK HAWK COLLEGE - LEARNING RESOURCES CENTER
6600 34th Ave.   Phone: (309) 796-1311
Moline, IL 61265   James Copas, Act.Chm.,Lib.Serv.

DEERE & COMPANY - LAW LIBRARY
John Deere Rd.   Phone: (309) 752-4165
Moline, IL 61265   Donna J. Eudaley, Adm.Sec.

DEERE & COMPANY - LIBRARY
John Deere Rd.   Phone: (309) 752-4442
Moline, IL 61265   Betty S. Hagberg, Mgr., Lib.Serv.

DEERE & COMPANY - TECHNICAL CENTER LIBRARY
3300 River Dr.   Phone: (309) 757-5363
Moline, IL 61265   Doris E. Starkey, Ref.Libn.

LUTHERAN HOSPITAL - MEDICAL STAFF LIBRARY AND SCHOOL FOR
    NURSES LIBRARY
501 10th Ave.   Phone: (309) 757-2912
Moline, IL 61265   Jeanne A. Gittings, Med.Libn.

(Moline) DAILY DISPATCH - LIBRARY
1720 5th Ave.   Phone: (309) 764-4344
Moline, IL 61265   Marlene Gantt, Libn.

NORTHERN PETROCHEMICAL COMPANY - TECHNICAL CENTER LIBRARY
                                                Phone: (815) 942-7558
Morris, IL 60450   Ingrid M. Voss, Libn.

CRANE PACKING COMPANY - TECHNICAL LIBRARY
6400 Oakton St.   Phone: (312) 967-3790
Morton Grove, IL 60053   Margaret W. Ashworth, Libn.

TRAVENOL LABORATORIES, INC. - INFORMATION RESOURCE CENTER
6301 Lincoln Ave.   Phone: (312) 965-4700
Morton Grove, IL 60053   Diane H. Sherry, Mgr., Info.Rsrc.Ctr.

INSTITUTE OF ENVIRONMENTAL SCIENCES - LIBRARY
940 E. Northwest Hwy.   Phone: (312) 255-1561
Mt. Prospect, IL 60056   Betty L. Peterson, Exec.Dir.

NORTHWEST MUNICIPAL CONFERENCE - GOVERNMENT INFORMATION
    CENTER
Mt. Prospect Public Library
10 S. Emerson St.   Phone: (312) 398-6460
Mt. Prospect, IL 60056   Kenneth L. Gross, Lib.Serv.Dir.

GOOD SAMARITAN HOSPITAL - HEALTH-SCIENCE LIBRARY
605 N. 12th St.   Phone: (618) 242-4600
Mt. Vernon, IL 62864   Debbie Greene, Libn.

ILLINOIS STATE - APPELLATE COURT, 5TH DISTRICT - LIBRARY
14th & Main St.   Phone: (618) 242-3120
Mt. Vernon, IL 62864   Walter T. Simmons, Ck. of Court

ST. MARY OF THE LAKE SEMINARY - FEEHAN MEMORIAL LIBRARY
                                                Phone: (312) 566-6401
Mundelein, IL 60060   Gloria Sieben, Libn.

AT & T BELL LABORATORIES - LIBRARY
                                                Phone: (312) 690-2550
Naperville, IL 60540   Robert E. Furlong, Lib. Group Supv.

NALCO CHEMICAL COMPANY - TECHNICAL CENTER - INFORMATION
    SERVICES
1601 W. Diehl Rd.   Phone: (312) 961-9500
Naperville, IL 60566   Stephen Boyle, Supv., Info.Serv.

NORTH CENTRAL COLLEGE - OESTERLE LIBRARY - SPECIAL COLLECTIONS
320 E. School Ave.   Phone: (312) 355-0597
Naperville, IL 60566   Harriet Arklie, Dir.

STANDARD OIL COMPANY OF INDIANA - CENTRAL RESEARCH LIBRARY
Amoco Research Center, Box 400   Phone: (312) 420-5545
Naperville, IL 60566   B. Camille Stryck, Res.Supv.

GARD - LIBRARY
7501 N. Natchez Ave.   Phone: (312) 647-9000
Niles, IL 60648   Ida Carter, Tech.Libn.

MEDICAL RESEARCH LABORATORIES - LIBRARY *
7450 Natchez Ave.   Phone: (312) 792-2666
Niles, IL 60648   Patrick Murphy, Libn.

TRIODYNE INC. CONSULTING ENGINEERS - INFORMATION CENTER
5950 W. Touhy Ave.   Phone: (312) 677-4730
Niles, IL 60648   Beth A. Hamilton, Sr.Info.Sci.

ILLINOIS STATE UNIVERSITY - MILNER LIBRARY - SPECIAL COLLECTIONS
                                                Phone: (309) 438-3675
Normal, IL 61761   Fred M. Peterson, Univ.Libn.

ABBOTT LABORATORIES - ABBOTT INFORMATION SERVICES
1400 Sheridan Rd.   Phone: (312) 688-2513
North Chicago, IL 60064   Dr. Ronald G. Wiegand, Mgr., Info.Serv.

U.S. VETERANS ADMINISTRATION (IL-North Chicago) - HOSPITAL LIBRARY
Phone: (312) 689-1900
North Chicago, IL 60064   Carl Worstell, Chf.Libn.

UNIVERSITY OF HEALTH SCIENCES/CHICAGO MEDICAL SCHOOL -
LIBRARY
3333 Green Bay Rd.   Phone: (312) 578-3655
North Chicago, IL 60064   Nancy W. Garn, Dir.

ALLSTATE INSURANCE COMPANY - LAW LIBRARY
Allstate Plaza, Bldg. E5   Phone: (312) 291-5407
Northbrook, IL 60062   Alice Bruemner, Lib.Serv.Supv.

DART & KRAFT, INC. - CORPORATE LIBRARY
2211 Sanders Rd.   Phone: (312) 498-8569
Northbrook, IL 60062   Mary E. Tyner, Corp.Libn.

EXTEL CORPORATION - TEHNICAL LIBRARY †
4000 Commercial Ave.   Phone: (312) 291-2766
Northbrook, IL 60062   Elizabeth Ziegler, Tech.Libn.

UNDERWRITERS LABORATORIES INC. - STANDARDS REFERENCE CENTER
333 Pfingsten Rd.   Phone: (312) 272-8800
Northbrook, IL 60062   A.N. Angonese, Sr.Assoc.Mng.Engr.

STEPAN COMPANY - TECHNICAL INFORMATION CENTER
Edens & Winnetka   Phone: (312) 446-7500
Northfield, IL 60093   Mary R. Davis, Supv.

GTE COMMUNICATION SYSTEMS - LIBRARY
400 N. Wolf Rd., A-6
Box 2317   Phone: (312) 681-7118
Northlake, IL 60164   Jane Yu Lee, Libn.

BETHANY AND NORTHERN BAPTIST THEOLOGICAL SEMINARIES - LIBRARY
Butterfield & Meyers Rds.   Phone: (312) 620-2214
Oak Brook, IL 60521   Murray L. Wagner, Hd.Libn.

CHICAGO BRIDGE & IRON COMPANY - TECHNICAL LIBRARY
800 Jorie Blvd.   Phone: (312) 654-7279
Oak Brook, IL 60521   Suzanne D. Beatty, Tech.Libn.

RADIOLOGICAL SOCIETY OF NORTH AMERICA, INC. - LIBRARY
1415 W. 22nd St.
Oak Brook Regency Towers, Suite 1150   Phone: (312) 920-2670
Oak Brook, IL 60521

SWIFT AND COMPANY - RESEARCH AND DEVELOPMENT INFORMATION
CENTER †
1919 Swift Dr.   Phone: (312) 325-9320
Oak Brook, IL 60521   Marcus Bornfleth, Hd., Info.Ctr.

TRI BROOK GROUP, INC. - LIBRARY
1100 Jorie Blvd., Suite 173   Phone: (312) 654-8070
Oak Brook, IL 60521   Sandra Rumbyrt, Asst.Libn.

OAK FOREST HOSPITAL - PROFESSIONAL LIBRARY †
15900 S. Cicero Ave.   Phone: (312) 928-4200
Oak Forest, IL 60452   Delores I. Quinn, Libn.

SLOVAK CATHOLIC CHARITABLE ORGANIZATION - SLOVAK CULTURAL
CENTER - LIBRARY
5900 W. 147th St.   Phone: (312) 687-2877
Oak Forest, IL 60452   Sr. M. Methodia Machalica, Dir.

CHRIST HOSPITAL - HOSPITAL LIBRARY
4440 W. 95th St.   Phone: (312) 425-8000
Oak Lawn, IL 60453   Gerald Dujsik, Lib.Mgr.

EVANGELICAL SCHOOL OF NURSING - WOJNIAK MEMORIAL LIBRARY
9345 S. Kilbourn   Phone: (312) 425-8000
Oak Lawn, IL 60453   Gerald Dujsik, Lib.Mgr.

OAK LAWN PUBLIC LIBRARY - LOCAL HISTORY ROOM
9427 S. Raymond Ave.   Phone: (312) 422-4990
Oak Lawn, IL 60453   Gerald R. Anderson, Local Hist.Libn.

EMMAUS BIBLE SCHOOL - LIBRARY
156 N. Oak Park Ave.   Phone: (312) 383-7000
Oak Park, IL 60301   John Rush, Libn.

INSTITUTE FOR ADVANCED PERCEPTION - LIBRARY
719 S. Clarence Ave.   Phone: (312) 386-1742
Oak Park, IL 60304   Harold S. Schroeppel, Exec.Sec.

OAK PARK PUBLIC LIBRARY - LOCAL AUTHOR AND LOCAL HISTORY
COLLECTIONS
834 Lake St.   Phone: (312) 383-8200
Oak Park, IL 60301   Barbara Ballinger, Hd.Libn.

WEST SUBURBAN HOSPITAL MEDICAL CENTER - WALTER LAWRENCE
MEMORIAL LIBRARY
Erie at Austin   Phone: (312) 383-6200
Oak Park, IL 60302   Julia B. Faust, Dir. of Lib. & Info.Serv.

OGLESBY HISTORICAL SOCIETY - LIBRARY
Oglesby Public Library
128 W. Walnut   Phone: (815) 883-3619
Oglesby, IL 61348   Albert Moyle, Pres.

RICHLAND MEMORIAL HOSPITAL - STAFF LIBRARY
800 East Locust   Phone: (618) 395-2131
Olney, IL 62450   Jan Nalin, Dir., Med.Rec.Dept.

CHICAGO COLLEGE OF OSTEOPATHIC MEDICINE - OLYMPIA FIELDS
OSTEOPATHIC MEDICAL CENTER LIBRARY
20201 S. Crawford   Phone: (312) 747-4000
Olympia Fields, IL 60461   Lois F. Hayes, Med.Libn.

NORTHERN ILLINOIS UNIVERSITY - TAFT FIELD CAMPUS -
INSTRUCTIONAL MATERIALS CENTER
Box 299   Phone: (815) 732-2111
Oregon, IL 61061   Elizabeth McKay, Dir.

ILLINOIS STATE - APPELLATE COURT, 3RD DISTRICT - LIBRARY
1004 Columbus St.   Phone: (815) 434-5050
Ottawa, IL 61350   Sharon Smith, Libn.

AMERICAN SOCIETY OF ARTISTS, INC. - RESOURCE CENTER
Box 1326   Phone: (312) 751-2500
Palatine, IL 60078   Donald Metcoff, Libn.

PALOS COMMUNITY HOSPITAL - MEDICAL LIBRARY
80th Ave. at McCarthy Rd.   Phone: (312) 361-4500
Palos Heights, IL 60463   Gail Waldoch, Libn.

OUTLOOK - OUTLOOK ACCESS CENTER *
105 Wolpers Rd.   Phone: (312) 481-6168
Park Forest, IL 60466   Elizabeth Hagens, Dir.

PARK FOREST PUBLIC LIBRARY - ORAL HISTORY OF PARK FOREST
COLLECTION
400 Lakewood Blvd.   Phone: (312) 748-3731
Park Forest, IL 60466   Neal Ney, Adm.Libn.

AMERICAN SOCIETY OF ANESTHESIOLOGISTS - WOOD LIBRARY-MUSEUM
OF ANESTHESIOLOGY
515 Busse Hwy.   Phone: (312) 825-5586
Park Ridge, IL 60068   Patrick Sim, Libn.

AMERICAN SOCIETY OF SAFETY ENGINEERS - TECHNICAL INFORMATION
CENTER
850 Busse Hwy.   Phone: (312) 692-4121
Park Ridge, IL 60068   N.J. Hudson, Mgr., Tech.Serv.

DAMES & MOORE - CHICAGO LIBRARY
1550 Northwest Highway   Phone: (312) 297-6120
Park Ridge, IL 60068   Patricia B. Krzysiak, Libn.

LUTHERAN GENERAL HOSPITAL - LIBRARY †
1775 Dempster St.   Phone: (312) 696-5494
Park Ridge, IL 60068   Joanne Crispen, Dir. of Lib.Serv.

DIRKSEN (Everett McKinley) CONGRESSIONAL LEADERSHIP RESEARCH
CENTER - LIBRARY
Broadway & Fourth St.   Phone: (309) 347-7113
Pekin, IL 61554   Frank H. Mackaman, II, Exec.Dir.

BAHAI REFERENCE LIBRARY OF PEORIA
5209 N. University   Phone: (309) 692-7597
Peoria, IL 61614   Carolyn Henderer, Libn.

BRADLEY UNIVERSITY - VIRGINIUS H. CHASE SPECIAL COLLECTIONS
    CENTER - APCO HISTORICAL COLLECTION
Cullom-Davis Library   Phone: (309) 676-7611
Peoria, IL 61625   Charles J. Frey, Spec.Coll.Libn.

BRADLEY UNIVERSITY - VIRGINIUS H. CHASE SPECIAL COLLECTIONS
    CENTER - CHARLES A. BENNETT COLLECTION
Cullom-Davis Library   Phone: (309) 676-7611
Peoria, IL 61625   Charles J. Frey, Spec.Coll.Libn.

BRADLEY UNIVERSITY - VIRGINIUS H. CHASE SPECIAL COLLECTIONS
    CENTER - CHASE COLLECTION
Cullom-Davis Library   Phone: (309) 676-7611
Peoria, IL 61625   Charles J. Frey, Spec.Coll.Libn.

BRADLEY UNIVERSITY - VIRGINIUS H. CHASE SPECIAL COLLECTIONS
    CENTER - LINCOLN COLLECTIONS
Cullom-Davis Library   Phone: (309) 676-7611
Peoria, IL 61625   Charles J. Frey, Spec.Coll.Libn.

CATERPILLAR TRACTOR COMPANY - BUSINESS LIBRARY †
100 N.E. Adams St.   Phone: (309) 675-4622
Peoria, IL 61629   Amy Wolf, Lib.Supv.

CATERPILLAR TRACTOR COMPANY - TECHNICAL INFORMATION CENTER
Technical Center   Phone: (309) 578-6118
Peoria, IL 61629   Carol E. Mulvaney, Tech.Libn.

METHODIST MEDICAL CENTER OF ILLINOIS - LEARNING RESOURCE
    CENTER
221 N.E. Glen Oak   Phone: (309) 672-5570
Peoria, IL 61636   Dorothy Mortimer, Libn.

METHODIST MEDICAL CENTER OF ILLINOIS - MEDICAL LIBRARY
221 N.E. Glen Oak   Phone: (309) 672-4937
Peoria, IL 61636   Trudy Landwirth, Dir.

PEORIA COUNTY LAW LIBRARY
Peoria County Court House, Rm. 209   Phone: (309) 672-6084
Peoria, IL 61602   Mary Louise Jacquin, Libn.

PEORIA HISTORICAL SOCIETY - HARRY L. SPOONER MEMORIAL LIBRARY
Bradley Univ., Cullom-Davis Library
Glenwood & Bradley Aves.   Phone: (309) 676-7611
Peoria, IL 61603   Charles Frey, Spec.Coll.Libn.

PROCTOR COMMUNITY HOSPITAL - MEDICAL LIBRARY
5409 N. Knoxville Ave.   Phone: (309) 691-4702
Peoria, IL 61614   Nancy Camacho, Libn.

ST. FRANCIS HOSPITAL - MEDICAL CENTER - MEDICAL LIBRARY *
530-616 N.E. Glen Oak Ave.   Phone: (309) 672-2210
Peoria, IL 61637   Mary Anne Parr, Med.Libn.

U.S.D.A. - AGRICULTURAL RESEARCH SERVICE - NORTHERN REGIONAL
    RESEARCH CENTER LIBRARY
1815 N. University St.   Phone: (309) 685-4011
Peoria, IL 61604   Donald L. Blevins, Libn.

UNIVERSITY OF ILLINOIS AT CHICAGO - HEALTH SCIENCES CENTER -
    LIBRARY OF THE HEALTH SCIENCES
Box 1649   Phone: (309) 671-3095
Peoria, IL 61656   Michele Johns, Br.Libn.

WABCO - CONSTRUCTION AND MINING EQUIPMENT - ENGINEERING
    TECHNICAL LIBRARY
2301 N.E. Adams St.   Phone: (309) 672-7143
Peoria, IL 61639   Marilyn G. Kopp, Libn.

ZELLER (George A.) MENTAL HEALTH CENTER - PROFESSIONAL LIBRARY
5407 N. University   Phone: (309) 691-2200
Peoria, IL 61614   Barbara Haun, Libn.

ST. JAMES HOSPITAL - MEDICAL LIBRARY
610 E. Water St.   Phone: (815) 842-2828
Pontiac, IL 61764   Jill A. Kresse, Lib.Mgr.

BUREAU COUNTY HISTORICAL SOCIETY - MUSEUM & LIBRARY
109 Park Ave., W.
Princeton, IL 61356   Mrs. D. Field Williams, Cur.

PERRY MEMORIAL HOSPITAL - DR. KENNETH O. NELSON LIBRARY OF THE
    HEALTH SCIENCES
530 Park Ave., E.   Phone: (815) 875-2811
Princeton, IL 61356   Mary Ann Butler, Lib.Coord.

HOUSEHOLD INTERNATIONAL - CORPORATE LIBRARY
2700 Sanders Rd.   Phone: (312) 564-5000
Prospect Heights, IL 60070   Win Sadecki, Corp.Libn.

HISTORICAL SOCIETY OF QUINCY AND ADAMS COUNTY - LIBRARY
425 S. 12th St.   Phone: (217) 222-1835
Quincy, IL 62301

SOCIETY FOR ACADEMIC ACHIEVEMENT - LIBRARY
220 WCU Bldg.
510 Maine St.   Phone: (217) 224-0570
Quincy, IL 62301   Leo W. Manning, Exec.Dir./Libn.

U.S. AIR FORCE HOSPITAL - MEDICAL LIBRARY (IL-Rantoul)
Chanute AFB   Phone: (217) 495-3068
Rantoul, IL 61868   R.M. Lucas, Med.Libn.

CONCORDIA COLLEGE - KLINCK MEMORIAL LIBRARY
7400 Augusta St.   Phone: (312) 771-8300
River Forest, IL 60305   Henry R. Latzke, Dir., Lib.Serv.

AUGUSTANA COLLEGE - DENKMANN MEMORIAL LIBRARY - SPECIAL
    COLLECTIONS
3520 7th Ave.   Phone: (309) 794-7266
Rock Island, IL 61201   John Caldwell, Dir.

BLACKHAWK GENEALOGICAL SOCIETY - LIBRARY *
Box 912
Rock Island, IL 61201   Mrs. F.A. Moseley, Lib.Chm.

SWENSON SWEDISH IMMIGRATION RESEARCH CENTER
Augustana College
Box 175   Phone: (309) 794-7204
Rock Island, IL 61201   Joel W. Lundeen, Act.Dir.

TRI-CITY JEWISH CENTER - JOSEPH AND BENJAMIN NEFF MEMORIAL
    LIBRARY
2715 30th St.
Box 679   Phone: (309) 788-3426
Rock Island, IL 61201

U.S. ARMY - ARMAMENT, MUNITIONS AND CHEMICAL COMMAND -
    TECHNICAL LIBRARY
HDQ AMCCOM
SMCAR-ESP-L   Phone: (309) 794-4208
Rock Island, IL 61299-6000   Philip E. Krouse, Chf.

U.S. ARMY - CORPS OF ENGINEERS - ROCK ISLAND DISTRICT -
    TECHNICAL LIBRARY
Clocktower Bldg.   Phone: (309) 788-6361
Rock Island, IL 61201

COMPREHENSIVE HEALTH PLANNING OF NORTHWEST ILLINOIS - LIBRARY
206 W. State St., Suite 1008   Phone: (815) 968-0720
Rockford, IL 61101   Barbara Lambert, Adm.Asst.

ROCKFORD MEMORIAL HOSPITAL - HEALTH SCIENCE LIBRARY
2400 N. Rockton Ave.   Phone: (815) 968-6861
Rockford, IL 61101   Prudence Dalrymple, Coord., Lib.Serv.

ROCKFORD PUBLIC LIBRARY - BUSINESS, SCIENCE AND TECHNOLOGY
    DIVISION †
215 N. Wyman   Phone: (815) 965-6731
Rockford, IL 61101   Marie Phillips, Hd.

ST. ANTHONY HOSPITAL MEDICAL CENTER - MEDICAL LIBRARY
5666 E. State St.   Phone: (815) 226-2000
Rockford, IL 61108   Nancy Dale, Libn.

ST. ANTHONY HOSPITAL MEDICAL CENTER - SCHOOL OF NURSING -
  BISHOP LANE LIBRARY
5666 E. State St.   Phone: (815) 226-2000
Rockford, IL 61108   Mary Patricia Pryor, Libn.

SINGER (H. Douglas) MENTAL HEALTH CENTER - LIBRARY
4402 North Main St.   Phone: (815) 987-7092
Rockford, IL 61105   Pat Ellison, Lib.Assoc.

SUNDSTRAND AVIATION - ENGINEERING LIBRARY
4747 Harrison Ave.
Box 7002   Phone: (815) 226-6753
Rockford, IL 61125   Mrs. Fran Genrich, Libn.

SWEDISH AMERICAN HOSPITAL - HEALTH CARE LIBRARY †
1400 Charles St.   Phone: (815) 968-4400
Rockford, IL 61101   Peggy Fuller, Med.Libn.

UNIVERSITY OF ILLINOIS - COLLEGE OF MEDICINE AT ROCKFORD -
  LIBRARY OF THE HEALTH SCIENCES
1601 Parkview Ave.   Phone: (815) 987-7377
Rockford, IL 61107   Stuart J. Kolner, Br.Libn.

WINNEBAGO COUNTY LAW LIBRARY
Courthouse Bldg., Suite 306
400 W. State St.   Phone: (815) 987-2514
Rockford, IL 61101   Roberta S. McGaw, Libn.

WOODWARD GOVERNOR CO. - WOODWARD LIBRARY
5001 N. Second St.   Phone: (815) 877-7441
Rockford, IL 61101   Ben Schleicher, Adm.Serv.Supv.

BANK ADMINISTRATION INSTITUTE - INFORMATION CENTER
60 Gould Center   Phone: (312) 228-6200
Rolling Meadows, IL 60008   Elissa Chovelak, Info.Spec.

CHEMPLEX COMPANY - LIBRARY
3100 Golf Rd.   Phone: (312) 437-7800
Rolling Meadows, IL 60008   Frieda R. Oetting, Libn.

GOULD INC. - GOULD INFORMATION CENTER
40 Gould Center   Phone: (312) 640-4423
Rolling Meadows, IL 60008   Terry Murphy, Mgr.

LEWIS UNIVERSITY - CANAL ARCHIVES AND SPECIAL COLLECTION OF
  HISTORY
Rte. 53   Phone: (815) 838-7316
Romeoville, IL 60441   John M. Lamb, Info.Dir.

LEWIS UNIVERSITY - LIBRARY
Rte. 53   Phone: (815) 838-0500
Romeoville, IL 60441   Fredereike A. Moskal, Lib.Dir.

DAIRY RESEARCH FOUNDATION - PRODUCT/PROCESS INFORMATION
  SERVICES
6300 N. River Rd.   Phone: (312) 696-1020
Rosemont, IL 60018   Diana Culbertson, Libn.

TRAVENOL LABORATORIES, INC. - INFORMATION RESOURCE CENTER
Route 120 and Wilson Rd.   Phone: (312) 546-6311
Round Lake, IL 60073   Barbara Petersen, Info.Spec.

AMERICAN VETERINARY MEDICAL ASSOCIATION - LIBRARY
930 N. Meacham Rd.   Phone: (312) 885-8070
Schaumburg, IL 60196   Janice Johnson, Libn.

MOTOROLA, INC. - COMMUNICATIONS SECTOR LIBRARY
1301 E. Algonquin Rd.   Phone: (312) 576-5940
Schaumburg, IL 60196   Marianna Sanderford, Mgr.

U.S. AIR FORCE COMMUNICATIONS COMMAND - TECHNICAL
  INFORMATION CENTER
HQ AFCC/DAPL
Bldg. 40, Fl 3114   Phone: (618) 256-4437
Scott AFB, IL 62225   Janet L. Schneider, Libn.

U.S. AIR FORCE ENVIRONMENTAL TECHNICAL APPLICATIONS CENTER -
  AIR WEATHER SERVICE TECHNICAL LIBRARY
FL 4414   Phone: (618) 256-2625
Scott AFB, IL 62225   Col. Lawrence R. French, Commander

U.S. AIR FORCE HOSPITAL MEDICAL CENTER - MEDICAL LIBRARY (IL-Scott
  AFB)
                                                      Phone: (618) 256-7437
Scott AFB, IL 62225   Blanche A. Savage, Health Sci.Libn.

HEBREW THEOLOGICAL COLLEGE - SAUL SILBER MEMORIAL LIBRARY
7135 N. Carpenter Rd.   Phone: (312) 267-9800
Skokie, IL 60077   Leah Mishkin, Hd.Libn. & Cur.

NILES TOWNSHIP JEWISH CONGREGATION - HILLMAN LIBRARY
4500 Dempster   Phone: (312) 675-4141
Skokie, IL 60076   Daniel Stuhlman, Libn.

PACKAGING CORPORATION OF AMERICA - INFORMATION SERVICES
  DEPARTMENT
5401 Old Orchard Rd.   Phone: (312) 470-0080
Skokie, IL 60077   Mary S. Senn, Info.Spec.

PORTLAND CEMENT ASSOCIATION/CONSTRUCTION TECHNOLOGY
  LABORATORIES - INFORMATION SERVICES SECTION
5420 Old Orchard Rd.   Phone: (312) 966-6200
Skokie, IL 60077   Marilynn Halasz, Mgr., Info.Serv.Sect.

RAND MC NALLY AND COMPANY - LIBRARY
8255 Central Park Ave.   Phone: (312) 673-9100
Skokie, IL 60076   Philip L. Forstall, Libn.

ST. PAUL LUTHERAN CHURCH AND SCHOOL - PARISH LIBRARY *
5201 Galitz   Phone: (312) 673-5030
Skokie, IL 60077   Paula Raabe, Libn.

SEARLE (G.D.) & CO. - RESEARCH LIBRARY
4901 Searle Pkwy.   Phone: (312) 982-8285
Skokie, IL 60077   Anthony Petrone, Mgr.

TEMPLE JUDEA MIZPAH - LIBRARY
8610 Niles Center Rd.   Phone: (312) 676-1566
Skokie, IL 60077   Claire Alport, Lib.Chm.

ALLSTATE INSURANCE COMPANY - COMMERCIAL LAW LIBRARY
51 W. Higgins Rd.   Phone: (312) 551-2093
South Barrington, IL 60010   Judith Hansel, Law Libn.

SOUTH SUBURBAN GENEALOGICAL & HISTORICAL SOCIETY - LIBRARY *
Box 96
South Holland, IL 60473   Marilyn Poe Laird, Hd.Libn.

AIRCHIVE - HISTORAIR FILE
326 S. MacArthur Blvd.   Phone: (217) 789-9754
Springfield, IL 62704   Job C. Conger, IV, Exec.Dir.

DAUGHTERS OF UNION VETERANS OF THE CIVIL WAR - NATIONAL
  HEADQUARTERS LIBRARY & MUSEUM
503 S. Walnut St.   Phone: (217) 544-0616
Springfield, IL 62704   Vivian Gertz, Natl.Treas.

DIOCESAN SEMINARY OF THE IMMACULATE CONCEPTION - LIBRARY
1903 E. Lake Dr.   Phone: (217) 529-2213
Springfield, IL 62707   Gale Pemberton, Libn.

HANSON ENGINEERS, INC. - TECHNICAL LIBRARY
1525 S. Sixth St.   Phone: (217) 788-2483
Springfield, IL 62703   Silvey W. Barge, Tech.Libn.

HORIZONS (The Illinois Career Information System)
217 E. Monroe, Suite 203   Phone: (217) 785-0789
Springfield, IL 62706   Dane R. Selby, Info.Dev.Mgr.

HOSPITAL SISTERS OF THIRD ORDER OF ST. FRANCIS - ARCHIVES
St. Francis Convent
Sangamon Ave.
Box 42   Phone: (217) 522-3386
Springfield, IL 62705   Sr. Dominica McGuire, Archv.

ILLINOIS STATE BOARD OF EDUCATION - MEDIA RESOURCES CENTER
100 N. First St.   Phone: (217) 782-4433
Springfield, IL 62777   William E. Lohman, Mgr.

ILLINOIS STATE BUREAU OF THE BUDGET - DIV. OF PLANNING AND
    FINANCIAL ANALYSIS - ILLINOIS STATE DATA CENTER
Stratton Office Bldg., Rm. 605   Phone: (217) 782-3500
Springfield, IL 62706   Jane Willey, Anl.

ILLINOIS STATE DEPARTMENT OF COMMERCE & COMMUNITY AFFAIRS -
    DCCA LIBRARY
620 E. Adams St.   Phone: (217) 785-6107
Springfield, IL 62701   Alice Kaige, Libn.

ILLINOIS STATE DEPARTMENT OF COMMERCE & COMMUNITY AFFAIRS -
    LIBRARY
620 E. Adams St.   Phone: (217) 785-6107
Springfield, IL 62701   Alice Kaige, Libn.

ILLINOIS STATE DEPARTMENT OF ENERGY AND NATURAL RESOURCES -
    ENERGY INFORMATION LIBRARY
325 W. Adams St., Rm. 300   Phone: (217) 785-2388
Springfield, IL 62706

ILLINOIS STATE DEPARTMENT OF TRANSPORTATION - TECHNICAL
    REFERENCE LIBRARY
338 Administration Bldg.
2300 S. Dirksen Pkwy.   Phone: (217) 782-6680
Springfield, IL 62764   Gisela Motzkus, Libn.

ILLINOIS STATE ENVIRONMENTAL PROTECTION AGENCY - LIBRARY
2200 Churchill Rd.   Phone: (217) 782-9691
Springfield, IL 62706   Nancy Simpson, Libn.

ILLINOIS STATE HISTORICAL LIBRARY
Old State Capitol   Phone: (217) 782-4836
Springfield, IL 62706   Olive S. Foster, State Hist.

ILLINOIS STATE LEGISLATIVE REFERENCE BUREAU
State House, Rm. 112   Phone: (217) 525-6625
Springfield, IL 62706   Patricia A. Coughlin, Law Libn.

ILLINOIS STATE LIBRARY
Centennial Bldg.   Phone: (217) 782-2994
Springfield, IL 62706   Bridget L. Lamont, Dir.

ILLINOIS STATE MUSEUM OF NATURAL HISTORY AND ART - TECHNICAL
    LIBRARY
                                    Phone: (217) 782-6623
Springfield, IL 62706   Orvetta Robinson, Libn.

ILLINOIS STATE - OFFICE OF THE AUDITOR GENERAL - LIBRARY
509 S. 6th St., 1st Fl.   Phone: (217) 782-1055
Springfield, IL 62701   Constance L. Etter, Libn.

ILLINOIS STATE - OFFICE OF THE SECRETARY OF STATE - STATE
    ARCHIVES
Illinois State Archives Bldg.   Phone: (217) 525-4682
Springfield, IL 62756   John Daly, Dir.

ILLINOIS STATE - SUPREME COURT LIBRARY
Supreme Court Bldg.   Phone: (217) 782-2424
Springfield, IL 62706   Catherine Bradley, Law Libn.

LINCOLN LIBRARY - SANGAMON VALLEY COLLECTION
326 S. 7th St.   Phone: (217) 753-4910
Springfield, IL 62701   Edward J. Russo, Hd.

MC FARLAND MENTAL HEALTH CENTER - STAFF LIBRARY
901 Southwind Rd.   Phone: (217) 786-6851
Springfield, IL 62703   Wanda Hesselberth, Lib.Coord.

MEMORIAL MEDICAL CENTER - KENNETH A. SCHNEPP MEDICAL LIBRARY
800 N. Rutledge St.   Phone: (217) 788-3336
Springfield, IL 62781   Myrtle Smarjesse, Med.Libn.

PROTESTANT EPISCOPAL CHURCH - EPISCOPAL DIOCESE OF
    SPRINGFIELD, ILLINOIS - DIOCESAN CENTER LIBRARY
821 S. 2nd St.   Phone: (217) 525-2827
Springfield, IL 62704   Philip L. Shutt, Registrar/Historiographer

ST. JOHN'S HOSPITAL - HEALTH SCIENCE LIBRARY
800 E. Carpenter   Phone: (217) 544-6464
Springfield, IL 62769   Kathryn Wrigley, Dir.

SANGAMON STATE UNIVERSITY - EAST CENTRAL NETWORK - LIBRARY
E22   Phone: (217) 786-6375
Springfield, IL 62708   Susie Shackleton, Libn.

SANGAMON STATE UNIVERSITY - ORAL HISTORY OFFICE - LIBRARY
Brookens Library, Rm. 377   Phone: (217) 786-6521
Springfield, IL 62708   Cullom Davis, Dir.

SOUTHERN ILLINOIS UNIVERSITY - SCHOOL OF MEDICINE - MEDICAL
    LIBRARY
801 N. Rutledge
Box 3926   Phone: (217) 782-2658
Springfield, IL 62708   Rick Dilley, Act.Dir.

SPRINGFIELD ART ASSOCIATION - MICHAEL VICTOR II ART LIBRARY
700 N. Fourth St.   Phone: (217) 523-2631
Springfield, IL 62702   Florence Irene Boyer, Libn.

SPRINGFIELD, ILLINOIS STATE JOURNAL & REGISTER - EDITORIAL
    LIBRARY
1 Copley Plaza   Phone: (217) 788-1300
Springfield, IL 62705   Sandra Vance, Libn.

MOULTRIE COUNTY HISTORICAL & GENEALOGICAL SOCIETY - MOULTRIE
    COUNTY HERITAGE CENTER
117 E. Harrison St.
Box MM   Phone: (217) 728-4085
Sullivan, IL 61951   Mary L. Storm, Libn.

TINLEY PARK MENTAL HEALTH CENTER - INSTRUCTIONAL MEDIA
    LIBRARY †
7400 W. 183rd St.   Phone: (312) 532-7000
Tinley Park, IL 60477   Sally M. Cole, Libn.

U.S. INDUSTRIAL CHEMICALS COMPANY - TUSCOLA PLANT TECHNICAL
    LIBRARY AND INFORMATION CENTER
Box 218   Phone: (217) 253-3311
Tuscola, IL 61953   Lois C. Bodoh, Tech.Libn.

ILLINOIS RAILWAY MUSEUM - TECHNICAL LIBRARY
Box 431   Phone: (815) 923-4391
Union, IL 60180   James E. Kehrein, Libn.

CARLE FOUNDATION HOSPITAL - LIBRARY
611 W. Park St.   Phone: (217) 337-3011
Urbana, IL 61801   Jane K. Olsgaard, Mgr., Lib.Serv.

CHAMPAIGN COUNTY HISTORICAL ARCHIVES
c/o Urbana Free Library
201 S. Race St.   Phone: (217) 367-4025
Urbana, IL 61801-3283   Barbara L. Roberts, Dir.

CLARK DIETZ ENGINEERS - LIBRARY
211 N. Race St.   Phone: (217) 384-1400
Urbana, IL 61801   Patricia E. Kirkwood, Libn.

ERIC CLEARINGHOUSE ON READING AND COMMUNICATIONS SKILLS
National Council of Teachers of English
1111 Kenyon Rd.   Phone: (217) 328-3870
Urbana, IL 61801   Charles Suhor, Dir.

MERCY HOSPITAL - LIBRARY
1400 W. Park St.   Phone: (217) 337-2283
Urbana, IL 61801   Harriet Williamson, Dir.

NATIONAL COUNCIL OF TEACHERS OF ENGLISH - LIBRARY
1111 Kenyon Rd.   Phone: (217) 328-3870
Urbana, IL 61801   Carolyn H. McMahon, Libn.

UNIVERSITY OF ILLINOIS - AGRICULTURE LIBRARY
226 Mumford Hall
1301 W. Gregory   Phone: (217) 333-2416
Urbana, IL 61801   Nancy Davis, Asst.Libn.

UNIVERSITY OF ILLINOIS - APPLIED LIFE STUDIES LIBRARY
Main Library, Rm. 146
1408 W. Gregory Dr.   Phone: (217) 333-3615
Urbana, IL 61801   Patricia McCandless, Libn.

UNIVERSITY OF ILLINOIS - ASIAN LIBRARY
325 Main Library
1408 W. Gregory Dr.   Phone: (217) 333-1501
Urbana, IL 61801   William S. Wong, Asst.Dir.

UNIVERSITY OF ILLINOIS - ASIAN LIBRARY - SOUTH AND WEST ASIAN
   DIVISION
329 Main Library
1408 W. Gregory Dr.   Phone: (217) 333-2492
Urbana, IL 61801   Narindar K. Aggarwal, Asst. Asian Libn.

UNIVERSITY OF ILLINOIS - BIOLOGY LIBRARY
101 Burrill Hall
407 S. Goodwin   Phone: (217) 333-3654
Urbana, IL 61801   Elisabeth B. Davis, Libn.

UNIVERSITY OF ILLINOIS - CHEMISTRY LIBRARY
257 Noyes Laboratory
505 S. Matthews   Phone: (217) 333-3737
Urbana, IL 61801   Dr. Lucille Wert, Chem.Libn.

UNIVERSITY OF ILLINOIS - CITY PLANNING AND LANDSCAPE
   ARCHITECTURE LIBRARY
203 Mumford Hall
1301 W. Gregory Dr.   Phone: (217) 333-0424
Urbana, IL 61801   Mary D. Ravenhall, Libn.

UNIVERSITY OF ILLINOIS - CLASSICS LIBRARY
419A Main Library
1408 W. Gregory Dr.   Phone: (217) 333-1124
Urbana, IL 61801   Suzanne Griffiths, Libn.

UNIVERSITY OF ILLINOIS - COLLEGE OF ENGINEERING - ENGINEERING
   DOCUMENTS CENTER
208 Engineering Hall
1308 W. Green St.   Phone: (217) 333-1510
Urbana, IL 61801   Mu-chin Cheng, Doc.Libn.

UNIVERSITY OF ILLINOIS - COMMERCE LIBRARY
Rm. 101, Main Library
1408 W. Gregory Dr.   Phone: (217) 333-3619
Urbana, IL 61801   M. Balachandran, Libn.

UNIVERSITY OF ILLINOIS - COMMUNICATIONS LIBRARY
122 Gregory Hall   Phone: (217) 333-2216
Urbana, IL 61801   Nancy Allen, Libn.

UNIVERSITY OF ILLINOIS - COORDINATED SCIENCE LABORATORY
   LIBRARY
1101 W. Springfield, Rm. 269 A   Phone: (217) 333-4368
Urbana, IL 61801

UNIVERSITY OF ILLINOIS - DEPARTMENT OF COMPUTER SCIENCE
   LIBRARY
260 Digital Computer Laboratory   Phone: (217) 333-6777
Urbana, IL 61801   Prof. S. Muroga, Chm., Lib.Comm.

UNIVERSITY OF ILLINOIS - DOCUMENTS LIBRARY
200d Main Library   Phone: (217) 333-1056
Urbana, IL 61801   Paula Watson, Hd.

UNIVERSITY OF ILLINOIS - EDUCATION AND SOCIAL SCIENCE LIBRARY
100 Main Library
1408 W. Gregory Dr.   Phone: (217) 333-2305
Urbana, IL 61801   Barton M. Clark, Libn.

UNIVERSITY OF ILLINOIS - ENGINEERING LIBRARY
221 Engineering Hall
1308 W. Green St.   Phone: (217) 333-3576
Urbana, IL 61801   William Mischo, Engr.Libn.

UNIVERSITY OF ILLINOIS - ENGLISH LIBRARY
321 Library
1408 W. Gregory Dr.   Phone: (217) 333-2220
Urbana, IL 61801   Melissa Cain, Libn.

UNIVERSITY OF ILLINOIS - GEOLOGY LIBRARY
223 Natural History Bldg.
1301 W. Green St.   Phone: (217) 333-1266
Urbana, IL 61801   Dederick C. Ward, Libn.

UNIVERSITY OF ILLINOIS - HIGHWAY TRAFFIC SAFETY CENTER -
   LIBRARY *
404 Engineering Hall   Phone: (217) 333-1270
Urbana, IL 61801   Dr. John Baerwald, Dir., Coll. of Engr.

UNIVERSITY OF ILLINOIS - HISTORY AND PHILOSOPHY LIBRARY
424 Main Library
1408 W. Gregory Dr.   Phone: (217) 333-1091
Urbana, IL 61801   Martha Friedman, Libn.

UNIVERSITY OF ILLINOIS - HOME ECONOMICS LIBRARY
905 S. Goodwin Ave.   Phone: (217) 333-0748
Urbana, IL 61801   Barbara C. Swain, Libn.

UNIVERSITY OF ILLINOIS - HOUSING RESEARCH & DEVELOPMENT
   PROGRAM - LIBRARY
1204 W. Nevada   Phone: (217) 333-7330
Urbana, IL 61801   Trudy Patton, Libn./Res.Assoc.

UNIVERSITY OF ILLINOIS - ILLINOIS HISTORICAL SURVEY LIBRARY
1A Main Library
1408 W. Gregory Dr.   Phone: (217) 333-1777
Urbana, IL 61801   John Hoffman, Libn.

UNIVERSITY OF ILLINOIS - LIBRARY AND INFORMATION SCIENCE
   LIBRARY
306 Main Library
1408 W. Gregory Dr.   Phone: (217) 333-3804
Urbana, IL 61801   Patricia Stenstrom, Libn.

UNIVERSITY OF ILLINOIS - MAP AND GEOGRAPHY LIBRARY
418 Main Library
1408 W. Gregory Dr.   Phone: (217) 333-0827
Urbana, IL 61801   David A. Cobb, Libn.

UNIVERSITY OF ILLINOIS - MATHEMATICS LIBRARY
216 Altgeld Hall
1409 W. Green St.   Phone: (217) 333-0258
Urbana, IL 61801   Nancy D. Anderson, Libn.

UNIVERSITY OF ILLINOIS - MODERN LANGUAGES AND LINGUISTICS
   LIBRARY
425 Main Library
1408 W. Gregory Dr.   Phone: (217) 333-0076
Urbana, IL 61801   Sara de Mundo Lo, Libn.

UNIVERSITY OF ILLINOIS - MUSIC LIBRARY
Music Bldg.   Phone: (217) 333-1173
Urbana, IL 61801   William M. McClellan, Music Libn.

UNIVERSITY OF ILLINOIS - NEWSPAPER LIBRARY
Main Library, Rm. 1
1408 W. Gregory Dr.   Phone: (217) 333-1509
Urbana, IL 61801

UNIVERSITY OF ILLINOIS - PHYSICS/ASTRONOMY LIBRARY
204 Loomis Laboratory
1110 W. Green St.   Phone: (217) 333-2101
Urbana, IL 61801   Bernice Lord Hulsizer, Libn.

UNIVERSITY OF ILLINOIS - RARE BOOK ROOM
346 Main Library
1408 W. Gregory Dr.   Phone: (217) 333-3777
Urbana, IL 61801   N. Frederick Nash, Libn.

UNIVERSITY OF ILLINOIS - RICKER LIBRARY OF ARCHITECTURE AND ART
208 Architecture Bldg.   Phone: (217) 333-0224
Urbana, IL 61801   Dee Wallace, Libn.

UNIVERSITY OF ILLINOIS - SLAVIC AND EAST EUROPEAN LIBRARY
225 Main Library   Phone: (217) 333-1349
Urbana, IL 61801   Marianna Choldin, Asst.Dir. of Gen.Serv.

UNIVERSITY OF ILLINOIS - SURVEY RESEARCH LABORATORY - SURVEY
    AND CENSUS DATA LIBRARY
1005 W. Nevada St.   Phone: (217) 333-7109
Urbana, IL 61801   Mary A. Spaeth, Survey Res.Info.Coord.

UNIVERSITY OF ILLINOIS - UNIVERSITY ARCHIVES
University Library, Rm. 19
1408 W. Gregory Dr.   Phone: (217) 333-0798
Urbana, IL 61801   Maynard Brichford, Univ.Archv.

UNIVERSITY OF ILLINOIS - VETERINARY MEDICINE LIBRARY
1257 Vet. Med. Basic Sciences Bldg.
2001 S. Lincoln Ave.   Phone: (217) 333-2193
Urbana, IL 61801   David Self, Libn.

UNIVERSITY OF ILLINOIS AT CHICAGO - HEALTH SCIENCES CENTER -
    LIBRARY OF THE HEALTH SCIENCES
506 S. Mathews
102 Medical Sciences Bldg.   Phone: (217) 333-4893
Urbana, IL 61801   Phyllis C. Self, Health Sci.Libn.

URBANA FREE LIBRARY - URBANA MUNICIPAL DOCUMENTS PROJECT
201 S. Race St.   Phone: (217) 384-0092
Urbana, IL 61801-3283   Jean E. Koch, Dir.

VANDALIA HISTORICAL SOCIETY - JAMES HALL LIBRARY
Little Brick House
621 St. Clair St.   Phone: (618) 283-0024
Vandalia, IL 62471   Mary Burtschi, Dir.

IROQUOIS COUNTY GENEALOGICAL SOCIETY - LIBRARY
103 W. Cherry St.
Watseka, IL 60970   Mary Ann Smith, Libn.

LAKE COUNTY MUSEUM - LIBRARY AND INFORMATION CENTER
Lakewood Forest Preserve
Rte. 176 & Fairfield Rd.   Phone: (312) 526-7878
Wauconda, IL 60084   Rebecca Goldberg, Dir.

LAKE COUNTY DEPARTMENT OF PLANNING, ZONING & ENVIRONMENTAL
    QUALITY - RESEARCH LIBRARY
803 County Bldg., Rm. A   Phone: (312) 689-6350
Waukegan, IL 60085   Mrs. Bhagwant Kaur Sidhu, Libn./Ed.

LAKE COUNTY LAW LIBRARY
18 N. County St.   Phone: (312) 689-6654
Waukegan, IL 60085   Joanne T. Baker, Law Libn.

VICTORY MEMORIAL HOSPITAL - MEDICAL LIBRARY
1324 N. Sheridan Rd.   Phone: (312) 688-3000
Waukegan, IL 60085   Helen Hewitt, Med.Lib.Tech.

WAUKEGAN HISTORICAL SOCIETY - JOHN RAYMOND MEMORIAL LIBRARY
1917 N. Sheridan Rd.   Phone: (312) 336-1859
Waukegan, IL 60087

WAUKEGAN NEWS-SUN - LIBRARY
100 Madison St.   Phone: (312) 689-6969
Waukegan, IL 60085   Barbara Apple, Libn.

NATIONAL EMPLOYEE SERVICES & RECREATION ASSOCIATION -
    INFORMATION CENTER
2400 S. Downing Ave.   Phone: (312) 562-8130
Westchester, IL 60153   Patrick B. Stinson, Exec.Dir.

C. BERGER AND COMPANY - LIBRARY
O-N. 469 Purnell St.   Phone: (312) 653-1115
Wheaton, IL 60187   Carol A. Berger, Owner

CANTIGNY WAR MEMORIAL MUSEUM OF THE FIRST DIVISION - ARCHIVES
    ROOM
1S151 Winfield Rd.   Phone: (312) 668-5161
Wheaton, IL 60187   Arthur Veysey, Gen.Mgr.

DU PAGE COUNTY LAW LIBRARY
Courthouse
201 Reber St.   Phone: (312) 682-7337
Wheaton, IL 60187   Charlean Eggert, Hd. Law Libn.

MARIANJOY REHABILITATION HOSPITAL - MEDICAL LIBRARY
26W171 Roosevelt Rd.
Box 795   Phone: (312) 653-7600
Wheaton, IL 60189   J. Zerwekh, Med.Libn.

THEOSOPHICAL SOCIETY IN AMERICA - OLCOTT LIBRARY & RESEARCH
    CENTER
1926 N. Main St.
Box 270   Phone: (312) 668-1571
Wheaton, IL 60187   Mary Jo Schneider, Lib.Hd.

WHEATON COLLEGE - BILLY GRAHAM CENTER - ARCHIVES
Wheaton, IL 60187   Robert Shuster, Dir.

WHEATON COLLEGE - BILLY GRAHAM CENTER - LIBRARY
                                            Phone: (312) 260-5194
Wheaton, IL 60187   Ferne L. Weimer, Dir.

WHEATON COLLEGE - BUSWELL MEMORIAL LIBRARY
501 E. Seminary   Phone: (312) 682-5101
Wheaton, IL 60187   P. Paul Snezek, Dir.

NORTH SUBURBAN LIBRARY SYSTEM - PROFESSIONAL INFORMATION
    CENTER
200 W. Dundee   Phone: (312) 459-1300
Wheeling, IL 60090   Dr. Elliott E. Kanner, Rsrcs.Coord./Info.Libn.

WILMETTE HISTORICAL MUSEUM - LIBRARY
565 Hunter Rd.   Phone: (312) 256-5838
Wilmette, IL 60091

COMMONWEALTH EDISON COMPANY - PRODUCTION TRAINING CENTER -
    LEARNING RESOURCE CENTER
R.R. 2, Box 120   Phone: (815) 458-3411
Wilmington, IL 60481   Carol Wolfe, Coord.

CENTRAL DU PAGE HOSPITAL - MEDICAL LIBRARY
0 North 025 Winfield Rd.   Phone: (312) 682-1600
Winfield, IL 60190   Dorothy B. Rowe, Libn.

MORTON THIOKOL INC. - MORTON CHEMICAL DIVISION - WOODSTOCK
    RESEARCH INFORMATION CENTER
1275 Lake Ave.   Phone: (815) 338-1800
Woodstock, IL 60098   Valentina M. Woodruff, Info.Sci.

WESTINGHOUSE ELECTRIC CORPORATION - WESTINGHOUSE NUCLEAR
    TRAINING CENTER - INFORMATION RSRC. CENTER †
505 Shiloh Blvd.   Phone: (312) 872-4585
Zion, IL 60099   Pat O'Rear, Info.Spec.

INDIANA

ALFORD HOUSE/ANDERSON FINE ARTS CENTER - ART REFERENCE
    LIBRARY
226 W. 8th St.
Anderson, IN 46016

ANDERSON COLLEGE - SCHOOL OF THEOLOGY - BYRD MEMORIAL LIBRARY
                                            Phone: (317) 649-9071
Anderson, IN 46012   Charles T. Kendall, Libn.

CENTER FOR MENTAL HEALTH - LIBRARY
2020 Brown St.
Box 1258   Phone: (317) 649-8161
Anderson, IN 46015   Paula Jarrett, Sec./Libn.

EAST CENTRAL LEGAL SERVICES - LIBRARY
1616 Meridian St.   Phone: (317) 644-2816
Anderson, IN 46016   Ben Jesudawson, Libn.

PARK PLACE CHURCH OF GOD - CARL KARDATZKE MEMORIAL LIBRARY
501 College Dr.
Anderson, IN 46012   Hazel Smith, Chm., Lib.Comm.

ST. JOHN'S MEDICAL CENTER - HEALTH SCIENCES LIBRARY
2015 Jackson St.   Phone: (317) 646-8264
Anderson, IN 46012   Scott S. Loman, Health Sci.Libn.

TRI-STATE UNIVERSITY - PERRY T. FORD MEMORIAL LIBRARY
S. Darling St.   Phone: (219) 665-3141
Angola, IN 46703   Mrs. Enriqueta G. Taboy, Lib.Dir.

AUBURN-CORD-DUESENBERG MUSEUM - TRI-KAPPA COLLECTION OF
    AUBURN AUTOMOTIVE LITERATURE
1600 S. Wayne St.
Box 271   Phone: (219) 925-1444
Auburn, IN 46706   Gregg Buttermore, Archv.

INDIANA LIMESTONE INSTITUTE OF AMERICA, INC. - LIBRARY AND
    INFORMATION CENTER
Stone City Bank Bldg., Suite 400   Phone: (812) 275-4426
Bedford, IN 47421   William H. McDonald, Exec.Dir.

INDIANA UNIVERSITY - AFRO-AMERICAN LEARNING RESOURCE CENTER
109 N. Jordan Ave.   Phone: (812) 335-3675
Bloomington, IN 47405   Leslie Denton, Supv.

INDIANA UNIVERSITY - ARCHIVES OF TRADITIONAL MUSIC
Maxwell Hall 057   Phone: (812) 335-8632
Bloomington, IN 47405   Anthony Seeger, Dir.

INDIANA UNIVERSITY - BIOLOGY LIBRARY
Jordan Hall   Phone: (812) 335-9791
Bloomington, IN 47405   Steven Sowell, Hd.

INDIANA UNIVERSITY - BUSINESS/SPEA LIBRARY
Business Bldg.   Phone: (812) 335-1957
Bloomington, IN 47405   Michael Parrish, Hd.

INDIANA UNIVERSITY - CHEMISTRY LIBRARY
                                                  Phone: (812) 335-9452
Bloomington, IN 47405   Gary Wiggins, Hd.

INDIANA UNIVERSITY - DEVELOPMENTAL TRAINING CENTER -
    INFORMATION AND MATERIALS SYSTEM (IMS)
2853 E. 10th St.   Phone: (812) 335-6508
Bloomington, IN 47405   Anne Beversdorf, Info. Dissemination Spec.

INDIANA UNIVERSITY - EAST ASIAN COLLECTION
                                                  Phone: (812) 335-9695
Bloomington, IN 47405   Shizue Matsuda, Libn.

INDIANA UNIVERSITY - EDUCATION LIBRARY
                                                  Phone: (812) 335-1798
Bloomington, IN 47405   Adele Dendy, Hd.

INDIANA UNIVERSITY - FINE ARTS LIBRARY
Fine Arts Ctr.   Phone: (812) 335-5743
Bloomington, IN 47405   Betty Jo Irvine, Hd.

INDIANA UNIVERSITY - FINE ARTS SLIDE LIBRARY
Fine Arts 415   Phone: (812) 335-6717
Bloomington, IN 47405   Eileen Fry, Slide Libn.

INDIANA UNIVERSITY - FOLKLORE ARCHIVES
510 N. Fess   Phone: (812) 335-3652
Bloomington, IN 47405   Timothy J. Kloberdanz, Hd.Archv.

INDIANA UNIVERSITY - FOLKLORE COLLECTION
10th and Jordan Sts.   Phone: (812) 335-1550
Bloomington, IN 47405   Polly S. Grimshaw, Libn./Cur.

INDIANA UNIVERSITY - GEOGRAPHY AND MAP LIBRARY
301 Kirkwood Hall   Phone: (812) 335-1108
Bloomington, IN 47405   Daniel Seldin, Hd.

INDIANA UNIVERSITY - GEOLOGY LIBRARY
Geology Bldg., 1005 E. Tenth St.   Phone: (812) 335-7170
Bloomington, IN 47405   Lois Heiser, Libn.

INDIANA UNIVERSITY - HEALTH, PHYSICAL EDUCATION & RECREATION
    LIBRARY
HPER Bldg. 031   Phone: (812) 335-4420
Bloomington, IN 47401   Linda Joachim, Hd.

INDIANA UNIVERSITY - INSTITUTE FOR URBAN TRANSPORTATION -
    RESOURCE CENTER
809 E. 9th St.   Phone: (812) 335-8143
Bloomington, IN 47401   Rachelle Reinhold, Sr. Staff Res.

INDIANA UNIVERSITY - JOURNALISM LIBRARY
Ernie Pyle Hall, 7th St.   Phone: (812) 335-3517
Bloomington, IN 47405   Frances Wilhoit

INDIANA UNIVERSITY - LAW LIBRARY
School of Law   Phone: (812) 335-9666
Bloomington, IN 47405   Colleen K. Pauwels, Dir.

INDIANA UNIVERSITY - LILLY LIBRARY
                                                  Phone: (812) 335-2452
Bloomington, IN 47405   William R. Cagle, Libn.

INDIANA UNIVERSITY - MEDICAL SCIENCES LIBRARY
251 Myers Hall   Phone: (812) 335-3347
Bloomington, IN 47405   Gwen Pershing, Hd.

INDIANA UNIVERSITY - MUSEUM - MUSEUM LIBRARY
Student Bldg., Rm. 209   Phone: (812) 335-7224
Bloomington, IN 47405

INDIANA UNIVERSITY - MUSIC LIBRARY
School of Music   Phone: (812) 335-8541
Bloomington, IN 47405   Dr. David Fenske, Hd.Libn.

INDIANA UNIVERSITY - NEAR EASTERN COLLECTION
                                                  Phone: (812) 335-3403
Bloomington, IN 47405

INDIANA UNIVERSITY - OPTOMETRY LIBRARY
Optometry Bldg.   Phone: (812) 335-8629
Bloomington, IN 47405   Roger Beckman, Hd.

INDIANA UNIVERSITY - ORAL HISTORY RESEARCH PROJECT - LIBRARY
512 N. Fess   Phone: (812) 335-2856
Bloomington, IN 47401   John Bodnar, Dir.

INDIANA UNIVERSITY - RESEARCH INSTITUTE FOR INNER ASIAN
    STUDIES - LIBRARY
Goodbody Hall 344   Phone: (812) 335-1605
Bloomington, IN 47405   Prof. Stephen Halkovic, Dir.

INDIANA UNIVERSITY - SCHOOL OF LIBRARY AND INFORMATION SCIENCE
    LIBRARY
                                                  Phone: (812) 335-5968
Bloomington, IN 47405   Patricia Steele, Hd.Libn.

INDIANA UNIVERSITY - SOCIAL STUDIES DEVELOPMENT CENTER -
    CURRICULUM RESOURCE CENTER
2805 E. 10th St.   Phone: (812) 337-3584
Bloomington, IN 47405   Linda Kelty, Libn.

INDIANA UNIVERSITY - SWAIN HALL LIBRARY
                                                  Phone: (812) 335-2758
Bloomington, IN 47405   Carol Hutchins, Hd.

INDIANA UNIVERSITY - WORKSHOP IN POLITICAL THEORY & POLICY
    ANALYSIS - WORKSHOP LIBRARY
515 N. Park St.   Phone: (812) 335-0441
Bloomington, IN 47405   Laura B. Miller, Libn.

KINSEY INSTITUTE FOR RESEARCH IN SEX, GENDER & REPRODUCTION,
    INC. - LIBRARY AND INFORMATION SERVICE
416 Morrison Hall
Indiana University   Phone: (812) 335-7686
Bloomington, IN 47405   Douglas K. Freeman, Hd., Coll.&Serv.

VISION INFORMATION PROGRAM, INC. *
Box 1208   Phone: (812) 332-4207
Bloomington, IN 47401   Dr. Gordon G. Heath, Pres.

CAYLOR-NICKEL CLINIC AND HOSPITAL - MEDICAL LIBRARY
311 S. Scott St.   Phone: (219) 824-3500
Bluffton, IN 46714   Patricia Niblick, Med.Libn.

MUSCATATUCK STATE HOSPITAL & TRAINING CENTER - RESIDENT AND
    STAFF DEVELOPMENT LIBRARY
Box 77   Phone: (812) 346-4401
Butlerville, IN 47223   Barbara Carter, Libn.

BARTHOLOMEW COUNTY HISTORICAL SOCIETY LIBRARY
524 Third St.   Phone: (812) 372-3541
Columbus, IN 47201   Renee Henry, Musm.Dir.

CUMMINS ENGINE CO., INC. - LIBRARIES
M/C 50120, Box 3005   Phone: (812) 379-6959
Columbus, IN 47201   W.E. Poor, Lib.Serv.Mgr.

IRWIN MANAGEMENT COMPANY, INC. - LIBRARY
235 Washington St.
Columbus, IN 47201

BLOMMEL HISTORIC AUTOMOTIVE DATA COLLECTION - LIBRARY AND
    INFORMATION CENTER
Rte. 5   Phone: (317) 825-9259
Connersville, IN 47331   Henry H. Blommel, Collector-Dir.

U.S. NAVY - NAVAL WEAPONS SUPPORT CENTER - LIBRARY †
Code 016   Phone: (812) 854-1615
Crane, IN 47522   Peggy Curran, Supv.Libn.

LAKE CIRCUIT COURT - LIBRARY *
2293 N. Main St.   Phone: (219) 663-0760
Crown Point, IN 46307   Beth Henderson, Libn.

EAST CHICAGO HISTORICAL SOCIETY - LIBRARY
East Chicago Public Library
2401 E. Columbus Dr.   Phone: (219) 397-2453
East Chicago, IN 46312   Ezelyn S. Johnston, Cat.

INLAND STEEL COMPANY - RESEARCH LABORATORIES - LIBRARY
3001 E. Columbus Dr.   Phone: (219) 392-5824
East Chicago, IN 46312   Barbara Minne Banek, Libn.

ST. CATHERINE HOSPITAL - MC GUIRE MEMORIAL LIBRARY
4321 Fir St.   Phone: (219) 392-7494
East Chicago, IN 46312   Madeline E. Downen, Dir., Lib.Serv.

ASSOCIATED MENNONITE BIBLICAL SEMINARIES - MENNONITE BIBLICAL
    SEMINARY - LIBRARY
3003 Benham Ave.   Phone: (219) 295-3726
Elkhart, IN 46514   Paul Roten, Libn.

MILES LABORATORIES, INC. - LIBRARY RESOURCES AND SERVICES
1127 Myrtle St.   Phone: (219) 264-8341
Elkhart, IN 46515   Alan K.E. Hagopian, Ph.D., Mgr.

OAKLAWN PSYCHIATRIC CENTER - PROFESSIONAL LIBRARY
2600 Oakland Ave.   Phone: (219) 294-3551
Elkhart, IN 46517   Nancy P. Price, Libn.

BRISTOL-MYERS COMPANY - PHARMACEUTICAL RESEARCH &
    DEVELOPMENT DIVISION - SCIENTIFIC INFO. DEPT. - EVANSVILLE
                                    Phone: (812) 426-6546
Evansville, IN 47721   Alice Weisling, Libn.

DEACONESS HOSPITAL - HEALTH SCIENCE LIBRARY
600 Mary St.   Phone: (812) 426-3385
Evansville, IN 47747   Millie H. Grunow, Med.Libn.

EVANSVILLE MUSEUM OF ARTS AND SCIENCE - LIBRARY
411 S.E. Riverside Dr.   Phone: (812) 425-2406
Evansville, IN 47713   Mary McNamee Schnepper, Cur. of Coll.

EVANSVILLE PSYCHIATRIC CHILDREN'S CENTER - STAFF LIBRARY
3330 E. Morgan Ave.   Phone: (812) 477-6436
Evansville, IN 47715   Juanita J. Massie, Med.Rec.Adm./Libn.

INDIANA STATE UNIVERSITY, EVANSVILLE - SPECIAL COLLECTIONS AND
    UNIVERSITY ARCHIVES
8600 University Blvd.   Phone: (812) 464-1896
Evansville, IN 47712-3595   Gina R. Walker, Act.Archv.

LEGAL SERVICES ORGANIZATION OF INDIANA, INC. - LIBRARY
101 Court St., Suite 102   Phone: (812) 426-1295
Evansville, IN 47708   Darlene Stewart, Off.Mgr.

MEAD JOHNSON AND COMPANY - MEAD JOHNSON INSTITUTE - LIBRARY *
2404 Pennsylvania   Phone: (812) 426-7042
Evansville, IN 47721   Larry H. Higgins, Mgr., Educ.

PLANNED PARENTHOOD OF SOUTHWESTERN INDIANA, INC. - LIBRARY
1610 S. Weinbach Ave.   Phone: (812) 473-8800
Evansville, IN 47714   Donna Reed, Health Educ.

ST. MARY'S MEDICAL CENTER - HERMAN M. BAKER, M.D. MEMORIAL
    LIBRARY
3700 Washington Ave.   Phone: (812) 479-4151
Evansville, IN 47750   Jane E. Saltzman, Dir.

SOUTHWESTERN INDIANA MENTAL HEALTH CENTER, INC. - LIBRARY
415 Mulberry St.   Phone: (812) 423-7791
Evansville, IN 47713   Donna Yuschak, Libn.

VANDERBURGH COUNTY LAW LIBRARY
City-County Courts Bldg., Rm. 207 Phone: (812) 426-5175
Evansville, IN 47708   Shirley Roll, Libn.

WILLARD LIBRARY OF EVANSVILLE - SPECIAL COLLECTIONS DEPARTMENT
21 First Ave.   Phone: (812) 425-4309
Evansville, IN 47710   Joan M. Elliott, Spec.Coll.Libn.

U.S. ARMY SOLDIER SUPPORT CENTER - MAIN LIBRARY †
Bldg. 400, Rm. 205   Phone: (317) 542-3891
Ft. Benjamin Harrison, IN 46216 Mrs. Marina Griner, Supv.Libn.

ALLEN COUNTY-FORT WAYNE HISTORICAL SOCIETY - LIBRARY AND
    MANUSCRIPT COLLECTIONS
302 E. Berry St.   Phone: (219) 426-2882
Fort Wayne, IN 46802   Walter Font, Cur.

ALLEN COUNTY LAW LIBRARY ASSOCIATION, INC.
Courthouse, Rm. 105   Phone: (219) 428-7638
Fort Wayne, IN 46802   Virginia B. Howell, Law Libn.

ALLEN COUNTY PUBLIC LIBRARY - BUSINESS AND TECHNOLOGY
    DEPARTMENT
900 Webster St.
Box 2270   Phone: (219) 424-7241
Fort Wayne, IN 46801   John N. Dickmeyer, Mgr.

ALLEN COUNTY PUBLIC LIBRARY - FRED J. REYNOLDS HISTORICAL
    GENEALOGY COLLECTION
900 Webster St.   Phone: (219) 424-7241
Fort Wayne, IN 46802   Michael B. Clegg, Mgr., Genealogy Dept.

AMERICAN INSTITUTE OF PARLIAMENTARIANS - LIBRARY
124 W. Washington Blvd., Suite 144 Phone: (219) 422-3680
Fort Wayne, IN 46802   Bob Leiman, Exec.Dir.

CENTRAL SOYA COMPANY, INC. - FOOD RESEARCH LIBRARY
Box 1400   Phone: (219) 489-1511
Fort Wayne, IN 46801-1400   Margaret Campbell, Libn.

CONCORDIA THEOLOGICAL SEMINARY - LIBRARY
6600 N. Clinton   Phone: (219) 482-9611
Fort Wayne, IN 46825   Cameron A. Mackenzie, Dir.

FIRST FEDERAL SAVINGS AND LOAN ASSOCIATION OF FORT WAYNE -
    LIBRARY *
719 Court St.   Phone: (219) 423-2377
Fort Wayne, IN 46801   Robert P. Norton, V.P.

FORT WAYNE BIBLE COLLEGE - S.A. LEHMAN MEMORIAL LIBRARY
919 W. Rudisill Blvd.   Phone: (219) 456-2111
Fort Wayne, IN 46807   Wava Bueschlen, Dir. of the Lib.

FORT WAYNE DEPARTMENT OF COMMUNITY DEVELOPMENT & PLANNING -
    PLANNING LIBRARY
One Main St., Rm. 800   Phone: (219) 427-1140
Fort Wayne, IN 46802   Roy Hossler, Asst. Planner/Lib.

FORT WAYNE JOURNAL-GAZETTE - NEWSPAPER LIBRARY
600 W. Main St.   Phone: (219) 461-8377
Fort Wayne, IN 46802   Rosalina Stier, Libn.

FRIENDS OF THE THIRD WORLD INC. - WHOLE WORLD BOOKS
611 W. Wayne St.   Phone: (219) 422-6821
Fort Wayne, IN 46802   Marian R. Waltz, Resource Coord.

INDIANA INSTITUTE OF TECHNOLOGY - MC MILLEN LIBRARY
1600 E. Washington Blvd.   Phone: (219) 422-5561
Fort Wayne, IN 46803   Jeanne Hickling, Libn.

INDIANA JEWISH HISTORICAL SOCIETY - LIBRARY
215 E. Berry St.   Phone: (219) 423-3862
Fort Wayne, IN 46802   Joseph Levine, Exec.Sec.

INDIANA UNIVERSITY/PURDUE UNIVERSITY AT FORT WAYNE - FINE
    ARTS LIBRARY †
1026 W. Berry St.   Phone: (219) 482-5201
Fort Wayne, IN 46804   Marilyn L. Murphy, Libn.

ITT CORPORATION - AEROSPACE/OPTICAL DIVISION - INFORMATION
    SERVICES CENTER
3700 E. Pontiac St.
Box 3700   Phone: (219) 423-9636
Fort Wayne, IN 46801   Carol L. Hilkey, Info. Data Spec.

LINCOLN NATIONAL CORPORATION - LAW LIBRARY
1300 S. Clinton St., 7th Fl.
Box 1110   Phone: (219) 427-3870
Fort Wayne, IN 46801   Mary A. McDonald, Adm., Info.Serv.

LINCOLN NATIONAL LIFE FOUNDATION - LOUIS A. WARREN LINCOLN
    LIBRARY AND MUSEUM
1300 S. Clinton St.
Box 1110   Phone: (219) 427-3864
Fort Wayne, IN 46801   Mark E. Neely, Jr., Dir.

LUTHERAN HOSPITAL OF FORT WAYNE, INC. - HEALTH SCIENCES LIBRARY
3024 Fairfield Ave.   Phone: (219) 458-2277
Fort Wayne, IN 46807-1697   Raisa Cherniv, Dir.

MAGNAVOX GOVERNMENT & INDUSTRIAL ELECTRONICS COMPANY -
    ENGINEERING LIBRARY †
2131 S. Coliseum Blvd.   Phone: (219) 429-6000
Fort Wayne, IN 46803   Lydia Peralta, Libn.

PARKVIEW MEMORIAL HOSPITAL - PARKVIEW-METHODIST SCHOOL OF
    NURSING - LIBRARY
2200 Randallia Dr.   Phone: (219) 484-6636
Fort Wayne, IN 46805   Phyllis Eckman, Libn.

ST. JOSEPH'S HOSPITAL - MEDICAL LIBRARY †
700 Broadway   Phone: (219) 423-2614
Fort Wayne, IN 46802   Michael Sheets, Dir., Med.Lib.

ST. JOSEPH'S HOSPITAL - SCHOOL OF NURSING LIBRARY
735 W. Berry St.   Phone: (219) 425-3950
Fort Wayne, IN 46804   Gloria Uptgraft, Libn.

U.S. VETERANS ADMINISTRATION (IN-Fort Wayne) - HOSPITAL LIBRARY
1600 Randalia Dr.   Phone: (219) 743-5431
Fort Wayne, IN 46805   Enolia L. Stalnaker, Chf., Lib.Serv.

FRANKLIN COLLEGE - SPECIAL COLLECTIONS
Library   Phone: (317) 736-8441
Franklin, IN 46131   Mary Alice Medlicott, Cur.

INDIANA UNIVERSITY NORTHWEST - CALUMET REGIONAL ARCHIVES
Library, 3400 Broadway   Phone: (219) 980-6628
Gary, IN 46408   Robert Moran

INDIANA VOCATIONAL-TECHNICAL COLLEGE - RESOURCE CENTER
1440 E. 35th Ave.   Phone: (219) 981-1111
Gary, IN 46409   John M. Niemann, Dir.

LAKE COUNTY SUPERIOR COURT LIBRARY †
400 Broadway, Rms. 3 & 4   Phone: (219) 886-3621
Gary, IN 46402-1286   Birdie Witson, Libn.

POST-TRIBUNE - LIBRARY
1065 Broadway   Phone: (219) 881-3134
Gary, IN 46402   Louise K. Tucker, Chf.Libn.

INDIANA NORTHERN GRADUATE SCHOOL OF PROFESSIONAL
    MANAGEMENT - LIBRARY
410 S. 10th St.
Box 1000
Gas City, IN 46933

GOSHEN COLLEGE - HAROLD AND WILMA GOOD LIBRARY - HARTZLER
    MUSIC COLLECTION
1700 S. Main   Phone: (219) 533-3161
Goshen, IN 46526   Devon J. Yoder, Libn.

HISTORICAL COMMITTEE OF THE MENNONITE CHURCH - ARCHIVES OF
    THE MENNONITE CHURCH
Goshen College   Phone: (219) 533-3161
Goshen, IN 46526   Leonard Gross, Archv.

MENNONITE HISTORICAL LIBRARY
Goshen College   Phone: (219) 533-3161
Goshen, IN 46526   John S. Oyer, Dir.

DE PAUW UNIVERSITY - ARCHIVES OF DE PAUW UNIVERSITY AND
    INDIANA UNITED METHODISM
Roy O. West Library   Phone: (317) 658-4501
Greencastle, IN 46135

PUTNAM COUNTY HISTORICAL SOCIETY - ARCHIVES
Roy O. West Library
DePauw University   Phone: (317) 658-4501
Greencastle, IN 46135

ELI LILLY AND COMPANY - GREENFIELD LABORATORIES - LIBRARY
    AGRICULTURAL SERVICE
Box 708   Phone: (317) 467-4482
Greenfield, IN 46140   Bernas Downing, Supv., Lit.Serv.

U.S. AIR FORCE BASE - GRISSOM BASE LIBRARY
FL 4654, Bldg. 575   Phone: (317) 689-2056
Grissom AFB, IN 46971   David S. English, Libn.

HAMMOND HISTORICAL SOCIETY - CALUMET ROOM
564 State St.   Phone: (219) 931-5100
Hammond, IN 46320   Kathryn Thegze, Libn.

LA SALLE STEEL COMPANY - RESEARCH AND DEVELOPMENT LIBRARY
1412 150th St.   Phone: (219) 853-6000
Hammond, IN 46327   Jerry Wilkes, Libn.

PURDUE UNIVERSITY, CALUMET - LIBRARY
2233 171st St.   Phone: (219) 844-0520
Hammond, IN 46323   Bernard H. Holicky, Dir.

ST. MARGARET HOSPITAL - SALLIE M. TYRRELL, M.D. MEMORIAL LIBRARY
5454 Hohman Ave.   Phone: (219) 932-2300
Hammond, IN 46320   Laurie Broadus, Libn.Coord.

BLACKFORD COUNTY HISTORICAL SOCIETY - MUSEUM AND BEESON
    LIBRARY *
321 N. High St.
Box 264   Phone: (317) 348-1905
Hartford City, IN 47348   Dwight Mikkelson, Pres.

THE NATIONAL RAILROAD CONSTRUCTION AND MAINTENANCE
    ASSOCIATION, INC. - TECHNICAL REFERENCE LIBRARY
9331 Waymond Ave.   Phone: (219) 924-1709
Highland, IN 46322   larry shields, Exec.Dir.

HOBART HISTORICAL SOCIETY, INC. - MARIAM J. PLEAK MEMORIAL
    LIBRARY AND ARCHIVE
706 E. Fourth St.
Box 24
Hobart, IN 46342   Elin B. Christianson, Cur.

ALL SOULS UNITARIAN CHURCH - E. BURDETTE BACKUS LIBRARY
5805 E. 56th St.   Phone: (317) 545-6005
Indianapolis, IN 46226   Marcia Blumenthal, Chm., Lib.Comm.

AMERICAN LEGION - NATIONAL HEADQUARTERS - LIBRARY
700 N. Pennsylvania St.
Box 1055   Phone: (317) 635-8411
Indianapolis, IN 46206   Thomas V. Hull, Dir.

AMERICAN STATES INSURANCE COMPANY - LIBRARY
500 N. Meridian St.
Box 1636   Phone: (317) 262-6560
Indianapolis, IN 46207   Sue Overstreet, Libn.

AT & T TECHNOLOGIES, INC. - LIBRARY
6612 E. 75th St.   Phone: (317) 352-3780
Indianapolis, IN 46250   Audrey M. Jackson, Lib. Group Supv.

BAKER & DANIELS - LAW LIBRARY
810 Fletcher Trust Bldg.   Phone: (317) 636-4535
Indianapolis, IN 46204   Paula Schmidt, Libn.

BARNES & THORNBURG - LIBRARY
1313 Merchants Bank Bldg.   Phone: (317) 638-1313
Indianapolis, IN 46204   Mary Ann Roman, Libn.

BOEHRINGER MANNHEIM CORPORATION - BMC INFORMATION CENTER *
8021 Knue Rd.
Box 50528   Phone: (317) 849-6635
Indianapolis, IN 46250   George L. Curran, III, Supv./Libn.

BUTLER UNIVERSITY - IRWIN LIBRARY - HUGH THOMAS MILLER RARE
   BOOK ROOM
46th & Sunset   Phone: (317) 283-9227
Indianapolis, IN 46208   Gisela Terrell, Rare Bks./Spec.Coll.Libn.

BUTLER UNIVERSITY - JORDAN COLLEGE OF FINE ARTS MUSIC LIBRARY
46th & Sunset   Phone: (317) 283-9243
Indianapolis, IN 46208   Phyllis J. Schoonover, Music Libn.

BUTLER UNIVERSITY - SCIENCE LIBRARY
46th & Sunset   Phone: (317) 283-9401
Indianapolis, IN 46208   Barbara Howes, Sci.Libn.

CARTER (Larue D.) MEMORIAL HOSPITAL - MEDICAL LIBRARY
1315 W. 10th St.   Phone: (317) 634-8401
Indianapolis, IN 46202   Philip I. Enz, Adm.Libn.

CATHOLIC SEMINARY FOUNDATION OF INDIANAPOLIS - LIBRARY
4545 Northwestern Ave.   Phone: (317) 925-9095
Indianapolis, IN 46208   Rev. Ivan W. Hughes, O.S.B., Dir., Lib.Serv.

CENTRAL STATE HOSPITAL - MEDICAL LIBRARY
3000 W. Washington St.   Phone: (317) 639-3927
Indianapolis, IN 46222   Aurelia S. Baker, Libn.

CHILDREN'S MUSEUM OF INDIANAPOLIS - RAUH MEMORIAL LIBRARY
Box 3000   Phone: (317) 924-5431
Indianapolis, IN 46206   Ng. George Hing, Libn./Archv.

CHRISTIAN CHURCH (Disciples of Christ), INC. - LIBRARY *
222 S. Downey Ave.
Box 1986   Phone: (317) 353-1491
Indianapolis, IN 46206   Doris Autrey Kennedy, Libn.

CHRISTIAN THEOLOGICAL SEMINARY - LIBRARY
1000 W. 42nd St.   Phone: (317) 924-1331
Indianapolis, IN 46208   Mr. Leslie R. Galbraith, Libn.

COMMUNITY HOSPITAL OF INDIANAPOLIS, INC. - LIBRARY
1500 N. Ritter Ave.   Phone: (317) 353-5591
Indianapolis, IN 46219   Jean Bonner, Dir.

DOW CHEMICAL COMPANY - RESEARCH CENTER LIBRARY †
Box 68511   Phone: (317) 873-7147
Indianapolis, IN 46268   Maxine Tomlin, Libn.

ELI LILLY AND COMPANY - BUSINESS LIBRARY
307 E. McCarty St.   Phone: (317) 261-3241
Indianapolis, IN 46285   Helen E. Loftus, Dept.Hd.

ELI LILLY AND COMPANY - LILLY ARCHIVES
Lilly Center
307 E. McCarty St.   Phone: (317) 261-2173
Indianapolis, IN 46285   Anita Martin, Archv.

ELI LILLY AND COMPANY - SCIENTIFIC LIBRARY
307 E. McCarty St.   Phone: (317) 261-4452
Indianapolis, IN 46285   Adele Hoskin, Chf.Libn.

ESTERLINE ANGUS INSTRUMENT CORPORATION - COMPANY LIBRARY
1201 Main St.   Phone: (317) 244-7611
Indianapolis, IN 46224   Kelli R. Norris, Co.Libn.

FIRST MERIDIAN HEIGHTS PRESBYTERIAN CHURCH - HUDELSON LIBRARY
4701 N. Central Ave.   Phone: (317) 283-1305
Indianapolis, IN 46205   Linda D. Finch, Chm., Lib.Comm.

GENERAL MOTORS CORPORATION - ALLISON GAS TURBINE DIVISION -
   LIBRARY
Mail Code 55
Box 420   Phone: (317) 242-5651
Indianapolis, IN 46206   W.H. Richardson, Libn.

GIRLS CLUBS OF AMERICA - NATIONAL RESOURCE CENTER
441 W. Michigan St.   Phone: (317) 634-7546
Indianapolis, IN 46202   Tom Rumer, Libn.

HARRISON (Benjamin) MEMORIAL HOME - LIBRARY *
1230 N. Delaware St.   Phone: (317) 631-1898
Indianapolis, IN 46202   Patricia Ronsheim, Cur.

HISTORIC LANDMARKS FOUNDATION OF INDIANA, INC. - INFORMATION
   CENTER
3402 Boulevard Pl.   Phone: (317) 926-2301
Indianapolis, IN 46208   Christine Connor, Dir. of Pubns./Pub.Info.

HURTY-PECK LIBRARY OF BEVERAGE LITERATURE
5600 W. Raymond St.
Indianapolis, IN 46241

INDIANA ACADEMY OF SCIENCE - JOHN SHEPARD WRIGHT MEMORIAL
   LIBRARY
State Library, 140 N. Senate Ave.   Phone: (317) 232-3686
Indianapolis, IN 46204   Lois Burton, Libn.

INDIANA HISTORICAL SOCIETY - WILLIAM HENRY SMITH MEMORIAL
   LIBRARY
315 W. Ohio St.   Phone: (317) 232-1879
Indianapolis, IN 46202   Robert K. O'Neill, Dir.

INDIANA STATE BOARD OF HEALTH - JACOB T. OLIPHANT LIBRARY *
1330 W. Michigan St.   Phone: (317) 633-8585
Indianapolis, IN 46206   Billy Smith, Dir.

INDIANA STATE CHAMBER OF COMMERCE - RESEARCH LIBRARY
One N. Capitol Ave., Suite 200   Phone: (317) 634-6407
Indianapolis, IN 46204   Max L. Moser, Dir., Res. & Spec.Proj.

INDIANA STATE COMMISSION ON PUBLIC RECORDS - ARCHIVES
   DIVISION
140 N. Senate Ave.   Phone: (317) 232-3737
Indianapolis, IN 46204   John J. Newman, Dp.Dir./Archv.

INDIANA STATE DEPARTMENT ON AGING & COMMUNITY SERVICES -
   NATE SALON RESOURCE CENTER
115 N. Pennsylvania Ave., Suite 1350   Phone: (317) 232-1260
Indianapolis, IN 46204   Joyce A. Smidley, Dir., Pub.Info. & Res.

INDIANA STATE DEPARTMENT OF COMMERCE - ENERGY LIBRARY
1 N. Capitol, Suite 700   Phone: (317) 232-8985
Indianapolis, IN 46204-2243   Shaukat A. Naeem, Res.Anl.

INDIANA STATE DEPARTMENT OF HIGHWAYS - PLANNING DIVISION -
   TECHNICAL REFERENCE LIBRARY *
State Office Bldg., Rm. 1205
100 N. Senate Ave.   Phone: (317) 232-5485
Indianapolis, IN 46204   Thomas E. Brethauer, Libn.

INDIANA STATE DEPARTMENT OF PUBLIC INSTRUCTION - PROFESSIONAL
  LIBRARY
229 State House   Phone: (317) 927-0295
Indianapolis, IN 46204   Phyllis M. Land Usher, Dir. of Fed.Res.

INDIANA STATE LEGISLATIVE SERVICES AGENCY - OFFICE OF CODE
  REVISION - LIBRARY
Rm. 302 State House   Phone: (317) 269-3728
Indianapolis, IN 46208   Nancy Thoms, Libn.

INDIANA STATE LIBRARY
140 N. Senate Ave.   Phone: (317) 232-3675
Indianapolis, IN 46204   C. Ray Ewick, Dir.

INDIANA STATE LIBRARY - INDIANA DIVISION
140 N. Senate Ave.   Phone: (317) 232-3668
Indianapolis, IN 46204   Robert Logsdon, Act.Hd.

INDIANA STATE SCHOOL FOR THE DEAF - LIBRARY
1200 E. 42nd St.   Phone: (317) 924-4374
Indianapolis, IN 46205   Irene Hodock, Libn.

INDIANA STATE SUPREME COURT - LAW LIBRARY
316 State House   Phone: (317) 633-4640
Indianapolis, IN 46204   Sally J. Sutton, Libn.

INDIANA UNIVERSITY, INDIANAPOLIS - SCHOOL OF DENTISTRY LIBRARY
1121 W. Michigan St.   Phone: (317) 264-7204
Indianapolis, IN 46202   Marie Sparks, Lib.Dir.

INDIANA UNIVERSITY, INDIANAPOLIS - SCHOOL OF LAW LIBRARY
735 W. New York St.   Phone: (317) 264-4028
Indianapolis, IN 46202   Prof. James F. Bailey, III, Dir., Law Lib.

INDIANA UNIVERSITY, INDIANAPOLIS - SCHOOL OF MEDICINE LIBRARY
635 Barnhill Dr.   Phone: (317) 264-7182
Indianapolis, IN 46223   Dana McDonald, Dir.

INDIANA UNIVERSITY, INDIANAPOLIS - UNIVERSITY LIBRARY/HERRON
  SCHOOL OF ART
1701 N. Pennsylvania   Phone: (317) 923-3651
Indianapolis, IN 46202   Maudine B. Williams, Hd.Libn.

INDIANA UNIVERSITY/PURDUE UNIVERSITY AT INDIANAPOLIS -
  ARCHIVES
815 W. Michigan St.   Phone: (317) 264-8278
Indianapolis, IN 46202

INDIANA UNIVERSITY/PURDUE UNIVERSITY AT INDIANAPOLIS - 38TH
  STREET CAMPUS LIBRARY
1201 E. 38th St.
Box 647   Phone: (317) 923-1325
Indianapolis, IN 46223   Jean M. Gnat, Hd., Pub.Serv.

INDIANA UNIVERSITY/PURDUE UNIVERSITY AT INDIANAPOLIS -
  UNIVERSITY LIBRARY
815 W. Michigan St.   Phone: (317) 264-8278
Indianapolis, IN 46202   Barbara B. Fischler, Dir. of Libs.

INDIANAPOLIS BAR ASSOCIATION - LIBRARY †
One Indiana Sq.   Phone: (317) 632-8240
Indianapolis, IN 46204   Mary Kramer, Libn.

INDIANAPOLIS CENTER FOR ADVANCED RESEARCH - ARAC - NASA
  TECHNICAL INFORMATION CENTER
611 N. Capitol   Phone: (317) 264-4644
Indianapolis, IN 46204   John M. Ulrich, Dir.

INDIANAPOLIS - DEPARTMENT OF METROPOLITAN DEVELOPMENT -
  DIVISION OF PLANNING - LIBRARY
2041 City-County Bldg.   Phone: (317) 633-3331
Indianapolis, IN 46204   Elizabeth Simmons, Libn.

INDIANAPOLIS-MARION COUNTY PUBLIC LIBRARY - ARTS DIVISION
40 E. St. Clair St.   Phone: (317) 269-1764
Indianapolis, IN 46204   Daniel Gann, Div.Hd.

INDIANAPOLIS-MARION COUNTY PUBLIC LIBRARY - BUSINESS, SCIENCE
  AND TECHNOLOGY DIVISION
40 E. St. Clair St.   Phone: (317) 269-1741
Indianapolis, IN 46204   Mark Leggett, Div.Hd.

INDIANAPOLIS-MARION COUNTY PUBLIC LIBRARY - FILM DIVISION
1435 N. Illinois St.   Phone: (317) 269-1821
Indianapolis, IN 46202   Jacqueline Ek, Div.Hd.

INDIANAPOLIS-MARION COUNTY PUBLIC LIBRARY - NEWSPAPER AND
  PERIODICAL DIVISION
40 E. St. Clair St.   Phone: (317) 269-1728
Indianapolis, IN 46204   Harriet Cohen, Div.Hd.

INDIANAPOLIS-MARION COUNTY PUBLIC LIBRARY - SOCIAL SCIENCE
  DIVISION
40 E. St. Clair St.   Phone: (317) 269-1733
Indianapolis, IN 46204   Lois Laube, Div.Hd.

INDIANAPOLIS MOTOR SPEEDWAY HALL OF FAME MUSEUM - LIBRARY
4790 W. 16th St.   Phone: (317) 241-2501
Indianapolis, IN 46222   Jack L. Martin, Dir.

INDIANAPOLIS MUSEUM OF ART - REFERENCE LIBRARY
1200 W. 38th St.   Phone: (317) 923-1331
Indianapolis, IN 46208   Martha G. Blocker, Hd.Libn.

INDIANAPOLIS MUSEUM OF ART - SLIDE COLLECTION
1200 W. 38th St.   Phone: (317) 923-1331
Indianapolis, IN 46208   Carolyn J. Metz, Dir., Vis.Rsrcs. & Serv.

INDIANAPOLIS NEWSPAPERS, INC. - INDIANAPOLIS STAR AND
  INDIANAPOLIS NEWS - REFERENCE LIBRARY
307 N. Pennsylvania St.   Phone: (317) 633-9293
Indianapolis, IN 46206   Sandra E. Fitzgerald, Hd.Libn.

INDIANAPOLIS POWER & LIGHT COMPANY - CORPORATE
  COMMUNICATIONS REFERENCE CENTER
25 Monument Circle
Box 1595B   Phone: (317) 261-8390
Indianapolis, IN 46206   Robert W. Golobish, Commun.Res.Coord.

INDIANAPOLIS PUBLIC SCHOOLS - KARL R. KALP LIBRARY
120 E. Walnut St.   Phone: (317) 266-4499
Indianapolis, IN 46204   Marjorie Percival, Hd.Libn.

KOSSUTH FOUNDATION - HUNGARIAN RESEARCH LIBRARY
Butler University
Indianapolis, IN 46208   Dr. Janos Horvath, Pres.

LEGAL SERVICES ORGANIZATION OF INDIANA, INC. - LIBRARY *
107 N. Pennsylvania, Suite 800   Phone: (317) 639-4151
Indianapolis, IN 46204   Sherry Englehart, Libn.

MARION COUNTY LAW LIBRARY
602 City County Bldg.   Phone: (317) 633-3643
Indianapolis, IN 46204   Lynn S. Connor, Libn.

METHODIST HOSPITAL OF INDIANA, INC. - LIBRARY SERVICES
1604 N. Capitol Ave.   Phone: (317) 929-8021
Indianapolis, IN 46202   Joyce S. Allen, Lib.Mgr.

MUSEUM OF INDIAN HERITAGE - LIBRARY
Eagle Creek Park
6040 De Long Rd.   Phone: (317) 293-4488
Indianapolis, IN 46254   Vicki Cummings, Act.Dir.

NATIONAL INTERFRATERNITY CONFERENCE - LIBRARY
3901 W. 86th St.
Box 689117   Phone: (317) 872-1112
Indianapolis, IN 46268   Jonathan J. Brant, Exec.Dir.

NATIONAL TRACK & FIELD HALL OF FAME - LIBRARY
Box 120   Phone: (317) 638-9555
Indianapolis, IN 46206   Ollan C. Cassell, Exec.Dir.

NORTH AMERICAN ISLAMIC TRUST, INC. - LIBRARY
10900 W. Washington St.   Phone: (317) 839-9248
Indianapolis, IN 46231

PLANNED PARENTHOOD OF CENTRAL INDIANA - RESOURCE CENTER
3209 N. Meridian St.   Phone: (317) 925-6686
Indianapolis, IN 46208   Katy Smith, Libn.

PROTESTANT EPISCOPAL CHURCH - DIOCESE OF INDIANAPOLIS, INDIANA
    - ARCHIVES
Indiana State Library
140 N. Senate Ave.   Phone: (317) 926-5454
Indianapolis, IN 46208

RCA CORPORATION - RCA CONSUMER ELECTRONICS DIVISION -
    ENGINEERING LIBRARY
600 N. Sherman Dr., Bldg. 6-223   Phone: (317) 267-5925
Indianapolis, IN 46201   Susan M. Tamer, Adm., Lib.Serv.

RCA CORPORATION - SELECTAVISION VIDEODISC OPERATIONS -
    TECHNICAL LIBRARY
Box 91079   Phone: (317) 273-3397
Indianapolis, IN 46291   Joan K. Griffitts, Libn.

RESEARCH AND REVIEW SERVICE OF AMERICA - LIBRARY
6213 La Pas Trail
Box 1727   Phone: (317) 297-4360
Indianapolis, IN 46206

ST. VINCENT'S HOSPITAL - GARCEAU LIBRARY
2001 W. 86th St.   Phone: (317) 871-2095
Indianapolis, IN 46260   Virginia Durkin, Mgr.,Lib.Serv.

SATURDAY EVENING POST SOCIETY - ARCHIVES
1100 Waterway Blvd.   Phone: (317) 634-1100
Indianapolis, IN 46202   Carol Brown McShane, Libn./Archv.

UNION CARBIDE CORPORATION - COATINGS SERVICE DEPARTMENT -
    LIBRARY
1500 Polco St.
Box 24166   Phone: (317) 240-2520
Indianapolis, IN 46224   Mary Ann Brady, Libn.

U.S. GEOLOGICAL SURVEY - WATER RESOURCES DIVISION -
    INFORMATION RESOURCE CENTER
6023 Guion Rd., Suite 201   Phone: (317) 927-8640
Indianapolis, IN 46254   Sharon S. Kuhnlein, IRC Supv.

U.S. NAVY - NAVAL AVIONICS CENTER - TECHNICAL LIBRARY
21st & Arlington Ave.   Phone: (317) 353-7765
Indianapolis, IN 46218   Louise Boyd, Supv.

U.S. VETERANS ADMINISTRATION (IN-Indianapolis) - MEDICAL CENTER
    LIBRARY
1481 W. Tenth St.   Phone: (317) 635-7401
Indianapolis, IN 46202   Judith Alfred, Lib.Serv.

WINONA MEMORIAL HOSPITAL - HEALTH SCIENCES LIBRARY †
3232 N. Meridian   Phone: (317) 927-2248
Indianapolis, IN 46208   Karen A. Davis, Med.Libn.

WISHARD (William N.) MEMORIAL HOSPITAL - PROFESSIONAL LIBRARY/
    MEDIA SERVICES †
1001 W. 10th St.   Phone: (317) 630-7028
Indianapolis, IN 46202   Jana Bradley, Dir.

CLARK COUNTY MEMORIAL HOSPITAL - MEDICAL LIBRARY
1220 Missouri Ave.   Phone: (812) 283-2358
Jeffersonville, IN 47130   Becky Lacefield Kelien, Med.Libn.

CABOT CORPORATION - TECHNICAL INFORMATION CENTER
1020 W. Park Ave.   Phone: (317) 456-6140
Kokomo, IN 46901   Betty S. Hollis, Tech.Libn.

GENERAL MOTORS CORPORATION - DELCO ELECTRONICS DIVISION -
    TECHNICAL LIBRARY
Box 797   Phone: (317) 459-7262
Kokomo, IN 46902   Cheryl K. Maris, Tech.Libn.

KOKOMO TRIBUNE - LIBRARY
300 N. Union   Phone: (317) 459-3121
Kokomo, IN 46901   Janice Johnson, Libn.

ST. JOSEPH MEMORIAL HOSPITAL - HEALTH SCIENCE LIBRARY
1907 W. Sycamore St.   Phone: (317) 452-5611
Kokomo, IN 46901   Dana Kemp, Med.Libn.

LAFAYETTE JOURNAL AND COURIER - LIBRARY
217 N. 6th St.   Phone: (317) 423-5511
Lafayette, IN 47901   Marlene Bailey, Libn.

ST. ELIZABETH HOSPITAL MEDICAL CENTER - BANNON HEALTH SCIENCE
    LIBRARY
1501 Hartford St.
Box 7501   Phone: (317) 423-6143
Lafayette, IN 47903   Ruth Pestalozzi Pape, Med.Libn.

ST. ELIZABETH MEDICAL CENTER - ST. ELIZABETH HOSPITAL SCHOOL OF
    NURSING - LIBRARY
1508 Tippecanoe St.   Phone: (317) 423-6125
Lafayette, IN 47904   Janet Stroud, Media & Instr.Serv.Coord.

TIPPECANOE COUNTY HISTORICAL ASSOCIATION - ALAMEDA MC
    COLLOUGH RESEARCH & GENEALOGY LIBRARY
909 South St.   Phone: (317) 742-8411
Lafayette, IN 47901   John M. Harris, Dir.

U.S. NATL. PARK SERVICE - LINCOLN BOYHOOD NATL. MEMORIAL -
    LIBRARY
                                                  Phone: (812) 937-4757
Lincoln City, IN 47552   Norman D. Hellmers, Supt.

LOGANSPORT STATE HOSPITAL - MEDICAL LIBRARY *
R.R. 2   Phone: (219) 722-4141
Logansport, IN 46947   Terra Newton, Libn.

MADISON STATE HOSPITAL - CRAGMONT MEDICAL LIBRARY *
                                                  Phone: (812) 265-2611
Madison, IN 47250   Lloyd Roberts, Libn.

MARION GENERAL HOSPITAL - MEDICAL LIBRARY †
Wabash & Euclid Avenues   Phone: (317) 662-4607
Marion, IN 46952   Rita J. Lone, Instr., Educ.Serv.

RCA CORPORATION - PICTURE TUBE DIVISION - LIBRARY *
3301 S. Adams St.   Phone: (317) 662-1411
Marion, IN 46952   Beth Dewitt, Libn.

U.S. VETERANS ADMINISTRATION (IN-Marion) - HOSPITAL MEDICAL
    LIBRARY
E. 38th St. at Home Ave.   Phone: (317) 674-3321
Marion, IN 46952   Joy E. Zuger

WESLEYAN CHURCH - ARCHIVES & HISTORICAL LIBRARY
Box 2000   Phone: (317) 674-3301
Marion, IN 46952   Paul W. Thomas, Dir.

AMERICAN CAMPING ASSOCIATION - LIBRARY
Bradford Woods   Phone: (317) 342-8456
Martinsville, IN 46151

BALL CORPORATION - CORPORATE INFORMATION CENTER AND LAW
    LIBRARY
345 S. High St.   Phone: (317) 747-6420
Muncie, IN 47302   Rebecca K. Shipley, Bus.Res.Asst.

BALL CORPORATION - RESEARCH LIBRARY
1509 S. Macedonia   Phone: (317) 747-6707
Muncie, IN 47302   Julia Mertens, Tech.Libn.

BALL MEMORIAL HOSPITAL - HEALTH SCIENCE LIBRARY
2401 University Ave.   Phone: (317) 747-3204
Muncie, IN 47303   Betty J. Daugherty, Dir. of Lib.Serv.

BALL STATE UNIVERSITY - BRACKEN LIBRARY - SPECIAL COLLECTIONS
Bracken Library, Rm. 210   Phone: (317) 285-5078
Muncie, IN 47306   David C. Tambo, Hd., Spec.Coll.

BALL STATE UNIVERSITY - CENTER FOR ENERGY RESEARCH/
    EDUCATION/SERVICE (CERES)
2000 University Ave., AB G19   Phone: (317) 285-4938
Muncie, IN 47306   Robert J. Koester, Dir.

BALL STATE UNIVERSITY - COLLEGE OF ARCHITECTURE & PLANNING - LIBRARY
Phone: (317) 285-4760
Muncie, IN 47306
Marjorie Joyner, Arch.Libn.

BALL STATE UNIVERSITY - DEPARTMENT OF LIBRARY SERVICE - MAP COLLECTION
Bracken Library, Rm. 218
Phone: (317) 285-1097
Muncie, IN 47306
Paul W. Stout, Map Libn.

BALL STATE UNIVERSITY - MUSIC LIBRARY
Phone: (317) 285-7356
Muncie, IN 47306
Dr. Nyal Williams, Music Libn.

MUNCIE STAR-PRESS LIBRARY
High & Jackson Sts.
Phone: (317) 747-5767
Muncie, IN 47302
Breena L. Wysong, Libn.

HENRY COUNTY HISTORICAL SOCIETY - LIBRARY
Henry County Historical Bldg.
606 S. 14th St.
Phone: (317) 529-4028
New Castle, IN 47362
Wilma Kern, Pres.

NEW CASTLE STATE HOSPITAL - MEDICAL LIBRARY
100 Van Nuys Rd.
Box 34
Phone: (317) 529-0900
New Castle, IN 47362
Jill Fitzhugh, Media Spec.

NEW HARMONY WORKINGMEN'S INSTITUTE - LIBRARY AND MUSEUM
407 W. Tavern St.
Box 368
Phone: (812) 682-4806
New Harmony, IN 47631
Mary Aline Cook, Libn.

CONNER PRAIRIE PIONEER SETTLEMENT - RESEARCH DEPARTMENT LIBRARY
13400 Allisonville Rd.
Phone: (317) 773-3633
Noblesville, IN 46060
David G. Vanderstel, Hist.

ENVIRONIC FOUNDATION INTERNATIONAL, INC. - LIBRARY AND FILES
Box 88
Phone: (219) 233-3357
Notre Dame, IN 46556
Patrick Horsbrugh, Chm.

MOREAU SEMINARY - LIBRARY
Congregation of Holy Cross
Phone: (219) 239-5046
Notre Dame, IN 46556
Rev. Joseph A. Rogusz, C.S.C., Libn.

SAINT MARY'S COLLEGE - CUSHWA-LEIGHTON LIBRARY - SPECIAL COLLECTIONS
Phone: (219) 284-5280
Notre Dame, IN 46556
Sr. Bernice Hollenhorts, CSC, Lib.Dir.

ST. MARY'S COLLEGE - MUSIC SEMINAR ROOM
Moreau Hall, Rm. 322
Phone: (219) 284-4638
Notre Dame, IN 46556
Sr. Rita Claire Lyons, C.S.C., Dir.

UNIVERSITY OF NOTRE DAME - ARCHITECTURE LIBRARY
210 Architectural Bldg.
Phone: (219) 239-6654
Notre Dame, IN 46556
Anton Masin, Libn.

UNIVERSITY OF NOTRE DAME - ARCHIVES
607 Memorial Library
Phone: (219) 239-6447
Notre Dame, IN 46556
Dr. Wendy Clauson Schlereth, Univ.Archv.

UNIVERSITY OF NOTRE DAME - CENTER FOR THE STUDY OF HUMAN RIGHTS - READING ROOM
Law School, Rm. 301
Notre Dame, IN 46556
Rita Kopezynski

UNIVERSITY OF NOTRE DAME - CHEMISTRY/PHYSICS LIBRARY
231 Nieuwland Science Hall
Phone: (219) 239-7203
Notre Dame, IN 46556
Karla P. Goold, Libn.

UNIVERSITY OF NOTRE DAME - ENGINEERING LIBRARY
149 Fitzpatrick Hall of Engineering
Phone: (219) 239-6665
Notre Dame, IN 46556
Robert J. Havlik, Engr.Libn.

UNIVERSITY OF NOTRE DAME - INTERNATIONAL DOCUMENTATION CENTER
213 Memorial Library
Phone: (219) 239-6587
Notre Dame, IN 46556
Theodore B. Ivanus, Hd.

UNIVERSITY OF NOTRE DAME - LAW SCHOOL LIBRARY
221 Memorial Library
Box 535
Phone: (219) 239-7024
Notre Dame, IN 46556
Kathleen Farmann, Law Libn.

UNIVERSITY OF NOTRE DAME - LIFE SCIENCES RESEARCH LIBRARY
Galvin Life Sciences Bldg.
Phone: (219) 239-7209
Notre Dame, IN 46556
Dorothy Coil, Libn.

UNIVERSITY OF NOTRE DAME - MATHEMATICS LIBRARY
200 Computing Center
Phone: (219) 239-7278
Notre Dame, IN 46556
Jennifer Helman, Supv.

UNIVERSITY OF NOTRE DAME - MEDIEVAL INSTITUTE LIBRARY
715 Memorial Library
Phone: (219) 239-7420
Notre Dame, IN 46556
Dr. Louis Jordan, Hd.

UNIVERSITY OF NOTRE DAME - RADIATION LABORATORY - RADIATION CHEMISTRY DATA CENTER
Phone: (219) 239-6527
Notre Dame, IN 46556
Dr. Alberta B. Ross, Supv.

UNIVERSITY OF NOTRE DAME - RARE BOOKS AND SPECIAL COLLECTIONS DEPARTMENT
102 Memorial Library
Phone: (219) 239-6489
Notre Dame, IN 46556
David E. Sparks, Hd.

UNIVERSITY OF NOTRE DAME - SNITE MUSEUM OF ART - LIBRARY
Phone: (219) 239-5466
Notre Dame, IN 46556
Lisa M. Stanczak, Libn.

INDIANA LAW ENFORCEMENT ACADEMY - DAVID F. ALLEN MEMORIAL LEARNING RESOURCES CENTER
Box 313
Phone: (317) 839-5191
Plainfield, IN 46168
Donna K. Zimmerman, Libn.

PLAINFIELD PUBLIC LIBRARY - GUILFORD TOWNSHIP HISTORICAL COLLECTION
1120 Stafford Rd.
Phone: (317) 839-6602
Plainfield, IN 46168
Susan Miller Carter, Hist.Libn.

MARSHALL COUNTY HISTORICAL SOCIETY MUSEUM - LIBRARY
317 W. Monroe St.
Phone: (219) 936-2306
Plymouth, IN 46563
Mary L. Durnan, Dir.

ART ASSOCIATION OF RICHMOND - LIBRARY
350 Whitewater Blvd.
Phone: (317) 966-0256
Richmond, IN 47374
Ruth Mills, Dir.

EARLHAM COLLEGE - JOSEPH MOORE MUSEUM - HADLEY LIBRARY
Box 68
Phone: (317) 962-6561
Richmond, IN 47374
John Iverson, Musm.Dir.

EARLHAM COLLEGE - QUAKER COLLECTION
Lilly Library
Phone: (317) 962-6561
Richmond, IN 47374
Philip Shore, Assoc.Libn.

HAYES (Stanley W.) RESEARCH FOUNDATION - LIBRARY
Box 1404
Phone: (317) 962-3745
Richmond, IN 47374
D.R. Hendricks, Pres.

WAYNE COUNTY HISTORICAL MUSEUM - LIBRARY
1150 North A St.
Phone: (317) 962-5756
Richmond, IN 47374
S. Anne Burcham, Dir.

FULTON COUNTY HISTORICAL SOCIETY - LIBRARY
7th & Pontiac
Phone: (219) 223-4436
Rochester, IN 46975
Shirley Willard, Dir.

ST. MEINRAD ARCHABBEY - COLLEGE & SCHOOL OF THEOLOGY - LIBRARY
Phone: (812) 357-6401
St. Meinrad, IN 47577
Rev. Simeon Daly, O.S.B., Libn.

WASHINGTON COUNTY HISTORICAL SOCIETY - LIBRARY
Stevens Memorial Musm.
307 E. Market St.
Salem, IN 47167
Lulie Davis, Sec.-Libn.

THERMARK CORPORATION - TECHNICAL INFORMATION SERVICES †
650 W. 67th Pl.   Phone: (219) 322-5030
Schererville, IN 46375   Irene Ganas, Tech.Info.Serv.Mgr.

INLOW CLINIC - LIBRARY *
Box 370
Shelbyville, IN 46176   Linda Stark, Libn.

ART CENTER, INC. - LIBRARY †
120 S. St. Joseph St.   Phone: (219) 284-9102
South Bend, IN 46601   Judy Oberhausen, Act.Dir./Cur.

BENDIX CORPORATION - BENDIX ENERGY CONTROLS DIVISION -
   ENGINEERING LIBRARY
717 Bendix Dr.   Phone: (219) 237-5976
South Bend, IN 46620   Mary Jane Brayfield, Libn.

DISCOVERY HALL MUSEUM - RESEARCH LIBRARY
120 S. St. Joseph St.   Phone: (219) 284-9714
South Bend, IN 46601   Julie Bennett, Archv.

MEMORIAL HOSPITAL OF SOUTH BEND - MEDICAL LIBRARY
615 N. Michigan   Phone: (219) 284-7389
South Bend, IN 46601   Jeanne M. Larson, Med.Libn.

NORTHERN INDIANA HISTORICAL SOCIETY - FREDERICK ELBEL LIBRARY
112 S. Lafayette Blvd.   Phone: (219) 284-9664
South Bend, IN 46601   Kathleen S. Stiso, Musm.Dir.

ST. JOSEPH COUNTY LAW LIBRARY
Court House   Phone: (219) 284-9657
South Bend, IN 46601   Conie J. Frank, Libn.

ST. JOSEPH'S MEDICAL CENTER - MEDICAL LIBRARY
811 E. Madison
Box 1935   Phone: (219) 237-7228
South Bend, IN 46634   Donna J. Bayless, Libn.

SOUTH BEND OSTEOPATHIC HOSPITAL - MEDICAL LIBRARY
2515 E. Jefferson Blvd.   Phone: (219) 288-8311
South Bend, IN 46615   Helga R. Wehrhan, Lib.Mgr.

DEBS (Eugene V.) FOUNDATION - LIBRARY
451 N. 8th St.   Phone: (812) 232-2163
Terre Haute, IN 47807   Noel Beasley, Exec.V.P.

INDIANA STATE UNIVERSITY - CENTER FOR GOVERNMENTAL SERVICES
HH 201   Phone: (812) 232-6311
Terre Haute, IN 47809   William H. Harader, Dir.

INDIANA STATE UNIVERSITY - CONTINUING EDUCATION AND EXTENDED
   SERVICES - LIBRARY
Alumni Ctr.   Phone: (812) 232-6311
Terre Haute, IN 47809   Dr. Louis R. Jensen, Asst. Dean

INDIANA STATE UNIVERSITY - DEPARTMENT OF RARE BOOKS AND
   SPECIAL COLLECTIONS
Cunningham Memorial Library   Phone: (812) 232-6311
Terre Haute, IN 47809   Dr. Lawrence J. McCrank, Hd., Rare Bks./Spec.Coll.

INDIANA STATE UNIVERSITY - SCIENCE LIBRARY
Science Bldg.   Phone: (812) 232-6311
Terre Haute, IN 47809   Susan J. Thompson, Sci.Libn.

INDIANA STATE UNIVERSITY - TEACHING MATERIALS AND SPECIAL
   SERVICES DIVISION
Cunningham Memorial Library   Phone: (812) 232-6311
Terre Haute, IN 47809   Rolland H. McGiverin, Hd.

INTERNATIONAL MINERALS & CHEMICALS CORPORATION - IMC
   RESEARCH & DEVELOPMENT LIBRARY
1331 S. First St.
Box 207   Phone: (812) 232-0121
Terre Haute, IN 47808   Mr. T.C. Shane, Jr., Dir., Info.Serv.

ROSE-HULMAN INSTITUTE OF TECHNOLOGY - JOHN A. LOGAN LIBRARY
5500 E. Wabash Ave.   Phone: (812) 877-1511
Terre Haute, IN 47803   Herman Cole, Jr., Dir.

VIGO COUNTY HISTORICAL SOCIETY - HISTORICAL MUSEUM OF THE
   WABASH VALLEY - LIBRARY
1411 S. 6th St.   Phone: (812) 235-9717
Terre Haute, IN 47802   Judy Calvert, Libn.

VIGO COUNTY PUBLIC LIBRARY - SPECIAL COLLECTIONS
One Library Square   Phone: (812) 232-1113
Terre Haute, IN 47807   Clarence Brink, Coord., Ref.Serv.

VIGO COUNTY SCHOOL CORPORATION - INSTRUCTIONAL MATERIALS
   CENTER
3000 College Ave.   Phone: (812) 238-4354
Terre Haute, IN 47803   Georgia R. Cole, Coord.

TAYLOR UNIVERSITY - AYRES ALUMNI MEMORIAL LIBRARY - SPECIAL
   COLLECTIONS
                                             Phone: (317) 998-2751
Upland, IN 46989   David Dickey, Lib.Dir.

HISTORICAL SOCIETY OF PORTER COUNTY - LIBRARY
Old Jail Museum
153 Franklin St.   Phone: (219) 464-8661
Valparaiso, IN 46383   Bertha Stalbaum, Dir./Cur.

LUTHERAN DEACONESS ASSOCIATION - DEACONESS HALL LIBRARY
Deaconess Hall, E. Union St.   Phone: (219) 464-5033
Valparaiso, IN 46383   Deaconess Louise Williams, Dir. of Serv.

VALPARAISO UNIVERSITY - LAW LIBRARY
Wesemann Hall   Phone: (219) 464-5438
Valparaiso, IN 46383   Chris Kirkwood, Act.Dir.

OLD CATHEDRAL PARISH CHURCH - BRUTE LIBRARY
205 Church St.   Phone: (812) 882-7016
Vincennes, IN 47591   Esther Cunningham, Guide/Archv.

VINCENNES UNIVERSITY - BYRON R. LEWIS HISTORICAL LIBRARY
                                             Phone: (812) 885-4330
Vincennes, IN 47591   Robert R. Stevens, Dir.

WABASH COUNTY HISTORICAL MUSEUM - HISTORICAL LIBRARY
Memorial Hall   Phone: (219) 563-5058
Wabash, IN 46992   Jack Miller, Cur.

ALLEN (J.C.) AND SON, INC. - PHOTO LIBRARY
Box 2061   Phone: (317) 463-9614
West Lafayette, IN 47906

PURDUE UNIVERSITY - AVIATION TECHNOLOGY LIBRARY
Purdue Univ. Airport   Phone: (317) 494-7640
West Lafayette, IN 47907   Dennis H. Parks, Libn.

PURDUE UNIVERSITY - BIOCHEMISTRY LIBRARY
Biochemistry Bldg.   Phone: (317) 494-1621
West Lafayette, IN 47907   Martha J. Bailey, Life Sci.Libn.

PURDUE UNIVERSITY - CHEMISTRY LIBRARY
Chemistry Bldg.   Phone: (317) 494-2862
West Lafayette, IN 47907   John Pinzelik, Chem.Libn.

PURDUE UNIVERSITY - CINDAS - ELECTRONIC PROPERTIES
   INFORMATION CENTER
2595 Yeager Rd.   Phone: (317) 494-6300
West Lafayette, IN 47906   C.Y. Ho, Dir.

PURDUE UNIVERSITY - CINDAS - THERMOPHYSICAL PROPERTIES
   RESEARCH CENTER - LIBRARY
2595 Yeager Rd.   Phone: (317) 494-6300
West Lafayette, IN 47906   C.Y. Ho, Dir.

PURDUE UNIVERSITY - CINDAS - UNDERGROUND EXCAVATION AND ROCK
   PROPERTIES INFORMATION CENTER
2595 Yeager Rd.
West Lafayette, IN 47906

PURDUE UNIVERSITY - CONSUMER AND FAMILY SCIENCES LIBRARY
Stone Hall   Phone: (317) 494-2914
West Lafayette, IN 47907   Judith Nixon, Libn.

PURDUE UNIVERSITY - ENGINEERING LIBRARY
Potter Bldg.   Phone: (317) 494-2867
West Lafayette, IN 47907   Edwin D. Posey, Engr.Libn.

PURDUE UNIVERSITY - FILM LIBRARY
Stewart Center   Phone: (317) 494-6742
West Lafayette, IN 47907   Carl E. Snow, Film Libn.

PURDUE UNIVERSITY - GEOSCIENCES LIBRARY
Geosciences Bldg.   Phone: (317) 494-3264
West Lafayette, IN 47907   Dennis H. Parks, Libn.

PURDUE UNIVERSITY - HUMANITIES, SOCIAL SCIENCE AND EDUCATION
    LIBRARY
                                                       Phone: (317) 494-2828
West Lafayette, IN 47907   Laszlo L. Kovacs, Hum.Libn.

PURDUE UNIVERSITY - LIFE SCIENCE LIBRARY
Lilly Hall of Life Sciences   Phone: (317) 494-2910
West Lafayette, IN 47907   Martha J. Bailey, Life Sci.Libn.

PURDUE UNIVERSITY - MANAGEMENT AND ECONOMICS LIBRARY
Krannert Grad.Sch. of Mgt.   Phone: (317) 494-2922
West Lafayette, IN 47907   Gordon Law, Libn.

PURDUE UNIVERSITY - MATHEMATICAL SCIENCES LIBRARY
Mathematical Sciences   Phone: (317) 494-2855
West Lafayette, IN 47907   Richard L. Funkhouser, Libn.

PURDUE UNIVERSITY - PHARMACY, NURSING AND HEALTH SCIENCES
    LIBRARY
Pharmacy Bldg.   Phone: (317) 494-1416
West Lafayette, IN 47907   Theodora Andrews, Libn.

PURDUE UNIVERSITY - PHYSICS LIBRARY
Physics Bldg.   Phone: (317) 494-2858
West Lafayette, IN 47907   Dennis H. Parks, Libn.

PURDUE UNIVERSITY - PSYCHOLOGICAL SCIENCES LIBRARY
Peirce Hall   Phone: (317) 494-2969
West Lafayette, IN 47907   Pam Baxter, Psych.Libn.

PURDUE UNIVERSITY - VETERINARY MEDICAL LIBRARY
C.V. Lynn Hall, Rm. 108   Phone: (317) 494-2852
West Lafayette, IN 47907   Gretchen Stephens, Libn.

UNION BIBLE SEMINARY - LIBRARY
434 S. Union St.   Phone: (317) 896-9324
Westfield, IN 46074   Michael Williams, Academic Dean

WESTVILLE CORRECTIONAL CENTER - STAFF LIBRARY
Box 473   Phone: (219) 785-2511
Westville, IN 46391   Catherine M. Mohlke, Dir., Lib.Serv.

RANDOLPH CIRCUIT COURT - LAW LIBRARY *
Courthouse, Rm. 307   Phone: (317) 584-7070
Winchester, IN 47394   Joan Benson, Libn.

FREE METHODIST CHURCH OF NORTH AMERICA - MARSTON MEMORIAL
    HISTORICAL LIBRARY
901 College Ave.   Phone: (219) 267-7656
Winona Lake, IN 46590   Evelyn Mottweiler, Libn./Exec.Dir.

GRACE THEOLOGICAL SEMINARY - LIBRARY
Wooster Rd.   Phone: (219) 267-8191
Winona Lake, IN 46590   Robert Ibach, Dir.

IOWA

AMANA HERITAGE SOCIETY - ARCHIVES
                                                       Phone: (319) 622-3567
Amana, IA 52203

AMES LABORATORY - DOCUMENT LIBRARY
Iowa State University   Phone: (515) 294-1856
Ames, IA 50011   Burton J. Gleason, Hd., Office of Info.

IOWA STATE DEPARTMENT OF TRANSPORTATION - LIBRARY
800 Lincoln Way   Phone: (515) 239-1200
Ames, IA 50010   Hank Zaletel, Libn.

IOWA STATE UNIVERSITY - ENERGY AND MINERAL RESOURCES
    RESEARCH INSTITUTE - RARE-EARTH INFORMATION CENTER
                                                       Phone: (515) 294-2272
Ames, IA 50011   Karl A. Gschneidner, Jr., Dir.

IOWA STATE UNIVERSITY - LIBRARY - DEPARTMENT OF SPECIAL
    COLLECTIONS
                                                       Phone: (515) 294-6672
Ames, IA 50011   Stanley M. Yates, Hd.

IOWA STATE UNIVERSITY - VETERINARY MEDICAL LIBRARY
                                                       Phone: (515) 294-2225
Ames, IA 50011   Sara Peterson, Hd.Libn.

U.S.D.A. - AGRICULTURAL RESEARCH SERVICE - NATL. ANIMAL DISEASE
    CENTER LIBRARY
Box 70   Phone: (515) 239-8200
Ames, IA 50010   Janice K. Eifling, Libn.

SOIL CONSERVATION SOCIETY OF AMERICA - H. WAYNE PRITCHARD
    LIBRARY
7515 N.E. Ankeny Rd.   Phone: (515) 289-2331
Ankeny, IA 50021   James L. Sanders, Asst.Ed.

EISENHOWER (Mamie Doud) BIRTHPLACE FOUNDATION, INC. - MUSEUM &
    LIBRARY
709 Carroll St.
Box 55   Phone: (515) 432-1896
Boone, IA 50036   Larry Adams, Cur.

BURLINGTON MEDICAL CENTER - LIBRARY
602 N. Third   Phone: (319) 753-3631
Burlington, IA 52601   Michael W. Wold, Libn.

CEDAR FALLS HISTORICAL SOCIETY - ROWND HISTORICAL LIBRARY
Cedar Falls Historical Museum
303 Clay St.   Phone: (319) 266-5149
Cedar Falls, IA 50613   Rosemary Beach, Dir.

UNIVERSITY OF NORTHERN IOWA - LIBRARY - SPECIAL COLLECTIONS
                                                       Phone: (319) 273-6307
Cedar Falls, IA 50613   Gerald L. Peterson, Spec.Coll.Libn.

CEDAR RAPIDS MUSEUM OF ART - HERBERT S. STAMATS ART LIBRARY
324 3rd St., S.E.   Phone: (319) 366-7503
Cedar Rapids, IA 52401

FIRST LUTHERAN CHURCH - ADULT LIBRARY
1000 3rd Ave., S.E.   Phone: (319) 365-1494
Cedar Rapids, IA 52403   Ortha R. Harstad, Libn.

GRAND LODGE OF IOWA, A.F. AND A.M. - IOWA MASONIC LIBRARY
813 First Ave., S.E.
Box 279   Phone: (319) 365-1438
Cedar Rapids, IA 52406   Tom Eggleston, Grand Sec./Libn.

LINN COUNTY BAR ASSOCIATION - LAW LIBRARY
Linn County Court House   Phone: (319) 398-3449
Cedar Rapids, IA 52401   Betty Dye, Law Libn.

MERCY HOSPITAL - HEALTH SERVICES LIBRARY
701 Tenth St., S.E.   Phone: (319) 398-6165
Cedar Rapids, IA 52403   Linda Miller, Libn.

ROCKWELL INTERNATIONAL - COLLINS DIVISIONS - INFORMATION
    CENTER
400 Collins Rd., N.E.   Phone: (319) 395-3070
Cedar Rapids, IA 52498   Judith A. Leavitt, Supv., Info.Ctr.

ST. LUKE'S METHODIST HOSPITAL - HEALTH SCIENCE LIBRARY
1026 A Ave., N.E.   Phone: (319) 398-7358
Cedar Rapids, IA 52402   Sally Harms, Dir.

MENTAL HEALTH INSTITUTE - HEALTH SCIENCE LIBRARY
1200 W. Cedar St.   Phone: (712) 225-2594
Cherokee, IA 51012   Tom Folkes, Health Sci.Libn.

SANFORD MUSEUM & PLANETARIUM - LIBRARY
117 E. Willow St.   Phone: (712) 225-3922
Cherokee, IA 51012   J. Terry Walker, Dir.

CLARINDA MENTAL HEALTH INSTITUTION - RESIDENTS AND STAFF
    LIBRARY *
Box 338   Phone: (712) 585-2161
Clarinda, IA 51632   Dorothy Horton, Libn.

CHEROKEE COUNTY HISTORICAL SOCIETY - RESEARCH CENTER
Box 247   Phone: (712) 436-2624
Cleghorn, IA 51014   Anne Wilberding, Pres.

THE BICKELHAUPT ARBORETUM - EDUCATION CENTER
340 S. Fourteenth St.   Phone: (319) 242-4771
Clinton, IA 52732   Frances B. Hill, Libn.

EDMUNDSON (Jennie) MEMORIAL HOSPITAL - LIBRARY *
933 E. Pierce St.   Phone: (712) 328-6130
Council Bluffs, IA 51501   Patricia A. Blanchard, Libn.

DAVENPORT ART GALLERY - ART REFERENCE LIBRARY
1737 W. 12th St.   Phone: (319) 326-7804
Davenport, IA 52804   Gladys Hitchings, Libn.

DAVENPORT OSTEOPATHIC HOSPITAL - MEDICAL STAFF LIBRARY
1111 W. Kimberly Rd.   Phone: (319) 383-0295
Davenport, IA 52806   Mary A. Vickery, Libn.

GRANT LAW LIBRARY
416 W. 4th St.   Phone: (319) 326-8741
Davenport, IA 52801   Ginger F. Wolfe, Libn.

MARYCREST COLLEGE - CONE LIBRARY
1607 West 12th St.   Phone: (319) 326-9254
Davenport, IA 52804   Sr. Joan Sheil, Dir., Lib.Serv.

PALMER COLLEGE OF CHIROPRACTIC - DAVID D. PALMER LIBRARY
1000 Brady St.   Phone: (319) 326-9641
Davenport, IA 52803   Dennis R. Peterson, Interim Dir.

PUTNAM MUSEUM - LIBRARY
1717 W. 12th St.   Phone: (319) 324-1933
Davenport, IA 52804   Michael J. Smith, Dir.

LUTHER COLLEGE - PREUS LIBRARY
                                           Phone: (319) 387-1163
Decorah, IA 52101   Leigh D. Jordahl, Hd.Libn.

NORWEGIAN-AMERICAN MUSEUM - REFERENCE LIBRARY
502 W. Water St.   Phone: (319) 382-9681
Decorah, IA 52101   Darrell D. Henning, Cur.

BROADLAWNS MEDICAL CENTER - HEALTH SCIENCES LIBRARY
18th & Hickman Rd.   Phone: (515) 282-2200
Des Moines, IA 50314   Charles Z. Hughes, Libn.

CHILD CARE RESOURCE CENTER
1044 7th St.
Des Moines, IA 50314   Emilie Duimstra, Training Coord.

DES MOINES ART CENTER - LIBRARY
Greenwood Park   Phone: (515) 277-4405
Des Moines, IA 50312   Margaret Buckley, Libn.

DRAKE UNIVERSITY - COLLEGE OF PHARMACY - LIBRARY
28th & Forest Ave.   Phone: (515) 271-2172
Des Moines, IA 50311   Margaret Daly Granberg, Libn.

DRAKE UNIVERSITY - COWLES LIBRARY - SPECIAL COLLECTIONS
28th St. & University Ave.   Phone: (515) 271-3993
Des Moines, IA 50311   J. Elias Jones, Bibliog./Archv.

DRAKE UNIVERSITY - LAW LIBRARY
Carnegie Hall
27th & Carpenter   Phone: (515) 271-2141
Des Moines, IA 50311   Juan F. Aguilar, Dir.

GRAND VIEW COLLEGE - ARCHIVES
1351 Grandview   Phone: (515) 263-2800
Des Moines, IA 50316   Thorvald Hansen, Archv.

IOWA GENEALOGICAL SOCIETY - LIBRARY
6000 Douglas
Box 3815   Phone: (515) 276-0287
Des Moines, IA 50322   Marilyn Schmitt, Libn.

IOWA HOSPITAL ASSOCIATION - LIBRARY
600 5th Ave. Plaza.   Phone: (515) 288-1955
Des Moines, IA 50309   Deborah Van Egdom, Libn.

IOWA LUTHERAN HOSPITAL - DEPARTMENT OF EDUCATIONAL MEDIA
University at Penn   Phone: (515) 263-5181
Des Moines, IA 50316   Wayne A. Pedersen, Dir., Educ. Media

IOWA METHODIST MEDICAL CENTER - OLIVER J. FAY MEMORIAL LIBRARY
1200 Pleasant St.   Phone: (515) 283-6490
Des Moines, IA 50308   Mary Wegner, Dir., Med.Lib.

IOWA METHODIST SCHOOL OF NURSING - MARJORIE GERTRUDE MORROW
    LIBRARY
1117 Pleasant St.   Phone: (515) 283-6453
Des Moines, IA 50309   Nancy O'Brien, Libn.

IOWA STATE COMMISSION FOR THE BLIND - LIBRARY FOR THE BLIND &
    PHYSICALLY HANDICAPPED
4th & Keosauqua Way   Phone: (515) 283-2601
Des Moines, IA 50309   Cathryn Ford, Libn.

IOWA STATE DEPARTMENT OF HEALTH - STATISTICAL SERVICES
Lucas State Office Bldg.   Phone: (515) 281-4945
Des Moines, IA 50319   Carson E. Whitlow, Dir.

IOWA STATE DEPARTMENT OF HUMAN SERVICES - LIBRARY
Hoover Bldg.   Phone: (515) 281-5925
Des Moines, IA 50319   Kay M. Elliott, Chf.Libn.

IOWA STATE DEPARTMENT OF PUBLIC INSTRUCTION - RESOURCE
    CENTER
Grimes State Office Bldg.   Phone: (515) 281-3770
Des Moines, IA 50319   D.A. Snyder, Libn.

IOWA STATE DEPARTMENT OF WATER, AIR AND WASTE MANAGEMENT -
    TECHNICAL LIBRARY
Henry A. Wallace Bldg.   Phone: (515) 281-8895
Des Moines, IA 50319   Cecilia Nelson, Rec.Ck.

IOWA (State) HISTORICAL DEPARTMENT LIBRARY
E. 12th & Grand Ave.
Historical Bldg.   Phone: (515) 281-5472
Des Moines, IA 50319   Lowell R. Wilbur, Libn.

IOWA STATE LAW LIBRARY
State House   Phone: (515) 281-5125
Des Moines, IA 50319   James H. Gritton, Law Libn.

IOWA STATE LEGISLATIVE SERVICE BUREAU - LIBRARY
State House   Phone: (515) 281-3312
Des Moines, IA 50319   Ruth D. McGhee, Libn.

IOWA STATE LIBRARY COMMISSION
E. 12th & Grand   Phone: (515) 281-4103
Des Moines, IA 50319   Claudya B. Muller, State Libn.

KIRKE VAN ORSDEL INC. - LIBRARY
400 Locust   Phone: (515) 243-1776
Des Moines, IA 50398   Ann Linquist, Libn.

LEAGUE OF IOWA MUNICIPALITIES - LIBRARY
900 Des Moines St., Suite 100   Phone: (515) 265-9961
Des Moines, IA 50316   Robert W. Harpster, Exec.Dir.

MERCY HOSPITAL - LEVITT HEALTH SCIENCES LIBRARY †
1165 5th Ave.
Des Moines, IA 50314
Phone: (515) 247-4189
Lenetta Atkins, Libn.

OPEN BIBLE COLLEGE - CARRIE HARDY MEMORIAL LIBRARY
2633 Fleur Dr.
Des Moines, IA 50321
Phone: (515) 283-0478
Linda Jones, Libn.

PIONEER HI-BRED INTERNATIONAL, INC. - CORPORATE LIBRARY
400 Locust, Suite 700
Des Moines, IA 50309
Phone: (515) 245-3518
Willona Graham Goers, Corp.Libn.

REED LIBRARY OF FOOT & ANKLE
6000 Waterbury Circle
Des Moines, IA 50312
Phone: (515) 277-5756
Stewart E. Reed, D.P.M.

U.S. DEPT. OF COMMERCE - INTERNATIONAL TRADE ADMINISTRATION - DES MOINES DISTRICT OFFICE LIBRARY *
817 Federal Bldg.
210 Walnut St.
Des Moines, IA 50309
Phone: (515) 284-4222
Jesse N. Durden, Dir.

U.S. VETERANS ADMINISTRATION (IA-Des Moines) - HOSPITAL LIBRARY
30th & Euclid Ave.
Des Moines, IA 50310
Phone: (515) 255-2173
Clare M. Jergens, Chf., Lib.Serv.

UNIVERSITY OF OSTEOPATHIC MEDICINE AND HEALTH SCIENCES - LIBRARY †
3200 Grand Ave.
Des Moines, IA 50312
Phone: (515) 271-1430
Mrs. Krishna Sahu, Dir.

AMERICAN LUTHERAN CHURCH - ARCHIVES
Wartburg Theological Seminary
Dubuque, IA 52001
Phone: (319) 556-8151
Robert C. Wiederaenders, Archv.

MERCY HEALTH CENTER - ANTHONY C. PFOHL HEALTH SCIENCE LIBRARY
Mercy Dr.
Dubuque, IA 52001
Phone: (319) 589-8000
James H. Lander, Lib.Mgr.

SCHOOLS OF THEOLOGY IN DUBUQUE - LIBRARIES
333 Wartburg Pl.
Dubuque, IA 52001
Phone: (319) 589-3215
Duncan Brockway, Dir. of Libs.

GLENWOOD STATE HOSPITAL-SCHOOL - STAFF LIBRARY
711 S. Vine
Glenwood, IA 51534
Phone: (712) 527-4811
Claire Osterholm, Assoc.Libn.

INDEPENDENCE MENTAL HEALTH INSTITUTE - MEDICAL LIBRARY
Box 111
Independence, IA 50644
Phone: (319) 334-2583
Lois J. Samek, Med.Libn.

AMERICAN COLLEGE TESTING PROGRAM - LIBRARY
Box 168
Iowa City, IA 52243
Phone: (319) 337-1165
Lois Renter, Hd.Libn.

STATE HISTORICAL SOCIETY OF IOWA - LIBRARY
402 Iowa Ave.
Iowa City, IA 52240
Phone: (319) 338-5471
Peter H. Curtis, Hd.Libn.

U.S. VETERANS ADMINISTRATION (IA-Iowa City) - HOSPITAL LIBRARY
Phone: (319) 338-0581
Iowa City, IA 52241
Marilyn J. Kraus, Med.Libn.

UNIVERSITY OF IOWA - ART LIBRARY
Art Bldg.
Iowa City, IA 52242
Phone: (319) 353-4440
Harlan Sifford, Libn.

UNIVERSITY OF IOWA - BOTANY-CHEMISTRY LIBRARY
Phone: (319) 353-3707
Iowa City, IA 52242
Sally Fry, Libn.

UNIVERSITY OF IOWA - BUSINESS LIBRARY
College of Business Administration
Phillips Hall
Iowa City, IA 52242
Phone: (319) 353-5803
Patricia H. Foley, Bus.Libn.

UNIVERSITY OF IOWA - COLLEGE OF EDUCATION - CURRICULUM RESOURCES LABORATORY
N140 Lindquist Center
Iowa City, IA 52242
Phone: (319) 353-4515
Paula O. Brandt, Coord.

UNIVERSITY OF IOWA - COLLEGE OF PHARMACY - IOWA DRUG INFORMATION SERVICE
Westlawn, Box 330
Iowa City, IA 52242
Phone: (319) 353-4639
Hazel H. Seaba, Dir.

UNIVERSITY OF IOWA - ENGINEERING LIBRARY
106 Engineering Bldg.
Iowa City, IA 52242
Phone: (319) 353-5224
John W. Forys, Libn.

UNIVERSITY OF IOWA - GEOLOGY LIBRARY
136 Trowbridge Hall
Iowa City, IA 52242
Phone: (319) 353-4225
Louise Zipp, Libn.

UNIVERSITY OF IOWA - HEALTH SCIENCES LIBRARY
Health Sciences Library Bldg.
Iowa City, IA 52242
Phone: (319) 353-5382
David S. Curry, Libn.

UNIVERSITY OF IOWA - INSTITUTE OF URBAN AND REGIONAL RESEARCH - LIBRARY
N222 Oakdale Campus
Iowa City, IA 52242
Phone: (319) 353-3862
John W. Fuller, Dir.

UNIVERSITY OF IOWA - IOWA URBAN COMMUNITY RESEARCH CENTER - REFERENCE LIBRARY
W170 Seashore Hall
Iowa City, IA 52242
Phone: (319) 353-4119
Lyle W. Shannon, Dir.

UNIVERSITY OF IOWA - LABORATORY FOR POLITICAL RESEARCH
345A Schaeffer Hall
Iowa City, IA 52242
Phone: (319) 353-3103
Prof. Greg Caldeira, Dir.

UNIVERSITY OF IOWA - LAW LIBRARY
Law Center
Iowa City, IA 52242
Phone: (319) 353-5968
George A. Strait, Dir.

UNIVERSITY OF IOWA - LIBRARY SCIENCE LIBRARY
Main Library
Iowa City, IA 52242
Phone: (319) 353-3946
Sandra S. Ballasch, Libn.

UNIVERSITY OF IOWA - MATHEMATICS LIBRARY
MacLean Hall
Iowa City, IA 52242
Phone: (319) 353-5939
Sally Fry, Libn.

UNIVERSITY OF IOWA - MUSIC LIBRARY
Music Bldg.
Iowa City, IA 52242
Phone: (319) 353-3797

UNIVERSITY OF IOWA - OFFICE OF THE STATE ARCHAEOLOGIST - DOCUMENT COLLECTION
317 Eastlawn
Iowa City, IA 52242
Phone: (319) 353-5175
Ruth Von Dracek, Docs.Cur.

UNIVERSITY OF IOWA - PHYSICS LIBRARY
Physics Research Center
Iowa City, IA 52242
Phone: (319) 353-4762
Jack W. Dickey, Libn.

UNIVERSITY OF IOWA - PSYCHOLOGY LIBRARY
Iowa City, IA 52242
Phone: (319) 353-5345
Dorothy M. Persson, Libn.

UNIVERSITY OF IOWA - SPECIAL COLLECTIONS DEPARTMENT
Main Library
Iowa City, IA 52242
Phone: (319) 353-4854
Frank Paluka, Hd.

UNIVERSITY OF IOWA - ZOOLOGY LIBRARY
301 Zoology Bldg.
Iowa City, IA 52242
Phone: (319) 353-5419
Jack W. Dickey, Libn.

WOMEN'S RESOURCE AND ACTION CENTER - SOJOURNER TRUTH WOMEN'S RESOURCE LIBRARY
130 N. Madison
Iowa City, IA 52242
Phone: (319) 353-6265
Kathy Lorz, Staff Libn.

IOWA LAW ENFORCEMENT ACADEMY - LIBRARY
Camp Dodge
Box 130
Johnston, IA 50131
Phone: (515) 278-9357
Jo Ellen Warne, Libn.

U.S. VETERANS ADMINISTRATION (IA-Knoxville) - MEDICAL CENTER
    LIBRARY
                                        Phone: (515) 842-3101
Knoxville, IA 50138

GRACELAND COLLEGE - FREDERICK MADISON SMITH LIBRARY
                                        Phone: (515) 784-3311
Lamoni, IA 50140   Volante H. Russell, Dir.

U.S. NATL. PARK SERVICE - EFFIGY MOUNDS NATL. MONUMENT - LIBRARY
Box K   Phone: (319) 873-2356
McGregor, IA 52157   Thomas A. Munson, Supt.

MARSHALLTOWN AREA COMMUNITY HOSPITAL - SCHOOL OF NURSING
    RESOURCE CENTER
3 S. 4th Ave.   Phone: (515) 754-5179
Marshalltown, IA 50158   Yvette Ferguson, Coord.

MONSANTO COMPANY - FISHER CONTROLS COMPANY - R.A. ENGEL
    TECHNICAL LIBRARY
R.A. Engel Technical Center, Box 11   Phone: (515) 754-2161
Marshalltown, IA 50158   Mark Heindselman, Sr.Res.Libn.

ST. JOSEPH MERCY HOSPITAL - MEDICAL LIBRARY
84 Beaumont Dr.   Phone: (515) 424-7699
Mason City, IA 50401   Judy I. Madson, Dir.

MIDWEST OLD SETTLERS AND THRESHERS ASSOCIATION - OLD
    THRESHERS OFFICE - LIBRARY
R.R. 1   Phone: (319) 385-9432
Mount Pleasant, IA 52641   Lennis Moore, Adm.

MOUNT PLEASANT MENTAL HEALTH INSTITUTE - PROFESSIONAL LIBRARY
1200 E. Washington St.   Phone: (319) 385-7231
Mount Pleasant, IA 52641   James Sommerville, Libn.

CORNELL COLLEGE - CHEMISTRY LIBRARY †
West Science Hall   Phone: (319) 895-8811
Mount Vernon, IA 52314   Stuart A. Stiffler, Dir., Lib.Serv.

GRAIN PROCESSING CORPORATION - TECHNICAL INFORMATION CENTER,
1600 Oregon St.
Box 349   Phone: (319) 264-4389
Muscatine, IA 52761   Maurene Failor, Libn.

STANLEY CONSULTANTS - TECHNICAL LIBRARY
Stanley Bldg.   Phone: (319) 264-6234
Muscatine, IA 52761   Kathy A. McNeal, Libn.

WILLIAM PENN COLLEGE - WILCOX LIBRARY - SPECIAL COLLECTIONS
                                        Phone: (515) 673-8311
Oskaloosa, IA 52577   Marion E. Rains, Libn.

AIRPOWER MUSEUM - LIBRARY
Antique Airfield
Rte. 2, Box 172
Ottumwa, IA 52501   David J. Sutton, Musm. Trustee

ST. JOSEPH HOSPITAL - LIBRARY *
312 E. Alta Vista   Phone: (515) 684-4651
Ottumwa, IA 52501   Sr. Mary Christine Conaway, Libn./Dir., Media Ctr.

CALHOUN COUNTY HISTORICAL MUSEUM - LIBRARY
680 Eighth St.
Rockwell City, IA 50579   Judy Webb, Libn.

DORDT COLLEGE - ARCHIVES AND DUTCH MEMORIAL COLLECTION
498 4th Ave., N.E.   Phone: (712) 722-3771
Sioux Center, IA 51250   Minnie Julia Dahm, Archv.

JEWISH COMMUNITY CENTER - LIBRARY
525 14th St.
Sioux City, IA 51105

ST. LUKE'S REGIONAL MEDICAL CENTER - LIBRARY-MEDIA CENTER
2720 Stone Park Blvd.   Phone: (712) 279-3156
Sioux City, IA 51104   Barbara Knight, Lib.-Media Coord.

SIOUX CITY ART CENTER ASSOCIATION - LIBRARY
513 Nebraska St.   Phone: (712) 279-6272
Sioux City, IA 51101   Marilyn Laufer, Educ.Cur.

WOODBURY COUNTY BAR ASSOCIATION - LAW LIBRARY
7th & Douglas Sts.
Woodbury County Courthouse, 6th Fl.   Phone: (712) 279-6609
Sioux City, IA 51101   Susan M. Dunn, Libn.

BUENA VISTA COLLEGE - L.E. & E.L. BALLOU LIBRARY - SPECIAL
    COLLECTIONS
                                        Phone: (712) 749-2141
Storm Lake, IA 50588   Dr. Barbara R. Palling, Hd.Libn.

ALLEN MEMORIAL HOSPITAL - HEALTH SCIENCES LIBRARY
1825 Logan Ave.   Phone: (319) 235-3681
Waterloo, IA 50703   Adele J. Harms, Libn.

GROUT MUSEUM OF HISTORY AND SCIENCE - GENEALOGY, ARCHIVES AND
    REFERENCE LIBRARY
503 South St.   Phone: (319) 234-6357
Waterloo, IA 50701   Mary B. Miller, Archv.

JOHN DEERE PRODUCT ENGINEERING CENTER - LIBRARY
Box 8000   Phone: (319) 292-8020
Waterloo, IA 50704   YangHoon Rhee, Libn.

LUTHERAN MUTUAL LIFE INSURANCE COMPANY - LIBRARY
Heritage Way   Phone: (319) 352-4090
Waverly, IA 50677   Marietta K. Rieken, Libn.

U.S. PRESIDENTIAL LIBRARIES - HERBERT HOOVER LIBRARY
                                        Phone: (319) 643-5301
West Branch, IA 52358   Robert Wood, Dir.

DELAVAN INC. - ENGINEERING LIBRARY
Box 100   Phone: (515) 274-1561
West Des Moines, IA 50265   Gwen Hartman, Libn.

WOODWARD STATE HOSPITAL SCHOOL - STAFF LIBRARY
                                        Phone: (515) 438-2600
Woodward, IA 50276   Joy Averill, Libn.

KANSAS

MUSEUM OF INDEPENDENT TELEPHONY - ARCHIVES COLLECTION
412 S. Campbell   Phone: (913) 263-2681
Abilene, KS 67410   Peg Chronister, Cur.

U.S. PRESIDENTIAL LIBRARIES - DWIGHT D. EISENHOWER LIBRARY
S.E. Fourth St.   Phone: (913) 263-4751
Abilene, KS 67410   Dr. John E. Wickman, Dir.

U.S. NATL. PARK SERVICE - CHEROKEE STRIP LIVING MUSEUM - DOCKING
    RESEARCH CENTER ARCHIVES LIBRARY
S. Summit Street Rd.
Box 230   Phone: (316) 442-6750
Arkansas City, KS 67005   Cheryl Voigtlander, Libn.

CLARK COUNTY HISTORICAL SOCIETY - PIONEER MUSEUM - LIBRARY
430 W. Fourth   Phone: (316) 635-2227
Ashland, KS 67831   Rosa Lee Mc Gee, Cur.

BAKER UNIVERSITY - ARCHIVES AND HISTORICAL LIBRARY
Collins Library   Phone: (913) 594-6451
Baldwin City, KS 66006

BAKER UNIVERSITY - QUAYLE RARE BIBLE COLLECTION
Baker University Library, Eighth St.   Phone: (913) 594-3422
Baldwin City, KS 66006   Dr. John M. Forbes, Dir. of Libs.

WYANDOTTE COUNTY HISTORICAL SOCIETY AND MUSEUM - HARRY M.
    TROWBRIDGE RESEARCH LIBRARY
631 N. 126th St.   Phone: (913) 721-1078
Bonner Springs, KS 66012   Stephen J. Allie, Archv.

CEDAR VALE REGIONAL HOSPITAL - LIBRARY *
Cedar St.
Box 398   Phone: (316) 758-2266
Cedar Vale, KS 67024   Mrs. Dera C. Brunstad, Libn.

MARTIN AND OSA JOHNSON SAFARI MUSEUM - STOTT EXPLORERS
    LIBRARY
16 S. Grant St.   Phone: (316) 431-2730
Chanute, KS 66720   Sondra Alden, Musm.Dir.

SOD TOWN PIONEER HOMESTEAD MUSEUM - LIBRARY *
U.S. Hwy. 24, East
Box 393   Phone: (913) 462-2021
Colby, KS 67701   Ronald E. Thiel, Dir.

THOMAS COUNTY HISTORICAL SOCIETY - LIBRARY
1525 W. Fourth   Phone: (913) 462-6972
Colby, KS 67701   Helen L. Smith, Dir.

CLOUD COUNTY HISTORICAL MUSEUM - LIBRARY
635 Broadway   Phone: (913) 243-2866
Concordia, KS 66901   Thelma Schroth, Cur.

KANSAS HERITAGE CENTER - LIBRARY
Box 1275   Phone: (316) 227-2823
Dodge City, KS 67801   Jeanie Covalt, Res.Libn.

BUTLER COUNTY HISTORICAL SOCIETY - OLIVE CLIFFORD STONE
    LIBRARY
381 E. Central
Box 696   Phone: (316) 321-9333
El Dorado, KS 67042   Anna Louise Borger, Libn.

EMPORIA STATE UNIVERSITY - BUTCHER TOY LENDING LIBRARY
1200 Commercial   Phone: (316) 343-1200
Emporia, KS 66801   Jeanne Frederickson, Media Spec.

EMPORIA STATE UNIVERSITY - WILLIAM ALLEN WHITE LIBRARY -
    SPECIAL COLLECTIONS
1200 Commercial   Phone: (316) 343-1200
Emporia, KS 66801   Mary E. Bogan, Spec.Coll.Libn.

FLINT HILLS AREA VOCATIONAL-TECHNICAL SCHOOL - LIBRARY
3301 W. 18th Ave.   Phone: (316) 342-6404
Emporia, KS 66801   Jane M. Birchard, Libn.

U.S. ARMY COMMAND AND GENERAL STAFF COLLEGE - COMBINED ARMS
    RESEARCH LIBRARY
Bell Hall   Phone: (913) 684-3282
Ft. Leavenworth, KS 66027   Martha A. Davis, Libn.

U.S. ARMY HOSPITALS - IRWIN ARMY HOSPITAL - MEDICAL LIBRARY
Bldg. 485   Phone: (913) 239-7874
Ft. Riley, KS 66442   Phyllis J. Whiteside, Med.Libn.

U.S. ARMY POST - FORT RILEY - LIBRARIES †
Bldg. 6   Phone: (913) 239-2460
Ft. Riley, KS 66442   Dan W. Viergever, Main Post Libn.

U.S. CAVALRY MUSEUM - LIBRARY
Bldg. 30   Phone: (913) 239-2737
Fort Riley, KS 66442   Terry Van Meter, Dir.

WILSON COUNTY HISTORICAL SOCIETY - MUSEUM LIBRARY
420 N. 7th   Phone: (316) 378-3965
Fredonia, KS 66736   Bonnie Forbes, Musm.Cur.

HERTZLER RESEARCH FOUNDATION LIBRARY *
3rd & Chestnut St.   Phone: (316) 835-2241
Halstead, KS 67056

ELLIS COUNTY HISTORICAL SOCIETY - ARCHIVES
100 W. 7th St.   Phone: (913) 628-2624
Hays, KS 67601   Rev. Blaine Burkey, Archv./Hist.

FORT HAYS STATE UNIVERSITY - FORSYTH LIBRARY - SPECIAL
    COLLECTIONS
600 Park St.   Phone: (913) 628-4431
Hays, KS 67601   Esta Lou Riley, Archv./Spec.Coll.

FORT HAYS STATE UNIVERSITY - STERNBERG MEMORIAL MUSEUM -
    LIBRARY
                                               Phone: (913) 628-4286
Hays, KS 67601   Dr. Richard J. Zakrzewski, Musm.Dir.

BETHANY MEDICAL CENTER - W.W. SUMMERVILLE MEDICAL LIBRARY
51 N. 12th St.   Phone: (913) 281-8770
Kansas City, KS 66102   Barbara Shannon, Med.Libn.

CENTRAL BAPTIST THEOLOGICAL SEMINARY - LIBRARY
Seminary Heights   Phone: (913) 371-1544
Kansas City, KS 66102   Dr. Henry R. Moeller, Libn.

PROVIDENCE-ST. MARGARET HEALTH CENTER - LIBRARY
8929 Parallel Pkwy.   Phone: (913) 596-4795
Kansas City, KS 66112   Pamela Drayson, Dir.

U.S. BUREAU OF THE CENSUS - INFORMATION SERVICES PROGRAM -
    KANSAS CITY REGIONAL OFFICE - LIBRARY
One Gateway Center, Suite 500   Phone: (816) 374-4601
Kansas City, KS 66101   John W. Dale, Prog.Coord.

UNIVERSITY OF KANSAS MEDICAL CTR. - COLLEGE OF HEALTH SCI. AND
    HOSPITAL - ARCHIE R. DYKES LIB. OF THE HEALTH SCI.
2100 W. 39th   Phone: (913) 588-7166
Kansas City, KS 66103   Earl Farley, Dir.

WYANDOTTE COUNTY LAW LIBRARY
County Courthouse
710 N. 7th St.   Phone: (913) 342-4225
Kansas City, KS 66101   Rita Hollecker Kancel, Law Libn.

FORT LARNED HISTORICAL SOCIETY, INC. - SANTA FE TRAIL CENTER
    LIBRARY
Rte. 3   Phone: (316) 285-2054
Larned, KS 67550   Kim Keiswetter, Archv./Educ.Dir.

LARNED STATE HOSPITAL - J.T. NARAMORE LIBRARY
Route 3, Box 89   Phone: (316) 285-2131
Larned, KS 67550   Virginia Brownlee, Dir., Nursing Educ.

U.S. NATL. PARK SERVICE - FORT LARNED NATL. HISTORIC SITE -
    LIBRARY
Rte. 3   Phone: (316) 285-3571
Larned, KS 67550   John B. Arnold, Supt.

GOLF COURSE SUPERINTENDENTS ASSOCIATION OF AMERICA - GCSAA
    LIBRARY
1617 St. Andrews Dr.   Phone: (913) 841-2240
Lawrence, KS 66044   Barbara L. Davis, Exec.Sec.

KANSAS STATE GEOLOGICAL SURVEY - MOORE HALL LIBRARY
1930 Ave. A, Campus W   Phone: (913) 864-3965
Lawrence, KS 66044   Janice H. Sorensen, Libn.

UNIVERSITY OF KANSAS - CENTER FOR PUBLIC AFFAIRS
607 Blake Hall   Phone: (913) 864-3701
Lawrence, KS 66045   Thelma Helyar, Libn.

UNIVERSITY OF KANSAS - DEPARTMENT OF SPECIAL COLLECTIONS
Spencer Research Library   Phone: (913) 864-4334
Lawrence, KS 66045   Alexandra Mason, Spencer Libn.

UNIVERSITY OF KANSAS - DOCUMENTS COLLECTION
117 Spencer Research Library   Phone: (913) 864-4662
Lawrence, KS 66045   Marion L. Howey, Doc.Libn.

UNIVERSITY OF KANSAS - EAST ASIAN LIBRARY
Watson Library   Phone: (913) 864-4669
Lawrence, KS 66045   Eugene Carvalho, Libn.

UNIVERSITY OF KANSAS - ENGINEERING LIBRARY
1012 Learned Hall   Phone: (913) 864-3866
Lawrence, KS 66045

UNIVERSITY OF KANSAS - JOURNALISM LIBRARY
William Allen White School of Journalism
210 Flint Hall   Phone: (913) 864-4755
Lawrence, KS 66045   Ethel Stewart, Libn.

UNIVERSITY OF KANSAS - KANSAS COLLECTION
220 Spencer Research Library   Phone: (913) 864-4274
Lawrence, KS 66045   Sheryl K. Williams, Cur.

UNIVERSITY OF KANSAS - MAP LIBRARY
110 Spencer Library   Phone: (913) 864-4420
Lawrence, KS 66045   Richard Embers, Map Lib.Assoc.

UNIVERSITY OF KANSAS - MURPHY LIBRARY OF ART HISTORY
Helen Foresman Spencer Museum of Art   Phone: (913) 864-3020
Lawrence, KS 66045   Susan V. Craig, Art Libn.

UNIVERSITY OF KANSAS - SCHOOL OF LAW LIBRARY
New Green Hall   Phone: (913) 864-3025
Lawrence, KS 66045   Peter C. Schanck, Dir.

UNIVERSITY OF KANSAS - SCIENCE LIBRARY
6040 Malott Hall   Phone: (913) 864-4928
Lawrence, KS 66045   Jeanne Richardson, Sci.Libn.

UNIVERSITY OF KANSAS - SLAVIC COLLECTION
Watson Library   Phone: (913) 864-3957
Lawrence, KS 66045   George Jerkovich, Dir./Cur.

UNIVERSITY OF KANSAS - THOMAS GORTON MUSIC LIBRARY
448 Murphy Hall   Phone: (913) 864-3496
Lawrence, KS 66045   Earl Gates, Libn.

UNIVERSITY OF KANSAS - UNIVERSITY ARCHIVES
422 Spencer Library   Phone: (913) 864-4188
Lawrence, KS 66045   John M. Nugent, Univ.Archv.

UNIVERSITY OF KANSAS - WEALTHY BABCOCK MATHEMATICS LIBRARY
209 Strong Hall   Phone: (913) 864-3440
Lawrence, KS 66045   Ruth D. Fauhl, Lib.Asst.

UNIVERSITY OF KANSAS - WILCOX COLLECTION OF CONTEMPORARY
POLITICAL MOVEMENTS
Kansas Collection, Spencer Library   Phone: (913) 864-4274
Lawrence, KS 66045   Sheryl K. Williams, Cur., Kansas Coll.

SAINT MARY COLLEGE - DE PAUL LIBRARY - SPECIAL COLLECTIONS
CENTER
                                               Phone: (913) 682-5151
Leavenworth, KS 66048   Sister Therese Deplazes, Spec.Coll.Libn.

U.S. VETERANS ADMINISTRATION (KS-Leavenworth) - CENTER MEDICAL
LIBRARY
                                               Phone: (913) 682-2000
Leavenworth, KS 66048   Bennett F. Lawson, Chf., Lib.Serv.

U.S. AIR FORCE BASE - MC CONNELL BASE LIBRARY
FL4621   Phone: (316) 681-5414
McConnell AFB, KS 67221   Mary E. Rinas, Libn.

MC PHERSON COLLEGE - MILLER LIBRARY
1600 E. Euclid
Box 1402   Phone: (316) 241-0731
McPherson, KS 67460-1402   Rowena Olsen, Libn.

AMERICAN INSTITUTE OF BAKING - LIBRARY
1213 Bakers Way   Phone: (913) 537-4750
Manhattan, KS 66502   Judith Hortin, Libn.

KANSAS ENERGY EXTENSION SERVICE
311 Umberger
Kansas State University   Phone: (913) 532-5804
Manhattan, KS 66506   Su Bacon, Ed.

KANSAS STATE UNIVERSITY - CHEMISTRY LIBRARY
                                               Phone: (913) 532-6530
Manhattan, KS 66506   Pat Parris, Libn.

KANSAS STATE UNIVERSITY - FARRELL LIBRARY
                                               Phone: (913) 532-6516
Manhattan, KS 66506   Brice G. Hobrock, Dean of Libs.

KANSAS STATE UNIVERSITY - FOOD AND FEED GRAIN INSTITUTE - POST-
HARVEST DOCUMENTATION SERVICE
Farrell Library   Phone: (913) 532-6516
Manhattan, KS 66502   Donna Schenck-Hamlin, Libn.

KANSAS STATE UNIVERSITY - GRAIN SCIENCE AND INDUSTRY -
SWANSON MEMORIAL LIBRARY
                                               Phone: (913) 532-6161
Manhattan, KS 66506   Diane LaBarbera, Libn.

KANSAS STATE UNIVERSITY - HERBARIUM LIBRARY
Bushnell Hall   Phone: (913) 532-6619
Manhattan, KS 66506   T.M. Barkley, Cur. of Herbarium

KANSAS STATE UNIVERSITY - INSTITUTE FOR ENVIRONMENTAL
RESEARCH - LIBRARY
Dept. of Mechanical Engineering   Phone: (913) 532-5620
Manhattan, KS 66506   Dr. F.H. Rohles

KANSAS STATE UNIVERSITY - INTERNATIONAL AGRICULTURAL
PROGRAMS - RESOURCES ON DEVELOPING COUNTRIES
Farrell Library   Phone: (913) 532-6516
Manhattan, KS 66506   Gretchen A. Graham, Libn.

KANSAS STATE UNIVERSITY - PAUL WEIGEL LIBRARY OF ARCHITECTURE
AND DESIGN
                                               Phone: (913) 532-5968
Manhattan, KS 66506   Patricia Weisenburger, Libn.

KANSAS STATE UNIVERSITY - PHYSICS LIBRARY
                                               Phone: (913) 532-6827
Manhattan, KS 66506   Calista McBride, Libn.

KANSAS STATE UNIVERSITY - POPULATION RESEARCH LABORATORY -
LIBRARY
                                               Phone: (913) 532-5984
Manhattan, KS 66506   Donald J. Adamchak, Dir.

KANSAS STATE UNIVERSITY - SPECIAL COLLECTIONS DEPARTMENT
Farrell Library   Phone: (913) 532-6516
Manhattan, KS 66506   John J. Vander Velde, Spec.Coll.Libn.

KANSAS STATE UNIVERSITY - UNIVERSITY ARCHIVES
Farrell Library   Phone: (913) 532-6516
Manhattan, KS 66506   Antonia Pigno, Coord., Spec.Coll./Archv.

KANSAS STATE UNIVERSITY - VETERINARY MEDICAL LIBRARY
                                               Phone: (913) 532-6006
Manhattan, KS 66506   E. Guy Coffee, Hd.Libn.

LEARNING RESOURCES NETWORK - PUBLICATIONS AND RESOURCES
1221 Thurston   Phone: (913) 539-5376
Manhattan, KS 66502   William A. Draves, Natl.Dir.

RILEY COUNTY GENEALOGICAL SOCIETY - LIBRARY
2005 Claflin Rd.   Phone: (913) 537-2205
Manhattan, KS 66502   Mildred Loeffler, Libn.

RILEY COUNTY HISTORICAL SOCIETY - SEATON MEMORIAL LIBRARY
2309 Claflin Rd.   Phone: (913) 537-2210
Manhattan, KS 66502   Cheryl Collins, Libn.

JOHNSON COUNTY MENTAL HEALTH CENTER - JOHN R. KEACH MEMORIAL
LIBRARY
6000 Lamar Ave.   Phone: (913) 384-1100
Mission, KS 66202   Krista Hilton-Ross, Libn.

BETHEL COLLEGE - MENNONITE LIBRARY AND ARCHIVES
                                               Phone: (316) 283-2500
North Newton, KS 67117   Robert Kreider, Dir.

MENNONITE CHURCH - WESTERN DISTRICT CONFERENCE - WESTERN
DISTRICT LOAN LIBRARY
Box 66
North Newton, KS 67117   Mrs. J. Lloyd Spaulding, Libn.

NORTON STATE HOSPITAL - PROFESSIONAL LIBRARY
Rte. 1   Phone: (913) 877-3301
Norton, KS 67654

JOHNSON COUNTY LAW LIBRARY
Courthouse
Olathe, KS 66061
Phone: (913) 782-5000
J.W. Breyfogle, III, Libn.

OSAWATOMIE STATE HOSPITAL - RAPAPORT PROFESSIONAL LIBRARY -
MENTAL HEALTH LIBRARY
Phone: (913) 755-3151
Osawatomie, KS 66064
Helen Porter, Libn.

EMPLOYEES REINSURANCE CORPORATION - JUNE AUSTIN PARRISH
MEMORIAL LIBRARY
5200 Metcalf
Box 2991
Overland Park, KS 66201
Phone: (913) 676-5681
Jeanne Wood, Libn.

PARSONS STATE HOSPITAL AND TRAINING CENTER - RESEARCH LIBRARY
Box 738
Parsons, KS 67357
Phone: (316) 421-6550
Banny P. Rucker, Asst.Libn.

PITTSBURG STATE UNIVERSITY - LEONARD H. AXE LIBRARY - SPECIAL
COLLECTIONS
S. Joplin
Pittsburg, KS 66762
Phone: (316) 231-7000
Eugene H. De Gruson, Spec.Coll.Libn.

LINN COUNTY HISTORICAL SOCIETY - LIBRARY
Box 137
Pleasanton, KS 66075
Phone: (913) 352-8739
Ola May Earnest, Pres.

KANSAS TECHNICAL INSTITUTE - TULLIS RESOURCE CENTER
1831 Crompton Rd.
Salina, KS 67401
Phone: (913) 825-0275
Eleen M. Owen, Libn.

BAYVET - LIBRARY †
12707 W. 63rd St.
Shawnee, KS 66201
Phone: (913) 631-4800
Cindy Stacy, Res.Data Coord.

SHAWNEE MISSION MEDICAL CENTER - MEDICAL LIBRARY
74th & Grandview
Box 2923
Shawnee Mission, KS 66201
Phone: (913) 676-2101
Clifford L. Nestell, Dir. of Lib.Serv.

UNIVERSITY OF KANSAS REGENTS CENTER - LIBRARY
9900 Mission Rd.
Shawnee Mission, KS 66206
Phone: (913) 341-4554
Nancy J. Burich, Libn.

AMERICAN LUNG ASSOCIATION OF KANSAS - INFORMATION CENTER *
Box 4426
Topeka, KS 66604
Phone: (913) 272-9290
Darrel Walton, Exec.Dir.

GRAND LODGE OF ANCIENT FREE AND ACCEPTED MASONS OF KANSAS -
GRAND LODGE MASONIC LIBRARY
320 W. 8th St.
Topeka, KS 66603
Phone: (913) 234-5518
Albert O. Arnold, Jr., Grand Sec.

KANSAS STATE DEPARTMENT OF SOCIAL & REHABILITATION SERVICES -
STAFF DEVELOPMENT TRAINING CENTER LIBRARY
2700 W. 6th St.
Topeka, KS 66606
Phone: (913) 296-4327
Jean Barton, Libn.

KANSAS STATE HISTORICAL SOCIETY - LIBRARY
120 W. 10th St.
Topeka, KS 66612
Phone: (913) 296-3251
Portia Allbert, Lib.Dir.

KANSAS STATE LIBRARY
Statehouse, 3rd Fl.
Topeka, KS 66612
Phone: (913) 296-3296
Duane F. Johnson, State Libn.

KANSAS STATE SUPREME COURT - LAW LIBRARY
Judicial Center
301 West 10th
Topeka, KS 66612
Phone: (913) 296-3257
Fred W. Knecht, Law Libn.

LONDON CLUB - ARCHIVES
Box 4527
Topeka, KS 66604
L.D. Baranski, Archv.

MENNINGER FOUNDATION - ARCHIVES
Box 829
Topeka, KS 66601
Phone: (913) 273-7500
Dr. Mark I. West, Archv.

MENNINGER FOUNDATION - PROFESSIONAL LIBRARY
Box 829
Topeka, KS 66601
Phone: (913) 273-7500
Alice Brand, Chf.Libn.

SECURITY BENEFIT LIFE INSURANCE COMPANY - LIBRARY
700 Harrison St.
Topeka, KS 66636
Phone: (913) 295-3000
Kathy Jones, Personnel Ck.

STORMONT-VAIL REGIONAL MEDICAL CENTER AND SHAWNEE COUNTY
MEDICAL SOCIETY - HEALTH SCIENCES LIBRARY
1500 S.W. 10th St.
Topeka, KS 66606
Phone: (913) 354-6090
Shirley Borglund, Hd.Libn.

TOPEKA STATE HOSPITAL - STAFF LIBRARY
2700 W. 6th St.
Topeka, KS 66606
Phone: (913) 296-4411
Laura E. Schafer, Libn.

U.S. VETERANS ADMINISTRATION (KS-Topeka) - DR. KARL A. MENNINGER
MEDICAL LIBRARY
2200 Gage Blvd.
Topeka, KS 66622
Phone: (913) 272-3111
Norma R. Godfrey, Chf., Lib.Serv.

WASHBURN UNIVERSITY OF TOPEKA - SCHOOL OF LAW LIBRARY
1700 College Ave.
Topeka, KS 66621
Phone: (913) 295-6688
John E. Christensen, Dir.

CHISHOLM TRAIL MUSEUM - ARCHIVES AND LIBRARY
502 N. Washington Ave.
Wellington, KS 67152
Phone: (316) 326-2174
Anita Busch, Libn.

BOEING MILITARY AIRPLANE COMPANY - LIBRARY
Box 7730
Wichita, KS 67277-7730
Phone: (316) 526-3801
C.H. Jones, Lib.Supv.

CESSNA AIRCRAFT COMPANY - WALLACE DIVISION - ENGINEERING
LIBRARY
Box 7704
Wichita, KS 67277
Phone: (316) 946-6575
Betty Parks, Libn.

FRIENDS UNIVERSITY - EDMUND STANLEY LIBRARY - SPECIAL
COLLECTIONS
2100 University Ave.
Wichita, KS 67213
Phone: (316) 261-5800
Marti Harris Allen, Dir., Lrng.Res.

INSTITUTE OF LOGOPEDICS - TECHNICAL LIBRARY
2400 Jardine Dr.
Wichita, KS 67219
Phone: (316) 262-8271
Clyde Cochran Berger, Tech.Libn.

INTERNATIONAL REFERENCE ORGANIZATION IN FORENSIC MEDICINE
AND SCIENCES - LIBRARY AND REFERENCE CENTER
Milton Helpern Center
Wichita State University
Box 95
Wichita, KS 67208
Phone: (316) 262-6211
Dr. William G. Eckert, Dir.

KANSAS STATE GEOLOGICAL SURVEY - WICHITA WELL SAMPLE LIBRARY
4150 Monroe St.
Wichita, KS 67209
Phone: (316) 943-2343
Lawrence H. Skelton, Geologist & Mgr.

MIDWEST HISTORICAL & GENEALOGICAL SOCIETY, INC. - LIBRARY
Box 1121
Wichita, KS 67201
Bill Pennington, Libn.

ST. FRANCIS REGIONAL MEDICAL CENTER - PROFESSIONAL LIBRARY
929 N. St. Francis
Wichita, KS 67214
Phone: (316) 268-5979
Betty B. Wood, Libn.

ST. JOSEPH MEDICAL CENTER - HOSPITAL LIBRARY
3600 E. Harry
Wichita, KS 67218
Phone: (316) 685-1111
Carol Matulka, Med.Libn.

SEDGWICK COUNTY LAW LIBRARY †
255 N. Market, Suite 210
Wichita, KS 67202
Phone: (316) 263-2251
Jonalou M. Pinnell, Libn.

U.S. VETERANS ADMINISTRATION (KS-Wichita) - MEDICAL CENTER
LIBRARY
5500 E. Kellogg St.
Wichita, KS 67208
Phone: (316) 685-2221

WESLEY MEDICAL CENTER - H.B. MC KIBBIN HEALTH SCIENCE LIBRARY
550 N. Hillside   Phone: (316) 685-2151
Wichita, KS 67214   Jan Braden, Dir., Lib.Serv.

WICHITA ART ASSOCIATION, INC. - REFERENCE LIBRARY
9112 E. Central   Phone: (316) 686-6687
Wichita, KS 67206   Irma Hobbs, Chm., Lib.Comm.

WICHITA ART MUSEUM - LIBRARY
619 Stackman Dr.   Phone: (316) 264-6251
Wichita, KS 67203   Lois F. Crane, Libn.

WICHITA EAGLE-BEACON - LIBRARY
825 E. Douglas   Phone: (316) 268-6575
Wichita, KS 67203   Sally Stratton, Chf.Libn.

WICHITA PUBLIC LIBRARY - BUSINESS AND TECHNOLOGY DIVISION
223 S. Main   Phone: (316) 262-0611
Wichita, KS 67202   Larry DePiesse, Hd.

WICHITA-SEDGWICK COUNTY HISTORICAL MUSEUM - LIBRARY &
    ARCHIVES
204 S. Main   Phone: (316) 265-9314
Wichita, KS 67202   Robert A. Puckett, Dir.

WICHITA STATE UNIVERSITY - DEPARTMENT OF CHEMISTRY - LLOYD MC
    KINLEY MEMORIAL CHEMISTRY LIBRARY
1845 Fairmount   Phone: (316) 689-3120
Wichita, KS 67208   B. Jack McCormick

WICHITA STATE UNIVERSITY - SPECIAL COLLECTIONS
1845 Fairmount   Phone: (316) 689-3590
Wichita, KS 67208   Michael T. Kelly, Cur.

WICHITA STATE UNIVERSITY - THURLOW LIEURANCE MEMORIAL MUSIC
    LIBRARY
Walter Duerksen Fine Arts Center   Phone: (316) 689-3029
Wichita, KS 67208   David L. Austin, Music Libn.

SNYDER (H.L.) MEMORIAL RESEARCH FOUNDATION - LIBRARY †
1407 Wheat Rd.   Phone: (316) 221-4080
Winfield, KS 67156   Barbara Smith, Libn.

UNITED METHODIST CHURCH - KANSAS WEST CONFERENCE - ARCHIVES
    AND HISTORY DEPOSITORY
Southwestern College Library   Phone: (316) 221-4150
Winfield, KS 67156   Irene Lively, Archv.

WINFIELD STATE HOSPITAL AND TRAINING CENTER - PROFESSIONAL
    AND MEDICAL LIBRARY
     Phone: (316) 221-1200
Winfield, KS 67156   Janis Beecham, Lib.Ck.

KENTUCKY

ASHLAND OIL, INC. - TECHNICAL INFORMATION CENTER
Box 391   Phone: (606) 739-4166
Ashland, KY 41101

BARTON MUSEUM OF WHISKEY HISTORY - LIBRARY *
Bardstown, KY 40004   Oscar Getz, Founder

BEREA COLLEGE - HUTCHINS LIBRARY - SPECIAL COLLECTIONS
     Phone: (606) 986-9341
Berea, KY 40404   Gerald F. Roberts, Spec.Coll.Libn.

WESTERN KENTUCKY UNIVERSITY - DEPARTMENT OF SPECIAL
    COLLECTIONS - FOLKLORE, FOLKLIFE & ORAL HISTORY ARCHIVES
Kentucky Bldg.   Phone: (502) 745-2592
Bowling Green, KY 42101   Patricia M. Hodges, Archv.

WESTERN KENTUCKY UNIVERSITY - DEPT. OF SPECIAL COLLECTIONS -
    KENTUCKY LIBRARY AND MUSEUM/UNIVERSITY ARCHIVES
     Phone: (502) 745-2592
Bowling Green, KY 42101   Riley Handy, Hd., Spec.Coll.Dept.

DIOCESE OF COVINGTON - ARCHIVES
1140 Madison Ave.   Phone: (606) 291-4240
Covington, KY 41012   Sr. Mary Philip Trauth, S.N.D., Archv.

KENTON COUNTY PUBLIC LIBRARY - KENTUCKY & LOCAL HISTORY
    DEPARTMENT
5th & Scott Sts.   Phone: (606) 491-0799
Covington, KY 41011   Mike Averdick, Assoc.Dir.

ST. ELIZABETH MEDICAL CENTER - NORTH - MEDICAL LIBRARY *
401 E. 20th St.   Phone: (606) 292-4048
Covington, KY 41014   Donald R. Smith, Libn.

ST. WALBURG CONVENT OF BENEDICTINE SISTERS OF COVINGTON,
    KENTUCKY - ARCHIVES
2500 Amsterdam Rd.   Phone: (606) 331-6771
Covington, KY 41016   Sr. Teresa Wolking, O.S.B., Archv.

CENTRE COLLEGE - GRACE DOHERTY LIBRARY - SPECIAL COLLECTIONS
     Phone: (606) 236-5211
Danville, KY 40422   Stanley Campbell, Dir.

KENTUCKY SCHOOL FOR THE DEAF - LEARNING RESOURCE CENTER
S. Second St.   Phone: (606) 236-5132
Danville, KY 40422-0027   George R. Benson, Dir. of Media Serv.

ST. ELIZABETH MEDICAL CENTER - SOUTH - LIBRARY
One Medical Village Dr.   Phone: (606) 344-2248
Edgewood, KY 41017   Donald R. Smith, Libn.

FERGUSON BAPTIST CHURCH - LIBRARY *
602 Gover Ln.   Phone: (606) 679-1690
Ferguson, KY 42533   Dorothy Holloway, Dir.

U.S. ARMY HOSPITALS - BLANCHFIELD ARMY COMMUNITY HOSPITAL -
    MEDICAL LIBRARY
     Phone: (502) 798-8014
Ft. Campbell, KY 42223   Ina L. Nesbitt, Med.Libn.

U.S. ARMY ARMOR SCHOOL - LIBRARY
Gaffey Hall, 2369
Old Ironsides Ave.   Phone: (502) 624-6231
Ft. Knox, KY 40121   William H. Hansen, Chf.Libn.

U.S. ARMY - PATTON MUSEUM OF CAVALRY & ARMOR - EMERT L. DAVIS
    MEMORIAL LIBRARY
4554 Fayette Ave.
Box 208   Phone: (502) 624-6350
Ft. Knox, KY 40121   Phyllis S. Cassler, Libn.

KENTUCKY COVERED BRIDGE ASSOCIATION - LIBRARY
62 Miami Pkwy.   Phone: (606) 441-7000
Fort Thomas, KY 41075   L.K. Patton, Exec.Dir.

KENTUCKY HISTORICAL SOCIETY - LIBRARY
Broadway, Old Capitol Annex
Box H   Phone: (502) 564-3016
Frankfort, KY 40601   Anne McDonnell, Lib.Mgr.

KENTUCKY STATE COUNCIL OF HIGHER EDUCATION - LIBRARY
U.S. 127 S.   Phone: (502) 564-3745
Frankfort, KY 40601   Jennie L. Carrigan, Libn.

KENTUCKY STATE DEPARTMENT OF COMMERCE - DIVISION OF RESEARCH
    - MAP LIBRARY *
133 Holmes St.   Phone: (502) 564-4715
Frankfort, KY 40601   Bill Howard, Chf.

KENTUCKY STATE DEPARTMENT OF ECONOMIC DEVELOPMENT -
    RESEARCH & PLANNING DIVISION - LIBRARY
Capitol Plaza Office Tower   Phone: (502) 564-4886
Frankfort, KY 40601   Doris Arnold, Libn.

KENTUCKY STATE DEPARTMENT OF EDUCATION - RESOURCE CENTER
Capital Plaza Tower   Phone: (502) 564-2000
Frankfort, KY 40601   Donna Swanson, Coord.

KENTUCKY STATE DEPARTMENT FOR HUMAN RESOURCES - LIBRARY
275 E. Main St.   Phone: (502) 564-4530
Frankfort, KY 40621   Douglas Raisor, Supv./Acq./ILL

KENTUCKY STATE DEPARTMENT FOR LIBRARIES & ARCHIVES - ARCHIVES
300 Coffee Tree Rd.
Box 537   Phone: (502) 875-7000
Frankfort, KY 40602   Dr. Lewis Bellardo, Dir.

KENTUCKY STATE DEPARTMENT FOR LIBRARIES & ARCHIVES - KENTUCKY
    TALKING BOOK LIBRARY
300 Coffee Tree Rd.
Box 818   Phone: (502) 875-7000
Frankfort, KY 40602   Richard Feindel, Br.Mgr.

KENTUCKY STATE DEPARTMENT FOR LIBRARIES AND ARCHIVES - STATE
    LIBRARY SERVICES DIVISION
300 Coffee Tree Rd.
Box 537   Phone: (502) 875-7000
Frankfort, KY 40602   Suzanne LeBarron, Dir.

KENTUCKY STATE DEPARTMENT OF PUBLIC ADVOCACY - LAW LIBRARY
State Office Bldg. Annex   Phone: (502) 564-5252
Frankfort, KY 40601   Karen C. McDaniel, Law Libn.

KENTUCKY STATE EXECUTIVE DEPARTMENT FOR FINANCE LIBRARY -
    OFFICE FOR POLICY AND MANAGEMENT *
Capitol Annex, Rm. 200   Phone: (502) 564-7300
Frankfort, KY 40601

KENTUCKY STATE FINANCE AND ADMINISTRATION CABINET -
    GOVERNMENT SERVICES CENTER LIBRARY
Kentucky State University
Academic Services Bldg., No. 407   Phone: (502) 564-8170
Frankfort, KY 40601   Norma Johnson, Adm.Spec.

KENTUCKY STATE LAW LIBRARY
State Capitol, Rm. 200   Phone: (502) 564-4848
Frankfort, KY 40601   Wesley Gilmer, Jr., State Law Libn.

KENTUCKY STATE LEGISLATIVE RESEARCH COMMISSION - LIBRARY
State Capitol, 4th Fl.   Phone: (502) 564-8100
Frankfort, KY 40601   Peggy D. King, Leg.Libn.

KENTUCKY CHRISTIAN COLLEGE - MEDIA CENTER *
College Ave.   Phone: (606) 474-6613
Grayson, KY 41143   Kenneth L. Beck, Libn.

HARRODSBURG HISTORICAL SOCIETY - MORGAN ROW LIBRARY
222 S. Chiles St.   Phone: (606) 734-9238
Harrodsburg, KY 40330   Amy Asbury Shewmaker, Pres.

NORTHERN KENTUCKY UNIVERSITY - SALMON P. CHASE COLLEGE OF LAW
    - LIBRARY
                                                  Phone: (606) 572-5394
Highland Heights, KY 41076   Carol B. Allred, Law Lib.Dir.

U.S. NATL. PARK SERVICE - ABRAHAM LINCOLN BIRTHPLACE NATL.
    HISTORIC SITE - LIBRARY
Rte. 1   Phone: (502) 358-3874
Hodgenville, KY 42748   Gary V. Talley, Chf., Interpretation

WESTERN STATE HOSPITAL - PROFESSIONAL LIBRARY
Russellville Rd.
Box 2200   Phone: (502) 886-4431
Hopkinsville, KY 42240   Margaret Crim Riley, Libn.

CELANESE PLASTICS & SPECIALTIES COMPANY - TECHNICAL CENTER -
    RESEARCH LIBRARY
9800 Bluegrass Pkwy.   Phone: (502) 585-8053
Jeffersontown, KY 40299   Elizabeth C. Hill, Info.Spec.

CENTRAL CHRISTIAN CHURCH - LIBRARY
205 E. Short St.
Box 1354   Phone: (606) 233-1551
Lexington, KY 40590   Walter A. Hehl, Hd.

COUNCIL OF STATE GOVERNMENTS - STATES INFORMATION CENTER
Iron Works Pike
Box 11910   Phone: (606) 252-2291
Lexington, KY 40578   Nanette D. Eichell, Info.Rsrcs.Coord.

EASTERN STATE HOSPITAL - RESOURCE LIBRARY
627 W. Fourth St.   Phone: (606) 255-1431
Lexington, KY 40508   Juanita H. Morrill, Libn.

EPISCOPAL THEOLOGICAL SEMINARY IN KENTUCKY - BROWNING
    MEMORIAL LIBRARY
544 Sayre Ave.   Phone: (606) 255-9591
Lexington, KY 40508   Nancy J. Metzner, Libn.

GOOD SAMARITAN HOSPITAL - MEDICAL LIBRARY
310 S. Limestone   Phone: (606) 252-6612
Lexington, KY 40508   Nelle T. Williams, Med.Libn.

HEADLEY-WHITNEY MUSEUM - LIBRARY
4435 Old Frankfort Pike   Phone: (606) 255-6653
Lexington, KY 40510   Anne Gobar, Musm.Dir.

IBM CORPORATION - INFORMATION PRODUCTS DIVISION - TECHNICAL
    LIBRARY/IC
Dept. D31, Bldg. 032
740 New Circle Rd., N.W.   Phone: (606) 232-6044
Lexington, KY 40511   Leo D. Burns, Mgr.

KEENELAND ASSOCIATION - LIBRARY
Keeneland Race Course
Box 1690   Phone: (606) 254-3412
Lexington, KY 40592   Doris Jean Waren, Libn.

LEXINGTON COMMUNITY COLLEGE - LIBRARY
Cooper Dr., Oswald Bldg.   Phone: (606) 258-4919
Lexington, KY 40506   Martha J. Birchfield, Dir.

LEXINGTON-FAYETTE URBAN COUNTY PLANNING COMMISSION -
    TECHNICAL INFORMATION LIBRARY
200 E. Main St.   Phone: (606) 252-8808
Lexington, KY 40507   Dale B. Thoma, Dir.

LEXINGTON HERALD-LEADER - LIBRARY
Main & Midland Ave.   Phone: (606) 231-3334
Lexington, KY 40507   David Reed, Dir., Lib.Serv.

LEXINGTON THEOLOGICAL SEMINARY - BOSWORTH MEMORIAL LIBRARY
631 S. Limestone   Phone: (606) 252-0361
Lexington, KY 40505   Philip N. Dare, Hd.Libn.

ST. JOSEPH HOSPITAL - MEDICAL LIBRARY
One St. Joseph Dr.   Phone: (606) 278-3436
Lexington, KY 40504   Jerri Trimble, Supv.

U.S. VETERANS ADMINISTRATION (KY-Lexington) - MEDICAL CENTER
    LIBRARY
                                                  Phone: (606) 233-4511
Lexington, KY 40511   Ethel F. Mullins, Chf., Lib.Serv.

UNIVERSITY OF KENTUCKY - AGRICULTURE LIBRARY
N 24 Agricultural Science Ctr., N.   Phone: (606) 258-2758
Lexington, KY 40546-0091   Antoinette P. Powell, Libn.

UNIVERSITY OF KENTUCKY - BIOLOGICAL SCIENCES LIBRARY
313 Thomas Hunt Morgan Bldg.   Phone: (606) 258-5889
Lexington, KY 40506-0225   Mildred A. Moore, Biological Sci.Libn.

UNIVERSITY OF KENTUCKY - CHEMISTRY-PHYSICS LIBRARY
150 Chemistry-Physics Bldg.   Phone: (606) 258-5954
Lexington, KY 40506-0055

UNIVERSITY OF KENTUCKY - EDUCATION LIBRARY
205 Dickey Hall   Phone: (606) 258-4939
Lexington, KY 40506-0017   Larry Greenwood, Educ.Libn.

UNIVERSITY OF KENTUCKY - GEORGE W. PIRTLE GEOLOGY LIBRARY
100 Bowman Hall   Phone: (606) 258-5730
Lexington, KY 40506-0059   Vivian S. Hall, Libn.

UNIVERSITY OF KENTUCKY - HUNTER M. ADAMS ARCHITECTURE LIBRARY
College of Architecture
200 Pence Hall   Phone: (606) 257-1533
Lexington, KY 40506-0041   Harry Gilbert, Libn.

UNIVERSITY OF KENTUCKY - INSTITUTE FOR MINING AND MINERALS
  RESEARCH - IMMR LIBRARY
Kentucky Energy Res. Laboratory
Iron Works Pike, Box 13015   Phone: (606) 252-5535
Lexington, KY 40512-3015   Theresa K. Wiley, Lib.Mgr.

UNIVERSITY OF KENTUCKY - LAW LIBRARY
College of Law   Phone: (606) 258-8686
Lexington, KY 40506-0048   William James, Dir.

UNIVERSITY OF KENTUCKY - MARGARET I. KING LIBRARY - ART LIBRARY
                                         Phone: (606) 257-3938
Lexington, KY 40506-0039   Meg Shaw, Art Libn.

UNIVERSITY OF KENTUCKY - MARGARET I. KING LIBRARY - GOVERNMENT
  PUBLICATIONS/MAP DEPARTMENT
                                         Phone: (606) 257-3139
Lexington, KY 40506   Sandra McAnich, Hd., Govt.Pubns.

UNIVERSITY OF KENTUCKY - MARGARET I. KING LIBRARY - GOVERNMENT
  PUBLICATIONS/MAP DEPARTMENT - MAP COLLECTION
                                         Phone: (606) 257-1853
Lexington, KY 40506-0039   Gwen Curtis, Hd.

UNIVERSITY OF KENTUCKY - MARGARET I. KING LIBRARY - SPECIAL
  COLLECTIONS AND ARCHIVES
11 King Library N.
Lexington, KY 40506-0039   Claire McCann, Mss.Libn.

UNIVERSITY OF KENTUCKY - MATHEMATICAL SCIENCES LIBRARY
OB-9 Patterson Office Tower   Phone: (606) 257-8365
Lexington, KY 40506-0027   Karen S. Croneis, Libn.

UNIVERSITY OF KENTUCKY - MUSIC LIBRARY/LISTENING CENTER
116 Fine Arts Bldg.   Phone: (606) 258-2800
Lexington, KY 40506-0022   Cathy S. Hunt, Music Libn.

UNIVERSITY OF KENTUCKY - ROBERT E. SHAVER LIBRARY OF
  ENGINEERING
355 Anderson Hall   Phone: (606) 258-2965
Lexington, KY 40506-0046   Russell H. Powell, Libn.

ALLIS-CHALMERS CORPORATION - AMERICAN AIR FILTER DIVISION -
  TECHNICAL LIBRARY
215 Central Ave.
Box 35260   Phone: (502) 637-0251
Louisville, KY 40232   Richard D. Rivers, Mgr. of Res.

BELLARMINE COLLEGE - THOMAS MERTON STUDIES CENTER
Newburg Rd.   Phone: (502) 452-8187
Louisville, KY 40205   Robert E. Daggy, Cur.

BROWN AND WILLIAMSON TOBACCO CORPORATION - RESEARCH LIBRARY
1600 W. Hill St.
Box 35090   Phone: (502) 568-7683
Louisville, KY 40232   Carol S. Lincoln, Res.Libn.

CONGREGATION OF THE PASSION - HOLY CROSS PROVINCE - PROVINCIAL
  LIBRARY *
1924 Newburg Rd.   Phone: (502) 451-2330
Louisville, KY 40205   Fr. Germain Legere, C.P., Libn.

COURIER-JOURNAL AND LOUISVILLE TIMES - LIBRARY
525 W. Broadway   Phone: (502) 582-4184
Louisville, KY 40202   Doris J. Batliner, Chf.Libn.

DOUGLASS BOULEVARD CHRISTIAN CHURCH - LIBRARY
2005 Douglass Blvd.   Phone: (502) 452-2620
Louisville, KY 40205   Clara C. Cruikshank, Libn.

FILSON CLUB - LIBRARY
118 W. Breckinridge St.   Phone: (502) 582-3727
Louisville, KY 40203   Dorothy C. Rush, Libn.

HUMANA HOSPITAL AUDUBON - MEDICAL LIBRARY
One Audubon Plaza   Phone: (502) 636-7296
Louisville, KY 40217   Elizabeth Fischer, Libn.

HUMANA HOSPITAL UNIVERSITY - GRADIE R. ROWNTREE MEDICAL
  LIBRARY
530 S. Jackson St.   Phone: (502) 562-3947
Louisville, KY 40202   Jody Branson, Med.Libn.

JEFFERSON COUNTY OFFICE OF HISTORIC PRESERVATION AND ARCHIVES
Fiscal Court Bldg., Rm. 100   Phone: (502) 581-5761
Louisville, KY 40202   Olivia Frederick, Cons.Archv.

JEFFERSON COUNTY PUBLIC LAW LIBRARY
Old Jail Bldg.
514 W. Liberty, Suite 240   Phone: (502) 581-5943
Louisville, KY 40202-2806   Linda D. Miller, Dir.

JEWISH HOSPITAL - MEDICAL LIBRARY SERVICES
217 E. Chestnut St.   Phone: (502) 587-4280
Louisville, KY 40202   Linda B. Reel, Dir.

KENTUCKY SCHOOL FOR THE BLIND - LIBRARY
1867 Frankfort Ave.   Phone: (502) 897-1583
Louisville, KY 40206   Cathy Hicks, Libn.

LOUISVILLE ACADEMY OF MUSIC - LIBRARY
2740 Frankfort Ave.   Phone: (502) 893-7885
Louisville, KY 40206   Robert B. French, Pres.

LOUISVILLE BAPTIST HOSPITALS - HAGAN LIBRARY
Highlands Baptist Hospital
810 Barret Ave.   Phone: (502) 566-3108
Louisville, KY 40204   Garry Johnson, Dir., Lib.Serv.

LOUISVILLE DEPARTMENT OF LAW - LIBRARY *
6th & Jefferson, Rm. 200   Phone: (502) 587-3511
Louisville, KY 40202   Marynell Haas, Libn.

LOUISVILLE FREE PUBLIC LIBRARY - FILM SERVICES †
301 W. York St.   Phone: (502) 584-4154
Louisville, KY 40203   Barbara Pickett, Mgr.

LOUISVILLE FREE PUBLIC LIBRARY - GOVERNMENT DOCUMENTS DIVISION
  †
Fourth & York Sts.   Phone: (502) 584-4154
Louisville, KY 40203   Kathleen Bullard, Hd.

LOUISVILLE FREE PUBLIC LIBRARY - KENTUCKY DIVISION †
Fourth & York Sts.   Phone: (502) 584-4154
Louisville, KY 40203   Mark Harris, Hd.

LOUISVILLE FREE PUBLIC LIBRARY - LIBRARY BROADCASTING †
301 W. York St.   Phone: (502) 584-4154
Louisville, KY 40203   Thomas A. Donoho, Dept.Hd.

LOUISVILLE AND JEFFERSON COUNTY PLANNING COMMISSION -
  LOUISVILLE METROPOLITAN PLANNING LIBRARY
900 Fiscal Court Bldg.   Phone: (502) 581-5860
Louisville, KY 40202   Biljon Slifer, Adm.Asst.

LOUISVILLE PRESBYTERIAN THEOLOGICAL SEMINARY - LIBRARY
1044 Alta Vista Rd.   Phone: (502) 895-3411
Louisville, KY 40205   Ernest M. White, Libn.

MEIDINGER, INC. - INFORMATION CENTER
2600 Meidinger Tower, Louisville Galleria   Phone: (502) 561-4500
Louisville, KY 40202   Herbert A. Miller, Jr., Mgr.

NATIONAL CRIME PREVENTION INSTITUTE - INFORMATION CENTER
University of Louisville, Shelby Campus   Phone: (502) 588-6987
Louisville, KY 40292   Barbara R. Bomar, Info.Mgr.

NATIONAL SOCIETY OF THE SONS OF THE AMERICAN REVOLUTION -
  GENEALOGY LIBRARY
1000 S. 4th St.   Phone: (502) 589-1776
Louisville, KY 40203   Martha A. Nellis, Libn.

NKC HOSPITALS, INC. - MEDICAL LIBRARY
Box 35070   Phone: (502) 562-8125
Louisville, KY 40232   Holly S. Buchanan, Dir.

OUR LADY OF PEACE HOSPITAL - MEDICAL LIBRARY
2020 Newburg Rd.   Phone: (502) 451-3330
Louisville, KY 40232   Sr. Margaret Siena, S.C.N., Dir.

ST. ANTHONY HOSPITAL - MEDICAL LIBRARY
1313 St. Anthony Pl.   Phone: (502) 587-1161
Louisville, KY 40204   Alma Hall Fielden, Adm.Asst., Med. Staff

STS. MARY AND ELIZABETH HOSPITAL - MEDICAL LIBRARY
4400 Churchman Ave.   Phone: (502) 361-6319
Louisville, KY 40215   Ruth Gendron, Libn.

SOUTHERN BAPTIST THEOLOGICAL SEMINARY - AUDIOVISUAL CENTER
2825 Lexington Rd.   Phone: (502) 897-4508
Louisville, KY 40280   Andrew B. Rawls, AV Libn.

SOUTHERN BAPTIST THEOLOGICAL SEMINARY - BILLY GRAHAM ROOM
2825 Lexington Rd.   Phone: (502) 897-4807
Louisville, KY 40280   Dr. Ronald F. Deering, Libn.

SOUTHERN BAPTIST THEOLOGICAL SEMINARY - CHURCH MUSIC LIBRARY
2825 Lexington Rd.   Phone: (502) 897-4712
Louisville, KY 40280   Martha C. Powell, Church Music Libn.

SOUTHERN BAPTIST THEOLOGICAL SEMINARY - JAMES P. BOYCE
  CENTENNIAL LIBRARY
2825 Lexington Rd.   Phone: (502) 897-4807
Louisville, KY 40280   Dr. Ronald F. Deering, Libn.

SPEED (J.B.) ART MUSEUM - LIBRARY
2035 S. Third St.   Phone: (502) 636-2893
Louisville, KY 40208   Mary Jane Benedict, Libn.

UNITED CATALYSTS, INC. - TECHNICAL LIBRARY
Box 32370   Phone: (502) 637-9751
Louisville, KY 40232   Betty B. Simms, Tech.Libn.

U.S. NAVY - NAVAL ORDNANCE STATION - TECHNICAL LIBRARY
50 D, MDS 50   Phone: (502) 367-5667
Louisville, KY 40214   Elizabeth T. Miles, Lib.Techn.

U.S. VETERANS ADMINISTRATION (KY-Louisville) - HOSPITAL LIBRARY
800 Zorn Ave.   Phone: (502) 895-3401
Louisville, KY 40202   James F. Kastner, Chf.Libn.

UNIVERSITY OF LOUISVILLE - ALLEN R. HITE ART INSTITUTE - MARGARET
  M. BRIDWELL ART LIBRARY
Belknap Campus   Phone: (502) 588-6741
Louisville, KY 40292   Gail R. Gilbert, Hd., Art Lib.

UNIVERSITY OF LOUISVILLE - DEPARTMENT OF RARE BOOKS AND SPECIAL
  COLLECTIONS
Belknap Campus   Phone: (502) 588-6762
Louisville, KY 40292   George T. McWhorter, Cur.

UNIVERSITY OF LOUISVILLE - DWIGHT ANDERSON MEMORIAL MUSIC
  LIBRARY †
2301 S. 3rd St.   Phone: (502) 588-5659
Louisville, KY 40292   Marion Korda, Libn.

UNIVERSITY OF LOUISVILLE - KERSEY LIBRARY
Belknap Campus   Phone: (502) 588-6297
Louisville, KY 40292   Carol S. Brinkman, Dir.

UNIVERSITY OF LOUISVILLE - KORNHAUSER HEALTH SCIENCES LIBRARY
                                             Phone: (502) 588-5771
Louisville, KY 40292   Leonard M. Eddy, Dir.

UNIVERSITY OF LOUISVILLE - PHOTOGRAPHIC ARCHIVES
Belknap Campus   Phone: (502) 588-6752
Louisville, KY 40292   James C. Anderson, Cur.

UNIVERSITY OF LOUISVILLE - SCHOOL OF LAW LIBRARY
Belknap Campus   Phone: (502) 588-6392
Louisville, KY 40292   Gene W. Teitelbaum, Law Libn.

UNIVERSITY OF LOUISVILLE - UNIVERSITY ARCHIVES AND RECORDS
  CENTER
Ekstrom Library   Phone: (502) 588-6674
Louisville, KY 40292   William J. Morison, Dir./Univ.Archv.

UNIVERSITY OF LOUISVILLE - UNIVERSITY ARCHIVES AND RECORDS
  CENTER - ORAL HISTORY CENTER
Belknap Campus   Phone: (502) 588-6674
Louisville, KY 40292

UNIVERSITY OF LOUISVILLE - URBAN STUDIES CENTER - LIBRARY
College of Urban and Public Affairs   Phone: (502) 588-6626
Louisville, KY 40292   Shirley Demos, Dir., Info.Rsrcs.

HOPKINS COUNTY - REGIONAL MEDICAL CENTER - LIBRARY ★
Hospital Dr.   Phone: (502) 825-5100
Madisonville, KY 42431   Mark A. Ingram, Med.Libn.

OUR LADY OF THE WAY HOSPITAL - MEDICAL LIBRARY
Box 910   Phone: (606) 285-5181
Martin, KY 41649   Mary Hogans, Act.Libn.

U.S. NATL. PARK SERVICE - CUMBERLAND GAP NATL. HISTORICAL PARK -
  LIBRARY
Box 840   Phone: (606) 248-2817
Middlesboro, KY 40965   Wes Leishman, Interpretation Chf.

MOREHEAD STATE UNIVERSITY - CAMDEN-CARROLL LIBRARY
                                             Phone: (606) 783-2142
Morehead, KY 40351   Dr. Jack D. Ellis, Dir. of Libs.

ST. CLAIRE MEDICAL CENTER - MEDICAL LIBRARY
222 Medical Circle   Phone: (606) 784-6661
Morehead, KY 40351   Patsy Wright, Libn.

MURRAY STATE UNIVERSITY - LIBRARY
                                             Phone: (502) 762-2291
Murray, KY 42071   Keith M. Heim, Interim Dean

KENTUCKY WESLEYAN COLLEGE - LIBRARY LEARNING CENTER - SPECIAL
  COLLECTIONS
3000 Frederica St.   Phone: (502) 926-3111
Owensboro, KY 42301   Andrew Dorfman, Act.Libn.

OWENSBORO AREA MUSEUM - LIBRARY
2829 S. Griffith Ave.   Phone: (502) 683-0296
Owensboro, KY 42301   Joseph M. Ford, Musm.Dir.

OWENSBORO-DAVIESS COUNTY PUBLIC LIBRARY - KENTUCKY ROOM
450 Griffith Ave.   Phone: (502) 684-0211
Owensboro, KY 42301   Shelia E. Heflin, Supv.

OWENSBORO MESSENGER-INQUIRER - LIBRARY
1401 Frederica St.   Phone: (502) 926-0123
Owensboro, KY 42301   Katherine Fiedler, Libn.

TEXAS GAS TRANSMISSION CORPORATION - LIBRARY
Box 1160   Phone: (502) 926-8686
Owensboro, KY 42301   Frieda Rhodes, Libn.

LOURDES HOSPITAL - HEALTH SCIENCES LIBRARY
1530 Lone Oak Rd.   Phone: (502) 444-2138
Paducah, KY 42001   Betsy Fusco, Libn.

MARTIN MARIETTA ENERGY SYSTEMS INC. - NUCLEAR DIV. - PADUCAH
  GASEOUS DIFFUSION PLANT INFO. CENTER
Box 1410   Phone: (502) 444-6311
Paducah, KY 42001   J.C. Gillespie, Libn.

LLOYD (Alice) COLLEGE - APPALACHIAN ORAL HISTORY PROJECT
                                             Phone: (606) 368-2101
Pippa Passes, KY 41844   Katherine Rosser Martin, Dir.

EASTERN KENTUCKY UNIVERSITY - JOHN GRANT CRABBE LIBRARY
                                             Phone: (606) 622-1778
Richmond, KY 40475   Ernest E. Weyhrauch, Dean, Libs. & Lrng.Rsrcs.

EASTERN KENTUCKY UNIVERSITY - JOHN GRANT CRABBE LIBRARY - JOHN
 WILSON TOWNSEND ROOM
                              Phone: (606) 622-1792
Richmond, KY 40475   Sharon McConnell, Cur.

EASTERN KENTUCKY UNIVERSITY - LAW ENFORCEMENT LIBRARY
Stratton Bldg.   Phone: (606) 622-1798
Richmond, KY 40475   Verna Casey, Libn.

EASTERN KENTUCKY UNIVERSITY - MUSIC LIBRARY
Foster Music Bldg.   Phone: (606) 622-1795
Richmond, KY 40475   Elizabeth K. Baker, Libn.

EASTERN KENTUCKY UNIVERSITY - ORAL HISTORY CENTER
University Bldg.   Phone: (606) 622-2446
Richmond, KY 40475   William H. Berge, Dir.

EASTERN KENTUCKY UNIVERSITY - UNIVERSITY ARCHIVES
Cammack Bldg., Rm. 26   Phone: (606) 622-2820
Richmond, KY 40475   Charles C. Hay, Dir.

MADISON COUNTY HISTORICAL SOCIETY, INC. - LIBRARY
Eastern Kentucky University
Box 876   Phone: (606) 623-1720
Richmond, KY 40475

GETHSEMANI ABBEY - LIBRARY
                              Phone: (502) 549-3117
Trappist, KY 40073   Fr. Hilarion Schmock, O.C.S.O., Libn.

KENTUCKY MOUNTAIN BIBLE INSTITUTE - GIBSON LIBRARY
                              Phone: (606) 666-5000
Vancleve, KY 41385   Ava Smith, Libn.

ASBURY THEOLOGICAL SEMINARY - B.L. FISHER LIBRARY
                              Phone: (606) 858-3581
Wilmore, KY 40390   D. William Faupel, Dir., Lib. Serv.

LOUISIANA

RAPIDES GENERAL HOSPITAL - MEDICAL LIBRARY †
Box 7146   Phone: (318) 487-8111
Alexandria, LA 71301   Mrs. B.T. Dawkins, Libn.

ST. FRANCES CABRINI HOSPITAL - MEDICAL LIBRARY
3330 Masonic Dr.   Phone: (318) 487-1122
Alexandria, LA 71301   Denise Dupont, Act.Libn.

TRUE VINE MISSIONARY BAPTIST CHURCH - LIBRARY †
831 Broadway Ave.
Box 1051   Phone: (318) 445-6730
Alexandria, LA 71301   Louise Humphrey, Libn.

U.S. VETERANS ADMINISTRATION (LA-Alexandria) - MEDICAL CENTER
 MEDICAL LIBRARY
                              Phone: (318) 473-0010
Alexandria, LA 71301   Nancy M. Guillet, Chf.Libn.

U.S. AIR FORCE BASE - BARKSDALE BASE LIBRARY
FL 4608   Phone: (318) 869-4449
Barksdale AFB, LA 71110   Ronald J. Ferland, Libn.

BATON ROUGE STATE-TIMES & MORNING ADVOCATE NEWSPAPERS -
 LIBRARY
525 Lafayette St.   Phone: (504) 383-1111
Baton Rouge, LA 70821   Lou Thomas, Lib.Dir.

ETHYL CORPORATION - INFORMATION & LIBRARY SERVICES LIBRARY
Box 2246   Phone: (504) 359-2182
Baton Rouge, LA 70821   Lois M. Skinner, Chem./Libn.

EXXON COMPANY, U.S.A. - EXXON RESEARCH & DEVELOPMENT
 LABORATORIES LIBRARY
Box 2226   Phone: (504) 359-7681
Baton Rouge, LA 70821   Barbara R. Biggs, Libn.

LONG (Earl K.) MEMORIAL HOSPITAL - MEDICAL LIBRARY
5825 Airline Highway   Phone: (504) 358-1089
Baton Rouge, LA 70805   Elaine P. O'Connor, Dir.

LOUISIANA STATE DEPT. OF COMMERCE - OFFICE OF COMMERCE &
 INDUSTRY - INDUSTRIAL DEVELOPMENT REFERENCE LIBRARY
Box 44185   Phone: (504) 342-5383
Baton Rouge, LA 70804   Gene Cretini, Info.Serv.Dir.

LOUISIANA STATE DEPARTMENT OF JUSTICE - OFFICE OF THE ATTORNEY
 GENERAL - HUEY P. LONG MEMORIAL LAW LIBRARY
State Capitol, 25th Fl. W.
Box 44005   Phone: (504) 342-7013
Baton Rouge, LA 70804   Patricia A. Oliver, Libn.

LOUISIANA STATE DEPARTMENT OF NATURAL RESOURCES - ENERGY,
 RESEARCH AND PLANNING DIVISION LIBRARY
Box 44156   Phone: (504) 342-1297
Baton Rouge, LA 70804   Diane Smith, Info.Dir.

LOUISIANA STATE DEPARTMENT OF TRANSPORTATION DEVELOPMENT -
 OFFICE OF PUBLIC WORKS - TECHNICAL LIBRARY *
Capitol Sta., Box 44155   Phone: (504) 342-7566
Baton Rouge, LA 70804   Dorothy D. McConnell, Libn.

LOUISIANA STATE HOUSE OF REPRESENTATIVES LEGISLATIVE SERVICES
 - RESEARCH LIBRARY
Box 44012   Phone: (504) 342-2431
Baton Rouge, LA 70804   Suzanne Hughes, Adm.

LOUISIANA STATE LIBRARY
Box 131   Phone: (504) 342-4923
Baton Rouge, LA 70821   Thomas F. Jaques, State Libn.

LOUISIANA STATE OFFICE OF THE SECRETARY OF STATE - STATE
 ARCHIVES AND RECORDS SERVICE - ARCHIVES SECTION
Box 44125   Phone: (504) 342-5440
Baton Rouge, LA 70804   Charlene C. Cain, Archv.

LOUISIANA STATE PLANNING OFFICE - LIBRARY - INFORMATION
 RESOURCES CENTER
Box 44426   Phone: (504) 342-7428
Baton Rouge, LA 70804   Kay W. McGinnis, Adm. & Info.Rsrcs.Spec.

LOUISIANA STATE UNIVERSITY - BUSINESS ADMINISTRATION/
 GOVERNMENT DOCUMENTS DEPARTMENT
Troy H. Middleton Library   Phone: (504) 388-2570
Baton Rouge, LA 70803   Myrtle S. Bolner, Act.Hd.

LOUISIANA STATE UNIVERSITY - CARTOGRAPHIC INFORMATION CENTER
Dept. of Geography & Anthropology
313 Geology Bldg.   Phone: (504) 388-5318
Baton Rouge, LA 70803   Joyce Nelson, Map Cur.

LOUISIANA STATE UNIVERSITY - CENTER FOR ENGINEERING & BUSINESS
 ADMINISTRATION READING ROOM
                              Phone: (504) 388-8221
Baton Rouge, LA 70803   Myrtle S. Bolner, Act.Hd.Bus.Adm./Govt.Doc.

LOUISIANA STATE UNIVERSITY - CHEMISTRY LIBRARY
Virginia Williams Hall   Phone: (504) 388-2530
Baton Rouge, LA 70803   Beth F. Warner, Libn.

LOUISIANA STATE UNIVERSITY - COASTAL INFORMATION REPOSITORY
Center for Wetland Resources Phone: (504) 388-8265
Baton Rouge, LA 70803   Norman Howden, Prog.Dir.

LOUISIANA STATE UNIVERSITY - COLLEGE OF DESIGN - DESIGN
 RESOURCE CENTER
104 Design Bldg.   Phone: (504) 388-2665
Baton Rouge, LA 70803   Doris A. Wheeler, Design Libn.

LOUISIANA STATE UNIVERSITY - DEPARTMENT OF ARCHIVES AND
 MANUSCRIPTS
Troy H. Middleton Library, Rm. 202   Phone: (504) 388-2240
Baton Rouge, LA 70803   M. Stone Miller, Jr., Hd.

LOUISIANA STATE UNIVERSITY - E.A. MC ILHENNY NATURAL HISTORY
COLLECTION
Library   Phone: (504) 388-6934
Baton Rouge, LA 70803   Kathryn Morgan, Cur.

LOUISIANA STATE UNIVERSITY - GOVERNMENTAL SERVICES INSTITUTE -
LIBRARY
385 Pleasant Hall   Phone: (504) 388-6746
Baton Rouge, LA 70803   Judith D. Smith, Libn.

LOUISIANA STATE UNIVERSITY - LAW LIBRARY
                                                     Phone: (504) 388-8802
Baton Rouge, LA 70803-1010   Lance E. Dickson, Dir.

LOUISIANA STATE UNIVERSITY - LIBRARY SCHOOL LIBRARY
Library, Rm. 263 Coates Hall   Phone: (504) 388-4576
Baton Rouge, LA 70803   Alma Dawson, Hd.

LOUISIANA STATE UNIVERSITY - LISTENING ROOMS
Library   Phone: (504) 388-2900
Baton Rouge, LA 70803   Glenn Walden, Hd.

LOUISIANA STATE UNIVERSITY - LOUISIANA ROOM
Library   Phone: (504) 388-2575
Baton Rouge, LA 70803   Evangeline Mills Lynch, Libn./Hd.

LOUISIANA STATE UNIVERSITY - MICROFORM ROOM
                                                     Phone: (504) 388-4662
Baton Rouge, LA 70803   Deborah Honeychurch, Hd.

LOUISIANA STATE UNIVERSITY - MUSEUM OF GEOSCIENCE -
ARCHAEOLOGY & GEOLOGY BOOK & REPRINT LIBRARIES
                                                     Phone: (504) 388-2931
Baton Rouge, LA 70803   June Dodd, Sec.

LOUISIANA STATE UNIVERSITY - RARE BOOK COLLECTION
Library   Phone: (504) 388-2575
Baton Rouge, LA 70803   Evangeline M. Lynch, Libn./Hd.

LOUISIANA STATE UNIVERSITY - REFERENCE SERVICES
                                                     Phone: (504) 388-8875
Baton Rouge, LA 70803   Joyce C. Werner, Hd.

LOUISIANA STATE UNIVERSITY - SCHOOL OF VETERINARY MEDICINE -
LIBRARY
                                                     Phone: (504) 346-3173
Baton Rouge, LA 70803   Sue Loubiere, Libn.

MC COLLISTER, MC CLEARY, FAZIO, MIXON, HOLLIDAY & HICKS - LAW
LIBRARY
One American Place, Suite 1800
Box 2706   Phone: (504) 387-5961
Baton Rouge, LA 70821   Anne Slaughter Towles, Law Libn.

OUR LADY OF THE LAKE REGIONAL MEDICAL CENTER - SCHOOL OF
NURSING LIBRARY
5000 Hennessy Blvd.   Phone: (504) 769-3100
Baton Rouge, LA 70809   Dorothy D. Romero, Libn.

PUBLIC AFFAIRS RESEARCH COUNCIL OF LOUISIANA - RESEARCH LIBRARY
Box 3118   Phone: (504) 343-9204
Baton Rouge, LA 70821   Jan Brashear, Res.Libn.

SOCIETY OF COSTA RICA COLLECTORS (SOCORICO) - EARL FOSSOM
MEMORIAL LIBRARY
Box 14831
Baton Rouge LA 70808   Hector R. Mena, Libn.

SOUTHERN UNIVERSITY - LAW SCHOOL LIBRARY
Southern Branch Post Office   Phone: (504) 771-4900
Baton Rouge, LA 70813   Ann Jones, Law Libn.

U.S. PUBLIC HEALTH SERVICE HOSPITAL - NATIONAL HANSEN'S DISEASE
CENTER - MEDICAL LIBRARY
                                                     Phone: (504) 642-7771
Carville, LA 70721   Anna Belle Steinbach, Med.Libn.

TULANE UNIVERSITY OF LOUISIANA - DELTA REGIONAL PRIMATE
RESEARCH CENTER - SCIENCE INFORMATION SERVICE
3 Rivers Rd.   Phone: (504) 892-2040
Covington, LA 70433   James L. Paysse, Ed.Asst.

U.S. AIR FORCE BASE - ENGLAND BASE LIBRARY †
FL 4805   Phone: (318) 448-5760
England AFB, LA 71301   Rupert C. Thom, Libn.

U.S. ARMY HOSPITALS - BAYNE JONES ARMY COMMUNITY HOSPITAL -
MEDICAL LIBRARY
                                                     Phone: (318) 535-3725
Ft. Polk, LA 71459   Mary K. Bradford, Med.Lib.Techn.

LOUISIANA STATE UNIVERSITY - SOUTHEAST RESEARCH STATION -
LIBRARY
Drawer 567   Phone: (504) 839-2322
Franklinton, LA 70438   Dr. Lee F. Mason, Resident Dir.

SOUTHEASTERN LOUISIANA UNIVERSITY - L.A. SIMS MEMORIAL LIBRARY
Drawer 896, Univ. Sta.   Phone: (504) 549-2234
Hammond, LA 70402   F. Landon Greaves, Jr., Lib.Dir.

DIOCESE OF LAFAYETTE, LOUISIANA - ARCHIVES *
Drawer 3387   Phone: (318) 361-5639
Lafayette, LA 70501   Rev. James F. Geraghty, Archv.

OUR LADY OF LOURDES REGIONAL MEDICAL & EDUCATION CENTER -
LEARNING RESOURCE CENTER †
611 St. Landry St.
Box 4027C   Phone: (318) 231-2141
Lafayette, LA 70502   Mary Lagroue, Med.Libn.

UNIVERSITY OF SOUTHWESTERN LOUISIANA - CENTER FOR LOUISIANA
STUDIES
Box 4-0831   Phone: (318) 231-6027
Lafayette, LA 70504   Glenn R. Conrad, Dir.

UNIVERSITY OF SOUTHWESTERN LOUISIANA - JEFFERSON CAFFERY
LOUISIANA ROOM
Dupre Library
302 E. St. Mary   Phone: (318) 231-6031
Lafayette, LA 70504   Cynthia J. Rice, Ref.Libn.

UNIVERSITY OF SOUTHWESTERN LOUISIANA - ORNAMENTAL
HORTICULTURE LIBRARY
Dept. of Agricultural Sciences
Box 44333   Phone: (318) 231-6064
Lafayette, LA 70504   Brenda Kosiba, Libn.

SOUTHEAST LOUISIANA HOSPITAL - PROFESSIONAL LIBRARY
Box 3850   Phone: (504) 626-8161
Mandeville, LA 70448   Carol C. Adams, Libn.

LOUISIANA STATE DEPT. OF CULTURE, RECREATION & TOURISM -
MANSFIELD STATE COMMEMORATIVE AREA - MUSEUM & LIB.
Rte. 2, Box 252   Phone: (318) 872-1474
Mansfield, LA 71052   Ernestiene Roundtree, Cur.

CONWAY (E.A.) MEMORIAL HOSPITAL - MEDICAL LIBRARY *
Box 1881   Phone: (318) 387-8460
Monroe, LA 71201   Linda Darnell, Libn.

NORTHEAST LOUISIANA UNIVERSITY - CENTER FOR BUSINESS &
ECONOMIC RESEARCH - LIBRARY
Administration Bldg. 2-104   Phone: (318) 342-2123
Monroe, LA 71209   Jerry L. Wall, Dir.

ALTON OCHSNER MEDICAL FOUNDATION - MEDICAL LIBRARY
1516 Jefferson Hwy.   Phone: (504) 838-3760
New Orleans, LA 70121   Joan M. Marcotte, Med.Libn.

AMISTAD RESEARCH CENTER - LIBRARY/ARCHIVES
400 Esplanade Ave.   Phone: (504) 522-0432
New Orleans, LA 70116   Dr. Clifton H. Johnson, Exec.Dir.

AMOCO PRODUCTION COMPANY - NEW ORLEANS REGION - LIBRARY
INFORMATION CENTER
Box 50879   Phone: (504) 586-6572
New Orleans, LA 70150   Louise M. Seidler, Supv.

ARCHDIOCESE OF NEW ORLEANS - ARCHIVES
1100 Chartres St.   Phone: (504) 529-2651
New Orleans, LA 70116   Msgr. Earl C. Woods, Chancellor

BUREAU OF GOVERNMENTAL RESEARCH - LIBRARY
1308 Richards Bldg.   Phone: (504) 525-4152
New Orleans, LA 70112   John Brewer, Lib. Contact

CHARITY HOSPITAL - SCHOOL OF NURSING - LIBRARY
450 S. Claiborne Ave.   Phone: (504) 568-6431
New Orleans, LA 70112   Bruce T. Abbott, Lib.Coord.

DEUTSCH, KERRIGAN AND STILES - LAW LIBRARY
755 Magazine St.   Phone: (504) 581-5141
New Orleans, LA 70130   Jean Sandel, Libn.

GULF SOUTH RESEARCH INSTITUTE - LIBRARY
Box 26518   Phone: (504) 283-4223
New Orleans, LA 70186-6518   Paul Bedverftig, Tech.Libn.

HISTORIC NEW ORLEANS COLLECTION - LIBRARY
533 Royal St.   Phone: (504) 523-4662
New Orleans, LA 70130   Florence M. Jumonville, Hd.Libn.

HOTEL DIEU HOSPITAL - LIBRARY
Box 61262   Phone: (504) 588-3470
New Orleans, LA 70161   Sarah C. von Rosenberg, Libn.

INTERNATIONAL HOUSE LIBRARY
Box 52020   Phone: (504) 522-3591
New Orleans, LA 70152   Mina L. Crais, Libn.

JONES, WALKER, WAECHTER, POITEVENT, CARRERE & DENEGRE - LAW
   LIBRARY
225 Baronne St.   Phone: (504) 581-6641
New Orleans, LA 70112   Teresa Neaves, Libn.

LAW LIBRARY OF LOUISIANA †
100 Supreme Court Bldg.
301 Loyola Ave.   Phone: (504) 568-5705
New Orleans, LA 70112   Carol D. Billings, Dir.

LOUISIANA STATE MUSEUM - LOUISIANA HISTORICAL CENTER
751 Chartres St.   Phone: (504) 568-8214
New Orleans, LA 70116   Rose Lambert, Libn.

LOUISIANA STATE UNIVERSITY MEDICAL CENTER - LIBRARY
1542 Tulane Ave.   Phone: (504) 568-6100
New Orleans, LA 70112   John P. Ische, Dir.

LOYOLA UNIVERSITY (New Orleans) - LAW LIBRARY
6363 St. Charles Ave.   Phone: (504) 865-3426
New Orleans, LA 70118   Win-Shin S. Chiang, Law Libn.

MC DERMOTT INC. - CORPORATE INFORMATION CENTER
1010 Common St.   Phone: (504) 587-5799
New Orleans, LA 70112   Karen L. Furlow, Corp.Libn.

MERCY HOSPITAL OF NEW ORLEANS - MEDICAL LIBRARY *
301 N. Jefferson Davis Pkwy.   Phone: (504) 486-7361
New Orleans, LA 70119   Jean Leonard, Med.Libn.

NEW ORLEANS BAPTIST THEOLOGICAL SEMINARY - JOHN T. CHRISTIAN
   LIBRARY
4110 Seminary Pl.   Phone: (504) 282-4455
New Orleans, LA 70126   Dr. Paul Gericke, Dir. of Lib.

NEW ORLEANS MUSEUM OF ART - FELIX J. DREYOUS LIBRARY
City Park
Box 19123   Phone: (504) 488-2631
New Orleans, LA 70179   Jeannette D. Downing, Libn.

NEW ORLEANS PSYCHOANALYTIC INSTITUTE, INC. - LIBRARY
3624 Coliseum St.   Phone: (504) 899-5815
New Orleans, LA 70115   Dr. Samuel Rubin, Chm.

NEW ORLEANS PUBLIC LIBRARY - ART, MUSIC & RECREATION DIVISION
219 Loyola Ave.   Phone: (504) 596-2565
New Orleans, LA 70140-1016   Marilyn Wilkins, Div.Hd.

NEW ORLEANS PUBLIC LIBRARY - BUSINESS AND SCIENCE DIVISION
219 Loyola Ave.   Phone: (504) 596-2580
New Orleans, LA 70140-1016   Elizabeth O. Bedikian, Div.Hd.

NEW ORLEANS PUBLIC LIBRARY - FOREIGN LANGUAGE DIVISION
219 Loyola Ave.   Phone: (504) 586-4943
New Orleans, LA 70140-1016   Norka Diaz, Div.Hd.

NEW ORLEANS PUBLIC LIBRARY - LOUISIANA DIVISION
219 Loyola Ave.   Phone: (504) 524-7382
New Orleans, LA 70140-1016   Collin B. Hamer, Jr., Div.Hd.

SOUTHERN BAPTIST HOSPITAL - LEARNING RESOURCE CENTER
2700 Napoleon Ave.   Phone: (504) 899-9311
New Orleans, LA 70115   Pauline Fulda, Dir.

SOUTHERN FOREST PRODUCTS ASSOCIATION - LIBRARY
Box 52468   Phone: (504) 443-4464
New Orleans, LA 70152   Ivy Riley, Libn.

STANDARD OIL OF CALIFORNIA - CHEVRON U.S.A., INC. - EASTERN
   REGION LIBRARY
935 Gravier St.   Phone: (504) 521-6292
New Orleans, LA 70112   Bob Hatten, Libn.

TOURO INFIRMARY - HOSPITAL LIBRARY SERVICES
1401 Foucher St., 10th Fl., M Bldg.   Phone: (504) 897-8102
New Orleans, LA 70115   Patricia J. Greenfield, Chf., Hosp.Lib.Serv.

TULANE UNIVERSITY OF LOUISIANA - ARCHITECTURE LIBRARY
Richardson Memorial Bldg.   Phone: (504) 865-4409
New Orleans, LA 70118   Frances E. Hecker, Hd.

TULANE UNIVERSITY OF LOUISIANA - HOWARD-TILTON MEMORIAL
   LIBRARY - LOUISIANA COLLECTION
                                         Phone: (504) 865-5643
New Orleans, LA 70118   Jane Stevens, Hd.

TULANE UNIVERSITY OF LOUISIANA - LATIN AMERICAN LIBRARY
Howard-Tilton Memorial Library   Phone: (504) 865-5681
New Orleans, LA 70118   Thomas Niehaus, Dir.

TULANE UNIVERSITY OF LOUISIANA - LAW LIBRARY
School of Law   Phone: (504) 866-2751
New Orleans, LA 70118   David A. Combe, Libn.

TULANE UNIVERSITY OF LOUISIANA - MATHEMATICS RESEARCH LIBRARY
Gibson Hall   Phone: (504) 865-5727
New Orleans, LA 70118   Dr. Terry Lawson, Prof., Mathematics

TULANE UNIVERSITY OF LOUISIANA - MAXWELL MUSIC LIBRARY
Howard-Tilton Memorial Library   Phone: (504) 865-4527
New Orleans, LA 70118   Liselotte Andersson, Libn.

TULANE UNIVERSITY OF LOUISIANA - SCHOOL OF BUSINESS
   ADMINISTRATION - NORMAN MAYER LIBRARY
                                         Phone: (504) 865-6111
New Orleans, LA 70118   Dorothy Whittemore, Dir.

TULANE UNIVERSITY OF LOUISIANA - SCHOOL OF MEDICINE - RUDOLPH
   MATAS MEDICAL LIBRARY †
1430 Tulane Ave.   Phone: (504) 588-5155
New Orleans, LA 70112   William D. Postell, Jr., Med.Libn.

TULANE UNIVERSITY OF LOUISIANA - SOUTHEASTERN ARCHITECTURAL
   ARCHIVE
7001 Freret St.
New Orleans, LA 70118   William R. Cullison, Cur.

TULANE UNIVERSITY OF LOUISIANA - SPECIAL COLLECTIONS DIVISION -
   MANUSCRIPTS AND RARE BOOKS SECTION
Howard-Tilton Memorial Library   Phone: (504) 865-5685
New Orleans, LA 70118   Wilbur E. Meneray, Ph.D., Hd.,Mss./Rare Bks.

TULANE UNIVERSITY OF LOUISIANA - WILLIAM RANSOM HOGAN JAZZ
   ARCHIVE
Howard-Tilton Memorial Library   Phone: (504) 865-5688
New Orleans, LA 70118   Curtis D. Jerde, Cur.

U.S. COURT OF APPEALS, 5TH CIRCUIT - LIBRARY
600 Camp St., Rm. 106
New Orleans, LA 70130
Phone: (504) 589-6510
Max G. Dodson, Circuit Libn.

U.S.D.A. - AGRICULTURAL RESEARCH SERVICE - SOUTHERN REGIONAL
RESEARCH CENTER
1100 Robert E. Lee Blvd.
Box 19687
New Orleans, LA 70179
Phone: (504) 589-7072
Dorothy B. Skau, Libn.

U.S. DEPT. OF COMMERCE - INTERNATIONAL TRADE ADMINISTRATION -
NEW ORLEANS DISTRICT OFFICE LIBRARY
International Trade Mart, Rm. 432
2 Canal St.
New Orleans, LA 70130
Phone: (504) 589-6546
Raymond E. Eveland, Dir.

U.S. FOREST SERVICE - SOUTHERN FOREST EXPERIMENT STATION
LIBRARY
Rm. T-10210 Postal Service Bldg.
701 Loyola Ave.
New Orleans, LA 70113
Phone: (504) 589-6798
Linda A. Korb, Libn.

U.S. VETERANS ADMINISTRATION (LA-New Orleans) - MEDICAL CENTER
LIBRARY
1601 Perdido St.
New Orleans, LA 70146
Phone: (504) 589-5272
Wilma B. Neveu, Chf., Lib.Serv.

UNIVERSITY OF NEW ORLEANS - EARL K. LONG LIBRARY - ARCHIVES &
MANUSCRIPTS/SPECIAL COLLECTIONS DEPT.
Lake Front
New Orleans, LA 70148
Phone: (504) 286-7273
D. Clive Hardy, Archv.

XAVIER UNIVERSITY OF LOUISIANA - COLLEGE OF PHARMACY - LIBRARY †
Palmetto & Pine Sts.
New Orleans, LA 70125
Phone: (504) 483-7428
Yvonne C. Hull, Libn.

CENTRAL LOUISIANA STATE HOSPITAL - MEDICAL AND PROFESSIONAL
LIBRARY
Box 31
Pineville, LA 71360
Phone: (318) 445-2421
Benton Carol McGee, Med.Libn.

DOW CHEMICAL U.S.A. - LOUISIANA DIVISION - LIBRARY
Box 400
Plaquemine, LA 70764-0400
Phone: (504) 389-8859
James H. Modeen, Mgr.

GREEN CLINIC - LIBRARY *
709 S. Vienna St.
Box 310
Ruston, LA 71270
Phone: (318) 255-3690
Louise M. Allen, Libn.

LOUISIANA TECH UNIVERSITY - COLLEGE OF EDUCATION - EDUCATIONAL
RESEARCH LIBRARY *
Tech Sta., Box 10108
Ruston, LA 71272
Phone: (318) 257-4683
Jeannette Robinson, Sec.

LOUISIANA TECH UNIVERSITY - RESEARCH DIVISION/COLLEGE OF
ADMINISTRATION AND BUSINESS - LIBRARY *
Tech Sta., Box 10318
Ruston, LA 71272
Phone: (318) 257-3701
Dr. James Robert Michael, Dir., Bus.Res.

ST. JOSEPH ABBEY - LIBRARY
St. Benedict, LA 70457
Phone: (504) 892-1800
Fr. Jules Tate, O.S.B., Libn.

ST. JOSEPH SEMINARY COLLEGE - PERE ROUQUETTE LIBRARY
St. Benedict, LA 70457
Phone: (504) 892-9895
Rev. Timothy J. Burnett, O.S.B., Dir. of Lib.

AMERICAN ROSE SOCIETY - LIBRARY
Box 30,000
Shreveport, LA 71130
Phone: (318) 938-5402
Harold S. Goldstein, Exec.Dir.

AT & T TECHNOLOGIES, INC. - TECHNICAL LIBRARY *
Box 31111
Shreveport, LA 71130
Phone: (318) 459-6850
Dorothy Wilson, Libn.

B'NAI ZION TEMPLE - MEMORIAL LIBRARY †
Box 5172
Shreveport, LA 71105
Phone: (318) 861-2122
Jean Stein, Adm. & Hd.

FIRST METHODIST CHURCH - BLISS MEMORIAL LIBRARY
Head of Texas St.
Shreveport, LA 71101
Phone: (318) 424-7771
Mrs. Dick Towery, Libn.

LOUISIANA STATE UNIVERSITY MEDICAL CENTER - SCHOOL OF MEDICINE
IN SHREVEPORT - LIBRARY
Box 33932
Shreveport, LA 71130
Phone: (318) 674-5446
Mr. Mayo Drake, Libn.

NORTHWESTERN STATE UNIVERSITY OF LOUISIANA - EUGENE P.
WATSON LIBRARY - SHREVEPORT DIVISION
1800 Warrington Pl.
Shreveport, LA 71101
Phone: (318) 424-1827
Dorcas M.C. McCormick, Div.Hd.

NORTON (R.W.) ART GALLERY - REFERENCE-RESEARCH LIBRARY
4747 Creswell Ave.
Shreveport, LA 71106
Phone: (318) 865-4201
Jerry M. Bloomer, Libn.

SCHUMPERT MEDICAL CENTER - MEDICAL LIBRARY
915 Margaret Place
Box 21976
Shreveport, LA 71120
Phone: (318) 227-4500
Marilyn Willis, Med.Libn.

THE (Shreveport) TIMES - LIBRARY
222 Lake St.
Shreveport, LA 71130
Phone: (318) 459-3283
Johnny L. King, Libn.

U.S. VETERANS ADMINISTRATION (LA-Shreveport) - MEDICAL CENTER
LIBRARY
510 E. Stoner
Shreveport, LA 71130
Phone: (318) 424-6036
Shirley B. Hegenwald, Chf., Lib.Serv.

MAINE

ANDROSCOGGIN COUNTY LAW LIBRARY
County Bldg.
Auburn, ME 04210
Phone: (207) 782-3121
Hon. Thomas E. Delahanty, Libn.

ANDROSCOGGIN HISTORICAL SOCIETY - CLARENCE E. MARCH LIBRARY
2 Turner St., County Bldg.
Auburn, ME 04210
Phone: (207) 784-0586
Leon M. Norris, Exec.Sec. & Cur.

CENTRE D'HERITAGE FRANCO-AMERICAIN - LIBRARY
27 1/2 Minot Ave.
Auburn, ME 04140
Phone: (207) 783-8143
JoAnne D. Lapointe, Cur.

CENTRAL MAINE POWER COMPANY - LIBRARY SERVICES
Edison Dr.
Augusta, ME 04336
Phone: (207) 623-3521
Cynthia Keating, Libn.

KENNEBEC COUNTY LAW LIBRARY
95 State St.
Augusta, ME 04330
Phone: (207) 622-9357
Matthew F. Dyer, Libn.

KENNEBEC VALLEY MEDICAL CENTER - MEDICAL LIBRARY
6 E. Chestnut St.
Augusta, ME 04330
Phone: (207) 623-4711
Mrs. Gabriel W. Kirkpatrick, Med.Libn.

MAINE STATE DEPARTMENT OF ENVIRONMENTAL PROTECTION &
DEPARTMENT OF CONSERVATION - DEP-DOC JOINT LIBRARY
State House, Station 17
Augusta, ME 04333
Phone: (207) 289-2811
Priscilla Bickford, Libn.

MAINE STATE DEPARTMENT OF HUMAN SERVICES - DEPARTMENTAL
LIBRARY
State House, Sta. No. 11
Augusta, ME 04333
Phone: (207) 289-3055
Mary J. Wandersee, Dept.Libn.

MAINE STATE DEPARTMENT OF TRANSPORTATION - LIBRARY *
Child St.
Augusta, ME 04333
Phone: (207) 289-2681
Richard Siroin, Libn.

MAINE STATE LAW AND LEGISLATIVE REFERENCE LIBRARY
State House, Station 43
Augusta, ME 04333
Phone: (207) 289-2648
Catherine A. Freehling, State Law Libn.

MAINE STATE LIBRARY
Cultural Bldg., State House Sta. 64   Phone: (207) 289-3561
Augusta, ME 04333   J. Gary Nichols, State Libn.

MAINE STATE MUSEUM - RESOURCE CENTER
State House, Station 83   Phone: (207) 289-2301
Augusta, ME 04333   Ronald J. Kley, Musm. Registrar/Cur.

MAINE STATE OFFICE OF ENERGY RESOURCES - LIBRARY *
State House Sta. 53   Phone: (207) 289-3811
Augusta, ME 04330   Robert Michaud, Libn.

MEDICAL CARE DEVELOPMENT, INC. - LIBRARY
11 Parkwood Dr.   Phone: (207) 622-7566
Augusta, ME 04330   Mary Anne Spindler Libby, Libn.

U.S. VETERANS ADMINISTRATION (ME-Augusta) - CENTER LIBRARY
Togus Br. (402/142D)   Phone: (207) 623-8411
Augusta, ME 04330   Melda W. Page, Chf.Libn.

U.S. VETERANS ADMINISTRATION (ME-Togus) - MEDICAL & REGIONAL OFFICE CENTER
    Phone: (207) 623-8411
Augusta, ME 04330   Melda W. Page, Chf.Libn.

BANGOR DAILY NEWS - LIBRARY
491 Main St.   Phone: (207) 942-4881
Bangor, ME 04401   Charles A. Campo, Hd.Libn.

BANGOR MENTAL HEALTH INSTITUTE - HEALTH SCIENCES MEDIA CENTER
Box 926   Phone: (207) 947-6981
Bangor, ME 04401   Wendy E. Troiano, Libn.

BANGOR THEOLOGICAL SEMINARY - MOULTON LIBRARY
300 Union St.   Phone: (207) 942-6781
Bangor, ME 04401   Clifton Davis, Libn.

BEAL COLLEGE - LIBRARY
629 Main St.   Phone: (207) 947-4591
Bangor, ME 04401   Ann Rea, Libn.

EASTERN MAINE MEDICAL CENTER - HEALTH SCIENCES LIBRARY
489 State St.   Phone: (207) 945-8228
Bangor, ME 04401   Suellen Jagels, Libn.

HUSSON COLLEGE - LIBRARY *
One College Circle   Phone: (207) 945-5641
Bangor, ME 04401   Berneice Thompson, Libn.

PENOBSCOT BAR LIBRARY ASSOCIATION - LIBRARY †
Penobscot County Court House
Bangor, ME 04401   Norman Minsky, Sec./Tres.

JACKSON LABORATORY - JOAN STAATS LIBRARY
    Phone: (207) 288-3371
Bar Harbor, ME 04609

BATH MEMORIAL HOSPITAL - HEALTH SCIENCES LIBRARY
23 Winship St.   Phone: (207) 443-5524
Bath, ME 04530   Ellen Johnstone, Health Sci.Libn.

MAINE MARITIME MUSEUM - LIBRARY/ARCHIVES
963 Washington St.   Phone: (207) 443-6311
Bath, ME 04530   Kathy Hudson, Adm.Asst.

SAGADAHOC COUNTY LAW LIBRARY *
County Court House
752 High St.   Phone: (207) 443-9734
Bath, ME 04530

WALDO COUNTY LAW LIBRARY
Waldo County Courthouse
73 Church St.   Phone: (207) 338-2512
Belfast, ME 04915   William Anderson, Libn.

FIBER MATERIALS, INC. - TECHNICAL LIBRARY
Biddeford Industrial Park   Phone: (207) 282-5911
Biddeford, ME 04005   Susan A. Walker, Tech.Libn.

UNIVERSITY OF NEW ENGLAND - COLLEGE OF OSTEOPATHIC MEDICINE - NECOM LIBRARY †
11 Hills Beach Rd.   Phone: (207) 283-0171
Biddeford, ME 04005   Rosemary G. Kelley, Med.Libn.

BOOTHBAY THEATRE MUSEUM
Corey Ln.   Phone: (207) 633-4536
Boothbay, ME 04537   Franklyn Lenthall, Cur.

ST. ANDREWS HOSPITAL - MEDICAL LIBRARY *
3 St. Andrews Lane   Phone: (207) 633-2121
Boothbay Harbor, ME 04538   Karen Roberts, Libn.

BOWDOIN COLLEGE - LIBRARY - SPECIAL COLLECTIONS
    Phone: (207) 725-8731
Brunswick, ME 04011   Dianne M. Gutscher, Cur.

REGIONAL MEMORIAL HOSPITAL - HEALTH SCIENCES LIBRARY
58 Baribeau Dr.   Phone: (207) 729-0181
Brunswick, ME 04011   Lynda K. Willis, Libn.

U.S. NAVY - NAVAL AIR STATION (ME-Brunswick) - LIBRARY
Box 21   Phone: (207) 921-2639
Brunswick, ME 04011   Judy A. Hoshaw, Libn.

CALAIS FREE LIBRARY
    Phone: (207) 454-3223
Calais, ME 04619   Helen R. Oliver, Libn.

CAMDEN-ROCKPORT HISTORICAL SOCIETY - ARCHIVES
Old Conway House and Cramer Museum
Box 897   Phone: (207) 236-2257
Camden, ME 04843

MAINE EDUCATIONAL RESOURCES, INC. - MID COAST TEACHERS' CENTER
Box 860   Phone: (207) 594-5428
Camden, ME 04843   John F. Parkman, Dir.

CARY MEDICAL CENTER - HEALTH SCIENCE LIBRARY
Van Buren Rd.
MRA Box 37   Phone: (207) 498-3131
Caribou, ME 04736   Donna E. Cote-Thibodeau, Libn.

NYLANDER MUSEUM - ARCHIVES
393 Main St.
Box 1062   Phone: (207) 493-4474
Caribou, ME 04736   Constance M. Simon, Dir.

MAINE MARITIME ACADEMY - NUTTING MEMORIAL LIBRARY
    Phone: (207) 326-4311
Castine, ME 04420   Marjorie T. Harrison, Hd.Libn.

DEER ISLE-STONINGTON HISTORICAL SOCIETY - LIBRARY
    Phone: (207) 348-2886
Deer Isle, ME 04627   Genice Welcome, Exec.Sec.

HAYSTACK MOUNTAIN SCHOOL OF CRAFTS - LIBRARY
    Phone: (207) 348-6946
Deer Isle, ME 04627

PISCATAQUIS COUNTY LAW LIBRARY
Court House Annex   Phone: (207) 564-2181
Dover-Foxcroft, ME 04426   Elaine H. Roberts, Libn.

HANCOCK COUNTY LAW LIBRARY, INC. *
60 State St.
Ellsworth, ME 04605   Margaret A. Cunningham, Libn.

MAINE AUDUBON SOCIETY - ENVIRONMENTAL INFORMATION SERVICE
Gilsland Farm
118 U.S. Rte. 1   Phone: (207) 781-2330
Falmouth, ME 04105   Miriam Schneider, Libn.

FRANKLIN MEMORIAL HOSPITAL - TURNER MEMORIAL LIBRARY
RFD No. 2
Wilton Rd.   Phone: (207) 778-6031
Farmington, ME 04938   Irene R. Pettengill, Med.Libn.

UNIVERSITY OF MAINE, FARMINGTON - MANTOR LIBRARY †
Phone: (207) 778-3501
Farmington, ME 04938   John P. Burnham, Hd.Libn.

HOULTON REGIONAL HOSPITAL - LIBRARY
20 Hartford St.   Phone: (207) 532-9471
Houlton, ME 04730   Cathy Bates, Med.Libn.

BRICK STORE MUSEUM - EDITH CLEAVES BARRY LIBRARY
117 Main St.
Box 117   Phone: (207) 985-4802
Kennebunk, ME 04043   Sandra S. Armentrout, Dir.

AMERICAN-CANADIAN GENEALOGICAL SOCIETY - FATHER LEO E. BEGIN
CHAPTER - LIBRARY
Box 2125
Lewiston, ME 04240   Bernadette Tardif, Libn.

BATES COLLEGE - GEORGE AND HELEN LADD LIBRARY - SPECIAL
COLLECTIONS
Phone: (207) 786-6272
Lewiston, ME 04240   Joseph J. Derbyshire, Libn.

CENTRAL MAINE MEDICAL CENTER - GERRISH-TRUE HEALTH SCIENCE
LIBRARY
300 Main St.   Phone: (207) 795-2376
Lewiston, ME 04240   Diane Carroll, Lib.Dir.

ST. MARY'S GENERAL HOSPITAL - HEALTH SCIENCES LIBRARY
45 Golder St.   Phone: (207) 786-2901
Lewiston, ME 04240   Evelyn A. Greenlaw, Libn.

U.S. AIR FORCE BASE - LORING BASE LIBRARY
FL 4678   Phone: (207) 999-2416
Loring AFB, ME 04751   Mary E. Bushey, Libn.

NATIONAL SOCIETY, DAUGHTERS OF THE AMERICAN REVOLUTION -
HANNAH WESTON CHAPTER - BURNHAM TAVERN MUSEUM
Main & Free Sts.   Phone: (207) 255-4432
Machias, ME 04654   Valdine C. Atwood, Chm.

LEARNING INCORPORATED - LIBRARY
Learning Place   Phone: (207) 244-5015
Manset-Seawall, ME 04656   A.L. Welles, Dir.

TRIGOM - RESEARCH LIBRARY *
Rampart Professional Complex
Rte. 302   Phone: (207) 846-3294
North Windham, ME 04062   Gregory M. Scott, Pres.

UNIVERSITY OF MAINE, ORONO - NORTHEAST ARCHIVES OF FOLKLORE
AND ORAL HISTORY
Dept. of Anthropology
S. Stevens Hall   Phone: (207) 581-1891
Orono, ME 04469   Edward D. Ives, Dir.

UNIVERSITY OF MAINE, ORONO - RAYMOND H. FOGLER LIBRARY -
SPECIAL COLLECTIONS DEPARTMENT
Phone: (207) 581-1686
Orono, ME 04469   Eric S. Flower, Dept.Hd.

PEMAQUID HISTORICAL ASSOCIATION - HARRINGTON MEETING HOUSE -
LIBRARY
Old Harrington Road   Phone: (207) 677-2587
Pemaquid, ME 04558   Stuart P. Gillespie, Pres.

UNITED SOCIETY OF BELIEVERS - THE SHAKER LIBRARY
Shaker Village, Sabbathday Lake   Phone: (207) 926-4865
Poland Spring, ME 04274   Bro. Theodore E. Johnson, Dir.

ANDOVER COLLEGE - LIBRARY
901 Washington Ave.   Phone: (207) 774-6126
Portland, ME 04103   Irene H. Tuttle, Libn.

BAXTER (Governor) SCHOOL FOR THE DEAF - LIBRARY
Box 799   Phone: (207) 781-2493
Portland, ME 04104   Russell Robinson, Media Spec./Libn.

CUMBERLAND BAR ASSOCIATION - NATHAN AND HENRY B. CLEAVES LAW
LIBRARY
County Court House, 142 Federal St.   Phone: (207) 773-9712
Portland, ME 04111   Lea Sutton, Libn.

GANNETT (Guy) PUBLISHING COMPANY - PRESS HERALD-EVENING
EXPRESS-MAINE SUNDAY TELEGRAM - LIBRARY
390 Congress St.   Phone: (207) 775-5811
Portland, ME 04104   Mary N. Sparrow, Chf.Libn.

JORDAN (Edward C.) CO., INC. - LIBRARY
Box 7050   Phone: (207) 775-5401
Portland, ME 04112   Rebecca F. Nutting, Libn.

MAINE CHARITABLE MECHANIC ASSOCIATION - LIBRARY
519 Congress St.   Phone: (207) 773-8396
Portland, ME 04111   Edith M. Riley, Libn.

MAINE HISTORICAL SOCIETY - LIBRARY
485 Congress St.   Phone: (207) 774-1822
Portland, ME 04101   Margaret J. McCain, Libn.

MAINE MEDICAL CENTER - LIBRARY
22 Bramhall St.   Phone: (207) 871-2201
Portland, ME 04102   Robin M. Rand, Dir., Lib.Serv.

MERCY HOSPITAL - HEALTH SCIENCES LIBRARY
144 State St.   Phone: (207) 774-1461
Portland, ME 04101   Mary Anne Toner, Libn.

PORTLAND SCHOOL OF ART - LIBRARY
619 Congress St.   Phone: (207) 761-1772
Portland, ME 04101   Joanne Waxman, Libn.

UNION MUTUAL LIFE INSURANCE COMPANY - CORPORATE INFORMATION
CENTER
2211 Congress St.   Phone: (207) 780-2347
Portland, ME 04122   Phillip C. Kalloch, Jr., Supv., Info.Serv.

UNIVERSITY OF MAINE SCHOOL OF LAW - DONALD L. GARBRECHT LAW
LIBRARY
246 Deering Ave.   Phone: (207) 780-4350
Portland, ME 04102   Dan J. Freehling, Law Libn.

UNIVERSITY OF SOUTHERN MAINE - CENTER FOR RESEARCH & ADVANCED
STUDY - RESEARCH CENTER LIBRARY
246 Deering Ave.   Phone: (207) 780-4411
Portland, ME 04102   Janet F. Brysh, Libn.

UNIVERSITY OF SOUTHERN MAINE - NEW ENTERPRISE INSTITUTE -
ENTERPRISE INFORMATION SERVICE
246 Deering Ave.   Phone: (207) 780-4420
Portland, ME 04102   Janet F. Brysh, Libn.

PINELAND CENTER - LIBRARY AND MEDIA CENTER
Box C   Phone: (207) 688-4811
Pownal, ME 04069   Sally Ward, Dir., Staff Dev.

AROOSTOOK MEDICAL CENTER - A.R. GOULD DIVISION - HEALTH
SCIENCES LIBRARY
151 Academy St.   Phone: (207) 768-4173
Presque Isle, ME 04769   Marilyn W. Dean, Lib.Supv.

NORTHERN MAINE RAISE - AROOSTOOK HEALTH INFORMATION AND
RESOURCE CONSORTIUM - LIBRARY
Box 1238   Phone: (207) 764-4178
Presque Isle, ME 04769

UNIVERSITY OF MAINE, PRESQUE ISLE - LIBRARY AND LEARNING
RESOURCES CENTER - SPECIAL COLLECTIONS
181 Main St.   Phone: (207) 764-0311
Presque Isle, ME 04769   John Vigle, Dir.

TRANET - LIBRARY
Box 567   Phone: (207) 864-2252
Rangeley, ME 04970   William N. Ellis, Exec.Dir.

FARNSWORTH (William A.) - LIBRARY AND ART MUSEUM
Phone: (207) 596-6457
Rockland, ME 04841   Marius B. Peladeau, Dir.

FMC CORPORATION - MARINE COLLOIDS DIVISION - LIBRARY
Box 308   Phone: (207) 594-4436
Rockland, ME 04841   Barbara Swift, Libn.

KNOX COUNTY LAW LIBRARY *
62 Union St.   Phone: (207) 594-2254
Rockland, ME 04841   Connie Campbell, Libn.

DYER-YORK LIBRARY AND MUSEUM
371-75 Main St.   Phone: (207) 283-3861
Saco, ME 04072   Stephen J. Podgajny, Exec.Dir.

MOUNT DESERT ISLAND BIOLOGICAL LABORATORY - LIBRARY
Phone: (207) 288-3605
Salsbury Cove, ME 04672

FOUNDATION FOR BLOOD RESEARCH - LIBRARY
Route 1
Box 428   Phone: (207) 883-4132
Scarborough, ME 04074   Maxine L. Brady, Libn.

PENOBSCOT MARINE MUSEUM - STEPHEN PHILLIPS MEMORIAL LIBRARY
Church St.
Box 403   Phone: (207) 548-6634
Searsport, ME 04974   Charles H. Howard, Libn.

SMITH (Margaret Chase) LIBRARY CENTER
Norridgewock Avenue
Box 366   Phone: (207) 474-8844
Skowhegan, ME 04976   James C. MacCampbell, Dir.

SOUTHERN MAINE VOCATIONAL TECHNICAL INSTITUTE - LIBRARY
Fort Rd.   Phone: (207) 799-7303
South Portland, ME 04106   Donald A. Bertsch, Jr., Libn.

UNIVERSITY OF MAINE, ORONO - IRA C. DARLING CENTER LIBRARY
Phone: (207) 563-3146
Walpole, ME 04573   Louise M. Dean, Libn.

COLBY COLLEGE - MILLER LIBRARY - SPECIAL COLLECTIONS
Phone: (207) 873-1131
Waterville, ME 04901   J. Fraser Cocks, III, Cur., Spec.Coll.

MAINE CRIMINAL JUSTICE ACADEMY - MEDIA RESOURCES
93 Silver St.   Phone: (207) 873-2651
Waterville, ME 04901   Linda J. Dwelley, Media Resource Supv.

MID-MAINE MEDICAL CENTER - CLARA HODGKINS MEMORIAL HEALTH
SCIENCES LIBRARY
Phone: (207) 873-0621
Waterville, ME 04901   Cora M. Damon, Libn.

THOMAS COLLEGE - MARRINER LIBRARY
W. River Rd.   Phone: (207) 873-0771
Waterville, ME 04901   Richard A. Boudreau, Libn.

WATERVILLE HISTORICAL SOCIETY - LIBRARY AND ARCHIVES
64 Silver St.   Phone: (207) 872-9439
Waterville, ME 04901

MAINE STATE DEPARTMENT OF MARINE RESOURCES - FISHERIES
RESEARCH STATION - LIBRARY
McKown Point   Phone: (207) 633-5572
West Boothbay Harbor, ME 04575   Pamela Shephard-Lupo, Libn.

SCOTT PAPER COMPANY - S.D. WARREN COMPANY - RESEARCH LIBRARY
Research Laboratory   Phone: (207) 856-6911
Westbrook, ME 04092   Deborah G. Chandler, Info.Spec.

LINCOLN COUNTY LAW LIBRARY †
Phone: (207) 882-7517
Wiscasset, ME 04578   George A. Cowan, Libn.

OLD YORK HISTORICAL SOCIETY - LIBRARY
George Marshall Store
Lindsay Rd.
Box 312   Phone: (207) 363-4974
York, ME 03909   Dr. Eldridge H. Pendleton, Dir., Coll. & Prog.

YORK HOSPITAL - HEALTH SCIENCES LIBRARY
15 Hospital Dr.   Phone: (207) 363-4321
York, ME 03909   Darryl Hamson, Med.Libn.

MARYLAND

U.S. ARMY - CHEMICAL RESEARCH & DEVELOPMENT CENTER -
INFORMATION SERVICES BRANCH - TECHNICAL LIBRARY
Phone: (301) 671-2934
Aberdeen Proving Ground, MD 21010   Edwin F. Gier, Chf., Tech.Lib.

U.S. ARMY - ENVIRONMENTAL HYGIENE AGENCY - LIBRARY
Bldg. E2100   Phone: (301) 671-4236
Aberdeen Proving Ground, MD 21010   Krishan S. Goel, Libn.

U.S. ARMY MEDICAL RESEARCH INSTITUTE OF CHEMICAL DEFENSE -
WOOD TECHNICAL LIBRARY
Bldg. E3100   Phone: (301) 671-4135
Aberdeen Proving Ground, MD 21010-5425 Patricia M. Pepin, Chf., Lib.Br.

U.S. ARMY ORDNANCE CENTER & SCHOOL - LIBRARY
Attn: ATSL-SE-LI, Bldg. 3071   Phone: (301) 278-4991
Aberdeen Proving Ground, MD 21005   Janice C. Weston, Chf.Libn.

U.S. ARMY POST - ABERDEEN PROVING GROUND - MORALE SUPPORT
ACTIVITIES DIVISION - POST LIBRARY
Bldg. 3320   Phone: (301) 278-3221
Aberdeen Proving Ground, MD 21005   Rose Marie Serbu, Adm.Libn.

U.S. ARMY - ELECTRONICS R & D COMMAND (ERADCOM) - HARRY
DIAMOND LABORATORIES - TECHNICAL INFORMATION BRANCH
2800 Powder Mill Rd. (DELHD-TA-L)   Phone: (202) 394-1010
Adelphi, MD 20783   Barbara L. McLaughlin, Chf.

U.S. PUBLIC HEALTH SERVICE - NATL. INSTITUTE OF MENTAL HEALTH -
MENTAL HEALTH STUDY CENTER LIBRARY †
2340 University Blvd., E.   Phone: (301) 436-6340
Adelphi, MD 20783   Ina Micas, Libn.

ANNE ARUNDEL COUNTY CIRCUIT COURT - LAW LIBRARY
Court House, Church Circle   Phone: (301) 224-1387
Annapolis, MD 21401   Joan B. Simison, Libn.

ANNE ARUNDEL COUNTY OFFICE OF PLANNING AND ZONING - LIBRARY
Arundel Center   Phone: (301) 224-1880
Annapolis, MD 21404   Alexander D. Speer, Planner

ANNE ARUNDEL GENERAL HOSPITAL - MEMORIAL LIBRARY
Franklin & Cathedral Sts.   Phone: (301) 267-1562
Annapolis, MD 21401   Joyce Richmond, Libn.

ARINC RESEARCH CORPORATION - TECHNICAL LIBRARY
2551 Riva Rd.   Phone: (301) 224-4000
Annapolis, MD 21401   William O. Lively, Libn.

ENVIRONMENTAL PROTECTION AGENCY - CENTRAL REGIONAL
LABORATORY - LIBRARY
839 Bestgate Rd.   Phone: (301) 224-2741
Annapolis, MD 21401   Michael R. Driscoll, Lib. Aide

HISTORIC ANNAPOLIS, INC. - LIBRARY
194 Prince George St.   /   Phone: (301) 267-7619
Annapolis, MD 21401   Mrs. John Symonds, Pres.

HISTORIC ANNAPOLIS, INC. - WILLIAM PACA GARDEN CONSERVATION
CENTER
3 Martin St.   Phone: (301) 269-0601
Annapolis, MD 21401   Lucy Dos Passos Coggin, Prog.Coord.

IIT RESEARCH INSTITUTE - ELECTROMAGNETIC COMPATIBILITY
ANALYSIS CENTER - TECHNICAL INFORMATION SERVICES
185 Admiral Cochrane   Phone: (301) 267-2251
Annapolis, MD 21402   Alison A. Storch, Mgr., Info.Serv.

MARYLAND MUNICIPAL LEAGUE - LIBRARY
76 Maryland Ave.   Phone: (301) 268-5514
Annapolis, MD 21401   Jon C. Burrell, Exec.Dir.

MARYLAND STATE DEPARTMENT OF LEGISLATIVE REFERENCE - LIBRARY
Legislative Services Bldg.
90 State Circle   Phone: (301) 841-3810
Annapolis, MD 21401   Lynda C. Davis, Chf., Lib.Div.

MARYLAND STATE DEPARTMENT OF NATURAL RESOURCES - LIBRARY
Tawes State Office Bldg.   Phone: (301) 269-3015
Annapolis, MD 21401   Shashi P. Thaper, Hd.Libn.

MARYLAND STATE HALL OF RECORDS COMMISSION - LIBRARY
College Ave. & St. John's St.   Phone: (301) 269-3915
Annapolis, MD 21404   Dr. Edward C. Papenfuse, Archv.

MARYLAND STATE LAW LIBRARY
361 Rowe Blvd.   Phone: (301) 269-3395
Annapolis, MD 21401   Michael S. Miller, Dir.

U.S. NAVY - NAVAL ACADEMY - NIMITZ LIBRARY
                                              Phone: (301) 267-2194
Annapolis, MD 21402   Professor Richard A. Evans, Lib.Dir.

U.S. NAVY - NAVAL INSTITUTE - ORAL HISTORY OFFICE
                                              Phone: (301) 268-6110
Annapolis, MD 21402   Paul Stillwell, Oral Hist.Dir.

U.S. NAVY - NAVAL INSTITUTE - REFERENCE & PHOTOGRAPHIC LIBRARY
                                              Phone: (301) 268-6110
Annapolis, MD 21402   Patty M. Maddocks, Dir.

POLISH NOBILITY ASSOCIATION - VILLA ANNESLIE ARCHIVES
529 Dunkirk Rd.   Phone: (301) 752-1087
Anneslie, MD 21212   Leonard Suligowski, Dir. of Heraldry

SOVEREIGN HOSPITALLER ORDER OF ST. JOHN - VILLA ANNESLIE -
ARCHIVES
529 Dunkirk Rd.   Phone: (301) 752-1087
Anneslie, MD 21212   Rev. Robert Woodside, H.O.S.J., Dir.

U.S. BUREAU OF MINES - AVONDALE RESEARCH CENTER LIBRARY
4900 La Salle Rd.   Phone: (301) 436-7552
Avondale, MD 20782   Paul F. Moran, Libn.

AAI CORPORATION - TECHNICAL LIBRARY
Box 6767   Phone: (301) 628-3193
Baltimore, MD 21204   Joyce F. Peacock, Libn.

ABELL (A.S.) PUBLISHING COMPANY INC. -THE BALTIMORE SUN - LIBRARY
501 N. Calvert
Box 1377   Phone: (301) 332-6253
Baltimore, MD 21278   Clement G. Vitek, Chf.Libn.

ADAMS EXPRESS COMPANY - LIBRARY
201 N. Charles St.   Phone: (301) 752-5900
Baltimore, MD 21201   Dorothy Marvel, Libn.

ALCOLAC, INC. - RESEARCH LIBRARY
3440 Fairfield Rd.   Phone: (301) 355-2600
Baltimore, MD 21226   Lydia Beyerlein, Res.Libn.

ALTERNATIVE PRESS CENTER - LIBRARY
Box 7229   Phone: (301) 243-2471
Baltimore, MD 21218   Peggy D'Adamo, Pres.

AT & T TECHNOLOGIES, INC. - TECHNICAL LIBRARY
2500 Broening Hwy., Rm. 200   Phone: (301) 563-6373
Baltimore, MD 21224   Miss R.M. Sawaryn, Libn.

BALTIMORE BRIEFING CENTER - LIBRARY
36 S. Charles St.   Phone: (301) 837-6068
Baltimore, MD 21201   Katherine Smith, Libn.

BALTIMORE CITY DEPARTMENT OF HOUSING AND COMMUNITY
DEVELOPMENT - RESEARCH LIBRARY
222 E. Saratoga St., Rm. 450   Phone: (301) 396-4248
Baltimore, MD 21202   Mrs. Shifra Cohen, Res.Anl.

BALTIMORE CITY - DEPARTMENT OF LEGISLATIVE REFERENCE - LIBRARY
City Hall   Phone: (301) 396-4733
Baltimore, MD 21202   Bernard F. Murphy, Dir.

BALTIMORE CITY DEPARTMENT OF PLANNING - LIBRARY
222 E. Saratoga St., 8th Fl.   Phone: (301) 396-5915
Baltimore, MD 21202   Nancy McLaughlin, Pub.Info.Off.

BALTIMORE CITY MAYOR'S OFFICE OF MANPOWER RESOURCES - LIBRARY
701 St. Paul St.   Phone: (301) 396-5586
Baltimore, MD 21202   Maxine Boodis, Libn.

BALTIMORE CITY PUBLIC SCHOOLS - PROFESSIONAL MEDIA CENTER *
181 North Bend Rd.   Phone: (301) 396-5348
Baltimore, MD 21229   Jacqueline M. Merchant, Libn.

BALTIMORE GAS AND ELECTRIC COMPANY - LIBRARY
2nd Fl., Monument St. Warehouse
Box 1475   Phone: (301) 234-6292
Baltimore, MD 21203   Agnes M. Lindemon, Libn.

BALTIMORE HEBREW COLLEGE - JOSEPH MEYERHOFF LIBRARY
5800 Park Heights Ave.   Phone: (301) 466-7900
Baltimore, MD 21215   Dr. Jesse Mashbaum, Dir.

BALTIMORE MUSEUM OF ART - REFERENCE LIBRARY
Art Museum Dr.   Phone: (301) 396-6317
Baltimore, MD 21218   Anita Gilden, Libn.

BALTIMORE NEWS AMERICAN - REFERENCE LIBRARY
301 E. Lombard St.   Phone: (301) 528-8196
Baltimore, MD 21203   Clark F. Ickes, Hd.Libn.

BALTIMORE POLICE DEPARTMENT - EDUCATION AND TRAINING DIVISION
- LIBRARY
601 E. Fayette St.   Phone: (301) 396-2518
Baltimore, MD 21202   Elaine B. Johnson, Libn.

BALTIMORE ZOO - ARTHUR R. WATSON LIBRARY
Druid Hill Pk.   Phone: (301) 396-7102
Baltimore, MD 21217   Ethel R. Hardee, Libn.

BENDIX CORPORATION - COMMUNICATIONS DIVISION - ENGINEERING
LIBRARY †
1300 E. Joppa Rd.   Phone: (301) 853-4383
Baltimore, MD 21204   Phyllis Davis, Libn.

BON SECOURS HOSPITAL - HEALTH SCIENCES LIBRARY
2000 W. Baltimore St.   Phone: (301) 362-3000
Baltimore, MD 21223   Marie Brown, Lib.Asst.

CARMELITE MONASTERY - LIBRARY AND ARCHIVES
1318 Dulaney Valley Rd.   Phone: (301) 823-7415
Baltimore, MD 21204   Sr. Constance Fitz Gerald, O.C.D., Archv.

CARNEGIE INSTITUTION OF WASHINGTON - DEPARTMENT OF
EMBRYOLOGY - LIBRARY *
115 W. University Pkwy.   Phone: (301) 467-1414
Baltimore, MD 21210

CENTER FOR URBAN ENVIRONMENTAL STUDIES, INC. - LIBRARY
516 N. Charles St., Suite 501   Phone: (301) 727-6212
Baltimore, MD 21201   Wayne Pulliam, Dir.

CHESSIE SYSTEM RAILROADS - TRAFFIC RESEARCH DEPARTMENT -
LIBRARY
One Charles Ctr., 16th Fl.   Phone: (301) 237-3742
Baltimore, MD 21201   R.M. Ruddle, Mgr., Traffic Res.

CHILDREN'S HOSPITAL, INC. - MEDICAL LIBRARY *
3825 Greenspring Ave.   Phone: (301) 462-6800
Baltimore, MD 21211   Janet E.N. Bush, Med.Rec.Adm.

COMMUNITY COLLEGE OF BALTIMORE - LIBRARIES/LEARNING
   RESOURCES CENTERS
Bard Library
2901 Liberty Heights Ave.   Phone: (301) 396-0432
Baltimore, MD 21213   Lloyd D. Mayfield, Dir.

CYLBURN ARBORETUM - LIBRARY
4915 Greenspring Ave.   Phone: (301) 396-0180
Baltimore, MD 21209   Adelaide C. Rackemann, Libn.

ENOCH PRATT FREE LIBRARY - AUDIO-VISUAL DEPARTMENT
400 Cathedral St.   Phone: (301) 396-4616
Baltimore, MD 21201   Helen W. Cyr, Hd.

ENOCH PRATT FREE LIBRARY - BUSINESS, SCIENCE AND TECHNOLOGY
   DEPARTMENT
400 Cathedral St.   Phone: (301) 396-5316
Baltimore, MD 21201   Sherry Ledbetter, Dept.Hd.

ENOCH PRATT FREE LIBRARY - FINE ARTS AND RECREATION
   DEPARTMENT
400 Cathedral St.   Phone: (301) 396-5491
Baltimore, MD 21201   Joan Stahl, Dept.Hd.

ENOCH PRATT FREE LIBRARY - JOB AND CAREER INFORMATION CENTER
400 Cathedral St.
Baltimore, MD 21201   Patricia Dougherty, Libn./Counselor

ENOCH PRATT FREE LIBRARY - MARYLAND DEPARTMENT
400 Cathedral St.   Phone: (301) 396-5468
Baltimore, MD 21201

ENOCH PRATT FREE LIBRARY - SOCIAL SCIENCE AND HISTORY
   DEPARTMENT
400 Cathedral St.   Phone: (301) 396-5430
Baltimore, MD 21201   Marva Belt, Hd.

FIDELITY & DEPOSIT COMPANY OF MARYLAND - LAW LIBRARY †
302 Fidelity Bldg.
Charles & Lexington Sts.   Phone: (301) 539-0800
Baltimore, MD 21203   Mary Teresa Jerscheid, Law Libn.

FLICKINGER FOUNDATION FOR AMERICAN STUDIES, INC. - LIBRARY
300 St. Dunstan's Rd.   Phone: (301) 323-6284
Baltimore, MD 21212   B. Floyd Flickinger, Pres.

FRANK, BERNSTEIN, CONAWAY & GOLDMAN - LIBRARY
300 E. Lombard St.   Phone: (301) 625-3503
Baltimore, MD 21202   Nina Ogden, Libn.

GENERAL REFRACTORIES COMPANY - U.S. REFRACTORIES DIVISION -
   RESEARCH CENTER LIBRARY
Box 1673   Phone: (301) 355-3400
Baltimore, MD 21203   Cathy Kamosa, Libn.

GOLDEN RADIO BUFFS OF MARYLAND, INC. - TAPE LIBRARY
7506 Iroquois Ave.   Phone: (301) 388-1976
Baltimore, MD 21219   Gene Leitner, Co-Founder

GRAND LODGE OF ANCIENT FREE AND ACCEPTED MASONS OF MARYLAND
   - LIBRARY
225 N. Charles St.   Phone: (301) 752-1198
Baltimore, MD 21201

GREATER BALTIMORE MEDICAL CENTER - DR. JOHN E. SAVAGE MEDICAL
   STAFF LIBRARY
6701 N. Charles St.   Phone: (301) 828-2530
Baltimore, MD 21204   Michael Houck, Libn.

HEALTH AND WELFARE COUNCIL OF CENTRAL MARYLAND, INC. - STAFF
   REFERENCE LIBRARY *
22 Light St.   Phone: (301) 752-4146
Baltimore, MD 21202   John G. Geist, Exec.Dir.

INSECT CONTROL AND RESEARCH, INC. - LIBRARY
1330 Dillon Heights Ave.   Phone: (301) 747-4500
Baltimore, MD 21228   Dr. Eugene J. Gerberg, Pres.

JEWISH HISTORICAL SOCIETY OF MARYLAND, INC. - ARCHIVES
3809 Clarks Ln.
Lower Level   Phone: (301) 358-9417
Baltimore, MD 21215   Cynthia H. Requardt, Archv.

JOHNS HOPKINS HOSPITAL - DEPARTMENT OF RADIOLOGY - LIBRARY
601 N. Broadway   Phone: (301) 955-6029
Baltimore, MD 21205   Elaine Pinkney, Libn.

JOHNS HOPKINS UNIVERSITY - CENTER FOR METROPOLITAN PLANNING
   AND RESEARCH - LIBRARY
Shriver Hall   Phone: (301) 338-7169
Baltimore, MD 21218   Dolores Sullivan, Adm.

JOHNS HOPKINS UNIVERSITY - DEPARTMENT OF EARTH AND PLANETARY
   SCIENCES - SINGEWALD READING ROOM
            Phone: (301) 366-3300
Baltimore, MD 21218   Hans P. Eugster, Chm.

JOHNS HOPKINS UNIVERSITY - FERDINAND HAMBURGER, JR. ARCHIVES
3400 North Charles St.   Phone: (301) 338-8323
Baltimore, MD 21218   Julia B. Morgan, Archv.

JOHNS HOPKINS UNIVERSITY - JOHN WORK GARRETT LIBRARY
Evergreen House
4545 N. Charles St.   Phone: (301) 338-7641
Baltimore, MD 21218   Jane Katz, Libn.

JOHNS HOPKINS UNIVERSITY - MILTON S. EISENHOWER LIBRARY -
   GEORGE PEABODY COLLECTION
17 E. Mt. Vernon Pl.   Phone: (301) 396-5540
Baltimore, MD 21202   Lyn Hart, Libn.

JOHNS HOPKINS UNIVERSITY - MILTON S. EISENHOWER LIBRARY -
   GOVERNMENT PUBN./MAPS/LAW LIBRARY
Charles & 34th Sts.   Phone: (301) 338-8360
Baltimore, MD 21218   James E. Gillispie, Libn.

JOHNS HOPKINS UNIVERSITY - MILTON S. EISENHOWER LIBRARY -
   SPECIAL COLLECTIONS DIVISION
3400 N. Charles St.   Phone: (301) 338-8348
Baltimore, MD 21218   Ann S. Gwyn, Asst.Dir., Spec.Coll.

JOHNS HOPKINS UNIVERSITY - POPULATION INFORMATION PROGRAM
624 N. Broadway   Phone: (301) 955-8200
Baltimore, MD 21205   Dr. Phyllis T. Piotrow, Dir.

JOHNS HOPKINS UNIVERSITY - RESEARCH & DEVELOPMENT CENTER -
   CENTER FOR SOCIAL ORGANIZATION OF SCHOOLS
3505 N. Charles St.   Phone: (301) 338-7570
Baltimore, MD 21218   John H. Hollifield, Asst.Dir.

JOHNS HOPKINS UNIVERSITY - SCHOOL OF HYGIENE AND PUBLIC HEALTH
   - INTERDEPARTMENTAL LIBRARY
615 N. Wolfe St.   Phone: (301) 955-3028
Baltimore, MD 21205   Edward S. Terry, Dir.

JOHNS HOPKINS UNIVERSITY-SCHOOL OF HYGIENE & PUBLIC HEALTH-
   MATERNAL & CHILD HEALTH/POPULATION DYNAMICS LIB.
615 N. Wolfe St.   Phone: (301) 955-3573
Baltimore, MD 21205   Camille D. Greenwald, Libn.

JOHNS HOPKINS UNIVERSITY - SCHOOL OF MEDICINE - DEPARTMENT OF
   PEDIATRICS - BAETJER MEMORIAL LIBRARY
CMSC 2-104 Johns Hopkins Hospital   Phone: (301) 955-3124
Baltimore, MD 21205   Patricia A. Nulle, Libn.

JOHNS HOPKINS UNIVERSITY - SCHOOL OF MEDICINE - JOSEPH L.
   LILIENTHAL LIBRARY
Blalock Bldg., 10th Fl.
601 N. Broadway   Phone: (301) 955-6641
Baltimore, MD 21205   Robin A. Kroft, Libn.

JOHNS HOPKINS UNIVERSITY - WILLIAM H. WELCH MEDICAL LIBRARY
1900 E. Monument St.   Phone: (301) 955-3411
Baltimore, MD 21205   Richard A. Polacsek, M.D., Dir./Libn.

JOHNS HOPKINS UNIVERSITY - WILMER OPHTHALMOLOGICAL INSTITUTE
- JONAS S. FRIEDENWALD LIBRARY
3/B 50 Woods Bldg.   Phone: (301) 955-3127
Baltimore, MD 21205   Maria Tama Maggio, Dept.Libn.

KENNEDY (John F.) INSTITUTE - INTERDISCIPLINARY MULTI-MEDIA
LIBRARY †
707 North Broadway   Phone: (301) 955-4240
Baltimore, MD 21205

KEY (Francis Scott) MEDICAL CENTER - HAROLD E. HARRISON LIBRARY
4940 Eastern Ave.   Phone: (301) 955-0678
Baltimore, MD 21224   Rebecca Charton, Libn.

LIBRARY COMPANY OF THE BALTIMORE BAR - LIBRARY
618 Court House West   Phone: (301) 727-0280
Baltimore, MD 21202   Kai-Yun Chiu, Law Libn.

LUTHERAN HOSPITAL OF MARYLAND - CHARLES G. REIGNER MEDICAL
LIBRARY
730 Ashburton St.   Phone: (301) 945-1600
Baltimore, MD 21216

MARTIN MARIETTA LABORATORIES - LIBRARY
1450 S. Rolling Rd.   Phone: (301) 247-0700
Baltimore, MD 21227-3898   Rosalind P. Cheslock, Mgr., Tech.Info.Serv.

MARYLAND GENERAL HOSPITAL - MEDICAL STAFF LIBRARY
827 Linden Ave.   Phone: (301) 728-7900
Baltimore, MD 21201   Monica Yang, Coord., Lib.Serv.

MARYLAND GENERAL HOSPITAL - SCHOOL OF NURSING LIBRARY
827 Linden Ave.   Phone: (301) 728-7900
Baltimore, MD 21201   Monica Yang, Coord., Lib.Serv.

MARYLAND HISTORICAL SOCIETY - LIBRARY
201 W. Monument St.   Phone: (301) 685-3750
Baltimore, MD 21201   William B. Keller, Hd.Libn.

MARYLAND INSTITUTE, COLLEGE OF ART - DECKER LIBRARY
1400 Cathedral St.   Phone: (301) 669-9200
Baltimore, MD 21201   John Stoneham, Dir.

MARYLAND PHARMACEUTICAL ASSOCIATION - LIBRARY
Kelly Memorial Bldg.
650 W. Lombard St.   Phone: (301) 727-0746
Baltimore, MD 21201   David A. Banta, Exec.Dir.

MARYLAND REHABILITATION CENTER - R.C. THOMPSON LIBRARY
2301 Argonne Dr.   Phone: (301) 366-8800
Baltimore, MD 21218   Jack Prial, Libn.

MARYLAND STATE DEPARTMENT OF EDUCATION - DIVISION OF LIBRARY
DEVELOPMENT & SERVICES - MEDIA SERVICES CENTER †
200 W. Baltimore St.   Phone: (301) 659-2113
Baltimore, MD 21201   Elsie A. Leonard, Sect.Chf.

MARYLAND STATE DEPARTMENT OF HEALTH & MENTAL HYGIENE -
LIBRARY †
201 W. Preston St.   Phone: (301) 383-2634
Baltimore, MD 21201   Yvette Dixon, Assoc.Libn.

MARYLAND STATE DEPARTMENT OF STATE PLANNING - LIBRARY
State Office Bldg., Rm. 1101
301 W. Preston St.   Phone: (301) 383-2439
Baltimore, MD 21201-2365   Helene W. Jeng, Libn.

MARYLAND STATE DIVISION OF LABOR AND INDUSTRY - OCCUPATIONAL
SAFETY AND HEALTH LIBRARY
501 St. Paul Pl.   Phone: (301) 659-4133
Baltimore, MD 21202   Stephen J. Rash, Health Planner

MARYLAND STATE ENERGY OFFICE - LIBRARY
301 W. Preston St., Suite 903   Phone: (301) 383-6810
Baltimore, MD 21201   Deborah Jones, Libn./Mgr.

MARYLAND STATE HIGHWAY ADMINISTRATION - LIBRARY
707 Calvert St.   Phone: (301) 659-1420
Baltimore, MD 21202   Ruby D. Weston, Libn.

MARYLAND STATE LAW DEPARTMENT - ATTORNEY GENERAL'S OFFICE -
LIBRARY
7 N. Calvert St., 1st Fl.   Phone: (301) 576-6300
Baltimore, MD 21202   Natalie Paymer Ellis, Law Libn.

MARYLAND STATE POLICE ACADEMY - LIBRARY
1200 Reisterstown Rd.   Phone: (301) 486-3101
Baltimore, MD 21208-3899   Marcia Abrams, Supv.

MEDICAL AND CHIRURGICAL FACULTY OF THE STATE OF MARYLAND -
LIBRARY
1211 Cathedral St.   Phone: (301) 539-0872
Baltimore, MD 21201   Joseph E. Jensen, Libn.

MERCY HOSPITAL - MC GLANNAN MEMORIAL LIBRARY
301 St. Paul Pl.   Phone: (301) 727-5400
Baltimore, MD 21202   Eileen W. Gillis, Libn.

MERCY HOSPITAL, INC. - NURSING LIBRARY
301 St. Paul Pl.   Phone: (301) 332-9228
Baltimore, MD 21202   Eileen W. Gillis, Libn.

MILES & STOCKBRIDGE, ATTORNEYS-AT-LAW - LIBRARY
10 Light St.   Phone: (301) 727-6464
Baltimore, MD 21202   Anna B. Cole, Libn.

NATIONAL INSTITUTE ON AGING - GERONTOLOGY RESEARCH CENTER
LIBRARY
4940 Eastern Ave.   Phone: (301) 396-9403
Baltimore, MD 21224   Joanna Chen, Libn.

NATIONAL INSTITUTE ON DRUG ABUSE - ADDICTION RESEARCH CENTER
LIBRARY
Box 5180   Phone: (301) 396-9680
Baltimore, MD 21224   Mary Pfeiffer, Libn.

NATURAL HISTORY SOCIETY OF MARYLAND - LIBRARY
2643 N. Charles St.   Phone: (301) 235-6116
Baltimore, MD 21218   C. Haven Kolb, Sec.

NER ISRAEL RABBINICAL COLLEGE - LIBRARY *
400 Mt. Wilson Lane   Phone: (301) 484-7200
Baltimore, MD 21208   Rabbi Jakowiski, Libn.

NORTH CHARLES GENERAL HOSPITAL - MEDICAL STAFF LIBRARY
2724 N. Charles St.   Phone: (301) 338-2306
Baltimore, MD 21218   Bertha J. Shub, Libn.

OBER, KALER, GRIMES & SHRIVER - LIBRARY
1600 Maryland National Bank Bldg.   Phone: (301) 685-1120
Baltimore, MD 21202   Madelyn H. Weschler, Libn.

PEABODY CONSERVATORY OF MUSIC - LIBRARY
21 E. Mt. Vernon Pl.   Phone: (301) 837-0600
Baltimore, MD 21202   Edwin A. Quist, Libn.

PEALE MUSEUM - REFERENCE CENTER
225 Holliday St.   Phone: (301) 396-3523
Baltimore, MD 21202   Richard Flint, Cur., Prints/Photographs

PIPER & MARBURY - LAW LIBRARY
36 S. Charles St., Suite 1100   Phone: (301) 576-1617
Baltimore, MD 21201   Loretta O. Yaller, Libn.

PROVIDENT HOSPITAL - HEALTH SCIENCES LIBRARY
2600 Liberty Heights Ave.
Baltimore, MD 21215

REGIONAL PLANNING COUNCIL - LIBRARY
2225 N. Charles St.   Phone: (301) 383-5864
Baltimore, MD 21218   Irva B. Nachlas-Gabin, Libn.

ST. AGNES HOSPITAL - L.P. GUNDRY HEALTH SCIENCES LIBRARY
900 Caton Ave.   Phone: (301) 368-7565
Baltimore, MD 21229   Joanne Sutt, Dir.

SCM CORPORATION - PIGMENTS DIVISION - LIBRARY
3901 Glidden Rd.   Phone: (301) 335-3600
Baltimore, MD 21226   Nancy Freeman, Libn.

SEMMES, BOWEN & SEMMES - LAW LIBRARY
10 Light St.   Phone: (301) 539-5040
Baltimore, MD 21202   Helen Y. Harris, Libn.

SINAI HOSPITAL OF BALTIMORE, INC. - EISENBERG MEDICAL STAFF
  LIBRARY
Belvedere & Greenspring   Phone: (301) 578-5015
Baltimore, MD 21215   Rita Matcher, Dir., Lib.Serv.

SOUTH BALTIMORE GENERAL HOSPITAL - MEDICAL LIBRARY
3001 S. Hanover St.   Phone: (301) 354-1000
Baltimore, MD 21230   Kristine M. Scannell, Med.Libn.

SPRING GROVE HOSPITAL CENTER - SULZBACHER MEMORIAL LIBRARY †
Wade Ave., Isidore Tuerk Bldg.   Phone: (301) 455-7824
Baltimore, MD 21228   Charles H. Johnson, Supv. of Lib.

UNION MEMORIAL HOSPITAL - DR. JOHN M.T. FINNEY, JR. MEMORIAL
  MEDICAL LIBRARY †
201 E. University Pkwy.   Phone: (301) 235-7200
Baltimore, MD 21218   Rena Snyder, Chf.Med.Libn.

UNION MEMORIAL HOSPITAL - NURSING LIBRARY
3301 N. Calvert St.   Phone: (301) 235-7200
Baltimore, MD 21218   Carolyn M. Daugherty, Libn.

UNITED METHODIST HISTORICAL SOCIETY - BALTIMORE ANNUAL
  CONFERENCE - LOVELY LANE MUSEUM LIBRARY
2200 St. Paul St.   Phone: (301) 889-4458
Baltimore, MD 21218   Rev. Edwin Schell, Exec.Sec./Libn.

U.S. DEPT. OF COMMERCE - INTERNATIONAL TRADE ADMINISTRATION -
  BALTIMORE DISTRICT OFFICE LIBRARY
415 U.S. Customhouse
Gay & Lombard Sts.   Phone: (301) 962-3560
Baltimore, MD 21202   Mary T. Conrad, Trade Spec.

U.S. NATL. PARK SERVICE - FORT MC HENRY NATL. MONUMENT - LIBRARY
End of Fort Ave.   Phone: (301) 962-4290
Baltimore, MD 21230   Paul E. Plamann, Hist.

U.S. SOCIAL SECURITY ADMINISTRATION - LIBRARY INFORMATION &
  GRAPHICS SERVICES BRANCH
6401 Security Blvd.
Altmeyer Bldg., Rm. 570   Phone: (301) 594-1650
Baltimore, MD 21235   Rowena S. Sadler, Chf., Lib.Info. & Br.

U.S. VETERANS ADMINISTRATION (MD-Baltimore) - MEDICAL CENTER
  LIBRARY SERVICE (142D)
3900 Loch Raven Blvd.   Phone: (301) 467-9932
Baltimore, MD 21218   Deborah A. Gustin, Chf., Lib.Serv.

UNIVERSITY OF BALTIMORE - LANGSDALE LIBRARY
1420 Maryland Ave.   Phone: (301) 625-3067
Baltimore, MD 21201   William Newman, Lib.Dir.

UNIVERSITY OF BALTIMORE - LANGSDALE LIBRARY - SPECIAL
  COLLECTIONS DEPARTMENT
1304 St. Paul St.   Phone: (301) 625-3135
Baltimore, MD 21202   Dr. W. Theodore Durr, Dir.

UNIVERSITY OF BALTIMORE - LAW LIBRARY
1415 Maryland Ave.   Phone: (301) 625-3400
Baltimore, MD 21201   Emily R. Greenberg, Dir.

UNIVERSITY OF MARYLAND, BALTIMORE - HEALTH SCIENCES LIBRARY
111 S. Greene St.   Phone: (301) 528-7545
Baltimore, MD 21201   Cyril C.H. Feng, Libn.

UNIVERSITY OF MARYLAND, BALTIMORE - SCHOOL OF LAW - MARSHALL
  LAW LIBRARY
20 N. Paca St.   Phone: (301) 528-7270
Baltimore, MD 21201   Barbara S. Gontrum, Dir.

VENABLE BAETJER & HOWARD - LIBRARY
2 Hopkins Plaza   Phone: (301) 752-6780
Baltimore, MD 21201   John S. Nixdorff, Libn.

WALTERS ART GALLERY - LIBRARY
600 N. Charles St.   Phone: (301) 547-9000
Baltimore, MD 21201   Muriel L. Toppan, Ref.Libn.

WEINBERG & GREEN, ATTORNEYS-AT-LAW - LIBRARY
100 S. Charles St.   Phone: (301) 332-8620
Baltimore, MD 21201   Sally J. Miles, Libn.

WESTINGHOUSE ELECTRIC CORPORATION - DEFENSE & ELECTRONIC
  CENTER - TECHNICAL INFORMATION CENTER
MS 1204, Box 1693   Phone: (301) 765-2858
Baltimore, MD 21203   Joan L. Doerr, Supv.

WYMAN PARK HEALTH SYSTEM, INC. - MEDICAL LIBRARY
3100 Wyman Park Dr.   Phone: (301) 338-3572
Baltimore, MD 21211-2895   Laurie A. Conway, Med.Libn.

EASTERN CHRISTIAN COLLEGE - LIBRARY
2410 Creswell Rd.
Box 629   Phone: (301) 879-9300
Bel Air, MD 21014   Thomas Joseph, Libn.

U.S.D.A. - NATIONAL AGRICULTURAL LIBRARY
10301 Baltimore Blvd.   Phone: (301) 344-3755
Beltsville, MD 20705   Joseph H. Howard, Dir.

U.S.D.A. - NATIONAL AGRICULTURAL LIBRARY - FOOD AND NUTRITION
  INFORMATION CENTER
10301 Baltimore Blvd., Rm. 304   Phone: (301) 344-3719
Beltsville, MD 20705   Robyn Frank, Dir.

U.S. NATL. PARK SERVICE - ASSATEAGUE ISLAND NATL. SEASHORE -
  LIBRARY
Rte. 2, Box 294   Phone: (301) 641-1441
Berlin, MD 21811   Larry G. Points, Chf., Interp.

AMERICAN COLLEGE OF HEALTH CARE ADMINISTRATORS - LIBRARY
4650 East-West Hwy.
Box 5890   Phone: (301) 652-8384
Bethesda, MD 20814   Helene Zubkoff, Serv.Spec.

AMERICAN NATIONAL METRIC COUNCIL - LIBRARY
5410 Grosvenor Lane   Phone: (301) 530-8333
Bethesda, MD 20814   Ruth E. Thaler, Ed.

ATOMIC INDUSTRIAL FORUM - LIBRARY
7101 Wisconsin Ave.   Phone: (301) 654-9260
Bethesda, MD 20814   Elizabeth A. Bourg, Libn.

BOOZ, ALLEN & HAMILTON, INC. - LIBRARY
4330 East-West Hwy.   Phone: (301) 951-2786
Bethesda, MD 20814   Linda Dodson, Libn.

BROWN (Earle Palmer) COMPANIES - THE SOURCE - LIBRARY
4733 Bethesda Ave.   Phone: (301) 986-0510
Bethesda, MD 20814   Susan Branzell Modak, Libn.

CONGRESSIONAL INFORMATION SERVICE, INC.
4520 East-West Hwy., Suite 800   Phone: (301) 654-1550
Bethesda MD 20814   Paul P. Massa, Pres.

DAMES & MOORE - LIBRARY
7101 Wisconsin Ave., Suite 700
Bethesda, MD 20814

DITTBERNER ASSOCIATES, INC. - LIBRARY
4903 Auburn Ave.   Phone: (301) 652-8350
Bethesda, MD 20814   Ingrid C.D. Mayr, Libn.

ERIC PROCESSING AND REFERENCE FACILITY
4833 Rugby Ave., Suite 301   Phone: (301) 656-9723
Bethesda, MD 20814   Ted Brandhorst, Dir.

HIGH BLOOD PRESSURE INFORMATION CENTER
120/80 Natl. Institutes of Health   Phone: (301) 496-1809
Bethesda, MD 20205   Barbara T. Kulawiec, Mgr.

INFORMATION SYSTEMS CONSULTANTS INC. - LIBRARY
Box 30212
Bethesda, MD 20814   Sue Pettipas, Adm.Asst.

INTERNATIONAL INSTITUTE FOR RESOURCE ECONOMICS - LIBRARY
6210 Massachusetts Ave.   Phone: (301) 229-6066
Bethesda, MD 20816

NATIONAL INSTITUTE OF ARTHRITIS, DIABETES, DIGESTIVE AND KIDNEY
    DISEASES - OFFICE OF HEALTH RESEARCH REPORTS
c/o Dr. Walter Stolz
Westwood Bldg., Rm 657   Phone: (301) 496-7277
Bethesda, MD 20205   Betsy Singer, Chf.

NATIONAL INSTITUTE OF DENTAL RESEARCH - DENTAL RESEARCH DATA
    OFFICE
                                                 Phone: (301) 496-7220
Bethesda, MD 20205   Kenneth C. Lynn, Data Off.

NATIONAL LIBRARY OF MEDICINE
                                                 Phone: (301) 496-6308
Bethesda, MD 20209   Harold M. Schoolman, M.D., Act.Dir.

NATIONAL STANDARDS ASSOCIATION, INC. - TECHINFO
5161 River Rd.   Phone: (301) 951-1389
Bethesda, MD 20816   Sonja Young, Mgr.

REFRIGERATION RESEARCH FOUNDATION - LIBRARY
Air Rights Bldg.
7315 Wisconsin Ave.   Phone: (301) 652-5674
Bethesda, MD 20814   J. William Hudson, Exec.Dir.

SOCIETY OF AMERICAN FORESTERS - LIBRARY
5400 Grosvenor Ln.   Phone: (301) 897-8720
Bethesda, MD 20814   Philip V. Petersen, Dir, Info./Member Serv.

U.S. ARMED FORCES RADIOBIOLOGY RESEARCH INSTITUTE (AFRRI) -
    LIBRARY SERVICES
National Naval Medical Ctr., Bldg.42   Phone: (301) 295-0428
Bethesda, MD 20814   Nannette M. Pope, Hd., Lib.Serv.

U.S. NATL. INSTITUTES OF HEALTH - DIVISION OF COMPUTER RESEARCH
    & TECHNOLOGY - LIBRARY
9000 Rockville Pike
Bldg. 12A, Rm. 3018   Phone: (301) 496-1658
Bethesda, MD 20205   Ellen M. Chu, Libn.

U.S. NATL. INSTITUTES OF HEALTH - LIBRARY
9000 Rockville Pike
Bldg. 10, Rm. 1L-25   Phone: (301) 496-2447
Bethesda, MD 20205   Carolyn P. Brown, Chf.

U.S. NATL. INSTITUTES OF HEALTH - NATIONAL CANCER INSTITUTE -
    CANCER INFORMATION CLEARINGHOUSE
Bldg. 31, Rm. 10A18   Phone: (301) 496-4070
Bethesda, MD 20205   Joseph Bangiolo, Dir.

U.S. NATL. INSTITUTES OF HEALTH - NATL. INST. OF NEUROLOGICAL &
    COMMUNICATIVE DISORDERS & STROKE - EPILEPSY LIB.
Federal Bldg., Rm. 114   Phone: (301) 496-6830
Bethesda, MD 20205   Judith L. Kirsch, Tech.Info.Spec.

U.S. NAVY - DAVID W. TAYLOR NAVAL SHIP RESEARCH AND
    DEVELOPMENT CENTER - TECHNICAL INFORMATION CENTER
Code 522   Phone: (202) 227-1309
Bethesda, MD 20084   Dr. Michael Dankewych, Libn.

U.S. NAVY - EDWARD RHODES STITT LIBRARY
Naval Hospital   Phone: (202) 295-1184
Bethesda, MD 20814-5011   Jerry Meyer, Adm.Libn.

U.S. NAVY - NAVAL MEDICAL COMMAND - NAVAL DENTAL CLINIC -
    NATIONAL CAPITAL REGION - WILLIAM L. DARNALL LIBRARY
                                                 Phone: (202) 295-0080
Bethesda, MD 20814   Patricia A. Evans, Chr., Lrng.Rsrcs.

U.S. NAVY - NAVAL MEDICAL RESEARCH INSTITUTE - INFORMATION
    SERVICES BRANCH
                                                 Phone: (202) 295-2186
Bethesda, MD 20814   Rosemary B. Spitzen, Adm.Libn.

U.S. NAVY - NAVAL SCHOOL OF HEALTH SCIENCES - LIBRARY
Bethesda, MD 20014   Phyllis R. Blum, Libn.

U.S. UNIFORMED SERVICES UNIVERSITY OF THE HEALTH SCIENCES -
    LEARNING RESOURCE CENTER
4301 Jones Bridge Rd.   Phone: (301) 295-3356
Bethesda, MD 20814   Chester J. Pleztke, Assoc.Prof. & Dir.

VEGETARIAN INFORMATION SERVICE, INC. - INFORMATION CENTER
Box 5888   Phone: (301) 530-1737
Bethesda MD 20814   Dr. Alex Hershaft, Libn.

EASTERN SHORE HOSPITAL CENTER - PROFESSIONAL LIBRARY
R.D. 1, Box 800   Phone: (301) 228-0800
Cambridge, MD 21613   Estella C. Clendaniel, Supv., Lib. & Files

TRANSPORTATION INSTITUTE - LIBRARY
5201 Auth Way   Phone: (301) 423-3335
Camp Springs, MD 20746   Chung-Tai Shen, Chf.Libn.

UNIVERSITY OF MARYLAND - SCHOOL OF MEDICINE - DEPT. OF
    PSYCHIATRY - HELEN C. TINGLEY MEMORIAL LIBRARY
Maryland Psychiatric Research Ctr.
Box 3235   Phone: (301) 747-1071
Catonsville, MD 21228   Edward D. French, Libn.

QUEEN ANNE'S COUNTY LAW LIBRARY
Court House   Phone: (301) 758-0216
Centreville, MD 21617   Mary F. Engle, Libn.

PRINCE GEORGE'S COUNTY HEALTH DEPARTMENT - PUBLIC HEALTH
    RESOURCE CENTER
Cheverly, MD 20778   Peggy H. Roeder, Libn.

PRINCE GEORGE'S GENERAL HOSPITAL & MEDICAL CENTER - SAUL
    SCHWARTZBACH MEMORIAL LIBRARY
                                                 Phone: (301) 341-2440
Cheverly, MD 20785   Eleanor Kleman, Med.Libn.

AUDUBON NATURALIST SOCIETY OF THE CENTRAL ATLANTIC STATES,
    INC. - LIBRARY
8940 Jones Mill Rd.   Phone: (301) 652-9188
Chevy Chase, MD 20815   Kathryn K. Rushing, Ed.

FAUCETT (Jack) ASSOCIATES - LIBRARY
5454 Wisconsin Ave., Suite 1155   Phone: (301) 657-8223
Chevy Chase, MD 20815   Ruth Geldon, Libn.

NATIONAL 4-H COUNCIL - COMMUNICATIONS DIVISION
7100 Connecticut Ave.
Chevy Chase, MD 20815   Mary Bedford, Rsrcs./Reporting Coord.

OHR KODESH CONGREGATION - SISTERHOOD LIBRARY
8402 Freyman Dr.   Phone: (301) 589-3880
Chevy Chase, MD 20015   Ethel E. Clemens, Libn.

RACHEL CARSON COUNCIL, INC. - LIBRARY
8940 Jones Mill Rd.   Phone: (301) 652-1877
Chevy Chase, MD 20815   Shirley A. Briggs, Exec.Dir.

UNIVERSITY RESEARCH CORPORATION - LIBRARY
5530 Wisconsin Ave.   Phone: (301) 654-8338
Chevy Chase, MD 20815   Patricia Place, Libn.

COMMUNICATIONS SATELLITE CORPORATION - COMSAT LABORATORIES
    TECHNICAL INFORMATION CENTER
22300 Comsat Dr.   Phone: (301) 428-4512
Clarksburg, MD 20871   Merilee Worsey, Libn., Tech.Info.Ctr.

MILBOURNE & TULL RESEARCH CENTER - LIBRARY
10605 Lakespring Way   Phone: (301) 628-2490
Cockeysville, MD 21030   Willis Clayton Tull, Jr., Libn.

UNITARIAN AND UNIVERSALIST GENEALOGICAL SOCIETY - LIBRARY
10605 Lakespring Way   Phone: (301) 628-2490
Cockeysville, MD 21030   Willis Clayton Tull, Jr., Libn.

AMERICAN CORRECTIONAL ASSOCIATION - LIBRARY
4321 Hartwick Rd., Suite L-208   Phone: (301) 699-7600
College Park, MD 20740   Diana Travisono, Res.

ASIAN STUDIES NEWSLETTER ARCHIVES
c/o East Asia Collection
McKeldin Library
University of Maryland   Phone: (301) 454-2819
College Park, MD 20742   Frank Joseph Shulman, Dir.

ASPHALT INSTITUTE - RESEARCH LIBRARY
Asphalt Institute Bldg.   Phone: (301) 277-4258
College Park, MD 20740   Helen E. Van Doren, Off.Serv.Coord.

UNIVERSITY OF MARYLAND, COLLEGE PARK - COLLEGE OF LIBRARY &
   INFORMATION SERVICES - LIBRARY
                                        Phone: (301) 454-6003
College Park, MD 20742   William G. Wilson, Libn.

UNIVERSITY OF MARYLAND, COLLEGE PARK - COMPUTER SCIENCE
   CENTER - PROGRAM LIBRARY
                                        Phone: (301) 454-4261
College Park, MD 20742   Barbara Rush, Program Libn.

UNIVERSITY OF MARYLAND, COLLEGE PARK - LIBRARIES - ARCHITECTURE
   LIBRARY
                                        Phone: (301) 454-4316
College Park, MD 20742   Berna E. Neal, Libn.

UNIVERSITY OF MARYLAND, COLLEGE PARK - LIBRARIES - ART LIBRARY
                                        Phone: (301) 454-2065
College Park, MD 20742   Courtney A. Shaw, Hd.

UNIVERSITY OF MARYLAND, COLLEGE PARK - LIBRARIES - CHARLES E.
   WHITE MEMORIAL LIBRARY
                                        Phone: (301) 454-2609
College Park, MD 20742   Elizabeth W. McElroy, Libn.

UNIVERSITY OF MARYLAND, COLLEGE PARK - LIBRARIES - EAST ASIA
   COLLECTION
                                        Phone: (301) 454-5459
College Park, MD 20742   Frank Joseph Shulman, Cur.

UNIVERSITY OF MARYLAND, COLLEGE PARK - LIBRARIES - ENGINEERING
   & PHYSICAL SCIENCES LIBRARY
                                        Phone: (301) 454-3037
College Park, MD 20742   Herbert N. Foerstel, Hd.Libn.

UNIVERSITY OF MARYLAND, COLLEGE PARK - LIBRARIES - HISTORICAL
   MANUSCRIPTS AND ARCHIVES DEPARTMENT
                                        Phone: (301) 454-2318
College Park, MD 20742   Lauren R. Brown, Cur.

UNIVERSITY OF MARYLAND, COLLEGE PARK - LIBRARIES - KATHERINE
   ANNE PORTER ROOM
                                        Phone: (301) 454-4020
College Park, MD 20742   Donald Farren, Assoc.Dir., Spec.Coll.

UNIVERSITY OF MARYLAND, COLLEGE PARK - LIBRARIES - MARYLANDIA
   DEPARTMENT
McKeldin Library   Phone: (301) 454-3035
College Park, MD 20742   Peter H. Curtis, Cur.

UNIVERSITY OF MARYLAND, COLLEGE PARK - LIBRARIES - MUSIC LIBRARY
                                        Phone: (301) 454-3036
College Park, MD 20742   Neil Ratliff, Fine Arts Libn.

UNIVERSITY OF MARYLAND, COLLEGE PARK - LIBRARIES - MUSIC LIBRARY
   - INTERNATIONAL PIANO ARCHIVES AT MARYLAND
Hornbake Library
College Park, MD 20742   Neil Ratliff, Fine Arts Lib.

UNIVERSITY OF MARYLAND, COLLEGE PARK - LIBRARIES NONPRINT
   MEDIA SERVICES
Hornbake Library   Phone: (301) 454-4723
College Park, MD 20742   Allan C. Rough, Hd., Nonprint Media Serv.

UNIVERSITY OF MARYLAND, COLLEGE PARK - LIBRARIES - RARE BOOKS
   AND LITERARY MANUSCRIPTS DEPARTMENT
                                        Phone: (301) 454-3035
College Park, MD 20742

UNIVERSITY OF MARYLAND, COLLEGE PARK - LIBRARIES - WOMEN'S
   STUDIES PAMPHLET COLLECTION
Reference Department
McKeldin Library   Phone: (301) 454-5704
College Park, MD 20742   Susan Cardinale, Coord.

UNIVERSITY OF MARYLAND, COLLEGE PARK - M. LUCIA JAMES
   CURRICULUM LABORATORY
College of Education   Phone: (301) 454-5466
College Park, MD 20742   Dr. Charles Brand, Dir.

UNIVERSITY OF MARYLAND, COLLEGE PARK - MARYLAND CENTER FOR
   PRODUCTIVITY AND QUALITY OF WORKING LIFE - LIB.
College of Business and Management   Phone: (301) 454-6688
College Park, MD 20742   Jan R. Lawrence, Commun.Mgr.

UNIVERSITY OF MARYLAND, COLLEGE PARK - NATIONAL CLEARINGHOUSE
   FOR COMMUTER PROGRAMS
1195 Adele H. Stamp Union   Phone: (301) 454-5274
College Park, MD 20742   Dr. Barbara Jacoby, Dir.

UNIVERSITY OF MARYLAND, COLLEGE PARK - U.S. INFORMATION CENTER
   FOR THE UNIVERSAL DECIMAL CLASSIFICATION
College of Library & Info.Serv.   Phone: (301) 454-3785
College Park, MD 20742   Hans H. Wellisch, Dir.

ALLIED CORPORATION - BENDIX AEROSPACE TECHNOLOGY CENTER
   LIBRARY
9140 Old Annapolis Rd., Rte. 108   Phone: (301) 964-4189
Columbia, MD 21045   T.A. Rupprecht, Supv., Lib.Serv.

GRACE (W.R.) AND COMPANY - RESEARCH DIVISION LIBRARY
7379 Route 32   Phone: (301) 531-4269
Columbia, MD 21044   Jeanette S. Hamilton, Supv., Info.Ctr.

HITTMAN ASSOCIATES, INC. - TECHNICAL INFORMATION DEPARTMENT -
   LIBRARY *
9190 Red Branch Rd.
Columbia, MD 21045

HOWARD COUNTY GENERAL HOSPITAL - HEALTH SCIENCES LIBRARY
5755 Cedar Lane   Phone: (301) 730-5000
Columbia, MD 21044   Marian G. Czajkowski, Dir. of Lib.Serv.

NATIONAL INSTITUTE FOR URBAN WILDLIFE - LIBRARY
10921 Trotting Ridge Way   Phone: (301) 596-3311
Columbia, MD 21044   Louise E. Dove, Wildlife Biologist

CROWNSVILLE HOSPITAL CENTER - PROFESSIONAL LIBRARY
                                        Phone: (301) 987-6200
Crownsville, MD 21032   Joyce Munsey, Supv. of Lib. & Files

ALLEGANY COUNTY CIRCUIT COURT - LIBRARY †
Court House, Washington St.   Phone: (301) 722-5633
Cumberland, MD 21502   Wanda Keller, Libn.

MEMORIAL HOSPITAL - MEDICAL AND NURSING LIBRARY
Memorial Ave.   Phone: (301) 777-4027
Cumberland, MD 21502   Mary E. Courtney, Libn.

SACRED HEART HOSPITAL - HEALTH SCIENCE LIBRARY *
900 Seton Dr.   Phone: (301) 759-5229
Cumberland, MD 21502   Sr. Martha, Libn.

MEMORIAL HOSPITAL - HEALTH SCIENCES LIBRARY
S. Washington St.   Phone: (301) 822-1000
Easton, MD 21601   Maureen Molter, Libn.

TALBOT COUNTY FREE LIBRARY - MARYLAND ROOM
100 W. Dover St.   Phone: (301) 822-1676
Easton, MD 21601   Mrs. Kenneth Harvey, Hd.

SMITHSONIAN INSTITUTION LIBRARIES - SMITHSONIAN
ENVIRONMENTAL RESEARCH CENTER LIBRARY-EDGEWATER
R.R. 4, Box 622   Phone: (202) 261-4190
Edgewater, MD 21037   Angela N. Haggins, Chf.

GORE (W.L.) & ASSOCIATES, INC. - TECHNICAL INFORMATION CENTER
2401 Singerly Rd.
Box 1220   Phone: (301) 368-5303
Elkton, MD 21921   Delcina Esser, Mgr., Tech.Info.Ctr.

NATIONAL EMERGENCY TRAINING CENTER - LIBRARY *
16825 S. Seton Ave.   Phone: (301) 447-6771
Emmitsburg, MD 21727   Adele M. Chiesa, Chf., Lrng.Rsrcs.Ctr.

U.S. ARMY - FORT MEADE MUSEUM - LIBRARY
                                              Phone: (301) 677-6966
Ft. George G. Meade, MD 20755   David C. Cole, Cur.

U.S. ARMY - LANGUAGE TRAINING FACILITY - LIBRARY
Bldg. 2509
USA Education Ctr.   Phone: (301) 677-7255
Ft. George G. Meade, MD 20755   Dorothy R. Kimball, Chf.

U.S. VETERANS ADMINISTRATION (MD-Fort Howard) - HOSPITAL LIBRARY
                                              Phone: (301) 477-1800
Fort Howard, MD 21052   Jacqueline Bird, Chf.Libn.

EAI CORPORATION - LIBRARY
198 Thomas Johnson Dr., Suite 16   Phone: (301) 662-8282
Frederick, MD 21701   Monica Borland, Libn.

FREDERICK COUNTY LAW LIBRARY
Court House   Phone: (301) 694-2019
Frederick, MD 21701   Janet D. Rippeon, Law Libn.

FREDERICK MEMORIAL HOSPITAL - WALTER F. PRIOR MEDICAL LIBRARY
Park Place & W. 7th St.   Phone: (301) 694-3459
Frederick, MD 21701   Linda A. Collenberg Bisaccia, Med.Libn.

U.S. ARMY MEDICAL BIOENGINEERING RESEARCH & DEVELOPMENT
LABORATORY - TECHNICAL REFERENCE LIBRARY
Fort Detrick, Bldg. 568   Phone: (301) 663-2502
Frederick, MD 21701   Edna M. Snyder, Libn.

U.S. ARMY MEDICAL RESEARCH INSTITUTE OF INFECTIOUS DISEASES -
MEDICAL LIBRARY
Fort Detrick   Phone: (301) 663-2720
Frederick, MD 21701   Ruth S. Janssen, Libn.

U.S. NATL. INSTITUTES OF HEALTH - NATIONAL CANCER INSTITUTE -
FREDERICK CANCER RES. FACILITY - SCIENTIFIC LIB.
Box B - Bldg. 426   Phone: (301) 663-7261
Frederick, MD 21701   Michele M. Sansbury, Mgr.

FROSTBURG STATE COLLEGE - LIBRARY
                                              Phone: (301) 689-4395
Frostburg, MD 21532

BECHTEL POWER CORPORATION - LIBRARY
15740 Shady Grove Rd.   Phone: (301) 258-3000
Gaithersburg, MD 20877   Carol A. Bell, Hd.Libn.

INTERNATIONAL ASSOCIATION OF CHIEFS OF POLICE - CENTER FOR LAW
ENFORCEMENT RESEARCH
11 Firstfield Rd.
Gaithersburg, MD 20760

NUS CORPORATION - LIBRARY
910 Clopper Rd.   Phone: (301) 258-6000
Gaithersburg, MD 20878   Jo Ann Merchant, Hd.Libn.

U.S. NATL. BUREAU OF STANDARDS - PHOTON AND CHARGED PARTICLE
DATA CENTER
Rm. 311, Radiation Physics Bldg., NBS   Phone: (301) 921-2685
Gaithersburg, MD 20899   Martin J. Berger, Mgr.

FAIRCHILD INDUSTRIES - TECHNICAL INFORMATION SERVICES LIBRARY
†
Sherman Fairchild Technology Ctr.
20301 Century Blvd.   Phone: (301) 428-6415
Germantown, MD 20874   Hazel M. More, Tech.Libn.

OAO CORPORATION - INFORMATION CENTER
7500 Greenway Ctr.   Phone: (301) 345-0750
Greenbelt, MD 20770   Joseph Langdon, Corp.Libn.

U.S. NASA - GODDARD SPACE FLIGHT CENTER - LIBRARY †
                                              Phone: (301) 344-6244
Greenbelt, MD 20771   Adelaide A. DelFrate, Hd., Lib.Br.

WORLD DATA CENTER A - ROCKETS & SATELLITES - NATIONAL SPACE
SCIENCE DATA CENTER (NSSDC)
Code 630.2, Goddard Space Flight Ctr.   Phone: (301) 344-6695
Greenbelt, MD 20771   Dr. James I. Vette, Dir.

BROOK LANE PSYCHIATRIC CENTER - MEDICAL LIBRARY †
Box 1945   Phone: (301) 733-0330
Hagerstown, MD 21740

MACK TRUCKS, INC. - TECHNICAL INFORMATION CENTER - ENGINEERING
DIVISION LIBRARY
1999 Pennsylvania Ave.   Phone: (301) 733-8308
Hagerstown, MD 21740   E.E. Stout, Engr.Adm.Coord.

REVIEW & HERALD PUBLISHING ASSOCIATION - LIBRARY
55 W. Oak Ridge Dr.   Phone: (301) 791-7000
Hagerstown, MD 21740   Betty F. Ullrich, Libn.

WASHINGTON COUNTY HOSPITAL - WROTH MEMORIAL LIBRARY
King & Antietam Sts.   Phone: (301) 824-8801
Hagerstown, MD 21740   Myra Binau, Coord., Lib.Serv.

WASHINGTON COUNTY LAW LIBRARY
Court House   Phone: (301) 791-3115
Hagerstown, MD 21740   Elizabeth F. Wilkinson, Libn.

WASHINGTON COUNTY MUSEUM OF FINE ARTS - LIBRARY
City Park, Box 423   Phone: (301) 739-5727
Hagerstown, MD 21740   Mabert E. Fox, Exec.Sec.

WESTERN MARYLAND PUBLIC LIBRARIES - REGIONAL LIBRARY
100 S. Potomac St.   Phone: (301) 739-3250
Hagerstown, MD 21740   Mary S. Mallery, Regional Libn.

MC CORMICK & CO. - R & D INFORMATION CENTER †
202 Wight Ave.   Phone: (301) 667-7485
Hunt Valley, MD 21031   Merle I. Eiss, Mgr.

NATIONAL CENTER FOR HEALTH STATISTICS - CLEARINGHOUSE ON
HEALTH INDEXES
3700 East West Hwy., Rm. 2-27   Phone: (301) 436-7035
Hyattsville, MD 20782   Pennifer Erickson, Chf.

U.S. NAVY - NAVAL EXPLOSIVE ORDNANCE DISPOSAL TECHNOLOGY
CENTER - TECHNICAL LIBRARY
                                              Phone: (301) 743-4738
Indian Head, MD 20640   Bonnie D. Davis, Adm.Libn.

U.S. NAVY - NAVAL ORDNANCE STATION - TECHNICAL LIBRARY (5246)
                                              Phone: (301) 743-4742
Indian Head, MD 20640   Charles F. Gallagher, Supv.Libn.

CAPITOL INSTITUTE OF TECHNOLOGY - JOHN G. PUENTE LIBRARY
11301 Springfield Rd.   Phone: (301) 953-0060
Kensington, MD 20895   Patricia H. Wissinger, Libn.

LITTON BIONETICS, INC. - SCIENTIFIC LIBRARY
5516 Nicholson Lane   Phone: (301) 881-5600
Kensington, MD 20895   E.M. Henderson, Libn.

NATIONAL EPILEPSY LIBRARY AND RESOURCE CENTER
4351 Garden City Dr.   Phone: (301) 459-3700
Landover, MD 20785   Sr. Ann Vivia Walton, Dir.

PRINCE GEORGE'S COUNTY PUBLIC SCHOOLS - PROFESSIONAL LIBRARY
8437 Landover Rd.   Phone: (301) 773-9790
Landover, MD 20785   Dr. Edward W. Barth, Supv., Lib. & Media Serv.

WASHINGTON BIBLE COLLEGE / CAPITAL BIBLE SEMINARY - OYER
MEMORIAL LIBRARY
6511 Princess Garden Pkwy.   Phone: (301) 552-1400
Lanham, MD 20706   Carol A. Satta, Dir., Lib.Serv.

JOHNS HOPKINS UNIVERSITY - APPLIED PHYSICS LABORATORY - CHEMICAL PROPULSION INFORMATION AGENCY
Johns Hopkins Rd.   Phone: (301) 953-7100
Laurel, MD 20707   Ronald D. Brown, Group Supv.

JOHNS HOPKINS UNIVERSITY - APPLIED PHYSICS LABORATORY - R.E. GIBSON LIBRARY AND INFORMATION CENTER
Johns Hopkins Rd.   Phone: (301) 953-7100
Laurel, MD 20810   Linda J. Kosmin, Dir.

U.S. FISH & WILDLIFE SERVICE - PATUXENT WILDLIFE RESEARCH CENTER LIBRARY
                                   Phone: (301) 498-0235
Laurel, MD 20708   Lynda Garrett, Libn.

WESTVACO CORPORATION - LAUREL RESEARCH LIBRARY
Johns Hopkins Rd.   Phone: (301) 792-9100
Laurel, MD 20707   Marie Liang, Res.Libn.

GENEALOGICAL PERIODICALS LIBRARY
709 E. Main St.   Phone: (301) 371-6293
Middletown, MD 21769   George Ely Russell, Genealogist

BIKELIBRARY
513 Williamsburg Ln.
Odenton MD 21113   Larry S. Bonura, Dir.

ROSEWOOD CENTER - MIRIAM LODGE PROFESSIONAL LIBRARY
                                   Phone: (301) 363-0300
Owings Mills, MD 21117   June M. Boardman, Supv., Lib./Files

U.S. NATL. MARINE FISHERIES SERVICE - NORTHEAST FISHERIES CENTER - OXFORD LAB. LIBRARY
                                   Phone: (301) 226-5193
Oxford, MD 21654   Susie K. Hines, Libn.

PRINCE GEORGE'S COUNTY MEMORIAL LIBRARY SYSTEM - SOJOURNER TRUTH ROOM
6200 Oxon Hill Rd.   Phone: (301) 839-2400
Oxon Hill, MD 20745   Cherie P. Barnett, Cur.

TWIRLY BIRDS - HELICOPTER ARCHIVE
Box 18029   Phone: (301) 567-4407
Oxon Hill, MD 20745   John M. Slattery, Hist.

U.S. NAVY - NAVAL AIR TEST CENTER - NAVAL AIR STATION - PATUXTENT RIVER CENTRAL LIBRARY
Bldg. 407   Phone: (301) 863-3686
Patuxent River, MD 20670   Suzanne M. Ryder, Dir.

U.S. NAVY - NAVAL TEST PILOT SCHOOL - RESEARCH LIBRARY
Naval Air Test Ctr.   Phone: (301) 863-4411
Patuxent River, MD 20670   Robert B. Richards, Hd. of Academics

U.S. VETERANS ADMINISTRATION (MD-Perry Point) - HOSPITAL MEDICAL LIBRARY
                                   Phone: (301) 642-2411
Perry Point, MD 21902   Mr. Lynn F. Delozier, Chf.Libn.

LUNDEBERG MARYLAND SEAMANSHIP SCHOOL - PAUL HALL LIBRARY AND MARITIME MUSEUM
                                   Phone: (301) 994-0010
Piney Point, MD 20674   Janice McAteer Smolek, Lib.Dir.

BALTIMORE COUNTY GENERAL HOSPITAL - HEALTH SCIENCES LIBRARY
5401 Old Court Rd.   Phone: (301) 521-2200
Randallstown, MD 21133   Bettie S. Holmes, Libn.

U.S. NATL. OCEANIC & ATMOSPHERIC ADMINISTRATION - NATL. OCEAN SERVICE - MAP LIBRARY
6501 Lafayette Ave.   Phone: (301) 436-6978
Riverdale, MD 20737   Gordon Allen, Tech.Info.Spec.

U.S. NATL. OCEANIC & ATMOSPHERIC ADM. - NATL. OCEAN SERVICE - PHYSICAL SCIENCE SERVICES SECT. - MAP LIB.
                                   Phone: (301) 436-5766
Riverdale, MD 20737   Henry L. Carter, Act.Chf.

AMERICAN OCCUPATIONAL THERAPY ASSOCIATION - REFERENCE LIBRARY
1383 Piccard Dr., Suite 201   Phone: (301) 948-9626
Rockville, MD 20850   Sheila A. Richard, Libn.

AMERICAN TYPE CULTURE COLLECTION - DONOVICK LIBRARY
12301 Parklawn Dr.   Phone: (301) 881-2600
Rockville, MD 20852   Mary Jane Gantt, Info.Sci.

ASPEN SYSTEMS CORPORATION - LAW LIBRARY & INFORMATION CENTER †
1600 Research Blvd.   Phone: (301) 251-5000
Rockville, MD 20850   Judy Meadows, Info.Mgr.

ASPEN SYSTEMS CORPORATION - PROJECT SHARE *
Box 2309   Phone: (301) 251-5170
Rockville, MD 20852   Eileen Wolff, Project Off.

BIOSPHERICS INC. - LIBRARY
4928 Wyaconda Rd.   Phone: (301) 770-7700
Rockville, MD 20852   Marlene S. Bobka, Chf., Lib.Serv.

EG&G, INC. - WASHINGTON ANALYTICAL SERVICES CENTER - INFORMATION CENTER
2150 Fields Rd.   Phone: (301) 840-3243
Rockville, MD 20850   Vanessa R.L. Schroader, Mgr.

FOI SERVICES, INC. - LIBRARY *
12315 Wilkins Ave.   Phone: (301) 881-0410
Rockville, MD 20852   John E. Carey, Gen.Mgr.

GEOMET TECHNOLOGIES INC. - INFORMATION CENTER †
1801 Research Blvd., 6th Fl.   Phone: (301) 424-9133
Rockville, MD 20850

GILLETTE MEDICAL EVALUATION LABORATORIES - INFORMATION CENTER
1413 Research Blvd.   Phone: (301) 424-2000
Rockville, MD 20850   Patrick J. Dexter, Info.Serv.Supv.

INFORMATICS GENERAL CORPORATION - FISH AND WILDLIFE REFERENCE
1887 E. Jefferson St., Suite 470 S
Rockville, MD 20852   Susan MacMullin, Proj.Mgr.

INFORMATICS GENERAL CORPORATION - LIBRARY SERVICES DIVISION
6011 Executive Blvd.   Phone: (301) 770-3000
Rockville, MD 20852   Lucinda E. Leonard, V.P.

INTERNATIONAL HIBERNATION SOCIETY
300 Dean Dr.
Rockville, MD 20851   Dr. Richard C. Simmonds, Exec.Sec.

JEWISH COMMUNITY CENTER OF GREATER WASHINGTON - KASS JUDAIC LIBRARY
6125 Montrose Rd.   Phone: (301) 881-0100
Rockville, MD 20852   T.K. Feldman, Dir., Literary Arts Dept.

KING RESEARCH, INC. - LIBRARY
6000 Executive Blvd.   Phone: (301) 881-6766
Rockville, MD 20852   Mary K. Yates, Libn.

MONTGOMERY COUNTY CIRCUIT COURT - LAW LIBRARY
Judicial Center
50 Courthouse Sq., Rm. 326   Phone: (301) 251-7165
Rockville, MD 20850   Karen D.M. Smith, Law Libn.

MONTGOMERY COUNTY HISTORICAL SOCIETY - LIBRARY
103 W. Montgomery Ave.   Phone: (301) 762-1492
Rockville, MD 20850   Jane C. Sween, Libn.

MONTGOMERY COUNTY PUBLIC SCHOOLS - PROFESSIONAL LIBRARY
850 N. Hungerford Dr.   Phone: (301) 279-3227
Rockville, MD 20850   Karen Dowling, Curric.Libn.

NATIONAL CLEARINGHOUSE FOR ALCOHOL INFORMATION - LIBRARY †
Box 2345   Phone: (301) 468-2600
Rockville, MD 20852   Sean O'Rourke, Dir.

NATIONAL CLEARINGHOUSE FOR FAMILY PLANNING INFORMATION *
Box 2225   Phone: (301) 881-9400
Rockville, MD 20852   Anita P. Cowan, Dir.

NATIONAL INSTITUTE ON DRUG ABUSE - RESOURCE CENTER
5600 Fishers Lane, Rm. 10A54   Phone: (301) 443-6614
Rockville, MD 20857   Ilse Vada, Libn.

NDC/FEDERAL SYSTEMS, INC. - LIBRARY
1300 Piccard Dr.   Phone: (301) 258-9200
Rockville, MD 20850   Renee R. Thaler, Libn.

OFFICE ON SMOKING AND HEALTH - TECHNICAL INFORMATION CENTER
Park Bldg., Rm. 1-16
5600 Fishers Lane   Phone: (301) 443-1690
Rockville, MD 20857   Donald R. Shopland, Tech.Info.Off.

SMITHSONIAN INSTITUTION LIBRARIES - SMITHSONIAN
   ENVIRONMENTAL RESEARCH CENTER LIBRARY-ROCKVILLE
12441 Parklawn Dr.   Phone: (301) 443-2307
Rockville, MD 20852   Angela Haggins, Chf.

TRACOR JITCO, INC. - RESEARCH RESOURCES INFORMATION CENTER
1776 E. Jefferson St.   Phone: (301) 881-4150
Rockville, MD 20852   Edward Post, Dir.

U.S. BUREAU OF ALCOHOL, TOBACCO AND FIREARMS - NATIONAL
   LABORATORY LIBRARY
1401 Research Blvd.   Phone: (301) 443-1195
Rockville, MD 20850

U.S. DEPT. OF JUSTICE - NATIONAL INSTITUTE OF JUSTICE - NATL.
   CRIMINAL JUSTICE REF. SERVICE
Box 6000   Phone: (301) 251-5500
Rockville, MD 20850   Harvey C. Byrd, III, Prog.Dir.

U.S. FOOD & DRUG ADMINISTRATION - BUREAU OF RADIOLOGICAL
   HEALTH - LIBRARY †
12720 Twinbrook Pkwy.   Phone: (301) 443-1038
Rockville, MD 20857   Mary G. Berkey, Libn.

U.S. FOOD & DRUG ADMINISTRATION - NATIONAL CENTER FOR DRUGS
   AND BIOLOGIES - MEDICAL LIBRARY/HFN-630
5600 Fishers Lane, Rm. 11B-40   Phone: (301) 443-3180
Rockville, MD 20857   Elizabeth C. Kelly, Dir., Med.Lib.

U.S. FOOD & DRUG ADMINISTRATION - NATL. CLEARINGHOUSE FOR
   POISON CONTROL CENTERS
5600 Fishers Lane
HDF 240, Rm. 1345   Phone: (301) 443-6260
Rockville, MD 20857   Mark I. Fow, Act.Dir.

U.S. NATL. OCEANIC & ATMOSPHERIC ADMINISTRATION - LIBRARY AND
   INFORMATION SERVICES DIVISION - MAIN LIBRARY
6009 Executive Blvd.   Phone: (301) 443-8330
Rockville, MD 20852   Elizabeth J. Yeates, Chf., LISD

U.S. PUBLIC HEALTH SERVICE - NATL. INSTITUTE OF MENTAL HEALTH -
   COMMUNICATION CENTER - LIBRARY †
Parklawn Bldg., Rm. 15C-05
5600 Fishers Lane   Phone: (301) 443-4506
Rockville, MD 20857   Angela Sirrocco, Chf.

U.S. PUBLIC HEALTH SERVICE - NATL. INSTITUTE OF MENTAL HEALTH -
   SCIENCE COMMUNICATION BRANCH - MENTAL HEALTH LIB.
5600 Fishers Lane, Rm. 15-99   Phone: (301) 443-4533
Rockville, MD 20857   Anne H. Rosenfeld, Chf.

U.S. PUBLIC HEALTH SERVICE - PARKLAWN HEALTH LIBRARY
5600 Fishers Ln., Rm. 13-12   Phone: (301) 443-2665
Rockville, MD 20857   Salvador B. Waller, Lib.Dir.

ST. MARY'S CITY COMMISSION - RESEARCH LIBRARY
Box 38   Phone: (301) 994-1614
St. Mary's City, MD 20686

CHESAPEAKE BAY MARITIME MUSEUM - HOWARD I. CHAPELLE MEMORIAL
   LIBRARY
Box 636   Phone: (301) 745-2916
St. Michaels, MD 21663   Mary Ruth Robertson, Libn.

SALISBURY STATE COLLEGE - BLACKWELL LIBRARY - SPECIAL
   COLLECTIONS
                                                   Phone: (301) 546-3261
Salisbury, MD 21801   James R. Thrash, Dir.

U.S. NATL. PARK SERVICE - ANTIETAM NATL. BATTLEFIELD - VISITOR
   CENTER LIBRARY
Box 158   Phone: (301) 432-5124
Sharpsburg, MD 21782   Betty J. Otto, Libn./Cur.

AMERICANS UNITED FOR SEPARATION OF CHURCH AND STATE -
   ARCHIVES
8120 Fenton St.   Phone: (301) 589-3707
Silver Spring, MD 20910   Morgan Dukes, Dir., Gen.Serv.

ASSOCIATION FOR INFORMATION AND IMAGE MANAGEMENT - RESOURCE
   CENTER
1100 Wayne Ave.   Phone: (301) 587-8202
Silver Spring, MD 20910   Nila Zynjuk, Info.Coord.

COMPUTER SCIENCES CORPORATION - SYSTEMS SCIENCES DIVISION -
   TECHNICAL INFORMATION CENTER
8728 Colesville Rd.   Phone: (301) 589-1545
Silver Spring, MD 20910   Tenna Morse, Mgr.

HAMMER, SILER, GEORGE ASSOCIATES - LIBRARY
1111 Bonifant St.   Phone: (301) 565-5200
Silver Spring, MD 20910   Shari Turner, Libn.

HOLY CROSS HOSPITAL OF SILVER SPRING - MEDICAL LIBRARY
1500 Forest Glen Road   Phone: (301) 565-1211
Silver Spring, MD 20910   Bernetta Payne, Libn.

INDUSTRIAL UNION OF MARINE AND SHIPBUILDING WORKERS OF
   AMERICA - RESEARCH LIBRARY
8121 Georgia Ave., Suite 700   Phone: (301) 589-8820
Silver Spring, MD 20910

INTERNATIONAL FABRICARE INSTITUTE - RESEARCH CENTER LIBRARY
12251 Tech Rd.   Phone: (301) 622-1900
Silver Spring, MD 20904   C. Busler, Dir., Res.

MARYLAND COLLEGE OF ART & DESIGN - LIBRARY
10500 Georgia Ave.   Phone: (301) 649-4454
Silver Spring, MD 20902   Laura C. Pratt, Libn.

MARYLAND NATIONAL CAPITAL PARK AND PLANNING COMMISSION -
   MONTGOMERY COUNTY PLANNING DEPARTMENT - LIBRARY
8787 Georgia Ave.   Phone: (301) 565-7507
Silver Spring, MD 20910-3760   Janice C. Holt, Hd.Libn.

MASONIC SERVICE ASSOCIATION OF THE UNITED STATES - LIBRARY
8120 Fenton St., Suite 203   Phone: (301) 588-4010
Silver Spring, MD 20910-4785   Stewart M.L. Pollard, Exec.Sec.

NATIONAL ASSOCIATION OF SOCIAL WORKERS - RESOURCE CENTER
7981 Eastern Ave.   Phone: (301) 565-0333
Silver Spring, MD 20910   Charlotte Reppy, Rsrc.Ctr.Coord.

NATIONAL CAPITAL HISTORICAL MUSEUM OF TRANSPORTATION -
   LIBRARY
Colesville Branch, Box 4007   Phone: (301) 384-9797
Silver Spring, MD 20904   Edmond Henderer, Libn.

NATIONAL FOUNDATION FOR CONSUMER CREDIT - LIBRARY
8701 Georgia Ave., Suite 601   Phone: (301) 589-5600
Silver Spring, MD 20910

NORTH AMERICAN TIDDLYWINKS ASSOCIATION - ARCHIVES
2701 Woodedge Rd.   Phone: (301) 933-3840
Silver Spring, MD 20906   Richard W. Tucker, Archv.

PRESBYTERIAN CHURCH OF THE ATONEMENT - LIBRARY
10613 Georgia Ave.   Phone: (301) 649-4131
Silver Spring, MD 20902   Lois Walker, Libn.

U.S. FOOD & DRUG ADMINISTRATION - NATIONAL CENTER FOR DEVICES &
   RADIOLOGICAL HEALTH - LIBRARY
8757 Georgia Ave., HFK-45   Phone: (301) 427-7755
Silver Spring, MD 20910   Harriet Albersheim, Libn.

U.S. NAVY - NAVAL SURFACE WEAPONS CENTER - WHITE OAK LIBRARY †
White Oak
Silver Spring, MD 20910
Phone: (202) 394-1922
Mary Jane Brewster, Hd.

VITRO CORPORATION - LIBRARY
14000 Georgia Ave.
Silver Spring, MD 20910
Phone: (301) 231-2553
James R. Griffin, Dept.Hd.

WASHINGTON THEOLOGICAL UNION - LIBRARY
9001 New Hampshire Ave.
Silver Spring, MD 20903-3699
Phone: (301) 439-0551
Carol R. Lange, Libn.

CALVERT MARINE MUSEUM - LIBRARY
Box 97
Solomons, MD 20688
Phone: (301) 326-3719
Ralph Eshelman, Dir.

UNIVERSITY OF MARYLAND, SOLOMONS - CTR. FOR ENVIRONMENT &
ENVIRONMENTAL STUD. - CHESAPEAKE BIOL. LAB. - LIB.
Box 38
Solomons, MD 20688
Phone: (301) 326-4281
Kathleen Heil-Zampier, Libn.

ECOLOGICAL ANALYSTS, INC. - LIBRARY
15 Loveton Circle
Sparks, MD 21152
Phone: (301) 771-4950
Vickilyn M. Gigante, Mgr., Lib. & Info.Serv.

U.S. NATL. ARCHIVES & RECORDS SERVICE - WASHINGTON NATL.
RECORDS CENTER
4205 Suitland
Suitland, MD 20409
Phone: (301) 763-7000
Ferris E. Stovel, Dir.

SPRINGFIELD HOSPITAL CENTER - MEDICAL LIBRARY
Sykesville, MD 21784
Phone: (301) 795-2100
Elizabeth D. Mercer, Libn.

COLUMBIA UNION COLLEGE - THEOFIELD G. WEIS LIBRARY
7600 Flower Ave.
Takoma Park, MD 20912
Phone: (301) 891-4217
Margaret J. von Hake, Libn.

WASHINGTON ADVENTIST HOSPITAL - MEDICAL LIBRARY
7600 Carroll Ave.
Takoma Park, MD 20012
Phone: (301) 891-5261
Loraine Sweetland, Libn./Supv.

TELEDYNE ENERGY SYSTEMS - LIBRARY
110 W. Timonium Rd.
Timonium, MD 21093
Phone: (301) 252-8220
Cathy Layne, Libn.

BALTIMORE COUNTY CIRCUIT COURT - LAW LIBRARY
401 Bosley Ave.
Towson, MD 21204
Phone: (301) 494-2621
Mary Seeley Barranco, Hd.Libn.

MARYLAND CRIMINAL JUSTICE COORDINATING COUNCIL - LIBRARY *
One Investment Pl., Suite 700
Towson, MD 21204
Patricia M. Donaho, Lib.Supv.

ST. JOSEPH HOSPITAL - SISTER MARY ALVINA NURSING LIBRARY
7620 York Rd.
Towson, MD 21204
Phone: (301) 337-1641
Mary Weihs, Libn.

ST. JOSEPH HOSPITAL - OTTO C. BRANTIGAN MEDICAL LIBRARY
7620 York Rd.
Towson, MD 21204
Phone: (301) 337-1210
Sr. Francis Marie, Libn.

TOWSON STATE UNIVERSITY - GERHARDT LIBRARY OF MUSICAL
INFORMATION
Towson State University
Towson, MD 21204
Phone: (301) 321-2839
Edwin L. Gerhardt, Cur.

TOWSON STATE UNIVERSITY - GERHARDT MARIMBA & XYLOPHONE
COLLECTION
Towson State University
Towson, MD 21204
Phone: (301) 321-2839
Edwin L. Gerhardt, Cur.

PRINCE GEORGE'S COUNTY CIRCUIT COURT - LAW LIBRARY
Courthouse
Box 580
Upper Marlboro, MD 20772
Phone: (301) 952-3438
Pamela J. Gregory, Law Libn.

PRINCE GEORGE'S COUNTY MEMORIAL LIBRARY SYSTEM - PUBLIC
DOCUMENTS REFERENCE LIBRARY
County Adm.Bldg., Rm. 2198
Upper Marlboro, MD 20772
Phone: (301) 952-3904
Marjorie M. Miller, Doc.Libn.

ACADEMY OF AMERICAN FRANCISCAN HISTORY - LIBRARY
Box 34440
West Bethesda, MD 20817
Phone: (301) 365-1763
Jesse Joseph Torres, Libn.

CARROLL COUNTY BAR ASSOCIATION - LIBRARY
Court House
Westminster, MD 21157
Phone: (301) 848-4500
Florence Green, Libn.

CARROLL COUNTY FARM MUSEUM - LANDON BURNS MEMORIAL LIBRARY
500 S. Center St.
Westminster, MD 21157
Phone: (301) 848-7775
JoAnn Hunter, Dir. of Musm.

MASSACHUSETTS

NEW ENGLAND DEPOSIT LIBRARY, INC.
135 Western Ave.
Allston, MA 02134
Phone: (617) 782-8441
Edward J. Sweny, Libn.

WHITTIER HOME ASSOCIATION - LIBRARY
86 Friend St.
Amesbury, MA 01913
Phone: (617) 388-1337
Debra Moore, Cur.

AMHERST COLLEGE - SCIENCE LIBRARY
Amherst, MA 01002
Phone: (413) 542-2076
Eleanor T. Brown, Hd.

AMHERST COLLEGE - SPECIAL COLLECTIONS DEPARTMENT AND
ARCHIVES
Amherst, MA 01002
Phone: (413) 542-2299
John Lancaster, Hd., Spec.Coll./Archv.

JONES LIBRARY, INC. - SPECIAL COLLECTIONS
43 Amity St.
Amherst, MA 01002
Phone: (413) 256-0246
Daniel J. Lombardo, Cur. of Spec.Coll.

NATIONAL YIDDISH BOOK CENTER, INC. - LIBRARY
Old East Street School
Box 969
Amherst, MA 01004
Phone: (413) 584-1142
Aaron Lansky, Exec.Dir.

UNIVERSITY OF MASSACHUSETTS, AMHERST - LABOR RELATIONS &
RESEARCH CENTER LIBRARY
Draper Hall
Amherst, MA 01003
Phone: (413) 545-2884
Janice Tausky, Libn.

UNIVERSITY OF MASSACHUSETTS, AMHERST - LIBRARY - DEPARTMENT
OF ARCHIVES
Amherst, MA 01003
Phone: (413) 545-2780
John Kendall, Act.Archv.

UNIVERSITY OF MASSACHUSETTS, AMHERST - LIBRARY - SPECIAL
COLLECTIONS AND RARE BOOKS
Amherst, MA 01003
Phone: (413) 545-0274
John D. Kendall, Hd.

UNIVERSITY OF MASSACHUSETTS, AMHERST - MORRILL BIOLOGICAL &
GEOLOGICAL SCIENCES LIBRARY
214 Morrill Science Ctr.
Amherst, MA 01003
Phone: (413) 545-2674
James L. Craig, Libn.

UNIVERSITY OF MASSACHUSETTS, AMHERST - MUSIC LIBRARY
Fine Arts Center, Rm. 149
Amherst, MA 01003
Phone: (413) 545-2870
Pamela Juengling, Mus.Libn.

UNIVERSITY OF MASSACHUSETTS, AMHERST - PHYSICAL SCIENCES
LIBRARY
Graduate Research Ctr.
Amherst, MA 01003
Phone: (413) 545-1370
Eric Esau, Libn.

ADDISON GALLERY OF AMERICAN ART - LIBRARY
Phillips Academy
Andover, MA 01810
Phone: (617) 475-7515

ALLIED CORPORATION - ALLIED ANALYTICAL SYSTEMS - LIBRARY
1 Burtt Rd.   Phone: (617) 470-1790
Andover, MA 01810   Jacqueline R. Kates, Corp.Libn.

ANDOVER HISTORICAL SOCIETY - CAROLINE M. UNDERHILL RESEARCH
   LIBRARY
97 Main St.   Phone: (617) 475-2236
Andover, MA 01810   Marsha Rooney, Dir./Cur.

DIGITAL EQUIPMENT CORPORATION - ANDOVER LIBRARY
100 Minuteman Rd.   Phone: (617) 689-1609
Andover, MA 01810   Nancy Sullivan, Tech.Libn.

HEWLETT-PACKARD COMPANY - ANDOVER DIVISION LIBRARY
3000 Minuteman Rd.   Phone: (617) 687-1501
Andover, MA 01810   Carol Miller, Libn.

PEABODY (Robert S.) FOUNDATION FOR ARCHEOLOGY - LIBRARY
Phillips Academy   Phone: (617) 475-0248
Andover, MA 01810   Dr. Donald W. McNemar, Act.Dir.

PHILLIPS ACADEMY - OLIVER WENDELL HOLMES LIBRARY - SPECIAL
   COLLECTIONS
                                               Phone: (617) 475-3400
Andover, MA 01810   Lynne C. Robbins, Dir.

ASHLAND HISTORICAL SOCIETY - LIBRARY
Box 321   Phone: (617) 881-3075
Ashland, MA 01721   Cynthia C. Winterhalter, Cur.

STURDY MEMORIAL HOSPITAL - HEALTH SCIENCES LIBRARY
211 Park St.   Phone: (617) 222-5200
Attleboro, MA 02703   Juliet I. Mansfield, Libn.

FIRST CONGREGATIONAL CHURCH OF AUBURN - LIBRARY
128 Central St.   Phone: (617) 832-2845
Auburn, MA 01501   Mrs. Leroy H. LaPlante, Chm.

NASHOBA COMMUNITY HOSPITAL - MEDICAL LIBRARY
200 Groton Rd.   Phone: (617) 772-0200
Ayer, MA 01432   Patricia Payton, Libn.

BABSON COLLEGE - HORN LIBRARY - SPECIAL COLLECTIONS †
                                               Phone: (617) 235-1200
Babson Park, MA 02157   Elizabeth DiBartolomeis, Spec.Coll.Cur.

BARNSTABLE LAW LIBRARY
First District Court House
Main St.   Phone: (617) 362-2511
Barnstable, MA 02630   Martha W. Brockington, Law Libn.

STURGIS LIBRARY †
Rte. 6A   Phone: (617) 362-6636
Barnstable, MA 02630   Susan R. Klein, Hd.Libn.

BAIRD CORPORATION - TECHNICAL LIBRARY †
125 Middlesex Tpke.   Phone: (617) 276-6390
Bedford, MA 01730   Frances G. Greene, Libn.

BEDFORD HISTORICAL SOCIETY - LIBRARY
15 The Great Road
Bedford, MA 01730   Mary S. Hafer, Cur.

GCA CORPORATION - TECHNOLOGY DIVISION - LIBRARY
213 Burlington Rd.   Phone: (617) 275-5444
Bedford, MA 01730   Josephine Silvestro, Libn.

MILLIPORE CORPORATION - INFORMATION CENTER
Ashby Rd.   Phone: (617) 275-9200
Bedford, MA 01730   Leslie R. Jacobs, Info.Spec.

MITRE CORPORATION - BEDFORD OPERATIONS LIBRARY
Burlington Rd.   Phone: (617) 271-7834
Bedford, MA 01730   Betsy F. Cogliano, Supv.

MITRE CORPORATION - TECHNICAL REPORT CENTER
Box 208   Phone: (617) 271-2351
Bedford, MA 01730   Patricia J. McNulty, Supv.

RAYTHEON COMPANY - MISSILE SYSTEMS DIVISION - BEDFORD
   LABORATORIES - TECHNICAL INFORMATION CENTER
Hartwell Rd.   Phone: (617) 274-7100
Bedford, MA 01730   Lorraine Bick-Gregoire, Mgr.

U.S. AIR FORCE - AIR FORCE SYSTEMS COMMAND - AIR FORCE
   GEOPHYSICS LABORATORY - RESEARCH LIBRARY
Hanscom Air Force Base   Phone: (617) 861-4895
Bedford, MA 01731   Ruth K. Seidman, Dir.

U.S. VETERANS ADMINISTRATION (MA-Bedford) - EDITH NOURSE ROGERS
   MEMORIAL VETERANS HOSPITAL - MEDICAL LIBRARY
200 Springs Rd.   Phone: (617) 275-7500
Bedford, MA 01730   Sanford S. Yagendorf, Libn.

VERBEX CORPORATION - LIBRARY
Two Oak Park   Phone: (617) 275-5160
Bedford, MA 01730   Frances Schutzberg, Tech.Libn.

ARMENIAN LIBRARY AND MUSEUM OF AMERICA
380 Concord Ave.
Belmont, MA 02178   Dr. Lucy Der Manuelian, Board Member

BETH EL TEMPLE CENTER - CARL KALES MEMORIAL LIBRARY *
2 Concord Ave.   Phone: (617) 484-6668
Belmont, MA 02178

EARTHWATCH - LIBRARY
10 Juniper Rd.
Box 127   Phone: (617) 489-3030
Belmont, MA 02178   Brian Rosborough, Pres.

HABITAT INSTITUTE - NATURAL HISTORY LIBRARY
10 Juniper Rd.
Box 136   Phone: (617) 489-3850
Belmont, MA 02178   Barbara B. Herzstein, Libn.

INSTITUTE OF ARAB STUDIES, INC. - LIBRARY
556 Trapelo Rd.   Phone: (617) 484-3262
Belmont, MA 02178

INTERNATIONAL SOCIETY FOR PHILOSOPHICAL ENQUIRY - ARCHIVES
307 Pleasant St.   Phone: (617) 489-3170
Belmont, MA 02178   Robert J. Davis, Hist.

MC LEAN HOSPITAL - MAILMAN RESEARCH CENTER LIBRARY
115 Mill St.   Phone: (617) 855-3241
Belmont, MA 02178   Lyn Dietrich, Libn.

MC LEAN HOSPITAL - MENTAL HEALTH SCIENCES LIBRARY
115 Mill St.   Phone: (617) 855-2460
Belmont, MA 02178   Rosanne Labree, Dir.

THE WORLD INSTITUTE FOR ADVANCED PHENOMENOLOGICAL RESEARCH
   AND LEARNING - LIBRARY AND ARCHIVES
348 Payson Rd.   Phone: (617) 489-3696
Belmont, MA 02178   Marie Lynch

BEVERLY HISTORICAL SOCIETY - LIBRARY AND ARCHIVES
Cabot House, 117 Cabot St.   Phone: (617) 922-1186
Beverly, MA 01915

BEVERLY HOSPITAL - LIBRARY
Herrick St.   Phone: (617) 922-3000
Beverly, MA 01915   Margaret A. Firth, Libn.

VARIAN ASSOCIATES - TECHNICAL LIBRARY †
Salem Rd.   Phone: (617) 922-6000
Beverly, MA 01915   Katherine R. MacGregor, Libn.

CABOT CORPORATION - TECHNICAL INFORMATION CENTER
Concord Rd.   Phone: (617) 663-3455
Billerica, MA 01821   Barbara M. Davis, Mgr.

AMERICAN CONGREGATIONAL ASSOCIATION - CONGREGATIONAL
   LIBRARY
14 Beacon St.   Phone: (617) 523-0470
Boston, MA 02108   Rev.Dr. Harold F. Worthley, Libn.

AMERICAN INSTITUTE OF MANAGEMENT - LIBRARY
45 Willard St.   Phone: (617) 536-2503
Boston, MA 02169   D. Ellis, Libn.

AMERICAN METEOROLOGICAL SOCIETY - ABSTRACTS PROJECT - LIBRARY
45 Beacon St.   Phone: (617) 227-2425
Boston, MA 02108   Kenneth C. Spengler, Exec.Dir.

AMERICAN METEOROLOGICAL SOCIETY - BROOKS LIBRARY
45 Beacon St.
Boston, MA 02108

AMERICAN SOCIETY OF LAW & MEDICINE - ELLIOT L. AND ANNETTE Y.
  SAGALL LIBRARY
765 Commonwealth Ave., 16th Fl.   Phone: (617) 262-4990
Boston, MA 02215   Kim Simmons, Lib.Dir.

ANCIENT AND HONORABLE ARTILLERY COMPANY OF MASSACHUSETTS -
  LIBRARY
Faneuil Hall   Phone: (617) 227-1638
Boston, MA 02109   Col. Charles F. Hoar, Exec.Sec.

ANTHROPOLOGY RESOURCE CENTER - CITIZENS INFORMATION CENTER
37 Temple Place, Rm. 521
Boston, MA 02111

APPALACHIAN MOUNTAIN CLUB - LIBRARY †
5 Joy St.   Phone: (617) 523-0636
Boston, MA 02108   C. Francis Belcher, Archv./Cons.

ART INSTITUTE OF BOSTON - LIBRARY
700 Beacon St.   Phone: (617) 262-1223
Boston, MA 02215   Andrea C. DesJardins, Libn.

ARTHUR ANDERSEN & CO. - LIBRARY
100 Federal St.   Phone: (617) 423-1400
Boston, MA 02110   Jean Fisher, Libn.

ASSOCIATED GRANTMAKERS OF MASSACHUSETTS, INC. - RESOURCE
  CENTER FOR PHILANTHROPY
294 Washington St., Suite 501   Phone: (617) 426-2608
Boston, MA 02108   Philip Conley, Libn.

BANK OF NEW ENGLAND - CORPORATION LIBRARY AND INFORMATION
  SERVICE †
1 Washington Mall, 16th Fl.   Phone: (617) 742-4000
Boston, MA 02108   Helen Mazareas, Libn.

BERKLEE COLLEGE OF MUSIC - LIBRARY
1140 Boylston St.   Phone: (617) 266-1400
Boston, MA 02215   John Voigt, Libn.

BETH ISRAEL HOSPITAL - LASSOR AGOOS LIBRARY
330 Brookline Ave.   Phone: (617) 735-4225
Boston, MA 02215   Martha F. Cole, Med.Libn.

BINGHAM, DANA AND GOULD - LAW LIBRARY
100 Federal St.   Phone: (617) 357-9300
Boston, MA 02110   Filippa Marullo Anzalone, Hd.Libn.

BOSTON ARCHITECTURAL CENTER - ALFRED SHAW AND EDWARD DURELL
  STONE LIBRARY
320 Newbury St.   Phone: (617) 536-9018
Boston, MA 02115   Susan Lewis, Hd.Libn.

BOSTON ATHENAEUM LIBRARY
10 1/2 Beacon St.   Phone: (617) 227-0270
Boston, MA 02108   Rodney Armstrong, Dir. & Libn.

BOSTON CITY HOSPITAL - MEDICAL LIBRARY †
818 Harrison Ave.   Phone: (617) 424-4198
Boston, MA 02118   Margie Dempsey, Sr.Med.Libn.

BOSTON CITY HOSPITAL - NURSING - MORSE-SLANGER LIBRARY
35 Northampton St.   Phone: (617) 424-4926
Boston, MA 02118   Jane Keating Latus, Hd.Libn.

BOSTON CONSERVATORY OF MUSIC - ALBERT ALPHIN MUSIC LIBRARY
8 The Fenway   Phone: (617) 536-6340
Boston, MA 02215   Reginald Didham, Hd.Libn.

BOSTON GLOBE NEWSPAPER COMPANY - LIBRARY
135 Morrissey Blvd.   Phone: (617) 929-2541
Boston, MA 02107   Shirley A. Jobe, Lib.Dir.

(Boston) METROPOLITAN DISTRICT COMMISSION - LIBRARY
20 Somerset St.   Phone: (617) 727-5218
Boston, MA 02108   Albert A. Swanson, Archv.

BOSTON MUNICIPAL RESEARCH BUREAU - LIBRARY
294 Washington St.   Phone: (617) 482-3626
Boston, MA 02108   Samuel R. Tyler, Exec.Dir.

BOSTON PSYCHOANALYTIC SOCIETY & INSTITUTE, INC. - LIBRARY
15 Commonwealth Ave.   Phone: (617) 266-0953
Boston, MA 02116   Ann V. Menashi, Libn.

BOSTON PUBLIC LIBRARY - FINE ARTS DEPARTMENT
Copley Sq.
Box 286   Phone: (617) 536-5400
Boston, MA 02117   Theresa Cederholm, Cur.

BOSTON PUBLIC LIBRARY - GOVERNMENT DOCUMENTS, MICROTEXT,
  NEWSPAPERS
Copley Sq.
Box 286   Phone: (617) 536-5400
Boston, MA 02117   V. Lloyd Jameson, Div.Coord.

BOSTON PUBLIC LIBRARY - HUMANITIES REFERENCE
Copley Sq.
Box 286   Phone: (617) 536-5400
Boston, MA 02117   Ms. Sally Beecher, Act.Coord.

BOSTON PUBLIC LIBRARY - KIRSTEIN BUSINESS BRANCH
20 City Hall Ave.   Phone: (617) 523-0860
Boston, MA 02108   Joseph E. Walsh, Bus.Br.Libn.

BOSTON PUBLIC LIBRARY - MUSIC DEPARTMENT
Copley Sq.
Box 286   Phone: (617) 536-5400
Boston, MA 02117   Ruth M. Bleecker, Cur. of Music

BOSTON PUBLIC LIBRARY - PRINTS
Copley Sq.
Box 286   Phone: (617) 536-5400
Boston, MA 02117   Sinclair H. Hitchings, Kpr. of Prints

BOSTON PUBLIC LIBRARY - RARE BOOKS AND MANUSCRIPTS
Copley Sq.
Box 286   Phone: (617) 536-5400
Boston, MA 02117   Dr. Laura V. Monti, Kpr.

BOSTON PUBLIC LIBRARY - SCIENCE REFERENCE
Copley Sq.
Box 286   Phone: (617) 536-5400
Boston, MA 02117

BOSTON PUBLIC LIBRARY - SOCIAL SCIENCES
Copley Sq.
Box 286   Phone: (617) 536-5400
Boston, MA 02117   Ed Sanford, Coord.

BOSTON REDEVELOPMENT AUTHORITY - STAFF LIBRARY
City Hall, 9th Fl.
One City Hall Sq.   Phone: (617) 722-4300
Boston, MA 02201   Rita M. Smith, Lib.Dir.

BOSTON SCHOOL COMMITTEE OF THE CITY OF BOSTON -
  ADMINISTRATION LIBRARY †
26 Court St.   Phone: (617) 726-6449
Boston, MA 02108   Elizabeth F. Scannell, Adm.Libn.

BOSTON STATE HOSPITAL - MEDICAL LIBRARY
591 Morton St.   Phone: (617) 436-6000
Boston, MA 02124   John B. Picott, Libn.

BOSTON UNIVERSITY - AFRICAN STUDIES LIBRARY
771 Commonwealth Ave.   Phone: (617) 353-3726
Boston, MA 02215   Gretchen Walsh, Hd.

BOSTON UNIVERSITY - CENTER FOR ARCHAEOLOGICAL STUDIES -
   LIBRARY
232 Bay State Rd., No. 523   Phone: (617) 353-3415
Boston, MA 02215   Conrad M. Goodwin, Libn.

BOSTON UNIVERSITY - DEPARTMENT OF SPECIAL COLLECTIONS
771 Commonwealth Ave.   Phone: (617) 353-3696
Boston, MA 02215   Dr. Howard B. Gotlieb, Dir.

BOSTON UNIVERSITY - DEPARTMENT OF SPECIAL COLLECTIONS -
   NURSING ARCHIVES
771 Commonwealth Ave.   Phone: (617) 353-3696
Boston, MA 02215   Dr. Nancy L. Noel, Cur.

BOSTON UNIVERSITY - EDUCATIONAL RESOURCES LIBRARY
605 Commonwealth Ave.   Phone: (617) 353-3734
Boston, MA 02215   John W. Collins, Hd.

BOSTON UNIVERSITY - GERONTOLOGY RESOURCE CENTER
730 Commonwealth Ave., 4th Fl.   Phone: (617) 738-1004
Boston, MA 02215   Gretchen Batra, Plan./Coord., Educ.

BOSTON UNIVERSITY - KRASKER MEMORIAL FILM LIBRARY
565 Commonwealth Ave.   Phone: (617) 353-3272
Boston, MA 02215   Earl E. Adreani, Dir.

BOSTON UNIVERSITY MEDICAL CENTER - ALUMNI MEDICAL LIBRARY
80 E. Concord St.   Phone: (617) 247-6187
Boston, MA 02118   Irene Christopher, Chf.Libn.

BOSTON UNIVERSITY - MUSIC LIBRARY
771 Commonwealth Ave.   Phone: (617) 353-3705
Boston, MA 02215   Francis L. Gramenz, Hd.

BOSTON UNIVERSITY - PAPPAS LAW LIBRARY
765 Commonwealth Ave.   Phone: (617) 353-3151
Boston, MA 02215   Virginia J. Wise, Dir./Assoc. Professor

BOSTON UNIVERSITY - SCHOOL OF THEOLOGY LIBRARY
745 Commonwealth Ave.   Phone: (617) 353-3034
Boston, MA 02215   William E. Zimpfer, Libn.

BOSTON UNIVERSITY - SCIENCE AND ENGINEERING LIBRARY
38 Cummington St.   Phone: (617) 353-3733
Boston, MA 02215   Ardelle F. Legg, Hd.

BOSTON UNIVERSITY - WOMEN'S CENTER - LIBRARY
775 Commonwealth Ave., North Tower   Phone: (617) 353-4202
Boston, MA 02215   Maureen Hurley, Adv.

BOSTONIAN SOCIETY - LIBRARY
Old State House
208 Washington St.   Phone: (617) 242-5614
Boston, MA 02109   Thomas W. Parker, Dir.

BOSTON'S MUSEUM OF TRANSPORTATION - LIBRARY
Museum Wharf
300 Congress St.
Boston, MA 02210

BROMFIELD STREET EDUCATIONAL FOUNDATION - GAY COMMUNITY
   NEWS - LIBRARY
167 Tremont St.   Phone: (617) 426-4469
Boston, MA 02111

THE C.T. MAIN CORPORATION - LIBRARY
Southeast Tower, Prudential Ctr.   Phone: (617) 262-3200
Boston, MA 02199   Hayden Mason, Libn.

CAMP DRESSER & MC KEE, INC. - HERMAN G. DRESSER LIBRARY
One Center Plaza   Phone: (617) 742-5151
Boston, MA 02108   Virginia L. Carroll, Libn.

CHARLES RIVER ASSOCIATES, INC. - LIBRARY
Box 708   Phone: (617) 266-0500
Boston, MA 02117   Nancy Jandl, Tech.Info.Mgr.

CHILDREN'S MUSEUM - RESOURCE CENTER
Museum Wharf
300 Congress St.   Phone: (617) 426-6501
Boston, MA 02210   Marie Ariel, Libn.

CHOATE, HALL AND STEWART - LAW LIBRARY †
60 State St.   Phone: (617) 227-5020
Boston, MA 02109   Joy Plunket, Libn.

CHRISTIAN SCIENCE MONITOR - RESEARCH LIBRARY
One Norway St.   Phone: (617) 262-2300
Boston, MA 02115   Geoffrey Fingland, Libn.

COMMERCIAL UNION INSURANCE COMPANIES - RISK CONTROL
   TECHNICAL RESOURCE CENTER
One Beacon St.   Phone: (617) 786-2155
Boston, MA 02108   Margaret Preston, Tech.Res.Assoc.

CONGREGATION ADATH ISRAEL - LIBRARY
Longwood Ave. & The Riverway   Phone: (617) 566-3960
Boston, MA 02215   Elaine B. Wilton, Libn.

COOPERS & LYBRAND - LIBRARY AND INFORMATION CENTER
One Post Office Sq.   Phone: (617) 574-5491
Boston, MA 02109   Kathleen Healy O'Donnell, Libn.

CRIME & JUSTICE FOUNDATION - MASCARELLO LIBRARY OF CRIMINAL
   JUSTICE
19 Temple Pl.   Phone: (617) 426-9800
Boston, MA 02111   Cynthia Brophy, Project Dir.

EARTHWORM, INC. - RECYCLING INFORMATION CENTER
186 Lincoln St.   Phone: (617) 426-7344
Boston, MA 02111   Jeffrey Coyne, Info.Dir.

EMERSON COLLEGE - LIBRARY
150 Beacon St.   Phone: (617) 262-2010
Boston, MA 02116   Mickey Moskowitz, Dir.

ENVIRONMENTAL PROTECTION AGENCY - REGION I LIBRARY
JFK Bldg.   Phone: (617) 223-5791
Boston, MA 02203   Peg Nelson, Libn.

ERNST & WHINNEY - INFORMATION CENTER
200 Clarendon St.   Phone: (617) 266-2000
Boston, MA 02116   Kathleen Driscoll, Mgr.

FEDERAL RESERVE BANK OF BOSTON - LAW LIBRARY
600 Atlantic Ave.
Boston, MA 02106

FEDERAL RESERVE BANK OF BOSTON - RESEARCH LIBRARY †
600 Atlantic Ave., T-28   Phone: (617) 973-3393
Boston, MA 02210   Mary C. Vlantikas, Libn.

FIDELITY MANAGEMENT & RESEARCH COMPANY - LIBRARY
82 Devonshire St.   Phone: (617) 726-0293
Boston, MA 02109   Catharine Schoellkopf, Hd.Libn.

FIRST CHURCH OF CHRIST SCIENTIST - ARCHIVES AND LIBRARY
Christian Science Ctr.   Phone: (617) 262-2300
Boston, MA 02115   Lee Z. Johnson, Archv.

FIRST NATIONAL BANK OF BOSTON - LIBRARY †
Box 1896   Phone: (617) 434-8440
Boston, MA 02105   Jane E. Gutowski-Connell, Libn.

FORSYTH DENTAL CENTER - PERCY HOWE MEMORIAL LIBRARY
140 The Fenway   Phone: (617) 262-5200
Boston, MA 02115   Roberta Oppenheim, Libn.

FRANKLIN INSTITUTE OF BOSTON - LIBRARY
41 Berkeley St.   Phone: (617) 423-4632
Boston, MA 02116   Bonnie L. Wilson, Libn.

FRENCH LIBRARY IN BOSTON, INC.
53 Marlborough St.   Phone: (617) 266-4351
Boston, MA 02116   Jane Stahl, Dir.

GARDNER (Isabella Stewart) MUSEUM, INC. - STAFF LIBRARY
2 Palace Rd.   Phone: (617) 566-1401
Boston, MA 02115   Susan Sinclair, Archv.

GASTON SNOW & ELY BARTLETT
One Federal St.   Phone: (617) 426-4600
Boston, MA 02110   Catherine F. Breen, Libn.

GENERAL THEOLOGICAL LIBRARY
14 Beacon St.   Phone: (617) 227-4557
Boston, MA 02108   Ruth Pragnell, Libn.

GILLETTE COMPANY - PERSONAL CARE DIVISION - INFORMATION
  CENTER †
Box 2131   Phone: (617) 463-2800
Boston, MA 02106   M. McDonough, Asst.Libn.

GOETHE INSTITUTE BOSTON - LIBRARY
170 Beacon St.   Phone: (617) 262-6050
Boston, MA 02116   Dorothee Burney, Hd.Libn.

GOODWIN, PROCTER & HOAR - LAW LIBRARY
28 State St., 22nd Fl.   Phone: (617) 523-5700
Boston, MA 02109   Mary Jo Poburko, Hd.Libn.

GRAND LODGE OF MASSACHUSETTS, A.F. AND A.M. - LIBRARY
Masonic Temple, 186 Tremont St.   Phone: (617) 426-6040
Boston, MA 02111   Roberta A. Hankamer, Libn.

GUILD OF BOOK WORKERS - LIBRARY
Boston Athenaeum
10 1/2 Beacon St.   Phone: (617) 227-0270
Boston, MA 02108   Stanley Ellis Cushing, Lib.Chm.

HALE AND DORR - LIBRARY
60 State St.   Phone: (617) 742-9100
Boston, MA 02109   Mary Catherine H. Crowley, Libn.

HARBRIDGE HOUSE, INC. - LIBRARY
12 Arlington St.   Phone: (617) 267-6410
Boston, MA 02116   Martha J. Berglund, Dir. of Lib.

HARVARD MUSICAL ASSOCIATION - LIBRARY
57A Chestnut St.   Phone: (617) 523-2897
Boston, MA 02108   Natalie Palme, Libn.

HARVARD UNIVERSITY - CENTER FOR POPULATION STUDIES LIBRARY
665 Huntington Ave.   Phone: (617) 732-1234
Boston, MA 02115   Wilma E. Winters, Libn.

HARVARD UNIVERSITY - HARVARD BUSINESS SCHOOL - BAKER LIBRARY
Soldiers Field   Phone: (617) 495-6395
Boston, MA 02163   Mary Chatfield, Libn.

HARVARD UNIVERSITY - SCHOOL OF MEDICINE - LUCIEN HOWE LIBRARY
  OF OPHTHALMOLOGY
243 Charles St.   Phone: (617) 523-7900
Boston, MA 02114   Chris Nims, Libn.

HARVARD UNIVERSITY - SCHOOL OF MEDICINE - SCHERING FOUNDATION
  LIBRARY OF HEALTH CARE
643 Huntington Ave.   Phone: (617) 732-2101
Boston, MA 02115   Anne Alach, Libn.

HARVARD UNIVERSITY - SCHOOL OF PUBLIC HEALTH - INSTITUTE FOR
  HEALTH RESEARCH - LIBRARY
677 Huntington Ave.   Phone: (617) 732-1060
Boston, MA 02115   Arnold Arzeno, Hd.

HARVARD UNIVERSITY - SCHOOL OF PUBLIC HEALTH - KRESGE CENTER
  LIBRARY
665 Huntington Ave.   Phone: (617) 732-1471
Boston, MA 02115   Betty Hauser, Libn.

HARVARD UNIVERSITY - SCHOOLS OF MEDICINE, DENTAL MED. & PUBLIC
  HEALTH, BOSTON MED.LIB. - FRANCIS A. COUNTWAY LIB.
10 Shattuck St.   Phone: (617) 732-2136
Boston, MA 02115   C. Robin LeSueur, Libn.

HERRICK AND SMITH - LAW LIBRARY
100 Federal St.   Phone: (617) 357-9000
Boston, MA 02110   Ann DiLoreto, Law Libn.

HILL AND BARLOW - LIBRARY
225 Franklin St.   Phone: (617) 423-6200
Boston, MA 02110   Carol S. Wellington, Libn.

HOUGHTON MIFFLIN COMPANY - LIBRARY
One Beacon St.   Phone: (617) 725-5270
Boston, MA 02107   Guest Perry, Dir.

INSTITUTE OF CONTEMPORARY ART - LIBRARY
955 Boylston St.   Phone: (617) 266-5152
Boston, MA 02115   Jennifer Bender, Hd., Pubns.

INSTITUTE FOR RESPONSIVE EDUCATION - NATIONAL CLEARINGHOUSE
  ON CITIZEN AND YOUTH PARTICIPATION
605 Commonwealth Ave.   Phone: (617) 353-3309
Boston, MA 02215   Rachel DiCarlo, Coord.

INSURANCE LIBRARY ASSOCIATION OF BOSTON
156 State St.   Phone: (617) 227-2087
Boston, MA 02109   Jean E. Lucey, Dir.

JENSEN ASSOCIATES, INC. - LIBRARY
84 State St.   Phone: (617) 227-8115
Boston, MA 02109   Janet C. Dwyer, Libn.

JOHN HANCOCK MUTUAL LIFE INSURANCE COMPANY - COMPANY LIBRARY
John Hancock Pl.
Box 111   Phone: (617) 421-4524
Boston, MA 02117   Amy C. Wang, Mgr., Lib.Serv.

JOSLIN DIABETES CENTER, INC. - MEDICAL LIBRARY
One Joslin Pl.   Phone: (617) 723-9065
Boston, MA 02215   Denise Corless, Libn.

KEYSTONE CUSTODIAN FUNDS, INC. - LIBRARY
99 High St.   Phone: (617) 338-3435
Boston, MA 02104   Kathleen Young, Libn.

LIBERTY MUTUAL INSURANCE COMPANY - EDUCATION/INFORMATION
  RESOURCES
175 Berkeley St.   Phone: (617) 357-9500
Boston, MA 02117   Ann M. McDonald, Mgr.

LIBERTY MUTUAL INSURANCE COMPANY - LAW LIBRARY
175 Berkeley St.   Phone: (617) 357-9500
Boston, MA 02117   C.E. Procopio, Dir. of Law Libs.

LINDEMANN (Erich) MENTAL HEALTH CENTER - LIBRARY
25 Staniford St.   Phone: (617) 727-7280
Boston, MA 02114   Vishakha Menta, Lib.Dir.

MARINE PRODUCTS COMPANY - LIBRARY
333 W. First St.
Boston, MA 02127

MASSACHUSETTS COLLEGE OF ART - LIBRARY
261 Huntington Ave.   Phone: (617) 232-1555
Boston, MA 02120   Benjamin Hopkins, Hd.Libn.

MASSACHUSETTS COLLEGE OF PHARMACY & ALLIED HEALTH SCIENCES -
  SHEPPARD LIBRARY
179 Longwood Ave.   Phone: (617) 732-2810
Boston, MA 02115   Barbara M. Hill, Libn.

MASSACHUSETTS FINANCIAL SERVICES, INC. - BUSINESS LIBRARY *
200 Berkeley St.   Phone: (617) 423-3500
Boston, MA 02116   Mrs. Kit Danskey, Libn.

MASSACHUSETTS GENERAL HOSPITAL - MGH HEALTH SCIENCES
LIBRARIES
Fruit St.   Phone: (617) 726-8600
Boston, MA 02114   Jacqueline Bastille, Dir.

MASSACHUSETTS HISTORICAL SOCIETY - RESEARCH LIBRARY
1154 Boylston St.   Phone: (617) 536-1608
Boston, MA 02215   John D. Cushing, Libn.

MASSACHUSETTS HORTICULTURAL SOCIETY - LIBRARY
300 Massachusetts Ave.
Boston, MA 02115

MASSACHUSETTS MENTAL HEALTH CENTER - CHARLES MAC FIE
CAMPBELL MEMORIAL LIBRARY
74 Fenwood Rd.   Phone: (617) 734-1300
Boston, MA 02115   Cynthia Doctoroff, Libn.

MASSACHUSETTS MUNICIPAL ASSOCIATION - RESEARCH LIBRARY *
131 Tremont St.   Phone: (617) 426-7272
Boston, MA 02111   James Segel, Exec.Dir.

MASSACHUSETTS REHABILITATION COMMISSION - LIBRARY
20 Park Plaza   Phone: (617) 727-1140
Boston, MA 02116   June C. Holt, Libn.

MASSACHUSETTS STATE BOARD OF LIBRARY COMMISSIONERS -
PROFESSIONAL AND REFERENCE LIBRARY
648 Beacon St.   Phone: (617) 267-9400
Boston, MA 02215   Catherine R. McCarthy, Hd.

MASSACHUSETTS STATE DEPARTMENT OF THE ATTORNEY GENERAL -
LIBRARY
McCormack Bldg., 20th Fl.
One Ashburton Pl.   Phone: (617) 727-1036
Boston, MA 02108   Ruth G. Matz, Chf.Libn.

MASSACHUSETTS STATE DEPARTMENT OF COMMERCE AND
DEVELOPMENT - RESEARCH LIBRARY
100 Cambridge St.   Phone: (617) 727-3206
Boston, MA 02202   Abbe Stephenson, Libn.

MASSACHUSETTS STATE DEPARTMENT OF COMMUNITY AFFAIRS -
LIBRARY *
100 Cambridge St.
Boston, MA 02202

MASSACHUSETTS STATE DEPARTMENT OF CORRECTION - CENTRAL
OFFICE STAFF LIBRARY
State Office Bldg., 22nd Fl.
100 Cambridge St.   Phone: (617) 727-3312
Boston, MA 02202   Daniel P. LeClair, Dp.Dir.

MASSACHUSETTS STATE DEPARTMENT OF PUBLIC HEALTH - CENTRAL
LIBRARY
150 Tremont St.   Phone: (617) 727-7022
Boston, MA 02111   Catherine Moore, Libn.

MASSACHUSETTS STATE LIBRARY
341 State House   Phone: (617) 727-2590
Boston, MA 02133   Gasper Caso, Act.State Libn.

MASSACHUSETTS STATE OFFICE OF THE SECRETARY OF STATE -
ARCHIVES DIVISION
55 State House   Phone: (617) 727-2816
Boston, MA 02133   Albert H. Whitaker, Jr., Archv.

MASSACHUSETTS STATE TRANSPORTATION LIBRARY
10 Park Plaza   Phone: (617) 973-7148
Boston, MA 02116   Ms. Toby Pearlstein, Chf.Libn. & Archv.

MASSACHUSETTS TAXPAYERS FOUNDATION, INC. - LIBRARY
One Federal St.   Phone: (617) 357-8500
Boston, MA 02110   Carol L. Cardozo, Libn.

METCALF & EDDY, INC. - LIBRARY
50 Staniford St.   Phone: (617) 367-4087
Boston, MA 02114   Mary E. Lydon, Corp.Libn.

MINTZ, LEVIN, COHN, FERRIS, GLOVSKY AND POPEO, P.C. - LAW LIBRARY
One Center Plaza   Phone: (617) 742-5800
Boston, MA 02108   Judy Rosen, Libn.

MUSEUM OF FINE ARTS - DEPARTMENT OF PHOTOGRAPHIC SERVICES -
SLIDE & PHOTOGRAPH LIBRARY
465 Huntington Ave.   Phone: (617) 267-9300
Boston, MA 02115   Janice Sorkow, Mgr., Photographic Serv.

MUSEUM OF FINE ARTS - SCHOOL LIBRARY
230 The Fenway   Phone: (617) 267-9300
Boston, MA 02115   Carol Bjork, Libn.

MUSEUM OF FINE ARTS - WILLIAM MORRIS HUNT MEMORIAL LIBRARY
465 Huntington Ave.   Phone: (617) 267-9300
Boston, MA 02115   Nancy S. Allen, Libn.

MUSEUM OF SCIENCE - LIBRARY
Science Pk.   Phone: (617) 723-2500
Boston, MA 02114-1099   Edward D. Pearce, Libn.

NEW ENGLAND AQUARIUM - LIBRARY
Central Wharf   Phone: (617) 742-8830
Boston, MA 02110   Marilyn Murphy, Libn.

NEW ENGLAND BAPTIST HOSPITAL - HELENE FULD LIBRARY *
220 Fisher Ave.   Phone: (617) 738-5800
Boston, MA 02120   Elizabeth Guiu, Libn.

NEW ENGLAND BAPTIST HOSPITAL - MEDICAL STAFF LIBRARY
91 Parker Hill Ave.   Phone: (617) 738-5800
Boston, MA 02120   Paul Esty Woodard, Ph.D., Chf.Med.Libn.

NEW ENGLAND COLLEGE OF OPTOMETRY - LIBRARY
420 Beacon St.   Phone: (617) 266-2030
Boston, MA 02115   F. Eleanor Warner, Hd.Libn.

NEW ENGLAND CONSERVATORY OF MUSIC - HARRIET M. SPAULDING
LIBRARY
33 Gainsborough St.   Phone: (617) 262-1120
Boston, MA 02115   Geraldine Ostrove, Lib.Dir.

NEW ENGLAND DEACONESS HOSPITAL - HORRAX LIBRARY †
185 Pilgrim Rd.   Phone: (617) 732-8311
Boston, MA 02215   Paul Vaiginas, Libn.

NEW ENGLAND GOVERNORS' CONFERENCE, INC. - REFERENCE LIBRARY
76 Summer St.   Phone: (617) 423-6900
Boston, MA 02110   Shirley M. Raynard, Ref.Libn.

NEW ENGLAND HISTORIC GENEALOGICAL SOCIETY - LIBRARY
101 Newbury St.   Phone: (617) 536-5740
Boston, MA 02116   Dr. Ralph J. Crandall, Dir./Ed.

NEW ENGLAND INSTITUTE OF APPLIED ARTS AND SCIENCES - NATIONAL
CENTER FOR DEATH EDUCATION
656 Beacon St.   Phone: (617) 536-6970
Boston, MA 02215   Gail Gruner, Dir.

NEW ENGLAND MUTUAL LIFE INSURANCE COMPANY - BUSINESS LIBRARY
501 Boylston St.   Phone: (617) 578-2307
Boston, MA 02117   Adrienne Korman, Libn.

NEW ENGLAND NUCLEAR CORPORATION - LIBRARY
549 Albany St.   Phone: (617) 482-9595
Boston, MA 02118   Pauline R. Leeds, Libn.

NEW ENGLAND RESOURCE CENTER FOR CHILDREN AND FAMILIES
Judge Baker Guidance Center - Gardner Library
295 Longwood Ave.   Phone: (617) 232-8390
Boston, MA 02115   Mary Lee Cox, Info.Spec.

NEW ENGLAND SCHOOL OF LAW - LIBRARY †
154 Stuart St.   Phone: (617) 451-0010
Boston, MA 02116   Frank S.H. Bae, Law Libn.

NEWS GROUP BOSTON, INC. - BOSTON HERALD LIBRARY
1 Herald Sq.   Phone: (617) 426-3000
Boston, MA 02106   John R. Cronin, Libn.

NORTHEASTERN UNIVERSITY - DANA RESEARCH CENTER - PHYSICS
ELECTRICAL ENGINEERING LIBRARY †
110 Forsyth St.   Phone: (617) 437-2363
Boston, MA 02115   Anastasija Cakste, Libn., Res.Ref.

NORTHEASTERN UNIVERSITY - LAW SCHOOL LIBRARY
400 Huntington Ave.   Phone: (617) 437-3350
Boston, MA 02115   Rajinder S. Walia, Law Libn./Prof. of Law

NORTHEASTERN UNIVERSITY - ROBERT GRAY DODGE LIBRARY †
360 Huntington Ave.   Phone: (617) 437-2350
Boston, MA 02115   Roland H. Moody, Dean

PAYETTE ASSOCIATES - LIBRARY †
40 Isabella St.   Phone: (617) 423-0070
Boston, MA 02116   Sonja M. Nielsen, Corp.Libn.

PORTUGUESE CONTINENTAL UNION OF THE U.S.A. - LIBRARY
899 Boylston St.   Phone: (617) 536-2916
Boston, MA 02115   Francisco J. Mendonca, Supreme Sec.-Libn.

PRICE WATERHOUSE - INFORMATION CENTER
One Federal St.   Phone: (617) 423-7330
Boston, MA 02110   Jean M. Scanlan, Mgr.

PROTESTANT EPISCOPAL CHURCH - EPISCOPAL DIOCESE OF
MASSACHUSETTS - DIOCESAN LIBRARY AND ARCHIVES
1 Joy St.   Phone: (617) 742-4720
Boston, MA 02108   Mark J. Duffy, Archv.

PUTNAM COMPANIES - INVESTMENT RESEARCH LIBRARY
One Post Office Sq.   Phone: (617) 292-1335
Boston, MA 02109   Susan L. Avitabile, Libn./Asst.V.P.

RELIGIOUS ARTS GUILD - MUSIC LIBRARY
25 Beacon St.   Phone: (617) 742-2100
Boston, MA 02108   Barbara M. Hutchins, Exec.Sec.

RETINA FOUNDATION - JOINT RESEARCH LIBRARY *
20 Staniford St.   Phone: (617) 742-3140
Boston, MA 02114   Rose M. Miller, Libn.

ROPES & GRAY - CENTRAL LIBRARY
225 Franklin St.   Phone: (617) 423-6100
Boston, MA 02110   Cornelia Trubey, Libn.

SCUDDER, STEVENS & CLARK - LIBRARY
175 Federal St.   Phone: (617) 482-3990
Boston, MA 02110   Helen Doikos, Libn.

SHAWMUT BANK OF BOSTON, N.A. - LIBRARY
1 Federal St., 8th Fl.   Phone: (617) 292-2550
Boston, MA 02211   Amy A. Ribuoli, Libn.

SIMMONS COLLEGE - GRADUATE SCHOOL OF LIBRARY AND INFORMATION
SCIENCE - LIBRARY
300 The Fenway   Phone: (617) 738-2226
Boston, MA 02115   Linda H. Watkins, Libn.

SIMMONS COLLEGE - SCHOOL OF SOCIAL WORK LIBRARY
51 Commonwealth Ave.   Phone: (617) 266-0806
Boston, MA 02116   Marilyn Smith Bregoli, Libn.

SOCIAL LAW LIBRARY
1200 Court House   Phone: (617) 523-0018
Boston, MA 02108   Edgar J. Bellefontaine, Libn.

SOCIETY FOR THE PRESERVATION OF NEW ENGLAND ANTIQUITIES -
LIBRARY
141 Cambridge St.   Phone: (617) 227-3956
Boston, MA 02114   Elinor Reichlin, Libn.

STATE STREET CONSULTANTS, INC. - INFORMATION CENTER
84 State St., Suite 905   Phone: (617) 720-2020
Boston, MA 02109   Denise Cloutier, Info.Mgr.

STONE AND WEBSTER ENGINEERING CORPORATION - TECHNICAL
INFORMATION CENTER
245 Summer St.   Phone: (617) 589-8891
Boston, MA 02110   Nancy M. Pellini, Div.Mgr.

SUFFOLK UNIVERSITY - LAW LIBRARY
41 Temple St.   Phone: (617) 723-4700
Boston, MA 02114   Edward Bander, Law Libn.

SUFFOLK UNIVERSITY - MILDRED F. SAWYER LIBRARY - COLLECTION OF
AFRO-AMERICAN LITERATURE
8 Ashburton Pl.   Phone: (617) 723-4700
Boston, MA 02108   E.G. Hamann, Dir.

SWEDENBORG LIBRARY AND BOOKSTORE
79 Newbury St.   Phone: (617) 262-5918
Boston, MA 02116   Rafael Guiu, Mgr.

THORNDIKE LIBRARY
1300 Court House   Phone: (617) 725-8078
Boston, MA 02108   Jean Roberts, Ed./Libn.

TUFTS UNIVERSITY - HEALTH SCIENCES LIBRARY
136 Harrison Ave.   Phone: (617) 956-6706
Boston, MA 02111   Elizabeth K. Eaton, Dir.

UNITARIAN-UNIVERSALIST ASSOCIATION - ARCHIVES
25 Beacon St.   Phone: (617) 742-2100
Boston, MA 02108   Carl Seaburg, Info.Off./Archv.

UNITED ENGINEERS & CONSTRUCTORS INC. - BOSTON OFFICE - LIBRARY
100 Summer St.   Phone: (617) 338-6000
Boston, MA 02110   Rocco Piccinino, Jr., Libn.

UNITED METHODIST CHURCH - SOUTHERN NEW ENGLAND CONFERENCE -
HISTORICAL SOCIETY LIBRARY
745 Commonwealth Ave.   Phone: (617) 353-3034
Boston, MA 02215   William E. Zimpfer, Libn.

U.S. BUREAU OF THE CENSUS - INFORMATION SERVICES PROGRAM -
BOSTON REGIONAL OFFICE - LIBRARY
441 Stuart St., 10th Fl.   Phone: (617) 223-2327
Boston, MA 02116   Arthur G. Dukakis, Regional Dir.

U.S. COURT OF APPEALS, 1ST CIRCUIT - LIBRARY
1208 McCormack P.O. & Court House   Phone: (617) 223-2891
Boston, MA 02109   Karen M. Moss, Circuit Libn.

U.S. DEPT. OF COMMERCE - INTERNATIONAL TRADE ADMINISTRATION -
BOSTON DISTRICT OFFICE LIBRARY
441 Stuart St., 10th Fl.   Phone: (617) 223-2312
Boston, MA 02116   Frank J. O'Connor, Dir.

U.S. DEPT. OF HEALTH AND HUMAN SERVICES - REGION I INFORMATION
CENTER
John F. Kennedy Bldg., Rm. 2411   Phone: (617) 223-7291
Boston, MA 02203   Robert Castricone, Info.Spec.

U.S. DEPT. OF HOUSING AND URBAN DEVELOPMENT - REGION I - LIBRARY
†
J.F.K. Federal Bldg.   Phone: (617) 223-4674
Boston, MA 02203   Christine A. Fraser, Libn.

U.S. GENERAL ACCOUNTING OFFICE - BOSTON REGIONAL OFFICE -
TECHNICAL LIBRARY
100 Summer St., Suite 1907   Phone: (617) 223-6536
Boston, MA 02110   Jennifer Arns, Tech.Info.Spec.

U.S. PRESIDENTIAL LIBRARIES - JOHN F. KENNEDY LIBRARY
Columbia Point on Dorchester Bay   Phone: (617) 929-4500
Boston, MA 02125   Dan H. Fenn, Jr., Dir.

U.S. VETERANS ADMINISTRATION (MA-Boston) - HOSPITAL MEDICAL
LIBRARY
150 S. Huntington Ave.   Phone: (617) 739-3434
Boston, MA 02130   Patricia J. McGrath, Chf., Lib.Serv.

U.S. VETERANS ADMINISTRATION (MA-Boston) - OUTPATIENT CLINIC
LIBRARY SERVICE (142D)
17 Court St.   Phone: (617) 223-2082
Boston, MA 02108   Carolyn B. Mathes, Chf., Lib.Serv.

WARNER & STACKPOLE - LAW LIBRARY *
28 State St.   Phone: (617) 523-6250
Boston, MA 02109   Brian J. Harkins, Libn.

WENTWORTH INSTITUTE OF TECHNOLOGY - LIBRARY
550 Huntington Ave.   Phone: (617) 442-9010
Boston, MA 02115   Ann Montgomery Smith, Dir. of Libs.

WIDETT, SLATER & GOLDMAN P.C. - LIBRARY
60 State St.   Phone: (617) 227-7200
Boston, MA 02109   Sarah G. Connell, Hd. Law Libn.

WILLIAM M. MERCER, INC. - LIBRARY/INFORMATION CENTER
200 Clarendon St.   Phone: (617) 421-0367
Boston, MA 02116   Holly W. Garner, Mgr., Info.Serv.

BRAINTREE HISTORICAL SOCIETY, INC. - LIBRARY
786 Washington St.   Phone: (617) 848-1640
Braintree, MA 02184   Mrs. Donald G. Maxham, Libn.

CAPE COD MUSEUM OF NATURAL HISTORY - LIBRARY AND INFORMATION
   CENTER
Main St.   Phone: (617) 896-3867
Brewster, MA 02631   Eileen R. Bush, Libn.

NEW ENGLAND FIRE & HISTORY MUSEUM - LIBRARY AND ARCHIVE
1439 Main St., Rte. 6A   Phone: (617) 896-5711
Brewster, MA 02631   Helen Berrien, Libn.

BRIDGEWATER STATE COLLEGE - CLEMENT C. MAXWELL LIBRARY
Shaw Rd.   Phone: (617) 697-1256
Bridgewater, MA 02434   Owen T.P. McGowan, Ph.D., Lib.Dir.

ARCHDIOCESE OF BOSTON - ARCHIVES
2121 Commonwealth Ave.   Phone: (617) 254-0100
Brighton, MA 02135   James M. O'Toole, Archv.

KENNEDY (Joseph P., Jr.) MEMORIAL HOSPITAL FOR CHILDREN - MEDICAL
   LIBRARY
30 Warren St.   Phone: (617) 254-3800
Brighton, MA 02135   Barbara L. McMurrough, Libn.

ST. ELIZABETH'S HOSPITAL - MEDICAL LIBRARY †
736 Cambridge St.   Phone: (617) 782-7000
Brighton, MA 02135   Deborah T. Almquist, Libn.

ST. ELIZABETH'S HOSPITAL - SCHOOL OF NURSING - LIBRARY
159 Washington St.   Phone: (617) 782-7000
Brighton, MA 02135   Robert L. Loud, Libn.

ST. JOHN'S SEMINARY - LIBRARY
99 Lake St.   Phone: (617) 254-2610
Brighton, MA 02135   Rev. L.W. McGrath, Hd.

BROCKTON ART MUSEUM - FULLER MEMORIAL LIBRARY
Oak St. on Upper Porters Pond   Phone: (617) 588-6000
Brockton, MA 02401   Linda Woolford, Ed.Supv.

BROCKTON DAILY ENTERPRISE AND BROCKTON TIMES-ENTERPRISE -
   LIBRARY *
60 Main St.   Phone: (617) 586-6200
Brockton, MA 02401   Bernice W. Johnson, Hd.Libn.

BROCKTON HOSPITAL - LIBRARY
680 Centre St.   Phone: (617) 586-2600
Brockton, MA 02402   Lovisa Kamenoff, Mgr., Lib.Serv.

CARDINAL CUSHING GENERAL HOSPITAL - STAFF LIBRARY
235 N. Pearl St.   Phone: (617) 588-4000
Brockton, MA 02401   Nancy Sezak, Med.Libn.

PLYMOUTH LAW LIBRARY †
Court House
72 Belmont St.   Phone: (617) 583-8250
Brockton, MA 02401   Kenneth E. MacMullen, Libn.

U.S. VETERANS ADMINISTRATION (MA-Brockton) - MEDICAL CENTER
   LIBRARY
Belmont St.   Phone: (617) 583-4500
Brockton, MA 02401   Suzanne Noyes, Chf., Lib.Serv.

BROOKLINE HOSPITAL - MEDICAL LIBRARY
165 Chestnut St.   Phone: (617) 734-1330
Brookline, MA 02146   Carole Foxman, Med.Libn.

HEBREW COLLEGE - JACOB AND ROSE GROSSMAN LIBRARY
43 Hawes St.   Phone: (617) 232-8710
Brookline, MA 02146   Maurice S. Tuchman, Libn.

HELLENIC COLLEGE AND HOLY CROSS GREEK ORTHODOX SCHOOL OF
   THEOLOGY - COTSIDAS-TONNA LIBRARY
50 Goddard Ave.   Phone: (617) 731-3500
Brookline, MA 02146   Rev. George. C. Papademetriou, Ph.D., Dir. of Lib.

INSTITUTE FOR DEFENSE AND DISARMAMENT STUDIES - LIBRARY
2001 Beacon St.   Phone: (617) 734-4216
Brookline, MA 02146   Elizabeth Bernstein, Libn./Pub.Info.Coord.

LONGYEAR HISTORICAL SOCIETY - MARY BAKER EDDY MUSEUM -
   LIBRARY
120 Seaver St.   Phone: (617) 277-8943
Brookline, MA 02146

PAN AMERICAN SOCIETY OF NEW ENGLAND - SHATTUCK MEMORIAL
   LIBRARY
1051 Beacon St.   Phone: (617) 277-9439
Brookline, MA 02146   Vivian P. Quiroga de Ingrao, Exec.Dir.

TEMPLE OHABEI SHALOM - SISTERHOOD LIBRARY
1187 Beacon St.   Phone: (617) 277-6610
Brookline, MA 02146   Mary R. Rosen, Libn.

TEMPLE SINAI - LIBRARY †
50 Sewall Ave.   Phone: (617) 277-5888
Brookline, MA 02146   Jane Taubenfield Cohen, Prin., Rel.Sch.

U.S. NATL. PARK SERVICE - FREDERICK LAW OLMSTED NATL. HISTORIC
   SITE - ARCHIVES
99 Warren St.   Phone: (617) 566-1689
Brookline, MA 02146   Elizabeth S. Banks, Coll.Mgr.

ANALYTICAL SYSTEMS ENGINEERING CORPORATION - LIBRARY
5 Old Concord Rd.   Phone: (617) 272-7910
Burlington, MA 01803   Rayna Lee Caplan, Libn.

DURACELL INC. - TECHNICAL INFORMATION CENTER
Northwest Industrial Pk.   Phone: (617) 272-4100
Burlington, MA 01803   Mildred Keller, Mgr., Tech.Info.Serv.

HIGH VOLTAGE ENGINEERING CORPORATION - LIBRARY
S. Bedford St.
Box 416
Burlington, MA 01803

LAHEY CLINIC MEDICAL CENTER - RICHARD B. CATTELL MEMORIAL
   LIBRARY
41 Mall Rd.   Phone: (617) 273-8253
Burlington, MA 01805   Carol Spencer, Med.Libn.

MICROWAVE ASSOCIATES, INC. - M/A COM LIBRARY
South Ave.   Phone: (617) 272-3000
Burlington, MA 01803   Christine S. Coburn, Libn.

RAYTHEON SERVICE COMPANY - INFORMATION CENTER
2 Wayside Rd., Spencer Laboratory   Phone: (617) 272-9300
Burlington, MA 01803   Jean Cameron, Info.Spec.

RCA CORPORATION - G & CS - AUTOMATED SYSTEMS - ENGINEERING
   LIBRARY
Box 588   Phone: (617) 272-4000
Burlington, MA 01803   Veronica Hsu, Tech.Libn.

MASSACHUSETTS MARITIME ACADEMY - CAPTAIN CHARLES H. HURLEY
   LIBRARY
Taylor's Point
Box D   Phone: (617) 759-5761
Buzzards Bay, MA 02532   Maurice H. Bosse, Dir. of Lib.Serv.

ABT ASSOCIATES INC. - LIBRARY
55 Wheeler St.   Phone: (617) 492-7100
Cambridge, MA 02138   Judy Weinberg, Libn.

AMERICAN ASSOCIATION OF VARIABLE STAR OBSERVERS - MC ATEER
   LIBRARY
187 Concord Ave.   Phone: (617) 354-0484
Cambridge, MA 02138   Janet A. Mattei, Dir.

ARCHITECTS COLLABORATIVE - LIBRARY †
46 Brattle St.   Phone: (617) 868-4200
Cambridge, MA 02138   Anne-Marie Hartmere, Libn.

ARTHUR D. LITTLE, INC. - BURLINGTON LIBRARY
17 Acorn Park   Phone: (617) 864-5770
Cambridge, MA 02140   Joanne C. Adamowicz, Libn.

ARTHUR D. LITTLE, INC. - LIFE SCIENCES LIBRARY
Acorn Park   Phone: (617) 864-5770
Cambridge, MA 02140   Margaret A. Miller, Dir.

ARTHUR D. LITTLE, INC. - MANAGEMENT LIBRARY †
35 Acorn Pk.   Phone: (617) 864-5770
Cambridge, MA 02140   Edith B. Mintz, Hd.Libn.

ARTHUR D. LITTLE, INC. - RESEARCH LIBRARY
25 Acorn Pk.   Phone: (617) 864-5770
Cambridge, MA 02140   Ethel M. Salonen, Hd.

BOLT BERANEK AND NEWMAN, INC. - LIBRARY
10 Moulton St.   Phone: (617) 491-1850
Cambridge, MA 02238

CAMBRIDGE ENERGY RESEARCH ASSOCIATES - LIBRARY
56 John F. Kennedy St.   Phone: (617) 497-6446
Cambridge, MA 02138   James Rosenfield, V.P.

CAMBRIDGE HISTORICAL COMMISSION - LIBRARY
City Hall Annex
57 Inman St.   Phone: (617) 498-9040
Cambridge, MA 02139   Charles M. Sullivan, Exec.Dir.

CAMBRIDGE HOSPITAL - MEDICAL LIBRARY
1493 Cambridge St.   Phone: (617) 498-1439
Cambridge, MA 02139   Therese Simeone, Med.Libn.

CAMBRIDGE SCHOOL DEPARTMENT - TEACHERS' RESOURCE CENTER
459 Broadway   Phone: (617) 492-8000
Cambridge, MA 02138   Sheila Morshead, Libn./Media Spec.

COM/ENERGY SERVICES CO. - LIBRARY †
675 Massachusetts Ave.   Phone: (617) 864-3100
Cambridge, MA 02139   Esther A. Reppucci, Supv., Lib./Rec.Ctr.

CULTURAL SURVIVAL, INC. - LIBRARY
11 Divinity Ave.   Phone: (617) 495-2562
Cambridge, MA 02138   Jason W. Clay, Dir. of Res./Ed.

DRAPER (Charles Stark) LABORATORY, INC. - TECHNICAL INFORMATION
   CENTER
555 Technology Sq., Mail Sta. 74   Phone: (617) 258-3555
Cambridge, MA 02139   M. Hope Coffman, Mgr.

DYNATECH RESEARCH DEVELOPMENT COMPANY - CORPORATION
   LIBRARY †
99 Erie St.   Phone: (617) 868-8050
Cambridge, MA 02139   Jane I. Petschaft, Libn.

ENERGY RESOURCES COMPANY - LIBRARY †
1 Alewife Pl.   Phone: (617) 661-3111
Cambridge, MA 02140

EVALUATION, DISSEMINATION & ASSESSMENT CENTER - EDAC RESEARCH
   LIBRARY
Lesley College
49 Washington Ave.   Phone: (617) 492-0505
Cambridge, MA 02140   Molly Leong, Bilingual Res.Libn.

GRACE (W.R.) AND COMPANY - INDUSTRIAL CHEMICALS GROUP - LIBRARY
62 Whittemore Ave.   Phone: (617) 876-1400
Cambridge, MA 02140   Marjorie Metcalf, Libn.

HARVARD UNIVERSITY - ARCHIVES
Pusey Library   Phone: (617) 495-2461
Cambridge, MA 02138   Harley P. Holden, Cur.

HARVARD UNIVERSITY - ARNOLD ARBORETUM & GRAY HERBARIUM -
   LIBRARY
22 Divinity Ave.   Phone: (617) 495-2366
Cambridge, MA 02138   Barbara A. Callahan, Libn.

HARVARD UNIVERSITY - BIOLOGICAL LABORATORIES LIBRARY
16 Divinity Ave.   Phone: (617) 495-3944
Cambridge, MA 02138   Dorothy J. Solbrig, Libn.

HARVARD UNIVERSITY - CARPENTER CENTER FOR THE VISUAL ARTS -
   PHOTOGRAPH COLLECTION
                                       Phone: (617) 495-3251
Cambridge, MA 02138   Barbara P. Norfleet, Cur.

HARVARD UNIVERSITY - CENTER FOR EUROPEAN STUDIES - LIBRARY
5 Bryant St.   Phone: (617) 495-4150
Cambridge, MA 02138   Loren Goldner, Libn.

HARVARD UNIVERSITY - CENTER FOR INTERNATIONAL AFFAIRS -
   LIBRARY
Coolidge Hall
1737 Cambridge St.   Phone: (617) 495-2173
Cambridge, MA 02138   Barbara A. Mitchell, Libn.

HARVARD UNIVERSITY - CENTER FOR MIDDLE EASTERN STUDIES -
   LIBRARY
Coolidge Hall
1737 Cambridge St.   Phone: (617) 495-2173
Cambridge, MA 02138   Barbara A. Mitchell, Libn.

HARVARD UNIVERSITY - CENTER FOR SCIENCE AND INTERNATIONAL
   AFFAIRS LIBRARY
79 Kennedy St.   Phone: (617) 495-1400
Cambridge, MA 02138   Jetta J. Cooper, Libn.

HARVARD UNIVERSITY - CHEMISTRY LIBRARY
Converse Memorial Laboratory   Phone: (617) 495-4079
Cambridge, MA 02138   Ludmila Birladeanu, Supv.

HARVARD UNIVERSITY - DIVINITY SCHOOL - ANDOVER-HARVARD
   THEOLOGICAL LIBRARY
45 Francis Ave.   Phone: (617) 495-5770
Cambridge, MA 02138   Maria Grossmann, Libn.

HARVARD UNIVERSITY - ECONOMIC BOTANY LIBRARY
Harvard University Herbaria
22 Divinity Ave.   Phone: (617) 495-2326
Cambridge, MA 02138   Wesley Wong

HARVARD UNIVERSITY - EDA KUHN LOEB MUSIC LIBRARY
                                       Phone: (617) 495-2794
Cambridge, MA 02138   Michael Ochs, Libn.

HARVARD UNIVERSITY - FARLOW REFERENCE LIBRARY
20 Divinity Ave.   Phone: (617) 495-2369
Cambridge, MA 02138   Geraldine C. Kaye, Libn.

HARVARD UNIVERSITY - FINE ARTS LIBRARY
Fogg Art Museum   Phone: (617) 495-3373
Cambridge, MA 02138   Wolfgang Freitag, Libn.

HARVARD UNIVERSITY - GEOLOGICAL SCIENCES LIBRARY
24 Oxford St.   Phone: (617) 495-2029
Cambridge, MA 02138   Constance S. Wick, Libn.

HARVARD UNIVERSITY - GODFREY LOWELL CABOT SCIENCE LIBRARY
Science Ctr., One Oxford St.   Phone: (617) 495-5353
Cambridge, MA 02138   Alan E. Erickson, Sci.Spec.

HARVARD UNIVERSITY - GORDON MC KAY LIBRARY - DIVISION OF
    APPLIED SCIENCES
Pierce Hall, 29 Oxford St.   Phone: (617) 495-2836
Cambridge, MA 02138   Julie Sandall Barlas, Libn.

HARVARD UNIVERSITY - GRADUATE SCHOOL OF DESIGN - FRANCES LOEB
    LIBRARY
Gund Hall   Phone: (617) 495-2574
Cambridge, MA 02138   James Hodgson, Libn.

HARVARD UNIVERSITY - GRADUATE SCHOOL OF EDUCATION - GUTMAN
    LIBRARY
Appian Way   Phone: (617) 495-4225
Cambridge, MA 02138   Inabeth Miller, Libn.

HARVARD UNIVERSITY - HARVARD UKRAINIAN RESEARCH INSTITUTE -
    REFERENCE LIBRARY
1583 Massachusetts Ave.   Phone: (617) 495-3341
Cambridge, MA 02138   Larisa A. Trolle, Act.Libn.

HARVARD UNIVERSITY - HARVARD-YENCHING LIBRARY
2 Divinity Ave.   Phone: (617) 495-2756
Cambridge, MA 02138   Eugene Wu, Libn.

HARVARD UNIVERSITY - HISTORY OF SCIENCE LIBRARY
Widener Library, Rm. 91
Cambridge, MA 02138   Barbara G. Rosenkrantz

HARVARD UNIVERSITY - HOUGHTON LIBRARY
                                              Phone: (617) 495-2440
Cambridge, MA 02138   Lawrence R. Dowler, Assoc.Libn.

HARVARD UNIVERSITY - INSTITUTE FOR INTERNATIONAL DEVELOPMENT
    - LIBRARY
Coolidge Hall
1737 Cambridge St.   Phone: (617) 495-2173
Cambridge, MA 02138   Barbara A. Mitchell, Libn.

HARVARD UNIVERSITY - JOHN FITZGERALD KENNEDY SCHOOL OF
    GOVERNMENT - LIBRARY
79 John F. Kennedy St.   Phone: (617) 495-1302
Cambridge, MA 02138   Malcolm C. Hamilton, Libn.

HARVARD UNIVERSITY - JOHN K. FAIRBANK CENTER FOR EAST ASIAN
    RESEARCH - LIBRARY
1737 Cambridge St.   Phone: (617) 495-5753
Cambridge, MA 02138   Nancy Hearst, Libn.

HARVARD UNIVERSITY - LAW SCHOOL LIBRARY
Langdell Hall   Phone: (617) 495-3170
Cambridge, MA 02138   Terry Martin, Dir.

HARVARD UNIVERSITY - LITTAUER LIBRARY
                                              Phone: (617) 495-2105
Cambridge, MA 02138   James Damaskos, Libn.

HARVARD UNIVERSITY - MAP COLLECTION
Pusey Library   Phone: (617) 495-2417
Cambridge, MA 02138   Frank E. Trout, Cur.

HARVARD UNIVERSITY - MATHEMATICAL LIBRARY
Science Center
1 Oxford St.   Phone: (617) 495-2147
Cambridge, MA 02138   Wilfried Schmid

HARVARD UNIVERSITY - MUSEUM OF COMPARATIVE ZOOLOGY - LIBRARY
Oxford St.   Phone: (617) 495-2475
Cambridge, MA 02138   Eva Jonas, Libn.

HARVARD UNIVERSITY - OAKES AMES ORCHID LIBRARY
University Herbarium   Phone: (617) 495-2360
Cambridge, MA 02138   Herman R. Sweet, Libn.

HARVARD UNIVERSITY - OBSERVATORY LIBRARY
60 Garden St.   Phone: (617) 495-5488
Cambridge, MA 02138   Estelle Karlin, Libn.

HARVARD UNIVERSITY - PHYSICS RESEARCH LIBRARY
450 Jefferson Library   Phone: (617) 495-2878
Cambridge, MA 02138   Nina McMaster, Libn.

HARVARD UNIVERSITY - PROGRAM ON NEGOTIATION: SPECIALIZED
    COLLECTION IN DISPUTE RESOLUTION AND NEGOTIATION
Pound Hall 500
Harvard Law School   Phone: (617) 495-1684
Cambridge, MA 02138   Bruce M. Patton, Assoc.Dir./Lib.Hd.

HARVARD UNIVERSITY - PSYCHOLOGY RESEARCH LIBRARY
33 Kirkland St.   Phone: (617) 495-3858
Cambridge, MA 02138   Annelise Katz, Libn.

HARVARD UNIVERSITY - RADCLIFFE COLLEGE - MORSE MUSIC LIBRARY
59 Shepard St.   Phone: (617) 495-8730
Cambridge, MA 02138   Cathy Balshone-Becze, Music Libn.

HARVARD UNIVERSITY - RADIO ASTRONOMY STATION - LIBRARY
60 Garden St.
Cambridge, MA 02138

HARVARD UNIVERSITY - ROBBINS LIBRARY
Emerson Hall   Phone: (617) 495-2193
Cambridge, MA 02138   Michael Pakaluk, Hd.Libn.

HARVARD UNIVERSITY - RUSSIAN RESEARCH CENTER - LIBRARY
Coolidge Hall Library
1737 Cambridge St.   Phone: (617) 495-4030
Cambridge, MA 02138   Susan Jo Gardos, Libn.

HARVARD UNIVERSITY - SOCIAL RELATIONS/SOCIOLOGY LIBRARY
33 Kirkland St.   Phone: (617) 495-3838
Cambridge, MA 02138   Annelise Katz, Libn.

HARVARD UNIVERSITY - STATISTICS LIBRARY
Science Center
1 Oxford St.   Phone: (617) 495-5496
Cambridge, MA 02138   John Carlin, Lib.Asst.

HARVARD UNIVERSITY - THEATRE COLLECTION
Pusey Library   Phone: (617) 495-2445
Cambridge, MA 02138   Jeanne T. Newlin, Cur.

HARVARD UNIVERSITY - TOZZER LIBRARY
21 Divinity Ave.   Phone: (617) 495-2253
Cambridge, MA 02138   Nancy J. Schmidt, Libn.

HARVARD UNIVERSITY - WOODBERRY POETRY ROOM
Lamont Library   Phone: (617) 495-2454
Cambridge, MA 02138   Stratis Haviaras, Cur.

INTERMETRICS INC. - LIBRARY
733 Concord Ave.   Phone: (617) 661-1840
Cambridge, MA 02138   Ann M. Wilson, Mgr., Lib.Serv.

JOHNSON (Carol R.) & ASSOCIATES, INC. - LIBRARY
15 Mount Auburn St.   Phone: (617) 868-6115
Cambridge, MA 02138   Rhonda Postrel, Libn.

KALBA BOWEN ASSOCIATES - LIBRARY
12 Arrow St.   Phone: (617) 661-2624
Cambridge, MA 02138   Beverly Hall Spencer, Libn./Info.Spec.

LINCOLN INSTITUTE OF LAND POLICY - LIBRARY
26 Trowbridge St.   Phone: (617) 661-3016
Cambridge, MA 02138   Mary J. O'Brien, Libn.

MASSACHUSETTS INSTITUTE OF TECHNOLOGY - AERONAUTICS AND
    ASTRONAUTICS LIBRARY
Rm. 33-316   Phone: (617) 253-5665
Cambridge, MA 02139   Beth Easter, Libn.

MASSACHUSETTS INSTITUTE OF TECHNOLOGY - BARKER ENGINEERING
    LIBRARY
Rm. 10-500   Phone: (617) 253-5663
Cambridge, MA 02139   James M. Kyed, Hd., Engr.Libs.

MASSACHUSETTS INSTITUTE OF TECHNOLOGY - CENTER FOR POLICY
    ALTERNATIVES - DOCUMENTS COLLECTION
Rm. E40-216   Phone: (617) 253-1659
Cambridge, MA 02139

MASSACHUSETTS INSTITUTE OF TECHNOLOGY - CENTER FOR SPACE
    RESEARCH - READING ROOM
Rm. 37-582   Phone: (617) 253-3746
Cambridge, MA 02139   Margaret E. Lania, Asst.Libn.

MASSACHUSETTS INSTITUTE OF TECHNOLOGY - CHEMISTRY READING
    ROOM
Rm. 18-480   Phone: (617) 253-1891
Cambridge, MA 02139

MASSACHUSETTS INSTITUTE OF TECHNOLOGY - CIVIL ENGINEERING
    DEPT. - RALPH M. PARSONS LABORATORY - REF. RM.
Bldg. 48-411   Phone: (617) 253-2994
Cambridge, MA 02139   Chiang C. Mei, Prof. Civil Engr.

MASSACHUSETTS INSTITUTE OF TECHNOLOGY - DEPARTMENT OF
    CHEMICAL ENGINEERING READING ROOM
Room 66-365   Phone: (617) 253-6521
Cambridge, MA 02139   Lisa Gould, Lib.Asst.

MASSACHUSETTS INSTITUTE OF TECHNOLOGY - DEPARTMENT OF
    NUTRITION AND FOOD SCIENCE - READING ROOM
Rm. 20A-213   Phone: (617) 253-7994
Cambridge, MA 02139   Margaret Mubirumusoke, Info.Spec.

MASSACHUSETTS INSTITUTE OF TECHNOLOGY - DEWEY LIBRARY
Hermann Bldg., E53-100   Phone: (617) 253-5677
Cambridge, MA 02139   Edgar W. Davy, Dewey Libn.

MASSACHUSETTS INSTITUTE OF TECHNOLOGY - DYNAMICS OF
    ATMOSPHERES AND OCEANS LIBRARY
Rm. 54-1427   Phone: (617) 253-2450
Cambridge, MA 02139   Ellen Silverberg, Libn.

MASSACHUSETTS INSTITUTE OF TECHNOLOGY - ENERGY LABORATORY
    INFORMATION CENTER
Rm. E40-498   Phone: (617) 253-3485
Cambridge, MA 02139   Shelley Rosenstein, Libn.

MASSACHUSETTS INSTITUTE OF TECHNOLOGY - ENVIRONMENTAL
    MEDICAL SERVICE - LIBRARY
77 Massachusetts Ave., Rm. 20B-238   Phone: (617) 253-7983
Cambridge, MA 02139   Margaret Mahoney, Libn.

MASSACHUSETTS INSTITUTE OF TECHNOLOGY - HUMANITIES LIBRARY
Rm. 14S-200   Phone: (617) 253-5683
Cambridge, MA 02139   David S. Ferriero, Libn.

MASSACHUSETTS INSTITUTE OF TECHNOLOGY - INFORMATION
    PROCESSING SERVICES - READING ROOM
Rm. 39-233   Phone: (617) 253-4105
Cambridge, MA 02139   Richard D. Scott, Mgr.

MASSACHUSETTS INSTITUTE OF TECHNOLOGY - INSTITUTE ARCHIVES
    AND SPECIAL COLLECTIONS
Hayden Library, Rm. 14N-118   Phone: (617) 253-5688
Cambridge, MA 02139   Helen W. Slotkin, Archv./Spec.Coll.Hd.

MASSACHUSETTS INSTITUTE OF TECHNOLOGY - LABORATORY FOR
    COMPUTER SCIENCE - READING ROOM
545 Technology Sq., Rm. 114   Phone: (617) 253-5896
Cambridge, MA 02139   Maria Sensale, Lib.Asst.

MASSACHUSETTS INSTITUTE OF TECHNOLOGY - LINDGREN LIBRARY
Rm. 54-200   Phone: (617) 253-5679
Cambridge, MA 02139   Jean Eaglesfield, Lindgren Libn.

MASSACHUSETTS INSTITUTE OF TECHNOLOGY - M.I.T. MUSEUM AND
    HISTORICAL COLLECTIONS
Bldg. N52   Phone: (617) 253-4440
Cambridge, MA 02139   Warren A. Seamans, Dir.

MASSACHUSETTS INSTITUTE OF TECHNOLOGY - MUSIC LIBRARY
Rm. 14E-109   Phone: (617) 253-5689
Cambridge, MA 02139   Linda I. Solow, Music Libn.

MASSACHUSETTS INSTITUTE OF TECHNOLOGY - PHYSICS READING ROOM
Rm. 26-152   Phone: (617) 253-1791
Cambridge, MA 02139   Gail M. Morchower, Supv.

MASSACHUSETTS INSTITUTE OF TECHNOLOGY - PLASMA FUSION CENTER
    - DAVID J. ROSE LIBRARY
NW16-153
167 Albany St.   Phone: (617) 253-8462
Cambridge, MA 02139   Beverly Colby, Libn.

MASSACHUSETTS INSTITUTE OF TECHNOLOGY - PSYCHOLOGY LIBRARY
Rm. E10-030   Phone: (617) 253-5755
Cambridge, MA 02139

MASSACHUSETTS INSTITUTE OF TECHNOLOGY - PURE MATHEMATICS
    READING ROOM
Rm. 2-285   Phone: (617) 253-4390
Cambridge, MA 02139   David A. Vogan, Assoc.Prof.

MASSACHUSETTS INSTITUTE OF TECHNOLOGY - RESEARCH LABORATORY
    OF ELECTRONICS - DOCUMENT ROOM
Rm. 36-412   Phone: (617) 253-2566
Cambridge, MA 02139   Janet E. Moore, Hd., Docs. & Pubns.

MASSACHUSETTS INSTITUTE OF TECHNOLOGY - ROTCH LIBRARY OF
    ARCHITECTURE AND PLANNING
Rm. 7-238   Phone: (617) 253-7052
Cambridge, MA 02139   Margaret DePopolo, Rotch Libn.

MASSACHUSETTS INSTITUTE OF TECHNOLOGY - ROTCH LIBRARY VISUAL
    COLLECTIONS - LOUIS SKIDMORE ROOM
Room 7-304   Phone: (617) 253-7098
Cambridge, MA 02139   Merrill W. Smith, Libn.

MASSACHUSETTS INSTITUTE OF TECHNOLOGY - SCHERING-PLOUGH
    LIBRARY
Rm. E25-131   Phone: (617) 253-3528
Cambridge, MA 02139

MASSACHUSETTS INSTITUTE OF TECHNOLOGY - SCIENCE FICTION
    SOCIETY - LIBRARY
Rm. W20-473   Phone: (617) 225-9144
Cambridge, MA 02139

MASSACHUSETTS INSTITUTE OF TECHNOLOGY - SCIENCE LIBRARY
Rm. 14S-100   Phone: (617) 253-5680
Cambridge, MA 02139   James M. Kyed, Act.Hd., Sci.Libs.

MASSACHUSETTS INSTITUTE OF TECHNOLOGY - SEA GRANT PROGRAM -
    SEA GRANT INFORMATION CENTER
E38-302, 292 Main St.   Phone: (617) 253-5944
Cambridge, MA 02139   Susan D. Stolz, Libn. & Info.Spec.

MASSACHUSETTS INSTITUTE OF TECHNOLOGY - TRI-SERVICE LIBRARY
U.S. AFROTC DET 365
Rm. 20E-122   Phone: (617) 253-4471
Cambridge, MA 02139   John Shannon, Tech.Instr.

MIDDLESEX LAW LIBRARY
Superior Court House
40 Thorndike St.   Phone: (617) 494-4148
Cambridge, MA 02141   Sandi Lindheimer, Lib.Dir.

MOUNT AUBURN HOSPITAL - HEALTH SCIENCES LIBRARY
330 Mt. Auburn St.   Phone: (617) 492-3500
Cambridge, MA 02138   M. Cherie Haitz, Dir.

POLAROID CORPORATION - RESEARCH LIBRARY
730 Main St.   Phone: (617) 577-3368
Cambridge, MA 02139   Jean M. Vnenchak, Dept.Mgr.

RADCLIFFE COLLEGE - ARTHUR AND ELIZABETH SCHLESINGER LIBRARY
    ON THE HISTORY OF WOMEN IN AMERICA
10 Garden St.   Phone: (617) 495-8647
Cambridge, MA 02138   Dr. Patricia M. King, Dir.

RADCLIFFE COLLEGE - HENRY A. MURRAY RESEARCH CENTER
10 Garden St.   Phone: (617) 495-8140
Cambridge, MA 02138   Anne Colby, Dir.

RAYTHEON COMPANY - BADGER AMERICA, INC. - LIBRARY
One Broadway   Phone: (617) 494-7565
Cambridge, MA 02142   Eleanor M. Rice, Libn.

SMITHSONIAN INSTITUTION LIBRARIES - ASTROPHYSICAL
   OBSERVATORY - LIBRARY †
60 Garden St.   Phone: (617) 495-7264
Cambridge, MA 02138   Joyce Rey, Libn.

U.S. DEPT. OF TRANSPORTATION - TRANSPORTATION SYSTEMS CENTER -
   TECHNICAL REFERENCE CENTER
Kendall Sq.   Phone: (617) 494-2783
Cambridge, MA 02142   Hadassah Linfield, Dir.

U.S. NATL. PARK SERVICE - LONGFELLOW NATL. HISTORIC SITE -
   LIBRARY
105 Brattle St.   Phone: (617) 876-4491
Cambridge, MA 02138   Kathleen Catalano, Cur.

WARNER-EDDISON ASSOCIATES, INC. - INFORMATION SERVICE
238 Broadway   Phone: (617) 661-8124
Cambridge, MA 02139   Elizabeth Bole Eddison, Pres.

WESTON SCHOOL OF THEOLOGY - LIBRARY
99 Brattle St.   Phone: (617) 868-3450
Cambridge, MA 02138   James Dunkly, Dir.

CANTON HISTORICAL SOCIETY - LIBRARY
1400 Washington St.
Canton, MA 02021

MASSACHUSETTS STATE HOSPITAL SCHOOL - MEDICAL LIBRARY *
Randolph St.   Phone: (617) 828-2440
Canton, MA 02021   Caroline Cento, Med.Rec.Techn.

U.S. COAST GUARD/AIR STATION - BASE LIBRARY
Otis AFB   Phone: (617) 968-5062
Cape Cod, MA 02542   Evelyn L. Norton, Act.Libn.

CHELMSFORD HISTORICAL SOCIETY - BARRETT-BYAM HOMESTEAD
   LIBRARY *
40 Byam Rd.   Phone: (617) 256-2311
Chelmsford, MA 01824   Mrs. Donald Fogg, Curator

MERRIMACK EDUCATION CENTER
101 Mill Rd.   Phone: (617) 256-3985
Chelmsford, MA 01824   Jean E. Sanders, Assoc.Dir.

CHESTERFIELD HISTORICAL SOCIETY - EDWARDS MUSEUM - LIBRARY
                                                 Phone: (413) 296-4759
Chesterfield, MA 01012

BOSTON COLLEGE - GRADUATE SCHOOL OF SOCIAL WORK LIBRARY
McGuinn Hall   Phone: (617) 552-3233
Chestnut Hill, MA 02167   Harriet Nemiccolo, Chf.Libn.

BOSTON COLLEGE - SPECIAL COLLECTIONS DEPARTMENT
St. Thomas More Hall, Rm. 216   Phone: (617) 552-3282
Chestnut Hill, MA 02167   Ralph Coffman, Hd., Spec.Coll.

CONGREGATION MISHKAN TEFILA - HARRY AND ANNA FEINBERG LIBRARY
300 Hammond Pond Pkwy.   Phone: (617) 332-7770
Chestnut Hill, MA 02167   Louise Lieberman, Libn.

ALCOTT (Louisa May) MEMORIAL ASSOCIATION - LIBRARY
Box 343   Phone: (617) 369-4118
Concord, MA 01742   Jayne Gordon, Dir.

CONCORD ANTIQUARIAN MUSEUM - LIBRARY OF RALPH WALDO EMERSON
200 Lexington Rd.   Phone: (617) 369-9609
Concord, MA 01742   Charmian Clark

ENVIRONMENTAL RESEARCH & TECHNOLOGY, INC. - INFORMATION
   CENTER
696 Virginia Rd.   Phone: (617) 369-8910
Concord, MA 01742   Brenda Y. Allen, Mgr.

GENRAD, INC. - LIBRARY †
300 Baker Ave., 3rd Fl.   Phone: (617) 369-4400
Concord, MA 01742

THOREAU LYCEUM - LIBRARY
156 Belknap St.   Phone: (617) 369-5912
Concord, MA 01742   Anne McGrath, Cur.

GTE SYLVANIA - ENGINEERING LIBRARY
100 Endicott St.   Phone: (617) 777-1900
Danvers, MA 01923   Mildred A. McKenna, Libn.

HUNT MEMORIAL HOSPITAL - GEORGE B. PALMER MEMORIAL LIBRARY
75 Lindall St.   Phone: (617) 774-4400
Danvers, MA 01923   Yvonne I. Cretecos, Med.Libn.

PEABODY INSTITUTE LIBRARY - DANVERS ARCHIVAL CENTER
15 Sylvan St.   Phone: (617) 774-0554
Danvers, MA 01923   Richard B. Trask, Town Archv.

DEDHAM HISTORICAL SOCIETY - LIBRARY
612 High St.   Phone: (617) 326-1385
Dedham, MA 02026   Electa Kane Tritsch, Exec.Dir.

NORFOLK LAW LIBRARY
Superior Court House
650 High St.   Phone: (617) 326-1600
Dedham, MA 02026   Louise C. Hoagland, Libn.

HISTORIC DEERFIELD, INC. - HENRY N. FLYNT LIBRARY - POCUMTUCK
   VALLEY MEMORIAL ASSOCIATION
Memorial St.
Box 53   Phone: (413) 774-5581
Deerfield, MA 01342   David R. Proper, Libn.

ICI AMERICAS INC. - PROCESS TECHNOLOGY DEPARTMENT LIBRARY
Main St.   Phone: (617) 669-6731
Dighton, MA 02715   Candace A. Fish, Libn.

CARNEY HOSPITAL - MEDICAL LIBRARY
2100 Dorchester Ave.   Phone: (617) 296-4000
Dorchester, MA 02124   Frances E. O'Brien, Med.Libn.

DORCHESTER HISTORICAL SOCIETY - ROBINSON-LEHANE LIBRARY
195 Boston St.   Phone: (617) 436-8367
Dorchester, MA 02125   Anthony Mitchell Sammarco, Vice Pres.

LEWIS (Elma) SCHOOL OF FINE ARTS - LIBRARY
122 Elm Hill Ave.   Phone: (617) 442-8820
Dorchester, MA 02121

NICHOLS COLLEGE - CONANT LIBRARY
                                                 Phone: (617) 943-1560
Dudley, MA 01570   Cheryl S. Nelson, Lib.Dir.

BATTELLE NEW ENGLAND MARINE RESEARCH LABORATORIES - LIBRARY
397 Washington St.
Box AH   Phone: (617) 934-5682
Duxbury, MA 02332   Joanne I. Lahey, Libn.

CONNECTICUT RIVER WATERSHED COUNCIL - LIBRARY
125 Combs Rd.   Phone: (413) 584-0057
Easthampton, MA 01027   Terry Blunt, Exec.Dir.

DUKES COUNTY HISTORICAL SOCIETY - LIBRARY
Cooke & School Sts.
Box 827   Phone: (617) 627-4441
Edgartown, MA 02539   Thomas E. Norton, Dir.

DUKES LAW LIBRARY
Box 1154
Edgartown, MA 02539

AVCO CORPORATION - AVCO-EVERETT RESEARCH LABORATORY -
   LIBRARY †
2385 Revere Beach Pkwy.   Phone: (617) 389-3000
Everett, MA 02149   Lorraine T. Nazzaro, Libn.

WHIDDEN MEMORIAL HOSPITAL - LIBRARY
103 Garland St.   Phone: (617) 389-6270
Everett, MA 02149   Selma W. Eigner, Libn.

FALL RIVER HISTORICAL SOCIETY - MUSEUM/LIBRARY
451 Rock St.   Phone: (617) 679-1071
Fall River, MA 02720   Florence C. Brigham, Cur.

FALL RIVER LAW LIBRARY
Superior Court House
441 N. Main St.   Phone: (617) 676-8971
Fall River, MA 02720   Mary L. Sullivan, Libn.

MARINE MUSEUM AT FALL RIVER, INC. - LIBRARY
Battleship Cove
Box 1147   Phone: (617) 674-3533
Fall River, MA 02722   John F. Gosson, Cur.

P.T. BOATS, INC. - LIBRARY, ARCHIVES & TECHNICAL INFORMATION
    CENTER
U.S.S. Massachusetts, Battleship Cove   Phone: (617) 678-1100
Fall River, MA 02721   Frank J. Szczepaniak, P.T. Boat Coord.

ST. ANNE'S HOSPITAL - SULLIVAN MEDICAL LIBRARY
795 Middle St.   Phone: (617) 674-5741
Fall River, MA 02722   Elaine M. Crites, Med.Libn.

TEMPLE BETH-EL - ZISKIND MEMORIAL LIBRARY
385 High St.   Phone: (617) 674-3529
Fall River, MA 02720   Ida C. Pollock, Libn.

U.S.S. MASSACHUSETTS MEMORIAL COMMITTEE, INC. - ARCHIVES &
    TECHNICAL LIBRARY
Battleship Cove   Phone: (617) 678-1100
Fall River, MA 02721   Mark Newton, Educ.Coord./Cur.

FALMOUTH HISTORICAL SOCIETY - RESOURCES CENTER - HISTORY &
    GENEALOGY ARCHIVES
Palmer Ave. at the Village Green
Box 174   Phone: (617) 548-4857
Falmouth, MA 02541   Charlotte S. Price, Archv.

FITCHBURG HISTORICAL SOCIETY - LIBRARY
50 Grove St.
Box 953
Fitchburg, MA 01420   Eleanora F. West, Cur. of Musm.

FITCHBURG LAW LIBRARY
Superior Court House
84 Elm St.   Phone: (617) 345-6726
Fitchburg, MA 01420   Ann E. O'Connor, Law Libn.

FITCHBURG STATE COLLEGE - LIBRARY
Pearl St.   Phone: (617) 345-2151
Fitchburg, MA 01420   William T. Casey, Lib.Dir.

U.S. ARMY HOSPITALS - CUTLER ARMY HOSPITAL - MEDICAL LIBRARY
                                            Phone: (617) 796-6750
Ft. Devens, MA 01433   Mrs. Leslie R. Seidel, Med.Libn.

U.S. ARMY INTELLIGENCE SCHOOL, DEVENS - LIBRARY †
                                            Phone: (617) 796-3413
Ft. Devens, MA 01433   Ornella L. Pensyl, Chf.

FOXBORO COMPANY - RD & E LIBRARY †
38 Neponset Ave.   Phone: (617) 543-8750
Foxboro, MA 02035   Helen E. Stevens, Tech.Libn.

CUSHING HOSPITAL - PROFESSIONAL LIBRARY
Dudley Rd.
Box 190   Phone: (617) 872-4301
Framingham, MA 01701   Susan M. Wald, Libn.

DENNISON MANUFACTURING COMPANY - RESEARCH LIBRARY
300 Howard St.   Phone: (617) 879-0511
Framingham, MA 01701   Eva M. Bonis, Mgr., Corp.Info.Rsrcs.

FRAMINGHAM UNION HOSPITAL - CESARE GEORGE TEDESCHI LIBRARY
115 Lincoln St.   Phone: (617) 879-7111
Framingham, MA 01701   Sandra Clevesy, Dir.Lib.Serv.

INTERNATIONAL DATA CORPORATION - INFORMATION CENTER
5 Speen St.   Phone: (617) 872-8200
Framingham, MA 01701   Mary Jo McSorley, Mgr.

MASSACHUSETTS SOCIETY FOR THE PREVENTION OF CRUELTY TO
    ANIMALS (SPCA) - HUMANE EDUCATION LIBRARY
450 Salem End Rd.   Phone: (617) 879-5345
Framingham, MA 01701   Marshall McKee, Libn./Cur. Designer

NEW ENGLAND WILD FLOWER SOCIETY, INC. - LAWRENCE NEWCOMB
    LIBRARY
Hemenway Rd.   Phone: (617) 877-7630
Framingham, MA 01701   Mary M. Walker, Libn.

PRIME COMPUTER, INC. - INFORMATION CENTER †
500 Old Connecticut Path   Phone: (617) 879-2960
Framingham, MA 01701   Linda Loring Shea, Corp.Libn.

RETORT, INC. - LIBRARY *
Tam O'Shanter Rd.   Phone: (617) 528-6404
Franklin, MA 02038   E.H. Rosenberg, Pres.

CAPE ANN HISTORICAL ASSOCIATION - LIBRARY
27 Pleasant St.   Phone: (617) 283-0455
Gloucester, MA 01930

AMERICAN INSTITUTE FOR ECONOMIC RESEARCH - E.C. HARWOOD
    LIBRARY
Division St.   Phone: (413) 528-1216
Great Barrington, MA 01230   Laura Tucker, Libn.

FRANKLIN LAW LIBRARY
Court House   Phone: (413) 772-6580
Greenfield, MA 01301   Marilyn M. Lee, Law Libn.

GREENFIELD COMMUNITY COLLEGE FOUNDATION - ARCHIBALD MAC
    LEISH COLLECTION
One College Dr.   Phone: (413) 774-3131
Greenfield, MA 01301   Margaret E.C. Howland, Cur.

GREENFIELD COMMUNITY COLLEGE - PIONEER VALLEY RESOURCE CENTER
One College Dr.   Phone: (413) 774-3131
Greenfield, MA 01301   Carol G. Letson, Libn.

HANDWRITING ANALYSIS RESEARCH LIBRARY
91 Washington St.   Phone: (413) 774-4667
Greenfield, MA 01301   Robert E. Backman, Cur.

U.S. AIR FORCE BASE - HANSCOM BASE LIBRARY
FL 2835   Phone: (617) 861-2177
Hanscom AFB, MA 01731   Gerald T. Griffin, Chf., Lib.Br.

FRUITLANDS MUSEUMS - LIBRARY
Prospect Hill Rd.
R.R. 2, Box 87   Phone: (617) 456-3924
Harvard, MA 01451   Richard S. Reed, Musm.Dir.

HOGAN (Charles V.) REGIONAL CENTER - REGIONAL RESOURCE LIBRARY
Box A   Phone: (617) 774-5000
Hathorne, MA 01937   Bonnie Stecher, Libn.

HOGAN (Charles V.) REGIONAL CENTER - STAFF LIBRARY
Box A   Phone: (617) 774-5000
Hathorne, MA 01937   Bonnie Stecher, Libn.

HAVERHILL MUNICIPAL (Hale) HOSPITAL - MEDICAL LIBRARY
40 Buttonwoods Ave.   Phone: (617) 372-7141
Haverhill, MA 01830   Eleanor Howard, Med.Libn.

HAVERHILL PUBLIC LIBRARY - SPECIAL COLLECTIONS DIVISION
99 Main St.   Phone: (617) 373-1586
Haverhill, MA 01830   Gregory H. Laing, Cur./Genealogist

DIGITAL EQUIPMENT CORPORATION - HUDSON LSI LIBRARY
HLO2-2/NO6
77 Reed Rd.   Phone: (617) 568-5258
Hudson, MA 01749   E. Ann Baker-Shear, Lib.Mgr.

FAULKNER HOSPITAL - INGERSOLL BOWDITCH LIBRARY
1153 Centre St.   Phone: (617) 522-5800
Jamaica Plain, MA 02130   Barbara P. Pastan, Lib.Dir.

SHATTUCK (Lemuel) HOSPITAL - MEDICAL LIBRARY
170 Morton St.   Phone: (617) 522-8110
Jamaica Plain, MA 02130   Beth C. Poisson, Libn.

LAKEVILLE HOSPITAL - HEALTH SCIENCES LIBRARY *
Main St.   Phone: (617) 947-1231
Lakeville, MA 02346   Janet Doherty, Libn.

LAWRENCE EAGLE TRIBUNE - LIBRARY
Box 100   Phone: (617) 685-1000
Lawrence, MA 01842   Cheryl Lynch, Libn.

LAWRENCE GENERAL HOSPITAL - HEALTH SCIENCE LIBRARY
One General Street   Phone: (617) 683-4000
Lawrence, MA 01842   Carmel M. Gram, Dir., Lib.Serv.

LAWRENCE LAW LIBRARY
Superior Court House
Appleton Way   Phone: (617) 687-7608
Lawrence, MA 01840   Natalie C. Ballard, Libn.

BERKSHIRE CHRISTIAN COLLEGE - DR. LINDEN J. CARTER LIBRARY
200 Stockbridge Rd.   Phone: (413) 637-0838
Lenox, MA 01240   Lois W. Jones, Dir. of Lib.

MASSACHUSETTS AUDUBON SOCIETY - BERKSHIRE SANCTUARIES -
    LIBRARY *
Pleasant Valley Wildlife Sanctuary   Phone: (413) 637-0320
Lenox, MA 01240   Lowell McAllister, Dir.

AMERICAN HOECHST CORPORATION - TECHNICAL INFORMATION CENTER
289 N. Main St.   Phone: (617) 534-2430
Leominster, MA 01720   Nancy Franzen Barringer, Libn.

ALLIED CORPORATION - INSTRUMENTATION LABORATORY - LIBRARY
113 Hartwell Ave.   Phone: (617) 861-0710
Lexington, MA 02173   Jacqueline R. Kates, Mgr., Lib.Serv.

HONEYWELL, INC. - ELECTRO-OPTICS DIVISION - TECHNICAL LIBRARY
2 Forbes Rd.   Phone: (617) 863-3756
Lexington, MA 02173   Kathleen A. Long, Mgr., Tech.Info.Serv.

ITEK CORPORATION - OPTICAL SYSTEMS DIVISION - LIBRARY
10 Maguire Rd.   Phone: (617) 276-2643
Lexington, MA 02173   Dorothy B. Cowe, Sr.Tech.Libn.

LEXINGTON HISTORICAL SOCIETY, INC. - LIBRARY
Box 514   Phone: (617) 861-0928
Lexington, MA 02173   S. Lawrence Whipple, Archv.

LEXINGTON PUBLIC SCHOOLS - CURRICULUM RESOURCE CENTER *
9 Philip Rd.   Phone: (617) 862-7500
Lexington, MA 02173   Martha Stanton, Coord.

MASSACHUSETTS INSTITUTE OF TECHNOLOGY - LINCOLN LABORATORY
    LIBRARY
Box 73   Phone: (617) 863-5500
Lexington, MA 02173-0073   Jane H. Katayama, Lib.Mgr.

MASSACHUSETTS VOCATIONAL CURRICULUM RESOURCE CENTER -
    MVCRC LIBRARY
758 Marrett Rd.   Phone: (617) 863-1863
Lexington, MA 02173-7398   Virginia M. Day, Libn.

MUSEUM OF OUR NATIONAL HERITAGE - VAN GORDEN-WILLIAMS
    LIBRARY
33 Marrett Rd.   Phone: (617) 861-6559
Lexington, MA 02173   Clement M. Silvestro, Dir./Libn.

RAYTHEON COMPANY - BUSINESS INFORMATION CENTER
141 Spring St.   Phone: (617) 862-6600
Lexington, MA 02173   Dayle Reilly, Mgr.

RAYTHEON COMPANY - LAW LIBRARY †
Office of the General Counsel
141 Spring St.   Phone: (617) 862-6600
Lexington, MA 02173   Joan Cook, Libn.

RAYTHEON COMPANY - RESEARCH DIVISION - LIBRARY
131 Spring St.   Phone: (617) 863-5300
Lexington, MA 02173   Martha C. Adamson, Hd.Libn.

WOMEN'S INTERNATIONAL NETWORK
187 Grant St.   Phone: (617) 862-9431
Lexington, MA 02173   Fran P. Hosken, Ed.

XEROX CORPORATION - GINN AND COMPANY LIBRARY
191 Spring St.   Phone: (617) 861-1670
Lexington, MA 02173   Constance J. LeBeau, Libn.

DE CORDOVA MUSEUM - LIBRARY
Sandy Pond Rd.   Phone: (617) 259-8355
Lincoln, MA 01773   Bee Warren, Libn.

MASSACHUSETTS AUDUBON SOCIETY - HATHEWAY RESOURCE CENTER
                                                   Phone: (617) 259-9500
Lincoln, MA 01773   Louise Maglione, Dir.

INFORONICS, INC. - TECHNICAL LIBRARY
550 Newton Rd.   Phone: (617) 486-8976
Littleton, MA 01460   Sandra Dennis, Mgr., Lib.Serv.

LOWELL GENERAL HOSPITAL - HEALTH SCIENCE LIBRARY
295 Varnum Ave.   Phone: (617) 454-0411
Lowell, MA 01854   Helen Sponseller, Libn.

LOWELL LAW LIBRARY
Superior Court House
360 Gorham St.   Phone: (617) 452-9301
Lowell, MA 01852   Karen J. Edwards, Law Libn.

ST. JOHN'S HOSPITAL - HEALTH SCIENCE LIBRARY
Hospital Dr.   Phone: (617) 458-1411
Lowell, MA 01852   Gale Cogan, Dir.

ST. JOSEPH'S HOSPITAL - HEALTH SCIENCE LIBRARY
220 Pawtucket St.   Phone: (617) 453-1761
Lowell, MA 01854   Anne C. Dick, Libn.

SOCIETY FOR THE PRESERVATION OF COLONIAL CULTURE - LIBRARY
c/o 10th Foot Royal
Lincolnshire Regimental Assn.
52 New Spalding St.
Lowell, MA 01851

UNIVERSITY OF LOWELL, NORTH CAMPUS - ALUMNI/LYDON LIBRARY †
1 University Ave.   Phone: (617) 452-5000
Lowell, MA 01854   Joseph V. Kopycinski, Dir.

UNIVERSITY OF LOWELL, NORTH CAMPUS - UNIVERSITY LIBRARIES -
    SPECIAL COLLECTIONS
1 University Ave.   Phone: (617) 454-7811
Lowell, MA 01854   Martha Mayo, Hd., Spec.Coll.

UNIVERSITY OF LOWELL, SOUTH CAMPUS - DANIEL H. O'LEARY LIBRARY -
    SPECIAL COLLECTIONS
Wilder St.   Phone: (617) 452-5000
Lowell, MA 01854   Rosanna Kowalewski, Act.Dir. of Univ.Libs.

INTERNATIONAL OLD LACERS, INC. - LIBRARY
Box 346   Phone: (413) 583-2040
Ludlow, MA 01056   Rachel E. Wareham, Libn.

GENERAL ELECTRIC COMPANY - AIRCRAFT ENGINE BUSINESS GROUP -
    DR. C.W. SMITH TECHNICAL INFORMATION CTR., 24001
1000 Western Ave.   Phone: (617) 594-5363
Lynn, MA 01910   Sandra S. Moltz, Supv.

HASTINGS & SONS PUBLISHERS - DAILY EVENING ITEM - NEWSPAPER
  MORGUE
38 Exchange St.   Phone: (617) 593-7700
Lynn, MA 01903   NancyAnn Rogers, Res.Libn.

LYNN HISTORICAL SOCIETY/MUSEUM - LIBRARY
125 Green St.   Phone: (617) 592-2465
Lynn, MA 01902   Joan Reynolds, Libn.

LYNN HOSPITAL - HEALTH SCIENCES LIBRARY
212 Boston St.   Phone: (617) 598-5100
Lynn, MA 01904   Elaine P. Rigby, Health Sci.Libn.

MALDEN HISTORICAL SOCIETY - LIBRARY
36 Salem St.   Phone: (617) 324-0220
Malden, MA 02148   Dorathy L. Rothe, Cur.

MALDEN HOSPITAL - MEDICAL LIBRARY
Hospital Rd.   Phone: (617) 322-7560
Malden, MA 02148   Elizabeth J. O'Brien, Libn.

MALDEN HOSPITAL - SCHOOL OF NURSING LIBRARY
Hospital Rd.   Phone: (617) 322-7560
Malden, MA 02148   Elizabeth O'Brien, Libn.

MANCHESTER HISTORICAL SOCIETY - LIBRARY
10 Union St.   Phone: (617) 526-7230
Manchester, MA 01944   Esther W. Proctor, Libn.

CODEX CORPORATION - CORPORATE LIBRARY
20 Cabot Blvd.   Phone: (617) 364-2000
Mansfield, MA 02048   Doris Friedeborn, Corp.Libn.

MARBLEHEAD HISTORICAL SOCIETY - JEREMIAH LEE MANSION - LIBRARY
161 Washington St.
Box 1048   Phone: (617) 631-1069
Marblehead, MA 01945

DIGITAL EQUIPMENT CORPORATION - MARLBORO LIBRARY
200 Forest St., MR01-2/A94   Phone: (617) 467-5040
Marlboro, MA 01752   Michelle Johnson, Lib.Mgr.

MARLBOROUGH HOSPITAL - HEALTH SCIENCE LIBRARY
57 Union St.   Phone: (617) 485-1121
Marlborough, MA 01752   Eleanor Kunen, Libn.

NEW ENGLAND TELEPHONE LEARNING CENTER - RESOURCE CENTER †
280 Locke Dr.   Phone: (617) 480-2331
Marlborough, MA 01572   Mark F. Mancevice, Dir., Resource Ctr.

DIGITAL EQUIPMENT CORPORATION - MAYNARD AREA INFORMATION
  SERVICES
146 Main St., MLO 4-3/A20   Phone: (617) 493-6231
Maynard, MA 01754-2571   Janice Eifrig

CORNING GLASS WORKS/CORNING MEDICAL & SCIENTIFIC - DAVID R.
  STEINBERG INFORMATION CENTER
63 North St.   Phone: (617) 359-7711
Medfield, MA 02052   Elizabeth Geiger, Info.Spec./Mkt.Res.

MEDFIELD HISTORICAL SOCIETY - LIBRARY
6 Pleasant St.
Box 233
Medfield, MA 02052   Connie Sabbag, Libn.

MEDFIELD STATE HOSPITAL - MEDICAL LIBRARY
Hospital Rd.   Phone: (617) 359-7312
Medfield, MA 02052   Jeanne Migliacci, Sr.Libn.

LAWRENCE MEMORIAL HOSPITAL OF MEDFORD - HEALTH SCIENCES
  LIBRARY
170 Governors Ave.   Phone: (617) 396-9250
Medford, MA 02155   Elaine V. LeGendre, Health Sci.Libn.

MEDFORD HISTORICAL SOCIETY - LIBRARY
10 Governor's Ave.   Phone: (617) 395-7863
Medford, MA 02155   Michael Bradford, Treas./Libn.

TUFTS UNIVERSITY - FLETCHER SCHOOL OF LAW & DIPLOMACY - EDWIN
  GINN LIBRARY
                                        Phone: (617) 628-5000
Medford, MA 02155   Natalie Schatz, Libn.

TUFTS UNIVERSITY - MATHEMATICS-PHYSICS LIBRARY
Robinson Hall, Rm. 251   Phone: (617) 628-5000
Medford, MA 02155   Pauline A. Boucher, Asst.Sci.Libn.

TUFTS UNIVERSITY - RICHARD H. LUFKIN LIBRARY
Anderson Hall   Phone: (617) 628-5000
Medford, MA 02155   Wayne B. Powell, Sci./Engr.Libn.

TUFTS UNIVERSITY - ROCKWELL CHEMISTRY LIBRARY
62 Talbot Ave.   Phone: (617) 628-5000
Medford, MA 02155   Pauline A. Boucher, Asst.Sci.Libn.

AMERICAN SOCIETY OF ABDOMINAL SURGEONS - DONALD COLLINS
  MEMORIAL LIBRARY
675 Main St.   Phone: (617) 665-6102
Melrose, MA 02176   Dr. Blaise F. Alfano, Hd.Libn.

FIRST BAPTIST CHURCH - LIBRARY ★
561 Main St.   Phone: (617) 665-4470
Melrose, MA 02176   Ruth Richardson, Libn.

BON SECOURS HOSPITAL - MEDICAL STAFF LIBRARY
70 East St.   Phone: (617) 687-0151
Methuen, MA 01844   Chin-Soon Han, Med.Libn.

ST. LUKE'S HOSPITAL OF MIDDLEBOROUGH - MEDICAL STAFF LIBRARY
52 Oak St.   Phone: (617) 947-6000
Middleboro, MA 02346   Gail Twomey, Med.Libn.

WATERS ASSOCIATES INC. - INFORMATION RESOURCE CENTER
Maple St.   Phone: (617) 478-2000
Milford, MA 01757   Carla J. Clayton, Mgr., Tech.Info.Serv.

CHINA TRADE MUSEUM - ARCHIVES
215 Adams St.   Phone: (617) 696-1815
Milton, MA 02186   Lisa L. Gwirtzman, Registrar/Cur.

CURRY COLLEGE - LOUIS R. LEVIN MEMORIAL LIBRARY - SPECIAL
  COLLECTIONS †
1071 Blue Hill Ave.   Phone: (617) 333-0500
Milton, MA 02186   Dr. Marshall Keys, Dir.

NORTHEASTERN UNIVERSITY - MARINE SCIENCE AND MARITIME
  STUDIES CENTER
East Point   Phone: (617) 581-7370
Nahant, MA 01908   E. Cole, Sec.

NANTUCKET HISTORICAL ASSOCIATION - PETER FOULGER LIBRARY
Broad St.
Nantucket, MA 02554   Edourd A. Stackpole, Hist.

NANTUCKET MARIA MITCHELL ASSOCIATION - LIBRARY
2 Vestal St.   Phone: (617) 228-9198
Nantucket, MA 02554   Dr. M. Jane Stroup, Libn.

LEONARD MORSE HOSPITAL - MEDICAL LIBRARY †
67 Union St.   Phone: (617) 653-3400
Natick, MA 01760   M. Margaret Cheney, Med.Libn.

U.S. ARMY - NATICK RESEARCH AND DEVELOPMENT CENTER - TECHNICAL
  LIBRARY
                                        Phone: (617) 651-4542
Natick, MA 01760   Carol J. Bursik, Chf.

ARCHIVES OF THE AIRWAVES
Box 4
Needham, MA 02192   Roger C. Paulson, Owner

GLOVER MEMORIAL HOSPITAL - MEDICAL LIBRARY
148 Chestnut St.   Phone: (617) 444-5600
Needham, MA 02192   Anita Loscalzo, Med.Libn.

GTE - COMMUNICATION SYSTEMS DIVISION - MAIN LIBRARY
77 A St.   Phone: (617) 449-2000
Needham Heights, MA 02194   Michael D. Snow, Supv., Lib.Serv.

INSTITUTE OF FAMILY HISTORY & GENEALOGY - LIBRARY
99 Ash St.   Phone: (617) 994-4616
New Bedford, MA 02740   Joseph M. Glynn, Jr., Dir./Libn.

IRISH GENEALOGICAL SOCIETY - LIBRARY
99 Ash St.   Phone: (617) 994-4616
New Bedford, MA 02740   Joseph M. Glynn, Jr., Dir./Libn.

ITALIAN FAMILY HISTORY SOCIETY - LIBRARY
99 Ash St.   Phone: (617) 994-4616
New Bedford, MA 02740   Joseph M. Glynn, Jr., Dir./Libn.

NEW BEDFORD FREE PUBLIC LIBRARY - GENEALOGY ROOM †
613 Pleasant St.   Phone: (617) 999-6291
New Bedford, MA 02740   Paul Cyr, Libn.

NEW BEDFORD FREE PUBLIC LIBRARY - MELVILLE WHALING ROOM †
613 Pleasant St.   Phone: (617) 999-6291
New Bedford, MA 02740   Paul Cyr, Cur.

NEW BEDFORD LAW LIBRARY
Superior Court House
441 County St.   Phone: (617) 992-8077
New Bedford, MA 02740   Margaretha E.H. Birknes, Law Libn.

NEW BEDFORD STANDARD-TIMES LIBRARY
555 Pleasant St.   Phone: (617) 997-7411
New Bedford, MA 02740   Maurice G. Lauzon, Libn.

OLD DARTMOUTH HISTORICAL SOCIETY - WHALING MUSEUM LIBRARY
18 Johnny Cake Hill   Phone: (617) 997-0046
New Bedford, MA 02740   Virginia M. Adams, Libn.

SWAIN SCHOOL OF DESIGN - LIBRARY
100 Madison St.   Phone: (617) 997-7831
New Bedford, MA 02740   Martha S. Maier, Lib.Dir.

HISTORICAL SOCIETY OF OLD NEWBURY - LIBRARY
Cushing House Museum
98 High St.   Phone: (617) 462-2681
Newburyport, MA 01950   Wilhelmina V. Lunt, Cur.

BETTERLEY CONSULTING GROUP - TECHNICAL INFORMATION CENTER
One Newton Executive Pk.   Phone: (617) 965-8420
Newton, MA 02162   Libn.

JACKSON HOMESTEAD - LIBRARY & MANUSCRIPT COLLECTION
527 Washington St.   Phone: (617) 552-7238
Newton, MA 02158   Duscha S. Scott, Dir.

NEWTON PUBLIC SCHOOLS - TEACHERS' PROFESSIONAL LIBRARY
100 Walnut St.   Phone: (617) 552-7630
Newton, MA 02160   David S. Whiting, Coord.Libn./Media

SWEDENBORG SCHOOL OF RELIGION - LIBRARY
48 Sargent St.   Phone: (617) 244-0504
Newton, MA 02158   Marian Kirven, Libn.

ANDOVER NEWTON THEOLOGICAL SCHOOL - TRASK LIBRARY
169 Herrick Rd.   Phone: (617) 964-1100
Newton Centre, MA 02159   Ellis E. O'Neal, Jr., Libn.

BOSTON COLLEGE - LAW SCHOOL LIBRARY †
885 Centre St.   Phone: (617) 969-0100
Newton Centre, MA 02159   Sharon Hamby, Dir.

NEWTON-WELLESLEY HOSPITAL - PAUL TALBOT BABSON MEMORIAL
   LIBRARY
2014 Washington St.   Phone: (617) 964-2800
Newton Lower Falls, MA 02162   Christine L. Bell, Dir., Lib.Serv.

ACTION FOR CHILDREN'S TELEVISION - ACT RESOURCE LIBRARY
46 Austin St.   Phone: (617) 527-7870
Newtonville, MA 02160   Paula Rohrlick, Rsrc.Dir.

MCI NORFOLK LAW LIBRARY
43 Clark St.   Phone: (617) 668-0800
Norfolk, MA 02067   Margaret M. Hayden, Law Libn.

SOUTHWOOD COMMUNITY HOSPITAL - MEDICAL LIBRARY
111 Dedham St.   Phone: (617) 668-0385
Norfolk, MA 02056   Isabella M. Callahan, Med.Libn.

NORTH ADAMS STATE COLLEGE - EUGENE L. FREEL LIBRARY - SPECIAL
   COLLECTIONS
Church St.   Phone: (413) 664-4511
North Adams, MA 01247   Ann B. Terryberry, Dir., Tech.Serv./Cur.

SPRAGUE ELECTRIC COMPANY - RESEARCH LIBRARY *
87 Marshall St.   Phone: (413) 664-4411
North Adams, MA 01247   Virginia Kemp, Libn.

AT & T BELL LABORATORIES & TECHNOLOGIES - LIBRARY
1600 Osgood St.   Phone: (617) 681-6752
North Andover, MA 01845   Mary E. Sexton, Lib. Group Supv.

MERRIMACK VALLEY TEXTILE MUSEUM - LIBRARY
800 Massachusetts Ave.   Phone: (617) 686-0191
North Andover, MA 01845   Clare M. Sheridan, Libn.

NATIONAL CENTER FOR STATE COURTS - NORTHEASTERN REGIONAL
   OFFICE - DONALD J. HURLEY LIBRARY
723 Osgood St.   Phone: (617) 687-0111
North Andover, MA 01845   Shirley Ann Conti, Adm.Asst.

NORTH ANDOVER HISTORICAL SOCIETY - LIBRARY
Merrimack Valley Textile Museum
800 Massachusetts Ave.   Phone: (617) 686-0191
North Andover, MA 01845   Mary Flinn, Soc.Adm.

STONEHILL COLLEGE - ARNOLD B. TOFIAS INDUSTRIAL ARCHIVES
Washington St.   Phone: (617) 238-1081
North Easton, MA 02356   Louise M. Kenneally, Archv.

FORBES LIBRARY
20 West St.   Phone: (413) 584-8550
Northampton, MA 01060   Blaise Bisaillon, Dir.

HAMPSHIRE LAW LIBRARY
Court House   Phone: (413) 586-2297
Northampton, MA 01060   Barbara Fell-Johnson, Law Libn.

NORTHAMPTON HISTORICAL SOCIETY - HISTORICAL COLLECTION
46 Bridge St.   Phone: (413) 584-6011
Northampton, MA 01060   Ruth E. Wilbur, Dir.

SMITH COLLEGE - ARCHIVES
                                            Phone: (413) 584-2700
Northampton, MA 01063

SMITH COLLEGE - CLARK SCIENCE LIBRARY
                                            Phone: (413) 584-2700
Northampton, MA 01063   David Vikre, Sci.Libn.

SMITH COLLEGE - HILLYER ART LIBRARY
Fine Arts Ctr.   Phone: (413) 584-2700
Northampton, MA 01063   Karen J. Harvey, Libn.

SMITH COLLEGE - RARE BOOK ROOM
                                            Phone: (413) 584-2700
Northampton, MA 01063   Ruth Mortimer, Cur.

SMITH COLLEGE - SOPHIA SMITH COLLECTION - WOMEN'S HISTORY
   ARCHIVE
                                            Phone: (413) 584-2700
Northampton, MA 01063

SMITH COLLEGE - WERNER JOSTEN LIBRARY OF THE PERFORMING ARTS
Mendenhall Ctr.   Phone: (413) 584-2700
Northampton, MA 01063   Marlene M. Wong, Libn.

U.S. VETERANS ADMINISTRATION (MA-Northampton) - MEDICAL CENTER
   LIBRARY
N. Main St.   Phone: (413) 584-4040
Northampton, MA 01060   Marjorie E. Sullivan, Chf., Lib.Serv.

NORTHBOROUGH HISTORICAL SOCIETY, INC. - LIBRARY
52 Main St.
Box 661   Phone: (617) 393-6298
Northborough, MA 01532

WHEATON COLLEGE - LIBRARY - FINE ARTS COLLECTION
                                      Phone: (617) 285-7722
Norton, MA 02766   Faith Dickhaut Kindness, Fine Arts Libn.

BRIGGS ENGINEERING & TESTING COMPANY, INC. - LIBRARY *
164 Washington St.   Phone: (617) 773-2780
Norwell, MA 02061   R. Wayne Crandlemere, Dir.

FACTORY MUTUAL SYSTEM - FACTORY MUTUAL RESEARCH CORPORATION
    - LIBRARY
1151 Boston-Providence Tpke.   Phone: (617) 762-4300
Norwood, MA 02062   Bruce P. Mattoon, V.P.

RAYTHEON DATA SYSTEMS COMPANY - LIBRARY
1415 Boston-Providence Tpke.   Phone: (617) 762-6700
Norwood, MA 02062   Vicary Maxant, Libn.

OXFORD MUSEUM - LIBRARY
339 Main St.   Phone: (617) 987-2882
Oxford, MA 01540   Gloria L. Edinburg, Hd.Libn.

OXFORD UNITED METHODIST CHURCH - OSCAR G. COOK MEMORIAL
    LIBRARY
465 Main St.   Phone: (617) 987-5378
Oxford, MA 01540

PEABODY HISTORICAL SOCIETY - LIBRARY AND ARCHIVES *
35 Washington St.   Phone: (617) 535-0805
Peabody, MA 01960

HARVARD UNIVERSITY - HARVARD FOREST LIBRARY
Shaler Hall   Phone: (617) 724-3285
Petersham, MA 01366   Catherine M. Danahar, Libn.

PETERSHAM HISTORICAL SOCIETY, INC. - LIBRARY
Main St.   Phone: (617) 724-3380
Petersham, MA 01366   Mrs. D. Gale Haines, Libn.

ART REFERENCE BUREAU, INC. *
Box 1324   Phone: (413) 443-4365
Pittsfield, MA 01202   Polly-Ann Duff, Hd. of Res.

BERKSHIRE ATHENAEUM - MUSIC AND ARTS DEPARTMENT
One Wendell Ave.   Phone: (413) 442-1559
Pittsfield, MA 01201   Mary Ann Knight, Dept.Hd.

BERKSHIRE EAGLE - LIBRARY
33 Eagle St.   Phone: (413) 447-7311
Pittsfield, MA 01201   Madeline F. Winter, Libn.

BERKSHIRE LAW LIBRARY
Court House
76 East St.   Phone: (413) 442-5059
Pittsfield, MA 01201   Jane M. Arvanites, Law Libn.

BERKSHIRE MEDICAL CENTER - MEDICAL LIBRARY
725 North St.   Phone: (413) 499-4161
Pittsfield, MA 01201   Jutta Luhde, Libn.

GENERAL ELECTRIC COMPANY - ORDNANCE SYSTEMS DIVISION -
    ENGINEERING LIBRARY
100 Plastics Ave., Rm. 2168   Phone: (413) 494-4207
Pittsfield, MA 01201   Ann B. Rauch, Tech.Libn.

GENERAL ELECTRIC COMPANY - PLASTICS BUSINESS GROUP -
    INFORMATION RESOURCE CENTER
One Plastics Ave.   Phone: (413) 494-7345
Pittsfield, MA 01201   Nancy J. Kane, Libn.

SHAKER COMMUNITY, INC. - LIBRARY
Box 898   Phone: (413) 447-7284
Pittsfield, MA 01202   Jerry V. Grant, Dir.

PILGRIM SOCIETY - PILGRIM HALL LIBRARY
75 Court St.   Phone: (617) 746-1620
Plymouth, MA 02360   Laurence R. Pizer, Dir.

PLIMOTH PLANTATION, INC. - LIBRARY
Warren Ave.
Box 1620   Phone: (617) 746-1622
Plymouth, MA 02360   James W. Baker, Res.Libn.

GENERAL DYNAMICS CORPORATION - QUINCY SHIPBUILDING DIVISION
    LIBRARY †
97 E. Howard St.   Phone: (617) 471-4200
Quincy, MA 02169   G. Richard Myers, Libn.

MASSACHUSETTS STATE DEPARTMENT OF EDUCATION - BUREAU OF
    OPERATIONAL SUPPORT - RESOURCE LIBRARY
1385 Hancock St.   Phone: (617) 727-5792
Quincy, MA 02169

NATIONAL FIRE PROTECTION ASSOCIATION - CHARLES S. MORGAN
    TECHNICAL LIBRARY
Batterymarch Park   Phone: (617) 770-3000
Quincy, MA 02269   Nancy Corrin, Mgr.

QUINCY HISTORICAL SOCIETY - LIBRARY
Adams Academy Bldg., 8 Adams St.   Phone: (617) 773-1144
Quincy, MA 02169   Lawrence J. Yerdon, Musm.Dir./Cur.

ADDISON-WESLEY PUBLISHING COMPANY - LIBRARY
Jacob Way   Phone: (617) 944-3700
Reading, MA 01867   Betsy Dupuis, Libn.

ANALYTIC SCIENCES CORPORATION - LIBRARY
1 Jacob Way   Phone: (617) 944-6850
Reading, MA 01867   Marian Farley, Dir.

SANDY BAY HISTORICAL SOCIETY AND MUSEUM - LIBRARY
40 King St.
Rockport, MA 01966   Dr. William D. Hoyt, Cur.

METROPOLITAN COUNCIL FOR EDUCATIONAL OPPORTUNITY - LIBRARY
55 Dimock St.   Phone: (617) 427-1545
Roxbury, MA 02119   J. Marcus Mitchell, Pub.Rel.Dir.

ESSEX INSTITUTE - JAMES DUNCAN PHILLIPS LIBRARY
132-134 Essex St.   Phone: (617) 744-3390
Salem, MA 01970   Mary M. Ritchie, Act.Libn.

ESSEX LAW LIBRARY
Superior Court House, 34 Federal St. Phone: (617) 741-0200
Salem, MA 01970   Richard E. Adamo, Law Libn.

PEABODY MUSEUM OF SALEM - PHILLIPS LIBRARY
East India Square   Phone: (617) 745-1876
Salem, MA 01970   Gregor Trinkaus-Randall, Libn.

SALEM HOSPITAL - MACK MEMORIAL HEALTH SCIENCES LIBRARY
81 Highland Ave.   Phone: (617) 744-6000
Salem, MA 01970   Nancy Fazzone, Dir., Lib.Serv.

SALEM STATE COLLEGE - LIBRARY - SPECIAL COLLECTIONS
352 Lafayette St.   Phone: (617) 745-0556
Salem, MA 01970   Neil B. Olson, Dir. of Libs.

SALEM STATE COLLEGE - PROFESSIONAL STUDIES RESOURCES CENTER
Library, 352 Lafayette St.   Phone: (617) 745-0556
Salem, MA 01970   Gertrude L. Fox, Libn.

SALEM STATE COLLEGE - STUDENT GOVERNMENT ASSOCIATION &
    LIBRARY - LIBRARY OF SOCIAL ALTERNATIVES
                                      Phone: (617) 745-0556
Salem, MA 01970   Margaret Andrews, Coord.

U.S. NATL. PARK SERVICE - SALEM MARITIME NATL. HISTORIC SITE -
    LIBRARY
Custom House, Derby St.   Phone: (617) 744-4323
Salem, MA 01970   John M. Frayler, Cur.

U.S. NATL. PARK SERVICE - SAUGUS IRON WORKS NATL. HISTORIC SITE - LIBRARY
244 Central St.
Saugus, MA 01906
Phone: (617) 233-0050
Frank Studinski, Supv. Park Ranger

SCITUATE HISTORICAL SOCIETY - LIBRARY *
Cudworth House, First Parish Rd.
Scituate, MA 02066
Mrs. Philip H. Wood, Libn.

KENDALL WHALING MUSEUM - LIBRARY
27 Everett St.
Box 297
Sharon, MA 02067
Phone: (617) 784-5642
Stuart M. Frank, Dir.

TEMPLE ISRAEL - LEONARD M. SANDHAUS MEMORIAL LIBRARY
125 Pond St.
Sharon, MA 02067
Phone: (617) 784-3986
Janet Perlin, Libn.

WORCESTER FOUNDATION FOR EXPERIMENTAL BIOLOGY - GEORGE F. FULLER LIBRARY
222 Maple St.
Shrewsbury, MA 01545
Phone: (617) 842-8921
Melinda Saffer, Lib.Dir.

SOMERVILLE HOSPITAL - CARR HEALTH SCIENCES LIBRARY
230 Highland Ave.
Somerville, MA 02143
Phone: (617) 666-4400
Celeste F. Kozlowski, Libn.

GORDON-CONWELL THEOLOGICAL SEMINARY - GODDARD LIBRARY
130 Essex St.
South Hamilton, MA 01982
Phone: (617) 468-7111

NATICK HISTORICAL SOCIETY - LIBRARY
Bacon Free Library Bldg.
South Natick, MA 01760
Phone: (617) 653-6730
Iola Scheufele, Dir.

BIRD MACHINE COMPANY, INC. - LIBRARY
Neponset St.
South Walpole, MA 02071
Phone: (617) 668-0400
Barbara E. Mangion, Libn.

U.S. NATL. PARK SERVICE - CAPE COD NATL. SEASHORE - LIBRARY
Marconi Station Site
South Wellfleet, MA 02663
Phone: (617) 349-3785
G. Franklin Ackerman, Chf., Interp.

HARVARD UNIVERSITY - NEW ENGLAND REGIONAL PRIMATE RESEARCH CENTER - LIBRARY
One Pine Hill Dr.
Southborough, MA 01772
Phone: (617) 481-0400
Sydney Fingold, Libn.

AMERICAN OPTICAL CORPORATION - RESEARCH CENTER LIBRARY
14 Mechanic St.
Southbridge, MA 01550
Phone: (617) 765-9711
Dr. Nori Chu, Lib.Adm.

EDWARDS (Jacob) LIBRARY - SPECIAL COLLECTIONS
236 Main St.
Southbridge, MA 01550
Phone: (617) 764-2544
Ronald B. Latham, Dir.

ST. JOSEPH'S ABBEY - LIBRARY
Rte. 31, N. Spencer Rd.
Spencer, MA 01562
Phone: (617) 885-3901
Fr. Basil Byrne, Libn.

AMERICAN INTERNATIONAL COLLEGE - ORAL HISTORY CENTER
1000 State St.
Springfield, MA 01109
Phone: (413) 737-7000
Susan R. Fox

BAYSTATE MEDICAL CENTER - HEALTH SCIENCES LIBRARY
759 Chestnut St.
Springfield, MA 01107
Phone: (413) 787-4293
Isabel Hunter, Dir.

CONNECTICUT VALLEY HISTORICAL MUSEUM - RESEARCH LIBRARY
194 State St.
Springfield, MA 01103
Phone: (413) 732-3080
Gregory Farmer, Dir.

HAMPDEN LAW LIBRARY
50 State St.
Box 559
Springfield, MA 01101
Phone: (413) 781-8100
Kathleen M. Flynn, Law Libn.

MASSACHUSETTS COLLEGE OF PHARMACY AND ALLIED HEALTH SCIENCES - LIBRARY
D'Amour Library
Western New England College
Springfield, MA 01119
Phone: (413) 782-3111
Mark J. Gazillo, Pharmacy Libn.

MASSACHUSETTS MUTUAL LIFE INSURANCE COMPANY - LAW LIBRARY
1295 State St.
Springfield, MA 01111
Phone: (413) 788-8411
Joyce H. Beaton, Legal Serv.Techn.

MASSACHUSETTS MUTUAL LIFE INSURANCE COMPANY - LIBRARY †
1295 State St.
Springfield, MA 01111
Phone: (413) 788-8411
Yvette M. Jensen, Libn.

MERCY HOSPITAL - MEDICAL & HOSPITAL INSERVICE LIBRARIES
Box 9012
Springfield, MA 01102
Phone: (413) 781-9100
Kathleen M. Zuiss, Libn.

MONSANTO POLYMER PRODUCTS COMPANY - RESEARCH LIBRARY-EAST
730 Worcester St.
Springfield, MA 01151
Phone: (413) 788-6911

NAISMITH MEMORIAL BASKETBALL HALL OF FAME - EDWARD J. AND GENA G. HICKOX LIBRARY
460 Alden St.
Highland Sta., Box 175
Springfield, MA 01109
Phone: (413) 781-6500
June Harrison Steitz, Subject Spec.

SMITH (George Walter Vincent) ART MUSEUM - LIBRARY
222 State St.
Springfield, MA 01103
Phone: (413) 733-4214
Richard Muhlberger, Dir.

SPRINGFIELD ACADEMY OF MEDICINE - HEALTH SCIENCE LIBRARY
1400 State St.
Springfield, MA 01109
Phone: (413) 734-5445
Margaret Stoler, Lib.Dir.

SPRINGFIELD CITY LIBRARY - FINE ARTS DEPARTMENT
220 State St.
Springfield, MA 01103
Phone: (413) 739-3871
Karen A. Dorval, Supv./Art Libn.

SPRINGFIELD CITY LIBRARY - WARTIME PROPAGANDA COLLECTION †
220 State St., Rice Hall
Springfield, MA 01103
Phone: (413) 739-3871
Joseph Carvalho, III, Coll.Libn.

SPRINGFIELD COLLEGE - BABSON LIBRARY - SPECIAL COLLECTIONS
263 Alden St.
Springfield, MA 01109
Phone: (413) 788-3307
Gerald F. Davis, Lib.Dir.

SPRINGFIELD LIBRARY AND MUSEUMS ASSOCIATION - CATHERINE E. HOWARD MEMORIAL LIBRARY
236 State St.
Springfield, MA 01103

SPRINGFIELD NEWSPAPERS - LIBRARY *
1860 Main St.
Springfield, MA 01101
Phone: (413) 787-2411
Diane A. Blais, Supv.

WESTERN NEW ENGLAND COLLEGE - SCHOOL OF LAW LIBRARY
1215 Wilbraham Rd.
Springfield, MA 01119
Phone: (413) 782-3111
Donald J. Dunn, Law Libn.

CHESTERWOOD - LIBRARY
Box 248
Stockbridge, MA 01262
Phone: (413) 298-3579
Susan Frisch Lehrer, Cur.

NORMAN ROCKWELL MUSEUM AT THE OLD CORNER HOUSE - REFERENCE DEPARTMENT
Main St.
Stockbridge, MA 01262
Phone: (413) 298-3869
Laurie Norton Moffatt, Cur.

RIGGS (Austen) CENTER, INC. - AUSTEN FOX RIGGS LIBRARY
Stockbridge, MA 01262
Phone: (413) 298-5511
Helen Linton, Libn.

STOCKBRIDGE LIBRARY ASSOCIATION - HISTORICAL ROOM
Main & Elm Sts.
Stockbridge, MA 01262
Phone: (413) 298-5501
Pauline D. Pierce, Cur.

OLD STURBRIDGE VILLAGE - RESEARCH LIBRARY
                                        Phone: (617) 347-3362
Sturbridge, MA 01566   Theresa Rini Percy, Libn.

RAYTHEON COMPANY - EQUIPMENT DIVISION - TECHNICAL
   INFORMATION CENTER
528 Boston Post Rd.   Phone: (617) 443-9521
Sudbury, MA 01776   Joan Dexter, Libn.

SPERRY - RESEARCH CENTER LIBRARY †
North Rd.   Phone: (617) 369-4000
Sudbury, MA 01776   H. Alan Steeves, Libn.

BRISTOL LAW LIBRARY
Superior Court House   Phone: (617) 824-7632
Taunton, MA 02780   Carol A. Francis, Libn.

OLD COLONY HISTORICAL SOCIETY - MUSEUM & LIBRARY
66 Church Green   Phone: (617) 822-1622
Taunton, MA 02780   Lisa A. Compton, Dir.

TAUNTON STATE HOSPITAL - MEDICAL LIBRARY *
60 Hodges Ave.
Box 151   Phone: (617) 824-7551
Taunton, MA 02780

DIGITAL EQUIPMENT CORPORATION - TEWKSBURY LIBRARY
1925 Andover St., TWO/BIO   Phone: (617) 851-5071
Tewksbury, MA 01876   Janet Slinn, Lib.Mgr.

WANG INSTITUTE OF GRADUATE STUDIES - LIBRARY
Tyng Rd.   Phone: (617) 649-9731
Tyngsboro, MA 01879   Eileen Baker, Libn.

MASSACHUSETTS COMPUTER ASSOCIATES, INC. - LIBRARY
26 Princess St.   Phone: (617) 245-9540
Wakefield, MA 01880   Arlene M. McGrane, Libn.

AMERICAN JEWISH HISTORICAL SOCIETY - LIBRARY
2 Thornton Rd.   Phone: (617) 891-8110
Waltham, MA 02154   Nathan M. Kaganoff, Libn.

BAYBANKS DATA SERVICES, INC. - TECHNICAL DATA LIBRARY
400 Fifth Ave.   Phone: (617) 890-2700
Waltham, MA 02154   Merrill Hench, Tech. Data Libn.

BENTLEY COLLEGE - SOLOMON R. BAKER LIBRARY
Beaver & Forest Sts.   Phone: (617) 891-2231
Waltham, MA 02154   John D. Cathcart, Act.Dir.

BRANDEIS UNIVERSITY - GERSTENZANG SCIENCE LIBRARY
415 South St.   Phone: (617) 647-2534
Waltham, MA 02254   Elizabeth Fitzpayne, Asst.Dir., Sci.Lib.

BRANDEIS UNIVERSITY - SPECIAL COLLECTIONS
415 South St.   Phone: (617) 647-2513
Waltham, MA 02272   Victor A. Berch, Spec.Coll.Libn.

CHARLES RIVER BROADCASTING COMPANY - WCRB LIBRARY
750 South St.   Phone: (617) 893-7080
Waltham, MA 02154   George C. Brown, Music Dir.

CORPORATE-TECH PLANNING - RESEARCH LIBRARY
275 Wyman St.   Phone: (617) 890-2600
Waltham, MA 02154   Katherine Blythe, Info.Spec.

GORE PLACE SOCIETY, INC. - LIBRARY
52 Gore St.   Phone: (617) 894-2798
Waltham, MA 02154   Charles Hammond, Dir.

GTE LABORATORIES - LIBRARY
40 Sylvan Rd.   Phone: (617) 890-8460
Waltham, MA 02254   David R. Jelley, Hd.Libn.

HELIX TECHNOLOGY CORPORATION - LIBRARY
266 Second Ave.   Phone: (617) 890-9400
Waltham, MA 02254   Carole B. Shutzer, Libn.

HEWLETT-PACKARD COMPANY - MEDICAL PRODUCTS GROUP - LIBRARY
175 Wyman St.   Phone: (617) 890-6300
Waltham, MA 02154   Susan Saraidaridis, Lib.Mgr.

HONEYWELL, INC. - HONEYWELL INFORMATION SYSTEMS - INFORMATION
   AND LIBRARY SERVICES
200 Smith St., MS 423   Phone: (617) 895-6370
Waltham, MA 02154   Melissa Brokalakis, Mgr., Info./Lib.Serv.

MOBIL SOLAR ENERGY CORPORATION - LIBRARY
16 Hickory Dr.   Phone: (617) 890-0909
Waltham, MA 02254   Dorothy O. Bergin, Libn.

SHRIVER (Eunice Kennedy) CENTER FOR MENTAL RETARDATION, INC. -
   LIBRARY
200 Trapelo Rd.   Phone: (617) 893-3500
Waltham, MA 02154   Jacklyn Collette, Libn.

TELEDYNE ENGINEERING SERVICES - INFORMATION CENTER
130 Second Ave.   Phone: (617) 890-3350
Waltham, MA 02254   Susan Fingerman, Mgr., Info.Serv.

U.S. ARMY - CORPS OF ENGINEERS - NEW ENGLAND DIVISION -
   TECHNICAL LIBRARY
Bldg. 116N
424 Trapelo Rd.   Phone: (617) 647-8118
Waltham, MA 02254   Timothy P. Hays, Chf., Tech.Lib.

U.S. NATL. ARCHIVES & RECORDS SERVICE - FEDERAL ARCHIVES AND
   RECORDS CENTER, REGION 1
380 Trapelo Rd.   Phone: (617) 647-8100
Waltham, MA 02154   Clifford Amsler, Jr., Dir.

WALTHAM HOSPITAL - MEDICAL LIBRARY
Hope Ave.   Phone: (617) 899-3300
Waltham, MA 02154   Alison Coolidge, Libn.

TOBEY HOSPITAL - STILLMAN LIBRARY
High St.   Phone: (617) 295-0880
Wareham, MA 02571   Bonnie C. Hsu, Libn.

GENERAL MICROFILM COMPANY - MICROFORM LIBRARY
70 Coolidge Hill Rd.   Phone: (617) 926-5557
Watertown, MA 02172   Cheryl A. Copeland, Dir., Micropubn.

IONICS, INC. - RESEARCH DEPARTMENT LIBRARY
65 Grove St.   Phone: (617) 926-2500
Watertown, MA 02172   Lorraine C. Baron, Libn.

PERKINS SCHOOL FOR THE BLIND - SAMUEL P. HAYES RESEARCH LIBRARY
175 N. Beacon St.   Phone: (617) 924-3434
Watertown, MA 02172   Kenneth A. Stuckey, Res.Libn.

SASAKI ASSOCIATES, INC. - LIBRARY
64 Pleasant St.   Phone: (617) 926-3300
Watertown, MA 02172   Jeanne M. Clancy, Libn.

U.S. ARMY - MATERIALS & MECHANICS RESEARCH CENTER - TECHNICAL
   LIBRARY
                                        Phone: (617) 923-5460
Watertown, MA 02172   Margaret M. Murphy, Chf., Tech.Lib.

RAYTHEON COMPANY - EQUIPMENT DIVISION - TECHNICAL
   INFORMATION CENTER
Boston Post Rd.   Phone: (617) 358-2721
Wayland, MA 01778   Joanne Portsch, Libn.

EDUCATIONAL RECORDS BUREAU - LIBRARY
Bardwell Hall
37 Cameron St.   Phone: (617) 235-8920
Wellesley, MA 02181   R. Bruce McGill, Pres.

EG&G, INC. - CORPORATE HEADQUARTERS - BUSINESS & FINANCIAL
   REFERENCE LIBRARY
45 William St.   Phone: (617) 237-5100
Wellesley, MA 02181   Raymond J. Champoux

INSTITUTE OF CERTIFIED TRAVEL AGENTS - LIBRARY
148 Linden St.   Phone: (617) 237-0280
Wellesley, MA 02181   Lois Tilles, Dir., Inst.Rel.

WELLESLEY COLLEGE - ARCHIVES
Wellesley College   Phone: (617) 235-0320
Wellesley, MA 02181   Wilma R. Slaight, Archv.

WELLESLEY COLLEGE - ART LIBRARY
Jewett Arts Center   Phone: (617) 235-0320
Wellesley, MA 02181   Katherine D. Finkelpearl, Art Libn.

WELLESLEY COLLEGE - MARGARET CLAPP LIBRARY - SPECIAL
   COLLECTIONS
Wellesley College   Phone: (617) 235-0320
Wellesley, MA 02181   Anne Anninger, Spec.Coll.Libn.

WELLESLEY COLLEGE - MUSIC LIBRARY
Jewett Arts Center   Phone: (617) 235-0320
Wellesley, MA 02181   Ross Wood, Music Libn.

WELLESLEY COLLEGE - SCIENCE LIBRARY
Science Ctr.   Phone: (617) 235-0320
Wellesley, MA 02181   Irene S. Laursen, Science Libn.

FIRST CONGREGATIONAL CHURCH IN WELLESLEY HILLS - LIBRARY
207 Washington St.   Phone: (617) 235-4424
Wellesley Hills, MA 02181   Dr. Lorraine E. Tolman, Lib.Coord.

SUN LIFE ASSURANCE COMPANY OF CANADA - REFERENCE LIBRARY
One Sun Life Executive Park   Phone: (617) 237-6030
Wellesley Hills, MA 02181   Pamela A. Mahaney, Libn.

GORDON COLLEGE - WINN LIBRARY
255 Grapevine Rd.   Phone: (617) 927-2300
Wenham, MA 01984   John Beauregard, Dir.

NEW ENGLAND BOARD OF HIGHER EDUCATION - LIBRARY
School St.   Phone: (617) 468-7341
Wenham, MA 01984   Joan Doucette, Libn./Archv.

WENHAM HISTORICAL ASSOCIATION AND MUSEUM - COLONEL TIMOTHY
   PICKERING LIBRARY
132 Main St.   Phone: (617) 468-2377
Wenham, MA 01984   Eleanor E. Thompson, Dir.

MASSACHUSETTS STATE DEPARTMENT OF LABOR & INDUSTRIES - DIV. OF
   OCCUPATIONAL HYGIENE - SPECIAL TECHNICAL LIBRARY
1001 Watertown St.   Phone: (617) 727-3982
West Newton, MA 02165   Mary Lim, Libn.

DATA GENERAL CORPORATION - CORPORATE LIBRARY
4400 Computer Dr., M.S. C-236   Phone: (617) 366-8911
Westborough, MA 01581   Roberta Ferguson, Sr.Res.Libn.

NEW ENGLAND POWER COMPANY - TECHNICAL INFORMATION CENTER
25 Research Dr.   Phone: (617) 366-9011
Westborough, MA 01581   William J. McCall, Sr.Tech.Libn.

BOSTON COLLEGE - WESTON OBSERVATORY - CATHERINE B. O'CONNOR
   LIBRARY †
    Phone: (617) 899-0950
Weston, MA 02193   F. Clifford McElroy, Sci.Libn.

CARDINAL SPELLMAN PHILATELIC MUSEUM, INC. - LIBRARY
235 Wellesley St.   Phone: (617) 894-6735
Weston, MA 02193   Ruth Koved, Libn.

CHURCH OF JESUS CHRIST OF LATTER-DAY SAINTS - BOSTON BRANCH
   GENEALOGICAL LIBRARY
Brown St. and South Ave.
Box 204   Phone: (617) 235-9892
Weston, MA 02193   Sue Winmill, Libn.

POPE JOHN XXIII NATIONAL SEMINARY - LIBRARY
558 South Ave.   Phone: (617) 899-5500
Weston, MA 02193   Rev. James L. Fahey, Libn.

CLARK (Sterling and Francine) ART INSTITUTE - LIBRARY
South St.
Box 8   Phone: (413) 458-8109
Williamstown, MA 01267   Michael Rinehart, Libn.

WILLIAMS COLLEGE - CENTER FOR ENVIRONMENTAL STUDIES - LIBRARY
    Phone: (413) 597-2500
Williamstown, MA 01267   Nancy E. Hanssen, Doc. & Env.Stud.Libn.

WILLIAMS COLLEGE - CHAPIN LIBRARY
Stetson Hall, 2nd Fl.
Box 426   Phone: (413) 597-2462
Williamstown, MA 01267   Robert L. Volz, Custodian

ABCOR, INC. - LIBRARY
850 Main St.   Phone: (617) 657-4250
Wilmington, MA 01887   Eileen P. Smith, Libn.

AVCO CORPORATION - SYSTEMS DIVISION - RESEARCH LIBRARY
201 Lowell St.   Phone: (617) 657-2632
Wilmington, MA 01887   Elizabeth M. Howard, Libn.

DYNAMICS RESEARCH CORPORATION - LIBRARY
60 Concord St.   Phone: (617) 658-7685
Wilmington, MA 01887   Sheila Elfman, Lib.Spec.

FLAG RESEARCH CENTER - LIBRARY
3 Edgehill Rd.   Phone: (617) 729-9410
Winchester, MA 01890   Whitney Smith, Dir.

U.S. FOOD AND DRUG ADMINISTRATION - WINCHESTER ENGINEERING &
   ANALYTICAL CENTER - LIBRARY
109 Holton St.   Phone: (617) 729-5700
Winchester, MA 01890   Lisa A. Leone, Ck.

MASSACHUSETTS STATE DISTRICT COURT - FOURTH EASTERN
   MIDDLESEX COURT - LAW LIBRARY
30 Pleasant St.   Phone: (617) 935-4000
Woburn, MA 01801   William Gavin, Law Libn.

NORTHERN RESEARCH & ENGINEERING CORPORATION - LIBRARY
39 Olympia Ave.   Phone: (617) 935-9050
Woburn, MA 01801   Mary Frances O'Brien, Libn.

MARINE BIOLOGICAL LABORATORY - LIBRARY
    Phone: (617) 548-3705
Woods Hole, MA 02543   Jane Fessenden, Libn.

U.S. NATL. MARINE FISHERIES SERVICE - NORTHEAST FISHERIES CENTER
   - LIBRARY
    Phone: (617) 548-5123
Woods Hole, MA 02543   Judith Brownlow, Libn.

WOODS HOLE OCEANOGRAPHIC INSTITUTION - RESEARCH LIBRARY
    Phone: (617) 548-1400
Woods Hole, MA 02543   Carolyn P. Winn, Res.Libn.

AMERICAN ANTIQUARIAN SOCIETY - LIBRARY
185 Salisbury St.   Phone: (617) 755-5221
Worcester, MA 01609   Marcus A. McCorison, Dir.

CLARK UNIVERSITY - GRADUATE SCHOOL OF GEOGRAPHY - GUY H.
   BURNHAM MAP-AERIAL PHOTOGRAPH LIBRARY
950 Main St.   Phone: (617) 793-7322
Worcester, MA 01610   Charlotte Slocum, Libn.

COLLEGE OF THE HOLY CROSS - FENWICK MUSIC LIBRARY
    Phone: (617) 793-2295
Worcester, MA 01610   Dawn R. Thistle, Music & Visual Arts Libn.

COLLEGE OF THE HOLY CROSS - SCIENCE LIBRARY
Science Center Complex   Phone: (617) 793-2643
Worcester, MA 01610   Tony Stankus, Sci.Libn.

EG&G, INC. - MASON RESEARCH INSTITUTE - LIBRARY
57 Union St.   Phone: (617) 791-0931
Worcester, MA 01608   Evelyn M. Brann, Libn.

HIGGINS ARMORY MUSEUM - MEMORIAL LIBRARY
100 Barber Ave.   Phone: (617) 853-6015
Worcester, MA 01606   Walter J. Karcheski, Jr., Assoc.Cur.

MEMORIAL HOSPITAL - HOMER GAGE LIBRARY
119 Belmont St.   Phone: (617) 793-6421
Worcester, MA 01605   Steve Hunter, Libn.

NORTON COMPANY - LIBRARY
One New Bond St.   Phone: (617) 853-1000
Worcester, MA 01606   Joan K. Chaffee, Libn.

RILEY STOKER CORPORATION - LIBRARY
Box 547   Phone: (617) 852-7100
Worcester, MA 01613   Cosette M. Kotseas, Info.Spec.

ST. VINCENT HOSPITAL - JOHN J. DUMPHY MEMORIAL LIBRARY
25 Winthrop St.   Phone: (617) 798-6117
Worcester, MA 01604   Theresa B. Davitt, Libn.

STATE MUTUAL LIFE ASSURANCE COMPANY OF AMERICA - LIBRARY
440 Lincoln St.   Phone: (617) 852-1000
Worcester, MA 01605   Mary F. Duffy, Assoc.Libn.

UNIVERSITY OF MASSACHUSETTS MEDICAL SCHOOL & WORCESTER
    DISTRICT MEDICAL SOCIETY - LIBRARY
55 N. Lake Ave.   Phone: (617) 856-2511
Worcester, MA 01605   Donald J. Morton, Dir.

WORCESTER ART MUSEUM - LIBRARY †
55 Salisbury St.   Phone: (617) 799-4406
Worcester, MA 01608   Kathy L. Berg, Libn.

WORCESTER CITY HOSPITAL - MEDICAL LIBRARY
26 Queen St.   Phone: (617) 799-8186
Worcester, MA 01610   Timothy D. Rivard, Med.Libn.

WORCESTER COUNTY HORTICULTURAL SOCIETY - LIBRARY
30 Elm St.   Phone: (617) 752-4274
Worcester, MA 01608   Wanda H. Sandberg, Libn.

WORCESTER HAHNEMANN HOSPITAL - MEDICAL LIBRARY
281 Lincoln St.   Phone: (617) 792-8567
Worcester, MA 01605   Roger S. Manahan, Libn.

WORCESTER HAHNEMANN HOSPITAL - SCHOOL OF NURSING LIBRARY
281 Lincoln St.   Phone: (617) 792-8567
Worcester, MA 01605   Roger S. Manahan, Libn.

WORCESTER HISTORICAL MUSEUM - LIBRARY
39 Salisbury St.   Phone: (617) 753-8278
Worcester, MA 01609   Jessica S. Goss, Hd.Libn.

WORCESTER LAW LIBRARY
County Court House   Phone: (617) 756-2441
Worcester, MA 01608   Mary A. Terpo, Law Libn.

WORCESTER POLYTECHNIC INSTITUTE - GEORGE C. GORDON LIBRARY
West St.   Phone: (617) 793-5411
Worcester, MA 01609   Albert G. Anderson, Jr., Hd.Libn.

WORCESTER PUBLIC LIBRARY - REFERENCE AND READER SERVICES
Salem Sq.   Phone: (617) 799-1655
Worcester, MA 01608   Penelope B. Johnson, Hd.

WORCESTER STATE COLLEGE - LEARNING RESOURCES CENTER
486 Chandler St.   Phone: (617) 793-8027
Worcester, MA 01602   Bruce Plummer, Dir.

WORCESTER TELEGRAM AND GAZETTE, INC. - LIBRARY
20 Franklin St.   Phone: (617) 793-9240
Worcester, MA 01613   Sharon C. Carter, Libn.

WORCESTER VOCATIONAL SCHOOLS - GEORGE I. ALDEN LIBRARY
26 Salisbury St.   Phone: (617) 799-1945
Worcester, MA 01608

MICHIGAN

BIXBY (Emma L.) HOSPITAL - PATMOS MEMORIAL LIBRARY
818 Riverside Ave.   Phone: (517) 263-0711
Adrian, MI 49221   Cinda Walton, Dir. of Med.Rec.

LENAWEE COUNTY HISTORICAL MUSEUM - LIBRARY
110 E. Church
Box 511   Phone: (517) 265-6071
Adrian, MI 49221   Charles N. Lindquist, Cur.

STAUFFER CHEMICAL COMPANY - SWS SILICONES - TECHNICAL LIBRARY
3301 Sutton Rd.   Phone: (517) 263-5711
Adrian, MI 49221   Dr. George Wolf, Libn.

U.S. VETERANS ADMINISTRATION (MI-Allen Park) - MEDICAL CENTER
    LIBRARY SERVICE (142D)
                                         Phone: (313) 562-6000
Allen Park, MI 48101   Arlene Devlin, Chf., Lib.Serv.

ALPENA COUNTY LAW LIBRARY
Courthouse   Phone: (517) 356-0395
Alpena, MI 49707   Joyce D. McLain, Law Libn.

BESSER (Jesse) MUSEUM - LIBRARY
491 Johnson St.   Phone: (517) 356-2202
Alpena, MI 49707   Dennis R. Bodem, Dir.

ADP NETWORK SERVICES - MARKETING SERVICES LIBRARY
175 Jackson Plaza   Phone: (313) 769-6800
Ann Arbor, MI 48106   Brenda Larison, Corp.Libn.

AMAX, INC. - CLIMAX MOLYBDENUM COMPANY OF MICHIGAN - AMAX
    MATERIALS RESEARCH CENTER
1600 Huron Parkway   Phone: (313) 761-2300
Ann Arbor, MI 48105   Eva Maria Di Giulio, Libn.

ANN ARBOR NEWS - LIBRARY
340 E. Huron St.   Phone: (313) 994-6953
Ann Arbor, MI 48106   Mary Meernik, Libn.

COMMUNITY SYSTEMS FOUNDATION - NUTRITION PLANNING
    INFORMATION SERVICE
1130 Hill St.   Phone: (313) 761-1357
Ann Arbor, MI 48103   Martha C. Gregg, Libn.

ENVIRONMENTAL PROTECTION AGENCY - MOTOR VEHICLE EMISSION
    LABORATORY - LIBRARY
2565 Plymouth Rd.   Phone: (313) 668-4311
Ann Arbor, MI 48105   Debra Talsma, Libn.

ENVIRONMENTAL RESEARCH INSTITUTE OF MICHIGAN - ERIM
    INFORMATION CENTER
Box 8618   Phone: (313) 994-1200
Ann Arbor, MI 48107   Corliss H. Allender, Mgr.

ENVIRONMENTAL RESEARCH INSTITUTE OF MICHIGAN - INFRARED
    INFORMATION AND ANALYSIS CENTER (IRIA)
Box 8618   Phone: (313) 994-1200
Ann Arbor, MI 48107   George J. Zissis, Dir.

ERIC CLEARINGHOUSE ON COUNSELING AND PERSONNEL SERVICES -
    LEARNING RESOURCES CENTER
School of Education Bldg., Rm. 2108
University of Michigan   Phone: (313) 764-9492
Ann Arbor, MI 48109-1259   Carol Mills, Coord., LRC

FIRST PRESBYTERIAN CHURCH - LIBRARY
1432 Washtenaw Ave.   Phone: (313) 662-4466
Ann Arbor, MI 48104

GUILD OF CARILLONNEURS IN NORTH AMERICA - ARCHIVES
900 Burton Memorial Tower
University of Michigan   Phone: (313) 764-2539
Ann Arbor, MI 48109   William De Turk, Archv.

INSTITUTE OF GERONTOLOGY - LEARNING RESOURCE CENTER
University of Michigan
300 N. Ingalls St., 9th Fl.   Phone: (313) 763-1325
Ann Arbor, MI 48109-2007   Willie M. Edwards, Hd.Libn.

KELSEY-HAYES COMPANY - RESEARCH & DEVELOPMENT CENTER LIBRARY
2500 Green Rd.   Phone: (313) 769-5890
Ann Arbor, MI 48105   Rita Van Assche Bueter, Libn.

KMS FUSION, INC. - FUSION LIBRARY †
3941 Research Park Dr.
Box 1567   Phone: (313) 769-8500
Ann Arbor, MI 48106   Christine Bennett, Tech.Libn.

LUTHERAN CHURCH - MISSOURI SYNOD - MICHIGAN DISTRICT ARCHIVES
4090 Geddes Rd.   Phone: (517) 772-1516
Ann Arbor, MI 48105   Rev. Edwin A. Mueckler, Archv.

MC AULEY (CATHERINE) HEALTH CENTER - RIECKER MEMORIAL LIBRARY
Box 995   Phone: (313) 572-3045
Ann Arbor, MI 48106   Metta T. Lansdale, Jr., Mgr., Lib.Serv.

MC NAMEE, PORTER & SEELEY - MPS ENGINEERING LIBRARY †
3131 S. State St.   Phone: (313) 665-6000
Ann Arbor, MI 48104   Elizabeth G. Brennan, Libn.

MATHEMATICAL REVIEWS - LIBRARY
611 Church St.   Phone: (313) 764-7228
Ann Arbor, MI 48104   Janice Seidler, Hd.Libn.

MICHIGAN MUNICIPAL LEAGUE - LIBRARY
1675 Green Rd.
Box 1487   Phone: (313) 662-3246
Ann Arbor, MI 48106   Carol Genco, Coord.Lib./Inquiry Serv.

MICHIGAN STATE DEPARTMENT OF NATURAL RESOURCES - INSTITUTE
   FOR FISHERIES RESEARCH - LIBRARY
Univ. Musms. Annex,
University of Michigan   Phone: (313) 663-3554
Ann Arbor, MI 48109   Grace M. Zurek, Libn.

NORTH AMERICAN STUDENTS OF COOPERATION - LIBRARY
Box 7715   Phone: (313) 663-0889
Ann Arbor, MI 48107   Karen Zimbelman, Dir., Trng. & Pubns.

U.S. FISH & WILDLIFE SERVICE - JOHN VAN OOSTEN GREAT LAKES
   FISHERY RESEARCH LIBRARY
Great Lakes Fishery Laboratory
1451 Green Rd.   Phone: (313) 994-3331
Ann Arbor, MI 48105   Cynthia McCauley, Libn.

U.S. NATL. OCEANIC & ATMOSPHERIC ADMINISTRATION - GREAT LAKES
   ENVIRONMENTAL RESEARCH LABORATORY LIBRARY †
2300 Washtenaw Ave.   Phone: (313) 668-2242
Ann Arbor, MI 48104   Barbara J. Carrick, Libn.

U.S. PRESIDENTIAL LIBRARIES - GERALD R. FORD LIBRARY
1000 Beal Ave.   Phone: (313) 668-2218
Ann Arbor, MI 48109   Dr. Don W. Wilson, Dir.

U.S. VETERANS ADMINISTRATION (MI-Ann Arbor) - HOSPITAL LIBRARY
2215 Fuller Rd.   Phone: (313) 769-7100
Ann Arbor, MI 48105   Vickie Smith, Lib.Techn.

UNIVERSITY OF MICHIGAN - AEROSPACE ENGINEERING DEPARTMENTAL
   LIBRARY
221 Aerospace Engineering Bldg.   Phone: (313) 764-7200
Ann Arbor, MI 48109   Jackie Kuczborski, Sec./Libn.

UNIVERSITY OF MICHIGAN - ALFRED TAUBMAN MEDICAL LIBRARY
1135 E. Catherine   Phone: (313) 764-1210
Ann Arbor, MI 48109   L. Yvonne Wulff, Hd.

UNIVERSITY OF MICHIGAN - ART & ARCHITECTURE LIBRARY
2106 Art & Architecture Bldg.   Phone: (313) 764-1303
Ann Arbor, MI 48109   Peggy Ann Kusnerz, Libn.

UNIVERSITY OF MICHIGAN - ASIA LIBRARY
Hatcher Graduate Library, 4th Fl.   Phone: (313) 764-0406
Ann Arbor, MI 48109   Weiying Wan, Hd.

UNIVERSITY OF MICHIGAN - BUREAU OF GOVERNMENT LIBRARY
100A Rackham Bldg.   Phone: (313) 763-3185
Ann Arbor, MI 48109

UNIVERSITY OF MICHIGAN - BURN CENTER - LIBRARY
200 N. Ingalls   Phone: (313) 763-0555
Ann Arbor, MI 48104   Julia L. Case, Libn.

UNIVERSITY OF MICHIGAN - CENTER FOR CONTINUING EDUCATION OF
   WOMEN - LIBRARY
350 S. Thayer   Phone: (313) 764-6555
Ann Arbor, MI 48109   Patricia Padala, Libn.

UNIVERSITY OF MICHIGAN - CENTER FOR RESEARCH ON ECONOMIC
   DEVELOPMENT
240 Lorch Hall   Phone: (313) 763-6609
Ann Arbor, MI 48109   Carol R. Wilson, Libn.

UNIVERSITY OF MICHIGAN - CHEMISTRY LIBRARY
2000 Chemistry Bldg.   Phone: (313) 764-7337
Ann Arbor, MI 48109-1055   Jack W. Weigel, Libn.

UNIVERSITY OF MICHIGAN - COOPERATIVE INFORMATION CENTER FOR
   HOSPITAL MANAGEMENT STUDIES
M3039 School of Public Health   Phone: (313) 764-1394
Ann Arbor, MI 48109   Gene Regenstreif, Libn.

UNIVERSITY OF MICHIGAN - DENTISTRY LIBRARY
1100 Dentistry   Phone: (313) 764-1526
Ann Arbor, MI 48109-1078   Susan I. Seger, Hd.Libn.

UNIVERSITY OF MICHIGAN - DEPARTMENT OF GEOLOGICAL SCIENCES -
   SUBSURFACE LABORATORY LIBRARY
1009 C.C. Little Bldg.   Phone: (313) 764-2434
Ann Arbor, MI 48109   Joyce M. Budai, Dir.

UNIVERSITY OF MICHIGAN - DEPARTMENT OF RARE BOOKS AND SPECIAL
   COLLECTIONS - LIBRARY
711 Hatcher Graduate Library   Phone: (313) 764-9377
Ann Arbor, MI 48109   Robert J. Starring, Hd.

UNIVERSITY OF MICHIGAN - ENGINEERING-TRANSPORTATION LIBRARY
Undergraduate Library Bldg.   Phone: (313) 764-7494
Ann Arbor, MI 48109   Maurita P. Holland, Libn.

UNIVERSITY OF MICHIGAN - ENGLISH LANGUAGE INSTITUTE - LIBRARY
1013 North University Bldg.   Phone: (313) 764-2413
Ann Arbor, MI 48109   Patricia M. Aldridge, Libn.

UNIVERSITY OF MICHIGAN - FINE ARTS LIBRARY
103 Tappan Hall   Phone: (313) 764-5405
Ann Arbor, MI 48109   Margaret P. Jensen, Hd.

UNIVERSITY OF MICHIGAN - HISTORY OF ART DEPARTMENT - ARCHIVES
   OF ASIAN ART
519 S. State
4 Tappan Hall   Phone: (313) 764-5555
Ann Arbor, MI 48109   Wendy Holden, Cur.

UNIVERSITY OF MICHIGAN - HISTORY OF ART DEPARTMENT -
   COLLECTION OF SLIDES AND PHOTOGRAPHS
107 Tappan Hall   Phone: (313) 764-5404
Ann Arbor, MI 48109   Joy Alexander, Cur.

UNIVERSITY OF MICHIGAN - HOPWOOD ROOM
1006 Angell Hall   Phone: (313) 764-6296
Ann Arbor, MI 48109   Andrea Beauchamp, Prog.Coord.

UNIVERSITY OF MICHIGAN - INST. FOR SOCIAL RESEARCH - INTER-
   UNIVERSITY CONSORTIUM FOR POLITICAL & SOC. RES.
Box 1248   Phone: (313) 764-2570
Ann Arbor, MI 48106   Maia I. Bergman, Archv.Libn.

UNIVERSITY OF MICHIGAN - INSTITUTE FOR SOCIAL RESEARCH -
    LIBRARY
426 Thompson St.
Box 1248   Phone: (313) 764-8513
Ann Arbor, MI 48109   Mrs. Adye Bel Evans, Libn.

UNIVERSITY OF MICHIGAN - KRESGE BUSINESS ADMINISTRATION
    LIBRARY
Graduate School of Business Adm.
Tappan & Monroe Sts.   Phone: (313) 764-1375
Ann Arbor, MI 48109-1234   Carol Holbrook, Dir.

UNIVERSITY OF MICHIGAN - LAW LIBRARY
Legal Research Bldg.   Phone: (313) 764-9322
Ann Arbor, MI 48109   Beverley J. Pooley, Dir.

UNIVERSITY OF MICHIGAN - LIBRARY SCIENCE LIBRARY
300 Hatcher Graduate Library   Phone: (313) 764-9375
Ann Arbor, MI 48109   James E. Crooks, Libn.

UNIVERSITY OF MICHIGAN - MAP ROOM
825 Hatcher Graduate Library   Phone: (313) 764-0407
Ann Arbor, MI 48109

UNIVERSITY OF MICHIGAN - MATHEMATICS LIBRARY
3027 Angell Hall   Phone: (313) 764-7266
Ann Arbor, MI 48109   Jack W. Weigel, Libn.

UNIVERSITY OF MICHIGAN - MATTHAEI BOTANICAL GARDENS - LIBRARY
1800 N. Dixboro Rd.   Phone: (313) 764-1168
Ann Arbor, MI 48105   Laurianne L. Hannan, Coll. Botanist

UNIVERSITY OF MICHIGAN - MEDICAL SCHOOL - LEARNING RESOURCE
    CENTER
1135 E. Catherine St.
Box 38   Phone: (313) 763-6770
Ann Arbor, MI 48109-0010   Judith G. Calhoun, Ph.D., Coord., LRC

UNIVERSITY OF MICHIGAN - MENTAL HEALTH RESEARCH INSTITUTE -
    LIBRARY
205 Washtenaw Pl.   Phone: (313) 764-4202
Ann Arbor, MI 48109   Anne C. Davis, Libn.

UNIVERSITY OF MICHIGAN - MICHIGAN HISTORICAL COLLECTIONS -
    BENTLEY HISTORICAL LIBRARY
1150 Beal   Phone: (313) 764-3482
Ann Arbor, MI 48109   Francis X. Blouin, Jr., Dir.

UNIVERSITY OF MICHIGAN - MICHIGAN INFORMATION TRANSFER
    SOURCE (MITS)
205 Harlan Hatcher Graduate Library   Phone: (313) 763-5060
Ann Arbor, MI 48109-1205   Anne K. Beaubien, Dir.

UNIVERSITY OF MICHIGAN - MUSEUMS LIBRARY
2500 Museums Bldg.   Phone: (313) 764-0467
Ann Arbor, MI 48109   Patricia B. Yocum, Hd.

UNIVERSITY OF MICHIGAN - MUSIC LIBRARY
3250 Earl V. Moore Bldg., N. Campus   Phone: (313) 764-2512
Ann Arbor, MI 48109   Peggy E. Daub, Music Libn.

UNIVERSITY OF MICHIGAN - NATURAL SCIENCE/NATURAL RESOURCES
    LIBRARY
3140 Natural Science Bldg.   Phone: (313) 764-1494
Ann Arbor, MI 48109   Patricia B. Yocum, Hd.

UNIVERSITY OF MICHIGAN - NORTH ENGINEERING LIBRARY
1002 I.S.T. Bldg.   Phone: (313) 764-5298
Ann Arbor, MI 48109   Maurita Petersen Holland, Hd.

UNIVERSITY OF MICHIGAN - PHYSICS-ASTRONOMY LIBRARY
290 Dennison Bldg.   Phone: (313) 764-3442
Ann Arbor, MI 48109   Jack W. Weigel, Libn.

UNIVERSITY OF MICHIGAN - SCHOOL OF EDUCATION & SCHOOL OF LIB.
    SCI. - INSTR. STRATEGY SERV.
3001 School of Education
Corner East and South University Avenues   Phone: (313) 764-0519
Ann Arbor, MI 48109   Elaine K. Didier, Ph.D., Dir.

UNIVERSITY OF MICHIGAN - SCHOOL OF PUBLIC HEALTH - CENTER FOR
    POPULATION PLANNING - REFERENCE COLLECTION
                                                  Phone: (313) 763-5732
Ann Arbor, MI 48109   Ellen Katzer, Libn.

UNIVERSITY OF MICHIGAN - SCHOOL OF PUBLIC HEALTH - PUBLIC
    HEALTH LIBRARY
M2030 School of Public Health   Phone: (313) 764-5473
Ann Arbor, MI 48109   Mary Townsend, Libn.

UNIVERSITY OF MICHIGAN - SOCIAL WORK LIBRARY
1548 Frieze Bldg.   Phone: (313) 764-5169
Ann Arbor, MI 48109   Christina W. Neal, Hd.

UNIVERSITY OF MICHIGAN - TRANSPORTATION RESEARCH INSTITUTE -
    LIBRARY
2901 Baxter Rd.   Phone: (313) 764-2171
Ann Arbor, MI 48109-2150   Ann C. Grimm, Libn.

UNIVERSITY OF MICHIGAN - TRANSPORTATION RESEARCH INSTITUTE -
    PUBLIC INFORMATION MATERIALS CENTER
2901 Baxter Rd.   Phone: (313) 764-2171
Ann Arbor, MI 48109-2150   Ann C. Grimm, Libn.

UNIVERSITY OF MICHIGAN - WILLIAM L. CLEMENTS LIBRARY
S. University Ave.   Phone: (313) 764-2347
Ann Arbor, MI 48109   John C. Dann, Dir.

WARNER-LAMBERT/PARKE-DAVIS - RESEARCH LIBRARY †
2800 Plymouth Rd.   Phone: (313) 994-3500
Ann Arbor, MI 48105   Katherine Owen, Mgr.

WASHTENAW COMMUNITY COLLEGE - LEARNING RESOURCE CENTER -
    SPECIAL COLLECTIONS
4800 Huron River Dr.   Phone: (313) 973-3300
Ann Arbor, MI 48106   Adella B. Scott, Dir. of LRC

WASHTENAW COUNTY METROPOLITAN PLANNING COMMISSION -
    LIBRARY
Court House, Rm. 305
Box 8645   Phone: (313) 994-2435
Ann Arbor, MI 48107   Eve Wuttke, Asst.Dir.

WILSON ORNITHOLOGICAL SOCIETY - JOSSELYN VAN TYNE MEMORIAL
    LIBRARY
Museum of Zoology
University of Michigan   Phone: (313) 764-0457
Ann Arbor, MI 48109   William A. Lunk, Chm. of Lib.Comm.

XEROX CORPORATION - UNIVERSITY MICROFILMS INTERNATIONAL -
    LIBRARY
300 N. Zeeb Rd.   Phone: (313) 761-4700
Ann Arbor, MI 48106   Joseph J. Fitzsimmons, Pres.

BATTLE CREEK ADVENTIST HOSPITAL - MEDICAL LIBRARY
165 N. Washington Ave.   Phone: (616) 964-7121
Battle Creek, MI 49016   Joni Wildman, Dir.

BATTLE CREEK ART CENTER - MICHIGAN ART ARCHIVES
265 E. Emmett   Phone: (616) 963-1219
Battle Creek, MI 49017   Linda Poirier, Cur. of Coll./Exhibitions

BATTLE CREEK ENQUIRER - EDITORIAL REFERENCE LIBRARY
155 W. Van Buren St.   Phone: (616) 964-7161
Battle Creek, MI 49016   Wanda G. Halsey, Libn.

COMMUNITY HOSPITAL ASSOCIATION - MEDICAL LIBRARY
183 West St.   Phone: (616) 963-5521
Battle Creek, MI 49016   Marilyn Cantrell, Dir., Med.Rec.

KELLOGG COMPANY - TECHNICAL LIBRARY SERVICES †
235 Porter St.   Phone: (616) 966-2291
Battle Creek, MI 49016   Emily Weingartz, Tech.Info.Spec.

KINGMAN MUSEUM OF NATURAL HISTORY - LIBRARY
West Michigan Ave. at 20th St.   Phone: (616) 965-5117
Battle Creek, MI 49017   Allison Van Nocker, Cur. of Coll.

LEILA HOSPITAL AND HEALTH CENTER - MEDICAL LIBRARY
300 North Ave.   Phone: (616) 962-8551
Battle Creek, MI 49016   Sr. Mary Georgia Brown, Med.Libn.

U.S. DEFENSE LOGISTICS AGENCY - DEFENSE LOGISTICS SERVICES
    CENTER - LIBRARY
Federal Ctr.
50 N. Washington St.   Phone: (616) 962-6511
Battle Creek, MI 49016   Anna K. Winger, Libn.

U.S. VETERANS ADMINISTRATION (MI-Battle Creek) - MEDICAL CENTER
    LIBRARY
                                                 Phone: (616) 966-5600
Battle Creek, MI 49016   Thomas Pyles, Jr., Chf., Lib.Serv.

BAY COUNTY HISTORICAL SOCIETY - LIBRARY *
1700 Center Ave.   Phone: (517) 893-5733
Bay City, MI 48706   Kathleen Krueger, Cur. of Coll.

BAY MEDICAL CENTER - HEALTH SCIENCES LIBRARY
1900 Columbus Ave.   Phone: (517) 894-3782
Bay City, MI 48706   Barbara Kormelink, Med.Libn.

HENDERSHOT BIBLIOGRAPHY & CONSULTANTS - LIBRARY
4114 Ridgewood Dr.
Bay City, MI 48706   Dr. Carl H. Hendershot, Publ.

WHIRLPOOL CORPORATION - TECHNICAL INFORMATION CENTER
Monte Rd.   Phone: (616) 926-5323
Benton Harbor, MI 49022   Clifford L. Tierney, Mgr.

ANDREWS UNIVERSITY - JAMES WHITE LIBRARY †
                                                 Phone: (616) 471-3264
Berrien Springs, MI 49104   Marley H. Soper, Dir.

FERRIS STATE COLLEGE - LIBRARY
901 S. State St.   Phone: (616) 796-0461
Big Rapids, MI 49307   Mary M. Bower, Dir.

FERRIS STATE COLLEGE - SCHOOL OF PHARMACY - PHARMACY READING
    ROOM
901 S. State St.   Phone: (616) 796-2641
Big Rapids, MI 49307   Mary M. Bower, Dir., Coll.Lib.

OUR LADY QUEEN OF MARTYRS - ST. LUCIAN LIBRARY
32460 S. Pierce   Phone: (313) 644-8620
Birmingham, MI 48009   Ruth E. Brady, Hd.Libn.

TEMPLE BETH EL - PRENTIS MEMORIAL LIBRARY
7400 Telegraph Rd.   Phone: (313) 851-1100
Birmingham, MI 48010   Marilyn R. Brenner, Libn.

CHURCH OF JESUS CHRIST OF LATTER-DAY SAINTS - DETROIT BRANCH
    GENEALOGICAL LIBRARY †
425 N. Woodward   Phone: (313) 647-5671
Bloomfield Hills, MI 48103

CRANBROOK ACADEMY OF ART - LIBRARY
500 Lone Pine Rd.
Box 801   Phone: (313) 645-3355
Bloomfield Hills, MI 48013   Linda Maberly, Temporary Libn.

CRANBROOK INSTITUTE OF SCIENCE - LIBRARY
500 Lone Pine Rd.
Box 801   Phone: (313) 645-3255
Bloomfield Hills, MI 48013   Christine Bartz, Hd.Libn.

D'ARCY, MAC MANUS, MASIUS - LIBRARY INFORMATION SERVICES
1725 N. Woodward Ave.
Box 811   Phone: (313) 646-1000
Bloomfield Hills, MI 48303   Lois W. Collet, Mgr.

IRON COUNTY MUSEUM - ARCHIVES
Box 272   Phone: (906) 265-3942
Caspian, MI 49915   Audrey Ridolphi, Mgr.

COLOMBIERE COLLEGE - LIBRARY
Box 139   Phone: (313) 625-5611
Clarkston, MI 48016   Rev. Stephen A. Meder, S.J., Libn.

JORDAN COLLEGE ENERGY INSTITUTE - LIBRARY
155 7-Mile Rd., N.W.   Phone: (616) 784-7595
Comstock Park, MI 49321   Alison S. Heins, Libn.

DEARBORN HISTORICAL MUSEUM - RESEARCH DIVISION - ARCHIVES AND
    LIBRARY †
915 S. Brady St.   Phone: (313) 565-3000
Dearborn, MI 48124

FORD MOTOR COMPANY - TECHNICAL INFORMATION SECTION
20000 Rotunda Dr.
Box 1602   Phone: (313) 323-1059
Dearborn, MI 48121   Douna Seiler Estry, Supv., Tech.Info.Sect.

HENRY FORD MUSEUM AND GREENFIELD VILLAGE - ARCHIVES &
    RESEARCH LIBRARY *
Village Rd.   Phone: (313) 271-1620
Dearborn, MI 48121   Douglas A. Bakken, Dir.

OAKWOOD HOSPITAL - MC LOUTH MEMORIAL HEALTH SCIENCE LIBRARY †
18101 Oakwood Blvd.   Phone: (313) 593-7685
Dearborn, MI 48124   Sharon A. Phillips, Dir.

SOCIETY OF MANUFACTURING ENGINEERS - SME LIBRARY
One SME Dr.
Box 930   Phone: (313) 271-1500
Dearborn, MI 48121   Paulette Groen, Libn.

AMERICAN CONCRETE INSTITUTE - LIBRARY
Box 19150   Phone: (313) 532-2600
Detroit, MI 48219   Betty Borschell, Libn.

ASSOCIATED GENERAL CONTRACTORS OF AMERICA - INFORMATION
    CENTER *
8100 Schaefer Hwy.   Phone: (313) 342-5100
Detroit, MI 48235   Joan Boram, Libn.

BURROUGHS CORPORATION - CORPORATE INFORMATION RESEARCH
    CENTER
Burroughs Place, Rm. 4C51   Phone: (313) 972-7350
Detroit, MI 48232   David R. Curry, Dir.

BURROUGHS CORPORATION - LAW LIBRARY
Burroughs Pl.   Phone: (313) 972-7895
Detroit, MI 48232   Bernice C. Frank, Law Libn.

BUSHNELL CONGREGATIONAL CHURCH - LIBRARY *
15000 Southfield Rd.   Phone: (313) 272-3550
Detroit, MI 48223   Mrs. George Unterburger, Lib.Cons.

CENTER FOR CREATIVE STUDIES/COLLEGE OF ART & DESIGN - LIBRARY
245 E. Kirby   Phone: (313) 872-3118
Detroit, MI 48202   Jean Peyrat, Libn.

CHARFOOS, CHRISTENSEN, GILBERT & ARCHER, P.C. - LIBRARY
4000 Penobscot Bldg.   Phone: (313) 963-8080
Detroit, MI 48226   Nora L.M. Shumake, Dir. of Libs.

CHILDREN'S HOSPITAL OF MICHIGAN - MEDICAL LIBRARY
3901 Beaubien   Phone: (313) 494-5322
Detroit, MI 48201   Michele S. Klein, Dir., Lib.Serv.

CHRYSLER CORPORATION - ENGINEERING DIVISION - ENGINEERING
    LIBRARY
Box 1118   Phone: (313) 956-4881
Detroit, MI 48288   Phyllis J. Sears, Supv.

CLARK, KLEIN AND BEAUMONT - LAW LIBRARY *
1600 First Federal Bldg.
1001 Woodward Ave.   Phone: (313) 962-6492
Detroit, MI 48226

COMERICA INCORPORATED - RESEARCH LIBRARY †
211 W. Fort   Phone: (313) 222-9377
Detroit, MI 48231   Carol Pollack, Asst. V.P./Mgr.

CONSTRUCTION CONSULTANTS, INC. - LIBRARY
900 Pallister   Phone: (313) 874-2770
Detroit, MI 48202   Joan M. Boram, Libn.

DETREX CHEMICAL INDUSTRIES, INC. - RESEARCH LABORATORIES -
   LIBRARY
Box 501   Phone: (313) 358-5800
Detroit, MI 48232   Sharon Bakaian, Libn.

DETROIT BAR ASSOCIATION FOUNDATION - LIBRARY †
600 Woodward Ave.   Phone: (313) 961-3507
Detroit, MI 48226   Elizabeth T. Stajniak, Dir.

DETROIT COLLEGE OF LAW - LIBRARY
130 E. Elizabeth St.   Phone: (313) 965-0150
Detroit, MI 48201   Mario A. Ceresa, Hd.Libn.

DETROIT EDISON COMPANY - REFERENCE SERVICES
2000 Second Ave.   Phone: (313) 237-9216
Detroit, MI 48226   Susan D. Clement, Supv., Ref.Serv.

DETROIT FREE PRESS - LIBRARY
321 W. Lafayette   Phone: (313) 222-6897
Detroit, MI 48231   Michele Ann Kapecky, Chief Libn.

DETROIT GARDEN CENTER - LIBRARY
1460 E. Jefferson Ave.   Phone: (313) 259-6363
Detroit, MI 48207   Margaret Grazier, Libn.

DETROIT INSTITUTE OF ARTS - RESEARCH LIBRARY
5200 Woodward Ave.   Phone: (313) 833-7926
Detroit, MI 48202   Constance Wall, Libn.

DETROIT JAZZ CENTER - JAZZ ARCHIVE
2626 Webb   Phone: (313) 867-4141
Detroit, MI 48206   Samuel Sanders, Jr., Dir.

DETROIT MACOMB HOSPITAL CORPORATION - HOSPITAL LIBRARY
690 Mullett   Phone: (313) 225-5185
Detroit, MI 48226   Lynn Sorensen Sutton, Corp.Dir. of Libs.

DETROIT NEWS - GEORGE B. CATLIN MEMORIAL LIBRARY
615 Lafayette Blvd.   Phone: (313) 222-2110
Detroit, MI 48231   Betty W. Havlena, Chf.Libn.

DETROIT PSYCHIATRIC INSTITUTE - LIBRARY
1151 Taylor   Phone: (313) 876-4170
Detroit, MI 48202   Rita H. Bigman, Libn.

DETROIT PUBLIC LIBRARY - BURTON HISTORICAL COLLECTION
5201 Woodward Ave.   Phone: (313) 833-1480
Detroit, MI 48202   Alice C. Dalligan, Chf.

DETROIT PUBLIC LIBRARY - BUSINESS AND FINANCE DEPARTMENT
5201 Woodward Ave.   Phone: (313) 833-1420
Detroit, MI 48202   Margaret Hammond, Chf.

DETROIT PUBLIC LIBRARY - FILM DEPARTMENT
5201 Woodward Ave.
Detroit, MI 48202

DETROIT PUBLIC LIBRARY - FINE ARTS DEPARTMENT
5201 Woodward Ave.   Phone: (313) 833-1467
Detroit, MI 48202   Shirley Solvick, Chf.

DETROIT PUBLIC LIBRARY - FOREIGN LANGUAGE COLLECTION
Downtown Library, 121 Gratiot   Phone: (313) 833-9800
Detroit, MI 48226   Celeste Chin, Foreign Lang.Spec.

DETROIT PUBLIC LIBRARY - GENERAL INFORMATION DEPARTMENT
5201 Woodward Ave.   Phone: (313) 833-1400
Detroit, MI 48202   Margaretta Sandula, Chf.

DETROIT PUBLIC LIBRARY - HISTORY AND TRAVEL DEPARTMENT
5201 Woodward Ave.   Phone: (313) 833-1445
Detroit, MI 48202   Anna DiPiazza, Chf.

DETROIT PUBLIC LIBRARY - LABOR COLLECTION
5201 Woodward Ave.   Phone: (313) 833-1440
Detroit, MI 48202   Doris Detwiler, Chf.

DETROIT PUBLIC LIBRARY - LANGUAGE AND LITERATURE DEPARTMENT
5201 Woodward Ave.   Phone: (313) 833-1470
Detroit, MI 48202   Ann Rabjohns, Chf.

DETROIT PUBLIC LIBRARY - MUNICIPAL REFERENCE LIBRARY
Rm. 1004, City County Bldg.
2 Woodward Ave.   Phone: (313) 224-3885
Detroit, MI 48226   Richard Maciejewski, Chf.

DETROIT PUBLIC LIBRARY - MUSIC AND PERFORMING ARTS DEPARTMENT
5201 Woodward Ave.   Phone: (313) 833-1460
Detroit, MI 48202   Agatha Pfeiffer Kalkanis, Chf.

DETROIT PUBLIC LIBRARY - NATIONAL AUTOMOTIVE HISTORY
   COLLECTION
5201 Woodward   Phone: (313) 833-1456
Detroit, MI 48202   Gloria Francis, Chf.

DETROIT PUBLIC LIBRARY - PHILOSOPHY, RELIGION AND EDUCATION
   DEPARTMENT
5201 Woodward Ave.   Phone: (313) 833-1430
Detroit, MI 48202   Geraldine Frenette, Chf.

DETROIT PUBLIC LIBRARY - RARE BOOK DIVISION
5201 Woodward Ave.
Detroit, MI 48202

DETROIT PUBLIC LIBRARY - SOCIOLOGY AND ECONOMICS DEPARTMENT
5201 Woodward Ave.   Phone: (313) 833-1440
Detroit, MI 48202   Doris Detwiler, Chf.

DETROIT PUBLIC LIBRARY - TECHNOLOGY AND SCIENCE DEPARTMENT
5201 Woodward Ave.   Phone: (313) 833-1450
Detroit, MI 48202   George Unterburger, Chf.

DETROIT PUBLIC SCHOOLS - PROFESSIONAL LIBRARY
5057 Woodward Ave.   Phone: (313) 494-1626
Detroit, MI 48202   Charles V. Partridge, Libn.

DETROIT RECEIVING HOSPITAL & UNIVERSITY HEALTH CENTER -
   LIBRARY
4201 St. Antoine   Phone: (313) 494-4475
Detroit, MI 48201   Cherrie M. Mudloff, Libn.

DETROIT SYMPHONY ORCHESTRA - LIBRARY
1 W. Jefferson   Phone: (313) 567-9000
Detroit, MI 48226   Elkhonon Yoffe, Libn.

DETROIT UNIVERSITY CLUB - LIBRARY *
1411 E. Jefferson   Phone: (313) 567-9280
Detroit, MI 48207

DICKINSON, WRIGHT, MOON, VAN DUSEN & FREEMAN - LIBRARY
800 First National Bldg.   Phone: (313) 223-3500
Detroit, MI 48226   Valerie Hanafee, Libn.

DWORMAN (Thomas J.) - LIBRARY
20210 Archer   Phone: (313) 255-2132
Detroit, MI 48219   Thomas J. Dworman

DYKEMA, GOSSETT, SPENCER, GOODNOW & TRIGG - LAW LIBRARY
400 Renaissance Center, 35th Fl.   Phone: (313) 568-6715
Detroit, MI 48243   Suzanne S. Schriefer, Mgr., Lib.Serv.

ERNST & WHINNEY - LIBRARY
200 Renaissance Center, Suite 2300   Phone: (313) 354-4600
Detroit, MI 48243   Brenda Crawford, Libn.

FRUEHAUF CORPORATION - RESEARCH AND DEVELOPMENT DIVISION -
   LIBRARY
10825 Harper   Phone: (313) 267-1504
Detroit, MI 48213   Rita Van Assche Bueter, Libn.

GALE RESEARCH COMPANY - LIBRARY
Penobscot Bldg.   Phone: (313) 961-2242
Detroit, MI 48226   Annie M. Brewer, Sr.Ed./Libn.

GENERAL ELECTRIC COMPANY - CARBOLOY SYSTEMS DEPARTMENT - CSD
LIBRARY
Box 237, G.P.O.
Detroit, MI 48232

GENERAL MOTORS CORPORATION - CADILLAC MOTOR CAR DIVISION -
ENGINEERING DIVISION LIBRARY
2860 Clark   Phone: (313) 554-7689
Detroit, MI 48232

GENERAL MOTORS CORPORATION - LEGAL STAFF LIBRARY †
14-224 General Motors Bldg.
3044 W. Grand Blvd.   Phone: (313) 556-4010
Detroit, MI 48202   Sheila M. Sweeny, Legal Staff Libn.

GENERAL MOTORS CORPORATION - PUBLIC RELATIONS STAFF LIBRARY
General Motors Bldg., Rm. 11-235
3044 W. Grand Blvd.   Phone: (313) 556-2051
Detroit, MI 48202   Nettie H. Seabrooks, Mgr.

GENERAL MOTORS CORPORATION - TAX STAFF LIBRARY
12-135 General Motors Bldg.   Phone: (313) 556-1567
Detroit, MI 48202   Geraldyne J. Musser, Asst.Libn.

GREAT LAKES MARITIME INSTITUTE - DOSSIN GREAT LAKES MUSEUM
INFORMATION CENTER
Belle Isle   Phone: (313) 824-3157
Detroit, MI 48207   John F. Polacsek, Cur.

HARPER-GRACE HOSPITALS - DRUG INFORMATION CENTER
8061 E. Harper   Phone: (313) 571-3140
Detroit, MI 48213   Vivian Terry, Dir.

HARPER-GRACE HOSPITALS - GRACE HOSPITAL DIVISION - OSCAR LE
SEURE PROFESSIONAL LIBRARY
18700 Meyers Rd.   Phone: (313) 927-3277
Detroit, MI 48235   Frances M. Phillips, Dir., Lib. & AV Serv.

HARPER-GRACE HOSPITALS - HARPER HOSPITAL DIVISION -
DEPARTMENT OF LIBRARIES
3990 John R St.   Phone: (313) 494-8264
Detroit, MI 48201   Barbara Coe Johnson, Dir. of Libs.

HENRY FORD HOSPITAL - FRANK J. SLADEN LIBRARY
2799 W. Grand Blvd.   Phone: (313) 876-2550
Detroit, MI 48202   Nardina L. Namath, Dir., Lib.Serv.

HOLY CROSS HOSPITAL - HEALTH SCIENCE LIBRARY
4777 E. Outer Dr.   Phone: (313) 369-9100
Detroit, MI 48234   Elaine Lynette Kissel, Med.Libn.

HONIGMAN MILLER SCHWARTZ & COHN - LAW LIBRARY
2290 First National Bldg.   Phone: (313) 256-7800
Detroit, MI 48202   Jane Williams, Hd.Libn.

HUTZEL HOSPITAL - MEDICAL LIBRARY
4707 St. Antoine   Phone: (313) 494-7179
Detroit, MI 48201   Caryl L. Scheuer, Dir., Lib.Serv.

INSTITUTE OF GERONTOLOGY - GERONTOLOGY LEARNING RESOURCES
CENTER *
Wayne State University
Knapp Bldg.
71-C East Ferry   Phone: (313) 577-2221
Detroit, MI 48202   H. Jean Owens, Dir.

LAFAYETTE CLINIC - LIBRARY
951 E. Lafayette   Phone: (313) 256-9596
Detroit, MI 48207   Nancy E. Ward, Libn.

METROPOLITAN HOSPITAL - MEDICAL LIBRARY
1800 Tuxedo Ave.   Phone: (313) 869-3600
Detroit, MI 48206   Carole M. Gilbert, Dir.

MICHIGAN BELL TELEPHONE COMPANY - CORPORATE REFERENCE CENTER
1365 Cass Ave., Rm. 1200   Phone: (313) 223-8040
Detroit, MI 48226   Karol S. Sprague, Human Rsrcs.Supv.

MICHIGAN CANCER FOUNDATION - LEONARD N. SIMONS RESEARCH
LIBRARY
110 E. Warren   Phone: (313) 833-0710
Detroit, MI 48201   C.J. Glodek, Dir.

MICHIGAN CONSOLIDATED GAS COMPANY - CORPORATE LIBRARY
500 Griswold St.   Phone: (313) 256-5470
Detroit, MI 48226   Kay L. Ames, Corp.Libn.

MICHIGAN OSTEOPATHIC MEDICAL CENTER, INC. - HEALTH SCIENCE
LIBRARY
2700 Martin Luther King Jr. Blvd.   Phone: (313) 494-0470
Detroit, MI 48208   Carolyn A. Hough, Mgr., Lib.Serv.

MICHIGAN STATE DEPARTMENT OF LABOR - MICHIGAN EMPLOYMENT
SECURITY COMMISSION - LIBRARY
7310 Woodward Ave., Rm. 5   Phone: (313) 876-5597
Detroit, MI 48202   Richard L. Daoust, Hd.Libn.

MILLER, CANFIELD, PADDOCK & STONE - LIBRARY
2500 Comerica Bldg.   Phone: (313) 963-6420
Detroit, MI 48226   Katherine A. Green, Hd.Libn.

MOTOR VEHICLE MANUFACTURERS ASSOCIATION (MVMA) -
COMMUNICATIONS LIBRARY
300 New Center Bldg.   Phone: (313) 872-4311
Detroit, MI 48202   Christina C. Kanabrodzki, Commun.Libn.

MOTOR VEHICLE MANUFACTURERS ASSOCIATION (MVMA) - PATENT
RESEARCH LIBRARY
320 New Center Bldg.   Phone: (313) 872-4311
Detroit, MI 48202   James A. Wren, Mgr.

MOTOR VEHICLE MANUFACTURERS ASSOCIATION (MVMA) - STATISTICS
INFORMATION CENTER
300 New Center Bldg.   Phone: (313) 872-4311
Detroit, MI 48202   Jacques J. Evers, Mgr.

MOTOR VEHICLE MANUFACTURERS ASSOCIATION (MVMA) - TECHNICAL
LIBRARY †
300 New Center Bldg.   Phone: (313) 872-4311
Detroit, MI 48202   M. Neil Massong, Info.Assoc.

MOUNT CARMEL MERCY HOSPITAL - MEDICAL LIBRARY
6071 W. Outer Dr.   Phone: (313) 927-7073
Detroit, MI 48235   Joan C. Luksik, Dir.

NATIONAL BANK OF DETROIT - MONEY MUSEUM LIBRARY
200 Renaissance Center, Street Level
Detroit, MI 48243

NATIONAL BANK OF DETROIT - RESEARCH LIBRARY
Box 116   Phone: (313) 225-2840
Detroit, MI 48232   Steven Wecker, Mgr., Lib.Serv.

NORTH DETROIT GENERAL HOSPITAL - MEDICAL LIBRARY
3105 Carpenter   Phone: (313) 369-3220
Detroit, MI 48212   Shirley Garber, Med.Libn.

REHABILITATION INSTITUTE, INC. - LEARNING RESOURCES CENTER
261 Mack Blvd.   Phone: (313) 494-9860
Detroit, MI 48201   Daria Shackelford, Med.Libn./Dir.

ROSS ROY, INC. - RESEARCH LIBRARY
2751 E. Jefferson Ave.   Phone: (313) 568-6117
Detroit, MI 48207   Eloise Lewis, Libn.

SACRED HEART SEMINARY - WARD MEMORIAL LIBRARY
2701 W. Chicago Blvd.   Phone: (313) 868-2700
Detroit, MI 48206   Arnold M. Rzepecki, Libn.

ST. JOHN HOSPITAL - MEDICAL LIBRARY
22101 Moross Rd.   Phone: (313) 343-3733
Detroit, MI 48236   Marie K. Bolanos, Dir.

SARATOGA GENERAL HOSPITAL - HEALTH SCIENCE LIBRARY
15000 Gratiot Ave.   Phone: (313) 245-1200
Detroit, MI 48205   Jean Brennan, Med.Libn.

SINAI HOSPITAL OF DETROIT - SAMUEL FRANK MEDICAL LIBRARY
6767 W. Outer Dr.   Phone: (313) 493-5140
Detroit, MI 48235   Barbara L. Finn, Dir. of Med.Lib.

SOUTHEAST MICHIGAN COUNCIL OF GOVERNMENTS - SEMCOG LIBRARY
800 Book Bldg.
1249 Washington Blvd.   Phone: (313) 961-4266
Detroit, MI 48226   Pamela L. Lazar, Libn.

UNITED AUTOMOBILE, AEROSPACE & AGRICULTURAL IMPLEMENT
    WORKERS OF AMERICA - RESEARCH LIBRARY
8000 E. Jefferson Ave.   Phone: (313) 926-5386
Detroit, MI 48214   Melba Kibildis, Libn.

U.S. ARMY - CORPS OF ENGINEERS - DETROIT DISTRICT - TECHNICAL
    LIBRARY
477 Federal McNamara Bldg., 6th Fl.
Box 1027   Phone: (313) 226-6231
Detroit, MI 48231   Monica Moffa, District Libn.

U.S. BUREAU OF THE CENSUS - INFORMATION SERVICES PROGRAM -
    DETROIT REGIONAL OFFICE - INFORMATION CENTER
231 W. Lafayette St., Rm. 565   Phone: (313) 226-4675
Detroit, MI 48226   Susan Hardy, Coord., Info.Serv.

U.S. DEPT. OF COMMERCE - INTERNATIONAL TRADE ADMINISTRATION -
    DETROIT DISTRICT OFFICE LIBRARY
445 Federal Bldg.
231 W. Lafayette   Phone: (313) 226-3650
Detroit, MI 48226   George R. Campbell, Act.Dir.

UNIVERSITY OF DETROIT - EVENING COLLEGE OF BUSINESS AND
    ADMINISTRATION - LIBRARY
651 E. Jefferson   Phone: (313) 927-1525
Detroit, MI 48226   JoAnn Chalmers, Libn.

UNIVERSITY OF DETROIT - LIBRARY MEDIA CENTER
4001 W. McNichols Rd.   Phone: (313) 927-1075
Detroit, MI 48221   Maris L. Cannon, Adm.Asst.

UNIVERSITY OF DETROIT - SCHOOL OF DENTISTRY LIBRARY
2931 E. Jefferson Ave.   Phone: (313) 446-1817
Detroit, MI 48207   Victor DeSchryver, Dir.

UNIVERSITY OF DETROIT - SCHOOL OF LAW LIBRARY
651 E. Jefferson Ave.   Phone: (313) 961-5444
Detroit, MI 48226   Byron D. Cooper, Dir.

WAYNE COUNTY CIRCUIT COURT - LAW LIBRARY †
1407 City-County Bldg.   Phone: (313) 224-5265
Detroit, MI 48226   Kathleen M. Friedman, Law Libn.

WAYNE STATE UNIVERSITY - ARCHIVES OF LABOR AND URBAN AFFAIRS/
    UNIVERSITY ARCHIVES
Walter P. Reuther Library   Phone: (313) 577-4024
Detroit, MI 48202   Philip P. Mason, Dir.

WAYNE STATE UNIVERSITY - ARTHUR NEEF LAW LIBRARY
468 W. Ferry Mall   Phone: (313) 577-3925
Detroit, MI 48202   Georgia A. Clark, Law Libn.

WAYNE STATE UNIVERSITY - EDUCATION LIBRARY
                                          Phone: (313) 577-4035
Detroit, MI 48202   Theodore Manheim, Hd.

WAYNE STATE UNIVERSITY - FOLKLORE ARCHIVE
448 Purdy Library   Phone: (313) 577-4053
Detroit, MI 48202   Janet L. Langlois, Dir.

WAYNE STATE UNIVERSITY - G. FLINT PURDY LIBRARY
                                          Phone: (313) 577-4040
Detroit, MI 48202   K.L. Kaul, Hd.

WAYNE STATE UNIVERSITY - SCHOOL OF MEDICINE - VERA PARSHALL
    SHIFFMAN MEDICAL LIBRARY
4325 Brush St.   Phone: (313) 577-1088
Detroit, MI 48201   Faith Van Toll, Act.Med.Libn.

WAYNE STATE UNIVERSITY - SCIENCE LIBRARY
5048 Gullen Mall   Phone: (313) 577-4066
Detroit, MI 48234   Emerson Hilker, Hd.

CHURCH OF JESUS CHRIST OF LATTER-DAY SAINTS - LANSING BRANCH
    GENEALOGICAL LIBRARY
431 E. Saginaw
Box 801   Phone: (517) 332-2932
East Lansing, MI 48823   Azalia Benjamin, Branch Libn.

MICHIGAN EDUCATION ASSOCIATION - LIBRARY
Box 673
East Lansing, MI 48823

MICHIGAN (State) DEPARTMENT OF AGRICULTURE - LIBRARY
1615 S. Harrison Rd.   Phone: (517) 373-6410
East Lansing, MI 48823   Kathleen E. Callahan, Lib.Asst.

MICHIGAN STATE UNIVERSITY - AGRICULTURAL ECONOMICS REFERENCE
    ROOM
29 Agriculture Hall   Phone: (517) 355-6650
East Lansing, MI 48824   Pauline Sondag, Libn.

MICHIGAN STATE UNIVERSITY - ANIMAL INDUSTRIES REFERENCE ROOM
208 Anthony Hall   Phone: (517) 355-8483
East Lansing, MI 48824   Carole S. Armstrong, Sci.Br.Coord.

MICHIGAN STATE UNIVERSITY - ART/MAPS LIBRARY
                                          Phone: (517) 353-4593
East Lansing, MI 48824   Shirlee A. Studt, Art Libn.

MICHIGAN STATE UNIVERSITY - BUSINESS LIBRARY
21 Eppley Ctr.   Phone: (517) 355-3380
East Lansing, MI 48824   William S. Stoddard, Bus.Libn.

MICHIGAN STATE UNIVERSITY - C.W. BARR PLANNING AND DESIGN
    LIBRARY
                                          Phone: (517) 353-3941
East Lansing, MI 48824   Dale E. Casper, Libn.

MICHIGAN STATE UNIVERSITY - CHEMISTRY LIBRARY
426 Chemistry Bldg.   Phone: (517) 355-8512
East Lansing, MI 48824   Bernice Wallace, Libn.

MICHIGAN STATE UNIVERSITY - CLINICAL CENTER LIBRARY
A-137, Clinical Ctr.   Phone: (517) 353-3037
East Lansing, MI 48823-1048   Leslie M. Behm, Libn.

MICHIGAN STATE UNIVERSITY - DOCUMENTS LIBRARY
                                          Phone: (517) 353-8707
East Lansing, MI 48824   Eleanor J. Boyles, Doc.Libn.

MICHIGAN STATE UNIVERSITY - ENGINEERING LIBRARY
308 Engineering Bldg.   Phone: (517) 355-8536
East Lansing, MI 48824   Jackson Yang, Engr./Sci.Libn.

MICHIGAN STATE UNIVERSITY - EXTERNAL COURSES AND PROGRAMS
    LIBRARY
Main Library, Rm. WG-5   Phone: (517) 355-2345
East Lansing, MI 48824-1048   Frank C. MacDougall, Libn.

MICHIGAN STATE UNIVERSITY - G. ROBERT VINCENT VOICE LIBRARY
Main Library Bldg., W433-W437   Phone: (517) 335-5122
East Lansing, MI 48824   Dr. Maurice A. Crane, Hd.

MICHIGAN STATE UNIVERSITY - GEOLOGY LIBRARY
5 Natural Sciences Bldg.   Phone: (517) 353-7988
East Lansing, MI 48824   Carole S. Armstrong, Sci.Br.Coord.

MICHIGAN STATE UNIVERSITY - HIGHWAY TRAFFIC SAFETY AND
    COMMUNITY DEVELOPMENT - LIBRARY
University Library   Phone: (517) 353-9309
East Lansing, MI 48824-1048   Frank C. MacDougall, Libn.

MICHIGAN STATE UNIVERSITY - INSTITUTE FOR RESEARCH ON
    TEACHING - INFORMATION CENTER
College of Education
133 Erickson Hall   Phone: (517) 355-1752
East Lansing, MI 48824   David Bolig, Info.Spec.

MICHIGAN STATE UNIVERSITY - INSTRUCTIONAL MEDIA CENTER - FILM
   LIBRARY
                                               Phone: (517) 353-7850
East Lansing, MI 48824   Sue Ann Wilt, Libn.

MICHIGAN STATE UNIVERSITY - INTERNATIONAL LIBRARY
W310-316 University Library   Phone: (517) 355-2366
East Lansing, MI 48824   Dr. Eugene de Benko, Hd., Intl.Lib.

MICHIGAN STATE UNIVERSITY - INTERNATIONAL LIBRARY - SAHEL
   DOCUMENTATION CENTER
W-312 University Library   Phone: (517) 355-2397
East Lansing, MI 48824   Dr. Learthen Dorsey, Libn. & Ed.

MICHIGAN STATE UNIVERSITY - LABOR AND INDUSTRIAL RELATIONS
   LIBRARY
Library E109   Phone: (517) 355-4647
East Lansing, MI 48824   Martha Jane Soltow, Libn.

MICHIGAN STATE UNIVERSITY - MICROFORMS LIBRARY
                                           Phone: (517) 353-3120
East Lansing, MI 48824   Sally A. Hiddinga, Br.Lib.Ck.

MICHIGAN STATE UNIVERSITY - MUSIC LIBRARY
                                           Phone: (517) 355-7660
East Lansing, MI 48824-1043   Roseann Hammill, Music Libn.

MICHIGAN STATE UNIVERSITY - NONFORMAL EDUCATION INFORMATION
   CENTER *
College of Education
513 Erickson Hall   Phone: (517) 355-5522
East Lansing, MI 48824   Joan M. Claffey, Dir.

MICHIGAN STATE UNIVERSITY - PHYSICS-ASTRONOMY LIBRARY
Rm. 229, Physics-Astronomy Bldg.   Phone: (517) 355-9704
East Lansing, MI 48824   Carole S. Armstrong, Sci.Br.Coord.

MICHIGAN STATE UNIVERSITY - SCIENCE LIBRARY
                                           Phone: (517) 355-2347
East Lansing, MI 48824   Carole S. Armstrong, Hd.

MICHIGAN STATE UNIVERSITY - SPECIAL COLLECTIONS LIBRARY
University Library   Phone: (517) 355-3770
East Lansing, MI 48824   Jannette Fiore, Libn.

MICHIGAN STATE UNIVERSITY - SPECIAL COLLECTIONS LIBRARY -
   RUSSEL B. NYE POPULAR CULTURE COLLECTION
University Library   Phone: (517) 355-3770
East Lansing, MI 48824   Jannette Fiore, Libn.

MICHIGAN STATE UNIVERSITY - UNIVERSITY ARCHIVES AND
   HISTORICAL COLLECTIONS
                                           Phone: (517) 355-2330
East Lansing, MI 48824   Dr. Frederick L. Honhart, Dir.

MICHIGAN STATE UNIVERSITY - UNIVERSITY CENTER FOR
   INTERNATIONAL REHABILITATION (UCIR) - RESOURCE LIB.
513 Erickson Hall   Phone: (517) 355-1824
East Lansing, MI 48824   William Frey, Dir.

MICHIGAN STATE UNIVERSITY - URBAN POLICY AND PLANNING LIBRARY
University Library   Phone: (517) 353-9304
East Lansing, MI 48824   Dale E. Casper, Libn.

MICHIGAN STATE UNIVERSITY - V.G. GROVE RESEARCH LIBRARY OF
   MATHEMATICS-STATISTICS
101-D Wells Hall   Phone: (517) 353-8852
East Lansing, MI 48824   Berle Reiter, Libn.

MICHIGAN STATE UNIVERSITY - VETERINARY CLINICAL CENTER LIBRARY
57 Veterinary Clinical Ctr.   Phone: (517) 353-5099
East Lansing, MI 48823-1048   Leslie M. Behm, Libn.

DELTA COUNTY HISTORICAL SOCIETY MUSEUM LIBRARY
Ludington Park, Box 1776
Escanaba, MI 49829   William G. Daniels, Pres.

BIRMINGHAM TEMPLE - LIBRARY †
28611 W. Twelve Mile Rd.   Phone: (313) 477-0177
Farmington, MI 48024

BOTSFORD GENERAL HOSPITAL, OSTEOPATHIC - HOSPITAL LIBRARY AND
   MEDIA CENTER
28050 Grand River Ave.   Phone: (313) 476-7600
Farmington, MI 48024   Deborah L. Adams, Dir.

FIRST PRESBYTERIAN CHURCH OF FLINT - PEIRCE MEMORIAL LIBRARY *
746 S. Saginaw St.   Phone: (313) 234-8673
Flint, MI 48502   Barbara Spaulding Westcott, Lib.Chm.

FLINT DEPARTMENT OF COMMUNITY DEVELOPMENT - LIBRARY
1101 S. Saginaw St., Rm. 6   Phone: (313) 766-7355
Flint, MI 48502   Dianne Montgomery, Adm. Aide

FLINT INSTITUTE OF ARTS - LIBRARY *
1120 E. Kearsley St.   Phone: (313) 234-1695
Flint, MI 48503   Diane Oliver, Act.Libn.

FLINT JOURNAL - EDITORIAL LIBRARY
200 E. First St.   Phone: (313) 767-0660
Flint, MI 48502   David W. Larzelere, Chf.Libn.

FLINT NEWMAN CENTER - LIBRARY AND CATHOLIC INFORMATION
   CENTER
609 E. 5th Ave.   Phone: (313) 239-9391
Flint, MI 48503   Rev. James B. Bettendorf, Dir.

FLINT OSTEOPATHIC HOSPITAL - DR. E. HERZOG MEMORIAL MEDICAL
   LIBRARY
3921 Beecher Rd.   Phone: (313) 762-4587
Flint, MI 48502   Doris M. Blauet, Dir.

FLINT PUBLIC LIBRARY - ART, MUSIC & DRAMA DEPARTMENT
1026 E. Kearsley St.   Phone: (313) 232-7111
Flint, MI 48502   James Kangas, Hd.

FLINT PUBLIC LIBRARY - AUTOMOTIVE HISTORY COLLECTION
1026 E. Kearsley St.   Phone: (313) 232-7111
Flint, MI 48502   Margaret E. Williams, Dept.Hd.

FLINT PUBLIC LIBRARY - BUSINESS AND INDUSTRY DEPARTMENT
1026 E. Kearsley St.   Phone: (313) 232-7111
Flint, MI 48502   Margaret E. Williams, Dept.Hd.

FLINT PUBLIC LIBRARY - CHILDREN'S DEPARTMENT
1026 E. Kearsley St.   Phone: (313) 232-7111
Flint, MI 48502   Marcia Carlsten, Hd.

FLINT PUBLIC LIBRARY - MICHIGAN ROOM
1026 E. Kearsley St.   Phone: (313) 232-7111
Flint, MI 48502   Judith J. Field, Hd., Gen.Ref.

GENERAL MOTORS CORPORATION - AC SPARK PLUG DIVISION -
   ENGINEERING LIBRARY
1300 N. Dort Hwy.   Phone: (313) 766-2655
Flint, MI 48556   Eileen L. Lane, Libn.

GENESEE COUNTY CIRCUIT COURT - LAW LIBRARY
County Court House
900 S. Saginaw St., Rm. 401   Phone: (313) 257-3253
Flint, MI 48502   Janet E. Patsy, Law Libn.

GENESEE-LAPEER-SHIAWASSEE REGION V PLANNING & DEVELOPMENT
   COMMISSION - LIBRARY
G3425 W. Bristol Rd., Suite 239   Phone: (313) 234-0340
Flint, MI 48507   Verna L. McColley, Lib.Techn.

GMI ENGINEERING & MANAGEMENT INSTITUTE - LIBRARY
1700 W. Third Ave.   Phone: (313) 762-7814
Flint, MI 48502   Emily R. Mobley, Dir.

HURLEY MEDICAL CENTER - HAMADY HEALTH SCIENCES LIBRARY
One Hurley Plaza   Phone: (313) 766-0427
Flint, MI 48502   Anthos Hungerford, Dir.

MC LAREN GENERAL HOSPITAL - MEDICAL LIBRARY
414 Chalmers   Phone: (313) 762-2141
Flint, MI 48502   Lea Ann McGaugh, Med.Libn.

MOTT (Charles Stewart) FOUNDATION - LIBRARY
Mott Foundation Bldg.   Phone: (313) 238-5651
Flint, MI 48502   Eve Brown, Rec.Mgt.Supv.

NATIONAL HAMILTONIAN PARTY - HAMILTONIAN LIBRARY
434 Chalmers St.   Phone: (313) 659-7384
Flint, MI 48503   Albert Victor, Libn.

ST. JOSEPH HOSPITAL - HEALTH SCIENCES LIBRARY
302 Kensington Ave.   Phone: (313) 762-8519
Flint, MI 48502   RoseMary Russo, Med.Libn.

SLOAN (Alfred P., Jr.) MUSEUM - MERLE G. PERRY ARCHIVES
1221 E. Kearsley St.   Phone: (313) 762-1170
Flint, MI 48503   Phillip C. Kwiatkowski, Dir.

FRANKENMUTH HISTORICAL ASSOCIATION MUSEUM - LIBRARY
613 S. Main St.   Phone: (517) 652-9701
Frankenmuth, MI 48734   Mary Nuechterlein, Registrar

GERBER PRODUCTS COMPANY - CORPORATE LIBRARY
445 State St.   Phone: (616) 928-2631
Fremont, MI 49412   Sherrie Anderson, Corp.Libn.

BLODGETT MEMORIAL MEDICAL CENTER - RICHARD ROOT SMITH
   LIBRARY
1840 Wealthy St., S.E.   Phone: (616) 774-7624
Grand Rapids, MI 49506   Brian Simmons, Med.Libn.

BUTTERWORTH HOSPITAL - HEALTH SCIENCES LIBRARY
100 Michigan, N.E.   Phone: (616) 774-1655
Grand Rapids, MI 49503   Eileen M. Dechow, Dir.

BUTTERWORTH HOSPITAL - SCHOOL OF NURSING LIBRARY *
335 Bostwick Ave., N.E.   Phone: (616) 774-1779
Grand Rapids, MI 49503   Betty Sherwood, Libn.

CALVIN COLLEGE AND SEMINARY - LIBRARY
3207 Burton St., S.E.   Phone: (616) 957-6297
Grand Rapids, MI 49506   Marvin E. Monsma, Dir.

GRACE BIBLE COLLEGE - BULTEMA MEMORIAL LIBRARY
1011 Aldon St., S.W.
Box 910   Phone: (616) 538-2332
Grand Rapids, MI 49509   Guni Olson, Hd.Libn.

GRAND RAPIDS ART MUSEUM - MC BRIDE LIBRARY
155 N. Division   Phone: (616) 459-4676
Grand Rapids, MI 49503   Luci King, Lib.Chm.

GRAND RAPIDS BAPTIST COLLEGE & SEMINARY - MILLER LIBRARY
1001 E. Beltline, N.E.   Phone: (616) 949-5300
Grand Rapids, MI 49505

GRAND RAPIDS LAW LIBRARY
200 Monroe, N.W., Suite 400   Phone: (616) 454-9493
Grand Rapids, MI 49503   Marjorie C. Wilcox, Exec.Dir.

GRAND RAPIDS PRESS - REFERENCE LIBRARY
155 Michigan St., N.W.   Phone: (616) 459-1474
Grand Rapids, MI 49503   Diane L. Buist, Libn.

GRAND RAPIDS PUBLIC LIBRARY - FOUNDATION CENTER REGIONAL
   COLLECTION
60 Library Plaza, N.E.   Phone: (616) 456-4411
Grand Rapids, MI 49503   James Langmo, Ref.Libn.

GRAND RAPIDS PUBLIC LIBRARY - FURNITURE DESIGN COLLECTION
60 Library Plaza, N.E.   Phone: (616) 456-4410
Grand Rapids, MI 49503   Lucija Skuja, Art Libn.

GRAND RAPIDS PUBLIC LIBRARY - MAY G. QUIGLEY COLLECTION
60 Library Plaza, N.E.   Phone: (616) 456-4403
Grand Rapids, MI 49503   Vicki Ford, Ch.Libn.

GRAND RAPIDS PUBLIC LIBRARY - MICHIGAN ROOM
60 Library Plaza, N.E.   Phone: (616) 456-4424
Grand Rapids, MI 49503   Gordon Olson, Hd.

GRAND RAPIDS PUBLIC MUSEUM - PICTORIAL MATERIALS COLLECTION
54 Jefferson St., S.E.   Phone: (616) 456-3977
Grand Rapids, MI 49503   Marilyn Merdzinski, Registrar

KENDALL SCHOOL OF DESIGN - LEARNING RESOURCE CENTER
1110 College N.E.   Phone: (616) 451-2787
Grand Rapids, MI 49503   Ruth Hornbach, Hd.Libn.

LEAR SIEGLER, INC. - INSTRUMENT DIVISION - ENGINEERING LIBRARY
4141 Eastern Ave., S.E.   Phone: (616) 241-7467
Grand Rapids, MI 49508   N. Scott Brackett, Tech.Libn.

PINE REST CHRISTIAN HOSPITAL - VAN NOORD HEALTH SCIENCES
   LIBRARY
6850 S. Division Ave.   Phone: (616) 455-5000
Grand Rapids, MI 49508   Thomas Van Dam, Libn.

REFORMED BIBLE COLLEGE - LIBRARY
1869 Robinson Rd., S.E.   Phone: (616) 458-0404
Grand Rapids, MI 49506   Joanne Boehm, Libn.

ST. MARY'S HOSPITAL - LIBRARY
200 Jefferson, S.E.   Phone: (616) 774-6243
Grand Rapids, MI 49503   Mary A. Hanson, Med.Libn.

WARNER, NORCROSS & JUDD - LIBRARY
900 Old Kent Bldg.   Phone: (616) 459-6121
Grand Rapids, MI 49503   Dianne Vander Kooy, Libn.

WESTVIEW CHRISTIAN REFORMED CHURCH - LIBRARY
2929 Leonard St., N.W.   Phone: (616) 453-3105
Grand Rapids, MI 49504   Beatrice Dahnke, Libn.

BON SECOURS HOSPITAL - HEALTH SCIENCE LIBRARY
468 Cadieux Rd.   Phone: (313) 343-1619
Grosse Pointe, MI 48230   Sr. M. Bernita, S.S.J., Lib.Dir.

COTTAGE HOSPITAL OF GROSSE POINTE - MEDICAL LIBRARY
159 Kercheval Ave.   Phone: (313) 884-8600
Grosse Pointe Farms, MI 48236   Carol Attar, Lib.Dir.

MACEDONIAN ETHNIC LIBRARY *
920 Shoreham Rd.   Phone: (313) 886-3361
Grosse Pointe Woods, MI 48236   Adrijana Panoska Randolph, Dir./Libn.

FINNISH-AMERICAN HISTORICAL ARCHIVES
Suomi College   Phone: (906) 482-5300
Hancock, MI 49930   Kenneth E. Niemi, Archv.Libn.

CHARLTON PARK HISTORIC VILLAGE & MUSEUM - LIBRARY
2545 S. Charlton Park Rd.   Phone: (616) 945-3775
Hastings, MI 49058   John Patterson, Dir.

PENNOCK HOSPITAL - MEDICAL LIBRARY
1009 W. Green St.   Phone: (616) 945-3451
Hastings, MI 49058   Mary Diane Hawkins, Med.Libn.

MICHIGAN STATE UNIVERSITY - W.K. KELLOGG BIOLOGICAL STATION -
   WALTER F. MOROFSKY MEMORIAL LIBRARY
3700 E. Gull Lake Dr.   Phone: (616) 671-5117
Hickory Corners, MI 49060   Carolyn Hammarskjold, Libn.

DETROIT OSTEOPATHIC HOSPITAL - MEDICAL LIBRARY
12523 Third Ave.   Phone: (313) 252-4830
Highland Park, MI 48203   Lucie Beard, Libn.

BASF WYANDOTTE CORPORATION - PIGMENTS LIBRARY
491 Columbia Ave.   Phone: (616) 392-2391
Holland, MI 49423   Mary K. Johnson, Libn.

DONNELLY MIRRORS, INC. - LIBRARY
414 East 40th St.   Phone: (616) 394-2268
Holland, MI 49423   Nancy Yetman, Tech.Libn.

HOLLAND COMMUNITY HOSPITAL - HOSPITAL AND MEDICAL STAFF
LIBRARY
602 Michigan Ave.   Phone: (616) 392-5141
Holland, MI 49423   Marge Kars, Dir.

NETHERLANDS MUSEUM - ARCHIVES AND LIBRARY
City Hall, 3rd Fl.   Phone: (616) 392-3129
Holland, MI 49423   Dr. Willard Wichers, Musm.Dir.

WESTERN THEOLOGICAL SEMINARY - BEARDSLEE LIBRARY
                                          Phone: (616) 392-8555
Holland, MI 49423   John R. Muether, Libn.

MICHIGAN TECHNOLOGICAL UNIVERSITY - INSTITUTE OF MINERAL
RESEARCH
                                          Phone: (906) 487-2600
Houghton, MI 49931   C.W. Schultz, Dir.

MICHIGAN TECHNOLOGICAL UNIVERSITY - INSTITUTE OF WOOD
RESEARCH INFORMATION CENTER
                                          Phone: (906) 487-2464
Houghton, MI 49931   Karen A. Antilla, Res.Info.Serv.

MICHIGAN TECHNOLOGICAL UNIVERSITY - LIBRARY
                                          Phone: (906) 487-2500
Houghton, MI 49931   Lee J. Lebbin, Dir.

INTERLOCHEN CENTER FOR THE ARTS - MUSIC LIBRARY
                                          Phone: (616) 276-9221
Interlochen, MI 49643   E. Delmer Weliver, Dir.

U.S. VETERANS ADMINISTRATION (MI-Iron Mountain) - MEDICAL CENTER
LIBRARY
East H St.   Phone: (906) 774-3300
Iron Mountain, MI 49801   Phyllis E. Goetz, Chf., Lib.Serv.

NATIONAL SKI HALL OF FAME AND MUSEUM - ROLAND PALMEDO
NATIONAL SKI LIBRARY
Box 191   Phone: (906) 486-9281
Ishpeming, MI 49849   Dr. Russell Magnaghi, Archv.

CONSUMERS POWER COMPANY - LAW LIBRARY
212 W. Michigan Ave.   Phone: (517) 788-1088
Jackson, MI 49201   Beulah I. Standish, Libn.

CONSUMERS POWER COMPANY - PARNALL TECHNICAL LIBRARY
1945 Parnall Rd.   Phone: (517) 788-0541
Jackson, MI 49201   Kay E. Stevens, Libn.

SHARP (Ella) MUSEUM - LIBRARY/ARCHIVES
3225 Fourth St.   Phone: (517) 787-2320
Jackson, MI 49203   Lynnea Loftis, Dir., Educ.

BORGESS MEDICAL CENTER - HEALTH INFORMATION LIBRARY
1521 Gull Rd.   Phone: (616) 383-4868
Kalamazoo, MI 49001   Jackie Mardikian, Dir.

BRONSON METHODIST HOSPITAL - HEALTH SCIENCES LIBRARY
252 Lovell St., E.   Phone: (616) 383-6318
Kalamazoo, MI 49007   Jeanne L. Hartenstein, Dir., Lib.Serv.

FIRST PRESBYTERIAN CHURCH - LIBRARY †
321 W. South St.   Phone: (616) 344-0119
Kalamazoo, MI 49006   Lillian B. Auducon

FIRST UNITED METHODIST CHURCH - ALLEN LIBRARY
212 S. Park St.   Phone: (616) 381-6340
Kalamazoo, MI 49007   Mildred S. Hedrick, Libn.

KALAMAZOO COLLEGE - UPJOHN LIBRARY - SPECIAL COLLECTIONS
Thompson & Academy Sts.   Phone: (616) 383-8481
Kalamazoo, MI 49007   Eleanor H. Pinkham, Coll.Libn.

KALAMAZOO COUNTY LAW LIBRARY - RAYMOND W. FOX MEMORIAL
LIBRARY
227 W. Michigan Ave.   Phone: (616) 383-8950
Kalamazoo, MI 49007   Jeffrey C. Brennan, Law Lib./Bar Assn.Dir.

KALAMAZOO INSTITUTE OF ARTS - ART CENTER LIBRARY
314 S. Park St.   Phone: (616) 349-7775
Kalamazoo, MI 49007   Helen Sheridan, Hd.Libn.

KALAMAZOO NATURE CENTER - REFERENCE LIBRARY
7000 N. Westnedge Ave.   Phone: (616) 381-1575
Kalamazoo, MI 49007   Linda Ormond, Libn.

KALSEC, INC. - LIBRARY
3713 W. Main   Phone: (616) 349-9711
Kalamazoo, MI 49005   Mary Sagar, Libn.

MICHIGAN AUDUBON SOCIETY - EDITH MUNGER LIBRARY
409 West E Ave.   Phone: (616) 344-8648
Kalamazoo, MI 49007   Patricia L. Adams, Off.Mgr.

UPJOHN COMPANY - BUSINESS LIBRARY 88-91
                                          Phone: (616) 323-6351
Kalamazoo, MI 49001   Valerie Noble, Hd.

UPJOHN COMPANY - CORPORATE TECHNICAL LIBRARY
                                          Phone: (616) 385-6414
Kalamazoo, MI 49001   Lorraine Schulte, Mgr.

UPJOHN COMPANY - PATENT LAW DEPARTMENT - LIBRARY
Bldg. 32-1   Phone: (616) 385-7569
Kalamazoo, MI 49001   Doreen B. Canton, Patent Law Libn.

WESTERN MICHIGAN UNIVERSITY - ARCHIVES AND REGIONAL HISTORY
COLLECTIONS
                                          Phone: (616) 383-1826
Kalamazoo, MI 49008   Wayne C. Mann, Dir.

WESTERN MICHIGAN UNIVERSITY - BUSINESS LIBRARY
                                          Phone: (616) 383-1926
Kalamazoo, MI 49008   David H. McKee, Hd.Libn.

WESTERN MICHIGAN UNIVERSITY - CENTER FOR WOMEN'S SERVICES -
LIBRARY
331 Ellsworth Hall   Phone: (616) 383-6097
Kalamazoo, MI 49008   Karen Lason, Lib.Cons.

WESTERN MICHIGAN UNIVERSITY - DOCUMENTS LIBRARY
Waldo Library   Phone: (616) 383-4952
Kalamazoo, MI 49008   Michael McDonnell, Ref.Libn., Maps & Docs.

WESTERN MICHIGAN UNIVERSITY - EDUCATIONAL LIBRARY
3300 Sangren Hall   Phone: (616) 383-1666
Kalamazoo, MI 49008   David Netz, Hd.Libn.

WESTERN MICHIGAN UNIVERSITY - HARPER C. MAYBEE MUSIC & DANCE
LIBRARY
3008 Dalton Center   Phone: (616) 383-1817
Kalamazoo, MI 49008   Gregory Fitzgerald, Hd.Libn.

WESTERN MICHIGAN UNIVERSITY - INSTITUTE OF CISTERCIAN STUDIES
LIBRARY
Hillside West   Phone: (616) 383-1969
Kalamazoo, MI 49008   Beatrice H. Beech, Hd.

WESTERN MICHIGAN UNIVERSITY - INST. OF PUBLIC AFFAIRS - ENV.
RESOURCE CENTER FOR COMMUNITY INFO.
                                          Phone: (616) 383-3983
Kalamazoo, MI 49008

WESTERN MICHIGAN UNIVERSITY - MAP LIBRARY
Waldo Library   Phone: (616) 383-4952
Kalamazoo, MI 49008   Michael McDonnell, Ref.Libn., Maps & Docs.

WESTERN MICHIGAN UNIVERSITY - PHYSICAL SCIENCES LIBRARY
3376 Rood Hall   Phone: (616) 383-4943
Kalamazoo, MI 49008   Beatrice Sichel, Hd.Libn.

HOUGHTON COUNTY HISTORICAL SOCIETY - LIBRARY
Highway M-26, Lock Box D   Phone: (906) 296-4121
Lake Linden, MI 49945   Flora O. Graham, Cur.

NORTH OAKLAND GENEALOGICAL SOCIETY - LIBRARY
845 S. Lapeer Rd.   Phone: (313) 693-1888
Lake Orion, MI 48035

MICHIGAN TECHNOLOGICAL UNIVERSITY - FORD FORESTRY CENTER -
    LIBRARY
Rt. 2, Box 736   Phone: (906) 524-6181
L'Anse, MI 49946   Stephen Shetron, Sr.Res.Sci.

COOLEY (Thomas M.) LAW SCHOOL - LIBRARY
217 S. Capitol Ave.
Box 13038   Phone: (517) 371-5140
Lansing, MI 48901   Peter M. Kempel, Dir., Res.Serv.

GREAT LAKES BIBLE COLLEGE - LOUIS M. DETRO MEMORIAL LIBRARY
Box 40060
Lansing, MI 48901   N.J. Olson, Hd.Libn.

INGHAM MEDICAL CENTER - JOHN W. CHI MEMORIAL MEDICAL LIBRARY
401 West Greenlawn Ave.   Phone: (517) 374-2270
Lansing, MI 48909   David G. Keddle, Dir., Med.Lib.

LANSING COMMUNITY COLLEGE - PROFESSIONAL RESOURCE CENTER
419 N. Capitol Ave.
Box 40010   Phone: (517) 483-1625
Lansing, MI 48901   James P. Platte, Dean/Div.Lrng.Rsrcs.

LANSING GENERAL HOSPITAL - OSTEOPATHIC - K.M. BAKER MEMORIAL
    LIBRARY
2800 Devonshire Ave.   Phone: (517) 377-8389
Lansing, MI 48909   Bethany A. Heinlen, Med.Libn.

MACKINAC ISLAND STATE PARK COMMISSION - HISTORICAL RESEARCH
    COLLECTION
Box 30028   Phone: (517) 322-1319
Lansing, MI 48909   Keith R. Widder, Cur.

MICHIGAN STATE DEPARTMENT OF MENTAL HEALTH - LIBRARY
Lewis Cass Bldg., 6th Fl.
Lansing, MI 48926

MICHIGAN STATE DEPARTMENT OF NATURAL RESOURCES - GEOLOGICAL
    SURVEY DIVISION - LIBRARY
Box 30028
Lansing, MI 48909

MICHIGAN STATE DEPARTMENT OF PUBLIC HEALTH - LIBRARY *
3500 N. Logan St.   Phone: (517) 373-1359
Lansing, MI 48909   Bill Nelton, Libn.

MICHIGAN STATE DEPARTMENT OF TRANSPORTATION -
    TRANSPORTATION LIBRARY
400 W. Ottawa
Box 30050   Phone: (517) 373-1545
Lansing, MI 48909   Jeanne F. Thomas, Libn.

MICHIGAN STATE HISTORY DIVISION - ARCHIVES
3405 N. Logan   Phone: (517) 373-0512
Lansing, MI 48918   David J. Johnson, State Archv.

MICHIGAN STATE LEGISLATIVE COUNCIL - LEGISLATIVE SERVICE
    BUREAU LIBRARY
125 W. Allegan, Suite 2
Box 30036   Phone: (517) 373-0472
Lansing, MI 48909   Elliott Smith, Dir.

MICHIGAN STATE - LIBRARY OF MICHIGAN
Box 30007   Phone: (517) 373-1580
Lansing, MI 48909   James W. Fry, State Libn.

MICHIGAN STATE - LIBRARY OF MICHIGAN - LAW LIBRARY
Law Bldg.
Box 30012   Phone: (517) 373-0630
Lansing, MI 48909   Charles B. Wolfe, State Law Libn.

ST. LAWRENCE HOSPITAL - MEDICAL LIBRARY
1210 West Saginaw   Phone: (515) 377-0354
Lansing, MI 48915   Jane B. Claytor, Med.Libn.

SPARROW (Edward W.) HOSPITAL - MEDICAL LIBRARY
1215 E. Michigan Ave.
Box 30480   Phone: (517) 483-2274
Lansing, MI 48909   Doris H. Asher, Med.Libn.

STATE BAR OF MICHIGAN - LIBRARY
306 Townsend St.   Phone: (517) 372-9030
Lansing, MI 48933   Douglas L. Sweet, Dir., R. & D.

TRI-COUNTY REGIONAL PLANNING COMMISSION - INFORMATION
    RESOURCE CENTER
913 W. Holmes Rd., Suite 201   Phone: (517) 393-0342
Lansing, MI 48901   Carrie Clinkscales, Exec.Asst.

OAKDALE REGIONAL CENTER FOR DEVELOPMENTAL DISABILITIES - STAFF
    LIBRARY
2995 W. Genesee St.   Phone: (313) 664-2951
Lapeer, MI 48446   Joanne Erskine, Lib.Coord.

LIVONIA PUBLIC SCHOOLS - CURRICULUM STUDY CENTER
18000 Newburgh Rd.
Livonia, MI 48152

MADONNA COLLEGE - CURRICULUM LIBRARY
36600 Schoolcraft Rd.   Phone: (313) 591-5149
Livonia, MI 48150   Sr. M. Martina, Ph.D., Dir.

ST. MARY HOSPITAL - MEDICAL LIBRARY
36475 Five Mile Road   Phone: (313) 464-4800
Livonia, MI 48154   Sister Mary Clementine, Libn.

SCHOOLCRAFT COLLEGE - WOMEN'S RESOURCE CENTER
18600 Haggerty Rd.   Phone: (313) 591-6400
Livonia, MI 48152   Virginia Wilhelm, Coord.

MASON COUNTY HISTORICAL SOCIETY - ROSE HAWLEY MUSEUM AND
    HISTORICAL LIBRARY
305 E. Filer St.   Phone: (616) 843-2001
Ludington, MI 49431   Molly Perry, Dir.

MEMORIAL MEDICAL CENTER OF WEST MICHIGAN - LIBRARY
One Atkinson Dr.   Phone: (616) 843-2591
Ludington, MI 49431   Julie A. Hall, Dir. of Med.Rec.

MANISTEE COUNTY HISTORICAL MUSEUM - FORTIER MEMORIAL LIBRARY
425 River St.   Phone: (616) 723-5531
Manistee, MI 49660   Steve Harold, Musm.Dir.

BISHOP BARAGA ASSOCIATION - ARCHIVES
444 S. Fourth St.
Marquette, MI 49855   Fr. N. Daniel Rupp, Archv.

MARQUETTE COUNTY HISTORICAL SOCIETY - J.M. LONGYEAR RESEARCH
    LIBRARY
213 N. Front St.   Phone: (906) 226-3571
Marquette, MI 49855   Frank O. Paull, Jr., Dir.

MARQUETTE GENERAL HOSPITAL - KEVIN F. O'BRIEN HEALTH SCIENCES
    LIBRARY
420 W. Magnetic   Phone: (906) 228-9440
Marquette, MI 49855   Mildred E. Kingsbury, Lib.Dir.

AMERICAN MUSEUM OF MAGIC - LIBRARY
107 E. Michigan   Phone: (616) 781-7666
Marshall, MI 49068   Robert Lund, Owner

CALHOUN COUNTY METROPOLITAN PLANNING COMMISSION - PLANNING
    LIBRARY *
County Bldg., 315 W. Green St.
Marshall, MI 49068

MARSHALL HISTORICAL SOCIETY - ARCHIVES *
Box 68   Phone: (616) 781-8544
Marshall, MI 49068   James Bryant, Pres.

MAYVILLE HISTORICAL MUSEUM - LIBRARY
22 Turner   Phone: (517) 843-6429
Mayville, MI 48744   Mrs. Willard Phelps, Dir. & Cur.

AUTOMOTIVE HALL OF FAME, INC. - LIBRARY
3225 Cook Rd.
Box 1742   Phone: (517) 631-5760
Midland, MI 48640   Dorothy M. Ross, Pres.

CITY OF MIDLAND - GRACE A. DOW MEMORIAL LIBRARY - SPECIAL
   COLLECTIONS
1710 W. St. Andrews Dr.   Phone: (517) 835-7151
Midland, MI 48640   Rosemarie Byers, Lib.Dir.

DOW CHEMICAL COMPANY - LEGAL LIBRARY
2030 Dow Center   Phone: (517) 636-6648
Midland, MI 48640   Doris L. Steiner, Supv.

DOW CHEMICAL COMPANY - TECHNICAL INFORMATION SERVICES -
   CENTRAL REPORT INDEX
566 Bldg.   Phone: (517) 636-3754
Midland, MI 48640   Paula B. Moses, Mgr.

DOW CHEMICAL COMPANY - TECHNICAL INFORMATION SERVICES -
   CHEMICAL LIBRARY
566 Bldg.
Box 1704   Phone: (517) 636-1098
Midland, MI 48640   Paula B. Moses, Mgr.

DOW CHEMICAL U.S.A. - BUSINESS INFORMATION CENTER
2020 Dow Center   Phone: (517) 636-3779
Midland, MI 48640   Phae H. Dorman, Mgr.

DOW CORNING CORPORATION - CORPORATE SITE INFORMATION CENTER
Box 1767   Phone: (517) 496-4941
Midland, MI 48640   Fred Lee, Supv.

DOW CORNING CORPORATION - INFORMATION CENTER - TECHNICAL
   LIBRARY (022)
                                        Phone: (517) 496-4957
Midland, MI 48640   Lori T. Karnath, Supv., Tech.Lib.

MEMORIAL PRESBYTERIAN CHURCH - LIBRARY
1310 Ashman St.   Phone: (517) 835-6759
Midland, MI 48640   Florence E. Hazlett, Chm., Lib.Bd.

MICHIGAN MOLECULAR INSTITUTE - LIBRARY
1910 W. St. Andrews Rd.   Phone: (517) 631-9450
Midland, MI 48640   Julia T. Lee, Libn.

MIDLAND COUNTY HISTORICAL SOCIETY - ARCHIVES
1801 W. St. Andrews Dr.   Phone: (517) 835-7401
Midland, MI 48640   Kathryn Cummins, Dir.

MIDLAND HOSPITAL CENTER - HEALTH SCIENCES LIBRARY
4005 Orchard Dr.   Phone: (517) 839-3262
Midland, MI 48670   Carole Colter, Health Sci.Libn.

MIDLAND PUBLIC SCHOOLS - INSTRUCTIONAL MEDIA CENTER
600 E. Carpenter St.   Phone: (517) 631-2311
Midland, MI 48640   Billy O. Robertson, Coord.

NORTHWOOD INSTITUTE - STROSACKER LIBRARY
3225 Cook Rd.   Phone: (517) 631-1600
Midland, MI 48640   Catherine Chen, Hd.Libn.

MONROE COUNTY HISTORICAL MUSEUM - ARCHIVES
126 S. Monroe St.   Phone: (313) 243-7137
Monroe, MI 48161   Christine L. Kull, Archv.

MONROE COUNTY LAW LIBRARY
Court House
Monroe, MI 48161   Margaret Weipert, Sec.

MONROE COUNTY LIBRARY SYSTEM - GENERAL GEORGE ARMSTRONG
   CUSTER COLLECTION
3700 S. Custer   Phone: (313) 241-5277
Monroe, MI 48161   Karen Stoll, Cur.

SOUTHEAST MICHIGAN REGIONAL FILM LIBRARY
c/o Monroe County Library System
3700 S. Custer Rd.   Phone: (313) 241-5277
Monroe, MI 48161   Bernard A. Margolis, Dir.

HARRISON COMMUNITY HOSPITAL - MEDICAL LIBRARY
26755 Ballard Rd.   Phone: (313) 465-5501
Mt. Clemens, MI 48045   Sr. Ursula Fabian, S.C., Med.Lib.Dir.

MACOMB INTERMEDIATE SCHOOL DISTRICT - BEAL LIBRARY
44001 Garfield Rd.   Phone: (313) 286-8800
Mt. Clemens, MI 48044   Richard J. Palmer, Libn.

MOUNT CLEMENS GENERAL HOSPITAL - STUCK MEDICAL LIBRARY
1000 Harrington Blvd.   Phone: (313) 466-8147
Mt. Clemens, MI 48043   Lynne L. Coles, Med.Libn.

ST. JOSEPH HOSPITAL OF MT. CLEMENS - MEDICAL LIBRARY
East Site, 215 North Ave.   Phone: (313) 286-8100
Mt. Clemens, MI 48043   Sandra A. Cryderman, Dir.

CENTRAL MICHIGAN UNIVERSITY - CLARKE HISTORICAL LIBRARY
                                        Phone: (517) 774-3352
Mt. Pleasant, MI 48859   William H. Mulligan, Jr., Dir.

FOREST PARK COVENANT CHURCH - LIBRARY
3815 Henry St.   Phone: (616) 728-5385
Muskegon, MI 49441   Mildred Peterson, Libn.

HACKLEY HOSPITAL - EDUCATION LIBRARY
1700 Clinton St.   Phone: (616) 728-4897
Muskegon, MI 49443   Betty Rogers, Libn.

MERCY HOSPITAL - HEALTH SCIENCES LIBRARY
1500 E. Sherman Blvd.   Phone: (616) 739-9341
Muskegon, MI 49443   Jean Parker, Libn.

MUSKEGON BUSINESS COLLEGE - LIBRARY
145 Apple Ave.   Phone: (616) 726-4904
Muskegon, MI 49442   Margaret Moon, Libn.

MUSKEGON CHRONICLE - EDITORIAL LIBRARY
981 Third St.   Phone: (616) 722-3161
Muskegon, MI 49443   Linda S. Thompson, Libn.

NORTHVILLE HISTORICAL SOCIETY - LIBRARY
No. 1 Griswold
Box 71   Phone: (313) 348-1845
Northville, MI 48167   Carol L. Butske, Libn.

NORTHVILLE REGIONAL PSYCHIATRIC HOSPITAL - PROFESSIONAL
   LIBRARY †
41001 W. 7 Mile Rd.   Phone: (313) 349-1800
Northville, MI 48167

CONGREGATION BETH SHALOM - RABBI MORDECAI S. HALPERN
   MEMORIAL LIBRARY *
14601 W. Lincoln Rd.   Phone: (313) 547-7970
Oak Park, MI 48237   Eleanor Smith, Libn.

UNIVERSITY OF MICHIGAN - BIOLOGICAL STATION LIBRARY
                                        Phone: (616) 539-8048
Pellston, MI 49769   Patricia B. Yocum, Hd.

BURNS (Dean C.) HEALTH SCIENCES LIBRARY
                                        Phone: (616) 348-4500
Petoskey, MI 49770   Kay Kelly, Med.Libn.

PIGEON DISTRICT LIBRARY - SPECIAL COLLECTIONS
7236 Nitz St.   Phone: (517) 453-2341
Pigeon, MI 48755   Roberta J. Richmond, Libn.

ADISTRA CORPORATION - R & D LIBRARY *
101 Union St.   Phone: (313) 425-2600
Plymouth, MI 48170   John H. Dillon, Mgr.

BURROUGHS CORPORATION - TECHNICAL INFORMATION CENTER
41100 Plymouth Rd.   Phone: (313) 451-4512
Plymouth, MI 48170   Dolores I. Schuller, Asst.Tech.Libn.

ST. JOHN'S PROVINCIAL SEMINARY - LIBRARY
44011 Five Mile Rd.   Phone: (313) 453-6200
Plymouth, MI 48170   Jean McGarty, Libn.

ADAMS-PRATT OAKLAND COUNTY LAW LIBRARY
1200 N. Telegraph Rd.   Phone: (313) 858-0011
Pontiac, MI 48054   Richard L. Beer, Dir.

OAKLAND COUNTY PIONEER AND HISTORICAL SOCIETY - LIBRARY &
    ARCHIVES
405 Oakland Ave.   Phone: (313) 338-6732
Pontiac, MI 48058   Mary Ann Treais, Adm.Coord.

OAKLAND COUNTY REFERENCE LIBRARY
1200 N. Telegraph Rd.   Phone: (313) 858-0738
Pontiac, MI 48053   Phyllis Jose, Dir.

OAKLAND SCHOOLS - EDUCATIONAL RESOURCE CENTER
2100 Pontiac Lake Rd.   Phone: (313) 858-1961
Pontiac, MI 48054   Dr. Robert N. Johnson, Dir.

PONTIAC GENERAL HOSPITAL - LIBRARY †
Seminole & W. Huron   Phone: (313) 857-7412
Pontiac, MI 48053   Naim K. Sahyoun, Dir. of Libs.

PONTIAC OSTEOPATHIC HOSPITAL - MEDICAL LIBRARY
50 N. Perry St.   Phone: (313) 338-5000
Pontiac, MI 48058   Janis M. Fox, Libn.

ST. JOSEPH MERCY HOSPITAL - EDUCATIONAL RESOURCES
900 Woodward   Phone: (313) 858-3495
Pontiac, MI 48053   Mollie S. Lynch, Lib.Mgr.

ACHESON INDUSTRIES, INC. - CORPORATE INFORMATION CENTER
315 Peoples Bank Bldg.
Box 8   Phone: (313) 984-5583
Port Huron, MI 48060   Myles T. Musgrave, Asst. to V.P.

PORT HURON TIMES HERALD - LIBRARY *
911 Military St.   Phone: (313) 985-7171
Port Huron, MI 48060   Joann M. Maxwell, Lib.Ck.

OAKLAND UNIVERSITY - LIBRARY - SPECIAL COLLECTIONS AND ARCHIVES
Kresge Library Building   Phone: (313) 377-2492
Rochester, MI 48063   Elizabeth A. Titus, Hd. of Archv./Spec.Coll.

BEAUMONT (William) HOSPITAL - MEDICAL LIBRARY
3601 W. Thirteen Mile Rd.   Phone: (313) 288-8340
Royal Oak, MI 48072   Joan M.B. Smith, Med.Libn.

AMERICAN ASSOCIATION OF CORRECTIONAL OFFICERS - LIBRARY
2309 State St., North Office   Phone: (517) 799-8208
Saginaw, MI 48602   Herbert Van Dusen, Libn.

MICHIGAN LUTHERAN SEMINARY - LIBRARY
2128 Court   Phone: (517) 793-1041
Saginaw, MI 48602   Milton P. Spaude, Libn. & Professor

SAGINAW COUNTY LAW LIBRARY
Courthouse, Rm. 215
111 S. Michigan Ave.   Phone: (517) 790-5490
Saginaw, MI 48602   Jannis Corley, Law Libn.

SAGINAW HEALTH SCIENCES LIBRARY
1000 Houghton St., Suite 2000   Phone: (517) 771-6846
Saginaw, MI 48602   Stephanie John, Dir.

SAGINAW NEWS - EDITORIAL LIBRARY
201-203 S. Washington Ave.   Phone: (517) 752-7171
Saginaw, MI 48605   Leland R. Watrous, Hd.Libn.

SAGINAW OSTEOPATHIC HOSPITAL - LIBRARY †
515 N. Michigan Ave.   Phone: (517) 771-5100
Saginaw, MI 48602   Patricia A. Wolfgram, Libn.

U.S. VETERANS ADMINISTRATION (MI-Saginaw) - MEDICAL CENTER
    LIBRARY
1500 Weiss St.   Phone: (517) 793-2340
Saginaw, MI 48602   Nancy R. Dingman, Chf.Libn.

FIRST CONGREGATIONAL CHURCH - LIBRARY *
2001 Niles Ave.   Phone: (616) 983-5519
St. Joseph, MI 49085   Arlene Emery, Libn.

GENEALOGICAL ASSOCIATION OF SOUTHWESTERN MICHIGAN - MAUD
    PRESTON PALENSKE MEMORIAL LIBRARY
Box 573
St. Joseph, MI 49085   Harold Atwood, Res.Chm.

LAKE SUPERIOR STATE COLLEGE - KENNETH J. SHOULDICE LIBRARY -
    MICHIGAN & MARINE COLLECTIONS
                                         Phone: (906) 635-2402
Sault Ste. Marie, MI 49783   Dr. Frederick A. Michels, Dir.

U.S. ARMY - TACOM SUPPORT ACTIVITY-SELFRIDGE - RECREATION
    SERVICES LIBRARY
Bldg. 169   Phone: (313) 466-5238
Selfridge Air Natl. Guard Base, MI 48045   JoAnn Bonnett, Chf., Lib.Br.

ALLIED CORPORATION - ALLIED AUTOMOTIVE SECTOR LIBRARY
Bendix Center
Box 5029   Phone: (313) 827-5618
Southfield, MI 48037   Mary C. Blaschak, Sr.Libn.

AUTOMOTIVE INFORMATION COUNCIL - LIBRARY
29200 Southfield Rd., No. 111   Phone: (313) 559-5922
Southfield, MI 48076   Peggy Pentecost, Info.Coord.

BURNETT (Leo) COMPANY, INC. - RESEARCH LIBRARY †
26555 Evergreen Rd.   Phone: (313) 355-1900
Southfield, MI 48076

CLAYTON ENVIRONMENTAL CONSULTANTS - LIBRARY AND INFORMATION
    CENTER
25711 Southfield Rd.   Phone: (313) 424-8860
Southfield, MI 48075   Marjorie Corey, Libn.

CONGREGATION BETH ACHIM - JOSEPH KATKOWSKY LIBRARY
21100 Twelve Mile Rd., W.   Phone: (313) 352-8670
Southfield, MI 48076   Dr. Israel Wiener, Lib.Chm./Libn.

CONGREGATION SHAAREY ZEDEK - LEARNING RESOURCE CENTER
27375 Bell Rd.   Phone: (313) 357-5544
Southfield, MI 48034

DUNS SCOTUS LIBRARY
20000 W. Nine Mile Rd.   Phone: (313) 357-3070
Southfield, MI 48075   Bro. Gabriel Balassone, Lib.Dir.

EATON CORPORATION - ENGINEERING & RESEARCH CENTER LIBRARY
Box 766   Phone: (313) 354-6979
Southfield, MI 48037   Mary E. Montgomery, Res.Libn.

FINNISH AMERICAN HISTORICAL SOCIETY OF MICHIGAN
19885 Melrose   Phone: (313) 354-1994
Southfield, MI 48075   Felix V. Jackonen, Pres.

GIFFELS ASSOCIATES, INC. - LIBRARY
Box 5025   Phone: (313) 355-4600
Southfield, MI 48037   William H. Dukes, Libn.

GULF & WESTERN MANUFACTURING COMPANY - MARKETING LIBRARY
26261 Evergreen Rd.
Box 999   Phone: (313) 355-8517
Southfield, MI 48037

INSTITUTE FOR ADVANCED PASTORAL STUDIES - REFERENCE LIBRARY
29129 Southfield Rd.   Phone: (313) 642-4401
Southfield, MI 48076

LAWRENCE INSTITUTE OF TECHNOLOGY - LIBRARY
21000 W. Ten Mile Rd.   Phone: (313) 356-0200
Southfield, MI 48075   Gary R. Cocozzoli, Dir.

MICHIGAN PSYCHOANALYTIC INSTITUTE - IRA MILLER MEMORIAL
    LIBRARY
16310 W. 12 Mile Rd., Suite 204   Phone: (313) 559-5855
Southfield, MI 48076   Alan Krohn, Ph.D., Chm., Lib.Comm.

MIDRASHA COLLEGE OF JEWISH STUDIES - LIBRARY †
21550 W. Twelve Mile Rd.   Phone: (313) 354-3130
Southfield, MI 48076   Sarah Bell, Libn.

PROVIDENCE HOSPITAL - PANZNER MEMORIAL LIBRARY
16001 W. Nine Mile Rd.
Box 2043   Phone: (313) 424-3294
Southfield, MI 48037   Sharon Cohen, Dir. of Lib.Serv.

SPILL CONTROL ASSOCIATION OF AMERICA - LIBRARY
17117 W. Nine Mile Rd., Suite 1040   Phone: (313) 552-0500
Southfield, MI 48075   Marc K. Shaye, General Counsel

FIRST BAPTIST CHURCH - LIBRARY *
Exchange & Meridian   Phone: (616) 842-1974
Spring Lake, MI 49456

PIONEER STUDY CENTER
Box 1108   Phone: (616) 946-3151
Traverse City, MI 49684   Steve Harold, Dir.

TRAVERSE CITY REGIONAL PSYCHIATRIC HOSPITAL - PROFESSIONAL
    RESOURCE LIBRARY
Elmwood & 11th Sts.   Phone: (616) 947-5550
Traverse City, MI 49684

RIVERSIDE OSTEOPATHIC HOSPITAL - RALPH F. LINDBERG MEMORIAL
    LIBRARY
150 Truax St.   Phone: (313) 676-4200
Trenton, MI 48183   Susan E. Skoglund, Dir. of Lib.Serv.

ROCKWELL INTERNATIONAL - HEAVY VEHICLES COMPONENTS
    OPERATION - REFERENCE CENTER
2135 W. Maple Rd.   Phone: (313) 435-1668
Troy, MI 48084   Cheryl Hull, Tech.Ref.Asst.

SANDY CORPORATION - LIBRARY
1500 W. Big Beaver Rd.   Phone: (313) 569-4000
Troy, MI 48084   Judith Wilson, Libn.

SCHERER (R.P.) CORPORATION - LIBRARY
2075 W. Big Beaver Rd.
Box 160   Phone: (313) 649-0900
Troy, MI 48099   Sandra Abrams, Libn.

WALSH COLLEGE OF ACCOUNTANCY AND BUSINESS ADMINISTRATION -
    LIBRARY
3838 Livernois   Phone: (313) 689-8282
Troy, MI 48084   Gloria B. Ellis, Lib.Dir.

CLINTON RIVER WATERSHED COUNCIL - LIBRARY
8215 Hall Rd.   Phone: (313) 739-1122
Utica, MI 48087   Peggy B. Johnson, Exec.Sec.

WILLIAMS INTERNATIONAL - LIBRARY
2280 W. Maple Rd.
Box 200   Phone: (313) 624-5200
Walled Lake, MI 48088   Lydia O. Johnstone, Hd.Libn.

BI-COUNTY COMMUNITY HOSPITAL - LIBRARY
13355 E. Ten Mile Rd.   Phone: (313) 756-1000
Warren, MI 48089   Gayle A. Williams, Dir.

CAMPBELL-EWALD COMPANY - REFERENCE CENTER
30400 Van Dyke   Phone: (313) 574-3400
Warren, MI 48093   Susan B. Stepek, V.P. & Mgr.

DETROIT MACOMB HOSPITAL CORPORATION - SOUTH MACOMB HOSPITAL
    LIBRARY
11800 Twelve Mile Rd.   Phone: (313) 573-5117
Warren, MI 48093   Lynn Sorensen Sutton, Corp.Dir. of Libs.

GENERAL DYNAMICS CORPORATION - LAND SYSTEMS DIVISION -
    TECHNICAL LIBRARY
Box 1901   Phone: (313) 497-7093
Warren, MI 48090   Margaret vonRosen, Chf.Libn.

GENERAL MOTORS CORPORATION - ADVANCED PRODUCT AND
    MANUFACTURING ENGINEERING STAFF - LIBRARY
GM Technical Center, A/MD-14
30300 Mound Rd.   Phone: (313) 575-0652
Warren, MI 48090-9040   Jean Schlage, Libn.

GENERAL MOTORS CORPORATION - CURRENT PRODUCT ENGINEERING -
    INFORMATION MANAGEMENT
WO-INFO MGMT
GM Engineering Bldg.
30200 Mound Rd.   Phone: (313) 575-1112
Warren, MI 48090-9010   John L. Thompson, Mgr.

GENERAL MOTORS CORPORATION - DESIGN STAFF LIBRARY
General Motors Technical Ctr.
30100 Mound Rd.   Phone: (313) 575-1957
Warren, MI 48090-9030   Mrs. Biljana Delevich, Design Libn.

GENERAL MOTORS CORPORATION - INFORMATION SYSTEMS &
    COMMUNICATIONS ACTIVITY - TECHNICAL INFORMATION CENTER *
2912 GMISCA Bldg.
7000 Chicago Rd.   Phone: (313) 492-3574
Warren, MI 48090   Patricia Cupoli, Libn.

GENERAL MOTORS CORPORATION - RESEARCH LABORATORIES LIBRARY
General Motors Technical Center
12 Mile & Mound Rd.   Phone: (313) 575-2736
Warren, MI 48090   Robert W. Gibson, Jr., Dept.Hd.

OMI INTERNATIONAL CORP. - LIBRARY
21441 Hoover Rd.   Phone: (313) 497-9100
Warren, MI 48089   Lynn M. Pefley

U.S. ARMY - TANK-AUTOMOTIVE COMMAND - TECHNICAL LIBRARY
    SERVICE BRANCH
28251 Van Dyke   Phone: (313) 573-2470
Warren, MI 48090   Louis X. Barbalas, Chf.

WAYNE HISTORICAL MUSEUM - HISTORICAL COMMISSION ARCHIVES
No. 1, Town Sq.   Phone: (313) 722-0113
Wayne, MI 48184   Mildred Hanchett, Dir./Supv.

JEWISH COMMUNITY CENTER OF METROPOLITAN DETROIT - HENRY
    MEYERS MEMORIAL LIBRARY
6600 W. Maple Rd.   Phone: (313) 661-1000
West Bloomfield, MI 48033   Adele Silver, Cultural Arts Dir.

TEMPLE ISRAEL - MAX AND EDITH WEINBERG LIBRARY
5725 Walnut Lake Rd.   Phone: (313) 661-5700
West Bloomfield, MI 48033   Bertha Wember, Libn.

WAYNE COUNTY GENERAL HOSPITAL - MEDICAL LIBRARY *
2345 Merriman   Phone: (313) 274-3000
Westland, MI 48185

BASF WYANDOTTE CORPORATION - RESEARCH LIBRARY
Box 111   Phone: (313) 282-3300
Wyandotte, MI 48192   Janice B. Spector, Res.Libn.

EASTERN MICHIGAN UNIVERSITY - CENTER OF EDUCATIONAL
    RESOURCES - ARCHIVES/SPECIAL COLLECTIONS
                                                Phone: (313) 487-3423
Ypsilanti, MI 48197   Margaret Eide, Soc.Sci.Libn.

EASTERN MICHIGAN UNIVERSITY - CENTER OF EDUCATIONAL
    RESOURCES - GOVERNMENT DOCUMENTS COLLECTION
                                                Phone: (313) 487-2280
Ypsilanti, MI 48197   Clare Beck, Govt.Doc.Libn.

EASTERN MICHIGAN UNIVERSITY - CENTER OF EDUCATIONAL
    RESOURCES - INSTRUCTIONAL MATERIALS CENTER
                                                Phone: (313) 487-0490
Ypsilanti, MI 48197   Margaret Best, Libn.

EASTERN MICHIGAN UNIVERSITY - CENTER OF EDUCATIONAL
    RESOURCES - MAP LIBRARY
                                                Phone: (313) 487-3191
Ypsilanti, MI 48197   Joanne Hansen, Sci. & Tech.Libn.

HUDSON ESSEX TERRAPLANE CLUB, INC. - LIBRARY
5765 Munger Rd.   Phone: (313) 434-3289
Ypsilanti, MI 48197   Charles Liskow, Libn.

YPSILANTI REGIONAL PSYCHIATRIC HOSPITAL - STAFF LIBRARY
Box A   Phone: (313) 434-3400
Ypsilanti, MI 48197   Penny Kirkman, Dir., Lib.Serv.

FIRST CHRISTIAN REFORMED CHURCH - LIBRARY
15 S. Church St.
Zeeland, MI 49464   Betty G. Shoemaker, Church Libn.

HERMAN MILLER, INC. - RESOURCE CENTER
                                           Phone: (616) 772-3629
Zeeland, MI 49464   Linda M. Wagenveld, Mgr.

MINNESOTA

NORMAN COUNTY HISTORICAL SOCIETY - MEMORIAL MUSEUM LIBRARY
404 W. 5th Ave.   Phone: (218) 784-4911
Ada, MN 56510   Lenora I. Johnson, Musm.Dir.

FREEBORN COUNTY HISTORICAL SOCIETY - NELSON LIBRARY
North Bridge St.
Box 105   Phone: (507) 373-8003
Albert Lea, MN 56007   Roger D. Lonning, Trustee

DOUGLAS COUNTY HOSPITAL - HEALTH SCIENCES LIBRARY
111 17th Ave., E.   Phone: (612) 762-1511
Alexandria, MN 56308   DiAnn Ness, Lib.Mgr.

ANOKA AREA VOCATIONAL TECHNICAL INSTITUTE - MEDIA CENTER
1355 W. Main St.   Phone: (612) 427-1880
Anoka, MN 55303   Deborah J. Brude, Media Serv.Coord.

ANOKA COUNTY HISTORICAL GENEALOGICAL SOCIETY - LIBRARY
1900 3rd Ave. S.   Phone: (612) 421-0600
Anoka, MN 55303   Pat Schwappach, Musm.Dir.

ANOKA STATE HOSPITAL - LIBRARY
3300 4th Ave., N.   Phone: (612) 422-4150
Anoka, MN 55303   Betty Palfalvi, Libn.

MINNESOTA ZOOLOGICAL GARDEN - LIBRARY
12101 Johnny Cake Ridge Rd.   Phone: (612) 432-9010
Apple Valley, MN 55124   Angie Norell, Libn.

PINE COUNTY HISTORICAL SOCIETY - LIBRARY *
Askov, MN 55704   Ron Nelson, Pres.

UNIVERSITY OF MINNESOTA - HORMEL INSTITUTE - LIBRARY
801 16th Ave., N.E.   Phone: (507) 433-8804
Austin, MN 55912   Jacqueline Budde, Libn.

SHERBURNE COUNTY SOCIAL SERVICES - THE BORROWING CORNER, INC.
County Office Building
1810 1st St. W.   Phone: (612) 441-1880
Becker, MN 55319   Christine Rudnicki, Coord.

NORTH CENTRAL MINNESOTA HISTORICAL CENTER - LIBRARY
Bemidji State University   Phone: (218) 755-3349
Bemidji, MN 56601   Ardis Wilander, Spec.Coll.Libn.

OAK HILLS BIBLE INSTITUTE - LIBRARY
Oak Hills   Phone: (218) 751-8670
Bemidji, MN 56601   John Sanders, Libn.

OUR REDEEMERS LUTHERAN CHURCH - LIBRARY
Tenth St., S. & Oakwood Ave.   Phone: (612) 843-3151
Benson, MN 56215   Marlene Skold, Libn.

HONEYWELL, INC. - PHYSICAL SCIENCES CENTER LIBRARY
10701 Lyndale Ave., S.   Phone: (612) 887-4321
Bloomington, MN 55420   Michael McClellan, Libn.

NORTHWESTERN COLLEGE OF CHIROPRACTIC - LIBRARY
2501 W. 84th St.   Phone: (612) 888-4777
Bloomington, MN 55431   Cheryl A. Bjerke, Dir.

BRAINERD STATE HOSPITAL - LIBRARY
East Oak St.   Phone: (218) 828-2357
Brainerd, MN 56401   David C. Bauer, Libn.

CROW WING COUNTY HISTORICAL SOCIETY - MUSEUM LIBRARY
320 Laurel St.
Box 722
Brainerd, MN 56401   Gail M. Christensen, Dir.

ST. FRANCIS HOSPITAL - COMMUNITY HEALTH SCIENCE LIBRARY
415 Oak St.
Breckenridge, MN 56520   Karen Engstrom, Dir. of Lib.Serv.

CAMBRIDGE STATE HOSPITAL - LIBRARY
                                           Phone: (612) 689-2121
Cambridge, MN 55008   Jean Peterson, Libn.

ISANTI COUNTY HISTORICAL SOCIETY - RESOURCE CENTER
Box 525   Phone: (612) 396-3957
Cambridge, MN 55008   Marilyn McGriff, Dir.

CANBY COMMUNITY HOSPITAL - MEDICAL LIBRARY
112 St. Olaf Ave., S.   Phone: (507) 223-7277
Canby, MN 56220   Janet Fransen, Med.Libn.

HAZELDEN FOUNDATION - STAFF LIBRARY †
Box 11   Phone: (612) 257-4010
Center City, MN 55012   Joan A. Frederickson, Libn.

UNIVERSITY OF MINNESOTA - LANDSCAPE ARBORETUM - ELMER L. &
   ELEANOR J. ANDERSEN HORTICULTURAL LIBRARY
3675 Arboretum Dr.   Phone: (612) 443-2460
Chaska, MN 55318   June Rogier, Libn.

CHATFIELD BRASS BAND INC. - FREE MUSIC LENDING LIBRARY
82 Library Ln.   Phone: (507) 867-3275
Chatfield, MN 55923   James A. Perkins, Pres.

IRON RANGE RESEARCH CENTER
Box 392   Phone: (218) 254-5733
Chisholm, MN 55719   Dana Miller, Dir.

ST. JOHN'S ABBEY AND UNIVERSITY - HILL MONASTIC MANUSCRIPT
   LIBRARY - BUSH CENTER
                                           Phone: (612) 363-3514
Collegeville, MN 56321   Dr. Julian G. Plante, Dir.

YAMAHA MOTOR CORPORATION USA - YAMAHA R&D MINNESOTA -
   RESEARCH LIBRARY
1255 Main St.   Phone: (612) 755-2743
Coon Rapids, MN 55433   William B. Seath, Info.Mgr.

UNIVERSITY OF MINNESOTA, CROOKSTON - KIEHLE LIBRARY - MEDIA
   RESOURCES
                                           Phone: (218) 281-6510
Crookston, MN 56716   Harold J. Opgrand, Dir., Media Rsrcs.

BECKER COUNTY HISTORICAL SOCIETY - WALTER D. BIRD MEMORIAL
   HISTORICAL LIBRARY
915 Lake Ave.   Phone: (218) 847-2938
Detroit Lakes, MN 56501   Merry J. Coleman, Dir.

(Duluth) NEWS-TRIBUNE & HERALD - LIBRARY
424 W. 1st St.   Phone: (218) 723-5309
Duluth, MN 55801   Lana Michelizzi, Libn.

MILLER-DWAN MEDICAL CENTER - TILDERQUIST MEMORIAL MEDICAL
   LIBRARY †
502 E. Second St.   Phone: (218) 727-8762
Duluth, MN 55805   Annelie Sober, Dir., Med.Lib.

NORTHEAST MINNESOTA HISTORICAL CENTER - LIBRARY
Library 375
University of Minnesota, Duluth   Phone: (218) 726-8526
Duluth, MN 55812   Pat Maus, Adm.

ST. LOUIS COUNTY LAW LIBRARY
515 St. Louis County Court House   Phone: (218) 723-3563
Duluth, MN 55802   Michele Milinovich, Law Libn.

ST. LUKE'S HOSPITAL - MEDICAL LIBRARY †
915 E. First St.   Phone: (218) 726-5320
Duluth, MN 55805   Kirsten Shelstad, Libn.

UNIVERSITY OF MINNESOTA, DULUTH - HEALTH SCIENCE LIBRARY
2400 Oakland Ave.   Phone: (218) 726-8585
Duluth, MN 55812   Diane C.P. Ebro, Dir.

UNIVERSITY OF MINNESOTA, DULUTH - LAKE SUPERIOR BASIN STUDIES
    CENTER - LAKE SUPERIOR REFERENCE LIBRARY
217 Research Lab. Bldg., Lower Campus
Duluth, MN 55812

INTERNATIONAL RESEARCH & EVALUATION (IRE) - INFORMATION &
    TECHNOLOGY TRANSFER RESOURCE CENTER
21098 IRE Control Ctr.   Phone: (612) 888-9635
Eagan, MN 55121   Randall L. Voight, Info.Dir.

MTS SYSTEMS CORPORATION - INFORMATION SERVICES
14000 Technology Dr.   Phone: (612) 937-4306
Eden Prairie, MN 55344   Kathleen M. Warner, Supv.

FAIRVIEW SOUTHDALE HOSPITAL - MARY ANN KING HEALTH SCIENCES
    LIBRARY †
6401 France Ave., S.   Phone: (612) 924-5005
Edina, MN 55435   Lisa C. Bjerken, Dir., Lib.Serv.

HONEYWELL, INC. - DEFENSE SYSTEMS DIVISION - ORDNANCE
    OPERATIONS ENGINEERING LIBRARY
5901 S. County Rd. 18   Phone: (612) 931-4204
Edina, MN 55436   Rachel Spiegel, Asst.Libn.

GRANT COUNTY HISTORICAL SOCIETY - LIBRARY
                                             Phone: (218) 685-4864
Elbow Lake, MN 56531   George M. Shervey, Cur.

LE SUEUR COUNTY HISTORICAL SOCIETY MUSEUM - LIBRARY
Box 557   Phone: (507) 267-4620
Elysian, MN 56028   Caroline Roessler, Asst.Cur.

U.S. HOCKEY HALL OF FAME - LIBRARY
Hat Trick Ave.
Box 657   Phone: (218) 749-5167
Eveleth, MN 55734   Earl Berglund, Exec.Dir.

HENNEPIN COUNTY PARK RESERVE DISTRICT - LOWRY NATURE CENTER -
    LIBRARY
Carver Park Reserve
7025 Victoria Dr.
Rt. 1, Box 690   Phone: (612) 472-4911
Excelsior, MN 55331   Dale Rock, Naturalist

"I LIKE MYSELF" EARLY CHILDHOOD & FAMILY EDUCATION PROGRAM -
    TOY LENDING LIBRARY
115 S. Park   Phone: (507) 235-6205
Fairmont, MN 56031   Elayne Hested

MARTIN COUNTY HISTORICAL SOCIETY, INC. - PIONEER MUSEUM -
    LIBRARY
304 E. Blue Earth Ave.   Phone: (507) 235-5178
Fairmont, MN 56031   Helen Simon, Cur.

ROSEVILLE EARLY CHILDHOOD/FAMILY PROGRAMS - PLAY 'N' LEARN
    LIBRARY
Falcon Heights Ctr.
1393 Garden Ave.   Phone: (612) 633-8150
Falcon Heights, MN 55113   Janet Robb, Lib.Mtls.Coord.

FARIBAULT STATE HOSPITAL - LIBRARY
                                             Phone: (507) 332-3274
Faribault, MN 55021   Mary K. Heltsley, Libn.

MINNESOTA LIBRARY FOR THE BLIND AND PHYSICALLY HANDICAPPED
                                             Phone: (507) 332-3279
Faribault, MN 55021   Myrna Wright, Libn.

RICE COUNTY HISTORICAL SOCIETY - ARCHIVES
1814 Second Ave.
Box 5   Phone: (507) 332-2121
Faribault, MN 55021   George Holey, Pres.

FERGUS FALLS STATE HOSPITAL - LIBRARY
Corner of Fir & Union
Box 157   Phone: (218) 739-7327
Fergus Falls, MN 56537   Elizabeth Swenson, Libn.

LUTHERAN BRETHREN SCHOOLS - BIBLE COLLEGE AND SEMINARY LIBRARY
815 W. Vernon Ave.
Box 317   Phone: (218) 739-3373
Fergus Falls, MN 56537   Donald W. Brue, Libn.

OTTER TAIL COUNTY HISTORICAL SOCIETY - LIBRARY
1110 Lincoln Ave., W.   Phone: (218) 736-6038
Fergus Falls, MN 56537   Pamela A. Brunfelt, Libn./Res.

OTTER TAIL POWER COMPANY - LIBRARY
215 S. Cascade   Phone: (218) 736-5411
Fergus Falls, MN 56537   Janet Johnson, Lib.Asst.

UNITY MEDICAL CENTER - LIBRARY
550 Osborne Rd.   Phone: (612) 786-2200
Fridley, MN 55432   Michael F. Winter, Med.Libn.

POPE COUNTY HISTORICAL SOCIETY & MUSEUM - LIBRARY
Hwy. No. 104 S. Glenwood   Phone: (612) 634-3293
Glenwood, MN 56334   Merlin Berglin, Off.Supv.

COURAGE CENTER LIBRARY
3915 Golden Valley Rd.   Phone: (612) 588-0811
Golden Valley, MN 55422   Mary Lindgren, Libn.

GOLDEN VALLEY HEALTH CENTER - MEDICAL LIBRARY
4101 Golden Valley Rd.   Phone: (612) 588-2771
Golden Valley, MN 55422   Carol Nordby, Lib.Ck.

HONEYWELL, INC. - RESIDENTIAL ENGINEERING RESOURCE AND
    LEARNING CENTER
MN10-2510
1985 Douglas Dr., N.   Phone: (612) 542-6828
Golden Valley, MN 55422   Karlan Kuhlmey-Williams, Tech.Libn.

COOK COUNTY HISTORICAL SOCIETY - GRAND MARAIS LIBRARY
                                             Phone: (218) 387-1678
Grand Marais, MN 55604   Mary Alice Harvey, Libn.

U.S. NATL. PARK SERVICE - GRAND PORTAGE NATL. MONUMENT -
    LIBRARY
Box 666   Phone: (218) 387-2788
Grand Marais, MN 55604   Donald W. Carney, Supv. Park Ranger

HONEYWELL, INC. - DEFENSE SYSTEMS DIVISION - ENGINEERING
    LIBRARY
600 Second St., N.   Phone: (612) 931-6603
Hopkins, MN 55343   Lawrence W. Werner, Libn.

HOPKINS HISTORICAL SOCIETY - LIBRARY
1010 1st St., S.   Phone: (612) 938-7315
Hopkins, MN 55343

KOOCHICHING COUNTY HISTORICAL SOCIETY - MUSEUM
Smokey Bear Park
214 6th St.
Box 1147   Phone: (218) 283-4316
International Falls, MN 56649   Mary Hilke, Exec.Sec. & Cur.

COUNCIL ON QUALITY EDUCATION - "BRINGING THE SCHOOL TO THE
    COMMUNITY" RESOURCE CENTER
Lewiston Elementary School   Phone: (507) 523-2194
Lewiston, MN 55952   Alice Duvall, Coord.

ST. GABRIEL'S HOSPITAL - LIBRARY
St. Joseph's Hall   Phone: (612) 632-5441
Little Falls, MN 56345   Peggy Martin, Dir. of Educ.

WEYERHAEUSER (Charles A.) MEMORIAL MUSEUM - LIBRARY
Box 239   Phone: (612) 632-4007
Little Falls, MN 56345   Jan Warner, Exec.Dir.

LAC QUI PARLE COUNTY HISTORICAL SOCIETY - MUSEUM LIBRARY
TH 75, S.   Phone: (612) 598-7678
Madison, MN 56256   Chris Schulstadt, Libn.

BETHANY LUTHERAN THEOLOGICAL SEMINARY - LIBRARY
447 N. Division St.   Phone: (507) 625-2977
Mankato, MN 56001   Prof. G.E. Reichwald, Act.Libn.

BLUE EARTH COUNTY HISTORICAL SOCIETY - MUSEUM ARCHIVES
606 S. Broad St.   Phone: (507) 345-4154
Mankato, MN 56001   Audrey K. Hicks, Staff Archv.

MANKATO STATE UNIVERSITY - BUREAU OF BUSINESS AND ECONOMIC
   RESEARCH - LIBRARY
Box 14   Phone: (507) 389-1623
Mankato, MN 56001   Ved P. Sharma, Dir.

MANKATO STATE UNIVERSITY - LIBRARY - SPECIAL COLLECTIONS
Memorial Library   Phone: (507) 389-6201
Mankato, MN 56001   Dale K. Carrison, Dean of Lib.

SOUTHERN MINNESOTA HISTORICAL CENTER - LIBRARY
Mankato State University   Phone: (507) 389-1029
Mankato, MN 56001   Dr. William E. Lass, Dir.

SOUTHWEST MINNESOTA HISTORICAL CENTER - LIBRARY
Southwest State University   Phone: (507) 537-7373
Marshall, MN 56258   Thaddeus Radzialowski, Dir.

ALTERNATIVE SOURCES OF ENERGY, INC. - LIBRARY AND REFERRAL
   SERVICE
107 S. Central Ave.   Phone: (612) 983-6892
Milaca, MN 56353   Donald Marier, Dir.

ABBOTT-NORTHWESTERN HOSPITAL CORPORATION - HEALTH SCIENCES
   RESOURCE CENTER
800 E. 28th St.   Phone: (612) 874-4312
Minneapolis, MN 55407   Donna Johnson, Dir, Rsrc.Ctr.

ADATH JESHURUN CONGREGATION - JENNY GROSS MEMORIAL LIBRARY
3400 Dupont, S.   Phone: (612) 824-2685
Minneapolis, MN 55408   Naomi Goldberg Honor, Libn.

AMERICAN COLLECTORS ASSOCIATION, INC. - ACA MEMORIAL LIBRARY
4040 W. 70th St.   Phone: (612) 926-6547
Minneapolis, MN 55435   Debra J. Ciskey, Libn.

AMERICAN HARDWARE MUTUAL INSURANCE COMPANY - LIBRARY
3033 Excelsior Blvd.   Phone: (612) 920-1400
Minneapolis, MN 55416   Sylvia Kamrud, Libn.

AMERICAN SWEDISH INSTITUTE - LIBRARY
2600 Park Ave., S.   Phone: (612) 871-4907
Minneapolis, MN 55407

ASSOCIATED COLLEGIATE PRESS/NATIONAL SCHOLASTIC PRESS
   ASSOCIATION - INFORMATION CENTER
University of Minnesota
620 Rarig Ctr.
330 21st Ave., S.   Phone: (612) 373-3180
Minneapolis, MN 55455   Tom Rolnicki, Exec.Dir.

AUGSBURG COLLEGE - GEORGE SVERDRUP LIBRARY AND MEDIA CENTER
731 21st Ave., S.   Phone: (612) 330-1017
Minneapolis, MN 55454   Margaret J. Anderson, Hd.Libn.

BAKKEN FOUNDATION - BAKKEN LIBRARY OF ELECTRICITY IN LIFE
3537 Zenith Ave., S.   Phone: (612) 927-6508
Minneapolis, MN 55416   Elizabeth Thrig, Hd.Libn.

BARR ENGINEERING COMPANY - LIBRARY
6800 France Ave. S.   Phone: (612) 920-0655
Minneapolis, MN 55435   Francine Creme, Tech.Libn.

BARTON-ASCHMAN ASSOCIATES, INC. - LIBRARY
10 Cedar Square West
1610 S. Sixth St.   Phone: (612) 332-0421
Minneapolis, MN 55454   Betsy Williams-Flores, Libn.

BIBLE SCIENCE ASSOCIATION - RESEARCH CENTER
2911 E. 42nd St.   Phone: (612) 724-1883
Minneapolis, MN 55406   Rev. Walter Lang, Exec.Dir.

CAMPBELL-MITHUN, INC. - INFORMATION SERVICES
110 S. 7th St.   Phone: (612) 347-1509
Minneapolis, MN 55402   Virginia Ferestad, Mgr., Info.Serv.

CARGILL, INC. - INFORMATION CENTER
Box 9300   Phone: (612) 475-6498
Minneapolis, MN 55440   Julia Peterson, Mgr.

CARLSON COMPANIES - LIBRARY
12755 State Hwy. 55   Phone: (612) 540-5236
Minneapolis, MN 55441   Stella M. Rosow, Libn.

CHILDREN'S THEATRE COMPANY AND SCHOOL - LIBRARY
2400 Third Ave. S.   Phone: (612) 874-0500
Minneapolis, MN 55404

CONTROL DATA BUSINESS ADVISORS, INC. - FACTFINDERS
3601 W. 77th St.
7th Fl. MNB07F   Phone: (612) 921-4222
Minneapolis, MN 55435   Crystal Clift, Lib.Dir.

CONTROL DATA CORPORATION - CORPORATE LIBRARY
8100 34th Ave. S.
Box O, HQW06Z   Phone: (612) 853-4229
Minneapolis, MN 55440   Gloria T. Andrew, Mgr.

DAIN BOSWORTH, INC. - LIBRARY
100 Dain Tower   Phone: (612) 371-2774
Minneapolis, MN 55402   Ruth Gadola, Libn.

DAYTON HUDSON CORPORATION - INFORMATION CENTER
777 Nicollet Mall   Phone: (612) 370-6769
Minneapolis, MN 55402   Douglas Schmidt, Info.Ctr.Coord.

DELOITTE HASKINS & SELLS - LIBRARY
625 Fourth Ave. S., Suite 1000   Phone: (612) 333-2900
Minneapolis, MN 55415   Richard G. Reynen, Libn.

DONALDSON COMPANY, INC. - INFORMATION CENTER
Box 1299   Phone: (612) 887-3019
Minneapolis, MN 55440   Arlene Louton, Supv., Info.Serv.

DORSEY & WHITNEY - LAW LIBRARY
2200 First Bank Place East   Phone: (612) 340-2613
Minneapolis, MN 55402   Ann M. Carter, Lib.Mgr.

DUNWOODY INDUSTRIAL INSTITUTE - JOHN A. BUTLER LEARNING
   CENTER
818 Wayzata Blvd.   Phone: (612) 374-5800
Minneapolis, MN 55403

EARTHWORK - CENTER FOR RURAL STUDIES
Box 8445
Minneapolis, MN 55408   Mark Ritchie

EDGEWATER BAPTIST CHURCH - LIBRARY *
5501 Chicago Ave.   Phone: (612) 827-3803
Minneapolis, MN 55417   Gordon Krantz, Libn.

EXPERIENCE, INC. - INFORMATION CENTER
1930 Dain Tower   Phone: (612) 333-5231
Minneapolis, MN 55402   Grieg Aspnes, Mgr., Info.Serv.

FAEGRE & BENSON - LAW LIBRARY
2300 Multifoods Tower
33 S. 6th St.   Phone: (612) 371-5300
Minneapolis, MN 55402   Carolyn Scott, Libn.

FAIRVIEW COMMUNITY HOSPITALS - HEALTH SCIENCES LIBRARY
2312 S. Sixth St.   Phone: (612) 371-6545
Minneapolis, MN 55454   Linda McIntosh, Dir.

FAIRVIEW DEACONESS HOSPITAL - MEDICAL LIBRARY †
1400 E. 24th St.   Phone: (612) 721-9475
Minneapolis, MN 55404   Susan Clark, Libn.

FAR EASTERN RESEARCH LIBRARY
5812 Knox Ave., S.   Phone: (612) 926-6887
Minneapolis, MN 55419   Dr. Jerome Cavanaugh, Dir.

FEDERAL RESERVE BANK OF MINNEAPOLIS - LAW LIBRARY
250 Marquette Ave.   Phone: (612) 340-2412
Minneapolis, MN 55480   Sheldon Azine, Dir.

FEDERAL RESERVE BANK OF MINNEAPOLIS - LIBRARY
250 Marquette, S.   Phone: (612) 340-2292
Minneapolis, MN 55480   Joanne E. Farley, Mgr., Lib.Serv.

FLUIDYNE ENGINEERING CORPORATION - TECHNICAL LIBRARY
5900 Olson Memorial Hwy.   Phone: (612) 544-2721
Minneapolis, MN 55422   Marlys J. Johnson, Tech.Libn.

GENERAL MILLS, INC. - JAMES FORD BELL TECHNICAL CENTER -
    TECHNICAL INFORMATION SERVICES
9000 Plymouth Ave., N.   Phone: (612) 540-3464
Minneapolis, MN 55427   Dr. Curtis H. Hallstrom, Mgr., Tech.Info.Serv.

GENERAL MILLS, INC. - LAW LIBRARY
Box 1113   Phone: (612) 540-2047
Minneapolis, MN 55440   Linda Rolontz, Law Libn.

GENERAL MILLS, INC. - MARKETING RESEARCH INFORMATION CENTER
Box 1113   Phone: (612) 540-2070
Minneapolis, MN 55440   Judith A. Galt, Mktg.Res.Info.Spec.

GENERAL MILLS, INC. - MGO LIBRARY/INFORMATION CENTER
Box 1113   Phone: (612) 540-3536
Minneapolis, MN 55440   Andrea C. Honebrink, Mgr.Lib./Info.Serv.

GOLDEN VALLEY LUTHERAN COLLEGE - LIBRARY †
6125 Olson Hwy.   Phone: (612) 542-1210
Minneapolis, MN 55422   Richard Serena, Libn.

GRAHAM (Billy) EVANGELISTIC ASSOCIATION - LIBRARY
1300 Harmon Place   Phone: (612) 338-0500
Minneapolis, MN 55403   Rev. Roger C. Palms, Ed.

GRAY, PLANT, MOOTY, MOOTY, AND BENNETT - LAW LIBRARY †
300 Roanoke Bldg.   Phone: (612) 343-2955
Minneapolis, MN 55402   Annette Jenson, Libn.

GUTHRIE THEATER FOUNDATION - GUTHRIE THEATER STAFF REFERENCE
    LIBRARY
725 Vineland Pl.   Phone: (612) 347-1133
Minneapolis, MN 55403   Katherine Ewald, Libn./Res.

HAMILTON ASSOCIATES, INC. - LIBRARY
2021 E. Hennepin   Phone: (612) 378-1700
Minneapolis, MN 55413   Marilynn R. Anderson, Libn.

HANSEN PRIVATE LIBRARY
3901 E. 49th St.
Minneapolis, MN 55417

HENKEL CORPORATION - HENNEPIN TECHNICAL CENTER LIBRARY
2010 E. Hennepin Ave.   Phone: (612) 378-8758
Minneapolis, MN 55413   Dr. R.R. Dueltgen, Dir., Info.Serv.

HENNEPIN COUNTY HISTORICAL SOCIETY - ARCHIVES
2303 Third Ave., S.   Phone: (612) 870-1329
Minneapolis, MN 55404   Donna Lind, Exec.Dir.

HENNEPIN COUNTY LAW LIBRARY †
C2451 Government Ctr.   Phone: (612) 348-3022
Minneapolis, MN 55487   Anne W. Grande, Dir.

HENNEPIN COUNTY LIBRARY SYSTEM - GOVERNMENT CENTER
    INFORMATION LIBRARY
C-2359 Government Center
300 S. Sixth St.   Phone: (612) 348-2024
Minneapolis, MN 55487   Carol LeDuc, Sr.Libn.

HENNEPIN COUNTY MEDICAL CENTER - HEALTH SCIENCES LIBRARY
701 Park Ave.   Phone: (612) 347-2710
Minneapolis, MN 55415   Patricia A. Williams, Sr.Libn.

HOLY TRINITY LUTHERAN CHURCH - LIBRARY
2730 E. 31st St.   Phone: (612) 729-8358
Minneapolis, MN 55406   Mae Cruys, Hd.Libn.

HONEYWELL, INC. - SYSTEMS & RESEARCH CENTER - LIBRARY
2600 Ridgeway Pkwy.
Box 312   Phone: (612) 378-4238
Minneapolis, MN 55440   Maro Theologides, Supv., Lib.Info.Serv.

IDS/AMERICAN EXPRESS, INC. - INVESTMENT LIBRARY
IDS Tower   Phone: (612) 372-3429
Minneapolis, MN 55402   Mel Kirkpatrick, Libn.

INTERNATIONAL DIABETES CENTER - LIBRARY
4959 Excelsior Blvd.   Phone: (612) 927-3393
Minneapolis, MN 55416   Helen R. Bowlin, Health Prof.Coord.

JEWISH COMMUNITY CENTER OF GREATER MINNEAPOLIS - LIBRARY
4330 S. Cedar Lake Rd.   Phone: (612) 377-8330
Minneapolis, MN 55416   Sharon Perwien, Lib.Coord.

JEWISH COMMUNITY RELATIONS COUNCIL - ANTI-DEFAMATION LEAGUE
    OF MINNESOTA-DAKOTAS - LIBRARY
15 S. 9th St. Bldg., Suite 400   Phone: (612) 338-7816
Minneapolis, MN 55402   Morton W. Ryweck, Dir.

LAND O'LAKES, INC. - RESEARCH & DEVELOPMENT LIBRARY
Box 116   Phone: (612) 481-2691
Minneapolis, MN 55440   Ann Becker, Libn.

LAWYERS' JOINT LAW LIBRARY †
3930 IDS Tower   Phone: (612) 338-4320
Minneapolis, MN 55402   Barbara E. Schmidt, Libn.

LUTHERAN BROTHERHOOD INSURANCE SOCIETY - LB LIBRARY
625 Fourth Ave., S.   Phone: (612) 340-7269
Minneapolis, MN 55415   Grete Hanson, Libn.

MARTIN/WILLIAMS ADVERTISING AGENCY - LIBRARY/INFORMATION
    CENTER
10 S. 5th St.   Phone: (612) 340-0800
Minneapolis, MN 55402   L. Bock, Dir., Info.Serv.

MEDTRONIC, INC. - LIBRARY †
3055 Old Hwy. 8
Box 1453   Phone: (612) 574-3497
Minneapolis, MN 55440   Leonard Bigelow, Mgr. of Lib.Serv.

MINITEX
S-33 Wilson Library, Univ. of Minnesota
309 19th Ave. S.   Phone: (612) 376-3925
Minneapolis, MN 55455-0414   William DeJohn, Dir.

MINNEAPOLIS COLLEGE OF ART AND DESIGN - LIBRARY AND MEDIA
    CENTER
200 E. 25th St.   Phone: (612) 870-3291
Minneapolis, MN 55404   Richard Kronstedt, Hd.Libn.

MINNEAPOLIS INSTITUTE OF ARTS - ARTS RESOURCE AND INFORMATION
    CENTER
2400 Third Ave., S.   Phone: (612) 870-3131
Minneapolis, MN 55404   Robert C. Booker, Supv.

MINNEAPOLIS INSTITUTE OF ARTS - LIBRARY
2400 Third Ave., S.   Phone: (612) 874-0200
Minneapolis, MN 55404   Harold Peterson, Libn.

MINNEAPOLIS PUBLIC LIBRARY & INFORMATION CENTER - ART, MUSIC &
    FILMS DEPARTMENT
300 Nicollet Mall   Phone: (612) 372-6520
Minneapolis, MN 55401   Richard Zgodava, Act.Dept.Hd.

MINNEAPOLIS PUBLIC LIBRARY & INFORMATION CENTER - BUSINESS AND
    ECONOMICS DEPARTMENT
300 Nicollet Mall   Phone: (612) 372-6552
Minneapolis, MN 55401   Mary Lawson, Dept.Hd.

MINNEAPOLIS PUBLIC LIBRARY & INFORMATION CENTER - GOVERNMENT
   DOCUMENTS
300 Nicollet Mall   Phone: (612) 372-6534
Minneapolis, MN 55401   Julia Copeland, Doc.Libn.

MINNEAPOLIS PUBLIC LIBRARY & INFORMATION CENTER - HISTORY
   DEPARTMENT
300 Nicollet Mall   Phone: (612) 372-6537
Minneapolis, MN 55401   Robert K. Bruce, Dept.Hd.

MINNEAPOLIS PUBLIC LIBRARY & INFORMATION CENTER - HUTTNER
   ABOLITION AND ANTI-SLAVERY COLLECTION
300 Nicollet Mall   Phone: (612) 372-6522
Minneapolis, MN 55401   Richard Hofstad, Athenaeum Libn.

MINNEAPOLIS PUBLIC LIBRARY & INFORMATION CENTER - KITTLESON
   WORLD WAR II COLLECTION
300 Nicollet Mall   Phone: (612) 372-6522
Minneapolis, MN 55401   Richard Hofstad, Athenaeum Libn.

MINNEAPOLIS PUBLIC LIBRARY & INFORMATION CENTER - LITERATURE
   AND LANGUAGE DEPARTMENT
300 Nicollet Mall   Phone: (612) 372-6540
Minneapolis, MN 55401   Dorothy D. Thews, Dept.Hd.

MINNEAPOLIS PUBLIC LIBRARY & INFORMATION CENTER - MINNEAPOLIS
   ATHENAEUM LIBRARY
300 Nicollet Mall   Phone: (612) 372-6522
Minneapolis, MN 55401   Richard Hofstad, Athenaeum Libn.

MINNEAPOLIS PUBLIC LIBRARY & INFORMATION CENTER - MUNICIPAL
   INFORMATION LIBRARY
City Hall, Rm. 302   Phone: (612) 348-8139
Minneapolis, MN 55415   Nancy Corcoran, Libn.

MINNEAPOLIS PUBLIC LIBRARY & INFORMATION CENTER - 19TH
   CENTURY AMERICAN STUDIES COLLECTION
N. Regional Library, Emerson Rm.
1315 Lowry Ave., N.   Phone: (612) 522-3333
Minneapolis, MN 55411   Richard Hofstad, Athenaeum Libn.

MINNEAPOLIS PUBLIC LIBRARY & INFORMATION CENTER - SOCIOLOGY
   DEPARTMENT
300 Nicollet Mall   Phone: (612) 372-6555
Minneapolis, MN 55401   Eileen Schwartzbauer, Dept.Hd.

MINNEAPOLIS PUBLIC LIBRARY & INFORMATION CENTER - TECHNOLOGY
   AND SCIENCE DEPARTMENT
300 Nicollet Mall   Phone: (612) 372-6570
Minneapolis, MN 55401   Edythe Abrahamson, Hd.

MINNEAPOLIS PUBLIC SCHOOLS - SPECIAL SCHOOL DISTRICT 1 - BOARD
   OF EDUCATION LIBRARY
807 N.E. Broadway   Phone: (612) 348-6048
Minneapolis, MN 55413

MINNEAPOLIS STAR AND TRIBUNE - LIBRARY
Fifth & Portland
Minneapolis, MN 55488   Robert H. Jansen, Hd.Libn.

MINNEAPOLIS TECHNICAL INSTITUTE/MINNEAPOLIS COMMUNITY
   COLLEGE - LIBRARY †
1415 Hennepin Ave. S.   Phone: (612) 341-7219
Minneapolis, MN 55403   David L. Jenson, Libn.

MINNEGASCO, INC. - LIBRARY
201 S. 7th St.   Phone: (612) 372-4824
Minneapolis, MN 55402   Virginia B. Shirk, Libn.

MINNESOTA CITIZENS COUNCIL ON CRIME AND JUSTICE
1427 Washington Ave., S.   Phone: (612) 340-5432
Minneapolis, MN 55454   Richard C. Ericson, Pres.

MINNESOTA HOSPITAL ASSOCIATION/MINNESOTA ASSOCIATION OF
   HOMES FOR THE AGING - LIBRARY
2221 University Ave., S.E., Suite 425   Phone: (612) 331-5571
Minneapolis, MN 55414   Mary Dolan, Res.Info.Spec.

MINNESOTA ORCHESTRA - MUSIC LIBRARY
1111 Nicollet Mall   Phone: (612) 371-5622
Minneapolis, MN 55403   James N. Berdahl, Libn.

MINNESOTA SCIENCE FICTION SOCIETY - LIBRARY
Loop Sta., Box 2128   Phone: (612) 722-5217
Minneapolis, MN 55402   Dennis Lien, Contact Person

MINNESOTA STATE DEPARTMENT OF HEALTH - ROBERT N. BARR PUBLIC
   HEALTH LIBRARY
717 Delaware St., S.E.
Box 9441   Phone: (612) 296-5240
Minneapolis, MN 55440   Lynne Siemers, Libn.

MOUNT OLIVET LUTHERAN CHURCH - LIBRARY
5025 Knox Ave., S.   Phone: (612) 926-7651
Minneapolis, MN 55419   Nancy Dahlquist, Lib.Adm.

MOUNT SINAI HOSPITAL - MEDICAL LIBRARY
2215 Park Ave.   Phone: (612) 871-3700
Minneapolis, MN 55404   Susan J. McIntyre, Med.Libn.

NATIONAL CAR RENTAL SYSTEM, INC. - BUSINESS INFORMATION CENTER
7700 France Ave., S.   Phone: (612) 893-6382
Minneapolis, MN 55435   Holly Hupfer, Info.Coord.

NATIONAL COUNCIL ON FAMILY RELATIONS - FAMILY RESOURCE &
   REFERRAL CENTER
1219 University Ave., S.E.   Phone: (612) 331-2774
Minneapolis, MN 55414   Margaret J. Bodley, Dir.

NATIONAL INDIAN EDUCATION ASSOCIATION - LIBRARY
Ivy Tower Bldg., 2nd Fl.
1115 Second Ave., S.   Phone: (612) 333-5341
Minneapolis, MN 55403   Joyce Yellowhammer, Libn./Data Anl.

NATIONAL PUBLICATIONS LIBRARY
7611 Oakland Ave.   Phone: (612) 861-2162
Minneapolis, MN 55423   Elmer Josephs, Libn.

NORTH CENTRAL BIBLE COLLEGE - T.J. JONES MEMORIAL LIBRARY †
910 Elliot Ave., S.   Phone: (612) 332-3491
Minneapolis, MN 55404   Marvin Smith, Lib.Dir.

NORTHERN STATES POWER COMPANY - COMMUNICATIONS DEPARTMENT
   - "ASK NSP" TAPE LIBRARY
414 Nicollet Mall   Phone: (612) 330-6000
Minneapolis, MN 55401

NORTHERN STATES POWER COMPANY - COMMUNICATIONS DEPARTMENT
   LIBRARY & INFORMATION CENTER
414 Nicollet Mall   Phone: (612) 330-6936
Minneapolis, MN 55401   Gwenn M. Solseth, Info.Anl.

NORTHWESTERN NATIONAL LIFE INSURANCE COMPANY - LIBRARY
20 Washington Ave., S.   Phone: (612) 372-5606
Minneapolis, MN 55440   Beth O'Connor, Libn.

NORWEST CORPORATION - LIBRARY
1200 Peavey Bldg.   Phone: (612) 372-8263
Minneapolis, MN 55479   Marilyn J. Schlee, Lib.Serv.Off.

ONAN CORPORATION - LIBRARY
1400 73rd Ave., N.E.   Phone: (612) 574-5000
Minneapolis, MN 55432   Valera L. Rohrer, Lib.Mgr.

PARK-NICOLLET MEDICAL FOUNDATION - ARNESON LIBRARY
5000 W. 39th St.   Phone: (612) 927-3097
Minneapolis, MN 55416   Barbara K. Latta, Dir.

PEAT, MARWICK, MITCHELL & CO. - LIBRARY
1700 IDS Center   Phone: (612) 341-2222
Minneapolis, MN 55402   Donna J. Harnden, Hd.Libn.

PILLSBURY COMPANY - BUSINESS REFERENCE LIBRARY
Pillsbury Center, 27th Fl.
Mail Station 2754   Phone: (612) 330-4047
Minneapolis, MN 55402   Rachel Berry, Mgr.

PILLSBURY COMPANY - TECHNICAL INFORMATION CENTER
311 Second St., S.E.   Phone: (612) 330-4750
Minneapolis, MN 55414   James B. Tchobanoff, Mgr.

PILOTS INTERNATIONAL ASSOCIATION - LIBRARY
Box 907   Phone: (612) 588-5175
Minneapolis, MN 55440   Laura E. Dirks, Libn.

RIDER, BENNETT, EGAN & ARUNDEL - LIBRARY
2500 First Bank Place W.   Phone: (612) 340-7960
Minneapolis, MN 55402   Janet A. Jacobson, Libn.

ST. MARY'S HOSPITAL - STAFF LIBRARY
2414 S. 7th St.   Phone: (612) 338-2229
Minneapolis, MN 55454   Jacquelynn Carlson, Chf.Libn.

ST. OLAF LUTHERAN CHURCH - CARLSEN MEMORIAL LIBRARY
29th & Emerson Ave., N.   Phone: (612) 529-7726
Minneapolis, MN 55411   Ruth Sivanich, Libn.

SONS OF NORWAY - NORTH STAR LIBRARY
1455 W. Lake St.   Phone: (612) 827-3611
Minneapolis, MN 55408   Bent Vanberg, Cons.

TEL-MED HEALTH INFORMATION SERVICE
Fairview-Southdale Hospital
6401 France Ave. S.   Phone: (612) 924-5959
Minneapolis, MN 55435   Glad Schlossman, Dir.

TEMPLE ISRAEL - LIBRARY
2324 Emerson Ave., S.   Phone: (612) 377-8680
Minneapolis, MN 55405   Georgia Kalman, Libn.

THERMO KING CORPORATION - LIBRARY
314 W. 90th St.   Phone: (612) 887-2336
Minneapolis, MN 55420   Mrs. Rougean Schoenborn, Corp.Libn.

UNITED METHODIST COMMN. ON ARCHIVES & HIST. - MINNESOTA
   ANNUAL CONFERENCE - ARCHIVES & HISTORICAL LIB.
122 W. Franklin Ave., Rm. 400   Phone: (612) 870-3657
Minneapolis, MN 55404   Thelma Boeder, Archv./Exec.Sec.

U.S. BUREAU OF MINES - TWIN CITIES RESEARCH CENTER - LIBRARY
5629 Minnehaha Ave., S.   Phone: (612) 725-4503
Minneapolis, MN 55417   Merle Bernstein, Libn.

U.S. DEPT. OF COMMERCE - INTERNATIONAL TRADE ADMINISTRATION -
   MINNEAPOLIS DISTRICT OFFICE LIBRARY
108 Federal Bldg.
110 S. Fourth St.   Phone: (612) 349-3338
Minneapolis, MN 55401   Mary Hobbs, Trade Spec.

U.S. VETERANS ADMINISTRATION (MN-Minneapolis) - MEDICAL CENTER
   LIBRARY SERVICE
54th St. & 48th Ave., S.   Phone: (612) 725-6767
Minneapolis, MN 55417   Lionelle Elsesser, Chf., Lib.Serv.

UNIVERSITY OF MINNESOTA - AMES LIBRARY OF SOUTH ASIA
Wilson Library s-10
309 19th Ave. S.   Phone: (612) 373-2890
Minneapolis, MN 55455   Henry Scholberg, Libn.

UNIVERSITY OF MINNESOTA - ARCHITECTURE LIBRARY
160 Architecture Bldg.
89 Church St., S.E.   Phone: (612) 373-2203
Minneapolis, MN 55455   A. Kristine Johnson, Hd.

UNIVERSITY OF MINNESOTA - ART COLLECTION
Wilson Library
309 19th Ave., S.   Phone: (612) 373-2875
Minneapolis, MN 55455   Herbert Scherer, Art Libn.

UNIVERSITY OF MINNESOTA - AUDIO VISUAL LIBRARY SERVICE
3300 University Ave., S.E.   Phone: (612) 373-5452
Minneapolis, MN 55414   Judith A. Gaston, Dir.

UNIVERSITY OF MINNESOTA - BELL MUSEUM OF NATURAL HISTORY -
   LIBRARY
10 Church St., S.E.   Phone: (612) 373-7771
Minneapolis, MN 55455   Tom English, Libn.

UNIVERSITY OF MINNESOTA - BIOMEDICAL LIBRARY
Diehl Hall
505 Essex St., S.E.   Phone: (612) 373-5584
Minneapolis, MN 55455   Sherrilynne Fuller, Dir.

UNIVERSITY OF MINNESOTA - BUSINESS REFERENCE SERVICE
Wilson Library, 2nd Fl.
309 19th Ave., S.   Phone: (612) 373-4109
Minneapolis, MN 55455   Judy Wells, Bus.Libn.

UNIVERSITY OF MINNESOTA - CHARLES BABBAGE INSTITUTE
   COLLECTION
104 Walter Library
117 Pleasant St., S.E.   Phone: (612) 376-9336
Minneapolis, MN 55455   Bruce Bruemmer, Archv.

UNIVERSITY OF MINNESOTA - CHEMISTRY LIBRARY
4 Walter Library
117 Pleasant St., S.E.   Phone: (612) 373-2375
Minneapolis, MN 55455   Beverly A. Lee, Libn.

UNIVERSITY OF MINNESOTA - CHILDREN'S LITERATURE RESEARCH
   COLLECTIONS
109 Walter Library
117 Pleasant St., S.E.   Phone: (612) 373-9731
Minneapolis, MN 55455   Karen Nelson Hoyle, Cur.

UNIVERSITY OF MINNESOTA - CLASSICS DEPARTMENT - SEMINAR
   LIBRARY
311 Folwell Hall
9 Pleasant St., S.E.   Phone: (612) 373-3924
Minneapolis, MN 55455   Prof. Jackson Hershbell, Libn.

UNIVERSITY OF MINNESOTA - DELOITTE HASKINS & SELLS TAX
   RESEARCH ROOM
Wilson Library, 2nd Fl.
309 19th Ave., S.   Phone: (612) 373-4109
Minneapolis, MN 55455   Judy Wells, Bus.Libn.

UNIVERSITY OF MINNESOTA - DEPARTMENT OF LINGUISTICS -
   LINGUISTICS LIBRARY
146 Klaeber Court
320 16th Ave., S.E.   Phone: (612) 373-5769
Minneapolis, MN 55455   Karen Frederickson, Sr.Sec.

UNIVERSITY OF MINNESOTA - DRUG INFORMATION SERVICES
3-106 Health Science Unit F
308 Harvard St., S.E.   Phone: (612) 376-7190
Minneapolis, MN 55455   Gary R. Gallo, Dir.

UNIVERSITY OF MINNESOTA - EAST ASIAN LIBRARY
Wilson Library, S-30
309 19th Ave., S.   Phone: (612) 373-3737
Minneapolis, MN 55455   Richard Wang, Hd.

UNIVERSITY OF MINNESOTA - ECONOMICS RESEARCH LIBRARY
525 Science Classroom Bldg.
222 Pleasant St., S.E.   Phone: (612) 373-5958
Minneapolis, MN 55455   Wendy Williamson, Lib.

UNIVERSITY OF MINNESOTA - EDUCATION-PSYCHOLOGY-LIBRARY
   SCIENCE COLLECTION
Walter Library, Rm. 206
117 Pleasant St., S.E.   Phone: (612) 376-4100
Minneapolis, MN 55455   Patricia Stark, Educ.Libn.

UNIVERSITY OF MINNESOTA - ENGINEERING LIBRARY
128 Lind Hall
207 Church St., S.E.   Phone: (612) 373-2957
Minneapolis, MN 55455   Raymond A. Bohling, Hd.

UNIVERSITY OF MINNESOTA - ERIC SEVAREID JOURNALISM LIBRARY
121 Murphy Hall
206 Church St., S.E.   Phone: (612) 373-3174
Minneapolis, MN 55455   Kathleen Hansen, Prof./Libn.

UNIVERSITY OF MINNESOTA - GEOLOGY LIBRARY
Pillsbury Hall, Rm. 204
310 Pillsbury Dr., S.E,   Phone: (612) 373-4052
Minneapolis, MN 55455   Marie Dvorzak, Hd.

UNIVERSITY OF MINNESOTA - GOVERNMENT PUBLICATIONS LIBRARY
409 Wilson Library
309 19th Ave., S.   Phone: (612) 373-7813
Minneapolis, MN 55455   William LaBissoniere, Libn.

UNIVERSITY OF MINNESOTA - HAROLD SCOTT QUIGLEY CENTER OF
  INTERNATIONAL STUDIES LIBRARY
1246 Social Sciences Bldg.
267 19th Ave., S.
Minneapolis, MN 55455

UNIVERSITY OF MINNESOTA - INDUSTRIAL RELATIONS CENTER -
  REFERENCE ROOM
309 Management & Economics, West Campus
271 19th Ave., S.   Phone: (612) 373-3681
Minneapolis, MN 55455   Georgianna Herman, Libn. & Supv.

UNIVERSITY OF MINNESOTA - INFORM
179 Wilson Library
309 19th Ave., S.   Phone: (612) 373-5938
Minneapolis, MN 55455

UNIVERSITY OF MINNESOTA - JAMES FORD BELL LIBRARY
Wilson Library 462
309 19th Ave., S.   Phone: (612) 373-2888
Minneapolis, MN 55455   John Parker, Cur.

UNIVERSITY OF MINNESOTA - LAW LIBRARY
229 19th Ave. S.   Phone: (612) 373-2737
Minneapolis, MN 55455   Kathleen Price, Dir.

UNIVERSITY OF MINNESOTA - LEARNING RESOURCES CENTER - NON-
  PRINT LIBRARY
111 Walter Library
117 Pleasant St., S.E.   Phone: (612) 373-2538
Minneapolis, MN 55455   Daniel Donnelly, Act.Hd.

UNIVERSITY OF MINNESOTA - LITZENBERG-LUND LIBRARY
Box 395, Mayo Memorial Bldg.
420 Delaware St., S.E.   Phone: (612) 373-8851
Minneapolis, MN 55455   Sandra Morrison, Libn.

UNIVERSITY OF MINNESOTA - MAP LIBRARY
Wilson Library, S-76
309 19th Ave. S.   Phone: (612) 373-2825
Minneapolis, MN 55455   J. Mai Treude, Libn.

UNIVERSITY OF MINNESOTA - MATHEMATICS LIBRARY
Vincent Hall, Rm. 310
206 Church St. S.E.   Phone: (612) 376-7207
Minneapolis, MN 55455   Margie L. Voelker, Libn.

UNIVERSITY OF MINNESOTA - MIDDLE EAST LIBRARY
S50 Wilson Library
309 19th Ave., S.   Phone: (612) 373-7804
Minneapolis, MN 55455   Nassif Youssif, Hd.

UNIVERSITY OF MINNESOTA - MINNESOTA CENTER FOR PHILOSOPHY OF
  SCIENCE - DEPARTMENTAL LIBRARY
309 Ford Hall
224 Church St., S.E.   Phone: (612) 373-2845
Minneapolis, MN 55455   Philip Kitcher, Dir.

UNIVERSITY OF MINNESOTA - MUSIC LIBRARY
204a Walter Library
117 Pleasant St., S.E.   Phone: (612) 373-3438
Minneapolis, MN 55455   Katharine Holum, Music Libn.

UNIVERSITY OF MINNESOTA - NEWMAN CENTER LIBRARY
1701 University Ave., S.E.   Phone: (612) 331-3437
Minneapolis, MN 55414   Christine Cundall, Libn.

UNIVERSITY OF MINNESOTA - OCCUPATIONAL INFORMATION LIBRARY
101 Eddy Hall
192 Pillsbury Dr., S.E.   Phone: (612) 373-4193
Minneapolis, MN 55455   Dr. Ellen Betz, Supv. of Lib.

UNIVERSITY OF MINNESOTA - PHYSICS LIBRARY
260 Tate Lab. of Physics
116 Church St. S.E.   Phone: (612) 373-3362
Minneapolis, MN 55455   Donald Marion, Libn.

UNIVERSITY OF MINNESOTA - PUBLIC ADMINISTRATION LIBRARY
365 Blegen Hall
269 19th Ave. S.   Phone: (612) 373-2892
Minneapolis, MN 55455   Eunice Bisbee Johnson, Sr.Lib.Asst.

UNIVERSITY OF MINNESOTA - ST. ANTHONY FALLS HYDRAULIC
  LABORATORY - LORENZ G. STRAUB MEMORIAL LIBRARY
Mississippi River at Third Ave., S.E.   Phone: (612) 373-2782
Minneapolis, MN 55414   Diana Dalbothen, Libn.

UNIVERSITY OF MINNESOTA - SCANDINAVIAN COLLECTION
Wilson Library
309 19th Ave. S.   Phone: (612) 376-2550
Minneapolis, MN 55455   Mariann Tiblin, Bibliog.

UNIVERSITY OF MINNESOTA - SOCIAL AND ADMINISTRATIVE PHARMACY
  READING ROOM
7-159 Health Sciences Unit F
308 Harvard St., S.E.   Phone: (612) 376-5326
Minneapolis, MN 55455   Dr. Albert I. Wertheimer, Dir.

UNIVERSITY OF MINNESOTA - SOCIAL WELFARE HISTORY ARCHIVES
109 Walter Library
117 Pleasant St., S.E.   Phone: (612) 373-4420
Minneapolis, MN 55455   David Klaassen, Cur.

UNIVERSITY OF MINNESOTA - SPECIAL COLLECTIONS AND RARE BOOKS
  LIBRARY
Wilson Library 466
309 19th Ave. S.   Phone: (612) 373-2897
Minneapolis, MN 55455   Austin J. McLean, Cur., Spec.Coll.

UNIVERSITY OF MINNESOTA - STATISTICS LIBRARY
270a Vincent Hall
206 Church St., S.E.   Phone: (612) 373-3035
Minneapolis, MN 55455   Seymour Geisser, Dir.

UNIVERSITY OF MINNESOTA - UNDERGROUND SPACE CENTER - LIBRARY
790 Civil and Mineral Engr.Bldg.
500 Pillsbury Dr., S.E.   Phone: (612) 376-5341
Minneapolis, MN 55455   Arlene R. Bennett, Adm.Sec.

UNIVERSITY OF MINNESOTA - UNIVERSITY ARCHIVES
10 Walter Library
117 Pleasant St. S.E.   Phone: (612) 373-2891
Minneapolis, MN 55455

WALKER ART CENTER - STAFF REFERENCE LIBRARY
Vineland Pl.   Phone: (612) 375-7680
Minneapolis, MN 55403   Rosemary Furtak, Dir.

WORKING OPPORTUNITIES FOR WOMEN - RESOURCE CENTER
2344 Nicollet Ave., Suite 140   Phone: (612) 874-6636
Minneapolis, MN 55404   Kate Wulf, Dir.

OAK TERRACE NURSING HOME - DPW LIBRARY
County Rd. 67   Phone: (612) 934-4100
Minnetonka, MN 55343   Susan F. Ager, Lib.Dir.

ROLLOFF (C.A.) FOUR COUNTY LAW LIBRARY
Chippewa County Courthouse   Phone: (612) 269-7733
Montevideo, MN 56265   C.A. Rolloff, Sec.

CLAY COUNTY HISTORICAL SOCIETY - ARCHIVES
22 N. 8th St.
Box 501   Phone: (218) 233-4604
Moorhead, MN 56560   John Schermeister, Exec.Dir.

NORTHWEST MINNESOTA HISTORICAL CENTER - LIBRARY
Moorhead State University Library   Phone: (218) 236-2922
Moorhead, MN 56560   Evelyn J. Swenson, Dir.

PLAINS ART MUSEUM - LIBRARY
521 Main Ave.
Moorhead, MN 56560
Phone: (218) 236-7171
Susan Talbot-Stanaway, Cur., Educ.

ST. ANSGAR HOSPITAL - HEALTH SCIENCE LIBRARY
715 N. 11th St.
Moorhead, MN 56560-2088
Phone: (218) 299-2252
Char Myhre, Libn./Educ.Coord.

TRINITY LUTHERAN CHURCH - LIBRARY
210 S. 7th St.
Moorhead, MN 56560
Phone: (218) 236-1333
Rodney Erickson, Comm.Chm.

MOOSE LAKE STATE HOSPITAL - STAFF LIBRARY
1000 Lake Shore Dr.
Moose Lake, MN 55767
Phone: (218) 485-4411
John C. Flynn, Libn.

WEST CENTRAL MINNESOTA HISTORICAL CENTER - LIBRARY
University of Minnesota, Morris
Morris, MN 56267
Phone: (612) 589-2211
Dr. Wilbert H. Ahern, Dir.

UNITED THEOLOGICAL SEMINARY OF THE TWIN CITIES - LIBRARY
3000 Fifth St., N.W.
New Brighton, MN 55112
Phone: (612) 633-4311
Arthur L. Merrill, Dir.

BROWN COUNTY HISTORICAL SOCIETY - MUSEUM LIBRARY
27 N. Broadway
Box 116
New Ulm, MN 56073
Phone: (507) 354-2016
Paul Klammer, Musm.Dir.

MANKATO AREA VOCATIONAL-TECHNICAL INSTITUTE - LIBRARY
1920 Lee Blvd.
North Mankato, MN 56001
Phone: (507) 625-3441
Diane Brennan, Libn.

CARLETON COLLEGE - SCIENCE LIBRARY
Northfield, MN 55057
Phone: (507) 663-4415
Elizabeth K. Tomlinson, Sci.Libn.

NORWEGIAN-AMERICAN HISTORICAL ASSOCIATION - ARCHIVES
St. Olaf College
Northfield, MN 55057
Phone: (507) 663-3221
Charlotte Jacobson, Cur. of Archv.

CROSIER SEMINARY - LIBRARY
Onamia, MN 56359
Phone: (612) 532-3103
Richard McGrath, Dir.

OWATONNA PUBLIC LIBRARY - TOY LIBRARY
105 N. Elm
Owatonna, MN 55060
Phone: (507) 451-4660
Andrea Hoslett, Hd., Children's Serv.

U.S. NATL. PARK SERVICE - PIPESTONE NATL. MONUMENT - LIBRARY &
  ARCHIVES
Box 727
Pipestone, MN 56164
Phone: (507) 825-5463
David L. Lane, Supt.

HONEYWELL, INC. - SOLID STATE ELECTRONICS DIVISION LIBRARY
12001 Hwy. 55
Plymouth, MN 55441
Phone: (612) 541-2075
Kathleen M. Knauer, Res.Libn.

FIRST LUTHERAN CHURCH OF THE LUTHERAN CHURCH IN AMERICA -
  SCHENDEL MEMORIAL LIBRARY
615 5th St.
Red Wing, MN 55066
Phone: (612) 388-9311
Mrs. Delma Rigelman, Libn.

GOODHUE COUNTY HISTORICAL SOCIETY - LIBRARY
1166 Oak St.
Red Wing, MN 55066
Phone: (612) 388-6024
Orville K. Olson, Cur. of Musm.

OAK GROVE LUTHERAN CHURCH - MEMORIAL LIBRARY †
71st & Lyndale Ave., S.
Richfield, MN 55423
Phone: (612) 869-4917
Mrs. Forrest Carpenter, Libn.

WOODLAKE LUTHERAN CHURCH - LIBRARY
7525 Oliver Ave., S.
Richfield, MN 55423
Phone: (612) 866-8449
Jean Ellefson, Church Libn.

NORTH MEMORIAL MEDICAL CENTER - MEDICAL LIBRARY
3300 Oakdale N.
Robbinsdale, MN 55422
Phone: (612) 520-5673
Donna Barbour-Talley, Dir., Med.Lib.

AMERICAN OTOLOGICAL SOCIETY, INC. - LIBRARY
200 First St., S.W.
Rochester, MN 55905
Jack D. Clemis, M.D., Ed.-Libn.

IBM CORPORATION - INFORMATION CENTER/LIBRARY
Dept. 205, Hwy. 52 & 37th St., N.W.
Rochester, MN 55901
Phone: (507) 286-4462
Ursula Shimek, Sr.Libn.

MAYO FOUNDATION - MAYO CLINIC LIBRARY
200 First St., S.W.
Rochester, MN 55905
Phone: (507) 284-2061
Jack D. Key, Libn.

MINNESOTA BIBLE COLLEGE - LIBRARY
920 Mayowood Rd., S.W.
Rochester, MN 55901
Phone: (507) 288-4563
Ardis C. Sawyer, Libn.

OLMSTED COUNTY HISTORICAL SOCIETY - LIBRARY AND ARCHIVES
Box 6411
Rochester, MN 55903
Phone: (507) 282-9447
Doris Blinks, Lib.Supv.

ROCHESTER METHODIST HOSPITAL - METHODIST KAHLER LIBRARY
Rochester, MN 55901
Phone: (507) 286-7425
Jean M. Brose, Hd.Libn.

ROCHESTER POST-BULLETIN - NEWS LIBRARY *
18 First Ave., S.E.
Rochester, MN 55901
Phone: (507) 285-7730
Marcy Sawyer, News Libn.

ST. MARY'S HOSPITAL - LIBRARY
1216 2nd St., S.W.
Rochester, MN 55902
Phone: (507) 285-5647
Elizabeth Warfield, Libn.

HONEYWELL, INC. - TECHNOLOGY STRATEGY CENTER - INFORMATION
  SERVICES
400 Rosedale Towers
1700 W. Hwy. 36
Roseville, MN 55113
Phone: (612) 378-5441
Denise Cumming, Info.Spec.

MINNESOTA STATE POLLUTION CONTROL AGENCY - LIBRARY
1935 W. County Road B-2
Roseville, MN 55113
Phone: (612) 296-7719
Elizabeth C. Gelbmann, Libn.

SPERRY COMPUTER SYSTEMS - ROSEVILLE INFORMATION CENTER
2276 Highcrest Rd.
Roseville, MN 55113
Phone: (612) 633-6170
Mary C. Steele, Mgr.

CENTRAL MINNESOTA HISTORICAL CENTER - LIBRARY
St. Cloud State University
St. Cloud, MN 56301
Phone: (612) 255-3254
Dr. Calvin W. Gower, Dir.

DIOCESE OF ST. CLOUD - BUREAU OF EDUCATION - MEDIA CENTER
305 7th Ave., N.
St. Cloud, MN 56301
Phone: (612) 252-1021
Sr. Mary Leone Furnstahl, Media Cons.

ST. CLOUD HOSPITAL - HEALTH SCIENCES LIBRARY *
1406 Sixth Ave., N.
St. Cloud, MN 56301
Phone: (612) 251-2700
Judy Heeter, Libn.

U.S. VETERANS ADMINISTRATION (MN-St. Cloud) - MEDICAL CENTER
  LIBRARY
St. Cloud, MN 56301
Phone: (612) 252-1670
Sanford J. Banker, Chf., Lib.Serv.

BETH EL SYNAGOGUE - MAX SHAPIRO LIBRARY
5224 W. 26th St.
St. Louis Park, MN 55416
Phone: (612) 920-3512
Arlene Kase, Libn.

METHODIST HOSPITAL - MEDICAL LIBRARY
6500 Excelsior Blvd.
St. Louis Park, MN 55426
Phone: (612) 932-5451
Pearly Rudin, Med.Libn.

THE ACID RAIN FOUNDATION, INC. - LIBRARY
1630 Blackhawk Hills Rd.
St. Paul, MN 55122
Phone: (612) 455-7719

AMERICAN HOIST & DERRICK CO. - ENGINEERING STANDARDS LIBRARY
63 S. Robert St.
St. Paul, MN 55107
Phone: (612) 293-4567
Jean Price

BAPTIST GENERAL CONFERENCE - ARCHIVES
3949 Bethel Dr.   Phone: (612) 638-6282
St. Paul, MN 55112   G. David Guston, Archv.

BETHEL THEOLOGICAL SEMINARY - RESOURCE CENTER
3949 Bethel Dr.   Phone: (612) 638-6184
St. Paul, MN 55112   Norris Magnuson, Dir.

BETHESDA LUTHERAN MEDICAL CENTER - MEDICAL-NURSING LIBRARY
570 Capitol Blvd.   Phone: (612) 221-2291
St. Paul, MN 55103   Eileen E. Glessner, Dir., Lib.Serv.

CENTRAL BAPTIST CHURCH - MEDIA CENTER
420 N. Roy   Phone: (612) 646-2751
St. Paul, MN 55104

CHAMPION INTERNATIONAL - TECHNICAL CENTER LIBRARY
2250 Wabash Ave.   Phone: (612) 641-4125
St. Paul, MN 55114   Jeanette Kustelski, Libn.

CHILDREN'S HOSPITAL, INC. - MEDICAL-NURSING LIBRARY
345 N. Smith Ave.   Phone: (612) 227-6521
St. Paul, MN 55102   Nancy W. Battaglia, Med.Libn.

COLLEGE OF ST. CATHERINE - LIBRARY - RUTH SAWYER COLLECTION
2004 Randolph Ave.   Phone: (612) 690-6553
St. Paul, MN 55105   Sr. Mary William Brady, Archv.

COLLEGE OF ST. CATHERINE - LIBRARY - WOMAN'S COLLECTION
2004 Randolph Ave.   Phone: (612) 690-6648
St. Paul, MN 55105   Margaret Conant, Hd., Rd.Serv. & ILL

COLLEGE OF ST. CATHERINE - PERFORMING ARTS LIBRARY
2004 Randolph Ave.   Phone: (612) 690-6696
St. Paul, MN 55105   Donald Bemis Jones, Libn.

COLLEGE OF ST. CATHERINE - SAINT CATHERINE LIBRARY
2004 Randolph Ave.   Phone: (612) 690-6650
St. Paul, MN 55105   Sr. Elizabeth Delmore, Lib.Dir.

COLLEGE OF ST. THOMAS - O'SHAUGHNESSY LIBRARY - SPECIAL
  COLLECTIONS
2115 Summit Ave.   Phone: (612) 647-5318
St. Paul, MN 55105   John B. Davenport, Spec.Coll.Libn.

COMO ZOO - LIBRARY
Midway Pkwy. & Kaufman Dr.   Phone: (612) 488-4041
St. Paul, MN 55103   Lala Byng, Libn.

CONCORDIA COLLEGE - BUENGER MEMORIAL LIBRARY
275 N. Syndicate   Phone: (612) 641-8240
St. Paul, MN 55104   Glenn W. Offermann, Hd.Libn.

CONWED CORPORATION - BUSINESS INFORMATION CENTER
444 Cedar St.
Box 64237   Phone: (612) 221-1271
St. Paul, MN 55164   Jean Marie Holles, Mgr.

DAYTONS BLUFF AREA EARLY CHILDHOOD & FAMILY EDUCATION
  PROGRAM - TOY & BOOK LIBRARY
262 Bates Ave.   Phone: (612) 774-5966
St. Paul, MN 55106   Mary Ann Cogelow, Prog.Dir.

ECONOMICS LABORATORY, INC. - CORPORATE INFORMATION CENTER
Osborn Bldg.   Phone: (612) 451-5651
St. Paul, MN 55102   D.M. Sontag Bradt, Mgr.

FIRST BAPTIST CHURCH - LIBRARY
Ninth & Wacouta Sts.   Phone: (612) 222-0718
St. Paul, MN 55101   Debbie Kessler, Libn.

GILLETTE CHILDREN'S HOSPITAL - PROFESSIONAL LIBRARY
200 E. University   Phone: (612) 291-2848
St. Paul, MN 55101   K. McCarty, Med. Staff Sec.

HAMLINE UNIVERSITY - BUSH MEMORIAL LIBRARY - SPECIAL
  COLLECTIONS
1536 Hewitt Ave.   Phone: (612) 641-2373
St. Paul, MN 55104

HAMLINE UNIVERSITY SCHOOL OF LAW - LIBRARY
1536 Hewitt Ave.   Phone: (612) 641-2119
St. Paul, MN 55104

HILL (James Jerome) REFERENCE LIBRARY
Fourth St. at Market   Phone: (612) 227-9531
St. Paul, MN 55102   Virgil F. Massman, Exec.Dir.

LEAGUE OF MINNESOTA CITIES - LIBRARY
183 University Ave., E.   Phone: (612) 227-5600
St. Paul, MN 55101   Peter Tritz, Res.Dir.

LUTHER NORTHWESTERN SEMINARY - LIBRARY
2375 Como Ave.   Phone: (612) 641-3225
St. Paul, MN 55108   Norman G. Wente, Chf.Libn.

MACALESTER COLLEGE - OLIN SCIENCE LIBRARY
1600 Grand Ave.   Phone: (612) 696-6344
St. Paul, MN 55105   Rosemary Salscheider, Supv.

MACALESTER COLLEGE - WEYERHAEUSER LIBRARY
Grand & Macalester Sts.   Phone: (612) 696-6345
St. Paul, MN 55105   Jean K. Archibald, Lib.Dir.

METROPOLITAN COUNCIL OF THE TWIN CITIES AREA - LIBRARY
300 Metro Sq.   Phone: (612) 227-9421
St. Paul, MN 55101   Mary D. Adams, Libn.

MIDWAY HOSPITAL - HEALTH SCIENCES LIBRARY
1700 University Ave.   Phone: (612) 641-5234
St. Paul, MN 55104   Carol Windham, Hd.Libn.

MIDWEST CHINA CENTER
2375 Como Ave., W.
Gullixson Hall, Rm. 308   Phone: (612) 641-3238
St. Paul, MN 55108   P. Richard Bohr, Dir.

MIDWEST CHINA CENTER - MIDWEST CHINA ORAL HISTORY ARCHIVES
  AND MUSEUM COLLECTION
2375 Como Ave.   Phone: (612) 641-3238
St. Paul, MN 55108   Jane Baker Koons, Dir., Prog.Dev.

MINNESOTA AGRICULTURAL STATISTICS SERVICE - LIBRARY
90 W. Plato Blvd.
Box 70068   Phone: (612) 296-2230
St. Paul, MN 55107   Linda Wright, Info.Spec.

MINNESOTA GEOLOGICAL SURVEY - LIBRARY
University of Minnesota
2642 University Ave.   Phone: (612) 373-3372
St. Paul, MN 55114-1057   Lynn Swanson, Sr.Lib.Asst.

MINNESOTA HISTORICAL SOCIETY - DIVISION OF ARCHIVES AND
  MANUSCRIPTS
1500 Mississippi St.   Phone: (612) 296-6980
St. Paul, MN 55101   Sue E. Holbert, State Archv.

MINNESOTA HISTORICAL SOCIETY - FORT SNELLING BRANCH LIBRARY
Fort Snelling History Center   Phone: (612) 726-1171
St. Paul, MN 55111

MINNESOTA HISTORICAL SOCIETY - REFERENCE LIBRARY
690 Cedar St.   Phone: (612) 296-2143
St. Paul, MN 55101   Patricia C. Harpole, Chf. of Ref.Lib.

MINNESOTA HISTORICAL SOCIETY - SPECIAL LIBRARIES
690 Cedar St.   Phone: (612) 296-2489
St. Paul, MN 55101   Bonnie Wilson, Hd.

MINNESOTA MUSEUM OF ART - LIBRARY
St. Peter St. at Kellogg Blvd.   Phone: (612) 292-4350
St. Paul, MN 55102   Leanne A. Klein, Assoc.Cur., Coll.Mgt.

MINNESOTA STATE ATTORNEY GENERAL - LAW LIBRARY
102 State Capitol Bldg.   Phone: (612) 296-8152
St. Paul, MN 55155   Anita Anderson, Libn.

MINNESOTA STATE BOARD OF ANIMAL HEALTH - LIBRARY
160 Agriculture Bldg.
90 W. Plato Blvd.   Phone: (612) 296-2942
St. Paul, MN 55107   J.G. Flint, Sec./Exec.Off.

MINNESOTA STATE DEPARTMENT OF ECONOMIC SECURITY - LIBRARY
690 American Center Bldg.   Phone: (612) 296-8810
St. Paul, MN 55101   Linda Woodstrom, Libn.

MINNESOTA STATE DEPARTMENT OF EDUCATION - INTERAGENCY
   RESOURCE AND INFORMATION CENTER
401-A Capitol Square Bldg.   Phone: (612) 296-6684
St. Paul, MN 55101   Pat Tupper, Lib.Prog.Dir.

MINNESOTA STATE DEPARTMENT OF EDUCATION - OFFICE OF PUBLIC
   LIBRARIES AND INTERLIBRARY COOPERATION - LIBRARY
Capitol Sq. Bldg.
550 Cedar St.   Phone: (612) 296-2821
St. Paul, MN 55101   Darlene M. Arnold, Sr.Libn.

MINNESOTA STATE DEPARTMENT OF ENERGY AND ECONOMIC
   DEVELOPMENT - ENERGY LIBRARY
150 E. Kellogg Blvd., Rm. 980   Phone: (612) 296-8902
St. Paul, MN 55101   Donna Slamkowski, Res.Libn.

MINNESOTA STATE DEPARTMENT OF PUBLIC SAFETY - FILM LIBRARY
Griggs Midway Bldg., Rm. 180 S.
1821 University Ave.   Phone: (612) 482-5925
St. Paul, MN 55104   Janet Weber, Supv.

MINNESOTA STATE DEPARTMENT OF REVENUE - TAX LIBRARY *
Centennial Office Bldg.
658 Cedar St.   Phone: (612) 296-1022
St. Paul MN 55145

MINNESOTA STATE DEPARTMENT OF TRANSPORTATION - LIBRARY AND
   INFORMATION SERVICES SECTION
B-26A State Transportation Bldg.   Phone: (612) 296-2385
St. Paul, MN 55155   Jerome C. Baldwin, Dir., Lib./Info.Serv.

MINNESOTA STATE HORTICULTURAL SOCIETY - LIBRARY
161 Alderman Hall
1970 Folwell Ave.   Phone: (612) 373-1031
St. Paul, MN 55108   Glenn Ray, Exec.Dir.

MINNESOTA STATE INFORMATION SYSTEMS DIVISION - LIBRARY
Centennial Office Bldg., 5th Fl.   Phone: (612) 296-4621
St. Paul, MN 55155   Arlene Kromminga, Libn.

MINNESOTA STATE LAW LIBRARY
117 University Ave.   Phone: (612) 296-2775
St. Paul, MN 55155   Marvin Roger Anderson, State Law Libn.

MINNESOTA STATE LEGISLATIVE REFERENCE LIBRARY
State Capitol, Rm. 111   Phone: (612) 296-8338
St. Paul, MN 55155   Linda S. Feist, Dir.

MINNESOTA STATE PLANNING AGENCY - CRIMINAL JUSTICE PROGRAM -
   LIBRARY
100 Hanover Bldg.
480 Cedar St.   Phone: (612) 296-2771
St. Paul, MN 55101   Marcia Anderson, Lib.Techn.

MINNESOTA STATE SERVICES FOR THE BLIND AND VISUALLY
   HANDICAPPED - COMMUNICATION CENTER
1745 University Ave.   Phone: (612) 296-6723
St. Paul, MN 55104   Joanne Jonson, Dir.

MINNESOTA STATE WATER RESOURCES BOARD - LIBRARY
555 Wabasha St.   Phone: (612) 296-2840
St. Paul, MN 55102   Mel Sinn, Dir.

MITCHELL (William) COLLEGE OF LAW - LIBRARY
871 Summit Ave.   Phone: (612) 227-9171
St. Paul, MN 55105   Madeleine J. Wilken, Lib.Dir.

MOUNDS PARK HOSPITAL - HEALTH SCIENCES LIBRARY
200 Earl St.   Phone: (612) 774-5901
St. Paul, MN 55106   Karen L. Brudvig, Libn.

MOUNT ZION HEBREW CONGREGATION - TEMPLE LIBRARY
1300 Summit Ave.   Phone: (612) 698-3881
St. Paul, MN 55105   Janice Leichter, Libn.

OPPENHEIMER, WOLFF, FOSTER, SHEPARD & DONNELLY - LIBRARY
W-1700 First Bank Bldg.   Phone: (612) 227-7271
St. Paul, MN 55101   Gretchen Haase, Libn.

ORPHAN VOYAGE - KAMMANDALE LIBRARY
57 N. Dale   Phone: (612) 224-5160
St. Paul, MN 55102   Jeanette G. Kamman, Dir.

PLANNED PARENTHOOD OF MINNESOTA - POPULATION RESOURCE
   CENTER
1965 Ford Pkwy.   Phone: (612) 698-2401
St. Paul, MN 55116   Phyllis Cooksey, Dir. of Educ. & Trng.

RAMSEY COUNTY HISTORICAL SOCIETY - JOSEPH E. KARTH RESEARCH
   CENTER - LIBRARY
75 W. Fifth St., Rm. 323   Phone: (612) 222-0701
St. Paul, MN 55102

RAMSEY COUNTY LAW LIBRARY
1815 Court House   Phone: (612) 298-5208
St. Paul, MN 55102   Carol C. Florin, Lib.Dir.

RAMSEY COUNTY MEDICAL SOCIETY - BOECKMANN LIBRARY
345 N. Smith Ave.   Phone: (612) 224-3346
St. Paul, MN 55102   Mary Sandra Tarman, Libn.

ST. JOHN'S HOSPITAL - FREDERICK J. PLONDKE MEDICAL LIBRARY
403 Maria Ave.   Phone: (612) 228-3255
St. Paul, MN 55106   Jan Walton, Lib.Serv.Dir.

ST. JOSEPH'S HOSPITAL - JEROME MEDICAL LIBRARY
69 W. Exchange St.   Phone: (612) 291-3193
St. Paul, MN 55102   Jacqueline Gionfriddo, Dir.

ST. PAUL CITY COUNCIL - RESEARCH LIBRARY
502 City Hall
15 W. Kellogg Blvd.   Phone: (612) 298-4163
St. Paul, MN 55102   Theresa M. Jungwirth, Ck.

ST. PAUL DISPATCH-PIONEER PRESS - LIBRARY
55 E. Fourth St.   Phone: (612) 222-5011
St. Paul, MN 55101   Judith Katzung, Hd.Libn.

ST. PAUL FIRE & MARINE INSURANCE COMPANY - LIBRARY
385 Washington St.   Phone: (612) 221-8226
St. Paul, MN 55102   Eleanor Hamilton, Lib.Supv.

ST. PAUL FIRE & MARINE INSURANCE COMPANY - RISK MANAGEMENT
   SERVICES DIVISION INFORMATION CENTER
385 Washington St.   Phone: (612) 221-7470
St. Paul, MN 55102   Sharon Carter, Info.Spec.

ST. PAUL PUBLIC LIBRARY - ART AND MUSIC
90 W. Fourth St.   Phone: (612) 292-6186
St. Paul, MN 55102   Delores Sundbye, Supv.

ST. PAUL PUBLIC LIBRARY - BUSINESS & SCIENCE ROOM
90 W. Fourth St.   Phone: (612) 292-6176
St. Paul, MN 55102   Virginia B. Stavn, Supv.

ST. PAUL PUBLIC LIBRARY - FILM & VIDEO CENTER
90 W. Fourth St.   Phone: (612) 292-6336
St. Paul, MN 55102   Annette Salo, Supv.

ST. PAUL PUBLIC LIBRARY - GOVERNMENT PUBLICATIONS OFFICE
90 W. 4th St.   Phone: (612) 292-6178
St. Paul, MN 55102   Rosamond T. Jacob, Libn.

ST. PAUL PUBLIC LIBRARY - HIGHLAND PARK BRANCH - PERRIE JONES
   MEMORIAL ROOM
1974 Ford Pkwy.   Phone: (612) 292-6622
St. Paul, MN 55116   Elizabeth McMonigal, Br.Libn.

ST. PAUL PUBLIC LIBRARY - REFERENCE ROOM
90 W. Fourth St.   Phone: (612) 224-3383
St. Paul, MN 55102   Judith W. Devine, Supv.

ST. PAUL PUBLIC LIBRARY - SOCIAL SCIENCES & LITERATURE
90 W. Fourth St.   Phone: (612) 292-6206
St. Paul, MN 55102   Ortha D. Robbins, Supv.

ST. PAUL PUBLIC SCHOOLS INDEPENDENT SCHOOL DISTRICT 625 -
   DISTRICT PROFESSIONAL LIBRARY
360 Colborne St.   Phone: (612) 293-7601
St. Paul, MN 55102   Walter M. Ostrem, Libn.

ST. PAUL RAMSEY MEDICAL CENTER - MEDICAL LIBRARY
640 Jackson St.   Phone: (612) 221-3607
St. Paul, MN 55101   Mary Dwyer, Hd.Libn.

ST. PAUL SEMINARY - JOHN IRELAND MEMORIAL LIBRARY
2260 Summit Ave.   Phone: (612) 690-4355
St. Paul, MN 55105   Rev. Leo J. Tibesar, Dir.

ST. PAUL TECHNICAL VOCATIONAL LIBRARY
235 Marshall Ave.   Phone: (612) 221-1410
St. Paul, MN 55102   Fred Berndt, Libn.

SCIENCE MUSEUM OF MINNESOTA - LOUIS S. HEADLEY MEMORIAL
   LIBRARY
30 E. 10th St.   Phone: (612) 221-9488
St. Paul, MN 55101   Mary S. Finlayson, Libn.

SISTERS OF ST. JOSEPH OF CARONDELET - ST. PAUL PROVINCE -
   ARCHIVES
1884 Randolph Ave.   Phone: (612) 690-7000
St. Paul, MN 55105   Mary E. Kraft, C.S.J., Archv.

SPERRY COMPUTER SYSTEMS - DEFENSE SYSTEMS DIVISION -
   INFORMATION SERVICE CENTER
M.S. UOR25, Box 43525   Phone: (612) 456-2580
St. Paul, MN 55164-0525   Faye V. Peterson, Supv.

3M - BUSINESS INFORMATION SERVICE
3M Center, 220-1C-02   Phone: (612) 733-9057
St. Paul, MN 55144   Aletta Moore, Supv.

3M - ENGINEERING INFORMATION SERVICES
Bldg. 21-BW-02   Phone: (612) 778-4406
St. Paul, MN 55144   William T. Greene, Mgr.

3M - LAW LIBRARY
Box 33428   Phone: (612) 733-1460
St. Paul, MN 55133   Virginia Groth, Libn.

3M - MERTLE LIBRARY
3M Center, Bldg. 235-1D
St. Paul, MN 55144

3M - PATENT AND TECHNICAL COMMUNICATIONS SERVICES
3M Center, 201 2C-12   Phone: (612) 733-7670
St. Paul, MN 55144   Victoria K. Veach, Supv.

3M - 201 TECHNICAL LIBRARY
3M Center, 201-2S   Phone: (612) 733-2447
St. Paul, MN 55144   Karen L. Flynn, Supv.

3M - 209 LIBRARY
3M Center, 209-BC-06   Phone: (612) 733-9794
St. Paul, MN 55144   Alice Bresnahan, Libn.

3M - 230 LIBRARY
3M Center, 230-1S-12   Phone: (612) 733-5017
St. Paul, MN 55144   Elizabeth Smith, Libn.

3M - 235 LIBRARY
3M Center, 234-1A-25   Phone: (612) 733-2592
St. Paul, MN 55144   Mariann Syr, Libn.

3M - 236 LIBRARY
3M Center, 236-1E-09   Phone: (612) 733-5751
St. Paul, MN 55144   Elaine L. Wardrop, Libn.

3M - 251 LIBRARY
3M Center, 251-2A-06   Phone: (612) 733-5236
St. Paul, MN 55144   Ramona Huppert, Libn.

3M - 270 LIBRARY
3M Center, 270-4A-06   Phone: (612) 733-3402
St. Paul, MN 55144   Eloise M. Jasken, Libn.

TOYS 'N THINGS, TRAINING & RESOURCE CENTER, INC.
906 N. Dale   Phone: (612) 488-7284
St. Paul, MN 55103   Elizabeth Overstad, Toy Lib.Dir.

U.S. ARMY - CORPS OF ENGINEERS - ST. PAUL DISTRICT - TECHNICAL
   LIBRARY
1135 U.S. Post Office & Custom House   Phone: (612) 725-5921
St. Paul, MN 55101   Jean Marie Schmidt, Libn.

U.S. COURT OF APPEALS, 8TH CIRCUIT - RESEARCH LIBRARY
590 Federal Bldg.
316 N. Robert St.   Phone: (612) 725-7177
St. Paul, MN 55101   Kathryn C. Kratz, Br.Libn.

U.S. FOREST SERVICE - NORTH CENTRAL FOREST EXPERIMENT STATION
   LIBRARY
1992 Folwell Ave.   Phone: (612) 642-5257
St. Paul, MN 55108   Floyd L. Henderson, Libn.

UNIVERSITY OF MINNESOTA - AGRICULTURAL EXTENSION SERVICE -
   DIAL-U INSECT AND PLANT INFORMATION CLINIC
155 Alderman Hall
1970 Folwell   Phone: (612) 376-3380
St. Paul, MN 55108   Dr. Mark Ascerno, Dial-U Coord.

UNIVERSITY OF MINNESOTA - AGRICULTURAL EXTENSION SERVICE -
   MINNESOTA ANALYSIS & PLANNING SYSTEM
475 Coffey Hall
1420 Eckles Ave.   Phone: (612) 376-7003
St. Paul, MN 55108   David M. Nelson, Dir.

UNIVERSITY OF MINNESOTA - CENTER FOR YOUTH DEVELOPMENT AND
   RESEARCH - RESOURCE ROOM
386 McNeal Hall
1985 Buford Ave.   Phone: (612) 376-7624
St. Paul, MN 55108   Paula Simon, Resource Rm.Coord.

UNIVERSITY OF MINNESOTA - FIRE CENTER
33 North Hall
2005 Buford Ave.   Phone: (612) 376-3535
St. Paul, MN 55108   Esther C.D. Doughty, Libn.

UNIVERSITY OF MINNESOTA - IMMIGRATION HISTORY RESEARCH
   CENTER COLLECTION
826 Berry St.   Phone: (612) 373-5581
St. Paul, MN 55114   Susan Grigg, Cur.

UNIVERSITY OF MINNESOTA - MANUSCRIPTS DIVISION
826 Berry St.   Phone: (612) 376-7271
St. Paul, MN 55114   Alan K. Lathrop, Cur.

UNIVERSITY OF MINNESOTA, ST. PAUL - BIOCHEMISTRY LIBRARY
406 Biological Sciences Ctr.
1445 Gortner Ave.   Phone: (612) 373-1582
St. Paul, MN 55108   Jeffrey Dains, Lib.Asst.

UNIVERSITY OF MINNESOTA, ST. PAUL - CENTRAL LIBRARY
1984 Buford Ave.   Phone: (612) 373-0904
St. Paul, MN 55108   Richard L. Rohrer, Dir.

UNIVERSITY OF MINNESOTA, ST. PAUL - DEPARTMENT OF VOCATIONAL &
   TECHNICAL EDUCATION - LEARNING RESOURCE CENTER
Vocational & Technical Educ. Bldg.
1954 Buford Ave.   Phone: (612) 373-3838
St. Paul, MN 55108   Dr. Jerome Moss, Dir.

UNIVERSITY OF MINNESOTA, ST. PAUL - ENTOMOLOGY, FISHERIES AND
   WILDLIFE LIBRARY
1980 Folwell Ave.
375 Hodson Hall   Phone: (612) 373-1741
St. Paul, MN 55108   Katherine S. Chiang, Hd.

UNIVERSITY OF MINNESOTA, ST. PAUL - FORESTRY LIBRARY
Green Hall
1530 N. Cleveland Ave.   Phone: (612) 373-1407
St. Paul, MN 55108   Jean Albrecht, Libn.

UNIVERSITY OF MINNESOTA, ST. PAUL - HERBARIUM COLLECTION
St. Paul Campus Library
1984 Buford Ave.
St. Paul, MN 55108

UNIVERSITY OF MINNESOTA, ST. PAUL - PLANT PATHOLOGY LIBRARY
202 Stakman Hall
1519 Gortner Ave.   Phone: (612) 373-1669
St. Paul, MN 55108   Erik Biever, Lib.Asst.

UNIVERSITY OF MINNESOTA, ST. PAUL - VETERINARY MEDICAL LIBRARY
450 Veterinary Science Bldg.
1971 Commonwealth Ave.   Phone: (612) 373-1455
St. Paul, MN 55108   Livija Carlson, Libn.

VOLUNTARY ACTION CENTER OF THE ST. PAUL AREA - LIBRARY
518 Bremer Bldg.
419 N. Robert St.   Phone: (612) 227-3938
St. Paul, MN 55101   Maggi Davern, Exec.Dir.

WANDERER PRESS - LIBRARY
201 Ohio St.   Phone: (612) 224-5733
St. Paul, MN 55107   Kathleen E. Walsh, Info.Mgr.

WESTERN LIFE INSURANCE COMPANY - LIBRARY
Box 43271   Phone: (612) 738-4589
St. Paul, MN 55164   Carole Steele, Libn.

GUSTAVUS ADOLPHUS COLLEGE - LUND MUSIC LIBRARY
                                                 Phone: (507) 931-7365
St. Peter, MN 56082   Mary Behrends, Music Lib.Asst.

NICOLLET COUNTY HISTORICAL SOCIETY - MUSEUM
400 S. 3rd St.   Phone: (507) 931-2160
St. Peter, MN 56082   Karen Mesrobian, Cur.

ST. PETER REGIONAL TREATMENT CENTER - STAFF LIBRARY
100 Freeman Dr.   Phone: (507) 931-3000
St. Peter, MN 56082   Richard Whitmore, Staff Libn.

LEWIS (Sinclair) INFORMATION & INTERPRETIVE CENTRE
Box 222   Phone: (612) 352-5201
Sauk Centre, MN 56378

NYBERG CARTOGRAPHIC COLLECTION
4946 Devonshire Circle   Phone: (612) 474-9011
Shorewood, MN 55331   Nancy Nyberg, Libn.

DAKOTA COUNTY HISTORICAL SOCIETY - RESEARCH CENTER
130 3rd Ave. N.   Phone: (612) 451-6260
South St. Paul, MN 55075   R.L. Zastrow, Dir.

STILLWATER PUBLIC LIBRARY - ST. CROIX VALLEY ROOM
223 N. 4th St.   Phone: (612) 439-1675
Stillwater, MN 55082   Sue Collins, Hist.

WASHINGTON COUNTY MUSEUM LIBRARY
602 N. Main St.   Phone: (612) 439-5956
Stillwater, MN 55082   Judith Payne, Cur.

WASHINGTON COUNTY TOY LENDING LIBRARY
223 N. 4th St.
Stillwater, MN 55082   Zantha LaFon-Horstmann, Coord.

U.S. FISH & WILDLIFE SERVICE - SCIENCE REFERENCE LIBRARY
Federal Bldg., Fort Snelling   Phone: (612) 725-3576
Twin Cities, MN 55111   Veronica Siedle, Libn.

RANGE MENTAL HEALTH CENTER - LIBRARY
624 South 13th St.   Phone: (218) 749-2881
Virginia, MN 55792   JoAnne Matson, Sec.

CARVER COUNTY HISTORICAL SOCIETY, INC. - LIBRARY
119 S. Cherry St.   Phone: (612) 442-4234
Waconia, MN 55387   Francis Klein, Pres.

UNIVERSITY OF MINNESOTA TECHNICAL COLLEGE, WASECA - LEARNING
   RESOURCES
                                                 Phone: (507) 835-1000
Waseca, MN 56093   Nan Wilhelmson, Dir.

GRACE LUTHERAN CHURCH - LIBRARY
18360 Minnetonka Blvd.   Phone: (612) 473-2362
Wayzata, MN 55391   Betty W. LeDell, Libn.

WHEATON COMMUNITY HOSPITAL - MEDICAL LIBRARY
401 12th St., N.   Phone: (612) 563-8226
Wheaton, MN 56296   Diana Johnson, Dir.

KANDIYOHI COUNTY HISTORICAL SOCIETY - VICTOR E. LAWSON
   RESEARCH LIBRARY
610 NE Hwy. 71   Phone: (612) 235-1881
Willmar, MN 56201   Mona R. Nelson, Prog.Dir.

RICE MEMORIAL HOSPITAL - HEALTH SCIENCE LIBRARY
301 Becker Ave., S.W.   Phone: (612) 235-4543
Willmar, MN 56201   Carol Conradi, Libn.

WILLMAR PUBLIC SCHOOLS - COMMUNITY EDUCATION TOY LIBRARY
c/o Pioneer Land Library System
410 S.W. 5th St.   Phone: (612) 235-3162
Willmar, MN 56201   Linda Cogelow, Coord.

WILLMAR STATE HOSPITAL - LIBRARY
Box 1128   Phone: (612) 235-3322
Willmar, MN 56201   Linda Bjornberg, Libn.

COTTONWOOD COUNTY HISTORICAL SOCIETY - LIBRARY
812 4th Ave.   Phone: (507) 831-1134
Windom, MN 56101   Lucille Stahl, Pres.

WESCHCKE (Carl L.) LIBRARY
1661 Woodbury Dr.   Phone: (612) 739-2490
Woodbury, MN 55125   Carl L. Weschcke, Pres.

MISSISSIPPI

DIVINE WORD SEMINARY OF ST. AUGUSTINE - LIBRARY
Ulman Ave.
Bay St. Louis, MS 39520

U.S. NAVY - NAVAL OCEANOGRAPHIC OFFICE - NAVY LIBRARY
NSTL   Phone: (601) 688-4597
Bay St. Louis, MS 39522   Katharine Wallace, Supv.Libn.

GULF PUBLISHING CO., INC. - EDITORIAL LIBRARY
Debuys Rd.
Box 4567   Phone: (601) 896-2314
Biloxi, MS 39531   Marilyn Pustay, Libn.

BLUE MOUNTAIN COLLEGE - MUSIC LIBRARY
                                                 Phone: (601) 685-5711
Blue Mountain, MS 38610   Carolyn Mounce, Libn.

FIRST BAPTIST CHURCH - LIBRARY
First at Church St.   Phone: (601) 728-6272
Booneville, MS 38825   Stanley Barnett, Libn.

MISSISSIPPI BAPTIST CONVENTION BOARD - MISSISSIPPI BAPTIST
   HISTORICAL COMMISSION
Box 51   Phone: (601) 924-6172
Clinton, MS 39056   Alice G. Cox, Libn.

LOWNDES COUNTY LAW LIBRARY
County Courthouse, Rm. 210   Phone: (601) 328-1056
Columbus, MS 39701   Brenda Dodson, Libn.

FIRST BAPTIST CHURCH - LIBRARY
2105 14th St.
Box 70   Phone: (601) 863-8501
Gulfport, MS 39501   Mrs. John K. Savell

HARRISON COUNTY LAW LIBRARY
1801 23rd Ave.   Phone: (601) 865-4004
Gulfport, MS 39501   Mary H. Ladner, Libn.

HERCULES, INC. - HATTIESBURG PLANT LABORATORY - LIBRARY
Box 1937   Phone: (601) 545-3450
Hattiesburg, MS 39401   Georgia Kay Carter, Supv. Chemist

UNIVERSITY OF SOUTHERN MISSISSIPPI - GEOLOGY DEPARTMENT -
    LIBRARY
Southern Sta., Box 5044   Phone: (601) 266-7196
Hattiesburg, MS 39406   Dr. Daniel A. Sundeen, Assoc.Prof.

UNIVERSITY OF SOUTHERN MISSISSIPPI - MC CAIN LIBRARY
Southern Sta., Box 5148   Phone: (601) 266-4347
Hattiesburg, MS 39406-5148   Claude E. Fike, Dir.

MISSISSIPPI VALLEY STATE UNIVERSITY - JAMES HERBERT WHITE
    LIBRARY - SPECIAL COLLECTIONS
                                      Phone: (601) 254-9041
Itta Bena, MS 38941   Dr. Robbye R. Henderson, Hd.Libn.

CAIN (J.B.) ARCHIVES OF MISSISSIPPI METHODISM AND MILLSAPS
    COLLEGE
Millsaps College Library   Phone: (601) 354-5201
Jackson, MS 39210   James F. Parks, Hd.Libn.

CENTRAL PRESBYTERIAN CHURCH - LIBRARY *
1100 W. Capitol   Phone: (601) 353-2757
Jackson, MS 39203

HINDS GENERAL HOSPITAL - WILLIAM M. SUTTLE MEDICAL LIBRARY
1850 Chadwick Dr.   Phone: (601) 376-1148
Jackson, MS 39204   Wanda W. King, Med.Libn.

JACKSON METROPOLITAN LIBRARY - INFORMATION AND REFERENCE
    DIVISION
301 N. State St.   Phone: (601) 352-3677
Jackson, MS 39201   Jack Mulkey, Dir.

MISSISSIPPI COLLEGE SCHOOL OF LAW - LAW LIBRARY
151 E. Griffith St.   Phone: (601) 944-1970
Jackson, MS 39201   Carol C. West, Dir./Professor of Law

MISSISSIPPI MUSEUM OF NATURAL SCIENCE - LIBRARY
111 N. Jefferson St.   Phone: (601) 354-7303
Jackson, MS 39202   Mary P. Stevens, Musm.Libn.

MISSISSIPPI STATE BUREAU OF GEOLOGY - LIBRARY
2525 N. West St.
Box 5348   Phone: (601) 354-6228
Jackson, MS 39216   Carolyn Woodley, Libn.

MISSISSIPPI STATE DEPARTMENT OF ARCHIVES AND HISTORY -
    ARCHIVES AND LIBRARY DIVISION
100 S. State St.
Box 571   Phone: (601) 359-1424
Jackson, MS 39205   Mrs. Madel J. Morgan, Dir., Archv. & Lib.Div.

MISSISSIPPI STATE DEPARTMENT OF EDUCATION - EDUCATIONAL MEDIA
    SERVICES
301 Walter Sillers Bldg.
Box 771   Phone: (601) 359-3553
Jackson, MS 39205   John Barlow, Info.Rsrcs.Spec.

MISSISSIPPI STATE DEPARTMENT OF HEALTH - AUDIOVISUAL LIBRARY
Box 1700   Phone: (601) 354-6639
Jackson, MS 39205   Nancy Kay Sullivan, Dir., Pub.Rel.

MISSISSIPPI STATE DEPARTMENT OF MENTAL HEALTH - LIBRARY
1027 Robert E. Lee Bldg.   Phone: (601) 359-1300
Jackson, MS 39201   Margueritte D. Ransom, Lib.Techn.

MISSISSIPPI STATE DEPARTMENT OF PUBLIC WELFARE - JEAN GUNTER
    SOCIAL WELFARE LIBRARY
515 E. Amite St.
Box 352   Phone: (601) 354-0341
Jackson, MS 39205   Mary Ellen Simpson, Welfare Libn.

MISSISSIPPI STATE LAW LIBRARY
Gartin Justice Bldg., 450 High St.
Box 1040   Phone: (601) 359-3672
Jackson, MS 39205   Merle Buckley Allen, Libn.

MISSISSIPPI STATE LIBRARY COMMISSION
Box 10700   Phone: (601) 359-1036
Jackson, MS 39209-0700   David M. Woodburn, Dir.

MISSISSIPPI STATE MEDICAL ASSOCIATION - LIBRARY
735 Riverside Dr.   Phone: (601) 354-5433
Jackson, MS 39216

MISSISSIPPI (State) RESEARCH AND DEVELOPMENT CENTER -
    INFORMATION SERVICES DIVISION
3825 Ridgewood Rd.   Phone: (601) 982-6324
Jackson, MS 39211   Natelle Isley, Mgr.

REFORMED THEOLOGICAL SEMINARY - LIBRARY
5422 Clinton Blvd.   Phone: (601) 922-4988
Jackson, MS 39209   Robert B. Ashlock, Act.Dir.

ST. DOMINIC-JACKSON MEMORIAL HOSPITAL - LUTHER MANSHIP
    MEDICAL LIBRARY †
969 Lakeland Drive   Phone: (601) 982-0121
Jackson, MS 39216   Clara Joorfetz, Libn.

U.S. VETERANS ADMINISTRATION (MS-Jackson) - CENTER LIBRARY
1500 E. Woodrow Wilson   Phone: (601) 362-4471
Jackson, MS 39216   Carol Sistrunk, Chf.Libn.

WESLEY BIBLICAL SEMINARY - LIBRARY
Box 9938   Phone: (601) 957-1315
Jackson, MS 39206   Wayne W. Woodward, Dir. of Lib.Serv.

U.S. AIR FORCE BASE - KEESLER BASE - MC BRIDE LIBRARY
FL 3010
Bldg. 2222, Larchler Blvd., 3380 ABG/SSL   Phone: (601) 377-2181
Keesler AFB, MS 39534   Elizabeth A. DeCoux, Adm.Libn.

U.S. AIR FORCE HOSPITAL MEDICAL CENTER - MEDICAL LIBRARY (MS-
    Keesler AFB)
SGEL   Phone: (601) 377-2042
Keesler AFB, MS 39534   Rita F. Smith, Med.Libn.

U.S. AIR FORCE - KEESLER TECHNICAL TRAINING CENTER - ACADEMIC
    LIBRARY
McClelland Hall, Bldg. 2818   Phone: (601) 377-4295
Keesler AFB, MS 39534   Verna Westerburg, Lib.Techn.

LAUREN ROGERS MUSEUM OF ART
5th Ave. at 7th St.   Phone: (601) 428-4875
Laurel, MS 39440   Betty Mulloy, Libn.

ALCORN STATE UNIVERSITY - JOHN DEWEY BOYD LIBRARY †
Box 539   Phone: (601) 877-6350
Lorman, MS 39096   Ms. Epsy Y. Hendricks, Lib.Dir.

MISSISSIPPI STATE UNIVERSITY - COLLEGE OF VETERINARY MEDICINE -
    LIBRARY †
Drawer V   Phone: (601) 325-3432
Mississippi State, MS 39762   Bruce A. Evans, Libn.

MISSISSIPPI STATE UNIVERSITY - MISSISSIPPI COOPERATIVE
    EXTENSION SERVICE - LAND USE CENTER LIBRARY
Box 5405   Phone: (601) 325-2112
Mississippi State, MS 39762

MISSISSIPPI STATE UNIVERSITY - MITCHELL MEMORIAL LIBRARY -
    SPECIAL COLLECTIONS *
Drawer 5408   Phone: (601) 325-4225
Mississippi State, MS 39762   Frances N. Coleman, Act.Hd., Spec.Coll.

U.S. GEOLOGICAL SURVEY - NATIONAL MAPPING DIVISION ASSISTANCE
    FACILITY - LIBRARY
National Space Technology Labs   Phone: (601) 688-3541
NSTL Station, MS 39529   Frank Beatty, Libn.

U.S. NASA - NATL. SPACE TECHNOLOGY LABORATORIES - RESEARCH
    LIBRARY
                                                 Phone: (601) 688-3244
NSTL Station, MS 39529   Mary Meighen, Chf.Libn.

GULF COAST RESEARCH LABORATORY - GORDON GUNTER LIBRARY
                                                 Phone: (601) 875-2244
Ocean Springs, MS 39564-0951   Malcolm S. Ware, Sr.Libn.

SINGING RIVER HOSPITAL - MEDICAL LIBRARY
2809 Denny Ave.   Phone: (601) 938-5040
Pascagoula, MS 39567   Mary Evelyn Dowell, Dir., Med.Lib.

U.S. NATL. MARINE FISHERIES SERVICE - FISHERIES LABORATORY -
    LIBRARY
Drawer 1207
Pascagoula, MS 39567

FIRST BAPTIST CHURCH - MATTIE D. HALL LIBRARY
Front St.
Box 655   Phone: (601) 759-6378
Rosedale, MS 38769   Beulah R. Lane, Media Dir.

MISSISSIPPI STATE AGRICULTURAL & FORESTRY EXPERIMENT STATION -
    DELTA BR. EXPERIMENT STA. LIBRARY
                                                 Phone: (601) 686-9311
Stoneville, MS 38776   Charlotte G. Pierce, Libn.

NORTH MISSISSIPPI MEDICAL CENTER - RESOURCE CENTER
830 S. Gloster St.   Phone: (601) 842-3632
Tupelo, MS 38801   Wanda Armstrong, Libn.

U.S. NATL. PARK SERVICE - NATCHEZ TRACE PARKWAY - LIBRARY &
    VISITOR CENTER
R.R. 1, NT-143   Phone: (601) 842-1572
Tupelo, MS 38801

UNIVERSITY OF MISSISSIPPI - ARCHIVES & SPECIAL COLLECTIONS/
    MISSISSIPPIANA
                                                 Phone: (601) 232-7408
University, MS 38677   Dr. Thomas M. Verich, Hd. of Archv. & Spec.Coll

UNIVERSITY OF MISSISSIPPI - BUREAU OF BUSINESS & ECONOMIC
    RESEARCH LIBRARY
School of Business Administration   Phone: (601) 232-7481
University, MS 38677

UNIVERSITY OF MISSISSIPPI - BUREAU OF GOVERNMENTAL RESEARCH
    LIBRARY
                                                 Phone: (601) 232-7401
University, MS 38677   Dorothy I. Wilson, Ed.Asst.

UNIVERSITY OF MISSISSIPPI - SCHOOL OF EDUCATION LIBRARY
School of Education Bldg.   Phone: (601) 232-7040
University, MS 38677   Joyce Taylor, Educ.Libn.

UNIVERSITY OF MISSISSIPPI - SCHOOL OF LAW LIBRARY
                                                 Phone: (601) 232-7361
University, MS 38677   Thomas M. Steele, Law Libn.

UNIVERSITY OF MISSISSIPPI - SCHOOL OF PHARMACY - AUSTIN A.
    DODGE PHARMACY LIBRARY
                                                 Phone: (601) 232-7381
University, MS 38677   Nancy F. Fuller, Libn.

MERCY REGIONAL MEDICAL CENTER LIBRARY
100 McAuley Dr.
Box 271   Phone: (601) 636-2131
Vicksburg, MS 39180   Frances Betts, Libn.

U.S. ARMY - CORPS OF ENGINEERS - LOWER MISSISSIPPI VALLEY DIV. -
    MISSISSIPPI RIVER COMMN. TECHNICAL LIB.
Box 80   Phone: (601) 634-5880
Vicksburg, MS 39180   Sherrie L. Moran, Libn.

U.S. ARMY - ENGINEER WATERWAYS EXPERIMENT STATION - COASTAL
    ENGINEERING INFORMATION ANALYSIS CENTER
Box 631   Phone: (601) 634-2017
Vicksburg, MS 39180   Andre Szuwalski, Dir.

U.S. ARMY - ENGINEER WATERWAYS EXPERIMENT STATION - CONCRETE
    TECHNOLOGY INFORMATION ANALYSIS CENTER
Box 631   Phone: (601) 634-3264
Vicksburg, MS 39180   Bryant Mather, Dir.

U.S. ARMY - ENGINEER WATERWAYS EXPERIMENT STATION - HYDRAULIC
    ENGINEERING INFORMATION ANALYSIS CENTER
Box 631   Phone: (601) 634-3368
Vicksburg, MS 39180   Bobby J. Brown, Dir.

U.S. ARMY - ENGINEER WATERWAYS EXPERIMENT STATION -
    PAVEMENTS & SOIL TRAFFICABILITY INFO. ANALYSIS CTR.
Box 631   Phone: (601) 634-2734
Vicksburg, MS 39180   Gerald W. Turnage, Dir.

U.S. ARMY - ENGINEER WATERWAYS EXPERIMENT STATION - SOIL
    MECHANICS INFORMATION ANALYSIS CENTER
Box 631   Phone: (601) 634-3475
Vicksburg, MS 39180   Paul F. Hadala, Dir.

U.S. ARMY - ENGINEER WATERWAYS EXPERIMENT STATION - TECHNICAL
    INFORMATION CENTER
Box 631   Phone: (601) 634-2533
Vicksburg, MS 39180   Al Sherlock, Chf., Tech.Info.Ctr.

U.S. NATL. PARK SERVICE - VICKSBURG NATL. MILITARY PARK - LIBRARY
Box 349   Phone: (601) 636-0583
Vicksburg, MS 39180-0349   David F. Riggs, Musm.Cur.

VICKSBURG HOSPITAL, INC. - MEDICAL LIBRARY *
3311 I-20 Frontage Rd.   Phone: (601) 636-2611
Vicksburg, MS 39180   Dinnie K. Johnston, Med.Libn.

VICKSBURG & WARREN COUNTY HISTORICAL SOCIETY - MC CARDLE
    LIBRARY
Old Court House Museum   Phone: (601) 636-0741
Vicksburg, MS 39180   Blanche Terry, Res.Dir.

MARY HOLMES COLLEGE - BARR LIBRARY - ORAL HISTORY COLLECTION †
                                                 Phone: (601) 494-6820
West Point, MS 39773

MISSOURI

DE PAUL HEALTH CENTER - MEDICAL LIBRARY
12303 DePaul Dr.   Phone: (314) 344-6397
Bridgeton, MO 63044   Joan Laneman, Lib.Dir.

ST. FRANCIS MEDICAL CENTER - CAPE COUNTY MEMORIAL MEDICAL
    LIBRARY, INC.
211 St. Francis Dr.   Phone: (314) 335-1251
Cape Girardeau, MO 63701   June Johnston, Med.Rec.Dir.

LOGAN COLLEGE OF CHIROPRACTIC - LIBRARY
1851 Schoettler Rd.
Box 100   Phone: (314) 227-2100
Chesterfield, MO 63107   Rosemary E. Buhr, Dir. of Lib.Serv.

ST. LOUIS COUNTY LAW LIBRARY *
St. Louis County Govt. Ctr.
7900 Carondelet Ave., Suite 545   Phone: (314) 889-2726
Clayton, MO 63105   Mary C. Dahm, Libn.

ELLIS FISCHEL STATE CANCER CENTER - LIBRARY & INFORMATION
    CENTER
Business Loop 70 & Garth Ave.   Phone: (314) 875-2100
Columbia, MO 65201   Charles A. O'Dell, Libn.

FIRST CHRISTIAN CHURCH - LIBRARY †
101 N. Tenth St.   Phone: (314) 449-7265
Columbia, MO 65201

INVESTIGATIVE REPORTERS AND EDITORS, INC. - PAUL WILLIAMS
    MEMORIAL RESOURCE CENTER
Box 838   Phone: (314) 882-2024
Columbia, MO 65205   Steve Weinberg, Exec.Dir.

NATIONAL ASSOCIATION OF ANIMAL BREEDERS - LIBRARY
401 Bernadette Dr.
Box 1033   Phone: (314) 445-4406
Columbia, MO 65205   Richard Antweiler, Dir. of Info.

NEW WAVE CORPORATION - AMERICAN AUDIO PROSE LIBRARY
915 E. Broadway   Phone: (314) 874-1139
Columbia, MO 65201   Kay Bonetti, Project Dir.

ORTHOPEDIC FOUNDATION FOR ANIMALS - OFA HIP DYSPLASIA
    REGISTRY
Middlebush Farms, Hwy. 63 S.   Phone: (314) 442-0418
Columbia, MO 65101   Dr. Al Corley, Project Dir.

STATE HISTORICAL SOCIETY OF MISSOURI - LIBRARY
1020 Lowry St.   Phone: (314) 882-7083
Columbia, MO 65201   Dr. Richard S. Brownlee, Dir.

U.S. FISH & WILDLIFE SERVICE - COLUMBIA NATIONAL FISHERIES
    RESEARCH LABORATORY LIBRARY
Route 1   Phone: (314) 875-5399
Columbia, MO 65201   Dr. Richard Shoettger, Dir.

U.S. NATL. OCEANIC & ATMOSPHERIC ADMINISTRATION - ASSESSMENT
    AND INFORMATION SERVICES CENTER
Federal Bldg., Rm. 212   Phone: (314) 875-5263
Columbia, MO 65201   Rita Terry

U.S. VETERANS ADMINISTRATION (MO-Columbia) - HOSPITAL LIBRARY
800 Stadium Rd.   Phone: (314) 443-2511
Columbia, MO 65201   Ray Starke, Chf., Lib.Serv.

UNIVERSITY OF MISSOURI - COLUMBIA MISSOURIAN - NEWSPAPER
    REFERENCE LIBRARY
9th & Elm   Phone: (314) 882-4876
Columbia, MO 65201   Robert Stevens, Newspaper Ref.Libn.

UNIVERSITY OF MISSOURI - ENGINEERING LIBRARY
2017 Engineering Bldg.   Phone: (314) 882-2379
Columbia, MO 65211   Alfred H. Jones, Libn.

UNIVERSITY OF MISSOURI - FREEDOM OF INFORMATION CENTER
223 Walter Williams Hall
Box 858   Phone: (314) 882-4856
Columbia, MO 65205   Dr. Paul L. Fisher, Dir.

UNIVERSITY OF MISSOURI - GEOLOGY LIBRARY
201 Geology Bldg.   Phone: (314) 882-4860
Columbia, MO 65211   Robert Heidlage, Lib.Asst.

UNIVERSITY OF MISSOURI - HEALTH CARE TECHNOLOGY CENTER &
    INFORMATION SCIENCE GROUP - INFORMATION CENTER
605 Lewis Hall   Phone: (314) 882-4906
Columbia, MO 65211   Arjun Reddy, Hd.

UNIVERSITY OF MISSOURI - HEALTH SCIENCES LIBRARY
Health Sciences Center   Phone: (314) 882-8086
Columbia, MO 65212   Dean Schmidt, Libn.

UNIVERSITY OF MISSOURI - JOURNALISM LIBRARY
117 Walter Williams Hall   Phone: (314) 882-7502
Columbia, MO 65202   Robert C. Hahn, Libn.

UNIVERSITY OF MISSOURI - MATH SCIENCES LIBRARY
206 Math Sciences Bldg.   Phone: (314) 882-7286
Columbia, MO 65211   Alfred H. Jones, Libn.

UNIVERSITY OF MISSOURI - MUSEUM LIBRARY
Pickard Hall   Phone: (314) 882-3591
Columbia, MO 65211   Forrest McGill, Dir. of Musm.

UNIVERSITY OF MISSOURI - RESEARCH PARK LIBRARY
132 Dalton Research Ctr.   Phone: (314) 882-3527
Columbia, MO 65211   Janice Dysart, Research Park Libn.

UNIVERSITY OF MISSOURI - SCHOOL OF LAW LIBRARY
Tate Hall   Phone: (314) 882-4597
Columbia, MO 65211   Susan D. Csaky, Prof./Law Libn.

UNIVERSITY OF MISSOURI - VETERINARY MEDICAL LIBRARY
W218 Veterinary Medicine   Phone: (314) 882-2461
Columbia, MO 65211   Trenton Boyd, Libn.

WESTERN HISTORICAL MANUSCRIPT COLLECTION/STATE HISTORICAL
    SOCIETY OF MISSOURI MANUSCRIPTS JOINT COLLECTION
University of Missouri
23 Ellis Library   Phone: (314) 882-6028
Columbia, MO 65201   Nancy Lankford, Assoc.Dir.

CONCEPTION ABBEY AND SEMINARY - LIBRARY
                                           Phone: (816) 944-2211
Conception, MO 64433   Rev. Aidan McSorley, Hd.Libn.

TEMPLE ISRAEL - PAUL PELTASON LIBRARY
10675 Ladue Rd.   Phone: (314) 432-8050
Creve Coeur, MO 63141   Mrs. Barry Katz

U.S. NATL. PARK SERVICE - GEORGE WASHINGTON CARVER NATL.
    MONUMENT - LIBRARY
Box 38   Phone: (417) 325-4151
Diamond, MO 64840   Gentry Davis, Supt.

KNOX COUNTY HISTORICAL SOCIETY - LIBRARY *
                                           Phone: (816) 397-2346
Edina, MO 63537   Brenton Karhoff, Pres.

MARITZ, INC. - LIBRARY
1355 N. Highway Dr.   Phone: (314) 225-4000
Fenton, MO 63026   Patty S. Slocombe, Libn.

MARITZ TRAVEL COMPANY - TRAVEL LIBRARY
1385 N. Highway Dr.   Phone: (314) 225-4000
Fenton, MO 63026   Sue Hamilton, Libn.

U.S. ARMY HOSPITALS - GENERAL LEONARD WOOD ARMY COMMUNITY
    HOSPITAL - MEDICAL LIBRARY
                                           Phone: (314) 368-9110
Ft. Leonard Wood, MO 65473   Mrs. Marian B. Strang, Med.Libn.

U.S. ARMY POST - FORT LEONARD WOOD - MAIN POST LIBRARY
Bldg. 1607   Phone: (314) 368-7169
Ft. Leonard Wood, MO 65473   Christine M. Reser, Chf.Libn.

FULTON STATE HOSPITAL - PROFESSIONAL LIBRARY
E. Fifth St., No. 102   Phone: (314) 642-3311
Fulton, MO 65251   Wilfrid S. Akiyama, Med.Libn.

WESTMINSTER COLLEGE - WINSTON CHURCHILL MEMORIAL AND LIBRARY
7th & Westminster Ave.   Phone: (314) 642-3361
Fulton, MO 65251-1299   Warren M. Hollrah, Musm.Mgr./Coll.Archv.

MARK TWAIN MUSEUM - LIBRARY
208 Hill St.   Phone: (314) 221-9010
Hannibal, MO 63401   Henry Sweets, Cur.

WORLD ARCHEOLOGICAL SOCIETY - INFORMATION CENTER
Lake Rd. 65-48
Star Rt. Box 445   Phone: (417) 334-2377
Hollister, MO 65672   Ron Miller, Dir.

ASSOCIATION OF INTERNATIONAL COLLEGES & UNIVERSITIES - AICU
    INTERNATIONAL EDUCATION LIBRARY
1301 S. Noland Rd.   Phone: (816) 931-6374
Independence, MO 64055   John W. Johnston, Dir.

BLUE SPRINGS HISTORICAL SOCIETY - LIBRARY
3929 Milton Dr.   Phone: (816) 373-5309
Independence, MO 64055   Larry Wiebusch, Musm.Chm.

THE INTERNATIONAL UNIVERSITY - INTERNATIONAL RELATIONS
    LIBRARY AND RESEARCH CENTER
1301 S. Noland Rd.   Phone: (816) 931-6374
Independence, MO 64055   Kathleen Thompson, Dir.

JACKSON COUNTY HISTORICAL SOCIETY - RESEARCH LIBRARY &
  ARCHIVES
Independence Sq. Courthouse, Rm.103   Phone: (816) 252-7454
Independence, MO 64050   Constance O. Soper, Archv.

REORGANIZED CHURCH OF JESUS CHRIST OF LATTER DAY SAINTS -
  LIBRARY & ARCHIVES
RLDS Auditorium
Box 1059   Phone: (816) 833-1000
Independence, MO 64051   Sara Hallier, Libn.

REORGANIZED CHURCH OF JESUS CHRIST OF LATTER DAY SAINTS -
  SERVICES TO THE BLIND
1001 Walnut
Box 1059   Phone: (816) 833-1000
Independence, MO 64051   Stephanie Kelley, Supv.

SPIRITUAL FRONTIERS FELLOWSHIP - LIBRARY
10819 Winner Rd.   Phone: (816) 254-8585
Independence, MO 64052

U.S. PRESIDENTIAL LIBRARIES - HARRY S TRUMAN LIBRARY
                                               Phone: (816) 833-1400
Independence, MO 64050   Dr. Benedict K. Zobrist, Dir.

COLE COUNTY HISTORICAL SOCIETY - MUSEUM AND LIBRARY
109 Madison   Phone: (314) 635-1850
Jefferson City, MO 65101   Cherie Montonyx Dowd, Cur.

LINCOLN UNIVERSITY OF MISSOURI - INMAN E. PAGE LIBRARY
                                               Phone: (314) 751-2325
Jefferson City, MO 65102   Catherine Long, Act.Libn.

MISSOURI STATE DIVISION OF COMMUNITY AND ECONOMIC
  DEVELOPMENT - RESEARCH LIBRARY
1014 Madison St.
Box 118   Phone: (314) 751-3674
Jefferson City, MO 65102

MISSOURI STATE LEGISLATIVE LIBRARY
State Capitol Bldg.   Phone: (314) 751-4633
Jefferson City, MO 65101   Anne Rottman, Libn.

MISSOURI STATE LIBRARY
Truman State Office Bldg.   Phone: (314) 751-3615
Jefferson City, MO 65102   Charles O'Halloran, State Libn.

MISSOURI STATE SUPREME COURT LIBRARY
Supreme Court Bldg., High St.   Phone: (314) 751-2636
Jefferson City, MO 65101   D.A. Divilbiss, Hd.Libn.

MESSENGER COLLEGE - LIBRARY
Box 850
Joplin, MO 64801   Judy Mitchell, Hd.Libn.

OZARK BIBLE COLLEGE - LIBRARY
1111 N. Main St.
Box 518   Phone: (417) 624-2518
Joplin, MO 64801   Loren L. Dickey, Libn.

POST (Winfred L. and Elizabeth C.) FOUNDATION - MEMORIAL ART
  REFERENCE LIBRARY
300 Main St.   Phone: (417) 782-5419
Joplin, MO 64801   Leslie Simpson, Libn./Dir.

AMERICAN ACADEMY OF FAMILY PHYSICIANS - INFORMATION RESOURCE
  DEPARTMENT
1740 W. 92nd St.   Phone: (816) 333-9700
Kansas City, MO 64114   Karen R. Carter, Mgr., Info.Rsrc.Dept.

AMERICAN ECONOMIC DEVELOPMENT COUNCIL - AEDC ECONOMIC
  DEVELOPMENT RESOURCES CENTER
Midwest Research Institute
425 Volker Blvd.   Phone: (816) 753-7600
Kansas City, MO 64110

BAPTIST MEDICAL CENTER - LIBRARY
6601 Rockhill Road   Phone: (816) 361-3500
Kansas City, MO 64131   Barbara Seiglar, Dir.

BELL & HOWELL EDUCATION GROUP - DE VRY INSTITUTE OF TECHNOLOGY
  - LEARNING RESOURCE CENTER
11224 Holmes Rd.   Phone: (913) 941-0430
Kansas City, MO 64131   Connie Jean Fogel, Dir.

BENDIX CORPORATION - KANSAS CITY DIVISION - TECHNICAL
  INFORMATION CENTER †
2000 E. 95th St.
Box 1159   Phone: (816) 997-2694
Kansas City, MO 64141   Lucile Stratton, Libn.

BETH SHALOM CONGREGATION - BLANCHE AND IRA ROSENBLUM
  MEMORIAL LIBRARY
9400 Wornall Rd.   Phone: (816) 363-3331
Kansas City, MO 64114   Frances Wolf, Libn.

BLACK & VEATCH CONSULTING ENGINEERS - CENTRAL LIBRARY
1500 Meadow Lake Pkwy.
Box 8405   Phone: (913) 967-2223
Kansas City, MO 64114   Leo M. Hack, Libn.

BURNS AND MC DONNELL ENGINEERING COMPANY - TECHNICAL LIBRARY
4600 E. 63rd St. Trafficway   Phone: (816) 333-4375
Kansas City, MO 64130   Adalene Stagner, Libn.

CALVARY BAPTIST CHURCH - LIBRARY *
3921 Baltimore   Phone: (816) 531-1208
Kansas City, MO 64111   Carroll O'Neal, Dir.

CHILDREN'S MERCY HOSPITAL - MEDICAL LIBRARY
24th at Gillham Rd.   Phone: (816) 234-3001
Kansas City, MO 64108   Judy Vermillion, Med.Libn.

CHURCH OF THE NAZARENE - INTERNATIONAL HEADQUARTERS -
  EDITORIAL LIBRARY
6401 The Paseo   Phone: (816) 333-7000
Kansas City, MO 64131   Patricia F. Christie, Ed.Libn.

CLEVELAND CHIROPRACTIC COLLEGE - LIBRARY
6401 Rockhill Rd.   Phone: (816) 333-8230
Kansas City, MO 64131   Marcia M. Thomas, Lib.Dir.

ENVIRONMENTAL PROTECTION AGENCY - REGION VII LIBRARY
324 E. 11th St., 16th Fl.   Phone: (816) 374-3497
Kansas City, MO 64106   Connie McKenzie, Libn.

FARMLAND INDUSTRIES, INC. - J.W. CUMMINS MEMORIAL LIBRARY
3315 N. Oak Trafficway
Box 7305   Phone: (816) 459-6606
Kansas City, MO 64116   Sarah Davidson, Info.Coord.

FEDERAL RESERVE BANK OF KANSAS CITY - LAW LIBRARY
925 Grand Ave.   Phone: (816) 881-2557
Kansas City, MO 64198   Jann Faltermeier, Law Libn.

FEDERAL RESERVE BANK OF KANSAS CITY - RESEARCH LIBRARY
                                               Phone: (816) 881-2676
Kansas City, MO 64198   Ellen M. Johnson, Libn.

GAGE & TUCKER - LIBRARY
2345 Grand Ave.   Phone: (816) 474-6460
Kansas City, MO 64108   Sharon O'Donoghue, Libn.

HALLMARK CARDS, INC. - CREATIVE RESEARCH LIBRARY
25th & McGee   Phone: (816) 274-5525
Kansas City, MO 64108   Jon M. Henderson, Mgr., Lib.Serv.

HEART OF AMERICA GENEALOGICAL SOCIETY & LIBRARY, INC.
311 E. 12th St.   Phone: (816) 221-2685
Kansas City, MO 64106   Glen L. Whitaker, Pres.

JACKSON COUNTY LAW LIBRARY
Jackson County Court House, 10th Fl.
415 E. 12th St.   Phone: (816) 881-3288
Kansas City, MO 64106   Vivian Shaw, Libn.

KANSAS CITY ART INSTITUTE - LIBRARY
4415 Warwick Blvd.
Box 10360   Phone: (816) 561-4852
Kansas City, MO 64111   Mary Lim Gamer, Dir.

KANSAS CITY - CITY DEVELOPMENT DEPARTMENT - LIBRARY *
City Hall, 414 E. 12th St.   Phone: (816) 274-1864
Kansas City, MO 64106   Alma Lee, Libn.

KANSAS CITY MUSEUM OF HISTORY AND SCIENCE - ARCHIVES
3218 Gladstone Blvd.   Phone: (816) 483-8300
Kansas City, MO 64123   Barbara M. Gorman, Cur. of Hist.

KANSAS CITY PUBLIC LIBRARY - ART AND MUSIC COLLECTION
311 E. 12th St.   Phone: (816) 221-2685
Kansas City, MO 64106

KANSAS CITY PUBLIC LIBRARY - BUSINESS AND TECHNICAL COLLECTION
311 E. 12th St.   Phone: (816) 221-2685
Kansas City, MO 64106

KANSAS CITY PUBLIC LIBRARY - MISSOURI VALLEY ROOM
311 E. 12th St.   Phone: (816) 221-2685
Kansas City, MO 64106

KANSAS CITY PUBLIC LIBRARY - PERIODICAL-MICROFILM COLLECTION
311 E. 12th St.
Kansas City, MO 64106

KANSAS CITY TIMES-STAR - LIBRARY
1729 Grand Ave.
Kansas City, MO 64108   John J. Springer, Libn.

LATHROP, KOONTZ, RIGHTER, CLAGETT & NORQUIST - LIBRARY
2600 Mutual Benefit Life Bldg.
2345 Grand Ave.   Phone: (816) 842-0820
Kansas City, MO 64108   Mary Ann Leahy, Libn.

LIBERTY MEMORIAL MUSEUM - LIBRARY
100 W. 26th St.   Phone: (816) 221-1918
Kansas City, MO 64108   Susan C. Wilkerson, Libn./Archv.

LINDA HALL LIBRARY
5109 Cherry St.   Phone: (816) 363-4600
Kansas City, MO 64110   Larry X. Besant, Dir.

MARION LABORATORIES, INC. - R & D LIBRARY
10236 Bunker Ridge Rd.   Phone: (816) 761-2500
Kansas City, MO 64137   Jane Stehlik-Kokker, Mgr., Sci.Info.Serv.

MENORAH MEDICAL CENTER - ROBERT UHLMAN MEDICAL LIBRARY
4949 Rockhill Rd.   Phone: (816) 276-8172
Kansas City, MO 64110   Marjorie L. Terrill, Med.Libn.

MIDWEST RESEARCH INSTITUTE - PATTERSON REFERENCE LIBRARY AND
    ECONOMICS REFERENCE CENTER
425 Volker Blvd.   Phone: (816) 753-7600
Kansas City, MO 64110   Harold Way, Hd.Libn.

MIDWESTERN BAPTIST THEOLOGICAL SEMINARY - LIBRARY †
5001 N. Oak St. Trafficway   Phone: (816) 453-4600
Kansas City, MO 64118   Dr. K. David Weekes, Dir.

MISSOURI STATE COURT OF APPEALS, WESTERN DISTRICT - LIBRARY
1300 Oak St.   Phone: (816) 474-5511
Kansas City, MO 64106   Vickie Selby, Libn.

MOBAY CHEMICAL CORPORATION - AGRICULTURAL CHEMICALS DIVISION
    - LIBRARY
Hawthorne Rd.
Box 4913   Phone: (816) 242-2236
Kansas City, MO 64120   Ty Webb, Act.Libn.

MODERN HANDCRAFT, INC. - RESEARCH LIBRARY
4251 Pennsylvania Ave.   Phone: (816) 531-5730
Kansas City, MO 64111

NATIONAL ASSOCIATION OF INSURANCE COMMISSIONERS - NAIC
    INFORMATION CENTER
1125 Grand Ave.   Phone: (816) 842-3600
Kansas City, MO 64106   Robin L. Tew, Libn.

NATIONAL ASSOCIATION OF PARLIAMENTARIANS - TECHNICAL
    INFORMATION CENTER
3706 Broadway, Suite 300   Phone: (816) 531-1735
Kansas City, MO 64111   Elaine Fulton, Exec.Sec.

NAZARENE THEOLOGICAL SEMINARY - WILLIAM BROADHURST LIBRARY
1700 E. Meyer Blvd.   Phone: (816) 333-6255
Kansas City, MO 64131   William C. Miller, Libn.

NELSON-ATKINS MUSEUM OF ART - SLIDE LIBRARY
4525 Oak St.   Phone: (816) 561-4000
Kansas City, MO 64111-1873   Jan McKenna, Slide Libn.

NELSON-ATKINS MUSEUM OF ART - SPENCER ART REFERENCE LIBRARY
4525 Oak St.   Phone: (816) 561-4000
Kansas City, MO 64111-1873   Stanley W. Hess, Libn.

OLD AMERICAN INSURANCE COMPANY - LIBRARY *
4900 Oak St.
Kansas City, MO 64112   Catherine Kufahl, Libn.

PANHANDLE EASTERN PIPE LINE COMPANY - TECHNICAL INFORMATION
    CENTER *
Box 1348   Phone: (816) 753-5600
Kansas City, MO 64141   GeorJane Simmons, Libn.

RESEARCH MEDICAL CENTER - LOCKWOOD MEMORIAL LIBRARY
Meyer Blvd. & Prospect Ave.   Phone: (816) 276-4159
Kansas City, MO 64132   Gerald R. Kruse, Dir.

ST. JOSEPH HOSPITAL - HEALTH SCIENCE LIBRARY
1000 Carondelet Dr.   Phone: (816) 942-4400
Kansas City, MO 64114   Janice Foster, Libn.

ST. LUKE'S HOSPITAL OF KANSAS CITY - MEDICAL LIBRARY
Spencer Center for Education
44th & Wornall Rd.   Phone: (816) 932-2333
Kansas City, MO 64111   Karen Horst, Dir. of Lib.Serv.

ST. MARY'S HOSPITAL - FAMILY PRACTICE & PATIENT EDUCATION
    LIBRARY †
2900 Baltimore   Phone: (816) 753-5700
Kansas City, MO 64108   Pamela Drayson, Libn.

ST. MARY'S HOSPITAL - LIBRARY
101 Memorial Dr.   Phone: (816) 753-5700
Kansas City, MO 64108   Cheryl A. Postlewait, Libn.

ST. MARY'S HOSPITAL MEDICAL EDUCATION FOUNDATION - MEDICAL
    LITERATURE INFORMATION CENTER
101 Memorial Dr.   Phone: (816) 753-5700
Kansas City, MO 64108   Dr. George X. Trimble, Dir.

ST. PAUL SCHOOL OF THEOLOGY - DANA DAWSON LIBRARY
5123 Truman Rd.   Phone: (816) 483-9600
Kansas City, MO 64127   Dr. William S. Sparks, Libn.

SHOOK, HARDY & BACON - LIBRARY
Mercantile Bank Tower, 20th Fl.
1101 Walnut   Phone: (816) 474-6550
Kansas City, MO 64106   Marianne L. Griffin, Libn.

TRINITY LUTHERAN HOSPITAL - FLORENCE L. NELSON MEMORIAL
    LIBRARY
31st & Wyandotte   Phone: (816) 753-4600
Kansas City, MO 64108   Cami L. Loucks, Dir.

U.S. COURT OF APPEALS, 8TH CIRCUIT - LIBRARY
U.S. Court House
811 Grand Ave., Rm. 845   Phone: (816) 842-9450
Kansas City, MO 64106   Margaret Tranne Pearce, Libn.

U.S. DEPT. OF EDUCATION - REFUGEE MATERIALS CENTER
324 E. 11th St., 9th Fl.   Phone: (816) 374-2276
Kansas City, MO 64106   Bud Tumy, Dir.

U.S. FEDERAL AVIATION ADMINISTRATION - CENTRAL REGION LIBRARY
Federal Bldg., Rm. 1556
601 E. 12th St.   Phone: (816) 374-5486
Kansas City, MO 64106   Judy Shifrin, Chf., Lib.Serv.

U.S. NATL. ARCHIVES & RECORDS SERVICE - FEDERAL ARCHIVES AND
  RECORDS CENTER, REGION 6
2306 E. Bannister Rd.   Phone: (816) 926-7271
Kansas City, MO 64131   Patrick Borders, Ctr.Dir.

U.S. NATL. WEATHER SERVICE - CENTRAL REGION HEADQUARTERS -
  LIBRARY
601 E. 12th St., Rm. 1844   Phone: (816) 374-5672
Kansas City, MO 64106   Dorothy Babich

U.S. VETERANS ADMINISTRATION (MO-Kansas City) - MEDICAL CENTER
  LIBRARY
4801 Linwood Blvd.   Phone: (816) 861-4700
Kansas City, MO 64128   Shirley C. Ting, Chf., Lib.Serv.

UNIVERSITY OF HEALTH SCIENCES - LIBRARY
2105 Independence Blvd.   Phone: (816) 283-2451
Kansas City, MO 64124   Marilyn J. DeGeus, Dir. of Libs.

UNIVERSITY OF MISSOURI, KANSAS CITY - CONSERVATORY LIBRARY
General Library
5100 Rockhill Rd.   Phone: (816) 276-1675
Kansas City, MO 64110

UNIVERSITY OF MISSOURI, KANSAS CITY - HEALTH SCIENCES LIBRARY
2411 Holmes   Phone: (816) 474-4100
Kansas City, MO 64108   Marilyn Sullivan, Chf.Libn.

UNIVERSITY OF MISSOURI, KANSAS CITY - LAW LIBRARY
School of Law
5100 Rockhill Rd.   Phone: (816) 276-1650
Kansas City, MO 64110   Charles R. Dyer, Law Libn.

UNIVERSITY OF MISSOURI, KANSAS CITY - SCHOOL OF DENTISTRY
  LIBRARY
650 E. 25th St.   Phone: (816) 234-0494
Kansas City, MO 64108   Ann Marie Corry, Dental Libn.

UNIVERSITY OF MISSOURI, KANSAS CITY - SNYDER COLLECTION OF
  AMERICANA
General Library
5100 Rockhill Rd.   Phone: (816) 276-1534
Kansas City, MO 64110

UNIVERSITY OF MISSOURI, KANSAS CITY - TEDROW TRANSPORTATION
  COLLECTION
General Library
5100 Rockhill Rd.   Phone: (816) 276-1534
Kansas City, MO 64110

WADDELL AND REED, INC. - RESEARCH LIBRARY
Box 1343   Phone: (816) 283-4072
Kansas City, MO 64141   Betty J. Howerton, Hd.Libn.

WESTERN HISTORICAL MANUSCRIPT COLLECTION/STATE HISTORICAL
  SOCIETY OF MISSOURI MANUSCRIPTS JOINT COLLECTION
University of Missouri
General Library 212
5100 Rockhill Rd.   Phone: (816) 276-1543
Kansas City, MO 64110   Gordon O. Hendrickson, Assoc.Dir.

WESTERN MISSOURI MENTAL HEALTH CENTER - LIBRARY †
600 E. 22nd St.   Phone: (816) 471-3000
Kansas City, MO 64108   Ellen Bull, Med.Libn.

FIRST BAPTIST CHURCH - LIBRARY
300 St. Francis St.   Phone: (314) 888-4689
Kennett, MO 63857   Pearl Young, Libn.

KIRKSVILLE COLLEGE OF OSTEOPATHIC MEDICINE - A.T. STILL MEMORIAL
  LIBRARY
                                         Phone: (816) 626-2345
Kirksville, MO 63501   Georgia Walter, Dir. of Lib.

NORTHEAST MISSOURI STATE UNIVERSITY - PICKLER MEMORIAL
  LIBRARY - SPECIAL COLLECTIONS
                                         Phone: (816) 785-4526
Kirksville, MO 63501   George N. Hartje, Dir. of Lib.

WATKINS WOOLEN MILL STATE HISTORIC SITE - RESEARCH LIBRARY *
Rte. 2, Box 270M   Phone: (816) 296-3357
Lawson, MO 64062   Ann M. Matthews, Historic Site Adm.

CLAY COUNTY ARCHIVES - FRANK HUGHES LIBRARY
Box 99   Phone: (816) 781-3611
Liberty, MO 64068   Jane Benson

MISSOURI BAPTIST HISTORICAL COMMISSION LIBRARY †
William Jewell College Library   Phone: (816) 781-3806
Liberty, MO 64068

NORTHWEST MISSOURI STATE UNIVERSITY - HORACE MANN LEARNING
  CENTER
                                         Phone: (816) 582-7141
Maryville, MO 64468   Nancy C. Hanks, Asst.Prof./Libn.

NORTHWEST MISSOURI STATE UNIVERSITY - OWENS LIBRARY - SPECIAL
  COLLECTIONS
                                         Phone: (816) 582-7141
Maryville, MO 64468   Charles W. Koch, Dir., Lrng.Rsrcs.

AUDRAIN COUNTY HISTORICAL SOCIETY - ROSS HOUSE LIBRARY/
  AMERICAN SADDLE HORSE MUSEUM LIBRARY
501 South Muldrow   Phone: (314) 581-3910
Mexico, MO 65265   Clara Kaiser, Libn./Genealogist

CENTRAL CHRISTIAN COLLEGE OF THE BIBLE - LIBRARY
1093 Urbandale Rd.   Phone: (816) 263-3900
Moberly, MO 65270   Gareth L. Reese, Libn.

MISSOURI STATE CHEST HOSPITAL - MEDICAL LIBRARY
                                         Phone: (417) 466-3711
Mount Vernon, MO 65712   Shirley Boucher, Libn.

FIRST BAPTIST CHURCH - LIBRARY
2205 Iron St.   Phone: (816) 842-1175
North Kansas City, MO 64116   Esther L. St. John, Hd.Libn.

MARK TWAIN RESEARCH FOUNDATION - LIBRARY
                                         Phone: (314) 565-3570
Perry, MO 63462   Chester L. Davis, Exec.Sec.

ST. MARY'S SEMINARY - ST. MARY'S OF THE BARRENS LIBRARY
                                         Phone: (314) 547-6533
Perryville, MO 63775   Sr. De Paul Schwinn, S.S.N.D., Hd.

SCHOOL OF THE OZARKS - RALPH FOSTER MUSEUM - LOIS BROWNELL
  RESEARCH LIBRARY
                                         Phone: (417) 334-6411
Point Lookout, MO 65726   Robert S. Esworthy, Dir.

U.S. VETERANS ADMINISTRATION (MO-Poplar Bluff) - MEDICAL CENTER
  LIBRARY (142D)
Highway 67 North   Phone: (314) 686-4151
Poplar Bluff, MO 63901   Kwang Hee Streiff, Chf., Lib.Serv.

MISSOURI STATE DIVISION OF GEOLOGY AND LAND SURVEY - LIBRARY
Box 250   Phone: (314) 364-1752
Rolla, MO 65401   Marcia Cussins, Libn.

U.S. BUREAU OF MINES - ROLLA RESEARCH CENTER - LIBRARY
1300 Bishop Ave.
Box 280   Phone: (314) 364-3169
Rolla, MO 65401

UNIVERSITY OF MISSOURI, ROLLA - CURTIS LAWS WILSON LIBRARY
                                         Phone: (314) 341-4227
Rolla, MO 65401   Ronald Bohley, Libn.

WESTERN HISTORICAL MANUSCRIPT COLLECTION/STATE HISTORICAL
  SOCIETY OF MISSOURI MANUSCRIPTS JOINT COLLECTION
University of Missouri
Rm. G-3 Library   Phone: (314) 341-4874
Rolla, MO 65401-0249   Mark C. Stauter, Assoc.Dir.

ST. CHARLES COUNTY HISTORICAL SOCIETY - ARCHIVES
101 S. Main St.   Phone: (314) 723-2939
St. Charles, MO 63301   Gertrude D. Johnson, Archv.

ST. JOSEPH HEALTH CENTER - HEALTH SCIENCE LIBRARY
300 First Capitol Dr.
St. Charles, MO 63301
Phone: (314) 724-2810
Lucille Dykas, Lib.Mgr.

HEARST (Phoebe Apperson) HISTORICAL SOCIETY, INC. - MUSEUM CENTER
850 Walton
Box 1842
St. Clair, MO 63077
Phone: (314) 629-3186
Mabel Reed, Sec. in Charge

BUCHANAN COUNTY LAW LIBRARY †
Buchanan County Courthouse
816 Corby Bldg.
St. Joseph, MO 64501
Phone: (816) 279-0274

FIRST CHRISTIAN CHURCH - LIBRARY *
Tenth & Faraon Sts.
St. Joseph, MO 64501
Phone: (816) 233-2556

FLETCHER, MAYO, ASSOCIATES, INC. - LIBRARY
Sta. E, Box B
St. Joseph, MO 64505
Phone: (816) 233-8261
Sandra Phillips, Libn.

HUFFMAN MEMORIAL UNITED METHODIST CHURCH - LIBRARY
2802 Renick
St. Joseph, MO 64507
Phone: (816) 233-0239
Dorothy Thomann, Libn.

METHODIST MEDICAL CENTER - SCHOOL OF NURSING LIBRARY
9th & Faraon Sts.
St. Joseph, MO 64501
Phone: (816) 271-7280
Sherril Garner, Libn.

PHILIPS ROXANE, INC. - TECHNICAL LIBRARY
2621 N. Belt Hwy.
St. Joseph, MO 64502
Phone: (816) 233-1385
Norma Barnes, Libn.

ST. JOSEPH HOSPITAL - MEDICAL LIBRARY
5325 Faraon
St. Joseph, MO 64506
Phone: (816) 271-6075
Jane Warren Carver, Med.Libn.

ST. JOSEPH MUSEUM - LIBRARY
Eleventh at Charles
St. Joseph, MO 64501
Phone: (816) 232-8471
Richard A. Nolf, Dir.

ST. JOSEPH NEWS-PRESS & GAZETTE - LIBRARY
9th & Edmond Sts.
St. Joseph, MO 64502
Phone: (816) 279-5671
Don E. Thornton, Dir.

ST. JOSEPH STATE HOSPITAL - PROFESSIONAL LIBRARY †
3400 Frederick Ave.
Box 263
St. Joseph, MO 64502
Phone: (816) 232-8431
Martha Godding, Libn.Dir.

AMERICAN ASSOCIATION OF BIOANALYSTS - SLIDE LIBRARY
81 Olive, Suite 918
St. Louis, MO 63101

AMERICAN SOYBEAN ASSOCIATION - LIBRARY
777 Craig Rd.
Box 27300
St. Louis, MO 63141
Phone: (314) 432-1600
Marianne Gibson, Libn.

ANHEUSER-BUSCH COMPANIES, INC. - CORPORATE LIBRARY
One Busch Pl.
St. Louis, MO 63118
Phone: (314) 577-2669
Ann Hunter, Corp.Libn.

AUTO CLUB OF MISSOURI - INFORMATION RESOURCE CENTER
Box 14611
St. Louis, MO 63178
Phone: (314) 576-7350
Muriel Lindsay, Libn.

AUTOMATED LOGISTIC MANAGEMENT SYSTEMS AGENCY - LIBRARY
210 N. Tucker St.
St. Louis, MO 63101
Phone: (314) 263-5955
Oneta M. Welch, Lib.Techn.

BARNES HOSPITAL - SCHOOL OF NURSING - LIBRARY & INSTRUCTIONAL
  RESOURCE LABORATORY
416 S. Kingshighway Blvd.
St. Louis, MO 63110
Phone: (314) 454-2554
Kim Uden Rutter, Libn.

BLISS (Malcolm) MENTAL HEALTH CENTER - ROBERT J. BROCKMAN
  MEMORIAL LIBRARY *
1420 Grattan St.
St. Louis, MO 63104
Phone: (314) 241-7600
William G. Heigold, Med.Libn.

BLUE CROSS HOSPITAL SERVICE, INC. - LIBRARY
4444 Forest Park Blvd.
St. Louis, MO 63108
Phone: (314) 658-4774
Mary Hebert, Libn.

BRODSKY (Saul) JEWISH COMMUNITY LIBRARY
12 Millstone Campus
St. Louis, MO 63146
Phone: (314) 432-5700
Lorraine K. Miller, Hd.Libn.

BRYAN, CAVE, MC PHEETERS & MC ROBERTS - LIBRARY †
500 N. Broadway
St. Louis, MO 63102
Phone: (314) 231-8600
Rose J. Garrett, Libn.

CATHOLIC CENTRAL UNION OF AMERICA - CENTRAL BUREAU LIBRARY
3835 Westminster Pl.
St. Louis, MO 63108
Phone: (314) 371-1653
Harvey J. Johnson, Dir.

CATHOLIC HEALTH ASSOCIATION OF THE UNITED STATES -
  INFORMATION RESOURCE CENTER
4455 Woodson Rd.
St. Louis, MO 63134
Phone: (314) 427-2500
Mark Unger, Dir., Info.Rsrcs.Ctr.

CENTER FOR REFORMATION RESEARCH - LIBRARY
6477 San Bonita Ave.
St. Louis, MO 63105
Phone: (314) 727-6655
Dr. William Maltby, Exec.Dir.

CENTRAL INSTITUTE FOR THE DEAF - EDUCATIONAL RESEARCH LIBRARY
818 S. Euclid
St. Louis, MO 63110
Phone: (314) 652-3200
Mary M. Sicking, Libn.

CHRISTIAN BOARD OF PUBLICATION - MARION STEVENSON LIBRARY †
2640 Pine St.
St. Louis, MO 63166
Phone: (314) 371-6900

CHRISTIAN CHURCH (Disciples of Christ), INC. - DIVISION OF HIGHER
  EDUCATION - LIBRARY
119 N. Jefferson Ave.
St. Louis, MO 63103
Phone: (314) 371-2050
Leslie P. Schroeder, Libn.

CONCORDIA HISTORICAL INSTITUTE - DEPARTMENT OF ARCHIVES AND
  HISTORY
801 DeMun Ave.
St. Louis, MO 63105
Phone: (314) 721-5934
August R. Suelflow, Dir.

CONCORDIA SEMINARY - LIBRARY
801 DeMun Ave.
St. Louis, MO 63105
Phone: (314) 721-5934
Dr. David P. Daniel, Act.Dir., Lib.Serv.

COVENANT THEOLOGICAL SEMINARY - J. OLIVER BUSWELL, JR. LIBRARY
12330 Conway Rd., Creve Coeur
St. Louis, MO 63141
Phone: (314) 434-4044
Dr. Joseph H. Hall, Libn.

D'ARCY, MAC MANUS, MASIUS - LIBRARY †
One S.Memorial Dr.
St. Louis, MO 63102
Phone: (314) 342-8818
Jean Kammer, Libn.

DEACONESS HOSPITAL - DRUSCH PROFESSIONAL LIBRARY
6150 Oakland Ave.
St. Louis, MO 63139
Phone: (314) 645-8510
Jane Whalen, Dir.

DOANE PUBLISHING - INFORMATION CENTER
11701 Borman Dr.
St. Louis, MO 63146

EAST-WEST GATEWAY COORDINATING COUNCIL - REFERENCE AREA
100 S. Tucker Blvd.
St. Louis, MO 63102
Phone: (314) 421-4220
Birdie Berry, Info.Serv.Coord.

EMERSON ELECTRIC COMPANY - SPACE AND ELECTRONICS DIVISION -
  ENGINEERING LIBRARY
8100 W. Florissant Ave.
St. Louis, MO 63136
Marian S. Shaffer, Tech.Libn.

ENVIRODYNE ENGINEERS, INC. - LIBRARY
12161 Lackland Rd.   Phone: (314) 434-6960
St. Louis, MO 63141   Kathryn L. Flowers, Libn./Info.Spec.

FEDERAL RESERVE BANK OF ST. LOUIS - RESEARCH LIBRARY
Box 442   Phone: (314) 444-8552
St. Louis, MO 63166   Carol J. Thaxton, Hd.Libn.

FIELD (Eugene) HOUSE AND TOY MUSEUM - LIBRARY
634 S. Broadway   Phone: (314) 421-4689
St. Louis, MO 63102   John Scholz, Dir.

GARDNER ADVERTISING COMPANY - INFORMATION CENTER
10 Broadway   Phone: (314) 444-2357
St. Louis, MO 63102   Debi Fingers, Info.Ctr.Mgr.

GENERAL DYNAMICS CORPORATION - PUBLIC AFFAIRS LIBRARY
Pierre Laclede Ctr.   Phone: (314) 889-8200
St. Louis, MO 63105   Barbara Elliott, Chf.Libn.

GREENSFELDER, HEMKER, WIESE, GALE & CHAPPELOW - LIBRARY
1800 Equitable Bldg.
10 S. Broadway   Phone: (314) 241-9090
St. Louis, MO 63102   Helen R. Gibson, Libn.

HARRIS-STOWE STATE COLLEGE LIBRARY
3026 Laclede Ave.   Phone: (314) 533-3366
St. Louis, MO 63103   Martin Knorr, Dir.

HELLMUTH, OBATA & KASSABAUM, INC. - HOK LIBRARY
100 N. Broadway   Phone: (314) 421-2000
St. Louis, MO 63102   Susan Baerwald, Libn.

INCARNATE WORD HOSPITAL - MEDICAL LIBRARY
3545 Lafayette Ave.   Phone: (314) 664-6500
St. Louis, MO 63104   Sr. Noeleen Hannigan, Med.Libn.

INTERNATIONAL BROTHERHOOD OF OLD BASTARDS, INC. - SIR THOMAS
   CRAPPER MEMORIAL ARCHIVES
2330 S. Brentwood Blvd., Suite 666   Phone: (314) 961-9825
St. Louis, MO 63144-2096   Bro. Jose "Bat" Guano, O.B., Chf., Archv./Kpr.

INTERNATIONAL CONSUMER CREDIT ASSOCIATION - DEPARTMENT OF
   EDUCATION LIBRARY
243 N. Lindbergh Blvd.
St. Louis, MO 63141

INTERNATIONAL LIBRARY, ARCHIVES & MUSEUM OF OPTOMETRY
243 N. Lindbergh Blvd.   Phone: (314) 991-0324
St. Louis, MO 63141   Maria Dablemont, Libn.

JEWISH HOSPITAL AT WASHINGTON UNIVERSITY MEDICAL CENTER -
   ROTHSCHILD MEDICAL LIBRARY
216 S. Kingshighway   Phone: (314) 454-7208
St. Louis, MO 63110   Ruth Kelly, Libn.

JEWISH HOSPITAL AT WASHINGTON UNIVERSITY MEDICAL CENTER -
   SCHOOL OF NURSING - MOSES SHOENBERG MEMORIAL LIBRARY
306 S. Kingshighway   Phone: (314) 454-8474
St. Louis, MO 63110   Alice Bruenjes, Hd.Libn.

JOHNSON (George) ADVERTISING - LIBRARY
763 New Ballas Rd., S.   Phone: (314) 569-3440
St. Louis, MO 63141   Marianne C. Goedeker, Libn.

KENRICK SEMINARY LIBRARY
7800 Kenrick Rd.   Phone: (314) 961-4320
St. Louis, MO 63119   Rev. Myron Gohmann, C.P., Hd.Libn.

KRUPNICK & ASSOCIATES, INC. - INFORMATION CENTER
135 N. Meramec
St. Louis, MO 63105

LAW LIBRARY ASSOCIATION OF ST. LOUIS
1300 Civil Courts Bldg.   Phone: (314) 622-4386
St. Louis, MO 63101   Rosa Gahn Wright, Libn.

LEGAL SERVICES OF EASTERN MISSOURI, INC. - LIBRARY
625 N. Euclid Ave.
Field Sta., Box 4999A   Phone: (314) 367-1700
St. Louis, MO 63108   Marjorie O'Blennis, Asst.Libn.

LEWIS & RICE - LAW LIBRARY
1400 Railway Exchange Bldg.
611 Olive St.   Phone: (314) 231-5833
St. Louis, MO 63101   Nancy M. Wiegand, Libn.

LUTHERAN CHURCH - MISSOURI SYNOD - CENTRAL LIBRARY
1333 S. Kirkwood Rd.   Phone: (314) 965-9000
St. Louis, MO 63122-7295   Linda C. Krueger, Libn.

LUTHERAN CHURCH - MISSOURI SYNOD - LUTHERAN LIBRARY FOR THE
   BLIND
1333 S. Kirkwood Rd.   Phone: (314) 965-9000
St. Louis, MO 63122   Marcia K. Seeger, Libn.

LUTHERAN MEDICAL CENTER - MEDICAL LIBRARY *
2639 Miami St.   Phone: (314) 772-1456
St. Louis, MO 63118   Jean Monsivais, Sec.

MC DONNELL DOUGLAS AUTOMATION COMPANY - MC AUTO CAMPUS
   LIBRARY
Dept. K222/300/2
Box 516   Phone: (314) 233-5194
St. Louis, MO 63166   Jenny Preston, Sect.Mgr.

MC DONNELL DOUGLAS CORPORATION - MC DONNELL AIRCRAFT LIBRARY
Dept. 022, Box 516   Phone: (314) 232-6134
St. Louis, MO 63166   C.E. Zoller, Mgr.

MALLINCKRODT, INC. - LIBRARY
Box 5439   Phone: (314) 695-5514
St. Louis, MO 63147   Juanita McCarthy, Corp.Libn.

MAY DEPARTMENT STORES COMPANY - INFORMATION CENTER
611 Olive St., Suite 1350   Phone: (314) 247-0329
St. Louis, MO 63101   Patricia A. Stepherson, Mgr.

MERCANTILE TRUST COMPANY - INTERNATIONAL LIBRARY
Box 14881   Phone: (314) 425-2867
St. Louis, MO 67178   Carrie L. Sallwasser, Libn.

MISSOURI BAPTIST HOSPITAL - MEDICAL LIBRARY
3015 N. Ballas Rd.   Phone: (314) 432-1212
St. Louis, MO 63131   Mildred Schupmann, Med.Libn.

MISSOURI BAPTIST HOSPITAL - SCHOOL OF NURSING LIBRARY
3015 N. Ballas Rd.   Phone: (314) 432-1212
St. Louis, MO 63131   Helen J. Seaton, Libn.

MISSOURI BOTANICAL GARDEN - LIBRARY
Box 299   Phone: (314) 577-5155
St. Louis, MO 63166   Constance P. Wolf, Dir. of Lib.

MISSOURI HISTORICAL SOCIETY - ARCHIVES AND MANUSCRIPTS
Jefferson Memorial Bldg.
Forest Park   Phone: (314) 361-1424
St. Louis, MO 63112   Stephanie Klein, Libn./Archv.

MISSOURI HISTORICAL SOCIETY - PICTORIAL HISTORY COLLECTION
Jefferson Memorial Bldg.
Forest Park   Phone: (314) 361-1424
St. Louis, MO 63112   Duane Sneddeker, Spec.Proj.Cur.

MISSOURI HISTORICAL SOCIETY - RESEARCH LIBRARY
Jefferson Memorial Bldg.
Forest Park   Phone: (314) 361-1424
St. Louis, MO 63112   Stephanie A. Klein, Libn./Archv.

MISSOURI INSTITUTE OF PSYCHIATRY LIBRARY
5400 Arsenal St.   Phone: (314) 644-8838
St. Louis, MO 63139   Mary E. Johnson, Libn.

MISSOURI STATE LIBRARY - WOLFNER MEMORIAL LIBRARY FOR THE
   BLIND & PHYSICALLY HANDICAPPED
1221 Locust St.   Phone: (314) 241-4227
St. Louis, MO 63103   Pennie D. Peterson, Coord.

MONSANTO COMPANY - CENTRAL ENGINEERING LIBRARY - CS71
800 N. Lindbergh Blvd.   Phone: (314) 694-7133
St. Louis, MO 63167   L.L. Holdman, Libn.

MONSANTO COMPANY - INFORMATION CENTER
800 N. Lindbergh Blvd.
Box 7090   Phone: (314) 694-4778
St. Louis, MO 63177   William A. Wilkinson, Mgr.

MONSANTO COMPANY - LAW LIBRARY
800 N. Lindbergh Blvd.   Phone: (314) 694-4306
St. Louis, MO 63166   Bette M. Buffa, Sr. Law Libn.

NATIONAL MUSEUM OF TRANSPORT - TRANSPORTATION REFERENCE
   LIBRARY
3015 Barrett Station Rd.   Phone: (314) 965-6885
St. Louis, MO 63122-3398   Dr. John P. Roberts, Sec.

NOOTER CORPORATION - TECHNICAL LIBRARY
Box 451   Phone: (314) 621-6000
St. Louis, MO 63166   Barry Heuer, Libn.

NORCLIFF THAYER MFG. FACILITY, DIVISION OF REVLON, INC. - LIBRARY
319 S. 4th St.   Phone: (314) 621-2304
St. Louis, MO 63102   Joann Aldridge, R.N., Libn.

PET, INC. - CORPORATE INFORMATION CENTER
Box 392   Phone: (314) 622-6134
St. Louis, MO 63166   Laurence R. Walton, Corp.Libn.

PETROLITE CORPORATION - INFORMATION CENTER
369 Marshall Ave.   Phone: (314) 968-6008
St. Louis, MO 63119   Pauline C. Beinbrech, Mgr.

PLANNED PARENTHOOD ASSOCIATION OF ST. LOUIS - FAMILY PLANNING
   LIBRARY
2202 S. Hanley Rd.   Phone: (314) 781-3800
St. Louis, MO 63144   Kathy Kurtz, Info.Ctr.Coord.

PROTESTANT EPISCOPAL CHURCH - MISSOURI DIOCESE - DIOCESAN
   ARCHIVES
1210 Locust St.   Phone: (314) 231-1220
St. Louis, MO 63103   Charles F. Rehkopf, Archv./Registrar

RALSTON PURINA COMPANY - INFORMATION CENTER
Checkerboard Square, 2RS   Phone: (314) 982-2150
St. Louis, MO 63164   Linda S. Lincks, Mgr.

ST. JOHN'S MERCY MEDICAL CENTER - JOHN YOUNG BROWN MEMORIAL
   LIBRARY
621 S. New Ballas Rd.   Phone: (314) 569-6340
St. Louis, MO 63141   Saundra H. Hudson, Dir.

ST. LOUIS ART MUSEUM - RICHARDSON MEMORIAL LIBRARY
Forest Pk.   Phone: (314) 721-0067
St. Louis, MO 63110   Ann B. Abid, Libn.

ST. LOUIS CHILDREN'S HOSPITAL - BORDEN S. VEEDER LIBRARY *
500 S. Kingshighway Blvd.
Box 14871   Phone: (314) 367-6880
St. Louis, MO 63178   Ileen R. Upton, Pediatric Libn.

ST. LOUIS CITY HOSPITAL - ST. LOUIS MUNICIPAL MEDICAL LIBRARY
1515 Lafayette Ave.   Phone: (314) 622-5255
St. Louis, MO 63104   Mrs. Bernie Ferrell, Libn.

ST. LOUIS COLLEGE OF PHARMACY - O.J. CLOUGHLY ALUMNI LIBRARY
4588 Parkview Pl.   Phone: (314) 367-8700
St. Louis, MO 63110   Helen F. Silverman, Libn.

ST. LOUIS - COMPTROLLERS OFFICE - MICROFILM DEPARTMENT
City Hall, Rm. 1
Tucker & Market Sts.   Phone: (314) 622-4274
St. Louis, MO 63103   Edward J. Machowski, Supv.

ST. LOUIS CONSERVATORY AND SCHOOLS FOR THE ARTS (CASA) - MAE M.
   WHITAKER LIBRARY
560 Trinity Ave.   Phone: (314) 863-3033
St. Louis, MO 63130   Marion Sherman, Libn.

ST. LOUIS HEARING AND SPEECH CENTER - LIBRARY
9526 Manchester   Phone: (314) 968-4710
St. Louis, MO 63119   Peggy Thompson, Exec.Dir.

ST. LOUIS MERCANTILE LIBRARY ASSOCIATION - LIBRARY
510 Locust St.
Box 633   Phone: (314) 621-0670
St. Louis, MO 63188   Elizabeth Kirchner, Dir./Libn.

ST. LOUIS METROPOLITAN MEDICAL SOCIETY - ST. LOUIS SOCIETY FOR
   MEDICAL AND SCIENTIFIC EDUCATION - LIBRARY
3839 Lindell Blvd.   Phone: (314) 371-5225
St. Louis, MO 63108   Audrey L. Berkley, Libn.

ST. LOUIS - POLICE LIBRARY
315 S. Tucker   Phone: (314) 444-5581
St. Louis, MO 63102   Cathy H. Reilly, Libn.

ST. LOUIS POST-DISPATCH - REFERENCE DEPARTMENT
900 N. Tucker Blvd.   Phone: (314) 621-1111
St. Louis, MO 63101   Nancy Williams Stoddard, Chf.Libn.

ST. LOUIS PSYCHOANALYTIC INSTITUTE - BETTY GOLDE SMITH
   MEMORIAL LIBRARY
4524 Forest Park Blvd.   Phone: (314) 361-7075
St. Louis, MO 63108   Rheba Symeonoglou, Libn.

ST. LOUIS PUBLIC LIBRARY - APPLIED SCIENCE DEPARTMENT
1301 Olive St.   Phone: (314) 241-2288
St. Louis, MO 63103   Therese F. Dawson, Supv.

ST. LOUIS PUBLIC LIBRARY - ART DEPARTMENT
1301 Olive St.   Phone: (314) 241-2288
St. Louis, MO 63103   Martha Hilligoss, Supv.

ST. LOUIS PUBLIC LIBRARY - CAROL MC DONALD GARDNER RARE BOOK
   ROOM
1301 Olive St.   Phone: (314) 241-2288
St. Louis, MO 63103   Julanne M. Good, Supv.

ST. LOUIS PUBLIC LIBRARY - CHILDREN'S LITERATURE ROOM
1301 Olive St.   Phone: (314) 241-2288
St. Louis, MO 63103   Julanne M. Good, Supv.

ST. LOUIS PUBLIC LIBRARY - FILM LIBRARY SERVICE
1624 Locust St.   Phone: (314) 241-2288
St. Louis, MO 63103   Rita Broughton, Supv.

ST. LOUIS PUBLIC LIBRARY - HISTORY AND GENEALOGY DEPARTMENT
1301 Olive St.   Phone: (314) 241-2288
St. Louis, MO 63103   Noel C. Holobeck, Supv.

ST. LOUIS PUBLIC LIBRARY - HUMANITIES AND SOCIAL SCIENCES
   DEPARTMENT
1301 Olive St.   Phone: (314) 241-2288
St. Louis, MO 63103   Edna J. Reinhold, Supv.

ST. LOUIS PUBLIC LIBRARY - POPULAR LIBRARY - MUSIC SECTION
1301 Olive St.   Phone: (314) 241-2288
St. Louis, MO 63103   Helen Taylor, Supv.

ST. LOUIS PUBLIC LIBRARY - READERS SERVICES/DOCUMENTS
   DEPARTMENT
1301 Olive St.   Phone: (314) 241-2288
St. Louis, MO 63103   Anne Watts, Supv.

ST. LOUIS PUBLIC SCHOOLS - LIBRARY SERVICES CENTER
1517 S. Theresa Ave.   Phone: (314) 865-4550
St. Louis, MO 63104   Robert G. Nador, Act.Dir.

ST. LOUIS SCIENCE CENTER - LIBRARY
5050 Oakland Ave.   Phone: (314) 652-5500
St. Louis, MO 63110   Paton R. White, Libn.

ST. LOUIS UNIVERSITY - COLLEGE OF PHILOSOPHY AND LETTERS - FUSZ
   MEMORIAL LIBRARY
3700 W. Pine Blvd.   Phone: (314) 652-3700
St. Louis, MO 63108   Rev. J. Eugene Coomes, S.J., Libn.

ST. LOUIS UNIVERSITY - DIVINITY LIBRARY
Pius XII Memorial Library
3655 W. Pine Blvd.   Phone: (314) 658-3082
St. Louis, MO 63108   Rev. W. Charles Heiser, S.J., Libn.

ST. LOUIS UNIVERSITY - KNIGHTS OF COLUMBUS VATICAN FILM LIBRARY
Pius XII Memorial Library
3655 West Pine Blvd.
St. Louis, MO 63108   Charles J. Ermatinger, Vatican Film Libn.

ST. LOUIS UNIVERSITY - MEDICAL CENTER LIBRARY
1402 S. Grand Blvd.   Phone: (314) 664-9800
St. Louis, MO 63104   Logan Ludwig, Dir.

ST. LOUIS UNIVERSITY - SCHOOL OF LAW - LIBRARY
3700 Lindell Blvd.   Phone: (314) 658-2755
St. Louis, MO 63108   Eileen H. Searls, Law Libn.

ST. LOUIS ZOOLOGICAL PARK - LIBRARY *
Forest Park
St. Louis, MO 63108   Charles Hoessle, Dir.

ST. LUKE'S HOSPITAL - LIBRARY
5535 Delmar Blvd.   Phone: (314) 361-1212
St. Louis, MO 63112   Kathy Mullen, Libn.

ST. LUKE'S HOSPITAL - SCHOOL OF NURSING LIBRARY
5555 Delmar Blvd.   Phone: (314) 361-1212
St. Louis, MO 63112   Sarah Deaver, Sch.Libn.

ST. MARY'S HEALTH CENTER - HEALTH SCIENCES LIBRARY
6420 Clayton Rd.   Phone: (314) 768-8112
St. Louis, MO 63117   Candace W. Thayer, Libn.

SOCIETY OF ST. VINCENT DE PAUL - LIBRARY
4140 Lindell Blvd.   Phone: (314) 371-4980
St. Louis, MO 63108   Dudley L. Baker, Exec.Sec.

SOUTHWESTERN BELL TELEPHONE COMPANY - BUSINESS INFORMATION
    RESOURCE SERVICE *
112 N. Fourth St., Rm. 1323   Phone: (314) 247-8696
St. Louis, MO 63102

SVERDRUP & PARCEL AND ASSOCIATES, INC. - TECHNICAL LIBRARY
801 N. 11th Blvd.   Phone: (314) 436-7600
St. Louis, MO 63101   R.A. Bodapati, Libn.

TEAM FOUR INC. - LIBRARY
14 N. Newstead Ave.   Phone: (314) 533-2200
St. Louis, MO 63108   Andrea Towell, Libn.

THIRD BAPTIST CHURCH - LIBRARY
620 N. Grand   Phone: (314) 533-7340
St. Louis, MO 63103

TRINITY UNITED CHURCH OF CHRIST - EDITH L. STOCK MEMORIAL
    LIBRARY
4700 S. Grand Blvd.   Phone: (314) 352-6645
St. Louis, MO 63111   Jean A. Allison, Chm., Lib.Comm.

UNIDYNAMICS/ST. LOUIS, INC. - LIBRARY
472 Paul Ave.
Box 11177   Phone: (314) 522-6700
St. Louis, MO 63135   Barbara Schulik, Libn.

UNION ELECTRIC COMPANY - LIBRARY
1901 Gratiot St.
Box 149   Phone: (314) 621-3222
St. Louis, MO 63166   Constance Ford, Chf.Libn.

UNITED NATIONS ASSOCIATION OF THE UNITED STATES OF AMERICA -
    GREATER ST. LOUIS CHAPTER - LIBRARY
7359 Forsyth Blvd.   Phone: (314) 721-1961
St. Louis, MO 63105   Alice W. Dunlop, Libn.

U.S. ARMY - CORPS OF ENGINEERS - ST. LOUIS DISTRICT - LIBRARY
210 Tucker Blvd., N.   Phone: (314) 263-5675
St. Louis, MO 63101   Katharine Hayes, District Libn.

U.S. ARMY - TROOP SUPPORT AND AVIATION MATERIEL READINESS
    COMMAND - STINFO AND REFERENCE LIBRARY †
4300 Goodfellow Blvd.   Phone: (314) 263-2345
St. Louis, MO 63120   Grace C. Feng, Supv.Libn.

U.S. COURT OF APPEALS, 8TH CIRCUIT - LIBRARY
U.S. Court & Customs House, Rm. 503   Phone: (314) 425-4930
St. Louis, MO 63101   David K. Brennan, Circuit Libn.

U.S. DEFENSE MAPPING AGENCY - AEROSPACE CENTER - TECHNICAL
    LIBRARY
3200 S. Second St.   Phone: (314) 263-4267
St. Louis, MO 63118   Russell E. Kappesser, Chf., Tech.Lib.

U.S. DEPT. OF COMMERCE - INTERNATIONAL TRADE ADMINISTRATION -
    ST. LOUIS DISTRICT OFFICE LIBRARY
120 S. Central Ave., Suite 400   Phone: (314) 425-3302
St. Louis, MO 63105

U.S. NATL. ARCHIVES & RECORDS SERVICE - NATL. PERSONNEL RECORDS
    CENTER
9700 Page Blvd.   Phone: (314) 263-7201
St. Louis, MO 63132   David L. Petree, Dir.

U.S. NATL. PARK SERVICE - JEFFERSON NATL. EXPANSION MEMORIAL -
    LIBRARY
11 N. Fourth St.   Phone: (314) 425-6023
St. Louis, MO 63102

U.S. VETERANS ADMINISTRATION (MO-St. Louis) - HOSPITAL LIBRARY
                                          Phone: (314) 652-4100
St. Louis, MO 63125   Larry Weitkemper, Chf., Lib.Serv.

UNIVERSITY OF MISSOURI, ST. LOUIS - EDUCATION LIBRARY
8001 Natural Bridge Rd.   Phone: (314) 553-5571
St. Louis, MO 63121   Virginia R. Workman, Hd., Educ.Lib.

UNIVERSITY OF MISSOURI, ST. LOUIS - HEALTH SCIENCES LIBRARY
8001 Natural Bridge Rd.   Phone: (314) 553-5909
St. Louis, MO 63121   Cheryle J. Cann, Health Sci.Libn.

UNIVERSITY OF MISSOURI, ST. LOUIS - THOMAS JEFFERSON LIBRARY -
    SPECIAL COLLECTIONS
8001 Natural Bridge Rd.   Phone: (314) 553-5053
St. Louis, MO 63121   Ron Krash, Dir.

UNIVERSITY OF MISSOURI, ST. LOUIS - WOMEN'S CENTER
107A Benton Hall
8001 Natural Bridge Rd.   Phone: (314) 553-5380
St. Louis, MO 63121   Cathy Burack, Dir.

WASHINGTON UNIVERSITY - ART & ARCHITECTURE LIBRARY
Steinberg Hall
Box 1061   Phone: (314) 889-5268
St. Louis, MO 63130   Imre Meszaros, Hd., Hum.Serv.

WASHINGTON UNIVERSITY - BIOLOGY LIBRARY
Life Sciences Bldg.   Phone: (314) 889-5405
St. Louis, MO 63130   Betty S. Galyon, Libn.

WASHINGTON UNIVERSITY - BUSINESS ADMINISTRATION LIBRARY
School of Business Adm., Prince Hall   Phone: (314) 889-6334
St. Louis, MO 63130   Magda Buday, Bus.Libn.

WASHINGTON UNIVERSITY - CENTER FOR THE STUDY OF DATA
    PROCESSING - CSDP LIBRARY
Cupples I, Rm. 15
Skinker & Lindell Blvds.   Phone: (314) 889-5366
St. Louis, MO 63130   Barbara Luszczynska, Lib.Assoc.

WASHINGTON UNIVERSITY - CHEMISTRY LIBRARY
Louderman Hall   Phone: (314) 889-6591
St. Louis, MO 63130   Eileen Horn, Chem.Libn.

WASHINGTON UNIVERSITY - COMPUTER LABORATORIES REFERENCE
    ROOM
700 S. Euclid Ave.   Phone: (314) 362-2275
St. Louis, MO 63110   Monica Shieh, Res.Libn.

WASHINGTON UNIVERSITY - DENTISTRY LIBRARY
School of Dental Medicine
4559 Scott Ave.   Phone: (314) 454-0385
St. Louis, MO 63110   Carol Murray, Libn.

WASHINGTON UNIVERSITY - DEPARTMENT OF SPECIAL COLLECTIONS
Olin Library   Phone: (314) 889-5495
St. Louis, MO 63130   Holly Hall, Hd.

WASHINGTON UNIVERSITY - DEPARTMENT OF TECHNOLOGY AND HUMAN
    AFFAIRS - LIBRARY
Box 1106   Phone: (314) 889-5494
St. Louis, MO 63130   Eric P. Rusten, Staff Assoc.

WASHINGTON UNIVERSITY - EARTH AND PLANETARY SCIENCES LIBRARY
Wilson Hall   Phone: (314) 889-5406
St. Louis, MO 63130   Deborah Hartwig, Libn.

WASHINGTON UNIVERSITY - EAST ASIAN LIBRARY
Box 1061   Phone: (314) 889-5155
St. Louis, MO 63130   Sachiko Morrell, Libn.

WASHINGTON UNIVERSITY - EDWARD MALLINCKRODT INSTITUTE OF
    RADIOLOGY LIBRARY
510 S. Kingshighway Blvd.   Phone: (314) 362-2978
St. Louis, MO 63110   Harriet Fieweger, Libn./Sec.

WASHINGTON UNIVERSITY - GAYLORD MUSIC LIBRARY
6500 Forsyth   Phone: (314) 889-5560
St. Louis, MO 63130   Susanne Bell, Music Libn.

WASHINGTON UNIVERSITY - GEORGE WARREN BROWN SCHOOL OF
    SOCIAL WORK - LIBRARY & LEARNING RESOURCES CENTER
Box 1196   Phone: (314) 889-6633
St. Louis, MO 63130   Michael E. Powell, Dir.

WASHINGTON UNIVERSITY - MATHEMATICS LIBRARY
Cupples I, Rm. 15
Skinker & Lindell Blvds.   Phone: (314) 889-5366
St. Louis, MO 63130   Barbara Luszczynska, Lib.Assoc.

WASHINGTON UNIVERSITY - PFEIFFER PHYSICS LIBRARY
Lindell & Skinker Blvds.   Phone: (314) 889-6215
St. Louis, MO 63130   B.M. Eickhoff, Physics Libn.

WASHINGTON UNIVERSITY - REGIONAL PLANETARY IMAGE FACILITY -
    LIBRARY
Dept. of Earth & Planetary Sciences
Campus Box 1169   Phone: (314) 889-5679
St. Louis, MO 63130   Betty L. Weiss, Libn./Data Mgr.

WASHINGTON UNIVERSITY - SCHOOL OF LAW - FREUND LAW LIBRARY
Mudd Bldg.
Box 1120   Phone: (314) 889-6459
St. Louis, MO 63130   Bernard D. Reams, Jr., Law Libn.

WASHINGTON UNIVERSITY - SCHOOL OF MEDICINE - DEPARTMENT OF
    PSYCHIATRY LIBRARY
4940 Audubon Ave.   Phone: (314) 362-2454
St. Louis, MO 63110

WASHINGTON UNIVERSITY - SCHOOL OF MEDICINE LIBRARY
660 S. Euclid Ave.   Phone: (314) 362-7080
St. Louis, MO 63110   Prof. Susan Y. Crawford, Dir.

WESTERN HISTORICAL MANUSCRIPT COLLECTION/STATE HISTORICAL
    SOCIETY OF MISSOURI MANUSCRIPTS JOINT COLL.
University of Missouri
Thomas Jefferson Library
8001 Natural Bridge Rd.   Phone: (314) 553-5143
St. Louis, MO 63121   Anne R. Kenney, Assoc.Dir.

ASSEMBLIES OF GOD GRADUATE SCHOOL - CORDAS C. BURNETT LIBRARY
    †
1445 Boonville Ave.   Phone: (417) 862-2781
Springfield, MO 65802   Larry L. Haight, Libn.

BAPTIST BIBLE COLLEGE - VICK MEMORIAL LIBRARY
628 E. Kearney St.   Phone: (417) 869-4130
Springfield, MO 65802   Ronald L. Walker, Dir.

BURGE SCHOOL OF NURSING - LIBRARY
1423 N. Jefferson   Phone: (417) 836-3460
Springfield, MO 65802

CENTRAL BIBLE COLLEGE - LIBRARY
3000 N. Grant   Phone: (417) 833-2551
Springfield, MO 65803   Gerard J. Flokstra, Jr., Lib.Dir.

COX MEDICAL CENTER-JEFFERSON - DOCTORS' LIBRARY
1423 N. Jefferson St.   Phone: (417) 836-3238
Springfield, MO 65802   Theresa Wimsatt, Asst.Dir., Med.Rec.

MISSOURI STATE COURT OF APPEALS, SOUTHERN DISTRICT - LAW
    LIBRARY
300 Sherman Pkwy.   Phone: (417) 864-4770
Springfield, MO 65806   Beverly Heist, Law Libn.

ST. JOHN'S HOSPITAL - MEDICAL LIBRARY
1235 E. Cherokee   Phone: (417) 881-8811
Springfield, MO 65804   Sr. Lillian Clare, Libn.

ST. JOHN'S HOSPITAL - SCHOOL OF NURSING LIBRARY
1930 S. National Ave.   Phone: (417) 885-2104
Springfield, MO 65804   Marty Osredker, Libn.

SOUTHWEST MISSOURI STATE UNIVERSITY - MAP COLLECTION
Box 175, Duane G. Meyer Library   Phone: (417) 836-5105
Springfield, MO 65804-0095   James A. Coombs, Map Libn.

SPRINGFIELD ART MUSEUM - ART REFERENCE LIBRARY
1111 E. Brookside Dr.   Phone: (417) 866-2716
Springfield, MO 65807   Alice Brooker, Libn.

SPRINGFIELD-GREENE COUNTY PUBLIC LIBRARIES - EDWARD M.
    SHEPARD MEMORIAL ROOM
397 E. Central   Phone: (417) 869-4621
Springfield, MO 65801   Michael D. Glenn, Ref.Libn.

MARK TWAIN BIRTHPLACE MUSEUM - RESEARCH LIBRARY
Box 54   Phone: (314) 565-3449
Stoutsville, MO 65283   Stanley Fast, Adm.

UNIVERSITY CITY PUBLIC LIBRARY - RECORD COLLECTION
6701 Delmar
University City, MO 63130   Robert L. Miller, Libn.

MORGAN COUNTY HISTORICAL SOCIETY - LIBRARY
210 N. Monroe St.
Versailles, MO 65084   Omega Hutchison, Supv.

CENTRAL MISSOURI STATE UNIVERSITY - WARD EDWARDS LIBRARY -
    SPECIAL COLLECTIONS
                                        Phone: (816) 429-4141
Warrensburg, MO 64093   Rosalie Schell, Dir., Rd.Serv.

JOHNSON COUNTY HISTORICAL SOCIETY - MARY MILLER SMISER
    HERITAGE LIBRARY
300 N. Main   Phone: (816) 747-9966
Warrensburg, MO 64093   Leona J. Sisson, Libn.

EDEN THEOLOGICAL SEMINARY - LIBRARY
475 E. Lockwood   Phone: (314) 961-3627
Webster Groves, MO 63119   Karen M. Leubbert, Dir.

EVANGELICAL AND REFORMED HISTORICAL SOCIETY - EDEN ARCHIVES
475 E. Lockwood Ave.   Phone: (314) 961-3627
Webster Groves, MO 63119   Gary W. Kwiatek, Archv.

U.S. AIR FORCE BASE - WHITEMAN BASE LIBRARY
FL 4625   Phone: (816) 687-3089
Whiteman AFB, MO 65305   Charlyne Van Oosbree, Base Libn.

MONTANA

BILLINGS GAZETTE - NEWS LIBRARY
401 N. Broadway
Box 2507   Phone: (406) 657-1271
Billings, MT 59103   Odelta A. Thomsen, Libn.

BILLINGS PUBLIC SCHOOLS - INSTRUCTIONAL MATERIALS CENTER *
504 North 29th St.   Phone: (406) 259-0291
Billings, MT 59101   W. Marshall Jones, Dir.

EASTERN MONTANA COLLEGE - LIBRARY - SPECIAL COLLECTIONS †
1500 N. 30th St.   Phone: (406) 657-2262
Billings, MT 59101   Ed Neroda, Dir., Lib.Serv.

HKM ASSOCIATES ENGINEERS/PLANNERS - LIBRARY
Airport Industrial Park, Box 31318   Phone: (406) 245-6354
Billings, MT 59107   Irene Nelson, Libn.

MERIDIAN LAND & MINERAL COMPANY - TECHNICAL SERVICES
800 First Northwestern Bank   Phone: (406) 256-4560
Billings, MT 59101   Margaret A. Lamberson, Supv., Rec.Mgt.

NORTHERN PLAINS RESOURCE COUNCIL - LIBRARY
419 Stapleton Bldg.   Phone: (406) 248-1154
Billings, MT 59101   John D. Smillie, Res.Coord.

PARMLY BILLINGS LIBRARY - MONTANA ROOM
510 N. Broadway   Phone: (406) 657-8290
Billings, MT 59101   Linda Weirather

SOUTH CENTRAL MONTANA REGIONAL MENTAL HEALTH CENTER -
  LIBRARY
1245 N. 29th St.   Phone: (406) 252-5658
Billings, MT 59101   ElRene A. Dorn, Libn.

U.S. BUREAU OF LAND MANAGEMENT - MONTANA STATE OFFICE LIBRARY
222 N. 32nd St.
Box 36800   Phone: (406) 657-6671
Billings, MT 59107   Carolyn M. Nelson, Libn.

MONTANA STATE UNIVERSITY - ROLAND R. RENNE LIBRARY - SPECIAL
  COLLECTIONS †
                                               Phone: (406) 994-4242
Bozeman, MT 59717

MONTANA STATE UNIVERSITY - UNIVERSITY ARCHIVES
Renne Library   Phone: (406) 994-4243
Bozeman, MT 59717   Jean Schmidt, Archv.

MONTANA STATE UNIVERSITY - VETERINARY RESEARCH LABORATORY -
  HUIDEKOPER LIBRARY
                                               Phone: (406) 994-4705
Bozeman, MT 59717   Kathryn Klingensmith, Libn.

MONTANA COLLEGE OF MINERAL SCIENCE AND TECHNOLOGY - LIBRARY
W. Park St.   Phone: (406) 496-4281
Butte, MT 59701   Elizabeth Morrissett, Hd.Libn.

THE MONTANA POWER COMPANY - LAW LIBRARY
40 E. Broadway St.   Phone: (406) 723-5421
Butte, MT 59701   Susan Nissen, Libn.

MOUNTAIN STATES ENERGY, INC. - CDIF TECHNICAL LIBRARY
Box 3767   Phone: (406) 494-7386
Butte, MT 59702   Carol Kirkpatrick, Lib.Ck.

MULTITECH - LIBRARY
225 S. Idaho
Box 4078
Butte, MT 59701   JoEllen Zeiler, Libn.

NATIONAL CENTER FOR APPROPRIATE TECHNOLOGY - RESEARCH
  LIBRARY
3040 Continental Dr.
Box 3838   Phone: (406) 494-4572
Butte, MT 59702   Rose C. Sullivan, Rsrc.Ctr.Spec.

ATLANTIC-RICHFIELD COMPANY - ANACONDA ALUMINUM COMPANY -
  COLUMBIA FALLS REDUCTION DIVISION - LIBRARY
Box 10   Phone: (406) 892-3261
Columbia Falls, MT 59912   Karen Green, Libn.

U.S. NATL. PARK SERVICE - CUSTER BATTLEFIELD NATL. MONUMENT -
  LIBRARY
Box 39   Phone: (406) 638-2622
Crow Agency, MT 59022   Neil C. Mangum, Park Hist.

U.S. NATL. PARK SERVICE - GRANT-KOHRS RANCH NATL. HISTORIC SITE
Box 790   Phone: (406) 846-2070
Deer Lodge, MT 59722   Neysa Dickey, Lead Park Techn.

CARTER COUNTY MUSEUM - LIBRARY
Ekalaka, MT 59324

U.S. VETERANS ADMINISTRATION (MT-Fort Harrison) - MEDICAL CENTER
  LIBRARY
                                               Phone: (406) 442-6410
Fort Harrison, MT 59636   Maurice C. Knutson, Chf., Lib.Serv.

U.S. NATL. PARK SERVICE - BIGHORN CANYON NATL. RECREATION AREA -
  LIBRARY *
Box 458   Phone: (406) 666-2412
Fort Smith, MT 59035   Theo D. Hugs, Park Techn.

FRONTIER GATEWAY MUSEUM - LIBRARY
Belle Prairie Frontage Rd.
Box 1181
Glendive, MT 59330   Louise Cross, Cur.

CASCADE COUNTY HISTORICAL SOCIETY - INFORMATION CENTER
1400 1st Ave. N.   Phone: (406) 452-3462
Great Falls, MT 59401   Mary T. Flanagan, Cur. of Hist.

COLUMBUS HOSPITAL - HEALTH SCIENCES LIBRARY
Box 5013   Phone: (406) 727-3333
Great Falls, MT 59403   Sr. Margaret LaPorte, Dir.

GREAT FALLS CLINIC - MEDICAL LIBRARY
1220 Central Ave.   Phone: (406) 454-2171
Great Falls, MT 59401   Carol Banas, Med.Libn.

GREAT FALLS GENEALOGY SOCIETY - LIBRARY
Paris Gibson Sq.
1400 First Ave., N.   Phone: (406) 727-8255
Great Falls, MT 59401   Thelma L. Marshall, Libn.

BITTER ROOT VALLEY HISTORICAL SOCIETY - RAVALLI COUNTY MUSEUM
205 Bedford Ave.   Phone: (406) 363-3338
Hamilton, MT 59840   Erma Owings, Dir.

U.S. NATL. INSTITUTES OF HEALTH - NATL. INSTITUTE OF ALLERGY &
  INFECTIOUS DISEASES - ROCKY MOUNTAIN LAB. LIB.
                                               Phone: (406) 363-3211
Hamilton, MT 59840   Liza Serha Hamby, Libn./Med.Sci.

ALTERNATIVE ENERGY RESOURCES ORGANIZATION (AERO) - LIBRARY
324 Fuller - C4   Phone: (406) 443-7272
Helena, MT 59601

CARROLL COLLEGE - LIBRARY
                                               Phone: (406) 442-1295
Helena, MT 59601   Lois A. Fitzpatrick, Dir.

CHURCH OF JESUS CHRIST OF LATTER-DAY SAINTS - HELENA BRANCH
  GENEALOGICAL LIBRARY
1610 E. Sixth Ave.
Box 811   Phone: (406) 443-1558
Helena, MT 59601   Esther M. Stratton, Br.Libn.

MONTANA HISTORICAL SOCIETY - LIBRARY/ARCHIVES
225 N. Roberts   Phone: (406) 444-2681
Helena, MT 59620

MONTANA STATE DEPARTMENT OF COMMERCE - CENSUS & ECONOMIC
  INFORMATION CENTER
1424 9th Ave.   Phone: (406) 444-2896
Helena, MT 59620-0401   Patricia A.B. Roberts, Prog.Mgr.

MONTANA STATE DEPARTMENT OF COMMERCE - MONTANA PROMOTION
    DIVISION
1424 9th Ave.   Phone: (406) 444-2654
Helena, MT 59620   John Wilson, Travel Dir.

MONTANA STATE DEPARTMENT OF NATURAL RESOURCES &
    CONSERVATION - RESEARCH & INFORMATION CENTER
32 S. Ewing   Phone: (406) 449-3647
Helena, MT 59601   Mildred Sullivan, Res.Spec.

MONTANA STATE LAW LIBRARY
Justice Bldg.
215 N. Sanders   Phone: (406) 444-3660
Helena, MT 59620   Claire Engel, State Law Libn.

MONTANA STATE LEGISLATIVE COUNCIL - RESEARCH DIVISION -
    REFERENCE LIBRARY
State Capitol, Rm. 101   Phone: (406) 444-3064
Helena, MT 59620   Sally Halverson, Res.Libn.

MONTANA STATE LIBRARY
1515 E. 6th Ave.   Phone: (406) 444-3115
Helena, MT 59620   Sara Parker, State Libn.

MONTANA STATE OFFICE OF PUBLIC INSTRUCTION - RESOURCE CENTER
    †
State Capitol, Rm. 106   Phone: (406) 449-2082
Helena, MT 59620   Cheri Bergeron, Libn.

SHODAIR CHILDREN'S HOSPITAL - MEDICAL REFERENCE LIBRARY
Box 5539   Phone: (406) 442-1980
Helena, MT 59604   Suzy Holt, Info.Spec.

KALISPELL REGIONAL HOSPITAL - MEDICAL LIBRARY
310 Sunnyview Ln.   Phone: (406) 755-5111
Kalispell, MT 59901   Susan Long, Med.Libn.

U.S. FOREST SERVICE - FLATHEAD NATL. FOREST CENTER
Box 147   Phone: (406) 755-5401
Kalispell, MT 59901

PARK COUNTY MUSEUM ASSOCIATION - MUSEUM LIBRARY
118 W. Chinook   Phone: (406) 222-3506
Livingston, MT 59047   Doris Whithorn, Caretaker

U.S. AIR FORCE BASE - MALMSTROM BASE LIBRARY
FL 4626   Phone: (406) 731-2748
Malmstrom AFB, MT 59402   Katherine V. Lex, Libn.

U.S. VETERANS ADMINISTRATION (MT-Miles City) - MEDICAL CENTER
    LIBRARY
                                            Phone: (406) 232-3060
Miles City, MT 59301   Donna B. Sweeney, Act.Chf., Lib.Serv.

MISSOULIAN NEWSPAPER - LIBRARY
Box 8029   Phone: (406) 721-5200
Missoula, MT 59807   Kathleen R. Kimble, Libn.

ST. PATRICK HOSPITAL - LIBRARY
500 W. Broadway
Box 4587   Phone: (406) 543-7271
Missoula, MT 59806   Jody Anderson, Libn.

UNIVERSITY OF MONTANA - BUREAU OF BUSINESS AND ECONOMIC
    RESEARCH - LIBRARY
School of Business Administration   Phone: (406) 243-5113
Missoula, MT 59812

UNIVERSITY OF MONTANA - MAUREEN & MIKE MANSFIELD LIBRARY - K.
    ROSS TOOLE ARCHIVES
                                            Phone: (406) 243-2053
Missoula, MT 59812   Dale L. Johnson, Archv.

UNIVERSITY OF MONTANA - OFFICE OF CAREER SERVICES - CAREER
    PLANNING & RESOURCE CENTER
Center for Student Development, Lodge 148   Phone: (406) 243-5460
Missoula, MT 59802   Richard McDonough, Career Counselor

UNIVERSITY OF MONTANA - SCHOOL OF FORESTRY - OXFORD
    COLLECTION
Science Division, Mansfield Library   Phone: (406) 243-6411
Missoula, MT 59812   Robert Schipf, Sci.Libn.

UNIVERSITY OF MONTANA - SCHOOL OF LAW - LAW LIBRARY
                                            Phone: (406) 243-6171
Missoula, MT 59801   Maurice M. Michel, Libn.

WESTERN MONTANA CLINIC - LIBRARY
501 W. Broadway   Phone: (406) 721-5600
Missoula, MT 59807   Patricia A. Manlove, Libn.

WESTERN MONTANA SCIENTISTS' COMMITTEE FOR PUBLIC
    INFORMATION - MONTANA ENVIRONMENTAL LIBRARY
Jeanette Rankin Hall
Univ. of Montana   Phone: (406) 243-2282
Missoula, MT 59812   William D. Tomlinson, Dir.

YELLOWSTONE-BIGHORN RESEARCH ASSOCIATION - LIBRARY
Red Lodge, MT 59068

UNITED METHODIST CHURCH - YELLOWSTONE ANNUAL CONFERENCE -
    ARCHIVES *
Box 297   Phone: (406) 745-3541
St. Ignatius, MT 59865   Rev. Ron Lang, Chm.

MONDAK HERITAGE CENTER - WILLO RALSTON MEMORIAL LIBRARY FOR
    HISTORICAL RESEARCH
Box 50   Phone: (406) 482-3500
Sidney, MT 59270   Anne Schneider, Musm.Dir.

U.S. NATL. PARK SERVICE - GLACIER NATL. PARK - GEORGE C. RUHLE
    LIBRARY
                                            Phone: (406) 888-5441
West Glacier, MT 59936   Beth Ladeau, Pk.Libn.

U.S. NATL. PARK SERVICE - BIG HOLE NATL. BATTLEFIELD - LIBRARY
Box 237   Phone: (406) 689-3155
Wisdom, MT 59761   Alfred W. Schulmeyer, Supt.

NEBRASKA

NEBRASKA STATE HISTORICAL SOCIETY - JOHN G. NEIHARDT CENTER -
    RESEARCH LIBRARY
Elm and Washington Sts.
Box 344   Phone: (402) 648-3388
Bancroft, NE 68004   John Lindahl, Cur./Libn.

BEATRICE STATE DEVELOPMENTAL CENTER - MEDIA RESOURCE CENTER
Box 808   Phone: (402) 223-2302
Beatrice, NE 68310   Sherrie Dux-Ideus, Training Off./Libn.

U.S. NATL. PARK SERVICE - HOMESTEAD NATL. MONUMENT - RESEARCH
    LIBRARY
R.R. 3, Box 47   Phone: (402) 223-3514
Beatrice, NE 68310-9416   Randall K. Baynes, Supt.

FONTENELLE FOREST NATURE CENTER - REFERENCE LIBRARY
1111 Bellevue Blvd., N.   Phone: (402) 731-3140
Bellevue, NE 68005   Robert W. Fluchel, Dir.

DANA COLLEGE - C.A. DANA-LIFE LIBRARY
College Dr.   Phone: (402) 426-4101
Blair, NE 68008   Ruth J. Rasmussen, Act.Lib.Dir.

FATHER FLANAGAN'S BOYS' HOME - INFORMATION SERVICES
Boys Town Center
14100 Crawford St.   Phone: (402) 498-1426
Boys Town, NE 68010   Donna L. Richardson, Info.Serv.Mgr.

CUSTER COUNTY HISTORICAL SOCIETY - LIBRARY
225 S. 10th Ave.   Phone: (308) 872-2203
Broken Bow, NE 68822   Mary Landkamer, Cur.

MERRICK COUNTY HISTORICAL MUSEUM - ARCHIVES
Phone: (308) 946-3309
Central City, NE 68826   T.C. Reeves, Pres.

U.S.D.A. - AGRICULTURAL RESEARCH SERVICE - MEAT ANIMAL RESEARCH
CENTER
Box 166   Phone: (402) 762-3241
Clay Center, NE 68933   Patricia L. Sheridan, Libn.

NEBRASKA STATE HISTORICAL SOCIETY - FORT ROBINSON MUSEUM -
RESEARCH LIBRARY
Box 304   Phone: (308) 665-2852
Crawford, NE 69339   Vance E. Nelson, Cur.

J-B PUBLISHING COMPANY - RESEARCH LIBRARY
430 Ivy Ave.   Phone: (402) 826-3356
Crete, NE 68333   William F. Rapp, Libn.

IOWA BEEF PROCESSORS, INC. - CORPORATE LIBRARY
Box 515
Dakota City, NE 68731

WASHINGTON COUNTY HISTORICAL ASSOCIATION - MUSEUM LIBRARY
14th & Monroe Sts.   Phone: (402) 468-5740
Fort Calhoun, NE 68023   Genevieve Slader, Libn./Cur.

DODGE COUNTY HISTORICAL SOCIETY - LOUIS E. MAY MUSEUM
1643 N. Nye   Phone: (402) 721-4515
Fremont, NE 68025   Loell R. Jorgensen, Musm.Dir.

EASTERN NEBRASKA GENEALOGICAL SOCIETY - LIBRARY
Box 541   Phone: (402) 721-9553
Fremont, NE 68025   Claire Mares, Ed.

U.S. NATL. PARK SERVICE - SCOTTS BLUFF NATL. MONUMENT - LIBRARY
Box 427   Phone: (308) 436-4340
Gerling, NE 69341   Russell Osborn, Chf. Ranger

HALL COUNTY MUSEUM BOARD - STUHR MUSEUM - LIBRARY AND
ARCHIVES
3133 W. Highway 34   Phone: (308) 384-1380
Grand Island, NE 68801   Dr. Robert Manley, Sr.Hist.

U.S. VETERANS ADMINISTRATION (NE-Grand Island) - HOSPITAL LIBRARY
2201 N. Broadwell St.   Phone: (308) 382-3660
Grand Island, NE 68801

ADAMS COUNTY HISTORICAL SOCIETY - ARCHIVES
1330 N. Burlington Ave.
Box 102   Phone: (402) 463-5838
Hastings, NE 68901

FIRST PRESBYTERIAN CHURCH - LIBRARY
7th at Lincoln Ave.   Phone: (402) 462-5147
Hastings, NE 68901   Joyce Ohlsen, Libn.

HASTINGS REGIONAL CENTER - MEDICAL LIBRARY
Phone: (402) 463-2471
Hastings, NE 68901   Ruth Swingle, Libn.

KEARNEY STATE COLLEGE - CALVIN T. RYAN LIBRARY - SPECIAL
COLLECTIONS
905 W. 25th   Phone: (308) 236-4218
Kearney, NE 68847   John Mayeski, Dir. of Lib.

BRYAN MEMORIAL HOSPITAL - MEDICAL LIBRARY
4848 Sumner St.   Phone: (402) 483-3141
Lincoln, NE 68506   Linda H. Coulter, Asst.Dir./Med.Rec.

BRYAN MEMORIAL HOSPITAL - SCHOOL OF NURSING - LIBRARY
5000 Sumner St.   Phone: (402) 483-3481
Lincoln, NE 68506   Susan P. Echols, Libn.

CHRISTIAN RECORD BRAILLE FOUNDATION, INC. - LENDING LIBRARY
4444 S. 52nd St.   Phone: (402) 488-0981
Lincoln, NE 68506   Wendell Carpenter, Coord., Rd.Serv.

CONTACT LITERACY CENTER - AAAA CONTACT CENTER
Box 81826   Phone: (402) 464-0602
Lincoln, NE 68501-1826   Rhonda Kadavy, Dir.

LINCOLN GENERAL HOSPITAL - HOSPITAL LIBRARY
2300 S. 16th St.   Phone: (402) 473-5332
Lincoln, NE 68502   Lucille Rosenberg, Hosp.Libn.

LINCOLN JOURNAL-STAR - LIBRARY
926 P St.
Box 81709   Phone: (402) 473-7293
Lincoln, NE 68501   Patricia R. Loos, Chf.Libn.

MADONNA PROFESSIONAL CARE CENTER - MEDICAL LIBRARY
2200 S. 52nd St.   Phone: (402) 489-7102
Lincoln, NE 68506   Donna Amedeo, Dir. of Educ.

NEBRASKA RESEARCH COORDINATING UNIT FOR VOCATIONAL
EDUCATION
511 E. Nebraska Hall
University of Nebraska   Phone: (402) 472-3337
Lincoln, NE 68588-0553   Elton. B. Mendenhall, Dir.

NEBRASKA STATE GAME AND PARKS COMMISSION - LIBRARY
2200 N. 33rd St.   Phone: (402) 464-0641
Lincoln, NE 68503   Recca A. Larson, Agency Libn.

NEBRASKA STATE HISTORICAL SOCIETY - ARCHIVES
Box 82554   Phone: (402) 471-4771
Lincoln, NE 68501   James E. Potter, State Archv.

NEBRASKA STATE HISTORICAL SOCIETY - LIBRARY
1500 R St.
Box 82554   Phone: (402) 471-3270
Lincoln, NE 68501   Ann Reinert, Libn.

NEBRASKA STATE LIBRARY
3rd. Floor S., Statehouse   Phone: (402) 471-3189
Lincoln, NE 68509   Reta Johnson, Dp.Libn.

NEBRASKA STATE LIBRARY COMMISSION
1420 P St.   Phone: (402) 471-2045
Lincoln, NE 68508   John Kopischke, Dir.

NEBRASKA STATE NATURAL RESOURCES COMMISSION - PLANNING
LIBRARY
301 Centennial Mall S.
Box 94876   Phone: (402) 471-2081
Lincoln, NE 68509   Jerry Wallin, Hd., Plan.Sect.

ST. ELIZABETH COMMUNITY HEALTH CENTER - MEDICAL LIBRARY
555 South 70th St.   Phone: (402) 483-9296
Lincoln, NE 68510   Leslee Shell, Dir.

UNION COLLEGE - ELLA JOHNSON CRANDALL MEMORIAL LIBRARY -
SPECIAL COLLECTIONS
3800 S. 48th St.   Phone: (402) 488-2331
Lincoln, NE 68506   Lawrence W. Onsager, Lib.Dir.

UNITED METHODIST CHURCH - NEBRASKA CONFERENCE - HISTORICAL
CENTER
Lucas Bldg.
Nebraska Wesleyan University
Box 4553   Phone: (402) 466-6769
Lincoln, NE 68504   Bernice Boilesen, Cur.

U.S. NATL. PARK SERVICE - MIDWEST ARCHEOLOGICAL CENTER -
RESEARCH LIBRARY *
Federal Bldg., Rm. 474
100 Centennial Mall N.   Phone: (402) 471-5392
Lincoln, NE 68508   Lynn M. Mitchell, Lib.Techn.

U.S. VETERANS ADMINISTRATION (NE-Lincoln) - MEDICAL CENTER
LIBRARY
600 S. 70th St.   Phone: (402) 489-3802
Lincoln, NE 68510   Jean Landfield, Chf.Libn.

UNIVERSITY OF NEBRASKA, LINCOLN - ARCHITECTURE LIBRARY
104 Architectural Hall   Phone: (402) 472-1208
Lincoln, NE 68588-0410   Kathleen A. Johnson, Assoc.Prof.

UNIVERSITY OF NEBRASKA, LINCOLN - BIOLOGICAL SCIENCES LIBRARY
Manter Hall 402   Phone: (402) 472-2756
Lincoln, NE 68588-0118   Richard E. Voeltz, Assoc. Professor

UNIVERSITY OF NEBRASKA, LINCOLN - C.Y. THOMPSON LIBRARY
East Campus   Phone: (402) 472-2802
Lincoln, NE 68583-0717   Lyle Schreiner, Professor

UNIVERSITY OF NEBRASKA, LINCOLN - CENTER FOR GREAT PLAINS
    STUDIES
205 Love Library   Phone: (402) 472-6220
Lincoln, NE 68588-0475   Jon Nelson, Cur.

UNIVERSITY OF NEBRASKA, LINCOLN - CHEMISTRY LIBRARY
Hamilton Hall 427   Phone: (402) 472-2739
Lincoln, NE 68588-0305   Richard E. Voeltz, Assoc. Professor

UNIVERSITY OF NEBRASKA, LINCOLN - COLLEGE OF LAW LIBRARY
East Campus   Phone: (402) 472-3548
Lincoln, NE 68583   John D. Nelson, Law Libn.

UNIVERSITY OF NEBRASKA, LINCOLN - DENTISTRY LIBRARY
College of Dentistry, East Campus, Rm. 8   Phone: (402) 472-1323
Lincoln, NE 68583-0740   Lyle Schreiner, Professor

UNIVERSITY OF NEBRASKA, LINCOLN - ENGINEERING LIBRARY
Nebraska Hall, 2nd Fl. W.   Phone: (402) 472-3411
Lincoln, NE 68588-0516   Alan V. Gould, Asst. Professor

UNIVERSITY OF NEBRASKA, LINCOLN - GEOLOGY LIBRARY
Morrill Hall, Rm. 303   Phone: (402) 472-2653
Lincoln, NE 68588-0341   Agnes Adams, Asst. Professor

UNIVERSITY OF NEBRASKA, LINCOLN - INSTRUCTIONAL MEDIA CENTER
421 Nebraska Hall   Phone: (402) 472-1910
Lincoln, NE 68583-0900

UNIVERSITY OF NEBRASKA, LINCOLN - MATHEMATICS LIBRARY
Oldfather Hall, Rm. 907   Phone: (402) 472-3731
Lincoln, NE 68588-0361   Agnes Adams, Asst. Professor

UNIVERSITY OF NEBRASKA, LINCOLN - MUSIC LIBRARY †
30 Westbrook Music Bldg.   Phone: (402) 472-6300
Lincoln, NE 68588-0101   Susan Messerli, Music Libn.

UNIVERSITY OF NEBRASKA, LINCOLN - PHYSICS LIBRARY
Behlen Laboratory, Rm. 263   Phone: (402) 472-1209
Lincoln, NE 68588-0112   Agnes Adams, Asst. Professor

UNIVERSITY OF NEBRASKA, LINCOLN - STATE MUSEUM - HAROLD W.
    MANTER LABORATORY - LIBRARY
W-529 Nebraska Hall
16th and W Sts.   Phone: (402) 472-3334
Lincoln, NE 68588-0514   Mary Hanson Pritchard, Prof. & Cur.

UNIVERSITY OF NEBRASKA, LINCOLN - UNIVERSITY ARCHIVES AND
    SPECIAL COLLECTIONS
303 Love Library   Phone: (402) 472-2531
Lincoln, NE 68588   Joseph G. Svoboda, Professor

WOODMEN ACCIDENT & LIFE COMPANY - LIBRARY
1526 K St.
Box 82288   Phone: (402) 476-6500
Lincoln, NE 68501   Virgene K. Sloan, Libn.

NORFOLK REGIONAL CENTER - STAFF LIBRARY
Box 1209   Phone: (402) 371-4343
Norfolk, NE 68701   Muriel V. Hillson, Libn.

U.S. AIR FORCE BASE - OFFUTT BASE LIBRARY †
FL 4600   Phone: (402) 294-2533
Offutt AFB, NE 68113   Margaret A. Byrne, Libn.

U.S. AIR FORCE HOSPITAL - EHRLING BERGQUIST REGIONAL HOSPITAL -
    MEDICAL LIBRARY
                                         Phone: (402) 294-7301
Offutt AFB, NE 68113   Jan Hatcher, Lib.Mgr.

U.S. AIR FORCE - STRATEGIC AIR COMMAND - LIBRARY SERVICES SAC
    (DPSOL)
Offutt AFB, NE 68113

BAIRD HOLM MC EACHEN PEDERSEN & HAMANN LAW OFFICES - LIBRARY
1500 Woodmen Tower   Phone: (402) 344-0500
Omaha, NE 68102   Patricia Carstens, Libn.

BERGAN MERCY HOSPITAL - MEDICAL LIBRARY
7500 Mercy Rd.   Phone: (402) 398-6092
Omaha, NE 68124   Ken Oyer, Libn.

BISHOP CLARKSON MEMORIAL HOSPITAL - PATHOLOGY/MEDICAL STAFF
    LIBRARY
Box 3328   Phone: (402) 559-2058
Omaha, NE 68103

CREIGHTON UNIVERSITY - HEALTH SCIENCES LIBRARY
California at 24th St.   Phone: (402) 280-2908
Omaha, NE 68178   Marjorie Wannarka, Dir.

CREIGHTON UNIVERSITY - LAW SCHOOL - KLUTZNICK LIBRARY †
2500 California St.   Phone: (402) 280-2875
Omaha, NE 68178   Robert Q. Kelly, Dir.

CREIGHTON UNIVERSITY - REINERT/ALUMNI MEMORIAL LIBRARY
2500 California St.   Phone: (402) 280-2705
Omaha, NE 68178   Ray B. Means, Lib.Dir.

DOUGLAS COUNTY LAW LIBRARY
Hall of Justice
17th & Farnam   Phone: (402) 444-7174
Omaha, NE 68183   Carol Gendler, Libn.

GRACE COLLEGE OF THE BIBLE - LIBRARY
1515 S. Tenth St.   Phone: (402) 342-3377
Omaha, NE 68108   Norma McWilliams, Hd.Libn.

IMMANUEL MEDICAL CENTER - PROFESSIONAL LIBRARY
6901 N. 72nd St.   Phone: (402) 572-2345
Omaha, NE 68122   Joan G. Kohout, Libn.

INTERNORTH - LAW LIBRARY
2223 Dodge St.   Phone: (402) 633-4000
Omaha, NE 68102   Janet Geist, Libn.

INTERNORTH - TECHNICAL INFORMATION CENTER
2223 Dodge St.   Phone: (402) 633-4298
Omaha, NE 68102   Marvin E. Lauver, Hd.Libn.

JEWISH FEDERATION OF OMAHA - LIBRARY
333 S. 132nd St.   Phone: (402) 334-8200
Omaha, NE 68154   Edythe Wolf, Dir.

JOSLYN ART MUSEUM - ART REFERENCE LIBRARY
2200 Dodge   Phone: (402) 342-3300
Omaha, NE 68102

KUTAK ROCK & HUIE - LAW LIBRARY
1650 Farnam St.   Phone: (402) 346-6000
Omaha, NE 68102   Avis B. Forsman, Libn.

MUTUAL OF OMAHA/UNITED OF OMAHA - LIBRARY †
Mutual of Omaha Plaza   Phone: (402) 978-2002
Omaha, NE 68175   Elizabeth Bremer, Hd.

NEBRASKA METHODIST HOSPITAL - LIBRARY
8303 Dodge St.   Phone: (402) 390-4611
Omaha, NE 68114   Angela Armer, Libn.

NEBRASKA PSYCHIATRIC INSTITUTE - LIBRARY
602 S. 45th St.   Phone: (402) 559-5124
Omaha, NE 68106   Pauline B. Allen, Libn.

NEBRASKA TESTING LABORATORIES - LIBRARY
4453 S. 67th St.
Elmwood Park Sta., Box 6075
Omaha, NE 68117   Phone: (402) 331-4453
                                            Dan McCarthy, Pres.

OMAHA-COUNCIL BLUFFS METROPOLITAN AREA PLANNING AGENCY
    (MAPA) - LIBRARY
7000 W. Center Rd., Suite 200   Phone: (402) 444-6866
Omaha, NE 68106   Dagnia Prieditis, Libn./Info.Off.

OMAHA PUBLIC LIBRARY - BUSINESS, SCIENCE & TECHNOLOGY
    DEPARTMENT
215 S. 15th St.   Phone: (402) 444-4817
Omaha, NE 68102   Bernice Johns, Hd.

OMAHA PUBLIC POWER DISTRICT - MANAGEMENT SYSTEMS SERVICES -
    LIBRARY
1623 Harney St.   Phone: (402) 536-4295
Omaha, NE 68102   Suzanne Forbes, Libn.

OMAHA WORLD-HERALD - LIBRARY
World Herald Square   Phone: (402) 444-1000
Omaha, NE 68102   Beverly Parisot, Lib.Mgr.

UNION PACIFIC RAILROAD COMPANY - LIBRARY
1416 Dodge St.   Phone: (402) 271-4785
Omaha, NE 68179   J.S. Boyer, Hd.Libn.

U.S. ARMY - CORPS OF ENGINEERS - OMAHA DISTRICT - LIBRARY
215 N. 17th St.
6014 U.S. Post Office & Courthouse   Phone: (402) 221-3230
Omaha, NE 68102-4978   Valetta Sharp, Libn.

U.S. NATL. PARK SERVICE - MIDWEST REGIONAL OFFICE LIBRARY †
1709 Jackson St.   Phone: (402) 221-3471
Omaha, NE 68102   Emily Bolton, Pub.Info.Asst.

U.S. VETERANS ADMINISTRATION (NE-Omaha) - HOSPITAL LIBRARY
4101 Woolworth Ave.   Phone: (402) 346-8800
Omaha, NE 68105   Lois J. Inskeep, Chf., Lib.Serv.

UNIVERSITY OF NEBRASKA MEDICAL CENTER - MC GOOGAN LIBRARY OF
    MEDICINE
42nd & Dewey Ave.   Phone: (402) 559-4006
Omaha, NE 68105   Robert M. Braude, Dir.

NEBRASKA STATE HISTORICAL SOCIETY - WILLA CATHER HISTORICAL
    CENTER - ARCHIVES
338 N. Webster St.   Phone: (402) 746-3285
Red Cloud, NE 68970   Ann E. Billesbach, Cur.

SHERIDAN COUNTY HISTORICAL SOCIETY, INC. - AGNES & CLARENCE
    BENSCHOTER MEMORIAL LIBRARY
Box 274   Phone: (308) 327-2961
Rushville, NE 69360   Robert Buchan, Cur.

CONCORDIA TEACHERS COLLEGE - LINK LIBRARY
800 N. Columbia Ave.   Phone: (402) 643-3651
Seward, NE 68434   Vivian A. Peterson, Dir., Lib.Serv.

WAYNE STATE COLLEGE - U.S. CONN LIBRARY
200 E. 10   Phone: (402) 375-2200
Wayne, NE 68787   Dr. Jack Middendorf, Dir.

NEVADA

U.S. BUREAU OF RECLAMATION - TECHNICAL LIBRARY
1404 Colorado St.
Box 427   Phone: (702) 293-8570
Boulder City, NV 89005   Cretha L. Riggle, Lib.Techn.

U.S. NATL. PARK SERVICE - LAKE MEAD NATL. RECREATION AREA -
    LIBRARY
601 Nevada Hwy.   Phone: (702) 293-4041
Boulder City, NV 89005   John S. Mohlenrich, Chf. Park Interp.

CARSON-TAHOE HOSPITAL - LAHONTAN BASIN MEDICAL LIBRARY
1201 N. Mountain St.
Box 2168   Phone: (702) 882-1361
Carson City, NV 89702   Mr. H. Pepper Sturm, Libn.

FORESTA INSTITUTE FOR OCEAN AND MOUNTAIN STUDIES -
    ENVIRONMENTAL STUDIES CENTER
6205 Franktown Rd.
Carson City, NV 89701

NEVADA STATE DEPARTMENT OF TRANSPORTATION - MAP INFORMATION
    LIBRARY
1263 S. Stewart St.   Phone: (702) 885-5400
Carson City, NV 89712   Dave Wise, Cart./Graphic Arts Des.

NEVADA STATE LIBRARY
Capitol Complex   Phone: (702) 885-5130
Carson City, NV 89710   Joseph J. Anderson, State Libn.

NEVADA STATE LIBRARY - DIVISION OF ARCHIVES
101 S. Fall St.   Phone: (702) 885-5210
Carson City, NV 89710   Guy L. Rocha, State Archv.

NEVADA STATE MUSEUM - LIBRARY
Capitol Complex
600 N. Carson St.   Phone: (702) 885-4810
Carson City, NV 89710   Robert A. Nylen, Registrar

NEVADA STATE SUPREME COURT - LIBRARY
Supreme Court Bldg., Capitol Complex   Phone: (702) 885-5140
Carson City, NV 89710   Susan Southwick, Law Libn.

CHURCH OF JESUS CHRIST OF LATTER-DAY SAINTS - ELKO BRANCH
    GENEALOGICAL LIBRARY
Box 651   Phone: (702) 738-4565
Elko, NV 89801   Mary Ann Meranda, Br.Libn.

ELKO MEDICAL CLINIC - LIBRARY *
762 14th St.   Phone: (702) 738-3111
Elko, NV 89801   Dr. George T. Manilla

NORTHEASTERN NEVADA MUSEUM - LIBRARY
1515 Idaho St.
Box 503   Phone: (702) 738-3418
Elko, NV 89801   Bevette Moore, Registrar

TITANIUM METALS CORPORATION OF AMERICA - HENDERSON TECHNICAL
    LIBRARY
Box 2128   Phone: (702) 564-2544
Henderson, NV 89015   Patricia A. Puckett, Tech.Libn.

AMERICAN SCIENCE FICTION ASSOCIATION - ASFA LIBRARY
421 E. Carson, Suite 95
Las Vegas, NV 89101   P.G. Silvers, Hd., Lib.Serv.

CER CORPORATION - LIBRARY
Desert Professional Plaza II
2225 E. Flamingo Rd.   Phone: (702) 735-7136
Las Vegas, NV 89109   Irene M. Voit, Libn.

CHURCH OF JESUS CHRIST OF LATTER-DAY SAINTS - LAS VEGAS BRANCH
    GENEALOGICAL LIBRARY
509 S. Ninth St.
Box 1360   Phone: (702) 382-9695
Las Vegas, NV 89101   Earl C. Brunner, Jr., Chf.Libn.

CLARK COUNTY DISTRICT HEALTH DEPARTMENT - LIBRARY
625 Shadow Ln.
Box 4426   Phone: (702) 385-1291
Las Vegas, NV 89127   Janet Dolan, Health Info.Spec.

CLARK COUNTY LAW LIBRARY
215 S. Third St.   Phone: (702) 386-4696
Las Vegas, NV 89101   Deniston J. Kay, Ph.D., Lib.Dir.

EG&G, INC. - TECHNICAL LIBRARY
680 E. Sunset Rd.
Box 1912   Phone: (702) 734-8181
Las Vegas, NV 89101   Anna Lee Kaighn, Libn.

HUMANA HOSPITAL SUNRISE - MEDICAL LIBRARY
3186 Maryland Pkwy.   Phone: (702) 731-8210
Las Vegas, NV 89109   Florence I. Jakus, Ed.D., Med.Libn.

LAS VEGAS - CITY MANAGER'S LIBRARY
City Hall, 10th Fl.
400 E. Stewart Ave.   Phone: (702) 386-6501
Las Vegas, NV 89101   Diane Ortiz, Mgt.Anl./Rec.Mgt.Coord.

LAS VEGAS REVIEW-JOURNAL - LIBRARY *
Box 70   Phone: (702) 383-0269
Las Vegas, NV 89125   Glenda Harris, Libn.

REYNOLDS ELECTRICAL AND ENGINEERING COMPANY, INC. -
   COORDINATION AND INFORMATION CENTER
Box 14400   Phone: (702) 295-1000
Las Vegas, NV 89114   Bernardo Maza, Supv.

REYNOLDS ELECTRICAL AND ENGINEERING COMPANY, INC. - TECHNICAL
   LIBRARY
Box 14400, M/S 707   Phone: (702) 295-6210
Las Vegas, NV 89114   Mona C. Lupo, Env.Sci.Tech.Libn.

SOUTHERN NEVADA MEMORIAL HOSPITAL - MEDICAL LIBRARY
2040 W. Charleston Blvd.   Phone: (702) 383-2368
Las Vegas, NV 89102   Aldona Lautenschlager, Dir., Lib.Serv.

U.S. DEPT. OF ENERGY - NEVADA OPERATIONS OFFICE - TECHNICAL
   LIBRARY
Box 14100   Phone: (702) 295-1274
Las Vegas, NV 89114   Cynthia Ortiz, Libn.

U.S. NATL. WEATHER SERVICE - WEATHER SERVICE NUCLEAR SUPPORT
   OFFICE - LIBRARY
Box 14985   Phone: (702) 734-3515
Las Vegas, NV 89114   Linda Schmith

UNIVERSITY OF NEVADA, LAS VEGAS - GAMING RESEARCH CENTER
4505 Maryland Pkwy.   Phone: (702) 739-3252
Las Vegas, NV 89154   Susan Dolin, Spec.Coll.Libn.

U.S. AIR FORCE BASE - NELLIS BASE LIBRARY
FL 4852, 554 CSG/SSL   Phone: (702) 643-2280
Nellis AFB, NV 89191   Dorothy Hart, Base Libn.

HARRAH'S AUTOMOTIVE LIBRARY
Box 10   Phone: (702) 786-3232
Reno, NV 89504   Helen King, Oper.Mgr.

NATIONAL JUDICIAL COLLEGE - LAW LIBRARY
University of Nevada   Phone: (702) 784-6747
Reno, NV 89557   Clara Kelly, Act.Libn.

NEVADA HISTORICAL SOCIETY - LIBRARY
1650 N. Virginia St.   Phone: (702) 789-0190
Reno, NV 89503   Peter L. Bandurraga, Dir.

NEVADA MENTAL HEALTH INSTITUTE - MEDICAL LIBRARY
480 Galletti Way   Phone: (702) 322-6961
Reno, NV 89512   Robert D. Armstrong, Libn.

ST. MARY'S HOSPITAL - MAX C. FLEISCHMANN MEDICAL LIBRARY
235 W. Sixth St.   Phone: (702) 789-3108
Reno, NV 89520   Kathleen L. Pratt, Libn.

U.S. BUREAU OF MINES - RENO RESEARCH CENTER - LIBRARY †
1605 Evans Ave.   Phone: (702) 784-5348
Reno, NV 89512   Janice Behers, Lib.Techn.

U.S. VETERANS ADMINISTRATION (NV-Reno) - MEDICAL CENTER -
   LEARNING CENTER
1000 Locust St.   Phone: (702) 786-7200
Reno, NV 89509   Janet F. Monk, Chf., Lib.Serv.

UNIVERSITY OF NEVADA, RENO - BASQUE STUDIES PROGRAM
Library   Phone: (702) 784-4854
Reno, NV 89557   William A. Douglass, Coord.

UNIVERSITY OF NEVADA, RENO - DESERT RESEARCH INSTITUTE -
   DANDINI PARK LIBRARY
7010 Dandini Blvd.
Reno, NV 89512   Roberta K. Orcutt, D.R.I. Libn.

UNIVERSITY OF NEVADA, RENO - DESERT RESEARCH INSTITUTE -
   LIBRARY
Box 60220   Phone: (702) 972-1676
Reno, NV 89506   Roberta K. Orcutt, D.R.I./Phys.Sci.Libn.

UNIVERSITY OF NEVADA, RENO - ENGINEERING LIBRARY
Scrugham Engineering Bldg., Rm. 228   Phone: (702) 784-6945
Reno, NV 89557   Mary B. Ansari, Libn.

UNIVERSITY OF NEVADA, RENO - LIFE AND HEALTH SCIENCES LIBRARY
Fleischmann College of Agriculture Bldg.   Phone: (702) 784-6616
Reno, NV 89557   Mary B. Ansari, Libn.

UNIVERSITY OF NEVADA, RENO - MACKAY SCHOOL OF MINES LIBRARY
                                             Phone: (702) 784-6596
Reno, NV 89557   Mary B. Ansari, Libn.

UNIVERSITY OF NEVADA, RENO - PHYSICAL SCIENCES LIBRARY
New Chemistry Bldg., Rm. 316   Phone: (702) 784-6716
Reno, NV 89557   Roberta K. Orcutt, Physical Sci.Libn.

UNIVERSITY OF NEVADA, RENO - RESEARCH AND EDUCATIONAL
   PLANNING CENTER
College of Education, Rm. 201   Phone: (702) 784-4921
Reno, NV 89557   Daniel Cline, Dir.

UNIVERSITY OF NEVADA, RENO - SAVITT MEDICAL LIBRARY
Savitt Medical Sciences Bldg.   Phone: (702) 784-4625
Reno, NV 89557   Joan S. Zenan, Libn.

UNIVERSITY OF NEVADA, RENO - SPECIAL COLLECTIONS DEPARTMENT/
   UNIVERSITY ARCHIVES
University Library   Phone: (702) 784-6538
Reno, NV 89557   Robert E. Blesse, Hd.

WASHOE COUNTY LAW LIBRARY
Court House
Box 11130   Phone: (702) 785-4188
Reno, NV 89520   Sandra Marz, Law Lib.Dir.

WASHOE MEDICAL CENTER - MEDICAL LIBRARY
77 Pringle Way   Phone: (702) 785-5693
Reno, NV 89520   Sherry A. McGee, Dir., Med.Lib.

NYE COUNTY LAW LIBRARY *
Court House, Box 1271   Phone: (702) 482-6666
Tonopah, NV 89049

NEW HAMPSHIRE

SALISBURY HISTORICAL SOCIETY - ARCHIVES
Box 91, R.D. 1   Phone: (603) 648-2431
Andover, NH 03216   Sylvia P. Barber, Cur.

ANDROSCOGGIN VALLEY HOSPITAL - MEDICAL LIBRARY
Page Hill Rd.   Phone: (603) 752-2200
Berlin, NH 03570   Clarisse Legere, Med.Rec.

NEW HAMPSHIRE VOCATIONAL-TECHNICAL COLLEGE - LIBRARY
Hanover St. Extension   Phone: (603) 542-7744
Claremont, NH 03743   Phil Prever, Libn.

NUMISMATICS INTERNATIONAL - LIBRARY
30 Pleasant St.
Colebrook, NH 03576   Granvyl Hulse, Libn.

FRANKLIN PIERCE LAW CENTER - LIBRARY
2 White St.   Phone: (603) 228-1541
Concord, NH 03301   Judith G. Norcross, Law Libn./Asst.Prof.

NEW HAMPSHIRE GOVERNOR'S COUNCIL ON ENERGY - ENERGY
INFORMATION CENTER *
2 1/2 Beacon St.   Phone: (603) 271-2711
Concord, NH 03301   Carol Waters, Dir. of Educ.

NEW HAMPSHIRE HISTORICAL SOCIETY - LIBRARY
30 Park St.   Phone: (603) 225-3381
Concord, NH 03301   William Copeley, Assoc.Libn.

NEW HAMPSHIRE HOSPITAL - PROFESSIONAL LIBRARY
105 Pleasant St.   Phone: (603) 224-6531
Concord, NH 03301   David R. Washburn, Prof. Staff Libn.

NEW HAMPSHIRE MUNICIPAL ASSOCIATION - LIBRARY
Box 617   Phone: (603) 224-7447
Concord, NH 03301   John B. Andrews, Exec.Dir.

NEW HAMPSHIRE PUBLIC UTILITIES COMMISSION - LIBRARY
8010 Suncook Rd.   Phone: (603) 271-2452
Concord, NH 03301   Paula M. Lebrocoguy, Lib.Asst.

NEW HAMPSHIRE STATE DEPARTMENT OF EDUCATION - COMPUTER &
STATISTICAL SERVICES
101 Pleasant St.   Phone: (603) 271-2778
Concord, NH 03301   Bruce G. Ryan, Supv.

NEW HAMPSHIRE STATE DEPARTMENT OF HEALTH & WELFARE - OFFICE
OF ALCOHOL & DRUG ABUSE PREVENTION - LIBRARY
Health & Welfare Bldg.
Hazen Dr.   Phone: (603) 271-4630
Concord, NH 03301   Susan Novak, Res.Asst.

NEW HAMPSHIRE STATE DEPARTMENT OF PUBLIC WORKS AND
HIGHWAYS - LIBRARY
Morton State Office Bldg., Rm. 101
Hazen Dr.
Box 483   Phone: (603) 271-2515
Concord, NH 03301-0483   William L. Rollins, Pub.Info.

NEW HAMPSHIRE STATE DEPARTMENT OF STATE - DIVISION OF
RECORDS MANAGEMENT & ARCHIVES
71 S. Fruit St.   Phone: (603) 271-2236
Concord, NH 03301   Frank C. Mevers, State Archv./Dir.

NEW HAMPSHIRE STATE FISH AND GAME DEPARTMENT - MANAGEMENT
AND RESEARCH DIVISION - LIBRARY
Concord, NH 03301

NEW HAMPSHIRE STATE LIBRARY
20 Park St.   Phone: (603) 271-2392
Concord, NH 03301   Shirley G. Adamovich, State Libn.

NEW HAMPSHIRE STATE LIBRARY - LAW LIBRARY
Supreme Court Bldg.
Loudon Rd.   Phone: (603) 271-3777
Concord, NH 03301   Constance T. Rinden, Law Libn.

NEW HAMPSHIRE STATE WATER SUPPLY AND POLLUTION CONTROL
COMMISSION - LIBRARY
Health and Welfare Bldg., Hazen Dr.
Box 95   Phone: (603) 271-3503
Concord, NH 03301

PATENT, TRADEMARK AND COPYRIGHT RESEARCH FOUNDATION -
LIBRARY
Franklin Pierce Law Ctr.   Phone: (603) 228-1541
Concord, NH 03301

UNIVERSITY OF NEW HAMPSHIRE - BIOLOGICAL SCIENCES LIBRARY
Kendall Hall   Phone: (603) 862-1018
Durham, NH 03824   Lloyd H. Heidgerd, Br.Libn.

UNIVERSITY OF NEW HAMPSHIRE - CHEMISTRY LIBRARY
Parsons Hall   Phone: (603) 862-1083
Durham, NH 03824   Edward Dauphinais, Libn.

UNIVERSITY OF NEW HAMPSHIRE - DAVID G. CLARK MEMORIAL PHYSICS
LIBRARY
DeMeritt Hall   Phone: (603) 862-2348
Durham, NH 03824   Edward Dauphinais, Libn.

UNIVERSITY OF NEW HAMPSHIRE - DEPARTMENT OF MEDIA SERVICES -
FILM LIBRARY
Dimond Library   Phone: (603) 862-2240
Durham, NH 03824   John D. Bardwell, Dir.

UNIVERSITY OF NEW HAMPSHIRE - ENGINEERING-MATH LIBRARY
Kingsbury Hall   Phone: (603) 862-1196
Durham, NH 03824   Edward Dauphinais, Libn.

UNIVERSITY OF NEW HAMPSHIRE - NEW HAMPSHIRE WATER RESOURCE
RESEARCH CENTER - LIBRARY
108 Pettee Hall   Phone: (603) 862-2144
Durham, NH 03824   Gayle J. Dorsey, Libn./Res.

UNIVERSITY OF NEW HAMPSHIRE - SPECIAL COLLECTIONS
Dimond Library   Phone: (603) 862-2714
Durham, NH 03824   Barbara A. White, Spec.Coll.Libn.

MOUNT WASHINGTON OBSERVATORY - LIBRARY
                                          Phone: (603) 466-3388
Gorham, NH 03581   Guy Gosselin, Dir.

MEETING HOUSE GREEN MEMORIAL AND HISTORICAL ASSOCIATION, INC.
- TUCK MEMORIAL MUSEUM - LIBRARY
Meeting House Green
40 Park Ave.
Hampton, NH 03842   Lester Cummings, Cur.

CREARE, INC. - LIBRARY
Box 71   Phone: (603) 643-3800
Hanover, NH 03755   Margaret Ackerson, Hd., Tech.Info.Serv.

DARTMOUTH COLLEGE - DANA BIOMEDICAL LIBRARY
Dartmouth-Hitchcock Medical Center   Phone: (603) 646-2858
Hanover, NH 03756   Shirley J. Grainger, Libn.

DARTMOUTH COLLEGE - FELDBERG LIBRARY
                                          Phone: (603) 646-2191
Hanover, NH 03755   James R. Fries, Libn.

DARTMOUTH COLLEGE - KRESGE PHYSICAL SCIENCES LIBRARY
                                          Phone: (603) 646-3564
Hanover, NH 03755   Susan C. George, Libn.

DARTMOUTH COLLEGE - MAP SECTION
Baker Library   Phone: (603) 646-2579
Hanover, NH 03755   John F. Berthelsen, Spec.Subj.Asst.

DARTMOUTH COLLEGE - ORIENTAL COLLECTION
Baker Library   Phone: (603) 646-3605
Hanover, NH 03755   Charles K.H. Chen, Far East Spec. and Cur.

DARTMOUTH COLLEGE - PADDOCK MUSIC LIBRARY
                                          Phone: (603) 646-3234
Hanover, NH 03755   Patricia B. Fisken, Libn.

DARTMOUTH COLLEGE - SANBORN HOUSE ENGLISH LIBRARY
                                          Phone: (603) 646-2312
Hanover, NH 03755   Charlotte S. McCanna, Branch Lib.Adm.Asst.

DARTMOUTH COLLEGE - SHERMAN ART LIBRARY
Carpenter Hall   Phone: (603) 646-2305
Hanover, NH 03755   Jeffrey L. Horrell, Libn.

DARTMOUTH COLLEGE - SPECIAL COLLECTIONS
Dartmouth College Library   Phone: (603) 646-2571
Hanover, NH 03755   Stanley W. Brown, Cur., Rare Books

U.S. ARMY - COLD REGIONS RESEARCH & ENGINEERING LABORATORY -
LIBRARY
72 Lyme Rd.   Phone: (603) 646-4221
Hanover, NH 03755   Nancy C. Liston, Libn.

NEW HAMPSHIRE STATE DIVISION OF FORESTS AND LANDS - FOX FOREST
LIBRARY
Fox State Forest   Phone: (603) 464-3453
Hillsboro, NH 03244   J.B. Cullen, Chf., Forest Info. & Plan

NEW HAMPSHIRE ANTIQUARIAN SOCIETY - LIBRARY
Main St.
Hopkinton Village, NH 03301   Rachael H. Johnson, Cur.

ANTIOCH/NEW ENGLAND GRADUATE SCHOOL - PROFESSIONAL RESOURCE
  CENTER
103 Roxbury St.   Phone: (603) 357-3122
Keene, NH 03431   James Craiglow, Assoc. Dean

CHESHIRE HOSPITAL - MAC GRATH FAMILY MEDICAL LIBRARY
580 Court St.   Phone: (603) 352-4111
Keene, NH 03431   Phyllis Askey, Med.Libn.

KEENE STATE COLLEGE - WALLACE E. MASON LIBRARY
Appian Way   Phone: (603) 352-1909
Keene, NH 03431   Edward A. Scott, Hd.Libn.

NEW HAMPSHIRE VOCATIONAL-TECHNICAL COLLEGE - LIBRARY
Prescott Hill   Phone: (603) 524-8084
Laconia, NH 03246   Patty Miller, Libn.

ACADIAN GENEALOGICAL & HISTORICAL ASSOCIATION - LIBRARY
Box 668
Manchester, NH 03105   Jean L. Pellerin, Assoc.Libn.

AMERICAN-CANADIAN GENEALOGICAL SOCIETY - LIBRARY
Box 668   Phone: (603) 623-1781
Manchester, NH 03105   Richard Gagnon, Libn.

ASSOCIATION CANADO-AMERICAINE - INSTITUT CANADO-AMERICAIN
Box 989   Phone: (603) 625-8577
Manchester, NH 03105   Robert A. Beaudoin, Chm., Archv.Comm.

CATHOLIC MEDICAL CENTER - HEALTH SCIENCE LIBRARY
100 McGregor St.   Phone: (603) 668-3545
Manchester, NH 03102   Marcia K. Allen, Libn.

MANCHESTER CITY LIBRARY - FINE ARTS DEPARTMENT
405 Pine St.   Phone: (603) 624-6550
Manchester, NH 03104   Theresa Snow Toy, Fine Arts Libn.

MANCHESTER CITY LIBRARY - NEW HAMPSHIRE ROOM
405 Pine St.   Phone: (603) 624-6550
Manchester, NH 03104   Cynthia O'Neil, Libn.

MANCHESTER HISTORIC ASSOCIATION - LIBRARY
129 Amherst St.   Phone: (603) 622-7531
Manchester, NH 03104   Elizabeth Lessard, Libn.

NEW HAMPSHIRE COLLEGE - SHAPIRO LIBRARY
2500 N. River Rd.   Phone: (603) 668-2211
Manchester, NH 03104   Richard Pantano, Dir.

ST. ANSELM'S COLLEGE - GEISEL LIBRARY
                                             Phone: (603) 669-1030
Manchester, NH 03102   James R. Kennedy, Libn.

U.S. VETERANS ADMINISTRATION (NH-Manchester) - MEDICAL CENTER
  LIBRARY
718 Smyth Rd.   Phone: (603) 624-4366
Manchester, NH 03104   Joan McGinnis, Chf.Libn.

KOLLSMAN INSTRUMENT COMPANY - KIC LIBRARY
Daniel Webster Hwy., S.   Phone: (603) 889-2500
Merrimack, NH 03054   Gerald W. Rice, Libn.

DANIEL WEBSTER COLLEGE - LIBRARY
University Dr.   Phone: (603) 883-3556
Nashua, NH 03063   Patience K. Jackson, Lib.Dir.

DIGITAL EQUIPMENT CORPORATION - SPIT BROOK LIBRARY
110 Spit Brook Rd.   Phone: (603) 881-1058
Nashua, NH 03062   Charles E. Matthews, Tech.Libn.

INGERSOLL-RAND COMPANY - ENGINEERING LIBRARY
150 Burke St.   Phone: (603) 882-2711
Nashua, NH 03061   M.D. Jewell, Mgr., Engr.Doc.

NASHUA CORPORATION - TECHNICAL LIBRARY †
44 Franklin St.   Phone: (603) 880-2537
Nashua, NH 03060   Kay Marquis, Tech.Lib.Supv.

NASHUA HOSPITAL ASSOCIATION - MEMORIAL HOSPITAL - HEALTH
  SCIENCES LIBRARY
8 Prospect St.   Phone: (603) 883-5521
Nashua, NH 03061-2014   Janis Isaacson Silver, Libn.

NASHUA PUBLIC LIBRARY - CHANDLER MEMORIAL LIBRARY AND ETHNIC
  CENTER
257 Main St.   Phone: (603) 882-4461
Nashua, NH 03060   Nelly Mitchell, Ethnic Coord.

NEW HAMPSHIRE VOCATIONAL-TECHNICAL COLLEGE - LIBRARY
505 Amherst St.   Phone: (603) 882-6923
Nashua, NH 03063   William A. McIntyre, Ed.D., Dir. of Lrng.Rsrcs

SANDERS ASSOCIATES, INC. - LIBRARY SERVICES
95 Canal St., NCA 1-1342   Phone: (603) 885-4143
Nashua, NH 03061-2004   Art Berlin, Mgr., Lib.Serv.

U.S. AIR FORCE BASE - PEASE BASE LIBRARY
FL 4623   Phone: (603) 430-3734
Pease AFB, NH 03801

PETERBOROUGH HISTORICAL SOCIETY - LIBRARY
Grove St.
Box 58   Phone: (603) 924-3235
Peterborough, NH 03458   Gloria Murray, Lib.Chm.

PLYMOUTH STATE COLLEGE - GEOGRAPHERS ON FILM COLLECTION
Ellen Reed House, Off. 4   Phone: (603) 536-1550
Plymouth, NH 03264   Prof. Maynard Weston Dow, Dir.

PLYMOUTH STATE COLLEGE - HERBERT H. LAMSON LIBRARY - ROBERT
  FROST COLLECTION †
                                             Phone: (604) 536-1550
Plymouth, NH 03264

PLYMOUTH STATE COLLEGE - HERBERT H. LAMSON LIBRARY - SPECIAL
  COLLECTIONS
                                             Phone: (603) 536-1550
Plymouth, NH 03264   Philip Wei, Dir.

ELEVENTH BOMBARDMENT GROUP (H) ASSOCIATION - ARCHIVES
1106 Maplewood Ave.   Phone: (603) 436-5835
Portsmouth, NH 03801   W.M. Cleveland, Hist.

MOSQUITO ASSOCIATION - ARCHIVES
1106 Maplewood Ave.   Phone: (603) 436-5835
Portsmouth, NH 03801   Mr. W.M. Cleveland, Hist.

PEARL HARBOR SURVIVORS ASSOCIATION - ARCHIVES
1106 Maplewood Ave.   Phone: (603) 436-5835
Portsmouth, NH 03801   Mr. W.M. Cleveland, Hist.

PORTSMOUTH ATHENAEUM - LIBRARY & MUSEUM
9 Market Sq.
Box 848   Phone: (603) 431-2538
Portsmouth, NH 03801-0848

STRAWBERY BANKE, INC. - THAYER CUMINGS HISTORICAL REFERENCE
  LIBRARY
454 Court St.   Phone: (603) 436-8010
Portsmouth, NH 03801   Nicole Osborn, Libn.

U.S. NAVY - NAVAL SHIPYARD (NH-Portsmouth) - TECHNICAL LIBRARY
Code 863   Phone: (603) 439-1000
Portsmouth, NH 03801   Josephine Rafferty, Tech.Libn.

GENERAL ELECTRIC COMPANY - METER BUSINESS DEPARTMENT -
  LIBRARY & DATA BUREAU *
130 Main St.   Phone: (603) 692-2100
Somersworth, NH 03878   Dave Weatherby

NEW HAMPSHIRE VOCATIONAL-TECHNICAL COLLEGE - LIBRARY
277R Portsmouth Ave.
Stratham, NH 03885   Nancy L. Dodge, Libn.

DIETRICH COLLECTION
West Farms Rd.
RR3, Box 35
West Canaan, NH 03741
Phone: (603) 632-7156
Dr. R. Krystyna Dietrich, Dir.

WOLFEBORO HISTORICAL SOCIETY - PLEASANT VALLEY SCHOOLHOUSE -
LIBRARY & FIRE ENGINE MUSEUM
S. Main St.
Wolfeboro, NH 03894
Phone: (603) 569-4997
Harrison D. Moore, Pres.

NEW JERSEY

EXXON RESEARCH AND ENGINEERING COMPANY - INFORMATION
SERVICES
Clinton Township
Rte. 22 East
Annandale, NJ 08801
Phone: (201) 730-3103
Margaret H. Graham, Mgr.

ATLANTIC CITY FREE PUBLIC LIBRARY - SPECIAL COLLECTIONS
Illinois & Pacific Aves.
Atlantic City, NJ 08401
Phone: (609) 345-2269
Maureen Sherr Frank, Lib.Dir.

ATLANTIC CITY MEDICAL CENTER - ATLANTIC CITY DIVISION - HEALTH
SCIENCE LIBRARY
1925 Pacific Ave.
Atlantic City, NJ 08401
Phone: (609) 344-4081
John P. Doesburgh, Med.Libn.

PRINCETON ANTIQUES BOOKFINDERS - ART MARKETING REFERENCE
LIBRARY
2915-17-31 Atlantic Ave.
Atlantic City, NJ 08401
Phone: (609) 344-1943
Robert Eugene, Cur.

U.S. FEDERAL AVIATION ADMINISTRATION - TECHNICAL INFORMATION
RESEARCH FACILITY (ACT 624)
Phone: (609) 484-5772
Atlantic City Airport, NJ 08405
Harry Kemp, Mgr.

AT & T COMMUNICATIONS - INFORMATION RESEARCH CENTER
295 N. Maple Ave., Rm. 4430C1
Basking Ridge, NJ 07920
Phone: (201) 221-4141
Melanie Z. Strub, Mgr.

CRUM AND FORSTER CORPORATION - BUSINESS INFORMATION CENTER
211 Mt. Airy Rd.
Basking Ridge, NJ 07920
Phone: (201) 953-3326
Melia M. Hoffman, Supv.

U.S. NATL. ARCHIVES & RECORDS SERVICE - FEDERAL ARCHIVES AND
RECORDS CENTER, REGION 2
Bldg. 22-MOT Bayonne
Bayonne, NJ 07002
Phone: (201) 858-7251
O.R. Whitelock, Dir.

AT & T COMMUNICATIONS - INFORMATION RESEARCH CENTER
Rm. 3B100
Bedminster, NJ 07921
Phone: (201) 234-3280
Melanie Z. Strub, Mgr.

CARRIER FOUNDATION - NOLAN D.C. LEWIS LIBRARY †
Box 147
Belle Mead, NJ 08502
Phone: (201) 874-4000
Sharon J. Geiger, Dir.

MAASS (Clara) MEDICAL CENTER - DOCTORS' LIBRARY †
Franklin Ave.
Belleville, NJ 07109
Phone: (201) 751-1000
Betty L. Garrison, Libn.

MAASS (Clara) MEDICAL CENTER - RADIOGRAPHY PROGRAM LIBRARY *
1 Franklin Ave.
Belleville, NJ 07109
Phone: (201) 751-1000
Willard Bell

OAKITE PRODUCTS INC. - CHEMICAL RESEARCH LIBRARY
50 Valley Rd.
Berkeley Heights, NJ 07922
Phone: (201) 464-6900
Mary Ann Derkach, Lib.Ck.

BLOOMFIELD COLLEGE - GEORGE TALBOT HALL LIBRARY - SPECIAL
COLLECTIONS
467 Franklin St.
Bloomfield, NJ 07003
Phone: (201) 748-9000
Dr. Painan R. Wu, Chf.Libn.

LUMMUS CREST, INC. - LUMMUS TECHNICAL CENTER - TECHNICAL
INFORMATION DEPARTMENT
1515 Broad St.
Bloomfield, NJ 07003
Phone: (201) 893-2251
Mary A. Ciaramella, Chf.Libn.

SCHERING-PLOUGH CORPORATION - PHARMACEUTICAL RESEARCH
DIVISION - LIBRARY INFORMATION CENTER
60 Orange St.
Bloomfield, NJ 07003
Phone: (201) 429-3727
Rita L. Goodemote, Assoc.Dir.

JOHNSTONE (E.R.) TRAINING & RESEARCH CENTER - PROFESSIONAL
LIBRARY
Burlington St.
Bordentown, NJ 08505
Phone: (609) 298-2500
Herman H. Spitz, Dir. of Res.

UNION CARBIDE CORPORATION - TECHNICAL INFORMATION SERVICE
Bldg. 200
Box 670
Bound Brook, NJ 08805
Phone: (201) 356-8000
Carol B. Klemm, Staff Coord.

BRIDGETON FREE PUBLIC LIBRARY - SPECIAL COLLECTIONS
150 E. Commerce St.
Bridgeton, NJ 08302
Phone: (609) 451-2620
Anthony M. Butler, Lib.Dir.

BRIDGETON HOSPITAL - HEALTH SCIENCES LIBRARY
Irving & Manheim Aves.
Bridgeton, NJ 08302
Phone: (609) 451-6600
Jeanne Garrison, Health Sci.Libn.

CUMBERLAND COUNTY DEPT. OF PLANNING & DEVELOPMENT -
TECHNICAL REFERENCE LIBRARY
800 E. Commerce St.
Bridgeton, NJ 08302
Phone: (609) 451-8000
Carl B. Holm, Prin. Planner

CUMBERLAND COUNTY LAW LIBRARY
County Court House
W. Broad & Fayette Sts.
Bridgeton, NJ 08302
Phone: (609) 451-8000
John R. Reinard, Law Libn.

BRIDGEWATER COURIER-NEWS - LIBRARY
1201 Route 22
Box 6600
Bridgewater, NJ 08807
Phone: (201) 722-8800
Linda H. Crow, Libn.

NATIONAL STARCH AND CHEMICAL CORPORATION - INFORMATION
RESOURCES
10 Finderne Ave.
Box 6500
Bridgewater, NJ 08807
Phone: (201) 685-5082
Marianne Vago, Info.Rsrcs.Supv.

DEBORAH HEART AND LUNG CENTER - MEDICAL LIBRARY
One Trenton Rd.
Browns Mills, NJ 08015
Phone: (609) 893-6611
Carol A. Harris, Med.Libn.

BURLINGTON COUNTY HISTORICAL SOCIETY - DELIA BIDDLE PUGH
LIBRARY
457 High St.
Burlington, NJ 08016
Phone: (609) 386-4773

CONVERSE CONSULTANTS - LIBRARY †
91 Roseland Ave.
Box 91
Caldwell, NJ 07006
Phone: (201) 226-9191
Roslyn M. Terry, Libn.

CAMDEN COUNTY BAR ASSOCIATION - LAW LIBRARY †
Camden County Courthouse, Rm. 500
Camden, NJ 08101
Phone: (609) 757-6703
Diane Hollingshead, Libn.

CAMDEN COUNTY HISTORICAL SOCIETY - LIBRARY
Park Blvd. & Euclid Ave.
Camden, NJ 08103
Phone: (609) 964-3333
Miriam Favorite, Libn.

CAMPBELL INSTITUTE FOR RESEARCH AND TECHNOLOGY - RESEARCH
DEVELOPMENT LIBRARY
Campbell Pl.
Camden, NJ 08101
Phone: (609) 342-4926
CarolAnn Vincent, Res.Libn.

COOPER HOSPITAL/UNIVERSITY MEDICAL CENTER - REUBEN L. SHARP
HEALTH SCIENCE LIBRARY
One Cooper Plaza
Camden, NJ 08103
Phone: (609) 342-2525
Patricia Solin, Dir.

HELENE FULD SCHOOL OF NURSING - LIBRARY †
Mt. Ephraim & Atlantic Aves.
                                    Phone: (609) 342-4599
Camden, NJ 08104   Barbara Some, Libn.

INSTITUTE FOR MEDICAL RESEARCH - LIBRARY
Copewood St.   Phone: (609) 966-7377
Camden, NJ 08103   Dorothy H. Gruber, Libn.

OUR LADY OF LOURDES MEDICAL CENTER - MEDICAL LIBRARY
1600 Haddon Ave.   Phone: (609) 757-3548
Camden, NJ 08103   Fred Kafes, Dir.

OUR LADY OF LOURDES MEDICAL CENTER - SCHOOL OF NURSING -
    LIBRARY
1565 Vesper Blvd.   Phone: (609) 757-3722
Camden, NJ 08103   Eleanor M. Kelly, Libn.

RCA CORPORATION - GSD - GOVERNMENT COMMUNICATIONS SYSTEMS -
    LIBRARY
Delaware Ave. & Cooper St., Bldg. 10-6-5   Phone: (609) 338-4046
Camden, NJ 08102   Nina R. Arrowood, Mgr., Lib.Rsrcs.

RUTGERS UNIVERSITY, THE STATE UNIVERSITY OF NEW JERSEY -
    SCHOOL OF LAW LIBRARY †
Fifth & Penn Sts.   Phone: (609) 757-6173
Camden, NJ 08102   Arno Liivak, Law Libn.

WHITMAN (Walt) HOUSE - LIBRARY
330 Mickle St.   Phone: (609) 964-5383
Camden, NJ 08103   Eleanor Ray, Caretaker

CAPE MAY COUNTY HISTORICAL & GENEALOGICAL SOCIETY - LIBRARY
DN 707
Rte. 9   Phone: (609) 465-3535
Cape May Court House, NJ 08210   Somers Corson, Act.Cur.

NEW YORK SOCIETY OF MODEL ENGINEERS - LIBRARY
341 Hoboken Rd.   Phone: (201) 939-9212
Caristadt, NJ 07072   Stephen Szewczuk, Libn.

SUN CHEMICAL CORPORATION - RESEARCH LIBRARY
631 Central Ave.   Phone: (201) 933-4500
Carlstadt, NJ 07072   Kendal Funk, Libn.

ESSEX COUNTY HOSPITAL CENTER - HAMILTON MEMORIAL LIBRARY
Box 500   Phone: (201) 228-8002
Cedar Grove, NJ 07009   Elizabeth B. Guarducci, Med.Libn.

BERLEX LABORATORIES, INC. - RESEARCH AND DEVELOPMENT DIVISION
    LIBRARY
110 E. Hanover Ave.   Phone: (201) 540-8700
Cedar Knolls, NJ 07927   Lorene Lingelbach, Libn.

CELANESE CORPORATION - CELANESE SPECIALTIES OPERATIONS -
    INFORMATION CENTER
26 Main St.   Phone: (201) 635-2600
Chatham, NJ 07928   Genevieve Spanacin, Info.Spec.

PHARMACO-MEDICAL DOCUMENTATION, INC. - RESEARCH LIBRARY †
205 Main St.
Box 401   Phone: (201) 822-9200
Chatham, NJ 07928   Miss G. Wold, Res.Libn.

COMPUTER HORIZONS, INC. - LIBRARY
1050 Kings Hwy., N.   Phone: (609) 779-0911
Cherry Hill, NJ 08034

KENNEDY MEMORIAL HOSPITALS - CHERRY HILL DIVISION - DR. BARNEY
    A. SLOTKIN MEMORIAL LIBRARY
Box 5009   Phone: (609) 665-2000
Cherry Hill, NJ 08034   Sharon Sobel, Libn.

TEMPLE EMANUEL - LIBRARY †
Cooper River Pkwy. at Donahue   Phone: (609) 665-0669
Cherry Hill, NJ 08034   Rene Batterman, Libn.

TRINITY PRESBYTERIAN CHURCH - NORMAN S. HJORTH MEMORIAL
    LIBRARY
Rte. 70 & W. Gate Dr.   Phone: (609) 428-2050
Cherry Hill, NJ 08034   Bernice Ahlquist, Chm., Lib.Comm.

TEMPLE SINAI - JACK BALABAN MEMORIAL LIBRARY
New Albany Rd.   Phone: (609) 829-0658
Cinnaminson, NJ 08077   Elaine Cohen, Libn.

AB BOOKMAN PUBLICATIONS, INC. - LIBRARY
Box AB   Phone: (201) 772-0020
Clifton, NJ 07015   Ellen Chernofsky, Libn.

AMERICAN CYANAMID COMPANY - CONSUMERS PRODUCTS RESEARCH
    DIVISION - LIBRARY
697 Rte. 46   Phone: (201) 365-6321
Clifton, NJ 07015   Linda M. Botti, Supv., Lib.Serv.

GIVAUDAN CORPORATION - LIBRARY
125 Delawanna Ave.   Phone: (201) 365-8563
Clifton, NJ 07014   Roberta F. Nugent, Chf.Libn.

UNITED TECHNOLOGIES CORPORATION - INMONT - LIBRARY
1255 Broad St.   Phone: (201) 365-3400
Clifton, NJ 07015   Joanne Freeman, Libn.

HUNTERDON DEVELOPMENTAL CENTER - ADAPTIVE LEARNING CENTER -
    LIBRARY
Pittstown Rd.
Box 5220   Phone: (201) 735-4031
Clinton, NJ 08809   Roger Schumacher, Dir.

BOROUGH OF COLLINGSWOOD - FREE PUBLIC LIBRARY - NEW JERSEY
    HISTORY ROOM
Haddon & Frazer Aves.   Phone: (609) 858-0649
Collingswood, NJ 08108   Peter P. Childs, Dir.

GENERAL DRAFTING COMPANY, INC. - MAP LIBRARY †
Canfield Rd.   Phone: (201) 538-7600
Convent Station, NJ 07961   Allan Freeman, Libn.

CARTER-WALLACE, INC. - LIBRARY
                                    Phone: (609) 655-6297
Cranbury, NJ 08512   Arthur Hilscher, Dir.

GENERAL FOODS CORPORATION - CRANBURY TECHNICAL INFORMATION
    CENTER
Prospect Plains Rd.   Phone: (609) 655-7186
Cranbury, NJ 08512   Grace Donnelly, Adm., Tech.Info.Rsrcs.

CRANFORD HISTORICAL SOCIETY - MUSEUM LIBRARY
124 N. Union Ave.   Phone: (201) 276-0082
Cranford, NJ 07016   Loretta A. Widdows, Cur.

CRANFORD UNITED METHODIST CHURCH - LIBRARY
201 E. Lincoln Ave.   Phone: (201) 276-0936
Cranford, NJ 07016   Laura Engel, Libn.

DAMES & MOORE - LIBRARY †
6 Commerce Dr.
Cranford, NJ 07016

ST. CLARE'S HOSPITAL - HEALTH SCIENCES LIBRARY
Pocono Rd.   Phone: (201) 625-6140
Denville, NJ 07834   Rosemary Murphy, Libn.

U.S. ARMY - ARMAMENT RESEARCH & DEVELOPMENT CENTER -
    SCIENTIFIC AND TECHNICAL INFORMATION DIVISION
ARRADCOM, Bldg. 59   Phone: (201) 724-2914
Dover, NJ 07801   Normand L. Varieur, Libn.

U.S. ARMY - PLASTICS TECHNICAL EVALUATION CENTER - LIBRARY
Armament Research and Development Center   Phone: (201) 724-2778
Dover, NJ 07801   Alfred M. Anzalone, Lib.Cons.

EAST BRUNSWICK PUBLIC LIBRARY - HOLOCAUST STUDIES COLLECTION
Two Jean Walling Civic Ctr.   Phone: (201) 390-6781
East Brunswick, NJ 08816   David P. Weill, Dir.

SANDOZ, INC. - LIBRARY
Route 10   Phone: (201) 386-8306
East Hanover, NJ 07936   Harriet W. Smith, Mgr., Lib.

SANDOZ PHARMACEUTICALS - INFORMATION SERVICES
Route 10   Phone: (201) 386-8105
East Hanover, NJ 07936   Joyce G. Koelle, Mgr.

EXXON CORPORATION - MEDICINE & ENVIRONMENTAL HEALTH DEPT. -
  RESEARCH & ENVIRONMENTAL HEALTH DIV.LIB.
Mettlers Rd.
Box 235   Phone: (201) 474-2506
East Millstone, NJ 08873   Patricia Hodge, Group Ldr., Lib./Off.Serv.

EAST ORANGE GENERAL HOSPITAL - HEALTH SERVICES LIBRARY
300 Central Ave.   Phone: (201) 672-8400
East Orange, NJ 07019   Joann Mehalick, Mgr. of Lib.Serv.

GLOBAL EDUCATION ASSOCIATES - CURRICULUM RESOURCE LIBRARY
552 Park Ave.   Phone: (201) 675-1409
East Orange, NJ 07017   Harriett Zullo, Dir.

U.S. VETERANS ADMINISTRATION (NJ-East Orange) - MEDICAL CENTER
  LIBRARY
                                          Phone: (201) 676-1000
East Orange, NJ 07019   Calvin A. Zamarelli, Chf.Libn.

LEVER RESEARCH AND DEVELOPMENT CENTER - RESEARCH LIBRARY
45 River Rd.   Phone: (201) 943-7100
Edgewater, NJ 07020   Terry Hauerstein, Info.Serv.Mgr.

ENGELHARD CORPORATION - TECHNICAL INFORMATION CENTER
Menlo Park   Phone: (201) 321-5271
Edison, NJ 08818   Roger L. Meyer, Mgr., Tech.Info.Serv.

ENVIRONMENTAL PROTECTION AGENCY - REGION II FIELD OFFICE -
  TECHNICAL LIBRARY
                                          Phone: (201) 321-6762
Edison, NJ 08837   Dorothy Szefczyk, Lib.Techn.

GENERAL CABLE COMPANY - RESEARCH CENTER LIBRARY
160 Fieldcrest Ave.   Phone: (201) 225-4780
Edison, NJ 08818   Benjamin L. De Witt, Mgr., Tech.Info.Serv.

KENNEDY (John F.) MEDICAL CENTER - LIBRARY
James St.   Phone: (201) 321-7181
Edison, NJ 08818   Maria C. Daly, Med.Libn.

MIDLANTIC NATIONAL BANK - TRUST DEPARTMENT LIBRARY
Metro Park Plaza
Box 600   Phone: (201) 321-8387
Edison, NJ 08818

MOBIL CHEMICAL COMPANY - RESEARCH & DEVELOPMENT -
  INFORMATION SERVICES
Box 240   Phone: (201) 321-6229
Edison, NJ 08818   Claire A. Holden, Supv., Info.Serv.

REVLON RESEARCH CENTER, INC. - LIBRARY
2121 Rte. 27   Phone: (201) 287-7649
Edison, NJ 08817   Lee J. Tanen, Mgr., Lib./Info.Serv.

ALEXIAN BROTHERS HOSPITAL - MEDICAL LIBRARY
655 E. Jersey St.   Phone: (201) 351-9000
Elizabeth, NJ 07206   Mary Conlon, Dir.

ELIZABETH GENERAL MEDICAL CENTER - CHARLES H. SCHLICHTER, M.D.
  HEALTH SCIENCE LIBRARY
925 E. Jersey St.   Phone: (201) 289-8600
Elizabeth, NJ 07201   Catherine M. Boss, Dir.

FREE PUBLIC LIBRARY OF ELIZABETH, NJ - ART AND MUSIC DEPARTMENT
11 S. Broad St.   Phone: (201) 354-6060
Elizabeth, NJ 07202   Roman A. Sawycky, Supv.Libn.

NATIONAL SOCIETY OF THE SONS OF THE AMERICAN REVOLUTION - NEW
  JERSEY SOCIETY - S.A.R. LIBRARY
1045 E. Jersey St.   Phone: (201) 355-1776
Elizabeth, NJ 07201   Howard W. Wiseman, Libn.

ST. ELIZABETH HOSPITAL - HEALTH SCIENCES LIBRARY
210 Williamson St.   Phone: (201) 527-5371
Elizabeth, NJ 07207   Sally Holdorf, Libn.

SEA-LAND SERVICE, INC. - CORPORATE INFORMATION CENTER †
General Office Port Authority Marine Terminal
Box 1050   Phone: (201) 558-6000
Elizabeth, NJ 07207

THORNTHWAITE (C.W.) ASSOCIATES LABORATORY OF CLIMATOLOGY -
  LIBRARY
Rural Delivery 1
Elmer, NJ 08318   William J. Superior, Pres.

AMERICAN LEPROSY MISSIONS, INC. - LIBRARY
One Broadway   Phone: (201) 794-8650
Elmwood Park, NJ 07407

ENGLEWOOD HOSPITAL - MEDICAL LIBRARY
350 Engle St.   Phone: (201) 894-3070
Englewood, NJ 07631   Katherine L. Lindner, Dir.

ENGLEWOOD HOSPITAL - SCHOOL OF NURSING LIBRARY
350 Engle St.   Phone: (201) 894-3326
Englewood, NJ 07631   Mary Alice Cesard, Libn.

LIPTON (Thomas J.), INC. - RESEARCH LIBRARY
800 Sylvan Ave.   Phone: (201) 567-8000
Englewood Cliffs, NJ 07632   Gloria S. Bernstein, Mgr., Lib.Info.Serv.

NORTHEASTERN BIBLE COLLEGE - LINCOLN MEMORIAL LIBRARY
12 Oak Lane   Phone: (201) 226-1074
Essex Fells, NJ 07021   Shirley N. Wood, Dir.

NABISCO BRANDS, INC. - FAIR LAWN TECHNICAL CENTER LIBRARY
2111 Rte. 208   Phone: (201) 797-6800
Fair Lawn, NJ 07410   Sonia D. Meurer, Libn.

AMERICAN PHONEMETER CORPORATION - CORPORATE LIBRARY
305 Fairfield Ave.   Phone: (201) 882-0640
Fairfield, NJ 07006

UNITED STATES GOLF ASSOCIATION - GOLF HOUSE LIBRARY
Golf House   Phone: (201) 234-2300
Far Hills, NJ 07931   Janet Seagle, Libn./Musm.Cur.

HUNTERDON COUNTY HISTORICAL SOCIETY - HIRAM E. DEATS MEMORIAL
  LIBRARY
114 Main St.   Phone: (201) 782-1091
Flemington, NJ 08822   Roxanne K. Carkhuff, Chm., Lib.Comm.

HUNTERDON COUNTY LAW LIBRARY
Court House
Main St.   Phone: (201) 788-1240
Flemington, NJ 08822   Gloria W. Peles, Law Libn.

HUNTERDON MEDICAL CENTER - MEDICAL LIBRARY
Rte. 31   Phone: (201) 782-2121
Flemington, NJ 08822   Joyce G. White, M.D., Libn.

REXHAM CORPORATION - PACKAGING TECHNICAL LIBRARY †
Church St. Extension
Box 111   Phone: (201) 782-4000
Flemington, NJ 08822   Anne T. Hand, Exec.Sec.

AUTOMATIC SWITCH COMPANY - ASCO LIBRARY †
50 Hanover Rd.   Phone: (201) 966-2479
Florham Park, NJ 07932   Nancy G. Garvey, Libn.

EXXON CORPORATION - COMMUNICATIONS AND COMPUTER SCIENCE
  DEPARTMENT- TECHNICAL LIBRARY †
180 Park Ave., Bldg. 102   Phone: (201) 765-5523
Florham Park, NJ 07932   P. Neubig, Ref.Sys.Supv.

EXXON RESEARCH AND ENGINEERING COMPANY - FLORHAM PARK
  INFORMATION CENTER †
Box 101   Phone: (201) 765-6704
Florham Park, NJ 07932   Martin Cosgrave, Sect.Hd.

GPU NUCLEAR - OYSTER CREEK TECHNICAL LIBRARY
Oyster Creek Nuclear Generating Sta.
Box 388
Forked River, NJ 08731   Kendall R. Wagner, Tech.Libn.

U.S. ARMY HOSPITALS - WALSON ARMY HOSPITAL - MEDICAL LIBRARY
Phone: (609) 562-5741
Ft. Dix, NJ 08640   Alice H. Gadsden, Med.Libn.

U.S. ARMY POST - FORT DIX - LIBRARY
Pennsylvania Ave., Bldg. 6501   Phone: (609) 562-4858
Fort Dix, NJ 08640   Valerie D. Fashion, Act.Dir.

FORT LEE PUBLIC LIBRARY - SILENT FILM PHOTO COLLECTION
320 Main St.   Phone: (201) 592-3614
Fort Lee, NJ 07024   Rita Altomara, Asst.Dir.

KWASHA LIPTON - LIBRARY
2100 N. Central Rd.   Phone: (201) 592-1300
Fort Lee, NJ 07024   Mary Seaman, Libn.

U.S. ARMY - COMMUNICATIONS-ELECTRONICS COMMAND - TECHNICAL
LIBRARY
DRSEL-ME-PSL   Phone: (201) 532-1298
Ft. Monmouth, NJ 07703

U.S. ARMY - COMMUNICATIONS SYSTEMS CENTER - ELECTRONICS
MUSEUM †
Myer Hall, Ave. of Memories   Phone: (201) 532-2445
Ft. Monmouth, NJ 07701   Edmond J. Norris, Dir.

U.S. ARMY - ELECTRONICS R & D COMMAND (ERADCOM) - TECHNICAL
LIBRARY DIVISION
Bldg. 2700, Attn: DELSD-L   Phone: (201) 544-2237
Ft. Monmouth, NJ 07703   William R. Werk, Chf.

IBM CORPORATION - BUSINESS INFORMATION LIBRARY
400 Parson's Pond Dr.
Franklin Lakes, NJ 07417   Ellen Feick, Mgr.

MONMOUTH COUNTY HISTORICAL ASSOCIATION - LIBRARY
70 Court St.   Phone: (201) 462-1466
Freehold, NJ 07728   Loretta M. Zwolak, Archv./Libn.

MONMOUTH COUNTY LAW LIBRARY
Court House   Phone: (201) 431-7079
Freehold, NJ 07728   Carolyn S. Geiling, Law Libn.

MONMOUTH COUNTY SOCIAL SERVICES - LIBRARY
Box 3000   Phone: (201) 431-6011
Freehold, NJ 07728   Francine Scheier, Libn.

GLASSBORO STATE COLLEGE - MUSIC BRANCH LIBRARY
Wilson Bldg. 615   Phone: (609) 445-7306
Glassboro, NJ 08028   Marjorie Travaline, Libn.

GLASSBORO STATE COLLEGE - SAVITZ LIBRARY - LLOYD V. MANWILLER
CURRICULUM LABORATORY
Rte. 322   Phone: (609) 863-5335
Glassboro, NJ 08028   Kathleen Kennedy, Asst.Dir./Bibliog./Ref.

GLASSBORO STATE COLLEGE - SAVITZ LIBRARY - STEWART ROOM
Phone: (609) 863-6303
Glassboro, NJ 08028   Clara M. Kirner, Spec.Coll.Libn.

ASSOCIATED TECHNICAL SERVICES, INC. - RESEARCH LIBRARY
855 Bloomfield Ave.   Phone: (201) 748-5673
Glen Ridge, NJ 07028   Leon Jacolev, Lib.Dir.

CUMBERLAND COUNTY HISTORICAL SOCIETY - PIRATE HOUSE LIBRARY
Box 16   Phone: (609) 455-8580
Greenwich, NJ 08323   Carl L. West, Hd.Libn.

GREYSTONE PARK PSYCHIATRIC HOSPITAL - HEALTH SCIENCE LIBRARY
Box A   Phone: (201) 538-1800
Greystone Park, NJ 07950   Brian C. Hamilton, Libn.

BERGEN COUNTY LAW LIBRARY †
Administrative Bldg.   Phone: (201) 646-2056
Hackensack, NJ 07601   Edna M. Oakley, Libn.

BERGEN COUNTY OFFICE ON AGING - REFERENCE LIBRARY OF
GERONTOLOGY
355 Main St.   Phone: (201) 646-2627
Hackensack, NJ 07624   Mildred Pere, Prin.Lib.Asst.

FAIRLEIGH DICKINSON UNIVERSITY - SCHOOL OF DENTISTRY LIBRARY
110 Fuller Pl.   Phone: (201) 692-2566
Hackensack, NJ 07601   Kathy Marousek, Dental Libn.

HACKENSACK MEDICAL CENTER - MEDICAL LIBRARY
Hospital Pl.   Phone: (201) 441-2326
Hackensack, NJ 07601   Duressa Pujat, Libn.

HACKETTSTOWN HISTORICAL SOCIETY - MUSEUM
106 Church St.   Phone: (201) 852-8797
Hackettstown, NJ 07840   Milton K. Thorp, Cur.

TEMPLE BETH SHOLOM - HERBERT GOLDBERG MEMORIAL LIBRARY †
Green St. & White Horse Pike
Haddon Heights, NJ 08035   Laura Olshan, Libn.

ARCHER & GREINER - LIBRARY
One Centennial Square   Phone: (609) 795-2121
Haddonfield, NJ 08033   Jean Newland, Libn.

HISTORICAL SOCIETY OF HADDONFIELD - LIBRARY *
343 King's Hwy. East   Phone: (609) 429-7375
Haddonfield, NJ 08033   Gertrude D. Hess, Libn.

ANCORA PSYCHIATRIC HOSPITAL - HEALTH SCIENCES LIBRARY
Phone: (609) 561-1700
Hammonton, NJ 08037   Norman T. Karchmer, Libn.

PUBLIC SERVICE ELECTRIC AND GAS COMPANY - NUCLEAR LIBRARY
Box 236, MC 150 A   Phone: (609) 339-4135
Hancocks Bridge, NJ 08308   Virginia L. Swichel, Libn.

STUDIO SUPPLIERS ASSOCIATION - BUSINESS LIBRARY
548 Goffle Rd.   Phone: (201) 427-9384
Hawthorne, NJ 07506   Donald Franz, Exec.Sec.

U.S. NATL. MARINE FISHERIES SERVICE - SANDY HOOK LABORATORY -
LIONEL A. WALFORD LIBRARY
Phone: (201) 872-0200
Highlands, NJ 07732   Claire L. Steimle, Libn.

BURR (Aaron) ASSOCIATION - LIBRARY
R.D. 1, Rte. 33, Box 429   Phone: (609) 448-2218
Hightstown, NJ 08520   Dr. Samuel Engle Burr, Jr., Act.Libn.

NL INDUSTRIES, INC. - MARKETING & TECHNICAL INFORMATION
SERVICE †
Box 420   Phone: (609) 443-2049
Hightstown, NJ 08520   Halina Kan, Libn.

BRISTOL-MYERS PRODUCTS - TECHNICAL INFORMATION CENTER
1350 Liberty Ave.   Phone: (201) 926-6691
Hillside, NJ 07207   Mary F. Bondarovich, Mgr., Tech.Info.Ctr.

WESTINGHOUSE ELECTRIC CORPORATION - LAMP DIVISIONS -
ENGINEERING LIBRARY †
1447 Chestnut Ave.   Phone: (201) 926-7940
Hillside, NJ 07205

GENERAL FOODS CORPORATION - MAXWELL HOUSE - TECHNICAL
INFORMATION CENTER †
1125 Hudson St.   Phone: (201) 420-3309
Hoboken, NJ 07030   Anne Marie Civinskas, Adm.

PLASTICS INSTITUTE OF AMERICA - LIBRARY
Stevens Institute of Technology
Castle Point Sta.   Phone: (201) 792-1839
Hoboken, NJ 07030   Albert Spaak, Exec.Dir.

STEVENS INSTITUTE OF TECHNOLOGY - SAMUEL C. WILLIAMS LIBRARY
Castle Point Sta.   Phone: (201) 420-5198
Hoboken, NJ 07030   Richard P. Widdicombe, Dir.

UNITED STATES TESTING COMPANY, INC. - LIBRARY †
1415 Park Ave.   Phone: (201) 792-2400
Hoboken, NJ 07030   Dorothy M. Campbell, Libn.

AT & T BELL LABORATORIES - LIBRARY
Phone: (201) 949-5236
Holmdel, NJ 07733   Mary Jane Miller, Lib. Group Supv.

AT & T TECHNOLOGIES, INC. - CORPORATE EDUCATION CENTER -
LIBRARY
Box 1000   Phone: (609) 639-4451
Hopewell, NJ 08525   S.M. Oderwald, Ref.Libn.

HOPEWELL MUSEUM - LIBRARY
28 E. Broad St.   Phone: (609) 466-0103
Hopewell, NJ 08525   Beverly Weidl, Cur.

CHRIST HOSPITAL - SCHOOL OF NURSING LIBRARY
169 Palisade Ave.
Jersey City, NJ 07306   Katherine Vargo, Libn.

HUDSON COUNTY LAW LIBRARY †
Hudson County Administration Bldg.
595 Newark Ave.   Phone: (201) 797-3737
Jersey City, NJ 07306

JERSEY CITY STATE COLLEGE - FORREST A. IRWIN LIBRARY - SPECIAL
COLLECTIONS
2039 Kennedy Blvd.   Phone: (201) 547-3027
Jersey City, NJ 07305-1597   Robert S. Nugent, Dir.

NATIONAL RAILWAY HISTORICAL SOCIETY - LIBRARY OF AMERICAN
TRANSPORTATION
Box 7   Phone: (609) 829-5204
Jobstown, NJ 08041   Earle P. Finkbiner, Libn.

AT & T TECHNOLOGIES, INC. - KEARNY INFORMATION RESOURCE CENTER
†
100 Central Ave.   Phone: (201) 465-4373
Kearny, NJ 07032   Anna-Elizabeth Vugrinecz, Ref.Libn.

SCHERING-PLOUGH CORPORATION - BUSINESS INFORMATION CENTER -
LIBRARY
Galloping Hill Rd.   Phone: (201) 558-5121
Kenilworth, NJ 07033   Esther M. Jankovics, Supv.

U.S. NAVY - NAVAL AIR ENGINEERING CENTER - TECHNICAL LIBRARY,
CODE 1115
Naval Air Engineering Center   Phone: (201) 323-2893
Lakehurst, NJ 08733   Deloris J. Swan, Lib.Off.

RIDER COLLEGE - FRANKLIN F. MOORE LIBRARY
2083 Lawrenceville Rd.   Phone: (609) 896-0800
Lawrenceville, NJ 08648   Ross Stephen, College Libn.

AT & T INFORMATION SYSTEMS - TECHNICAL LIBRARY
307 Middletown-Lincroft Rd.   Phone: (201) 576-3116
Lincroft, NJ 07738   Joseph A. Canose, Lib. Group Supv.

SOCIETY FOR THE INVESTIGATION OF THE UNEXPLAINED - LIBRARY
Box 265   Phone: (201) 842-5229
Little Silver, NJ 07739   N. Warth, Sec.

BELL COMMUNICATIONS RESEARCH, INC. - INFORMATION RESOURCES
SERVICES CENTER
290 W. Mount Pleasant Ave.   Phone: (201) 740-6206
Livingston, NJ 07039   L.C. Schneider, Staff Mgr.

BELL COMMUNICATIONS RESEARCH, INC. - INFORMATION RESOURCES &
SERVICES DISTRICT
290 W. Mount Pleasant Ave.   Phone: (201) 740-6205
Livingston, NJ 07039   A.M. Buck, Dist.Mgr.

C.I.T. FINANCIAL CORPORATION - BUSINESS/LEGAL INFORMATION
CENTER
650 C.I.T. Drive, Rm. 3332   Phone: (201) 740-5415
Livingston, NJ 07039

FOSTER WHEELER DEVELOPMENT CORPORATION - JOHN BLIZARD
RESEARCH CENTER - INFORMATION CENTER AND LIBRARY
12 Peach Tree Hill Rd.   Phone: (201) 533-3663
Livingston, NJ 07039   Karlo J. Mirth, Mgr.

MOTION PICTURE SERVICES
Box 252   Phone: (201) 992-8194
Livingston, NJ 07039   Murray Mankowitz, Dir.

ST. BARNABAS MEDICAL CENTER - MEDICAL LIBRARY
Old Short Hills Rd.   Phone: (201) 533-5050
Livingston, NJ 07039   A. Christine Connor, Lib.Dir.

MONMOUTH MEDICAL CENTER - ALTSCHUL MEDICAL LIBRARY
Third & Pavilion Aves.   Phone: (201) 870-5170
Long Branch, NJ 07740   John Conway, Dir.

PENICK CORPORATION - PPT LIBRARY
530 New York Ave.   Phone: (201) 438-6000
Lyndhurst, NJ 07071

U.S. VETERANS ADMINISTRATION (NJ-Lyons) - HOSPITAL LIBRARY
Knollcroft Rd.   Phone: (201) 647-0180
Lyons, NJ 07939   James G. Delo, Chf./Med.Libn.

U.S. AIR FORCE BASE - MC GUIRE BASE LIBRARY
FL 4484   Phone: (609) 724-2079
McGuire AFB, NJ 08641   Barbara-Ann Bomgardner, Base Libn.

DREW UNIVERSITY - LIBRARY
Phone: (201) 377-3000
Madison, NJ 07940   Dr. Arthur E. Jones, Jr., Dir.

UNITED METHODIST CHURCH - GENERAL COMMISSION ON ARCHIVES AND
HISTORY - LIBRARY AND ARCHIVES
Box 127
Madison, NJ 07940   Kenneth E. Rowe, Libn.

IMMACULATE CONCEPTION SEMINARY - LIBRARY
671 Ramapo Valley Rd.   Phone: (201) 327-0300
Mahwah, NJ 07430   Rev. James C. Turro, Dir., Lib.Serv.

HAMMOND, INC. - EDITORIAL DIVISION LIBRARY
515 Valley St.   Phone: (201) 763-6000
Maplewood, NJ 07040   E.J. Dupuy, Libn.

MADISON TOWNSHIP HISTORICAL SOCIETY - THOMAS WARNE
HISTORICAL MUSEUM AND LIBRARY
RD 1, Box 150   Phone: (201) 566-0348
Matawan, NJ 07747   Alvia D. Martin, Cur.

CONGREGATION BETH JACOB - GOODWIN FAMILY LIBRARY
109 E. Maple Ave.   Phone: (609) 662-4509
Merchantville, NJ 08109   Linda Strauss, Libn.

ROOSEVELT HOSPITAL - HEALTH SCIENCE LIBRARY
Box 151   Phone: (201) 321-6833
Metuchen, NJ 08840   Karen Rubin, Libn.

CHICOPEE, INC. - RESEARCH DIVISION - LIBRARY †
2 Ford Ave.
Box 8   Phone: (201) 524-7872
Milltown, NJ 08850   Judith A. Hassert, Res.Libn.

PERSONAL PRODUCTS COMPANY - RESEARCH & DEVELOPMENT LIBRARY
Van Liew Ave.   Phone: (201) 524-7544
Milltown, NJ 08850   Kathryn Hummer, Res.Libn.

WHEATON HISTORICAL ASSOCIATION - LIBRARY & RESEARCH OFFICE
Wheaton Village   Phone: (609) 825-6800
Millville, NJ 08332   Gay Le Cleire Taylor

MONTCLAIR ART MUSEUM - LE BRUN LIBRARY
3 S. Mountain Ave.
Box 1582   Phone: (201) 746-5555
Montclair, NJ 07042   Edith A. Rights, Libn.

MONTCLAIR PUBLIC LIBRARY - LOCAL HISTORY FILE
50 S. Fullerton Ave.   Phone: (201) 744-0500
Montclair, NJ 07042   Michael Connell, Dir.

MOUNTAINSIDE HOSPITAL - SCHOOL OF NURSING LIBRARY
Bay & Highland Aves.   Phone: (201) 746-6000
Montclair, NJ 07042   Ann Vreeland, Libn.

MOUNTAINSIDE HOSPITAL - ASSMANN HEALTH SCIENCES LIBRARY
Bay & Highland Aves.   Phone: (201) 429-6240
Montclair, NJ 07042   Patricia Regenberg, Dir.

GRANDMET USA, INC. - CORPORATE LIBRARY
100 Paragon Dr.   Phone: (212) 573-4111
Montvale, NJ 07645   A.J. Jerashen, Mgr.

HALCON SD GROUP, INC. - HALCON RESEARCH - LIBRARY
1 Philips Pkwy.   Phone: (201) 573-8100
Montvale, NJ 07645   Amy Feller, Libn./Info.Spec.

LEHN & FINK PRODUCTS GROUP - LIBRARY
225 Summit Ave.   Phone: (201) 573-5339
Montvale, NJ 07645   Ujwal Ranadive, Libn.

HENRY (J.J.) CO., INC. - ENGINEERING LIBRARY
West Park Dr.
Mt. Laurel Ind. Pk.   Phone: (609) 234-3880
Moorestown, NJ 08057   Lorraine Ulmer, Libn.

RCA CORPORATION - ENGINEERING LIBRARY †
Borton Landing Rd., Bldg. 101-222   Phone: (609) 778-3394
Moorestown, NJ 08057   Natalie J. Mamchur, Mgr., Lib.Res.

AT & T COMMUNICATIONS - INFORMATION RESEARCH CENTER
Atrium 1, Rm. 1J21
202 Johnson Rd.   Phone: (201) 993-5415
Morris Plains, NJ 07950   Jack Borbely, Mgr.

WARNER-LAMBERT COMPANY - CORPORATE LIBRARY
170 Tabor Rd.   Phone: (201) 540-2875
Morris Plains, NJ 07950   Nedra Behringer, Mgr., Corp.Lib.

ALLIED CORPORATION - LAW LIBRARY
Box 2245R   Phone: (201) 455-4445
Morristown, NJ 07960   Jeanne C. Seigle, Law Libn.

ALLIED CORPORATION - LIBRARY & INFORMATION SERVICES
Box 1021R   Phone: (201) 455-3014
Morristown, NJ 07960   Linnea Ditchey, Mgr.

AT & T INFORMATION SYSTEMS - LIBRARY
1776 On the Green   Phone: (201) 898-6264
Morristown, NJ 07960   Alfred Giraldi, Supv.Libn.

BELL COMMUNICATIONS RESEARCH, INC. - INFORMATION RESOURCES
SERVICES CENTER
445 South St.   Phone: (201) 829-4603
Morristown, NJ 07960

BENEFICIAL MANAGEMENT CORPORATION - LIBRARY †
Beneficial Bldg.
200 South St.   Phone: (201) 538-5500
Morristown, NJ 07208   Patricia A. Moffat, Libn.

CANAL SOCIETY OF NEW JERSEY - MUSEUM
Box 737   Phone: (201) 584-7297
Morristown, NJ 07960

CHURCH OF JESUS CHRIST OF LATTER-DAY SAINTS - MORRISTOWN, NEW
JERSEY BRANCH GENEALOGICAL LIBRARY
283 James St.   Phone: (201) 539-5362
Morristown, NJ 07960   Warner Hauer, Hd.Libn.

DIAMOND SHAMROCK CORPORATION - PROCESS CHEMICALS DIVISION -
LIBRARY †
350 Mt. Kemble Ave.
Box 2386-R   Phone: (201) 267-1000
Morristown, NJ 07960   Marilyn Swetell, Libn.

FINANCIAL EXECUTIVES RESEARCH FOUNDATION - LIBRARY
10 Madison Ave.
Box 1938
Morristown, NJ 07960   Judith Donaldson, Libn.

KEUFFEL AND ESSER COMPANY - CHEMICAL RESEARCH AND
DEVELOPMENT LIBRARY
20 Whippany Rd.   Phone: (201) 285-5530
Morristown, NJ 07960   Kaye Streppone, Libn.

MORRIS COUNTY HISTORICAL SOCIETY - VICTORIAN RESOURCE LIBRARY
68 Morris Ave.   Phone: (201) 267-3465
Morristown, NJ 07960   Naomi C. Stevens, Libn.

MORRIS COUNTY LAW LIBRARY
Morris County Court House
Washington St.   Phone: (201) 285-6497
Morristown, NJ 07960   Karen B. Brunner, Law Libn.

MORRIS MUSEUM OF ARTS AND SCIENCE - REFERENCE LIBRARY
Morristown, NJ 07960   Mrs. James C. Pitney

MORRISTOWN JEWISH COMMUNITY CENTER - THE LIBRARY
177 Speedwell Ave.   Phone: (201) 538-9292
Morristown, NJ 07960   Frances Tillinger, Libn.

MORRISTOWN MEMORIAL HOSPITAL - LATHROPE HEALTH SCIENCES
LIBRARY
100 Madison Ave., Rm. JB-80   Phone: (201) 540-5657
Morristown, NJ 07960   JoAnne M. Searle, Dir.

PITNEY, HARDIN, KIPP & SZUCH - LAW LIBRARY
163 Madison Ave.
CN 1945   Phone: (201) 267-3333
Morristown, NJ 07960   Julie L. von Schrader, Libn.

SILVER BURDETT COMPANY - EDITORIAL LIBRARY
250 James St.   Phone: (201) 538-0400
Morristown, NJ 07960   Jane Marie Schrader, Hd.Libn.

U.S. NATL. PARK SERVICE - MORRISTOWN NATL. HISTORICAL PARK -
LIBRARY
Washington Place   Phone: (201) 539-2017
Morristown, NJ 07960   Thomas O.C. Smith, Libn.

BURLINGTON COUNTY LYCEUM OF HISTORY AND NATURAL SCIENCE -
MOUNT HOLLY LIBRARY
307 High St.   Phone: (609) 267-7111
Mt. Holly, NJ 08060   Donald H. Dederick, Lib.Dir.

MEMORIAL HOSPITAL OF BURLINGTON COUNTY - HEALTH SCIENCES
LIBRARY
175 Madison Ave.   Phone: (609) 267-0700
Mt. Holly, NJ 08060   Betsy O'Connor, Libn.

CHILDREN'S SPECIALIZED HOSPITAL - MEDICAL LIBRARY
150 New Providence Rd.   Phone: (201) 233-3720
Mountainside, NJ 07090   Emily L. Snitow, Med.Libn.

MC GRAW-EDISON COMPANY - WORTHINGTON DIVISION - INFORMATION
CENTER
270 Sheffield St.   Phone: (201) 654-3300
Mountainside, NJ 07092   Larissa Palyvoda, Info.Spec.

AT & T BELL LABORATORIES - LIBRARIES AND INFORMATION SYSTEMS
CENTER
600 Mountain Ave.   Phone: (201) 582-2525
Murray Hill, NJ 07974   W.D. Penniman, Dir.

AT & T BELL LABORATORIES - LIBRARY
600 Mountain Ave.   Phone: (201) 582-4612
Murray Hill, NJ 07974   Ann W. Talcott, Lib. Group Supv.

THE BOC GROUP INC. - TECHNICAL CENTER - INFORMATION CENTER
                                              Phone: (201) 464-8100
Murray Hill, NJ 07974   Loretta J. Kiersky, Mgr.

BRAUN (C.F.) COMPANY - MURRAY HILL DIVISION - ENGINEERING
LIBRARY †
Diamond Hill Rd. & Mountain Ave.   Phone: (201) 665-6093
Murray Hill, NJ 07974   Marion C. Bale, Libn.

KRUPP WILPUTTE CORPORATION - LIBRARY †
152 Floral Ave.   Phone: (201) 464-5900
Murray Hill, NJ 07974   Roberta K. Sager, Supv.

JERSEY SHORE MEDICAL CENTER - ANN MAY SCHOOL OF NURSING
   LIBRARY & MEDIA CENTER
1945 Corlies Ave.   Phone: (201) 775-5500
Neptune, NJ 07753   Elsalyn P. Drucker, Lib.Dir.

JERSEY SHORE MEDICAL CENTER - MEDICAL LIBRARY
1945 Corlies Ave.   Phone: (201) 775-5500
Neptune, NJ 07753   Mr. Gian C. Hasija, Med.Libn.

CENTER FOR THE AMERICAN WOMAN & POLITICS - LIBRARY
Eagleton Institute, Rutgers University
Wood Lawn, Neilson Campus   Phone: (201) 932-9384
New Brunswick, NJ 08901   Kathy Stanwick, Asst.Dir.

GENEALOGICAL SOCIETY OF NEW JERSEY - MANUSCRIPT COLLECTIONS
Alexander Library
Rutgers University   Phone: (201) 932-7006
New Brunswick, NJ 08903   Ruth J. Simmons, Hd., Spec.Coll. & Archv.

HOME NEWS PUBLISHING COMPANY - LIBRARY
123 How Ln.   Phone: (201) 246-5529
New Brunswick, NJ 08901   Dr. Koit Ojamaa, Dir.

MIDDLESEX COUNTY LAW LIBRARY
County Court House, 2nd Fl., E. Wing
1 Kennedy Square   Phone: (201) 745-3357
New Brunswick, NJ 08901   Roland A. Winter, Libn.

MIDDLESEX COUNTY PLANNING BOARD - DATA MANAGEMENT &
   TECHNICAL SERVICES SECTION - LIBRARY
40 Livingston Ave.   Phone: (201) 745-3062
New Brunswick, NJ 08901   Louis Mattei, Supv.Plan.

NEW BRUNSWICK THEOLOGICAL SEMINARY - GARDNER A. SAGE LIBRARY
21 Seminary Pl.   Phone: (201) 247-5243
New Brunswick, NJ 08901   D. LeRoy Engelhardt, Libn.

RUTGERS UNIVERSITY, THE STATE UNIVERSITY OF NEW JERSEY -
   ALEXANDER LIBRARY - EAST ASIAN LIBRARY
College Ave.   Phone: (201) 932-7161
New Brunswick, NJ 08903   Dr. Nelson Chou, Libn.

RUTGERS UNIVERSITY, THE STATE UNIVERSITY OF NEW JERSEY - ART
   LIBRARY
Voorhees Hall   Phone: (201) 932-7739
New Brunswick, NJ 08903   Ferris Olin, Art Libn.

RUTGERS UNIVERSITY, THE STATE UNIVERSITY OF NEW JERSEY -
   BLANCHE AND IRVING LAURIE MUSIC LIBRARY
Mabel Smith Douglass Library   Phone: (201) 932-9783
New Brunswick, NJ 08903   Jan R. Cody, Music Libn.

RUTGERS UNIVERSITY, THE STATE UNIVERSITY OF NEW JERSEY -
   DEPARTMENT OF SPECIAL COLLECTIONS AND ARCHIVES
Alexander Library
College Ave. & Huntington St.   Phone: (201) 932-1766
New Brunswick, NJ 08903   Ruth J. Simmons, Sr.Archv./Coord.

RUTGERS UNIVERSITY, THE STATE UNIVERSITY OF NEW JERSEY -
   INSTITUTE OF MANAGEMENT/LABOR RELATIONS LIBRARY
                                                   Phone: (201) 932-9513
New Brunswick, NJ 08903   Bernard F. Downey, Libn.

ST. PETER'S MEDICAL CENTER - LIBRARY †
254 Easton Ave.   Phone: (201) 745-8545
New Brunswick, NJ 08903   Elizabeth McMullen, Mgr., Lib.Serv.

SQUIBB (E.R.) & SONS, INC. - SQUIBB INST. FOR MEDICAL RES. - SCIENCE
   INFO. DEPT. - NEW BRUNSWICK LIBRARY
Georges Rd.   Phone: (201) 545-1300
New Brunswick, NJ 08903   Muriel S. George, Supv., Lib.Oper.

UNIV. OF MEDICINE & DENTISTRY OF NJ - RUTGERS MED. SCHOOL -
   MIDDLESEX GENERAL-UNIV. HOSPITAL - HEALTH SCI.LIB.
CN 19   Phone: (201) 937-7606
New Brunswick, NJ 08903   Mary R. Scanlon, Libn.

NEW PROVIDENCE HISTORICAL SOCIETY - LIBRARY
1350 Springfield Ave.   Phone: (201) 464-5798
New Providence, NJ 07974   Dorothy Mason, Hd.Libn.

COLUMBUS HOSPITAL - MEDICAL LIBRARY
495 N. 13th St.   Phone: (201) 268-2074
Newark, NJ 07107   N. Milszyn, Libn.

ESSEX COUNTY LAW LIBRARY
512 County Courts Bldg.
50 W. Market St.   Phone: (201) 961-7293
Newark, NJ 07102   Jill Wright, Law Libn.

LUM, HOENS, ABELES, CONANT & DANZIS - LAW LIBRARY
550 Broad St.   Phone: (201) 622-7000
Newark, NJ 07102   Mr. Tae J. Yoo, Hd. Law Libn.

MC CARTER & ENGLISH - LAW LIBRARY †
550 Broad St.   Phone: (201) 622-4444
Newark, NJ 07102   Carol Lee Discavage, Libn.

NEW JERSEY HISTORICAL SOCIETY - LIBRARY
230 Broadway   Phone: (201) 483-3939
Newark, NJ 07104   Barbara Smith Irwin, Lib.Dir.

NEW JERSEY INSTITUTE OF TECHNOLOGY - ROBERT W. VAN HOUTEN
   LIBRARY
323 High St.   Phone: (201) 645-5306
Newark, NJ 07102   Morton Snowhite, Libn.

NEWARK BETH ISRAEL MEDICAL CENTER - DR. VICTOR PARSONNET
   MEMORIAL LIBRARY
201 Lyons Ave.   Phone: (201) 926-7233
Newark, NJ 07112   Lillian Bernstein, Libn.

NEWARK BOARD OF EDUCATION - TEACHERS' PROFESSIONAL LIBRARY
2 Cedar St.   Phone: (201) 733-7136
Newark, NJ 07102   Elberta H. Stone, Libn.

NEWARK MUSEUM - MUSEUM LIBRARY
49 Washington St.
Box 540   Phone: (201) 733-6640
Newark, NJ 07101   Margaret Di Salvi, Libn.

NEWARK PUBLIC LIBRARY - ART AND MUSIC DEPARTMENT
5 Washington St.
Box 630   Phone: (201) 733-7840
Newark, NJ 07101-0630   William J. Dane, Supv.

NEWARK PUBLIC LIBRARY - BUSINESS LIBRARY
34 Commerce St.   Phone: (201) 733-7849
Newark, NJ 07102   Leslie P. Rupprecht, Supv.

NEWARK PUBLIC LIBRARY - EDUCATION DIVISION
5 Washington St.
Box 630   Phone: (201) 733-7793
Newark, NJ 07101-0630   Frances Beiman, Prin.Libn.

NEWARK PUBLIC LIBRARY - HUMANITIES DIVISION
5 Washington St.
Box 630   Phone: (201) 733-7820
Newark, NJ 07101-0630   Sallie Hannigan, Prin.Libn., Ref.

NEWARK PUBLIC LIBRARY - NEW JERSEY REFERENCE DIVISION
5 Washington St.
Box 630   Phone: (201) 733-7776
Newark, NJ 07101-0630   Charles F. Cummings, Supv.Libn.

NEWARK PUBLIC LIBRARY - SCIENCE AND TECHNOLOGY DIVISION
5 Washington St.
Box 630   Phone: (201) 733-7815
Newark, NJ 07101-0630   Nicholas W. Patton, Prin.Libn.

NEWARK PUBLIC LIBRARY - SOCIAL SCIENCE DIVISION
5 Washington St.
Box 630   Phone: (201) 733-7782
Newark, NJ 07101-0630   Donald Fostel, Prin.Libn.

PRUDENTIAL INSURANCE COMPANY OF AMERICA - DRYDEN BUSINESS LIBRARY
Prudential Plaza - 2W
Newark, NJ 07101
Phone: (201) 877-6749
Robert P. Fallon, Libn.

PRUDENTIAL INSURANCE COMPANY OF AMERICA - FINANCIAL RESEARCH CENTER
4 Prudential Plaza
Newark, NJ 07107
Phone: (201) 877-6529
Debra R.A. Bowne, Res.Cons.

PRUDENTIAL INSURANCE COMPANY OF AMERICA - LAW LIBRARY
Gibralter Bldg., 5th Fl.
Newark, NJ 07101
Phone: (201) 877-6804
Vickie Riccardo-Markot, Law Libn.

PRUDENTIAL INSURANCE COMPANY OF AMERICA - MARKETING RESEARCH CENTER
14 Prudential Plaza
Newark, NJ 07101
Phone: (201) 877-7583
Barbara Gurdon Ciccone, Marketing Res.Cons.

PUBLIC SERVICE ELECTRIC AND GAS COMPANY - LIBRARY
80 Park Plaza, P3C
Box 570
Newark, NJ 07101
Phone: (201) 430-7333
Florine E. Hunt, Corp.Libn.

RUTGERS UNIVERSITY, THE STATE UNIVERSITY OF NEW JERSEY - CRIMINAL JUSTICE/NCCD COLLECTION
John Cotton Dana Library
185 University Ave.
Newark, NJ 07102
Phone: (201) 648-5522
Phyllis A. Schultze, Libn.

RUTGERS UNIVERSITY, THE STATE UNIVERSITY OF NEW JERSEY - JUSTICE HENRY ACKERSON LIBRARY OF LAW & CRIMINAL JUSTICE
Samuel I. Newhouse Ctr.
for Law & Justice
15 Washington St.
Newark, NJ 07102
Phone: (201) 648-5675
Charlie Harvey, Law Libn.

RUTGERS UNIVERSITY, THE STATE UNIVERSITY OF NEW JERSEY - INSTITUTE OF JAZZ STUDIES
Bradley Hall
Warren St. and Martin Luther King Blvd.
Newark, NJ 07102
Phone: (201) 648-5595
Dan Morgenstern, Dir.

ST. MICHAEL MEDICAL CENTER - AQUINAS MEDICAL LIBRARY
268 Dr. Martin Luther King Jr. Blvd.
Newark, NJ 07102
Phone: (201) 877-5471
Betty L. Garrison, Dir., Med.Lib.

SETON HALL UNIVERSITY - SCHOOL OF LAW - LAW LIBRARY
1111 Raymond Blvd.
Newark, NJ 07102
Phone: (201) 642-8766
Richard G. Hutchins, Dir.

SHANLEY & FISHER - LAW LIBRARY
550 Broad St.
Newark, NJ 07102
Phone: (201) 643-1220
Susan C. Cunningham, Libn.

UNITED HOSPITALS MEDICAL CENTER OF NEWARK - LIBRARY/ INFORMATION SERVICES
15 S. Ninth St.
Newark, NJ 07107
Phone: (201) 268-8774
Rosary S. Gilheany, Dir./Lib. & Ref.Serv.

U.S. COURT OF APPEALS, 3RD CIRCUIT - BRANCH LIBRARY
U.S. Post Office & Court House
Box 1068
Newark, NJ 07101
Phone: (201) 645-3034
Gerry Saletta, Libn.

U.S. DEPT. OF JUSTICE - UNITED STATES ATTORNEY, DISTRICT OF NEW JERSEY - LAW LIBRARY †
970 Broad St.
Newark, NJ 07102
Phone: (201) 645-2387
Martha Bomgardner, Libn.

UNIVERSITY OF MEDICINE AND DENTISTRY OF NEW JERSEY AT NEWARK - GEORGE F. SMITH LIBRARY
100 Bergen St.
Newark, NJ 07103
Phone: (201) 456-4580
Philip Rosenstein, Dir. of Libs.

UNEXPECTED WILDLIFE REFUGE - LIBRARY
Unexpected Rd.
Newfield, NJ 08344
Hope Sawyer Buyukmihci, Sec.

SUSSEX COUNTY HISTORICAL SOCIETY - LIBRARY †
82 Main St.
Newton, NJ 07860
Phone: (201) 383-6010
Howard E. Case

SUSSEX COUNTY LAW LIBRARY
Court House, 3 High St.
Newton, NJ 07860
Phone: (201) 383-4590
Barbara J. Smith, Ck. to Jury Comm.

DURO-TEST CORPORATION - TECHNICAL LIBRARY †
2321 Kennedy Blvd.
North Bergen, NJ 07047
Phone: (201) 867-7000
Dorothy K. Jakubczak, Tech.Libn.

HOFFMANN-LA ROCHE, INC. - BUSINESS INFORMATION CENTER
340 Kingsland St.
Nutley, NJ 07110
Phone: (201) 235-3901
Goldie Rosenberg, Mgr.

HOFFMANN-LA ROCHE, INC. - SCIENTIFIC LIBRARY
Nutley, NJ 07110
Phone: (201) 235-3091
Phyllis Deline, Mgr.

ITT CORPORATION - ITT AVIONICS/DEFENSE COMMUNICATIONS DIVISION - TECHNICAL LIBRARY
492 River Rd., Dept. 39212
Nutley, NJ 07110
Phone: (201) 284-2096
Terry T. Ladner, Hd.Libn.

NUTLEY HISTORICAL SOCIETY MUSEUM - ALICE J. BICKERS LIBRARY
65 Church St.
Nutley, NJ 07110
Phone: (201) 667-5239

WITCO CHEMICAL CORPORATION - TECHNICAL CENTER LIBRARY
100 Bauer Dr.
Oakland, NJ 07436
Phone: (201) 337-5812
Miss Jo Therese Smith, Mgr., Info.Serv.

OCEAN CITY HISTORICAL MUSEUM - LIBRARY
409 Wesley Ave.
Ocean City, NJ 08226
Phone: (609) 399-1801
Alberta E. Lamphear, Libn.

RUTGERS UNIVERSITY, THE STATE UNIVERSITY OF NEW JERSEY - NEW JERSEY VOCATIONAL EDUCATION RESOURCE CENTER
200 Old Matawan Rd.
Old Bridge, NJ 08857
Phone: (201) 390-1191
Beverly Genetta, Info.Ctr.Dir.

BURNS AND ROE, INC. - TECHNICAL LIBRARY
800 Kinderkamack Rd.
Oradell, NJ 07649
Phone: (201) 265-2000
Patricia Bernstein, Tech.Lib.Asst.

NATIONAL ASSOCIATION OF PURCHASING MANAGEMENT, INC. - INFORMATION CENTER
496 Kinderkamack Rd.
Box 418
Oradell, NJ 07649
Phone: (201) 967-8585
Sharon Gray, Mgr.

HOSPITAL CENTER AT ORANGE - WILLIAM PIERSON MEDICAL LIBRARY
188 S. Essex Ave.
Orange, NJ 07051
Phone: (201) 266-2000
Jeanette Merkl, Libn.

BECTON, DICKINSON & COMPANY - CORPORATE INFORMATION CENTER
Mack Centre Dr.
Paramus, NJ 07652
Phone: (201) 967-3928
Barbara L. Swan, Mgr.

BERGEN PINES COUNTY HOSPITAL - MEDICAL LIBRARY
E. Ridgewood Ave.
Paramus, NJ 07652
Phone: (201) 967-4000
Victoria Gonzalez, Med.Libn.

ALLEN (John E.), INC. - MOTION PICTURE ARCHIVES
116 North Ave.
Park Ridge, NJ 07656
Phone: (201) 391-3464
Robert A. Summers, Archv.

DU PONT DE NEMOURS (E.I.) & COMPANY, INC. - PHOTO PRODUCTS DEPARTMENT - INFORMATION CENTER
Parlin, NJ 08859
Phone: (201) 257-4600
Peggy J. Joplin, Supv.

BASF WYANDOTTE CORPORATION - BUSINESS INFORMATION CENTER
100 Cherry Hill Rd.
Parsippany, NJ 07821
Phone: (201) 263-3466
Ingrid Memming, Bus.Info.Anl./Mgr.

BEECHAM PRODUCTS - WESTERN HEMISPHERE RESEARCH - LIBRARY
1500 Littleton Rd.   Phone: (201) 267-1200
Parsippany, NJ 07504   Caroline Perkons, Info.Serv.Spec.

GPU NUCLEAR - HEADQUARTERS LIBRARY
100 Interpace Pkwy.   Phone: (201) 263-6185
Parsippany, NJ 07054   Jan Thompson, Sys.Libn.

GPU NUCLEAR - TECHNICAL LIBRARY
100 Interpace Pkwy.   Phone: (201) 299-2159
Parsippany, NJ 07054   Toby E. Hecht, Libn.

ST. MARY'S HOSPITAL - MEDICAL ALLIED HEALTH LIBRARY †
211 Pennington Ave.   Phone: (201) 473-1000
Passaic, NJ 07055   Sister Gertrude, S.C., Libn.

PASSAIC COUNTY HISTORICAL SOCIETY - LIBRARY
Lambert Castle, Valley Rd.   Phone: (201) 881-2761
Paterson, NJ 07503   Catherine Keene, Dir.

PATERSON NEWS - LIBRARY/NEWSPAPER MORGUE
1 News Plaza   Phone: (201) 684-3000
Paterson, NJ 07509   Sheldon Matson, Libn.

ST. JOSEPH'S HOSPITAL AND MEDICAL CENTER - HEALTH SCIENCES
   LIBRARY
703 Main St.   Phone: (201) 977-2104
Paterson, NJ 07503   Patricia May, Lib.Serv.

MOBIL RESEARCH & DEVELOPMENT CORPORATION - PAULSBORO
   LABORATORY - TECHNICAL INFORMATION SERVICES
Box 300   Phone: (609) 423-1040
Paulsboro, NJ 08066   Phillip Q. Stumpf, Jr., Mgr.

AUERBACH PUBLISHERS INC. - INFORMATION CENTER
6560 North Park Dr.   Phone: (609) 662-2070
Pennsauken, NJ 08109   Clare M. Appenzeller, Info.Res.Supv.

DATA SYSTEMS ANALYSTS - TECHNICAL LIBRARY
North Park Dr. & Airport Hwy.   Phone: (609) 665-6088
Pennsauken, NJ 08109   Elizabeth Colabrese, Libn.

PERTH AMBOY GENERAL HOSPITAL - HEALTH SCIENCE LIBRARY
530 New Brunswick Ave.   Phone: (201) 442-3700
Perth Amboy, NJ 08861   Catherine A. Hilman, Health Sci.Libn.

BAKER (J.T.) CHEMICAL COMPANY - RESEARCH LIBRARY
                                      Phone: (201) 859-2151
Phillipsburg, NJ 08865   Janie E. Welty, Tech.Libn.

INGERSOLL-RAND COMPANY - TECHNICAL LIBRARY
Memorial Pkwy.   Phone: (201) 859-8288
Phillipsburg, NJ 08865   Sharon L. Shiner, Libn.

WARREN HOSPITAL - MEDICAL LIBRARY
185 Roseberry St.   Phone: (201) 859-1500
Phillipsburg, NJ 08865   Mary K. Shipley, Staff Sec.

GUIDA (Pat) ASSOCIATES - LIBRARY
346 Changebridge Rd.   Phone: (201) 227-7418
Pine Brook, NJ 07058   Pat Guida, Pres.

AT & T BELL LABORATORIES - AT & T RESOURCE MANAGEMENT -
   CORPORATE RESEARCH CENTER
330 S. Randolphville Rd., Rm. 5LF164 Phone: (201) 562-2563
Piscataway, NJ 08854   Marianne Benjamin, Rsrc.Mgr.

AT & T COMMUNICATIONS - INFORMATION RESEARCH CENTER
30 Knightsbridge Rd.
Piscataway, NJ 08854   Melanie Z. Strub, Mgr.

BELL COMMUNICATIONS RESEARCH, INC. - INFORMATION RESOURCES
   SERVICES CENTER
6 Corporate Pl.   Phone: (201) 981-7676
Piscataway, NJ 08854

BELL COMMUNICATIONS RESEARCH, INC. - INFORMATION RESOURCES
   SERVICES CENTER
444 Hoes Ln.   Phone: (201) 699-2283
Piscataway, NJ 08854   A. Wang, Staff Mgr.

BELL COMMUNICATIONS RESEARCH, INC. - INFORMATION RESOURCES
   SERVICES CENTER
33 Knightsbridge Rd.   Phone: (201) 885-7790
Piscataway, NJ 08854

COLGATE PALMOLIVE COMPANY - TECHNICAL INFORMATION CENTER
909 River Rd.   Phone: (201) 463-1212
Piscataway, NJ 08854   Monica Grover, Sect.Hd.

NUODEX, INC. - LIBRARY
Box 365   Phone: (201) 981-5252
Piscataway, NJ 08854   Joan A. Carnahan, Mgr., Lib. & Info.Ctr.

RUTGERS UNIVERSITY, THE STATE UNIVERSITY OF NEW JERSEY -
   CENTER FOR COMPUTER AND INFORMATION SERVICES
Busch Campus
Computer Reference Ctr.
Box 879 Hill Center   Phone: (201) 932-2296
Piscataway, NJ 08854   Christopher P. Jarocha-Ernst, Coord.

RUTGERS UNIVERSITY, THE STATE UNIVERSITY OF NEW JERSEY -
   CENTER FOR URBAN POLICY RESEARCH LIBRARY
Kilmer Area, Bldg. 4051   Phone: (201) 932-3136
Piscataway, NJ 08854   Edward E. Duensing, Jr., Info.Mgr.

RUTGERS UNIVERSITY, THE STATE UNIVERSITY OF NEW JERSEY -
   CHEMISTRY LIBRARY
Busch Campus
Wright-Riemann Laboratories   Phone: (201) 932-2625
Piscataway, NJ 08854   Dr. Louis P. Torre, Physical Sci.Libn.

RUTGERS UNIVERSITY, THE STATE UNIVERSITY OF NEW JERSEY -
   GOTTSCHO PACKAGING INFORMATION CENTER
College of Engineering
Box 909   Phone: (201) 932-3044
Piscataway, NJ 08854   Darrell R. Morrow, Dir.

RUTGERS UNIVERSITY, THE STATE UNIVERSITY OF NEW JERSEY -
   LIBRARY OF SCIENCE & MEDICINE
Box 1029   Phone: (201) 932-3850
Piscataway, NJ 08854   Dr. Frank Polach, Dir.

RUTGERS UNIVERSITY, THE STATE UNIVERSITY OF NEW JERSEY -
   MATHEMATICAL SCIENCES LIBRARY
                                      Phone: (201) 932-3735
Piscataway, NJ 08854   Sylvia Walsh, Libn.

RUTGERS UNIVERSITY, THE STATE UNIVERSITY OF NEW JERSEY -
   PHYSICS LIBRARY
Busch Campus
Serin Physics Laboratory   Phone: (201) 932-2500
Piscataway, NJ 08854   Dr. Louis P. Torre, Physical Sci.Libn.

RUTGERS UNIVERSITY, THE STATE UNIVERSITY OF NEW JERSEY -
   RUTGERS CENTER OF ALCOHOL STUDIES - LIBRARY
Busch Campus
Smithers Hall   Phone: (201) 932-4442
Piscataway, NJ 08854   Penny B. Page, Libn.

RUTGERS UNIVERSITY, THE STATE UNIVERSITY OF NEW JERSEY -
   WAKSMAN INSTITUTE OF MICROBIOLOGY LIBRARY
Box 759   Phone: (201) 932-2906
Piscataway, NJ 08854   Helen Hoffman, Libn.

UNIVERSITY OF MEDICINE AND DENTISTRY OF NEW JERSEY - RUTGERS
   MEDICAL SCHOOL - MEDIA LIBRARY
University Heights   Phone: (201) 463-4460
Piscataway, NJ 08854   Adrienne Berenbaum, Libn.

BURROUGHS CORPORATION - ELECTRONIC COMPONENTS DIVISION -
   ENGINEERING LIBRARY †
Mt. Bethel Rd.
Box 1226   Phone: (201) 757-5000
Plainfield, NJ 07061

CRESCENT AVENUE PRESBYTERIAN CHURCH - LIBRARY *
716 Watchung Ave.   Phone: (201) 756-2469
Plainfield, NJ 07060   Mary McDougall

LOCKHEED ELECTRONICS COMPANY, INC. - TECHNICAL INFORMATION CENTER
1501 U.S. Hwy. 22, C.S. No. 1   Phone: (201) 757-1600
Plainfield, NJ 07061   Linda Gabriel, Supv.

MUHLENBERG HOSPITAL - E. GORDON GLASS, M.D., MEMORIAL LIBRARY
Park Ave. & Randolph Rd.   Phone: (201) 668-2005
Plainfield, NJ 07061   Jane McCarthy, Libn.

TEMPLE BETH EL - LIBRARY †
225 E. Seventh St.   Phone: (201) 756-2333
Plainfield, NJ 07060   Irving Olian, Libn.

PRINCETON POLYMER LABORATORIES, INC. - LIBRARY
501 Plainsboro Rd.   Phone: (609) 799-2060
Plainsboro, NJ 08536   Carol Troy, Libn.

ATLANTIC CITY MEDICAL CENTER - MAINLAND DIVISION - HEALTH SCIENCE LIBRARY
Jim Leeds Rd.   Phone: (609) 652-1000
Pomona, NJ 08240   John P. Doesburgh, Med.Libn.

BACHARACH (Betty) REHABILITATION HOSPITAL - MEDICAL AND CLINICAL STAFF LIBRARY
Jim Leeds Rd.   Phone: (609) 652-7000
Pomona, NJ 08240   Greta Glessner, Dir., Med.Rec.

CHILTON MEMORIAL HOSPITAL - MEDICAL LIBRARY
97 West Parkway   Phone: (201) 835-3700
Pompton Plains, NJ 07444   Janice Sweeton, Med.Libn.

AMERICAN CAN COMPANY - PRINCETON RESEARCH INFORMATION CENTER *
Box 50
Princeton, NJ 08540   Kathleen A. Giovannini, Info.Sci.

AMERICAN CYANAMID COMPANY - AGRICULTURAL RESEARCH DIVISION - TECHNICAL INFORMATION SERVICES
Box 400   Phone: (609) 799-0400
Princeton, NJ 08540   Judith C. Leondar, Mgr.

AT & T BELL LABORATORIES & TECHNOLOGIES - ENGINEERING RESEARCH CENTER - TECHNICAL LIBRARY
Carter Rd.
Box 900   Phone: (609) 639-2512
Princeton, NJ 08540   William H. Fisher, Sect.Chf.

CARNEGIE FOUNDATION FOR THE ADVANCEMENT OF TEACHING - LIBRARY
5 Ivy Lane   Phone: (609) 452-1780
Princeton NJ 08540   Lisa Cziffra, Libn./Archv.

EDUCATIONAL TESTING SERVICE - CARL CAMPBELL BRIGHAM LIBRARY
Rosedale Rd.   Phone: (609) 734-5672
Princeton, NJ 08541   Janet Williams, Libn.

EDUCATIONAL TESTING SERVICE - TEST COLLECTION
Rosedale Rd.   Phone: (609) 734-5686
Princeton, NJ 08541   Marilyn Halpern, Hd., Test Coll.

EDUCOM, INTERUNIVERSITY COMMUNICATIONS COUNCIL, INC. - LIBRARY †
Rosedale Rd.
Box 364   Phone: (609) 921-7575
Princeton, NJ 08540   Eleanor G. Sayles, Libn.

ERIC CLEARINGHOUSE ON TESTS, MEASUREMENT AND EVALUATION
Educational Testing Service
Rosedale Rd.   Phone: (609) 734-5181
Princeton, NJ 08541   Dr. S. Donald Melville, Dir.

FMC CORPORATION - CHEMICAL RESEARCH & DEVELOPMENT CENTER - TECHNICAL INFORMATION SERVICES
Box 8   Phone: (609) 452-2300
Princeton, NJ 08540   Paul Garwig, Mgr., Tech.Info.Serv.

FOUNDATION FOR STUDENT COMMUNICATION - LIBRARY AND RESOURCE CENTER
305 Aaron Burr Hall
Princeton University
Princeton, NJ 08540

HEALTH RESEARCH AND EDUCATIONAL TRUST OF NEW JERSEY - LEARNING CENTER †
760 Alexander Rd. (CN-1)   Phone: (609) 452-9280
Princeton, NJ 08540   Michelle Pentland, Program Coord.

HISTORICAL SOCIETY OF PRINCETON - LIBRARY
158 Nassau St.   Phone: (609) 921-6817
Princeton, NJ 08542

INGERSOLL-RAND RESEARCH, INC. - TECHNICAL LIBRARY
Box 301   Phone: (609) 921-9103
Princeton, NJ 08540   Diane M. Kliminski, Tech.Libn.

INSTITUTE FOR ADVANCED STUDY - LIBRARIES
                                                 Phone: (609) 734-8000
Princeton, NJ 08540

INSTITUTE FOR DEFENSE ANALYSES - COMMUNICATIONS RESEARCH DIVISION - LIBRARY
Thanet Rd.   Phone: (609) 924-4600
Princeton, NJ 08540   Jane P. Ciosek, Libn.

JOHNSON (Robert Wood) FOUNDATION - LIBRARY
Box 2316   Phone: (609) 452-8701
Princeton, NJ 08540   Philip J. Gallagher, Libn.

MEDICAL CENTER AT PRINCETON - MEDICAL CENTER LIBRARY
253 Witherspoon St.   Phone: (609) 921-7700
Princeton, NJ 08540   Louise M. Yorke, Med.Libn.

METAL POWDER INDUSTRIES FEDERATION - TECHNICAL INFORMATION CENTER
105 College Rd., E.   Phone: (609) 452-7700
Princeton, NJ 08540   Kempton H. Roll, Exec.Dir.

MOBIL OIL CORPORATION - TOXICOLOGY INFORMATION CENTER
Box 1029   Phone: (609) 737-5583
Princeton, NJ 08540   Yvonne B. Smith, Tech.Info.Spec.

MOBIL RESEARCH & DEVELOPMENT CORPORATION - CENTRAL RESEARCH DIVISION LIBRARY
Box 1025   Phone: (609) 737-4328
Princeton, NJ 08540   Jean B. Clarke, Libn.

MOBIL RESEARCH & DEVELOPMENT CORPORATION - ENGINEERING DEPARTMENT - INFORMATION CENTER
Box 1026   Phone: (609) 737-4192
Princeton, NJ 08540   Elizabeth N. Mailloux, Mgr.

NORTH PRINCETON DEVELOPMENTAL CENTER - PROFESSIONAL LIBRARY
Box 1000   Phone: (609) 466-0400
Princeton, NJ 08540   Donald W. Biggs, Sr.Libn.

PRINCETON THEOLOGICAL SEMINARY - SPEER LIBRARY
Mercer St. & Library Pl.
Box 111   Phone: (609) 921-8300
Princeton, NJ 08540   Dr. Charles Willard, Libn.

PRINCETON UNIVERSITY - ASTRONOMY LIBRARY
Peyton Hall   Phone: (609) 452-3820
Princeton, NJ 08544   Peter Cziffra, Libn.

PRINCETON UNIVERSITY - BIOLOGY LIBRARY
Guyot Hall   Phone: (609) 452-3235
Princeton, NJ 08544   Helen Y. Zimmerberg, Libn.

PRINCETON UNIVERSITY - CHEMISTRY & BIOCHEMISTRY LIBRARY
Frick Chemical Laboratory   Phone: (609) 452-3238
Princeton, NJ 08544   Dr. David Goodman, Libn.

PRINCETON UNIVERSITY - DEPARTMENT OF ART & ARCHAEOLOGY - INDEX OF CHRISTIAN ART
McCormick Hall   Phone: (609) 452-3773
Princeton, NJ 08544   Nigel Morgan, Act.Dir.

PRINCETON UNIVERSITY - ENGINEERING LIBRARY
Engineering Quadrangle   Phone: (609) 452-3200
Princeton, NJ 08544   Dolores M. Hoelle, Libn.

PRINCETON UNIVERSITY - GEOLOGY LIBRARY
Guyot Hall   Phone: (609) 452-3267
Princeton, NJ 08544   David C. Stager, Geology Libn.

PRINCETON UNIVERSITY - GEST ORIENTAL LIBRARY AND EAST ASIAN
   COLLECTIONS
317 Palmer Hall   Phone: (609) 452-3182
Princeton, NJ 08544   Diane Perushek, Cur.

PRINCETON UNIVERSITY - INDUSTRIAL RELATIONS LIBRARY
                                                    Phone: (609) 452-4936
Princeton, NJ 08544   Katherine Bagin, Libn.

PRINCETON UNIVERSITY - MARQUAND LIBRARY †
McCormick Hall   Phone: (609) 452-3783
Princeton, NJ 08544   Mary M. Schmidt, Libn.

PRINCETON UNIVERSITY - MATHEMATICS, PHYSICS AND STATISTICS
   LIBRARY
                                                    Phone: (609) 452-3188
Princeton, NJ 08544   Peter Cziffra, Libn.

PRINCETON UNIVERSITY - MUSIC COLLECTION †
Firestone Library   Phone: (609) 452-3230
Princeton, NJ 08544   Paula Morgan, Music Libn.

PRINCETON UNIVERSITY - NEAR EAST COLLECTIONS †
Firestone Library   Phone: (609) 452-3279
Princeton, NJ 08544   Eric Ormsby, Cur.

PRINCETON UNIVERSITY - OFFICE OF POPULATION RESEARCH - LIBRARY
21 Prospect Ave.   Phone: (609) 452-4874
Princeton, NJ 08544   Thomas Holzmann, Libn.

PRINCETON UNIVERSITY - PHONOGRAPH RECORD LIBRARY
Woolworth Center of Musical Studies   Phone: (609) 452-4251
Princeton, NJ 08544   Marjorie Hassen, Record Libn.

PRINCETON UNIVERSITY - PLASMA PHYSICS LIBRARY
Box 451   Phone: (609) 452-3567
Princeton, NJ 08544   Elizabeth Graydon, Libn.

PRINCETON UNIVERSITY - PLINY FISK LIBRARY OF ECONOMICS AND
   FINANCE †
Firestone Library   Phone: (609) 452-3211
Princeton, NJ 08544   Louise Tompkins, Libn.

PRINCETON UNIVERSITY - PSYCHOLOGY LIBRARY †
Green Hall   Phone: (609) 452-3239
Princeton, NJ 08544   Janice D. Welburn, Psych.Libn.

PRINCETON UNIVERSITY - PUBLIC ADMINISTRATION COLLECTION †
Firestone Library   Phone: (609) 452-3209
Princeton, NJ 08544   Rosemary Allen Little, Libn.

PRINCETON UNIVERSITY - RARE BOOKS AND SPECIAL COLLECTIONS
Firestone Library   Phone: (609) 452-3184
Princeton, NJ 08544   Richard M. Ludwig, Asst.Libn.

PRINCETON UNIVERSITY - RICHARD HALLIBURTON MAP COLLECTION
Firestone Library   Phone: (609) 452-3214
Princeton, NJ 08544   Lawrence E. Spellman, Cur. of Maps

PRINCETON UNIVERSITY - SCHOOL OF ARCHITECTURE LIBRARY
                                                    Phone: (609) 452-3256
Princeton, NJ 08544   Frances Chen, Libn.

PRINCETON UNIVERSITY - WILLIAM SEYMOUR THEATRE COLLECTION
Firestone Library   Phone: (609) 452-3223
Princeton, NJ 08544   Mary Ann Jensen, Cur.

PRINCETON UNIVERSITY - WOODROW WILSON SCHOOL OF PUBLIC AND
   INTERNATIONAL AFFAIRS - LIBRARY
                                                    Phone: (609) 452-4848
Princeton, NJ 08544   Linda Oppenheim, Libn.

RCA CORPORATION - ASTRO-ELECTRONICS-GOVERNMENT SYSTEMS
   DIVISION - LIBRARY
Box 800   Phone: (609) 448-3400
Princeton, NJ 08540   Mary L. Pfann, Libn.

RCA CORPORATION - DAVID SARNOFF LIBRARY
201 Washington Rd.
Box 432   Phone: (609) 452-2700
Princeton, NJ 08540   Wendy Chu, Mgr., Lib.Serv.

RCA CORPORATION - RCA LABORATORIES - DAVID SARNOFF RESEARCH
   CENTER - LIBRARY
                                                    Phone: (609) 734-2608
Princeton, NJ 08540   Wendy Chu, Mgr.

RECORDING FOR THE BLIND, INC. - MASTER TAPE LIBRARY
20 Roszel Rd.   Phone: (609) 452-0606
Princeton, NJ 08540   Anne H. Parkison, Dir. of Lib.Serv.

RESPONSE ANALYSIS CORPORATION - LIBRARY
Research Park
Rte. 206, Box 158   Phone: (609) 921-3333
Princeton, NJ 08542   Anne R. Frihart, Libn.

SANGAMO WESTON GROUP - EMR PHOTOELECTRIC DIVISION -
   INFORMATION CENTER
Box 44   Phone: (609) 799-1000
Princeton, NJ 08542   Joyce Jordan, Tech.Libn.

SQUIBB (E.R.) AND SONS, INC. - SQUIBB INSTITUTE FOR MEDICAL
   RESEARCH - SCIENCE INFORMATION DEPARTMENT
Box 4000   Phone: (609) 921-4844
Princeton, NJ 08540   Dr. Frank L. Weisenborn, Dir.

TEXTILE RESEARCH INSTITUTE - LIBRARY
601 Prospect Ave.
Box 625   Phone: (609) 924-3150
Princeton, NJ 08540

UNION CAMP CORP. - R & D DIVISION LIBRARY †
Box 412   Phone: (609) 896-1200
Princeton, NJ 08540   Helen Lee, Libn.

U.S. NATL. OCEANIC & ATMOSPHERIC ADMINISTRATION - GEOPHYSICAL
   FLUID DYNAMICS LABORATORY - LIBRARY
Box 308   Phone: (609) 452-6550
Princeton, NJ 08542   Philip Fraulino, Libn.

WESTMINSTER CHOIR COLLEGE - TALBOTT LIBRARY
Hamilton Ave. at Walnut Ln.   Phone: (609) 921-3658
Princeton, NJ 08540   Sherry L. Vellucci, Dir., Lib.Serv.

M AND T CHEMICALS, INC. - TECHNICAL & BUSINESS INFORMATION
   CENTER
Box 1104   Phone: (201) 499-2437
Rahway, NJ 07065   Marguerite K. Moran, V.P. & Dir.

MERCK & COMPANY, INC. - LAW LIBRARY
Box 2000   Phone: (201) 574-5805
Rahway, NJ 07065   Elizabeth H. Penman, Libn.

MERCK & COMPANY, INC. - MERCK SHARP & DOHME RESEARCH
   LABORATORIES - LITERATURE RESOURCES
                                                    Phone: (201) 574-6713
Rahway, NJ 07065   Jerome E. Holtz, Mgr.

MERCK & COMPANY, INC. - MERCK SHARP & DOHME RESEARCH
   LABORATORIES - RESEARCH INFORMATION SYSTEMS
126 E. Lincoln Ave.   Phone: (201) 574-4726
Rahway, NJ 07065   Arlene C. Peterson, Asst.Dir., Res.Info.Sys.

ORTHO PHARMACEUTICAL CORPORATION - HARTMAN LIBRARY
U.S. Hwy. 202   Phone: (201) 524-2240
Raritan, NJ 08869   June Bente, Mgr.

BELL COMMUNICATIONS RESEARCH, INC. - INFORMATION RESOURCES
   SERVICES CENTER
331 Newman Springs Rd.   Phone: (201) 758-2407
Red Bank, NJ 07701   Molly Collins, Staff Mgr.

RIVERVIEW HOSPITAL - MEDICAL LIBRARY
35 Union St.   Phone: (201) 741-2700
Red Bank, NJ 07701   Cheryl Newman, Med.Libn.

VALLEY HOSPITAL - LIBRARY
Linwood Ave.   Phone: (201) 447-8285
Ridgewood, NJ 07451   Wanda Borgen, Med.Libn.

BERGEN COUNTY HISTORICAL SOCIETY - JOHNSON LIBRARY
Box 55
River Edge, NJ 07661   Richard Goerner, Libn.

PQA ENGINEERING - LIBRARY †
90 Riverdale Rd.   Phone: (201) 831-1500
Riverdale, NJ 07457   Kathryn Sullivan, Libn.

TIMEPLEX, INC. - ENGINEERING LIBRARY
1 Communications Plaza
Rochelle Park, NJ 07662   Florence Gerardi, Libn.

BYELORUSSIAN INSTITUTE OF ARTS AND SCIENCES, INC. - LIBRARY
230 Springfield Ave.   Phone: (201) 933-6807
Rutherford, NJ 07070   Zora Kipel, Libn.

FAIRLEIGH DICKINSON UNIVERSITY - MESSLER LIBRARY - NEW JERSEY
    ROOM
Montross Ave.   Phone: (201) 933-5000
Rutherford, NJ 07070   Catharine M. Fogarty, NJ Rm.Libn.

PUBLIC SERVICE ELECTRIC AND GAS COMPANY - NUCLEAR TRAINING
    CENTER LIBRARY
244 Chestnut St.   Phone: (609) 339-3773
Salem, NJ 08079   Richard E. Bater, Lrng.Rsrcs.Spec.

SALEM COUNTY HISTORICAL SOCIETY - LIBRARY
79-83 Market St.   Phone: (609) 935-5004
Salem, NJ 08079   Alice G. Boggs

SALEM COUNTY LAW LIBRARY *
Salem County Court House
92 Market St.   Phone: (609) 935-7510
Salem, NJ 08079   Albert Telsey, Law Ck./Libn.

SALEM COUNTY MEMORIAL HOSPITAL - DAVID W. GREEN MEDICAL
    LIBRARY †
                                         Phone: (609) 935-1000
Salem, NJ 08079   Marion E. Schultz, Med.Libn.

SALEM FREE PUBLIC LIBRARY - SPECIAL COLLECTIONS
112 W. Broadway   Phone: (609) 935-0526
Salem, NJ 08079   Elizabeth C. Fogg, Dir.

MOSS ARCHIVES
Box 336   Phone: (201) 842-0336
Sea Bright, NJ 07760   George H. Moss, Jr.

AT & T BELL LABORATORIES - LIBRARY
150 J.F. Kennedy Parkway
Short Hills, NJ 07078   Margaret L. McSpiritt, Lib.Supv.

SHREWSBURY DAILY-SUNDAY REGISTER - LIBRARY
One Register Plaza   Phone: (201) 542-4000
Shrewsbury, NJ 07701   Olga Boeckel, Hd.Libn.

JOHNSON AND JOHNSON BABY PRODUCTS COMPANY - RESEARCH
    INFORMATION CENTER
Grandview Rd.   Phone: (201) 874-1439
Skillman, NJ 08558   Marilyn H. Rondelli, Mgr.

ATLANTIC COUNTY HISTORICAL SOCIETY - LIBRARY
907 Shore Rd.
Box 301   Phone: (609) 927-5218
Somers Point, NJ 08244   Barbara E. Koedel, Libn.

ETHICON, INC. - SCIENTIFIC INFORMATION SERVICES
Rte. 22   Phone: (201) 524-3402
Somerville, NJ 08076   Dr. Charles G. Fritz, Dir.

HOECHST-ROUSSEL PHARMACEUTICALS, INC. - LIBRARY
Route 202-206, North   Phone: (201) 231-2394
Somerville, NJ 08876   Loretta F. Stangs, Mgr., Lib.Serv.

RCA CORPORATION - SOLID STATE DIVISION - LIBRARY
Rte. 202   Phone: (201) 685-6017
Somerville, NJ 08876   Halina S. Kan, Libn.

SOMERSET COUNTY LAW LIBRARY
Court House   Phone: (201) 231-7000
Somerville, NJ 08876   Helen W. Leavitt, Law Libn.

ARCHAEOLOGICAL SOCIETY OF NEW JERSEY - LIBRARY †
Rm. 106, Humanities Bldg.
Seton Hall University   Phone: (201) 762-6690
South Orange, NJ 07079   Joan E. Kraft, Chm., Lib.Comm.

SETON HALL UNIVERSITY - MC LAUGHLIN LIBRARY
405 South Orange Ave.   Phone: (201) 762-9000
South Orange, NJ 07079   Rev. James C. Sharp, Univ.Libn.

SETON HALL UNIVERSITY - MAC MANUS COLLECTION
McLaughlin Library
405 South Orange Ave.   Phone: (201) 762-9000
South Orange, NJ 07079   Rev. William Noe Field, Cur., Spec.Coll.

SETON HALL UNIVERSITY - UNIVERSITY ARCHIVES
McLaughlin Library
405 South Orange Ave.   Phone: (201) 762-7052
South Orange, NJ 07079   Peter J. Wosh, Univ.Archv.

SOUTH MOUNTAIN LABORATORIES, INC. - LIBRARY
380 Lackawanna Pl.   Phone: (201) 762-0045
South Orange, NJ 07079   C.N. Mangieri, Dir.

TEMPLE SHAREY TEFILO-ISRAEL - EDWARD EHRENKRANTZ/ELCHANAN
    ECHIKSON MEMORIAL LIBRARY
432 Scotland Rd.   Phone: (201) 763-4116
South Orange, NJ 07079   Ann R. Zeve, Libn.

ASARCO INC. - LIBRARY
Central Research Dept.
901 Oak Tree Rd.   Phone: (201) 756-4800
South Plainfield, NJ 07080   Betty E. Hurlbert, Libn.

SPRINGFIELD HISTORICAL SOCIETY - LIBRARY
126 Morris Ave.
Box 124   Phone: (201) 376-7737
Springfield, NJ 07081   Kenneth D. Hendrix, Pres.

VESTIGIA - LIBRARY
56 Brookwood Rd.   Phone: (201) 347-3638
Stanhope, NJ 07874   Robert E. Jones, Pres.

UNIV. OF MEDICINE AND DENTISTRY OF NEW JERSEY - SCHOOL OF
    OSTEOPATHIC MED. - DR. JERROLD S. SCHWARTZ MEM. LIB.
Kennedy Memorial Hospital
University Medical Ctr. - Stratford Div.
18 E. Laurel Rd.   Phone: (609) 784-4000
Stratford, NJ 08084   Judith Schuback, Libn.

CELANESE CORPORATION - SUMMIT RESEARCH LABORATORIES -
    TECHNICAL INFORMATION CENTER
86 Morris Ave.   Phone: (201) 522-7500
Summit, NJ 07901   Dr. Bernice I. Feuer, Supv.

CIBA-GEIGY CORPORATION - PHARMACEUTICALS DIVISION - SCIENTIFIC
    INFORMATION CENTER †
566 Morris Ave.   Phone: (201) 277-5544
Summit, NJ 07901   Dr. Karl Doebel, Dir.

FAIR OAKS HOSPITAL - MEDICAL LIBRARY
19 Prospect St.   Phone: (201) 522-7000
Summit, NJ 07901   Miriam Rosenstein, Libn.

OVERLOOK HOSPITAL - HEALTH SCIENCES LIBRARY
193 Morris Ave.   Phone: (201) 522-2119
Summit, NJ 07901   Kathleen A. Moeller, Dir., Lib.Serv.

FAIRLEIGH DICKINSON UNIVERSITY - WEINER LIBRARY - REFERENCE/
    GOVERNMENT DOCUMENTS DEPARTMENT
1000 River Rd.   Phone: (201) 692-2290
Teaneck, NJ 07666   Sandra V. Gage, Hd.

HOLY NAME HOSPITAL - MEDICAL LIBRARY
Teaneck Rd.   Phone: (201) 833-3395
Teaneck, NJ 07666   Leila M. Hover, Dir.

TEANECK PUBLIC LIBRARY - ORAL AND LOCAL HISTORY PROJECT
840 Teaneck Rd.   Phone: (201) 837-4171
Teaneck, NJ 07666   Hilda Lipkin, Dir.

BENDIX CORPORATION - ENGINEERING LIBRARY
                                               Phone: (201) 288-2000
Teterboro, NJ 07608   Beth Charnley Owen, Libn.

PERKIN-ELMER DATA SYSTEMS GROUP - LIBRARY
106 Apple St.   Phone: (201) 747-7300
Tinton Falls, NJ 07724   Nancy B. Lynott, Libn.

CIBA-GEIGY CORPORATION - CHEMICAL LIBRARY
Box 71   Phone: (201) 349-5200
Toms River, NJ 08753   Irmine Pilmes, Res.Libn.

OCEAN COUNTY LAW LIBRARY †
118 Washington St.   Phone: (201) 244-2121
Toms River, NJ 08753   James P. Rutigliano, Asst.Ct.Adm.

CONGOLEUM CORPORATION - RESILIENT FLOORING DIVISION -
   TECHNICAL RESEARCH LIBRARY
Box 3127   Phone: (609) 587-1000
Trenton, NJ 08619   Daniel W. Schutter, Supv., Analytical Group

DELAWARE RIVER BASIN COMMISSION - TECHNICAL LIBRARY
25 State Police Dr.
Box 7360   Phone: (609) 883-9500
Trenton, NJ 08628   Betty A. Lin, Libn.

HAMILTON HOSPITAL - MEDICAL LIBRARY
Box H   Phone: (609) 586-7900
Trenton, NJ 08690   Olga S. Dytyniak, Dir.

HELENE FULD MEDICAL CENTER - HEALTH SCIENCES LIBRARY
750 Brunswick Ave.   Phone: (609) 394-6065
Trenton, NJ 08638   Carol R. Glatt, Dir.

MERCER MEDICAL CENTER - DAVID B. ACKLEY MEDICAL LIBRARY
446 Bellevue Ave.
Box 1658   Phone: (609) 394-4125
Trenton, NJ 08607   Catherine W. Marchok, Lib.Dir.

MERCER MEDICAL CENTER - SCHOOL OF NURSING - LIBRARY
446 Bellevue Ave.   Phone: (609) 394-4282
Trenton, NJ 08607   Kerry Birnbaum, Libn.

MOTOR BUS SOCIETY, INC. - LIBRARY
Box 7058
Trenton, NJ 08628   Gerald L. Squier, Pres.

NEW JERSEY EDUCATION ASSOCIATION - RESEARCH LIBRARY
180 W. State St.
Box 1211   Phone: (609) 599-4561
Trenton, NJ 08607   E. Lynne Van Buskirk, Assoc.Dir., Res.

NEW JERSEY GEOLOGICAL SURVEY - INFORMATION CENTER
CN 029   Phone: (609) 292-2576
Trenton, NJ 08625

NEW JERSEY OPTOMETRIC ASSOCIATION - DR. E.C. NUROCK LIBRARY †
684 Whitehead Rd.   Phone: (609) 695-3456
Trenton, NJ 08648   David L. Knowlton, Exec.Dir.

NEW JERSEY STATE DEPARTMENT OF ENVIRONMENTAL PROTECTION -
   DIVISION OF WATER RESOURCES - LIBRARY *
1474 Prospect St.
Box CN029   Phone: (609) 292-5519
Trenton, NJ 08625   Angelo R. Papa, Lib.Techn.

NEW JERSEY STATE DEPARTMENT OF ENVIRONMENTAL PROTECTION -
   OFFICE OF SCIENCE & RESEARCH - INFO. RESEARCH CTR.
CN-402   Phone: (609) 984-2249
Trenton, NJ 08625   Barbara E. Sergeant, Sr.Env.Spec.

NEW JERSEY STATE DEPARTMENT OF HEALTH - LIBRARY †
CN 360   Phone: (609) 292-5693
Trenton, NJ 08625   Cathy A. Stout, Libn.

NEW JERSEY STATE DEPARTMENT OF LABOR - LIBRARY
CN 110   Phone: (609) 292-2035
Trenton, NJ 08625   Stuart H. Anderson, Libn.

NEW JERSEY STATE DEPARTMENT OF LAW AND PUBLIC SAFETY -
   ATTORNEY GENERAL'S LIBRARY
Hughes Justice Complex, CN115   Phone: (609) 292-4958
Trenton, NJ 08625   Moira O. Strong, Chf.Libn.

NEW JERSEY STATE LEAGUE OF MUNICIPALITIES - LIBRARY
407 W. State St.   Phone: (609) 695-3481
Trenton, NJ 08618   Albert J. Wolfe, Res.Assoc.

NEW JERSEY STATE LIBRARY
185 W. State St.   Phone: (609) 292-6220
Trenton, NJ 08625-0520   Barbara F. Weaver, State Libn.

NEW JERSEY STATE LIBRARY - BUREAU OF LAW AND REFERENCE
185 W. State St.   Phone: (609) 292-6210
Trenton, NJ 08625-0520   Susan Roumfort, Hd.

NEW JERSEY STATE MUSEUM - LIBRARY
State Cultural Ctr., W. State St.
CN 530   Phone: (609) 292-6308
Trenton, NJ 08625   Leah P. Sloshberg, Dir. of Musm.

ST. FRANCIS MEDICAL CENTER - HEALTH SCIENCES LIBRARY
601 Hamilton Ave.   Phone: (609) 599-5068
Trenton, NJ 08629   Anita k. Johnson, Dir.

TRANSAMERICA DE LAVAL INC. - TECHNICAL LIBRARY
Box 8788   Phone: (609) 890-5445
Trenton, NJ 08650   Ann C. Hunt, Libn.

TRENTON FREE PUBLIC LIBRARY - ART & MUSIC DEPARTMENT
120 Academy St.
Box 2448   Phone: (609) 392-7188
Trenton, NJ 08608   Alice F. Fullam, Dept.Hd.

TRENTON FREE PUBLIC LIBRARY - BUSINESS AND TECHNOLOGY
   DEPARTMENT
120 Academy St.   Phone: (609) 392-7188
Trenton, NJ 08608   Richard D. Rebecca, Dept.Hd.

TRENTON FREE PUBLIC LIBRARY - GOVERNMENT DOCUMENTS
   COLLECTION
120 Academy St.   Phone: (609) 392-7188
Trenton, NJ 08608   Nan Wright, Hd., Ref.Dept.

TRENTON FREE PUBLIC LIBRARY - TRENTONIANA COLLECTION
120 Academy St.   Phone: (609) 392-7188
Trenton, NJ 08608   Nan Wright, Hd., Ref.Dept.

TRENTON STATE COLLEGE - ROSCOE L. WEST LIBRARY - SPECIAL
   COLLECTIONS
Hillwood Lakes CN550   Phone: (609) 771-2346
Trenton, NJ 08625   Richard P. Matthews, Spec.Coll.Libn.

TRENTON TIMES - LIBRARY
500 Perry St.   Phone: (609) 396-3232
Trenton, NJ 08605   Susan E. Connery, Dir.

U.S. NAVY - NAVAL AIR PROPULSION CENTER - TECHNICAL LIBRARY
Box 7176   Phone: (609) 896-5600
Trenton, NJ 08628   Robert Malone, Libn.

CPC INTERNATIONAL - BEST FOODS RESEARCH CENTER - INFORMATION
   CENTER
1120 Commerce Ave.
Box 1534   Phone: (201) 688-9000
Union, NJ 07083   Anne Troop, Mgr., Info.Serv.

KEAN COLLEGE OF NEW JERSEY - EVE ADULT ADVISORY SERVICES
                                               Phone: (201) 527-2210
Union, NJ 07083   Phyllis Shaunesey

KEAN COLLEGE OF NEW JERSEY - INSTRUCTIONAL RESOURCE CENTER
Morris Ave.   Phone: (201) 527-2073
Union, NJ 07083   Vincent V. Merlo, Dir., Media & Tech.

KEAN COLLEGE OF NEW JERSEY - NANCY THOMPSON LIBRARY †
       Phone: (201) 527-2017
Union, NJ 07083   Dr. Louis N. Nagy, Dir.

MEMORIAL GENERAL HOSPITAL - MEDICAL LIBRARY
1000 Galloping Hill Rd.   Phone: (201) 687-1900
Union, NJ 07083   Aileen Z. Tannenbaum, Med.Libn.

INTERNATIONAL FLAVORS AND FRAGRANCES, INC. - TECHNICAL
    INFORMATION CENTER
1515 Hwy. 36   Phone: (201) 264-4500
Union Beach, NJ 07735   Bernard J. Mayers, Supv.

MONTCLAIR STATE COLLEGE - HARRY A. SPRAGUE LIBRARY - SPECIAL
    COLLECTIONS
       Phone: (201) 893-4291
Upper Montclair, NJ 07035   Blanche W. Haller, Dir. of Lib.Serv.

MONTCLAIR STATE COLLEGE - NATIONAL ADULT EDUCATION
    CLEARINGHOUSE/MULTIMEDIA CENTER
Montclair State College   Phone: (201) 893-4353
Upper Montclair, NJ 07043   Frances M. Spinelli, Dir.

MONTCLAIR STATE COLLEGE - WOMEN'S CENTER LIBRARY
       Phone: (201) 893-5106
Upper Montclair, NJ 07043   Dr. Constance Waller, Dir.

WESTERN UNION CORPORATION - LIBRARY †
One Lake St.   Phone: (201) 825-5850
Upper Saddle River, NJ 07458   Alice Critchley, Libn.

BETH ISRAEL CONGREGATION - LIBRARY
1015 E. Park Ave.   Phone: (609) 691-0852
Vineland, NJ 08360   Ruth Greenblatt, Dir.

BIOVIVAN RESEARCH INSTITUTE - LIBRARY
9 S. Eighth St.   Phone: (609) 692-1499
Vineland, NJ 08360   Herbert Schwartz, Res.Coord.

VINELAND HISTORICAL AND ANTIQUARIAN SOCIETY - LIBRARY
108 S. 7th St.
Box 35   Phone: (609) 691-1111
Vineland, NJ 08360   Joseph E. Sherry, Libn.

SOUTH JERSEY REGIONAL FILM LIBRARY
Echelon Urban Ctr., Laurel Rd.   Phone: (609) 772-1642
Voorhees, NJ 08043   Katherine Schalk-Greene, Dir.

WEST JERSEY HOSPITAL, EASTERN DIVISION - STAFF MEDICAL LIBRARY
Evesham Rd.   Phone: (609) 795-3000
Voorhees, NJ 08043   Jean I. Belsterling, Med.Libn.

AMERICAN CYANAMID COMPANY - BUSINESS INFORMATION CENTER
One Cyanamid Plaza   Phone: (201) 831-3592
Wayne, NJ 07470   Marilyn M. Lukas, Mgr.

AMERICAN CYANAMID COMPANY - ENVIRONMENTAL HEALTH LIBRARY †
One Cyanamid Plaza   Phone: (201) 831-4379
Wayne, NJ 07470   Kaarin Kolbre, Supv.

GAF CORPORATION - LEGAL DEPARTMENT LIBRARY
1361 Alps Rd.   Phone: (201) 628-3000
Wayne, NJ 07470

GAF CORPORATION - TECHNICAL INFORMATION SERVICES †
1361 Alps Rd.   Phone: (201) 628-3321
Wayne, NJ 07470   Ira Naznitsky, Mgr.

SINGER COMPANY - KEARFOTT DIVISION - TECHNICAL INFORMATION
    CENTER
150 Totowa Rd.   Phone: (201) 785-6462
Wayne, NJ 07470   B.R. Meade, Supv.

WILLIAM PATERSON COLLEGE OF NEW JERSEY - SARAH BYRD ASKEW
    LIBRARY - SPECIAL COLLECTIONS
300 Pompton Rd.   Phone: (201) 595-2116
Wayne, NJ 07470   Robert Lopresti, Docs./Spec.Coll.Libn.

WOODWARD-CLYDE CONSULTANTS, EASTERN REGION - WCC LIBRARY
201 Willowbrook Blvd.   Phone: (201) 785-0700
Wayne, NJ 07470   Aida R. Green, Libn.

INTERNATIONAL UNION OF OPERATING ENGINEERS TRAINING CENTER -
    LOCAL 68, 68A, 68B - LIBRARY
14 Fairfield Pl.
Box 534   Phone: (201) 227-6426
West Caldwell, NJ 07006   Ann L. Maiara, Libn.

AT & T BELL LABORATORIES - LIBRARY
185 Monmouth Parkway   Phone: (201) 870-7823
West Long Branch, NJ 07764   Wing Chan, Info.Libn.

ORGANON, INC. - MEDICAL LIBRARY
375 Mt. Pleasant Ave.   Phone: (201) 325-4614
West Orange, NJ 07052   Jane E. Farrands, Libn.

U.S. NATL. PARK SERVICE - EDISON NATL. HISTORIC SITE - ARCHIVES
Main St. and Lakeside Ave.   Phone: (201) 736-0550
West Orange, NJ 07052   Mary Bowling, Archv.

TRENTON PSYCHIATRIC HOSPITAL - MEDICAL LIBRARY
Box 7500   Phone: (609) 396-8261
West Trenton, NJ 08628   Elaine Scheuerer, Lib.Coord.

BAKER (H.M.) ASSOCIATES - RESEARCH COLLECTION
266 E. Dudley Ave.
Westfield, NJ 07090   Helen M.B. Cushman, Dir.

PASCACK VALLEY HOSPITAL - DAVID GOLDBERG MEMORIAL MEDICAL
    LIBRARY †
Old Hook Rd.   Phone: (201) 664-4000
Westwood, NJ 07675   Margaret F. DeMarrais, Libn.

TELEDYNE ISOTOPES - BUSINESS LIBRARY
50 Vanburen Ave.   Phone: (201) 664-7070
Westwood, NJ 07675   Helen Principe, Res.Libn./Adm.Asst.

AT & T BELL LABORATORIES - LIBRARY
Whippany Rd.   Phone: (201) 386-2604
Whippany, NJ 07981   Don T. Ho, Lib. Group Supv.

KNOLL PHARMACEUTICAL COMPANY - SCIENCE INFORMATION CENTER
30 N. Jefferson Rd.   Phone: (201) 887-8300
Whippany, NJ 07981   Joanne Lustig, Mgr., Med./Sci.Info.

MORRIS COUNTY FREE LIBRARY - NEW JERSEY COLLECTION
30 East Hanover Ave.   Phone: (201) 285-6130
Whippany, NJ 07981   Evelyn L. Klingler, Ref.Libn.

NATIONAL ASSOCIATION OF PRECANCEL COLLECTORS, INC. - CHESTER
    DAVIS MEMORIAL LIBRARY
5121 Park Blvd.   Phone: (609) 522-2569
Wildwood, NJ 08260   Glenn W. Dye, Sec.-Treas.

WILDWOOD HISTORICAL COMMISSION - WILDWOOD LIBRARY OF NEW
    JERSEY HISTORY
4400 New Jersey Ave., Rm. 214   Phone: (609) 522-2444
Wildwood, NJ 08260   Ethel T. Holmes, Attendant

BURLINGTON COUNTY TIMES - LIBRARY
Route 130   Phone: (609) 871-8000
Willingboro, NJ 08046   Helen Rosser, Libn.

GLOUCESTER COUNTY HISTORICAL SOCIETY - LIBRARY
17 Hunter St.   Phone: (609) 845-4771
Woodbury, NJ 08096   Edith Hoelle, Libn.

UNDERWOOD-MEMORIAL HOSPITAL - MEDICAL LIBRARY
N. Broad St. & W. Redbank Ave.   Phone: (609) 845-0100
Woodbury, NJ 08096   Ellen K. Tiedrich, Libn.

NEW MEXICO

GHOST RANCH CONFERENCE CENTER - GHOST RANCH LIBRARY
Phone: (505) 685-4333
Abiquiu, NM 87510   Lidie Miller, Libn.

NEW MEXICO SCHOOL FOR THE VISUALLY HANDICAPPED - LIBRARY AND
MEDIA CENTER
1900 White Sands Blvd.   Phone: (505) 347-3505
Alamogordo, NM 88310   Bill Davis, Media Spec. & Coord.

ALBUQUERQUE MUSEUM OF ART, HISTORY & SCIENCE - LIBRARY †
2000 Mountain Rd.
Box 1293   Phone: (505) 766-7878
Albuquerque, NM 87103   James C. Moore, Dir.

AMERICAN CLASSICAL COLLEGE - LIBRARY
Box 4526   Phone: (505) 843-7749
Albuquerque, NM 87106   Dr. C.M. Flumiani, Dir.

AMERICAN CLASSICAL COLLEGE - STOCK MARKET LIBRARY
Box 4526   Phone: (505) 843-7749
Albuquerque, NM 87106   Dr. C.M. Flumiani, Dir.

BERNALILLO COUNTY - DISTRICT COURT LAW LIBRARY
415 Tijeras, N.W.
Box 488   Phone: (505) 841-7408
Albuquerque, NM 87103   Donna Freels, Asst.Libn.

CHURCH OF JESUS CHRIST OF LATTER-DAY SAINTS - ALBUQUERQUE
BRANCH GENEALOGICAL LIBRARY
Box 3568   Phone: (505) 255-1227
Albuquerque, NM 87110   David W. Seegmiller, Libn.

FIRST UNITED PRESBYTERIAN CHURCH - LIBRARY
215 Locust St., N.E.   Phone: (505) 247-9594
Albuquerque, NM 87102   Anita Odermann, Dir., Christian Educ.

LOVELACE BIOMEDICAL & ENVIRONMENTAL RESEARCH INSTITUTE, INC. -
INHALATION TOXICOLOGY RESEARCH INST. - LIB. †
Box 5890   Phone: (505) 844-2600
Albuquerque, NM 87115   Julia D. Grimes, Libn.

NATIONAL INFORMATION CENTER FOR EDUCATIONAL MEDIA (NICEM)
Box 40130   Phone: (505) 265-3591
Albuquerque, NM 87196   Jay Johnstone, Dir.

NATIONAL INFORMATION CENTER FOR SPECIAL EDUCATION MATERIALS
(NICSEM)
Box 40130   Phone: (800) 421-8711
Albuquerque, NM 87196   Susan Reinke, Act.Dir.

PRESBYTERIAN HOSPITAL - MEDICAL LIBRARY
1100 Central Ave., S.E.   Phone: (505) 243-9411
Albuquerque, NM 87102   Helen Saylor, Med.Libn.

ST. JOSEPH HOSPITAL - MEDICAL LIBRARY *
400 Walter, N.E.   Phone: (505) 243-8811
Albuquerque, NM 87102   Melba Clark, Libn.

ST. THOMAS AQUINAS NEWMAN CENTER - LIBRARY
1815 Las Lomas Rd., N.E.   Phone: (505) 247-1094
Albuquerque, NM 87106   Betty Innerst, Libn.

SANDIA NATIONAL LABORATORIES - TECHNICAL LIBRARY
Dept. 3140   Phone: (505) 844-2869
Albuquerque, NM 87185   Danielle K. Brown, Mgr.

SOUTHWEST RESEARCH & INFORMATION CENTER
Box 4524   Phone: (505) 262-1862
Albuquerque, NM 87106   Paul Robinson, Exec.Dir.

SOUTHWESTERN INDIAN POLYTECHNIC INSTITUTE - INSTRUCTIONAL
MATERIALS CENTER
9169 Coors Rd., N.W.   Phone: (505) 766-3266
Albuquerque, NM 87184   Dollie D. Watson, Dir., Spec.Serv.

TINGLEY (Carrie) CRIPPLED CHILDREN'S HOSPITAL - MEDICAL LIBRARY
1128 University Blvd., N.E.
Albuquerque, NM 87102   Dr. Charles F. Eberle, Med.Dir.

U.S. DEPT. OF COMMERCE - INTERNATIONAL TRADE ADMINISTRATION -
ALBUQUERQUE DISTRICT OFFICE LIBRARY *
505 Marquette Ave., N.W., Suite 1015   Phone: (505) 766-2386
Albuquerque, NM 87102   William E. Dwyer, Dir.

U.S. DEPT. OF ENERGY - ALBUQUERQUE OPERATIONS OFFICE - LIBRARY
AND PUBLIC DOCUMENT ROOM
Box 5400   Phone: (505) 844-4378
Albuquerque, NM 87115   Philip Larragoite, Libn.

U.S. GEOLOGICAL SURVEY - WATER RESOURCES DIVISION - READING
ROOM
Western Bank, Rm. 714
505 Marquette N.W.   Phone: (505) 766-2810
Albuquerque, NM 87102   Janie S. Jones, Libn.

U.S. NATL. PARK SERVICE - CHACO CENTER - LIBRARY
Box 26176   Phone: (505) 766-3545
Albuquerque, NM 87125   Thomas C. Windes, Supv.Archeo.

U.S. VETERANS ADMINISTRATION (NM-Albuquerque) - MEDICAL CENTER
LIBRARY
2100 Ridgecrest Dr., S.E.   Phone: (505) 265-1711
Albuquerque, NM 87108   Nancy Myer, Chf., Lib.Serv.

UNIVERSITY OF NEW MEXICO - BUNTING MEMORIAL SLIDE LIBRARY
Fine Arts Center   Phone: (505) 277-6415
Albuquerque, NM 87131   A. Zelda Richardson, Dir.

UNIVERSITY OF NEW MEXICO - BUREAU OF BUSINESS & ECONOMIC
RESEARCH DATA BANK
1920 Lomas Blvd., N.E.   Phone: (505) 277-6626
Albuquerque, NM 87131   Betsie Kasner, Hd., Info.Serv.

UNIVERSITY OF NEW MEXICO - DEPARTMENT OF ANTHROPOLOGY -
CLARK FIELD ARCHIVES AND LIBRARY
Roma & University, N.E.   Phone: (505) 277-4524
Albuquerque, NM 87131   E. Mickel, Off.Mgr.

UNIVERSITY OF NEW MEXICO - FINE ARTS LIBRARY
Phone: (505) 277-2357
Albuquerque, NM 87131   James B. Wright, Hd.

UNIVERSITY OF NEW MEXICO - JONSON GALLERY - LIBRARY
1909 Las Lomas Rd., N.E.   Phone: (505) 243-4667
Albuquerque, NM 87106

UNIVERSITY OF NEW MEXICO - MEDICAL CENTER LIBRARY
North Campus   Phone: (505) 277-2548
Albuquerque, NM 87131   Erika Love, Dir.

UNIVERSITY OF NEW MEXICO - SCHOOL OF LAW LIBRARY
1117 Stanford, N.E.   Phone: (505) 277-6236
Albuquerque, NM 87131   Myron Fink, Libn.

UNIVERSITY OF NEW MEXICO - SPECIAL COLLECTIONS DEPARTMENT
General Library   Phone: (505) 277-6451
Albuquerque, NM 87131   William E. Tydeman, Hd.

UNIVERSITY OF NEW MEXICO - TECHNOLOGY APPLICATION CENTER
Phone: (505) 277-3622
Albuquerque, NM 87131   Stanley A. Morain, Dir.

UNIVERSITY OF NEW MEXICO - TIREMAN LEARNING MATERIALS LIBRARY
Phone: (505) 277-3854
Albuquerque, NM 87131   Eileen E. Schroeder, Hd.

UNIVERSITY OF NEW MEXICO - WILLIAM J. PARISH MEMORIAL LIBRARY
Phone: (505) 277-5912
Albuquerque, NM 87131   Judith Bernstein, Bus.Adm.Libn.

WESTINGHOUSE ELECTRIC CORPORATION - WIPP TECHNICAL LIBRARY
Box 40039   Phone: (505) 766-3030
Albuquerque, NM 87196   Elaine K. Bickerstaff, Libn.

ARTESIA HISTORICAL MUSEUM AND ART CENTER - LIBRARY
505 W. Richardson   Phone: (505) 748-2390
Artesia, NM 88210   Terry R. Koenig, Dir. of Musm.

U.S. NATL. PARK SERVICE - AZTEC RUINS NATL. MONUMENT - LIBRARY
Box U   Phone: (505) 334-6174
Aztec, NM 87410

U.S. NATL. PARK SERVICE - CHACO CANYON NATL. MONUMENT - STUDY
    LIBRARY
Chaco Star Rte. 4
Box 6500   Phone: (505) 786-5384
Bloomfield, NM 87413   Ellen Boling, Pk.Techn.

U.S. AIR FORCE BASE - CANNON BASE LIBRARY *
FL 4855   Phone: (505) 784-2786
Cannon AFB, NM 88101   M. Edith Pierce, Libn.

GUADALUPE MEDICAL CENTER - MEDICAL STAFF LIBRARY
2430 W. Pierce St.   Phone: (505) 887-6633
Carlsbad, NM 88220   Dorothy Eswein, Med. Staff Libn.

U.S. NATL. PARK SERVICE - CARLSBAD CAVERNS NATL. PARK - LIBRARY
3225 National Parks Hwy.   Phone: (505) 885-8884
Carlsbad, NM 88220   Robert W. Peters, Interp.Spec.

SETON MEMORIAL LIBRARY
Philmont Scout Ranch & Explorer Base
Cimarron, NM 87714

SAN JUAN COUNTY ARCHAEOLOGICAL RESEARCH CENTER & LIBRARY
975 Hwy. 64   Phone: (505) 632-2013
Farmington, NM 87401   Ouida Steward, Libn.

GALLUP INDIAN MEDICAL CENTER - MEDICAL LIBRARY
East Nizhoni Blvd.
Box 1337   Phone: (505) 722-1119
Gallup, NM 87301   Patricia V. Bradley, Med.Libn.

U.S. AIR FORCE - AIR FORCE SYSTEMS COMMAND - TECHNICAL
    INFORMATION CENTER †
6585th Test Group/TSL   Phone: (505) 479-6511
Holloman AFB, NM 88330   Elizabeth Mohr, Libn.

U.S. AIR FORCE BASE - HOLLOMAN BASE LIBRARY †
FL 4801   Phone: (505) 479-3939
Holloman AFB, NM 88310   Wanda M. Goecke, Libn.

U.S. AIR FORCE BASE - KIRTLAND BASE LIBRARY
FL 4469   Phone: (505) 844-0795
Kirtland AFB, NM 87117   Alice R. Roy, Chf.Libn.

U.S. AIR FORCE HOSPITAL - MEDICAL LIBRARY (NM-Kirtland AFB)
                                     Phone: (505) 844-1086
Kirtland AFB, NM 87117   Alice T. Lee, Libn.

U.S. AIR FORCE WEAPONS LABORATORY - TECHNICAL LIBRARY
                                     Phone: (505) 844-7449
Kirtland AFB, NM 87117

ERIC CLEARINGHOUSE ON RURAL EDUCATION AND SMALL SCHOOLS
New Mexico State University
Box 3AP   Phone: (505) 646-2623
Las Cruces, NM 88003   Dr. Jack Cole, Dir.

LAS CRUCES PUBLIC SCHOOL TEACHERS' CENTER - TOY LENDING LIBRARY
    & EARLY CHILDHOOD RESOURCE CENTER
301 W. Amador   Phone: (505) 523-9220
Las Cruces, NM 88001   Susan Tetrault, Libn.

NEW MEXICO STATE UNIVERSITY - LIBRARY - RIO GRANDE HISTORICAL
    COLLECTIONS
Box 3475   Phone: (505) 646-4727
Las Cruces, NM 88003

NEW MEXICO STATE DEPARTMENT OF HOSPITALS - STATE HOSPITAL -
    ELLA P. KIEF MEMORIAL LIBRARY
Hot Springs Blvd.
Box 1388   Phone: (505) 425-6711
Las Vegas, NM 87701   Hazel Hurley, Libn.

IMMACULATE HEART OF MARY - PARISH LIBRARY
3700 Canyon Rd.   Phone: (505) 662-6193
Los Alamos, NM 87544

LOS ALAMOS COUNTY HISTORICAL MUSEUM - ARCHIVES
Fuller Lodge Cultural Ctr.
Box 43   Phone: (505) 662-6272
Los Alamos, NM 87544   Linda K. Aldrich, Archv.

UNITED CHURCH OF LOS ALAMOS - LIBRARY
2525 Canyon Rd.
Box 1286   Phone: (505) 662-2971
Los Alamos, NM 87544   Martha C. MacMillan, Libn.

U.S. NATL. PARK SERVICE - BANDELIER NATL. MONUMENT - LIBRARY
                                     Phone: (505) 672-3861
Los Alamos, NM 87544   Edward J. Greene, Supv.Pk.Ranger

UNIVERSITY OF CALIFORNIA - LOS ALAMOS NATIONAL LABORATORY -
    LIBRARY
MS-P362, Box 1663   Phone: (505) 667-4448
Los Alamos, NM 87545   J. Arthur Freed, Hd.Libn.

LOS LUNAS HOSPITAL AND TRAINING SCHOOL - LIBRARY AND RESOURCE
    CENTER †
Box 1269   Phone: (505) 865-9611
Los Lunas, NM 87031   Sarah Knox Morley, Libn.

EASTERN NEW MEXICO UNIVERSITY - GOLDEN LIBRARY - SPECIAL
    COLLECTIONS
                                     Phone: (505) 562-2624
Portales, NM 88130   Peggy M. Tozer, Lib.Dir.

SOUTHERN METHODIST UNIVERSITY - FORT BURGWIN RESEARCH
    CENTER - LIBRARY & HERBARIUM *
Box 314   Phone: (505) 758-8322
Ranchos de Taos, NM 87557

CHAVES COUNTY DISTRICT COURT - LIBRARY *
Box 1776   Phone: (505) 622-2212
Roswell, NM 88201

FIRST BAPTIST CHURCH - MEDIA LIBRARY
Box 1996   Phone: (505) 623-2640
Roswell, NM 88201   L. Jeannine Miller, Dir., Lib.Serv.

ROSWELL MUSEUM AND ART CENTER - ART LIBRARY
100 W. 11th St.   Phone: (505) 622-4700
Roswell, NM 88201   Wendell Ott, Dir.

BROTHERS THREE OF MORIARTY - LIBRARY
1917 Fort Union Dr.   Phone: (505) 982-2947
Santa Fe, NM 87501   John Bennett Shaw, Owner

EPISCOPAL CHURCH OF THE HOLY FAITH - PARISH LIBRARY
311 E. Palace Ave.   Phone: (505) 982-4447
Santa Fe, NM 87501   Katherine Landers, Libn.

INSTITUTE OF AMERICAN INDIAN ARTS - LIBRARY
College of Santa Fe Campus
St. Michael's Dr.   Phone: (505) 988-6356
Santa Fe, NM 87501   Karen Highfill, Libn.

MUSEUM OF NEW MEXICO - HISTORY LIBRARY
Box 2087   Phone: (505) 827-2343
Santa Fe, NM 87503   Orlando Romero, Res.Libn.

MUSEUM OF NEW MEXICO - LABORATORY OF ANTHROPOLOGY - LIBRARY †
Box 2087   Phone: (505) 827-3241
Santa Fe, NM 87503   Laura J. Holt, Libn.

MUSEUM OF NEW MEXICO - MUSEUM OF FINE ARTS - LIBRARY
Box 2087   Phone: (505) 827-3165
Santa Fe, NM 87501   Sue Critchfield, Hd.Libn.

MUSEUM OF NEW MEXICO - MUSEUM OF INTERNATIONAL FOLK ART -
    LIBRARY
Box 2087   Phone: (505) 827-8353
Santa Fe, NM 87504-2087   Judith Sellars, Libn.

MUSEUM OF NEW MEXICO - PHOTOGRAPHIC ARCHIVES
Box 2087   Phone: (505) 827-6472
Santa Fe, NM 87503   Arthur L. Olivas, Photographic Archv.

NEW MEXICO ENERGY RESEARCH AND DEVELOPMENT INSTITUTE -
    LIBRARY
1220 S. St. Francis Dr., Rm. 358   Phone: (505) 827-5886
Santa Fe, NM 87501   Dr. Dal Sepner, Planner

NEW MEXICO STATE COMMISSION OF PUBLIC RECORDS AND ARCHIVES -
    ARCHIVAL SERVICES DIVISION
404 Montezuma St.   Phone: (505) 827-2321
Santa Fe, NM 87503   Sherry Smith-Gonzales, Chf., Archv.Serv.

NEW MEXICO STATE DEPARTMENT OF HEALTH & ENVIRONMENT -
    ENVIRONMENTAL IMPROVEMENT DIVISION - LIBRARY
Box 577   Phone: (505) 984-0020
Santa Fe, NM 87504-0968   Jacqueline M. Calligan, Libn. II

NEW MEXICO STATE ENERGY AND MINERALS DEPARTMENT - LIBRARY
525 Camino de los Marquez   Phone: (505) 827-5913
Santa Fe, NM 87501   Glennis Hinshaw, Libn.

NEW MEXICO STATE LEGISLATIVE COUNCIL SERVICE - LIBRARY
325 Don Gaspar St.   Phone: (505) 827-3800
Santa Fe, NM 87503   Virginia Downing, State Libn.

NEW MEXICO STATE LIBRARY
325 Don Gaspar   Phone: (505) 827-3800
Santa Fe, NM 87503   Virginia Downing, State Libn.

NEW MEXICO STATE SUPREME COURT - LAW LIBRARY
Supreme Court Bldg.
Drawer L   Phone: (505) 827-2515
Santa Fe, NM 87501   John P. Blum, Dir.

SCHOOL OF AMERICAN RESEARCH - LIBRARY
Box 2188   Phone: (505) 982-3583
Santa Fe, NM 87501   Elizabeth Y. Kingman, Libn.

SOUTHWEST FOUNDATION FOR AUDIOVISUAL RESOURCES - AV
    COLLECTION
Box 522
Santa Fe, NM 87501

U.S. BUREAU OF LAND MANAGEMENT - NEW MEXICO STATE OFFICE
    LIBRARY
Box 1449   Phone: (505) 988-6047
Santa Fe, NM 87501   M. Ferne Bridgford, Supv.Mgt.Asst.

WHEELRIGHT MUSEUM - LIBRARY †
704 Camino Lejo
Box 5153   Phone: (505) 982-4636
Santa Fe, NM 87501   Susan McGreevy, Dir.

U.S. NATL. PARK SERVICE - GILA CLIFF DWELLINGS NATL. MONUMENT -
    VISITOR CENTER LIBRARY *
Rte. 11, Box 100   Phone: (505) 534-9461
Silver City, NM 88061

NEW MEXICO INSTITUTE OF MINING AND TECHNOLOGY - MARTIN
    SPEARE MEMORIAL LIBRARY
Campus Station   Phone: (505) 835-5614
Socorro, NM 87801   Betty Reynolds, Dir.

NATIONAL SOLAR OBSERVATORY - TECHNICAL LIBRARY
                                                  Phone: (505) 434-1390
Sunspot, NM 88349   John Cornett, Libn.

CARSON (Kit) MEMORIAL FOUNDATION - HISTORICAL RESEARCH LIBRARY
    AND ARCHIVES
E. Kit Carson Ave.
Box B   Phone: (505) 758-4741
Taos, NM 87571   Jack K. Boyer, Dir.

HARWOOD FOUNDATION LIBRARY OF THE UNIVERSITY OF NEW MEXICO
25 Ledoux St.
Box 766   Phone: (505) 758-3063
Taos, NM 87571   David Caffey, Dir.

ROGERS (Millicent) MUSEUM - LIBRARY
Box A   Phone: (505) 758-2462
Taos, NM 87571   May Harrover, Libn.

U.S. NATL. PARK SERVICE - FORT UNION NATL. MONUMENT - LIBRARY
                                                  Phone: (505) 425-8025
Watrous, NM 87753   Carol M. Kruse, Unit Mgr.

U.S. ARMY - TRADOC SYSTEMS ANALYSIS ACTIVITY - TRASANA
    TECHNICAL LIBRARY
Attn: ATOR-TSL   Phone: (505) 678-3135
White Sands Missile Range, NM 88002   Julie A. Gibson, Adm.Libn.

U.S. ARMY - WHITE SANDS MISSILE RANGE - TECHNICAL LIBRARY
    DIVISION
                                                  Phone: (505) 678-1317
White Sands Missile Range, NM 88002   Laurel B. Saunders, Chf.

NEW YORK

ALBANY BUSINESS COLLEGE - LIBRARY †
130 Washington Ave.   Phone: (518) 449-7163
Albany, NY 12210   Richard C. Matturro, Libn.

ALBANY INSTITUTE OF HISTORY AND ART - MC KINNEY LIBRARY
125 Washington Ave.   Phone: (518) 463-4478
Albany, NY 12210   Daryl J. Severson, Act.Libn.

CAPITAL DISTRICT PSYCHIATRIC CENTER - LIBRARY
75 New Scotland Ave.   Phone: (518) 445-6608
Albany, NY 12208   Bill McKewen, Libn.

FIRST CHURCH IN ALBANY (Reformed) - LIBRARY
N. Pearl & Clinton Sq.   Phone: (518) 463-4449
Albany, NY 12210   E. Helen Gardner, Libn.

HISTORICAL SOCIETY OF EARLY AMERICAN DECORATION, INC. - LIBRARY
19 Dove St.   Phone: (518) 462-1676
Albany, NY 12210   Mrs. Charles Coffin, Libn.

HOSPITAL EDUCATIONAL AND RESEARCH FUND - LILLIAN R. HAYT
    MEMORIAL LIBRARY
Center for Health Initiatives
15 Computer Dr., W.   Phone: (518) 458-7940
Albany, NY 12205   Elaine C. Rotman, Dir., Lib.Serv.

KEY BANK N.A. - INFORMATION CENTER
60 State St.   Phone: (518) 447-3594
Albany, NY 12207   Joy Longo, Libn.

MEMORIAL HOSPITAL - MEDICAL LIBRARY
Northern Blvd.   Phone: (518) 471-3264
Albany, NY 12204   G.A. McNamara, Libn.

NATIONAL CATHOLIC STEWARDSHIP COUNCIL - INFORMATION CENTER
1 Columbia Place   Phone: (518) 465-0233
Albany, NY 12207   Rev. James M. Mackey, Exec.Dir.

NEW YORK STATE CONFERENCE OF MAYORS AND MUNICIPAL OFFICIALS -
    LIBRARY
119 Washington Ave.   Phone: (518) 463-1185
Albany, NY 12210   John Lauber, Exec.Dir.

NEW YORK STATE COURT OF APPEALS - LIBRARY
Eagle St.   Phone: (518) 474-3624
Albany, NY 12207   Francis B. Waters, Libn.

NEW YORK STATE DEPARTMENT OF AUDIT CONTROL - LIBRARY *
Alfred E. Smith Office Bldg.   Phone: (518) 474-3419
Albany, NY 12236   Rita Wiers, Sr. Typist

NEW YORK STATE DEPARTMENT OF CIVIL SERVICE - LIBRARY *
State Office Bldg. Campus, Bldg. No. 1   Phone: (518) 457-6494
Albany, NY 12239   Virginia McCarthy, Libn.

NEW YORK STATE DEPARTMENT OF COMMERCE - LIBRARY
1 Commerce Plaza   Phone: (518) 474-5664
Albany, NY 12245   John J. Kilrain, Libn.

NEW YORK STATE DEPARTMENT OF ENVIRONMENTAL CONSERVATION -
  OFFICE OF PUBLIC AFFAIRS - INFORMATION SERVICE
50 Wolf Rd.   Phone: (518) 457-2344
Albany, NY 12233   Edward S. Feldman, Assoc.Dir., Info.Serv.

NEW YORK STATE DEPARTMENT OF HEALTH - CENTER FOR
  LABORATORIES AND RESEARCH LIBRARY
Empire State Plaza   Phone: (518) 474-6172
Albany, NY 12201   Thomas Flynn, Dir.

NEW YORK STATE DEPARTMENT OF LAW - LIBRARY
The Capitol   Phone: (518) 474-3840
Albany, NY 12224   Claire Engel, Chf., Lib.Serv.

NEW YORK STATE DEPARTMENT OF MOTOR VEHICLES - RESEARCH
  LIBRARY
Swan St. Bldg., Empire State Plaza   Phone: (518) 473-5467
Albany, NY 12228   Frances A. Miller, Sr.Libn.

NEW YORK STATE DEPARTMENT OF STATE - INFORMATION RESOURCE
  CENTER
162 Washington Ave.   Phone: (518) 474-4324
Albany, NY 12231   M.L. Johnson, Asst.Libn.

NEW YORK STATE DEPARTMENT OF TAXATION & FINANCE - TAX LIBRARY
Bureau of Research & Statistics
Taxation & Finance Bldg.   Phone: (518) 457-3512
Albany, NY 12227   Janet Snay, Act.Libn.

NEW YORK STATE DEPARTMENT OF TRANSPORTATION - MAP
  INFORMATION UNIT
State Office Campus
Bldg. 4, Rm. 105   Phone: (518) 457-3555
Albany, NY 12232   Paul G. Hein, Sr. Cartographer

NEW YORK STATE DEPARTMENT OF TRANSPORTATION - PUBLIC
  TRANSPORTATION - LIBRARY
1220 Washington Ave.
Bldg. 4, Rm. 209   Phone: (518) 457-6143
Albany, NY 12232   Carol R. Olson, Asst.Libn.

NEW YORK STATE LEGISLATIVE LIBRARY
State Capitol, Rm. 337   Phone: (518) 463-5683
Albany, NY 12224   John T. Hagy, Adm.Off.

NEW YORK STATE LIBRARY
Cultural Education Center
Empire State Plaza   Phone: (518) 474-7646
Albany, NY 12230   Peter Paulson, Dir.

NEW YORK STATE LIBRARY FOR THE BLIND AND VISUALLY HANDICAPPED
Cultural Education Center
Empire State Plaza   Phone: (518) 474-5935
Albany, NY 12230   Audrey Smith, Assoc.Libn.

NEW YORK STATE LIBRARY - HUMANITIES REFERENCE SECTION
Cultural Education Center
Empire State Plaza   Phone: (518) 474-5958
Albany, NY 12230   Lee Stanton, Act.Assoc.Libn.

NEW YORK STATE LIBRARY - LAW/SOCIAL SCIENCE REFERENCE
  SERVICES
Cultural Education Center
Empire State Plaza   Phone: (518) 474-5943
Albany, NY 12230   Stephanie Welden, State Law Libn.

NEW YORK STATE LIBRARY - LEGISLATIVE AND GOVERNMENTAL
  SERVICES
Cultural Education Center
Empire State Plaza   Phone: (518) 474-3940
Albany, NY 12230   Mary Redmond, Principal Libn.

NEW YORK STATE LIBRARY - MANUSCRIPTS AND SPECIAL COLLECTIONS
Cultural Education Center
Empire State Plaza   Phone: (518) 474-4461
Albany, NY 12230   Peter R. Christoph, Assoc.Libn.

NEW YORK STATE LIBRARY - SCIENCES/HEALTH SCIENCES/TECHNOLOGY
  REFERENCE SERVICES
Cultural Education Center
Empire State Plaza   Phone: (518) 474-7040
Albany, NY 12230   Christine A. Bain, Assoc.Libn.

NEW YORK STATE MUSEUM AND SCIENCE SERVICE - MUSEUM LIBRARY
State Education Dept., Rm.3128 CEC
Empire State Plaza   Phone: (518) 474-5878
Albany, NY 12230   Eleanor A. Gossen, Libn.

NEW YORK STATE OFFICE OF MENTAL HEALTH - RESEARCH RESOURCE
  CENTER *
44 Holland Ave.   Phone: (518) 474-7167
Albany, NY 12229   Paul G. Hillengas, Libn.

NEW YORK STATE OFFICE OF MENTAL RETARDATION AND
  DEVELOPMENTAL DISABILITIES - REFERENCE CENTER
44 Holland Ave.   Phone: (518) 474-0951
Albany, NY 12208   Yolanda Kendris, Libn.

NEW YORK STATE PARKS AND RECREATION - DIVISION FOR HISTORIC
  PRESERVATION - FIELD SERVICES BUREAU - LIBRARY
Agencies Tower No. 1
Empire State Plaza   Phone: (518) 474-0479
Albany, NY 12238   Kathleen LaFrank, Prog.Anl.

NEW YORK STATE SUPREME COURT - APPELLATE DIVISION, 3RD
  JUDICIAL DEPARTMENT - LAW LIBRARY
Justice Bldg., Empire State Plaza
Capitol Station, Box 7288
Albany, NY 12224   Ronald J. Milkins

ST. PETER'S HOSPITAL - MEDICAL STAFF LIBRARY
315 S. Manning Blvd.   Phone: (518) 454-1490
Albany, NY 12208   Lynn Siegelman, Libn.

SUNY AT ALBANY - GRADUATE LIBRARY FOR PUBLIC AFFAIRS AND POLICY
Hawley Library
1400 Washington Ave.   Phone: (518) 455-6178
Albany, NY 12222   Ruth A. Fraley, Hd.Libn.

SUNY - CENTRAL ADMINISTRATION RESEARCH LIBRARY
State University Plaza, Rm. S540   Phone: (518) 473-1070
Albany, NY 12246   M. Joan Tauber, Libn.

UNION UNIVERSITY - ALBANY COLLEGE OF PHARMACY - LIBRARY
106 New Scotland Ave.   Phone: (518) 445-5217
Albany, NY 12208   John B. Hall, Libn.

UNION UNIVERSITY - ALBANY LAW SCHOOL - LIBRARY
80 New Scotland Ave.   Phone: (518) 445-2340
Albany, NY 12208   Robert T. Begg, Dir.

UNION UNIVERSITY - ALBANY MEDICAL COLLEGE - SCHAFFER LIBRARY OF
  THE HEALTH SCIENCES
47 New Scotland Ave.   Phone: (518) 445-5586
Albany, NY 12208   Ursula H. Poland, Libn.

U.S. GEOLOGICAL SURVEY - WATER RESOURCES DIVISION - NEW YORK
  DISTRICT - LIBRARY
343 Court House
Box 1350   Phone: (518) 472-3107
Albany, NY 12201   Denise A. Wiltshire, Libn.

U.S. VETERANS ADMINISTRATION (NY-Albany) - MEDICAL CENTER
  LIBRARY (500/142-D)
113 Holland Ave.   Phone: (518) 462-3311
Albany, NY 12208   John F. Connors, Adm.Libn.

HUMAN RESOURCES CENTER - RESEARCH LIBRARY
I.U. Willets & Searingtown Rds.   Phone: (516) 747-5400
Albertson, NY 11507   Ruth A. Velleman, Lib.Dir.

ALFRED UNIVERSITY - HERRICK MEMORIAL LIBRARY - OPENHYM
  COLLECTION
                                              Phone: (607) 871-2184
Alfred, NY 14802   Norma Higgins, Spec.Coll.Tech.Spec.

ALFRED UNIVERSITY - HERRICK MEMORIAL LIBRARY - SPECIAL
   COLLECTIONS
                                                      Phone: (607) 871-2184
Alfred, NY 14802   Norma B. Higgins, Univ.Archv.

NEW YORK STATE COLLEGE OF CERAMICS AT ALFRED UNIVERSITY -
   SAMUEL R. SCHOLES LIBRARY OF CERAMICS
Harder Hall   Phone: (607) 871-2492
Alfred, NY 14802-1297   Bruce E. Connolly, Dir.

SUNY - AGRICULTURAL AND TECHNICAL COLLEGE AT ALFRED - WALTER C.
   HINKLE MEMORIAL LIBRARY
                                                      Phone: (607) 871-6313
Alfred, NY 14802   Barry Lash, Hd.Libn.

SUNY AT BUFFALO - CENTER FOR CURRICULUM PLANNING
Faculty of Educational Studies
17 Baldy Hall   Phone: (716) 636-2488
Amherst, NY 14260   Dr. William Eller, Dir.

TEMPLE SHAAREY ZEDEK - LIBRARY
Hartford & Getzville Rds.   Phone: (716) 838-3232
Amherst, NY 14226   Grace Stern, Libn.

CIBA-GEIGY CORPORATION - CORPORATE LIBRARY
Saw Mill River Rd.   Phone: (914) 478-3131
Ardsley, NY 10502   Paul M. McIlvaine, Libn.

AUBURN MEMORIAL HOSPITAL - LIBRARY/RESOURCE CENTER
5-19 Lansing St.   Phone: (315) 255-7231
Auburn, NY 13021   Anne Costello Tomlin, Dir.

CAYUGA COUNTY HISTORICAL RESEARCH CENTER - LIBRARY
County Office Bldg.   Phone: (315) 253-1300
Auburn, NY 13021   Mary M. Pinckney, Asst. County Hist.

CAYUGA MUSEUM OF HISTORY AND ART - LIBRARY & ARCHIVES
203 Genesee St.   Phone: (315) 253-8051
Auburn, NY 13021   Prof. Walter K. Long, Dir.

FOUNDATION HISTORICAL ASSOCIATION - SEWARD HOUSE
33 South St.   Phone: (315) 252-1283
Auburn, NY 13021   Betty Mae Lewis, Cur.

NEW YORK STATE SUPREME COURT - 7TH JUDICIAL DISTRICT - LAW
   LIBRARY
Cayuga County Court House   Phone: (315) 253-1279
Auburn, NY 13021

SARATOGA COUNTY HISTORICAL SOCIETY - LIBRARY
Brookside   Phone: (518) 885-4000
Ballston Spa, NY 12020

GENESEE COUNTY - DEPARTMENT OF HISTORY - RESEARCH LIBRARY
131 W. Main St.   Phone: (716) 343-2550
Batavia, NY 14020   Susan L. Conklin, Hist.

U.S. VETERANS ADMINISTRATION (NY-Batavia) - MEDICAL CENTER
   LIBRARY
Redfield Pkwy.   Phone: (716) 343-7500
Batavia, NY 14020   Madeline A. Coco, Chf.Libn.

NEW YORK STATE SUPREME COURT - 7TH JUDICIAL DISTRICT - LAW
   LIBRARY
13 Surrogates Court
Pulteney Sq.   Phone: (607) 776-7126
Bath, NY 14810   Cynthia A. Grimshaw, Law Libn.

U.S. VETERANS ADMINISTRATION (NY-Bath) - MEDICAL CENTER LIBRARY
                                                      Phone: (607) 776-2111
Bath, NY 14810   Norma W. Haskins, Chf., Lib.Serv.

SOUTHSIDE HOSPITAL - MEDICAL LIBRARY
Montauk Hwy.   Phone: (516) 859-3111
Bay Shore, NY 11706   May Chariton, Libn.

BEAR MOUNTAIN TRAILSIDE MUSEUMS - LIBRARY
Bear Mountain State Park   Phone: (914) 786-2701
Bear Mountain, NY 10911   John H. Mead, Musm.Dir.

QUEENS CHILDREN'S PSYCHIATRIC CENTER - LAURETTA BENDER STAFF
   LIBRARY *
74-03 Commonwealth Blvd.   Phone: (718) 464-2900
Bellerose, NY 11426   Mr. L. Feher, Libn.

DAMIEN DUTTON SOCIETY FOR LEPROSY AID, INC. - LIBRARY
616 Bedford Ave.   Phone: (516) 221-5829
Bellmore, NY 11710   Howard E. Crouch, Pres.

LONG ISLAND LIBRARY RESOURCES COUNCIL, INC. (LILRC)
Box 31   Phone: (516) 286-0400
Bellport, NY 11713   Herbert Biblo, Dir.

SUFFOLK COOPERATIVE LIBRARY SYSTEM - AUDIOVISUAL DEPARTMENT
Box 187   Phone: (516) 286-1600
Bellport, NY 11713   Philip Levering, AV Cons.

ALLEGANY COUNTY MUSEUM - LIBRARY
Court House   Phone: (716) 268-7612
Belmont, NY 14813   Bill Greene, Hist.

GRUMMAN AEROSPACE CORPORATION - TECHNICAL INFORMATION
   CENTER
Plant 35   Phone: (516) 575-3912
Bethpage, NY 11714   Harold B. Smith, Mgr., Lib. & Info.Serv.

BINGHAMTON GENERAL HOSPITAL - STUART B. BLAKELY MEMORIAL
   LIBRARY *
Mitchell Ave.   Phone: (607) 771-2200
Binghamton, NY 13903   Maryanne Mattimore, Med.Libn.

BINGHAMTON PRESS AND SUN BULLETIN - LIBRARY
Vestal Pkwy., E.
Box 1270   Phone: (607) 798-1159
Binghamton, NY 13902   Jorette Martin, Lib.Dir.

BINGHAMTON PSYCHIATRIC CENTER - PROFESSIONAL LIBRARY
425 Robinson St.   Phone: (607) 773-4052
Binghamton, NY 13901   Martha A. Mason, Sr.Libn.

BROOME COUNTY HISTORICAL SOCIETY - RESEARCH CENTER - JOSIAH T.
   NEWCOMB LIBRARY
30 Front St.   Phone: (607) 772-0660
Binghamton, NY 13905   Marjory B. Hinman, Libn.

BROOME DEVELOPMENTAL SERVICES - STAFF LIBRARY
Glenwood Rd.   Phone: (607) 770-0410
Binghamton, NY 13905   Mary Jeanne Perlmutter, Asst.Libn.

INSTITUTE FOR DEVELOPMENT ANTHROPOLOGY - LIBRARY
99 Collier St., Suite 302
Box 818   Phone: (607) 772-6244
Binghamton, NY 13902   Vera F. Beers, Adm.Off.

NEW YORK STATE ELECTRIC AND GAS CORPORATION - CORPORATE
   LIBRARY
4500 Vestal Pkwy., E.   Phone: (607) 729-2551
Binghamton, NY 13902   Melba H. Lewis, Libn.

NEW YORK STATE SUPREME COURT - 6TH JUDICIAL DISTRICT - LAW
   LIBRARY
107 Court House   Phone: (607) 772-2119
Binghamton, NY 13901   Judy A. Lauer, Law Libn.

SAVIN CORPORATION - ENGINEERING AND MANUFACTURING DIVISION -
   SAVIN TECHNICAL INFORMATION CENTER
33 Lewis Rd.   Phone: (607) 729-6531
Binghamton, NY 13902   Catherine S. Rybicki,, Lib.Spec.

SINGER COMPANY - LINK FLIGHT SIMULATION DIVISION - INFORMATION
   CENTER
Colesville Rd.
Binghamton, NY 13902   Eileen M. Hamlin, Supv.

SUNY AT BINGHAMTON - CENTER FOR MEDIEVAL AND EARLY
   RENAISSANCE STUDIES
Binghamton, NY 13901   Paul E. Szarmach, Dir.

SUNY AT BINGHAMTON - FINE ARTS LIBRARY
Vestal Pkwy. E.   Phone: (607) 798-4927
Binghamton, NY 13901   Marion Hanscom, Spec.Coll./Fine Arts Libn

SUNY AT BINGHAMTON - SCIENCE LIBRARY
Vestal Pkwy. E.   Phone: (607) 798-2528
Binghamton, NY 13901

SUNY AT BINGHAMTON - SPECIAL COLLECTIONS
Glenn G. Bartle Library
Vestal Pkwy. E.   Phone: (607) 798-4844
Binghamton, NY 13901   Marion Hanscom, Spec.Coll.Libn.

ADIRONDACK HISTORICAL ASSOCIATION - ADIRONDACK MUSEUM -
    RESEARCH LIBRARY
                                                   Phone: (518) 352-7311
Blue Mountain Lake, NY 12812   Craig Gilborn, Dir.

NORTH AMERICAN PHILIPS CORPORATION - PHILIPS LABORATORIES
    RESEARCH LIBRARY
345 Scarborough Rd.   Phone: (914) 945-6195
Briarcliff Manor, NY 10510   Betsy McIlvaine, Hd.Libn.

SUNY - COLLEGE AT BROCKPORT - DRAKE MEMORIAL LIBRARY
                                                   Phone: (716) 395-2141
Brockport, NY 14420   Dr. George W. Cornell, Dir. of Lib.Serv.

BETH ABRAHAM HOSPITAL - PATIENT LIBRARY
612 Allerton Ave.   Phone: (212) 920-5856
Bronx, NY 10467   Amy J. Kishinsky, Therapeutic Rec.Spec.

BRONX COUNTY BAR ASSOCIATION - LAW LIBRARY †
851 Grand Concourse   Phone: (212) 293-5600
Bronx, NY 10451

BRONX COUNTY HISTORICAL SOCIETY - THEODORE KAZIMIROFF
    RESEARCH LIBRARY
3309 Bainbridge Ave.   Phone: (212) 881-8900
Bronx, NY 10469   Laura Tosi, Assoc.Libn.

BRONX-LEBANON HOSPITAL CENTER - CONCOURSE DIVISION MEDICAL
    LIBRARY
1650 Grand Concourse   Phone: (212) 588-7000
Bronx, NY 10457   Gerardo Gomez, Libn.

CALVARY HOSPITAL - MEDICAL LIBRARY
1740-1770 Eastchester Rd.   Phone: (212) 430-4983
Bronx, NY 10461   Dorothy M. Maucione, Med.Libn.

FORDHAM UNIVERSITY - MULCAHY SCIENCE LIBRARY
Mulcahy Hall, Rm. 420   Phone: (212) 933-2233
Bronx, NY 10458   Edmund P. Maloney, Circ.Libn.

FORDHAM UNIVERSITY - SPECIAL COLLECTIONS
Duane Library   Phone: (212) 933-2233
Bronx, NY 10458   Mary Riley, Chf.Ref.Libn.

HUNTINGTON FREE LIBRARY - MUSEUM OF THE AMERICAN INDIAN -
    LIBRARY
9 Westchester Sq.   Phone: (212) 829-7770
Bronx, NY 10461   Mary B. Davis, Libn.

JOHN XXIII ECUMENICAL CENTER, INC. - CENTER FOR EASTERN
    CHRISTIAN STUDIES
2502 Belmont Ave.   Phone: (212) 365-8752
Bronx, NY 10458   Rev. Thomas F. Sable, S.J., Dir.

LINCOLN HOSPITAL - MEDICAL LIBRARY
234 E. 149th St.   Phone: (212) 579-5745
Bronx, NY 10451   Miss Milagros M. Paredes, Med.Libn.

MANHATTAN COLLEGE - GROVER M. HERMANN ENGINEERING LIBRARY
Corlear Ave. & 238th St.   Phone: (212) 920-0165
Bronx, NY 10471   Richard A. Barry, Engr.-Ref.Libn.

MANHATTAN COLLEGE - SONNTAG LIBRARY
Engineering Bldg.
Corlear Ave. & 238th St.   Phone: (212) 920-0266
Bronx, NY 10471   Harry E. Welsh, Lib.Dir.

MISERICORDIA HOSPITAL - MEDICAL LIBRARY †
600 E. 233rd St.   Phone: (212) 920-9869
Bronx, NY 10466   Denise L. Kirk, Dir., Libs.

MONTEFIORE MEDICAL CENTER - KARL CHERKASKY SOCIAL MEDICINE
    LIBRARY
111 E. 210th St.   Phone: (212) 920-5508
Bronx, NY 10467   Dr. Victor W. Sidel, Chm., Dept.Soc.Med.

MONTEFIORE MEDICAL CENTER - MEDICAL LIBRARY
111 E. 210 St.   Phone: (212) 920-4666
Bronx, NY 10467   Debra Cassel, Dir.

NEW YORK BOTANICAL GARDEN - LIBRARY †
                                                   Phone: (212) 220-8749
Bronx, NY 10458   Charles R. Long, Dir.

NEW YORK INSTITUTE FOR THE EDUCATION OF THE BLIND - WALTER
    BROOKS LIBRARY
999 Pelham Pkwy.   Phone: (212) 547-1234
Bronx, NY 10469   Helen C. Isherwood, Libn.

NEW YORK PUBLIC LIBRARY - BELMONT REGIONAL LIBRARY - ENRICO
    FERMI CULTURAL CENTER
610 E. 186th St.   Phone: (212) 933-6410
Bronx, NY 10458   Theresa K. Casile, Principal Libn.

NEW YORK STATE OFFICE OF COURT ADMINISTRATION - BRONX
    CRIMINAL-FAMILY COURT - LIBRARY
215 E. 161st St., Rm. 9-5A   Phone: (212) 590-2931
Bronx, NY 10451   Mary T. Rooney, Libn.

NEW YORK ZOOLOGICAL SOCIETY - LIBRARY
185th St. & Southern Blvd.   Phone: (212) 220-5125
Bronx, NY 10460   Steven P. Johnson, Archv.-Libn.

NORTH CENTRAL BRONX HOSPITAL - J.L. AMSTER HEALTH SCIENCES
    LIBRARY
3424 Kossuth Ave., RM. 14A-04   Phone: (212) 920-7868
Bronx, NY 10467   Ms. Padma Chittampalli, Med.Libn.

SUNY - MARITIME COLLEGE - STEPHEN B. LUCE LIBRARY
Fort Schuyler   Phone: (212) 409-7231
Bronx, NY 10465   Richard H. Corson, Libn.

U.S. VETERANS ADMINISTRATION (NY-Bronx) - MEDICAL CENTER LIBRARY
130 W. Kingsbridge Rd.
Bronx, NY 10468   Margaret M. Kinney, Chf.Libn.

YESHIVA UNIVERSITY - ALBERT EINSTEIN COLLEGE OF MEDICINE - D.
    SAMUEL GOTTESMAN LIBRARY
1300 Morris Park Ave.   Phone: (212) 430-3108
Bronx, NY 10461   Charlotte K. Lindner, Dir. of Lib.

YESHIVA UNIVERSITY - ALBERT EINSTEIN COLLEGE OF MEDICINE -
    DEPARTMENT OF ANESTHESIOLOGY - LIBRARY
Eastchester Rd. & Morris Park Ave.
Bldg. J, Rm. 1226
Bronx, NY 10461   Agnes Klein, Adm.

YESHIVA UNIVERSITY - ALBERT EINSTEIN COLLEGE OF MEDICINE - DEPT.
    OF PSYCHIATRY - J. THOMPSON PSYCHIATRY LIB.
Bronx Municipal Hospital Center
NR 2E7A   Phone: (212) 430-5571
Bronx, NY 10461   Silvia Davidson, Libn.

YESHIVA UNIVERSITY - ALBERT EINSTEIN COLLEGE OF MEDICINE -
    SURGERY LIBRARY
Jacobi Hospital, Rm. 613
Pelham Pkwy. & Eastchester Rd.   Phone: (212) 430-5800
Bronx, NY 10461

LAWRENCE HOSPITAL - ASHLEY BAKER MORRILL LIBRARY †
55 Palmer Ave.   Phone: (914) 337-7300
Bronxville, NY 10708   Judith M. Topper, Med.Libn.

AMERICAN ASSOCIATION OF CRIMEAN TURKS, INC. - ISMAIL GASPIRALI
    LIBRARY
4509 New Utrecht Ave.   Phone: (718) 438-9567
Brooklyn, NY 11219   Halim Saylik, Mgr.

AMSTAR CORPORATION - RESEARCH AND DEVELOPMENT LIBRARY
266 Kent Ave.   Phone: (718) 387-6800
Brooklyn, NY 11211   Joseph X. Cavano, Info.Spec.

ANTIQUE PHONOGRAPH MONTHLY - APM LIBRARY OF RECORDED SOUND
502 E. 17th St.   Phone: (718) 941-6835
Brooklyn, NY 11226   Allen Koenigsberg, Dir.

BROOKDALE HOSPITAL MEDICAL CENTER - MARIE SMITH SCHWARTZ
    MEDICAL LIBRARY
Linden Blvd. & Rockaway Pkwy.   Phone: (718) 240-5312
Brooklyn, NY 11212   Sophie Winston, Chf.Med.Libn.

BROOKLYN BAR ASSOCIATION FOUNDATION, INC. - LIBRARY
123 Remsen St.
Brooklyn, NY 11201

BROOKLYN BOTANIC GARDEN - LIBRARY
1000 Washington Ave.   Phone: (718) 622-4433
Brooklyn, NY 11225   Brenda Weisman, Dir., Info.Serv.

BROOKLYN CHILDREN'S MUSEUM - CHILDREN'S RESOURCE LIBRARY
145 Brooklyn Ave.   Phone: (718) 735-4400
Brooklyn, NY 11213   Susan J. Pober, Libn.

BROOKLYN CHILDREN'S MUSEUM - STAFF RESEARCH LIBRARY
145 Brooklyn Ave.   Phone: (718) 735-4400
Brooklyn, NY 11213   Cindy Schofield-Bodt, Staff Libn.

BROOKLYN COLLEGE OF THE CITY UNIVERSITY OF NEW YORK - CENTER
    FOR RESPONSIVE PSYCHOLOGY - LIBRARY
Rm. 5111, James Hall   Phone: (718) 780-5960
Brooklyn, NY 11210   Robert Buckhout, Prof. of Psychology

BROOKLYN COLLEGE OF THE CITY UNIVERSITY OF NEW YORK - HARRY D.
    GIDEONSE LIBRARY - SPECIAL COLLECTIONS
Bedford Ave. & Ave. H   Phone: (718) 780-5335
Brooklyn, NY 11210   Lillian Lester, Spec.Coll.Libn.

BROOKLYN COLLEGE OF THE CITY UNIVERSITY OF NEW YORK - MUSIC
    LIBRARY
417 Gershwin Hall   Phone: (718) 780-5289
Brooklyn, NY 11210   Prof. Dee Baily, Music Libn.

BROOKLYN DAILY LIBRARY
338 3rd Ave.   Phone: (718) 858-3300
Brooklyn, NY 11215   Lionel Klass, Ed. & Libn.

BROOKLYN HOSPITAL - MEDICAL LIBRARY *
121 DeKalb Ave.   Phone: (718) 270-4367
Brooklyn, NY 11201   Saul Kuchinsky, Libn.

BROOKLYN LAW SCHOOL - LAW LIBRARY
250 Joralemon St.   Phone: (718) 780-7974
Brooklyn, NY 11201   Charlotte L. Levy, Libn.

BROOKLYN MUSEUM - ART REFERENCE LIBRARY
188 Eastern Pkwy.   Phone: (718) 638-5000
Brooklyn, NY 11238   Deirdre E. Lawrence, Prin.Libn.

BROOKLYN MUSEUM - WILBOUR LIBRARY OF EGYPTOLOGY
188 Eastern Pkwy.   Phone: (718) 638-5000
Brooklyn, NY 11238   Diane Guzman, Libn.

BROOKLYN PUBLIC LIBRARY - ART AND MUSIC DIVISION
Grand Army Plaza   Phone: (718) 780-7784
Brooklyn, NY 11238   Sue Sharma, Div.Chf.

BROOKLYN PUBLIC LIBRARY - AUDIO VISUAL DIVISION
Grand Army Plaza   Phone: (718) 780-7793
Brooklyn, NY 11238   Kenneth W. Axthelm, Div.Chf.

BROOKLYN PUBLIC LIBRARY - BUSINESS LIBRARY
280 Cadman Plaza W.   Phone: (718) 780-7800
Brooklyn, NY 11201   Sylvia Mechanic, Bus.Libn.

BROOKLYN PUBLIC LIBRARY - HISTORY, TRAVEL, RELIGION AND
    BIOGRAPHY DIVISION
Grand Army Plaza   Phone: (718) 780-7794
Brooklyn, NY 11238   Henri Veit, Div.Chf.

BROOKLYN PUBLIC LIBRARY - LANGUAGE AND LITERATURE DIVISION
Grand Army Plaza   Phone: (718) 780-7733
Brooklyn, NY 11238   Monte Olenick, Div.Chf.

BROOKLYN PUBLIC LIBRARY - SCIENCE AND INDUSTRY DIVISION
Grand Army Plaza   Phone: (718) 780-7745
Brooklyn, NY 11238   Walter Wolff, Div.Chf.

BROOKLYN PUBLIC LIBRARY - SOCIAL SCIENCE AND PHILOSOPHY
    DIVISION
Grand Army Plaza   Phone: (718) 780-7746
Brooklyn, NY 11238   M.K. Gunning, Div.Chf.

CATHOLIC MEDICAL CENTER OF BROOKLYN & QUEENS, INC. - ST. MARY'S
    HOSPITAL - MEDICAL ADMINISTRATIVE LIBRARY
170 Buffalo Ave.   Phone: (718) 774-3600
Brooklyn, NY 11213   Jo-Anne Richardson, Med.Lib.Asst.

CENTER FOR HOLOCAUST STUDIES - DOCUMENTATION & RESEARCH
1610 Ave. J
Brooklyn, NY 11230   Bonnie Gurewitsch, Res.Libn.

CONEY ISLAND HOSPITAL - HAROLD FINK MEMORIAL LIBRARY
Ocean & Shore Pkwys.   Phone: (718) 743-4100
Brooklyn, NY 11235   Ronnie Joan Mark, Dir.

CUNY - NEW YORK CITY TECHNICAL COLLEGE LIBRARY/LEARNING
    RESOURCE CENTER
300 Jay St.   Phone: (718) 643-5240
Brooklyn, NY 11201   Catherine T. Brody, Chf.Libn.

DI CYAN - LIBRARY
1486 E. 33rd St.   Phone: (718) 252-8844
Brooklyn, NY 11234

INTERFAITH MEDICAL CENTER - BROOKLYN JEWISH SITE - MEDICAL &
    NURSING LIBRARY
555 Prospect Pl.   Phone: (718) 240-1795
Brooklyn, NY 11238   Sharon R. Peterson, Med.Libn.

INTERFAITH MEDICAL CENTER - ST. JOHN'S EPISCOPAL HOSPITAL -
    NURSING AND MEDICAL LIBRARY
1545 Atlantic Ave.   Phone: (718) 467-7000
Brooklyn, NY 11213   Dallas C. Hopson, Med.Libn.

KINGSBORO PSYCHIATRIC CENTER - MEDICAL LIBRARY
681 Clarkson Ave.   Phone: (718) 735-1273
Brooklyn, NY 11203   Dr. Abby P. Reiss, Dir., Quality Assurance

KINGSBOROUGH COMMUNITY COLLEGE - KINGSBOROUGH HISTORICAL
    SOCIETY †
2001 Oriental Blvd.   Phone: (718) 934-5417
Brooklyn, NY 11235   John B. Manbeck, Archv.

KINGSBROOK JEWISH MEDICAL CENTER - MEDICAL LIBRARY *
585 Schenectady Ave.   Phone: (718) 756-9700
Brooklyn, NY 11203   Mary E. Buchheit, Dir., Med.Lib.

LONG ISLAND COLLEGE HOSPITAL - HOAGLAND MEDICAL LIBRARY
340 Henry St.   Phone: (718) 780-1077
Brooklyn, NY 11201   Gabriel Bakcsy, Dir.

LONG ISLAND HISTORICAL SOCIETY - LIBRARY
128 Pierrepont St.   Phone: (718) 624-0890
Brooklyn, NY 11201   Lucinda Manning, Libn.

LONG ISLAND UNIV. - ARNOLD & MARIE SCHWARTZ COLLEGE OF
    PHARMACY & HEALTH SCIENCES - PHARMACEUTICAL STUDY CENTER
75 DeKalb Ave.   Phone: (718) 834-6000
Brooklyn, NY 11201   Lisa M. Livingston, Dir.

LUTHERAN MEDICAL CENTER - MEDICAL LIBRARY
150 55th St.   Phone: (718) 630-7200
Brooklyn, NY 11220   Mary Fugle, Libn.

MAIMONIDES MEDICAL CENTER - GEORGE A. DEGENSHEIN, M.D.
    MEMORIAL LIBRARY
4802 Tenth Ave.   Phone: (718) 270-7406
Brooklyn, NY 11219   Lydia Friedman, Chf.Med.Libn.

METHODIST HOSPITAL - HEALTH SCIENCES LIBRARY
506 6th St.   Phone: (718) 780-3368
Brooklyn, NY 11215   Martha E. Lynch, Dir. of Libs.

METROPOLITAN JEWISH GERIATRIC CENTER - MAX B. & LOUISA S.
   MARKS MEMORIAL MEDICAL LIBRARY
4915 Tenth Ave.   Phone: (718) 853-2800
Brooklyn, NY 11219   Gracie Cooper, Libn.

NEW YORK CITY TRANSIT AUTHORITY - LAW LIBRARY
370 Jay St., Rm. 1333   Phone: (718) 330-4330
Brooklyn, NY 11201   James P. McMahon, Exec.Asst.Gen. Counsel

NEW YORK STATE SUPREME COURT - 2ND JUDICIAL DISTRICT - LAW
   LIBRARY
360 Adams St.   Phone: (718) 643-8080
Brooklyn, NY 11201   Jatindra N. Mukerji, Prin. Law Libn.

NOVOCOL CHEMICAL MANUFACTURING COMPANY, INC. - LIBRARY *
2921 Atlantic Ave.   Phone: (718) 277-5400
Brooklyn, NY 11207   Elias Epstein, Dir. of Res.

OFFICE OF BILINGUAL EDUCATION - RESOURCE LIBRARY AND
   INFORMATION UNIT
131 Livingston St., Rm. 204   Phone: (718) 858-5505
Brooklyn, NY 11201   Carmen Gloria Burgos, Libn.

OSBORN LABORATORIES OF MARINE SCIENCES - NEW YORK AQUARIUM
   LIBRARY
Boardwalk & W. 8th St.   Phone: (718) 266-8500
Brooklyn, NY 11224   G.D. Ruggieri, Ph.D., Dir.

POLYTECHNIC INSTITUTE OF NEW YORK - SPICER LIBRARY
333 Jay St.   Phone: (718) 643-8690
Brooklyn, NY 11201   James Jarman, Act.Dir. of Libs.

PRATT INSTITUTE - LIBRARY
200 Willoughby Ave.   Phone: (718) 636-3545
Brooklyn, NY 11205   George Lowy, Dean of Libs.

ST. FRANCIS COLLEGE - JAMES A. KELLY INSTITUTE FOR LOCAL
   HISTORICAL STUDIES - LIBRARY
180 Remsen St.   Phone: (718) 522-2300
Brooklyn, NY 11201   Arthur J. Konop, Dir.-Archv.

SUNY - DOWNSTATE MEDICAL CENTER - DEPARTMENT OF PSYCHIATRY
   LIBRARY
606 Winthrop St.   Phone: (718) 735-3915
Brooklyn, NY 11203   Patricia Tomasulo, Libn.

SUNY - DOWNSTATE MEDICAL CENTER - MEDICAL RESEARCH LIBRARY OF
   BROOKLYN †
450 Clarkson Ave.
Box 14   Phone: (718) 270-1041
Brooklyn, NY 11203   Kenneth E. Moody, Dir.

TEMPLE AHAVATH SHOLOM - RABBI A. ALAN STEINBACH LIBRARY
1010 Ave. M
Brooklyn, NY 11230

THIRD WORLD WOMEN'S EDUCATIONAL RESOURCES, INC. - THIRD
   WORLD WOMEN'S ARCHIVES
Bush Terminal, Box 159   Phone: (718) 308-5389
Brooklyn, NY 11232

U.S. ARMY POST - FORT HAMILTON - LIBRARY
Bldg. 404   Phone: (718) 836-4100
Brooklyn, NY 11252   Amelia K. Sefton, Libn. I

U.S. DISTRICT COURT - EASTERN DISTRICT OF NEW YORK - LIBRARY
225 Cadman Plaza E.   Phone: (718) 330-7483
Brooklyn, NY 11201   Lillian B. Garrell, Law Libn.

U.S. VETERANS ADMINISTRATION (NY-Brooklyn) - MEDICAL CENTER
   LIBRARY
800 Poly Place   Phone: (718) 836-6600
Brooklyn, NY 11209   Barbara B. Goldberg, Chf.Libn.

WOODHULL MEDICAL AND MENTAL HEALTH CENTER - HEALTH SCIENCES
   LIBRARY
760 Broadway, Rm. 3A160   Phone: (718) 963-8397
Brooklyn, NY 11206   Leon Elveson, Med.Libn.

WORLD JEWISH GENEALOGY ORGANIZATION - LIBRARY
1533 60th St.
Box FF   Phone: (718) 435-0500
Brooklyn, NY 11219   Rabbi N. Halberstam, Libn.

YESHIVA TORAH VODAATH AND MESIFTA - TORAH VODAATH LIBRARY
425 E. Ninth St.   Phone: (718) 941-8000
Brooklyn, NY 11218

ACRES AMERICAN INC. - LIBRARY
1000 Liberty Bldg.   Phone: (716) 853-7525
Buffalo, NY 14202   Susan C. Doughtie, Libn.

ALBRIGHT-KNOX ART GALLERY - ART REFERENCE LIBRARY
1285 Elmwood Ave.   Phone: (716) 882-8700
Buffalo, NY 14222   Annette Masling, Libn.

ALLIED CORPORATION - ALLIED CHEMICAL - LIBRARY
20 Peabody St.   Phone: (716) 827-6229
Buffalo, NY 14210   Dr. J. Northcott, Supv.

BELL AEROSPACE TEXTRON - LAWRENCE D. BELL MEMORIAL LIBRARY
Box 1   Phone: (716) 297-1000
Buffalo, NY 14240   Lester M. Breslauer, Chf.Libn.

BRYANT AND STRATTON BUSINESS INSTITUTE - LIBRARY
1028 Main St.   Phone: (716) 884-9120
Buffalo, NY 14202   Shirley R. Rowland, Media Supv.

BUFFALO COURIER-EXPRESS - LIBRARY *
795 Main St.   Phone: (716) 855-6583
Buffalo, NY 14240   Cynthia Hayes, Libn.

BUFFALO & ERIE COUNTY HISTORICAL SOCIETY - LIBRARY †
25 Nottingham Ct.   Phone: (716) 873-9644
Buffalo, NY 14216   Robert L. Damm, Dir.

BUFFALO & ERIE COUNTY PUBLIC LIBRARY - BUSINESS AND LABOR
   DEPARTMENT
Lafayette Sq.   Phone: (716) 856-7525
Buffalo, NY 14203   Joyce M. Davoli, Hd.

BUFFALO & ERIE COUNTY PUBLIC LIBRARY - EDUCATION, SOCIOLOGY,
   PHILOSOPHY & RELIGION DEPARTMENT
Lafayette Sq.   Phone: (716) 856-7525
Buffalo, NY 14203   Ann P. Miller, Hd.

BUFFALO & ERIE COUNTY PUBLIC LIBRARY - FILM DEPARTMENT
Lafayette Sq.   Phone: (716) 856-7525
Buffalo, NY 14203   Robert M. Gurn, Hd.

BUFFALO & ERIE COUNTY PUBLIC LIBRARY - HISTORY, TRAVEL AND
   GOVERNMENT DEPARTMENT
Lafayette Sq.   Phone: (716) 856-7525
Buffalo, NY 14203   Ruth Willet, Dept.Hd.

BUFFALO & ERIE COUNTY PUBLIC LIBRARY - LANGUAGE, LITERATURE AND
   ARTS DEPARTMENT
Lafayette Sq.   Phone: (716) 856-7525
Buffalo, NY 14203   Ann P. Miller, Hd.

BUFFALO & ERIE COUNTY PUBLIC LIBRARY - MUSIC DEPARTMENT
Lafayette Sq.   Phone: (716) 856-7525
Buffalo, NY 14203   Norma Jean Lamb, Hd.

BUFFALO & ERIE COUNTY PUBLIC LIBRARY - RARE BOOK ROOM
Lafayette Sq.   Phone: (716) 856-7525
Buffalo, NY 14203   William H. Loos, Cur.

BUFFALO & ERIE COUNTY PUBLIC LIBRARY - SCIENCE AND TECHNOLOGY
   DEPARTMENT
Lafayette Sq.   Phone: (716) 856-7525
Buffalo, NY 14203   Stanley P. Zukowski, Hd.

BUFFALO GENERAL HOSPITAL, INC. - A.H. AARON MEDICAL LIBRARY †
100 High St.   Phone: (716) 845-2878
Buffalo, NY 14203   Wentsing Liu, Dir.

BUFFALO NEWS - LIBRARY
One News Plaza   Phone: (716) 849-4401
Buffalo, NY 14240   Sally G. Schlaerth, Hd.Libn.

BUFFALO PSYCHIATRIC CENTER - BPC LIBRARY *
400 Forest Ave.   Phone: (716) 885-2261
Buffalo, NY 14213   Margaret Litzenberger, Asst.Libn.

BUFFALO SOCIETY OF NATURAL SCIENCES - RESEARCH LIBRARY
Buffalo Musm. of Science
Humboldt Pkwy.   Phone: (716) 896-5200
Buffalo, NY 14211   Marcia Morrison, Libn.

CALSPAN CORPORATION - TECHNICAL INFORMATION CENTER
4455 Genesee St.   Phone: (716) 632-7500
Buffalo, NY 14225   Betty Miller, Supv.

CHILDREN'S HOSPITAL OF BUFFALO - MEDICAL LIBRARY
219 Bryant St.   Phone: (716) 878-7304
Buffalo, NY 14222   Lucy Wargo, Med.Libn.

DEACONESS HOSPITAL - MEDICAL LIBRARY
1001 Humboldt Parkway   Phone: (716) 886-4400
Buffalo, NY 14208   Donna Browning, Med.Libn.

ECOLOGY & ENVIRONMENT, INC. - LIBRARY
195 Sugg Rd.
Box D   Phone: (716) 632-4491
Buffalo, NY 14225   Theresa L. Wolfe, Info.Spec.

ERIE COUNTY MEDICAL CENTER - MEDICAL LIBRARY †
462 Grider St.   Phone: (716) 898-3939
Buffalo, NY 14215   Anthony Ciko, Sr.Med.Libn.

EVERYWOMAN OPPORTUNITY CENTER, INC. - LIBRARY
237 Main St., Suite 330
Buffalo, NY 14203

FILLMORE (Millard) HOSPITAL - KIDENEY HEALTH SCIENCES LIBRARY *
3 Gates Circle   Phone: (716) 887-4848
Buffalo, NY 14209   Aniela Lichtenstein, Hd.Libn.

MARINE MIDLAND BANK - TECHNICAL INFORMATION CENTER
One Marine Midland Ctr., 4th Fl., W. Wing   Phone: (716) 843-5011
Buffalo, NY 14240   Eva M. Saintcross, Stat.Libn.

MERCY HOSPITAL - MEDICAL LIBRARY
565 Abbott Rd.   Phone: (716) 826-7000
Buffalo, NY 14220   Linda S. Karch, Libn.

NEW YORK STATE SUPREME COURT - 8TH JUDICIAL DISTRICT - LAW
   LIBRARY †
92 Franklin St.   Phone: (716) 852-0712
Buffalo, NY 14202   James R. Sahlem, Principal Law Libn.

PENNWALT CORPORATION - LUCIDOL DIVISION - RESEARCH LIBRARY †
1740 Military Rd.   Phone: (716) 877-1740
Buffalo, NY 14240   David C. Noller, Tech.Info.Spec.

PHILLIPS, LYTLE, HITCHCOCK, BLAINE AND HUBER - LIBRARY
3400 Maine Midland Ctr.   Phone: (716) 847-8400
Buffalo, NY 14203   Ellen M. Reen, Libn.

RESEARCH INSTITUTE ON ALCOHOLISM - LIBRARY
1021 Main St.   Phone: (716) 887-2511
Buffalo, NY 14203   Diane Augustino, Res.Sci. I

ROSWELL PARK MEMORIAL INSTITUTE - LIBRARY AND INFORMATION
   MANAGEMENT SERVICES
666 Elm St.   Phone: (716) 845-5966
Buffalo, NY 14263   Ann P. Hutchinson, Lib.Dir.

ST. MARY'S SCHOOL FOR THE DEAF - INFORMATION CENTER
2253 Main St.   Phone: (716) 834-7200
Buffalo, NY 14214   Collette Sangster, Dir.

SISTERS OF CHARITY HOSPITAL - MEDICAL STAFF LIBRARY
2157 Main St.   Phone: (716) 862-2846
Buffalo, NY 14214   Anne Cohen, Med.Libn.

SUNY AT BUFFALO - ARCHITECTURE & ENVIRONMENTAL DESIGN LIBRARY
Hayes Hall
Main Street Campus   Phone: (716) 831-3505
Buffalo, NY 14214   Norma Segal, Hd.

SUNY AT BUFFALO - CENTER FOR INTEGRATIVE STUDIES - LIBRARY
108 Hayes Hall
3435 Main St.   Phone: (716) 831-3727
Buffalo, NY 14214   Magda Cordell McHale, Dir.

SUNY AT BUFFALO - CHARLES B. SEARS LAW LIBRARY
O'Brian Hall, Amherst Campus   Phone: (716) 636-2048
Buffalo, NY 14260   Professor Wade J. Newhouse, Dir.

SUNY AT BUFFALO - HEALTH SCIENCES LIBRARY
Main St. Campus   Phone: (716) 831-3337
Buffalo, NY 14214   Mr. C.K. Huang, Dir.

SUNY AT BUFFALO - MUSIC LIBRARY
Baird Hall   Phone: (716) 636-2923
Buffalo, NY 14260   James Coover, Dir.

SUNY AT BUFFALO - POETRY/RARE BOOKS COLLECTION
University Libraries, 420 Capen Hall   Phone: (716) 636-2918
Buffalo, NY 14260   Robert J. Bertholf, Cur.

SUNY AT BUFFALO - SCIENCE AND ENGINEERING LIBRARY
                                                    Phone: (716) 636-2946
Buffalo, NY 14260   Diane C. Parker, Dir.

SUNY AT BUFFALO - UNIVERSITY ARCHIVES
420 Capen Hall   Phone: (716) 636-2916
Buffalo, NY 14260   Shonnie Finnegan, Univ.Archv.

SUNY - COLLEGE AT BUFFALO - BURCHFIELD CENTER-WESTERN NEW
   YORK FORUM FOR AMERICAN ART
1300 Elmwood Ave.   Phone: (716) 878-6011
Buffalo, NY 14222   Nancy M. Weekly, Libn./Archv.

SUNY - COLLEGE AT BUFFALO - EDWARD H. BUTLER LIBRARY
1300 Elmwood Ave.   Phone: (716) 878-6302
Buffalo, NY 14222   Dr. George C. Newman, Dir.

SUNY - COLLEGE AT BUFFALO - GREAT LAKES LABORATORY - LIMNOLOGY
   LIBRARY
1300 Elmwood Ave.
Buffalo, NY 14222

SUNY - SCHOOL OF PHARMACY - DRUG INFORMATION SERVICE - LIBRARY
Erie County Medical Center
462 Grider St.   Phone: (716) 898-3927
Buffalo, NY 14215   Dr. Sue Rozek

TEMPLE BETH ZION - LIBRARY
805 Delaware Ave.   Phone: (716) 886-7151
Buffalo, NY 14209   Donna J. Davidoff, Hd.Libn.

TEXTRON, INC. - SPENCER KELLOGG DIVISION - RESEARCH CENTER
   LIBRARY
4201 Genesee St.
Box 210   Phone: (716) 852-5850
Buffalo, NY 14225   Pamela G. Kobelski, Tech.Info.Supv.

U.S. DEPT. OF COMMERCE - INTERNATIONAL TRADE ADMINISTRATION -
   BUFFALO DISTRICT OFFICE LIBRARY *
1312 Federal Bldg.
111 W. Huron St.   Phone: (716) 846-4191
Buffalo, NY 14202   Robert F. Magee, Dir.

U.S. VETERANS ADMINISTRATION (NY-Buffalo) - MEDICAL CENTER
   LIBRARY SERVICE
3495 Bailey Ave.   Phone: (716) 834-9200
Buffalo, NY 14215   Joyce Kaupa, Libn.

ONTARIO COUNTY HISTORICAL SOCIETY, INC. - ARCHIVES
55 N. Main St.   Phone: (716) 394-4975
Canandaigua, NY 14424   Robert Donald Muller, Dir.

U.S. VETERANS ADMINISTRATION (NY-Canandaigua) - MEDICAL CENTER
   LIBRARY (142D)
                                     Phone: (315) 394-2000
Canandaigua, NY 14424   Peter Fleming, Chf., Lib.Serv.

NORTH COUNTRY REFERENCE & RESEARCH RESOURCES COUNCIL -
   LIBRARY
Box 568   Phone: (315) 386-4569
Canton, NY 13617   Richard H. Kimball, Exec.Dir.

ST. LAWRENCE COUNTY HISTORICAL ASSOCIATION - ARCHIVES
3 E. Main St.
Box 8   Phone: (315) 386-2780
Canton, NY 13617   John A. Baule, Dir.

ST. LAWRENCE UNIVERSITY - SPECIAL COLLECTIONS
Owen D. Young Library   Phone: (315) 379-6398
Canton, NY 13617   Lynn Ekfelt, Cur.

BOARD OF COOPERATIVE EDUCATIONAL SERVICES OF NASSAU COUNTY
   (BOCES) - NASSAU EDUC. RSRCS. CTR. (NERC)
234 Glen Cove Rd.   Phone: (516) 877-1190
Carle Place, NY 11514

U.S. VETERANS ADMINISTRATION (NY-Castle Point) - MEDICAL CENTER
   LIBRARY
                                     Phone: (914) 831-2000
Castle Point, NY 12511   William E. Kane, Chf., Lib.Serv.

NEW YORK STATE SUPREME COURT - 3RD JUDICIAL DISTRICT - EMORY
   A. CHASE MEMORIAL LIBRARY
Greene County Court House, Main St.
Box 65   Phone: (518) 943-3130
Catskill, NY 12414   Mrs. Armida M. Marafioti, Libn.

FRANKLIN (H.H.) CLUB - LIBRARY *
Cazenovia College
Cazenovia, NY 13035   Lee Schopmeier, Libn.

NEW YORK BARTOK ARCHIVE
2 Tulip St.   Phone: (516) 569-1468
Cedarhurst, NY 11516   Dr. Benjamin Suchoff, Trustee

TEMPLE BETH EL - BUDDY BERMAN MEMORIAL LIBRARY *
Broadway & Locust Ave.   Phone: (516) 569-2700
Cedarhurst, NY 11516   Mirel Touger, Libn.

CENTRAL ISLIP PSYCHIATRIC CENTER - HEALTH SCIENCE LIBRARY †
Carlton Ave., Station H   Phone: (516) 234-6262
Central Islip, NY 11722   Mary Avlon, Libn.

FALKIRK HOSPITAL - LIBRARY *
Box 194   Phone: (914) 928-2256
Central Valley, NY 10917   Maria Gern

SMITH MEMORIAL LIBRARY
Pratt & Miller Ave.   Phone: (716) 357-5844
Chautauqua, NY 14722   Mrs. Torrey Isaac, Libn.

MINER (Alice T.) COLONIAL COLLECTION - LIBRARY
Box 330   Phone: (518) 846-7336
Chazy, NY 12921   Lucille L. Czarnetzky, Cur.

MINER CENTER LIBRARY
SUNY College at Plattsburgh   Phone: (518) 564-2178
Chazy, NY 12921   Linda J. Masters, Lib.Tech.Asst.

ST. JOSEPH INTERCOMMUNITY HOSPITAL - MEDICAL STAFF LIBRARY
2605 Harlem Rd.   Phone: (716) 896-6300
Cheektowaga, NY 14225   Sr. M. Tiburtia Gorecki, F.S.S.J., Cons.

THOUSAND ISLANDS MUSEUM, INC. - LIBRARY
750 Mary St.   Phone: (315) 686-4104
Clayton, NY 13624   Frederick P. Schmitt, Asst.Dir.

CLIFTON SPRINGS HOSPITAL AND CLINIC - MEDICAL LIBRARY
2 Coulter Rd.   Phone: (315) 462-9561
Clifton Springs, NY 14432   Amy H. Ballard, Dir., Med.Rec.

SUNY - AGRICULTURAL AND TECHNICAL COLLEGE AT COBLESKILL - JARED
   VAN WAGENEN, JR. LEARNING RESOURCE CENTER †
                                     Phone: (518) 234-5841
Cobleskill, NY 12043   Eleanor M. Carter, Dir.

PUTNAM COUNTY HISTORICAL SOCIETY - FOUNDRY SCHOOL MUSEUM -
   REFERENCE LIBRARY
63 Chestnut St.   Phone: (914) 265-2781
Cold Spring, NY 10516   Carol F. Morse, Libn.

COLD SPRING HARBOR LABORATORY - MAIN LIBRARY
Box 100   Phone: (516) 692-6660
Cold Spring Harbor, NY 11724   Susan Gensel, Dir., Libs. & Marketing

NATURE CONSERVANCY - LONG ISLAND CHAPTER - UPLANDS FARM
   ENVIRONMENTAL CENTER
Lawrence Hill Rd.
Box 72   Phone: (516) 367-3281
Cold Spring Harbor, NY 11724   Margo S. Myles, Dir.

WHALING MUSEUM SOCIETY, INC. - LIBRARY
Main St.
Box 25   Phone: (516) 367-3418
Cold Spring Harbor, NY 11724   Robert D. Farwell, Exec.Dir.

EDO CORPORATION - ENGINEERING LIBRARY
14-04 111th St.   Phone: (718) 445-6000
College Point, NY 11356   Robin I. Praver, Libn.

BASSETT (Mary Imogene) HOSPITAL - MEDICAL LIBRARY
Atwell Rd.   Phone: (607) 547-3115
Cooperstown, NY 13326   Wendy E. Rice, Med.Libn.

NATIONAL BASEBALL HALL OF FAME AND MUSEUM, INC. - NATIONAL
   BASEBALL LIBRARY
Box 590   Phone: (607) 547-9988
Cooperstown, NY 13326   Thomas R. Heitz, Libn.

NEW YORK STATE HISTORICAL ASSOCIATION - LIBRARY
                                     Phone: (607) 547-2509
Cooperstown, NY 13326   Amy Barnum, Libn.

COLLEGE CENTER OF THE FINGER LAKES - LIBRARY †
22 W. Third St.   Phone: (607) 962-3134
Corning, NY 14830   Julia Lonnberg, Libn.

CORNING GLASS WORKS - TECHNICAL INFORMATION CENTER
Sullivan Pk.   Phone: (607) 974-3258
Corning, NY 14831   Raymond R. Barber, Libn.

CORNING MUSEUM OF GLASS - LIBRARY
Museum Way   Phone: (607) 937-5371
Corning, NY 14831   Dr. John H. Martin, Dir.

HARVARD UNIVERSITY - HARVARD BLACK ROCK FOREST LIBRARY
                                     Phone: (914) 534-4517
Cornwall, NY 12518   Jack J. Karnig, Forest Mgr.

QUEENS BOROUGH PUBLIC LIBRARY - LANGSTON HUGHES COMMUNITY
   LIBRARY AND CULTURAL CENTER
102-09 Northern Blvd.   Phone: (718) 651-1100
Corona, NY 11368   Andrew P. Jackson, Exec.Dir.

CORTLAND COUNTY HISTORICAL SOCIETY - LIBRARY
25 Homer Ave.   Phone: (607) 756-6071
Cortland, NY 13045   Shirley G. Heppell, Libn.

SUNY - COLLEGE AT CORTLAND - MEMORIAL LIBRARY
Prospect Terrace
Box 2000   Phone: (607) 753-2221
Cortland, NY 13045   Selby U. Gration, Dir. of Libs.

U.S. FISH & WILDLIFE SERVICE - TUNISON LABORATORY OF FISH
   NUTRITION - LIBRARY
28 Gracie Rd.   Phone: (607) 753-9391
Cortland, NY 13045   Gary L. Rumsey, Dir.

GREENE COUNTY HISTORICAL SOCIETY - VEDDER MEMORIAL LIBRARY
R.D. 1, Box 10A   Phone: (518) 731-6822
Coxsackie, NY 12051   Raymond Beecher, Libn.

HUDSON INSTITUTE - LIBRARY
Quaker Ridge Rd.   Phone: (914) 762-0700
Croton-On-Hudson, NY 10520   Mildred Schneck, Libn.

TCR SERVICE, INC. - COMMON LAW LIBRARY
One Prickly Pear Hill   Phone: (201) 461-7475
Croton-on-Hudson, NY 10520   Anne Dartnell, Supv.

WORLD MODELING ASSOCIATION - WMA LIBRARY
Box 100   Phone: (914) 737-8512
Croton-on-Hudson, NY 10520   Ruth Tolman, Pres.

MUSICAL MUSEUM - RESEARCH LIBRARY
Main St.   Phone: (315) 841-8774
Deansboro, NY 13328   Arthur H. Sanders, Cur.

NEW YORK STATE SUPREME COURT - 6TH JUDICIAL DISTRICT - LAW
    LIBRARY
Court House   Phone: (607) 746-2603
Delhi, NY 13753   Katherine Flint, Lib.Ck.

O'CONNOR (Lindsay A. & Olive B.) HOSPITAL - LIBRARY
Andes Road, Route 28   Phone: (607) 746-2371
Delhi, NY 13753   Barbara Green, Libn.

SUNY - AGRICULTURAL AND TECHNICAL COLLEGE AT DELHI - LIBRARY †
                                                         Phone: (607) 746-4107
Delhi, NY 13753   Herbert J. Sorgen, Libn.

PARAPSYCHOLOGY SOURCES OF INFORMATION CENTER
2 Plane Tree Ln.   Phone: (516) 271-1243
Dix Hills, NY 11746   Rhea A. White, Dir.

STAUFFER CHEMICAL COMPANY - EASTERN RESEARCH CENTER
    INFORMATION SERVICES
Livingstone Ave.   Phone: (914) 693-1200
Dobbs Ferry, NY 10522   Ramona C.T. Crosby, Supv.Info./Comp.Serv.

DUNKIRK OBSERVER - LIBRARY
8 E. Second St.   Phone: (716) 366-3000
Dunkirk, NY 14048

AURORA HISTORICAL SOCIETY - ELBERT HUBBARD LIBRARY AND MUSEUM
    †
Main & Pine Sts.
East Aurora, NY 14052   Genevieve M. Steffen, Cur.

CHRIST THE KING SEMINARY - LIBRARY
711 Knox Rd.   Phone: (716) 652-8959
East Aurora, NY 14052   Rev. Bonaventure F. Hayes, O.F.M., Lib.Dir.

EAST HAMPTON FREE LIBRARY - LONG ISLAND COLLECTION
159 Main St.   Phone: (516) 324-0222
East Hampton, NY 11937   Dorothy T. King, Libn.

NASSAU COUNTY MEDICAL CENTER - HEALTH SCIENCES LIBRARY
2201 Hempstead Turnpike   Phone: (516) 542-3542
East Meadow, NY 11554   Paul G. Merrigan, Lib.Dir.

NASSAU COUNTY MUSEUM REFERENCE LIBRARY
Dwight D. Eisenhower Memorial Pk.   Phone: (516) 542-4516
East Meadow, NY 11554   Edward J. Smits, Dir.

SUNY AT STONY BROOK - HEALTH SCIENCES LIBRARY
Box 66   Phone: (516) 444-2512
East Setauket, NY 11733   Ruth Marcolina, Dir.

GALSON & GALSON, P.C., AND GALSON TECHNICAL SERVICES, INC. -
    INFORMATION CENTER
6601 Kirkville Rd.   Phone: (315) 437-7181
East Syracuse, NY 13057   Mary P. Young, Info.Spec.

EASTCHESTER HISTORICAL SOCIETY - LIBRARY
Box 37   Phone: (914) 793-1900
Eastchester, NY 10709   Madeline Schaeffer, Libn.

EDEN HISTORICAL SOCIETY - TOWN HISTORIAN'S OFFICE AND
    HISTORICAL SOCIETY LIBRARY
8584 S. Main St.   Phone: (716) 992-9141
Eden, NY 14057   Nathalie B. Leonard, Town Hist./Cur.

ESSEX COUNTY HISTORICAL SOCIETY - LIBRARY
Court St.   Phone: (518) 873-6466
Elizabethtown, NY 12932   Dorothy A. Plum, Libn.

MOUNT SINAI HOSPITAL SERVICES - CITY HOSPITAL CENTER AT
    ELMHURST - MEDICAL LIBRARY
79-01 Broadway   Phone: (718) 830-1538
Elmhurst, NY 11373   Stacey Saley, Chf.Med.Libn.

ARNOT-OGDEN MEMORIAL HOSPITAL - WEY MEMORIAL LIBRARY
600 Roe Ave.   Phone: (607) 737-4101
Elmira, NY 14901   Katherine F. Mekos, Med.Libn.

CHEMUNG COUNTY HISTORICAL SOCIETY, INC. - MRS. ARTHUR W. BOOTH
    LIBRARY
415 E. Water St.   Phone: (607) 734-4167
Elmira, NY 14901   Richard Warters, Pres.

ELMIRA PSYCHIATRIC CENTER - PROFESSIONAL LIBRARY
Caller 1527   Phone: (607) 737-4769
Elmira, NY 14902   Consuelo R. Madumba, Act.Dir., Educ. & Trng.

ELMIRA STAR GAZETTE - LIBRARY
201 Baldwin St.   Phone: (607) 734-5151
Elmira, NY 14902   Jean M. Strong, Libn.

NATIONAL SOARING MUSEUM - LIBRARY & ARCHIVES
Harris Hill, R.D. 3   Phone: (607) 734-3128
Elmira, NY 14903   Shirley Sliwa, Dir.

NEW YORK STATE SUPREME COURT - 6TH JUDICIAL DISTRICT - LAW
    LIBRARY
Hazlett Bldg.   Phone: (607) 737-2983
Elmira, NY 14901   Julie H. McDowell, Libn.

ST. JOSEPH'S HOSPITAL - HELENE FULD LEARNING RESOURCE CENTER
555 E. Market St.   Phone: (607) 733-6541
Elmira, NY 14902   Arlene C. Pien, Libn.

THATCHER GLASS CORPORATION - RESEARCH CENTER LIBRARY
Box 1505   Phone: (607) 737-3162
Elmira, NY 14902   Jenny C. Dean

PERGAMON INSTITUTE - LIBRARY
Maxwell House   Phone: (914) 592-7700
Elmsford, NY 10523   Maureen Lyon, Libn.

IBM CORPORATION - SYSTEMS TECHNOLOGY DIVISION - LIBRARY
Dept. E 50
Rte. 17C & Glendale Dr.   Phone: (607) 752-3601
Endicott, NY 13760   Dr. John W. Forman, Mgr.

MOUNT ST. ALPHONSUS THEOLOGICAL SEMINARY - LIBRARY †
                                                         Phone: (914) 384-6550
Esopus, NY 12429   Joan W. Durand, Libn.

INTERFAITH MEDICAL CENTER - ST. JOHN'S EPISCOPAL HOSPITAL (South
    Shore Division) - MEDICAL LIBRARY
327 Beach 19th St.   Phone: (718) 471-8100
Far Rockaway, NY 11691   Esther Skolnik, Med.Libn.

PENINSULA HOSPITAL CENTER - MEDICAL LIBRARY
51-15 Beach Channel Dr.   Phone: (718) 945-7100
Far Rockaway, NY 11691   Edith Rubinstein, Lib.Dir.

FAIRCHILD INDUSTRIES - FAIRCHILD REPUBLIC COMPANY - TECHNICAL
    INFORMATION CENTER
Conklin St.   Phone: (516) 531-3497
Farmingdale, NY 11735   George A. Mauter, Supv.

FARMINGDALE PUBLIC SCHOOLS - PROFESSIONAL LIBRARY *
East Memorial at Mill Lane School
Mill Lane   Phone: (516) 752-6553
Farmingdale, NY 11735   Geoffrey L. Mattocks, Adm.Dir.

SUNY - AGRICULTURAL AND TECHNICAL COLLEGE AT FARMINGDALE -
   THOMAS D. GREENLEY LIBRARY
Melville Rd.   Phone: (516) 420-2040
Farmingdale, NY 11735   Michael G. Knauth, Chf.Libn.

VAN WYCK HOMESTEAD MUSEUM - LIBRARY
Rte. 9, Box 133   Phone: (914) 896-9560
Fishkill, NY 12524   Ruth B. Polhill, Libn.

ACADEMY OF AERONAUTICS - LIBRARY
LaGuardia Airport Sta.   Phone: (718) 429-6600
Flushing, NY 11371   JoAnn Jayne, Hd.Libn.

ATLAS TRAFFIC CONSULTANTS CORPORATION - TARIFF DEPARTMENT
   LIBRARY
18-42 College Point Blvd.   Phone: (718) 461-0556
Flushing, NY 11356   Diana Otero, Tariff Libn.

BOOTH MEMORIAL MEDICAL CENTER - HEALTH EDUCATION LIBRARY
Main St. at Booth Memorial Ave.   Phone: (718) 670-1118
Flushing, NY 11355   Rita S. Maier, Lib.Dir.

FLUSHING HOSPITAL AND MEDICAL CENTER - MEDICAL LIBRARY
4500 Parsons Blvd.   Phone: (718) 670-5653
Flushing, NY 11355-9980   Maria Czechowicz, Dir.

QUEENS COLLEGE OF THE CITY UNIVERSITY OF NEW YORK - CTR. FOR
   BYZANTINE & MODERN GREEK STUD. - LIB.
                                          Phone: (718) 520-7035
Flushing, NY 11367   Prof. Harry J. Psomiades, Dir.

QUEENS COLLEGE OF THE CITY UNIVERSITY OF NEW YORK - ETHNIC
   MATERIALS INFORMATION CENTER
Graduate School of Lib. & Info. Studies
64-15 Kissena Blvd.   Phone: (718) 520-7194
Flushing, NY 11367   David Cohen, Prog.Dir.

QUEENS COLLEGE OF THE CITY UNIVERSITY OF NEW YORK - PAUL
   KLAPPER LIBRARY - ART LIBRARY
                                          Phone: (718) 520-7243
Flushing, NY 11367   Suzanna Simor, Hd.

QUEENS COLLEGE OF THE CITY UNIVERSITY OF NEW YORK - PAUL
   KLAPPER LIBRARY - HISTORICAL DOCUMENTS COLLECTION
                                          Phone: (718) 520-7482
Flushing, NY 11367

QUEENS COLLEGE OF THE CITY UNIVERSITY OF NEW YORK - SCIENCE
   LIBRARY
65-30 Kissena Blvd.   Phone: (718) 520-7254
Flushing, NY 11367   Jackson B. Cohen, Hd., Sci.Lib.

MOHAWK-CAUGHNAWAGA MUSEUM - LIBRARY
R.D. 1
Box 554   Phone: (518) 853-3678
Fonda, NY 12068   Rev. Nicholas Weiss, Dir.

MONTGOMERY COUNTY - DEPARTMENT OF HISTORY AND ARCHIVES
Old Court House   Phone: (518) 853-3431
Fonda, NY 12068

GOLDWATER MEMORIAL HOSPITAL - HEALTH SCIENCES LIBRARY
New York Univ. Medical Center Affiliate   Phone: (212) 750-6749
Franklin D. Roosevelt Island, NY 10044   Martin M. Leibovici, Lib.Dir.

NOSTALGIA PRESS, INC. - ARCHIVES AND ART LIBRARY *
Box 293   Phone: (516) 488-4747
Franklin Square, NY 11010   Martin F. Jackson, Info.Dir.

SUNY - COLLEGE AT FREDONIA - MUSIC LIBRARY
                                          Phone: (716) 673-3183
Fredonia, NY 14063   Joseph Chouinard, Music Libn.

HALL (Lydia E.) HOSPITAL - MEDICAL LIBRARY
320 W. Merrick Rd.   Phone: (516) 378-8500
Freeport, NY 11520   Edith T. Hyman, Libn.

PHOTO TRENDS - LIBRARY
Box 650   Phone: (516) 379-1440
Freeport, NY 11520   R. Eugene Keesee, Owner

WESTRECO, INC. - FOOD RESEARCH AND DEVELOPMENT - LIBRARY
555 S. Fourth St.
Box 274   Phone: (315) 598-1234
Fulton, NY 13069   Janice Burns, Res.Libn.

ADELPHI UNIVERSITY - FINE ARTS LIBRARY - SPECIAL COLLECTIONS -
   ARCHIVES †
South Ave.   Phone: (516) 663-1042
Garden City, NY 11530   Erica Doctorow, Hd.

ADELPHI UNIVERSITY - SCIENCE LIBRARY †
                                          Phone: (516) 663-1043
Garden City, NY 11530   Liselotte Matzka, Hd., Sci.Lib.

ADELPHI UNIVERSITY - SOCIAL WORK LIBRARY †
                                          Phone: (516) 560-8040
Garden City, NY 11530   Rita Edwards, Hd.

ENDO LABORATORIES, INC. - LIBRARY †
1000 Stewart Ave.   Phone: (516) 832-2113
Garden City, NY 11530   Virginia Steinberger, Mgr.

MERCER (George, Jr.) SCHOOL OF THEOLOGY - LIBRARY
65 Fourth St.   Phone: (516) 248-4800
Garden City, NY 11530   Elizabeth D. Dupont, Libn.

NASSAU COMMUNITY COLLEGE - NEW YORK STATE HEALTH FILM
   COLLECTION
                                          Phone: (516) 222-7413
Garden City, NY 11530   Arthur L. Friedman, Media Libn.

NASSAU COUNTY MEDICAL SOCIETY - NASSAU ACADEMY OF MEDICINE -
   JOHN N. SHELL LIBRARY
1200 Stewart Ave.   Phone: (516) 832-2320
Garden City, NY 11530   Mary L. Westermann, Med.Libn.

FRIARS OF THE ATONEMENT - CARDINAL SPELLMAN LIBRARY
Graymoor   Phone: (914) 424-3671
Garrison, NY 10524   Rev. Alexander Kelliher, S.A., Mgr.

LIVINGSTON COUNTY LAW LIBRARY
2 Court St.   Phone: (716) 243-2500
Geneseo, NY 14454   Patricia Mothersell, Libn.

SUNY - COLLEGE AT GENESEO - COLLEGE LIBRARIES
Fraser Library   Phone: (716) 245-5591
Geneseo, NY 14454   Richard C. Quick, Dir. of Coll.Libs.

CORNELL UNIVERSITY - NEW YORK STATE AGRICULTURAL EXPERIMENT
   STATION - LIBRARY
W. North St.   Phone: (315) 787-2214
Geneva, NY 14456   Mary Van Buren, Libn.

GENEVA HISTORICAL SOCIETY AND MUSEUM - JAMES D. LUCKETT
   MEMORIAL ARCHIVES
543 S. Main St.   Phone: (315) 789-5151
Geneva, NY 14456   Eleanore R. Clise, Chf.Archv.

BUREAU OF JEWISH EDUCATION - COMMUNITY LIBRARY
2640 N. Forest Rd.   Phone: (716) 689-8844
Getzville, NY 14068   Abraham F. Yanover, Exec.Dir.

COMMUNITY HOSPITAL AT GLEN COVE - MEDICAL LIBRARY
St. Andrews Ln.   Phone: (516) 676-5000
Glen Cove, NY 11542   Kathryn M. Gegan, Libn.

PALL CORPORATION - LIBRARY
30 Sea Cliff Ave.   Phone: (516) 671-4000
Glen Cove, NY 11724   Patricia J. Iannucci, Mkt.Res.Mgr.

WEBB INSTITUTE OF NAVAL ARCHITECTURE - LIVINGSTON LIBRARY
Crescent Beach Rd.   Phone: (516) 671-0439
Glen Cove, NY 11542   Fred H. Forrest, Libn.

NEW YORK CHIROPRACTIC COLLEGE - LIBRARY
255 Valentines Ln., Old Brookville   Phone: (516) 686-7657
Glen Head, NY 11545   Michele L. Barrett, Libn./Dir.

LONG ISLAND JEWISH-HILLSIDE MEDICAL CENTER - HILLSIDE DIVISION -
    HEALTH SCIENCES LIBRARY †
Box 38   Phone: (718) 470-4406
Glen Oaks, NY 11004   Joan L. Kauff, Chf.Med.Libn.

GLENS FALLS-QUEENSBURY HISTORICAL ASSN., INC. - CHAPMAN
    HISTORICAL MUSM. - RUSSELL M.L. CARSON MEMORIAL LIB.
348 Glen St.   Phone: (518) 793-2826
Glens Falls, NY 12801   Joseph A. Cutshall King, Dir.

HYDE COLLECTION
161 Warren St.   Phone: (518) 792-1761
Glens Falls, NY 12801

FIRST UNITED METHODIST CHURCH - JENNIE E. WEAVER MEMORIAL
    LIBRARY
7 Elm St.   Phone: (518) 725-9313
Gloversville, NY 12078   Nancy Naish, Asst.Libn.

TROTTING HORSE MUSEUM - PETER D. HAUGHTON MEMORIAL LIBRARY
240 Main St.   Phone: (914) 294-6330
Goshen, NY 10924   Philip A. Pines, Dir.

MOORE BUSINESS FORMS, INC. - RESEARCH CENTER LIBRARY
300 Lang Blvd.   Phone: (716) 773-0557
Grand Island, NY 14072   Betsy M. Waters, Lib.Supv.

CONTEL INFORMATION SYSTEMS - LIBRARY
130 Steamboat Rd.   Phone: (516) 829-5900
Great Neck, NY 11024

SPERRY - SPERRY ELECTRONIC SYSTEMS - TECHNICAL INFORMATION
    CENTER
Lakeville Rd. & Marcus Ave.   Phone: (516) 574-1001
Great Neck, NY 11020   Catherine L. Marcoux, Libn.

TEMPLE BETH-EL OF GREAT NECK - ARNOLD & MARIE SCHWARTZ
    LIBRARY
5 Old Mill Rd.   Phone: (516) 487-0900
Great Neck, NY 11023   Linda Insler, Libn.

U.S.D.A. - AGRICULTURAL RESEARCH SERVICE - PLUM ISLAND ANIMAL
    DISEASE CENTER LIBRARY
Box 848   Phone: (516) 323-2500
Greenport, NY 11944   Stephen Perlman, Libn.

LONG ISLAND UNIVERSITY - C.W. POST CAMPUS - CENTER FOR BUSINESS
    RESEARCH
B. Davis Schwartz Memorial Library   Phone: (516) 299-2932
Greenvale, NY 11548   Mary McNierney Grant, Mgr.

LONG ISLAND UNIVERSITY - C.W. POST CAMPUS - PALMER SCHOOL OF
    LIBRARY AND INFORMATION SCIENCE - LIBRARY
B. Davis Schwartz Memorial Library   Phone: (516) 299-2826
Greenvale, NY 11548   Ellen Weinstein, Hd.

U.S. AIR FORCE - ROME AIR DEVELOPMENT CENTER - DATA & ANALYSIS
    CENTER FOR SOFTWARE
RADC/ISISI   Phone: (315) 336-0937
Griffiss AFB, NY 13441   Thomas Robbins, DACS Prog.Mgr.

U.S. AIR FORCE - ROME AIR DEVELOPMENT CENTER - TECHNICAL
    LIBRARY
RADC TST   Phone: (315) 330-7607
Griffiss AFB, NY 13441   Linda Evans, Chf., Tech.Lib.

NEW YORK STATE NURSES ASSOCIATION - LIBRARY
2113 Western Ave.   Phone: (518) 456-5371
Guilderland, NY 12084   Barbara Van Nortwick, Lib.Dir.

HILBERT COLLEGE - MC GRATH LIBRARY - SPECIAL COLLECTIONS
5200 S. Park Ave.   Phone: (716) 649-7900
Hamburg, NY 14075   Sr. M. Tiburtia Gorecki, Dir.

WESTERN NEW YORK GENEALOGICAL SOCIETY, INC. - LIBRARY
Box 338   Phone: (716) 649-4440
Hamburg, NY 14075   Donald C. Shaw, Libn.

AMERICAN MANAGEMENT ASSOCIATIONS - D.W. MITCHELL MEMORIAL
    LIBRARY
Box 88   Phone: (315) 824-2000
Hamilton, NY 13346   Madge Snyder, Libn.

COLGATE UNIVERSITY - EVERETT NEEDHAM CASE LIBRARY - ARCHIVES
    Phone: (315) 824-1000
Hamilton, NY 13346   Bruce M. Brown, Univ.Archv.

CURTISS (Glenn H.) MUSEUM OF LOCAL HISTORY - MINOR SWARTHOUT
    MEMORIAL LIBRARY
Lake & Main St.   Phone: (607) 569-2160
Hammondsport, NY 14840   Merrill Stickler, Dir./Cur.

AFRAM ASSOCIATES, INC. - AFRAMAILIBRARY
Beatrice Lewis Bldg.
68-72 E. 131st St.   Phone: (212) 690-5903
Harlem, NY 10037   Mr. Wilcox, Dir.

ST. VINCENT'S HOSPITAL AND MEDICAL CENTER OF NEW YORK,
    WESTCHESTER BRANCH - MEDICAL LIBRARY
240 North St.   Phone: (914) 967-6500
Harrison, NY 10528   Ethel Eisenberg, Med.Libn.

HASTINGS CENTER LIBRARY - INSTITUTE OF SOCIETY, ETHICS & THE
    LIFE SCIENCES
360 Broadway   Phone: (914) 478-0500
Hastings-on-Hudson, NY 10706   Marna Howarth, Libn.

SUFFOLK ACADEMY OF MEDICINE - LIBRARY
850 Veterans Memorial Hwy.   Phone: (516) 724-7970
Hauppauge, NY 11787   Isabel V. Hathorn, Libn.

GOWANDA PSYCHIATRIC CENTER - HEALTH SCIENCES LIBRARY
Rte. 62   Phone: (716) 532-3311
Helmuth, NY 14079   Mark Wudyka, Libn.

HEMPSTEAD PUBLIC LIBRARY - SPECIAL COLLECTIONS
115 Nichols Ct.   Phone: (516) 481-6990
Hempstead, NY 11550   Irene A. Duskiewicz, Dir.

HOFSTRA UNIVERSITY - LIBRARY - SPECIAL COLLECTIONS
1000 Fulton Ave.   Phone: (516) 560-5974
Hempstead, NY 11550   Marguerite Regan, Asst. to Dean

HOFSTRA UNIVERSITY - SCHOOL OF LAW LIBRARY
    Phone: (516) 560-5900
Hempstead, NY 11550   Eugene M. Wypyski, Dir.

INDUSTRIAL HOME FOR THE BLIND - NASSAU-SUFFOLK BRAILLE LIBRARY
320 Fulton Ave.   Phone: (516) 485-1234
Hempstead, NY 11550   Helen Lomax, Libn.

LONG ISLAND CATHOLIC - RESEARCH LIBRARY
Box 700   Phone: (516) 538-8800
Hempstead, NY 11551   Doris S. Bader, Libn.

NASSAU COUNTY DEPARTMENT OF HEALTH - DIVISION OF LABORATORIES
    & RESEARCH - MEDICAL LIBRARY
209 Main St.   Phone: (516) 483-9158
Hempstead, NY 11550   Madeline H. Burston, Pub. Health Adm.

HERKIMER COUNTY LAW LIBRARY
Court House, Main St.   Phone: (315) 867-1172
Herkimer, NY 13350   Jane C. Gilbert, Law Lib.Ck.

TEMPLE BETH JOSEPH - ROSE BASLOE LIBRARY
North Prospect St.   Phone: (315) 866-4270
Herkimer, NY 13350

GENERAL INSTRUMENT CORPORATION, GOVERNMENT SYSTEMS DIVISION
    - ENGINEERING LIBRARY
600 West John St.   Phone: (516) 733-3000
Hicksville, NY 11802   Hilda N. Shevack, Logistics/Data Mgr.

LONG ISLAND LIGHTING COMPANY - CORPORATE LIBRARY †
175 E. Old Country Rd.   Phone: (516) 733-4264
Hicksville, NY 11801   Patricia Clancy, Libn.

AKWESASNE LIBRARY CULTURAL CENTER
                                            Phone: (518) 358-2240
Hogansburg, NY 13655   Margaret M. Jacobs, Dir.

ANTIQUE WIRELESS ASSOCIATION, INC. - LIBRARY
Main St. (East Bloomfield)   Phone: (716) 657-7489
Holcomb, NY 14469   Bruce Kelley, Dir./Cur.

LEIBIGER (O.W.) RESEARCH LABORATORIES, INC. - TECHNICAL
   INFORMATION CENTER
48 Classic St.
Hoosick Falls, NY 12090   I. Leibiger, Hd.

IBM CORPORATION - GENERAL TECHNOLOGY DIVISION - EAST FISHKILL
   FACILITY - LIBRARY
Rte. 52   Phone: (914) 894-6219
Hopewell Junction, NY 12533   Karen A. Murley, Mgr.

COLUMBIA MEMORIAL HOSPITAL - SCHOOL OF NURSING LIBRARY
Prospect Ave.   Phone: (518) 828-7601
Hudson, NY 12534   Gail Nagel, Libn.

NEW YORK STATE SUPREME COURT - 3RD JUDICIAL DISTRICT - LAW
   LIBRARY
Court House
Hudson, NY 12534   Emily M. Wildey, Libn.

OLANA STATE HISTORIC SITE - LIBRARY
R.D. 2   Phone: (518) 828-0135
Hudson, NY 12534   James Ryan, Site Mgr.

HUNTINGTON HISTORICAL SOCIETY - LIBRARY
209 Main St.   Phone: (516) 427-7045
Huntington, NY 11743

HUNTINGTON HOSPITAL - MEDICAL LIBRARY
270 Park Ave.   Phone: (516) 351-2283
Huntington, NY 11743   Ruth I. Glick, Dir.

SEMINARY OF THE IMMACULATE CONCEPTION - LIBRARY
West Neck Rd.   Phone: (516) 423-0483
Huntington, NY 11743   Jiri (George) Lipa, Ph.D., Libn.

KLD ASSOCIATES, INC. - LIBRARY †
300 Broadway   Phone: (516) 549-9803
Huntington Station, NY 11746

WHITMAN (Walt) BIRTHPLACE ASSOCIATION - LIBRARY AND MUSEUM
246 Walt Whitman Rd.   Phone: (516) 427-5240
Huntington Station, NY 11746   Betsy Vondrasek, Cur.

CULINARY INSTITUTE OF AMERICA - KATHARINE ANGELL LIBRARY
North Rd.   Phone: (914) 452-9600
Hyde Park, NY 12538   Eileen De Vries, Libn.

ULRICH (Edwin A.) MUSEUM - LIBRARY/ARCHIVES
"Wave Crest" On-The-Hudson
Albany Post Rd.   Phone: (914) 229-7107
Hyde Park, NY 12583   Edwin A. Ulrich, Dir. and Owner

U.S. NATL. PARK SERVICE - ROOSEVELT-VANDERBILT NATL. HISTORIC
   SITES - MUSEUMS
                                            Phone: (914) 229-9115
Hyde Park, NY 12538   Franceska Macsali, Site Libn./Park Ranger

U.S. PRESIDENTIAL LIBRARIES - FRANKLIN D. ROOSEVELT LIBRARY
259 Albany Post Rd.   Phone: (914) 229-8114
Hyde Park, NY 12538   William R. Emerson, Dir.

FOUNDATION FOR ECONOMIC EDUCATION - LIBRARY
30 S. Broadway   Phone: (914) 591-7230
Irvington-On-Hudson, NY 10533   Brian Summers, Libn.

CENTER FOR RELIGION, ETHICS & SOCIAL POLICY - ANNE CARRY
   DURLAND MEMORIAL ALTERNATIVES LIBRARY
Cornell University
122 Anabel Taylor Hall   Phone: (607) 256-6486
Ithaca, NY 14853   Louise T. Fry, Libn.

CORNELL INSTITUTE FOR SOCIAL AND ECONOMIC RESEARCH (CISER) -
   DATA ARCHIVE
Cornell University
323 Uris Hall   Phone: (607) 256-4801
Ithaca, NY 14853   Ann E. Gerken, Data Archv.

CORNELL UNIVERSITY - AFRICANA STUDIES AND RESEARCH CENTER
   LIBRARY
310 Triphammer Rd.   Phone: (607) 256-3822
Ithaca, NY 14853   Marvin Williams, Adm.Supv.

CORNELL UNIVERSITY - ALBERT R. MANN LIBRARY
                                            Phone: (607) 256-2285
Ithaca, NY 14853   Jan Olsen, Libn.

CORNELL UNIVERSITY - AUDIO-VISUAL RESOURCE CENTER
8 Research Park   Phone: (607) 256-2091
Ithaca, NY 14850   Carol Doolittle, AV Coord.

CORNELL UNIVERSITY - BAILEY HORTORIUM LIBRARY
Mann Library, Rm. 467   Phone: (607) 256-2132
Ithaca, NY 14853   D.A. Young, Dir.

CORNELL UNIVERSITY - DEPARTMENT OF MANUSCRIPTS AND
   UNIVERSITY ARCHIVES
101 Olin Research Library   Phone: (607) 256-3530
Ithaca, NY 14853   H. Thomas Hickerson, Chm.

CORNELL UNIVERSITY - ENGINEERING LIBRARY
Carpenter Hall   Phone: (607) 256-4318
Ithaca, NY 14853   Susan Markowitz, Engr.Libn.

CORNELL UNIVERSITY - ENTOMOLOGY LIBRARY
Comstock Hall   Phone: (607) 256-3265
Ithaca, NY 14853   Edwin Spragg, Entomology Libn.

CORNELL UNIVERSITY - FINE ARTS LIBRARY
Sibley Dome   Phone: (607) 256-3710
Ithaca, NY 14853   Judith E. Holliday, Libn.

CORNELL UNIVERSITY - FLOWER VETERINARY LIBRARY
Schurman Hall   Phone: (607) 256-5454
Ithaca, NY 14853   Susanne K. Whitaker, Libn.

CORNELL UNIVERSITY - GRADUATE SCHOOL OF MANAGEMENT - LIBRARY
Malott Hall   Phone: (607) 256-3389
Ithaca, NY 14853   Betsy Ann Olive, Libn.

CORNELL UNIVERSITY - HERBERT F. JOHNSON MUSEUM OF ART -
   REFERENCE LIBRARY
                                            Phone: (607) 256-6464
Ithaca, NY 14853   Suzette Lane, Cur.Asst.

CORNELL UNIVERSITY - HISTORY OF SCIENCE COLLECTIONS
215 Olin Research Library   Phone: (607) 256-4033
Ithaca, NY 14853   David W. Corson, Hist. of Sci.Libn.

CORNELL UNIVERSITY - ICELANDIC COLLECTION
Olin Research Library   Phone: (607) 256-6462
Ithaca, NY 14853   Louis A. Pitschmann, Libn.

CORNELL UNIVERSITY - JOHN M. ECHOLS COLLECTION ON SOUTHEAST
   ASIA
Olin Library   Phone: (607) 256-4189
Ithaca, NY 14853   Giok Po Oey, Cur.

CORNELL UNIVERSITY - LABORATORY OF ORNITHOLOGY - LIBRARY
159 Sapsucker Woods Rd.   Phone: (607) 256-4319
Ithaca, NY 14850

CORNELL UNIVERSITY - LABORATORY OF ORNITHOLOGY - LIBRARY OF
   NATURAL SOUNDS
159 Sapsucker Woods Rd.   Phone: (607) 256-4035
Ithaca, NY 14850   Dr. James L. Gulledge, Dir.

CORNELL UNIVERSITY - LAW LIBRARY
Myron Taylor Hall   Phone: (607) 256-7236
Ithaca, NY 14853   Jane L. Hammond, Law Libn.

CORNELL UNIVERSITY - MAPS, MICROTEXTS, NEWSPAPERS DEPARTMENT
Olin Research Library   Phone: (607) 256-5258
Ithaca, NY 14853   Marie Gast, Libn.

CORNELL UNIVERSITY - MARTIN P. CATHERWOOD LIBRARY OF
    INDUSTRIAL AND LABOR RELATIONS
Ives Hall   Phone: (607) 256-2277
Ithaca, NY 14853   Shirley F. Harper, Libn.

CORNELL UNIVERSITY - MATHEMATICS LIBRARY
White Hall   Phone: (607) 256-5076
Ithaca, NY 14853   Steven W. Rockey, Supv.

CORNELL UNIVERSITY - MUSIC LIBRARY
225 Lincoln Hall   Phone: (607) 256-4011
Ithaca, NY 14853   Lenore Coral, Music Libn.

CORNELL UNIVERSITY - PHYSICAL SCIENCES LIBRARY
Clark Hall   Phone: (607) 256-4016
Ithaca, NY 14853   Ellen Thomas, Libn.

CORNELL UNIVERSITY - PROGRAM ON PARTICIPATION AND LABOR-
    MANAGED SYSTEMS - DOCUMENTATION CENTER
490 Uris Hall   Phone: (607) 256-4070
Ithaca, NY 14853

CORNELL UNIVERSITY - RARE BOOKS DEPARTMENT
Olin Research Library   Phone: (607) 256-4211
Ithaca, NY 14853   Donald Eddy, Libn.

CORNELL UNIVERSITY - RESOURCE INFORMATION LABORATORY
Box 22, Roberts Hall   Phone: (607) 256-6520
Ithaca, NY 14853   Eugenia M. Barnaba, Mgr., Tech.Serv.

CORNELL UNIVERSITY - SCHOOL OF HOTEL ADMINISTRATION LIBRARY
Statler Hall   Phone: (607) 256-3673
Ithaca, NY 14853   Margaret J. Oaksford, Libn.

CORNELL UNIVERSITY - SHOALS MARINE LABORATORY - LIBRARY
G14 Stimson Hall   Phone: (607) 256-3717
Ithaca, NY 14853

CORNELL UNIVERSITY - SOUTHEAST ASIA PROGRAM - CORNELL MODERN
    INDONESIA PROJECT
102 West Ave.   Phone: (607) 256-4359
Ithaca, NY 14850   Audrey Kahin

CORNELL UNIVERSITY - WASON COLLECTION
Olin Library   Phone: (607) 256-4357
Ithaca, NY 14853   James H. Cole, Cur.

DEWITT HISTORICAL SOCIETY OF TOMPKINS COUNTY - ARCHIVE/
    LIBRARY/MUSEUM
116 N. Cayuga St.   Phone: (607) 273-8284
Ithaca, NY 14850   Margaret C. Hobbie, Dir.

HINCKLEY FOUNDATION MUSEUM - LIBRARY
410 E. Seneca St.   Phone: (607) 273-7053
Ithaca, NY 14850   Ellen Baker Wikotrom, Dir.

PALEONTOLOGICAL RESEARCH INSTITUTION - LIBRARY
1259 Trumansburg Rd.   Phone: (607) 273-6623
Ithaca, NY 14850   Peter R. Hoover, Dir.

THOMPSON (Boyce) INSTITUTE - LIBRARY
Cornell University
Tower Rd.   Phone: (607) 257-2030
Ithaca, NY 14853   Greta Colavito, Lib.Hd.

TOMPKINS COMMUNITY HOSPITAL - ROBERT BROAD MEDICAL LIBRARY
1285 Trumansburg Rd.   Phone: (607) 274-4407
Ithaca, NY 14850   Sally Van Idistine, Libn.

LEXINGTON SCHOOL FOR THE DEAF - LIBRARY MEDIA CENTER *
26-26 75th St.   Phone: (718) 899-8800
Jackson Heights, NY 11370   Marie-Ann Marchese, Lib.Coord.

CATHOLIC MEDICAL CENTER OF BROOKLYN & QUEENS, INC. - CENTRAL
    MEDICAL LIBRARY
88-25 153rd St.   Phone: (718) 657-6800
Jamaica, NY 11432   Sr. Regina Clare Woods, O.P., Coord./Med.Libs.

JAMAICA HOSPITAL - MEDICAL LIBRARY
89th Ave. & Van Wyck Expy.   Phone: (718) 657-1800
Jamaica, NY 11418   Carolyn Mansbach, Dir.

LONG ISLAND JEWISH-HILLSIDE MEDICAL CENTER - QUEENS HOSPITAL
    CENTER - HEALTH SCIENCE LIBRARY
82-68 164th St.   Phone: (718) 990-2795
Jamaica, NY 11432   Helen M. Pilikian, Chf.Med.Libn.

NEW YORK STATE SUPREME COURT - 11TH JUDICIAL DISTRICT - LAW
    LIBRARY
General Court House
88-11 Sutphin Blvd.   Phone: (718) 520-3140
Jamaica, NY 11435   Andrew J. Tschinkel, Prin. Law Libn.

PASSIONIST MONASTIC SEMINARY - LIBRARY
86-45 178th St.   Phone: (718) 739-6502
Jamaica, NY 11432   Br. James G. Johnson, C.P., Libn.

QUEENS BOROUGH PUBLIC LIBRARY - ART AND MUSIC DIVISION
89-11 Merrick Blvd.   Phone: (718) 990-0755
Jamaica, NY 11432   Dorothea Wu, Div.Hd.

QUEENS BOROUGH PUBLIC LIBRARY - HISTORY, TRAVEL & BIOGRAPHY
    DIVISION
89-11 Merrick Blvd.   Phone: (718) 990-0762
Jamaica, NY 11432   Deborah Hammer, Div.Hd.

QUEENS BOROUGH PUBLIC LIBRARY - LANGUAGE & LITERATURE DIVISION
89-11 Merrick Blvd.   Phone: (718) 990-0763
Jamaica, NY 11432   Inge M. Judd, Div.Hd.

QUEENS BOROUGH PUBLIC LIBRARY - LONG ISLAND DIVISION
89-11 Merrick Blvd.   Phone: (718) 990-0770
Jamaica, NY 11432   Nicholas Falco, Div.Hd.

QUEENS BOROUGH PUBLIC LIBRARY - SCIENCE & TECHNOLOGY DIVISION
89-11 Merrick Blvd.   Phone: (718) 990-0760
Jamaica, NY 11432   John D. Brady, Jr., Div.Hd.

QUEENS BOROUGH PUBLIC LIBRARY - SOCIAL SCIENCES DIVISION
89-11 Merrick Blvd.   Phone: (718) 990-0761
Jamaica, NY 11432   Nathan Shoengold, Div.Hd.

ST. JOHN'S UNIVERSITY - ARCHIVES
Grand Central & Utopia Pkwys.   Phone: (718) 990-6161
Jamaica, NY 11439   Rev. John E. Young, C.M., Archv.

ST. JOHN'S UNIVERSITY - ASIAN COLLECTION - LIBRARY
Grand Central & Utopia Pkwys.   Phone: (718) 990-6161
Jamaica, NY 11439   Mr. Hou Ran Ferng, Hd.Libn.

ST. JOHN'S UNIVERSITY - COLLEGE OF PHARMACY & ALLIED HEALTH
    PROFESSIONS - HEALTH EDUCATION RESOURCE CENTER
Grand Central & Utopia Pkwys.   Phone: (718) 990-6162
Jamaica, NY 11439   Mary A. Grant, Dir.

ST. JOHN'S UNIVERSITY - GOVERNMENT DOCUMENTS DEPARTMENT
Grand Central & Utopia Pkwys.   Phone: (718) 990-6161
Jamaica, NY 11439   Shu-fang Lin, Libn./Assoc.Prof.

ST. JOHN'S UNIVERSITY - INSTRUCTIONAL MATERIALS CENTER
Grand Central & Utopia Pkwys.   Phone: (718) 990-6161
Jamaica, NY 11439   Sharon Krauss, Libn./Asst.Prof.

ST. JOHN'S UNIVERSITY - LAW LIBRARY
Fromkes Hall
Grand Central & Utopia Pkwys.   Phone: (718) 990-6161
Jamaica, NY 11439   Ralph Monaco, Assoc. Law Libn.

ST. JOHN'S UNIVERSITY - LIBRARY AND INFORMATION SCIENCE LIBRARY
Grand Central & Utopia Pkwys.　　　　　　Phone: (718) 990-6161
Jamaica, NY 11439　　　　　　Szilvia Szmuk, Libn./Assoc.Prof.

ST. JOHN'S UNIVERSITY - SPECIAL COLLECTIONS
Grand Central & Utopia Pkwys.　　　　　　Phone: (718) 990-6161
Jamaica, NY 11439　　　　　　Szilvia E. Szmuk, Spec.Coll.Libn.

U.S. FEDERAL AVIATION ADMINISTRATION - EASTERN REGION LIBRARY
Federal Bldg.
J.F. Kennedy Intl. Airport　　　　　　Phone: (718) 995-3325
Jamaica, NY 11430　　　　　　Shirley Sheard, Libn.

FENTON HISTORICAL SOCIETY - LIBRARY
67 Washington St.　　　　　　Phone: (716) 661-2296
Jamestown, NY 14701　　　　　　Mark E. Allnatt, Cur./Mss.

TRW, INC. - BEARINGS DIVISION - RESEARCH & DEVELOPMENT
　　TECHNICAL LIBRARY
402 Chandler St.　　　　　　Phone: (716) 661-2894
Jamestown, NY 14701　　Harold E. Munson, Supv., Project Engr.

UNITED HEALTH SERVICES/WILSON HOSPITAL - LEARNING RESOURCES
　　DEPARTMENT
33-57 Harrison St.　　　　　　Phone: (607) 773-6030
Johnson City, NY 13790　　　　　　Shirley Edsall, Mgr.

JOHNSTOWN HISTORICAL SOCIETY - LIBRARY REFERENCE CENTER
17 N. William St.　　　　　　Phone: (518) 762-7076
Johnstown, NY 12095　　　　　　Dr. Charles J. Noxon, Cur.

AUTHENTICATED NEWS INTERNATIONAL - PHOTO LIBRARY
29 Katohah Ave.　　　　　　Phone: (914) 232-7726
Katonah, NY 10536　　　　　　Sidney Polinsky, Mng.Ed.

GARIBALDI AND MEUCCI MEMORIAL MUSEUM - LIBRARY OF THE ITALIAN
　　RISORGIMENTO
John Jay Homestead, Box AH　　　　　　Phone: (914) 232-3667
Katonah, NY 10536　　　　Lino S. Lipinsky de Orlov, Dir.

JAY (John) HOMESTEAD - LIBRARY
Box A.H.　　　　　　Phone: (914) 232-5651
Katonah, NY 10536　　　　　　Linda M. Connelly, Mgr.

KENMORE MERCY HOSPITAL - HEALTH SCIENCES RESOURCE CENTER
2950 Elmwood Ave.　　　　　　Phone: (716) 879-6253
Kenmore, NY 14217　　　　　　Grace C. Loree, Libn.

SISTERS OF ST. MARY OF NAMUR - MOUNT ST. MARY RESEARCH CENTER
3756 Delaware Ave.　　　　　　Phone: (716) 875-4705
Kenmore, NY 14217　　　Sr. M. Xavier Hefner, Archv./Libn.

NEW YORK STATE SUPREME COURT - 11TH JUDICIAL DISTRICT - LAW
　　LIBRARY
Supreme Court Bldg.
125-01 Queens Blvd.　　　　　　Phone: (718) 520-3541
Kew Gardens, NY 11415　　　　　　Andrew Tschinkel, Libn.

COLUMBIA COUNTY HISTORICAL SOCIETY - HOUSE OF HISTORY LIBRARY
　　　　　　Phone: (518) 758-9265
Kinderhook, NY 12106　　　　　　Ruth Piwonka, Exec.Dir.

KINGS PARK PSYCHIATRIC CENTER - LIBRARY
Box A　　　　　　Phone: (516) 544-2671
Kings Park, NY 11754　　　　James W. Macinick, Sr.Libn.

U.S. MARITIME ADMINISTRATION - NATL. MARITIME RESEARCH CENTER
　　- STUDY CENTER
　　　　　　Phone: (516) 482-8200
Kings Point, NY 11024　　　　Rayma Feldman, Sr.Info.Spec.

U.S. MERCHANT MARINE ACADEMY - SCHUYLER OTIS BLAND MEMORIAL
　　LIBRARY
　　　　　　Phone: (516) 482-8200
Kings Point, NY 11024　　　　　　George J. Billy, Libn.

IBM CORPORATION - DSD SITE LIBRARY *
Dept. 65P/840
Neighborhood Rd.　　　　　　Phone: (914) 383-3574
Kingston, NY 12401　　　　Frank von Rekowski, Mgr.

KINGSTON HOSPITAL - LIBRARY
396 Broadway　　　　　　Phone: (914) 331-3131
Kingston, NY 12401　　　　　　Linda Stopard, Libn.

NEW YORK STATE SUPREME COURT - 3RD JUDICIAL DISTRICT - LAW
　　LIBRARY
Court House
Kingston, NY 12401　　　　　　Harriett Straus, Libn.

SENATE HOUSE STATE HISTORIC SITE - LIBRARY & ARCHIVES
296 Fair St.　　　　　　Phone: (914) 338-2786
Kingston, NY 12401　　　Leigh R. Jones, Historic Site Mgr.

ULSTER COUNTY PLANNING BOARD - LIBRARY
244 Fair St.
Box 1800　　　　　　Phone: (914) 331-9300
Kingston, NY 12401　　　　　　Dennis Doyle, Planner

OUR LADY OF VICTORY HOSPITAL - HOSPITAL LIBRARY
55 Melroy at Ridge Rd.　　　　　　Phone: (716) 825-8000
Lackawanna, NY 14218　　　　　　Ann Hassett, Lib.Ck.

NEW YORK STATE SUPREME COURT - 4TH JUDICIAL DISTRICT - LAW
　　LIBRARY
Warren County Municipal Ctr.　　　　　　Phone: (518) 761-6442
Lake George, NY 12845　　　James D. Summa, Law Lib.Ck.

JONES (W. Alton) CELL SCIENCE CENTER - GEORGE AND MARGARET GEY
　　LIBRARY
Old Barn Rd.　　　　　　Phone: (518) 523-2427
Lake Placid, NY 12946　　　　A. Kathleen Bonham, Libn.

LAKE PLACID ASSOCIATION FOR MUSIC, DRAMA & ART - NETTIE MARIE
　　JONES FINE ARTS LIBRARY
Saranac Ave. at Fawn Ridge
Lake Placid, NY 12946

MEDICAL SOCIETY OF THE STATE OF NEW YORK - ALBION O. BERNSTEIN
　　LIBRARY
420 Lakeville Rd.　　　　　　Phone: (516) 488-6100
Lake Success, NY 11042　　　　　　Ella Abney, Libn.

PRC SPEAS - TECHNICAL LIBRARY *
3003 New Hyde Park Rd.　　　　　　Phone: (516) 488-6930
Lake Success, NY 11042　　　　Maria D. Ferri, Tech.Libn.

CAPITAL DISTRICT LIBRARY COUNCIL FOR REFERENCE AND RESEARCH
　　RESOURCES - BIBLIOGRAPHIC CENTER
91 Fiddlers Lane　　　　　　Phone: (518) 785-0798
Latham, NY 12110　　　Charles D. Custer, Exec.Dir.

MECHANICAL TECHNOLOGY INC. - TECHNICAL INFORMATION SERVICES
968 Albany-Shaker Rd.　　　　　　Phone: (518) 785-2265
Latham, NY 12110　　　　　　Terri Sierra, Adm.

TEMPLE ISRAEL - LIBRARY
140 Central Ave.　　　　　　Phone: (516) 239-1140
Lawrence, NY 11559　　　　　　Donna Z. Lifland, Libn.

LE ROY HISTORICAL SOCIETY - LIBRARY
23 E. Main St.
Box 176　　　　　　Phone: (716) 768-7433
Le Roy, NY 14482　　　Wilfred Vasile, Village Hist.

CATTARAUGUS COUNTY MEMORIAL AND HISTORICAL MUSEUM - LIBRARY
Court St.　　　　　　Phone: (716) 938-9111
Little Valley, NY 14755　　　　　　Lorna Spencer, Cur.

SCHUMANN MEMORIAL FOUNDATION, INC. - LIBRARY
2904 E. Lake Rd.　　　　　　Phone: (716) 346-2745
Livonia, NY 14487　　　　June M. Dickinson, Pres.

NIAGARA COUNTY HISTORICAL SOCIETY - LIBRARY AND ARCHIVES
215 Niagara St.　　　　　　Phone: (716) 434-7433
Lockport, NY 14094　　　　　　Jan J. Losi, Cur.

TEMPLE EMANU-EL - LIBRARY
455 Neptune Blvd.　　　　　　Phone: (516) 431-4060
Long Beach, NY 11561　　　　　　Beth Moscowitz, Libn.

POLYTECHNIC INSTITUTE OF NEW YORK - LONG ISLAND CENTER LIBRARY
Phone: (516) 694-5500
Long Island, NY 11735   Lorraine Schein, Br.Libn.

NEW YORK STATE SUPREME COURT - 11TH JUDICIAL DISTRICT - LAW
LIBRARY *
Supreme Court Bldg.
25-10 Court Sq.   Phone: (718) 520-3921
Long Island City, NY 11101

WAYNE COUNTY HISTORICAL SOCIETY MUSEUM - LIBRARY
21 Butternut St.   Phone: (315) 946-4943
Lyons, NY 14489   Marjory Allen Perez, County Hist.

MOBIL CHEMICAL COMPANY - PLASTICS DIVISION - INFORMATION
CENTER
Technical Center   Phone: (315) 986-6375
Macedon, NY 14502   Violanda O. Burns, Info.Anl.

HISTORICAL SOCIETY OF THE TOWN OF NORTH HEMPSTEAD - LIBRARY *
220 Plandome Rd.   Phone: (516) 627-0590
Manhasset, NY 11030   F.J. Pistone, Pres.

MANHASSET PUBLIC LIBRARY - SPECIAL COLLECTIONS
30 Onderdonk Ave.   Phone: (516) 627-2300
Manhasset, NY 11030   Sylvia Levin, Dir.

NORTH SHORE UNIVERSITY HOSPITAL - DANIEL CARROLL PAYSON
MEDICAL LIBRARY
Community Dr.   Phone: (516) 562-4324
Manhasset, NY 11030   Elsie Wilensky, Med.Libn.

NORTH SHORE UNIVERSITY HOSPITAL - OFFICE OF HEALTH EDUC. - WE
CARE ABOUT SPECIAL CHILDREN MOBIL RESOURCE LIB.
400 Community Dr.   Phone: (516) 562-3045
Manhasset, NY 11030   Linda Haberman, Health Educator

MARYKNOLL FATHERS - PHOTO LIBRARY
Pines Bridge Rd.   Phone: (914) 941-7590
Maryknoll, NY 10545   Penny Ann Sandoval, Photo Libn.

MARYKNOLL SEMINARY - LIBRARY
Maryknoll, P.O.   Phone: (914) 941-7590
Maryknoll, NY 10545   Rev. Arthur E. Brown, M.M., Libn.

CHAUTAUQUA COUNTY LAW LIBRARY
Gerace Office Bldg.   Phone: (716) 753-4247
Mayville, NY 14757   Peggy J. Cross

EATON CORPORATION - AIL DIVISION - RESEARCH LIBRARY
Walt Whitman Rd.   Phone: (516) 595-4400
Melville, NY 11747   Laurel D. Meyerhoff, Libn.

NEWSDAY, INC. - LIBRARY
235 Pinelawn Rd.   Phone: (516) 454-2335
Melville, NY 11747   Andrew V. Ippolito, Dir. of Lib. & Res.

HORTON MEMORIAL HOSPITAL - MEDICAL LIBRARY
60 Prospect Ave.   Phone: (914) 342-5561
Middletown, NY 10940   Laura Leese, Med.Libn.

MIDDLETOWN PSYCHIATRIC CENTER - MEDICAL LIBRARY
141 Monhagen Ave.
Box 1453   Phone: (914) 342-5511
Middletown, NY 10940   Frank C. Appell, Jr., Asst.Libn.

INSTITUTE OF ECOSYSTEM STUDIES - LIBRARY
Cary Arboretum
New York Botanical Garden
Box AB   Phone: (914) 677-5343
Millbrook, NY 12545   Charles R. Long, Adm.Libn.

NASSAU COUNTY DEPARTMENT OF HEALTH - OFFICE OF PUBLIC HEALTH -
LIBRARY
240 Old Country Rd., Rm. 613   Phone: (516) 535-3368
Mineola, NY 11501   Irena Robkoff, Lib.Asst.

NASSAU COUNTY PLANNING COMMISSION - LIBRARY
222 Willis Ave.   Phone: (516) 535-2244
Mineola, NY 11501   Robert Gaiser, Plan.

NASSAU COUNTY SUPREME COURT - LAW LIBRARY
100 Supreme Court Dr.   Phone: (516) 535-3883
Mineola, NY 11501   James J. Lodato, Prin. Law Libn.

NASSAU HOSPITAL - BENJAMIN WHITE SEAMAN MEDICAL LIBRARY
259 First St.   Phone: (516) 663-2280
Mineola, NY 11501   Virginia I. Cook, Med.Libn.

NEW YORK STATE SUPREME COURT - 3RD JUDICIAL DISTRICT -
HAMILTON ODELL LIBRARY
Sullivan County Court House
Monticello, NY 12701   Edith Schop, Libn.

NEW YORK STATE DEPARTMENT OF STATE - FIRE ACADEMY LIBRARY
600 College Ave.
Box 811   Phone: (607) 535-7136
Montour Falls, NY 14865   Diana Zell, Asst.Libn.

SCHUYLER COUNTY HISTORICAL SOCIETY - LEE SCHOOL MUSEUM
Rte. 14 South
Box 651   Phone: (607) 535-9741
Montour Falls, NY 14865   Alice M. Wixson, Dir.

SCHUYLER COUNTY HISTORICAL SOCIETY - OLD BRICK TAVERN MUSEUM
- RESEARCH LIBRARY
108 N. Catharine St.
Box 651   Phone: (607) 535-9741
Montour Falls, NY 14865   Alice M. Wixson, Dir.

U.S. VETERANS ADMINISTRATION (NY-Montrose) - HOSPITAL LIBRARY
Phone: (914) 737-4400
Montrose, NY 10548   Eileen J. Liberty, Chf., Lib.Serv.

SUNY - AGRICULTURAL AND TECHNICAL COLLEGE AT MORRISVILLE -
LIBRARY
Phone: (315) 684-7055
Morrisville, NY 13408   Michael Gieryic, Hd.Libn.

NORTHERN WESTCHESTER HOSPITAL CENTER - HEALTH SCIENCES
LIBRARY
Phone: (914) 666-1259
Mount Kisco, NY 10549   Nona C. Willoughby, Hd.Libn.

CONSUMERS UNION OF UNITED STATES, INC. - LIBRARY
256 Washington St.   Phone: (914) 664-6400
Mount Vernon, NY 10553   Sara Ingram, Mgr.

MOUNT VERNON HOSPITAL - LIBRARY AND INFORMATION SERVICES
12 N. Seventh Ave.
Mount Vernon, NY 10550   Mary L. Coan, Dir.

AUSTEN (Jane) SOCIETY OF NORTH AMERICA - ARCHIVES
Box 621   Phone: (914) 425-9548
Nanuet, NY 10954   Joseph J. Costa, Pres.

HISTORICAL SOCIETY OF ROCKLAND COUNTY - LIBRARY *
20 Zukor Rd.   Phone: (914) 634-9629
New City, NY 10956

CENTRAL NEW YORK ACADEMY OF MEDICINE - LIBRARY
210 Clinton St.   Phone: (315) 735-2204
New Hartford, NY 13413   Mildred D. Timmerman, Libn.

SPECIAL METALS CORPORATION - TECHNICAL LIBRARY/INFORMATION
CENTER
Middle Settlement Rd.   Phone: (315) 798-2936
New Hartford, NY 13413   Elizabeth A. Lazore, Libn.

UTICA MUTUAL INSURANCE COMPANY - RESOURCE CENTER
180 Genesee St.   Phone: (315) 735-3321
New Hartford, NY 13413   Therese C. Kinney, Rsrcs.Coord.

LONG ISLAND JEWISH-HILLSIDE MEDICAL CENTER - HEALTH SCIENCES
LIBRARY
270-05 76th Ave.   Phone: (212) 470-2673
New Hyde Park, NY 11042   Mark-Allen Taylor, Dir., Lib.Serv.

GEBBIE PRESS, INC. - HOUSE MAGAZINE LIBRARY *
Phone: (914) 255-7560
New Paltz, NY 12561   A. Gebbie, Pres.

HUGUENOT HISTORICAL SOCIETY, NEW PALTZ - LIBRARY
18 Brodhead Ave.
Box 339   Phone: (914) 255-1660
New Paltz, NY 12561   Kenneth E. Hasbrouck, Dir.

HUGUENOT-THOMAS PAINE HISTORICAL ASSOCIATION OF NEW
    ROCHELLE - HUFELAND MEMORIAL LIBRARY
893 North Ave.   Phone: (914) 632-5376
New Rochelle, NY 10804   Ruth M. Phillips, Chm.

MEDICAL LETTER - LIBRARY
56 Harrison St.   Phone: (914) 235-0500
New Rochelle, NY 10801   Donna Goodstein, Libn.

NEW ROCHELLE HOSPITAL MEDICAL CENTER - J. MARSHALL PERLEY
    HEALTH SCIENCE LIBRARY
Iselin Hall   Phone: (914) 632-5000
New Rochelle, NY 10802   Helene D. Lambert, Med.Libn.

ACADEMY FOR EDUCATIONAL DEVELOPMENT, INC. - EDUCATIONAL
    FACILITIES LABORATORIES DIVISION - LIBRARY *
680 Fifth Ave.   Phone: (212) 397-0040
New York, NY 10019   S. De Camp, Prog.Dir.

ACKERMAN INSTITUTE FOR FAMILY THERAPY, INC. - LIBRARY *
149 E. 78th St.   Phone: (212) 879-4900
New York, NY 10021   Ruth Perl

ACME, INC. - THE ASSOCIATION OF MANAGEMENT CONSULTING FIRMS -
    LIBRARY
230 Park Ave.   Phone: (212) 697-9693
New York, NY 10169   Joseph J. Brady, Pres.

ADAMS & RINEHART, INC. - LIBRARY
708 Third Ave.   Phone: (212) 557-0100
New York, NY 10022   Joan M. Reicherter, Libn.

ADVERTISING RESEARCH FOUNDATION - LIBRARY
3 E. 54th St.   Phone: (212) 751-5656
New York, NY 10022   Elisabeth R. Proudfit, Mgr., Info.Ctr.

ADVISORY GROUP ON ELECTRON DEVICES - LIBRARY *
201 Varick St., 11th Fl.   Phone: (212) 620-3374
New York, NY 10014   David Slater, Sec.

AESTHETIC REALISM FOUNDATION, INC. - LIBRARY
141 Greene St.   Phone: (212) 777-4490
New York, NY 10012   Margot Carpenter, Cons.

AFRICAN-AMERICAN INSTITUTE - AFRICA POLICY INFORMATION CENTER
833 United Nations Plaza   Phone: (212) 949-5730
New York, NY 10017   Jason Zweig

AIR FRANCE - PUBLIC RELATIONS DEPARTMENT - LIBRARY
1350 Ave. of the Americas, 16th Fl.   Phone: (212) 841-7300
New York, NY 10019   Gail Muntner, Stud. & Doc.Adm.

ALLIANCE OF RESIDENT THEATRES/NEW YORK - LIBRARY
325 Spring St., Rm. 315   Phone: (212) 989-5257
New York, NY 10013   Kate Busch, Dir., Member Serv.

ALLY AND GARGANO, INC. - INFORMATION CENTER
805 3rd Ave.   Phone: (212) 688-5300
New York, NY 10022   Marsha Cohen, Mgr., Info.Serv.

AMALGAMATED CLOTHING & TEXTILE WORKERS UNION, AFL-CIO -
    RESEARCH DEPARTMENT LIBRARY
15 Union Sq.   Phone: (212) 255-7800
New York, NY 10003

AMATEUR ASTRONOMERS ASSOCIATION - JANE H. DOUGLAS MEMORIAL
    LIBRARY
1010 Park Ave.   Phone: (212) 535-2922
New York, NY 10028   John Pazmino, Libn.

AMERICAN ACADEMY OF DRAMATIC ARTS - LIBRARY
120 Madison Ave.   Phone: (212) 686-9244
New York, NY 10016   John Barrow, Libn.

AMERICAN ACADEMY AND INSTITUTE OF ARTS AND LETTERS - LIBRARY
633 W. 155th St.   Phone: (212) 368-5900
New York, NY 10032   Casindania P. Eaton, Libn.

AMERICAN ALPINE CLUB - LIBRARY
113 E. 90th St.   Phone: (212) 722-1628
New York, NY 10128   Margo McKee, Chm., Lib.Comm.

AMERICAN ARBITRATION ASSOCIATION - EASTMAN ARBITRATION
    LIBRARY
140 W. 51st St.   Phone: (212) 484-4127
New York, NY 10020   Laura Ferris Brown, Chf.Libn.

AMERICAN ASSOCIATION OF ADVERTISING AGENCIES - MEMBER
    INFORMATION SERVICE
666 3rd Ave.   Phone: (212) 682-2500
New York, NY 10017   Marilyn M. Bockman, V.P.

AMERICAN ASSOCIATION FOR THE INTERNATIONAL COMMISSION OF
    JURISTS, INC. - LIBRARY
777 United Nations Plaza   Phone: (212) 972-0883
New York, NY 10017

AMERICAN BANKER, INC. - LIBRARY
One State St. Plaza   Phone: (212) 943-4844
New York, NY 10004   Patricia Y. Bluestein, Hd.Libn.

AMERICAN BIBLE SOCIETY - LIBRARY
1865 Broadway   Phone: (212) 581-7400
New York, NY 10023-9980   Dr. Boyd L. Daniels, Coord. of Lib.Serv.

AMERICAN BROADCASTING COMPANIES, INC. - ABC NEWS INFORMATION
    CENTER
1926 Broadway   Phone: (212) 887-3796
New York, NY 10023   Madeline Cohen, Mgr., Lib.Serv.

AMERICAN CANCER SOCIETY - AUDIO VISUAL LIBRARIES
4 W. 35th St.
New York, NY 10001   Stefan Bodnariuk, Supv. Film Ed.

AMERICAN CANCER SOCIETY - MEDICAL LIBRARY
4 W. 35th St.   Phone: (212) 736-3030
New York, NY 10001   Dr. Sourya Henderson, Med.Libn.

AMERICAN CIVIL LIBERTIES UNION - LIBRARY/ARCHIVES
132 W. 43rd St.   Phone: (212) 944-9800
New York, NY 10036   Barbara J. Eichman, Libn.

AMERICAN COUNCIL FOR THE ARTS - LIBRARY
570 Seventh Ave.   Phone: (212) 354-6655
New York, NY 10018   Robert Porter, Mgr., Info.Serv.

AMERICAN COUNCIL FOR NATIONALITIES SERVICE - LIBRARY AND
    INFORMATION CENTER
20 W. 40th St.   Phone: (212) 398-9142
New York, NY 10018   Wells C. Klein, Exec.Dir.

AMERICAN COUNCIL OF VOLUNTARY AGENCIES FOR FOREIGN SERVICE,
    INC. - TECH. ASSISTANCE INFO. CLEARING HOUSE
200 Park Ave. S., 11th Fl.   Phone: (212) 777-8210
New York, NY 10003   Leon O. Marion, Exec.Dir.

AMERICAN CRAFT COUNCIL - LIBRARY
45 W. 45th St.   Phone: (212) 869-9423
New York, NY 10036   Joanne Polster, Libn.

AMERICAN DRUGGIST MAGAZINE LIBRARY
224 W. 57th St.
New York, NY 10019

AMERICAN ELECTRIC POWER SERVICE CORP. - LIBRARY †
2 Broadway   Phone: (212) 440-9000
New York, NY 10004   Janet T. Bulger, Act.Libn.

AMERICAN EXPRESS COMPANY - CARD INFORMATION CENTER *
American Express Plaza
New York, NY 10004
Phone: (212) 323-4146
Joan B. Lurye, Mgr.

AMERICAN EXPRESS COMPANY - CORPORATE SYSTEMS &
TELECOMMUNICATIONS INFORMATION CENTER *
125 Broad St., 11th Fl.
New York, NY 10004
Phone: (212) 323-4063
Stephanie Morrell, Corp.Tech.Libn.

AMERICAN EXPRESS COMPANY - PSD TECHNICAL INFORMATION CENTER
125 Broad St., 10th Fl.
New York, NY 10004
Phone: (212) 323-4182
Sarika Mahant, Supv., Info.Sys.Adm.

AMERICAN FEDERATION OF STATE, COUNTY AND MUNICIPAL
EMPLOYEES, AFL-CIO (AFSCME) - DC37 RESEARCH LIBRARY
140 Park Place
New York, NY 10007
Phone: (212) 766-1032
Evelyn Seinfeld, Libn.

AMERICAN FOUNDATION FOR THE BLIND - HELEN KELLER ARCHIVES
15 W. 16th St.
New York, NY 10011
Phone: (212) 620-2157
Margeurite L. Levine, Archv.

AMERICAN FOUNDATION FOR THE BLIND - M.C. MIGEL MEMORIAL
LIBRARY
15 W. 16th St.
New York, NY 10011
Phone: (212) 620-2161
Judith M. Kaplan, Hd.Libn.

AMERICAN HERITAGE PUBLISHING COMPANY, INC. - LIBRARY
10 Rockefeller Plaza
New York, NY 10020
Phone: (212) 399-8931
Patrick Bunyan, Libn.

AMERICAN HUNGARIAN LIBRARY AND HISTORICAL SOCIETY
213 E. 82nd St.
New York, NY 10028
Phone: (212) 744-5298
Paul E. Vesenyi, Pres.

AMERICAN INSTITUTE OF AERONAUTICS AND ASTRONAUTICS -
TECHNICAL INFORMATION SERVICE
555 W. 57th St.
New York, NY 10019
Patricia Marshall, Dir., Lib.Rsrcs.

AMERICAN INSTITUTE OF AERONAUTICS AND ASTRONAUTICS -
TECHNICAL INFORMATION SERVICE
555 W. 57th St.
New York, NY 10019
Phone: (212) 247-6500
B. Lawrence, Adm.

AMERICAN INSTITUTE OF CERTIFIED PUBLIC ACCOUNTANTS - LIBRARY
SERVICES
1211 Ave. of the Americas
New York, NY 10036-8775
Phone: (800) 223-4155
Karen Hegge Simmons, Chf.Libn.

AMERICAN INSTITUTE FOR MARXIST STUDIES - LIBRARY
85 E. 4th St.
New York, NY 10003
Phone: (212) 982-6751
Henry Klein, Libn.

AMERICAN INSTITUTE OF PHYSICS - CENTER FOR HISTORY OF PHYSICS -
NIELS BOHR LIBRARY
335 E. 45th St.
New York, NY 10017-3483
Phone: (212) 661-9404
John C. Aubry, Archv./Libn.

AMERICAN INSURANCE ASSOCIATION - LAW LIBRARY
85 John St.
New York, NY 10038
Phone: (212) 433-4400
Lorna L. Beasley, Libn.

AMERICAN INSURANCE SERVICES GROUP, INC. - ENGINEERING & SAFETY
DEPARTMENT LIBRARY
85 John St.
New York, NY 10038
Phone: (212) 669-0478
Donna Handville, Libn.

AMERICAN IRISH HISTORICAL SOCIETY - LIBRARY
991 Fifth Ave.
New York, NY 10028
Phone: (212) 288-2263
Dr. William Griffin, Libn./Archv.

AMERICAN JEWISH COMMITTEE - BLAUSTEIN LIBRARY
165 E. 56th St.
New York, NY 10022
Phone: (212) 751-4000
Cyma M. Horowitz, Lib.Dir.

AMERICAN JEWISH COMMITTEE - WILLIAM E. WIENER ORAL HISTORY
LIBRARY
165 E. 56th St.
New York, NY 10022
Phone: (212) 751-4000
Irma Kopp Krents, Dir.

AMERICAN JEWISH CONGRESS - CHARLES AND BERTIE G. SCHWARTZ
JUDAICA READING ROOM & LIBRARY
Martin Steinberg Ctr. for Jewish Artists
15 E. 84th St.
New York, NY 10028

AMERICAN JEWISH CONGRESS-COMMISSION ON LAW AND SOCIAL
ACTION - SHAD POLIER MEMORIAL LIBRARY
15 E. 84th St.
New York, NY 10028
Phone: (212) 879-4500
Laraine C. Spector, Libn.

AMERICAN JEWISH JOINT DISTRIBUTION COMMITTEE - ARCHIVES
60 E. 42nd St., Suite 1914
New York, NY 10645
Phone: (212) 687-6200
Rose Klepfisz, Dir., Archv.

AMERICAN JEWISH JOINT DISTRIBUTION COMMITTEE - LIBRARY
60 E. 42nd St., Suite 1914
New York, NY 10645
Phone: (212) 687-6200
Micha F. Oppenheim, Libn.

AMERICAN JOURNAL OF NURSING COMPANY - SOPHIA F. PALMER LIBRARY
555 W. 57th St.
New York, NY 10019
Phone: (212) 582-8820
Frederick W. Pattison, Libn.

AMERICAN KENNEL CLUB - LIBRARY
51 Madison Ave.
New York, NY 10010
Phone: (212) 696-8245
Roberta A. Vesley, Lib.Dir.

AMERICAN MANAGEMENT ASSOCIATIONS - LIBRARY
135 W. 50th St.
New York, NY 10020
Phone: (212) 903-8182
Claire A. Lambkin, Chf.Libn.

AMERICAN MERCHANT MARINE LIBRARY ASSOCIATION - PUBLIC LIBRARY
OF THE HIGH SEAS
One World Trade Center, Suite 2601
New York, NY 10048
Phone: (212) 775-1038
Sally-Ann Coash, Dir.

AMERICAN MIME, INC. - LIBRARY
61 4th Ave.
New York, NY 10003
Phone: (212) 677-9276
Paul J. Curtis, Dir.

AMERICAN MUSEUM OF NATURAL HISTORY - DEPARTMENT OF
ICHTHYOLOGY - DEAN MEMORIAL LIBRARY
Central Park W. at 79th St.
New York, NY 10024
Phone: (212) 873-1300
Dr. Gareth Nelson, Cur.

AMERICAN MUSEUM OF NATURAL HISTORY - DEPARTMENT OF LIBRARY
SERVICES
Central Park W. at 79th St.
New York, NY 10024
Phone: (212) 873-1300
Nina J. Root, Chairperson

AMERICAN MUSEUM OF NATURAL HISTORY - HAYDEN PLANETARIUM -
RICHARD S. PERKIN LIBRARY
Central Park W. at 81st St.
New York, NY 10024
Phone: (212) 873-1300
Sandra Kitt, Libn.

AMERICAN MUSEUM OF NATURAL HISTORY - OSBORN LIBRARY OF
VERTEBRATE PALEONTOLOGY
Central Park W. at 79th St.
New York, NY 10024
Phone: (212) 873-1300
Charlotte Holton, Libn.

AMERICAN MUSIC CENTER - LIBRARY
250 W. 54th St., Rm. 300
New York, NY 10019
Phone: (212) 265-8190
Eero Richmond, Hd.Libn.

AMERICAN NUMISMATIC SOCIETY - LIBRARY
Broadway at 155th St.
New York, NY 10032
Phone: (212) 234-3130
Francis D. Campbell, Jr., Libn.

AMERICAN PAPER INSTITUTE - LIBRARY
260 Madison Ave.
New York, NY 10016
Phone: (212) 340-0612
Miriam A. Meehan, Libn.

AMERICAN-SCANDINAVIAN FOUNDATION - WILLIAM HENRY SCHOFIELD
MEMORIAL LIBRARY
127 E. 73rd St.
New York, NY 10021

AMERICAN-SCOTTISH FOUNDATION, INC. - SCOTTISH RESEARCH
　LIBRARY
174 E. 74th St.
Lenox Hill Sta., Box 537　　　　　　　Phone: (212) 249-5556
New York, NY 10021　　　　Lady Malcolm Douglas-Hamilton, Pres.

AMERICAN SOCIETY OF CIVIL ENGINEERS - INFORMATION SERVICES
345 E. 47th St.　　　　　　　　　　Phone: (212) 705-7520
New York, NY 10017　　　　Melanie G. Edwards, Mgr., Ref.Pubns.

AMERICAN SOCIETY FOR PSYCHICAL RESEARCH - LIBRARY
5 W. 73rd St.　　　　　　　　　　Phone: (212) 799-5050
New York, NY 10023　　　　　　Laura F. Knipe, Exec.Sec.

AMERICAN STANDARDS TESTING BUREAU, INC. - SAM TOUR LIBRARY
40 Water St.　　　　　　　　　　Phone: (212) 943-3157
New York, NY 10004　　　　　　　Mr. C. Chavis, Libn.

AMERICAN STOCK EXCHANGE - MARTIN J. KEENA MEMORIAL LIBRARY
86 Trinity Pl.　　　　　　　　　　Phone: (212) 306-1290
New York, NY 10006　　　　　　Margie A. Balogh, Supv.

ANALYTICAL PSYCHOLOGY CLUB OF NEW YORK - KRISTINE MANN
　LIBRARY
28 E. 39th St.　　　　　　　　　　Phone: (212) 697-7877
New York, NY 10016　　　　　　Peggy Brooks, Lib.Chm.

ANCHOR FOUNDATION - LIBRARY OF SOCIAL HISTORY
410 West St.　　　　　　　　　　Phone: (212) 255-1767
New York, NY 10014　　　　　　　Reba Hausen, Dir.

ANIMAL LIBERATION, INC. - LIBRARY
319 W. 74th St.　　　　　　　　　Phone: (212) 874-1792
New York, NY 10023　　　　　　　Dudley Giehl, Pres.

ANIMAL MEDICAL CENTER - LIBRARY
510 E. 62nd St.　　　　　　　　　Phone: (212) 838-8100
New York, NY 10021　　　　A. Christine MacMurray, Ed./Libn.

ANTHOLOGY FILM ARCHIVES - LIBRARY
491 Broadway　　　　　　　　　　Phone: (212) 226-0010
New York, NY 10012

ANTI-DEFAMATION LEAGUE OF B'NAI B'RITH - JACOB ALSON MEMORIAL
　LIBRARY
823 United Nations Plaza　　　　　　Phone: (212) 689-7400
New York, NY 10017　　　　　　Florence Lummer, Libn.

ARCHIVES OF AMERICAN ART/SMITHSONIAN INSTITUTION - NATIONAL
　HEADQUARTERS
41 E. 65th St.　　　　　　　　　　Phone: (212) 826-5722
New York, NY 10021　　　　　　Richard N. Murray, Dir.

ARGUS ARCHIVES, INC.
228 E. 49th St.　　　　　　　　　Phone: (212) 355-6140
New York, NY 10017　　　　　Julie Van Ness, Res.Assoc.

ARGUS RESEARCH CORPORATION - LIBRARY
42 Broadway　　　　　　　　　　Phone: (212) 425-7500
New York, NY 10004　　　　　　Laurie Wiehle, Libn.

ARICA INSTITUTE, INC. - LIBRARY AND ARCHIVES
235 Park Ave., S.
New York, NY 10003　　　　David J. Johnson, Libn./Archv.

ARNHOLD AND S. BLEICHROEDER, INC. - LIBRARY
30 Broad St.　　　　　　　　　　Phone: (212) 943-9200
New York, NY 10004　　　　　　David E. Genna, Libn.

ART INFORMATION CENTER, INC.
280 Broadway, Suite 412　　　　　　Phone: (212) 725-0335
New York, NY 10007　　　　　　Dan R. Concholar, Dir.

ART STUDENTS LEAGUE OF NEW YORK - LIBRARY
215 W. 57th St.　　　　　　　　　Phone: (212) 247-4510
New York, NY 10019　　　　　　R.A. Florio, Exec.Dir.

ARTHUR ANDERSEN & CO. - LIBRARY †
1345 Ave. of the Americas　　　　　Phone: (212) 956-2815
New York, NY 10019　　　　　　Louise Wagner, Libn.

ARTHUR YOUNG & COMPANY - LIBRARY
277 Park Ave.　　　　　　　　　　Phone: (212) 407-1975
New York, NY 10172　　　　　　Jeanne F. Mellon, Libn.

ARTISTS SPACE - COMMITTEE FOR THE VISUAL ARTS - UNAFFILIATED
　ARTISTS FILE
105 Hudson St.　　　　　　　　　Phone: (212) 226-3970
New York, NY 10013　　　　　　Linda Shearer, Exec.Dir.

ASSOCIATED PRESS - NEWSPHOTO LIBRARY
50 Rockefeller Plaza　　　　　　　Phone: (212) 621-1913
New York, NY 10020　　　　　　Joan A. Kearney, Dir.

ASSOCIATION OF AMERICAN PUBLISHERS - STEPHEN GREENE MEMORIAL
　LIBRARY AND INFORMATION CENTER
One Park Ave.　　　　　　　　　　Phone: (212) 689-8920
New York, NY 10016　　　　　　Sandra Math, Libn.

ASSOCIATION OF THE BAR OF THE CITY OF NEW YORK - LIBRARY *
42 W. 44th St.　　　　　　　　　　Phone: (212) 840-3550
New York, NY 10036　　　　　　Anthony P. Grech, Libn.

ASSOCIATION OF JUNIOR LEAGUES, INC. - RESOURCE CENTER
825 Third Ave.　　　　　　　　　　Phone: (212) 355-4380
New York, NY 10022　　　　　　Thomas Littler, Libn.

ASSOCIATION OF NATIONAL ADVERTISERS - LIBRARY
155 E. 44th St.　　　　　　　　　Phone: (212) 697-5950
New York, NY 10017　　　　　　Rosemary Collins, Mgr.

ASSOCIATION OF PHILIPPINE COCONUT DESICCATORS - LIBRARY *
Times Sq. Sta., Box 787　　　　　　Phone: (212) 929-0104
New York, NY 10036　　　　Conrado A. Escudero, U.S. Rep.

AT & T COMMUNICATIONS - INFORMATION RESEARCH CENTER
22 Cortlandt St., 17th Fl.　　　　　Phone: (212) 393-9800
New York, NY 10005　　　　　　Melanie Z. Strub, Mgr.

AT & T - CORPORATE RESEARCH CENTER
550 Madison Ave., 5th Fl.　　　　　Phone: (212) 605-7733
New York, NY 10022　　　Marianne V. Benjamin, Rsrc.Mgr.

AT & T - EDITORIAL RESEARCH CENTER †
550 Madison Ave., 250022
New York, NY 10022　　　　　　Marcie Chapin, Ed.

AT & T - LAW LIBRARY
550 Madison Ave., Rm. 2239　　　　Phone: (212) 605-6598
New York, NY 10022　　　　　Lorraine Fricke, Law Libn.

AT & T TECHNOLOGIES, INC. - HEADQUARTERS LIBRARY †
222 Broadway　　　　　　　　　　Phone: (212) 669-3491
New York, NY 10038　　　　　　Mary-Jo Jones, Libn.

AUSTRALIAN INFORMATION SERVICE - REFERENCE LIBRARY/
　INFORMATION SERVICE
636 5th Ave.　　　　　　　　　　Phone: (212) 245-4000
New York, NY 10020　　　G. Dixon, Dp. Consul-General/Info.

AUSTRIAN PRESS AND INFORMATION SERVICE
31 E. 69th St.　　　　　　　　　　Phone: (212) 737-6400
New York, NY 10021　　　　　　Krista Lewis, Asst.Dir.

AVON PRODUCTS, INC. - CENTRAL LIBRARY †
9 W. 57th St.　　　　　　　　　　Phone: (212) 593-5375
New York, NY 10019　　　Regina E. Gottesman, Lib.Coord.

AYER (NW) INCORPORATED - AYER INFORMATION CENTER (AIC)
1345 Ave. of the Americas　　　　　Phone: (212) 708-5181
New York, NY 10105　　　　Holly J. Bussey, Mgr. of AIC

AYERST LABORATORIES - INFORMATION CENTER
685 Third Ave.　　　　　　　　　Phone: (212) 878-5587
New York, NY 10017　　　　　　Mimi Golob, Mgr.

B.E.A. ASSOCIATES, INC. - LIBRARY
153 E. 53rd St.
New York, NY 10022
Phone: (212) 832-2626
Anita B. Collins, Info.Mgr./Libn.

BAECK (Leo) INSTITUTE - LIBRARY
129 E. 73rd St.
New York, NY 10021
Phone: (212) 744-6400
Stephanie Stern, Chf.Libn.

BAKER & MC KENZIE - LAW LIBRARY
805 Third Ave.
New York, NY 10022
Phone: (212) 751-5700
Janet S. Zagorin, Libn.

BANK STREET COLLEGE OF EDUCATION - LIBRARY
610 W. 112 St.
New York, NY 10025
Phone: (212) 663-7200
Eleanor Kulleseid, Lib.Dir.

BANKERS TRUST COMPANY - CORPORATE FINANCE DEPARTMENT -
INFORMATION CENTER
280 Park Ave., 9th Fl. West
New York, NY 10017
Phone: (212) 850-1496
Carol L. Ginsburg, Asst. V.P./Info.Off.

BARNARD COLLEGE WOMEN'S CENTER - BIRDIE GOLDSMITH AST
RESOURCE COLLECTION
100 Barnard Hall
3001 Broadway
New York, NY 10027
Phone: (212) 280-2067
Temma Kaplan, Dir., Women's Ctr.

BARRETT SMITH SCHAPIRO SIMON & ARMSTRONG - LIBRARY
26 Broadway
New York, NY 10004
Phone: (212) 422-8180
Alice Arant-Cousins, Dir.

BARUCH COLLEGE OF THE CITY UNIVERSITY OF NEW YORK - ELIAS
LIEBERMAN HIGHER EDUC. CONTRACT LIB. †
17 Lexington Ave.
New York, NY 10010
Phone: (212) 725-3390
Lisa Flanzraich, Libn.

BARUCH COLLEGE OF THE CITY UNIVERSITY OF NEW YORK -
LIBRARY †
156 E. 25th St.
New York, NY 10010
Phone: (212) 725-3112
Harold Eiberson, Chf.Libn.

BATES (Ted) ADVERTISING - INFORMATION CENTER
1515 Broadway
New York, NY 10036
Phone: (212) 869-3131
Ms. Bert Schachter, Mgr./V.P.

BATTEN, BARTON, DURSTINE, OSBORN, INC. - INFORMATION RETRIEVAL
CENTER †
383 Madison Ave.
New York, NY 10017
Phone: (212) 355-5800
Paula Brown, Mgr.

BELGIAN CONSULATE GENERAL - LIBRARY
50 Rockefeller Plaza
New York, NY 10020
Phone: (212) 586-5110
Moureau Lorette

BELLEVUE HOSPITAL - MEDICAL LIBRARY
1st Ave. at 27th St.
New York, NY 10016
Phone: (212) 561-6535
Paul Barth, Dir.

BENDER (Matthew) AND COMPANY, INC. - LIBRARY
235 E. 45th St.
New York, NY 10017
Phone: (212) 661-5050
Rudolph Caughman, Chf.Libn.

BENTON AND BOWLES, INC. - LIBRARY
909 3rd Ave.
New York, NY 10022
Phone: (212) 758-6200
Lois Burke, Libn.

BERNSTEIN (Sanford C.) & COMPANY, INC. - RESEARCH LIBRARY
767 5th Ave.
New York, NY 10153
Phone: (212) 486-5899
Mr. Rene D. Alcid, Corp.Libn.

BESSEMER TRUST COMPANY, N.A. - INVESTMENT LIBRARY
630 Fifth Ave.
New York, NY 10111
Phone: (212) 708-9184
Merrill H. Lishan, Libn.

BETH ISRAEL MEDICAL CTR. - HOSPITAL FOR JOINT DISEASES
ORTHOPAEDIC INST. - SEYMOUR J. PHILLIPS HEALTH SCI.LIB.
10 Nathan D. Perlman Pl.
New York, NY 10003
Phone: (212) 420-2168
Arlene L. Freedman, Dir. of Lib.Serv.

BETTMANN ARCHIVE
136 E. 57th St.
New York, NY 10022
Phone: (212) 758-0362
David Greenstein, Dir.

BIGHAM, ENGLAR, JONES AND HOUSTON - LIBRARY †
14 Wall St.
New York, NY 10005
Phone: (212) 732-4646
Sharon M. Kallop, Libn.

BISHOP, LIBERMAN & COOK - LAW LIBRARY
1155 Ave. of the Americas, Suite 2400
New York, NY 10036
Ben Schneberg, Law Libn.

BLUE CROSS AND BLUE SHIELD OF GREATER NEW YORK - CORPORATE
REFERENCE INFORMATION SERVICES
3 Park Ave., 19th Fl.
New York, NY 10016
Phone: (212) 481-2385
Iona Prilop, Libn.

BOARD OF JEWISH EDUCATION OF GREATER NEW YORK - EDUCATIONAL
RESOURCE LIBRARY
426 W. 58th St.
New York, NY 10019
Phone: (212) 245-8200
Benjamin Miller, Chf.Libn.

BOOZ, ALLEN & HAMILTON, INC. - RESEARCH SERVICE
101 Park Ave.
New York, NY 10178
Phone: (212) 697-1900
Ellen L. Miller, Mgr., Res.Serv.

BORICUA COLLEGE - LIBRARY - SPECIAL COLLECTIONS
3755 Broadway
New York, NY 10032
Phone: (212) 865-9000
Aurora Gomez, Libn.

BOTEIN, HAYS, SKLAR & HERZBERG - LIBRARY
200 Park Ave., Suite 3014
New York, NY 10166
Phone: (212) 867-5500
Donald Wecht, Libn.

BOWKER (R.R.) COMPANY - FREDERIC G. MELCHER LIBRARY
205 E. 42nd St.
New York, NY 10017
Phone: (212) 916-1960
Nancy Dvorin, Libn.

BRANT PUBLICATIONS, INC. - THE ANTIQUES MAGAZINE - LIBRARY
551 Fifth Ave.
New York, NY 10176
Phone: (212) 922-1818
Allison Eckardt, Assoc.Ed.

BREED, ABBOTT & MORGAN - LIBRARY
153 E. 53rd St.
New York, NY 10022
Phone: (212) 888-0800
Carol H. Barra, Hd.Libn.

BRIGER & ASSOCIATES - LIBRARY †
299 Park Ave.
New York, NY 10017
Phone: (212) 758-4000
Jacqueline Granek, Libn.

BRITISH INFORMATION SERVICES - LIBRARY
845 Third Ave.
New York, NY 10022
Phone: (212) 752-8400
Margaret J. Gale, Libn.

BROWN BROTHERS HARRIMAN & CO. - RESEARCH LIBRARY
59 Wall St.
New York, NY 10005
Phone: (212) 483-5517
Kelly Mattis, Libn.

BROWN, WOOD, IVEY, MITCHELL & PETTY - LIBRARY
One World Trade Center
New York, NY 10048
Phone: (212) 839-5444
Connie L. Kluever, Libn.

BRUNDAGE, STORY & ROSE, INVESTMENT COUNSEL - LIBRARY
1 Broadway
New York, NY 10004
Phone: (212) 269-3050
Julie L. Halston, Hd.Libn.

BURKE & BURKE - LAW LIBRARY
529 Fifth Ave.
New York, NY 10017
Phone: (212) 661-6600
Peter Bartucca, Libn.

BURSON-MARSTELLER - INFORMATION SERVICE
866 Third Ave.
New York, NY 10022
Phone: (212) 752-6500
Gayle Haring, Mgr., Info.Serv.

BUSINESS INTERNATIONAL - RESEARCH LIBRARY
One Dag Hammarskjold Plaza
Second Ave. & 47th St.
New York, NY 10017
Phone: (212) 750-6383
Audrey L. Bott, Dir. of Lib.Serv.

BUTTERICK COMPANY, INC. - ARCHIVES
161 Ave. of the Americas   Phone: (212) 620-2670
New York, NY 10013   Barbara Luby, Archv.Ck.

CABRINI MEDICAL CENTER - DR. MASSIMO BAZZINI MEMORIAL LIBRARY
227 E. 19th St.   Phone: (212) 725-6631
New York, NY 10003   Jeanne Becker, Med.Libn.

CAHILL GORDON & REINDEL - LAW LIBRARY
80 Pine St.   Phone: (212) 825-0100
New York, NY 10005   Margaret J. Davenport, Libn.

CANADIAN CONSULATE GENERAL - LIBRARY
1251 Ave. of the Americas   Phone: (212) 586-2400
New York, NY 10020   Sheila Purse, Hd.Libn.

CARPENTER (Guy) & COMPANY, INC. - LIBRARY AND INFORMATION
    SERVICES
110 William St.   Phone: (212) 791-8665
New York, NY 10038   John Cocke, Libn.

CARTER, LEDYARD AND MILBURN - LIBRARY †
2 Wall St.   Phone: (212) 732-3200
New York, NY 10005   Julius M. Pomerantz, Libn.

CATALYST - INFORMATION CENTER
14 E. 60th St.   Phone: (212) 759-9700
New York, NY 10022   Gurley Turner, Dir. of Info.Serv.

CATHEDRAL OF ST. JOHN THE DIVINE - CATHEDRAL LIBRARY
Cathedral Heights   Phone: (212) 678-6910
New York, NY 10025   Madeleine L'Engle Franklin, Writer in Residence

CATHOLIC CENTER AT NEW YORK UNIVERSITY - CATHOLIC CENTER
    LIBRARY
58 Washington Sq., S.   Phone: (212) 674-7236
New York, NY 10012

CBS INC. - CBS LAW LIBRARY
51 W. 52nd St.   Phone: (212) 975-4260
New York, NY 10019   Susan Bieber, Law Libn.

CBS INC. - CBS NEWS AUDIO ARCHIVES
524 W. 57th St.   Phone: (212) 975-6489
New York, NY 10019

CBS INC. - CBS NEWS REFERENCE LIBRARY
524 W. 57th St.   Phone: (212) 975-2877
New York, NY 10019   Laura B. Kapnick, Dir.

CBS RECORDS - ARCHIVES
49 E. 52nd St.   Phone: (212) 975-4949
New York, NY 10019   Martine Vinces, Archv.

CENTER FOR LIBERTARIAN STUDIES
200 Park Ave., S., Suite 1314
New York, NY 10003

CENTER FOR MEDICAL CONSUMERS AND HEALTH INFORMATION -
    LIBRARY
237 Thompson St.   Phone: (212) 674-7105
New York, NY 10012   Arthur Levin, Dir.

CENTER FOR MODERN PSYCHOANALYTIC STUDIES - LIBRARY
16 W. 10th St.   Phone: (212) 260-7050
New York, NY 10011   C.Z. Meadow, Dir.

CENTER FOR NONPROFIT ORGANIZATIONS, INC. - LIBRARY
203 W. 25th St., 3rd Fl.   Phone: (212) 989-9026
New York, NY 10001   Howard E. Fischer, Dir.

CENTER FOR RUSSIAN & EAST EUROPEAN JEWRY/STUDENTS STRUGGLE
    FOR SOVIET JEWRY - ARCHIVES
210 W. 91st St.   Phone: (212) 799-8900
New York, NY 10024   Glenn Richter, Natl.Coord.

CENTER ON SOCIAL WELFARE POLICY AND LAW - LIBRARY
95 Madison Ave., Rm. 701   Phone: (212) 679-3709
New York, NY 10016   Henry A. Freedman, Dir.

CENTER FOR THE STUDY OF HUMAN RIGHTS - LIBRARY
Columbia University
704 International Affairs Bldg.   Phone: (212) 280-2479
New York, NY 10027   Jane Callaghy, Adm.Asst.

CENTER FOR THE STUDY OF THE PRESIDENCY - LIBRARY
208 E. 75th St.   Phone: (212) 240-1200
New York, NY 10021   Sabrina Boothe, Libn.

CENTRAL OPERA SERVICE - INFORMATION CENTER AND LIBRARY
c/o Metropolitan Opera
Lincoln Center   Phone: (212) 957-9871
New York, NY 10023   Maria F. Rich, Exec.Dir.

CENTURY ASSOCIATION - LIBRARY
7 W. 43rd St.   Phone: (212) 944-0090
New York, NY 10036   Andrew Zaremba, Libn.

CHADBOURNE, PARKE, WHITESIDE, & WOLFF - LIBRARY
30 Rockefeller Plaza, 24th Fl.   Phone: (212) 344-8900
New York, NY 10112   Jeannine R. Thomasch, Libn.

CHASE MANHATTAN BANK, N.A. - INFORMATION CENTER
One Chase Manhattan Plaza, 9th Fl.   Phone: (212) 552-0014
New York, NY 10081   Catherine R. Reilly, 2nd V.P., Mgr.

CHEMICAL BANK - RESEARCH LIBRARY
20 Pine St., Rm. 1915   Phone: (212) 770-3127
New York, NY 10015   Helen Traina, Chf.Libn.

CHEMISTS' CLUB LIBRARY - CHEMICAL INTERNATIONAL INFORMATION
    CENTER
52 E. 41st St.   Phone: (212) 679-6383
New York, NY 10017   Elsie Lim, Libn.

CHILD WELFARE LEAGUE OF AMERICA, INC. - INFORMATIONAL RESOURCE
    SERVICES - DOROTHY L. BERNHARD LIBRARY
67 Irving Pl.   Phone: (212) 254-7410
New York, NY 10003   Marilyn Katz, Libn.

CHILDREN'S BOOK COUNCIL - LIBRARY
67 Irving Pl.   Phone: (212) 254-2666
New York, NY 10003

CHINESE CULTURAL CENTER - INFORMATION & COMMUNICATION
    DIVISION - LIBRARY
159 Lexington Ave.   Phone: (212) 725-4950
New York, NY 10016   Ming-Tien Tsai, Libn.

CHURCH OF THE BELOVED DISCIPLE - HOMOPHILE RESEARCH LIBRARY *
348 W. 14th St.   Phone: (212) 242-6616
New York, NY 10014   Thor Wood, Libn.

CITIBANK, N.A. - CITICORP LAW LIBRARY
399 Park Ave., 37th Fl.   Phone: (212) 559-2503
New York, NY 10043   Evelyn Sokol, Law Libn.

CITIBANK, N.A. LIBRARY
153 E. 53rd St.   Phone: (212) 559-9000
New York, NY 10043   Conchita J. Pineda, Mgr.

CITIZENS FORUM ON SELF-GOVERNMENT/NATIONAL MUNICIPAL LEAGUE,
    INC. - MURRAY SEASONGOOD LIBRARY
55 W. 44th St.   Phone: (212) 535-5700
New York, NY 10036   Joan A. Casey, Dir., Lib./Pubns.

CITIZENS HOUSING AND PLANNING COUNCIL OF NEW YORK - LIBRARY
20 W. 40th St.   Phone: (212) 391-9030
New York, NY 10018   Marian Sameth, Assoc.Dir.

CITIZENS UNION OF THE CITY OF NEW YORK - LIBRARY
198 Broadway   Phone: (212) 227-0342
New York, NY 10038   Vance Benguiat, Exec.Dir.

CLARK (William H.) ASSOCIATES, INC. - RESEARCH LIBRARY *
330 Madison Ave.   Phone: (212) 661-8760
New York, NY 10017   Judith Stein, Dir. of Res.

CLEARINGHOUSE FOR ARTS INFORMATION - CENTER FOR ARTS
  INFORMATION
625 Broadway   Phone: (212) 677-7548
New York, NY 10012   Jana Jevnikar, Info.Coord.

CLEARY, GOTTLIEB, STEEN & HAMILTON - LIBRARY
One State St. Plaza   Phone: (212) 344-0600
New York, NY 10004   Karol M. Sokol, Libn.

COLER MEMORIAL HOSPITAL - MEDICAL LIBRARY †
Roosevelt Island   Phone: (212) 688-9400
New York, NY 10044   Gina Buika, Ph.D., Dir., Med.Lib.

COLLECTORS CLUB - LIBRARY
22 E. 35th St.   Phone: (212) 683-0559
New York, NY 10016   Werner Elias, Libn.

COLLEGE FOR HUMAN SERVICES - LIBRARY
345 Hudson St.   Phone: (212) 989-2002
New York, NY 10014   Hibbert W. Moss, Hd.Libn.

COLLEGE OF INSURANCE - INSURANCE SOCIETY OF NEW YORK - LIBRARY
123 William St.   Phone: (212) 962-4111
New York, NY 10038   Donald Carson, Chf.Libn.

COLLEGE RETIREMENT EQUITIES FUND - CREF RESEARCH LIBRARY
730 Third Ave.   Phone: (212) 916-4009
New York, NY 10017   Linda K. Bashover, Libn.

COLLEGIATE REFORMED DUTCH CHURCH - LIBRARY
45 John St.   Phone: (212) 233-1960
New York, NY 10038   Robert F. Williams, Chf.

COLUMBIA UNIVERSITY - AMBROSE MONELL ENGINEERING LIBRARY
422 Mudd   Phone: (212) 280-2976
New York, NY 10027

COLUMBIA UNIVERSITY - AVERY ARCHITECTURAL AND FINE ARTS
  LIBRARY
Broadway & 116th St.   Phone: (212) 280-3501
New York, NY 10027   Angela Giral, Libn.

COLUMBIA UNIVERSITY - BIOLOGICAL SCIENCES LIBRARY
601 Fairchild Bldg.   Phone: (212) 280-4715
New York, NY 10027   Barbara List, Ref./Coll.Dev.Libn.

COLUMBIA UNIVERSITY - BURGESS-CARPENTER LIBRARY
406 Butler Library   Phone: (212) 280-4710
New York, NY 10027   Frederick Byrne, Libn.

COLUMBIA UNIVERSITY - BUTLER LIBRARY CIRCULATION DEPARTMENT
303 Butler Library   Phone: (212) 280-2235
New York, NY 10027   Robert Pepin, Hd.

COLUMBIA UNIVERSITY - C.V. STARR EAST ASIAN LIBRARY
300 Kent   Phone: (212) 280-4318
New York, NY 10027   James Reardon-Anderson, Libn.

COLUMBIA UNIVERSITY CANCER CENTER - INSTITUTE OF CANCER
  RESEARCH
701 W. 168th St.   Phone: (212) 694-6948
New York, NY 10032   Betty Rose Moore, Lib.Serv.Coord.

COLUMBIA UNIVERSITY - CENTER FOR POPULATION & FAMILY HEALTH -
  LIBRARY/INFORMATION PROGRAM
60 Haven Ave.   Phone: (212) 694-6960
New York, NY 10032   Susan K. Pasquariella, Hd.Libn.

COLUMBIA UNIVERSITY - CHEMISTRY LIBRARY
454 Chandler Hall   Phone: (212) 280-4709
New York, NY 10027   Mary Kay, Ref./Coll.Dev.Libn.

COLUMBIA UNIVERSITY - COLUMBIA COLLEGE LIBRARY
225 Butler Library   Phone: (212) 280-3534
New York, NY 10027   Frederick Byrne, Libn.

COLUMBIA UNIVERSITY - COLUMBIANA
210 Low Memorial Library   Phone: (212) 280-3786
New York, NY 10027   Paul R. Palmer, Cur.

COLUMBIA UNIVERSITY - DEPARTMENT OF ART HISTORY &
  ARCHAEOLOGY - PHOTOGRAPH COLLECTION
420 Schermerhorn Hall   Phone: (212) 280-5203
New York, NY 10027   Prof. Jane Rosenthal, Rep.

COLUMBIA UNIVERSITY - GEOLOGY LIBRARY
601 Schermerhorn   Phone: (212) 280-4522
New York, NY 10027   Susan Klimley, Libn.

COLUMBIA UNIVERSITY - HEALTH SCIENCES LIBRARY
701 W. 168th St.   Phone: (212) 694-3692
New York, NY 10032   Rachael K. Goldstein, Libn.

COLUMBIA UNIVERSITY - HERBERT H. LEHMAN LIBRARY
Intl. Affairs Bldg.
420 W. 118th St.   Phone: (212) 280-4170
New York, NY 10027   David B. Lewis, Libn.

COLUMBIA UNIVERSITY - LAW LIBRARY
Law School
435 W. 116th St.   Phone: (212) 280-3737
New York, NY 10027   James L. Hoover, Law Libn.

COLUMBIA UNIVERSITY - LIBRARY SERVICE LIBRARY
606 Butler Library   Phone: (212) 280-3543
New York, NY 10027   Olha della Cava, Libn.

COLUMBIA UNIVERSITY - MATHEMATICS/SCIENCE LIBRARY
303 Mathematics   Phone: (212) 280-4712
New York, NY 10027   Suzanne Fedunok, Hd., Ref. & Coll.Dev.

COLUMBIA UNIVERSITY - MUSIC LIBRARY
701 Dodge   Phone: (212) 280-4711
New York, NY 10027   Kathleen Haefliger, Libn.

COLUMBIA UNIVERSITY - ORAL HISTORY COLLECTION
Butler Library
Box 20   Phone: (212) 280-2273
New York, NY 10027   Ronald J. Grele, Dir.

COLUMBIA UNIVERSITY - PATERNO LIBRARY
Casa Italiana, 1161 Amsterdam Ave.   Phone: (212) 280-2307
New York, NY 10027   Robert Connolly, Lib.Asst.

COLUMBIA UNIVERSITY - PHILOSOPHY LIBRARY
228 Butler Library   Phone: (212) 280-2259
New York, NY 10027   Frederick Byrne, Libn.

COLUMBIA UNIVERSITY - PHYSICS LIBRARY
810 Pupin Laboratories   Phone: (212) 280-3943
New York, NY 10027   Mary Kay, Ref./Coll.Dev.Libn.

COLUMBIA UNIVERSITY - PSYCHOLOGY LIBRARY
409 Schermerhorn Hall   Phone: (212) 280-4714
New York, NY 10027   Barbara List, Ref./Coll.Dev.Libn.

COLUMBIA UNIVERSITY - RARE BOOK AND MANUSCRIPT LIBRARY
654 Butler Library   Phone: (212) 280-2231
New York, NY 10027   Kenneth A. Lohf, Libn.

COLUMBIA UNIVERSITY - SULZBERGER JOURNALISM LIBRARY
304 Journalism Bldg.
Broadway & 116th St.   Phone: (212) 280-3860
New York, NY 10027   Wade A. Doares, Journalism Libn.

COLUMBIA UNIVERSITY - THOMAS J. WATSON LIBRARY OF BUSINESS AND
  ECONOMICS
130 Uris Hall   Phone: (212) 280-4000
New York, NY 10027   Jane E. Winland, Bus.Libn.

COLUMBIA UNIVERSITY - WHITNEY M. YOUNG, JR. MEMORIAL LIBRARY
  OF SOCIAL WORK
309 International Affairs Bldg.   Phone: (212) 280-5159
New York, NY 10027   Tyrone H. Cannon, Soc. Work Libn.

COMICS MAGAZINE ASSOCIATION OF AMERICA, INC. - LIBRARY
60 E. 42nd St., Suite 511   Phone: (212) 682-8144
New York, NY 10165   J. Dudley Waldner, Exec.Sec.

COMPOSERS AND CHOREOGRAPHERS THEATRE, INC. - MASTER TAPE
  LIBRARY
Lincoln Center   Phone: (212) 925-3721
New York, NY 10012   Laura Foreman, Pres.

COMPTON ADVERTISING INC. - RESEARCH LIBRARY
625 Madison Ave.   Phone: (212) 350-1570
New York, NY 10022   Shirley Damon, Hd.Libn.

CONDE NAST PUBLICATIONS, INC. - LIBRARY
350 Madison Ave., 11th Fl.   Phone: (212) 880-8244
New York, NY 10017   Dianne Weber Spoto, Sr.Libn.

CONFERENCE BOARD, INC. - INFORMATION SERVICE
845 3rd Ave.   Phone: (212) 759-0900
New York, NY 10022   Tamsen M. Hernandez, Dir.

CONGREGATION EMANU-EL - IVAN M. STETTENHEIM LIBRARY
1 E. 65th St.   Phone: (212) 744-1400
New York, NY 10021   Robin Meng, Libn.

CONGREGATION SHEARITH ISRAEL - SOPHIE AND IVAN SALOMON
  LIBRARY COLLECTION
8 W. 70th St.   Phone: (212) 873-0300
New York, NY 10023   Richard P. Simmonds, Libn.

CONSOLIDATED EDISON COMPANY OF NEW YORK, INC. - LIBRARY
4 Irving Pl., Rm. 1650-S   Phone: (212) 460-4228
New York, NY 10003   Steven Jaffe, Libn.

CONSULATE GENERAL OF DENMARK - DANISH INFORMATION OFFICE
280 Park Ave.   Phone: (212) 697-5107
New York, NY 10017   Else Rothe, Libn.

CONSULATE GENERAL OF INDIA - INFORMATION SERVICE OF INDIA
  LIBRARY
3 E. 64th St.   Phone: (212) 879-7800
New York, NY 10021   Mrs. Pushpa Gupta, Libn.

CONSULATE GENERAL OF ISRAEL - LT. DAVID TAMIR LIBRARY AND
  READING ROOM
800 Second Ave.   Phone: (212) 697-5500
New York, NY 10017   Evelyn Musher, Dir., Community Rel.

CONSULATE GENERAL OF JAPAN - JAPAN INFORMATION CENTER -
  LIBRARY †
3 E. 64th St.   Phone: (212) 986-1600
New York, NY 10021   Masakatsio Wajima, Libn.

CONSULATE GENERAL OF THE NETHERLANDS - PRESS AND CULTURAL
  SECTION
One Rockefeller Plaza
New York, NY 10020

COOPER UNION FOR THE ADVANCEMENT OF SCIENCE AND ART - LIBRARY
41 Cooper Sq.   Phone: (212) 254-6300
New York, NY 10003   Elizabeth A. Vajda, Hd.Libn.

COOPERS & LYBRAND - NATIONAL LIBRARY †
1251 Ave. of the Americas   Phone: (212) 536-2858
New York, NY 10020   Dorothy Kasman, Chf.Libn.

COORDINATING COUNCIL OF LITERARY MAGAZINES - LIBRARY
2 Park Ave.   Phone: (212) 481-5245
New York, NY 10016   Jennifer Moyer, Dir.

CORNELL UNIVERSITY - MEDICAL COLLEGE - SAMUEL J. WOOD LIBRARY
1300 York Ave.   Phone: (212) 472-5300
New York, NY 10021   Erich Meyerhoff, Libn.

CORNELL UNIVERSITY - SANFORD V. LENZ LIBRARY
3 E. 43rd St.   Phone: (212) 599-4693
New York, NY 10033   Mike Donovan, Libn.

COSSACK LIBRARY IN NEW YORK
208 E. 9th St.
Box 3   Phone: (212) 475-4789
New York, NY 10003   Dr. W.G. Glaskow, Cur.

COUDERT BROTHERS - LIBRARY
200 Park Ave.   Phone: (212) 880-4796
New York, NY 10166   Jane C. Rubens, Libn.

COUNCIL FOR FINANCIAL AID TO EDUCATION - FOUNDERS ROOM LIBRARY
680 Fifth Ave.   Phone: (212) 924-8137
New York, NY 10019   Frances C. Burns, Dir., Lib. & Info.Serv.

COUNCIL ON FOREIGN RELATIONS - LIBRARY
58 E. 68th St.   Phone: (212) 734-0400
New York, NY 10021   Janet Rigney, Libn.

COUNCIL OF JEWISH FEDERATIONS - LIBRARY †
575 Lexington Ave.   Phone: (212) 751-1311
New York, NY 10022   Zalman Alpert, Libn.

CRAVATH, SWAINE, & MOORE - LAW LIBRARY
1 Chase Manhattan Plaza   Phone: (212) 422-3000
New York, NY 10005   Arlene Eis, Libn.

CRESAP, MC CORMICK, AND PAGET, INC. - LIBRARY †
245 Park Ave., 30th Fl.   Phone: (212) 953-7157
New York, NY 10167   Helen Garvey, Libn.

CULVER PICTURES, INC. - LIBRARY
660 First Ave.   Phone: (212) 684-5054
New York, NY 10016   Harriet L. Culver, Pres.

CUNNINGHAM AND WALSH, INC. - INFORMATION CENTER
260 Madison Ave.   Phone: (212) 683-4900
New York, NY 10016   Ruth Fromkes, Hd., Info.Ctr.

CUNY - CENTRO DE ESTUDIOS PUERTORRIQUENOS
695 Park Ave.   Phone: (212) 772-5685
New York, NY 10021   Nelida Perez, Libn.

CUNY - CITY COLLEGE LIBRARY - ARCHITECTURE LIBRARY
3300 Broadway, Rm. 206   Phone: (212) 690-5329
New York, NY 10031   Sylvia H. Wright, Libn.-in-Charge

CUNY - CITY COLLEGE LIBRARY - COLLEGE ARCHIVES
North Academic Center
Convent Ave. & W. 137th St.   Phone: (212) 690-5367
New York, NY 10031   Barbara J. Dunlap, Archv.

CUNY - CITY COLLEGE LIBRARY - MUSIC LIBRARY
Shepard Hall, Rm. 318A
Convent Ave. & W. 138th St.   Phone: (212) 690-4174
New York, NY 10031   Melva Peterson, Chf., Music Lib.

CUNY - CITY COLLEGE LIBRARY - SCIENCE/ENGINEERING DIVISION
Science Bldg., Rm. 29   Phone: (212) 690-8243
New York, NY 10031   Anabel Meister, Lib.Chf.

CUNY - CITY COLLEGE LIBRARY - SPECIAL COLLECTIONS
North Academic Center
Convent Ave. & W. 137th St.   Phone: (212) 690-5367
New York, NY 10031   Barbara Jane Dunlap, Chf., Archv. & Spec.Coll.

CUNY - GRADUATE SCHOOL AND UNIVERSITY CENTER - LIBRARY
33 W. 42nd St.   Phone: (212) 790-4541
New York, NY 10036   Jane R. Moore, Chf.Libn.

CURTIS, MALLET-PREVOST, COLT AND MOSLE - LIBRARY
101 Park Ave.   Phone: (212) 248-8111
New York, NY 10178   Janet P. Tidwell, Libn.

CYRUS J. LAWRENCE, INC. - LIBRARY †
115 Broadway   Phone: (212) 962-2200
New York, NY 10006   Joan Grant, Libn.

DANCE FILMS ASSOCIATION, INC.
241 E. 34th St., Rm. 301   Phone: (212) 686-7019
New York, NY 10016   Susan Braun, Pres.

DANCER FITZGERALD SAMPLE, INC. - INFORMATION CENTER
405 Lexington Ave.   Phone: (212) 661-0800
New York, NY 10174   Irene H. Kossowsky, Mgr., Info.Ctr.

DAVIS POLK & WARDWELL - LIBRARY
One Chase Manhattan Plaza
New York, NY 10005
Phone: (212) 530-4267
Nuchine Nobari, Chf.Libn.

DCA FOOD INDUSTRIES, INC. - RESEARCH & DEVELOPMENT DIVISION -
    SCIENTIFIC INFORMATION CENTER
330 W. 34th St.
New York, NY 10001
Phone: (212) 239-6852
Helene S. Pandelakis, Info.Sci.

DEAN WITTER REYNOLDS, INC. - LIBRARY
2 World Trade Center
New York, NY 10048
Phone: (212) 524-2745
Barbara C. White, Chf.Libn.

DEAN WITTER REYNOLDS, INC. - RESEARCH DEPARTMENT LIBRARY
5 World Trade Center
New York, NY 10048
Phone: (212) 524-2222
Eileen Elizabeth Rourke, Res.Libn.

DEBEVOISE & PLIMPTON - LAW LIBRARY
875 Third Ave.
New York, NY 10022
Phone: (212) 909-6275
Denis R. O'Connor, Libn.

DELL PUBLISHING COMPANY, INC. - LIBRARY
One Dag Hammarskjold Plaza
New York, NY 10017
Phone: (212) 605-3000
Jaine Fabian, Libn.

DELOITTE HASKINS & SELLS - EXECUTIVE OFFICE LIBRARY
1114 Ave. of the Americas
New York, NY 10036
Phone: (212) 790-0639
Rhea Tabakin, Exec.Off.Libn.

DELOITTE HASKINS & SELLS - LIBRARY
One World Trade Center
New York, NY 10048
Phone: (212) 669-5160
Janine J. Kaplan, Hd.Libn.

DEWEY, BALLANTINE, BUSHBY, PALMER & WOOD - LIBRARY
140 Broadway
New York, NY 10005
Phone: (212) 820-1300
Gitelle Seer, Libn.

DIEBOLD GROUP, INC. - LIBRARY
475 Park Ave., S.
New York, NY 10016
Phone: (212) 684-4700

DILLON, READ & COMPANY, INC. - LIBRARY
535 Madison Ave.
New York, NY 10022
Phone: (212) 906-7082
Nancy J. Bowles, Lib.Dir.

DIRECT MARKETING ASSOCIATION, INC. - INFORMATION CENTER
6 E. 43rd St., 12th Fl.
New York, NY 10017
Phone: (212) 689-4977
Glenda Shasho, Dir., Info. & Res.

DOCUMENTS PLUS, INC.
853 Broadway, Rm. 1606
New York, NY 10003
Phone: (212) 505-8787
Linda S. Rosenberg, Pres.

DONALDSON, LUFKIN AND JENRETTE, INC. - CORPORATE INFORMATION
    CENTER
140 Broadway, 47th Fl.
New York, NY 10005
Phone: (212) 902-2371
Leslie A. Wheaton, Asst. V.P./Mgr.

DONALDSON, LUFKIN AND JENRETTE, INC. - PERSHING DIVISION -
    RESEARCH LIBRARY †
120 Broadway
New York, NY 10005
Phone: (212) 902-3325
Joanne Deluca, Libn.

DONOVAN, LEISURE, NEWTON & IRVINE - LIBRARY
30 Rockefeller Plaza
New York, NY 10112
Phone: (212) 489-4293
Albert P. Borner, Libn.

DOVER PUBLICATIONS, INC. - PICTORIAL ARCHIVES LIBRARY †
180 Varick St.
New York, NY 10014
Phone: (212) 255-3755

DOW JONES & CO. - LIBRARY
22 Cortlandt
New York, NY 10007
Phone: (212) 285-5075
Lottie Lindberg, Libn.

DOYLE DANE BERNBACH INC. - LIBRARY
437 Madison Ave.
New York, NY 10022
Phone: (212) 826-2000
Sandra A. Sutliff, Chf.Libn.

DREXEL BURNHAM LAMBERT INC. - RESEARCH LIBRARY
60 Broad St.
New York, NY 10004
Phone: (212) 480-6475
Laura G. Ripin, Lib.Dir.

DREYFUS CORPORATION - INFORMATION CENTER
767 Fifth Ave.
New York, NY 10153
Phone: (212) 935-8405
Cytheria Theodos, Dir.Info.Serv.

DUN AND BRADSTREET CORP. - BUSINESS LIBRARY
99 Church St.
New York, NY 10007
Phone: (212) 285-7304
Carol Stankiewicz, Libn.

E.F. HUTTON & COMPANY, INC. - RESEARCH LIBRARY
One Battery Park Plaza
New York, NY 10004
Phone: (212) 742-6563
Sheila Sterling, Chf.Libn.

EBASCO SERVICES, INC. - CORPORATE LIBRARY
2 World Trade Ctr., 92nd Fl.
New York, NY 10048
Phone: (212) 839-2021
Veronica C. Pidala, Lib./Rec.Adm.

EBERSTADT (F.) AND COMPANY - BUSINESS LIBRARY
61 Broadway
New York, NY 10006
Phone: (212) 480-0807
Mrs. Pat Salandy, Libn.

ECUMENICAL LIBRARY
475 Riverside Dr., Rm. 1372
New York, NY 10115
Phone: (212) 870-3600
Betty Ljungberg, Libn.

EDITOR & PUBLISHER - LIBRARY
575 Lexington Ave.
New York, NY 10022
Phone: (212) 752-7050
Juanita Hatcher, Libn.

EDUCATIONAL BROADCASTING CORPORATION - THIRTEEN RESEARCH
    LIBRARY
356 W. 58th St.
New York, NY 10019
Phone: (212) 560-3063
Victoria A. Dawson, Mgr., Res.Lib.

EDUCATIONAL FILM LIBRARY ASSOCIATION - LIBRARY AND
    INFORMATION CENTER
45 John St., Suite 301
New York, NY 10036
Phone: (212) 227-5599
Lisa Flanzraich, Film Info.Spec.

EIC/INTELLIGENCE, INC.
48 W. 38th St.
New York, NY 10018
Phone: (212) 944-8500
James G. Kollegger, Pres. & Pub.

EMBASE (Excerpta Medica Online)
Elsevier Science Publishers, Inc.
52 Vanderbilt Ave.
New York, NY 10017
Jeffrey Gold, Educ.Off.

EMBROIDERERS' GUILD OF AMERICA, INC. - LIBRARY
6 E. 45th St.
New York, NY 10017
Phone: (212) 986-0460
Carol Algie, Libn.

ENGINEERING SOCIETIES LIBRARY
United Engineering Ctr.
345 E. 47th St.
New York, NY 10017
Phone: (212) 705-7611
S.K. Cabeen, Dir.

ENGLISH-SPEAKING UNION OF THE U.S.A. - BOOKS ACROSS THE SEA
    LIBRARY
16 E. 69th St.
New York, NY 10021
Phone: (212) 879-6800
Catherine Nolan, Libn.

ENVIRONMENTAL ACTION COALITION - LIBRARY/RESOURCE CENTER
417 Lafayette St.
New York, NY 10003
Phone: (212) 677-1601
Lori Klamner, Libn.

ENVIRONMENTAL PROTECTION AGENCY - REGION II LIBRARY
26 Federal Plaza, Rm. 1002
New York, NY 10007
Phone: (212) 264-2881
Audrey Thomas, Regional Libn.

EQUITABLE LIFE ASSURANCE SOCIETY OF THE U.S. - INFORMATION
    SERVICES DIVISION
1285 Ave. of the Americas
New York, NY 10019
Phone: (201) 554-2491
Jean Carrigan, Dir.

EQUITABLE LIFE ASSURANCE SOCIETY OF THE U.S. - TECHNICAL
    INFORMATION CENTER
1285 Ave. of the Americas, Rm. 3I   Phone: (212) 554-4064
New York, NY 10019   Kathryn Marsala, Mgr., Tech.Info.Ctr.

ERIC CLEARINGHOUSE ON URBAN EDUCATION
Box 40, Teachers College
Columbia University   Phone: (212) 678-3437
New York, NY 10027   Dr. Erwin Flaxman, Dir.

ERNST & WHINNEY - INFORMATION CENTER
153 E. 53rd St.   Phone: (212) 888-9100
New York, NY 10022   Janet How, Dir., Info.Serv.

ERNST & WHINNEY - INTERNATIONAL LIBRARY
153 E. 53rd St.   Phone: (212) 888-9100
New York, NY 10022

EUROPEAN ART COLOR - PETER ADELBERG ARCHIVE
120 W. 70th St.   Phone: (212) 877-9654
New York, NY 10023   Greta Adelberg, Pict.Libn.

EUROPEAN COMMUNITY INFORMATION SERVICE - LIBRARY
245 E. 47th St.   Phone: (212) 371-3804
New York, NY 10017   Elizabeth Grant, Chf.Info.Off.

EXPLORERS CLUB - JAMES B. FORD MEMORIAL LIBRARY
46 E. 70th St.   Phone: (212) 628-8383
New York, NY 10021   Janet E. Baldwin, Libn.

EXXON CORPORATION - LAW-TAX LIBRARY
1251 Ave. of the Americas, 45th Fl.   Phone: (212) 398-3247
New York, NY 10020   Mary K. Moynihan, Libn.

EXXON CORPORATION - MEDICAL LIBRARY †
1251 Ave. of the Americas   Phone: (212) 398-2504
New York, NY 10020   Constance M. Lima, Med.Libn.

FAMILY SERVICE AMERICA - LIBRARY
44 E. 23rd St.   Phone: (212) 674-6100
New York, NY 10010   Joan Fenton, Libn.

FASHION INSTITUTE OF TECHNOLOGY - LIBRARY †
227 W. 27th St.   Phone: (212) 760-7695
New York, NY 10001

FEDERAL RESERVE BANK OF NEW YORK - COMPUTER SCIENCES LIBRARY
59 Maiden Ln., 24th Fl.   Phone: (212) 791-5766
New York, NY 10038   Myra F. Van Vactor, Sr.Comp.Sci.Libn.

FEDERAL RESERVE BANK OF NEW YORK - LAW LIBRARY DIVISION
33 Liberty St.   Phone: (212) 791-5012
New York, NY 10045   Rodney H. Congdon, Chf. Law Libn.

FEDERAL RESERVE BANK OF NEW YORK - RESEARCH LIBRARY
33 Liberty St.
New York, NY 10045   Jean Deuss, Chf.Libn.

FEDERATION EMPLOYMENT & GUIDANCE SERVICE - RICHARD J.
    BERNHARD MEMORIAL LIBRARY
510 6th Ave.   Phone: (212) 741-7151
New York, NY 10011   Otto Kanocz, Chf.Libn.

FEHL (Fred) PHOTOGRAPHER - INFORMATION CENTER
415 W. 115th St.   Phone: (212) 662-2253
New York, NY 10025

FIDUCIARY TRUST COMPANY OF NEW YORK - RESEARCH LIBRARY
2 World Trade Ctr., 94th Fl.   Phone: (212) 466-4100
New York, NY 10048   Marilyn Armeit, Libn.

FIND/SVP - LIBRARY
500 Fifth Ave.   Phone: (212) 354-2424
New York, NY 10110   Anne Dennis, Dir., Info.Rsrcs.

FIRST BOSTON CORPORATION - INFORMATION CENTER
Park Avenue Plaza   Phone: (212) 825-7781
New York, NY 10055   Regina M. Galligan, Asst.V.P./Mgr.

FISH AND NEAVE - LIBRARY
875 Third Ave.   Phone: (212) 715-0672
New York, NY 10022   Janet M. Stark, Libn.

FOOTE CONE & BELDING - CREATIVE ARCHIVES *
101 Park Ave.   Phone: (212) 907-1577
New York, NY 10178   Barbara Hogenson, Dir.

FORBES, INC. - LIBRARY †
60 Fifth Ave.   Phone: (212) 620-2237
New York, NY 10011   Dolores Lataniotis, Libn.

FORD FOUNDATION - INVESTMENT RESEARCH LIBRARY
320 E. 43rd St., 9th Fl.   Phone: (212) 573-5221
New York, NY 10017   Nick Sayward, Investment Serv.Libn.

FORD FOUNDATION - LIBRARY
320 E. 43rd St.   Phone: (212) 573-5155
New York, NY 10017   Susan T. Newman, Libn.

FORDHAM UNIVERSITY - LIBRARY AT LINCOLN CENTER
W. 60th St. and Columbus Ave.   Phone: (212) 841-5130
New York, NY 10023   Clement J. Anzul, Libn.

FORDHAM UNIVERSITY - SCHOOL OF LAW LIBRARY
Lincoln Sq.
140 W. 62nd St.   Phone: (212) 841-5223
New York, NY 10023   Dr. Ludwik A. Teclaff, Prof./Law Libn.

FOUNDATION CENTER - NEW YORK - LIBRARY
79 Fifth Ave., 8th Fl.   Phone: (212) 620-4230
New York, NY 10003   Candace Kuhta, Coord., Pub.Serv./Dir.

FOUNDATION FOR CITIZEN EDUCATION - ANNA LORD STRAUSS LIBRARY *
817 Broadway   Phone: (212) 677-5050
New York, NY 10003   Alice Vielehr, Libn.

FPG, INTERNATIONAL CORPORATION
251 Park Ave., S.   Phone: (212) 777-4210
New York, NY 10010   Howard A. Eskenazi, Natl. Sales Mgr.

FRANKLIN FURNACE ARCHIVES, INC. - LIBRARY
112 Franklin St.   Phone: (212) 925-4671
New York, NY 10013   Matthew Hogan, Cur.

FREEDOM HOUSE - INFORMATION CENTER
20 W. 40th St.   Phone: (212) 730-7744
New York, NY 10018   Leonard R. Sussman, Exec.Dir.

FRENCH AMERICAN CULTURAL SERVICES AND EDUCATIONAL AID
    (FACSEA)
972 Fifth Ave.   Phone: (212) 570-4440
New York, NY 10021   Anne Marie Morotte, Exec.Dir.

FRENCH INSTITUTE/ALLIANCE FRANCAISE - LIBRARY
22 E. 60th St.   Phone: (212) 355-6100
New York, NY 10022   Fred J. Gitner, Libn.

FRICK ART REFERENCE LIBRARY
10 E. 71st St.   Phone: (212) 288-8700
New York, NY 10021   Helen Sanger, Libn.

FRIED FRANK HARRIS SHRIVER JACOBSON - LIBRARY & INFORMATION
    CENTER
1 New York Plaza   Phone: (212) 820-8000
New York, NY 10004   Warren Gordon, Hd.Libn.

FRITZSCHE, DODGE AND OLCOTT, INC. - RESEARCH LIBRARY
76 Ninth Ave.   Phone: (212) 929-4100
New York, NY 10011   Rita Intal, Libn.

FUND FOR MODERN COURTS - LIBRARY
36 W. 44th St., Rm. 310   Phone: (212) 575-1577
New York, NY 10036   Dr. M.L. Henry, Jr., Exec.Dir.

GEERS GROSS ADV. INC. - LIBRARY
220 E. 42nd St.   Phone: (212) 916-8242
New York, NY 10017   Janet Jacquette, Libn.

GELBERG & ABRAMS - LAW LIBRARY †
711 Third Ave.   Phone: (212) 599-3200
New York, NY 10017   Jennifer L. Elden, Libn.

GENERAL AMERICAN INVESTORS CO., INC. - LIBRARY
330 Madison Ave.   Phone: (212) 916-8430
New York, NY 10017   Jennifer Jones, Libn.

GENERAL MOTORS CORPORATION - ECONOMICS STAFF LIBRARY *
767 Fifth Ave., 26th Fl.   Phone: (212) 486-5092
New York, NY 10153   Lourdes P. Lim, Libn.

GENERAL SOCIETY OF MECHANICS AND TRADESMEN OF THE CITY OF
      NEW YORK - LIBRARY
20 W. 44th St.   Phone: (212) 921-1767
New York, NY 10036   Margery Peters, Libn.

GENERAL THEOLOGICAL SEMINARY OF THE PROTESTANT EPISCOPAL
      CHURCH IN THE U.S.A. - ST. MARK'S LIBRARY
175 Ninth Ave.   Phone: (212) 243-5150
New York, NY 10011   David Green, Lib.Dir.

GEORGESON & COMPANY - LIBRARY
Wall St. Plaza   Phone: (212) 440-9949
New York, NY 10005   Aileen V. Burnes, Libn.

GERMAN INFORMATION CENTER - FEDERAL REPUBLIC OF GERMANY
410 Park Ave.   Phone: (212) 888-9840
New York, NY 10022

GIBBS AND COX, INC. - TECHNICAL INFORMATION CENTER
119 W. 31st St.   Phone: (212) 613-1300
New York, NY 10001   J.W. Hoffman, Jr., Mgr.

GIBBS & HILL, INC. - LIBRARY
11 Penn Plaza
393 Seventh Ave.   Phone: (212) 760-5062
New York, NY 10001   M. Pellegrino, Chf.Libn.

GIRL SCOUTS OF THE USA - LIBRARY/ARCHIVES
830 Third Ave. & 51st St.   Phone: (212) 940-7500
New York, NY 10022   Juana Alers-Quinones, Adm., Lib. & Archv.

GLOBE PHOTOS, INC. - LIBRARY
275 7th Ave., 21st Fl.   Phone: (212) 689-1340
New York, NY 10001

GOETHE HOUSE NEW YORK - LIBRARY
1014 Fifth Ave.   Phone: (212) 744-8310
New York, NY 10028   Freya Jeschke, Libn.

GOLD INFORMATION CENTER
900 Third Ave.   Phone: (212) 688-0474
New York, NY 10022   Diana Shiel, Mgr.

GOLDMAN, SACHS AND COMPANY - LIBRARY
85 Broad St.   Phone: (212) 676-7400
New York, NY 10004   Elizabeth O'Mahoney, V.P.

GOLDOME BANK - INFORMATION CENTER
1230 Ave. of the Americas   Phone: (212) 841-6919
New York, NY 10020   Mary L. Callinan, Mgr.

GRAND LODGE OF NEW YORK, F. AND A.M. - ROBERT R. LIVINGSTON
      LIBRARY AND MUSEUM
71 W. 23rd St.   Phone: (212) 741-4500
New York, NY 10010   Allan Boudreau, Dir. & Cur.

GRANGER COLLECTION
1841 Broadway   Phone: (212) 586-0971
New York, NY 10023   William Glover, Dir.

GREY ADVERTISING, INC. - INFORMATION CENTER
777 3rd Ave.   Phone: (212) 546-2511
New York, NY 10017   Janet K. Barnett, Dir.

GROLIER CLUB OF NEW YORK - LIBRARY
47 E. 60th St.   Phone: (212) 838-6690
New York, NY 10022   Robert Nikirk, Libn.

GUGGENHEIM (Solomon R.) MUSEUM - LIBRARY
1071 Fifth Ave.   Phone: (212) 860-1338
New York, NY 10128   Sonja Bay, Libn.

HACKETT (G.D.) PHOTO AGENCY AND ARCHIVES
130 W. 57th St.   Phone: (212) 265-6842
New York, NY 10019   Gabriel D. Hackett, Owner, Ed.

HAIGHT, GARDNER, POOR AND HAVENS - LIBRARY
One State St. Plaza   Phone: (212) 344-6800
New York, NY 10004   Cheryl S. Bennin, Libn.

HALCON SD GROUP, INC. - TECHNICAL INFORMATION CENTER
2 Park Ave.   Phone: (212) 689-3000
New York, NY 10016   R. Rosen, Hd.Libn.

HAMPDEN-BOOTH THEATRE LIBRARY
The Players, 16 Gramercy Pk.   Phone: (212) 228-7610
New York, NY 10003   Louis A. Rachow, Cur.Libn.

HANDY ASSOCIATES, INC. - RESEARCH LIBRARY
245 Park Ave.   Phone: (212) 867-8444
New York, NY 10167   Ann Barry, Dir. of Res.

HARKNESS (Edward S.) EYE INSTITUTE - JOHN M. WHEELER LIBRARY
635 W. 165th St.   Phone: (212) 694-2916
New York, NY 10032   Albertina F. Mount, Lib.Supv.

HARLEM HOSPITAL MEDICAL CENTER - HEALTH SCIENCES LIBRARY
506 Lenox Ave., KP 6108   Phone: (212) 491-8264
New York, NY 10037   Mr. Manny Chowdhury, Chf.Libn.

HARPER & ROW, PUBLISHERS, INC. - SCHOOL DIVISION LIBRARY
10 E. 53rd St., 16th Fl.   Phone: (212) 593-7379
New York, NY 10022   Beth Murphy, Mgr., Lib.

HARRIS (Louis) & ASSOCIATES, INC. - INFORMATION SERVICES
630 Fifth Ave.   Phone: (212) 975-1695
New York, NY 10111   Barbara Winokur, Sr.Libn.

HARVARD LIBRARY IN NEW YORK
27 W. 44th St.   Phone: (212) 840-6600
New York, NY 10036   Adrienne G. Fischier, Libn.

HASHOMER HATZAIR-ZIONIST YOUTH MOVEMENT - LIBRARY
150 Fifth Ave.   Phone: (212) 929-4955
New York, NY 10011   Natan Gottesman, Pres.

HATCH-BILLOPS COLLECTION, INC.
491 Broadway, 7th Fl.   Phone: (212) 966-3231
New York, NY 10012   Camille Billops, Exec.Dir.

HAWKINS, DELAFIELD & WOOD - LIBRARY
67 Wall St.   Phone: (212) 820-9444
New York, NY 10005   Debra Glessner, Libn.

HAWORTH PRESS, INC. - EDITORIAL DEPARTMENT ARCHIVE
28 E. 22nd St.   Phone: (212) 228-2800
New York, NY 10010   Faye Zucker, Ed.

HEARST METROTONE NEWS - FILM LIBRARY
235 E. 45th St.   Phone: (212) 682-7690
New York, NY 10017   Ted Troll, Chf.Libn.

HEBREW UNION COLLEGE - JEWISH INSTITUTE OF RELIGION - KLAU
      LIBRARY
1 W. Fourth St.   Phone: (212) 674-5300
New York, NY 10012   Philip E. Miller, Libn.

HISPANIC INSTITUTE - LIBRARY
Casa Hispanica, Columbia University
612 W. 116th St.   Phone: (212) 280-4187
New York, NY 10027

HISPANIC SOCIETY OF AMERICA - DEPARTMENT OF ICONOGRAPHY -
      GENERAL REFERENCE FILE
Broadway & 155th St.   Phone: (212) 926-2234
New York, NY 10032   Lydia Dufour, Assoc.Cur., Iconography

HISPANIC SOCIETY OF AMERICA - LIBRARY
Broadway & 155th St.   Phone: (212) 926-2234
New York, NY 10032   Jean R. Longland, Cur.

HODES (Bernard) ADVERTISING - INFORMATION CENTER
555 Madison Ave., 16th Fl.   Phone: (212) 758-2600
New York, NY 10022   Roberta J. Gardner, Dir., Info.Serv.

HOLLAND SOCIETY OF NEW YORK - LIBRARY
122 E. 58th St.   Phone: (212) 758-1675
New York, NY 10022   John Vander Veer, Pres.

HOLY LAND MUSEUM & LIBRARY
Marble Collegiate Church
1 W. 29th St.   Phone: (212) 686-2770
New York, NY 10001   Cleo Monson, Cur.

HOME LIFE INSURANCE COMPANY - LIBRARY
253 Broadway   Phone: (212) 233-6400
New York, NY 10007   Jeannette L. Secunda, Libn.

HORTICULTURAL SOCIETY OF NEW YORK - PUBLIC REFERENCE LIBRARY
128 W. 58th St.   Phone: (212) 757-0915
New York, NY 10019   Heidi S. Friedman, Libn.

HOSPITAL FOR SPECIAL SURGERY - KIM BARRETT MEMORIAL LIBRARY
535 E. 70th St.   Phone: (212) 606-1210
New York, NY 10021   Munir U. Din, Med.Libn.

HOUSE BEAUTIFUL - STAFF LIBRARY
1700 Broadway   Phone: (212) 903-5241
New York, NY 10019   Carolyn E. Chesney, Libn.

HUGHES, HUBBARD, AND REED - LIBRARY
One Wall St.   Phone: (212) 709-7777
New York, NY 10005   John S. Fitzgerald, Libn.

HUGUENOT SOCIETY OF AMERICA - LIBRARY
122 E. 58th St.   Phone: (212) 755-0592
New York, NY 10022   Mrs. Nicholas P. Christy, Exec.Sec.

HUNTER COLLEGE OF THE CITY UNIVERSITY OF NEW YORK - HEALTH
   PROFESSIONS LIBRARY
425 E. 25th St.   Phone: (212) 481-4326
New York, NY 10010   Samuel J. Waddell, Assoc.Prof./Libn.

HUNTER COLLEGE OF THE CITY UNIVERSITY OF NEW YORK - HUNTER
   COLLEGE SCHOOL OF SOCIAL WORK - LIBRARY
129 E. 79th St.   Phone: (212) 570-5072
New York, NY 10021   Charles W. Elder, Hd.Libn.

IF EVERY FOOL, INC. - PERFORMING ARTS LIBRARY
143 Chambers St.   Phone: (212) 964-7240
New York, NY 10007

INCO UNITED STATES, INC. - BUSINESS LIBRARY
One New York Plaza   Phone: (212) 742-4141
New York, NY 10004   Karen Nash, Lib.Coord.

INCO UNITED STATES, INC. - LIBRARY
One New York Plaza   Phone: (212) 742-4061
New York, NY 10004   Linda G. Doty, Lib.Adm.

INFORMATION TECHNOLOGY CENTER - LIBRARY *
One World Trade Center
New York, NY 10048   Richard VanAuken, Dir.

INSTITUTE OF INTERNATIONAL EDUCATION - LIBRARY/
   COMMUNICATIONS
809 UN Plaza   Phone: (212) 883-8470
New York, NY 10017   Dulcie L. Schackman, Sr.Info.Adm.

INSTITUTE OF JUDICIAL ADMINISTRATION - LIBRARY
One Washington Square Village   Phone: (212) 598-7721
New York, NY 10012   Calvin Hudson, Act.Libn.

INSTITUTE OF PUBLIC ADMINISTRATION - LIBRARY
55 W. 44th St.   Phone: (212) 730-5632
New York, NY 10036   Xenia W. Duisin, Libn.

INSTITUTE FOR RATIONAL-EMOTIVE THERAPY - RESEARCH LIBRARY
45 E. 65th St.   Phone: (212) 535-0822
New York, NY 10021   J. Wolf, Assoc.Dir.

INSTITUTE FOR RESEARCH IN HYPNOSIS - BERNARD B. RAGINSKY
   RESEARCH LIBRARY
10 W. 66th St.   Phone: (212) 874-5290
New York, NY 10023   Dr. Milton V. Kline, Dir. of Institute

INSTITUTES OF RELIGION AND HEALTH - LIBRARY
3 W. 29th St.   Phone: (212) 725-7842
New York, NY 10001   Frank De Georges, Libn.

INSURANCE INFORMATION INSTITUTE - LIBRARY
110 William St.   Phone: (212) 669-9200
New York, NY 10038   Carol A. Fraser, Libn.

INTERNATIONAL ADVERTISING ASSOCIATION - LIBRARY
475 Fifth Ave.   Phone: (212) 684-1583
New York, NY 10017

INTERNATIONAL CENTER FOR THE DISABLED (ICD) - BRUCE BARTON
   MEMORIAL LIBRARY
340 E. 24th St.   Phone: (212) 679-0100
New York, NY 10010   Helen Stonehill, Mgr., Lib./Info.Ctr.

INTERNATIONAL CENTER OF PHOTOGRAPHY - LIBRARY RESOURCE
   CENTER
1130 Fifth Ave.   Phone: (212) 860-1787
New York, NY 10028   Lee C. Sievan, Resource Libn.

INTERNATIONAL CENTER OF PHOTOGRAPHY - RICHARD A. HILLMAN
   RESEARCH COLLECTIONS
1130 Fifth Ave.   Phone: (212) 860-1750
New York, NY 10028   Miles Barth, Cur., Archv. & Coll.

INTERNATIONAL COPPER RESEARCH ASSOCIATION, INC. - LIBRARY
708 Third Ave.   Phone: (212) 697-9355
New York, NY 10017

INTERNATIONAL COUNCIL OF SHOPPING CENTERS - LIBRARY
665 Fifth Ave.   Phone: (212) 421-8181
New York, NY 10022   Mary Ann D'Aho, Libn.

INTERNATIONAL GAY INFORMATION CENTER, INC.
Village Sta., Box 2   Phone: (212) 473-5884
New York, NY 10014   Keith McKinney, Libn.

INTERNATIONAL LADIES' GARMENT WORKERS UNION - RESEARCH
   DEPARTMENT LIBRARY
1710 Broadway   Phone: (212) 265-7000
New York, NY 10019

INTERNATIONAL PAPER COMPANY - CORPORATE INFORMATION CENTER
77 W. 45th St., 2nd Fl.   Phone: (212) 536-5549
New York, NY 10036   Elizabeth Skerritt, Corp.Libn.

INTERNATIONAL PLANNED PARENTHOOD FEDERATION - WESTERN
   HEMISPHERE REGION - DOCUMENTATION & PUBLICATIONS CTR.
105 Madison Ave.   Phone: (212) 679-2230
New York, NY 10016   Mr. Rene Jaimes, Hd.

INTERNATIONAL SOCIETY FOR REHABILITATION OF THE DISABLED/
   REHABILITATION INTERNATIONAL - LIBRARY
25 E. 21st St.   Phone: (212) 420-1500
New York, NY 10010   Barbara Duncan, Dir. of Info.

INTERNATIONAL THEATRE INSTITUTE OF THE UNITED STATES, INC. -
   INTERNATIONAL THEATRE COLLECTION
1860 Broadway, Suite 1510   Phone: (212) 245-3950
New York, NY 10023   Elizabeth B. Burdick, Dir.

INTERNATIONAL THOMSON EDUCATIONAL PUBLISHING, INC. - EDITORIAL
   LIBRARY *
135 W. 50th St.   Phone: (212) 265-8700
New York, NY 10020   David Brown

INTERPUBLIC GROUP OF COMPANIES - CENTER FOR ADVERTISING
    SERVICES
1271 Ave. of the Americas   Phone: (212) 399-8222
New York, NY 10020   Robin Feuerstein, Dir., Info.Prog./Anl.

IRELAND CONSULATE GENERAL - LIBRARY *
580 Fifth Ave.   Phone: (212) 382-2525
New York, NY 10036   Hon. Sean Oh'Uiginn, Consul Gen.

IRI RESEARCH INSTITUTE, INC. - LIBRARY
One Rockefeller Plaza, Rm. 1401   Phone: (212) 581-1942
New York, NY 10020

IRVING TRUST COMPANY - BUSINESS LIBRARY
One Wall St.   Phone: (212) 487-6431
New York, NY 10015   Susan Stewart, Asst.Sec./Hd.Libn.

ISLANDS RESEARCH FOUNDATION, INC. - INFORMATION CENTER
108 Prospect Tower
45 Tudor City Pl.
New York, NY 10017

ITALIAN CULTURAL INSTITUTE - LIBRARY
686 Park Ave.   Phone: (212) 879-4242
New York, NY 10021   Dr. Maria A. Gargotta, Hd.Libn.

ITT CORPORATION - HEADQUARTERS LIBRARY
320 Park Ave.   Phone: (212) 752-6000
New York, NY 10022   Margaret M. DeLorme, Mgr., Res. & Lib.Serv.

ITT CORPORATION - LEGAL DEPARTMENT LIBRARY
320 Park Ave.
New York, NY 10022   Beryl White, Law Libn.

IVIMEY (Muriel) LIBRARY
329 E. 62nd St.   Phone: (212) 752-5267
New York, NY 10021   Eleanor Yachnes, M.D., Chm., Lib.Comm.

JAPAN SOCIETY, INC. - LIBRARY
333 E. 47th St.   Phone: (212) 832-1155
New York, NY 10017   Tomie Mochizuki, Libn.

JEWISH BOARD OF FAMILY & CHILDREN SERVICES - MARY & LOUIS
    ROBINSON LIBRARY
120 W. 57th St.   Phone: (212) 582-9100
New York, NY 10019   Teresa Kremer, Libn.

JEWISH BRAILLE INSTITUTE OF AMERICA, INC. - LIBRARY
110 E. 30th St.   Phone: (212) 889-2525
New York, NY 10016   Richard Borgersen, Lib.Dir.

JEWISH EDUCATION SERVICE OF NORTH AMERICA, INC. - LIBRARY
114 Fifth Ave.   Phone: (212) 675-5656
New York, NY 10011   Dr. Shimon Frost, Dir.

JEWISH EDUCATION SERVICE OF NORTH AMERICA, INC. - NATIONAL
    EDUCATIONAL RESOURCE CENTER
114 Fifth Ave.   Phone: (212) 675-5656
New York, NY 10011   Carolyn S. Hessel, Coord.

JEWISH GUILD FOR THE BLIND - YOUNG MEN'S PHILANTHROPIC LEAGUE -
    CASSETTE LIBRARY
15 W. 65th St.   Phone: (212) 595-2000
New York, NY 10023   Bruce E. Massis, Dir.

JEWISH HISTORICAL SOCIETY OF NEW YORK, INC. - LIBRARY
8 W. 70th St.   Phone: (212) 873-0300
New York, NY 10023   Steven W. Siegel, Exec.Sec.

JEWISH LABOR BUND - BUND ARCHIVES OF THE JEWISH LABOR
    MOVEMENT
25 E. 21st St.   Phone: (212) 505-8970
New York, NY 10010   Eleonora Golobic, Archv.

JEWISH MEMORIAL HOSPITAL - IRVING DORFMAN MEMORIAL MEDICAL
    LIBRARY †
4600 Broadway   Phone: (212) 569-4700
New York, NY 10040   Theodora L.D. Lindt, Dir.

JEWISH MUSEUM - LIBRARY
1109 Fifth Ave.   Phone: (212) 860-1888
New York, NY 10028

JEWISH THEOLOGICAL SEMINARY OF AMERICA - LIBRARY
3080 Broadway   Phone: (212) 749-8000
New York, NY 10027   Dr. Menahem Schmelzer, Libn.

JOCKEY CLUB - LIBRARY
380 Madison Ave.   Phone: (212) 599-1919
New York, NY 10017   Robert L. Melican, Exec.Dir.

JOHN JAY COLLEGE OF CRIMINAL JUSTICE OF THE CITY UNIVERSITY OF
    NEW YORK - REISMAN MEMORIAL LIBRARY
445 W. 59th St.   Phone: (212) 489-5169
New York, NY 10019   Professor Eileen Rowland, Chf.Libn.

JOHNSON & HIGGINS - EBP RESEARCH LIBRARY †
95 Wall St.   Phone: (212) 482-6570
New York, NY 10005   Renee Sanders, Libn.

JOINT DISEASES/NORTH GENERAL HOSPITAL - MEDICAL LIBRARY
1919 Madison Ave.   Phone: (212) 650-4000
New York, NY 10035   Jana Martin, Med.Libn.

JONES LANG WOOTTON - INFORMATION CENTER
499 Park Ave.   Phone: (212) 688-8181
New York, NY 10022   Susan Courtney, Lib.Dir.

JOURNAL OF COMMERCE - EDITORIAL LIBRARY
110 Wall St.   Phone: (212) 208-0241
New York, NY 10005   Christine Karpevych, Info.Mgr./Libn.

JUILLIARD SCHOOL - LILA ACHESON WALLACE LIBRARY
Lincoln Center Plaza   Phone: (212) 799-5000
New York, NY 10023   Brinton Jackson, Libn.

JULIEN, SCHLESINGER & FINZ, P.C., ATTORNEYS-AT-LAW - LIBRARY *
2 Lafayette St., Suite 1006   Phone: (212) 962-8020
New York, NY 10007

KAYE, SCHOLER, FIERMAN, HAYS & HANDLER - LAW LIBRARY
425 Park Ave.   Phone: (212) 407-8312
New York, NY 10022   Gerald Goodhartz, Libn.

KELLEY, DRYE & WARREN - LAW LIBRARY
101 Park Ave.   Phone: (212) 808-7800
New York, NY 10178   Martha Goldman, Libn.

KENNEDY GALLERIES - ART LIBRARY
40 W. 57th St.   Phone: (212) 541-9600
New York, NY 10019   Cynthia Seibels, Libn.

KENYON & ECKHARDT ADVERTISING - INFORMATION CENTER *
200 Park Ave.   Phone: (212) 880-2361
New York, NY 10017   Aina Geske, Hd.Libn.

KEYSTONE PRESS AGENCY, INC. - PICTURE LIBRARY
202 E. 42nd St.   Phone: (212) 924-8123
New York, NY 10017   Brian F. Alpert, Mng.Ed.

KIDDER, PEABODY AND COMPANY, INC. - LIBRARY
10 Hanover Sq., 21st Fl.   Phone: (212) 747-2504
New York, NY 10005   Joanne Ultang, Libn.

KNOEDLER (M.) AND COMPANY, INC. - LIBRARY
19 E. 70th St.   Phone: (212) 794-0569
New York, NY 10021   Nancy C. Little, Libn.

KOSCIUSZKO FOUNDATION - REFERENCE LIBRARY
15 E. 65th St.
New York, NY 10021

LABOR RESEARCH ASSOCIATION - LIBRARY
80 E. 11th St.   Phone: (212) 473-1042
New York, NY 10003   Greg Tarpinian, Dir.

LANDAUER ASSOCIATES, INC. - INFORMATION CENTER
335 Madison Ave.   Phone: (212) 687-2323
New York, NY 10017   Paula Nelson, Hd.Libn.

LANE & MITTENDORF - LAW LIBRARY
26 Broadway   Phone: (212) 943-3000
New York, NY 10004   Joel L. Solomon, Libn.

LAZARD FRERES & COMPANY - FINANCIAL LIBRARY
One Rockefeller Plaza   Phone: (212) 489-6600
New York, NY 10020   Anne Mintz, Mgr., Lib.Serv.

LEAGUE OF ARAB STATES - ARAB INFORMATION CENTER
747 Third Ave.   Phone: (212) 838-8700
New York, NY 10017   Marwan Kanafani, Info.Off.

LEAGUE FOR YIDDISH - LIBRARY
200 W. 72nd St.   Phone: (212) 787-6675
New York, NY 10023   Leybl Kahn, Libn.

LEBER KATZ, INC. - MARKETING INFORMATION CENTER LIBRARY
767 Fifth Ave.   Phone: (212) 705-1000
New York, NY 10022   Catherine Preston, Dir.

LEBHAR-FRIEDMAN, INC. - CHAIN STORE AGE - READER SERVICE
   RESEARCH LIBRARY
425 Park Ave.   Phone: (212) 371-9400
New York, NY 10022   Ruth Weselteer, Libn.

LEBOEUF, LAMB, LEIBY & MAC RAE - LIBRARY
520 Madison Ave.   Phone: (212) 715-8000
New York, NY 10022   Ruth V. Mortensen, Libn.

LEGAL AID SOCIETY - LIBRARIES
15 Park Row   Phone: (212) 577-3333
New York, NY 10038   David Donaldson, Hd.Libn.

LENOX HILL HOSPITAL - HEALTH SCIENCES LIBRARY
100 E. 77th St.   Phone: (212) 794-4266
New York, NY 10021   Shirley E. Dansker, Dir.

LESBIAN HERSTORY EDUCATIONAL FOUNDATION, INC. - ARCHIVES
Box 1258   Phone: (212) 874-7232
New York, NY 10116

LEWIS (Frederic) INC. - PHOTOGRAPHIC LIBRARY
15 W. 38th St.   Phone: (212) 921-2850
New York, NY 10018   David Perton, Pres.

LIONEL D. EDIE AND COMPANY, INC. - LIBRARY †
600 Fifth Ave.   Phone: (212) 957-1400
New York, NY 10020   Kay Stock, Sr.Lib.Asst.

LORD, DAY & LORD - LIBRARY
25 Broadway   Phone: (212) 344-8480
New York, NY 10004   Cecelia B. Scotti, Hd.Libn.

LOWENSTEIN (M.) CORPORATION - DESIGN RESEARCH LIBRARY
1430 Broadway   Phone: (212) 930-5610
New York, NY 10018   Colleen Ryan-McIntyre, Libn.

LOWER EAST SIDE FAMILY RESOURCE CENTER
137 East 2nd St.   Phone: (212) 677-6602
New York, NY 10009

LUTHERAN COUNCIL IN THE U.S.A. - RECORDS AND INFORMATION
   CENTER - REFERENCE LIBRARY
360 Park Ave., S.   Phone: (212) 532-6350
New York, NY 10010   Alice M. Kendrick, Dir.

MC ADAMS, WILLIAM DOUGLAS, INC. - MEDICAL LIBRARY
110 E. 59th St.   Phone: (212) 759-6300
New York, NY 10022   Molly Garfin, Mgr., Lib.

MC GRAW-HILL, INC. - AVIATION WEEK & SPACE TECHNOLOGY LIBRARY
1221 Ave. of the Americas   Phone: (212) 997-4117
New York, NY 10020   Mark Padnos, Libn.

MC GRAW-HILL, INC. - BUSINESS WEEK MAGAZINE LIBRARY †
1221 Ave. of the Americas   Phone: (212) 997-3297
New York, NY 10020   Tessie Mantzoros, Libn.

MC GRAW-HILL, INC. - LIBRARY
1221 Ave. of the Americas   Phone: (212) 997-6829
New York, NY 10020   George W. Barlow, Chf.Libn.

MC GRAW-HILL PUBLICATIONS COMPANY - MARKETING INFORMATION
   CENTER
1221 Ave. of the Americas   Phone: (212) 997-3222
New York, NY 10020   Ranulph F. Norman, Dir.

MC KINSEY & COMPANY, INC. - INFORMATION SERVICES
55 E. 52nd St.   Phone: (212) 909-8400
New York, NY 10022   Ellen Shedlarz, Mgr.

MACKAY - SHIELDS FINANCIAL CORPORATION - RESEARCH LIBRARY
551 Fifth Ave.   Phone: (212) 210-0462
New York, NY 10017   Ann Hally, Libn.

MAGAZINE PUBLISHERS ASSOCIATION - MAGAZINE INFORMATION
   CENTER
575 Lexington Ave.   Phone: (212) 752-0055
New York, NY 10022   Annmaria Di Cesare, Mgr., Info.Serv.

MAIN HURDMAN - LIBRARY
Park Avenue Plaza
55 E. 52nd St.   Phone: (212) 909-5600
New York, NY 10055   Marjorie Moyal, Libn.

MANHATTAN SCHOOL OF MUSIC - FRANCES HALL BALLARD LIBRARY †
120 Claremont Ave.   Phone: (212) 749-2802
New York, NY 10027   Nina Davis-Millis, Libn.

MANNES COLLEGE OF MUSIC - HARRY SCHERMAN LIBRARY
150 W. 85th St.   Phone: (212) 580-0210
New York, NY 10024   Jane Gottlieb, Hd.Libn.

MANUFACTURERS HANOVER TRUST COMPANY - CORPORATE LIBRARY/
   FINANCIAL LIBRARY DIVISION †
270 Park Ave.   Phone: (212) 350-4733
New York, NY 10017   Ann Little, Libn.

MANUFACTURERS HANOVER TRUST COMPANY - CORPORATE LIBRARY/
   INVESTMENT LIBRARY DIVISION †
600 Fifth Ave.   Phone: (212) 957-1356
New York, NY 10020   Ann Little, Libn.

MANUFACTURERS HANOVER TRUST COMPANY - INTERNATIONAL
   ECONOMICS DEPARTMENT - LIBRARY
Two Grand Central Tower
140 E. 43rd St., 23rd Fl.   Phone: (212) 808-8703
New York, NY 10017   Halina Osysko, Libn.

MARINE MIDLAND BANK - LIBRARY
140 Broadway, 15th Fl.   Phone: (212) 440-1966
New York, NY 10015   Joan W. Glazier, Lib.Off.

MARLBOROUGH GALLERY - LIBRARY
40 W. 57th St.   Phone: (212) 541-4900
New York, NY 10019   Dorothy W. Herman, Libn.

MARSCHALK COMPANY, INC. - LIBRARY †
1345 Ave. of the Americas   Phone: (212) 708-8800
New York, NY 10019

MARSH AND MC LENNAN, INC. - INFORMATION CENTER
1221 Ave. of the Americas   Phone: (212) 997-7800
New York, NY 10020   Susan Kucsma, Mgr.

MATERNITY CENTER ASSOCIATION - REFERENCE LIBRARY
48 E. 92nd St.   Phone: (212) 369-7300
New York, NY 10028   Esther Hanchett, Act.Libn.

MEDICAL LIBRARY CENTER OF NEW YORK †
5 E. 102nd St.   Phone: (212) 427-1630
New York, NY 10029   William D. Walker, Dir.

MEMORIAL SLOAN-KETTERING CANCER CENTER - LEE COOMBE
MEMORIAL LIBRARY
1275 York Ave.   Phone: (212) 794-7439
New York, NY 10021   Angelina Harmon, Libn.

MEMORY SHOP, INC. - MOVIE MEMORABILIA STILLS *
109 E. 12th St.   Phone: (212) 473-2404
New York, NY 10003   Mark Ricci, Mgr.

MERCANTILE LIBRARY ASSOCIATION - MERCANTILE LIBRARY
17 E. 47th St.   Phone: (212) 755-6710
New York, NY 10017   Claire J. Roth, Lib.Dir.

MERRILL LYNCH PIERCE FENNER & SMITH, INC. - LIBRARY †
One Liberty Plaza
165 Broadway   Phone: (212) 637-7420
New York, NY 10080   Rita A. Hughes, Chf. Libn.

MERRILL LYNCH WHITE WELD - CAPITAL MARKETS GROUP - LIBRARY †
One Liberty Plaza, 42nd Fl.   Phone: (212) 637-2085
New York, NY 10080   Eva Vanek, Mgr., Lib.Serv.

METROMEDIA INC. - CORPORATE RESEARCH LIBRARY †
205 E. 67th St.   Phone: (212) 682-9100
New York, NY 10021   Francine Holzer, Hd.Libn.

METROPOLITAN HOSPITAL CENTER - DRAPER HALL LIBRARY *
1918 First Ave.   Phone: (212) 360-6957
New York, NY 10029   Walter Klivcks, Libn.

METROPOLITAN HOSPITAL CENTER - FREDERICK M. DEARBORN MEDICAL
LIBRARY
1901 First Ave.   Phone: (212) 360-6270
New York, NY 10029   Vivienne Whitson, Chf.Libn.

METROPOLITAN HOSPITAL CENTER - PSYCHIATRY LIBRARY
1901 First Ave., Rm. 10M13   Phone: (212) 360-7285
New York, NY 10029   Lorna Macdonald, Libn.

METROPOLITAN LIFE INSURANCE COMPANY - CORPORATE INFORMATION
CENTER AND LIBRARY
One Madison Ave., 1 M-R   Phone: (212) 578-3700
New York, NY 10010   Elizabeth McCloat, Libn.

METROPOLITAN LIFE INSURANCE COMPANY - LAW LIBRARY
One Madison Ave.   Phone: (212) 578-3111
New York, NY 10010   Rita Barone, Law Libn.

METROPOLITAN MUSEUM OF ART - CLOISTERS LIBRARY
Fort Tryon Pk.   Phone: (212) 923-3700
New York, NY 10040   Suse Childs, Libn.

METROPOLITAN MUSEUM OF ART - DEPARTMENT OF PRINTS AND
PHOTOGRAPHS
Fifth Ave. & 82nd St.   Phone: (212) 879-5500
New York, NY 10028   Colta Ives, Cur.

METROPOLITAN MUSEUM OF ART - IRENE LEWISOHN COSTUME
REFERENCE LIBRARY *
Fifth Ave. & 82nd St.   Phone: (212) 879-5500
New York, NY 10028   Gordon Stone, Assoc.Musm.Libn.

METROPOLITAN MUSEUM OF ART - PHOTOGRAPH AND SLIDE LIBRARY
Fifth Ave. & 82nd St.   Phone: (212) 879-5500
New York, NY 10028   Margaret P. Nolan, Chf.Libn.

METROPOLITAN MUSEUM OF ART - ROBERT GOLDWATER LIBRARY
Fifth Ave. & 82nd St.   Phone: (212) 879-5500
New York, NY 10028   Allan D. Chapman, Musm.Libn.

METROPOLITAN MUSEUM OF ART - ROBERT LEHMAN COLLECTION -
LIBRARY *
Fifth Ave. & 82nd St.   Phone: (212) 879-5500
New York, NY 10028   Victoria S. Galban, Asst.Cur., Res.

METROPOLITAN MUSEUM OF ART - THOMAS J. WATSON LIBRARY
Fifth Ave. & 82nd St.   Phone: (212) 879-5500
New York, NY 10028   William B. Walker, Chf.Libn.

METROPOLITAN MUSEUM OF ART - URIS LIBRARY AND RESOURCE CENTER
Fifth Ave. & 82nd St.   Phone: (212) 879-5500
New York, NY 10028   Roberta M. Paine, Musm. Educator

METROPOLITAN OPERA ASSOCIATION - ARCHIVES
Lincoln Ctr. Plaza   Phone: (212) 799-3100
New York, NY 10023   Robert Tuggle, Dir. of Archv.

MILBANK, TWEED, HADLEY & MC CLOY - LIBRARY
1 Chase Manhattan Plaza   Phone: (212) 530-5200
New York, NY 10005   Gina Resnick, Libn.

MINORITY BUSINESS INFORMATION INSTITUTE, INC. - LIBRARY
130 Fifth Ave.   Phone: (212) 242-8000
New York, NY 10011   Earl G. Graves, Dir.

MOBIL OIL CORPORATION - PUBLIC AFFAIRS SECRETARIAT
150 E. 42nd St., Rm. 606   Phone: (212) 883-2155
New York, NY 10017   E. Holmes Bearden, Mgr.

MODERN LANGUAGE ASSOCIATION - CENTER FOR BIBLIOGRAPHICAL
SERVICES
62 Fifth Ave.   Phone: (212) 741-5590
New York, NY 10011   Eileen M. Mackesy, Dir./Mng.Ed.

MONKMEYER PRESS PHOTO SERVICE
118 E. 28th St.   Phone: (212) 689-2242
New York, NY 10016   Hilde R. Monkmeyer

MOODY'S INVESTORS SERVICE, INC. - INFORMATION CENTER
99 Church St.   Phone: (212) 553-0525
New York, NY 10007   Angelica Carroll, Mgr.

MORGAN GUARANTY TRUST COMPANY OF NEW YORK - LIBRARY
23 Wall St.   Phone: (212) 483-2180
New York, NY 10015   Mary S. DePasquale, Hd.Libn.

MORGAN, LEWIS & BOCKIUS - LIBRARY
101 Park Ave.   Phone: (212) 309-6000
New York, NY 10178   Huguette Streuli, Libn.

MORGAN STANLEY & COMPANY, INC. - LIBRARY SERVICES
1251 Ave. of the Americas   Phone: (212) 974-4369
New York, NY 10020   Sarah C. Jones, Dir., Lib.Serv.

MOTION PICTURE ASSOCIATION OF AMERICA - LIBRARY
522 Fifth Ave.   Phone: (212) 840-6161
New York, NY 10036   Robert A. Franklin, Ph.D., Dir. of Res.

MOUNT SINAI SCHOOL OF MEDICINE OF THE CITY UNIVERSITY OF NEW
YORK - GUSTAVE L. & JANET W. LEVY LIBRARY
One Gustave L. Levy Pl.   Phone: (212) 650-7793
New York, NY 10029   Lynn Kasner Morgan, Dir.

MOVIE STAR NEWS - PHOTOGRAPH COLLECTION
134 W. 18th St.   Phone: (212) 620-8160
New York, NY 10011   Paula Klaw, Pres.

MUDGE, ROSE, GUTHRIE, ALEXANDER & FERDON - LIBRARY
180 Maiden Ln.   Phone: (212) 510-7000
New York, NY 10038   Peggy Martin, Libn.

MUNICIPAL ART SOCIETY OF NEW YORK - INFORMATION EXCHANGE
457 Madison Ave.   Phone: (212) 980-1297
New York, NY 10022   Darlene McCloud, Dir.

MUSCULAR DYSTROPHY ASSOCIATION - LIBRARY
810 Seventh Ave.   Phone: (212) 586-0808
New York, NY 10019

MUSEUM OF THE CITY OF NEW YORK - LIBRARY
Fifth Ave. at 103rd St.   Phone: (212) 534-1672
New York, NY 10029   Nancy Kessler-Post, Libn.

MUSEUM OF THE CITY OF NEW YORK - THEATRE COLLECTION
103rd St. & Fifth Ave.   Phone: (212) 534-1672
New York, NY 10029   Dr. Mary C. Henderson, Cur.

MUSEUM OF MODERN ART - DEPARTMENT OF RIGHTS AND
  REPRODUCTIONS - PHOTOGRAPHIC ARCHIVES
11 W. 53rd St.   Phone: (212) 708-9458
New York, NY 10019   Esther M. Carpenter, Archv.

MUSEUM OF MODERN ART - FILM STUDY CENTER
11 W. 53rd St.   Phone: (212) 708-9613
New York, NY 10019   Charles Silver, Supv.

MUSEUM OF MODERN ART - LIBRARY
11 W. 53rd St.   Phone: (212) 708-9433
New York, NY 10019   Clive Phillpot, Dir.

MUTUAL OF NEW YORK (MONY) - CORPORATE LIBRARY / INFORMATION
  SERVICE
1740 Broadway   Phone: (212) 708-2139
New York, NY 10019   Marion Koshar, Corp.Libn.

MUTUAL OF NEW YORK (MONY) - LAW LIBRARY
1740 Broadway   Phone: (212) 708-2235
New York, NY 10019   Marion Koshar, Libn.

MYSTERY WRITERS OF AMERICA, INC. - MYSTERY LIBRARY
150 E. 19th St.   Phone: (212) 255-7005
New York, NY 10003   Harold Q. Masur, Exec. V.P.

NATIONAL ACADEMY OF DESIGN - LIBRARY AND ARCHIVES
1083 Fifth Ave.   Phone: (212) 369-4880
New York, NY 10128   Abigail Booth Gerdts, Archv.

NATIONAL ASSOCIATION OF ACCOUNTANTS - LIBRARY
919 Third Ave.   Phone: (212) 754-9736
New York, NY 10022   Miriam J. Redrick, Mgr., Lib.Serv.

NATIONAL AUDUBON SOCIETY - LIBRARY
950 Third Ave.
New York, NY 10022

NATIONAL BROADCASTING COMPANY, INC. - INFORMATION SERVICES -
  RESEARCH DEPARTMENT
30 Rockefeller Plaza, Rm. 1640   Phone: (212) 664-4243
New York, NY 10020   Doris B. Katz, Mgr.

NATIONAL BROADCASTING COMPANY, INC. - NEWS ARCHIVAL
  OPERATIONS
30 Rockefeller Plaza   Phone: (212) 664-3271
New York, NY 10020   Joann T. O'Dowd, Mgr.

NATIONAL BROADCASTING COMPANY, INC. - RECORDS ADMINISTRATION
  INFORMATION AND ARCHIVES
30 Rockefeller Plaza, Rm. 2M1W   Phone: (212) 664-2690
New York, NY 10020   Vera Mayer, V.P., Info. & Archv.

NATIONAL BROADCASTING COMPANY, INC. - REFERENCE LIBRARY
30 Rockefeller Plaza   Phone: (212) 664-5307
New York, NY 10020   Vera Mayer, V.P., Info. & Archv.

NATIONAL CENTER FOR THE STUDY OF COLLECTIVE BARGAINING IN
  HIGHER EDUCATION AND THE PROFESSIONS
Elias Lieberman Higher Education
Contract Library
17 Lexington Ave.
Box 322   Phone: (212) 725-3390
New York, NY 10012   Joel M. Douglas, Dir.

NATIONAL CENTER ON WOMEN AND FAMILY LAW, INC. - INFORMATION
  CENTER
799 Broadway, Rm. 402   Phone: (212) 674-8200
New York, NY 10003   Laurie Woods, Exec.Dir.

NATIONAL CHAMBER OF COMMERCE FOR WOMEN - ELIZABETH LEWIN
  BUSINESS LIBRARY & INFORMATION CENTER
Box 1132   Phone: (212) 532-6408
New York, NY 10159   Madeline Reynolds, Dir.

NATIONAL CONFERENCE OF CHRISTIANS AND JEWS - PAULA K. LAZRUS
  LIBRARY OF INTERGROUP RELATIONS
71 Fifth Ave.   Phone: (212) 206-0006
New York, NY 10011   Edith G. Selig, Adm.Asst.

NATIONAL CONFERENCE ON SOVIET JEWRY (NCSJ) - RESEARCH BUREAU
10 E. 40th St., Suite 907   Phone: (212) 679-6122
New York, NY 10016   Myrna Shinbaum, Assoc.Dir.

NATIONAL COUNCIL ON ALCOHOLISM, INC. - YVELIN GARDNER
  ALCOHOLISM LIBRARY
733 Third Ave.   Phone: (212) 986-4433
New York, NY 10017   Betty Gold, Libn.

NATIONAL COUNCIL OF CHURCHES - INTERFAITH CENTER ON CORPORATE
  RESPONSIBILITY
475 Riverside Dr., Rm. 566   Phone: (212) 870-2293
New York, NY 10115

NATIONAL EMPLOYMENT LAW PROJECT, INC. - LIBRARY
475 Riverside Dr., Suite 240   Phone: (212) 870-2121
New York, NY 10027   Deborah Hassan, Lib.Info.Mgr.

NATIONAL ENERGY FOUNDATION - ENERGY REFERENCE AND RESOURCE
  CENTER
330 W. 58th St.   Phone: (212) 246-8223
New York, NY 10019   Ann Borden, Exec.V.P.

NATIONAL FILM BOARD OF CANADA - FILM LIBRARY
1251 Ave. of the Americas, 16th Fl.   Phone: (212) 586-5131
New York, NY 10020   Ken Shere, U.S. Gen.Mgr.

NATIONAL LEAGUE FOR NURSING, INC. - LIBRARY/RECORDS CENTER
10 Columbus Circle   Phone: (212) 582-1022
New York, NY 10019   Beryl Gilkes, Supv.

NATIONAL MULTIPLE SCLEROSIS SOCIETY - MEDICAL LIBRARY
205 E. 42nd St.   Phone: (212) 986-3240
New York, NY 10017   Margaret Calvano, Med.Info.Spec.

NATIONAL PSYCHOLOGICAL ASSOCIATION FOR PSYCHOANALYSIS -
  GEORGE LAWTON MEMORIAL LIBRARY
150 W. 13th St.   Phone: (212) 924-7440
New York, NY 10011   M. Shute, Libn.

NATIONAL RECORDS MANAGEMENT COUNCIL - LIBRARY
60 E. 42nd St.   Phone: (212) 697-0290
New York, NY 10165   Robert A. Shiff, Chm.

NATIONAL SOCIETY TO PREVENT BLINDNESS - CONRAD BERENS LIBRARY
79 Madison Ave.   Phone: (212) 684-3505
New York, NY 10016   Dede Silverston, Med.Libn.

NATIONAL TRAINING CENTER OF POLYGRAPH SCIENCE - LIBRARY
200 W. 57th St.
New York, NY 10019   Richard O. Arther, Dir.

NEEDHAM, HARPER & STEERS ADVERTISING, INC. - RESEARCH LIBRARY †
909 Third Ave., 18th Fl.   Phone: (212) 758-7600
New York, NY 10022   Alice Vallinos, Res.Libn.

NEIGHBORHOOD PLAYHOUSE SCHOOL OF THE THEATRE - IRENE
  LEWISOHN LIBRARY †
340 E. 54th St.   Phone: (212) 688-3770
New York, NY 10022   Alice G. Owen, Libn.

NEW SCHOOL FOR SOCIAL RESEARCH - RAYMOND FOGELMAN LIBRARY
65 Fifth Ave.   Phone: (212) 741-7902
New York, NY 10003   Michael Lordi, Lib.Dir.

NEW YORK ACADEMY OF MEDICINE - LIBRARY
2 E. 103rd St.   Phone: (212) 876-8200
New York, NY 10029   Brett A. Kirkpatrick, Libn.

NEW YORK ASSOCIATION FOR THE BLIND - LIGHTHOUSE LIBRARY
111 E. 59th St.   Phone: (212) 355-2200
New York, NY 10022   Agnes Beck, Coord., Ancillary Serv.

NEW YORK CITY BOARD OF EDUCATION - DIVISION OF SPECIAL
  EDUCATION - MANHATTAN REGIONAL RESOURCE CENTER
55 E. 120th St.   Phone: (212) 686-6120
New York, NY 10035   Roberta Berger, Asst.Libn.

NEW YORK CITY COMMISSION ON HUMAN RIGHTS - LIBRARY
52 Duane St.
New York, NY 10007

NEW YORK CITY - DEPARTMENT OF RECORDS AND INFORMATION
   SERVICES - MUNICIPAL ARCHIVES
52 Chambers St.   Phone: (212) 566-5292
New York, NY 10007   Idilio Gracia-Pena, Dir.

NEW YORK CITY HUMAN RESOURCES ADMINISTRATION - LIBRARY
109 E. 16th St.   Phone: (212) 420-7652
New York, NY 10003   Harold W. Benson, Libn.

NEW YORK CITY HUMAN RESOURCES ADMINISTRATION - MEDICAL
   ASSISTANCE PROGRAM - MEDICAID LIBRARY
330 W. 34th St., 10th Fl. South   Phone: (212) 790-2811
New York, NY 10001   Barry L. Cohen, MAP Libn.

NEW YORK CITY - LAW DEPARTMENT - CORPORATION COUNSEL'S
   LIBRARY †
100 Church St., Rm. 6B1   Phone: (212) 566-4418
New York, NY 10007   Jacob Wexler, Libn.

NEW YORK CITY - MUNICIPAL REFERENCE AND RESEARCH CENTER
31 Chambers St.   Phone: (212) 566-4284
New York, NY 10007   Anne M. Gordon, Dir.

NEW YORK CITY - MUNICIPAL REFERENCE AND RESEARCH CENTER -
   HAVEN EMERSON PUBLIC HEALTH LIBRARY
125 Worth St., Rm. 223   Phone: (212) 566-5169
New York, NY 10013   Shirley Paris, Chf.Libn.

NEW YORK CITY - OFFICE OF CHIEF MEDICAL EXAMINER - MILTON
   HELPERN LIBRARY OF LEGAL MEDICINE
520 First Ave.   Phone: (212) 340-0102
New York, NY 10016   Barry W. Seaver, Libn.

NEW YORK CITY POLICE DEPARTMENT - POLICE ACADEMY LIBRARY
235 E. 20th St.   Phone: (212) 477-9723
New York, NY 10003   John D. Preston, Libn.

NEW YORK CITY - PUBLIC HEALTH LABORATORIES - WILLIAM HALLOCK
   PARK MEMORIAL LIBRARY
455 First Ave.   Phone: (212) 340-4700
New York, NY 10016   Shirley Chapin, Libn.

NEW YORK COLLEGE OF PODIATRIC MEDICINE - MEDICAL LIBRARY
53-55 E. 124th St., 3rd Fl.   Phone: (212) 427-8400
New York, NY 10035   Marshall J. Giannotti, Adm. of Libs.

NEW YORK COUNTY - DISTRICT ATTORNEY'S OFFICE LIBRARY
One Hogan Pl.   Phone: (212) 553-9344
New York, NY 10013   Madeleine Fenster, Libn.

NEW YORK COUNTY LAWYERS' ASSOCIATION - LIBRARY
14 Vesey St.   Phone: (212) 267-6646
New York, NY 10007   Edward M. O'Connell, Law Libn.

NEW YORK COUNTY SURROGATE'S COURT - LAW LIBRARY *
31 Chambers St., Rm. 401   Phone: (212) 374-8275
New York, NY 10007   Nadine A. Dubson, Libn.

NEW YORK DAILY NEWS - LIBRARY †
220 E. 42nd St.   Phone: (212) 949-3569
New York, NY 10017   John C. Hodgson, Chf.Libn.

NEW YORK EYE AND EAR INFIRMARY - BERNARD SAMUELS LIBRARY
310 E. 14th St.   Phone: (212) 598-1431
New York, NY 10003   Carol Strauss, Med.Libn.

NEW YORK GENEALOGICAL AND BIOGRAPHICAL SOCIETY -
   GENEALOGICAL RESEARCH LIBRARY
122 E. 58th St.   Phone: (212) 755-8532
New York, NY 10022   Gunther Pohl, Libn.

NEW-YORK HISTORICAL SOCIETY - LIBRARY
170 Central Park W.   Phone: (212) 873-3400
New York, NY 10024   Dr. Larry E. Sullivan, Libn.

NEW YORK HOSPITAL-CORNELL MEDICAL CENTER - MEDICAL ARCHIVES
1300 York Ave.   Phone: (212) 472-5759
New York, NY 10021   Adele A. Lerner, Archv.

NEW YORK HOSPITAL-CORNELL MEDICAL CENTER - OSKAR DIETHELM
   HISTORICAL LIBRARY
525 E. 68th St.   Phone: (212) 472-6434
New York, NY 10021   Phyllis Rubinton, Libn.

NEW YORK INFIRMARY BEEKMAN DOWNTOWN HOSPITAL - ELISHA
   WALKER STAFF LIBRARY
170 William St.   Phone: (212) 233-5300
New York, NY 10038   Lois Sook, Dir., Med.Lib.

NEW YORK LAW INSTITUTE - LIBRARY
120 Broadway, Rm. 932   Phone: (212) 732-8720
New York, NY 10271   Sieglinde H. Rothschild, Libn.

NEW YORK LAW SCHOOL - LIBRARY
57 Worth St.   Phone: (212) 966-3500
New York, NY 10013   Joyce D. Saltalamachia, Lib.Dir.

NEW YORK LIFE INSURANCE COMPANY - LAW LIBRARY
51 Madison Ave., Rm. 10SB   Phone: (212) 576-6458
New York, NY 10010   Margaret Butler, Law Libn.

NEW YORK LIFE INSURANCE COMPANY - MEDICAL DEPARTMENT LIBRARY
51 Madison Ave.   Phone: (212) 576-6246
New York, NY 10010   Thomas Jernigan, M.D., Med.Dir.

NEW YORK LIFE INSURANCE COMPANY - NEW YORK LIFE LIBRARY
51 Madison Ave.   Phone: (212) 576-6738
New York, NY 10010   Lola M. McComb, Sr.Libn.

NEW YORK METROPOLITAN TRANSPORTATION COUNCIL - LIBRARY
One World Trade Ctr., 82nd Fl. E.
New York, NY 10048

NEW YORK ORTHOPAEDIC HOSPITAL - RUSSELL A. HIBBS MEMORIAL
   LIBRARY
622 W. 168th St.   Phone: (212) 694-3294
New York, NY 10032   Jack E. Termine, Med.Libn.

NEW YORK POST - LIBRARY
210 South St.   Phone: (212) 349-5000
New York, NY 10002   Merrill F. Sherr, Hd.Libn.

NEW YORK PSYCHOANALYTIC INSTITUTE - ABRAHAM A. BRILL LIBRARY
247 E. Eighty-Second St.   Phone: (212) 879-6900
New York, NY 10028   Ellen Gilbert, Libn.

NEW YORK PUBLIC LIBRARY - ANNEX SECTION - NEWSPAPERS AND
   OTHER RESEARCH MATERIALS COLLECTION
521 W. 43rd St.   Phone: (212) 930-0847
New York, NY 10036   Richard L. Hill, First Asst., Annex

NEW YORK PUBLIC LIBRARY - ANNEX SECTION - PATENTS COLLECTION
521 W. 43rd St.   Phone: (212) 930-0850
New York, NY 10036   Richard L. Hill, First Asst., Annex

NEW YORK PUBLIC LIBRARY - ARENTS COLLECTION OF BOOKS IN PARTS
Fifth Ave. & 42nd St., Rm. 324   Phone: (212) 930-0801
New York, NY 10018   Bernard McTigue, Cur., Arents Coll.

NEW YORK PUBLIC LIBRARY - ARENTS TOBACCO COLLECTION
Fifth Ave. & 42nd St., Rm. 324   Phone: (212) 930-0801
New York, NY 10018   Bernard McTigue, Cur., Arents Coll.

NEW YORK PUBLIC LIBRARY - ART, PRINTS & PHOTOGRAPHS DIVISION -
   ART AND ARCHITECTURE COLLECTION
Fifth Ave. & 42nd St., Rm. 313   Phone: (212) 930-0834
New York, NY 10018

NEW YORK PUBLIC LIBRARY - ART, PRINTS & PHOTOGRAPHS DIVISION -
   PRINTS & PHOTOGRAPHS ROOM
Fifth Ave. & 42nd St., Rm. 308   Phone: (212) 930-0817
New York, NY 10018

NEW YORK PUBLIC LIBRARY - BERG COLLECTION
Fifth Ave. & 42nd St., Rm. 318, 320   Phone: (212) 930-0802
New York, NY 10018   Dr. Lola L. Szladits, Cur.

NEW YORK PUBLIC LIBRARY - DONNELL LIBRARY CENTER
20 W. 53rd St.   Phone: (212) 621-0613
New York, NY 10019   Philip Gerrard, Prin.Coord.Libn.

NEW YORK PUBLIC LIBRARY - DONNELL LIBRARY CENTER - CENTRAL
   CHILDREN'S ROOM
20 W. 53rd St.   Phone: (212) 621-0636
New York, NY 10019   Angeline Moscatt, Supv.Libn.

NEW YORK PUBLIC LIBRARY - DONNELL LIBRARY CENTER - FOREIGN
   LANGUAGE LIBRARY
20 W. 53rd St.   Phone: (212) 621-0641
New York, NY 10019   Bosiljka Stevanovic, Supv.Libn.

NEW YORK PUBLIC LIBRARY - DONNELL LIBRARY CENTER - MEDIA
   CENTER - FILM/VIDEO COLLECTION
20 W. 53rd St.   Phone: (212) 621-0609
New York, NY 10019   Marie Nesthus, Principal Libn.

NEW YORK PUBLIC LIBRARY - DONNELL LIBRARY CENTER - MEDIA
   CENTER - RECORD COLLECTION
20 W. 53rd St.   Phone: (212) 621-0624
New York, NY 10019   Louise Spain, Supv.Libn.

NEW YORK PUBLIC LIBRARY - DONNELL LIBRARY CENTER - NATHAN
   STRAUS YOUNG ADULT LIBRARY
20 W. 53rd St.   Phone: (212) 621-0633
New York, NY 10019   Beryl Eber, Supv.Libn.

NEW YORK PUBLIC LIBRARY - EARLY CHILDHOOD RESOURCE AND
   INFORMATION CENTER
66 Leroy St.   Phone: (212) 929-0815
New York, NY 10014   Hannah Nuba Scheffler, Dir.

NEW YORK PUBLIC LIBRARY - ECONOMIC AND PUBLIC AFFAIRS DIVISION
Fifth Ave. & 42nd St., Rm. 228   Phone: (212) 930-0750
New York, NY 10018   Edward Di Roma, Div.Chf.

NEW YORK PUBLIC LIBRARY - GENERAL LIBRARY OF THE PERFORMING
   ARTS
111 Amsterdam Ave.   Phone: (212) 870-1630
New York, NY 10023   George L. Mayer, Coord.

NEW YORK PUBLIC LIBRARY - GENERAL RESEARCH DIVISION
Fifth Ave. & 42nd St.   Phone: (212) 930-0831
New York, NY 10011   Rodney Phillips, Chf.

NEW YORK PUBLIC LIBRARY - JEWISH DIVISION
Fifth Ave. & 42nd St., Rm. 84   Phone: (212) 930-0601
New York, NY 10018   Leonard S. Gold, Div.Chf.

NEW YORK PUBLIC LIBRARY - MAP DIVISION
Fifth Ave. & 42nd St., Rm. 117   Phone: (212) 930-0587
New York, NY 10018   Alice C. Hudson, Div.Chf.

NEW YORK PUBLIC LIBRARY - MICROFORMS DIVISION
Fifth Ave. & 42nd St.   Phone: (212) 930-0838
New York, NY 10018   Thomas Bourke, Chf.

NEW YORK PUBLIC LIBRARY - MID-MANHATTAN LIBRARY
455 Fifth Ave.   Phone: (212) 340-0833
New York, NY 10016   Julia J. Brody, Chf. & Assoc.Dir.

NEW YORK PUBLIC LIBRARY - MID-MANHATTAN LIBRARY - ART LIBRARY
455 Fifth Ave.   Phone: (212) 340-0871
New York, NY 10016

NEW YORK PUBLIC LIBRARY - MID-MANHATTAN LIBRARY - GENERAL
   REFERENCE SERVICE/EDUCATION
455 Fifth Ave.   Phone: (212) 340-0863
New York, NY 10016   Eleanor Radwan, Sr.Prin.Libn.

NEW YORK PUBLIC LIBRARY - MID-MANHATTAN LIBRARY - HISTORY AND
   SOCIAL SCIENCES DEPARTMENT
455 Fifth Ave.   Phone: (212) 340-0887
New York, NY 10016   Robert C. Sheehan, Sr. Principal Libn.

NEW YORK PUBLIC LIBRARY - MID-MANHATTAN LIBRARY - JOB
   INFORMATION CENTER
455 Fifth Ave.   Phone: (212) 340-0836
New York, NY 10016   Barbara Shapiro, Prin.Libn.

NEW YORK PUBLIC LIBRARY - MID-MANHATTAN LIBRARY - LEARNER'S
   ADVISORY SERVICE
455 Fifth Ave.   Phone: (212) 340-0835
New York, NY 10016   Barbara Shapiro, Prin.Libn.

NEW YORK PUBLIC LIBRARY - MID-MANHATTAN LIBRARY - LITERATURE
   AND LANGUAGE DEPARTMENT
455 Fifth Ave.   Phone: (212) 340-0873
New York, NY 10016   Eric Steele, Sr. Principal Libn.

NEW YORK PUBLIC LIBRARY - MID-MANHATTAN LIBRARY - PICTURE
   COLLECTION
455 Fifth Ave.   Phone: (212) 340-0877
New York, NY 10016

NEW YORK PUBLIC LIBRARY - MID-MANHATTAN LIBRARY - PROJECT
   ACCESS
455 Fifth Ave.   Phone: (212) 340-0843
New York, NY 10016   Rebecca Adler, Sr.Libn.

NEW YORK PUBLIC LIBRARY - MID-MANHATTAN LIBRARY - READERS'
   ADVISER'S OFFICE
455 Fifth Ave.   Phone: (212) 340-0866
New York, NY 10016   Adele Greenberg, Rd.Adv.

NEW YORK PUBLIC LIBRARY - MID-MANHATTAN LIBRARY - SCIENCE/
   BUSINESS DEPARTMENT
455 Fifth Ave.   Phone: (212) 340-0882
New York, NY 10016   Frederick Dusold, Sr.Prin.Libn.

NEW YORK PUBLIC LIBRARY - ORIENTAL DIVISION
Fifth Ave. & 42nd St., Rm. 219   Phone: (212) 930-0716
New York, NY 10018   E. Christian Filstrup, Div.Chf.

NEW YORK PUBLIC LIBRARY - PERFORMING ARTS RESEARCH CENTER -
   BILLY ROSE THEATRE COLLECTION
111 Amsterdam Ave.   Phone: (212) 870-1639
New York, NY 10023   Dorothy L. Swerdlove, Cur.

NEW YORK PUBLIC LIBRARY - PERFORMING ARTS RESEARCH CENTER -
   DANCE COLLECTION
111 Amsterdam Ave.   Phone: (212) 870-1657
New York, NY 10023   Genevieve Oswald, Cur.

NEW YORK PUBLIC LIBRARY - PERFORMING ARTS RESEARCH CENTER -
   MUSIC DIVISION
111 Amsterdam Ave.   Phone: (212) 870-1650
New York, NY 10023   Frank C. Campbell, Chf.

NEW YORK PUBLIC LIBRARY - PERFORMING ARTS RESEARCH CENTER -
   RODGERS & HAMMERSTEIN ARCHIVES OF RECORDED SOUND
111 Amsterdam Ave.   Phone: (212) 870-1663
New York, NY 10023

NEW YORK PUBLIC LIBRARY - RARE BOOKS & MANUSCRIPTS DIVISION -
   MANUSCRIPTS AND ARCHIVES COLLECTION
476 Fifth Ave., Rm. 319   Phone: (212) 930-0804
New York, NY 10018   Susan E. Davis, Cur. of Mss.

NEW YORK PUBLIC LIBRARY - RARE BOOKS & MANUSCRIPTS DIVISION -
   RARE BOOK COLLECTION
Fifth Ave. & 42nd St.   Phone: (212) 930-0820
New York, NY 10018   Francis O. Mattson, Cur. of Rare Bks.

NEW YORK PUBLIC LIBRARY - REGIONAL LIBRARY FOR THE BLIND AND
   PHYSICALLY HANDICAPPED
166 Ave. of the Americas   Phone: (212) 925-1014
New York, NY 10013   Barbara Nugent, Regional Br.Libn.

NEW YORK PUBLIC LIBRARY - SCHOMBURG CENTER FOR RESEARCH IN
   BLACK CULTURE
515 Lenox Ave.   Phone: (212) 862-4000
New York, NY 10037   Catherine J. Lenix Hooker, Interim Adm.

NEW YORK PUBLIC LIBRARY - SCIENCE AND TECHNOLOGY RESEARCH
CENTER
Fifth Ave. & 42nd St., Rm. 121   Phone: (212) 930-0573
New York, NY 10018   Vitaut Kipel, Act.Chf.

NEW YORK PUBLIC LIBRARY - SLAVONIC DIVISION
Fifth Ave. & 42nd St., Rm. 217   Phone: (212) 930-0714
New York, NY 10018   Edward Kasinec, Div.Chf.

NEW YORK PUBLIC LIBRARY - SPENCER COLLECTION
Fifth Ave. & 42nd St., Rm. 308   Phone: (212) 930-0818
New York, NY 10018

NEW YORK PUBLIC LIBRARY - UNITED STATES HISTORY, LOCAL HISTORY
AND GENEALOGY DIVISION
Fifth Ave. & 42nd St., Rm. 315N   Phone: (212) 930-0828
New York, NY 10018   Gunther E. Pohl, Div.Chf.

NEW YORK ROAD RUNNERS CLUB - INTERNATIONAL RUNNING CENTER
LIBRARY
FDR Sta., Box 881   Phone: (212) 860-4455
New York, NY 10150   Mimi Fahnestock, Libn.

NEW YORK SOCIETY LIBRARY
53 E. 79th St.   Phone: (212) 288-6900
New York, NY 10021   Mark Piel, Libn.

NEW YORK STATE DEPARTMENT OF LABOR - LIBRARY
2 World Trade Ctr., Rm. 6826   Phone: (212) 488-6295
New York, NY 10047   Gloria Weinrich, Sr.Libn.

NEW YORK STATE DEPARTMENT OF LABOR - WORKERS' COMPENSATION
BOARD - LIBRARY †
2 World Trade Ctr.
39th Fl., Rm. 3901   Phone: (212) 488-3103
New York, NY 10047   Donald H. Holley, Assoc. Attorney

NEW YORK STATE DEPARTMENT OF LAW - NEW YORK CITY LIBRARY
2 World Trade Center, Rm. 4749   Phone: (212) 488-7445
New York, NY 10047   Fran Sheinwald, Sr.Libn.

NEW YORK STATE DIVISION OF HOUSING AND COMMUNITY RENEWAL -
REFERENCE ROOM †
2 World Trade Center, 60th Fl.   Phone: (212) 488-4968
New York, NY 10047   William T. Mikell, Sr. Clerk

NEW YORK STATE DIVISION OF HUMAN RIGHTS - REFERENCE LIBRARY
2 World Trade Center, Rm.5356   Phone: (212) 488-5750
New York, NY 10047   James E. Capel, Comm. of Adm.

NEW YORK STATE DIVISION OF SUBSTANCE ABUSE SERVICES - BUREAU
OF TRAINING & RESOURCE DEVELOPMENT - RESOURCE CENTER
350 Broadway, 4th Fl.   Phone: (212) 966-7600
New York, NY 10013   Betty Gee, Res.Ctr.Coord.

NEW YORK STATE METROPOLITAN TRANSPORTATION AUTHORITY -
LIBRARY
347 Madison Ave., 10th Fl.   Phone: (212) 878-7414
New York, NY 10017   Carlotta Rossi, Libn.

NEW YORK STATE OFFICE OF MENTAL HEALTH - NEW YORK STATE
PSYCHIATRIC INSTITUTE - LIBRARY
722 W. 168 St.   Phone: (212) 960-5670
New York, NY 10032

NEW YORK STATE SUPREME COURT - APPELLATE DIVISION, 1ST
JUDICIAL DEPARTMENT - LAW LIBRARY †
27 Madison Ave.   Phone: (212) 532-1000
New York, NY 10010   Stephen R. Grotsky, Libn.

NEW YORK STATE SUPREME COURT - 1ST JUDICIAL DISTRICT -
CRIMINAL BRANCH - LAW LIBRARY
100 Centre St., 17th Fl.   Phone: (212) 374-5615
New York, NY 10013   David G. Badertscher, Prin. Law Libn.

NEW YORK STATE TRIAL LAWYERS ASSOCIATION - LIBRARY
132 Nassau St., Suite 200   Phone: (212) 349-5890
New York, NY 10038   Anne J. Quashen, Exec.Dir.

NEW YORK STOCK EXCHANGE - RESEARCH LIBRARY †
11 Wall St., Rm. 1702   Phone: (212) 623-5049
New York, NY 10005   Jean E. Tobin, Libn.

NEW YORK TELEPHONE COMPANY - LEGAL DEPARTMENT LIBRARY
1095 Ave. of the Americas   Phone: (212) 395-6158
New York, NY 10036   Cornelia E. Mahon, Law Libn.

NEW YORK THEOLOGICAL SEMINARY - LIBRARY
5 W. 29th St.   Phone: (212) 532-4012
New York, NY 10001   Eleanor Soler, Libn.

NEW YORK UNIVERSITY - COURANT INSTITUTE OF MATHEMATICAL
SCIENCES - LIBRARY
251 Mercer St.   Phone: (212) 460-7301
New York, NY 10012   Nancy Gubman, Dir.

NEW YORK UNIVERSITY - DENTAL CENTER - JOHN & BERTHA E.
WALDMANN MEMORIAL LIBRARY
345 E. 24th St.   Phone: (212) 481-5874
New York, NY 10010   Roy C. Johnson, Libn.

NEW YORK UNIVERSITY - ELMER HOLMES BOBST LIBRARY - FROST
LIBRARY
70 Washington Square South   Phone: (212) 598-3756
New York, NY 10012   Frank Walker, Cur.

NEW YORK UNIVERSITY - FALES LIBRARY - DIVISION OF SPECIAL
COLLECTIONS
Bobst Library
70 Washington Sq., S.   Phone: (212) 598-3756
New York, NY 10012   Frank Walker, Cur.

NEW YORK UNIVERSITY - FILM LIBRARY
26 Washington Pl.   Phone: (212) 598-2251
New York, NY 10003   Joyce McGuinnes, Dir.

NEW YORK UNIVERSITY - GRADUATE SCHOOL OF BUSINESS
ADMINISTRATION - LIBRARY
19 Rector St., 2nd Fl.   Phone: (212) 285-6230
New York, NY 10006   Carol Falcione, Dir.

NEW YORK UNIVERSITY - INSTITUTE OF FINE ARTS - SLIDE AND
PHOTOGRAPHIC COLLECTION
1 East 78th St.   Phone: (212) 772-5800
New York, NY 10021   Suzanne Babineau-Simenauer, Cur.

NEW YORK UNIVERSITY MEDICAL CENTER - FREDERICK L. EHRMAN
MEDICAL LIBRARY
550 First Ave.   Phone: (212) 340-5393
New York, NY 10016   Gilbert J. Clausman, Libn.

NEW YORK UNIVERSITY - SALOMON BROTHERS CENTER FOR THE STUDY
OF FINANCIAL INSTITUTIONS - LIBRARY
90 Trinity Pl.   Phone: (212) 285-6100
New York, NY 10006   Margie Guinyard, Libn.

NEW YORK UNIVERSITY - SCHOOL OF CONTINUING EDUC. - REAL ESTATE
INSTITUTE - JACK BRAUSE LIBRARY & INFO. CENTER
11 W. 42nd St.   Phone: (212) 790-1300
New York, NY 10036   Laura Harris, Info.Spec.

NEW YORK UNIVERSITY - SCHOOL OF LAW LIBRARY
40 Washington Sq., S.   Phone: (212) 598-3040
New York, NY 10012   Diana Vincent-Daviss, Law Libn.

NEW YORK UNIVERSITY - STEPHEN CHAN LIBRARY OF FINE ARTS †
1 E. 78th St.   Phone: (212) 988-5550
New York, NY 10021   Evelyn Samuel, Hd.Libn.

NEW YORK UNIVERSITY - TAMIMENT LIBRARY
70 Washington Sq., S.   Phone: (212) 598-3708
New York, NY 10012   Dorothy Swanson, Libn.

NEW YORK UNIVERSITY - UNITED NATIONS COLLECTION
Bobst Library
70 Washington Sq., S.   Phone: (212) 598-3609
New York, NY 10012   Peter B. Allison, Hd., Soc.Sci./Docs.

NEW ZEALAND CONSULATE GENERAL - LIBRARY
630 Fifth Ave., Suite 530   Phone: (212) 586-0060
New York, NY 10111   Nicholas Lorimer, Info. Officer

NEWMONT MINING CORPORATION - TECHNICAL ENGINEERING LIBRARY
300 Park Ave.   Phone: (212) 980-1111
New York, NY 10022   Loretta Herrmann, Libn.

NEWSPAPER ADVERTISING BUREAU, INC. - INFORMATION CENTER
1180 Ave. of the Americas   Phone: (212) 557-1822
New York, NY 10036   Ann Brady, Hd., Info.Ctr.

NEWSWEEK, INC. - LIBRARY
444 Madison Ave.   Phone: (212) 350-2494
New York, NY 10022-6999   Ted Slate, Lib.Dir.

92ND STREET YOUNG MEN'S AND YOUNG WOMEN'S HEBREW
    ASSOCIATION - ARCHIVES
1395 Lexington Ave.   Phone: (212) 427-6000
New York, NY 10028   Steven W. Siegel, Dir., Lib. & Archv.

92ND STREET YOUNG MEN'S AND YOUNG WOMEN'S HEBREW
    ASSOCIATION - BUTTENWIESER LIBRARY
1395 Lexington Ave.   Phone: (212) 427-6000
New York, NY 10028   Steven W. Siegel, Dir., Lib. & Archv.

NORTH AMERICAN JEWISH STUDENTS' NETWORK - LIBRARY
1 Park Ave., Suite 418   Phone: (212) 689-0790
New York, NY 10016   Eric L. Jacobs, Dir.

OGILVY & MATHER, INC. - RESEARCH LIBRARY †
2 E. 48th St.   Phone: (212) 907-3502
New York, NY 10017   Joanne Winiarski, Hd.Libn.

OLWINE, CONNELLY, CHASE, O'DONNELL & WEYHER - LAW LIBRARY
299 Park Ave.   Phone: (212) 207-1800
New York, NY 10171   James T. Roscher, Libn.

ONE TO ONE - RESOURCE CENTER *
One Lincoln Plaza
63rd & Broadway   Phone: (212) 874-2410
New York, NY 10023   Mariette Bates, Resource Ctr.Coord.

OPPENHEIMER & CO., INC. - LIBRARY
One New York Plaza, 32nd Fl.   Phone: (212) 825-4264
New York, NY 10004   Carter Crawford, Libn.

ORGANIZATION RESOURCES COUNSELORS, INC. - INFORMATION CENTER
1211 Ave. of the Americas   Phone: (212) 719-3400
New York, NY 10036   Mary J. DuVal, Libn.

OXFORD UNIVERSITY PRESS, INC. - LIBRARY
200 Madison Ave.   Phone: (212) 679-7300
New York, NY 10016   Clare Marie Hess, Hd.Libn.

PACE UNIVERSITY - LIBRARY
Pace Plaza   Phone: (212) 488-1331
New York, NY 10038   Henry Birnbaum, Univ.Libn.

PACKAGING INSTITUTE, USA - LIBRARY AND RESOURCE CENTER
20 E. 46th St., Suite 603
New York, NY 10017

PAINE WEBBER INC. - PAINE WEBBER BLYTH EASTMAN - LIBRARY
1221 Ave. of the Americas   Phone: (212) 730-8839
New York, NY 10020   Barbara A. Fody, Asst. V.P.

PAINE WEBBER INC. - PAINE WEBBER MITCHELL HUTCHINS - LIBRARY
140 Broadway   Phone: (212) 437-7465
New York, NY 10005   June Fackler, Libn.

PAN AMERICAN WORLD AIRWAYS - CORPORATE LIBRARY
200 Park Ave., Rm. 904   Phone: (212) 880-1917
New York, NY 10166   Liwa Chiu, Libn.

PANNELL KERR FORSTER - LIBRARY
420 Lexington Ave.   Phone: (212) 867-8000
New York, NY 10170   Pam Wells Newton, Libn.

PARADE PUBLICATIONS, INC. - LIBRARY
750 Third Ave., 7th Fl.   Phone: (212) 573-7188
New York, NY 10017   Paul Cook, Lib.Dir.

PARAPSYCHOLOGY FOUNDATION - EILEEN J. GARRETT LIBRARY
228 E. 71st St.   Phone: (212) 628-1550
New York, NY 10021   Wayne Norman, Libn.

PARK AVENUE SYNAGOGUE - ROTHSCHILD LIBRARY
50 E. 87th St.   Phone: (212) 369-2600
New York, NY 10128   Susan Vogelstein, Hd.Libn.

PARKER, CHAPIN, FLATTAU AND KLIMPL - LIBRARY
530 Fifth Ave.   Phone: (212) 840-6200
New York, NY 10036   Helene W. Nelson, Mgr., Files/Lib.

PARSONS, BRINCKERHOFF, QUADE & DOUGLAS - LIBRARY
250 W. 34th St.   Phone: (212) 613-5290
New York, NY 10119   Jeanne I. Brown, Libn.

PARSONS SCHOOL OF DESIGN - ADAM AND SOPHIE GIMBEL DESIGN
    LIBRARY
66 Fifth Ave.   Phone: (212) 741-8914
New York, NY 10011   Sharon Chickanzeff, Lib.Dir.

PATTERSON, BELKNAP, WEBB & TYLER - LIBRARY
30 Rockefeller Plaza   Phone: (212) 541-4000
New York, NY 10112   Penny Tarpley, Chf.Libn.

PAUL, WEISS, RIFKIND, WHARTON AND GARRISON - LIBRARY
345 Park Ave.   Phone: (212) 644-8235
New York, NY 10154   Deborah S. Panella, Chf.Libn.

PAYNE WHITNEY PSYCHIATRIC CLINIC LIBRARY
New York Hospital-
Cornell University Medical College
525 E. 68th St.   Phone: (212) 472-6442
New York, NY 10021   Phyllis Rubinton, Libn.

PEAT, MARWICK, MITCHELL & CO. - INFORMATION AND RESEARCH
    CENTER
345 Park Ave.   Phone: (212) 872-6531
New York, NY 10154   Michael J. Ready, Hd.Libn.

PEN AND BRUSH INC. - LIBRARY
16 E. Tenth St.   Phone: (212) 475-3669
New York, NY 10003   Evelyn C. Kelley, Pres.

PENNEY (J.C.) COMPANY, INC. - LAW LIBRARY
1301 Ave. of the Americas   Phone: (212) 957-8488
New York, NY 10019   Eleanor A. Sabo, Legal Libn.

PENNIE & EDMONDS - LAW LIBRARY
330 Madison Ave.   Phone: (212) 986-8686
New York, NY 10017   Alfred Baman, Libn.

P'EYLIM-AMERICAN YESHIVA STUDENT UNION - LIBRARY
3 W. 16th St.
New York, NY 10011

PFIZER, INC. - N.Y.O. LIBRARY
235 E. 42nd St.   Phone: (212) 573-2966
New York, NY 10017   Veronica Plucinski, Chf.Libn.

PFORZHEIMER (Carl & Lily) FOUNDATION, INC. - CARL H. PFORZHEIMER
    LIBRARY
41 E. 42nd St., Rm. 815   Phone: (212) 697-7217
New York, NY 10017

PHILATELIC FOUNDATION - ARCHIVES AND LIBRARY
270 Madison Ave.   Phone: (212) 889-6483
New York, NY 10016   John F. Dunn, Dir. of Educ.

PHOTO RESEARCHERS, INC. - LIBRARY
60 E. 56th St.   Phone: (212) 758-3420
New York, NY 10022   Jane S. Kinne, Pres.

PICTORIAL PARADE INC. - LIBRARY
130 W. 42nd St.   Phone: (212) 840-2026
New York, NY 10036   Baer M. Frimer, Pres.

PIERPONT MORGAN LIBRARY
29 E. 36th St.   Phone: (212) 685-0008
New York, NY 10016   Charles A. Ryskamp, Dir.

PILSUDSKI (Jozef) INSTITUTE OF AMERICA FOR RESEARCH IN THE
    MODERN HISTORY OF POLAND - LIBRARY
381 Park Ave., S., Suite 701   Phone: (212) 683-4342
New York, NY 10016   Stanislaw Jordanowski, Pres.

PLANNED PARENTHOOD FEDERATION OF AMERICA, INC. - KATHARINE
    DEXTER MC CORMICK LIBRARY
810 Seventh Ave.   Phone: (212) 541-7800
New York, NY 10019   Gloria A. Roberts, Hd.Libn.

POETRY SOCIETY OF AMERICA - VAN VOORHIS LIBRARY †
15 Gramercy Park   Phone: (212) 254-9628
New York, NY 10003   Deborah Gimelson, Adm.Dir.

POINT OF PURCHASE ADVERTISING INSTITUTE - INFORMATION CENTER
60 E. 42nd St.   Phone: (212) 682-7041
New York, NY 10165   John Kawula

POLISH INSTITUTE OF ARTS AND SCIENCES IN AMERICA, INC. -
    RESEARCH LIBRARY
59 E. 66th St.   Phone: (212) 988-4338
New York, NY 10021   Krystyna Baron, Libn.

POLISH SINGERS ALLIANCE OF AMERICA - LIBRARY
180 Second Ave.   Phone: (212) 254-6642
New York, NY 10003   Walter Witkowicki, Libn.

POPULATION COUNCIL - LIBRARY
1 Dag Hammarskjold Plaza   Phone: (212) 644-1620
New York, NY 10017   H. Neil Zimmerman, Libn.

PORT AUTHORITY OF NEW YORK AND NEW JERSEY - LIBRARY
55 N., One World Trade Ctr.   Phone: (212) 466-4062
New York, NY 10048   Jane M. Janiak, Chf.Libn.

POSTGRADUATE CENTER FOR MENTAL HEALTH - EMIL A. GUTHEIL
    MEMORIAL LIBRARY
124 E. 28th St.   Phone: (212) 689-7700
New York, NY 10016   Mrs. Lee Mackler, Dir., Lib. & Info.Serv.

PRACTISING LAW INSTITUTE - LIBRARY
810 Seventh Ave.   Phone: (212) 765-5700
New York, NY 10019   Henry W. Enberg, II, Legal Ed.

PRATT INSTITUTE - PRATT/PHOENIX SCHOOL OF DESIGN LIBRARY
160 Lexington Ave.   Phone: (212) 685-2973
New York, NY 10016   Sharon Lewis, Libn.

PRICE WATERHOUSE - NATIONAL INFORMATION CENTER
1251 Ave. of the Americas   Phone: (212) 489-8900
New York, NY 10020   Masha Zipper, Mgr.

PRICE WATERHOUSE - NEW YORK OFFICE INFORMATION CENTER
153 E. 53rd St.   Phone: (212) 371-2000
New York, NY 10022   Patricia R. Pauth, Adm.

PRICE WATERHOUSE - TAX LIBRARY †
153 E. 53rd St.   Phone: (212) 371-2000
New York, NY 10022   Barbara Ferrante, Tax Libn.

PRINCETON LIBRARY IN NEW YORK
15 W. 43rd St.   Phone: (212) 840-6400
New York, NY 10036   Paula Matta, Libn.

PROGRAM PLANNERS, INC. - LIBRARY/INFORMATION CENTER
230 W. 41st St.   Phone: (212) 840-2600
New York, NY 10036   Patricia Virga, Info.Off.

PROJECT FOR PUBLIC SPACES - LIBRARY
153 Waverly Place   Phone: (212) 581-6553
New York, NY 10014   Steven Davies, Project Dir.

PROSKAUER, ROSE, GOETZ & MENDELSOHN - LIBRARY
300 Park Ave.   Phone: (212) 909-7208
New York, NY 10022   Marsha Pront, Hd.Libn.

PROTESTANT EPISCOPAL CHURCH - EPISCOPAL DIOCESE OF NEW YORK -
    ARCHIVES
1047 Amsterdam Ave.   Phone: (212) 678-6977
New York, NY 10025   James E. Templar, Archv.

PROTESTANT EPISCOPAL CHURCH EXECUTIVE COUNCIL - HENRY KNOX
    SHERRILL RESOURCE CENTER
Episcopal Church Center
815 Second Ave.   Phone: (212) 867-8400
New York, NY 10017   Avis E. Harvey, Rsrcs./Info.Off.

PRUDENTIAL-BACHE SECURITIES INC. - CORPORATE FINANCE
    DEPARTMENT LIBRARY
100 Gold St., 7th Fl.   Phone: (212) 791-3988
New York, NY 10292   Anne M. Bladstrom, Corp.Fin.Libn.

PUBLIC AFFAIRS INFORMATION SERVICE
11 W. 40th St.   Phone: (212) 736-6629
New York, NY 10018   Wilhelm Bartenbach, Exec.Dir.

PUBLIC EDUCATION ASSOCIATION - LIBRARY AND ARCHIVES
20 W. 40th St.   Phone: (212) 354-6100
New York, NY 10018   Judith Baum, Dir., Info.Serv.

PUBLIC RELATIONS SOCIETY OF AMERICA - INFORMATION CENTER
845 Third Ave.   Phone: (212) 826-1776
New York, NY 10022   Mary W. Wilson, Dir.

PUTNEY, TWOMBLY, HALL & HIRSON - LAW LIBRARY
250 Park Ave.   Phone: (212) 661-8700
New York, NY 10017   Lois Liss, Libn.

RACQUET AND TENNIS CLUB - LIBRARY
370 Park Ave.   Phone: (212) 753-9700
New York, NY 10022   Gerard J. Belliveau, Jr., Libn.

RADIO ADVERTISING BUREAU - MARKETING INFORMATION CENTER
485 Lexington Ave.   Phone: (212) 599-6666
New York, NY 10017   Erwyn Khan, Dir.

RADIO FREE EUROPE/RADIO LIBERTY INC. - REFERENCE LIBRARY
1775 Broadway   Phone: (212) 397-5343
New York, NY 10019   Irene V. Dutikow, Ref.Libn.

RAILROAD ENTHUSIASTS NEW YORK DIVISION, INC. - WILLIAMSON
    LIBRARY
Box 1318
New York, NY 10017   Charles Grossman, Libn.

READER'S DIGEST - ADVERTISING AND MARKETING LIBRARY
200 Park Ave.   Phone: (212) 972-3730
New York, NY 10166   Helen Fledderus, Libn.

RECORDING INDUSTRY ASSOCIATION OF AMERICA - REFERENCE LIBRARY
888 7th Ave., 9th Fl.   Phone: (212) 765-4330
New York, NY 10019   James Fishel, Exec.Dir.

REGIONAL PLAN ASSOCIATION, INC. - LIBRARY
1040 Ave. of the Americas   Phone: (212) 398-1140
New York, NY 10018   Peter Haskel, Libn.

REID AND PRIEST - LAW LIBRARY
40 W. 57th St.   Phone: (212) 603-2000
New York, NY 10019   Morton Barad, Libn.

RELIANCE GROUP HOLDINGS, INC. - CORPORATE LIBRARY
Park Ave. Plaza
New York, NY 10055   Ellen Rubin, Corp.Libn.

RELIGIOUS NEWS SERVICE - LIBRARY AND MORGUE
104 W. 56th St.   Phone: (212) 688-7094
New York, NY 10019

RELIGIOUS NEWS SERVICE - PHOTOGRAPH LIBRARY
106 W. 56th St.   Phone: (212) 688-7094
New York, NY 10019   Jim Hansen, Photo Ed.

REPERTOIRE INTERNATIONAL D'ICONOGRAPHIE MUSICALE - RESEARCH
   CENTER FOR MUSICAL ICONOGRAPHY - LIBRARY
Grad. Ctr., CUNY, Dept. of Music
33 W. 42nd St.   Phone: (212) 790-4282
New York, NY 10036   Dr. Barry S. Brook, Dir.

RESEARCH CENTER FOR RELIGION & HUMAN RIGHTS IN CLOSED
   SOCIETIES - INFORMATION CENTER *
475 Riverside Dr., Suite 448   Phone: (212) 870-2481
New York, NY 10115   Rev. B.S. Hruby, Exec.Dir.

RESEARCH & EDUCATION ASSOCIATION - LIBRARY
505 Eighth Ave.   Phone: (212) 695-9487
New York, NY 10018   Carl Fuchs, Libn.

RESEARCH FOUNDATION FOR JEWISH IMMIGRATION, INC. - ARCHIVES
570 7th Ave., 16th Fl.   Phone: (212) 921-3871
New York, NY 10018   Herbert A. Strauss, Coord. of Res.

RESEARCH INSTITUTE OF AMERICA - INFORMATION SERVICES CENTER
589 Fifth Ave.   Phone: (212) 755-8900
New York, NY 10017   Mary Summers, Adm. of Info.Serv.

RESEARCH INSTITUTE FOR THE STUDY OF MAN - LIBRARY
162 E. 78th St.   Phone: (212) 535-8448
New York, NY 10021   Judith Selakoff, Libn.

ROBINSON, SILVERMAN, PEARCE, ARONSOHN & BERMAN - LIBRARY &
   INFORMATION CENTER
230 Park Ave.   Phone: (212) 687-0400
New York, NY 10169   Mary Cosgrove, Libn.

ROCKEFELLER FOUNDATION - LIBRARY
1133 Ave. of the Americas   Phone: (212) 869-8500
New York, NY 10036   Marie Dooling, Libn.

ROCKEFELLER UNIVERSITY - LIBRARY
1230 York Ave.
RU Box 263   Phone: (212) 570-8901
New York, NY 10021-6399   Sonya Wohl Mirsky, Univ.Libn./Spec.Coll.Cur.

ROCKEFELLER UNIVERSITY - NEUROSCIENCES RESEARCH PROGRAM -
   LIBRARY *
100 York Ave.
New York, NY 10021   Dr. Einar Gall

ROGERS & WELLS - LAW LIBRARY
200 Park Ave.   Phone: (212) 878-8210
New York, NY 10166   Raphael Gonzalez, Libn.

ROMANIAN LIBRARY
200 E. 38th St.   Phone: (212) 687-0180
New York, NY 10016   Aurelian Paraipan, Dir.

ROOSEVELT HOSPITAL - MEDICAL LIBRARY
428 W. 59th St.   Phone: (212) 554-6872
New York, NY 10019   Winifred Lieber, Libn.

ROSENMAN, COLIN, FREUND, LEWIS & COHEN - LAW LIBRARY
575 Madison Ave.   Phone: (212) 940-8598
New York, NY 10022   Denise Hasil, Hd.Libn.

RUSSELL SAGE FOUNDATION - LIBRARY
112 E. 64th St.   Phone: (212) 750-6008
New York, NY 10021   Pauline M. Rothstein, Dir., Info.Serv.

ST. CLARE'S HOSPITAL & HEALTH CENTER - MEDICAL LIBRARY
415 W. 51st St.   Phone: (212) 586-1500
New York, NY 10019   James H. Kirk, Libn.

ST. LUKE'S HOSPITAL CENTER - NURSING LIBRARY *
Amsterdam Ave. at 114th St.   Phone: (212) 870-6195
New York, NY 10025   Geraldine Allerman, Dir., Staff Educ.

ST. LUKE'S HOSPITAL CENTER - RICHARD WALKER BOLLING MEMORIAL
   MEDICAL LIBRARY †
Amsterdam Ave. & 114th St.   Phone: (212) 870-1861
New York, NY 10025   Nancy Mary Panella, Libn.

ST. MATTHEW'S & ST. TIMOTHY'S NEIGHBORHOOD CENTER, INC. -
   TUTORIAL PROGRAM LIBRARY
26 W. 84th St.   Phone: (212) 362-6750
New York, NY 10024   Delfa Castillo, Lib.Dir.

ST. VINCENT'S HOSPITAL AND MEDICAL CENTER - MEDICAL LIBRARY
153 W. Eleventh St.   Phone: (212) 790-7811
New York, NY 10011   Agnes T. Frank, Dir.

ST. VINCENT'S HOSPITAL - SCHOOL OF NURSING LIBRARY
27 Christopher St.   Phone: (212) 790-8486
New York, NY 10014   Marie C. Medici, Libn.

SALES AND MARKETING MANAGEMENT - LIBRARY
633 Third Ave.   Phone: (212) 986-4800
New York, NY 10017   J. D. Roberts, Libn.

SALMAGUNDI CLUB - LIBRARY
47 Fifth Ave.   Phone: (212) 255-7740
New York, NY 10003   Joseph Levenson, Libn.

SALOMON BROTHERS - CORPORATE FINANCE LIBRARY
One New York Plaza, 46th Fl.   Phone: (212) 747-7933
New York, NY 10004   Lydia P. Davies, Lib.Mgr.

SALVATION ARMY - ARCHIVES AND RESEARCH CENTER
145 W. 15th St.   Phone: (212) 620-4392
New York, NY 10011   Thomas Wilsted, Archv./Adm.

SALVATION ARMY - EDUCATION DEPARTMENT LIBRARY
120-130 W. 14th St.   Phone: (212) 620-4994
New York, NY 10011   Mrs. Marjorie Sharp

SANGER (Margaret) CENTER-PLANNED PARENTHOOD NEW YORK CITY -
   ABRAHAM STONE LIBRARY
380 Second Ave.   Phone: (212) 677-6474
New York, NY 10010   Jeanne Swinton, Libn.

SCHOLASTIC MAGAZINES & BOOK SERVICES - GENERAL LIBRARY
730 Broadway   Phone: (212) 505-3000
New York, NY 10003   Lucy Evankow, Chf.Libn.

SCHOOL OF VISUAL ARTS - LIBRARY
209 E. 23rd St.   Phone: (212) 679-7350
New York, NY 10010   Zuki Landau, Chf.Libn.

SCHRODER (J. Henry) BANK & TRUST COMPANY - LIBRARY
One State St.   Phone: (212) 269-6500
New York, NY 10015   Juliette Levinton, Libn.

SCIENCE ASSOCIATES/INTERNATIONAL, INC. - LIBRARY
1841 Broadway   Phone: (212) 265-4995
New York, NY 10023   Roxy Bauer, Libn.

SCUDDER, STEVENS & CLARK - LIBRARY
345 Park Ave.   Phone: (212) 350-8371
New York, NY 10154   Linda Osborn, Libn.

SEAGRAM (Joseph E.) & SONS, INC. - CORPORATE LIBRARY
800 Third Ave.   Phone: (212) 572-7873
New York, NY 10022   Alice Gross, Mgr., Lib.Serv.

SEAMEN'S CHURCH INSTITUTE OF NEW YORK - JOSEPH CONRAD LIBRARY
15 State St.   Phone: (212) 269-2710
New York, NY 10004   Bonnie Golightly, Libn.

SELIGMAN (J. & W.) & CO. INCORPORATED - RESEARCH LIBRARY
One Bankers Trust Pl.   Phone: (212) 488-0456
New York, NY 10006   Paula A. Gray, Libn.

SEWARD & KISSEL - LIBRARY
Wall Street Plaza   Phone: (212) 248-2800
New York, NY 10005   Robert J. Davis, Libn.

SEX INFORMATION & EDUCATION COUNCIL OF THE U.S. - SIECUS
    INFORMATION SERVICE AND LIBRARY
715 Broadway, Rm. 213   Phone: (212) 673-3850
New York, NY 10003   Leigh Hallingby, Libn.

SEYFARTH, SHAW, FAIRWEATHER & GERALDSON - LIBRARY
520 Madison Ave.   Phone: (212) 715-9635
New York, NY 10022   Catherine Inglis, Libn.

SHEARMAN & STERLING - LIBRARY
53 Wall St., Rm. 718   Phone: (212) 483-1000
New York, NY 10005   Jack S. Ellenberger, Libn.

SHEARSON LEHMAN/AMERICAN EXPRESS INC. - LIBRARY
55 Water St.   Phone: (212) 558-2134
New York, NY 10041   Ronald F. Dow, Mgr., Lib.Serv.

SHEARSON LEHMAN/AMERICAN EXPRESS INC. - RESEARCH LIBRARY
2 World Trade Ctr., 101st Fl.   Phone: (212) 321-5745
New York, NY 10048   Elizabeth R. Boutinon, Chf.Libn.

SHERMAN GRINBERG FILM LIBRARIES, INC.
630 Ninth Ave.   Phone: (212) 765-5170
New York, NY 10036   Bernard Chertok, Pres.

SHEVCHENKO SCIENTIFIC SOCIETY, INC. - LIBRARY AND ARCHIVES
63 4th Ave.   Phone: (212) 254-5130
New York, NY 10003   Svetlana Andrushkiv, Dir.

SHOSTAL ASSOCIATES, INC.
164 Madison Ave.   Phone: (212) 686-8850
New York, NY 10016

SIMAT, HELLIESEN AND EICHNER - LIBRARY
708 Third Ave., 17th Fl.   Phone: (212) 682-8455
New York, NY 10017   William J. Ehlers, Libn.

SIMPSON, THACHER & BARTLETT - LIBRARY †
1 Battery Park Plaza   Phone: (212) 483-9000
New York, NY 10004   John S. Marsh, Libn.

SKADDEN, ARPS, SLATE, MEAGHER & FLOM - LIBRARY †
919 3rd Ave.   Phone: (212) 371-6000
New York, NY 10022   Carrie Hirtz, Libn.

SKIDMORE, OWINGS & MERRILL - INFORMATION SERVICES DEPARTMENT
220 E. 42nd St.   Phone: (212) 309-9500
New York, NY 10017   Frances C. Gretes, Mgr., Info.Serv.

SMITH BARNEY, HARRIS UPHAM & COMPANY, INC. - LIBRARY
1345 Ave. of the Americas   Phone: (212) 399-6294
New York, NY 10105   Morton R. Brown, Libn.

SMITHSONIAN INSTITUTION LIBRARIES - COOPER-HEWITT MUSEUM OF
    DESIGN - DORIS & HENRY DREYFUSS MEMORIAL STUDY CENTER
2 E. 91st St.   Phone: (212) 860-6887
New York, NY 10128   Katharine Martinez, Chf.Libn.

SMYTHE (R.M.) AND COMPANY - OBSOLETE AND INACTIVE SECURITIES
    LIBRARY
24 Broadway   Phone: (212) 668-1880
New York, NY 10004   Diana E. Herzog, Vice Pres.

SOAP AND DETERGENT ASSOCIATION - LIBRARY
475 Park Ave., S.   Phone: (212) 725-1262
New York, NY 10016   Rose D. Api, Off.Mgr.

SOCIETE CULINAIRE PHILANTHROPIQUE DE NEW YORK, INC. - LIBRARY
250 W. 57th St., Rm. 1532   Phone: (212) 246-6754
New York, NY 10019   Henri Deltieure, Pres.

SOCIETY OF COSMETIC CHEMISTS - LIBRARY
1995 Broadway, 17th Fl.   Phone: (212) 532-7320
New York, NY 10023   George L. Cohen, Ph.D., Chm., Lib.Comm.

SOCIETY OF FRIENDS - NEW YORK YEARLY MEETING - RECORDS
    COMMITTEE - HAVILAND RECORDS ROOM
15 Rutherford Pl.   Phone: (212) 673-6866
New York, NY 10003   Elizabeth Haas Moger, Kpr.

SOCIETY OF WOMEN ENGINEERS - INFORMATION CENTER
345 E. 47th St., Rm. 305   Phone: (212) 705-7855
New York, NY 10017

SOHO CENTER FOR VISUAL ARTISTS - LIBRARY
110 Prince St.   Phone: (212) 226-1993
New York, NY 10012   Rhonda Wall, Libn.

SONS OF THE REVOLUTION IN THE STATE OF NEW YORK - LIBRARY
Fraunces Tavern Museum
Broad & 54 Pearl Sts.   Phone: (212) 425-1776
New York, NY 10004   Patricia Kesling, Act.Adm.

SOUTH STREET SEAPORT MUSEUM - LIBRARY
207 Front St.   Phone: (212) 669-9422
New York, NY 10038   Norman J. Brouwer, Ship Hist.

SPECIAL LIBRARIES ASSOCIATION - INFORMATION RESOURCES CENTER
235 Park Ave., S.   Phone: (212) 477-9250
New York, NY 10003   Mr. Chris R. Ikehara, Mgr., Info.Rsrcs.

SPENCE-CHAPIN SERVICES TO FAMILIES AND CHILDREN - CHARLOTTE
    TOWLE MEMORIAL LIBRARY
6 E. 94th St.   Phone: (212) 369-0300
New York, NY 10028   Leilani Straw, Asst.Dir.

SPERRY - BUSINESS PLANNING LIBRARY
1290 Avenue of the Americas   Phone: (212) 956-3476
New York, NY 10104   William C. Patterson, Dir.

SPERRY AND HUTCHINSON COMPANY - MARKET RESEARCH LIBRARY
330 Madison Ave., 9th Fl.
New York, NY 10017

SPERRY - LAW LIBRARY
1290 Avenue of the Americas   Phone: (212) 484-4444
New York, NY 10104   Rosemarie Scirica, Lib.Adm.

SPERRY - TECHNICAL LIBRARY
1290 Avenue of the Americas   Phone: (212) 484-4444
New York, NY 10104   Graham Gurney, Dist.Mgr.

STACK'S RARE COIN COMPANY OF NEW YORK - TECHNICAL
    INFORMATION CENTER
123 W. 57th St.   Phone: (212) 582-2580
New York, NY 10019   James C. Risk, Mgr., Tech.Oper.

STANDARD & POOR'S CORPORATION - RESEARCH LIBRARY
25 Broadway   Phone: (212) 208-8514
New York, NY 10004   Dennis F. Jensen, Lib.Mgr.

STEP FAMILY FOUNDATION, INC. - LIBRARY
333 West End Ave.   Phone: (212) 877-3244
New York, NY 10023   Jeannette Lofas, Exec.Dir.

STERLING DRUG, INC. - WINTHROP LABORATORIES - MEDICAL LIBRARY
90 Park Ave.   Phone: (212) 972-6256
New York, NY 10016   Irene Frisch, Lib.Dir.

STOCKPHOTOS, INC. - LIBRARY *
275 Seventh Ave.
New York, NY 10001   Robert Werner, Dir.

STONE AND WEBSTER MANAGEMENT CONSULTANTS, INC. -
    INFORMATION CENTER/LIBRARY
One Penn Plaza   Phone: (212) 290-6377
New York, NY 10119

SULLIVAN AND CROMWELL - LIBRARY †
125 Broad St.   Phone: (212) 558-4000
New York, NY 10004   Helene A. Weatherill, Libn.

SUNY - COLLEGE OF OPTOMETRY - HAROLD KOHN MEMORIAL VISUAL
    SCIENCE LIBRARY
100 E. 24th St.   Phone: (212) 477-7965
New York, NY 10010-3677   Margaret Lewis, Libn.

SWEDENBORG FOUNDATION - LIBRARY
139 E. 23rd St.   Phone: (212) 673-7310
New York, NY 10010   Darrell Ruhl, Exec.Dir.

SWEDISH CONSULATE GENERAL - SWEDISH INFORMATION SERVICE
825 Third Ave.   Phone: (212) 751-5900
New York, NY 10022   Elisabeth Halvarsson-Stapen, Lib.Asst.

SYMMERS, FISH AND WARNER - RESEARCH LIBRARY
111 E. 50th St.   Phone: (212) 751-6400
New York, NY 10022   Eileen Finnegan, Libn.

TAMS ENGINEERS, ARCHITECTS & PLANNERS - LIBRARY
655 Third Ave.   Phone: (212) 867-1777
New York, NY 10017

TAYLOR BUSINESS INSTITUTE - LIBRARY
One Penn Plaza   Phone: (212) 279-0510
New York, NY 10019   Roslyn Arnstein, Libn.

TEACHERS COLLEGE - MILBANK MEMORIAL LIBRARY
Columbia University
Box 307   Phone: (212) 678-3494
New York, NY 10027   Jane P. Franck, Dir.

TEACHERS INSURANCE AND ANNUITY ASSOCIATION OF AMERICA -
    BUSINESS LIBRARY
730 Third Ave.   Phone: (212) 490-9000
New York, NY 10017   Kathleen Kelleher, Libn.

TELEVISION INFORMATION OFFICE OF THE NATIONAL ASSOCIATION OF
    BROADCASTERS - RESEARCH SERVICES †
745 Fifth Ave., 17th Fl.   Phone: (212) 759-6800
New York, NY 10151   James Poteat, Mgr., Res.Serv.

THOMPSON (J. Walter) COMPANY - INFORMATION CENTER
466 Lexington Ave.   Phone: (212) 210-7000
New York, NY 10017   Nancy Terry Munger, Mgr., Info.Serv.

THREE LIONS, INC. - LIBRARY
145 E. 32nd St., 9th Fl.   Phone: (212) 725-2242
New York, NY 10016

TIME, INC. - LIBRARY
Time & Life Bldg.
Rockefeller Center   Phone: (212) 556-3746
New York, NY 10020   Benjamin Lightman, Chf.Libn.

TIME, INC. - SPORTS LIBRARY
Radio City Sta.
Box 614   Phone: (212) 841-3397
New York, NY 10019   Lester Annenberg, Hd.Libn.

TOBACCO MERCHANTS ASSOCIATION OF THE U.S. - HOWARD S. CULLMAN
    LIBRARY
1220 Broadway   Phone: (212) 239-4435
New York, NY 10001   R. Robert Sengstacken, Dir., Info.Serv.

TOUCHE ROSS AND COMPANY - INFORMATION CENTER
1633 Broadway   Phone: (212) 489-1600
New York, NY 10019   Harold W. Miller, Mgr., Info.Serv.

TOWERS, PERRIN, FORSTER & CROSBY, INC. - INFORMATION CENTER
600 Third Ave.   Phone: (212) 309-3482
New York, NY 10016   Joseph M. Simmons, Mgr.

TOWNLEY & UPDIKE - LAW LIBRARY
405 Lexington Ave.   Phone: (212) 682-4567
New York, NY 10174   Josephine A. DiGiovanna, Libn.

TOWNSEND-GREENSPAN & COMPANY, INC. - LIBRARY
120 Wall St., 26th Fl.   Phone: (212) 943-9515
New York, NY 10005   Blanche Siegel, Libn.

TRANS WORLD AIRLINES, INC. - CORPORATE LIBRARY
605 Third Ave.   Phone: (212) 557-6055
New York, NY 10158   Esther L. Giles, Corp.Libn.

TRAPHAGEN SCHOOL OF FASHION - ETHEL TRAPHAGEN LEIGH MEMORIAL
    LIBRARY
257 Park Ave., S.   Phone: (212) 673-0300
New York, NY 10010   Allyn Rice Bloeme, Chf.Libn.

TURKISH TOURISM AND INFORMATION OFFICE
821 United Nations Plaza   Phone: (212) 687-2194
New York, NY 10017   C. Kamil Muren, Dir.

TURTLE BAY MUSIC SCHOOL - LIBRARY
244 E. 52nd St.   Phone: (212) 753-8811
New York, NY 10022   Lilien Weintraub, Libn.

TWENTIETH CENTURY FUND - LIBRARY
41 E. 70th St.   Phone: (212) 535-4441
New York, NY 10021   Nettie Gerduk, Libn.

UKRAINIAN ENGINEERS SOCIETY OF AMERICA - LIBRARY
2 East 79th St.   Phone: (212) 535-7676
New York, NY 10021   Mr. E.B. Zmyj, Pres.

UNION OF AMERICAN HEBREW CONGREGATIONS - SYNAGOGUE
    ARCHITECTURAL AND ART LIBRARY †
838 Fifth Ave.   Phone: (212) 249-0100
New York, NY 10021   Myron E. Schoen, Dir.

UNION CLUB - LIBRARY
101 E. 69th St.   Phone: (212) 734-5400
New York, NY 10021   Helen M. Allen, Libn.

UNION LEAGUE CLUB LIBRARY
38 E. 37th St.   Phone: (212) 685-3800
New York, NY 10016   Jane Reed, Libn.

UNION THEOLOGICAL SEMINARY - BURKE LIBRARY
3041 Broadway at Reinhold Niebuhr Place   Phone: (212) 662-7100
New York, NY 10027   Richard D. Spoor, Dir.

UNITED CEREBRAL PALSY OF NEW YORK CITY, INC. - LIBRARY
122 E. 23rd St.   Phone: (212) 677-7400
New York, NY 10010   Richard Gordon, Lib.Mgr.

UNITED CHURCH BOARD FOR WORLD MINISTRIES - LIBRARY
475 Riverside Dr., 16th Fl.
New York, NY 10115   Virginia Stowe, Libn.

UNITED HOSPITAL FUND OF NEW YORK - REFERENCE LIBRARY
3 E. 54th St.   Phone: (212) 754-1080
New York, NY 10022   Christine Bahr, Libn.

UNITED LODGE OF THEOSOPHISTS - THEOSOPHY HALL - LIBRARY
347 E. 72nd St.   Phone: (212) 535-2230
New York, NY 10021

UNITED NATIONS - CENTRE ON TRANSNATIONAL CORPORATIONS -
    LIBRARY
United Nations   Phone: (212) 754-3352
New York, NY 10017   Samuel K.B. Asante, Dir.,Adv./Info.Serv.Div.

UNITED NATIONS FUND FOR POPULATION ACTIVITIES - LIBRARY
220 E. 42nd St., Rm. DN-1710   Phone: (212) 850-5809
New York, NY 10017   Avi Green, Chf.

UNITED NATIONS HEADQUARTERS - DAG HAMMARSKJOLD LIBRARY
United Nations   Phone: (212) 754-7412
New York, NY 10017   Vladimir Orlov, Dir.

UNITED NEGRO COLLEGE FUND, INC. - DEPARTMENT OF ARCHIVES AND
    HISTORY
500 E. 62nd St.   Phone: (212) 644-9672
New York, NY 10021   Gregory S. Hunter, Dir. of Archv.Prog.

U.S. ARMY IN EUROPE (USAREUR) - LIBRARY AND RESOURCE CENTER
HQ USAREUR and Seventh Army
APO New York, NY 09403   Duane G. Nahley, Supv.Libn.

U.S. BUREAU OF THE CENSUS - INFORMATION SERVICES PROGRAM - NEW
    YORK REGIONAL OFFICE - LIBRARY
26 Federal Plaza, Rm. 37-100   Phone: (212) 264-4730
New York, NY 10278   William F. Hill, Regional Dir.

U.S. COAST GUARD - SUPPORT CENTER LIBRARY
Governors Island, Bldg. S251
New York, NY 10004
Phone: (212) 264-8694
Bessie Seymour, Libn.

UNITED STATES COMMITTEE FOR REFUGEES - LIBRARY
20 W. 40th St.
New York, NY 10018
Phone: (212) 398-9142
Roger Winter, Dir.

U.S. COMMITTEE FOR UNICEF - INFORMATION CENTER ON CHILDREN'S
CULTURES
331 E. 38th St.
New York, NY 10016
Phone: (212) 686-5522
Melinda Greenblatt, Chf.Libn.

U.S. COURT OF APPEALS, 2ND CIRCUIT - LIBRARY
U.S. Court House, Rm. 2501, Foley Sq.
New York, NY 10007
Phone: (212) 791-1052
Margaret J. Evans, Chf.Libn.

U.S. COURT OF INTERNATIONAL TRADE - LAW LIBRARY
One Federal Plaza
New York, NY 10007
Phone: (212) 264-2816
Abraham Montekio, Libn.

U.S. CUSTOMS SERVICE - REGION II - LAW LIBRARY *
6 World Trade Ctr., Rm. 732
New York, NY 10048
Phone: (212) 466-4579
Ann Marie D'Ambrosio, Lib.Techn.

U.S. DEPT. OF COMMERCE - INTERNATIONAL TRADE ADMINISTRATION -
NEW YORK DISTRICT OFFICE LIBRARY
26 Federal Plaza
New York, NY 10278
Phone: (212) 264-0630
Stuart Werner, Tech.Info.Spec.

U.S. DEPT. OF ENERGY - ENVIRONMENTAL MEASUREMENTS LABORATORY
LIBRARY
376 Hudson St.
New York, NY 10014
Phone: (212) 620-3606
Michael P. Durso, Libn.

U.S. DEPT. OF HOUSING AND URBAN DEVELOPMENT - REGION II -
LIBRARY
26 Federal Plaza, Rm. 1304
New York, NY 10278
Phone: (212) 264-8175
Susan J. Heller, Regional Libn.

U.S. DEPT. OF JUSTICE - UNITED STATES ATTORNEY, SOUTHERN
DISTRICT OF NEW YORK - LIBRARY
One St. Andrew's Plaza, 6th Fl.
New York, NY 10007
Phone: (212) 791-0029
Barbara J. Zelenko, Hd.Libn.

U.S. DEPT. OF LABOR - BUREAU OF LABOR STATISTICS - INFORMATION
AND ADVISORY SECTION
1515 Broadway, Rm. 3400
New York, NY 10036
Phone: (212) 944-3121
Martin Karlin, Chf.

U.S. NASA - GODDARD INSTITUTE FOR SPACE STUDIES - LIBRARY
2880 Broadway
New York, NY 10025
Phone: (212) 678-5613
Sarah Scott, Lib.Mgr.

U.S. NATL. PARK SERVICE - STATUE OF LIBERTY NATL. MONUMENT -
AMERICAN MUSEUM OF IMMIGRATION - LIBRARY
Liberty Island
New York, NY 10004
Phone: (212) 732-1236
Paul J. Kinney, Musm.Cur.

UNITED STATES TRADEMARK ASSOCIATION - LAW LIBRARY
6 E. 45th St.
New York, NY 10017
Phone: (212) 986-5880
Charlotte Jones, Mng.Ed./Libn.

UNITED STATES TRUST COMPANY - INVESTMENT LIBRARY
45 Wall St.
New York, NY 10005
Phone: (212) 806-4500
Trudy Daley, Chf.Libn.

U.S. VETERANS ADMINISTRATION (NY-New York) - MEDICAL LIBRARY
408 First Ave.
New York, NY 10010
Phone: (212) 686-7500
Malvin Vitriol, Chf.Libn.

U.S. VETERANS ADMINISTRATION (NY-New York) - OFFICE OF
TECHNOLOGY TRANSFER - REFERENCE COLLECTION
252 Seventh Ave., 3rd Fl.
New York, NY 10001
Phone: (212) 620-6670
Lily W. Hom, Tech.Info.Spec.

UNIVERSITY CLUB LIBRARY
1 W. 54th St.
New York, NY 10019
Phone: (212) 572-3418
Guy St. Clair, Dir.

VALUE LINE INC. - BUSINESS LIBRARY
711 Third Ave.
New York, NY 10017
Phone: (212) 687-3965
Gloria Napoli, Chf.Libn.

VIDEO TAPE NETWORK, INC. - LIBRARY
33 E. 68th St.
New York, NY 10021
Phone: (212) 570-1200
John A. Friede, Pres.

WALL STREET JOURNAL - LIBRARY
22 Cortlandt St.
New York, NY 10007
Phone: (212) 285-5075
Lottie Lindberg, Libn.

WALTER, CONSTON & SCHURTMAN, P.C. - LAW LIBRARY
90 Park Ave.
New York, NY 10016
Phone: (212) 210-9526
Nina Cerny, Hd.Libn.

WEBSTER & SHEFFIELD - LIBRARY
One Rockefeller Plaza
New York, NY 10020
Phone: (212) 957-9800
Christine Wierzba, Libn.

WENDER, MURASE & WHITE - LIBRARY
400 Park Ave.
New York, NY 10022
Phone: (212) 832-3333
Karen A. Shea, Libn.

WENNER-GREN FOUNDATION FOR ANTHROPOLOGICAL RESEARCH -
LIBRARY
1865 Broadway
New York, NY 10023-7596
Phone: (212) 957-8750
Annetherese Hirth, Off./Prog.Mgr.

WERTHEIM AND COMPANY, INC. - RESEARCH LIBRARY †
200 Park Ave.
New York, NY 10166
Phone: (212) 578-0427
Joanne Johannessen, Libn.

WEST END COLLEGIATE CHURCH - LIBRARY
West End Ave. at 77th St.
New York, NY 10024

WHITE AND CASE - LIBRARY
14 Wall St.
New York, NY 10005
Phone: (212) 732-1040
John J. Banta, Chf. Law Libn.

WHITMAN & RANSOM - LIBRARY
522 Fifth Ave.
New York, NY 10036
Phone: (212) 575-5800

WHITNEY COMMUNICATIONS CORPORATION - RESEARCH LIBRARY
Time & Life Bldg., Rm. 4600
110 W. 51st St.
New York, NY 10020
Phone: (212) 582-2300
Christine P. Leamon, Res.Dir.

WHITNEY MUSEUM OF AMERICAN ART - LIBRARY
945 Madison Ave.
New York, NY 10021
Phone: (212) 570-3649
May FitzGerald, Libn.

WIDE WORLD PHOTOS, INC.
50 Rockefeller Plaza
New York, NY 10020
Phone: (212) 621-1930
Jim Donna, Gen. Sales Mgr.

WILEY AND SONS, INC. - LIBRARY
605 Third Ave.
New York, NY 10158

WILLKIE FARR & GALLAGHER - LIBRARY
153 E. 53rd St.
New York, NY 10022
Phone: (212) 935-8000
Marilyn E. Maney, Hd.Libn.

WINDELS, MARX, DAVIES & IVES - LIBRARY
51 W. 51st St.
New York, NY 10019
Phone: (212) 977-9600
Huguette Streuli, Libn.

WINTHROP, STIMSON, PUTNAM AND ROBERTS - LIBRARY
40 Wall St.
New York, NY 10005
Phone: (212) 530-7567
Nancy J. Haab, Libn.

WOMEN ARTISTS NEWS - ARCHIVES
Grand Central Sta., Box 3304
New York, NY 10163
Phone: (212) 666-6990
Rena Hansen, Adm.

WOMEN'S ACTION ALLIANCE, INC. - LIBRARY
370 Lexington Ave., Suite 603   Phone: (212) 532-8330
New York, NY 10017   Jane Ordway, Info.Serv.Coord.

WOOD GUNDY INC. - LIBRARY
100 Wall St.   Phone: (212) 344-0633
New York, NY 10005   Anne Bowman

WORLD ZIONIST ORGANIZATION - AMERICAN SECTION - ZIONIST
    ARCHIVES AND LIBRARY
515 Park Ave.   Phone: (212) 753-2167
New York, NY 10022   Sylvia Landress, Dir. & Libn.

XAVIER SOCIETY FOR THE BLIND - NATIONAL CATHOLIC PRESS AND
    LIBRARY FOR THE VISUALLY HANDICAPPED
154 E. 23rd St.
New York, NY 10010   Anthony F. LaBau, Dir.

YALE CLUB OF NEW YORK CITY - LIBRARY
50 Vanderbilt Ave.   Phone: (212) 661-2070
New York, NY 10017   David T. Dale, Libn.

YESHIVA UNIVERSITY - HEDI STEINBERG LIBRARY
Stern College for Women
245 Lexington Ave.   Phone: (212) 481-0570
New York, NY 10016   Edith Lubetski, Hd.Libn.

YESHIVA UNIVERSITY - MENDEL GOTTESMAN LIBRARY OF HEBRAICA AND
    JUDAICA
500 W. 185th St.   Phone: (212) 960-5382
New York, NY 10033   Pearl Berger, Hd.Libn.

YESHIVA UNIVERSITY - POLLACK LIBRARY - LANDOWNE-BLOOM
    COLLECTION
500 W. 185th St.   Phone: (212) 960-5378
New York, NY 10033   Pearl Berger, Hd.Libn.

YIVO INSTITUTE FOR JEWISH RESEARCH - LIBRARY AND ARCHIVES
1048 Fifth Ave.   Phone: (212) 535-6700
New York, NY 10028   Marek Web, Chf.Archv.

YOUNG (Morris N. & Chesley V.) MNEMONICS LIBRARY
270 Riverside Dr.   Phone: (212) 233-2344
New York, NY 10025   Morris N. Young, M.D., Dir.

YOUNG AND RUBICAM INTERNATIONAL - LIBRARY
285 Madison Ave., 10th Fl.   Phone: (212) 953-3075
New York, NY 10017   Celestine G. Frankenberg, Dir. of Lib.Serv.

YOUNG WOMEN'S CHRISTIAN ASSOCIATION - NATIONAL BOARD -
    LIBRARY
726-730 Broadway
New York, NY 10003   Elizabeth D. Norris, Libn./Hist.

ZIFF-DAVIS PUBLISHING COMPANY - TRANSPORTATION DIVISION -
    LIBRARY
One Park Ave.   Phone: (212) 503-5300
New York, NY 10016   Amelia Schwartz, Dir., Lib.Serv.

ZINC INSTITUTE - INFORMATION SERVICE
292 Madison Ave.   Phone: (212) 578-4750
New York, NY 10017   Mary W. Covington, Mgr., Info.Serv.

HISTORICAL SOCIETY OF NEWBURGH BAY AND THE HIGHLANDS -
    LIBRARY
189 Montgomery St.   Phone: (914) 561-2585
Newburgh, NY 12550   Helen VerNooy Gearn, Chm. of Lib.Comm.

NEW YORK STATE BUREAU OF HISTORIC SITES - WASHINGTON'S
    HEADQUARTERS STATE HISTORIC SITE - LIBRARY
84 Liberty St.   Phone: (914) 562-1195
Newburgh, NY 12550   Mel Johnson, Hist.Site Asst.

NEW YORK STATE SUPREME COURT - 9TH JUDICIAL DISTRICT - LAW
    LIBRARY
104 Second St.
Newburgh, NY 12550   Ann McClean, Law Lib.Ck.

SUNY - COLLEGE OF ENVIRONMENTAL SCIENCE & FORESTRY -
    HUNTINGTON WILDLIFE FOREST LIBRARY
                    Phone: (518) 582-4551
Newcomb, NY 12852   Donald Webster, Dir. of Libs.

AIRCO CARBON - RESEARCH LIBRARY
Packard Rd. & 47th St.   Phone: (716) 286-0328
Niagara Falls, NY 14302

MOUNT CARMEL SPIRITUAL CENTER - TOELLE MEMORIAL LIBRARY
Box 767   Phone: (416) 356-4113
Niagara Falls, NY 14302

OCCIDENTAL CHEMICAL CORPORATION - TECHNICAL INFORMATION
    CENTER
Box 8   Phone: (716) 773-8531
Niagara Falls, NY 14302   Dr. Irving Gordon, Supv.

ROCKEFELLER UNIVERSITY - ROCKEFELLER ARCHIVE CENTER
Hillcrest, Pocantico Hills   Phone: (914) 631-4505
North Tarrytown, NY 10591   Dr. Joseph W. Ernst, Dir.

NORTHPORT-EAST NORTHPORT SCHOOL DISTRICT - TEACHERS'
    PROFESSIONAL LIBRARY *
110 Elwood Rd.
Northport, NY 11768   Edwin Sorensen, Hd.

U.S. VETERANS ADMINISTRATION (NY-Northport) - HEALTH SCIENCE
    LIBRARY
                    Phone: (516) 261-4400
Northport, NY 11768   Deborah Lewek, Chf., Lib.Serv.

CHENANGO MEMORIAL HOSPITAL - MEDICAL LIBRARY
179 N. Broad St.   Phone: (607) 335-4159
Norwich, NY 13815   Ann L. Slocum, Med.Libn.

NEW YORK STATE SUPREME COURT - 6TH JUDICIAL DISTRICT - LAW
    LIBRARY
West Park Pl.
Norwich, NY 13815   Margaret S. Reed, Libn.

NORWICH EATON PHARMACEUTICALS, INC. - RESEARCH AND
    DEVELOPMENT LIBRARY
Box 191   Phone: (607) 335-2678
Norwich, NY 13815   Donald A. Windsor, Info.Sup. Group

FELLOWSHIP OF RECONCILIATION - LIBRARY
Box 171   Phone: (914) 358-4601
Nyack, NY 10960

NYACK COLLEGE - LIBRARY
                    Phone: (914) 358-1710
Nyack, NY 10960   May K. Leo, Libn.

NYACK HOSPITAL - MEMORIAL LIBRARY
N. Midland Ave.   Phone: (914) 358-6200
Nyack, NY 10960   Daniel J. Heenan, Dir.

ROCKLAND COUNTY GUIDANCE CENTER - LIBRARY
83 Main St.
Nyack, NY 10960   Henrietta Hendrick, Career Info.Asst.

STIEFEL LABORATORIES, INC. - RESEARCH INSTITUTE LIBRARY
                    Phone: (518) 239-6901
Oak Hill, NY 12460   Loretta Lounsbury, Act.Libn.

SOUTH NASSAU COMMUNITIES HOSPITAL - JULES REDISH MEMORIAL
    MEDICAL LIBRARY
Oceanside Rd.   Phone: (516) 536-1600
Oceanside, NY 11572   Claire Joseph, Dir.

DIOCESE OF OGDENSBURG - ARCHIVES
622 Washington St.
Box 369   Phone: (315) 393-2920
Ogdensburg, NY 13669   Rev. Lawrence E. Cotter, Archv.

HEPBURN (A. Barton) HOSPITAL - MEDICAL LIBRARY †
214 King St.   Phone: (315) 393-3600
Ogdensburg, NY 13669   M. Bridget Doyle, Med.Libn.

Geographic Index

NEW YORK STATE OFFICE OF MENTAL HEALTH - ST. LAWRENCE
  PSYCHIATRIC CENTER - LIBRARY
Station A
Ogdensburg, NY 13669
Phone: (315) 393-3000
Wayne Miller, Libn.

WADHAMS HALL SEMINARY - COLLEGE LIBRARY
Riverside Dr.
Ogdensburg, NY 13669
Phone: (315) 393-4231
Jonas Barciauskas, Hd.Libn.

SHAKER MUSEUM FOUNDATION - EMMA B. KING LIBRARY
Phone: (518) 794-9100
Old Chatham, NY 12136
Ann Kelly, Libn./Archv.

NEW YORK COLLEGE OF OSTEOPATHIC MEDICINE - MEDICAL LIBRARY
c/o New York Institute of Technology
Old Westbury, NY 11568
Phone: (516) 686-7786
Ruth W. Schmitz, Chf.Med.Libn.

NEW YORK INSTITUTE OF TECHNOLOGY - CENTER FOR ENERGY POLICY
  AND RESEARCH - ENERGY INFORMATION CENTER †
Phone: (516) 686-7765
Old Westbury, NY 11568
Mickie Watterson, Assoc.Dir., Info.Sys.

NEW YORK INSTITUTE OF TECHNOLOGY - EDUCATION HALL - ART &
  ARCHITECTURE LIBRARY
Wheatley Rd.
Old Westbury, NY 11568
Phone: (516) 686-7579
Stephen H. Van Dyk, Libn.

NEW YORK INSTITUTE OF TECHNOLOGY - LIBRARY
Wheatley Rd.
Old Westbury, NY 11568
Phone: (516) 686-7657
Dr. Constance Woo, Dir. of Libs.

MADISON COUNTY HISTORICAL SOCIETY - LIBRARY
435 Main St.
Box 415
Oneida, NY 13421
Phone: (315) 363-4136
Barbara J. Giambastiani, Dir.

HARTWICK COLLEGE - LIBRARY - NORTH AMERICAN INDIAN COLLECTION
Phone: (607) 432-4200
Oneonta, NY 13820
Eric von Brockdorff, Lib.Dir.

SUNY - COLLEGE AT ONEONTA - JAMES M. MILNE LIBRARY - SPECIAL
  COLLECTIONS
Phone: (607) 431-2723
Oneonta, NY 13820
Martha Chambers, Spec.Coll.Libn.

BECTON, DICKINSON IMMUNODIAGNOSTICS - TECHNICAL RESEARCH AND
  DEVELOPMENT LIBRARY
Mountain View Ave.
Orangeburg, NY 10962
Phone: (914) 359-2700
Dr. Jean Armstrong, Asst.Dir., R & D

KLINE (Nathan S.) INSTITUTE FOR PSYCHIATRIC RESEARCH - ROCKLAND
  HEALTH SCIENCES LIBRARY
Bldg. 37
Orangeburg, NY 10962
Phone: (914) 359-1050
Lois Cohan, Lib.Dir.

OYSTERPONDS HISTORICAL SOCIETY - LIBRARY
Village Lane
Orient, NY 11957
Phone: (516) 323-2480
Constance J. Terry, Archv.

OSSINING HISTORICAL SOCIETY MUSEUM - LIBRARY
196 Croton Ave.
Ossining, NY 10562
Phone: (914) 941-0001
John B. Drittler, Libn.

FORT ONTARIO - LIBRARY *
Phone: (315) 343-4711
Oswego, NY 13126
Wallace Workmaster, Historic Site Mgr.

NEW YORK STATE SUPREME COURT - 4TH JUDICIAL DISTRICT - LAW
  LIBRARY
Court House, E. Oneida St.
Oswego, NY 13126
Phone: (315) 342-0550
Janice Drumm Matthews, Law Lib.Ck.

SUNY - COLLEGE AT OSWEGO - PENFIELD LIBRARY - SPECIAL
  COLLECTIONS
Phone: (315) 341-3122
Oswego, NY 13126

IBM CORPORATION - FEDERAL SYSTEMS DIVISION - AVIONICS SYSTEMS -
  LIBRARY
Phone: (607) 751-2721
Owego, NY 13827
J.J. Cambridge, Project Mgr.

TIOGA COUNTY HISTORICAL SOCIETY MUSEUM - LIBRARY
110-112 Front St.
Owego, NY 13827
Phone: (607) 687-2460
William Lay, Jr., Musm.Cur.

PLANTING FIELDS ARBORETUM - HORTICULTURAL LIBRARY
Planting Fields Rd.
Oyster Bay, NY 11771
Phone: (516) 922-9024
Elizabeth K. Reilley, Dir.

COLUMBIA UNIVERSITY - LAMONT-DOHERTY GEOLOGICAL OBSERVATORY
  - GEOSCIENCE LIBRARY
Phone: (914) 359-2900
Palisades, NY 10964
Susan Klimley, Libn.

BROOKHAVEN MEMORIAL HOSPITAL MEDICAL CENTER - MEDICAL
  LIBRARY
101 Hospital Rd.
Patchogue, NY 11772
Phone: (516) 654-7774
Mrs. Freddie Borock, Med.Libn.

U.S. NATL. PARK SERVICE - FIRE ISLAND NATL. SEASHORE -
  HEADQUARTERS LIBRARY
120 Laurel St.
Patchogue, NY 11772
Phone: (516) 289-4810
Neal Bullington, Asst.Chf. Ranger

PAUL SMITH'S COLLEGE OF ARTS AND SCIENCES - FRANK L. CUBLEY
  LIBRARY
Phone: (518) 327-6313
Paul Smiths, NY 12970
Theodore D. Mack, Libn.

AKIN HALL ASSOCIATION - AKIN FREE LIBRARY
Quaker Hill
Pawling, NY 12564
Phone: (914) 855-5099
James Mandracchia, Libn.

AMERICAN CYANAMID COMPANY - LEDERLE LABORATORIES DIVISION -
  SUBBAROW MEMORIAL LIBRARY †
N. Middletown Rd.
Pearl River, NY 10965
Phone: (914) 735-5000
Dr. M.G. Howell, Hd., Tech.Info.Serv.

LAWLER MATUSKY & SKELLY ENGINEERS - LIBRARY
One Blue Hill Plaza
Pearl River, NY 10965
Phone: (914) 735-8300
Katharine S. Thomas, Info.Sci.

ORANGE AND ROCKLAND UTILITIES, INC. - LIBRARY
1 Blue Hill Plaza
Pearl River, NY 10965
Phone: (914) 627-2680
Esther B. Clifford, Libn.

ROSENBERG (Paul) ASSOCIATES - LIBRARY
330 Fifth Ave.
Pelham, NY 10803
Phone: (914) 738-2266
M. Hill, Libn.

CHAMPLAIN VALLEY - PHYSICIANS HOSPITAL MEDICAL CENTER -
  MEDICAL LIBRARY
100 Beekman St.
Plattsburgh, NY 12901
Phone: (518) 561-2000
Judith El Reedy, Med.Libn.

SUNY - COLLEGE AT PLATTSBURGH - BENJAMIN F. FEINBERG LIBRARY -
  SPECIAL COLLECTIONS
Phone: (518) 564-3180
Plattsburgh, NY 12901
Joseph G. Swinyer, Dir.

PACE UNIVERSITY, PLEASANTVILLE/BRIARCLIFF - EDWARD AND DORIS
  MORTOLA LIBRARY
861 Bedford Rd.
Pleasantville, NY 10570
Phone: (914) 769-3200
William J. Murdock, Lib.Dir.

READER'S DIGEST - INDEX
Phone: (914) 769-7000
Pleasantville, NY 10570
Adrienne M. Bova, Ed.

LIFE SAVERS, INC. - RESEARCH AND DEVELOPMENT DIVISION -
  TECHNICAL INFORMATION CENTER †
N. Main St.
Port Chester, NY 10573
Phone: (914) 937-3200
Clare Adamo, Libn.

NEWSPAPER COMICS COUNCIL - LIBRARY INFORMATION CENTER
Ward Castle
Comly Ave.   Phone: (914) 939-3919
Port Chester, NY 10573   Catherine T. Prentice, Libn.

MINISINK VALLEY HISTORICAL SOCIETY - LIBRARY
138 Pike St.
Box 659   Phone: (914) 856-2375
Port Jervis, NY 12771   Peter Osborne, III, Exec.Dir.

GRAVURE RESEARCH INSTITUTE - LIBRARY
22 Manhasset Ave.   Phone: (516) 883-6670
Port Washington, NY 11050   Harvey F. George, Exec. V.P./Res.Dir.

GREENVALE EDITORIAL SERVICES, INC. - LIBRARY *
2 Haven Ave.   Phone: (516) 944-8066
Port Washington, NY 11050   Joan Casson Sauer, Libn.

CLARKSON UNIVERSITY - EDUCATIONAL RESOURCES CENTER
                                              Phone: (315) 268-2292
Potsdam, NY 13676   Martin P. Wilson, Assoc.Dir.

SUNY - COLLEGE AT POTSDAM - CRANE MUSIC LIBRARY
                                              Phone: (315) 268-3019
Potsdam, NY 13676   Sally Skyrm, Music Libn.

SUNY - COLLEGE AT POTSDAM - FREDERICK W. CRUMB MEMORIAL
   LIBRARY
Pierrepont Ave.   Phone: (315) 268-4991
Potsdam, NY 13676   Dr. Thomas M. Peischl, Dir. of Libs.

DUTCHESS COUNTY DEPARTMENT OF PLANNING - INFORMATION CENTER
47 Cannon St.   Phone: (914) 485-9890
Poughkeepsie, NY 12601   Charles J. Murphy, Pub.Info.Off.

DUTCHESS COUNTY GENEALOGICAL SOCIETY - LIBRARY *
LDS Church
Spackenkill Rd., Box 708
Poughkeepsie, NY 12602

DUTCHESS COUNTY MENTAL HEALTH LIBRARY
230 North Rd.   Phone: (914) 485-9700
Poughkeepsie, NY 12601   Barbara B. Pantridge, Libn.

HUDSON RIVER PSYCHIATRIC CENTER - MEDICAL LIBRARY *
                                              Phone: (914) 452-8000
Poughkeepsie, NY 12601   Joyce Cunningham, Libn.

IBM CORPORATION - DSD LIBRARY/LEARNING CENTER
Dept. 261/701
Box 390   Phone: (914) 463-1630
Poughkeepsie, NY 12602   Gabrielle S. Nelson, Mgr.

NEW YORK STATE SUPREME COURT - 9TH JUDICIAL DISTRICT - JOSEPH
   F. BARNARD MEMORIAL LAW LIBRARY ASSOCIATION
Court House
10 Market St.   Phone: (914) 431-1815
Poughkeepsie, NY 12601   Catherine A. Maher, Sr. Law Lib.Ck.

ST. FRANCIS HOSPITAL - HEALTH SCIENCE LIBRARY
North Rd.   Phone: (914) 471-2000
Poughkeepsie, NY 12601   Carol Page, Med.Libn.

VASSAR BROTHERS HOSPITAL - MEDICAL LIBRARY
Reade Pl.   Phone: (914) 454-8500
Poughkeepsie, NY 12601   Mrs. Howard A. Wilson, Med.Libn.

VASSAR COLLEGE - ART LIBRARY
                                              Phone: (914) 452-7000
Poughkeepsie, NY 12601   Janet Clarke-Hazlett, Art Libn.

VASSAR COLLEGE - GEORGE SHERMAN DICKINSON MUSIC LIBRARY
                                              Phone: (914) 452-7000
Poughkeepsie, NY 12601   Sabrina L. Weiss, Music Libn.

FEDERATED CONSERVATIONISTS OF WESTCHESTER COUNTY - FCWC
   OFFICE RESOURCE LIBRARY
Natural Science Bldg., Rm. 1002
SUNY   Phone: (914) 253-8046
Purchase, NY 10577   Carolyn Cunningham, Exec.Dir.

MANHATTANVILLE COLLEGE - LIBRARY - SPECIAL COLLECTIONS AND
   ARCHIVES
                                              Phone: (914) 946-9600
Purchase, NY 10577   Donna L. Nickerson, Spec.Coll.Libn.

CREEDMOOR PSYCHIATRIC CENTER - HEALTH SCIENCES LIBRARY
80-45 Winchester Blvd.   Phone: (718) 464-7500
Queens Village, NY 11427   Susan Taubman, Lrng.Rsrcs.Coord.

BASF WYANDOTTE CORPORATION - DEVELOPMENT LABORATORY -
   LIBRARY *
36 Riverside Ave.   Phone: (518) 465-4511
Rensselaer, NY 12144

ST. ANTHONY-ON-HUDSON THEOLOGICAL LIBRARY
St. Anthony-On-Hudson   Phone: (518) 463-2261
Rensselaer, NY 12144   Bro. James J. Doyle, Libn.

STERLING DRUG, INC. STERLING-WINTHROP RESEARCH INSTITUTE -
   LIBRARY
Columbia Turnpike   Phone: (518) 445-8259
Rensselaer, NY 12144   Carol Bekar, Sr.Adm., Lib.Serv.

IN-FACT - RESEARCH AND INFORMATION SERVICE
Righter Rd.
Rural Delivery Box 35D   Phone: (518) 797-5154
Rensselaerville, NY 12147   Katherine H. Storms, Info.Spec.

ASTOR HOME FOR CHILDREN - PROFESSIONAL LIBRARY
36 Mill St.   Phone: (914) 876-4081
Rhinebeck, NY 12572   William J. Nichols, Libn.

CENTRAL SUFFOLK HOSPITAL - MEDICAL LIBRARY †
1300 Roanoke Ave.   Phone: (516) 369-6088
Riverhead, NY 11901   Anne Kirsch, Med.Libn.

LONG ISLAND HORTICULTURAL RESEARCH LABORATORY - LIBRARY
39 Sound Ave.   Phone: (516) 727-3595
Riverhead, NY 11901   Margery Daughtrey, Extension Assoc.

NEW YORK STATE SUPREME COURT - 10TH JUDICIAL DISTRICT - LAW
   LIBRARY
Court House, Rm. 210
Griffing Ave.   Phone: (516) 548-3766
Riverhead, NY 11901   Lynn C. Fullshire, Sr. Law Libn.

SUFFOLK COUNTY HISTORICAL SOCIETY - LIBRARY
300 W. Main St.   Phone: (516) 727-2881
Riverhead, NY 11901   Betty M. Carpenter, Libn.

AMERICAN BAPTIST HISTORICAL SOCIETY - SAMUEL COLGATE BAPTIST
   HISTORICAL LIBRARY
1106 S. Goodman St.   Phone: (716) 473-1740
Rochester, NY 14620   William H. Brackney, Exec.Dir.

BAUSCH & LOMB, INC. - LIBRARY RESOURCE CENTER
1400 N. Goodman St.   Phone: (716) 338-6053
Rochester, NY 14692   Delsa I. Benz, Corp.Libn.

CENTER FOR ENVIRONMENTAL INFORMATION, INC. - ACID RAIN
   REFERENCE COLLECTION
33 S. Washington St.   Phone: (716) 546-3796
Rochester, NY 14608   Frederick W. Stoss, Mgr., Info.Serv.

CENTER FOR ENVIRONMENTAL INFORMATION, INC. - HARTWELL LIBRARY
33 S. Washington St.   Phone: (716) 546-3796
Rochester, NY 14608   Frederick W. Stoss, Mgr., Info.Serv.

CENTER FOR GOVERNMENTAL RESEARCH, INC. - LIBRARY
37 S. Washington St.   Phone: (716) 325-6360
Rochester, NY 14608   Dianne Salopek, Libn.

COLGATE ROCHESTER/BEXLEY HALL/CROZER THEOLOGICAL SEMINARIES
   - AMBROSE SWASEY LIBRARY
1100 S. Goodman St.   Phone: (716) 271-1320
Rochester, NY 14620   Norman J. Kansfield, Dir. of Lib.Serv.

COMBUSTION ENGINEERING, INC. - TAYLOR INSTRUMENT TECHNICAL
   INFORMATION CENTER
95 Ames St.   Phone: (716) 235-5000
Rochester, NY 14601   Mary Jo Eiser, Libn.

CONVALESCENT HOSPITAL FOR CHILDREN - LIBRARY
2075 Scottsville Rd.   Phone: (716) 436-4442
Rochester, NY 14623   Christine A. Sabin, Libn.

DANISH BAPTIST GENERAL CONFERENCE OF AMERICA - ARCHIVES
American Baptist Historical Society
1106 S. Goodman St.   Phone: (716) 473-1740
Rochester, NY 14620   William H. Brackney, Exec.Dir.

EASTMAN DENTAL CENTER - BASIL G. BIBBY LIBRARY
625 Elmwood Ave.   Phone: (716) 275-5010
Rochester, NY 14620   June Glaser, Libn.

EASTMAN KODAK COMPANY - BUSINESS INFORMATION CENTER
343 State St.   Phone: (716) 724-3041
Rochester, NY 14650   M. Lois Gauch, Libn.

EASTMAN KODAK COMPANY - ENGINEERING LIBRARY
Kodak Park Division, Bldg. 23   Phone: (716) 722-2356
Rochester, NY 14650   Raymond W. Curtin, Libn.

EASTMAN KODAK COMPANY - HEALTH AND ENVIRONMENT LABORATORIES
   - LIBRARY
Kodak Park Division, Bldg. 320   Phone: (716) 588-3619
Rochester, NY 14650   Rita B. Stack, Libn.

EASTMAN KODAK COMPANY - MANAGEMENT SERVICES - LIBRARY
Kodak Park, Bldg. 56   Phone: (716) 722-1184
Rochester, NY 14650   Deborah Mourey, Libn.

EASTMAN KODAK COMPANY - PHOTOGRAPHIC TECHNOLOGY DIVISION -
   LIBRARY
Kodak Park Division   Phone: (716) 477-5462
Rochester, NY 14650   Kathy M. Bushart, Lib.Asst.

EASTMAN KODAK COMPANY - RESEARCH LIBRARY
Kodak Park, Bldg. 83   Phone: (716) 722-2723
Rochester, NY 14650   Elizabeth W. Kraus, Info.Assoc./Lib.Mgr.

EASTMAN KODAK COMPANY - U.S. APPARATUS DIVISION - TECHNICAL
   LIBRARY
901 Elmgrove Rd.   Phone: (716) 726-2127
Rochester, NY 14650   Marie Jean Bonn, Supv.Libn.

FRENCH (R.T.) COMPANY - TECHNICAL LIBRARY
Box 23450   Phone: (716) 482-8000
Rochester, NY 14692   Mary Frances Mullin, Libn.

GARDEN CENTER OF ROCHESTER - LIBRARY
5 Castle Park   Phone: (716) 473-5130
Rochester, NY 14620   Mrs. Robert Baschnagel, Libn.

GAY ALLIANCE OF GENESEE VALLEY INC. - LIBRARY
713 Monroe Ave.   Phone: (716) 244-8640
Rochester, NY 14607   Rosemary Cahill, Ed.

GENERAL RAILWAY SIGNAL CO. - TECHNICAL LIBRARY
801 West Ave.
Box 600   Phone: (716) 436-2020
Rochester, NY 14692   Kathy Zuidema, Tech.Libn.

GENESEE HOSPITAL - SAMUEL J. STABINS, M.D., HEALTH SCIENCES
   LIBRARY
224 Alexander St.   Phone: (716) 263-6305
Rochester, NY 14607   Sally M. Gerling, Chf.Libn.

HIGHLAND HOSPITAL - JOHN R. WILLIAMS, SR., HEALTH SCIENCES
   LIBRARY
South Ave. at Bellevue Dr.   Phone: (716) 473-2200
Rochester, NY 14620   Helen King Murphy, Dir.

HIGHLAND PARK HERBARIUM - LIBRARY
375 Westfall Rd.   Phone: (716) 244-4640
Rochester, NY 14620   James W. Kelly, Cur.

INTERNATIONAL MUSEUM OF PHOTOGRAPHY AT GEORGE EASTMAN
   HOUSE - LIBRARY
900 East Ave.   Phone: (716) 271-3361
Rochester, NY 14607   Rachel Stuhlman, Hd.Libn.

IRONDEQUOIT TOWN HISTORIAN - PHOTOGRAPH COLLECTION
2158 East Ridge Rd.   Phone: (716) 467-8840
Rochester, NY 14622

LANDMARK SOCIETY OF WESTERN NEW YORK - WENRICH MEMORIAL
   LIBRARY
130 Spring St.   Phone: (716) 546-7029
Rochester, NY 14608   Ann B. Parks, Asst.Dir.

LINCOLN FIRST BANK, NA, INC. - LINCOLN FIRST LIBRARY †
One Lincoln First Square   Phone: (716) 258-6460
Rochester, NY 14643   Alla F. Levi, Dir. of Lib.Serv.

MIXING EQUIPMENT COMPANY, INC. - MIXCO R&D LIBRARY †
135 Mt. Read Blvd.   Phone: (716) 436-5550
Rochester, NY 14611   Maryann Kerwin, Libn.

MONROE COMMUNITY HOSPITAL - T.F. WILLIAMS HEALTH SCIENCES
   LIBRARY
435 E. Henrietta Rd.   Phone: (716) 473-4080
Rochester, NY 14603   Elinor Reynolds, Lib.Dir.

MONROE COUNTY DEPARTMENT OF HEALTH - HEALTH EDUCATION
   LIBRARY
111 Westfall Rd.   Phone: (716) 442-4000
Rochester, NY 14692   Mary Coykendall, Libn.

MONROE COUNTY HISTORIAN'S DEPARTMENT - LIBRARY
115 South Ave.
Rochester, NY 14604   Shirley C. Husted, County Hist.

MONROE DEVELOPMENTAL CENTER - STAFF/PARENT LIBRARY
620 Westfall Rd.   Phone: (716) 461-2800
Rochester, NY 14620   Mary Ann H. Clark, Staff Libn.

NAZARETH COLLEGE OF ROCHESTER - LORETTE WILMOT LIBRARY -
   SPECIAL COLLECTIONS
Box 10996   Phone: (716) 586-2525
Rochester, NY 14610-0996   Richard A. Matzek, Dir.

NEW YORK STATE ARCHEOLOGICAL ASSOCIATION - LIBRARY
657 East Ave.
Box 1480   Phone: (716) 271-4320
Rochester, NY 14603   Charles F. Hayes, III, Res.Dir.

NEW YORK STATE SUPREME COURT - APPELLATE DIVISION, 4TH
   JUDICIAL DEPARTMENT - LAW LIBRARY
525 Hall of Justice   Phone: (716) 428-5480
Rochester, NY 14614   Joseph T. Pascucci, Libn.

NIXON, HARGRAVE, DEVANS & DOYLE - LAW LIBRARY *
Lincoln First Tower
Box 1051   Phone: (716) 546-8000
Rochester, NY 14603   Sharon A. Hayden, Libn.

PARK RIDGE HOSPITAL - LIBRARY
1555 Long Pond Rd.   Phone: (716) 225-7150
Rochester, NY 14626   Eileen P. Shirley, Libn.

PENNWALT CORPORATION - PENNWALT PHARMACEUTICAL DIVISION -
   RESEARCH LIBRARY
755 Jefferson Rd.
Box 1710   Phone: (716) 475-9000
Rochester, NY 14603   Angela Scarfia, Libn.

ROCHESTER ACADEMY OF MEDICINE - LIBRARY †
1441 East Ave.   Phone: (716) 271-1313
Rochester, NY 14610

ROCHESTER BUSINESS INSTITUTE - BETTY CRONK MEMORIAL LIBRARY
107 Clinton Ave., N.   Phone: (716) 325-7290
Rochester, NY 14604   Shirley Nagg, Lib.Aide

ROCHESTER GAS AND ELECTRIC CORPORATION - TECHNICAL
  INFORMATION CENTER
89 East Ave.   Phone: (716) 546-2700
Rochester, NY 14649   Linda L. Phillips, Supv., Off.Serv./Doc.Ctr.

ROCHESTER GENERAL HOSPITAL - LILLIE B. WERNER HEALTH SCIENCES
  LIBRARY
1425 Portland Ave.   Phone: (716) 338-4743
Rochester, NY 14621   Bernie Todd Smith, Lib.Dir.

ROCHESTER HISTORICAL SOCIETY - LIBRARY
485 East Ave.   Phone: (716) 271-2705
Rochester, NY 14607   Mary Widger, Libn.

ROCHESTER INSTITUTE OF TECHNOLOGY - CHEMISTRY GRADUATE
  RESEARCH LIBRARY
One Lomb Memorial Dr.   Phone: (716) 475-2520
Rochester, NY 14623   Christine DeGolyer, Chem.Libn.

ROCHESTER INSTITUTE OF TECHNOLOGY - MELBERT B. CARY, JR.
  GRAPHIC ARTS COLLECTION †
School of Printing   Phone: (716) 475-2408
Rochester, NY 14623   David Pankow, Libn.

ROCHESTER INSTITUTE OF TECHNOLOGY - NATIONAL TECHNICAL
  INSTITUTE FOR THE DEAF - STAFF RESOURCE CENTER
Lyndon Baines Johnson Bldg., Rm. 2490
1 Lomb Memorial Dr.   Phone: (716) 475-6823
Rochester, NY 14623   Audrey Ritter, Rsrcs.Spec.

ROCHESTER INSTITUTE OF TECHNOLOGY - TECHNICAL & EDUCATION
  CENTER FOR THE GRAPHIC ARTS - GRAPHIC ARTS INFO.SERV.
One Lomb Memorial Dr.   Phone: (716) 475-2791
Rochester, NY 14623   Susan Clark, Tech.Libn.

ROCHESTER INSTITUTE OF TECHNOLOGY - WALLACE MEMORIAL LIBRARY
One Lomb Memorial Dr.   Phone: (716) 475-2565
Rochester, NY 14623   Patricia A. Pitkin, Dir.

ROCHESTER MUSEUM AND SCIENCE CENTER - LIBRARY
657 East Ave.
Box 1480   Phone: (716) 271-4320
Rochester, NY 14603   Leatrice M. Kemp, Libn.

ROCHESTER MUSEUM AND SCIENCE CENTER - STRASENBURGH
  PLANETARIUM - TODD LIBRARY
657 East Ave.   Phone: (716) 244-6060
Rochester, NY 14607

ROCHESTER PSYCHIATRIC CENTER - PROFESSIONAL LIBRARY †
1600 South Ave.   Phone: (716) 473-3230
Rochester, NY 14620

ROCHESTER PUBLIC LIBRARY - ART DIVISION
115 South Ave.   Phone: (716) 428-7332
Rochester, NY 14604   Mary Lee Miller, Hd.

ROCHESTER PUBLIC LIBRARY - BUSINESS, ECONOMICS AND LEGISLATION
  DIVISION
115 South Ave.   Phone: (716) 428-7328
Rochester, NY 14604   Carolyn Johnson, Hd.

ROCHESTER PUBLIC LIBRARY - EDUCATION, SOCIOLOGY AND RELIGION
  DIVISION
115 South Ave.   Phone: (716) 428-7330
Rochester, NY 14604   Robert D. Murphy, Hd.

ROCHESTER PUBLIC LIBRARY - HISTORY, GOVERNMENT AND TRAVEL
  DIVISION
115 South Ave.   Phone: (716) 428-7323
Rochester, NY 14604   Winn McCray, Hd.

ROCHESTER PUBLIC LIBRARY - LITERATURE, BIOGRAPHY AND SPORTS
  DIVISION
115 South Ave.   Phone: (716) 428-7315
Rochester, NY 14604   William J. Cuseo, Hd.

ROCHESTER PUBLIC LIBRARY - LOCAL HISTORY AND GENEALOGY
  DIVISION
115 South Ave.   Phone: (716) 428-7338
Rochester, NY 14604   Wayne Arnold, Hd.

ROCHESTER PUBLIC LIBRARY - REYNOLDS AUDIO-VISUAL DEPARTMENT
115 South Ave.   Phone: (716) 428-7335
Rochester, NY 14604   Robert Barnes, Hd.

ROCHESTER PUBLIC LIBRARY - SCIENCE AND TECHNOLOGY DIVISION
115 South Ave.   Phone: (716) 428-7327
Rochester, NY 14604   Judith Prevratil, Hd.

ROCHESTER TIMES-UNION AND ROCHESTER DEMOCRAT & CHRONICLE -
  LIBRARY
55 Exchange St.   Phone: (716) 232-7100
Rochester, NY 14614   Peter Ford, Lib.Dir.

ST. BERNARD'S INSTITUTE - LIBRARY
1100 S. Goodman   Phone: (716) 271-1320
Rochester, NY 14620   Rev. Sebastian A. Falcone, Dean

SEAR-BROWN ASSOCIATES, P.C. - INFORMATION CENTER
85 Metro Park   Phone: (716) 475-1440
Rochester, NY 14623   Michele Shipley, Info.Ctr.Mgr.

SENECA ZOOLOGICAL SOCIETY - LIBRARY
2222 St. Paul St.   Phone: (716) 342-2744
Rochester, NY 14621   Daniel R. Michalowski, Zoological Pk.Dir.

SINGER COMPANY - EDUCATION DIVISION - TECHNICAL LIBRARY *
3750 Monroe Ave.
Rochester, NY 14603

STANDARD OIL COMPANY OF OHIO - THE PFAUDLER COMPANY -
  TECHNICAL LIBRARY
1000 West Ave.
Box 1600   Phone: (716) 235-1000
Rochester, NY 14692   Candice M. Johnson, Libn.

STRONG (Margaret Woodbury) MUSEUM - LIBRARY
One Manhattan Square   Phone: (716) 263-2700
Rochester, NY 14607   Elaine M. Challacombe, Libn.

TEMPLE BETH EL - LIBRARY
139 Winton Rd., S.   Phone: (716) 473-1770
Rochester, NY 14610   Anne Kirshenbaum, Libn.

TEMPLE B'RITH KODESH - LIBRARY
2131 Elmwood Ave.   Phone: (716) 244-7060
Rochester, NY 14618   Bertha Cravets, Libn.

UNIVERSITY OF ROCHESTER - ASIA LIBRARY
Rush Rhees Library, River Campus   Phone: (716) 275-4489
Rochester, NY 14627   Datta S. Kharbas, Libn.

UNIVERSITY OF ROCHESTER - CARLSON LIBRARY
Hutchison Hall, River Campus   Phone: (716) 275-4465
Rochester, NY 14627   Michael Poulin, Libn.

UNIVERSITY OF ROCHESTER - CHARLOTTE WHITNEY ALLEN LIBRARY
Memorial Art Gallery
490 University Ave.   Phone: (716) 275-4765
Rochester, NY 14607   Stephanie Frontz, Libn.

UNIVERSITY OF ROCHESTER - DEPARTMENT OF RARE BOOKS AND
  SPECIAL COLLECTIONS
River Campus   Phone: (716) 275-4477
Rochester, NY 14627   Peter Dzwonkoski, Hd.

UNIVERSITY OF ROCHESTER - EASTMAN SCHOOL OF MUSIC - SIBLEY
  MUSIC LIBRARY
44 Swan St.   Phone: (716) 275-3018
Rochester, NY 14604   Mary Wallace Davidson, Libn.

UNIVERSITY OF ROCHESTER - EDUCATION LIBRARY
Rush Rhees Library   Phone: (716) 275-4481
Rochester, NY 14627   Kathleen McGowan, Ref.Libn.

UNIVERSITY OF ROCHESTER - ENGINEERING LIBRARY
Gavett Hall
Rochester, NY 14627   Phone: (716) 275-4486
                                                         Isabel Kaplan, Libn.

UNIVERSITY OF ROCHESTER - FINE ARTS LIBRARY
Rush Rhees Library, River Campus   Phone: (716) 275-4476
Rochester, NY 14627   Stephanie Frontz, Libn.

UNIVERSITY OF ROCHESTER - GEOLOGY/MAP LIBRARY
Rush Rhees Library
Rochester, NY 14627   Arleen Somerville, Libn.

UNIVERSITY OF ROCHESTER - LABORATORY FOR LASER ENERGETICS -
   LIBRARY
250 E. River Rd.   Phone: (716) 275-5768
Rochester, NY 14623   Loretta Caren, Libn.

UNIVERSITY OF ROCHESTER - MANAGEMENT LIBRARY
Rush Rhees Library, River Campus   Phone: (716) 275-4482
Rochester, NY 14627   Edward P. Wass, Libn.

UNIVERSITY OF ROCHESTER - PHYSICS-OPTICS-ASTRONOMY LIBRARY
374 Bausch & Lomb Bldg.   Phone: (716) 275-4469
Rochester, NY 14627   Loretta Caren, Hd.

UNIVERSITY OF ROCHESTER - SCHOOL OF MEDICINE & DENTISTRY -
   EDWARD G. MINER LIBRARY
601 Elmwood Ave.   Phone: (716) 275-3364
Rochester, NY 14642   Lucretia McClure, Med.Libn.

WOMEN'S CAREER CENTER - LIBRARY
30 N. Clinton Ave.   Phone: (716) 325-2274
Rochester, NY 14604   Sarah I. Hartwell, Coord. of Info. & Rsrcs.

CENTRAL SYNAGOGUE OF NASSAU COUNTY - HELEN BLAU MEMORIAL
   LIBRARY
430 DeMott Ave.   Phone: (516) 766-4300
Rockville Centre, NY 11570   Barbara Gresack, Libn.

MERCY HOSPITAL - MEDICAL/NURSING LIBRARY
1000 N. Village Ave.   Phone: (516) 255-2255
Rockville Centre, NY 11570   Carol L. Reid, Med./Nursing Libn.

IIT RESEARCH INSTITUTE - RELIABILITY ANALYSIS CENTER
RADC (RAC)
Griffiss Air Force Base   Phone: (315) 330-4151
Rome, NY 13441   Steve Flint, Tech.Dir.

JERVIS PUBLIC LIBRARY
613 N. Washington St.   Phone: (315) 336-4570
Rome, NY 13440   William A. Dillon, Dir.

ROME HISTORICAL SOCIETY - ELAINE & WILLIAM E. SCRIPTURE
   MEMORIAL LIBRARY
200 Church St.   Phone: (315) 336-5870
Rome, NY 13440   Joseph C. Di Giovanni, Adm.

U.S. AIR FORCE HOSPITAL - MEDICAL LIBRARY (NY-Rome) *
Griffiss AFB   Phone: (315) 330-7713
Rome, NY 13441   Susan Ho, Med.Libn.

BRYANT LIBRARY - LOCAL HISTORY COLLECTION
Paper Mill Rd.   Phone: (516) 621-2240
Roslyn, NY 11576   Anthony M. Cucchiara, Archv.

ST. FRANCIS HOSPITAL - MEDICAL LIBRARY
Port Washington Blvd.   Phone: (516) 627-6200
Roslyn, NY 11576   John Dwyer, Med.Libn.

AYERST LABORATORIES, INC. - INFORMATION CENTER
Maple St.   Phone: (518) 297-6611
Rouses Point, NY 12979   Christina Ransom, Mgr.Info.Ctr.

ITT CONTINENTAL BAKING COMPANY - RESEARCH LABORATORIES
   LIBRARY
Halstead Ave.
Box 731   Phone: (914) 899-0380
Rye, NY 10580   Jocelyn Rosen, Supv., Tech.Info.Serv.

SLOAN-KETTERING INSTITUTE FOR CANCER RESEARCH - DONALD S.
   WALKER LABORATORY - C.P. RHOADS MEMORIAL LIBRARY
145 Boston Post Rd.   Phone: (914) 698-1100
Rye, NY 10580   Virginia Gregory, Libn.

MUSEUM OF CARTOON ART - LIBRARY
Comly Ave.   Phone: (914) 939-0234
Rye Brook, NY 10573   Lorraine Schilling, Mgr.

SUFFOLK COUNTY WHALING MUSEUM - LIBRARY
Main St.   Phone: (516) 725-0770
Sag Harbor, NY 11963   George A. Finckenor, Sr., Cur.

FRANCISCAN INSTITUTE - LIBRARY
St. Bonaventure University   Phone: (716) 375-2105
St. Bonaventure, NY 14778   Dr. Louis J. Reith, Rare Book Libn.

BOCES - ORLEANS-NIAGARA EDUCATIONAL COMMUNICATIONS CENTER *
4124 Saunders Settlement Rd.
Niagara East - Box 310D   Phone: (716) 731-4146
Sanborn, NY 14132   Douglas David, Supv., Instr.Serv.

HELEN KELLER NATIONAL CENTER - REFERENCE LIBRARY
111 Middle Neck Rd.   Phone: (516) 944-8900
Sands Point, NY 11050   Gertrude Queen, Libn.

TRUDEAU INSTITUTE IMMUNOBIOLOGICAL RESEARCH LABORATORIES -
   LIBRARY
Algonquin Ave.
Box 59   Phone: (518) 891-3080
Saranac Lake, NY 12983   Joyce Ward, Libn.

ESPEY MFG. & ELECTRONICS CORP. - COMPONENT SPECIFICATIONS
   LIBRARY
Ballston at Congress Ave.
Box 422   Phone: (518) 584-4100
Saratoga Springs, NY 12866   Cathi Jackson, Libn.

HISTORICAL SOCIETY OF SARATOGA SPRINGS - MUSEUM AND LIBRARY
Casino, Congress Park
Box 216   Phone: (518) 584-6920
Saratoga Springs, NY 12866   Heidi A. Fuge, Dir.

NEW YORK STATE SUPREME COURT - 4TH JUDICIAL DISTRICT - LAW
   LIBRARY
2 City Hall   Phone: (518) 584-4862
Saratoga Springs, NY 12866   Linda E. Macica, Sr. Law Lib.Ck.

SUNY - EMPIRE STATE COLLEGE - CENTER FOR DISTANCE LEARNING
2 Union Ave.   Phone: (518) 587-2100
Saratoga Springs, NY 12866   Daniel Granger, Dir.

WEINBERG NATURE CENTER - LIBRARY
455 Mamaroneck Rd.   Phone: (914) 723-4784
Scarsdale, NY 10583   Peter J. Woodcock, Naturalist/Dir.

WORK IN AMERICA INSTITUTE, INC. - LIBRARY
700 White Plains Rd.   Phone: (914) 472-9600
Scarsdale, NY 10583   Ellen Daniels, Mgr., Info.Serv.

ELLIS HOSPITAL - MAC MILLAN LIBRARY
1101 Nott St.   Phone: (518) 382-4381
Schenectady, NY 12308   Dorothy Dralle, Libn.

GENERAL ELECTRIC COMPANY - CORPORATE RESEARCH & DEVELOPMENT
   - WHITNEY INFORMATION SERVICES
Box 8   Phone: (518) 385-8791
Schenectady, NY 12345   Maryde Fahey King, Mgr.

GENERAL ELECTRIC COMPANY - MAIN LIBRARY
One River Rd.   Phone: (518) 385-3652
Schenectady, NY 12345   Julia F. Hewitt, Mgr.

GENERAL ELECTRIC COMPANY - TECHNICAL INFORMATION EXCHANGE
Bldg. 5, Rm. 321
One River Rd.   Phone: (518) 385-3615
Schenectady, NY 12345   P.A. Oliver, Mgr.

KNOLLS ATOMIC POWER LABORATORY - LIBRARIES
Box 1072   Phone: (518) 393-6611
Schenectady, NY 12301   Elizabeth A. DeSimone, Act.Supv.

NATIONAL RAILWAY HISTORICAL SOCIETY - MOHAWK AND HUDSON
  CHAPTER - LAWRENCE R. LEE MEMORIAL LIBRARY
Schenectady YMCA
Schenectady, NY 12305   Clarence Langley, Jr., Libn.

NEW YORK STATE SUPREME COURT - 4TH JUDICIAL DISTRICT - LAW
  LIBRARY
612 State St.   Phone: (518) 382-3310
Schenectady, NY 12307   Patricia L. North, Law Libn.

SCHENECTADY CHEMICALS, INC. - W. HOWARD WRIGHT RESEARCH
  CENTER - LIBRARY
2750 Balltown Rd.   Phone: (518) 370-4200
Schenectady, NY 12309   Elizabeth H. Groot, Mgr., Tech.Info.Serv.

SCHENECTADY COUNTY HISTORICAL SOCIETY - LIBRARY AND ARCHIVES
32 Washington Ave.   Phone: (518) 374-0263
Schenectady, NY 12305   Mrs. C.A. Church, Archv.

SCHENECTADY GAZETTE - LIBRARY
332 State St.   Phone: (518) 374-4141
Schenectady, NY 12301   Colleen J. Daze, Libn.

SCHENECTADY MUSEUM - LIBRARY
Nott Terrace Heights   Phone: (518) 382-7890
Schenectady, NY 12308

UNION COLLEGE - SCHAFFER LIBRARY - SPECIAL COLLECTIONS
                                                Phone: (518) 370-6278
Schenectady, NY 12308   Ann M. Seeman, Act.Dir.

UNION UNIVERSITY - DUDLEY OBSERVATORY - LIBRARY
69 Union Ave.   Phone: (518) 382-7583
Schenectady, NY 12308   Rita A. Spenser, Act.Libn.

SCHOHARIE COUNTY HISTORICAL SOCIETY - REFERENCE LIBRARY
Old Stone Fort Museum, N. Main St.   Phone: (518) 295-7192
Schoharie, NY 12157   Helene S. Farrell, Dir.

TACKAPAUSHA MUSEUM - LIBRARY
Washington Ave.   Phone: (516) 785-2802
Seaford, NY 11783   Richard D. Ryder, Cur.

SENECA FALLS HISTORICAL SOCIETY - LIBRARY
55 Cayuga St.   Phone: (315) 568-8412
Seneca Falls, NY 13148   Lisa F. Johnson, Exec.Dir.

SHELTER ISLAND HISTORICAL SOCIETY - ARCHIVES *
Havens House   Phone: (516) 749-0025
Shelter Island, NY 11964   Margaret Joyce, Chairwoman

ROGERS ENVIRONMENTAL EDUCATION CENTER - GEORGE W. HOTCHKIN
  MEMORIAL LIBRARY
Box Q   Phone: (607) 674-2861
Sherburne, NY 13460

BENDIX CORPORATION - ELECTRICAL COMPONENTS DIVISION -
  ENGINEERING LIBRARY
                                                Phone: (607) 563-5605
Sidney, NY 13838   Betty L. Burnham, Libn.

SMITHTOWN HISTORICAL SOCIETY - LIBRARY †
Route 25A
Box 69   Phone: (516) 265-6768
Smithtown, NY 11787   Louise P. Hall, Dir.

SMITHTOWN LIBRARY - SPECIAL COLLECTIONS
1 North Country Rd.   Phone: (516) 265-2072
Smithtown, NY 11787   Peter McCann Gillard, Dir.

ALLIED CORPORATION - ALLIED CHEMICAL - SYRACUSE RESEARCH
  LABORATORY - LIBRARY
Box 6   Phone: (315) 487-4151
Solvay, NY 13209   Howard A. Fraenkel, Supv., Info. & Comp.Serv.

SOMERS HISTORICAL SOCIETY - LIBRARY AND ARCHIVES
Box 336   Phone: (914) 277-4977
Somers, NY 10589   Florence S. Oliver, Archv.

CRAIG DEVELOPMENTAL CENTER - MARGARET A. KENNGOTT MEMORIAL
  LIBRARY OF THE HEALTH SCIENCES
                                                Phone: (716) 658-2221
Sonyea, NY 14556   Audrey Algier, Dir., Staff Dev.

PARRISH ART MUSEUM - LIBRARY
25 Job's Ln.   Phone: (516) 283-2118
Southampton, NY 11968   Eva D. Balamuth, Chm., Lib.Comm.

SOUTHOLD HISTORICAL SOCIETY MUSEUM - LIBRARY
Main Rd. & Maple Ln.   Phone: (516) 765-5500
Southold, NY 11971   George D. Wagoner, Dir.

HUDSON RIVER ENVIRONMENTAL SOCIETY - RICHARD W. BARNETT
  MEMORIAL LIBRARY
Norrie Point Environmental Ctr.   Phone: (914) 889-4830
Staatsburg, NY 12580   Allen Beebe, Tech.Mgr.

BAYLEY SETON HOSPITAL - CHARLES FERGUSON MEDICAL LIBRARY
Bay St. & Vanderbilt Ave.   Phone: (718) 447-3010
Staten Island, NY 10304   Marie A. Sheldon, Med.Lib.Asst.

CENTER FOR MIGRATION STUDIES - CMS DOCUMENTATION CENTER
209 Flagg Pl.   Phone: (718) 351-8800
Staten Island, NY 10304   Diana J. Zimmerman, Libn.

MARCHAIS (Jacques) CENTER OF TIBETAN ARTS, INC. - LIBRARY
338 Lighthouse Ave.   Phone: (718) 987-3478
Staten Island, NY 10306   Sigrid Sidrow, Libn.

NEW YORK STATE INSTITUTE FOR BASIC RESEARCH IN DEVELOPMENTAL
  DISABILITIES - LIBRARY
1050 Forest Hill Rd.   Phone: (718) 494-5119
Staten Island, NY 10314   Lawrence Black, Sr.Libn.

NEW YORK STATE SUPREME COURT - 2ND JUDICIAL DISTRICT - LAW
  LIBRARY
County Court House   Phone: (718) 390-5291
Staten Island, NY 10301   Philip A. Klingle, Sr. Law Libn.

ST. JOHN'S UNIVERSITY, NOTRE DAME CAMPUS - LIBRARY †
300 Howard Ave.   Phone: (718) 447-4343
Staten Island, NY 10301   William V. Stone, Libn.

SEA VIEW HOSPITAL AND HOME - MEDICAL LIBRARY
460 Brielle Ave.   Phone: (718) 390-8689
Staten Island, NY 10314   Selma Amtzis, Med.Libn.

STATEN ISLAND COOPERATIVE CONTINUUM - EDUCATIONAL RESOURCE
  CENTER
130 Stuyvesant Pl., Rm. 704   Phone: (718) 390-7985
Staten Island, NY 10301   John Gino, Prog.Dir.

STATEN ISLAND HISTORICAL SOCIETY - LIBRARY
Court & Center Sts.   Phone: (718) 351-1611
Staten Island, NY 10306   Stephen C. Barto, Res.Assoc.

STATEN ISLAND HOSPITAL - MEDICAL STAFF LIBRARY
475 Seaview Ave.   Phone: (718) 390-9000
Staten Island, NY 10305   Song Ja Oh, Libn.

STATEN ISLAND INSTITUTE OF ARTS AND SCIENCES - ARCHIVES AND
  LIBRARY
75 Stuyvesant Pl.   Phone: (718) 727-1135
Staten Island, NY 10301   Eloise Beil, Archv./Libn.

STATEN ISLAND INSTITUTE OF ARTS AND SCIENCES - HIGH ROCK PARK
  CONSERVATION CENTER - LIBRARY
200 Nevada Ave.   Phone: (718) 987-6233
Staten Island, NY 10306   Evelyn Hare, Libn.

STATEN ISLAND ZOOLOGICAL SOCIETY - LIBRARY
614 Broadway   Phone: (718) 442-3101
Staten Island, NY 10310   Vincent Gattullo, Dir.

STEAMSHIP HISTORICAL SOCIETY OF AMERICA COLLECTION
414 Pelton Ave.　　Phone: (718) 727-9583
Staten Island, NY 10310　　Alice S. Wilson, Sec./Libn.

WAGNER COLLEGE - HORRMANN LIBRARY
631 Howard Ave.　　Phone: (718) 390-3401
Staten Island, NY 10301　　Y. John Auh, Chf.Libn.

U.S. NATL. PARK SERVICE - SARATOGA NATL. HISTORICAL PARK -
　LIBRARY
R.D. 2, Box 33　　Phone: (518) 664-9821
Stillwater, NY 12170　　S. Paul Okey, Pk.Hist.

INSTITUTE FOR ADVANCED STUDIES OF WORLD RELIGIONS - LIBRARY
Melville Memorial Library, 5th Fl.
SUNY at Stony Brook　　Phone: (516) 246-8366
Stony Brook, NY 11794-3383　　C.T. Shen, Pres.

MUSEUMS AT STONY BROOK - KATE STRONG HISTORICAL LIBRARY
Rte. 25A　　Phone: (516) 751-0066
Stony Brook, NY 11790　　Janice Gray Armstrong, Libn.

SUNY AT STONY BROOK - BIOLOGICAL SCIENCES LIBRARY
　　Phone: (516) 246-5662
Stony Brook, NY 11794　　Doris Williams, Libn.

SUNY AT STONY BROOK - CHEMISTRY LIBRARY
　　Phone: (516) 246-5664
Stony Brook, NY 11794　　Esther C. Linkletter, Hd.

SUNY AT STONY BROOK - DEPARTMENT OF SPECIAL COLLECTIONS
　　Phone: (516) 246-3615
Stony Brook, NY 11794　　Evert Volkersz, Libn.

SUNY AT STONY BROOK - EARTH AND SPACE SCIENCES LIBRARY
　　Phone: (516) 246-3616
Stony Brook, NY 11794　　Rosalind Walcott, ESS Libn.

SUNY AT STONY BROOK - ENGINEERING LIBRARY
　　Phone: (516) 246-7724
Stony Brook, NY 11794　　Kenneth W. Furst, Libn.

SUNY AT STONY BROOK - ENVIRONMENTAL INFORMATION SERVICE
　　Phone: (516) 246-5975
Stony Brook, NY 11794　　David Allen, Libn.

SUNY AT STONY BROOK - MAP LIBRARY
　　Phone: (516) 246-5975
Stony Brook, NY 11794　　Barbara A. Shupe, Libn.

SUNY AT STONY BROOK - MATHEMATICS-PHYSICS LIBRARY
Physics Bldg., C Fl.　　Phone: (516) 246-5666
Stony Brook, NY 11794　　Sherry Chang, Libn.

SUNY AT STONY BROOK - MUSIC LIBRARY
　　Phone: (516) 246-5660
Stony Brook, NY 11794　　Judith Kaufman, Libn.

SUNY AT STONY BROOK - POETRY COLLECTION
　　Phone: (516) 246-5654
Stony Brook, NY 11794　　Paul B. Wiener, AV Libn.

AVON PRODUCTS, INC. - RESEARCH LIBRARY
Division St.　　Phone: (914) 357-2000
Suffern, NY 10901　　Rosa K. Conlon, Sect.Mgr.

HARRIS CORPORATION - GOVERNMENT SUPPORT SYSTEMS DIVISION -
　INFORMATION CENTER
6801 Jericho Tpke.　　Phone: (516) 496-8700
Syosset, NY 11791　　Eleanor Pienitz, Libn./Info.Spec.

NATIONAL VIDEO CLEARINGHOUSE, INC. - NVC LIBRARY AND
　INFORMATION SERVICE
100 Lafayette Dr.　　Phone: (516) 364-3686
Syosset, NY 11791　　David J. Weiner, Dir.

NORTH SHORE SYNAGOGUE - CHARLES COHN MEMORIAL LIBRARY
83 Muttontown Rd.　　Phone: (516) 921-2282
Syosset, NY 11791　　Elaine Charnow, Libn.

ORTHODOX CHURCH IN AMERICA - DEPARTMENT OF HISTORY AND
　ARCHIVES
Rte. 25A, Box 675　　Phone: (516) 922-0550
Syosset, NY 11791　　Rev. Dennis R. Rhodes, Archv.

U.S. GEOLOGICAL SURVEY - WATER RESOURCES DIVISION - NEW YORK
　SUBDISTRICT - LIBRARY
5 Aerial Way　　Phone: (516) 938-8830
Syosset, NY 11791　　Joan M. Bachmann, Adm.Asst.

WATER INFORMATION CENTER, INC.
The North Shore Atrium
6800 Jericho Tpke.　　Phone: (516) 921-7690
Syosset, NY 11791　　Fred Troise, Vice-Pres.

AGWAY, INC. - CORPORATE LIBRARY
Box 4766　　Phone: (315) 477-6408
Syracuse, NY 13221　　Ron Herrgesell, Libn.

BORDEN INC. - RESEARCH CENTRE - LIBRARY
600 N. Franklin St.　　Phone: (315) 474-8526
Syracuse, NY 13204　　Carol Lenz Taylor, Libn.

BRISTOL-MYERS COMPANY - SCIENTIFIC INFORMATION DEPARTMENT
Box 4755　　Phone: (315) 432-2232
Syracuse, NY 13221-4755　　Dr. John E. MacNintch, Dir.

CANAL MUSEUM - RESEARCH LIBRARY AND DOCUMENTATION CENTER
Canal Museum Administration Bldg.
315 E. Water St.　　Phone: (315) 471-0593
Syracuse, NY 13202　　Todd S. Weseloh, Libn./Archv.

CARRIER CORPORATION - LOGAN LEWIS LIBRARY
Research Division, Carrier Pkwy.
Box 4808　　Phone: (315) 432-6306
Syracuse, NY 13221　　J. Huitfeldt, Mgr., Info.Res.

CENTRAL NEW YORK REGIONAL PLANNING BOARD - LIBRARY &
　INFORMATION CENTER
90 Presidential Plaza, Suite 122　　Phone: (315) 422-8276
Syracuse, NY 13202　　Paul Jasek, Res.Asst.

COMMUNITY-GENERAL HOSPITAL OF GREATER SYRACUSE - STAFF
　LIBRARY
Broad Rd.　　Phone: (315) 492-5500
Syracuse, NY 13215　　Jessica Boysen, Staff Libn.

CROUSE-IRVING MEMORIAL HOSPITAL - LIBRARY
736 Irving Ave.　　Phone: (315) 424-6380
Syracuse, NY 13210　　Frances Shelander, Hd.

ERIC CLEARINGHOUSE ON INFORMATION RESOURCES
Syracuse Univ., School of Education
150 Marshall St.　　Phone: (315) 423-3640
Syracuse, NY 13210　　Dr. Donald Ely, Dir.

EVERSON MUSEUM OF ART - LIBRARY
401 Harrison St.　　Phone: (315) 474-6064
Syracuse, NY 13202　　Jeffrey J. York, Libn.

GENERAL ELECTRIC COMPANY - INFORMATION RESOURCES CENTER
Electronics Park, Bldg. 3, Rm. 154　　Phone: (315) 456-2023
Syracuse, NY 13221　　C.S. Webb, Mgr., Info.Rsrcs.

HANCOCK & ESTABROOK - LAW LIBRARY
One Mony Plaza　　Phone: (315) 471-3151
Syracuse, NY 13202　　Paula G. Niemi, Libn.

LAUBACH LITERACY INTERNATIONAL, INC. - LIBRARY
1320 Jamesville Ave.
Box 131　　Phone: (315) 422-9121
Syracuse, NY 13210　　Jenny L. Ryan, Libn.

LE MOYNE COLLEGE - LIBRARY - SPECIAL COLLECTIONS
Le Moyne Heights　　Phone: (315) 446-2882
Syracuse, NY 13214　　Annette M. Monaco, Spec.Coll.Libn.

LITERACY VOLUNTEERS OF AMERICA, INC. - LIBRARY
404 Oak St.   Phone: (315) 474-7039
Syracuse, NY 13203   Frances J. Farnsworth, Supv.

MAC KENZIE, SMITH, LEWIS, MICHELL & HUGHES - LAW LIBRARY
600 Onondaga Savings Bank Bldg.   Phone: (315) 474-7571
Syracuse, NY 13202   Cynthia J. Kesler, Libn.

MANUFACTURERS ASSOCIATION OF CENTRAL NEW YORK - LIBRARY
770 James St.   Phone: (315) 474-4201
Syracuse, NY 13203   Elaine R. Reilley, Lib.Assoc.

NEW YORK STATE SUPREME COURT - APPELLATE DIVISION, 4TH
   JUDICIAL DEPARTMENT - LAW LIBRARY
500 Court House   Phone: (315) 425-2063
Syracuse, NY 13202   Susan M. Wood, Prin. Law Libn.

ONONDAGA COUNTY PUBLIC LIBRARY - ART AND MUSIC DEPARTMENT
335 Montgomery St.   Phone: (415) 473-4492
Syracuse, NY 13202   Beatrice N. Marble, Dept.Hd.

ONONDAGA COUNTY PUBLIC LIBRARY - BUSINESS AND INDUSTRIAL
   DEPARTMENT
335 Montgomery St.   Phone: (315) 473-4493
Syracuse, NY 13202   Evelyn B. Phelps, Dept.Hd.

ONONDAGA COUNTY PUBLIC LIBRARY - LOCAL HISTORY AND GENEALOGY
   DEPARTMENT
335 Montgomery St.   Phone: (315) 473-6801
Syracuse, NY 13202   Gerald J. Parsons, Dept.Hd.

ONONDAGA HISTORICAL ASSOCIATION - LIBRARY *
311 Montgomery St.   Phone: (315) 422-9948
Syracuse, NY 13202

ST. JOSEPH'S HOSPITAL HEALTH CENTER - MEDICAL AND SCHOOL OF
   NURSING LIBRARIES
301 Prospect Ave.   Phone: (315) 424-5053
Syracuse, NY 13203   Mr. V. Juchimek, Hd.Libn.

SUNY - COLLEGE OF ENVIRONMENTAL SCIENCE AND FORESTRY - F.
   FRANKLIN MOON LIBRARY
                                        Phone: (315) 470-6716
Syracuse, NY 13210   Donald F. Webster, Libn.

SUNY - SYRACUSE EDUCATIONAL OPPORTUNITY CENTER - PAUL ROBESON
   LIBRARY
100 New St.   Phone: (315) 472-0130
Syracuse, NY 13202   Florence Beer, Libn.

SUNY - UPSTATE MEDICAL CENTER LIBRARY
766 Irving Ave.   Phone: (315) 473-4580
Syracuse, NY 13210   Evelyn L. Hoey, Dir.

SYRACUSE RESEARCH CORPORATION - LIBRARY
Merrill Lane   Phone: (315) 425-5200
Syracuse, NY 13210   Mary E. O'Neill, Res.Libn.

SYRACUSE UNIVERSITY - E.S. BIRD LIBRARY - AREA STUDIES
   DEPARTMENT
                                        Phone: (315) 423-4176
Syracuse, NY 13210   Gurnek Singh, Hd./Asian Bibliog.

SYRACUSE UNIVERSITY - E.S. BIRD LIBRARY - FINE ARTS DEPARTMENT
                                        Phone: (315) 423-2440
Syracuse, NY 13210   Donald Seibert, Dept.Hd./Music Bibliog.

SYRACUSE UNIVERSITY - E.S. BIRD LIBRARY - HUMANITIES DEPARTMENT
                                        Phone: (315) 423-4243
Syracuse, NY 13210

SYRACUSE UNIVERSITY - E.S. BIRD LIBRARY - MEDIA SERVICES
   DEPARTMENT
B101 Bird Library   Phone: (315) 423-2438
Syracuse, NY 13210   George Abbott, Hd.

SYRACUSE UNIVERSITY - E.S. BIRD LIBRARY - SOCIAL SCIENCES
   DEPARTMENT
                                        Phone: (315) 423-3715
Syracuse, NY 13210   Carl Braun, Dept.Hd.

SYRACUSE UNIVERSITY - GEOLOGY LIBRARY
300 Heroy Geology Lab   Phone: (315) 423-3337
Syracuse, NY 13210   Eileen Snyder, Libn.

SYRACUSE UNIVERSITY - GEORGE ARENTS RESEARCH LIBRARY FOR
   SPECIAL COLLECTIONS
E.S. Bird Library   Phone: (315) 423-2585
Syracuse, NY 13210   Metod M. Milac, Act.Hd.

SYRACUSE UNIVERSITY - LAW LIBRARY
E.I. White Hall   Phone: (315) 423-2528
Syracuse, NY 13210   Thomas C. Kingsley, Libn.

SYRACUSE UNIVERSITY - MATHEMATICS LIBRARY
308 Carnegie Bldg.   Phone: (315) 423-2092
Syracuse, NY 13210   Mary Elling, Bibliog.

SYRACUSE UNIVERSITY - PHYSICS LIBRARY
208 Physics Bldg.   Phone: (315) 423-2692
Syracuse, NY 13210   Eileen Snyder, Libn.

SYRACUSE UNIVERSITY - SCHOOL OF EDUCATION - EDUCATIONAL
   RESOURCE CENTER
150 Marshall St.   Phone: (315) 423-3800
Syracuse, NY 13210   Dr. Tom Rusk Vickery, Dir.

SYRACUSE UNIVERSITY - SCIENCE AND TECHNOLOGY LIBRARY
105 Carnegie   Phone: (315) 423-2160
Syracuse, NY 13210   Pauline M. Miller, Hd., Sci. & Tech.Dept.

U.S. VETERANS ADMINISTRATION (NY-Syracuse) - MEDICAL CENTER
   LIBRARY
Irving Ave. & University Pl.   Phone: (315) 476-7461
Syracuse, NY 13210   June M. Mitchell, Chf., Lib./LRC Serv.

CHEM SYSTEMS INC. - INFORMATION CENTER
303 S. Broadway   Phone: (914) 631-2828
Tarrytown, NY 10591   Maryann M. Grandy, Mgr., Info.Serv.

HISTORICAL SOCIETY OF THE TARRYTOWNS - HEADQUARTERS LIBRARY
19 Grove St. & 1 Grove St.   Phone: (914) 631-8374
Tarrytown, NY 10591   Adelaide R. Smith, Cur.

RAYMOND, PARISH, PINE & WEINER, INC. - LIBRARY
555 White Plains Rd.   Phone: (914) 631-9003
Tarrytown, NY 10591   Bertha R. Dwyer, Libn.

SLEEPY HOLLOW RESTORATIONS, INC. - SPECIAL LIBRARY & ARCHIVES
150 White Plains Rd.   Phone: (914) 631-8200
Tarrytown, NY 10591   Hollee Haswell, Libn.

TECHNICON INSTRUMENTS CORPORATION - LIBRARY
511 Benedict Ave.   Phone: (914) 681-2338
Tarrytown, NY 10591   Gitta Benglas, Libn.

UNION CARBIDE CORPORATION - I.S. INFORMATION CENTER
Saw Mill River Rd.   Phone: (914) 789-2000
Tarrytown, NY 10591   Joan Schechtman, Mgr.

UNION CARBIDE CORPORATION - LIBRARY & TECHNICAL INFORMATION
   SERVICE
Tarrytown Technical Center   Phone: (914) 789-3700
Tarrytown, NY 10591   Joan Schechtman, Mgr.

LETCHWORTH VILLAGE DEVELOPMENTAL CENTER - ISAAC N. WOLFSON
   LIBRARY
                                        Phone: (914) 947-1000
Thiells, NY 10984   Eleanor Flaherty, Sr.Ck.

FORT TICONDEROGA ASSOCIATION, INC. - LIBRARY
Box 390   Phone: (518) 585-2821
Ticonderoga, NY 12883   Jane M. Lape, Cur.-Libn.

TICONDEROGA HISTORICAL SOCIETY - LIBRARY
Hancock House
Moses Circle   Phone: (518) 585-7868
Ticonderoga, NY 12883

TEMPLE BETH EL OF GREATER BUFFALO - LIBRARY
2368 Eggert Rd. Phone: (716) 836-3762
Tonawanda, NY 14150 Sandra Freed Gralnick, Libn.

UNION CARBIDE CORPORATION - LINDE DIVISION - TECHNICAL LIBRARY
Box 44 Phone: (716) 879-2031
Tonawanda, NY 14151 Sandra C. Anderson, Tech.Libn.

HUDSON VALLEY COMMUNITY COLLEGE - DWIGHT MARVIN LEARNING
RESOURCES CENTER
80 Vandenburgh Ave. Phone: (518) 283-1100
Troy, NY 12180 James F. McCoy, Dir.

NEW YORK STATE SUPREME COURT - 3RD JUDICIAL DISTRICT - LAW
LIBRARY
Court House, 2nd St. Annex
Rensselaer County Phone: (518) 270-3717
Troy, NY 12180 Karlye Ann Gill Pillai, Law Libn.

NORTON COMPANY - COATED ABRASIVE DIVISION - TECHNICAL LIBRARY
Box 808 Phone: (518) 273-0100
Troy, NY 12181 P.E. Smith, Tech.Info.Spec.

RENSSELAER COUNTY HISTORICAL SOCIETY - LIBRARY
59 Second St. Phone: (518) 272-7232
Troy, NY 12180 Mrs. Frederick R. Walsh, Dir.

RENSSELAER POLYTECHNIC INSTITUTE - ARCHITECTURE LIBRARY
Phone: (518) 270-6465
Troy, NY 12181 Virginia S. Bailey

RENSSELAER POLYTECHNIC INSTITUTE - FOLSOM LIBRARY
Phone: (518) 270-6673
Troy, NY 12181 James C. Andrews, Dir. of Lib.

ST. MARY'S HOSPITAL - MEDICAL STAFF LIBRARY
1300 Massachusetts Ave. Phone: (518) 272-5000
Troy, NY 12180 Audna T. Clum, Libn.

SAMARITAN HOSPITAL - MEDICAL LIBRARY
2215 Burdett Ave. Phone: (518) 271-3200
Troy, NY 12180 Annie J. Smith, Med.Libn.

TROY TIMES RECORD - LIBRARY
501 Broadway Phone: (518) 272-2000
Troy, NY 12181 Ingrid Sharke, Libn.

REVLON HEALTH CARE GROUP - INFORMATION SERVICES
1 Scarsdale Rd. Phone: (914) 779-6300
Tuckahoe, NY 10707 Rena Radovich, Mgr., Info.Serv.

ST. VLADIMIR'S ORTHODOX THEOLOGICAL SEMINARY - FR. GEORGES
FLOROVSKY LIBRARY
575 Scarsdale Rd. Phone: (914) 961-8313
Tuckahoe, NY 10707 Paul D. Garrett, Libn.

INTERNATIONAL PAPER COMPANY - CORPORATE RESEARCH &
DEVELOPMENT DIVISION - TECHNICAL INFORMATION CENTER
Box 797 Phone: (914) 351-2101
Tuxedo, NY 10987 Bernadette Marasco, Sr.Tech.Info.Spec.

NEW YORK UNIVERSITY MEDICAL CENTER - INSTITUTE OF
ENVIRONMENTAL MEDICINE - LIBRARY
Long Meadow Rd., Sterling Forest Phone: (914) 351-4232
Tuxedo, NY 10987 Christine M. Singleton, Res.Libn.

CINTICHEM, INC. - LIBRARY
Long Meadow Rd. Phone: (914) 351-2131
Tuxedo Park, NY 10987 Shirley Sollinger, Tech.Libn.

BROOKHAVEN NATIONAL LABORATORY - NATIONAL NUCLEAR DATA
CENTER
Bldg. 197 D Phone: (516) 282-2901
Upton, NY 11973 Sol Pearlstein, Dir.

BROOKHAVEN NATIONAL LABORATORY - NUCLEAR SAFEGUARDS LIBRARY
Bldg. 197C Phone: (516) 282-2909
Upton, NY 11973 Donna M. Albertus, Mgr.

BROOKHAVEN NATIONAL LABORATORY - NUCLEAR SAFETY LIBRARY
Bldg. 130 Phone: (516) 282-2398
Upton, NY 11973 Helen K. Todosow, Sr.Libn.

BROOKHAVEN NATIONAL LABORATORY - NUCLEAR WASTE MANAGEMENT
LIBRARY
Bldg. 830 Phone: (516) 282-7159
Upton, NY 11973 Sandra G. Lane, Sr.Libn.

BROOKHAVEN NATIONAL LABORATORY - TECHNICAL INFORMATION
DIVISION
Phone: (516) 282-3489
Upton, NY 11973 Ken Ryan, Mgr., Tech.Info.Div.

GENERAL ELECTRIC COMPANY - AIRCRAFT EQUIPMENT DIV. -
AEROSPACE ELECTRONIC SYSTEMS DEPT. - INFO.RSRCS. CENTER
French Rd. Phone: (315) 793-5716
Utica, NY 13503 Catherine Walsh, Supv.

GENERAL ELECTRIC COMPANY - INFORMATION RESOURCES
French Rd., MD300 Phone: (315) 793-7875
Utica, NY 13503 Catherine Walsh, Supv.

HERKIMER-ONEIDA COUNTIES COMPREHENSIVE PLANNING PROGRAM -
LIBRARY *
800 Park Ave. Phone: (315) 798-5721
Utica, NY 13501 Michael Gapin, Prog.Dir.

MASONIC MEDICAL RESEARCH LABORATORY - LIBRARY
2150 Bleecker St. Phone: (315) 735-2217
Utica, NY 13503 Irma S. Tuttle, Libn.

MOHAWK VALLEY COMMUNITY COLLEGE LIBRARY - SPECIAL
COLLECTIONS *
1101 Sherman Dr. Phone: (315) 792-5408
Utica, NY 13501 Alice B. Griffith, Lib.Dir.

MUNSON-WILLIAMS-PROCTOR INSTITUTE - ART REFERENCE AND MUSIC
LIBRARY
310 Genesee St. Phone: (315) 797-0000
Utica, NY 13502 Linda Lott, Libn.

NEW YORK STATE SUPREME COURT - 5TH JUDICIAL DISTRICT - LAW
LIBRARY †
Oneida County Court House Phone: (315) 798-5703
Utica, NY 13501 Constance Zogby, Libn.

ONEIDA HISTORICAL SOCIETY - LIBRARY
318 Genesee St. Phone: (315) 797-0000
Utica, NY 13502 Alice C. Dodge, Libn.

ST. ELIZABETH'S HOSPITAL - NURSING SCHOOL LIBRARY
2215 Genesee St. Phone: (315) 798-5209
Utica, NY 13503 Ann M. Kelly, Libn.

UTICA/MARCY PSYCHIATRIC CENTER - MARCY CAMPUS PROFESSIONAL
LIBRARY
1213 Court St. Phone: (315) 736-3301
Utica, NY 13502 Janina Strife, Sr.Libn.

UTICA/MARCY PSYCHIATRIC CENTER - UTICA CAMPUS LIBRARY
SERVICES
1213 Court St. Phone: (315) 797-6800
Utica, NY 13502 Toms E. Smith, Sr.Libn.

UTICA OBSERVER DISPATCH & UTICA DAILY PRESS - LIBRARY †
221-3 Oriskany Plaza Phone: (315) 797-9150
Utica, NY 13502 Virginia Malecki, Libn.

AMERICAN HEALTH FOUNDATION - NAYLOR DANA INSTITUTE FOR
DISEASE PREVENTION - LIBRARY
Dana Rd. Phone: (914) 592-2600
Valhalla, NY 10595 Patricia B. Isom, Libn.

NEW YORK MEDICAL COLLEGE AND THE WESTCHESTER ACADEMY OF
MEDICINE - WESTCHESTER MEDICAL CENTER LIBRARY
New York Medical College
Basic Sciences Bldg. Phone: (914) 347-5237
Valhalla, NY 10595 Donald E. Roy, Dir.

PEPSICO TECHNICAL CENTER - INFORMATION CENTER
100 Stevens Ave.   Phone: (914) 683-0500
Valhalla, NY 10595   Helen Regan, Libn.

WESTCHESTER COUNTY HISTORICAL SOCIETY - LIBRARY
75 Grasslands Rd.   Phone: (914) 592-4338
Valhalla, NY 10595   Elizabeth G. Fuller, Libn.

WESTCHESTER COUNTY MEDICAL CENTER - HEALTH SCIENCES LIBRARY
                                          Phone: (914) 347-7033
Valhalla, NY 10595   Charlene Sikorski, Med.Libn.

TOLSTOY FOUNDATION INC. - ALEXANDRA TOLSTOY MEMORIAL LIBRARY
Lake Rd.   Phone: (914) 268-9208
Valley Cottage, NY 10989   Tatiana Kalinin, Act.Libn.

FRANKLIN GENERAL HOSPITAL - MEDICAL LIBRARY
900 Franklin Ave.   Phone: (516) 825-8800
Valley Stream, NY 11582   Kathryn A. Boccieri, Libn.

VAN HORNESVILLE COMMUNITY CORPORATION - OWEN D. YOUNG
    COLLECTION
                                          Phone: (315) 858-0030
Van Hornesville, NY 13475   Josephine Young Case, Pres.

MADISON COUNTY LAW LIBRARY
Court House
Wampsville, NY 13163   Edward M. Kane, Libn.

WARSAW HISTORICAL SOCIETY - LIBRARY *
15 Perry Ave.
Warsaw, NY 14569

GENERAL ELECTRIC COMPANY - SILICONE PRODUCTS DIVISION -
    LIBRARY
                                          Phone: (518) 237-2264
Waterford, NY 12188   Marianne K. Pouliott, Libn.

WATERLOO LIBRARY AND HISTORICAL SOCIETY †
31 E. Williams St.   Phone: (315) 539-3313
Waterloo, NY 13165   Elizabeth A. Stetz, Libn.

JEFFERSON COUNTY HISTORICAL SOCIETY - LIBRARY
228 Washington St.   Phone: (315) 782-3491
Watertown, NY 13601   Margaret W.M. Shaeffer, Dir.

MERCY HOSPITAL OF WATERTOWN - HEALTH SCIENCE LIBRARY
218 Stone St.   Phone: (315) 782-7400
Watertown, NY 13601   Jeffrey M. Garvey, Libn.

NEW YORK STATE SUPREME COURT - 5TH JUDICIAL DISTRICT -
    WATERTOWN LAW LIBRARY
Court House   Phone: (315) 782-9100
Watertown, NY 13601   Patrica B. Donaldson, Libn.

U.S. ARMY - ARMAMENT RESEARCH & DEVELOPMENT CENTER - BENET
    WEAPONS LABORATORY - TECHNICAL LIBRARY
Watervliet Arsenal
Attn: DRSMC-LCB-TL   Phone: (518) 266-5613
Watervliet, NY 12189   Philip M. Casey, Chf., Sci./Tech.Info.

AMERICAN LIFE FOUNDATION - PRANG-MARK SOCIETY - LIBRARY
Old Irelandville   Phone: (607) 535-4004
Watkins Glen, NY 14891   L. M. Goodman, Coord.

AMERICAN LIFE FOUNDATION AND STUDY INSTITUTE - AMERICANA
    RESEARCH LIBRARY
Old Irelandville
Box 349   Phone: (607) 535-4737
Watkins Glen, NY 14891   John Crosby Freeman, Dir.

XEROX CORPORATION - TECHNICAL INFORMATION CENTER
Box 305   Phone: (716) 422-3505
Webster, NY 14580   Michael D. Majcher, Mgr., Tech.Info.Ctr.

OLD BRUTUS HISTORICAL SOCIETY, INC. - LIBRARY
8943 N. Seneca St.   Phone: (315) 834-6779
Weedsport, NY 13166   Howard J. Finley, Dir.

PILGRIM PSYCHIATRIC CENTER - HEALTH SCIENCES LIBRARY
Bldg. 23
Box A   Phone: (516) 231-8000
West Brentwood, NY 11717   Aime Atlas, Sr.Libn.

HELEN HAYES HOSPITAL - LIBRARY
Route 9W   Phone: (914) 947-3000
West Haverstraw, NY 10993   Kathleen Kuczynski, Lib.Dir.

GOOD SAMARITAN HOSPITAL - MEDICAL LIBRARY
1000 Montauk Hwy.   Phone: (516) 669-6670
West Islip, NY 11795   Helen Matlin, Libn.

ST. REGIS CORPORATION - TECHNICAL CENTER LIBRARY
W. Nyack Rd.   Phone: (914) 578-7102
West Nyack, NY 10994   Mary Ruth Bateman, Mgr., Tech.Info.

CONSTITUTION ISLAND ASSOCIATION, INC. - WARNER HOUSE LIBRARY
Box 41   Phone: (914) 446-8676
West Point, NY 10996

U.S. ARMY - MILITARY ACADEMY - ARCHIVES
                                          Phone: (914) 938-2017
West Point, NY 10996

U.S. ARMY - MILITARY ACADEMY - LIBRARY
                                          Phone: (914) 938-3833
West Point, NY 10966   Egon A. Weiss, Libn.

SUFFOLK MARINE MUSEUM - HERVEY GARRETT SMITH RESEARCH
    LIBRARY
Montauk Hwy.
Box 144   Phone: (516) 567-1733
West Sayville, NY 11796   Ruth Dougherty Jennings, Libn.

HOUGHTON COLLEGE - BUFFALO SUBURBAN CAMPUS - ADA M. KIDDER
    MEMORIAL LIBRARY
910 Union Rd.   Phone: (716) 674-6363
West Seneca, NY 14224   Ruth G. Butler, Libn.

METCO INC. - ENGINEERING LIBRARY
1101 Prospect Ave.   Phone: (516) 334-1300
Westbury, NY 11590   Peter H. Leonard, Dir.

CHAUTAUQUA COUNTY HISTORICAL SOCIETY - LIBRARY
Village Park   Phone: (716) 326-2977
Westfield, NY 14787   Maxine Smith, Hostess/Libn.

AMERICAN TEILHARD ASSOCIATION FOR THE FUTURE OF MAN - LIBRARY
Box 67   Phone: (212) 920-0114
White Plains, NY 10604   Donald P. Gray

GENERAL FOODS CORPORATION - FINANCIAL INFORMATION CENTER
250 North St.   Phone: (914) 335-0972
White Plains, NY 10625   Nancy Kiehnle, Libn.

GENERAL FOODS CORPORATION - INFORMATION MANAGEMENT
    DEPARTMENT - INFORMATION CENTER
250 North St., RA-3S   Phone: (914) 335-1040
White Plains, NY 10625   Theresa Maylone, Lib.Serv.Spec.

GENERAL FOODS CORPORATION - MARKETING INFORMATION CENTER
250 North St.   Phone: (914) 683-3911
White Plains, NY 10625   Lois Seulowitz, Mgr.

GENERAL FOODS CORPORATION - TECHNICAL CENTER - TARRYTOWN
    TECHNICAL INFORMATION CENTER
                                          Phone: (914) 683-6827
White Plains, NY 10625   Elinor Cohen, Adm., Tech.Info.Serv.

IBM CORPORATION - NAD COMMUNICATIONS LIBRARY
1133 Westchester Ave.   Phone: (914) 696-2384
White Plains, NY 10604   Anne A. Austin, Manager

LEGAL AID SOCIETY OF WESTCHESTER - LIBRARY *
1 North Broadway   Phone: (914) 682-0250
White Plains, NY 10601   Mina Pease, Dir.

MALCOLM PIRNIE, INC. - TECHNICAL LIBRARY
2 Corporate Park Dr.
Box 751   Phone: (914) 694-2100
White Plains, NY 10602   Myron E. Menewitch, Tech.Libn.

MANTELL AND MARTIN COMPANY, INC. - LIBRARY †
40 Mamaroneck Ave.   Phone: (914) 949-2544
White Plains, NY 10601

MARCH OF DIMES BIRTH DEFECTS FOUNDATION - REFERENCE ROOM
1275 Mamaroneck Ave.   Phone: (914) 428-7100
White Plains, NY 10605   Sandra Schepis, Libn.

MENTAL HEALTH ASSOCIATION OF WESTCHESTER COUNTY - LIBRARY
29 Sterling Ave.   Phone: (914) 949-6741
White Plains, NY 10606   Mary H. Johnson, Libn.

NATIONAL ECONOMIC RESEARCH ASSOCIATES, INC. - LIBRARY
123 Main St., 8th Fl.   Phone: (914) 681-7200
White Plains, NY 10601   Dolores Colgan, Libn.

NEW YORK HOSPITAL-CORNELL MEDICAL CENTER, WESTCHESTER
   DIVISION - MEDICAL LIBRARY
21 Bloomingdale Rd.   Phone: (914) 682-9100
White Plains, NY 10605   Lillian A. Wahrow, Med.Libn.

NEW YORK STATE SUPREME COURT - 9TH JUDICIAL DISTRICT - LAW
   LIBRARY
Westchester County Court House
111 Grove St., 9th Fl.   Phone: (914) 682-2574
White Plains, NY 10601   Harriet E. Smith, Prin. Law Libn.

PACE UNIVERSITY - SCHOOL OF LAW LIBRARY
78 N. Broadway   Phone: (914) 681-4273
White Plains, NY 10603   Bardie C. Wolfe, Jr., Law Libn./Prof.

TEXACO INC. - ARCHIVES
2000 Westchester Ave.   Phone: (914) 253-7129
White Plains, NY 10650   Stafford Acher, Hist.

TEXACO INC. - CORPORATE LIBRARY
2000 Westchester Ave.   Phone: (914) 253-6382
White Plains, NY 10650   Holly J. Furman, Corp.Lib.Adm.

WHITE PLAINS HOSPITAL - BERTON LATTIN MEMORIAL MEDICAL
   LIBRARY
E. Post Rd. at Davis Ave.   Phone: (914) 681-1231
White Plains, NY 10601   Joan Giordano, Mgr., Med.Lib.

COUNCIL ON NATIONAL LITERATURES - INFORMATION CENTER
Box 81   Phone: (212) 767-8380
Whitestone, NY 11357   Anne Paolucci, Pres./Exec.Dir.

WILLARD PSYCHIATRIC CENTER - HATCH LIBRARY
Hatch Bldg.   Phone: (607) 869-3111
Willard, NY 14588   Helen Bunting, Sr.Libn.

NASSAU COUNTY POLICE DEPARTMENT - POLICE ACADEMY - LIBRARY
Cross St.   Phone: (516) 535-7580
Williston Park, NY 11596   Dolores Hauner, Ck.

HARLEM VALLEY PSYCHIATRIC CENTER - INTERDISCIPLINARY LIBRARY
                                               Phone: (914) 832-6611
Wingdale, NY 12594   Virginia Lewandowski, Libn.

BULOVA (Joseph) SCHOOL - LIBRARY
40-24 62nd St.   Phone: (718) 424-2929
Woodside, Queens, NY 11377   James M. Devaney, Dir.

MIDDLEBURY HISTORICAL SOCIETY - MIDDLEBURY ACADEMY MUSEUM
   LIBRARY
22 S. Academy St.   Phone: (716) 495-6495
Wyoming, NY 14591   Mrs. Robert Gordon, Sec.

LORAL ELECTRONIC SYSTEMS - TECHNICAL INFORMATION CENTER
Ridge Hill   Phone: (914) 968-2500
Yonkers, NY 10710-0800   Terry Mozorosky, Mgr.

POLYCHROME CORPORATION - RESEARCH & DEVELOPMENT LIBRARY †
137 Alexander St.   Phone: (914) 965-8800
Yonkers, NY 10702   Peg Otis, Libn.

ST. JOHN'S RIVERSIDE HOSPITAL - MEDICAL LIBRARY
967 N. Broadway   Phone: (914) 963-3535
Yonkers, NY 10701   Helen A. Vocasek, Dir., Med.Rec.

ST. JOSEPH'S MEDICAL CENTER - MEDICAL LIBRARY
127 S. Broadway   Phone: (914) 965-6700
Yonkers, NY 10701   Ann Gorghan, Med.Libn.

ST. JOSEPH'S SEMINARY - ARCHBISHOP CORRIGAN MEMORIAL LIBRARY *
Dunwoodie   Phone: (914) 968-6200
Yonkers, NY 10704   Paul J. Fullam, Lib.Dir.

TEMPLE EMANU-EL OF YONKERS - LEVITAS LIBRARY
306 Rumsey Rd.   Phone: (914) 963-0575
Yonkers, NY 10705   Irving Levitas, Libn.

YONKERS GENERAL HOSPITAL - MEDICAL LIBRARY
127 Ashburton Ave.   Phone: (914) 965-8200
Yonkers, NY 10701   Lucila R. Samson, Med.Libn.

YONKERS HISTORICAL SOCIETY - LIBRARY
Hudson River Museum
511 Warburton Ave.   Phone: (914) 969-5622
Yonkers, NY 10701   Olga C. Kourre, Libn.

YONKERS PUBLIC LIBRARY - FINE ARTS DEPARTMENT
1500 Central Park Ave.   Phone: (914) 337-1500
Yonkers, NY 10710   Joan W. Stevenson, Dept.Hd.

YONKERS PUBLIC LIBRARY - INFORMATION SERVICES - TECHNICAL &
   BUSINESS DIVISION
7 Main St.   Phone: (914) 476-1255
Yonkers, NY 10701   Marta Schwarz, Dept.Hd.

IBM CORPORATION - THOMAS J. WATSON RESEARCH CENTER LIBRARY
Box 218   Phone: (914) 945-1415
Yorktown Heights, NY 10598   J.W. Leonard, Mgr.

OLD FORT NIAGARA ASSOCIATION - LIBRARY
Box 169   Phone: (716) 745-7611
Youngstown, NY 14174   Brian Leigh Dunnigan, Exec.Dir.

NORTH CAROLINA

MOORE, GARDNER & ASSOCIATES, INC., CONSULTING ENGINEERS -
   LIBRARY
Box 728   Phone: (919) 672-3600
Asheboro, NC 27203   Pamela A. Mattson, Libn.

MOUNTAIN AREA HEALTH EDUCATION CENTER - INFORMATION & MEDIA
   SERVICES
501 Biltmore Ave.   Phone: (704) 258-0881
Asheville, NC 28801   Patricia L. Thibodeau, Dir.

SOUTHERN HIGHLAND HANDICRAFT GUILD - FOLK ART CENTER LIBRARY
Box 9545   Phone: (704) 298-7928
Asheville, NC 28815   James Gentry, Dir.

U.S. NATL. OCEANIC & ATMOSPHERIC ADMINISTRATION - NATIONAL
   CLIMATIC DATA CENTER LIBRARY
Federal Bldg., OA/D542x2   Phone: (704) 258-2850
Asheville, NC 28801   R.L. Money, Chf., User Serv.Br.

U.S. VETERANS ADMINISTRATION (NC-Asheville) - MEDICAL CENTER
   LIBRARY
                                               Phone: (704) 298-7911
Asheville, NC 28805   Richard Haver, Chf.Libn.

UNIVERSITY OF NORTH CAROLINA, ASHEVILLE - SOUTHERN HIGHLANDS
   RESEARCH CENTER
                                               Phone: (704) 258-6414
Asheville, NC 28814   Dr. Milton Ready, Dir.

WORLD DATA CENTER A - METEOROLOGY
Natl. Environmental Satellite, Data & Info.Serv.
Natl. Climatic Data Ctr.
Federal Bldg.   Phone: (704) 258-2850
Asheville, NC 28801   Dr. L. Ray Hoxit, Act.Dir.

COUNTRY DOCTOR MUSEUM - LIBRARY
Vance St.
Box 34   Phone: (919) 235-4165
Bailey, NC 27807   Paul Crellin, Cur.

DUKE UNIVERSITY - MARINE LABORATORY - A.S. PEARSE MEMORIAL
   LIBRARY
                                           Phone: (919) 728-2111
Beaufort, NC 28516   Jean S. Williams, Lib.Assoc.

NORTH CAROLINA MARITIME MUSEUM - LIBRARY
315 Front St.   Phone: (919) 728-7317
Beaufort, NC 28516   Jean Potter

U.S. NATL. MARINE FISHERIES SERVICE - SOUTHEAST FISHERIES CENTER
   - BEAUFORT LABORATORY LIBRARY †
                                           Phone: (919) 728-4595
Beaufort, NC 28516   Ann Bowman Hall, Libn.

U.S. NATL. PARK SERVICE - CAPE LOOKOUT NATL. SEASHORE - LIBRARY
415 Front St.
Box 378   Phone: (919) 728-2121
Beaufort, NC 28516   William T. Springer, Chf., Park Oper.

BELMONT ABBEY COLLEGE - ABBOT VINCENT TAYLOR LIBRARY - SPECIAL
   COLLECTIONS
                                           Phone: (704) 825-3711
Belmont, NC 28012   Marjorie McDermott, Dir., Lrng.Rsrcs.

GULF RESOURCES AND CHEMICAL CORPORATION - LITHIUM
   CORPORATION OF AMERICA, INC. - RESEARCH LIBRARY
Box 795   Phone: (704) 629-2282
Bessemer City, NC 28016   JoAnn Trull, Libn.

APPALACHIAN STATE UNIVERSITY - BELK LIBRARY - JUSTICE-QUERY
   INSTRUCTIONAL MATERIALS CENTER
                                           Phone: (704) 262-2186
Boone, NC 28608   Pat Farthing, Libn.

APPALACHIAN STATE UNIVERSITY - BELK LIBRARY - SPECIAL
   COLLECTIONS
                                           Phone: (704) 262-2186
Boone, NC 28608   Richard T. Barker, Univ.Libn.

APPALACHIAN STATE UNIVERSITY - MUSIC LIBRARY
Broyhill Music Ctr.   Phone: (704) 262-2292
Boone, NC 28608   Joan O. Falconer, Music Libn.

NORTHWEST AREA HEALTH EDUCATION CENTER - NW AHEC LIBRARY *
Watauga County Hospital
Deerfield Rd.   Phone: (704) 264-2431
Boone, NC 28607   Jill Byerly, AHEC Libn./Coord.

FIRST BAPTIST CHURCH - MEDIA CENTER
122 Gaston St.   Phone: (704) 883-8251
Brevard, NC 28712   Ann Allen, Chm., Media Ctr.

CAMPBELL UNIVERSITY - SCHOOL OF LAW - LAW LIBRARY
Box 458   Phone: (919) 893-4111
Buies Creek, NC 27506   Karen C. Sorvari, Dir. of Res.

MEMORIAL HOSPITAL OF ALAMANCE COUNTY, INC. - MEDICAL LIBRARY
730 Hermitage Rd.   Phone: (919) 229-2680
Burlington, NC 27215   Rebecca Brown, Libn.

UMSTEAD (John) HOSPITAL - LEARNING RESOURCE CENTER
Twelfth St.   Phone: (919) 575-7259
Butner, NC 27509   Brenda M. Ellis, Libn.

U.S. NAVY - NAVAL HOSPITAL (NC-Camp Lejeune) - MEDICAL LIBRARY
                                           Phone: (919) 451-4076
Camp Lejeune, NC 28542   Betty Frazelle, Lib.Techn.

UNIVERSITY OF NORTH CAROLINA, CHAPEL HILL - CENTER FOR EARLY
   ADOLESCENCE - INFORMATION SERVICES DIVISION
Carr Mill Mall, Suite 223   Phone: (919) 966-1148
Carrboro, NC 27510   Susan Rosenzweig, Info.Mgr.

ASSOCIATION FOR POPULATION/FAMILY PLANNING LIBRARIES &
   INFORMATION CENTERS INTERNATIONAL
c/o Carolina Population Center Library
University Square - East 300A
Chapel Hill, NC 27514   Susan K. Pasquariella, Pres.

CAROLINA LIBRARY SERVICES, INC.
106 Henderson St.   Phone: (919) 929-4870
Chapel Hill, NC 27514   Eva C. Metzger, Dir.

CAROLINA LIBRARY SERVICES, INC. - WOMEN'S BOOK EXCHANGE
106 Henderson St.   Phone: (919) 942-7430
Chapel Hill, NC 27514   Melody Ivins, Libn.

CAROLINA POPULATION CENTER - LIBRARY
University Sq.
123 W. Franklin St.   Phone: (919) 933-3081
Chapel Hill, NC 27514   Patricia E. Shipman, Hd.Libn.

KXE6S VEREIN CHESS SOCIETY - SPECIAL/RESEARCH LIBRARY - EAST
   DIVISION
Box 2204
Chapel Hill, NC 27514   Steven Leslie Buntin, Bibliothecar

PSYCHICAL RESEARCH FOUNDATION - DAVID WAYNE HOOKS MEMORIAL
   LIBRARY
214 Pittsboro St.   Phone: (919) 968-4956
Chapel Hill, NC 27514

SOUTHEAST INSTITUTE - LIBRARY
Edwards Mountain
Box 2183   Phone: (919) 929-1171
Chapel Hill, NC 27514   Vann Joines, Pres.

UNIVERSITY OF NORTH CAROLINA, CHAPEL HILL - ALFRED T. BRAVER
   LIBRARY
Phillips Hall 039A   Phone: (919) 962-2323
Chapel Hill, NC 27514   Dana M. Sally, Math/Physics Libn.

UNIVERSITY OF NORTH CAROLINA, CHAPEL HILL - ART LIBRARY
Art Classroom Studio Bldg.   Phone: (919) 933-2397
Chapel Hill, NC 27514   Philip A. Rees, Art Libn.

UNIVERSITY OF NORTH CAROLINA, CHAPEL HILL - CENTER FOR ALCOHOL
   STUDIES - LIBRARY
Wing B Medical School 207-H   Phone: (919) 966-5678
Chapel Hill, NC 27514   Myra A. Carpenter, Soc.Res.Asst.

UNIVERSITY OF NORTH CAROLINA, CHAPEL HILL - GEOLOGY LIBRARY
Mitchell Hall 029-A   Phone: (919) 962-2386
Chapel Hill, NC 27514   Miriam L. Sheaves, Libn.

UNIVERSITY OF NORTH CAROLINA, CHAPEL HILL - HEALTH SCIENCES
   LIBRARY
                                           Phone: (919) 966-2111
Chapel Hill, NC 27514   Samuel Hitt, Dir.

UNIVERSITY OF NORTH CAROLINA, CHAPEL HILL - HIGHWAY SAFETY
   RESEARCH CENTER - LIBRARY
Trailer 13, CTP, 197 A   Phone: (919) 933-2202
Chapel Hill, NC 27514   Beth A. Boone, Libn.

UNIVERSITY OF NORTH CAROLINA, CHAPEL HILL - INSTITUTE OF
   GOVERNMENT - LIBRARY
Knapp Bldg. 059A   Phone: (919) 966-5381
Chapel Hill, NC 27514   Rebecca S. Ballentine, Libn.

UNIVERSITY OF NORTH CAROLINA, CHAPEL HILL - INSTITUTE OF
   OUTDOOR DRAMA - ARCHIVES
202 Graham Memorial Hall   Phone: (919) 962-1328
Chapel Hill, NC 27514   Mark R. Sumner, Dir.

UNIVERSITY OF NORTH CAROLINA, CHAPEL HILL - INSTITUTE FOR
RESEARCH IN SOCIAL SCIENCE - DATA LIBRARY
Manning Hall 026A, Rm. 10   Phone: (919) 966-3346
Chapel Hill, NC 27514   Diana McDuffee, Dir.

UNIVERSITY OF NORTH CAROLINA, CHAPEL HILL - JOHN N. COUCH
LIBRARY
301 Coker Hall 010-A   Phone: (919) 962-3783
Chapel Hill, NC 27514   William R. Burk, Botany Libn.

UNIVERSITY OF NORTH CAROLINA, CHAPEL HILL - KENAN CHEMISTRY
LIBRARY
269 Venable Hall 045-A   Phone: (919) 933-1188
Chapel Hill, NC 27514   Jimmy Dickerson, Chem.Libn.

UNIVERSITY OF NORTH CAROLINA, CHAPEL HILL - LAW LIBRARY
Van Hecke-Wettach Bldg.   Phone: (919) 933-1321
Chapel Hill, NC 27514   Mary W. Oliver, Law Libn.

UNIVERSITY OF NORTH CAROLINA, CHAPEL HILL - MAPS COLLECTION
Wilson Library 024A   Phone: (919) 933-3028
Chapel Hill, NC 27514   Celia D. Poe, Map Libn.

UNIVERSITY OF NORTH CAROLINA, CHAPEL HILL - MUSIC LIBRARY
Hill Hall   Phone: (919) 933-1030
Chapel Hill, NC 27514

UNIVERSITY OF NORTH CAROLINA, CHAPEL HILL - NORTH CAROLINA
COLLECTION
Wilson Library 024-A   Phone: (919) 933-1172
Chapel Hill, NC 27514   H.G. Jones, Cur.

UNIVERSITY OF NORTH CAROLINA, CHAPEL HILL - RARE BOOK
COLLECTION
Wilson Library 024A   Phone: (919) 962-1143
Chapel Hill, NC 27514   Paul S. Koda, Cur.

UNIVERSITY OF NORTH CAROLINA, CHAPEL HILL - SCHOOL OF LIBRARY
SCIENCE LIBRARY
114 Manning Hall   Phone: (919) 962-8361
Chapel Hill, NC 27514   Ellen D. Sutton, Interim Libn.

UNIVERSITY OF NORTH CAROLINA, CHAPEL HILL - SOUTHERN HISTORICAL
COLLECTION & MANUSCRIPTS DEPARTMENT
Wilson Library 024A   Phone: (919) 933-1345
Chapel Hill, NC 27514   Carolyn A. Wallace, Dir./Cur.

UNIVERSITY OF NORTH CAROLINA, CHAPEL HILL - ZOOLOGY LIBRARY
213 Wilson Hall 046A   Phone: (919) 962-2264
Chapel Hill, NC 27514   John B. Darling, Libn.

CHARLOTTE LAW BUILDING ASSN. - CHARLOTTE LAW LIBRARY
730 E. Trade St.   Phone: (704) 334-4912
Charlotte, NC 28202   Elizabeth F. Ledford, Libn.

CHARLOTTE AND MECKLENBURG COUNTY PUBLIC LIBRARY - CAROLINA
ROOM
310 N. Tryon St.   Phone: (704) 374-2980
Charlotte, NC 28202   Mary Louise Phillips, Local Hist.Libn.

CHARLOTTE AND MECKLENBURG COUNTY PUBLIC LIBRARY - TEXTILE
COLLECTION
310 N. Tryon St.   Phone: (704) 374-2725
Charlotte, NC 28202   Mae S. Tucker, Asst.Dir., Main Lib.Serv.

CHARLOTTE-MECKLENBURG SCHOOLS - CURRICULUM RESEARCH CENTER
428 W. Boulevard   Phone: (704) 376-0122
Charlotte, NC 28203   Beth M. Rountree, Hd., Media Spec.

CHARLOTTE MEMORIAL HOSPITAL AND MEDICAL CENTER - MEDICAL
LIBRARY OF MECKLENBURG COUNTY/LRC OF CHARLOTTE AHEC
Box 32681   Phone: (704) 331-3129
Charlotte, NC 28232   Donna Keklock, Chf.Libn.

CHARLOTTE OBSERVER AND THE CHARLOTTE NEWS - LIBRARY
600 S. Tryon St.
Box 32188   Phone: (704) 369-6889
Charlotte, NC 28232   Sara Gesler Klemmer, Hd.Libn.

DUKE POWER COMPANY - DAVID NABOW LIBRARY
                                   Phone: (704) 373-4095
Charlotte, NC 28242   Peggy B. Lambert, Libn.

MARTIN MARIETTA CHEMICALS - SODYECO DIVISION - TECHNICAL
LIBRARY
Box 669246   Phone: (704) 827-4351
Charlotte, NC 28266-9246   Jacqueline N. Kirkman, Tech.Libn.

MERCY SCHOOL OF NURSING - LIBRARY
1921 Vail Ave.   Phone: (704) 379-5845
Charlotte, NC 28207   Barbara Duval, Libn.

MIDREX CORPORATION - LIBRARY
One NCNB Plaza   Phone: (704) 373-1600
Charlotte, NC 28280   Josef Schmid, Jr., Libn.

MINT MUSEUM OF ART - LIBRARY *
501 Hempstead Pl.
Box 6011   Phone: (704) 334-9723
Charlotte, NC 28207   Sara H. Wolf, Libn.

MINT MUSEUM OF HISTORY - LASSITER LIBRARY
3500 Shamrock Dr.   Phone: (704) 568-1774
Charlotte, NC 28215   Phyllis Russell, Libn.

NATIONAL ASSOCIATION OF HOSIERY MANUFACTURERS - LIBRARY
447 S. Sharon Amity Rd.   Phone: (704) 365-0913
Charlotte, NC 28211   Sid Smith, Pres.

NCNB - LIBRARY
One NCNB Plaza
Box 120   Phone: (704) 374-5842
Charlotte, NC 28255   Barbara Mesimer, Libn.

PRESBYTERIAN HOSPITAL - LEARNING RESOURCE CENTER
Box 33549   Phone: (704) 371-4258
Charlotte, NC 28233   Ellen Cooper, Libn.

SANDOZ COLORS & CHEMICALS - LIBRARY
4000 Monroe Rd.   Phone: (704) 372-0210
Charlotte, NC 28205   Carol D. Zwingli, Libn.

U.S. BUREAU OF THE CENSUS - INFORMATION SERVICES PROGRAM -
CHARLOTTE REGIONAL OFFICE - LIBRARY
230 S. Tryon St., Suite 800   Phone: (704) 371-6144
Charlotte, NC 28202   Frank Ambrose, Info.Serv.Spec.

DUKE POWER COMPANY - PRODUCTION DEPARTMENTS - INFORMATION
RESOURCE CENTER (IRC)
Box 670   Phone: (704) 875-1686
Cornelius, NC 28031   Ella Butler Scarborough, Supv., IRC

WESTERN CAROLINA UNIVERSITY - HUNTER MEMORIAL LIBRARY -
SPECIAL COLLECTIONS
                                   Phone: (704) 227-7474
Cullowhee, NC 28723   James B. Lloyd, Cur. of Spec.Coll.

U.S. NATL. PARK SERVICE - MOORES CREEK NATL. BATTLEFIELD -
LIBRARY
Box 69   Phone: (919) 283-5591
Currie, NC 28435   John W. Stockert, Supt.

BLUE CROSS AND BLUE SHIELD OF NORTH CAROLINA - INFORMATION
CENTER
Box 2291   Phone: (919) 489-7431
Durham, NC 27702   Tera B. White, Mgr., Corp.Info.Serv.

DUKE UNIVERSITY - ARCHIVES
341 Perkins   Phone: (919) 684-5637
Durham, NC 27706   William E. King, Univ.Archv.

DUKE UNIVERSITY - BIOLOGY-FORESTRY LIBRARY
                                   Phone: (919) 684-2381
Durham, NC 27706   Bertha Livingstone, Libn.

DUKE UNIVERSITY - CENTER FOR DEMOGRAPHIC STUDIES - REFERENCE
LIBRARY
2117 Campus Dr.   Phone: (919) 684-6126
Durham, NC 27706   Michael McFee, Libn.

DUKE UNIVERSITY - CHEMISTRY LIBRARY
Phone: (919) 684-3004
Durham, NC 27706   Kitty Porter, Libn.

DUKE UNIVERSITY - DIVINITY SCHOOL LIBRARY †
Phone: (919) 684-3691
Durham, NC 27706   Donn Michael Farris, Libn.

DUKE UNIVERSITY - MANUSCRIPT DEPARTMENT
344 Perkins Library   Phone: (919) 684-3372
Durham, NC 27706   Mattie Underwood Russell, Cur. of Mss.

DUKE UNIVERSITY - MATH-PHYSICS LIBRARY
233 Physics Bldg.   Phone: (919) 684-8118
Durham, NC 27706   Mary Ann W. Southern, Libn.

DUKE UNIVERSITY - MEDICAL CENTER LIBRARY
Phone: (919) 684-2092
Durham, NC 27710   Warren Bird, Dir.

DUKE UNIVERSITY - MUSIC LIBRARY
College Sta., Box 6695   Phone: (919) 684-6449
Durham, NC 27708   J. Samuel Hammond, Libn.

DUKE UNIVERSITY - SCHOOL OF ENGINEERING LIBRARY
Phone: (919) 684-2371
Durham, NC 27706   Eric J. Smith, Engr.Libn.

DUKE UNIVERSITY - SCHOOL OF LAW LIBRARY
Phone: (919) 684-2847
Durham, NC 27706   Richard Danner, Dir.

DURHAM COUNTY HOSPITAL CORPORATION - WATTS SCHOOL OF
NURSING - LIBRARY
3643 N. Roxboro Rd.   Phone: (919) 471-3411
Durham, NC 27704   Priscilla W. Hoover, Libn.

DURHAM HERALD-SUN NEWSPAPER - LIBRARY
115 Market St.   Phone: (919) 682-8181
Durham, NC 27702   Barbara P. Semonche, Chf.Libn.

FOREST HISTORY SOCIETY, INC. - LIBRARY AND ARCHIVES
701 Vickers Ave.   Phone: (919) 682-9319
Durham, NC 27701   Mary E. Johnson, Libn.

FOUNDATION FOR RESEARCH ON THE NATURE OF MAN - INSTITUTE FOR
PARAPSYCHOLOGY - RESEARCH LIBRARY
College Station
Box 6847   Phone: (919) 688-8241
Durham, NC 27708   Mrs. Farilla A. David, Libn.

LIGGETT & MYERS TOBACCO CO. - INFORMATION SERVICES
Research Department
Box 1572   Phone: (919) 683-8985
Durham, NC 27702   Sandra S. Harris, Libn.

NORTH CAROLINA CENTRAL UNIVERSITY - LAW LIBRARY
Phone: (919) 683-6244
Durham, NC 27707   Douglas W. Martin, Law Libn.

NORTH CAROLINA CENTRAL UNIVERSITY - SCHOOL OF LIBRARY SCIENCE
- LIBRARY
J.E. Shepard Library   Phone: (919) 683-6400
Durham, NC 27707   Alice S. Richmond, Libn.

U.S. VETERANS ADMINISTRATION (NC-Durham) - MEDICAL CENTER
LIBRARY
508 Fulton St.   Phone: (919) 286-0411
Durham, NC 27705   Leola H. Jenkins, Chf.Libn.

AMERICAN ENKA COMPANY - BUSINESS AND TECHNICAL LIBRARY †
Phone: (704) 667-6936
Enka, NC 28728   Ruth H. Easter, Libn.

FIRST BAPTIST CHURCH - STINCEON IVEY MEMORIAL LIBRARY
Box 663   Phone: (919) 628-6844
Fairmont, NC 28340   Mrs. Jack Waters, Lib.Asst.

CUMBERLAND COUNTY HOSPITAL SYSTEM, INC. - CAPE FEAR VALLEY
HOSPITAL - LIBRARY SERVICES
Box 2000   Phone: (919) 323-6601
Fayetteville, NC 28302   Barbara C. Beattie, Dir., Lib.Serv.

CUMBERLAND COUNTY PUBLIC LIBRARY - NORTH CAROLINA FOREIGN
LANGUAGE CENTER
328 Gillespie St.   Phone: (919) 483-5022
Fayetteville, NC 28301   Patrick M. Valentine, Coord./Libn.

FAYETTEVILLE AREA HEALTH EDUCATION CENTER - LIBRARY
1601 Owen Dr.   Phone: (919) 323-1152
Fayetteville, NC 28304   Barbara Wright, Dir.

FAYETTEVILLE PUBLISHING COMPANY - NEWSPAPER LIBRARY
Box 849   Phone: (919) 323-4848
Fayetteville, NC 28302   Daisy D. Maxwell, Libn.

METHODIST COLLEGE, INC. - DAVIS MEMORIAL LIBRARY - SPECIAL
COLLECTIONS
Raleigh Rd.   Phone: (919) 488-7110
Fayetteville, NC 28301   Norma C. Womack, Libn./Cur.

U.S. VETERANS ADMINISTRATION (NC-Fayetteville) - HOSPITAL LIBRARY
Phone: (919) 488-2120
Fayetteville, NC 28301   Nancy A. Clark, Chf., Lib.Serv.

U.S. NATL. PARK SERVICE - CARL SANDBURG HOME NATL. HISTORIC SITE
- MUSEUM/LIBRARY
Box 395   Phone: (704) 693-4178
Flat Rock, NC 28731   Benjamin Davis, Supt.

U.S. ARMY HOSPITALS - WOMACK ARMY COMMUNITY HOSPITAL -
MEDICAL LIBRARY
Phone: (919) 396-1819
Ft. Bragg, NC 28307   Cecilia C. Edwards, Med.Libn.

U.S. ARMY - JFK SPECIAL WARFARE CENTER - MARQUAT MEMORIAL
LIBRARY
Rm. 140, Kennedy Hall   Phone: (919) 396-9383
Ft. Bragg, NC 28307   Frank M. London, Supv.Libn.

U.S. ARMY POST - FORT BRAGG - LIBRARY
HQ, XVIII Airborne Corps & Fort Bragg
AFZA-PA-MS   Phone: (919) 396-1691
Ft. Bragg, NC 28307   Barbara A. Eller, Chf.Libn.

SCHIELE MUSEUM OF NATURAL HISTORY AND PLANETARIUM - LIBRARY
1500 E. Garrison Blvd.
Box 953   Phone: (704) 864-3962
Gastonia, NC 28052   Jackie Ramseur, Registrar/Libn.

CARTER (William) COLLEGE & EVANGELICAL THEOLOGICAL SEMINARY -
WAGNER-KEVETTER LIBRARY
2306 E. Ash St.   Phone: (919) 735-0831
Goldsboro, NC 27530   Doris Byrd Thomas, Libn.

CHERRY HOSPITAL - LEARNING RESOURCE CENTER
Phone: (919) 731-3447
Goldsboro, NC 27530   Maxim Tabory, Libn./Dir. of LRC

WAYNE COMMUNITY COLLEGE - LEARNING RESOURCE CENTER
Caller Box 8002   Phone: (919) 735-5151
Goldsboro, NC 27530   Dr. Shirley T. Jones, LRC Dean

ALAMANCE COUNTY PLANNING DEPARTMENT - LIBRARY
124 W. Elm St.
Graham, NC 27253

AT & T TECHNOLOGIES, INC. - GUILFORD CENTER LIBRARY
I-85 & Mt. Hope Church Rd.
Box 25000   Phone: (919) 697-5012
Greensboro, NC 27420   Edward H. Uhler, Libn.

BENNETT COLLEGE - THOMAS F. HOLGATE LIBRARY - SPECIAL
COLLECTIONS
Phone: (919) 273-4431
Greensboro, NC 27420   Ednita W. Bullock, Hd.Libn.

BURLINGTON INDUSTRIES, INC. - LIBRARY INFORMATION SERVICES
Box 20288
Greensboro, NC 27420   Darlene L. Ball, Mgr.

CENTER FOR CREATIVE LEADERSHIP - LIBRARY
5000 Laurinda Dr.   Phone: (919) 288-7210
Greensboro, NC 27402   Frank H. Freeman, Dir.

CIBA-GEIGY CORPORATION - TECHNICAL INFORMATION SERVICE
410 Swing Rd.   Phone: (919) 292-7100
Greensboro, NC 27409

CONE MILLS CORPORATION - LIBRARY
1106 Maple St.   Phone: (919) 379-6215
Greensboro, NC 27405   Arletta M. Kluttz, Libn.

CONE (Moses H.) MEMORIAL HOSPITAL - MEDICAL LIBRARY
1200 N. Elm St.   Phone: (919) 379-4484
Greensboro, NC 27420   Leslie G. Mackler, Dir., Med.Lib.

FIRST BAPTIST CHURCH - LIBRARY
1000 W. Friendly
Box 5443   Phone: (919) 274-3286
Greensboro, NC 27403   Charlotte M. Bell, Dir., Media Serv.

GREENSBORO DAILY NEWS AND RECORD - LIBRARY
Box 20848   Phone: (919) 373-7044
Greensboro, NC 27420   R.L. Beall, Lib.Dir.

GREENSBORO HISTORICAL MUSEUM - ARCHIVES
130 Summit Ave.   Phone: (919) 373-2043
Greensboro, NC 27401   Karen Carroll, Archv.

GREENSBORO MASONIC MUSEUM LIBRARY
426 W. Market St.
Box 466
Greensboro, NC 27402   Robert A. Pinnix, Cur.

GREENSBORO PLANNING & COMMUNITY DEVELOPMENT DEPARTMENT -
   LIBRARY
Drawer W-2   Phone: (919) 373-2144
Greensboro, NC 27402   Arthur Davis, III, Data & Anl.Spec.

GREENSBORO PUBLIC LIBRARY - BUSINESS LIBRARY
201 N. Greene St.   Phone: (919) 373-2471
Greensboro, NC 27402   Ms. Lebby B. Lamb, Bus.Libn.

GUILFORD COLLEGE - LIBRARY - SPECIAL COLLECTIONS
5800 W. Friendly Ave.   Phone: (919) 292-5511
Greensboro, NC 27410   Dr. Herbert Poole, Dir.

LORILLARD RESEARCH CENTER LIBRARY
420 English St.
Box 21688   Phone: (919) 373-6895
Greensboro, NC 27420   Lawrence M. Skladanowski, Lib.Supv.

NORTH CAROLINA AGRICULTURAL & TECHNICAL STATE UNIVERSITY -
   F.D. BLUFORD LIBRARY
312 Market St.   Phone: (919) 379-7783
Greensboro, NC 27411   Alene C. Young, Act.Dir., Lib.Serv.

TRANSPORTATION INSTITUTE - RESEARCH DOCUMENTATION CENTER
301-303 Merrick Bldg.
North Carolina Agricultural & Tech. State Univ.   Phone: (919) 379-7745
Greensboro, NC 27411   Joyce H. Johnson, Adm.Off.

U.S. DEPT. OF COMMERCE - INTERNATIONAL TRADE ADMINISTRATION -
   GREENSBORO DISTRICT OFFICE LIBRARY
203 Federal Bldg., West Market St.   Phone: (919) 378-5345
Greensboro, NC 27402   Jack F. Whiteley, Dp.Dir.

UNIVERSITY OF NORTH CAROLINA, GREENSBORO - DANCE COLLECTION
Jackson Library, Special Collections   Phone: (919) 379-5246
Greensboro, NC 27412   Emilie Mills, Spec.Coll.Libn.

UNIVERSITY OF NORTH CAROLINA, GREENSBORO - EUGENIE SILVERMAN
   BAIZERMAN ARCHIVE
Jackson Library, Special Collections   Phone: (919) 379-5246
Greensboro, NC 27412

UNIVERSITY OF NORTH CAROLINA, GREENSBORO - GEORGE HERBERT
   COLLECTION
Jackson Library, Special Collections   Phone: (919) 379-5246
Greensboro, NC 27412

UNIVERSITY OF NORTH CAROLINA, GREENSBORO - GIRLS BOOKS IN
   SERIES
Jackson Library, Special Collections   Phone: (919) 379-5246
Greensboro, NC 27412   Emilie Mills, Spec.Coll.Libn.

UNIVERSITY OF NORTH CAROLINA, GREENSBORO - LOIS LENSKI
   COLLECTION
Jackson Library, Special Collections   Phone: (919) 379-5246
Greensboro, NC 27412

UNIVERSITY OF NORTH CAROLINA, GREENSBORO - LUIGI SILVA
   COLLECTION
Jackson Library, Special Collections   Phone: (919) 379-5246
Greensboro, NC 27412

UNIVERSITY OF NORTH CAROLINA, GREENSBORO - PHYSICAL EDUCATION
   HISTORY COLLECTION
Jackson Library, Special Collections   Phone: (919) 379-5246
Greensboro, NC 27412

UNIVERSITY OF NORTH CAROLINA, GREENSBORO - PRINTING
   COLLECTION
Jackson Library, Special Collections   Phone: (919) 379-5246
Greensboro, NC 27412

UNIVERSITY OF NORTH CAROLINA, GREENSBORO - RANDALL JARRELL
   COLLECTION
Jackson Library, Special Collections   Phone: (919) 379-5246
Greensboro, NC 27412

UNIVERSITY OF NORTH CAROLINA, GREENSBORO - SAUL BAIZERMAN
   ARCHIVE
Jackson Library, Special Collections   Phone: (919) 379-5246
Greensboro, NC 27412

UNIVERSITY OF NORTH CAROLINA, GREENSBORO - WAY & WILLIAMS
   COLLECTION
Jackson Library, Special Collections   Phone: (919) 379-5246
Greensboro, NC 27412

UNIVERSITY OF NORTH CAROLINA, GREENSBORO - WOMAN'S
   COLLECTION
Jackson Library, Special Collections   Phone: (919) 379-5246
Greensboro, NC 27412

UNIVERSITY OF NORTH CAROLINA, GREENSBORO - WOMEN DETECTIVES
   FICTION COLLECTION
Jackson Library, Special Collections   Phone: (919) 379-5246
Greensboro, NC 27412

BURROUGHS WELLCOME COMPANY - PLANT LIBRARY
Box 1887   Phone: (919) 758-3436
Greenville, NC 27834   Laura Ann Bollinger, Plant Libn.

EAST CAROLINA UNIVERSITY - EAST CAROLINA MANUSCRIPT
   COLLECTION
J.Y. Joyner Library   Phone: (919) 757-6671
Greenville, NC 27834   Donald R. Lennon, Coll.Dir.

EAST CAROLINA UNIVERSITY - HEALTH SCIENCES LIBRARY
                                           Phone: (919) 757-2212
Greenville, NC 27834   JoAnn Bell, Ph.D., Dir.

EAST CAROLINA UNIVERSITY - MUSIC LIBRARY
School of Music   Phone: (919) 757-6250
Greenville, NC 27834   Geraldine Laudati, Music Libn.

TECHNICAL COLLEGE OF ALAMANCE - TECHNICAL LIBRARY
Box 623   Phone: (919) 578-2002
Haw River, NC 27265

NORTHWEST AREA HEALTH EDUCATION CENTER - NW AHEC LIBRARY
Catawba Memorial Hospital   Phone: (704) 322-0662
Hickory, NC 28601   Phyllis C. Gillikin, Dir., AHEC Lib.

SIECOR CORPORATION - TECHNICAL INFORMATION CENTER
1928 Main Ave., S.E.
Box 489   Phone: (704) 328-2171
Hickory, NC 28601   Nola V. Callahan, Tech.Libn.

FURNITURE LIBRARY ASSOCIATION
1009 N. Main St.   Phone: (919) 883-4011
High Point, NC 27262   N. I. Bienenstock, Cur.

GUILFORD TECHNICAL COMMUNITY COLLEGE - LEARNING RESOURCE
    CENTER
Box 309   Phone: (919) 292-1101
Jamestown, NC 27282   Mertys W. Bell, Dean of Lrng.Rsrcs.

NORTH AMERICAN YOUTH SPORT INSTITUTE - INFORMATION CENTER
4985 Oak Garden Dr., Suite G   Phone: (919) 784-4926
Kernersville, NC 27284   Dr. Jack Hutslar, Exec.Dir.

U.S. NATL. PARK SERVICE - KINGS MOUNTAIN NATL. MILITARY PARK -
    LIBRARY
Box 31   Phone: (803) 936-7921
Kings Mountain, NC 28086   James J. Anderson, Chf.Interp. & Rsrcs.Mgt.

DU PONT DE NEMOURS (E.I.) & COMPANY, INC. - DACRON RESEARCH
    LABORATORY - TECHNICAL LIBRARY
Box 800   Phone: (919) 522-6406
Kinston, NC 28501

ST. ANDREWS PRESBYTERIAN COLLEGE - MUSIC LIBRARY *
Laurinburg, NC 28352

SOUTHEASTERN GENERAL HOSPITAL, INC. - LIBRARY
300 W. 27th St.
Box 1408   Phone: (919) 738-6441
Lumberton, NC 28358   Ann Stephens, Libn.

U.S. NATL. PARK SERVICE - CAPE HATTERAS NATL. SEASHORE LIBRARY
Rte. 1, Box 675   Phone: (919) 473-2111
Manteo, NC 27954   Sue Swanson, Sec./Libn.

HISTORICAL FOUNDATION OF THE PRESBYTERIAN AND REFORMED
    CHURCHES - LIBRARY AND ARCHIVES
Box 847   Phone: (704) 669-7061
Montreat, NC 28757   Jerrold Lee Brooks, Dir.

UNIVERSITY OF NORTH CAROLINA - INSTITUTE OF MARINE SCIENCES -
    LIBRARY
3407 Arendell St.   Phone: (919) 726-6841
Morehead City, NC 28557   Brenda B. Bright, Libn.

BROUGHTON HOSPITAL - MEDICAL LIBRARY †
1000 S. Sterling St.   Phone: (704) 433-2303
Morganton, NC 28655   Mary E. Bush, Libn.

MOUNT OLIVE COLLEGE - FREE WILL BAPTIST HISTORICAL COLLECTION
Moye Library   Phone: (919) 658-2502
Mount Olive, NC 28365   Gary Fenton Barefoot, Libn.

COMMITTEE ON DIAGNOSTIC READING TESTS, INC. - LIBRARY
                  Phone: (704) 693-5223
Mountain Home, NC 28758   Dr. Frances Oralind Triggs, Chm.

NORTH CAROLINA STATE DEPARTMENT OF CULTURAL RESOURCES -
    TRYON PALACE RESTORATION - LIBRARY
613 Pollock St.
Box 1007   Phone: (919) 638-5109
New Bern, NC 28560   Kay P. Williams, Adm.

CATAWBA COUNTY HISTORICAL MUSEUM - LIBRARY
U.S. Hwy. 321   Phone: (704) 465-0383
Newton, NC 28658   Sidney Halma, Dir.

OLIN CORPORATION - ECUSTA PAPER AND FILM GROUP - TECHNICAL
    LIBRARY †
Box 200   Phone: (704) 877-2339
Pisgah Forest, NC 28768   Martha M. Sellers, Tech.Libn.

NATIONAL SHARECROPPERS FUND/RURAL ADVANCEMENT FUND - F.P.
    GRAHAM RESOURCE CENTER
Box 1029   Phone: (704) 851-9346
Pittsboro, NC 27312   Cary Fowler, Prog.Dir.

U.S. AIR FORCE BASE - POPE BASE LIBRARY
FL 4488   Phone: (919) 394-2791
Pope AFB, NC 28308   Jean L. Hort, Base Libn.

CAROLINA POWER & LIGHT COMPANY - TECHNICAL LIBRARY
411 Fayetteville St.
Box 1551   Phone: (919) 836-6790
Raleigh, NC 27602   A.P. Carmichael, Corp.Libn.

DOROTHEA DIX HOSPITAL - F.T. FULLER STAFF LIBRARY
                  Phone: (919) 733-5111
Raleigh, NC 27611   Spanola M. Eubanks, Dir., Lib.Serv.

NEWS AND OBSERVER PUBLISHING COMPANY - LIBRARY
215 S. McDowell St.   Phone: (919) 821-1234
Raleigh, NC 27602   Lany W. McDonald, Libn.

NORTH CAROLINA GEOLOGICAL SURVEY - LIBRARY
Box 27687   Phone: (919) 733-2424
Raleigh, NC 27611

NORTH CAROLINA MUSEUM OF ART - ART REFERENCE LIBRARY
Cultural Resources Dept.
2110 Blue Ridge Blvd.   Phone: (919) 833-1935
Raleigh, NC 27607   Dr. Anna Dvorak, Libn.

NORTH CAROLINA STATE DEPT. OF CULTURAL RESOURCES - DIV. OF
    ARCHIVES AND HISTORY - ARCHIVES & RECORDS SECTION
109 E. Jones St.   Phone: (919) 733-3952
Raleigh, NC 27611   David J. Olson, State Archv.

NORTH CAROLINA STATE DEPARTMENT OF CULTURAL RESOURCES -
    DIVISION OF THE STATE LIBRARY
109 E. Jones St.   Phone: (919) 733-2570
Raleigh, NC 27611   David N. McKay, Dir./State Libn.

NORTH CAROLINA STATE DEPARTMENT OF CULTURAL RESOURCES -
    LIBRARY FOR THE BLIND AND PHYSICALLY HANDICAPPED
1811 North Blvd.   Phone: (919) 733-4376
Raleigh, NC 27635   Charles H. Fox, Chf., Spec.Serv.Sect.

NORTH CAROLINA STATE DEPARTMENT OF HUMAN RESOURCES -
    DIVISION OF HEALTH SERVICES - PUBLIC HEALTH LIBRARY
Bath Bldg., Rm. 215
306 N. Wilmington St.
Box 2091   Phone: (919) 733-7389
Raleigh, NC 27602   Elnora H. Turner, Pub. Health Libn.

NORTH CAROLINA STATE DEPT. OF NATURAL RESOURCES & COMMUNITY
    DEVELOPMENT - DIV. OF COMMUNITY ASSISTANCE LIB.
Box 27687   Phone: (919) 733-2850
Raleigh, NC 27611   Julie Torrey, Libn.

NORTH CAROLINA STATE DEPT. OF NATURAL RESOURCES & COMMUNITY
    DEVELOPMENT - ENVIRONMENTAL MGT. LIBRARY
512 N. Salisbury St., Rm. 702
Box 27687   Phone: (919) 733-7015
Raleigh, NC 27611   Jane Basnight, Libn.

NORTH CAROLINA STATE DEPARTMENT OF PUBLIC INSTRUCTION -
    EDUCATION INFORMATION CENTER
Education Bldg.   Phone: (919) 733-7094
Raleigh, NC 27611   Ann Fowler, Coord.

NORTH CAROLINA STATE LEGISLATIVE LIBRARY
Legislative Off. Bldg.   Phone: (919) 733-7778
Raleigh, NC 27611   Vivian Payne Halperen, Libn.

NORTH CAROLINA STATE MUSEUM OF NATURAL HISTORY - H.H. BRIMLEY
    MEMORIAL LIBRARY
102 N. Salisbury St.
Box 27647   Phone: (919) 733-7450
Raleigh, NC 27611   John B. Funderburg, Dir.

NORTH CAROLINA STATE SUPREME COURT LIBRARY
Box 28006   Phone: (919) 733-3425
Raleigh, NC 27611   Frances H. Hall, Libn.

NORTH CAROLINA STATE UNIVERSITY - BURLINGTON TEXTILES LIBRARY
Box 8301   Phone: (919) 737-3043
Raleigh, NC 27695-8301   Georgia H. Rodeffer, Textiles Libn.

NORTH CAROLINA STATE UNIVERSITY - D.H. HILL LIBRARY
Box 7111   Phone: (919) 737-2843
Raleigh, NC 27695-7111   Isaac T. Littleton, Dir.

NORTH CAROLINA STATE UNIVERSITY - D.H. HILL LIBRARY - DOCUMENTS
    DEPARTMENT
Box 7111   Phone: (919) 737-3280
Raleigh, NC 27695-7111   Jean Porter, Docs.Libn./Dept.Hd.

NORTH CAROLINA STATE UNIVERSITY - D.H. HILL LIBRARY - TECHNICAL
    INFORMATION CENTER
Box 7111   Phone: (919) 737-2830
Raleigh, NC 27695-7111   M. Ronald Simpson, Hd.

NORTH CAROLINA STATE UNIVERSITY - FOREST RESOURCES LIBRARY
Box 8001   Phone: (919) 737-2306
Raleigh, NC 27695-8001   Pamela E. Puryear, Hd.

NORTH CAROLINA STATE UNIVERSITY - HARRYE LYONS DESIGN LIBRARY
209 Brooks Hall
Box 7701   Phone: (919) 737-2207
Raleigh, NC 27695-7701   Maryellen LoPresti, Libn.

NORTH CAROLINA STATE UNIVERSITY - TOBACCO LITERATURE SERVICE
2314 D.H. Hill Library
Box 7111   Phone: (919) 737-2837
Raleigh, NC 27695   Carmen M. Marin, Dir.

NORTH CAROLINA STATE UNIVERSITY - VETERINARY MEDICAL LIBRARY
School of Veterinary Medicine   Phone: (919) 737-3910
Raleigh, NC 27606   Thea J. Fischer, Veterinary Med.Libn.

REX HOSPITAL - LIBRARY
4420 Lake Boone Trail   Phone: (919) 755-3100
Raleigh, NC 27607   Dorothy T. McCallum, Libn.

SMITH, ANDERSON, BLOUNT, DORSETT, MITCHELL & JERNIGAN - LIBRARY
1300 St. Mary's St.
Box 12807   Phone: (919) 821-1220
Raleigh, NC 27605   Constance M. Matzen, Libn.

WAKE COUNTY MEDICAL CENTER - MEDICAL LIBRARY
3000 New Bern Ave.   Phone: (919) 755-8528
Raleigh, NC 27610   Karen K. Grandage, Dir., Med.Lib.

PENN (Annie) MEMORIAL HOSPITAL - MEDICAL LIBRARY
618 S. Main St.   Phone: (919) 349-8461
Reidsville, NC 27320   Susan Bray, Libn.

AMERICAN ASSOCIATION OF TEXTILE CHEMISTS AND COLORISTS -
    LIBRARY
Box 12215   Phone: (919) 549-8141
Research Triangle Park, NC 27709   George J. Mandikos, Tech.Dir.

BECTON, DICKINSON & COMPANY - RESEARCH CENTER LIBRARY
Box 12016   Phone: (919) 549-8641
Research Triangle Park, NC 27709   Dora Zia, Res.Libn.

BURROUGHS WELLCOME COMPANY - LIBRARY
3030 Cornwallis Rd.   Phone: (919) 541-9090
Research Triangle Park, NC 27709   Ildiko Trombitas, Hd., Tech.Info.Dept.

ENVIRONMENTAL PROTECTION AGENCY - DIVISION OF METEOROLOGY -
    INFORMATION SERVICE CENTER
                                             Phone: (919) 541-4536
Research Triangle Park, NC 27711   Evelyn M. Poole-Kober, Tech.Info.Ck.

ENVIRONMENTAL PROTECTION AGENCY - LIBRARY SERVICES
MD 35   Phone: (919) 541-2777
Research Triangle Park, NC 27711   Libby Smith, Libn.

FAMILY HEALTH INTERNATIONAL - LIBRARY
Triangle Dr.   Phone: (919) 549-0517
Research Triangle Park, NC 27709   William Barrows, Info.Coord.

IBM CORPORATION - COMMUNICATION PRODUCTS DIVISION - LIBRARY
Dept. 609/Bldg. 060
Box 12195   Phone: (919) 543-5942
Research Triangle Park, NC 27709   Dorothy Huey, Libn.

INSTRUMENT SOCIETY OF AMERICA - LIBRARY
67 Alexander Dr.
Box 12277   Phone: (919) 549-8411
Research Triangle Park, NC 27709   Charles D. McAlister, Tech.Dir.

NATIONAL HUMANITIES CENTER - LIBRARY
Box 12256   Phone: (919) 549-0661
Research Triangle Park, NC 27709   Walter Alan Tuttle, Libn.

NATIONAL INSTITUTE OF ENVIRONMENTAL HEALTH SCIENCES - LIBRARY
Box 12233   Phone: (919) 541-3426
Research Triangle Park, NC 27709   W. Davenport Robertson, Hd.Libn.

NATL.INST. OF ENVIRONMENTAL HEALTH SCI. - NATL. TOXICOLOGY
    PROGRAM - ENVIRONMENTAL TERATOLOGY INFO.CTR.
Box 12233   Phone: (919) 541-3214
Research Triangle Park, NC 27709   Florence E. Jordan, Proj.Off.

NORTH CAROLINA STATE SCIENCE AND TECHNOLOGY RESEARCH CENTER
Box 12235   Phone: (919) 549-0671
Research Triangle Park, NC 27709   Dr. James E. Vann, Dir.

UNION CARBIDE AGRICULTURAL PRODUCTS COMPANY, INC. - LIBRARY
T.W. Alexander Dr.
Box 12014   Phone: (919) 549-2649
Research Triangle Park, NC 27709   Constance J. Lavoy, Lib.Serv.Supv.

U.S. ARMY RESEARCH OFFICE - TECHNICAL LIBRARY
Box 12211   Phone: (919) 549-0641
Research Triangle Park, NC 27709   Brenda Mann, Tech.Libn.

NORTH CAROLINA STATE JUSTICE ACADEMY - LEARNING RESOURCE
    CENTER
Drawer 99   Phone: (919) 525-4151
Salemburg, NC 28385   Donald K. Stacy, Libn.

HOOD THEOLOGICAL SEMINARY - LIVINGSTONE COLLEGE - LIBRARY *
W.J. Walls Ctr.
800 W. Thomas St.   Phone: (704) 633-7960
Salisbury, NC 28144   Mrs. Willie L. Aldrich, Hd.Libn.

LUTHERAN CHURCH IN AMERICA - NORTH CAROLINA SYNOD - ARCHIVES
Box 2049   Phone: (704) 633-4861
Salisbury, NC 28145   James A. Chesky, Sec./Archv.

ROWAN MEMORIAL HOSPITAL - MC KENZIE MEMORIAL LIBRARY
612 Mocksville Ave.   Phone: (704) 636-3311
Salisbury, NC 28144   Mary J. Peck, AHEC Lib.Dir.

ROWAN PUBLIC LIBRARY - EDITH M. CLARK HISTORY ROOM
201 W. Fisher St.
Box 4039   Phone: (704) 633-5578
Salisbury, NC 28144

U.S. VETERANS ADMINISTRATION (NC-Salisbury) - MEDICAL CENTER
    LIBRARY
1601 Brenner Ave.   Phone: (704) 636-2351
Salisbury, NC 28144   Mara R. Wilhelm, Chf., Lib.Serv.

CENTRAL CAROLINA TECHNICAL COLLEGE - LEARNING RESOURCE CENTER
1105 Kelly Dr.   Phone: (919) 775-5401
Sanford, NC 27330   Jim Foster, Dir., LRC

SWANSBORO HISTORICAL ASSOCIATION, INC. - RESEARCH FILES
Box 414   Phone: (919) 326-5361
Swansboro, NC 28584

MONTGOMERY TECHNICAL COLLEGE - LEARNING RESOURCES CENTER
Drawer 487   Phone: (919) 572-3691
Troy, NC 27371   Gay R. Russell, Libn.

ST. JOHN'S MUSEUM OF ART, INC. - LIBRARY
114 Orange St.   Phone: (919) 763-0281
Wilmington, NC 28401   Alan Aiches, Dir.

UNIVERSITY OF NORTH CAROLINA, WILMINGTON - WILLIAM MADISON
   RANDALL LIBRARY - HELEN HAGAN RARE BOOK ROOM
Box 3725   Phone: (919) 791-4330
Wilmington, NC 28401

WILMINGTON AREA HEALTH EDUCATION CENTER - HEALTH SCIENCES
   LIBRARY
2131 S. 17th St.   Phone: (919) 343-0161
Wilmington, NC 28402-9990   Ms. Spencer Kearns Sexton, Libn.

WILMINGTON STAR-NEWS NEWSPAPERS, INC. - LIBRARY
1103 S. 17th St.
Box 840   Phone: (919) 343-2309
Wilmington, NC 28402   Shirley A. Moore, Libn.

WILSON MEMORIAL HOSPITAL - LIBRARY/LEARNING CENTER
1705 S. Tarboro St.   Phone: (919) 399-8253
Wilson, NC 27893   Marian H. Spencer, Lib.Dir.

FORSYTH MEMORIAL HOSPITAL - JOHN C. WHITAKER LIBRARY
3333 Silas Creek Pkwy.   Phone: (919) 773-3995
Winston-Salem, NC 27103-3090   Margaret L. Cobb, Med.Libn.

FORSYTH TECHNICAL INSTITUTE - LIBRARY
2100 Silas Creek Pkwy.   Phone: (919) 723-0371
Winston-Salem, NC 27103   Audrey B. Zablocki, Dir.

MORAVIAN CHURCH IN AMERICA - SOUTHERN PROVINCE - MORAVIAN
   ARCHIVES
Salem Sta., Drawer M   Phone: (919) 722-1742
Winston-Salem, NC 27108   Mary Creech, Archv.

MORAVIAN MUSIC FOUNDATION, INC. - PETER MEMORIAL LIBRARY
20 Cascade Ave.   Phone: (919) 725-0651
Winston-Salem, NC 27107   James Boeringer, Dir.

OLD SALEM, INC. - LIBRARY
Drawer F, Salem Sta.   Phone: (919) 723-3688
Winston-Salem, NC 27108   Gene T. Capps, Dir., Dept. of Educ.

OLD SALEM, INC. - MUSEUM OF EARLY SOUTHERN DECORATIVE ARTS
   (MESDA) - LIBRARY
Box 10310   Phone: (919) 722-6148
Winston-Salem, NC 27108   Bradford L. Rauschenberg

PIEDMONT BIBLE COLLEGE - GEORGE M. MANUEL MEMORIAL LIBRARY
716 Franklin St.   Phone: (919) 725-8345
Winston-Salem, NC 27101   William P. Thompson, Libn.

REYNOLDA HOUSE, INC. - LIBRARY *
Reynolda Rd.
Box 11765   Phone: (919) 725-5325
Winston-Salem, NC 27106   Ruth Mullen, Libn.

REYNOLDS (R.J.) INDUSTRIES, INC. - RJR CORPORATE LIBRARY-PLAZA
Plaza Bldg., 1st Fl.   Phone: (919) 777-2092
Winston-Salem, NC 27102   Molly C. Barnett, Plaza Libn.

REYNOLDS (R.J.) INDUSTRIES, INC. - RJR WORLD HEADQUARTERS
   CORPORATE LIBRARY
B4102 World Headquarters Bldg.   Phone: (919) 773-2652
Winston-Salem, NC 27102   Barry K. Miller, Corp.Libn.

REYNOLDS (R.J.) TOBACCO COMPANY - ENGINEERING - TECHNICAL
   INFORMATION/RECORDS SECTION
RJR Plaza, 11th Fl.   Phone: (919) 777-5842
Winston-Salem, NC 27102   Pansy D. Broughton, Ref.Libn.

REYNOLDS (R.J.) TOBACCO COMPANY - R&D SCIENTIFIC INFORMATION
   SERVICES LIBRARY
Chestnut at Belews St.   Phone: (919) 773-4360
Winston-Salem, NC 27102   Randy D. Ralph, Sr.Lit.Sci., R&D

WAKE FOREST UNIVERSITY - BABCOCK GRADUATE SCHOOL OF
   MANAGEMENT - LIBRARY
Box 7689, Reynolda Sta.   Phone: (919) 761-5414
Winston-Salem, NC 27109   Jean B. Hopson, Lib.Dir.

WAKE FOREST UNIVERSITY - BAPTIST COLLECTION
University Library   Phone: (919) 761-5472
Winston-Salem, NC 27109   John R. Woodard, Jr., Dir.

WAKE FOREST UNIVERSITY - BOWMAN GRAY SCHOOL OF MEDICINE - COY
   C. CARPENTER LIBRARY
300 S. Hawthorne Rd.   Phone: (919) 748-4691
Winston-Salem, NC 27103   Michael D. Sprinkle, Dir.

WAKE FOREST UNIVERSITY - LAW LIBRARY
Reynolda Sta., Box 7206   Phone: (919) 761-5438
Winston-Salem, NC 27109   Kenneth A. Zick, II, Dir.

WINSTON-SALEM FOUNDATION - FOUNDATION CENTER REGIONAL
   LIBRARY
229 First Union Bldg.   Phone: (919) 725-2382
Winston-Salem, NC 27101   Sara N. Willard, Libn.

WINSTON-SALEM JOURNAL AND SENTINEL - REFERENCE DEPARTMENT
418 N. Marshall   Phone: (919) 727-7275
Winston-Salem, NC 27102   Marilyn H. Rollins, Ref.Dept.Mgr.

WINSTON-SALEM STATE UNIVERSITY - O'KELLY LIBRARY - SPECIAL
   COLLECTIONS
                                       Phone: (919) 761-2128
Winston-Salem, NC 27110   Mae L. Holt, Dir. of Lib.Serv.

YADKIN COUNTY HISTORICAL SOCIETY - LIBRARY
Yadkin County Public Library
E. Main St.
Box 1250   Phone: (919) 679-8792
Yadkinville, NC 27055   Mildred Matthew, Pres.

NORTH DAKOTA

BISMARCK TRIBUNE - NEWS LIBRARY
707 E. Front Ave.
Box 1498   Phone: (701) 223-2500
Bismarck, ND 58502   Elizabeth A. Simes, Libn.

MARY COLLEGE - LIBRARY
Apple Creek Rd.   Phone: (701) 255-4681
Bismarck, ND 58501   Cheryl M. Bailey, Dir.

NORTH DAKOTA STATE DEPARTMENT OF HEALTH - DIVISION OF HEALTH
   EDUCATION
Capitol Bldg.
Judicial Wing, 2nd Fl.   Phone: (701) 224-2368
Bismarck, ND 58505

NORTH DAKOTA STATE LIBRARY
Liberty Memorial Bldg.
Capitol Grounds   Phone: (701) 224-2490
Bismarck, ND 58505   Ruth Mahan, State Libn.

NORTH DAKOTA STATE SUPREME COURT LAW LIBRARY
State Capitol, 2nd Fl.   Phone: (701) 224-2227
Bismarck, ND 58505   Elmer J. Dewald, Law Libn.

QUAIN AND RAMSTAD CLINIC - MEDICAL LIBRARY
622 Ave. A East   Phone: (701) 222-5390
Bismarck, ND 58501   Harriet Kling, Med.Libn.

STATE HISTORICAL SOCIETY OF NORTH DAKOTA - STATE ARCHIVES AND
   HISTORICAL RESEARCH LIBRARY
Heritage Center   Phone: (701) 224-2668
Bismarck, ND 58505   Gerald Newborg, State Archv.

NORTH DAKOTA STATE UNIVERSITY - BOTTINEAU BRANCH AND
   INSTITUTE OF FORESTRY - LIBRARY
First & Simrall Blvd.   Phone: (701) 228-2277
Bottineau, ND 58318   Mary Claire Thorleifson, Libn.

DICKINSON STATE COLLEGE - STOXEN LIBRARY
Phone: (701) 227-2135
Dickinson, ND 58601   Bernnett Reinke, Lib.Dir.

ST. JOSEPH'S HOSPITAL AND HEALTH CENTER - MEDICAL LIBRARY
7th St. W.   Phone: (701) 225-7200
Dickinson, ND 58601   Sr. Salome, Libn.

TRINITY BIBLE COLLEGE - GRAHAM LIBRARY
Phone: (701) 349-3408
Ellendale, ND 58436   Esther Zink, Libn.

DAKOTA HOSPITAL - FRANCIS J. BUTLER HEALTH SCIENCE LIBRARY
1720 S. University Dr.   Phone: (701) 280-4187
Fargo, ND 58103   Ardis Haaland, Med.Libn.

FORUM PUBLISHING CO. - LIBRARY
Box 2020   Phone: (701) 235-7311
Fargo, ND 58102   Andrea H. Halgrimson, Hd.Libn.

LUTHERAN HOSPITALS AND HOMES SOCIETY OF AMERICA - LIBRARY
Box 2087   Phone: (701) 293-9053
Fargo, ND 58107   Mary L. Littlefield, Sec., Lib.Comm.

NEUROPSYCHIATRIC INSTITUTE - LIBRARY
700 1st Ave. S.   Phone: (701) 235-5354
Fargo, ND 58103   Diane Nordeng, Libn.

NORTH DAKOTA STATE FILM LIBRARY
Box 5036, State University Sta.   Phone: (701) 237-8907
Fargo, ND 58105   Lillian M. Wadnizak, Lib.Mgr.

NORTH DAKOTA STATE UNIVERSITY - ARCHITECTURE RESOURCE CENTER
University Sta.   Phone: (701) 237-8616
Fargo, ND 58105   Susan Wee, Supv.

NORTH DAKOTA STATE UNIVERSITY - CHEMISTRY RESOURCE CENTER
University Sta.   Phone: (701) 237-8293
Fargo, ND 58105   Linda Schultz, Supv.

NORTH DAKOTA STATE UNIVERSITY - INSTITUTE FOR REGIONAL
  STUDIES
State University Sta.   Phone: (701) 237-8914
Fargo, ND 58105   John E. Bye, Archv.

NORTH DAKOTA STATE UNIVERSITY - PHARMACY RESOURCE CENTER
University Sta.   Phone: (701) 237-7748
Fargo, ND 58105   Linda Schultz, Supv.

NORTH DAKOTA STATE UNIVERSITY - UPPER GREAT PLAINS
  TRANSPORTATION INSTITUTE - INFORMATION CENTER *
Phone: (701) 237-7767
Fargo, ND 58105   Gene C. Griffin, Dir.

ST. LUKE'S HOSPITAL - LIBRARY
5th St. N. at Mills Ave.   Phone: (701) 280-5571
Fargo, ND 58122   Marcia Stephens, Dir. of Lib.Serv.

SOUTHEAST HUMAN SERVICES CENTER - LIBRARY
700 1st Ave., S.   Phone: (701) 235-5354
Fargo, ND 58103   Diane Nordeng, Libn.

TEMPLE BETH EL - MAX & ANN GOLDBERG LIBRARY
809 11th Ave., S.   Phone: (701) 232-0441
Fargo, ND 58103   Susan Plambeck, Libn.

U.S. VETERANS ADMINISTRATION (ND-Fargo) - CENTER LIBRARY
Phone: (701) 232-3241
Fargo, ND 58102

UNITED HOSPITAL - LIBRARY
1200 S. Columbia Rd.   Phone: (701) 780-5187
Grand Forks, ND 58201   Janise Paulson Dorman, Libn.

UNIVERSITY OF NORTH DAKOTA - CHEMISTRY LIBRARY
224 Abbott Hall   Phone: (701) 777-2741
Grand Forks, ND 58202   Evelyn Cole, Sec.

UNIVERSITY OF NORTH DAKOTA - DEPARTMENT OF SPECIAL
  COLLECTIONS
Chester Fritz Library   Phone: (701) 777-4625
Grand Forks, ND 58202   Dan Rylance, Coord. of Spec.Coll.

UNIVERSITY OF NORTH DAKOTA - ENERGY RESEARCH CENTER - ENERGY
  LIBRARY
University Sta., Box 8213   Phone: (701) 777-5132
Grand Forks, ND 58202   Mary W. Scott, Libn.

UNIVERSITY OF NORTH DAKOTA - ENGINEERING LIBRARY
Harrington Hall, University Sta.   Phone: (701) 777-3040
Grand Forks, ND 58202   Ruth Peterson, Libn.

UNIVERSITY OF NORTH DAKOTA - GEOLOGY LIBRARY
Leonard Hall, University Sta.   Phone: (701) 777-3221
Grand Forks, ND 58202   Holly Gilbert, Ref.Libn.

UNIVERSITY OF NORTH DAKOTA - INSTITUTE FOR ECOLOGICAL STUDIES
  - ENVIRONMENTAL RESOURCE CENTER - LIBRARY
Box 8278   Phone: (701) 777-2851
Grand Forks, ND 58202   Rod Sayler, Dir.

UNIVERSITY OF NORTH DAKOTA - MATH-PHYSICS LIBRARY
211 Witmer Hall   Phone: (701) 777-2911
Grand Forks, ND 58202   Monica Bednarz, Sec.

UNIVERSITY OF NORTH DAKOTA - MUSIC LIBRARY
Hughes Fine Arts Center
Grand Forks, ND 58202   Julie Reiman, Libn.

UNIVERSITY OF NORTH DAKOTA - OLAF H. THORMODSGARD LAW LIBRARY
Phone: (701) 777-2204
Grand Forks, ND 58201   Rita T. Reusch, Dir.

UNIVERSITY OF NORTH DAKOTA - SCHOOL OF MEDICINE - HARLEY E.
  FRENCH MEDICAL LIBRARY
Phone: (701) 777-3993
Grand Forks, ND 58202   David Boilard, Dir.

U.S. AIR FORCE - STRATEGIC AIR COMMAND - 321 CSG/SS - LIBRARY †
FL 4659   Phone: (701) 594-6725
Grand Forks AFB, ND 58205   Teresa M. Hathaway, Adm.Libn.

STEELE COUNTY HISTORICAL SOCIETY - ARCHIVES
Box 144   Phone: (701) 945-2394
Hope, ND 58230   Helen Parkman, Cur.

NORTH DAKOTA FARMERS UNION - LULU EVANSON RESOURCE LIBRARY
Box 651   Phone: (701) 252-2340
Jamestown, ND 58401   Myra Spilde, Lib.Sec.

NORTH DAKOTA STATE HOSPITAL - HEALTH SCIENCE LIBRARY
Box 476   Phone: (701) 253-2679
Jamestown, ND 58401   Gertrude Berndt, Libn.

U.S. FISH & WILDLIFE SERVICE - NORTHERN PRAIRIE WILDLIFE
  RESEARCH CENTER LIBRARY
Box 1747   Phone: (701) 252-5363
Jamestown, ND 58401   Angie Kokott, Libn.

U.S. NATL. PARK SERVICE - THEODORE ROOSEVELT NATL. PARK - LIBRARY
Phone: (701) 623-4466
Medora, ND 58645   Michele Hellickson, Interpretation Chf.

MINOT DAILY NEWS - LIBRARY *
301-303 Fourth St., S.E.   Phone: (701) 852-3341
Minot, ND 58701   Betty Rogstad, Libn.

MINOT STATE COLLEGE - MEMORIAL LIBRARY - SPECIAL COLLECTIONS
Phone: (701) 857-3200
Minot, ND 58701   Ronald J. Rudser, Dir.

NORTHWEST BIBLE COLLEGE - LIBRARY †
1900 8th Ave., S.E.   Phone: (701) 852-3781
Minot, ND 58701   Clyde R. Root, Hd.Libn.

TRINITY MEDICAL CENTER - ANGUS L. CAMERON MEDICAL LIBRARY †
Trinity Professional Bldg.
20 Fourth Ave., S.W.   Phone: (701) 857-5435
Minot, ND 58701   Frances E. Cockrum, AHEC Libn.

TRINITY MEDICAL CENTER - SCHOOL OF NURSING LIBRARY †
S. Main and 4th Ave.   Phone: (701) 857-5621
Minot, ND 58701   Mildred A. Morgan, Libn.

U.S. AIR FORCE BASE - MINOT BASE LIBRARY *
91 CSG/SSL   Phone: (701) 727-4761
Minot AFB, ND 58705   Geraldine Y. Brosman, Libn.

ASSUMPTION ABBEY - LIBRARY *
                    Phone: (701) 974-3315
Richardton, ND 58652   Bro. Paul Nyquist, Hd.Libn.

MERCY HOSPITAL - MEDICAL LIBRARY
570 Chautauqua Blvd.   Phone: (701) 845-0440
Valley City, ND 58072   Pam Lacher, Lib.Mgr.

NORTH DAKOTA STATE SCHOOL OF SCIENCE - MILDRED JOHNSON
    LIBRARY
                    Phone: (701) 671-2298
Wahpeton, ND 58075   Jerald Stewart, Lib.Dir.

OHIO

OHIO NORTHERN UNIVERSITY - COLLEGE OF LAW - JAY P. TAGGART
    MEMORIAL LAW LIBRARY
                    Phone: (419) 772-2250
Ada, OH 45810   Lynn Foster, Dir./Hd.Libn.

OHIO NORTHERN UNIVERSITY - HETERICK MEMORIAL LIBRARY
                    Phone: (419) 772-2180
Ada, OH 45810   Jane Weimer, Act.Lib.Dir.

AKRON ART MUSEUM - LIBRARY
70 E. Market St.   Phone: (216) 376-9185
Akron, OH 44308   Marcianne Herr, Cur. of Educ.

AKRON BEACON JOURNAL - REFERENCE LIBRARY
44 E. Exchange St.   Phone: (216) 375-8514
Akron, OH 44328   Catherine M. Tierney, Chf.Libn.

AKRON CITY HEALTH DEPARTMENT - PUBLIC HEALTH LIBRARY *
177 S. Broadway   Phone: (216) 375-2960
Akron, OH 44308   Dr. C. William Keck, Dir. of Health

AKRON CITY HOSPITAL - MEDICAL LIBRARY
525 E. Market St.   Phone: (216) 375-3360
Akron, OH 44309   Marilee S. Creelan, Dir. of Hosp.Libs.

AKRON - DEPARTMENT OF PLANNING AND URBAN DEVELOPMENT -
    LIBRARY
403 Municipal Bldg.   Phone: (216) 375-2091
Akron, OH 44308   Louise A. Morris, Libn.

AKRON GENERAL MEDICAL CENTER - J.D. SMITH MEMORIAL LIBRARY
400 Wabash Ave.   Phone: (216) 384-6242
Akron, OH 44307   Lois Arnold, Med.Libn.

AKRON LAW LIBRARY
Summit County Court House, 4th Fl.   Phone: (216) 379-5734
Akron, OH 44308-1675   Rosemarie Chrisant, Lib.Dir.

AKRON-SUMMIT COUNTY PUBLIC LIBRARY - BUSINESS, LABOR AND
    GOVERNMENT DIVISION
55 S. Main St.   Phone: (216) 762-7621
Akron, OH 44326   William G. Johnson, Div.Hd.

AKRON-SUMMIT COUNTY PUBLIC LIBRARY - SCIENCE AND TECHNOLOGY
    DIVISION
55 S. Main St.   Phone: (216) 762-7621
Akron, OH 44326   Joyce A. McKnight, Div.Hd.

AMERICAN CHEMICAL SOCIETY, INC. - RUBBER DIVISION - JOHN H.
    GIFFORD MEMORIAL LIBRARY & INFORMATION CTR.
Bierce Library, University of Akron   Phone: (216) 375-7197
Akron, OH 44325   Ruth Murray, Info.Spec.

CHILDREN'S MEDICAL CENTER - MARY A. HOWER MEDICAL LIBRARY
281 Locust St.   Phone: (216) 379-8250
Akron, OH 44308   Sandra Strozier, Dir.

FIRESTONE TIRE AND RUBBER COMPANY - BUSINESS LIBRARY
1200 Firestone Pkwy.   Phone: (216) 379-6650
Akron, OH 44317   Shirley Evans, Libn.

FIRESTONE TIRE AND RUBBER COMPANY - CENTRAL RESEARCH LIBRARY
1200 Firestone Pkwy.   Phone: (216) 379-7430
Akron, OH 44317   S. Koo, Sr.Res.Libn.

GENERAL TIRE AND RUBBER COMPANY - RESEARCH DIVISION
    INFORMATION CENTER
2990 Gilchrist Rd.   Phone: (216) 798-3000
Akron, OH 44305   B.D. Farah, Hd., Info.Ctr.

GOODRICH (B.F.) COMPANY - AKRON INFORMATION CENTER
500 S. Main St.   Phone: (216) 374-4368
Akron, OH 44318   Virginia Gallicchio, Mgr.

GOODYEAR AEROSPACE CORPORATION - LIBRARY
1210 Massillon Rd.   Phone: (216) 796-2557
Akron, OH 44315   Louise Lariccia, Libn.

GOODYEAR TIRE AND RUBBER COMPANY - BUSINESS INFORMATION
    CENTER
1144 E. Market St.   Phone: (216) 796-6986
Akron, OH 44316   Robin Waynesboro, Bus.Info.Spec.

GOODYEAR TIRE AND RUBBER COMPANY - TECHNICAL INFORMATION
    CENTER
142 Goodyear Blvd.   Phone: (216) 796-6539
Akron, OH 44316   Judy E. Hale, Mgr., Info.Serv.

HIGH STREET CHRISTIAN CHURCH - H.A. VALENTINE MEMORIAL LIBRARY
131 S. High St.   Phone: (216) 434-1039
Akron, OH 44308   Evelyn R. Ling, Libn.

INTERNATIONAL SOAP BOX DERBY - LIBRARY
Derby Downs
Box 7233   Phone: (216) 733-8723
Akron, OH 44306   Jeff Iula, Asst.Gen.Mgr.

MONSANTO COMPANY - RUBBER CHEMICALS RESEARCH LIBRARY †
260 Springside Dr.   Phone: (216) 666-4111
Akron, OH 44313   Paul Ferrin, Libn.

NORTHEAST OHIO FOUR COUNTY REGIONAL PLANNING & DEVELOPMENT
    ORGANIZATION - TECHNICAL INFORMATION CENTER
969 Copley Rd.   Phone: (216) 253-4196
Akron, OH 44320

NORTON COMPANY - CHAMBERLAIN LABORATORIES - TECHNICAL
    LIBRARY
Box 350   Phone: (216) 673-5860
Akron, OH 44309   Jan York, Libn.

OHIO EDISON COMPANY - CORPORATE LIBRARY
76 S. Main St.   Phone: (216) 384-5367
Akron, OH 44308   Sharon M. Malumphy, Corp.Libn.

ST. THOMAS HOSPITAL - MEDICAL LIBRARY
444 N. Main St.   Phone: (216) 379-1111
Akron, OH 44310   Linda E. Bunyan, Med.Libn.

UNIVERSITY OF AKRON - ARCHIVES OF THE HISTORY OF AMERICAN
    PSYCHOLOGY
                    Phone: (216) 375-7285
Akron, OH 44325   John A. Popplestone, Dir.

UNIVERSITY OF AKRON - CENTER FOR PEACE STUDIES - LIBRARY
                    Phone: (216) 375-7008
Akron, OH 44325   Warren F. Kuehl, Dir.

UNIVERSITY OF AKRON - SCHOOL OF LAW - C. BLAKE MC DOWELL LAW
   LIBRARY
Law Center   Phone: (216) 375-7447
Akron, OH 44325   Paul Richert, Law Libn.

BABCOCK AND WILCOX COMPANY - RESEARCH CENTER LIBRARY
Box 835   Phone: (216) 821-9110
Alliance, OH 44601   James W. Carter, Supv.

MOUNT UNION COLLEGE - STURGEON MUSIC LIBRARY
Cope Music Hall   Phone: (216) 823-3206
Alliance, OH 44601   Becky C. Thomas, Music Libn.

STARK COUNTY LAW LIBRARY ASSOCIATION - ALLIANCE BRANCH LAW
   LIBRARY *
City Hall
470 E. Market   Phone: (216) 823-6181
Alliance, OH 44601

MC GILL & SMITH ENGINEERS, ARCHITECTS & PLANNERS - LIBRARY
119 W. Main St.   Phone: (513) 753-4430
Amelia, OH 45102

ASHLAND THEOLOGICAL SEMINARY - ROGER DARLING MEMORIAL
   LIBRARY
910 Center St.   Phone: (419) 289-4126
Ashland, OH 44805   Rev. Bradley E. Weidenhamer, Libn.

ATHENS COUNTY LAW LIBRARY *
Courthouse, 3rd Fl.   Phone: (614) 594-2234
Athens, OH 45701   Fran Ridge, Libn.

ATHENS MENTAL HEALTH CENTER - STAFF LIBRARY
Richland Ave.   Phone: (614) 592-3031
Athens, OH 45701   Judy McGinn, Staff Libn.

OHIO UNIVERSITY - DEPARTMENT OF ARCHIVES AND SPECIAL
   COLLECTIONS
Alden Library   Phone: (614) 594-5755
Athens, OH 45701   Gary A. Hunt, Hd.

OHIO UNIVERSITY - FINE ARTS COLLECTION
Alden Library   Phone: (614) 594-5065
Athens, OH 45701   Anne Braxton, Fine Arts Libn.

OHIO UNIVERSITY - HEALTH SCIENCES LIBRARY
                                                    Phone: (614) 594-6731
Athens, OH 45701   Anne S. Goss, Hd.Libn.

OHIO UNIVERSITY - MAP COLLECTION
Alden Library   Phone: (614) 594-5240
Athens, OH 45701   Theodore Foster, Map Libn.

OHIO UNIVERSITY - MUSIC/DANCE LIBRARY
Music Bldg.   Phone: (614) 594-5733
Athens, OH 45701   Dan O. Clark, Libn.

OHIO UNIVERSITY - SOUTHEAST ASIA COLLECTION
Alden Library   Phone: (614) 594-6958
Athens, OH 45701   Lian The-Mulliner, Hd.

OHIO VALLEY HEALTH SERVICES FOUNDATION, INC. - LIBRARY
One Blue Line Ave.   Phone: (614) 592-4457
Athens, OH 45701   Sandra L. Porter, Adm.Asst.

GOODRICH (B.F.) COMPANY - GOODRICH CHEMICAL DIVISION TECHNICAL
   CENTER - INFORMATION CENTER
Box 122   Phone: (216) 933-6181
Avon Lake, OH 44012   Carol Ann Lioce, Mgr., Info.Ctr.

BARBERTON CITIZENS HOSPITAL - MEDICAL LIBRARY *
Tuscora Pk.   Phone: (216) 745-1611
Barberton, OH 44203   Helen Young, Adm.Coord.

BARBERTON PUBLIC LIBRARY - SPECIAL COLLECTIONS
602 W. Park Ave.   Phone: (216) 745-1194
Barberton, OH 44203   Phyllis Taylor, Hd., Tech.Proc.

PPG INDUSTRIES, INC. - CHEMICAL DIVISION - RESEARCH LIBRARY
Box 31   Phone: (216) 848-4161
Barberton, OH 44203   Diana M. Danko, Supv., Info.Serv.

CLERMONT COUNTY LAW LIBRARY ASSOCIATION
Main St., Courthouse   Phone: (513) 732-7109
Batavia, OH 45103   Carol A. O'Connor, Law Libn.

CLEVELAND COLLEGE OF JEWISH STUDIES - AARON GARBER LIBRARY
26500 Shaker Blvd.   Phone: (216) 464-5581
Beachwood, OH 44122   Jean Loeb Lettofsky, Dir., Lib.Serv.

BEDFORD HISTORICAL SOCIETY - LIBRARY
30 S. Park St.
Box 46282   Phone: (216) 232-0796
Bedford, OH 44146   Dona Basel, Libn.

FERRO CORPORATION - FERRO CHEMICAL DIVISION - FERRO CHEMICAL
   LIBRARY
7040 Krick Rd.   Phone: (216) 641-8580
Bedford, OH 44146   Mary Jane Campbell, Libn.

BALDWIN-WALLACE COLLEGE - RIEMENSCHNEIDER BACH INSTITUTE -
   BACH LIBRARY
Merner-Pfeiffer Hall
49 Seminary St.   Phone: (216) 826-2207
Berea, OH 44017   Dr. Elinore Barber, Dir., Bach Inst.

BLUFFTON COLLEGE - MENNONITE HISTORICAL LIBRARY
                                                   Phone: (419) 358-8015
Bluffton, OH 45817   Delbert L. Gratz, Libn.

BOWLING GREEN STATE UNIVERSITY - CENTER FOR ARCHIVAL
   COLLECTIONS
Library, 5th Fl.   Phone: (419) 372-2411
Bowling Green, OH 43403   Paul D. Yon, Dir.

BOWLING GREEN STATE UNIVERSITY - INSTITUTE FOR GREAT LAKES
   RESEARCH
Jerome Library   Phone: (419) 372-0012
Bowling Green, OH 43403   Dr. Richard J. Wright, Dir.

BOWLING GREEN STATE UNIVERSITY - MAP LIBRARY
Jerome Library   Phone: (419) 372-2156
Bowling Green, OH 43403   Miss Evron Collins, Map Libn.

BOWLING GREEN STATE UNIVERSITY - MUSIC LIBRARY
Jerome Library   Phone: (419) 372-2307
Bowling Green, OH 43403   Linda M. Fidler, Hd., Mus.Lib.

BOWLING GREEN STATE UNIVERSITY - POPULAR CULTURE LIBRARY
                                                   Phone: (419) 372-2450
Bowling Green, OH 43403   Evron Collins, Hd.Libn.

WOOD COUNTY HISTORICAL SOCIETY - HISTORICAL MUSEUM LIBRARY
13660 County Home Rd.   Phone: (419) 352-0967
Bowling Green, OH 43402   Lyle Fletcher, Archv.

WOOD COUNTY LAW LIBRARY
County Office Bldg., 1st Fl.   Phone: (419) 353-3921
Bowling Green, OH 43402   Marianne Mason, Law Libn.

GOODRICH (B.F.) COMPANY - RESEARCH AND DEVELOPMENT CENTER -
   BRECKSVILLE INFORMATION CENTER
9921 Brecksville Rd.   Phone: (216) 447-5299
Brecksville, OH 44141   Carol A. Lioce, Mgr., Info.Ctr.

U.S. VETERANS ADMINISTRATION (OH-Brecksville) - HOSPITAL LIBRARY
10000 Brecksville Rd.   Phone: (216) 526-3030
Brecksville, OH 44141   Nancy S. Tesmer, Chf., Lib.Serv.

NORTHEAST OHIO DEVELOPMENTAL CENTER-BROADVIEW CAMPUS -
   REGIONAL STAFF LIBRARY
9543 Broadview Rd.   Phone: (216) 526-5000
Broadview Heights, OH 44147   Noreen M. Kenney, Regional Staff Libn.

GEAUGA COUNTY HISTORICAL SOCIETY - LIBRARY
14653 E. Park St.   Phone: (216) 834-4012
Burton, OH 44021   Marlene F. Collins, Off.Mgr.

CAMBRIDGE MENTAL HEALTH & DEVELOPMENTAL CENTER - RESOURCE
CENTER
County Rd. 35
Cambridge, OH 43725
Phone: (614) 439-1371
Jill R. Warren, Dir., Lib.Serv.

GUERNSEY COUNTY LAW LIBRARY
Court House
Cambridge, OH 43725
Phone: (614) 439-3916
Frank C. Leyshon, Libn.

AULTMAN HOSPITAL - MEDICAL LIBRARY
2600 6th St., S.W.
Canton, OH 44710
Phone: (216) 452-9911
Leah R. Lloyd, Libn.

AULTMAN HOSPITAL - SCHOOL OF NURSING LIBRARY
2614 6th St., S.W.
Canton, OH 44710
Phone: (216) 452-9911
Violet E. Russell, Libn.

CANTON ART INSTITUTE - PURDY MEMORIAL LIBRARY
1001 Market Ave. N.
Canton, OH 44702
Phone: (216) 453-7666
M.J. Albacete, Assoc.Dir.

MC KINLEY MUSEUM OF HISTORY, SCIENCE AND EDUCATION - RALPH K.
RAMSAYER, M.D. LIBRARY
749 Hazlett Ave., N.W.
Box 483
Canton, OH 44701
Phone: (216) 455-7043
Eva Sparrowgrove

OHIO POWER COMPANY - LIBRARY
Box 400
Canton, OH 44701
Phone: (216) 456-8173
James M. Beck, Libn.

PRO FOOTBALL HALL OF FAME - LIBRARY/RESEARCH CENTER
2121 Harrison Ave., N.W.
Canton, OH 44708
Phone: (216) 456-8207
Anne Mangus, Libn.

STARK COUNTY LAW LIBRARY ASSOCIATION - LAW LIBRARY
Court House, Fourth Fl.
Canton, OH 44702
Phone: (216) 456-2330
Martha M. Cox, Dir.

TIMKEN COMPANY - RESEARCH LIBRARY
1835 Deuber Ave.
Canton, OH 44706
Phone: (216) 497-2049
Joellen A. Hadbavny, Info.Techn.

TIMKEN MERCY HOSPITAL - MEDICAL LIBRARY
1320 Timken Mercy Dr.
Canton, OH 44708
Phone: (216) 489-1462
Jane L. Clark, Dir., Med.Lib.Serv.

ST. CHARLES SEMINARY - LIBRARY
Carthagena, OH 45822

MERCER COUNTY LAW LIBRARY
Court House
Celina, OH 45822
Phone: (419) 586-2122
Carolyn Leffler, Law Libn.

GEAUGA COUNTY LAW LIBRARY
Court House
Chardon, OH 44024
Phone: (216) 285-2222
Violet R. Amnasan, Libn.

MEAD CORPORATION - LIBRARY
Central Research Laboratories
8th & Hickory Sts.
Chillicothe, OH 45601
Phone: (614) 772-3524
Sheldon T. Miller, Supv., Lib.Serv.

U.S. NATL. PARK SERVICE - MOUND CITY GROUP NATL. MONUMENT -
LIBRARY
16062 State Route 104
Chillicothe, OH 45601
Phone: (614) 774-1125
Kenneth Apschnikat, Supt.

U.S. VETERANS ADMINISTRATION (OH-Chillicothe) - HOSPITAL LIBRARY
Phone: (614) 773-1141
Chillicothe, OH 45601
Barbara A. Schultz, Chf., Lib.Serv.

AMERICAN WATCHMAKERS INSTITUTE - LIBRARY
3700 Harrison Ave.
Cincinnati, OH 45211
Phone: (513) 661-3838
Mrs. Michael Danner, Libn.

ARCHDIOCESE OF CINCINNATI - ARCHIVES
6616 Beechmont Ave.
Cincinnati, OH 45230
Phone: (513) 731-9229
Rev. Gerard P. Hiland, Dir.

AT & T COMMUNICATIONS - INFORMATION RESEARCH CENTER
15 W. Sixth St.
Cincinnati, OH 45202
Phone: (513) 352-8400
Melanie Z. Strub, Mgr.

ATE MANAGEMENT AND SERVICE COMPANY, INC. - RESOURCE CENTER
617 Vine St., Suite 800
Cincinnati, OH 45202
Phone: (513) 381-7424
Jean M. Lucas, Libn.

ATHENAEUM OF OHIO - MOUNT ST. MARY'S SEMINARY OF THE WEST -
EUGENE H. MALY MEMORIAL LIBRARY
6616 Beechmont Ave.
Cincinnati, OH 45230
Phone: (513) 231-1516
Sr. Loretta Driscoll, C.D.P., Hd.Libn.

BETHESDA HOSPITAL - INFORMATION RESOURCE CENTER †
619 Oak St.
Cincinnati, OH 45206
Phone: (513) 559-6337
Margaret Gomien, Libn.

CARSTAB CORPORATION - RESEARCH LIBRARY
West St.
Cincinnati, OH 45215
Phone: (513) 733-2171
Diana L. Waid, Res.Libn.

CHILDREN'S HOSPITAL RESEARCH FOUNDATION - RESEARCH LIBRARY
Elland & Bethesda Sts.
Cincinnati, OH 45229
Phone: (513) 559-4300
Margaret L. Moutseous, Lib.Dir.

CINCINNATI ART MUSEUM - LIBRARY
Eden Pk.
Cincinnati, OH 45202
Phone: (513) 721-5204
Patricia P. Rutledge, Libn.

CINCINNATI CITY PLANNING COMMISSION - OFFICE OF PLANNING AND
MANAGEMENT SUPPORT - LIBRARY
City Hall, Rm. 141
801 Plum St.
Cincinnati, OH 45202
Phone: (513) 352-3441
Lawrence P. Annett, Libn./City Planner

CINCINNATI COLLEGE OF MORTUARY SCIENCE - LIBRARY
2220 Victory Pkwy.
Cincinnati, OH 45206
Phone: (513) 861-3240
Dan L. Flory, Registrar

CINCINNATI ELECTRONICS CORPORATION - TECHNICAL LIBRARY
2630 Glendale-Milford Rd.
Cincinnati, OH 45241
Phone: (513) 563-6000
Lois D. Hammond, Chf.Tech.Libn.

CINCINNATI HISTORICAL SOCIETY - LIBRARY
Eden Park
Cincinnati, OH 45202
Phone: (513) 241-4622
Laura L. Chace, Libn.

CINCINNATI LAW LIBRARY ASSOCIATION
601 Courthouse
Cincinnati, OH 45202
Phone: (513) 632-8372
Carol E. Meyer, Law Libn.

CINCINNATI MILACRON INDUSTRIES, INC. - CORPORATE INFORMATION
CENTER
4701 Marburg Ave.
Cincinnati, OH 45209
Phone: (513) 841-8879
Rory L. Chase, Corp.Libn.

CINCINNATI MUSEUM OF NATURAL HISTORY - LIBRARY
1720 Gilbert Ave.
Cincinnati, OH 45202
Phone: (513) 621-3889
DeVere Burt, Musm.Dir.

CINCINNATI POST - LIBRARY
800 Broadway
Cincinnati, OH 45202
Phone: (513) 352-2785
Elmer L. Geers, Libn.

CINCINNATI PSYCHOANALYTIC INSTITUTE - FREDERIC T. KAPP
MEMORIAL LIBRARY
3001 Highland Ave.
Cincinnati, OH 45219
Phone: (513) 961-8886
Cynthia I. Meisner, Libn.

CINCINNATI PUBLIC SCHOOLS - PROFESSIONAL LIBRARY †
230 E. Ninth St.
Cincinnati, OH 45202
Phone: (513) 369-4734
Paul J. Lee, Libn.

CORVA LIBRARY
35 E. 7th St., Suite 608
Cincinnati, OH 45252

DEACONESS HOSPITAL - SCHOOL OF NURSING - RICHARD W. ANGERT
    MEMORIAL LIBRARY
415 Straight St.   Phone: (513) 559-2285
Cincinnati, OH 45219   Valerie J. Eliot, Libn.

DINSMORE & SHOHL - LIBRARY
2100 Fountain Sq. Plaza
511 Walnut St.   Phone: (513) 621-6747
Cincinnati, OH 45202   Sharon A. Huge, Libn.

DOW CHEMICAL COMPANY - MERRELL DOW PHARMACEUTICALS, INC. -
    RESEARCH CENTER LIBRARY
2110 E. Galbraith Rd.   Phone: (513) 948-9111
Cincinnati, OH 45215   Elaine Besterman, Mgr., Lib.Serv.

DRACKETT COMPANY - RESEARCH AND DEVELOPMENT LIBRARY
5020 Spring Grove Ave.   Phone: (513) 632-1449
Cincinnati, OH 45232   Patricia Beck, Res.Libn.

EMERY INDUSTRIES - RESEARCH LIBRARY
4900 Este Ave.   Phone: (513) 482-2157
Cincinnati, OH 45232   B.A. Bernard, Res.Libn.

ENVIRONMENTAL PROTECTION AGENCY - ANDREW W. BREIDENBACH
    ENVIRONMENTAL RESEARCH CTR., CINCINNATI - TECH.LIB.
26 W. St. Clair Ave.   Phone: (513) 684-7701
Cincinnati, OH 45268   JoAnn Johnson, Chf., Lib.Serv.

FROST & JACOBS - LIBRARY
2500 Central Trust Ctr.
201 E. 5th St.   Phone: (513) 651-6810
Cincinnati, OH 45202   Connie S. Whipple, Libn.

GAMBLE (James N.) INSTITUTE OF MEDICAL RESEARCH - LIBRARY
2141 Auburn Ave.   Phone: (513) 369-2540
Cincinnati, OH 45219   Lisa L. McCormick, Res.Libn.

GENERAL ELECTRIC COMPANY - AIRCRAFT ENGINE GROUP - LAW
    LIBRARY †
Mail Drop F17   Phone: (513) 243-2298
Cincinnati, OH 45215   Peggy Edwards

GENERAL ELECTRIC COMPANY - AIRCRAFT ENGINE GROUP - TECHNICAL
    INFORMATION CENTER
Bldg. 700, N-32   Phone: (513) 243-4333
Cincinnati, OH 45215   J.J. Brady, Mgr.

GOOD SAMARITAN HOSPITAL - MEDICAL LIBRARY
3217 Clifton Ave.   Phone: (513) 872-2433
Cincinnati, OH 45220   Rosalie V. Zajac, Med.Libn.

GREATER CINCINNATI CHAMBER OF COMMERCE - RESEARCH LIBRARY
120 W. Fifth St.   Phone: (513) 579-3182
Cincinnati, OH 45202   Marge Rotte, Mgr., Res.Info.

HEBREW UNION COLLEGE - JEWISH INSTITUTE OF RELIGION - AMERICAN
    JEWISH ARCHIVES
3101 Clifton Ave.   Phone: (513) 221-1875
Cincinnati, OH 45220   Fannie Zelcer, Archv.

HEBREW UNION COLLEGE - JEWISH INSTITUTE OF RELIGION - AMERICAN
    JEWISH PERIODICAL CENTER
3101 Clifton Ave.   Phone: (513) 221-1875
Cincinnati, OH 45220   Jacob R. Marcus, Dir.

HEBREW UNION COLLEGE - JEWISH INSTITUTE OF RELIGION - KLAU
    LIBRARY
3101 Clifton Ave.   Phone: (513) 221-1875
Cincinnati, OH 45220   Herbert C. Zafren, Lib.Dir.

HOME MISSIONERS OF AMERICA - GLENMARY NOVITIATE LIBRARY *
Box 46404   Phone: (513) 874-8900
Cincinnati, OH 45246   Thomas J. Meehan, Libn.

INTERNATIONAL THESPIAN SOCIETY - LIBRARY
3368 Central Pkwy.   Phone: (513) 559-1996
Cincinnati, OH 45225   Ronald L. Longstreth, Exec.Sec.

JEWISH HOSPITAL OF CINCINNATI - MEDICAL LIBRARY
3200 Burnet Ave.   Phone: (513) 569-2014
Cincinnati, OH 45229   Barb Lucas, Med.Libn.

JEWISH HOSPITAL OF CINCINNATI SCHOOL OF NURSING - NURSE'S
    REFERENCE LIBRARY
3161 Harvey Ave.   Phone: (513) 872-3534
Cincinnati, OH 45229   Alice M. Warner, Instr./Media Coord.

K.K. BENE ISRAEL/ROCKDALE TEMPLE - SIDNEY G. ROSE MEMORIAL
    LIBRARY
8501 Ridge Rd.   Phone: (513) 891-9900
Cincinnati, OH 45236   Mrs. Seymour Miller, Libn.

KINNEY (A.M.) INC. - LIBRARY
2900 Vernon Place   Phone: (513) 281-2900
Cincinnati, OH 45219   Ann Guy, Libn.

KZF, INC. - KZF LIBRARY
111 Merchant St.   Phone: (513) 772-1117
Cincinnati, OH 45246   Dennis O. Hamilton, Lib.Dir.

LLOYD LIBRARY AND MUSEUM
917 Plum St.   Phone: (513) 721-3707
Cincinnati, OH 45202   John B. Griggs, Libn.

METCUT RESEARCH ASSOCIATES, INC. - MACHINABILITY DATA CENTER
3980 Rosslyn Dr.   Phone: (513) 271-9510
Cincinnati, OH 45209   John F. Kahles, Dir.

MIAMI PURCHASE ASSOCIATION FOR HISTORIC PRESERVATION -
    LIBRARY AND INFORMATION CENTER
812 Dayton St.   Phone: (513) 721-4506
Cincinnati, OH 45214   Marian Apking, Libn.

NATIONAL ASSOCIATION FOR CREATIVE CHILDREN AND ADULTS (NACCA)
    - LIBRARY
8080 Springvalley Dr.   Phone: (513) 631-1777
Cincinnati, OH 45236   Ann Fabe Isaacs, Hd.

NLO, INC. - LIBRARY
Box 39158   Phone: (513) 738-1151
Cincinnati, OH 45239   Rosemary H. Gardewing, Lib.Asst.

OHIO COVERED BRIDGE COMMITTEE - LIBRARY *
18 Elm Ave.   Phone: (513) 761-1789
Cincinnati, OH 45215   John A. Diehl, Libn.

PEDCO GROUP LIBRARY
Chester Towers
11499 Chester Rd.   Phone: (513) 782-4700
Cincinnati, OH 45246   Janet L. Zieleniewski, Libn.

PROCTER & GAMBLE COMPANY - IVORYDALE TECHNICAL CENTER -
    LIBRARY *
Cincinnati, OH 45217

PROCTER & GAMBLE COMPANY - LIBRARY
Box 599
Cincinnati, OH 45201   Marcia Cahall, Libn.

PROCTER & GAMBLE COMPANY - MIAMI VALLEY LABORATORIES -
    TECHNICAL LIBRARY
Box 39175
Cincinnati, OH 45247   Emelyn L. Hiland, Lib.Mgr.

PROCTER & GAMBLE COMPANY - WINTON HILL TECHNICAL CENTER -
    TECHNICAL LIBRARY
6090 Center Hill Rd.   Phone: (513) 977-7257
Cincinnati, OH 45224   Irene L. Myers, Sect.Hd.

PUBLIC LIBRARY OF CINCINNATI AND HAMILTON COUNTY - ART AND
    MUSIC DEPARTMENT
800 Vine St.   Phone: (513) 369-6955
Cincinnati, OH 45202   R. Jayne Craven, Hd., Art & Music

PUBLIC LIBRARY OF CINCINNATI AND HAMILTON COUNTY - CHILDREN'S
    DEPARTMENT
800 Vine St.   Phone: (513) 369-6900
Cincinnati, OH 45202   Consuelo W. Harris, Dept.Hd.

PUBLIC LIBRARY OF CINCINNATI AND HAMILTON COUNTY - DEPARTMENT
OF RARE BOOKS & SPECIAL COLLECTIONS
800 Vine St.   Phone: (513) 369-6957
Cincinnati, OH 45202   Yeatman Anderson, III, Cur.

PUBLIC LIBRARY OF CINCINNATI AND HAMILTON COUNTY - EDUCATION
AND RELIGION DEPARTMENT
800 Vine St.   Phone: (513) 369-6940
Cincinnati, OH 45202   Susan F. Hettinger, Hd.

PUBLIC LIBRARY OF CINCINNATI AND HAMILTON COUNTY - EXCEPTIONAL
CHILDREN'S DIVISION
800 Vine St.   Phone: (513) 369-6065
Cincinnati, OH 45202   Miss Coy K. Hunsucker, Hd.

PUBLIC LIBRARY OF CINCINNATI AND HAMILTON COUNTY - FILMS AND
RECORDINGS CENTER
800 Vine St.   Phone: (513) 369-6924
Cincinnati, OH 45202   Robert Hudzik, Hd.

PUBLIC LIBRARY OF CINCINNATI AND HAMILTON COUNTY - GOVERNMENT
AND BUSINESS DEPARTMENT
800 Vine St.   Phone: (513) 369-6932
Cincinnati, OH 45202   Carl G. Marquette, Jr., Hd.

PUBLIC LIBRARY OF CINCINNATI AND HAMILTON COUNTY - HISTORY
DEPARTMENT
800 Vine St.   Phone: (513) 369-6905
Cincinnati, OH 45202   J. Richard Abell, Hd.

PUBLIC LIBRARY OF CINCINNATI AND HAMILTON COUNTY - HISTORY
DEPARTMENT - MAP UNIT
800 Vine St.   Phone: (513) 369-6909
Cincinnati, OH 45202   Gardner Neely, Map Libn.

PUBLIC LIBRARY OF CINCINNATI AND HAMILTON COUNTY -
INSTITUTIONS/BOOKS BY MAIL
800 Vine St., Library Sq.   Phone: (513) 369-6070
Cincinnati, OH 45202   Cynthia Whitt-Covalcine, Hd.

PUBLIC LIBRARY OF CINCINNATI AND HAMILTON COUNTY - LIBRARY FOR
THE BLIND AND PHYSICALLY HANDICAPPED
800 Vine St., Library Sq.   Phone: (513) 369-6075
Cincinnati, OH 45202   Carol Heideman, Regional Libn.

PUBLIC LIBRARY OF CINCINNATI AND HAMILTON COUNTY - LITERATURE
DEPARTMENT
800 Vine St.   Phone: (513) 369-6991
Cincinnati, OH 45202   Donna S. Monnig, Hd.

PUBLIC LIBRARY OF CINCINNATI AND HAMILTON COUNTY - MUNICIPAL
REFERENCE LIBRARY
801 Plum St.   Phone: (513) 369-6076
Cincinnati, OH 45202   Sharon Huge

PUBLIC LIBRARY OF CINCINNATI AND HAMILTON COUNTY - SCIENCE AND
TECHNOLOGY DEPARTMENT
800 Vine St.   Phone: (513) 369-6936
Cincinnati, OH 45202   Rosemary Gaiser, Hd.

ST. FRANCIS-ST. GEORGE HOSPITAL - HEALTH SCIENCES LIBRARY *
3131 Queen City Ave.   Phone: (513) 389-5118
Cincinnati, OH 45238   Carol Mayor, Libn.

ST. THOMAS INSTITUTE - LIBRARY
1842 Madison Rd.   Phone: (513) 861-3460
Cincinnati, OH 45206   Sr. M. Virgil Ghering, O.P., Libn.

SISTERS OF NOTRE DAME DE NAMUR - OHIO PROVINCE - ARCHIVES
Provincial House
701 E. Columbia Ave.   Phone: (513) 821-7448
Cincinnati, OH 45215

STERLING DRUG, INC. - HILTON-DAVIS CHEMICAL COMPANY DIVISION -
LIBRARY
2235 Langdon Farm Rd.   Phone: (513) 841-4074
Cincinnati, OH 45237   Carol Heusner, Libn.

TAFT MUSEUM - LIBRARY
316 Pike St.   Phone: (513) 241-0343
Cincinnati, OH 45202   Ruth K. Meyer, Dir.

TAFT, STETTINIUS & HOLLISTER - LAW LIBRARY
First National Bank Ctr.   Phone: (513) 381-2838
Cincinnati, OH 45202   Maureen T. Willig, Libn.

U.S. COURT OF APPEALS, 6TH CIRCUIT - LIBRARY
617 U.S. Court House & Post Office Bldg.   Phone: (513) 684-2678
Cincinnati, OH 45202   Kathy Joyce Welker, Circuit Libn.

U.S. DEPT. OF COMMERCE - INTERNATIONAL TRADE ADMINISTRATION -
CINCINNATI DISTRICT OFFICE LIBRARY *
10504 Federal Office Bldg.
550 Main St.   Phone: (513) 684-2944
Cincinnati, OH 45202   Gordon B. Thomas, Dir.

U.S. INDUSTRIAL CHEMICALS COMPANY - RESEARCH DEPARTMENT
LIBRARY
1275 Section Rd.   Phone: (513) 761-4130
Cincinnati, OH 45237   Michelle M. Rudy, Tech.Libn.

U.S. NATL. INSTITUTE FOR OCCUPATIONAL SAFETY & HEALTH -
TECHNICAL INFORMATION BRANCH
Robert A. Taft Laboratory
4676 Columbia Pkwy.   Phone: (513) 684-8321
Cincinnati, OH 45226   Vivian Morgan, Sect.Chf.

U.S. VETERANS ADMINISTRATION (OH-Cincinnati) - MEDICAL CENTER
LIBRARY
3200 Vine St.
Cincinnati, OH 45220   Cynthia R. Sterling, Libn.

UNIVERSITY AFFILIATED CINCINNATI CENTER FOR DEVELOPMENTAL
DISORDERS - RESEARCH LIBRARY
Pavilion Bldg.
3300 Elland Ave.   Phone: (513) 559-4626
Cincinnati, OH 45229   Dorothy A. Gilroy, Chf.Res.Libn.

UNIVERSITY OF CINCINNATI - ARCHIVES AND RARE BOOKS DEPARTMENT
Carl Blegen Library, 8th Fl.   Phone: (513) 475-6459
Cincinnati, OH 45221   Alice M. Vestal, Hd.

UNIVERSITY OF CINCINNATI - COLLEGE CONSERVATORY OF MUSIC -
GORNO MEMORIAL MUSIC LIBRARY
Carl Blegen Library, Rm. 417   Phone: (513) 475-4471
Cincinnati, OH 45221   Robert O. Johnson, Hd.

UNIVERSITY OF CINCINNATI - DEPARTMENT OF ENVIRONMENTAL
HEALTH LIBRARY
Kettering Laboratory Library
3223 Eden Ave.   Phone: (513) 872-5771
Cincinnati, OH 45267   Evelyn M. Widner, Sr.Res.Assoc.

UNIVERSITY OF CINCINNATI - DESIGN, ARCHITECTURE, ART & PLANNING
LIBRARY
800 Alms Bldg.   Phone: (513) 475-3238
Cincinnati, OH 45221-0016   Elizabeth D. Byrne, Hd.

UNIVERSITY OF CINCINNATI - ENGINEERING LIBRARY
880 Baldwin Hall   Phone: (513) 475-3761
Cincinnati, OH 45221   Dorothy F. Byers, Hd.

UNIVERSITY OF CINCINNATI - GEOLOGY LIBRARY
103 Old Tech Bldg.
ML 13   Phone: (513) 475-4332
Cincinnati, OH 45221   Richard A. Spohn, Hd.

UNIVERSITY OF CINCINNATI - GEORGE ELLISTON POETRY COLLECTION
646 Central Library   Phone: (513) 475-4709
Cincinnati, OH 45221   James Cummins, Cur.

UNIVERSITY OF CINCINNATI - JOHN MILLER BURNAM CLASSICAL
LIBRARY
Carl Blegen Library, Rm. 320   Phone: (513) 475-6724
Cincinnati, OH 45221   Jean Susorney Wellington, Hd.

UNIVERSITY OF CINCINNATI - MATHEMATICS LIBRARY
840 Old Chemistry Bldg.   Phone: (513) 475-4449
Cincinnati, OH 45221   Joyce Pons, Hd.

UNIVERSITY OF CINCINNATI - MEDICAL CENTER LIBRARIES - COLLEGE
   OF NURSING & HEALTH - LEVI MEMORIAL LIBRARY
Vine St. & St. Clair Ave.   Phone: (513) 872-5543
Cincinnati, OH 45219   Ava Fried, Dir.

UNIVERSITY OF CINCINNATI - MEDICAL CENTER LIBRARIES - HEALTH
   SCIENCES LIBRARY †
231 Bethesda Ave.   Phone: (513) 872-5627
Cincinnati, OH 45267   Richard Lucier, Dir., Media/Lib.Serv.

UNIVERSITY OF CINCINNATI - MEDICAL CENTER LIBRARIES - HISTORY
   OF HEALTH SCIENCES LIBRARY AND MUSEUM
Eden & Bethesda Aves., Wherry Hall   Phone: (513) 872-5120
Cincinnati, OH 45267   Billie Broaddus, Dir.

UNIVERSITY OF CINCINNATI - OBSERVATORY LIBRARY
Observatory Pl.
High Park   Phone: (513) 475-2331
Cincinnati, OH 45208   Marianne Wells, Hd., Physics Lib.

UNIVERSITY OF CINCINNATI - OESPER CHEMISTRY-BIOLOGY LIBRARY
Brodie A-3, Rm. 503 (151)   Phone: (513) 475-4524
Cincinnati, OH 45221   Dorice Des Chene, Hd.

UNIVERSITY OF CINCINNATI - OMI COLLEGE OF APPLIED SCIENCE -
   TIMOTHY C. DAY TECHNICAL LIBRARY
100 E. Central Pkwy.   Phone: (513) 475-6553
Cincinnati, OH 45210   John P. Hiestand, Libn.

UNIVERSITY OF CINCINNATI - PHYSICS LIBRARY
406 Braunstein Hall   Phone: (513) 475-2331
Cincinnati, OH 45221   Marianna Wells, Hd.

UNIVERSITY OF CINCINNATI - RAYMOND WALTERS COLLEGE - LIBRARY
9555 Plainfield Rd.   Phone: (513) 745-4313
Cincinnati, OH 45236   Lucy Wilson, Coll.Libn.

UNIVERSITY OF CINCINNATI - ROBERT S. MARX LAW LIBRARY
Law School   Phone: (513) 472-3016
Cincinnati, OH 45221   Jorge L. Carro, Hd.Libn.

WESTERN AND SOUTHERN LIFE INSURANCE CO. - LIBRARY
400 Broadway   Phone: (513) 629-1393
Cincinnati, OH 45202   Virginia Custer, Libn.

WESTMINSTER PRESBYTERIAN CHURCH - JOHN H. HOLMES LIBRARY
4991 Cleves Warsaw Pike   Phone: (513) 921-1623
Cincinnati, OH 45238   Emma Reeves, Libn.

WESTWOOD FIRST PRESBYTERIAN CHURCH - WALTER LORENZ
   MEMORIAL LIBRARY
3011 Harrison Ave.   Phone: (513) 661-6846
Cincinnati, OH 45211   Marian B. McNair, Libn.

WISE (Isaac M.) TEMPLE - RALPH COHEN MEMORIAL LIBRARY
8329 Ridge Rd.   Phone: (513) 793-2556
Cincinnati, OH 45236   Judith S. Carsch, Libn.

YOUNG MEN'S MERCANTILE LIBRARY ASSOCIATION - LIBRARY †
414 Walnut St.   Phone: (513) 621-0717
Cincinnati, OH 45202   Jean M. Springer, Exec.Dir.

ZOOLOGICAL SOCIETY OF CINCINNATI - MEDIA CENTER
3400 Vine St.   Phone: (513) 281-3700
Cincinnati, OH 45220   MiMi Hilarius, Media Ctr.Coord.

PICKAWAY COUNTY LAW LIBRARY †
Courthouse
Box 87   Phone: (614) 474-6026
Circleville, OH 43113   William Ammer, Treas.

AFRO-AMERICAN CULTURAL AND HISTORICAL SOCIETY MUSEUM -
   LIBRARY
1765 Crawford Rd.   Phone: (216) 231-2131
Cleveland, OH 44106   Icabod Flewellen, Dir.

ALCAN ALUMINUM CORPORATION - CORPORATE LIBRARY
100 Erieview Plaza   Phone: (216) 523-6860
Cleveland, OH 44114   Winifred B. Bowes, Libn.

THE AUSTIN COMPANY - LIBRARY
3650 Mayfield Rd.   Phone: (216) 291-6636
Cleveland, OH 44121   Helen M. Makela, Info.Rsrcs.Coord.

BAKER AND HOSTETLER - LIBRARY
3200 National City Ctr.   Phone: (216) 621-0200
Cleveland, OH 44114   Alvin M. Podboy, Libn.

BRENTWOOD HOSPITAL - LIBRARY
4110 Warrensville Center Rd.   Phone: (216) 283-2900
Cleveland, OH 44122   Barbara S. Schur, Dir. of Lib.Serv.

BRUSH WELLMAN, INC. - TECHNICAL LIBRARY
17876 St. Clair Ave.   Phone: (216) 486-4200
Cleveland, OH 44110   Nancie J. Skonezny, Libn.

CARROLL (John) UNIVERSITY - SEISMOLOGICAL LIBRARY
                                                  Phone: (216) 491-4361
Cleveland, OH 44118   Susan A. Dimonski, Libn.

CASE WESTERN RESERVE UNIVERSITY - APPLIED SOCIAL SCIENCES
   LIBRARY
School of Applied Social Sciences
2035 Abington Rd.   Phone: (216) 368-2302
Cleveland, OH 44106   Vlatka Ivanisevic, Libn.

CASE WESTERN RESERVE UNIVERSITY - KULAS MUSIC LIBRARY
Haydn Hall
11118 Bellflower Rd.   Phone: (216) 368-2403
Cleveland, OH 44106   Timothy D. Robson, Music Libn.

CASE WESTERN RESERVE UNIVERSITY - LAW SCHOOL LIBRARY †
11075 East Blvd.   Phone: (216) 368-2792
Cleveland, OH 44106   Simon L. Goren, Law Libn.

CASE WESTERN RESERVE UNIVERSITY - MATTHEW A. BAXTER SCHOOL OF
   LIBRARY & INFORMATION SCIENCE
Newton D. Baker Bldg.
10950 Euclid Ave.   Phone: (216) 368-3524
Cleveland, OH 44106   Bettina R. MacAyeal, Libn.

CASE WESTERN RESERVE UNIVERSITY - SEARS LIBRARY
10900 Euclid Ave.   Phone: (216) 368-4244
Cleveland, OH 44106   Robert R. Garland, Hd.Libn.

CASE WESTERN RESERVE UNIVERSITY - UNIVERSITY ARCHIVES
2040 Adelbert Rd.
Cleveland, OH 44106   Ruth Helmuth, Archv.

CATHOLIC UNIVERSE BULLETIN - LIBRARY
Chancery Bldg.
1027 Superior Ave.   Phone: (216) 696-6525
Cleveland, OH 44114   Edgar V. Barmann, Ed.

CENTER FOR HEALTH AFFAIRS - LIBRARY
Playhouse Square
1226 Huron Rd.   Phone: (216) 696-6900
Cleveland, OH 44115   Jean Dreifort, Libn.

CLEVELAND CLINIC EDUCATION FOUNDATION - MEDICAL LIBRARY/
   AUDIOVISUAL CENTER †
9500 Euclid Ave.   Phone: (216) 444-5698
Cleveland, OH 44106   Elizabeth Joy, Hd.Med.Libn.

CLEVELAND COUNCIL ON WORLD AFFAIRS - LIBRARY
601 Rockwell Ave.   Phone: (216) 781-3730
Cleveland, OH 44114   Gayle A. Williams, Prog.Off.

CLEVELAND DEPARTMENT OF LAW LIBRARY
100 City Hall
601 Lakeside Ave.   Phone: (216) 664-2656
Cleveland, OH 44114   Jan Ryan Novak, Libn.

CLEVELAND ELECTRIC ILLUMINATING COMPANY - LAW LIBRARY
Public Square
Box 5000   Phone: (216) 622-9800
Cleveland, OH 44101   Judith A. Coll, Law Libn.

CLEVELAND ELECTRIC ILLUMINATING COMPANY - LIBRARY
Public Square, Rm. 504
Box 5000   Phone: (216) 622-9800
Cleveland, OH 44101   Paula Scalley, Assoc.Libn.

CLEVELAND HEALTH SCIENCES LIBRARY
2119 Abington Rd.   Phone: (216) 368-3426
Cleveland, OH 44106   Robert G. Cheshier, Dir.

CLEVELAND HEALTH SCIENCES LIBRARY - ALLEN MEMORIAL LIBRARY
11000 Euclid Ave.   Phone: (216) 368-3640
Cleveland, OH 44106   Lydia T. Holian, Assoc.Dir.

CLEVELAND HEALTH SCIENCES LIBRARY - HEALTH CENTER LIBRARY
2119 Abington Rd.   Phone: (216) 368-3426
Cleveland, OH 44106   Marjorie Saunders, Assoc.Dir.

CLEVELAND HEALTH SCIENCES LIBRARY - HISTORICAL DIVISION
11000 Euclid Ave.   Phone: (216) 368-3648
Cleveland, OH 44106   Dr. Patsy A. Gerstner, Chf.Cur.

CLEVELAND HEARING AND SPEECH CENTER - LUCILE DAUBY GRIES
MEMORIAL LIBRARY *
11206 Euclid Ave.   Phone: (216) 231-8787
Cleveland, OH 44106   Mildred P. Grant, Libn.

CLEVELAND INSTITUTE OF ART - JESSICA R. GUND MEMORIAL LIBRARY
11141 East Blvd.   Phone: (216) 421-4322
Cleveland, OH 44106   Karen D. Tschudy, Lib.Dir.

CLEVELAND INSTITUTE OF MUSIC - LIBRARY
11021 East Blvd.   Phone: (216) 791-5165
Cleveland, OH 44106   Karen K. Griffith, Dir., Lib.

CLEVELAND LAW LIBRARY ASSOCIATION †
404 County Court House   Phone: (216) 861-5070
Cleveland, OH 44113   Arthur W. Fiske, Libn.

CLEVELAND METROPARKS ZOO - LIBRARY
3900 Brookside Park Dr.   Phone: (216) 661-6500
Cleveland, OH 44109   Charles R. Voracek, Sr.Educ.Spec.

CLEVELAND METROPOLITAN GENERAL HOSPITAL - HAROLD H.
BRITTINGHAM MEMORIAL LIBRARY
3395 Scranton Rd.   Phone: (216) 459-5623
Cleveland, OH 44109   Christine Dziedzina, Chf.Libn.

CLEVELAND MUSEUM OF ART - INGALLS LIBRARY
11150 East Blvd.   Phone: (216) 421-7340
Cleveland, OH 44106   Jack Perry Brown, Libn.

CLEVELAND MUSEUM OF NATURAL HISTORY - HAROLD TERRY CLARK
LIBRARY
Wade Oval, University Circle   Phone: (216) 231-4600
Cleveland, OH 44106   Mary Baum, Libn.

CLEVELAND MUSIC SCHOOL SETTLEMENT - KULAS LIBRARY
11125 Magnolia Dr.
Cleveland, OH 44106

CLEVELAND PSYCHIATRIC INSTITUTE - KARNOSH LIBRARY
1708 Aiken Ave.   Phone: (216) 661-6200
Cleveland, OH 44109   Anna L. Harris, Libn.

CLEVELAND PSYCHOANALYTIC SOCIETY - LIBRARY
11328 Euclid Ave., No. 205   Phone: (216) 229-2111
Cleveland, OH 44106   Murray A. Goldstone, M.D., Chm., Lib.Comm.

CLEVELAND PUBLIC LIBRARY - BUSINESS, ECONOMICS & LABOR
DEPARTMENT
325 Superior Ave.   Phone: (216) 623-2927
Cleveland, OH 44114-1271   Joan Sorger, Dept.Hd.

CLEVELAND PUBLIC LIBRARY - CHILDREN'S LITERATURE DEPARTMENT
325 Superior Ave.   Phone: (216) 623-2834
Cleveland, OH 44114-1271   Ruth M. Hadlow, Dept.Hd.

CLEVELAND PUBLIC LIBRARY - DOCUMENTS COLLECTION
325 Superior Ave.   Phone: (216) 623-2870
Cleveland, OH 44114-1271   Siegfried Weinhold, Dept.Hd.

CLEVELAND PUBLIC LIBRARY - FINE ARTS AND SPECIAL COLLECTIONS
DEPARTMENT - FINE ARTS SECTION
325 Superior Ave.   Phone: (216) 623-2848
Cleveland, OH 44114-1271   Alice N. Loranth, Dept.Hd.

CLEVELAND PUBLIC LIBRARY - FOREIGN LITERATURE DEPARTMENT
325 Superior Ave.   Phone: (216) 623-2895
Cleveland, OH 44114-1271   Natalia B. Bezugloff, Dept.Hd.

CLEVELAND PUBLIC LIBRARY - GENERAL REFERENCE DEPARTMENT
325 Superior Ave.   Phone: (216) 623-2856
Cleveland, OH 44114-1271   Donald Tipka, Dept.Hd.

CLEVELAND PUBLIC LIBRARY - HISTORY AND GEOGRAPHY DEPARTMENT
325 Superior Ave.   Phone: (216) 623-2864
Cleveland, OH 44114-1271   JoAnn Petrello, Dept.Hd.

CLEVELAND PUBLIC LIBRARY - JOHN G. WHITE COLLECTION OF FOLKLORE,
ORIENTALIA, & CHESS
325 Superior Ave.   Phone: (216) 623-2818
Cleveland, OH 44114-1271   Alice N. Loranth, Dept.Hd.

CLEVELAND PUBLIC LIBRARY - LITERATURE DEPARTMENT
325 Superior Ave.   Phone: (216) 623-2881
Cleveland, OH 44114-1271   Evelyn M. Ward, Dept.Hd.

CLEVELAND PUBLIC LIBRARY - POPULAR LIBRARY DEPARTMENT
325 Superior Ave.   Phone: (216) 623-2842
Cleveland, OH 44114-1271   John Philip Ferguson, Dept.Hd.

CLEVELAND PUBLIC LIBRARY - PUBLIC ADMINISTRATION LIBRARY
601 Lakeside Ave., Rm. 100   Phone: (216) 623-2919
Cleveland, OH 44114-1271   Jan Ryan Novak, Dept.Hd.

CLEVELAND PUBLIC LIBRARY - SCIENCE AND TECHNOLOGY DEPARTMENT
325 Superior Ave.   Phone: (216) 623-2932
Cleveland, OH 44114-1271   Jean Z. Piety, Hd.

CLEVELAND PUBLIC LIBRARY - SOCIAL SCIENCES DEPARTMENT
325 Superior Ave.   Phone: (216) 623-2860
Cleveland, OH 44114-1271   Thelma J. Morris, Dept.Hd.

CLEVELAND STATE UNIVERSITY - COLLEGE OF URBAN AFFAIRS - URBAN
CENTER - DOCUMENT CENTER
1935 Euclid Ave.   Phone: (216) 687-2134
Cleveland, OH 44114

CLEVELAND STATE UNIVERSITY - JOSEPH W. BARTUNEK III LAW LIBRARY
Euclid Ave. at E. 18th St.   Phone: (216) 687-2250
Cleveland, OH 44115   W. Nicholas Pope, Asst.Prof./Law Libn.

CONSOLIDATED NATURAL GAS SERVICE CO., INC. - RESEARCH
DEPARTMENT LIBRARY
11001 Cedar Ave.   Phone: (216) 421-6310
Cleveland, OH 44106   Carol A. Brown, Supv., Info.Serv.

CUYAHOGA COUNTY REGIONAL PLANNING COMMISSION - LIBRARY
415 The Arcade   Phone: (216) 861-6805
Cleveland, OH 44114   Robert Parry, Dp.Dir.

DALTON-DALTON-NEWPORT - RESOURCE CENTER
3605 Warrensville Center Rd.   Phone: (216) 283-4000
Cleveland, OH 44122   Patricia A. Rice, Libn.

DANA CORPORATION - WEATHERHEAD DIVISION - LIBRARY AND
TECHNICAL INFORMATION CENTER †
767 Beta Dr.   Phone: (216) 449-6500
Cleveland, OH 44143   Dorothy Schaberl, Libn.

DUNHAM TAVERN MUSEUM - LIBRARY
6709 Euclid Ave.
Cleveland, OH 44103
Phone: (216) 431-1060
Elizabeth Martel, Libn.

ERNST & WHINNEY - NATIONAL OFFICE LIBRARY
2000 National City Ctr.
Cleveland, OH 44114
Phone: (216) 861-5000
Naomi Clifford, Natl.Off.Libn.

FAIRMOUNT TEMPLE - SAM AND EMMA MILLER LIBRARY
23737 Fairmount Blvd.
Cleveland, OH 44122
Phone: (216) 464-1330
Merrily F. Hart, Libn.

FAIRVIEW GENERAL HOSPITAL - HEALTH MEDIA CENTER
18101 Lorain Ave.
Cleveland, OH 44111
Phone: (216) 476-7118
Susan L. Favorite, Dir.

FEDERAL RESERVE BANK OF CLEVELAND - RESEARCH LIBRARY
Box 6387
Cleveland, OH 44101
Phone: (216) 241-2800
Elizabeth Maynard, Libn.

FIRST CATHOLIC SLOVAK UNION OF U.S.A. AND CANADA
3289 E. 55th St.
Cleveland, OH 44127
Phone: (216) 341-3355
Joseph R. Vehec, Exec.Sec.

FOUNDATION CENTER - CLEVELAND - KENT H. SMITH LIBRARY
1442 Hanna Bldg.
Cleveland, OH 44115-2001
Phone: (216) 861-1933
Jeanne Bohlen, Dir.

GARDEN CENTER OF GREATER CLEVELAND - ELEANOR SQUIRE LIBRARY
East Blvd.
Cleveland, OH 44106
Phone: (216) 721-1600
Richard T. Isaacson, Libn.

GENERAL ELECTRIC COMPANY - LIGHTING RESEARCH AND TECHNICAL
    SERVICES OPERATIONS - LIBRARY
Nela Park
Cleveland, OH 44112
Phone: (216) 266-3216
Sue Haase, Info.Spec.

GENERAL ELECTRIC COMPANY - REFRACTORY METAL PRODUCTS
    DEPARTMENT - LIBRARY *
21800 Tungsten Rd.
Cleveland, OH 44117
Phone: (216) 266-3736
Patricia A. Loucka, Libn.

GOULD, INC. - OCEAN SYSTEMS INFORMATION CENTER
Dept. 749, Plant 2
18901 Euclid Ave.
Cleveland, OH 44117
Phone: (216) 486-8300
Robert J. Rittenhouse, Tech.Info.Spec. & Mgr.

HAYES (Max S.) VOCATIONAL SCHOOL - LIBRARY
4600 Detroit Ave.
Cleveland, OH 44102
Phone: (216) 631-1528
Robert Stephen, Libn.

HOLZHEIMER INTERIORS - RESEARCH CENTER
10901 Carnegie Ave.
Cleveland, OH 44106
Phone: (216) 791-9292
Steven J. Grove, Hd.Libn.

HOUSING ADVOCATES - LAW AND CONSUMER AFFAIRS LIBRARY
353 Leader Bldg.
526 Superior Ave.
Cleveland, OH 44114
Phone: (216) 579-0575
Jim Buchanan, Dir.

HURON ROAD HOSPITAL - LIBRARY AND AUDIOVISUAL CENTER
13951 Terrace Rd.
Cleveland, OH 44112
Phone: (216) 261-8106
Sara W. Baker, Dir., Lib.Serv.

IMPERIAL CLEVITE INC. - IC INFORMATION CENTER
540 E. 105th St.
Cleveland, OH 44108
Phone: (216) 851-5500
Barbara Sanduleak, Mgr.

THE INFORMATION SPECIALISTS, INC. - THE A.F. MEMORIAL LIBRARY
2490 Lee Blvd.
Cleveland, OH 44118
Phone: (216) 321-7500
Gary Hirsch

THE INFORMATION SPECIALISTS, INC. - APPLE MICROCOMPUTER
    LIBRARY
2490 Lee Blvd.
Cleveland, OH 44118
Phone: (216) 321-7500
Jim Yanella

JONES, DAY, REAVIS & POGUE - LIBRARY
1700 Huntington Bldg.
Cleveland, OH 44115
Phone: (216) 696-3939
Sharon R. McIntyre, Libn.

KAISER FOUNDATION HOSPITALS - MEDICAL LIBRARY *
11203 Fairhill Rd.
Cleveland, OH 44104
Phone: (216) 795-8000
Marlene Saul, Med.Libn.

LUTHERAN MEDICAL CENTER - C.W. NEVEL MEMORIAL LIBRARY
2609 Franklin Blvd.
Cleveland, OH 44113
Phone: (216) 363-2143
Irene B. Szentkiralyi, Libn.

MC GEAN-ROHCO, INC. - RESEARCH LIBRARY
2910 Harvard Ave.
Box 09087
Cleveland, OH 44109
Phone: (216) 441-4900
Charlotte L. Conklin, Libn.

MC KEE (Arthur) CORPORATION - INFORMATION RESOURCE CENTER †
6200 Oak Tree Blvd.
Cleveland, OH 44131
Phone: (216) 524-9300
Ruth W. Parratt, Libn.

MARSCHALK COMPANY, INC. - LIBRARY †
601 Rockwell Ave.
Cleveland, OH 44114
Phone: (216) 687-8859
Mildred Mitchell, Libn.

MELDRUM AND FEWSMITH, INC. - BUSINESS INFORMATION LIBRARY
1220 Huron Rd.
Cleveland, OH 44115
Phone: (216) 241-2141
John Skutnik, Jr., Supv.

MIDLAND-ROSS CORPORATION - LIBRARY
20600 Chagrin Blvd.
Cleveland, OH 44122
Phone: (216) 491-8400
Diane Greenbaum, Chf.Libn.

MOUNT SINAI MEDICAL CENTER OF CLEVELAND - GEORGE H. HAYS
    MEMORIAL LIBRARY
University Circle
Cleveland, OH 44106
Phone: (216) 421-5615
Pamela Alderman, Chf.Med.Libn.

NORTHEAST OHIO AREAWIDE COORDINATING AGENCY - RESEARCH
    LIBRARY †
1501 Euclid Ave.
Cleveland, OH 44115
Phone: (216) 241-2414
Kenneth Goldberg, Res.Libn.

OHIO BELL - CORPORATE LIBRARY
100 Erieview Plaza, Rm. 112
Cleveland, OH 44114
Phone: (216) 822-2740
Adele R. Kurka, Asst.Mgr.-Libn.

OHIO COLLEGE OF PODIATRIC MEDICINE - LIBRARY/MEDIA CENTER
10515 Carnegie Ave.
Cleveland, OH 44106
Phone: (216) 231-3300
Judy Mehl Cowell, Dir.

PENTON/IPC - MARKETING INFORMATION CENTER
1111 Chester Ave.
Cleveland, OH 44114
Phone: (216) 696-7000
Kenneth Long, Mgr.

PLAIN DEALER PUBLISHING COMPANY - LIBRARY
1801 Superior Ave.
Cleveland, OH 44114
Phone: (216) 344-4195
Patti A. Graziano, Lib.Dir.

PLANNED PARENTHOOD OF CLEVELAND, INC. - LIBRARY
1501 Euclid Ave., Suite 300
Cleveland, OH 44115
Phone: (216) 781-0410
Lyn Cooper Gill, Exec.Dir.

PREFORMED LINE PRODUCTS - RESEARCH & ENGINEERING LIBRARY
Box 91129
Cleveland, OH 44101
Phone: (216) 461-5200
Edwina T. Barron, Libn.

REPUBLIC STEEL CORPORATION - RESEARCH CENTER LIBRARY
6801 Brecksville Rd.
Cleveland, OH 44131
Phone: (216) 524-5100
Kathryn A. Woolard, Libn.

ST. ALEXIS HOSPITAL - HEALTH SCIENCES LIBRARY
5163 Broadway Ave.
Cleveland, OH 44127
Phone: (216) 641-3300
Stephen C. Johnson, Dir., Lib.Serv.

ST. LUKE'S HOSPITAL - MEDICAL LIBRARY
11311 Shaker Blvd.
Cleveland, OH 44104
Phone: (216) 368-7691
Pam Billick, Dir.

ST. MARY SEMINARY - JOSEPH M. BRUENING LIBRARY
1227 Ansel Rd.   Phone: (216) 721-2100
Cleveland, OH 44108   Steven A. Kiczek, Libn.

ST. VINCENT CHARITY HOSPITAL - LIBRARY
2351 E. 22nd St.   Phone: (216) 861-6200
Cleveland, OH 44115   Joanne Billiar, Hd.Libn.

SHERWIN-WILLIAMS COMPANY - INFORMATION CENTER
13 Midland Bldg.
101 Prospect Ave., N.W.   Phone: (216) 234-6444
Cleveland, OH 44115   Gary Weske, Info.Ctr.Dir.

SLOVAK WRITERS AND ARTISTS ASSOCIATION - SLOVAK INSTITUTE -
    LIBRARY
St. Andrew's Abbey
2900 East Blvd.   Phone: (216) 521-7288
Cleveland, OH 44104   Fr. Nicholas Sprinc, Sec.

SOHIO CHEMCIAL COMPANY - INFORMATION CENTER
1875 Guildhall Bldg.   Phone: (216) 575-5715
Cleveland, OH 44115   Christine Kikta, Mgr., Info.Serv.

SQUIRE, SANDERS & DEMPSEY - LAW LIBRARY
1800 Union Commerce Bldg.   Phone: (216) 696-9200
Cleveland, OH 44115   Vivian S. Balester, Hd.Libn.

STANDARD OIL COMPANY OF OHIO - CORPORATE ENGINEERING LIBRARY
Midland Bldg., 826HB   Phone: (216) 575-8006
Cleveland, OH 44115   Dorothy A. Jankowski, Supv., Tech.Info.Serv.

TEMPLE LIBRARY
University Circle & Silver Pk.   Phone: (216) 791-7755
Cleveland, OH 44106   Beth Dwoskin, Libn.

TRW, INC. - AIRCRAFT COMPONENTS GROUP LIBRARY
23555 Euclid Ave.   Phone: (216) 383-3417
Cleveland, OH 44117   Sharon K. DeLong, Libn.

UKRAINIAN MUSEUM - ARCHIVES, INC.
1202 Kenilworth Ave.   Phone: (216) 781-4329
Cleveland, OH 44113   Stepan Kikta, Pres.

UNION CARBIDE CORPORATION - PARMA TECHNICAL CENTER -
    TECHNICAL INFORMATION SERVICE
Box 6116   Phone: (216) 676-2120
Cleveland, OH 44101   Joan C. Long, Mgr.

U.S. DEPT. OF COMMERCE - INTERNATIONAL TRADE ADMINISTRATION -
    CLEVELAND DISTRICT OFFICE LIBRARY
666 Euclid Ave., Rm. 600   Phone: (216) 522-4750
Cleveland, OH 44114   Zelda W. Milner, Dir.

U.S. NASA - LEWIS RESEARCH CENTER - LIBRARY †
21000 Brookpark Rd.   Phone: (216) 433-4000
Cleveland, OH 44135   Dorothy Morris, Chf., Lib.

U.S. VETERANS ADMINISTRATION (OH-Cleveland) - HOSPITAL LIBRARY
10701 East Blvd.   Phone: (216) 791-3800
Cleveland, OH 44106   Nancy S. Tesmer, Chf.Libn.

UNIVERSITY HOSPITALS OF CLEVELAND & CASE WESTERN RESERVE
    UNIVERSITY - DEPT. OF PATHOLOGY - LIBRARY
2085 Adelbert Rd.   Phone: (216) 368-2482
Cleveland, OH 44106   Jeanette W. Nagy, Dir.

WESTERN RESERVE HISTORICAL SOCIETY - LIBRARY
10825 E. Blvd.   Phone: (216) 721-5722
Cleveland, OH 44106   Kermit J. Pike, Dir.

WOMAN'S GENERAL HOSPITAL - MEDICAL LIBRARY
1940 E. 101st St.   Phone: (216) 421-3100
Cleveland, OH 44106   Dzwinka Komarjanski, Circuit Libn.

CONGREGATION BETH AM - DOROTHY G. FELDMAN LIBRARY
3557 Washington Blvd.   Phone: (216) 321-1000
Cleveland Heights, OH 44118   Mrs. Louis L. Powers, Libn.

PARK SYNAGOGUE LIBRARY - KRAVITZ MEMORIAL LIBRARY
3300 Mayfield Rd.   Phone: (216) 371-2244
Cleveland Heights, OH 44118   Sharon R. Merklin, Libn.

ACCURAY CORPORATION - ENGINEERING LIBRARY
650 Ackerman Rd.   Phone: (614) 261-2000
Columbus, OH 43202   Carol Staudenheimer, Libn.

AGUDAS ACHIM CONGREGATION - STEIN MEMORIAL LIBRARY
2767 E. Broad St.   Phone: (614) 237-2747
Columbus, OH 43209   Virginia Gold, Libn.

AMERICAN CERAMIC SOCIETY - LIBRARY
65 Ceramic Dr.   Phone: (614) 268-8645
Columbus, OH 43214-0387   Jessica Edwards, Libn.

AMERICAN SOCIETY FOR NONDESTRUCTIVE TESTING - LIBRARY AND
    INFORMATION CENTER
Caller 28518
Columbus, OH 43228

ASHLAND CHEMICAL COMPANY - TECHNICAL INFORMATION CENTER
Box 2219   Phone: (614) 889-3281
Columbus, OH 43216   Priscilla Ratliff, Supv.

AT & T BELL LABORATORIES & TECHNOLOGIES - LIBRARY
6200 E. Broad St.   Phone: (614) 868-3696
Columbus, OH 43213   Beverly A. Kaushagen, Lib. Group Supv.

BATTELLE-COLUMBUS LABORATORIES - COPPER DATA CENTER
505 King Ave.   Phone: (614) 424-7679
Columbus, OH 43201   Ross A. Gubiotti, Project Mgr.

BATTELLE-COLUMBUS LABORATORIES - LIBRARY
505 King Ave.   Phone: (614) 424-6424
Columbus, OH 43201   Carol A. Feltes, Mgr., Lib.Serv.

BATTELLE-COLUMBUS LABORATORIES - METALS AND CERAMICS
    INFORMATION CENTER
505 King Ave.   Phone: (614) 424-5000
Columbus, OH 43201   Harold Mindlin, Prog.Mgr.

BATTELLE-COLUMBUS LABORATORIES - RAPIDLY SOLIDIFIED MATERIALS
    (RaSoMat) - RESOURCE CENTER
505 King Ave.   Phone: (614) 424-4324
Columbus, OH 43201   Dr. R.S. Carbonara, Assoc.Mgr.

BATTELLE-COLUMBUS LABORATORIES - STACK GAS EMISSION CONTROL
    COORDINATION CENTER - LIBRARY
505 King Ave.   Phone: (614) 424-7885
Columbus, OH 43201   Joseph H. Oxley, Mgr.

BATTELLE-COLUMBUS LABORATORIES - TACTICAL TECHNOLOGY CENTER
505 King Ave.   Phone: (614) 424-5047
Columbus, OH 43201   Dr. Larry W. Williams, Mgr.

BATTELLE MEMORIAL INSTITUTE - LIBRARY
505 King Ave.   Phone: (614) 424-7697
Columbus, OH 43201-2693   P.G. Johnson, Libn.

BELL & HOWELL EDUCATION GROUP - DE VRY INSTITUTE OF TECHNOLOGY
    - LIBRARY
1350 Alum Creek Dr.   Phone: (614) 253-7291
Columbus, OH 43209   Susan F. Blaine, Dir., LRC

CAPITAL UNIVERSITY - CHEMISTRY LIBRARY
2199 E. Main St.   Phone: (614) 236-6500
Columbus, OH 43209   Albert F. Maag, Univ.Libn.

CAPITAL UNIVERSITY - LAW SCHOOL LIBRARY
665 S. High St.   Phone: (614) 445-8634
Columbus, OH 43215   Leverett L. Preble, III, J.D., Hd. Law Libn.

CENTER FOR HUMANE OPTIONS IN CHILDBIRTH EXPERIENCES (CHOICE) -
    LIBRARY
2862 Johnstown Rd.   Phone: (614) 476-1474
Columbus, OH 43219   Abby Kinne, Founder

CENTRAL OHIO TRANSIT AUTHORITY - LIBRARY
1600 McKinley Ave.
Phone: (614) 275-5800
Columbus, OH 43222
John T. Kniesner, Libn.

CHEMICAL ABSTRACTS SERVICE - LIBRARY
Box 3012
Phone: (614) 421-3600
Columbus, OH 43210
Robert S. Tannehill, Jr., Lib.Mgr.

CIRCUS HISTORICAL SOCIETY - LIBRARY
2515 Dorset Rd.
Columbus, OH 43221
Fred D. Pfening, Jr.

COLUMBIA GAS SYSTEM SERVICE CORPORATION - RESEARCH LIBRARY
1600 Dublin Rd.
Phone: (614) 486-3681
Columbus, OH 43215
Patricia Daley, Res.Libn.

COLUMBUS COLLEGE OF ART AND DESIGN - PACKARD LIBRARY
47 N. Washington Ave.
Phone: (614) 224-9101
Columbus, OH 43215
Chilin Yu, Hd.Libn.

COLUMBUS DEVELOPMENTAL CENTER - GOVE SCHOOL LIBRARY
1601 W. Broad St.
Phone: (614) 272-0509
Columbus, OH 43223

COLUMBUS DISPATCH - EDITORIAL LIBRARY
34 S. Third St.
Phone: (614) 461-5039
Columbus, OH 43216
James Hunter, Libn.

COLUMBUS LAW LIBRARY ASSOCIATION
Franklin County Hall of Justice
369 S. High St., 10th Fl.
Phone: (614) 221-4181
Columbus, OH 43215
Keith Blough, Law Libn.

COLUMBUS MUSEUM OF ART - RESOURCE CENTER
480 E. Broad St.
Phone: (614) 221-6801
Columbus, OH 43215
Martha Morford, Coord.

COLUMBUS PUBLIC SCHOOLS - PROFESSIONAL LIBRARY
889 E. 17th Ave.
Phone: (614) 225-2815
Columbus, OH 43211
Hugh A. Durbin, Dir.

COLUMBUS TECHNICAL INSTITUTE - EDUCATIONAL RESOURCES CENTER
550 E. Spring St.
Box 1609
Phone: (614) 227-2400
Columbus, OH 43216
Linda Landis, Dir., ERC

DOCTORS HOSPITAL - W.S. KONOLD MEMORIAL LIBRARY
1087 Dennison Ave.
Phone: (614) 297-4113
Columbus, OH 43201
Joseph Muzzo, Dir.

ERIC CLEARINGHOUSE ON ADULT, CAREER AND VOCATIONAL EDUCATION - NATL. CTR. FOR RESEARCH IN VOCATIONAL EDUC.
Ohio State University
1960 Kenny Rd.
Phone: (614) 486-3655
Columbus, OH 43210
Juliet V. Miller, Dir.

ERIC CLEARINGHOUSE FOR SCIENCE, MATHEMATICS AND ENVIRONMENTAL EDUCATION
Ohio State University
1200 Chambers Rd.
Phone: (614) 422-6717
Columbus, OH 43212
Robert W. Howe, Dir.

FEDERATION FOR UNIFIED SCIENCE EDUCATION - FUSE CENTER LIBRARY
231 Battelle Hall of Science
Capital University
Phone: (614) 236-6816
Columbus, OH 43209
Dr. Victor M. Showalter, Dir.

FRANKLIN COUNTY HISTORICAL SOCIETY - CENTER OF SCIENCE & INDUSTRY - CLEMENTS HISTORY MEMORIAL LIBRARY
280 E. Broad St.
Phone: (614) 488-4335
Columbus, OH 43215
Daniel F. Prugh, Dir., Hist./Pub.Rel.

FRANKLIN UNIVERSITY - LIBRARY
201 S. Grant Ave.
Phone: (614) 224-6237
Columbus, OH 43215
Mr. Allyn Ehrhardt, Libn.

GRANT HOSPITAL - MEDICAL LIBRARY
309 E. State St.
Phone: (614) 461-3467
Columbus, OH 43215
Nancy Cohen, Med.Libn.

GUITAR FOUNDATION OF AMERICA - ARCHIVE
C/O Music Library, Sullivant Hall
The Ohio State University
Phone: (614) 422-2310
Columbus, OH 43210
Thomas F. Heck, Archv.

ITT TELECOM NSD - LIBRARY
Box 20345
Phone: (614) 548-4301
Columbus, OH 43220
Gerald M. Hay, Libn.

MOUNT CARMEL MEDICAL CENTER - MOTHER M. CONSTANTINE MEMORIAL LIBRARY
793 W. State St.
Phone: (614) 225-5214
Columbus, OH 43222
Pamela M. Elwell, Libn.

NATIONAL CENTER FOR RESEARCH IN VOCATIONAL EDUCATION - RESEARCH LIBRARY
Ohio State University
1960 Kenny Rd.
Phone: (614) 486-3655
Columbus, OH 43212
Naomi Jacobs, Res.Libn.

NATIONWIDE MUTUAL INSURANCE COMPANY - LIBRARY/CORPORATE ARCHIVES
1 Nationwide Plaza
Phone: (614) 227-6154
Columbus, OH 43216
Karen Benedict, Chf.Libn. & Corp.Archv.

OHIO DOMINICAN COLLEGE - SPANGLER LIBRARY
1216 Sunbury Rd.
Phone: (614) 253-2741
Columbus, OH 43219
Sr. Rosalie Graham, Dir.

OHIO HISTORICAL SOCIETY - ARCHIVES-LIBRARY
I-71 & 17th Ave.
Phone: (614) 466-1500
Columbus, OH 43211
Dr. Dennis East, Hd.

OHIO POETRY THERAPY CENTER - WELCH LIBRARY
2384 Hardesty Dr., S.
Phone: (614) 279-4188
Columbus, OH 43204
Jennifer Groce Welch, Dir.

OHIO STATE ATTORNEY GENERAL'S OFFICE - LAW LIBRARY
30 E. Broad St., 17th Fl.
Phone: (614) 466-2465
Columbus, OH 43215
Deborah T. Byers, Libn.

OHIO STATE DEPARTMENT OF DEVELOPMENT - DIVISION OF ENERGY - ENERGY LIBRARY
30 E. Broad St., 34th Fl.
Phone: (614) 466-7915
Columbus, OH 43215
Riek A. Oldenquist, Libn.

OHIO STATE DEPARTMENT OF DEVELOPMENT - RESEARCH LIBRARY
Box 1001
Phone: (614) 466-2115
Columbus, OH 43204
Jean Fisher, Libn.

OHIO STATE DEPARTMENT OF MENTAL HEALTH - EDUCATIONAL MEDIA CENTER
2401 W. Walnut St.
Phone: (614) 466-6013
Columbus, OH 43223
Portia McDade, Libn.

OHIO STATE DEPARTMENT OF TAXATION - RESEARCH AND STATISTICS LIBRARY
State Office Tower
Box 530
Columbus, OH 43216
S.L. Shriver, Res.

OHIO (State) DEPARTMENT OF TRANSPORTATION - LIBRARY
25 S. Front St.
Box 899
Phone: (614) 466-7680
Columbus, OH 43216
Ellen Haider, Libn.

OHIO (State) DIVISION OF GEOLOGICAL SURVEY - LIBRARY
Fountain Sq., Bldg. B
Phone: (614) 265-6605
Columbus, OH 43224
Merrianne Hackathorn, Geologist

OHIO STATE ENVIRONMENTAL PROTECTION AGENCY - ENVIRONMENTAL TECHNICAL INFORMATION CENTER
361 E. Broad St.
Phone: (614) 466-6058
Columbus, OH 43215
Donna Pittman, Libn.

OHIO STATE INDUSTRIAL COMMISSION - DIVISION OF SAFETY AND HYGIENE - RESOURCE CENTER
246 N. High St.
Box 16512
Phone: (614) 466-7388
Columbus, OH 43215
Rosemary Larkins, Libn.

OHIO STATE LEGISLATIVE SERVICE COMMISSION - RESEARCH LIBRARY
State House
Phone: (614) 466-7434
Columbus, OH 43215
Barbara J. Laughon, Lib.Adm.

OHIO STATE SCHOOL FOR THE BLIND - LIBRARY
5220 N. High St.
Phone: (614) 888-8211
Columbus, OH 43214
Beverly Kessler, Libn.

OHIO STATE SUPREME COURT LAW LIBRARY
30 E. Broad St., 4th Fl.
Phone: (614) 466-2044
Columbus, OH 43215
Paul S. Fu, Law Libn.

OHIO STATE UNIVERSITY - AGRICULTURE LIBRARY
2120 Fyffe Rd.
Phone: (614) 422-6125
Columbus, OH 43210
Mary P. Key, Hd.Libn.

OHIO STATE UNIVERSITY - ARCHIVES
2121 Tuttle Park Pl.
Phone: (614) 422-2409
Columbus, OH 43210
Dr. Raimund E. Goerler, Univ.Archv.

OHIO STATE UNIVERSITY - BIOLOGICAL SCIENCES LIBRARY
1735 Neil Ave.
Phone: (614) 422-1744
Columbus, OH 43210
Victoria Welborn, Hd.Libn.

OHIO STATE UNIVERSITY - BLACK STUDIES LIBRARY
1858 Neil Ave.
Phone: (614) 422-8403
Columbus, OH 43210
Eleanor M. Daniel, Hd.Libn.

OHIO STATE UNIVERSITY - CENTER FOR LAKE ERIE AREA RESEARCH -
LAKE ERIE PROGRAM LIBRARY
484 W. 12th Ave.
Phone: (614) 422-8949
Columbus, OH 43210
Charles E. Herdendorf, Dir.

OHIO STATE UNIVERSITY - CHEMISTRY LIBRARY
140 W. 18th Ave.
Phone: (614) 422-1118
Columbus, OH 43210
Virginia E. Yagello, Hd.Libn.

OHIO STATE UNIVERSITY - CHILDREN'S HOSPITAL LIBRARY
700 Children's Drive
Phone: (614) 461-2375
Columbus, OH 43205
Mary Pat Wilhem, Hd.

OHIO STATE UNIVERSITY - CLASSICS, GERMAN, LINGUISTICS AND
ROMANCE LANGUAGES GRADUATE LIBRARY
1858 Neil Ave.
Phone: (614) 422-2594
Columbus, OH 43210

OHIO STATE UNIVERSITY - COLE MEMORIAL LIBRARY OF THE PHYSICS
AND ASTRONOMY DEPARTMENT
174 W. 18th Ave.
Phone: (614) 422-7894
Columbus, OH 43210
Virginia E. Yagello, Hd.Libn.

OHIO STATE UNIVERSITY - COMMERCE LIBRARY
1810 College Rd.
Phone: (614) 422-2136
Columbus, OH 43210
Charles Popovich, Hd.Libn.

OHIO STATE UNIVERSITY - EAST ASIAN COLLECTION
1858 Neil Ave. Mall
Phone: (614) 422-3502
Columbus, OH 43210
David Y. Hu, Bibliog.

OHIO STATE UNIVERSITY - EAST EUROPEAN AND SLAVIC READING ROOM
Main Library, Rm. 300
1858 Neil Ave. Mall
Phone: (614) 422-2073
Columbus, OH 43210
G. Koolemans Beynen, Slavic Bibliog.

OHIO STATE UNIVERSITY - EDGAR DALE EDUCATIONAL MEDIA &
INSTRUCTIONAL MATERIALS LABORATORY
260 Ramseyer Hall
29 W. Woodruff Ave.
Phone: (614) 422-1177
Columbus, OH 43210
Dr. Betty P. Cleaver, Dir.

OHIO STATE UNIVERSITY - EDUCATION/PSYCHOLOGY LIBRARY
1945 N. High St.
Phone: (614) 422-6275
Columbus, OH 43210
Laura Blomquist, Hd.Libn.

OHIO STATE UNIVERSITY - ENGINEERING LIBRARY
112 Caldwell Lab.
2024 Neil Ave.
Phone: (614) 422-2852
Columbus, OH 43210
Mary Jo Arnold, Hd.Libn.

OHIO STATE UNIVERSITY - ENGLISH DEPARTMENT LIBRARY
Derby Hall
154 N. Oval Mall
Phone: (614) 422-6357
Columbus, OH 43210
Louise H. Smith, Libn.

OHIO STATE UNIVERSITY - ENGLISH, THEATRE AND COMMUNICATION
GRADUATE LIBRARY
Main Library
1858 Neil Ave. Mall
Phone: (614) 422-2786
Columbus, OH 43210
Richard Centing, Hd.

OHIO STATE UNIVERSITY - FINE ARTS LIBRARY
Sullivant Hall
1813 N. High St.
Phone: (614) 422-6184
Columbus, OH 43210
Susan Wyngaard, Hd.Libn.

OHIO STATE UNIVERSITY - HEALTH SCIENCES LIBRARY
376 W. 10th Ave.
Phone: (614) 422-9810
Columbus, OH 43210
Elizabeth J. Sawyers, Dir.

OHIO STATE UNIVERSITY - HILANDAR ROOM
308 Main Library
1858 Neil Ave.
Phone: (614) 422-0634
Columbus, OH 43210
Dr. Predrag Matejic, Cur.

OHIO STATE UNIVERSITY - HISTORY, POLITICAL SCIENCE, AND
PHILOSOPHY GRADUATE LIBRARY
Main Library
1858 Neil Ave.
Phone: (614) 422-2393
Columbus, OH 43210
A. Robert Thorson, Hd.Libn.

OHIO STATE UNIVERSITY - HOME ECONOMICS LIBRARY
Campbell Hall
1787 Neil Ave.
Phone: (614) 422-4220
Columbus, OH 43210
Neosha Mackey, Hd.Libn.

OHIO STATE UNIVERSITY - INSTITUTE OF POLAR STUDIES -
GOLDTHWAIT POLAR LIBRARY
125 S. Oval Mall
Phone: (614) 422-6531
Columbus, OH 43210
Lynn B. Lay, Libn.

OHIO STATE UNIVERSITY - JOURNALISM LIBRARY
242 W. 18th Ave.
Phone: (614) 422-8747
Columbus, OH 43210
Eleanor Block, Hd.Libn.

OHIO STATE UNIVERSITY - JUDAICA LIBRARY
1858 Neil Ave. Mall
Phone: (614) 422-3362
Columbus, OH 43210
Amnon Zipin, Jewish Stud.Libn.

OHIO STATE UNIVERSITY - LATIN AMERICAN STUDIES READING ROOM
AND LIBRARY
Main Library
1858 Neil Ave.
Phone: (614) 422-8959
Columbus, OH 43210
Dr. Laurence Hallewell, Bibliog.

OHIO STATE UNIVERSITY - LAW LIBRARY
College of Law
1659 N. High St.
Phone: (614) 422-6691
Columbus, OH 43210
Ruth Kessler, Act.Dir.

OHIO STATE UNIVERSITY - LIBRARY FOR COMMUNICATION AND GRAPHIC
ARTS
242 W. 18th Ave., Rm. 147
Phone: (614) 422-0538
Columbus, OH 43210
Lucy S. Caswell, Cur.

OHIO STATE UNIVERSITY - MAP GRADUATE LIBRARY
1858 Neil Ave.
Phone: (614) 422-2393
Columbus, OH 43210
A. Robert Thorson, Hd.Libn.

OHIO STATE UNIVERSITY - MATERIALS ENGINEERING LIBRARY
2041 N. College Rd.
Phone: (614) 422-9614
Columbus, OH 43210
Mary Jo Arnold, Hd.Libn.

OHIO STATE UNIVERSITY - MATHEMATICS LIBRARY
231 W. 18th St.
Phone: (614) 422-2009
Columbus, OH 43210

OHIO STATE UNIVERSITY - MECHANIZED INFORMATION CENTER (MIC)
1858 Neil Ave. Mall
Columbus, OH 43210
Phone: (614) 422-3480
Bernard Bayer, Hd.

OHIO STATE UNIVERSITY - MIDDLE EAST/ISLAMICA READING ROOM
Thompson Library, Rm. 320
1858 Neil Ave. Mall
Columbus, OH 43210
Phone: (614) 422-3362
Dona S. Straley, Middle East Libn.

OHIO STATE UNIVERSITY - MUSIC LIBRARY
186 Sullivant Hall
1813 N. High St.
Columbus, OH 43210
Phone: (614) 422-2319
Thomas Heck, Hd.Libn.

OHIO STATE UNIVERSITY - OHIO COOPERATIVE WILDLIFE RESEARCH
UNIT - LIBRARY
1735 Neil Ave.
Columbus, OH 43210
Phone: (614) 422-6112
Dr. Theodore A. Bookhout, Unit Leader

OHIO STATE UNIVERSITY - ORTON MEMORIAL LIBRARY OF GEOLOGY
155 S. Oval Dr.
Columbus, OH 43210
Phone: (614) 422-2428
Regina Brown, Hd.Libn.

OHIO STATE UNIVERSITY - PERSONNEL AND CAREER EXPLORATION
(PACE) RESOURCE CENTER
Ohio Union, Fl. 4
1739 N. High St.
Columbus, OH 43210
Phone: (614) 422-5766
Jean Brethauer, Career Libn.

OHIO STATE UNIVERSITY - PHARMACY LIBRARY
Pharmacy Bldg.
500 W. 12th Ave.
Columbus, OH 43210
Phone: (614) 422-6078

OHIO STATE UNIVERSITY - SOCIAL WORK LIBRARY
1947 College Rd.
Columbus, OH 43210
Phone: (614) 422-6627
Mrs. Toyo S. Kawakami, Hd.Libn.

OHIO STATE UNIVERSITY - THEATRE RESEARCH INSTITUTE
1089 Drake Union
1849 Cannon Dr.
Columbus, OH 43210
Phone: (614) 422-6614
Alan Woods, Dir.

OHIO STATE UNIVERSITY - TOPAZ MEMORIAL LIBRARY
College of Optometry
338 W. Tenth Ave.
Columbus, OH 43210
Phone: (614) 422-1888
Molly A. Phillips, Libn. Media Tech.Asst.

OHIO STATE UNIVERSITY - VETERINARY MEDICINE LIBRARY
1900 Coffey Rd.
Columbus, OH 43210
Phone: (614) 422-6107
Bruce Evans, Hd.Libn.

OHIO STATE UNIVERSITY - WOMEN'S STUDIES LIBRARY
1858 Neil Ave. Mall
Columbus, OH 43210
Phone: (614) 422-3035
Adrienne Zahniser, Hd.Libn.

OHIOANA LIBRARY ASSOCIATION - OHIOANA LIBRARY AND ARCHIVES
1105 Ohio Departments Bldg.
65 S. Front St.
Columbus, OH 43215
Phone: (614) 466-3831
Kathy A. Babeaux, Libn.

OTTAWA INSTITUTE - IRENE HOLM MEMORIAL LIBRARY
1465 Osborn Dr.
Columbus, OH 43221
Phone: (614) 486-5028
Ms. Bobbi Wilson, Libn.

PONTIFICAL COLLEGE JOSEPHINUM - A.T. WEHRLE MEMORIAL LIBRARY
7625 N. High St.
Columbus, OH 43085
Phone: (614) 885-5585
Peter G. Veracka, Dir./Coll.Libn.

PUBLIC UTILITIES COMMISSION OF OHIO - LIBRARY
180 E. Broad St.
Columbus, OH 43215
Phone: (614) 466-5082
Elza O. Fodor, Libn.

RIVERSIDE METHODIST HOSPITAL - D.J. VINCENT MEDICAL LIBRARY
3535 Olentangy River Rd.
Columbus, OH 43214
Phone: (614) 261-5230
Josephine W. Yeoh, Dir.

ROCKWELL INTERNATIONAL - TECHNICAL INFORMATION CENTER
4300 E. Fifth Ave.
Box 1259
Columbus, OH 43216
Phone: (614) 239-3131

ROSS LABORATORIES - LIBRARY
625 Cleveland Ave.
Columbus, OH 43216
Phone: (614) 227-3503
Linda Mitro Hopkins, Mgr.

ST. ANTHONY HOSPITAL - PHILIP B. HARDYMON LIBRARY
1450 Hawthorne Ave.
Columbus, OH 43203
Phone: (614) 251-3248
James S. Rucker, Chf.Med.Libn.

SOCIETY OF FRIENDS - OHIO YEARLY MEETING - WESTGATE FRIENDS
LIBRARY
3750 Sullivant Ave.
Columbus, OH 43228
Phone: (614) 274-5131
William T. Peters, Lit.Coord.

STATE LIBRARY OF OHIO
65 S. Front St.
Columbus, OH 43215
Phone: (614) 462-7061
Richard M. Cheski, State Libn.

TIN RESEARCH INSTITUTE, INC. - LIBRARY & INFORMATION CENTER
1353 Perry St.
Columbus, OH 43201
Phone: (614) 424-6200
Daniel J. Maykuth, Mgr.

TRINITY LUTHERAN SEMINARY - HAMMA LIBRARY
2199 E. Main St.
Columbus, OH 43209
Phone: (614) 236-7116
Donald L. Huber, Libn.

U.S. DEFENSE LOGISTICS AGENCY - DEFENSE CONSTRUCTION SUPPLY
CTR. - TECH. DATA PROCESSING BRANCH - LIBRARY
3990 E. Broad St.
Columbus, OH 43216-5000
Phone: (614) 238-3549
Joseph S. Cohen, Chf.

FALLSVIEW PSYCHIATRIC HOSPITAL - STAFF LIBRARY
330 Broadway E.
Cuyahoga Falls, OH 44221
Phone: (216) 929-8301
David Allen, Libn.

AULLWOOD AUDUBON CENTER AND FARM - LIBRARY
1000 Aullwood Rd.
Dayton, OH 45414
Phone: (513) 890-7360
Evelyn Pereny, Libn.

CHEMINEER, INC. - LIBRARY
Box 1123
Dayton, OH 45401
Phone: (513) 229-7000
Dr. David S. Dickey, Tech.Dir.

CHILDREN'S MEDICAL CENTER - LIBRARY †
One Children's Plaza
Dayton, OH 45404
Phone: (513) 226-8307
Jane R. Bottoms, Libn.

DAYTON ART INSTITUTE - LIBRARY
Forest & Riverview Aves.
Box 941
Dayton, OH 45401
Phone: (513) 223-5277
Helen L. Pinkney, Libn.

DAYTON LAW LIBRARY ASSOCIATION †
505 Montgomery County Courts Bldg.
41 N. Perry St.
Dayton, OH 45422
Phone: (513) 225-4505
Betty Busch, Libn.

DAYTON MENTAL HEALTH CENTER - STAFF LIBRARY
2611 Wayne Ave.
Dayton, OH 45420
Phone: (513) 258-0440
Leonard Skonecki, Libn.

DAYTON AND MONTGOMERY COUNTY PUBLIC LIBRARY - INDUSTRY AND
SCIENCE DIVISION
215 E. Third St.
Dayton, OH 45402
Phone: (513) 224-1651
Martha A. Overwein, Div.Hd.

DAYTON AND MONTGOMERY COUNTY PUBLIC LIBRARY - LITERATURE AND
FINE ARTS DIVISION
215 E. Third St.
Dayton, OH 45402
Phone: (513) 224-1651
Donald T. Paul, Hd.

DAYTON AND MONTGOMERY COUNTY PUBLIC LIBRARY - NON-PRINT
MEDIA CENTER
215 E. Third St.
Dayton, OH 45402
Phone: (513) 224-1651
Theodore J. Nunn, Jr., Hd.

DAYTON AND MONTGOMERY COUNTY PUBLIC LIBRARY - SOCIAL
  SCIENCES DIVISION
215 E. Third St.   Phone: (513) 224-1651
Dayton, OH 45402   Laura J. Smith, Div.Hd.

DAYTON NEWSPAPERS INC. - REFERENCE LIBRARY
37 S. Ludlow St.   Phone: (513) 225-2430
Dayton, OH 45402   Mr. Harish Trivedi, Ref. & Res.Dir.

ENGINEERS' CLUB OF DAYTON - LIBRARY *
110 E. Monument Ave.   Phone: (513) 228-2148
Dayton, OH 45402   Susan Marks, Libn.

GOOD SAMARITAN HOSPITAL - SHANK MEMORIAL LIBRARY
2222 Philadelphia Dr.   Phone: (513) 278-2612
Dayton, OH 45406   Elizabeth A. Robinson, Libn.

GRANDVIEW HOSPITAL - MEDICAL LIBRARY
405 Grand Ave.   Phone: (513) 226-3379
Dayton, OH 45405   Loma Pallman, Dir.

MEAD CORPORATION - CORPORATE LIBRARY
Corporate Plaza N.E.   Phone: (513) 222-6323
Dayton, OH 45463   Susan Kremer, Corp.Libn./Anl.

MIAMI VALLEY HOSPITAL - EDUCATIONAL RESOURCES CENTER - MEDICAL
  LIBRARY
One Wyoming St.   Phone: (513) 223-6192
Dayton, OH 45409   Margaret C. Hardy, Dir.

MIAMI VALLEY REGIONAL PLANNING COMMISSION - LIBRARY
117 S. Main St., Suite 200   Phone: (513) 223-6323
Dayton, OH 45402   Nora Lake, Exec.Dir.

NCR CORPORATION - TECHNICAL LIBRARY
Engineering & Manufacturing-Dayton
Building EMD, 3rd Fl.   Phone: (513) 445-7032
Dayton, OH 45479   Vicki Anderson, Libn.

ST. ELIZABETH MEDICAL CENTER - HEALTH SCIENCES LIBRARY †
601 Miami Blvd., W.   Phone: (513) 229-6061
Dayton, OH 45408   Ann L. Lewis, Med.Libn.

SOCIETY OF MARY - CINCINNATI PROVINCE - ARCHIVES
University of Dayton
Box 445   Phone: (513) 229-2724
Dayton, OH 45469   Bro. Bernard Laurinaitis, S.M., Archv.

STANDARD REGISTER COMPANY - CORPORATE LIBRARY
Box 1167   Phone: (513) 223-6181
Dayton, OH 45401   Dorothea P. Adkinson, Libn.

TEMPLE ISRAEL - RABBI LOUIS WITT MEMORIAL LIBRARY
1821 Emerson Ave.   Phone: (513) 278-9621
Dayton, OH 45406   Jeanne B. Goldzwig, Libn.

U.S. AIR FORCE - WRIGHT-PATTERSON TECHNICAL LIBRARY
Wright-Patterson AFB, Bldg. 22   Phone: (513) 255-3630
Dayton, OH 45433   Dorothy E. Siegfried, Chf.

U.S. VETERANS ADMINISTRATION (OH-Dayton) - CENTER LIBRARY
4100 W. Third St.   Phone: (513) 268-6511
Dayton, OH 45428   Lendell Beverly, Chf., Lib.Serv.

UNITED THEOLOGICAL SEMINARY - LIBRARY
1810 Harvard Blvd.   Phone: (513) 278-5817
Dayton, OH 45406   Elmer J. O'Brien, Libn.

UNIVERSITY OF DAYTON - LAW SCHOOL LIBRARY
300 College Park   Phone: (513) 229-2314
Dayton, OH 45469   Prof. Thomas L. Hanley, Dir.

UNIVERSITY OF DAYTON - MARIAN LIBRARY
300 College Park   Phone: (513) 229-4214
Dayton, OH 45469   Rev. Theodore Koehler, S.M., Dir.

UNIVERSITY OF DAYTON - ROESCH LIBRARY - SPECIAL COLLECTIONS/
  RARE BOOKS
300 College Park Ave.   Phone: (513) 229-4221
Dayton, OH 45469   Cecilia Mushenheim, Archv./Spec.Coll.Libn.

UNIVERSITY OF DAYTON - SCHOOL OF EDUCATION - CURRICULUM
  MATERIALS CENTER
300 College Park, Chaminade Hall   Phone: (513) 229-3140
Dayton, OH 49469   Sr. Catherine Rudolph, O.S.F., Dir.

WRIGHT STATE UNIVERSITY - ARCHIVES & SPECIAL COLLECTIONS
                                           Phone: (513) 873-2092
Dayton, OH 45435   Dr. Patrick B. Nolan, Hd. of Archv.

WRIGHT STATE UNIVERSITY - HEALTH SCIENCES LIBRARY
3640 Colonel Glenn Hwy.   Phone: (513) 873-2266
Dayton, OH 45435   Mary Ann Hoffman, Act. Health Sci.Libn.

DELAWARE COUNTY LAW LIBRARY
Court House
N. Sandusky St.   Phone: (614) 363-4632
Delaware, OH 43015   Maryanne W. Stewart, Law Libn.

METHODIST THEOLOGICAL SCHOOL IN OHIO - JOHN W. DICKHAUT
  LIBRARY
Box 1204   Phone: (614) 363-1146
Delaware, OH 43015   M. Edward Hunter, Libn.

OCLC, INC. - LIBRARY
Box 7777   Phone: (614) 764-6000
Dublin, OH 43017   Ann T. Dodson, Mgr.

GOULD INC. - FOIL DIVISION - TECHNICAL INFORMATION CENTER
35129 Curtis Blvd.   Phone: (216) 953-5117
Eastlake, OH 44094   Martha C. Walunis, Libn.

ELYRIA MEMORIAL HOSPITAL - LIBRARY †
630 E. River St.   Phone: (216) 323-3221
Elyria, OH 44035   Linda Masek, Hd.Libn.

LORAIN COUNTY HISTORICAL SOCIETY - GERALD HICKS MEMORIAL
  LIBRARY
509 Washington Ave.   Phone: (216) 322-3341
Elyria, OH 44035   Mary Jeffries, Cat.

LORAIN COUNTY LAW LIBRARY ASSOCIATION - LIBRARY
Courthouse, 3rd Fl.   Phone: (216) 322-5024
Elyria, OH 44035

LORAIN COUNTY PRINTING & PUBLISHING COMPANY - ELYRIA
  CHRONICLE-TELEGRAM - LIBRARY
225 East Ave.   Phone: (216) 329-7000
Elyria, OH 44036   Marie Banks, Hd.Libn.

CUYAHOGA COUNTY PUBLIC LIBRARY - FAIRVIEW PARK REGIONAL
  BRANCH - SPECIAL COLLECTIONS
4449 W. 213th St.   Phone: (216) 333-4700
Fairview Park, OH 44126   John Lonsak, Regional Mgr.

COURIER - LIBRARY
701 W. Sandusky St.   Phone: (419) 422-5151
Findlay, OH 45840   Kathy Drummond, Libn.

HANCOCK COUNTY LAW LIBRARY ASSOCIATION
Hancock County Courthouse   Phone: (419) 424-7077
Findlay, OH 45840   Ruth A. Long, Asst. Law Libn.

MARATHON OIL COMPANY - LAW LIBRARY
539 S. Main St., Rm. 854-M   Phone: (419) 422-2121
Findlay, OH 45840   Durand S. Dudley, Sr. Law Libn.

WINEBRENNER THEOLOGICAL SEMINARY - LIBRARY
701 E. Melrose Ave.
Box 478   Phone: (419) 422-4824
Findlay, OH 45839-0478   Oscar C. Schultz, Jr., Hd.Libn.

HAYES (Rutherford B.) PRESIDENTIAL CENTER - LIBRARY
Spiegel Grove   Phone: (419) 332-2081
Fremont, OH 43420   Leslie H. Fishel, Jr., Dir.

SANDUSKY COUNTY LAW LIBRARY
Courthouse, 100 N. Park Ave.   Phone: (419) 332-6411
Fremont, OH 43420

HOLZER MEDICAL CENTER - MEDICAL LIBRARY
385 Jackson Pike   Phone: (614) 446-5057
Gallipolis, OH 45631   Beverly J. Jackson, Lib.Ck.

OWENS-CORNING FIBERGLAS CORPORATION - TECHNICAL DATA CENTER
Granville, OH 43023   Betty Nethers, Mgr.

GREENVILLE LAW LIBRARY
Court House   Phone: (513) 547-1420
Greenville, OH 45331   Helen V. Pierce, Libn.

BUTLER COUNTY LAW LIBRARY ASSOCIATION
Court House Annex   Phone: (513) 867-5714
Hamilton, OH 45011   Anita K. Shew, Law Libn.

CHAMPION INTERNATIONAL - CHAMPION PAPERS TECHNICAL LIBRARY
Knightsbridge Dr.   Phone: (513) 868-4578
Hamilton, OH 45020   Paul F. Bryant, Tech.Libn.

FORT HAMILTON-HUGHES MEMORIAL HOSPITAL CENTER - SOHN
   MEMORIAL HEALTH SERVICES LIBRARY
630 Eaton Ave.   Phone: (513) 867-2310
Hamilton, OH 45013   Lois Protzman, Libn.

MERCY NORTH HOSPITAL - HEALTH SCIENCES LIBRARY
116 Dayton St.   Phone: (513) 867-6458
Hamilton, OH 45011   Frances McCullough, Libn.

BLESSED SACRAMENT SEMINARY - LIBRARY
5384 Wilson Mills Rd.   Phone: (216) 442-3410
Highland Heights, OH 44143

HIGHLAND COUNTY LAW LIBRARY
High & Main Sts., Court House   Phone: (513) 393-4863
Hillsboro, OH 45133   Michelle Vanzant, Law Libn.

SOUTHERN OHIO GENEALOGICAL SOCIETY - REFERENCE LIBRARY
879 W. Main St.
Box 414   Phone: (513) 393-2452
Hillsboro, OH 45133   Marie A. Knott, Libn.

HIRAM COLLEGE - TEACHOUT-PRICE MEMORIAL LIBRARY
                                          Phone: (216) 569-5359
Hiram, OH 44234   Joanne M. Sawyer, Archv.

HUDSON LIBRARY AND HISTORICAL SOCIETY
22 Aurora St.   Phone: (216) 653-6658
Hudson, OH 44236   Thomas L. Vince, Libn. & Cur.

FERRO CORPORATION - LIBRARY
7500 E. Pleasant Valley Rd.   Phone: (216) 641-8580
Independence, OH 44131   Kathleen Fuller, Hd.Libn.

JACKSON COUNTY LAW LIBRARY
Court House
Jackson, OH 45640   Martha E. Murphy, Lib. Custodian

KENT STATE UNIVERSITY - AMERICAN HISTORY RESEARCH CENTER
Library   Phone: (216) 672-2411
Kent, OH 44242   Stephen C. Morton, Archv.

KENT STATE UNIVERSITY - ARCHIVES
Library   Phone: (216) 672-2411
Kent, OH 44242   Stephen C. Morton, Univ.Archv.

KENT STATE UNIVERSITY - AUDIOVISUAL SERVICES
330 University Library   Phone: (216) 672-3456
Kent, OH 44242   Charles Hunger, Dir., AV Serv.

KENT STATE UNIVERSITY - AUDIOVISUAL SERVICES - SELF INSTRUCTION
   CENTER
330 Library   Phone: (216) 672-2889
Kent, OH 44242

KENT STATE UNIVERSITY - CENTER FOR THE STUDY OF ETHNIC
   PUBLICATIONS IN THE UNITED STATES
University Library, Rm. 318   Phone: (216) 672-2782
Kent, OH 44242   Dr. Lubomyr Wynar, Dir.

KENT STATE UNIVERSITY - CHEMISTRY/PHYSICS LIBRARY
312 Williams Hall   Phone: (216) 672-2532
Kent, OH 44242   Joy Woodson, Libn.

KENT STATE UNIVERSITY - DEPARTMENT OF SPECIAL COLLECTIONS
University Library   Phone: (216) 672-2270
Kent, OH 44242   Dean H. Keller, Cur.

KENT STATE UNIVERSITY - DOCUMENTS UNIT
370 Library   Phone: (216) 672-2388
Kent, OH 44242   Liese Adams, Doc.Libn.

KENT STATE UNIVERSITY - MAP LIBRARY
406 McGilvery Hall   Phone: (216) 672-2017
Kent, OH 44242   Julia Cannan, Supv.

KENT STATE UNIVERSITY - MUSIC LIBRARY
D5 Music & Speech Bldg.   Phone: (216) 672-2004
Kent, OH 44242   Judith B. McCarron, Music Lib.Supv.

NATIONAL ASSOCIATION FOR CORE CURRICULUM, INC. - LIBRARY
316 White Hall
Kent State University   Phone: (216) 672-7977
Kent, OH 44242   Dr. Gordon F. Vars, Exec.Sec.-Treas.

KETTERING COLLEGE OF MEDICAL ARTS - LEARNING RESOURCES CENTER
3737 Southern Blvd.   Phone: (513) 296-7201
Kettering, OH 45429   Edward Collins, Libn.

KETTERING MEDICAL CENTER HOSPITAL - MEDICAL LIBRARY
3535 Southern Blvd.   Phone: (513) 298-4331
Kettering, OH 45429   Joseph P. Stoia, Med.Libn.

LAKEWOOD HISTORICAL SOCIETY - LIBRARY
14710 Lake Ave.   Phone: (216) 221-7343
Lakewood, OH 44107   Bertha M. Noe, Cur.

LAKEWOOD HOSPITAL - MEDICAL LIBRARY *
14519 Detroit Ave.   Phone: (216) 521-4200
Lakewood, OH 44107   Dorothy Jorgens, Dir.

ANCHOR HOCKING CORPORATION - CORPORATE LIBRARY †
2980 W. Fair Ave.   Phone: (614) 687-2344
Lancaster, OH 43130   Peggy J. Myers, Corp.Libn.

ARCAIR COMPANY - LIBRARY †
Box 406   Phone: (614) 653-5618
Lancaster, OH 43130   Dottie Young, Libn.

WARREN COUNTY HISTORICAL SOCIETY - MUSEUM AND LIBRARY
105 S. Broadway
Box 223   Phone: (513) 932-1817
Lebanon, OH 45036   Victoria Visintainer, Dir.

WARREN COUNTY LAW LIBRARY †
500 Justice Dr.   Phone: (614) 932-4040
Lebanon, OH 45036   Barbara Bronson, Libn.

ALLEN COUNTY HISTORICAL SOCIETY - ELIZABETH M. MAC DONELL
   MEMORIAL LIBRARY
620 W. Market St.   Phone: (419) 222-9426
Lima, OH 45801   Anna B. Selfridge, Asst.Cur./Mss., Archv.

ALLEN COUNTY LAW LIBRARY *
Court House, 4th Fl.
Lima, OH 45801   Ruth Laudahn, Act.Libn.

LIMA MEMORIAL HOSPITAL - HEALTH SCIENCES LIBRARY
Linden & Mobel Sts.   Phone: (419) 228-3335
Lima, OH 45804   Margaret D. Cutter, Health Sci.Libn.

LIMA STATE HOSPITAL - OAKWOOD FORENSIC CENTER
3200 N. West St. Rd.   Phone: (419) 227-4631
Lima, OH 45801   Mary Bice, Libn.

ST. RITA'S MEDICAL CENTER - MEDICAL LIBRARY
730 W. Market St.   Phone: (419) 227-3361
Lima, OH 45801   Sharon Bilopavlovich, Libn.

WESTINGHOUSE ELECTRIC CORPORATION - ELECTRICAL SYSTEMS
   DIVISION - TECHNICAL LIBRARY †
1501 S. Dixie   Phone: (419) 226-3121
Lima, OH 45804   Russel J. Heine, Tech.Pub.Anl.

COLUMBIANA COUNTY LAW LIBRARY
Court House   Phone: (216) 424-9511
Lisbon, OH 44432

WAGNALLS MEMORIAL LIBRARY
150 E. Columbus St.   Phone: (614) 837-4765
Lithopolis, OH 43136   Jerry W. Neff, Exec.Dir.

MADISON COUNTY LAW LIBRARY
Court House   Phone: (614) 852-9515
London, OH 43140   Janet C. Kronk, Libn.

LORAIN COMMUNITY HOSPITAL - MEDICAL STAFF LIBRARY
3700 Kolbe Rd.   Phone: (216) 282-9121
Lorain, OH 44053   Mrs. Tory Wagner, Med.Libn.

ST. JOSEPH HOSPITAL - MEDICAL STAFF LIBRARY
205 W. 20th St.   Phone: (216) 245-6851
Lorain, OH 44052   Sue Van Atta, Dir.

MORGAN COUNTY BAR ASSOCIATION - LIBRARY
Court House
McConnelsville, OH 43756   Mary Woodward, Law Libn.

KINGWOOD CENTER - LIBRARY
900 Park Ave. W.   Phone: (419) 522-0211
Mansfield, OH 44906 Timothy J. Gardner, Horticulturist

OHIO GENEALOGICAL SOCIETY - LIBRARY
Box 2625   Phone: (419) 522-9077
Mansfield, OH 44906   Mrs. Carl Main, Libn.

RICHLAND COUNTY LAW LIBRARY †
Court House
50 Park Ave., E.   Phone: (419) 524-9944
Mansfield, OH 44902   Arthur W. Negin, Libn./V.P.

OHIO HISTORICAL SOCIETY - CAMPUS MARTIUS MUSEUM - LIBRARY
601 Second St.   Phone: (614) 373-3750
Marietta, OH 45750   John B. Briley, Mgr.

WASHINGTON COUNTY LAW LIBRARY
Court House
201 Putnam St.
Marietta, OH 45750   Patricia Wheeler, Libn.

MARION COUNTY LAW LIBRARY
Court House   Phone: (614) 387-5871
Marion, OH 43302   Hazel Aldrich, Ck.

MARION GENERAL HOSPITAL - MEDICAL LIBRARY
McKinley Park Dr.   Phone: (614) 387-8810
Marion, OH 43302   Doris P. Hurn, Libn.

SMITH (Frederick C.) CLINIC - MEDICAL LIBRARY
1040 Delaware Ave.   Phone: (614) 387-0850
Marion, OH 43302   Doris P. Hurn, Libn.

SCOTT (O.M.) AND SONS - INFORMATION SERVICES
Dwight G. Scott Research Center   Phone: (513) 644-0011
Marysville, OH 43041   Betty Seitz, Supv., Info.Serv.

DOCTORS HOSPITAL INC. OF STARK COUNTY - MEDICAL LIBRARY
400 Austin Ave., N.W.   Phone: (216) 837-7371
Massillon, OH 44646 Christine J. Williams, Dir.Lib.Serv.

STARK COUNTY LAW LIBRARY ASSOCIATION - MASSILLON BRANCH LAW
   LIBRARY *
City Hall   Phone: (216) 837-4271
Massillon, OH 44646

THE ANDERSONS - MARKET RESEARCH LIBRARY
Box 119   Phone: (419) 893-5050
Maumee, OH 43537   Mary Nesper, Libn.

MEDINA COUNTY LAW LIBRARY ASSOCIATION
Court House, 93 Public Sq.   Phone: (216) 723-3641
Medina, OH 44256   Jeffrey L. Bramley, Libn.

HOLDEN ARBORETUM - WARREN H. CORNING LIBRARY
Sperry Rd.   Phone: (216) 946-4400
Mentor, OH 44060   Paul C. Spector, Dir.

LAKE COUNTY HISTORICAL SOCIETY - PERCY KENDALL SMITH LIBRARY
   FOR HISTORICAL RESEARCH
8095 Mentor Ave.   Phone: (216) 255-8722
Mentor, OH 44060   Carl Thomas Engel, Libn.

LIBRARY OF HENRY J. GRUND †
4897 Corduroy Rd.
Mentor Headlands
Mentor, OH 44060   Henry J. Grund, II, Dir.

AMERICAN SOCIETY FOR METALS - METALS INFORMATION
                    Phone: (216) 338-5151
Metals Park, OH 44073   William A. Weida, Libn.

MONARCH MARKING SYSTEMS - TECHNICAL LIBRARY
1 Kohnle Dr.   Phone: (513) 865-2082
Miamisburg, OH 45342 Mrs. Artence Walton, Tech.Dir.

MONSANTO RESEARCH CORPORATION - MOUND TECHNICAL
   INFORMATION CENTER
Box 32   Phone: (513) 865-3942
Miamisburg, OH 45342 Hermina Brinkmeier, Supv., Lib. & Rec.

ARMCO, INC. - TECHNICAL INFORMATION CENTER
703 Curtis St.   Phone: (513) 425-2596
Middletown, OH 45043   David C. Heckard, Mgr.

MIDDLETOWN HOSPITAL ASSOCIATION - ADA I. LEONARD MEMORIAL
   LIBRARY
105 McKnight Dr.   Phone: (513) 422-2111
Middletown, OH 45042   Ursula S. Boettcher, Libn.

HOLMES COUNTY LAW LIBRARY
Court House   Phone: (216) 674-5086
Millersburg, OH 44654 Thomas D. Gindlesberger, Law Libn.

KNOX COMMUNITY HOSPITAL - MEDICAL LIBRARY
1330 Coshocton Rd.   Phone: (614) 393-9000
Mount Vernon, OH 43050   Havilah Phelps, Libn.

HENRY COUNTY LAW LIBRARY
Court House
Napoleon, OH 43545   James Donovan, Libn.

HOCKING TECHNICAL COLLEGE - LIBRARY
Rt. 1   Phone: (614) 753-3591
Nelsonville, OH 45764   Margy L. Kramer, Libn.

TUSCARAWAS COUNTY GENEALOGICAL SOCIETY - LIBRARY
Box 141
New Philadelphia, OH 44663   Marjorie Degen, Libn.

TUSCARAWAS COUNTY LAW LIBRARY ASSOCIATION
Court House   Phone: (216) 364-3703
New Philadelphia, OH 44663   Diana L. Tripp, Libn.

DAWES ARBORETUM - LIBRARY
7770 Jacksontown Rd., S.E.   Phone: (614) 323-2355
Newark, OH 43055   Alan D. Cook, Sr. Horticulturist

HEISEY COLLECTORS OF AMERICA, INC. - HCA LIBRARY & ARCHIVES
Sixth & Church Sts.
Box 27   Phone: (614) 345-2932
Newark, OH 43055   Thomas H. Bredehoft, Pres.

LICKING COUNTY LAW LIBRARY ASSOCIATION †
22 1/2 N. Second St.   Phone: (614) 345-6400
Newark, OH 43055   Hon. Virginia Weiss, Libn.

LICKING MEMORIAL HOSPITAL - MEDICAL LIBRARY
1320 W. Main St.   Phone: (614) 344-0331
Newark, OH 43055   Kathleen M. Martin, Lib.Asst.

SAGAMORE HILLS CHILDREN'S PSYCHIATRIC HOSPITAL - STAFF MEDICAL
    LIBRARY
11910 Dunham Rd.   Phone: (614) 467-7955
Northfield, OH 44067   Karen Parsons, Libn.

WESTERN RESERVE PSYCHIATRIC HABILITATION CENTER - STAFF
    LIBRARY
1756 Sagamore Rd.
Box 305   Phone: (216) 467-7131
Northfield, OH 44067   Pearlie McAlpine, Libn.

GILFORD INSTRUMENT LABORATORIES, INC. - TECHNICAL LIBRARY
132 Artino St.   Phone: (216) 774-1041
Oberlin, OH 44074   Marjorie Mulder, Libn.

OBERLIN COLLEGE - CLARENCE WARD ART LIBRARY
Allen Art Bldg.   Phone: (216) 775-8635
Oberlin, OH 44074   Jeffrey Weidman, Art Libn.

OBERLIN COLLEGE - CONSERVATORY OF MUSIC LIBRARY
                                         Phone: (216) 775-8280
Oberlin, OH 44074   John E. Druesedow, Jr., Dir.

OBERLIN COLLEGE - SCIENCE LIBRARY
Kettering Hall   Phone: (216) 775-8310
Oberlin, OH 44074   Alison Ricker, Sci.Libn.

MC GUFFEY (William Holmes) HOUSE AND MUSEUM - LIBRARY
Spring & Oak Sts.   Phone: (513) 529-4917
Oxford, OH 45056   Sterling Cook, Cur.

MIAMI UNIVERSITY - ART AND ARCHITECTURE LIBRARY
Alumni Hall   Phone: (513) 529-3219
Oxford, OH 45056   Joann Olson, Hum.Libn.

MIAMI UNIVERSITY - BRILL SCIENCE LIBRARY
                                         Phone: (513) 529-7527
Oxford, OH 45056   Marian C. Winner, Hd.Sci.Libn.

MIAMI UNIVERSITY - MUSIC LIBRARY
Ctr. for Performing Arts   Phone: (513) 529-2017
Oxford, OH 45056

MIAMI UNIVERSITY - WALTER HAVIGHURST SPECIAL COLLECTIONS
    LIBRARY
King Library   Phone: (513) 529-2537
Oxford, OH 45056   Helen Ball, Cur. of Spec.Coll.

LAKE COUNTY MEMORIAL HOSPITALS - MEDICAL LIBRARIES (East and
    West)
Washington at Liberty   Phone: (216) 354-2400
Painesville, OH 44077   Vicki L. Edick, Health Sci.Libn.

SDS BIOTECH CORPORATION - CORPORATE LIBRARY
Box 348   Phone: (216) 357-3475
Painesville, OH 44077   L. Violet Forgach, Supv., Bus.Info.

KAISER FOUNDATION HOSPITALS - MEDICAL LIBRARY *
12301 Snow Rd.   Phone: (216) 362-2086
Parma, OH 44130   Dianne McCutcheon, Med.Libn.

PENINSULA LIBRARY AND HISTORICAL SOCIETY †
6105 Riverview Rd.   Phone: (216) 657-2291
Peninsula, OH 44264   Edith M. Minns, Libn.

B'NAI JESHURUN TEMPLE ON THE HEIGHTS - JACOBSON LIBRARY
27501 Fairmount Blvd.   Phone: (216) 831-6555
Pepper Pike, OH 44124

GOODYEAR TIRE AND RUBBER COMPANY - GOODYEAR ATOMIC
    CORPORATION - TECHNICAL LIBRARY
Box 628   Phone: (614) 289-2331
Piketon, OH 45661   Robert P. Holland, Supv.

MEIGS COUNTY LAW LIBRARY *
Court House   Phone: (614) 992-7430
Pomeroy, OH 45769   Karen Story, Libn.

PORTSMOUTH BAR AND LAW LIBRARY †
Scioto County Court House, 3rd Fl.   Phone: (614) 353-5111
Portsmouth, OH 45662   Otha Sanderlin, Libn.

PORTSMOUTH RECEIVING HOSPITAL - MEDICAL LIBRARY
25th & Elmwood   Phone: (614) 354-2804
Portsmouth, OH 45662   Jack W. Haffner, Educ.Coord.

OHIO STATE UNIVERSITY - FRANZ THEODORE STONE LABORATORY -
    LIBRARY
Box 119   Phone: (419) 285-2341
Put-In-Bay, OH 43456   Victoria Welborn, Hd.

U.S. NATL. PARK SERVICE - PERRY'S VICTORY & INTERNATIONAL PEACE
    MEMORIAL - LIBRARY
Box 549   Phone: (419) 285-2184
Put-In-Bay, OH 43456   Harry C. Myers, Supt.

PORTAGE COUNTY HISTORICAL SOCIETY, INC. - LIBRARY AND MUSEUM
6549-51 N. Chestnut St.   Phone: (216) 296-3523
Ravenna, OH 44266

GENERAL ELECTRIC COMPANY - LAMP GLASS & COMPONENTS LIBRARY *
24400 Highland Rd.   Phone: (216) 266-3653
Richmond Heights, OH 44143   Jeanne Parker

NORTHEASTERN OHIO UNIVERSITIES COLLEGE OF MEDICINE - BASIC
    MEDICAL SCIENCES LIBRARY
                                         Phone: (216) 325-2511
Rootstown, OH 44272   Karen Brewer, Dir.

BELMONT COUNTY LAW LIBRARY *
Court House   Phone: (614) 695-2121
St. Clairsville, OH 43950   John W. Greenlee, Libn.

JENNINGS LIBRARY
437 Jennings Ave.   Phone: (216) 337-3348
Salem, OH 44460   Dale E. Shaffer, Lib.Cons. & Dir.

ERIE COUNTY LAW LIBRARY
Court House, 1st Fl.   Phone: (419) 626-4823
Sandusky, OH 44870   Robin A. Muratori, Ck.

PROVIDENCE HOSPITAL - SCHOOL OF NURSING MEDIA CENTER
1912 Hayes Ave.   Phone: (419) 625-8450
Sandusky, OH 44870

INSTITUTE FOR CENTRAL EUROPEAN RESEARCH - LIBRARY
2950 Warrensville Ctr. Rd.   Phone: (216) 752-9927
Shaker Heights, OH 44122   W.K. Von Uhlenhorst-Ziechmann, Dir.

SHAKER HEIGHTS CITY SCHOOL DISTRICT - GARVIN LIBRARY
15600 Parkland Dr.   Phone: (216) 921-1400
Shaker Heights, OH 44120   Ellen M. Stepanian, Dir. of Lib. Media

MSC CENTER LIBRARY *
Route 4   Phone: (419) 747-4772
Shelby, OH 44875   Rev. Mark McDonald, M.S.C., Dir.

SHELBY COUNTY LAW LIBRARY *
Courthouse   Phone: (513) 498-4541
Sidney, OH 45365   Rita Miller, Libn.

BENDIX CORPORATION - AUTOMATION GROUP - RESEARCH DIVISION
    LIBRARY
28999 Aurora Rd.   Phone: (216) 432-6144
Solon, OH 44139   Carla S. Newsome, Libn.

CLARK COUNTY HISTORICAL SOCIETY - LIBRARY
Memorial Hall, 300 W. Main St.   Phone: (513) 324-0657
Springfield, OH 45504   Floyd A. Barmann, Dir.

COMMUNITY HOSPITAL OF SPRINGFIELD & CLARK COUNTY - HEALTH
    SCIENCES LIBRARY
2615 E. High St.   Phone: (513) 325-0531
Springfield, OH 45501   Jane Violet, Libn.

MERCY MEDICAL CENTER - HEALTH SCIENCES LIBRARY
1343 Fountain   Phone: (513) 390-5000
Springfield, OH 45501   Marietta Wilson, Libn.

SPRINGFIELD ART CENTER - LIBRARY
107 Cliff Park Rd.   Phone: (513) 325-4673
Springfield, OH 45501   Mary McG. Miller, Chm. of Lib.Comm.

SPRINGFIELD BAR AND LAW LIBRARY ASSOCIATION - LIBRARY †
Clark County Court House, 3rd Fl.   Phone: (513) 428-2478
Springfield, OH 45502   Rita M. Harnish, Libn.

WITTENBERG UNIVERSITY - THOMAS LIBRARY
                                           Phone: (513) 327-7016
Springfield, OH 45501   Betty Beatty, Act.Dir.

BARIUM AND CHEMICALS, INC. - RESEARCH LIBRARY †
County Rd. 44
Box 218   Phone: (614) 282-9776
Steubenville, OH 43952   Eleanor R. Naylor, Libn.

JEFFERSON COUNTY LAW LIBRARY
Courthouse   Phone: (614) 283-4111
Steubenville, OH 43952   C. Kay Firm, Libn.

OHIO VALLEY HOSPITAL - HEALTH SCIENCES LIBRARY
380 Summit Ave.   Phone: (614) 283-7400
Steubenville, OH 43952   Kathie Pasquarella, Med.Libn.

SCM CORPORATION - GLIDDEN COATINGS & RESINS DIVISION/DURKEE
   FOODS DIVISION - TECHNICAL INFORMATION SERVICES
Dwight P. Joyce Research Ctr.
16651 Sprague Rd.   Phone: (216) 826-5260
Strongsville, OH 44136   Ann J. Yancura, Mgr.

TALLMADGE HISTORICAL SOCIETY - LIBRARY & ARCHIVES *
One Tallmadge Circle   Phone: (216) 630-9760
Tallmadge, OH 44278   James B. Hillegas, Pres.

ANTIQUE AND HISTORIC GLASS FOUNDATION - LIBRARY
Box 7413   Phone: (419) 531-5679
Toledo, OH 43615   Carl U. Fauster, Dir.

FARM LABOR ORGANIZING COMMITTEE - LIBRARY
714 1/2 S. St. Clair St.   Phone: (419) 243-3456
Toledo, OH 43609   Ernesto Reza, Coord.

FULLER & HENRY - LIBRARY
12th Fl., Edison Plaza
300 Madison Ave.   Phone: (419) 255-8220
Toledo, OH 43604   Melvia A. Scott, Libn.

LIBBEY-OWENS-FORD COMPANY - CORPORATE LIBRARY †
811 Madison Ave.   Phone: (419) 247-4862
Toledo, OH 43695   Patricia B. Jones, Corp.Libn.

LIBBEY-OWENS-FORD COMPANY - TECHNICAL CENTER LIBRARY
1701 E. Broadway   Phone: (419) 247-4367
Toledo, OH 43605   Jeanne M. Keogh, Tech.Libn.

MARSHALL & MELHORN LAW FIRM - LIBRARY
Four Sea Gate, Suite 800   Phone: (419) 243-4200
Toledo, OH 43604   Polly Jo Snider, Libn.

MEDICAL COLLEGE OF OHIO AT TOLEDO - RAYMON H. MULFORD LIBRARY
3000 Arlington Ave.   Phone: (419) 381-4223
Toledo, OH 43614   R.M. Watterson, Libn.

MERCY HOSPITAL - EDWARD L. BURNS HEALTH SCIENCES LIBRARY
2200 Jefferson Ave.   Phone: (419) 259-1327
Toledo, OH 43624   Thomas R. Sink, Dir. of Lib.Serv.

MIDLAND-ROSS CORPORATION - ENERGY TECHNOLOGY DIVISION -
   LIBRARY
900 N. Westwood Ave.
Box 985   Phone: (419) 537-6449
Toledo, OH 43696   Beverly Zielinski, Libn.

OWENS-CORNING FIBERGLAS CORPORATION - LAW DEPARTMENT
   LIBRARY
Fiberglas Tower 26   Phone: (419) 248-7787
Toledo, OH 43659   Sandra Sanderson, Law Libn.

OWENS-ILLINOIS - INFORMATION RESEARCH DEPARTMENT
One Seagate   Phone: (419) 247-1788
Toledo, OH 43666   Ilga I. Ozolins, Coord.

PARKVIEW OSTEOPATHIC HOSPITAL - LIBRARY *
1920 Parkwood Ave.   Phone: (419) 242-8471
Toledo, OH 43624   Donna McLain, Lib.Cons.

RIVERSIDE HOSPITAL - SARAH AND JULIUS STEINBERG MEMORIAL
   LIBRARY
1600 N. Superior St.   Phone: (419) 729-6712
Toledo, OH 43604   Kathryn Maluchnik, Libn.

ST. VINCENT MEDICAL CENTER - HEALTH SCIENCE LIBRARY
2213 Cherry St.   Phone: (419) 259-4324
Toledo, OH 43608   Jack W. Shaffer, Dir.

SAMBORN, STEKETEE, OTIS & EVANS, INC. - RESOURCE & INFORMATION
   CENTER
1001 Madison Ave.   Phone: (419) 255-3830
Toledo, OH 43624   Mary Jo Coates

SHUMAKER, LOOP & KENDRICK - LIBRARY
1000 Jackson   Phone: (419) 241-4201
Toledo, OH 43624   Martha Esbin, Law Libn.

TELEDYNE CAE CORPORATION - ENGINEERING LIBRARY
1330 Laskey Rd.   Phone: (419) 470-3027
Toledo, OH 43612   Marlene S. Dowdell, Dept.Hd., Data Mgt.

TOLEDO BLADE - LIBRARY
541 Superior St.   Phone: (419) 245-6188
Toledo, OH 43660   Mary E. Reddington, Hd.Libn.

TOLEDO EDISON COMPANY - LIBRARY
Edison Plaza   Phone: (419) 259-5279
Toledo, OH 43652   Catherine Witker, Libn.Techn.

TOLEDO HOSPITAL - LIBRARY
2142 N. Cove Blvd.   Phone: (419) 471-5437
Toledo, OH 43606   Linda Fankhauser Tillman, Dir.

TOLEDO LAW ASSOCIATION LIBRARY
Lucas County Court House   Phone: (419) 245-4747
Toledo, OH 43624   Brenda Woodruff, Libn./Dir.

TOLEDO-LUCAS COUNTY PLAN COMMISSIONS - LIBRARY
One Government Ctr., Suite 1620
Jackson Street
Toledo, OH 43604

TOLEDO-LUCAS COUNTY PUBLIC LIBRARY - BUSINESS DEPARTMENT
325 Michigan St.   Phone: (419) 255-7055
Toledo, OH 43624   Margaret Danziger, Dept.Hd.

TOLEDO-LUCAS COUNTY PUBLIC LIBRARY - FINE ARTS AND AUDIO
   SERVICE DEPARTMENT
325 Michigan St.   Phone: (419) 255-7055
Toledo, OH 43624   Paula J. Baker, Dept.Hd.

TOLEDO-LUCAS COUNTY PUBLIC LIBRARY - HISTORY-TRAVEL-BIOGRAPHY
   DEPARTMENT
325 Michigan St.   Phone: (419) 255-7055
Toledo, OH 43624   Donald C. Barnette, Jr., Dept.Hd.

TOLEDO-LUCAS COUNTY PUBLIC LIBRARY - LITERATURE/FICTION
   DEPARTMENT
325 Michigan St.   Phone: (419) 255-7055
Toledo, OH 43624   William S. Granger, Dept.Hd.

TOLEDO-LUCAS COUNTY PUBLIC LIBRARY - LOCAL HISTORY & GENEALOGY
   DEPARTMENT
325 Michigan St.   Phone: (419) 255-7055
Toledo, OH 43624   James Marshall, Dept.Hd.

TOLEDO-LUCAS COUNTY PUBLIC LIBRARY - SCIENCE AND TECHNOLOGY
  DEPARTMENT
325 Michigan St.   Phone: (419) 255-7055
Toledo, OH 43624   Mary B. Hubbard, Dept.Hd.

TOLEDO-LUCAS COUNTY PUBLIC LIBRARY - SOCIAL SCIENCE
  DEPARTMENT
325 Michigan St.   Phone: (419) 255-7055
Toledo, OH 43624   Marcia Learned Au, Dept.Hd.

TOLEDO MUSEUM OF ART - ART REFERENCE LIBRARY †
Box 1013   Phone: (419) 255-8000
Toledo, OH 43697   Anne O. Reese, Hd.Libn.

UNIVERSITY OF TOLEDO - COLLEGE OF LAW LIBRARY
2801 W. Bancroft St.   Phone: (419) 537-2733
Toledo, OH 43606   Janet L. Wallin, Law Libn.

UNIVERSITY OF TOLEDO - WARD M. CANADAY CENTER
William S. Carlson Library   Phone: (419) 537-2443
Toledo, OH 43606   David J. Martz, Jr., Dir.

HOBART BROTHERS TECHNICAL CENTER - JOHN H. BLANKENBUEHLER
  MEMORIAL LIBRARY
Trade Square E.   Phone: (513) 339-6011
Troy, OH 45373   Martha A. Baker, Libn.

MIAMI COUNTY LAW LIBRARY
201 W. Main St.   Phone: (513) 335-8341
Troy, OH 45373   Carolyn Bolin, Libn.

WYANDOT COUNTY HISTORICAL SOCIETY - WYANDOT MUSEUM -
  LIBRARY
130 S. 7th St.   Phone: (419) 294-3857
Upper Sandusky, OH 43351   Garnett Hudson, Cur.

CHAMPAIGN COUNTY LAW LIBRARY
County Court House   Phone: (513) 652-2222
Urbana, OH 43078   Judy K. Burnett, Libn.

URBANA COLLEGE - SWEDENBORG MEMORIAL LIBRARY - SPECIAL
  COLLECTIONS
College Way   Phone: (513) 652-1301
Urbana, OH 43078   Connie Salyers, Libn.

VAN WERT COUNTY LAW LIBRARY
Court of Common Pleas, 3rd Fl.   Phone: (419) 238-6935
Van Wert, OH 45891   Richard Atwood, Libn.

GREAT LAKES HISTORICAL SOCIETY - CLARENCE METCALF RESEARCH
  LIBRARY
480 Main St.   Phone: (216) 967-3467
Vermilion, OH 44089   Dr. Robert M. Hosler

UNITED CHURCH OF CHRIST (Evangelical and Reformed) - CHURCH LIBRARY
Grand & Ohio Sts.   Phone: (216) 967-3559
Vermilion, OH 44089   Doris M. Feiszli, Lib.Chm.

AUGLAIZE COUNTY LAW LIBRARY *
Court House   Phone: (419) 738-2961
Wapakoneta, OH 45895   Ron Miller, Att.

TRUMBULL MEMORIAL HOSPITAL - SCHOOL OF NURSING LIBRARY
1350 East Market St.   Phone: (216) 841-9371
Warren, OH 44484   Dorothy Stambaugh, Libn.

TRUMBULL MEMORIAL HOSPITAL - WEAN MEDICAL LIBRARY
1350 E. Market St.   Phone: (216) 841-9379
Warren, OH 44482   Linda Bundy, Med.Libn.

WARREN GENERAL HOSPITAL - MEDICAL STAFF LIBRARY
667 Eastland Ave., S.E.   Phone: (216) 399-7541
Warren, OH 44484   Nancy L. Bindas, Med.Libn.

FAYETTE COUNTY LAW LIBRARY
Fayette County Court House
Washington Court House, OH 43160   Barbara A. Zoodsma, Asst.Libn.

FULTON COUNTY LAW LIBRARY ASSOCIATION - LAW LIBRARY
Court House   Phone: (419) 335-8863
Wauseon, OH 43567   Laura A. N. Nieber, Libn.

ADAMS COUNTY LAW LIBRARY
Courthouse, Rm. 207   Phone: (513) 544-5155
West Union, OH 45693   Roy E. Gabbert, Libn.

MERRILL (Charles E.) PUBLISHING COMPANY - LIBRARY
936 Eastwind Dr.   Phone: (614) 890-1111
Westerville, OH 43081

CHURCH OF JESUS CHRIST OF LATTER-DAY SAINTS - CLEVELAND, OHIO
  STAKE BRANCH GENEALOGICAL LIBRARY
25000 Westwood Rd.   Phone: (216) 777-1518
Westlake, OH 44145   J. Ashbury, Supv.

NORDSON CORPORATION WORLD HEADQUARTERS - TECHNICAL
  INFORMATION DEPARTMENT
28601 Clemens Rd.   Phone: (216) 892-1580
Westlake, OH 44145   Rosemary Davidson, Corp.Libn./Dept.Hd.

ST. JOHN AND WEST SHORE HOSPITAL - MEDIA CENTER
29000 Center Ridge Rd.   Phone: (216) 835-6020
Westlake, OH 44145   Jung Gallant, Dir.

UNION CARBIDE CORPORATION - BATTERY PRODUCTS DIVISION -
  TECHNICAL INFORMATION CENTER
25225 Detroit Rd.   Phone: (216) 835-7631
Westlake, OH 44145   Claire Marie Langkau, Mgr., Tech.Info.

LUBRIZOL CORPORATION - CHEMICAL LIBRARY
29400 Lakeland Blvd.   Phone: (216) 943-4200
Wickliffe, OH 44092   Dr. Horton Dunn, Jr., Supv., Info.Serv.

TELSHE YESHIVA - RABBI A.N. SCHWARTZ LIBRARY
28400 Euclid Ave.   Phone: (216) 943-5300
Wickliffe, OH 44092   Rabbi Binyomin Grunwald, Hd.Libn.

PAYNE THEOLOGICAL SEMINARY - R.C. RANSOM MEMORIAL LIBRARY †
Wilberforce-Clifton Rd.   Phone: (513) 376-2946
Wilberforce, OH 45384   Barbara L. Tyiska, Hd.Libn.

WILBERFORCE UNIVERSITY - REMBERT-STOKES LEARNING CENTER -
  ARCHIVES AND SPECIAL COLLECTIONS
                                              Phone: (513) 376-2911
Wilberforce, OH 45384   Jean Mulhern, Chf.Libn.

SCHOOL OF FINE ARTS - LIBRARY
38660 Mentor Ave.   Phone: (216) 951-7500
Willoughby, OH 44094   Edith Reed, Act.Libn.

WILMINGTON COLLEGE - CURRICULUM MATERIALS CENTER *
                                              Phone: (513) 382-6661
Wilmington, OH 45177   George Winsor, Prof. of Educ.

BELL & HOWELL COMPANY - MICRO PHOTO DIVISION - MICROFORMS
  ARCHIVE †
Old Mansfield Rd.   Phone: (216) 264-6666
Wooster, OH 44691

LATHROP (Norman) ENTERPRISES - LIBRARY
2342 Star Dr.
Box 198   Phone: (216) 262-5587
Wooster, OH 44691   Norman Lathrop, Mgr.

OHIO (State) AGRICULTURAL RESEARCH AND DEVELOPMENT CENTER -
  LIBRARY
                                              Phone: (216) 263-3773
Wooster, OH 44691   Constance J. Britton, Libn.

OHIO STATE UNIVERSITY - AGRICULTURAL TECHNICAL INSTITUTE -
  LIBRARY
                                              Phone: (216) 264-3911
Wooster, OH 44691   Phoebe F. Phillips, Hd.Libn.

WAYNE COUNTY LAW LIBRARY ASSOCIATION
Wayne County Courthouse   Phone: (216) 262-5561
Wooster, OH 44691   Betty K. Schuler, Libn.

AVIATION SAFETY INSTITUTE - ASI TECHNICAL LABS. - LIBRARY
893 High St., Suite J
Box 304
Worthington, OH 43085   Phone: (614) 885-4242
                                         John B. Galipault, Pres.

NATIONAL WATER WELL ASSOCIATION - NATIONAL GROUND WATER
   INFORMATION CENTER
500 W. Wilson Bridge Rd.   Phone: (614) 846-9355
Worthington, OH 43085   Valerie J. Orr, Info.Dir.

OHIO STATE UNIVERSITY - CENTER FOR HUMAN RESOURCE RESEARCH -
   LIBRARY
5701 N. High St.   Phone: (614) 422-7337
Worthington, OH 43085   Julian Larson, Libn.

WORTHINGTON HISTORICAL SOCIETY - LIBRARY
50 W. New England Ave.   Phone: (614) 885-1247
Worthington, OH 43085   Lillian Skeele, Libn.

U.S. AIR FORCE BASE - WRIGHT-PATTERSON GENERAL LIBRARY *
FL 2300, Kittyhawk Ctr.   Phone: (513) 257-4815
Wright-Patterson AFB, OH 45433   Theresa J. Knasiak, Adm.Libn.

U.S. AIR FORCE HOSPITAL MEDICAL CENTER - MEDICAL LIBRARY (OH-
   Wright-Patterson AFB)
SGEL/Bldg. 830A   Phone: (513) 257-4506
Wright-Patterson AFB, OH 45433   Cheryl Harris, Biomed.Libn.

U.S. AIR FORCE INSTITUTE OF TECHNOLOGY - LIBRARY
Bldg. 640, Area B   Phone: (513) 255-5894
Wright-Patterson AFB, OH 45433   Virginia E. Eckel, Dir.

U.S. AIR FORCE MUSEUM - RESEARCH DIVISION LIBRARY
Bldg. 489, Area B   Phone: (513) 255-3284
Wright-Patterson AFB, OH 45433   Charles G. Worman, Chf., Res.Div.

U.S. AIR FORCE - WRIGHT AERONAUTICAL LABORATORIES - AEROSPACE
   STRUCTURES INFORMATION & ANALYSIS CENTER
AFWAL/FIBRA/ASIAC   Phone: (513) 255-6688
Wright-Patterson AFB, OH 45433   Gordon R. Negaard, Dir.

GREENE COUNTY DISTRICT LIBRARY - GREENE COUNTY ROOM
76 E. Market St.
Box 520   Phone: (513) 376-2995
Xenia, OH 45385   Julie M. Overton, Coord., Local Hist.

GREENE COUNTY LAW LIBRARY †
Court House   Phone: (513) 376-5115
Xenia, OH 45385   Jill LeSourd, Libn.

BATTELLE-COLUMBUS LABORATORIES - CHARLES F. KETTERING
   LABORATORY - LIBRARY
150 E. South College St.   Phone: (513) 767-7271
Yellow Springs, OH 45387   Janice Williams, Libn.

COMMUNITY SERVICE, INC. - LIBRARY
114 E. Whiteman St.   Phone: (513) 767-2161
Yellow Springs, OH 45387   Jane Morgan, Exec.Dir.

FELLOWSHIP OF RELIGIOUS HUMANISTS - LIBRARY
Box 278
Yellow Springs, OH 45387   Edwin H. Wilson, Hist.

GLEN HELEN ASSOCIATION - LIBRARY
Glen Helen Bldg.
405 Corry St.   Phone: (513) 767-7375
Yellow Springs, OH 45387   Mrs. George Asakawa, Libn.

AMERICAN AMBULANCE ASSOCIATION - INFORMATION CENTER
1919 Market St.   Phone: (216) 744-4161
Youngstown, OH 44507   Daniel Becker

BUTLER INSTITUTE OF AMERICAN ART - LIBRARY
524 Wick Ave.
Youngstown, OH 44502

MAHONING LAW LIBRARY
Court House
120 Market St.   Phone: (216) 747-2000
Youngstown, OH 44503   Lucille G. DeMoss, Law Libn.

PUBLIC LIBRARY OF YOUNGSTOWN AND MAHONING COUNTY - SCIENCE
   AND INDUSTRY COLLECTION
305 Wick Ave.   Phone: (216) 744-8636
Youngstown, OH 44503   Orin D. Cole, Hd.

ST. ELIZABETH HOSPITAL MEDICAL CENTER - MEDICAL LIBRARY †
1044 Belmont Ave.   Phone: (216) 746-7231
Youngstown, OH 44501   Barbara G. Rosenthal, Med.Libn.

ST. ELIZABETH HOSPITAL MEDICAL CENTER SCHOOL OF NURSING -
   LIBRARY
1044 Belmont Ave.   Phone: (216) 746-7211
Youngstown, OH 44501   Doris L. Crawford, Libn.

WOODSIDE RECEIVING HOSPITAL - STAFF RESOURCE LIBRARY/
   PATIENTS' LIBRARY
800 E. Indianola Ave.   Phone: (216) 788-8712
Youngstown, OH 44502   Carol L. Homrighausen, Libn.

YOUNGSTOWN HOSPITAL ASSOCIATION - HEALTH SCIENCES LIBRARY
345 Oak Hill Ave.   Phone: (216) 747-0751
Youngstown, OH 44501   Christine S. Roeder, Supv., Health Sci.Lib.

BETHESDA HOSPITAL - LIBRARY AND EDUCATION SERVICES
2951 Maple Ave.   Phone: (614) 454-4220
Zanesville, OH 43701   Patty Y. Hartley, Dir.

MUSKINGUM LAW LIBRARY
Court House   Phone: (614) 452-9143
Zanesville, OH 43701   Helen Porter, Libn.

ZANESVILLE ART CENTER - LIBRARY
620 Military Rd.   Phone: (614) 452-0741
Zanesville, OH 43701   Mrs. Joseph Howell, Libn.

OKLAHOMA

EAST CENTRAL OKLAHOMA STATE UNIVERSITY - OKLAHOMA
   ENVIRONMENTAL INFORMATION/MEDIA CENTER
                                         Phone: (405) 332-8000
Ada, OK 74820   Cynthia M. Coulter, Dir.

ENVIRONMENTAL PROTECTION AGENCY - ROBERT S. KERR
   ENVIRONMENTAL RESEARCH CENTER - LIBRARY
Box 1198   Phone: (405) 332-8800
Ada, OK 74820   Ms. LoRene Fuller, Libn.

U.S. AIR FORCE BASE - ALTUS BASE LIBRARY †
FL 4419   Phone: (405) 482-8670
Altus AFB, OK 73523   A. Lucille Lowrie, Libn.

NORTHWESTERN OKLAHOMA STATE UNIVERSITY - LIBRARY
                                         Phone: (405) 327-1700
Alva, OK 73717   Ray D. Lau, Lib.Dir.

SAMUEL ROBERTS NOBLE FOUNDATION, INC. - BIOMEDICAL DIVISION
   LIBRARY
2510 Hwy. 70 East
Box 2180   Phone: (405) 223-5810
Ardmore, OK 73402   Loretta Cook, Libn.

BARTLESVILLE PUBLIC LIBRARY - HISTORY ROOM
6th & Johnstone   Phone: (918) 336-2133
Bartlesville, OK 74003   Susan C. Box, Hist.Rm.Cur.

NATIONAL INSTITUTE FOR PETROLEUM & ENERGY RESEARCH (NIPER) -
   LIBRARY
Box 2128   Phone: (918) 337-4371
Bartlesville, OK 74005   Josh Stroman, Hd.Libn.

PHILLIPS (Frank) FOUNDATION, INC. - WOOLAROC MUSEUM - LIBRARY
Rte. 3   Phone: (918) 336-0307
Bartlesville, OK 74003   Linda Stone, Cur. of Art

PHILLIPS PETROLEUM COMPANY - ENGINEERING LIBRARY
8 A3 Phillips Bldg.   Phone: (918) 661-5911
Bartlesville, OK 74004   Norma Benefiel, Off.Serv.Supv.

PHILLIPS PETROLEUM COMPANY - EXPLORATION & PRODUCTION GROUP - LIBRARY
439 Frank Phillips Bldg.
Bartlesville, OK 74004
Phone: (918) 661-5514
Annabeth Robin, Mgr.

PHILLIPS PETROLEUM COMPANY - GAS & GAS LIQUIDS GROUP - LIBRARY
3 D4 Home Savings & Loan Bldg.
Bartlesville, OK 74004
Phone: (918) 661-5803
Ollie Mae Burdett, Rec.Mgt.Supv.

PHILLIPS PETROLEUM COMPANY - RESEARCH & DEVELOPMENT DEPARTMENT - TECHNICAL INFORMATION BRANCH
Phillips Research Ctr.
Bartlesville, OK 74004
Phone: (918) 661-0535
David R. Weiser, Mgr.

DAVIS (J.M.) GUN MUSEUM - RESEARCH LIBRARY
333 N. Lynn Riggs Blvd.
Box 966
Claremore, OK 74017
Phone: (918) 341-5707
Sue E. Cook, Adm.Off.

WILL ROGERS LIBRARY †
121 N. Weenonah
Claremore, OK 74017
Phone: (918) 341-1564
Geraldine Warmack, Libn.

ST. FRANCIS OF THE WOODS LTD. - EASTERN ORTHODOX CATHOLIC CHURCH IN AMERICA - LIBRARY
Rt. 1
Coyle, OK 73027
Phone: (405) 466-3774
Kay Adair, Libn.

KERR INDUSTRIAL APPLICATIONS CENTER
Southeastern Oklahoma State University
Durant, OK 74701
Phone: (405) 924-6822
Dr. Tom J. McRorey, Dir.

CENTRAL STATE UNIVERSITY - LIBRARY - MICROFORMS RESEARCH CENTER
100 N. University Dr.
Edmond, OK 73034
Phone: (405) 341-2980
Dr. John L. Lolley, Dir., Lib.Serv.

CANADIAN COUNTY HISTORICAL MUSEUM - LIBRARY
Wade & Grand Sts.
El Reno, OK 73036
Phone: (405) 232-5121
Mrs. Frank C. Ball, Cur.

PHILLIPS UNIVERSITY - GRADUATE SEMINARY LIBRARY
University Sta., Box 2218
Enid, OK 73701
Phone: (405) 237-4433
John L. Sayre, Dir.

ST. MARY'S HOSPITAL - MEDICAL LIBRARY
305 S. Fifth St.
Box 232
Enid, OK 73701
Phone: (405) 233-6100
Jean McDaniel, Med.Libn.

U.S. ARMY FIELD ARTILLERY SCHOOL - MORRIS SWETT TECHNICAL LIBRARY
Snow Hall, Rm. 16
Ft. Sill, OK 73503
Phone: (405) 351-4525
Lester L. Miller, Jr., Supv.Libn.

WESTERN STATE HOSPITAL - MEDICAL LIBRARY
Fort Supply, OK 73841
Phone: (405) 766-2311
Vi Thomas, Lib.Techn.

PANHANDLE STATE UNIVERSITY - NO MAN'S LAND HISTORICAL MUSEUM - LIBRARY
Sewel St.
Box 278
Goodwell, OK 73939
Phone: (405) 349-2670
Dr. Harold S. Kachel, Cur.

UNIVERSITY OF OKLAHOMA - BIOLOGICAL STATION LIBRARY
Star Route B
Kingston, OK 73439
Loren G. Hill, Dir.

LANGSTON UNIVERSITY - MELVIN B. TOLSON BLACK HERITAGE CENTER †
2nd Fl., Page Hall Annex
Langston, OK 73050
Phone: (405) 466-2231
Rosalind Savage, Cur.

MUSEUM OF THE GREAT PLAINS - GREAT PLAINS RESEARCH LIBRARY AND ARCHIVES
601 Ferris
Box 68
Lawton, OK 73502
Phone: (405) 353-5675
Steve Wilson, Dir.

OKLAHOMA GEOLOGICAL SURVEY - OKLAHOMA GEOPHYSICAL OBSERVATORY LIBRARY
Box 8
Leonard, OK 74043-0008
Phone: (918) 366-4152
Charles J. Mankin, Dir.

BACONE COLLEGE - LIBRARY - SPECIAL COLLECTIONS
East Shawnee
Muskogee, OK 74403
Phone: (918) 683-4581
Frances A. Donelson, Libn.

OKLAHOMA SCHOOL FOR THE BLIND - PARKVIEW LIBRARY
3300 Gibson St.
Box 309
Muskogee, OK 74402-0309
Phone: (918) 682-6641
Marjorie Moske, Libn.

U.S. VETERANS ADMINISTRATION (OK-Muskogee) - MEDICAL CENTER LIBRARY
1101 Honor Height Dr.
Muskogee, OK 74401
Phone: (918) 683-3261
Larry L. Shea, Chf., Lib.Serv.

CENTRAL STATE HOSPITAL - PROFESSIONAL LIBRARY *
Box 151
Norman, OK 73069
Phone: (405) 321-4880
Jane Marie Hamilton, Med.Libn.

NORMAN MUNICIPAL HOSPITAL - HEALTH SCIENCE LIBRARY
901 N. Porter
Box 1308
Norman, OK 73070
Phone: (405) 321-1700
Michelyn McKnight, Libn.

U.S. POSTAL SERVICE - TRAINING & DEVELOPMENT INSTITUTE - TECHNICAL TRAINING CENTER LIBRARY
Box 1400
Norman, OK 73070-7810
Phone: (405) 366-2121

UNIVERSITY OF OKLAHOMA - ART LIBRARY †
Jacobson Hall, Rm. 203
Norman, OK 73019
Phone: (405) 325-2841
Donald E. Koozer, Supv.

UNIVERSITY OF OKLAHOMA - CENTER FOR ECONOMIC AND MANAGEMENT RESEARCH *
307 W. Brooks St., Rm. 4
Norman, OK 73019
Phone: (405) 325-2931

UNIVERSITY OF OKLAHOMA - CHEMISTRY-MATHEMATICS LIBRARY
Physical Sciences Center, 207
Norman, OK 73019
Phone: (405) 325-5628
Jeanne G. Howard, Libn.

UNIVERSITY OF OKLAHOMA - ENGINEERING LIBRARY
Norman, OK 73019
Phone: (405) 325-2941
Jean Poland, Libn.

UNIVERSITY OF OKLAHOMA - GEOLOGY LIBRARY
830 Van Vleet Oval, Rm. 103
Norman, OK 73019
Phone: (405) 325-6451
Claren M. Kidd, Libn.

UNIVERSITY OF OKLAHOMA - HARRY W. BASS COLLECTION IN BUSINESS HISTORY
401 W. Brooks
Norman, OK 73019
Phone: (405) 325-3941
Dr. Daniel A. Wren, Cur.

UNIVERSITY OF OKLAHOMA - HISTORY OF SCIENCE COLLECTIONS
401 W. Brooks, Rm. 339
Norman, OK 73019
Phone: (405) 325-2741
Duane H.D. Roller, Cur.

UNIVERSITY OF OKLAHOMA - LAW LIBRARY
300 Timberdell Rd.
Norman, OK 73019
Phone: (405) 325-4311
Laura N. Gasaway, Dir.

UNIVERSITY OF OKLAHOMA - LIMITED ACCESS COLLECTION
401 W. Brooks, Rm. 440
Norman, OK 73019
Phone: (405) 325-2048
Duane H.D. Roller, Cur.

UNIVERSITY OF OKLAHOMA - MUSIC LIBRARY
Norman, OK 73019
Phone: (405) 325-4243
Jan Seifert, Fine Arts Libn.

UNIVERSITY OF OKLAHOMA - PHYSICS-ASTRONOMY LIBRARY
219 Neilsen Hall
Norman, OK 73019
Phone: (405) 325-3961
Jeanne Howard, Libn.

UNIVERSITY OF OKLAHOMA - SCHOOL OF ARCHITECTURE LIBRARY
Phone: (405) 325-5521
Norman, OK 73019   Ilse Davis, Lib.Techn.

UNIVERSITY OF OKLAHOMA - SCIENCE AND PUBLIC POLICY PROGRAM -
LIBRARY
601 Elm Ave., Rm. 431   Phone: (405) 325-2554
Norman, OK 73019   Emily T. Terrell, Libn.

UNIVERSITY OF OKLAHOMA - WESTERN HISTORY COLLECTIONS
630 Parrington Oval, Rm. 452   Phone: (405) 325-3641
Norman, OK 73019   John S. Ezell, Cur.

UNIVERSITY OF OKLAHOMA - WESTERN HISTORY COLLECTIONS -
LIBRARY DIVISION
Monnet Hall, Rm. 300
630 Parrington Oval   Phone: (405) 325-3641
Norman, OK 73019   John S. Ezell, Cur.

AMATEUR SOFTBALL ASSOCIATION - ASA RESEARCH CENTER AND
LIBRARY
2801 N.E. 50th St.   Phone: (405) 424-5266
Oklahoma City, OK 73111   Bill Plummer, III, Commun.Dir.

ANTA CORPORATION - LIBRARY
101 N. Robinson, Suite 1400   Phone: (405) 272-9321
Oklahoma City, OK 73102   Virginia Milam, Res.Asst.

BAPTIST MEDICAL CENTER - WANN LANGSTON MEMORIAL LIBRARY
3300 Northwest Expy.   Phone: (405) 949-3766
Oklahoma City, OK 73112   Cheryl Suttles, Dir., Med.Lib.

BENHAM GROUP - INFORMATION RESOURCE CENTER
9400 N. Broadway
Box 20400   Phone: (405) 478-5353
Oklahoma City, OK 73156   Nevine Butcher, Mgr.

HTB, INC. - TECHNICAL INFORMATION CENTER
Box 1845   Phone: (405) 525-7451
Oklahoma City, OK 73101   Retha Robertson, Libn.

INTERSTATE OIL AND GAS COMPACT COMMISSION - LIBRARY
900 N.E. 23rd St.
Box 53127   Phone: (405) 525-3556
Oklahoma City, OK 73152   W. Timothy Dowd, Exec.Dir.

KERR-MC GEE CORPORATION - MC GEE LIBRARY
Box 25861   Phone: (405) 270-3358
Oklahoma City, OK 73125   Tom W. Harrison, Mgr.

MERCY HEALTH CENTER - MEDICAL LIBRARY
4300 W. Memorial Rd.   Phone: (405) 755-1515
Oklahoma City, OK 73118   Sr. Mary Eileen Durnell, Hd.Libn.

NATIONAL COWBOY HALL OF FAME & WESTERN HERITAGE CENTER -
RESEARCH LIBRARY OF WESTERN AMERICANA
1700 N.E. 63rd St.   Phone: (405) 478-2250
Oklahoma City, OK 73111   Mr. A.J. Tytgat, Educ.Dir.

NINETY-NINES, INC. - LIBRARY
Will Rogers World Airport
Box 59965   Phone: (405) 685-7969
Oklahoma City, OK 73159   Dorothy Niekamp, Libn.

OKLAHOMA ART CENTER - LIBRARY
3113 Pershing Blvd.   Phone: (405) 946-4477
Oklahoma City, OK 73107   Michael Sanden, Dir.

OKLAHOMA CITY METROPOLITAN LIBRARY SYSTEM - BUSINESS-SCIENCE
SECTION *
131 Dean A. McGee Ave.   Phone: (405) 235-0571
Oklahoma City, OK 73102   Elsie Bell, Chf., Main Lib.

OKLAHOMA CITY UNIVERSITY - LAW LIBRARY
Phone: (405) 521-5271
Oklahoma City, OK 73106   William J. Beintema, Law Libn.

OKLAHOMA CORPORATION COMMISSION - ENERGY CONSERVATION
SERVICES DIVISION - TECHNICAL INFORMATION CENTER
4400 N. Lincoln Blvd., Suite 251   Phone: (405) 521-3941
Oklahoma City, OK 73105   Steven Boggs, Prog.Mgr.

OKLAHOMA COUNTY LAW LIBRARY
County Courthouse, Rm. 247   Phone: (405) 236-2727
Oklahoma City, OK 73102   Betty A. Skaggs, Libn.

OKLAHOMA GAS AND ELECTRIC COMPANY - LIBRARY
Box 321   Phone: (405) 272-3191
Oklahoma City, OK 73102   Ms. Pat Tucker, Libn.

OKLAHOMA HISTORICAL SOCIETY - ARCHIVES AND MANUSCRIPT
DIVISION
Historical Bldg.   Phone: (405) 521-2491
Oklahoma City, OK 73105   Mary Lee Ervin Boyle, Sr.Archv.

OKLAHOMA HISTORICAL SOCIETY - DIVISION OF LIBRARY RESOURCES
Historical Bldg.   Phone: (405) 521-2491
Oklahoma City, OK 73105   Andrea Cantrell Clark, Dir., Lib.Rsrcs.

OKLAHOMA REGIONAL LIBRARY FOR THE BLIND AND PHYSICALLY
HANDICAPPED
1108 N.E. 36th St.   Phone: (405) 521-3514
Oklahoma City, OK 73111   Bill McIlvain, Adm.Libn.

OKLAHOMA STATE DEPARTMENT OF HEALTH - INFORMATION & REFERRAL
HEALTHLINE †
N.E. 10th & Stonewall
Box 53551   Phone: (405) 271-4725
Oklahoma City, OK 73152   Dorothy Hall, Dir.

OKLAHOMA STATE DEPARTMENT OF LIBRARIES
200 N.E. 18th St.   Phone: (405) 521-2502
Oklahoma City, OK 73105   Robert L. Clark, Jr., Dir.

OKLAHOMA STATE UNIVERSITY - OKLAHOMA CITY BRANCH - TECHNICAL
INSTITUTE LIBRARY
900 N. Portland   Phone: (405) 947-4421
Oklahoma City, OK 73107   Annette Duffy, Hd.Libn.

OKLAHOMA WATER RESOURCES BOARD - LIBRARY
1000 N.E. 10th, 12th Fl.
Box 53585   Phone: (405) 271-2555
Oklahoma City, OK 73152   Susan E. Lutz, Libn.

PRESBYTERIAN HOSPITAL - MEDICAL LIBRARY
N.E. 13th and Lincoln Blvd.   Phone: (405) 271-4266
Oklahoma City, OK 73104   Dorothy Williams, Lib.Dir.

RAINBOW FLEET, INC. - LIBRARY
3016 Paseo   Phone: (405) 521-1426
Oklahoma City, OK 73103   Susan Moore Myers, Exec.Dir.

ST. ANTHONY HOSPITAL - O'DONOGHUE MEDICAL LIBRARY
1000 N. Lee St.   Phone: (405) 272-6284
Oklahoma City, OK 73102   Robert J. Lefkowitz, Dir.

ST. FRANCIS CENTER FOR CHRISTIAN RENEWAL - ECUMENICAL LIBRARY
Box 32180
Oklahoma City, OK 73123

U.S. COURT OF APPEALS, 10TH CIRCUIT - OKLAHOMA CITY GENERAL
LIBRARY
200 N.W. 4th St.   Phone: (405) 232-7441
Oklahoma City, OK 73102   Sharon Ware, Sec.

U.S. FEDERAL AVIATION ADMINISTRATION - AERONAUTICAL CENTER
LIBRARY, AAC-64D
6500 S. MacArthur
Box 25082   Phone: (405) 686-4709
Oklahoma City, OK 73125   Virginia C. Hughes, Libn.

U.S. VETERANS ADMINISTRATION (OK-Oklahoma City) - MEDICAL CENTER
LIBRARY
921 N.E. 13th St.   Phone: (405) 272-9876
Oklahoma City, OK 73104   Verlean Delaney, Chf.Libn.

UNIVERSITY OF OKLAHOMA - HEALTH SCIENCES CENTER - DEAN A. MC
  GEE EYE INSTITUTE - LIBRARY
Department of Ophthalmology
608 Stanton L. Young Blvd.   Phone: (405) 271-6085
Oklahoma City, OK 73104   Sheri Taylor, Libn.

UNIVERSITY OF OKLAHOMA - HEALTH SCIENCES CENTER - DEPARTMENT
  OF SURGERY LIBRARY
Oklahoma Memorial Hospital
Box 26307   Phone: (405) 271-5506
Oklahoma City, OK 73126   Linda R. O'Rourke, Med.Libn.

UNIVERSITY OF OKLAHOMA - HEALTH SCIENCES CENTER LIBRARY
1000 Stanton L. Young Blvd.
Box 26901   Phone: (405) 271-2285
Oklahoma City, OK 73190   C.M. Thompson, Dir.

WESTMINSTER PRESBYTERIAN CHURCH - LIBRARY
4400 N. Shartel   Phone: (405) 524-2204
Oklahoma City, OK 73118   J. Richard Hershberger, Assoc. Minister

WILSON FOODS, INC. - RESEARCH LIBRARY †
4545 Lincoln Blvd.   Phone: (405) 525-4781
Oklahoma City, OK 73105   Joy Jones

CREEK INDIAN MEMORIAL ASSOCIATION - CREEK COUNCIL HOUSE
  MUSEUM - LIBRARY
Town Square
106 W. 6th St.   Phone: (918) 756-2324
Okmulgee, OK 74447   Bruce M. Shackelford, Cur./Dir.

OKLAHOMA STATE UNIVERSITY - SCHOOL OF TECHNICAL TRAINING -
  OKMULGEE BRANCH LIBRARY
                                              Phone: (918) 756-6211
Okmulgee, OK 74447   Becky Kirkbride, Libn.

CONOCO, INC. - RESEARCH AND DEVELOPMENT DEPARTMENT -
  TECHNICAL INFORMATION SERVICES
                                              Phone: (405) 767-4719
Ponca City, OK 74603   Dr. Harold H. Eby, Dir., Corp.Serv.Sect.

PONCA CITY CULTURAL CENTER & MUSEUMS - LIBRARY
1000 E. Grand Ave.   Phone: (405) 762-6123
Ponca City, OK 74601   LaWanda French, Supv.

NATIONAL CLEARING HOUSE OF REHABILITATION TRAINING MATERIALS
  - REFERENCE COLLECTION
115 Old USDA Bldg.
Oklahoma State University   Phone: (405) 624-7650
Stillwater, OK 74074   Paul G. Gaines, Proj.Dir.

NATIONAL WRESTLING HALL OF FAME - LIBRARY
405 W. Hall of Fame Ave.   Phone: (405) 377-5243
Stillwater, OK 74075   Tereasa Stewart, Libn.

OKLAHOMA STATE DEPARTMENT OF VOCATIONAL AND TECHNICAL
  EDUCATION - CURRICULUM DIVISION - LIBRARY
1500 W. 7th Ave.   Phone: (405) 377-2000
Stillwater, OK 74074   Susan K. Hedrick, Libn.

OKLAHOMA STATE UNIVERSITY - AUDIO VISUAL CENTER
                                              Phone: (405) 624-7212
Stillwater, OK 74078   Dr. Woodfin G. Harris, Dir.

OKLAHOMA STATE UNIVERSITY - BIOLOGICAL SCIENCES DIVISION
University Library   Phone: (405) 624-6309
Stillwater, OK 74078   Sheila G. Johnson, Hd.

OKLAHOMA STATE UNIVERSITY - CURRICULUM MATERIALS LABORATORY
University Library   Phone: (405) 624-6310
Stillwater, OK 74078

OKLAHOMA STATE UNIVERSITY - DOCUMENTS DEPARTMENT
University Library   Phone: (405) 624-6546
Stillwater, OK 74078   Vicki W. Phillips, Hd.

OKLAHOMA STATE UNIVERSITY - HUMANITIES DIVISION
University Library   Phone: (405) 624-6544
Stillwater, OK 74078   Kim Fisher, Hd.

OKLAHOMA STATE UNIVERSITY - PHYSICAL SCIENCES AND ENGINEERING
  DIVISION
University Library   Phone: (405) 624-6305
Stillwater, OK 74078   Calvin Brewer, Hd.

OKLAHOMA STATE UNIVERSITY - SOCIAL SCIENCE DIVISION
University Library   Phone: (405) 624-6540
Stillwater, OK 74078   Edward G. Hollman, Hd.

OKLAHOMA STATE UNIVERSITY - SPECIAL COLLECTIONS AND MAPS
University Library   Phone: (405) 624-6311
Stillwater, OK 74078   Heather M. Lloyd, Hd., Gen.Ref.Dept.

OKLAHOMA STATE UNIVERSITY - VETERINARY MEDICINE LIBRARY
University Library   Phone: (405) 624-6655
Stillwater, OK 74078   LaVerne K. Jones, Libn.

U.S. NATL. PARK SERVICE - CHICKASAW NATL. RECREATION AREA -
  TRAVERTINE NATURE CENTER LIBRARY
Box 201   Phone: (405) 622-3165
Sulphur, OK 73086   Bert L. Speed, Chf.Pk. Interpreter

CHEROKEE NATIONAL HISTORICAL SOCIETY, INC. - CHEROKEE NATIONAL
  ARCHIVES
Box 515
TSA-LA-GI   Phone: (918) 456-6007
Tahlequah, OK 74464   Duane King, Exec.Dir.

NORTHEASTERN OKLAHOMA STATE UNIVERSITY - JOHN VAUGHAN
  LIBRARY/LRC - SPECIAL COLLECTIONS
                                              Phone: (918) 456-5511
Tahlequah, OK 74464   Dr. J. Richard Madaus, Dir.

OKLAHOMA VETERANS CENTER - TALIHINA DIVISION - LIBRARY
Box 488   Phone: (918) 567-2251
Talihina, OK 74571   Betty L. Davis, Libn.

U.S. AIR FORCE BASE - TINKER BASE LIBRARY
2854 ABG/SSL, Bldg. 5702   Phone: (405) 734-3083
Tinker AFB, OK 73145   Doris Haglund, Base Libn.

U.S. AIR FORCE HOSPITAL - MEDICAL LIBRARY (OK-Tinker AFB)
                                              Phone: (405) 734-8373
Tinker AFB, OK 73145   Mary B. Mills, Lib.Techn.

OKLAHOMA HISTORICAL SOCIETY - CHICKASAW COUNCIL HOUSE
  LIBRARY
Court House Sq.
Box 717   Phone: (405) 371-3351
Tishomingo, OK 73460   Beverly J. Wyatt, Site Dir.

AMERICAN AIRLINES, INC. - ENGINEERING LIBRARY
3800 N. Mingo Rd.   Phone: (918) 832-3313
Tulsa, OK 74151   O.F. Redding, Mgr., Engr.Tech.Serv.

AMERICAN ASSOCIATION OF PETROLEUM GEOLOGISTS - LIBRARY'
1444 S. Boulder
Box 979   Phone: (918) 584-2555
Tulsa, OK 74101   Kathy Shanks, Libn.

AMOCO PRODUCTION COMPANY - LAW DEPARTMENT LIBRARY
Box 591   Phone: (918) 581-3523
Tulsa, OK 74102   Sally Shipley, Libn.

AMOCO PRODUCTION COMPANY - RESEARCH CENTER LIBRARY
Box 591   Phone: (918) 664-3238
Tulsa, OK 74102   Carolyn Beson, Supv., Tech.Info.Serv.

CITIES SERVICE COMPANY - ERG - RESEARCH LIBRARY
4500 S. 129 E. Ave.
Box 3908   Phone: (918) 561-5271
Tulsa, OK 74102   Linda L. Hill, Mgr.

CITIES SERVICE OIL & GAS CORPORATION - LEGAL DIVISION LIBRARY
110 W. Seventh St.
Box 300   Phone: (918) 561-2272
Tulsa, OK 74102   Alberta Baker, Law Libn.

FIRST UNITED METHODIST CHURCH - LIBRARY
1115 S. Boulder   Phone: (918) 587-9481
Tulsa, OK 74119   Marie Tongue, Dir. of Lib.Serv.

GETTY REFINING AND MARKETING COMPANY - LAW LIBRARY
Box 1650   Phone: (918) 560-6136
Tulsa, OK 74102   Margaret A. Brookfield, Law Libn.

GILCREASE (Thomas) INSTITUTE OF AMERICAN HISTORY AND ART -
    LIBRARY
1400 N. 25th West Ave.   Phone: (918) 531-5311
Tulsa, OK 74127   Sarah Hirsch, Libn.

HILLCREST MEDICAL CENTER - LIBRARY
1120 S. Utica   Phone: (918) 584-1351
Tulsa, OK 74104   Peggy Cook, Libn.

OKLAHOMA COLLEGE OF BUSINESS AND TECHNOLOGY - LEARNING
    RESOURCE CENTER
4821 S. 72nd E. Ave.   Phone: (918) 742-3311
Tulsa, OK 74145   Carolyn S. McCauley, Dir. of Lrng.Rsrcs.

OKLAHOMA COLLEGE OF OSTEOPATHIC MEDICINE & SURGERY - LIBRARY
1111 W. 17th St.   Phone: (918) 582-1972
Tulsa, OK 74107   Linda L. Roberts, Coll.Libn.

OKLAHOMA OSTEOPATHIC HOSPITAL - L.C. BAXTER MEDICAL LIBRARY
Ninth St. at Jackson Ave.   Phone: (918) 599-5297
Tulsa, OK 74127   S. Jane Cooper, Hd.Med.Libn.

OKLAHOMA WELL LOG LIBRARY, INC.
837 Mayo Bldg.   Phone: (918) 582-6188
Tulsa, OK 74103   Jan Jennings, Mgr./Libn.

ORAL ROBERTS UNIVERSITY - GRADUATE THEOLOGY LIBRARY - JOHN
    MESSICK LEARNING RESOURCE CENTER
7777 S. Lewis   Phone: (918) 495-6723
Tulsa, OK 74171   Dr. William W. Jernigan, Dir.

ORAL ROBERTS UNIVERSITY - HEALTH SCIENCES LIBRARY
7777 S. Lewis
Box 2187   Phone: (918) 495-6897
Tulsa, OK 74171   Timothy C. Judkins, Asst.Dir.

ORAL ROBERTS UNIVERSITY - LIBRARY - HOLY SPIRIT RESEARCH CENTER
Box 2187   Phone: (918) 495-6898
Tulsa, OK 74171   Karen Robinson, Libn.

ORAL ROBERTS UNIVERSITY - O.W. COBURN LAW LIBRARY †
School of Law
7777 S. Lewis
Box 2187   Phone: (918) 495-7155
Tulsa, OK 74171   Prof. David W. Dunn, Law Libn.

OZARK-MAHONING COMPANY - RESEARCH LIBRARY
1870 S. Boulder Ave.   Phone: (918) 585-2661
Tulsa, OK 74119   Judy Tibson, Libn.

PHILBROOK ART CENTER - LIBRARY
Box 52510   Phone: (918) 741-7941
Tulsa, OK 74152   Thomas E. Young, Libn.

PUBLIC SERVICE COMPANY OF OKLAHOMA - REFERENCE CENTER
212 E. 6th St.
Box 201   Phone: (918) 599-2367
Tulsa, OK 74119   Carol Hayhurst, Supv.

ROCKWELL INTERNATIONAL - TECHNICAL INFORMATION CENTER
2000 N. Memorial Dr.
Box 51308   Phone: (918) 835-3111
Tulsa, OK 74151   Mary B. Sewell, Adm.

ST. FRANCIS HOSPITAL - HEALTH SCIENCES LIBRARY †
6161 S. Yale Ave.   Phone: (918) 494-1210
Tulsa, OK 74177   Darryl Logan, Med.Libn.

ST. JOHN MEDICAL CENTER - HEALTH SCIENCES LIBRARY †
1923 S. Utica   Phone: (918) 744-2970
Tulsa, OK 74104   Geneva N. Norvell, Libn.

TULSA CITY-COUNTY LIBRARY SYSTEM - BUSINESS AND TECHNOLOGY
    DEPARTMENT
400 Civic Ctr.   Phone: (918) 581-5211
Tulsa, OK 74103   J. Craig Buthod, Dept.Hd.

TULSA COUNTY HISTORICAL SOCIETY - LIBRARY
Tulsa City-County Library
400 Civic Ctr.   Phone: (918) 592-2595
Tulsa, OK 74103

TULSA COUNTY LAW LIBRARY †
Tulsa County Court House, Rm. 242
500 S. Denver   Phone: (918) 584-0471
Tulsa, OK 74103   Rena C. Hanton, Libn.

TULSA WORLD-TULSA TRIBUNE - LIBRARY DEPARTMENT
315 S. Boulder Ave.
Box 1770   Phone: (918) 583-2161
Tulsa, OK 74102   Lucy Towry, Libn.

TULSA ZOOLOGICAL PARK - LIBRARY
5701 E. 36th St., N.   Phone: (918) 835-8471
Tulsa, OK 74115   Carol Eames, Educ.Cur.

UNIVERSITY OF OKLAHOMA - TULSA MEDICAL COLLEGE - LIBRARY
2808 S. Sheridan   Phone: (918) 838-3464
Tulsa, OK 74129   Janet Minnerath, Hd.Libn.

UNIVERSITY OF TULSA - COLLEGE OF LAW LIBRARY
3120 E. Fourth Pl.   Phone: (918) 592-6000
Tulsa, OK 74104   Marian Parker, Dir./Asst.Prof.

UNIVERSITY OF TULSA - DIVISION OF INFORMATION SERVICES
600 S. College Ave.   Phone: (918) 592-6000
Tulsa, OK 74104   John Dowgray, Dir.

UNIVERSITY OF TULSA - MC FARLIN LIBRARY - RARE BOOKS AND SPECIAL
    COLLECTIONS
600 S. College Ave.   Phone: (918) 592-6000
Tulsa, OK 74120   Dr. David Farmer, Dir., Rare Bks./Spec.Coll

WILLIAMS BROTHERS ENGINEERING COMPANY - TECHNICAL
    INFORMATION CENTER †
6600 S. Yale Ave.   Phone: (918) 496-5020
Tulsa, OK 74177   Kay Kittrell, Mgr.

U.S. AIR FORCE BASE - VANCE BASE LIBRARY ★
FL 3029   Phone: (405) 237-2121
Vance AFB, OK 73702   Tom L. Kirk, Chf.Libn.

SOUTHWESTERN OKLAHOMA STATE UNIVERSITY - AL HARRIS LIBRARY
                                   Phone: (405) 772-6611
Weatherford, OK 73096   Sheila Wilder Hoke, Lib.Dir.

OREGON

ALBANY GENERAL HOSPITAL - HEALTH SCIENCES LIBRARY
1046 W. 6th   Phone: (503) 926-2244
Albany, OR 97321   Arleen Libertini, Libn.

U.S. BUREAU OF MINES - ALBANY TECHNICAL LIBRARY
Box 70   Phone: (503) 967-5864
Albany, OR 97321   Eleanor Abshire, Libn.

INTEL CORPORATION - TECHNICAL INFORMATION CENTER
3585 S.W. 198th   Phone: (503) 642-6598
Aloha, OR 97007   Colleen Sobieski, Mgr., Tech.Info.Ctr.

SOUTHERN OREGON STATE COLLEGE - LIBRARY
1250 Siskiyou Blvd.   Phone: (503) 482-6445
Ashland, OR 97520   Ruth Monical, Act.Lib.Dir.

COLUMBIA RIVER MARITIME MUSEUM - LIBRARY
1792 Marine Dr.   Phone: (503) 325-2323
Astoria, OR 97103   Larry D. Gilmore, Cur.

FLOATING POINT SYSTEMS, INC. - INFORMATION CENTER/LIBRARY
3601 S.W. Murray Blvd.   Phone: (503) 641-3151
Beaverton, OR 97005   Richard Grahner, Mgr.

OREGON GRADUATE CENTER FOR STUDY AND RESEARCH - LIBRARY
19600 N.W. Walker Rd.   Phone: (503) 645-1121
Beaverton, OR 97006   Maureen G. Seaman, Libn.

OREGON REGIONAL PRIMATE RESEARCH CENTER - LIBRARY
505 N.W. 185th Ave.   Phone: (503) 645-1141
Beaverton, OR 97006   Isabel McDonald, Libn.

TEKTRONIX, INC. - CORPORATE LIBRARY
Box 500, MS 50-210   Phone: (503) 627-5388
Beaverton, OR 97077   Julianne Williams, Lib.Mgr.

TEKTRONIX, INC. - WALKER ROAD BRANCH LIBRARY
MS 94-501
Box 4600   Phone: (503) 629-1062
Beaverton, OR 97075   Yan Y. Soucie, Br.Libn.

UNIVERSITY OF OREGON - OREGON INSTITUTE OF MARINE BIOLOGY -
    LIBRARY
                    Phone: (503) 888-5534
Charleston, OR 97420   Jean Hanna, Libn.

KAISER SUNNYSIDE MEDICAL CENTER - LIBRARY
10180 S.E. Sunnyside Rd.
Clackamas, OR 97015   Ann H. Haines, Med.Libn.

OREGON STATE DEPARTMENT OF FISH AND WILDLIFE - LIBRARY
17330 S.E. Evelyn St.
Clackamas, OR 97015   Shirley M. McKinney, Libn.

CH2M HILL, INC. - CORVALLIS REGIONAL OFFICE LIBRARY
2300 N.W. Walnut Blvd.
Box 428   Phone: (503) 752-4271
Corvallis, OR 97339   Mary O'Brien, Libn.

ENVIRONMENTAL PROTECTION AGENCY - ENVIRONMENTAL RESEARCH
    LABORATORY, CORVALLIS - LIBRARY
200 S.W. 35th St.   Phone: (503) 757-4731
Corvallis, OR 97330   Betty M. McCauley, Libn.

HEWLETT-PACKARD COMPANY - PORTABLE COMPUTER DIVISION -
    TECHNICAL INFORMATION CENTER
1000 N.E. Circle Blvd.   Phone: (503) 757-2000
Corvallis, OR 97330   Shari Morwood, Dir.

NEPTUNE MICROFLOC, INC. - RESEARCH AND TECHNICAL LIBRARY
Box 612   Phone: (503) 754-7654
Corvallis, OR 97339   Marilyn Curteman, Doc.Coord.

OREGON STATE UNIVERSITY - ARCHIVES
Ad.Bldg., BO94   Phone: (503) 754-2165
Corvallis, OR 97331   Lauren K. Filson, Archv.

OREGON STATE UNIVERSITY - DEPARTMENT OF CROP SCIENCE - HOP
    RESEARCH CENTER - WORKING COLLECTION
                    Phone: (503) 754-2964
Corvallis, OR 97331   Dr. Alfred Hacinold, Res.Sci.

OREGON STATE UNIVERSITY - SCHOOL OF FORESTRY - FRL LIBRARY
                    Phone: (503) 753-9166
Corvallis, OR 97331   Mary B. Scroggins, Libn.

OREGON STATE UNIVERSITY - WILLIAM JASPER KERR LIBRARY
                    Phone: (503) 754-3411
Corvallis, OR 97331   Melvin R. George, Dir. Of Libs.

U.S. NATL. PARK SERVICE - CRATER LAKE NATL. PARK - LIBRARY
Box 7
Crater Lake, OR 97604   Henry M. Tanski, Jr., Asst.Interp.

CHURCH OF JESUS CHRIST OF LATTER-DAY SAINTS - EUGENE, OREGON
    BRANCH GENEALOGICAL LIBRARY
3550 W. 18th Ave.   Phone: (503) 343-3741
Eugene, OR 97402   Irma Best, Libn.

ERIC CLEARINGHOUSE ON EDUCATIONAL MANAGEMENT
College of Education
University of Oregon   Phone: (503) 686-5043
Eugene, OR 97403   Dr. Philip K. Piele, Prof./Dir.

EUGENE HEARING AND SPEECH CENTER - LIBRARY *
1202 Almaden
Box 2087   Phone: (503) 485-8521
Eugene, OR 97402   Ned Risbrough, Exec.Dir.

EUGENE HOSPITAL AND CLINIC - DOCTORS' LIBRARY *
1162 Willamette St.   Phone: (503) 687-6000
Eugene, OR 97401   Dr. Byron Musa, Chm., Lib.Comm.

LANE COUNCIL OF GOVERNMENTS - LIBRARY
125 E. 8th Ave.   Phone: (503) 687-4283
Eugene, OR 97401   Claire Van Bloem, Res.Asst.

LANE COUNTY LAW LIBRARY
Courthouse   Phone: (503) 687-4337
Eugene, OR 97401   Mary E. Clayton, Law Libn.

LANE COUNTY MUSEUM - SPECIAL COLLECTIONS & ARCHIVES
740 W. 13th Ave.   Phone: (503) 687-4239
Eugene, OR 97402   Marty West, Cur., Spec.Coll.

NORTHWEST CHRISTIAN COLLEGE - LEARNING RESOURCE CENTER
828 E. 11th   Phone: (503) 343-1641
Eugene, OR 97401   Margaret W. Hewitt, Dir.

OCEAN AND COASTAL LAW CENTER - LIBRARY
School of Law
University of Oregon   Phone: (503) 686-3845
Eugene, OR 97403   Andrea G. Coffman, Libn.

OREGON RESEARCH INSTITUTE - LIBRARY
195 W. 12th Ave.
Eugene, OR 97401   Linda Rangus, Lib.Mgr.

REGISTER-GUARD - LIBRARY
975 High St.
Box 10188   Phone: (503) 485-1234
Eugene, OR 97440   Marijoy Rubaloff, Libn.

SACRED HEART GENERAL HOSPITAL AND MEDICAL CENTER - LIBRARY
    SERVICES
1255 Hilyard
Box 10905   Phone: (503) 686-6837
Eugene, OR 97440   Deborah Graham, Dir., Lib.Serv.

UNIVERSITY OF OREGON - ARCHITECTURE AND ALLIED ARTS BRANCH
    LIBRARY
                    Phone: (503) 686-3637
Eugene, OR 97403   Rayburn R. McCready, Hd.Libn.

UNIVERSITY OF OREGON - BUREAU OF GOVERNMENTAL RESEARCH AND
    SERVICE LIBRARY
Box 3177   Phone: (503) 686-3048
Eugene, OR 97403   Katherine G. Eaton, Libn.

UNIVERSITY OF OREGON - CAREER INFORMATION CENTER
221 Hendricks Hall
Box 3257   Phone: (503) 686-3235
Eugene, OR 97403   Lawrence H. Smith, Dir.

UNIVERSITY OF OREGON - CAREER INFORMATION SYSTEM
1787 Agate St.   Phone: (503) 686-3872
Eugene, OR 97403   Bruce McKinlay, Dir.

UNIVERSITY OF OREGON - COLLEGE OF BUSINESS ADMINISTRATION -
    DIVISION OF RESEARCH †
140 Gilbert Hall
Eugene, OR 97403

UNIVERSITY OF OREGON - DEPARTMENT OF ENGLISH - RANDALL V. MILLS
    ARCHIVES OF NORTHWEST FOLKLORE
                    Phone: (503) 686-3925
Eugene, OR 97403   Janet M. Cliff, Archv.

UNIVERSITY OF OREGON - ENVIRONMENTAL STUDIES CENTER
Phone: (503) 686-5006
Eugene, OR 97403　　　　　　　　Pamela Vorachek, Libn.

UNIVERSITY OF OREGON - GOVERNMENT DOCUMENTS SECTION
University Library　　　　　　　Phone: (503) 686-3070
Eugene, OR 97403　　　　　　　　John A. Shuler, Act.Hd.

UNIVERSITY OF OREGON - INSTITUTE OF RECREATION RESEARCH AND
　　SERVICE
180 Esslinger Hall　　　　　　　Phone: (503) 686-3602
Eugene, OR 97403　　　　　　　　Larry L. Neal, Dir.

UNIVERSITY OF OREGON - INSTRUCTIONAL MEDIA CENTER
University Library　　　　　　　Phone: (503) 686-3091
Eugene, OR 97403　　　　　　　　George E. Bynon, Dir.

UNIVERSITY OF OREGON - LAW LIBRARY
Phone: (503) 686-3088
Eugene, OR 97403　　　　　　　　Dennis R. Hyatt, Libn.

UNIVERSITY OF OREGON - MAP LIBRARY
165 Condon Hall　　　　　　　Phone: (503) 686-3051
Eugene, OR 97403　　　　　　　　Peter L. Stark, Hd.

UNIVERSITY OF OREGON - MATHEMATICS LIBRARY
University Library　　　　　　　Phone: (503) 686-3023
Eugene, OR 97403　　　　　　　　Isabel A. Stirling, Hd.Libn.

UNIVERSITY OF OREGON - MICROFORMS AND RECORDINGS DEPARTMENT
University Library　　　　　　　Phone: (503) 686-3080
Eugene, OR 97403　　　　　　　　Rory Funke, Hd.

UNIVERSITY OF OREGON - ORIENTALIA COLLECTION
University Library　　　　　　　Phone: (503) 686-3114
Eugene, OR 97403　　　　　　　　Wen-Kai Kung, Bibliog.

UNIVERSITY OF OREGON - SCIENCE LIBRARY
University Library　　　　　　　Phone: (503) 686-3075
Eugene, OR 97403　　　　　　　　Isabel A. Stirling, Hd.Libn.

UNIVERSITY OF OREGON - SPECIAL COLLECTIONS DIVISION
University Library　　　　　　　Phone: (503) 686-3068
Eugene, OR 97403　　　　　　　　Kenneth Duckett, Cur.

OREGON ELECTRIC RAILWAY HISTORICAL SOCIETY, INC. - TROLLEY PARK
　- LIBRARY
HCR 71
Box 1318 Glenwood　　　　　　　Phone: (503) 357-3574
Forest Grove, OR 97116　　　　　　　William Hayes, Hist.

PACIFIC UNIVERSITY - MUSIC DEPARTMENT - LIBRARY
College Way　　　　　　　Phone: (503) 357-6151
Forest Grove, OR 97116　　　　　　　Norma M. Cooper, Music Libn.

JOSEPHINE COUNTY HISTORICAL SOCIETY - RESEARCH LIBRARY
508 S.W. 5th St.　　　　　　　Phone: (503) 479-7827
Grants Pass, OR 97526　　　　　　　Martha Murphy, Res.Libn.

JOSEPHINE COUNTY LAW LIBRARY
Courthouse　　　　　　　Phone: (503) 474-5181
Grants Pass, OR 97526　　　　　　　Steven P. Medley, Libn.

TUALITY COMMUNITY HOSPITAL - HEALTH SCIENCES LIBRARY
335 S.E. 8th Ave.　　　　　　　Phone: (503) 681-1121
Hillsboro, OR 97123　　　　　　　Robin Braun, Health Sci.Libn.

WASHINGTON COUNTY LAW LIBRARY †
Courthouse　　　　　　　Phone: (503) 648-8880
Hillsboro, OR 97123　　　　　　　Ann Karlen, Libn.

SOUTHERN OREGON HISTORICAL SOCIETY - RESEARCH LIBRARY
206 N. 5th St.
Box 480　　　　　　　Phone: (503) 899-1847
Jacksonville, OR 97530　　　　　　　Alan C. Miller, Libn./Archv.

COLLIER STATE PARK LOGGING MUSEUM - LIBRARY
Box 428　　　　　　　Phone: (503) 884-5145
Klamath Falls, OR 97601　　　　　　　Alfred D. Collier, Cur.

KLAMATH COUNTY - LOYD DELAP LAW LIBRARY
Court House　　　　　　　Phone: (503) 882-2501
Klamath Falls, OR 97601　　　　　　　Ruth Rice, Law Libn.

OREGON INSTITUTE OF TECHNOLOGY - LEARNING RESOURCES CENTER
Oretech Branch P.O.　　　　　　　Phone: (503) 882-6321
Klamath Falls, OR 97601　　　　　　　Charles H. Kemp, Dir.

PROTESTANT EPISCOPAL CHURCH - EPISCOPAL DIOCESE OF EASTERN
　　OREGON - ARCHIVES
Box 1091　　　　　　　Phone: (503) 568-4898
LaGrande, OR 97850　　　　　　　Rev. Louis L. Perkins

JACKSON COUNTY LAW LIBRARY
Jackson County Justice Bldg.　　　　　　　Phone: (503) 776-7214
Medford, OR 97501　　　　　　　Pamela Pfeil, Libn.

MEDFORD MAIL TRIBUNE - LIBRARY
Box 1108　　　　　　　Phone: (503) 776-4493
Medford, OR 97501　　　　　　　Kathryn Harper, Libn.

WESTERN EVANGELICAL SEMINARY - GEORGE HALLAUER MEMORIAL
　　LIBRARY
4200 S.E. Jennings Ave.　　　　　　　Phone: (503) 654-5182
Milwaukie, OR 97222　　　　　　　Gary Metzenbacher, Dir. of Lib.

WESTERN OREGON STATE COLLEGE - LIBRARY
234 Monmouth Ave.　　　　　　　Phone: (503) 838-1220
Monmouth, OR 97361　　　　　　　Dr. Clarence Gorchels, Dir.

OREGON STATE UNIVERSITY - HATFIELD MARINE SCIENCE CENTER -
　　LIBRARY
Phone: (503) 867-3011
Newport, OR 97365　　　　　　　Marilyn Guin, Libn.

AMERICAN-NEPAL EDUCATION FOUNDATION - WOOD NEPAL LIBRARY
Box ANEF　　　　　　　Phone: (503) 842-4024
Oceanside, OR 97134　　　　　　　Hugh B. Wood, Libn.

CLACKAMAS COUNTY, OREGON - ALDEN E. MILLER LAW LIBRARY
Clackamas County Courthouse, Rm. 101　　　　　　　Phone: (503) 655-8248
Oregon City, OR 97045　　　　　　　Ailsa Mackenzie Werner, Law Libn.

EASTERN OREGON HOSPITAL AND TRAINING CENTER - PROFESSIONAL
　　LIBRARY *
Box A　　　　　　　Phone: (503) 276-1711
Pendleton, OR 97801

AMERICAN INSTITUTE OF ARCHITECTS - PORTLAND CHAPTER - AIA
　　LIBRARY
615 S.W. Park Ave.　　　　　　　Phone: (503) 223-8757
Portland, OR 97209　　　　　　　Kit Whittaker, Libn.

BASSIST COLLEGE - LIBRARY
2000 S.W. Fifth Ave.　　　　　　　Phone: (503) 228-6528
Portland, OR 97201　　　　　　　Norma H. Bassist, Libn.

CH2M HILL, INC. - LIBRARY
2020 S.W. 4th Ave., 2nd Fl.　　　　　　　Phone: (503) 224-9190
Portland, OR 97201　　　　　　　Bette L. Stewart, Libn.

COLUMBIA CHRISTIAN COLLEGE - LIBRARY - SPECIAL COLLECTIONS
200 N.E. 91st Ave.　　　　　　　Phone: (503) 255-7060
Portland, OR 97220　　　　　　　Dr. Richard Lee, Libn.

CONTEMPORARY CRAFTS ASSOCIATION - LIBRARY *
3934 S.W. Corbett Ave.　　　　　　　Phone: (503) 223-2654
Portland, OR 97201　　　　　　　LaVerne Kuchler, Act.Libn.

EASTMORELAND GENERAL HOSPITAL - HEALTH SCIENCES LIBRARY
2900 S.E. Steele St.　　　　　　　Phone: (503) 234-0411
Portland, OR 97202　　　　　　　Ann H. Haines, Med.Libn.

EMANUEL HOSPITAL - LIBRARY SERVICES
2801 N. Gantenbein Ave.　　　　　　　Phone: (503) 280-3558
Portland, OR 97227　　　　　　　Katherine W. Rouzie, Dir., Lib.Serv.

ESCO CORP. - LIBRARY *
2141 N.W. 25th Ave.   Phone: (503) 228-2141
Portland, OR 97210   Leroy Finch, Sr. Metallurgist

FIRST INTERSTATE BANK - LIBRARY
1300 S.W. 5th
Box 3131   Phone: (503) 225-4193
Portland, OR 97208   Carol Dick, Libn.

GENEALOGICAL FORUM OF PORTLAND, OREGON, INC. - LIBRARY
1410 S.W. Morrison St.   Phone: (503) 227-2398
Portland, OR 97205

GEORGIA-PACIFIC CORPORATION - HISTORICAL MUSEUM
900 S.W. 5th Ave.   Phone: (503) 222-5561
Portland, OR 97204   Richard M. Thompson, Musm.Dir.

GOLDEN AGE RADIO - THE BEST OF OLD TIME RADIO COLLECTION
Box 25215   Phone: (503) 297-6231
Portland, OR 97225   Rex E. Bills, Owner

GOOD SAMARITAN HOSPITAL AND MEDICAL CENTER - LIBRARY
1015 N.W. 22nd Ave.   Phone: (503) 229-7336
Portland, OR 97210   Melvina Stell, Dir.

HYSTER COMPANY - ENGINEERING LIBRARY
2902 N.E. Clackamas   Phone: (503) 280-7405
Portland, OR 97208   Ruth Jahnke, Libn.

INDUSTRIAL FORESTRY ASSOCIATION - LIBRARY
225 S.W. Broadway, Rm. 400   Phone: (503) 222-9505
Portland, OR 97205   Michael D. Sullivan, Dir., Pub.Aff.

KAISER FOUNDATION HOSPITALS - HEALTH SERVICES RESEARCH CENTER
   LIBRARY
4610 S.E. Belmont St.   Phone: (503) 233-5631
Portland, OR 97215   Leslie Webb Wykoff, Libn.

KAISER-PERMANENTE MEDICAL CENTER - MEDICAL LIBRARY
5055 N. Greeley Ave.   Phone: (503) 285-9321
Portland, OR 97217   Patricia Hanley, Med.Libn.

LAMB-WESTON - BUSINESS RESEARCH CENTER
Box 23517   Phone: (503) 639-8612
Portland, OR 97223   Anne Isbell, Bus.Res.Supv.

LEWIS AND CLARK LAW SCHOOL - NORTHWESTERN SCHOOL OF LAW -
   PAUL L. BOLEY LAW LIBRARY
10015 S.W. Terwilliger Blvd.   Phone: (503) 244-1181
Portland, OR 97219   Professor Peter S. Nycum, Law Libn.

LIBRARY ASSOCIATION OF PORTLAND - ART AND MUSIC DEPARTMENT
801 S.W. Tenth Ave.   Phone: (503) 223-7201
Portland, OR 97205   Barbara K. Padden, Hd.

LIBRARY ASSOCIATION OF PORTLAND - GENERAL INFORMATION
   DEPARTMENT - FOUNDATION CENTER
801 S.W. 10th Ave.   Phone: (503) 223-7201
Portland, OR 97205   Meg Eisemann, Coll.Supv.

LIBRARY ASSOCIATION OF PORTLAND - LITERATURE AND HISTORY
   DEPARTMENT
801 S.W. Tenth Ave.   Phone: (503) 223-7201
Portland, OR 97205   Barbara J. Kahl, Dept.Hd.

LIBRARY ASSOCIATION OF PORTLAND - OREGON COLLECTION
801 S.W. Tenth Ave.   Phone: (503) 223-7201
Portland, OR 97205   Barbara J. Kahl

LIBRARY ASSOCIATION OF PORTLAND - SOCIAL SCIENCE AND SCIENCE
   DEPARTMENT
801 S.W. Tenth Ave.   Phone: (503) 223-7201
Portland, OR 97205   Jim Takita, Dept.Hd.

LUTHERAN CHURCH - MISSOURI SYNOD - NORTHWEST DISTRICT
   ARCHIVES
1700 N.E. Knott   Phone: (503) 288-8383
Portland, OR 97212   C. Nitz, Archv.

MAZAMAS - LIBRARY
909 N.W. Nineteenth Ave.   Phone: (503) 227-2345
Portland, OR 97209

MILLER, NASH, WIENER, HAGER & CARLSEN - LIBRARY
111 S.W. Fifth Ave.   Phone: (503) 224-5858
Portland, OR 97204-3699   Leslie Meserve, Libn.

MULTNOMAH LAW LIBRARY
Court House   Phone: (503) 248-3394
Portland, OR 97204   Jacquelyn J. Jurkins, Law Libn.

MULTNOMAH SCHOOL OF THE BIBLE - JOHN AND MARY MITCHELL
   LIBRARY
8435 N.E. Glisan St.   Phone: (503) 255-0332
Portland, OR 97220   James F. Scott, Lib.Dir.

NATIONAL COLLEGE OF NATUROPATHIC MEDICINE - LIBRARY
510 S.W. 3rd Ave.   Phone: (503) 226-3745
Portland, OR 97204   Friedhelm Kirchfeld, Libn.

NERCO, INC. - LIBRARY
111 S.W. Columbia, Suite 800   Phone: (503) 796-6631
Portland, OR 97201   Peggy Castlen, Off.Serv.Supv.

NORTHWEST POWER PLANNING COUNCIL - LIBRARY/PUBLIC READING
   ROOM
700 S.W. Taylor, Suite 200   Phone: (503) 222-5161
Portland, OR 97205   Ruth L. Curtis, Info.Coord.

NORTHWEST REGIONAL EDUCATIONAL LABORATORY - INFORMATION
   CENTER/LIBRARY
300 S.W. Sixth Ave.   Phone: (503) 248-6800
Portland, OR 97204   M. Margaret Rogers, Dir.Info.Serv.

OREGON HEALTH SCIENCES UNIVERSITY - DENTAL BRANCH LIBRARY
611 S.W. Campus Dr.   Phone: (503) 225-8822
Portland, OR 97201   Dolores Judkins, Dental Libn.

OREGON HEALTH SCIENCES UNIVERSITY - LIBRARY
3181 S.W. Sam Jackson Park Rd.
Box 573   Phone: (503) 225-8026
Portland, OR 97207   James E. Morgan, Dir.

OREGON HISTORICAL SOCIETY - LIBRARY
1230 S.W. Park Ave.   Phone: (503) 222-1741
Portland, OR 97205   Louis Flannery, Chf.Libn.

OREGON SCHOOL OF ARTS AND CRAFTS - LIBRARY
8245 S.W. Barnes Rd.   Phone: (503) 297-5544
Portland, OR 97225   Kristin L. Koester, Libn.

OREGON STATE DEPARTMENT OF GEOLOGY AND MINERAL INDUSTRIES -
   LIBRARY
1400 S.W. 5th Ave.   Phone: (503) 229-5580
Portland, OR 97201   Klaus Neuendorf, Ed./Libn.

OREGONIAN LIBRARY
1320 S.W. Broadway   Phone: (503) 221-8131
Portland, OR 97201   Doris N. Smith, Hd.Libn.

PACIFIC POWER AND LIGHT COMPANY - LIBRARY
920 S.W. Sixth Ave.   Phone: (503) 243-4095
Portland, OR 97204   Susan Jackson, Libn.

PORT OF PORTLAND - LIBRARY
700 N.E. Multnomah   Phone: (503) 231-5000
Portland, OR 97232   Jo Dwyer, Lib.Acq.

PORTLAND ART ASSOCIATION - NORTHWEST FILM STUDY CENTER -
   CIRCULATING FILM LIBRARY
1219 S.W. Park Ave.   Phone: (503) 221-1156
Portland, OR 97205   Karen Karbo, Regional Serv.

PORTLAND ART MUSEUM - LIBRARY
1219 S.W. Park   Phone: (503) 226-2811
Portland, OR 97205   Emily Evans Elsner, Libn.

PORTLAND BUREAU OF PLANNING - LIBRARY
1120 S.W. 5th Ave., 10th Fl.   Phone: (503) 796-7717
Portland, OR 97204

PORTLAND GENERAL ELECTRIC - CORPORATE AND TECHNICAL LIBRARIES
121 S.W. Salmon St.   Phone: (503) 226-8695
Portland, OR 97204   Mary K. Devlin-Willis, Br.Mgr., Lib.Serv.

PORTLAND PUBLIC SCHOOLS - PROFESSIONAL LIBRARY
501 N. Dixon St.
Box 3107   Phone: (503) 249-2000
Portland, OR 97208   Connie Stanton, Libn.

PORTLAND STATE UNIVERSITY - AUDIO-VISUAL SERVICES
Box 1151   Phone: (503) 229-4514
Portland, OR 97207   Frank F. Kuo, Dir.

PORTLAND STATE UNIVERSITY - CONTINUING EDUCATION FILM LIBRARY
1633 S.W. Park Ave.   Phone: (503) 229-4890
Portland, OR 97207   Anthony J. Midson, Dir.

PORTLAND STATE UNIVERSITY - MIDDLE EAST STUDIES CENTER
Box 751
Portland, OR 97207

PORTLAND STATE UNIVERSITY - SCIENCE LIBRARY
Box 1151   Phone: (503) 229-4735
Portland, OR 97207   Robert L. Lockerby, Engr.Libn.

PRECISION CASTPARTS CORPORATION - TECHNICAL INFORMATION
   CENTER
4600 S.E. Harney Dr.   Phone: (503) 777-3881
Portland, OR 97206   Pat Spurlock, Tech.Info.Spec.

PROVIDENCE MEDICAL CENTER - MEDICAL LIBRARY
4805 N.E. Glisan   Phone: (503) 230-6075
Portland, OR 97213   Miriam Palmer, Med.Libn.

RADER COMPANIES, INC. - INFORMATION CENTER †
6005 N.E. 82nd Ave.
Portland, OR 97220

REED COLLEGE - PHYSICS LIBRARY *
Dept. of Physics   Phone: (503) 771-1112
Portland, OR 97202   Nicholas A. Wheeler, Prof.

ST. VINCENT HOSPITAL AND MEDICAL CENTER - HEALTH SCIENCES
   LIBRARY
9205 S.W. Barnes Rd.   Phone: (503) 299-2257
Portland, OR 97225   Edith H. Throckmorton, Dir.

SETON, JOHNSON & ODELL, INC. - TECHNICAL INFORMATION CENTER
133 S.W. 2nd Ave.   Phone: (503) 226-3921
Portland, OR 97204   Denise Hiatt, Sec.

SPEARS, LUBERSKY, CAMPBELL, BLEDSOE, ANDERSON & YOUNG - LIBRARY
800 Pacific Bldg.
520 S.W. Yamhill St.   Phone: (503) 226-6151
Portland, OR 97204   Bob Newby, Libn.

STOEL, RIVES, BOLEY, ET AL - LIBRARY
900 S.W. Fifth Ave.   Phone: (503) 224-3380
Portland, OR 97204   Larry W. Piper, Libn.

THE STRATEGIC CORPORATION - STRATEGIC MOVES LIBRARY
2165 S.W. Main St.   Phone: (503) 222-9028
Portland, OR 97205   Susan Limper, Staff Futurist

UNION PACIFIC RAILROAD COMPANY - LAW LIBRARY
1515 S.W. 5th Ave., Suite 400   Phone: (503) 249-2519
Portland, OR 97201   L. James Bergmann, Gen. Solicitor

U.S. ARMY - CORPS OF ENGINEERS - PORTLAND DISTRICT - LIBRARY
Box 2946   Phone: (503) 221-6016
Portland, OR 97208   Christian P. Hurd, District Libn.

U.S. BANCORP - RESOURCE LIBRARY
555 S.W. Oak St.   Phone: (503) 225-5816
Portland, OR 97204

U.S. COURT OF APPEALS, 9TH CIRCUIT - LIBRARY
Pioneer Courthouse   Phone: (503) 221-6042
Portland, OR 97204   Scott M. McCurdy, Libn.

U.S. DEPT. OF ENERGY - BONNEVILLE POWER ADMINISTRATION -
   LIBRARY
1002 N.E. Holladay St.
Box 3621   Phone: (503) 234-3361
Portland, OR 97208   Karen L. Hadman, Chf., Lib.Br.

U.S. DISTRICT COURT - DISTRICT OF OREGON - LIBRARY
529 U.S. Courthouse
620 S.W. Main   Phone: (503) 221-6042
Portland, OR 97219   Scott McCurdy, Libn.

U.S. VETERANS ADMINISTRATION (OR-Portland) - MEDICAL LIBRARY
3710 S.W. U.S. Veterans Hospital Rd.
Box 1035   Phone: (503) 222-9221
Portland, OR 97207   Mrs. Nymah L. Trued, Chf., Lib.Serv.

WALLA WALLA COLLEGE - SCHOOL OF NURSING PROFESSIONAL LIBRARY
10345 S.E. Market   Phone: (503) 251-6115
Portland, OR 97216   Shirley A. Cody, Libn.

WARNER-PACIFIC COLLEGE - OTTO F. LINN LIBRARY
2219 S.E. 68th Ave.   Phone: (503) 775-4368
Portland, OR 97215   Dr. William M. Orr, Gen.Lib.Adm.

WASHINGTON COUNTY MUSEUM - LIBRARY
17677 N.W. Springville Rd.   Phone: (503) 645-6606
Portland, OR 97229   Dr. Robert W. Keeler, Cur. of Coll.

WASHINGTON PARK ZOO - LIBRARY
4001 S.W. Canyon Rd.   Phone: (503) 226-1561
Portland, OR 97221   Warren J. Iliff, Dir.

WESTERN CONSERVATIVE BAPTIST SEMINARY - CLINE-TUNNELL LIBRARY
5511 S.E. Hawthorne Blvd.   Phone: (503) 233-8561
Portland, OR 97215   R.A. Krupp, Lib.Dir.

WESTERN STATES CHIROPRACTIC COLLEGE - W.A. BUDDEN MEMORIAL
   LIBRARY
2900 N.E. 132nd Ave.   Phone: (503) 256-3180
Portland, OR 97230   Kay Irvine, Hd.Libn.

DOUGLAS COUNTY MUSEUM - LAVOLA BAKKEN MEMORIAL LIBRARY
Box 1550   Phone: (503) 440-4507
Roseburg, OR 97470   Ella Mae Young, Res.Libn.

FIRST PRESBYTERIAN CHURCH - LIBRARY †
823 S.E. Lane St.   Phone: (503) 673-5559
Roseburg, OR 97470   Nancy Nixon, Libn.

U.S. VETERANS ADMINISTRATION (OR-Roseburg) - MEDICAL CENTER
   LIBRARY SERVICE
Garden Valley Blvd.   Phone: (503) 672-4411
Roseburg, OR 97470

COLUMBIA COUNTY HISTORICAL SOCIETY - MUSEUM
Old Courthouse   Phone: (503) 397-2805
St. Helens, OR 97051   Mildred Lain, Hist.

OREGON STATE DEPARTMENT OF AGRICULTURE - INFORMATION SERVICE
   - LIBRARY
Agriculture Bldg.
635 Capitol St., N.E.   Phone: (503) 378-3773
Salem, OR 97310

OREGON STATE DEPARTMENT OF EDUCATION - RESOURCE/
   DISSEMINATION CENTER
700 Pringle Parkway, S.E.   Phone: (503) 378-8471
Salem, OR 97310   Juanita Maloney, Lib.Asst.

OREGON STATE DEPARTMENT OF HUMAN RESOURCES - SENIOR SERVICES
   DIVISION - LIBRARY
313 Public Service Bldg.   Phone: (503) 378-4728
Salem, OR 97310

OREGON STATE DEPARTMENT OF LAND CONSERVATION AND
DEVELOPMENT - LIBRARY
1175 Court St., N.E.   Phone: (503) 378-2980
Salem, OR 97310   Bonnie Putman, Libn./Sec.

OREGON STATE DEPARTMENT OF REVENUE - RESEARCH LIBRARY
955 Center St., N.E., Rm. 452   Phone: (503) 378-3727
Salem, OR 97310   Marty Orr, Libn.

OREGON STATE DEPARTMENT OF TRANSPORTATION - LIBRARY
127 Transportation Bldg.   Phone: (503) 378-6268
Salem, OR 97310   Marie Elefante, Libn.

OREGON STATE HOSPITAL - MEDICAL LIBRARY
2600 Center St., N.E.   Phone: (503) 378-2266
Salem, OR 97310   Sharon R. Paulsen, Libn.

OREGON STATE LIBRARY
State Library Bldg.
Summer and Court Sts.   Phone: (503) 378-4274
Salem, OR 97310   Wesley A. Doak, State Libn.

OREGON STATE LIBRARY - SERVICES FOR THE BLIND AND PHYSICALLY
HANDICAPPED
555 13th St., N.E.   Phone: (503) 378-3849
Salem, OR 97301   Margaret Rader, Act.Dir.

OREGON STATE SCHOOL FOR THE BLIND - MEDIA CENTER
700 Church St., S.E.   Phone: (503) 378-8025
Salem, OR 97310   Delphie Schuberg, Media Coord.

OREGON STATE SCHOOL FOR THE DEAF - LIBRARY
999 Locust St., N.E.   Phone: (503) 378-6252
Salem, OR 97310   Adoracion A. Alvarez, Curric.Dir.

OREGON STATE SECRETARY OF STATE - ARCHIVES AND RECORDS
CENTER
1005 Broadway, N.E.   Phone: (503) 378-4240
Salem, OR 97310

OREGON STATE SUPREME COURT LIBRARY
                                        Phone: (503) 378-6030
Salem, OR 97310   Roger Andrus, Law Libn.

OREGON STATE WATER RESOURCES DEPARTMENT - LIBRARY &
INFORMATION CENTER
555 13th St., N.E.   Phone: (503) 378-3739
Salem, OR 97310   Darnell Learn, Adm., Policy & Plan.

SALEM HOSPITAL - HEALTH SCIENCES LIBRARY AND INFORMATION
CENTER
665 Winter St., S.E.
Box 14001   Phone: (503) 370-5377
Salem, OR 97309   Susan Dyer, Health Sci.Libn.

WILLAMETTE UNIVERSITY - LAW LIBRARY
250 Winter St., S.E.   Phone: (503) 370-6386
Salem, OR 97301   Richard F. Breen, Jr., Law Libn.

AMUNDSON ASSOCIATES - PLANNING REFERENCE LIBRARY
200 S. Mill
Springfield, OR 97477

NICHOLS MUSEUM - LIBRARY
400 E. Scenic Dr.
The Dalles, OR 97058

TILLAMOOK COUNTY PIONEER MUSEUM - LIBRARY
2106 Second St.   Phone: (503) 842-4553
Tillamook, OR 97141   M. Wayne Jensen, Jr., Dir.

U.S. VETERANS ADMINISTRATION (OR-White City) - LIBRARY
VA Domiciliary   Phone: (503) 826-2111
White City, OR 97503   Sarah Fitzpatrick, Chf., Lib.Serv.

TEKTRONIX, INC. - WILSONVILLE BRANCH LIBRARY
Box 1000   Phone: (503) 685-3986
Wilsonville, OR 97070   Linda K. Appel, Br.Libn.

PENNSYLVANIA

ABINGTON MEMORIAL HOSPITAL - SCHOOL OF NURSING LIBRARY
1942 Horace Ave.   Phone: (215) 576-2598
Abington, PA 19001   Carol Paskowsky, Libn.

ABINGTON MEMORIAL HOSPITAL - WILMER MEMORIAL MEDICAL LIBRARY
1200 York Rd.   Phone: (215) 576-2096
Abington, PA 19001   Marion C. Chayes, Libn.

ALUMINUM COMPANY OF AMERICA - ALCOA TECHNICAL CENTER -
INFORMATION DEPARTMENT
                                        Phone: (412) 337-2283
Alcoa Center, PA 15069   P.W. Morton, Mgr., Info.Dept.

AIR PRODUCTS AND CHEMICALS, INC. - BUSINESS LIBRARY
Box 538   Phone: (215) 481-7442
Allentown, PA 18105   Michelle A. Burylo, Bus.Libn.

AIR PRODUCTS AND CHEMICALS, INC. - CRSD INFORMATION SERVICES
Box 538   Phone: (215) 481-7292
Allentown, PA 18105   Valerie K. Tucci, Mgr., Info.Serv.

ALLENTOWN ART MUSEUM - RESEARCH LIBRARY
5th & Court Sts.
Box 117   Phone: (215) 432-4333
Allentown, PA 18105   Peter F. Blume, Dir.

ALLENTOWN CALL-CHRONICLE - NEWSPAPER LIBRARY
6th & Linden Sts.
Box 1260   Phone: (215) 820-6523
Allentown, PA 18105   Lois A. Doncevic, Dir. of Lib.Serv.

THE ALLENTOWN HOSPITAL - HEALTH SCIENCES LIBRARY
17th & Chew Sts.   Phone: (215) 821-2263
Allentown, PA 18102   Barbara J. Iobst, Dir. of Lib.Serv.

ALLENTOWN STATE HOSPITAL - HEIM MEMORIAL LIBRARY
1600 Hanover Ave.   Phone: (215) 821-6265
Allentown, PA 18103   Margaret M. Caffrey, Libn.

AT & T BELL LABORATORIES & TECHNOLOGIES - LIBRARY
555 Union Blvd.   Phone: (215) 439-7648
Allentown, PA 18103   R.A. Di Cuollo, Group Supv.

CEDAR CREST COLLEGE - WOMEN'S CENTER †
                                        Phone: (215) 437-4471
Allentown, PA 18104   Ginny Pityo Mihalik, Dir.

CONGREGATION KENESETH ISRAEL - LIBRARY †
2227 Chew St.   Phone: (215) 435-9074
Allentown, PA 18104   Ruth Y. Radin, Lib. Chairperson

LEHIGH COUNTY HISTORICAL SOCIETY - SCOTT ANDREW TREXLER II
MEMORIAL LIBRARY
Old Court House
Fifth & Hamilton Sts.   Phone: (215) 435-1072
Allentown, PA 18101   Mrs. A. Foster Allen, Libn.

LEHIGH COUNTY LAW LIBRARY †
County Court House
5th & Hamilton Sts.
Box 1548   Phone: (215) 820-3308
Allentown, PA 18105   James L. Weirbach, Esq., Law Libn.

LEHIGH VALLEY COMMITTEE AGAINST HEALTH FRAUD, INC. - LIBRARY
Box 1602   Phone: (215) 437-1795
Allentown, PA 18105   Dr. Stephen Barrett

LEHIGH VALLEY HOSPITAL CENTER - HEALTH SCIENCES LIBRARY
1200 S. Cedar Crest Blvd.   Phone: (215) 776-8410
Allentown, PA 18105   Carolyn C. Nippert, Dir.

MUHLENBERG COLLEGE - JOHN A.W. HAAS LIBRARY
                                        Phone: (215) 433-3191
Allentown, PA 18104   Patricia Ann Sacks, Dir. of Libs.

RAILWAYS TO YESTERDAY, INC. - LEHIGH VALLEY TRANSPORTATION
   RESEARCH CENTER *
12th and Cumberland Sts.
2nd Fl., General Office   Phone: (215) 797-3242
Allentown, PA 18103   Douglas E. Peters, Hist./Libn.

SACRED HEART HOSPITAL - WILLIAM A. HAUSMAN MEDICAL LIBRARY
4th & Chew Sts.   Phone: (215) 821-3280
Allentown, PA 18102   Sylvia B. Cesanek, Libn.

TREXLER (Harry C.) MASONIC LIBRARY
1524 Linden St.   Phone: (215) 432-2618
Allentown, PA 18102   Paul R. Breitenstein, Libn.

PPG INDUSTRIES, INC. - C & R GROUP - RESEARCH CENTER LIBRARY
Rosanna Dr.
Box 1009   Phone: (412) 487-4500
Allison Park, PA 15101   Helen Lamrey, Supv., Info.Serv.

ALTOONA AREA PUBLIC LIBRARY & DISTRICT CENTER - PENNSYLVANIA
   ROOM
1600 Fifth Ave.   Phone: (814) 946-0417
Altoona, PA 16602   Alberta Y. Haught, Ref.Libn.

ALTOONA HOSPITAL - GLOVER MEMORIAL MEDICAL AND NURSING
   LIBRARY
Howard Ave. & 7th St.   Phone: (814) 946-2318
Altoona, PA 16603   Caryn J. Carr, Chf. of Lib.Serv.

ALTOONA MIRROR - LIBRARY
1000 Green Ave.
Box 2008   Phone: (814) 946-7457
Altoona, PA 16603   John T. Doyle, Libn.

MERCY HOSPITAL - SCHOOL OF NURSING LIBRARY
2621 8th Ave.   Phone: (814) 944-1681
Altoona, PA 16602   Patricia Shirley, Libn.

U.S. VETERANS ADMINISTRATION (PA-Altoona) - JAMES E. VAN ZANDT
   MEDICAL CENTER LIBRARY
     Phone: (814) 943-8164
Altoona, PA 16603   Rose Altberg, Chf.Libn.

TEMPLE UNIVERSITY - CENTRAL LIBRARY SYSTEM - AMBLER CAMPUS
   LIBRARY
Meetinghouse Rd.   Phone: (215) 643-1200
Ambler, PA 19002

PENNSYLVANIA STATE HISTORICAL & MUSEUM COMMISSION - OLD
   ECONOMY VILLAGE - LIBRARY
14th & Church Sts.   Phone: (412) 266-4500
Ambridge, PA 15003   Raymond V. Shepherd, Jr., Dir.

UNITED METHODIST CHURCH - HISTORICAL SOCIETY OF THE EASTERN
   PENNSYLVANIA CONFERENCE - ARCHIVES ROOM
Gossard Memorial Library
Lebanon Valley College   Phone: (717) 867-4411
Annville, PA 17003   Rev. Robert Curry, Archv.-Libn.

FAIRCHILD-WESTON SYSTEMS INC. - WESTON CONTROLS DIVISION -
   TECHNICAL LIBRARY
Kennedy Dr.   Phone: (717) 876-1500
Archbald, PA 18403   Arlene F. Kohl, Tech.Libn.

HEWLETT-PACKARD COMPANY - AVONDALE DIVISION LIBRARY
Route 41 & Starr Rd.   Phone: (215) 268-2281
Avondale, PA 19311   Shirley Lamkin, Clerk

PHILADELPHIA ASSOCIATION FOR PSYCHOANALYSIS - LOUIS S. KAPLAN
   MEMORIAL LIBRARY
15 St. Asaph's Rd.
Bala Cynwyd, PA 19004   June M. Strickland, Libn.

BAKER (Michael, Jr.), INC. - LIBRARY
4301 Dutch Ridge Rd.
Box 280   Phone: (412) 495-7711
Beaver, PA 15009   Ruth J. Williams, Libn.

BEAVER COUNTY LAW LIBRARY
Court House   Phone: (412) 728-5700
Beaver, PA 15009   Bette Sue Dengel, Law Libn.

BEAVER COUNTY TIMES - LIBRARY
400 Fair Ave.
Box 400   Phone: (412) 775-3200
Beaver, PA 15009   Dorothy L. Basar, Hd.Libn.

MEDICAL CENTER OF BEAVER COUNTY - HEALTH SCIENCES LIBRARY
1000 Dutch Ridge Rd.   Phone: (412) 728-7000
Beaver, PA 15009   Patricia M. Coghlan, Dir.

RESOURCE & RESEARCH CENTER FOR BEAVER COUNTY & LOCAL HISTORY
Carnegie Free Library
1301 7th Ave.   Phone: (412) 846-4340
Beaver Falls, PA 15010   Vivian C. McLaughlin, Dir.

CENTRE COUNTY LAW LIBRARY
Centre County Courthouse, Rm. 305   Phone: (814) 355-2861
Bellefonte, PA 16823   Lawrence C. Bickford, Court Adm.

PENNSYLVANIA STATE FISH COMMISSION LIBRARY - BENNER SPRING
   FISH RESEARCH STATION
R.D. 1, Box 200 C   Phone: (814) 355-4837
Bellefonte, PA 16823   Thomas R. Bender, Jr., Biologist

CHRIST UNITED METHODIST CHURCH - LIBRARY *
44 Highland Rd.   Phone: (412) 835-6621
Bethel Park, PA 15102

BETHLEHEM STEEL CORPORATION - BERNARD D. BROEKER LAW LIBRARY
Martin Tower Bldg., Rm. 2027   Phone: (215) 694-5002
Bethlehem, PA 18016   David D. Hendley, Law Libn.

BETHLEHEM STEEL CORPORATION - HERTY TECHNICAL INFORMATION
   CENTER
Homer Research Laboratories   Phone: (215) 694-6441
Bethlehem, PA 18016   L.M. Austen, Libn.

BETHLEHEM STEEL CORPORATION - SCHWAB INFORMATION CENTER
Martin Tower   Phone: (215) 694-3325
Bethlehem, PA 18016   Darla L. Wagner, Dir. of Lib.Serv.

COLLEGE PLACEMENT COUNCIL, INC. - RESOURCE INFORMATION CENTER
62 Highland Ave.   Phone: (215) 868-1421
Bethlehem, PA 18017   Linda M. Pengilly, Rsrc.Info.Ctr.Coord.

DIOCESE OF ALLENTOWN - PRO-LIFE LIBRARY
1135 Stefko Blvd.   Phone: (215) 691-0380
Bethlehem, PA 18017   Sr. M. Irene, O.S.F., Libn.

HISTORIC BETHLEHEM INC. - LIBRARY/ARCHIVES
501 Main St.   Phone: (215) 868-6311
Bethlehem, PA 18018   Becky Hoskins, Cur.

LEHIGH UNIVERSITY - FRITZ ENGINEERING LABORATORY LIBRARY
Bldg. 13, Rm. 601   Phone: (215) 861-3520
Bethlehem, PA 18015   Eleanor S. Nothelfer, Libn.

LEHIGH UNIVERSITY - MART SCIENCE AND ENGINEERING LIBRARY
15 East Packer Ave., Bldg. 8   Phone: (215) 861-3075
Bethlehem, PA 18015   Sharon Siegler, Asst.Dir., Sci. & Engr.

MORAVIAN CHURCH IN AMERICA - NORTHERN PROVINCE - MORAVIAN
   ARCHIVES
41 W. Locust St.   Phone: (215) 866-3255
Bethlehem, PA 18018   Vernon H. Nelson, Archv.

MORAVIAN COLLEGE - REEVES LIBRARY
Main St. at Elizabeth Ave.   Phone: (215) 865-0741
Bethlehem, PA 18018

MUHLENBERG MEDICAL CENTER - MEDICAL LIBRARY
Schoenersville Rd.   Phone: (215) 861-2237
Bethlehem, PA 18017   Carole Mazzeo, Libn.

ST. LUKE'S HOSPITAL OF BETHLEHEM, PENNSYLVANIA - AUDIOVISUAL
  LIBRARY
801 Ostrum St.   Phone: (215) 691-4341
Bethlehem, PA 18015   Robert Fields, Techn.

ST. LUKE'S HOSPITAL OF BETHLEHEM, PENNSYLVANIA - SCHOOL OF
  NURSING - TREXLER NURSES' LIBRARY
Bishopthorpe & Ostrum Sts.   Phone: (215) 691-4355
Bethlehem, PA 18015   Diane Frantz, Libn.

ST. LUKE'S HOSPITAL OF BETHLEHEM, PENNSYLVANIA - W.L. ESTES, JR.
  MEMORIAL LIBRARY
801 Ostrum St.   Phone: (215) 691-4227
Bethlehem, PA 18015   Maria D. Collette, Libn.

BLOOMSBURG UNIVERSITY OF PENNSYLVANIA - HARVEY A. ANDRUSS
  LIBRARY - SPECIAL COLLECTIONS
                                                    Phone: (717) 389-4216
Bloomsburg, PA 17815   William V. Ryan, Dir., Lib.Serv.

CERTAINTEED CORPORATION - CORPORATE LIBRARY/INFORMATION
  CENTER
1400 Union Meeting Rd.   Phone: (215) 542-0500
Blue Bell, PA 19422   Karola Rac, Chf.Libn.

SPERRY COMPUTER SYSTEMS - INFORMATION CENTER †
Township Line & Union Meeting Rds.
Box 500   Phone: (215) 542-2458
Blue Bell, PA 19424   Alma B. Campbell, Mgr.

ALLEGHENY LUDLUM STEEL CORPORATION - RESEARCH CENTER
  TECHNICAL LIBRARY
Alabama & Pacific Aves.
Brackenridge, PA 15014   Eileen W. Gallagher, Libn.

BRADFORD HOSPITAL - HUFF MEMORIAL LIBRARY
Interstate Pkwy.   Phone: (814) 368-4761
Bradford, PA 16701   Genevieve R. Killen, Dir., Med.Rec.

PENNSYLVANIA STATE DEPARTMENT OF PUBLIC WELFARE - MAYVIEW
  STATE HOSPITAL - MENTAL HEALTH AND MEDICAL LIBRARY
1601 Mayview Rd.   Phone: (412) 221-7500
Bridgeville, PA 15017-1599   William A. Suvak, Jr., Libn.Supv. I

UNIVERSAL-CYCLOPS SPECIALTY STEEL DIVISION - TECHNICAL
  INFORMATION CENTER
Mayer St.
Bridgeville, PA 15017

DELAWARE VALLEY MEDICAL CENTER - JOHN A. WHYTE MEDICAL
  LIBRARY †
Wilson Ave. & Pond St.   Phone: (215) 245-2335
Bristol, PA 19007   Marian C. Moran, Med.Libn.

ROHM & HAAS COMPANY - RESEARCH DIVISION - INFORMATION
  SERVICES DEPARTMENT - LIBRARY
Box 718   Phone: (215) 785-8055
Bristol, PA 19007   Barbara G. Prewitt, Res.Lib.Mgr.

BROCKWAY GLASS COMPANY, INC. - ENGINEERING AND RESEARCH
  CENTER LIBRARY *
                                                    Phone: (814) 261-5275
Brockway, PA 15824   Ed McKinley

U.S. FOREST SERVICE - NORTHEASTERN FOREST EXPERIMENT STATION
  LIBRARY
370 Reed Rd.   Phone: (215) 461-3105
Broomall, PA 19008   Thomas L. Baucom, Pub.Aff.Off.

ACADEMY OF THE NEW CHURCH - LIBRARY
2815 Huntingdon Pike
Box 278-68   Phone: (215) 947-0203
Bryn Athyn, PA 19009   Mary Alice Carswell, Dir.

AMERICAN COLLEGE - VANE B. LUCAS MEMORIAL LIBRARY
270 S. Bryn Mawr Ave.   Phone: (215) 896-4507
Bryn Mawr, PA 19010   Judith L. Hill, Libn.

AMERICAN COLLEGE - VANE B. LUCAS MEMORIAL LIBRARY - ORAL
  HISTORY CENTER & ARCHIVES
270 Bryn Mawr Ave.   Phone: (215) 896-4506
Bryn Mawr, PA 19010   Marjorie Amos Fletcher, Dir.

BRYN MAWR COLLEGE - GEOLOGY LIBRARY
                                                    Phone: (215) 645-5118
Bryn Mawr, PA 19010   Anne Pringle, Hd., Sci. & Psych.Libs.

BRYN MAWR HOSPITAL - MEDICAL LIBRARY
                                                    Phone: (215) 896-3160
Bryn Mawr, PA 19010   L.D. Gundry, Chf.Med.Libn.

BRYN MAWR HOSPITAL - MEDICAL LIBRARY - NURSING DIVISION
Lindsay Ave.   Phone: (215) 896-3084
Bryn Mawr, PA 19010   L.D. Gundry, Chf.Med.Libn.

COMBS COLLEGE OF MUSIC - LIBRARY
464 S. Roberts Rd.   Phone: (215) 527-6900
Bryn Mawr, PA 19010   Rosemarie B. LaFollette, Libn.

BUTLER COUNTY LAW LIBRARY
Court House   Phone: (412) 285-4731
Butler, PA 16001   Kate Geiger, Law Libn.

BUTLER MEMORIAL HOSPITAL - RUTH ARMSTRONG MEMORIAL MEDICAL
  LIBRARY
911 E. Brady St.   Phone: (412) 284-4240
Butler, PA 16001   Rita V. Liebler, Med.Libn.

U.S. VETERANS ADMINISTRATION (PA-Butler) - MEDICAL CENTER LIBRARY
                                                    Phone: (412) 287-4781
Butler, PA 16001   Dianne Hohn, Chf., Lib.Serv.

BRANDYWINE HOSPITAL - HEALTH SCIENCES LIBRARY AND
  INFORMATION RESOURCE CENTER
201 Reeceville Rd.   Phone: (215) 383-8147
Caln Township, PA 19320   John F. Kelley, Dir.

ALLIANCE COLLEGE - LIBRARY - SPECIAL COLLECTIONS
Washington Hall
Fullerton Ave.   Phone: (814) 398-2098
Cambridge Springs, PA 16403   Stanley J. Kozaczka, Hd.Libn.

HOSPITAL ASSOCIATION OF PENNSYLVANIA - LIBRARY SERVICES
Box 608   Phone: (717) 763-7053
Camp Hill, PA 17011   Alice Wiley, Libn.

PENNSYLVANIA BLUE SHIELD - RESEARCH LIBRARY
1800 Center St.   Phone: (717) 763-3151
Camp Hill, PA 17011   Charlene Mezellin, Sec.

WESTERN CENTER - LIBRARY
333 Curry Hill Rd.   Phone: (412) 745-0700
Canonsburg, PA 15317   Nicholas L. Liguori, Libn.

CUMBERLAND COUNTY HISTORICAL SOCIETY & HAMILTON LIBRARY
21 N. Pitt St.
Box 626   Phone: (717) 249-7610
Carlisle, PA 17013   Ann Kramer Hoffer, Pres.

CUMBERLAND COUNTY LAW LIBRARY †
Court House, S. Hanover St.   Phone: (717) 249-1133
Carlisle, PA 17013   Mary S. Rykoskey, Libn.

DICKINSON COLLEGE - LIBRARY - SPECIAL COLLECTIONS †
College Library   Phone: (717) 245-1399
Carlisle, PA 17013   Martha Calvert Slotten, Cur.

DICKINSON SCHOOL OF LAW - SHEELY-LEE LAW LIBRARY
150 S. College St.   Phone: (717) 243-4611
Carlisle, PA 17013   James R. Fox, Law Libn.

U.S. ARMY MILITARY HISTORY INSTITUTE
                                                    Phone: (717) 245-4139
Carlisle Barracks, PA 17013-5008   Col. Donald P. Shaw, Dir.

U.S. ARMY WAR COLLEGE - LIBRARY
Phone: (717) 245-3660
Carlisle Barracks, PA 17013   Barbara E. Stevens, Dir.

NATIONAL STANDARDS COUNCIL OF AMERICAN EMBROIDERERS - NSCAE
LIBRARY
Carnegie Office Park
600 Bell Ave.   Phone: (412) 279-0299
Carnegie, PA 15106   June H. Haulk, Libn.

WOODVILLE STATE HOSPITAL - PROFESSIONAL LIBRARY †
Phone: (412) 279-2000
Carnegie, PA 15106   Mary Thompson, Libn.

BRANDYWINE RIVER MUSEUM LIBRARY
Box 141   Phone: (215) 388-7601
Chadds Ford, PA 19317   Ruth Bassett, Libn.

MOTORCYCLE SAFETY FOUNDATION - INFORMATION RESOURCE CENTER
Box 120   Phone: (215) 388-1555
Chadds Ford, PA 19317   Cynthia A. Griffin, Libn.

FRANKLIN COUNTY LAW LIBRARY
Court House   Phone: (717) 263-4809
Chambersburg, PA 17201   Paula S. Rabinowitz, Libn.

CROZER CHESTER MEDICAL CENTER - MEDICAL LIBRARY
15th St. & Upland Ave.   Phone: (215) 447-2600
Chester, PA 19013   Elizabeth R. Warner, Med.Libn.

DELAWARE COUNTY HISTORICAL SOCIETY - LIBRARY
Box 1036, Widener University   Phone: (215) 874-6444
Chester, PA 19013   Judith L. Buck, Cur.

LINDSAY LAW LIBRARY
Wolfgram Memorial Library
Widener Univ.   Phone: (215) 872-3821
Chester, PA 19013

WIDENER UNIVERSITY - WOLFGRAM MEMORIAL LIBRARY
17th & Walnut Sts.   Phone: (215) 499-4066
Chester, PA 19013   Theresa Taborsky, Lib.Dir.

SPRING GARDEN COLLEGE - LIBRARY
102 E. Mermaid Ln.   Phone: (215) 242-3700
Chestnut Hill, PA 19118   Mildred Glushakow, Dir.

CHEYNEY UNIVERSITY OF PENNSYLVANIA - LESLIE PINCKNEY HILL
LIBRARY - SPECIAL COLLECTIONS
Phone: (215) 399-2062
Cheyney, PA 19319   Floyd C. Hardy, Ph.D., Dir. of Lib.Serv.

HERCULES, INC. - PICCO RESINS DIVISION - LIBRARY
120 State St.   Phone: (412) 233-8600
Clairton, PA 15025   Norman E. Daughenbaugh, Tech.Libn.

CLARION COUNTY HISTORICAL SOCIETY - LIBRARY/MUSEUM
18 Grant St.   Phone: (814) 226-4450
Clarion, PA 16214   Carla R. Henry, Libn.

CLARION UNIV. OF PENNSYLVANIA - COLL. OF LIBRARY SCIENCE - CTR.
FOR THE STUDY OF RURAL LIBRARIANSHIP - LIB.
Phone: (814) 226-2383
Clarion, PA 16214   Dr. Bernard Vavrek, Coord.

CLARION UNIVERSITY OF PENNSYLVANIA - RENA M. CARLSON LIBRARY
Phone: (814) 226-2343
Clarion, PA 16214-1232   Gerard B. McCabe, Dir. of Libs.

BAPTIST BIBLE COLLEGE OF PENNSYLVANIA - RICHARD J. MURPHY
MEMORIAL LIBRARY
538 Venard Rd.   Phone: (717) 587-1172
Clarks Summit, PA 18411   David C. McClain, Hd.Libn.

CLEARFIELD LAW LIBRARY
Court House   Phone: (814) 765-9511
Clearfield, PA 16830   Carl Soderlund, Libn.

BRANDYWINE HOSPITAL - SCHOOL OF NURSING - LIBRARY
300 Strode Ave.   Phone: (215) 383-9003
Coatesville, PA 19320   John F. Kelley, Dir.

LUKENS STEEL COMPANY - TECHNICAL LIBRARY
Phone: (215) 383-2675
Coatesville, PA 19320   Gloria R. Hartley, Tech.Libn.

U.S. VETERANS ADMINISTRATION (PA-Coatesville) - MEDICAL CENTER
LIBRARY
Phone: (215) 384-7711
Coatesville, PA 19320   Alice M. VonderLindt, Chf., Lib.Serv.

NATIONAL ASSOCIATION OF WATCH AND CLOCK COLLECTORS MUSEUM -
LIBRARY
514 Poplar St.
Box 33   Phone: (717) 684-8261
Columbia, PA 17512   G.L. Bagwell, Pres.

QUAKER CHEMICAL CORPORATION - INFORMATION RESOURCES CENTER
Phone: (215) 828-4250
Conshohocken, PA 19428   Ellen B. Morrow, Mgr.

PITTSBURGH-DES MOINES CORPORATION - ENGINEERING LIBRARY
410 Rouser Rd.   Phone: (412) 262-9114
Coraopolis, PA 15108   Louise Franz, Libn.

CORRY AREA HISTORICAL SOCIETY - LIBRARY
Box 107
Corry, PA 16407   Mrs. Keppel Tiffany, Libn.

U.S. NATL. PARK SERVICE - ALLEGHENY PORTAGE RAILROAD NATL.
HISTORIC SITE - LIBRARY
Lemon House
Box 247   Phone: (814) 886-8176
Cresson, PA 16630   Dean R. Garrett, Chf.

DANVILLE STATE HOSPITAL - MEDICAL LIBRARY *
Phone: (717) 275-7011
Danville, PA 17821

GEISINGER MEDICAL CENTER - MEDICAL LIBRARY
N. Academy Ave.   Phone: (717) 275-6463
Danville, PA 17822   Britain G. Roth, Mgr., Lrng.Rsrcs.

GEISINGER MEDICAL CENTER - SCHOOL OF NURSING LIBRARY
Phone: (717) 271-6288
Danville, PA 17822   Claire A. Huntington, Libn.

MERCY CATHOLIC MEDICAL CENTER - HEALTH SCIENCES LIBRARY
Lansdowne & Baily Rd.   Phone: (215) 586-2050
Darby, PA 19023   Janet Clinton, Chf. of Lib.Serv.

DEVEREUX FOUNDATION - PROFESSIONAL LIBRARY
19 S. Waterloo Rd.
Box 400   Phone: (215) 296-6901
Devon, PA 19333   Annetta Zulick, Libn.

BUCKS COUNTY HISTORICAL SOCIETY - SPRUANCE LIBRARY
Pine St.   Phone: (215) 345-0210
Doylestown, PA 18901   Terry A. McNealy, Lib.Dir.

BUCKS COUNTY LAW LIBRARY
Court House   Phone: (215) 348-2911
Doylestown, PA 18901   Katharine P. Lehnig, Law Libn.

BUCKS COUNTY PLANNING COMMISSION STAFF LIBRARY
22-28 S. Main St.   Phone: (215) 348-2911
Doylestown, PA 18901   Jeffrey A. Vey, Info.Spec.

DELAWARE VALLEY COLLEGE OF SCIENCE AND AGRICULTURE - JOSEPH
KRAUSKOPF MEMORIAL LIBRARY
Phone: (215) 345-1500
Doylestown, PA 18901   Constance R. Shook, Hd.Libn.

EARLY AMERICAN INDUSTRIES ASSOCIATION - LIBRARY
Bucks County Historical Society
Pine St.   Phone: (215) 345-0210
Doylestown, PA 18901   Terry A. McNealy, Libn.

AMERICAN SOCIETY OF ANCIENT INSTRUMENTS - LIBRARY
1205 Blythe Ave.   Phone: (215) 789-1205
Drexel Hill, PA 19026   Frederick Stad, Pres.

EAGLEVILLE HOSPITAL - HENRY S. LOUCHHEIM LIBRARY
100 Eagleville Rd.   Phone: (215) 539-6000
Eagleville, PA 19408   Harold Selix, Mgr. of Lib.Serv.

EAST STROUDSBURG UNIVERSITY - KENT LIBRARY †
                                              Phone: (717) 424-3465
East Stroudsburg, PA 18301   Russell J. Emele, Dir. of Lib.

POCONO HOSPITAL - MARSHALL R. METZGAR MEDICAL LIBRARY
206 E. Brown St.   Phone: (717) 421-4000
East Stroudsburg, PA 18301   Ellen P. Woodhead, Dir.

EASTON HOSPITAL - MEDICAL LIBRARY
21st & Lehigh Sts.   Phone: (215) 250-4130
Easton, PA 18042   Mary James, Libn.

FOUNDATION FOR DISABILITY INTERCHANGE - LIBRARY
Box 602   Phone: (215) 258-6663
Easton, PA 18042   Yisrael Mayer, Sec.

HIVE PUBLISHING COMPANY - MANAGEMENT HISTORY LIBRARY
Alpha Bldg.   Phone: (215) 258-6663
Easton, PA 18042   Kiva Perkins, Cur.

LAFAYETTE COLLEGE - AMERICAN FRIENDS OF LAFAYETTE COLLECTION
David Bishop Skillman Library   Phone: (215) 253-6281
Easton, PA 18042

LAFAYETTE COLLEGE - KIRBY LIBRARY OF GOVERNMENT AND LAW †
Kirby Hall   Phone: (215) 250-5399
Easton, PA 18042   Mercedes Benitez Sharpless, Libn.

NORTHAMPTON COUNTY HISTORICAL AND GENEALOGICAL SOCIETY -
   HISTORICAL MUSEUM AND LIBRARY
101 S. Fourth St.   Phone: (215) 253-1222
Easton, PA 18042   Bruce Drinkhouse, Pres.

NORTHAMPTON COUNTY LAW LIBRARY
7th & Washington Sts.   Phone: (215) 253-4111
Easton, PA 18042   George A. Gollub, Law Libn.

PENNSYLVANIA CANAL SOCIETY - CANAL MUSEUM - RESEARCH LIBRARY *
Hugo Moore Park
200 S. Delaware Dr.
Box 877   Phone: (215) 258-7155
Easton, PA 18042   Marsha L. Kleedorfer, Cur.

CAMBRIA COUNTY FREE LAW LIBRARY
Courthouse   Phone: (814) 427-5440
Ebensburg, PA 15931   Judy Patterson, Libn.

CAMBRIA COUNTY HISTORICAL SOCIETY - MUSEUM & LIBRARY
521 W. High St.   Phone: (814) 472-6674
Ebensburg, PA 15931   Sara Leishman, Cur.

BISHOP'S MILL HISTORICAL INSTITUTE - SOL FEINSTONE LIBRARY
Ridley Creek State Park   Phone: (215) 566-1725
Edgemont, PA 19028   Betty Arnett

EDINBORO UNIVERSITY OF PENNSYLVANIA - BARON-FORNESS LIBRARY
                                           Phone: (814) 732-2780
Edinboro, PA 16444   Saul Weinstein, Dir.

ENSANIAN PHYSICOCHEMICAL INSTITUTE - INFORMATION CENTER FOR
   GRAVITATION CHEMISTRY
Box 98   Phone: (814) 225-3296
Eldred, PA 16731   Elizabeth A. Ensanian, Chf.Libn.

ELIZABETHTOWN COLLEGE - ZUG MEMORIAL LIBRARY - ARCHIVES
                                           Phone: (717) 367-1151
Elizabethtown, PA 17022   Anna M. Carper, Dir.

UNITED STATES SPACE EDUCATION ASSOCIATION - USSEA MEDIA
   CENTER
746 Turnpike Rd.   Phone: (717) 367-3265
Elizabethtown, PA 17022   Stephen M. Cobaugh, Intl.Pres.

BETH SHOLOM CONGREGATION - JOSEPH & ELIZABETH SCHWARTZ
   LIBRARY
Foxcroft & Old York Rd.   Phone: (215) 887-1342
Elkins Park, PA 19117   David J. Salaman, Libn.

CONGREGATION ADATH JESHURUN - GOTTLIEB MEMORIAL LIBRARY
York & Ashbourne Rds.   Phone: (215) 635-1337
Elkins Park, PA 19117   Carole G. Ozeroff, Libn.

REFORM CONGREGATION KENESETH ISRAEL - MEYERS LIBRARY
York Rd. & Township Line   Phone: (215) 887-8700
Elkins Park, PA 19117

U.S. NATL. PARK SERVICE - HOPEWELL VILLAGE NATL. HISTORIC SITE -
   LIBRARY
R.D. 2, Box 345   Phone: (215) 582-8773
Elverson, PA 19520   Elizabeth E. Disrude, Supt.

ELWYN INSTITUTES - LIBRARY
                                          Phone: (215) 358-6487
Elwyn, PA 19063   Joyce Lentz, Libn.

CAMERON COUNTY HISTORICAL SOCIETY - LITTLE MUSEUM
R.R. 2, Box 54   Phone: (814) 483-3636
Emporium, PA 15834   Mrs. Merle L. Bowser, Pres.

HISTORICAL SOCIETY OF THE COCALICO VALLEY - MUSEUM AND LIBRARY
249 W. Main St.   Phone: (717) 733-1616
Ephrata, PA 17522   Clarence E. Spohn, Cur.

PENNSYLVANIA STATE HISTORICAL & MUSEUM COMMISSION - EPHRATA
   CLOISTER - LIBRARY
632 W. Main St.   Phone: (717) 733-6600
Ephrata, PA 17522   James A. Lewars, Act.Adm.

AMERICAN STERILIZER COMPANY - LIBRARY
2424 W. 23rd St.   Phone: (814) 452-3100
Erie, PA 16512   Janis M. Ruben, Info.Spec.

ANSHE HESED TEMPLE - LIBRARY †
930 Liberty St.   Phone: (814) 454-2426
Erie, PA 16502   Rose Tanner, Chm.

CONGREGATION BRITH SHALOM - MORRIS P. RADOV JEWISH CENTER
   LIBRARY *
3207 State St.   Phone: (814) 454-2431
Erie, PA 16508

ERIE COUNTY HISTORICAL SOCIETY
Cashiers House, 417 State St.   Phone: (814) 454-1813
Erie, PA 16501   Robert F. Taft, Pres.

ERIE COUNTY LAW LIBRARY
Court House   Phone: (814) 452-3333
Erie, PA 16501   Max C. Peaster, Libn.

FIRST UNITED PRESBYTERIAN CHURCH OF THE COVENANT - BRITTAIN
   LIBRARY *
250 W. 7th St.   Phone: (814) 456-4243
Erie, PA 16501   Louise Loesel, Libn.

GENERAL ELECTRIC COMPANY - DIRECT CURRENT MOTOR AND
   GENERATOR DEPARTMENT - LIBRARY
3001 E. Lake Rd.
Erie, PA 16531

GENERAL ELECTRIC COMPANY - TRANSPORTATION TECHNOLOGY CENTER
   - TECHNICAL INFORMATION CENTER *
Bldg. 14, Rm. 123A
2901 E. Lake Rd.   Phone: (814) 455-5466
Erie, PA 16531   Robert H. Berry, Tech.Info.Spec.

HAMMERMILL PAPER COMPANY - CORPORATE RESEARCH TECHNICAL
   LIBRARY
1540 East Lake Rd.
Box 10050   Phone: (814) 456-8811
Erie, PA 16533   Patricia D. Schmitt, Tech.Libn.

HAMOT MEDICAL CENTER - LIBRARY SERVICES
201 State St.   Phone: (814) 455-6711
Erie, PA 16550   Jean A. Tauber, Dir., Lib.Serv.

LORD CORPORATION - INFORMATION CENTERS
Box 10039   Phone: (814) 456-8511
Erie, PA 16514

MERCYHURST COLLEGE - LIBRARY - ARCHIVES
501 E. 38th St.   Phone: (814) 825-4000
Erie, PA 16546   Joanne S. Cooper, Dir.

ST. VINCENT HEALTH CENTER - HEALTH SCIENCE LIBRARY
232 W. 25th St.   Phone: (814) 459-4000
Erie, PA 16512   Joni M. Alex, Med.Libn.

MINE SAFETY APPLIANCES COMPANY - MSA RESEARCH CORPORATION -
    CALLERY CHEMICAL COMPANY - LIBRARY
                                                            Phone: (412) 538-3510
Evans City, PA 16033   Paula L. Lindey, Libn.

FOOTE MINERAL COMPANY - RESEARCH AND ENGINEERING DEPARTMENT
    LIBRARY
Rte. 100   Phone: (215) 363-6500
Exton, PA 19341   M.R. Abernathy, Mgr., Lib.

NEWCOMEN SOCIETY OF THE UNITED STATES - THOMAS NEWCOMEN LIB.
    IN STEAM TECHNOLOGY & INDUSTRIAL HISTORY
412 Newcomen Rd.   Phone: (215) 363-6600
Exton, PA 19335   Nancy Arnold, Libn./Cur.

U.S. NATL. PARK SERVICE - FORT NECESSITY NATL. BATTLEFIELD -
    LIBRARY
The National Pike   Phone: (412) 329-5512
Farmington, PA 15437   Robert Warren, Supt.

SHENANGO VALLEY OSTEOPATHIC HOSPITAL - MEDICAL LIBRARY
2200 Memorial Dr. Extended   Phone: (412) 981-3500
Farrell, PA 16121   Ethelnel Baron, Staff Sec.

BUDD COMPANY TECHNICAL LIBRARY
375 Commerce Dr.   Phone: (215) 643-2950
Fort Washington, PA 19034   Herbert A. Johnle, Mgr.

HONEYWELL, INC. - PROCESS CONTROLS DIVISION - INFORMATION
    CENTER, M.S. 221
Virginia Dr.   Phone: (215) 641-3982
Fort Washington, PA 19034   Dawn Chrisman, Lib.Ck.

MC NEIL LABORATORIES - LIBRARY *
Camp Hill Rd.   Phone: (215) 233-7000
Fort Washington, PA 19034   M.E. Rountree, Hd.Libn.

WILLIAM H. RORER, INC. - RESEARCH LIBRARY
500 Virginia Dr.   Phone: (215) 628-6358
Fort Washington, PA 19034   Catherine M. Heslin, Info.Sci.

FRANKLIN REGIONAL MEDICAL CENTER - MEDICAL LIBRARY
1 Spruce St.   Phone: (814) 437-7000
Franklin, PA 16323   Mr. L.P. Gilliland, Libn.

VENANGO COUNTY LAW LIBRARY
Court House
Corner 12th & Liberty Sts.   Phone: (814) 437-6871
Franklin, PA 16323   Julia I. McNamara, Law Libn.

FRANKLIN MINT - INFORMATION RESEARCH SERVICES
                                                            Phone: (215) 459-6374
Franklin Center, PA 19091   Nancy Davis, Dir.

PENNSYLVANIA STATE HISTORICAL & MUSEUM COMMISSION -
    PENNSYLVANIA LUMBER MUSEUM - LIBRARY
Box K   Phone: (814) 435-2652
Galeton, PA 16922   Dolores M. Buchsen, Cur.

ADAMS COUNTY HISTORICAL SOCIETY - LIBRARY
Drawer A, Schmucker Hall
Seminary Campus   Phone: (717) 334-4723
Gettysburg, PA 17325   Dr. Charles H. Glatfelter, Dir.

ADAMS COUNTY LAW LIBRARY
Court House   Phone: (717) 334-6781
Gettysburg, PA 17325   Mr. Claire S. Weaver, Law Libn.

GETTYSBURG COLLEGE - DEPARTMENT OF CHEMISTRY - LIBRARY
Breidenbaugh Hall
Gettysburg, PA 17325   Lillian S. Jackson, Chem. Faculty

GETTYSBURG COLLEGE - MUSSELMAN LIBRARY - SPECIAL COLLECTIONS
                                                            Phone: (717) 334-3131
Gettysburg, PA 17325   Nancy Scott, Spec.Coll.Libn./Archv.

LUTHERAN THEOLOGICAL SEMINARY - A.R. WENTZ LIBRARY
66 W. Confederate Ave.   Phone: (717) 334-6286
Gettysburg, PA 17325   Donald N. Matthews, Libn.

U.S. NATL. PARK SERVICE - GETTYSBURG NATL. MILITARY PARK -
    CYCLORAMA CENTER LIBRARY
                                                            Phone: (717) 334-1124
Gettysburg, PA 17325   Kathleen R. Georg, Coord.

DEACONESS COMMUNITY LUTHERAN CHURCH OF AMERICA - LUTHERAN
    DEACONESS COMMUNITY LIBRARY
801 Merion Sq. Rd.
Gladwyne, PA 19035

FAIR ACRES GERIATRIC CENTER - MEDICAL LIBRARY
Rte. 352   Phone: (215) 891-5717
Glen Riddle-Lima, PA 19037   Lisa A. Maffei, Health Info.Coord.

CARMEL PRESBYTERIAN CHURCH - MEMORIAL LIBRARY
100 Edge Hill Rd.   Phone: (215) 887-1074
Glenside, PA 19038   Mrs. James T. Eaton, Libn.

CHILD CUSTODY EVALUATION SERVICES, INC. - RESOURCE CENTER
Box 202   Phone: (215) 576-0177
Glenside, PA 19038   Dr. Ken Lewis, Dir.

BRETHREN IN CHRIST CHURCH AND MESSIAH COLLEGE - ARCHIVES
Messiah College   Phone: (717) 766-2511
Grantham, PA 17027   Dr. E. Morris Sider, Archv.

CITIZENS LAW LIBRARY †
202 Courthouse Sq.   Phone: (412) 834-2191
Greensburg, PA 15601   Peter P. Cherellia, Libn.

WESTMORELAND COUNTY HISTORICAL SOCIETY - CALVIN E. POLLINS
    MEMORIAL LIBRARY
Museum of Art Building
221 N. Main St.   Phone: (412) 836-1800
Greensburg, PA 15601   Linda E. Forish, Adm.Sec.

WESTMORELAND HOSPITAL - LIBRARY AND HEALTH RESOURCE CENTER
532 W. Pittsburgh St.   Phone: (412) 832-4088
Greensburg, PA 15601-2282   Janet C. Petrak, Libn.

WESTMORELAND MUSEUM OF ART - ART REFERENCE LIBRARY
221 N. Main St.   Phone: (412) 837-1500
Greensburg, PA 15601   Jeannine Earley, Musm.Asst.

HAMBURG CENTER FOR THE MENTALLY RETARDED - STAFF DEVELOPMENT
    LIBRARY
Hamburg, PA 19526

AMP, INC. - TECHNICAL INFORMATION CENTER
Box 3608, Res. Div.
Harrisburg, PA 17105

DAUPHIN COUNTY LAW LIBRARY
Dauphin County Court House
Front & Market Sts.   Phone: (717) 255-2797
Harrisburg, PA 17101   Brenda Mull, Libn.

HARRISBURG HOSPITAL - LIBRARY/MEDIA SERVICES
S. Front St.   Phone: (717) 782-5511
Harrisburg, PA 17101   Cheryl A. Capitani, Dir., Lib./Media Serv.

HARRISBURG STATE HOSPITAL - STAFF LIBRARY
Cameron & Maclay Sts.
Pouch A   Phone: (717) 787-9215
Harrisburg, PA 17105   Glenn Wayne Miller, Staff Libn.

HISTORICAL SOCIETY OF DAUPHIN COUNTY - ARCHIVES/LIBRARY
219 S. Front St.   Phone: (717) 233-3462
Harrisburg, PA 17104   Thomas L. Schaefer, Archv.

MC NEES, WALLACE AND NURICK - LIBRARY
100 Pine St.
Box 1166   Phone: (717) 232-8000
Harrisburg, PA 17108   Mary E. Rinesmith, Libn.

PATRIOT NEWS COMPANY - NEWS LIBRARY
812 Market St.
Box 2265   Phone: (717) 255-8402
Harrisburg, PA 17105   Deanna S. Beeching, Libn.

PENNSYLVANIA PUBLIC UTILITY COMMISSION - LIBRARY
Box 3265   Phone: (717) 787-4466
Harrisburg, PA 17120   Thais Gardy, Libn.

PENNSYLVANIA STATE DEPARTMENT OF ENVIRONMENTAL RESOURCES -
    BUREAU OF TOPOGRAPHIC & GEOLOGIC SURVEY LIB.
916 Executive House Apts.
Second & Chestnut Sts.   Phone: (717) 783-8077
Harrisburg, PA 17120   Sandra Blust, Libn.

PENNSYLVANIA STATE DEPT. OF ENVIRONMENTAL RESOURCES -
    ENVIRONMENTAL PROTECTION TECHNICAL REFERENCE LIBRARY
Fulton Bldg., 17th Fl.
Box 2063   Phone: (717) 787-9647
Harrisburg, PA 17120   Wanda R. Bell, Libn.

PENNSYLVANIA STATE DEPARTMENT OF TRANSPORTATION -
    TRANSPORTATION INFORMATION CENTER
903 Transportation & Safety Bldg.   Phone: (717) 787-6527
Harrisburg, PA 17120   Judy H. Gutshall, Libn.

PENNSYLVANIA STATE HISTORICAL & MUSEUM COMMISSION - DIVISION
    OF ARCHIVES AND MANUSCRIPTS
William Penn Memorial Museum
& Archives Bldg.
Box 1026   Phone: (717) 787-3051
Harrisburg, PA 17120   Harry E. Whipkey, State Archv.

PENNSYLVANIA STATE HISTORICAL & MUSEUM COMMISSION -
    REFERENCE LIBRARY
William Penn Memorial Museum & Archives Bldg.
Box 1026   Phone: (717) 783-9898
Harrisburg, PA 17108-1026   Carol W. Tallman, Lib.Techn.

PENNSYLVANIA STATE - JOINT STATE GOVERNMENT COMMISSION -
    LIBRARY
108 Finance Bldg.   Phone: (717) 787-6803
Harrisburg, PA 17120   Donna Dort, Libn.

PENNSYLVANIA STATE - LEGISLATIVE REFERENCE BUREAU LIBRARY
Box 1127   Phone: (717) 787-4816
Harrisburg, PA 17120   Susan K. Zavacky, Libn.

PENNSYLVANIA STATE LIBRARY
Forum Bldg.
Walnut St. & Commonwealth Ave.   Phone: (717) 783-5968
Harrisburg, PA 17105   Elliot L. Shelkrot, State Libn.

PENNSYLVANIA STATE - OFFICE OF ATTORNEY GENERAL - LAW LIBRARY
1525 Strawberry Square   Phone: (717) 787-3176
Harrisburg, PA 17120   Ellen R. Chack, Libn.

POLYCLINIC MEDICAL CENTER - MEDICAL STAFF LIBRARY
Third & Radnor Sts.
Box 3410   Phone: (717) 782-4292
Harrisburg, PA 17105   Suzanne M. Shultz, Libn.

HATBORO BAPTIST CHURCH - LIBRARY
32 N. York Ave.   Phone: (215) 675-8400
Hatboro, PA 19040   Carolyn A. Zimmerman, Libn.

BIBLICAL THEOLOGICAL SEMINARY - LIBRARY
200 N. Main St.   Phone: (215) 368-5000
Hatfield, PA 19440   James C. Pakala, Libn.

CATHOLIC LIBRARY ASSOCIATION - NATIONAL HEADQUARTERS -
    LIBRARY
461 W. Lancaster Ave.   Phone: (215) 649-5250
Haverford, PA 19041   Matthew R. Wilt, Exec.Dir.

HAVERFORD COLLEGE - TREASURE ROOM AND QUAKER COLLECTION
Haverford College Library   Phone: (215) 896-1161
Haverford, PA 19041   Edwin B. Bronner, Cur.

HAVERFORD STATE HOSPITAL - HEALTH SCIENCES LIBRARY †
3500 Darby Rd.   Phone: (215) 525-9620
Haverford, PA 19041   Joyce Matheson, Dir., Lib.Serv.

HAVERFORD TOWNSHIP HISTORICAL SOCIETY - LIBRARY
Box 825
Havertown, PA 19083   Margaret E. Johnston, Cur.

GILMAN MUSEUM - LIBRARY
At the Cave   Phone: (215) 838-8767
Hellertown, PA 18055   Naomi P. Gilman, Info.Dir.

AACA LIBRARY & RESEARCH CENTER, INC.
501 W. Governor Rd.
Box 417   Phone: (717) 534-1910
Hershey, PA 17033   Kim M. Miller, Libn.

HERSHEY FOODS CORPORATION - COMMUNICATIONS CENTER
1025 Reese Ave.   Phone: (717) 534-5106
Hershey, PA 17033   William M. Woodruff, Mgr., Commun.Ctr.

PENNSYLVANIA STATE UNIVERSITY - COLLEGE OF MEDICINE - GEORGE T.
    HARRELL LIBRARY
Milton S. Hershey Medical Center   Phone: (717) 534-8629
Hershey, PA 17033   Lois J. Lehman, Libn.

BLAIR COUNTY LAW LIBRARY †
County Court House   Phone: (814) 695-5541
Hollidaysburg, PA 16648   June C. Ringdal, Law Libn.

SWIGART MUSEUM - LIBRARY
Museum Pk., Box 214   Phone: (814) 643-3000
Huntingdon, PA 16652   William E. Swigart, Jr., Exec.Dir.

SERVANTS OF THE IMMACULATE HEART OF MARY - ARCHIVES
Villa Maria House of Studies   Phone: (215) 647-2160
Immaculata, PA 19345   Sr. Genevieve Mary, Archv.

HISTORICAL AND GENEALOGICAL SOCIETY OF INDIANA COUNTY -
    LIBRARY AND ARCHIVES
Silas M. Clark House
S. Sixth & Wayne Ave.   Phone: (412) 463-9600
Indiana, PA 15701   Margaret Rees Derwart, Libn.

INDIANA COUNTY LAW LIBRARY
Court House
Eighth & Philadelphia   Phone: (412) 465-2661
Indiana, PA 15701   Bonnie Brady, Law Libn.

INDIANA UNIVERSITY OF PENNSYLVANIA - COGSWELL MUSIC LIBRARY
Cogswell Hall   Phone: (412) 357-2892
Indiana, PA 15705   Calvin Elliker, Music Libn.

INDIANA UNIVERSITY OF PENNSYLVANIA - UNIVERSITY LIBRARY
                                           Phone: (412) 357-2330
Indiana, PA 15705   William E. Lafranchi, Dir., Libs./Media Rsrcs.

MONSOUR MEDICAL CENTER - HEALTH SERVICES LIBRARY *
70 Lincoln Way, East   Phone: (412) 527-1511
Jeannette, PA 15644   Edith Gross, Med.Libn.

UNITED TECHNOLOGIES CORPORATION - ELLIOTT COMPANY - LIBRARY
N. Fourth St.   Phone: (412) 527-8054
Jeannette, PA 15644   Geri K. Keitzer, Libn.

GELLMAN RESEARCH ASSOCIATES, INC. - GRA LIBRARY
100 West Ave.   Phone: (215) 884-7500
Jenkintown, PA 19046   Janet W. Appleton, Libn.

JENKINTOWN LIBRARY - PENNSYLVANIA COLLECTION
York & Vista Rds.   Phone: (215) 884-0593
Jenkintown, PA 19046   Joan Greenberg, Hd.Libn.

MANOR JUNIOR COLLEGE - BASILEIAD LIBRARY - SPECIAL COLLECTIONS
Fox Chase Manor   Phone: (215) 885-2360
Jenkintown, PA 19046   Anna Maksymowych, Spec.Coll.Libn.

OLD YORK ROAD HISTORICAL SOCIETY - ARCHIVES
Abington Library Society   Phone: (215) 884-8058
Jenkintown, PA 19046   Warren Hilton, Libn.

SPS TECHNOLOGIES, INC. - RESEARCH AND DEVELOPMENT
   LABORATORIES - CORPORATE TECHNICAL LIBRARY
Highland Ave.   Phone: (215) 572-3564
Jenkintown, PA 19046   Michele R. Thomas, Corp.Libn./Editor

CARBON COUNTY LAW LIBRARY †
Court House   Phone: (717) 325-3111
Jim Thorpe, PA 18229   Benjamin A. Lesniak, Libn.

CAMBRIA LIBRARY ASSOCIATION - PRESCHOOL ADVENTURE LIBRARY
248 Main St.   Phone: (814) 536-5131
Johnstown, PA 15901   Sue Hensel, Children's Libn.

CONEMAUGH VALLEY MEMORIAL HOSPITAL - HEALTH SCIENCES LIBRARY
1086 Franklin St.   Phone: (814) 536-6671
Johnstown, PA 15905   Fred L. Wilson, Jr., Med. Staff Libn.

FIRST LUTHERAN CHURCH - PARISH LIBRARY
415 Vine St.   Phone: (814) 536-7521
Johnstown, PA 15901   Elizabeth J. Will, Libn.

LONGWOOD GARDENS, INC. - LIBRARY
      Phone: (215) 388-6741
Kennett Square, PA 19348   Enola Jane N. Teeter, Libn.

TAYLOR (Bayard) MEMORIAL LIBRARY
216 E. State St.   Phone: (215) 444-2702
Kennett Square, PA 19348   Joseph A. Lordi, Dir.

UNIVERSITY OF PENNSYLVANIA - NEW BOLTON CENTER - JEAN AUSTIN
   DU PONT LIBRARY
382 W. Street Rd.   Phone: (215) 444-5800
Kennett Square, PA 19348   Alice K. Holton, Lib.Serv.Asst.

PENNSYLVANIA RESOURCES AND INFORMATION CENTER FOR SPECIAL
   EDUCATION
200 Anderson Rd.   Phone: (215) 265-7321
King Of Prussia, PA 19406   Dr. Marianne Price, Dir.

PENNSYLVANIA STATE UNIVERSITY - KING OF PRUSSIA CENTER -
   LIBRARY
650 S. Henderson Rd.   Phone: (215) 265-7645
King Of Prussia, PA 19406   Vera Hospodka, Hd.Libn.

PENNWALT CORPORATION - INFORMATION SERVICES DEPARTMENT
900 First Ave.   Phone: (215) 337-6776
King Of Prussia, PA 19406   Kathryn M. Donovan, Mgr.

RESEARCH & INFORMATION SERVICES FOR EDUCATION - MONTGOMERY
   COUNTY INTERMEDIATE UNIT LIBRARY
725 Caley Rd.
King of Prussia, PA 19406   Richard R. Brickley, Dir.

NESBITT MEMORIAL HOSPITAL - LIBRARY
562 Wyoming Ave.   Phone: (717) 288-1411
Kingston, PA 18704   Katherine L. McCrea, Libn.

KUTZTOWN UNIVERSITY - ROHRBACH LIBRARY
      Phone: (215) 683-4480
Kutztown, PA 19530   John K. Amrhein, Univ.Libn.

PQ CORPORATION - RESEARCH LIBRARY
Box 258   Phone: (215) 825-5000
Lafayette Hill, PA 19444   Geraldine R. James, Libn.

ARMSTRONG WORLD INDUSTRIES, INC. - MANAGEMENT REFERENCE
   SERVICES
Liberty & Charlotte Sts.
Box 3001   Phone: (717) 397-0611
Lancaster, PA 17604   Margaret B. Boyer, Libn.

ARMSTRONG WORLD INDUSTRIES, INC. - TECHNICAL CENTER -
   TECHNICAL INFORMATION SERVICES
2500 Columbia Ave.   Phone: (717) 397-0611
Lancaster, PA 17604   Dr. Joseph M. Judge, Mgr.

EVANGELICAL AND REFORMED HISTORICAL SOCIETY - LANCASTER
   CENTRAL ARCHIVES AND LIBRARY
Lancaster Theological Seminary
555 W. James St.   Phone: (717) 393-0654
Lancaster, PA 17603   Florence M. Bricker, Archv.

FRANKLIN AND MARSHALL COLLEGE - BIOLOGY READING ROOM
      Phone: (717) 291-4118
Lancaster, PA 17604   Kathleen Spencer, Lib.Dir.

FRANKLIN AND MARSHALL COLLEGE - CHEMISTRY DEPARTMENT -
   WILLIAM SHAND, JR. MEMORIAL LIBRARY
      Phone: (717) 291-4123
Lancaster, PA 17604   Kathleen Spencer, Lib.Dir.

FRANKLIN AND MARSHALL COLLEGE - DEPARTMENT OF GEOLOGY -
   READING ROOM
      Phone: (717) 291-4133
Lancaster, PA 17604   Kathleen Spencer, Lib.Dir.

FRANKLIN AND MARSHALL COLLEGE - DEPARTMENT OF PHYSICS -
   READING ROOM
      Phone: (717) 291-4136
Lancaster, PA 17604   Kathleen Spencer, Lib.Dir.

FRANKLIN AND MARSHALL COLLEGE - PSYCHOLOGY READING ROOM
      Phone: (717) 291-4202
Lancaster, PA 17604   Kathleen Spencer, Lib.Dir.

FRANKLIN AND MARSHALL COLLEGE - SHADEK-FACKENTHAL LIBRARY -
   SPECIAL COLLECTIONS
      Phone: (717) 291-4216
Lancaster, PA 17604   Kathleen Moretto Spencer, Dir.

JAMES BUCHANAN FOUNDATION FOR THE PRESERVATION OF WHEATLAND
   - LIBRARY
1120 Marietta Ave.   Phone: (717) 392-8721
Lancaster, PA 17603   Sally Smith Cahalan, Dir.

LANCASTER BIBLE COLLEGE - STOLL MEMORIAL LIBRARY
901 Eden Rd.   Phone: (717) 569-7071
Lancaster, PA 17601   Mary L. Walters, Lib.Dir.

LANCASTER COUNTY HISTORICAL SOCIETY - LIBRARY
Willson Bldg.
230 N. President Ave.   Phone: (717) 392-4633
Lancaster, PA 17603   Salinda M. Matt, Chf.Libn.

LANCASTER COUNTY LAW LIBRARY
50 N. Duke St.
Box 3480   Phone: (717) 299-8090
Lancaster, PA 17603   Eleanor Lloyd, Libn.

LANCASTER GENERAL HOSPITAL - MUELLER HEALTH SCIENCES LIBRARY
555 N. Duke St.
Box 3555   Phone: (717) 299-5511
Lancaster, PA 17603   Claudette Strohm, Libn.

LANCASTER MENNONITE HISTORICAL SOCIETY - LIBRARY
2215 Millstream Rd.   Phone: (717) 393-9745
Lancaster, PA 17602   Carolyn C. Wenger, Dir.

LANCASTER NEWSPAPERS - LIBRARY
8 W. King St.
Lancaster, PA 17603
Phone: (717) 291-8773
Helen L. Everts, Libn.

LANCASTER THEOLOGICAL SEMINARY OF THE UNITED CHURCH OF
CHRIST - PHILIP SCHAFF LIBRARY
555 W. James St.
Lancaster, PA 17603
Phone: (717) 393-0654
Anne-Marie Salgat, Dir. of Lib.Serv.

PENNSYLVANIA FARM MUSEUM OF LANDIS VALLEY - LIBRARY
2451 Kissel Hill Rd.
Lancaster, PA 17601
Phone: (717) 569-0401
Robert N. Sieber, Dir.

RCA CORPORATION - LIBRARY
New Holland Pike
Lancaster, PA 17604
Phone: (717) 397-7661
Mary K. Noll, Libn.

ST. JOSEPH HOSPITAL - HOSPITAL LIBRARY
250 College Ave.
Box 3509
Lancaster, PA 17604
Phone: (717) 291-8119
Eileen B. Doudna, Libn.

TECHNOMIC PUBLISHING CO., INC. (TPC) - BUSINESS LIBRARY
851 New Holland Ave.
Box 3535
Lancaster, PA 17604
Richard Dunn, Lib.Dir.

PHILADELPHIA COLLEGE OF BIBLE - LIBRARY
Langhorne Manor
Langhorne, PA 19047
Phone: (215) 752-5800
Julius C. Bosco, Dir.

CALVARY BAPTIST THEOLOGICAL SEMINARY - LIBRARY
Valley Forge Rd. & Sumneytown Pike
Lansdale, PA 19446
Phone: (215) 368-7538
James F. Stitzinger, Libn.

MENNONITE HISTORICAL LIBRARY OF EASTERN PENNSYLVANIA
1000 Forty Foot Rd.
Lansdale, PA 19446
Phone: (215) 362-0203
Joseph S. Miller, Adm.

LATROBE AREA HOSPITAL - MEDICAL & NURSING LIBRARIES
W. Second Ave.
Latrobe, PA 15650
Phone: (412) 537-1275
Marsha E. Gelman, Med.Libn.

ST. VINCENT COLLEGE AND ARCHABBEY - LIBRARIES
Latrobe, PA 15650
Phone: (412) 539-9761
Rev. Chrysostom V. Schlimm, O.S.B., Dir.

ST. VINCENT COLLEGE AND ARCHABBEY - MUSIC LIBRARY
Latrobe, PA 15650

ST. VINCENT COLLEGE AND ARCHABBEY - PHYSICS DEPARTMENTAL
LIBRARY
Latrobe, PA 15650

LAURELTON CENTER - LIBRARY
Laurelton, PA 17835
Phone: (717) 922-3311
Jane G. Slack, Libn.

GOOD SAMARITAN HOSPITAL - KROHN MEMORIAL LIBRARY
4th & Walnut Sts.
Lebanon, PA 17042
Phone: (717) 272-7611
Susan Foltz, Libn.

LEBANON COUNTY HISTORICAL SOCIETY - LIBRARY
924 Cumberland St.
Lebanon, PA 17042
Phone: (717) 272-1473

U.S. VETERANS ADMINISTRATION (PA-Lebanon) - MEDICAL CENTER
LIBRARY
State Drive
Lebanon, PA 17042
Phone: (717) 272-6621
David E. Falger, Chf., Lib.Serv.

LEHIGH-NORTHAMPTON COUNTIES JOINT PLANNING COMMISSION -
LIBRARY
Allentown-Bethlehem-Easton Airport
Government Bldg.
Lehigh Valley, PA 18103
Phone: (215) 264-4544
Penn Clissold, Libn.

LITERATURE SERVICE ASSOCIATES
Rd. 3, Box 442A
Lehighton, PA 18235

PENNSYLVANIA DUTCH FOLK CULTURE SOCIETY, INC. - BAVER MEMORIAL
LIBRARY
Lenhartsville, PA 19534
Phone: (215) 562-4803
Florence Baver, Mgr.

BUCKS COUNTY COURIER TIMES - LIBRARY
8400 Rte. 13
Levittown, PA 19057
Phone: (215) 752-6877
Susan Y. Ditterline, Libn./Supv.

BUCKNELL UNIVERSITY - ARCHIVES
Lewisburg, PA 17837
Phone: (717) 524-1493
William B. Weist, Univ.Archv.

BUCKNELL UNIVERSITY - ELLEN CLARKE BERTRAND LIBRARY
Lewisburg, PA 17837
Phone: (717) 524-1661
George M. Jenks, Coll.Dev.Libn.

UNION COUNTY HISTORICAL SOCIETY - JOHN B. DEANS MEMORIAL
LIBRARY
2nd & St. Louis Sts.
Lewisburg, PA 17837
Phone: (717) 524-4461
Gary W. Slear, Chm., Archv. & Musm.

LEWISTOWN HOSPITAL - MEDICAL LIBRARY †
Highland Ave.
Lewistown, PA 17044
Phone: (717) 248-5411
Jane B. Karn, Med.Libn.

MIFFLIN COUNTY HISTORICAL SOCIETY - LIBRARY AND MUSEUM †
The McCoy House
17 N. Main St.
Lewistown, PA 17044
Helen McNitt, Libn.

MIFFLIN COUNTY LAW LIBRARY
20 N. Wayne St.
Lewistown, PA 17044
Phone: (717) 248-7332

CONOCO INC. - COAL RESEARCH DIVISION - TECHNICAL LIBRARY
4000 Brownsville Rd.
Library, PA 15129
Phone: (412) 831-6688
Nancy Barley, Tech.Libn.

FORT LIGONIER MEMORIAL FOUNDATION - HENRY BOUQUET ROOM *
S. Market St.
Ligonier, PA 15658
Phone: (412) 238-9701
J. Martin West, Dir./Cur.

DELAWARE COUNTY PLANNING COMMISSION - LIBRARY AND DATA
SECTION †
Watkins Bldg.
350 N. Middletown Rd.
Lima, PA 19037
Phone: (215) 891-5656
Jane Taggart Quinn, Libn.

LINCOLN UNIVERSITY - LANGSTON HUGHES MEMORIAL LIBRARY -
SPECIAL COLLECTIONS †
Lincoln University, PA 19352
Phone: (215) 932-8300
Sophy H. Cornwell, Spec.Coll.Libn.

UNIVERSITY OF PITTSBURGH - PYMATUNING LABORATORY OF ECOLOGY -
TRYON LIBRARY
R.R. 1, Box 7
Linesville, PA 16424
Phone: (814) 683-5813
Dr. Richard T. Hartman, Dir.

PENNSYLVANIA STATE DEPARTMENT OF HEALTH - BUREAU OF
LABORATORIES - HERBERT FOX MEMORIAL LIBRARY
Pickering Way & Welsh Pool Rd.
Lionville, PA 19353
Phone: (215) 363-8500
Leonard Sideman, Libn.

AMERICAN COLOR AND CHEMICAL CORPORATION, INC. - LIBRARY *
Mt. Vernon St.
Lock Haven, PA 17745
Phone: (717) 748-6747

LOCK HAVEN STATE COLLEGE - GEORGE B. STEVENSON LIBRARY -
ARCHIVES
Lock Haven, PA 17745
Phone: (717) 893-2371
Charles Robert Kent, Archv.

FULTON COUNTY HISTORICAL SOCIETY - LIBRARY
Box 115
McConnellsburg, PA 17233

OHIO VALLEY GENERAL HOSPITAL - PROFESSIONAL LIBRARY
Heckel Rd.   Phone: (412) 777-6159
McKee's Rock, PA 15136   Mary Evans, Libn.

MC KEESPORT HOSPITAL - HEALTH SERVICES LIBRARY
1500 Fifth Ave.   Phone: (412) 664-2363
McKeesport, PA 15132   Kate Kearney, Dir.

WESTINGHOUSE ELECTRIC CORPORATION - NUCLEAR ENERGY SYSTEMS -
    ADVANCED REACTORS DIVISION - LIBRARY †
Waltz Mill Site
Box 158   Phone: (412) 722-5301
Madison, PA 15663   Ann Chernega, Lib.Mgr.

AMERICAN INSTITUTE FOR PROPERTY & LIABILITY UNDERWRITERS -
    INSURANCE INSTITUTE OF AMERICA - LIBRARY
Providence & Sugartown Rds.   Phone: (215) 644-2100
Malvern, PA 19355   Kim Holston, Libn.

MANSFIELD UNIVERSITY - AUDIO VISUAL CENTER
Retan   Phone: (717) 662-4138
Mansfield, PA 16933   Ronald E. Remy, Dir.

MANSFIELD UNIVERSITY - BUTLER CENTER LIBRARY
                                    Phone: (717) 662-4365
Mansfield, PA 16933-1198   Holly Gardinier, Music Libn.

AIR PRODUCTS AND CHEMICALS, INC. - HOUDRY LABORATORIES -
    INFORMATION SERVICES
Box 427
Marcus Hook, PA 19061

SUN TECH, INC. - LIBRARY & INFORMATION SERVICE
Box 1135   Phone: (215) 485-1121
Marcus Hook, PA 19061   Norman D. Morphet, Sect.Chf.

ALLEGHENY COLLEGE - WALTER M. SMALL GEOLOGY LIBRARY †
Alden Hall   Phone: (814) 724-2350
Meadville, PA 16335   Margaret L. Moser, Libn.

CRAWFORD COUNTY BAR ASSOCIATION - LAW LIBRARY †
Court House, Rm. 212   Phone: (814) 336-1151
Meadville, PA 16335   William K. Reid, Libn.

CRAWFORD COUNTY HISTORICAL SOCIETY - LIBRARY AND ARCHIVES
848 N. Main St.   Phone: (814) 724-6080
Meadville, PA 16335   Robert Ilisevich, Libn.

MEADVILLE CITY HOSPITAL - HUMMER LIBRARY
751 Liberty St.   Phone: (814) 336-3121
Meadville, PA 16335   Barbara Ewing, Libn.

DELAWARE COUNTY LAW LIBRARY *
Courthouse   Phone: (215) 891-2380
Media, PA 19063   Charlotte H. Hewlings, Libn.

MERCER COUNTY HISTORICAL SOCIETY - LIBRARY AND ARCHIVES
119 S. Pitt St.   Phone: (412) 662-3490
Mercer, PA 16137   Mark Brown, Pres.

MERCER COUNTY LAW LIBRARY
Court House
Mercer, PA 16137   Olive L. Griffin, Libn.

AKIBA HEBREW ACADEMY - JOSEPH M. FIRST LIBRARY
N. Highland Ave. & Old Lancaster Rd.
Merion, PA 19066   Jane E. Schofer, Libn.

BUTEN MUSEUM - LIBRARY
246 N. Bowman Ave.   Phone: (215) 664-6601
Merion, PA 19066   Caroline M. Stuckert, Dir.

DROPSIE COLLEGE - LIBRARY
250 Highland Ave.   Phone: (215) 667-1831
Merion, PA 19066   Sarah N. Levy, Lib.Dir.

TEMPLE ADATH ISRAEL - RUBEN LIBRARY
Old Lancaster Rd. & Highland Ave.   Phone: (215) 664-5150
Merion, PA 19066   Joan Furey, Libn.

SNYDER COUNTY HISTORICAL SOCIETY, INC. - LIBRARY
30 E. Market St.
Box 276   Phone: (717) 837-6191
Middleburg, PA 17842   Kathryn Gift, Libn.

GPU NUCLEAR - TMI TECHNICAL LIBRARY
Three Mile Island Nuclear Generating Sta.
Box 480   Phone: (717) 948-8105
Middletown, PA 17057   Joan H. Slavin, Tech.Libn.

MILLERSVILLE UNIVERSITY OF PENNSYLVANIA - HELEN A. GANSER
    LIBRARY - SPECIAL COLLECTIONS
                                    Phone: (717) 872-3607
Millersville, PA 17551   Robert E. Coley, Hd., Archv./Spec.Coll.

ST. JOE MINERALS CORPORATION - INFORMATION CENTER
Box A   Phone: (412) 774-1020
Monaca, PA 15061   Sallie Smith, Tech.Libn.

BITUMINOUS COAL RESEARCH, INC. - LIBRARY †
350 Hochberg Rd.
Box 278   Phone: (412) 327-1600
Monroeville, PA 15146   Mary Ann Sakoian, Libn.

FORBES HEALTH SYSTEM - FORBES REGIONAL HEALTH CENTER - MEDICAL
    LIBRARY
2570 Haymaker Rd.   Phone: (412) 273-2422
Monroeville, PA 15146   Barbara Brooks, Med.Libn.

KOPPERS COMPANY, INC. - TECHNICAL INFORMATION GROUP
440 College Park Dr.   Phone: (412) 327-3000
Monroeville, PA 15146   Eugene P. Meckly, Libn.

UNITED STATES STEEL CORPORATION - TECHNICAL INFORMATION
    CENTER
MS 88   Phone: (412) 825-2344
Monroeville, PA 15146   Angela R. Pollis, Staff Supv.

SUSQUEHANNA COUNTY HISTORICAL SOCIETY AND FREE LIBRARY
    ASSOCIATION
Monument Square   Phone: (717) 278-1881
Montrose, PA 18801   Mary O. Garm, Libn.

MUNCY HISTORICAL SOCIETY AND MUSEUM OF HISTORY - HISTORICAL
    LIBRARY
Muncy Public Library
108 S. Main St.   Phone: (717) 546-5014
Muncy, PA 17756   Kathleen Vellam, Libn.

EVANGELICAL SCHOOL OF THEOLOGY - ROSTAD LIBRARY
121 S. College St.   Phone: (717) 866-5775
Myerstown, PA 17067   Terry M. Heisey, Libn.

FIRST CHRISTIAN CHURCH - LIBRARY
On The Diamond
New Castle, PA 16101   Mrs. H.E. McEwen, Libn.

HIGHLAND UNITED PRESBYTERIAN CHURCH - LIBRARY
708 Highland Ave.   Phone: (412) 654-7391
New Castle, PA 16101   Elizabeth Milholland, Libn.

JAMESON MEMORIAL HOSPITAL - SCHOOL OF NURSING LIBRARY
W. Garfield Ave.   Phone: (412) 658-9001
New Castle, PA 16105   Joan T. Whitman, Libn.

LYON'S SCHOOL OF BUSINESS - LIBRARY †
316 Rhodes Pl.   Phone: (412) 658-9066
New Castle, PA 16103   Grace Lyon, Hd.Libn.

NEW CASTLE PUBLIC LIBRARY - PENNSYLVANIA HISTORY ROOM
207 E. North St.   Phone: (412) 658-6659
New Castle, PA 16101   Helen M. Roux, Dir.

NORTHMINSTER UNITED PRESBYTERIAN CHURCH - LIBRARY
2434 Wilmington Rd.   Phone: (412) 658-9051
New Castle, PA 16105   Helen Sloat, Church Libn.

SPERRY - NEW HOLLAND ENGINEERING LIBRARY
500 Diller Ave.   Phone: (717) 354-1358
New Holland, PA 17557   Tammy A. Houck, Libn.

NEWTOWN HISTORIC ASSOCIATION, INC. - RESEARCH CENTER OF
   NEWTOWN AREA HISTORY
Box 303   Phone: (215) 968-4004
Newton, PA 18940   Elizabeth Gish, Info.Dir.

ATLANTIC-RICHFIELD COMPANY - ARCO CHEMICAL COMPANY -
   RESEARCH & DEVELOPMENT LIBRARY
3801 West Chester Pike   Phone: (215) 359-2903
Newton Square, PA 19073   Dori Whitehurst, Supv.Lib.Serv.

MONTGOMERY COUNTY LAW LIBRARY †
Court House   Phone: (215) 278-3806
Norristown, PA 19404   Arthur S. Zanan, Law Libn.

MONTGOMERY COUNTY PLANNING COMMISSION - RESEARCH LIBRARY *
Court House   Phone: (215) 278-3726
Norristown, PA 19404   Florence Bailey, Supv.

MONTGOMERY HOSPITAL - MEDICAL LIBRARY
Powell & Fornance St.   Phone: (215) 631-3232
Norristown, PA 19401   Alberta T. O'Brien, Med.Libn.

PENNSYLVANIA STATE DEPARTMENT OF PUBLIC WELFARE -
   NORRISTOWN STATE HOSPITAL - PROFESSIONAL/STAFF SERVICES LIB.
c/o Central Professional Library, Bldg. 11   Phone: (215) 270-1369
Norristown, PA 19401   Raymond Frank Roedell, Jr., Dir.

LEEDS AND NORTHRUP COMPANY - TECHNICAL CENTER LIBRARY
Dickerson Rd.   Phone: (215) 643-2000
North Wales, PA 19454   Sandra Davis, Mgr., Lib.Serv.

MARY IMMACULATE SEMINARY - LIBRARY
R.D. 1, Cherryville Rd.
Box 27   Phone: (215) 262-7866
Northampton, PA 18067   Rev. Michael V. Thornton, C.M., Libn.

COLUMBIA COUNTY HISTORICAL SOCIETY - LIBRARY
Box 197   Phone: (717) 683-6011
Orangeville, PA 17859   Edna Lynn, Exec.Dir.

PAOLI MEMORIAL HOSPITAL - ROBERT M. WHITE MEMORIAL LIBRARY
Lancaster Pike   Phone: (215) 648-1218
Paoli, PA 19301   Doris J. Rickards, Med.Libn.

MID-VALLEY HOSPITAL - PHYSICIAN'S LIBRARY
1400 Main St.   Phone: (717) 489-7546
Peckville, PA 18452   Arline Ham, Dir.

HAR ZION TEMPLE - IDA AND MATTHEW RUDOFKER LIBRARY
Hagys Ford & Hollow Rds.   Phone: (215) 839-1250
Penn Valley, PA 19072   Jessie Rubenstone, Hd.Libn.

SCHWENKFELDER LIBRARY
                                                            Phone: (215) 679-7175
Pennsburg, PA 18073   D.K. Moyer, Dir.

ACADEMY OF NATURAL SCIENCES - LIBRARY
19th & The Parkway   Phone: (215) 299-1040
Philadelphia, PA 19103   Sylva Baker, Hd.Libn.

ADOPTION CENTER OF DELAWARE VALLEY - LIBRARY
1218 Chestnut St.   Phone: (215) 925-0200
Philadelphia, PA 19107   Vernice W. Berry, Libn.

AMERICAN ASSOCIATION OF MEDICO-LEGAL CONSULTANTS - LIBRARY
Park Towne Pl., N-105
2200 Benjamin Franklin Pkwy.   Phone: (215) 561-2121
Philadelphia, PA 19130   Arlene Goldman, Libn.

AMERICAN HOME PRODUCTS CORPORATION - WYETH LABORATORIES
   DIVISION LIBRARY
Box 8299   Phone: (215) 688-4400
Philadelphia, PA 19101   Larry D. Taylor, Supv., Lib.Serv.

AMERICAN LAW INSTITUTE - LIBRARY
4025 Chestnut St.   Phone: (215) 243-1658
Philadelphia, PA 19104   Loretta U. McConnell, Libn.

AMERICAN PHILOSOPHICAL SOCIETY - LIBRARY
105 S. Fifth St.   Phone: (215) 627-0706
Philadelphia, PA 19106-3386   Dr. Edward C. Carter, II, Libn.

AMERICAN SOCIETY FOR TESTING AND MATERIALS - INFORMATION
   CENTER
1916 Race St.   Phone: (215) 299-5474
Philadelphia, PA 19103   Dolores G. Collyer, Adm.

AMERICAN SWEDISH HISTORICAL MUSEUM - NORD LIBRARY
1900 Pattison Ave.   Phone: (215) 389-1776
Philadelphia, PA 19145   Katarina Cerny, Cur.

ANTIOCH UNIVERSITY - RESOURCE CENTER
1811 Spring Garden St.   Phone: (215) 629-1370
Philadelphia, PA 19130   William B. Saunders, Libn./External Coord.

ARCHDIOCESE OF PHILADELPHIA - CATHOLIC INFORMATION CENTER
936 Market St.   Phone: (215) 587-3520
Philadelphia, PA 19107   Rev. Paul F. Curran, Dir.

AREA COUNCIL FOR ECONOMIC EDUCATION (ACEE) - LIBRARY *
254 Suburban Sta. Bldg.
1617 John F. Kennedy Blvd.   Phone: (215) 564-3504
Philadelphia, PA 19103

ATHENAEUM OF PHILADELPHIA
219 S. Sixth St.   Phone: (215) 925-2688
Philadelphia, PA 19106   Dr. Roger W. Moss, Jr., Exec.Dir.

BALCH INSTITUTE FOR ETHNIC STUDIES - LIBRARY
18 S. 7th St.
Philadelphia, PA 19106   R. Joseph Anderson, Lib.Dir.

BALLARD, SPAHR, ANDREWS AND INGERSOLL - LAW LIBRARY *
30 S. 17th St., 20th Fl.   Phone: (215) 564-1800
Philadelphia, PA 19103   Shari Y. Liu, Libn.

BELLET (Samuel) LIBRARY OF LAW, MEDICINE AND BEHAVIORAL SCIENCE
201E Piersol Bldg. H.U.P.   Phone: (215) 662-2848
Philadelphia, PA 19104

BEREAN INSTITUTE - LIBRARY
1901 W. Girard Ave.   Phone: (215) 763-4833
Philadelphia, PA 19130   Pamela Theus, Hd.Libn.

BETH DAVID REFORM CONGREGATION - JEWEL K. MARKOWITZ LIBRARY †
5220 Wynnefield Ave.   Phone: (215) 473-8438
Philadelphia, PA 19131   Mrs. Jerome Apfel, Chm.

BIOSCIENCES INFORMATION SERVICE - BIOLOGICAL ABSTRACTS -
   LIBRARY
2100 Arch St.   Phone: (215) 587-4864
Philadelphia, PA 19103   Janet S. Zimmerman, Group Ldr.

BLUE CROSS OF GREATER PHILADELPHIA - E.A. VAN STEENWYK
   MEMORIAL LIBRARY
1333 Chestnut St.
16th Fl., Widener Bldg.   Phone: (215) 448-5400
Philadelphia, PA 19107   Judith Delbaum, Libn.

B'NAI B'RITH CAREER & COUNSELING SERVICES - LIBRARY
1405 Locust St.   Phone: (215) 545-1455
Philadelphia, PA 19102   Julius S. Romanoff, Exec.Dir.

BOCKUS RESEARCH INSTITUTE - LIBRARY
Office of Research Administration
Graduate Hospital
One Graduate Plaza   Phone: (215) 893-7497
Philadelphia, PA 19146   Robert F. Lovelace, Dir.

BOEING VERTOL COMPANY - LYDIA RANKIN TECHNICAL LIBRARY
Box 16858
Phone: (215) 522-2536
Philadelphia, PA 19142
Bonnie Hahn, Tech.Libn.

CHESTNUT HILL COLLEGE - LOGUE LIBRARY - SPECIAL COLLECTIONS
Germantown & Northwestern Aves.   Phone: (215) 248-7055
Philadelphia, PA 19118

CHESTNUT HILL HOSPITAL - SCHOOL OF NURSING LIBRARY
8835 Germantown Ave.
Phone: (215) 248-8394
Philadelphia, PA 19118
Maude H. Meyerend, Libn.

CHILDREN'S HOSPITAL OF PHILADELPHIA - MEDICAL LIBRARY
34th & Civic Center Blvd.
Phone: (215) 596-9673
Philadelphia, PA 19104   Mrs. Swaran Lata Chopra, Adm.Supv./Dir.

CHINATOWN BUILDING AND EDUCATION FOUNDATION - CHINESE
   CULTURAL AND COMMUNITY CENTER
125 N. Tenth St.
Phone: (215) 923-6767
Philadelphia, PA 19107

CIGNA CORPORATION - PHILADELPHIA LIBRARY
1600 Arch St.
Phone: (215) 241-4677
Philadelphia, PA 19101
Joan C. Divor, Mgr.

CLIVEDEN - LIBRARY
6401 Germantown Ave.
Phone: (215) 848-1777
Philadelphia, PA 19144   Hope Coppage Hendrickson, Exec.Dir.

COHEN, SHAPIRO, POLISHER, SHIEKMAN AND COHEN - LIBRARY
12 S. 12th St.
Phone: (215) 922-1300
Philadelphia, PA 19107

COLLEGE OF PHYSICIANS OF PHILADELPHIA - LIBRARY AND MEDICAL
   DOCUMENTATION SERVICE
19 S. 22nd St.
Phone: (215) 561-6050
Philadelphia, PA 19103
Anthony Aguirre, Lib.Dir.

COLONIAL PENN GROUP, INC. - INFORMATION RESEARCH CENTER
5 Penn Center Plaza
Phone: (215) 988-3796
Philadelphia, PA 19181
Lee Fishman, Sr.Info.Spec.

COMMUNITY COLLEGE OF PHILADELPHIA - EDUCATION RESOURCES
   CENTER †
34 S. 11th St.
Phone: (215) 972-7256
Philadelphia, PA 19107
Sidney August, Dir.

COMMUNITY LEGAL SERVICES, INC. - LAW LIBRARY
Sylvania House
Juniper & Locust Sts.
Phone: (215) 893-5368
Philadelphia, PA 19107
Barbara L. Krauss, Libn.

CONGREGATION MIKVEH ISRAEL - ARCHIVES
Independence Mall East
Phone: (215) 922-5446
Philadelphia, PA 19106

CONGREGATION RODEPH SHALOM - LIBRARY
1338 Mount Vernon St.
Phone: (215) 627-6747
Philadelphia, PA 19123
Mildred Kurland, Libn.

CONSERVATION AND RENEWABLE ENERGY INQUIRY AND REFERRAL
   SERVICE
Franklin Research Center
20th & Race Sts.
Phone: (800) 523-2929
Philadelphia, PA 19103
Ken Bordner, Dir.

CURTIS INSTITUTE OF MUSIC - LIBRARY
Rittenhouse Sq.
1726 Locust St.
Phone: (215) 893-5265
Philadelphia, PA 19103
Elizabeth Walker, Libn.

CUSHMAN (Charlotte) CLUB - THEATRE RESEARCH LIBRARY
239 S. Camac St.
Phone: (215) 735-4676
Philadelphia, PA 19107
Jean Rapp, Lib.Chm.

DAY & ZIMMERMANN, INC. - LIBRARY
1818 Market St., 21st Fl.
Phone: (215) 299-8222
Philadelphia, PA 19103
Maureen Szwajkowski, Libn.

DECHERT, PRICE AND RHOADS - LIBRARY
3400 Centre Sq., W.
1500 Market St.
Phone: (215) 972-3453
Philadelphia, PA 19102
Susan Jane Gibbons, Libn.

DELOITTE HASKINS & SELLS - LIBRARY
2500 Three Girard Plaza
Phone: (215) 569-3500
Philadelphia, PA 19102
Lenka Berlin, Libn.

DREXEL UNIVERSITY - SCIENCE AND TECHNOLOGY LIBRARY
32nd & Chestnut Sts.
Phone: (215) 895-2765
Philadelphia, PA 19104   William Page, Hd., Sci. & Tech.Lib.

DREXEL UNIVERSITY - W.W. HAGERTY LIBRARY - SPECIAL COLLECTIONS
32nd & Chestnut Sts.
Phone: (215) 895-2755
Philadelphia, PA 19104
Tim Laborie, Hd.

DRINKER, BIDDLE & REATH - LAW LIBRARY
1100 Philadelphia National Bank Bldg.
Broad & Chestnut Sts.
Phone: (215) 988-2951
Philadelphia, PA 19107
Nancy H. Nance, Libn.

DU PONT DE NEMOURS (E.I.) & COMPANY, INC. - MARSHALL LABORATORY
   LIBRARY
3500 Grays Ferry Ave.
Box 3886
Phone: (215) 339-6314
Philadelphia, PA 19146
Virginia L. Maier, Libn.

DUANE, MORRIS & HECKSCHER - LAW LIBRARY
1500 One Franklin Plaza
Phone: (215) 854-6248
Philadelphia, PA 19102
Teresa N. Clarkson, Libn.

EASTERN BAPTIST THEOLOGICAL SEMINARY - LIBRARY
Lancaster Ave. & City Line
Phone: (215) 896-5000
Philadelphia, PA 19151   Rev. R. David Koch, Assoc.Libn./Tech.Serv.

EINSTEIN (Albert) MEDICAL CENTER - MT. SINAI-DAROFF DIVISION -
   MEDICAL LIBRARY
5th & Reed Sts.
Phone: (215) 339-3780
Philadelphia, PA 19147
Marian E. Schaner, Lib.Dir.

EINSTEIN (Albert) MEDICAL CENTER - NORTHERN DIVISION - LURIA
   MEDICAL LIBRARY †
York & Tabor Roads
Phone: (215) 456-6345
Philadelphia, PA 19141
Marion H. Silverman, Dir.

EINSTEIN (Albert) MEDICAL CENTER - SCHOOL OF NURSING LIBRARY
11th & Tabor Rds.
Phone: (215) 456-7319
Philadelphia, PA 19141
Judith E. Schaeffer, Libn.

ENVIRONMENTAL PROTECTION AGENCY - REGION III LIBRARY
Curtis Bldg., 6th & Walnut Sts.
Phone: (215) 597-0580
Philadelphia, PA 19106
Diane M. McCreary, Libn.

EPISCOPAL HOSPITAL - MEDICAL LIBRARY
Front St. & Lehigh Ave.
Phone: (215) 427-7487
Philadelphia, PA 19125
Margaret Flanagan, Med.Libn.

FARM JOURNAL, INC. - MARKETING RESEARCH LIBRARY
230 W. Washington Sq.
Phone: (215) 574-1360
Philadelphia, PA 19105
Kandace Herzog, Libn.

FARNHAM (Frank C.) COMPANY, INC. - LIBRARY †
1930 Chestnut St., 8th Fl.
Phone: (215) 567-1500
Philadelphia, PA 19103
Katherine C. Jordan, Sci.Ed.

FEDERAL RESERVE BANK OF PHILADELPHIA - LIBRARY
Box 66
Phone: (215) 574-6540
Philadelphia, PA 19105
Aileen C. Boer, Mgr.

FIRST PENNSYLVANIA BANK, N.A. - MARKETING INFORMATION CENTER
Center Sq. Tower, 42nd Fl.
1500 Market St.
Phone: (215) 786-8316
Philadelphia, PA 19101
Larry Felzer, Mgr.

FOOTWEAR INDUSTRIES OF AMERICA, INC. - LIBRARY
3700 Market St.
Phone: (215) 222-1484
Philadelphia, PA 19104
Ruth Schachter, Commun.Coord.

FOREIGN POLICY RESEARCH INSTITUTE - LIBRARY
3508 Market St., Suite 350   Phone: (215) 382-2054
Philadelphia, PA 19104

FOX, ROTHSCHILD, O'BRIEN AND FRANKEL - LIBRARY
2000 Market St., 10th Fl.   Phone: (215) 299-2108
Philadelphia, PA 19103   Diane B. Abazarnia, Libn.

FRANKFORD HOSPITAL - HOSPITAL LIBRARIES
Frankford Ave. & Wakeling St.   Phone: (215) 831-2182
Philadelphia, PA 19124   Dianne E. Rose, Med.Libn.

FRANKFORD HOSPITAL - SCHOOL OF NURSING - STUDENT LIBRARY
4918 Penn St.   Phone: (215) 831-2372
Philadelphia, PA 19124   Dianne Rose, Med.Libn.

FRANKLIN INSTITUTE - FRANKLIN RESEARCH CENTER - INFORMATION
   MANAGEMENT DEPARTMENT
20th & Race Sts.   Phone: (215) 448-1227
Philadelphia, PA 19103   J. Lifsey, V.P.

FRANKLIN INSTITUTE - LIBRARY
20th & Race Sts.   Phone: (215) 448-1239
Philadelphia, PA 19103   Miriam D. Padusis, Libn.

FREE LIBRARY OF PHILADELPHIA - ART DEPARTMENT
Logan Sq.   Phone: (215) 686-5403
Philadelphia, PA 19103   Marianne Promos, Hd.

FREE LIBRARY OF PHILADELPHIA - BUSINESS, SCIENCE AND INDUSTRY
   DEPARTMENT
Logan Sq.   Phone: (215) 686-5394
Philadelphia, PA 19103   Alex S. Weinbaum, Hd.

FREE LIBRARY OF PHILADELPHIA - EDUCATION, PHILOSOPHY, RELIGION
   DEPARTMENT
Logan Sq.   Phone: (215) 686-5392
Philadelphia, PA 19103   Esther J. Maurer, Hd.

FREE LIBRARY OF PHILADELPHIA - EDWIN A. FLEISHER COLLECTION OF
   ORCHESTRAL MUSIC
Logan Sq.   Phone: (215) 686-5313
Philadelphia, PA 19103   Sam Dennison, Cur.

FREE LIBRARY OF PHILADELPHIA - FILMS DEPARTMENT
Logan Sq.   Phone: (215) 686-5367
Philadelphia, PA 19103   Elizabeth O. Levin, Lib. Film Oper.Supv.

FREE LIBRARY OF PHILADELPHIA - GOVERNMENT PUBLICATIONS
   DEPARTMENT
Logan Sq.   Phone: (215) 686-5330
Philadelphia, PA 19103   William A. Felker, Hd.

FREE LIBRARY OF PHILADELPHIA - LIBRARY FOR THE BLIND AND
   PHYSICALLY HANDICAPPED
919 Walnut St.   Phone: (215) 925-3213
Philadelphia, PA 19107   Michael P. Coyle, Hd.

FREE LIBRARY OF PHILADELPHIA - LITERATURE DEPARTMENT
Logan Sq.   Phone: (215) 686-5402
Philadelphia, PA 19103   Maryann Baker, Hd.

FREE LIBRARY OF PHILADELPHIA - MERCANTILE LIBRARY
1021 Chestnut St.   Phone: (215) 627-1231
Philadelphia, PA 19107   James B. Woy, Hd.

FREE LIBRARY OF PHILADELPHIA - MICROFORMS AND NEWSPAPERS
   DEPARTMENT
Logan Sq.   Phone: (215) 686-5431
Philadelphia, PA 19103   Bernard F. Pasqualini, Hd.

FREE LIBRARY OF PHILADELPHIA - MUSIC DEPARTMENT
Logan Sq.   Phone: (215) 686-5316
Philadelphia, PA 19103   Frederick J. Kent, Hd.

FREE LIBRARY OF PHILADELPHIA - MUSIC DEPARTMENT - DRINKER
   LIBRARY OF CHORAL MUSIC
Logan Sq.   Phone: (215) 686-5364
Philadelphia, PA 19103   Frederick J. Kent, Hd.

FREE LIBRARY OF PHILADELPHIA - PRINT AND PICTURE COLLECTION
Logan Sq.   Phone: (215) 686-5405
Philadelphia, PA 19103   Robert F. Looney, Cur.

FREE LIBRARY OF PHILADELPHIA - RARE BOOK DEPARTMENT
Logan Sq.   Phone: (215) 686-5416
Philadelphia, PA 19103   Marie Korey, Rare Book Libn.

FREE LIBRARY OF PHILADELPHIA - SOCIAL SCIENCE & HISTORY
   DEPARTMENT
Logan Sq.
Philadelphia, PA 19103   William Handley, Hd.

FREE LIBRARY OF PHILADELPHIA - SOCIAL SCIENCE & HISTORY
   DEPARTMENT - MAP COLLECTION
Logan Sq.   Phone: (215) 686-5397
Philadelphia, PA 19103   Richard C. Boardman, Map Libn.

FREE LIBRARY OF PHILADELPHIA - THEATRE COLLECTION
Logan Sq.   Phone: (215) 686-5427
Philadelphia, PA 19103   Geraldine Duclow, Libn.-In-Charge

FRIENDS HOSPITAL - NORMAN D. WEINER PROFESSIONAL LIBRARY
Roosevelt Blvd. & Adams Ave.   Phone: (215) 831-4763
Philadelphia, PA 19124   Donna M. Zoccola Soultoukis, Libn./Search Anl.

GAY TASK FORCE - INFORMATION CENTER
Box 2383   Phone: (215) 471-3322
Philadelphia, PA 19103   Barbara Gittings, Coord.

GENEALOGICAL SOCIETY OF PENNSYLVANIA - LIBRARY
1300 Locust St.   Phone: (215) 545-0391
Philadelphia, PA 19107

GENERAL ELECTRIC COMPANY - SPACE/SYSTEMS DIVISION LIBRARIES
Box 8555   Phone: (215) 962-4700
Philadelphia, PA 19101   Larry Chasen, Mgr.

GEOGRAPHICAL SOCIETY OF PHILADELPHIA - LIBRARY †
21 S. 12th St., Rm. 909   Phone: (215) 563-0127
Philadelphia, PA 19107

GERMAN SOCIETY OF PENNSYLVANIA - JOSEPH HORNER MEMORIAL
   LIBRARY
611 Spring Garden St.   Phone: (215) 627-4365
Philadelphia, PA 19123   Russell C. Spruance, Act.Lib.Comm.Chr.

GERMANTOWN FRIENDS MEETING - FRIENDS FREE LIBRARY †
5418 Germantown Ave.   Phone: (215) 438-6023
Philadelphia, PA 19144   Sara G. Woy, Hd.Libn.

GERMANTOWN HISTORICAL SOCIETY - LIBRARY
5214 Germantown Ave.   Phone: (215) 844-0514
Philadelphia, PA 19144   Patricia A. Henning, Libn.

GERMANTOWN HOSPITAL AND MEDICAL CENTER - LIBRARY
One Penn Blvd.   Phone: (215) 438-9700
Philadelphia, PA 19144   Kathleen A. Leigh, Libn.

GIUFFRE MEDICAL CENTER - LIBRARY
8th & Girard Ave.   Phone: (215) 787-2228
Philadelphia, PA 19122   Allathea Ames, Libn.

GRADUATE HOSPITAL - LIBRARY
One Graduate Plaza   Phone: (215) 893-2401
Philadelphia, PA 19146   Diane M. Farny, Dir. of Lib.Serv.

GRAND LODGE OF FREE AND ACCEPTED MASONS OF PENNSYLVANIA -
   LIBRARY
Masonic Temple
1 N. Broad St.   Phone: (215) 988-1933
Philadelphia, PA 19107   Frank W. Bobb, Libn. & Cur.

GRATZ COLLEGE - ELSIE AND WILLIAM CHOMSKY EDUCATIONAL
   RESOURCE CENTER (CERC)
10th St. & Tabor Rd.   Phone: (215) 329-3363
Philadelphia, PA 19141   Eileen L. Samuelson, Dir.

GRATZ COLLEGE - LIBRARY
10th St. & Tabor Rd.
Phone: (215) 329-3363
Philadelphia, PA 19141
Michael Grunberger, Libn.

GRAY PANTHERS - NATIONAL OFFICE LIBRARY
3635 Chestnut St.
Philadelphia, PA 19104
Jean G. Hopper, Libn.

GREAT LAKES COLLEGES ASSOCIATION - PHILADELPHIA URBAN
SEMESTER - LIBRARY
1227-29 Walnut St.
Phone: (215) 574-9490
Philadelphia, PA 19107
Lisa M. Dyckman, Prog.Asst./Libn.

HAHNEMANN UNIVERSITY - WARREN H. FAKE LIBRARY †
245 N. 15th St.
Phone: (215) 448-7631
Philadelphia, PA 19102
Eleanora M. Kenworthy, Dir.

HAY ASSOCIATES - RESEARCH LIBRARY
229 S. 18th St., Rittenhouse Sq.
Phone: (215) 875-2300
Philadelphia, PA 19103
Barbara Mattscheck, Res.Libn.

HISTORICAL SOCIETY OF PENNSYLVANIA - LIBRARY
1300 Locust St.
Phone: (215) 732-6200
Philadelphia, PA 19107
David Fraser, Hd.Libn.

HOLY FAMILY COLLEGE - LIBRARY - SPECIAL COLLECTIONS
Grant & Frankford Aves.
Phone: (215) 637-7703
Philadelphia, PA 19114
Sr. M. Kathryn Dobbs, C.S.F.N., Dir.

HOSPITAL OF THE UNIVERSITY OF PENNSYLVANIA - ROBERT DUNNING
DRIPPS LIBRARY OF ANESTHESIA
Department of Anesthesia
3400 Spruce St.
Phone: (215) 662-3784
Philadelphia, PA 19104
Joan Meranze, Dir.

HOUSING ASSOCIATION OF DELAWARE VALLEY - LIBRARY
1317 Filbert St., Suite 523
Phone: (215) 563-4050
Philadelphia, PA 19107
Anthony Lewis, Managing Dir.

HUEBNER (S.S.) FOUNDATION FOR INSURANCE EDUCATION - LIBRARY
Steinberg Hall-Dietrich Hall/CC
Suite 1400
University of Pennsylvania
Phone: (215) 898-7621
Philadelphia, PA 19104
Elizabeth W. Gillies, Libn.

HUMAN RESOURCES NETWORK - INFORMATION CENTER †
2011 Chancellor St.
Phone: (215) 299-2928
Philadelphia, PA 19103
Eleanor Mitchell, Dir.

INSTITUTE FOR CANCER RESEARCH - LIBRARY
Fox Chase Cancer Center
Phone: (215) 728-2711
Philadelphia, PA 19111
Jane M. Bosley, Libn.

INSTITUTE OF THE PENNSYLVANIA HOSPITAL - MEDICAL LIBRARY
111 N. 49th St.
Phone: (215) 471-2013
Philadelphia, PA 19139
June M. Strickland, Libn.

INSTITUTE FOR SCIENTIFIC INFORMATION
3501 Market St.
University City Science Ctr.
Phone: (215) 386-0100
Philadelphia, PA 19104
Mary Ann Mangravite, Mgr., Jrnl. Liaison

JEFFERSON (Thomas) UNIVERSITY - CARDEZA FOUNDATION - TOCANTINS
MEMORIAL LIBRARY
1015 Walnut St.
Phone: (215) 928-8474
Philadelphia, PA 19107
A.J. Erslev, M.D., Found.Dir.

JEFFERSON (Thomas) UNIVERSITY - SCOTT MEMORIAL LIBRARY
11th & Walnut Sts.
Phone: (215) 928-6994
Philadelphia, PA 19107
John A. Timour, Univ.Libn.

JENKINS (Theodore F.) MEMORIAL LAW LIBRARY COMPANY - LIBRARY
Widener Bldg., 10th Fl.
1339 Chestnut St.
Phone: (215) 686-5692
Philadelphia, PA 19107
Regina A. Smith, Dir.

KEAN ARCHIVES *
1320 Locust St.
Phone: (215) 735-1812
Philadelphia, PA 19107
Manuel Kean, Owner

KLAUDER (Louis T.) & ASSOCIATES - LIBRARY
Pennsylvania Bldg.
1500 Chestnut St.
Phone: (215) 563-2570
Philadelphia, PA 19102
Nancy C. Todd, Libn.

LAMBERT (Harold M.) STUDIOS - LIBRARY
2801 W. Cheltenham Ave.
Box 27310
Phone: (215) 224-1400
Philadelphia, PA 19150
Raymond Lambert, Owner

LANKENAU HOSPITAL - MEDICAL LIBRARY
Lancaster & City Line Aves.
Phone: (215) 645-2698
Philadelphia, PA 19151
Marie A. Norton, Med.Libn.

LANKENAU HOSPITAL - SCHOOL OF NURSING LIBRARY
City Ave. & 64th St.
Phone: (215) 642-3931
Philadelphia, PA 19151
Sr. Alma Koder, Libn.

LAVENTHOL AND HORWATH - NATIONAL INFORMATION CENTER
1845 Walnut St.
Phone: (215) 299-1606
Philadelphia, PA 19103
Marjorie Hill, Dir.

LIBRARY COMPANY OF PHILADELPHIA
1314 Locust St.
Phone: (215) 546-3181
Philadelphia, PA 19107
Edwin Wolf, II, Libn.

LUTHERAN CHURCH IN AMERICA - BOARD OF PUBLICATION - LIBRARY
2900 Queen Ln.
Phone: (215) 848-6800
Philadelphia, PA 19129
Judi Fahnestock, Ed.

LUTHERAN THEOLOGICAL SEMINARY - KRAUTH MEMORIAL LIBRARY
7301 Germantown Ave.
Phone: (215) 248-4616
Philadelphia, PA 19119
Rev. David J. Wartluft, Lib.Dir.

MAGEE MEMORIAL REHABILITATION HOSPITAL - MAGEE MEMORIAL
MEDICAL LIBRARY *
1513 Race St.
Phone: (215) 864-7100
Philadelphia, PA 19102

MARQUETTE COPPERSMITHING COMPANY - LIBRARY
Box 4584
Phone: (215) 877-9362
Philadelphia, PA 19131
T.T. Hill, Libn.

MARRIAGE COUNCIL OF PHILADELPHIA - DIVISION OF FAMILY STUDY AND
MARRIAGE COUNCIL LIBRARY
4025 Chestnut St., 2nd Fl.
Phone: (215) 382-6680
Philadelphia, PA 19104
Ellen M. Berman, Dir. of Clinical Trng.

MEDICAL COLLEGE OF PENNSYLVANIA - ARCHIVES AND SPECIAL
COLLECTIONS ON WOMEN IN MEDICINE
3300 Henry Ave.
Phone: (215) 842-7124
Philadelphia, PA 19129
Sandra L. Chaff, Dir., Archv.

MEDICAL COLLEGE OF PENNSYLVANIA - EASTERN PENNSYLVANIA
PSYCHIATRIC INST. - MENTAL HEALTH AND NEUROSCIENCES LIB.
Henry Ave. & Abbottsford Rd.
Phone: (215) 842-4510
Philadelphia, PA 19129
Etheldra Templeton, Dir.

MELLON BANK EAST - INFORMATION CENTER
14-4 Mellon Bank Ctr.
Phone: (215) 585-3313
Philadelphia, PA 19101
Lee Ann Dean, Mgr.

MERCY CATHOLIC MEDICAL CENTER - MISERICORDIA DIVISION LIBRARY
54th and Cedar Ave.
Phone: (215) 748-9415
Philadelphia, PA 19143
Janet C. Clinton, Chf. of Lib.Serv.

METHODIST HOSPITAL - LIBRARY
2301 S. Broad St.
Phone: (215) 952-9404
Philadelphia, PA 19148
Sara J. Richardson, Libn.

METROPOLITAN HOSPITAL - CENTRAL DIVISION - LEVIN MEMORIAL
LIBRARY
201 N. Eighth St.
Phone: (215) 238-2312
Philadelphia, PA 19106-1098
Marjorie Greenfield, Libn.

METROPOLITAN HOSPITAL - PARKVIEW DIVISION - MEDICAL LIBRARY
1331 E. Wyoming Ave.
Phone: (215) 537-7684
Philadelphia, PA 19124
Nina F. Galpern, Libn.

MICRODOC - TECHNICAL DOCUMENTATION COLLECTION
815 Carpenter Ln.   Phone: (215) 848-4545
Philadelphia, PA 19119   Thomas F. Deahl, Info.Sys.Engr.

MILITARY ORDER OF THE LOYAL LEGION OF THE UNITED STATES - WAR
  LIBRARY AND MUSEUM
1805 Pine St.   Phone: (215) 735-8196
Philadelphia, PA 19103   Karla M. Steffen, Libn.

MONELL CHEMICAL SENSES CENTER - LIBRARY
3500 Market St.   Phone: (215) 898-6666
Philadelphia, PA 19104

MONTGOMERY, MC CRACKEN, WALKER & RHOADS - LIBRARY
3 Pkwy.   Phone: (215) 563-0650
Philadelphia, PA 19102   G.H. Brown, Libn.

MOORE COLLEGE OF ART - LIBRARY
20th & the Parkway   Phone: (215) 568-4515
Philadelphia, PA 19103   Lorraine Baggett-Heuser, Lib.Dir.

MORGAN, LEWIS & BOCKIUS - LIBRARY
123 S. Broad St.   Phone: (215) 491-9633
Philadelphia, PA 19109   Linda C. Roach, Libn.

MORRIS (Robert) ASSOCIATES - LIBRARY
1616 Philadelphia Natl. Bank Bldg.   Phone: (215) 665-2850
Philadelphia, PA 19107   Susan M. Kelsay, Asst.Dir.

MUTUAL ASSURANCE COMPANY - LIBRARY/ARCHIVES
240 S. 4th St.   Phone: (215) 925-0609
Philadelphia, PA 19106

NATIONAL ACTION/RESEARCH ON THE MILITARY-INDUSTRIAL COMPLEX
  - LIBRARY
1501 Cherry St.   Phone: (215) 241-7175
Philadelphia, PA 19102   David Goodman

NATIONAL ASSOCIATION OF SELF-INSTRUCTIONAL LANGUAGE PROGRAMS
  - NASILP INFORMATION CENTER & ARCHIVES
Critical Languages 022-38
Temple University   Phone: (215) 787-1715
Philadelphia, PA 19122   Dr. John B. Means, Exec.Dir.

NATIONAL CENTER FOR THE STUDY OF CORPORAL PUNISHMENT &
  ALTERNATIVES IN THE SCHOOLS - LIBRARY
253 Ritter Annex   Phone: (215) 787-6091
Philadelphia, PA 19122   Irwin A. Hyman, Dir.

NATIONAL FEDERATION OF ABSTRACTING AND INFORMATION SERVICES
112 S. 16th St.   Phone: (215) 563-2406
Philadelphia, PA 19102   M. Lynne Neufeld, Exec.Dir.

NAZARETH HOSPITAL - MEDICAL LIBRARY
2601 Holme Ave.   Phone: (215) 335-6000
Philadelphia, PA 19152   Shirley M. Betz, Dir.

NEW SCHOOL OF MUSIC, INC. - ALICE TULLY LIBRARY
301 S. 21st St.   Phone: (215) 732-3966
Philadelphia, PA 19103   Susan L. Koenig, Libn.

NORTHEASTERN HOSPITAL - SCHOOL OF NURSING LIBRARY
2301 E. Allegheny Ave.   Phone: (215) 291-3168
Philadelphia, PA 19134   James W. Osborne, Libn.

OVERBROOK SCHOOL FOR THE BLIND - LIBRARY
64th St. & Malvern Ave.   Phone: (215) 877-0313
Philadelphia, PA 19151   Edith L. Willoughby, Libn.

PEIRCE JUNIOR COLLEGE - LIBRARY - SPECIAL COLLECTIONS
1420 Pine St.   Phone: (215) 545-6400
Philadelphia, PA 19102   James R. McAuliffe, Hd.Libn.

PENN MUTUAL LIFE INSURANCE COMPANY - LAW LIBRARY
Independence Sq.   Phone: (215) 629-0600
Philadelphia, PA 19172   Doris Nardin, Asst.Libn.

PENN VIRGINIA CORPORATION - LIBRARY
2500 Fidelity Bldg.   Phone: (302) 545-6600
Philadelphia, PA 19109   Ben Payne, Libn.

PENNSYLVANIA ACADEMY OF THE FINE ARTS - LIBRARY
Broad & Cherry Sts.   Phone: (215) 972-7611
Philadelphia, PA 19102   Marietta P. Bushnell, Libn.

PENNSYLVANIA AREA LIBRARY NETWORK AND UNION LIBRARY
  CATALOGUE OF PENNSYLVANIA
3401 Market St., Suite 262   Phone: (215) 382-7031
Philadelphia, PA 19104   Dr. James G. Schoenung, Exec.Dir.

PENNSYLVANIA COLLEGE OF OPTOMETRY - ALBERT FITCH MEMORIAL
  LIBRARY
1200 W. Godfrey Ave.   Phone: (215) 276-6270
Philadelphia, PA 19141   Marita J. Krivda, Lib.Dir.

PENNSYLVANIA COLLEGE OF PODIATRIC MEDICINE - CENTER FOR THE
  HISTORY OF FOOT CARE AND FOOT WEAR
Charles E. Krausz Library
Eighth St. at Race   Phone: (215) 629-0300
Philadelphia, PA 19107   Lisabeth M. Holloway, Dir.

PENNSYLVANIA COLLEGE OF PODIATRIC MEDICINE - CHARLES E. KRAUSZ
  LIBRARY
Eighth St. at Race   Phone: (215) 629-0300
Philadelphia, PA 19107   John C. Harris, Coll.Libn.

PENNSYLVANIA ECONOMY LEAGUE - EASTERN DIVISION - LIBRARY
1211 Chestnut St.   Phone: (215) 864-9562
Philadelphia, PA 19107   Ellen Brennan, Libn.

PENNSYLVANIA HORTICULTURAL SOCIETY - LIBRARY
325 Walnut St.   Phone: (215) 625-8268
Philadelphia, PA 19106   Mary Lou Wolfe, Libn.

PENNSYLVANIA HOSPITAL - DEPARTMENT FOR SICK AND INJURED -
  HISTORICAL LIBRARY
Eighth & Spruce Sts.   Phone: (215) 829-3998
Philadelphia, PA 19107   Caroline Morris, Libn.-Archv.

PENNSYLVANIA HOSPITAL - DEPARTMENT FOR SICK AND INJURED -
  MEDICAL LIBRARY
Eighth & Spruce Sts.   Phone: (215) 829-3998
Philadelphia, PA 19107   Caroline Morris, Libn.-Archv.

PENNSYLVANIA SCHOOL FOR THE DEAF - LIBRARY
7500 Germantown Ave.   Phone: (215) 247-9700
Philadelphia, PA 19119   Catherine Lawlor-Fennell, Libn.

PENNSYLVANIA STATE SUPERIOR COURT - APPELLATE COURTS LIBRARY
2061 Old Federal Courthouse   Phone: (215) 351-5840
Philadelphia, PA 19107   Renee Allard Betts, Supv.Libn.

PEPPER, HAMILTON AND SCHEETZ - LAW LIBRARY
123 S. Broad St.   Phone: (215) 893-3080
Philadelphia, PA 19109   Robyn L. Beyer, Dir., Lib.Serv.

PERELMAN ANTIQUE TOY MUSEUM - LIBRARY
270 S. 2nd St.   Phone: (215) 922-1070
Philadelphia, PA 19106   Harriet Goldfarb, Cur.

PHILADELPHIA BOARD OF EDUCATION - PEDAGOGICAL LIBRARY †
22nd St. & Parkway
Adm. Bldg., Rm. 301   Phone: (215) 299-7783
Philadelphia, PA 19103   Helen E. Howe, Hd.Libn.

PHILADELPHIA - CITY ARCHIVES
Dept. of Records
Rm. 523, City Hall Annex   Phone: (215) 686-2272
Philadelphia, PA 19107   Allen Weinberg, City Archv.

PHILADELPHIA CITY PLANNING COMMISSION - LIBRARY
City Hall Annex, 14th Fl.
Juniper & Filbert Sts.   Phone: (215) 686-4637
Philadelphia, PA 19103

PHILADELPHIA COLLEGE OF ART - AUDIOVISIUAL DEPARTMENT - FILM LIBRARY
Broad & Spruce Sts.
Philadelphia, PA 19102
Phone: (215) 893-3204
Richard Sassaman, AV Coord.

PHILADELPHIA COLLEGE OF ART - SLIDE LIBRARY
Broad & Spruce Sts., Anderson Hall
Philadelphia, PA 19102
Phone: (215) 893-3117
John Caldwell, Libn.

PHILADELPHIA COLLEGE OF OSTEOPATHIC MEDICINE - O.J. SNYDER MEMORIAL MEDICAL LIBRARY
4150 City Ave.
Philadelphia, PA 19131
Phone: (215) 581-6526
Dr. Shanker H. Vyas, Prof./Dir. of Libs.

PHILADELPHIA COLLEGE OF THE PERFORMING ARTS - LIBRARY
250 S. Broad St.
Philadelphia, PA 19102
Phone: (215) 875-2200
Phoebe Law, Hd.Libn.

PHILADELPHIA COLLEGE OF PHARMACY AND SCIENCE - JOSEPH W. ENGLAND LIBRARY
42nd St. & Woodland Ave.
Philadelphia, PA 19104
Phone: (215) 596-8960
Carol Hansen Fenichel, Dir., Lib.Serv.

PHILADELPHIA COLLEGE OF TEXTILES AND SCIENCE - PASTORE LIBRARY
School House Lane & Henry Ave.
Philadelphia, PA 19144
Phone: (215) 951-2840
J. Thomas Vogel, Dir. of Lib.Serv.

PHILADELPHIA COMMUNITY LEGAL SERVICES, INC. - LAW LIBRARY
Sylvania House
1324 Locust at Juniper St.
Philadelphia, PA 19107
Phone: (215) 893-5368
Barbara L. Krauss, Libn.

PHILADELPHIA CORPORATION FOR AGING - LIBRARY
Penn Square Bldg.
1317 Filbert St., Rm. 415
Philadelphia, PA 19107
Phone: (215) 241-8207
Steven J. Bell, Ref.Libn.

PHILADELPHIA COURT OF COMMON PLEAS - LAW LIBRARY
City Hall, Rm. 600
Philadelphia, PA 19107
Phone: (215) 686-3799
James M. Clark, Libn.

PHILADELPHIA ELECTRIC COMPANY - LIBRARY
2301 Market St.
Philadelphia, PA 19101
Phone: (215) 841-4358
Sabina D. Tannenbaum, Libn.

PHILADELPHIA GERIATRIC CENTER - LIBRARY
5307 N. 13th St.
Philadelphia, PA 19141
Phone: (215) 455-6100
Barbara Halpern, Libn.

PHILADELPHIA HISTORICAL COMMISSION - LIBRARY
1313 City Hall Annex
Philadelphia, PA 19107
Phone: (215) 686-4543
Dr. Richard Tyler, Hist.

PHILADELPHIA JEWISH ARCHIVES CENTER
625 Walnut St.
Philadelphia, PA 19106
Phone: (215) 923-2729
Lee B. Leopold, Archv.

PHILADELPHIA MARITIME MUSEUM - LIBRARY
321 Chestnut St.
Philadelphia, PA 19106
Phone: (215) 925-5439
Dorothy H. Mueller, Libn.

PHILADELPHIA MUSEUM OF ART - LIBRARY
Box 7646
Philadelphia, PA 19101
Phone: (215) 763-8100
Barbara Sevy, Libn.

PHILADELPHIA MUSEUM OF ART - SLIDE LIBRARY
Parkway at 26th St.
Box 7646
Philadelphia, PA 19101
Phone: (215) 763-8100
Thomas Donio, Slide Libn.

PHILADELPHIA NEWSPAPERS, INC. - INQUIRER AND DAILY NEWS LIBRARY
400 N. Broad St.
Philadelphia, PA 19101
Phone: (215) 854-2000
Mary Jo Crowley, Mgr., Lib./Info.Ctr.

PHILADELPHIA ORCHESTRA ASSOCIATION - LIBRARY
Academy of Music
1420 Locust St.
Philadelphia, PA 19102
Phone: (215) 893-1929
Clinton F. Nieweg, Principal Libn.

PHILADELPHIA PSYCHIATRIC CENTER - PROFESSIONAL LIBRARY
Ford Rd. & Monument Ave.
Philadelphia, PA 19131
Phone: (215) 877-2000
Ann Vosbergh, Libn.

PHILADELPHIA STATE HOSPITAL - STAFF LIBRARY †
Research & Education Bldg.
14000 Roosevelt Blvd.
Philadelphia, PA 19114
Phone: (215) 671-4111
Greta Clark, Libn.

PLANNED PARENTHOOD OF SOUTHEASTERN PENNSYLVANIA - RESOURCE CENTER
1220 Sansom St.
Philadelphia, PA 19107
Phone: (215) 629-2828
Roslyn R. Wright, Dir.

PRESBYTERIAN CHURCH (U.S.A). - PRESBYTERIAN HISTORICAL SOCIETY - LIBRARY
425 Lombard St.
Philadelphia, PA 19147
Phone: (215) 627-1852
William B. Miller, Dir.

PRESBYTERIAN-UNIVERSITY OF PENNSYLVANIA MEDICAL CENTER - MARY ELLEN BROWN MEDICAL CENTER LIBRARY
51 N. 39th St.
Philadelphia, PA 19104
Phone: (215) 662-9181
Kathleen M. Ahrens, Libn.

PROTESTANT EPISCOPAL CHURCH - DIOCESE OF PENNSYLVANIA - INFORMATION CENTER
IVB Bldg., Suite 2616
1700 Market St.
Philadelphia, PA 19103
Phone: (215) 567-6650

PROVIDENT MUTUAL LIFE INSURANCE COMPANY OF PHILADELPHIA - LIBRARY †
46th & Market Sts.
Box 7378
Philadelphia, PA 19101
Phone: (215) 474-7000
Tikvah S. Shulman, Libn.

PUBLIC/PRIVATE VENTURES - RESOURCE CENTER
1701 Arch St.
Philadelphia, PA 19103
Phone: (215) 564-4815
Carol Thomson, Dir. of Pub.Aff.

RAHENKAMP & ASSOCIATES, INC. - RSWA PLANNING LIBRARY
1717 Spring Garden St.
Philadelphia, PA 19130

RAWLE AND HENDERSON - LAW LIBRARY
211 S. Broad St.
Philadelphia, PA 19107
Phone: (215) 875-4000
Hope S. Ridge, Libn.

REFORMED EPISCOPAL CHURCH - THEOLOGICAL SEMINARY - KUEHNER MEMORIAL LIBRARY
4225 Chestnut St.
Philadelphia, PA 19104
Phone: (215) 222-5158
Walter G. Truesdell, Libn.

RESEARCH FOR BETTER SCHOOLS, INC. - RESOURCE CENTER
444 N. Third St.
Philadelphia, PA 19123
Phone: (215) 574-9300
Marian L. Chapman, Dir.

ROBERTS (H. Armstrong) INC. - STOCK PHOTOGRAPHY LIBRARY
4203 Locust St.
Philadelphia, PA 19104
Phone: (215) 386-6300
H. Armstrong Roberts, III, Pres.

ROHM & HAAS COMPANY - HOME OFFICE LIBRARY
Independence Mall, W.
Philadelphia, PA 19105
Phone: (215) 592-3631
Sandra F. Hostetter, Bus.Libn./Info.Spec.

ROSENBACH MUSEUM & LIBRARY
2010 De Lancey Pl.
Philadelphia, PA 19103
Phone: (215) 732-1600
Ellen S. Dunlap, Dir.

ROXBOROUGH MEMORIAL HOSPITAL - SCHOOL OF NURSING AND MEDICAL STAFF LIBRARY
5800 Ridge Ave.
Philadelphia, PA 19128
Phone: (215) 483-9900
Linda C. Stanley, Libn.

SADTLER RESEARCH LABORATORIES - LIBRARY
3316 Spring Garden St.
Philadelphia, PA 19104
Phone: (215) 382-7800
Bernadette Steiner, Libn.

ST. AGNES MEDICAL CENTER - HEALTH SCIENCE LIBRARY
1900 S. Broad St.
Phone: (215) 339-4448
Philadelphia, PA 19145
Angelina Caponigro, Hd.Libn.

ST. CHARLES BORROMEO SEMINARY - RYAN MEMORIAL LIBRARY
Overbrook
Phone: (215) 839-3760
Philadelphia, PA 19151
Rev. John B. DeMayo, Dir. of Libs.

ST. CHRISTOPHER'S HOSPITAL FOR CHILDREN - MEDICAL LIBRARY
2600 N. Lawrence St.
Phone: (215) 427-5374
Philadelphia, PA 19133
Frances B. Pinnel, Med.Libn.

ST. JOSEPH'S UNIVERSITY - ACADEMY OF FOOD MARKETING - CAMPBELL
LIBRARY
54th & City Line Ave.
Phone: (215) 879-7489
Philadelphia, PA 19131
Anna Mae Penrose, Libn.

SAUL, EWING, REMICK & SAUL - LAW LIBRARY
3800 Centre Square W.
Phone: (215) 972-7873
Philadelphia, PA 19102
Judith A. Wishner, Libn.

SCHEIE EYE INSTITUTE - LIBRARY
Myrin Circle, 51 N. 39th St.
Phone: (215) 662-8148
Philadelphia, PA 19104
Michael P. Toner, Lib.Dir.

SCHNADER, HARRISON, SEGAL & LEWIS - LIBRARY
1600 Market St., Suite 3600
Phone: (215) 751-2111
Philadelphia, PA 19103
Carol Lee Williamson, Libn.

SCHUYLKILL VALLEY NATURE CENTER - LIBRARY
8480 Hagy's Mill Rd.
Phone: (215) 482-7300
Philadelphia, PA 19128
Karin James, Libn.

SCOTT PAPER COMPANY - MARKETING LIBRARY
Scott Plaza
Phone: (215) 522-6262
Philadelphia, PA 19113
Eva K. Butler, Libn.

SCOTT PAPER COMPANY - RESEARCH LIBRARY & TECHNICAL
INFORMATION SERVICE
Scott Plaza 3
Phone: (215) 522-6416
Philadelphia, PA 19113
George Burna, Mgr.

SETTLEMENT MUSIC SCHOOL - BLANCHE WOLF KOHN LIBRARY
416 Queen St.
Phone: (215) 336-0400
Philadelphia, PA 19147
Alicia Randisi Hooker, Hd.Libn.

SISTERS OF THE HOLY FAMILY OF NAZARETH - IMMACULATE
CONCEPTION B.V.M. - ARCHIVES
Grant & Frankford Aves.
Phone: (215) 637-6464
Philadelphia, PA 19114
Sr. M. Theodosette, Archv.

SMITH, KLINE & FRENCH LABORATORIES - MARKETING RESEARCH
DEPARTMENT - INFORMATION CENTER
1500 Spring Garden St.
Phone: (215) 854-5328
Philadelphia, PA 19101
Anna M. Smyth, Info.Ctr.Coord.

SMITH, KLINE & FRENCH LABORATORIES - RESEARCH AND DEVELOPMENT
LIBRARY
F-121
1500 Spring Garden St.
Phone: (215) 751-5593
Philadelphia, PA 19101
Penny Young, Libn.

SOCIETY OF FRIENDS - PHILADELPHIA YEARLY MEETING - LIBRARY
1515 Cherry St.
Phone: (215) 241-7220
Philadelphia, PA 19102
Mary Davidson, Libn.

SOUTHEASTERN PENNSYLVANIA TRANSPORTATION AUTHORITY - SEPTA
LIBRARY
841 Chestnut St., 11th Fl.
Phone: (215) 472-1287
Philadelphia, PA 19107
Rena E. Hawes, Libn.

STEARNS CATALYTIC CORPORATION - PHILADELPHIA LIBRARY
Centre Square West
1500 Market St.
Phone: (215) 864-8567
Philadelphia, PA 19102
Mary J. Kober, Dir.

STRADLEY, RONON, STEVENS & YOUNG - LAW LIBRARY
1100 One Franklin Plaza
Phone: (215) 564-8190
Philadelphia, PA 19102
Linda-Jean Smith, Libn.

TEMPLE UNIVERSITY - CENTER FOR THE STUDY OF FEDERALISM -
LIBRARY
Gladfelter Hall, 10th Fl.
Phone: (215) 787-1480
Philadelphia, PA 19122
Gail L. Charette, Hd.Libn.

TEMPLE UNIVERSITY - CENTRAL LIBRARY SYSTEM - AUDIO UNIT
Broad & Montgomery
Philadelphia, PA 19122

TEMPLE UNIVERSITY - CENTRAL LIBRARY SYSTEM - BIOLOGY LIBRARY
248 Life Science Bldg.
Phone: (215) 787-8878
Philadelphia, PA 19122
Jocelyn McCrae, Bibliog.Asst.

TEMPLE UNIVERSITY - CENTRAL LIBRARY SYSTEM - CENTER CITY
LIBRARY
1619 Walnut St.
Phone: (215) 787-6950
Philadelphia, PA 19103
Cornelia Tucker, Hd.Libn.

TEMPLE UNIVERSITY - CENTRAL LIBRARY SYSTEM - CHARLES L.
BLOCKSON AFRO-AMERICAN HISTORICAL COLL.
13th & Berks Sts.
Phone: (215) 787-6632
Philadelphia, PA 19122
Charles L. Blockson, Cur.

TEMPLE UNIVERSITY - CENTRAL LIBRARY SYSTEM - CHEMISTRY LIBRARY
Beury Hall, 1st Fl.
Phone: (215) 787-7120
Philadelphia, PA 19122
Dolores Michalak, Bibliog.Asst.

TEMPLE UNIVERSITY - CENTRAL LIBRARY SYSTEM - COLLEGE OF
ENGINEERING AND ARCHITECTURE - LIBRARY
12th & Norris Sts.
Phone: (215) 787-7828
Philadelphia, PA 19122
Raelaine Ballou, Libn.

TEMPLE UNIVERSITY - CENTRAL LIBRARY SYSTEM - CONTEMPORARY
CULTURE COLLECTION
13th & Berks Sts.
Phone: (215) 787-8667
Philadelphia, PA 19122
Patricia J. Case, Cur.

TEMPLE UNIVERSITY - CENTRAL LIBRARY SYSTEM - CONWELLANA-
TEMPLANA COLLECTION
13th & Berks Sts.
Phone: (215) 787-8240
Philadelphia, PA 19122
Miriam I. Crawford, Cur.

TEMPLE UNIVERSITY - CENTRAL LIBRARY SYSTEM - MATHEMATICAL
SCIENCES LIBRARY
407 Computer Sciences Bldg.
Phone: (215) 787-8434
Philadelphia, PA 19122
Sandra Thompson, Bibliog.Asst.

TEMPLE UNIVERSITY - CENTRAL LIBRARY SYSTEM - NATIONAL
IMMIGRATION ARCHIVES
Balch Institute Bldg.
18 S. 7th St.
Phone: (215) 922-3454
Philadelphia, PA 19106
Stephanie A. Morris, Cur.

TEMPLE UNIVERSITY - CENTRAL LIBRARY SYSTEM - PHOTO-JOURNALISM
COLLECTION
13th & Berks St.
Phone: (215) 787-8230
Philadelphia, PA 19122

TEMPLE UNIVERSITY - CENTRAL LIBRARY SYSTEM - PHYSICS LIBRARY
209A Barton Hall
Phone: (215) 787-7649
Philadelphia, PA 19122
Rhea Mihalisin, Bibliog.Asst.

TEMPLE UNIVERSITY - CENTRAL LIBRARY SYSTEM - RARE BOOK &
MANUSCRIPT COLLECTION
13th & Berks St.
Phone: (215) 787-8230
Philadelphia, PA 19122
Thomas M. Whitehead, Hd., Spec.Coll.Dept.

TEMPLE UNIVERSITY - CENTRAL LIBRARY SYSTEM - REFERENCE
DEPARTMENT MAP UNIT
Paley Library
13th & Berks Sts.
Phone: (215) 787-8213
Philadelphia, PA 19122
Ida G. Ginsburgs, Map Libn.

TEMPLE UNIVERSITY - CENTRAL LIBRARY SYSTEM - SCIENCE FICTION
COLLECTION
13th & Berks St.
Phone: (215) 787-8230
Philadelphia, PA 19122
Thomas M. Whitehead, Hd., Spec.Coll.Dept.

TEMPLE UNIVERSITY - CENTRAL LIBRARY SYSTEM - TYLER SCHOOL OF
FINE ARTS - LIBRARY
Beech & Penrose Aves.
Philadelphia, PA 19126
Phone: (215) 224-7575
Mary Ivy Bayard, Libn.

TEMPLE UNIVERSITY - CENTRAL LIBRARY SYSTEM - TYLER SCHOOL OF
FINE ARTS - SLIDE LIBRARY
Beech & Penrose Aves.
Philadelphia, PA 19126
Phone: (215) 224-7575
Edith Zuckerman, Hd. Slide Cur.

TEMPLE UNIVERSITY - CENTRAL LIBRARY SYSTEM - URBAN ARCHIVES
13th & Berks Sts.
Philadelphia, PA 19122
Phone: (215) 787-8257
Dr. Fredric Miller, Cur.

TEMPLE UNIVERSITY - CENTRAL LIBRARY SYSTEM - ZAHN
INSTRUCTIONAL MATERIALS CTR./SOCIAL ADM. LIB.
Ritter Annex 139
13th & Columbia Ave.
Philadelphia, PA 19122
Phone: (215) 787-8481
Linda Cotilla, Hd.Libn.

TEMPLE UNIVERSITY - HEALTH SCIENCES CENTER - LIBRARY
N. Broad & Tioga Sts.
Philadelphia, PA 19140
Phone: (215) 221-4032
Ruth Y. Diamond, Dir.

TEMPLE UNIVERSITY HOSPITAL - HEALTH SCIENCES CENTER -
DEPARTMENT OF DIAGNOSTIC IMAGING - LIBRARY
3401 N. Broad St.
Philadelphia, PA 19140
Phone: (215) 221-4226
Shirley T.L. Ding, Libn.

TEMPLE UNIVERSITY - LAW LIBRARY
N. Broad St. & Montgomery Ave.
Philadelphia, PA 19122
Phone: (215) 787-7892
John M. Lindsey, Law Prof./Law Libn.

TRW, INC. - ELECTRONIC COMPONENTS - RESEARCH & DEVELOPMENT
LIBRARY
401 N. Broad St.
Philadelphia, PA 19108
Phone: (215) 922-8900
Barbara Welsh, Libn.

UNION LEAGUE OF PHILADELPHIA - LIBRARY
140 S. Broad St.
Philadelphia, PA 19102
Phone: (215) 563-6500
James G. Mundy, Jr., Libn.

UNITED ENGINEERS & CONSTRUCTORS INC. - LIBRARY
30 S. 17th St.
Box 8223
Philadelphia, PA 19101
Phone: (215) 422-3374
Marie S. Knap, Hd.Libn.

UNITED METHODIST CHURCH - PHILADELPHIA ANNUAL CONFERENCE -
HISTORICAL SOCIETY LIBRARY
326 New St.
Philadelphia, PA 19106
Phone: (215) 925-7788
Brian McCloskey, Adm.

U.S. ARMY - CORPS OF ENGINEERS - PHILADELPHIA DISTRICT -
TECHNICAL LIBRARY
2nd & Chestnut Sts.
Philadelphia, PA 19106
Phone: (215) 597-3610
Jeanne Marie Turner, Lib.Techn.

U.S. BUREAU OF THE CENSUS - INFORMATION SERVICES PROGRAM -
PHILADELPHIA REGIONAL OFFICE - LIBRARY
Federal Bldg., Rm. 9244
600 Arch St.
Philadelphia, PA 19106
Phone: (215) 597-8314
David C. Lewis, Chf.

U.S. COURT OF APPEALS, 3RD CIRCUIT - LIBRARY
22409 U.S. Court House
601 Market St.
Philadelphia, PA 19106
Phone: (215) 597-2009
Dorothy A. Cozzolino, Chf.Libn.

U.S. DEFENSE LOGISTICS AGENCY - DEFENSE INDUSTRIAL SUPPLY
CENTER - TECHNICAL DATA MANAGEMENT OFFICE
700 Robbins Ave.
Philadelphia, PA 19111
Phone: (215) 697-2757
William Helkowski, Chf.Tech. Data Mgr.

U.S. DEFENSE LOGISTICS AGENCY - DEFENSE PERSONNEL SUPPORT CTR. -
DIRECTORATE OF MED. MATERIEL TECH. LIBRARY
2800 S. 20th St., Bldg. 9-3-F
Philadelphia, PA 19101
Phone: (215) 952-2110
Gerald J. Ziccardi, Med.Libn.

U.S.D.A. - AGRICULTURAL RESEARCH SERVICE - EASTERN REGIONAL
RESEARCH CENTER LIBRARY
600 E. Mermaid Lane
Philadelphia, PA 19118
Phone: (215) 233-6602
Wendy H. Kramer, Adm.Libn.

U.S. DEPT. OF COMMERCE - INTERNATIONAL TRADE ADMINISTRATION -
PHILADELPHIA DISTRICT OFFICE LIBRARY *
9448 Federal Bldg.
600 Arch St.
Philadelphia, PA 19106
Phone: (215) 597-2850
Robert Kistler, Dir.

U.S. DEPT. OF HOUSING AND URBAN DEVELOPMENT - REGION III -
LIBRARY †
6th and Walnut St.
Curtis Bldg., Rm. 989
Philadelphia, PA 19106
Phone: (215) 597-2608
Beverly R. Taplinger, Lib.Techn.

U.S. DEPT. OF JUSTICE - UNITED STATES ATTORNEY, DISTRICT OF
PENNSYLVANIA - LIBRARY
3310 U.S. Courthouse
601 Market St.
Philadelphia, PA 19106
Phone: (215) 597-2161
Pamela M. Ward, Law Libn.

U.S. DEPT. OF LABOR - OSHA - REGION III LIBRARY
3535 Market St.
Philadelphia, PA 19104
Phone: (215) 596-1201
Barbara Goodman, Libn.

U.S. GENERAL ACCOUNTING OFFICE - PHILADELPHIA REGIONAL
RESOURCE CENTER
434 Walnut St., 11th Fl.
Philadelphia, PA 19106
Phone: (215) 597-7360
Linda Carnevale Skale, Tech.Info.Spec.

U.S. INTERAGENCY ADVANCED POWER GROUP - POWER INFORMATION
CENTER
Franklin Research Center
20th & Race Sts.
Philadelphia, PA 19103
Phone: (215) 448-1034
Joyce E. Michelfelder, Dp.Dir.

U.S. NATL. ARCHIVES & RECORDS SERVICE - FEDERAL ARCHIVES AND
RECORDS CENTER, REGION 3
5000 Wissahickon Ave.
Philadelphia, PA 19144
Phone: (215) 951-5588
Charles T. Glessner, Dir.

U.S. NATL. PARK SERVICE - INDEPENDENCE NATL. HISTORICAL PARK -
LIBRARY †
313 Walnut St.
Philadelphia, PA 19106
Phone: (215) 597-8047
David C. Dutcher, Chf.Pk.Hist.

U.S. NAVY - NAVAL FACILITIES ENGINEERING COMMAND - NORTHERN
DIVISION - DESIGN DIVISION LIBRARY
Bldg. 77-L
Philadelphia Naval Base
Philadelphia, PA 19112
Phone: (215) 897-6043
Mary Crum, Engr.Libn.

U.S. NAVY - NAVAL HOSPITAL (PA-Philadelphia) - MEDICAL LIBRARY
17th & Pattison Aves.
Philadelphia, PA 19145
Phone: (215) 755-8314
Giovina Cavacini, Libn.

U.S. NAVY - NAVAL SHIP SYSTEMS ENGINEERING STATION
HEADQUARTERS - TECHNICAL LIBRARY
Bldg. 619, Naval Base
Philadelphia, PA 19112
Phone: (215) 952-7078
Pearl O. Robinson, Libn.

U.S. NAVY - NAVAL SHIPYARD (PA-Philadelphia) - TECHNICAL LIBRARY
Philadelphia Naval Base
Philadelphia, PA 19112
Phone: (215) 897-3657
Alice R. Murray, Dir.

U.S. VETERANS ADMINISTRATION (PA-Philadelphia) - MEDICAL CENTER
LIBRARY
University & Woodland Aves.
Philadelphia, PA 19104
Phone: (215) 823-5860
Robert S. Lyle, Chf., Lib.Serv.

UNIVERSITY OF PENNSYLVANIA - ANNENBERG SCHOOL OF
COMMUNICATIONS - LIBRARY †
3620 Walnut St./C5
Philadelphia, PA 19104
Phone: (215) 898-7027
Sandra B. Grilikhes, Hd.Libn.

UNIVERSITY OF PENNSYLVANIA - ARCHIVES AND RECORDS CENTER
North Arcade, Franklin Field   Phone: (215) 898-7024
Philadelphia, PA 19104   Mark Frazier Lloyd, Univ.Archv.

UNIVERSITY OF PENNSYLVANIA - BIDDLE LAW LIBRARY
3400 Chestnut St./I4   Phone: (215) 898-7478
Philadelphia, PA 19104   Elizabeth S. Kelly, Libn.

UNIVERSITY OF PENNSYLVANIA - BIOMEDICAL LIBRARY
Johnson Pavilion/G2
36th & Hamilton Walk   Phone: (215) 898-4223
Philadelphia, PA 19104   Eleanor Goodchild, Biomed.Libn.

UNIVERSITY OF PENNSYLVANIA - CENTER FOR THE HISTORY OF
    CHEMISTRY
Van Pelt Library, 6th Fl.   Phone: (215) 898-7553
Philadelphia, PA 19104   Dr. Arnold W. Thackray, Dir.

UNIVERSITY OF PENNSYLVANIA - DEPARTMENT OF FOLKLORE & FOLKLIFE
    - ARCHIVE
417 Logan Hall   Phone: (215) 898-7352
Philadelphia, PA 19104   Dr. Kenneth Goldstein, Hd.

UNIVERSITY OF PENNSYLVANIA - EDGAR FAHS SMITH MEMORIAL
    COLLECTION IN THE HISTORY OF CHEMISTRY
Van Pelt Library/CH   Phone: (215) 898-7088
Philadelphia, PA 19104   Dr. Arnold W. Thackray, Cur.

UNIVERSITY OF PENNSYLVANIA - FINE ARTS LIBRARY
Furness Bldg./CK   Phone: (215) 898-8325
Philadelphia, PA 19104   Alan E. Morrison, Libn.

UNIVERSITY OF PENNSYLVANIA - GEOLOGY MAP LIBRARY
Hayden Hall
240 S. 33rd St.   Phone: (215) 898-5630
Philadelphia, PA 19104   Carol Faul, Map Libn.

UNIVERSITY OF PENNSYLVANIA - HENRY CHARLES LEA LIBRARY
Van Pelt Library
3420 Walnut St.   Phone: (215) 898-7088
Philadelphia, PA 19104

UNIVERSITY OF PENNSYLVANIA - HORACE HOWARD FURNESS MEMORIAL
    LIBRARY
Van Pelt Library
3420 Walnut St./CH   Phone: (215) 898-7552
Philadelphia, PA 19104   Georgiana Ziegler, Cur.

UNIVERSITY OF PENNSYLVANIA - JOHN PENMAN WOOD LIBRARY OF
    NATIONAL DEFENSE
3000 South St.   Phone: (215) 898-7757
Philadelphia, PA 19104   Margaret Brinkley, Adm.Asst.

UNIVERSITY OF PENNSYLVANIA - JOHNSON RESEARCH FOUNDATION
    LIBRARY
Richards Bldg.
37th & Hamilton Walk   Phone: (215) 898-4387
Philadelphia, PA 19104

UNIVERSITY OF PENNSYLVANIA - LIPPINCOTT LIBRARY
3420 Walnut St./CH   Phone: (215) 898-5924
Philadelphia, PA 19104   Michael Halperin, Hd.Libn.

UNIVERSITY OF PENNSYLVANIA - MATHEMATICS-PHYSICS-ASTRONOMY
    LIBRARY
Rittenhouse Laboratory/E1   Phone: (215) 898-8173
Philadelphia, PA 19104   Marion A. Kreiter, Libn.

UNIVERSITY OF PENNSYLVANIA - MORRIS ARBORETUM LIBRARY
9414 Meadowbrook Ave.   Phone: (215) 247-5777
Philadelphia, PA 19118

UNIVERSITY OF PENNSYLVANIA - MUSEUM LIBRARY
33rd & Spruce Sts./F1   Phone: (215) 898-7840
Philadelphia, PA 19104   Jean S. Adelman, Libn.

UNIVERSITY OF PENNSYLVANIA - POPULATION STUDIES CENTER -
    DEMOGRAPHY LIBRARY
3718 Locust Walk   Phone: (215) 898-5375
Philadelphia, PA 19174   Cindi S. Posner, Res.Bibliog.

UNIVERSITY OF PENNSYLVANIA - RARE BOOK COLLECTION †
Van Pelt Library, 3420 Walnut St.   Phone: (215) 898-7088
Philadelphia, PA 19104   Lyman W. Riley, Asst.Dir. of Libs.

UNIVERSITY OF PENNSYLVANIA - SCHOOL OF DENTAL MEDICINE - LEON
    LEVY LIBRARY
4001 Spruce St./A1   Phone: (215) 898-8969
Philadelphia, PA 19104   John M. Whittock, Jr., Libn.

UNIVERSITY OF PENNSYLVANIA - SCHOOL OF ENGINEERING AND APPLIED
    SCIENCE - MOORE LIBRARY
200 South 33rd St./D2   Phone: (215) 898-8135
Philadelphia, PA 19104   Charles J. Myers, Libn.

UNIVERSITY OF PENNSYLVANIA - SCHOOL OF ENGINEERING AND APPLIED
    SCIENCE - TOWNE LIBRARY
220 S. 33rd St./D3   Phone: (215) 898-7266
Philadelphia, PA 19104   Charles J. Myers, Libn.

UNIVERSITY OF PENNSYLVANIA - SCHOOL OF SOCIAL WORK - SMALLEY
    LIBRARY OF SOCIAL WORK †
Caster Bldg./C3
3701 Locust Walk   Phone: (215) 898-5508
Philadelphia, PA 19104   Evelyn Butler, Libn.

UNIVERSITY OF PENNSYLVANIA - SCHOOL OF VETERINARY MEDICINE -
    C.J. MARSHALL MEMORIAL LIBRARY
3800 Spruce St./H1   Phone: (215) 898-8874
Philadelphia, PA 19104   Lillian Bryant, Libn.

UNIVERSITY OF PENNSYLVANIA - UNIVERSITY HOSPITAL LIBRARY †
3400 Spruce St./G1   Phone: (215) 662-2571
Philadelphia, PA 19104   Susan Cleveland, Dir.

UNIVERSITY OF PENNSYLVANIA - WISTAR INSTITUTE OF ANATOMY &
    BIOLOGY - LIBRARY
36th & Spruce Sts.   Phone: (215) 898-3508
Philadelphia, PA 19104   J.A. Hunter, Libn.

WAGNER FREE INSTITUTE OF SCIENCE - LIBRARY *
17th St. & Montgomery Ave.   Phone: (215) 763-6529
Philadelphia, PA 19121   John Graham, Dir.

WESTMINSTER THEOLOGICAL SEMINARY - MONTGOMERY LIBRARY †
Chestnut Hill   Phone: (215) 887-5511
Philadelphia, PA 19118   Robert J. Kepple, Libn.

WHITE & WILLIAMS - LIBRARY
1234 Market St.   Phone: (215) 854-7126
Philadelphia, PA 19107   Margaret S. Fallon, Libn.

WILLET STAINED GLASS STUDIOS - LIBRARY
10 E. Moreland Ave.   Phone: (215) 247-5721
Philadelphia, PA 19118   Helene Weis, Libn.

WILLS EYE HOSPITAL AND RESEARCH INSTITUTE - ARTHUR J. BEDELL
    MEMORIAL LIBRARY
Ninth & Walnut Sts.   Phone: (215) 928-3288
Philadelphia, PA 19107   Fleur Weinberg, Libn.

WOLF, BLOCK, SCHORR & SOLIS-COHEN - LIBRARY
Packard Bldg., 12th Fl.   Phone: (215) 977-2000
Philadelphia, PA 19102   John Duckett, Libn.

ZOOLOGICAL SOCIETY OF PHILADELPHIA - LIBRARY
34th St. & Girard Ave.   Phone: (215) 243-1100
Philadelphia, PA 19104   Alyssa N. Scheuermann, Libn.

PENNSYLVANIA STATE DEPARTMENT OF PUBLIC WELFARE - PHILIPSBURG
    STATE GENERAL HOSPITAL - LIBRARY
Loch Lomond Rd.   Phone: (814) 342-3320
Philipsburg, PA 16866   Elaine G. Filsinger, Libn.

FIRST PRESBYTERIAN CHURCH - LIBRARY
Main and Morgan St.   Phone: (215) 933-8816
Phoenixville, PA 19460   Elizabeth Holden, Libn.

VALLEY FORGE CHRISTIAN COLLEGE - LIBRARY
Phone: (215) 935-0450
Phoenixville, PA 19460   Dorsey Reynolds, Libn.

ACTION-HOUSING, INC. - LIBRARY & HOUSING INFORMATION CENTER
2 Gateway Ctr.   Phone: (412) 281-2102
Pittsburgh, PA 15222   Terri F. Gould, Dir. of Educ.

AIR POLLUTION CONTROL ASSOCIATION - LIBRARY
Box 2861   Phone: (412) 621-1090
Pittsburgh, PA 15230

ALLEGHENY COUNTY - DEPARTMENT OF PLANNING - LIBRARY
429 Forbes Ave., 12th Fl.   Phone: (412) 355-4353
Pittsburgh, PA 15219   Mary Ann Munsch, Lib.Cons.

ALLEGHENY COUNTY HEALTH DEPARTMENT - LIBRARY
40th St. & Penn Ave.   Phone: (412) 578-8028
Pittsburgh, PA 15224   Carol Schmitt, Libn.

ALLEGHENY COUNTY LAW LIBRARY †
921 City-County Bldg.   Phone: (412) 355-5353
Pittsburgh, PA 15219   Joel H. Fishman, Law Libn.

ALLEGHENY GENERAL HOSPITAL - HEALTH SCIENCES LIBRARY
320 E. North Ave.   Phone: (412) 359-3040
Pittsburgh, PA 15212   Jennifer J. Angier, Mgr.

ALUMINUM COMPANY OF AMERICA - CORPORATE LIBRARY
1501 Alcoa Bldg.   Phone: (412) 553-4482
Pittsburgh, PA 15219   Nancy J. Furlan, Info.Serv.Adm.

BLUE CROSS OF WESTERN PENNSYLVANIA - IN-HOUSE BUSINESS LIBRARY
1 Smithfield St.   Phone: (412) 255-8220
Pittsburgh, PA 15222   Connie Ferguson, Libn.

CARNEGIE LIBRARY OF PITTSBURGH - BUSINESS DIVISION
Frick Bldg. Mezzanine
437 Grant St.   Phone: (412) 281-5945
Pittsburgh, PA 15219   Miriam S. Lerch, Div.Hd.

CARNEGIE LIBRARY OF PITTSBURGH - CENTRAL CHILDREN'S ROOM
   HISTORICAL COLLECTION
4400 Forbes Ave.   Phone: (412) 622-3122
Pittsburgh, PA 15213   Amy Kellman, Hd., Ch.Dept.

CARNEGIE LIBRARY OF PITTSBURGH - MUSIC AND ART DEPARTMENT
4400 Forbes Ave.   Phone: (412) 622-3105
Pittsburgh, PA 15213   Ida Reed, Dept.Hd.

CARNEGIE LIBRARY OF PITTSBURGH - PENNSYLVANIA DIVISION
4400 Forbes Ave.   Phone: (412) 622-3154
Pittsburgh, PA 15213   Maria Zini, Hd.

CARNEGIE LIBRARY OF PITTSBURGH - SCIENCE AND TECHNOLOGY
   DEPARTMENT
4400 Forbes Ave.   Phone: (412) 622-3138
Pittsburgh, PA 15213   Catherine Brosky, Hd.

CARNEGIE-MELLON UNIVERSITY - AUDIO VISUAL SERVICES
Hunt Library
Schenley Park   Phone: (412) 578-2430
Pittsburgh, PA 15213   Stan Yoder, Hd., AV Serv.

CARNEGIE-MELLON UNIVERSITY - ENGINEERING & SCIENCE LIBRARY
Schenley Park   Phone: (412) 578-2428
Pittsburgh, PA 15213   Patricia FitzGerald, Hd., Engr. & Sci.Lib.

CARNEGIE-MELLON UNIVERSITY - HUNT INSTITUTE FOR BOTANICAL
   DOCUMENTATION
Schenley Park   Phone: (412) 578-2434
Pittsburgh, PA 15213   Robert W. Kiger, Dir.

CARNEGIE-MELLON UNIVERSITY - MELLON INSTITUTE LIBRARY
4400 Fifth Ave.   Phone: (412) 578-3172
Pittsburgh, PA 15213   Patricia FitzGerald, Hd., Engr. & Sci.Libs.

CARNEGIE-MELLON UNIVERSITY - SPECIAL COLLECTIONS
Hunt Library
Schenley Park   Phone: (412) 578-2447
Pittsburgh, PA 15213   Mary Catherine Schall, Hd., Spec.Coll.

CARNEGIE MUSEUM OF NATURAL HISTORY - LIBRARY
4400 Forbes Ave.   Phone: (412) 622-3264
Pittsburgh, PA 15213   Gerard McKiernan, Libn.

CENTER FOR THE HISTORY OF AMERICAN NEEDLEWORK - LIBRARY
Carlow College
3333 Fifth Ave.   Phone: (412) 266-6440
Pittsburgh, PA 15213   Virginia Suplee, Info. & Res.Dir.

CHILDREN'S HOSPITAL OF PITTSBURGH - BLAXTER MEMORIAL LIBRARY †
125 De Soto St.   Phone: (412) 647-5288
Pittsburgh, PA 15213   Nancy Dunn, Libn.

COLT INDUSTRIES - CRUCIBLE RESEARCH CENTER - LIBRARY
Box 88   Phone: (412) 923-2955
Pittsburgh, PA 15230   Patricia J. Aducci, Tech.Libn.

CONSOLIDATION COAL COMPANY - EXPLORATION LIBRARY †
Consol Plaza
1800 Washington Rd.   Phone: (412) 831-4513
Pittsburgh, PA 15241   Eva Marie Tomassetti, Land Ck.

DIOCESE OF PITTSBURGH - LEARNING MEDIA CENTER
111 Blvd. of the Allies   Phone: (412) 456-3120
Pittsburgh, PA 15222   Carole Obrokta, Dir.

DRAVO ENGINEERS INC. - LIBRARY
1 Oliver Plaza   Phone: (412) 566-5075
Pittsburgh, PA 15222   Alice Patience, Lib.Mgr.

DUQUESNE UNIVERSITY - LAW LIBRARY
600 Forbes Ave.   Phone: (412) 434-6293
Pittsburgh, PA 15282   Frank Yining Liu, Law Libn.

EAST LIBERTY PRESBYTERIAN CHURCH - LIBRARY
116 S. Highland Mall   Phone: (412) 441-3800
Pittsburgh, PA 15217   Katherine Hackney, Libn.

EYE AND EAR HOSPITAL OF PITTSBURGH - BLAIR-LIPPINCOTT LIBRARY
230 Lothrop St.   Phone: (412) 647-2287
Pittsburgh, PA 15213   Bruce Johnston, Med.Libn.

FEDERAL RESERVE BANK OF CLEVELAND - PITTSBURGH BRANCH LIBRARY
717 Grant St.   Phone: (412) 261-7915
Pittsburgh, PA 15230   Dolores Craft, Act.Libn.

FORBES HEALTH SYSTEM - CORPORATE OFFICE LIBRARY
500 Finley St.   Phone: (412) 665-3570
Pittsburgh, PA 15206   Susan V. Reber, Libn.

FORBES HEALTH SYSTEM - FORBES CENTER FOR GERONTOLOGY - LIBRARY
Frankstown Ave. & Washington Blvd.   Phone: (412) 665-3050
Pittsburgh, PA 15206   Susan V. Reber, Libn.

FORBES HEALTH SYSTEM - FORBES METROPOLITAN HEALTH CENTER
   LIBRARY
225 Penn Ave.   Phone: (412) 247-2422
Pittsburgh, PA 15221   Susan V. Reber, Libn.

FOUNDATION FOR THE STUDY OF CYCLES INC. - LIBRARY
124 S. Highland Ave.   Phone: (412) 441-1666
Pittsburgh, PA 15206   Gertrude F. Shirk, Ed.

GRAPHIC ARTS TECHNICAL FOUNDATION - E.H. WADEWITZ MEMORIAL
   LIBRARY
4615 Forbes Ave.   Phone: (412) 621-6941
Pittsburgh, PA 15213   Janice L. Lloyd, Libn.

GULF OIL CORPORATION - BUSINESS RESEARCH LIBRARY
Box 1166   Phone: (412) 263-6040
Pittsburgh, PA 15230   Phyllis McCanna, Lib.Supv.

GULF RESEARCH AND DEVELOPMENT COMPANY - TECHNICAL
  INFORMATION SERVICES †
Drawer 2038   Phone: (412) 665-4678
Pittsburgh, PA 15230   Tina B. Ross, Dir., Tech.Info.Serv.

HARBISON-WALKER REFRACTORIES COMPANY - GARBER RESEARCH
  CENTER LIBRARY *
Box 98037   Phone: (412) 469-3880
Pittsburgh, PA 15227   Harriet Gillespie, Res.Libn.

HARMARVILLE REHABILITATION CENTER - STAFF LIBRARY
Guys Run Rd.
Box 11460   Phone: (412) 781-5700
Pittsburgh, PA 15238   Alice B. Kuller, Dir.

HEALTH EDUCATION CENTER LIBRARY
200 Ross St.   Phone: (412) 392-3165
Pittsburgh, PA 15219   Susan Stapley Walko, Libn.

HEALTH AND WELFARE PLANNING ASSOCIATION OF ALLEGHENY COUNTY -
  LIBRARY
200 Ross St.   Phone: (412) 392-3150
Pittsburgh, PA 15219   Mary Lou Charlton, Libn.

HEBREW INSTITUTE OF PITTSBURGH - SOL ROSENBLOOM LIBRARY
6401 Forbes Ave.   Phone: (412) 521-1100
Pittsburgh, PA 15217   Michella Segall, Libn.

HEINZ (H.J.) COMPANY - LIBRARY
1062 Progress St.
Box 57   Phone: (412) 237-5948
Pittsburgh, PA 15230   Nancy M. Wright, Libn.

HISTORICAL SOCIETY OF WESTERN PENNSYLVANIA - LIBRARY
4338 Bigelow Blvd.   Phone: (412) 681-5533
Pittsburgh, PA 15213   Helen M. Wilson, Libn.

INDUSTRIAL HEALTH FOUNDATION, INC. - LIBRARY
34 Penn Circle W.   Phone: (412) 687-2100
Pittsburgh, PA 15206   Jane F. Brislin, Dir., Info.Serv.

JONES AND LAUGHLIN STEEL CORPORATION - COMMERCIAL LIBRARY †
1600 W. Carson St.   Phone: (412) 227-4354
Pittsburgh, PA 15263   Nancy Winstanley, Libn.

JONES AND LAUGHLIN STEEL CORPORATION - GRAHAM LIBRARY
900 Agnew Rd.   Phone: (412) 884-1000
Pittsburgh, PA 15227   Joanne S. Klein, Tech.Libn.

KETCHUM COMMUNICATIONS INC. - LIBRARY SERVICES
Four Gateway Ctr.   Phone: (412) 456-3600
Pittsburgh, PA 15222   Florence V. Merkel, Lib.Supv.

KNOW, INC.
Box 86031   Phone: (412) 241-4844
Pittsburgh, PA 15221   Phyllis Wetherby, Pres.

KOPPERS COMPANY, INC. - ENGINEERING AND CONSTRUCTION DIVISION
  - INFORMATION SERVICE - LIBRARY
C806 Chamber of Commerce Bldg.
Pittsburgh, PA 15219

KTA-TATOR, INC. - LIBRARY
115 Technology Dr.   Phone: (412) 788-1300
Pittsburgh, PA 15275   Dwight Weldon, Lab.Dir.

LIBERTY MUTUAL INSURANCE COMPANY - BUSINESS REFERENCE LIBRARY
600 Grant St.   Phone: (412) 391-6555
Pittsburgh, PA 15219   Dorothy Fornof, Supv., Lib.Serv.

MAGEE-WOMENS HOSPITAL - HOWARD ANDERSON POWER MEMORIAL
  LIBRARY
Forbes Ave. & Halket St.   Phone: (412) 647-4288
Pittsburgh, PA 15213   Velma H. Axelrod, Med.Libn.

MELLON BANK, N.A. - LIBRARY †
Mellon Sq., Rm. 2825   Phone: (412) 234-4100
Pittsburgh, PA 15230   Patricia H. Riordan, Libn.

MERCK & COMPANY, INC. - CALGON CORPORATION - INFORMATION
  CENTER
Box 1346   Phone: (412) 777-8203
Pittsburgh, PA 15230   Betty P. Schwarz, Mgr.

MERCY HOSPITAL - MEDICAL STAFF LIBRARY †
Pride & Locust Sts.   Phone: (412) 232-7520
Pittsburgh, PA 15219   Suzanne A. Gabarry, Libn.

MERCY HOSPITAL - SCHOOL OF NURSING LIBRARY
1401 Blvd. of the Allies   Phone: (412) 232-7963
Pittsburgh, PA 15219   Veronica C. Harrison, Libn.

METROPOLITAN PITTSBURGH PUBLIC BROADCASTING, INC. - WQED
  LIBRARY
4802 Fifth Ave.   Phone: (412) 622-1524
Pittsburgh, PA 15213   Deborah Barrett, Libn.

MINE SAFETY APPLIANCES COMPANY - BUSINESS LIBRARY
600 Penn Ctr. Blvd.   Phone: (412) 273-5131
Pittsburgh, PA 15235   Barbara Boutwell, Libn.

MINE SAFETY APPLIANCES COMPANY - TECHNICAL LIBRARY
201 N. Braddock Ave.   Phone: (412) 273-5600
Pittsburgh, PA 15208   Barbara Boutwell, Supv., Lib.Serv.

MOBAY CHEMICAL CORPORATION - RESEARCH CENTER LIBRARY †
Penn Lincoln Pkwy., W.   Phone: (412) 777-2782
Pittsburgh, PA 15205   Nancy R. Alstadt, Libn.

NATIONAL FLAG FOUNDATION - FLAG PLAZA LIBRARY
Flag Plaza   Phone: (412) 261-1776
Pittsburgh, PA 15219   George F. Cahill, Pres.

NORTH HILLS PASSAVANT HOSPITAL - MEDICAL LIBRARY
9100 Babcock Blvd.   Phone: (412) 367-6320
Pittsburgh, PA 15237   Margaret U. Trevanion, Med.Libn.

NUS CORPORATION - TECHNICAL LIBRARY
Parkwest Two
Cliff Mine Rd.   Phone: (412) 788-1080
Pittsburgh, PA 15275   Kathryn E. Marlow, Libn.

PENNSYLVANIA ECONOMY LEAGUE - WESTERN DIVISION - LIBRARY
Two Gateway Ctr.   Phone: (412) 471-1477
Pittsburgh, PA 15222   Judith A. Eves, Libn.

PENNSYLVANIA STATE HISTORICAL & MUSEUM COMMISSION - FORT PITT
  MUSEUM - LIBRARY
Point State Park   Phone: (412) 281-9284
Pittsburgh, PA 15222   Robert J. Trombetta, Dir.

PEOPLES NATURAL GAS COMPANY - LAW LIBRARY
2 Gateway Ctr.   Phone: (412) 471-5100
Pittsburgh, PA 15222   Edison W. Keener, Att.

PITTSBURGH BOARD OF EDUCATION - PROFESSIONAL LIBRARY
635 Ridge Ave.   Phone: (412) 323-4146
Pittsburgh, PA 15212   Dorothy Hopkins, Libn.

PITTSBURGH CORNING CORPORATION - TECHNICAL LIBRARY †
800 Presque Isle Dr.
Pittsburgh, PA 15239

PITTSBURGH HISTORY & LANDMARKS FOUNDATION - JAMES D. VAN
  TRUMP LIBRARY †
One Landmarks Sq.   Phone: (412) 322-1204
Pittsburgh, PA 15212   Arthur P. Ziegler, Jr., Pres.

PITTSBURGH POST-GAZETTE PUBLISHING COMPANY - LIBRARY
50 Blvd. of the Allies   Phone: (412) 263-1397
Pittsburgh, PA 15222   Angelika Kane, Libn.

PITTSBURGH PRESS - LIBRARY
Boulevard of the Allies   Phone: (412) 263-1480
Pittsburgh, PA 15230   Eileen E. Finster, Libn.

PITTSBURGH THEOLOGICAL SEMINARY - CLIFFORD E. BARBOUR LIBRARY
616 N. Highland Ave.   Phone: (412) 362-5610
Pittsburgh, PA 15206   Dikran Y. Hadidian, Libn.

PORT AUTHORITY OF ALLEGHENY COUNTY - TRANSIT RESEARCH LIBRARY
Beaver & Island Ave.   Phone: (412) 237-7334
Pittsburgh, PA 15233

PPG INDUSTRIES, INC. - FIBER GLASS RESEARCH CENTER - LIBRARY *
Box 2844   Phone: (412) 782-5130
Pittsburgh, PA 15230   Jacqueline A. Maxin, Supv., Info.Serv.

PPG INDUSTRIES, INC. - GLASS RESEARCH CENTER - INFORMATION
   SERVICES
Box 11472   Phone: (412) 665-8566
Pittsburgh, PA 15238   Jane Bookmyer, Supv.

PSYCHOLOGICAL SERVICE OF PITTSBURGH - LIBRARY
429 Forbes Ave.   Phone: (412) 261-1333
Pittsburgh, PA 15219   Dina J. Fulmer, Libn.

REED, SMITH, SHAW AND MC CLAY - LAW LIBRARY
747 Union Trust Bldg.   Phone: (412) 288-3377
Pittsburgh, PA 15219   Barbara Rose Stewart, Hd.Libn.

REFORMED PRESBYTERIAN THEOLOGICAL SEMINARY - LIBRARY
7418 Penn Ave.   Phone: (412) 731-8690
Pittsburgh, PA 15208   Rachel George, Libn.

ROCKWELL INTERNATIONAL - BUSINESS RESEARCH CENTER
600 Grant St.   Phone: (412) 565-5880
Pittsburgh, PA 15219   Ruth T. Gunning, Mgr., Bus.Info.Serv.

ROCKWELL INTERNATIONAL - FLOW CONTROL DIVISION - TECHNICAL
   INFORMATION CENTER
400 N. Lexington Ave.   Phone: (412) 247-3095
Pittsburgh, PA 15208   Kathleen M. Witkowski, Lib.Coord.

ST. CYRIL AND METHODIUS BYZANTINE CATHOLIC SEMINARY - LIBRARY
3605 Perrysville Ave.   Phone: (412) 321-8383
Pittsburgh, PA 15214   Rev. Gary Powell, O.F.M.Cap., Libn.

ST. MARGARET MEMORIAL HOSPITAL - PAUL TITUS MEMORIAL LIBRARY
   AND SCHOOL OF NURSING LIBRARY
4631 Davison St.   Phone: (412) 622-7090
Pittsburgh, PA 15201   Dorothy Schiff, Libn.

SHADYSIDE HOSPITAL - JAMES FRAZER HILLMAN HEALTH SCIENCES
   LIBRARY
5230 Centre Ave.   Phone: (412) 622-2415
Pittsburgh, PA 15232   Malinda Fetkovich, Dir.

SOUTH HILLS HEALTH SYSTEM - BEHAN HEALTH SCIENCE LIBRARY
Coal Valley Rd.
Box 18119   Phone: (412) 664-5786
Pittsburgh, PA 15236   William Rose, Dir., Lib./Media Serv.

U.S. BUREAU OF MINES - BOEING SERVICES INTERNATIONAL - LIBRARY
4800 Forbes Ave.   Phone: (412) 621-4500
Pittsburgh, PA 15213   Kathleen M. Stabryla, Lead Libn.

U.S. COURT OF APPEALS, 3RD CIRCUIT - PITTSBURGH BRANCH LIBRARY
512 U.S. Courthouse   Phone: (412) 644-6485
Pittsburgh, PA 15219   Linda Schneider, Libn.

U.S. DEPT. OF COMMERCE - INTERNATIONAL TRADE ADMINISTRATION -
   PITTSBURGH DISTRICT OFFICE LIBRARY
2002 Federal Bldg.
1000 Liberty Ave.   Phone: (412) 644-2850
Pittsburgh, PA 15222   William M. Bradley, Dir.

UNITED STATES STEEL CORPORATION - INFORMATION CENTER
600 Grant St.   Phone: (412) 433-3459
Pittsburgh, PA 15230   Nancy J. Suvak, Supv.

U.S. VETERANS ADMINISTRATION (PA-Pittsburgh) - HOSPITAL LIBRARY
Highland Dr.   Phone: (412) 363-4900
Pittsburgh, PA 15206   Pauline M. Mason, Chf., Lib.Serv.

U.S. VETERANS ADMINISTRATION (PA-Pittsburgh) - MEDICAL CENTER
   LIBRARY SERVICE (142D)
University Dr. C   Phone: (412) 683-3000
Pittsburgh, PA 15240   Tuula Beazell, Chf., Lib.Serv.

UNIVERSITY HEALTH CENTER OF PITTSBURGH - CENTER FOR EMERGENCY
   MEDICINE - LIBRARY
190 Lothrop St., Suite 113   Phone: (412) 624-2858
Pittsburgh, PA 15213   R.D. Stewart, M.D., Dir.

UNIVERSITY OF PITTSBURGH - AFRO-AMERICAN LIBRARY
Hillman Library   Phone: (412) 624-4447
Pittsburgh, PA 15260   Arthur C. Gunn, Libn.

UNIVERSITY OF PITTSBURGH - ALLEGHENY OBSERVATORY - LIBRARY
159 Riverview Airway   Phone: (412) 321-2400
Pittsburgh, PA 15260

UNIVERSITY OF PITTSBURGH - ARCHIVES
363 Hillman Library   Phone: (412) 624-4428
Pittsburgh, PA 15260   Dr. Marilyn P. Whitmore, Univ.Archv.

UNIVERSITY OF PITTSBURGH - ARCHIVES OF INDUSTRIAL SOCIETY
363-H., Hillman Library
Univ. of Pittsburgh   Phone: (412) 624-4429
Pittsburgh, PA 15260   Frank A. Zabrosky, Cur.

UNIVERSITY OF PITTSBURGH - BEVIER ENGINEERING LIBRARY
126 Benedum Hall   Phone: (412) 624-4484
Pittsburgh, PA 15261   Sandra S. Kerbel, Libn.

UNIVERSITY OF PITTSBURGH - BIOLOGICAL SCIENCES AND PSYCHOLOGY
   LIBRARY
A-217 Langley Hall   Phone: (412) 624-4489
Pittsburgh, PA 15260   D.L. Johnston, Hd.

UNIVERSITY OF PITTSBURGH - CHEMISTRY LIBRARY
200 Alumni Hall   Phone: (412) 624-5026
Pittsburgh, PA 15260   Paul J. Kobulnicky, Libn.

UNIVERSITY OF PITTSBURGH - CIOCCO LIBRARY
130 De Soto St.   Phone: (412) 624-3016
Pittsburgh, PA 15261   Suzanne O. Paul, Dir.

UNIVERSITY OF PITTSBURGH - COMPUTER SCIENCE LIBRARY
200 Alumni Hall   Phone: (412) 624-6699
Pittsburgh, PA 15260   Paul Kobulnicky, Libn.

UNIVERSITY OF PITTSBURGH - DARLINGTON MEMORIAL LIBRARY
Cathedral of Learning   Phone: (412) 624-4491
Pittsburgh, PA 15260   Dennis Lambert, Libn.

UNIVERSITY OF PITTSBURGH - EAST ASIAN LIBRARY
234 Hillman Library   Phone: (412) 624-4457
Pittsburgh, PA 15260   Dr. Thomas Kuo, Cur.

UNIVERSITY OF PITTSBURGH - ECONOMICS/COLLECTION IN REGIONAL
   ECONOMICS
Mervis Hall, Rm. 430
139 University Pl.   Phone: (412) 624-4492
Pittsburgh, PA 15260   Patricia Suozzi, Econ.Libn.

UNIVERSITY OF PITTSBURGH - FALK LIBRARY OF THE HEALTH SCIENCES
Scaife Hall, 2nd Fl.   Phone: (412) 624-2521
Pittsburgh, PA 15261   Laurabelle Eakin, Dir.

UNIVERSITY OF PITTSBURGH - FOSTER HALL COLLECTION
Stephen Foster Memorial
Forbes Ave.   Phone: (412) 624-4100
Pittsburgh, PA 15260   Dr. Deane L. Root, Cur.

UNIVERSITY OF PITTSBURGH - GRADUATE SCHOOL OF BUSINESS LIBRARY
1501 Cathedral of Learning   Phone: (412) 624-6408
Pittsburgh, PA 15260   Susan Neuman, Dir.

UNIVERSITY OF PITTSBURGH - GRADUATE SCHOOL OF PUBLIC &
   INTERNATIONAL AFFAIRS LIBRARY
Forbes Quadrangle, 1st Fl. West   Phone: (412) 624-4738
Pittsburgh, PA 15260   Nicholas C. Caruso, Libn.

UNIVERSITY OF PITTSBURGH - HENRY CLAY FRICK FINE ARTS LIBRARY
Phone: (412) 624-4124
Pittsburgh, PA 15260
Anne W. Gordon, Hd.

UNIVERSITY OF PITTSBURGH - HUMAN RELATIONS AREA FILES
G16 Hillman Library
Phone: (412) 624-4449
Pittsburgh, PA 15260
Jean R. Aiken, Info.Libn.

UNIVERSITY OF PITTSBURGH - LATIN AMERICAN COLLECTION
171 Hillman Library
Phone: (412) 624-4425
Pittsburgh, PA 15260
Eduardo Lozano, Bibliog.

UNIVERSITY OF PITTSBURGH - LAW LIBRARY
3900 Forbes Ave.
Phone: (412) 624-6213
Pittsburgh, PA 15260
Jenni Parrish, Dir.

UNIVERSITY OF PITTSBURGH - MATHEMATICS LIBRARY
809 William Pitt Union
Phone: (412) 624-4488
Pittsburgh, PA 15260
Sandra S. Kerbel, Hd.

UNIVERSITY OF PITTSBURGH - NASA INDUSTRIAL APPLICATIONS CENTER
(NIAC)
8th Fl., William Pitt Union
Phone: (412) 624-5212
Pittsburgh, PA 15260
Paul A. McWilliams, Exec.Dir.

UNIVERSITY OF PITTSBURGH - PENNSYLVANIA ETHNIC HERITAGE
STUDIES CENTER †
4G31 Forbes Quad
Phone: (412) 624-4936
Pittsburgh, PA 15260
Frank Zabrosky, Archv./Libn.

UNIVERSITY OF PITTSBURGH - PHYSICS LIBRARY
208 Engineering Hall
Phone: (412) 624-4482
Pittsburgh, PA 15260
Paul J. Kobulnicky, Libn.

UNIVERSITY OF PITTSBURGH - PRESBYTERIAN-UNIVERSITY HOSPITAL -
MEDICAL STAFF LIBRARY
DeSoto at O'Hara Sts.
Phone: (412) 647-3287
Pittsburgh, PA 15213
Mrs. Bianka M. Hesz, Med.Libn.

UNIVERSITY OF PITTSBURGH - SCHOOL OF EDUCATION - INTERNATIONAL
& DEVELOPMENT EDUCATION PROGRAM CLEARINGHOUSE
5A01 Forbes Quadrangle
Phone: (412) 624-1281
Pittsburgh, PA 15260
Carmelita Lavayna-Portugal, Dir.

UNIVERSITY OF PITTSBURGH - SCHOOL OF LIBRARY & INFORMATION
SCIENCE - INTERNATIONAL LIB. INFO. CTR.
135 N. Bellefield Ave.
Phone: (412) 624-3394
Pittsburgh, PA 15260
Dr. Richard Krzys, Dir.

UNIVERSITY OF PITTSBURGH - SCHOOL OF LIBRARY & INFORMATION
SCIENCE - LIBRARY †
135 N. Bellefield Ave.
LIS Bldg., 3rd Fl.
Phone: (412) 624-5238
Pittsburgh, PA 15260
Jean Kindlin, Dir., Lib. & Media Serv.

UNIVERSITY OF PITTSBURGH - SCHOOL OF SOCIAL WORK - BUHL LIBRARY
Hillman Library
Phone: (412) 624-4456
Pittsburgh, PA 15260
Patricia Miles Carle

UNIVERSITY OF PITTSBURGH - SPECIAL COLLECTIONS DEPARTMENT
363 Hillman Library
Phone: (412) 624-4430
Pittsburgh, PA 15260
Charles E. Aston, Jr., Coord.

UNIVERSITY OF PITTSBURGH - THEODORE M. FINNEY MUSIC LIBRARY
Music Bldg.
Phone: (412) 624-4130
Pittsburgh, PA 15260
Norris L. Stephens, Libn.

UNIVERSITY OF PITTSBURGH - UNIVERSITY CENTER FOR
INSTRUCTIONAL RESOURCES
G-20 Hillman Library
Phone: (412) 624-4468
Pittsburgh, PA 15260
Dr. J. Fred Gage, Dir.

UNIVERSITY OF PITTSBURGH - WESTERN PSYCHIATRIC INSTITUTE AND
CLINIC - LIBRARY
3811 O'Hara St.
Phone: (412) 624-2378
Pittsburgh, PA 15213
Lucile S. Stark, Dir.

WESTERN PENNSYLVANIA GENEALOGICAL SOCIETY - LIBRARY
4338 Bigelow Blvd.
Phone: (412) 681-5533
Pittsburgh, PA 15213
Helen M. Wilson, Libn.

WESTINGHOUSE ELECTRIC CORPORATION - RESEARCH AND
DEVELOPMENT CENTER - RESEARCH LIBRARY
1310 Beulah Rd.
Phone: (412) 256-1610
Pittsburgh, PA 15235
Anita Newell, Mgr.

WESTINGHOUSE ELECTRIC CORPORATION - WATER REACTOR DIVISIONS
- INFORMATION RESOURCE CENTER
Box 355
Phone: (412) 373-4200
Pittsburgh, PA 15230
Cynthia A. Hodgson, Mgr.

WESTMINSTER PRESBYTERIAN CHURCH - LIBRARY *
2040 Washington Rd.
Phone: (412) 835-6630
Pittsburgh, PA 15241
Mrs. R.L. Hutchison, Libn.

EMERGENCY CARE RESEARCH INSTITUTE - LIBRARY
5200 Butler Pike
Phone: (215) 825-6000
Plymouth Meeting, PA 19462
June P. Katucki, Hd.Libn.

POTTSTOWN MEMORIAL MEDICAL CENTER - MEDICAL STAFF LIBRARY
1600 E. High St.
Phone: (215) 327-7000
Pottstown, PA 19464
Marilyn D. Chapis, Med. Staff Libn.

SANDERS & THOMAS, INC. - LIBRARY
11 Robinson St.
Phone: (215) 326-4600
Pottstown, PA 19464
Carol S. Leh, Tech.Libn.

OHEB ZEDECK SYNAGOGUE CENTER - LIBRARY *
2300 Mahantongo St.
Phone: (717) 622-4320
Pottsville, PA 17901

POTTSVILLE HOSPITAL AND WARNE CLINIC - MEDICAL LIBRARY
Jackson & Mauch Chunk Sts.
Phone: (717) 622-6120
Pottsville, PA 17901
Dorothy Rice, Libn.

SCHUYLKILL COUNTY LAW LIBRARY
Court House
Phone: (717) 622-5570
Pottsville, PA 17901
Patricia G. Kellet, Law Libn.

ROSICRUCIAN FRATERNITY - LIBRARY
Beverly Hall
Box 220
Phone: (215) 536-5168
Quakertown, PA 18951
Gerald E. Poesnecker, Pres.

RESSLER (Martin E.) - PRIVATE MUSIC LIBRARY
R.D. 2, Box 173
Phone: (717) 529-2463
Quarryville, PA 17566
Martin E. Ressler, Owner

FIDELITY MUTUAL LIFE INSURANCE COMPANY - LIBRARY ARCHIVES †
Fidelity Mutual Life Bldg.
250 King of Prussia Rd.
Phone: (215) 964-7000
Radner, PA 19087

CHILTON COMPANY - MARKETING & ADVERTISING INFORMATION
CENTER
One Chilton Way
Phone: (215) 964-4496
Radnor, PA 19089
Louise Cupelli, Dir., Info. & Commun.

TRIANGLE PUBLICATIONS, INC. - TV GUIDE MICROFILM LIBRARY
Four Radnor Corporate Center
Phone: (215) 293-8947
Radnor, PA 19088
Cathy Johnson, Microfilm Coord.

AT & T LABORATORIES & TECHNOLOGIES - LIBRARY
2525 N. 11th St.
Phone: (215) 929-7990
Reading, PA 19603
Ina A. Brown, Lib. Group Supv.

BERKS COUNTY LAW LIBRARY
Court House
Phone: (215) 375-6121
Reading, PA 19601
Linda Fuerle Fisk, Law Libn.

CABOT CORPORATION - READING TECHNOLOGY LIBRARY
Box 1296
Phone: (215) 921-5262
Reading, PA 19603
Pamela L. Hehr, Libn.

CARPENTER TECHNOLOGY CORPORATION - RESEARCH AND
  DEVELOPMENT CENTER LIBRARY
Box 662   Phone: (215) 371-2583
Reading, PA 19603   Wendy M. Holt, Libn.

CROMPTON & KNOWLES CORPORATION - DYES AND CHEMICALS DIVISION
  - GIBRALTAR RESEARCH LIBRARY
Box 341   Phone: (215) 582-8765
Reading, PA 19603   Betty Hanf, Sr.Info.Chem.

GILBERT/COMMONWEALTH, INC. - LIBRARY AND INFORMATION
  SERVICES
Box 1498   Phone: (215) 775-2600
Reading, PA 19603   Deborah M. Bosler, Supv., Lib.Serv.

GPU NUCLEAR - LIBRARY *
Rte. 183 & Van Reed Rd.   Phone: (215) 371-1001
Reading, PA 19601   Jan Thompson, Libn.

HISTORICAL SOCIETY OF BERKS COUNTY - LIBRARY
940 Centre Ave.   Phone: (215) 375-4375
Reading, PA 19601   Aimee Devine Sanders, Lib.Cons.

KESHER ZION SYNAGOGUE AND SISTERHOOD - LIBRARY
1245 Perkiomen Ave.   Phone: (215) 372-3818
Reading, PA 19602   Rachel Yaffee, Libn.

METROPOLITAN EDISON COMPANY - SYSTEM LIBRARY
2800 Pottsville Pike
Box 542   Phone: (215) 929-6203
Reading, PA 19640   Diane L. Pawling, Libn.

PENNSYLVANIA STATE UNIVERSITY, BERKS CAMPUS - MEMORIAL
  LIBRARY
R.D. 5, Tulpehocken Rd.
Box 2150   Phone: (215) 375-4211
Reading, PA 19608   Sally S. Small, Hd.Libn.

POLYMER CORPORATION - LIBRARY †
501 Crescent Ave.   Phone: (215) 929-5858
Reading, PA 19603

READING HOSPITAL & MEDICAL CENTER - MEDICAL LIBRARY
Sixth & Spruce Sts.   Phone: (215) 378-6418
Reading, PA 19603   Melinda Robinson Paquette, Med.Libn.

READING HOSPITAL & MEDICAL CENTER - SCHOOL OF NURSING LIBRARY
                                     Phone: (215) 378-6359
Reading, PA 19603   Carolyn V. Unruh, Libn.

READING PUBLIC MUSEUM AND ART GALLERY - REFERENCE LIBRARY †
500 Museum Rd.   Phone: (215) 371-5850
Reading, PA 19611   Bruce L. Dietrich, Dir.

READING REHABILITATION HOSPITAL - MEDICAL LIBRARY
Rte. 1, Box 250, Morgantown Rd.   Phone: (215) 777-7615
Reading, PA 19607   Toni Wlasniewski, Libn.

READING SCHOOL DISTRICT PLANETARIUM - LIBRARY
1211 Parkside Dr., S.   Phone: (215) 371-5854
Reading, PA 19611   Bruce L. Dietrich, Dir. of Planetarium

ST. JOSEPH HOSPITAL - HEALTH SCIENCES LIBRARY
12th & Walnut Sts.   Phone: (215) 378-2390
Reading, PA 19603   Kathleen A. Izzo, Libn.

DELTIOLOGISTS OF AMERICA - LIBRARY
10 Felton Ave.   Phone: (215) 353-1689
Ridley Park, PA 19078   James L. Lowe, Dir.

ROSEMONT COLLEGE - GERTRUDE KISTLER MEMORIAL LIBRARY - SPECIAL
  COLLECTIONS
                                     Phone: (215) 527-0200
Rosemont, PA 19010   Sr. M. Dennis Lynch, S.H.C.J., Lib.Dir.

NATIONAL STEREOSCOPIC ASSOCIATION - OLIVER WENDELL HOLMES
  STEREOSCOPIC RESEARCH LIBRARY
Eastern College   Phone: (215) 688-3300
St. Davids, PA 19087   Dr. William Allen Zulker, Cur./Libn.

PURE CARBON CO., INC. - ENGINEERING LIBRARY
441 Hall Ave.   Phone: (814) 781-1573
St. Marys, PA 15857   Betty J. Clark, Libn.

PACKER (Robert) HOSPITAL - MEDICAL LIBRARY *
Guthrie Sq.   Phone: (717) 888-6666
Sayre, PA 18840   E. Jean Antes, Med.Ref.Libn.

HISTORIC SCHAEFFERSTOWN, INC. - THOMAS R. BRENDLE MEMORIAL
  LIBRARY & MUSEUM
N. Market St.
Schaefferstown, PA 17088   Violet Webber

JOHNSON SCHOOL OF TECHNOLOGY - LIBRARY
3427 N. Main Ave.   Phone: (717) 342-6404
Scranton, PA 18508   Esther K. Friedman, Lib.Dir.

LACKAWANNA BAR ASSOCIATION - LAW LIBRARY
Court House   Phone: (717) 342-8089
Scranton, PA 18503   Marita E. Paparelli, Law Libn.

LACKAWANNA HISTORICAL SOCIETY - LIBRARY AND ARCHIVES
232 Monroe Ave.   Phone: (717) 344-3841
Scranton, PA 18510   William P. Lewis, Exec.Dir.

MERCY HOSPITAL - MEDICAL LIBRARY
746 Jefferson Ave.   Phone: (717) 348-7800
Scranton, PA 18510   Sr. Elizabeth Anne Brandreth, Libn.

MERCY HOSPITAL - SCHOOL OF NURSING - LIBRARY †
520 Jefferson Ave.   Phone: (717) 344-8571
Scranton, PA 18501   Marie McAndrew, Libn.

PARMAR ELDALIEVA LIBRARY
1846 Bundy St.
Scranton, PA 18508   Rumil of Cameloford, Libn.

ST. ANN'S PASSIONIST MONASTERY - LIBRARY
1230 St. Ann St.
Scranton, PA 18504

SCRANTON TRIBUNE AND SCRANTONIAN - LIBRARY *
338 N. Washington Ave.   Phone: (717) 344-7221
Scranton, PA 18503   Hal Lewis, Libn.

TAYLOR (Moses) HOSPITAL - LIBRARY
700 Quincy Ave.   Phone: (717) 969-4057
Scranton, PA 18411   Jo-Ann M. Babish, Dir., Lib.Serv.

GRAND VIEW HOSPITAL - EDWARD F. BURROW MEMORIAL LIBRARY
700 Lawn Ave.   Phone: (215) 257-3611
Sellersville, PA 18960   Linda M. Beach, Med.Libn.

DIXMONT STATE HOSPITAL - PERSONNEL LIBRARY †
                                     Phone: (412) 761-1780
Sewickley, PA 15143   Ta-Liang Daisy Yao Tang, Libn.

SHARON GENERAL HOSPITAL - MEDICAL STAFF LIBRARY
740 E. State St.   Phone: (412) 983-3911
Sharon, PA 16146   Eugenia Christenson, Libn.

SHARON GENERAL HOSPITAL - SCHOOL OF NURSING - LIBRARY
740 E. State St.   Phone: (412) 983-3911
Sharon, PA 16146   Eugenia Christenson, Libn.

WESTINGHOUSE ELECTRIC CORPORATION - MEDIUM POWER
  TRANSFORMER DIV. - SHARON ENGINEERING LIBRARY †
469 Sharpsville Ave.
Sharon, PA 16146

MERCER COUNTY REGIONAL PLANNING COMMISSION - LIBRARY
Sharpsville Ctr. Plaza
94 E. Shenango St.   Phone: (412) 962-5787
Sharpsville, PA 16150   Leslie E. Spaulding, Libn.

SHIPPENSBURG HISTORICAL SOCIETY - ARCHIVES *
Shippensburg Public Library
West King St.   Phone: (717) 532-4508
Shippensburg, PA 17257

SHIPPENSBURG UNIVERSITY - EZRA LEHMAN LIBRARY
Phone: (717) 532-1463
Shippensburg, PA 17257   Gene Hanson, Dir., Lib. & Media Serv.

MC KEAN COUNTY LAW LIBRARY
Court House   Phone: (814) 887-5571
Smethport, PA 16749   Phyllis P. Anderson, Libn.

HISTORICAL AND GENEALOGICAL SOCIETY OF SOMERSET COUNTY -
    COUNTY HISTORICAL LIBRARY AND RESEARCH CENTER
Somerset Historical Ctr.
R.F.D. 2, Box 238   Phone: (814) 445-6077
Somerset, PA 15501   Mark D. Ware, Musm.Asst.

PENNSYLVANIA STATE DEPARTMENT OF PUBLIC WELFARE - SOMERSET
    STATE HOSPITAL - LIBRARY
Box 631   Phone: (814) 445-6501
Somerset, PA 15501   Eve Kline, Libn./Dir.

SOMERSET COUNTY LAW LIBRARY *
Phone: (814) 445-5545
Somerset, PA 15501   Irene Coffroth, Libn.

UNION NATIONAL BANK AND TRUST COMPANY - LIBRARY
14 Main St.   Phone: (215) 721-2400
Souderton, PA 18964   Gladys Detweiler, Libn.

ZION MENNONITE CHURCH - LIBRARY
149 Cherry Lane   Phone: (215) 723-5605
Souderton, PA 18964   Gwen N. Hartzel, Chm., Lib.Comm.

ST. TIKHON'S SEMINARY - LIBRARY
Phone: (717) 937-4411
South Canaan, PA 18459   Father John Udics, Libn.

PENNHURST CENTER - STAFF LIBRARY
324 Buchanan Bldg.
Spring City, PA 19475

GLATFELTER (P.H.) COMPANY - RESEARCH LIBRARY
Phone: (717) 225-4711
Spring Grove, PA 17362   Jean M. Bailey, Libn.

ROHM & HAAS COMPANY - RESEARCH DIVISION - INFORMATION
    SERVICES DEPARTMENT
727 Norristown Rd.   Phone: (215) 641-7816
Spring House, PA 19477   Dr. Frederick H. Owens, Mgr., Info.Serv.

SPRINGHOUSE CORPORATION - CORPORATE LIBRARY
1111 Bethlehem Pike   Phone: (215) 646-8700
Spring House, PA 19477   Vonda Heller, Libn./Rec.Coord.

METROPOLITAN HOSPITAL - SPRINGFIELD DIVISION - MEDICAL LIBRARY
Sproul & Thomson Rds.
Springfield, PA 19064   Karen R. Stesis, Libn.

AMERICAN PHILATELIC RESEARCH LIBRARY
Box 8338   Phone: (814) 237-3803
State College, PA 16803

CENTRE COMMUNITY HOSPITAL - HEALTH SCIENCES LIBRARY
Orchard Rd.   Phone: (814) 234-6191
State College, PA 16803   Gloria Durbin Venett, Libn.

PENNSYLVANIA STATE UNIVERSITY - APPLIED RESEARCH LABORATORY -
    LIBRARY
Box 30   Phone: (814) 865-6621
State College, PA 16804   Charles G. Murphy, Sr.Asst.Libn.

SINGER COMPANY - HRB-SINGER, INC. - TECHNICAL INFORMATION
    CENTER
Science Pk.   Phone: (814) 238-4311
State College, PA 16804   Peggy A. Hayden, Tech.Libn.

SLAVIA LIBRARY
418 W. Nittany Ave.   Phone: (814) 238-5215
State College, PA 16801   Dr. W.O. Luciw, Dir.

BROWN BROTHERS - PHOTOGRAPH COLLECTION
Phone: (717) 689-9688
Sterling, PA 18463   Meredith M. Collins, Pres.

HUTCHINSON ROSS PUBLISHING COMPANY - REFERENCE LIBRARY †
523 Sarah St.
Box 699
Stroudsburg, PA 18360

MONROE COUNTY HISTORICAL SOCIETY - LIBRARY AND MUSEUM
Ninth & Main Sts.
Stroud Community House
Box 488   Phone: (717) 421-7703
Stroudsburg, PA 18360   Vertie Knapp, Cur./Libn.

MONROE COUNTY LAW LIBRARY
Court House   Phone: (717) 424-5100
Stroudsburg, PA 18360   Kirby Upright, Esq., Chm., Lib.Comm.

NORTHUMBERLAND COUNTY LAW LIBRARY
Court House   Phone: (717) 286-0147
Sunbury, PA 17801   Pauline M. Sokalzuk, Law Libn.

FOX RESEARCH AND LIBRARY SERVICE
309 Yale Ave.   Phone: (215) 543-2801
Swarthmore, PA 19081   Jane G. Fox, Libn.

SWARTHMORE COLLEGE - CORNELL LIBRARY OF SCIENCE AND
    ENGINEERING
Phone: (215) 447-7261
Swarthmore, PA 19081   Emi K. Horikawa, Libn.

SWARTHMORE COLLEGE - DANIEL UNDERHILL MUSIC LIBRARY
Phone: (215) 447-7232
Swarthmore, PA 19081   George K. Huber, Music Libn.

SWARTHMORE COLLEGE - FRIENDS HISTORICAL LIBRARY
Phone: (215) 447-7496
Swarthmore, PA 19081   J. William Frost, Dir.

SWARTHMORE COLLEGE - FRIENDS HISTORICAL LIBRARY - PEACE
    COLLECTION
McCabe Library   Phone: (215) 447-7557
Swarthmore, PA 19081   Jean R. Soderlund, Cur.

SWARTHMORE COLLEGE - SPROUL OBSERVATORY LIBRARY
Phone: (215) 447-7261
Swarthmore, PA 19081   Emi K. Horikawa, Libn.

ATLAS POWDER COMPANY - RESEARCH & DEVELOPMENT LABORATORY -
    LIBRARY
Box 271   Phone: (717) 386-4121
Tamaqua, PA 18252   Charlotte D. Fisler, Libn.

PENNSYLVANIA STATE HISTORICAL & MUSEUM COMMISSION - DRAKE
    WELL MUSEUM - LIBRARY
R.D. 3   Phone: (814) 827-2797
Titusville, PA 16354

BETZ LABORATORIES, INC. - RESEARCH LIBRARY
4636 Somerton Rd.   Phone: (215) 355-3300
Trevose, PA 19047   Joan E. Goldberg, Tech.Libn.

EASTERN STATE SCHOOL AND HOSPITAL - STAFF LIBRARY
3740 Lincoln Hwy.   Phone: (215) 671-3389
Trevose, PA 19047   Elizabeth Sorg, Libn.

RMS - VS PROGRAM LIBRARY
One Neshaminy
Interplex Suite 306
Trevose, PA 19047   Karen Anderson, Tech.Libn.

FAYETTE COUNTY LAW LIBRARY
Court House
Uniontown, PA 15401   Elnora E. Mullooly, Libn.

UNIONTOWN HOSPITAL ASSOCIATION - MEDICAL LIBRARY *
500 W. Berkeley St.   Phone: (412) 430-5178
Uniontown, PA 15401   Nina M. Stith, Med.Libn.

PENNSYLVANIA STATE UNIVERSITY - ARCHITECTURE READING ROOM
207 Engineering Unit C   Phone: (814) 863-0511
University Park, PA 16802   Jean Smith, Libn.

PENNSYLVANIA STATE UNIVERSITY - ARTS LIBRARY
University Library, Rm. E405   Phone: (814) 865-6481
University Park, PA 16802   Jean Smith, Arts & Arch.Libn.

PENNSYLVANIA STATE UNIVERSITY - AUDIOVISUAL SERVICES
Special Services Bldg.   Phone: (814) 865-6314
University Park, PA 16802   Robert L. Allen, Dir.

PENNSYLVANIA STATE UNIVERSITY - CENTER FOR AIR ENVIRONMENT
    STUDIES - CAES INFORMATION SERVICES
225 Fenske Laboratory   Phone: (814) 865-1415
University Park, PA 16802   Elizabeth J. Carroll, Adm.Asst.

PENNSYLVANIA STATE UNIVERSITY - COLLEGE OF BUSINESS
    ADMINISTRATION - CENTER FOR RESEARCH - RES. WORKING COLL.
807 Business Administration Bldg.   Phone: (814) 863-0598
University Park, PA 16802   Lydia W. Wasylenko, Libn.

PENNSYLVANIA STATE UNIVERSITY - EARTH AND MINERAL SCIENCES
    LIBRARY
105 Deike Bldg.   Phone: (814) 865-9517
University Park, PA 16802   Emilie T. McWilliams, Hd.

PENNSYLVANIA STATE UNIVERSITY - ENGINEERING LIBRARY
325 Hammond Bldg.   Phone: (814) 865-3451
University Park, PA 16802   Thomas W. Conkling, Hd.

PENNSYLVANIA STATE UNIVERSITY - FROST ENTOMOLOGICAL MUSEUM -
    TAXONOMIC RESEARCH LIBRARY
106 Patterson Bldg.   Phone: (814) 865-1895
University Park, PA 16802   Ke Chung Kim, Cur.

PENNSYLVANIA STATE UNIVERSITY - INSTITUTE FOR POLICY RESEARCH
    AND EVALUATION - LIBRARY
N253 Burrowes   Phone: (814) 865-5541
University Park, PA 16802   Mary Jane Johnson, Sec.

PENNSYLVANIA STATE UNIVERSITY - INSTITUTE OF PUBLIC
    ADMINISTRATION - LIBRARY
205 Burrowes Bldg.   Phone: (814) 865-2536
University Park, PA 16802   Robert D. Lee, Jr.

PENNSYLVANIA STATE UNIVERSITY - INSTITUTE FOR RESEARCH ON LAND
    AND WATER RESOURCES - LIBRARY
Land & Water Research Bldg.   Phone: (814) 863-0140
University Park, PA 16802   Eunice Roe, Info.Anl.

PENNSYLVANIA STATE UNIVERSITY - LIFE SCIENCES LIBRARY
E205 E. Pattee Library   Phone: (814) 865-7056
University Park, PA 16802   Keith Roe, Hd.

PENNSYLVANIA STATE UNIVERSITY - MAPS SECTION
Pattee Library   Phone: (814) 863-0094
University Park, PA 16802   Karl H. Proehl, Map Libn.

PENNSYLVANIA STATE UNIVERSITY - MATHEMATICS LIBRARY
109 McAllister Bldg.   Phone: (814) 865-6822
University Park, PA 16802   Miriam Pierce, Hd.

PENNSYLVANIA STATE UNIVERSITY - PHYSICAL SCIENCES LIBRARY
230 Davey Laboratory   Phone: (814) 865-7617
University Park, PA 16802   C.J. McKown, Hd.

PENNSYLVANIA STATE UNIVERSITY - TRANSPORTATION INSTITUTE
    WORKING COLLECTION
Research Bldg. B   Phone: (814) 863-3953
University Park, PA 16802   Del Sweeney, Info.Spec.

SPORTS RESEARCH INSTITUTE - LIBRARY
109 Sports Research Bldg.
Pennsylvania State University   Phone: (814) 865-9543
University Park, PA 16802   Patricia McMullen, Sec.

AMERICAN BAPTIST CHURCHES IN THE U.S.A. - BOARD OF EDUCATIONAL
    MINISTRIES - EDITORIAL LIBRARY
                                         Phone: (215) 768-2378
Valley Forge, PA 19481   William H. Brackney, Exec.Dir.

AMERICAN BAPTIST CHURCHES IN THE U.S.A. - BOARD OF
    INTERNATIONAL MINISTRIES - LIBRARY AND CENTRAL FILES
                                         Phone: (215) 768-2365
Valley Forge, PA 19481   Priscilla B. Shaw, Libn.

AMERICAN BAPTIST CHURCHES IN THE U.S.A. - BOARD OF NATIONAL
    MINISTRIES - RECORDS MANAGEMENT & CENTRAL FILES
                                         Phone: (215) 768-2383
Valley Forge, PA 19481   Madeline M. Williams, Dir., Word Mgt.

FREEDOMS FOUNDATION AT VALLEY FORGE - LIBRARY
                                         Phone: (215) 933-8825
Valley Forge, PA 19481   Harold Badger, Libn.

HOUGHTON (E.F.) TECHNICAL CENTER - LIBRARY
Madison & Van Buren Aves.   Phone: (215) 666-4000
Valley Forge, PA 19482   Margaret C. Schweitzer, Libn.

PHILADELPHIA QUARTZ COMPANY - BUSINESS/CHEMISTRY
    INFORMATION CENTER
Valley Forge Executive Mall
Box 840   Phone: (215) 293-7363
Valley Forge, PA 19482   Frieda S. Mecray, Info.Spec.

VALLEY FORGE HISTORICAL SOCIETY - LIBRARY
                                         Phone: (215) 783-0535
Valley Forge, PA 19481   John F. Reed, Cur., Doc.

WELLINGTON MANAGEMENT COMPANY - RESEARCH LIBRARY
Box 823   Phone: (215) 647-6000
Valley Forge, PA 19482   Jeanne Wilmer, Libn.

AUGUSTINIAN HISTORICAL INSTITUTE - LIBRARY
Villanova University, Falvey Hall   Phone: (215) 645-7590
Villanova, PA 19085   Rev. Joseph C. Schnaubelt, O.S.A., Dir.

VILLANOVA UNIVERSITY - LIBRARY SCIENCE LIBRARY
Graduate Dept. of Library Science   Phone: (215) 645-4672
Villanova, PA 19085   Carolyn C. Walsh, Libn.

VILLANOVA UNIVERSITY - PULLING LAW LIBRARY
Garey Hall   Phone: (215) 645-7020
Villanova, PA 19085   Alan Holoch, Dir./Asst.Prof.

OHEV SHALOM SYNAGOGUE - RAY DOBLITZ MEMORIAL LIBRARY
2 Chester Rd.   Phone: (215) 874-1465
Wallingford, PA 19086   Evelyn Schott, Libn.

PENDLE HILL - LIBRARY
                                         Phone: (215) 566-4507
Wallingford, PA 19086   Yuki T. Brinton, Libn.

FISCHER & PORTER CO. - CORPORATE ENGINEERING LIBRARY
125 E. County Line Rd.   Phone: (215) 674-6834
Warminster, PA 18974   Cheryl A. Cherry, Libn.

U.S. NAVY - NAVAL AIR DEVELOPMENT CENTER - TECHNICAL
    INFORMATION BRANCH
Technical Services Dept.   Phone: (215) 441-2429
Warminster, PA 18974   Dora Huang, Br.Hd.Libn.

WARREN COUNTY HISTORICAL SOCIETY - LIBRARY AND ARCHIVES
Box 427   Phone: (814) 723-1795
Warren, PA 16365   Mrs. Conrad Brunke, Libn.

WARREN LIBRARY ASSOCIATION - LIBRARY
205 Market St.   Phone: (814) 723-4650
Warren, PA 16365   Mary Elizabeth Richardson, Ref.Libn.

WARREN STATE HOSPITAL - MEDICAL LIBRARY
Box 249   Phone: (814) 723-5500
Warren, PA 16365   Daryl G. Ellsworth, Libn.

SOCIETY OF AUTOMOTIVE ENGINEERS - SAE LIBRARY
400 Commonwealth Dr.   Phone: (412) 776-4841
Warrendale, PA 15096   Janet Jedlicka, Libn./Res.Ck.

WASHINGTON COUNTY HISTORICAL AND MUSEUM SOCIETY - LE MOYNE
    HOUSE LIBRARY
LeMoyne House
49 E. Maiden St.   Phone: (412) 225-6740
Washington, PA 15301   Nancy Berry Saxon, Dir.

WASHINGTON COUNTY LAW LIBRARY
Court House   Phone: (412) 228-6747
Washington, PA 15301   Jane M. Fulcher, Law Libn.

WASHINGTON HOSPITAL - HEALTH SCIENCES LIBRARY
155 Wilson Ave.   Phone: (412) 225-7000
Washington, PA 15301   Mary D. Leif, Libn.

DAVID LIBRARY OF THE AMERICAN REVOLUTION
River Rd.
Box 48   Phone: (215) 493-6776
Washington Crossing, PA 18977   Joseph J. Felcone, Libn.

PENNSYLVANIA STATE HISTORICAL & MUSEUM COMMISSION - FORT LE
    BOEUF MUSEUM - LIBRARY
123 S. High St.   Phone: (814) 796-4113
Waterford, PA 16441   Patricia P. Leiphart, Hist. Site Mgr.

RADNOR HISTORICAL SOCIETY - RESEARCH LIBRARY
Finley House
113 W. Beech Tree Ln.   Phone: (215) 688-2668
Wayne, PA 19087   K.H. Cummin, Pres.

WAYNE PRESBYTERIAN CHURCH - LIBRARY
125 E. Lancaster Ave.   Phone: (215) 688-8700
Wayne, PA 19087   Natalie Veitch, Libn.

GREENE COUNTY HISTORICAL SOCIETY - LIBRARY AND MUSEUM
R.F.D. 2   Phone: (412) 627-3204
Waynesburg, PA 15370   Kathryn Gooden, Libn.

GREENE COUNTY LAW LIBRARY
Court House   Phone: (412) 852-1171
Waynesburg, PA 15370   Wanda B. Smith, Libn.

SOLDIERS AND SAILORS MEMORIAL HOSPITAL - HEALTH SCIENCE
    LIBRARY
Central Ave.   Phone: (717) 724-1631
Wellsboro, PA 16901   Charlean Patterson, Libn.

AMERICAN HOME PRODUCTS CORPORATION - WYETH LABORATORIES
    DIVISION - ANTIBIOTICS LABORATORIES LIBRARY
611 E. Nield St.   Phone: (215) 696-3100
West Chester, PA 19380   Beverly L. Cantor, Tech.Libn.

CHESTER COUNTY HISTORICAL SOCIETY - LIBRARY
225 N. High St.   Phone: (215) 692-4800
West Chester, PA 19380   Rosemary B. Philips, Libn.

CHESTER COUNTY HOSPITAL - MEDICAL STAFF & SCHOOL OF NURSING
    LIBRARIES
                                             Phone: (215) 431-5204
West Chester, PA 19380

CHESTER COUNTY LAW AND MISCELLANEOUS LIBRARY ASSOCIATION
Court House   Phone: (215) 431-6166
West Chester, PA 19380   Christine C. Harvan, Libn.

WEST CHESTER UNIVERSITY - FRANCIS HARVEY GREEN LIBRARY -
    SPECIAL COLLECTIONS
                                             Phone: (215) 436-3456
West Chester, PA 19383   R. Gerald Schoelkopf, Spec.Coll.Libn./Archv.

WEST CHESTER UNIVERSITY - SCHOOL OF MUSIC LIBRARY
Francis Harvey Green Library   Phone: (215) 436-2430
West Chester, PA 19383   Ruth Weidner, Music Libn./Assoc.Prof.

WESTON (Roy F.), INC. - TECHNICAL INFORMATION CENTER AND LIBRARY
    †
Weston Way   Phone: (215) 692-3030
West Chester, PA 19380   Margo Dinniman, Sr.Info.Spec.

WESTINGHOUSE ELECTRIC CORPORATION - BETTIS ATOMIC POWER
    LABORATORY - LIBRARY †
Box 79   Phone: (412) 462-5000
West Mifflin, PA 15122-0079   Mary Louise Frazee, Libn.

MERCK & COMPANY, INC. - MERCK SHARP & DOHME RESEARCH
    LABORATORIES - LITERATURE RESOURCES
                                             Phone: (215) 661-6026
West Point, PA 19486   Karen J. Messick, Supv.

WHITE HAVEN CENTER - STAFF LIBRARY
Oley Valley Rd.   Phone: (717) 443-9564
White Haven, PA 18661   Frances M. McSpedon, Libn.

KING'S COLLEGE - D. LEONARD CORGAN LIBRARY
14 W. Jackson St.   Phone: (717) 824-9931
Wilkes-Barre, PA 18711   Judith Tierney, Spec.Coll.Libn.

MERCY HOSPITAL - MEDICAL LIBRARY
25 Church St.   Phone: (717) 826-3699
Wilkes-Barre, PA 18765   Barbara Nanstiel, Dir. of Lib.Serv.

ROSENN, JENKINS & GREENWALD, ATTORNEYS AT LAW - LIBRARY
15 S. Franklin St.   Phone: (717) 826-5663
Wilkes-Barre, PA 18711   Sarah P. Carr, Libn.

U.S. VETERANS ADMINISTRATION (PA-Wilkes-Barre) - MEDICAL CENTER
    LIBRARY
1111 E. End Blvd.   Phone: (717) 824-3521
Wilkes-Barre, PA 18711   Bruce D. Reid, Chf., Lib.Serv.

WILKES-BARRE GENERAL HOSPITAL - HOSPITAL LIBRARY
Auburn & River Sts.   Phone: (717) 829-8111
Wilkes-Barre, PA 18764   Rosemarie Kazda Taylor, Dir., Lib.Serv.

WILKES-BARRE LAW AND LIBRARY ASSOCIATION *
Courthouse, Rm. 23   Phone: (717) 822-6712
Wilkes-Barre, PA 18711   Lawrence H. Sindaco, Libn.

WILKES COLLEGE - EARTH AND ENVIRONMENTAL SCIENCES READING
    ROOM
Box 111   Phone: (717) 824-4651
Wilkes-Barre, PA 18766   Brian Redmond, Chm.

WILKES COLLEGE - INSTITUTE OF REGIONAL AFFAIRS - LIBRARY
165 S. Franklin St.
Box 111   Phone: (717) 824-4651
Wilkes-Barre, PA 18766   Dr. Andrew Shaw, Jr., Dir.

WYOMING HISTORICAL AND GEOLOGICAL SOCIETY - BISHOP MEMORIAL
    LIBRARY
49 S. Franklin St.   Phone: (717) 823-6244
Wilkes-Barre, PA 18701   Margaret E. Craft, Libn.

DIVINE PROVIDENCE HOSPITAL - MEDICAL LIBRARY *
1100 Grampian Blvd.   Phone: (717) 326-8153
Williamsport, PA 17701   Janet Anderson, Med.Rec.Adm.

LYCOMING COUNTY LAW LIBRARY †
Court House, 3rd Fl.   Phone: (717) 323-9811
Williamsport, PA 17701   Charles Hunt, Law Libn.

WILLIAMSPORT AREA COMMUNITY COLLEGE - SLOAN FINE ARTS LIBRARY
1005 W. 3rd St.   Phone: (717) 326-3761
Williamsport, PA 17701   Kate D. Hickey, Dir., Lib.Serv.

WILLIAMSPORT HOSPITAL - LEARNING RESOURCES CENTER
777 Rural Ave.   Phone: (717) 322-7861
Williamsport, PA 17701-3198   Michael Heyd, Dir.

RECONSTRUCTIONIST RABBINICAL COLLEGE - MORDECAI M. KAPLAN
    LIBRARY
Church Rd. & Greenwood Ave.   Phone: (215) 576-0800
Wyncote, PA 19095   Jennifer Gabriel, Libn.

MAIN LINE REFORM TEMPLE - LIBRARY
410 Montgomery Ave.   Phone: (215) 649-7800
Wynnewood, PA 19096   Betty Graboyes, Libn.

BORG-WARNER CORPORATION - YORK DIVISION - ENGINEERING LIBRARY
Box 1592   Phone: (717) 771-7553
York, PA 17405   Doris Kline, Libn.

HISTORICAL SOCIETY OF YORK COUNTY - LIBRARY AND ARCHIVES
250 E. Market St.   Phone: (717) 848-1587
York, PA 17403   Landon C. Reisinger, Libn.

SCHOOL OF LIVING - RALPH BORSODI MEMORIAL LIBRARY
R.D. 7
Box 388   Phone: (717) 755-2666
York, PA 17402   M.J. Loomis, Libn.

YORK COUNTY LAW LIBRARY
Court House   Phone: (717) 854-0754
York, PA 17401   Gail A. Davis, Libn.

YORK COUNTY PLANNING COMMISSION - LIBRARY
118 Pleasant Acres Rd.   Phone: (717) 757-2647
York, PA 17402   Trudy Stockton, Libn.

YORK HOSPITAL - LIBRARY
1001 S. George St.   Phone: (717) 771-2495
York, PA 17405   Barbara H. Bevan, Libn.

RHODE ISLAND

BARRINGTON COLLEGE - LIBRARY
Middle Hwy.   Phone: (401) 246-1200
Barrington, RI 02806   Eleanor C. Wilson, Libn.

BRISTOL HISTORICAL AND PRESERVATION SOCIETY - LIBRARY *
48 Court St.   Phone: (401) 253-8825
Bristol, RI 02809   Helene L. Tessler, Cur.-Libn.

JOHNSON & WALES COLLEGE - PAUL FRITZSCHE LIBRARY
1150 Narragansett Blvd.   Phone: (401) 456-1174
Cranston RI 02905   Margaret A. Thomas, Libn.

RHODE ISLAND STATE DEPARTMENT OF SOCIAL AND REHABILITATIVE
  SERVICES - STAFF DEVELOPMENT LIBRARY
600 New London Ave.   Phone: (401) 464-3111
Cranston, RI 02920   Joyce McGee

NEW ENGLAND WIRELESS & STEAM MUSEUM, INC. - LIBRARY
697 Tillinghast Rd.   Phone: (401) 884-1710
East Greenwich, RI 02818   Robert W. Merriam, Dir.

ALLENDALE MUTUAL INSURANCE COMPANY - LIBRARY
Allendale Park
Box 7500   Phone: (401) 275-4500
Johnston, RI 02919   Carol Emby, Libn.

METASCIENCE FOUNDATION - LIBRARY
Box 32   Phone: (401) 783-8683
Kingston, RI 02881   Marc Seifer, Dir.

PETTAQUAMSCUTT HISTORICAL SOCIETY - LIBRARY
1348 Kingstown Rd.   Phone: (401) 783-1328
Kingston, RI 02881

UNIVERSITY OF RHODE ISLAND - ART DEPARTMENT - SLIDE LIBRARY
Fine Arts Center
Kingston, RI 02881

UNIVERSITY OF RHODE ISLAND - INTERNATIONAL CENTER FOR MARINE
  RESOURCE DEVELOPMENT - LIBRARY
Main Library   Phone: (401) 792-2938
Kingston, RI 02881   Mary Jane Beardsley, Libn.

UNIVERSITY OF RHODE ISLAND - RHODE ISLAND ORAL HISTORY PROJECT
Library - Special Collections   Phone: (401) 792-2594
Kingston, RI 02881   David C. Maslyn, Hd., Spec.Coll.

UNIVERSITY OF RHODE ISLAND - SPECIAL COLLECTIONS
Library   Phone: (401) 792-2594
Kingston, RI 02881   David C. Maslyn, Hd.

ISOCHEM RESINS COMPANY - TECHNICAL INFORMATION CENTER †
99 Cook St.   Phone: (401) 723-2100
Lincoln, RI 02865   Herman C. Selya, Pres.

ENVIRONMENTAL PROTECTION AGENCY - ENVIRONMENTAL RESEARCH
  LABORATORY, NARRAGANSETT - LIBRARY †
South Ferry Rd.   Phone: (401) 789-1071
Narragansett, RI 02882   Rose Ann Gamache, Libn.

UNIVERSITY OF RHODE ISLAND, NARRAGANSETT BAY - PELL MARINE
  SCIENCE LIBRARY †
                                             Phone: (401) 792-6161
Narragansett, RI 02882   Kenneth T. Morse, Chf.Libn.

INTERNATIONAL TENNIS HALL OF FAME AND TENNIS MUSEUM - LIBRARY
Newport Casino
194 Bellevue Ave.   Phone: (401) 846-4567
Newport, RI 02840   Jane G. Brown, Exec.Dir.

NEWPORT HISTORICAL SOCIETY - LIBRARY
82 Touro St.   Phone: (401) 846-0813
Newport, RI 02840   T.G. Brennan, Libn./Cur.

NEWPORT HOSPITAL - INA MOSHER HEALTH SCIENCES LIBRARY
Friendship St.   Phone: (401) 846-6400
Newport, RI 02840   Tosca N. Carpenter, Hd.Libn.

U.S. NAVY - NAVAL EDUCATION AND TRAINING CENTER - LIBRARY
  SYSTEM
Main Library Bldg. 114   Phone: (401) 841-3044
Newport, RI 02841   James F. Aylward, Adm.

U.S. NAVY - NAVAL HOSPITAL (RI-Newport) - MEDICAL LIBRARY
Cypress & Third Sts.   Phone: (401) 841-1180
Newport, RI 02840   Winifred M. Jacome, Lib.Techn.

U.S. NAVY - NAVAL UNDERWATER SYSTEMS CENTER - NEWPORT
  TECHNICAL LIBRARY †
                                             Phone: (401) 841-4338
Newport, RI 02840   Mary Barravecchia, Hd.Libn.

U.S. NAVY - NAVAL WAR COLLEGE - LIBRARY
                                             Phone: (401) 841-2641
Newport, RI 02841   Earl R. Schwass, Dir.

ST. JOSEPH HOSPITAL - HEALTH SCIENCE LIBRARY *
200 High Service Ave.   Phone: (401) 456-3060
North Providence, RI 02904   Kathleen C. McAvoy, Libn.

PAWTUCKET MEMORIAL HOSPITAL - HEALTH SCIENCES LIBRARY *
Prospect & Pond Sts.   Phone: (401) 722-6000
Pawtucket, RI 02860   Carol-Ann Rausch, Med.Libn.

SLATER MILL HISTORIC SITE - RESEARCH LIBRARY
Roosevelt Ave.
Box 727   Phone: (401) 725-8638
Pawtucket, RI 02862   T.E. Leary, Cur.

RAYTHEON COMPANY - SUBMARINE SIGNAL DIVISION - TECHNICAL
  INFORMATION CENTER
1847 W. Main Rd.
Box 360   Phone: (401) 847-8000
Portsmouth, RI 02871   Mark F. Baldwin, Mgr., Tech.Info.Ctr.

ADLER POLLOCK & SHEEHAN, INC. - LAW LIBRARY
One Hospital Trust Plaza   Phone: (401) 274-7200
Providence, RI 02903   Paul R. Dumaine, Law Libn.

AUDUBON SOCIETY OF RHODE ISLAND - HARRY S. HATHAWAY LIBRARY OF
  NATURAL HISTORY AND CONSERVATION
40 Bowen St.   Phone: (401) 521-1670
Providence, RI 02903   Tim Rumage, Libn.

BROWN UNIVERSITY - ART DEPARTMENT SLIDE ROOM
Box 1861, List Art Bldg.
64 College St.   Phone: (401) 863-3218
Providence, RI 02912   Norine Duncan Cashman, Cur.

BROWN UNIVERSITY - JOHN CARTER BROWN LIBRARY
Box 1894   Phone: (401) 863-2725
Providence, RI 02912   Norman Fiering, Dir./Libn.

BROWN UNIVERSITY - POPULATION STUDIES AND TRAINING CENTER -
    DEMOGRAPHY LIBRARY
Sociology Dept., Box 1916   Phone: (401) 863-2668
Providence, RI 02912   Sidney Goldstein, Dir.

BROWN UNIVERSITY - SCIENCES LIBRARY
Brown Univ. Library, Box I   Phone: (401) 863-2405
Providence, RI 02912   Florence Kell Doksansky, Asst.Univ.Libn.

BROWN UNIVERSITY - SPECIAL COLLECTIONS
John Hay Library
20 Prospect St.   Phone: (401) 863-2146
Providence, RI 02912   Samuel A. Streit, Asst.Univ.Libn./Spec.Coll

BUTLER HOSPITAL - ISAAC RAY MEDICAL LIBRARY
345 Blackstone Blvd.   Phone: (401) 456-3869
Providence, RI 02906   Erika Schmidt, Libn.

HINCKLEY & ALLEN - LAW LIBRARY
2200 Fleet National Bank Building   Phone: (401) 274-2000
Providence, RI 02903   Elizabeth K. Labedz, Hd.Libn.

INTERNATIONAL RAILROAD & TRANSPORTATION POSTCARD COLLECTORS
    CLUB - LIBRARY
Box 6782
Providence, RI 02940   Robert J. Andrews, Pres.

KEYES ASSOCIATES - LIBRARY
321 S. Main St.   Phone: (401) 861-2900
Providence, RI 02903   Carole E. Twombly, Libn.

MIRIAM HOSPITAL - MEDICAL LIBRARY
164 Summit Ave   Phone: (401) 274-3700
Providence, RI 02906   Ann LeClaire, Dir., Lib.Serv.

PROVIDENCE ATHENAEUM - LIBRARY
251 Benefit St.   Phone: (401) 421-6970
Providence, RI 02903   Sally Duplaix, Dir.

PROVIDENCE COLLEGE - PHILLIPS MEMORIAL LIBRARY
River Ave. at Eaton St.   Phone: (401) 865-2242
Providence, RI 02918   Joseph H. Doherty, Dir.

PROVIDENCE JOURNAL COMPANY - NEWS LIBRARY
75 Fountain St.   Phone: (401) 277-7390
Providence, RI 02902   Joseph O. Mehr, Libn.

PROVIDENCE PUBLIC LIBRARY - ART AND MUSIC DEPARTMENT
150 Empire St.   Phone: (401) 521-7722
Providence, RI 02903   Susan R. Waddington, Dept.Hd.

PROVIDENCE PUBLIC LIBRARY - BUSINESS-INDUSTRY-SCIENCE
    DEPARTMENT
150 Empire St.   Phone: (401) 521-7722
Providence, RI 02903   Marcia DiGregorio, Dept.Hd.

RHODE ISLAND HISTORICAL SOCIETY - LIBRARY
121 Hope St.   Phone: (401) 331-0448
Providence, RI 02906

RHODE ISLAND HOSPITAL - PETERS HEALTH SCIENCES LIBRARY
                                                  Phone: (401) 277-4671
Providence, RI 02902   Irene Lathrop, Dir. of Lib.Serv.

RHODE ISLAND JEWISH HISTORICAL ASSOCIATION - LIBRARY
130 Sessions St.   Phone: (401) 331-1360
Providence, RI 02906   Eleanor F. Horvitz, Libn./Archv.

RHODE ISLAND MEDICAL SOCIETY - LIBRARY
106 Francis St.   Phone: (401) 331-3208
Providence, RI 02903   Marion Sabella, Libn.

RHODE ISLAND PUBLIC EXPENDITURE COUNCIL - LIBRARY
126 N. Main St.   Phone: (401) 521-6320
Providence, RI 02903   Gary S. Sasse, Exec.Dir.

RHODE ISLAND SCHOOL OF DESIGN - LIBRARY
2 College St.   Phone: (401) 331-3511
Providence, RI 02903   James A. Findlay, Dir.

RHODE ISLAND STATE ARCHIVES
State House, Rm. 43, Smith St.   Phone: (401) 277-2353
Providence, RI 02903   Phyllis Peloquin Silva, Dir.

RHODE ISLAND STATE DEPARTMENT OF COMMUNITY AFFAIRS -
    REFERENCE LIBRARY
150 Washington St.   Phone: (401) 277-2857
Providence, RI 02903   Donald J. Boisvert, Libn.

RHODE ISLAND STATE DEPARTMENT OF ECONOMIC DEVELOPMENT -
    RESEARCH DIVISION LIBRARY
7 Jackson Walkway   Phone: (401) 277-2601
Providence, RI 02903   John A. Iemma, Asst.Dir., DED

RHODE ISLAND STATE DEPARTMENT OF ELDERLY AFFAIRS - LIBRARY
79 Washington St.   Phone: (401) 277-2858
Providence, RI 02903   Eve M. Goldberg, Libn.

RHODE ISLAND STATE DEPARTMENT OF HEALTH - GERTRUDE E. STURGES
    MEMORIAL LIBRARY
75 Davis St., Rm. 407   Phone: (401) 277-2506
Providence, RI 02908   A. William Pett, Libn.

RHODE ISLAND STATE DEPARTMENT OF STATE LIBRARY SERVICES
95 Davis St.   Phone: (401) 277-2726
Providence, RI 02908   Fay Zipkowitz, Dir.

RHODE ISLAND STATE LAW LIBRARY
Providence County Court House
250 Benefit St.   Phone: (401) 277-3275
Providence, RI 02903   Kendall F. Svengalis, State Law Libn.

RHODE ISLAND STATE LIBRARY
State House   Phone: (401) 277-2473
Providence, RI 02903   Beth I. Perry, State Libn.

ROGER WILLIAMS GENERAL HOSPITAL - HEALTH SCIENCES LIBRARY
825 Chalkstone Ave.   Phone: (401) 456-2036
Providence, RI 02908   Hadassah Stein, Libn.

ROGER WILLIAMS PARK - PARK MUSEUM OF NATURAL HISTORY &
    PLANETARIUM - MUSEUM LIBRARY/RESOURCE CENTER
Providence, RI 02905

ST. FRANCIS MONASTERY AND CHAPEL - ST. FRANCIS CHAPEL
    INFORMATION CENTER & FREE-LENDING LIBRARY
20 Page St.   Phone: (401) 331-6510
Providence, RI 02903   Fr. John Bosco Valente, O.F.M., Libn.

ST. JOSEPH HOSPITAL, OUR LADY OF PROVIDENCE UNIT - HEALTH
    SCIENCE LIBRARY
21 Peace St.   Phone: (401) 456-4035
Providence, RI 02907   Ruth E. Szabo, Coord., Lib.Serv.

SOCIETY OF FRIENDS - NEW ENGLAND YEARLY MEETING OF FRIENDS -
    ARCHIVES

121 Hope St.   Phone: (401) 331-8575
Providence, RI 02906   Rosalind Wiggins, Cur.

TECHNIC INC. - LIBRARY
1 Spectacle St.   Phone: (401) 781-6100
Providence, RI 02910   James V. Elliott, Jr., Pub.Rel.Off.

TEMPLE BETH-EL - WILLIAM G. BRAUDE LIBRARY
70 Orchard Ave.   Phone: (401) 331-6070
Providence, RI 02906   Allan Metz, Libn.

TEMPLE EMANU-EL - CONGREGATIONAL LIBRARY
99 Taft Ave.   Phone: (401) 331-1616
Providence, RI 02906   Lillian Schwartz, Libn.

U.S. VETERANS ADMINISTRATION (RI-Providence) - HEALTH SCIENCES
LIBRARY
Davis Park   Phone: (401) 273-7100
Providence, RI 02908   Lynn A. Lloyd, Chf., Lib.Serv.

WOMEN & INFANTS HOSPITAL OF RHODE ISLAND - HEALTH SCIENCES
INFORMATION CENTER
50 Maude St.   Phone: (401) 274-1100
Providence, RI 02908   Christine Chapman, Libn.

BRADLEY (Emma Pendleton) HOSPITAL - AUSTIN T. AND JUNE ROCKWELL
LEVY LIBRARY
1011 Veterans Memorial Pkwy.   Phone: (401) 434-3400
Riverside, RI 02915   Carolyn A. Waller, Med.Libn.

BRYANT COLLEGE OF BUSINESS ADMINISTRATION - EDITH M. HODGSON
MEMORIAL LIBRARY
    Phone: (401) 231-1200
Smithfield, RI 02917   Dr. John P. Hannon, Dir.

KENT COUNTY MEMORIAL HOSPITAL - MEDICAL LIBRARY
455 Toll Gate Rd.   Phone: (401) 737-7000
Warwick, RI 02886   Jo-Anne M. Aspri, Libn.

LEESONA CORPORATION - LIBRARY
333 Strawberry Field Rd.
Warwick, RI 02887

METROPOLITAN PROPERTY & LIABILITY INSURANCE COMPANY - LAW &
CORPORATE INFORMATION CENTER
700 Quaker Ln.   Phone: (401) 827-2658
Warwick, RI 02886   Kevin J. Carty, Libn.

NATIONAL FOUNDATION FOR GIFTED AND CREATIVE CHILDREN -
LIBRARY
395 Diamond Hill Rd.   Phone: (401) 942-2253
Warwick, RI 02886   Marie Friedel, Exec.Dir.

WARWICK PUBLIC LIBRARY - CENTRAL CHILDREN'S LIBRARY
600 Sandy Lane   Phone: (401) 739-5440
Warwick, RI 02886   Alice E. Forsstrom, Hd. of Children's Serv.

WESTERLY HOSPITAL - MEDICAL LIBRARY
Wells St.   Phone: (401) 596-4961
Westerly, RI 02891   Natalie V. Lawton, Libn.

UNION SAINT-JEAN-BAPTISTE - MALLET LIBRARY
One Social St.   Phone: (401) 769-0520
Woonsocket, RI 02895   Bro. Felician, S.C., Libn.

SOUTH CAROLINA

SAVANNAH RIVER PLANT - TECHNICAL LIBRARY
E.I. Du Pont de Nemours & Company   Phone: (803) 725-2707
Aiken, SC 29808   C. Tom Sutherland, Supv.

CAMDEN DISTRICT HERITAGE FOUNDATION - HISTORIC CAMDEN
Box 710   Phone: (803) 432-0764
Camden, SC 29020   Stephen Smith, Dir.

CAROLINA ART ASSOCIATION - LIBRARY
Gibbes Art Gallery
135 Meeting St.   Phone: (803) 722-2706
Charleston, SC 29401   Martha Severens, Cur. of Coll.

CHARLESTON EVENING POST/NEWS AND COURIER - LIBRARY
134 Columbus St.
Box 758   Phone: (803) 577-7111
Charleston, SC 29402   Mary S. Crockett, Chf.Libn.

CHARLESTON LIBRARY SOCIETY
164 King St.   Phone: (803) 723-9912
Charleston, SC 29401   Catherine E. Sadler, Libn.

CHARLESTON MUSEUM - LIBRARY †
360 Meeting St.   Phone: (803) 722-2996
Charleston, SC 29403   K. Sharon Bennett, Libn.

CITADEL - THE MILITARY COLLEGE OF SOUTH CAROLINA - ARCHIVES/
MUSEUM
The Citadel   Phone: (803) 792-6846
Charleston, SC 29409   CDR Mal J. Collet, Dir.

CITADEL - THE MILITARY COLLEGE OF SOUTH CAROLINA - DANIEL
LIBRARY
    Phone: (803) 723-0711
Charleston, SC 29409   James M. Hillard, Dir. of Libs.

COLLEGE OF CHARLESTON - ROBERT SCOTT SMALL LIBRARY - SPECIAL
COLLECTIONS
66 George St.   Phone: (803) 792-5530
Charleston, SC 29424   Dr. Ralph Melnick, Hd., Spec.Coll.

DALCHO HISTORICAL SOCIETY OF THE PROTESTANT EPISCOPAL CHURCH
IN SOUTH CAROLINA - LIBRARY AND ARCHIVES
Box 2127   Phone: (803) 722-4075
Charleston, SC 29403   George W. Williams, Pres.

HUGUENOT SOCIETY OF SOUTH CAROLINA - LIBRARY
25 Chalmers St.   Phone: (803) 723-3235
Charleston, SC 29401

MEDICAL UNIVERSITY OF SOUTH CAROLINA - ARTHRITIS CENTER
LIBRARY
Division of Rheumatology and Immunology
171 Ashley Ave.   Phone: (803) 792-2001
Charleston, SC 29464   E.C. LeRoy, M.D., Dir.

MEDICAL UNIVERSITY OF SOUTH CAROLINA - LIBRARY
171 Ashley Ave.   Phone: (803) 792-2374
Charleston, SC 29425   Warren A. Sawyer, Dir.

MEDICAL UNIVERSITY OF SOUTH CAROLINA - MARINE BIOMEDICAL
RESEARCH CENTER
Fort Johnson
Box 12559   Phone: (803) 795-7480
Charleston, SC 29412   Dr. John T. Sullivan, Asst.Prof.

SOUTH CAROLINA HISTORICAL SOCIETY - LIBRARY
Fireproof Bldg.
Meeting & Chalmers Sts.   Phone: (803) 723-3225
Charleston, SC 29401   Gene Waddell, Dir.

SOUTH CAROLINA STATE WILDLIFE AND MARINE RESOURCES
DEPARTMENT - LIBRARY
P.O. Box 12559   Phone: (803) 795-6350
Charleston, SC 29412   Marilyn L. Lewis, Marine Rsrcs.Libn.

U.S. NAVY - NAVAL SHIPYARD (SC-Charleston) - TECHNICAL LIBRARY
Naval Base   Phone: (803) 743-3843
Charleston, SC 29408   D.C. Woody, Act.Techn.

U.S. AIR FORCE BASE - CHARLESTON BASE LIBRARY
FL 4418   Phone: (803) 554-3134
Charleston AFB, SC 29404   William E. Darcy, Libn.

CLEMSON UNIVERSITY - EMERY A. GUNNIN ARCHITECTURAL LIBRARY
Lee Hall   Phone: (803) 656-3081
Clemson, SC 29631   Leslie Abrams, Arch.Libn.

CLEMSON UNIVERSITY - ROBERT MULDROW COOPER LIBRARY
    Phone: (803) 656-3026
Clemson, SC 29631   Joseph Boykin, Dir.

SOUTH CAROLINA STATE DEPARTMENT OF MENTAL RETARDATION -
WHITTEN CENTER LIBRARY & MEDIA RESOURCE SERVICES
Box 239   Phone: (803) 833-2736
Clinton, SC 29325   Mr. Hsiu-Yun Keng, Dir.

BAPTIST MEDICAL CENTER - AMELIA WHITE PITTS MEMORIAL LIBRARY †
Taylor at Marion St.   Phone: (803) 771-5281
Columbia, SC 29220   Lois W. Smith, Libn.

BARUCH (Belle W.) INSTITUTE FOR MARINE BIOLOGY AND COASTAL
    RESEARCH - LIBRARY
University of South Carolina   Phone: (803) 777-5288
Columbia, SC 29208   Ms. V. Smith, Adm.Asst.

BRYAN (G. Werber) PSYCHIATRIC HOSPITAL - PROFESSIONAL LIBRARY
220 Faison Dr.   Phone: (803) 758-4839
Columbia, SC 29203   Virginia S. McEachern, Libn.

CHEM-NUCLEAR SYSTEMS, INC. - INFORMATION CENTER
240 Stoneridge Dr., Suite 100   Phone: (803) 256-0450
Columbia, SC 29210   Robin L. Deal, Doc. Control Adm.

COLUMBIA BIBLE COLLEGE - LEARNING RESOURCES CENTER
7435 Monticello Rd.
Box 3122   Phone: (803) 754-4100
Columbia, SC 29230   Laura Braswell, Dir.

COLUMBIA MUSEUMS OF ART & SCIENCE - LIBRARY
1112 Bull St.   Phone: (803) 799-2810
Columbia, SC 29201   William B. Gordon, Hd.

HALL (William S.) PSYCHIATRIC INSTITUTE - PROFESSIONAL LIBRARY
Box 202   Phone: (803) 758-5370
Columbia, SC 29202   Mrs. Neeta N. Shah, Chf.Med.Libn.

INTERNATIONAL ASSOCIATION FOR IDENTIFICATION - LIBRARY
Box 90259   Phone: (803) 776-2001
Columbia, SC 29290   Walter G. Hoetzer, Sec./Treas.

LUTHERAN THEOLOGICAL SOUTHERN SEMINARY - LINEBERGER MEMORIAL
    LIBRARY *
4201 Main St.   Phone: (803) 786-5150
Columbia, SC 29203   William Richard Fritz, Sr., Libn.

MUNICIPAL ASSOCIATION OF SOUTH CAROLINA - LIBRARY AND
    REFERENCE CENTER
1529 Washington   Phone: (803) 799-9574
Columbia, SC 29201   Anne Dixon

NATIONAL ASSOCIATION FOR SPORT & PHYSICAL EDUCATION (NASPE) -
    MEDIA RESOURCE CENTER
Dept. of Physical Education
University of South Carolina   Phone: (803) 777-3172
Columbia, SC 29208   Dr. Richard C. Hohn, Dir.

RICHLAND MEMORIAL HOSPITAL - JOSEY MEMORIAL MEDICAL LIBRARY
3301 Harden St.   Phone: (803) 765-6312
Columbia, SC 29203   Kay F. Harwood, Libn.

SOUTH CAROLINA CONFEDERATE RELIC ROOM & MUSEUM - LIBRARY
World War Memorial Bldg.
920 Sumter St.   Phone: (803) 758-2144
Columbia, SC 29201

SOUTH CAROLINA STATE ATTORNEY GENERAL'S OFFICE - LEGAL LIBRARY
1000 Assembly St., Suite 701
Box 11549   Phone: (803) 758-3094
Columbia, SC 29211   Susan Husman, Libn.

SOUTH CAROLINA STATE COMMISSION ON ALCOHOL AND DRUG ABUSE -
    RESOURCE CENTER
3700 Forest Dr.   Phone: (803) 758-3866
Columbia, SC 29204   Sarah B. Clarkson, Libn.

SOUTH CAROLINA STATE DEPARTMENT OF ARCHIVES & HISTORY -
    ARCHIVES SEARCH ROOM
Capitol Sta., Box 11669   Phone: (803) 758-5816
Columbia, SC 29211   Charles E. Lee, Dir.

SOUTH CAROLINA STATE DEPARTMENT OF HEALTH & ENVIRONMENTAL
    CONTROL - EDUCATIONAL RESOURCE CENTER
2600 Bull St.   Phone: (803) 758-5448
Columbia, SC 29201   Michael Kronenfeld, Dir.

SOUTH CAROLINA STATE DEPARTMENT OF MENTAL RETARDATION -
    MIDLANDS CENTER LIBRARY †
8301 Farrow Rd.   Phone: (803) 758-4434
Columbia, SC 29203   Mrs. Clannie H. Washington, Libn.

SOUTH CAROLINA STATE ENERGY EXTENSION SERVICE - ENERGY
    INFORMATION CENTER
111 Executive Center Dr., Rm. 118   Phone: (803) 758-6925
Columbia, SC 29210   Debbie Bowdler, Energy Info.Spec.

SOUTH CAROLINA (State) GEOLOGICAL SURVEY - LIBRARY
Harbison Forest Rd.   Phone: (803) 758-6431
Columbia, SC 29210   Alan-Jun Zupan, Prin. Geologist

SOUTH CAROLINA STATE LIBRARY
1500 Senate St.
Box 11469   Phone: (803) 758-3181
Columbia, SC 29211   Betty E. Callaham, State Libn.

SOUTH CAROLINA STATE SUPREME COURT - LIBRARY
Box 11330   Phone: (803) 758-3741
Columbia, SC 29211   Elizabeth A. Tomlinson, Libn.

U.S. VETERANS ADMINISTRATION (SC-Columbia) - WILLIAM JENNINGS
    BRYAN-DORN VETERANS HOSPITAL - LIBRARY
Garners Ferry Rd.   Phone: (803) 776-4000
Columbia, SC 29201   Charletta P. Felder, Chf., Lib.Serv.

UNIVERSITY OF SOUTH CAROLINA - BUREAU OF GOVERNMENTAL
    RESEARCH AND SERVICE - LIBRARY
                                                     Phone: (803) 777-8156
Columbia, SC 29208   Sandra T. Cowen, Chf., Info.Serv.

UNIVERSITY OF SOUTH CAROLINA - COLEMAN KARESH LAW LIBRARY
Law Center   Phone: (803) 777-5942
Columbia, SC 29208   Joseph R. Cross, Jr., Act.Hd. Law Lib.

UNIVERSITY OF SOUTH CAROLINA - MAP LIBRARY
James F. Byrnes Ctr.   Phone: (803) 777-2802
Columbia, SC 29208   David C. McQuillan, Map Libn.

UNIVERSITY OF SOUTH CAROLINA - SCHOOL OF MEDICINE LIBRARY
                                                     Phone: (803) 733-3344
Columbia, SC 29208   R. Thomas Lange, Chf.Med.Libn.

UNIVERSITY OF SOUTH CAROLINA - SOUTH CAROLINIANA LIBRARY
                                                     Phone: (803) 777-3131
Columbia, SC 29208   Allen H. Stokes, Libn.

UNIVERSITY OF SOUTH CAROLINA - THOMAS COOPER LIBRARY - RARE
    BOOKS & SPECIAL COLLECTIONS DEPARTMENT
                                                     Phone: (803) 777-8154
Columbia, SC 29208   Roger Mortimer, Hd., Spec.Coll.

UNIVERSITY OF SOUTH CAROLINA - UNIVERSITY ARCHIVES
McKissick Museums   Phone: (803) 777-7251
Columbia, SC 29208   George D. Terry, Dir./Archv.

WILBUR SMITH AND ASSOCIATES - LIBRARY
1301 Gervais St.
Box 92   Phone: (803) 738-0580
Columbia, SC 29202   Jasper Salmond, Info.Dir.

DARLINGTON COUNTY HISTORICAL COMMISSION - DARLINGTON COUNTY
    ARCHIVES
Court House, Rm. 307
Darlington, SC 29532   Horace Fraser Rudisill, Hist.

GRACE (W.R.) AND COMPANY - CRYOVAC DIVISION - TECHNICAL LIBRARY
    †
Box 464   Phone: (803) 433-2000
Duncan, SC 29334   Margaret M. Ezell, Tech.Libn.

TOMPKINS (D.A.) MEMORIAL LIBRARY
104 Courthouse Square
Box 468   Phone: (803) 637-6480
Edgefield, SC 29824   Nancy C. Mims, Archv./Cur.

FLORENCE CITY PLANNING AND DEVELOPMENT LIBRARY
City-County Complex, Drawer FF   Phone: (803) 665-3141
Florence, SC 29501   Elizabeth Shaw, Libn.

FLORENCE-DARLINGTON TECHNICAL COLLEGE - LIBRARY
Drawer 8000
Florence, SC 29501
Phone: (803) 662-8151
Jeronell White, Lib.Coord.

PEE DEE AREA HEALTH EDUCATION CENTER LIBRARY
McLeod Regional Medical Ctr.
555 E. Cheves St.
Florence, SC 29501
Phone: (803) 667-2275
Lillian Fisher, Regional Libn.

U.S. ARMY POST - FORT JACKSON - LIBRARY
Bldg. 4679
Ft. Jackson, SC 29207
Phone: (803) 751-4816
Marilyn E. Mize, Adm.Libn.

BOB JONES UNIVERSITY - CHURCH MINISTRIES RESOURCE LAB
Phone: (803) 242-5100
Greenville, SC 29614
Mrs. James Berg, Supv.

BOB JONES UNIVERSITY - MUSIC LIBRARY †
Phone: (803) 242-5100
Greenville, SC 29614
Dr. Karen S. Wilson, Music Libn.

BOB JONES UNIVERSITY - SCHOOL OF EDUCATION - MEDIA CENTER
Phone: (803) 242-5100
Greenville, SC 29614
Charles Joss, Supv.

FURMAN UNIVERSITY LIBRARY - SPECIAL COLLECTIONS
Phone: (803) 294-2194
Greenville, SC 29613
Dr. J. Glen Clayton, Spec.Coll.Libn.

GREENVILLE COUNTY PLANNING COMMISSION - PLANNING TECHNICAL
LIBRARY
Courthouse Annex, Box 1947
Greenville, SC 29602
Phone: (803) 298-8671
Tom Meeks, Dir. of Plan.Serv.

GREENVILLE HOSPITAL SYSTEM - HEALTH SCIENCE LIBRARY †
701 Grove Rd.
Greenville, SC 29605
Phone: (803) 242-7176
Susan Chappell, Med.Libn.

GREENVILLE MENTAL HEALTH CENTER - LIBRARY
715 Grove Rd.
Greenville, SC 29605-4280
Phone: (803) 235-0184
Laura F. Pitzer, Libn.

GREENVILLE TECHNICAL COLLEGE - LEARNING RESOURCES CENTER
Box 5539
Greenville, SC 29606
Phone: (803) 242-3170
Elizabeth B. Olinger, Libr.Dir.

HOLLINGSWORTH (John D.) ON WHEELS, INC. - INFORMATION SERVICES *
Box 516
Greenville, SC 29602
Phone: (803) 297-1000
Rick Carter, Info.Spec.

J.P. STEVENS AND CO., INC. - TECHNICAL LIBRARY
400 E. Stone Ave.
Box 2850
Greenville, SC 29602
Phone: (803) 239-4211
Dr. B.M. Latta, Dir.

PLATT SACO LOWELL CORPORATION - ENGINEERING LIBRARY
Drawer 2327
Greenville, SC 29602
Phone: (803) 859-3211
Donald H. Feldman, Mgr.

POLYMER INDUSTRIES - LIBRARY
Roberts Road
Box 2184
Greenville, SC 29602
Phone: (803) 244-5351
Linda F. Gentry, Libn.

MONSANTO FIBERS & INTERMEDIATES COMPANY - LIBRARY
Box 1057
Greenwood, SC 29648
Phone: (803) 223-4241
Mildred Upton, Libn.

PIEDMONT TECHNICAL COLLEGE - LIBRARY
Emerald Rd.
P.O. Drawer 1467
Greenwood, SC 29648
Phone: (803) 223-8357
Daniel D. Koenig, Dir., Lrng.Rscs.

UPPER SAVANNAH AREA HEALTH EDUCATION CONSORTIUM - LIBRARY
Self Memorial Hospital
Spring St.
Greenwood, SC 29646
Phone: (803) 227-4851
Nancy Morrow, Libn.

AMERICAN HOECHST CORPORATION - FILMS DIVISION - TECHNICAL
INFORMATION CENTER
Box 1400
Greer, SC 29651
Phone: (803) 877-8471
Judith Duffie, Info.Spec.

UNITED MERCHANTS AND MANUFACTURING COMPANY - RESEARCH
CENTER LIBRARY
Box 64
Langley, SC 29834
Phone: (803) 593-4461
Larry G. Smith, Mgr., Res.Serv.

MARION COUNTY MEMORIAL HOSPITAL - LIBRARY
1108 N. Main St.
Marion, SC 29571
Phone: (803) 423-3210
Ann Finney, Educ.Dir.

BROOKGREEN GARDENS - LIBRARY
Phone: (803) 237-4218
Murrells Inlet, SC 29576
G.L. Tarbox, Jr., Dir.

U.S. AIR FORCE BASE - MYRTLE BEACH BASE LIBRARY *
FL 4806
Myrtle Beach AFB, SC 29577
Phone: (803) 238-7086
Jean L. Cady, Base Libn.

TRIDENT TECHNICAL COLLEGE - NORTH CAMPUS LIBRARY
Box 10367
North Charleston, SC 29411
Phone: (803) 572-6089
Marion L. Vogel, Dir., Lrng.Rsrcs.

WESTVACO CORPORATION - INFORMATION SERVICES CENTER
Box 5207
North Charleston, SC 29406
Phone: (803) 744-8231
Elizabeth de Liesseline, Info.Spec.

ORANGEBURG-CALHOUN TECHNICAL COLLEGE - GRESSETTE LEARNING
RESOURCE CENTER
3250 Matthews Rd.
Orangeburg, SC 29115
Phone: (803) 536-0311
Margaret F. Huff, Dean, LRC

PENDLETON DISTRICT HISTORICAL AND RECREATIONAL COMMISSION -
REFERENCE LIBRARY
125 E. Queen St.
Box 565
Pendleton, SC 29670
Phone: (803) 646-3782
Hurley Badders, Commn.Dir.

TRI-COUNTY TECHNICAL COLLEGE - LEARNING RESOURCE CENTER
Box 587
Pendleton, SC 29670
Phone: (803) 646-8361
Dr. Stephen B. Walter, Dir., L.R.C.

CELANESE CORPORATION - CELANESE FIBERS COMPANY - TECHNICAL
LIBRARY †
Cherry Rd. Sta.
Rock Hill, SC 29730

MUSEUM OF YORK COUNTY - EDUCATIONAL LIBRARY
4621 Mt. Gallant Rd.
Rock Hill, SC 29730
Phone: (803) 329-2121
Ms. Chris Houmes, Exec.Dir.

YORK TECHNICAL COLLEGE - LIBRARY
U.S. 21 Bypass
Rock Hill, SC 29730
Phone: (803) 324-3130
Amanda Yu, Libn.

CALHOUN COUNTY MUSEUM - ARCHIVES AND LIBRARY *
303 Butler St.
St. Matthews, SC 29135
Phone: (803) 874-3964
Virginia D. Carroll, Libn.

MILLIKEN RESEARCH CORPORATION - RESEARCH LIBRARY
Box 1927
Spartanburg, SC 29304
Phone: (803) 573-2340
Trudy W. Craven, Libn.

SHERMAN COLLEGE OF STRAIGHT CHIROPRACTIC - TOM AND MAE BAHAN
LIBRARY
Box 1452
Spartanburg, SC 29304
Phone: (803) 578-8770
Susan Matusak, Hd.Libn.

SPARTANBURG GENERAL HOSPITAL - HEALTH SCIENCES LIBRARY
101 E. Wood St.
Spartanburg, SC 29303
Phone: (803) 573-6220
Fay J. Towell, Dir., Lib.Serv.

UNITED METHODIST COMMN. ON ARCHIVES & HISTORY - SOUTH
CAROLINA CONFERENCE - HISTORICAL LIBRARY
Wofford College
Spartanburg, SC 29301
Phone: (803) 585-4821
Herbert Hucks, Jr., Cur.

WOFFORD COLLEGE - SANDOR TESZLER LIBRARY - ARCHIVES
N. Church St.
Spartanburg, SC 29301
Phone: (803) 585-4821
Herbert Hucks, Jr., Archv.

WOFFORD COLLEGE - SANDOR TESZLER LIBRARY - LITTLEJOHN RARE
   BOOK ROOM
N. Church St.   Phone: (803) 585-4821
Spartanburg, SC 29301   Frank J. Anderson, Libn.

OLD SLAVE MART MUSEUM - LIBRARY
Box 446   Phone: (803) 883-3797
Sullivan's Island, SC 29482   Judith Wragg Chase, Lib.Dir.

U.S. NATL. PARK SERVICE - FORT SUMTER NATL. MONUMENT - LIBRARY
1214 Middle St.   Phone: (803) 883-3123
Sullivan's Island, SC 29482   Brien Varnado, Supt.

SUMTER AREA TECHNICAL COLLEGE - LIBRARY
506 N. Guignard Dr.   Phone: (803) 773-9371
Sumter, SC 29150   Fannie M. Davis, Libn.

NCR CORPORATION - TECHNICAL LIBRARY
3325 Platt Springs Rd.   Phone: (803) 796-9250
West Columbia, SC 29169   Trudy Katz Cook, Tech.Libn.

SOUTH DAKOTA

BETHLEHEM LUTHERAN CHURCH - LIBRARY
Fourth Ave. & Jay St.   Phone: (605) 225-9740
Aberdeen, SD 57401   Bernice Theeler, Libn.

DACOTAH PRAIRIE MUSEUM - ARCHIVES
21 S. Main St.
Box 395   Phone: (605) 229-1608
Aberdeen, SD 57401   Evearad Stelfax, Dir.

PRESENTATION COLLEGE - LIBRARY
1500 North Main   Phone: (605) 225-0420
Aberdeen, SD 57401   Ellen F. Hall, Lib.Dir.

SOUTH DAKOTA STATE UNIVERSITY - DEPARTMENT OF WILDLIFE &
   FISHERIES SCIENCES - RESEARCH LIBRARY
Brookings, SD 57007

SOUTH DAKOTA STATE UNIVERSITY - HILTON M. BRIGGS LIBRARY
Box 2115   Phone: (605) 688-5106
Brookings, SD 57007-1098   Dr. Leon Raney, Dean of Lib.

U.S. VETERANS ADMINISTRATION (SD-Fort Meade) - MEDICAL CENTER
   LIBRARY
                                                   Phone: (605) 347-2511
Fort Meade, SD 57741   Eugene A. Stevens, Chf., Lib.Serv.

U.S. VETERANS ADMINISTRATION (SD-Hot Springs) - CENTER LIBRARY
                                                   Phone: (605) 745-4101
Hot Springs, SD 57747   Carole W. Miles, Med.Libn.

U.S. NATL. PARK SERVICE - BADLANDS NATL. PARK - LIBRARY
Box 6   Phone: (605) 433-5361
Interior, SD 57750   Midge Johnston, Bus.Mgr.

DAKOTA STATE COLLEGE - KARL E. MUNDT LIBRARY
                                                   Phone: (605) 256-3551
Madison, SD 57042   Joseph T. Paulukonis, Dir.

MADISON COMMUNITY HOSPITAL - HEALTH-SCIENCE LIBRARY
917 N. Washington Ave.   Phone: (605) 256-6551
Madison, SD 57042   Donna Sullivan, Lib.Mgr.

BLUE CLOUD ABBEY - LIBRARY †
                                                   Phone: (605) 432-5528
Marvin, SD 57251   Rev. John David McMullen, O.S.B., Hd.Libn.

UNITED METHODIST CHURCH - SOUTH DAKOTA CONFERENCE -
   COMMITTEE ON ARCHIVES AND HISTORY - LIBRARY
1331 W. University Ave.
Box 460   Phone: (605) 996-6552
Mitchell, SD 57301   Barbara Rich Sorenson, Archv.

ST. MARY'S HOSPITAL - MEDICAL LIBRARY
803 E. Dakota Ave.
Pierre, SD 57501   DeAnn DeKay Hilmoe, Med.Libn.

SOUTH DAKOTA STATE HISTORICAL RESOURCE CENTER
Memorial Bldg.   Phone: (605) 773-3615
Pierre, SD 57501   Rosemary Evetts, Libn.

SOUTH DAKOTA STATE LIBRARY & ARCHIVES
800 N. Illinois St.   Phone: (605) 773-3131
Pierre, SD 57501   Clarence L. Coffindaffer, State Libn.

SOUTH DAKOTA STATE LIBRARY & ARCHIVES - SOUTH DAKOTA STATE
   ARCHIVES
800 N. Illinois St.   Phone: (605) 773-3173
Pierre, SD 57501   Lawrence E. Hibpshman, State Archv.

SOUTH DAKOTA STATE SUPREME COURT - LIBRARY †
State Capitol
Pierre, SD 57501   V. Biddle, Asst.Libn.

NATIONAL COLLEGE - THOMAS JEFFERSON LEARNING RESOURCE CENTER
Box 1780   Phone: (605) 394-4943
Rapid City, SD 57709   Linda L. Watson, Dir.

RUSHMORE NATIONAL HEALTH SYSTEM - HEALTH SCIENCES LIBRARY
353 Fairmont Blvd.   Phone: (605) 341-7101
Rapid City, SD 57701   Bonnie R. Mack, Dept.Mgr./Lib.Serv.

SOUTH DAKOTA SCHOOL OF MINES & TECHNOLOGY - DEVEREAUX LIBRARY
500 St. Joseph St.   Phone: (605) 394-2418
Rapid City, SD 57701   Bernice E. McKibben, Dir.

AMERICAN LUTHERAN CHURCH - SOUTH DAKOTA DISTRICT - ARCHIVES
Center for Western Studies
Augustana College
Sioux Falls, SD 57197

AUGUSTANA COLLEGE - CENTER FOR WESTERN STUDIES
29th & Summit Sts.   Phone: (605) 336-4007
Sioux Falls, SD 57102   Sven Froiland, Dir.

FIRST BAPTIST CHURCH - LIBRARY
1401 S. Covell   Phone: (605) 336-0966
Sioux Falls, SD 57105   Chris Carstensen, Libn.

GREAT PLAINS ZOO & MUSEUM - REFERENCE LIBRARY
600 E. 7th St.   Phone: (605) 339-7059
Sioux Falls, SD 57102-0496   Roger Shepherd, Mgr.

LUTHERAN CHURCH - MISSOURI SYNOD - SOUTH DAKOTA DISTRICT
   ARCHIVES
101 E. 38th St.   Phone: (605) 336-0811
Sioux Falls, SD 57105   E.F. Shaefer, Archv.

MC KENNAN HOSPITAL - MEDICAL LIBRARY
800 E. 21st St.   Phone: (605) 339-8088
Sioux Falls, SD 57101   Carol Galganski, Med.Libn.

NORTH AMERICAN BAPTIST SEMINARY - KAISER-RAMAKER LIBRARY
1321 W. 22nd St.   Phone: (605) 336-6805
Sioux Falls, SD 57105   George W. Lang, Lib.Adm.

PROTESTANT EPISCOPAL CHURCH - EPISCOPAL DIOCESE OF SOUTH
   DAKOTA - ARCHIVES
Center for Western Studies
Augustana College   Phone: (605) 336-4007
Sioux Falls, SD 57197   Harry F. Thompson, Archv.

SIOUX FALLS ARGUS-LEADER - LIBRARY *
200 S. Minnesota   Phone: (605) 331-2300
Sioux Falls, SD 57102

SIOUX VALLEY HOSPITAL - MEDICAL LIBRARY
1100 S. Euclid Ave.
Box 5039   Phone: (605) 333-1000
Sioux Falls, SD 57117   Kay Hasegawa, Libn.

SIOUXLAND HERITAGE MUSEUMS - PETTIGREW MUSEUM - LIBRARY
131 N. Duluth Ave.   Phone: (605) 339-7097
Sioux Falls, SD 57104   Ms. Lee N. McLaird, Cur. of Collections

U.S. GEOLOGICAL SURVEY - EROS DATA CENTER - TECHNICAL REFERENCE
    UNIT
EROS Data Center   Phone: (605) 594-6511
Sioux Falls, SD 57198   Karen Tramp, Customer Serv.Techn.

U.S. VETERANS ADMINISTRATION (SD-Sioux Falls) - HOSPITAL LIBRARY
2501 W. 22nd St.   Phone: (605) 336-3230
Sioux Falls, SD 57101   Lori Klein, Chf., Lib.Serv.

BLACK HILLS STATE COLLEGE - E.Y. BERRY LIBRARY-LEARNING CENTER -
    CURRICULUM LIBRARY
Berry Library-Learning Ctr.
University St.   Phone: (605) 642-6833
Spearfish, SD 57783   Barbra J. Cram, Curric.Libn.

BLACK HILLS STATE COLLEGE - E.Y. BERRY LIBRARY-LEARNING CENTER -
    SPECIAL COLLECTIONS
1200 University Ave.   Phone: (605) 642-6833
Spearfish, SD 57783   Dora Ann Jones, Spec.Coll.Libn.

UNIVERSITY OF SOUTH DAKOTA, SPRINGFIELD - CARL G. LAWRENCE
    LIBRARY †
    Phone: (605) 369-2296
Springfield, SD 57062

AMERICAN INDIAN RESEARCH PROJECT - LIBRARY
17 Dakota Hall
University of South Dakota   Phone: (605) 677-5208
Vermillion, SD 57069   Leonard Bruguier, Assoc.Dir.

OVER (W.H.) MUSEUM - LIBRARY
University of South Dakota   Phone: (605) 677-5228
Vermillion, SD 57069   Julia R. Vodicka, Musm.Dir.

SHRINE TO MUSIC MUSEUM
University of South Dakota
Box 194   Phone: (605) 677-5306
Vermillion, SD 57069   Andre P. Larson, Dir.

UNIVERSITY OF SOUTH DAKOTA - BUSINESS RESEARCH BUREAU
School of Business   Phone: (605) 677-5287
Vermillion, SD 57069   Dr. Jerry Johnson, Dir.

UNIVERSITY OF SOUTH DAKOTA - CHEMISTRY LIBRARY
Pardee Laboratory   Phone: (605) 677-5487
Vermillion, SD 57069

UNIVERSITY OF SOUTH DAKOTA - CHRISTIAN P. LOMMEN HEALTH
    SCIENCES LIBRARY
School of Medicine   Phone: (605) 677-5347
Vermillion, SD 57069   David A. Hulkonen, Dir.

UNIVERSITY OF SOUTH DAKOTA - GOVERNMENTAL RESEARCH LIBRARY
    Phone: (605) 677-5242
Vermillion, SD 57069   Russell L. Smith, Dir.

UNIVERSITY OF SOUTH DAKOTA - I.D. WEEKS LIBRARY - RICHARDSON
    ARCHIVES
    Phone: (605) 677-5371
Vermillion, SD 57069   Elizabeth Lang, Archv.

UNIVERSITY OF SOUTH DAKOTA - MC KUSICK LAW LIBRARY
    Phone: (605) 677-5259
Vermillion, SD 57069   Eileen Collier Bouniol, Hd. Law Libn.

SACRED HEART HOSPITAL - MEDICAL LIBRARY
W. 4th St.   Phone: (605) 665-9371
Yankton, SD 57078   Roxie Olson, Med.Libn.

SOUTH DAKOTA HUMAN SERVICES CENTER - MEDICAL LIBRARY
Box 76   Phone: (605) 665-3671
Yankton, SD 57078   Mary Lou Kostel, Libn.

TENNESSEE

ARLINGTON DEVELOPMENTAL CENTER - PROFESSIONAL LIBRARY
11293 Memphis-Arlington Rd.   Phone: (901) 867-2921
Arlington, TN 38002   Christine B. Gavin, Instr. Media Spec.

ARNOLD ENGINEERING DEVELOPMENT CENTER TECHNICAL LIBRARY
Mail Stop 100   Phone: (615) 455-2611
Arnold Air Force Sta., TN 37389   Gay D. Goethert, Lib.Supv.

BEECHAM, INC. - BEECHAM LABORATORIES - MEDICAL LIBRARY
501 5th St.   Phone: (615) 764-5141
Bristol, TN 37620   Peggy Rutsis, Med.Libn.

OLIN CORPORATION - CHEMICALS - CHARLESTON TECHNICAL
    INFORMATION CENTER
    Phone: (615) 336-2251
Charleston, TN 37310   Barbara C. Suttles, Supv.

CHATTANOOGA-HAMILTON COUNTY BICENTENNIAL LIBRARY - LOCAL
    HISTORY AND GENEALOGICAL COLLECTIONS
1001 Broad St.   Phone: (615) 757-5317
Chattanooga, TN 37402   Clara W. Swann, Hd.

CHATTANOOGA-HAMILTON COUNTY REGIONAL PLANNING COMMISSION -
    LIBRARY
100 E. 11th St.
City Hall Annex, Rm. 200   Phone: (615) 757-5216
Chattanooga, TN 37402

CHATTANOOGA TIMES - LIBRARY
117 E. 10th St.
Box 951   Phone: (615) 756-1234
Chattanooga, TN 37402   Tom Cotter, Libn.

CHATTEM DRUG AND CHEMICAL COMPANY - RESEARCH LIBRARY †
175 W. 38th St.   Phone: (615) 821-4571
Chattanooga, TN 37409   Tilda Wall, Libn.

COMBUSTION ENGINEERING, INC. - METALLURGICAL AND MATERIALS
    LIBRARY
911 W. Main St.   Phone: (615) 752-7132
Chattanooga, TN 37402   Nell T. Holder, Libn.

ERLANGER MEDICAL CENTER - MEDICAL LIBRARY †
975 E. Third St.   Phone: (615) 778-7498
Chattanooga, TN 37403   Margarette D. Koplan, Chf.Libn.

ERLANGER MEDICAL CENTER - SCHOOL OF NURSING - SARAH C. BARTON
    LIBRARY *
975 E. Third St.   Phone: (615) 265-3254
Chattanooga, TN 37403   Margarette D. Koplan, Chf.Libn.

HUNTER MUSEUM OF ART - REFERENCE LIBRARY
Bluff View   Phone: (615) 267-0968
Chattanooga, TN 37403   William T. Henning, Jr., Cur. of Coll.

TENNESSEE VALLEY AUTHORITY - MAPS AND SURVEYS BRANCH - MAP
    INFORMATION AND RECORDS UNIT
101 Haney Bldg.   Phone: (615) 751-5404
Chattanooga, TN 37401   J.L. Dodd, Supv.

TENNESSEE VALLEY AUTHORITY - TECHNICAL LIBRARY
100-401 Bldg.   Phone: (615) 751-4913
Chattanooga, TN 37401   Dean Robinson, Supv., Lib.Serv.

CLARKSVILLE LEAF-CHRONICLE COMPANY - LIBRARY
200 Commerce St.   Phone: (615) 552-1808
Clarksville, TN 37040   Judi Vaughn, Libn.

SOUTHERN MISSIONARY COLLEGE - MC KEE LIBRARY - SPECIAL
    COLLECTIONS
Box 629   Phone: (615) 396-4290
Collegedale, TN 37315   Charles E. Davis, Dir. of Libs./Archv.

POLK (James K.) ANCESTRAL HOME - LIBRARY
301 S. Seventh St.
Box 741   Phone: (615) 388-2354
Columbia, TN 38401   W.H. Bass, Dir.

GREAT LAKES RESEARCH CORPORATION - RESEARCH LIBRARY
Box 1031   Phone: (615) 543-3111
Elizabethton, TN 37643   Joan Warden, Libn.

U.S. NATL. PARK SERVICE - GREAT SMOKY MOUNTAINS NATL. PARK -
    SUGARLANDS VISITOR CENTER
                                                     Phone: (615) 436-5615
Gatlinburg, TN 37738   Claryse D. Myers, Libn.

TUSCULUM COLLEGE - INSTRUCTIONAL MATERIALS CENTER
Box 88   Phone: (615) 639-3751
Greeneville, TN 37743   Dr. Shirley S. Beck, Chm., Div. of Prof.Educ.

U.S. NATL. PARK SERVICE - ANDREW JOHNSON NATL. HISTORIC SITE -
    LIBRARY
College & Depot Sts.
Box 1088   Phone: (615) 474-2006
Greeneville, TN 37744-1088   Edward G. Speer, Park Tech.

LINCOLN MEMORIAL UNIVERSITY - ABRAHAM LINCOLN LIBRARY AND
    MUSEUM
Harrogate, TN 37752   Edgar G. Archer, Dir.

JACKSON-MADISON COUNTY GENERAL HOSPITAL - LEARNING CENTER
708 W. Forest Ave.   Phone: (901) 424-0424
Jackson, TN 38301   Linda G. Farmer, Med.Libn.

CARSON-NEWMAN COLLEGE LIBRARY - SPECIAL COLLECTIONS
Russell Ave.   Phone: (615) 475-9061
Jefferson City, TN 37760   Dr. William N. Nelson, Dir.

EAST TENNESSEE STATE UNIVERSITY - ARCHIVES OF APPALACHIA
Sherrod Library   Phone: (615) 929-4338
Johnson City, TN 37614   Dr. Ellen Garrison, Dir.

EAST TENNESSEE STATE UNIVERSITY, QUILLEN-DISHNER COLLEGE OF
    MEDICINE - DEPT. OF LEARNING RSRCS. - MEDICAL LIBRARY †
Box 23290A   Phone: (615) 928-6426
Johnson City, TN 37614   Janet S. Fisher, Asst. Dean

NATIONAL STORYTELLING RESOURCE CENTER
Box 112   Phone: (615) 753-2171
Jonesboro, TN 37659   Jean Smith, Dir.

EASTMAN KODAK COMPANY - EASTMAN CHEMICALS DIVISION -
    RESEARCH LIBRARY
Box 1972   Phone: (615) 229-3870
Kingsport, TN 37662   Michael W. Ubaldini, Sr.Libn.

EASTMAN KODAK COMPANY - TENNESSEE EASTMAN COMPANY -
    BUSINESS LIBRARY
Box 431   Phone: (615) 229-2071
Kingsport, TN 37662   Sandra H. Boyd, Lib.Asst.

HOLSTON VALLEY HOSPITAL AND MEDICAL CENTER - HEALTH SCIENCE
    LIBRARY
Ravine St.   Phone: (615) 246-3322
Kingsport, TN 37662   Angela C. England, Med.Libn.

COOPER INSTITUTE, INC. - KNOXVILLE BUSINESS COLLEGE - LIBRARY
720 N. 5th Ave.   Phone: (615) 637-3573
Knoxville, TN 37917   Meredith J. Keyser, Dir., Lib.Serv.

EAST TENNESSEE BAPTIST HOSPITAL - HEALTH SCIENCES LIBRARY
Box 1788   Phone: (615) 632-5618
Knoxville, TN 37920   Mary Evelyn Lynn, Libn.

FIRST CHRISTIAN CHURCH - WINONA ROEHL LIBRARY
211 W. 5th Ave.   Phone: (615) 522-0545
Knoxville, TN 37917

FORT SANDERS REGIONAL MEDICAL CENTER - MEDICAL/NURSING
    LIBRARY
1915 White Ave.   Phone: (615) 971-1293
Knoxville, TN 37916   Nedra Cook, Libn.

JOHNSON BIBLE COLLEGE - GLASS MEMORIAL LIBRARY
                                                     Phone: (615) 573-4517
Knoxville, TN 37998   Helen E. Lemmon, Libn.

KNOX COUNTY GOVERNMENTAL LIBRARY
M-47, City-County Bldg.
Main Ave.   Phone: (615) 521-2368
Knoxville, TN 37902   Meredith Douglas, Libn.

KNOX COUNTY PUBLIC LIBRARY SYSTEM - MC CLUNG HISTORICAL
    COLLECTION
East Tennesee Historical Center
600 Market St.   Phone: (615) 523-0781
Knoxville, TN 37902   William J. MacArthur, Jr., Hd.

KNOXVILLE-KNOX COUNTY METROPOLITAN PLANNING COMMISSION -
    LIBRARY
City-County Bldg., Suite 403
400 Main St.   Phone: (615) 521-2500
Knoxville, TN 37902   Gretchen F. Beal, Libn.

KNOXVILLE STATE TECHNICAL INSTITUTE - EDUCATIONAL RESOURCE
    CENTER
Box 19802   Phone: (615) 584-6103
Knoxville, TN 37939   Nina Hayden, Hd.Libn.

MUNICIPAL TECHNICAL ADVISORY SERVICE - LIBRARY
                                                     Phone: (615) 974-1008
Knoxville, TN 37996-4400   Carol C. Hewlett, Libn.

ST. MARY'S MEDICAL CENTER, INC. - MEDICAL LIBRARY
Oak Hill Ave.   Phone: (615) 971-7916
Knoxville, TN 37917   Glenda Clark, Libn.

ST. MARY'S MEDICAL CENTER, INC. - SCHOOL OF NURSING LIBRARY
Celeste Hall, Emerald Ave.   Phone: (615) 971-7839
Knoxville, TN 37917   Beth Barret, Libn.

STUDENTS' MUSEUM, INC. - LIBRARY
516 Beaman St.
Chilhowee Pk., Box 6108   Phone: (615) 637-1121
Knoxville, TN 37914   David R. Sincerbox, Dir.

TENNESSEE STATE SUPREME COURT - LAW LIBRARY
Supreme Court Bldg.
719 Locust St.   Phone: (615) 673-6128
Knoxville, TN 37902   Mamie H. Winstead, Libn.

TENNESSEE VALLEY AUTHORITY - CONTRACT SERVICES
400 W. Summit Hill Dr., WPA3   Phone: (615) 632-2717
Knoxville, TN 37902   Mr. G.V. Rogers, Jr., Supv.

TENNESSEE VALLEY AUTHORITY - LAW LIBRARY
400 W. Summit Hill Dr., E4A20   Phone: (615) 632-4391
Knoxville, TN 37902   Bonnie M. Holmes, Supv., Law Lib.Serv.

TENNESSEE VALLEY AUTHORITY - TECHNICAL LIBRARY
400 Commerce Ave.   Phone: (615) 632-3464
Knoxville, TN 37902   Jesse C. Mills, Chf.Libn.

UNIVERSITY OF TENNESSEE - AGRICULTURE-VETERINARY MEDICINE
    LIBRARY
Veterinary Medicine Teaching Hospital   Phone: (615) 974-7338
Knoxville, TN 37996-4500   Don Jett, Libn.

UNIVERSITY OF TENNESSEE - COLLEGE OF LAW LIBRARY
1505 W. Cumberland Ave.   Phone: (615) 974-4381
Knoxville, TN 37996-1800   D. Cheryl Picquet, Act.Dir.

UNIVERSITY OF TENNESSEE - ENERGY, ENVIRONMENT & RESOURCES
    CENTER - JOINT RESEARCH CENTERS' LIBRARY
327 S. Stadium Hall   Phone: (615) 974-4251
Knoxville, TN 37996-0710   Alan B. Johns, Libn.

UNIVERSITY OF TENNESSEE - MEMORIAL RESEARCH CENTER AND
    HOSPITAL - PRESTON MEDICAL LIBRARY
1924 Alcoa Hwy.   Phone: (615) 971-3305
Knoxville, TN 37920   Martha C. Childs, Libn.

UNIVERSITY OF TENNESSEE - MUSIC LIBRARY
Music Bldg., Rm. 301
Knoxville, TN 37796-2600
Phone: (615) 974-3474
Pauline S. Bayne, Libn.

UNIVERSITY OF TENNESSEE - SPECIAL COLLECTIONS
Phone: (615) 974-4480
Knoxville, TN 37996-1000
John Dobson, Spec.Coll.Libn.

OKRA RIDGE FARM - TENNESSEE LESBIAN ARCHIVES
Rte. 2, Box 252
Luttrell, TN 37779
Phone: (615) 992-8423
Catherine R. Moirai, Coord.

BLOUNT MEMORIAL HOSPITAL - LESLIE R. LINGEMAN MEMORIAL MEDICAL
LIBRARY
New Walland Highway
Maryville, TN 37801
Phone: (615) 977-5520
Miriam B. Williamson, Libn.

AMERICAN BLAKE FOUNDATION - RESEARCH LIBRARY
Dept. of English
Memphis State University
Memphis, TN 38152
Phone: (901) 454-2653
Dr. Roger R. Easson, Exec.Dir.

AMERICAN CONTRACT BRIDGE LEAGUE - ALBERT H. MOREHEAD
MEMORIAL LIBRARY
2200 Democrat Rd.
Box 161192
Memphis, TN 38186
Phone: (901) 332-5586
Fran Braden Downing, Libn.

BAPTIST MEMORIAL HOSPITAL - JOHN L. MC GEHEE LIBRARY
899 Madison Ave.
Memphis, TN 38146
Phone: (901) 522-5140
Donna L. Davis, Med.Libn.

BAPTIST MEMORIAL HOSPITAL - SCHOOL OF NURSING - LIBRARY *
999 Monroe
Memphis, TN 38104
Phone: (901) 522-4309
Sherry Young, Libn.

BARTHOLOMEW (Harland) AND ASSOCIATES, INC. - LIBRARY
2701 Union Extended
Memphis, TN 38112
Phone: (901) 327-4222
Jennifer B. Fox, Libn.

CENTER FOR SOUTHERN FOLKLORE - ARCHIVES
1216 Peabody Ave.
Box 40105
Memphis, TN 38104
Phone: (901) 726-4205
Diane Yacoubian, Archv.

DIXON GALLERY AND GARDENS - LIBRARY
4339 Park Ave.
Memphis, TN 38117
Phone: (901) 761-5250
Moussa M. Domit, Dir.

GRACE (W.R.) AND COMPANY - AGRICULTURAL CHEMICALS GROUP -
PLANNING SERVICES LIBRARY
100 N. Main Bldg.
Box 277
Memphis, TN 38101
Phone: (901) 522-2385
Carolyn A. Wilhite, Libn.

HARDING GRADUATE SCHOOL OF RELIGION - L.M. GRAVES MEMORIAL
LIBRARY
1000 Cherry Rd.
Memphis, TN 38117
Phone: (901) 761-1354
Don L. Meredith, Libn.

HOLIDAY INNS, INC. - CORPORATE RESOURCE CENTER
3742 Lamar Ave.
Memphis, TN 38195
Phone: (901) 369-5993
Vanessa Patterson, Supv., Res.Serv.

LE BONHEUR CHILDREN'S MEDICAL CENTER - HEALTH SCIENCES LIBRARY
One Children's Plaza
Memphis, TN 38103
Phone: (901) 522-3167
Jan Hawkins, Libn.

MEMPHIS ACADEMY OF ARTS - G. PILLOW LEWIS MEMORIAL LIBRARY
Overton Pk.
Memphis, TN 38112
Phone: (901) 726-4085
Robert M. Scarlett, Libn.

MEMPHIS BOTANIC GARDEN FOUNDATION, INC. - GOLDSMITH CIVIC
GARDEN CTR. - SYBILE MALLOY MEMORIAL LIBRARY
750 Cherry Rd.
Memphis, TN 38117
Phone: (901) 685-1566
Clara M. Wright, Adm.Ck.

MEMPHIS BROOKS MUSEUM OF ART - LIBRARY
Overton Pk.
Memphis, TN 38112
Phone: (901) 726-5266
Letitia B. Proctor, Libn.

MEMPHIS COMMERCIAL APPEAL - LIBRARY
495 Union Ave.
Memphis, TN 38107
Phone: (901) 529-2781
Eugene G. Brady, Jr., Libn.

MEMPHIS MENTAL HEALTH INSTITUTE - JAMES A. WALLACE LIBRARY
865 Poplar Ave.
Box 40966
Memphis, TN 38174-0966
Phone: (901) 521-1261
Josephine Maddry, Lib.Techn.

MEMPHIS PINK PALACE MUSEUM - LIBRARY
3050 Central Ave.
Memphis, TN 38111
Phone: (901) 454-5600
Coralu D. Buddenbohm, Libn.

MEMPHIS-SHELBY COUNTY BAR ASSOCIATION - LAW LIBRARY
Court House
Adams Ave., Rm. 315
Memphis, TN 38103
Phone: (901) 527-7041
Barbara F. Moore, Law Libn.

MEMPHIS-SHELBY COUNTY OFFICE OF PLANNING AND DEVELOPMENT -
LIBRARY
City Hall, Rm. 419
125 N. Main St.
Memphis, TN 38103-2084
Phone: (901) 528-2601
Marilyn A. Meeks, Libn.

MEMPHIS-SHELBY COUNTY PUBLIC LIBRARY AND INFORMATION CENTER -
MEMPHIS ROOM COLLECTIONS
1850 Peabody Ave.
Memphis, TN 38104
Phone: (901) 528-2961
James R. Johnson, Hd., Hist. & Travel

MEMPHIS-SHELBY COUNTY PUBLIC LIBRARY AND INFO. CTR. - SCIENCE/
BUSINESS/SOCIAL SCI.DEPT.
1850 Peabody Ave.
Memphis, TN 38104
Phone: (901) 528-2984
Barbara C. Shultz, Dept.Hd.

MEMPHIS STATE UNIVERSITY - GRADUATE DEPT. OF PLANNING &
REGIONAL ECONOMIC DEVELOPMENT CTR. - PLANNING LIBRARY
226 Johnson Hall
Memphis, TN 38152
Phone: (901) 454-2056
Luchy S. Burrell, Supv.

MEMPHIS STATE UNIVERSITY LIBRARIES - ART SLIDE LIBRARY
Department of Art
Jones Hall, Rm. 220
Memphis, TN 38152
Phone: (901) 454-2216
Belinda C. Patterson, Slide Cur.

MEMPHIS STATE UNIVERSITY LIBRARIES - BUREAU OF EDUCATIONAL
RESEARCH AND SERVICES - LIBRARY
College of Education
302 Ball Bldg.
Memphis, TN 38152
Phone: (901) 454-2362
John R. Petry, Res.Assoc./Assoc.Prof.

MEMPHIS STATE UNIVERSITY LIBRARIES - C.H. NASH MUSEUM LIBRARY
1987 Indian Village Dr.
Memphis, TN 38109
Phone: (901) 785-3160
Gerald P. Smith, Cur.

MEMPHIS STATE UNIVERSITY LIBRARIES - CHEMISTRY LIBRARY
Phone: (901) 454-2625
Memphis, TN 38152
Aletris Scott, Lib.Asst.

MEMPHIS STATE UNIVERSITY LIBRARIES - ENGINEERING LIBRARY
Central Ave.
Memphis, TN 38152
Phone: (901) 454-2179
Sue Ward, Libn.

MEMPHIS STATE UNIVERSITY LIBRARIES - MUSIC LIBRARY
Central Ave.
Memphis, TN 38152
Phone: (901) 454-2556
Ann Viles, Music Libn.

MEMPHIS STATE UNIVERSITY LIBRARIES - RADIO PROGRAM HISTORY
COLLECTION
Brister Library Learning Media Center
Memphis, TN 38152
Phone: (901) 454-2001
Dr. Marvin R. Bensman, Assoc.Prof.

MEMPHIS STATE UNIVERSITY LIBRARIES - SCHOOL OF LAW LIBRARY
Phone: (901) 454-2426
Memphis, TN 38152
Sara Turley Cole, Law Libn.

MEMPHIS STATE UNIVERSITY LIBRARIES - SPECIAL COLLECTIONS
Phone: (901) 454-2210
Memphis, TN 38152

MEMPHIS STATE UNIVERSITY LIBRARIES - SPEECH AND HEARING
CENTER LIBRARY
807 Jefferson Ave.   Phone: (901) 525-2682
Memphis, TN 38104

MEMPHIS THEOLOGICAL SEMINARY - LIBRARY †
168 E. Pkwy. S.   Phone: (901) 458-8232
Memphis, TN 38104   Bobbie E. Oliver, Adm.Libn.

METHODIST HOSPITAL SCHOOL OF NURSING - LESLIE M. STRATTON
NURSING LIBRARY
251 S. Claybrook   Phone: (901) 726-8862
Memphis, TN 38104   Joanne S. Guyton, Libn.

NATIONAL COTTON COUNCIL OF AMERICA - LIBRARY
1918 N. Parkway   Phone: (901) 274-9030
Memphis, TN 38112   Carolyn Robertson, Libn.

P.T. BOATS, INC. - LIBRARY, ARCHIVES & TECHNICAL INFORMATION
CENTER - NATIONAL HEADQUARTERS
Box 109   Phone: (901) 272-9980
Memphis, TN 38101   J.M. "Boats" Newberry, Founder & Dir.

PLOUGH, INC. - RESEARCH LIBRARY
Box 377   Phone: (901) 320-2702
Memphis, TN 38151   Martha Hurst, Libn.

PROCTER & GAMBLE COMPANY - BUCKEYE CELLULOSE CORPORATION -
CELLULOSE & SPECIALTIES DIV. TECH. INFO.SERV.
949 Tillman Ave.   Phone: (901) 454-8310
Memphis, TN 38108   Ruth S. McLallen, Tech.Info.Mgr.

ST. JOSEPH HOSPITAL - HEALTH SCIENCE LIBRARY
220 Overton
Box 178   Phone: (901) 529-2874
Memphis, TN 38101   Denise Fesmire, Libn.

ST. JUDE CHILDREN'S RESEARCH HOSPITAL - RESEARCH LIBRARY
332 N. Lauderdale
Box 318   Phone: (901) 525-0388
Memphis, TN 38101   Mary Edith Walker, Med.Libn.

SEMMES-MURPHEY CLINIC - LIBRARY
920 Madison Ave., Suite 201   Phone: (901) 522-7700
Memphis, TN 38103   Charles M. Prest, Libn.

SHILOH MILITARY TRAIL, INC. - LIBRARY
Box 17386   Phone: (901) 454-5600
Memphis, TN 38117   Edward F. Williams, III, Res.Hist.

SOUTHERN COLLEGE OF OPTOMETRY - WILLIAM P. MAC CRACKEN, JR.
MEMORIAL LIBRARY
1245 Madison Ave.   Phone: (901) 725-0180
Memphis, TN 38104   Nancy Gatlin, Dir.

STATE TECHNICAL INSTITUTE AT MEMPHIS - GEORGE E. FREEMAN
LIBRARY
5983 Macon Cove   Phone: (901) 377-4111
Memphis, TN 38134   Rosa S. Burnett, Libn.

U.S. ARMY - CORPS OF ENGINEERS - MEMPHIS DISTRICT - LIBRARY
B-314 Clifford Davis Federal Bldg.   Phone: (901) 521-3584
Memphis, TN 38103   Jacque Patterson, Libn.

U.S. DEPT. OF DEFENSE - DEFENSE INDUSTRIAL PLANT EQUIPMENT
CENTER - TECHNICAL DATA REPOSITORY & LIBRARY *
Airways Blvd.   Phone: (901) 744-5549
Memphis, TN 38114   Johnny F. Murray, Chf., Lib.

U.S. VETERANS ADMINISTRATION (TN-Memphis) - MEDICAL CENTER
LIBRARY
1030 Jefferson Ave.   Phone: (901) 523-8990
Memphis, TN 38104   Mary Virginia Taylor, Chf., Lib.Serv.

UNIVERSITY OF TENNESSEE - CENTER FOR THE HEALTH SCIENCES
LIBRARY
800 Madison Ave.   Phone: (901) 528-5638
Memphis, TN 38163   Jess A. Martin, Dir.

WEST TENNESSEE HISTORICAL SOCIETY - LIBRARY
Memphis State University
Box 111046   Phone: (901) 458-4696
Memphis, TN 38111

U.S. NAVY - NAVAL AIR STATION (TN-Memphis) - LIBRARY
S-78   Phone: (901) 872-5683
Millington, TN 38054   Relda D. Hale, Libn.

U.S. NAVY - NAVAL HOSPITAL (TN-Memphis) - GENERAL AND MEDICAL
LIBRARY
                                                       Phone: (901) 872-5846
Millington, TN 38054   Virginia C. Masner, Libn.

U.S. VETERANS ADMINISTRATION (TN-Johnson City) - MEDICAL CENTER
LIBRARY
                                                       Phone: (615) 926-1171
Mountain Home, TN 37684   Mary Jane Crutchfield, Chf., Lib.Serv.

U.S. NATL. PARK SERVICE - STONES RIVER NATL. BATTLEFIELD - LIBRARY
Old Nashville Hwy.
Rte. 10, Box 401   Phone: (615) 893-9501
Murfreesboro, TN 37130   Donald E. Magee, Pk.Supt.

U.S. VETERANS ADMINISTRATION (TN-Murfreesboro) - MEDICAL CENTER
LIBRARY
                                                       Phone: (615) 893-1360
Murfreesboro, TN 37130   Joy W. Hunter, Chf., Lib.Serv.

ALADDIN INDUSTRIES INC. - LIBRARY
703 Murfreesboro Rd.   Phone: (615) 748-3427
Nashville, TN 37210   Nancy S. Rumsey, Info.Spec.

AMERICAN BAPTIST THEOLOGICAL SEMINARY - T.L. HOLCOMB LIBRARY
1800 White's Creek Pike   Phone: (615) 228-7877
Nashville, TN 37207   Dorothy B. Lucas, Libn.

AVCO CORPORATION - AEROSTRUCTURES DIVISION - ENGINEERING
LIBRARY
Box 210   Phone: (615) 360-4043
Nashville, TN 37202   Julie A. McDole, Libn.

BAPTIST HOSPITAL - LIBRARY †
2000 Church St.   Phone: (615) 329-5373
Nashville, TN 37236   Vickie A. Overstreet, Med.Libn.

BIOMEDICAL COMPUTING TECHNOLOGY INFORMATION CENTER
R-1302
Vanderbilt Medical Center   Phone: (615) 322-2385
Nashville, TN 37232

COMMERCE UNION BANK - LIBRARY
One Commerce Pl.   Phone: (615) 749-3227
Nashville, TN 37219   Susan B. Holmes, Mgt.Info.Spec.

COUNTRY MUSIC FOUNDATION - LIBRARY AND MEDIA CENTER
4 Music Square E.   Phone: (615) 256-7008
Nashville, TN 37203   Charlie Seemann, Dp.Dir., Coll. & Res.

CRAWFORD (F. Marion) MEMORIAL SOCIETY - BIBLIOTHECA
CRAWFORDIANA
Saracinesca House
3610 Meadowbrook Ave.   Phone: (615) 292-9695
Nashville, TN 37205   John C. Moran, Dir.

CUMBERLAND MUSEUM AND SCIENCE CENTER - DYER MEMORIAL LIBRARY
800 Ridley Ave.   Phone: (615) 242-1858
Nashville, TN 37203   Mary S. Thieme, Cur.

DARGAN-CARVER LIBRARY
127 Ninth Ave., N.   Phone: (615) 251-2134
Nashville, TN 37234   Howard Gallimore, Supv.

DISCIPLES OF CHRIST HISTORICAL SOCIETY - LIBRARY
1101 19th Ave., S.
Nashville, TN 37212   David I. McWhirter, Dir. of Lib./Archv.

FISK UNIVERSITY - MOLECULAR SPECTROSCOPY RESEARCH LABORATORY
    - LIBRARY
Box 15   Phone: (615) 329-8620
Nashville, TN 37203   E. Silberman, Prof./Dir.

FISK UNIVERSITY - SPECIAL COLLECTIONS DEPARTMENT
17th at Jackson St.   Phone: (615) 329-8646
Nashville, TN 37203   Ann Allen Shockley, Assoc.Libn./Archv.

HOSPITAL CORPORATION OF AMERICA - RESEARCH/INFORMATION
    SERVICES
One Park Plaza
Box 550   Phone: (615) 327-9551
Nashville, TN 37202-0550   Mary Wester-House, Mgr.

INTERNATIONAL ROCK AND ROLL MUSIC ASSOCIATION, INC. - LIBRARY
Box 50111   Phone: (615) 352-1443
Nashville, TN 37205   Bernard G. Walters, Pres.

JEWISH COMMUNITY CENTER - LIBRARY
815 Percy Warner Blvd.   Phone: (615) 297-3588
Nashville, TN 37205   Annette R. Levy, Libn.

JEWISH FEDERATION OF NASHVILLE AND MIDDLE TENNESSEE -
    ARCHIVES
815 Percy Warner Blvd.   Phone: (615) 297-3588
Nashville, TN 37205   Annette R. Levy, Dir.

MEHARRY MEDICAL COLLEGE - MEDICAL LIBRARY - LEARNING
    RESOURCES CENTER
1005 D.B. Todd   Phone: (615) 327-6319
Nashville, TN 37208   Leslie J. Goodale, Lib.Dir.

NASHVILLE BANNER - LIBRARY
1100 Broadway   Phone: (615) 255-5401
Nashville, TN 37202   Sally P. Moran, Libn.

NASHVILLE AND DAVIDSON COUNTY METROPOLITAN PLANNING
    COMMISSION - LIBRARY
Lindsley Hall
730 Second Ave. S.   Phone: (615) 259-6268
Nashville, TN 37201   Wanda Lucia Moore, Libn. I

NASHVILLE - METROPOLITAN DEPARTMENT OF PUBLIC HEALTH - LENTZ
    HEALTH CENTER LIBRARY
311 23rd Ave., N.   Phone: (615) 327-9313
Nashville, TN 37203   Jenny Patterson, Libn.

NASHVILLE METROPOLITAN GENERAL HOSPITAL - HEALTH SCIENCE
    LIBRARY
72 Hermitage Ave.   Phone: (615) 259-5657
Nashville, TN 37210   Evelyn H. Forbes, Libn.

NASHVILLE STATE TECHNICAL INSTITUTE - EDUCATIONAL RESOURCE
    CENTER
120 White Bridge Rd.   Phone: (615) 741-1229
Nashville, TN 37209   Carolyn Householder, Hd.

PEABODY (George) COLLEGE FOR TEACHERS OF VANDERBILT UNIVERSITY
    - KENNEDY CENTER - MATERIALS LIBRARY
Box 62   Phone: (615) 322-8184
Nashville, TN 37203   Mrs. Jamesie Rodney, Mgr.

PUBLIC LIBRARY OF NASHVILLE AND DAVIDSON COUNTY - BUSINESS
    INFORMATION SERVICE
222 Eighth Ave., N.   Phone: (615) 244-4700
Nashville, TN 37203   Alyne R. Gundlach, Chf.

SCARRITT COLLEGE FOR CHRISTIAN WORKERS - VIRGINIA DAVIS LASKEY
    LIBRARY
1104 19th Ave., S.   Phone: (615) 327-2700
Nashville, TN 37203   Dale E. Bilbrey, Libn.

SOUTHERN BAPTIST CONVENTION - HISTORICAL COMMISSION -
    SOUTHERN BAPTIST HISTORICAL LIBRARY & ARCHIVES
901 Commerce St.   Phone: (615) 251-2660
Nashville, TN 37203   A. Ronald Tonks, Asst.Exec.Dir.

TEMPLE OHABAI SHALOM - LIBRARY
5015 Harding Rd.   Phone: (615) 352-7620
Nashville, TN 37205   Annette R. Levy, Libn.

TENNESSEAN NEWSPAPER - LIBRARY
1100 Broadway   Phone: (615) 259-8007
Nashville, TN 37202   Annette Morrison, Hd.Libn.

TENNESSEE BOTANICAL GARDENS & FINE ARTS CENTER - FINE ARTS
    CENTER LIBRARY
Cheekwood-Forrest Park Dr.   Phone: (615) 352-8632
Nashville, TN 37205

TENNESSEE BOTANICAL GARDENS & FINE ARTS CENTER - MINNIE
    RITCHEY & JOEL OWSLEY CHEEK LIBRARY
Cheekwood-Forrest Park Dr.   Phone: (615) 356-3306
Nashville, TN 37205   Muriel H. Connell, Libn.

TENNESSEE STATE COMMISSION ON AGING - LIBRARY
700 Tennessee Bldg.
535 Church St.   Phone: (615) 741-2056
Nashville, TN 37219   Mason Rowe, Res.Anl.

TENNESSEE STATE COMMISSION FOR HUMAN DEVELOPMENT - RESOURCE
    LIBRARY
208 Tennessee Bldg.
535 Church St.   Phone: (615) 741-2424
Nashville, TN 37219

TENNESSEE STATE DEPARTMENT OF AGRICULTURE - LOU WALLACE
    LIBRARY
Ellington Agricultural Center
Melrose Sta., Box 40627   Phone: (615) 741-1456
Nashville, TN 37204   Mark McBride, Adm.Asst., Pub.Aff.

TENNESSEE STATE DEPARTMENT OF CONSERVATION - DIVISION OF
    GEOLOGY - CONSERVATION RESOURCE CENTER
701 Broadway   Phone: (615) 741-2726
Nashville, TN 37203   Robert A. Hershey, Dir./State Geologist

TENNESSEE STATE DEPARTMENT OF ECONOMIC & COMMUNITY
    DEVELOPMENT - LIBRARY
1014 Andrew Jackson Office Bldg.   Phone: (615) 741-1995
Nashville, TN 37219   Edith Snider, Libn.

TENNESSEE STATE DEPARTMENT OF EMPLOYMENT SECURITY -
    RESEARCH & STATISTICS SECTION
519 Cordell Hull Bldg.   Phone: (615) 741-2284
Nashville, TN 37219   Joe Cummings, Chf., Res. & Stat.

TENNESSEE STATE DEPARTMENT OF HEALTH AND ENVIRONMENT - FILM
    LIBRARY
State Office Bldg.
Ben Allen Rd.   Phone: (615) 741-7276
Nashville, TN 37216   Randall Brady, Dir.

TENNESSEE STATE DEPARTMENT OF PUBLIC HEALTH - MCH/HWP
    RESOURCE CENTER †
TDPH State Office Bldg.
Ben Allen Rd.   Phone: (615) 741-7276
Nashville, TN 37216   Randall Brady, Dir., Resource Ctr.

TENNESSEE STATE DEPARTMENT OF TRANSPORTATION - LIBRARY
James K. Polk Bldg., Suite 900   Phone: (615) 741-2330
Nashville, TN 37219   Ruth S. Letson, Libn.

TENNESSEE STATE LAW LIBRARY
Supreme Court Bldg.
401 Seventh Ave., N.   Phone: (615) 741-2016
Nashville, TN 37219   G. Alvis Winstead, Dir. & Libn.

TENNESSEE STATE LEGISLATIVE LIBRARY
G-16 War Memorial Bldg.   Phone: (615) 741-3091
Nashville, TN 37219   Julie J. McCown, Leg.Libn.

TENNESSEE STATE LIBRARY AND ARCHIVES - ARCHIVES & MANUSCRIPTS
  SECTION
403 Seventh Ave., N.   Phone: (615) 741-2561
Nashville, TN 37219   Jean B. Waggener, Dir.

TENNESSEE STATE LIBRARY - LIBRARY FOR THE BLIND AND PHYSICALLY
  HANDICAPPED
403 Seventh Ave. N.   Phone: (615) 741-3915
Nashville, TN 37219   Miss Francis H. Ezell, Dir.

TENNESSEE STATE LIBRARY - STATE LIBRARY DIVISION
403 7th Ave., N.   Phone: (615) 741-2764
Nashville, TN 37219   Miss Kendall Cram, Dir.

TENNESSEE STATE PLANNING OFFICE - LIBRARY
1800 Polk Bldg.
505 Deaderick St.   Phone: (615) 741-2363
Nashville, TN 37219-5082   Eleanor J. Burt, Libn.

TENNESSEE STATE PUBLIC SERVICE COMMISSION - LEGAL DEPARTMENT
  - LIBRARY
C1-103 Cordell Hull Bldg.   Phone: (615) 741-3191
Nashville, TN 37219   Henry Walker, Gen. Counsel

TENNESSEE WESTERN HISTORY AND FOLKLORE SOCIETY - LIBRARY
Box 60072   Phone: (615) 226-1890
Nashville, TN 37206   Steve Eng, Cur.

UNITED METHODIST PUBLISHING HOUSE - LIBRARY
201 Eighth Ave., S.   Phone: (615) 749-6335
Nashville, TN 37202   Rosalyn Lewis, Libn.

U.S. DEPT. OF COMMERCE - INTERNATIONAL TRADE ADMINISTRATION -
  NASHVILLE DISTRICT OFFICE LIBRARY
One Commerce Pl., Suite 1427   Phone: (615) 251-5161
Nashville, TN 37239   Martha Broadway, Trade Ref.Asst.

U.S. VETERANS ADMINISTRATION (TN-Nashville) - MEDICAL CENTER
  LIBRARY SERVICE
1310 24th Ave., S.   Phone: (615) 327-4751
Nashville, TN 37203   Barbara A. Meadows, Chf., Lib.Serv.

UPPER ROOM DEVOTIONAL LIBRARY, MUSEUM AND ARCHIVES
1908 Grand Ave.
Box 189   Phone: (615) 327-2700
Nashville, TN 37202   Julie L. Julian, Libn./Res.Asst.

VANDERBILT UNIVERSITY - ALYNE QUEENER MASSEY LAW LIBRARY
School of Law   Phone: (615) 322-2568
Nashville, TN 37203   Igor I. Kavass, Dir.

VANDERBILT UNIVERSITY - JEAN AND ALEXANDER HEARD LIBRARY -
  CENTRAL DIVISION - ARTS LIBRARY
419 21st Ave., S.   Phone: (615) 322-3485
Nashville, TN 37203   Jack Robertson, Arts Libn.

VANDERBILT UNIVERSITY - JEAN AND ALEXANDER HEARD LIBRARY -
  CENTRAL DIV. - SARA SHANNON STEVENSON SCI. LIB.
419 21st Ave. S.   Phone: (615) 322-2775
Nashville, TN 37203

VANDERBILT UNIVERSITY - JEAN AND ALEXANDER HEARD LIBRARY -
  DIVINITY LIBRARY
419 21st Ave., S.   Phone: (615) 322-2865
Nashville, TN 37203   Dorothy Ruth Parks, Dir.

VANDERBILT UNIVERSITY - JEAN AND ALEXANDER HEARD LIBRARY -
  DIVINITY LIBRARY - KESLER CIRCULATING LIBRARY
419 21st Ave., S.   Phone: (615) 322-2865
Nashville, TN 37203   Dorothy Ruth Parks, Dir.

VANDERBILT UNIVERSITY - JEAN AND ALEXANDER HEARD LIBRARY -
  DYER OBSERVATORY
Sta. B
Box 1803   Phone: (615) 373-4897
Nashville, TN 37235   Ellen Ellis, Libn.

VANDERBILT UNIVERSITY - JEAN AND ALEXANDER HEARD LIBRARY -
  EDUCATION LIBRARY
Box 325   Phone: (615) 322-8095
Nashville, TN 37203   Mary Beth Blalock, Act.Dir.

VANDERBILT UNIVERSITY - JEAN AND ALEXANDER HEARD LIBRARY -
  EDUCATION LIB. - PEABODY COLL. OF BOOKS ON CHILDREN
Box 325   Phone: (615) 322-8095
Nashville, TN 37203   Pamela Estes, Libn.

VANDERBILT UNIVERSITY - JEAN AND ALEXANDER HEARD LIBRARY -
  MUSIC LIBRARY
                                               Phone: (615) 322-8222
Nashville, TN 37203   Shirley Marie Watts, Libn.

VANDERBILT UNIVERSITY - JEAN AND ALEXANDER HEARD LIBRARY -
  SPECIAL COLLECTIONS DEPARTMENT
21st Ave., S.   Phone: (615) 322-2807
Nashville, TN 37203   Marice Wolfe, Hd.

VANDERBILT UNIVERSITY - JEAN AND ALEXANDER HEARD LIBRARY -
  TELEVISION NEWS ARCHIVES
                                               Phone: (615) 322-2927
Nashville, TN 37203   James P. Pilkington, Adm.

VANDERBILT UNIVERSITY - JEAN AND ALEXANDER HEARD LIBRARY -
  WALKER MANAGEMENT LIBRARY
401 21st Ave. S.   Phone: (615) 322-2970
Nashville, TN 37203   Shirley Hallblade, Dir.

VANDERBILT UNIVERSITY - MEDICAL CENTER LIBRARY
                                               Phone: (615) 322-2292
Nashville, TN 37232   T. Mark Hodges, Dir.

WEST END SYNAGOGUE - LIBRARY
3810 West End Ave.   Phone: (615) 269-4592
Nashville, TN 37205   Annette R. Levy, Dir.

TENNESSEE VALLEY AUTHORITY - DIVISION OF LAND AND FOREST
  RESOURCES - NATURAL RESOURCES LIBRARY †
Forestry Bldg.   Phone: (615) 494-7173
Norris, TN 37828   Janice P. McDonnell, Libn.

MARTIN MARIETTA ENERGY SYSTEMS INC. - ORGDP INFORMATION
  RESOURCE CENTER
Bldg. K-1002, MS 221
Box P   Phone: (615) 574-9694
Oak Ridge, TN 37830   John T. Phillips, Mgr.

NATIONAL LIBRARY OF MEDICINE - TOXICOLOGY DATA BANK
Oak Ridge Natl. Laboratory   Phone: (615) 574-7805
Oak Ridge, TN 37830   Dr. Po-Yung Lu, Dir.

OAK RIDGE ASSOCIATED UNIVERSITIES - MANPOWER EDUCATION,
  RESEARCH, AND TRAINING DIVISION - LIBRARY
Bldg. 2714-F, Rm. E-1
246 Laboratory Rd.
Box 117   Phone: (615) 576-3408
Oak Ridge, TN 37831-0117   Harry T. Burn, Libn.

OAK RIDGE ASSOCIATED UNIVERSITIES - MEDICAL HEALTH SCIENCES
  DIVISION LIBRARY
Box 117   Phone: (615) 576-3490
Oak Ridge, TN 37830   Randa Yalcintas, Info.Dir.

OAK RIDGE NATIONAL LABORATORY - CONTROLLED FUSION ATOMIC
  DATA CENTER
Bldg. 6003, Box X   Phone: (615) 574-4704
Oak Ridge, TN 37830   D.H. Crandall, Dir.

OAK RIDGE NATIONAL LABORATORY - INFORMATION CENTER FOR
  INTERNAL EXPOSURE
Box X   Phone: (615) 574-6261
Oak Ridge, TN 37830   S.R. Bernard, Dir.

OAK RIDGE NATIONAL LABORATORY - INFORMATION DIVISION -
  ENVIRONMENTAL MUTAGEN INFORMATION CENTER
Box Y   Phone: (615) 574-7871
Oak Ridge, TN 37830   John S. Wassom, Dir.

OAK RIDGE NATIONAL LABORATORY - LIBRARIES †
Box X   Phone: (615) 574-6722
Oak Ridge, TN 37830   R.R. Dickison, Chf.Libn.

OAK RIDGE NATIONAL LABORATORY - NUCLEAR DATA PROJECT
Box X   Phone: (615) 574-4699
Oak Ridge, TN 37830   M.J. Martin, Dir.

OAK RIDGE NATIONAL LABORATORY - NUCLEAR SAFETY INFORMATION
    CENTER
Bldg. 9711-1, Box Y   Phone: (615) 483-8611
Oak Ridge, TN 37830   J.R. Buchanan, Dir.

OAK RIDGE NATIONAL LABORATORY - RADIATION SHIELDING
    INFORMATION CENTER
Box X   Phone: (615) 574-6176
Oak Ridge, TN 37830   Betty F. Maskewitz, Dir.

OAK RIDGE NATIONAL LABORATORY - TOXICOLOGY INFORMATION
    RESPONSE CENTER
Bldg. 2024, Box X   Phone: (615) 576-1743
Oak Ridge, TN 37830   Susan G. Winslow, Dir.

U.S. DEPT. OF ENERGY - OFFICE OF SCIENTIFIC AND TECHNICAL
    INFORMATION (OSTI) - TECHNICAL INFORMATION CENTER
Box 62   Phone: (615) 576-6837
Oak Ridge, TN 37831   Nancy Hardin

U.S. NATL. OCEANIC & ATMOSPHERIC ADMINISTRATION - ATMOSPHERIC
    TURBULENCE & DIFFUSION LABORATORY - LIBRARY
Box E   Phone: (615) 576-1236
Oak Ridge, TN 37830   Ruth A. Green

UNIVERSITY OF TENNESSEE - ARBORETUM SOCIETY - LIBRARY
Univ. of Tenn. Experiment Station & Arboretum
901 Kerr Hollow Rd.   Phone: (615) 483-3571
Oak Ridge, TN 37830   Richard M. Evans, Supv., Forestry Sta.

ROCKY MOUNT HISTORICAL ASSOCIATION - LIBRARY
Route 2, Box 70   Phone: (615) 538-7396
Piney Flats, TN 37686   Cindy Penix, Libn.

HUGHES (Thomas) LIBRARY
Box 8   Phone: (615) 628-2441
Rugby, TN 37733   Barbara Stagg, Exec.Dir.

UNIVERSITY OF THE SOUTH - ARCHIVES
duPont Library   Phone: (615) 598-5931
Sewanee, TN 37375   Gertrude Mignery, Univ.Archv.

UNIVERSITY OF THE SOUTH - SCHOOL OF THEOLOGY LIBRARY
                                         Phone: (615) 598-5931
Sewanee, TN 37375   Thomas E. Camp, Libn.

U.S. NATL. PARK SERVICE - SHILOH NATL. MILITARY PARK - LIBRARY
Box 61   Phone: (901) 689-5275
Shiloh, TN 38376   George A. Reaves, Chf.Interp. & Rsrcs.Mgt.

UNIVERSITY OF TENNESSEE - SPACE INSTITUTE LIBRARY
                                         Phone: (615) 455-0631
Tullahoma, TN 37388   Helen B. Mason, Libn.

TEXAS

ABILENE REPORTER-NEWS - LIBRARY
Box 30   Phone: (915) 673-4271
Abilene, TX 79604   Anne Bell, Libn.

ABILENE STATE SCHOOL - SPECIAL LIBRARY
Box 451   Phone: (915) 692-4053
Abilene, TX 79604   Peggy G. Allen, Libn.

CRESCENT HEIGHTS BAPTIST CHURCH - LIBRARY †
1902 N. Mockingbird Ln.   Phone: (915) 677-3749
Abilene, TX 79603   Mrs. Bill Jonas, Dir. of Lib.Serv.

FIRST BAPTIST CHURCH - MEDIA LIBRARY
Box 85   Phone: (915) 673-5031
Abilene, TX 79604   Karin Richardson, Lib.Dir.

HENDRICK MEDICAL CENTER - MARY MEEK SCHOOL OF NURSING - MEEK
    LIBRARY EDUCATIONAL PROGRAMS
N. 19th & Hickory Sts.   Phone: (915) 677-3551
Abilene, TX 79601   Frances Brookreson, Libn.

UNITED METHODIST COMMISSION ON ARCHIVES & HISTORY -
    NORTHWEST TEXAS ANNUAL CONFERENCE - ARCHIVES
McMurry College
Jay-Rollins Library
Box 296   Phone: (915) 692-4130
Abilene, TX 79697   Jewell Posey, Archv.

AMARILLO COLLEGE - LEARNING RESOURCE CENTER - SPECIAL
    COLLECTIONS †
Box 447   Phone: (806) 376-5111
Amarillo, TX 79178   George E. Huffman, Dir.

AMARILLO GENEALOGICAL SOCIETY - LIBRARY
Amarillo Public Library
Box 2171   Phone: (806) 378-3054
Amarillo, TX 79189   Mary Kay Snell, Hd.Libn.

AMARILLO GLOBE-NEWS LIBRARY
900 Harrison   Phone: (806) 376-4488
Amarillo, TX 79166   Bobbie Fortenberry, Libn.

AMARILLO PUBLIC LIBRARY - LOCAL HISTORY COLLECTION
413 E. 4th
Box 2171   Phone: (806) 378-3050
Amarillo, TX 79189   Mary Kay Snell, Libn.

DIOCESE OF AMARILLO - DIOCESAN ARCHIVES
1800 N. Spring St.
Box 5644   Phone: (806) 383-2243
Amarillo, TX 79107   Sr. Charles Marie Forster, Archv.

M.P.K. OMEGA COMPANY - B.O.T.I. SPECIAL RESEARCH COLLECTION *
3615 Carson   Phone: (806) 355-9369
Amarillo, TX 79109   Jacques Cantrell, Libn.

M.P.K. OMEGA COMPANY - BIOSCIENCE LIBRARY *
3615 Carson   Phone: (806) 355-9369
Amarillo, TX 79109   Jacques Cantrell, Corp.Libn.

MASON & HANGER-SILAS MASON COMPANY, INC. - PANTEX PLANT -
    TECHNICAL LIBRARY
Box 30020   Phone: (806) 381-3547
Amarillo, TX 79177   Sue Sutphin, Tech.Libn.

SOUTHWESTERN PUBLIC SERVICE COMPANY - LIBRARY
Box 1261   Phone: (806) 378-2741
Amarillo, TX 79170   Gloria Branham, Libn.

TEXAS STATE - COURT OF APPEALS - 7TH SUPREME JUDICIAL DISTRICT
    AND POTTER COUNTY - LAW LIBRARY
Potter County Courthouse   Phone: (806) 379-2470
Amarillo, TX 79101   Janis N. Thorne, Law Libn.

TEXAS STATE TECHNICAL INSTITUTE, MID-CONTINENT CAMPUS -
    LIBRARY
Box 11117   Phone: (806) 335-2316
Amarillo, TX 79111   Cynthia Sadler, Hd.Libn.

U.S. VETERANS ADMINISTRATION (TX-Amarillo) - HOSPITAL LIBRARY
                                         Phone: (806) 355-9703
Amarillo, TX 79106   Cheryl A. Latham, Chf., Lib.Serv.

ARLINGTON BAPTIST COLLEGE - EARL K. OLDHAM LIBRARY
3001 W. Division   Phone: (817) 461-8741
Arlington, TX 76012   Sandra J. Tanner, Libn.

BAUDER FASHION COLLEGE - LIBRARY
508 S. Center St.   Phone: (817) 277-6666
Arlington, TX 76010   Ronald L. Tester, Libn.

COMPUTER AIDED MANUFACTURING-INTERNATIONAL, INC. (CAM-I) - LIBRARY
611 Ryan Plaza Dr., Suite 1107
Arlington, TX 76011
Phone: (817) 860-1654
Joanne E. Cruz, Lib.Coord.

JET RESEARCH CENTER, INC. - TECHNICAL INFORMATION AND SCIENCE LIBRARY
Box 246
Arlington, TX 76010
Phone: (817) 483-0933
Karan Mathes, Engr.Sec.

NORTH CENTRAL TEXAS COUNCIL OF GOVERNMENTS - REGIONAL INFORMATION SERVICE CENTER *
Drawer COG
1201 N. Watson Rd., Suite 270
Arlington, TX 76011
Phone: (817) 640-3300
Teri S. Wiseman

SURGIKOS - TECHNICAL INFORMATION CENTER
2500 Arbrook Blvd.
Box 130
Arlington, TX 76010
Phone: (817) 465-3141
W.B. Scroggs, Tech.Info.Coord.

UNIVERSITY OF TEXAS, ARLINGTON - LIBRARY - DIVISION OF SPECIAL COLLECTIONS AND ARCHIVES
Box 19497
Arlington, TX 76019
Phone: (817) 273-3393
Dr. Charles C. Colley, Dir.

AUSTIN AMERICAN STATESMAN - LIBRARY
Box 670
Austin, TX 78767
Phone: (512) 445-3676
Karen Anderson, Hd.Libn.

AUSTIN COMMUNITY COLLEGE - HEALTH SCIENCES LIBRARY
Box 2285
Austin, TX 78768
Phone: (512) 495-7054
Margaret Peloquin, Med.Libn.

AUSTIN PRESBYTERIAN THEOLOGICAL SEMINARY - STITT LIBRARY
106 W. 27th St.
Austin, TX 78705
Phone: (512) 472-6736
Calvin Klemt, Libn.

AUSTIN PUBLIC LIBRARY - AUSTIN HISTORY CENTER
810 Guadalupe
Austin, TX 78701
Phone: (512) 472-5433
Audray Bateman, Cur.

AUSTIN STATE HOSPITAL - STAFF LIBRARY
4110 Guadalupe St.
Austin, TX 78751
Phone: (512) 452-0381
Nancy H. Dobson, Libn.

CHRIST SEMINARY - SEMINEX LIBRARY
c/o Episcopal Theological Seminary
of the Southwest
Box 2243
Austin, TX 78768
Lucille Hager, Dir.

CITE RESOURCE CENTER
211 E. 7th St.
Southwest Tower
Austin, TX 78701
Phone: (512) 476-6861
Jan B. Anderson, Mgr.

EPISCOPAL THEOLOGICAL SEMINARY OF THE SOUTHWEST - LIBRARY
Box 2247
Austin, TX 78768
Phone: (512) 472-4134
Harold H. Booher, Libn.

IBM CORPORATION - SITE TECHNICAL LIBRARY/INFORMATION CENTER
11400 Burnet Rd., Dept. 449 045-3
Austin, TX 78758
Maye A. Bartlett, Libn.

INTERNATIONAL OIL SCOUTS ASSOCIATION - LIBRARY
Box 2121
Austin, TX 78768
Phone: (512) 472-3357
Barbara Lockstedt, Mgr.

MOTOROLA, INC. - MOS INTEGRATED CIRCUITS GROUP - INFORMATION CENTER
3501 Ed Bluestein Blvd.
Austin, TX 78721
Phone: (512) 928-6089
Thomas Fairbrother, Dir., Info.Serv.

NEY (Elisabet) MUSEUM - LIBRARY
304 E. 44th
Austin, TX 78751
Phone: (512) 458-2255
Lynn L. Lichtenfels, Cur.

PROTESTANT EPISCOPAL CHURCH - ARCHIVES
Box 2247
Austin, TX 78768
Phone: (512) 472-6816
Dr. Virginia Nelle Bellamy, Archv.

PUBLIC UTILITY COMMISSION OF TEXAS - LIBRARY
7800 Shoal Creek Blvd.
Austin, TX 78757
Phone: (512) 458-0251
Martha M. Bartow, Hd.Libn.

RADIAN CORPORATION - LIBRARY
8500 Shoal Creek Blvd.
Box 9948
Austin, TX 78766
Phone: (512) 454-4797
Barbara J. Maxey, Sr.Libn.

SMALL, CRAIG & WERKENTHIN - LIBRARY
2500 Interfirst Tower
Austin, TX 78701
Phone: (512) 472-8355
Candice Cortes Kennington, Libn.

SOCIETY OF SEPARATIONISTS - CHARLES E. STEVENS AMERICAN ATHEIST LIBRARY AND ARCHIVES INC.
2210 Hancock Dr.
Austin, TX 78756
Phone: (512) 458-1244
R. Murray-O'Hair, Dir.

TEXACO CHEMICAL COMPANY, INC. - TECHNICAL LITERATURE SECTION
Box 15730
Austin, TX 78761
Phone: (512) 459-6543
Mary E. Reese, Sr.Res.Libn.

TEXAS ADVISORY COMMISSION ON INTERGOVERNMENTAL RELATIONS - INFORMATION CENTER
Box 13206
Austin, TX 78711
Phone: (512) 475-3728
Catherine K. Harris, Libn.

TEXAS CATHOLIC HISTORICAL SOCIETY - CATHOLIC ARCHIVES OF TEXAS
Capitol Sta., Box 13327
Austin, TX 78711
Phone: (512) 476-4888
Sr. M. Dolores Kasner, O.P., Dir.

TEXAS EDUCATION AGENCY - RESOURCE CENTER LIBRARY
201 E. 11th St.
Austin, TX 78701
Phone: (512) 834-4070
Linda Kemp, Libn.

TEXAS INSTRUMENTS, INC. - DATA SYSTEMS GROUP - SITE LIBRARY †
Box 2909, MS 2146
Austin, TX 78769
Phone: (512) 250-7421
James R. Neaves, Mgr., Site Lib.

TEXAS MEDICAL ASSOCIATION - MEMORIAL LIBRARY
1801 Lamar Blvd.
Austin, TX 78701
Phone: (512) 477-6704
Betty Afflerbach, Lib.Dir.

TEXAS MEMORIAL MUSEUM - LIBRARY †
24th & Trinity
Austin, TX 78705
Phone: (512) 471-1604
Terry Lee Morse, Libn.

TEXAS MUNICIPAL LEAGUE - LIBRARY
1020 Southwest Tower
Austin, TX 78701
Phone: (512) 478-6601
Ted Willis, Exec.Dir.

TEXAS RESEARCH LEAGUE - LIBRARY
1117 Red River
Austin, TX 78701
Phone: (512) 472-3127
Claire Oxley, Res.Libn.

TEXAS STATE AERONAUTICS COMMISSION - LIBRARY & INFORMATION CENTER
Capitol Sta., Box 12607
Austin, TX 78711
Phone: (512) 476-9262
Nonie Mitchel, Libn.

TEXAS STATE AIR CONTROL BOARD - LIBRARY
6330 Hwy. 290 E.
Austin, TX 78723
Phone: (512) 451-5711
Kerry Williams, Libn.

TEXAS STATE BUREAU OF ECONOMIC GEOLOGY - WELL SAMPLE AND CORE LIBRARY
Balcones Research Center
10100 Burnet Rd.
Austin, TX 78758-4497
Phone: (512) 835-3042
George Donaldson, Cur.

TEXAS STATE - COURT OF APPEALS - 3RD SUPREME JUDICIAL DISTRICT - LAW LIBRARY
Capitol Sta., Box 12547
Austin, TX 78711
Phone: (512) 475-2441

TEXAS STATE DEPARTMENT OF AGRICULTURE - LIBRARY
Stephen F. Austin Bldg., Rm. 915
Box 12847   Phone: (512) 475-6467
Austin, TX 78711   Virginia Hall, Libn.

TEXAS STATE DEPARTMENT OF HEALTH - LIBRARY
1100 W. 49th St.   Phone: (512) 458-7559
Austin, TX 78756   John Burlinson, Libn.

TEXAS STATE DEPARTMENT OF HUMAN RESOURCES - LIBRARY
Box 2960   Phone: (512) 458-8568
Austin, TX 78769   Diana Boardman Houston, Libn.

TEXAS STATE DEPARTMENT OF MENTAL HEALTH & MENTAL
   RETARDATION - CENTRAL OFFICE LIBRARY
Box 12668   Phone: (512) 465-4621
Austin, TX 78711   Becky S. Renfro, Libn.

TEXAS STATE DEPARTMENT OF WATER RESOURCES - WATER RESOURCES
   RESEARCH LIBRARY
Stephen F. Austin Bldg., Rm. 511
Capitol Sta., Box 13087   Phone: (512) 475-3781
Austin, TX 78711   Sylvia Von Fange, Hd.Libn.

TEXAS STATE EMPLOYMENT COMMISSION - TEC LIBRARY
15th & Congress   Phone: (512) 397-4987
Austin, TX 78778   Kaye Hanson, Libn.

TEXAS STATE INDUSTRIAL COMMISSION - RESEARCH LIBRARY
Capitol Sta., Box 12728   Phone: (512) 472-5059
Austin, TX 78711   Laura Koenig, Libn.

TEXAS STATE LAW LIBRARY
Supreme Court Bldg.
Box 12367   Phone: (512) 475-3807
Austin, TX 78711   James Hambleton, Dir.

TEXAS STATE LEGISLATIVE REFERENCE LIBRARY
Capitol Sta., Box 12488   Phone: (512) 475-4626
Austin, TX 78711   James R. Sanders, Dir.

TEXAS STATE LIBRARY
1201 Brazos
Capitol Sta., Box 12927   Phone: (512) 475-2996
Austin, TX 78711   Dr. Dorman H. Winfrey, Dir. & Libn.

TEXAS STATE LIBRARY - INFORMATION SERVICES DIVISION
Box 12927   Phone: (512) 475-2996
Austin, TX 78711   Allan S. Quinn, Div.Dir.

TEXAS STATE LIBRARY - LIBRARY SCIENCE COLLECTION
Box 12927   Phone: (512) 475-3564
Austin, TX 78711   Anne Ramos, Libn.

TEXAS STATE LIBRARY - REGIONAL HISTORICAL RESOURCES
   DEPOSITORIES & LOCAL RECORDS DIVISION
Box 12927   Phone: (512) 475-2449
Austin, TX 78711   Marilyn von Kohl, Dir.

TEXAS STATE LIBRARY - TEXAS ARCHIVES DIVISION
1201 Brazos St.
Box 12927   Phone: (512) 475-2445
Austin, TX 78711   Dr. David B. Gracy, II, Dir.

TEXAS STATE PARKS & WILDLIFE DEPARTMENT - LIBRARY
4200 Smith School Rd.   Phone: (512) 479-4960
Austin, TX 78744

TEXAS STATE - RAILROAD COMMISSION OF TEXAS - CENTRAL RECORDS
1124 South IH 35   Phone: (512) 445-1318
Austin, TX 78711   Mark Browning, Mgr.

TRACOR, INC. - TECHNICAL LIBRARY
6500 Tracor Ln.   Phone: (512) 926-2800
Austin, TX 78721   Sara Jane Lee, Libn.

UNITED DAUGHTERS OF THE CONFEDERACY - TEXAS CONFEDERATE
   MUSEUM LIBRARY
112 E. 11th   Phone: (512) 472-2596
Austin, TX 78701   Florence Odom, Musm.Cur.

U.S. GEOLOGICAL SURVEY - LIBRARY
Federal Bldg.
300 E. 8th St.   Phone: (512) 482-5520
Austin, TX 78701   Patricia Tenner, Libn.

U.S. PRESIDENTIAL LIBRARIES - LYNDON B. JOHNSON LIBRARY
2313 Red River   Phone: (512) 482-5137
Austin, TX 78705   Harry J. Middleton, Dir.

UNIVERSITY OF TEXAS, AUSTIN - ARCHITECTURE & PLANNING LIBRARY
General Libraries, BTL 200   Phone: (512) 471-1844
Austin, TX 78712-7330   Eloise E. McDonald, Arch. & Plan.Libn.

UNIVERSITY OF TEXAS, AUSTIN - ASIAN COLLECTION
General Libraries, MAI 316   Phone: (512) 471-3135
Austin, TX 78712-7330   Kevin Lin, Libn.

UNIVERSITY OF TEXAS, AUSTIN - BENSON LATIN AMERICAN COLLECTION
General Libraries, SRH 1.108   Phone: (512) 471-3818
Austin, TX 78712-7330   Laura Gutierrez-Witt, Libn.

UNIVERSITY OF TEXAS, AUSTIN - BUREAU OF BUSINESS RESEARCH -
   INFORMATION SERVICES
Box 7459, University Sta.   Phone: (512) 471-1616
Austin, TX 78713   Rita J. Wright, Libn.

UNIVERSITY OF TEXAS, AUSTIN - BUREAU OF ECONOMIC GEOLOGY
   READING ROOM/DATA CENTER
Balcones Research Center
10100 Burnet Road
Austin, TX 78758-4497   Kay Forward, Mgr.

UNIVERSITY OF TEXAS, AUSTIN - CENTER FOR ENERGY STUDIES -
   ENERGY INFORMATION SERVICE
ENS 143   Phone: (512) 471-4946
Austin, TX 78712   Carol J. Wallin, Res.Assoc.

UNIVERSITY OF TEXAS, AUSTIN - CENTER FOR INTERCULTURAL STUDIES
   IN FOLKLORE AND ETHNOMUSICOLOGY - LIBRARY
Student Services Bldg., Rm. 3.106 Phone: (512) 471-1288
Austin, TX 78712   Dr. Richard Bauman, Dir.

UNIVERSITY OF TEXAS, AUSTIN - CENTER FOR TRANSPORTATION
   RESEARCH
ECJ 2.510   Phone: (512) 471-1414
Austin, TX 78712   Betty Hudman, Libn.

UNIVERSITY OF TEXAS, AUSTIN - CHEMISTRY LIBRARY
General Libraries, WEL 2.132   Phone: (512) 471-1303
Austin, TX 78712-7330   Aubrey E. Skinner, Libn.

UNIVERSITY OF TEXAS, AUSTIN - CLASSICS LIBRARY
General Libraries, WAG 1   Phone: (512) 471-5742
Austin, TX 78712-7330   Bernice M. Dawson, Lib.Asst.

UNIVERSITY OF TEXAS, AUSTIN - DOCUMENTS COLLECTION
General Libraries, PCL 2.400   Phone: (512) 471-3813
Austin, TX 78712-7330   Kathleen Eisenbeis, Libn.

UNIVERSITY OF TEXAS, AUSTIN - ENGINEERING LIBRARY
General Libraries, ECJ 1.300   Phone: (512) 471-1610
Austin, TX 78712-7330   Susan B. Ardis, Libn.

UNIVERSITY OF TEXAS, AUSTIN - EUGENE C. BARKER TEXAS HISTORY
   CENTER
General Libraries, SRH 2.109   Phone: (512) 471-5961
Austin, TX 78712-7330   Dr. Don E. Carleton, Hd.Libn./Archv.

UNIVERSITY OF TEXAS, AUSTIN - FILM LIBRARY
General Libraries, EDA G-12
Box W   Phone: (512) 471-3572
Austin, TX 78712-7448   Jane Hazelton, Media Coord.

UNIVERSITY OF TEXAS, AUSTIN - FINE ARTS LIBRARY
General Libraries, FAB 3.200   Phone: (512) 471-4777
Austin, TX 78712-7330   Carole Cable, Fine Arts Libn.

UNIVERSITY OF TEXAS, AUSTIN - GEOLOGY LIBRARY
General Libraries, GEO 302   Phone: (512) 471-1257
Austin, TX 78712   Chestalene Pintozzi, Libn.

UNIVERSITY OF TEXAS, AUSTIN - HARRY RANSOM HUMANITIES
  RESEARCH CENTER
Box 7219   Phone: (512) 471-1833
Austin, TX 78712   Decherd Turner, Dir.

UNIVERSITY OF TEXAS, AUSTIN - HOGG FOUNDATION FOR MENTAL
  HEALTH - LIBRARY
W.C. Hogg Bldg., Rm. 301   Phone: (512) 471-5041
Austin, TX 78712   Anita Faubion, Libn.

UNIVERSITY OF TEXAS, AUSTIN - HUMANITIES RESEARCH CENTER -
  THEATRE ARTS COLLECTIONS
Box 7219   Phone: (512) 471-9122
Austin, TX 78712

UNIVERSITY OF TEXAS, AUSTIN - INSTITUTE FOR GEOPHYSICS - LIBRARY
4920 North IH 35
Austin, TX 78751   Josefa A. York, Libn.

UNIVERSITY OF TEXAS, AUSTIN - MAP COLLECTION
General Libraries, PCL 1.306   Phone: (512) 471-5944
Austin, TX 78712-7330   Dennis Dillon, Map Libn.

UNIVERSITY OF TEXAS, AUSTIN - MIDDLE EAST COLLECTION
General Libraries, MAI 316   Phone: (512) 471-4675
Austin, TX 78712-7330   Abazar Sepehri, Libn.

UNIVERSITY OF TEXAS, AUSTIN - NATURAL FIBERS INFORMATION
  CENTER *
University Sta., Box 8180   Phone: (512) 471-1063
Austin, TX 78712   Mary P. Green, Act.Dir.

UNIVERSITY OF TEXAS, AUSTIN - PHYSICS-MATHEMATICS-ASTRONOMY
  LIBRARY
General Libraries, RLM 4.200   Phone: (512) 471-7539
Austin, TX 78712-7330   John H. Sandy, Libn.

UNIVERSITY OF TEXAS, AUSTIN - POPULATION RESEARCH CENTER
  LIBRARY
1800 Main Bldg.   Phone: (512) 471-5514
Austin, TX 78712   Doreen S. Goyer, Dir., Lib. Core

UNIVERSITY OF TEXAS, AUSTIN - SCHOOL OF LAW - TARLTON LAW
  LIBRARY
727 E. 26th St.   Phone: (512) 471-7726
Austin, TX 78705   Roy M. Mersky, Dir. of Res.

UNIVERSITY OF TEXAS, AUSTIN - SCIENCE LIBRARY
General Libraries, MAI 220   Phone: (512) 471-1475
Austin, TX 78712-7330   Nancy Elder, Libn.

UNIVERSITY OF TEXAS, AUSTIN - WASSERMAN PUBLIC AFFAIRS LIBRARY
General Libraries
Sid Richardson Hall, 3.243   Phone: (512) 471-4486
Austin, TX 78712-7330   Olive Forbes, Hd.Libn.

EXXON CHEMICAL AMERICAS - TECHNICAL INFORMATION CENTER
Box 4004   Phone: (713) 425-1239
Baytown, TX 77522   Martha S. Fellabaum, Libn.

EXXON COMPANY, U.S.A. - REFINERY LIBRARY
Box 3950   Phone: (713) 425-4487
Baytown, TX 77522   Bethany Picard, Libn.

EXXON RESEARCH AND ENGINEERING COMPANY - LIBRARY
Box 4178   Phone: (713) 425-5100
Baytown, TX 77520   Geraldine Gieger, Res.Libn.

BAPTIST HOSPITAL OF SOUTHEAST TEXAS - MEDICAL LIBRARY *
Box 1591   Phone: (409) 839-5160
Beaumont, TX 77704   Deloris Blake, Med.Libn.

BEAUMONT ART MUSEUM - LIBRARY †
1111 9th St.   Phone: (409) 832-3432
Beaumont, TX 77702   Julie Redding, Asst.Cur. of Educ.

BEAUMONT ENTERPRISE & JOURNAL - LIBRARY *
380 Walnut
Box 3071   Phone: (409) 833-3311
Beaumont, TX 77704   Jeanne E. Houston, Libn.

BEAUMONT PUBLIC LIBRARY SYSTEM - TYRRELL HISTORICAL LIBRARY
695 Pearl St.
Box 3827   Phone: (409) 838-0780
Beaumont, TX 77704   Mabel Leyda, Libn.

DU PONT DE NEMOURS (E.I.) & COMPANY, INC. - POLYMER PRODUCTS
  LIBRARY
Hwy. 347
Box 3269   Phone: (409) 727-9606
Beaumont, TX 77704   Roberta L. Howard, Tech.Libn.

EAST TEXAS LEGAL SERVICES - LIBRARY
527 Forsythe   Phone: (409) 835-4971
Beaumont, TX 77701   Lana Caswell Garcia, Law Libn./Res.Spec.

GULF STATES UTILITIES COMPANY - CORPORATE LIBRARY
Box 2951   Phone: (409) 838-6631
Beaumont, TX 77704   Karen S. McConnell, Corp.Libn.

GULF STATES UTILITIES COMPANY - FINANCE LIBRARY
350 Pine St.   Phone: (409) 838-6631
Beaumont, TX 77701   Hal G. Tierney, Supv. of Adm.

GULF STATES UTILITIES COMPANY - LAW LIBRARY
350 Pine St.
Box 2951   Phone: (409) 838-6631
Beaumont, TX 77704   Barbara Penry, Legal Asst.

GULF STATES UTILITIES COMPANY - NUCLEAR LIBRARY
Box 2951   Phone: (409) 839-2811
Beaumont, TX 77704   Katherine N. Pfeiffer, Licensing Anl./Libn.

ST. ELIZABETH HOSPITAL - HEALTH SCIENCES LIBRARY †
2830 Calder Ave.
Box 5405   Phone: (409) 892-7171
Beaumont, TX 77702   Deborah West, Health Sci.Libn.

U.S. AIR FORCE BASE - BERGSTROM BASE LIBRARY
FI 4857   Phone: (512) 479-4100
Bergstrom AFB, TX 78743   Louise St. John, Base Libn.

AMBASSADOR COLLEGE - LIBRARY - SPECIAL COLLECTIONS
Box 111
Big Sandy, TX 75755   Luren E. Dickinson, Dir.

U.S. VETERANS ADMINISTRATION (TX-Big Spring) - HOSPITAL LIBRARY
2400 S. Gregg St.   Phone: (915) 263-7361
Big Spring, TX 79720   Donald D. Fortner

RAYBURN (Sam) FOUNDATION - SAM RAYBURN LIBRARY
                                                    Phone: (214) 583-2455
Bonham, TX 75418   H.G. Dulaney, Lib.Dir.

U.S. VETERANS ADMINISTRATION (TX-Bonham) - SAM RAYBURN
  MEMORIAL VETERANS CENTER MEDICAL LIBRARY
9th & Lipscomb Sts.   Phone: (214) 583-2111
Bonham, TX 75418   Dorothea C. Linn, Chf., Lib.Serv.

HUBER (J.M.) CORPORATION - RESEARCH LIBRARY
Box 2831   Phone: (806) 274-6331
Borger, TX 79007   Wanetca Reynolds, Libn.

BRAZOSPORT MUSEUM OF NATURAL SCIENCE - LIBRARY
400 College Dr.   Phone: (409) 265-7831
Brazosport, TX 77566

TEXAS BAPTIST HISTORICAL CENTER/MUSEUM - LIBRARY
Rt. 5
Box 222   Phone: (409) 836-5117
Brenham, TX 77833   Jesse E. Bigbee, Dir.

U.S. AIR FORCE - AEROSPACE MEDICAL DIVISION - SCHOOL OF
  AEROSPACE MEDICINE - STRUGHOLD AEROMEDICAL LIBRARY
                                                    Phone: (512) 536-3322
Brooks AFB, TX 78235   Fred W. Todd, Chf.Libn.

U.S. AIR FORCE - HUMAN RESOURCES LABORATORY - LIBRARY
Phone: (512) 536-2651
Brooks AFB, TX 78235   Orrine L. Woinowsk, Adm.Libn.

PANHANDLE-PLAINS HISTORICAL MUSEUM - RESEARCH CENTER
Wt. Sta., Box 967   Phone: (806) 655-7191
Canyon, TX 79016   Claire R. Kuehn, Archv./Libn.

WEST TEXAS STATE UNIVERSITY - CORNETTE LIBRARY - SPECIAL
    COLLECTIONS
W.T. Sta., Box 748   Phone: (806) 656-2761
Canyon, TX 79016   Dr. John G. Veenstra, Univ.Libn.

U.S. AIR FORCE BASE - CARSWELL BASE LIBRARY
FL 4689   Phone: (817) 735-5230
Carswell AFB, TX 76127   Christine R. Lain, Libn.

U.S. AIR FORCE HOSPITAL - MEDICAL LIBRARY (TX-Carswell AFB) *
Phone: (817) 735-7579
Carswell AFB, TX 76127   Jean Robbins, Med.Libn.

EAST TEXAS GENEALOGICAL ASSOCIATION - LIBRARY
4121 W. College St.
Carthage, TX 75633

NORTHWOOD INSTITUTE OF TEXAS - FREEDOM EDUCATION CENTER
Box 58   Phone: (214) 291-7466
Cedar Hill, TX 75104   James R. Bromley, Dir.

NORTHWOOD INSTITUTE OF TEXAS - LIBRARY
Box 58   Phone: (214) 291-1541
Cedar Hill, TX 75104   Jennifer Cope, Libn.

NORTHWOOD INSTITUTE OF TEXAS - ROSALIND KRESS HALEY LIBRARY
Box 58   Phone: (214) 291-7466
Cedar Hill, TX 75104   JoAnn Seguin, Registrar

ATLANTIC-RICHFIELD COMPANY - ARCO CHEMICAL COMPANY - LYONDELL
    PLANT LIBRARY
Box 777   Phone: (409) 452-8147
Channelview, TX 77530   Virginia Wood, Lib.Supv.

FOOD PROTEIN RESEARCH AND DEVELOPMENT CENTER - LIBRARY
Texas A & M University, F.E. Box 183
College Station, TX 77843

TEXAS A & M UNIVERSITY - ARCHIVES & MANUSCRIPTS COLLECTIONS
Sterling C. Evans Library   Phone: (409) 845-1815
College Station, TX 77843   Dr. Charles R. Schultz, Univ.Archv.

TEXAS A & M UNIVERSITY - DEPARTMENTS OF OCEANOGRAPHY AND
    METEOROLOGY - WORKING COLLECTION
Dept. of Oceanography   Phone: (409) 845-7327
College Station, TX 77843   Gloria Guffy, Resource Ctr.Supv.

TEXAS A & M UNIVERSITY - MAP DEPARTMENT
Sterling C. Evans Library   Phone: (409) 845-1024
College Station, TX 77843   Judy Rieke, Map Libn.

TEXAS A & M UNIVERSITY - MEDICAL SCIENCES LIBRARY
Veterinary Adm. Bldg., Rm. 101   Phone: (409) 845-7427
College Station, TX 77843   Virginia L. Algermissen, Dir.

TEXAS A & M UNIVERSITY - NAUTICAL ARCHAEOLOGY LIBRARY
Dept. of Anthropology   Phone: (409) 845-6398
College Station, TX 77843-4352   Vicki Reid, Libn.

TEXAS A & M UNIVERSITY - REFERENCE DIVISION
Sterling C. Evans Library   Phone: (409) 845-5741
College Station, TX 77843   Katherine M. Jackson, Hd., Ref.Div.

TEXAS A & M UNIVERSITY - SPECIAL COLLECTIONS DIVISION
Sterling C. Evans Library   Phone: (409) 845-1951
College Station, TX 77843   Donald A. Dyal, Hd., Spec.Coll.Div.

TEXAS A & M UNIVERSITY - TECHNICAL REPORTS DEPARTMENT
Sterling C. Evans Library   Phone: (409) 845-2551
College Station, TX 77843   Lisa Abbott, Tech.Rpts.Libn.

TEXAS A & M UNIVERSITY - THERMODYNAMICS RESEARCH CENTER
Texas Engineering Experiment Station   Phone: (409) 845-4940
College Station, TX 77843   Dr. Kenneth R. Hall, Dir.

TEXAS (State) FOREST SERVICE - LIBRARY
Texas A & M University   Phone: (409) 845-2641
College Station, TX 77843

AMERICAN NAME SOCIETY - PLACE NAME SURVEY OF THE UNITED
    STATES - LIBRARY
James Gilliam Gee Library
East Texas State University   Phone: (214) 886-5251
Commerce, TX 75428   Dr. Fred Tarpley, Natl.Dir.

EAST TEXAS STATE UNIVERSITY - JAMES GILLIAM GEE LIBRARY
East Texas Sta.   Phone: (214) 886-5717
Commerce, TX 75428   Mary E. Cook, Dir. of Lib.Serv.

EAST TEXAS STATE UNIVERSITY - ORAL HISTORY PROGRAM
James Gilliam Gee Library
East Texas Sta.   Phone: (214) 886-5738
Commerce, TX 75428   James Conrad, Coord.

ART MUSEUM OF SOUTH TEXAS - LIBRARY
1902 N. Shoreline   Phone: (512) 884-3844
Corpus Christi, TX 78401   Margaret Kadoyama, Asst.Cur.

CELANESE CORPORATION - CELANESE CHEMICAL COMPANY, INC. -
    TECHNICAL CENTER - LIBRARY †
Box 9077   Phone: (512) 241-2343
Corpus Christi, TX 78408   Betty Goodridge, Info.Ctr.Coord.

CORPUS CHRISTI CALLER-TIMES - LIBRARY
Box 9136   Phone: (512) 884-2011
Corpus Christi, TX 78469-9136   Margaret J. Neu, Hd.Libn.

CORPUS CHRISTI MUSEUM - STAFF LIBRARY
1900 N. Chaparral   Phone: (512) 883-2862
Corpus Christi, TX 78401   Aalbert Heine, Musm.Dir.

DEL MAR COLLEGE - MUSIC LIBRARY
Music Dept.   Phone: (512) 881-6386
Corpus Christi, TX 78404   Ralph Thibodeau, Prof. of Music/Libn.

DRISCOLL FOUNDATION CHILDREN'S HOSPITAL - MEDICAL LIBRARY
3533 Alameda
Box 6530   Phone: (512) 854-5341
Corpus Christi, TX 78411   Becky Melton, Med.Libn.

MEMORIAL MEDICAL CENTER - HEALTH SCIENCES LIBRARY *
2606 Hospital Blvd.
Box 5280   Phone: (512) 881-4197
Corpus Christi, TX 78405   Charles A. Brown, Dir. of Lib.

PPG INDUSTRIES, INC. - CHEMICAL DIVISION - RESEARCH LIBRARY *
Box 4026   Phone: (512) 883-4301
Corpus Christi, TX 78408   Ivan C. Trombley, Res.Libn.

SPOHN HOSPITAL - MEDICAL LIBRARY
600 Elizabeth St.   Phone: (512) 881-3261
Corpus Christi, TX 78404   Linda Neargardner-Shake, Med.Libn.

U.S. NAVY - NAVAL AIR STATION (TX-Corpus Christi) - LIBRARY
Station Library, Bldg. 5   Phone: (512) 939-3574
Corpus Christi, TX 78419   Eugene V. Lopez, Libn.

U.S. NAVY - NAVAL HOSPITAL (TX-Corpus Christi) - MEDICAL LIBRARY
Phone: (512) 939-3863
Corpus Christi, TX 78419   Dorothy Reichenstein, Med.Libn.

CROSBY COUNTY PIONEER MEMORIAL - CCPM HISTORICAL COLLECTION/
    MUSEUM LIBRARY
101 Main St.
Box 386   Phone: (806) 675-2331
Crosbyton, TX 79322   Verna Anne Wheeler, Exec.Dir.

AKIN, GUMP, STRAUSS, HAUER & FELD LAW LIBRARY
2800 Republic Bank Bldg.   Phone: (214) 655-2800
Dallas, TX 75201   Joan Hass, Hd.Libn.

AMERICAN HEART ASSOCIATION - LIBRARY/RECORDS CENTER
7320 Greenville Ave.   Phone: (214) 750-5408
Dallas, TX 75231   Barbara Arie Lightfoot, Mgr.

ATLANTIC-RICHFIELD COMPANY - ARCO OIL AND GAS COMPANY -
   RESEARCH & DEVELOPMENT TECHNICAL INFORMATION CENTER
Box 2819   Phone: (214) 422-6965
Dallas, TX 75221   Inge Loncaric, Supv.

BAYLOR UNIVERSITY, DALLAS - LIBRARY
3402 Gaston Ave.   Phone: (214) 820-2372
Dallas, TX 75246   Marcel C. Carol, Libn.

BISHOP COLLEGE - ZALE LIBRARY - BANKS AFRO-AMERICAN HERITAGE
   COLLECTION
3837 Simpson-Stuart Rd.   Phone: (214) 372-8734
Dallas, TX 75241   E.K. Berg, Dir. of Pub.Serv.

BURGESS INDUSTRIES - ENGINEERING LIBRARY †
8101 John W. Carpenter Fwy.   Phone: (214) 631-1410
Dallas, TX 75247   Ernest L. Black, Mgr.

CALTEX PETROLEUM CORPORATION - CORPORATE LIBRARY †
Box 61500   Phone: (214) 830-1006
Dallas, TX 75261   Muriel H. Hummel, Libn.

CAMPBELL TAGGART, INC. - RESEARCH DIVISION - LIBRARY
3401 Haggar Way   Phone: (214) 358-9211
Dallas, TX 75222   Sue Hammond, Libn.

CARRINGTON, COLEMAN, SLOMAN & BLUMENTHAL - LIBRARY
2500 South Tower
Plaza of the Americas   Phone: (214) 741-2121
Dallas, TX 75201   Sue H. Johnson, Libn.

CHURCH OF THE INCARNATION - MARMION LIBRARY
3966 McKinney Ave.   Phone: (214) 521-5101
Dallas, TX 75204-2099   Willa H. Johnson, Libn.

CITIZENS ASSOCIATION FOR SOUND ENERGY (CASE) - LIBRARY *
Box 4123   Phone: (214) 946-9446
Dallas, TX 75208   Juanita Ellis, Pres.

CORE LABORATORIES, INC. - LIBRARY
7501 Stemmons
Box 47547   Phone: (214) 631-8270
Dallas, TX 75247   Allison C.V. Owen, Libn.

CRISWELL CENTER FOR BIBLICAL STUDIES - LIBRARY †
525 N. Ervay, 10th Fl.   Phone: (214) 742-3111
Dallas, TX 75201   John A. Burns, Libn.

DALLAS BIBLE COLLEGE - GOULD MEMORIAL LIBRARY
8733 LaPrada Dr.   Phone: (214) 328-7171
Dallas, TX 75228   John R. Stanley, Libn.

DALLAS CHRISTIAN COLLEGE - LIBRARY
2700 Christian Pkwy.   Phone: (214) 241-3371
Dallas, TX 75234   Richard Hathaway, Libn.

DALLAS CITY SECRETARY - DALLAS CITY ARCHIVES
City Hall   Phone: (214) 670-3741
Dallas, TX 75201   Robert S. Sloan, City Sec.

DALLAS CIVIC GARDEN CENTER - HORTICULTURE LIBRARY
Fair Park
First at Martin Luther King Blvd.   Phone: (214) 428-7476
Dallas, TX 75226   Susan Miller, Libn.

DALLAS COUNTY LAW LIBRARY
Government Ctr. Bldg., 2nd Fl.   Phone: (214) 749-8481
Dallas, TX 75202   Lawrence E. Hood, Dir.

DALLAS HISTORICAL SOCIETY - RESEARCH CENTER
Hall of State, Fair Park
Box 26038   Phone: (214) 421-5136
Dallas, TX 75226   Casey Edward Greene, Dir., Lib./Archv.

DALLAS MORNING NEWS - REFERENCE DEPARTMENT
Communications Center   Phone: (214) 745-8302
Dallas, TX 75265   Judy Metcalf, Ref.Ed.

DALLAS MUSEUM OF ARTS - REFERENCE LIBRARY
1717 N. Harwood   Phone: (214) 421-4187
Dallas, TX 75201   Donna E. Rhein, Dir.

DALLAS POWER AND LIGHT COMPANY - RESEARCH LIBRARY †
1506 Commerce St., Rm. 1801   Phone: (214) 698-7000
Dallas, TX 75201   Mrs. I. Naraine, Libn.

DALLAS PUBLIC LIBRARY - BUSINESS AND TECHNOLOGY DIVISION
1515 Young St.   Phone: (214) 749-4100
Dallas, TX 75201   Sarabeth Allen, Div.Mgr.

DALLAS PUBLIC LIBRARY - FILM SERVICE
1515 Young St.   Phone: (214) 749-4474
Dallas, TX 75201   Julie Travis, Mgr.

DALLAS PUBLIC LIBRARY - FINE ARTS DIVISION
1515 Young St.   Phone: (214) 749-4236
Dallas, TX 75201   Jane Holahan, Div.Hd.

DALLAS PUBLIC LIBRARY - FINE BOOKS DIVISION
1515 Young St.   Phone: (214) 749-4154
Dallas, TX 75201   Marvin H. Stone, Fine Bks.Libn.

DALLAS PUBLIC LIBRARY - GENEALOGY COLLECTION
1515 Young St.   Phone: (214) 749-4129
Dallas, TX 75201   Lloyd DeWitt Bockstruck, Div.Hd.

DALLAS PUBLIC LIBRARY - GENERAL REFERENCE DEPARTMENT
1515 Young St.   Phone: (214) 749-4321
Dallas, TX 75201   Marsha Fleckenstein, Mgr.

DALLAS PUBLIC LIBRARY - GOVERNMENT PUBLICATIONS DIVISION
1515 Young St.   Phone: (214) 749-4176
Dallas, TX 75201   Frank Lee, Mgr.

DALLAS PUBLIC LIBRARY - HISTORY AND SOCIAL SCIENCES DIVISION
1515 Young St.   Phone: (214) 749-4123
Dallas, TX 75201   Thomas M. Bogie, Mgr.

DALLAS PUBLIC LIBRARY - HUMANITIES DIVISION
1515 Young St.   Phone: (214) 749-4100
Dallas, TX 75201   Frances Bell, Div.Hd.

DALLAS PUBLIC LIBRARY - TEXAS/DALLAS HISTORY AND ARCHIVES
   DIVISION
1515 Young St.   Phone: (214) 749-4151
Dallas, TX 75201   Wayne Gray, Mgr.

DALLAS PUBLIC LIBRARY - URBAN INFORMATION CENTER
1515 Young St.   Phone: (214) 749-4170
Dallas, TX 75201   Mary Tod, Mgr.

DALLAS THEOLOGICAL SEMINARY - MOSHER LIBRARY
3909 Swiss Ave.   Phone: (214) 824-3094
Dallas, TX 75204   Dr. John A. Witmer, Dir.

DALLAS TIMES-HERALD - LIBRARY
1101 Pacific St.
Box 5445   Phone: (214) 744-6240
Dallas, TX 75202   Elaine B. Walden, Libn.

DEGOLYER AND MAC NAUGHTON - LIBRARY
One Energy Sq.   Phone: (214) 368-6391
Dallas, TX 75206   Eleanor Maclay, Libn.

E-SYSTEMS, INC. - GARLAND DIVISION - TECHNICAL LIBRARY
Box 226118   Phone: (214) 272-0515
Dallas, TX 75266   Charlene Morris, Tech.Libn.

EAST DALLAS CHRISTIAN CHURCH - HAGGARD MEMORIAL LIBRARY †
629 N. Peak St.   Phone: (214) 542-8441
Dallas, TX 75246   Mrs. Alfred C. Grosse, Lib.Chm.

EL CENTRO JOBS TRAINING CENTER - LEARNING RESOURCE CENTER
1403 Corinth
Dallas, TX 75215   Cynthia A. Teter, Lrng.Ctr.Instr.

ENVIRONMENTAL PROTECTION AGENCY - REGION VI LIBRARY †
First International Bldg.
1201 Elm St.   Phone: (214) 767-7341
Dallas, TX 75270

FEDERAL RESERVE BANK OF DALLAS - RESEARCH LIBRARY
400 S. Akard St.   Phone: (214) 651-6392
Dallas, TX 75222   Jane B. Freeman, Sr.Libn.

FIRST BAPTIST CHURCH OF DALLAS - FIRST BAPTIST ACADEMY - GEORGE
   W. TRUETT MEMORIAL LIBRARY †
1707 San Jacinto   Phone: (214) 742-3111
Dallas, TX 75201   Mildred L. Lively, Dir. of Lib.Serv.

FORD, BACON & DAVIS, INC. - LIBRARY
Box 38209   Phone: (214) 238-6500
Dallas, TX 75238

FRITO-LAY, INC. - LIBRARY *
6400 Harry Hines
Box 35034   Phone: (214) 351-7298
Dallas, TX 75235   Rosemary Barrett, Libn.

FRITO-LAY, INC. - TECHNICAL INFORMATION CENTER
7929 Brookriver Dr.   Phone: (214) 689-1708
Dallas, TX 75247   Suzanne M. Ogden, Tech.Libn.

GEOLOGICAL INFORMATION LIBRARY OF DALLAS (GILD)
One Energy Sq., Suite 100
4925 Greenville Ave.   Phone: (214) 363-1078
Dallas, TX 75206   G. Frederick Shepherd, Dir.

GEOTRONICS LABORATORIES, INC. - LIBRARY †
1314 Cedar Hill Ave.   Phone: (214) 946-7573
Dallas, TX 75208

GRACE (W.R.) AND COMPANY - NATURAL RESOURCES GROUP -
   INFORMATION CENTER
3400 Interfirst Two   Phone: (214) 658-1030
Dallas, TX 75270   Mary Thomas Sullivan, Mgr.

HIGHLAND PARK PRESBYTERIAN CHURCH - MADELINE ROACH
   MEYERCORD LIBRARY
3821 University Blvd.   Phone: (214) 526-7457
Dallas, TX 75205   Mrs. David P. Smith, Chm.

HIGHLAND PARK UNITED METHODIST CHURCH - LIBRARY
3300 Mockingbird Ln.   Phone: (214) 521-3111
Dallas, TX 75205   Adele Ervine, Libn.

HUGHES & HILL - LIBRARY
1000 Mercantile Dallas Bldg.   Phone: (214) 651-0477
Dallas, TX 75201   Ann Jeter, Libn.

JOHNSON & SWANSON - LIBRARY
900 Jackson St.   Phone: (214) 746-7059
Dallas, TX 75202   Catherine Pennington, Law Libn.

JONES, DAY, REAVIS & POGUE - LAW LIBRARY
2001 Bryan Tower, Suite 2700   Phone: (214) 748-3939
Dallas, TX 75201   Edward E. Carraway, Hd.Libn.

LIFE PLANNING/HEALTH SERVICES - LIBRARY/MEDIA SERVICES
2727 Oaklawn, Suite 228   Phone: (214) 522-0290
Dallas, TX 75219   Martha Brewer, Dp.Dir.

LONE STAR GAS COMPANY - RESEARCH LIBRARY †
301 S. Harwood St.   Phone: (214) 741-3711
Dallas, TX 75201   Charlotte W. Vinson, Chf.Libn.

LTV AEROSPACE AND DEFENSE COMPANY - VOUGHT MISSILES AND
   ADVANCED PROGRAMS DIVISION - LIBRARY 3-58200
M.S. MSF-60
Box 225907   Phone: (214) 266-4660
Dallas, TX 75265   T.P. McGinty, Chf.Libn.

MARY KAY COSMETICS, INC. - TECHNICAL INFORMATION CENTER
1330 Regal Row   Phone: (214) 638-6750
Dallas, TX 75247   Susan M. Wilson, Tech.Info.Coord.

METHODIST HOSPITALS OF DALLAS - MEDICAL LIBRARY
301 W. Colorado   Phone: (214) 946-8181
Dallas, TX 75222   Mary J. Jarvis, Med.Libn.

MOBIL EXPLORATION AND PRODUCING SERVICES INC. - MEPSI LIBRARY
Box 900   Phone: (214) 658-4779
Dallas, TX 75221   Mary Lee Freeman, Libn.

MOBIL PIPE LINE COMPANY - ENGINEERING LIBRARY
Box 900   Phone: (214) 658-2039
Dallas, TX 75221   K.E. Anderson, Mgr. of Engr.

MOBIL RESEARCH & DEVELOPMENT CORPORATION - DALLAS RESEARCH
   DIVISION - LIBRARY
Box 819047   Phone: (214) 333-6111
Dallas, TX 75381   Ammarette Roberts, Mgr., Tech.Info.Serv.

MOBIL RESEARCH & DEVELOPMENT CORPORATION - OFFSHORE
   ENGINEERING INFORMATION CENTER †
Box 900   Phone: (214) 333-6312
Dallas, TX 75221   R.S. Thomson, Tech.Info.Spec.

MURRAY PROPERTIES COMPANY - RESOURCE CENTER †
5520 LBJ Fwy., Suite 600
Box 401650   Phone: (214) 386-9900
Dallas, TX 75240   Joan Davis, Rsrcs.Ctr.Mgr.

NORTHERN TELECOM, INC. - BUSINESS INFORMATION CENTER
1001 E. Arapaho Rd.   Phone: (214) 234-5300
Dallas, TX 75081

PEAT, MARWICK, MITCHELL & CO. - INFORMATION SERVICES
1601 Elm St., Suite 1400   Phone: (214) 747-8911
Dallas, TX 75201   Celia S. Ellingson, Info.Serv.Dir.

REPUBLICBANK CORPORATION - ECONOMIC RESEARCH LIBRARY
Box 222105   Phone: (214) 653-5807
Dallas, TX 75222   John W. Brewster, Economic Libn.

RICHLAND COLLEGE - EVERYWOMAN PROGRAM - ADULT RESOURCE
   CENTER
12800 Abrams Rd.   Phone: (214) 238-6034
Dallas, TX 75243   Jean Yale, Coord.

ROCKWELL INTERNATIONAL - ELECTRONICS OPERATIONS - DALLAS
   INFORMATION CENTER
Dallas Information Center 407-120   Phone: (214) 996-6022
Dallas, TX 75207   Wanda J. Fox, Supv.

ST. PAUL HOSPITAL - C.B. SACHER LIBRARY
5909 Harry Hines Blvd.   Phone: (214) 689-2390
Dallas, TX 75235   Barbara J. Miller, Dir.

SOUTHERN METHODIST UNIVERSITY - BRIDWELL LIBRARY - CENTER FOR
   METHODIST STUDIES
                                            Phone: (214) 692-2363
Dallas, TX 75275   Rev. Roger L. Loyd, Assoc.Libn.

SOUTHERN METHODIST UNIVERSITY - DEGOLYER LIBRARY - FIKES HALL
   OF SPECIAL COLLECTIONS
Central University Libraries, SMU Sta.   Phone: (214) 692-2253
Dallas, TX 75275   Clifton H. Jones, Dir.

SOUTHERN METHODIST UNIVERSITY - MC CORD THEATER COLLECTION
Fondren Library   Phone: (214) 692-2400
Dallas, TX 75275   Edyth Renshaw, Cur.

SOUTHERN METHODIST UNIVERSITY - PERKINS SCHOOL OF THEOLOGY -
   LIBRARY
Bridwell Library   Phone: (214) 692-3483
Dallas, TX 75275   Jerry D. Campbell, Libn.

SOUTHERN METHODIST UNIVERSITY - SCIENCE/ENGINEERING LIBRARY
                                            Phone: (214) 692-2276
Dallas, TX 75275   Devertt D. Bickston, Libn.

SOUTHERN METHODIST UNIVERSITY - UNDERWOOD LAW LIBRARY
Phone: (214) 692-3258
Dallas, TX 75275
Earl C. Borgeson, Libn.

SOUTHERN UNION COMPANY - LEGAL LIBRARY
InterFirst Two, Suite 1800
Phone: (214) 748-8511
Dallas, TX 75270

SOUTHERN UNION COMPANY - PLANNING RESEARCH LIBRARY
InterFirst Two, Suite 1800
Phone: (214) 748-8511
Dallas, TX 75270
Charles B. Woodard, Res.Libn.

SOUTHLAND CORPORATION - CORPORATE BUSINESS RESEARCH CENTER
2828 N. Haskell
Phone: (214) 828-7840
Dallas, TX 75204
Debra H. Marshall, Mgr.

SOUTHWEST MUSEUM OF SCIENCE & TECHNOLOGY/THE SCIENCE PLACE -
LIBRARY
Fair Park, Box 11158
Dallas, TX 75223

SUMMER INSTITUTE OF LINGUISTICS - DALLAS/NORMAN LIBRARY
7500 W. Camp Wisdom Rd.
Phone: (214) 298-3331
Dallas, TX 75236
Melinda L. Lyons, Hd.Libn.

TEMPLE EMANU-EL - ALEX F. WEISBERG LIBRARY
8500 Hillcrest
Phone: (214) 368-3613
Dallas, TX 75225
Donna Berliner, Libn.

TEXAS EMPLOYERS INSURANCE ASSOCIATION - ENGINEERING
INFORMATION CENTER
Box 2759
Phone: (214) 653-8100
Dallas, TX 75221
Gay Bethel, Info.Res.Spec.

TEXAS INSTRUMENTS, INC. - INFORMATION SYSTEMS & SERVICES
LIBRARY
Box 226015, MS 3610
Phone: (214) 343-7954
Dallas, TX 75266
Cecilia Tung, Libn.

TEXAS INSTRUMENTS, INC. - NORTH BUILDING LIBRARY
Box 226015, MS 211
Phone: (214) 995-2803
Dallas, TX 75266
Frances Dort, Libn.

TEXAS INSTRUMENTS, INC. - RESEARCH BUILDING LIBRARY
Box 225936, MS 135
Phone: (214) 995-2407
Dallas, TX 75265
Olga Paradis, Libn.

TEXAS INSTRUMENTS, INC. - SEMICONDUCTOR BUILDING LIBRARY
Box 225012, MS 20
Phone: (214) 995-2511
Dallas, TX 75265
Kathy L. Nordhaus, Libn.

TEXAS MID-CONTINENT OIL & GAS ASSOCIATION - LIBRARY
United Bank Tower, Suite 500
400 W. 15th St.
Phone: (214) 478-6631
Dallas, TX 78701
Cheryl Stacy, Libn.

TEXAS SCOTTISH RITE HOSPITAL FOR CRIPPLED CHILDREN - BRANDON
CARRELL, M.D., MEDICAL LIBRARY
2222 Welborn St.
Phone: (214) 521-3168
Dallas, TX 75219-0567
Mary Peters, Med.Libn.

TEXAS STATE - COURT OF APPEALS - 5TH SUPREME JUDICIAL DISTRICT -
LAW LIBRARY ∗
Dallas County Courthouse
Phone: (214) 749-8011
Dallas, TX 75202

TEXAS WOMAN'S UNIVERSITY, DALLAS CENTER - F.W. AND BESSIE DYE
MEMORIAL LIBRARY
1810 Inwood Rd.
Phone: (214) 638-0084
Dallas, TX 75235
M. Virginia Kimzey, Coord., Health Sci.Lib.

THOMPSON & KNIGHT - LIBRARY
3300 First City Ctr.
Phone: (214) 655-7568
Dallas, TX 75201
Jane Ward, Libn.

TRACY-LOCKE/BBDO ADVERTISING - INFORMATION SERVICES
DEPARTMENT
Texas Commerce Bank Tower
Plaza of the Americas
Box 50129
Phone: (214) 742-3131
Dallas, TX 75250
Ellen Shapley, Mgr., Info.Serv.

TRINITY UNIVERSITY - DALLAS THEATER CENTER LIBRARY
3636 Turtle Creek Blvd.
Dallas, TX 75219

U.S. ARMY AND AIR FORCE EXCHANGE SERVICE - CENTRAL LIBRARY AD-M
Phone: (214) 330-3337
Dallas, TX 75222
Linda McVey, Lib.Tech.

U.S. ARMY - CORPS OF ENGINEERS - SOUTHWESTERN DIVISION -
LIBRARY
1114 Commerce St.
Phone: (214) 767-2325
Dallas, TX 75242
Maxine C. Smith, Libn.

U.S. BUREAU OF THE CENSUS - INFORMATION SERVICES PROGRAM -
DALLAS REGIONAL OFFICE - LIBRARY
Earle Caball Federal Bldg.
1100 Commerce St.
Phone: (214) 767-0625
Dallas, TX 75242
Brooks Sitton, Coord.

U.S. DEPT. OF COMMERCE - INTERNATIONAL TRADE ADMINISTRATION -
DALLAS DISTRICT OFFICE LIBRARY
1110 Commerce St., Rm. 7A5
Phone: (214) 767-0542
Dallas, TX 75242
C. Carmon Stiles, Dir.

U.S. VETERANS ADMINISTRATION (TX-Dallas) - MEDICAL CENTER LIBRARY
(142D)
4500 S. Lancaster Rd.
Phone: (214) 372-7025
Dallas, TX 75080
Barbara W. Huckins, Chf., Lib.Serv.

UNIVERSITY OF TEXAS, DALLAS - CALLIER CENTER FOR
COMMUNICATIONS DISORDERS - LIBRARY
1966 Inwood Rd.
Phone: (214) 783-3143
Dallas, TX 75235
Edward James Earle, Libn.

UNIVERSITY OF TEXAS HEALTH SCIENCE CENTER, DALLAS - LIBRARY
5323 Harry Hines Blvd.
Phone: (214) 688-3368
Dallas, TX 75235
Jean K. Miller, Dir.

WADLEY INSTITUTES OF MOLECULAR MEDICINE - RESEARCH INSTITUTE
LIBRARY †
9000 Harry Hines Blvd.
Phone: (214) 351-8648
Dallas, TX 75235
Kathryn Manning, Libn.

XEROX CORPORATION - INFORMATION PRODUCTS DIVISION - LIBRARY
SERVICES
1341 W. Mockingbird Ln.
Phone: (214) 689-6027
Dallas, TX 75247
Marjorie A. Henderson, Mgr., Lib.Serv.

AMERICAN AIRLINES, INC. - CORPORATE LIBRARY
Box 619616
Phone: (817) 355-1464
Dallas-Fort Worth Airport, TX 75261-9616
Christine Dobson, Corp.Libn.

WISE COUNTY HISTORICAL COMMISSION ARCHIVE
1602 S. College
Box 427
Phone: (817) 627-5586
Decatur, TX 76234
Rosalie Gregg, Exec.Dir.

SHELL OIL COMPANY - DEER PARK MANUFACTURING COMPLEX - LIBRARY
SERVICES †
Box 999
Phone: (713) 476-6565
Deer Park, TX 77536
Julia C. Smith, Libn.

AMERICAN DONKEY AND MULE SOCIETY - INFORMATION OFFICE
Rte. 5, Box 65
Phone: (817) 382-6845
Denton, TX 76201
Betsy Hutchins, Info.Off.

NORTH TEXAS STATE UNIVERSITY LIBRARIES - MEDIA LIBRARY
Box 12898
Phone: (817) 565-2691
Denton, TX 76203
George D. Mitchell, III, Media Lib.Dir.

NORTH TEXAS STATE UNIVERSITY LIBRARIES - ORAL HISTORY
COLLECTION
University Sta., Box 13734
Phone: (817) 788-2558
Denton, TX 76203
Dr. Ronald E. Marcello, Coord.

NORTH TEXAS STATE UNIVERSITY LIBRARIES - RARE BOOK ROOM
North Texas Sta.
Box 5188
Phone: (817) 788-2411
Denton, TX 76203
Dr. Kenneth Lavender, Univ.Bibliog.

TEXAS WOMAN'S UNIVERSITY - CENTER FOR THE STUDY OF LEARNING -
  LIBRARY
Box 11300   Phone: (817) 382-3522
Denton, TX 76204   Dr. Mario C. Di Nello, Dir.

TEXAS WOMAN'S UNIVERSITY - LIBRARY SCIENCE LIBRARY
School of Library Science   Phone: (817) 387-2418
Denton, TX 76204   James L. Thomas, Libn.

TEXAS WOMAN'S UNIVERSITY - LIBRARY SCIENCE LIBRARY - PROYECTO
  LEER
School of Library Science
Denton, TX 76204   Ali Mattei-Mejia, Coord.

TEXAS WOMAN'S UNIVERSITY - SPECIAL COLLECTIONS
Bralley Memorial Library
TWU Sta., Box 23715   Phone: (817) 566-6415
Denton, TX 76204   Metta Nicewarner, Spec.Coll.Libn.

U.S. AIR FORCE BASE - DYESS BASE LIBRARY
FL 4661   Phone: (915) 696-2618
Dyess AFB, TX 79607   Edith V. Roebuck, Libn.

TEXAS STATE - COURT OF APPEALS - 11TH SUPREME JUDICIAL DISTRICT
  - LAW LIBRARY
                                      Phone: (817) 629-2638
Eastland, TX 76448

HIDALGO COUNTY LAW LIBRARY †
Courthouse, Box 215   Phone: (512) 383-2751
Edinburg, TX 78539   Aurora Rutledge, Libn.

CHURCH OF JESUS CHRIST OF LATTER-DAY SAINTS - EL PASO BRANCH
  GENEALOGICAL LIBRARY
3651 Douglas Ave.   Phone: (915) 565-9711
El Paso, TX 79903   H. Leroy Taylor, Libn.

EL PASO COUNTY LAW LIBRARY
508 City-County Bldg.
500 San Antonio St.   Phone: (915) 543-2917
El Paso, TX 79901   June D. Walker, Libn.

EL PASO HERALD-POST - LIBRARY
401 Mills St.   Phone: (915) 747-6950
El Paso, TX 79999   Trinidad B. Acosta, Libn.

EL PASO NATURAL GAS COMPANY - TECHNICAL INFORMATION CENTER
Box 1492   Phone: (915) 541-3085
El Paso, TX 79978   Anne S. Wise, Coord.

EL PASO PUBLIC LIBRARY - GENEALOGY SECTION
501 N. Oregon St.   Phone: (915) 541-4873
El Paso, TX 79901   Janet Fisher, Genealogy Libn.

EL PASO PUBLIC LIBRARY - SOUTHWEST RESEARCH COLLECTION
501 N. Oregon St.   Phone: (915) 543-3815
El Paso, TX 79901   Mary A. Sarber, Hd., S.W. Coll.

FIRST PRESBYTERIAN CHURCH - LIBRARY *
1340 Murchison Dr.   Phone: (915) 533-7551
El Paso, TX 79902

TEXAS TECH UNIVERSITY - HEALTH SCIENCES CENTER - REGIONAL
  ACADEMIC HEALTH CENTER LIBRARY
4800 Alberta Ave.   Phone: (915) 533-3020
El Paso, TX 79905   Dona Roush, Assoc.Dir.

U.S. ARMY HOSPITALS - WILLIAM BEAUMONT ARMY MEDICAL CENTER -
  MEDICAL LIBRARY †
Bldg. 7777   Phone: (915) 569-3121
El Paso, TX 79920   Merle I. Alexander, Med.Libn.

U.S. NATL. PARK SERVICE - CHAMIZAL NATL. MEMORIAL - LIBRARY
109 N. Oregon, Suite 1316
Box 722   Phone: (915) 541-7780
El Paso, TX 79944   Richard Razo, Interp.Spec.

UNIVERSITY OF TEXAS, EL PASO - INSTITUTE OF ORAL HISTORY
Liberal Arts 339   Phone: (915) 747-5488
El Paso, TX 79968   Vicki L. Ruiz, Ph.D., Dir.

UNIVERSITY OF TEXAS, EL PASO - LIBRARY - DOCUMENTS/MAPS LIBRARY
Library Annex   Phone: (915) 747-5685
El Paso, TX 79968   Brenda McDonald, Hd.

UNIVERSITY OF TEXAS, EL PASO - LIBRARY - S.L.A. MARSHALL MILITARY
  HISTORY COLLECTION
Rm. 139   Phone: (915) 747-5697
El Paso, TX 79968-0582   Thomas B. Burdett, Cur.

UNIVERSITY OF TEXAS, EL PASO - LIBRARY - SPECIAL COLLECTIONS
                                      Phone: (915) 747-5684
El Paso, TX 79968   Fred W. Hanes, Dir. of Libs.

UNIVERSITY OF TEXAS, EL PASO - NURSING/MEDICAL LIBRARY
                                      Phone: (915) 533-6094
El Paso, TX 79968   Esperanza A. Moreno, Hd.Libn.

UNIVERSITY OF TEXAS, EL PASO - SCIENCE/ENGINEERING/
  MATHEMATICS LIBRARY
Library Annex   Phone: (915) 747-5138
El Paso, TX 79968   Fletcher C. Newman, Hd.

UNIVERSITY OF TEXAS, EL PASO - TEACHING MATERIALS CENTER
College of Education   Phone: (915) 747-5417
El Paso, TX 79968   Jean Stevens, Hd.

U.S. ARMY AIR DEFENSE SCHOOL - LIBRARY †
Bldg. 2, Wing E
Box 5040   Phone: (915) 568-5781
Ft. Bliss, TX 79916   Delfina C. Galloway, Chf.Libn.

U.S. ARMY SERGEANTS MAJOR ACADEMY - OTHON O. VALENT LEARNING
  RESOURCES CENTER
Bldg. 11203   Phone: (915) 568-8176
Ft. Bliss, TX 79918   Marijean Murray, Supv.Libn.

U.S. NATL. PARK SERVICE - FORT DAVIS NATL. HISTORIC SITE - LIBRARY
Box 1456   Phone: (915) 426-3225
Fort Davis, TX 79734   Douglas C. McChristian, Supt.

U.S. ARMY HOSPITALS - DARNALL ARMY HOSPITAL - MEDICAL LIBRARY
                                      Phone: (817) 288-8368
Ft. Hood, TX 76544   Frank M. Norton, Adm.Libn.

U.S. ARMY - LANGUAGE TRAINING FACILITY - LIBRARY
Bldg. 4404   Phone: (817) 287-7506
Ft. Hood, TX 76544   Else B. d'Emery, Libn.

U.S. ARMY POST - FORT HOOD - MSA DIVISION - CASEY MEMORIAL
  LIBRARY
Bldg. 18000   Phone: (817) 685-5202
Ft. Hood, TX 76544   M.F. Hardin, Chf.Libn.

U.S. ARMY - ACADEMY OF HEALTH SCIENCES - STIMSON LIBRARY
Bldg. 2840   Phone: (512) 221-2116
Ft. Sam Houston, TX 78234   Norma L. Sellers, Chf.Libn.

U.S. ARMY HOSPITALS - BROOKE ARMY MEDICAL CENTER - MEDICAL
  LIBRARY
Bldg. 1001   Phone: (512) 221-4119
Ft. Sam Houston, TX 78234   Ida E. Davis, Adm.Libn.

ALCON LABORATORIES, INC. - RESEARCH & DEVELOPMENT LIBRARY
6201 S. Fwy.
Box 1959   Phone: (817) 293-0450
Fort Worth, TX 76101   Sharon L. McAllister, Sci.Libn.

ALL SAINTS EPISCOPAL HOSPITAL - F.M. CORSELIUS LIBRARY
1400 Enderly Pl.
Box 31   Phone: (817) 926-2544
Fort Worth, TX 76101   Alma Enis, Libn.

BELL HELICOPTER TEXTRON - ENGINEERING TECHNICAL LIBRARY
Box 482   Phone: (817) 280-3608
Fort Worth, TX 76101   Carol A. Barrett, Libn.

CARTER (Amon) MUSEUM - LIBRARY
3501 Camp Bowie Blvd.
Box 2365   Phone: (817) 738-1933
Fort Worth, TX 76113   Nancy G. Wynne, Libn.

CARTER & BURGESS, INC. ENGINEERS & PLANNERS - LIBRARY
1100 Macon   Phone: (817) 335-2611
Fort Worth, TX 76102   Julia W. Sweet, Libn.

COASTAL ECOSYSTEMS MANAGEMENT, INC. - LIBRARY *
3600 Hulen St.   Phone: (817) 731-3727
Fort Worth, TX 76107   Elizabeth L. Parker, Libn.

FORT WORTH ART MUSEUM - LIBRARY
1309 Montgomery St.   Phone: (817) 738-9215
Fort Worth, TX 76107   David Ryan, Dir.

FORT WORTH PUBLIC LIBRARY - ARTS DEPARTMENT
300 Taylor St.   Phone: (817) 870-7739
Fort Worth, TX 76102   Heather L. Goebel, Unit Mgr.

FORT WORTH PUBLIC LIBRARY - BUSINESS AND TECHNOLOGY
    DEPARTMENT
300 Taylor St.   Phone: (817) 870-7727
Fort Worth, TX 76102   John McCracken, Sect.Mgr.

FORT WORTH PUBLIC LIBRARY - BUSINESS AND TECHNOLOGY
    DEPARTMENT - EARTH SCIENCE LIBRARY
300 Taylor St.   Phone: (817) 870-7727
Fort Worth, TX 76102   John McCracken, Sect.Mgr.

FORT WORTH PUBLIC LIBRARY - GENEALOGY AND LOCAL HISTORY
    DEPARTMENT
300 Taylor St.   Phone: (817) 870-7740
Fort Worth, TX 76102   Patricia Chadwell, Unit Mgr., Soc.Sci.Div.

FORT WORTH STAR-TELEGRAM - LIBRARY
400 W. 7th St.   Phone: (817) 390-7740
Fort Worth, TX 76102   Hettie Arleth, Chf.Libn.

GEARHART INDUSTRIES, INC. - TECHNICAL LIBRARY
Box 1936   Phone: (817) 293-1300
Fort Worth, TX 76101   Randall Coffman, Libn.

GENERAL DYNAMICS CORPORATION - FORT WORTH DIVISION -
    TECHNICAL LIBRARY
Grant's Lane, MZ2246
Box 748   Phone: (817) 732-4811
Fort Worth, TX 76101   P. Roger de Tonnancour, Chf.Libn.

HARRIS HOSPITAL - MEDICAL LIBRARY
1300 W. Cannon St.   Phone: (817) 334-6474
Fort Worth, TX 76104   Vaida Durham, Libn.

HYMN SOCIETY OF AMERICA, INC. - NATIONAL HEADQUARTERS LIBRARY
Texas Christian University
Fort Worth, TX 76129   W. Thomas Smith, Exec.Dir.

INTERFIRST BANK FORT WORTH, N.A. - LIBRARY
Box 2260   Phone: (817) 390-6381
Fort Worth, TX 76113   Nancy Bean, Libn.

JOHN PETER SMITH HOSPITAL - MARIETTA MEMORIAL MEDICAL LIBRARY
1500 S. Main   Phone: (817) 921-3431
Fort Worth, TX 76104   M. June Bowman, Med.Libn.

KIMBELL ART MUSEUM - LIBRARY
Will Rogers Rd., W.
Box 9440   Phone: (817) 332-8451
Fort Worth, TX 76107

RESEARCH SERVICES CORPORATION - THE O.A. BATTISTA RESEARCH
    INSTITUTE - LIBRARY
3863 Southwest Loop   Phone: (817) 292-4272
Fort Worth, TX 76133   Naomi L. Matous, Libn.

ST. JOSEPH HOSPITAL - MEDICAL AND NURSING LIBRARY
1401 S. Main St.   Phone: (817) 336-9371
Fort Worth, TX 76104   Jesse Pierrard, Libn.

SOUTHWESTERN BAPTIST THEOLOGICAL SEMINARY - A. WEBB ROBERTS
    LIBRARY
Box 22000-2E   Phone: (817) 923-1921
Fort Worth, TX 76122   Keith C. Wills, Dir. of Libs.

TARRANT COUNTY LAW LIBRARY
420 Courthouse   Phone: (817) 334-1481
Fort Worth, TX 76196   Frances Perry, Law Libn.

TEXAS CHRISTIAN UNIVERSITY - MARY COUTS BURNETT LIBRARY -
    BRITE DIVINITY SCHOOL COLLECTION
                                Phone: (817) 921-7106
Fort Worth, TX 76129   Robert A. Olsen, Jr., Libn.

TEXAS CHRISTIAN UNIVERSITY - MARY COUTS BURNETT LIBRARY -
    MUSIC LIBRARY AND AUDIO CENTER
                                Phone: (817) 921-7000
Fort Worth, TX 76129   Sheila Madden, Music Libn.

TEXAS COLLEGE OF OSTEOPATHIC MEDICINE - HEALTH SCIENCES
    LIBRARY
Camp Bowie at Montgomery   Phone: (817) 735-2464
Fort Worth, TX 76107   Bobby R. Carter, Dir., Lib.Serv.

TEXAS ELECTRIC SERVICE COMPANY - LIBRARY
115 W. 7th St.
Box 970   Phone: (817) 336-9454
Fort Worth, TX 76101   Melba Connelley, Libn.

TRAVIS AVENUE BAPTIST CHURCH - MAURINE HENDERSON LIBRARY
3041 Travis Ave.   Phone: (817) 924-4266
Fort Worth, TX 76110   Mrs. S.H. Henderson, Libn.

U.S. ARMY - CORPS OF ENGINEERS - FORT WORTH DISTRICT -
    TECHNICAL LIBRARY †
819 Taylor St.
Box 17300   Phone: (817) 334-2138
Fort Worth, TX 76102   Robin A. Osborne, Libn.

U.S. DEPT. OF HOUSING AND URBAN DEVELOPMENT - REGION VI -
    LIBRARY
221 W. Lancaster, 8th Fl.
Box 2905   Phone: (817) 870-5431
Fort Worth, TX 76113   Susan M. Hayes, Regional Libn.

U.S. NATL. ARCHIVES & RECORDS SERVICE - FEDERAL ARCHIVES AND
    RECORDS CENTER, REGION 7
501 Felix at Hemphill, Bldg. 1
Box 6216   Phone: (817) 334-5525
Fort Worth, TX 76115   Kent Carter, Chf., Archv.Br.

DOW CHEMICAL U.S.A. - TEXAS DIVISION - LIBRARY
                                Phone: (409) 238-3512
Freeport, TX 77541   G.S. Layne, Res.Assoc.

INTERMEDICS, INC. - LIBRARY
240 W. 2nd St.
Box 617   Phone: (409) 233-8611
Freeport, TX 77541   Catherine Rogers, Tech.Info.Spec.

ROSENBERG LIBRARY - GALVESTON AND TEXAS HISTORY CENTER
2310 Sealy Ave.   Phone: (409) 763-8854
Galveston, TX 77550   Jane A. Kenamore, Archv.

TEMPLE B'NAI ISRAEL - LASKER MEMORIAL LIBRARY
3006 Ave. O   Phone: (409) 765-5796
Galveston, TX 77550   Mrs. Sidney R. Kay

TEXAS A & M UNIVERSITY AT GALVESTON - LIBRARY
Mitchell Campus
Pelican Island, Box 1675   Phone: (409) 766-3366
Galveston, TX 77553   Natalie W. Shipman, Lib.Dir.

U.S. ARMY - CORPS OF ENGINEERS - GALVESTON DISTRICT - LIBRARY
Box 1229   Phone: (409) 766-3196
Galveston, TX 77553   Gail M. Henderson, Libn.

U.S. NATL. MARINE FISHERIES SERVICE - SOUTHEAST FISHERIES CENTER
- GALVESTON LABORATORY LIBRARY
4700 Avenue U   Phone: (409) 766-3506
Galveston, TX 77550   Patricia Torrefranca, Libn.

UNIVERSITY OF TEXAS MEDICAL BRANCH - MOODY MEDICAL LIBRARY
                                                 Phone: (409) 765-1971
Galveston, TX 77550   Emil F. Frey, Dir.

GENERAL ELECTRODYNAMICS CORPORATION - LIBRARY *
4430 Forest Ln.   Phone: (214) 276-1161
Garland, TX 75040

U.S. AIR FORCE BASE - GOODFELLOW BASE LIBRARY †
FL 3030, Bldg. 712   Phone: (915) 653-3231
Goodfellow AFB, TX 76908   Elaine C. Penner, Libn.

DALLAS-FORT WORTH MEDICAL CENTER - LIBRARY
2709 Hospital Blvd.   Phone: (214) 641-5086
Grand Prairie, TX 75051

E-SYSTEMS, INC. - DIVISION LIBRARY
Box 1056   Phone: (214) 454-4580
Greenville, TX 75401   Joleta Moore, Supv.

MORGAN (J. Harris) LAW OFFICE - LAW LIBRARY
Box 556   Phone: (214) 455-3183
Greenville, TX 75401   Almarine Morgan, Libn.

TEXAS STATE TECHNICAL INSTITUTE, HARLINGEN CAMPUS - LIBRARY
                                                 Phone: (512) 425-4922
Harlingen, TX 78551-2628   David J. Diehl, Dir. of Lib.

TEXAS BAPTIST INSTITUTE/SEMINARY - LIBRARY
1300 Longview Dr.
Box 570   Phone: (214) 657-6543
Henderson, TX 75652   James A. Kirkland, Libn.

DEAF SMITH GENERAL HOSPITAL - LIBRARY *
801 E. 3rd St.   Phone: (806) 364-2141
Hereford, TX 79045   Vicky L. Higgins, Dir., Med.Rec.

HILL JUNIOR COLLEGE - CONFEDERATE RESEARCH CENTER AND GUN
MUSEUM
                                                 Phone: (817) 582-2555
Hillsboro, TX 76645   Peggy Fox, Libn.

AMERICAN BRAHMAN BREEDERS ASSOCIATION - LIBRARY
1313 La Concha Ln.   Phone: (713) 795-4444
Houston, TX 77054   Cecilia Cowart, Dir., Commun.

AMERICAN CAPITAL ASSET MANAGEMENT, INC. - RESEARCH LIBRARY
Box 3121   Phone: (713) 529-0600
Houston, TX 77253   Betty J. Mohrman, Libn.

AMERICAN PRODUCTIVITY CENTER - INFORMATION SERVICES
123 N. Post Oak Lane   Phone: (713) 681-4020
Houston, TX 77024   Emmy Crawford, Mgr., Info.Serv.

AMERICAN SOCIETY FOR MEDICAL TECHNOLOGY - LIBRARY
330 Meadowfern Dr.   Phone: (713) 893-7072
Houston, TX 77067

AMOCO PRODUCTION COMPANY INTERNATIONAL - LIBRARY
INFORMATION CENTER
16825 Northchase Dr.   Phone: (713) 931-2584
Houston, TX 77060   Eloise F. Martinez, Supv.

ARNOLD, WHITE & DURKEE - LIBRARY
Box 4433   Phone: (713) 621-9100
Houston, TX 77210   Genel F. Moran, Libn.

ARTHUR ANDERSEN & CO. - BUSINESS LIBRARY
711 Louisiana, Suite 1300   Phone: (713) 237-2718
Houston, TX 77338   Ann Ghist, Libn.

ASHLAND EXPLORATION, INC. - INFORMATION CENTER
900 Threadneedle, Suite 800   Phone: (713) 531-2930
Houston, TX 77079   Teresa A. Matlock, Info.Coord.

ATLAS TRAVEL, INC. - LIBRARY
3411 Montrose   Phone: (713) 527-4555
Houston, TX 77006   William C. Morrison, Libn.

BAKER & BOTTS - LAW LIBRARY †
3000 One Shell Plaza   Phone: (713) 229-1412
Houston, TX 77002   Melissa Colbert, Libn.

BECHTEL POWER CORPORATION - LIBRARY
Box 2166   Phone: (713) 235-4130
Houston, TX 77001   Sheila Carter, Libn.

BONNER & MOORE ASSOCIATES, INC. - LIBRARY
2727 Allen Pkwy., 17th Fl.   Phone: (713) 522-6800
Houston, TX 77019   J. Lawton, Corp.Libn.

BRACEWELL & PATTERSON - LAW LIBRARY
2900 South Tower, Pennzoil Place   Phone: (713) 221-1129
Houston, TX 77002   Susan Mims Yancey, Libn.

BROWN & ROOT, INC. - TECHNICAL LIBRARY
Box 4574   Phone: (713) 676-8693
Houston, TX 77210   Kathy Hubbard, Lib.Mgr.

BUTLER & BINION - LAW LIBRARY
1600 Allied Bank Plaza   Phone: (713) 237-3655
Houston, TX 77002   Lea Black, Libn.

CAMERON IRON WORKS, INC. - LIBRARY
Box 1212   Phone: (713) 939-4332
Houston, TX 77251   Norma A. Willoughby, Libn.

CENTRAL PRESBYTERIAN CHURCH - LIBRARY
3788 Richmond Ave.   Phone: (713) 621-2424
Houston, TX 77027   J.J. Britton, Libn.

CHEVRON GEOSCIENCES COMPANY - LIBRARY †
8435 Westglen
Box 36487   Phone: (713) 781-3030
Houston, TX 77063   Francine Rorabaugh, Libn.

COLUMBIA GULF TRANSMISSION COMPANY - ENGINEERING LIBRARY
Box 683   Phone: (713) 621-1200
Houston, TX 77001   Vance Benoit, Engr.Libn.

CONOCO, INC. - INTERNATIONAL PRODUCTION - CENTRAL FILES/
LIBRARY
Conoco Tower, Suite 1821
Greenway Plaza E.   Phone: (713) 965-2499
Houston, TX 77046   Frances A. Nowak, Supv.

CONOCO, INC. - LEGAL INFORMATION CENTER
5 Greenway Plaza E., Suite 1614
Box 2197   Phone: (713) 965-2592
Houston, TX 77252   Robert S. Grundy, Law Libn./Att.

CONTINENTAL CARBON COMPANY - TECHNICAL LIBRARY †
10500 Richmond Ave.
Box 42817   Phone: (713) 975-5802
Houston, TX 77042   Linda M. Malisheski, Libn./Sec.

CRS SIRRINE, INC. - LIBRARY
1111 W. Loop S.
Box 22427   Phone: (713) 621-9600
Houston, TX 77027   Nancy Acker Fleshmen, Res.Libn.

DAMES & MOORE - LIBRARY AND INFORMATION CENTER
4321 Directors Row, Suite 200
Houston, TX 77092

DELTA ENGINEERING CORPORATION - LIBRARY †
7400 Harwin
Box 36255   Phone: (713) 783-9120
Houston, TX 77036   Jacquelyn D. Davis, Libn.

DOW CHEMICAL U.S.A. - HOUSTON DOW CENTER LIBRARY
400 West Belt South   Phone: (713) 978-2694
Houston, TX 77042   Cynthia J. Crosby, Libn.

DRESSER INDUSTRIES, INC. - MAGCOBAR RESEARCH LIBRARY
10201 Westheimer, Bldg. 1A, Rm. 100   Phone: (713) 972-6611
Houston, TX 77042   Dr. Aliyah Von Nussbaumer, Res.Libn.

ESOTERIC PHILOSOPHY CENTER, INC. - LIBRARY
9441 Roark Rd., Suite 110   Phone: (713) 271-1863
Houston, TX 77099

EXXON COMPANY, U.S.A. - EXPLORATION LIBRARY
Box 4279   Phone: (713) 591-5257
Houston, TX 77210-4279   Roza Ekimov, Libn.

EXXON COMPANY, U.S.A. - LAW LIBRARY
Box 2180   Phone: (713) 656-2019
Houston, TX 77001   Mrs. Del Wherry, Libn.

FIRST PRESBYTERIAN CHURCH - EWING MEMORIAL LIBRARY
5300 Main St.   Phone: (713) 526-2525
Houston, TX 77005   Mary Carter, Libn.

FLUOR ENGINEERS, INC. - OCEAN SERVICES DIVISION - LIBRARY
6200 Hillcroft
Box 36878   Phone: (713) 776-4369
Houston, TX 77036   Letty E. Killingsworth, Lib.Tech.

FOSTER WHEELER ENERGY CORPORATION - HOUSTON ENGINEERING
   CENTER LIBRARY
Box 22395   Phone: (713) 961-6275
Houston, TX 77227   Laura Pilgrim, Libn.

FUGRO INTER, INC. - LIBRARY
10165 Harwin, Suite 170   Phone: (713) 777-2641
Houston, TX 77036   Gloria Bellis, Libn.

FULBRIGHT & JAWORSKI - LIBRARY
Bank of the Southwest Bldg.   Phone: (713) 651-5151
Houston, TX 77002   Jane D. Holland, Libn.

GENERAL ELECTRIC COMPANY - APOLLO SYSTEMS - TECHNICAL AND
   SERVICES SUPPORT LIBRARY *
1830 Nasa Blvd.
Box 58408   Phone: (713) 332-4511
Houston, TX 77058   C.E. Colburn, Libn.

GETTY OIL COMPANY, INC. - RESEARCH CENTER LIBRARY
3901 Briarpark Dr.
Box 770070   Phone: (713) 972-6000
Houston, TX 77215-0070   Debra J. Clay, Supv., Lib.Serv.

GULF COMPANIES - LAW LIBRARY
Box 4553   Phone: (713) 754-3172
Houston, TX 77210   Frederick A. Riemann, Law Libn.

GULF OIL CHEMICALS COMPANY - POLYMER RESEARCH LIBRARY †
Box 3766   Phone: (713) 754-2000
Houston, TX 77001   R.C. Sartorius, Info.Anl.

GULF OIL CORPORATION - LIBRARY AND INFORMATION CENTER
Box 2100   Phone: (713) 754-8973
Houston, TX 77252   Stanley E. Brewer, Hd.Libn.

GULF OIL PRODUCTS COMPANY - CHEMICAL INFORMATION CENTER
Suite 833, Gulf Tower
Box 3766   Phone: (713) 754-1485
Houston, TX 77253   Joel A. Beale, Dir.

HARRIS COUNTY HERITAGE SOCIETY - LIBRARY *
1100 Bagby St.   Phone: (713) 223-8367
Houston, TX 77002   Mrs. T.J. Burnett, Jr., Chm.

HARRIS COUNTY LAW LIBRARY
101 Civil Courts Bldg.   Phone: (713) 221-5183
Houston, TX 77002   Eugene Chambers, Dir., Law Lib.

HERMANN HOSPITAL - SCHOOL OF VOCATIONAL NURSING LIBRARY *
1203 Ross Sterling   Phone: (713) 797-4080
Houston, TX 77030   Helen C. Harrell, Dir.

HOUSTON ACADEMY OF MEDICINE - TEXAS MEDICAL CENTER LIBRARY
1133 M.D. Anderson Blvd.   Phone: (713) 797-1230
Houston, TX 77030   Richard Lyders, Exec.Dir.

HOUSTON CHRONICLE - EDITORIAL LIBRARY
Box 4260   Phone: (713) 220-7313
Houston, TX 77210   Sherry Adams, Libn.

HOUSTON CITY AVIATION DEPARTMENT - LIBRARY
Box 60106   Phone: (713) 443-1714
Houston, TX 77205

HOUSTON - CITY LEGAL DEPARTMENT - LAW LIBRARY
4th Fl. City Hall
Box 1562   Phone: (713) 222-5151
Houston, TX 77063   Mary Vela-Creixell, Law Libn.

HOUSTON LIGHTING & POWER COMPANY - LIBRARY
Box 1700   Phone: (713) 228-9211
Houston, TX 77001   Alicia B. Quinn, Supv.

HOUSTON MUSEUM OF NATURAL SCIENCE - REFERENCE LIBRARY *
1 Hermann Circle Dr.   Phone: (713) 526-4273
Houston, TX 77030   Carl H. Ailsen, Act.Dir.

HOUSTON POST - LIBRARY/INFORMATION CENTER
                                            Phone: (713) 840-5830
Houston, TX 77001   Kathy Foley, Chf.Libn.

HOUSTON PUBLIC LIBRARY - ARCHIVES AND MANUSCRIPT DEPARTMENT
500 McKinney St.   Phone: (713) 224-5441
Houston, TX 77002   Dr. Louis J. Marchiafava, Archv.

HOUSTON PUBLIC LIBRARY - BUSINESS, SCIENCE & TECHNOLOGY
   DEPARTMENT
500 McKinney Ave.   Phone: (713) 224-5441
Houston, TX 77002   Brenda Peabody Tirrell, Dept.Hd.

HOUSTON PUBLIC LIBRARY - CLAYTON LIBRARY - CENTER FOR
   GENEALOGICAL RESEARCH
5300 Caroline St.   Phone: (713) 524-0101
Houston, TX 77004   Maxine Alcorn, Hd., Clayton Lib.

HOUSTON PUBLIC LIBRARY - COMMUNITY INFORMATION SERVICE
500 McKinney Ave.   Phone: (713) 229-9195
Houston, TX 77002   Charles Masling, Coord.

HOUSTON PUBLIC LIBRARY - FILM COLLECTION DEPARTMENT
500 McKinney Ave.   Phone: (713) 224-5441
Houston, TX 77002   Syma Zerkow, Dept.Hd.

HOUSTON PUBLIC LIBRARY - FINE ARTS & RECREATION DEPARTMENT
500 McKinney Ave.   Phone: (713) 224-5441
Houston, TX 77002   John Harvath, Dept.Hd.

HOUSTON PUBLIC LIBRARY - SPECIAL COLLECTIONS DEPARTMENT
500 McKinney Ave.   Phone: (713) 224-5441
Houston, TX 77002   Donna Grove, Dept.Hd.

HOUSTON PUBLIC LIBRARY - TEXAS AND LOCAL HISTORY DEPARTMENT
500 McKinney Ave.   Phone: (713) 224-5441
Houston, TX 77002   Dorothy Glasser, Dept.Hd.

HUGHES TOOL COMPANY - BUSINESS AND TECHNICAL LIBRARY
Box 2539   Phone: (713) 924-2990
Houston, TX 77001   Melody M. Morningstar, Div.Libn.

I/H INCORPORATED - GAY AND LESBIAN ARCHIVES OF TEXAS †
802 Westheimer   Phone: (713) 529-7014
Houston, TX 77006   Charles Gillis, Info.Dir.

IBM CORPORATION - NATIONAL ACCOUNTS DIVISION - LIBRARY
Two Riverway   Phone: (713) 940-2554
Houston, TX 77056   Agnete V. Katherman, Libn.

THE INSTITUTE FOR REHABILITATION AND RESEARCH (TIRR) -
   INFORMATION SERVICES CENTER
1333 Moursund Ave.
Box 20095   Phone: (713) 797-1440
Houston, TX 77225   Kay Lindloff, Info.Sci.

INSTITUTE FOR STORM RESEARCH - LIBRARY
4104 Mt. Vernon   Phone: (713) 529-4891
Houston, TX 77006   Dr. John C. Freeman, Hd.

JACOBS ENGINEERING GROUP - TECHNICAL INFORMATION SERVICES
  DEPARTMENT
Box 53495   Phone: (713) 626-2020
Houston, TX 77052   Carolyn A. Meanley, Mgr., Tech.Info.

JOHNSON (Bernard) INC. - TECHNICAL LIBRARY
5050 Westheimer   Phone: (713) 622-1400
Houston, TX 77056   C. David Rushbrook, Libn.

KELLOGG (M.W.) - RESEARCH INFORMATION DIVISION
16200 Park Row
Industrial Park Ten   Phone: (713) 492-2500
Houston, TX 77084   Una M. Gourlay, Mgr.

LOCKWOOD, ANDREWS & NEWNAM, INC. - INFORMATION CENTER
1500 CityWest Blvd.   Phone: (713) 266-6900
Houston, TX 77042   Diane E. Walker, Info.Ctr.Coord.

LUMMUS CREST, INC. - TECHNICAL LIBRARY
3000 Post Oak Blvd.
Houston, TX 77056

LUNAR AND PLANETARY INSTITUTE - LIBRARY/INFORMATION CENTER
3303 NASA Rd., No. 1   Phone: (713) 486-2135
Houston, TX 77058   Frances B. Waranius, Lib./Info.Ctr.Mgr.

LUNAR AND PLANETARY INSTITUTE - PLANETARY IMAGE CENTER †
3303 NASA Rd., No. 1   Phone: (713) 486-2172
Houston, TX 77058   Ron Weber, Mgr.

MC CLELLAND ENGINEERS, INC. - CORPORATE TECHNICAL LIBRARY
6100 Hillcroft
Box 740010   Phone: (713) 772-3700
Houston, TX 77274   Pat M. Johnson, Dir., Libs./Rec.

MENTAL HEALTH AND MENTAL RETARDATION AUTHORITY OF HARRIS
  COUNTY - INFORMATION RESOURCE CENTER *
2850 Fannin   Phone: (713) 759-1010
Houston, TX 77002   Jacqueline M. Woods, Adm.Techn. III

MICHIGAN WISCONSIN PIPELINE COMPANY - LIBRARY *
5075 Westheimer, Suite 1100 W.   Phone: (713) 623-0300
Houston, TX 77056   Donna Heard, Rec.Supv.

MOBIL PRODUCING TEXAS & NEW MEXICO INC. - INFORMATION
  RESOURCE CENTER
Nine Greenway Plaza, Suite 2700   Phone: (713) 871-5621
Houston, TX 77046   Denise Hampton, Coord.

MOORE (Walter P.) & ASSOCIATES - LIBRARY
3203 W. Alabama
Houston, TX 77098   Joan Ferry, Libn.

MUSEUM OF FINE ARTS, HOUSTON - HIRSCH LIBRARY
1001 Bissonnet   Phone: (713) 526-1361
Houston, TX 77005   Linda Nelson Shearouse, Libn.

NATIONAL COLLEGE OF DISTRICT ATTORNEYS - RESOURCE CENTER
College of Law
University of Houston   Phone: (713) 749-1571
Houston, TX 77004   Mary Ann Freeman, Commun.Mgr.

NL BAROID/NL INDUSTRIES, INC. - TECHNICAL LIBRARY
2404 Southwest Freeway
Box 1675   Phone: (713) 527-1282
Houston, TX 77251   Bilha Wieczner, Info.Rsrcs.Supv.

NL INDUSTRIES, INC. - INFORMATION CENTER
Box 60087   Phone: (713) 987-4544
Houston, TX 77205   Leah A. Bartlett-Cahill, Tech.Info.Supv.

PANNELL KERR FORSTER - LIBRARY
601 Jefferson, Suite 745   Phone: (713) 654-1881
Houston, TX 77002   Megan W. Trauth, Off.Serv.Mgr.

PEAT, MARWICK, MITCHELL & CO. - LIBRARY
3000 Republic Bank Center   Phone: (713) 224-4262
Houston, TX 77002   Charlotte Kohrs, Supv., Info.Serv.

PENNZOIL EXPLORATION AND PRODUCTION COMPANY - TECHNICAL
  INFORMATION SERVICES
700 Milam
Box 2967   Phone: (713) 546-8793
Houston, TX 77001   Joan K. Baldwin, Libn.

PIERCE/GOODWIN/ALEXANDER - LIBRARY/RESOURCE CENTER
800 Bering Dr.
Box 13319   Phone: (713) 977-5777
Houston, TX 77219   Peggy Kelly, Libn.

PRUDENTIAL INSURANCE COMPANY OF AMERICA - BUSINESS LIBRARY
24 Greenway Plaza, Suite 1900   Phone: (713) 993-3526
Houston, TX 77046   Fred Suza

RICE UNIVERSITY - ART LIBRARY
Box 1892   Phone: (713) 527-4832
Houston, TX 77251-1892   Jet Marie Prendeville, Art Libn.

RICE UNIVERSITY - GOVERNMENT DOCUMENTS AND MICROFORMS
  DEPARTMENT
Fondren Library
Box 1892   Phone: (713) 527-8101
Houston, TX 77251-1892   Barbara Kile, Hd.

RICE UNIVERSITY - JONES GRADUATE SCHOOL OF ADMINISTRATION -
  BUSINESS INFORMATION CENTER
Herring Hall
Houston, TX 77251   Mary S. Barnard, Bus.Libn.

RICE UNIVERSITY - MUSIC LIBRARY
Fondren Library
Box 1892   Phone: (713) 527-8101
Houston, TX 77251-1892   Ellen J. Burns, Music Libn.

RICE UNIVERSITY - WOODSON RESEARCH CENTER
Fondren Library, Box 1892   Phone: (713) 527-8101
Houston, TX 77251-1892   Nancy Boothe Parker, Dir.

ST. JOSEPH HOSPITAL - HOSPITAL HEALTH SCIENCE LIBRARY
1919 LaBranch   Phone: (713) 757-1000
Houston, TX 77002   Shelley G. Mao, Dir.

ST. LUKE'S EPISCOPAL & TEXAS CHILDREN'S HOSPITALS - MEDICAL
  LIBRARY
6621 Fannin St.   Phone: (715) 791-3054
Houston, TX 77030   Robert C. Park, Dir. of Lib.Serv.

ST. MARY'S SEMINARY - CARDINAL BERAN LIBRARY
9845 Memorial Dr.   Phone: (713) 681-5544
Houston, TX 77024   Constance Walker, Libn.

SCHLUMBERGER WELL SERVICES - ENGINEERING LIBRARY
5000 Gulf Fwy.
Box 4594   Phone: (713) 928-4411
Houston, TX 77210   Margaret Kuo, Engr.Libn.

SHELL DEVELOPMENT COMPANY - BELLAIRE RESEARCH CENTER LIBRARY
Box 481   Phone: (713) 663-2293
Houston, TX 77001   Aphrodite Mamoulides, Lib.Supv.

SHELL DEVELOPMENT COMPANY - WESTHOLLOW RESEARCH CENTER
  LIBRARY †
3333 Hwy. 6 S.
Box 1380   Phone: (713) 493-7530
Houston, TX 77001   Esther Ando, Supv. of Lib.

SHELL OIL COMPANY - INFORMATION & LIBRARY SERVICES
Box 587   Phone: (713) 241-1017
Houston, TX 77001   Jane C. Rodgers, Supv.

SHRINERS HOSPITAL FOR CRIPPLED CHILDREN - ORTHOPEDIC LIBRARY *
1402 Outerbelt Dr.   Phone: (713) 797-1616
Houston, TX 77030   Lillian Nicholson, Libn.

SOUTH TEXAS COLLEGE OF LAW - LIBRARY
1220 Polk St.   Phone: (713) 659-8040
Houston, TX 77002   F.H. Thompson, Law Libn.

TAUB (Ben) GENERAL HOSPITAL - DOCTOR'S MEDICAL LIBRARY *
1502 Taub Loop   Phone: (713) 791-7441
Houston, TX 77025   Angie Ortiz, Lib.Ck.

TENNECO, INC. - CORPORATE LIBRARY
1010 Milam St., Suite 2143
Box 2511   Phone: (713) 757-2788
Houston, TX 77001   Linda S. Shults, Libn.

TENNECO OIL EXPLORATION AND PRODUCTION - GEOLOGICAL RESEARCH
   LIBRARY
1100 Milam Bldg., Rm. 1460   Phone: (713) 757-8832
Houston, TX 77001

TEXAS EASTERN TRANSMISSION CORPORATION - LIBRARY
1221 McKinney
Box 2521   Phone: (713) 759-3533
Houston, TX 77252   Kay Bailey, Libn.

TEXAS INSTRUMENTS, INC. - HOUSTON SITE LIBRARY
Box 1443, MS 695   Phone: (713) 490-2981
Houston, TX 77001   Helen Manning, Libn.

TEXAS RESEARCH INSTITUTE OF MENTAL SCIENCES - LIBRARY
1300 Moursund   Phone: (713) 797-1976
Houston, TX 77030   Felicia S. Chuang, Libn.

TEXAS SOUTHERN UNIVERSITY - LAW LIBRARY †
3200 Cleburne   Phone: (713) 527-7125
Houston, TX 77004   David D. Melillo, Law Libn.

TEXAS SOUTHERN UNIVERSITY - LIBRARY - HEARTMAN COLLECTION
3201 Wheeler   Phone: (713) 527-7149
Houston, TX 77004   Dorothy H. Chapman, Cur.

TEXAS SOUTHERN UNIVERSITY - PHARMACY LIBRARY
3201 Wheeler Ave.   Phone: (713) 527-7160
Houston, TX 77004   Norma Bean, Assoc.Dir.

TEXAS STATE - COURT OF APPEALS - 1ST SUPREME JUDICIAL DISTRICT -
   LAW LIBRARY
1307 San Jacinto, 10th Fl.   Phone: (713) 228-8311
Houston, TX 77002

TRANSCONTINENTAL GAS PIPE LINE CORPORATION - LIBRARY
Box 1396   Phone: (713) 871-2321
Houston, TX 77251   Cheryl L. Watson, Libn.

TRUNKLINE GAS COMPANY - EMPLOYEE RESOURCE CENTER
Box 1642   Phone: (713) 664-3401
Houston, TX 77001   Hershall Stair, Libn.

TURNER, COLLIE & BRADEN, INC. - LIBRARY AND INFORMATION SERVICES
Box 13089   Phone: (713) 780-4100
Houston, TX 77219   Jean Steinhardt, Libn.

UNDERWOOD, NEUHAUS & COMPANY INC. - CORPORATE FINANCE
   LIBRARY
724 Travis St.   Phone: (713) 221-2086
Houston, TX 77002

UNION TEXAS PETROLEUM CORPORATION - LIBRARY
Box 2120   Phone: (713) 960-7044
Houston, TX 77252   Betty J. Backus, Supv., Lib.

U.S. DEPT. OF COMMERCE - INTERNATIONAL TRADE ADMINISTRATION -
   HOUSTON DISTRICT OFFICE LIBRARY †
515 Rusk Ave., Rm. 2625   Phone: (713) 226-4231
Houston, TX 77002   Felicito C. Guerrero, Dir.

U.S. NASA - LYNDON B. JOHNSON SPACE CENTER - TECHNICAL LIBRARY
                                                 Phone: (713) 483-4048
Houston, TX 77058   Martin P. McDonough, Lead Libn.

U.S. VETERANS ADMINISTRATION (TX-Houston) - MEDICAL CENTER
   LIBRARY
2002 Holcombe Blvd.   Phone: (713) 795-4411
Houston, TX 77211   Jerry E. Barrett

UNIVERSITY OF HOUSTON - AUDIOVISUAL SERVICES
University Park Campus   Phone: (713) 749-2361
Houston, TX 77004   Joseph R. Schroeder, Dir.

UNIVERSITY OF HOUSTON - COLLEGE OF OPTOMETRY LIBRARY
                                                 Phone: (713) 749-2411
Houston, TX 77004   Suzanne Ferimer, Dir., Lrng.Rsrcs.

UNIVERSITY OF HOUSTON - COLLEGE OF PHARMACY LIBRARY
University Park Campus   Phone: (713) 749-1566
Houston, TX 77004   Derral Parkin, Libn.

UNIVERSITY OF HOUSTON - FRANZHEIM ARCHITECTURE LIBRARY
University Park Campus   Phone: (713) 749-1193
Houston, TX 77004   Margaret Culbertson, Libn.

UNIVERSITY OF HOUSTON - LAW LIBRARY
University Park Campus   Phone: (713) 749-3191
Houston, TX 77004   Jon S. Schultz, Dir.

UNIVERSITY OF HOUSTON - LIBRARIES - SPECIAL COLLECTIONS
University Park Campus   Phone: (713) 749-2725
Houston, TX 77004   Dr. David Farmer, Cur. of Spec.Coll.

UNIVERSITY OF HOUSTON - MUSIC LIBRARY
University Park Campus   Phone: (713) 749-2534
Houston, TX 77004   Samuel R. Hyde, Libn.

UNIVERSITY OF TEXAS - M.D. ANDERSON HOSPITAL AND TUMOR
   INSTITUTE - RESEARCH MEDICAL LIBRARY
Texas Medical Center   Phone: (713) 792-2282
Houston, TX 77030   Marie Harvin, Res.Med.Libn.

UNIVERSITY OF TEXAS HEALTH SCIENCE CENTER, HOUSTON - DENTAL
   BRANCH LIBRARY
Box 20068   Phone: (713) 792-4094
Houston, TX 77225   Lorrayne B. Webb, Libn.

VINSON & ELKINS - LAW LIBRARY
First City Tower   Phone: (713) 651-2678
Houston, TX 77002   Karl T. Gruben, Libn.

WESTERN GEOPHYSICAL COMPANY OF AMERICA - R & D LIBRARY
Box 2469   Phone: (713) 789-9600
Houston, TX 77001   Ching-Cheng C. Ting, R & D Libn.

WITCO CHEMICAL CORPORATION - LIBRARY
3200 Brookfield   Phone: (713) 433-7281
Houston, TX 77045   Helen K. Kim, Tech.Libn./Res.Chem.

HUNTSVILLE MEMORIAL HOSPITAL - SCHOOL OF VOCATIONAL NURSING -
   EARNESTINE CANNON MEMORIAL LIBRARY †
3000 I-45
Box 479   Phone: (409) 291-3411
Huntsville, TX 77340   J. Martin, Dir.

SAM HOUSTON STATE UNIVERSITY - LIBRARY - SPECIAL COLLECTIONS
                                                 Phone: (409) 294-1613
Huntsville, TX 77341   Charles L. Dwyer, Hd., Thomason/Spec.Coll.

BELL & HOWELL EDUCATION GROUP - DE VRY INSTITUTE OF TECHNOLOGY
   - LEARNING RESOURCE CENTER
4250 N. Beltline Rd.   Phone: (214) 258-6767
Irving, TX 75038   Carolyn Cochran, Dir., LRC

BOY SCOUTS OF AMERICA - LIBRARY
1325 Walnut Hill Ln.   Phone: (214) 659-2280
Irving, TX 75038-3096   Ann L. McVicar, Libn.

GENSTAR-FLINTKOTE BUILDING PRODUCTS COMPANY - CORPORATE R&D
   LIBRARY
3241 W. Story Rd.   Phone: (214) 659-9800
Irving, TX 75062   Lawrence A. Wilson, Act.Libn.

GRUY (H.J.) & ASSOCIATES, INC. - LIBRARY
150 W. Carpenter Fwy.   Phone: (214) 659-3200
Irving, TX 75062   Nancy Cooper, Dir., Lib./Info.Serv.

NEC AMERICA - SWITCHING SYSTEMS DIVISON - TECHNICAL DOCUMENT
   CENTER
1525 Walnut Hill Lane   Phone: (214) 257-9239
Irving, TX 75062   Michiko K. Adams, Supv.

BAPTIST MISSIONARY ASSOCIATION THEOLOGICAL SEMINARY - KELLAR
   LIBRARY
1410 E. Pine St.
Box 1797   Phone: (214) 586-2501
Jacksonville, TX 75766   James C. Blaylock, Libn.

JEFFERSON HISTORICAL SOCIETY AND MUSEUM - ARCHIVES
223 Austin St.
Drawer G   Phone: (214) 665-2775
Jefferson, TX 75657   Mrs. Jack Bullard, Cur.

U.S. NATL. PARK SERVICE - LYNDON B. JOHNSON NATL. HISTORICAL PARK
   - LIBRARY
Box 329   Phone: (512) 868-7128
Johnson City, TX 78636   John T. Tiff, Hist.

U.S. AIR FORCE BASE - KELLY BASE - SPECIAL SERVICES LIBRARY *
FL 2050   Phone: (512) 925-3214
Kelly AFB, TX 78241   Melvin P. McElfresh, Libn.

U.S. VETERANS ADMINISTRATION (TX-Kerrville) - HEALTH SCIENCES
   LIBRARY
Memorial Blvd.   Phone: (512) 896-2020
Kerrville, TX 78028   Lawrence M. Larimer, Chf., Lib.Serv.

SAN JACINTO MUSEUM OF HISTORY ASSOCIATION - LIBRARY
3800 Park Rd.   Phone: (409) 479-2421
La Porte, TX 77571   Winston Atkins, Libn.

U.S. AIR FORCE BASE - LAUGHLIN BASE LIBRARY *
FL 3099   Phone: (512) 298-5119
Laughlin AFB, TX 78840   William Darcy, Base Libn.

CONSERVATION DISTRICTS FOUNDATION - DAVIS CONSERVATION
   LIBRARY
408 E. Main St.
Box 776   Phone: (409) 332-3404
League City, TX 77573   Mary M. Wooley, Libn.

AMERICAN SUFFOLK HORSE ASSOCIATION (ASHA) - LIBRARY
Rte. 1, Box 212
Ledbetter, TX 78946   Mary Margaret M. Read, Sec.

TEXAS INSTRUMENTS, INC. - LEWISVILLE TECHNICAL LIBRARY
Box 405, M/S 3411   Phone: (214) 462-5425
Lewisville, TX 75067   Stephanie S. Mutty, Libn.

TEXAS STATE LIBRARY - LOCAL RECORDS DIVISION - SAM HOUSTON
   REGIONAL LIBRARY AND RESEARCH CENTER
Farm Road 1011
Box 989   Phone: (409) 336-7097
Liberty, TX 77575   Robert L. Schaadt, Dir./Archv.

CHURCH OF JESUS CHRIST OF LATTER-DAY SAINTS - LONGVIEW BRANCH
   GENEALOGICAL LIBRARY
1700 Blueridge Pkwy.   Phone: (214) 759-7911
Longview, TX 75605

EASTMAN KODAK COMPANY - TEXAS EASTMAN COMPANY - BUSINESS
   LIBRARY
Box 7444   Phone: (214) 757-6611
Longview, TX 75607   Carol Kinsey, Bus.Libn.

EASTMAN KODAK COMPANY - TEXAS EASTMAN COMPANY - RESEARCH &
   DEVELOPMENT LIBRARY
Box 7444   Phone: (214) 236-5000
Longview, TX 75607   Jack T. Buchanan, Res.Libn.

FIRST BAPTIST CHURCH - JOHN L. WHORTON MEDIA CENTER
209 E. South St.   Phone: (214) 758-0681
Longview, TX 75601   Sandra Kay Trippett, Dir.

LE TOURNEAU COLLEGE - MARGARET ESTES LIBRARY
Box 7001   Phone: (214) 753-0231
Longview, TX 75607   Paul Gray, Dir., Lib.Serv.

HIGHLAND HOSPITAL, INC. - MEDICAL LIBRARY
2412 50th St.   Phone: (806) 795-8251
Lubbock, TX 79412   Margaret Bussey, Med.Libn./Dir., Med.Rec.

LUBBOCK CHRISTIAN COLLEGE - MOODY LIBRARY
5601 W. 19th St.   Phone: (806) 792-3221
Lubbock, TX 79407

METHODIST HOSPITAL AND SCHOOL OF NURSING - LIBRARY
3615 19th St.   Phone: (806) 793-4180
Lubbock, TX 79410   June Rayburn, Libn.

TEXAS TECH UNIVERSITY - HEALTH SCIENCES CENTER - LIBRARY OF THE
   HEALTH SCIENCES
                                       Phone: (806) 743-2203
Lubbock, TX 79430   Charles W. Sargent, Ph.D., Dir.

TEXAS TECH UNIVERSITY - LIBRARY
                                       Phone: (806) 742-2261
Lubbock, TX 79409   Dr. E. Dale Cluff, Dir. of Libs.

TEXAS TECH UNIVERSITY - LIBRARY - DOCUMENTS DEPARTMENT
                                       Phone: (806) 742-2268
Lubbock, TX 79409   Mary Ann Higdon, Doc.Libn.

TEXAS TECH UNIVERSITY - SCHOOL OF LAW LIBRARY
                                       Phone: (806) 742-3794
Lubbock, TX 79409   Jane G. Olm, Dir.

TEXAS TECH UNIVERSITY - SOUTHWEST COLLECTION
Box 4090   Phone: (806) 742-3749
Lubbock, TX 79409   Dr. David Murrah, Dir.

U.S. AIR FORCE BASE - REESE BASE LIBRARY
Reese AFB
3060   Phone: (806) 885-4511
Lubbock, TX 79489

MEMORIAL HOSPITAL - MEDICAL LIBRARY *
Box 1447   Phone: (409) 634-8111
Lufkin, TX 75902   Nancy Anderson, Dir., Med.Rec.

TEXAS (State) FOREST SERVICE - TEXAS FOREST PRODUCTS LABORATORY
   - LIBRARY
Box 310   Phone: (409) 632-6666
Lufkin, TX 75901   Kim Mericle, Libn.

FIRST BAPTIST CHURCH - E.F. WALKER MEMORIAL LIBRARY
218 N. Magnolia
Box 90   Phone: (512) 875-2227
Luling, TX 78648   Mrs. Raymond Matthews, Libn.

FIRST BAPTIST CHURCH - LIBRARY *
1200 Beech St.   Phone: (512) 686-7418
McAllen, TX 78501   Mrs. Hans Wells, Dir.

HERCULES, INC. - AEROSPACE DIVISION - MC GREGOR TECHNICAL
   INFORMATION CENTER
Box 548   Phone: (817) 840-2811
McGregor, TX 76657   D.A. Browne, Pubn.Coord.

MC KINNEY JOB CORPS - LIBRARY
1501 N. Church St.
Box 750   Phone: (214) 542-2623
McKinney, TX 75069   Lois Stewart, Libn.

NORTH TEXAS MEDICAL CENTER - MEDICAL LIBRARY
1800 N. Graves St.
Box 370   Phone: (214) 542-2641
McKinney, TX 75069   Joan L. Thomas, Dir., Med.Rec.

U.S. VETERANS ADMINISTRATION (TX-Marlin) - MEDICAL CENTER
LIBRARY SERVICE (142D)
1016 Ward St.   Phone: (817) 883-3511
Marlin, TX 76661   Lewis Koster, Chf., Lib.Serv.

EAST TEXAS BAPTIST UNIVERSITY - MAMYE JARRETT LEARNING CENTER
1209 North Grove   Phone: (214) 935-7963
Marshall, TX 75670   E.M. Adams, Jr., Dir.

HARRISON COUNTY HISTORICAL MUSEUM - INEZ HATLEY HUGHES
RESEARCH CENTER
Peter Whetstone Sq.   Phone: (214) 938-2680
Marshall, TX 75670   Inez H. Hughes, Musm.Dir.

ICI AMERICAS INC. - DARCO EXPERIMENTAL LABORATORY LIBRARY †
Box 790   Phone: (214) 938-9211
Marshall, TX 75670   S. Neafus, Libn.

MIDLAND COUNTY PUBLIC LIBRARY - PETROLEUM DEPARTMENT LIBRARY
Box 1191   Phone: (915) 683-2708
Midland, TX 79702   Sandra Wegner, Petroleum Dept.Libn.

PALOMINO HORSE BREEDERS OF AMERICA - LIBRARY
Box 249   Phone: (817) 325-2513
Mineral Wells, TX 76067   Robert J. Shiflet, Exec. V.P.

STEPHEN F. AUSTIN STATE UNIVERSITY - STEEN LIBRARY - SPECIAL
COLLECTIONS DEPARTMENT
SFA Sta., Box 13055   Phone: (409) 569-4101
Nacogdoches, TX 75962   Linda Cheves Nicklas, Spec.Coll.Libn.

FORT BELKNAP ARCHIVES, INC. - LIBRARY
Route 1, Box 27   Phone: (817) 549-1856
Newcastle, TX 76372   K.F. Neighbours, Archv.

EL PASO PRODUCTS COMPANY - RESEARCH AND DEVELOPMENT LIBRARY
Box 3986   Phone: (915) 333-8497
Odessa, TX 79760

ODESSA AMERICAN - EDITORIAL LIBRARY
Box 2952   Phone: (915) 337-4661
Odessa, TX 79760   Jo Jones, Libn.

U.S. PRESIDENTIAL MUSEUM - LIBRARY OF THE PRESIDENTS
622 N. Lee   Phone: (915) 332-7123
Odessa, TX 79761

DU PONT DE NEMOURS (E.I.) & COMPANY, INC. - POLYMER PRODUCTS
DEPARTMENT - TECHNICAL LIBRARY
Sabine River Works
Box 1089   Phone: (409) 886-6418
Orange, TX 77630   Patsy Holland, Tech.Libn.

CABOT CORPORATION - RESEARCH & DEVELOPMENT LIBRARY †
Box 5001   Phone: (806) 669-2596
Pampa, TX 79065   Delores Martin, Libn./Off.Mgr.

CARSON COUNTY SQUARE HOUSE MUSEUM - INFORMATION CENTER
Box 276   Phone: (806) 537-3118
Panhandle, TX 79068   P.J. Pronger, III, Dir.

TEXAS CHIROPRACTIC COLLEGE - MAE HILTY MEMORIAL LIBRARY
5912 Spencer Hwy.   Phone: (409) 487-1170
Pasadena, TX 77505   Mara Umpierre, Hd.Libn.

UNIVERSITY OF TEXAS - PORT ARANSAS MARINE LABORATORY - LIBRARY
                                       Phone: (512) 749-6723
Port Aransas, TX 78373   Ruth Grundy, Libn.

ST. MARY HOSPITAL - HEALTH SCIENCE LIBRARY
3600 Gates Blvd.
Box 3696   Phone: (409) 985-7431
Port Arthur, TX 77642   Sister Mary Patricius, Dir.

PRAIRIE VIEW A & M COLLEGE OF TEXAS - W.R. BANKS LIBRARY -
SPECIAL COLLECTIONS †
Third St.
Box T   Phone: (409) 857-2012
Prairie View, TX 77445   Joyce Stimage, Spec.Coll.

U.S. AIR FORCE - AIR FORCE MANPOWER & PERSONNEL CENTER -
MORALE, WELFARE & RECREATION DIVISION - LIBRARY SERVICES BR.
AFMPC/MPCSOL   Phone: (512) 652-3037
Randolph AFB, TX 78150   Tony Dakan, Dir., USAF Libs.

U.S. AIR FORCE - AIR TRAINING COMMAND - LIBRARY PROGRAM
HQ ATC/DPSOL   Phone: (512) 652-3410
Randolph AFB, TX 78150   Duane A. Johnson, Command Libn.

U.S. AIR FORCE BASE - RANDOLPH BASE LIBRARY *
FL 3089   Phone: (512) 652-2617
Randolph AFB, TX 78150   Nova C. Maddox, Chf.Libn.

U.S. AIR FORCE HOSPITAL - MEDICAL LIBRARY (TX-Reese AFB)
SGAS/35   Phone: (806) 885-4511
Reese AFB, TX 79489   Dorothy F. Haynes, Med.libn.

ANDERSON CLAYTON FOODS - W.L. CLAYTON RESEARCH CENTER
3333 N. Central Expy.   Phone: (214) 231-6121
Richardson, TX 75080   Irmgarde Martin, Libn.

DALLAS COUNTY LAW LIBRARY - RICHARDSON BRANCH
Richardson Public Library
900 Civic Center Dr.   Phone: (214) 238-8251
Richardson, TX 75080   Larry Hood, Law Libn.

SUN EXPLORATION & PRODUCTION COMPANY - INFORMATION
RESOURCES CENTER
1201 Exchange
Box 936   Phone: (214) 699-3148
Richardson, TX 75080   Margaret Anderson, Libn.

TEXAS STATE PARKS & WILDLIFE DEPARTMENT - MARINE LABORATORY
LIBRARY
Box 1717   Phone: (512) 729-2328
Rockport, TX 78382   T.L. Heffernan, Lab.Supv.

WINEDALE HISTORICAL CENTER - LIBRARY
Box 11   Phone: (409) 278-3530
Round Top, TX 78954   Gloria Jaster, Off.Supv.

FORT CONCHO MUSEUM - REFERENCE LIBRARY
213 E. Ave. D   Phone: (915) 655-9121
San Angelo, TX 76903   Wayne Daniel, Libn./Archv.

GENERAL TELEPHONE COMPANY OF THE SOUTHWEST - E.H. DANNER
LIBRARY OF TELEPHONY
2701 S. Johnson St.
Box 1001   Phone: (915) 944-5149
San Angelo, TX 76904   Aline H. Taylor, Libn.

ARCHDIOCESE OF SAN ANTONIO - CATHOLIC ARCHIVES
9123 Lorene Ln.   Phone: (512) 344-2331
San Antonio, TX 78284   Ofelia Tennant, Archv.

ASSUMPTION SEMINARY - LIBRARY †
2600 W. Woodlawn   Phone: (512) 734-5137
San Antonio, TX 78284   John R. McGrath, Libn.

BAPTIST MEMORIAL HOSPITAL SYSTEM - BRUCE A. GARRETT MEMORIAL
LIBRARY & MEDIA CENTER
111 Dallas St.   Phone: (512) 222-8431
San Antonio, TX 78286   Ruth R. Libby, Chf.Libn.

BEXAR COUNTY LAW LIBRARY
Court House, 5th Fl.   Phone: (512) 227-8822
San Antonio, TX 78205   Jimmy Alleson, Libn.

BEXAR COUNTY MEDICAL LIBRARY ASSOCIATION
202 W. French Place
Box 12678   Phone: (512) 734-6691
San Antonio, TX 78212   Priscilla D. Siniff, Info.Coord.

CONGREGATION AGUDAS ACHIM - BERNARD RUBENSTEIN LIBRARY
1201 Donaldson Ave.   Phone: (512) 736-4216
San Antonio, TX 78228   Marie Bartman, Libn.

DATAPOINT CORPORATION - INFORMATION RESOURCE CENTER
9725 Datapoint Dr., Mail Sta. M-15   Phone: (512) 699-7151
San Antonio, TX 78284   Susan K. Hughes, Corp.Libn.

DAUGHTERS OF THE REPUBLIC OF TEXAS - LIBRARY
Box 2599   Phone: (512) 225-1071
San Antonio, TX 78299   Sharon R. Crutchfield, Dir.

FIRST BAPTIST CHURCH - LIBRARY
515 McCullough Ave.   Phone: (512) 226-0363
San Antonio, TX 78215   Virginia Patterson, Libn.

FUNDING INFORMATION CENTER
507 Brooklyn   Phone: (512) 227-4333
San Antonio, TX 78215   Candes Chumney, Supv.

MC NAY (Marion Koogler) ART MUSEUM - LIBRARY
Box 6069   Phone: (512) 824-5368
San Antonio, TX 77509   Mrs. John P. Leeper, Libn.

MATTHEWS & BRANSCOMB - LAW LIBRARY
One Alamo Center
106 S. St. Mary's St.   Phone: (512) 226-4211
San Antonio, TX 78205   Noreen McGee, Libn.

MIND SCIENCE FOUNDATION - LIBRARY
102 W. Rector, Suite 215   Phone: (512) 349-5127
San Antonio, TX 78216   Diane Morton Holmes, Lib.Dir.

OBLATE SCHOOL OF THEOLOGY - LIBRARY
285 Oblate Dr.   Phone: (512) 341-1366
San Antonio, TX 78216-6693   James Maney, Lib.Dir.

**OUR LADY OF THE LAKE UNIVERSITY - OLD SPANISH MISSIONS
HISTORICAL RESEARCH LIBRARY**
411 S.W. 24th St.   Phone: (512) 434-6711
San Antonio, TX 78285   Fr. Benedict Leutenegger, Archv.

**OUR LADY OF THE LAKE UNIVERSITY - WORDEN SCHOOL OF SOCIAL
SERVICE - LIBRARY**
411 S.W. 24th St.   Phone: (512) 434-6711
San Antonio, TX 78285   Margaret Pittman Munke, Libn.

PLANNED PARENTHOOD CENTER OF SAN ANTONIO - LIBRARY
104 Babcock Rd.   Phone: (512) 736-2244
San Antonio, TX 78201   Karen Glenney, Pub.Aff.Dir.

**PROTESTANT EPISCOPAL CHURCH - EPISCOPAL DIOCESE OF WEST TEXAS
- CATHEDRAL HOUSE ARCHIVES**
111 Torcido Dr.
Box 6885   Phone: (512) 824-5387
San Antonio, TX 78209   Zethyl T. LeStourgeon, Dir.

ST. MARY'S UNIVERSITY - LAW LIBRARY †
One Camino Santa Maria   Phone: (512) 436-3435
San Antonio, TX 78284   Robert L. Summers, Jr., Dir.

SAN ANTONIO COLLEGE - SPECIAL COLLECTIONS
1001 Howard St.   Phone: (512) 734-7311
San Antonio, TX 78284   James O. Wallace, Dir., Lrng.Rsrcs.

SAN ANTONIO CONSERVATION SOCIETY - FOUNDATION LIBRARY
107 King William St.   Phone: (512) 224-6163
San Antonio, TX 78204   Marianna C. Jones, Libn.

SAN ANTONIO EXPRESS AND NEWS - LIBRARY †
Ave. E. & Third
Box 2171   Phone: (512) 225-7411
San Antonio, TX 78205   Judy Robinson, Hd.Libn.

SAN ANTONIO MUSEUM ASSOCIATION - LIBRARIES
3801 Broadway
Box 2601   Phone: (512) 226-5544
San Antonio, TX 78299-2601   George Anne Cormier, Asst.Libn.

**SAN ANTONIO PUBLIC LIBRARY AND INFORMATION CENTER - ART, MUSIC
AND FILMS DEPARTMENT**
203 S. St. Mary's St.   Phone: (512) 299-7795
San Antonio, TX 78205   Mary A. Wright, Hd.

**SAN ANTONIO PUBLIC LIBRARY AND INFORMATION CENTER - BUSINESS,
SCIENCE AND TECHNOLOGY DEPARTMENT**
203 S. St. Mary's St.   Phone: (512) 299-7800
San Antonio, TX 78205   James Sosa, Hd.

**SAN ANTONIO PUBLIC LIBRARY AND INFORMATION CENTER - HARRY
HERTZBERG CIRCUS COLLECTION**
210 W. Market St.   Phone: (512) 299-7810
San Antonio, TX 78205   Betty Claire King, Hd.

**SAN ANTONIO PUBLIC LIBRARY AND INFORMATION CENTER - HISTORY,
SOCIAL SCIENCE & GENERAL REFERENCE DEPT.**
203 S. St. Mary's St.   Phone: (512) 299-7813
San Antonio, TX 78205   Marie Berry, Hd.

**SAN ANTONIO PUBLIC LIBRARY AND INFORMATION CENTER -
LITERATURE, PHILOSOPHY AND RELIGION DEPARTMENT**
203 S. St. Mary's St.   Phone: (512) 299-7817
San Antonio, TX 78205   Helen K. Halloran, Hd.

SAN ANTONIO STATE CHEST HOSPITAL - HEALTH SCIENCE LIBRARY
Highland Hills Sta.
Box 23340   Phone: (512) 534-8857
San Antonio, TX 78223   Patricia Beaman, Libn.

SAN ANTONIO STATE HOSPITAL - STAFF LIBRARY
Box 23310, Highland Hills Sta.   Phone: (512) 532-8811
San Antonio, TX 78223   Patricia Small, Med.Libn.

SAN ANTONIO SYMPHONY ORCHESTRA - SYMPHONY LIBRARY
109 Lexington Ave., Suite 207   Phone: (512) 222-8573
San Antonio, TX 78205   Gregory Vaught, Libn.

SANTA ROSA MEDICAL CENTER - HEALTH SCIENCE LIBRARY
519 W. Houston St.
Sta. A, Box 7330   Phone: (512) 228-2284
San Antonio, TX 78285   Marjorie McFarland, Libn.

**SOUTHWEST FOUNDATION FOR BIOMEDICAL RESEARCH - PRESTON G.
NORTHROP MEMORIAL LIBRARY**
Box 28147   Phone: (512) 674-1410
San Antonio, TX 78284   Maureen D. Funnell, Libn.

**SOUTHWEST RESEARCH INSTITUTE - NONDESTRUCTIVE TESTING
INFORMATION ANALYSIS CENTER**
Drawer 28510   Phone: (512) 684-5111
San Antonio, TX 78284   George A. Matzkanin, Dir.

**SOUTHWEST RESEARCH INSTITUTE - THOMAS BAKER SLICK MEMORIAL
LIBRARY**
Drawer 28510   Phone: (512) 684-5111
San Antonio, TX 78284   Robert D. Armor, Libn.

SOUTHWEST TEXAS METHODIST HOSPITAL - LIBRARY
7700 Floyd Curl Dr.   Phone: (512) 696-4583
San Antonio, TX 78229   Eileen T. Lively, Libn.

**TRINITY UNIVERSITY - ELIZABETH COATES MADDUX LIBRARY - SPECIAL
COLLECTIONS**
715 Stadium Dr.
Box 56   Phone: (512) 736-8121
San Antonio, TX 78284   Richard Hume Werking, Lib.Dir.

UNITED SERVICES AUTOMOBILE ASSOCIATION - CORPORATE LIBRARY
USAA Bldg.   Phone: (512) 690-2900
San Antonio, TX 78229   Frances Bethea Day, Mgr., Corp.Lib.

U.S. AIR FORCE - ELECTRONIC SECURITY COMMAND - GENERAL LIBRARY
6923 SPTS/SSL   Phone: (512) 925-2617
San Antonio, TX 78243   Dale T. Ogden, Libn.

**U.S. AIR FORCE HOSPITAL - WILFORD HALL U.S.A.F. MEDICAL CENTER -
MEDICAL LIBRARY (SGEL) ***
Lackland AFB   Phone: (512) 670-7204
San Antonio, TX 78236   Royden R. Jones, Med.Libn.

**U.S. VETERANS ADMINISTRATION (TX-San Antonio) - MEDICAL CENTER
LIBRARY SERVICE (142D)**
7400 Merton Minter Blvd.   Phone: (512) 696-9660
San Antonio, TX 78284   Elosia Mitchell, Chf.

UNIVERSITY OF TEXAS - INSTITUTE OF TEXAN CULTURES AT SAN
ANTONIO - LIBRARY
801 S. Bowie St.
Box 1226
San Antonio, TX 78294
Phone: (512) 226-7651
Deborah S. Large, Dir.Lib.Serv.

UNIVERSITY OF TEXAS HEALTH SCIENCE CENTER, SAN ANTONIO -
BRADY/GREEN EDUCATIONAL RESOURCES CENTER
4502 Medical Dr.
San Antonio, TX 78284
Phone: (512) 223-6361
Rajia C. Tobia, Libn.

UNIVERSITY OF TEXAS HEALTH SCIENCE CENTER, SAN ANTONIO -
LIBRARY
7703 Floyd Curl Dr.
San Antonio, TX 78284
Phone: (512) 691-6271
Dr. David A. Kronick, Libn.

VALERO ENERGY CORPORATION - CORPORATE RESOURCE CENTER
530 McCullough
Box 500
San Antonio, TX 78292
Phone: (512) 246-2869
Mary S. Woods, Supv.

ZACHRY (H.B.) COMPANY - CENTRAL RECORDS AND LIBRARY
Box 21130
San Antonio, TX 78285
Phone: (512) 922-1213
Janice Burger, Libn.

FIRST UNITED METHODIST CHURCH - GERTRUDE CALLIHAN MEMORIAL
LIBRARY *
129 W. Hutchinson
Box 2490
San Marcos, TX 78666
Phone: (512) 392-6001
Hilda Carlisle, Lib.Chm.

U.S. AIR FORCE BASE - SHEPPARD BASE LIBRARY
FL 3020
Sheppard AFB, TX 76311
Phone: (817) 851-2687
Linda Fryar, Libn.

U.S. AIR FORCE HOSPITAL - SHEPPARD REGIONAL HOSPITAL - MEDICAL
LIBRARY
Sheppard AFB, TX 76311
Phone: (817) 851-6647
Maxine Gustafson, Lib.Techn.

U.S. AIR FORCE SCHOOL OF HEALTH CARE SCIENCES - ACADEMIC
LIBRARY
MSTL/114, Bldg. 1900
Sheppard AFB, TX 76311
Phone: (817) 851-2256
Theodore C. Kennedy, Supv.Libn.

AUSTIN COLLEGE - HOPKINS LIBRARY - SPECIAL COLLECTIONS
900 N. Grand
Sherman, TX 75090
Phone: (214) 892-9101
Imogene Gibson, Coll.Libn.

NORTH PARK BAPTIST CHURCH - LIBRARY
2605 Rex Cruse Dr.
Sherman, TX 75090
Phone: (214) 892-8429
Mrs. Jack Raidt, Dir. of Lib.Serv.

WELDER (Rob & Bessie) WILDLIFE FOUNDATION - LIBRARY
Box 1400
Sinton, TX 78387
Phone: (512) 364-2643
J.G. Teer, Dir.

FLUOR ENGINEERS, INC. - FLUOR HOUSTON LIBRARY
1 Fluor Dr.
Sugar Land, TX 77478
Phone: (713) 662-3960
Robin Holab-Abelman, Tech.Libn.

SUNSET TRADING POST-OLD WEST MUSEUM - LIBRARY
Rte. 1
Sunset, TX 76270
Phone: (817) 872-2027
Jack Glover, Owner

RAILROAD AND PIONEER MUSEUM, INC. - LIBRARY
Box 5126
Temple, TX 76501
Phone: (817) 778-6873
Mary Pat McLaughlin, Libn. & Dir.

SCOTT & WHITE MEMORIAL HOSPITAL - MEDICAL LIBRARY
2401 S. 31st St.
Temple, TX 76508
Phone: (817) 774-2228
Mary H. Spoede, Dir.

SLAVONIC BENEVOLENT ORDER OF THE STATE OF TEXAS - LIBRARY,
ARCHIVES, MUSEUM
520 N. Main St.
Temple, TX 76501
Phone: (817) 773-1575
Otto Hanus, Libn./Cur.

TEXAS CENTRAL COUNTIES CENTER FOR MENTAL HEALTH & MENTAL
RETARDATION SERVICES - INFO. RESOURCE CENTER
Box 518
Temple, TX 76503

U.S. VETERANS ADMINISTRATION (TX-Temple) - MEDICAL CENTER
MEDICAL LIBRARY
Olin E. Teague Veterans Adm. Ctr.
1901 S. First St.
Temple, TX 76501
Phone: (817) 778-4811
Mary E. Curtis-Kellett, Chf., Lib.Serv.

TERRELL STATE HOSPITAL - STAFF LIBRARY
Box 70
Terrell, TX 75160
Phone: (214) 563-6452
Lillian Squires, Libn.

TEXARKANA HISTORICAL SOCIETY & MUSEUM - LIBRARY
219 State Line Ave.
Box 2343
Texarkana, TX 75501
Phone: (214) 793-4831
Katy Caver, Cur.

TEXAS STATE - COURT OF APPEALS - 6TH SUPREME JUDICIAL DISTRICT -
LAW LIBRARY *
401 Texas City Hall
Third & Texas
Texarkana, TX 75501
Phone: (214) 794-2576

U.S. ARMY - MATERIEL DEVELOPMENT & READINESS COMMAND (DARCOM)
- INTERN TRAINING CENTER LIBRARY
Red River Army Depot
Texarkana, TX 75507
Phone: (214) 838-3430
Lelia K. Vollman, Lib.Tech.Supv.

MONSANTO FIBERS & INTERMEDIATES COMPANY - TECHNOLOGY CENTER
LIBRARY
Box 1311
Texas City, TX 77590
Phone: (409) 945-4431
Robert J. Bodre, Info.Supv.

UNION CARBIDE CORPORATION - SOLVENTS & INTERMEDIATES DIVISION
- PLANT LIBRARY
3300 Fifth Ave., S.
Box 471
Texas City, TX 77590
Phone: (409) 948-5562
Jean Croix, Hd.

CHAPARRAL GENEALOGICAL SOCIETY - LIBRARY
310 N. Live Oak
Box 606
Tomball, TX 77375
Phone: (409) 372-3738
Joy A. Blake, Libn.

MEDICAL CENTER HOSPITAL - BELL-MARSH MEMORIAL LIBRARY
1000 Beckham Ave.
Box 6400
Tyler, TX 75701
Phone: (214) 597-0357
Mrs. Rae Dowdy, Med. Staff Coord.

TYLER COURIER-TIMES-TELEGRAPH - LIBRARY
Box 2030
Tyler, TX 75710
Phone: (214) 597-8111
Leoma Pratt, Libn.

DU PONT DE NEMOURS (E.I.) & COMPANY, INC. - VICTORIA PLANT
LIBRARY
Box 2626
Victoria, TX 77901
Phone: (512) 572-1349
Debbie A. Ganem, Libn.

VICTORIA COLLEGE/UNIVERSITY OF HOUSTON, VICTORIA - LIBRARY -
SPECIAL COLLECTIONS
2602 N. Ben Jordan
Victoria, TX 77901
Phone: (512) 576-3157
Dr. S. Joe McCord, Lib.Dir.

BAYLOR UNIVERSITY - ARMSTRONG BROWNING LIBRARY
Box 6336
Waco, TX 76706
Phone: (817) 755-3566

BAYLOR UNIVERSITY - CONGRESSIONAL COLLECTION
Box 245
Waco, TX 76798
Phone: (817) 755-3530
Phillip Thompson, Archv.

BAYLOR UNIVERSITY - CROUCH MUSIC LIBRARY
Moody Memorial Library
Box 6307
Waco, TX 76706
Phone: (817) 755-1366
Dr. Avery T. Sharp, Music Libn.

BAYLOR UNIVERSITY - DEPARTMENT OF GEOLOGY - FERDINAND ROEMER
  GEOLOGICAL LIBRARY
Moody Library   Phone: (817) 755-2361
Waco, TX 76703   H.H. Beaver, Chm., Dept. of Geol.

BAYLOR UNIVERSITY - J.M. DAWSON CHURCH-STATE RESEARCH CENTER
  - LIBRARY
Box 380   Phone: (817) 755-1519
Waco, TX 76798   James E. Wood, Dir.

BAYLOR UNIVERSITY - LAW LIBRARY
Box 6342   Phone: (817) 755-2168
Waco, TX 76706   Della M. Geyer, Law Libn.

BAYLOR UNIVERSITY - STRECKER MUSEUM LIBRARY
Richardson Bldg.   Phone: (817) 755-1110
Waco, TX 76798   Calvin B. Smith, Musm.Dir.

BAYLOR UNIVERSITY - TEXAS COLLECTION
Carroll Library Bldg.
Box 6396   Phone: (817) 755-1268
Waco, TX 76706   Kent Keeth, Dir.

FIRST BAPTIST CHURCH - I.C. ANDERSON MEMORIAL LIBRARY & MEDIA
  CENTER
Fifth & Webster Sts.
Box 1847   Phone: (817) 752-3000
Waco, TX 76703   Esther Davis, Dir. of Lib.Serv.

MC LENNAN COUNTY LAW LIBRARY †
Box 1606   Phone: (817) 753-7341
Waco, TX 76703   Mary Padgett

MASONIC GRAND LODGE LIBRARY AND MUSEUM OF TEXAS
Box 446   Phone: (817) 753-7395
Waco, TX 76703   Janet Melton, Libn.

TEXAS STATE TECHNICAL INSTITUTE, WACO CAMPUS - LIBRARY
                                           Phone: (817) 799-3611
Waco, TX 76705   Linda S. Koepf, Dir., Lib.

U.S. VETERANS ADMINISTRATION (TX-Waco) - MEDICAL CENTER LIBRARY
Memorial Dr.   Phone: (817) 752-6581
Waco, TX 76703   Barbara H. Hobbs, Chf., Lib.Serv.

WACO-MC LENNAN COUNTY LIBRARY - SPECIAL COLLECTIONS
  DEPARTMENT
1717 Austin Ave.   Phone: (817) 754-4694
Waco, TX 76701   Sue Kethley, Libn.

STAR OF THE REPUBLIC MUSEUM - LIBRARY
Box 317   Phone: (409) 878-2461
Washington, TX 77880   D. Ryan Smith, Dir.

SOUTHWESTERN ASSEMBLIES OF GOD COLLEGE - P.C. NELSON MEMORIAL
  LIBRARY
1200 Sycamore   Phone: (214) 937-4010
Waxahachie, TX 75165   Mr. Murl M. Winters, Dir.

OIL INFORMATION LIBRARY OF WICHITA FALLS
813 Hamilton Bldg.   Phone: (817) 322-4241
Wichita Falls, TX 76301   Dorothy Shilts, Libn.

WICHITA FALLS STATE HOSPITAL - PATIENTS AND MEDICAL LIBRARY
Box 300   Phone: (817) 692-1220
Wichita Falls, TX 76307   Grace E. Smith, Libn.

WICHITA GENERAL HOSPITAL - MEDICAL LIBRARY *
1600 8th St.   Phone: (817) 723-1461
Wichita Falls, TX 76301   Marge Bohack, Hd.Libn.

UTAH

U.S. NATL. PARK SERVICE - TIMPANOGOS CAVE NATL. MONUMENT -
  LIBRARY
R.R. 3, Box 200   Phone: (801) 756-4497
American Fork, UT 84003   James Boll, Supv.Pk. Ranger

BRIGHAM CITY MUSEUM-GALLERY - RENTMEISTER WESTERN AMERICANA
  LIBRARY
Box 583   Phone: (801) 723-6769
Brigham City, UT 84302   Larry Douglass, Musm.Dir.

SOUTHERN UTAH STATE COLLEGE - LIBRARY - SPECIAL COLLECTIONS
  DEPARTMENT
300 W. Center St.   Phone: (801) 586-7945
Cedar City, UT 84720

U.S. ARMY - DUGWAY PROVING GROUND - TECHNICAL LIBRARY
                                           Phone: (801) 522-3565
Dugway, UT 84022   Duane Williamson, Chf., Tech.Lib.

U.S. NATL. PARK SERVICE - DINOSAUR NATL. MONUMENT - QUARRY
  VISITOR CENTER - LIBRARY †
Box 128   Phone: (801) 789-2115
Jensen, UT 84035   Dennis B. Davies, Chf. Naturalist-Dir.

UTAH WATER RESEARCH LABORATORY - LIBRARY
Utah State Univ.   Phone: (801) 752-4100
Logan, UT 84322   Tammy Bachman-Gabbert, Libn.

HERCULES, INC. - AEROSPACE DIVISION - BACCHUS WORKS LIBRARY
  INFORMATION CENTER
Box 98   Phone: (801) 250-5911
Magna, UT 84044   Cathleen F. Partridge, Lib.Supv.

BROWNING ARMS COMPANY - LIBRARY †
6175 Cottonwood Canyon Rd.
Mountain Green, UT 84121

COMPUTERIZED GENEALOGY LIBRARY
Box 174   Phone: (801) 486-3111
North Salt Lake, UT 84054   David S. Barss, Mgr.

MC KAY DEE HOSPITAL CENTER - LIBRARY
3939 Harrison Blvd.   Phone: (801) 399-4141
Ogden, UT 84409   Mark Meldrum, Lib.Dir.

ST. BENEDICT'S HOSPITAL - HEALTH SCIENCES LIBRARY
5475 S. 500 East   Phone: (801) 479-2055
Ogden, UT 84403   Sandy Eckersley, Med.Libn.

U.S. FOREST SERVICE - INTERMOUNTAIN FOREST & RANGE EXPERIMENT
  STATION - LIBRARY
Forest Service Bldg.
507 25th St.   Phone: (801) 625-5444
Ogden, UT 84401   Elizabeth G. Close, Tech.Info.Off.

WEBER COUNTY LAW LIBRARY
Municipal Bldg.   Phone: (801) 399-8466
Ogden, UT 84401   Grace A. Rost, Libn.

GSG, INC. - CTI LIBRARY SYSTEMS, INC. *
1455 S. State St., Suite 3   Phone: (801) 224-1390
Orem, UT 84057   Paul Sybrowsky, Pres.

BRIGHAM YOUNG UNIVERSITY - ARCHIVES AND MANUSCRIPTS DIVISION
  - ARCHIVES OF RECORDED SOUND
5030 Harold B. Lee Library   Phone: (801) 378-6373
Provo, UT 84602   John F. Bluth, Cur.

BRIGHAM YOUNG UNIVERSITY - BEAN MUSEUM - RESEARCH LIBRARY
390 MLBM   Phone: (801) 378-4585
Provo, UT 84602   Jody Chandler, Lib.Supv.

BRIGHAM YOUNG UNIVERSITY - HUMANITIES AND ARTS DIVISION
  LIBRARY
University Library   Phone: (801) 378-4005
Provo, UT 84602   Blaine H. Hall, Div.Coord.

BRIGHAM YOUNG UNIVERSITY - J. REUBEN CLARK LAW SCHOOL LIBRARY
B.Y.U.   Phone: (801) 378-3593
Provo, UT 84602   David A. Thomas, Law Libn.

BRIGHAM YOUNG UNIVERSITY - MUSEUM OF PEOPLES AND CULTURES
  LIBRARY
Allen Hall   Phone: (801) 378-6112
Provo, UT 84602   Dale L. Berge, Dir.

BRIGHAM YOUNG UNIVERSITY - RELIGION AND HISTORY DIVISION
   LIBRARY
University Library   Phone: (801) 378-6198
Provo, UT 84602   Donald H. Howard, Div.Coord.

BRIGHAM YOUNG UNIVERSITY - SCIENCE DIVISION LIBRARY
University Library   Phone: (801) 378-2986
Provo, UT 84602   Richard Jensen, Div.Coord.

BRIGHAM YOUNG UNIVERSITY - SOCIAL SCIENCE DIVISION LIBRARY
University Library   Phone: (801) 378-3809
Provo, UT 84602   Aftar Miner, Div.Coord.

BRIGHAM YOUNG UNIVERSITY - SPECIAL COLLECTIONS
University Library   Phone: (801) 378-2932
Provo, UT 84602   Chad Flake, Cur.

BRIGHAM YOUNG UNIVERSITY - TANNER SCHOOL OF MANAGEMENT -
   LIBRARY
410 TNRB
Box 188   Phone: (801) 378-3924
Provo, UT 84602   Gordon C. Casper, Bus.Libn.

BRIGHAM YOUNG UNIVERSITY - UTAH VALLEY BRANCH GENEALOGICAL
   LIBRARY
Harold B. Lee Library, Rm. 4385   Phone: (801) 378-3934
Provo, UT 84602   Donald H. Howard, Div.Coord.

HIGH PRESSURE DATA CENTER *
Box 7246
Provo, UT 84602   Dr. Leo Merrill, Dir.

UTAH STATE HOSPITAL - LIBRARY
East Center St.
Box 270   Phone: (801) 373-4400
Provo, UT 84601   Janina Chilton, Libn.

UTAH VALLEY HOSPITAL - MEDICAL LIBRARY
1034 N. 500 W.   Phone: (801) 373-7850
Provo, UT 84601   Gregory R. Patterson, Dir., Med.Lib.

CHURCH OF JESUS CHRIST OF LATTER-DAY SAINTS - ST. GEORGE BRANCH
   GENEALOGICAL LIBRARY
Box 417
St. George, UT 84770   Dr. David R. Morris, Libn.

AMERICAN ACADEMY OF PSYCHOTHERAPISTS - TAPE LIBRARY
585 Third Ave.   Phone: (801) 532-2839
Salt Lake City, UT 84103   James H. Magleby, Dir.

AMERICAN EXPRESS COMPANY - TRAVELERS CHEQUE DIVISION - T/C
   SYSTEMS LIBRARY
4315 S. 2700 W.   Phone: (801) 965-5000
Salt Lake City, UT 84184   Louise Pollard, Sys.Libn.

CHURCH OF JESUS CHRIST OF LATTER-DAY SAINTS - GENEALOGICAL
   LIBRARY
50 E. North Temple St.   Phone: (801) 531-2331
Salt Lake City, UT 84150   David M. Mayfield, Dir.

CHURCH OF JESUS CHRIST OF LATTER-DAY SAINTS - HISTORICAL
   DEPARTMENT - CHURCH LIBRARY-ARCHIVES
50 E. North Temple St.   Phone: (801) 531-2745
Salt Lake City, UT 84150   Donald T. Schmidt, Dir., Lib.Archv.

DESERET NEWS PUBLISHING CO. - DESERET NEWS LIBRARY &
   INFORMATION
30 East 100 S.
Box 1257   Phone: (801) 237-2155
Salt Lake City, UT 84110   Audrey M. Clark, Hd.Libn.

EIMCO PROCESS EQUIPMENT COMPANY - TECHNICAL LIBRARY †
Box 300   Phone: (801) 526-2492
Salt Lake City, UT 84110

HOLY CROSS HOSPITAL - MEDICAL LIBRARY
1045 E. First South St.   Phone: (801) 350-4060
Salt Lake City, UT 84102   Sr. M. Fidelia, Med.Libn.

INTERGALACTIC CORP. - LIBRARY
3585 Via Terra
Box 15752   Phone: (801) 262-0094
Salt Lake City, UT 84115   Douglas MacGregor, Dir.

L.D.S. HOSPITAL - LIBRARY
325 Eighth Ave.   Phone: (801) 321-1054
Salt Lake City, UT 84143   Mr. Terry L. Heyer, Lib.Dir.

MOUNTAIN FUEL SUPPLY COMPANY - CORPORATE LIBRARY
180 E. 100 South   Phone: (801) 534-5691
Salt Lake City, UT 84139   Vicky York, Corp.Libn.

NORTH AMERICAN WEATHER CONSULTANTS - TECHNICAL LIBRARY †
1141 E. 3900 S. A230
Salt Lake City, UT 84117   Carol Robinson Simpson, Libn.

PROTESTANT EPISCOPAL CHURCH - EPISCOPAL DIOCESE OF UTAH -
   ARCHIVES
231 E. First St.   Phone: (801) 322-3400
Salt Lake City, UT 84111

ST. MARK'S HOSPITAL - LIBRARY
1200 East 3900 South St.   Phone: (801) 268-7004
Salt Lake City, UT 84117   Kerry F. Skidmore, Libn.

SALT LAKE CITY SCHOOLS - DISTRICT LEARNING CENTER
1575 S. State   Phone: (801) 328-7279
Salt Lake City, UT 84115   Marian Karpisek, Hd.

SALT LAKE COUNTY LAW LIBRARY
240 E. 400 South, Rm. 219   Phone: (801) 535-7518
Salt Lake City, UT 84111   Jean Ann McMurrin, Law Libn.

SALT LAKE TRIBUNE - LIBRARY
143 S. Main St.   Phone: (801) 237-2001
Salt Lake City, UT 84117   Laurene A. Sowby, Hd.Libn.

SPERRY COMPUTER SYSTEMS - LIBRARY/TECHNICAL INFORMATION
   CENTER
322 North 2200 West   Phone: (801) 539-5222
Salt Lake City, UT 84116   Phyllis J. Nye, Libn.

STOVE KING - LIBRARY
1116 Capistrano Dr.   Phone: (801) 363-7143
Salt Lake City, UT 84116   Clarence Froman, Owner

TERRA TEK RESEARCH - TECHNICAL LIBRARY
420 Wakara Way
University Research Park   Phone: (801) 584-2400
Salt Lake City, UT 84108   Sharlene Ivie, Libn.

U.S. BUREAU OF MINES - SALT LAKE CITY RESEARCH CENTER - LIBRARY
729 Arapeen Dr.   Phone: (801) 524-6112
Salt Lake City, UT 84108   W.I. Nissen, Tech.Supv.

U.S. DEPT. OF COMMERCE - INTERNATIONAL TRADE ADMINISTRATION -
   SALT LAKE CITY DISTRICT OFFICE LIBRARY
340 U.S. Post Office Bldg.
350 S. Main St.   Phone: (801) 524-5116
Salt Lake City, UT 84101   Stephen P. Smoot, Dir.

U.S. VETERANS ADMINISTRATION (UT-Salt Lake City) - HOSPITAL
   MEDICAL LIBRARY
500 Foothill Dr.   Phone: (801) 582-1209
Salt Lake City, UT 84148   Cherryi M. Povey, Chf., Lib.Serv.

UNIVERSITY OF UTAH - AUDIO-VISUAL SERVICES
Marriott Library, 4th Fl.   Phone: (801) 581-6283
Salt Lake City, UT 84112   Ralph E. Kranz, AV Libn.

UNIVERSITY OF UTAH - CENTER FOR PUBLIC AFFAIRS AND
   ADMINISTRATION - RESEARCH LIBRARY
214 Orson Spencer Hall   Phone: (801) 581-6781
Salt Lake City, UT 84112   Bryna Pocock, Libn.

UNIVERSITY OF UTAH - DOCUMENTS DIVISION
Marriott Library   Phone: (801) 581-8394
Salt Lake City, UT 84112   Julianne P. Hinz, Doc.Libn.

UNIVERSITY OF UTAH - HUMAN RELATIONS AREA FILES
Marriott Library
Salt Lake City, UT 84112
Phone: (801) 581-7024
Mark W. Emery, Ref.Libn.

UNIVERSITY OF UTAH - INSTRUCTIONAL MEDIA SERVICES
207 Milton Bennion Hall
Salt Lake City, UT 84112
Phone: (801) 581-6112
Stephen H. Hess, Dir.

UNIVERSITY OF UTAH - LAW LIBRARY
College of Law
Salt Lake City, UT 84112
Phone: (801) 581-6438
Ms. Lane Wilkins, Dir.

UNIVERSITY OF UTAH - MAP LIBRARY
158 Marriott Library
Salt Lake City, UT 84112
Phone: (801) 581-7533
Barbara Cox, Map Libn.

UNIVERSITY OF UTAH - MATHEMATICS LIBRARY
121 JWB
Salt Lake City, UT 84112
Phone: (801) 581-6208
Christine Zeidner, Sci. & Engr.Libn.

UNIVERSITY OF UTAH - MIDDLE EAST LIBRARY
Marriott Library
Salt Lake City, UT 84112
Phone: (801) 581-6311
Ragai N. Makar, Libn.

UNIVERSITY OF UTAH - SPECIAL COLLECTIONS DEPARTMENT
Marriott Library
Salt Lake City, UT 84112
Phone: (801) 581-8863
Gregory C. Thompson, Asst.Dir., Spec.Coll.

UNIVERSITY OF UTAH - SPENCER S. ECCLES HEALTH SCIENCES LIBRARY
Bldg. 89
10 N. Medical Dr.
Salt Lake City, UT 84112
Phone: (801) 581-8771
Priscilla M. Mayden, Dir.

UPPER COLORADO RIVER COMMISSION - LIBRARY
355 S. Fourth East St.
Salt Lake City, UT 84111
Phone: (801) 531-1150
Gerald R. Zimmerman, Exec.Dir.

UTAH STATE ARCHIVES
Archives Bldg.
Capitol Hill
Salt Lake City, UT 84114
Phone: (801) 533-5250
M. Liisa Fagerlund, State Archv.

UTAH STATE BOARD OF EDUCATION - UTAH INFORMATION TECHNICAL
DEMONSTRATION CENTER
Curriculum and Instruction Program
250 E. Fifth, S.
Salt Lake City, UT 84111
Phone: (801) 533-5061
Robert Olson, Mgr.

UTAH STATE HISTORICAL SOCIETY - RESEARCH LIBRARY
300 Rio Grande
Salt Lake City, UT 84105
Phone: (801) 533-5808
Jay M. Haymond, Libn.

UTAH STATE LAW LIBRARY
332 State Capitol Bldg.
Salt Lake City, UT 84114
Phone: (801) 533-5280
Geoffrey J. Butler, Law Libn.

UTAH STATE LIBRARY
2150 South 300 West, Suite 16
Salt Lake City, UT 84115
Phone: (801) 533-5875
Russell L. Davis, Dir.

UTAH STATE LIBRARY - BLIND AND PHYSICALLY HANDICAPPED PROGRAM
- REGIONAL LIBRARY
2150 South 300 West, Suite 16
Salt Lake City, UT 84115
Phone: (801) 533-5855
Gerald Buttars, Dir.

UTAH STATE LIBRARY - FILM PROGRAM
2150 South 300 West, Suite 9
Salt Lake City, UT 84115
Phone: (801) 533-5875
David Mann, Hd.

U.S. NATL. PARK SERVICE - ZION NATL. PARK - LIBRARY
Springdale, UT 84767
Phone: (801) 772-3256
Marion Hilkey, Libn.

DINOSAUR NATURAL HISTORY MUSEUM - REFERENCE LIBRARY
235 E. Main St.
Vernal, UT 84078
Phone: (801) 789-3799
Alden H. Hamblin, Dir./Park Mgr.

VERMONT

CANFIELD MEMORIAL LIBRARY - RUSSELL VERMONTIANA COLLECTION
Arlington, VT 05250
Phone: (802) 375-6153
Mary Henning, Libn.

CARMELITE MONASTERY - LIBRARY OF THE IMMACULATE HEART OF
MARY
Beckley Hill
Barre, VT 05641
Phone: (802) 476-8362
Sr. Jeanne M. Gonyon, Libn.

CENTRAL VERMONT HOSPITAL - MEDICAL LIBRARY
Box 547
Barre, VT 05641
Phone: (802) 229-9121
Betty-Jean Eastman, Med.Libn.

ASSOCIATION OF NORTH AMERICAN DIRECTORY PUBLISHERS - PRICE &
LEE COMPANY DIRECTORY LIBRARY
Box 317
Bellows Falls, VT 05101
Pat Lentocha

BENNINGTON MUSEUM - GENEALOGICAL LIBRARY
W. Main St.
Bennington, VT 05201
Phone: (802) 442-2180
P.N. Kennedy, Libn.

BLACKMER (Samuel H.) MEMORIAL LIBRARY *
County Court House
207 South St.
Bennington, VT 05201
Phone: (802) 442-8528

PUTNAM (Henry W.) MEMORIAL HOSPITAL - MEDICAL LIBRARY *
100 Hospital Dr.
Bennington, VT 05201
Phone: (802) 442-6361
Jack Hall, Med.Libn.

BRANDON TRAINING SCHOOL - LIBRARY
Brandon, VT 05733
Phone: (802) 247-5711
John J. Choppa, Staff Dev.Coord.

AUSTINE SCHOOL - LIBRARY
120 Maple St.
Brattleboro, VT 05301
Phone: (802) 254-4571
John I. Enola, Libn.

BRATTLEBORO MEMORIAL HOSPITAL - MEDICAL LIBRARY
9 Belmont Ave.
Brattleboro, VT 05301
Phone: (802) 257-0341
Martha J. Fenn, Libn.

BRATTLEBORO RETREAT - MEDICAL LIBRARY
75 Linden St.
Brattleboro, VT 05301
Phone: (802) 257-7785
Jane Rand, Dir. of Lib.Serv.

EXPERIMENT IN INTERNATIONAL LIVING - SCHOOL FOR INTERNATIONAL
TRAINING - DONALD B. WATT LIBRARY
Kipling Rd.
Brattleboro, VT 05301
Phone: (802) 257-7751
Shirley Capron, Pub.Serv.Libn.

NEW ENGLAND SOLAR ENERGY ASSOCIATION - LIBRARY
14 Green St.
Box 541
Brattleboro, VT 05301
Phone: (802) 254-2386
Larry Sherwood, Assoc.Dir.

MUSEUM OF THE AMERICAS - LIBRARY
Brookfield, VT 05036
Phone: (802) 276-3386
Earle W. Newton, Dir.

GENERAL ELECTRIC COMPANY - AIRCRAFT EQUIPMENT DIV. - ARMAMENT
& ELECTRICAL SYSTEMS DEPT. ENGINEERING LIBRARY
Lakeside Ave.
Burlington, VT 05402
Phone: (802) 657-6598
Raymond M. Palmer, Tech.Libn.

UNIVERSITY OF VERMONT - CHEMISTRY/PHYSICS LIBRARY
Burlington, VT 05405
Phone: (802) 656-2268
Craig A. Robertson, Chem./Physics Libn.

UNIVERSITY OF VERMONT - DIVISION OF HEALTH SCIENCES - CHARLES A.
DANA MEDICAL LIBRARY
Given Bldg.
Burlington, VT 05405
Phone: (802) 656-2200
Ellen Nagle, Med.Libn.

UNIVERSITY OF VERMONT - PRINGLE HERBARIUM - LIBRARY
Botany Dept.
Phone: (802) 656-3221
Burlington, VT 05405   David S. Barrington, Cur.

UNIVERSITY OF VERMONT - WILBUR COLLECTION OF VERMONTIANA
Bailey/Howe Library
Phone: (802) 656-2138
Burlington, VT 05405   John Buechler, Asst.Dir., Spec.Coll.

CASTLETON HISTORICAL SOCIETY - MUSEUM LIBRARY *
Main St.
Phone: (802) 468-2226
Castleton, VT 05735   Mrs. Finley Shepard, Cur.

CASTLETON STATE COLLEGE - CALVIN COOLIDGE LIBRARY - LEARNING
  RESOURCES CENTER
Phone: (802) 468-5611
Castleton, VT 05735

AMERICAN SOCIETY OF DOWSERS, INC. - LIBRARY
Phone: (802) 684-3417
Danville, VT 05828   Paul J. Sevigny, Pres.

IBM CORPORATION - GENERAL TECHNOLOGY DIVISION - INFORMATION
  CENTER/LEARNING CENTER
Phone: (802) 769-2331
Essex Junction, VT 05452   David C. Palmer, Mgr.

WALKER MUSEUM - LIBRARY
Fairlee, VT 05045

CHAPMAN (Bruce) COMPANY - LIBRARY
Phone: (802) 843-2321
Grafton, VT 05146   William Chapman, Libn.

GRAFTON HISTORICAL MUSEUM
Main St.
Phone: (802) 843-2388
Grafton, VT 05146   Helen M. Pettengill, Musm.Dir.

AMERICAN MUSEUM OF FLY FISHING, INC. - LIBRARY
Phone: (802) 362-3300
Manchester, VT 05254   JoAnna Sheridan, Registrar

PORTER MEDICAL CENTER - MEDICAL LIBRARY AND INFORMATION
  SERVICE
South St.
Phone: (802) 388-7901
Middlebury, VT 05753   Simone Rollin Lazarus, Libn.

SHELDON ART MUSEUM - GOVERNOR JOHN W. STEWART & MR. & MRS.
  CHARLES M. SWIFT RESEARCH CENTER LIBRARY
1 Park St.
Phone: (802) 388-2117
Middlebury, VT 05753   Polly C. Darnell, Libn.

NATIONAL LIFE INSURANCE COMPANY - LIBRARY
National Life Dr.
Phone: (802) 229-3278
Montpelier, VT 05602   Saba L. Foster, Chf.Libn.

VERMONT HISTORICAL SOCIETY - LIBRARY
Pavilion Bldg., 109 State St.
Phone: (802) 828-2291
Montpelier, VT 05602   Mrs. Reidun D. Nuquist, Libn.

VERMONT STATE AGENCY OF ADMINISTRATION - PUBLIC RECORDS
  DIVISION
State Administrative Bldg.
Phone: (802) 828-3288
Montpelier, VT 05602   A. John Yacavoni, Asst.Dir.

VERMONT STATE DEPARTMENT OF EDUCATION - VERMONT
  EDUCATIONAL RESOURCE CENTER (VERC)
120 State St.
Phone: (802) 828-3124
Montpelier, VT 05602   David D. Joslyn, Libn.

VERMONT STATE DEPARTMENT OF LIBRARIES
State Office Bldg. Post Office
Phone: (802) 828-3261
Montpelier, VT 05602   Patricia E. Klinck, State Libn.

VERMONT STATE OFFICE OF THE SECRETARY OF STATE - VERMONT
  STATE PAPERS
Redstone Bldg.
27 Terrace St.
Phone: (802) 828-2363
Montpelier, VT 05602   D. Gregory Sanford, State Archv.

NORTH COUNTRY HOSPITAL - MEDICAL LIBRARY
Prouty Dr.
Phone: (802) 334-7331
Newport, VT 05855   Janet Miller, Med.Libn.

NORWICH UNIVERSITY - CHAPLIN MEMORIAL LIBRARY - SPECIAL
  COLLECTIONS
Phone: (802) 485-5011
Northfield, VT 05663   Jacqueline S. Painter, Doc.Libn./Univ.Archv.

GIFFORD MEMORIAL HOSPITAL - HEALTH INFORMATION CENTER
44 S. Main St.
Phone: (802) 728-3366
Randolph, VT 05060   Patience L. Crowley, Dir.

VERMONT TECHNICAL COLLEGE - HARTNESS LIBRARY
Phone: (802) 728-3391
Randolph Center, VT 05061   Dewey F. Patterson, Lib.Dir.

CENTRAL VERMONT PUBLIC SERVICE CORPORATION - CORPORATE
  LIBRARY
77 Grove St.
Phone: (802) 773-2711
Rutland, VT 05701   Linda G. Cameron, Libn.

RUTLAND REGIONAL MEDICAL CENTER - HEALTH SCIENCE LIBRARY
Allen St.
Phone: (802) 775-7111
Rutland, VT 05701   Cherie L. Goderwis, R.N., Dir.

NORTHWESTERN MEDICAL CENTER - INFORMATION CENTER
Fairfield St.
Phone: (802) 524-5911
St. Albans, VT 05478   June C. Wakefield, Info.Ctr.Dir.

FAIRBANKS MUSEUM AND PLANETARIUM - LIBRARY
Main and Prospect Sts.
Phone: (802) 748-2378
St. Johnsbury, VT 05819   Howard B. Reed, Act. Co-Dir., Musm.Coll.

NORTHEASTERN VERMONT REGIONAL HOSPITAL - INFORMATION
  CENTER/LIBRARY
Hospital Dr.
Phone: (802) 748-8141
St. Johnsbury, VT 05819   Eleanor Simons, Libn.

SHELBURNE MUSEUM, INC. - RESEARCH LIBRARY
Phone: (802) 985-3346
Shelburne, VT 05482   Leslie A. Hasker, Lib.Asst.

VERMONT LAW SCHOOL - LIBRARY
Chelsea St.
Phone: (802) 763-8303
South Royalton, VT 05068   W. Leslie Peat, Law Libn.

SPRINGFIELD HOSPITAL - INFORMATION CENTER LIBRARY
25 Ridgewood Rd.
Phone: (802) 885-2151
Springfield, VT 05156   Holly H. Eddy, Med.Libn.

MILLHOUSE BUNDY PERFORMING & FINE ARTS CENTER - LIBRARY
Phone: (802) 496-3713
Waitsfield, VT 05673

VERMONT STATE HOSPITAL - AGENCY OF HUMAN SERVICES LIBRARY
103 S. Main St.
Waterbury, VT 05676   Susan Maywood, Chf.Libn.

U.S. VETERANS ADMINISTRATION (VT-White River Junction) - ALLIED
  HEALTH SCIENCES LIBRARY
Phone: (802) 295-9369
White River Junction, VT 05001   John A. Package, Chf.Libn.

FANNY ALLEN HOSPITAL - INFORMATION CENTER
101 College Pkwy.
Phone: (802) 655-1234
Winooski, VT 05404   Ann M. Bousquet, Med.Libn.

CENTER FOR NORTHERN STUDIES - LIBRARY
Town Hill
Phone: (802) 888-4331
Wolcott, VT 05680   William E. Osgood, Libn.

VERMONT INSTITUTE OF NATURAL SCIENCES - LIBRARY
Church Hill Rd.
Phone: (802) 457-2779
Woodstock, VT 05091   Sarah B. Laughlin, Dir.

WOODSTOCK HISTORICAL SOCIETY, INC. - JOHN COTTON DANA LIBRARY
26 Elm St.
Phone: (802) 457-1822
Woodstock, VT 05091   John Martin, Pres.

VIRGINIA

AIR AND SPACE MARKETING - INFORMATION CENTER
6203 Yellowstone Dr.   Phone: (703) 941-4724
Alexandria, VA 22312   Douglas Campbell, Dir.

ALEXANDRIA CITY PUBLIC SCHOOLS - EDUCATIONAL MEDIA CENTER -
   NICHOLS PROFESSIONAL LIBRARY
3801 W. Braddock Rd.   Phone: (703) 998-9045
Alexandria, VA 22302   Dale W. Brown, Dir., Lib. & Media Serv.

ALEXANDRIA GAZETTE - LIBRARY *
Box 119
Alexandria, VA 22313

ALEXANDRIA HOSPITAL - HEALTH SCIENCES LIBRARY
4320 Seminary Rd.   Phone: (703) 379-3126
Alexandria, VA 22304   Libby Hamilton, Libn.

ALEXANDRIA LIBRARY - LLOYD HOUSE
220 N. Washington St.   Phone: (703) 838-4577
Alexandria, VA 22314   Jeanne G. Plitt, Dir.

AMERICAN ASSOCIATION FOR COUNSELING AND DEVELOPMENT -
   PROFESSIONAL INFORMATION SERVICE
5999 Stevenson Ave.   Phone: (703) 823-9800
Alexandria, VA 22304   Sylvia Nisenoff, Prof.Info.Spec.

AMERICAN GEOLOGICAL INSTITUTE - GEOREF INFORMATION SYSTEM
4220 King St.   Phone: (703) 379-2480
Alexandria, VA 22302   John Mulvihill, Dir.

AMERICAN HELICOPTER SOCIETY - TECHNICAL INFORMATION
217 N. Washington St.   Phone: (703) 684-6777
Alexandria, VA 22314   John F. Zugschwert, Exec.Dir.

AMERICAN ORTHOTIC AND PROSTHETIC ASSOCIATION - LIBRARY
717 Pendleton St.   Phone: (703) 836-7114
Alexandria, VA 22314   William L. McCulloch, Exec.Dir.

AMERICAN TRUCKING ASSOCIATIONS, INC. - LIBRARY
2200 Mill Rd.
Alexandria, VA 22314   Linda Rothbart, Dir., Lib.Serv.

ATLANTIC RESEARCH CORPORATION - LIBRARY †
5390 Cherokee Ave.   Phone: (703) 642-4178
Alexandria, VA 22314   Ellen Levin, Libn.

CABLE TELEVISION INFORMATION CENTER
1500 N. Beauregard St., Suite 205   Phone: (703) 845-1700
Alexandria, VA 22311   Harold E. Horn, Pres.

CONTROL DATA CORPORATION - GOVERNMENT SYSTEMS LIBRARY
1800 N. Beauregard St.   Phone: (703) 998-4606
Alexandria, VA 22311   Barbara H. Carey, Libn.

FIRST CHRISTIAN CHURCH - LIBRARY *
2723 King St.   Phone: (703) 549-3911
Alexandria, VA 22302   Sue Solomon, Libn.

FORT WARD MUSEUM - DOROTHY C.S. STARR CIVIL WAR RESEARCH
   LIBRARY
4301 W. Braddock Rd.   Phone: (703) 838-4848
Alexandria, VA 22304   Wanda S. Dowell, Cur.

HUMAN RESOURCES RESEARCH ORGANIZATION - VAN EVERA LIBRARY
1100 S. Washington St.   Phone: (703) 549-3611
Alexandria, VA 22314   Josephine R. Hunter, Libn.

IFI/PLENUM DATA COMPANY - LIBRARY
302 Swann Ave.   Phone: (703) 683-1085
Alexandria, VA 22301   Harry M. Allcock, V.P.

INSTITUTE FOR DEFENSE ANALYSES - TECHNICAL INFORMATION
   SERVICES
1801 N. Beauregard St.   Phone: (703) 845-2043
Alexandria, VA 22311   Cathryn C. Lyon, Mgr., Tech.Info.Serv.

JHK & ASSOCIATES - TECHNICAL LIBRARY - EAST
4660 Kenmore Ave.   Phone: (703) 370-2411
Alexandria, VA 22304   Richard Presby, Dir.

NATIONAL RECREATION AND PARK ASSOCIATION - JOSEPH LEE
   MEMORIAL LIBRARY AND INFORMATION CENTER
3101 Park Ctr. Dr., 12th Fl.
Alexandria, VA 22302

OCTAMERON ASSOCIATES, INC. - RESEARCH LIBRARY
820 Fontaine St.   Phone: (703) 836-1019
Alexandria, VA 22302   Karen Stokstad, Libn.

TIME-LIFE BOOKS INC. - REFERENCE LIBRARY
777 Duke St.   Phone: (703) 960-5353
Alexandria, VA 22314   Louise D. Forstall, Hd.Libn.

UNITED FRESH FRUIT AND VEGETABLE ASSOCIATION - LIBRARY
N. Washington at Madison   Phone: (703) 836-3410
Alexandria, VA 22314   Charles Magoon, Dir. of Res.

U.S. ARMY - THE INSTITUTE OF HERALDRY - LIBRARY
Cameron Station
5010 Duke St., Bldg. 15   Phone: (202) 274-6544
Alexandria, VA 22314   Herbert M. Pastan, Libn.

U.S. ARMY - MATERIEL DEVELOPMENT & READINESS COMMAND -
   HEADQUARTERS - TECHNICAL LIBRARY
5001 Eisenhower Ave.   Phone: (202) 274-8152
Alexandria, VA 22333   Phyllis Ortutay, Chf.

U.S. ARMY - OFFICE OF THE ADJUTANT GENERAL - MORALE SUPPORT
   DIRECTORATE - LIBRARY ACTIVITIES DIVISION
Hoffman Bldg. I, Rm. 1450   Phone: (703) 325-9700
Alexandria, VA 22331   Nellie B. Strickland, Div.Chf.

U.S. BUREAU OF LAND MANAGEMENT - EASTERN STATES OFFICE LIBRARY
350 S. Pickett St.
Alexandria, VA 22304   M. Willette Proctor, Mgt.Asst.

U.S. DEFENSE LOGISTICS AGENCY - HEADQUARTERS LIBRARY
Cameron Sta.   Phone: (202) 274-6055
Alexandria, VA 22304-6100   Barbara Ralston, Chf.Libn.

U.S. DEFENSE TECHNICAL INFORMATION CENTER
Cameron Sta.   Phone: (202) 274-7633
Alexandria, VA 22314   Hubert E. Sauter, Adm.

U.S. DEFENSE TECHNICAL INFORMATION CENTER - TECHNICAL LIBRARY
Cameron Sta., Bldg. 5   Phone: (202) 274-6833
Alexandria, VA 22314   Robert Billingsley, Libn.

U.S. NAVY - CENTER FOR NAVAL ANALYSES - LIBRARY
2000 N. Beauregard St.   Phone: (703) 998-3580
Alexandria, VA 22311   Jill C. Hanna, Chf.Libn.

U.S. NAVY - NAVAL FACILITIES ENGINEERING COMMAND - TECHNICAL
   LIBRARY
Hoffman Bldg. 2, 200 Stovall St.   Phone: (202) 325-8507
Alexandria, VA 22332   Cynthia K. Neyland, Libn.

U.S. NAVY - OFFICE OF THE JUDGE ADVOCATE GENERAL - LAW LIBRARY
Hoffman Bldg. No. 2
200 Stovall St.   Phone: (202) 325-9565
Alexandria, VA 22332   Richard S. Barrows, Libn.

UNITED WAY OF AMERICA - INFORMATION CENTER
701 N. Fairfax St.   Phone: (703) 836-7100
Alexandria, VA 22314-2088   Henry M. Smith, Dir.

VIRGINIA THEOLOGICAL SEMINARY - BISHOP PAYNE LIBRARY
Seminary Rd. & Quaker Ln.   Phone: (703) 370-6602
Alexandria, VA 22304   J.H. Goodwin, Libn.

VSE CORPORATION - TECHNICAL LIBRARY
2550 Huntington Ave.   Phone: (703) 960-4600
Alexandria, VA 22303   Merriel T. Whitehead, Libn.

WESTMINSTER PRESBYTERIAN CHURCH - LIBRARY
2701 Cameron Mills Rd.   Phone: (703) 549-4766
Alexandria, VA 22302   Esther M. Cook, Libn.

AMELIA HISTORICAL LIBRARY - JACKSON MEMORIAL LIBRARY
Box 113
Amelia, VA 23002   W. Cary McConnaughey, Chm.

U.S. NATL. PARK SERVICE - APPOMATTOX COURT HOUSE NATL.
    HISTORICAL PARK - LIBRARY
Box 218   Phone: (703) 352-8987
Appomattox, VA 24522   Ronald G. Wilson, Pk.Hist.

AMERICAN ACADEMY OF PHYSICIAN ASSISTANTS - INFORMATION
    CENTER
1117 N. 19th St., Suite 300   Phone: (703) 525-4200
Arlington, VA 22209   Karen L. LaViolette, Info. & Pub.Asst.

AMERICAN GAS ASSOCIATION - LIBRARY
1515 Wilson Blvd.   Phone: (703) 841-8415
Arlington, VA 22209   Steven J. Dorner, Mgr., Lib.Serv.

AMERICAN GEAR MANUFACTURERS ASSOCIATION - LIBRARY
1901 N. Fort Myer Dr., Suite 1000   Phone: (703) 525-1600
Arlington, VA 22209

AMERICAN PATENT LAW ASSOCIATION - PATENT LAW LIBRARY
2001 Jefferson Davis Hwy., Suite 203   Phone: (703) 521-1680
Arlington, VA 22202   Gail D. Durant, Dir. of Adm.

AMERICAN PSYCHOLOGICAL ASSOCIATION - ARTHUR W. MELTON
    LIBRARY
1400 N. Uhle St.   Phone: (202) 833-7590
Arlington, VA 22201   Rick A. Sample, Hd.Libn.

AMERICAN WATERWAYS OPERATORS, INC. - LIBRARY
1600 Wilson Blvd., Suite 1000
Arlington, VA 22209

ANSER - TECHNICAL LIBRARY
400 Army-Navy Dr.   Phone: (703) 979-0700
Arlington, VA 22202   Francie G. Binion, Mgr.

ARCHITECTURAL WOODWORK INSTITUTE - LIBRARY
2310 S. Walter Reed Dr.   Phone: (703) 671-9100
Arlington, VA 22206

ARLINGTON COUNTY CENTRAL LIBRARY - VIRGINIANA COLLECTION
1015 N. Quincy St.   Phone: (703) 527-4777
Arlington, VA 22201   Sara Collins, Virginiana Libn.

ARLINGTON HOSPITAL - DOCTORS' LIBRARY †
1701 N. George Mason Dr.   Phone: (703) 558-6524
Arlington, VA 22205   Olga Taylor, Libn.

ARLINGTON PUBLIC SCHOOLS - PROFESSIONAL LIBRARY
1426 N. Quincy St.   Phone: (703) 558-2836
Arlington, VA 22207   Luke Yaeger, Supv., School Lib.Serv.

ARTHRITIS INFORMATION CLEARINGHOUSE
Box 9782   Phone: (703) 558-8250
Arlington, VA 22209   Lois Lunin, Project Dir.

ASBESTOS INFORMATION ASSOCIATION/NORTH AMERICA - TECHNICAL
    AND MEDICAL FILES
1745 Jefferson Davis Hwy., Suite 509   Phone: (703) 979-1150
Arlington, VA 22202   B.J. Pigg, Exec.Dir.

ASSOCIATION OF UNIVERSITY PROGRAMS IN HEALTH ADMINISTRATION -
    RESOURCE CTR. FOR HEALTH SERVICES ADM. EDUCATION
1911 N. Fort Myer Dr., Suite 503   Phone: (703) 524-5500
Arlington, VA 22209

CACI, INC. - LIBRARY AND TECHNICAL INFORMATION CENTER
1815 N. Fort Myer Dr.   Phone: (703) 841-4425
Arlington, VA 22209   William E. Baxter, Libn.

DATA USE AND ACCESS LABORATORIES (DUALABS) - LIBRARY †
1515 Wilson Blvd., Suite 607   Phone: (703) 525-1480
Arlington, VA 22209   Deborah S. Pomerance, Libn.

EDUCATIONAL RESEARCH SERVICE - LIBRARY
1800 N. Kent St.   Phone: (703) 243-2100
Arlington, VA 22209   Josephine Franklin, Coord., Info.Serv.

ENERGY & ENVIRONMENTAL ANALYSIS, INC. - LIBRARY
1655 N. Fort Myer Dr., Suite 600   Phone: (703) 528-1900
Arlington, VA 22209   Tracy Flood, Libn.

GEORGE MASON UNIVERSITY - SCHOOL OF LAW - LIBRARY
3401 N. Fairfax Dr.   Phone: (703) 841-2652
Arlington, VA 22201   Stephen L. Burnett, Dir.

GREEN THUMB LIBRARY *
1401 Wilson Blvd., Suite 100   Phone: (703) 276-0750
Arlington, VA 22209   Fred Twombley, Sr.Adm.Asst.

HARRIS & GIFFORD - LIBRARY
2037 N. Glebe Rd.   Phone: (202) 628-8700
Arlington, VA 22207   R.A. Gifford, Owner

HERNER AND COMPANY - LIBRARY
1700 N. Moore St.   Phone: (703) 558-8200
Arlington, VA 22209   Nancy D. Wright, V.P. for Lib.Serv.

INTERAMERICA RESEARCH ASSOCIATES, INC. - NATIONAL
    CLEARINGHOUSE FOR BILINGUAL EDUCATION
1555 Wilson Blvd., Suite 605   Phone: (703) 522-0710
Arlington, VA 22209   Deborah Sauve, Info.Serv.Mgr.

INTERNATIONAL BUSINESS FORMS INDUSTRIES INC. - LIBRARY
1730 N. Lynn St., Suite 501
Arlington, VA 22209

INTERNATIONAL FORTEAN ORGANIZATION - INFO RESEARCH LIBRARY
Box 367
Arlington, VA 22210-0367   Paul J. Willis, Archv.

KETRON, INC. - LIBRARY
1700 N. Moore St.   Phone: (703) 558-8700
Arlington, VA 22209   Joann Poindexter, Off.Mgr.

MC CARTHY (Walter T.) LAW LIBRARY †
1400 N. Courthouse Rd.
Court House, Rm. 501   Phone: (703) 558-2243
Arlington, VA 22201   Betty J. Waldow, Exec.Dir.

NATIONAL ALLIANCE OF SENIOR CITIZENS - LIBRARY
2525 Wilson Blvd.   Phone: (703) 528-4380
Arlington, VA 22201   C.C. Clinkscales, III, Natl.Dir.

NATIONAL CENTER FOR EMPLOYEE OWNERSHIP - LIBRARY
927 S. Walter Reed Dr., Suite 6   Phone: (703) 979-2375
Arlington, VA 22204   Corey Rosen, Exec.Dir.

NATIONAL CONFERENCE ON MINISTRY TO THE ARMED FORCES -
    CHAPLAINS MEMORIAL LIBRARY
4141 N. Henderson Rd., Suite 13
Arlington, VA 22203

NATIONAL GRADUATE UNIVERSITY - LIBRARY
1101 N. Highland St.   Phone: (703) 527-4800
Arlington, VA 22201   Dr. Jean K. Boek, Chm., Lib.Comm.

NATIONAL MENTAL HEALTH ASSOCIATION - CLIFFORD BEERS MEMORIAL
    LIBRARY
1021 Prince St.   Phone: (703) 684-7722
Arlington, VA 22314   Joshua Hammond, Dir., Commun.

SRI INTERNATIONAL - STRATEGIC CENTER LIBRARY
1611 N. Kent St.   Phone: (703) 524-2053
Arlington, VA 22209   Helga Brennan, Res.Anl.

STRAYER COLLEGE - LEARNING RESOURCES CENTER
3045 Columbia Pike   Phone: (703) 892-5100
Arlington, VA 22204   David A. Moulton, Dir.

SYSTEM PLANNING CORPORATION - TECHNICAL LIBRARY
1500 Wilson Blvd.   Phone: (703) 841-3661
Arlington, VA 22209   Nicholas E. Mercury, Mgr.

TAX EXECUTIVES INSTITUTE, INC. - LIBRARY
1300 N. 17th St., Suite 1300   Phone: (703) 522-3535
Arlington, VA 22209   Edward A. Sprague, Exec.Dir.

TRW, INC. - INFORMATION CENTER/GOVERNMENT RELATIONS
1000 Wilson Blvd., Suite 2700   Phone: (703) 276-5016
Arlington, VA 22209   Kathleen Galiher Ott, Mgr.

U.S. AGENCY FOR INTERNATIONAL DEVELOPMENT - WATER &
  SANITATION FOR HEALTH PROJECT - INFORMATION CENTER
1611 N. Kent St., Rm. 1002   Phone: (703) 243-8200
Arlington, VA 22209   James E. Beverly, Info.Dir.

U.S. ARMY - INTELLIGENCE AND THREAT ANALYSIS CENTER - TECHNICAL
  INFORMATION CENTER
Bldg. A, Rm. 2204
Arlington Hall Station   Phone: (202) 692-1428
Arlington, VA 22212   Dean A. Burns, Chf.

U.S. NAVY - OFFICE OF NAVAL RESEARCH - LIBRARY
633 Ballston Tower, No. 1
800 N. Quincy St.   Phone: (202) 696-4415
Arlington, VA 22217   Mrs. Dorcas E. Tabor, Lib.Techn.

U.S. PATENT & TRADEMARK OFFICE - SCIENTIFIC LIBRARY †
Crystal Plaza Bldg. 3
2021 Jefferson Davis Hwy.   Phone: (703) 557-2955
Arlington, VA 22202   Henry Rosicky, Prog.Mgr.

VOLUNTEER - THE NATIONAL CENTER FOR CITIZEN INVOLVEMENT -
  LIBRARY
1111 N. 19th St., Suite 500   Phone: (703) 276-0542
Arlington, VA 22209   Sharee Morris, Mgr., Info.Serv.

VIRGINIA-MARYLAND REGIONAL COLLEGE OF VETERINARY MEDICINE -
  LIBRARY
Virginia Polytechnic Inst. & State Univ.
CVM, Phase II   Phone: (703) 961-7666
Blacksburg, VA 24061   Naomi V. Tuttle, Veterinary Med.Lib.Asst.

VIRGINIA POLYTECHNIC INSTITUTE AND STATE UNIVERSITY -
  ARCHITECTURE LIBRARY
Cowgill Hall   Phone: (703) 961-6182
Blacksburg, VA 24061   Robert E. Stephenson, Arch.Libn.

VIRGINIA POLYTECHNIC INSTITUTE AND STATE UNIVERSITY - CAROL M.
  NEWMAN LIBRARY
                                         Phone: (703) 961-5593
Blacksburg, VA 24061   Thomas A. Souter, Act.Dir.

VIRGINIA POLYTECHNIC INSTITUTE AND STATE UNIVERSITY - CENTER
  FOR THE STUDY OF SCIENCE IN SOCIETY - LIBRARY
Price House   Phone: (703) 961-7687
Blacksburg, VA 24061   Ann LaBerge, Asst.Dir.

VIRGINIA POLYTECHNIC INSTITUTE AND STATE UNIVERSITY - GEOLOGY
  LIBRARY
3040 Derring Hall   Phone: (703) 961-6101
Blacksburg, VA 24061   John D. Crissinger, Geology & Map Libn.

AMERICAN SECURITY COUNCIL FOUNDATION - SOL FEINSTONE LIBRARY
                                        Phone: (703) 547-1776
Boston, VA 22713   John M. Fisher, Pres.

UNIVERSITY OF VIRGINIA - BLANDY EXPERIMENTAL FARM LIBRARY
Box 175   Phone: (703) 837-1758
Boyce, VA 22620   Thomas E. Ewert, Dir.

BRIDGEWATER COLLEGE - ALEXANDER MACK MEMORIAL LIBRARY -
  SPECIAL COLLECTIONS
                                        Phone: (703) 828-2501
Bridgewater, VA 22812   Ruth Greenawalt, Dir.

ARMED FORCES COMMUNICATIONS AND ELECTRONICS ASSOCIATION -
  C3I LIBRARY
5641 Burke Centre Pkwy.   Phone: (703) 425-8500
Burke, VA 22015   M.L. Peterson

GENERAL ELECTRIC COMPANY - INDUSTRIAL ELECTRONICS
  INFORMATION CENTER
Box 8106   Phone: (804) 978-5427
Charlottesville, VA 22906   Tina Cox, Mgr.

INSTITUTE OF CHARTERED FINANCIAL ANALYSTS - LIBRARY
University of Virginia
Box 3668   Phone: (804) 977-6600
Charlottesville, VA 22903

INSTITUTE OF TEXTILE TECHNOLOGY - TEXTILE INFORMATION SERVICES
  - ROGER MILLIKEN TEXTILE LIBRARY
Rte. 250 W.
Box 391   Phone: (804) 296-5511
Charlottesville, VA 22902   Linda Justus Cahill, Mgr.

MICHIE COMPANY - LIBRARY
914 Emmet St.   Phone: (804) 295-6171
Charlottesville, VA 22903   Marion J. Samuels, Libn.

NATIONAL RADIO ASTRONOMY OBSERVATORY - LIBRARY
Edgemont Rd.   Phone: (804) 296-0211
Charlottesville, VA 22901   Ellen N. Bouton, Libn.

SPERRY ELECTRONIC SYSTEMS - ENGINEERING LIBRARY
Rte. 29 North   Phone: (804) 973-0100
Charlottesville, VA 22906   Ora Bray, Libn.

U.S. ARMY - JUDGE ADVOCATE GENERAL'S SCHOOL - LIBRARY
                                         Phone: (804) 293-9824
Charlottesville, VA 22903-1781   R. Vivian Hebert, Law Libn.

UNIVERSITY OF VIRGINIA - ARTHUR J. MORRIS LAW LIBRARY
School of Law   Phone: (804) 924-3384
Charlottesville, VA 22901   Larry B. Wenger

UNIVERSITY OF VIRGINIA - BIOLOGY/PSYCHOLOGY LIBRARY
Gilmer Hall   Phone: (804) 924-0678
Charlottesville, VA 22901   Sandra Dulaney, Libn.

UNIVERSITY OF VIRGINIA - CHEMISTRY LIBRARY
Chemistry Bldg.   Phone: (804) 924-3159
Charlottesville, VA 22901   Robert LaRue, Libn.

UNIVERSITY OF VIRGINIA - CLIFTON WALLER BARRETT LIBRARY
Alderman Library   Phone: (804) 924-3366
Charlottesville, VA 22901   Joan S. Crane, Cur.Amer.Lit.

UNIVERSITY OF VIRGINIA - COLGATE DARDEN GRADUATE SCHOOL OF
  BUSINESS ADMINISTRATION - LIBRARY
Box 6550   Phone: (804) 924-7321
Charlottesville, VA 22906   Henry Wingate, Libn.

UNIVERSITY OF VIRGINIA - EDUCATION LIBRARY
Ruffner Hall
405 Emmet St.
Charlottesville, VA 22903   Betsy Anthony, Libn.

UNIVERSITY OF VIRGINIA - FISKE KIMBALL FINE ARTS LIBRARY
Bayly Dr.   Phone: (804) 924-7024
Charlottesville, VA 22903   Mary C. Dunnigan, Libn.

UNIVERSITY OF VIRGINIA - LIBRARY - MANUSCRIPTS DEPARTMENT &
  UNIVERSITY ARCHIVES
                                         Phone: (804) 924-3025
Charlottesville, VA 22901   Edmund Berkeley, Jr., Cur. of Archv.

UNIVERSITY OF VIRGINIA - LIBRARY - RARE BOOK DEPARTMENT
                                         Phone: (804) 924-3366
Charlottesville, VA 22901   Julius P. Barclay, Cur. of Rare Bks.

UNIVERSITY OF VIRGINIA - MATHEMATICS-ASTRONOMY LIBRARY
Mathematics-Astronomy Bldg.   Phone: (804) 924-7806
Charlottesville, VA 22901   Roma Reed, Libn.

UNIVERSITY OF VIRGINIA - MEDICAL CENTER - CLAUDE MOORE HEALTH
    SCIENCES LIBRARY
Box 234   Phone: (804) 924-5464
Charlottesville, VA 22908   Terry A. Thorkildson, Dir. & Assoc.Prof.

UNIVERSITY OF VIRGINIA - MEDICAL CENTER - DEPARTMENT OF
    NEUROLOGY - ELIZABETH J. OHRSTROM LIBRARY
Box 394   Phone: (804) 924-2676
Charlottesville, VA 22908   Janice Reynolds, Libn.

UNIVERSITY OF VIRGINIA - MID ATLANTIC CENTER FOR COMMUNITY
    EDUCATION - LIBRARY
School of Education
217 Ruffner Hall, 405 Emmet St.
Charlottesville, VA 22903

UNIVERSITY OF VIRGINIA - MUSIC LIBRARY
Old Cabell Hall   Phone: (804) 924-7041
Charlottesville, VA 22901   Evan Bonds, Music Libn.

UNIVERSITY OF VIRGINIA - PHYSICS LIBRARY
Physics Bldg.   Phone: (804) 924-6589
Charlottesville, VA 22901   Violetta Mercado, Libn.

UNIVERSITY OF VIRGINIA - SCIENCE & ENGINEERING LIBRARY
Clark Hall   Phone: (804) 924-7209
Charlottesville, VA 22901   Edwina H. Pancake, Dir.

UNIVERSITY OF VIRGINIA - TRACY W. MC GREGOR LIBRARY
Alderman Library   Phone: (804) 924-3366
Charlottesville, VA 22901   William H. Runge, Cur.

VIRGINIA STATE DEPARTMENT OF CONSERVATION & ECONOMIC
    DEVELOPMENT - NATIONAL CARTOGRAPHIC INFORMATION CENTER
Virginia State Division of Mineral Resources Library
Box 3667
Charlottesville, VA 22903   Avon L. Hudson, Libn.

VSE CORPORATION - TECHNICAL LIBRARY †
1417 N. Battlefield Blvd.   Phone: (804) 449-0608
Chesapeake, VA 23320   Patricia L. Alderman, Tech.Libn.

U.S. NAVY - NAVAL SURFACE WEAPONS CENTER - CENTER LIBRARY
Mail Code E43   Phone: (703) 663-8994
Dahlgren, VA 22448   Dr. J. Marshal Hughes, II, Ctr.Libn.

DAN RIVER, INC. - RESEARCH LIBRARY
                                                Phone: (804) 799-7103
Danville, VA 24541

MEMORIAL HOSPITAL - MEDICAL LIBRARY
142 S. Main St.   Phone: (804) 799-4418
Danville, VA 24541   Ann B. Sasser, Med.Libn.

MEMORIAL HOSPITAL - SCHOOL OF PROFESSIONAL NURSING - LIBRARY
Simpson Hall
Danville, VA 24541   Daisy Reynolds, Lib.Tech.

NATIONAL TOBACCO-TEXTILE MUSEUM - LIBRARY AND INFORMATION
    CENTER
614 Lynn St.   Phone: (804) 797-9437
Danville, VA 24541   Samuel W. Price, Exec.Dir.

COAL EMPLOYMENT PROJECT (CEP) - ARCHIVES
16221 Sunny Knoll Court   Phone: (703) 670-3416
Dumfries, VA 22026   Jeri Smerick

EMORY AND HENRY COLLEGE - APPALACHIAN ORAL HISTORY COLLECTION
Drawer S   Phone: (703) 944-3121
Emory, VA 24327   George Stevenson, Dir.

BOOTHE, PRICHARD & DUDLEY - LAW LIBRARY
4103 Chain Bridge Rd.
Box 338   Phone: (703) 273-4600
Fairfax, VA 22030   Margarita A. Bull, Libn.

FAIRFAX COUNTY - COMPREHENSIVE PLANNING LIBRARY
4100 Chain Bridge Rd.
Fairfax, VA 22030   James L. Linard, Libn./Pub.Info.Off.

FAIRFAX COUNTY PUBLIC LIBRARY - FAIRFAX CITY REGIONAL LIBRARY -
    BUSINESS SPECIALTY
3915 Chain Bridge Rd.   Phone: (703) 691-2741
Fairfax, VA 22030   Judith P. Anderson, Br.Mgr.

FAIRFAX COUNTY PUBLIC LIBRARY - FAIRFAX CITY REGIONAL LIBRARY -
    VIRGINIA ROOM
3915 Chain Bridge Rd.   Phone: (703) 691-2123
Fairfax, VA 22030   Suzanne S. Levy, Libn.

FAIRFAX COUNTY PUBLIC SCHOOLS - PROFESSIONAL REFERENCE LIBRARY
    IN EDUCATION
3500 Old Lee Hwy.   Phone: (703) 591-4514
Fairfax, VA 22030   Betty H. Chilton, Staff Lib.Spec.

FAIRFAX LAW LIBRARY
4110 Chain Bridge Rd.   Phone: (703) 691-2170
Fairfax, VA 22030   Judith A. Meadows, Law Libn.

GEORGE MASON UNIVERSITY - FENWICK LIBRARY - SPECIAL
    COLLECTIONS
4400 University Dr.   Phone: (703) 323-2251
Fairfax, VA 22030   Ruth Kerns, Pub.Serv.Libn/Archv.

MOBIL OIL CORPORATION - LIBRARY/SECRETARIAT
3225 Gallows Rd., Rm. BN507   Phone: (703) 849-4647
Fairfax, VA 22037   Mary E. Oldham, Res.Serv.Anl.

NATIONAL INSTITUTE FOR PUBLIC POLICY - NIPP RESEARCH LIBRARY
8408 Arlington Blvd.   Phone: (703) 698-0563
Fairfax, VA 22031

VINNELL CORPORATION - CORPORATE/PROGRAM DEVELOPMENT LIBRARY
    *
10530 Rosehaven St., Suite 600   Phone: (703) 385-4544
Fairfax, VA 22030   Sylvia A. Keys, Libn.

AMERICAN AUTOMOBILE ASSOCIATION - LIBRARY
8111 Gatehouse Rd.   Phone: (703) 222-6466
Falls Church, VA 22047   Sue Williams, Libn.

AMERICAN SOCIETY OF PHOTOGRAMMETRY - HEINZ GRUNER LIBRARY
210 Little Falls St.   Phone: (703) 534-6617
Falls Church, VA 22046   William D. French, Exec.Dir.

ARCANE ORDER - LIBRARY
Studio of Contemplation
2904 Rosemary Lane
Falls Church, VA 22042   Jennifer E. O'Neill, Cur.

COMPUTER SCIENCES CORPORATION - TECHNICAL LIBRARY
6565 Arlington Blvd.   Phone: (703) 237-2000
Falls Church, VA 22046   Ramona Sheftel, Mgr.Tech.Lib.

E-SYSTEMS, INC. - MELPAR DIVISION - TECHNICAL LIBRARY
7700 Arlington Blvd.   Phone: (703) 560-5000
Falls Church, VA 22046   Mary A. Albertson, Div.Libn.

FAIRFAX HOSPITAL - JACOB D. ZYLMAN MEMORIAL LIBRARY
3300 Gallows Rd.   Phone: (703) 698-3234
Falls Church, VA 22046   Alice J. Sheridan, Dir.

STYLES (Mary Riley) PUBLIC LIBRARY - LOCAL HISTORY COLLECTION
120 N. Virginia Ave.   Phone: (703) 241-5030
Falls Church, VA 22046   Anna Rups, Virginia Coll.Libn.

TECHNOLOGY APPLICATIONS, INC. - TECHNICAL LIBRARY
5201 Leesburg Pike   Phone: (703) 931-2000
Falls Church, VA 22041   Frances M. Oliver, Tech.Libn.

U.S. ARMY OPERATIONAL TEST & EVALUATION AGENCY (OTEA) -
    TECHNICAL LIBRARY
5600 Columbia Pike   Phone: (202) 756-2234
Falls Church, VA 22041   Ava Dell Headley, Libn.

FRANKLIN COUNTY HISTORICAL SOCIETY - STANLEY LIBRARY †
Ferrum College   Phone: (703) 365-2121
Ferrum, VA 24088   J.B. Mitchell, Hd.Libn.

U.S. ARMY - BELVOIR RESEARCH & DEVELOPMENT CENTER - TECHNICAL LIBRARY
Bldg. 315
Ft. Belvoir, VA 22060
Phone: (703) 664-5179
Gloria R. James, Chf., Tech.Lib.Div.

U.S. ARMY COMPUTER SYSTEMS COMMAND - TECHNICAL LIBRARY †
ACSC-DST (Annex), Stop H-9
Ft. Belvoir, VA 22060
Phone: (703) 756-5491
Grace Corbin, Tech.Info.Spec.

U.S. ARMY - CORPS OF ENGINEERS - HUMPHREY'S ENGINEERING CENTER - TECHNICAL LIBRARY
Kingman Bldg., Rm. 3C02
Ft. Belvoir, VA 22060
Phone: (202) 325-7375
Bennie F. Maddox, Chf., Lib.Br.

U.S. ARMY ENGINEER SCHOOL - LIBRARY
Bldg. 270
Ft. Belvoir, VA 22060
Phone: (703) 664-2524
Madge J. Busey, Lib.Dir.

U.S. ARMY - ENGINEER TOPOGRAPHIC LABORATORIES - SCIENTIFIC & TECHNICAL INFORMATION CENTER
Ft. Belvoir, VA 22060
Phone: (703) 664-3834
Mildred Stiger, Chf.

U.S. ARMY POST - FORT BELVOIR - VAN NOY LIBRARY
Bldg. 1024
Ft. Belvoir, VA 22060
Phone: (703) 664-1045
Madge J. Busey, Dir.

U.S. ARMY - ARMY TRANSPORTATION MUSEUM - LIBRARY
Drawer D
Fort Eustis, VA 23604
Phone: (804) 878-3603
Dennis P. Mroczkowski, Dir.

U.S. ARMY HOSPITALS - MC DONALD USA COMMUNITY HOSPITAL - MEDICAL LIBRARY †
Ft. Eustis, VA 23604
Phone: (804) 878-2897
Helen O. Hearn, Lib.Mgr.

U.S. ARMY - RESEARCH AND TECHNOLOGY LABS (AVRADCOM) - APPLIED TECH. LABORATORY - TECHNICAL LIB.
Ft. Eustis, VA 23604
Phone: (804) 878-2963
Mrs. Lealer M. Hughes, Libn.

U.S. ARMY TRANSPORTATION - TECHNICAL INFORMATION AND RESEARCH CENTER
Bldg. 705
Ft. Eustis, VA 23604
Phone: (804) 878-5563
Jo An I. Stolley, Chf.Libn.

U.S. ARMY HOSPITALS - KENNER ARMY HOSPITAL - MEDICAL LIBRARY *
Ft. Lee, VA 23801
Phone: (804) 734-1339
Betty K. Lewis, Libn.

U.S. ARMY - LOGISTICS LIBRARY
Attn: ATSM - OSL
Bldg. P-12500
Ft. Lee, VA 23801
Phone: (703) 734-4286
Raymon Trisdale, Chf.Libn.

CASEMATE MUSEUM - LIBRARY
Box 341
Ft. Monroe, VA 23651
Phone: (804) 727-3935
R. Cody Phillips, Musm.Cur.

U.S. ARMY - HEADQUARTERS TRADOC/FORT MONROE LIBRARY & INTERN TRAINING CENTER
Bldg. 133
Ft. Monroe, VA 23651
Phone: (804) 727-2821
Frances M. Doyle, Supv.Libn.

U.S. ARMY POST - FORT STORY - LIBRARY
Bldg. T-530
Ft. Story, VA 23459
Phone: (804) 422-7548
Patricia L. Alderman, Libn.

KENMORE ASSOCIATION, INC. - ARCHIVES
1201 Washington Ave.
Fredericksburg, VA 22401
Phone: (703) 373-3381

MONROE (James) LAW OFFICE - MUSEUM AND MEMORIAL LIBRARY
908 Charles St.
Fredericksburg, VA 22401
Phone: (703) 373-8426
Rosalie Mercein Sullivan, Act.Dir.

U.S. NATL. PARK SERVICE - FREDERICKSBURG & SPOTSYLVANIA NATL. MILITARY PARK - LIBRARY
Box 679
Fredericksburg, VA 22401
Phone: (703) 373-4461
Robert K. Krick, Chf.Hist.

WASHINGTON (Mary) HOSPITAL - MEDICAL LIBRARY
2300 Fall Hill Ave.
Fredericksburg, VA 22401
Phone: (703) 373-4110
Joan S. Bulley, Med.Libn.

ATLANTIC RESEARCH CORPORATION - TECHNICAL INFORMATION CENTER
7511 Wellington Rd.
Gainesville, VA 22065
Phone: (703) 642-6416
Joyce Doering, Tech.Info.Spec.

VIRGINIA INSTITUTE OF MARINE SCIENCE LIBRARY
Gloucester Point, VA 23062
Phone: (804) 642-2111
Susan O. Barrick, Lib.Dir.

HAMPTON GENERAL HOSPITAL - MEDICAL LIBRARY
P.O. Drawer 640
Hampton, VA 23669
Phone: (804) 727-7102
Ruth Kelley, Med.Libn.

HAMPTON INSTITUTE - COLLIS P. HUNTINGTON MEMORIAL LIBRARY - SPECIAL COLLECTIONS †
Hampton, VA 23668
Phone: (804) 727-5371
Jason C. Grant, III, Dir.

U.S. NASA - LANGLEY RESEARCH CENTER - TECHNICAL LIBRARY MS 185 †
Hampton, VA 23665
Phone: (804) 827-2786
Jane S. Hess, Hd., Tech.Lib.Br.

U.S. VETERANS ADMINISTRATION (VA-Hampton) - MEDICAL CENTER LIBRARY
Hampton, VA 23667
Phone: (804) 722-9961
Nancy J. Smith, Chf., Lib.Serv.

U.S. NATL. PARK SERVICE - BOOKER T. WASHINGTON NATL. MONUMENT - LIBRARY
Rte. 1, Box 195
Hardy, VA 24101
Phone: (703) 721-2094
Richard Saunders, Chf.Interp. & Rsrcs.Mgt.

EASTERN MENNONITE COLLEGE - MENNO SIMONS HISTORICAL LIBRARY AND ARCHIVES
Harrisonburg, VA 22801
Phone: (703) 433-2771
Grace Showalter, Libn.

HARRISONBURG-ROCKINGHAM HISTORICAL SOCIETY AND MUSEUM - JOHN W. WAYLAND LIBRARY
301 S. Main St.
Harrisonburg, VA 22801
Phone: (703) 434-4762
Mary H. Geisler, Adm.

ROCKINGHAM MEMORIAL HOSPITAL - HEALTH SCIENCES LIBRARY
235 Cantrell Ave.
Harrisonburg, VA 22801-3293
Phone: (703) 433-8311
Ilene N. Smith, Med.Libn.

HOLLINS COLLEGE - MUSIC DEPARTMENT - ERICH RATH LIBRARY - LISTENING CENTER
Hollins College, VA 24020
Phone: (703) 362-6511
John Diercks, Chm.

AMERICAN BRANDS, INC. - AMERICAN TOBACCO COMPANY - DEPARTMENT OF RESEARCH & DEVELOPMENT LIBRARY
Box 899
Hopewell, VA 23860
Phone: (804) 748-4561
Dorothy D. Robben, Supv., Lib. & Rec.

MARY BALL WASHINGTON MUSEUM AND LIBRARY, INC.
Box 97
Lancaster, VA 22503
Phone: (804) 462-7280
Ann Lewis Burrows, Exec.Dir.

U.S. AIR FORCE BASE - LANGLEY BASE LIBRARY
FL 4800
Langley AFB, VA 23665
Phone: (804) 764-3078
David A.L. Smith, Base Libn.

U.S. AIR FORCE - TACTICAL AIR COMMAND - LANGLEY BASE LIBRARY
FL 4800
Langley AFB, VA 23665
Phone: (804) 764-2906
David A.L. Smith, Chf.Libn.

HISTORIC LEXINGTON FOUNDATION - GARLAND GRAY RESEARCH CENTER & LIBRARY
Stonewall Jackson House
8 E. Washington St.
Lexington, VA 24450
Phone: (703) 463-2552
Ms. Michael Anne Lynn, Musm.Dir.

MARSHALL (George C.) RESEARCH FOUNDATION - GEORGE C. MARSHALL
RESEARCH LIBRARY †
Box 1600   Phone: (703) 463-7103
Lexington, VA 24450   Dr. Fred L. Hadsel, Dir.

ROCKBRIDGE HISTORICAL SOCIETY - LIBRARY/ARCHIVES
Randolph St.   Phone: (703) 911-1403
Lexington, VA 24450   Charles W. Turner, Soc.Libn.

VIRGINIA MILITARY INSTITUTE - PRESTON LIBRARY
                                                      Phone: (703) 463-6228
Lexington, VA 24450   James E. Gaines, Hd.Libn.

WASHINGTON & LEE UNIVERSITY - LAW LIBRARY
Lewis Hall   Phone: (703) 463-3157
Lexington, VA 24450   Sarah K. Wiant, Dir.

GUNSTON HALL PLANTATION - HOUSE MUSEUM - LIBRARY
                                                      Phone: (703) 550-9220
Lorton, VA 22079   Bennie Brown, Jr., Libn.

BABCOCK AND WILCOX COMPANY - UTILITY POWER GENERATION
DIVISION - LIBRARY
3315 Old Forest Rd.   Phone: (804) 385-2475
Lynchburg, VA 24501   Ruth H. Johnson, Hd.Libn.

CENTRAL VIRGINIA COMMUNITY COLLEGE - LIBRARY - SPECIAL
COLLECTIONS
3506 Wards Rd.   Phone: (803) 239-0321
Lynchburg, VA 24503   John B. St. Leger, Coord.

CENTRAL VIRGINIA TRAINING CENTER - PROFESSIONAL LIBRARY
Box 1098   Phone: (804) 528-6171
Lynchburg, VA 24505   Helen Hester, Libn.

LYNCHBURG GENERAL MARSHALL LODGE HOSPITAL - HEALTH SCIENCES
LIBRARY
Tate Springs Rd.   Phone: (804) 528-2147
Lynchburg, VA 24506   Sybil A. Sturgis, Health Sci.Libn.

VIRGINIA BAPTIST HOSPITAL - BARKSDALE MEDICAL LIBRARY
3300 Rivermont Ave.   Phone: (804) 522-4608
Lynchburg, VA 24503   Anne M. Nurmi, Libn.

BDM CORPORATION - CORPORATE LIBRARY
7915 Jones Branch Dr.   Phone: (703) 821-5328
McLean, VA 22102   Dana D. Mallett, Corp.Libn.

DECISIONS AND DESIGNS, INC. - LIBRARY
8400 Westpark Dr., Suite 600
Box 907
McLean, VA 22101

DEFENSE SYSTEMS, INC. - LIBRARY
7903 Westpark Dr.   Phone: (703) 883-1000
McLean, VA 22102   Mary Sue Conaway, Libn./Res.Assoc.

GENERAL RESEARCH CORPORATION - LIBRARY
7655 Old Springhouse Rd.   Phone: (703) 893-5900
McLean, VA 22102   Luci Bugg, Dir., Facility Serv.

HONEYWELL, INC. - AEROSPACE AND DEFENSE LIBRARY
7900 Westpark Dr., Rm. 407   Phone: (703) 827-3327
McLean, VA 22102   Betsey Capraro, Res.Anl.

MITRE CORPORATION - LIBRARY
1820 Dolley Madison Blvd.   Phone: (703) 827-6484
McLean, VA 22102   Paula M. Strain, Mgr., Info.Serv.

PLANNING RESEARCH CORPORATION - TECHNICAL LIBRARY
1500 Planning Research Dr.   Phone: (703) 556-1131
McLean, VA 22102   Marion C. Kersey, Lib.Mgr.

QUEST RESEARCH CORPORATION - LIBRARY
6858 Old Dominion Dr.   Phone: (703) 821-3200
McLean, VA 22101   Stacey McKinley, Libn.

SAI/JRB LIBRARY
8400 Westpark Dr.   Phone: (703) 827-8108
McLean, VA 22102   Madeleine Hahn, Libn.

SAN MARTIN SOCIETY OF WASHINGTON, DC - INFORMATION CENTER
Box 33   Phone: (703) 883-0950
McLean, VA 22101-0033   Dr. Christian Garcia-Godoy, Pres.

TRW, INC. - DEFENSE SYSTEMS GROUP - SEAD TECHNICAL LIBRARY
7600 Colshire Dr.   Phone: (703) 734-6243
McLean, VA 22102   Mary Drew, Lib.Mgr.

U.S. NATL. PARK SERVICE - ARLINGTON HOUSE, THE ROBERT E. LEE
MEMORIAL - LIBRARY
Turkey Run Park   Phone: (703) 557-0613
McLean, VA 22101   Agnes D. Mullins, Cur.

IBM CORPORATION - MANASSAS LIBRARY AND INFORMATION CENTER
887/039
9500 Godwin Dr.   Phone: (703) 367-3156
Manassas, VA 22110   Ruth Doucette, Sr.Libn.

PRINCE WILLIAM COUNTY SCHOOLS - STAFF LIBRARY
Box 389   Phone: (703) 791-7334
Manassas, VA 22110   Dr. Bobbie J. Bowyer, Staff Libn.

U.S. NATL. PARK SERVICE - MANASSAS NATL. BATTLEFIELD PARK -
LIBRARY
Box 1830   Phone: (703) 754-7107
Manassas, VA 22110   Haywood S. Harrell, Chf.Hist.

SOUTHWESTERN STATE HOSPITAL - PROFESSIONAL LIBRARY
E. Main St.
Box 670   Phone: (703) 783-3171
Marion, VA 24354   Kathleen G. Overbay, Dir., Lib.Serv.

MEMORIAL HOSPITAL OF MARTINSVILLE - MEDICAL LIBRARY
Commonwealth Blvd.   Phone: (703) 632-2911
Martinsville, VA 24112   Mary Alice Sherrard, Libn.

NATIONAL SPORTING LIBRARY, INC.
Box 1335   Phone: (703) 687-6542
Middleburg, VA 22117   Judith Ozment, Libn.

AMERICAN HORTICULTURAL SOCIETY - LIBRARY
Box 0105   Phone: (703) 768-5700
Mount Vernon, VA 22121   Raymond J. Rogers, Educ.Supv.

MOUNT VERNON LADIES' ASSOCIATION OF THE UNION - RESEARCH AND
REFERENCE LIBRARY
                                                      Phone: (703) 780-2000
Mount Vernon, VA 22121   Ellen McCallister Clark, Libn.

CHESAPEAKE & OHIO HISTORICAL SOCIETY, INC. - C&O ARCHIVAL
COLLECTION
Christopher Newport College
50 Shoe Lane
Newport News VA 23606   Thomas W. Dixon, Jr., Pres.

COLLEGE OF WILLIAM AND MARY - VIRGINIA ASSOCIATED RESEARCH
CAMPUS LIBRARY
12070 Jefferson Ave.   Phone: (804) 877-9231
Newport News, VA 23606   Gail L. Wilson, Libn.

MARINERS MUSEUM - LIBRARY
                                                      Phone: (804) 595-0368
Newport News, VA 23606   Ardie L. Kelly, Libn.

NEWPORT NEWS DAILY PRESS, INC. - LIBRARY
7505 Warwick Blvd.
Box 746   Phone: (804) 244-8421
Newport News, VA 23607   Theresa M. Hammond, Dir., Lib.Serv.

NEWPORT NEWS SHIPBUILDING AND DRY DOCK COMPANY - LIBRARY
SERVICES DEPARTMENT
                                                      Phone: (804) 380-2610
Newport News, VA 23607   R.M. Norton, Supv., Info.Serv.

RIVERSIDE HOSPITAL - HEALTH SCIENCES LIBRARY
J. Clyde Morris Blvd.   Phone: (804) 599-2175
Newport News, VA 23601

SCHUYLER TECHNICAL LIBRARY
615 Brandywine Dr.   Phone: (804) 877-5860
Newport News, VA 23602   Gilbert S. Bahn, Hd.

WAR MEMORIAL MUSEUM OF VIRGINIA - RESEARCH LIBRARY
9285 Warwick Blvd.   Phone: (804) 247-8523
Newport News, VA 23607   Eliza E. Embrey, Libn.

CHILDREN'S HOSPITAL OF THE KING'S DAUGHTERS - MEDICAL LIBRARY
800 W. Olney Rd.   Phone: (804) 628-3180
Norfolk, VA 23507   Dolores M. Roberts, Dir. of Med.Rec.

CHRYSLER MUSEUM - JEAN OUTLAND CHRYSLER LIBRARY
Olney Rd. & Mowbray Arch   Phone: (804) 622-1211
Norfolk, VA 23510   Amy Navratil Ciccone, Libn.

DE PAUL HOSPITAL - DR. HENRY BOONE MEMORIAL LIBRARY
Kingsley Ln. & Granby St.   Phone: (804) 489-5270
Norfolk, VA 23505   Ramona C. Parrish, Libn.

DE PAUL HOSPITAL - SCHOOL OF NURSING LIBRARY
150 Kingsley Ln.   Phone: (804) 489-5386
Norfolk, VA 23505   Elinor B. Arsic, Libn.

EASTERN VIRGINIA MEDICAL SCHOOL - MOORMAN MEMORIAL LIBRARY
700 Olney Rd.
Box 1980   Phone: (804) 446-5845
Norfolk, VA 23501   Anne Cramer, Dir.

MAC ARTHUR (General Douglas) MEMORIAL - LIBRARY AND ARCHIVES
MacArthur Sq.   Phone: (804) 441-2965
Norfolk, VA 23510   Lyman H. Hammond, Jr., Dir.

NORFOLK BOTANICAL GARDENS - LIBRARY
Airport Rd.   Phone: (804) 855-0194
Norfolk, VA 23518   Marian G. Cole, Libn.

NORFOLK AND PORTSMOUTH BAR ASSOCIATION - LAW LIBRARY
1105 Virginia National Bank Bldg.   Phone: (804) 622-3152
Norfolk, VA 23510   William J. Davis, Exec.Dir.

NORFOLK PUBLIC LIBRARY - SARGEANT MEMORIAL ROOM
301 E. City Hall Ave.   Phone: (804) 441-2503
Norfolk, VA 23507   John A. Parker, Hd.Cur.

NORFOLK STATE COLLEGE - W.K. KELLOGG SOCIAL SCIENCE RESEARCH
    CENTER - LIBRARY
2401 Corprew Ave.   Phone: (804) 623-8435
Norfolk, VA 23504   Angela Perkins, Coord.

SOVRAN BANK, N.A. - LIBRARY
Two Commercial Pl.
Box 600   Phone: (804) 441-4419
Norfolk, VA 23501   Victoria Strickland-Cordial, Libn.

U.S. ARMED FORCES SCHOOL OF MUSIC - REFERENCE LIBRARY
NAVPHI Base, Little Creek   Phone: (703) 464-7511
Norfolk, VA 23521

U.S. ARMED FORCES STAFF COLLEGE - LIBRARY
7800 Hampton Blvd.   Phone: (804) 444-5155
Norfolk, VA 23511   Margaret J. Martin, Libn.

U.S. NAVY - FLEET ANTI-SUBMARINE WARFARE TRAINING CENTER,
    ATLANTIC - TACTICAL LIBRARY
    Phone: (804) 444-1660
Norfolk, VA 23511   Elizabeth H. Evans, Libn.

U.S. NAVY - NAVAL AMPHIBIOUS SCHOOL - JOHN SIDNEY MC CAIN
    AMPHIBIOUS WARFARE LIBRARY
Bldg. 3504   Phone: (804) 464-7467
Norfolk, VA 23521   Carolyn G. Jones, Dir., Lib.Serv.

VIRGINIAN-PILOT & LEDGER-STAR - LIBRARY
150 W. Brambleton Ave.   Phone: (804) 446-2242
Norfolk, VA 23510   Ann Kinken Johnson, Hd.Libn.

UNITY OF FAIRFAX - LIBRARY
2854 Hunter Mill Rd.
Oakton, VA 22124   Lorna Barnes, Libn.

AMERICAN WORK HORSE MUSEUM - LIBRARY
Box 88   Phone: (703) 338-6290
Paeonian Springs, VA 22129   Frank Joy Hopkins, Chf.Libn.

ALLIED CORPORATION - FIBERS & PLASTICS COMPANY - TECHNICAL
    CENTER LIBRARY
Box 31   Phone: (804) 520-3617
Petersburg, VA 23804   Mrs. R.P. Murphy, Libn.

CENTRAL STATE HOSPITAL - HEALTH SCIENCES LIBRARY
Box 4030   Phone: (804) 861-7517
Petersburg, VA 23803   Mr. P.D. Upadhyaya, Med.Libn.

PETERSBURG GENERAL HOSPITAL - MEDICAL LIBRARY MEDIA SERVICES
801 S. Adams St.   Phone: (804) 732-7220
Petersburg, VA 23803   Mary Grace H. Brown, Med.Lib./Media Serv.Dir.

U.S. NATL. PARK SERVICE - PETERSBURG NATL. BATTLEFIELD - LIBRARY
Box 549   Phone: (804) 732-3531
Petersburg, VA 23803   Christopher M. Calkins, Hist./Park Ranger

VIRGINIA STATE UNIVERSITY - JOHNSTON MEMORIAL LIBRARY - SPECIAL
    COLLECTIONS
Box JJ   Phone: (804) 520-6171
Petersburg, VA 23803   Catherine V. Bland, Dir., Lib.Serv.

MARYVIEW HOSPITAL - HEALTH SCIENCES LIBRARY
3636 High St.   Phone: (804) 398-2330
Portsmouth, VA 23707   Katherine A. Yatrofsky, Libn.

PORTSMOUTH GENERAL HOSPITAL - MEDICAL LIBRARY
850 Crawford Pkwy.   Phone: (804) 398-4000
Portsmouth, VA 23704   Linda Wilkinson, Sec.

PORTSMOUTH PUBLIC LIBRARY - LOCAL HISTORY ROOM
601 Court St.   Phone: (804) 393-8501
Portsmouth, VA 23704   Octavia Parrish, Lib.Asst.

PORTSMOUTH PUBLIC LIBRARY - MUNICIPAL REFERENCE
601 Court St.
Portsmouth, VA 23704

U.S. NAVY - NAVAL HOSPITAL (VA-Portsmouth) - MEDICAL LIBRARY
    Phone: (804) 398-5386
Portsmouth, VA 23708   Suad Jones, Med.Libn.

U.S. NAVY - NAVAL SHIPYARD (VA-Norfolk) - TECHNICAL LIBRARY †
Code 202.3, Bldg. 29, 2nd Fl.   Phone: (703) 393-5580
Portsmouth, VA 23709   Carolyn B. Orr, Libn.

VIRGINIA CENTER FOR PSYCHIATRY - MEDICAL LIBRARY
301 Fort Lane   Phone: (804) 393-0061
Portsmouth, VA 23704   Renee E. Mansheim, Med.Libn.

VIRGINIA CHEMICALS, INC. - LIBRARY
3340 W. Norfolk Rd.   Phone: (703) 483-7213
Portsmouth, VA 23703   Barbara Smith, Libn.

U.S. DEPT. OF JUSTICE - FEDERAL BUREAU OF INVESTIGATION - F.B.I.
    ACADEMY - LIBRARY
    Phone: (703) 640-6131
Quantico, VA 22135   Robert L. Keadle, Unit Chf.

U.S. MARINE CORPS - EDUCATION CENTER - JAMES CARSON
    BRECKINRIDGE LIBRARY & AMPHIBIOUS WARFARE RESEARCH FACILITY
Marine Corps Development &
Education Command   Phone: (703) 640-2248
Quantico, VA 22134   David C. Brown, Adm.Libn.

U.S. NAVY - NAVAL REGIONAL MEDICAL CLINIC - MEDICAL LIBRARY
Phone: (703) 640-2887
Quantico, VA 22134   Mrs. F.B. Starr, Libn.

RADFORD UNIVERSITY - LIBRARY - VIRGINIA ROOM AND SPECIAL
   COLLECTIONS
Phone: (703) 731-5471
Radford, VA 24142   Ann Swain, Lib.Asst.

AEROSPACE EDUCATION ASSOCIATION
1910 Association Dr.   Phone: (703) 476-0990
Reston, VA 22091   Julie Bettenberg, Rsrcs.Ed.

AMERICAN ALLIANCE FOR HEALTH, PHYSICAL EDUCATION, RECREATION
   & DANCE - UNIT ON PROGRAMS FOR THE HANDICAPPED
1900 Association Dr.   Phone: (202) 833-5547
Reston, VA 22091   Mary Coscarelli, Dir.

AMERICAN NEWSPAPER PUBLISHERS ASSOCIATION - LIBRARY
The Newspaper Center
11600 Sunrise Valley Dr.   Phone: (703) 620-9500
Reston, VA 22091   Yvonne L. Egertson, Libn.

ANPA - TECHNICAL RESEARCH DEPARTMENT - LIBRARY
The Newspaper Center
11600 Sunrise Valley Dr.   Phone: (703) 620-9500
Reston, VA 22091   George R. Cashau, Dir., Tech.Res.

ERIC CLEARINGHOUSE ON HANDICAPPED & GIFTED CHILDREN - CEC
   INFORMATION SERVICES
Council for Exceptional Children
1920 Association Dr.   Phone: (703) 620-3660
Reston, VA 22091   Lynn Smarte, Asst.Dir./User Serv.

FUTURE HOMEMAKERS OF AMERICA - NATIONAL HEADQUARTERS &
   LEADERSHIP CENTER - RESOURCE CENTER
1910 Association Drive
Reston, VA 22091

HARDWOOD PLYWOOD MANUFACTURERS ASSOCIATION - LIBRARY
1825 Michael Faraday Dr.
Box 2789   Phone: (703) 435-2900
Reston, VA 22090   Myrna Downey, Libn.

NATIONAL COUNCIL OF TEACHERS OF MATHEMATICS - TEACHER/
   LEARNING CENTER
1906 Association Dr.   Phone: (703) 620-9840
Reston, VA 22091   Joseph R. Caravella, Dir., Prof.Serv.

NATIONAL GROCERS ASSOCIATION - LIBRARY
1825 Samuel Morse Dr.   Phone: (703) 437-5300
Reston, VA 22090   Jane Arnwine, Info.Mgr.

U.S. GEOLOGICAL SURVEY - LIBRARY
National Ctr., Mail Stop 950   Phone: (703) 860-6671
Reston, VA 22092   George H. Goodwin, Jr., Chf.Libn.

U.S. GEOLOGICAL SURVEY - NATL. CARTOGRAPHIC INFORMATION CENTER
   (NCIC)
507 National Center   Phone: (703) 860-6045
Reston, VA 22092   Alan R. Stevens, Chf.

U.S. GEOLOGICAL SURVEY - WATER RESOURCES DIVISION - NATL. WATER
   DATA STORAGE & RETRIEVAL SYSTEM
National Ctr., Mail Stop 437   Phone: (703) 860-6871
Reston, VA 22092   Philip Cohen, Chf. Hydrologist

BLUE CROSS AND BLUE SHIELD OF VIRGINIA - PLANS LIBRARY
2015 Staples Mill Rd.
Box 27401   Phone: (804) 359-7177
Richmond, VA 23279   Frank Johns, Libn.

BRAILLE CIRCULATING LIBRARY, INC.
2700 Stuart Ave.   Phone: (804) 359-3743
Richmond, VA 23220   Robert N. Gordon, Exec.Dir.

CONFEDERATE MEMORIAL LITERARY SOCIETY - MUSEUM OF THE
   CONFEDERACY - ELEANOR S. BROCKENBROUGH LIBRARY
1201 E. Clay St.   Phone: (804) 649-1861
Richmond, VA 23219   Cathleen A. Carlson, Cur. of Mss.

FEDERAL RESERVE BANK OF RICHMOND - RESEARCH LIBRARY
Box 27622   Phone: (804) 643-1250
Richmond, VA 23261   Ruth M.E. Cannon, Libn.

FIRST BAPTIST CHURCH OF RICHMOND - LIBRARY *
Monument & Boulevard   Phone: (804) 355-8637
Richmond, VA 23220

HUNTON & WILLIAMS - LAW LIBRARY †
707 E. Main St.
Box 1535   Phone: (804) 788-8245
Richmond, VA 23212   Mr. Beverley Butler, Hd.Libn.

MC GUIRE, WOODS AND BATTLE - INFORMATION CENTER
1400 Ross Bldg.   Phone: (804) 644-4131
Richmond, VA 23219   Ann B. Roberts, Mgr.

PHILIP MORRIS, U.S.A. - RESEARCH CENTER LIBRARY
Box 26583   Phone: (804) 274-2877
Richmond, VA 23261   Marian Z. DeBardeleben, Res.Libn.

REVEILLE UNITED METHODIST CHURCH - REVEILLE MEMORIAL LIBRARY
4200 Cary Street Rd.   Phone: (804) 359-6041
Richmond, VA 23221   Janet P. Sigman, Adult Libn.

REYNOLDS METALS COMPANY - CORPORATE LIBRARY SERVICES
6601 W. Broad St.   Phone: (804) 281-2804
Richmond, VA 23261   Carla L. Gregory, Corp.Libn.

REYNOLDS METALS COMPANY - PACKAGING DIVISION - TECHNOLOGY
   LIBRARY †
2101 Reymet Rd.   Phone: (804) 743-6649
Richmond, VA 23234   Lorna K. Joyner, Adm.

REYNOLDS METALS COMPANY - TECHNICAL INFORMATION SERVICES
   LIBRARY
Fourth & Canal Sts.
Box 27003   Phone: (804) 788-7409
Richmond, VA 23261   Mary R. Cameron, Libn.

RICHMOND MEMORIAL HOSPITAL - MEDICAL AND NURSING SCHOOL
   LIBRARY
1300 Westwood Ave.   Phone: (804) 254-6008
Richmond, VA 23227   Lynne Turman, Libn.

RICHMOND NEWSPAPERS, INC. - LIBRARY
333 E. Grace St.   Phone: (703) 649-6283
Richmond, VA 23213   Charles D. Saunders, Libn.

RICHMOND PUBLIC LIBRARY - ART AND MUSIC DEPARTMENT
101 E. Franklin St.   Phone: (804) 780-4740
Richmond, VA 23219   Helen M. Ogden, Hd.

RICHMOND PUBLIC LIBRARY - BUSINESS, SCIENCE & TECHNOLOGY
   DEPARTMENT
101 E. Franklin St.   Phone: (804) 780-8223
Richmond, VA 23219   Alice L. DeCamps, Hd.

RICHMOND PUBLIC SCHOOLS - CURRICULUM MATERIALS CENTER *
301 N. Ninth St.   Phone: (804) 780-5370
Richmond, VA 23219   Delores Z. Pretlow, Coord., Media Serv.

ST. MARY'S HOSPITAL - HEALTH SCIENCES LIBRARY
5801 Bremo Rd.   Phone: (804) 285-2011
Richmond, VA 23226

ST. PAUL'S EPISCOPAL CHURCH - LIBRARY
815 E. Grace St.   Phone: (804) 643-3589
Richmond, VA 23219   Leigh S. Hulcher, Lib.Cons.

SOUTHERN BAPTIST CONVENTION - FOREIGN MISSION BOARD -
   ARCHIVES CENTER
3806 Monument Ave.
Box 6767
Richmond, VA 23230   Mary Virginia Currie Jones, Mgr., Rec.Mgt.Sect.

SOUTHERN BAPTIST CONVENTION - FOREIGN MISSION BOARD - JENKINS
   RESEARCH CENTER
3806 Monument Ave.
Box 6767   Phone: (804) 353-0151
Richmond, VA 23230   Mary Virginia Currie Jones, Mgr.

SOUTHERN BAPTIST CONVENTION - FOREIGN MISSION BOARD -
    MISSIONARY LEARNING CENTER LIBRARY
Box 6767
Richmond, VA 23230   Cary Ann Geron, Libn.

UNION THEOLOGICAL SEMINARY IN VIRGINIA - LIBRARY
3401 Brook Rd.   Phone: (804) 355-0671
Richmond, VA 23227   Dr. John B. Trotti, Libn.

UNITED DAUGHTERS OF THE CONFEDERACY - CAROLINE MERIWETHER
    GOODLETT LIBRARY
U.D.C. Headquarters Bldg.
328 North Blvd.   Phone: (804) 355-1636
Richmond, VA 23220   Dorothy L. Barrett, Chm., Lib.Comm.

U.S. COURT OF APPEALS, 4TH CIRCUIT - LIBRARY
U.S. Courthouse, Rm. 424
Tenth & Main Sts.   Phone: (804) 771-2219
Richmond, VA 23219   Iris C. Stevenson, Circuit Libn.

U.S. DEFENSE LOGISTICS AGENCY - DEFENSE GENERAL SUPPLY CENTER -
    CENTER LIBRARY
                                   Phone: (804) 275-3215
Richmond, VA 23297   Yvonne H. Oakley, Ctr.Libn.

U.S. DEPT. OF COMMERCE - INTERNATIONAL TRADE ADMINISTRATION -
    RICHMOND DISTRICT OFFICE LIBRARY
8010 Federal Bldg.
400 N. 8th St.   Phone: (804) 771-2246
Richmond, VA 23240   Philip A. Ouzts, Dir.

U.S. NATL. PARK SERVICE - RICHMOND NATL. BATTLEFIELD PARK -
    LIBRARY
3215 E. Broad St.   Phone: (804) 226-1981
Richmond, VA 23223   Keithel C. Morgan, Chf.Interp.

U.S. VETERANS ADMINISTRATION (VA-Richmond) - HOSPITAL LIBRARY
1201 Broad Rock Blvd.   Phone: (804) 231-9011
Richmond, VA 23249   Eleanor Rollins, Chf., Lib.Serv.

UNITED VIRGINIA BANK - INFORMATION CENTER
Box 26665   Phone: (804) 782-7452
Richmond, VA 23261   Marion D. George, V.P., Info.Serv/Corp.Rec.

UNIVERSITY OF RICHMOND - E. CLAIBORNE ROBINS SCHOOL OF BUSINESS
    LIBRARY
Boatwright Library   Phone: (804) 285-6394
Richmond, VA 23173   Littleton M. Maxwell, Libn.

UNIVERSITY OF RICHMOND - MUSIC LIBRARY
                                   Phone: (804) 285-6398
Richmond, VA 23173   Bonlyn G. Hall, Libn.

UNIVERSITY OF RICHMOND - WILLIAM T. MUSE MEMORIAL LAW LIBRARY
                                   Phone: (804) 285-6239
Richmond, VA 23173   Susan B. English, Law Libn.

VALENTINE MUSEUM - LIBRARY
1015 E. Clay St.   Phone: (804) 649-0711
Richmond, VA 23219   Sarah Shields, Cur.

VIRGINIA BAPTIST HISTORICAL SOCIETY - LIBRARY
University of Richmond
Box 34   Phone: (804) 285-6324
Richmond, VA 23173   Fred Anderson, Exec.Dir.

VIRGINIA COMMONWEALTH UNIVERSITY - JAMES BRANCH CABELL
    LIBRARY - SPECIAL COLLECTIONS
901 Park Ave.   Phone: (804) 257-1108
Richmond, VA 23284   Daniel A. Yanchisin, Spec.Coll.Libn.

VIRGINIA COMMONWEALTH UNIVERSITY - MEDICAL COLLEGE OF
    VIRGINIA - TOMPKINS-MC CAW LIBRARY
MCV Sta., Box 667   Phone: (804) 786-0823
Richmond, VA 23298   William J. Judd, Dir., Univ.Lib.Serv.

VIRGINIA ELECTRIC AND POWER COMPANY - LIBRARY AND
    INFORMATION SERVICES
One James River Plaza
Box 26666   Phone: (804) 771-3657
Richmond, VA 23233   Jeanne E. Varteressian, Supv.

VIRGINIA HISTORIC LANDMARKS COMMISSION - ARCHIVES
221 Governor St.   Phone: (804) 786-3143
Richmond, VA 23219

VIRGINIA HISTORICAL SOCIETY - LIBRARY
428 North Blvd.
Box 7311   Phone: (804) 358-4901
Richmond, VA 23221   Paul C. Nagel, Dir.

VIRGINIA MUSEUM OF FINE ARTS - LIBRARY
Boulevard & Grove Ave.
Box 7260   Phone: (804) 257-0827
Richmond, VA 23221   Betty A. Stacy, Libn.

VIRGINIA STATE DEPARTMENT OF CRIMINAL JUSTICE SERVICES -
    LIBRARY
805 E. Broad St.   Phone: (804) 786-8478
Richmond, VA 23219   Stephen E. Squire, Libn.

VIRGINIA STATE DEPT. OF EDUCATION - DIVISION OF MANAGEMENT
    INFORMATION SERVICES - DATA UTILIZATION & REPORTING
Box 6Q   Phone: (804) 225-2101
Richmond, VA 23216   Dr. Jan L. Harris, Supv.

VIRGINIA STATE DEPARTMENT OF GENERAL SERVICES - DIVISION OF
    CONSOLIDATED LABORATORY SERVICES LIBRARY
1 N. 14th St., Rm. 274   Phone: (804) 786-1155
Richmond, VA 23219   Susan Childress

VIRGINIA STATE DEPARTMENT OF TRANSPORTATION SAFETY - FILM
    LIBRARY *
300 Turner Rd.   Phone: (804) 276-9600
Richmond, VA 23225   Nancy T. Arrowood, Film Libn.

VIRGINIA STATE DIVISION OF LEGISLATIVE SERVICES - REFERENCE
    LIBRARY
State Capitol, Box 3-AG   Phone: (804) 786-1861
Richmond, VA 23208

VIRGINIA STATE LAW LIBRARY
Supreme Court Bldg., 2nd Fl.
100 N. Ninth St.   Phone: (804) 786-2075
Richmond, VA 23219   Gail Warren, State Law Libn.

VIRGINIA STATE LIBRARY
12th & Capitol St.   Phone: (804) 786-8929
Richmond, VA 23219   Donald Haynes, State Libn.

VIRGINIA STATE LIBRARY FOR THE VISUALLY AND PHYSICALLY
    HANDICAPPED
1901 Roane St.   Phone: (804) 786-8016
Richmond, VA 23222   Constance J.M. Tracy, Reg.Libn.

VIRGINIA STATE OFFICE OF EMERGENCY & ENERGY SERVICES - ENERGY
    INFORMATION AND SERVICES CENTER
310 Turner Rd.   Phone: (804) 745-3245
Richmond, VA 23225   Kathy Erickson, Supv.

VIRGINIA STATE WATER CONTROL BOARD - LIBRARY
2111 N. Hamilton St.
Box 11143   Phone: (804) 257-6340
Richmond, VA 23230   Patricia G. Vanderland, Libn.

VIRGINIA UNION UNIVERSITY - WILLIAM J. CLARK LIBRARY - SPECIAL
    COLLECTIONS
1500 N. Lombardy St.   Phone: (804) 257-5820
Richmond, VA 23220   Verdelle V. Bradley, Libn.

COLLEGE OF HEALTH SCIENCES - LEARNING RESOURCES CENTER
920 S. Jefferson St., Rm. 611   Phone: (703) 985-8270
Roanoke, VA 24016   Hope Reenstjerna, Dir.

HAYES, SEAY, MATTERN & MATTERN - TECHNICAL LIBRARY
1315 Franklin Rd., S.W.
Box 13446   Phone: (703) 343-6971
Roanoke, VA 24034   Nancy H. Seamans, Libn.

ROANOKE LAW LIBRARY
315 Church Ave., S.W.
Roanoke, VA 24016
Phone: (703) 981-2268
Clayne Calhoun, Libn.

ROANOKE MEMORIAL HOSPITALS - MEDICAL LIBRARY
Belleview at Jefferson St.
Box 13367
Roanoke, VA 24033
Phone: (703) 981-7371
Lucy D. Glenn, Chf.Med.Libn.

ROANOKE VALLEY HISTORICAL SOCIETY - LIBRARY
1 Market Square, Center in The Square
Roanoke, VA 24011
Phone: (703) 342-5770
Clare White, Hd.Libn.

TIMES-WORLD CORPORATION - NEWSPAPER LIBRARY
Box 2491
Roanoke, VA 24010
Phone: (703) 981-3279
Richard Hancock, Libn.

CONSUMER EDUCATION RESOURCE NETWORK (CERN) †
1555 Wilson Blvd., Suite 600
Rosslyn, VA 22209
Phone: (703) 522-4616
Celia Szarejko, Mgr., Info.Sys. & Lib.

LEWIS-GALE HOSPITAL CORPORATION - LEWIS-GALE MEDICAL LIBRARY
1900 Electric Rd.
Salem, VA 24153
Phone: (703) 989-4261
Audrey D. Lachowicz, Med.Libn.

U.S. VETERANS ADMINISTRATION (VA-Salem) - MEDICAL CENTER
LIBRARY
Salem, VA 24153
Phone: (703) 982-2463
Jean A. Kennedy, Chf.Libn.

SPOTSYLVANIA HISTORICAL ASSOCIATION, INC. - RESEARCH MUSEUM
AND LIBRARY
Court House, Box 64
Spotsylvania, VA 22553
Phone: (703) 582-5672
Frances L.N. Waller, Dir.

ENSCO, INC. - TECHNICAL LIBRARY
5400 Port Royal Rd.
Springfield, VA 22151
Phone: (703) 321-4604
Sue E. Littlepage, Mgr.

U.S. DEPT. OF COMMERCE - NATL. TECHNICAL INFORMATION SERVICE
5285 Port Royal Rd.
Springfield, VA 22161
Phone: (703) 487-4600

U.S. NATL. PARK SERVICE - HARPERS FERRY CENTER - BRANCH OF
GRAPHICS RESEARCH - PICTURE LIBRARY
5508 Port Royal Rd.
Springfield, VA 22151-2393
Phone: (703) 756-6138
Thomas A. DuRant, Pict.Libn.

WASHINGTON GAS LIGHT COMPANY - CORPORATE LIBRARY †
6801 Industrial Rd.
Springfield, VA 22151
Phone: (703) 750-7927
Jan Magnusson, Corp.Libn.

WESTERN STATE HOSPITAL - MEDICAL LIBRARY
Box 2500
Staunton, VA 24401
Phone: (703) 885-9387
Richard D. Wills, Libn.

WILSON (Woodrow) BIRTHPLACE FOUNDATION, INC. - RESEARCH LIBRARY
& ARCHIVES
20 N. Coalter St.
Box 24
Staunton, VA 24401
Phone: (703) 885-0897
Dr. Katharine L. Brown, Exec.Dir.

SYSTEMATICS GENERAL CORPORATION - LIBRARY *
1606 Old Ox Rd.
Sterling, VA 22170
Phone: (703) 471-2200
Robin Posten, Libn.

STRATFORD HALL PLANTATION - JESSIE BALL DUPONT MEMORIAL
LIBRARY
Stratford Post Office
Stratford, VA 22558
Phone: (804) 493-8572
Dr. Ralph Draughon, Jr., Libn./Hist.

OBICI (Louise) MEMORIAL HOSPITAL - LIBRARY *
Box 1100
Suffolk, VA 23434
Phone: (804) 539-1511
Patricia D. Herzfeldt, Supv., Med.Rec.

BOEING COMPUTER SERVICES COMPANY - TECHNICAL LIBRARY
7980 Gallows Ct.
Vienna, VA 22180
Phone: (703) 821-6062
Marian Ulincy Starr, Lib.Mgr.

CONTINENTAL PAGE ENGINEERS, INC. - TECHNICAL LIBRARY
801 Follin Ln.
Vienna, VA 22180
Phone: (703) 255-4262
Eileen C. Durham, Libn.

INTERNATIONAL MICROWAVE POWER INSTITUTE - REFERENCE LIBRARY
301 Maple Ave., W., Tower Suite 520
Vienna, VA 22180
Phone: (703) 281-1515
Robert C. LaGasse, Exec.Dir.

ASSOCIATION FOR RESEARCH AND ENLIGHTENMENT - EDGAR CAYCE
FOUNDATION - LIBRARY
Box 595
Virginia Beach, VA 23451
Phone: (804) 428-3588
Stephen Jordan, Lib.Dir.

VIRGINIA BEACH PUBLIC LIBRARY SYSTEM - MUNICIPAL REFERENCE
LIBRARY
Municipal Ctr.
Virginia Beach, VA 23456
Phone: (804) 427-4644
Kathleen G. Hevey, Municipal Ref.Coord.

VIRGINIA BEACH PUBLIC LIBRARY SYSTEM - ROBERT S. WAHAB, JR.
PUBLIC LAW LIBRARY
Municipal Ctr.
Virginia Beach, VA 23456-9002
Phone: (804) 427-4419
Robert P. Miller, Jr., Law Lib.Coord.

VIRGINIA STATE TRUCK AND ORNAMENTALS RESEARCH STATION -
LIBRARY
1444 Diamond Springs Rd.
Virginia Beach, VA 23455
Phone: (804) 464-3528
Amy DesRoches, Libn.

U.S. NASA - WALLOPS FLIGHT CENTER - TECHNICAL LIBRARY
Wallops Island, VA 23337
Phone: (804) 824-3411
Jane N. Foster, Lib.Adm.

INTERTECHNOLOGY/SOLAR CORPORATION - LIBRARY *
100 Main St.
Warrenton, VA 22186
Sherry L. Crocker, Libn.

DU PONT DE NEMOURS (E.I.) & COMPANY, INC. - BENGER LABORATORY -
LIBRARY
Waynesboro, VA 22980
Phone: (703) 949-2485
Virginia G. Mize, Libn.

VIRGINIA STATE DEPARTMENT OF CORRECTIONS - ACADEMY FOR STAFF
DEVELOPMENT - LIBRARY
500 N. Winchester Ave.
Box 2215
Waynesboro, VA 22980
Phone: (703) 943-3141
Elizabeth A. Robson, Libn.

ABBY ALDRICH ROCKEFELLER FOLK ART CENTER - LIBRARY
307 S. England St.
Drawer C
Williamsburg, VA 23185
Phone: (804) 229-1000
Anne E. Watkins, Registrar/Libn.

BADISCHE CORPORATION - LIBRARY
Drawer D
Williamsburg, VA 23187
Phone: (804) 887-6335
Carmalita J. Beasley, Libn.

COLLEGE OF WILLIAM AND MARY - EARL GREGG SWEM LIBRARY -
SPECIAL COLLECTIONS
Williamsburg, VA 23185
Phone: (804) 253-4404
Clifford Currie, Libn.

COLLEGE OF WILLIAM AND MARY - MARSHALL-WYTHE LAW LIBRARY
Williamsburg, VA 23185
Phone: (804) 253-4680
Edmund P. Edmonds, Law Libn.

COLONIAL WILLIAMSBURG - AUDIO-VISUAL LIBRARY †
Williamsburg, VA 23185
Phone: (804) 229-1000
Patricia G. Maccubbin, Chf.Libn.

COLONIAL WILLIAMSBURG - RESEARCH LIBRARY & ARCHIVES †
Box C
Williamsburg, VA 23185
Phone: (804) 229-1000
Louise A. Merriam, Res.Libn.

EASTERN STATE HOSPITAL - STAFF LIBRARY
Drawer A
Williamsburg, VA 23187
Phone: (804) 253-5457
Paula Greenwood, Staff Libn.

INSTITUTE OF EARLY AMERICAN HISTORY AND CULTURE - KELLOCK
    LIBRARY
College of William and Mary
Box 220   Phone: (804) 229-2771
Williamsburg, VA 23187   Patricia V. Higgs, Supv.

MARQUANDIA SOCIETY FOR STUDIES IN HISTORY AND LITERATURE -
    LIBRARY
421 Scotland St., No. 6   Phone: (804) 229-7049
Williamsburg, VA 23185   John Thelin, Co-Dir.

NATIONAL CENTER FOR STATE COURTS - LIBRARY
300 Newport Ave.   Phone: (804) 253-2000
Williamsburg, VA 23185   Erick Baker Low, Libn.

SHENANDOAH COLLEGE & CONSERVATORY OF MUSIC - HOWE LIBRARY
                                      Phone: (703) 667-8714
Winchester, VA 22601   Nancy H. Moore, Dir.

WINCHESTER MEMORIAL HOSPITAL - HEALTH SCIENCES LIBRARY
South Stewart St.   Phone: (703) 665-5124
Winchester, VA 22601   Beth A. Layton, Libn.

WYTHEVILLE COMMUNITY COLLEGE - KEGLEY LIBRARY - SPECIAL
    COLLECTIONS
1000 E. Main St.   Phone: (703) 228-5541
Wytheville, VA 24382   Anna Ray Roberts, Coord., Lib.Serv.

U.S. NAVY - NAVAL WEAPONS STATION - LIBRARY
Bldg. 705   Phone: (804) 887-4726
Yorktown, VA 23691   Eleanor Lacy Sorokatch, Libn.

WASHINGTON

WHITE RIVER VALLEY HISTORICAL SOCIETY MUSEUM - LIBRARY
918 H St., S.E.   Phone: (206) 939-2783
Auburn, WA 98002   LaVerna J. Conrad, Libn.

CH2M HILL, INC. - TECHNICAL INFORMATION CENTER
1500 114th Ave., S.E.   Phone: (206) 453-5000
Bellevue, WA 98004-6922   Kay M. Pflug-Felder, Rec.Mgt.Supv.

ENI COMPANIES - INFORMATION CENTER *
110 110th Ave., N.E.   Phone: (206) 451-4000
Bellevue, WA 98009   Wendy Doty, Hd.

NORTHWEST PULP AND PAPER ASSOCIATION - TECHNICAL INFORMATION
    CENTER
555 116th Ave., N.E., Suite 266
Bellevue, WA 98004

PUGET SOUND POWER AND LIGHT COMPANY LIBRARY
                                      Phone: (206) 454-6363
Bellevue, WA 98009   Susan Campbell Ball, Libn.

HUXLEY COLLEGE OF ENVIRONMENTAL STUDIES - ENVIRONMENTAL
    RESOURCE LIBRARY
ESC 535, Huxley College   Phone: (206) 676-3974
Bellingham, WA 98225   Steve Menthe, Lib. Coord.

SPIE - THE INTERNATIONAL SOCIETY FOR OPTICAL ENGINEERING -
    LIBRARY
Box 10   Phone: (206) 676-3290
Bellingham, WA 98227-0010   Joseph Yaver, Exec.Dir.

WESTERN WASHINGTON UNIVERSITY - CENTER FOR PACIFIC
    NORTHWEST STUDIES
Bellingham, WA 98225   Dr. James W. Scott, Dir.

WESTERN WASHINGTON UNIVERSITY - DEPARTMENT OF GEOGRAPHY
    AND REGIONAL PLANNING - MAP LIBRARY
Arntzen Hall 101   Phone: (206) 676-3272
Bellingham, WA 98225   Karl Thompson, Act. Map Cur.

WHATCOM/ISLAND HEALTH SERVICES - LIBRARY
3201 Ellis St.   Phone: (206) 734-5400
Bellingham, WA 98225   Betty Jo Jensen, Med.Libn.

HAKLUYT MINOR - LIBRARY
9206 N.E. 180th St.   Phone: (206) 485-2124
Bothell, WA 98011   Richard G. McCloskey, Dir.

HARRISON MEMORIAL HOSPITAL - HEALTH SCIENCES LIBRARY *
2520 Cherry St.   Phone: (206) 377-3911
Bremerton, WA 98310   Selma Kannel, Med.Libn.

U.S. NAVY - NAVAL HOSPITAL (WA-Bremerton) - MEDICAL LIBRARY
                                      Phone: (206) 478-9316
Bremerton, WA 98314   Jane Easley, Libn.

WASHINGTON STATE LIBRARY - RAINIER SCHOOL STAFF LIBRARY
Rainier School
Box 600   Phone: (206) 829-1111
Buckley, WA 98321   Lynn Red, Module Supv.

CROWN ZELLERBACH CORPORATION - CENTRAL RESEARCH LIBRARY
349 N.W. Seventh Ave.   Phone: (206) 834-4444
Camas, WA 98607

WEYERHAEUSER COMPANY - WESTERN FORESTRY RESEARCH CENTER -
    LIBRARY
Box 420   Phone: (206) 736-8241
Centralia, WA 98531   Donna Loucks, Libn.

LEWIS COUNTY HISTORICAL MUSEUM - LIBRARY
599 N.W. Front St.   Phone: (206) 748-0831
Chehalis, WA 98532   Jill Kangas, Musm.Dir.

LEWIS COUNTY LAW LIBRARY
Box 357   Phone: (206) 748-9121
Chehalis, WA 98532   Jan Draper, Law Libn.

EASTERN WASHINGTON UNIVERSITY - INSTRUCTIONAL MEDIA CENTER
                                      Phone: (509) 359-2265
Cheney, WA 99004   Jerome S. Donen, Dir.

EASTERN WASHINGTON UNIVERSITY - MUSIC LIBRARY
Music Bldg.   Phone: (509) 359-7843
Cheney, WA 99004   Karen Olson, Libn.

WALLA WALLA COLLEGE - CURRICULUM LIBRARY
Smith Hall   Phone: (509) 527-2221
College Place, WA 99324   Camille Wood, Dir.

U.S. NATL. PARK SERVICE - COULEE DAM NATL. RECREATION AREA - FORT
    SPOKANE VISITOR CENTER *
Star Rte., Box 51   Phone: (509) 725-2715
Davenport, WA 99122-0051   Steve Shrader, District Ranger

CENTRAL WASHINGTON UNIVERSITY - LIBRARY - CURRICULUM
    LABORATORY
                                      Phone: (509) 963-1641
Ellensburg, WA 98926   Ann Donovan, Curric.Libn.

CENTRAL WASHINGTON UNIVERSITY - LIBRARY DOCUMENTS
    DEPARTMENT
                                      Phone: (509) 963-1541
Ellensburg, WA 98926   Ruth Dahlgren Hartman, Govt.Doc.Libn.

CENTRAL WASHINGTON UNIVERSITY - MAP LIBRARY
                                      Phone: (509) 963-1541
Ellensburg, WA 98926   Susanne Villar, Asst.Doc.Libn.

CENTRAL WASHINGTON UNIVERSITY - MEDIA LIBRARY SERVICES
Instructional Media Center   Phone: (509) 963-2861
Ellensburg, WA 98926   Charles Vlcek, Dir.

CENTRAL WASHINGTON UNIVERSITY - MUSIC LIBRARY
                                      Phone: (509) 963-1841
Ellensburg, WA 98926   Paul Emmons, Music Libn.

EVERETT PUBLIC LIBRARY - NORTHWEST HISTORY COLLECTION
2702 Hoyt   Phone: (206) 259-8858
Everett, WA 98201

FLUKE (John) MANUFACTURING CO., INC. - LIBRARY
Box C9090
Everett, WA 98206   Barbara Meiser, Corp.Info.Rsrcs.Mgr.

PROVIDENCE HOSPITAL, EVERETT - HEALTH INFORMATION NETWORK
   SERVICES (HINS)
Pacific & Nassau
Box 1067   Phone: (206) 258-7558
Everett, WA 98206   Shirley C. Lewis, Dir., Lib.Serv.

SNOHOMISH COUNTY LAW LIBRARY
County Court House   Phone: (206) 259-5326
Everett WA 98201   Betty Z. Scott, Libn.

U.S. AIR FORCE BASE - FAIRCHILD BASE LIBRARY
FL 4620   Phone: (509) 247-5556
Fairchild AFB, WA 99011   Nancy M. Bemis, Libn.

U.S. AIR FORCE HOSPITAL - MEDICAL LIBRARY (WA - Fairchild AFB)
                                        Phone: (509) 247-2801
Fairchild AFB, WA 99011   Linda M. Norton, Libn.

RHODODENDRON SPECIES FOUNDATION - LAWRENCE J. PIERCE
   RHODODENDRON LIBRARY
2525 S. 336th St.
Box 3798   Phone: (206) 927-6960
Federal Way, WA 98063-3798   Mrs. George Harrison, Chm.

FORT LEWIS MILITARY MUSEUM - MUSEUM RESEARCH LIBRARY
Main St., Bldg. 4320   Phone: (206) 967-7206
Fort Lewis, WA 98433   Barbara A. Bower, Dir.

U.S. ARMY POST - FORT LEWIS - LIBRARY SYSTEM
Bldg. 2109   Phone: (206) 967-7736
Ft. Lewis, WA 98433-5000   Patricia A. Louderback, Chf.Libn.

WASHINGTON STATE LIBRARY - WESTERN STATE HOSPITAL - STAFF
   LIBRARY
                                        Phone: (206) 756-9635
Fort Steilacoom, WA 98494   Neal Van Der Voorn, Libn.

UNIVERSITY OF WASHINGTON - FRIDAY HARBOR LABORATORIES -
   LIBRARY
NJ-22   Phone: (206) 378-2501
Friday Harbor, WA 98250   Kathy M. Carr, Libn.

LUTHERAN BIBLE INSTITUTE - LIBRARY
Providence Heights   Phone: (206) 392-0400
Issaquah, WA 98027   Mary E. Porter, Hd.Libn.

VALLEY NEWSPAPERS - LIBRARY
600 S. Washington St.
Box 130   Phone: (206) 872-6674
Kent, WA 98031   Frances Wright, Libn.

KENWORTH TRUCK CO. - DIVISION LIBRARY
Box 1000   Phone: (206) 828-5255
Kirkland, WA 98033

NORTHWEST COLLEGE OF THE ASSEMBLIES OF GOD - HURST LIBRARY †
11102 N.E. 53rd Ave.
Box 579   Phone: (206) 822-8266
Kirkland, WA 98033   Ruth Petty, Libn.

SKAGIT COUNTY HISTORICAL MUSEUM - HISTORICAL REFERENCE
   LIBRARY
Box 818   Phone: (206) 466-3365
La Conner, WA 98257   David J. van Meer, Cur.

WASHINGTON STATE DEPARTMENT OF NATURAL RESOURCES - DIVISION
   OF GEOLOGY AND EARTH RESOURCES - LIBRARY
Bldg. One, Rowe 6
4224 6th Ave., S.E.   Phone: (206) 753-3647
Lacey, WA 98503   Connie J. Manson, Sr.Libn.

MONTICELLO MEDICAL CENTER - MEDICAL STAFF LIBRARY
Box 638   Phone: (206) 423-5850
Longview, WA 98632   Margaret B. Geering, Coord., Med. Staff Serv.

U.S. FISH & WILDLIFE SERVICE - ABERNATHY SALMON CULTURAL
   DEVELOPMENT CENTER - RESEARCH & INFO. CENTER
1440 Abernathy Rd.   Phone: (206) 425-6072
Longview, WA 98632   David A. Leith, Dir.

U.S. AIR FORCE BASE - MC CHORD BASE LIBRARY
62 ABG/SSL   Phone: (206) 984-3454
McChord AFB, WA 98438   Margaret Ono, Base Libn.

WASHINGTON STATE LIBRARY - EASTERN STATE HOSPITAL LIBRARY
Box A   Phone: (509) 299-4276
Medical Lake, WA 99022   Mary E. Mims, Libn.

WASHINGTON STATE LIBRARY - LAKELAND VILLAGE BRANCH LIBRARY
Box 200   Phone: (509) 299-5089
Medical Lake, WA 99022   Kathy Butler, Inst.Libn.

GRAYS HARBOR COUNTY LAW LIBRARY †
Courthouse, 2nd Fl.   Phone: (206) 249-5311
Montesano, WA 98563   E. Urquhart, Libn.

SKAGIT COUNTY LAW LIBRARY
County Court House, 2nd Fl.   Phone: (206) 336-9313
Mount Vernon, WA 98273   Pat Ryan, Libn.

ST. PETER HOSPITAL - PROFESSIONAL LIBRARY
413 N. Lilly Rd.   Phone: (206) 456-7222
Olympia, WA 98506   Edean Berglund, Dir., Lib.Serv.

STATE CAPITAL HISTORICAL ASSOCIATION - LIBRARY AND PHOTO
   ARCHIVES
211 W. 21st Ave.   Phone: (206) 753-2580
Olympia, WA 98501   Derek R. Valley, Dir.

WASHINGTON STATE ATTORNEY GENERAL'S LIBRARY
Temple of Justice   Phone: (206) 753-2681
Olympia, WA 98504   Phil Bunker, Law Libn.

WASHINGTON STATE DEPARTMENT OF COMMERCE AND ECONOMIC
   DEVELOPMENT - TOURISM DEVELOPMENT DIVISION
101 General Administration Bldg.   Phone: (206) 753-5600
Olympia, WA 98504   Leslie Sluman, Dir.

WASHINGTON STATE DEPARTMENT OF ECOLOGY - TECHNICAL LIBRARY
PV-11   Phone: (206) 459-6150
Olympia, WA 98504

WASHINGTON STATE DEPARTMENT OF REVENUE - RESEARCH AND
   INFORMATION DIVISION
414 Gen.Adm.Bldg. AX-02   Phone: (206) 753-5516
Olympia, WA 98504   Gary O'Neil, Dir. of Res.

WASHINGTON STATE DEPARTMENT OF TRANSPORTATION - LIBRARY
Transportation Bldg.   Phone: (206) 753-2107
Olympia, WA 98504   Barbara Russo, Libn.

WASHINGTON STATE ENERGY OFFICE - LIBRARY
400 E. Union St.   Phone: (206) 754-0778
Olympia, WA 98504   Ginger Alexander, Libn.

WASHINGTON STATE LAW LIBRARY
Temple of Justice   Phone: (206) 753-6524
Olympia, WA 98504   C.E. Bolden, Dir.

WASHINGTON STATE LIBRARY
State Library Bldg.   Phone: (206) 753-5592
Olympia, WA 98504   Roderick G. Swartz, State Libn.

WASHINGTON STATE OFFICE OF SECRETARY OF STATE - DIVISION OF
   ARCHIVES AND RECORD MANAGEMENT
Archives & Records Ctr.
12th & Washington   Phone: (206) 753-5467
Olympia, WA 98504   Sidney McAlpin, State Archv.

WASHINGTON STATE SUPERINTENDENT OF PUBLIC INSTRUCTION -
   RESOURCE INFORMATION CENTER
Old Capitol Bldg., Fg-11   Phone: (206) 753-6731
Olympia, WA 98504   Mrs. Bobbie J. Patterson, Coord.

NORTH OLYMPIC LIBRARY SYSTEM - PORT ANGELES BRANCH - PACIFIC
  NORTHWEST ROOM
207 S. Lincoln St.   Phone: (206) 452-9253
Port Angeles, WA 98362   Peggy M. Brady, Hd., Ref.Dept.

U.S. NATL. PARK SERVICE - OLYMPIC NATL. PARK - PIONEER MEMORIAL
  MUSEUM - LIBRARY
3002 Mount Angeles Rd.   Phone: (206) 452-4501
Port Angeles, WA 98362   Henry C. Warren, Chf.Pk. Naturalist

KITSAP COUNTY LAW LIBRARY
614 Division St.   Phone: (206) 876-7140
Port Orchard, WA 98366

ABUNDANT LIFE SEED FOUNDATION - LIBRARY
1029 Lawrence   Phone: (206) 385-5660
Port Townsend, WA 98368   Forest Shomer, Dir.

JEFFERSON COUNTY HISTORICAL SOCIETY - MUSEUM
City Hall   Phone: (206) 385-1003
Port Townsend, WA 98368

INFORMATION FUTURES - INFORMATION CENTER
2217 College Station   Phone: (509) 332-5726
Pullman, WA 99163   Gerald R. Brong, Pres.

WASHINGTON ARCHAEOLOGICAL RESEARCH CENTER - LIBRARY
Washington State Univ.
Commons Hall 322   Phone: (509) 335-8566
Pullman, WA 99164   Alice Gronski, Rec.Libn.

WASHINGTON STATE UNIVERSITY - EDUCATION LIBRARY
130 Cleveland Hall   Phone: (509) 335-1591
Pullman, WA 99164-2110   Barbara Kemp, Hd., Hum./Soc.Pub.Serv.

WASHINGTON STATE UNIVERSITY - MANUSCRIPTS, ARCHIVES, &
  SPECIAL COLLECTIONS
                                          Phone: (509) 335-6691
Pullman, WA 99164-5610   John F. Guido, Hd.

WASHINGTON STATE UNIVERSITY - OWEN SCIENCE AND ENGINEERING
  LIBRARY
                                          Phone: (509) 335-2671
Pullman, WA 99164-3200   Elizabeth P. Roberts, Hd.

WASHINGTON STATE UNIVERSITY - PRIMATE RESEARCH CENTER
  LIBRARY
                                          Phone: (509) 335-1507
Pullman, WA 99164   Francis A. Young, Dir.

WASHINGTON STATE UNIVERSITY - VETERINARY MEDICAL/PHARMACY
  LIBRARY
170 Wegner Hall   Phone: (509) 335-9556
Pullman, WA 99164-6512   Vicki F. Croft, Hd.

GOOD SAMARITAN HOSPITAL - DR. THOMAS CLARK HEALTH SERVICES
  LIBRARY
407 14th Ave., S.E.   Phone: (206) 848-6661
Puyallup, WA 98371   Linda Ziemke, Dir.

SUNDSTRAND DATA CONTROL, INC. - LIBRARY
Overlake Industrial Pk.   Phone: (206) 885-8420
Redmond, WA 98052   Peggy Lucero, Tech.Libn.

VALLEY GENERAL HOSPITAL - LIBRARY
400 S. 43rd St.   Phone: (206) 228-3450
Renton, WA 98055   Dr. Douglas R. Currin, Chm., Lib.Comm.

WASHINGTON STATE DEPARTMENT OF VETERANS AFFAIRS - STAFF &
  MEMBER LIBRARY
Washington Veterans' Home   Phone: (206) 876-7512
Retsil, WA 98378   Cherie J. Mastro, Staff Libn.

BATTELLE-NORTHWEST - PACIFIC NORTHWEST LABORATORY - HANFORD
  TECHNICAL LIBRARY
Box 999   Phone: (509) 376-5451
Richland, WA 99352   W.A. Snyder, Mgr., Tech.Info.

CHURCH OF JESUS CHRIST OF LATTER-DAY SAINTS - TRI-CITIES BRANCH
  GENEALOGICAL LIBRARY
1720 Thayer   Phone: (509) 943-0921
Richland, WA 99352   Jess Crinkerhoff, Hd.Libn.

ROCKWELL INTERNATIONAL - ROCKWELL HANFORD OPERATIONS -
  BASALT WASTE ISOLATION PROJECT - LIBRARY
PBB/1100 Area   Phone: (509) 376-6898
Richland, WA 99352   Betty Jeanne King, Anl.Libn.Res.

ROCKWELL INTERNATIONAL - ROCKWELL HANFORD OPERATIONS - LEGAL
  LIBRARY
Federal Bldg., Rm. 146   Phone: (509) 376-6807
Richland, WA 99352   Bonnie Jean Brown, Libn.

UNIVERSITY OF WASHINGTON - GRADUATE SCHOOL - JOINT CENTER FOR
  GRADUATE STUDY - LIBRARY
100 Sprout Rd.   Phone: (509) 943-3176
Richland, WA 99352   Beverly Jane Cooper, Libn.

WASHINGTON PUBLIC POWER SUPPLY SYSTEM - LIBRARY
3000 George Washington Way
Box 968   Phone: (509) 372-6337
Richland, WA 99352   Betty J. Hodges, Lib.Spec.

BATTELLE MEMORIAL INSTITUTE - HUMAN AFFAIRS RESEARCH CENTER -
  SEATTLE RESEARCH CENTERS LIBRARY
4000 N.E. 41st St.   Phone: (206) 525-3130
Seattle, WA 98105   Brenna Louzin, Libn.

BECK (R.W.) & ASSOCIATES - LIBRARY
Tower Bldg., 7th Ave. at Olive Way   Phone: (206) 622-5000
Seattle, WA 98101   Enid Miller Slivka, Libn.

BOEING COMPANY - SEATTLE SERVICES DIVISION - TECHNICAL
  LIBRARIES †
Box 3707, MS 74-60   Phone: (206) 237-8314
Seattle, WA 98124   Diana K. Carey, Mgr.

BROWN & CALDWELL - SEATTLE BRANCH OFFICE LIBRARY
100 W. Harrison   Phone: (206) 281-4000
Seattle, WA 98119   Marilyn Burwell, Libn.

CHILDREN'S ORTHOPEDIC HOSPITAL & MEDICAL CENTER - HOSPITAL
  LIBRARY
4800 Sand Point Way, N.E.   Phone: (206) 526-2118
Seattle, WA 98105   Tamara A. Turner, Dir.

CORNISH INSTITUTE - LIBRARY
710 E. Roy St.   Phone: (206) 323-1400
Seattle, WA 98102   Ronald G. McComb, Hd.Libn.

DAMES & MOORE - SEATTLE OFFICE LIBRARY
155 N.E. 100th St., Suite 500   Phone: (206) 523-0560
Seattle, WA 98125   Lyn F. Sauter, Libn.

ENVIRONMENTAL PROTECTION AGENCY - REGION X LIBRARY
1200 Sixth Ave.   Phone: (206) 442-1289
Seattle, WA 98101   Julienne Sears, Regional Libn.

FOSTER, PEPPER & RIVIERA - LAW LIBRARY
1111 Third Ave. Bldg.   Phone: (206) 447-4400
Seattle, WA 98101   Karen Braucht, Libn.

FRYE (Charles and Emma) ART MUSEUM - LIBRARY
Box 3005   Phone: (206) 622-9250
Seattle, WA 98114   Mrs. W.S. Greathouse, Pres.

GROUP HEALTH COOPERATIVE OF PUGET SOUND - MEDICAL LIBRARY
200 15th Ave., E.   Phone: (206) 326-6093
Seattle, WA 98112   Dick Pride, Dir.

HISTORICAL SOCIETY OF SEATTLE & KING COUNTY - SOPHIE FRYE BASS
  LIBRARY OF NORTHWEST AMERICANA
Museum of History & Industry
2700 24th Ave. E.   Phone: (206) 324-1125
Seattle, WA 98112   Rick Caldwell, Libn.

HONEYWELL, INC. - HONEYWELL MARINE SYSTEMS OPERATIONS -
   TECHNICAL INFORMATION CENTER
5303 Shilshole Ave., N.W.   Phone: (206) 789-2000
Seattle, WA 98107   Christine Mackey, Tech.Libn.

KARR, TUTTLE, KOCH, CAMPBELL, MAWER & MORROW - LAW LIBRARY
1111 Third Ave., Suite 2500   Phone: (206) 223-1313
Seattle, WA 98101   Barbara Cornwell Holt, Libn.

KING COUNTY LAW LIBRARY
601 County Courthouse
Seattle, WA 98104   James J. McArdle, Libn.

KING COUNTY MASONIC LIBRARY ASSOCIATION - LIBRARY *
Harvard & E. Pine St.   Phone: (206) 322-9535
Seattle, WA 98122   Erwin L. Hippe, Libn.

KING COUNTY YOUTH SERVICE CENTER - LIBRARY
1211 E. Alder   Phone: (206) 323-9500
Seattle, WA 98122   Julie Ann Oiye, Libn.

KRAMER CHIN AND MAYO INC. - LIBRARY
1917 First Ave.   Phone: (206) 447-5301
Seattle, WA 98101   Patrick A. Hall, Libn.

LE BEACON PRESSE - SMALL PRESS COLLECTION
2921 E. Madison St., Suite 7   Phone: (206) 322-1431
Seattle, WA 98112-4237   Keith S. Gormezano, Dir./Coord.

MUNICIPAL RESEARCH AND SERVICES CENTER OF WASHINGTON -
   LIBRARY
4719 Brooklyn Ave., N.E.   Phone: (206) 543-9050
Seattle, WA 98105   Lynne DeMerritt, Libn.

MUNICIPALITY OF METROPOLITAN SEATTLE - METRO LIBRARY
821 Second Ave.
Seattle, WA 98104   Bonnie Mattson, Libn.

NORDIC HERITAGE MUSEUM - WALTER JOHNSON LIBRARY
3014 N.W. 67th St.   Phone: (206) 789-5707
Seattle, WA 98107   Marianne Forssblad, Dir./Hd.Libn.

NORTHWEST HOSPITAL - EFFIE M. STOREY LEARNING CENTER
1550 North 115th   Phone: (206) 364-0500
Seattle, WA 98133   Edith Sutton, Libn.

PACIFIC COAST BANKING SCHOOL - LIBRARY
2001 Sixth Ave., Suite 1710   Phone: (206) 624-7618
Seattle, WA 98121   Mrs. Marciel Tomich, Registrar

PACIFIC SCIENCE CENTER FOUNDATION - LIBRARY
200 Second Ave., N.
Seattle, WA 98109

PERKINS, COIE, STONE, OLSEN & WILLIAMS - LAW LIBRARY
1900 Washington Bldg.   Phone: (206) 682-8770
Seattle, WA 98101   Jane Stewart, Librarian

PLYMOUTH CONGREGATIONAL CHURCH - VIDA B. VAREY LIBRARY
1217 6th Ave.
Seattle, WA 98101   Anna F. Chiong, Libn.

POPULATION DYNAMICS, INC. - INFORMATION CENTER
3829 Aurora Ave., N.   Phone: (206) 632-5030
Seattle, WA 98103

PRESTON, THORGRIMSON, ELLIS & HOLMAN - LIBRARY
2000 IBM Bldg.
Box 2927   Phone: (206) 623-7580
Seattle, WA 98111   Margaret Chillingworth, Libn.

PROTESTANT EPISCOPAL CHURCH OF WESTERN WASHINGTON - DIOCESE
   OF OLYMPIA - ARCHIVES
1551 Tenth Ave., E.
Box 12126   Phone: (206) 325-4200
Seattle, WA 98102   Peggy Ann Hansen, Archv.

PROTESTANT EPISCOPAL CHURCH OF WESTERN WASHINGTON - DIOCESE
   OF OLYMPIA - EDUCATION RESOURCE CENTER
1551 Tenth Ave., E.
Box 12126   Phone: (206) 325-4200
Seattle, WA 98102   Anita Steury, Libn.

PROVIDENCE MEDICAL CENTER - HORTON HEALTH SCIENCES LIBRARY
500 17th Ave., C-34008   Phone: (206) 326-5621
Seattle, WA 98124   Kathleen Murray, Dir., Lib.Serv.

PSYCHOANALYTIC ASSOCIATION OF SEATTLE - EDITH BUXBAUM LIBRARY
4029 E. Madison St.   Phone: (206) 324-6614
Seattle, WA 98112   Adolph M. Gruhn, Chm., Lib.Comm.

PUGET SOUND COUNCIL OF GOVERNMENTS - INFORMATION CENTER
Grand Central on the Park
216 First Ave., S.   Phone: (206) 464-7090
Seattle, WA 98104   Cam McIntosh, Info.Spec.

RAINIER NATIONAL BANK - INFORMATION CENTER
Box 3966
Seattle, WA 98124   Vivienne C. Burke, Asst.V.P./Mgr.

SAFECO INSURANCE COMPANY - LIBRARY
Safeco Plaza   Phone: (206) 545-5505
Seattle, WA 98185   Esther J. Delaney, Libn.

SCHICK SHADEL HOSPITAL - MEDICAL LIBRARY
Box 48149   Phone: (206) 244-8100
Seattle, WA 98148   Mary Jane McInturff, Med.Libn.

SEATTLE ART MUSEUM - LIBRARY
Volunteer Park   Phone: (206) 447-4686
Seattle, WA 98112   Elizabeth De Fato, Libn.

SEATTLE-FIRST NATIONAL BANK - LIBRARY
Box 3586   Phone: (206) 583-4056
Seattle, WA 98124   Jeannette M. Privat, A.V.P. & Mgr.

SEATTLE POST-INTELLIGENCER - NEWSPAPER LIBRARY
6th & Wall Sts.   Phone: (206) 628-8000
Seattle, WA 98111   Lytton Smith, Chf.Libn.

SEATTLE PUBLIC HEALTH HOSPITAL - MEDICAL SERVICE LIBRARY *
1131 14th Ave. S.   Phone: (206) 324-7650
Seattle, WA 98114   Seungja Song, Chf.Libn.

SEATTLE PUBLIC LIBRARY - ART AND MUSIC DEPARTMENT †
1000 Fourth Ave.   Phone: (206) 625-2665
Seattle, WA 98104   Carolyn J. Holmquist, Hd.

SEATTLE PUBLIC LIBRARY - BUSINESS AND SCIENCE DEPARTMENT †
1000 Fourth Ave.   Phone: (206) 625-2665
Seattle, WA 98104

SEATTLE PUBLIC LIBRARY - DOUGLASS-TRUTH BRANCH LIBRARY
23rd Ave. & E. Yesler Way   Phone: (206) 625-4874
Seattle, WA 98122   Marcia Myers, South Reg.Libn.

SEATTLE PUBLIC LIBRARY - EDUCATION, PSYCHOLOGY, SOCIOLOGY,
   SPORTS DEPARTMENT †
1000 Fourth Ave.   Phone: (206) 625-2665
Seattle, WA 98104   Lonita M. Walton, Mng.Libn.

SEATTLE PUBLIC LIBRARY - GOVERNMENTAL RESEARCH ASSISTANCE
   LIBRARY †
Municipal Bldg.
600 Fourth Ave.   Phone: (206) 625-2665
Seattle, WA 98104   Barbara Guptill, Mng.Libn.

SEATTLE PUBLIC LIBRARY - HISTORY, GOVERNMENT AND BIOGRAPHY
   DEPARTMENT †
1000 Fourth Ave.   Phone: (206) 625-2665
Seattle, WA 98104   Jean Coberly, Hd., History Dept.

SEATTLE PUBLIC LIBRARY - LITERATURE, LANGUAGES, PHILOSOPHY &
   RELIGION DEPARTMENT †
1000 Fourth Ave.   Phone: (206) 625-2665
Seattle, WA 98104   Nancy Wildin, Hd.

SEATTLE PUBLIC LIBRARY - MEDIA & PROGRAM SERVICES †
1000 Fourth Ave.   Phone: (206) 625-2665
Seattle, WA 98104   Kandy B. Brandt, Hd.

SEATTLE PUBLIC LIBRARY - WASHINGTON LIBRARY FOR THE BLIND AND
    PHYSICALLY HANDICAPPED
821 Lenora St.   Phone: (206) 464-6930
Seattle, WA 98121   Jan Ames, Regional Libn.

SEATTLE TIMES - LIBRARY †
Fairview N. & John
Box 70
Seattle, WA 98111   Phone: (206) 464-2311
                                          Beverly Russell, Libn.

SEATTLE TRUST & SAVINGS BANK - LIBRARY
804 Second Ave.   Phone: (206) 223-2052
Seattle, WA 98104   Dorothy S. Hughes, Libn.

SEATTLE WEAVERS' GUILD - LIBRARY
1245 10th Ave. E.
Seattle, WA 98102

SHANNON & WILSON, INC. - TECHNICAL LIBRARY †
1105 N. 38th St.
Box C-30313   Phone: (206) 632-8020
Seattle, WA 98103   Phyllis Jean Boucher, Libn.

SISTERS OF PROVIDENCE - SACRED HEART PROVINCE - ARCHIVES
4800 37th Ave., S.W.   Phone: (206) 937-4600
Seattle, WA 98126   Sr. Rita Bergamini, S.P., Archv.

SWEDISH HOSPITAL MEDICAL CENTER - REFERENCE LIBRARY
747 Summit Ave.   Phone: (206) 292-2484
Seattle, WA 98104   Jean C. Anderson, Chf.Libn.

TEMPLE DE HIRSCH SINAI - LIBRARY
1511 E. Pike
Seattle, WA 98122   Kathryn K. Crane, Libn.

TRA ARCHITECTURE ENGINEERING PLANNING INTERIORS - LIBRARY
215 Columbia   Phone: (206) 682-1133
Seattle, WA 98104   Dan Trefethen, Libn.

U.S. ARMY - CORPS OF ENGINEERS - SEATTLE DISTRICT - LIBRARY
Box C-3755   Phone: (206) 764-3728
Seattle, WA 98124   Pat J. Perry, District Libn.

U.S. ARMY POST - FORT GREELY - LIBRARY
Bldg. 663   Phone: (907) 873-3217
APO Seattle, WA 98733   Bonnie Ricks, Lib.Dir.

U.S. BUREAU OF THE CENSUS - INFORMATION SERVICES PROGRAM -
    SEATTLE REGIONAL OFFICE - LIBRARY
1700 Westlake Ave., N.   Phone: (206) 442-7080
Seattle, WA 98174   Betty J. Owens, Libn.

U.S. DEPT. OF LABOR - EMPLOYMENT & TRAINING ADMINISTRATION -
    REGION X RESOURCE CENTER *
909 First Ave., No. 1145   Phone: (206) 442-1078
Seattle, WA 98174   Ellen Kampel, Info.Dir.

U.S. DEPT. OF LABOR - OSHA - REGIONAL LIBRARY
6003 Federal Office Bldg.
909 First Ave.   Phone: (206) 442-5930
Seattle, WA 98174   Donna M. Hoffman, Libn.

U.S. NATL. ARCHIVES & RECORDS SERVICE - FEDERAL ARCHIVES AND
    RECORDS CENTER, REGION 10
6125 Sand Point Way   Phone: (206) 442-4502
Seattle, WA 98115   David Piff, Chf., Archv.Br.

U.S. NATL. MARINE FISHERIES SERVICE - NATIONAL MARINE MAMMAL
    LABORATORY - LIBRARY *
7600 Sand Point Way N.E., Bldg. 32   Phone: (206) 442-4580
Seattle, WA 98115   Sherry Pearson, Tech.Info.Spec.

U.S. NATL. MARINE FISHERIES SERVICE - NORTHWEST & ALASKA
    FISHERIES CENTER - LIBRARY
2725 Montlake Blvd., E.   Phone: (206) 442-7795
Seattle, WA 98112   Patricia Cook, Libn.

U.S. NATL. OCEANIC & ATMOSPHERIC ADMINISTRATION - SEATTLE
    CENTER
7600 Sand Point Way, N.E., Bin C15700, Bldg. 3   Phone: (206) 527-6241
Seattle, WA 98115   Bruce Keck, Libn.

U.S. NAVY - NAVAL SUPPORT ACTIVITY - LIBRARY
Bldg. 47   Phone: (206) 526-3577
Seattle, WA 98115   Bob Kinsedahl, Libn.

U.S. VETERANS ADMINISTRATION (WA-Seattle) - HOSPITAL MEDICAL
    LIBRARY
4435 Beacon Ave., S.   Phone: (206) 762-1010
Seattle, WA 98108   Martha Leredu, Chf., Lib.Serv.

UNIVERSITY CONGREGATIONAL CHURCH - LIBRARY
4515 16th Ave., N.E.   Phone: (206) 524-2322
Seattle, WA 98105   Gertrude Wulfekoetter, Libn.

UNIVERSITY OF WASHINGTON - ARCHITECTURE-URBAN PLANNING
    LIBRARY
334 Gould Hall, JO-30   Phone: (206) 543-4067
Seattle, WA 98195   Betty L. Wagner, Libn.

UNIVERSITY OF WASHINGTON - ART LIBRARY
101 Art Bldg., DM-10   Phone: (206) 543-0648
Seattle, WA 98195   Connie T. Okada, Libn.

UNIVERSITY OF WASHINGTON - ART SLIDE COLLECTION
120 Art Bldg., DM-10   Phone: (206) 543-0649
Seattle, WA 98195   Marietta S. Foubert, Preparator

UNIVERSITY OF WASHINGTON - BUSINESS ADMINISTRATION LIBRARY
100 Balmer Hall, DJ-10   Phone: (206) 543-4360
Seattle, WA 98195   Anne B. Passarelli, Hd.Libn.

UNIVERSITY OF WASHINGTON - CENTER FOR LAW & JUSTICE - CLJ/
    NCADBIP INFORMATION SERVICE
1107 N.E. 45th St., Suite 505   Phone: (206) 543-1485
Seattle, WA 98105   Janette H. Schueller, Info.Spec.

UNIVERSITY OF WASHINGTON - CENTER FOR STUDIES IN DEMOGRAPHY
    AND ECOLOGY - LIBRARY
102 Savery Hall, DK-40   Phone: (206) 543-5035
Seattle, WA 98195   Thomas W. Pullum, Dir.

UNIVERSITY OF WASHINGTON - CHEMISTRY-PHARMACY LIBRARY
192 Bagley Hall, BG-10   Phone: (206) 543-1603
Seattle, WA 98195   Heidi Mercado

UNIVERSITY OF WASHINGTON - COMPUTING INFORMATION CENTER
3737 Brooklyn N.E., HG-45   Phone: (206) 543-8519
Seattle, WA 98105   Myers Hildebrandt, Mgr.

UNIVERSITY OF WASHINGTON - CURRICULUM MATERIALS SECTION
Suzzallo Library, FM-25   Phone: (206) 543-2725
Seattle, WA 98195

UNIVERSITY OF WASHINGTON - DRAMA LIBRARY
25 Drama-TV Bldg., BH-20   Phone: (206) 543-5148
Seattle, WA 98195   Liz Fugate, Libn.

UNIVERSITY OF WASHINGTON - EAST ASIA LIBRARY
322 Gowen Hall, DO-27   Phone: (206) 543-4490
Seattle, WA 98195   Karl Lo, Hd.

UNIVERSITY OF WASHINGTON - ENGINEERING LIBRARY
Engineering Library Bldg., FH-15   Phone: (206) 543-0740
Seattle, WA 98195   Harold N. Wiren, Hd.Libn.

UNIVERSITY OF WASHINGTON - FISHERIES-OCEANOGRAPHY LIBRARY
151 Oceanography Teaching Bldg., WB-30   Phone: (206) 543-4279
Seattle, WA 98195   Thomas D. Moritz, Hd.Libn.

UNIVERSITY OF WASHINGTON - FISHING VESSEL SAFETY CENTER -
    LIBRARY
326 Mechanical Engineering Bldg.
Mail Stop FU-10   Phone: (206) 543-7446
Seattle, WA 98195   Bruce H. Adee, Dir.

UNIVERSITY OF WASHINGTON - FOREST RESOURCES LIBRARY
60 Bloedel Hall, AQ-15   Phone: (206) 543-2758
Seattle, WA 98195   Barbara B. Gordon, Hd.

UNIVERSITY OF WASHINGTON - GEOGRAPHY LIBRARY
415 Smith Hall, DP-10   Phone: (206) 543-5244
Seattle, WA 98195   Joan E. Christ, Libn.

UNIVERSITY OF WASHINGTON - GOVERNMENT PUBLICATIONS DIVISION
Suzzalo Library, FM-25   Phone: (206) 543-1937
Seattle, WA 98195   Eleanor L. Chase, Hd.Libn.

UNIVERSITY OF WASHINGTON - HEALTH SCIENCES LIBRARY
T-231 Health Sciences, SB-55   Phone: (206) 543-5530
Seattle, WA 98195   Gerald J. Oppenheimer, Dir.

UNIVERSITY OF WASHINGTON - HEALTH SCIENCES LIBRARY - K.K.
   SHERWOOD LIBRARY
Harborview Medical Ctr.
325 9th Ave., ZA-43   Phone: (206) 223-3360
Seattle, WA 98104   Sharon Babcock, Lib.Supv.

UNIVERSITY OF WASHINGTON - HENRY ART GALLERY TEXTILE
   COLLECTION
51 Drama-TV Bldg., DL-10   Phone: (206) 543-1739
Seattle, WA 98195   Judy Sourakli, Registrar

UNIVERSITY OF WASHINGTON - MAP SECTION
Suzzalo Library, FM-25   Phone: (206) 543-9392
Seattle, WA 98195   Steven Z. Hiller, Hd.

UNIVERSITY OF WASHINGTON - MARIAN GOULD GALLAGHER LAW
   LIBRARY
School of Law
1100 N.E. Campus Pkwy., JB-20   Phone: (206) 543-4089
Seattle, WA 98105   Elizabeth R. Wilkins, Law Libn.

UNIVERSITY OF WASHINGTON - MATHEMATICS RESEARCH LIBRARY
C306 Padelford, GN-50   Phone: (206) 543-7296
Seattle, WA 98195   Martha Tucker Murdoch, Hd.

UNIVERSITY OF WASHINGTON - MUSIC LIBRARY
113 Music Bldg., DN-10   Phone: (206) 543-1168
Seattle, WA 98195   David A. Wood, Hd.Libn.

UNIVERSITY OF WASHINGTON - NATURAL SCIENCES LIBRARY
Suzzalo Library, FM-25   Phone: (206) 543-1243
Seattle, WA 98195   Nancy G. Blase, Hd.

UNIVERSITY OF WASHINGTON - PACIFIC NORTHWEST LONG-TERM CARE
   CENTER - INFORMATION CLEARINGHOUSE
University of Washington JM-20
Seattle, WA 98195

UNIVERSITY OF WASHINGTON - PHILOSOPHY LIBRARY
331 Savery, DK-50   Phone: (206) 543-5856
Seattle, WA 98195   Joan E. Christ, Libn.

UNIVERSITY OF WASHINGTON - PHYSICS-ASTRONOMY LIBRARY
219 Physics Bldg., FM-15   Phone: (206) 543-2988
Seattle, WA 98195   Martha Austin, Hd.Libn.

UNIVERSITY OF WASHINGTON - POLITICAL SCIENCE LIBRARY
220 Smith Hall, DP 25   Phone: (206) 543-2389
Seattle, WA 98195   Al Fritz, Libn.

UNIVERSITY OF WASHINGTON - REGIONAL PRIMATE RESEARCH CENTER -
   PRIMATE INFORMATION CENTER
SJ-50   Phone: (206) 543-4376
Seattle, WA 98195   Benella Caminiti, Mgr.

UNIVERSITY OF WASHINGTON - SOCIAL WORK LIBRARY
Social Work/Speech-Hearing Bldg., JH-30   Phone: (206) 545-2180
Seattle, WA 98195   Guela G. Johnson, Libn.

UNIVERSITY OF WASHINGTON - SPECIAL COLLECTIONS DIVISION -
   PACIFIC NORTHWEST COLLECTION
Suzzalo Library, FM-25   Phone: (206) 543-1929
Seattle, WA 98195   Carla Rickerson, Hd.

UNIVERSITY OF WASHINGTON - SPECIAL COLL.DIV. - PACIFIC
   NORTHWEST COLLECTION - ARCHITECTURAL HISTORY COLL.
Suzzallo Library, FM-25   Phone: (206) 543-0742
Seattle, WA 98195   Richard H. Engeman, Asst.Libn.

UNIVERSITY OF WASHINGTON - SPECIAL COLL.DIV. - PACIFIC
   NORTHWEST COLLECTION - HISTORICAL PHOTOGRAPHY COLL.
Suzzallo Library, FM-25   Phone: (206) 543-1929
Seattle, WA 98195   Richard H. Engeman, Asst.Libn.

UNIVERSITY OF WASHINGTON - UNIVERSITY ARCHIVES & MANUSCRIPT
   DIVISION - MANUSCRIPT COLLECTION
Suzzallo Library, FM-25   Phone: (206) 543-1879
Seattle, WA 98195   Richard Berner, Hd.Libn.

UNIVERSITY OF WASHINGTON - UNIVERSITY ARCHIVES & MANUSCRIPT
   DIVISION - UNIVERSITY ARCHIVES
3902 Cowlitz Rd., HO-10   Phone: (206) 543-6509
Seattle, WA 98195   Richard C. Berner, Univ.Archv.

WALDO GENERAL HOSPITAL - MEDICAL LIBRARY
10560 5th, N.E.
Box 25167   Phone: (206) 364-2050
Seattle, WA 98125   Janet Schnall, Consulting Libn.

WASHINGTON MUTUAL SAVINGS BANK - INFORMATION CENTER &
   DIETRICH SCHMITZ MEMORIAL LIBRARY
Box 834   Phone: (206) 464-4494
Seattle, WA 98111   Marcella C. Gaar, Info.Off.

WOODLAND PARK ZOOLOGICAL GARDENS - LIBRARY *
5500 Phinney Ave., N.   Phone: (206) 625-4550
Seattle, WA 98103   Mary C. Hopkins, Libn.

ITT RAYONIER, INC. - RESEARCH CENTER - LIBRARY
409 E. Harvard St.   Phone: (206) 426-4461
Shelton, WA 98584   Patricia A. Tostevin, Libn.

KITSAP COUNTY HISTORICAL MUSEUM - LIBRARY
3343 N.W. Byron St.   Phone: (206) 692-1949
Silverdale, WA 98383   Suzanne T. Anest, Musm.Dir.

DIOCESE OF SPOKANE - DIOCESAN CHANCERY ARCHIVES
1023 W. Riverside Ave.
Box 1453   Phone: (509) 456-7100
Spokane, WA 99210   Rev. Edward J. Kowrach, Archv.

EASTERN WASHINGTON STATE HISTORICAL SOCIETY - LIBRARY
Cheney Cowles Memorial Museum
W. 2316 First Ave.   Phone: (509) 456-3931
Spokane, WA 99204   Douglas A. Olson, Libn.

GONZAGA UNIVERSITY - CROSBY LIBRARY
502 E. Boone Ave.   Phone: (509) 328-4220
Spokane, WA 99258   Robert L. Burr, Dir.

GONZAGA UNIVERSITY SCHOOL OF LAW - LIBRARY
E. 600 Sharp Ave.
Box 3528   Phone: (509) 328-4220
Spokane, WA 99220   James M. Murray, Law Libn.

HOLLISTER-STIER - LIBRARY
Box 3145, Terminal Annex   Phone: (509) 489-5656
Spokane, WA 99220   Kitty Torgerson, Libn.

INTERCOLLEGIATE CENTER FOR NURSING EDUCATION - LIBRARY
W. 2917 Ft. George Wright Dr.   Phone: (509) 326-7270
Spokane, WA 99204   Robert M. Pringle, Jr., Hd.Libn.

MOLDENHAUER ARCHIVES
1011 Comstock Ct.   Phone: (509) 747-4555
Spokane, WA 99203   Dr. Hans Moldenhauer, Dir.

SACRED HEART MEDICAL CENTER - HEALTH SCIENCES LIBRARY
W. 101 8th Ave.   Phone: (509) 455-3094
Spokane, WA 99204   Elizabeth J. Guilfoil, Dir.

ST. LUKE'S MEMORIAL HOSPITAL - A.M. JOHNSON MEMORIAL MEDICAL
  LIBRARY
711 S. Cowley St.   Phone: (509) 838-4771
Spokane, WA 99210   Loren A. Gothberg, Chm., Lib.Comm.

SOCIETY OF JESUS - OREGON PROVINCE ARCHIVES
Crosby Library, Gonzaga University
E. 502 Boone Ave.   Phone: (509) 328-4220
Spokane, WA 92588   Rev. Clifford Carroll, S.J., Archv.

SPOKANE COUNTY LAW LIBRARY
1020 Paulsen Bldg.   Phone: (509) 456-3680
Spokane, WA 99201   Emily E. Wadden, Law Libn.

SPOKANE MEDICAL LIBRARY
W. 35 8th Ave.   Phone: (509) 747-5777
Spokane, WA 99204   Lisa Veium, Dir.

SPOKANE SPOKESMAN-REVIEW AND SPOKANE CHRONICLE - NEWSPAPER
  REFERENCE LIBRARY †
508 Chronicle Bldg.   Phone: (509) 455-6891
Spokane, WA 99210   Robert A. Neswick, Mgr.

U.S. GEOLOGICAL SURVEY - WESTERN MINERAL RESOURCES LIBRARY
656 U.S. Court House
920 W. Riverside Ave.   Phone: (509) 456-4677
Spokane, WA 99201   Anita W. Tarbert, Lib.Techn.

U.S. VETERANS ADMINISTRATION (WA-Spokane) - MEDICAL CENTER
  LIBRARY
N. 4815 Assembly St.   Phone: (509) 328-4521
Spokane, WA 99205   Ruth A. Jones, Chf.Libn.

WHITWORTH COLLEGE - SCIENCE LIBRARY †
                                              Phone: (509) 489-3550
Spokane, WA 99251

ABAM ENGINEERS, INC. - TECHNICAL LIBRARY
500 S. 336th, Suite 200
Federal Way   Phone: (206) 241-6100
Tacoma, WA 98003   Ann Kennedy, Tech.Libn.

AMERICAN PLYWOOD ASSOCIATION - INFORMATION CENTER
Box 11700   Phone: (206) 565-6600
Tacoma, WA 98411   June Packer, Rec.Mgr.

ASBURY UNITED METHODIST CHURCH - LIBRARY
5601 S. Puget Sound
Box 9448   Phone: (206) 472-4239
Tacoma, WA 98409   Crystal M. Parks, Libn.

CHURCH OF JESUS CHRIST OF LATTER-DAY SAINTS - TACOMA BRANCH
  GENEALOGY LIBRARY
1102 S. Pearl   Phone: (206) 564-1103
Tacoma, WA 98465   Wallace Johnson, Hd.Libn.

FAITH EVANGELICAL LUTHERAN SEMINARY - LIBRARY
3504 N. Pearl
Box 7186   Phone: (206) 752-2020
Tacoma, WA 98407   Rev. Osborne Y. Bruland, Libn.

PIERCE COUNTY LAW LIBRARY †
123 County-City Bldg.   Phone: (206) 593-4346
Tacoma, WA 98402   Faye L. Reese, Libn.

PIERCE COUNTY MEDICAL LIBRARY
315 South K St.
Box 5277   Phone: (206) 572-5340
Tacoma, WA 98405   Ms. Marion VonBruck, Med.Libn.

REICHHOLD CHEMICALS, INC. - TECHNICAL LIBRARY
2340 Taylor Way   Phone: (206) 572-5600
Tacoma, WA 98401   Deirdre R. Preston, Info. Resource Spec.

ST. JOSEPH HOSPITAL AND HEALTH CARE CENTER - HOSPITAL LIBRARY
1718 South I St.
Box 2197   Phone: (206) 627-4101
Tacoma, WA 98401   Cheryl M. Goodwin, Libn.

TACOMA ART MUSEUM - LIBRARY
12th & Pacific Ave.   Phone: (206) 272-4258
Tacoma, WA 98402   Sally Norris, Libn.

TACOMA NEWS TRIBUNE - LIBRARY
Box 11000   Phone: (206) 597-8626
Tacoma, WA 98411   Paula F. Stevens, Libn.

TACOMA PUBLIC LIBRARY - SPECIAL COLLECTIONS
1102 Tacoma Ave. S.   Phone: (206) 591-5622
Tacoma, WA 98402   Kevin Hegarty, Dir.

U.S. ARMY HOSPITALS - MADIGAN ARMY MEDICAL CENTER - MEDICAL
  LIBRARY
Box 375   Phone: (206) 967-6782
Tacoma, WA 98431   Elizabeth C. Bolden, Libn.

U.S. ARMY HOSPITALS - MADIGAN ARMY MEDICAL CENTER - MORALE
  SUPPORT LIBRARY
                                              Phone: (206) 967-6198
Tacoma, WA 98431   Marganne Weathers, Adm.Libn.

U.S. VETERANS ADMINISTRATION (WA-Tacoma) - MEDICAL CENTER
  LIBRARY
American Lake   Phone: (206) 582-8440
Tacoma, WA 98493   Dennis L. Levi, Chf., Lib.Serv.

UNIVERSITY OF PUGET SOUND - SCHOOL OF LAW LIBRARY
950 Broadway Plaza   Phone: (206) 756-3326
Tacoma, WA 98402   Anita M. Steele, Dir.

WASHINGTON STATE HISTORICAL SOCIETY - LIBRARY
315 N. Stadium Way   Phone: (206) 593-2830
Tacoma, WA 98403   Frank L. Green, Libn.

WEYERHAEUSER COMPANY - ARCHIVES
                                              Phone: (206) 924-5051
Tacoma, WA 98477   Donnie Crespo, Archv.

WEYERHAEUSER COMPANY - CORPORATE LIBRARY
CH 1-W   Phone: (206) 924-3030
Tacoma, WA 98477   Karin H. Williams, Mgr., Corp.Lib.

WEYERHAEUSER COMPANY - TECHNICAL INFORMATION CENTER
                                              Phone: (206) 924-6265
Tacoma, WA 98477   L.W. Martinez, Mgr.

BOISE CASCADE CORPORATION - PULP & PAPER RESEARCH LIBRARY
909 W. Seventh St.   Phone: (206) 695-4477
Vancouver, WA 98660   Vernon N. Gagnon, Libn.

CLARK COUNTY LAW LIBRARY
Court House, Rm. 302
Box 5000   Phone: (206) 699-2268
Vancouver, WA 98668   Barbara Rowland, Libn.

CLARK COUNTY REGIONAL PLANNING COUNCIL - LIBRARY
1408 Franklin
Box 5000   Phone: (206) 699-2361
Vancouver, WA 98668   Mary Legry, Data Coord.

ST. JOSEPH COMMUNITY HOSPITAL - LIBRARY
600 N.E. 92nd Ave.
Box 1687   Phone: (206) 256-2045
Vancouver, WA 98668   Sylvia E. MacWilliams, Lib.Coord.

U.S. NATL. PARK SERVICE - FORT VANCOUVER NATL. HISTORIC SITE -
  LIBRARY
1501 E. Evergreen Blvd.   Phone: (206) 696-7655
Vancouver, WA 98661   Kent J. Taylor, Supv./Pk. Ranger

U.S. VETERANS ADMINISTRATION (WA-Vancouver) - HOSPITAL LIBRARY
Fourth Plain & O Sts.   Phone: (206) 696-4061
Vancouver, WA 98661   Mrs. Nymah L. Trued, Chf., Lib.Serv.

VANCOUVER MEMORIAL HOSPITAL - R.D. WISWALL MEMORIAL LIBRARY
3400 Main St.
Box 1600   Phone: (206) 696-5143
Vancouver, WA 98668   Sylvia E. MacWilliams, Lib.Coord.

WASHINGTON STATE SCHOOL FOR THE DEAF - LEARNING RESOURCE
   CENTER
611 Grand Blvd.   Phone: (206) 696-6223
Vancouver, WA 98661   James Randall, Dir.

U.S. VETERANS ADMINISTRATION (WA-Walla Walla) - HOSPITAL LIBRARY
77 Wainwright Dr.   Phone: (509) 525-5200
Walla Walla, WA 99362   Max J. Merrell, Chf.Libn.

WALLA WALLA COUNTY LAW LIBRARY
Court House   Phone: (509) 529-9520
Walla Walla, WA 99362   Ben R. Forcier, Jr., Libn.

WHITMAN COLLEGE - EELLS NORTHWEST COLLECTION AND NORTHWEST
   ARCHIVES
Penrose Memorial Library
345 Boyer St.   Phone: (509) 527-5191
Walla Walla, WA 99362   Lawrence L. Dodd, Cur. of Mss. & Spec.Coll.

CENTRAL WASHINGTON HOSPITAL - HEMINGER HEALTH SCIENCES
   LIBRARY
1211 Rosewood
Box 1887   Phone: (509) 662-1511
Wenatchee, WA 98801   Jane Belt, Med.Libn.

ST. ELIZABETH MEDICAL CENTER - HEALTH SCIENCES LIBRARY
110 S. 9th Ave.   Phone: (509) 575-5000
Yakima, WA 98902   Sr. Irene Charron, S.P., Med.Libn.

YAKIMA COUNTY LAW LIBRARY
Yakima County Court House   Phone: (509) 457-5452
Yakima, WA 98901   Linda Von Essen, Law Libn.

YAKIMA VALLEY GENEALOGICAL SOCIETY - LIBRARY
Box 445   Phone: (509) 248-1328
Yakima, WA 98907   Ellen Brzoska, Libn.

YAKIMA VALLEY MUSEUM AND HISTORICAL ASSOCIATION - ARCHIVES
2105 Tieton Dr.   Phone: (509) 248-0747
Yakima, WA 98902   Frances A. Hare, Archv.

WEST VIRGINIA

APPALACHIAN REGIONAL HOSPITAL - MEDICAL LIBRARY
306 Stanaford Rd.   Phone: (304) 255-3261
Beckley, WV 25801   Thelma Wilson, Dir. of Educ.

U.S. NATIONAL MINE HEALTH AND SAFETY ACADEMY - LEARNING
   RESOURCE CENTER
Airport Rd.
Box 1166   Phone: (304) 255-0451
Beckley, WV 25801   Dr. Leslie E. Woelflin, Chf., Lrng.Res.Ctr.

U.S. VETERANS ADMINISTRATION (WV-Beckley) - MEDICAL CENTER
   LIBRARY
200 Veterans Ave.   Phone: (304) 255-2121
Beckley, WV 25801   Shelley C. Doman, Chf., Lib.Serv.

BETHANY COLLEGE - CHEMISTRY LIBRARY
Richardson Hall of Science   Phone: (304) 829-7711
Bethany, WV 26032   Rosalie S. Draper, Ck.

BLUEFIELD DAILY TELEGRAPH - LIBRARY
412 Bland St.   Phone: (304) 327-6171
Bluefield, WV 24701   Karen Kaplan, Info.Dir.

APPALACHIAN BIBLE COLLEGE - LIBRARY
                                             Phone: (304) 877-6428
Bradley, WV 25818   John Van Puffelen, Libn.

WEST VIRGINIA WESLEYAN COLLEGE - ANNIE MERNER PFEIFFER LIBRARY
College Ave.   Phone: (304) 473-8013
Buckhannon, WV 26201   Benjamin F. Crutchfield, Jr., Dir., Lib.Serv.

OLD CHARLES TOWN LIBRARY, INC.
200 E. Washington St.   Phone: (304) 725-2208
Charles Town, WV 25414   Anna M. Shewbridge, Libn.

APPALACHIA EDUCATIONAL LABORATORY - RESEARCH & INFORMATION
   CENTER ★
Box 1348   Phone: (304) 347-0428
Charleston, WV 25325   Louise Kinzy, Libn.

CHARLESTON GAZETTE-MAIL - LIBRARY
1001 Virginia St., E.   Phone: (304) 348-4888
Charleston, WV 25330   Ron Miller, Hd.Libn.

COLUMBIA GAS TRANSMISSION CORPORATION - LAW LIBRARY
Box 1273   Phone: (304) 346-0951
Charleston, WV 25325   Nina K. Angle, Law Libn.

FIRST PRESBYTERIAN CHURCH OF CHARLESTON - LIBRARY
16 Broad St.   Phone: (304) 343-8961
Charleston, WV 25301   Susan Perkins, Dir., Educ.Rsrcs.

JACKSON, KELLY, HOLT & O'FARRELL - LIBRARY
1500 One Valley Sq.
Box 553   Phone: (304) 347-7500
Charleston, WV 25322   Holley M. Blair, Libn.

SUNRISE MUSEUMS, INC. - LIBRARY
746 Myrtle Rd.   Phone: (304) 344-8035
Charleston, WV 25314

SURFACE MINING RESEARCH LIBRARY
Box 5024   Phone: (304) 342-0717
Charleston, WV 25311   Norman Kilpatrick, Dir.

U.S. DEPT. OF COMMERCE - INTERNATIONAL TRADE ADMINISTRATION -
   CHARLESTON DISTRICT OFFICE LIBRARY
3000 New Federal Office Bldg.
500 Quarrier St.   Phone: (304) 347-5123
Charleston, WV 25301   Roger L. Fortner, Dir.

WEST VIRGINIA STATE ATTORNEY GENERAL - LAW LIBRARY
Rm. 26E, State Capitol   Phone: (304) 348-2021
Charleston, WV 25305

WEST VIRGINIA STATE COMMISSION ON AGING - LIBRARY
State Capitol   Phone: (304) 348-2241
Charleston, WV 25305   Eleanor M. Keenan, Libn.

WEST VIRGINIA STATE DEPARTMENT OF AGRICULTURE - PLANT PEST
   CONTROL & LABORATORY SERVICES DIVISION LIBRARY
Capitol Bldg.   Phone: (304) 348-2212
Charleston, WV 25305   Maria Gyulahazi, Libn.

WEST VIRGINIA STATE DEPARTMENT OF CULTURE AND HISTORY -
   ARCHIVES AND HISTORY LIBRARY
Cultural Center, Capitol Complex   Phone: (304) 348-0230
Charleston, WV 26505   Rodney A. Pyles, Dir.

WEST VIRGINIA STATE DEPARTMENT OF EDUCATION - EDUCATIONAL
   MEDIA CENTER
1900 Washington St., Rm. B346   Phone: (304) 348-3925
Charleston, WV 25305   Carolyn R. Skidmore, Lib.Dir.

WEST VIRGINIA STATE DEPARTMENT OF HIGHWAYS - RIGHT OF WAY
   DIVISION LIBRARY
1900 Washington St., E.   Phone: (304) 348-3195
Charleston, WV 25305

WEST VIRGINIA STATE DEPARTMENT OF NATURAL RESOURCES -
   DIVISION OF WATER RESOURCES - LIBRARY
1201 Greenbrier St.
Charleston, WV 25311

WEST VIRGINIA STATE LEGISLATIVE REFERENCE LIBRARY
Rm. 206 W, Capitol Bldg.   Phone: (304) 348-2153
Charleston, WV 25305   Mary Del Cont, Libn.

WEST VIRGINIA STATE LIBRARY COMMISSION - FILM SERVICES
   DEPARTMENT
Science and Cultural Ctr.   Phone: (304) 348-3976
Charleston, WV 25305   Steve Fesenmaier, Film Libn.

WEST VIRGINIA STATE LIBRARY COMMISSION - REFERENCE LIBRARY
Science and Cultural Center   Phone: (304) 348-2045
Charleston, WV 25305   Karen E. Goff, Ref.Libn.

WEST VIRGINIA STATE SUPREME COURT OF APPEALS - STATE LAW
   LIBRARY
E-404 Capitol Bldg.   Phone: (304) 348-2607
Charleston, WV 25309   Richard Rosswurm, Supreme Court Law Libn.

WEST VIRGINIA UNIVERSITY MEDICAL CENTER - CHARLESTON DIVISION
   - LEARNING RESOURCES CENTER
3110 Mac Corkle Ave., S.E.   Phone: (304) 347-1285
Charleston, WV 25304   Patricia Powell, Libn.

SPACE AND UNEXPLAINED CELESTIAL EVENTS RESEARCH SOCIETY -
   LIBRARY
Box 2228   Phone: (304) 269-2719
Clarksburg, WV 26301   Gray Barker, Dir.

UNITED HOSPITAL CENTER INC. - MEDICAL LIBRARY
3 Hospital Plaza   Phone: (304) 624-2230
Clarksburg, WV 26301   Brenda J. Curry, Libn.

U.S. VETERANS ADMINISTRATION (WV-Clarksburg) - MEDICAL CENTER
   LIBRARY SERVICE
                                           Phone: (304) 623-3461
Clarksburg, WV 26301   Edward J. Poletti, Chf., Lib.Serv.

U.S. NATL. PARK SERVICE - HARPERS FERRY CENTER LIBRARY
                                           Phone: (304) 535-6371
Harpers Ferry, WV 25425   David Nathanson, Chf.Libn.

U.S. NATL. PARK SERVICE - HARPERS FERRY NATL. HISTORICAL PARK -
   LIBRARY
Box 65   Phone: (304) 535-6371
Harpers Ferry, WV 25425   Hilda E. Staubs, Musm.Techn.

BOONE COUNTY GENEALOGICAL SOCIETY - LIBRARY *
Box 10   Phone: (304) 369-4675
Hewett, WV 25108   Sue Roberts, Sec.

BUCK (Pearl S.) BIRTHPLACE FOUNDATION - LIBRARY
Box 126   Phone: (304) 653-4430
Hillsboro, WV 24946   David C. Hyer, Exec.Dir.

CABELL HUNTINGTON HOSPITAL - HEALTH SCIENCE LIBRARY
1340 Hal Greer Blvd.   Phone: (304) 696-2605
Huntington, WV 25701   Deborah L. Woodburn, Health Sci.Libn.

HUNTINGTON ALLOYS, INC. - TECHNOLOGY LIBRARY
Guyan River Rd.
Box 1958   Phone: (304) 696-6260
Huntington, WV 25720   Lola W. McClure, Tech.Libn.

HUNTINGTON ART GALLERIES - LIBRARY
Park Hills   Phone: (304) 529-2701
Huntington, WV 25701   Mary L. McKernon, Libn.

MARSHALL UNIVERSITY - JAMES E. MORROW LIBRARY - SPECIAL
   COLLECTIONS
                                           Phone: (304) 696-2320
Huntington, WV 25701   Lisle G. Brown, Cur.

MARSHALL UNIVERSITY - RESEARCH COORDINATING UNIT FOR
   VOCATIONAL EDUCATION *
                                           Phone: (304) 696-3180
Huntington, WV 25701   Kristine Standifur, Res.Asst.

MARSHALL UNIVERSITY - SCHOOL OF MEDICINE - HEALTH SCIENCE
   LIBRARIES
Marshall University Campus   Phone: (304) 696-6426
Huntington, WV 25701   Edward Dzierzak, Dir.

ST. MARY'S HOSPITAL - MEDICAL LIBRARY (6E)
                                           Phone: (304) 696-6807
Huntington, WV 25701-5501   Kay Gibson, Med.Libn.

U.S. ARMY - CORPS OF ENGINEERS - HUNTINGTON DISTRICT - LIBRARY
502 8th St.   Phone: (304) 529-5713
Huntington, WV 25721   Sandra V. Morris, Libn.

U.S. VETERANS ADMINISTRATION (WV-Huntington) - MEDICAL CENTER
   LIBRARY
1540 Spring Valley Dr.   Phone: (304) 429-6741
Huntington, WV 25704

WEST VIRGINIA STATE BOARD OF VOCATIONAL EDUC. - DIV. OF
   VOCATIONAL REHABILITATION - STAFF DEVELOPMENT LIBRARY
Rehabilitation Center   Phone: (304) 768-8861
Institute, WV 25112   Mrs. Jo Skiles, Libn.

U.S. FISH & WILDLIFE SERVICE - NATIONAL FISHERIES CENTER -
   TECHNICAL INFORMATION SERVICES
Box 700   Phone: (304) 725-8461
Kearneysville, WV 25430   Joyce A. Mann-Grim, Tech.Info.Off.

GREENBRIER HISTORICAL SOCIETY - ARCHIVES *
North House, Church St.   Phone: (304) 645-3503
Lewisburg, WV 24901   Frances A. Swope, Archv.

WEST VIRGINIA SCHOOL OF OSTEOPATHIC MEDICINE - WVSOM LIBRARY
400 N. Lee St.   Phone: (304) 645-6270
Lewisburg, WV 24901-0827   Donna M. Hudson, Libn.

U.S. VETERANS ADMINISTRATION (WV-Martinsburg) - CENTER MEDICAL
   LIBRARY
                                           Phone: (304) 263-0811
Martinsburg, WV 25401   Barbara S. Adams, Chf.Libn.

AMERICAN ASSOCIATION OF COST ENGINEERS - LIBRARY
308 Monongahela Bldg.   Phone: (304) 296-8444
Morgantown, WV 26505   Kenneth K. Humphreys, Exec.Dir.

U.S. DEPT. OF ENERGY - MORGANTOWN ENERGY TECHNOLOGY CENTER
   LIBRARY †
Box 880   Phone: (304) 599-7183
Morgantown, WV 26505   S. Elaine Pasini, Libn.

WEST VIRGINIA STATE GEOLOGICAL AND ECONOMIC SURVEY - LIBRARY
Box 879   Phone: (304) 292-6331
Morgantown, WV 26505   Ruth I. Hayhurst, Libn.

WEST VIRGINIA UNIVERSITY - COLLEGE OF BUSINESS AND ECONOMICS -
   BUREAU OF BUSINESS RESEARCH
Box 6025   Phone: (304) 293-5837
Morgantown, WV 26506   Stanley J. Kloc, Act.Dir.

WEST VIRGINIA UNIVERSITY - CREATIVE ARTS CENTER - MUSIC
   LIBRARY
                                           Phone: (304) 293-4505
Morgantown, WV 26506   Ruby M. Canning, Supv.

WEST VIRGINIA UNIVERSITY - LAW LIBRARY
Law School
Box 6130   Phone: (304) 293-5309
Morgantown, WV 26506-6130   William E. Johnson, Law Libn./Professor

WEST VIRGINIA UNIVERSITY - MEDICAL CENTER LIBRARY
Basic Sciences Bldg.
Box 6306   Phone: (304) 293-2113
Morgantown, WV 26506-6306   Robert Murphy, Dir.

WEST VIRGINIA UNIVERSITY - WEST VIRGINIA AND REGIONAL
   COLLECTION
University Library   Phone: (304) 293-3240
Morgantown, WV 26506   George Parkinson, Cur.

MOBAY CHEMICAL CORPORATION - RESEARCH LIBRARY
                                           Phone: (304) 455-4400
New Martinsville, WV 26155   Douglas A. Portmann, Tech.Libn.

PPG INDUSTRIES, INC. - CHEMICAL DIVISION - NATRIUM RESEARCH AND
   DEVELOPMENT LIBRARY
Box 191   Phone: (304) 455-2200
New Martinsville, WV 26155   Alice K. Johnson, Libn.

WEST VIRGINIA SCHOOLS FOR THE DEAF AND BLIND - WV SCHOOL FOR
   THE BLIND LIBRARY
                                        Phone: (304) 822-3521
Romney, WV 26757   Leslie Durst, Libn.

UNION CARBIDE CORPORATION - ENGINEERING DEPARTMENT LIBRARY
Box 8361   Phone: (304) 747-4608
South Charleston, WV 25303   Julia Adkins, Libn.

UNION CARBIDE CORPORATION - RESEARCH AND DEVELOPMENT
   INFORMATION CENTER
Bldg. 770
Box 8361   Phone: (304) 747-5119
South Charleston, WV 25303   Alice S. Behr, Tech.Libn.

WEST VIRGINIA STATE DEPARTMENT OF HEALTH - STATE HYGIENIC
   LABORATORY - LIBRARY
167 11th Ave.   Phone: (304) 348-3530
South Charleston, WV 25303   Jennifer J. Graley, Stenographer

BORG-WARNER CHEMICALS, INC. - LIBRARY
Box 68   Phone: (304) 863-7335
Washington, WV 26181   Sharon D. Watson, Libn.

NATIONAL STEEL CORPORATION - RESEARCH CENTER LIBRARY
500 Three Springs Dr.   Phone: (304) 723-5800
Weirton, WV 26062-4988   Elizabeth W. Fulton, Sr.Res.Libn.

STEVENS CLINIC HOSPITAL - LIBRARY
U.S. 52, East   Phone: (304) 436-3161
Welch, WV 24801   Karen Peery, Libn.

WEST LIBERTY STATE COLLEGE - ELBIN LIBRARY
                                        Phone: (304) 336-8035
West Liberty, WV 26074   Donald R. Strong, Libn.

OGLEBAY INSTITUTE - MANSION MUSEUM LIBRARY
Oglebay Park   Phone: (304) 242-7272
Wheeling, WV 26003   T. Patrick Brennan, Cur.

OHIO COUNTY LAW LIBRARY
City-County Bldg.
1500 Chapline St.   Phone: (304) 234-3634
Wheeling, WV 26003   Nancy C. Obecny, Law Libn.

OHIO VALLEY MEDICAL CENTER - HUPP MEDICAL LIBRARY
2000 Eoff St.   Phone: (304) 234-8771
Wheeling, WV 26003   Eleanor Shonn, Med.Libn.

WHEELING HOSPITAL, INC. - HENRY G. JEPSON MEMORIAL LIBRARY
Medical Pk.   Phone: (304) 243-3308
Wheeling, WV 26003   Rosella M. Saseen, Med.Libn.

WISCONSIN

AID ASSOCIATION FOR LUTHERANS - CORPORATE LIBRARY
4321 N. Ballard Rd.   Phone: (414) 734-5721
Appleton, WI 54919   Ordelle Aaker, Libn.

INSTITUTE OF PAPER CHEMISTRY - LIBRARY
1043 E. South River St.
Box 1039   Phone: (414) 738-3384
Appleton, WI 54912   Craig S. Booher, Libn.

JUSTICE SYSTEM TRAINING ASSOCIATION - PSYCHO-MOTOR SKILL
   DESIGN ARCHIVE
Box 356   Phone: (414) 731-8893
Appleton, WI 54912   Kevin Parsons, Dir.

OUTAGAMIE COUNTY LAW LIBRARY
410 S. Walnut St.   Phone: (414) 735-5347
Appleton, WI 54911   Diane M. Ebert, Law Ck.

ST. ELIZABETH HOSPITAL - HEALTH SCIENCE LIBRARY
1506 S. Oneida St.   Phone: (414) 738-2324
Appleton, WI 54915   Mary M. Bayorgeon, Dir., Lib.Serv.

CIRCUS WORLD MUSEUM - LIBRARY
415 Lynn St.   Phone: (608) 356-8341
Baraboo, WI 53913   Robert L. Parkinson, Chf.Libn. & Hist.

INTERNATIONAL CRANE FOUNDATION - LIBRARY
Shady Lane Rd.
Rt. 1, Box 230C   Phone: (608) 356-9462
Baraboo, WI 53913   Joan A. Fordham, Adm.

SAUK COUNTY HISTORICAL SOCIETY, INC. - HISTORICAL MUSEUM
   LIBRARY
531 Fourth Ave.   Phone: (608) 356-6549
Baraboo, WI 53913   Nijole Etzwiler, Cur.

BELOIT COLLEGE - HERBERT V. KOHLER SCIENCE LIBRARY
                                        Phone: (608) 365-3391
Beloit, WI 53511   Glenn Remelts, Hd., Pub.Serv./Br.Lib.

BELOIT COLLEGE - LOGAN MUSEUM OF ANTHROPOLOGY - LIBRARY
                                        Phone: (608) 365-3391
Beloit, WI 53511   Dr. J. Edson Way, Dir.

BELOIT HISTORICAL SOCIETY - BARTLETT HISTORICAL LIBRARY
2149 St. Lawrence Ave.   Phone: (608) 365-3811
Beloit, WI 53511   Evelyn T. Wehrle, Dir.

COLT INDUSTRIES - FM ENGINE DIVISION LIBRARY
701 Lawton St.   Phone: (608) 364-4411
Beloit, WI 53511   Wesley A. Brill, Act.Adm.

HOLY FAMILY CONVENT - LIBRARY
Benet Lake, WI 53102

ST. BENEDICT'S ABBEY - BENET LIBRARY *
                                        Phone: (414) 396-4311
Benet Lake, WI 53102   Bro. Vincent Wedig, O.S.B., Libn.

MONROE, JUNEAU, JACKSON COUNTY, WISCONSIN GENEALOGY
   WORKSHOP - LIBRARY
Rte. 3, Box 253   Phone: (608) 378-4388
Black River Falls, WI 54615   Carolyn Habelman, Pres.

ELMBROOK MEMORIAL HOSPITAL - MARY BETH CURTIS HEALTH SCIENCE
   LIBRARY
19333 W. North Ave.   Phone: (414) 785-2091
Brookfield, WI 53005   Harvada Oitzinger, Med.Libn.

INTERNATIONAL FOUNDATION OF EMPLOYEE BENEFIT PLANS -
   INFORMATION CENTER
18700 W. Bluemound Rd.   Phone: (414) 786-6700
Brookfield, WI 53005   Jack Baltes, Dir., Info.Serv.

COOPERATIVE EDUCATIONAL SERVICE AGENCY (CESA) NO. 6 -
   INSTRUCTIONAL MATERIALS CENTER
725 W. Park Ave.   Phone: (715) 723-0341
Chippewa Falls, WI 54729   Linda Simenson, Libn.

NORTHERN WISCONSIN CENTER FOR THE DEVELOPMENTALLY DISABLED -
   LIBRARY/INSTRUCTIONAL MATERIALS CENTER
E. Park Ave.
Box 340   Phone: (715) 723-5542
Chippewa Falls, WI 54729   Robert Carlsen, Teacher-Libn.

ST. JOSEPH'S HOSPITAL - HEALTH SCIENCE LIBRARY *
2661 County Trunk I   Phone: (715) 723-1811
Chippewa Falls, WI 54729   Carolyn Kowalkowski, Dir.

LAKESHORE TECHNICAL INSTITUTE - EDUCATIONAL RESOURCE CENTER
1290 North Ave.   Phone: (414) 458-4183
Cleveland, WI 53015   Linda McCabe, Lib.Mgr.

LADISH CO. - METALLURGICAL DEPARTMENT LIBRARY †
5481 S. Packard Ave.   Phone: (414) 747-2611
Cudahy, WI 53110   Patrick Berry, Libn.

TRINITY MEMORIAL HOSPITAL - LIBRARY
5900 S. Lake Dr.   Phone: (414) 769-9000
Cudahy, WI 53110   Mrs. Pat Cameron, Libn.

ST. NORBERT ABBEY - AUGUSTINE LIBRARY
1016 N. Broadway   Phone: (414) 336-1321
De Pere, WI 54115   Rev. Aaron Walschinski, Libn.

WISCONSIN SCHOOL FOR THE DEAF - JOHN R. GANT LIBRARY
309 W. Walworth Ave.   Phone: (414) 728-6477
Delavan, WI 53115   Betty E. Watkins, Libn.

CHIPPEWA VALLEY MUSEUM, INC. - LIBRARY
9 Carson Park Dr.
Box 1204   Phone: (715) 834-7871
Eau Claire, WI 54701   Alberta Rommelmeyer, Archv.

DISTRICT ONE TECHNICAL INSTITUTE - LIBRARY - EDUCATIONAL
    RESOURCE CENTER
620 W. Clairemont Ave.   Phone: (715) 836-4756
Eau Claire, WI 54701   Lorraine Kearney, Coord., Lib.Serv.

LUTHER HOSPITAL - LIBRARY SERVICES
1221 Whipple St.   Phone: (715) 839-3248
Eau Claire, WI 54701   Eileen Emberson, Dir., Lib.Serv.

SACRED HEART HOSPITAL - MEDICAL LIBRARY
900 W. Clairemont Ave.   Phone: (715) 839-4330
Eau Claire, WI 54701   Bruno Warner, Libn.

UNIVERSITY OF WISCONSIN, EAU CLAIRE - AREA RESEARCH CENTER AND
    UNIVERSITY ARCHIVES
McIntyre Library   Phone: (715) 836-2739
Eau Claire, WI 54701   Richard L. Pifer, Archv.

UNIVERSITY OF WISCONSIN, EAU CLAIRE - SIMPSON GEOGRAPHIC
    RESEARCH CENTER - MAP LIBRARY
Department of Geography   Phone: (715) 836-3244
Eau Claire, WI 54701   Adam Cahow, Cur., Geographic Mtls.

LAKELAND COUNSELING CENTER - LIBRARY †
Hwy. NN
Box 1005   Phone: (414) 723-5400
Elkhorn, WI 53121   Ruby Bill, Libn.

LAKELAND HOSPITAL - MEDICAL LIBRARY
Hwy. NN
Box 1002   Phone: (414) 723-2960
Elkhorn, WI 53121   Mary Bray, Libn.

SOUTHWEST WISCONSIN VOCATIONAL-TECHNICAL INSTITUTE -
    LEARNING RESOURCES CENTER
Bronson Blvd.
Rte. 1, Box 500   Phone: (608) 822-3262
Fennimore, WI 53809   Patricia Payson, Libn.

WISCONSIN STATE DEPARTMENT OF NATURAL RESOURCES - BUREAU OF
    RESEARCH - TECHNICAL LIBRARY
3911 Fish Hatchery Rd.   Phone: (608) 266-9725
Fitchburg, WI 53711   Rose B. Smith, Libn.

FOND DU LAC COUNTY HISTORICAL SOCIETY - HISTORIC GALLOWAY
    HOUSE AND VILLAGE - ARCHIVES
336 Old Pioneer Rd.
Box 131   Phone: (414) 922-6390
Fond du Lac, WI 54935   Ruth Worthing, Hist.

MORAINE PARK TECHNICAL INSTITUTE - LEARNING RESOURCE CENTER
235 N. National Ave.   Phone: (414) 922-8611
Fond du Lac, WI 54935   Judy Denor, Libn.

ST. AGNES HOSPITAL - LIBRARY
430 E. Division St.   Phone: (414) 921-2300
Fond du Lac, WI 54935   Sr. Mary David Boyle, C.S.A., Libn.

WISCONSIN STATE - FOND DU LAC COUNTY LAW LIBRARY
Court House   Phone: (414) 921-5600
Fond du Lac, WI 54935   Mary E. Scharf, Law Libn.

HOARD HISTORICAL MUSEUM - LIBRARY
407 Merchant Ave.   Phone: (414) 563-4521
Fort Atkinson, WI 53538   Hannah W. Swart, Cur.

NORLAND CORPORATION - TECHNICAL LIBRARY
R4 Norland Dr.   Phone: (414) 563-8456
Fort Atkinson, WI 53538   Oma Dixon, Doc.Libn.

BELLIN MEMORIAL HOSPITAL - HEALTH SCIENCES LIBRARY
744 S. Webster Ave.
Box 1700   Phone: (414) 433-3693
Green Bay, WI 54305   Cynthia Reinl, Health Sci.Libn.

BROWN COUNTY MENTAL HEALTH CENTER - H.H. HUMPHREY MEMORIAL
    STAFF LIBRARY *
2900 St. Anthony Dr.   Phone: (414) 468-1136
Green Bay, WI 54301   Nancy Hillen, Lib.Mgr.

DURANT FAMILY REGISTRY - LIBRARY
2700 Timber Ln.   Phone: (414) 499-8797
Green Bay, WI 54303   Jeff Gillis, Pres.

GREEN BAY PRESS-GAZETTE - LIBRARY *
435 E. Walnut St.   Phone: (414) 435-4411
Green Bay, WI 54305   Diane L. Laes, Libn.

NEVILLE PUBLIC MUSEUM - LIBRARY
210 Museum Pl.   Phone: (414) 497-3767
Green Bay, WI 54303

NORTHEAST WISCONSIN TECHNICAL INSTITUTE - LEARNING RESOURCE
    CENTER
2740 W. Mason   Phone: (414) 497-3190
Green Bay, WI 54303   Mary Parrott, Libn.

ST. VINCENT HOSPITAL - MEDICAL LIBRARY
835 S. VanBuren St.
Box 1221   Phone: (414) 433-8171
Green Bay, WI 54305   Margaret Warpinski, Hd.Libn.

SCHREIBER FOODS, INC. - LIBRARY
425 Pine St.
Box 610   Phone: (414) 437-7601
Green Bay, WI 54305   Karen K. Braatz, Info.Spec.

UNIVERSITY OF WISCONSIN, GREEN BAY - AREA RESEARCH CENTER
2420 Nicolet Dr.   Phone: (414) 465-2539
Green Bay, WI 54301-7001   Marian A. Gould, Act.Dir., Spec.Coll.

UNIVERSITY OF WISCONSIN, GREEN BAY - WOMEN'S EDUCATIONAL
    PROGRAMS - WOMEN'S STUDIES RESOURCE LIBRARY
LC 750   Phone: (414) 465-2136
Green Bay, WI 54302   Patricia Maguire, Spec.

SACRED HEART MONASTERY - LEO DEHON LIBRARY †
7331 S. Lovers Lane Rd.   Phone: (414) 425-8300
Hales Corners, WI 53130   Sr. Agnese Jasko, P.H.J.C., Libn.

BLACKHAWK TECHNICAL INSTITUTE, JANESVILLE - LEARNING
    MATERIALS CENTER
Prairie Ave., Rte. 3   Phone: (608) 756-4121
Janesville, WI 53545   Grace Sweeney, Libn.

MERCY HOSPITAL - MEDICAL LIBRARY
1000 Mineral Point   Phone: (608) 756-6749
Janesville, WI 53545   Lois J. Zuehlke, Lib.Dir.

ROCK COUNTY HEALTH CARE CENTER - STAFF LIBRARY
Box 351   Phone: (608) 755-2543
Janesville, WI 53547   Louise Jilbert, Libn.

ROCK COUNTY HISTORICAL SOCIETY - ARCHIVES OF ROCK COUNTY
    HISTORY
10 S. High
Box 896   Phone: (608) 756-4509
Janesville, WI 53545   Maurice J. Montgomery, Archv.

SEVENTH DAY BAPTIST HISTORICAL SOCIETY - LIBRARY
Box 1678   Phone: (608) 752-5055
Janesville, WI 53547   D. Scott Smith, Hist.

WISCONSIN STATE DEPARTMENT OF PUBLIC INSTRUCTION - SCHOOL FOR
THE VISUALLY HANDICAPPED - LIBRARY
1700 W. State St.   Phone: (608) 755-2967
Janesville, WI 53545   Jean Wolski, Libn.

COUNTRYSIDE HOME - STAFF LIBRARY
1425 Wisconsin Dr.   Phone: (414) 674-3170
Jefferson, WI 53549   Catherine M. Rueth, Sec./Libn.

GATEWAY VOCATIONAL TECHNICAL & ADULT EDUCATION DISTRICT -
LEARNING RESOURCES CENTER
3520 30th Ave.   Phone: (414) 656-6924
Kenosha, WI 53141   Gerald F. Perona, District Libn.

KENOSHA ACHIEVEMENT CENTER - LIBRARY *
1218 79th St.   Phone: (414) 658-1687
Kenosha, WI 53140   Betty Anderson

KENOSHA COUNTY HISTORICAL MUSEUM - HISTORICAL RESEARCH
LIBRARY
6300 Third Ave.   Phone: (414) 654-5770
Kenosha, WI 53140   Lois Stein, Archv.

KENOSHA MEMORIAL HOSPITAL - HEALTH SCIENCES LIBRARY
6308 Eighth Ave.   Phone: (414) 656-2120
Kenosha, WI 53140   Esther L. Puhek, Libn.

KENOSHA NEWS - NEWSPAPER LIBRARY *
715 58th St.   Phone: (414) 657-1000
Kenosha, WI 53141   Bernice L. Nagy, Libn.

KENOSHA PUBLIC MUSEUM - LIBRARY
Civic Center, 5608 10th Ave.   Phone: (414) 656-8026
Kenosha, WI 53140   Paula Touhey, Interim Dir./Cur. of Educ

ST. CATHERINE'S HOSPITAL - MEDICAL LIBRARY
3556 Seventh Ave.   Phone: (414) 656-3230
Kenosha, WI 53140   Mary Sipsma, Med.Libn.

SOCIETY FOR THE PRESERVATION AND ENCOURAGEMENT OF BARBER
SHOP QUARTET SINGING IN AMERICA - OLD SONGS LIBRARY
6315 Third Ave.
Box 575   Phone: (414) 654-9111
Kenosha, WI 53141   Ruth Marks, Harmony Found.Adm.

UNIVERSITY OF WISCONSIN, PARKSIDE - UNIVERSITY ARCHIVES AND
AREA RESEARCH CENTER
Box 2000   Phone: (414) 553-2411
Kenosha, WI 53141   Nicholas C. Burckel, Dir.

DAIRYLAND POWER COOPERATIVE - LIBRARY
2615 E. Ave. South   Phone: (608) 788-4000
La Crosse, WI 54601   Dolly Matthes, Rec.Coord.

DIOCESE OF LA CROSSE - ARCHIVES
4238 Mormon Coulee Rd.
Box 69   Phone: (608) 788-7700
La Crosse, WI 54601

LA CROSSE LUTHERAN HOSPITAL - HEALTH SCIENCES LIBRARY
1910 South Ave.   Phone: (608) 785-0530
La Crosse, WI 54601   LaVerne Samb, Libn.

ST. FRANCIS MEDICAL CENTER - HEALTH SCIENCES LIBRARY
615 S. 10th St.   Phone: (608) 785-0940
La Crosse, WI 54601   Sr. Louise Therese Lotze, Lib.Supv.

U.S. FISH & WILDLIFE SERVICE - NATIONAL FISHERY RESEARCH
LABORATORY LIBRARY
Box 818   Phone: (608) 783-6451
La Crosse, WI 54602-0818   Rosalie A. Schnick, Tech.Info.Spec.

UNIVERSITY OF WISCONSIN, LA CROSSE - AUDIOVISUAL CENTER - FILM
LIBRARY
1705 State St.   Phone: (608) 785-8040
La Crosse, WI 54601   Gary Goorough, Coord., Film Lib.

UNIVERSITY OF WISCONSIN, LA CROSSE - CENTER FOR CONTEMPORARY
POETRY
Murphy Library
1631 Pine St.   Phone: (608) 785-8511
La Crosse, WI 54601   Edwin L. Hill, Spec.Coll.Libn.

UNIVERSITY OF WISCONSIN, LA CROSSE - CURRICULUM AND
INSTRUCTION CENTER
College of Education
Morris Hall   Phone: (608) 785-8651
La Crosse, WI 54601   Ed Zeimet, Libn.

UNIVERSITY OF WISCONSIN, LA CROSSE - MURPHY LIBRARY
1631 Pine St.   Phone: (608) 785-8505
La Crosse, WI 54601   Dale Montgomery, Dir., Instr.Serv.

VITERBO COLLEGE - ZOELLER FINE ARTS LIBRARY
815 S. Ninth   Phone: (608) 784-0040
La Crosse, WI 54601

WESLEY UNITED METHODIST CHURCH - LIBRARY
721 King St.   Phone: (608) 782-3018
La Crosse, WI 54601   Ms. Johnie Wardwell, Libn.

WESTERN WISCONSIN TECHNICAL INSTITUTE - LIBRARY
6th & Vine Sts.   Phone: (608) 785-9142
La Crosse, WI 54601   Thuan T. Tran, Hd.Libn.

AMERICAN SOCIETY OF AGRONOMY - INFORMATION CENTER
677 S. Segoe Rd.   Phone: (608) 274-1212
Madison, WI 53711   Keith R. Schlesinger, Dir., P.R. & Info.

CAPITAL TIMES NEWSPAPER - LIBRARY
1901 Fish Hatchery Rd.
Box 8060   Phone: (608) 252-6412
Madison, WI 53708   Ann Lund, Libn.

CREDIT UNION NATIONAL ASSOCIATION - INFORMATION RESOURCE
CENTER
5710 W. Mineral Point Rd.
Box 431   Phone: (608) 231-4170
Madison, WI 53701   Judith Sayrs, Ref.Libn.

DANE COUNTY LAW LIBRARY
230 City-County Bldg.
210 Monona Ave.   Phone: (608) 266-4230
Madison, WI 53709   Ann Waidelich, Libn.

DANE COUNTY REGIONAL PLANNING COMMISSION - LIBRARY
City-County Bldg., Rm. 114   Phone: (608) 266-4137
Madison, WI 53709

EDGEWOOD COLLEGE - MAUDE WEBSTER MIDDLETON NURSING LIBRARY
1010 Mound St.   Phone: (608) 267-6313
Madison, WI 53715   Vicki Schluge, Instr.Rsrcs.Mgr.

FOREST PRODUCTS RESEARCH SOCIETY - FOREST INFORMATION
RETRIEVAL SYSTEM
2801 Marshall Ct.   Phone: (608) 231-1361
Madison, WI 53705   Mary Gordon, AIDS Abstractor

GRAND ARMY OF THE REPUBLIC MEMORIAL HALL MUSEUM - ARCHIVES
AND LIBRARY
Capitol 419 North   Phone: (608) 266-1680
Madison, WI 53702   Lynnette M. Wolfe, Musm.Prog.Asst.

GREATER MADISON CHAMBER OF COMMERCE - MATERIALS REFERENCE
LIBRARY
Box 71   Phone: (608) 256-8348
Madison, WI 53701   Robert Brennan, Pres.

HAZELTON LABS AMERICA, INC. - LIBRARY
3301 Kinsman Blvd.
Box 7545   Phone: (608) 241-4471
Madison, WI 53707   Patricia Riese, Libn.

MADISON AREA TECHNICAL COLLEGE - TECHNICAL CENTER LIBRARY
2125 Commercial Ave.   Phone: (608) 266-5025
Madison, WI 53704   Janet B. Jeffcott, Tech.Libn.

MADISON BUSINESS COLLEGE - LIBRARY
1110 Spring Harbor Dr.　　　　　　　Phone: (608) 238-4266
Madison, WI 53705　　　　　　　　　　Mary T. Boyd, Libn.

MADISON GENERAL HOSPITAL - MEDICAL LIBRARY
202 South Park St.　　　　　　　　　Phone: (608) 267-6234
Madison, WI 53715　　　　　　　　Dona Bowman, Med.Libn.

MADISON METROPOLITAN SCHOOL DISTRICT - EDUCATION REFERENCE
　　LIBRARY
545 W. Dayton St.　　　　　　　　　Phone: (608) 266-6188
Madison, WI 53703　　　　　Joanne Lenburg, Educ.Ref.Libn.

MADISON PUBLIC LIBRARY - ART AND MUSIC DIVISION
201 W. Mifflin St.　　　　　　　　Phone: (608) 266-6311
Madison, WI 53703　　　　　　Beverly J. Brager, Supv.

MADISON PUBLIC LIBRARY - BUSINESS AND SCIENCE DIVISION
201 W. Mifflin St.　　　　　　　　Phone: (608) 266-6333
Madison, WI 53703　　　　　　　Philip Sullivan, Supv.

MADISON PUBLIC LIBRARY - LITERATURE AND SOCIAL SCIENCES
201 W. Mifflin St.　　　　　　　　Phone: (608) 266-6350
Madison, WI 53703　　　　　　Natalie Tinkham, Supv.

MADISON PUBLIC LIBRARY - MUNICIPAL REFERENCE SERVICE
City-County Bldg., Rm. 230
210 Monona Ave.　　　　　　　　Phone: (608) 266-6316
Madison, WI 53710　　　　　　　Ann Waidelich, Libn.

MAYER (Oscar) FOODS CORPORATION - R&D LIBRARY
Box 7188　　　　　　　　　　　　Phone: (608) 241-3311
Madison, WI 53707　　　　Thomas R. Whitemarsh, R&D Libn.

MENDOTA MENTAL HEALTH INSTITUTE - LIBRARY MEDIA CENTER †
301 Troy Dr.　　　　　　　　　　Phone: (608) 244-2411
Madison, WI 53704　　　Margaret Tielke Grinnell, Act.Dir.

METHODIST HOSPITAL - LIBRARY
309 W. Washington Ave.
Madison, WI 53703　　　　Mary Alice Kuehling, Libn.

RAY-O-VAC CORP. - TECHNOLOGY CENTER LIBRARY
630 Forward Dr.　　　　　　　　Phone: (608) 252-7400
Madison, WI 53711　　　　　　C. Saxe, Sr.Tech.Adv.

RESIDUALS MANAGEMENT TECHNOLOGY, INC. - LIBRARY
1406 E. Washington Ave., Suite 124　　Phone: (608) 255-2134
Madison, WI 53703　　　　　Mary Jane Kayes, Libn.

ST. MARIA GORETTI CHURCH LIBRARY *
5405 Flad Ave.　　　　　　　　　Phone: (608) 271-8244
Madison, WI 53711

STATE HISTORICAL SOCIETY OF WISCONSIN - ARCHIVES DIVISION
816 State St.　　　　　　　　　　Phone: (608) 262-3338
Madison, WI 53706　　　F. Gerald Ham, State Archv. & Dir.

STATE HISTORICAL SOCIETY OF WISCONSIN - LIBRARY
816 State St.　　　　　　　　　　Phone: (608) 262-3421
Madison, WI 53706　　　James H. Sweetland, Hd.Libn.

TRINITY LUTHERAN CHURCH - LIBRARY
1904 Winnebago St.　　　　　　　Phone: (608) 249-8527
Madison, WI 53704　　　　　Sharon Kenyon, Libn.

U.S. FOREST SERVICE - FOREST PRODUCTS LABORATORY LIBRARY
Box 5130　　　　　　　　　　　Phone: (608) 264-5712
Madison, WI 53705　　　　　Roger Scharmer, Libn.

U.S. GEOLOGICAL SURVEY - WATER RESOURCES DIVISION - LIBRARY
1815 University Ave.　　　　　　　Phone: (608) 262-2488
Madison, WI 53705-4042　　Rachel Lansing, Adm.Oper.Asst.

U.S. VETERANS ADMINISTRATION (WI-Madison) - WILLIAM S. MIDDLETON
　　MEMORIAL VETERANS HOSPITAL - LIBRARY
2500 Overlook Terrace　　　　　　Phone: (608) 256-1901
Madison, WI 53705　　　　Anne M. Taylor, Chf., Lib.Serv.

UNIVERSITY OF WISCONSIN, MADISON - AFRICAN STUDIES
　　INSTRUCTIONAL MATERIALS CENTER †
Teachers Education Bldg.
225 N. Mills St.　　　　　　　　　Phone: (608) 263-4178
Madison, WI 53706　　Dr. Joseph Adjaye, Outreach Coord.

UNIVERSITY OF WISCONSIN, MADISON - ARCHIVES
B134 Memorial Library
728 State St.　　　　　　　　　　Phone: (608) 262-3290
Madison, WI 53706　　　　　　J. Frank Cook, Dir.

UNIVERSITY OF WISCONSIN, MADISON - BIOLOGY LIBRARY
Birge Hall
430 Lincoln Dr.　　　　　　　　　Phone: (608) 262-2740
Madison, WI 53706　　　　　Silvia Watson, Act.Libn.

UNIVERSITY OF WISCONSIN, MADISON - BOTANY DEPARTMENT -
　　HERBARIUM LIBRARY
158 Birge Hall　　　　　　　　　Phone: (608) 262-2792
Madison, WI 53706　　　H.H. Iltis, Dir. of Herbarium

UNIVERSITY OF WISCONSIN, MADISON - BUREAU OF AUDIOVISUAL
　　INSTRUCTION - LIBRARY
1327 University Ave.
Box 2093　　　　　　　　　　　Phone: (608) 262-1644
Madison, WI 53701　　　　　Dr. Hal F. Riehle, Dir.

UNIVERSITY OF WISCONSIN, MADISON - CARTOGRAPHIC LABORATORY -
　　ARTHUR H. ROBINSON MAP LIBRARY
310 Science Hall
550 N. Park St.　　　　　　　　　Phone: (608) 262-1471
Madison, WI 53706　　　　　Mary Galneder, Map Libn.

UNIVERSITY OF WISCONSIN, MADISON - CENTER FOR HEALTH SCIENCES
　　LIBRARIES †
1305 Linden Dr.　　　　　　　　　Phone: (608) 262-6594
Madison, WI 53706　　　　　　Virginia Holtz, Dir.

UNIVERSITY OF WISCONSIN, MADISON - CENTER FOR LIMNOLOGY -
　　LIBRARY
680 N. Park　　　　　　　　　　Phone: (608) 262-3304
Madison, WI 53706　　　　　　Jane Colwin, Libn.

UNIVERSITY OF WISCONSIN, MADISON - CHEMISTRY LIBRARY
Chemistry Bldg.　　　　　　　　Phone: (608) 262-2942
Madison, WI 53706　　　　Kendall Rouse, Chem.Libn.

UNIVERSITY OF WISCONSIN, MADISON - COLLEGE OF ENGINEERING -
　　TECHNICAL REPORTS CENTER
Kurt F. Wendt Library
215 N. Randall Ave.　　　　　　　Phone: (608) 262-6845
Madison, WI 53706　　　　　Jean Gilbertson, Libn.

UNIVERSITY OF WISCONSIN, MADISON - COOPERATIVE CHILDREN'S
　　BOOK CENTER (CCBC)
Helen C. White Hall, Rm. 4289-4290
600 N. Park St.　　　　　　　　　Phone: (608) 263-3721
Madison, WI 53706　　　　　Ginny Moore Kruse, Dir.

UNIVERSITY OF WISCONSIN, MADISON - DATA AND PROGRAM LIBRARY
　　SERVICE
4452 Social Science Bldg.　　　　　Phone: (608) 262-7962
Madison, WI 53706　　　　　　Alice Robbin, Hd.

UNIVERSITY OF WISCONSIN, MADISON - DEPARTMENT OF PSYCHIATRY -
　　LITHIUM INFORMATION CENTER
600 Highland Ave.　　　　　　　　Phone: (608) 263-6171
Madison, WI 53792　　Margaret G. Baudhuin, Libn./Info.Spec.

UNIVERSITY OF WISCONSIN, MADISON - DEPARTMENT OF RURAL
　　SOCIOLOGY - APPLIED POPULATION LAB. - LIBRARY
Agriculture Hall, Rm. 316　　　　　Phone: (608) 262-3029
Madison, WI 53706　　　　　Stephen J. Tordella, Spec.

UNIVERSITY OF WISCONSIN, MADISON - DEPARTMENT OF URBAN AND
　　REGIONAL PLANNING - GRADUATE RESEARCH CENTER
Music Hall
925 Lathrop Dr.　　　　　　　　　Phone: (608) 262-1004
Madison, WI 53706　　　　　Irwin Weintraub, Libn.

UNIVERSITY OF WISCONSIN, MADISON - F.B. POWER PHARMACEUTICAL
   LIBRARY
School of Pharmacy
425 N. Charter St.   Phone: (608) 262-2894
Madison, WI 53706   Dolores Nemec, Libn.

UNIVERSITY OF WISCONSIN, MADISON - GEOGRAPHY LIBRARY
280 Science Hall   Phone: (608) 262-1706
Madison, WI 53706   Miriam E. Kerndt, Geog.Libn.

UNIVERSITY OF WISCONSIN, MADISON - GEOLOGY-GEOPHYSICS LIBRARY
440 Weeks Hall   Phone: (608) 262-8956
Madison, WI 53706   Nancy L. Crossfield, Libn.

UNIVERSITY OF WISCONSIN, MADISON - GERALD G. SOMERS GRADUATE
   REFERENCE ROOM
8432 Social Science Bldg.
1180 Observatory Dr.   Phone: (608) 262-6195
Madison, WI 53706   Mary L. Crompton, Libn.

UNIVERSITY OF WISCONSIN, MADISON - INSTITUTE FOR RESEARCH IN
   THE HUMANITIES - LIBRARY
Old Observatory   Phone: (608) 262-3855
Madison, WI 53706   Loretta Freiling, Prog.Asst.

UNIVERSITY OF WISCONSIN, MADISON - KOHLER ART LIBRARY
Elvehjem Museum of Art
800 University Ave.   Phone: (608) 263-2256
Madison, WI 53706   William C. Bunce, Dir. & Hd.Libn.

UNIVERSITY OF WISCONSIN, MADISON - LAND TENURE CENTER -
   LIBRARY
434 Steenbock Memorial Library
550 Babcock Dr.   Phone: (608) 262-1240
Madison, WI 53706   Teresa J. Anderson, Libn.

UNIVERSITY OF WISCONSIN, MADISON - LAW SCHOOL LIBRARY
                           Phone: (608) 262-1128
Madison, WI 53706   Anita Morse, Dir.

UNIVERSITY OF WISCONSIN, MADISON - LAW SCHOOL LIBRARY -
   CRIMINAL JUSTICE REFERENCE & INFORMATION CENTER
L140 Law Library   Phone: (608) 262-1499
Madison, WI 53706   Sue L. Center, Asst.Dir.

UNIVERSITY OF WISCONSIN, MADISON - LIBRARY SCHOOL LIBRARY
600 N. Park St.   Phone: (608) 263-2960
Madison, WI 53706   Sally Davis, Libn.

UNIVERSITY OF WISCONSIN, MADISON - MATHEMATICS LIBRARY
B224 Van Vleck Hall   Phone: (608) 262-3596
Madison, WI 53706   Shirley Tan Shen, Libn.-Spec.

UNIVERSITY OF WISCONSIN, MADISON - MEMORIAL LIBRARY -
   DEPARTMENT OF RARE BOOKS & SPECIAL COLLECTIONS
728 State St.   Phone: (608) 262-3243
Madison, WI 53706   John Tedeschi, Cur.

UNIVERSITY OF WISCONSIN, MADISON - MILLS MUSIC LIBRARY
B162 Memorial Library
728 State St.   Phone: (608) 263-1884
Madison, WI 53706   Arne J. Arneson, Music Libn.

UNIVERSITY OF WISCONSIN, MADISON - NIEMAN-GRANT JOURNALISM
   READING ROOM
2130 Vilas Communication Hall
821 University Ave.   Phone: (608) 263-3387
Madison, WI 53706   Mary Kay Nagel, Libn.

UNIVERSITY OF WISCONSIN, MADISON - PHYSICS LIBRARY
1150 University Ave.   Phone: (608) 262-9500
Madison, WI 53706   Sandra Moline, Libn.

UNIVERSITY OF WISCONSIN, MADISON - PLANT PATHOLOGY MEMORIAL
   LIBRARY
1630 Linden Dr.   Phone: (608) 262-1410
Madison, WI 53706   Helen H. Kuntz, Libn.

UNIVERSITY OF WISCONSIN, MADISON - POULTRY SCIENCE
   DEPARTMENT - HALPIN MEMORIAL LIBRARY
Animal Science Bldg., Rm. 214
1675 Observatory Dr.   Phone: (608) 262-1243
Madison, WI 53706   Louis C. Arrington, Prof.

UNIVERSITY OF WISCONSIN, MADISON - SCHOOL OF EDUCATION -
   INSTRUCTIONAL MATERIALS CENTER
Teacher Education Bldg.
225 N. Mills St.   Phone: (608) 263-4750
Madison, WI 53706   Deane W. Hill, Dir.

UNIVERSITY OF WISCONSIN, MADISON - SCHOOL OF SOCIAL WORK -
   VIDEO RESOURCE LIBRARY
425 Henry Mall, Suite 163   Phone: (608) 263-3663
Madison, WI 53706   Rebecca Roberts, Supv.

UNIVERSITY OF WISCONSIN, MADISON - SCHOOL OF SOCIAL WORK -
   VIRGINIA L. FRANKS MEMORIAL LIBRARY
425 Henry Mall, Rm. 230   Phone: (608) 263-3840
Madison, WI 53706   Thurston Davini, Libn.

UNIVERSITY OF WISCONSIN, MADISON - SEMINARY OF MEDIEVAL
   SPANISH STUDIES - LIBRARY
1120 Van Hise Hall   Phone: (608) 262-2529
Madison, WI 53706   Lloyd Kasten, Prof.

UNIVERSITY OF WISCONSIN, MADISON - SMALL BUSINESS DEVELOPMENT
   & RECREATION CENTER - LIBRARY
602 State St.   Phone: (608) 263-3166
Madison, WI 53703   Susan Awe, Info.Coord.

UNIVERSITY OF WISCONSIN, MADISON - STEENBOCK MEMORIAL LIBRARY
550 Babcock Dr.   Phone: (608) 262-9990
Madison, WI 53706   Daisy T. Wu, Dir.

UNIVERSITY OF WISCONSIN, MADISON - THEORETICAL CHEMISTRY
   INSTITUTE - LIBRARY
1101 University Ave., Rm. 8326   Phone: (608) 262-1511
Madison, WI 53706   Barbara Kelly, Prog.Asst./Supv.

UNIVERSITY OF WISCONSIN, MADISON - TRACE R & D CENTER - LIBRARY
314 Waisman
1500 Highland Ave.   Phone: (608) 262-6966
Madison, WI 53706   Mary Brady, Proj.Dir.

UNIVERSITY OF WISCONSIN, MADISON - UNIVERSITY CENTER FOR
   COOPERATIVES - COOPERATIVE LIBRARY
Lowell Hall, Rm. 514
610 Langdon St.   Phone: (608) 262-3251
Madison, WI 53706   MaryJean McGrath, Act.Libn.

UNIVERSITY OF WISCONSIN, MADISON - WASHBURN OBSERVATORY -
   WOODMAN ASTRONOMICAL LIBRARY
6521 Sterling Hall
475 N. Charter St.   Phone: (608) 262-1320
Madison, WI 53706   Marcia Lynn Cooke, Libn.

UNIVERSITY OF WISCONSIN, MADISON - WATER RESOURCES CENTER -
   LIBRARY
1975 Willow Dr.   Phone: (608) 262-3069
Madison, WI 53706   Sarah L. Calcese, Libn.

UNIVERSITY OF WISCONSIN, MADISON - WILLIAM A. SCOTT BUSINESS
   LIBRARY
Bascom Hall   Phone: (608) 262-5935
Madison, WI 53706   Marilyn Hicks, Bus.Libn.

UNIVERSITY OF WISCONSIN, MADISON - WISCONSIN CENTER FOR FILM
   AND THEATER RESEARCH
6039 Vilas Communication Hall   Phone: (608) 262-9706
Madison, WI 53706   Russell Merritt, Dir.

UNIVERSITY OF WISCONSIN, MADISON - WISCONSIN REGIONAL PRIMATE
   RESEARCH CENTER - PRIMATE CENTER LIBRARY
1223 Capitol Court   Phone: (608) 263-3512
Madison, WI 53706   Lawrence Jacobsen, Hd.Libn.

UNIVERSITY OF WISCONSIN, MADISON - ZOOLOGICAL MUSEUM LIBRARY
L.E. Noland Bldg.
250 N. Mills St.   Phone: (608) 262-3766
Madison, WI 53706   John A.W. Kirsch, Dir.

VESTERHEIM GENEALOGICAL CENTER/NORWEGIAN-AMERICAN MUSEUM
   - LIBRARY
4909 Sherwood Rd.   Phone: (608) 271-8826
Madison, WI 53711   Gerhard B. Naeseth, Libn.

VISITING NURSE SERVICE, INC. - LIBRARY
328 E. Lakeside St.   Phone: (608) 257-6710
Madison, WI 53715   Ruth M. Hanson, Exec.Dir.

WISCONSIN ALUMNI RESEARCH FOUNDATION - LIBRARY
614 N. Walnut St.
Box 7365   Phone: (608) 263-2848
Madison, WI 53707   Lila N. Hillyer, Libn.

WISCONSIN HOSPITAL ASSOCIATION - MEMORIAL LIBRARY †
5721 Odana Rd.   Phone: (608) 274-1820
Madison, WI 53719   Pat Craven, Libn.

WISCONSIN STATE BOARD OF VOCATIONAL, TECHNICAL & ADULT
   EDUCATION - RESEARCH COORDINATING UNIT RESOURCE CTR.
4802 Sheboygan Ave., HFSOB, 7th Fl.
Box 7874   Phone: (608) 266-3705
Madison, WI 53707   Roland J. Krogstad, Dir.

WISCONSIN (State) DEPARTMENT OF DEVELOPMENT - LIBRARY
123 W. Washington Ave.
Box 7970   Phone: (608) 266-2423
Madison, WI 53707   Judith Royster, Libn.

WISCONSIN STATE DEPARTMENT OF EMPLOYEE TRUST FUNDS - LIBRARY
201 E. Washington Ave., Rm. 171
Box 7931   Phone: (608) 266-7387
Madison, WI 53707   John R. Wendorf, Prog.Asst./Libn.

WISCONSIN STATE DEPARTMENT OF HEALTH & SOCIAL SERVICES -
   LIBRARY
1 W. Wilson St., Rm. 655
Box 7850   Phone: (608) 266-7473
Madison, WI 53707   Mary Gusse Sanchez, Libn.

WISCONSIN STATE DEPARTMENT OF INDUSTRY, LABOR & HUMAN
   RELATIONS - JOB SERVICE LIBRARY
201 E. Washington Ave.
Box 7944   Phone: (608) 266-2832
Madison, WI 53707   Janet D. Pugh, Libn.

WISCONSIN STATE DEPARTMENT OF JUSTICE - LAW LIBRARY
123 W. Washington, Rm. 349
Box 7857   Phone: (608) 266-0325
Madison, WI 53707   Michael F. Bemis, Law Libn.

WISCONSIN STATE DEPARTMENT OF NATURAL RESOURCES - LIBRARY
Box 7921   Phone: (608) 266-8933
Madison, WI 53707   Patricia Parsons, Dept.Libn.

WISCONSIN STATE DEPARTMENT OF PUBLIC INSTRUCTION - D.P.I.
   LIBRARY
125 S. Webster St., 3rd Fl.
Box 7841   Phone: (608) 266-2529
Madison, WI 53707   Marjorie D. Westergard, Libn.

WISCONSIN STATE DEPARTMENT OF PUBLIC INSTRUCTION - WISCONSIN
   DISSEMINATION PROGRAM (WDP)
125 S. Webster St.
Box 7841   Phone: (608) 266-2127
Madison, WI 53707   Dianne Hopkins, Dir.

WISCONSIN STATE DEPARTMENT OF TRANSPORTATION - LIBRARY
4802 Sheboygan Ave., Rm. 901
Box 7913   Phone: (608) 266-0724
Madison, WI 53707   Cordell Klyve, Libn.

WISCONSIN STATE DIVISION FOR LIBRARY SERVICES - REFERENCE AND
   LOAN LIBRARY
2109 S. Stoughton Rd.   Phone: (608) 266-1081
Madison, WI 53716   Sally J. Drew, Dir.

WISCONSIN STATE JOURNAL - LIBRARY
Box 8058   Phone: (608) 252-6112
Madison, WI 53708   Ronald J. Larson, Hd.Libn.

WISCONSIN STATE LEGISLATIVE REFERENCE BUREAU
State Capitol, Rm. 201 North   Phone: (608) 266-0341
Madison, WI 53702   H. Rupert Theobald, Chf., Lib. & Ref.Sects.

WISCONSIN STATE MEDICAL SOCIETY - LIBRARY
330 E. Lakeside St.
Box 1109   Phone: (608) 257-6781
Madison, WI 53701   Mary Angell, Mng.Ed./Libn.

WISCONSIN STATE OFFICE OF THE COMMISSIONER OF INSURANCE -
   LIBRARY
Box 7873   Phone: (608) 266-3585
Madison, WI 53707   Jan Angell

WISCONSIN STATE SUPREME COURT - WISCONSIN STATE LAW LIBRARY
Box 7881   Phone: (608) 266-1424
Madison, WI 53707   Marcia J. Koslov, State Law Libn.

HOLY FAMILY HOSPITAL - HEALTH SCIENCE LIBRARY
21st & Western Ave.   Phone: (414) 684-2260
Manitowoc, WI 54220   Dan Eckert, Libn.

MANITOWOC MARITIME MUSEUM - LIBRARY
809 S. 8th St.   Phone: (414) 684-0218
Manitowoc, WI 54220   David Pamperin, Dir.

RAHR-WEST MUSEUM - LIBRARY
Park St. at N. 8th
Manitowoc, WI 54220

MARINETTE COUNTY LAW LIBRARY
Court House
1926 Hall Ave.   Phone: (715) 735-3371
Marinette, WI 54143   Don E. Phillips, Ck. of Court

MARSHFIELD CLINIC - MEDICAL LIBRARY
1000 N. Oak   Phone: (715) 387-5183
Marshfield, WI 54449   Albert Zimmermann, Libn./Med.Ed.

ST. JOSEPH'S HOSPITAL - SCHOOL OF NURSING - LEARNING RESOURCE
   CENTER
611 St. Joseph Ave.   Phone: (715) 387-7374
Marshfield, WI 54449   Margaret A. Allen, Libn.

COMMUNITY MEMORIAL HOSPITAL OF MENOMONEE FALLS - MC KAY
   MEMORIAL LIBRARY
W180 N8085 Town Hall Rd.
Box 408   Phone: (414) 251-1000
Menomonee Falls, WI 53051   Sunja Shaikh, Libn.

MEDICAL ASSOCIATES - HEALTH CENTER - LIBRARY
W180 N7950 Town Hall Rd.   Phone: (414) 255-2500
Menomonee Falls, WI 53051   Carol J. McIlveen, Libn.

WISCONSIN LUTHERAN SEMINARY - LIBRARY
6633 W. Wartburg Circle   Phone: (414) 242-2331
Mequon, WI 53092   Rev. Martin O. Westerhaus, Libn.

ALLEN-BRADLEY COMPANY - CORPORATE LIBRARY
1201 S. 2nd St.
Box 2086   Phone: (414) 671-2000
Milwaukee, WI 53201   Agnes G. Rice, Libn.

ALLIS-CHALMERS CORPORATION - ADVANCED TECHNOLOGY CENTER -
   LIBRARY
Box 512   Phone: (414) 475-2102
Milwaukee, WI 53201   R.A. Schlueter, Libn.

ALVERNO COLLEGE - RESEARCH CENTER ON WOMEN
3401 S. 39th St.   Phone: (414) 671-5400
Milwaukee, WI 53215   Lola Stuller, Libn.

AMERICAN APPRAISAL COMPANY - LIBRARY
525 E. Michigan St.   Phone: (414) 271-7240
Milwaukee, WI 53201   Stella Lorenz, Libn.

AMERICAN GEOGRAPHICAL SOCIETY COLLECTION OF THE UNIVERSITY OF
   WISCONSIN, MILWAUKEE - GOLDA MEIR LIBRARY
Box 399   Phone: (414) 963-6282
Milwaukee, WI 53201   Roman Drazniowsky, Cur.

AMERICAN SOCIETY FOR QUALITY CONTROL - LIBRARY
230 W. Wells St., Suite 7000   Phone: (414) 272-8575
Milwaukee, WI 53203   Debra Owens, Dir., Tech.Serv.

ASCENSION LUTHERAN CHURCH - LIBRARY
1236 S. Layton Blvd.   Phone: (414) 671-5066
Milwaukee, WI 53215   Lorraine H. Pike, Libn.

BEIHOFF MUSIC CORPORATION - SHEET MUSIC DEPARTMENT
5040 W. North Ave.   Phone: (414) 442-3920
Milwaukee, WI 53208   Robert F. Loomer, Mgr.

CATHOLIC SOCIAL SERVICES - LIBRARY *
206 E. Michigan St.   Phone: (414) 271-2881
Milwaukee, WI 53202   Anne Kozlowski, Coord.

CITIZENS' GOVERNMENTAL RESEARCH BUREAU, INC.
125 E. Wells St., Rm. 616   Phone: (414) 276-8240
Milwaukee, WI 53202   Norman N. Gill, Exec.Dir.

COLUMBIA HOSPITAL - COLLEGE OF NURSING - LIBRARY
2121 E. Newport Ave.   Phone: (414) 961-3533
Milwaukee, WI 53211   Shirley S. Chan, Libn.

COLUMBIA HOSPITAL - MEDICAL LIBRARY
2025 E. Newport Ave.   Phone: (414) 961-3858
Milwaukee, WI 53211   Ruth Holst, Dir., Lib.Serv.

COMMUNITY RELATIONS-SOCIAL DEVELOPMENT COMMISSION -
   RESEARCH LIBRARY
161 W. Wisconsin Ave., Rm. 7146   Phone: (414) 272-5600
Milwaukee, WI 53203   Pat Waddell, Res.Spec.

CONGREGATION EMANU-EL B'NE JESHURUN - RABBI DUDLEY WEINBERG
   LIBRARY
2419 E. Kenwood Blvd.   Phone: (414) 964-4100
Milwaukee, WI 53211   Paula H. Fine, Libn.

CONGREGATION SHALOM - SHERMAN PASTOR MEMORIAL LIBRARY
7630 N. Santa Monica Blvd.   Phone: (414) 352-9288
Milwaukee, WI 53217   Ellen Mandelman, Libn.

EATON CORPORATION - CUTLER-HAMMER LIBRARY
4201 N. 27th St.
Box 463-464   Phone: (414) 449-7679
Milwaukee, WI 53201   Herbert J. Seuss, Libn.

FOLEY & LARDNER - LIBRARY
777 E. Wisconsin Ave.   Phone: (414) 271-2400
Milwaukee, WI 53202   Noreen Link, Libn.

GOOD SAMARITAN MEDICAL CENTER - DEACONESS HOSPITAL CAMPUS -
   HEALTH SCIENCE LIBRARY †
620 N. 19th St.   Phone: (414) 933-9600
Milwaukee, WI 53233   Julia Woodward Schleif, Libn.

GOOD SAMARITAN MEDICAL CENTER - EVANS MEMORIAL LIBRARY
2000 W. Kilbourn Ave.
Milwaukee, WI 53233   Ann Towell, Med.Libn.

HARLEY-DAVIDSON MOTOR CO., INC. - ENGINEERING LIBRARY
3700 W. Juneau Ave.
Box 653
Milwaukee, WI 53201   P.A. Lodde, Libn.

HISTORIC WALKER'S POINT, INC. - LIBRARY *
734 S. 5th St.   Phone: (414) 645-6681
Milwaukee, WI 53204   Diane Kealty, Pres.

HOPE LUTHERAN CHURCH - LIBRARY
1115 N. 35th St.
Milwaukee, WI 53208   Esther Damkoehler, Libn.

JOHNSON CONTROLS, INC. - CORPORATE INFO. CTR./LIBRARY M47
507 E. Michigan St.
Box 423   Phone: (414) 274-4687
Milwaukee, WI 53201   Mary F. Kaczmarek, Libn.

JOHNSON CONTROLS, INC. - CORPORATE AND TECHNICAL LIBRARY
5757 N. Green Bay Ave.   Phone: (414) 228-2382
Milwaukee, WI 53201   Marian Rauch, Tech.Libn.

KALMBACH PUBLISHING COMPANY - INFORMATION CENTER
1027 N. Seventh St.   Phone: (414) 272-2060
Milwaukee, WI 53233   George H. Drury, Info.Chf.

KRAUSE MILLING COMPANY - TECHNICAL LIBRARY
4222 W. Burnham St.   Phone: (414) 355-7500
Milwaukee, WI 53215   Virginia M. Gamache, Lib.Asst.

MARQUETTE UNIVERSITY - DEPARTMENT OF SPECIAL COLLECTIONS AND
   UNIVERSITY ARCHIVES
Memorial Library
1415 W. Wisconsin Ave.   Phone: (414) 224-7256
Milwaukee, WI 53233   Charles B. Elston, Dept.Hd.

MARQUETTE UNIVERSITY - FOUNDATION CENTER REGIONAL REFERENCE
   COLLECTION
Memorial Library
1415 W. Wisconsin Ave.   Phone: (414) 224-1515
Milwaukee, WI 53233   Susan Hopwood, Found.Coll.Libn.

MARQUETTE UNIVERSITY - LEGAL RESEARCH CENTER
1103 W. Wisconsin Ave.   Phone: (414) 224-7031
Milwaukee, WI 53233   Robert L. Starz, Law Libn.

MARQUETTE UNIVERSITY - MEMORIAL LIBRARY
1415 W. Wisconsin Ave.   Phone: (414) 224-7214
Milwaukee, WI 53233   William M. Gardner, Dir. of Libs.

MARQUETTE UNIVERSITY - SCIENCE LIBRARY
560 N. Sixteenth St.   Phone: (414) 224-3396
Milwaukee, WI 53233   Jay H. Kirk, Hd., Sci.Lib.

MEDICAL COLLEGE OF WISCONSIN - LIBRARIES
8701 Watertown Plank Rd.   Phone: (414) 257-8323
Milwaukee, WI 53226   Patrick W. Brennen, Dir.

MGIC INVESTMENT CORPORATION - CORPORATE LIBRARY
MGIC Plaza   Phone: (414) 347-6409
Milwaukee, WI 53202   Peg Peterson, Corp.Libn.

MICHAEL, BEST & FRIEDRICH - LAW LIBRARY
250 E. Wisconsin Ave.   Phone: (414) 271-6560
Milwaukee, WI 53202   Mary Wood, Libn.

MILLER BREWING COMPANY - SCIENTIFIC TECHNICAL INFORMATION
   FACILITY
3939 W. Highland Blvd.   Phone: (414) 931-3640
Milwaukee, WI 53201   Joanne L. Schwarz, Ldr.

MILWAUKEE ACADEMY OF MEDICINE - LIBRARY
8701 Watertown Plank Rd.
Box 26509
Milwaukee, WI 53226   Leonard Weistrop, M.D., Libn.

MILWAUKEE AREA TECHNICAL COLLEGE - RASCHE MEMORIAL LIBRARY
1015 N. Sixth St.   Phone: (414) 278-6205
Milwaukee, WI 53203   Richard E. Meerdink, District Libn.

MILWAUKEE ART MUSEUM - LIBRARY
750 N. Lincoln Memorial Dr.   Phone: (414) 271-9508
Milwaukee, WI 53202   Betty Karow, Libn.

MILWAUKEE CHILDREN'S HOSPITAL - HEALTH SCIENCES LIBRARY
Box 1997   Phone: (414) 931-4121
Milwaukee, WI 53201   Margaret Wold, Health Sci.Libn.

MILWAUKEE COUNTY BOARD OF SUPERVISORS - RESEARCH LIBRARY *
901 N. 9th St., Rm. 201
Milwaukee, WI 53233

MILWAUKEE COUNTY HISTORICAL SOCIETY - LIBRARY AND ARCHIVES
910 N. Third St.   Phone: (414) 273-8288
Milwaukee, WI 53203   Charles W. Cooney, Jr., Cur., Res.Coll.

MILWAUKEE COUNTY LAW LIBRARY
Rm. 307, Courthouse
901 N. 9th St.   Phone: (414) 278-4321
Milwaukee, WI 53233   Divinia J. Astraquillo, Law Libn.

MILWAUKEE COUNTY MENTAL HEALTH COMPLEX - MICHAEL KASAK
   LIBRARY
9455 Watertown Plank Rd.   Phone: (414) 257-7381
Milwaukee, WI 53226   Anna M. Green, Libn.

MILWAUKEE INSTITUTE OF ART & DESIGN - LIBRARY
207 N. Milwaukee St.   Phone: (414) 276-7889
Milwaukee, WI 53202   Terry Marcus, Libn.

MILWAUKEE - LEGISLATIVE REFERENCE BUREAU - LEGISLATIVE LIBRARY
City Hall, Rm. 404
200 E. Wells St.   Phone: (414) 278-2295
Milwaukee, WI 53202   Ronald D. Leonhardt, Dir.

MILWAUKEE PUBLIC LIBRARY - ART, MUSIC AND RECREATION SECTION
814 W. Wisconsin Ave.   Phone: (414) 278-3043
Milwaukee, WI 53233   Ruth Ruege, Coord., Fine Arts

MILWAUKEE PUBLIC LIBRARY - HUMANITIES DIVISION - LOCAL HISTORY
   AND MARINE ROOM
814 W. Wisconsin Ave.   Phone: (414) 278-3074
Milwaukee, WI 53233   Paul Woehrmann, Local Hist.Libn.

MILWAUKEE PUBLIC LIBRARY - SCIENCE & BUSINESS DIVISION
814 W. Wisconsin Ave.   Phone: (414) 278-3043
Milwaukee, WI 53233   Theodore Cebula, Coord.Sci./Bus.Div.

MILWAUKEE PUBLIC LIBRARY - WISCONSIN ARCHITECTURAL ARCHIVE
814 W. Wisconsin Ave.   Phone: (414) 278-3897
Milwaukee, WI 53233   Ruth Ruege, Coord., Fine Arts

MILWAUKEE PUBLIC MUSEUM - REFERENCE LIBRARY
800 W. Wells St.   Phone: (414) 278-2736
Milwaukee, WI 53233   Judith Campbell Turner, Sect.Hd., Libn.

MILWAUKEE SCHOOL OF ENGINEERING - WALTER SCHROEDER LIBRARY
500 E. Kilbourn Ave.
Box 644   Phone: (412) 277-7180
Milwaukee, WI 53201   Mary Ann Schmidt, Lib.Dir.

MOUNT CARMEL LUTHERAN CHURCH - LIBRARY
8424 W. Center St.   Phone: (414) 771-1270
Milwaukee, WI 53222   Verna A. Weller, Libn.

MOUNT SINAI MEDICAL CENTER - MEDICAL LIBRARY
Box 342   Phone: (414) 289-8318
Milwaukee, WI 53201   Deborah A. Hall, Dir.

NATIONAL FLUID POWER ASSOCIATION - FLUID POWER NATIONAL
   INFORMATION CENTER
3333 N. Mayfair Rd.   Phone: (414) 259-0990
Milwaukee, WI 53222

NEWSPAPERS, INC. - EDITORIAL LIBRARY
333 W. State St.   Phone: (414) 224-2376
Milwaukee, WI 53203   Jo Reitman, Libn.

NORTH PRESBYTERIAN CHURCH - LIBRARY
3410 W. Silver Spring Dr.   Phone: (414) 466-1870
Milwaukee, WI 53209-4092

NORTHWEST GENERAL HOSPITAL - MEDICAL LIBRARY
5310 W. Capitol Dr.   Phone: (414) 447-8599
Milwaukee, WI 53216   Coralyn Marks, Lib.Dir.

NORTHWESTERN MUTUAL LIFE INSURANCE COMPANY - LAW LIBRARY
720 E. Wisconsin Ave.   Phone: (414) 271-1444
Milwaukee, WI 53202   Jane Marshall, Law Libn.

NORTHWESTERN MUTUAL LIFE INSURANCE COMPANY - MEDICAL LIBRARY
720 E. Wisconsin Ave.   Phone: (414) 271-1444
Milwaukee, WI 53202   Virginia Murphy, Med.Libn.

NORTHWESTERN MUTUAL LIFE INSURANCE COMPANY - REFERENCE
   LIBRARY
720 E. Wisconsin Ave.   Phone: (414) 271-1444
Milwaukee, WI 53202   Patricia H. Ehr, Hd.Libn.

OUR SAVIOR'S LUTHERAN CHURCH - LIBRARY
3022 W. Wisconsin Ave.   Phone: (414) 342-5252
Milwaukee, WI 53208   Kenneth E. Nordby, Lay Asst.

OUTBOARD MARINE CORPORATION - RESEARCH CENTER LIBRARY †
4109 N. 27th
Box 663   Phone: (414) 447-5400
Milwaukee, WI 53201   Cynthia Meinhardt, Libn.

PALLOTTINE PROVINCIALATE LIBRARY
5424 W. Blue Mound Rd.   Phone: (414) 258-0653
Milwaukee, WI 53208   Rev. Jerome Kuskowski, S.A.C., Libn.

PHARMACIA P-L BIOCHEMICALS, INC. - RESEARCH LIBRARY
2202 N. Bartlett Ave.   Phone: (414) 225-2601
Milwaukee, WI 53202   Marie Fendry, Res.Libn.

PLANNED PARENTHOOD OF WISCONSIN - MAURICE RITZ RESOURCE
   CENTER
1135 W. State St.   Phone: (414) 271-8116
Milwaukee, WI 53233   Ann H. McIntyre, Libn.

PRINCE OF PEACE LUTHERAN CHURCH - LIBRARY
4419 S. Howell Ave.   Phone: (414) 483-3828
Milwaukee, WI 53207   Mrs. Robert Heinritz, Hd.Libn.

QUARLES & BRADY - LIBRARY
780 N. Water St.   Phone: (414) 277-5000
Milwaukee, WI 53202   Susan H. Jankowski, Libn.

REINHART, BOERNER, VAN DEUREN, NORRIS & RIESELBACH - LIBRARY
1800 Marine Plaza   Phone: (414) 271-1190
Milwaukee, WI 53202   Carol Bannen, Libn.

REXNORD INC. - TECHNICAL LIBRARY †
5101 W. Beloit Rd.
Box 2022   Phone: (414) 643-2725
Milwaukee, WI 53214   Linda L. LeVeille, Info.Spec.

ROA FILMS - LIBRARY
914 N. 4th St.
Box 661   Phone: (414) 271-0861
Milwaukee, WI 53202   Jean Larson, Exec. V.P.

ST. FRANCIS HOSPITAL - HEALTH SCIENCE LEARNING CENTER
3237 S. 16th St.   Phone: (414) 647-5156
Milwaukee, WI 53215   Joy Shong, Coord.

ST. FRANCIS SEMINARY - SALZMANN LIBRARY
3257 South Lake Dr.   Phone: (414) 483-1979
Milwaukee, WI 53207   Rev. Lawrence K. Miech, Lib.Dir.

ST. JOSEPH'S HOSPITAL - SAMUEL ROSENTHAL MEMORIAL LIBRARY
5000 W. Chambers St.   Phone: (414) 447-2194
Milwaukee, WI 53210   M. Frances McManimon, Med.Libn.

ST. LUKE'S HOSPITAL - MEDICAL LIBRARY
2900 W. Oklahoma Ave.   Phone: (414) 649-7357
Milwaukee, WI 53215   Midge Wos, Hd.Libn.

ST. MARY'S HOSPITAL - HEALTH SCIENCES LIBRARY
2323 N. Lake Dr.
Box 503   Phone: (414) 289-7000
Milwaukee, WI 53201   Carolyn J. Barloga, Libn.

ST. MICHAEL'S HOSPITAL - REGNER HEALTH SCIENCES LIBRARY †
2400 W. Villard Ave.   Phone: (414) 263-8477
Milwaukee, WI 53209   Joan Yanicke, Dir., Lib.Serv.

SMITH (A.O.) CORPORATION - TECHNICAL LIBRARY
Box 584   Phone: (414) 447-4683
Milwaukee, WI 53201   Larry Medley, Libn.

SOUTHEASTERN WISCONSIN HEALTH SYSTEMS AGENCY - RESOURCE
    INFORMATION CENTER
735 W. Wisconsin Ave., Suite 600   Phone: (414) 271-9788
Milwaukee, WI 53211   Suzy Weisman, Coord.

SQUARE D COMPANY - LIBRARY
4041 N. Richards St.   Phone: (414) 332-2000
Milwaukee, WI 53212   Julie Schwartz, Libn.

U.S. DEFENSE CONTRACT ADMINISTRATION SERVICES OF MILWAUKEE
    AREA - LIBRARY
310 W. Wisconsin Ave., Suite 340   Phone: (414) 291-4327
Milwaukee, WI 53204   Nancy Slowinski, QA Data Ck.

U.S. DEPT. OF COMMERCE - INTERNATIONAL TRADE ADMINISTRATION -
    MILWAUKEE DISTRICT OFFICE LIBRARY *
Federal Bldg.
517 E. Wisconsin Ave.   Phone: (414) 291-3473
Milwaukee, WI 53202   Russell H. Leitch, Dir.

UNIVERSAL FOODS CORPORATION - TECHNICAL INFORMATION CENTER
6143 N. 60th St.   Phone: (414) 535-4307
Milwaukee, WI 53218   Aileen Mundstock, Tech.Info.Spec.

UNIVERSITY OF WISCONSIN, MILWAUKEE - AREA RESEARCH CENTER
2311 E. Hartford Ave.   Phone: (414) 963-5402
Milwaukee, WI 53201   Allan Kovan, Cur.

UNIVERSITY OF WISCONSIN, MILWAUKEE - FEMINIST CENTER - LIBRARY
    *
Student Union Box 189
P.O. Box 413   Phone: (414) 963-5683
Milwaukee, WI 53201   Julie A. Jorgensen, Dir.

UNIVERSITY OF WISCONSIN, MILWAUKEE - GOLDA MEIR LIBRARY -
    CURRICULUM COLLECTION
Box 604   Phone: (414) 963-4074
Milwaukee, WI 53201   Julie Czisny, Educ.Libn.

UNIVERSITY OF WISCONSIN, MILWAUKEE - GRADUATE SCHOOL - OFFICE
    OF RESEARCH - INFORMATION LIBRARY
Box 340   Phone: (414) 963-4063
Milwaukee, WI 53201   Victor J. Larson, Info.Spec.

UNIVERSITY OF WISCONSIN, MILWAUKEE - GREENE MEMORIAL MUSEUM
    - LIBRARY
3367 N. Downer Ave.
Milwaukee, WI 53201

UNIVERSITY OF WISCONSIN, MILWAUKEE - INSTITUTE OF WORLD
    AFFAIRS - RESOURCE CENTER
Bolton 659
Box 413   Phone: (414) 963-4251
Milwaukee, WI 53201   David Garnham, Coord.

UNIVERSITY OF WISCONSIN, MILWAUKEE - MORRIS FROMKIN MEMORIAL
    COLLECTION
2311 E. Hartford Ave.   Phone: (414) 963-5402
Milwaukee, WI 53201   Stanley Mallach, Bibliog.

UNIVERSITY OF WISCONSIN, MILWAUKEE - MUSIC COLLECTION
2311 E. Hartford Ave.
Box 604   Phone: (414) 963-5529
Milwaukee, WI 53201   Richard E. Jones, Music Libn.

VALUATION RESEARCH CORPORATION - CORPORATE RESEARCH AND
    REFERENCE LIBRARY
250 E. Wisconsin Ave.   Phone: (414) 271-8662
Milwaukee, WI 53202   Don F. Schwamb, Corp.Libn.

WISCONSIN CONSERVATORY OF MUSIC - LIBRARY
1584 N. Prospect Ave.   Phone: (414) 276-5760
Milwaukee, WI 53202-2394   Brian Jonathan Gerl, Dir.

WISCONSIN GAS COMPANY - CORPORATE AND LAW LIBRARY
626 E. Wisconsin Ave.   Phone: (414) 291-6666
Milwaukee, WI 53202   Carolyn A. Simpson, Coord. of Regulatory Info

WISCONSIN INFORMATION SERVICE
161 W. Wisconsin Ave., Rm. 7071   Phone: (414) 276-0760
Milwaukee, WI 53203   Judith H. Cohen, Dir.

WISCONSIN STATE DEPARTMENT OF NATURAL RESOURCES - SOUTHEAST
    DISTRICT LIBRARY
2300 N. 3rd St.   Phone: (414) 562-9536
Milwaukee, WI 53212   Kathleen Schultz, Libn.

MINERAL POINT HISTORICAL SOCIETY - ARCHIVES
Gundry House
234 Madison St.   Phone: (608) 987-3800
Mineral Point, WI 53565   Patrick Ripp

ST. LAWRENCE SEMINARY - LIBRARY
                                                 Phone: (414) 753-3911
Mount Calvary, WI 53057   Sr. Elaine Basche, Libn.

NASHOTAH HOUSE - LIBRARY
2777 Mission Rd.   Phone: (414) 646-3371
Nashotah, WI 53058   Dr. Linda Hartig, Act.Libn.

BERGSTROM-MAHLER MUSEUM - REFERENCE LIBRARY *
165 N. Park Ave.
Neenah, WI 54956

JAMES RIVER CORPORATION - NEENAH TECHNICAL CENTER - TECHNICAL
    INFORMATION CENTER
1915 Marathon Ave.
Box 899   Phone: (414) 729-8169
Neenah, WI 54956   Cheryl Lamb, Info.Sci.

KELLER (J.J.) & ASSOCIATES, INC. - RESEARCH & TECHNICAL LIBRARY
145 W. Wisconsin Ave.   Phone: (414) 722-2848
Neenah, WI 54956   John K. Breese, Mgr., RTL

KIMBERLY-CLARK CORPORATION - LIBRARY †
N. Lake St.   Phone: (414) 721-5261
Neenah, WI 54956   Mary E. Sutliff, Tech.Libn.

THEDA CLARK REGIONAL MEDICAL CENTER - HEALTH SCIENCES LIBRARY
130 2nd St.   Phone: (414) 729-2190
Neenah, WI 54956   Nancy Berth Campbell, Supv., Lib.

NEW BERLIN MEMORIAL HOSPITAL - LIBRARY
13750 W. National Ave.   Phone: (414) 782-2700
New Berlin, WI 53151   June Regis, Staff Libn.

WISCONSIN INDIANHEAD TECHNICAL INSTITUTE, NEW RICHMOND
    CAMPUS - LEARNING RESOURCE CENTER
1019 S. Knowles Ave.   Phone: (715) 246-6561
New Richmond, WI 54017   David D. Hartung, Libn.

MID-CONTINENT RAILWAY HISTORICAL SOCIETY, INC. - MUSEUM
    LIBRARY
                                                 Phone: (608) 522-4261
North Freedom, WI 53951   Donald W. Gimter, Cur.

MILWAUKEE AREA TECHNICAL COLLEGE - SOUTH CAMPUS LIBRARY
6665 S. Howell Ave.   Phone: (414) 762-2500
Oak Creek, WI 53154   Elizabeth Conrad, Lib.Techn.

MEMORIAL HOSPITAL AT OCONOMOWOC - HEALTH SCIENCES LIBRARY
791 East Summit Ave.   Phone: (414) 567-0371
Oconomowoc, WI 53066   Mary Kaye Lintner, Health Sci.Libn.

EXPERIMENTAL AIRCRAFT ASSOCIATION - AVIATION FOUNDATION -
   LIBRARY
EAA Aviation Center
Oshkosh, WI 54901

OSHKOSH PUBLIC MUSEUM - LIBRARY & ARCHIVES
1331 Algoma Blvd.   Phone: (414) 424-0452
Oshkosh, WI 54901   Kitty A. Hobson, Archv.

PAINE ART CENTER AND ARBORETUM - GEORGE P. NEVITT LIBRARY
1410 Algoma Blvd.   Phone: (414) 235-4530
Oshkosh, WI 54901   Corinne H. Spoo, Hd.

UNIVERSITY OF WISCONSIN, OSHKOSH - UNIVERSITY LIBRARIES AND
   LEARNING RESOURCES - SPECIAL COLLECTIONS
800 Algoma Blvd.   Phone: (414) 424-3333
Oshkosh, WI 54901   J. Daniel Vann, Exec.Dir.

WAUKESHA COUNTY TECHNICAL INSTITUTE - WCTI LIBRARY
800 Main St.   Phone: (414) 691-5316
Pewaukee, WI 53072   Ruth Ahl, District Libn.

UNIVERSITY OF WISCONSIN, PLATTEVILLE - KARRMANN LIBRARY -
   SPECIAL COLLECTIONS
725 W. Main St.   Phone: (608) 342-1688
Platteville, WI 53818   Jerome P. Daniels, Dir.

WISCONSIN STATE DEPARTMENT OF NATURAL RESOURCES - MAC KENZIE
   ENVIRONMENTAL EDUCATION CENTER
Rte. 2, Box 825   Phone: (608) 635-4498
Poynette, WI 53955   Robert Wallen, Prog.Spec.

FRANCISCAN FRIARS - ASSUMPTION FRIARY LIBRARY *
Franciscan Center
143 E. Pulaski St.   Phone: (414) 822-3291
Pulaski, WI 54162   Joseph Krymkowski, O.F.M., Libn.

INTERNATIONAL BANK NOTE SOCIETY - LIBRARY
Box 1222
Racine, WI 53405   Milan Alusic, Sec.

JOHNSON (S.C.) AND SON, INC. - TECHNICAL & BUSINESS INFORMATION
   CENTER
M.S. 123
1525 Howe St.   Phone: (414) 631-2372
Racine, WI 53403   Mara Teranis, Sr.Info.Sci.

RACINE COUNTY HISTORICAL SOCIETY AND MUSEUM, INC. - LOCAL
   HISTORY AND GENEALOGICAL REFERENCE LIBRARY
701 Main St.   Phone: (414) 637-8585
Racine, WI 53403   Jeffrey R. Schultz, Dir.

RACINE JOURNAL TIMES - LIBRARY *
212 4th St.   Phone: (414) 634-3322
Racine, WI 53403   Karolyn Cotton, Libn.

WALKER MANUFACTURING CO. - LIBRARY
1201 Michigan Blvd.
Racine, WI 53402   Dennis Otwaska, Supv., Adm.Serv.

WESTERN PUBLISHING COMPANY, INC. - CORPORATE TRAINING CENTER
   LIBRARY
1220 Mound Ave.   Phone: (414) 633-2431
Racine, WI 53404   Richard H. Popp, Mgr., Corp. Training

WISCONSIN STATE - RACINE COUNTY LAW LIBRARY
730 Wisconsin Ave.   Phone: (414) 636-3862
Racine, WI 53403   Lawrence E. Flynn, Ck. of Courts

YOUNG RADIATOR COMPANY - LIBRARY †
2825 Four Mile Rd.   Phone: (414) 639-1011
Racine, WI 53404   Sandra Kraft, Libn.

RIPON HISTORICAL SOCIETY - LIBRARY *
508 Watson St.
Box 274   Phone: (414) 748-5354
Ripon, WI 54971   George H. Miller, Cur.

UNIVERSITY OF WISCONSIN, RIVER FALLS - CHALMER DAVEE LIBRARY
120 E. Cascade Ave.   Phone: (715) 425-3321
River Falls, WI 54022   Richard A. Cooklock, Dir.

UNIVERSITY OF WISCONSIN, RIVER FALLS - CHALMER DAVEE LIBRARY -
   AREA RESEARCH CENTER
                                               Phone: (715) 425-3567
River Falls, WI 54022   Timothy L. Ericson, Archv.

REED LIGNIN INC. - LIGNIN RESEARCH LIBRARY
100 Hwy. 51, S.   Phone: (715) 359-6544
Rothschild, WI 54474-1198   Julie M. Stephany, Libn.

STERLING DRUG, INC. - ZIMPRO INC. - REFERENCE AND RESOURCE
   CENTER
Military Rd.   Phone: (715) 359-7211
Rothschild, WI 54474

LAND, INC. - LIBRARY
Route 1
525 River Rd.   Phone: (715) 423-7996
Rudolph, WI 54475   Naomi Jacobson, Co-Chm.

ST. NICHOLAS HOSPITAL - HEALTH SCIENCES LIBRARY †
1601 N. Taylor Dr.   Phone: (414) 459-4713
Sheboygan, WI 53081   Kathleen Blaser, Libn.

SHEBOYGAN PRESS LIBRARY
632 Center Ave.   Phone: (414) 457-7711
Sheboygan, WI 53081   Janice Hildebrand, Libn.

DOMINICAN EDUCATION CENTER - LIBRARY
                                               Phone: (608) 748-4411
Sinsinawa, WI 53824   Sr. Coronata Harvey, Dir.

MONROE COUNTY LOCAL HISTORY ROOM & LIBRARY
Community Services Bldg.
Rte. 2, Box 21   Phone: (608) 269-8680
Sparta, WI 54656   Audrey Johnson, Act. County Hist.

AMERICAN PLAYERS THEATRE, INC. (APT) - LIBRARY
Route 3   Phone: (608) 588-7401
Spring Green, WI 53588   Margaret L. Hayes, Libn.

ST. MICHAEL'S HOSPITAL - HEALTH SCIENCES LIBRARY
900 Illinois Ave.   Phone: (715) 344-4400
Stevens Point, WI 54481   Barbara DeWeerd, Libn.

SENTRY INSURANCE COMPANY - LIBRARY †
1800 N. Point Dr.   Phone: (715) 346-6788
Stevens Point, WI 54481   Irene A. Dobbert, Corp.Libn.

UNIVERSITY OF WISCONSIN, STEVENS POINT - JAMES H. ALBERTSON
   CENTER FOR LEARNING RESOURCES
                                               Phone: (715) 346-2540
Stevens Point, WI 54481   Allen F. Barrows, Dir. of Pub.Serv.

UNIVERSITY OF WISCONSIN, STEVENS POINT - UNIVERSITY ARCHIVES &
   PORTAGE COUNTY HISTORICAL SOCIETY COLLECTION
012 Old Main Bldg.   Phone: (705) 346-2586
Stevens Point, WI 54481   William G. Paul, Univ.Archv.

UNITED METHODIST CHURCH - WISCONSIN CONFERENCE - ARCHIVES
750 Windsor St., Suite 302   Phone: (608) 837-7320
Sun Prairie, WI 53590   Mary E. Schroeder, Archv./Hist.Libn.

DOUGLAS COUNTY HISTORICAL SOCIETY - FAIRLAWN MUSEUM LIBRARY
906 E. 2nd St.   Phone: (715) 394-5712
Superior, WI 54880   Florence Walde, Chm., Lib.Comm.

DOUGLAS COUNTY LAW LIBRARY †
1313 Belknap St.
Court House   Phone: (715) 394-0239
Superior, WI 54880   Carol Wittke, Libn.

WISCONSIN INDIANHEAD TECHNICAL INSTITUTE, SUPERIOR CAMPUS -
   LIBRARY †
600 N. 21st St.   Phone: (715) 394-6677
Superior, WI 54880   Donald Rantala, LRC Spec.

U.S. VETERANS ADMINISTRATION (WI-Tomah) - HOSPITAL LIBRARY
Phone: (608) 372-3971
Tomah, WI 54660   William E. Nielsen, Chf., Lib.Serv.

SOUTHERN WISCONSIN CENTER FOR THE DEVELOPMENTALLY DISABLED -
LIBRARY *
2145 Spring St.
Box 100   Phone: (414) 878-2411
Union Grove, WI 53182   Joyce Dabbs

WATERTOWN HISTORICAL SOCIETY - ARCHIVES
919 Charles St.
Watertown, WI 53094

MALEDICTA: INTERNATIONAL RESEARCH CENTER FOR VERBAL
AGGRESSION, INC. - ARCHIVES
331 S. Greenfield Ave.   Phone: (414) 542-5853
Waukesha, WI 53186   Dr. Reinhold A. Aman, Pres.

SOUTHEASTERN WISCONSIN REGIONAL PLANNING COMMISSION -
REFERENCE LIBRARY
916 N. East Ave.
Box 769   Phone: (414) 547-6721
Waukesha, WI 53187-1607   Edell M. Peters, Libn.

WAUKESHA COUNTY HISTORICAL MUSEUM - RESEARCH CENTER
101 W. Main St.   Phone: (414) 548-7186
Waukesha, WI 53186   Jean Penn Loerke, Musm.Dir./Hist.

WAUKESHA FREEMAN - NEWSPAPER LIBRARY
200 Park Pl.   Phone: (414) 542-2501
Waukesha, WI 53186   Steven Walter, Mng.Ed.

WAUKESHA MEMORIAL HOSPITAL - MEDICAL LIBRARY
725 American Ave.   Phone: (414) 544-2150
Waukesha, WI 53186   Linda Oddan, Med.Libn.

RIVERSIDE COMMUNITY MEMORIAL HOSPITAL - HEALTH SCIENCE
LIBRARY
500 Riverside Dr.   Phone: (715) 258-1049
Waupaca, WI 54981   Mary Hanegraaf, Libn.

LUTHERAN CHURCH - MISSOURI SYNOD - NORTH WISCONSIN DISTRICT
ARCHIVES
3103 Seymour Ln.   Phone: (715) 845-8241
Wausau, WI 54401   Rev. Ronald W. Goetsch, Archv.

MARATHON COUNTY HISTORICAL MUSEUM - LIBRARY
403 McIndoe St.   Phone: (715) 848-6143
Wausau, WI 54401   Maryanne C. Norton, Libn.

WAUSAU INSURANCE COMPANIES - LIBRARY
2000 Westwood Dr.   Phone: (715) 847-8504
Wausau, WI 54401   Douglas H. Lay, Dir., Lib.Serv.

BETHANY UNITED METHODIST CHURCH - LIBRARY
7265 W. Center St.   Phone: (414) 258-2868
Wauwatosa, WI 53210   Barbara A. Jones, Libn.

CURATIVE REHABILITATION CENTER - LEARNING RESOURCE CENTER
9001 W. Watertown Plank Rd.   Phone: (414) 259-1414
Wauwatosa, WI 53226   Terry Bochte, Libn.

MILWAUKEE PSYCHIATRIC HOSPITAL - LIBRARY
1220 Dewey Ave.   Phone: (414) 258-2600
Wauwatosa, WI 53213   Darlyne Ritter, Libn.

WEST ALLIS MEMORIAL HOSPITAL - MEDICAL LIBRARY
8901 W. Lincoln Ave.   Phone: (414) 546-6162
West Allis, WI 53227   Joan A. Clausz, Med.Libn.

WEST BEND GALLERY OF FINE ARTS - LIBRARY
300 S. 6th Ave.   Phone: (414) 334-9638
West Bend, WI 53095   Thomas Lidtke, Exec.Dir.

UNIVERSITY OF CHICAGO - YERKES OBSERVATORY LIBRARY
Phone: (414) 245-5555
Williams Bay, WI 53191   J.A. Lola, Asst. in Chg.

WINNEBAGO MENTAL HEALTH INSTITUTE - MEDICAL LIBRARY
Box 9   Phone: (414) 235-4910
Winnebago, WI 54985-0009   Mary Campfield, Dir. of Lib.Serv.

CONSOLIDATED PAPERS, INC. - RESEARCH AND DEVELOPMENT LIBRARY
Box 50   Phone: (715) 422-3768
Wisconsin Rapids, WI 54494   Helen W. Sanborn, Supv., Info.Serv.

MIDSTATE TECHNICAL INSTITUTE - EDUCATIONAL RESOURCE CENTER-
LIBRARY
500 32nd St. N.   Phone: (715) 423-5650
Wisconsin Rapids, WI 54494   Harriet L. Broom, Libn.

U.S. VETERANS ADMINISTRATION (WI-Wood) - MEDICAL CENTER
LIBRARY
Phone: (414) 384-2000
Wood, WI 53193   Maureen Farmer, Med.Libn.

HOWARD YOUNG MEDICAL CENTER - HEALTH SCIENCE LIBRARY
Box 470   Phone: (715) 356-8000
Woodruff, WI 54568   Debra L. Nordgren, Libn.

WYOMING

GULF OIL CORPORATION - EXPLORATION AND PRODUCTION COMPANY -
INFORMATION CENTER
Box 2619   Phone: (307) 235-1311
Casper, WY 82602   Sarah A. Garrett, Unit Supv.

MEMORIAL HOSPITAL OF NATRONA COUNTY - MEDICAL LIBRARY
1233 E. 2nd St.   Phone: (307) 577-2450
Casper, WY 82601   Jeanette Murrell, Med.Libn.

U.S. BUREAU OF LAND MANAGEMENT - CASPER DISTRICT OFFICE -
LIBRARY
951 Rancho Rd.   Phone: (307) 261-5591
Casper, WY 82601   Trudy Closson, Rec.Mgr.

UNIVERSITY OF WYOMING - COLLEGE OF HUMAN MEDICINE - FAMILY
PRACTICE RESIDENCY PROGRAM - LEARNING RESOURCES CENTER
1522 East A St.   Phone: (307) 266-3076
Casper, WY 82601   Naomi Lange, Med.Libn.

FAMILY PRACTICE RESIDENCY PROGRAM AT CHEYENNE - FAMILY
PRACTICE LIBRARY AT CHEYENNE
821 E. 18th St.   Phone: (307) 777-7911
Cheyenne, WY 82001-4797   Carol Seebaum, Med.Libn.

GRAND LODGE OF ANCIENT FREE AND ACCEPTED MASONS OF WYOMING -
GRAND LODGE LIBRARY
1820 Capitol Ave.   Phone: (307) 635-5666
Cheyenne, WY 82001   Fred B. Sellin, Grand Libn.

U.S. VETERANS ADMINISTRATION (WY-Cheyenne) - CENTER LIBRARY
2360 E. Pershing Blvd.   Phone: (307) 778-7550
Cheyenne, WY 82001   Edwina M. Hubbard, Libn.

WYOMING STATE ARCHIVES MUSEUMS & HISTORICAL DEPARTMENT
Barrett Bldg.   Phone: (307) 777-7518
Cheyenne, WY 82002   Robert D. Bush, Dir.

WYOMING STATE DEPARTMENT OF ECONOMIC PLANNING AND
DEVELOPMENT - LIBRARY
Barrett Bldg.   Phone: (307) 777-6430
Cheyenne, WY 82002   Anne W. McGowan, Lib.Mgr.

WYOMING (State) DEPARTMENT OF EDUCATION - INSTRUCTIONAL
RESOURCE CENTER
Hathaway Bldg.   Phone: (307) 777-6254
Cheyenne, WY 82002   Jack Prince, Coord., Instr.Rsrcs.

WYOMING STATE DEPARTMENT OF HEALTH & SOCIAL SERVICE - PUBLIC
HEALTH FILM LIBRARY
Hathaway Bldg., Rm. 518   Phone: (307) 777-7363
Cheyenne, WY 82002   Cindy G. Stephens, Film Libn.

WYOMING STATE LAW LIBRARY
Supreme Court Bldg.   Phone: (307) 777-7509
Cheyenne, WY 82002   Albert W. St.Clair, Law Libn.

WYOMING STATE LIBRARY
Supreme Court & State Library Bldg.   Phone: (307) 777-7281
Cheyenne, WY 82002   Wayne H. Johnson, State Libn.

BUFFALO BILL HISTORICAL CENTER - HAROLD MC CRACKEN RESEARCH
   LIBRARY
Box 1000   Phone: (307) 587-4771
Cody, WY 82414   Albert C. Minnick, Libn./Archv.

PARK COUNTY BAR ASSOCIATION - LAW LIBRARY
Court House
1002 Sheridan Ave.   Phone: (307) 587-2204
Cody, WY 82414   Ernest F. Fuller, Jr., Chm.

GRAND ENCAMPMENT MUSEUM, INC. - LIBRARY
                                                 Phone: (307) 327-5310
Encampment, WY 82325   Vera Oldman, Pres., Musm.Corp.

WYOMING STATE HOSPITAL - MEDICAL LIBRARY *
Box 177   Phone: (307) 789-3464
Evanston, WY 82930   Charles D. Bright, Supv.

U.S. NATL. PARK SERVICE - FORT LARAMIE NATL. HISTORIC SITE -
   LIBRARY
Box 178   Phone: (307) 837-2221
Fort Laramie, WY 82212   Phillip J. Gomez, Park Techn.

SWEETWATER COUNTY HISTORICAL MUSEUM - INFORMATION CENTER
50 W. Flaming Gorge Ave.
Box 25   Phone: (307) 875-2611
Green River, WY 82935   Henry F. Chadey, Dir.

NATIONAL OUTDOOR LEADERSHIP SCHOOL - OUTDOOR EDUCATION
   RESOURCE LIBRARY
Box AA   Phone: (307) 332-4381
Lander, WY 82520   Kevin Hildebrant, Chf.Instr.

GEOLOGICAL SURVEY OF WYOMING - PUBLIC RECORDS SECTION
Box 3008, University Sta.   Phone: (307) 742-2054
Laramie, WY 82071   Gary B. Glass, Dir./State Geologist

LARAMIE PLAINS MUSEUM ASSOCIATION - LIBRARY
603 Ivinson   Phone: (307) 742-4448
Laramie, WY 82070   Eugene E. Dunn, Dir.

U.S.D.A. - AGRICULTURAL RESEARCH SERVICE - HONEY BEE PESTICIDES/
   DISEASES RESEARCH LABORATORY - LIBRARY
University of Wyoming
University Sta., Box 3168   Phone: (307) 766-2281
Laramie, WY 82071   W.T. Wilson, Res. Entomologist

U.S. DEPT. OF ENERGY - LARAMIE PROJECTS LIBRARY
University Sta., Box 3395   Phone: (307) 721-2201
Laramie, WY 82071   B.J. Davidson, Libn.

UNIVERSITY OF WYOMING - ANIMAL SCIENCE DIVISION - WOOL LIBRARY
University Sta.
Box 3354   Phone: (307) 766-5212
Laramie, WY 82071   Robert Stobart, Dir.

UNIVERSITY OF WYOMING - GEOLOGY LIBRARY †
S.H. Knight Geology Bldg.   Phone: (307) 766-3374
Laramie, WY 82071   Josephine Battisti, Libn.

UNIVERSITY OF WYOMING - LAW LIBRARY
College of Law   Phone: (307) 766-5175
Laramie, WY 82071   Catherine Mealey, Law Libn./Prof.

UNIVERSITY OF WYOMING - PETROLEUM HISTORY AND RESEARCH
   CENTER LIBRARY *
William Robertson Coe Library
Univ. Sta., Box 3334   Phone: (307) 766-4114
Laramie, WY 82071   Dr. Gene M. Gressley, Dir.

UNIVERSITY OF WYOMING - SCIENCE AND TECHNOLOGY LIBRARY
University Sta., Box 3262   Phone: (307) 766-5165
Laramie, WY 82071   Linda S. Keiter, Asst. Dir., Sci.Libs.

UNIVERSITY OF WYOMING - WATER RESEARCH CENTER - LIBRARY
Laramie, WY 82071

UNIVERSITY OF WYOMING - WESTERN HISTORY RESEARCH CENTER
   LIBRARY *
William Robertson Coe Library
Univ. Sta., Box 3334   Phone: (307) 766-4114
Laramie, WY 82071   Dr. Gene M. Gressley, Dir.

UNIVERSITY OF WYOMING - WYOMING CAREER INFORMATION SYSTEM
Div. of Student Educational Opportunity
Box 3808, University Sta.   Phone: (307) 766-6189
Laramie, WY 82701   Karen P. Scott, Dir.

CHURCH OF JESUS CHRIST OF LATTER-DAY SAINTS - LOVELL, WYOMING
   BRANCH GENEALOGICAL LIBRARY
50 W. Main St.   Phone: (307) 548-2963
Lovell, WY 82431   Barbara C. Bassett, Libn.

U.S. NATL. PARK SERVICE - GRAND TETON NATL. PARK - LIBRARY
Drawer 170   Phone: (307) 733-2880
Moose, WY 83012

WESTON COUNTY HISTORICAL SOCIETY - ANNA MILLER MUSEUM -
   LIBRARY
Box 698   Phone: (307) 746-4188
Newcastle, WY 82701   Helen Larsen, Musm.Dir.

U.S. VETERANS ADMINISTRATION (WY-Sheridan) - MEDICAL CENTER
   LIBRARY
                                                 Phone: (307) 672-3473
Sheridan, WY 82801   Donna Homewood, Chf., Lib.Serv.

U.S. NATL. PARK SERVICE - YELLOWSTONE LIBRARY AND MUSEUM
   ASSOCIATION *
                                                 Phone: (307) 344-7381
Yellowstone National Park, WY 82190   Geri Hape, Bus.Mgr.

U.S. Territories & Possessions

AMERICAN SAMOA

FELETI PACIFIC LIBRARY
Box 1329   Phone: (684) 633-1181
Pago Pago, AS 96799   Manisesa Apelu, Lib.Ck.

GUAM

FLORES (Nieves M.) MEMORIAL LIBRARY
254 Martyr St.   Phone: (471) 472-6417
Agana, GU 96910   Magdalena S. Taitano, Territorial Libn.

GUAM TERRITORIAL LAW LIBRARY
141 San Ramon Rd.   Phone: (671) 477-7623
Agana, GU 96910   Darlene Weingarth, Territorial Law Libn.

UNIVERSITY OF GUAM - MICRONESIAN AREA RESEARCH CENTER -
  PACIFIC COLLECTION
U.O.G. Sta.   Phone: (717) 734-2921
Mangilao, GU 96913   Albert L. Williams, Libn.

GUAM MEMORIAL HOSPITAL AUTHORITY - MEDICAL LIBRARY
850 Gov. Carlos Camacho Rd.   Phone: (671) 646-5801
Tamuning, GU 96911   Juliana C. Salumbides, Med.Libn.

PUERTO RICO

CORNELL UNIVERSITY - ARECIBO OBSERVATORY - LIBRARY
Box 995   Phone: (809) 878-2612
Arecibo, PR 00613   Carmen G. Segarra, Libn.

PUERTO RICAN CULTURE INSTITUTE - LUIS MUNOZ RIVERA LIBRARY AND
  MUSEUM
Luis Munoz Rivera St. No.10
Barranquitas, PR 00618   Leticia del Rosario, Inst.Dir.

CONSERVATORIO DE MUSICA DE PUERTO RICO - BIBLIOTECA
Ave. Roosevelt, Esquina Lamar   Phone: (809) 751-0160
Hato Rey, PR 00918   Alberto H. Hernandez, Hd.Libn.

EVANGELICAL SEMINARY OF PUERTO RICO - JUAN DE VALDES LIBRARY
Ave. Ponce de Leon 776   Phone: (809) 751-6483
Hato Rey, PR 00918   Hector Ruben Sanchez, Lib.Dir.

PUERTO RICO - GENERAL COURT OF JUSTICE - OFFICE OF COURT
  ADMINISTRATION - LIBRARY DIVISION
Call Box 22-A   Phone: (809) 764-2739
Hato Rey, PR 00919   Nidia Miranda Graterole, Dir.

U.S. DEPT. OF COMMERCE - INTERNATIONAL TRADE ADMINISTRATION -
  SAN JUAN DISTRICT OFFICE LIBRARY
Federal Office Bldg., Rm. 659   Phone: (809) 753-4555
Hato Rey, PR 00918   Enrique Vilella, Dir.

UNIVERSITY OF PUERTO RICO - HUMACAO UNIVERSITY COLLEGE -
  LIBRARY
Bo. Tejas, CUH-Sta.   Phone: (809) 852-2525
Humacao, PR 00661   Ileana D. Martinez, Dir.

CENTER FOR ENERGY AND ENVIRONMENT - RESEARCH COLLECTION
College Sta.   Phone: (809) 832-1408
Mayaguez, PR 00708   Sandra A. Enriquez, Asst.Libn.

PUERTO RICO - DEPARTMENT OF HEALTH - RAMON EMETERIO BETANCES
  MEDICAL LIBRARY
Bo. Sabalos, Carr. no. 2
Box 1868   Phone: (809) 832-8686
Mayaguez, PR 00708   Myrna Y. Ramirez, Libn.

UNIVERSITY OF PUERTO RICO - MAYAGUEZ CAMPUS LIBRARY - MARINE
  SCIENCES COLLECTION
                                            Phone: (809) 832-3150
Mayaguez, PR 00708   Sheila Dunstan, Libn.

UNIVERSITY OF PUERTO RICO - MAYAGUEZ CAMPUS LIBRARY - SPECIAL
  COLLECTIONS
Main Library   Phone: (809) 834-4040
Mayaguez, PR 00708   Grace Quinones, Spec.Coll.Libn.

CATHOLIC UNIVERSITY OF PUERTO RICO - MONSIGNOR JUAN FREMIOT
  TORRES OLIVER LAW LIBRARY
Ave. Las Americas   Phone: (809) 844-4150
Ponce, PR 00732   Noelia Padua, Dir.

PONCE SCHOOL OF MEDICINE - LIBRARY ✶
Box 7004   Phone: (809) 844-4150
Ponce, PR 00732   Margarita Arroyo, Libn.

U.S. FOREST SERVICE - INSTITUTE OF TROPICAL FORESTRY - LIBRARY
Box AQ   Phone: (809) 763-3939
Rio Piedras, PR 00928   JoAnne Feheley, Lib.Techn.

UNIVERSITY OF PUERTO RICO - AGRICULTURAL EXPERIMENT STATION -
  LIBRARY ✶
Box H   Phone: (809) 767-9705
Rio Piedras, PR 00928   Joan P. Hayes, Libn.

UNIVERSITY OF PUERTO RICO - COLLEGE OF EDUCATION - SELLES SOLA
  MEMORIAL COLLECTION †
                                            Phone: (809) 764-0000
Rio Piedras, PR 00931   Lina B. Morales, Hd.Libn.

UNIVERSITY OF PUERTO RICO - GRADUATE SCHOOL OF PLANNING -
  LIBRARY †
UPR Sta., Box BE   Phone: (809) 764-0000
Rio Piedras, PR 00931   Martha Torres-Irizarry, Libn.

UNIVERSITY OF PUERTO RICO - HISTORICAL RESEARCH CENTER ✶
University Sta., Box 22802   Phone: (809) 764-0000
Rio Piedras, PR 00931   Dr. Aida R. Caro Costas, Dir.

UNIVERSITY OF PUERTO RICO - LAW SCHOOL LIBRARY
Box L   Phone: (809) 764-0000
Rio Piedras, PR 00931   Carmelo Delgado Cintron, Law Libn.

UNIVERSITY OF PUERTO RICO - MEDICAL SCIENCES CAMPUS - LIBRARY
Box 5067   Phone: (809) 767-9626
Rio Piedras, PR 00936   Aura J. Panepinto, Dir.

UNIVERSITY OF PUERTO RICO - NATURAL SCIENCE LIBRARY ✶
Box 22446   Phone: (809) 764-0000
Rio Piedras, PR 00931   Giovanna Del Pilar Barber, Hd.

UNIVERSITY OF PUERTO RICO - PUERTO RICAN COLLECTION †
UPR Sta., Box C   Phone: (809) 764-0000
Rio Piedras, PR 00931   Denise Perez

UNIVERSITY OF PUERTO RICO - SCHOOL OF PUBLIC ADMINISTRATION -
  LIBRARY †
                                            Phone: (809) 764-0000
Rio Piedras, PR 00931   Perfecto Camacho, Libn.

ASHFORD MEMORIAL COMMUNITY HOSPITAL - MEDICAL LIBRARY ✶
1451 Ashford Ave.
Box 32   Phone: (809) 721-2160
San Juan, PR 00902

CARIBBEAN REGIONAL LIBRARY
UPR Sta., Box 21927   Phone: (809) 764-0000
San Juan, PR 00931   Carmen M. Costa-Ramos, Dir.

PUERTO RICO - ATENEO PUERTORRIQUENO - BIBLIOTECA
Ave. Ponce de Leon
Parada 2, Apartado 1180   Phone: (809) 722-1258
San Juan, PR 00902   Clara S. Lergier, Chf.Libn.

PUERTO RICO - DEPARTMENT OF HEALTH - MEDICAL LIBRARY *
Ant. Hospital de Psiquiatria -
Bo. Monacillos
Call Box 70184   Phone: (809) 767-6060
San Juan, PR 00936   Esther Rosario Hernandez, Libn.

PUERTO RICO - DEPARTMENT OF HEALTH - MENTAL HEALTH LIBRARY *
Asst. Secretariat for Mental Health
Box G.P.O. 61   Phone: (809) 781-5660
San Juan, PR 00936   Consuelo Serrano Romero, Libn.

PUERTO RICO - DEPARTMENT OF JUSTICE - LIBRARY
Box 192   Phone: (809) 721-2900
San Juan, PR 00902   Antonio Nadal, Hd. Law Libn.

PUERTO RICO - INSTITUTE OF PUERTO RICAN CULTURE - ARCHIVO
    GENERAL DE PUERTO RICO
Ponce de Leon 500, Apartado 4184   Phone: (809) 722-2113
San Juan, PR 00905   Miguel Angel Nieves, Dir.

PUERTO RICO - INSTITUTE OF PUERTO RICAN CULTURE - LA CASA DEL
    LIBRO
Calle Del Cristo 225
Box 2265   Phone: (809) 723-0354
San Juan, PR 00903   David Jackson McWilliams, Dir.

PUERTO RICO - OFFICE OF BUDGET & MANAGEMENT - LIBRARY
254 Cruz St.
Box 3228   Phone: (809) 725-9420
San Juan, PR 00904   Gladys Santiago, Hd.Libn.

PUERTO RICO - SUPREME COURT - LAW LIBRARY
Box 2392   Phone: (809) 723-3863
San Juan, PR 00903   Doris Asencio-Toro, Hd.Libn.

U.S. DISTRICT COURT - LEGAL LIBRARY *
Box 3671   Phone: (809) 725-9229
San Juan, PR 00904   Ana Milagros Rodriguez, Libn.

U.S. VETERANS ADMINISTRATION (PR-San Juan) - HOSPITAL LIBRARY
VA Medical & Regional Office Center
Box 4867   Phone: (809) 765-3185
San Juan, PR 00936   Raquel A. Walters, Chf., Lib.Serv.

UNIVERSITY OF PUERTO RICO - GENERAL LIBRARY - SPECIAL
    COLLECTIONS †
Jose M. Lazaro Memorial Library
Box C   Phone: (809) 764-0000
San Juan, PR 00931   Raquel Sarraga, Hd., Spec.Coll.

UNIVERSITY OF PUERTO RICO - GRADUATE SCHOOL OF LIBRARIANSHIPS -
    LIBRARY
Box 21906   Phone: (809) 764-0000
San Juan, PR 00931   Vilma Rivera Bayron, Libn.

CARIBBEAN CENTER FOR ADVANCED STUDIES - LIBRARY
Minillas Sta., Box 41246   Phone: (809) 725-2458
Santurce, PR 00940   Betsaida Velez, Hd.Libn.

INTERAMERICAN UNIVERSITY OF PUERTO RICO - SCHOOL OF LAW -
    DOMINGO TOLEDO ALAMO LAW LIBRARY †
1610 Fernandez Juncos Ave.
Box 8897   Phone: (809) 727-1930
Santurce, PR 00910   Prof. Carlos J.R. Davis, Dir.

PUERTO RICO - CENTRAL OFFICE OF PERSONNEL ADMINISTRATION -
    INSTITUTE OF PERSONNEL DEVELOPMENT - LIBRARY *
Fernandez Juncos Sta.
Box 8476   Phone: (809) 721-4300
Santurce, PR 00910   Jose A. Fonseca Molina, Libn.

PUERTO RICO - STATE DEPARTMENT OF CONSUMER AFFAIRS - LIBRARY *
Minillas Govt. Center
North Tower, 5th Fl.   Phone: (809) 726-7555
Santurce, PR 00940   Israel Rivera, Libn.

VIRGIN ISLANDS

COLLEGE OF THE VIRGIN ISLANDS - CARIBBEAN RESEARCH INSTITUTE -
    LIBRARY
CRI Library   Phone: (809) 774-1252
St. Thomas, VI 00801   Anna Mae Brown-Comment, Adm.Asst.

COLLEGE OF THE VIRGIN ISLANDS - FOUNDATION CENTER REGIONAL
    COLLECTION
Ralph M. Paiewonsky Library   Phone: (809) 774-9200
St. Thomas, VI 00802   F. Keith Bingham, Assoc.Libn.

VIRGIN ISLANDS - DEPARTMENT OF CONSERVATION & CULTURAL
    AFFAIRS - BUREAU OF LIBRARIES AND MUSEUMS
Box 390   Phone: (809) 774-3407
St. Thomas, VI 00850   Dr. Henry C. Chang, Dir.

Canada

ALBERTA

ALPINE CLUB OF CANADA - LIBRARY
Box 160
Phone: (403) 762-2291
Banff, AB T0L 0C0
Mary Andrews, Act.Libn.

ARCHIVES OF THE CANADIAN ROCKIES
Box 160
Phone: (403) 762-2291
Banff, AB T0L 0C0
Edward J. Hart, Dir.

BANFF CENTRE FOR CONTINUING EDUCATION - LIBRARY
Box 1020
Phone: (403) 762-6265
Banff, AB T0L 0C0
Bob Foley, Hd.Libn.

MINERAL SPRINGS HOSPITAL - MEDICAL LIBRARY
Box 1050
Phone: (403) 762-2222
Banff, AB T0L 0C0
Mrs. E. Heikkila, Dir., Med.Rec.

CANADA - AGRICULTURE CANADA - RESEARCH STATION, BEAVERLODGE -
    LIBRARY
Box 29
Phone: (403) 354-2212
Beaverlodge, AB T0H 0C0
Dr. L.P.S. Spangelo, Dir.

ALBERTA ALCOHOLISM AND DRUG ABUSE COMMISSION - LIBRARY
3rd Fl., 1177 11th Ave., S.W.
Phone: (403) 244-2727
Calgary, AB T2R 0G5
Linda Scott, Libn.

ALBERTA - DEPARTMENT OF THE ATTORNEY GENERAL - JUDGES' LAW
    LIBRARY
611 4th St., S.W.
Phone: (403) 261-7475
Calgary, AB T2P 1T5
Melody M. Hainsworth, Libn.

ALBERTA - DEPARTMENT OF THE SOLICITOR GENERAL - CALGARY
    CORRECTIONAL CENTRE - STAFF LIBRARY *
P.O. Box 3250, Sta. B
Phone: (403) 239-0010
Calgary, AB T2M 4L9
Marcia G. Kennedy, Regional Libn./South

ALBERTA - ENERGY RESOURCES CONSERVATION BOARD - LIBRARY
640 5th Ave., S.W.
Phone: (403) 261-8242
Calgary, AB T2P 3G4
Liz Johnson, Libn.

ALBERTA HEART FOUNDATION - LIBRARY †
2011 10th Ave., S.W.
Phone: (403) 244-0786
Calgary, AB T3C 0K4
Emily Alstad, Educ.Coord.

ALBERTA HISTORICAL RESOURCES FOUNDATION - LIBRARY
102 8th Ave., S.E.
Phone: (403) 261-7320
Calgary, AB T2G 0K6
Esther Brown, Project Asst.

ALBERTA MENTAL HEALTH SERVICES - MENTAL HEALTH SYSTEMS
    LIBRARY
1000 8th Ave., S.W., 2nd Fl.
Phone: (403) 297-7311
Calgary, AB T2P 3M7
Hanne Tribe, Lib. Chairperson

ALBERTA PETROLEUM MARKETING COMMISSION - LIBRARY
250 6th Ave., S.W., No. 1900
Phone: (403) 262-8808
Calgary, AB T2P 3H7
T. Armanious, Libn.

ALBERTA AND SOUTHERN GAS COMPANY LTD. - LIBRARY
425 1st St., S.W., 25th Fl.
Phone: (403) 260-9919
Calgary, AB T2P 3L8
Marian Eagen, Libn.

AMOCO CANADA PETROLEUM COMPANY, LTD. - LIBRARY/INFORMATION
    CENTER
Amoco Canada Bldg.
444 7th Ave., S.W., Rm. 1012
Phone: (403) 233-1963
Calgary, AB T2P 0Y2
Frances M. Drummond, Supv.

ANGLICAN CHURCH OF CANADA - DIOCESE OF CALGARY - ANGLICAN
    ARCHIVES
Special Collections Library
University of Calgary
Phone: (403) 269-1905
Calgary, AB T2N 1N4
David Carter, Archv.

ARCTIC INSTITUTE OF NORTH AMERICA - LIBRARY †
University of Calgary Library
2500 University Dr., N.W.
Phone: (403) 284-5966
Calgary, AB T2N 1N4
Hazel Fry, Northern Stud.Libn.

ATKINS (Gordon) AND ASSOCIATES ARCHITECTS LTD. - LIBRARY
1909 17th Ave., S.W.
Phone: (403) 245-4545
Calgary, AB T2T 0E9
Robert Wenton, Libn.

BAPTIST UNION OF WESTERN CANADA - BAPTIST LEADERSHIP TRAINING
    SCHOOL LIBRARY
4330 - 16th St., S.W.
Phone: (403) 243-3770
Calgary, AB T2T 4H9
Tom Geddes, Libn.

BENNETT JONES - LIBRARY
3200 Shell Centre
400 4th Ave., S.W.
Phone: (403) 267-3226
Calgary, AB T2P 0X9
Jennifer Martison, Libn.

BURNET, DUCKWORTH & PALMER, BARRISTERS & SOLICITORS - LIBRARY
425 1st St., S.W., 32nd Fl.
Phone: (403) 260-0179
Calgary, AB T2P 3L8
Kathy Kurceba, Libn.

CALGARY BOARD OF EDUCATION - PROFESSIONAL LIBRARY
3610 9th St. S.E.
Phone: (403) 294-8581
Calgary, AB T2G 3C5
M. Jane Webb, Hd.Libn.

CALGARY CENTENNIAL PLANETARIUM & AERO-SPACE SCIENCE CENTRE -
    LIBRARY & ARCHIVES †
Mewata Park
Phone: (403) 264-2030
Calgary, AB T2P 2M5
S. Wieser, Dir.

CALGARY CITY ELECTRIC SYSTEM - RESOURCE CENTRE
2808 Spiller Rd., S.E.
P.O. Box 2100
Phone: (403) 268-1100
Calgary, AB T2P 2M5

CALGARY GENERAL HOSPITAL - LIBRARY SERVICES
841 Centre Ave., E.
Phone: (403) 268-9234
Calgary, AB T2E 0A1
Elizabeth Kirchner, Chf.Med.Libn.

CALGARY HERALD - LIBRARY
215 16th St., S.E.
Phone: (403) 235-7361
Calgary, AB T2G 3P2
Karen Liddiard, Chf.Libn.

CALGARY PLANNING DEPARTMENT - INFORMATION SERVICES
Box 2100
Phone: (403) 268-5449
Calgary, AB T2P 2M5

CALGARY SOCIAL SERVICE DEPARTMENT - LIBRARY
Box 2100
Phone: (403) 268-5111
Calgary, AB T2P 2M5
Tahani Sarophim, Lib.Ck.

CALGARY SUN - LIBRARY
2615 12th St., N.E.
Phone: (403) 250-4135
Calgary, AB T2E 7W9
Jennifer Anderson, Chf.Libn.

CANADA - GEOLOGICAL SURVEY OF CANADA - INSTITUTE OF
    SEDIMENTARY & PETROLEUM GEOLOGY - LIBRARY
3303 33rd St., N.W.
Phone: (403) 284-0301
Calgary, AB T2L 2A7
Flora Fritz, Libn.

CANADA - NATIONAL FILM BOARD OF CANADA - FILM LIBRARY
222 First St., S.E.
Box 2959, Sta. M
Phone: (403) 231-5414
Calgary, AB T2P 3C3
Doris Ostergaard, Libn.

CANADA - PARKS CANADA, WESTERN REGION - LIBRARY
220 4th Ave., S.E., Rm. 520
P.O. Box 2989, Sta. M
Phone: (403) 231-4455
Calgary, AB T2P 3H8
R.P. Morgan, Libn.

CANADIAN ETHNIC STUDIES ASSOCIATION - RESEARCH CENTRE
University of Calgary
2500 University Dr., N.W.
Phone: (403) 284-7257
Calgary, AB T2N 1N4
Dr. James S. Frideres, Dir.

CANADIAN MENTAL HEALTH ASSOCIATION - SUICIDE INFORMATION AND
   EDUCATION CENTRE
723 14th St., N.W., Suite 103   Phone: (403) 283-3031
Calgary, AB T2N 2A4   Donna J. Sim, Dir.

CANADIAN MUSIC CENTRE - PRAIRIE REGION LIBRARY
911 Library Tower
2500 University Dr., N.W.   Phone: (403) 284-7403
Calgary, AB T2N 1N4   Mr. Clare Richman, Regional Dir.

CANADIAN WESTERN NATURAL GAS COMPANY LIMITED - LIBRARY
909 11th Ave., S.W.   Phone: (403) 245-7403
Calgary, AB T2R 1L8   Shelley J. Weatherhead, Libn.

CANTERRA ENERGY LTD. - LIBRARY
555 4th Ave., S.W.
Box 1051   Phone: (403) 267-9017
Calgary, AB T2P 2K7   Mary Proudfoot, Coord., Info.Serv.

CENTRE FOR RESEARCH AND DEVELOPMENT IN MASONRY (CRDM) -
   LIBRARY
4528 6A St., N.E., No. 105   Phone: (403) 277-3024
Calgary, AB T2E 4B2   Mrs. Zaytoon Janjua, Libn./Info.Off.

CHEVRON CANADA RESOURCES LTD. - LIBRARY
500 5th Ave., S.W.   Phone: (403) 234-5577
Calgary, AB T2P 0L7   Terri Pieschel, Supv., Lib.

CHURCH OF JESUS CHRIST OF LATTER-DAY SAINTS - CALGARY
   INSTITUTE OF RELIGION - LIBRARY
3120 32nd Ave., N.W.   Phone: (403) 282-5516
Calgary, AB T2N 1N7   John Livingstone, Dir.

CLARKSON GORDON/WOODS GORDON - LIBRARY
707 7th Ave., S.W., 13th Fl.   Phone: (403) 290-4183
Calgary, AB T2P 3H6   Cheryl DeWolf, Mgr., Lib.Serv.

DOME PETROLEUM LIMITED - CORPORATE LIBRARY
P.O. Box 200   Phone: (403) 234-4304
Calgary, AB T2P 2H8   Kolette L. Taber, Corp.Libn.

ESSO RESOURCES CANADA LIMITED - LIBRARY INFORMATION CENTRE
237 4th Ave., S.W.   Phone: (403) 237-4500
Calgary, AB T2P 0H6   Terri A. Harris, Supv.

ESSO RESOURCES CANADA LIMITED - RESEARCH LIBRARY
339 50th Ave., S.E.   Phone: (403) 259-0303
Calgary, AB T2G 2B3   Heather A. Wharton, Libn.

FOOTHILLS CHRISTIAN COLLEGE - LIBRARY
460 31st Ave., N.W.   Phone: (403) 230-3424
Calgary, AB T2M 2P4   J. Ray Doerksen, Dir. of Lib.Serv.

FOOTHILLS HOSPITAL EDUCATIONAL SERVICES CENTER
1403 29th St. N.W.   Phone: (403) 270-1460
Calgary, AB T2N 2T9   Ruth MacRae, Coord.

GLENBOW-ALBERTA INSTITUTE - LIBRARY & ARCHIVES
130 9th Ave., S.E.   Phone: (403) 264-8300
Calgary, AB T2G 0P3   Leonard J. Gottselig, Chf.Libn.

GULF CANADA RESOURCES INC. - LIBRARY
P.O. Box 130   Phone: (403) 233-3804
Calgary, AB T2P 2H7   Ms. S. Crozier-Parkinson, Sr.Libn.

HOLY CROSS HOSPITAL OF CALGARY - DEPARTMENT OF LIBRARY
   SERVICES
2210 2nd St., S.W.   Phone: (403) 266-7231
Calgary, AB T2S 1S6   Mumtaz Jivraj, Hd.Libn.

HOME OIL COMPANY, LTD. - TECHNICAL INFORMATION CENTER
2300 Home Oil Tower
324 8th Ave., S.W.   Phone: (403) 232-5018
Calgary, AB T2P 2Z5   Rodney A. Muir, Coord.

HUSKY OIL OPERATIONS LTD. - LIBRARY/RECORDS MANAGEMENT
Sta. D, Box 6525   Phone: (403) 298-7061
Calgary, AB T2P 3G7   Wanda Oleszkiewicz, Libn.

INSURANCE INSTITUTE OF SOUTHERN ALBERTA - LIBRARY †
630 8th Ave., S.W., No. 601   Phone: (403) 266-3427
Calgary, AB T2P 1G6   Carolyn Geary, Sec.

LAW SOCIETY OF ALBERTA - CALGARY LIBRARY
Court House
611 4th St., S.W.   Phone: (403) 261-6148
Calgary, AB T2P 1T5   Melody M. Hainsworth, Libn.

MC KINNON, ALLEN & ASSOCIATES (Western), LTD. - RESEARCH LIBRARY
1115 46th Ave., S.E.   Phone: (403) 243-4345
Calgary, AB T2G 2A5   Janice Lore, Res.Assoc.

MC KINNON (I.N.) MEMORIAL LIBRARY
3512 33rd St., N.W.   Phone: (403) 282-1211
Calgary, AB T2L 2A6   L. Nugent, Libn.

MC LAWS & COMPANY - LIBRARY
407 8th Ave., S.W.   Phone: (403) 294-7057
Calgary, AB T2P 1E6   Susan L. Ross, Libn.

MASON, MAC LEOD, LYLE, SMITH - BARRISTERS AND SOLICITORS -
   LIBRARY
2200 Bow Valley Sq. IV
205 6th Ave., S.W.   Phone: (403) 263-2190
Calgary, AB T2P 3H7   Judy Reynard, Libn.

MOBIL OIL CANADA, LTD. - LIBRARY
P.O. Box 800   Phone: (403) 268-7785
Calgary, AB T2P 2J7   Pat Munro, Libn.

MONENCO CONSULTANTS LIMITED - LIBRARY
400 Monenco Pl.
801 6th Ave., S.W.   Phone: (403) 263-1680
Calgary, AB T2P 3W3   Beverley Bendell, Libn.

NORCEN ENERGY RESOURCES LIMITED - LIBRARY
715 5th Ave., S.W.   Phone: (403) 231-0887
Calgary, AB T2P 2X7   Susan Anderson, Libn.

NOVA - CORPORATE LIBRARY
P.O. Box 2535   Phone: (403) 290-6718
Calgary, AB T2P 2N6   M.W. Genoe, Corp.Libn.

PANARCTIC OILS LTD. - LIBRARY
815 8th Ave., S.W.
Box 190   Phone: (403) 269-0329
Calgary, AB T2P 2H6   Susan J. Tyrrell, Libn.

PCL-BRAUN-SIMONS LTD. - PBS LIBRARY †
1015 4th St., S.W.   Phone: (403) 260-1592
Calgary, AB T2R 1J4   Kathleen Robertson, Libn.

PETRO-CANADA - LIBRARY SERVICES
P.O. Box 2844   Phone: (403) 296-8000
Calgary, AB T2P 3E3   Beverly Gref, Hd.Libn.

ROYAL BANK OF CANADA - LIBRARY
335 8th Ave., S.W.
P.O. Box 2534   Phone: (403) 268-3722
Calgary, AB T2P 2N5   Ms. Myrla J. Koenderink, Libn.

ST. DAVID'S UNITED CHURCH - LIBRARY *
3303 Capitol Hill Crescent, N.W.   Phone: (403) 284-2276
Calgary, AB T2M 2R2   Molly Webb

ST. VLADIMIR'S UKRAINIAN ORTHODOX CULTURAL CENTRE - LIBRARY
   AND ARCHIVES
400 Meredith Rd., N.E.   Phone: (403) 264-3437
Calgary, AB T2E 5A6   Mykola Woron, Hd.Libn.

SALVATION ARMY GRACE HOSPITAL - MEDICAL STAFF LIBRARY †
1402 8th Ave., N.W.   Phone: (403) 284-1141
Calgary, AB T2N 1B9   Dr. A. Rothwell, Chm., Lib.Comm.

SHELL CANADA RESOURCES LIMITED - TECHNICAL LIBRARY
400 4th Ave., S.W.   Phone: (403) 232-3512
Calgary, AB T2P 2H5   Mila E. Carozzi, Sr.Libn.

SOUTHERN ALBERTA INSTITUTE OF TECHNOLOGY - LEARNING
   RESOURCES CENTRE
1301 16th Ave., N.W.   Phone: (403) 284-8647
Calgary, AB T2M 0L4   R.F. Peters, Hd., LRC

SOUTHERN ALBERTA INSTITUTE OF TECHNOLOGY - LEARNING
   RESOURCES CENTRE - ALBERTA COLLEGE OF ART BRANCH
1301 16th Ave., N.W.   Phone: (403) 284-8665
Calgary, AB T2M 0L4   Christine E. Sammon, Libn.

STOCKMEN'S MEMORIAL FOUNDATION - LIBRARY
2116 27th Ave., N.E., No. 126   Phone: (403) 230-3338
Calgary, AB T2E 7A6   Helgi Leesment, Cons.Libn.

SUNCOR INC. - LIBRARY
500 4th Ave., S.W.
P.O. Box 38   Phone: (403) 269-8128
Calgary, AB T2P 2V5   Pat Strong, Libn.

SWAN WOOSTER CONSULTANTS LIMITED - LIBRARY
202 Kensington House
1167 Bowness Rd., N.W.   Phone: (403) 283-3601
Calgary, AB T2N 3J6   W. Daunine Kemp, Libn.

SWEDISH CONSULATE - LIBRARY †
420 47th Ave., S.W.   Phone: (403) 243-1093
Calgary, AB T2S 1C4   R. Zoumer, Consul

TOM BAKER CANCER CENTER - LIBRARY
1331 - 29th St., N.W.   Phone: (403) 270-1765
Calgary, AB T2N 4N2   Judy Flax, Libn.

TOTAL PETROLEUM CANADA, LTD. - LIBRARY
639 5th Ave., S.W., 12th Fl.   Phone: (403) 265-9080
Calgary, AB T2P 0M9   Cheryl Fishleigh, Libn.

TOUCHE ROSS AND COMPANY - LIBRARY
700 2nd St., S.W., Suite 3500   Phone: (403) 263-4800
Calgary, AB T2P 0S7   L. Herman, Libn.

TOUCHE ROSS AND COMPANY - LIBRARY
715 5th Ave., S.W.   Phone: (403) 264-4441
Calgary, AB T2P 2X6   L. Herman, Libn.

TRANS CANADA PIPELINES LTD. - LIBRARY
530 8th Ave., S.W.
P.O. Box 500, Sta. M   Phone: (403) 269-5792
Calgary, AB T2P 3V6   Elizabeth A. Winter, Libn.

TRANSALTA UTILITIES CORPORATION - LIBRARY
110 12th Ave., S.W.
P.O. Box 1900   Phone: (403) 267-7388
Calgary, AB T2P 2M1   Shamim Kassam, Libn.

UNION OIL COMPANY OF CANADA, LTD. - LIBRARY
335 8th Ave., S.W.
P.O. Box 999   Phone: (403) 268-0303
Calgary, AB T2P 2K6   Julie Graham, Libn.

UNIVERSITY OF CALGARY - ARTS AND HUMANITIES LIBRARY †
2500 University Dr., N.W.   Phone: (403) 284-5976
Calgary, AB T2N 1N4   Kathy Zimon, Asst. Area Hd./Arts Libn.

UNIVERSITY OF CALGARY - CANADIAN INSTITUTE OF RESOURCES LAW -
   LIBRARY
BioSciences Bldg., Rm. 430M   Phone: (403) 282-2569
Calgary, AB T2N 1N4   Evangeline S. Case, Pubn.Off.

UNIVERSITY OF CALGARY - EDUCATION MATERIALS CENTER *
2500 University Dr., N.W.   Phone: (403) 284-5637
Calgary, AB T2N 1N4   Dr. Philomena Hauck, Dir.

UNIVERSITY OF CALGARY - ENVIRONMENT-SCIENCE-TECHNOLOGY
   LIBRARY †
2500 University Dr., N.W.   Phone: (403) 284-5966
Calgary, AB T2N 1N4   Hazel Fry, Area Hd.

UNIVERSITY OF CALGARY - LAW LIBRARY †
2500 University Dr., N.W.   Phone: (403) 284-5090
Calgary, AB T2N 1N4   Georgia Macrae, Law Libn.

UNIVERSITY OF CALGARY - MEDIA UTILIZATION UNIT & FILM LIBRARY *
2500 University Dr., N.W.   Phone: (403) 284-6146
Calgary, AB T2N 1N4   Jennie Paine, Mgr.

UNIVERSITY OF CALGARY - MEDICAL LIBRARY †
Health Sciences Centre   Phone: (403) 284-6858
Calgary, AB T2N 1N4   Andras Kirchner, Med.Libn.

UNIVERSITY OF CALGARY - SOCIAL SCIENCES LIBRARY †
2500 University Dr., N.W.   Phone: (403) 284-5965
Calgary, AB T2N 1N4   Gretchen Ghent, Area Hd.

UNIVERSITY OF CALGARY - SPECIAL COLLECTIONS DIVISION †
2500 University Dr., N.W.   Phone: (403) 284-5972
Calgary, AB T2N 1N4   Apollonia Steele, Spec.Coll.Libn.

WALSH YOUNG - LIBRARY
1500 Guinness House   Phone: (403) 263-8490
Calgary, AB T2P 0Z8   Susan L. Ross, Libn.

CAMROSE LUTHERAN COLLEGE - LIBRARY
4503 50th St.   Phone: (403) 672-3381
Camrose, AB T4V 2R3   Asgeir Ingibergsson, Hd.Libn.

CANADIAN UNION COLLEGE - LIBRARY
Box 430   Phone: (403) 782-6461
College Heights, AB T0C 0Z0   Keith H. Clouten, Lib.Serv.Dir.

MOUNTAIN VIEW BIBLE COLLEGE - LIBRARY
Box 190   Phone: (403) 335-3337
Didsbury, AB T0M 0W0   A. Chris Beldan, Libn.

AFRICAN LITERATURE ASSOCIATION - SECRETARIAT LIBRARY
University of Alberta
Dept. of Comparative Literature   Phone: (403) 432-5535
Edmonton, AB T6G 2E6   Stephen H. Arnold, Sec.-Treas., Ed.

ALBERTA ALCOHOLISM AND DRUG ABUSE COMMISSION - LIBRARY
10909 Jasper Ave., 7th Fl.   Phone: (403) 427-7303
Edmonton, AB T5J 3M9   Bette Reimer, Libn.

ALBERTA ASSOCIATION OF REGISTERED NURSES - LIBRARY
10256 112th St.   Phone: (403) 426-0160
Edmonton, AB T5K 1M6   Lloanne G. Walker, Libn.

ALBERTA - DEPARTMENT OF ADVANCED EDUCATION - LIBRARY
9th Fl., East Tower
11160 Jasper Ave.   Phone: (403) 427-5590
Edmonton, AB T5K 0L1   Cynthia K. Ryan, Hd.Libn.

ALBERTA - DEPARTMENT OF AGRICULTURE - LIBRARY
7000 113th St.   Phone: (403) 422-1302
Edmonton, AB T6H 5T6   M.E. Bhatnagar, Dept.Libn.

ALBERTA - DEPARTMENT OF THE ATTORNEY GENERAL - ATTORNEY
   GENERAL LAW LIBRARY
4th Fl., N. Wing
9833 109th St.   Phone: (403) 427-5021
Edmonton, AB T5K 2E8   Andrew Balazs, Dept.Libn.

ALBERTA - DEPARTMENT OF CONSUMER AND CORPORATE AFFAIRS -
   RESOURCE CENTRE
Main Fl., 11044 82nd Ave.   Phone: (403) 427-5215
Edmonton, AB T6G 0T2   Linda Giffen, Oper.Mgr.

ALBERTA - DEPARTMENT OF CULTURE - DEPARTMENTAL LIBRARY
CN Tower, 11th Fl.
10004 104th Ave.   Phone: (403) 427-2571
Edmonton, AB T5J 0K5   Lucy M. Pana, Dept.Libn.

ALBERTA - DEPARTMENT OF CULTURE - HISTORICAL RESOURCES LIBRARY
12845 102nd Ave.   Phone: (403) 427-1750
Edmonton, AB T5N 0M6   Mrs. Jo Toon, Hd.Libn.

ALBERTA - DEPARTMENT OF ECONOMIC DEVELOPMENT - LIBRARY
11th Fl., Pacific Plaza
10909 Jasper Ave.   Phone: (403) 427-4957
Edmonton, AB T5J 3M8   Donna M. Gordon, Libn.

ALBERTA - DEPARTMENT OF EDUCATION - LIBRARY SERVICES
4th Fl., West Wing, Devonian Bldg.
11160 Jasper Ave.   Phone: (403) 427-2985
Edmonton, AB T5K 0L2   Shirley Wolodko, Adm., Lib.Serv.

ALBERTA - DEPARTMENT OF ENERGY AND NATURAL RESOURCES -
    LIBRARY
9th Fl., South Tower, Petroleum Plaza
9915 108th St.   Phone: (403) 427-7425
Edmonton, AB T5K 2C9   Peter K. Mutchler, Chf.Libn.

ALBERTA - DEPARTMENT OF ENERGY AND NATURAL RESOURCES - MAP &
    AIR PHOTO REFERENCE LIBRARY
2nd Fl. W., North Tower, Petroleum Plaza
9945 108th St.   Phone: (403) 427-7417
Edmonton, AB T5K 2G6   Alice S. Chen, Supv.

ALBERTA - DEPARTMENT OF THE ENVIRONMENT - LIBRARY
14th Fl., Oxbridge Place
9820 106th St.   Phone: (403) 427-6132
Edmonton, AB T5K 2J6   Marilyn Corbett, Hd., Lib.Serv.

ALBERTA - DEPARTMENT OF FEDERAL AND INTERGOVERNMENTAL
    AFFAIRS - LIBRARY
14th Fl., Seventh Street Plaza
10030 107th St.   Phone: (403) 427-2611
Edmonton, AB T5J 3E4   Anita E. Duncan, Lib.Techn.

ALBERTA - DEPARTMENT OF HOSPITALS AND MEDICAL CARE - HOSPITAL
    SERVICES LIBRARY
11010 101st St., 5th Fl.
Box 2222   Phone: (403) 427-8720
Edmonton, AB T5J 2P4   Margaret Bradfield, Lib.Techn.

ALBERTA - DEPARTMENT OF HOUSING AND PUBLIC WORKS - HOUSING
    LIBRARY *
10050 112th St., 4th Fl.   Phone: (403) 427-8144
Edmonton, AB T5K 1L9   Dolores Ogilvie, Libn.

ALBERTA - DEPARTMENT OF LABOUR - BUILDING STANDARDS BRANCH
    RESOURCE CENTRE
10808 99th Ave., Rm. 705   Phone: (403) 427-8265
Edmonton, AB T5K 0G2   W. Steinhausen, Info.Dir.

ALBERTA - DEPARTMENT OF LABOUR - LIBRARY SERVICES
10808 99th Ave., Rm. 501   Phone: (403) 427-8531
Edmonton, AB T5K 0G2   Wendy Kinsella, Hd.Libn.

ALBERTA - DEPARTMENT OF MUNICIPAL AFFAIRS - LIBRARY
9925 107th St., 9th Fl.   Phone: (403) 427-4829
Edmonton, AB T5K 2H9   Bettie Bayrak, Libn.

ALBERTA - DEPARTMENT OF PUBLIC WORKS, SUPPLY & SERVICES -
    LIBRARY
6950 113th St.   Phone: (403) 427-2353
Edmonton, AB T6H 5V7   Danielle Bugeaud, Coord.

ALBERTA - DEPARTMENT OF RECREATION & PARKS - LIBRARY
Standard Life Centre, 8th Fl.
10405 Jasper Ave.   Phone: (403) 427-7638
Edmonton, AB T5J 3N4   Michael N. Aston, Dept.Libn.

ALBERTA - DEPARTMENT OF SOCIAL SERVICES AND COMMUNITY HEALTH
    - LIBRARY
6th Fl., Seventh St. Plaza
10030 107th St.   Phone: (403) 427-7272
Edmonton, AB T5J 3E4   Pauline Howatt, Dept.Libn.

ALBERTA - DEPARTMENT OF THE SOLICITOR GENERAL - LIBRARY
Melton Bldg., 5th Fl.
10310 Jasper Ave.   Phone: (403) 427-3421
Edmonton, AB T5J 2W4   Aileen Wright, Dept.Libn.

ALBERTA - DEPARTMENT OF TOURISM AND SMALL BUSINESS - LIBRARY
15th Fl., Capitol Sq.
10065 Jasper Ave.   Phone: (403) 427-3299
Edmonton, AB T5J 0H4   Glenna Winter, Libn.

ALBERTA - DEPARTMENT OF TRANSPORTATION - LIBRARY
Main Fl., Twin Atria Bldg.
4999 98th Ave.   Phone: (403) 427-8802
Edmonton, AB T6B 2X3   D.L. Smith, Dept.Libn.

ALBERTA - DEPARTMENT OF TREASURY - BUREAU OF STATISTICS
    LIBRARY
7th Fl., Sir Frederick W. Haultain Bldg.
9811 109th St.   Phone: (403) 427-3058
Edmonton, AB T5K 0C8   Christine Minailo, Lib.Techn.

ALBERTA - DEPARTMENT OF TREASURY - CORPORATE TAX
    ADMINISTRATION LIBRARY
Sir Fredrick Haultain Bldg., 8th Fl.
9811 109th St.   Phone: (403) 427-9400
Edmonton, AB T5K 2L5   Johanna H. Breijer, Lib.Techn. II

ALBERTA - DEPARTMENT OF TREASURY - LIBRARY SERVICES
404 Terrace Bldg.
9515 107th St.   Phone: (403) 427-7595
Edmonton, AB T5K 2C3   J. Robin Brown, Dept.Libn.

ALBERTA - ENVIRONMENT COUNCIL - INFORMATION CENTRE
8th Fl., Weber Centre
5555 Calgary Trail, S.   Phone: (403) 427-5792
Edmonton, AB T6H 5P9   Terry Forbes, Lib.Techn.

ALBERTA HOSPITAL ASSOCIATION - RESOURCE CENTRE
10025 108th St., 6th Fl.   Phone: (403) 423-1776
Edmonton, AB T5J 1K9   Patricia Baxter, Libn.

ALBERTA HOSPITAL - LIBRARY
Box 307   Phone: (403) 973-2268
Edmonton, AB T5J 2J7   Margaret Pierre, Med.Lib.Techn.

ALBERTA - LEGISLATIVE ASSEMBLY OF ALBERTA - LEGISLATURE LIBRARY
216 Legislature Bldg.   Phone: (403) 427-2473
Edmonton, AB T5K 2B6   D.B. McDougall, Leg.Libn.

ALBERTA MENTAL HEALTH SERVICES - CLINIC LIBRARY
5th Fl., 9942 108th St.
Edmonton, AB T5K 2J5   Shirley Lea, Lib.Techn.

ALBERTA - OFFICE OF THE OMBUDSMAN - OMBUDSMAN'S LIBRARY
1630 Phipps-McKinnon Bldg.
10020 101A Ave.   Phone: (403) 427-2756
Edmonton, AB T5J 3G2   Mrs. A. Matthews, Supv.

ALBERTA - PERSONNEL ADMINISTRATION OFFICE - LIBRARY
3rd Fl., Kensington Place
10011 109th St.   Phone: (403) 422-1131
Edmonton, AB T5J 3S8   Jasveer Jhass, Lib.Techn.

ALBERTA - PUBLIC UTILITIES BOARD - LIBRARY
Manulife House, 11th Fl.
10055 106th St.   Phone: (403) 427-4901
Edmonton, AB T5J 2Y2   James E. McKee, Lib.Techn.

ALBERTA RESEARCH COUNCIL - ALBERTA OIL SANDS INFORMATION
    CENTRE
6th Fl., Highfield Pl.
10010 106th St.   Phone: (403) 427-8382
Edmonton, AB T5J 3L8   Helga Radvanyi, Mgr.

ALBERTA RESEARCH COUNCIL - LIBRARY SERVICES
Terrace Plaza
4445 Calgary Trail, S.   Phone: (403) 438-1810
Edmonton, AB T6H 5R7   Sharon M. Gee, Mgr.

ALBERTA RESEARCH COUNCIL - SOLAR & WIND ENERGY RESEARCH
    PROGRAM (SWERP) INFORMATION CENTRE
5th Fl., Terrace Plaza
4445 Calgary Trail, S.   Phone: (403) 438-1666
Edmonton, AB T6H 5R7   Karen D. Beliveau, Coord.

ALBERTA SCHOOL FOR THE DEAF - L.A. BROUGHTON LIBRARY
6240 113th St.   Phone: (403) 434-1481
Edmonton, AB T6H 3L2   Charmaine Muise, Teacher/Libn.

ALBERTA SOCIETY FOR AUTISTIC CHILDREN - LIBRARY
Edmonton School for Autistic Children
11728 King's Way Ave.   Phone: (403) 451-6173
Edmonton, AB T5G 0X5   Gary Sorensen, Prog.Dir.

ALBERTA TEACHERS' ASSOCIATION - LIBRARY
11010 142nd St., Barnett House   Phone: (403) 453-2411
Edmonton, AB T5N 2R1   Maria Loranger, Libn.

ALBERTA - WORKERS' HEALTH SAFETY & COMPENSATION -
    OCCUPATIONAL HEALTH & SAFETY LIBRARY
5th Fl., 10709 Jasper Ave.   Phone: (403) 427-4671
Edmonton, AB T5J 3N3   W. Keith McLaughlin, Hd.Libn.

AME ENGINEERING LTD. - LIBRARY
700-10160 112th St.   Phone: (403) 425-1710
Edmonton, AB T5K 1M3   D. Elias, Lib.Supv.

ASSOCIATED ENGINEERING SERVICES, LTD. - INFORMATION CENTRE
13220 St. Albert Trail   Phone: (403) 453-8111
Edmonton, AB T5L 4W5   Gloria Heemeryck, Libn.

BISHOP & MC KENZIE, BARRISTERS & SOLICITORS - LIBRARY
Canadian Commercial Bank Tower   Phone: (403) 426-5550
Edmonton, AB T5J 1V3   Katherine McKenney, Libn.

CAMSELL (Charles) GENERAL HOSPITAL - PETER WILCOCK LIBRARY
12815 115th Ave.   Phone: (403) 452-8770
Edmonton, AB T5M 3A4   Donna Dryden, Med.Libn.

CANADA - ATMOSPHERIC ENVIRONMENT SERVICE - WESTERN REGION
    HEADQUARTERS LIBRARY
Argyll Centre
6325 103rd St.   Phone: (403) 437-1250
Edmonton, AB T6H 5H6   Hilda E. Gutzmann, Sec.

CANADA - CANADIAN FORESTRY SERVICE - NORTHERN FOREST
    RESEARCH CENTRE - LIBRARY
5320 122nd St.   Phone: (403) 435-7323
Edmonton, AB T6H 3S5   D. Robinson, Libn.

CANADA - CANADIAN WILDLIFE SERVICE - WESTERN AND NORTHERN
    REGION LIBRARY
9942 108th St., Suite 1000   Phone: (403) 425-5891
Edmonton, AB T5K 2J5   Peter A. Jordan, Regional Libn.

CANADA - NATIONAL FILM BOARD OF CANADA - EDMONTON DISTRICT
    OFFICE - FILM LIBRARY
Centennial Bldg.
10031 103rd Ave.   Phone: (403) 420-3010
Edmonton, AB T5J 0G9

CANADA - STATISTICS CANADA - ADVISORY SERVICES - EDMONTON
    REFERENCE CENTRE
215 Hy's Centre
11010 101st St.   Phone: (403) 420-3027
Edmonton, AB T5H 4C5   Lynn Brochu, Data Dissemination Off.

CANADA - TRANSPORT CANADA - CANADIAN AIR TRANSPORTATION
    ADMINISTRATION - WESTERN REGIONAL LIBRARY
Federal Bldg.
9820 107th St., Rm. 10-76   Phone: (403) 420-3801
Edmonton, AB T5K 1G3   P.J. Nelson, Regional Libn.

CANADIAN UTILITIES LIMITED - LIBRARY
10035 105th St.   Phone: (403) 420-7039
Edmonton, AB T5J 2V6   Donna I. Humphries, Libn.

CONSULATE-GENERAL OF JAPAN - JAPANESE CONSULATE LIBRARY †
10020 100th St., Suite 2600   Phone: (403) 422-3752
Edmonton, AB T5J 0N4

CROSS CANCER INSTITUTE - LIBRARY
11560 University Ave.   Phone: (403) 432-8593
Edmonton, AB T6G 1Z2   Katherine Sharma, Libn.

EDMONTON ART GALLERY - REFERENCE LIBRARY
2 Sir Winston Churchill Sq.   Phone: (403) 422-6223
Edmonton, AB T5J 2C1   Brenda Banks, Libn.

EDMONTON CITY ARCHIVES
10105 112th Ave.   Phone: (403) 479-2069
Edmonton, AB T5G 0H1   Helen LaRose, Supv., Archv.

EDMONTON CITY ENGINEERING DEPARTMENT - MATERIALS & TESTING
    LIBRARY
2950 Parsons Rd.   Phone: (403) 428-2919
Edmonton, AB T6N 1B1   Dawn Dalcourt, Lib.Techn.

EDMONTON CITY PLANNING DEPARTMENT - LIBRARY/RESOURCE CENTRE
11th Fl., Phipps-McKinnon Bldg.
10020 101A Ave.   Phone: (403) 428-2665
Edmonton, AB T5J 3G2   Coreen Douglas, Libn.

EDMONTON GENERAL HOSPITAL - HEALTH SCIENCES LIBRARY
11111 Jasper Ave.   Phone: (403) 482-8301
Edmonton, AB T5K 0L4   Jake Vande Brink, Lib.Mgr.

EDMONTON JOURNAL - LIBRARY
101st St. & 100th Ave.
Box 2421   Phone: (403) 420-1919
Edmonton, AB T5J 2S6   Patricia Garneau, Libn.

EDMONTON POWER - LIBRARY
10250 101st St., 7th Fl.   Phone: (403) 428-4302
Edmonton, AB T5J 3P4   Ronald Friesen, Libn.

EDMONTON PUBLIC SCHOOLS - LEARNING RESOURCES PROFESSIONAL
    LIBRARY
10010 107A Ave.   Phone: (403) 429-5621
Edmonton, AB T5H 0Z8   Marilyn Elliott, Libn.

EDMONTON SEPARATE SCHOOL BOARD - PROFESSIONAL LIBRARY
9807 106th St.   Phone: (403) 422-6376
Edmonton, AB T5K 1C2   C. Hornby, Res.Libn.

EDMONTON SOCIAL SERVICES DEPARTMENT - STAFF LIBRARY †
CN Tower, 6th Fl.
10004 104th Ave.   Phone: (403) 428-5918
Edmonton, AB T5J 0K1

EDMONTON SUN - NEWSPAPER LIBRARY
9405 50th St.   Phone: (403) 468-5111
Edmonton, AB T6B 2T4   John M. Sinclair, Libn.

GCG ENGINEERING PARTNERSHIP - LIBRARY *
17420 Stony Plain Rd.   Phone: (403) 483-8094
Edmonton, AB T5S 1K6   Heather Grimble, Lib.Techn.

GENSTAR CEMENT, LTD. - TECHNICAL LIBRARY
Sta. D, P.O. Box 3961   Phone: (403) 470-1450
Edmonton, AB T5L 4P8   Miss L. Froud, Sec.

GOOD SAMARITAN SOCIETY - LIBRARY
Good Samaritan Auxiliary Hospital
9649 71st Ave.   Phone: (403) 439-6381
Edmonton, AB T6E 5J2   Geraldine Ridge, Libn.

HANSON MATERIALS ENGINEERING (Western) LTD. - CORPORATE LIBRARY
7450 18th St.   Phone: (403) 464-7916
Edmonton, AB T6P 1N8   Irene J. Caine, Corp.Libn.

HARDY ASSOCIATES (1978) LTD. - LIBRARY †
4810 93rd St.
Box 746   Phone: (403) 436-2152
Edmonton, AB T5J 2L4   Alice R. Lechelt, Lib.Techn.

HEALTH COMPUTER INFORMATION BUREAU
10504A 169th St.   Phone: (403) 489-4553
Edmonton, AB T5P 3X6   Steven A. Huesing, HCIB Secretariat

INSTITUTE OF LAW RESEARCH AND REFORM - LIBRARY
402 Law Centre
University of Alberta   Phone: (403) 432-5291
Edmonton, AB T6G 2H5

INTERNATIONAL OMBUDSMAN INSTITUTE - I.O.I. LIBRARY
Faculty of Law
University of Alberta   Phone: (403) 432-3196
Edmonton, AB T6G 2H5   Diane Conlon, Asst. to Exec.Dir.

LAW SOCIETY OF ALBERTA - EDMONTON LIBRARY
Law Courts Bldg., 1A Churchill Sq.   Phone: (403) 423-7601
Edmonton, AB T5J 0R2   Shih-Sheng Hu, Chf.Prov. Law Libn.

MILNER & STEER, BARRISTERS & SOLICITORS - LAW LIBRARY †
2900 Manulife Place
10180 101st St.   Phone: (403) 425-8830
Edmonton, AB T5J 3V5   A. Verwijk-O'Sullivan, Libn.

MISERICORDIA HOSPITAL - WEINLOS MEDICAL LIBRARY
16940 87th Ave.   Phone: (403) 484-8811
Edmonton, AB T5R 4H5   Francine Lapointe, Dir., Lib.Serv.

NEWMAN THEOLOGICAL COLLEGE - LIBRARY
15611 St. Albert Trail   Phone: (403) 459-6656
Edmonton, AB T5L 4H8   Shirley Anne Threndyle, Libn.

NORTH AMERICAN BAPTIST COLLEGE AND DIVINITY SCHOOL - LIBRARY
11523 23rd Ave.   Phone: (403) 988-5571
Edmonton, AB T6J 4T3   Arnold Rapske, Libn.

NORTHERN ALBERTA INSTITUTE OF TECHNOLOGY - LEARNING RESOURCE
  CENTRE
11762 106th St.   Phone: (403) 477-4375
Edmonton, AB T5G 2R1   Helga Kinnaird, Chf.Libn.

NORTHWEST BIBLE COLLEGE - J.C. COOKE LIBRARY
11617 106th Ave.   Phone: (403) 452-0808
Edmonton, AB T5H 0S1   Braden S. Fawcett, Libn.

NORTHWEST INDUSTRIES LTD. - TECHNICAL DATA CONTROL CENTRE
Edmonton Intl. Airport
P.O. Box 9864   Phone: (403) 955-6300
Edmonton, AB T5J 2T2   C.E. Buckley, Supv.

QUEEN'S BENCH - COURT OF APPEAL JUDGES' LIBRARY
Law Courts Bldg.
1A Churchill Sq.
Edmonton, AB T5J 0R2   Shih-Sheng Hu, Chf.Prov. Law Libn.

ROYAL ALEXANDRA HOSPITAL - MEDICAL LIBRARY
10240 Kingsway Ave.   Phone: (403) 474-3431
Edmonton, AB T5H 3V9   Deana Dryden, Libn.

ROYAL ALEXANDRA HOSPITAL - SCHOOL OF NURSING LIBRARY
10240 Kingsway Ave.   Phone: (403) 474-3431
Edmonton, AB T5H 3V9   E. Pass, Libn.

ST. STEPHEN'S COLLEGE - LIBRARY
University of Alberta   Phone: (403) 439-7311
Edmonton, AB T6G 2J6   Carol Mundie, Act.Libn.

STANLEY ASSOCIATES ENGINEERING, LTD. - LIBRARY
10512 169th St.   Phone: (403) 483-4777
Edmonton, AB T5P 3X6   Patricia Wilson, Libn.

SYNCRUDE CANADA, LTD. - RESEARCH AND DEVELOPMENT LIBRARY
P.O. Box 5790   Phone: (403) 464-8400
Edmonton, AB T6C 4G3   Peter J. Bates, Info.Spec.

UKRAINIAN MUSEUM OF CANADA - LIBRARY †
10611 110th Ave.   Phone: (403) 424-1530
Edmonton, AB T5H 1H7   Mrs. J. Verchomin, Dir.

UNDERWOOD MC LELLAN LTD. - INFORMATION SERVICES
17007 107th Ave.   Phone: (403) 483-7722
Edmonton, AB T5S 1G3   Jacquie Fenton, Hd., Info.Serv.

UNIVERSITY OF ALBERTA - BOREAL INSTITUTE FOR NORTHERN STUDIES -
  LIBRARY
CW 401 Biological Sciences Bldg.   Phone: (403) 432-4409
Edmonton, AB T6G 2E9   Mrs. G.A. Cooke, Libn.

UNIVERSITY OF ALBERTA - BRUCE PEEL SPECIAL COLLECTIONS LIBRARY
Rutherford South   Phone: (403) 432-5998
Edmonton, AB T6G 2J8   John W. Charles, Spec.Coll.Libn.

UNIVERSITY OF ALBERTA - CENTRE FOR THE STUDY OF MENTAL
  RETARDATION - LIBRARY
6-123A Education II   Phone: (403) 432-4439
Edmonton, AB T6G 2E1   Heidi Julien, Sec.

UNIVERSITY OF ALBERTA - COMPUTING SCIENCE READING ROOM
604 General Services Bldg.   Phone: (403) 432-3977
Edmonton, AB T6G 2H1   Jennifer Penny, Libn.

UNIVERSITY OF ALBERTA - DEPT. OF SOCIOLOGY - STANLEY TAYLOR
  SOCIOLOGY READING ROOM
Dept. of Sociology   Phone: (403) 439-1604
Edmonton, AB T6G 2H4   Kerri Calvert, Lib.Asst.

UNIVERSITY OF ALBERTA - DIVISION OF EDUCATIONAL RESEARCH -
  TECHNICAL LIBRARY
3-104 Education North   Phone: (403) 432-3762
Edmonton, AB T6G 2G5   Dr. Steve Hunka, Coord.

UNIVERSITY OF ALBERTA - FACULTE ST-JEAN - BIBLIOTHEQUE
8406 91st St.   Phone: (403) 468-1254
Edmonton, AB T6C 4G9   Juliette J. Henley, Act.Hd.Libn.

UNIVERSITY OF ALBERTA - H.T. COUTTS LIBRARY
Faculty of Education Bldg.   Phone: (403) 432-2371
Edmonton, AB T6G 2G5   Madge MacGown, Hd.

UNIVERSITY OF ALBERTA - HUMANITIES AND SOCIAL SCIENCES LIBRARY
Rutherford North   Phone: (403) 432-3794
Edmonton, AB T6G 2J4   B.J. Busch, Area Coord.

UNIVERSITY OF ALBERTA - HUMANITIES AND SOCIAL SCIENCES LIBRARY
  - GOVERNMENT PUBLICATIONS
                                             Phone: (403) 432-3776
Edmonton, AB T6G 2J8   Sally Manwaring, Hd., Govt.Pubn.Lib.

UNIVERSITY OF ALBERTA - JOHN W. SCOTT HEALTH SCIENCES LIBRARY
                                             Phone: (403) 432-3791
Edmonton, AB T6G 2B7   Sylvia R. Chetner, Act. Area Coord.

UNIVERSITY OF ALBERTA - LAW LIBRARY
Law Centre   Phone: (403) 432-5560
Edmonton, AB T6G 2H5   Lillian MacPherson, Law Libn.

UNIVERSITY OF ALBERTA - NUCLEAR PHYSICS LIBRARY
Nuclear Research Center   Phone: (403) 432-3637
Edmonton, AB T6G 2N5   G.M.T. Tratt, Sec.

UNIVERSITY OF ALBERTA - SCIENCE AND TECHNOLOGY LIBRARY
                                             Phone: (403) 432-2728
Edmonton, AB T6G 2J8   Margo Young, Area Coord.

UNIVERSITY OF ALBERTA - UNIVERSITY MAP COLLECTION
B-7 H.M. Tory Bldg.   Phone: (403) 432-4760
Edmonton, AB T6G 2H4 Ron Whistance-Smith, Univ. Map Curator

FAIRVIEW COLLEGE - LEARNING RESOURCES CENTRE
Box 3000   Phone: (403) 835-2213
Fairview, AB T0H 1L0   Olive V. Lancaster, Chm., LRC

SYNCRUDE CANADA, LTD. - OPERATIONS LIBRARY
Postal Bag 4009, Zone 3060   Phone: (403) 790-8773
Fort McMurray, AB T9H 3L1   Marcella Dankow, Lib.Techn.

SHERRITT GORDON MINES, LTD. - RESEARCH CENTRE LIBRARY
                                             Phone: (403) 998-6419
Fort Saskatchewan, AB T8L 2P2   J. Derek Sim, Libn.

QUEEN ELIZABETH II HOSPITAL - MEDICAL LIBRARY
10409 98th St.
Postal Bag 2600   Phone: (403) 538-7100
Grande Prairie, AB T8V 2E8

CANADA - AGRICULTURE CANADA - RESEARCH STATION, LACOMBE -
LIBRARY
Phone: (403) 782-3316
Lacombe, AB T0C 1S0   D.E. Waldern, Dir.

ALBERTA - DEPARTMENT OF THE ATTORNEY GENERAL - LAW SOCIETY
LIBRARY
Court House
320 4th St., S.   Phone: (403) 329-5639
Lethbridge, AB T1J 1Z8   Robert Leigh, Libn.

CANADA - AGRICULTURE CANADA - RESEARCH STATION, LETHBRIDGE -
LIBRARY
Phone: (403) 327-4561
Lethbridge, AB T1J 4B1   C.M. Cutler, Lib. Area Coord.

OLDS COLLEGE - LEARNING RESOURCES CENTRE - SPECIAL COLLECTIONS
Phone: (403) 556-8243
Olds, AB T0M 1P0   Garry Grisak, Coord., Lib.Serv.

ALBERTA HOSPITAL PONOKA - AHP LIBRARY
P.O. Box 1000   Phone: (403) 783-3351
Ponoka, AB T0C 2H0   Peter Managhan, Staff Libn.

CANADA - DEFENCE RESEARCH ESTABLISHMENT SUFFIELD -
INFORMATION SERVICES †
Phone: (403) 544-3701
Ralston, AB T0J 2N0   John G. Currie, Hd., Info.Serv.

MICHENER CENTRE - STAFF LIBRARY
Box 5002   Phone: (403) 343-5936
Red Deer, AB T4N 5Y5   Judith Benson, Libn.

RED DEER ADVOCATE - NEWSPAPER LIBRARY
2950 Bremner Ave.   Phone: (403) 343-2400
Red Deer, AB T4N 5G3   Patricia J. Goulet, Libn.

UNIVERSITY OF CALGARY - KANANASKIS ENVIRONMENTAL SCIENCES
CENTRE - LIBRARY
Phone: (403) 284-5355
Seebe, AB T0L 1X0   Grace LeBel, Libn.

PRAIRIE BIBLE INSTITUTE - LIBRARY
Phone: (403) 443-5511
Three Hills, AB T0M 2A0   Ron Jordahl, Libn.

ALBERTA ENVIRONMENTAL CENTRE - LIBRARY
Bag 4000   Phone: (403) 632-6767
Vegreville, AB T0B 4L0   Diana Lee, Hd., Info.Serv.

WAINWRIGHT GENERAL HOSPITAL - MEDICAL LIBRARY
Box 820   Phone: (403) 842-3324
Wainwright, AB T0B 4P0   Loretta Haire, Health Rec.Adm.

REYNOLDS MUSEUM - LIBRARY
4118 57th St.   Phone: (403) 352-5201
Wetaskiwin, AB T9A 2B6   Stanley G. Reynolds, Cur.

BRITISH COLUMBIA

WESTERN CANADIAN UNIVERSITIES - MARINE BIOLOGICAL SOCIETY -
DEVONIAN LIBRARY
Bamfield Marine Sta.   Phone: (604) 728-3301
Bamfield, BC V0R 1B0   Christine Milliken, Libn.

BRITISH COLUMBIA INSTITUTE OF TECHNOLOGY - LIBRARY SERVICES
DIVISION
3700 Willingdon Ave.   Phone: (604) 434-5734
Burnaby, BC V5G 3H2   Joseph E. Carver, Inst.Libn.

BRITISH COLUMBIA - MINISTRY OF HEALTH - MENTAL HEALTH SERVICES
LIBRARY
3405 Willingdon Ave.   Phone: (604) 434-4247
Burnaby, BC V5G 3H4   Joy Fourchalk, Libn.

BRITISH COLUMBIA TELEPHONE COMPANY - BUSINESS LIBRARY
3777 Kingsway, 5th Fl.   Phone: (604) 432-2671
Burnaby, BC V5H 3Z7   Elizabeth B. Murray, Libn.

BURNABY GENERAL HOSPITAL - DR. H.H.W. BROOKE MEMORIAL LIBRARY
3935 Kincaid St.   Phone: (604) 434-4211
Burnaby, BC V5G 2X6   Mr. Hoong Lim, Libn.

BURNABY AND NEW WESTMINSTER SCHOOL BOARDS - REGIONAL FILM
LIBRARY SERVICES
Schou Education Centre
4041 Canada Way   Phone: (604) 437-4511
Burnaby, BC V5G 1G6   R. Donald Lyon, Coord.

BURNABY SCHOOL BOARD - MEDIA LOANS
Schou Education Centre
4041 Canada Way   Phone: (604) 437-4511
Burnaby, BC V5G 1G6   R. Donald Lyon, Coord.

BURNABY SCHOOL BOARD - TEACHERS' PROFESSIONAL LIBRARY
Schou Education Centre
4041 Canada Way   Phone: (604) 437-4511
Burnaby, BC V5G 1G6

MICROTEL PACIFIC RESEARCH LTD. - TECHNICAL LIBRARY *
8999 Nelson Way   Phone: (604) 294-1471
Burnaby, BC V5A 4B5   V. Renzetti, Tech.Libn.

SIMON FRASER UNIVERSITY - LIBRARY - SPECIAL COLLECTIONS
Phone: (604) 291-3261
Burnaby, BC V5A 1S6   Percilla Groves, Spec.Coll.Libn.

CANADIAN MILITARY ENGINEERS MUSEUM - LIBRARY †
M.P.O. 612   Phone: (604) 858-3311
C.F.B. Chilliwack, BC V0X 2E0

WESTERN PENTECOSTAL BIBLE COLLEGE - LIBRARY
Box 1000   Phone: (604) 853-7491
Clayburn, BC V0X 1E0   Rev. Laurence M. Van Kleek, Libn.

CANADA - AGRICULTURE CANADA - RESEARCH STATION, KAMLOOPS -
LIBRARY †
3015 Ord Rd.   Phone: (604) 376-5565
Kamloops, BC V2B 8A9   J.D. McElgunn, Dir.

KOOTENAY LAKE HISTORICAL SOCIETY - LIBRARY
Box 537   Phone: (604) 353-2525
Kaslo, BC V0G 1M0   June Griswold, Cur.

YASODHARA ASHRAM SOCIETY - LIBRARY
Box 9   Phone: (604) 227-9224
Kootenay Bay, BC V0B 1X0   Dawn Spickler, Libn.

LANGLEY SCHOOL DISTRICT - RESOURCE CENTRE
19740 32nd Ave.   Phone: (604) 530-5151
Langley, BC V3A 4S1   Jean Gregson, Libn.

WESTMINSTER ABBEY - LIBRARY
Mission, BC V2V 4J2   Boniface Aicher, O.S.B., Libn.

CANADA - FISHERIES & OCEANS - PACIFIC BIOLOGICAL STATION -
LIBRARY
Phone: (604) 756-7071
Nanaimo, BC V9R 5K6   G. Miller, Hd., Lib.Serv.

NANAIMO CENTENNIAL MUSEUM - ARCHIVES
100 Cameron Rd.   Phone: (604) 753-1821
Nanaimo, BC V9R 2X1   Dick Ferre, Adm.

NANAIMO DAILY FREE PRESS - LIBRARY
223 Commercial St.
Box 69   Phone: (604) 753-3451
Nanaimo, BC V94 5K5   Richard Dunstan, City Editor

BRITISH COLUMBIA - MINISTRY OF FORESTS - NELSON FOREST REGION
LIBRARY
518 Lake St.   Phone: (604) 354-4181
Nelson, BC V1L 4C6   Jo White, Regional Rsrcs.Info.Ck.

CHAMBER OF MINES OF EASTERN BRITISH COLUMBIA - BUREAU OF
　　INFORMATION *
215 Hall St.　　　　　　　　　　　　　Phone: (604) 352-5242
Nelson, BC V1L 5X4　　　　　　　　　　George Murray, Mgr.

DAVID THOMPSON UNIVERSITY CENTRE - SPECIAL COLLECTIONS †
820 Tenth St.　　　　　　　　　　　　Phone: (604) 352-2241
Nelson, BC V1L 3C7　　　　　　　Ronald J. Welwood, Chm.

CANOCEAN RESOURCES LTD. - ENGINEERING LIBRARY
610 Derwent Way
New Westminster, BC V3M 5P8　　　　　Ronald V. Simmer, Libn.

INTERNATIONAL PACIFIC SALMON FISHERIES COMMISSION - LIBRARY
Box 30　　　　　　　　　　　　　　　Phone: (604) 521-3771
New Westminster, BC V3L 4X9　　　　　Mrs. Fumi Sato, Libn.

ROYAL COLUMBIAN HOSPITAL - LIBRARY
330 E. Columbia St.　　　　　　　　Phone: (604) 520-4255
New Westminster, BC V3L 3W7　　　　　Ms. S. Abzinger, Libn.

INSURANCE CORPORATION OF BRITISH COLUMBIA - LAW LIBRARY
151 W. Esplanade, Rm. 505　　　　　Phone: (604) 661-6288
North Vancouver, BC V7M 3H9　　　Norman Churchland, Hd.Libn.

LIONS GATE HOSPITAL - DR. H. CARSON GRAHAM MEMORIAL LIBRARY
15th St. at St. Georges Ave.　　　　　Phone: (604) 988-3131
North Vancouver, BC V7L 2L7　　　Sharon M. Robertson, Libn.

CANADA - NATIONAL RESEARCH COUNCIL - CISTI - DOMINION RADIO
　　ASTROPHYSICAL OBSERVATORY BRANCH
Box 248　　　　　　　　　　　　　Phone: (604) 497-5321
Penticton, BC V2A 6K3　　　　　　　　W. Gully, Libn.

RIVERVIEW HOSPITAL - STAFF REFERENCE LIBRARY
500 Lougheed Hwy.　　　　　　　　Phone: (604) 521-1911
Port Coquitlam, BC V3C 1J0　　Min-Ja Laubental, Dir., Lib.Serv.

PRINCE GEORGE CITIZEN - NEWSPAPER LIBRARY
150 Brunswick St.　　　　　　　　　Phone: (604) 562-2441
Prince George, BC V2L 4T1　　　　　Sheryl Timmer, Libn.

PRINCE GEORGE CITY PLANNING DEPARTMENT - PLANNING LIBRARY
1100 Patricia Blvd.　　　　　　　　Phone: (604) 564-5151
Prince George, BC V2L 3V9　　　　Kent Sedgwick, Libn.

BRITISH COLUMBIA GENEALOGICAL SOCIETY - REFERENCE LIBRARY
Box 94371　　　　　　　　　　　　Phone: (604) 274-3659
Richmond, BC V6Y 2A8　　　　　　Alice Marwood, Libn.

BRITISH COLUMBIA - MINISTRY OF EDUCATION - PROVINCIAL
　　EDUCATIONAL MEDIA CENTRE
7351 Elmbridge Way　　　　　　　　Phone: (604) 278-4961
Richmond, BC V6X 1B8　　　　　　　B.A. Black, Dir.

BRITISH COLUMBIA - WORKER'S COMPENSATION BOARD - LIBRARY
6951 Westminster Hwy.　　　　　　　Phone: (604) 273-2266
Richmond, BC V7C 1C6　　　　　　Barbara L. Nield, Libn.

ROSSLAND HISTORICAL MUSEUM ASSOCIATION - ARCHIVES
Box 26　　　　　　　　　　　　　　Phone: (604) 362-7722
Rossland, BC V0G 1Y0　　　　　　Joyce Tadevic, Archv.

CANADA - AGRICULTURE CANADA - SAANICHTON RESEARCH & PLANT
　　QUARANTINE STATION - LIBRARY
8801 E. Saanich Rd.　　　　　　　　Phone: (604) 656-1173
Sidney, BC V8L 1H3　　　　　　　Peggy Watson, Libn.

INSTITUTE OF OCEAN SCIENCES - LIBRARY *
9860 W. Saanich Rd.
Box 6000　　　　　　　　　　　　　Phone: (604) 656-8392
Sidney, BC V8L 4B2　　　　　　　Sharon Thomson, Libn.

CANADA - AGRICULTURE CANADA - RESEARCH STATION, SUMMERLAND -
　　LIBRARY
　　　　　　　　　　　　　　　　Phone: (604) 494-7711
Summerland, BC V0H 1Z0　　　　　Kathleen Neer, Libn.

SURREY MUSEUM - ARCHIVES
Cloverdale
Box 1006　　　　　　　　　　　　　Phone: (604) 574-5744
Surrey, BC V3S 4P5　　　　　　　D.R. Hooser, Cur.

COMINCO LTD. - CENTRAL TECHNICAL LIBRARY
　　　　　　　　　　　　　　　　Phone: (604) 364-4409
Trail, BC V1R 4L8　　　　　　Robert G. Lewis, Lib.Supv.

WILLIAMS (C.S.) CLINIC - LIBRARY
901 Helena St.　　　　　　　　　　Phone: (604) 368-5211
Trail, BC V1R 3X4　　　　　Dr. L. Simonetta, Lib.Chm.

ANGLICAN CHURCH OF CANADA - ECCLESIASTICAL PROV. OF BRITISH
　　COLUMBIA & DIOCESE OF NEW WESTMINSTER - ARCHV.
6050 Chancellor Blvd.　　　　　　　Phone: (604) 228-9031
Vancouver, BC V6T 1X3　　　　　R. Garth Walker, Archv.

ASSOCIATION OF BOOK PUBLISHERS OF BRITISH COLUMBIA - LIBRARY
1622 W. 7th Ave.　　　　　　　　　Phone: (604) 734-1611
Vancouver, BC V6J 1S5　　　Barbara Pulling, Project Coord.

B.C. HYDRO - ENGINEERING LIBRARY
555 W. Hastings St.
Box 12121　　　　　　　　　　　　Phone: (604) 663-2894
Vancouver, BC V6B 4T6　　　　Judith Bradshaw, Asst.Libn.

B.C. HYDRO - LIBRARY
970 Burrard St.　　　　　　　　　　Phone: (604) 663-2416
Vancouver, BC V6Z 1Y3　　　　Elizabeth McLaren, Libn.

BARBEAU, MC KERCHER & COLLINGWOOD, BARRISTERS & SOLICITORS -
　　LIBRARY
1066 W. Hastings St., 24th Fl.　　　Phone: (604) 688-9411
Vancouver, BC V6E 2E6　　　　Johanna Sigurdson, Libn.

BRITISH COLUMBIA ALCOHOL AND DRUG PROGRAMS - LIBRARY †
1755 W. Broadway, 2nd Fl.　　　　Phone: (604) 731-9121
Vancouver, BC V6J 4S5　　　　W. Holmes, Lib.Techn.

BRITISH COLUMBIA CENTRAL CREDIT UNION - RESOURCE CENTRE
P.O. Box 2038　　　　　　　　　　Phone: (604) 734-2511
Vancouver, BC V6B 3R9　　　　Paula Murray, Lib.Techn.

BRITISH COLUMBIA - COUNCIL OF FOREST INDUSTRIES OF BRITISH
　　COLUMBIA - LIBRARY
1055 W. Hastings St., Suite 1800　　Phone: (604) 684-0211
Vancouver, BC V6E 2H1　　　　　Sheila Foley, Libn.

BRITISH COLUMBIA HEALTH ASSOCIATION (BCHA) - LIBRARY
440 Cambie St.　　　　　　　　　　Phone: (604) 683-7421
Vancouver, BC V6B 2N6　　　　Carolyn Hall, Lib.Techn.

BRITISH COLUMBIA - JUDGES' LIBRARY - SUPERIOR & COUNTY COURTS
Law Courts, 800 Smithe St.　　　　Phone: (604) 668-2799
Vancouver, BC V6Z 2E1　　　　　A. Rector, Libn.

BRITISH COLUMBIA LAW LIBRARY FOUNDATION - VANCOUVER
　　COURTHOUSE LIBRARY
800 Smithe St.　　　　　　　　　　Phone: (604) 689-7295
Vancouver, BC V6Z 2E1　　　Maureen B. McCormick, Exec.Dir.

BRITISH COLUMBIA - MINISTRY OF HUMAN RESOURCES - LIBRARY
800 Cassiar St.　　　　　　　　　　Phone: (604) 387-6415
Vancouver, BC V5K 4N6　　　　　M.J. Love, Libn.

BRITISH COLUMBIA RESEARCH COUNCIL - LIBRARY
3650 Wesbrook Mall　　　　　　　Phone: (604) 224-4331
Vancouver, BC V6S 2L2　　　　　Viona Esen, Libn.

BRITISH COLUMBIA RESEARCH COUNCIL - URANIUM INFORMATION
　　CENTRE
3650 Wesbrook Mall　　　　　　　Phone: (604) 224-4331
Vancouver, BC V6S 2L2　　　　Viona Esen, Res.Libn.

BRITISH COLUMBIA RESOURCES INVESTMENT CORPORATION -
　　CORPORATE INFORMATION CENTER
2600-1177 W. Hastings St.　　　　Phone: (604) 687-2600
Vancouver, BC V6E 4B9

BRITISH COLUMBIA TEACHERS' FEDERATION - RESOURCES CENTRE
2235 Burrard St.   Phone: (604) 731-8121
Vancouver, BC V6J 3H9   Teresa M. Murphy, Libn.

BRITISH COLUMBIA UTILITIES COMMISSION - LIBRARY
2100-1177 W. Hastings St.   Phone: (604) 689-1831
Vancouver, BC V6E 2L3   C. Brian Tu, Mgr., Info.Serv.

BRITISH COLUMBIA AND YUKON CHAMBER OF MINES - LIBRARY
840 W. Hastings St.   Phone: (604) 681-5328
Vancouver, BC V6C 1C8   Jack M. Patterson, Mgr.

BULL, HOUSSER AND TUPPER - LIBRARY
3000 Royal Centre
1055 W. Georgia
P.O. Box 11130   Phone: (604) 687-6575
Vancouver, BC V6E 3R3   Susan Daly, Libn.

CANADA - AGRICULTURE CANADA - RESEARCH STATION, VANCOUVER -
    LIBRARY
6660 N.W. Marine Dr.   Phone: (604) 224-4355
Vancouver, BC V6T 1X2   C.M. Cutler, Lib. Area Coord.

CANADA - ATMOSPHERIC ENVIRONMENT SERVICE - PACIFIC REGION -
    LIBRARY
700-1200 W. 73rd Ave.   Phone: (604) 732-4830
Vancouver, BC V6P 6H9   D.A. Faulkner, Meteorologist

CANADA - FISHERIES & OCEANS - FISHERIES MANAGEMENT REGIONAL
    LIBRARY
1090 W. Pender St.   Phone: (604) 666-3851
Vancouver, BC V6E 2P1   Paulette Westlake, Hd., Lib.Serv.

CANADA - GEOLOGICAL SURVEY OF CANADA - CORDILLERAN GEOLOGY
    LIBRARY
100 W. Pender St., 5th Fl.   Phone: (604) 666-3812
Vancouver, BC V6B 1R8   Mary Akehurst, Libn.

CANADA - HEALTH AND WELFARE CANADA - HEALTH PROTECTION
    BRANCH - REGIONAL LIBRARY
1001 W. Pender St., 6th Fl.   Phone: (604) 666-3147
Vancouver, BC V6E 2M7   Elizabeth Hardacre, Lib.Techn.

CANADA - STATISTICS CANADA - ADVISORY SERVICES - VANCOUVER
    REFERENCE CENTRE
1145 Robson St.   Phone: (604) 666-3695
Vancouver, BC V6E 3W8   C.G. Lenoski, Asst. Regional Dir.

CANADIAN MUSIC CENTRE - BRITISH COLUMBIA REGIONAL OFFICE -
    LIBRARY
2007 W. 4th Ave.   Phone: (604) 734-4622
Vancouver, BC V6J 1N3   Colin Miles, Regional Dir.

CANCER CONTROL AGENCY OF BRITISH COLUMBIA - LIBRARY
2656 Heather St.   Phone: (604) 873-6212
Vancouver, BC V5Z 3J3   David Noble, Libn.

CARR (Emily) COLLEGE OF ART - LIBRARY
1399 Johnston St.
Granville Island   Phone: (604) 687-2345
Vancouver, BC V6H 3R9   Ken Chamberlain, Hd.Libn.

CHINESE NATIONALIST LEAGUE OF CANADA - LIBRARY †
529 Gore Ave.   Phone: (604) 681-6022
Vancouver, BC V6A 2Z6   James K. Cheng, Chf.Libn.

COLLEGE OF PHYSICIANS AND SURGEONS OF BRITISH COLUMBIA -
    MEDICAL LIBRARY SERVICE
Keith Library
1807 W. 10th Ave.   Phone: (604) 736-5551
Vancouver, BC V6J 2A9   C. William Fraser, Dir.

COMINCO LTD. - INFORMATION SERVICES
200 Granville Sq., 24th Fl.   Phone: (604) 682-0611
Vancouver, BC V6C 2R2   Grace E. Rogozinska, Info.Anl.

CP AIR - ENGINEERING LIBRARY
One Grant McConachie Way
Vancouver International Airport
Vancouver, BC V7B 1V1   Phone: (604) 270-5211

DAVIS & COMPANY - LAW LIBRARY
1400-1030 W. Georgia St.   Phone: (604) 687-9444
Vancouver, BC V6E 3C2   Joan Mulholland, Libn.

FARRIS, VAUGHAN, WILLS & MURPHY - LIBRARY
700 W. Georgia St.
Box 10026   Phone: (604) 684-9151
Vancouver, BC V7Y 1B3   Fiona Anderson, Libn.

FORINTEK CANADA CORPORATION - WESTERN LABORATORY - LIBRARY
6620 N.W. Marine Dr.   Phone: (604) 224-3221
Vancouver, BC V6T 1X2   Mrs. Marion E. Johnson, Hd., Info.Rsrcs.

FRASER HYNDMAN, BARRISTERS & SOLICITORS - LAW LIBRARY
32nd Fl., Four Bentall Centre
1055 Dunsmuir St.
P.O. Box 49360   Phone: (604) 687-3216
Vancouver, BC V7X 1P2   Gillian Crabtree, Law Libn.

GREATER VANCOUVER REGIONAL DISTRICT - LIBRARY
2294 W. 10th Ave.   Phone: (604) 731-1155
Vancouver, BC V6K 2H9   Frances Christopherson, Libn.

THE MC ELHANNEY GROUP LTD. - INFORMATION CENTRE
1166 Alberni St., Suite 200   Phone: (604) 683-8521
Vancouver, BC V6E 3Z3   Patricia B. Daum, Info.Coord.

MAC MILLAN BLOEDEL RESEARCH LIMITED - LIBRARY
3350 E. Broadway   Phone: (604) 254-5151
Vancouver, BC V5M 4E6   Diana Wilimovsky, Supv., Info.Serv.

NORTHWEST BAPTIST THEOLOGICAL COLLEGE AND SEMINARY - LIBRARY
3358 S.E. Marine Dr.   Phone: (604) 433-2475
Vancouver, BC V5S 3W3   W.B. Badke, Libn.

PACIFIC PRESS, LTD. - PRESS LIBRARY
2250 Granville St.   Phone: (604) 732-2519
Vancouver, BC V6H 3G2   Shirley E. Mooney, Libn.

PLACER DEVELOPMENT, LTD. - LIBRARY
Bentall Postal Sta., P.O. Box 49330   Phone: (604) 682-7082
Vancouver, BC V7X 1P1   Linda Martin, Libn.

PRICE WATERHOUSE - AUDIT LIBRARY
1075 W. Georgia St., No. 1500   Phone: (604) 682-4711
Vancouver, BC V6E 3G1   Janet A. Parkinson, Libn.

REGISTERED NURSES' ASSOCIATION OF BRITISH COLUMBIA - LIBRARY
2855 Arbutus St.   Phone: (604) 736-7331
Vancouver, BC V6J 3Y8   Ilka Abbott, Libn.

RUSSELL AND DUMOULIN - LIBRARY
MacMillan Bloedel Bldg., 17th Fl.
1075 W. Georgia St.   Phone: (604) 688-3411
Vancouver, BC V6E 3G2   Diana E. Hunt, Libn.

SATELLITE VIDEO EXCHANGE SOCIETY - VIDEO INN LIBRARY
261 Powell St.   Phone: (604) 688-4336
Vancouver, BC V6A 1G3   Julie Healy

TECK MINING GROUP LTD. - LIBRARY
1199 W. Hastings St.   Phone: (604) 687-1117
Vancouver, BC V6E 2K5   Elizabeth Watson

TOUCHE, ROSS AND COMPANY - LIBRARY AND INFORMATION CENTER
Suite 700 Board of Trade
1177 W. Hastings   Phone: (604) 669-3343
Vancouver, BC V6E 2L2   C. Iona Douglas, Libn.

UNITED NATIONS - CENTRE FOR HUMAN SETTLEMENTS - INFORMATION
    OFFICE
University of British Columbia
2206 E. Mall   Phone: (604) 228-5095
Vancouver, BC V6T 1W5   James Carney, Info.Off.

UNITED WAY OF THE LOWER MAINLAND - SOCIAL PLANNING AND
    RESEARCH DEPARTMENT LIBRARY
1625 W. 8th Ave.   Phone: (604) 731-7781
Vancouver, BC V6J 1T9   Jeanette Hall, Asst.Libn.

UNIVERSITY OF BRITISH COLUMBIA - ASIAN STUDIES LIBRARY
1871 W. Mall   Phone: (604) 228-2427
Vancouver, BC V6T 1W5   Tung-King Ng, Hd.

UNIVERSITY OF BRITISH COLUMBIA - BIOMEDICAL BRANCH LIBRARY
Vancouver General Hospital
700 W. 10th Ave.   Phone: (604) 875-4505
Vancouver, BC V5Z 1L5   George C. Freeman, Hd., Biomed.Br.

UNIVERSITY OF BRITISH COLUMBIA - CHARLES CRANE MEMORIAL
  LIBRARY
1874 East Mall   Phone: (604) 228-6111
Vancouver, BC V6T 1W5   Paul E. Thiele, Libn. & Hd.

UNIVERSITY OF BRITISH COLUMBIA - CURRICULUM LABORATORY
Scarfe Bldg., 2125 Main Mall   Phone: (604) 228-5378
Vancouver, BC V6T 1Z5   Howard Hurt, Hd.

UNIVERSITY OF BRITISH COLUMBIA - DATA LIBRARY
6356 Agricultural Rd., Rm. 206   Phone: (604) 228-5587
Vancouver, BC V6T 1W5   Ms. Laine Ruus, Hd., Data Lib.

UNIVERSITY OF BRITISH COLUMBIA - DEPARTMENT OF GEOGRAPHY -
  MAP AND AIR PHOTO CENTRE
2075 Wesbrook Pl.   Phone: (604) 228-3048
Vancouver, BC V6T 1W5   Rosemary J. Hadley, Map Libn.

UNIVERSITY OF BRITISH COLUMBIA - ERIC W. HAMBER LIBRARY
Children's Hospital
4480 Oak St.   Phone: (604) 875-2154
Vancouver, BC V6H 3V4   Ann M.A. Nelson, Libn.

UNIVERSITY OF BRITISH COLUMBIA - FINE ARTS DIVISION
University Library, 1956 Main Mall Phone: (604) 228-2720
Vancouver, BC V6T 1Y3   Melva J. Dwyer, Hd.

UNIVERSITY OF BRITISH COLUMBIA - GOVERNMENT PUBLICATIONS &
  MICROFORMS DIVISIONS
University Library   Phone: (604) 228-2584
Vancouver, BC V6T 1Y3   Suzanne Dodson, Hd.

UNIVERSITY OF BRITISH COLUMBIA - HUMANITIES AND SOCIAL
  SCIENCES DIVISION
University Library   Phone: (604) 228-2411
Vancouver, BC V6T 1Y3   Charles F. Forbes, Hd.

UNIVERSITY OF BRITISH COLUMBIA - LAW LIBRARY
1822 East Mall   Phone: (604) 228-2275
Vancouver, BC V6T 1W5   Thomas J. Shorthouse, Law Libn.

UNIVERSITY OF BRITISH COLUMBIA - MAC MILLAN FORESTRY/
  AGRICULTURE LIBRARY
MacMillan Bldg., 2357 Main Mall   Phone: (604) 228-3445
Vancouver, BC V6T 2A2   Mary W. Macaree, Hd.

UNIVERSITY OF BRITISH COLUMBIA - MAP DIVISION
University Library   Phone: (604) 228-2231
Vancouver, BC V6T 1Y3   Maureen F. Wilson, Hd.

UNIVERSITY OF BRITISH COLUMBIA - MARJORIE SMITH LIBRARY
School of Social Work
6201 Cecil Green Pk. Rd.   Phone: (604) 228-2242
Vancouver, BC V6T 1W5   Judith Frye, Hd.

UNIVERSITY OF BRITISH COLUMBIA - MATHEMATICS LIBRARY
1984 Main Mall   Phone: (604) 228-2667
Vancouver, BC V6T 1W5   Rein J. Brongers, Hd.

UNIVERSITY OF BRITISH COLUMBIA - MINING & METALLURGICAL
  READING ROOM
6350 Stores Rd.   Phone: (604) 228-2540
Vancouver, BC V6V 1E4   A.E. Hall, Asst.Prof.

UNIVERSITY OF BRITISH COLUMBIA - MUSIC LIBRARY
6361 Memorial Rd.   Phone: (604) 228-3589
Vancouver, BC V6T 1W5   Hans Burndorfer, Hd.

UNIVERSITY OF BRITISH COLUMBIA - ST. PAUL'S HOSPITAL HEALTH
  SCIENCES LIBRARY
1081 Burrard St.   Phone: (604) 682-2344
Vancouver, BC V6Z 1Y6   Barbara J. Saint, Hd.

UNIVERSITY OF BRITISH COLUMBIA - SCHOOL OF LIBRARIANSHIP
  READING ROOM
1956 Main Mall, Rm. 831   Phone: (604) 228-2446
Vancouver, BC V6T 1Y3   Margaret Burke, Libn.

UNIVERSITY OF BRITISH COLUMBIA - SCIENCE DIVISION
University Library   Phone: (604) 228-3295
Vancouver, BC V6T 1Y3   Rein J. Brongers, Hd.

UNIVERSITY OF BRITISH COLUMBIA - SPECIAL COLLECTIONS DIVISION
University Library
1956 Main Mall   Phone: (604) 228-2521
Vancouver, BC V6T 1Y3   Anne Yandle, Hd.

UNIVERSITY OF BRITISH COLUMBIA - SPENCER ENTOMOLOGICAL
  MUSEUM - LIBRARY
Dept. of Zoology   Phone: (604) 228-3379
Vancouver, BC V6T 2A9   G.G.E. Scudder, Dir.

UNIVERSITY OF BRITISH COLUMBIA - WILSON RECORDINGS COLLECTION
1958 Main Mall   Phone: (604) 228-2534
Vancouver, BC V6T 1W5   Doug Kaye, Hd.

UNIVERSITY OF BRITISH COLUMBIA - WOODWARD BIOMEDICAL LIBRARY
2198 Health Sciences Mall   Phone: (604) 228-2762
Vancouver, BC V6T 1W5   Anna R. Leith, Hd.

VANCOUVER ART GALLERY - LIBRARY
750 Hornby St.   Phone: (604) 682-5621
Vancouver, BC V6Z 2H7   Catherine Cowan, Libn.

VANCOUVER BOARD OF TRADE - RESOURCE LIBRARY †
5th Fl., 1177 W. Hastings St.   Phone: (604) 681-2111
Vancouver, BC V6E 2K3   Maureen W. Devine, Res.Libn.

VANCOUVER MUSEUMS & PLANETARIUM ASSOCIATION - LIBRARY AND
  RESOURCE CENTRE
1100 Chestnut St.   Phone: (604) 736-4431
Vancouver, BC V6J 3J9   Norah J. McLaren, Libn.

VANCOUVER PUBLIC LIBRARY - BUSINESS & ECONOMICS DIVISION
750 Burrard St.   Phone: (604) 682-5911
Vancouver, BC V6Z 1X5   Barbara Bell, Hd.

VANCOUVER SCHOOL OF THEOLOGY - LIBRARY
6050 Chancellor Blvd.   Phone: (604) 228-9031
Vancouver, BC V6T 1X3   Elizabeth Hannon, Libn.

VANCOUVER TALMUD TORAH SCHOOL - LIBRARY
998 W. 26th Ave.   Phone: (604) 736-7307
Vancouver, BC V5Z 2G1   Marylile Gill, Teacher/Libn.

VANCOUVER TEACHERS' PROFESSIONAL LIBRARY
Teacher Centre, 123 E. 6th Ave.   Phone: (604) 874-2617
Vancouver, BC V5T 1J6   Linda Dunbar, Lib.Techn.

VANCOUVER VOCATIONAL INSTITUTE - LIBRARY
250 West Pender St.   Phone: (604) 681-8111
Vancouver, BC V6B 1S9   Ross M. Henderson, Campus Libn.

WESTCOAST TRANSMISSION COMPANY LIMITED - LIBRARY
1333 W. Georgia St., 14th Fl.   Phone: (604) 664-5517
Vancouver, BC V6E 3K9   Beatrice P. Yakimchuk, Libn.

ART GALLERY OF GREATER VICTORIA - LIBRARY
1040 Moss St.   Phone: (604) 384-4101
Victoria, BC V8V 4P1   Jean Paige, Libn.

BRITISH COLUMBIA - JUDGES' LIBRARY - SUPERIOR & COUNTY COURTS *
Law Courts, 850 Burdett Ave.
Victoria, BC V8W 1B4

BRITISH COLUMBIA - LEGISLATIVE LIBRARY
Parliament Bldgs. Phone: (604) 387-6510
Victoria, BC V8V 1X4

BRITISH COLUMBIA - MINISTRY OF CONSUMER AND CORPORATE AFFAIRS
- LIBRARY SERVICES
940 Blanshard St., 3rd Fl. Phone: (604) 387-1251
Victoria, BC V8W 3E6 Frances Baskerville, Hd.Libn.

BRITISH COLUMBIA - MINISTRY OF EDUCATION - LIBRARY
Parliament Bldgs. Phone: (604) 387-6279
Victoria, BC V8V 2M4 Norma Lofthouse, Libn.

BRITISH COLUMBIA - MINISTRY OF ENERGY, MINES AND PETROLEUM
RESOURCES - LIBRARY †
Douglas Bldg., Rm. 430 Phone: (604) 387-6407
Victoria, BC V8V 1X4 S.E. Ferris, Libn.

BRITISH COLUMBIA - MINISTRY OF ENVIRONMENT - LIBRARY
780 Blanshard St. Phone: (604) 387-5194
Victoria, BC V8V 1X5 Marg Palmer, Ministry Libn.

BRITISH COLUMBIA - MINISTRY OF ENVIRONMENT - MAPS-B.C.
Parliament Bldgs.
553 Superior St., Rm. 110 Phone: (604) 387-1441
Victoria, BC V8V 1X5 C. Reich, Supv.

BRITISH COLUMBIA - MINISTRY OF FORESTS - LIBRARY
Parliament Bldgs.
1450 Government St. Phone: (604) 387-3628
Victoria, BC V8W 3E7 S.E. Barker, Mgr.

BRITISH COLUMBIA - MINISTRY OF HEALTH - LIBRARY
1515 Blanshard St., 5th Fl. Phone: (604) 386-3166
Victoria, BC V8W 3C8 Elizabeth M. Woodworth, Libn.

BRITISH COLUMBIA - MINISTRY OF INDUSTRY & SMALL BUSINESS
DEVELOPMENT - LIBRARY
Legislative Bldgs. Phone: (604) 387-3765
Victoria, BC V8V 1X4 Helen G. Bruce, Libn.

BRITISH COLUMBIA - MINISTRY OF LANDS, PARKS AND HOUSING - PARKS
LIBRARY
Parliament Bldgs. Phone: (604) 387-1067
Victoria, BC V8V 1X4 Shirley Desrosiers, Libn.

BRITISH COLUMBIA - MINISTRY OF PROVINCIAL SEC. & GOVERNMENT
SERV. - HERITAGE CONSRV. BR. - RESOURCE INFO. CTR.
1016 Langley St. Phone: (604) 387-6956
Victoria, BC V8W 1V8 Anne Morgan, Br.Libn.

BRITISH COLUMBIA - MINISTRY OF PROVINCIAL SECRETARY &
GOVERNMENT SERVICES - PROVINCIAL ARCHIVES
Parliament Bldgs. Phone: (604) 387-5885
Victoria, BC V8V 1X4 John A. Bovey, Prov.Archv.

BRITISH COLUMBIA - MINISTRY OF PROVINCIAL SEC. & GOVERNMENT
SERV. - PROVINCIAL ARCHIVES - MAP COLLECTION
Parliament Bldgs. Phone: (604) 387-6516
Victoria, BC V8V 1X4 David R. Chamberlin, Hd., Lib. & Maps Sect.

BRITISH COLUMBIA - MINISTRY OF TOURISM - PHOTOGRAPHIC LIBRARY
†
1117 Wharf St., 3rd Fl. Phone: (604) 387-6490
Victoria, BC V8W 2Z2 K.L. Gibbs, Act.Dir.

BRITISH COLUMBIA SYSTEMS CORPORATION - LIBRARY
4000 Seymour Place Phone: (604) 389-3941
Victoria, BC V8X 4S8 Wendie A. McHenry, Coord., Lib.Serv.

CANADA - CANADIAN FORESTRY SERVICE - PACIFIC FOREST RESEARCH
CENTRE - LIBRARY
506 W. Burnside Rd. Phone: (604) 388-3811
Victoria, BC V8Z 1M5 Alice Solyma, Libn.

CANADA - DEFENCE RESEARCH ESTABLISHMENT PACIFIC - LIBRARY
Forces Mail Office Phone: (604) 388-1665
Victoria, BC V0S 1B0 L.B. Jensen, Act.Hd., Info.Serv.

CANADA - NATIONAL RESEARCH COUNCIL - CISTI - DOMINION
ASTROPHYSICAL OBSERVATORY BRANCH
5071 W. Saanich Rd.
R.R. 5 Phone: (604) 388-0298
Victoria, BC V8X 3X3 Eric S. LeBlanc, Libn.

MARITIME MUSEUM OF BRITISH COLUMBIA - LIBRARY
28-30 Bastion Square Phone: (604) 385-4222
Victoria, BC V8W 1H9 C.H. Shaw, Dir.

PEARSON (Lester B.) COLLEGE OF THE PACIFIC - LIBRARY
RR 1 Phone: (604) 478-5591
Victoria, BC V8X 3W9 Margaret McAvity, Libn.

ROYAL ROADS MILITARY COLLEGE - LIBRARY †
Phone: (604) 388-1483
Victoria, BC V0S 1B0 C.C. Whitlock, Chf.Libn.

UNIVERSITY OF VICTORIA - KATHARINE MALTWOOD COLLECTION
P.O. Box 1700 Phone: (604) 477-6911
Victoria, BC V8W 2Y2 Martin Segger, Cur.

UNIVERSITY OF VICTORIA - LAW LIBRARY
P.O. Box 2300 Phone: (604) 477-6911
Victoria, BC V8W 3B1 Diana M. Priestly, Law Libn.

UNIVERSITY OF VICTORIA - MC PHERSON LIBRARY - CURRICULUM
LABORATORY
P.O. Box 1800 Phone: (604) 477-6911
Victoria, BC V8W 3H5 Donald E. Hamilton, Educ.Libn.

UNIVERSITY OF VICTORIA - MC PHERSON LIBRARY - MUSIC & AUDIO
COLLECTION
P.O. Box 1800 Phone: (604) 477-6911
Victoria, BC V8W 3H5 Sandra Benet, Music Libn.

UNIVERSITY OF VICTORIA - MC PHERSON LIBRARY - SPECIAL
COLLECTIONS
Box 1800 Phone: (604) 477-6911
Victoria, BC V8W 3H5 Howard B. Gerwing, Rare Bks.Libn.

UNIVERSITY OF VICTORIA - MC PHERSON LIBRARY - UNIVERSITY MAP
COLLECTION
P.O. Box 1800 Phone: (604) 477-6911
Victoria, BC V8W 3H5 M.A. Brian Turnbull, Map Cur.

VICTORIA CONSERVATORY OF MUSIC - LIBRARY
839 Academy Close Phone: (604) 386-5311
Victoria, BC V8V 2X8 Larry de la Haye, Libn.

VICTORIA GENERAL HOSPITAL (North) - HEALTH SCIENCES LIBRARY *
35 Helmecken Rd. Phone: (604) 727-4212
Victoria, BC V8Z 6R5 George E.A. Zizka, Libn.

VICTORIA GENERAL HOSPITAL (South) - GERIATRIC MEDICINE AND
GERONTOLOGY †
841 Fairfield Rd. Phone: (604) 388-9121
Victoria, BC V8V 2VD George E.A. Zizka, Health Sci.Libn.

VICTORIA MEDICAL SOCIETY/ROYAL JUBILEE HOSPITAL - LIBRARY
1900 Fort St. Phone: (604) 595-9723
Victoria, BC V8R 1J8 Johann van Reenen, Libn.

VICTORIA TIMES-COLONIST - LIBRARY
P.O. Box 300 Phone: (604) 382-7211
Victoria, BC V8W 2N4 Corinne Wong, Libn.

BAROQUE STRINGS OF VANCOUVER - LIBRARY
104-1425 Esquimalt Ave. Phone: (604) 922-4849
West Vancouver, BC V7T 1L1 Ronald L. Milne, Libn.

CANADA - ENVIRONMENTAL PROTECTION SERVICE - PACIFIC REGION
LIBRARY
2nd Fl., Kapilano 100
Park Royal South Phone: (604) 666-6711
West Vancouver, BC V7M 2N2 Andrew Fabro, Libn.

MANITOBA

BRANDON GENERAL HOSPITAL - LIBRARY SERVICES
150 McTavish Ave., E.   Phone: (204) 728-3321
Brandon, MB R7A 2B3   Kathy Eagleton, Dir.

BRANDON MENTAL HEALTH CENTRE - REFERENCE AND LENDING LIBRARY
Box 420   Phone: (204) 728-7110
Brandon, MB R7A 5Z5   Marjorie G. McKinnon, Lib.Techn.

BRANDON SUN - LIBRARY
501 Rosser Ave.   Phone: (204) 727-2451
Brandon, MB R7A 5Z6   Gloria Yakimenko, Libn.

BRANDON UNIVERSITY - CHRISTIE EDUCATION LIBRARY *
Eighteenth St.   Phone: (204) 728-9520
Brandon, MB R7A 6A9   Mrs. M. Nichols, Libn.

BRANDON UNIVERSITY - MUSIC LIBRARY *
Music Bldg.   Phone: (204) 728-9520
Brandon, MB R7A 6A9   June D. Jones, Music Libn.

CANADA - AGRICULTURE CANADA - RESEARCH STATION, MORDEN -
LIBRARY
P.O. Box 3001   Phone: (204) 822-4471
Morden, MB R0G 1J0   Mrs. D. Martinook, Sec.

WINNIPEG BIBLE COLLEGE/WINNIPEG THEOLOGICAL SEMINARY -
LIBRARY
                                         Phone: (204) 284-2923
Otterburne, MB R0A 1G0   Karen Friesen, Libn.

ATOMIC ENERGY OF CANADA, LTD. - WNRE LIBRARY *
Whiteshell Nuclear Research Establishment   Phone: (204) 753-2311
Pinawa, MB R0E 1L0   Gladys Gibson, Chf.Libn.

DELTA WATERFOWL RESEARCH STATION - DAVID WINTON BELL
MEMORIAL LIBRARY
R.R. 1   Phone: (204) 239-1900
Portage La Prairie, MB R1N 3A1   Shirley Rutledge, Libn.

MANITOBA - DEPARTMENT OF COMMUNITY SERVICES & CORRECTIONS -
MANITOBA SCHOOL - MEMORIAL LIBRARY
Box 1190   Phone: (204) 239-6435
Portage La Prairie, MB R1N 3C6   Connie McCorrister, Lib.Ck.

COLLEGE UNIVERSITAIRE DE ST. BONIFACE - BIBLIOTHEQUE ALFRED-
MONNIN
200 Ave. de la Cathedrale   Phone: (204) 233-0210
Saint-Boniface, MB R2H 0H7   Marcel Boulet, Hd.Libn.

MANITOBA - DEPT. OF EDUCATION - BUREAU DE L'EDUCATION
FRANCAISE - DIRECTION DES RESSOURCES EDUCATIVES FRANCAISES
200, ave. de la Cathedrale   Phone: (204) 237-6671
Saint-Boniface, MB R2H 0H7   Arsene Huberdeau, Dir.

SELKIRK MENTAL HEALTH CENTRE - CENTRAL LIBRARY
Box 9600   Phone: (204) 482-3810
Selkirk, MB R1A 2B5   John English, Chm., Lib.Comm.

ROYAL CANADIAN ARTILLERY MUSEUM - LIBRARY
Canadian Forces Base   Phone: (204) 765-2282
Shilo, MB R0K 2A0   CWO Lunan, Chf.Libn.

MENNONITE VILLAGE MUSEUM (Canada) INC. - LIBRARY
Box 1136   Phone: (204) 326-9661
Steinbach, MB R0A 2A0   Peter Goertzen, Mgr.

ALCOHOLISM FOUNDATION OF MANITOBA - WILLIAM POTOROKA
MEMORIAL LIBRARY
1031 Portage Ave.   Phone: (204) 775-8601
Winnipeg, MB R3G 0R8   Diana Ringstrom, Libn.

CANADA - AGRICULTURE CANADA - CANADIAN GRAIN COMMISSION -
LIBRARY
303 Main St., Rm. 1001   Phone: (204) 949-3360
Winnipeg, MB R3C 3G7   J. Blanchard, Libn.

CANADA - AGRICULTURE CANADA - RESEARCH STATION, WINNIPEG -
LIBRARY †
195 Dafoe Rd.   Phone: (204) 269-2100
Winnipeg, MB R3T 2M9   M. Malyk, Libn.

CANADA - ATMOSPHERIC ENVIRONMENT SERVICE - CENTRAL REGION
LIBRARY †
266 Graham Ave., Suite 1000   Phone: (204) 949-6224
Winnipeg, MB R3C 3V4   R.R. Tortorelli, Sci.Serv.Techn.

CANADA - EMPLOYMENT & IMMIGRATION CANADA - PUBLIC AFFAIRS -
MANITOBA REGIONAL OFFICE LIBRARY
330 Graham Ave., Rm. 710   Phone: (204) 949-2868
Winnipeg, MB R3C 4B9   Win Kennedy, Regional Mgr.

CANADA - FISHERIES & OCEANS - FRESHWATER INSTITUTE LIBRARY
501 University Crescent   Phone: (204) 949-5170
Winnipeg, MB R3T 2N6   K. Eric Marshall, Hd., Lib.Serv.

CANADA - NATIONAL FILM BOARD OF CANADA - FILM LIBRARY †
245 Main St.   Phone: (204) 949-4131
Winnipeg, MB R3C 1A7   Janine Vandale, Hd.Libn.

CANADA - STATISTICS CANADA - ADVISORY SERVICES - WINNIPEG
REFERENCE CENTRE
600 General Post Office
266 Graham Ave.   Phone: (204) 949-4020
Winnipeg, MB R3C 0K4   Mr. W.S. Pawluk, Asst. Regional Dir.

CANADIAN BROADCASTING CORPORATION - MUSIC & RECORD LIBRARY
541 Portage Ave.
P.O. Box 160   Phone: (204) 775-8351
Winnipeg, MB R3C 2H1   Don R. McLaren, Sr.Libn.

CANADIAN JEWISH CONGRESS - JEWISH HISTORICAL SOCIETY OF
WESTERN CANADA - ARCHIVES
402-365 Hargrave St.   Phone: (204) 942-4822
Winnipeg, MB R3B 2K3   Esther Nisenholt, Archv.

CRAFTS GUILD OF MANITOBA - LIBRARY
183 Kennedy St.   Phone: (204) 943-6281
Winnipeg, MB R2M 3T5   Helga Miller, Chm.

DEER LODGE CENTRE - LIBRARY
2109 Portage Ave.   Phone: (204) 837-1301
Winnipeg, MB R3J 0L3   J.L. Saunders, Lib.Dir.

DUCKS UNLIMITED CANADA - LIBRARY
1190 Waverley St.   Phone: (204) 477-1760
Winnipeg, MB R3T 2E2   Marlene Hilland, Adm.Sec.

GERMAN SOCIETY OF WINNIPEG - LIBRARY
121 Charles St.   Phone: (204) 589-7724
Winnipeg, MB R2W 4A6

GRAND LODGE OF MANITOBA, A.F. AND A.M. - MASONIC LIBRARY †
Masonic Memorial Temple
420 Corydon Ave.   Phone: (204) 453-7410
Winnipeg, MB R3L 0N8   W.F.L. Hyde, Grand Libn.

GREAT-WEST LIFE ASSURANCE COMPANY - LIBRARY
60 Osborne St., N.   Phone: (204) 946-7225
Winnipeg, MB R3C 3A5

HUDSON'S BAY COMPANY ARCHIVES
Provincial Archives of Manitoba
Manitoba Archives Bldg.
200 Vaughan St.   Phone: (204) 944-4949
Winnipeg, MB R3C 1T5   Shirlee Anne Smith, Kpr.

HUDSON'S BAY COMPANY - LIBRARY
Hudson's Bay House
77 Main St.   Phone: (204) 934-1465
Winnipeg, MB R3C 2R1   Carol Preston, Libn.

LAW SOCIETY OF MANITOBA - LIBRARY †
155 Carlton St.   Phone: (204) 942-5571
Winnipeg, MB R3C 3H8   Garth Niven, Chf.Libn.

MANITOBA ASSOCIATION OF REGISTERED NURSES - LIBRARY
647 Broadway   Phone: (204) 774-3477
Winnipeg, MB R3C 0X2   Eleanor Gowerluk, Lib.Techn.

MANITOBA CANCER TREATMENT AND RESEARCH FOUNDATION - LIBRARY
700 Bannatyne Ave.   Phone: (204) 787-2136
Winnipeg, MB R3C 1N7   Isobel M. Steedman, Libn.

MANITOBA - DEPARTMENT OF EDUCATION - LIBRARY
1181 Portage Ave., Main Fl.
Box 3   Phone: (204) 945-7832
Winnipeg, MB R3G 0T3   John Tooth, Chf.Libn.

MANITOBA - DEPT. OF ENVIRONMENTAL & WORKPLACE SAFETY & HEALTH
    - CONSUMER AFFAIRS LIBRARY
1023-405 Broadway Ave.
Winnipeg, MB R3C 3L6

MANITOBA - DEPT. OF ENVIRONMENTAL & WORKPLACE SAFETY & HEALTH
    - ENVIRONMENTAL MANAGEMENT LIBRARY
139 Tuxedo Ave.
Box 7
Winnipeg, MB R3N 0H6   S. Norma Godavari, Hd.Libn.

MANITOBA - DEPARTMENT OF FINANCE - FEDERAL-PROVINCIAL
    RELATIONS AND RESEARCH DIVISION LIBRARY
Legislative Bldg., Rm. 4   Phone: (204) 944-3757
Winnipeg, MB R3C OV8   Beatrice Miller, Lib.Ck.

MANITOBA - DEPARTMENT OF HEALTH - INFORMATION RESOURCES
202-880 Portage Ave.   Phone: (204) 786-5867
Winnipeg, MB R3G 0P1   Marilyn J. Hernandez, Coord. of Info.Rsrcs.

MANITOBA - DEPARTMENT OF INDUSTRY, TRADE AND TECHNOLOGY -
    BUSINESS LIBRARY
648-155 Carlton St.   Phone: (204) 944-2036
Winnipeg, MB R3C 3H8   F. Helen Paine, Libn.

MANITOBA - DEPARTMENT OF MUNICIPAL AFFAIRS - LIBRARY
1438-405 Broadway   Phone: (204) 944-4129
Winnipeg, MB R3C 3L6   Judy Stephenson, Libn.

MANITOBA - DEPARTMENT OF NATURAL RESOURCES - LIBRARY †
1495 St. James St.
Box 26   Phone: (204) 786-9299
Winnipeg, MB R3H 0W9   Irene Hamerton, Libn.

MANITOBA - HEALTH SERVICES COMMISSION - LIBRARY
599 Empress St.
P.O. Box 925   Phone: (204) 786-7398
Winnipeg, MB R3C 2T6   Vera Ott, Libn.

MANITOBA HYDRO - LIBRARY
Box 815   Phone: (204) 474-3614
Winnipeg, MB R3C 2P4   Rhona Lapierre, Corp.Libn.

MANITOBA INDIAN CULTURAL EDUCATION CENTRE - PEOPLES LIBRARY
119 Sutherland Ave.   Phone: (204) 942-0228
Winnipeg, MB R2W 3C9   V.J. Chalmers, Lib.Dir.

MANITOBA - LEGISLATIVE LIBRARY
200 Vaughan St., Main Fl.   Phone: (204) 944-4330
Winnipeg, MB R3C 1T8   F.B. "Rick" MacLowick, Hd., Info.Serv.

MANITOBA MUSEUM OF MAN AND NATURE - LIBRARY
190 Rupert Ave.   Phone: (204) 956-2830
Winnipeg, MB R3B 0N2   Valerie Hatten, Libn.

MANITOBA - PROVINCIAL ARCHIVES OF MANITOBA
Manitoba Archives Bldg.
200 Vaughan St.   Phone: (204) 944-3971
Winnipeg, MB R3C OV8   Peter Bower, Prov.Archv.

MENNONITE BRETHREN BIBLE COLLEGE - LIBRARY
77 Henderson Hwy.   Phone: (204) 667-9560
Winnipeg, MB R2L 1L1   Herbert Giesbrecht, College Libn.

MISERICORDIA GENERAL HOSPITAL - HOSPITAL LIBRARY
99 Cornish Ave.   Phone: (204) 786-8109
Winnipeg, MB R3C 1A2   Sharon Allentuck, Hosp.Libn.

RICHARDSON GREENSHIELDS OF CANADA, LTD. - RESEARCH LIBRARY
One Lombard Place, 29th Fl.   Phone: (204) 988-5940
Winnipeg, MB R3B 0Y2   Agnes Unger, Libn.

ST. AMANT CENTRE INC. - MEDICAL LIBRARY
440 River Rd.
Winnipeg, MB R2M 3Z9   Pauline Dufresne, Techn.

SOCIETY FOR CRIPPLED CHILDREN AND ADULTS OF MANITOBA - STEPHEN
    SPARLING LIBRARY
825 Sherbrook St.   Phone: (204) 786-5601
Winnipeg, MB R3A 1M5   Barbara Wolfe, Libn.

UKRAINIAN CULTURAL AND EDUCATIONAL CENTRE (Oserdok) - LIBRARY
184 Alexander Ave., E.   Phone: (204) 942-0218
Winnipeg, MB R3B 0L6   Orysia Tracz, Hd.Libn.

UNITED GRAIN GROWERS LTD. - LIBRARY
433 Main St.
Box 6600   Phone: (204) 944-5572
Winnipeg, MB R3C 3A7   Carole Rogers, Libn.

UNIVERSITY OF MANITOBA - ADMINISTRATIVE STUDIES LIBRARY
             Phone: (204) 474-8440
Winnipeg, MB R3T 2N2   Judith Head, Hd.Libn.

UNIVERSITY OF MANITOBA - AGRICULTURE LIBRARY
             Phone: (204) 474-9457
Winnipeg, MB R3T 2N2   Judith Harper, Hd.

UNIVERSITY OF MANITOBA - ARCHITECTURE & FINE ARTS LIBRARY
206 Architecture Bldg.   Phone: (204) 474-9216
Winnipeg, MB R3T 2N2   Peter Anthony, Hd.Libn.

UNIVERSITY OF MANITOBA - ARCHIVES AND SPECIAL COLLECTIONS
331 Elizabeth Dafoe Library   Phone: (204) 474-9986
Winnipeg, MB R3T 2N2   Richard E. Bennett, Hd.

UNIVERSITY OF MANITOBA - D.S. WOODS EDUCATION LIBRARY
228 Education Bldg.   Phone: (204) 474-9976
Winnipeg, MB R3T 2N2   Doreen Shanks, Hd.Libn.

UNIVERSITY OF MANITOBA - DENTAL LIBRARY
780 Bannatyne Ave.   Phone: (204) 786-3635
Winnipeg, MB R3E 0W3   Doris Pritchard, Hd.Libn.

UNIVERSITY OF MANITOBA - E.K. WILLIAMS LAW LIBRARY
Robson Hall   Phone: (204) 474-9995
Winnipeg, MB R3T 2N2   Denis Marshall, Hd.Libn.

UNIVERSITY OF MANITOBA - ENGINEERING LIBRARY
351 Engineering Bldg.   Phone: (204) 474-9445
Winnipeg, MB R3T 2N2   Patricia Routledge, Act.Hd.

UNIVERSITY OF MANITOBA - MEDICAL LIBRARY
Medical College Bldg.
770 Bannatyne Ave.   Phone: (204) 786-4342
Winnipeg, MB R3T 0W3   Audrey M. Kerr, Hd.Med.Libn.

UNIVERSITY OF MANITOBA - MUSIC LIBRARY
223 Music Bldg.   Phone: (204) 474-9567
Winnipeg, MB R3T 2N2   Vladimir Simosko, Adm.Hd.

UNIVERSITY OF MANITOBA - ST. JOHN'S COLLEGE - LIBRARY
400 Dysart Rd.   Phone: (204) 474-8542
Winnipeg, MB R3T 2M5   Patrick D. Wright, Libn.

UNIVERSITY OF MANITOBA - ST. PAUL'S COLLEGE - LIBRARY
             Phone: (204) 474-8585
Winnipeg, MB R3T 2M6   Fr. Harold Drake, Hd.

UNIVERSITY OF MANITOBA - SCIENCE LIBRARY
             Phone: (204) 474-8171
Winnipeg, MB R3T 2N2   Yong Cha Jo, Hd.

UNIVERSITY OF WINNIPEG - LIBRARY - SPECIAL COLLECTIONS
515 Portage Ave.   Phone: (204) 786-7811
Winnipeg, MB R3B 2E9   Dr. W.R. Converse, Chf.Libn.

WINNIPEG ART GALLERY - CLARA LANDER LIBRARY
300 Memorial Blvd.   Phone: (204) 786-6641
Winnipeg, MB R3C 1V1   David W. Rozniatowski, Libn.

WINNIPEG CLINIC - LIBRARY
425 St. Mary Ave.   Phone: (204) 957-1900
Winnipeg, MB R3C 0N2   S. Loeppky, Libn.

WINNIPEG DEPARTMENT OF ENVIRONMENTAL PLANNING - LIBRARY †
395 Main St.   Phone: (204) 985-5174
Winnipeg, MB R3B 3E1   Mrs. A. Thiesson, Libn.

WINNIPEG FREE PRESS - LIBRARY
300 Carlton St.   Phone: (204) 943-9331
Winnipeg, MB R3C 3C1   Mrs. E. Langer, Libn.

WINNIPEG HEALTH SCIENCES CENTRE - LIBRARY SERVICES
700 McDermot Ave.   Phone: (204) 787-2743
Winnipeg, MB R3E 0T2   Barbara Greeniaus, Dir., Lib.Serv.

WINNIPEG SCHOOL DIVISION NO. 1 - TEACHERS LIBRARY AND RESOURCE
    CENTRE
1180 Notre Dame Ave.   Phone: (204) 943-3541
Winnipeg, MB R3E 0P2   Gerald R. Brown, Chf.Libn.

WINNIPEG SOCIAL PLANNING COUNCIL - LIBRARY
412 McDermot Ave.   Phone: (204) 943-2561
Winnipeg, MB R3A 0A9   E.T. Sale, Exec.Dir.

NEW BRUNSWICK

FRASER INC. - CENTRAL TECHNICAL DEPARTMENT LIBRARY
                                              Phone: (506) 735-5551
Edmundston, NB E3V 1S9   Elizabeth Kennedy, Libn.

BARRISTERS' SOCIETY OF NEW BRUNSWICK - LAW LIBRARY †
Justice Bldg., Rm. 305
Queen St.   Phone: (506) 453-2500
Fredericton, NB E3B 5C2   Diane Hanson, Prov. Law Libn.

CANADA - AGRICULTURE CANADA - RESEARCH STATION, FREDERICTON -
    LIBRARY
Box 20280   Phone: (506) 452-3260
Fredericton, NB E3B 4Z7   Donald B. Gammon, Area Coord. Atlantic

CANADA - CANADIAN FORESTRY SERVICE - MARITIMES FOREST
    RESEARCH CENTRE - LIBRARY
P.O. Box 4000   Phone: (506) 452-3541
Fredericton, NB E3B 5P7   Barry Barner, Libn.

CHALMERS (Dr. Everett) HOSPITAL - DR. GARFIELD MOFFATT HEALTH
    SCIENCES LIBRARY
Box 9000   Phone: (506) 452-5431
Fredericton, NB E3B 5N5   Kathryn M. Smith, Libn.

NEW BRUNSWICK ASSOCIATION OF REGISTERED NURSES - LIBRARY
231 Saunders St.   Phone: (506) 454-5591
Fredericton, NB E3B 1N6   Barbara Thompson, Libn.

NEW BRUNSWICK - DEPARTMENT OF AGRICULTURE & RURAL
    DEVELOPMENT - LIBRARY †
P.O. Box 6000   Phone: (506) 453-2258
Fredericton, NB E3B 5H1

NEW BRUNSWICK - DEPARTMENT OF COMMERCE & DEVELOPMENT -
    CENTRAL FILES & LIBRARY
P.O. Box 6000   Phone: (506) 453-2187
Fredericton, NB E3B 5H1   Jane Phillips, Supv.

NEW BRUNSWICK - DEPARTMENT OF EDUCATION - LIBRARY
3rd Fl., King's Place
P.O. Box 6000   Phone: (506) 453-3739
Fredericton, NB E3B 5H1   Germaine Burns, Supv.

NEW BRUNSWICK - DEPARTMENT OF THE ENVIRONMENT - LIBRARY
P.O. Box 6000   Phone: (506) 453-3700
Fredericton, NB E3B 5H1   Gail Darby, Lib.Asst.

NEW BRUNSWICK - DEPARTMENT OF HEALTH - LIBRARY
Third Fl., Carleton Place
P.O. Box 6000   Phone: (506) 453-2536
Fredericton, NB E3B 5H1   Faith Fairweather, Libn.

NEW BRUNSWICK - DEPARTMENT OF HISTORICAL AND CULTURAL
    RESOURCES - NEW BRUNSWICK LIBRARY SERVICE
P.O. Box 6000   Phone: (506) 453-2224
Fredericton, NB E3B 5H1   Jocelyne LeBel, Act.Dir.

NEW BRUNSWICK - DEPARTMENT OF NATURAL RESOURCES - FORESTS
    BRANCH LIBRARY
P.O. Box 6000   Phone: (506) 453-2485
Fredericton, NB E3B 5H1   Irma R. Long, Lib.Asst.

NEW BRUNSWICK ELECTRIC POWER COMMISSION - REFERENCE CENTER
    †
527 King St.
P.O. Box 2000   Phone: (506) 453-4353
Fredericton, NB E3B 4X1   Aileen W. Humes, Libn.

NEW BRUNSWICK - LEGISLATIVE LIBRARY
Legislative Bldg.
P.O. Box 6000   Phone: (506) 453-2338
Fredericton, NB E3B 5H1   Jocelyn LeBel, Dir.

NEW BRUNSWICK - PROVINCIAL ARCHIVES OF NEW BRUNSWICK
Box 6000   Phone: (506) 453-2637
Fredericton, NB E3B 5H1   Marion Beyea, Prov.Archv.

NEW BRUNSWICK RESEARCH AND PRODUCTIVITY COUNCIL - LIBRARY
P.O. Box 6000   Phone: (506) 452-8994
Fredericton, NB E3B 5H1   Valerie Owen, Lib.Supv.

UNIVERSITY OF NEW BRUNSWICK - EDUCATION RESOURCE CENTRE
D'Avray Hall
P.O. Box 7500   Phone: (506) 453-3516
Fredericton, NB E3B 5H5   Andrew Pope, Educ.Libn.

UNIVERSITY OF NEW BRUNSWICK - ENGINEERING LIBRARY
Sir Edmund Head Hall
P.O. Box 7500   Phone: (506) 453-4747
Fredericton, NB E3B 5H5   Everett R. Dunfield, Engr.Libn.

UNIVERSITY OF NEW BRUNSWICK - LAW LIBRARY
Ludlow Hall
Bag Service No. 44999   Phone: (506) 453-4669
Fredericton, NB E3B 6C9   Anne Crocker, Law Libn.

UNIVERSITY OF NEW BRUNSWICK - SCIENCE LIBRARY
P.O. Box 7500   Phone: (506) 453-4601
Fredericton, NB E3B 5H5   Eszter L.K. Schwenke, Hd.

MONCTON HOSPITAL - HEALTH SCIENCES LIBRARY
135 MacBeath Ave.   Phone: (506) 855-1600
Moncton, NB E1C 6Z8   Susan P. Libby, Hosp.Libn.

UNIVERSITE DE MONCTON - BIBLIOTHEQUE DE DROIT
                                              Phone: (506) 858-4569
Moncton, NB E1A 3E9   Simonne Clermont, Law Libn.

UNIVERSITE DE MONCTON - CENTRE D'ETUDES ACADIENNES
                                              Phone: (506) 858-4085
Moncton, NB E1A 3E9   Ronald Leblanc, Libn.

UNIVERSITE DE MONCTON - FACULTE DES SCIENCES DE L'EDUCATION -
    CENTRE DE RESSOURCES PEDAGOGIQUES
                                              Phone: (506) 858-4356
Moncton, NB E1A 3E9   Berthe Boudreau, Dir.

MIRAMICHI HOSPITAL - HEALTH SCIENCES LIBRARY
P.O. Box 420   Phone: (506) 622-1340
Newcastle, NB E1V 3M5   Audrey D. Somers, Educ.Coord.

OLD MANSE LIBRARY
225 Mary St.
Newcastle, NB E1V 1Z3
Phone: (506) 622-0453
Catherine Bryan, Libn.

CANADA - CANADIAN WILDLIFE SERVICE - ATLANTIC REGION LIBRARY
Box 1590
Sackville, NB E0A 3C0
Phone: (506) 536-3025
Jean Sealy, Libn.

MOUNT ALLISON UNIVERSITY - ALFRED WHITEHEAD MEMORIAL MUSIC
LIBRARY
Sackville, NB E0A 3C0
Phone: (506) 536-2040
Bert Meerveld, Music Libn.

MOUNT ALLISON UNIVERSITY - WINTHROP P. BELL COLLECTION OF
ACADIANA
Ralph Pickard Bell Library
Sackville, NB E0A 3C0
Phone: (506) 536-2040
Margaret Fancy, Spec.Coll.Libn.

ATLANTIC SALMON FEDERATION - J. KENNETH STALLMAN MEMORIAL
LIBRARY
P.O. Box 429
St. Andrews, NB E0G 2X0
Phone: (506) 529-8899
Kevin B. Murchie, Libn.

CANADA - FISHERIES & OCEANS - BIOLOGICAL STATION LIBRARY
Phone: (506) 529-8854
St. Andrews, NB E0G 2X0
Ms. C.R. Garnett, Libn.

SUNBURY SHORES ARTS AND NATURE CENTRE, INC. - SUNBURY SHORES
LIBRARY
139 Water St.
P.O. Box 100
St. Andrews, NB E0G 2X0
Phone: (506) 529-3386
Mary Blatherwick, Prog.Dir./Art Cons.

CHURCH OF ENGLAND INSTITUTE - LIBRARY
116 Princess St.
Saint John, NB E2L 1K4
Phone: (506) 693-2295
Mrs. F.H. Burton, Mgr.

NEW BRUNSWICK MUSEUM - LIBRARY AND ARCHIVES DEPARTMENT
277 Douglas Ave.
Saint John, NB E2K 1E5
Phone: (506) 693-1196
Carol Rosevear, Hd.

PALMER, O'CONNELL, LEGER, TURNBULL & TURNBULL - LAW LIBRARY †
One Brunswick Sq., Suite 1600
P.O. Box 1324
Saint John, NB E2L 4H8
Phone: (506) 642-2700
Peter R. Forestell, Libn.

CARLETON MEMORIAL HOSPITAL - HEALTH SCIENCES LIBRARY
Box 400
Woodstock, NB E0J 2B0
Phone: (506) 328-3391
Joanne E. Rosevear, Dir.

NEWFOUNDLAND

WESTERN MEMORIAL REGIONAL HOSPITAL - HEALTH SCIENCE LIBRARY †
West Valley Rd.
Box 2005
Corner Brook, NF A2H 6J7
Phone: (709) 634-5101
Walter S. MacPherson, Libn.

LABRADOR CITY COLLEGIATE - LIBRARY
213 Matthew Ave.
Labrador City, NF A2V 2J9
Phone: (709) 944-5953
Bruce Dyer, Libn.

CANADA - AGRICULTURE CANADA - RESEARCH STATION, ST. JOHN'S
WEST - LIBRARY
Brookfield Rd.
P.O. Box 7098
St. John's, NF A1E 3Y3
Phone: (709) 772-4619
H.M. Stevenson, Off.Mgr.

CANADA - CANADIAN FORESTRY SERVICE - NEWFOUNDLAND FOREST
RESEARCH CENTRE - LIBRARY
P.O. Box 6028
St. John's, NF A1C 5X8
Phone: (709) 772-4672
Catherine E. Philpott, Libn.

CANADA - FISHERIES & OCEANS - NEWFOUNDLAND REGIONAL LIBRARY
P.O. Box 5667
St. John's, NF A1C 5X1
Phone: (709) 737-2022
Audrey Conroy, Libn.

CANADA - STATISTICS CANADA - ADVISORY SERVICES - ST. JOHN'S
REFERENCE CENTRE †
Viking Bldg., 3rd Fl., Crosbie Rd.
Box 8556
St. John's, NF A1B 3P2
Phone: (709) 772-4073

COLLEGE OF FISHERIES, NAVIGATION, MARINE ENGINEERING AND
ELECTRONICS - LIBRARY
Parade St.
P.O. Box 4920
St. John's, NF A1C 5R3
Phone: (709) 726-5272
Mabel Farmer, Libn.

COLLEGE OF TRADES AND TECHNOLOGY - LIBRARY
P.O. Box 1693
St. John's, NF A1C 5P7
Phone: (709) 753-9360
Patricia Rahal, Libn.

COLLEGE OF TRADES AND TECHNOLOGY - MEDICAL LIBRARY
Topsail Campus
P.O. Box 1693
St. John's, NF A1C 5P7
Phone: (709) 368-2001
Patricia Rahal, Libn.

GRACE GENERAL HOSPITAL - CHESLEY A. PIPPY, JR. MEDICAL LIBRARY
LeMarchant Rd.
St. John's, NF A1E 1P9
Phone: (709) 778-6796
Elizabeth Duggan, Med.Libn.

GRACE GENERAL HOSPITAL - SCHOOL OF NURSING LIBRARY
LeMarchant Rd.
St. John's, NF A1E 1P9
Phone: (709) 778-6645
Catherine Ryan, Libn.

JANEWAY (Dr. Charles A.) CHILD HEALTH CENTRE - JANEWAY MEDICAL
LIBRARY
Pleasantville
St. John's, NF A1A 1R8
Phone: (709) 778-4344
Joan E. Wheeler, Med.Libn.

LAW SOCIETY OF NEWFOUNDLAND - LIBRARY
Court House, Duckworth St.
P.O. Box 1028
St. John's, NF A1C 5M3
Phone: (709) 753-7770
Susanna P. Duke, Libn.

MEMORIAL UNIVERSITY OF NEWFOUNDLAND - FOLKLORE AND LANGUAGE
ARCHIVE
St. John's, NF A1C 5S7
Phone: (709) 737-8401
Neil V. Rosenberg, Dir.

MEMORIAL UNIVERSITY OF NEWFOUNDLAND - HEALTH SCIENCES
LIBRARY
Health Science Centre
300 Prince Philip Dr.
St. John's, NF A1B 3V6
Phone: (709) 737-6672
Shelagh Wotherspoon, Act.Hd.

MEMORIAL UNIVERSITY OF NEWFOUNDLAND - INTERNATIONAL
REFERENCE CENTRE FOR AVIAN HAEMATOZOA
Department of Biology
St. John's, NF A1B 3X9
Phone: (709) 737-8141
Madonna Whiteway, Res.Asst.

MEMORIAL UNIVERSITY OF NEWFOUNDLAND - OCEAN ENGINEERING
INFORMATION CENTRE
St. John's, NF A1B 3X5
Phone: (709) 737-8377
Judith A. Whittick, Info.Res.

MEMORIAL UNIVERSITY OF NEWFOUNDLAND - QUEEN ELIZABETH II
LIBRARY - CENTRE FOR NEWFOUNDLAND STUDIES
St. John's, NF A1B 3Y1
Phone: (709) 737-7475
Anne Hart, Hd.

MEMORIAL UNIVERSITY OF NEWFOUNDLAND - QUEEN ELIZABETH II
LIBRARY - MAP LIBRARY
St. John's, NF A1B 3Y1
Phone: (709) 737-8892
Alberta Auringer Wood, Map Libn.

NEWFOUNDLAND - DEPARTMENT OF EDUCATION - INSTRUCTIONAL
MATERIALS LIBRARY
Bldg. 951, Pleasantville
St. John's, NF A1A 1R2
Phone: (709) 737-2619
D. Nanayakkara, Libn.

NEWFOUNDLAND - DEPARTMENT OF JUSTICE - LAW LIBRARY
Confederation Bldg.
St. John's, NF A1C 5T7
Phone: (709) 737-2861
Mona B. Pearce, Libn.

NEWFOUNDLAND - DEPARTMENT OF MINES AND ENERGY - MINERAL
DEVELOPMENT DIVISION - LIBRARY
95 Bonaventure Ave.   Phone: (709) 737-3159
St. John's, NF A1C 5T7   Genie Power, Lib.Techn.

NEWFOUNDLAND - DEPARTMENT OF RURAL DEVELOPMENT - RESOURCE
CENTRE
Atlantic Place   Phone: (709) 737-3172
St. John's, NF A1C 5T7   Philip I. Mullett, Info.Spec.

NEWFOUNDLAND AND LABRADOR DEVELOPMENT CORPORATION LTD. -
LIBRARY
136 Crosbie Rd.
P.O. Box 8630   Phone: (709) 753-3560
St. John's, NF A1B 3T1   Patricia Wilson, Libn.

NEWFOUNDLAND - LEGISLATIVE LIBRARY
House of Assembly, Confederation Bldg.
P.O. Box 4750   Phone: (709) 737-3604
St. John's, NF A1C 5T7   N.J. Richards, Legislative Libn.

NEWFOUNDLAND LIGHT & POWER COMPANY, LTD. - CENTRAL RECORDS
LIBRARY
P.O. Box 8910, Kenmount Road   Phone: (709) 737-5645
St. John's, NF A1B 3P6

NEWFOUNDLAND - PROVINCIAL ARCHIVES OF NEWFOUNDLAND AND
LABRADOR
Colonial Bldg., Military Rd.   Phone: (709) 753-9390
St. John's, NF A1C 2C9   David J. Davis, Prov.Archv.

NEWFOUNDLAND - PUBLIC LIBRARY SERVICES
Arts & Culture Centre
Allandale Rd.   Phone: (709) 737-3964
St. John's, NF A1B 3A3   Pearce J. Penney, Chf.Prov.Libn.

ST. CLARE'S MERCY HOSPITAL - MEDICAL LIBRARY
St. Clare Ave.   Phone: (709) 778-3414
St. John's, NF A1C 5B8   Eileen E. Woll, Lib.Techn.

WATERFORD HOSPITAL - HEALTH SERVICES LIBRARY
Waterford Bridge Rd.   Phone: (709) 364-0269
St. John's, NF A1E 4J8   Maisie Young, Libn.

NORTHWEST TERRITORIES

CANADA - INDIAN & NORTHERN AFFAIRS CANADA - INUVIK SCIENTIFIC
RESOURCE CENTRE - LIBRARY †
P.O. Box 1430   Phone: (403) 979-3838
Inuvik, NT X0E 0T0   D.A. Sherstone, Scientist-in-Charge

CANADA - NATIONAL DEFENCE - NORTHERN REGION HEADQUARTERS
LIBRARY
Evans Block, P.O. Box 6666   Phone: (403) 873-4011
Yellowknife, NT X1A 2R3   Capt. B. Brighton

NORTHWEST TERRITORIES - GOVERNMENT LIBRARY
Laing No. 1
P.O. Box 1320   Phone: (403) 873-7628
Yellowknife, NT X1A 2L9   Margaret Orr, Govt.Libn.

NORTHWEST TERRITORIES - SAFETY DIVISION - OCCUPATIONAL HEALTH
& SAFETY RESOURCE CENTRE
Box 1320   Phone: (403) 873-7470
Yellowknife, NT X1A 2L9   Diane Thompson, Ck.

NOVA SCOTIA

COUNCIL OF MARITIME PREMIERS - ATLANTIC COASTAL RESOURCE
INFORMATION CENTRE LIBRARY
Box 310   Phone: (902) 667-7231
Amherst, NS B4H 3Z5   Margaret E. Campbell, Libn.

COUNCIL OF MARITIME PREMIERS - MARITIME RESOURCE MANAGEMENT
SERVICE - INFORMATION CENTRE
P.O. Box 310   Phone: (902) 667-7231
Amherst, NS B4H 3Z5   Margaret E. Campbell, Libn.

ST. FRANCIS XAVIER UNIVERSITY - COADY INTERNATIONAL INSTITUTE -
MARIE MICHAEL LIBRARY †
                                           Phone: (902) 867-3964
Antigonish, NS B2G 1C0   Sr. Berthold Mackey, Chf.Libn.

ST. MARTHA'S HOSPITAL - SCHOOL OF NURSING LIBRARY
25 Bay St.   Phone: (902) 863-2830
Antigonish, NS B2G 2G5   Sr. Marilyn Curry, Libn.

CANADA - ATMOSPHERIC ENVIRONMENT SERVICE - ATLANTIC REGIONAL
LIBRARY
5th Fl., 1496 Bedford Hwy.   Phone: (902) 835-9529
Bedford, NS B4A 1E5   B.L. Taylor

BEDFORD INSTITUTE OF OCEANOGRAPHY - LIBRARY
Box 1006   Phone: (902) 426-3675
Dartmouth, NS B2Y 4A2   J. Elizabeth Sutherland, Hd., Lib.Serv.

CANADA - DEFENCE RESEARCH ESTABLISHMENT ATLANTIC - LIBRARY
P.O. Box 1012   Phone: (902) 426-3100
Dartmouth, NS B2Y 3Z7   Donna I. Richardson, Hd.Info.Serv. Group

CANADA - TRANSPORT CANADA - CANADIAN COAST GUARD, MARITIMES
REGION - REGIONAL LIBRARY
46 Portland St.
P.O. Box 1013   Phone: (902) 426-5182
Dartmouth, NS B2Y 4K2   Mrs. Gaylan Ritchie, Regional Libn.

HERMES ELECTRONICS LTD. - LIBRARY
Box 1005   Phone: (902) 466-7491
Dartmouth, NS B2Y 4A1   Vaila S. Mowat, Libn.

NOVA SCOTIA HOSPITAL - HEALTH SCIENCE LIBRARY
P.O. Box 1004   Phone: (902) 469-7500
Dartmouth, NS B2Y 3Z9   Marjorie A. Cox

NOVA SCOTIA RESEARCH FOUNDATION CORPORATION - LIBRARY †
100 Fenwick St.
P.O. Box 790   Phone: (902) 424-8670
Dartmouth, NS B2Y 3Z7   Helen I. Hendry, Libn.

CAPE BRETON MINERS' MUSEUM - LIBRARY
Quarry Point   Phone: (902) 849-4522
Glace Bay, NS B1A 5T8   Thomas Miller, Cat.

ATLANTIC PROVINCES ECONOMIC COUNCIL - LIBRARY
5121 Sackville St., Suite 500   Phone: (902) 422-6516
Halifax, NS B3J 1K1

ATLANTIC SCHOOL OF THEOLOGY - LIBRARY †
640 Francklyn St.   Phone: (902) 423-7986
Halifax, NS B3H 3B5   Alice W. Harrison, Libn.

CAMP HILL HOSPITAL - DRUG INFORMATION CENTRE
1763 Robie St.   Phone: (902) 423-1371
Halifax, NS B3H 3G2   C. Brian Tuttle, Asst.Dir.

CAMP HILL HOSPITAL - HEALTH SCIENCES LIBRARY
1763 Robie St.   Phone: (902) 423-1371
Halifax, NS B3H 3G2   Verona Hall, Lib./Drug Info.Asst.

CANADA - FISHERIES & OCEANS - SCOTIA-FUNDY REGIONAL LIBRARY
P.O. Box 550   Phone: (902) 426-3972
Halifax, NS B3J 2S7   Anna Oxley, Regional Libn.

CANADA - NATIONAL DEFENCE - CAMBRIDGE MILITARY LIBRARY †
Royal Artillery Pk.
1565 Queen St.   Phone: (902) 426-5142
Halifax, NS B3J 2H9

CANADA - NATIONAL FILM BOARD OF CANADA - ATLANTIC FILM & VIDEO
CENTER - REFERENCE LIBRARY
1572 Barrington St.   Phone: (902) 426-6157
Halifax, NS B3J 1Z6   Harold Rennie, Info.Off.

CANADA - NATIONAL RESEARCH COUNCIL - ATLANTIC RESEARCH
LABORATORY - LIBRARY
1411 Oxford St.   Phone: (902) 426-8250
Halifax, NS B3H 3Z1   Annabelle Taylor, Libn.

CANADA - STATISTICS CANADA - ADVISORY SERVICES - HALIFAX
REFERENCE CENTRE
1256 Barrington St., 3rd Fl.   Phone: (902) 426-5331
Halifax, NS B3J 1Y6

CANADIAN BROADCASTING CORPORATION - MUSIC & RECORD LIBRARY
5600 Sackville St.
Box 3000   Phone: (902) 422-8311
Halifax, NS B3J 3E9   David S. Leadbeater, Sr.Rec.Libn.

DALHOUSIE OCEAN STUDIES PROGRAMME - LIBRARY
1321 Edward St.   Phone: (902) 424-6557
Halifax, NS B3H 4H9   Judy Reade, Libn.

DALHOUSIE UNIVERSITY - BACON COLLECTION
University Library   Phone: (902) 424-3615
Halifax, NS B3H 4H8   Karen Smith, Hd., Spec.Coll.

DALHOUSIE UNIVERSITY - CANADIAN LITERATURE COLLECTION
                                         Phone: (902) 424-3601
Halifax, NS B3H 4H8   Karen Smith, Hd., Spec.Coll.

DALHOUSIE UNIVERSITY - COCKERELL COLLECTION
University Library   Phone: (902) 424-3615
Halifax, NS B3H 4H8   Karen Smith, Hd., Spec.Coll.

DALHOUSIE UNIVERSITY - INSTITUTE OF PUBLIC AFFAIRS - LIBRARY
6086 University Ave.   Phone: (902) 424-2526
Halifax, NS B3H 3J5   Faustina Chen, Libn.

DALHOUSIE UNIVERSITY - INSTITUTE FOR RESOURCE AND
ENVIRONMENTAL STUDIES - LIBRARY
1312 Robie St.   Phone: (902) 424-3632
Halifax, NS B3H 3E2   J.G. Reade, Libn.

DALHOUSIE UNIVERSITY - KIPLING COLLECTION
University Library   Phone: (902) 424-3615
Halifax, NS B3H 4H8   Karen Smith, Hd., Spec.Coll.

DALHOUSIE UNIVERSITY - LAW LIBRARY
Weldon Law Bldg.   Phone: (902) 424-2124
Halifax, NS B3H 4H9   Christian L. Wiktor, Law Libn.

DALHOUSIE UNIVERSITY - MACDONALD SCIENCE LIBRARY
University Library   Phone: (902) 424-2059
Halifax, NS B3H 4J3   Sylvia J. Fullerton, Asst.Univ.Libn., Sci.

DALHOUSIE UNIVERSITY - MARITIME SCHOOL OF SOCIAL WORK -
LIBRARY
6420 Coburg Rd.   Phone: (902) 424-6433
Halifax, NS B3H 3J5   Linda MacLeod, Libn.

DALHOUSIE UNIVERSITY - W.K. KELLOGG HEALTH SCIENCES LIBRARY
Sir Charles Tupper Medical Bldg.   Phone: (902) 424-2458
Halifax, NS B3H 4H7   Ann Manning, Health Sci.Libn.

GRACE MATERNITY HOSPITAL - MEDICAL LIBRARY
5821 University Ave.   Phone: (902) 422-6501
Halifax, NS B3H 1W3   Donna M. Gallivan, Dir., Med.Rec.Dept.

HALIFAX BOARD OF TRADE - LIBRARY *
Suite 400, 5251 Duke St.   Phone: (902) 422-6447
Halifax, NS B3J 1P3   G.H. Lummis, Exec.V.P.

HALIFAX HERALD LTD. - LIBRARY
1650 Argyle St.   Phone: (902) 426-3080
Halifax, NS B3J 2T2   Dorothy Leadbetter, Hd.Libn.

HALIFAX INFIRMARY - HEALTH SERVICES LIBRARY †
1335 Queen St.   Phone: (902) 428-3058
Halifax, NS B3J 2H6   Dr. Anitra Laycock, Libn.

HALIFAX REGIONAL VOCATIONAL SCHOOL - LIBRARY
1825 Bell Rd.   Phone: (902) 422-8301
Halifax, NS B3H 2Z4   Joann Morris, Libn.

IZAAK WALTON KILLAM HOSPITAL FOR CHILDREN - MEDICAL STAFF
LIBRARY *
5850 University Ave.   Phone: (902) 424-3055
Halifax, NS B3J 3G9   Hilda van Rooyen, Med.Libn.

MARITIME MUSEUM OF THE ATLANTIC - LIBRARY
1675 Lower Water St.   Phone: (902) 429-8210
Halifax, NS B3J 1S3   M. Blackford, Libn.

MARITIME TELEGRAPH & TELEPHONE CO. LTD. - INFORMATION
RESOURCE CENTRE
P.O. Box 880   Phone: (902) 421-4570
Halifax, NS B3J 2W3   Joan E. Fage, Libn.

MOUNT SAINT VINCENT UNIVERSITY - LIBRARY
166 Bedford Hwy.   Phone: (902) 443-4450
Halifax, NS B3M 2J6   Mr. L. Bianchini, Hd.Libn.

NOVA SCOTIA - ATTORNEY GENERAL'S LIBRARY
Provincial Bldg.
P.O. Box 7   Phone: (902) 424-7699
Halifax, NS B3J 2L6   Margaret Murphy, Libn.

NOVA SCOTIA BARRISTERS' SOCIETY - LIBRARY
Law Courts, 1815 Upper Water St.   Phone: (902) 422-1491
Halifax, NS B3J 1S7   Barbara Campbell, Libn.

NOVA SCOTIA COLLEGE OF ART AND DESIGN - LIBRARY
5163 Duke St.   Phone: (902) 422-7381
Halifax, NS B3J 3J6   John Murchie, Lib.Dir.

NOVA SCOTIA COMMISSION ON DRUG DEPENDENCY - LIBRARY AND
INFORMATION CENTRE
Lord Nelson Bldg., Suite 314
5675 Spring Garden Rd.   Phone: (902) 424-4270
Halifax, NS B3J 1H1   Patricia MacNeil, Libn.

NOVA SCOTIA - DEPARTMENT OF CULTURE, RECREATION AND FITNESS -
LIBRARY
P.O. Box 864   Phone: (902) 424-7734
Halifax, NS B3J 2V2   Genni Archibald, Lib.Off.

NOVA SCOTIA - DEPARTMENT OF DEVELOPMENT - LIBRARY
5151 George St., 8th Fl.
P.O. Box 519   Phone: (902) 424-5807
Halifax, NS B3J 2R7   Donald Purcell, Libn.

NOVA SCOTIA - DEPARTMENT OF EDUCATION - EDUCATION MEDIA
SERVICES
6955 Bayers Rd.   Phone: (902) 453-2810
Halifax, NS B3J 1E8   Audrey McSweeney, Libn.

NOVA SCOTIA - DEPARTMENT OF LABOUR AND MANPOWER - LIBRARY
P.O. Box 697   Phone: (902) 424-4313
Halifax, NS B3J 2T8   Marie DeYoung, Libn.

NOVA SCOTIA - DEPARTMENT OF MINES & ENERGY - LIBRARY †
P.O. Box 1087   Phone: (902) 424-8633
Halifax, NS B3J 2X1   Valerie Brisco, Res.Asst.

NOVA SCOTIA - DEPARTMENT OF SOCIAL SERVICES - LIBRARY
P.O. Box 696   Phone: (902) 424-4383
Halifax, NS B3J 2T7   Jane Phillips, Libn.

NOVA SCOTIA INSTITUTE OF TECHNOLOGY - LEARNING RESOURCES
CENTER
5685 Leeds St.
P.O. Box 2210   Phone: (902) 424-4224
Halifax, NS B3J 3C4   Nola Brennan, Libn.

NOVA SCOTIA - LEGISLATIVE LIBRARY
Province House   Phone: (902) 424-5932
Halifax, NS B3J 2P8   Ilga Leja, Legislative Libn.

NOVA SCOTIA MUSEUM - LIBRARY
1747 Summer St.   Phone: (902) 429-4610
Halifax, NS B3H 3A6   S. Whiteside, Libn.

NOVA SCOTIA POWER CORPORATION - CORPORATE RESEARCH AND
    INFORMATION CENTRE
Box 910   Phone: (902) 424-2928
Halifax, NS B3J 2W5   Barbara N. MacKenzie, Libn.

NOVA SCOTIA - PROVINCIAL LIBRARY
6955 Bayers Rd.   Phone: (902) 453-2810
Halifax, NS B3L 4S4   Mrs. Carin Somers, Dir.

NOVA SCOTIA - PUBLIC ARCHIVES OF NOVA SCOTIA
6016 University Ave.   Phone: (902) 423-9115
Halifax, NS B3H 1W4   Phyllis R. Blakeley, Prov.Archv.

ST. MARY'S UNIVERSITY - PATRICK POWER LIBRARY
                                               Phone: (902) 429-9780
Halifax, NS B3H 3C3   Ronald A. Lewis, Univ.Libn.

TECHNICAL UNIVERSITY OF NOVA SCOTIA - LIBRARY
Barrington & Bishop St.
P.O. Box 1000   Phone: (902) 429-8300
Halifax, NS B3J 2X4   Mohammad Riaz Hussain, Libn.

UNITED CHURCH OF CANADA - MARITIME CONFERENCE ARCHIVES
Pine Hill Divinity Hall   Phone: (902) 429-4819
Halifax, NS B3H 3B5   Rev. Neil A. MacLeod, Archv.

UNIVERSITY OF KING'S COLLEGE - KING'S COLLEGE LIBRARY
                                               Phone: (902) 423-8428
Halifax, NS B3H 2A1   Dr. W.J. Hankey, Chf.Libn.

VICTORIA GENERAL HOSPITAL - HEALTH SCIENCES LIBRARY
                                               Phone: (902) 428-3497
Halifax, NS B3H 2Y9   Joyce A. Kublin, Libn.

CANADA - AGRICULTURE CANADA - RESEARCH STATION, KENTVILLE -
    LIBRARY
                                               Phone: (902) 678-2171
Kentville, NS B4N 1J5   Jerry Miner, Libn.

FORTRESS OF LOUISBOURG NATIONAL HISTORIC PARK - LIBRARY †
P.O. Box 160   Phone: (902) 733-2280
Louisbourg, NS B0A 1M0   Judith-Marie Romard, Archv./Lib.Techn.

CANADA - TRANSPORT CANADA - CANADIAN COAST GUARD COLLEGE -
    LIBRARY
P.O. Box 4500   Phone: (902) 562-8550
Sydney, NS B1P 6L1   David N. MacSween, Libn.

UNIVERSITY OF CAPE BRETON - BEATON INSTITUTE ARCHIVES
Box 5300   Phone: (902) 564-6343
Sydney, NS B1P 6L2   Dr. R.J. Morgan, Dir.

NOVA SCOTIA AGRICULTURAL COLLEGE - LIBRARY
Box 550   Phone: (902) 895-1571
Truro, NS B2N 5E3   Bhagat Sodhi, Chf.Libn.

ACADIA UNIVERSITY - SCIENCE LIBRARY
                                               Phone: (902) 542-2201
Wolfville, NS B0P 1X0   Dr. Nirmal K. Jain, Hd., Sci.Lib.

FIREFIGHTERS' MUSEUM OF NOVA SCOTIA - LIBRARY & INFORMATION
    CENTER
451 Main St.   Phone: (902) 742-5525
Yarmouth, NS B5A 1G9   R. Bruce Hopkins, Cur.

YARMOUTH COUNTY HISTORICAL SOCIETY - RESEARCH LIBRARY AND
    ARCHIVES
P.O. Box 39   Phone: (902) 742-5539
Yarmouth, NS B5A 4B1   Helen Hall, Archv.

ONTARIO

MISSISSIPPI VALLEY CONSERVATION AUTHORITY - R. TAIT MC KENZIE
    RESEARCH LIBRARY *
R.R. 1, The Mill of Kintail   Phone: (613) 256-3610
Almonte, ON K0A 1A0

FORT MALDEN NATIONAL HISTORIC PARK - LIBRARY & ARCHIVES
100 Laird Ave.
Box 38   Phone: (519) 736-5416
Amherstburg, ON N9V 2Z2   Sally Snyder, Libn.

ONTARIO POLICE COLLEGE - LIBRARY
Box 1190   Phone: (519) 773-5361
Aylmer West, ON N5H 2T2   Mr. Yen-pin Chao, Libn.

SIMCOE COUNTY LAW ASSOCIATION - LIBRARY †
30 Poyntz St.   Phone: (715) 728-1221
Barrie, ON L4M 1M1   Eleanor Garner, Act.Libn.

LOYALIST COLLEGE OF APPLIED ARTS & TECHNOLOGY - ANDERSON
    RESOURCE CENTRE †
Loyalist-Wallbridge Rd.
Box 4200   Phone: (613) 962-9501
Belleville, ON K8N 5B9   Ronald H. Boyce, Hd., Lib.Serv.

CANADA - NATIONAL DEFENCE - CANADIAN FORCES MEDICAL SERVICES
    SCHOOL - LIBRARY †
Canadian Forces Base   Phone: (705) 424-1200
Borden, ON L0M 1C0   Mrs. Marion Thomson, Libn.

BRANT COUNTY MUSEUM - LIBRARY
57 Charlotte St.   Phone: (519) 752-2483
Brantford, ON N3T 2W6   William R. Robbins

BRANT (Joseph) MEMORIAL HOSPITAL - HOSPITAL LIBRARY †
1230 Northshore Blvd.   Phone: (416) 632-3730
Burlington, ON L7R 4C4   Janice McMillan, Hosp.Libn.

CANADA CENTRE FOR INLAND WATERS - LIBRARY †
867 Lakeshore Rd.
Box 5050   Phone: (416) 637-4282
Burlington, ON L7R 4A6   Eve Dowie, Hd., Lib.Serv.

CANADIAN CANNERS, LTD. - RESEARCH CENTRE - LIBRARY
1101 Walker's Line   Phone: (416) 335-9700
Burlington, ON L7N 2G4   Gisela Smithson, Tech.Libn.

WESTINGHOUSE CANADA LTD. - ELECTRONICS DIVISION LIBRARY †
777 Walker's Lane
P.O. Box 5009   Phone: (416) 528-8811
Burlington, ON L7R 4B3   E. Jackson, Libn.

NORWICH-EATON - FILM LIBRARY
P.O. Box 819   Phone: (519) 442-6361
Cambridge, ON N1R 5W6   Nicole Delplace

LEIGH INSTRUMENTS, LTD. - ENGINEERING & AEROSPACE DIVISION -
    TECHNICAL LIBRARY
P.O. Box 82   Phone: (613) 257-3883
Carleton Place, ON K7C 3P3   Betty G. Robertson, Info.Sec.

ATOMIC ENERGY OF CANADA, LTD. - TECHNICAL INFORMATION BRANCH -
    MAIN LIBRARY
Chalk River Nuclear Labs.   Phone: (613) 687-5581
Chalk River, ON K0J 1J0   H. Greenshields, Chf.Libn.

CANADA - CANADIAN FORESTRY SERVICE - PETAWAWA NATIONAL
    FORESTRY INSTITUTE - LIBRARY
                                               Phone: (613) 589-2880
Chalk River, ON K0J 1J0   Mary Mitchell, Libn.

UNION GAS, LTD. - LIBRARY SERVICE †
50 Keil Dr., N.   Phone: (519) 352-3100
Chatham, ON N7M 5M1   Mrs. A. Steen

CANADIAN NUMISMATIC ASSOCIATION - LIBRARY
P.O. Box 112
Cookstown, ON L0L 1L0
Phone: (705) 458-9242
Carol Gregory, Libn.

CANADA - PARKS CANADA, ONTARIO REGION - LIBRARY
132 Second St., E.
Cornwall, ON K6H 5V4
Phone: (613) 933-9712
Joan M. Lipscombe, Libn.

CANADA - TRANSPORT CANADA - TRAINING INSTITUTE - TECHNICAL
INFORMATION CENTRE
1950 Montreal Rd.
Bag Service 5400
Cornwall, ON K6H 6L2
Phone: (613) 938-4344
Cathy Pickard, Supv.

ST. LAWRENCE COLLEGE SAINT-LAURENT - LEARNING RESOURCE CENTRE
†
2 Belmont St.
Cornwall, ON K6H 4Z1
Phone: (613) 933-6080
Norah Fourney, Hd.Libn.

CANADIAN REAL ESTATE ASSOCIATION - LIBRARY †
99 Duncan Mill Rd.
Don Mills, ON M3B 1Z2

CIVIC GARDEN CENTRE - LIBRARY
777 Lawrence Ave., E.
Don Mills, ON M3C 1P2
Phone: (416) 445-1552
Pamela MacKenzie, Libn.

IBM CANADA, LTD. - LABORATORY LIBRARY
1150 Eglinton Ave., E.
Don Mills, ON M3C 1H7
Phone: (416) 443-3136
Barbara Wallace, Lab.Libn.

IBM CANADA, LTD. - MARKETING LIBRARY
105 Moatfield Dr.
Don Mills, ON M3B 3L9
Phone: (416) 443-2043
Marjorie Lauer, Libn.

MARSHALL MACKLIN MONAGHAN LIMITED - LIBRARY †
275 Duncan Mill Rd.
Don Mills, ON M3B 2N1

NORANDA MINES LTD. - INFORMATION SERVICES - RESOURCE CENTRE
1300 Don Mills Rd.
Don Mills, ON M3B 2W6
Phone: (416) 449-0145
Anna Takashiba, Sys.Libn.

ONTARIO FEDERATION OF LABOUR - RESOURCE CENTRE
15 Gervais Dr., Suite 202
Don Mills, ON M3C 1Y8
Phone: (416) 441-2731
Dr. Jo Surich, Res.Coord.

ONTARIO FILM INSTITUTE - LIBRARY & INFORMATION CENTRE
770 Don Mills Rd.
Don Mills, ON M3C 1T3
Phone: (416) 429-4100
Sherie Brethour, Libn.

ONTARIO HOSPITAL ASSOCIATION - LIBRARY
150 Ferrand Dr.
Don Mills, ON M3C 1H6
Phone: (416) 429-2661
John Tagg, Supv.

ONTARIO SCIENCE CENTRE - LIBRARY
770 Don Mills Rd.
Don Mills, ON M3C 1T3
Phone: (416) 429-4100
Jeanne Duperreault, Libn.

ORTHO PHARMACEUTICAL (Canada), LTD. - LIBRARY
19 Green Belt Dr.
Don Mills, ON M3C 1L9
Phone: (416) 449-9444
Marta Bodnar, Libn.

PROCTOR & REDFERN, CONSULTING ENGINEERS - LIBRARY
45 Green Belt Dr.
Don Mills, ON M3C 3K3
Phone: (416) 486-5225
Linda Rogachevsky, Hd.Libn.

SOUTHAM COMMUNICATIONS LTD. - LIBRARY
1450 Don Mills Rd.
Don Mills, ON M3B 2X7
Phone: (416) 445-6641
Eileen M. Wise, Libn.

CANADA - ATMOSPHERIC ENVIRONMENT SERVICE - LIBRARY
4905 Dufferin St.
Downsview, ON M3H 5T4
Phone: (416) 667-4500
Janice M. Glover, Chf., Lib.Serv.Div.

CANADA - DEFENCE AND CIVIL INSTITUTE OF ENVIRONMENTAL
MEDICINE - SCIENTIFIC INFORMATION CENTRE
1133 Sheppard Ave., W.
P.O. Box 2000
Downsview, ON M3M 3B9
Phone: (416) 635-2000
Anthony Cheung, Chf.Libn.

DE HAVILLAND AIRCRAFT OF CANADA, LTD. - ENGINEERING LIBRARY
Garratt Blvd.
Downsview, ON M3K 1Y5
Phone: (416) 633-7310
Catherine Parsons, Libn.

DELLCREST CHILDREN'S CENTRE - LIBRARY
1645 Sheppard Ave. W.
Downsview, ON M3M 2X4
Phone: (416) 633-0515
Lois Elliott, Libn.

NATIONAL INSTITUTE ON MENTAL RETARDATION - NATIONAL
REFERENCE SERVICE LIBRARY
Kinsmen Bldg., York University
4700 Keele St.
Downsview, ON M3J 1P3
Phone: (416) 661-9611
Mary Ann Hutton, Coord., Libs.

ONTARIO - MINISTRY OF TRANSPORTATION AND COMMUNICATIONS -
LIBRARY AND INFORMATION CENTRE
Central Bldg., Rm. 149
1201 Wilson Ave.
Downsview, ON M3M 1J8
Phone: (416) 248-3591
Stefanie A. Pavlin, Hd., Lib.Serv.

UNIVERSITY OF TORONTO - INSTITUTE FOR AEROSPACE STUDIES -
LIBRARY
4925 Dufferin St.
Downsview, ON M3H 5T6
Phone: (416) 667-7712
Asta Luik, Libn.

WORKER'S COMPENSATION BOARD OF ONTARIO - HOSPITAL &
REHABILITATION CENTRE - MEDICAL LIBRARY
115 Torbarrie Rd.
Downsview, ON M3L 1G8
Phone: (416) 244-1761
Catherine W. Wilson, Libn.

YORK-FINCH GENERAL HOSPITAL - DR. THOMAS J. MALCHO MEMORIAL
LIBRARY
2111 Finch Ave., W.
Downsview, ON M3N 1N1
Phone: (416) 744-2583
Mona Kakoschke, Med.Libn.

YORK UNIVERSITY - CENTRE FOR RESEARCH ON LATIN AMERICA AND THE
CARIBBEAN - CERLAC-LARU DOCUMENTATION CENTRE
204B Founders College
4700 Keele St.
Downsview, ON M3J 1P3
Phone: (416) 667-3085
Peter Landstreet, Dp.Dir., CERLAC.

YORK UNIVERSITY - FACULTY OF ARTS - PROGRAMME IN ENGLISH AS A
SECOND LANGUAGE - ESL RESOURCE COLLECTION
306 Strong College
4700 Keele St.
Downsview, ON M3J 1P3
Phone: (416) 667-3926
Merlin Homer, ESL Coord.

YORK UNIVERSITY - FACULTY OF ARTS - WRITING WORKSHOP LIBRARY
208 Strong College
4700 Keele St.
Downsview, ON M3J 1P3
Phone: (416) 667-3737
Sylvia Meade, Adm.Sec.

YORK UNIVERSITY - FACULTY OF EDUCATION - EDUCATION CENTRE *
S166 Ross Bldg.
4700 Keele St.
Downsview, ON M3J 1P3
Phone: (416) 667-2395
Prof. Laura Ford, Supv.

YORK UNIVERSITY - FILM LIBRARY
Scott Library
4700 Keele St.
Downsview, ON M3J 2R2
Phone: (416) 667-2546
Kathryn Elder, Libn.

YORK UNIVERSITY - GOVERNMENT DOCUMENTS/ADMINISTRATIVE
STUDIES LIBRARY
113 Administrative Studies Bldg.
4700 Keele St.
Downsview, ON M3J 2R6
Phone: (416) 667-2545
Vivienne Monty, Libn.

YORK UNIVERSITY - INSTITUTE FOR SOCIAL RESEARCH - DATA BANK
4700 Keele St.
Downsview, ON M3J 2R6
Phone: (416) 667-3026
Prof. Gordon Darroch

YORK UNIVERSITY - LAW LIBRARY
4700 Keele St.
Downsview, ON M3J 2R5
Phone: (416) 667-3939
Prof. B.J. Halevy, Libn.

YORK UNIVERSITY - LISTENING ROOM
Scott Library, Rm. 409
4700 Keele St.
Downsview, ON M3J 2R2
Phone: (416) 667-3694
Julie Stockton, Hd.

YORK UNIVERSITY - MAP LIBRARY
Scott Library, Rm. 115
4700 Keele St.   Phone: (416) 667-3353
Downsview, ON M3J 2R2   Janet Allin, Hd.

YORK UNIVERSITY - SPECIAL COLLECTIONS
Scott Library, Rm. 305
4700 Keele St.   Phone: (416) 667-2457
Downsview, ON M3J 2R2

YORK UNIVERSITY - STEACIE SCIENCE LIBRARY
4700 Keele St.   Phone: (416) 667-3927
Downsview, ON M3J 2R3   Brian B. Wilks, Sci.Libn.

YORK UNIVERSITY - UNIVERSITY ARCHIVES
105 Scott Library
4700 Keele St.   Phone: (416) 667-3306
Downsview, ON M3J 2R2   Hartwell Bowsfield, Univ.Archv.

CONSUMERS GLASS COMPANY LIMITED - LIBRARY
401 The West Mall, Suite 900   Phone: (416) 232-3275
Etobicoke, ON M9C 5J7   Barbara Presho, Libn.

ETOBICOKE BOARD OF EDUCATION - RESOURCE LIBRARY
1 Civic Centre Court   Phone: (416) 626-4360
Etobicoke, ON M9C 2B3   Alice Churchman, Coord.

HOFFMANN-LA ROCHE, LTD. - CORPORATE LIBRARY
401 The West Mall, Suite 700
Etobicoke, ON M9C 5J4   Mr. C.G.D. Hoare, Supv., Sci.Info.

NORTHERN PIGMENT LIMITED - TECHNICAL LIBRARY †
35 Towns Rd.
P.O. Box One, Station N   Phone: (416) 251-1161
Etobicoke, ON M8V 3S5   W. Nord, V.P., Oper.

VARIAN CANADA INC. - TECHNICAL LIBRARY †
45 River Dr.   Phone: (416) 877-0161
Georgetown, ON L7G 2J4   Rhonda Barber, Libn.

CHRISTIAN FARMERS FEDERATION OF ONTARIO - JUBILEE FOUNDATION
    FOR AGRICULTURAL RESEARCH - LIBRARY
115 Woolwich St.
Guelph, ON N1H 3V1   Elbert van Donkersgoed, Res. & Policy Dir.

CONESTOGA COLLEGE OF APPLIED ARTS & TECHNOLOGY, GUELPH CENTRE
    - HEALTH SCIENCES DIV. LEARNING RESOURCE CENTRE
70 Westmount Rd.   Phone: (519) 824-9390
Guelph, ON N1H 5H7   Joy Weiss, Libn.

UNIROYAL, LTD. - RESEARCH LABORATORIES LIBRARY
120 Huron St.   Phone: (519) 822-3790
Guelph, ON N1H 6N3   Lorna P. Cole, Mgr., Info.Serv.

UNIVERSITY OF GUELPH - HUMANITIES AND SOCIAL SCIENCES DIVISION
    - MAP COLLECTION †
McLaughlin Library   Phone: (519) 824-4120
Guelph, ON N1G 2W1   Mrs. F. Francis, Ref.Libn.

UNIVERSITY OF GUELPH - LIBRARY
McLaughlin Library   Phone: (519) 824-4120
Guelph, ON N1G 2W1   Margaret L. Beckman, Chf.Libn.

WELLINGTON COUNTY BOARD OF EDUCATION - EDUCATION LIBRARY
500 Victoria Rd., N.   Phone: (519) 822-4420
Guelph, ON N1E 6K2   R.E. Monkhouse, Educ. Media Cons.

NORTHERN COLLEGE - HAILEYBURY SCHOOL OF MINES - LIBRARY
Latchford St.   Phone: (705) 672-3376
Haileybury, ON P0J 1K0   Maureen Taeger, Libn.

ART GALLERY OF HAMILTON - MURIEL ISABEL BOSTWICK LIBRARY
123 King St., W.   Phone: (416) 527-6610
Hamilton, ON L8P 4S8   Andrew J. Oko, Cur.

BAPTIST CONVENTION OF ONTARIO AND QUEBEC - CANADIAN BAPTIST
    ARCHIVES
McMaster Divinity College   Phone: (416) 525-9140
Hamilton, ON L8S 4K1   Judith Colwell, Libn.

CANADIAN CENTRE FOR OCCUPATIONAL HEALTH AND SAFETY -
    DOCUMENTATION SERVICES/SERVICE DE DOCUMENTATION
250 Main St. E.   Phone: (416) 523-2981
Hamilton, ON L8N 1H6   Marilyn Moore, Dir.

DOFASCO INC. - MAIN OFFICE LIBRARY
1330 Burlington St. E.
P.O. Box 460   Phone: (416) 544-3761
Hamilton, ON L8N 3J5   Mrs. Mina Gucma, Libn.

DOFASCO INC. - RESEARCH INFORMATION CENTRE
1390 Burlington St., E.
Box 460   Phone: (416) 544-3761
Hamilton, ON L8N 3J5   Ann M. Duff, Res.Libn.

HAMILTON ACADEMY OF MEDICINE - LIBRARY
286 Victoria Ave., N.   Phone: (416) 528-1611
Hamilton, ON L8L 5G4   Bessie J. McKinlay, Med.Libn.

HAMILTON BOARD OF EDUCATION - EDUCATION CENTRE LIBRARY †
100 Main St., W.   Phone: (416) 527-5092
Hamilton, ON L8P 1H6   E. Birgit Langhammer, Libn.

HAMILTON CITY HALL - LIBRARY
71 Main St., W.   Phone: (416) 526-4645
Hamilton, ON L8N 3T4   S.G. Hollowell, Rec.Adm.

HAMILTON LAW ASSOCIATION - LAW LIBRARY
50 Main St., E.   Phone: (416) 522-1563
Hamilton, ON L8N 1E9   W. Hearder-Moan, Libn.

HAMILTON PSYCHIATRIC HOSPITAL - LIBRARY RESOURCE CENTRE
P.O. Box 585   Phone: (416) 388-2511
Hamilton, ON L9C 3N6   Mary McManus, Libn.

HAMILTON PUBLIC LIBRARY - SPECIAL COLLECTIONS
55 York Blvd.   Phone: (416) 529-8111
Hamilton, ON L8R 3K1   Kathleen Mathews, Coord.

HAMILTON PUBLIC LIBRARY - URBAN/MUNICIPAL COLLECTION
55 York Blvd.   Phone: (416) 529-8111
Hamilton, ON L8R 3K1   Ann Von Rosenbach, Urban/Municipal Libn.

HAMILTON SPECTATOR - REFERENCE LIBRARY †
44 Frid St.   Phone: (416) 526-3315
Hamilton, ON L8N 3G3   Jean M. Tebbutt, Chf.Libn.

MC MASTER UNIVERSITY - ARCHIVES AND RESEARCH COLLECTIONS
    DIVISION
Mills Memorial Library   Phone: (416) 525-9140
Hamilton, ON L8S 4L6   Charlotte Stewart, Dir., Archv. & Res.Coll.

MC MASTER UNIVERSITY - BUSINESS LIBRARY
Innis Room, Kenneth Taylor Hall 108   Phone: (416) 525-9140
Hamilton, ON L8S 4M4   Sheila Pepper, Bus.Libn.

MC MASTER UNIVERSITY - HEALTH SCIENCES LIBRARY
1400 Main St., W.   Phone: (416) 525-9140
Hamilton, ON L8N 3Z5   Dorothy Fitzgerald, Health Sci.Libn.

MC MASTER UNIVERSITY - MAP LIBRARY
Burke Science Bldg. 137   Phone: (416) 525-9140
Hamilton, ON L8S 4K1   Kate Donkin, Map Cur.

MC MASTER UNIVERSITY - THODE LIBRARY OF SCIENCE & ENGINEERING
                                        Phone: (416) 525-9140
Hamilton, ON L8S 4P5   Harold Siroonian, Sci. & Engr.Libn.

MC MASTER UNIVERSITY - URBAN DOCUMENTATION CENTRE
1280 Main St. West   Phone: (416) 525-9140
Hamilton, ON L8S 4K1   Cathy Moulder, Documentalist

MOHAWK COLLEGE OF APPLIED ARTS AND TECHNOLOGY - HEALTH
    SCIENCES LIBRARY RESOURCE CENTRE
P.O. Box 2034   Phone: (416) 389-4461
Hamilton, ON L8N 3T2   June Shore, Lib.Supv.

MOHAWK COLLEGE OF APPLIED ARTS AND TECHNOLOGY - MOHAWK
    LIBRARY RESOURCE CENTRE
P.O. Box 2034   Phone: (416) 389-4461
Hamilton, ON L8N 3T2   Sandra M. Black, Chf.Libn.

ROYAL BOTANICAL GARDENS - LIBRARY
Box 399   Phone: (416) 527-1158
Hamilton, ON L8N 3H8   Ina Vrugtman, Botanical Libn.

ST. JOSEPH'S HOSPITAL - DRUG INFORMATION CENTRE
50 Charlton Ave., E.   Phone: (416) 522-4941
Hamilton, ON L8N 1Y4   Mrs. D.A. Thompson, Dir. of Pharmacy Serv.

ST. JOSEPH'S HOSPITAL - HOSPITAL LIBRARY
50 Charlton Ave., E.   Phone: (416) 522-4941
Hamilton, ON L8N 1Y4   Mrs. S.L. Rogers, Hosp.Libn.

ST. PETER'S HOSPITAL - PROFESSIONAL LIBRARY
88 Maplewood Ave.
Hamilton, ON L8M 1W9   Joan Osburn, Libn.

SOCIETY OF MANAGEMENT ACCOUNTANTS OF CANADA - RESOURCE
    CENTRE
154 Main St., E.
Box 176   Phone: (416) 525-4100
Hamilton, ON L8N 3C3   Helen Hill, Libn.

STELCO INC. - RESEARCH AND DEVELOPMENT LIBRARY
P.O. Box 2030   Phone: (416) 528-2511
Hamilton, ON L8N 3T1   David Rosenplot, Libn.

CANADA - AGRICULTURE CANADA - RESEARCH STATION, HARROW -
    LIBRARY †
                                                 Phone: (519) 738-2251
Harrow, ON N0R 1G0   Eric A. Champagne, Libn.

CIP RESEARCH LTD. - LIBRARY
179 Main St., W.   Phone: (613) 632-4121
Hawkesbury, ON K6A 2H4   M. Higginson, Lib.Asst.

NOTRE DAME HOSPITAL - LIBRARY
1405 Edward St.   Phone: (705) 362-4291
Hearst, ON P0L 1N0   Mary Kellie, Inservice Coord.

ERCO INDUSTRIES, LTD. - LIBRARY
2 Gibbs Rd.   Phone: (416) 239-7111
Islington, ON M9B 1R1   Douglas G. Suarez, Corp.Libn.

NORTHERN TELECOM CANADA, LTD. - BUSINESS SYSTEMS LIBRARY
304 The East Mall   Phone: (416) 232-2000
Islington, ON M9B 6E4   Karen J. Ryan, Jr., Data Base Anl.

KEMPTVILLE COLLEGE OF AGRICULTURAL TECHNOLOGY - PURVIS LIBRARY
                                                 Phone: (613) 258-3411
Kemptville, ON K0G 1J0   Alison Meikle, Libn.

ONTARIO - MINISTRY OF AGRICULTURE AND FOOD - VETERINARY
    SERVICES LABORATORY LIBRARY
P.O. Box 2005   Phone: (613) 258-3804
Kemptville, ON K0G 1J0   Dr. Peter Lusis, Hd.

ALCAN INTERNATIONAL LTD. - KINGSTON LABORATORIES - LIBRARY
P.O. Box 8400   Phone: (613) 549-4500
Kingston, ON K7L 4Z4   Miss E.M. Vanags, Hd.

CANADA - NATIONAL DEFENCE - FORT FRONTENAC LIBRARY
Fort Frontenac   Phone: (613) 545-5829
Kingston, ON K7K 2X8   Mr. S.K. Kamra, Chf.Libn.

CANADIAN INSTITUTE OF GUIDED GROUND TRANSPORT - INFORMATION
    CENTRE
Queen's University   Phone: (613) 547-5777
Kingston, ON K7L 3N6   Jane Law, Info.Off.

DU PONT CANADA, INC. - CUSTOMER TECHNICAL CENTRE LIBRARY
P.O. Box 3500   Phone: (613) 544-6000
Kingston, ON K7L 5A1   L.A. Collins, Lib.Asst.

DU PONT CANADA, INC. - RESEARCH CENTRE LIBRARY
P.O. Box 5000   Phone: (613) 544-6400
Kingston, ON K7L 5A5   Henry R. Meyer, Sr.Res.Sci.-Info.Off.

KINGSTON GENERAL HOSPITAL - HOSPITAL LIBRARY
Stuart St.   Phone: (613) 547-5023
Kingston, ON K7L 2V7   Enid M. Scott, Libn.

KINGSTON PSYCHIATRIC HOSPITAL - STAFF LIBRARY
Bag 603   Phone: (613) 546-1101
Kingston, ON K7L 4X3   Mae Morley, Libn.

ONGWANADA HOSPITAL - PENROSE & HOPKINS DIVISIONS - PENROSE
    DIVISION LIBRARY †
117 Park St.   Phone: (613) 544-9611
Kingston, ON K7L 1J9   Margaret Garrigan

QUEEN'S UNIVERSITY AT KINGSTON - ART LIBRARY
Ontario Hall   Phone: (613) 547-2633
Kingston, ON K7L 5C4   Eve Albrich, Music/Art Libn.

QUEEN'S UNIVERSITY AT KINGSTON - BIOLOGY LIBRARY
Earl Hall, Barrie St.   Phone: (613) 547-2896
Kingston, ON K7L 5C4   Mrs. J. Stevenson, Lib.Asst.

QUEEN'S UNIVERSITY AT KINGSTON - BRACKEN LIBRARY
                                                 Phone: (613) 547-5753
Kingston, ON K7L 3N6   Gwen Wright, Libn.

QUEEN'S UNIVERSITY AT KINGSTON - CHEMISTRY LIBRARY
Frost Wing, Gordon Hall   Phone: (613) 547-2636
Kingston, ON K7L 5C4   Janet Innis, Lib.Asst.

QUEEN'S UNIVERSITY AT KINGSTON - CIVIL ENGINEERING LIBRARY
Ellis Hall   Phone: (613) 547-5546
Kingston, ON K7L 5C4   Stewart Renfrew, Lib.Techn.

QUEEN'S UNIVERSITY AT KINGSTON - DOCUMENTS LIBRARY
Mackintosh-Corry Hall   Phone: (613) 547-6138
Kingston, ON K7L 3N6   Peter Girard, Doc.Libn.

QUEEN'S UNIVERSITY AT KINGSTON - DUPUIS HALL LIBRARY
Division & Clergy Sts.
Kingston, ON K7L 5C4   Mrs. B. Walls, Lib.Asst.

QUEEN'S UNIVERSITY AT KINGSTON - EDUCATION LIBRARY
Duncan McArthur Hall   Phone: (613) 547-6286
Kingston, ON K7L 3N6   Sandra Casey, Educ.Libn.

QUEEN'S UNIVERSITY AT KINGSTON - ELECTRICAL ENGINEERING
    LIBRARY
Fleming Hall
Kingston, ON K7L 5C4   Christine Bruce, Lib.Asst.

QUEEN'S UNIVERSITY AT KINGSTON - GEOLOGICAL SCIENCES LIBRARY
Miller Hall, Bruce Wing   Phone: (613) 547-2653
Kingston, ON K7L 5C4   Mary Mayson, Sr.Lib.Techn.

QUEEN'S UNIVERSITY AT KINGSTON - INDUSTRIAL RELATIONS CENTRE -
    LIBRARY
                                                 Phone: (613) 547-6917
Kingston, ON K7L 3N6   Carol Williams, Libn.

QUEEN'S UNIVERSITY AT KINGSTON - LAW LIBRARY
Sir John A. Macdonald Hall   Phone: (613) 547-5934
Kingston, ON K7L 3N6   Irene Bessette, Libn.

QUEEN'S UNIVERSITY AT KINGSTON - MAP AND AIR PHOTO LIBRARY
Mackintosh-Corry Hall   Phone: (613) 547-6193
Kingston, ON K7L 5C4   Kathy Harding, Sr.Lib.Asst.

QUEEN'S UNIVERSITY AT KINGSTON - MATHEMATICS LIBRARY
Jeffery Hall   Phone: (613) 547-5720
Kingston, ON K7L 5C4   Mrs. D. Nuttall, Lib.Asst.

QUEEN'S UNIVERSITY AT KINGSTON - MECHANICAL ENGINEERING
    LIBRARY
McLaughlin Hall, Stuart St.   Phone: (613) 547-2714
Kingston, ON K7L 5C4   Hilary Richardson, Lib.Asst.

QUEEN'S UNIVERSITY AT KINGSTON - MUSIC LIBRARY
Harrison-LeCaine Hall
Kingston, ON K7L 5C4
Phone: (613) 547-2873
Eve Albrich, Music/Art Libn.

QUEEN'S UNIVERSITY AT KINGSTON - PHYSICS LIBRARY
Stirling Hall, Queen's Crescent
Kingston, ON K7L 5C4
Phone: (613) 547-2739
Catherine Johnson, Lib.Asst.

QUEEN'S UNIVERSITY AT KINGSTON - PSYCHOLOGY LIBRARY
Humphrey Hall
Kingston, ON K7L 5C4
Phone: (613) 547-3172
Barbara Astbury, Lib.Techn.

QUEEN'S UNIVERSITY AT KINGSTON - SPECIAL COLLECTIONS
Douglas Library
Kingston, ON K7L 5C4
Phone: (613) 547-3030
William F.E. Morley, Cur., Spec.Coll.

ROYAL MILITARY COLLEGE OF CANADA - MASSEY LIBRARY & SCIENCE/
ENGINEERING LIBRARY
Phone: (613) 545-7330
Kingston, ON K7L 2W3
Keith Crouch, Chf.Libn.

ST. LAWRENCE COLLEGE SAINT-LAURENT - LEARNING RESOURCE CENTRE
King & Portsmouth
Box 6000
Kingston, ON K7L 5A6
Phone: (613) 544-5400
Sherwin Raichman, Hd.

ST. MARY'S OF THE LAKE HOSPITAL - GIBSON MEDICAL RESOURCE
CENTRE
340 Union St., W.
Box 3600
Kingston, ON K7L 5A2
Phone: (613) 544-5220
Penny G. Levi, Libn.

URBAN TRANSPORTATION DEVELOPMENT CORPORATION - METRO
CANADA LIBRARY
Box 70, Sta. A.
Kingston, ON K7M 6P9
Phone: (613) 384-3100
Theresa Brennan, Mgr., Rec./Off.Sys.

KITCHENER-WATERLOO ART GALLERY - ELEANOR CALVERT MEMORIAL
LIBRARY
101 Queen St. N.
Kitchener, ON N2H 6P7
Phone: (519) 579-5860
Nancy E. Francis, Libn.

KITCHENER-WATERLOO HOSPITAL - HEALTH SCIENCES LIBRARY †
835 King St., W.
Kitchener, ON N2G 1G3
Phone: (519) 742-3611
Thelma Bisch, Libn.

KITCHENER-WATERLOO OVERSEAS AID INC. - GLOBAL COMMUNITY
CENTRE - LIBRARY
94 Queen St. S.
Kitchener, ON N2G 1V9
Phone: (519) 743-7111
Jane Reble, Rsrc.Coord.

KITCHENER-WATERLOO RECORD - LIBRARY
225 Fairway Rd., S.
Kitchener, ON N2G 4E5
Phone: (519) 894-2231
Penny Coates, Libn.

ST. MARY'S HOSPITAL - MEDICAL LIBRARY †
911B Queen's Blvd.
Kitchener, ON N2M 1B2
Phone: (519) 744-3311
Marilyn Mathews, Libn.

WATERLOO HISTORICAL SOCIETY - LIBRARY
Box 552, Sta. C
Kitchener, ON N2G 4A2
Phone: (519) 743-0271
Erich Schultz, Pres.

GLENGARRY GENEALOGICAL SOCIETY - HIGHLAND HERITAGE RESEARCH
LIBRARY
P.O. Box 460
Lancaster, ON K0C 1N0
Alex W. Fraser, Pres.

POINT PELEE NATIONAL PARK - LIBRARY
R.R. 1
Leamington, ON N8H 3V4
Phone: (519) 326-1161
Rob Watt, Chf.Pk. Naturalist

AULT FOODS, LTD. - RESEARCH & DEVELOPMENT LIBRARY
Box 2185
London, ON N6A 4E5
Phone: (519) 672-9111
Dr. W.S. Cheng, Dir., R & D Lab.

CANADA - AGRICULTURE CANADA - LONDON RESEARCH CENTRE LIBRARY
University Sub Post Office
London, ON N6A 5B7
Phone: (519) 679-4452
Dorothy Drew, Libn.

COLLEGE OF FAMILY PHYSICIANS OF CANADA - CANADIAN LIBRARY OF
FAMILY MEDICINE
Sciences Library
Natural Sciences Centre
University of Western Ontario
London, ON N6A 5B7
Phone: (519) 679-2537
Lynn Dunikowski, Libn.

DIVINE WORD INTERNATIONAL RELIGIOUS EDUCATION CENTRE -
LIBRARY
Box 2400
London, ON N6A 4G3

FANSHAWE COLLEGE OF APPLIED ARTS AND TECHNOLOGY - MAIN
LIBRARY
P.O. Box 4005
London, ON N5W 5H1
Phone: (519) 452-4350
Annette K. Frost, Mgr., Lib.Serv.

HURON COLLEGE - SILCOX MEMORIAL LIBRARY
1349 Western Rd.
London, ON N6G 1H3
Phone: (519) 438-7224
Pamela MacKay, Chf.Libn.

LABATT BREWING COMPANY LIMITED - CENTRAL RESEARCH LIBRARY
150 Simcoe St.
Box 5050
London, ON N6A 4M3
Phone: (519) 673-5324
Marliese Lehwaldt, Hd.Libn.

LONDON FREE PRESS PUBLISHING COMPANY, LTD. - EDITORIAL LIBRARY
369 York St.
London, ON N6A 4G1
Phone: (519) 679-1111
Edythe Cusack, Libn.

LONDON PUBLIC LIBRARIES AND MUSEUMS - LONDON ROOM
305 Queens Ave.
London, ON N6B 3L7
Phone: (519) 432-7166
W. Glen Curnoe, Libn.

MIDDLESEX LAW ASSOCIATION - LIBRARY
80 Dundas St.
Box 5600
London, ON N6A 1P3
Phone: (519) 679-7046
Marjorie Martin, Libn.

ST. JOSEPH'S HOSPITAL - MEDICAL LIBRARY
268 Grosvenor St.
London, ON N6A 4V2
Phone: (519) 439-3271
Louise Lin, Coord., Lib.Serv.

ST. PETER'S SEMINARY - LIBRARY
1040 Waterloo St., N.
London, ON N6A 3Y1
Phone: (519) 432-1824
Lois Cote, Libn.

3M CANADA - TECHNICAL INFORMATION CENTRE
Box 5757
London, ON N6A 4T1
Phone: (519) 451-2500
Lorraine Busby, Tech.Libn.

UNIVERSITY OF WESTERN ONTARIO - CPRI LIBRARY
Box 2460, Terminal A
London, ON N6A 4G6
Phone: (519) 471-2540
Asta Hansen, Libn.

UNIVERSITY OF WESTERN ONTARIO - D.B. WELDON LIBRARY -
DEPARTMENT OF SPECIAL COLLECTIONS
Phone: (519) 679-6289
London, ON N6A 3K7
Beth Miller, Libn.

UNIVERSITY OF WESTERN ONTARIO - D.B. WELDON LIBRARY - REGIONAL
COLLECTION
Phone: (519) 679-6213
London, ON N6A 3K7
Edward Phelps, Libn.

UNIVERSITY OF WESTERN ONTARIO - DEPARTMENT OF GEOGRAPHY -
MAP LIBRARY
Phone: (519) 679-3424
London, ON N6A 5C2
Serge A. Sauer, Map Cur.

UNIVERSITY OF WESTERN ONTARIO - ENGINEERING LIBRARY
Phone: (519) 679-6120
London, ON N6A 5B9
Bogdana Brajsa, Libn.

UNIVERSITY OF WESTERN ONTARIO - FACULTY OF EDUCATION LIBRARY
Althouse College
1137 Western Rd.
London, ON N6G 1G7
Phone: (519) 679-3488
Anna Holman, Libn.

UNIVERSITY OF WESTERN ONTARIO - LAW LIBRARY
Phone: (519) 679-2857
London, ON N6A 3K7   Dr. Margaret A. Banks, Libn.

UNIVERSITY OF WESTERN ONTARIO - MUSIC LIBRARY
Phone: (519) 679-2466
London, ON N6A 3K7   William Guthrie, Libn.

UNIVERSITY OF WESTERN ONTARIO - SCHOOL OF BUSINESS
ADMINISTRATION - BUSINESS LIBRARY & INFORMATION CENTRE
Phone: (519) 679-3255
London, ON N6A 3K7   Jerry Mulcahy, Libn.

UNIVERSITY OF WESTERN ONTARIO - SCHOOL OF LIBRARY &
INFORMATION SCIENCE - LIBRARY
Phone: (519) 679-3542
London, ON N6A 1H1   Victoria Ripley, Academic Sup.Serv.Coord.

UNIVERSITY OF WESTERN ONTARIO - SCIENCES LIBRARY
Natural Sciences Centre   Phone: (519) 679-6601
London, ON N6A 5B7   Larry C. Lewis, Sci.Libn.

WESTMINSTER INSTITUTE FOR ETHICS AND HUMAN VALUES - LIBRARY
361 Windermere Rd.   Phone: (519) 673-0046
London, ON N6G 2K3   Gwen Fraser, Asst. for Pub.Educ.

DU PONT CANADA, INC. - MAITLAND WORKS LIBRARY
P.O. Box 611   Phone: (613) 348-3611
Maitland, ON K0E 1P0   H.M. Perrott, Libn.

ONTARIO - MINISTRY OF NATURAL RESOURCES - NATURAL RESOURCES
LIBRARY - MAPLE †
Southern Research Sta.   Phone: (416) 832-2761
Maple, ON L0J 1E0   Sandra Louet, Mgr.

CROWNTEK INC. - LIBRARY SERVICES
3000 Steeles Ave., E.
Markham, ON L3R 4T9   Lucille Slack, Mgr., Lib.Serv.

IBM CANADA, LTD. - HEADQUARTERS LIBRARY
31/761
3500 Steeles Ave. E.   Phone: (416) 474-2348
Markham, ON L3R 2Z1   Anne F. Martin, Libn.

INDUSMIN, LTD. - TECHNICAL CENTRE LIBRARY
2651 John St., Unit 5
Markham, ON L3R 2W5

HURONIA HISTORICAL PARKS - RESOURCE CENTRE
P.O. Box 160   Phone: (705) 526-7838
Midland, ON L4R 4K8   Mrs. M. Quealey, Supv., Lib.Serv.

SIMCOE COUNTY ARCHIVES
R.R. 2   Phone: (705) 726-9300
Minesing, ON L0L 1Y0   Peter P. Moran, Archv.

ABITIBI-PRICE INC. - RESEARCH CENTRE LIBRARY
Sheridan Park   Phone: (416) 822-4770
Mississauga, ON L5K 1A9   Joy A. Armstrong, Libn.

AES DATA INC. - ATRIUM LIBRARY
1900 Minnesota Court   Phone: (416) 821-9190
Mississauga, ON L5N 3C9   Stella J. Cybruch, Supv., Lib./Info.Serv.

ATOMIC ENERGY OF CANADA, LTD. - CANDU OPERATIONS LIBRARY
Sheridan Park Research Community   Phone: (416) 823-9040
Mississauga, ON L5K 1B2   Christine C. Byrne, Hd.

C-I-L INC. - CHEMICALS RESEARCH LABORATORY LIBRARY
2101 Hadwen Rd.
Sheridan Park   Phone: (416) 823-7160
Mississauga, ON L5K 2L3   Joan L. Leishman, Libn.

CANADA SYSTEMS GROUP - REFERENCE LIBRARY
2599 Speakman Dr.   Phone: (416) 822-5200
Mississauga, ON L5K 1B1   Janet Bycio, Libn.

CANADIAN FILM INSTITUTE - NATIONAL SCIENCE FILM LIBRARY
211 Watline Ave.   Phone: (416) 272-3840
Mississauga, ON L4Z 1P3   Peter Dyson-Bonter, Dir., N.S.F.L.

CIBA-GEIGY (Canada) LTD. - PHARMACEUTICAL LIBRARY
6860 Century Ave.
Mississauga, ON L5N 2W5   Heather Dansereau, Med.Libn.

COMINCO LTD. - PRODUCT RESEARCH CENTRE LIBRARY
Sheridan Park   Phone: (416) 822-2022
Mississauga, ON L5K 1B4   Pat Doyle, Tech.Libn.

COMMONWEALTH MICROFILM LIBRARY
3395 American Dr., Unit 11   Phone: (416) 671-4173
Mississauga, ON L4V 1T5   K.W. (Bill) Hayden, Mktg.Dir.

DOMGLAS INC. - CORPORATE LIBRARY
2070 Hadwen Rd.   Phone: (416) 823-3860
Mississauga, ON L5K 2C9   Mary MacKinnon

DU PONT CANADA, INC. - CENTRAL LIBRARY
Streetsville Postal Sta., Box 2300   Phone: (416) 821-5781
Mississauga, ON L5M 2J4   Martha Pettit, Libn.

DU PONT CANADA, INC. - PATENT DIVISION LIBRARY
Box 2200, Streetsville   Phone: (416) 821-5504
Mississauga, ON L5M 2H3

DUNLOP RESEARCH CENTRE - LIBRARY
Sheridan Park   Phone: (416) 822-4711
Mississauga, ON L5K 1Z8   Shirley A. Morrison, Libn.

DURACELL INC. - RESEARCH LIBRARY
2333 N. Sheridan Way
Sheridan Park   Phone: (416) 823-4410
Mississauga, ON L5K 1A7   Gail J. Robertson, Libn.

GOLDER (H.Q.) & ASSOCIATES - LIBRARY
3151 Wharton Way   Phone: (416) 625-0094
Mississauga, ON L4X 2B6   Mary Anne Smyth, Lib.Techn.

GULF CANADA LIMITED - RESEARCH & DEVELOPMENT DEPARTMENT -
LIBRARY †
2489 N. Sheridan Way
Sheridan Park   Phone: (416) 822-6770
Mississauga, ON L5K 1A8   Ann Neilson, Libn.

IEC BEAK CONSULTANTS LTD. - LIBRARY
6870 Goreway Dr.   Phone: (416) 671-2600
Mississauga, ON L4V 1P1   R.K. Suri, Libn.

INCO LIMITED - J. ROY GORDON RESEARCH LABORATORY
Sheridan Park   Phone: (416) 822-3322
Mississauga, ON L5K 1Z9   L. Green, Libn.

NCR CANADA LTD. - MIRS LIBRARY
6865 Century Ave.   Phone: (416) 826-9000
Mississauga, ON L5N 2E2   Ms. Tye Hofmeister, MIRS Libn.

NORTHERN TELECOM, LTD. - NT LIBRARY
33 City Centre Dr.   Phone: (416) 232-2000
Mississauga, ON L5B 3A2   Eileen Daniel, Libn.

ONTARIO RESEARCH FOUNDATION - LIBRARY
Sheridan Park   Phone: (416) 822-4111
Mississauga, ON L5K 1B3   Carl K. Wei, Libn.

PEEL COUNTY BOARD OF EDUCATION - J.A. TURNER PROFESSIONAL
LIBRARY
73 King St., W.   Phone: (416) 279-6010
Mississauga, ON L5B 1H5   Dr. K. Kirkwood, Chf.Res.Off.

SHERIDAN COLLEGE OF APPLIED ARTS AND TECHNOLOGY - SCHOOL OF
DESIGN - LIBRARY
1460 S. Sheridan Way   Phone: (416) 274-3685
Mississauga, ON L5H 1Z7   Madeleine La Pointe, Lib.Techn.

SMITH, KLINE & FRENCH CANADA, LTD. - MEDICAL/MARKETING LIBRARY
1940 Argentia Rd.　　　　　　　　　Phone: (416) 821-2200
Mississauga, ON L5N 2V7　　　　　　Janet B. Hillis, Lib.Techn.

SPERRY COMPUTER SYSTEMS - LIBRARY *
55 City Centre Dr.　　　　　　　　　Phone: (416) 270-3030
Mississauga, ON L5B 1M4　　　　　　Laurie Bennett, Libn.

UNITED COOPERATIVES OF ONTARIO - HARMAN LIBRARY
Sta. A, P.O. Box 527　　　　　　　　Phone: (416) 270-3560
Mississauga, ON L5A 3A4　　　　　　Audrey Ferger, Libn.

XEROX RESEARCH CENTRE OF CANADA - TECHNICAL INFORMATION
　　CENTRE
2660 Speakman Dr.　　　　　　　　　Phone: (416) 823-7091
Mississauga, ON L5K 2L1　　Betty A. Bassett, Mgr., Tech.Info.Ctr.

LENNOX AND ADDINGTON COUNTY MUSEUM - LIBRARY & ARCHIVES
97 Thomas St., E.
Postal Bag 1000　　　　　　　　　Phone: (613) 354-3027
Napanee, ON K7R 3S9　　　　　　　Jane Foster, Dir.

ONTARIO - MINISTRY OF AGRICULTURE AND FOOD - VETERINARY
　　SERVICES LABORATORY LIBRARY
Box 790　　　　　　　　　　　　Phone: (705) 647-6701
New Liskeard, ON P0J 1P0

ACRES CONSULTING SERVICES, LTD. - LIBRARY
5259 Dorchester Rd.
Box 1001　　　　　　　　　　　Phone: (416) 354-3831
Niagara Falls, ON L2E 6W1　　　　　Mrs. A. McKay, Libn.

NIAGARA PARKS COMMISSION - SCHOOL OF HORTICULTURE -
　　HORTICULTURAL LIBRARY
P.O. Box 150　　　　　　　　　　Phone: (416) 356-8554
Niagara Falls, ON L2E 6T2　　　　Ruth Stoner, Lib.Techn.

NORTON RESEARCH CORPORATION (Canada) LTD. - LIBRARY
8001 Daly St.　　　　　　　　　　Phone: (416) 295-4311
Niagara Falls, ON L2G 6S2　　Wende Cournoyea, Exec.Sec.

NIAGARA HISTORICAL SOCIETY - LIBRARY
43 Castlereagh St.
Box 208
Niagara on the Lake, ON L0S 1J0

FOREST PRODUCTS ACCIDENT PREVENTION ASSOCIATION - LIBRARY
Box 270　　　　　　　　　　　Phone: (705) 472-4120
North Bay, ON P1B 8H2　　　　　　James Nugent

NORTH BAY COLLEGE EDUCATION CENTRE - LIBRARY
Box 5001, Gormanville Rd.　　　　　Phone: (705) 474-7600
North Bay, ON P1B 8K9　　　　　　J.G. Poff, Hd.Libn.

C-I-L INC. - CENTRAL LIBRARY
P.O. Box 200　　　　　　　　　　Phone: (416) 229-8047
North York, ON M2N 6H2　　　　　M.R. Weaver, Libn.

C-I-L INC. - PATENT LIBRARY
P.O. Box 200　　　　　　　　　　Phone: (416) 229-8186
North York, ON M2N 6H2　　　　　Yolande D' Souza, Libn.

NORTH YORK BOARD OF EDUCATION - F.W. MINKLER LIBRARY
Education Administration Ctr.
5050 Yonge St.　　　　　　　　　Phone: (416) 225-4661
North York, ON M2N 5N8　　　　　H.P. Greaves, Chf.Libn.

NORTH YORK PUBLIC LIBRARY - MULTILINGUAL MATERIALS DEPARTMENT
120 Martin Ross Ave.　　　　　　　Phone: (416) 667-7618
North York, ON M3J 2L4　　　Diane Dragasevich, Libn./Supv.

NORTH YORK PUBLIC LIBRARY - URBAN AFFAIRS SECTION
5126 Yonge St.　　　　　　　　　Phone: (416) 225-8891
North York, ON M2N 5N9　　Clara J. "Callie" Stacey, Libn.Supv.

SEARLE (G.D.) & CO. OF CANADA, LIMITED - LIBRARY
400 Iroquois Shore Rd.　　　　　　Phone: (416) 844-1040
Oakville, ON L6H 1M5

SHELL CANADA LIMITED - OAKVILLE RESEARCH CENTRE - SHELL
　　RESEARCH CENTRE LIBRARY
P.O. Box 2100　　　　　　　　　Phone: (416) 827-1141
Oakville, ON L6J 5C7　　　　　　Mr. Lan C. Sun, Libn.

WELDING INSTITUTE OF CANADA - LIBRARY
391 Burnhamthorpe Rd. E.　　　　　Phone: (416) 487-5415
Oakville, ON L6J 6C9　　Bruce F. Bryan, Info.Off. & Res.Engr.

HURONIA REGIONAL CENTRE - LIBRARY
Box 1000　　　　　　　　　　　Phone: (705) 326-7361
Orillia, ON L3V 6L2　　　　　　　Maureen Maguire, Libn.

LEACOCK (Stephen) MEMORIAL HOME - LIBRARY
Old Brewery Bay
P.O. Box 625　　　　　　　　　　Phone: (705) 324-9357
Orillia, ON L3V 6K5　　　　　　　Jay Cody, Dir./Cur.

DURHAM COLLEGE OF APPLIED ARTS AND TECHNOLOGY - MAIN LIBRARY &
　　SIMCOE RESOURCE CENTRE
Simcoe St., N.
Box 385　　　　　　　　　　　　Phone: (416) 576-0210
Oshawa, ON L1H 7L7　　　　　　Susan Barclay, Coll.Libn.

MC LAUGHLIN (Robert) GALLERY - LIBRARY
Civic Centre　　　　　　　　　　Phone: (416) 576-3000
Oshawa, ON L1H 3Z3　　　Patricia Glaxton-Oldfield, Libn.

ONTARIO - MINISTRY OF REVENUE - LIBRARY
33 King St. W.
P.O. Box 627　　　　　　　　　　Phone: (416) 433-6135
Oshawa, ON L1H 8H5　　　　　　Penni Lee, Act.Libn.

AGUDATH ISRAEL CONGREGATION - MALCA PASS MEMORIAL LIBRARY
1400 Coldrey Ave.
Ottawa, ON K1Z 7P9　　　　　　　Frieda Lauterman, Libn.

ALGONQUIN COLLEGE OF APPLIED ARTS & TECHNOLOGY - RESOURCE
　　CENTRES †
1385 Woodroffe Ave.　　　　　　　Phone: (613) 725-7301
Ottawa, ON K2G 1V8　　　　　　　James Feeley, Dir.

ATOMIC ENERGY OF CANADA, LTD. - COMMERCIAL PRODUCTS LIBRARY *
Sta. J, P.O. Box 6300　　　　　　　Phone: (613) 592-2790
Ottawa, ON K2A 3W3　　　　　　　Herb Fletcher, Libn.

ATOMIC ENERGY CONTROL BOARD - LIBRARY
P.O. Box 1046　　　　　　　　　Phone: (613) 995-1359
Ottawa, ON K1P 5S9

BANK OF CANADA - LIBRARY
245 Sparks St.　　　　　　　　　Phone: (613) 563-8201
Ottawa, ON K1A 0G9　　　　　　Jane E. King, Chf.Libn.

BELL-NORTHERN RESEARCH LTD. - INFORMATION RESOURCE CENTRE
P.O. Box 3511, Station C　　　　　　Phone: (613) 596-2467
Ottawa, ON K1Y 4H7　　　Grant Birks, Mgr., Info.Rsrc.Ctr.

BOY SCOUTS OF CANADA - MUSEUM & ARCHIVES OF CANADIAN
　　SCOUTING
1345 Base Line Rd.
Sta. F, Box 5151　　　　　　　　　Phone: (613) 224-5131
Ottawa, ON K2C 3G7　　Melanie E. Crampton, Cur./Libn.

BOY SCOUTS OF CANADA - NATIONAL LIBRARY
1345 Base Line Rd.
Sta. F, Box 5151　　　　　　　　　Phone: (613) 224-5131
Ottawa, ON K2C 3G7　　　　　Melanie Crampton, Libn.

BREWERS ASSOCIATION OF CANADA - LIBRARY
151 Sparks St., Suite 805　　　　　Phone: (613) 232-9601
Ottawa, ON K1P 5E3　　　　　　Edwin Gregory, Libn.

CANADA - AGRICULTURE CANADA - ANIMAL DISEASES RESEARCH
　　INSTITUTE LIBRARY
Sta. H., P.O. Box 11300　　　　　　Phone: (613) 998-9320
Ottawa, ON K2H 8P9　　　　　　P. Atherton, Libn.

CANADA - AGRICULTURE CANADA - ANIMAL RESEARCH CENTRE LIBRARY
Genetics Bldg.   Phone: (613) 994-9719
Ottawa, ON K1A 0C6

CANADA - AGRICULTURE CANADA - ENTOMOLOGY RESEARCH LIBRARY
K.W. Neatby Bldg., Rm. 4061
Central Experimental Farm   Phone: (613) 996-1665
Ottawa, ON K1A 0C6   Marie-Josee Boisvenue, Entomology Res.Libn.

CANADA - AGRICULTURE CANADA - LIBRARIES DIVISION
Sir John Carling Bldg., Rm. 245   Phone: (613) 995-7829
Ottawa, ON K1A 0C5   M.L. Morton, Dir., Lib.Div.

CANADA - AGRICULTURE CANADA - NEATBY LIBRARY
K.W. Neatby Bldg., Rm. 3032
Central Experimental Farm   Phone: (613) 995-5011
Ottawa, ON K1A 0C6   Marcel Charette, Ck. in Charge

CANADA - AGRICULTURE CANADA - PLANT RESEARCH LIBRARY
Biosystematics Research Inst., Bldg. 49   Phone: (613) 996-1665
Ottawa, ON K1A 0C6   Eva Gavora, Libn.

CANADA - AGRICULTURE CANADA - RESEARCH STATION, OTTAWA -
   LIBRARY
                                                       Phone: (613) 995-9428
Ottawa, ON K1A 0C6

CANADA - CANADA CENTRE FOR REMOTE SENSING - TECHNICAL
   INFORMATION SERVICE
240 Bank St., 5th Fl.   Phone: (613) 995-5645
Ottawa, ON K1A 0Y7   Brian McGurrin, Hd.

CANADA - CANADA POST CORPORATION - LIBRARY
Sir Alexander Campbell Bldg.
Riverside Dr.   Phone: (613) 998-4463
Ottawa, ON K1A 0B1   Jean Weerasinghe, Corp.Libn.

CANADA - CANADIAN ADVISORY COUNCIL ON THE STATUS OF WOMEN -
   DOCUMENTATION CENTRE
Sta. B, Box 1541   Phone: (613) 995-8284
Ottawa, ON K1P 5R5   Nicole Proulx, Libn.

CANADA - CANADIAN RADIO-TELEVISION AND TELECOMMUNICATIONS
   COMMISSION - LIBRARY
                                                       Phone: (613) 997-0313
Ottawa, ON K1A 0N2   Ms. M.A. Anschutz, Libn.

CANADA - CANADIAN TRANSPORT COMMISSION - LIBRARY
                                                       Phone: (819) 997-7160
Ottawa, ON K1A 0N9   Marty H. Lovelock, Libn.

CANADA - CANADIAN WILDLIFE SERVICE - ONTARIO REGION LIBRARY †
1725 Woodward Dr., 5th Fl.   Phone: (613) 998-4693
Ottawa, ON K1A 0E7   Katherine L. Mahoney, Libn.

CANADA - CONSUMER AND CORPORATE AFFAIRS CANADA -
   DEPARTMENTAL LIBRARY
                                                       Phone: (819) 997-1632
Ottawa, ON K1A 0C9   Corinne K. MacLaurin, Chf.Libn.

CANADA - CONSUMER AND CORPORATE AFFAIRS CANADA - PATENT
   OFFICE LIBRARY
Place du Portage   Phone: (613) 997-2525
Ottawa, ON K1A 0E1   William Berdnikoff, Hd.

CANADA - DEFENCE RESEARCH ESTABLISHMENT OTTAWA - LIBRARY †
                                                       Phone: (613) 596-9386
Ottawa, ON K1A 0Z4   Tina Matiisen, Hd., Info.Serv.

CANADA - DEPARTMENT OF COMMUNICATIONS - COMMUNICATIONS
   RESEARCH CENTRE LIBRARY
Box 11490, Sta. H   Phone: (613) 596-9250
Ottawa, ON K2H 8S2   Callista Kelly, Libn.

CANADA - DEPARTMENT OF COMMUNICATIONS - INFORMATION
   SERVICES
300 Slater St., Rm. 1420   Phone: (613) 995-8883
Ottawa, ON K1A 0C8   Monique Perrier, Act.Chf.Libn.

CANADA - DEPARTMENT OF FINANCE - FINANCE/TREASURY BOARD
   LIBRARY
Place Bell Canada, 17th Fl.
160 Elgin St.   Phone: (613) 996-5491
Ottawa, ON K1A 0G5   J.E.T. Reid, Chf.Libn.

CANADA - DEPARTMENT OF INSURANCE - LIBRARY
140 O'Connor St., 16th Fl.
East Tower   Phone: (613) 996-5162
Ottawa, ON K1A 0H2   Luanne Larose, Lib.Techn.

CANADA - DEPARTMENT OF JUSTICE - LIBRARY
Justice Bldg.
Kent & Wellington Sts.   Phone: (613) 995-0144
Ottawa, ON K1A 0H8   Susan Jackson, Dir., Lib.Serv.

CANADA - ECONOMIC COUNCIL OF CANADA - LIBRARY
Sta. B., P.O. Box 527   Phone: (613) 993-1253
Ottawa, ON K1P 5V6   Irene Lackner, Libn.

CANADA - EMPLOYMENT & IMMIGRATION CANADA - LIBRARY
                                                       Phone: (819) 994-2603
Ottawa, ON K1A 0J9   P.E. Sunder-Raj, Dir., Lib.Serv.

CANADA - ENERGY, MINES & RESOURCES CANADA - CANMET - LIBRARY †
555 Booth St.   Phone: (613) 995-4132
Ottawa, ON K1A 0G1   Gloria M. Peckham, Chf.Libn.

CANADA - ENERGY, MINES & RESOURCES CANADA - EARTH PHYSICS
   BRANCH LIBRARY
1 Observatory Crescent   Phone: (613) 995-5558
Ottawa, ON K1A 0Y3   W.M. Tsang, Chf.Libn.

CANADA - ENERGY, MINES & RESOURCES CANADA - GEOGRAPHICAL
   SERVICES DIRECTORATE - MAP RESOURCE CENTRE
580 Booth St.
Ottawa, ON K1A 0E9

CANADA - ENERGY, MINES & RESOURCES CANADA - HEADQUARTERS
   LIBRARY
580 Booth St.   Phone: (613) 996-0825
Ottawa, ON K1A 0E4   F.B. Scollie, Chf.Libn.

CANADA - ENERGY, MINES & RESOURCES CANADA - SURVEYS & MAPPING
   BRANCH - LIBRARY
615 Booth St.   Phone: (613) 995-4071
Ottawa, ON K1A 0E9   Valerie E. Hoare, Chf.Libn.

CANADA - ENERGY, MINES & RESOURCES CANADA - SURVEYS & MAPPING
   BRANCH - NATIONAL AIR PHOTO LIBRARY
615 Booth St.   Phone: (613) 995-4560
Ottawa, ON K1A 0E9   Dianne Rombough, Hd.

CANADA - ENVIRONMENT CANADA - LIBRARY SERVICES BRANCH
                                                       Phone: (613) 997-1767
Ottawa, ON K1A 1C7   Mrs. A.M. Bystram, Dir., Lib.Serv.Br.

CANADA - EXTERNAL AFFAIRS CANADA - LIBRARY
Lester B. Pearson Bldg.
Sussex Dr.   Phone: (613) 996-8691
Ottawa, ON K1A 0G2   Ruth Margaret Thompson, Dir.

CANADA - FARM CREDIT CORPORATION CANADA - LIBRARY
Sta. D, Box 2314   Phone: (613) 996-6606
Ottawa, ON K1P 6J9   Susan Moore, P.R. Asst.

CANADA - FISHERIES & OCEANS - LIBRARY †
240 Sparks St., 8th Fl. W.   Phone: (613) 995-9991
Ottawa, ON K1A 0E6   C.S. Boyle, Dir., Lib.Serv.

CANADA - GEOLOGICAL SURVEY OF CANADA - LIBRARY
601 Booth St., Rm. 350   Phone: (613) 995-4151
Ottawa, ON K1A 0E8   Miss A.E. Bourgeois, Hd., Lib.Serv.

CANADA - HEALTH AND WELFARE CANADA - DEPARTMENTAL LIBRARY
   SERVICES
Brooke Claxton Bldg., Rm. 374
Tunney's Pasture   Phone: (613) 992-5743
Ottawa, ON K1A 0K9   B.A. Stableford, Act.Chf.

CANADA - HEALTH AND WELFARE CANADA - LIBRARY SERVICES
Sir F.G. Banting Research Centre, 3rd Fl., E.
Ross Ave., Tunney's Pasture   Phone: (613) 593-7603
Ottawa, ON K1A 0L2   Bonita Stableford, Chf., Lib.Serv.

CANADA - IMMIGRATION APPEAL BOARD - LIBRARY
116 Lisgar St.   Phone: (613) 995-6486
Ottawa, ON K1A 0K1   Philippa Wall, Hd.

CANADA - INDIAN & NORTHERN AFFAIRS CANADA - DEPARTMENTAL
  LIBRARY
                                     Phone: (819) 997-0799
Ottawa, ON K1A 0H4   Kamra Ramma, Hd.Libn.

CANADA - LABOUR CANADA - LIBRARY SERVICES †
                                     Phone: (819) 997-3540
Ottawa, ON K1A 0J2   V.S. MacKelvie, Dir., Lib.Serv.

CANADA - LABOUR RELATIONS BOARD - LIBRARY
C.D. Howe Bldg., 4th Fl. West
240 Sparks St.   Phone: (613) 995-0895
Ottawa, ON K1A 0X8   Alan Crawford, Libn.

CANADA - LAW REFORM COMMISSION OF CANADA - LIBRARY
130 Albert St., Rm. 809   Phone: (613) 995-8648
Ottawa, ON K1A 0L6   Judith Rubin, Libn.

CANADA - LIBRARY OF PARLIAMENT
Parliament Bldgs.   Phone: (613) 995-7113
Ottawa, ON K1A 0A9   Erik J. Spicer, Parliamentary Libn.

CANADA - METRIC COMMISSION CANADA - REFERENCE SERVICE
255 Argyle Ave.   Phone: (613) 995-2294
Ottawa, ON K1A 0C9   Ms. J. Findley, Doc.Asst.

CANADA - MINISTRY OF STATE FOR ECONOMIC & REGIONAL
  DEVELOPMENT - LIBRARY
270 Albert St.   Phone: (613) 996-0326
Ottawa, ON K1A 1E7   Carol P. Barton, Libn.

CANADA - MORTGAGE AND HOUSING CORPORATION - CANADIAN
  HOUSING INFORMATION CENTRE
Ground Fl., Annex, Montreal Rd.   Phone: (613) 746-4611
Ottawa, ON K1A 0P7   Leslie Jones, Mgr.

CANADA - NATIONAL DEFENCE - DIRECTORATE OF HISTORY LIBRARY
National Defence Headquarters   Phone: (613) 992-7849
Ottawa, ON K1A 0K2   Dr. W.A.B. Douglas, Dir.

CANADA - NATIONAL DEFENCE - MAPPING AND CHARTING
  ESTABLISHMENT TECHNICAL LIBRARY
615 Booth St.
Ottawa, ON K1A 0K2

CANADA - NATIONAL DEFENCE - NATIONAL DEFENCE MEDICAL CENTRE -
  MEDICAL LIBRARY
Alta Vista Dr.   Phone: (613) 733-6600
Ottawa, ON K1A 0K6   Philip B. Allan, Med.Libn.

CANADA - NATIONAL DEFENCE - NDHQ CHIEF CONSTRUCTION AND
  PROPERTIES LIBRARY
101 Colonel By Drive
8th North Tower   Phone: (613) 992-5710
Ottawa, ON K1A 0K2   Mr. L. Monuk, Hd.

CANADA - NATIONAL DEFENCE - NDHQ COMPUTER CENTRE LIBRARY
Canadian Bldg., 14th Fl.
219 Laurier Ave., W.   Phone: (613) 996-6296
Ottawa, ON K1A 0K2   Hazel D. Rolland, Hd.

CANADA - NATIONAL DEFENCE - NDHQ LAND TECHNICAL LIBRARY
305 Rideau St.
Constitution Bldg., Rm. 741   Phone: (613) 992-9862
Ottawa, ON K1A 0K2   D.J. Moyle, Hd.

CANADA - NATIONAL DEFENCE - NDHQ LIBRARY
101 Colonel By Drive, 2NT   Phone: (613) 996-0831
Ottawa, ON K1A 0K2   Mr. R. Van Den Berg, Dept.Libn.

CANADA - NATIONAL DEFENCE - NDHQ MARITIME TECHNICAL LIBRARY
101 Colonel By Drive, 7ST   Phone: (613) 996-2324
Ottawa, ON K1A 0K2   D. Shaver, Hd.

CANADA - NATIONAL DEFENCE - NDHQ TECHNICAL LIBRARY
Bldg. 155W, CFB Ottawa (N)   Phone: (613) 993-2105
Ottawa, ON K1A 0K2   L. McKim, Libn.

CANADA - NATIONAL DEFENCE - OFFICE OF THE JUDGE ADVOCATE
  GENERAL - LIBRARY
National Defence Headquarters   Phone: (613) 996-3380
Ottawa, ON K1A 0K2   W.J. Kenney, Law Ck.

CANADA - NATIONAL ENERGY BOARD - LIBRARY
473 Albert St., Rm. 962   Phone: (613) 996-0375
Ottawa, ON K1A 0E5   Ms. N.R. Park, Mgr.

CANADA - NATIONAL FILM BOARD OF CANADA - PHOTOTHEQUE
Tunney's Pasture   Phone: (613) 593-5826
Ottawa, ON K1A 0M9   David Barbour, Photo Ed.

CANADA - NATIONAL GALLERY OF CANADA - LIBRARY
75 Albert St., 4th Fl.   Phone: (613) 995-6245
Ottawa, ON K1A 0M8   J.E.B. Hunter, Chf.Libn.

CANADA - NATIONAL MUSEUMS OF CANADA - CANADIAN CONSERVATION
  INSTITUTE LIBRARY
                                     Phone: (613) 998-3721
Ottawa, ON K1A 0M8   Mrs. M. Anderson, Libn.

CANADA - NATIONAL MUSEUMS OF CANADA - CANADIAN WAR MUSEUM -
  LIBRARY
330 Sussex Dr.   Phone: (613) 996-4708
Ottawa, ON K1A 0M8   Mr. L. Kosche, Libn.

CANADA - NATIONAL MUSEUMS OF CANADA - LIBRARY SERVICES
  DIRECTORATE
                                     Phone: (613) 998-3923
Ottawa, ON K1A 0M8   Valerie Monkhouse, Dir.

CANADA - NATIONAL MUSEUMS OF CANADA - NATIONAL MUSEUM OF
  SCIENCE AND TECHNOLOGY - LIBRARY
                                     Phone: (613) 998-9520
Ottawa, ON K1A 0M8   Minda Bojin, Libn.

CANADA - NATIONAL RESEARCH COUNCIL - CANADA INSTITUTE FOR
  SCIENTIFIC AND TECHNICAL INFORMATION (CISTI)
Montreal Rd.   Phone: (613) 993-1600
Ottawa, ON K1A 0S2   Elmer V. Smith, Dir.

CANADA - NATIONAL RESEARCH COUNCIL - CISTI - ADMINISTRATION
  BRANCH
Montreal Rd.   Phone: (613) 993-1517
Ottawa, ON K1A 0R6   Dene McColm, Hd.

CANADA - NATIONAL RESEARCH COUNCIL - CISTI - AERONAUTICAL &
  MECHANICAL ENGINEERING BRANCH
Montreal Rd., Bldg M-2   Phone: (613) 993-2431
Ottawa, ON K1A 0R6

CANADA - NATIONAL RESEARCH COUNCIL - CISTI - BUILDING RESEARCH
  BRANCH
Montreal Rd.   Phone: (613) 993-2466
Ottawa, ON K1A 0R6   Joyce Waudby-Smith, Libn.

CANADA - NATIONAL RESEARCH COUNCIL - CISTI - CHEMISTRY BRANCH
Montreal Rd. Laboratories   Phone: (613) 993-2266
Ottawa, ON K1A 0R9   Nancy Ross, Libn.

CANADA - NATIONAL RESEARCH COUNCIL - CISTI - ELECTRICAL
  ENGINEERING BRANCH
Montreal Rd.   Phone: (613) 993-2006
Ottawa, ON K1A 0R6   Jane Dyment, Libn.

CANADA - NATIONAL RESEARCH COUNCIL - CISTI - ENERGY BRANCH
Bldg. M-55, Montreal Rd.   Phone: (613) 993-3861
Ottawa, ON K1A 0S2   Susan Suart, Libn.

CANADA - NATIONAL RESEARCH COUNCIL - CISTI - PHYSICS BRANCH
Division of Physics, Bldg. M-36   Phone: (613) 993-2483
Ottawa, ON K1A 0S1   Raymond Jacyna, Libn.

CANADA - NATIONAL RESEARCH COUNCIL - CISTI - SUSSEX BRANCH
100 Sussex Dr.   Phone: (613) 992-9151
Ottawa, ON K1A 0R6   Margaret Schade, Libn.

CANADA - NATIONAL RESEARCH COUNCIL - CISTI - UPLANDS BRANCH
Montreal Rd.   Phone: (613) 998-3327
Ottawa, ON K1A 0R6   Debbie Dumouchel, Hd.

CANADA - OFFICE OF THE COMMISSIONER OF OFFICIAL LANGUAGES -
   LIBRARY
66 Slater St., 20th Fl.   Phone: (613) 995-7717
Ottawa, ON K1A 0T8   Beryl M. Hunter, Libn.

CANADA - PRIVY COUNCIL OFFICE - LIBRARY
Blackburn Bldg.   Phone: (613) 992-7608
Ottawa, ON K1A 0A3   Margot Ryan, Libn.

CANADA - PUBLIC ARCHIVES OF CANADA - FEDERAL ARCHIVES DIVISION
395 Wellington St.   Phone: (613) 996-8507
Ottawa, ON K1A 0N3   E. Frost, Dir.

CANADA - PUBLIC ARCHIVES OF CANADA - LIBRARY
395 Wellington St.   Phone: (613) 992-2669
Ottawa, ON K1A 0N3   Normand St. Pierre, Dir.

CANADA - PUBLIC ARCHIVES OF CANADA - MANUSCRIPT DIVISION
395 Wellington St.   Phone: (613) 995-8094
Ottawa, ON K1A 0N3

CANADA - PUBLIC ARCHIVES OF CANADA - NATL. FILM, TELEVISION &
   SOUND ARCHIVES - DOCUMENTATION & PUB. SERV.
395 Wellington St.   Phone: (613) 995-1311
Ottawa, ON K1A 0N3   Jana Vosikovska, Chf.

CANADA - PUBLIC ARCHIVES OF CANADA - NATIONAL MAP COLLECTION
395 Wellington St.   Phone: (613) 995-1077
Ottawa, ON K1A 0N3   Betty Kidd, Dir.

CANADA - PUBLIC SERVICE COMMISSION - LIBRARY SERVICES DIVISION
Esplanade-Laurier Bldg., Rm. 930, Tower 2
300 Laurier Ave.   Phone: (613) 996-6365
Ottawa, ON K1A 0M7   A. Campbell, Libn.

CANADA - PUBLIC SERVICE STAFF RELATIONS BOARD - LIBRARY
Sta. B, P.O. Box 1525   Phone: (613) 992-3584
Ottawa, ON K1P 5V2   Lucie Molgat, Lib.Mgr.

CANADA - PUBLIC WORKS CANADA - INFORMATION, RESEARCH &
   LIBRARY SERVICES
Sir Charles Tupper Bldg.   Phone: (613) 998-8350
Ottawa, ON K1A 0M2   Mr. R. Gagnon, Chf.Libn.

CANADA - PUBLIC WORKS CANADA - OFFICE OF THE FIRE COMMISSIONER
   OF CANADA - RESOURCE CENTRE
Riverside Drive   Phone: (613) 998-4617
Ottawa, ON K1A 0M2   Mrs. M.L. Levesque, Fire Res.Off.

CANADA - REGIONAL INDUSTRIAL EXPANSION - CANADIAN GOVERNMENT
   OFFICE OF TOURISM
Tourism Reference & Data Centre
235 Queen St.   Phone: (613) 995-2754
Ottawa, ON K1A 0H6   Rae Bradford, Mgr.

CANADA - REGIONAL INDUSTRIAL EXPANSION - LIBRARY
235 Queen St.   Phone: (613) 992-4947
Ottawa, ON K1A 0H6   Stephan Rush, Mgr., Dept.Lib.

CANADA - REVENUE CANADA - CUSTOMS & EXCISE - LEGAL SERVICES
   LIBRARY †
3rd Fl. Connaught Bldg.
MacKenzie Ave.   Phone: (613) 996-9208
Ottawa, ON K1A 0L5   Diana Millar, Law Ck.

CANADA - REVENUE CANADA - CUSTOMS & EXCISE LIBRARY
Connaught Bldg., 2nd Fl.   Phone: (613) 995-0007
Ottawa, ON K1A 0L5   Dianne L. Parsonage, Dept.Libn.

CANADA - REVENUE CANADA - CUSTOMS & EXCISE - SCIENTIFIC AND
   TECHNICAL INFORMATION CENTRE
79 Bentley Ave.   Phone: (613) 998-8510
Ottawa, ON K1A 0L5   Althea Sproule, Hd., Info.Ctr.

CANADA - REVENUE CANADA - TAXATION LIBRARY
Head Office, 875 Heron Rd.   Phone: (613) 996-9896
Ottawa, ON K1A 0L8   Lorraine Wilkinson, Chf., Lib.Serv.

CANADA SAFETY COUNCIL (CSC) - LIBRARY
1765 St. Laurent Blvd.   Phone: (613) 521-6881
Ottawa, ON K1G 3V4   Charles James, Libn.

CANADA - SCIENCE COUNCIL OF CANADA - LIBRARY †
100 Metcalfe St.   Phone: (613) 996-3818
Ottawa, ON K1P 5M1   Ms. Frances Bonney, Libn.

CANADA - SECRETARY OF STATE - TRANSLATION BUREAU -
   DOCUMENTATION DIRECTORATE †
                                                   Phone: (819) 997-3857
Ottawa, ON K1A 0M5   Suzanne Richer, Dir.

CANADA - SOLICITOR GENERAL CANADA - MINISTRY LIBRARY &
   REFERENCE CENTRE
340 Laurier Ave. W.   Phone: (613) 995-4811
Ottawa, ON K1A 0P8   Heather Moore, Chf.

CANADA - STATISTICS CANADA - LIBRARY
R.H. Coats Bldg., Tunney's Pasture   Phone: (613) 992-2365
Ottawa, ON K1A 0T6   Georgia Ellis, Dir., Lib.Serv.

CANADA - SUPREME COURT OF CANADA - LIBRARY
Supreme Court Bldg.
Kent & Wellington Sts.   Phone: (613) 995-4330
Ottawa, ON K1A 0J1   F. Diane Teeple, Chf.Libn.

CANADA - TAX COURT OF CANADA - TAX LIBRARY
Centennial Towers
200 Kent St.   Phone: (613) 996-4763
Ottawa, ON K1A 0M1   Mrs. N.C. Mecher

CANADA - TELESAT CANADA - COMPANY LIBRARY
333 River Rd.   Phone: (613) 746-5920
Ottawa, ON K1L 8B9   Eileen Foster, Lib.Mgr.

CANADA - TRANSPORT CANADA - LIBRARY & INFORMATION CENTRE
Place de Ville, Tower C   Phone: (613) 992-4529
Ottawa, ON K1A 0N5   Serge G. Campion, Chf.Libn.

CANADA - TRANSPORT CANADA - ST. LAWRENCE SEAWAY AUTHORITY -
   INFORMATION OFFICE
Place de Ville, 320 Queen St.   Phone: (613) 992-3949
Ottawa, ON K1R 5A3   G. Hemsley, Info.Off.

CANADA - VETERANS AFFAIRS CANADA - LIBRARY
284 Wellington St.   Phone: (613) 593-4155
Ottawa, ON K1A 0P4

CANADIAN AUTOMOBILE ASSOCIATION - LIBRARY
1775 Courtwood Crescent   Phone: (613) 226-7631
Ottawa, ON K2C 3J2   V.L. Aronson, Libn.

CANADIAN BROADCASTING CORPORATION - HEAD OFFICE LIBRARY
1500 Bronson Ave.
P.O. Box 8478   Phone: (613) 731-3111
Ottawa, ON K1G 3J5   N. Deschamps, Ref.Libn.

CANADIAN COUNCIL ON SOCIAL DEVELOPMENT - LIBRARY
55 Parkdale Ave.
Box 3505, Sta. C   Phone: (613) 728-1865
Ottawa, ON K1Y 4G1   Odette Gosselin, Lib. & Info.Off.

CANADIAN DENTAL ASSOCIATION - SYDNEY WOOD BRADLEY MEMORIAL
   LIBRARY
1815 Alta Vista Dr.   Phone: (613) 523-1770
Ottawa, ON K1G 3Y6   Trudi Di Trolio, Libn.

CANADIAN EXPORT ASSOCIATION - LIBRARY
99 Bank St., Suite 250   Phone: (613) 238-8888
Ottawa, ON K1P 6B9   J.D. Moore, Sec.

CANADIAN HOSPITAL ASSOCIATION - INFORMATION CENTRE
17 York St.
Ottawa, ON K1N 9J6

CANADIAN LABOUR CONGRESS - LIBRARY
2841 Riverside Dr.   Phone: (613) 521-3400
Ottawa, ON K1V 8X7   Dawn Dobson, Libn.

CANADIAN LAW INFORMATION COUNCIL - RESOURCE CENTRE FOR
    COMPUTERS AND LAW
Place de Ville, Suite 2010
112 Kent St.   Phone: (613) 236-9766
Ottawa, ON K1P 5P2   Lorna K. Rees-Potter, Dir. of Res.

CANADIAN MEDICAL ASSOCIATION - LIBRARY
1867 Alta Vista Dr.
P.O. Box 8650   Phone: (613) 731-9331
Ottawa, ON K1G 0G8   Kathleen Beaudoin, Libn.

CANADIAN NURSES ASSOCIATION - HELEN K. MUSSALLEM LIBRARY
50 The Driveway   Phone: (613) 237-2133
Ottawa, ON K2P 1E2   Linda Solomon Shiff, Chf.Libn.

CANADIAN TEACHERS' FEDERATION - GEORGE G. CROSKERY MEMORIAL
    LIBRARY
110 Argyle Ave.   Phone: (613) 232-1505
Ottawa, ON K2P 1B4   Geraldine Channon, Dir., Res. & Info.Serv.

CANADIAN WILDLIFE FEDERATION - REFERENCE LIBRARY &
    INFORMATION CENTRE
1673 Carling Ave.   Phone: (613) 725-2191
Ottawa, ON K2A 1C4   Luba Mycio, Pub.Aff.

CANADIAN WOOD COUNCIL - LIBRARY
85 Albert St., Suite 800   Phone: (613) 235-7221
Ottawa, ON K1P 6A4   Thomas Moryto, Dir. of Educ.

CARLETON UNIVERSITY - MACODRUM LIBRARY - MAP LIBRARY
D299 Loeb Bldg., Colonel By Drive   Phone: (613) 231-4392
Ottawa, ON K1S 5B6   Barbara E. Farrell, Map Libn.

CARLETON UNIVERSITY - NORMAN PATERSON SCHOOL OF
    INTERNATIONAL AFFAIRS - RESOURCE CENTRE *
Colonel By Drive   Phone: (613) 231-7182
Ottawa, ON K1B 5B6   Rede Widstrand, Coord.

CHILDREN'S HOSPITAL OF EASTERN ONTARIO - MEDICAL LIBRARY
401 Smyth Rd.   Phone: (613) 737-2206
Ottawa, ON K1H 8L1   Margaret P.J. Taylor, Dir., Lib.Serv.

COLLEGE DOMINICAIN DE PHILOSOPHIE ET DE THEOLOGIE -
    BIBLIOTHEQUE
96 Empress Ave.   Phone: (613) 233-5696
Ottawa, ON K1R 7G2   Jean-Jacques Robillard, Chf.Libn./Info.Dir.

CONFERENCE BOARD OF CANADA - INFORMATION RESOURCE CENTER
25 McArthur Rd., Suite 100   Phone: (613) 746-1261
Ottawa, ON K1L 6R3   George Khoury, Dir., Info.Serv.

COUNTY OF CARLETON LAW ASSOCIATION - LAW LIBRARY
Court House, 2 Daly Ave.   Phone: (613) 233-7386
Ottawa, ON K1N 6E2   Wanda T. Walsh, Libn.

ELDORADO RESOURCES LTD. - RESEARCH & DEVELOPMENT LIBRARY
400-255 Albert St.   Phone: (613) 238-5222
Ottawa, ON K1P 6A9   Peggy Nash, Lib.Techn.

EXPORT DEVELOPMENT CORPORATION - LIBRARY
110 O'Connor St.
Box 655   Phone: (613) 598-2701
Ottawa, ON K1P 5T9   Ann James, Libn.

FORINTEK CANADA CORPORATION - EASTERN LABORATORY - LIBRARY
800 Montreal Rd.   Phone: (613) 744-0963
Ottawa, ON K1G 3Z5   Marjorie Wickens, Libn.

GOETHE INSTITUTE OTTAWA - LIBRARY
192 Laurier E.   Phone: (613) 235-5124
Ottawa, ON K1N 6N5

INFORMETRICA LTD. - BUSINESS LIBRARY
350 Sparks, Suite 1007   Phone: (613) 238-4831
Ottawa, ON K1P 5P9   Diane Purdie, Libn.

INSTITUT CANADIEN-FRANCAIS D'OTTAWA - LIBRARY
316 Dalhousie St.   Phone: (613) 234-1288
Ottawa, ON K1N 7E7   Roland P. Lamarche, Sec.

INTERNATIONAL DEVELOPMENT RESEARCH CENTRE - LIBRARY †
Box 8500   Phone: (613) 996-2321
Ottawa, ON K1G 3H9   Charles A. Godfrey, Assoc.Dir.

INTERNATIONAL JOINT COMMISSION - LIBRARY
100 Metcalfe St., 18th Fl.   Phone: (613) 995-2984
Ottawa, ON K1P 5M1

JEWISH COMMUNITY CENTRE - LIBRARY
151 Chapel St.   Phone: (613) 232-7306
Ottawa, ON K1N 7Y2   Miriam Paghis, Libn.

LE DROIT - CENTRE DE DOCUMENTATION
375, Rue Rideau   Phone: (613) 237-3050
Ottawa, ON K1N 5Y7   Alice Mimeault, Documentaliste

METROPOLITAN LIFE INSURANCE COMPANY - RESEARCH & REFERENCE
    CENTRE
99 Bank St.
Ottawa, ON K1P 5A3

NATIONAL LIBRARY OF CANADA/BIBLIOTHEQUE NATIONALE DU CANADA
395 Wellington St.   Phone: (613) 995-9481
Ottawa, ON K1A 0N4   Marianne Scott, Natl.Libn.

NATIONAL LIBRARY OF CANADA - CANADIAN BOOK EXCHANGE CENTRE
    (CBEC)
85 Bentley Ave.   Phone: (613) 995-2317
Ottawa, ON K2E 6T7   Ergun Camlioglu, Chf.

NATIONAL LIBRARY OF CANADA - CHILDREN'S LITERATURE SERVICE
395 Wellington St.   Phone: (613) 996-2300
Ottawa, ON K1A 0N4   Irene E. Aubrey, Chf.

NATIONAL LIBRARY OF CANADA - LIBRARY DOCUMENTATION CENTRE
395 Wellington St.   Phone: (613) 995-8717
Ottawa, ON K1A 0N4   Beryl L. Anderson, Chf.

NATIONAL LIBRARY OF CANADA - LITERARY MANUSCRIPTS COLLECTION
395 Wellington St.   Phone: (613) 995-3364
Ottawa, ON K1A 0N4   Claude LeMoine, Cur.

NATIONAL LIBRARY OF CANADA - MULTILINGUAL BIBLIOSERVICE
                                          Phone: (819) 997-9930
Ottawa, ON K1A 0N4   Marie F. Zielinska, Chf.

NATIONAL LIBRARY OF CANADA - MUSIC DIVISION
395 Wellington St.   Phone: (613) 996-3377
Ottawa, ON K1A 0N4   Dr. Helmut Kallmann, Chf.

NATIONAL LIBRARY OF CANADA - NEWSPAPER DIVISION
395 Wellington St.   Phone: (613) 996-1338
Ottawa, ON K1A 0N4   Lois Burrell, Chf.

NATIONAL LIBRARY OF CANADA - OFFICIAL PUBLICATIONS DIVISION
395 Wellington St.   Phone: (613) 996-3842
Ottawa, ON K1A 0N4   Doreen A. Guenter, Chf.

NATIONAL LIBRARY OF CANADA - RARE BOOK DIVISION
395 Wellington St.   Phone: (613) 996-1318
Ottawa, ON K1A 0N4   Liana Van der Bellen, Chf.

NATIONAL LIBRARY OF CANADA - REFERENCE SERVICES SECTION
395 Wellington St.   Phone: (613) 995-9481
Ottawa, ON K1A 0N4   Wendy Scott, Sect.Hd.

NATIONAL LIBRARY OF CANADA - SERVICE FOR HANDICAPPED PERSONS
395 Wellington St.   Phone: (613) 992-7811
Ottawa, ON K1A 0N4

NAVY LEAGUE OF CANADA - NATIONAL OFFICE - LIBRARY
4 Queen Elizabeth Dr.   Phone: (613) 232-2784
Ottawa, ON K2P 2H9   W.J. Hodge, Gen.Mgr.

OBLATE FATHERS - BIBLIOTHEQUE DESCHATELETS
175 Main   Phone: (613) 237-0580
Ottawa, ON K1S 1C3   Leo Laberge, Dir.

OTTAWA CITIZEN - LIBRARY
1101 Baxter Rd.
Box 5020
Box 5020   Phone: (613) 829-9100
Ottawa, ON K2C 3M4   Steven Proulx, Chf.Libn.

OTTAWA CIVIC HOSPITAL - DR. GEORGE S. WILLIAMSON HEALTH
   SCIENCES LIBRARY
1053 Carling Ave.   Phone: (613) 725-4450
Ottawa, ON K1Y 4E9   Mabel C. Brown, Dir., Lib.Serv.

OTTAWA GENERAL HOSPITAL - MEDICAL LIBRARY
501 Smyth Rd.   Phone: (613) 737-8530
Ottawa, ON K1H 8L6   Diane R. Couture, Supv.

OTTAWA PUBLIC LIBRARY - OTTAWA ROOM
120 Metcalfe St.
Ottawa, ON K1P 5M2   Jean de Temple, Asst.Dir.

RIVERSIDE HOSPITAL - SCOBIE MEMORIAL LIBRARY
1967 Riverside Dr.   Phone: (613) 731-6710
Ottawa, ON K1H 7W9   Jean E. White, Libn.

ROADS AND TRANSPORTATION ASSOCIATION OF CANADA - TECHNICAL
   INFORMATION SERVICE
1765 St. Laurent Blvd.   Phone: (613) 521-4052
Ottawa, ON K1G 3V4   Charles James, Tech.Info.Off.

ROYAL CANADIAN MOUNTED POLICE - LAW ENFORCEMENT REFERENCE
   CENTRE
1200 Alta Vista Dr.   Phone: (613) 993-3225
Ottawa, ON K1A 0R2   Mrs. G. Wyatt, Mgr.

ROYAL SOCIETY OF CANADA - LIBRARY
344 Wellington St.   Phone: (613) 992-3468
Ottawa, ON K1A 0N4   E.H.P. Garneau, Exec.Sec.

ST. VINCENT HOSPITAL - MEDICAL LIBRARY
60 Cambridge St., N.   Phone: (613) 233-4041
Ottawa, ON K1R 7A5   Sr. Germaine Lafleur, Hd. of Dept.

SPORT INFORMATION RESOURCE CENTRE
333 River Rd.   Phone: (613) 746-5357
Ottawa, ON K1L 8H9   Gilles Chiasson, Mgr.

STANDARDS COUNCIL OF CANADA - STANDARDS INFORMATION DIVISION
350 Sparks St., Suite 1210   Phone: (613) 238-3222
Ottawa, ON K1R 7S8   M. Crainey, Mgr.

TELECOM CANADA - INFORMATION RESOURCE CENTRE
410 Laurier Ave., W.   Phone: (613) 560-3953
Ottawa, ON K1P 6H5   Joan Chinkiwsky, Mgr.

TRAFFIC INJURY RESEARCH FOUNDATION OF CANADA (TIRF) -
   TECHNICAL INFORMATION CENTRE
171 Nepean St., 6th Fl.   Phone: (613) 238-5235
Ottawa, ON K2P 0B4   Joseph M. Grabetz, Libn.

UNITED STATES INFORMATION SERVICE - LIBRARY SERVICE
150 Wellington St., 3rd Fl.   Phone: (613) 238-5335
Ottawa, ON K1P 5A4   Brenda Brady, Supv.Libn.

UNIVERSITE ST-PAUL - BIBLIOTHEQUE
223 Main   Phone: (613) 236-1393
Ottawa, ON K1S 1C4   Gaston Rioux, O.M.I., Chf.Libn.

UNIVERSITY OF OTTAWA - HEALTH SCIENCES LIBRARY
451 Smyth Rd.   Phone: (613) 737-6521
Ottawa, ON K1H 8M4   Myra Owen, Dir.

UNIVERSITY OF OTTAWA - LAW LIBRARY
Fauteux Hall
57 Copernicus St.   Phone: (613) 231-4943
Ottawa, ON K1N 6N5   Raymond Dicaire, Act.Libn.

UNIVERSITY OF OTTAWA - MAP LIBRARY
Morisset Library
65 Hastey St., Rm. 353   Phone: (613) 231-6830
Ottawa, ON K1N 9A5   Aileen Desbarats, Hd.

UNIVERSITY OF OTTAWA - MORISSET LIBRARY
65 Hastey St.   Phone: (613) 231-6880
Ottawa, ON K1N 9A5   Yvon Richer, Univ.Chf.Libn.

UNIVERSITY OF OTTAWA - MUSIC LIBRARY
One Stewart St.   Phone: (613) 231-5717
Ottawa, ON K1N 6H7   Debra Begg, Libn.

UNIVERSITY OF OTTAWA - TEACHER EDUCATION LIBRARY
651 Cumberland St.   Phone: (613) 231-5986
Ottawa, ON K2P 1L3   Jan Kolaczek, Libn.

UNIVERSITY OF OTTAWA - VANIER SCIENCE & ENGINEERING LIBRARY
11 Somerset St., E.   Phone: (613) 231-2324
Ottawa, ON K1N 9A4   Blanca Stead, Act.Dir.

VANIER INSTITUTE OF THE FAMILY - RESOURCE & INFORMATION CENTRE
151 Slater St., Suite 207   Phone: (613) 232-7115
Ottawa, ON K1P 5H3   Susan L. Campbell, Libn./Res.

CANADIAN GENERAL ELECTRIC COMPANY, LTD. - ENGINEERING LIBRARY
107 Park St., N.   Phone: (705) 748-7745
Peterborough, ON K9J 7B5   Leida Madisso, Act.Libn.

SIR SANDFORD FLEMING COLLEGE OF APPLIED ARTS & TECHNOLOGY -
   EDUCATIONAL RESOURCE CENTER
Sutherland Campus
Brealey Bldg.   Phone: (705) 743-5610
Peterborough, ON K9J 7B1   Janice Coughlin, Dir.

PRINCE EDWARD HEIGHTS - RESIDENT RECORDS LIBRARY
Box 440   Phone: (613) 476-2104
Picton, ON K0K 2T0   Deborah Norton, Health Rec.Adm.

CANADIAN STANDARDS ASSOCIATION - INFORMATION CENTRE
178 Rexdale Blvd.   Phone: (416) 744-4058
Rexdale, ON M9W 1R3   Cameron D. Macdonald, Supv.

CANADIAN THOROUGHBRED HORSE SOCIETY - LIBRARY
Box 172   Phone: (416) 675-3602
Rexdale, ON M9W 5L1   C.R. McEwan, Mgr.

ETOBICOKE GENERAL HOSPITAL - MEDICAL LIBRARY
101 Humber College Blvd.   Phone: (416) 744-3334
Rexdale, ON M9V 1R8   Joyce Gitt, Lib.Techn.

GARRETT MANUFACTURING, LTD. - ENGINEERING LIBRARY
255 Attwell Dr.   Phone: (416) 675-1411
Rexdale, ON M9W 5B8   Louis J. Hale, Standards Engr.

HUMBER COLLEGE OF APPLIED ARTS & TECHNOLOGY - LIBRARY - SPECIAL
   COLLECTIONS
205 Humber College Blvd.   Phone: (416) 675-3111
Rexdale, ON M9W 5L7   Audrey MacLellan, Chf.Libn.

THISTLETOWN REGIONAL CENTRE - LIBRARY
51 Panorama Court   Phone: (416) 741-1210
Rexdale, ON M9V 4L8   Joy Shanfield, Libn.

RIDGETOWN COLLEGE OF AGRICULTURAL TECHNOLOGY - LIBRARY
                                            Phone: (519) 674-5456
Ridgetown, ON N0P 2C0   Mrs. I.R. Roadhouse, Libn.

BROCK UNIVERSITY - DEPARTMENT OF GEOGRAPHY - MAP LIBRARY
Decew Campus   Phone: (416) 688-5550
St. Catharines, ON L2S 3A1   Olga Slachta, Map Libn.

RODMAN HALL ARTS CENTRE - ART LIBRARY
109 St. Paul Crescent   Phone: (416) 684-2925
St. Catharines, ON L2S 1M3   Debra Attenborough, Educ.Off.

ST. CATHARINES HISTORICAL MUSEUM - LIBRARY
343 Merritt St.   Phone: (416) 227-2962
St. Catharines, ON L2T 1K7   Mr. Arden Phair, Dir.

SHAVER HOSPITAL FOR CHEST DISEASES - HEALTH SCIENCES LIBRARY
541 Glenridge Ave.   Phone: (416) 685-1381
St. Catharines, ON L2R 6S5   Ruth Servos, Dir.

ST. THOMAS PSYCHIATRIC HOSPITAL - LIBRARY SERVICES
Box 2004   Phone: (519) 631-8510
St. Thomas, ON N5P 3V9   Lisa McInnis, Libn.

DOW CHEMICAL CANADA INC. - LIBRARY
1086 Modeland Rd.
P.O. Box 1012   Phone: (519) 339-3663
Sarnia, ON N7T 7K7   Barbara R. Buchanan, Libn.

ESSO PETROLEUM CANADA - RESEARCH TECHNICAL INFORMATION
  CENTRE
Box 3004   Phone: (519) 339-2471
Sarnia, ON N7T 7M1   N.J. Gaspar, Hd., Info.Serv.

POLYSAR, LTD. - INFORMATION CENTRE
Vidal St., S.   Phone: (519) 337-8251
Sarnia, ON N7T 7M2   Dorothy J. Clarkson, Supv.

CANADA - CANADIAN FORESTRY SERVICE - GREAT LAKES FOREST
  RESEARCH CENTRE - LIBRARY
P.O. Box 490   Phone: (705) 949-9461
Sault Ste. Marie, ON P6A 5M7   Sandra Burt, Libn.

CANADA - FISHERIES & OCEANS - SEA LAMPREY CONTROL CENTRE -
  LIBRARY
Huron St., Ship Canal P.O.   Phone: (705) 949-1102
Sault Ste. Marie, ON P6A 1P0   B.G.H. Johnson, Biologist

GENERAL HOSPITAL - HEALTH SCIENCES LIBRARY
941 Queen St. E.   Phone: (705) 254-5181
Sault Ste. Marie, ON P6A 2B8   Kathy You, Libn.

PLUMMER MEMORIAL PUBLIC HOSPITAL - MEDICAL LIBRARY
969 Queen St., E.   Phone: (705) 254-5161
Sault Ste. Marie, ON P6A 2C4   Kathy You, Libn.

ALCOHOL AND DRUG CONCERNS, INC. - AUDIOVISUAL LIBRARY
11 Progress Ave., Suite 200   Phone: (416) 293-3400
Scarborough, ON M1P 4S7   Rev. Karl N. Burden, Exec.Dir.

BANK OF MONTREAL - TECHNICAL INFORMATION CENTRE
Box 7000   Phone: (416) 498-8800
Scarborough, ON M1S 4M5   Carol M. Diakun, Mgr., Tech.Info.Serv.

BANK OF NOVA SCOTIA - TECHNICAL LIBRARY/RESEARCH CENTRE
2201 Eglinton Ave. E.   Phone: (416) 288-3571
Scarborough, ON M1L 4S2   Cathy Kealey, Tech.Res.Libn.

CANADA - HEALTH AND WELFARE CANADA - HEALTH PROTECTION
  BRANCH - TORONTO REGIONAL LIBRARY †
2301 Midland Ave.   Phone: (416) 291-4231
Scarborough, ON M1P 4R7   S. Brockhurst, Lib.Techn.

CENTENNIAL COLLEGE OF APPLIED ARTS & TECHNOLOGY - ASHTONBEE
  CAMPUS RESOURCE CENTRE
Sta. A, P.O. Box 631   Phone: (416) 752-4444
Scarborough, ON M1K 5E9   Wendy Scott, Campus Libn.

CENTENNIAL COLLEGE OF APPLIED ARTS & TECHNOLOGY - EAST YORK
  CAMPUS RESOURCE CENTRE
Sta. A, P.O. Box 631   Phone: (416) 469-5981
Scarborough, ON M1K 5E9   Ron Wood, Campus Libn.

CENTENNIAL COLLEGE OF APPLIED ARTS & TECHNOLOGY - PROGRESS
  CAMPUS RESOURCE CENTRE
Sta. A, P.O. Box 631   Phone: (416) 439-7180
Scarborough, ON M1K 5E9   Judy Downs, Campus Libn.

CENTENNIAL COLLEGE OF APPLIED ARTS & TECHNOLOGY - WARDEN
  WOODS CAMPUS RESOURCE CENTRE
Sta. A, P.O. Box 631   Phone: (416) 694-3241
Scarborough, ON M1K 5E9   Annetta Turner, Campus Libn.

CONSUMERS' GAS COMPANY - LIBRARY SERVICES †
P.O. Box 650   Phone: (416) 492-5490
Scarborough, ON M1K 5E3   Donna M. Ivey, Supv., Lib.Serv.

GINN AND COMPANY - EDITORIAL LIBRARY
3771 Victoria Park Ave.   Phone: (416) 497-4600
Scarborough, ON M1W 2P9   Eleanor Taylor, Libn.

ST. AUGUSTINE'S SEMINARY - LIBRARY
2661 Kingston Rd.   Phone: (416) 261-7207
Scarborough, ON M1M 1M3   Sr. Madeline Connolly, Libn.

SCARBOROUGH BOARD OF EDUCATION - A.B. PATTERSON PROFESSIONAL
  LIBRARY
140 Borough Dr., Level 2   Phone: (416) 296-7515
Scarborough, ON M1P 4N6   MaryLu Brennan, Supv.

SCARBOROUGH GENERAL HOSPITAL - HEALTH SCIENCES LIBRARY
3050 Lawrence Ave., E.   Phone: (416) 438-2911
Scarborough, ON M1P 2V5

SCARBOROUGH PUBLIC LIBRARY - FILM SERVICES
Campbell District Library
496 Birchmount Rd.   Phone: (416) 698-1191
Scarborough, ON M1K 1N8   Kathy Therrien, Film Coord.

SCARBOROUGH RESOURCE CENTRE
Scarborough Civic Centre
150 Borough Dr.   Phone: (416) 296-7215
Scarborough, ON M1P 4N7   Dave Hawkins, Mgr.

WARNER-LAMBERT CANADA INC. - LIBRARY †
2200 Eglinton Ave., E.   Phone: (416) 750-2360
Scarborough, ON M1K 5C9   Edna Allen, Libn.

WARNER-LAMBERT CANADA INC. - TECHNICAL INFORMATION CENTRE
2200 Eglinton Ave., E.   Phone: (416) 750-2402
Scarborough, ON M1K 5C9   Susan W. Underdown, Tech.Libn.

MC NEIL LABORATORIES (Canada) LIMITED - LIBRARY
600 Main St., W.   Phone: (416) 640-6900
Stouffville, ON L0H 1L0   Karen Connell, Libn.

GALLERY/STRATFORD - JOHN MARTIN LIBRARY
54 Romeo St.   Phone: (519) 271-5271
Stratford, ON N5A 4S9

STRATFORD SHAKESPEAREAN FESTIVAL FOUNDATION OF CANADA -
  STRATFORD FESTIVAL ARCHIVES
Box 520   Phone: (519) 271-4040
Stratford, ON N5A 6V2   Daniel W. Ladell, Archv.

CAMBRIAN COLLEGE OF APPLIED ARTS AND TECHNOLOGY - LEARNING
  RESOURCES CENTRE
1400 Barrydowne Rd., Station A   Phone: (705) 566-8101
Sudbury, ON P3A 3V8   Chris Bartlett, Dir., LRC

LAURENTIAN HOSPITAL - MEDICAL LIBRARY
41 Ramsey Lake Rd.   Phone: (705) 522-2200
Sudbury, ON P3E 5J1   Simone Hamilton, Supv.

LAURENTIAN UNIVERSITY - MAIN LIBRARY
Ramsey Lake Rd.   Phone: (705) 675-1151
Sudbury, ON P3E 2C6   Andrzej H. Mrozewski, Chf.Libn.

LAURENTIAN UNIVERSITY - SCHOOL OF EDUCATION - LIBRARY
Ramsey Lake Rd.   Phone: (705) 675-1151
Sudbury, ON P3E 2C6   Lionel Bonin, Libn.

LAURENTIAN UNIVERSITY - SCIENCE AND ENGINEERING LIBRARY
Ramsey Lake Rd.   Phone: (705) 675-1151
Sudbury, ON P3E 2C6   Robert M. Wilson, Lib.Hd.

ONTARIO - MINISTRY OF EDUCATION - EDUCATION CENTER LIBRARY
199 Larch St., 7th Fl.   Phone: (705) 675-4427
Sudbury, ON P3E 5P9   George Whalen, Libn.

SUDBURY GENERAL HOSPITAL - HOSPITAL LIBRARY
700 Paris St., Station B   Phone: (705) 674-3181
Sudbury, ON P3E 3B5   D.M. Hawryliuk, Libn.

UNIVERSITY OF SUDBURY - JESUIT ARCHIVES
                                                          Phone: (705) 673-5661
Sudbury, ON P3E 2C6   Robert Toupin, S.J., Dir.

UNIVERSITY OF SUDBURY - LIBRARY
                                                          Phone: (705) 673-5661
Sudbury, ON P3E 2C6   Stanislaw Chojnacki, Dir. of Lib.

FALCONBRIDGE NICKEL MINES, LTD. - METALLURGICAL LABORATORIES
   INFORMATION SERVICES †
Box 900   Phone: (416) 889-6221
Thornhill, ON L3T 4A8   Doris George, Libn.

ONTARIO PAPER COMPANY, LTD. - LIBRARY
Allanburg Rd.   Phone: (416) 227-1121
Thorold, ON L2V 3Z5   Isabelle Ridgway, Libn.

CANADA - NATIONAL FILM BOARD OF CANADA - FILM LIBRARY
910 Victoria Ave.   Phone: (807) 623-5224
Thunder Bay, ON P7C 1B4   William Murphy, Film Off.

CONFEDERATION COLLEGE OF APPLIED ARTS & TECHNOLOGY - RESOURCE
   CENTRE
Box 398   Phone: (807) 475-6241
Thunder Bay, ON P7C 4W1   J.R. Rapino, Dir.

LAKEHEAD UNIVERSITY - CHANCELLOR PATERSON LIBRARY
Oliver Rd.   Phone: (807) 345-2121
Thunder Bay, ON P7B 5E1   Marshall Clinton, Chf.Libn.

LAKEHEAD UNIVERSITY - EDUCATION LIBRARY
Oliver Road   Phone: (807) 345-2121
Thunder Bay, ON P7B 5E1   Mr. J. Arnot, Educ.Libn.

ST. JOSEPH'S GENERAL HOSPITAL - MEDICAL LIBRARY
P.O. Box 3251   Phone: (807) 344-2431
Thunder Bay, ON P7B 5G7   Laurie J. Hill, Libn.

ACADEMY OF MEDICINE, TORONTO - WILLIAM BOYD LIBRARY
288 Bloor St., W.   Phone: (416) 964-7088
Toronto, ON M5S 1V8   Sheila Swanson, Libn.

ACRES CONSULTING SERVICES, LTD. - TORONTO LIBRARY †
480 University Ave.   Phone: (416) 595-2000
Toronto, ON M5G 1V2

AIRD & BERLIS - LAW LIBRARY
145 King St., W., 15th Fl.   Phone: (416) 364-1241
Toronto, ON M5H 2J3   Carol Malcolm, Libn.

ALCOHOLISM AND DRUG ADDICTION RESEARCH FOUNDATION - LIBRARY
33 Russell St.   Phone: (416) 595-6144
Toronto, ON M5S 2S1   D. Fridenberg, Mgr., Lib.Serv.

AMERICAN STANDARD - ENGINEERING LIBRARY
80 Ward St.   Phone: (416) 536-1078
Toronto, ON M6H 4A7   Nora Hollands, Libn.

ANGLICAN CHURCH ARMY IN CANADA - COWAN MEMORIAL LIBRARY
397 Brunswick Ave.   Phone: (416) 924-9279
Toronto, ON M5R 2Z2   Sr. Victoria Gilmor, Libn.

ANGLICAN CHURCH OF CANADA - CHURCH HOUSE LIBRARY
600 Jarvis St.   Phone: (416) 924-9192
Toronto, ON M4Y 2J6   Alice Marie Hedderick, Libn.

ANGLICAN CHURCH OF CANADA - DIOCESE OF TORONTO - DIOCESAN
   LIBRARY & RESOURCE CENTRE †
135 Adelaide St., E.   Phone: (416) 924-9121
Toronto, ON M5C 1L8   Anne Tanner, Diocesan Libn.

ANGLICAN CHURCH OF CANADA - GENERAL SYNOD ARCHIVES
600 Jarvis St.   Phone: (416) 924-9192
Toronto, ON M4Y 2J6   Mrs. Terry Thompson, Archv.

ANTHROPOSOPHICAL SOCIETY IN CANADA - RUDOLPH STEINER LIBRARY
   †
81 Lawton Blvd.   Phone: (416) 488-2886
Toronto, ON M4V 1Z6   Barbara Gunther, Libn.

ANTIQUE AND CLASSIC CAR CLUB OF CANADA - LIBRARY *
27 Queen St., E., Suite 404   Phone: (416) 621-9743
Toronto, ON M5C 2M6   Peter Weatherhead, Pubn.Chm.

ART GALLERY OF ONTARIO - EDWARD P. TAYLOR AUDIO-VISUAL CENTRE
317 Dundas St., W.   Phone: (416) 977-0414
Toronto, ON M5T 1G4   Catherine Jonasson, Hd.

ART GALLERY OF ONTARIO - EDWARD P. TAYLOR REFERENCE LIBRARY
317 Dundas St. W.   Phone: (416) 361-0414
Toronto, ON M5T 1G4   Karen McKenzie, Chf.Libn.

ARTHRITIS SOCIETY - NATIONAL OFFICE LIBRARY
920 Yonge St., Suite 420   Phone: (416) 967-1414
Toronto, ON M4W 3J7   Joan-Mary Attwood, Libn.

ARTHUR ANDERSEN & CO. - LIBRARY †
Toronto Dominion Ctr.
Box 29   Phone: (416) 863-1540
Toronto, ON M5K 1B9   Mary O'Neill, Libn.

BANK OF NOVA SCOTIA - LIBRARY
44 King St., W.   Phone: (416) 866-6257
Toronto, ON M5H 1E2   Beverley Kent, Chf.Libn.

BECHTEL CANADA LIMITED - ENGINEERING CONSULTANTS - LIBRARY
250 Bloor St., E., 15th Fl.   Phone: (416) 928-1671
Toronto, ON M4W 3K5   Irene Cairns, Libn.

BELL CANADA - O.R. INFORMATION RESOURCE CENTRE
Bell Trinity Square
North Tower, 1st Fl.   Phone: (416) 581-4258
Toronto, ON M5G 2E1   Vivian Lung, Libn.

BELL-NORTHERN RESEARCH LTD. - TECHNICAL INFORMATION CENTRE
522 University Ave.   Phone: (416) 598-0196
Toronto, ON M5G 1W7   D. Masseau, Info.Spec.

BETH TZEDEC CONGREGATION - MAX & BEATRICE WOLFE LIBRARY
1700 Bathurst St.   Phone: (416) 781-5658
Toronto, ON M5P 3K3   Samuel Simchovitch, Libn.

BLAKE, CASSELS & GRAYDON - LIBRARY
Commerce Court West
P.O. Box 25   Phone: (416) 863-2650
Toronto, ON M5L 1A9   Vicki L. Whitmell, Libn.

BLANEY, PASTERNAK, SMELA & WATSON - LAW LIBRARY
20 Queen St. W., Suite 1400   Phone: (416) 364-9421
Toronto, ON M5H 2V3   Rowan J. Amott, Libn.

BOARD OF TRADE OF METROPOLITAN TORONTO - RESOURCE CENTRE
3 First Canadian Pl.
Box 60   Phone: (416) 366-6811
Toronto, ON M5X 1C1   M.J. de Reus, Res.Libn.

BRINCO LIMITED - LIBRARY †
20 King St. W., 10th Fl.   Phone: (416) 868-6970
Toronto, ON M5H 1C4   Deborah M. Kelly, Corp.Libn.

BUILT ENVIRONMENT COORDINATORS LIMITED - BEC INFORMATION
   SYSTEM (BIS) †
76 Richmond St. E.   Phone: (416) 864-0486
Toronto, ON M5C 1P1   Jill Roughley, Dir.

BURNS FRY LIMITED - RESEARCH LIBRARY
1 First Canadian Place
P.O. Box 150   Phone: (416) 365-4444
Toronto, ON M5X 1H3   Ann Rait, Libn.

C-I-L PAINTS INC. - PAINT RESEARCH LABORATORY LIBRARY
1330 Castlefield Ave.   Phone: (416) 787-2411
Toronto, ON M6B 1G5   M. Elaine Fitzpatrick, Libn.

CAMPBELL, GODFREY & LEWTAS - LIBRARY
Toronto Dominion Centre
Box 36   Phone: (416) 362-2401
Toronto, ON M5K 1C5   Vernon Russell, Libn.

CANADA - ENVIRONMENTAL PROTECTION SERVICE - LIBRARY
25 St. Clair Ave., E.   Phone: (416) 966-5840
Toronto, ON M4T 1M2   Catherine Graham, Libn.

CANADA LIFE ASSURANCE COMPANY - LIBRARY
330 University Ave.   Phone: (416) 597-1456
Toronto, ON M5G 1R8   Gloria F.L. Johns, Libn.

CANADA - NATIONAL DEFENCE - CANADIAN FORCES COLLEGE - KEITH HODSON MEMORIAL LIBRARY †
215 Yonge Blvd.   Phone: (416) 484-5742
Toronto, ON M5M 3H9   Mary Ash, Chf.Libn.

CANADA - NATIONAL DEFENCE - CANADIAN FORCES COLLEGE - STAFF SCHOOL LIBRARY †
1107 Avenue Rd.   Phone: (416) 484-5645
Toronto, ON M5N 2E4   Coby Oates, Techn.-in-Charge

CANADA - STATISTICS CANADA - ADVISORY SERVICES - TORONTO REFERENCE CENTRE
25 St. Clair Ave., E., 10th Fl.   Phone: (416) 966-6586
Toronto, ON M4T 1M4   Sandra McIntyre, Hd., Inquiries

CANADA WIRE AND CABLE, LTD. - TECHNICAL LIBRARY
22 Commercial Rd.   Phone: (416) 421-0440
Toronto, ON M4G 1Z4   Dianne Crompton, Lib.Techn.

CANADIAN ASSOCIATION - LATIN AMERICA AND CARIBBEAN - INFORMATION CENTRE
42 Charles St., E.   Phone: (416) 964-6068
Toronto, ON M4Y 1T4   Maria A. Escriu, Chf.Libn.

CANADIAN BANKERS ASSOCIATION - LIBRARY
2 First Canadian Place, Suite 600
Box 348   Phone: (416) 362-6092
Toronto, ON M5X 1E1   Jane Leamen, Libn.

CANADIAN BOOK INFORMATION CENTRE - NATIONAL OFFICE
70 the Esplanade, 3rd Fl.   Phone: (416) 362-6555
Toronto, ON M5E 1A6   Gordon Montador, Natl.Mgr.

CANADIAN BOOK PUBLISHERS' COUNCIL - LIBRARY
45 Charles St., E., 7th Fl.   Phone: (416) 964-7231
Toronto, ON M4Y 1S2   Veronica Keely, Off.Mgr.

CANADIAN BROADCASTING CORPORATION - MUSIC LIBRARY
Sta. A., Box 500   Phone: (416) 925-3311
Toronto, ON M5W 1E6   John P. Lawrence, Coord., Music Lib.

CANADIAN BROADCASTING CORPORATION - PROGRAM ARCHIVES (Sound)
Sta. A, Box 500   Phone: (416) 925-3311
Toronto, ON M5W 1E6   John P. Lawrence, Coord., Prog.Archv.

CANADIAN BROADCASTING CORPORATION - RECORD LIBRARY
Sta. A, Box 500   Phone: (416) 925-3311
Toronto, ON M5W 1E6   John P. Lawrence, Coord.

CANADIAN BROADCASTING CORPORATION - REFERENCE LIBRARY
365 Church St.
Sta. A, Box 500   Phone: (416) 925-3311
Toronto, ON M5W 1E6   Leone Earls, Hd.Libn.

CANADIAN BROADCASTING CORPORATION - TV CURRENT AFFAIRS LIBRARY †
Sta. A, Box 500   Phone: (416) 925-3311
Toronto, ON M5W 1E6   Diana Redegeld, Lib.Techn.

CANADIAN COUNCIL OF CHRISTIANS AND JEWS - JOHN D. HAYES LIBRARY OF HUMAN RELATIONS
49 Front St., E.
Toronto, ON M5E 1B3

CANADIAN CREDIT INSTITUTE - CREDIT RESEARCH AND LENDING LIBRARY
931 Yonge St.   Phone: (416) 962-9911
Toronto, ON M4W 2H6   A.L. Peterman, Registrar

CANADIAN DIABETES ASSOCIATION - NATIONAL OFFICE ARCHIVES
78 Bond St.   Phone: (416) 362-4440
Toronto, ON M5B 2J8   Thora Mills, Chm., Archv.Comm.

CANADIAN EDUCATION ASSOCIATION - LIBRARY
252 Bloor St., W., Suite 8-200   Phone: (416) 924-7721
Toronto, ON M5S 1V5   Diane Sibbett, Libn.

CANADIAN FEDERATION OF INDEPENDENT BUSINESS (CFIB) - RESEARCH LIBRARY
4141 Yonge St.   Phone: (416) 222-8022
Toronto, ON M2P 2A6   Ryla Snider Lightman, Libn.

CANADIAN FOUNDATION FOR ECONOMIC EDUCATION - RESOURCE CENTRE
252 Bloor St. W., Suite 560   Phone: (416) 968-2236
Toronto, ON M5S 1V5   Judith Jackson, Rsrc.Ctr.Dir.

CANADIAN GAY ARCHIVES - LIBRARY
Sta. A, Box 639   Phone: (416) 364-2763
Toronto, ON M5W 1G2

CANADIAN GENERAL ELECTRIC COMPANY, LTD. - CORPORATE INFORMATION CENTRE
Commerce Court Postal Station
P.O. Box 417   Phone: (416) 365-6598
Toronto, ON M5L 1J2   Anne Pashley, Mgr.

CANADIAN HEARING SOCIETY - LIBRARY
60 Bedford Rd.   Phone: (416) 964-9595
Toronto, ON M5R 2K2   Pat Stewart, Libn.

CANADIAN IMPERIAL BANK OF COMMERCE - INFORMATION CENTRE
Head Office - Commerce Court   Phone: (416) 862-3053
Toronto, ON M5L 1A2   Susan A. Merry, Mgr./Chf.Libn.

CANADIAN INSTITUTE OF CHARTERED ACCOUNTANTS - RESEARCH DEPARTMENT LIBRARY †
150 Bloor St. W.   Phone: (416) 962-1242
Toronto, ON M5S 2Y2   Gerald B. Gerard, Libn.

CANADIAN INSTITUTE OF INTERNATIONAL AFFAIRS - LIBRARY
15 King's College Circle   Phone: (416) 979-1851
Toronto, ON M5S 2V9   Jane R. Barrett, Libn.

CANADIAN JEWELLERS INSTITUTE - GERSTEIN/TIFFANY LIBRARY
Howard Bldg.
1491 Yonge St.   Phone: (416) 368-8372
Toronto, ON M4T 1Z4   Jacqui Tuli, Educ.Coord.

CANADIAN MEMORIAL CHIROPRACTIC COLLEGE - C.C. CLEMMER LIBRARY
1900 Bayview Ave.   Phone: (416) 482-2340
Toronto, ON M4G 3E6   J. Claire Callaghan, Dir., Lib.Serv.

CANADIAN MUSIC CENTRE - LIBRARY
20 St. Joseph St.   Phone: (416) 961-6601
Toronto, ON M4Y 1J9   Mark Hand, Libn.

CANADIAN NATIONAL INSTITUTE FOR THE BLIND - NATIONAL LIBRARY SERVICES - SHERMAN SWIFT REFERENCE LIBRARY
1929 Bayview Ave.   Phone: (416) 486-2579
Toronto, ON M4G 3E8   Francoise Hebert, Exec.Dir.

CANADIAN NATIONAL RAIL - GREAT LAKES REGION LIBRARY *
20 York St.   Phone: (416) 860-2418
Toronto, ON M5J 1E7   Shirley K. Smith, Libn.

CANADIAN NUCLEAR ASSOCIATION - CNA LIBRARY †
111 Elizabeth St., 11th Fl.   Phone: (416) 977-6152
Toronto, ON M5G 1P7

CANADIAN OPERA COMPANY - ARCHIVES
417 Queen's Quay West   Phone: (416) 363-6671
Toronto, ON M5V 1A2   Joan L. Baillie, Archv./Rec.Mgr.

CANADIAN PARAPLEGIC ASSOCIATION - LIBRARY
520 Sutherland Dr.   Phone: (416) 422-5640
Toronto, ON M4G 3V9   Peter Bernauer, Res.Libn.

CANADIAN PRESS - LIBRARY
36 King St., E.   Phone: (416) 364-0321
Toronto, ON M5C 2L9   Elizabeth Shewan, Libn.

CANADIAN RED CROSS SOCIETY - LIBRARY
95 Wellesley St., E.   Phone: (416) 923-6692
Toronto, ON M4Y 1H6   Deborah Chalmers, Libn.

CANADIAN REHABILITATION COUNCIL FOR THE DISABLED - CRCD
   RESOURCE CENTRE
One Yonge St., Suite 2110   Phone: (416) 862-0340
Toronto, ON M5E 1E5   Maureen Vasey, Dir., Info.Serv.

CANADIAN REHABILITATION COUNCIL FOR THE DISABLED - NATIONAL
   INFORMATION RESOURCE CENTRE
One Yonge St., Suite 2110   Phone: (416) 862-0340
Toronto, ON M5E 1E5   Ms. Gartley Wagner, Libn.

CANADIAN RESTAURANT & FOODSERVICES ASSOCIATION - RESOURCE
   CENTRE
80 Bloor St., W., Suite 904   Phone: (416) 923-8416
Toronto, ON M5S 2V1   Karen Graves, Mgr., Info.Serv.

CANADIAN TAX FOUNDATION - LIBRARY
130 Adelaide St., W.   Phone: (416) 863-9784
Toronto, ON M5H 3P5   Marjorie Robinson, Libn.

CANADIAN TROTTING ASSOCIATION - STANDARDBRED CANADA LIBRARY
233 Evans Ave.   Phone: (416) 252-3565
Toronto, ON M8Z 1J6   Margaret Neal, Coord. & Info.Spec.

CENTRAL BAPTIST SEMINARY - DR. W. GORDON BROWN MEMORIAL
   LIBRARY
95 Jonesville Crescent   Phone: (416) 752-1976
Toronto, ON M4A 1H3   Marjory Knaap, Libn.

CENTRE FOR CHRISTIAN STUDIES - LIBRARY †
77 Charles St., W.   Phone: (416) 923-1168
Toronto, ON M5S 1K5   Mrs. Elfa M. Davidson, Libn.

CITADEL GENERAL ASSURANCE COMPANY - INFORMATION CENTRE
1075 Bay St.   Phone: (416) 928-8539
Toronto, ON M5S 2W5   Christine Macdonald, Mgr., Plan. & Res.

CITY OF TORONTO ARCHIVES
City Hall
100 Queen St., W.   Phone: (416) 367-7483
Toronto, ON M5H 2N2   Robert Halifax, Dir. of Rec./City Archv.

CITY-TV - CITY PULSE LIBRARY
99 Queen St. E.   Phone: (416) 367-5757
Toronto, ON M5C 2M1   Joy George, Hd.Libn.

CLARKE INSTITUTE OF PSYCHIATRY - FARRAR LIBRARY †
250 College St.   Phone: (416) 979-2221
Toronto, ON M5T 1R8   Dawn Stewardson, Libn./Archv.

CLARKSON, GORDON/WOODS, GORDON - LIBRARY
Box 251, Toronto Dominion Centre   Phone: (416) 864-1234
Toronto, ON M5K 1J7   Karen Melville, Libn.

COLLINS CANADA - TIC LIBRARY
150 Bartley Dr.   Phone: (416) 757-1101
Toronto, ON M4A 1C7   Joan Ann Hall, Libn.

COMMUNITY INFORMATION CENTRE OF METROPOLITAN TORONTO
34 King St. E., 3rd Fl.   Phone: (416) 863-0505
Toronto, ON M5C 1E5   Elizabeth Wray, Exec.Dir.

CONFEDERATION LIFE INSURANCE COMPANY - LIBRARY
321 Bloor St., E.   Phone: (416) 967-8326
Toronto, ON M4W 1H1   Lynne M. Sugden, Libn.

CONSERVATION COUNCIL OF ONTARIO - LIBRARY
74 Victoria St., Suite 202   Phone: (416) 362-2218
Toronto, ON M5C 2A5   Harvey H. Clare, Sec./Treas.

COUNTY OF YORK LAW ASSOCIATION - COURT HOUSE LIBRARY †
361 University Ave.   Phone: (416) 965-7488
Toronto, ON M5G 1T3   Anna M. MacIver, Libn./Adm.

CRANE (J.W.) MEMORIAL LIBRARY
351 Christie St.   Phone: (416) 537-6000
Toronto, ON M6G 3C3   Madeline Grant, Libn.

CRAVEN FOUNDATION - AUTOMOTIVE REFERENCE LIBRARY †
760 Lawrence Ave., W.   Phone: (416) 789-3432
Toronto, ON M6A 1B8   Frank Francis, Gen.Mgr.

CROWN LIFE INSURANCE COMPANY - CORPORATE INFORMATION CENTRE
120 Bloor St., E.   Phone: (416) 928-4650
Toronto, ON M4W 1B8   Nancy Hamilton, Corp.Libn.

CROWN LIFE INSURANCE COMPANY - LAW LIBRARY
120 Bloor St., E.   Phone: (416) 928-4563
Toronto, ON M4W 1B8   Mari White, Law Libn.

CURRIE, COOPERS & LYBRAND, LTD. - LIBRARY/INFORMATION CENTRE
145 King St., W.   Phone: (416) 366-1921
Toronto, ON M5H 1J8   Stephen K. Abram, Libn.

DENISON MINES LTD. - LIBRARY
Royal Bank Plaza, South Tower
P.O. Box 40   Phone: (416) 865-1991
Toronto, ON M5J 2K2   Mary Anne Wilflin, Libn.

DOCTORS HOSPITAL - ALEXANDER RAXLER LIBRARY
45 Brunswick Ave.   Phone: (416) 963-5464
Toronto, ON M5S 2M1   Margy Chan, Libn.

EAST YORK BOARD OF EDUCATION - PROFESSIONAL LIBRARY †
840 Coxwell Ave.   Phone: (416) 465-4631
Toronto, ON M4C 2V3   Martha Pluscauskas, Coord.

FALCONBRIDGE NICKEL MINES, LTD. - FALCONBRIDGE INFORMATION
   CENTRE †
Commerce Court West
P.O. Box 40   Phone: (416) 863-7227
Toronto, ON M5L 1B4   Stewart Collett, Mgr.

FASKEN & CALVIN, BARRISTERS AND SOLICITORS - LIBRARY †
Toronto Dominion Centre, Box 30   Phone: (416) 366-8381
Toronto, ON M5K 1C1   Bettina Hakala, Libn.

FENCO ENGINEERS, INC. - LIBRARY
33 Yonge St.   Phone: (416) 365-9955
Toronto, ON M5E 1E7   Agnes M. Croxford, Chf.Libn.

FINANCIAL TIMES OF CANADA - LIBRARY
920 Yonge St., Suite 500   Phone: (416) 922-1133
Toronto, ON M4W 3L5   Jane Wachna, Libn.

FRASER AND BEATTY - LIBRARY
Box 100, First Canadian Place   Phone: (416) 863-4527
Toronto, ON M5X 1B2   Jan Barrett, Libn.

GENERAL FOODS, LTD. - INFORMATION CENTRE †
Terminal A, P.O. Box 4019   Phone: (416) 481-4211
Toronto, ON M5W 1J6   Carol Symon, Supv., Info.Ctr.

GEORGE BROWN COLLEGE OF APPLIED ARTS & TECHNOLOGY - ARCHIVES
Sta. B, Box 1015   Phone: (416) 967-1212
Toronto, ON M5T 2T9   John L. Hardy, Archv.

GEORGE BROWN COLLEGE OF APPLIED ARTS & TECHNOLOGY - LIBRARY
Sta. B, Box 1015   Phone: (416) 967-1212
Toronto, ON M5T 2T9   Rita L. Edwards, Dir./Lib. & AV Serv.

GLAXO CANADA, LTD. - LIBRARY
1025 The Queensway   Phone: (416) 252-2281
Toronto, ON M8Z 5S6   Dr. V. Chivers Wilson, Dir., Res./Dev.

GOETHE INSTITUTE TORONTO - LIBRARY
1067 Yonge St.   Phone: (416) 924-3327
Toronto, ON M4W 2L2   Ulla Habekost, Libn.

GOODMAN AND CARR - LIBRARY
145 King St., W., Suite 2800   Phone: (416) 868-1234
Toronto, ON M5H 3K1   Arlene Levy, Libn.

GOODMAN AND GOODMAN - LIBRARY
20 Queen St., W.
Box 30   Phone: (416) 979-2211
Toronto, ON M5H 1V5   Michele L. Miles, Libn.

GULF CANADA LIMITED - CENTRAL LIBRARY †
800 Bay St.
Sta. A, P.O. Box 460   Phone: (416) 924-4141
Toronto, ON M5W 1E5   Wendy A. Davis, Sr.Libn.

HAWKER SIDDELEY CANADA INC. - ORENDA DIVISION - ENGINEERING
  LIBRARY
Box 6001, A.M.F.
Toronto, ON L5P 1B3

HAYHURST ADVERTISING, LTD. - MEDIA RESEARCH LIBRARY
55 Eglinton Ave., East   Phone: (416) 487-4371
Toronto, ON M4P 1G9   J. Marcotte, Media Supv.

HOCKEY HALL OF FAME AND MUSEUM - LIBRARY
Exhibition Place   Phone: (416) 595-1345
Toronto, ON M6K 3C3   M.H. (Lefty) Reid, Dir. & Cur.

HOSPITAL FOR SICK CHILDREN - HOSPITAL LIBRARY
555 University Ave.   Phone: (416) 597-1500
Toronto, ON M5G 1X8   Irene Jeryn, Libn.

HOWE (C.D.) INSTITUTE - LIBRARY
Glendon Hall
2275 Bayview Ave.   Phone: (416) 485-4310
Toronto, ON M4N 3M6   Barry A. Norris, Libn.

IMPERIAL LIFE ASSURANCE COMPANY - LIBRARY
95 St. Clair Ave., W.   Phone: (416) 923-6661
Toronto, ON M4V 1N7

IMPERIAL OIL, LTD. - AUDIO-VISUAL RESOURCE CENTRE
111 St. Clair Ave., W.
Toronto, ON M5W 1K3   Linda Scott, Lib.Techn.

IMPERIAL OIL, LTD. - BUSINESS INFORMATION CENTRE
111 St. Clair Ave., W.   Phone: (416) 968-4866
Toronto, ON M5W 1K3   Susan Reid, Mgr.

IMPERIAL OIL, LTD. - ESSO PETROLEUM INFORMATION CENTRE
55 St. Clair Ave., W.   Phone: (416) 968-4645
Toronto, ON M4V 2Y2   Fran Krayewski, Supv.

INCO LIMITED - BUSINESS LIBRARY
1 First Canadian Pl.
Box 44   Phone: (416) 361-7533
Toronto, ON M5X 1C4   Neftalie Abrenica, Info.Serv.

INCO LIMITED - EXPLORATION LIBRARY
1 First Canadian Place
Box 44   Phone: (416) 361-7533
Toronto, ON M5X 1C4   Neftalie Abrenica, Libn.

INDUSTRIAL ACCIDENT PREVENTION ASSOCIATION - RESOURCE LIBRARY
  & INFORMATION SERVICE
2 Bloor St., E.   Phone: (416) 965-8888
Toronto, ON M4W 3C2   Marion Frank, Libn.-in-Charge

INSTITUTE OF CHARTERED ACCOUNTANTS OF ONTARIO - THE MERRILEES
  LIBRARY
69 Bloor St., E.   Phone: (416) 962-1841
Toronto, ON M4W 1B3   Theresa Wolak, Libn.

INTERGOVERNMENTAL COMMITTEE ON URBAN AND REGIONAL RESEARCH
  (ICURR) - INFORMATION EXCHANGE SERVICE
123 Edward St., Suite 625   Phone: (416) 966-5629
Toronto, ON M5G 1E2   Tanya Wanio, Info.Coord.

LAW SOCIETY OF UPPER CANADA - GREAT LIBRARY
Osgoode Hall, 130 Queen St., W.   Phone: (416) 947-3400
Toronto, ON M5H 2N6   Glen W. Howell, Chf.Libn.

MC CARTHY AND MC CARTHY - LIBRARY
Toronto Dominion Ctr.
P.O. Box 48   Phone: (416) 362-1812
Toronto, ON M5K 1E6   Mary Percival, Libn.

MC KIM ADVERTISING, LTD. - INFORMATION CENTRE
Commerce Court East
P.O. Box 99   Phone: (416) 863-5300
Toronto, ON M5L 1E1   Patricia L. Petruga, Libn.

MC KINSEY & COMPANY, INC. - INFORMATION CENTRE
80 Bloor St., W., 8th Fl.   Phone: (416) 922-2200
Toronto, ON M5S 2V1   Marie Gadula, Supv., Info.Serv.

MC LEOD YOUNG WEIR LIMITED - INFORMATION CENTRE
Commercial Union Tower
Toronto-Dominion Centre, Box 433   Phone: (416) 863-7737
Toronto, ON M5K 1M2   Angela Agostino, Libn.

MC MILLAN, BINCH - LIBRARY
Royal Bank Plaza
P.O. Box 38   Phone: (416) 865-7031
Toronto, ON M5J 2J7   JoAnne Gulliver, Mgr., Lib.Serv.

MACLEAN HUNTER/FINANCIAL POST - LIBRARY
Maclean Hunter Bldg.
777 Bay St.   Phone: (416) 596-5244
Toronto, ON M5W 1A7   Theresa M. Butcher, Lib.Mgr.

MANUFACTURERS LIFE INSURANCE COMPANY - BUSINESS LIBRARY
200 Bloor St., E.   Phone: (416) 928-4104
Toronto, ON M4W 1E5   Julie Citroen, Libn.

MASSEY COLLEGE - ROBERTSON DAVIES LIBRARY
4 Devonshire Place   Phone: (416) 978-2893
Toronto, ON M5S 2E1   Desmond G. Neill, Libn.

MERCANTILE GENERAL REINSURANCE COMPANY - LIBRARY
University Place
123 Front St., W.   Phone: (416) 360-8340
Toronto, ON M5J 2M7   Jeanette Cornish, Libn.

METROPOLITAN TORONTO ASSOCIATION FOR THE MENTALLY RETARDED
  - HOWARD E. BACON MEMORIAL LIBRARY
8 Spadina Rd.   Phone: (416) 968-0650
Toronto, ON M5R 2S7   M. McPherson, Libn.

METROPOLITAN TORONTO LIBRARY - BOOK INFORMATION AND
  INTERLOAN DEPARTMENT
789 Yonge St.   Phone: (416) 928-5182
Toronto, ON M4W 2G8   Robert H.S. Yu, Hd.

METROPOLITAN TORONTO LIBRARY - BUSINESS DEPARTMENT
789 Yonge St.   Phone: (416) 928-5256
Toronto, ON M4W 2G8   Patricia Dye, Hd.

METROPOLITAN TORONTO LIBRARY - CANADIAN HISTORY DEPARTMENT
789 Yonge St.   Phone: (416) 928-5275
Toronto, ON M4W 2G8   David B. Kotin, Hd.

METROPOLITAN TORONTO LIBRARY - FINE ART DEPARTMENT
789 Yonge St.   Phone: (416) 928-5214
Toronto, ON M4W 2G8   Alan Suddon, Hd.

METROPOLITAN TORONTO LIBRARY - GENERAL REFERENCE DEPARTMENT
789 Yonge St.   Phone: (416) 928-5211
Toronto, ON M4W 2G8   Anne Mack, Hd.

METROPOLITAN TORONTO LIBRARY - HISTORY DEPARTMENT
789 Yonge St.   Phone: (416) 928-5267
Toronto, ON M4W 2G8   Michael Pearson, Hd.

METROPOLITAN TORONTO LIBRARY - LANGUAGES DEPARTMENT
789 Yonge St.   Phone: (416) 928-5280
Toronto, ON M4W 2G8   Barbara Gunther, Hd.

METROPOLITAN TORONTO LIBRARY - LITERATURE DEPARTMENT
789 Yonge St.   Phone: (416) 928-5284
Toronto, ON M4W 2G8   Katherine McCook, Hd.

METROPOLITAN TORONTO LIBRARY - MUNICIPAL REFERENCE
    DEPARTMENT
City Hall, Nathan Phillips Square   Phone: (416) 928-5357
Toronto, ON M5H 2N1   Margot Hewings, Hd.

METROPOLITAN TORONTO LIBRARY - MUSIC DEPARTMENT
789 Yonge St.   Phone: (416) 928-5224
Toronto, ON M4W 2G8   Isabel Rose, Hd.

METROPOLITAN TORONTO LIBRARY - NEWSPAPER UNIT
789 Yonge St.   Phone: (416) 928-5254
Toronto, ON M4W 2G8   Alan Suddon, Hd. of Unit

METROPOLITAN TORONTO LIBRARY - REGIONAL AUDIO VISUAL
    DEPARTMENT
789 Yonge St.   Phone: (416) 928-5185
Toronto, ON M4W 2G8   Laura Murray, Hd.

METROPOLITAN TORONTO LIBRARY - SCIENCE & TECHNOLOGY
    DEPARTMENT
789 Yonge St.   Phone: (416) 928-5234
Toronto, ON M4W 2G8   Margaret Walshe, Hd.

METROPOLITAN TORONTO LIBRARY - SOCIAL SCIENCES DEPARTMENT
789 Yonge St.   Phone: (416) 928-5246
Toronto, ON M4W 2G8   Abdus Salam, Hd.

METROPOLITAN TORONTO LIBRARY - THEATRE DEPARTMENT
789 Yonge St.   Phone: (416) 928-5230
Toronto, ON M4W 2G8   Heather McCallum, Hd.

METROPOLITAN TORONTO PLANNING DEPARTMENT - LIBRARY †
City Hall, 11th Fl., East Tower   Phone: (416) 367-8101
Toronto, ON M5H 2N1   Pamela J. Smith, Libn.

METROPOLITAN (Toronto) SEPARATE SCHOOL BOARD - CATHOLIC
    EDUCATION CENTRE LIBRARY
80 Sheppard Ave., E.   Phone: (416) 222-8282
Toronto, ON M2N 6E8   Rev. William J. Brown, Asst.Supt., Curric.

MIDLAND DOHERTY, LTD. - LIBRARY
Box 25, Commercial Union Tower
Toronto Dominion Centre   Phone: (416) 361-6063
Toronto, ON M5K 1B5   Gwynne Tucker, Libn.

MIGRAINE FOUNDATION - LIBRARY †
390 Brunswick Ave.   Phone: (416) 920-4916
Toronto, ON M5R 2Z4   David Jones, Chm., Lib.Comm.

MOUNT SINAI HOSPITAL - SIDNEY LISWOOD LIBRARY
600 University Ave.   Phone: (416) 596-4614
Toronto, ON M5G 1X5   Eleanor Hayes, Libn.

NATIONAL YOUTH ORCHESTRA ASSOCIATION OF CANADA - LIBRARY
76 Charles St., W.   Phone: (416) 922-5031
Toronto, ON M5S 1K8   Paul Hawkshaw, Artistic Coord.

NEEDHAM, HARPER & STEERS OF CANADA, LTD. - INFORMATION
    SERVICES CENTRE
130 Adelaide St., W.   Phone: (416) 364-1492
Toronto, ON M5H 1T3   Hilary Livingstone, Res.Asst.

NORANDA SALES CORPORATION, LTD. - SALES LIBRARY
Commerce Court W.
Box 45   Phone: (416) 867-7036
Toronto, ON M5L 1B6   Karen L. Hammond, Mgr., Info.Rsrcs.

NORTH AMERICAN LIFE ASSURANCE COMPANY - LIBRARY
105 Adelaide St., W.   Phone: (416) 362-6011
Toronto, ON M5H 1R1   Kitty MacMillan, Libn.

NORTHERN MINER - LIBRARY
7 Labatt Ave.   Phone: (416) 368-3481
Toronto, ON M5A 1Z1   Mrs. M. Murray, Libn.

ONTARIO - ARCHIVES OF ONTARIO - LIBRARY
Ministry of Citizenship & Culture
77 Grenville St.   Phone: (416) 965-4030
Toronto, ON M7A 2R9   Ethelyn Harlow, Libn.

ONTARIO CANCER INSTITUTE - LIBRARY
500 Sherbourne St.   Phone: (416) 926-4482
Toronto, ON M4X 1K9   Carol A. Morrison, Libn.

ONTARIO CHORAL FEDERATION - LIBRARY
Maison Chalmers House
20 St. Joseph St.
Toronto, ON M5Y 1J9   Norah Bolton, Exec.Adm.

ONTARIO COLLEGE OF ART - LIBRARY/AUDIOVISUAL CENTRE
100 McCaul St.   Phone: (416) 977-5311
Toronto, ON M5T 1W1   Ian Carr-Harris, Dir.

ONTARIO CRAFTS COUNCIL - CRAFT RESOURCE CENTRE
346 Dundas St., W.   Phone: (416) 977-3551
Toronto, ON M5T 1G5   Ted Rickard, Mgr.

ONTARIO ECONOMIC COUNCIL - LIBRARY
81 Wellesley St. E.   Phone: (416) 965-4315
Toronto, ON M4Y 1H6   Diane Wenzel, Libn.

ONTARIO ENERGY BOARD - LIBRARY
14 Carlton St., 9th Fl.   Phone: (416) 598-4000
Toronto, ON M5B 1J2   Rita Piazza, Lib.Mgr.

ONTARIO HYDRO - LIBRARY
700 University Ave.   Phone: (416) 592-2719
Toronto, ON M5G 1X6   Doreen Taylor, Chf.Libn.

ONTARIO INSTITUTE FOR STUDIES IN EDUCATION (OISE) - MODERN
    LANGUAGE CENTRE - LANGUAGE TEACHING LIBRARY †
252 Bloor St., W.   Phone: (416) 923-6641
Toronto, ON M5S 1V6   Alice Weinrib, Res.Assoc./Libn.

ONTARIO INSTITUTE FOR STUDIES IN EDUCATION (OISE) - R.W.B.
    JACKSON LIBRARY
252 Bloor St., W.   Phone: (416) 923-6641
Toronto, ON M5S 1V6   Shirley K. Wigmore, Chf.Libn.

ONTARIO - LEGISLATIVE ASSEMBLY - LEGISLATIVE LIBRARY RESEARCH
    AND INFORMATION SERVICES
Legislative Bldg., Queen's Park   Phone: (416) 965-4545
Toronto, ON M7A 1A2   R. Brian Land, Dir.

ONTARIO LOTTERY CORPORATION - LIBRARY
2 Bloor St., W., 24th Fl.   Phone: (416) 961-6262
Toronto, ON M4W 3H8   Suzanne Kemper, Libn.

ONTARIO MEDICAL ASSOCIATION - LIBRARY
240 St. George St.   Phone: (416) 925-3264
Toronto, ON M5R 2P4   Jan Greenwood, Libn.

ONTARIO - MINISTRY OF AGRICULTURE AND FOOD - LIBRARY
801 Bay St., 3rd Fl.   Phone: (416) 965-1816
Toronto, ON M7A 2B2   Ken Sundquist, Ministry Libn.

ONTARIO - MINISTRY OF THE ATTORNEY GENERAL - LIBRARY
18 King St., E., 12th Fl.   Phone: (416) 965-4714
Toronto, ON M5C 1C5   Sharon Day-Feldman, Libn.

ONTARIO - MINISTRY OF CITIZENSHIP AND CULTURE - LIBRARIES AND
   COMMUNITY INFORMATION
7th Fl., 77 Bloor St., W.   Phone: (416) 965-2696
Toronto, ON M7A 2R9   Wil Vanderelst, Dir.

ONTARIO - MINISTRY OF CITIZENSHIP AND CULTURE - MAP LIBRARY
77 Grenville St.   Phone: (416) 965-4030
Toronto, ON M7A 2R9   John W. Fortier, Archv.

ONTARIO - MINISTRY OF CITIZENSHIP AND CULTURE - MINISTRY OF
   TOURISM AND RECREATION - LIBRARY/RESOURCE CENTRE
77 Bloor St., W., 9th Fl.   Phone: (416) 965-6763
Toronto, ON M7A 2R9   Marjorie Howard, Coord.

ONTARIO - MINISTRY OF CITIZENSHIP AND CULTURE - PLANNING AND
   TECHNICAL SERVICES
77 Bloor St., W., 4th Fl.   Phone: (416) 965-0322
Toronto, ON M7A 2R9   Brian Forsyth, Sr.Arch.Adv.

ONTARIO - MINISTRY OF COMMUNITY AND SOCIAL SERVICES - MINISTRY
   LIBRARY †
880 Bay St., Rm. 663   Phone: (416) 965-2314
Toronto, ON M7A 2B2   Sandra Walsh, Mgr., Lib.Serv.

ONTARIO - MINISTRY OF CONSUMER AND COMMERCIAL RELATIONS -
   CONSUMER INFORMATION CENTRE
555 Yonge St., 1st Fl.   Phone: (416) 963-1111
Toronto, ON M7A 2H6   Sarah Coombs, Mgr.

ONTARIO - MINISTRY OF CORRECTIONAL SERVICES - LIBRARY SERVICES
2001 Eglinton Ave., E.   Phone: (416) 750-3481
Toronto, ON M1L 4P1   T.J.B. Anderson, Chf.Libn.

ONTARIO - MINISTRY OF EDUCATION - INFORMATION CENTRE
Mowat Block, 13th Fl., Queen's Park   Phone: (416) 965-1451
Toronto, ON M7A 1L2

ONTARIO - MINISTRY OF ENERGY - LIBRARY
56 Wellesley St., W., 12th Fl.   Phone: (416) 965-9175
Toronto, ON M7A 2B7   Nancy Pierobon, Hd.Libn.

ONTARIO - MINISTRY OF THE ENVIRONMENT - LIBRARY †
135 St. Clair Ave., W., 1st Fl.   Phone: (416) 965-7978
Toronto, ON M4V 1P5   N.J. McIlroy, Libn.

ONTARIO - MINISTRY OF GOVERNMENT SERVICES - TECHNICAL
   REFERENCE LIBRARY *
1200 Bay St., 4th Fl.   Phone: (416) 965-2965
Toronto, ON M5R 2A5   Lynda Magistrale, Educ.Serv.Off.

ONTARIO - MINISTRY OF HEALTH - LIBRARY
15 Overlea Blvd., 7th Fl.   Phone: (416) 965-7881
Toronto, ON M4H 1A9   Veronica Brunka, Lib.Supv.

ONTARIO - MINISTRY OF HEALTH - PUBLIC HEALTH LABORATORIES -
   LIBRARY
Postal Terminal A, Box 9000   Phone: (416) 248-3165
Toronto, ON M5W 1R5   Doris A. Standing, Libn.

ONTARIO - MINISTRY OF INDUSTRY AND TRADE - INFORMATION CENTRE
Hearst Block, Queen's Park   Phone: (416) 965-3365
Toronto, ON M7A 2E1   Dee Phillips, Mgr.

ONTARIO - MINISTRY OF LABOUR - LIBRARY
400 University Ave.   Phone: (416) 965-1641
Toronto, ON M7A 1T7   Jean Collins-Williams, Act.Hd.Libn.

ONTARIO - MINISTRY OF LABOUR - ONTARIO LABOUR RELATIONS BOARD
   - LIBRARY
400 University Ave., 4th Fl.   Phone: (416) 965-0206
Toronto, ON M7A 1V4   Clare Lyons, Libn.

ONTARIO - MINISTRY OF MUNICIPAL AFFAIRS & HOUSING - LIBRARY
2-777 Bay St.   Phone: (416) 965-9720
Toronto, ON M5G 2E5   Frank Szucs, Libn.

ONTARIO - MINISTRY OF NATURAL RESOURCES - MINES LIBRARY
77 Grenville St.   Phone: (416) 965-1352
Toronto, ON M5S 1B3   Nancy Thurston, Libn.

ONTARIO - MINISTRY OF NATURAL RESOURCES - NATURAL RESOURCES
   LIBRARY
Whitney Block, Rm. 4540
Queen's Park   Phone: (416) 965-6319
Toronto, ON M7A 1W3   Sandra Louet, Mgr.

ONTARIO - MINISTRY OF NORTHERN AFFAIRS - LIBRARY AND RECORDS
10 Wellesley St. E., 8th Fl.   Phone: (416) 965-1417
Toronto, ON M4Y 1G2   Susan Baumann, Coord.

ONTARIO - MINISTRY OF THE SOLICITOR GENERAL - CENTRE OF
   FORENSIC SCIENCES - H. WARD SMITH LIBRARY
25 Grosvenor St., 2nd Fl.   Phone: (416) 965-2561
Toronto, ON M7A 2G8   Eva Gulbinowicz, Libn.

ONTARIO - MINISTRY OF THE SOLICITOR GENERAL - OFFICE OF THE FIRE
   MARSHAL LIBRARY
7 Overlea Blvd., 3rd Fl.   Phone: (416) 965-4855
Toronto, ON M4H 1A8   Iris Becker-Zawadowski, Libn.

ONTARIO - MINISTRY OF TOURISM AND RECREATION - PHOTO LIBRARY
10th Fl., Hearst Block
900 Bay St.   Phone: (416) 965-5411
Toronto, ON M7A 2E1   Linda M. Goodwin, Photo Libn.

ONTARIO - MINISTRY OF TREASURY AND ECONOMICS - LIBRARY
   SERVICES BRANCH
Frost Bldg. North, 1st Fl.
Queen's Park   Phone: (416) 965-2314
Toronto, ON M7A 1Y7   Barbara Weatherhead, Dir.

ONTARIO - MUNICIPAL BOARD - LIBRARY
180 Dundas St., W.   Phone: (416) 598-2266
Toronto, ON M5G 1E5   B.C. Alty, Asst.Sec. & Adm.Off.

ONTARIO NURSES ASSOCIATION - ONA LIBRARY
415 Yonge St., 14th Fl.   Phone: (416) 977-1975
Toronto, ON M5B 2E7   Kathy Bennett O'Hara, Lib.Techn.

ONTARIO PROVINCIAL POLICE HEADQUARTERS - CAREER MANAGEMENT
   BRANCH - LIBRARY
90 Harbour St.   Phone: (416) 965-4468
Toronto, ON M7A 2S1   Lorna E. Brown, Libn.

ONTARIO - SUPREME COURT OF ONTARIO - JUDGES' LIBRARY †
Osgoode Hall
130 Queen St., W.   Phone: (416) 363-4101
Toronto, ON M5H 2N5   Anne Brown, Mgr.

ORTHOPAEDIC AND ARTHRITIC HOSPITAL - LIBRARY
43 Wellesley St., E.   Phone: (416) 967-8545
Toronto, ON M4Y 1H1   Sheila M. Lethbridge, Libn.

PEAT, MARWICK & PARTNERS - LIBRARY
Commerce Court West   Phone: (416) 863-3440
Toronto, ON M5L 1B2   Mrs. S.A. Layton, Libn.

POLAR GAS PROJECT - LIBRARY
Commerce Court W.
Box 90   Phone: (416) 869-2675
Toronto, ON M5L 1H3   Carolyn Giovanetti, Libn.

PRICE WATERHOUSE - NATIONAL/TORONTO OFFICE LIBRARY
Toronto Dominion Centre
P.O. Box 51   Phone: (416) 863-1133
Toronto, ON M5K 1G1   Dorothy L. Sedgwick, Hd.Libn.

PRUDENTIAL LIFE INSURANCE COMPANY OF AMERICA - BUSINESS
   LIBRARY †
King & Yonge Sts.   Phone: (416) 366-6971
Toronto, ON M5H 1B7   J. Ireland, Libn.

QUEEN STREET MENTAL HEALTH CENTRE - HEALTH SCIENCES LIBRARY
1001 Queen St., W.   Phone: (416) 535-8501
Toronto, ON M6J 1H3   Mary Ann Georges, Staff Libn.

REED STENHOUSE, LTD. - RESEARCH DEPARTMENT LIBRARY
Toronto Dominion Centre
P.O. Box 250   Phone: (416) 868-5520
Toronto, ON M5K 1J6   G.R.E. Bromwich, V.P., Res. & Info.Dept.

REED INC. - TECHNICAL INFORMATION CENTRE
207 Queen's Quay W.   Phone: (416) 862-5006
Toronto, ON M5J 1A7   Jim Drake, Info.Spec.

REGIS COLLEGE - LIBRARY †
15 St. Mary St.   Phone: (416) 922-0536
Toronto, ON M4Y 2R5   Rev. Vincent MacKenzie, S.J., Chf.Libn.

REGISTERED NURSES' ASSOCIATION OF ONTARIO - LIBRARY
33 Price St.   Phone: (416) 923-3523
Toronto, ON M4W 1Z2   Mary Boite, Libn.

RIO ALGOM, LTD. - LIBRARY
120 Adelaide St., W.   Phone: (416) 365-6800
Toronto, ON M5H 1W5   Penny Lipman, Libn.

ROYAL ASTRONOMICAL SOCIETY OF CANADA - NATIONAL LIBRARY
136 Dupont St.   Phone: (416) 924-7973
Toronto, ON M5R 1V2   Phil Mozel, Libn.

ROYAL BANK OF CANADA - INFORMATION RESOURCES
Royal Bank Plaza, 4th Fl.   Phone: (416) 865-2780
Toronto, ON M5H 2J5   Jane Dysart, Chf.Libn.

ROYAL BANK OF CANADA - TAXATION LIBRARY/INTERNATIONAL
Royal Bank Plaza
Toronto, ON M5J 2J5   Franki Elliott, Tax Libn.

ROYAL CANADIAN MILITARY INSTITUTE - LIBRARY
426 University Ave.   Phone: (416) 597-0286
Toronto, ON M5G 1S9   Lt.Col. W.G. Heard, Cur.

ROYAL ONTARIO MUSEUM - CANADIANA GALLERY LIBRARY †
14 Queen's Park Crescent, W.   Phone: (416) 978-6738
Toronto, ON M5S 2C6   Janet Holmes, Cur.Asst.

ROYAL ONTARIO MUSEUM - FAR EASTERN LIBRARY *
100 Queen's Park   Phone: (416) 978-3653
Toronto, ON M5S 2C6   John Howard, Assoc.Libn.

ROYAL ONTARIO MUSEUM - LIBRARY †
100 Queen's Park   Phone: (416) 928-3671
Toronto, ON M5S 2C6   Gene Wilburn, Hd.Libn.

ROYAL TRUST CORPORATION OF CANADA - INVESTMENT RESEARCH
   LIBRARY
P.O. Box 7500, Sta. A   Phone: (416) 867-2928
Toronto, ON M5W 1P9   Anita Frank, Libn.

RYERSON POLYTECHNICAL INSTITUTE - LEARNING RESOURCES CENTRE
350 Victoria St.   Phone: (416) 595-5322
Toronto, ON M5B 2K3   John North, Dir.

ST. JOSEPH'S HEALTH CENTRE - GEORGE PENNAL LIBRARY
30 The Queensway   Phone: (416) 530-6726
Toronto, ON M6R 1B5   Julia Chan, Med.Libn.

ST. MICHAEL'S HOSPITAL - HEALTH SCIENCE LIBRARY
30 Bond St.   Phone: (416) 360-4941
Toronto, ON M5B 1W8   Anita Wong, Dir.

ST. VLADIMIR INSTITUTE - UKRAINIAN LIBRARY †
620 Spadina Ave.   Phone: (416) 923-8266
Toronto, ON M5S 2H4   Vera Skop, Libn.

SHAWINIGAN GROUP INCORPORATED - ENERGY LIBRARY
620 University Ave.   Phone: (416) 365-7290
Toronto, ON M5G 2C1   Pearl H. Weisbaum, Libn.

SHELL CANADA LIMITED - TECHNICAL LIBRARY
505 University Ave.
Toronto, ON M5G 1X4   Miss S. Tattershall, Hd., Lib.Sect.

SOCIETY OF FRIENDS - FRIENDS HOUSE LIBRARY
60 Lowther Ave.   Phone: (416) 921-0368
Toronto, ON M5R 1C7   Jane Sweet, Lib.Coord.

STRATHY, ARCHIBALD AND SEAGRAM - LAW LIBRARY
3801 Commerce Court W.
Box 438   Phone: (416) 863-7525
Toronto, ON M5L 1J3   Alison J. Colvin, Libn.

SUN LIFE OF CANADA - INVESTMENT LIBRARY
Box 4084, Sta. A   Phone: (416) 595-7894
Toronto, ON M5W 2K9   Elizabeth Gibson, Libn.

SUN LIFE OF CANADA - REFERENCE LIBRARY
200 University Ave.   Phone: (416) 595-7890
Toronto, ON M5H 3C7   Mrs. Trinidad B. Espiritu, Ref.Libn.

SUNNYBROOK MEDICAL CENTRE - HEALTH SCIENCES LIBRARY
2075 Bayview Ave.   Phone: (416) 486-3880
Toronto, ON M4N 3M5   Linda McFarlane, Health Sci.Libn.

THOMSON, ROGERS, BARRISTERS & SOLICITORS - LIBRARY †
390 Bay St., Suite 3100   Phone: (416) 868-3100
Toronto, ON M5H 1W2   Dianne D. Sydij, Libn.

TOMENSON SAUNDERS WHITEHEAD LTD./TA ASSOCIATES - RESOURCE
   CENTRE
Toronto-Dominion Center
P.O. Box 439   Phone: (416) 361-6830
Toronto, ON M5K 1M3   Glen Miller

TORONTO BOARD OF EDUCATION - EDUCATION CENTRE LIBRARY
155 College St.   Phone: (416) 591-8183
Toronto, ON M5T 1P6   F. Eugene Gattinger, Coord., Lib.Serv.

TORONTO CITY PLANNING AND DEVELOPMENT DEPARTMENT - LIBRARY
City Hall   Phone: (416) 947-7185
Toronto, ON M5H 2N2   Georgina Moravec, Libn.

TORONTO DOMINION BANK - DEPARTMENT OF ECONOMIC RESEARCH -
   LIBRARY
55 King St., W.   Phone: (416) 866-8068
Toronto, ON M5K 1A2   Ruth P. Smith, Libn.

TORONTO EAST GENERAL HOSPITAL - HEALTH SCIENCES LIBRARY
825 Coxwell Ave.   Phone: (416) 461-8272
Toronto, ON M4C 3E7   Roger Smithies, Libn.

TORONTO GENERAL HOSPITAL - FUDGER MEDICAL LIBRARY
101 College St.   Phone: (416) 595-3549
Toronto, ON M5G 1L7   Mrs. D. Cowper, Libn.

TORONTO GLOBE AND MAIL, LTD. - LIBRARY
444 Front St., W.   Phone: (416) 598-5075
Toronto, ON M5V 2S9   Amanda Valpy, Chf.Libn.

TORONTO INSTITUTE OF MEDICAL TECHNOLOGY - LIBRARY
222 St. Patrick St.   Phone: (416) 596-3123
Toronto, ON M5T 1V4   Patricia Fortin, Libn.

TORONTO PUBLIC LIBRARY - CANADIANA COLLECTION OF CHILDREN'S
   BOOKS
40 St. George St.
Boys and Girls House   Phone: (416) 593-5350
Toronto, ON M5S 2E4   Margaret Crawford Maloney, Hd.

TORONTO PUBLIC LIBRARY - LILLIAN H. SMITH COLLECTION OF
   CHILDREN'S BOOKS
40 St. George St.
Boys And Girls House   Phone: (416) 593-5350
Toronto, ON M5S 2E4   Margaret Crawford Maloney, Hd.

TORONTO PUBLIC LIBRARY - MARGUERITE G. BAGSHAW COLLECTION †
40 St. George St.
Boys and Girls House   Phone: (416) 593-5162
Toronto, ON M5S 2E4   Stephen Lee, Bagshaw Comm.Chm.

TORONTO PUBLIC LIBRARY - OSBORNE COLLECTION OF EARLY
   CHILDREN'S BOOKS
40 St. George St.
Boys and Girls House   Phone: (416) 593-5350
Toronto, ON M5S 2E4   Margaret Crawford Maloney, Hd.

TORONTO PUBLIC LIBRARY - SPACED-OUT LIBRARY
40 St. George St.   Phone: (416) 593-5351
Toronto, ON M5S 2E4   Doris Mehegan, Hd.

TORONTO STAR NEWSPAPERS LTD. - LIBRARY
One Yonge St.   Phone: (416) 367-2420
Toronto, ON M5E 1E6   Carol Lindsay, Chf.Libn.

TORONTO STOCK EXCHANGE - LIBRARY
The Exchange Tower
2 First Canadian Pl., 3rd Fl.   Phone: (416) 868-5326
Toronto, ON M5X 1J2   Shirley Foster, Libn.

TORONTO SUN - LIBRARY
333 King St., E.   Phone: (416) 947-2257
Toronto, ON M5A 3X5   Julie Kirsh, Chf.Libn.

TORONTO TRANSIT COMMISSION - ENGINEERING & CONSTRUCTION
    LIBRARY
1900 Yonge St.   Phone: (416) 534-9511
Toronto, ON M4S 1Z2   Frances Villanti, Lib.Techn.

TORONTO TRANSIT COMMISSION - HEAD OFFICE LIBRARY †
1900 Yonge St.   Phone: (416) 481-4252
Toronto, ON M4S 1Z2   Adrian Gehring, Lib.Techn.

TORONTO WESTERN HOSPITAL - R.C. LAIRD HEALTH SCIENCES LIBRARY
399 Bathurst St.   Phone: (416) 369-5750
Toronto, ON M5T 2S8   Elizabeth A. Reid, Dir.

TORY, TORY, DESLAURIERS & BINNINGTON - LIBRARY
Royal Bank Plaza, Suite 3400
P.O. Box 20   Phone: (416) 865-0040
Toronto, ON M5J 2K1   Janet Darby, Libn.

TOUCHE, ROSS & COMPANY/TOUCHE ROSS & PARTNERS - INFORMATION
    CENTRE
100 King St. W.
Box 12, First Canadian Pl.   Phone: (416) 364-4242
Toronto, ON M5X 1B3   Barbara Dance, Libn.

TOWERS, PERRIN, FORSTER & CROSBY LTD. - INFORMATION CENTRE
250 Bloor St., E., Suite 1100
Toronto, ON M4W 3N3   Sari Bercovitch, Dir. of Info.Serv.

TRANS CANADA PIPELINES LTD. - LIBRARY
Box 54, Commerce Court West   Phone: (416) 869-2678
Toronto, ON M5L 1C2   Nancy L. Urbankiewicz, Sr.Libn.

TV ONTARIO - LIBRARY
P.O. Box 200, Station Q   Phone: (416) 484-2600
Toronto, ON M4T 2T1   Ms. Rechilde Volpatti, Supv.

UNION CARBIDE CANADA, LTD. - REFERENCE LIBRARY
123 Eglinton Ave., E.   Phone: (416) 488-1444
Toronto, ON M4P 1J3   K. Martha Nagata, Libn.

UNITED CHURCH OF CANADA - CENTRAL ARCHIVES †
Birge-Carnegie Bldg., Victoria Univ.
73 Queen's Park Crescent, E.   Phone: (416) 978-3832
Toronto, ON M5S 2C4   Rev. Glenn Lucas, Archv./Hist.

UNIVERSITY OF TORONTO - A.E. MAC DONALD OPHTHALMIC LIBRARY
1 Spadina Crescent   Phone: (416) 978-2635
Toronto, ON M5S 2J5   Amy Reszczynski, Sec.

UNIVERSITY OF TORONTO - ANTHROPOLOGY READING ROOM
Sidney Smith Hall, Rm. 560A
100 St. George St.   Phone: (416) 978-3296
Toronto, ON M5S 1A1   Tessa J. Ireland, Sec.

UNIVERSITY OF TORONTO - ASTRONOMY LIBRARY
60 St. George St., Rm. 1306   Phone: (416) 884-2112
Toronto, ON M5S 187   Lynda Colbeck, Libn.

UNIVERSITY OF TORONTO - AUDIO-VISUAL LIBRARY
                    Phone: (416) 978-6084
Toronto, ON M5S 2E8   Liz Avison, Hd.Libn.

UNIVERSITY OF TORONTO - CENTRE OF CRIMINOLOGY - LIBRARY
130 St. George St., Suite 8055   Phone: (416) 978-7068
Toronto, ON M5S 1A5   Catherine J. Matthews, Libn.

UNIVERSITY OF TORONTO - CENTRE FOR INDUSTRIAL RELATIONS -
    INFORMATION SERVICE
                    Phone: (416) 978-2928
Toronto, ON M5S 2E8   Elizabeth Perry, Libn.

UNIVERSITY OF TORONTO - CENTRE FOR URBAN AND COMMUNITY
    STUDIES - RESOURCE ROOM
455 Spadina Ave.   Phone: (416) 978-4478
Toronto, ON M5S 2G8   Judith Kjellberg, Info.Off.

UNIVERSITY OF TORONTO - DEPARTMENT OF BOTANY LIBRARY
Botany Bldg., Rm. 202
6 Queen's Pk.   Phone: (416) 978-3538
Toronto, ON M5S 1A1   Ellen Chamberlain, Sec.

UNIVERSITY OF TORONTO - DEPARTMENT OF CHEMISTRY LIBRARY
Lash-Miller Bldg., Rms. 429-433
Willcocks & St. George Sts.   Phone: (416) 978-3587
Toronto, ON M5S 2T4   Donna Allen, Sec.

UNIVERSITY OF TORONTO - DEPARTMENT OF COMPUTER SCIENCE
    LIBRARY
McLennan Physical Labs.
60 St. George St.   Phone: (416) 978-2987
Toronto, ON M5S 2E7   Stephanie Johnston, Libn.

UNIVERSITY OF TORONTO - DEPARTMENT OF GEOLOGY - COLEMAN
    LIBRARY
Mining Bldg., Rm. 316
170 College St.   Phone: (416) 978-3024
Toronto, ON M5S 1A1   L.A. Eschenauer, Sec.

UNIVERSITY OF TORONTO - DEPARTMENT OF MEDICAL RESEARCH
    LIBRARY
Banting & Best Institute, Rm. 304
112 College St.   Phone: (416) 978-2588
Toronto, ON M5G 1L6   Colin Savage

UNIVERSITY OF TORONTO - DEPARTMENT OF PHYSICS LIBRARY
McLennan Physical Labs., Rm. 211
Russell & Huron Sts.   Phone: (416) 978-5788
Toronto, ON M5S 1A7   B. Chu, Libn.

UNIVERSITY OF TORONTO - DEPARTMENT OF ZOOLOGY LIBRARY
Ramsey-Wright Bldg., Rm. 225
St. George & Harbord Sts.   Phone: (416) 978-3515
Toronto, ON M5S 1A1   R. O'Grady, Sec.

UNIVERSITY OF TORONTO - EAST ASIAN LIBRARY
280 Huron St.   Phone: (416) 928-3300
Toronto, ON M5S 1A1   Anna U, Libn.

UNIVERSITY OF TORONTO - FACULTY OF APPLIED SCIENCE AND
    ENGINEERING - CENTRE FOR BUILDING SCIENCE - LIBRARY
35 St. George St.   Phone: (416) 978-5053
Toronto, ON M5S 1A4   Mr. A. Seskus, Res.Off.

UNIVERSITY OF TORONTO - FACULTY OF DENTISTRY LIBRARY
124 Edward St., Rm. 202   Phone: (416) 978-2796
Toronto, ON M5G 1G6   Susan Goddard, Faculty Libn.

UNIVERSITY OF TORONTO - FACULTY OF EDUCATION LIBRARY
371 Bloor St., W.   Phone: (416) 978-3224
Toronto, ON M5S 2R7   Mary Shortt, Chf.Libn.

UNIVERSITY OF TORONTO - FACULTY OF ENGINEERING LIBRARY
Sandford Fleming Bldg., Rm 2402
10 King's College Rd.   Phone: (416) 978-6109
Toronto, ON M5S 1A4   E.S. Brown

UNIVERSITY OF TORONTO - FACULTY OF FORESTRY LIBRARY
Forestry Bldg., Rm. 102
45 St. George St.   Phone: (416) 978-6016
Toronto, ON M5S 1A1   Jean Bohne, Libn.

UNIVERSITY OF TORONTO - FACULTY OF LAW LIBRARY
78 Queen's Park   Phone: (416) 978-3719
Toronto, ON M5S 1A1   Christine Attalai, Act.Chf.Libn.

UNIVERSITY OF TORONTO - FACULTY OF LIBRARY SCIENCE LIBRARY
140 St. George St.   Phone: (416) 978-7060
Toronto, ON M5S 1A1   Diane Henderson, Chf.Libn.

UNIVERSITY OF TORONTO - FACULTY OF MANAGEMENT STUDIES LIBRARY
246 Bloor St., W.   Phone: (416) 978-3421
Toronto, ON M5S 1V4   Margaret McKay, Libn.

UNIVERSITY OF TORONTO - FACULTY OF MUSIC LIBRARY
Edward Johnson Bldg.   Phone: (416) 978-3734
Toronto, ON M5S 1A1   Kathleen McMorrow, Libn.

UNIVERSITY OF TORONTO - FACULTY OF PHARMACY - R.O. HURST
   LIBRARY
25 Russell St.   Phone: (416) 978-2870
Toronto, ON M5S 1A1   Barbara A. Gallivan, Libn.

UNIVERSITY OF TORONTO - FINE ARTS LIBRARY
100 St. George St.   Phone: (416) 978-3290
Toronto, ON M5S 1A1   Andrea Retfalvi, Libn.

UNIVERSITY OF TORONTO - GENERAL LIBRARY - SCIENCE AND MEDICINE
   DEPARTMENT
                                             Phone: (416) 978-2284
Toronto, ON M5S 1A5   Ms. G. Heaton, Hd.

UNIVERSITY OF TORONTO - INSTITUTE OF CHILD STUDY - LIBRARY
45 Walmer Rd.   Phone: (416) 978-5086
Toronto, ON M5R 2X2   Miriam Herman, Lib.Techn.

UNIVERSITY OF TORONTO - INSTITUTE FOR POLICY ANALYSIS - LIBRARY
150 St. George St.   Phone: (416) 928-8623
Toronto, ON M5S 2E9   U. Gutenburg, Lib.Techn.

UNIVERSITY OF TORONTO - KNOX COLLEGE - CAVEN LIBRARY
59 St. George St.   Phone: (416) 979-2532
Toronto, ON M5S 2E6   A. Burgess, Libn.

UNIVERSITY OF TORONTO - MAP LIBRARY
130 St. George St., Rm. 1001   Phone: (416) 978-3372
Toronto, ON M5S 1A5   Joan Winearls, Map Libn.

UNIVERSITY OF TORONTO - MATHEMATICS LIBRARY
Sidney Smith Hall, Rm. 2124
100 St. George St.   Phone: (416) 978-8624
Toronto, ON M5S 1A1   Chibeck Graham, Libn.

UNIVERSITY OF TORONTO - PATHOLOGY LIBRARY
Banting Institute, Rms. 108-109
100 College St.   Phone: (416) 978-2558
Toronto, ON M5G 1L5   Sophia Duda, Libn.

UNIVERSITY OF TORONTO - PONTIFICAL INSTITUTE OF MEDIAEVAL
   STUDIES - LIBRARY
113 St. Joseph   Phone: (416) 926-7146
Toronto, ON M5S 1J4   Rev. D.F. Finlay, Libn.

UNIVERSITY OF TORONTO - ST. MICHAEL'S COLLEGE - JOHN M. KELLY
   LIBRARY
113 St. Joseph St.   Phone: (416) 926-7111
Toronto, ON M5S 1J4   Rev. J. Bernard Black, Libn.

UNIVERSITY OF TORONTO - SCHOOL OF ARCHITECTURE AND PLANNING
   LIBRARY
230 College St.   Phone: (416) 978-2649
Toronto, ON M5S 1A1   Pamela Manson-Smith, Libn.

UNIVERSITY OF TORONTO - THOMAS FISHER RARE BOOK LIBRARY
120 St. George St.   Phone: (416) 978-5285
Toronto, ON M5S 1A5   Richard G. Landon, Dept.Hd.

UNIVERSITY OF TORONTO - UNIVERSITY ARCHIVES
Fisher Library
120 St. George St.   Phone: (416) 978-2277
Toronto, ON M5S 1A5   Harold A. Averill, Act.Univ.Archv.

UNIVERSITY OF TORONTO - UNIVERSITY OF TRINITY COLLEGE - LIBRARY
6 Hoskin Ave.   Phone: (416) 978-2653
Toronto, ON M5S 1H8   Linda Wilson Corman, Hd.Libn.

UNIVERSITY OF TORONTO - VICTORIA UNIVERSITY - LIBRARY
71 Queen's Park Crescent, E.   Phone: (416) 978-3821
Toronto, ON M5S 1K7   Dr. Robert C. Brandeis, Chf.Libn.

UNIVERSITY OF TORONTO - WYCLIFFE COLLEGE - LEONARD LIBRARY
Hoskin Ave.   Phone: (416) 979-2870
Toronto, ON M5S 1H7   Adrienne Taylor, Coll.Libn.

UPPER CANADA RAILWAY SOCIETY, INC. - LIBRARY
Box 122, Sta. A
Toronto, ON M5W 1A2

WELLESLEY HOSPITAL - LIBRARY
160 Wellesley St., E.   Phone: (416) 966-6617
Toronto, ON M4Y 1J3   Verla E. Empey, Dir.

WESTON RESEARCH CENTRE - INFORMATION RESOURCE CENTRE
1047 Yonge St.   Phone: (416) 922-5100
Toronto, ON M4W 2L3   Lusi Wong, Info.Mgr.

WILLIAM M. MERCER, LTD. - INFORMATION CENTRE
1 First Canadian Pl., 56th Fl.
P.O. Box 59   Phone: (416) 868-2989
Toronto, ON M5X 1G3   Laurence Pellan, Libn.

WOMEN'S COLLEGE HOSPITAL - MEDICAL LIBRARY
76 Grenville St.   Phone: (416) 966-7468
Toronto, ON M5S 1B2   Margaret Robins, Med.Libn.

WOMEN'S COLLEGE HOSPITAL - PSORIASIS EDUCATION AND RESEARCH
   CENTRE
60 Grosvenor St.   Phone: (416) 964-0247
Toronto, ON M5S 1B6   Dr. R. Schachter, Dir.

WOMEN'S MOVEMENT ARCHIVES
Sta. Q, P.O. Box 928   Phone: (416) 597-8865
Toronto, ON M4T 2P1   Sandra Fox, Proj.Mgr.

WOOD GUNDY LTD. - LIBRARY
Royal Trust Tower
P.O. Box 274   Phone: (416) 869-8100
Toronto, ON M5K 1M7   Anne Baumann, Libn.

WORLD TRADE CENTRE TORONTO - LIBRARY
60 Harbour St.   Phone: (416) 863-2153
Toronto, ON M5J 1B7   Wendy Vosberg, Dir.

YORK BOROUGH BOARD OF EDUCATION - PROFESSIONAL LIBRARY
2 Trethewey Dr.   Phone: (416) 653-2270
Toronto, ON M6M 4A8

YORK UNIVERSITY - DEPARTMENT OF VISUAL ARTS - SLIDE LIBRARY
Fine Arts Phase II, Rm. 274   Phone: (416) 667-3749
Toronto, ON M3J 1P3   Michele Metraux, Coord.

CANADA - AGRICULTURE CANADA - RESEARCH STATION, VINELAND
   STATION - LIBRARY
                                             Phone: (416) 562-4113
Vineland Station, ON L0R 2E0   Ms. M.-J. Boisvenue, Libn.

ONTARIO - MINISTRY OF AGRICULTURE AND FOOD - HORTICULTURAL
   RESEARCH INSTITUTE OF ONTARIO - LIBRARY
                                             Phone: (416) 562-4141
Vineland Station, ON L0R 2E0   Judith Wanner, Libn.

CANADIAN INDUSTRIAL INNOVATION CENTRE/WATERLOO - RESOURCE
   CENTRE
156 Columbia St., W.   Phone: (519) 885-5870
Waterloo, ON N2L 3L3

CONRAD GREBEL COLLEGE - LIBRARY/ARCHIVES
                                             Phone: (519) 885-0220
Waterloo, ON N2L 3G6   Samuel Steiner, Libn. & Archv.

MUTUAL LIFE ASSURANCE COMPANY OF CANADA - LIBRARY
227 King St.   Phone: (519) 888-2262
Waterloo, ON N2J 1R2   Leslie Day, Libn.

SEAGRAM MUSEUM - ARCHIVES AND LIBRARY
57 Erb St. W.
P.O. Box 1605   Phone: (519) 885-1857
Waterloo, ON N2J 4N6   Sandra Lowman, Archv./Libn.

UNIVERSITY OF WATERLOO - DANA PORTER ARTS LIBRARY
                                                Phone: (519) 885-1211
Waterloo, ON N2L 3G1   Murray C. Shepherd, Univ.Libn.

UNIVERSITY OF WATERLOO - ENGINEERING, MATHEMATICS & SCIENCE
    DIVISIONAL LIBRARY
                                                Phone: (519) 885-1211
Waterloo, ON N2L 3G1

UNIVERSITY OF WATERLOO - ONLINE INFO. RETRIEVAL SYSTEM FOR THE
    SOCIOLOGY OF LEISURE & SPORT (SIRLS)
                                                Phone: (519) 885-1211
Waterloo, ON N2L 3G1   Betty Smith, Database Mgr./Cons.

UNIVERSITY OF WATERLOO - UNIVERSITY MAP AND DESIGN LIBRARY
Environmental Studies Bldg., Rm. 246   Phone: (519) 885-1211
Waterloo, ON N2L 3G1   Richard Hugh Pinnell, Map Libn.

WILFRID LAURIER UNIVERSITY - LIBRARY
75 University Ave., W.   Phone: (519) 884-1970
Waterloo, ON N2L 3C5   Erich R.W. Schultz, Univ.Libn.

NIAGARA COLLEGE OF APPLIED ARTS AND TECHNOLOGY - LEARNING
    RESOURCE CENTRE
Woodlawn Rd.
Box 1005   Phone: (416) 735-2211
Welland, ON L3B 5S2

ALGONQUIN PARK MUSEUM - LIBRARY & ARCHIVES
Box 219   Phone: (705) 633-5592
Whitney, ON K0J 2M0   Ronald G. Tozer, Interp.Serv.Supv.

BANK OF MONTREAL - TECHNICAL INFORMATION CENTRE
245 Consumers Rd.   Phone: (416) 493-2440
Willowdale, ON M2J 1S2   Janice Reynolds, Tech.Libn.

CANADA - PUBLIC WORKS CANADA - ONTARIO REGIONAL LIBRARY
4900 Yonge St.   Phone: (416) 224-4235
Willowdale, ON M2N 6A6   Rocco Cornacchia, Reg.Libn.

CANADIAN JEWISH CONGRESS - TORONTO JEWISH CONGRESS - ONTARIO
    REGION ARCHIVES
4600 Bathurst St.   Phone: (416) 977-3811
Willowdale, ON M2R 3V2   Dr. Stephen A. Speisman, Dir.

CONNAUGHT LABORATORIES, LTD. - BALMER NEILLY LIBRARY
1755 Steeles Ave., W.   Phone: (416) 667-2921
Willowdale, ON M2R 3T4   Leanne Johnson, Libn.

LATNER (Albert J.) JEWISH PUBLIC LIBRARY
4600 Bathurst St.   Phone: (416) 635-2996
Willowdale, ON M2R 3V3   Rabbi Z. Wolkenstein, Exec.Dir.

METROPOLITAN TORONTO SCHOOL BOARD - LIBRARY
45 York Mills Rd.   Phone: (416) 598-4620
Willowdale, ON M2P 1B6   Carol Williams, Libn.

NORTH YORK GENERAL HOSPITAL - W. KEITH WELSH LIBRARY
4001 Leslie St.   Phone: (416) 492-4748
Willowdale, ON M2K 1E1   Majrory L. Morphy, Hosp.Libn.

NORTH YORK PUBLIC LIBRARY - CANADIANA COLLECTION
35 Fairview Mall Dr.   Phone: (416) 494-6838
Willowdale, ON M2J 4S4   Ian Ross, Hd.

ONTARIO BIBLE COLLEGE/ONTARIO THEOLOGICAL SEMINARY - J.
    WILLIAM HORSEY LIBRARY
25 Ballyconnor Ct.   Phone: (416) 226-6380
Willowdale, ON M2M 4B3   James Johnson, Libn.

ONTARIO GENEALOGICAL SOCIETY - LIBRARY
c/o Canadiana Collection
North York Public Library
35 Fairview Mall Dr.   Phone: (416) 494-6838
Willowdale, ON M2J 4S4   Grant Brown, Libn.

ONTARIO PUPPETRY ASSOCIATION CENTRE - RESOURCE LIBRARY
171 Avondale Ave.   Phone: (416) 222-9029
Willowdale, ON M2N 2V4   Michael Sam Cronk, Musm.Dir./Cur.

SENECA COLLEGE OF APPLIED ARTS AND TECHNOLOGY - LESLIE CAMPUS
    RESOURCE CENTRE
1255 Sheppard Ave. E.   Phone: (416) 494-8900
Willowdale, ON M2K 1E2   Vinh P. Le, Ref.Libn.

ESSEX LAW ASSOCIATION - LIBRARY
County Court House
245 Windsor Ave.   Phone: (519) 252-8418
Windsor, ON N9A 1J2   Anne Matthewman, Libn.

HOTEL-DIEU OF ST. JOSEPH HOSPITAL - MEDICAL LIBRARY
1030 Ouellette Ave.   Phone: (519) 252-3631
Windsor, ON N9A 1E1   Toni Janik, Hosp.Libn.

INTERNATIONAL JOINT COMMISSION - GREAT LAKES REGIONAL OFFICE
    LIBRARY
100 Ouellette Ave., 7th Fl.   Phone: (519) 256-7821
Windsor, ON N9A 6T3   Patricia Murray, Libn./Tech.Ed.

SALVATION ARMY GRACE HOSPITAL - LIBRARY
339 Crawford Ave.   Phone: (519) 255-2245
Windsor, ON N9A 5C6   Maureen Richards, Act.Libn.

UNITED CHURCH OF CANADA - ESSEX PRESBYTERY - RESOURCE CENTRE
208 Sunset Ave.   Phone: (519) 252-0353
Windsor, ON N9B 3A7   Jean Fanson

UNIVERSITY OF WINDSOR - FACULTY OF EDUCATION LIBRARY
600 Third Concession Rd.   Phone: (519) 969-0520
Windsor, ON N9E 1A5   Thomas J. Robinson, Educ.Libn.

UNIVERSITY OF WINDSOR - PAUL MARTIN LAW LIBRARY
                                                Phone: (519) 253-4232
Windsor, ON N9B 3P4   Paul T. Murphy, Law Libn.

WALKER (Hiram) HISTORICAL MUSEUM - REFERENCE LIBRARY
254 Pitt St., W.   Phone: (519) 253-1812
Windsor, ON N9A 5L5   Alan Douglas, Cur.

WINDSOR COALITION FOR DEVELOPMENT - THIRD WORLD RESOURCE
    CENTRE *
125 Tecumseh, W.   Phone: (519) 252-1517
Windsor, ON N8X 1E8   Sr. Gabrielle Morin, SNJM, Coord. of Rsrcs.

WINDSOR STAR - LIBRARY
167 Ferry St.   Phone: (519) 256-5511
Windsor, ON N9A 4M5   Mary Jane Handy, Libn.

ONTARIO - MINISTRY OF COMMUNITY AND SOCIAL SERVICES -
    RESOURCE LIBRARY
Highway 59N
P.O. Box 310   Phone: (519) 539-1251
Woodstock, ON N4S 7X9   Frances Thompson, Libn.

WESTERN ONTARIO BREEDERS, INC. - LIBRARY
Hwy. 59 N.
P.O. Box 457   Phone: (519) 539-9831
Woodstock, ON N4S 7Y7   Howard D. Start, Dir.

PRINCE EDWARD ISLAND

CANADA - AGRICULTURE CANADA - RESEARCH STATION,
    CHARLOTTETOWN - LIBRARY
P.O. Box 1210   Phone: (902) 892-5461
Charlottetown, PE C1A 7M8   Barrie Stanfield, Libn.

CONFEDERATION CENTRE ART GALLERY AND MUSEUM - ART REFERENCE
    LIBRARY
P.O. Box 848   Phone: (902) 892-2464
Charlottetown, PE C1A 7L9   David Webber, Dir.

PRINCE EDWARD ISLAND - DEPARTMENT OF EDUCATION - MEDIA
    CENTRE
202 Richmond St.   Phone: (902) 892-3504
Charlottetown, PE C1A 1J2   Bill Ledwell, Chf. of Educ. Media

PRINCE EDWARD ISLAND MUSEUM AND HERITAGE FOUNDATION -
    GENEALOGICAL COLLECTION
2 Kent St.   Phone: (902) 892-9127
Charlottetown, PE C1A 1M6   Miss Orlo Jones, Prov.Geneal.

PRINCE EDWARD ISLAND - PLANNING LIBRARY
Box 2000   Phone: (902) 892-3504
Charlottetown, PE C1A 7N8   Marilyn Bell, Libn.

PRINCE EDWARD ISLAND - PUBLIC ARCHIVES
P.O. Box 1000   Phone: (902) 892-7949
Charlottetown, PE C1A 7M4   N.J. de Jong, Prov.Archv.

UNIVERSITY OF PRINCE EDWARD ISLAND - ROBERTSON LIBRARY
                                               Phone: (902) 892-1243
Charlottetown, PE C1A 4P3   M.C. Crockett, Chf.Libn.

PRINCE COUNTY HOSPITAL - MEDICAL LIBRARY
                                               Phone: (902) 436-9131
Summerside, PE C1N 2A9   Dr. J.P. Schaefer, Dir.

QUEBEC

HOTEL-DIEU D'ARTHABASKA - MEDICAL LIBRARY-DOCUMENTATION
    SERVICE †
5 Quesnel St.   Phone: (819) 357-2031
Arthabaska, PQ G6P 6N2   Micheline LeClair, Lib.Techn.

CENTRE HOSPITALIER ROBERT-GIFFARD - BIBLIOTHEQUE
    PROFESSIONNELLE
2601, de la Canardiere   Phone: (418) 663-6300
Beauport, PQ G1J 2G3   Yolande Plamondon, Techn.

CANADA - NATIONAL RESEARCH COUNCIL - CISTI - INDUSTRIAL
    MATERIALS RESEARCH BRANCH
75 Blvd. de Mortagne   Phone: (514) 935-8513
Boucherville, PQ J4B 6Y4   Louise Venne, Libn.

JARDIN ZOOLOGIQUE DE QUEBEC - BIBLIOTHEQUE
8191 Ave. du Zoo   Phone: (418) 622-0312
Charlesbourg, PQ G1G 4G4   Philippe Demers, Dir.

HOPITAL DE CHICOUTIMI INC. - BIBLIOTHEQUE †
305, rue St-Vallier
C.P. 5006   Phone: (418) 549-2195
Chicoutimi, PQ G7H 5H6   Angele Tremblay, Bibliothecaire

SEMINAIRE DE CHICOUTIMI - BIBLIOTHEQUE
679 Rue Chabanel   Phone: (418) 549-1786
Chicoutimi, PQ G7H 1Z7   Clement-Jacques Simard, Dir.

SOCIETE HISTORIQUE DU SAGUENAY - BIBLIOTHEQUE
C.P. 456
Chicoutimi, PQ G7H 5C8   Roland Belanger, Archv.

JEWISH CONVALESCENT HOSPITAL CENTRE - HEALTH SCIENCES
    INFORMATION CENTRE
3205 Alton Goldbloom   Phone: (514) 688-9550
Chomedey, Laval, PQ H7V 1R2   Irene Deborah Shanefield, Med.Libn.

SIDBEC-DOSCO INC. - CENTRE DE DOCUMENTATION
C.P. 1000   Phone: (514) 587-2091
Contrecoeur, PQ J0L 1C0   L. Seguin, Coord.

CANADA - DEFENCE RESEARCH ESTABLISHMENT VALCARTIER - LIBRARY
P.O. Box 8800   Phone: (418) 844-4271
Courcelette, PQ G0A 1R0   Real Menard, Chf.Libn.

CONSOLIDATED-BATHURST INC. - RESEARCH CENTRE LIBRARY
                                               Phone: (819) 538-3341
Grand Mere, PQ G9T 5L2   Gilberte Angel, Libn.

CENTRE HOSPITALIER DE L'HOTEL-DIEU DE GASPE - MEDICAL LIBRARY
                                               Phone: (418) 368-3301
Havre de Gaspe, PQ G0C 1S0   Mathilda Adams, Responsable

CANADA - CANADIAN INTERNATIONAL DEVELOPMENT AGENCY -
    DEVELOPMENT INFORMATION CENTRE
Place du Centre
200 Promenade du Portage   Phone: (819) 997-6212
Hull, PQ K1A 0G4   Nicole Smith, Dir.

CANADA - LABOUR CANADA - LIBRARY SERVICES - OCCUPATIONAL
    SAFETY AND HEALTH BRANCH - RESOURCE CENTRE
165 Hotel de Ville   Phone: (819) 997-3100
Hull, PQ K1A 0J2   Francine Frappier, Br.Libn.

CANADA - SECRETARY OF STATE - LIBRARY
15 Eddy St., 2nd Fl.   Phone: (819) 997-5467
Hull, PQ K1A 0M5   Claire Renaud-Frigon, Chf.Libn.

EDDY (E.B.) FOREST PRODUCTS, LTD. - LIBRARY
P.O. Box 600
Hull, PQ J8X 3Y7   J.D. Hall, Mgr., R & D

UNIVERSITE DU QUEBEC A HULL - BIBLIOTHEQUE
C.P. 1250, Succursale B   Phone: (819) 776-8381
Hull, PQ J8X 3X7   Andre Chenier, Directeur

CENTRE HOSPITALIER REGIONAL DE LANAUDIERE - BIBLIOTHEQUE
    MEDICALE
1000 Ste-Anne Blvd.   Phone: (514) 759-8222
Joliette, PQ J6E 6J2   Francine Garneau, Bibliothecaire

MUSEE D'ART DE JOLIETTE - BIBLIOTHEQUE †
145 rue Wilfrid-Corbeil   Phone: (514) 756-0311
Joliette, PQ J6E 3Z3   Carmen Delorme Toupin, Animator

ALCAN INTERNATIONAL, LTD. - TECHNICAL INFORMATION CENTRE
P.O. Box 1250   Phone: (418) 548-1121
Jonquiere, PQ G7S 4K8   Ms. P. Leclerc, Chf.Libn.

BURROUGHS WELLCOME COMPANY - MEDICAL INFORMATION CENTER
16751 Trans Canada Rd.   Phone: (514) 694-8220
Kirkland, PQ H9H 4J4   Anna Maria Caranci, Med.Info.Off.

BROME COUNTY HISTORICAL SOCIETY - ARCHIVES
P.O. Box 690   Phone: (514) 243-6782
Knowlton, PQ J0E 1V0   Marion L. Phelps, Cur. & Archv.

CANADA - AGRICULTURE CANADA - EXPERIMENTAL FARM LIBRARY
C.P. 400   Phone: (418) 856-3141
La Pocatiere, PQ G0R 1Z0   J. Deschenes

COLLEGE DE STE-ANNE-DE-LA-POCATIERE - BIBLIOTHEQUE
100 Ave. Painchaud   Phone: (418) 856-3082
La Pocatiere, PQ G0R 1Z0   Marcel Mignault, Hd.

COLLEGE DE STE-ANNE-DE-LA-POCATIERE - SOCIETE HISTORIQUE-DE-
    LA-COTE-DU-SUD - BIBLIOTHEQUE
C.P. 937   Phone: (418) 856-2104
La Pocatiere, PQ G0R 1Z0   Guy Theberge, Sec.

INSTITUT DE TECHNOLOGIE AGRICOLE - RESEARCH LIBRARY †
                                               Phone: (418) 856-1110
La Pocatiere, PQ G0R 1Z0   Rene-Daniel Langlois, Libn.

WARNOCK HERSEY PROFESSIONAL SERVICES LTD. - LIBRARY
128 Elmslie St.   Phone: (514) 366-3100
LaSalle, PQ H8R 1V8   Andre Blain, Gen.Mgr.

CONFEDERATION DES CAISSES POPULAIRES ET D'ECONOMIE DESJARDINS
    DU QUEBEC - SERVICE DE DOCUMENTATION
100 Ave. Des Commandeurs   Phone: (418) 835-2468
Levis, PQ G6V 7N5   Louise Tremblay

HOTEL-DIEU DE LEVIS - BIBLIOTHEQUE MEDICALE †
143 rue Wolfe   Phone: (418) 833-7121
Levis, PQ G6V 3Y9   Colette Pasquis-Audant, Libn.

INSTITUT NAZARETH ET LOUIS-BRAILLE - BIBLIOTHEQUE PUBLIQUE
1255 Beauregard   Phone: (514) 463-1710
Longeuil, PQ J4K 2M3   Suzanne Olivier, Chief

CANADA - HEALTH AND WELFARE CANADA - HEALTH PROTECTION
   BRANCH - REGIONAL LIBRARY
1001 Ouest Boul. St. Laurent, Ch. 321   Phone: (514) 283-5472
Longueuil, PQ J4K 1C7   Eleanora Ferenczy, Techn.

PRATT AND WHITNEY CANADA, INC. - LIBRARY
P.O. Box 10   Phone: (514) 677-9411
Longueuil, PQ J4K 4X9   Joyce C. Charlebois, Chf.Libn.

HOPITAL DE MONT-JOLI, INC. - BIBLIOTHEQUE *
800 Sanatorium   Phone: (418) 775-7261
Mont-Joli, PQ G5H 3L6   Sylvie Dupuis, Lib.Techn.

ABBOTT LABORATORIES, LTD. - COMPANY LIBRARY
Sta. A, P.O. Box 6150   Phone: (514) 342-6244
Montreal, PQ H3C 3K6   Genevieve Heroux, Lib.Techn.

AIR CANADA - LIBRARY
Place Air Canada   Phone: (514) 879-7733
Montreal, PQ H2Z 1X5   Iris L. Land, Mgr., Lib.Serv.

ALCAN ALUMINUM, LTD. - INFORMATION CENTRE
1188 Sherbrooke St., W.
Box 6077   Phone: (514) 877-2610
Montreal, PQ H3C 3A7   Ellen A. Johnston, Chf.Libn.

ANGLICAN CHURCH OF CANADA - DIOCESE OF MONTREAL - ARCHIVES
Synod Office, 1444 Union Ave.   Phone: (514) 845-6211
Montreal, PQ H3A 2B8   Rev. Canon M.A. Hughes, Adm.Off.

ASSELIN, BENOIT, BOUCHER, DUCHARME, LAPOINTE, INC. - LIBRARY
   DEPARTMENT
85 W. Ste. Catherine   Phone: (514) 287-8546
Montreal, PQ H2X 3P4   Diane Mercier, Libn.

ASSOCIATION PARITAIRE DE PREVENTION POUR LA SANTE ET LA
   SECURITE DU TRAVAIL DU QUEBEC - TECH.INFO. CENTER *
1016 St. Alexandre   Phone: (514) 866-1871
Montreal, PQ H2P 1P5   Lise Locas, Doc. Recherchiste

ASSOCIATION DES UNIVERSITES PARTIELLEMENT OU ENTIEREMENT DE
   LANGUE FRANCAISE - BIBLIOTHEQUE
Universite de Montreal
B.P. 6128, Succ. A   Phone: (514) 343-6630
Montreal, PQ H3C 3J7   Francoise Sorieul

ATOMIC ENERGY OF CANADA, LTD. - ENGINEERING COMPANY LIBRARY *
1600 Dorchester Blvd. W.   Phone: (514) 934-4811
Montreal, PQ H3H 1P9   Susan Nish, Techn.

AVIATION ELECTRIC, LTD. - TECHNICAL DATA SECTION LIBRARY
St. Laurent
P.O. Box 2140   Phone: (514) 744-2811
Montreal, PQ H4L 4X8   T.R. Warrick, Mgr., Tech.Serv.

AYERST, MC KENNA & HARRISON, INC. - LIBRARY
1025 Laurentian Blvd.   Phone: (514) 744-6771
Montreal, PQ H4R 1J6   Nicole Barrette-Pilon, Libn.

BANK OF MONTREAL - BUSINESS INFORMATION CENTRE
Postal Sta. A., P.O. Box 6002   Phone: (514) 877-1470
Montreal, PQ H3C 3B1   Richard Orlando, Supv.

BANK OF MONTREAL - TECHNICAL INFORMATION CENTRE
Box 6002
Place d'Armes Montreal   Phone: (514) 877-8235
Montreal, PQ H2Y 3S8   Sylvia E.A. Piggott, Tech.Libn.

BARREAU DE MONTREAL - BIBLIOTHEQUE
Palais de Justice   Phone: (514) 873-3083
Montreal, PQ H2Y 1B6   Arthur Perrault, Libn.

BEAUCHEMIN-BEATON-LAPOINTE, INC. - BBL LIBRARY
1134 Ste-Catherine St., W.   Phone: (514) 871-9555
Montreal, PQ H3B 1H4   Danielle Dallaire, Libn.

BELL CANADA - INFORMATION RESOURCE CENTRE
1050 Beaver Hall Hill, 1st Fl.   Phone: (514) 870-8500
Montreal, PQ H2Z 1S4

BELL CANADA - LAW LIBRARY
1050 Beaver Hall Hill, Rm. 1500   Phone: (514) 861-6550
Montreal, PQ H2Z 1S4   Patricia M. Young, Law Libn.

BELL CANADA - TELEPHONE HISTORICAL COLLECTION
1050 Beaver Hall Hill, Rm. 820   Phone: (514) 870-5214
Montreal, PQ H2Z 1S4   Stephanie L. Sykes, Hist.

BIBLIOTHEQUE DE LA VILLE DE MONTREAL - CINEMATHEQUE
880 Roy St. E., Suite 200   Phone: (514) 872-3680
Montreal, PQ H2L 1E6   Lise Depatie-Bourassa, Coord., AV Serv.

BIBLIOTHEQUE DE LA VILLE DE MONTREAL - COLLECTION GAGNON
1210 Sherbrooke St., E.   Phone: (514) 872-5923
Montreal, PQ H2L 1L9   Carmen Catelli, Hd.

BIBLIOTHEQUE DE LA VILLE DE MONTREAL - SONOTHEQUE
880 Roy St., E., Suite 300   Phone: (514) 872-3680
Montreal, PQ H2L 1E6   Lise Depatie-Bourassa, Coord., AV Serv.

B'NAI BRITH HILLEL FOUNDATION AT MC GILL UNIVERSITY - LIBRARY *
3460 Stanley St.   Phone: (514) 845-9171
Montreal, PQ H3A 1R8

C.I. POWER SERVICES - INFORMATION CENTRE *
2020 University St., Suite 1800   Phone: (514) 285-1414
Montreal, PQ H3A 2A5   Judith Joba, Info.Spec.

CANADA - EMPLOYMENT & IMMIGRATION CANADA - QUEBEC REGIONAL
   LIBRARY †
550 Sherbrooke St., W., 4th Fl.
C.P. 7500, Sta. A   Phone: (514) 283-4695
Montreal, PQ H3C 3L4   Claudine Lussier, Dir.

CANADA - NATIONAL FILM BOARD OF CANADA - ARCHIVES
Sta. A, P.O. Box 6100   Phone: (514) 333-3087
Montreal, PQ H3C 3H5

CANADA - NATIONAL FILM BOARD OF CANADA - FILM PREVIEW LIBRARY
3155 Cote de Liesse Rd.   Phone: (514) 333-3180
Montreal, PQ H3C 3H5   Jeannine Hopfinger, Film Off.

CANADA - NATIONAL FILM BOARD OF CANADA - REFERENCE LIBRARY
Sta. A, P.O. Box 6100   Phone: (514) 333-3141
Montreal, PQ H3C 3H5   Rose-Aimee Todd, Chf.Libn.

CANADA - REGIONAL INDUSTRIAL EXPANSION - GOVERNMENT
   DOCUMENTATION CENTRE
800 Square Victoria
C.P. 247   Phone: (514) 283-7266
Montreal, PQ H4Z 1E8   Carole Laplante, Libn.

CANADA - SECRETARY OF STATE - TRANSLATION BUREAU - LIBRARY
Complexe Guy-Favreau
200 W. Dorchester Blvd., Rm. 307   Phone: (514) 283-7519
Montreal, PQ H2Z 1X4   Cecile Mondou, Hd.Libn.

CANADA - STATISTICS CANADA - ADVISORY SERVICES - MONTREAL
   REFERENCE CENTRE
Complexe Guy Favreau
200 Dorchester Blvd. W., Suite 412   Phone: (514) 283-5725
Montreal, PQ H2Z 1X4   Nicole Benoit, Data Dissem.Off.

CANADA - TRANSPORT CANADA - TRANSPORTATION DEVELOPMENT
   CENTRE - LIBRARY
1000 Sherbrooke St., W.
P.O. Box 549   Phone: (514) 283-4084
Montreal, PQ H3A 2R3   Judith Nogrady, Hd.

CANADAIR, LTD. - COMPANY LIBRARY †
P.O. Box 6087
Montreal, PQ H3C 3G9
Phone: (514) 744-1511
Margaret Levesque

CANADIAN AMATEUR MUSICIANS-MUSICIENS AMATEURS DU CANADA
(CAMMAC) - MUSIC LIBRARY
4450 Sherbrooke St., W.
Montreal, PQ H3Z 1E6
Phone: (514) 932-8755
Diane Duguay, Adm.

CANADIAN BROADCASTING CORPORATION - ENGINEERING
HEADQUARTERS LIBRARY
7925 Cote St. Luc Rd.
Montreal, PQ H4W 1R5
Phone: (514) 488-2551
Lysanne St-Laurent, Lib.Techn.

CANADIAN BROADCASTING CORPORATION - LIBRARY
C.P. 6000
Montreal, PQ H3C 3A8
Phone: (514) 285-3854
Michelle Bachand, Hd.Libn.

CANADIAN BROADCASTING CORPORATION - MUSIC SERVICES LIBRARY
1400 Dorchester Blvd., E.
P.O. Box 6000
Montreal, PQ H3C 3A8
Phone: (514) 285-3900
Claude Gagnon, Hd., Music Serv.

CANADIAN CENTRE FOR ECUMENISM - LIBRARY
2065 W. Sherbrooke
Montreal, PQ H3H 1G6
Phone: (514) 937-9176
Reginald Goulet, S.J., Dir.

CANADIAN JEWISH CONGRESS - NATIONAL ARCHIVES
1590 Ave. Docteur Penfield
Montreal, PQ H3G 1C5
Phone: (514) 931-7531
Judith Nefsky, Archv.

CANADIAN MARCONI COMPANY - LIBRARY †
2442 Trenton Ave.
Montreal, PQ H3P 1Y9
Phone: (514) 341-7630
Mrs. M. Benjamin, Libn.

CANADIAN MUSIC CENTRE - LIBRARY
430 rue St-Pierre, Suite 300
Montreal, PQ H2Y 2M5
Phone: (514) 849-9175
Mireille Gagne, Regional Dir.

CANADIAN NATIONAL INSTITUTE FOR THE BLIND - QUEBEC DIVISION
LIBRARY †
1181 Guy St.
Montreal, PQ H3H 2K6
Phone: (514) 931-7221
Jeannine Tardif, Lib.Supv.

CANADIAN NATIONAL RAILWAYS - DECHIEF LIBRARY
935 Lagauchetiere St., W.
B.P. 8100
Montreal, PQ H3C 3N4
Phone: (514) 877-4407
Gilda Martinello, Sr.Sys.Libn.

CANADIAN NATIONAL RAILWAYS - PHOTOGRAPHIC LIBRARY
P.O. Box 8100
Montreal, PQ H3C 3N4
Phone: (514) 877-5465
Connie Romani, Photo Libn.

CANADIAN NATIONAL RAILWAYS - PUBLIC AFFAIRS DEPARTMENT
LIBRARY
935 Lagauchetiere St., W.
Sta. A, P.O. Box 8100
Montreal, PQ H3C 3N4

CANADIAN OLYMPIC ASSOCIATION - LIBRARY/INFORMATION SERVICES
Olympic House, Cite du Havre
Montreal, PQ H3C 3R4
Phone: (514) 861-3371
Sylvia Doucette, Lib.Asst.

CANADIAN PACIFIC, LTD. - CORPORATE LIBRARY/INFORMATION CENTRE
Windsor Station
Sta. A, P.O. Box 6042
Montreal, PQ H3C 3E4
Phone: (514) 395-6617
A.A. DiIorio, Corp.Libn.

CANADIAN PSYCHOANALYTIC SOCIETY - LIBRARY
7000 Cote des Neiges Rd.
Montreal, PQ H3S 2C1
Phone: (514) 738-6105
Nadia Gargour, Adm.Dir.

CANADIAN RAILROAD HISTORICAL ASSOCIATION - LIBRARY *
Canadian Railway Museum
Sta. B, P.O. Box 22
Montreal, PQ H3B 3J5
Phone: (514) 632-2410
Dr. R.V.V. Nicholls, Archv./Libn.

CANADIAN TELEPHONE EMPLOYEES' ASSOCIATION - LIBRARY *
Place du Canada, Rm. 1465
Montreal, PQ H3B 2N2
Phone: (514) 861-9963
Miss E.A. Fenton, Gen.Sec.

CANADIAN TOBACCO MANUFACTURERS COUNCIL - INFORMATION
CENTER
1808 Sherbrooke St., W.
Montreal, PQ H3H 1E5
Phone: (514) 937-7428
Myrna Cain, Info.Spec.

CANATOM INC. - LIBRARY
Tour de la Bourse, C.P. 420
Montreal, PQ H4Z 1K3

CEGEP DU VIEUX-MONTREAL - LIBRARY
255 Ontario St. E.
Station N, P.O. Box 1444
Montreal, PQ H2X 3M8
Phone: (514) 284-7315
Flavius Pelletier, Media Ctr.Dir.

CENTRE D'ANIMATION, DE DEVELOPPEMENT ET DE RECHERCHE EN
EDUCATION - BIBLIOTHEQUE
1940 Blvd. Henri-Bourassa Est
Montreal, PQ H2B 1S2
Phone: (514) 381-8891
Jean-Luc Roy, Libn.

CENTRE D'ETUDES DU TOURISME - TECHNICAL INFORMATION CENTRE
1420 Saint Denis
Montreal, PQ H2X 3J8
Phone: (514) 282-9613
Mureille Bourque, Documentaliste

CENTRE HOSPITALIER COTE-DES-NEIGES - CENTRE DE DOCUMENTATION
4565 Chemin de la Reine-Marie
Montreal, PQ H3W 1W5
Phone: (514) 344-3905
Jocelyne Blain-Juneau, Chf.Libn.

CENTRE HOSPITALIER JACQUES-VIGER - CENTRE DE DOCUMENTATION
1051 St. Hubert St.
Montreal, PQ H2L 3Y5
Phone: (514) 842-7181
Conrad Tessier, Lib.Techn.

CENTRE HOSPITALIER STE. JEANNE D'ARC - BIBLIOTHEQUE MEDICALE *
3570 rue St. Urbain
Montreal, PQ H2X 2N8
Phone: (514) 842-6141
Louise Lemay, Chf.Libn.

CENTRE INTERCULTUREL MONCHANIN - BIBLIOTHEQUE
4917 St-Urbain
Montreal, PQ H2T 2W1
Phone: (514) 288-7229
Real Bathalon, Libn.

CENTRE DE READAPTATION CONSTANCE-LETHBRIDGE - MEDICAL
LIBRARY
7005 blvd. de Maisonneuve W.
Montreal, PQ H4B 1T3
Phone: (514) 487-1770
Jane Petrov, Libn.

CENTRE DE RECHERCHES EN RELATIONS HUMAINES - BIBLIOTHEQUE
2715 Cote St. Catherine Rd.
Montreal, PQ H3T 1B6
Phone: (514) 738-8076
Noel Mailloux, Dir./Prof. Emeritus

CENTRE DE SERVICES SOCIAUX DU MONTREAL METROPOLITAIN (CSSMM)
- BIBLIOTHEQUE *
1001 Est Boul. de Maisonneuve, 8th Fl.
Montreal, PQ H2L 4R5
Phone: (514) 527-7261
Micheline Gaudette, Bibliotechnicienne

CHAIT SALOMON - LIBRARY
1 Place Ville Marie, Suite 1901
Montreal, PQ H3B 2C3
Phone: (514) 879-1353
Shake Hagopian, Libn.

CHAMBRE DES NOTAIRES DU QUEBEC - CENTRE DE DOCUMENTATION *
630 Dorchester Blvd. W., Suite 1658
Montreal, PQ H3B 1T6
Phone: (514) 879-1793
Lise Lachance, Documentaliste

CHARETTE, FORTIER, HAWEY/TOUCHE, ROSS - LIBRARY
One Place Ville Marie
Royal Bank Bldg.
Montreal, PQ H3B 2A3
Phone: (514) 861-8531
Nancy Bouchard, Libn.

CINEMATHEQUE QUEBECOISE - ARCHIVES & FILM MUSEUM
335 Blvd. de Maisonneuve E.
Montreal, PQ H2X 1K1
Phone: (514) 842-9763
Robert Daudelin, Exec.Dir.

CINEMATHEQUE QUEBECOISE - CENTRE DE DOCUMENTATION
CINEMATOGRAPHIQUE
335 Blvd. de Maisonneuve E.
Montreal, PQ H2X 1K1
Phone: (514) 842-9763
Rene Beauclair, Hd.Libn.

CLARKSON GORDON - BUSINESS LIBRARY
630 Dorchester Blvd., W.
Phone: (514) 875-6060
Montreal, PQ H3B 1T9
Margaret Cameron, Libn.

CLINICAL RESEARCH INSTITUTE OF MONTREAL - MEDICAL LIBRARY
110 Pine Ave., W.
Phone: (514) 842-1481
Montreal, PQ H2W 1R7
Lorraine Bielmann, Hd.Libn.

COMMISSION DES ECOLES CATHOLIQUES DE MONTREAL - BIBLIOTHEQUE
    CENTRALE †
3737 Sherbrooke E.
Montreal, PQ H1X 3B3

COMPAGNIE DE JESUS - BIBLIOTHEQUE DE THEOLOGIE
5605 Decelles Ave.
Phone: (514) 737-1465
Montreal, PQ H3T 1W4
Claude-Roger Nadeau, S.J., Dir.

CONCORDIA UNIVERSITY - SIR GEORGE WILLIAMS CAMPUS - GUIDANCE
    INFORMATION CENTRE
1455 de Maisonneuve Blvd., W.
Phone: (514) 879-4443
Montreal, PQ H3G 1M8
Marlis Hubbard, Libn.

CONCORDIA UNIVERSITY - SIR GEORGE WILLIAMS CAMPUS - SCIENCE &
    ENGINEERING LIBRARY
1455 De Maisonneuve Blvd., W.
Phone: (514) 879-4184
Montreal, PQ H3G 1M8
Z. Jirkovsky, Hd., Sci. & Engr.Lib.

CONCORDIA UNIVERSITY - LOYOLA CAMPUS - DRUMMOND SCIENCE
    LIBRARY
7141 Sherbrooke St., W.
Phone: (514) 482-0320
Montreal, PQ H4B 1R6
Tatiana Slivitzky, Supv.

CONCORDIA UNIVERSITY - LOYOLA CAMPUS - GEORGES P. VANIER
    LIBRARY
7141 Sherbrooke St., W.
Phone: (514) 482-0320
Montreal, PQ H4B 1R6
Irene Sendek, Hd., Loyola Libs.

CONFERENCE DES RECTEURS ET DES PRINCIPAUX DES UNIVERSITES DU
    QUEBEC - CENTRE DE DOCUMENTATION
2 Complexe Desjardins, Suite 1817
C.P. 124
Phone: (514) 288-8524
Montreal, PQ H3B 1B3
Marie Brie-Berard, Documentaliste

CONSERVATOIRE DE MUSIQUE DE MONTREAL - CENTRE DE
    DOCUMENTATION
100 rue Notre-Dame est
Phone: (514) 873-4031
Montreal, PQ H2Y 1C1
Nicole Boisclair, Directrice

CORPORATION PROFESSIONNELLE DES MEDECINS DU QUEBEC -
    INFORMATHEQUE
1440 Ste. Catherine St., W., Rm. 914
Phone: (514) 878-4441
Montreal, PQ H3G 1S5
Marthe Dumont Salvail, Hd.Libn.

CULINAR FOODS INC. - LIBRARY
4945 Ontario St., E.
Phone: (514) 255-2811
Montreal, PQ H1V 1M2
Louise Pichet, Lib.Techn.

CURRIE, COOPERS & LYBRAND, LTD. - INFORMATION CENTRE
630 Dorchester Blvd., W.
Phone: (514) 866-3721
Montreal, PQ H3B 1W5
Johan Mady, Libn.

DESJARDINS DUCHARME DESJARDINS & BOURQUE - LAW LIBRARY †
635 W. Dorchester Blvd., Suite 1200
Phone: (514) 878-9411
Montreal, PQ H3B 1R9
Jacques Cartier, Law Libn.

DISADA PRODUCTIONS LTD. - WALT DISNEY MEMORIAL LIBRARY
5788 Notre Dame de Grace Ave.
Phone: (514) 489-0527
Montreal, PQ H4A 1M4
Sherrill Barth, Libn.

DOMINICAINS DE ST-ALBERT-LE-GRAND, MONTREAL - INSTITUT
    D'ETUDES MEDIEVALES - BIBLIOTHEQUE *
2715 Chemin de la Cote Ste-Catherine
Phone: (514) 739-9868
Montreal, PQ H3T 1B6
Yvon-D. Gelinas, O.P., Hd.Libn.

DOMTAR, INC. - CENTRAL LIBRARY
P.O. Box 7210
Phone: (514) 282-5039
Montreal, PQ H3C 3M1
Elyse Therrien, Libn.

DOUGLAS HOSPITAL CENTRE - STAFF LIBRARY
6875 La Salle Blvd.
Montreal, PQ H4H 1R3
Elaine Mancina, Chf.Libn.

ECOLE DES HAUTES ETUDES COMMERCIALES DE MONTREAL -
    BIBLIOTHEQUE
5255 Decelles Ave.
Phone: (514) 343-4481
Montreal, PQ H3T 1V6
Rodolphe Lavergne, Chf.Libn.

ECOLE POLYTECHNIQUE - BIBLIOTHEQUE
C.P. 6079, Succursale A
Phone: (514) 344-4847
Montreal, PQ H3C 3A7
Olivier Paradis, Dir.

FEDERAL BUSINESS DEVELOPMENT BANK - DOCUMENTATION CENTRE
P.O. Box 6021, Succursale A
Phone: (514) 283-7632
Montreal, PQ H3C 3C3
Julia E. McIntosh, Hd.Libn.

FEDERATION DES ADMINISTRATEURS DES SERVICES DE SANTE ET DES
    SERVICES SOCIAUX DU QUEBEC - BIBLIOTHEQUE
4237 rue de Bordeaux
Phone: (514) 526-0875
Montreal, PQ H2H 1Z4
Robert Savard, Dir.Gen.

FEDERATION DES MEDECINS OMNIPRACTICIENS DU QUEBEC -
    DOCUMENTATION CENTRE
1440 Ouest Ste-Catherine, Suite 1100
Phone: (514) 878-1911
Montreal, PQ H3G 1R8
Ghislaine Lincourt, Adm.

FONDATION QUEBECOISE D'EDUCATION ECONOMIQUE - CENTRE
    D'INFORMATION SUR LES RESSOURCES EN EDUCATION ECONOMIQUE
P.O. Box 8891
Phone: (514) 282-7703
Montreal, PQ H3C 3P3
Jean Francois Doutrelepont, Dir.

FRASER-HICKSON INSTITUTE, MONTREAL - FREE LIBRARY - SPECIAL
    COLLECTIONS
4855 Kensington Ave.
Phone: (514) 489-5301
Montreal, PQ H3X 3S6
Jeanne B. Randle, Chf.Libn.

GESTAS INC. - DOCUMENTATION CENTER
410 St. Nicolas St.
Phone: (514) 288-5611
Montreal, PQ H2Y 2P5
Monique Dumont, Mgr.

GOETHE INSTITUTE MONTREAL - GERMAN CULTURAL CENTRE - LIBRARY
Place Bonaventure
P.O. Box 428
Phone: (514) 866-1081
Montreal, PQ H5A 1B8
Elisabeth Morf, Libn.

GRAND SEMINAIRE DE MONTREAL - BIBLIOTHEQUE
2065 Sherbrooke, W.
Phone: (514) 932-9918
Montreal, PQ H3H 1G6
Rev. Jacques Viger, S.S., Hd.Libn.

HOPITAL JEAN-TALON - BIBLIOTHEQUE MEDICALE
1385 E. Jean-Talon
Phone: (514) 273-5151
Montreal, PQ H2E 1S6
Pierrette Galarneau, Med.Libn.

HOPITAL LOUIS H. LAFONTAINE - BIBLIOTHEQUE
7401 Rue Hochelaga
Phone: (514) 253-8200
Montreal, PQ H1N 3M5
Camil Lemire, Med.Libn.

HOPITAL MAISONNEUVE-ROSEMONT - SERVICE DES BIBLIOTHEQUES
5415 de l'Assomption Blvd.
Phone: (514) 254-8341
Montreal, PQ H1T 2M4
Helene Lauzon, Hd.Libn.

HOPITAL NOTRE DAME - MEDICAL LIBRARY
C.P. 1560, Succ. C.
Phone: (514) 876-6862
Montreal, PQ H2L 4K8
Marcelle L'Esperance, Chf.Libn.

HOPITAL REINE ELIZABETH - A. HOLLIS MARDEN BIBLIOTHEQUE
2100 Marlowe Ave.
Phone: (514) 488-2311
Montreal, PQ H4A 3L6
Ms. S.L. Mullan, Lib.Techn.

HOPITAL RIVIERE-DES-PRAIRIES - BIBLIOTHEQUE DU PERSONNEL
7070 Blvd. Perras E.
Phone: (514) 323-7260
Montreal, PQ H1E 1A4
Robert Aubin, Med.Libn.

HOPITAL DU SACRE COEUR - PAVILLON ALBERT-PREVOST - MEDICAL
    LIBRARY †
5400 Gouin Blvd., W.
Phone: (514) 333-4284
Montreal, PQ H4J 1C5
Margareth Page, Techn., Docs.

HOPITAL STE-JUSTINE - CENTRE D'INFORMATION SUR LA SANTE DE
  L'ENFANT
3175, Chemin Cote Ste-Catherine   Phone: (514) 731-4931
Montreal, PQ H3T 1C5   Louis-Lue Lecompte, Hd.

HOPITAL ST-LUC - BIBLIOTHEQUE MEDICALE †
1058 St. Denis St.   Phone: (514) 285-1525
Montreal, PQ H2X 3J4   Rene Cote, Chf.Libn.

HOPITAL SANTA CABRINI - BIBLIOTHEQUE MEDICALE
5655 E. St-Zotique St.   Phone: (514) 252-6488
Montreal, PQ H1T 1P7   Diane Seguin, Lib.Techn.

HORNER (Frank W.), LTD. - RESEARCH LIBRARY
5485 Ferrier St.   Phone: (514) 731-3931
Montreal, PQ H4P 1M6   Miss R. Robinson, Libn.

HOTEL-DIEU DE MONTREAL - SERVICE DE DOCUMENTATION
3840 Rue St-Urbain   Phone: (514) 844-0161
Montreal, PQ H2W 1T8   Ginette Boyer, Libn.

HYDRO-QUEBEC - BIBLIOTHEQUE
75 Dorchester Blvd., W., Mezzanine Fl.   Phone: (514) 289-2145
Montreal, PQ H2Z 1A4   Claude-Andre Bonin, Info.Mgr.

HYDRO-QUEBEC - V.P. PLANIFICATION GENERALE - CENTRE DE
  DOCUMENTATION
870 Blvd. de Maisonneuve, 4th Fl.   Phone: (514) 289-6787
Montreal, PQ H2L 4S8   Sylvie Perron, Analyste

IBM CANADA, LTD. - EASTERN REGION REFERENCE LIBRARY †
5 Place Ville Marie, 2nd Fl.   Phone: (514) 874-6123
Montreal, PQ H3B 2G2   Catherine Bourgeois, Libn.

IMPERIAL TOBACCO LTD. - CORPORATE LIBRARY
P.O. Box 6500   Phone: (514) 932-6161
Montreal, PQ H3C 3L6   Yolande Mukherjee, Corp.Libn.

IMPERIAL TOBACCO LTD. - RESEARCH LIBRARY
734 Bourget St.   Phone: (514) 932-6161
Montreal, PQ H4C 2M7   Miss R.A. Ayoung, Res.Libn.

INDUSTRIAL GRAIN PRODUCTS, LTD. - RESEARCH & DEVELOPMENT
  LIBRARY †
995 Mill St.
P.O. Box 6089   Phone: (514) 866-1838
Montreal, PQ H3C 3H1   Muriel Henri, Libn.

INSTITUT CANADIEN D'EDUCATION DES ADULTES ET RELAIS-FEMMES DE
  MONTREAL - CENTRE DE DOCUMENTATION
506 rue Ste-Catherine, Suite 800   Phone: (514) 842-2766
Montreal, PQ H2L 2C7

INSTITUT D'HISTOIRE DE L'AMERIQUE FRANCAISE (1970) - RESEARCH
  CENTRE LIBRARY
257-261 Ave. Bloomfield   Phone: (514) 271-4759
Montreal, PQ H2V 3R6   Rene Hardy, Pres.

INSTITUT NATIONAL DE LA RECHERCHE SCIENTIFIQUE - CARTOTHEQUE
3465 Durocher, Local 225   Phone: (514) 842-4191
Montreal, PQ H2X 2C6   Christiane Desmarais, Cartothecaire

INSTITUT PHILIPPE PINEL - LIBRARY †
10905 Henri-Bourassa Blvd., E.   Phone: (514) 648-8461
Montreal, PQ H1C 1H1   Normand Beaudet, Bibliotechnicien

INSTITUT DE READAPTATION DE MONTREAL - BIBLIOTHEQUE MEDICALE
  †
6300 Darlington Ave.   Phone: (514) 735-3741
Montreal, PQ H3S 2J4   Maryse Boyer, Lib.Techn.

INSTITUTE OF OCCUPATIONAL AND ENVIRONMENTAL HEALTH -
  ARCHIVES
Crown Trust Bldg., Suite 410
1130 Sherbrooke St., W.   Phone: (514) 844-4955
Montreal, PQ H3A 2M8   Therese Brien, Exec.Sec.

INSTITUTION DES SOURDS DE MONTREAL - CENTRE DE RESSOURCES
  MULTI-MEDIA
360 rue Berri   Phone: (514) 284-2581
Montreal, PQ H2L 4G9   Sylvie Laverdiere, Libn.

INTERNATIONAL CIVIL AVIATION ORGANIZATION - LIBRARY
1000 Sherbrooke St., W., Suite 400   Phone: (514) 285-8208
Montreal, PQ H3A 2R2   Mrs. Fathia Ismail, Libn.

INTERNATIONAL INSTITUTE OF STRESS - LIBRARY AND DOCUMENTATION
  CENTER
659 Milton St.
Montreal, PQ H2X 1W6

ITALIAN CULTURAL SERVICE - LIBRARY
1200 Dr. Penfield Ave.   Phone: (514) 849-3473
Montreal, PQ H3A 1A9   Dr. Guido Bistolfi, Dir.

J&HWF INC. - EMPLOYEE BENEFIT PLAN DEPARTMENT LIBRARY
Tour de la Bourse, Suite 2300
Place Victoria   Phone: (514) 878-1781
Montreal, PQ H4Z 1E2   Mary J. Norton, Libn.

JARDIN BOTANIQUE DE MONTREAL - BIBLIOTHEQUE
4101 Sherbrooke St., E.   Phone: (514) 252-8765
Montreal, PQ H1X 2B2   Celine Arseneault, Botanist/Libn.

JEWISH PUBLIC LIBRARY OF MONTREAL
5151 Cote St. Catherine Rd.   Phone: (514) 735-6535
Montreal, PQ H3W 1M6   Zipporah Dunsky-Shnay, Dir.

JOHNSON AND JOHNSON, INC. - RESEARCH LIBRARY
7101 Notre Dame St., E.   Phone: (514) 252-5029
Montreal, PQ H1N 2G4   Lilian Smyth, Res.Libn.

KLOCKNER STADLER HURTER LTD. - LIBRARY
1600 Dorchester Blvd., W.   Phone: (514) 932-4611
Montreal, PQ H3H 1P9   D.S.L. Monstad-Ozolins, Libn.

LA PRESSE, LTEE. - CENTRE DE DOCUMENTATION †
7 Ouest, Rue St-Jacques   Phone: (514) 285-7007
Montreal, PQ H2Y 1K9   Fernand Drouin, Dir.

LA SOCIETE LA HAYE OUELLET - LIBRAIRIE *
2500 Bates Rd.
Montreal, PQ H3S 1A6   Claude La Haye, Documentaliste

LAVALIN - CENTRE DE DOCUMENTATION
1130 Sherbrooke St. W., 16th Fl.   Phone: (514) 288-1294
Montreal, PQ H3A 2R5   Nicole Goyette, Libn.

LE DEVOIR - CENTRE DE DOCUMENTATION
211, Rue du St-Sacrement   Phone: (514) 844-3361
Montreal, PQ H2Y 1X1   Gilles Pare, Libn.

LIQUID AIR ENGINEERING CORPORATION - E & C LIBRARY
1155 Sherbrooke St., W.   Phone: (514) 842-5431
Montreal, PQ H3A 1H8   C. Tremblay, Libn.

LIVESTOCK FEED BOARD OF CANADA - LIBRARY
Snowdon Sta., P.O. Box 177   Phone: (514) 283-7505
Montreal, PQ H3X 3T4   A. Douglas Mutch

LOVELL LITHO & PUBLICATIONS INC. - LIBRARY †
423 St. Nicholas St.
Montreal, PQ H2Y 2P4

MC GILL UNIVERSITY - ALLAN MEMORIAL INSTITUTE OF PSYCHIATRY -
  LIBRARY
1025 Pine Ave., W.   Phone: (514) 842-1251
Montreal, PQ H3A 1A1   Julia Main, Libn.

MC GILL UNIVERSITY - BLACKADER LIBRARY OF ARCHITECTURE/
  LAUTERMAN LIBRARY OF ART
3459 McTavish St.   Phone: (514) 392-4960
Montreal, PQ H3A 1Y1   Irena Murray, Libn.

MC GILL UNIVERSITY - BLACKER/WOOD LIBRARY OF ZOOLOGY AND
  ORNITHOLOGY
Redpath Library Bldg.
3459 McTavish St.   Phone: (514) 392-4955
Montreal, PQ H3A 1Y1   Eleanor MacLean, Libn.

MC GILL UNIVERSITY - BOTANY-GENETICS LIBRARY
Stewart Biological Sciences Bldg.
1205 Dr. Penfield Ave.   Phone: (514) 392-5829
Montreal, PQ H3A 1B1

MC GILL UNIVERSITY - CENTRE FOR DEVELOPING AREA STUDIES -
  DOCUMENTATION CENTRE
815 Sherbrooke St., W.   Phone: (514) 392-5342
Montreal, PQ H3A 2K6   Marjorie Neilson, Documentalist

MC GILL UNIVERSITY - DENTISTRY LIBRARY
Strathcona Anatomy & Dentistry Bldg.
3640 University St.   Phone: (514) 392-4926
Montreal, PQ H3A 2B2   Christine Izmirlian, Lib.Asst.

MC GILL UNIVERSITY - DEPARTMENT OF RARE BOOKS & SPECIAL
  COLLECTIONS
McLennan Library Bldg.
3459 McTavish St.   Phone: (514) 392-4973
Montreal, PQ H3A 1Y1   Elizabeth Lewis, Rare Book Libn.

MC GILL UNIVERSITY - EDUCATION LIBRARY
3700 McTavish St.   Phone: (514) 392-8849
Montreal, PQ H3A 1Y2   Joan Gagne, Educ.Libn.

MC GILL UNIVERSITY - EDUCATION LIBRARY - SAM RABINOVITCH
  MEMORIAL COLLECTION
3700 McTavish St.   Phone: (514) 392-8849
Montreal, PQ H3A 1Y2   Joan Gagne, Educ.Libn.

MC GILL UNIVERSITY - EXPERIMENTAL SURGERY LIBRARY
Donner Bldg.
740 Dr. Penfield Ave.   Phone: (514) 392-4858
Montreal, PQ H3A 1A4   Brenda Bewick, Libn.

MC GILL UNIVERSITY - HOWARD ROSS LIBRARY OF MANAGEMENT
Bronfman Bldg.
1001 Sherbrooke St., W.   Phone: (514) 392-5795
Montreal, PQ H3A 1G5   Marjorie Judah, Libn.

MC GILL UNIVERSITY - ISLAMIC STUDIES LIBRARY
Stephen Leacock Bldg., 9th Fl.
855 Sherbrooke St., W.   Phone: (514) 392-5197
Montreal, PQ H3A 2T7   Norma Johnston, Libn.

MC GILL UNIVERSITY - LABOUR AGREEMENTS DATA BANK
1001 Sherbrooke St., W.   Phone: (514) 392-3076
Montreal, PQ H3A 1G5   Dr. Charles Steinberg, Dir.

MC GILL UNIVERSITY - LAW LIBRARY
New Chancellor Day Hall
3644 Peel St.   Phone: (514) 392-5060
Montreal, PQ H3A 1W9   Michael Renshawe, Area Libn., Law

MC GILL UNIVERSITY - LIBRARY SCIENCE LIBRARY
McLennan Library Bldg.
3459 McTavish St.   Phone: (514) 392-5931
Montreal, PQ H3A 1Y1   Stephanie Both, Libn.

MC GILL UNIVERSITY - MAP AND AIR PHOTO LIBRARY
524 Burnside Hall
805 Sherbrooke St., W.   Phone: (514) 392-5492
Montreal, PQ H3A 2K6   Lorraine Dubreuil, Map Cur.

MC GILL UNIVERSITY - MARVIN DUCHOW MUSIC LIBRARY
Strathcona Music Bldg.
555 Sherbrooke St., W.   Phone: (514) 392-4530
Montreal, PQ H3A 1E3   Kathleen M. Toomey, Libn.

MC GILL UNIVERSITY - MATHEMATICS LIBRARY
1105 Burnside Hall
805 Sherbrooke St., W.   Phone: (514) 392-8273
Montreal, PQ H3A 2K6   Allan Youster, Lib.Supv.

MC GILL UNIVERSITY - MEDICAL LIBRARY
McIntyre Medical Sciences Bldg.
3655 Drummond St.   Phone: (514) 392-3056
Montreal, PQ H3G 1Y6   Frances Groen, Life Sci. Area Libn.

MC GILL UNIVERSITY - METEOROLOGY LIBRARY
704 Burnside Hall
805 Sherbrooke St., W.   Phone: (514) 392-8237
Montreal, PQ H3A 2K6   Keston Forde, Lib.Supv.

MC GILL UNIVERSITY - NURSING/SOCIAL WORK LIBRARY
Wilson Hall
3506 University St.   Phone: (514) 392-5027
Montreal, PQ H3A 2A7   Wendy Patrick, Hd.Libn.

MC GILL UNIVERSITY - OCEANOGRAPHY LIBRARY
3620 University St.   Phone: (514) 392-5723
Montreal, PQ H3A 2B2   Yvonne Mattocks, Lib.Supv.

MC GILL UNIVERSITY - OSLER LIBRARY
McIntyre Medical Sciences Bldg.
3655 Drummond St.   Phone: (514) 392-4329
Montreal, PQ H3G 1Y6   Philip Teigen, Osler Libn.

MC GILL UNIVERSITY - PHYSICAL SCIENCES AND ENGINEERING LIBRARY
809 Sherbrooke St., W.   Phone: (514) 392-5914
Montreal, PQ H3A 2K6   Robert T. Freese, Area Libn.

MC GILL UNIVERSITY - RELIGIOUS STUDIES LIBRARY
William & Henry Birks Bldg.
3520 University St.   Phone: (514) 392-4832
Montreal, PQ H3A 2A7   Norma Johnston, Hd.Libn.

MC GILL UNIVERSITY - RUTHERFORD PHYSICS LIBRARY
3600 University St.   Phone: (514) 392-4785
Montreal, PQ H3A 2T8   Valerie Oboruns, Lib.Supv.

MC GILL UNIVERSITY - SCHOOL OF HUMAN COMMUNICATION DISORDERS
  - LIBRARY
1266 Pine Ave., W.   Phone: (514) 392-5966
Montreal, PQ H3G 1A8   Dr. Kirti K. Charan, Assoc.Prof. & Dir.

MCMASTER MEIGHEN - LAW LIBRARY
630 Dorchester Blvd. W., 7th Fl.   Phone: (514) 879-1212
Montreal, PQ H3B 4H7   Elenore Hubscher, Libn.

MAIMONIDES HOSPITAL GERIATRIC CENTRE - POLLACK LIBRARY
5795 Caldwell Ave.   Phone: (514) 483-2121
Montreal, PQ H4W 1W3   Sheindel Bresinger, Libn.

MAISON BELLARMIN LIBRARY
25 W. Jarry   Phone: (514) 387-2541
Montreal, PQ H2P 1S6   Edmond E. Desrochers, Dir.

MARIANOPOLIS COLLEGE - LIBRARY - SPECIAL COLLECTIONS
3880 Cote des Neiges Rd.   Phone: (514) 931-8792
Montreal, PQ H3H 1W1   Dr. Roman R. Grodzicky, Chf.Libn.

MECHANICS' INSTITUTE OF MONTREAL - ATWATER LIBRARY
1200 Atwater Ave.   Phone: (514) 935-7344
Montreal, PQ H3Z 1X4   Brenda Pym, Chf.Libn.

MOLSON BREWERIES OF CANADA, LTD. - INFORMATION CENTRE
1555 Notre Dame St., E.   Phone: (514) 521-1786
Montreal, PQ H2L 2R5   Ann Hawley, Res.Libn.

MONTREAL ASSOCIATION FOR THE MENTALLY RETARDED -
  DOCUMENTATION CENTRE †
8605 rue Berri, 3rd Fl.   Phone: (514) 381-2307
Montreal, PQ H2P 2G5   Michelle Jacques, Documentalist

MONTREAL BOARD OF TRADE - INFORMATION CENTRE
1080 Beaver Hall Hill, 7th Fl.   Phone: (514) 878-4651
Montreal, PQ H2Z 1S9   Carole Peters, Mgr., Info.Serv.

MONTREAL CANCER INSTITUTE - LIBRARY
1560 Sherbrooke St., E.   Phone: (514) 876-7078
Montreal, PQ H2L 4M1   Dr. Roger Daoust, Info.Dir.

MONTREAL CHEST HOSPITAL CENTRE - MEDICAL LIBRARY
3650 St. Urbain St.   Phone: (514) 849-5201
Montreal, PQ H2X 2P4   Marianne Constantine, Med.Libn.

MONTREAL CHILDREN'S HOSPITAL - MEDICAL LIBRARY
2300 Tupper St.   Phone: (514) 937-8511
Montreal, PQ H3H 1P3   Dorothy Sirois, Med.Libn.

MONTREAL CITY PLANNING DEPARTMENT - LIBRARY †
85 Notre-Dame St., E.
Montreal, PQ H2Y 1B5

MONTREAL ENGINEERING COMPANY, LTD. - LIBRARY
Sta. A, Box 6088   Phone: (514) 286-3519
Montreal, PQ H3C 3Z8   Penelope H. Kamichaitis, Libn.

MONTREAL GAZETTE - LIBRARY
250 St. Antoine St. W.
P.O. Box 4300, Place d'Armes   Phone: (514) 282-2771
Montreal, PQ H2Y 3S1   Agnes McFarlane, Libn.

MONTREAL GENERAL HOSPITAL - MEDICAL LIBRARY
1650 Cedar Ave.   Phone: (514) 937-6011
Montreal, PQ H3G 1A4   Kathryn Vaughn, Chf.Med.Libn.

MONTREAL GENERAL HOSPITAL - NURSES LIBRARY
1650 Cedar Ave., Rm. 3808   Phone: (514) 937-6011
Montreal, PQ H3G 1A4   Mrs. B.A. Covington, Lib.Techn.

THE MONTREAL MUSEUM OF FINE ARTS - LIBRARY †
3400 Ave. du Musee   Phone: (514) 285-1600
Montreal, PQ H3G 1K3   Juanita M. Toupin, Libn.

MONTREAL NEUROLOGICAL INSTITUTE - LIBRARY †
3801 University St.   Phone: (514) 284-4651
Montreal, PQ H3A 2B4   Marina M. Boski, Libn.

MONTREAL URBAN COMMUNITY TRANSIT COMMISSION - LIBRARY
159 St. Antoine St., W., Rm. 912   Phone: (514) 877-6046
Montreal, PQ H2Z 1H3   Victor Itesco, Hd.Libn.

MONTREAL YOUNG WOMEN'S CHRISTIAN ASSOCIATION - LIBRARY *
1355 Dorchester Blvd., W.   Phone: (514) 866-9941
Montreal, PQ H3G 1T3

MUSEE D'ART CONTEMPORAIN - CENTRE DE DOCUMENTATION †
Cite du Havre   Phone: (514) 873-2878
Montreal, PQ H3C 3R4   Isabelle Montplaisir, Libn.

NATIONAL THEATRE SCHOOL OF CANADA - THEATRICAL LIBRARY
5030 St. Denis St.   Phone: (514) 842-7954
Montreal, PQ H2J 2L8   Beatrice De-Vreeze, Hd.Libn.

NESBITT THOMSON BONGARD INC. - RESEARCH LIBRARY
355 St. James St., W.   Phone: (514) 844-0131
Montreal, PQ H2Y 1P1   Ms. L. Cahill, Libn.

NORANDA MINES LTD. - CCR DIVISION - PROCESS DEVELOPMENT
  LIBRARY *
Place d'Armes
P.O. Box 338   Phone: (514) 645-8861
Montreal, PQ H2Y 3H2   Pierce Frattolillo, Process Dev.Supt.

NORTHERN TELECOM CANADA, LTD. - LIBRARY & TECHNICAL
  INFORMATION CENTRE
P.O. Box 6122, Sta. A   Phone: (514) 634-3511
Montreal, PQ H3C 3J4   Miss M.Y. Pollock, Mgr.

OGILVY, RENAULT - LIBRARY †
1981 McGill College Ave.   Phone: (514) 286-5424
Montreal, PQ H3A 3C1   Mrs. M. Elvidge, Libn.

ORATOIRE ST-JOSEPH - CENTRE DE DOCUMENTATION
3800 Queen Mary Rd.   Phone: (514) 733-8211
Montreal, PQ H3V 1H6   Aime Trottier, Libn.

ORDRE DES INFIRMIERES ET DES INFIRMIERS DU QUEBEC - CENTRE DE
  DOCUMENTATION †
4200 Dorchester, W.   Phone: (514) 935-2501
Montreal, PQ H3Z 1V4   Denise Mailhot, Libn.

PEAT, MARWICK, MITCHELL & CO. - INFORMATION RESOURCES/CENTRE
  DE DOCUMENTATAION
1155 Dorchester Blvd., W., 20th Fl.   Phone: (514) 879-3428
Montreal, PQ H3B 2J9   Judy Macfarlane, Mgr.

POLISH INSTITUTE OF ARTS AND SCIENCES IN CANADA - POLISH
  LIBRARY
McGill University
3479 Peel St.   Phone: (514) 392-5958
Montreal, PQ H3A 1W7   Dr. Anna Poray-Wybranowski, Chf.Libn.

PRESBYTERIAN COLLEGE - LIBRARY
3495 University St.   Phone: (514) 288-5257
Montreal, PQ H3A 2A8   Rev. Daniel Shute, Libn.

PRICE WATERHOUSE - LIBRARY
1200 McGill College Ave.   Phone: (514) 879-9050
Montreal, PQ H3B 2G4   Martha Nugent

PROTESTANT SCHOOL BOARD OF GREATER MONTREAL - PROFESSIONAL
  LIBRARY
6000 Fielding Ave.   Phone: (514) 482-6000
Montreal, PQ H3X 1T4   M.E. Montague, Lib.Techn.

QUEBEC PROVINCE - BIBLIOTHEQUE NATIONALE DU QUEBEC
1700, rue St-Denis   Phone: (514) 873-4553
Montreal, PQ H2X 3K6   M. Jean-Remi Brault, Conservateur en Chef

QUEBEC PROVINCE - BIBLIOTHEQUE NATIONALE DU QUEBEC - SERVICE
  DES COLLECTIONS SPECIALES - SECTEUR MUSIQUE
1700 rue Saint-Denis   Phone: (514) 873-4512
Montreal, PQ H2X 3K6   Gabrielle Bourbonnais, Hd.

QUEBEC PROVINCE - CAISSE DE DEPOT ET PLACEMENT DU QUEBEC -
  LIBRARY †
C.P. 74, Tour de la Bourse   Phone: (514) 873-2460
Montreal, PQ H4Z 1B4   Pauline Lefebvre Gour, Libn.

QUEBEC PROVINCE - CENTRALE DES BIBLIOTHEQUES - CENTRE
  DOCUMENTAIRE
1685 Est, Rue Fleury   Phone: (514) 382-0895
Montreal, PQ H2C 1T1   Gertrude S. DeCarufel, Hd.Libn.

QUEBEC PROVINCE - COMMISSION DE LA SANTE ET DE LA SECURITE DU
  TRAVAIL - CENTRE DE DOCUMENTATION
C.P. 6067, Succ. A   Phone: (514) 873-3160
Montreal, PQ H3C 4E2   Suzanne Heureux

QUEBEC PROVINCE - DIRECTION GENERALE DES MOYENS
  D'ENSEIGNEMENT - CENTRE DE DOCUMENTATION *
600 rue Fullum, 5th Fl.   Phone: (514) 873-3973
Montreal, PQ H2K 4L1   Chantal Robinson, Assoc.Dir.

QUEBEC PROVINCE - MINISTERE DES AFFAIRES SOCIALES - SERVICE DE
  LA DOCUMENTATION
6161 rue Saint-Denis, R.C. 07   Phone: (514) 873-3695
Montreal, PQ H2S 2R5   Gerard Darlington, Libn.

QUEBEC PROVINCE - MINISTERE DU LOISIR, DE LA CHASSE ET DE LA
  PECHE - BIBLIOTHEQUE DE LA FAUNE
6255 13th Ave.   Phone: (514) 374-5840
Montreal, PQ H1X 3E6   Richard Mathieu, Chf.Libn.

QUEBEC PROVINCE - OFFICE DES COMMUNICATIONS SOCIALES -
  BIBLIOTHEQUE ET CENTRE DE DOCUMENTATION
4005 De Bellechasse   Phone: (514) 729-6391
Montreal, PQ H1X 1J6   Lucien Labille, Dir.

QUEBEC PROVINCE - REGIE DE L'ELECTRICITE ET DU GAZ -
  BIBLIOTHEQUE
2100, rue Drummond   Phone: (514) 873-2452
Montreal, PQ H3G 1X1   Marielle Bernard, Lib.Techn.

RADIO QUEBEC - CENTRE DES RESSOURCES DOCUMENTAIRES
1000 Fullum   Phone: (514) 521-2424
Montreal, PQ H2K 3L7   Nicole Charest, Dir.

READER'S DIGEST MAGAZINES LIMITED - EDITORIAL LIBRARY
215 Redfern Ave.   Phone: (514) 934-0751
Montreal, PQ H3Z 2V9   Colette Nishizaki, Libn.

ROBINSON, SHEPPARD, BORENSTEIN, SHAPIRO - LAW LIBRARY
800 Place Victoria, Suite 4700   Phone: (514) 878-2631
Montreal, PQ H4Z 1H6   Angela Belle Tietolman, Law Libn.

ROYAL BANK OF CANADA - INFORMATION RESOURCES
P.O. Box 6001   Phone: (514) 874-2452
Montreal, PQ H3C 3A9   Anthea Downing, Chf.Libn.

ROYAL CANADIAN ORDNANCE CORPS MUSEUM - LIBRARY
6560 Hochelaga St.
P.O. Box 6109   Phone: (514) 255-8811
Montreal, PQ H3C 3H7   Leo Lavigne, Cur.

ROYAL VICTORIA HOSPITAL - MEDICAL LIBRARY †
687 Pine Ave., W., Rm. H4.01   Phone: (514) 842-1231
Montreal, PQ H3A 1A1   Sandra R. Duchow, Chf.Med.Libn.

ROYAL VICTORIA HOSPITAL - WOMEN'S PAVILION LIBRARY
687 Pine Ave., W.   Phone: (514) 842-1251
Montreal, PQ H3A 1A1   Elaine Waddington, Libn.

S.E.R.U. NUCLEAIRE (Canada) LTEE. - LIBRARY
2000 Mansfield, Suite 400   Phone: (514) 282-9369
Montreal, PQ H3A 2Z1   Elisabeth Lavigueur, Libn.

ST. HELEN'S ISLAND MUSEUM MONTREAL - DAVID M. STEWART LIBRARY
  †
Sta. A, P.O. Box 1024   Phone: (514) 861-6738
Montreal, PQ H3C 2W9   Elizabeth F. Hale, Libn.Cons.

ST. MARY'S HOSPITAL - MEDICAL LIBRARY
3830 Lacombe   Phone: (514) 344-3317
Montreal, PQ H3T 1M5   Lucile Lavigueur, Libn.

SHAWINIGAN CONSULTANTS INC. - LIBRARY
620 Dorchester West   Phone: (514) 878-6294
Montreal, PQ H3B 1N8   Carol Lacourte, Libn.

SIR MORTIMER B. DAVIS JEWISH GENERAL HOSPITAL - INSTITUTE OF
  COMMUNITY & FAMILY PSYCHIATRY - LIBRARY
4333 Cote St. Catherine Rd.   Phone: (514) 341-6211
Montreal, PQ H3T 1E2   Ruth Stilman, Libn.

SIR MORTIMER B. DAVIS JEWISH GENERAL HOSPITAL - LADY DAVIS
  INSTITUTE FOR MEDICAL RESEARCH - RESEARCH LIBRARY
3755 Cote St. Catherine Rd.   Phone: (514) 342-3620
Montreal, PQ H3T 1E2   Arlene Greenberg, Chf.Med.Libn.

SIR MORTIMER B. DAVIS JEWISH GENERAL HOSPITAL - MEDICAL LIBRARY
3755 Cote St. Catherine Rd.   Phone: (514) 342-3111
Montreal, PQ H3T 1E2   Arlene Greenberg, Chf.Med.Libn.

SNC GROUP - LIBRARY
1 Complexe Desjardins
C.P. 10   Phone: (514) 282-9551
Montreal, PQ H5B 1C8   Andree Nicole, Lib.Supv.

SOCIETE D'ARCHEOLOGIE ET DE NUMISMATIQUE DE MONTREAL -
  BIBLIOTHEQUE †
280 est, rue Notre-Dame   Phone: (514) 861-7182
Montreal, PQ H2Y 1C5   Margot Albert, Sec.

SOCIETE DE DEVELOPPEMENT DE LA BAIE JAMES - DOCUMENTATION
  CENTRE
800 de Maisonneuve Blvd., E.   Phone: (514) 284-0270
Montreal, PQ H2L 4M6   Diane Lefebvre, Dir.

SQUIBB CANADA INC. - MEDICAL LIBRARY
2365 Cote de Liesse Rd.   Phone: (514) 337-7423
Montreal, PQ H4N 2M7   Carole Schneider, Sec./Libn.

SUN LIFE OF CANADA - REFERENCE LIBRARY
Box 6075, Sta. A   Phone: (514) 866-6411
Montreal, PQ H3C 3G5   France Payant, Libn.

TA ASSOCIATES - INFORMATION CENTER
1801 McGill College Ave.   Phone: (514) 281-2753
Montreal, PQ H3A 2N4   Line St-Pierre, Libn.

TOWERS, PERRIN, FORSTER & CROSBY - INFORMATION CENTRE
800 Dorchester W., Suite 3010   Phone: (514) 866-7652
Montreal, PQ H3B 1X9   Amy L. Scowen, Info.Serv.Spec.

TRANS QUEBEC & MARITIMES INC. - CENTRE DE DOCUMENTATION
870 de Maisonneuve Blvd., E., 6th Fl.   Phone: (514) 286-5067
Montreal, PQ H2L 1Y6

UNIVERSITE DE MONTREAL - AMENAGEMENT-BIBLIOTHEQUE
C.P. 6128, Succursale A   Phone: (514) 343-7177
Montreal, PQ H3C 3J7   Jacqueline Pelletier, Libn.

UNIVERSITE DE MONTREAL - AUDIOVIDEOTHEQUE
C.P. 6128, Succursale A   Phone: (514) 343-7344
Montreal, PQ H3C 3J7   Ginette Gagnier, Libn.

UNIVERSITE DE MONTREAL - BIBLIOTHECONOMIE-BIBLIOTHEQUE
C.P. 6128, Succursale A   Phone: (514) 343-6047
Montreal, PQ H3C 3J7   Georges Clonda, Libn.

UNIVERSITE DE MONTREAL - BIBLIOTHEQUE PARA-MEDICALE
C.P. 6128, Succursale A   Phone: (514) 343-7490
Montreal, PQ H3C 3J7   Johanne Hopper, Libn.

UNIVERSITE DE MONTREAL - BIBLIOTHEQUE DE LA SANTE
C.P. 6128, Succursale A   Phone: (514) 343-6826
Montreal, PQ H3C 3J7   Therese Peternell, Libn.

UNIVERSITE DE MONTREAL - BIOLOGIE-BIBLIOTHEQUE
C.P. 6128, Succursale A   Phone: (514) 343-6801
Montreal, PQ H3C 3J7   Vesna Blazina, Libn.

UNIVERSITE DE MONTREAL - BOTANIQUE-BIBLIOTHEQUE
4101 Est, Rue Sherbrooke   Phone: (514) 256-9441
Montreal, PQ H1X 2B2   Nicole Taillefer-Witty, Libn.

UNIVERSITE DE MONTREAL - CENTRE D'ETUDES ET DE DOCUMENTATION
  EUROPEENNES
3150 Rue Jean-Brillant
C.P. 6128, Succursale A   Phone: (514) 343-7870
Montreal, PQ H3C 3J7   Lucie Bouchard, Documentaliste

UNIVERSITE DE MONTREAL - CENTRE INTERNATIONAL DE CRIMINOLOGIE
  COMPAREE - DOCUMENTATION CENTRE
C.P. 6128, Succursale A   Phone: (514) 343-6534
Montreal, PQ H3C 3J7   Jacqueline DePlaen, Hd., Doc.

UNIVERSITE DE MONTREAL - CENTRE DE RECHERCHE SUR LES
  TRANSPORTS - DOCUMENTATION CENTRE
C.P. 6128, Succursale A   Phone: (514) 343-6949
Montreal, PQ H3C 3J7   Sylvie Hetu, Libn.

UNIVERSITE DE MONTREAL - CENTRE DE RECHERCHES CARAIBES -
  BIBLIOTHEQUE ★
C.P. 6128   Phone: (514) 343-5807
Montreal, PQ H3C 3J7   Michelle Cote, Documentaliste

UNIVERSITE DE MONTREAL - CHIMIE-BIBLIOTHEQUE
C.P. 6128, Succursale A   Phone: (514) 343-6459
Montreal, PQ H3C 3J7   Corinne Haumont, Libn.

UNIVERSITE DE MONTREAL - COLLECTIONS SPECIALES
C.P. 6128, Succursale A   Phone: (514) 343-7753
Montreal, PQ H3C 3J7   Genevieve Bazin, Libn.

UNIVERSITE DE MONTREAL - DEPARTEMENT DE DEMOGRAPHIE - SERVICE
  DE LA RECHERCHE DOCUMENTATION
C.P. 6128, Succursale A   Phone: (514) 343-7567
Montreal, PQ H3C 3J7   Isabelle Laperle, Documentaliste

UNIVERSITE DE MONTREAL - DROIT-BIBLIOTHEQUE
C.P. 6206, Succursale A   Phone: (514) 343-6132
Montreal, PQ H3C 3T6   Paquerette Ranger, Libn.

UNIVERSITE DE MONTREAL - EDUCATION PHYSIQUE-BIBLIOTHEQUE
C.P. 6128, Succursale A   Phone: (514) 343-6765
Montreal, PQ H3C 3J7   Lise Mayrand, Libn.

UNIVERSITE DE MONTREAL - EDUCATION/PSYCHOLOGIE/
   COMMUNICATION-BIBLIOTHEQUE
C.P. 6128, Succursale A   Phone: (514) 343-6638
Montreal, PQ H3C 3J7   Marielle Durand, Libn.

UNIVERSITE DE MONTREAL - GEOGRAPHIE-BIBLIOTHEQUE
C.P. 6128, Succursale A   Phone: (514) 270-3727
Montreal, PQ H3C 3J7   Francine Caplette, Hd.

UNIVERSITE DE MONTREAL - GEOLOGIE-BIBLIOTHEQUE
C.P. 6128, Succursale A   Phone: (514) 343-6831
Montreal, PQ H3C 3J7   Clement Arwas, Libn.

UNIVERSITE DE MONTREAL - INFORMATIQUE-BIBLIOTHEQUE
C.P. 6128, Succursale A   Phone: (514) 343-6819
Montreal, PQ H3C 3J7   Louis Sarrasin, Libn.

UNIVERSITE DE MONTREAL - MATHEMATIQUES-BIBLIOTHEQUE
C.P. 6128, Succursale A   Phone: (514) 343-6703
Montreal, PQ H3C 3J7   Rita Paquette, Libn.

UNIVERSITE DE MONTREAL - MUSIQUE-BIBLIOTHEQUE
C.P. 6128, Succursale A   Phone: (514) 343-6432
Montreal, PQ H3C 3J7   Monique Lecavalier, Libn.

UNIVERSITE DE MONTREAL - OPTOMETRIE-BIBLIOTHEQUE
C.P. 6128, Succursale A   Phone: (514) 343-7674
Montreal, PQ H3C 3J7   Denise Lacroix, Libn.

UNIVERSITE DE MONTREAL - PHYSIQUE-BIBLIOTHEQUE
C.P. 6128, Succursale A   Phone: (514) 343-6613
Montreal, PQ H3C 3J7   Janine Cadet, Libn.

UNIVERSITE DE MONTREAL - PSYCHO-EDUCATION-BIBLIOTHEQUE
750 Est, Boul. Gouin   Phone: (514) 382-2977
Montreal, PQ H2C 1A6   Yolande Beaudoin, Libn.

UNIVERSITE DE MONTREAL - SCIENCES HUMAINES ET SOCIALES-
   BIBLIOTHEQUE
C.P. 6202, Succursale A   Phone: (514) 343-7424
Montreal, PQ H3C 3T2   Richard Greene, Libn.

UNIVERSITE DE MONTREAL - THEOLOGIE-PHILOSOPHIE BIBLIOTHEQUE
C.P. 6128, Succursale A   Phone: (514) 343-6592
Montreal, PQ H3C 3J7   Francoise Beaudet

UNIVERSITE DU QUEBEC A MONTREAL - AUDIOVIDEOTHEQUE
C.P. 8889   Phone: (514) 282-4332
Montreal, PQ H3C 3P3   Huguette Tanguay, Audiovideothecaire

UNIVERSITE DU QUEBEC A MONTREAL - BIBLIOTHEQUE DES ARTS
C.P. 8889, Succursale A   Phone: (514) 282-6134
Montreal, PQ H3C 3P3   Daphne Dufresne, Chf.Libn.

UNIVERSITE DU QUEBEC A MONTREAL - BIBLIOTHEQUE DE MUSIQUE
C.P. 8889, Succursale A   Phone: (514) 282-3934
Montreal, PQ H3C 3P3   Renald Beaumier, Dir.

UNIVERSITE DU QUEBEC A MONTREAL - BIBLIOTHEQUE DES SCIENCES
C.P. 8889, Succursale A   Phone: (514) 282-6164
Montreal, PQ H3C 3P3   Conrad Corriveau, Dir.

UNIVERSITE DU QUEBEC A MONTREAL - BIBLIOTHEQUE DES SCIENCES DE
   L'EDUCATION
C.P. 8889, Succursale A   Phone: (514) 282-6174
Montreal, PQ H3C 3P3   Denis Rousseau, Dir.

UNIVERSITE DU QUEBEC A MONTREAL - BIBLIOTHEQUES DES SCIENCES
   JURIDIQUES
C.P. 8889, Succursale A   Phone: (514) 282-6184
Montreal, PQ H3C 3P3   Micheline Drapeau, Dir.

UNIVERSITE DU QUEBEC A MONTREAL - CARTOTHEQUE
C.P. 8889, Succursale A   Phone: (514) 282-3133
Montreal, PQ H3C 3P8   Leon-Pierre Sciamma, Responsable

UNIVERSITE DU QUEBEC A MONTREAL - CENTRE DE DOCUMENTATION
   ECONOMIE-ADMINISTRATION
C.P. 8889, Succursale A   Phone: (514) 282-6136
Montreal, PQ H3C 3P8   Monique Cote, Libn.

UNIVERSITE DU QUEBEC A MONTREAL - CENTRE DE DOCUMENTATION EN
   SCIENCES HUMAINES
C.P. 8889, Succursale A   Phone: (514) 282-6138
Montreal, PQ H3C 3P3   Louis LeBorgne, Documentaliste

VILLE MARIE SOCIAL SERVICE CENTRE - LIBRARY
4018 St. Catherine, W.   Phone: (514) 989-1885
Montreal, PQ H3Z 1P2   Janet Sand-Steinhouse, Libn.

ZITTRER, SIBLIN, STEIN, LEVINE - LIBRARY
4115 Sherbrooke St., W.   Phone: (514) 933-1112
Montreal, PQ H3Z 1K9   Norman Daitchman

UNION CARBIDE CANADA, LTD. - TECHNICAL CENTRE LIBRARY
10555 Metropolitan Blvd., E.
C.P. 700   Phone: (514) 645-5311
Pointe-Aux-Trembles, PQ H1B 5K8   A.M. de Jesus, Libn.

FOREST ENGINEERING RESEARCH INSTITUTE OF CANADA - LIBRARY
143 Place Frontenac   Phone: (514) 694-1140
Pointe Claire, PQ H9R 4Z7   Linda Cobbett, Libn.

NORANDA RESEARCH CENTRE - LIBRARY
240 Hymus Blvd.   Phone: (514) 697-6640
Pointe Claire, PQ H9R 1G5   Shirley Courtis, Libn.

PULP AND PAPER RESEARCH INSTITUTE OF CANADA - LIBRARY
570 St. John's Blvd.   Phone: (514) 697-4110
Pointe Claire, PQ H9R 3J9   Alison Finnemore, Libn.

MERCK FROSST CANADA INC. - RESEARCH LIBRARY
P.O. Box 1005   Phone: (514) 695-7920
Pointe Claire-Dorval, PQ H9R 4P8   Claire B. Kelly, Res.Libn.

PFIZER CANADA INC. - MEDICAL LIBRARY
P.O. Box 800   Phone: (514) 695-0500
Pointe Claire-Dorval, PQ H9R 4V2   Miriam Hayward, Sci.Info.Coord.

FOREIGN MISSIONS SOCIETY OF QUEBEC - LIBRARY
180, place Juge-Desnoyers   Phone: (514) 667-4190
Pont-Viau, Ville Laval, PQ I17G 1A4   Florian Vachon, Lib.Dir.

ASSOCIATION DE PARALYSIE CEREBRALE DU QUEBEC, INC. - CENTRE DE
   DOCUMENTATION *
525 Boul. Hamel Est, Suite A-50   Phone: (418) 529-5371
Quebec, PQ G1M 2S8

CENTRALE DE L'ENSEIGNEMENT DU QUEBEC - CENTRE DE
   DOCUMENTATION
2336 Chemin Ste-Foy   Phone: (418) 658-5711
Quebec, PQ G1V 4E5   Guy Duchesne

CENTRE HOSPITALIER CHRIST-ROI - BIBLIOTHEQUE MEDICALE
300, Boul. Wilfrid-Hamel   Phone: (418) 687-1711
Quebec, PQ G1M 2R9   Gratien Gelinas, Bibliothecaire

CONSERVATOIRE D'ART DRAMATIQUE DE QUEBEC - BIBLIOTHEQUE *
30 St-Denis   Phone: (418) 643-2139
Quebec, PQ G1R 4B6   Georgette Laki, Bibliothecaire

HOPITAL DE L'ENFANT-JESUS - BIBLIOTHEQUE MEDICALE
1401 18eme Rue   Phone: (418) 694-5686
Quebec, PQ G1J 1Z4   Madeleine Dumais, Responsable

HOPITAL ST-FRANCOIS D'ASSISE - BIBLIOTHEQUE MEDICALE ET
   ADMINISTRATIVE †
10 rue de l'Espinay   Phone: (418) 529-7311
Quebec, PQ G1L 3L5   Ulric Lefebvre, Chief

HOPITAL DU ST-SACREMENT - BIBLIOTHEQUE MEDICALE †
1050 Chemin Ste-Foy   Phone: (418) 688-7560
Quebec, PQ G1S 4L8   Bernadette Drolet, Chf.Libn.

HOTEL-DIEU DU SACRE-COEUR DE JESUS - BIBLIOTHEQUE MEDICALE
1, Ave. du Sacre-Coeur   Phone: (418) 529-6851
Quebec, PQ G1N 2W1   Christian Martel, Lib.Techn.

INDUSTRIAL GENERAL INSURANCE COMPANY - LIBRARY
1080 St. Louis Rd.
Box 1907   Phone: (418) 688-8210
Quebec, PQ G1K 7M3   M. Robichaud, Sec.

LA LAURENTIENNE COMPAGNIE D'ASSURANCES GENERALES - LIBRARY †
425 St-Amable   Phone: (418) 647-5151
Quebec, PQ G1K 7X5   Louise de Bellefeville, Tech.Libn.

LITERARY AND HISTORICAL SOCIETY OF QUEBEC - LIBRARY †
44 St. Stanislas St.   Phone: (418) 694-9147
Quebec, PQ G1R 4H3   Cynthia Dooley, Libn.

MONASTERE DES URSULINES - ARCHIVES DES URSULINES DE QUEBEC
C.P. 760   Phone: (418) 692-2523
Quebec, PQ G1R 4T1   Sr. Marcelle Boucher, Archv.

MUSEE DU QUEBEC - BIBLIOTHEQUE
Parc des Champs de Bataille   Phone: (418) 643-7134
Quebec, PQ G1S 1C8   Francois Lafortune, Chf.Libn.

QUEBEC PROVINCE - BIBLIOTHEQUE DE L'ASSEMBLEE NATIONALE
Edifice Pamphile-Lemay   Phone: (418) 643-2896
Quebec, PQ G1A 1A5   Jacques Premont, Dir.

QUEBEC PROVINCE - L'INSPECTEUR GENERAL DES INSTITUTIONS
  FINANCIERES - BIBLIOTHEQUE
800 Place D'Youville, 7th Fl.   Phone: (418) 643-5236
Quebec, PQ G1R 4Y5   Sylvie Nadeau, Bibliotechnicienne

QUEBEC PROVINCE - MINISTERE DES AFFAIRES CULTURELLES - CENTRE
  DE DOCUMENTATION †
225 Grande-Allee Est   Phone: (418) 643-6330
Quebec, PQ G1R 5G5   Real Dumoulin, Chf.

QUEBEC PROVINCE - MINISTERE DES AFFAIRES MUNICIPALES - CENTRE
  DE DOCUMENTATION
20, rue Chauveau   Phone: (418) 643-6570
Quebec, PQ G1R 4J3   Ernest Bertrand Roy, Responsable

QUEBEC PROVINCE - MINISTERE DES AFFAIRES SOCIALES - SERVICE DE
  LA DOCUMENTATION
1075 Chemin Ste-Foy   Phone: (418) 643-6392
Quebec, PQ G1S 2M1   Yvon Papillon, Hd.Libn.

QUEBEC PROVINCE - MINISTERE DE L'AGRICULTURE, DES PECHERIES ET
  DE L'ALIMENTATION - CENTRE DE DOCUMENTATION
200-A, Chemin Ste-Foy   Phone: (418) 643-2428
Quebec, PQ G1R 4X6   Michele Audette, Responsable

QUEBEC PROVINCE - MINISTERE DES COMMUNICATIONS - BIBLIOTHEQUE
  ADMINISTRATIVE
1037 de la Chevrotiere, Edifice G Phone: (418) 643-1515
Quebec, PQ G1R 4Y7   Monique Charbonneau, Lib.Dir.

QUEBEC PROV. - MIN. DE L'ENERGIE ET DES RESSOURCES - SERVICE DE
  DOCUMENTATION ET DE RENSEIGNEMENTS
200B Chemin Ste-Foy, 7th Fl.   Phone: (418) 643-6004
Quebec, PQ G1R 4X7   Normand Guerette, Dir.

QUEBEC PROVINCE - MINISTERE DE L'INDUSTRIE, DU COMMERCE ET DU
  TOURISME - BIBLIOTHEQUE MINISTERIELLE
710 Place d'Youville, local 203   Phone: (418) 643-5081
Quebec, PQ G1R 4Y4   Mario Day, Responsable

QUEBEC PROVINCE - MINISTERE DU LOISIR, DE LA CHASSE ET DE LA
  PECHE - BIBLIOTHEQUE
150 est, Blvd. St-Cyrille   Phone: (418) 643-5300
Quebec, PQ G1R 4Y3

QUEBEC PROVINCE - OFFICE DE PLANIFICATION ET DE DEVELOPPEMENT
  DU QUEBEC - BIBLIOTHEQUE †
1060 Rue Conroy
Complexe G, Bloc 2, 3rd Fl.   Phone: (418) 643-1607
Quebec, PQ G1R 5E6   Suzanne Plante-Garneau

QUEBEC PROVINCE - REGIE DES RENTES - CENTRE DE DOCUMENTATION
C.P. 5200   Phone: (418) 643-8250
Quebec, PQ G1K 7S9   Michel Dupuis, Libn.

REED INC. - R&D LIBRARY
Box 1487   Phone: (418) 694-7990
Quebec, PQ G1K 7H9   Jim Drake, Libn.

SEMINAIRE DE QUEBEC - ARCHIVES *
Box 460   Phone: (418) 692-3981
Quebec, PQ G1R 4R7   Rev. Georges Drouin, Archiviste

SOLEIL LIMITEE - CENTRE DE DOCUMENTATION
390 E. St. Vallier   Phone: (418) 647-3369
Quebec, PQ G1K 7J6   Mr. Berthold Landry, Adm.Asst.

TELE-UNIVERSITE - CENTRE DE DOCUMENTATION
214, Ave. St-Sacrement   Phone: (418) 657-2262
Quebec, PQ G1N 4M6   Claude Tousignant, Hd.Libn.

CANADA - FISHERIES & OCEANS - LIBRARY
901 Cap Diamant
Box 15,500   Phone: (418) 694-3010
Quebec City, PQ G1K 7Y7   Christine Roy,, Libn.

CANADA - REVENUE CANADA - CUSTOMS & EXCISE - COLLEGE LIBRARY †
                                  Phone: (514) 451-5357
Rigaud, PQ J0P 1P0   Luc Filiatreault, Lib.Ck.

UNIVERSITE DU QUEBEC A RIMOUSKI - CARTOTHEQUE
300, Avenue des Ursulines   Phone: (418) 724-1669
Rimouski, PQ G5L 3A1   Yves Michaud, Map Libn.

COLLEGE DE L'ABITIBI-TEMISCAMINGUE - BIBLIOTHEQUE - SPECIAL
  COLLECTIONS
425 College Blvd.
Box 8000   Phone: (819) 762-0931
Rouyn, PQ J9X 5M5   Serge Allard, Dir.

UNIVERSITE DU QUEBEC EN ABITIBI-TEMISCAMINGUE - BIBLIOTHEQUE
446, rue Gagne
Box 8000   Phone: (819) 762-0971
Rouyn, PQ J9X 5M5   Serge Allard, Dir.

SEMINAIRE ST-ALPHONSE - BIBLIOTHEQUE
10026 Rue Royale   Phone: (418) 827-2751
Ste. Anne de Beaupre, PQ G0A 3C0   Robert Boucher, Dir.

CANADA - FISHERIES & OCEANS - R&D DIRECTORATE - ARCTIC
  BIOLOGICAL STATION LIBRARY
555 St. Pierre Blvd.   Phone: (514) 457-3660
Ste. Anne-de-Bellevue, PQ H9X 3R4   June Currie, Libn.

CANADIAN INSTITUTE OF HYPNOTISM - LIBRARY
P.O. Box 60   Phone: (514) 457-3377
Ste. Anne de Bellevue, PQ H9X 3L4   Jeanne Rigaud, Coord.

MC GILL UNIVERSITY - MACDONALD CAMPUS - BRACE RESEARCH
  INSTITUTE LIBRARY
P.O. Box 900   Phone: (514) 457-2000
Ste. Anne de Bellevue, PQ H9X 1C0 Mrs. A. Ives, Adm. & Info.Serv.

MC GILL UNIVERSITY - MACDONALD CAMPUS - INSTITUTE OF
  PARASITOLOGY - LIBRARY
                                  Phone: (514) 457-2000
Ste. Anne de Bellevue, PQ H9X 1C0 Dr. G.M. Faubert, Assoc.Prof.

MC GILL UNIVERSITY - MACDONALD COLLEGE - LIBRARY
Barton Bldg.
2111 Lakeshore Rd.   Phone:,(514) 457-2000
Ste. Anne de Bellevue, PQ H9X 1C0   Janet Finlayson, Hd.Libn.

SPAR AEROSPACE LTD. - LIBRARY
21025 Trans Canada Hwy.   Phone: (514) 457-2150
Ste. Anne de Bellevue, PQ H9X 3R2   Margaret B. Gross, Libn.

CANADA - AGRICULTURE CANADA - RESEARCH STATION, STE-FOY -
  LIBRARY
2560 Hochelaga Blvd.   Phone: (418) 694-4017
Ste. Foy, PQ G1V 2J3   Paul R. Venne, Area Coord., Quebec

CANADA - CANADIAN FORESTRY SERVICE - LAURENTIAN FOREST
  RESEARCH CENTRE - LIBRARY
C.P. 3800, 1080 Route Du Vallon   Phone: (418) 694-3989
Ste. Foy, PQ G1V 4C7   Claudine Lussier, Libn.

CENTRE HOSPITALIER DE L'UNIVERSITE LAVAL - BIBLIOTHEQUE DES
  SCIENCES DE LA SANTE †
2705 Blvd. Sir Wilfred Laurier   Phone: (418) 656-8188
Ste. Foy, PQ G1V 4G2   Beatrice Dionne, Chf.

CENTRE DE RECHERCHE INDUSTRIELLE DU QUEBEC - DIRECTION DE
  L'INFORMATION TECHNOLOGIQUE
333 Rue Franquet   Phone: (418) 659-1550
Ste. Foy, PQ G1V 4C7   Claude Lafrance, Dir.

COMPLEXE SCIENTIFIQUE DU QUEBEC - SERVICE DE DOCUMENTATION ET
  DE BIBLIOTHEQUE
2700 Einstein C-1-1   Phone: (418) 643-9730
Ste. Foy, PQ G1P 3W8   M. Levesque, Hd.Libn.

QUEBEC PROVINCE - ARCHIVES NATIONALES DU QUEBEC - BIBLIOTHEQUE
C.P. 10450   Phone: (418) 643-2167
Ste. Foy, PQ G1V 4N1   Colette Barry, Libn.

QUEBEC PROVINCE - MINISTERE DE LA JUSTICE - BIBLIOTHEQUE
1200, Route de l'Eglise
Edifice Delta, 4th Fl.   Phone: (418) 643-8409
Ste. Foy, PQ G1V 4M1   Michel Ricard, Agent de Recherche

QUEBEC PROVINCE - MINISTERE DU REVENU - BIBLIOTHEQUE
3800, Rue Marly   Phone: (418) 644-6835
Ste. Foy, PQ G1X 4A5   Pierre-Paul Blais, Dir.

SOCIETE QUEBECOISE D'INITIATIVES PETROLIERES - DOCUMENTATION
  CENTRE †
1175 de Lavigerie   Phone: (418) 651-9543
Ste. Foy, PQ G1V 4P1   Gilles Dion, Chf.

UNIVERSITE LAVAL - BIBLIOTHEQUE
Cite Universitaire   Phone: (418) 656-3343
Ste. Foy, PQ G1K 7P4   Celine R. Cartier, Dir.

UNIVERSITE LAVAL - INTERNATIONAL CENTRE FOR RESEARCH ON
  BILINGUALISM
Pavillon Casault, 6th Fl.   Phone: (418) 656-3232
Ste. Foy, PQ G1K 7P4   Guy Teasdale, Lib.Techn.

UNIVERSITE DU QUEBEC - ECOLE NATIONALE D'ADMINISTRATION
  PUBLIQUE - CENTRE DE DOCUMENTATION
945 Ave. Wolfe   Phone: (418) 657-2485
Ste. Foy, PQ G1V 3J9   Michel Gelinas, Libn.

UNIVERSITE DU QUEBEC - MEDIATHEQUE †
2875, Boul. Laurier   Phone: (418) 657-2578
Ste. Foy, PQ G1V 2M3   Yvon Isabel, Directeur

CANADA - NATIONAL DEFENCE - MOBILE COMMAND HQ LIBRARY
                                                   Phone: (514) 671-3711
St. Hubert, PQ J3Y 5T5   Mary Finlay, Chf.Libn.

CEGEP ST-JEAN SUR RICHELIEU - BIBLIOTHEQUE
30 Blvd. Du Seminaire
C.P. 1018   Phone: (514) 347-5301
St. Jean, PQ J3B 5J4   Michel Robert, Chf.Libn.

COLLEGE MILITAIRE ROYAL DE ST-JEAN - LIBRARY
                                                   Phone: (514) 346-2131
St. Jean, PQ J0J 1R0   Armand Lamirande, Chf.Libn.

CANADA - AGRICULTURE CANADA - RESEARCH STATION, ST-JEAN -
  LIBRARY
P.O. Box 457   Phone: (514) 346-4494
St. Jean-Sur-Richelieu, PQ J3B 6Z8   Ian Wallace, Libn.

COMPAGNIE DE JESUS - JESUITS LIBRARY
C.P. 130   Phone: (514) 438-3593
St. Jerome, PQ J7Z 5T8   Joseph Cossette, S.J., Lib.Dir.

CAE ELECTRONICS, LTD. - ENGINEERING REFERENCE LIBRARY
P.O. Box 1800   Phone: (514) 341-6780
St. Laurent, PQ H4L 4X4   Ellen Sharpe, Libn.

CANADA - ATMOSPHERIC ENVIRONMENT SERVICE - QUEBEC REGION -
  BIBLIOTHEQUE REGIONALE †
100 Blvd. Alexis-Nihon, 3rd Fl.   Phone: (514) 333-3020
St. Laurent, PQ H4M 2N8   Jacques Miron, Off.-in-Charge

CENTRE HOSPITALIER DE ST-LAURENT - BIBLIOTHEQUE †
1275 Chemin Cote Vertu   Phone: (514) 747-4771
St. Laurent, PQ H4L 4V2   Sr. Gemma Emond, Med.Libn.

COLLEGE DE MUSIQUE SAINTE-CROIX - BIBLIOTHEQUE
637 Sainte-Croix Blvd.   Phone: (514) 747-6521
St. Laurent, PQ H4L 3X7   Lucienne Nadeau, Dir.

SOCIETE NATIONALE DE DIFFUSION EDUCATIVE ET CULTURELLE -
  SERVICE D'INFORMATION SONDEC
8770 Langelier, Suite 230   Phone: (514) 324-4010
St. Leonard, PQ H1P 3E8   Micheline Lestage, Dir.

MC GILL UNIVERSITY - SUB-ARCTIC RESEARCH STATION LIBRARY
Box 790   Phone: (418) 585-2489
Schefferville, PQ G0G 2T0   Douglas R. Barr, Sta.Mgr.

DOMTAR, INC. - RESEARCH CENTRE LIBRARY
C.P. 300   Phone: (514) 457-6810
Senneville, PQ H9X 3L7   Barbara G. Bolton, Libn.

CENTRE HOSPITALIER HOTEL-DIEU DE SHERBROOKE - BIBLIOTHEQUE
580 S. Bowen St.   Phone: (819) 569-2551
Sherbrooke, PQ J1G 2E8   Louise Cadieux, Chf.Libn.

GRAND SEMINAIRE DES SAINTS APOTRES - BIBLIOTHEQUE
130 Cathedrale
C.P. 430   Phone: (819) 562-2440
Sherbrooke, PQ J1H 5K1   Raynald Provencher, Sec.

MONASTERE DES PERES REDEMPTORISTES - BIBLIOTHEQUE †
871 Rue Ontario   Phone: (819) 562-2677
Sherbrooke, PQ J1J 3S1   Laurent Tousegnant, Libn.

SOCIETE D'HISTOIRE DES CANTONS DE L'EST - BIBLIOTHEQUE
C.P. 2117   Phone: (819) 562-0616
Sherbrooke, PQ J1J 3Y1   Andree Desilets, Pres.

UNIVERSITE DE SHERBROOKE - FACULTE DE MEDECINE - BIBLIOTHEQUE
  DES SCIENCES DE LA SANTE
Centre Hospitalier Universitaire   Phone: (819) 565-2096
Sherbrooke, PQ J1H 5N4   Germain Chouinard, Dir.

Q.I.T. - FER ET TITANE INC. - BIBLIOTHEQUE
B.P. 560   Phone: (514) 742-6671
Sorel, PQ J3P 5P6   C. Stroemgren, Libn.

UNIVERSITE DE MONTREAL - MEDECINE VETERINAIRE-BIBLIOTHEQUE
C.P. 5000   Phone: (514) 773-8521
St-Hyacinthe, PQ J2S 7C6   Jean-Paul Jette, Dir.

HOPITAL DU HAUT-RICHELIEU - BIBLIOTHEQUE MEDICALE
920, boul. du Seminaire   Phone: (514) 348-6101
St-Jean, PQ J3A 1B7   Helene Heroux-Bouchard, Bibliotechnicienne

MISSISQUOI HISTORICAL SOCIETY - CORNELL MILL MUSEUM -
  REFERENCE LIBRARY & ARCHIVES
Box 186
Stanbridge East, PQ J0J 2H0   M. J. Cockerline Laduke, Archv.

ASBESTOS CORPORATION, LTD. - PRODUCT RESEARCH & DEVELOPMENT
  LIBRARY
835 Mooney St.
P.O. Box 9
Thetford Mines, PQ G6G 5S1

CEGEP DE TROIS-RIVIERES - BIBLIOTHEQUE
3500 De Courval   Phone: (819) 376-1721
Trois-Rivieres, PQ G9A 5E6   Denis Simard, Dir.

CENTRE HOSPITALIER COOKE - BIBLIOTHEQUE MEDICALE ET
    ADMINISTRATIVE †
3450 rue Ste-Marguerite   Phone: (819) 375-7713
Trois-Rivieres, PQ G8Z 1X3   Helene H. Bouchard, Bibliotechnicienne

CENTRE HOSPITALIER ST-JOSEPH - BIBLIOTHEQUE MEDICALE ET
    ADMINISTRATIVE
731 Rue Ste-Julie   Phone: (819) 379-8112
Trois-Rivieres, PQ G9A 1Y1   Solange De-Rouyn, Chf.

SEMINAIRE ST-JOSEPH - BIBLIOTHEQUE
858 Laviolette
C.P. 548   Phone: (819) 378-5167
Trois-Rivieres, PQ G9A 5J1   Claude Aubin, Dir.

SEMINAIRE DES TROIS RIVIERES - ARCHIVES *
858 Laviolette
C.P. 548
Trois-Rivieres, PQ G9A 5J1   Jules Bettez, Dir.

UNIVERSITE DU QUEBEC A TROIS-RIVIERES - CARTOTHEQUE
Pavillon Leon-Provancher
C.P. 500   Phone: (819) 376-5351
Trois-Rivieres, PQ G9A 5H7   Marie Lefebvre, Cartothecaire

HYDRO-QUEBEC - INSTITUT DE RECHERCHE - BIBLIOTHEQUE
1800, Montee Ste-Julie   Phone: (514) 652-8324
Varennes, PQ J0L 2P0   Louise Pelletier, Hd.

BELL-NORTHERN RESEARCH LTD. - TECHNICAL INFORMATION CENTRE
3 Place du Commerce   Phone: (514) 761-5831
Verdun, PQ H3E 1H6   Ghislaine Gauthier, Info.Spec.

CENTRE HOSPITALIER DE VERDUN - BIBLIOTHEQUE MEDICALE
4000 blvd. LaSalle   Phone: (514) 761-3551
Verdun, PQ H4G 2A3   Mrs. Andree N. Mandeville, Libn.

SASKATCHEWAN

BATTLEFORD NATIONAL HISTORIC PARK - CAMPBELL INNES MEMORIAL
    LIBRARY
Box 70   Phone: (306) 937-2621
Battleford, SK S0M 0E0   Mrs. M.A. Simpson, Supt.

ST. CHARLES SCHOLASTICATE - LIBRARY
Box 99   Phone: (306) 937-2355
Battleford, SK S0M 0E0   Ron Zimmer

BRIERCREST BIBLE COLLEGE - ARCHIBALD LIBRARY
                                           Phone: (306) 756-2321
Caronport, SK S0H 0S0   Allan R. Johnson, Lib.Dir.

PRAIRIE AGRICULTURAL MACHINERY INSTITUTE - LIBRARY
Box 1900   Phone: (306) 682-2555
Humboldt, SK S0K 2A0   Bernadette Jansen, Lib.Techn.

ALDERSGATE COLLEGE - WILSON MEMORIAL LIBRARY
Box 460   Phone: (306) 693-7773
Moose Jaw, SK S6H 4P1   Lillian Friesen, Dir., Lib.Serv.

MOOSE JAW LAW SOCIETY - LIBRARY *
Court House
64 Ominica St., W.   Phone: (306) 693-6105
Moose Jaw, SK S6H 4P1   Lola Sharp, Libn.

ST. PETER'S ABBEY & COLLEGE - LIBRARY
Box 10   Phone: (306) 682-5431
Muenster, SK S0K 2Y0   Andrew M. Britz, Libn.

SASKATCHEWAN HOSPITAL - DEPARTMENT OF PSYCHIATRIC SERVICES -
    STAFF LIBRARY
P.O. Box 39   Phone: (306) 445-9411
North Battleford, SK S9A 2X8   Doris Allan, Libn.

SASKATCHEWAN - DEPARTMENT OF PARKS AND RENEWABLE RESOURCES
    - FISH ENHANCEMENT DIVISION LIBRARY †
Government Bldg.
Prince Albert, SK S6V 1B5   Brian Christensen, Fisheries Geologist

SASKATCHEWAN - DEPARTMENT OF PARKS AND RENEWABLE RESOURCES
    - FORESTRY DIVISION LIBRARY
P.O. Box 3003   Phone: (306) 922-3133
Prince Albert, SK S6V 6G1   Janelle D. Johnston, Clerk

VICTORIA UNION HOSPITAL - MEDICAL LIBRARY
1200 24th St.   Phone: (306) 764-1551
Prince Albert, SK S6V 5T4   Joan I. Ryan, Med.Rec.Libn.

CAMPION COLLEGE - LIBRARY
University of Regina   Phone: (306) 586-4242
Regina, SK S4S 0A2   Myfanwy Truscott, Libn.

CANADA - AGRICULTURE CANADA - REGIONAL DEVELOPMENT BRANCH
    LIBRARY
101-2050 Cornwall St.   Phone: (306) 359-5545
Regina, SK S4P 2K5   S. Yanosik, Lib.Techn.

CANADA - AGRICULTURE CANADA - RESEARCH STATION, REGINA -
    LIBRARY
5000 Wascana Pkwy.
Box 440   Phone: (306) 585-0255
Regina, SK S4P 3A2   S. Yanosik, Lib.Techn.

CANADA - PRAIRIE FARM REHABILITATION ADMINISTRATION - LIBRARY
Motherwell Bldg.   Phone: (306) 359-5100
Regina, SK S4P 0R5   Charlene Kosack, Hd., Lib.Sect.

CANADA - STATISTICS CANADA - ADVISORY SERVICES - REGINA
    REFERENCE CENTRE
530 Midtown Centre   Phone: (306) 359-5405
Regina, SK S4P 2B6   D. Lawrance, Regional Adv.

CANADIAN BIBLE COLLEGE/CANADIAN THEOLOGICAL SEMINARY -
    ARCHIBALD FOUNDATION LIBRARY
4400 Fourth Ave.   Phone: (306) 545-1515
Regina, SK S4T 0H8   Marguerite E. Porter, Dir., Lib.Serv.

LAW SOCIETY OF SASKATCHEWAN - LIBRARY †
Woodbine Plaza, No. 201
2212 Scarth St.
Box 4320   Phone: (306) 569-8020
Regina, SK S4P 3W6   Douglass T. MacEllven, Dir.

MACKENZIE (Norman) ART GALLERY - RESOURCE CENTRE
University of Regina   Phone: (306) 584-4847
Regina, SK S4S 0A2   Patricia Roulston, Coord.

PASQUA HOSPITAL - HEALTH SCIENCES LIBRARY †
4101 Dewdney Ave.   Phone: (306) 527-9641
Regina, SK S4T 1A5   Leona Lang, Dir.

PLAINS HEALTH CENTRE - DR. W.A. RIDDELL HEALTH SCIENCES LIBRARY
4500 Wascana Pkwy.   Phone: (306) 584-6426
Regina, SK S4S 5W9   Beth Silzer, Dir.

REGINA CITY - PLANNING DEPARTMENT - LIBRARY
P.O. Box 1790   Phone: (306) 569-7533
Regina, SK S4P 3C8   Beth Wignall, Lib.Techn.

REGINA GENERAL HOSPITAL - HEALTH SCIENCES LIBRARY
1440 14th Ave.   Phone: (306) 359-4314
Regina, SK S4P 0W5   Mrs. A. Belva Park, Med.Libn.

ROYAL CANADIAN MOUNTED POLICE - CENTENNIAL MUSEUM LIBRARY
P.O. Box 6500   Phone: (306) 359-5837
Regina, SK S4P 3J7   Malcolm J.H. Wake, Musm.Dir.

SASKATCHEWAN ALCOHOLISM COMMISSION - LIBRARY
3475 Albert St.   Phone: (306) 565-4656
Regina, SK S4S 6X6   Karen P. King, Libn.

SASKATCHEWAN ARCHIVES BOARD
University of Regina   Phone: (306) 565-4068
Regina, SK S4S 0A2   Ian E. Wilson, Prov.Archv.

SASKATCHEWAN ARTS BOARD - LIBRARY
2550 Broad St.   Phone: (306) 565-4056
Regina, SK S4P 3V7

SASKATCHEWAN CANCER FOUNDATION - ALLAN BLAIR MEMORIAL CLINIC
  - LIBRARY
4101 Dewdney Ave.   Phone: (306) 359-2203
Regina, SK S4T 7T1   Barbara Karchewski, Libn.

SASKATCHEWAN - DEPARTMENT OF ADVANCED EDUCATION AND
  MANPOWER - WOMEN'S SERVICES - BRANCH RESOURCE CENTRE
1855 Victoria Ave.   Phone: (306) 565-2452
Regina, SK S4P 3V5   Betty Doucette, Educ.Ext.Coord.

SASKATCHEWAN - DEPARTMENT OF AGRICULTURE - LIBRARY
Walter Scott Bldg.
3085 Albert St.   Phone: (306) 565-5151
Regina, SK S4S 0B1   Helene Stewart, Libn.

SASKATCHEWAN - DEPARTMENT OF THE ATTORNEY GENERAL - COURT OF
  APPEAL LIBRARY
Court House, 2425 Victoria Ave.   Phone: (306) 565-5411
Regina, SK S4P 0S8   Shirley A. Hurnard, Libn.

SASKATCHEWAN - DEPARTMENT OF CONSUMER AND COMMERICAL
  AFFAIRS - CONSUMER INFORMATION CENTRE
1871 Smith St.   Phone: (306) 565-5549
Regina, SK S4P 3V7   Edith Berg, Coord.

SASKATCHEWAN - DEPARTMENT OF CO-OPERATION - LIBRARY
2055 Albert St.   Phone: (306) 565-5807
Regina, SK S4P 3V7   Rae French, Resource Ctr.Coord.

SASKATCHEWAN - DEPARTMENT OF EDUCATION - RESOURCE CENTRE
2220 College Ave.   Phone: (306) 565-5977
Regina, SK S4P 3V7   Jane Naisbitt, Libn.

SASKATCHEWAN - DEPARTMENT OF THE ENVIRONMENT - LIBRARY
5th Fl., 1855 Victoria Ave.   Phone: (306) 565-6125
Regina, SK S4P 3V5   Shannon G. Bellamy, Libn.

SASKATCHEWAN - DEPARTMENT OF HEALTH - LIBRARY
3475 Albert St.   Phone: (306) 565-3090
Regina, SK S4S 6X6   M. Smigarowski, Lib.Supv.

SASKATCHEWAN - DEPARTMENT OF HIGHWAYS AND TRANSPORTATION -
  PLANNING BRANCH LIBRARY
1855 Victoria Ave.   Phone: (306) 565-4777
Regina, SK S4P 3V5   Dr. M.U. Hassan, Libn.

SASKATCHEWAN - DEPARTMENT OF LABOUR - LIBRARY
1914 Hamilton St.   Phone: (306) 565-2429
Regina, SK S4P 4V4   Fraser Russell, Libn.

SASKATCHEWAN - DEPARTMENT OF LABOUR - OCCUPATIONAL HEALTH
  AND SAFETY DIVISION - LIBRARY
1150 Rose St.   Phone: (306) 565-4494
Regina, SK S4P 3V7   Susan Johnson, Libn.

SASKATCHEWAN - DEPARTMENT OF SOCIAL SERVICES - LIBRARY
1920 Broad St.   Phone: (306) 565-3605
Regina, SK S4P 3V6   Janice Szuch, Lib.Techn.

SASKATCHEWAN - DEPARTMENT OF SUPPLY & SERVICES -
  PHOTOGRAPHIC SERVICES AGENCY - LIBRARY †
Walter Scott Bldg., Rm. 306
3085 Albert St.   Phone: (306) 565-6298
Regina, SK S4S 0B1

SASKATCHEWAN - DEPARTMENT OF SUPPLY & SERVICES - SYSTEMS
  CENTRE LIBRARY
3rd Fl., T.C. Douglas Bldg.
3475 Albert St.   Phone: (306) 565-2090
Regina, SK S4S 6X6   Heather D. Henley, Lib.Techn.

SASKATCHEWAN - DEPARTMENT OF TOURISM & SMALL BUSINESS -
  BUSINESS INFORMATION CENTRE
Bank of Montreal Bldg., 4th Fl.
2103 11th Ave.   Phone: (306) 565-2254
Regina, SK S4P 3V7   Rochelle Smith, Coord.

SASKATCHEWAN - DEPARTMENT OF URBAN AFFAIRS - LIBRARY
2151 Scarth St.
Regina, SK S4P 3V7

SASKATCHEWAN GENEALOGICAL SOCIETY - LIBRARY
Box 1894
Regina, SK S4P 3E1   Laura M. Hanowski, Libn.

SASKATCHEWAN INDIAN FEDERATED COLLEGE - LIBRARY
University of Regina
C-4, Classroom Bldg.   Phone: (306) 584-8333
Regina, SK S4S 0A2   Heather West, Libn.

SASKATCHEWAN - LEGISLATIVE LIBRARY †
234 Legislative Bldg.   Phone: (306) 565-2277
Regina, SK S4S 0B3   Christine MacDonald, Legislative Libn.

SASKATCHEWAN MUSEUM OF NATURAL HISTORY - LIBRARY
Dept. of Culture and Recreation
Wascana Park   Phone: (306) 565-2808
Regina, SK S4P 3V7   Ruby Apperley, Supv., Museum Serv.

SASKATCHEWAN PIPING INDUSTRY JOINT TRAINING BOARD - LIBRARY
1366 Cornwall St.   Phone: (306) 522-4237
Regina, SK S4R 2H5   Darlene Pellerin

SASKATCHEWAN POWER CORPORATION - LIBRARY †
2025 Victoria Ave.   Phone: (306) 566-2697
Regina, SK S4P 0S1   H. Philley, Lib.Ck.

SASKATCHEWAN - PROVINCIAL LIBRARY
1352 Winnipeg St.   Phone: (306) 565-2972
Regina, SK S4P 3V7   Stan Skrzeszewski, Act.Prov.Libn.

SASKATCHEWAN TELECOMMUNICATIONS - CORPORATE LIBRARY
2121 Saskatchewan Dr., 2nd Fl.   Phone: (306) 347-2229
Regina, SK S4P 3Y2   Basil G. Pogue, Corp.Libn.

SASKATCHEWAN WHEAT POOL - REFERENCE LIBRARY
2625 Victoria Ave.   Phone: (306) 569-4480
Regina, SK S4T 7T9   A.D. McLeod, Res.Dir.

UNIVERSITY OF REGINA - BILINGUAL CENTRE - LIBRARY
College West No. 218   Phone: (306) 584-4177
Regina, SK S4S 0A2

UNIVERSITY OF REGINA - CANADIAN PLAINS RESEARCH CENTER
  INFORMATION SYSTEM
                                               Phone: (306) 584-4758
Regina, SK S4S 0A2   Carol MacDonald, Coord., Info.Serv.

UNIVERSITY OF REGINA - EDUCATION BRANCH LIBRARY
                                               Phone: (306) 584-4642
Regina, SK S4S 0A2   Del Affleck, Hd.

UNIVERSITY OF REGINA - MAP LIBRARY
                                               Phone: (306) 584-4401
Regina, SK S4S 0A2

WASCANA HOSPITAL - HEALTH SCIENCES LIBRARY
Ave. G & 23rd Ave.   Phone: (306) 359-9230
Regina, SK S4S 0A5   Darlene Jones, Dir.

WASCANA INSTITUTE OF APPLIED ARTS AND SCIENCES - RESOURCE &
  INFORMATION CENTRE
4635 Wascana Pkwy.
Box 556   Phone: (306) 565-4321
Regina, SK S4P 3A3   Pran Vohra, Supv./Chf.Libn.

CANADA - AGRICULTURE CANADA - RESEARCH STATION, SASKATOON -
  LIBRARY
107 Science Cresc.   Phone: (306) 343-8214
Saskatoon, SK S7N 0X2   Diana Kichuk, Libn.

CANADA - CANADIAN WILDLIFE SERVICE - PRAIRIE MIGRATORY BIRD
  RESEARCH CENTRE - LIBRARY
115 Perimeter Rd.   Phone: (306) 665-4087
Saskatoon, SK S7N 0X4   Colleen Haichert, Lib.Techn.

CANADA - NATIONAL FILM BOARD OF CANADA - FILM LIBRARY
424 21st St. E.   Phone: (306) 665-4246
Saskatoon, SK S7K 0C2   Cindy Ives Bigeau, Distribution Rep.

CANADA - NATIONAL RESEARCH COUNCIL - PLANT BIOTECHNOLOGY
   INSTITUTE - LIBRARY
110 Gymnasium Rd.   Phone: (306) 665-5256
Saskatoon, SK S7N 0W9   Flora Chen, Libn.

CO-OPERATIVE COLLEGE OF CANADA - LIBRARY SERVICES
141 105th St., W.   Phone: (306) 373-0474
Saskatoon, SK S7N 1N3   Leona Olson, Lib.Supv.

ELIASON (Frank) CENTRE - HEALTH SCIENCES LIBRARY
2003 Arlington Ave.   Phone: (306) 373-2151
Saskatoon, SK S7J 2H6   Kristine Wisser, Dir. of Med.Rec.

KELSEY INSTITUTE OF APPLIED ARTS AND SCIENCES - LEARNING
   RESOURCES CENTRE
Idylwyld Dr. & 33rd St. W.
P.O. Box 1520   Phone: (306) 664-6417
Saskatoon, SK S7K 3R5   D.F. Robertson, Dir.

LAW SOCIETY OF SASKATCHEWAN - BARRISTERS LIBRARY
Court House
520 Spadina Crescent, E.   Phone: (306) 664-5141
Saskatoon, SK S7K 3G7   Peta Bates, Libn.

MOHYLA INSTITUTE - LIBRARY AND ARCHIVES
1240 Temperance St.   Phone: (306) 653-1944
Saskatoon, SK S7N 0P1   Henry Leson, Rector

SASKATCHEWAN INDIAN CULTURAL COLLEGE - LIBRARY
Box 3085   Phone: (306) 244-1146
Saskatoon, SK S7K 3S9   David L. Sparvier, Coord./Libn.

SASKATCHEWAN RESEARCH COUNCIL - INFORMATION CENTRE
30 Campus Dr.   Phone: (306) 664-5488
Saskatoon, SK S7N 0X1   Margaret Samms, Info.Ctr.Mgr.

SASKATCHEWAN TEACHERS' FEDERATION - STEWART RESOURCES
   CENTRE
2317 Arlington Ave.
Box 1108   Phone: (306) 373-1660
Saskatoon, SK S7K 3N3   Ms. S.M. Dyer, Libn.

SASKATCHEWAN WESTERN DEVELOPMENT MUSEUM - GEORGE SHEPHERD
   LIBRARY
2935 Melville St.   Phone: (306) 934-1400
Saskatoon, SK S7K 3S5   Warren A. Clubb, Res.Coord.

SASKATOON CANCER CLINIC - LIBRARY
University Hospital   Phone: (306) 343-9565
Saskatoon, SK S7N 0X0   Mrs. A. Oatway, Libn.

SASKATOON GALLERY AND CONSERVATORY CORPORATION - MENDEL ART
   GALLERY - LIBRARY
950 Spadina Crescent E.
P.O. Box 569   Phone: (306) 664-9610
Saskatoon, SK S7K 3L6   Joan Steel, Libn.

SASKATOON PUBLIC LIBRARY - FINE AND PERFORMING ARTS
   DEPARTMENT
311 23rd St., E.   Phone: (306) 664-5579
Saskatoon, SK S7K 0J6   Frances Bergles, Dept.Hd.

SASKATOON STAR-PHOENIX - LIBRARY
204 5th Ave., N.   Phone: (306) 664-8223
Saskatoon, SK S7K 2P1   Lori Hoveland

UKRAINIAN MUSEUM OF CANADA - LIBRARY
910 Spadina Crescent, E.   Phone: (306) 244-3800
Saskatoon, SK S7K 3H5   Albert Kachkowski, Dir.

UNIVERSITY OF SASKATCHEWAN - EDUCATION BRANCH LIBRARY
         Phone: (306) 343-3793
Saskatoon, SK S7N 0W0   Margaret Baldock, Libn.

UNIVERSITY OF SASKATCHEWAN - ENGINEERING BRANCH LIBRARY
         Phone: (306) 343-2062
Saskatoon, SK S7N 0W0   David Salt, Engr. & Sci.Libn.

UNIVERSITY OF SASKATCHEWAN - GEOLOGY BRANCH LIBRARY
         Phone: (306) 343-4358
Saskatoon, SK S7N 0W0   Marilyn Lapp, Lib.Asst.

UNIVERSITY OF SASKATCHEWAN - HEALTH SCIENCES LIBRARY
         Phone: (306) 343-3168
Saskatoon, SK S7N 0W0   Dr. Wilma Sweaney, Libn.

UNIVERSITY OF SASKATCHEWAN - LAW LIBRARY
         Phone: (306) 343-4273
Saskatoon, SK S7N 0W0   E. Stanek, Law Libn.

UNIVERSITY OF SASKATCHEWAN - LUTHERAN THEOLOGICAL SEMINARY -
   OTTO OLSON MEMORIAL LIBRARY
114 Seminary Crescent   Phone: (306) 343-8204
Saskatoon, SK S7N 0X3   Mary Mitchell, Libn.

UNIVERSITY OF SASKATCHEWAN - PHYSICS BRANCH LIBRARY
         Phone: (306) 343-4934
Saskatoon, SK S7N 0W0   Lori Nizinkevitch, Lib.Asst.

UNIVERSITY OF SASKATCHEWAN - ST. ANDREW'S COLLEGE - LIBRARY
1121 College Dr.   Phone: (306) 343-6631
Saskatoon, SK S7N 0W3   Jo-Anne Coulic, Asst.Libn.

UNIVERSITY OF SASKATCHEWAN - ST. THOMAS MORE COLLEGE -
   SHANNON LIBRARY
1437 College Dr.   Phone: (306) 343-4561
Saskatoon, SK S7N 0W6   Dr. Margot King, Libn.

UNIVERSITY OF SASKATCHEWAN - SPECIAL COLLECTIONS - SHORTT
   LIBRARY OF CANADIANA
University Library   Phone: (306) 343-4514
Saskatoon, SK S7N 0W0   Shirley Perkins, Hd.

UNIVERSITY OF SASKATCHEWAN - THORVALDSON LIBRARY
Thorvaldson Bldg.   Phone: (306) 343-2956
Saskatoon, SK S7N 0W0   Connie Fendelet, Lib.Asst.

UNIVERSITY OF SASKATCHEWAN - WESTERN COLLEGE OF VETERINARY
   MEDICINE - LIBRARY
         Phone: (306) 343-3249
Saskatoon, SK S7N 0W0   John V. James, Libn.

CANADA - AGRICULTURE CANADA - RESEARCH STATION, SWIFT
   CURRENT - LIBRARY
Box 1030   Phone: (306) 773-4621
Swift Current, SK S9H 3X2   Karen E. Wilton, Libn.

PSYCHIATRIC CENTRE - STAFF LIBRARY
Box 1056   Phone: (306) 842-5461
Weyburn, SK S4H 2L4   Merle St. Onge, Ck. Stenographer II

SOURIS VALLEY REGIONAL CARE CENTER - MEDICAL & HEALTH SCIENCES
   LIBRARY
Box 2001   Phone: (306) 842-7481
Weyburn, SK S4H 2L7   Melva Cooke, Libn.

UNITED STATES SPACE EDUCATION ASSOCIATION - G.L. BORROWMAN
   ASTRONAUTICS LIBRARY
P.O. Box 1032
Weyburn, SK S4H 2L3   Gerald L. Borrowman, Chf.Libn.

NOTRE DAME COLLEGE - LANE HALL MEMORIAL LIBRARY - SPECIAL
   COLLECTIONS
Box 220   Phone: (306) 732-2080
Wilcox, SK S0G 5E0   Louis Stoeckle, College Sec.

YUKON TERRITORY

YUKON TERRITORY - DEPARTMENT OF TOURISM, RECREATION AND
   CULTURE - YUKON ARCHIVES
Box 2703   Phone: (403) 667-5321
Whitehorse, YT Y1A 2C6   Miriam McTiernan, Territorial Archv.

Section 2

PERSONNEL INDEX

PERSONNEL INDEX

This is an alphabetical arrangement by surname of professional librarians and information specialists employed by organizations listed in the Geographic Index and in Vol. 1.

A

Aaker, Ordelle, Libn.
AID ASSOCIATION FOR LUTHERANS - CORPORATE LIBRARY □ Appleton, WI

Aaron, Celeste M., Info.Sci.
MILES LABORATORIES, INC. - LIBRARY RESOURCES AND SERVICES □ Elkhart, IN

Aaronson, Janet, Music Cat.Libn.
RUTGERS UNIVERSITY, THE STATE UNIVERSITY OF NEW JERSEY - BLANCHE AND IRVING LAURIE MUSIC LIBRARY □ New Brunswick, NJ

Abatelli, Carol, Asst.Libn., Slides
COOPER UNION FOR THE ADVANCEMENT OF SCIENCE AND ART - LIBRARY □ New York, NY

Abazarnia, Diane B., Libn.
FOX, ROTHSCHILD, O'BRIEN AND FRANKEL - LIBRARY □ Philadelphia, PA

Abbasi, Sherie A., Law Libn.
U.S. FEDERAL HIGHWAY ADMINISTRATION - OFFICE OF THE CHIEF COUNSEL - LEGISLATIVE/REFERENCE LIBRARY □ Washington, DC

Abbe, Elizabeth, Libn.
CONNECTICUT HISTORICAL SOCIETY - LIBRARY □ Hartford, CT

Abbey, Eugenia H., Chf.Libn.
U.S. VETERANS ADMINISTRATION (GA-Atlanta) - HOSPITAL MEDICAL LIBRARY □ Decatur, GA

Abbey, Sue, Archv.
SHARLOT HALL/PRESCOTT HISTORICAL SOCIETIES - LIBRARY/ARCHIVES □ Prescott, AZ

Abbott, Bruce T., Lib.Coord.
CHARITY HOSPITAL - SCHOOL OF NURSING - LIBRARY □ New Orleans, LA

Abbott, George, Hd.
SYRACUSE UNIVERSITY - E.S. BIRD LIBRARY - MEDIA SERVICES DEPARTMENT □ Syracuse, NY

Abbott, Ilka, Libn.
REGISTERED NURSES' ASSOCIATION OF BRITISH COLUMBIA - LIBRARY □ Vancouver, BC

Abbott, John, Sci.Ref.Libn.
TEXAS A & M UNIVERSITY - REFERENCE DIVISION □ College Station, TX

Abbott, Lisa, Tech.Rpts.Libn.
TEXAS A & M UNIVERSITY - TECHNICAL REPORTS DEPARTMENT □ College Station, TX

Abbott, Sidney M., Cur.
ANCIENT AND HONORABLE ARTILLERY COMPANY OF MASSACHUSETTS - LIBRARY □ Boston, MA

Abbruzzese, Marie Grace, Libn.
SETON MEDICAL CENTER - LIBRARY □ Daly City, CA

Abdel-Malek, Laila, Cat.
MUSEUM OF FINE ARTS - WILLIAM MORRIS HUNT MEMORIAL LIBRARY □ Boston, MA

Abel, Blanche, Libn.
CARNEGIE LIBRARY OF PITTSBURGH - BUSINESS DIVISION □ Pittsburgh, PA

Abel, Marge, Asst.Dir.
WEST VIRGINIA UNIVERSITY - MEDICAL CENTER LIBRARY □ Morgantown, WV

Abell, J. Richard, Hd.
PUBLIC LIBRARY OF CINCINNATI AND HAMILTON COUNTY - HISTORY DEPARTMENT □ Cincinnati, OH

Abell, Joan, Chf., Pub. Inquiries Sect
U.S. PUBLIC HEALTH SERVICE - NATL. INSTITUTE OF MENTAL HEALTH - SCIENCE COMMUNICATION BRANCH - MENTAL HEALTH LIB. □ Rockville, MD

Abell, Millicent D., Univ.Libn.
UNIVERSITY OF CALIFORNIA, SAN DIEGO - UNIVERSITY LIBRARIES □ La Jolla, CA

Abelow, Ruth M., Libn.
TEMPLE EMANU-EL - LIBRARY □ Miami Beach, FL

Abelson, Rabbi Kassel, Supv.
BETH EL SYNAGOGUE - MAX SHAPIRO LIBRARY □ St. Louis Park, MN

Abend, Beth, Libn.
TIMEX GROUP, LTD. - LEGAL & CORPORATE LIBRARY □ Middlebury, CT

Abernathy, M.R., Mgr., Lib.
FOOTE MINERAL COMPANY - RESEARCH AND ENGINEERING DEPARTMENT LIBRARY □ Exton, PA

Abid, Ann B., Libn.
ST. LOUIS ART MUSEUM - RICHARDSON MEMORIAL LIBRARY □ St. Louis, MO

Ables, Linda, Libn.
OKLAHOMA REGIONAL LIBRARY FOR THE BLIND AND PHYSICALLY HANDICAPPED □ Oklahoma City, OK

Ablove, Gayle, Cat.
ROSWELL PARK MEMORIAL INSTITUTE - LIBRARY AND INFORMATION MANAGEMENT SERVICES □ Buffalo, NY

Abney, Ella, Libn.
MEDICAL SOCIETY OF THE STATE OF NEW YORK - ALBION O. BERNSTEIN LIBRARY □ Lake Success, NY

Abols, Edite, Law Cat.
CANADA - DEPARTMENT OF JUSTICE - LIBRARY □ Ottawa, ON

Abonyi, Malvina, Archv.
WAYNE STATE UNIVERSITY - ARCHIVES OF LABOR AND URBAN AFFAIRS/UNIVERSITY ARCHIVES □ Detroit, MI

Abraham, Lynn, Assoc.Libn.
SIMPSON, THACHER & BARTLETT - LIBRARY† □ New York, NY

Abraham, Mildred K., Libn., Rd.Serv.
UNIVERSITY OF VIRGINIA - LIBRARY - RARE BOOK DEPARTMENT □ Charlottesville, VA

Abrahamson, Edythe, Hd.
MINNEAPOLIS PUBLIC LIBRARY & INFORMATION CENTER - TECHNOLOGY AND SCIENCE DEPARTMENT □ Minneapolis, MN

Abram, Stephen K., Libn.
CURRIE, COOPERS & LYBRAND, LTD. - LIBRARY/INFORMATION CENTRE □ Toronto, ON

Abramowicz, Dina, Chf.Libn.
YIVO INSTITUTE FOR JEWISH RESEARCH - LIBRARY AND ARCHIVES □ New York, NY

Abrams, Douglas, Tech.Serv.Dir.
UTAH STATE LIBRARY □ Salt Lake City, UT

Abrams, F., Hd., Ref./Coll.Dev.
UNIVERSITY OF WATERLOO - ENGINEERING, MATHEMATICS & SCIENCE DIVISIONAL LIBRARY □ Waterloo, ON

Abrams, Jeanne, Archv.
ROCKY MOUNTAIN JEWISH HISTORICAL SOCIETY - IRA M. BECK MEMORIAL LIBRARY □ Denver, CO

Abrams, Leslie, Arch.Libn.
CLEMSON UNIVERSITY - EMERY A. GUNNIN ARCHITECTURAL LIBRARY □ Clemson, SC

Abrams, Marcia, Supv.
MARYLAND STATE POLICE ACADEMY -
LIBRARY □ Baltimore, MD

Abrams, Sandra, Libn.
SCHERER (R.P.) CORPORATION - LIBRARY □
Troy, MI

Abrenica, Neftalie, Info.Serv.
INCO LIMITED - BUSINESS LIBRARY □ Toronto,
ON

Abrenica, Neftalie, Libn.
INCO LIMITED - EXPLORATION LIBRARY □
Toronto, ON

Abshire, Eleanor, Libn.
U.S. BUREAU OF MINES - ALBANY TECHNICAL
LIBRARY □ Albany, OR

Abzinger, Ms. S., Libn.
ROYAL COLUMBIAN HOSPITAL - LIBRARY □
New Westminster, BC

Achenbach, Erna, Hd.Libn.
KROTONA INSTITUTE OF THEOSOPHY -
KROTONA LIBRARY - BETTY WARRINGTON
MEMORIAL† □ Ojai, CA

Acher, Stafford, Hist.
TEXACO INC. - ARCHIVES □ White Plains, NY

Ackerman, Sr. Colette, Libn.
CARMELITE MONASTERY - LIBRARY AND
ARCHIVES □ Baltimore, MD

Ackerman, Dorothy P., Per.
U.S. ARMY POST - FORT JACKSON - LIBRARY □
Ft. Jackson, SC

Ackerman, Ellen, Supv., Ref.Serv.
CONFERENCE BOARD, INC. - INFORMATION
SERVICE □ New York, NY

Ackerman, G. Franklin, Chf., Interp.
U.S. NATL. PARK SERVICE - CAPE COD NATL.
SEASHORE - LIBRARY □ South Wellfleet, MA

Ackerman, Pat M., Sect.Mgr.
MC DONNELL DOUGLAS CORPORATION -
DOUGLAS AIRCRAFT COMPANY - TECHNICAL
LIBRARY □ Long Beach, CA

Ackerson, Margaret, Hd., Tech.Info.Serv.
CREARE, INC. - LIBRARY □ Hanover, NH

Acosta, Trinidad B., Libn.
EL PASO HERALD-POST - LIBRARY □ El Paso, TX

Acre, Judi, Act.Libn.
DENVER POST - LIBRARY □ Denver, CO

Acton, Anne, Asst.Libn.
NEW ENGLAND SCHOOL OF LAW - LIBRARY† □
Boston, MA

Adach, Ms. S., Data Lib. Programmer
UNIVERSITY OF BRITISH COLUMBIA - DATA
LIBRARY □ Vancouver, BC

Adair, Galina V., Law Libn.
C.I.T. FINANCIAL CORPORATION - BUSINESS/
LEGAL INFORMATION CENTER □ Livingston, NJ

Adair, Kay, Libn.
ST. FRANCIS OF THE WOODS LTD. - EASTERN
ORTHODOX CATHOLIC CHURCH IN AMERICA -
LIBRARY □ Coyle, OK

Adair, Sunny, Libn.
ROCKY MOUNTAIN ENERGY - LIBRARY □
Broomfield, CO

Adam, Mrs., Asst. Genealogist
LEBANON COUNTY HISTORICAL SOCIETY -
LIBRARY □ Lebanon, PA

Adam, Mrs. Rohini, Pub.Serv.Libn.
MC GILL UNIVERSITY - PHYSICAL SCIENCES
AND ENGINEERING LIBRARY □ Montreal, PQ

Adamchak, Donald J., Dir.
KANSAS STATE UNIVERSITY - POPULATION
RESEARCH LABORATORY - LIBRARY □
Manhattan, KS

Adamo, Clare, Libn.
LIFE SAVERS, INC. - RESEARCH AND
DEVELOPMENT DIVISION - TECHNICAL
INFORMATION CENTER† □ Port Chester, NY

Adamo, Marilyn, Corp.Info.Spec.
CRAVATH, SWAINE, & MOORE - LAW LIBRARY
□ New York, NY

Adamo, Richard E., Law Libn.
ESSEX LAW LIBRARY □ Salem, MA

Adamovich, Shirley G., State Libn.
NEW HAMPSHIRE STATE LIBRARY □ Concord,
NH

Adamowicz, Joanne C., Libn.
ARTHUR D. LITTLE, INC. - BURLINGTON
LIBRARY □ Cambridge, MA

Adams, Agnes, Asst. Professor
UNIVERSITY OF NEBRASKA, LINCOLN -
GEOLOGY LIBRARY □ Lincoln, NE

Adams, Agnes, Asst. Professor
UNIVERSITY OF NEBRASKA, LINCOLN -
MATHEMATICS LIBRARY □ Lincoln, NE

Adams, Agnes, Asst. Professor
UNIVERSITY OF NEBRASKA, LINCOLN -
PHYSICS LIBRARY □ Lincoln, NE

Adams, Barbara M., Asst.Libn./Mss./Microfilm
DU PONT (Henry Francis) WINTERTHUR
MUSEUM - LIBRARY □ Winterthur, DE

Adams, Barbara S., Chf.Libn.
U.S. VETERANS ADMINISTRATION (WV-
Martinsburg) - CENTER MEDICAL LIBRARY □
Martinsburg, WV

Adams, Brenda, Assoc.Libn./Cat.
SYRACUSE UNIVERSITY - LAW LIBRARY □
Syracuse, NY

Adams, Carol C., Libn.
SOUTHEAST LOUISIANA HOSPITAL -
PROFESSIONAL LIBRARY □ Mandeville, LA

Adams, Cindy, Libn.
LONG & ALDRIDGE - LAW LIBRARY □ Atlanta,
GA

Adams, Dawn, Asst.Libn./Cat.
TOCCOA FALLS COLLEGE - SEBY JONES
LIBRARY □ Toccoa Falls, GA

Adams, Deborah L., Dir.
BOTSFORD GENERAL HOSPITAL, OSTEOPATHIC
- HOSPITAL LIBRARY AND MEDIA CENTER □
Farmington, MI

Adams, E.M., Jr., Dir.
EAST TEXAS BAPTIST UNIVERSITY - MAMYE
JARRETT LEARNING CENTER □ Marshall, TX

Adams, Eleanor, Sch.Libn.
SOUTH CHICAGO COMMUNITY HOSPITAL -
DEPARTMENT OF LIBRARY SERVICES □
Chicago, IL

Adams, Evelyn, Tech.Libn.
VENTURA COUNTY RESOURCE MANAGEMENT
AGENCY - TECHNICAL LIBRARY □ Ventura, CA

Adams, Geraldine, Acq.
OKLAHOMA STATE DEPARTMENT OF
LIBRARIES □ Oklahoma City, OK

Adams, J. Emily, Tech.Serv.Libn.
INTERCOLLEGIATE CENTER FOR NURSING
EDUCATION - LIBRARY □ Spokane, WA

Adams, Jacqueline, Hd., Acq.Sect.
NORTHWESTERN UNIVERSITY - HEALTH
SCIENCES LIBRARY† □ Chicago, IL

Adams, Joe A., Ph.D., Dir.
NATIONAL FOUNDATION OF FUNERAL SERVICE
- BERYL L. BOYER LIBRARY □ Evanston, IL

Adams, John, Univ. Photographer
UNIVERSITY OF NEW HAMPSHIRE -
DEPARTMENT OF MEDIA SERVICES - FILM
LIBRARY □ Durham, NH

Adams, John C., Mng.Ed.
RUTGERS UNIVERSITY, THE STATE
UNIVERSITY OF NEW JERSEY - GOTTSCHO
PACKAGING INFORMATION CENTER □
Piscataway, NJ

Adams, Katherine, Asst.Hd.Libn./Archv.
UNIVERSITY OF TEXAS, AUSTIN - EUGENE C.
BARKER TEXAS HISTORY CENTER □ Austin, TX

Adams, Larry, Cur.
EISENHOWER (Mamie Doud) BIRTHPLACE
FOUNDATION, INC. - MUSEUM & LIBRARY □
Boone, IA

Adams, Laura, Co-Libn.
OXFORD UNITED METHODIST CHURCH -
OSCAR G. COOK MEMORIAL LIBRARY □ Oxford,
MA

Adams, Liese, Doc.Libn.
KENT STATE UNIVERSITY - DOCUMENTS UNIT
□ Kent, OH

Adams, Louis M., Ref.Libn.
SETON HALL UNIVERSITY - SCHOOL OF LAW -
LAW LIBRARY □ Newark, NJ

Adams, Louise, Circuit-Rider Libn.
UNIVERSITY OF SOUTHERN CALIFORNIA -
HEALTH SCIENCES CAMPUS - NORRIS
MEDICAL LIBRARY □ Los Angeles, CA

Adams, Margaret B., Cur.
U.S. ARMY MUSEUM, PRESIDIO OF MONTEREY
- LIBRARY □ Monterey, CA

Adams, Marjorie, Archv.
BOSTON COLLEGE - SPECIAL COLLECTIONS
DEPARTMENT □ Chestnut Hill, MA

Adams, Mary D., Libn.
METROPOLITAN COUNCIL OF THE TWIN
CITIES AREA - LIBRARY □ St. Paul, MN

Adams, Mathilda, Responsable
CENTRE HOSPITALIER DE L'HOTEL-DIEU DE
GASPE - MEDICAL LIBRARY □ Havre de Gaspe,
PQ

Adams, Michiko K., Supv.
NEC AMERICA - SWITCHING SYSTEMS
DIVISON - TECHNICAL DOCUMENT CENTER □
Irving, TX

Adams, Patricia L., Off.Mgr.
MICHIGAN AUDUBON SOCIETY - EDITH
MUNGER LIBRARY □ Kalamazoo, MI

Adams, Patricia L., Sr.Ms.Spec.
WESTERN HISTORICAL MANUSCRIPT
COLLECTION/STATE HISTORICAL SOCIETY OF
MISSOURI MANUSCRIPTS JOINT COLL. □ St.
Louis, MO

Adams, Ruth C., Libn.
EASTER SEAL REHABILITATION CENTER OF
SOUTHWESTERN CONNECTICUT - FRANCIS M.
HARRISON MEMORIAL LIBRARY† □ Stamford,
CT

Adams, Sherry, Libn.
HOUSTON CHRONICLE - EDITORIAL LIBRARY □
Houston, TX

Adams, Tommy, Archv.Proc.
TENNESSEE STATE LIBRARY AND ARCHIVES -
ARCHIVES & MANUSCRIPTS SECTION □
Nashville, TN

Adams, Virginia, Info.Spec.
FIDELITY MANAGEMENT & RESEARCH
COMPANY - LIBRARY □ Boston, MA

Adams, Virginia, Off.Mgr., Pubn.
FUND FOR PEACE - CENTER FOR
INTERNATIONAL POLICY □ Washington, DC

Adams, Virginia M., Libn.
OLD DARTMOUTH HISTORICAL SOCIETY -
WHALING MUSEUM LIBRARY □ New Bedford,
MA

Adams-Malone, Bernadette, Asst.Libn.
ROCKEFELLER FOUNDATION - LIBRARY □ New
York, NY

Adamson, L. Kurt, Hd., Pub.Serv.
BOSTON UNIVERSITY - PAPPAS LAW LIBRARY
□ Boston, MA

Adamson, Martha C., Hd.Libn.
RAYTHEON COMPANY - RESEARCH DIVISION -
LIBRARY □ Lexington, MA

Addis, Louise, Assoc.Hd.Libn.
STANFORD LINEAR ACCELERATOR CENTER -
LIBRARY □ Stanford, CA

Addison, Barbara, Cat.
SWARTHMORE COLLEGE - FRIENDS
HISTORICAL LIBRARY - PEACE COLLECTION □
Swarthmore, PA

Addison, Marion, Libn.
METROPOLITAN TORONTO LIBRARY - HISTORY
DEPARTMENT □ Toronto, ON

Addy, Mary, Info.Spec.
TEXACO INC. - CORPORATE LIBRARY □ White
Plains, NY

Ade, Cheryl L., Asst.Libn./Tech.Serv.
NORTHEASTERN UNIVERSITY - LAW SCHOOL
LIBRARY □ Boston, MA

Adee, Bruce H., Dir.
UNIVERSITY OF WASHINGTON - FISHING
VESSEL SAFETY CENTER - LIBRARY □ Seattle,
WA

Adelberg, Greta, Pict.Libn.
EUROPEAN ART COLOR - PETER ADELBERG ARCHIVE □ New York, NY
Adelman, Jean S., Libn.
UNIVERSITY OF PENNSYLVANIA - MUSEUM LIBRARY □ Philadelphia, PA
Adelsperger, Robert, Hd., Spec.Coll./Archv.
UNIVERSITY OF ILLINOIS AT CHICAGO - HEALTH SCIENCES CENTER - LIBRARY OF THE HEALTH SCIENCES □ Chicago, IL
Adinolfi, Susan, Database Mgr.
MERRILL LYNCH WHITE WELD - CAPITAL MARKETS GROUP - LIBRARY† □ New York, NY
Adjaye, Dr. Joseph, Outreach Coord.
UNIVERSITY OF WISCONSIN, MADISON - AFRICAN STUDIES INSTRUCTIONAL MATERIALS CENTER† □ Madison, WI
Adkins, Julia, Libn.
UNION CARBIDE CORPORATION - ENGINEERING DEPARTMENT LIBRARY □ South Charleston, WV
Adkins, Rosemarie, Tech.Serv.Libn.
U.S. VETERANS ADMINISTRATION (KS-Topeka) - DR. KARL A. MENNINGER MEDICAL LIBRARY □ Topeka, KS
Adkinson, Dorothea P., Libn.
STANDARD REGISTER COMPANY - CORPORATE LIBRARY □ Dayton, OH
Adler, Betty J., Off.Mgr.
INSTITUTE OF INTERNAL AUDITORS, INC. - LIBRARY □ Altamonte Springs, FL
Adler, Estelle C., Mgr.
AMERICAN CAN COMPANY - BUSINESS INFORMATION CENTER □ Greenwich, CT
Adler, Naomi, Lib.Supv.
FIRST NATIONAL BANK OF CHICAGO - INFORMATION TECHNOLOGY LIBRARY □ Chicago, IL
Adler, Rebecca, Sr.Libn.
NEW YORK PUBLIC LIBRARY - MID-MANHATTAN LIBRARY - PROJECT ACCESS □ New York, NY
Adreani, Earl E., Dir.
BOSTON UNIVERSITY - KRASKER MEMORIAL FILM LIBRARY □ Boston, MA
Adrian-Neufeld, Audrey, Asst.Libn.
WINNIPEG BIBLE COLLEGE/WINNIPEG THEOLOGICAL SEMINARY - LIBRARY □ Otterburne, MB
Aducci, Patricia J., Tech.Libn.
COLT INDUSTRIES - CRUCIBLE RESEARCH CENTER - LIBRARY □ Pittsburgh, PA
Aeschliman, Jim, Libn.
ALLEN COUNTY PUBLIC LIBRARY - BUSINESS AND TECHNOLOGY DEPARTMENT □ Fort Wayne, IN
Affleck, Del, Hd.
UNIVERSITY OF REGINA - EDUCATION BRANCH LIBRARY □ Regina, SK
Afflerbach, Betty, Lib.Dir.
TEXAS MEDICAL ASSOCIATION - MEMORIAL LIBRARY □ Austin, TX
Affolter, Dr. James, Cur.
UNIVERSITY OF CALIFORNIA, BERKELEY - BOTANICAL GARDEN - LIBRARY □ Berkeley, CA
Africano, Theresa, Asst.Libn.
ST. AGNES MEDICAL CENTER - HEALTH SCIENCE LIBRARY □ Philadelphia, PA
Agajanian, A.H., Bibliog.
IBM CORPORATION - GENERAL TECHNOLOGY DIVISION - EAST FISHKILL FACILITY - LIBRARY □ Hopewell Junction, NY
Agar, Mrs. W.S., Hist.Stud.Libn.
INSTITUTE FOR ADVANCED STUDY - LIBRARIES □ Princeton, NJ
Ager, Susan F., Lib.Dir.
OAK TERRACE NURSING HOME - DPW LIBRARY □ Minnetonka, MN
Aggarwal, Narindar, Asst. Asian Libn.
UNIVERSITY OF ILLINOIS - ASIAN LIBRARY □ Urbana, IL

Aggarwal, Narindar K., Asst. Asian Libn.
UNIVERSITY OF ILLINOIS - ASIAN LIBRARY - SOUTH AND WEST ASIAN DIVISION □ Urbana, IL
Agnes, Mother, O.S.B., Libn.
ABBEY OF REGINA LAUDIS, ORDER OF ST. BENEDICT - LIBRARY □ Bethlehem, CT
Agnew, James C., Tech.Serv.
NEW ENGLAND HISTORIC GENEALOGICAL SOCIETY - LIBRARY □ Boston, MA
Agostino, Angela, Libn.
MC LEOD YOUNG WEIR LIMITED - INFORMATION CENTRE □ Toronto, ON
Agriesti, Kim, Res.Asst.
REYNOLDS (Russell) ASSOCIATES, INC. - LIBRARY □ Chicago, IL
Agriesti, Paul A., Dp. State Libn.
NEW MEXICO STATE LIBRARY □ Santa Fe, NM
Aguece, Debra, Ref.Libn.
NEW YORK PUBLIC LIBRARY - BELMONT REGIONAL LIBRARY - ENRICO FERMI CULTURAL CENTER □ Bronx, NY
Aguilar, Juan F., Dir.
DRAKE UNIVERSITY - LAW LIBRARY □ Des Moines, IA
Aguilar, Dr. William, Dir.
CENTRAL CONNECTICUT STATE UNIVERSITY - ELIHU BURRITT LIBRARY □ New Britain, CT
Aguirre, Anthony, Lib.Dir.
COLLEGE OF PHYSICIANS OF PHILADELPHIA - LIBRARY AND MEDICAL DOCUMENTATION SERVICE □ Philadelphia, PA
Aguirre, Margaret, Lib.Asst.
UNIVERSITY OF CALIFORNIA, IRVINE - BIOLOGICAL SCIENCES LIBRARY □ Irvine, CA
Agyeman, Akwasi, Adm.Libn.
HOWARD UNIVERSITY - SCHOOL OF LAW - ALLEN MERCER DANIEL LAW LIBRARY □ Washington, DC
Ahearn, Carolyn P., Libn.
SHAW, PITTMAN, POTTS & TROWBRIDGE - LIBRARY □ Washington, DC
Ahearn, Judith A., Asst.Libn.
SAGINAW NEWS - EDITORIAL LIBRARY □ Saginaw, MI
Ahearn, Marg, Chf., Ref.Serv.
CANADA - MORTGAGE AND HOUSING CORPORATION - CANADIAN HOUSING INFORMATION CENTRE □ Ottawa, ON
Ahern, Camille, Ref./Ser.
NEW HAMPSHIRE COLLEGE - SHAPIRO LIBRARY □ Manchester, NH
Ahern, Robin
ERNST & WHINNEY - INFORMATION CENTER □ New York, NY
Ahern, Dr. Wilbert H., Dir.
WEST CENTRAL MINNESOTA HISTORICAL CENTER - LIBRARY □ Morris, MN
Ahl, Ruth, District Libn.
WAUKESHA COUNTY TECHNICAL INSTITUTE - WCTI LIBRARY □ Pewaukee, WI
Ahlborn, Joy W., Libn.
WELD COUNTY DISTRICT COURT - LAW LIBRARY† □ Greeley, CO
Ahlers, Glen Peter, Asst.Libn.
WASHBURN UNIVERSITY OF TOPEKA - SCHOOL OF LAW LIBRARY □ Topeka, KS
Ahlin, Nancy, Libn.
ORLANDO MUNICIPAL REFERENCE LIBRARY □ Orlando, FL
Ahlquist, Bernice, Chm., Lib.Comm.
TRINITY PRESBYTERIAN CHURCH - NORMAN S. HJORTH MEMORIAL LIBRARY □ Cherry Hill, NJ
Ahlquist, Nancy, Search Anl./Libn.
WISCONSIN STATE DEPARTMENT OF PUBLIC INSTRUCTION - WISCONSIN DISSEMINATION PROGRAM (WDP) □ Madison, WI
Ahn, Herbert, Ref.Libn.
UNIVERSITY OF CALIFORNIA, IRVINE - BIOMEDICAL LIBRARY □ Irvine, CA
Ahnquist, Elwyn T., Pres.
AMERICAN RAILWAY CAR INSTITUTE - LIBRARY □ Chicago, IL

Ahrens, Kathleen M., Libn.
PRESBYTERIAN-UNIVERSITY OF PENNSYLVANIA MEDICAL CENTER - MARY ELLEN BROWN MEDICAL CENTER LIBRARY □ Philadelphia, PA
Aicher, Boniface, O.S.B., Libn.
WESTMINSTER ABBEY - LIBRARY □ Mission, BC
Aiches, Alan, Dir.
ST. JOHN'S MUSEUM OF ART, INC. - LIBRARY □ Wilmington, NC
Aiello, JoAnne, Mgr.
CONTRA COSTA CHILDREN'S COUNCIL - EAST BRANCH LIBRARY □ Pittsburg, CA
Aiken, Jean R., Info.Libn.
UNIVERSITY OF PITTSBURGH - HUMAN RELATIONS AREA FILES □ Pittsburgh, PA
Aiken, Linda S., Acq.Libn.
DALHOUSIE UNIVERSITY - LAW LIBRARY □ Halifax, NS
Aiken, Michael, Libn.
CONFEDERATION LIFE INSURANCE COMPANY - LIBRARY □ Atlanta, GA
Ailsen, Carl H., Act.Dir.
HOUSTON MUSEUM OF NATURAL SCIENCE - REFERENCE LIBRARY □ Houston, TX
Aimone, Alan C., Military Hist.Libn.
U.S. ARMY - MILITARY ACADEMY - LIBRARY □ West Point, NY
Ainsworth, Mary Lynn, Mgr., Tech.Info.Ctr.
PITNEY BOWES - TECHNICAL INFORMATION CENTER† □ Stamford, CT
Aitel, Grace, Libn.
U.S. DEFENSE COMMUNICATIONS AGENCY - TECHNICAL AND MANAGEMENT INFORMATION CENTER □ Washington, DC
Aitro, Vincent P., Tech.Proc.Anl.
U.S. FOREST SERV. - PACIFIC SOUTHWEST FOREST & RANGE EXPERIMENT STA. - WESTFORNET-BERKELEY SERV.CTR. □ Berkeley, CA
Ajemian, Mrs. P.A., Mgr.
OWENS-ILLINOIS - INFORMATION RESEARCH DEPARTMENT □ Toledo, OH
Akanful, John, Hd., Adm.Serv.
NORTH CAROLINA AGRICULTURAL & TECHNICAL STATE UNIVERSITY - F.D. BLUFORD LIBRARY □ Greensboro, NC
Akehurst, Mary, Libn.
CANADA - GEOLOGICAL SURVEY OF CANADA - CORDILLERAN GEOLOGY LIBRARY □ Vancouver, BC
Akey, Sharon, Sr.Libn.
CALIFORNIA STATE DEPARTMENT OF CORPORATIONS - LAW LIBRARY □ Los Angeles, CA
Akin, Donna, Lib.Tech.Asst.
SANTA CLARA COUNTY OFFICE OF EDUCATION - CENTRAL CALIFORNIA CENTER FOR EDUCATIONAL IMPROVEMENT - LIBRARY □ San Jose, CA
Akins, Diana, Search Anl.
U.S. AIR FORCE - AEROSPACE MEDICAL DIVISION - SCHOOL OF AEROSPACE MEDICINE - STRUGHOLD AEROMEDICAL LIBRARY □ Brooks AFB, TX
Akins, John, Ref.Libn.
ALASKA (State) COURT SYSTEM - ALASKA COURT LIBRARIES □ Anchorage, AK
Akiyama, Emi, Assoc.Libn.
CORNELL UNIVERSITY - MEDICAL COLLEGE - SAMUEL J. WOOD LIBRARY □ New York, NY
Akiyama, Wilfrid S., Med.Libn.
FULTON STATE HOSPITAL - PROFESSIONAL LIBRARY □ Fulton, MO
Alach, Anne, Libn.
HARVARD UNIVERSITY - SCHOOL OF MEDICINE - SCHERING FOUNDATION LIBRARY OF HEALTH CARE □ Boston, MA
Alan, Adrienne, Tech.Proc.
UNIVERSITY OF CALIFORNIA, LOS ANGELES - LAW LIBRARY □ Los Angeles, CA

Alarie, Maurice, Ref.
UNIVERSITY OF OTTAWA - VANIER SCIENCE & ENGINEERING LIBRARY □ Ottawa, ON

Albacete, M.J., Assoc.Dir.
CANTON ART INSTITUTE - PURDY MEMORIAL LIBRARY □ Canton, OH

Albala, Monica, Musm.Cur.
NASSAU COUNTY MUSEUM REFERENCE LIBRARY □ East Meadow, NY

Albee, Rev. Lowell, Jr., Libn.
LUTHERAN SCHOOL OF THEOLOGY AT CHICAGO - KRAUSS LIBRARY† □ Chicago, IL

Albee, Mary, Bus.Mgr.
YALE UNIVERSITY - OBSERVATORY LIBRARY □ New Haven, CT

Albersheim, Harriet, Libn.
U.S. FOOD & DRUG ADMINISTRATION - NATIONAL CENTER FOR DEVICES & RADIOLOGICAL HEALTH - LIBRARY □ Silver Spring, MD

Albert, Karen, Ref.Libn./Search Anl.
PHILADELPHIA COLLEGE OF PHARMACY AND SCIENCE - JOSEPH W. ENGLAND LIBRARY □ Philadelphia, PA

Albert, Margot, Sec.
SOCIETE D'ARCHEOLOGIE ET DE NUMISMATIQUE DE MONTREAL - BIBLIOTHEQUE† □ Montreal, PQ

Albertson, Mary A., Div.Libn.
E-SYSTEMS, INC. - MELPAR DIVISION - TECHNICAL LIBRARY □ Falls Church, VA

Albertus, Donna M., Mgr.
BROOKHAVEN NATIONAL LABORATORY - NUCLEAR SAFEGUARDS LIBRARY □ Upton, NY

Albrecht, Doris, Libn.
ANALYTICAL PSYCHOLOGY CLUB OF NEW YORK - KRISTINE MANN LIBRARY □ New York, NY

Albrecht, Jean, Libn.
UNIVERSITY OF MINNESOTA, ST. PAUL - FORESTRY LIBRARY □ St. Paul, MN

Albrecht, Starla, Asst.Libn.
PIGEON DISTRICT LIBRARY - SPECIAL COLLECTIONS □ Pigeon, MI

Albrich, Eve, Music/Art Libn.
QUEEN'S UNIVERSITY AT KINGSTON - ART LIBRARY □ Kingston, ON

Albrich, Eve, Music/Art Libn.
QUEEN'S UNIVERSITY AT KINGSTON - MUSIC LIBRARY □ Kingston, ON

Albright, Ernest, Info.Spec.
KERR-MC GEE CORPORATION - MC GEE LIBRARY □ Oklahoma City, OK

Albright, Jane, Ref.Libn.
CARSON-NEWMAN COLLEGE LIBRARY - SPECIAL COLLECTIONS □ Jefferson City, TN

Albright, Nancy, Genealogy Ref.Libn.
NORTH CAROLINA STATE DEPARTMENT OF CULTURAL RESOURCES - DIVISION OF THE STATE LIBRARY □ Raleigh, NC

Albright, Sue R., Lib.Supv.
IMED CORPORATION - LIBRARY □ San Diego, CA

Alburger, T.P., Acq.Libn.
ATOMIC ENERGY OF CANADA, LTD. - TECHNICAL INFORMATION BRANCH - MAIN LIBRARY □ Chalk River, ON

Alcid, Mr. Rene D., Corp.Libn.
BERNSTEIN (Sanford C.) & COMPANY, INC. - RESEARCH LIBRARY □ New York, NY

Alcorn, Cynthia, Hd., Coll.Dev.
EMERSON COLLEGE - LIBRARY □ Boston, MA

Alcorn, Marianne, Circ. & Ref.Libn.
ARIZONA STATE UNIVERSITY - COLLEGE OF LAW - LIBRARY □ Tempe, AZ

Alcorn, Maxine, Hd., Clayton Lib.
HOUSTON PUBLIC LIBRARY - CLAYTON LIBRARY - CENTER FOR GENEALOGICAL RESEARCH □ Houston, TX

Alcott, Colleen, Asst.Libn.
BECKMAN INSTRUMENTS, INC. - RESEARCH LIBRARY □ Fullerton, CA

Alcott, Marilynn, Supv. Radio Talking BkNet
MINNESOTA STATE SERVICES FOR THE BLIND AND VISUALLY HANDICAPPED - COMMUNICATION CENTER □ St. Paul, MN

Alday, Caroline, Libn.
NORTHEAST GEORGIA MEDICAL CENTER AND HALL SCHOOL OF NURSING/BRENAU COLLEGE - LIBRARY □ Gainesville, GA

Alden, Sondra, Musm.Dir.
MARTIN AND OSA JOHNSON SAFARI MUSEUM - STOTT EXPLORERS LIBRARY □ Chanute, KS

Alderman, Pamela, Chf.Med.Libn.
MOUNT SINAI MEDICAL CENTER OF CLEVELAND - GEORGE H. HAYS MEMORIAL LIBRARY □ Cleveland, OH

Alderman, Patricia L., Libn.
U.S. ARMY POST - FORT STORY - LIBRARY □ Ft. Story, VA

Alderman, Patricia L., Tech.Libn.
VSE CORPORATION - TECHNICAL LIBRARY† □ Chesapeake, VA

Alderson, Calvin, O.C., Dir.
CARMELITANA COLLECTION □ Washington, DC

Aldous, Mary, Libn.
U.S. NAVY - NAVAL HEALTH RESEARCH CENTER - WALTER L. WILKINS BIO-MEDICAL LIBRARY □ San Diego, CA

Aldred, Richard, Cat./Acq.Supv.
HAHNEMANN UNIVERSITY - WARREN H. FAKE LIBRARY† □ Philadelphia, PA

Aldrich, Hazel, Ck.
MARION COUNTY LAW LIBRARY □ Marion, OH

Aldrich, Linda, Ref.Libn.
WELLS FARGO BANK - LIBRARY 888 □ San Francisco, CA

Aldrich, Linda K., Archv.
LOS ALAMOS COUNTY HISTORICAL MUSEUM - ARCHIVES □ Los Alamos, NM

Aldrich, Mrs. Willie L., Hd.Libn.
HOOD THEOLOGICAL SEMINARY - LIVINGSTONE COLLEGE - LIBRARY □ Salisbury, NC

Aldridge, Joann, R.N., Libn.
NORCLIFF THAYER MFG. FACILITY, DIVISION OF REVLON, INC. - LIBRARY □ St. Louis, MO

Aldridge, Patricia M., Libn.
UNIVERSITY OF MICHIGAN - ENGLISH LANGUAGE INSTITUTE - LIBRARY □ Ann Arbor, MI

Alers-Quinones, Juana, Adm., Lib. & Archv.
GIRL SCOUTS OF THE USA - LIBRARY/ARCHIVES □ New York, NY

Alesse, Constance Ryan, Asst.Libn.
NEW YORK STATE LIBRARY - LAW/SOCIAL SCIENCE REFERENCE SERVICES □ Albany, NY

Alex, Joni M., Med.Libn.
ST. VINCENT HEALTH CENTER - HEALTH SCIENCE LIBRARY □ Erie, PA

Alexander, Barbara, Asst.Libn.
U.S. COURT OF APPEALS, 3RD CIRCUIT - PITTSBURGH BRANCH LIBRARY □ Pittsburgh, PA

Alexander, C.A., Tech.Info.Spec.
ATLANTIC-RICHFIELD COMPANY - INFORMATION RESEARCH CENTER □ Los Angeles, CA

Alexander, Carolyn, Act.Coord.
ST. LOUIS PUBLIC SCHOOLS - LIBRARY SERVICES CENTER □ St. Louis, MO

Alexander, Carolyn I., Chf.Libn.
U.S. ARMY COMBAT DEVELOPMENTS EXPERIMENTATION COMMAND - TECHNICAL INFORMATION CENTER† □ Ft. Ord, CA

Alexander, Colleen, Info.Spec.
GENERAL DYNAMICS CORPORATION - CONVAIR DIVISION - RESEARCH LIBRARY □ San Diego, CA

Alexander, Elizabeth, Libn.
UNIVERSITY OF FLORIDA - P.K. YONGE LIBRARY OF FLORIDA HISTORY □ Gainesville, FL

Alexander, Gary, Law Libn.
AMAX, INC. - LAW LIBRARY □ Golden, CO

Alexander, Georgia, Tech.Serv.Libn.
MILBANK, TWEED, HADLEY & MC CLOY - LIBRARY □ New York, NY

Alexander, Ginger, Libn.
WASHINGTON STATE ENERGY OFFICE - LIBRARY □ Olympia, WA

Alexander, Herbert E., Dir.
CITIZENS' RESEARCH FOUNDATION - LIBRARY □ Los Angeles, CA

Alexander, Jill M., Act.Dir., Tech.Serv.
FLORIDA INSTITUTE OF TECHNOLOGY - LIBRARY □ Melbourne, FL

Alexander, Joy, Cur.
UNIVERSITY OF MICHIGAN - HISTORY OF ART DEPARTMENT - COLLECTION OF SLIDES AND PHOTOGRAPHS □ Ann Arbor, MI

Alexander, Merle I., Med.Libn.
U.S. ARMY HOSPITALS - WILLIAM BEAUMONT ARMY MEDICAL CENTER - MEDICAL LIBRARY† □ El Paso, TX

Alexander, Rondal, Data Anl. Planner
GREENSBORO PLANNING & COMMUNITY DEVELOPMENT DEPARTMENT - LIBRARY □ Greensboro, NC

Alexander, Mr. S., Hd., Tech.Serv.
CANADA - GEOLOGICAL SURVEY OF CANADA - LIBRARY □ Ottawa, ON

Alexander, Sarah, Libn.
ATLANTA FULTON PUBLIC LIBRARY - SPECIAL COLLECTIONS DEPARTMENT □ Atlanta, GA

Alexander, Terri, AV
UNIVERSITY OF HEALTH SCIENCES - LIBRARY □ Kansas City, MO

Alexander, Thomas J., Hd.
UNIVERSITY OF CALIFORNIA, BERKELEY - PUBLIC HEALTH LIBRARY □ Berkeley, CA

Alexander, Vera, Archv.
LOUISIANA STATE OFFICE OF THE SECRETARY OF STATE - STATE ARCHIVES AND RECORDS SERVICE - ARCHIVES SECTION □ Baton Rouge, LA

Alexanian, Ann, Asst. to Mgr.
PRICE WATERHOUSE - NATIONAL INFORMATION CENTER □ New York, NY

Alexis, Donald G., Supv.Libn./Bus.Coll.
NEW YORK PUBLIC LIBRARY - MID-MANHATTAN LIBRARY - SCIENCE/BUSINESS DEPARTMENT □ New York, NY

Alfano, Dr. Blaise F., Hd.Libn.
AMERICAN SOCIETY OF ABDOMINAL SURGEONS - DONALD COLLINS MEMORIAL LIBRARY □ Melrose, MA

Alfonsi-Gini, Mary Ann, Libn.
MC BRIDE, BAKER, WIENKE - LAW LIBRARY† □ Chicago, IL

Alford, Carolyn S., Lib.Techn.
U.S. ARMS CONTROL AND DISARMAMENT AGENCY - LIBRARY □ Washington, DC

Alford, Marydel, Media Spec.
FLORIDA SCHOOL FOR THE DEAF AND BLIND - LIBRARY FOR THE DEAF □ St. Augustine, FL

Alfred, Judith, Lib.Serv.
U.S. VETERANS ADMINISTRATION (IN-Indianapolis) - MEDICAL CENTER LIBRARY □ Indianapolis, IN

Algermissen, Virginia L., Dir.
TEXAS A & M UNIVERSITY - MEDICAL SCIENCES LIBRARY □ College Station, TX

Algie, Carol, Libn.
EMBROIDERERS' GUILD OF AMERICA, INC. - LIBRARY □ New York, NY

Algier, Audrey, Dir., Staff Dev.
CRAIG DEVELOPMENTAL CENTER - MARGARET A. KENNGOTT MEMORIAL LIBRARY OF THE HEALTH SCIENCES □ Sonyea, NY

Algon, Jacqueline, Sr.Pubn.Coord.
MERCK & COMPANY, INC. - MERCK SHARP & DOHME RESEARCH LABORATORIES - RESEARCH INFORMATION SYSTEMS □ Rahway, NJ

Alig, Katharine, Sr.Info.Spec.
THE BOC GROUP INC. - TECHNICAL CENTER - INFORMATION CENTER □ Murray Hill, NJ

Alkes, Doris, Hd., Acq.Sect.
BROOKHAVEN NATIONAL LABORATORY - TECHNICAL INFORMATION DIVISION □ Upton, NY

Allain, Carmel, Cat.
UNIVERSITE DE MONCTON - BIBLIOTHEQUE DE DROIT □ Moncton, NB

Allamian, Barbara P., Supv.
A.G. BECKER PARIBAS, INC. - LIBRARY □ Chicago, IL

Allan, Doris, Libn.
SASKATCHEWAN HOSPITAL - DEPARTMENT OF PSYCHIATRIC SERVICES - STAFF LIBRARY □ North Battleford, SK

Allan, Ferne C., Supv., Lib.
LOCKHEED-CALIFORNIA COMPANY - TECHNICAL INFORMATION CENTER □ Burbank, CA

Allan, Michael F., Sr.Info.Spec.
UNION CARBIDE CORPORATION - BATTERY PRODUCTS DIVISION - TECHNICAL INFORMATION CENTER □ Westlake, OH

Allan, Philip B., Med.Libn.
CANADA - NATIONAL DEFENCE - NATIONAL DEFENCE MEDICAL CENTRE - MEDICAL LIBRARY □ Ottawa, ON

Allard, Dr. Dean C., Dir.
U.S. NAVY - NAVAL HISTORICAL CENTER - OPERATIONAL ARCHIVES □ Washington, DC

Allard, Francois, Ref. & Acq.Libn.
QUEBEC PROVINCE - MINISTERE DES AFFAIRES SOCIALES - SERVICE DE LA DOCUMENTATION □ Quebec, PQ

Allard, Serge, Dir.
COLLEGE DE L'ABITIBI-TEMISCAMINGUE - BIBLIOTHEQUE - SPECIAL COLLECTIONS □ Rouyn, PQ

Allard, Serge, Dir.
UNIVERSITE DU QUEBEC EN ABITIBI-TEMISCAMINGUE - BIBLIOTHEQUE □ Rouyn, PQ

Allbert, Portia, Lib.Dir.
KANSAS STATE HISTORICAL SOCIETY - LIBRARY □ Topeka, KS

Allcock, Harry M., V.P.
IFI/PLENUM DATA COMPANY - LIBRARY □ Alexandria, VA

Allen, Mrs. A. Foster, Libn.
LEHIGH COUNTY HISTORICAL SOCIETY - SCOTT ANDREW TREXLER II MEMORIAL LIBRARY □ Allentown, PA

Allen, Ann, Chm., Media Ctr.
FIRST BAPTIST CHURCH - MEDIA CENTER □ Brevard, NC

Allen, Barbara, Cat.Libn.
UNIVERSITY OF DENVER - COLLEGE OF LAW - WESTMINSTER LAW LIBRARY □ Denver, CO

Allen, Barbara A., Libn.
OLIN CORPORATION - BRASS GROUP LIBRARY† □ East Alton, IL

Allen, Beverly E., Dir.
MOREHOUSE SCHOOL OF MEDICINE - MULTI-MEDIA CENTER □ Atlanta, GA

Allen, Brenda Y., Mgr.
ENVIRONMENTAL RESEARCH & TECHNOLOGY, INC. - INFORMATION CENTER □ Concord, MA

Allen, Brian, Dir.
FAIRBANKS ENVIRONMENTAL CENTER - LIBRARY □ Fairbanks, AK

Allen, Bryce, Coll.Dev.Libn.
LAKEHEAD UNIVERSITY - CHANCELLOR PATERSON LIBRARY □ Thunder Bay, ON

Allen, David, Libn.
FALLSVIEW PSYCHIATRIC HOSPITAL - STAFF LIBRARY □ Cuyahoga Falls, OH

Allen, David, Libn.
SUNY AT STONY BROOK - ENVIRONMENTAL INFORMATION SERVICE □ Stony Brook, NY

Allen, Donna, Sec.
UNIVERSITY OF TORONTO - DEPARTMENT OF CHEMISTRY LIBRARY □ Toronto, ON

Allen, Dorothy, Marine Stud.Lib.Supv.
UNIVERSITY OF DELAWARE, NEWARK - COLLEGE OF MARINE STUDIES - MARINE STUDIES COMPLEX LIBRARY □ Lewes, DE

Allen, Doug, Circ.&Ser.
PARSONS SCHOOL OF DESIGN - OTIS ART INSTITUTE - LIBRARY □ Los Angeles, CA

Allen, Edna, Libn.
WARNER-LAMBERT CANADA INC. - LIBRARY† □ Scarborough, ON

Allen, Faith A., Asst.Libn.
KANSAS CITY TIMES-STAR - LIBRARY □ Kansas City, MO

Allen, Farrell J., Supv., Lib.Sys.
MONSANTO FIBERS & INTERMEDIATES COMPANY - TECHNICAL LIBRARY □ Pensacola, FL

Allen, Gordon, Tech.Info.Spec.
U.S. NATL. OCEANIC & ATMOSPHERIC ADMINISTRATION - NATL. OCEAN SERVICE - MAP LIBRARY □ Riverdale, MD

Allen, Helen M., Libn.
UNION CLUB - LIBRARY □ New York, NY

Allen, Jacquelyn, Cat.
TRINITY EVANGELICAL DIVINITY SCHOOL - ROLFING MEMORIAL LIBRARY □ Deerfield, IL

Allen, Jane D., Sr.Libn., Rd.Serv.
NEW YORK STATE DEPARTMENT OF HEALTH - CENTER FOR LABORATORIES AND RESEARCH LIBRARY □ Albany, NY

Allen, Joan, Cat.
OLD STURBRIDGE VILLAGE - RESEARCH LIBRARY □ Sturbridge, MA

Allen, Joe H., Dir.
WORLD DATA CENTER A - SOLAR-TERRESTRIAL PHYSICS □ Boulder, CO

Allen, Joyce S., Lib.Mgr.
METHODIST HOSPITAL OF INDIANA, INC. - LIBRARY SERVICES □ Indianapolis, IN

Allen, Kimberly M., Tech.Info.Spec.
NATL.INST. OF ENVIRONMENTAL HEALTH SCI. - NATL. TOXICOLOGY PROGRAM - ENVIRONMENTAL TERATOLOGY INFO.CTR. □ Research Triangle Park, NC

Allen, Louise M., Libn.
GREEN CLINIC - LIBRARY □ Ruston, LA

Allen, Luella, Hd., Media Rsrcs.Ctr.
SUNY AT BUFFALO - HEALTH SCIENCES LIBRARY □ Buffalo, NY

Allen, Marcia K., Libn.
CATHOLIC MEDICAL CENTER - HEALTH SCIENCE LIBRARY □ Manchester, NH

Allen, Margaret A., Libn.
ST. JOSEPH'S HOSPITAL - SCHOOL OF NURSING - LEARNING RESOURCE CENTER □ Marshfield, WI

Allen, Marjorie, Media Spec.
HUDSON VALLEY COMMUNITY COLLEGE - DWIGHT MARVIN LEARNING RESOURCES CENTER □ Troy, NY

Allen, Martha, Archv., Still Photographs
ALLEN (John E.), INC. - MOTION PICTURE ARCHIVES □ Park Ridge, NJ

Allen, Marti Harris, Dir., Lrng.Res.
FRIENDS UNIVERSITY - EDMUND STANLEY LIBRARY - SPECIAL COLLECTIONS □ Wichita, KS

Allen, Mary Lou
ST. LOUIS PUBLIC LIBRARY - POPULAR LIBRARY - MUSIC SECTION □ St. Louis, MO

Allen, Mary W., Libn.
WASHINGTON PSYCHOANALYTIC SOCIETY - ERNEST E. HADLEY MEMORIAL LIBRARY □ Washington, DC

Allen, Merle Buckley, Libn.
MISSISSIPPI STATE LAW LIBRARY □ Jackson, MS

Allen, Nancy, Libn.
UNIVERSITY OF ILLINOIS - COMMUNICATIONS LIBRARY □ Urbana, IL

Allen, Nancy S., Libn.
MUSEUM OF FINE ARTS - WILLIAM MORRIS HUNT MEMORIAL LIBRARY □ Boston, MA

Allen, Pam, Asst.Libn.
PENINSULA TIMES TRIBUNE - LIBRARY □ Palo Alto, CA

Allen, Pat, Instr.Techn.
BILLINGS PUBLIC SCHOOLS - INSTRUCTIONAL MATERIALS CENTER □ Billings, MT

Allen, Pauline B., Libn.
NEBRASKA PSYCHIATRIC INSTITUTE - LIBRARY □ Omaha, NE

Allen, Peggy G., Libn.
ABILENE STATE SCHOOL - SPECIAL LIBRARY □ Abilene, TX

Allen, Rachel M., Asst.Dir.
SMITHSONIAN INSTITUTION - NATIONAL MUSEUM OF AMERICAN ART - OFFICE OF VISUAL RSRCS. - SLIDE/PHOTOGRAPH ARCHIVE □ Washington, DC

Allen, Reginald, Cur., Gilbert & Sullivan
PIERPONT MORGAN LIBRARY □ New York, NY

Allen, Robert L., Dir.
PENNSYLVANIA STATE UNIVERSITY - AUDIOVISUAL SERVICES □ University Park, PA

Allen, Ruth, Libn.
CHURCH OF JESUS CHRIST OF LATTER-DAY SAINTS - EUREKA, CALIFORNIA STAKE BRANCH GENEALOGICAL LIBRARY □ Eureka, CA

Allen, Sarabeth, Div.Mgr.
DALLAS PUBLIC LIBRARY - BUSINESS AND TECHNOLOGY DIVISION □ Dallas, TX

Allen, Stephanie, Ref.Libn.
UNIVERSITY OF KENTUCKY - MEDICAL CENTER LIBRARY □ Lexington, KY

Allen, Susan, Ref.Libn.
THE CLAREMONT COLLEGES - ELLA STRONG DENISON LIBRARY □ Claremont, CA

Allen, Valentine, ILL
UNIVERSITY OF MEDICINE AND DENTISTRY OF NEW JERSEY AT NEWARK - GEORGE F. SMITH LIBRARY □ Newark, NJ

Allen, Virginia M., Ships Plans Libn.
MYSTIC SEAPORT, INC. - G.W. BLUNT WHITE LIBRARY □ Mystic, CT

Allender, Corliss H., Mgr.
ENVIRONMENTAL RESEARCH INSTITUTE OF MICHIGAN - ERIM INFORMATION CENTER □ Ann Arbor, MI

Allentuck, Sharon, Hosp.Libn.
MISERICORDIA GENERAL HOSPITAL - HOSPITAL LIBRARY □ Winnipeg, MB

Allerman, Geraldine, Dir., Staff Educ.
ST. LUKE'S HOSPITAL CENTER - NURSING LIBRARY □ New York, NY

Alleson, Jimmy, Libn.
BEXAR COUNTY LAW LIBRARY □ San Antonio, TX

Alley, Dorothy H., Lit.Chem.
HERCULES, INC. - AEROSPACE DIVISION - BACCHUS WORKS LIBRARY INFORMATION CENTER □ Magna, UT

Alley, Mark A., Instr. Media Spec.
ABRAHAM BALDWIN AGRICULTURAL COLLEGE - LIBRARY □ Tifton, GA

Allie, Stephen J., Archv.
WYANDOTTE COUNTY HISTORICAL SOCIETY AND MUSEUM - HARRY M. TROWBRIDGE RESEARCH LIBRARY □ Bonner Springs, KS

Alligood, Elaine C., Asst.Dir., Pub.Serv.
UNIVERSITY OF VIRGINIA - MEDICAL CENTER - CLAUDE MOORE HEALTH SCIENCES LIBRARY □ Charlottesville, VA

Allin, Janet, Hd.
YORK UNIVERSITY - MAP LIBRARY □ Downsview, ON

Allingham, Margot
BRITISH COLUMBIA INSTITUTE OF TECHNOLOGY - LIBRARY SERVICES DIVISION □ Burnaby, BC

Allinson, Sally G., Libn.
U.S. ARMED FORCES INSTITUTE OF PATHOLOGY - ASH LIBRARY† □ Washington, DC

Allison, Brent, Acq./Ref.Spec.
NEW YORK PUBLIC LIBRARY - MAP DIVISION □ New York, NY

Allison, Estaline, Dir.
HOBE SOUND BIBLE COLLEGE - LIBRARY □ Hobe Sound, FL

Allison, Jean A., Chm., Lib.Comm.
TRINITY UNITED CHURCH OF CHRIST - EDITH L. STOCK MEMORIAL LIBRARY □ St. Louis, MO

Allison, Peter B., Hd., Soc.Sci./Docs.
NEW YORK UNIVERSITY - UNITED NATIONS COLLECTION □ New York, NY

Allman, Miriam, Asst.Libn./Coll.Dev.& Mgt
HARVARD UNIVERSITY - SCHOOLS OF MEDICINE, DENTAL MED. & PUBLIC HEALTH, BOSTON MED.LIB. - FRANCIS A. COUNTWAY LIB. □ Boston, MA

Allman, Myron K., Circ.
U.S. ARMED FORCES RADIOBIOLOGY RESEARCH INSTITUTE (AFRRI) - LIBRARY SERVICES □ Bethesda, MD

Allnatt, Mark E., Cur./Mss.
FENTON HISTORICAL SOCIETY - LIBRARY □ Jamestown, NY

Allred, Carol B., Law Lib.Dir.
NORTHERN KENTUCKY UNIVERSITY - SALMON P. CHASE COLLEGE OF LAW - LIBRARY □ Highland Heights, KY

Allsop, Mary Beth, Asst.Libn.
JOHNSON CONTROLS, INC. - CORPORATE INFO. CTR./LIBRARY M47 □ Milwaukee, WI

Allyn, Judy L., Rd.Serv.
UNIVERSITY OF KANSAS MEDICAL CTR. - COLLEGE OF HEALTH SCI. AND HOSPITAL - ARCHIE R. DYKES LIB. OF THE HEALTH SCI. □ Kansas City, KS

Almagro, Bertha R., Asst.Libn./Proc.
UNIVERSITY OF ARIZONA - ARIZONA HEALTH SCIENCES CENTER LIBRARY □ Tucson, AZ

Almeida, Carlos, Dir.
U.P.E.C. CULTURAL CENTER - J.A. FREITAS LIBRARY □ San Leandro, CA

Almeida, Maria F., Supv.
U.P.E.C. CULTURAL CENTER - J.A. FREITAS LIBRARY □ San Leandro, CA

Almquist, Deborah T., Libn.
ST. ELIZABETH'S HOSPITAL - MEDICAL LIBRARY† □ Brighton, MA

Aloisa, Francine, Asst.Dir.
KENT MEMORIAL LIBRARY - HISTORICAL ROOM □ Suffield, CT

Alonzo, Anna M., Libn.
ARIZONA STATE OFFICE OF ECONOMIC PLANNING AND DEVELOPMENT - RESEARCH LIBRARY □ Phoenix, AZ

Aloyse, Sr. M. John, R.S.M., Rare Bk.Libn.
ST. CHARLES BORROMEO SEMINARY - RYAN MEMORIAL LIBRARY □ Philadelphia, PA

Alpert, Brian F., Mng.Ed.
KEYSTONE PRESS AGENCY, INC. - PICTURE LIBRARY □ New York, NY

Alpert, Carol, Media Libn.
NEW YORK UNIVERSITY - SCHOOL OF LAW LIBRARY □ New York, NY

Alpert, Diane, Cur./Adm.Off.
WESTERN KENTUCKY UNIVERSITY - DEPT. OF SPECIAL COLLECTIONS - KENTUCKY LIBRARY AND MUSEUM/UNIVERSITY ARCHIVES □ Bowling Green, KY

Alpert, Satoko, Photo Libn.
KEYSTONE PRESS AGENCY, INC. - PICTURE LIBRARY □ New York, NY

Alpert, Zalman, Libn.
COUNCIL OF JEWISH FEDERATIONS - LIBRARY† □ New York, NY

Alport, Claire, Lib.Chm.
TEMPLE JUDEA MIZPAH - LIBRARY □ Skokie, IL

Alsbach, George, Cat.
SOUTHWESTERN OKLAHOMA STATE UNIVERSITY - AL HARRIS LIBRARY □ Weatherford, OK

Alsbrooks, Helen, Asst.Libn.
FLORENCE-DARLINGTON TECHNICAL COLLEGE - LIBRARY □ Florence, SC

Alsobrook, Dr. David E., Supv.Archv.
U.S. PRESIDENTIAL LIBRARIES - CARTER PRESIDENTIAL MATERIALS PROJECT □ Atlanta, GA

Alsop, Rosemary, Asst.Libn.
NEW HARMONY WORKINGMEN'S INSTITUTE - LIBRARY AND MUSEUM □ New Harmony, IN

Alstad, Emily, Educ.Coord.
ALBERTA HEART FOUNDATION - LIBRARY† □ Calgary, AB

Alstadt, Nancy R., Libn.
MOBAY CHEMICAL CORPORATION - RESEARCH CENTER LIBRARY† □ Pittsburgh, PA

Alston, Mornee, Asst.Libn.
LEGAL AID SOCIETY - LIBRARIES □ New York, NY

Altberg, Rose, Chf.Libn.
U.S. VETERANS ADMINISTRATION (PA-Altoona) - JAMES E. VAN ZANDT MEDICAL CENTER LIBRARY □ Altoona, PA

Alten, Diana, Mss.Cat.
HAVERFORD COLLEGE - TREASURE ROOM AND QUAKER COLLECTION □ Haverford, PA

Altman, Burton, Assoc.Libn./Pepper Coll.
FLORIDA STATE UNIVERSITY - SPECIAL COLLECTIONS □ Tallahassee, FL

Altner, Patricia, Ref.Libn.
U.S. NATL. DEFENSE UNIVERSITY - LIBRARY □ Washington, DC

Altomara, Rita, Asst.Dir.
FORT LEE PUBLIC LIBRARY - SILENT FILM PHOTO COLLECTION □ Fort Lee, NJ

Altshiller, Donald, Asst.Libn.
AMERICAN JEWISH HISTORICAL SOCIETY - LIBRARY □ Waltham, MA

Alty, B.C., Asst.Sec. & Adm.Off.
ONTARIO - MUNICIPAL BOARD - LIBRARY □ Toronto, ON

Alusic, Milan, Sec.
INTERNATIONAL BANK NOTE SOCIETY - LIBRARY □ Racine, WI

Alvarado, Ruby G., Cat.
AMERICAN CHEMICAL SOCIETY, INC. - LIBRARY □ Washington, DC

Alvarez, Adoracion A., Curric.Dir.
OREGON STATE SCHOOL FOR THE DEAF - LIBRARY □ Salem, OR

Alvarez, Octavio, Libn.
U.S. SOCIAL SECURITY ADMINISTRATION - BRANCH LIBRARY □ Washington, DC

Alvarez, Octavio, Br.Libn.
U.S. SOCIAL SECURITY ADMINISTRATION - LIBRARY INFORMATION & GRAPHICS SERVICES BRANCH □ Baltimore, MD

Alvarez, Sonia, Info.Dir.
THIRD WORLD WOMEN'S EDUCATIONAL RESOURCES, INC. - THIRD WORLD WOMEN'S ARCHIVES □ Brooklyn, NY

Alves, C. Douglas, Jr., Dir.
WETHERSFIELD HISTORICAL SOCIETY - OLD ACADEMY MUSEUM LIBRARY □ Wethersfield, CT

Alyn, Janet, Educ.Coord.
PLANNED PARENTHOOD CENTER OF SAN ANTONIO - LIBRARY □ San Antonio, TX

Aman, Dr. Reinhold A., Pres.
MALEDICTA: INTERNATIONAL RESEARCH CENTER FOR VERBAL AGGRESSION, INC. - ARCHIVES □ Waukesha, WI

Amantia, Anne Marie B., Libn.
POPULATION CRISIS COMMITTEE/DRAPER FUND - LIBRARY □ Washington, DC

Amara, Margaret, Libn.
CENTER FOR ADVANCED STUDY IN THE BEHAVIORAL SCIENCES - LIBRARY □ Stanford, CA

Amaral, Anne, Info.Spec.
UNIVERSITY OF NEVADA, RENO - ENGINEERING LIBRARY □ Reno, NV

Amaral, Anne, Info.Spec.
UNIVERSITY OF NEVADA, RENO - LIFE AND HEALTH SCIENCES LIBRARY □ Reno, NV

Amaral, Anne, Info.Spec.
UNIVERSITY OF NEVADA, RENO - MACKAY SCHOOL OF MINES LIBRARY □ Reno, NV

Amaya, Rene, Spanish Lang.Libn.
BRAILLE INSTITUTE OF AMERICA - LIBRARY □ Los Angeles, CA

Ambrose, Frank, Info.Serv.Spec.
U.S. BUREAU OF THE CENSUS - INFORMATION SERVICES PROGRAM - CHARLOTTE REGIONAL OFFICE - LIBRARY □ Charlotte, NC

Ambrose, Karen, Lib.Cons.
ST. ANTHONY HOSPITAL - SPRAFKA MEMORIAL HEALTH SCIENCE LIBRARY □ Chicago, IL

Ambush, Gary D., Chf. of Doc. Control
DRAPER (Charles Stark) LABORATORY, INC. - TECHNICAL INFORMATION CENTER □ Cambridge, MA

Amdahl, Ruth, Libn.
PARK-NICOLLET MEDICAL FOUNDATION - ARNESON LIBRARY □ Minneapolis, MN

Amedeo, Donna, Dir. of Educ.
MADONNA PROFESSIONAL CARE CENTER - MEDICAL LIBRARY □ Lincoln, NE

Ameel, Henrietta
RILEY COUNTY HISTORICAL SOCIETY - SEATON MEMORIAL LIBRARY □ Manhattan, KS

Ames, Allathea, Libn.
GIUFFRE MEDICAL CENTER - LIBRARY □ Philadelphia, PA

Ames, Jan, Regional Libn.
SEATTLE PUBLIC LIBRARY - WASHINGTON LIBRARY FOR THE BLIND AND PHYSICALLY HANDICAPPED □ Seattle, WA

Ames, Kay L., Corp.Libn.
MICHIGAN CONSOLIDATED GAS COMPANY - CORPORATE LIBRARY □ Detroit, MI

Ames, L.A., Tech.Info.Spec.
U.S. DEFENSE TECHNICAL INFORMATION CENTER - DTIC ON-LINE SERVICE FACILITY □ Los Angeles, CA

Ames, Louise Bates, Ph.D.
GESELL INSTITUTE OF HUMAN DEVELOPMENT - LIBRARY □ New Haven, CT

Ames, Mary M., Asst.Libn.
HINCKLEY & ALLEN - LAW LIBRARY □ Providence, RI

Amese, Robert, Asst.Libn.
CANADA - TRANSPORT CANADA - TRAINING INSTITUTE - TECHNICAL INFORMATION CENTRE □ Cornwall, ON

Amirault, Mary Lou, Libn.
NATURE CENTER FOR ENVIRONMENTAL ACTIVITIES - REFERENCE LIBRARY □ Westport, CT

Ammer, William, Treas.
PICKAWAY COUNTY LAW LIBRARY† □ Circleville, OH

Ammons, Betty, Asst.Libn.
UNITED METHODIST HISTORICAL SOCIETY - BALTIMORE ANNUAL CONFERENCE - LOVELY LANE MUSEUM LIBRARY □ Baltimore, MD

Amnasan, Violet R., Libn.
GEAUGA COUNTY LAW LIBRARY □ Chardon, OH

Amon, Jane, Libn.
MORRISON & FOERSTER - BRANCH LAW LIBRARY □ Washington, DC

Amor, Badia, Libn.
MONTEREY INSTITUTE OF INTERNATIONAL STUDIES - LIBRARY □ Monterey, CA

Amott, Rowan J., Libn.
BLANEY, PASTERNAK, SMELA & WATSON - LAW LIBRARY □ Toronto, ON

Amrhein, John K., Univ.Libn.
KUTZTOWN UNIVERSITY - ROHRBACH LIBRARY □ Kutztown, PA

Amsler, Clifford, Jr., Dir.
U.S. NATL. ARCHIVES & RECORDS SERVICE - FEDERAL ARCHIVES AND RECORDS CENTER, REGION 1 □ Waltham, MA

Amtzis, Selma, Med.Libn.
SEA VIEW HOSPITAL AND HOME - MEDICAL LIBRARY □ Staten Island, NY

Amundson, Jean, Cat.
NAZARENE THEOLOGICAL SEMINARY -
WILLIAM BROADHURST LIBRARY □ Kansas City,
MO

An, Suei, Monograph Cat.
MAYO FOUNDATION - MAYO CLINIC LIBRARY □
Rochester, MN

Anaclerio, C.R., Chf., Info.Serv.Br.
U.S. ARMY - CHEMICAL RESEARCH &
DEVELOPMENT CENTER - INFORMATION
SERVICES BRANCH - TECHNICAL LIBRARY □
Aberdeen Proving Ground, MD

Ananda, Peter, Hd.
UNIVERSITY OF CALIFORNIA, BERKELEY -
SOUTH/SOUTHEAST ASIA LIBRARY SERVICE □
Berkeley, CA

Ancelet, Barry Jean
UNIVERSITY OF SOUTHWESTERN LOUISIANA -
CENTER FOR LOUISIANA STUDIES □ Lafayette,
LA

Andel, June, Ref.
MUHLENBERG COLLEGE - JOHN A.W. HAAS
LIBRARY □ Allentown, PA

Anders, Ora, Ref.
KENNEDY-KING COLLEGE - LIBRARY† □
Chicago, IL

Anders, Vicki, Hd., Bibliog.Instr.
TEXAS A & M UNIVERSITY - REFERENCE
DIVISION □ College Station, TX

Andersen, Jeffrey W., Dir.
LYME HISTORICAL SOCIETY, INC. - ARCHIVES
□ Old Lyme, CT

Andersen, Valerie, Doc.Libn.
NEVADA STATE LIBRARY □ Carson City, NV

Anderson, Alan B., Asst.Libn.
KING COUNTY LAW LIBRARY □ Seattle, WA

Anderson, Albert G., Jr., Hd.Libn.
WORCESTER POLYTECHNIC INSTITUTE -
GEORGE C. GORDON LIBRARY □ Worcester, MA

Anderson, Anita, Chf., Ref.Dept.
ILLINOIS INSTITUTE OF TECHNOLOGY -
INFORMATION AND LIBRARY RESOURCES
CENTER† □ Chicago, IL

Anderson, Anita, Libn.
MINNESOTA STATE ATTORNEY GENERAL -
LAW LIBRARY □ St. Paul, MN

Anderson, Anna Mary, Pres./Cur.
MARISKA ALDRICH MEMORIAL FOUNDATION,
INC. - ALDRICH LIBRARY OF MUSIC □
Wrightwood, CA

Anderson, Barbara, Mgr., Customer Serv.
DIALOG INFORMATION SERVICES, INC. □ Palo
Alto, CA

Anderson, Beryl L., Chf.
NATIONAL LIBRARY OF CANADA - LIBRARY
DOCUMENTATION CENTRE □ Ottawa, ON

Anderson, Betty
KENOSHA ACHIEVEMENT CENTER - LIBRARY □
Kenosha, WI

Anderson, Bruce, AV Prod.
ANOKA AREA VOCATIONAL TECHNICAL
INSTITUTE - MEDIA CENTER □ Anoka, MN

Anderson, Christine, Chf., Med.Res.Lib.
U.S. VETERANS ADMINISTRATION (CA-Los
Angeles) - MEDICAL RESEARCH LIBRARY □ Los
Angeles, CA

Anderson, Connie, Ref.Libn.
BA INVESTMENT MANAGEMENT
CORPORATION - LIBRARY □ San Francisco, CA

Anderson, David C., Tech.Serv.Libn.
UNIVERSITY OF CALIFORNIA, DAVIS - HEALTH
SCIENCES LIBRARY □ Davis, CA

Anderson, David N., Exec.Dir.
GEOTHERMAL RESOURCES COUNCIL - LIBRARY
□ Davis, CA

Anderson, Debbie, Res./Writer
SEA WORLD, INC. - LIBRARY □ San Diego, CA

Anderson, Delburna, Tech.Info.Spec.
U.S. CENTERS FOR DISEASE CONTROL -
CHAMBLEE FACILITY LIBRARY □ Atlanta, GA

Anderson, Dixie, Ref.
ALBERTA - DEPARTMENT OF EDUCATION -
LIBRARY SERVICES □ Edmonton, AB

Anderson, E. Sue, Libn.
U.S.D.A. - AGRICULTURAL RESEARCH SERVICE
- SOUTHWEST RANGELAND WATERSHED
RESEARCH CENTER □ Tucson, AZ

Anderson, Fiona, Libn.
FARRIS, VAUGHAN, WILLS & MURPHY -
LIBRARY □ Vancouver, BC

Anderson, Frank J., Libn.
WOFFORD COLLEGE - SANDOR TESZLER
LIBRARY - LITTLEJOHN RARE BOOK ROOM □
Spartanburg, SC

Anderson, Fred, Exec.Dir.
VIRGINIA BAPTIST HISTORICAL SOCIETY -
LIBRARY □ Richmond, VA

Anderson, Gail C., Search Anl.
MEDICAL COLLEGE OF GEORGIA - LIBRARY □
Augusta, GA

Anderson, Gerald R., Local Hist.Libn.
OAK LAWN PUBLIC LIBRARY - LOCAL HISTORY
ROOM □ Oak Lawn, IL

Anderson, Glenda E., Res.Libn.
SAVANNAH (City) - MUNICIPAL RESEARCH
LIBRARY† □ Savannah, GA

Anderson, Glenda E., Res.Libn.
SAVANNAH (City) - POLICE DEPARTMENT -
LIBRARY† □ Savannah, GA

Anderson, Grace, Libn.
SPARKS REGIONAL MEDICAL CENTER -
REGIONAL HEALTH SCIENCES LIBRARY □ Fort
Smith, AR

Anderson, James C., Cur.
UNIVERSITY OF LOUISVILLE - PHOTOGRAPHIC
ARCHIVES □ Louisville, KY

Anderson, James J., Chf.Interp. & Rsrcs.Mgt.
U.S. NATL. PARK SERVICE - KINGS MOUNTAIN
NATL. MILITARY PARK - LIBRARY □ Kings
Mountain, NC

Anderson, Jan B., Mgr.
CITE RESOURCE CENTER □ Austin, TX

Anderson, Janet, Med.Rec.Adm.
DIVINE PROVIDENCE HOSPITAL - MEDICAL
LIBRARY □ Williamsport, PA

Anderson, Janice, Asst.Libn.Tech.Serv.
GEORGETOWN UNIVERSITY - FRED O. DENNIS
LAW LIBRARY □ Washington, DC

Anderson, Jean C., Chf.Libn.
SWEDISH HOSPITAL MEDICAL CENTER -
REFERENCE LIBRARY □ Seattle, WA

Anderson, Jennifer, Chf.Libn.
CALGARY SUN - LIBRARY □ Calgary, AB

Anderson, Joan, Cat./Music Libn.
CALIFORNIA INSTITUTE OF THE ARTS -
LIBRARY □ Valencia, CA

Anderson, Joan, Libn.
CARNEGIE LIBRARY OF PITTSBURGH -
SCIENCE AND TECHNOLOGY DEPARTMENT □
Pittsburgh, PA

Anderson, Joanne, Sr.Libn.
SAN DIEGO PUBLIC LIBRARY - SCIENCE &
INDUSTRY SECTION □ San Diego, CA

Anderson, Jody, Libn.
ST. PATRICK HOSPITAL - LIBRARY □ Missoula,
MT

Anderson, Joseph J., State Libn.
NEVADA STATE LIBRARY □ Carson City, NV

Anderson, Judith P., Br.Mgr.
FAIRFAX COUNTY PUBLIC LIBRARY - FAIRFAX
CITY REGIONAL LIBRARY - BUSINESS
SPECIALTY □ Fairfax, VA

Anderson, K.E., Mgr. of Engr.
MOBIL PIPE LINE COMPANY - ENGINEERING
LIBRARY □ Dallas, TX

Anderson, Karen, Hd.Libn.
AUSTIN AMERICAN STATESMAN - LIBRARY □
Austin, TX

Anderson, Karen, Tech.Libn.
RMS - VS PROGRAM LIBRARY □ Trevose, PA

Anderson, LeMoyne W., Dir. of Lib.
COLORADO STATE UNIVERSITY - WILLIAM E.
MORGAN LIBRARY □ Fort Collins, CO

Anderson, Mrs. M., Libn.
CANADA - NATIONAL MUSEUMS OF CANADA -
CANADIAN CONSERVATION INSTITUTE
LIBRARY □ Ottawa, ON

Anderson, M. Sharon, Doc.Dept.Libn.
UNIVERSITY OF CALIFORNIA, SAN DIEGO -
UNIVERSITY LIBRARIES □ La Jolla, CA

Anderson, Madeline, Ref.Libn.
BOULDER PUBLIC LIBRARY - CARNEGIE
BRANCH LIBRARY FOR LOCAL HISTORY □
Boulder, CO

Anderson, Marcia, Lib.Techn.
MINNESOTA STATE PLANNING AGENCY -
CRIMINAL JUSTICE PROGRAM - LIBRARY □ St.
Paul, MN

Anderson, Marcia, Extramural Coord.
OHIO STATE UNIVERSITY - HEALTH SCIENCES
LIBRARY □ Columbus, OH

Anderson, Margaret, Libn.
SUN EXPLORATION & PRODUCTION COMPANY -
INFORMATION RESOURCES CENTER □
Richardson, TX

Anderson, Margaret J., Hd.Libn.
AUGSBURG COLLEGE - GEORGE SVERDRUP
LIBRARY AND MEDIA CENTER □ Minneapolis,
MN

Anderson, Margaret R., Mgr.
R & D ASSOCIATES - TECHNICAL
INFORMATION SERVICES □ Marina Del Rey, CA

Anderson, Marilynn R., Libn.
HAMILTON ASSOCIATES, INC. - LIBRARY □
Minneapolis, MN

Anderson, Marvin Roger, State Law Libn.
MINNESOTA STATE LAW LIBRARY □ St. Paul,
MN

Anderson, Mary Elizabeth, Libn.
U.S. NASA - HEADQUARTERS LIBRARY □
Washington, DC

Anderson, Mary G., Div.Libn.
U.S. ARMY - CORPS OF ENGINEERS - SOUTH
PACIFIC DIVISION - LIBRARY □ San Francisco,
CA

Anderson, Michael, Chf., Archv.Br.
U.S. NATL. ARCHIVES & RECORDS SERVICE -
FEDERAL ARCHIVES AND RECORDS CENTER,
REGION 9 □ San Bruno, CA

Anderson, Nancy, Dir., Med.Rec.
MEMORIAL HOSPITAL - MEDICAL LIBRARY □
Lufkin, TX

Anderson, Nancy D., Libn.
UNIVERSITY OF ILLINOIS - MATHEMATICS
LIBRARY □ Urbana, IL

Anderson, Norman E., Assoc.Libn.
GORDON-CONWELL THEOLOGICAL SEMINARY -
GODDARD LIBRARY □ South Hamilton, MA

Anderson, Orvis, Cur.
MERCER COUNTY HISTORICAL SOCIETY -
LIBRARY AND ARCHIVES □ Mercer, PA

Anderson, Paul, Archv.
WASHINGTON UNIVERSITY - SCHOOL OF
MEDICINE LIBRARY □ St. Louis, MO

Anderson, Phyllis P., Libn.
MC KEAN COUNTY LAW LIBRARY □ Smethport,
PA

Anderson, R. Joseph, Lib.Dir.
BALCH INSTITUTE FOR ETHNIC STUDIES -
LIBRARY □ Philadelphia, PA

Anderson, Dr. Ric, Chm./Chf.Exec.Off.
MARISKA ALDRICH MEMORIAL FOUNDATION,
INC. - ALDRICH LIBRARY OF MUSIC □
Wrightwood, CA

Anderson, Ron, Field Serv.Libn./AV
SOUTH CAROLINA STATE LIBRARY □ Columbia,
SC

Anderson, Ross, Libn.
METROPOLITAN TORONTO LIBRARY - SOCIAL
SCIENCES DEPARTMENT □ Toronto, ON

Anderson, S., Libn.
RAYTHEON COMPANY - ELECTROMAGNETIC
SYSTEMS DIVISION - ENGINEERING LIBRARY □
Goleta, CA

Anderson, Sandra C., Tech.Libn.
UNION CARBIDE CORPORATION - LINDE
DIVISION - TECHNICAL LIBRARY □ Tonawanda,
NY

Anderson, Sarah, Libn.
NORTHROP CORPORATION - VENTURA
DIVISION - TECHNICAL INFORMATION
CENTER □ Newbury Park, CA

Anderson, Sharon, Ref.Libn.
DICKINSON SCHOOL OF LAW - SHEELY-LEE
LAW LIBRARY □ Carlisle, PA

Anderson, Sherrie, Corp.Libn.
GERBER PRODUCTS COMPANY - CORPORATE
LIBRARY □ Fremont, MI

Anderson, Sherry, Assoc.Dir.
WAKE FOREST UNIVERSITY - BOWMAN GRAY
SCHOOL OF MEDICINE - COY C. CARPENTER
LIBRARY □ Winston-Salem, NC

Anderson, Stuart H., Libn.
NEW JERSEY STATE DEPARTMENT OF LABOR -
LIBRARY □ Trenton, NJ

Anderson, Sue, Libn.
ONTARIO HYDRO - LIBRARY □ Toronto, ON

Anderson, Susan, Assoc.Libn.
COLUMBIA HOSPITAL - MEDICAL LIBRARY □
Milwaukee, WI

Anderson, Susan, Ref.Libn.
GEORGETOWN UNIVERSITY - MEDICAL
CENTER - DAHLGREN MEMORIAL LIBRARY □
Washington, DC

Anderson, Susan, Libn.
NORCEN ENERGY RESOURCES LIMITED -
LIBRARY □ Calgary, AB

Anderson, T.J.B., Chf.Libn.
ONTARIO - MINISTRY OF CORRECTIONAL
SERVICES - LIBRARY SERVICES □ Toronto, ON

Anderson, Teresa J., Libn.
UNIVERSITY OF WISCONSIN, MADISON - LAND
TENURE CENTER - LIBRARY □ Madison, WI

Anderson, Thomas E., Asst.Libn.
SAN DIEGO COUNTY LAW LIBRARY □ San Diego,
CA

Anderson, Vicki, Libn.
NCR CORPORATION - TECHNICAL LIBRARY □
Dayton, OH

Anderson, Virginia, Asst.Libn.
INDIANA STATE UNIVERSITY - TEACHING
MATERIALS AND SPECIAL SERVICES DIVISION
□ Terre Haute, IN

Anderson, Virginia N., Libn.
CALIFORNIA INSTITUTE OF TECHNOLOGY -
AERONAUTICS LIBRARY □ Pasadena, CA

Anderson, William, Libn.
WALDO COUNTY LAW LIBRARY □ Belfast, ME

Anderson, Yeatman, III, Cur.
PUBLIC LIBRARY OF CINCINNATI AND
HAMILTON COUNTY - DEPARTMENT OF RARE
BOOKS & SPECIAL COLLECTIONS □ Cincinnati,
OH

Andersson, Liselotte, Libn.
TULANE UNIVERSITY OF LOUISIANA -
MAXWELL MUSIC LIBRARY □ New Orleans, LA

Anderton, Lois, Libn./Archv.
BOULDER PUBLIC LIBRARY - CARNEGIE
BRANCH LIBRARY FOR LOCAL HISTORY □
Boulder, CO

Ando, Esther, Supv. of Lib.
SHELL DEVELOPMENT COMPANY -
WESTHOLLOW RESEARCH CENTER LIBRARY† □
Houston, TX

Andre-Angers, Francine, Bibliotechnicienne
QUEBEC PROVINCE - CENTRALE DES
BIBLIOTHEQUES - CENTRE DOCUMENTAIRE □
Montreal, PQ

Andres, Gerry, Support Staff
LOS ANGELES COUNTY SUPERINTENDENT OF
SCHOOLS - SOUTHERN CALIFORNIA CENTER
FOR EDUCATIONAL IMPROVEMENT □ Downey,
CA

Andresen, LTC Martin W., Chf., Oral Hist.Br.
U.S. ARMY MILITARY HISTORY INSTITUTE □
Carlisle Barracks, PA

Andress, Loretta, Libn. I
UNIVERSITY OF ALASKA, ANCHORAGE -
ALASKA HEALTH SCIENCES LIBRARY □
Anchorage, AK

Andrew, Gloria T., Mgr.
CONTROL DATA CORPORATION - CORPORATE
LIBRARY □ Minneapolis, MN

Andrews, Claire, Doc./Bibliog.Instr.Libn.
KUTZTOWN UNIVERSITY - ROHRBACH
LIBRARY □ Kutztown, PA

Andrews, Elizabeth, Asst.Libn.
NEW ENGLAND COLLEGE OF OPTOMETRY -
LIBRARY □ Boston, MA

Andrews, Helen, Libn.
ERIE COUNTY HISTORICAL SOCIETY □ Erie, PA

Andrews, James C., Dir. of Lib.
RENSSELAER POLYTECHNIC INSTITUTE -
FOLSOM LIBRARY □ Troy, NY

Andrews, Joanna, Cat.
MC GILL UNIVERSITY - PHYSICAL SCIENCES
AND ENGINEERING LIBRARY □ Montreal, PQ

Andrews, Dr. John, Dir. of Res.
FOLGER SHAKESPEARE LIBRARY □ Washington,
DC

Andrews, John B., Exec.Dir.
NEW HAMPSHIRE MUNICIPAL ASSOCIATION -
LIBRARY □ Concord, NH

Andrews, Johnnie, Jr., Dir.
PRICHARD (Cleveland) MEMORIAL LIBRARY □
Prichard, AL

Andrews, Judith K., Sci.Libn.
UNIVERSITY OF THE PACIFIC - SCIENCE
LIBRARY† □ Stockton, CA

Andrews, Karen L., Hd.Libn.
UNIVERSITY OF CALIFORNIA, LOS ANGELES -
ENGINEERING & MATHEMATICAL SCIENCES
LIBRARY □ Los Angeles, CA

Andrews, Margaret, Coord.
SALEM STATE COLLEGE - STUDENT
GOVERNMENT ASSOCIATION & LIBRARY -
LIBRARY OF SOCIAL ALTERNATIVES □ Salem,
MA

Andrews, Martha, Prof.Res.Asst.
UNIVERSITY OF COLORADO, BOULDER -
INSTITUTE OF ARCTIC & ALPINE RESEARCH -
READING ROOM □ Boulder, CO

Andrews, Martha Shipman, Coord.
SMITHSONIAN INSTITUTION - NATL. MUSEUM
OF AMERICAN ART - INVENTORY OF
AMERICAN PAINTINGS EXECUTED BEFORE
1914 □ Washington, DC

Andrews, Mary, Act.Libn.
ALPINE CLUB OF CANADA - LIBRARY □ Banff,
AB

Andrews, Mary, Libn.
ARCHIVES OF THE CANADIAN ROCKIES □
Banff, AB

Andrews, Michael W., Rd.Serv.Libn.
ELIZABETHTOWN COLLEGE - ZUG MEMORIAL
LIBRARY - ARCHIVES □ Elizabethtown, PA

Andrews, Nancy J., Libn.
SAN DIEGO MUSEUM OF ART - REFERENCE
LIBRARY □ San Diego, CA

Andrews, Robert J., Pres.
INTERNATIONAL RAILROAD &
TRANSPORTATION POSTCARD COLLECTORS
CLUB - LIBRARY □ Providence, RI

Andrews, Roberta, Libn.
U.S. NATL. INSTITUTE FOR OCCUPATIONAL
SAFETY & HEALTH - TECHNICAL INFORMATION
BRANCH □ Cincinnati, OH

Andrews, Sara, Ref.Hd.
UNIVERSITY OF VERMONT - DIVISION OF
HEALTH SCIENCES - CHARLES A. DANA
MEDICAL LIBRARY □ Burlington, VT

Andrews, Shelley, Lib.Techn./Res.Asst
PEEL COUNTY BOARD OF EDUCATION - J.A.
TURNER PROFESSIONAL LIBRARY □
Mississauga, ON

Andrews, Theodora, Libn.
PURDUE UNIVERSITY - PHARMACY, NURSING
AND HEALTH SCIENCES LIBRARY □ West
Lafayette, IN

Andrews-Zike, Lysbeth, Ref.Libn.
NEW HAVEN COLONY HISTORICAL SOCIETY -
WHITNEY LIBRARY □ New Haven, CT

Andrle, Lorna, Libn.
U.S. ARMY POST - FORT MC PHERSON -
LIBRARY SYSTEM □ Ft. McPherson, GA

Andrus, Kay L., Rd.Serv.Libn.
SOUTHERN ILLINOIS UNIVERSITY,
CARBONDALE - SCHOOL OF LAW LIBRARY □
Carbondale, IL

Andrus, Mike, Archv.
U.S. NATL. PARK SERVICE - MANASSAS NATL.
BATTLEFIELD PARK - LIBRARY □ Manassas, VA

Andrus, Roger, Law Libn.
OREGON STATE SUPREME COURT LIBRARY □
Salem, OR

Andrushkiv, Svetlana, Dir.
SHEVCHENKO SCIENTIFIC SOCIETY, INC. -
LIBRARY AND ARCHIVES □ New York, NY

Anduha, Isabel T., Court Libn.
U.S. DISTRICT COURT - LIBRARY □ Honolulu, HI

Anest, Suzanne T., Musm.Dir.
KITSAP COUNTY HISTORICAL MUSEUM -
LIBRARY □ Silverdale, WA

Angel, Gilberte, Libn.
CONSOLIDATED-BATHURST INC. - RESEARCH
CENTRE LIBRARY □ Grand Mere, PQ

Angeletti, Lois, Libn.
RICHMOND PUBLIC LIBRARY - ART AND MUSIC
DEPARTMENT □ Richmond, VA

Angelini, A., Hd.Cat.
EAST STROUDSBURG UNIVERSITY - KENT
LIBRARY† □ East Stroudsburg, PA

Angell, Jan
WISCONSIN STATE OFFICE OF THE
COMMISSIONER OF INSURANCE - LIBRARY □
Madison, WI

Angell, Mary, Mng.Ed./Libn.
WISCONSIN STATE MEDICAL SOCIETY -
LIBRARY □ Madison, WI

Angier, Jennifer J., Mgr.
ALLEGHENY GENERAL HOSPITAL - HEALTH
SCIENCES LIBRARY □ Pittsburgh, PA

Angiletta, Anthony A., Soc.Sci.Bibliog.
YALE UNIVERSITY - SOCIAL SCIENCE LIBRARY
□ New Haven, CT

Angle, Joanne, Proj.Dir.
NATIONAL HEALTH INFORMATION
CLEARINGHOUSE □ Washington, DC

Angle, Nina K., Law Libn.
COLUMBIA GAS TRANSMISSION CORPORATION
- LAW LIBRARY □ Charleston, WV

Angonese, A.N., Sr.Assoc.Mng.Engr.
UNDERWRITERS LABORATORIES INC. -
STANDARDS REFERENCE CENTER □ Northbrook,
IL

Angstadt, Ernest, Res.Libn.
NATIONAL BROADCASTING COMPANY, INC. -
REFERENCE LIBRARY □ New York, NY

Angus, Jacqueline, Supv., Lib.Sec.
GENERAL MILLS, INC. - JAMES FORD BELL
TECHNICAL CENTER - TECHNICAL
INFORMATION SERVICES □ Minneapolis, MN

Angus, Sheri, Ref.Libn.
BATTLE CREEK ADVENTIST HOSPITAL -
MEDICAL LIBRARY □ Battle Creek, MI

Anilosky, Judith, Asst.Libn.
PENNSYLVANIA STATE UNIVERSITY - LIFE
SCIENCES LIBRARY □ University Park, PA

Anish, Michele, Asst.Libn.
AMERICAN JEWISH COMMITTEE - BLAUSTEIN
LIBRARY □ New York, NY

Anker, Anita, MULS Coord.
MINITEX □ Minneapolis, MN

Annand, Stewart, Libn.
MC CUTCHEN, BLACK, VERLEGER AND SHEA -
LAW LIBRARY □ Los Angeles, CA

Annenberg, Lester, Hd. of Sports Br.
TIME, INC. - LIBRARY □ New York, NY

Annenberg, Lester, Hd.Libn.
TIME, INC. - SPORTS LIBRARY □ New York, NY

Annett, Lawrence P., Libn./City Planner
CINCINNATI CITY PLANNING COMMISSION -
OFFICE OF PLANNING AND MANAGEMENT
SUPPORT - LIBRARY □ Cincinnati, OH

Annicharico, Ralph J., Asst. to Cur.
CATHOLIC UNIVERSITY OF AMERICA -
OLIVEIRA LIMA LIBRARY □ Washington, DC

Anninger, Anne, Spec.Coll.Libn.
WELLESLEY COLLEGE - MARGARET CLAPP
LIBRARY - SPECIAL COLLECTIONS □ Wellesley,
MA

Annino, Harriet, Libn.
WOODWARD-CLYDE CONSULTANTS -
ENVIRONMENTAL SYSTEMS DIVISION -
INFORMATION CENTER† □ Walnut Creek, CA

Ansari, Mary B., Libn.
UNIVERSITY OF NEVADA, RENO -
ENGINEERING LIBRARY □ Reno, NV

Ansari, Mary B., Libn.
UNIVERSITY OF NEVADA, RENO - LIFE AND
HEALTH SCIENCES LIBRARY □ Reno, NV

Ansari, Mary B., Libn.
UNIVERSITY OF NEVADA, RENO - MACKAY
SCHOOL OF MINES LIBRARY □ Reno, NV

Anschutz, Ms. M.A., Libn.
CANADA - CANADIAN RADIO-TELEVISION AND
TELECOMMUNICATIONS COMMISSION -
LIBRARY □ Ottawa, ON

Ansel, Phyllis, Govt.Docs./Circ.Libn.
NEW ENGLAND SCHOOL OF LAW - LIBRARY† □
Boston, MA

Ansley, Beth, Lib.Serv.Supv.
GEORGIA POWER COMPANY - LIBRARY
SERVICES □ Atlanta, GA

Ansley, Josephine, Govt.Doc.
OHIO NORTHERN UNIVERSITY - COLLEGE OF
LAW - JAY P. TAGGART MEMORIAL LAW
LIBRARY □ Ada, OH

Anspach, Judith F., Assoc.Libn.
UNIVERSITY OF CONNECTICUT - LAW SCHOOL
LIBRARY □ Hartford, CT

Anstaett, Herbert B., Exec.Sec.
EVANGELICAL AND REFORMED HISTORICAL
SOCIETY - LANCASTER CENTRAL ARCHIVES
AND LIBRARY □ Lancaster, PA

Anstine, Francesca, Asst.Libn.
UNIVERSITY OF ILLINOIS AT CHICAGO -
HEALTH SCIENCES CENTER - LIBRARY OF THE
HEALTH SCIENCES □ Urbana, IL

Antes, E. Jean, Med.Ref.Libn.
PACKER (Robert) HOSPITAL - MEDICAL
LIBRARY □ Sayre, PA

Antevil, Virginia, Asst.Coord., Info.Serv.
EDUCATIONAL RESEARCH SERVICE - LIBRARY
□ Arlington, VA

Anthony, Betsy, Libn.
UNIVERSITY OF VIRGINIA - EDUCATION
LIBRARY □ Charlottesville, VA

Anthony, Mary, Law Libn.
NEW YORK STATE SUPREME COURT -
APPELLATE DIVISION, 4TH JUDICIAL
DEPARTMENT - LAW LIBRARY □ Syracuse, NY

Anthony, Peter, Hd.Libn.
UNIVERSITY OF MANITOBA - ARCHITECTURE
& FINE ARTS LIBRARY □ Winnipeg, MB

Anthony, Robert, Lit.Res.Anl.
AEROSPACE CORPORATION - CHARLES C.
LAURITSEN LIBRARY □ Los Angeles, CA

Anthony, Robert, Group Ldr.
GEORGE BROWN COLLEGE OF APPLIED ARTS &
TECHNOLOGY - LIBRARY □ Toronto, ON

Anthony, Susan, Dir., Info.Serv.
UNIVERSITY OF CINCINNATI - MEDICAL
CENTER LIBRARIES - HEALTH SCIENCES
LIBRARY† □ Cincinnati, OH

Anthony, Walter, C.S.P., Dir.
OLD ST. MARY'S CHURCH - PAULIST LIBRARY □
San Francisco, CA

Antill, Ellen, Adm.Asst.
OCEANIC INSTITUTE - WORKING LIBRARY □
Waimanalo, HI

Antilla, Karen A., Res.Info.Serv.
MICHIGAN TECHNOLOGICAL UNIVERSITY -
INSTITUTE OF WOOD RESEARCH
INFORMATION CENTER □ Houghton, MI

Antonelli, Claudio, Ref.Libn.
UNIVERSITE DU QUEBEC A MONTREAL -
BIBLIOTHEQUES DES SCIENCES JURIDIQUES □
Montreal, PQ

Antonetz, Delores, Libn.
SHEARSON LEHMAN/AMERICAN EXPRESS INC.
- LIBRARY □ New York, NY

Antonietti, Reno, Dir., Media Serv.
ROCHESTER INSTITUTE OF TECHNOLOGY -
WALLACE MEMORIAL LIBRARY □ Rochester, NY

Antony, A.A., Info.Anl.
CHEVRON RESEARCH COMPANY - TECHNICAL
INFORMATION CENTER □ Richmond, CA

Antos, Curtis, Info.Spec.
NATIONAL ACADEMY OF SCIENCES -
NATIONAL RESEARCH COUNCIL - HIGHWAY
RESEARCH INFORMATION SERVICE □
Washington, DC

Anttila, Faith, Per.Libn.
FITCHBURG STATE COLLEGE - LIBRARY □
Fitchburg, MA

Antweiler, Richard, Dir. of Info.
NATIONAL ASSOCIATION OF ANIMAL
BREEDERS - LIBRARY □ Columbia, MO

Anzalone, Alfred M., Lib.Cons.
U.S. ARMY - PLASTICS TECHNICAL
EVALUATION CENTER - LIBRARY □ Dover, NJ

Anzalone, Filippa Marullo, Hd.Libn.
BINGHAM, DANA AND GOULD - LAW LIBRARY □
Boston, MA

Anzul, Clement J., Libn.
FORDHAM UNIVERSITY - LIBRARY AT LINCOLN
CENTER □ New York, NY

Aoki, Toshiyuki, Asst.Libn./Japanese Sect.
HARVARD UNIVERSITY - HARVARD-YENCHING
LIBRARY □ Cambridge, MA

Apelu, Manisesa, Lib.Ck.
FELETI PACIFIC LIBRARY □ Pago Pago, AS

Apfel, Mrs. Jerome, Chm.
BETH DAVID REFORM CONGREGATION -
JEWEL K. MARKOWITZ LIBRARY† □
Philadelphia, PA

Api, Rose D., Off.Mgr.
SOAP AND DETERGENT ASSOCIATION -
LIBRARY □ New York, NY

Apking, Marian, Libn.
MIAMI PURCHASE ASSOCIATION FOR
HISTORIC PRESERVATION - LIBRARY AND
INFORMATION CENTER □ Cincinnati, OH

Apostle, Lynne, Ref.Libn.
UNIVERSITY OF CALIFORNIA, DAVIS - HEALTH
SCIENCES LIBRARY □ Davis, CA

Apostolos, Margaret M., Microforms & Per.Libn.
KUTZTOWN UNIVERSITY - ROHRBACH
LIBRARY □ Kutztown, PA

Apostolos, Paul M., Evening Libn.
KUTZTOWN UNIVERSITY - ROHRBACH
LIBRARY □ Kutztown, PA

Appel, Joan, Info.Spec.
NATIONAL REHABILITATION INFORMATION
CENTER □ Washington, DC

Appel, Linda K., Br.Libn.
TEKTRONIX, INC. - WILSONVILLE BRANCH
LIBRARY □ Wilsonville, OR

Appel, Marsha, Staff Exec. & Mgr.
AMERICAN ASSOCIATION OF ADVERTISING
AGENCIES - MEMBER INFORMATION SERVICE
□ New York, NY

Appell, Frank C., Jr., Asst.Libn.
MIDDLETOWN PSYCHIATRIC CENTER -
MEDICAL LIBRARY □ Middletown, NY

Appenzeller, Clare M., Info.Res.Supv.
AUERBACH PUBLISHERS INC. - INFORMATION
CENTER □ Pennsauken, NJ

Apperley, Ruby, Supv., Museum Serv.
SASKATCHEWAN MUSEUM OF NATURAL
HISTORY - LIBRARY □ Regina, SK

Apple, Barbara, Libn.
WAUKEGAN NEWS-SUN - LIBRARY □ Waukegan,
IL

Appleby, Judy, Ref.Libn.
CONCORDIA UNIVERSITY - LOYOLA CAMPUS -
GEORGES P. VANIER LIBRARY □ Montreal, PQ

Appleton, Janet W., Libn.
GELLMAN RESEARCH ASSOCIATES, INC. - GRA
LIBRARY □ Jenkintown, PA

Appleton, Margaret, Tech.Proc.
OHIO NORTHERN UNIVERSITY - COLLEGE OF
LAW - JAY P. TAGGART MEMORIAL LAW
LIBRARY □ Ada, OH

Appleyard, James, Dir.
DMS, INC. - TECHNICAL LIBRARY □ Greenwich,
CT

Apschnikat, Kenneth, Supt.
U.S. NATL. PARK SERVICE - MOUND CITY
GROUP NATL. MONUMENT - LIBRARY □
Chillicothe, OH

Aquilino, Magdelene, ILL Libn.
U.S. VETERANS ADMINISTRATION (NY-
Northport) - HEALTH SCIENCE LIBRARY □
Northport, NY

Aragon, Bill, Cur.
CHEYENNE MOUNTAIN ZOOLOGICAL PARK -
LIBRARY □ Colorado Springs, CO

Araki, Nancy, Exec.Dir.
VISUAL COMMUNICATIONS - ASIAN PACIFIC
AMERICAN PHOTOGRAPHIC ARCHIVES □ Los
Angeles, CA

Aranda-Coddou, Patricio, Assoc.Libn., Ref./Res.
UNIVERSITY OF NEBRASKA, LINCOLN -
COLLEGE OF LAW LIBRARY □ Lincoln, NE

Arango, Xiomara, Acq.Libn.
MOREHOUSE SCHOOL OF MEDICINE - MULTI-
MEDIA CENTER □ Atlanta, GA

Arant-Cousins, Alice, Dir.
BARRETT SMITH SCHAPIRO SIMON &
ARMSTRONG - LIBRARY □ New York, NY

Arany, Ruth Ann, Staff Libn.
COMMUNITY HOSPITAL OF INDIANAPOLIS,
INC. - LIBRARY □ Indianapolis, IN

Arbach, Edith, Ref.
UNIVERSITY OF OTTAWA - VANIER SCIENCE &
ENGINEERING LIBRARY □ Ottawa, ON

Arbelius, Deborah, Libn.
NATIONAL SKI HALL OF FAME AND MUSEUM -
ROLAND PALMEDO NATIONAL SKI LIBRARY □
Ishpeming, MI

Arbogast, Judith, Media Supv.
SAN DIEGO STATE UNIVERSITY - MEDIA &
CURRICULUM CENTER† □ San Diego, CA

Arcari, Ralph, Dir. of Lib.
UNIVERSITY OF CONNECTICUT - HEALTH
CENTER - LYMAN MAYNARD STOWE LIBRARY □
Farmington, CT

Arceneaux, Pamela D., Ref.Libn.
HISTORIC NEW ORLEANS COLLECTION -
LIBRARY □ New Orleans, LA

Archambault, Christine, Cat.Libn.
WESTERN NEW ENGLAND COLLEGE - SCHOOL
OF LAW LIBRARY □ Springfield, MA

Archer, David, Libn.
MERCY HOSPITAL - MEDICAL LIBRARY □ Miami,
FL

Archer, Edgar G., Dir.
LINCOLN MEMORIAL UNIVERSITY - ABRAHAM
LINCOLN LIBRARY AND MUSEUM □ Harrogate,
TN

Archer, Robert F., Libn.
AMERICAN INSTITUTES FOR RESEARCH -
LIBRARY □ Washington, DC

Archibald, Genni, Lib.Off.
NOVA SCOTIA - DEPARTMENT OF CULTURE,
RECREATION AND FITNESS - LIBRARY □
Halifax, NS

Archibald, Jane, Coll.Dev./User Educ.
ST. MARY'S UNIVERSITY - PATRICK POWER
LIBRARY □ Halifax, NS

Archibald, Jean K., Lib.Dir.
MACALESTER COLLEGE - WEYERHAEUSER
LIBRARY □ St. Paul, MN

Archor, Sandra, Asst.Libn.
ACADEMY OF MOTION PICTURE ARTS AND
SCIENCES - MARGARET HERRICK LIBRARY □
Beverly Hills, CA

Archuleta, Alyce, Sr.Libn.
SAN DIEGO PUBLIC LIBRARY - LITERATURE &
LANGUAGES SECTION □ San Diego, CA

Archuleta, Julian, Circ.Libn.
DALLAS COUNTY LAW LIBRARY □ Dallas, TX

Arden, Sylvia, Hd.Libn./Archv.
SAN DIEGO HISTORICAL SOCIETY - RESEARCH
ARCHIVES □ San Diego, CA

Ardis, Bruce, Dir.
SOUTH CHICAGO COMMUNITY HOSPITAL -
DEPARTMENT OF LIBRARY SERVICES □
Chicago, IL

Ardis, Susan B., Libn.
UNIVERSITY OF TEXAS, AUSTIN -
ENGINEERING LIBRARY □ Austin, TX

Arenberg, Gerald, Exec.Dir.
AMERICAN FEDERATION OF POLICE RESEARCH
CENTER AND LIBRARY □ North Miami, FL

Argentati, Ron, Libn.
U.S. NAVY - NAVAL STATION LIBRARY (FL-
Mayport) □ Mayport, FL

Arguimbau, Ellie, Asst.Archv.
MONTANA HISTORICAL SOCIETY - LIBRARY/
ARCHIVES □ Helena, MT

Ariel, Marie, Libn.
CHILDREN'S MUSEUM - RESOURCE CENTER □
Boston, MA

Aristoff, Eugene, Info.Spec.
ATLANTIC-RICHFIELD COMPANY - ARCO
CHEMICAL COMPANY - RESEARCH &
DEVELOPMENT LIBRARY □ Newton Square, PA

Arkin, Cynthia, Assoc.Libn.
UNIVERSITY OF PENNSYLVANIA - BIDDLE LAW
LIBRARY □ Philadelphia, PA

Arklie, Harriet, Dir.
NORTH CENTRAL COLLEGE - OESTERLE
LIBRARY - SPECIAL COLLECTIONS □ Naperville,
IL

Arlen, Shelley, Photo Archv.
UNIVERSITY OF OKLAHOMA - WESTERN
HISTORY COLLECTIONS □ Norman, OK

Arleth, Hettie, Chf.Libn.
FORT WORTH STAR-TELEGRAM - LIBRARY □
Fort Worth, TX

Armanious, T., Libn.
ALBERTA PETROLEUM MARKETING
COMMISSION - LIBRARY □ Calgary, AB

Armeit, Marilyn, Libn.
FIDUCIARY TRUST COMPANY OF NEW YORK -
RESEARCH LIBRARY □ New York, NY

Armentrout, Sandra S., Dir.
BRICK STORE MUSEUM - EDITH CLEAVES
BARRY LIBRARY □ Kennebunk, ME

Armer, Angela, Libn.
NEBRASKA METHODIST HOSPITAL - LIBRARY □
Omaha, NE

Armes, Patricia, Assoc.Dir.
UNIVERSITY OF TEXAS HEALTH SCIENCE
CENTER, DALLAS - LIBRARY □ Dallas, TX

Armistead, Henry T., Hd., Coll.Dept.
JEFFERSON (Thomas) UNIVERSITY - SCOTT
MEMORIAL LIBRARY □ Philadelphia, PA

Armor, Robert D., Libn.
SOUTHWEST RESEARCH INSTITUTE - THOMAS
BAKER SLICK MEMORIAL LIBRARY □ San
Antonio, TX

Armstead, Bernice, Cat.Libn.
MEHARRY MEDICAL COLLEGE - MEDICAL
LIBRARY - LEARNING RESOURCES CENTER □
Nashville, TN

Armstrong, B. June, Ref.Libn.
UNIVERSITY OF CALIFORNIA, LOS ANGELES -
ENGINEERING & MATHEMATICAL SCIENCES
LIBRARY □ Los Angeles, CA

Armstrong, Carole S., Sci.Br.Coord.
MICHIGAN STATE UNIVERSITY - ANIMAL
INDUSTRIES REFERENCE ROOM □ East Lansing,
MI

Armstrong, Carole S., Sci.Br.Coord.
MICHIGAN STATE UNIVERSITY - GEOLOGY
LIBRARY □ East Lansing, MI

Armstrong, Carole S., Sci.Br.Coord.
MICHIGAN STATE UNIVERSITY - PHYSICS-
ASTRONOMY LIBRARY □ East Lansing, MI

Armstrong, Carole S., Hd.
MICHIGAN STATE UNIVERSITY - SCIENCE
LIBRARY □ East Lansing, MI

Armstrong, Dr. Cesar J., Res.Libn.
BLACKWELL, WALKER, GRAY, POWERS, FLICK
& HOEHL - LAW LIBRARY □ Miami, FL

Armstrong, Diane, Night Supv.
LE TOURNEAU COLLEGE - MARGARET ESTES
LIBRARY □ Longview, TX

Armstrong, Dr. HelenJane, Map Libn.
UNIVERSITY OF FLORIDA - MAP LIBRARY □
Gainesville, FL

Armstrong, J.W., Res.Transl.
CHEVRON RESEARCH COMPANY - TECHNICAL
INFORMATION CENTER □ Richmond, CA

Armstrong, Janice Gray, Libn.
MUSEUMS AT STONY BROOK - KATE STRONG
HISTORICAL LIBRARY □ Stony Brook, NY

Armstrong, Dr. Jean, Asst.Dir., R & D
BECTON, DICKINSON IMMUNODIAGNOSTICS -
TECHNICAL RESEARCH AND DEVELOPMENT
LIBRARY □ Orangeburg, NY

Armstrong, John W., Selection Libn.
U.S. AIR FORCE - AIR FORCE SYSTEMS
COMMAND - AIR FORCE GEOPHYSICS
LABORATORY - RESEARCH LIBRARY □ Bedford,
MA

Armstrong, Joy A., Libn.
ABITIBI-PRICE INC. - RESEARCH CENTRE
LIBRARY □ Mississauga, ON

Armstrong, M.A., Libn.
LIQUID CARBONIC CORPORATION - LIBRARY □
Chicago, IL

Armstrong, Marolyn, Asst.Libn.
HINSDALE SANITARIUM AND HOSPITAL - A.C.
LARSON LIBRARY □ Hinsdale, IL

Armstrong, Nancy, Asst.Libn.
ILLINOIS AGRICULTURAL ASSOCIATION - IAA
AND AFFILIATED COMPANIES LIBRARY □
Bloomington, IL

Armstrong, Robert D., Libn.
NEVADA MENTAL HEALTH INSTITUTE -
MEDICAL LIBRARY □ Reno, NV

Armstrong, Rodney, Dir. & Libn.
BOSTON ATHENAEUM LIBRARY □ Boston, MA

Armstrong, Wanda, Libn.
NORTH MISSISSIPPI MEDICAL CENTER -
RESOURCE CENTER □ Tupelo, MS

Arndal, Robert E., Info.Spec.
GENERAL DYNAMICS CORPORATION -
CONVAIR DIVISION - RESEARCH LIBRARY □
San Diego, CA

Arndt, Clinton, Libn.
OAKLAND PUBLIC LIBRARY - ART, MUSIC,
RECREATION □ Oakland, CA

Arndt, John, Ref./Coll.Libn.
WILFRID LAURIER UNIVERSITY - LIBRARY □
Waterloo, ON

Arneson, Arne J., Music Libn.
UNIVERSITY OF WISCONSIN, MADISON -
MILLS MUSIC LIBRARY □ Madison, WI

Arnett, Betty
BISHOP'S MILL HISTORICAL INSTITUTE - SOL
FEINSTONE LIBRARY □ Edgemont, PA

Arnold, Albert O., Jr., Grand Sec.
GRAND LODGE OF ANCIENT FREE AND
ACCEPTED MASONS OF KANSAS - GRAND
LODGE MASONIC LIBRARY □ Topeka, KS

Arnold, Carol W., Hd.Libn.
UNIVERSITY OF HAWAII - SCHOOL OF PUBLIC
HEALTH - LIBRARY □ Honolulu, HI

Arnold, Darlene M., Sr.Libn.
MINNESOTA STATE DEPARTMENT OF
EDUCATION - OFFICE OF PUBLIC LIBRARIES
AND INTERLIBRARY COOPERATION - LIBRARY
□ St. Paul, MN

Arnold, Doris, Libn.
KENTUCKY STATE DEPARTMENT OF
ECONOMIC DEVELOPMENT - RESEARCH &
PLANNING DIVISION - LIBRARY □ Frankfort, KY

Arnold, Gary J., Hd., Ref.
OHIO HISTORICAL SOCIETY - ARCHIVES-
LIBRARY □ Columbus, OH

Arnold, Jessie, Dir.,Pub.Serv./Doc.
ALCORN STATE UNIVERSITY - JOHN DEWEY
BOYD LIBRARY† □ Lorman, MS

Arnold, Joan, Cat.
SCHOOL OF VISUAL ARTS - LIBRARY □ New
York, NY

Arnold, John B., Supt.
U.S. NATL. PARK SERVICE - FORT LARNED
NATL. HISTORIC SITE - LIBRARY □ Larned, KS

Arnold, Lee, Libn.
WORLD ASSOCIATION OF DOCUMENT
EXAMINERS - WADE LIBRARY □ Chicago, IL

Arnold, Lois, Med.Libn.
AKRON GENERAL MEDICAL CENTER - J.D.
SMITH MEMORIAL LIBRARY □ Akron, OH

Arnold, Mary Jo, Hd.Libn.
OHIO STATE UNIVERSITY - ENGINEERING
LIBRARY □ Columbus, OH

Arnold, Mary Jo, Hd.Libn.
OHIO STATE UNIVERSITY - MATERIALS
ENGINEERING LIBRARY □ Columbus, OH

Arnold, Nancy, Libn./Cur.
NEWCOMEN SOCIETY OF THE UNITED STATES
- THOMAS NEWCOMEN LIB. IN STEAM
TECHNOLOGY & INDUSTRIAL HISTORY □ Exton,
PA

Arnold, Rose, Libn.
WISCONSIN STATE LEGISLATIVE REFERENCE
BUREAU □ Madison, WI

Arnold, Stephen H., Sec.-Treas., Ed.
AFRICAN LITERATURE ASSOCIATION -
SECRETARIAT LIBRARY □ Edmonton, AB

Arnold, Suzanne R., Asst.Libn.
ST. VINCENT CHARITY HOSPITAL - LIBRARY □
Cleveland, OH

Arnold, Wayne, Hd.
ROCHESTER PUBLIC LIBRARY - LOCAL
HISTORY AND GENEALOGY DIVISION □
Rochester, NY

Arnot, Mr. J., Educ.Libn.
LAKEHEAD UNIVERSITY - EDUCATION LIBRARY
□ Thunder Bay, ON

Arnott, Barbara A., Adm.Libn.
U.S. NAVY - NAVAL AIR STATION (CA-Alameda)
- LIBRARY □ Alameda, CA

Arnott, Julie, Supv.
WASHINGTON UNIVERSITY - ART &
ARCHITECTURE LIBRARY □ St. Louis, MO

Arns, Jennifer, Tech.Info.Spec.
U.S. GENERAL ACCOUNTING OFFICE - BOSTON
REGIONAL OFFICE - TECHNICAL LIBRARY □
Boston, MA

Arnsan, Daniel, Pub.Serv.
PALOMAR COMMUNITY COLLEGE - LIBRARY -
SPECIAL COLLECTIONS □ San Marcos, CA

Arnstein, Roslyn, Libn.
TAYLOR BUSINESS INSTITUTE - LIBRARY □
New York, NY

Arnwine, Jane, Info.Mgr.
NATIONAL GROCERS ASSOCIATION - LIBRARY
□ Reston, VA

Arny, Linda Ray, Ref./Asst.Br.Libn.
UNIVERSITY OF MASSACHUSETTS, AMHERST -
PHYSICAL SCIENCES LIBRARY □ Amherst, MA

Aronson, Shirley C., Doc.Libn.
MARYLAND STATE LAW LIBRARY □ Annapolis,
MD

Aronson, V.L., Libn.
CANADIAN AUTOMOBILE ASSOCIATION -
LIBRARY □ Ottawa, ON

Arora, Ved P., Hd., Bibliog.Serv.
SASKATCHEWAN - PROVINCIAL LIBRARY □
Regina, SK

Arries, Donald, Chf., Data Acq.Br.
U.S. GEOLOGICAL SURVEY - NATL. CARTOGRAPHIC INFORMATION CENTER (NCIC) □ Reston, VA

Arrington, James, Chf., Circ. & ILL
U.S. DEPT. OF HEALTH AND HUMAN SERVICES - DEPARTMENT LIBRARY† □ Washington, DC

Arrington, Louis C., Prof.
UNIVERSITY OF WISCONSIN, MADISON - POULTRY SCIENCE DEPARTMENT - HALPIN MEMORIAL LIBRARY □ Madison, WI

Arrington, Susan J., Spec. Projects Libn.
U.S. CUSTOMS SERVICE - LIBRARY AND INFORMATION CENTER □ Washington, DC

Arrowood, Nancy T., Film Libn.
VIRGINIA STATE DEPARTMENT OF TRANSPORTATION SAFETY - FILM LIBRARY □ Richmond, VA

Arrowood, Nina R., Mgr., Lib.Rsrcs.
RCA CORPORATION - GSD - GOVERNMENT COMMUNICATIONS SYSTEMS - LIBRARY □ Camden, NJ

Arroyo, Margarita, Libn.
PONCE SCHOOL OF MEDICINE - LIBRARY □ Ponce, PR

Arsenault, Cori, Firm Libn.
WELBORN, DUFFORD, BROWN & TOOLEY - LAW LIBRARY □ Denver, CO

Arseneault, Celine, Botanist/Libn.
JARDIN BOTANIQUE DE MONTREAL - BIBLIOTHEQUE □ Montreal, PQ

Arsenoff, Mary M., Br.Chf.
U.S. GENERAL SERVICES ADMINISTRATION - CONSUMER INFORMATION CENTER □ Washington, DC

Arsic, Elinor B., Libn.
DE PAUL HOSPITAL - SCHOOL OF NURSING LIBRARY □ Norfolk, VA

Arterbery, Vivian J., Lib.Dir.
RAND CORPORATION - LIBRARY† □ Santa Monica, CA

Arther, Richard O., Dir.
NATIONAL TRAINING CENTER OF POLYGRAPH SCIENCE - LIBRARY □ New York, NY

Arthur, John, Info.Sci.
AMERICAN CYANAMID COMPANY - AGRICULTURAL RESEARCH DIVISION - TECHNICAL INFORMATION SERVICES □ Princeton, NJ

Arthur, Mary, Ref.Libn.
SUFFOLK UNIVERSITY - MILDRED F. SAWYER LIBRARY - COLLECTION OF AFRO-AMERICAN LITERATURE □ Boston, MA

Artz, Theodora, Hd., Acq.Dept.
UNIVERSITY OF DAYTON - LAW SCHOOL LIBRARY □ Dayton, OH

Artzberger, John A., Dir. Mansion Musm.
OGLEBAY INSTITUTE - MANSION MUSEUM LIBRARY □ Wheeling, WV

Arvanites, Jane M., Law Libn.
BERKSHIRE LAW LIBRARY □ Pittsfield, MA

Arwas, Clement, Libn.
UNIVERSITE DE MONTREAL - GEOLOGIE-BIBLIOTHEQUE □ Montreal, PQ

Ary, Noel, Asst.Dir.
KANSAS HERITAGE CENTER - LIBRARY □ Dodge City, KS

Arzeno, Arnold, Hd.
HARVARD UNIVERSITY - SCHOOL OF PUBLIC HEALTH - INSTITUTE FOR HEALTH RESEARCH - LIBRARY □ Boston, MA

Arzigan, Arleen, Asst.Musm.Libn.
METROPOLITAN MUSEUM OF ART - PHOTOGRAPH AND SLIDE LIBRARY □ New York, NY

Arzu, Bernard
U.S. BUREAU OF THE CENSUS - INFORMATION SERVICES PROGRAM - KANSAS CITY REGIONAL OFFICE - LIBRARY □ Kansas City, KS

Asadorian, William, Ref.
QUEENS BOROUGH PUBLIC LIBRARY - LONG ISLAND DIVISION □ Jamaica, NY

Asakawa, Mrs. George, Libn.
GLEN HELEN ASSOCIATION - LIBRARY □ Yellow Springs, OH

Asante, Samuel K.B., Dir.,Adv./Info.Serv.Div.
UNITED NATIONS - CENTRE ON TRANSNATIONAL CORPORATIONS - LIBRARY □ New York, NY

Asawa, Edward E., Libn.
LOS ANGELES COUNTY - DEPARTMENT OF MENTAL HEALTH - LIBRARY □ Los Angeles, CA

Asbell, Mary M., Ext.Libn.
UNIVERSITY OF TEXAS MEDICAL BRANCH - MOODY MEDICAL LIBRARY □ Galveston, TX

Asbell, Mildred, Med.Libn.
CONNECTICUT VALLEY HOSPITAL - HALLOCK MEDICAL LIBRARY □ Middletown, CT

Asbury, Herbert, Prog.Mgr., NASA
UNIVERSITY OF SOUTHERN CALIFORNIA - NASA INDUSTRIAL APPLICATION CENTER (NIAC) □ Los Angeles, CA

Ascerno, Dr. Mark, Dial-U Coord.
UNIVERSITY OF MINNESOTA - AGRICULTURAL EXTENSION SERVICE - DIAL-U INSECT AND PLANT INFORMATION CLINIC □ St. Paul, MN

Asencio-Toro, Doris, Hd.Libn.
PUERTO RICO - SUPREME COURT - LAW LIBRARY □ San Juan, PR

Ash, Joan, Assoc.Dir.
OREGON HEALTH SCIENCES UNIVERSITY - LIBRARY □ Portland, OR

Ash, Mary, Chf.Libn.
CANADA - NATIONAL DEFENCE - CANADIAN FORCES COLLEGE - KEITH HODSON MEMORIAL LIBRARY† □ Toronto, ON

Ashburn, Dorothy, Asst.Libn.
SAFECO INSURANCE COMPANY - LIBRARY □ Seattle, WA

Ashbury, J., Supv.
CHURCH OF JESUS CHRIST OF LATTER-DAY SAINTS - CLEVELAND, OHIO STAKE BRANCH GENEALOGICAL LIBRARY □ Westlake, OH

Ashby, Anna Lou, Hd., Ref. & Lib.Serv.
PIERPONT MORGAN LIBRARY □ New York, NY

Ashe, Kathleen, Tech.Serv.Libn.
UNIVERSITY OF MINNESOTA TECHNICAL COLLEGE, WASECA - LEARNING RESOURCES □ Waseca, MN

Asher, Doris H., Med.Libn.
SPARROW (Edward W.) HOSPITAL - MEDICAL LIBRARY □ Lansing, MI

Asher, Lester, Asst.Libn.
ILLINOIS RAILWAY MUSEUM - TECHNICAL LIBRARY □ Union, IL

Ashford, C. Denise, Sr.Libn. & Mgr.
MOTOROLA, INC. - BIPOLAR INTEGRATED CIRCUITS DIVISION - TECHNICAL LIBRARY □ Phoenix, AZ

Ashford, C. Denise, Sr.Libn. & Mgr.
MOTOROLA, INC. - SEMICONDUCTOR PRODUCTS SECTOR - TECHNICAL LIBRARY □ Phoenix, AZ

Ashford, Marguerite K., Ref.Libn.
BISHOP (Bernice P.) MUSEUM - LIBRARY □ Honolulu, HI

Ashin, Elizabeth R., Dental Ref.Libn.
LOUISIANA STATE UNIVERSITY MEDICAL CENTER - LIBRARY □ New Orleans, LA

Ashley, Elizabeth, Dir. of Tech.Serv.
GOLDEN GATE BAPTIST THEOLOGICAL SEMINARY - LIBRARY □ Mill Valley, CA

Ashley, Pamela, ILL
LOUISIANA STATE UNIVERSITY MEDICAL CENTER - SCHOOL OF MEDICINE IN SHREVEPORT - LIBRARY □ Shreveport, LA

Ashley, Rudine, Libn.
ATLANTA FULTON PUBLIC LIBRARY - SPECIAL COLLECTIONS DEPARTMENT □ Atlanta, GA

Ashlock, Robert B., Act.Dir.
REFORMED THEOLOGICAL SEMINARY - LIBRARY □ Jackson, MS

Ashton, Elizabeth H., Res.Libn.
CHEVRON OIL FIELD RESEARCH COMPANY - TECHNICAL INFORMATION SERVICES □ La Habra, CA

Ashworth, Margaret W., Libn.
CRANE PACKING COMPANY - TECHNICAL LIBRARY □ Morton Grove, IL

Askey, Phyllis, Med.Libn.
CHESHIRE HOSPITAL - MAC GRATH FAMILY MEDICAL LIBRARY □ Keene, NH

Aspnes, Grieg, Mgr., Info.Serv.
EXPERIENCE, INC. - INFORMATION CENTER □ Minneapolis, MN

Aspri, Jo-Anne M., Libn.
KENT COUNTY MEMORIAL HOSPITAL - MEDICAL LIBRARY □ Warwick, RI

Aspry, Robert, Libn.
U.S. NAVY - NAVAL UNDERWATER SYSTEMS CENTER - NEWPORT TECHNICAL LIBRARY† □ Newport, RI

Assad, William, Govt.Doc.Libn./Asst.Libn.
ACADEMY OF AERONAUTICS - LIBRARY □ Flushing, NY

Assadourian, Lynn, Libn.
DU PONT CANADA, INC. - PATENT DIVISION LIBRARY □ Mississauga, ON

Assanheimer, Judy, Libn.
NEW JERSEY STATE DEPARTMENT OF LAW AND PUBLIC SAFETY - ATTORNEY GENERAL'S LIBRARY □ Trenton, NJ

Assenmacher, Kaye, Archv.
LUNDEBERG MARYLAND SEAMANSHIP SCHOOL - PAUL HALL LIBRARY AND MARITIME MUSEUM □ Piney Point, MD

Astbury, Barbara, Lib.Techn.
QUEEN'S UNIVERSITY AT KINGSTON - PSYCHOLOGY LIBRARY □ Kingston, ON

Astheimer, Bernice, Br.Libn.
NORDEN SYSTEMS, INC. - TECHNICAL LIBRARY □ Norwalk, CT

Aston, Charles E., Jr., Coord.
UNIVERSITY OF PITTSBURGH - SPECIAL COLLECTIONS DEPARTMENT □ Pittsburgh, PA

Aston, Jane, Supv., Graphics
OKLAHOMA STATE UNIVERSITY - AUDIO VISUAL CENTER □ Stillwater, OK

Aston, Michael N., Dept.Libn.
ALBERTA - DEPARTMENT OF RECREATION & PARKS - LIBRARY □ Edmonton, AB

Astraquillo, Divinia J., Law Libn.
MILWAUKEE COUNTY LAW LIBRARY □ Milwaukee, WI

Astroza, Maria Tereza, Ref.Libn.
PAN AMERICAN HEALTH ORGANIZATION - BIBLIOGRAPHIC INFORMATION OFFICE† □ Washington, DC

Atherton, P., Libn.
CANADA - AGRICULTURE CANADA - ANIMAL DISEASES RESEARCH INSTITUTE LIBRARY □ Ottawa, ON

Atik, Shifra, Hd., Tech.Serv.
MEDICAL LIBRARY CENTER OF NEW YORK† □ New York, NY

Atiyeh, George N., Hd., Near East Sect.
LIBRARY OF CONGRESS - AFRICAN & MIDDLE EASTERN DIVISION □ Washington, DC

Atkins, Eleanor E., Asst.Cur.
FIREFIGHTERS' MUSEUM OF NOVA SCOTIA - LIBRARY & INFORMATION CENTER □ Yarmouth, NS

Atkins, Lenetta, Libn.
MERCY HOSPITAL - LEVITT HEALTH SCIENCES LIBRARY† □ Des Moines, IA

Atkins, Martha, Pub.Serv.Libn.
SUNY - COLLEGE AT CORTLAND - MEMORIAL LIBRARY □ Cortland, NY

Atkins, Thomas, Hd., Instr.Serv.
BARUCH (Bernard M.) COLLEGE OF THE CITY UNIVERSITY OF NEW YORK - LIBRARY† □ New York, NY

Atkins, Winston, Libn.
SAN JACINTO MUSEUM OF HISTORY ASSOCIATION - LIBRARY □ La Porte, TX

Atkinson, Calberta O., Libn.
RUST INTERNATIONAL CORPORATION -
LIBRARY □ Birmingham, AL

Atkinson, Jean, Chf.Med.Libn.
EISENHOWER MEDICAL CENTER - DEL E. WEBB
MEMORIAL MEDICAL INFORMATION CENTER □
Rancho Mirage, CA

Atkinson, Rose Marie, Asst.Dir.
U.S. NEWS & WORLD REPORT - LIBRARY □
Washington, DC

Atlas, Aime, Sr.Libn.
PILGRIM PSYCHIATRIC CENTER - HEALTH
SCIENCES LIBRARY □ West Brentwood, NY

Atman, Skye, Pres.
DOCUMENTATION ASSOCIATES □ Los Angeles,
CA

Atmore, Colleen E.
BONNER COUNTY HISTORICAL SOCIETY, INC. -
RESEARCH LIBRARY □ Sandpoint, ID

Atson, Elsa B., Asst.Libn., Tech.Serv.
JENKINS (Theodore F.) MEMORIAL LAW
LIBRARY COMPANY - LIBRARY □ Philadelphia,
PA

Attalai, Christine, Act.Chf.Libn.
UNIVERSITY OF TORONTO - FACULTY OF LAW
LIBRARY □ Toronto, ON

Attar, Carol, Lib.Dir.
COTTAGE HOSPITAL OF GROSSE POINTE -
MEDICAL LIBRARY □ Grosse Pointe Farms, MI

Attenborough, Debra, Educ.Off.
RODMAN HALL ARTS CENTRE - ART LIBRARY □
St. Catharines, ON

Attinello, Salvatore J., Ref.
KENNEDY-KING COLLEGE - LIBRARY† □
Chicago, IL

Attwood, J.M., Libn.-Archv.
CANADIAN DIABETES ASSOCIATION -
NATIONAL OFFICE ARCHIVES □ Toronto, ON

Attwood, Joan-Mary, Libn.
ARTHRITIS SOCIETY - NATIONAL OFFICE
LIBRARY □ Toronto, ON

Atwater, Virginia, Libn.
U.S. ARMY SERGEANTS MAJOR ACADEMY -
OTHON O. VALENT LEARNING RESOURCES
CENTER □ Ft. Bliss, TX

Atwood, Harold, Res.Chm.
GENEALOGICAL ASSOCIATION OF
SOUTHWESTERN MICHIGAN - MAUD PRESTON
PALENSKE MEMORIAL LIBRARY □ St. Joseph,
MI

Atwood, Karen P., Cur.
HISTORICAL SOCIETY OF DAUPHIN COUNTY -
ARCHIVES/LIBRARY □ Harrisburg, PA

Atwood, Richard, Libn.
VAN WERT COUNTY LAW LIBRARY □ Van Wert,
OH

Atwood, Valdine C., Chm.
NATIONAL SOCIETY, DAUGHTERS OF THE
AMERICAN REVOLUTION - HANNAH WESTON
CHAPTER - BURNHAM TAVERN MUSEUM □
Machias, ME

Au, Eleanor, Hd., Spec.Coll.
UNIVERSITY OFHAWAII - SPECIAL
COLLECTIONS - JEAN CHARLOT COLLECTION □
Honolulu, HI

Au, Eleanor C., Hd., Spec.Coll.
UNIVERSITY OF HAWAII - SPECIAL
COLLECTIONS - RARE BOOKS □ Honolulu, HI

Au, Jeannette Chin Chun, Hd., Tech.Serv.
ARIZONA STATE UNIVERSITY - COLLEGE OF
LAW - LIBRARY □ Tempe, AZ

Au, Marcia Learned, Dept.Hd.
TOLEDO-LUCAS COUNTY PUBLIC LIBRARY -
SOCIAL SCIENCE DEPARTMENT □ Toledo, OH

Aubert, Bernadine, Asst.Chf.Libn.
DETROIT FREE PRESS - LIBRARY □ Detroit, MI

Aubin, Claude, Dir.
SEMINAIRE ST-JOSEPH - BIBLIOTHEQUE □
Trois-Rivieres, PQ

Aubin, Robert, Med.Libn.
HOPITAL RIVIERE-DES-PRAIRIES -
BIBLIOTHEQUE DU PERSONNEL □ Montreal, PQ

Aubrey, Irene E., Chf.
NATIONAL LIBRARY OF CANADA - CHILDREN'S
LITERATURE SERVICE □ Ottawa, ON

Aubry, John C., Archv./Libn.
AMERICAN INSTITUTE OF PHYSICS - CENTER
FOR HISTORY OF PHYSICS - NIELS BOHR
LIBRARY □ New York, NY

Audet, Louise, Asst. to Dir.
LA PRESSE, LTEE. - CENTRE DE
DOCUMENTATION† □ Montreal, PQ

Audette, Michele, Responsable
QUEBEC PROVINCE - MINISTERE DE
L'AGRICULTURE, DES PECHERIES ET DE
L'ALIMENTATION - CENTRE DE
DOCUMENTATION □ Quebec, PQ

Audino, Nancy, Res.Mgr.
AT & T COMMUNICATIONS - INFORMATION
RESEARCH CENTER □ Morris Plains, NJ

Auducon, Lillian B.
FIRST PRESBYTERIAN CHURCH - LIBRARY† □
Kalamazoo, MI

Auer, Grace, Coord., Lib. & Archv.
COOK COUNTY HOSPITAL - HEALTH SCIENCE
LIBRARY AND ARCHIVES □ Chicago, IL

Auer, Grace, Hd.Med.Libn.
COOK COUNTY HOSPITAL - TICE MEMORIAL
LIBRARY □ Chicago, IL

Auer, Mary A., Cat.
U.S. ARMY - NATICK RESEARCH AND
DEVELOPMENT CENTER - TECHNICAL LIBRARY
□ Natick, MA

Auerbach, Judith, Acq.Libn.
HARVARD UNIVERSITY - GRADUATE SCHOOL
OF DESIGN - FRANCES LOEB LIBRARY □
Cambridge, MA

Auerbach, Stevanne, Ph.D., Dir.
INSTITUTE FOR CHILDHOOD RESOURCES -
LIBRARY □ San Francisco, CA

Auerbach, Wanda, Ref.Libn.
UNIVERSITY OF WISCONSIN, MADISON -
CENTER FOR HEALTH SCIENCES LIBRARIES† □
Madison, WI

Auger, Roland, Dir., Coll.Dev. & Cons.
QUEBEC PROVINCE - BIBLIOTHEQUE
NATIONALE DU QUEBEC □ Montreal, PQ

Aughey, Kathleen, Lit.Sci.
AMERICAN CYANAMID COMPANY -
CONSUMERS PRODUCTS RESEARCH DIVISION -
LIBRARY □ Clifton, NJ

Augliera, Rosemary, Ref.Libn.
MC GRAW-HILL, INC. - LIBRARY □ New York,
NY

August, Sidney, Dir.
COMMUNITY COLLEGE OF PHILADELPHIA -
EDUCATION RESOURCES CENTER† □
Philadelphia, PA

Augustine, Patricia, Med.Libn.
YOUNGSTOWN HOSPITAL ASSOCIATION -
HEALTH SCIENCES LIBRARY □ Youngstown, OH

Augustine, Sheryl, Libn., Tech.Serv.
BETH ISRAEL MEDICAL CTR. - HOSPITAL FOR
JOINT DISEASES ORTHOPAEDIC INST. -
SEYMOUR J. PHILLIPS HEALTH SCI.LIB. □ New
York, NY

Augustino, Diane, Res.Sci. I
RESEARCH INSTITUTE ON ALCOHOLISM -
LIBRARY □ Buffalo, NY

Augustyniak, Rebecca, Libn.
FLORIDA STATE UNIVERSITY - CTR. FOR
STUDIES IN VOCATIONAL EDUC. - FLORIDA
EDUCATIONAL INFO. SERV. □ Tallahassee, FL

Auh, Y. John, Chf.Libn.
WAGNER COLLEGE - HORRMANN LIBRARY □
Staten Island, NY

Aulf, Lydia
UNIVERSITY OF PUERTO RICO - NATURAL
SCIENCE LIBRARY □ Rio Piedras, PR

Aulffo, Pier R., Tech.Info.Spec.
GENERAL DYNAMICS CORPORATION - FORT
WORTH DIVISION - TECHNICAL LIBRARY □
Fort Worth, TX

Aum, Kyung Eun, Libn.
KOREAN CULTURAL SERVICE - LIBRARY □ Los
Angeles, CA

Austen, L.M., Libn.
BETHLEHEM STEEL CORPORATION - HERTY
TECHNICAL INFORMATION CENTER □
Bethlehem, PA

Austin, Ann, Res.
EARTHWATCH - LIBRARY □ Belmont, MA

Austin, Sr. Ann Marie, R.S.M., Asst.Libn.
MERCY HOSPITAL - MEDICAL LIBRARY □
Wilkes-Barre, PA

Austin, Anne A., Manager
IBM CORPORATION - NAD COMMUNICATIONS
LIBRARY □ White Plains, NY

Austin, Barbara J., Asst. to Dir.
ATLANTA BUREAU OF PLANNING - LIBRARY □
Atlanta, GA

Austin, Carol, Lib.Techn.
U.S. AIR FORCE BASE - HOLLOMAN BASE
LIBRARY† □ Holloman AFB, NM

Austin, David L., Music Libn.
WICHITA STATE UNIVERSITY - THURLOW
LIEURANCE MEMORIAL MUSIC LIBRARY □
Wichita, KS

Austin, Dennis, Dp. Law Libn.
WISCONSIN STATE SUPREME COURT -
WISCONSIN STATE LAW LIBRARY □ Madison,
WI

Austin, Jean, Supv., Indexing
BELL & HOWELL COMPANY - MICRO PHOTO
DIVISION - MICROFORMS ARCHIVE† □
Wooster, OH

Austin, Judith, Ed./Res.Hist./Archv.
IDAHO STATE HISTORICAL SOCIETY -
LIBRARY AND ARCHIVES □ Boise, ID

Austin, Judith P., Hd.
LIBRARY OF CONGRESS - GEN. READING
ROOMS DIV. - LOCAL HISTORY & GENEALOGY
READING ROOM SECTION □ Washington, DC

Austin, Linda Swann, Libn.
THORNDIKE, DORAN, PAINE AND LEWIS INC. -
RESEARCH LIBRARY □ Atlanta, GA

Austin, Loretta E., Tech.Lib.Asst.
CALIFORNIA STATE - COLORADO RIVER BOARD
OF CALIFORNIA - LIBRARY □ Los Angeles, CA

Austin, Martha, Hd.Libn.
UNIVERSITY OF WASHINGTON - PHYSICS-
ASTRONOMY LIBRARY □ Seattle, WA

Austin, Nancy, Cat.
UNIVERSITY OF NORTH DAKOTA - SCHOOL OF
MEDICINE - HARLEY E. FRENCH MEDICAL
LIBRARY □ Grand Forks, ND

Austin, Ralph, Chf., Lit.
U.S. ARMY - WHITE SANDS MISSILE RANGE -
TECHNICAL LIBRARY DIVISION □ White Sands
Missile Range, NM

Austin, Terry, Dir., Spec.Coll.
AMERICAN MEDICAL ASSOCIATION -
DIVISION OF LIBRARY AND ARCHIVAL
SERVICES □ Chicago, IL

Austin, William, Supv.
AT & T BELL LABORATORIES - LIBRARY □
Holmdel, NJ

Austin, William, Circ.Libn.
FORDHAM UNIVERSITY - LIBRARY AT LINCOLN
CENTER □ New York, NY

Auten, Anne, User Serv.Coord.
ERIC CLEARINGHOUSE ON READING AND
COMMUNICATIONS SKILLS □ Urbana, IL

Avallone, Cynthia A., Chf.Libn.
U.S. VETERANS ADMINISTRATION (CA-San
Francisco) - MEDICAL CENTER LIBRARY □ San
Francisco, CA

Avaloz, Faustino, Newspaper Cur.
MINNESOTA HISTORICAL SOCIETY -
REFERENCE LIBRARY □ St. Paul, MN

Avant, John Alfred, Fiction Libn.
BROOKLYN PUBLIC LIBRARY - LANGUAGE AND
LITERATURE DIVISION □ Brooklyn, NY

Avdzej, Tamara, Acq.Libn.
KEAN COLLEGE OF NEW JERSEY - NANCY
THOMPSON LIBRARY† □ Union, NJ

Avens, Irene, Art Libn.
QUEENS COLLEGE OF THE CITY UNIVERSITY
OF NEW YORK - PAUL KLAPPER LIBRARY - ART
LIBRARY □ Flushing, NY
Avera, Victoria, Chf., Auto.Bibliog.Cont.
SMITHSONIAN INSTITUTION LIBRARIES □
Washington, DC
Averdick, Mike, Assoc.Dir.
KENTON COUNTY PUBLIC LIBRARY -
KENTUCKY & LOCAL HISTORY DEPARTMENT □
Covington, KY
Averill, Harold, Collective Member
CANADIAN GAY ARCHIVES - LIBRARY □
Toronto, ON
Averill, Harold A., Act.Univ.Archv.
UNIVERSITY OF TORONTO - UNIVERSITY
ARCHIVES □ Toronto, ON
Averill, Joy, Libn.
WOODWARD STATE HOSPITAL SCHOOL -
STAFF LIBRARY □ Woodward, IA
Averill, Laurie, Rd.Serv.Libn.
RHODE ISLAND SCHOOL OF DESIGN - LIBRARY
□ Providence, RI
Averill, M.S., Libn.
LUTHERAN MEDICAL CENTER - MEDICAL
LIBRARY □ Brooklyn, NY
Avers-Fejes, Susan, Libn.
MOBIL CHEMICAL COMPANY - RESEARCH &
DEVELOPMENT - INFORMATION SERVICES □
Edison, NJ
Avery, Carol, Cat.
UNIVERSITY OF NORTH CAROLINA, CHAPEL
HILL - LAW LIBRARY □ Chapel Hill, NC
Avery, May S., Info.Spec.
STANDARD OIL COMPANY OF INDIANA -
CENTRAL RESEARCH LIBRARY □ Naperville, IL
Avery, Shelley, Res.Libn.
BANCROFT, AVERY AND MC ALISTER - LAW
LIBRARY □ San Francisco, CA
Avetria, Arsenia Q., Tech.Serv.Libn.
MEMORIAL SLOAN-KETTERING CANCER
CENTER - LEE COOMBE MEMORIAL LIBRARY □
New York, NY
Avey, Edward M., Tech.Serv.Libn.
CANADA - PUBLIC WORKS CANADA - ONTARIO
REGIONAL LIBRARY □ Willowdale, ON
Avgikos, Jan, Visual Coll.Cur.
ATLANTA COLLEGE OF ART - LIBRARY □
Atlanta, GA
Avila, Marian, Libn.
SAN DIEGO PUBLIC LIBRARY - SOCIAL
SCIENCES SECTION □ San Diego, CA
Avis, Joel L., Jr., Local Church Hist.
HISTORICAL FOUNDATION OF THE
PRESBYTERIAN AND REFORMED CHURCHES -
LIBRARY AND ARCHIVES □ Montreat, NC
Avison, Liz, Hd.Libn.
UNIVERSITY OF TORONTO - AUDIO-VISUAL
LIBRARY □ Toronto, ON
Avitabile, Susan L., Libn./Asst.V.P.
PUTNAM COMPANIES - INVESTMENT
RESEARCH LIBRARY □ Boston, MA
Avlon, Mary, Libn.
CENTRAL ISLIP PSYCHIATRIC CENTER -
HEALTH SCIENCE LIBRARY† □ Central Islip, NY
Avner, Sylvia, Libn.
92ND STREET YOUNG MEN'S AND YOUNG
WOMEN'S HEBREW ASSOCIATION -
BUTTENWIESER LIBRARY □ New York, NY
Awe, Susan, Info.Coord.
UNIVERSITY OF WISCONSIN, MADISON -
SMALL BUSINESS DEVELOPMENT &
RECREATION CENTER - LIBRARY □ Madison,
WI
Axel-Lute, Paul, Coll.Dev.
RUTGERS UNIVERSITY, THE STATE
UNIVERSITY OF NEW JERSEY - JUSTICE
HENRY ACKERSON LIBRARY OF LAW &
CRIMINAL JUSTICE □ Newark, NJ
Axelrod, Jane, U.S. Tax Spec.
PRICE WATERHOUSE - NATIONAL
INFORMATION CENTER □ New York, NY

Axelrod, Nancy, Unit Hd.
UNIVERSITY OF CALIFORNIA, BERKELEY -
ENTOMOLOGY LIBRARY □ Berkeley, CA
Axelrod, Velma H., Med.Libn.
MAGEE-WOMENS HOSPITAL - HOWARD
ANDERSON POWER MEMORIAL LIBRARY □
Pittsburgh, PA
Axelroth, Joan L., Libn.
CROWELL & MORING - LIBRARY □ Washington,
DC
Axford, Lavonne, Libn.
PRYOR, CARNEY AND JOHNSON - LIBRARY □
Englewood, CO
Axilrod, Paula, Circ.
MARYLAND INSTITUTE, COLLEGE OF ART -
DECKER LIBRARY □ Baltimore, MD
Axthelm, Kenneth W., Div.Chf.
BROOKLYN PUBLIC LIBRARY - AUDIO VISUAL
DIVISION □ Brooklyn, NY
Ayala, John L., Lib.Dir./Assoc.Prof.
LONG BEACH CITY COLLEGE - PACIFIC COAST
CAMPUS LIBRARY □ Long Beach, CA
Ayala, Orietta, Hd., Acq.Dept.
UNIVERSITY OF PUERTO RICO - LAW SCHOOL
LIBRARY □ Rio Piedras, PR
Aycock, Margaret, Oceans/Intl. Law Libn.
UNIVERSITY OF VIRGINIA - ARTHUR J.
MORRIS LAW LIBRARY □ Charlottesville, VA
Aycock, Martha, Ref.Libn.
UNION THEOLOGICAL SEMINARY IN VIRGINIA
- LIBRARY □ Richmond, VA
Ayer, Carol A., Libn.
U.S. FOREST SERVICE - PACIFIC NORTHWEST
FOREST & RANGE EXPERIMENT STATION -
FORESTRY SCI. LAB. LIB. □ Juneau, AK
Ayer, Suzanne, Govt.Doc.Libn.
UNION UNIVERSITY - ALBANY LAW SCHOOL -
LIBRARY □ Albany, NY
Ayers, Janet, Geology Libn.
NORTHWESTERN UNIVERSITY - GEOLOGY
LIBRARY □ Evanston, IL
Ayers, Janet, Physical Sci. & Engr.Libn
NORTHWESTERN UNIVERSITY - SEELEY G.
MUDD LIBRARY FOR SCIENCE AND
ENGINEERING □ Evanston, IL
Aylward, James F., Adm.
U.S. NAVY - NAVAL EDUCATION AND TRAINING
CENTER - LIBRARY SYSTEM □ Newport, RI
Ayotte, Richard, Pub.Serv.Libn.
ORANGE COUNTY LAW LIBRARY □ Santa Ana,
CA
Ayoung, Miss R.A., Res.Libn.
IMPERIAL TOBACCO LTD. - RESEARCH
LIBRARY □ Montreal, PQ
Azine, Sheldon, Dir.
FEDERAL RESERVE BANK OF MINNEAPOLIS -
LAW LIBRARY □ Minneapolis, MN
Azzani, Eunice J., Libn.
DELOITTE HASKINS & SELLS - AUDIT/MAS &
TAX LIBRARY □ San Francisco, CA
Azzarello, Mary Ann, Law Libn.
IMPERIAL COUNTY LAW LIBRARY† □ El Centro,
CA

B

Baacke, Ruth K., Libn.
MIDDLE EAST INSTITUTE - GEORGE CAMP
KEISER LIBRARY □ Washington, DC
Babcock, Sharon, Lib.Supv.
UNIVERSITY OF WASHINGTON - HEALTH
SCIENCES LIBRARY - K.K. SHERWOOD LIBRARY
□ Seattle, WA
Babeaux, Kathy A., Libn.
OHIOANA LIBRARY ASSOCIATION - OHIOANA
LIBRARY AND ARCHIVES □ Columbus, OH
Babian, Mary C., Staff Libn.
GENERAL MOTORS CORPORATION - RESEARCH
LABORATORIES LIBRARY □ Warren, MI

Babich, Dorothy
U.S. NATL. WEATHER SERVICE - CENTRAL
REGION HEADQUARTERS - LIBRARY □ Kansas
City, MO
Babilot, Dr. George, Dir.
SAN DIEGO STATE UNIVERSITY - CENTER FOR
PUBLIC ECONOMICS LIBRARY □ San Diego, CA
Babin, Pamela, Tech.Serv.Libn.
GOLDMAN, SACHS AND COMPANY - LIBRARY □
New York, NY
Babineau-Simenauer, Suzanne, Cur.
NEW YORK UNIVERSITY - INSTITUTE OF FINE
ARTS - SLIDE AND PHOTOGRAPHIC
COLLECTION □ New York, NY
Babish, Jo-Ann M., Dir., Lib.Serv.
TAYLOR (Moses) HOSPITAL - LIBRARY □
Scranton, PA
Babitch, Marianne, Ref.
UNIVERSITY OF TEXAS HEALTH SCIENCE
CENTER, DALLAS - LIBRARY □ Dallas, TX
Baboyant, Marie, Ref.Libn.
BIBLIOTHEQUE DE LA VILLE DE MONTREAL -
COLLECTION GAGNON □ Montreal, PQ
Baca, Dan, Supv., Rpt.Lib.
UNIVERSITY OF CALIFORNIA - LOS ALAMOS
NATIONAL LABORATORY - LIBRARY □ Los
Alamos, NM
Bachand, Michelle, Hd.Libn.
CANADIAN BROADCASTING CORPORATION -
LIBRARY □ Montreal, PQ
Bachman-Gabbert, Tammy, Libn.
UTAH WATER RESEARCH LABORATORY -
LIBRARY □ Logan, UT
Bachmann, Joan M., Adm.Asst.
U.S. GEOLOGICAL SURVEY - WATER
RESOURCES DIVISION - NEW YORK
SUBDISTRICT - LIBRARY □ Syosset, NY
Bachrach, Amy, Asst.
BARNARD COLLEGE WOMEN'S CENTER -
BIRDIE GOLDSMITH AST RESOURCE
COLLECTION □ New York, NY
Bachrach, Joseph, Asst.Libn.
HEBREW THEOLOGICAL COLLEGE - SAUL
SILBER MEMORIAL LIBRARY □ Skokie, IL
Back, Julia G., Rd.Serv.Libn.
FEDERAL RESERVE SYSTEM - BOARD OF
GOVERNORS - RESEARCH LIBRARY □
Washington, DC
Backes, James C., Asst.Libn.
NEW YORK LAW INSTITUTE - LIBRARY □ New
York, NY
Backhus, Carol, Engr.Libn.
LAWRENCE BERKELEY LABORATORY - LIBRARY
□ Berkeley, CA
Backlund, Caroline H., Hd., Rd.Serv.
NATIONAL GALLERY OF ART - LIBRARY □
Washington, DC
Backman, Prudence K., Mss.Libn.
ESSEX INSTITUTE - JAMES DUNCAN PHILLIPS
LIBRARY □ Salem, MA
Backman, Robert E., Cur.
HANDWRITING ANALYSIS RESEARCH LIBRARY
□ Greenfield, MA
Backovsky, Ljuba, Assoc.Musm.Libn.
METROPOLITAN MUSEUM OF ART - THOMAS J.
WATSON LIBRARY □ New York, NY
Backsen, Marcella, Libn.
IMMACULATE HEART OF MARY - PARISH
LIBRARY □ Los Alamos, NM
Backus, Betty J., Supv., Lib.
UNION TEXAS PETROLEUM CORPORATION -
LIBRARY □ Houston, TX
Bacon, Ethel, Libn.
UNIVERSITY OF HARTFORD - HARTT SCHOOL
OF MUSIC - ALLEN MEMORIAL LIBRARY □ West
Hartford, CT
Bacon, Isabelle, Founder
HOLY LAND MUSEUM & LIBRARY □ New York,
NY
Bacon, Su, Ed.
KANSAS ENERGY EXTENSION SERVICE □
Manhattan, KS

Bacon, Viola, Hd. Lending Libn.
CHATFIELD BRASS BAND INC. - FREE MUSIC
LENDING LIBRARY □ Chatfield, MN
Bacsanyi, Karen, Ref.Libn.
WAYNE STATE UNIVERSITY - EDUCATION
LIBRARY □ Detroit, MI
Badders, Hurley, Commn.Dir.
PENDLETON DISTRICT HISTORICAL AND
RECREATIONAL COMMISSION - REFERENCE
LIBRARY □ Pendleton, SC
Bader, Doris S., Libn.
LONG ISLAND CATHOLIC - RESEARCH LIBRARY
□ Hempstead, NY
Bader, Hazel, Libn.
RUTAN AND TUCKER - LIBRARY □ Costa Mesa,
CA
Bader, Shelley A., Dir.
GEORGE WASHINGTON UNIVERSITY -
MEDICAL CENTER - PAUL HIMMELFARB
HEALTH SCIENCES LIBRARY □ Washington, DC
Bader, Susan, Ref.
UNIVERSITY OF TEXAS HEALTH SCIENCE
CENTER, DALLAS - LIBRARY □ Dallas, TX
Badertscher, David A., Tech.Serv.Libn.
VIRGINIA MILITARY INSTITUTE - PRESTON
LIBRARY □ Lexington, VA
Badertscher, David G., Prin. Law Libn.
NEW YORK STATE SUPREME COURT - 1ST
JUDICIAL DISTRICT - CRIMINAL BRANCH -
LAW LIBRARY □ New York, NY
Badger, Harold, Libn.
FREEDOMS FOUNDATION AT VALLEY FORGE -
LIBRARY □ Valley Forge, PA
Badke, W.B., Libn.
NORTHWEST BAPTIST THEOLOGICAL COLLEGE
AND SEMINARY - LIBRARY □ Vancouver, BC
Bae, Frank S.H., Law Libn.
NEW ENGLAND SCHOOL OF LAW - LIBRARY† □
Boston, MA
Baer, D. Richard, Dir.
HOLLYWOOD FILM ARCHIVE - LIBRARY □
Hollywood, CA
Baer, Steven, Dir. of Educ.
AMERICANS UNITED FOR LIFE - AUL LEGAL
DEFENSE FUND - INFORMATION CENTER □
Chicago, IL
Baerwald, Dr. John, Dir., Coll. of Engr.
UNIVERSITY OF ILLINOIS - HIGHWAY TRAFFIC
SAFETY CENTER - LIBRARY □ Urbana, IL
Baerwald, Susan, Libn.
HELLMUTH, OBATA & KASSABAUM, INC. - HOK
LIBRARY □ St. Louis, MO
Bagby, Felicia, Tech.Libn.
LEAR SIEGLER, INC. - ASTRONICS DIVISION -
TECHNICAL LIBRARY □ Santa Monica, CA
Bagdoyan, Helen, Asst.Libn./Pub.Serv.
GEORGETOWN UNIVERSITY - MEDICAL
CENTER - DAHLGREN MEMORIAL LIBRARY □
Washington, DC
Baggett-Heuser, Lorraine, Lib.Dir.
MOORE COLLEGE OF ART - LIBRARY □
Philadelphia, PA
Baggott, Vickey, Cat.Libn.
MISSISSIPPI COLLEGE SCHOOL OF LAW - LAW
LIBRARY □ Jackson, MS
Bagin, Katherine, Libn.
PRINCETON UNIVERSITY - INDUSTRIAL
RELATIONS LIBRARY □ Princeton, NJ
Bagley, Marcy, Hd.Libn.
PHOENIX NEWSPAPERS, INC. - LIBRARY □
Phoenix, AZ
Bagnerise, Charles, Asst.Libn.
U.S. VETERANS ADMINISTRATION (LA-New
Orleans) - MEDICAL CENTER LIBRARY □ New
Orleans, LA
Bagwell, G.L., Pres.
NATIONAL ASSOCIATION OF WATCH AND
CLOCK COLLECTORS MUSEUM - LIBRARY □
Columbia, PA
Baher-Simpon, Vaughn
UNIVERSITY OF SOUTHWESTERN LOUISIANA -
CENTER FOR LOUISIANA STUDIES □ Lafayette,
LA

Bahn, Gilbert S., Hd.
SCHUYLER TECHNICAL LIBRARY □ Newport
News, VA
Bahr, Christine, Libn.
UNITED HOSPITAL FUND OF NEW YORK -
REFERENCE LIBRARY □ New York, NY
Bailey, Cheryl M., Dir.
MARY COLLEGE - LIBRARY □ Bismarck, ND
Bailey, Mr. Chris H., Mng.Dir.
AMERICAN CLOCK AND WATCH MUSEUM -
EDWARD INGRAHAM LIBRARY □ Bristol, CT
Bailey, Clint, Archv.
UNIVERSITY OF UTAH - SPECIAL COLLECTIONS
DEPARTMENT □ Salt Lake City, UT
Bailey, Dreama Jil, Asst.
CHARLESTON GAZETTE-MAIL - LIBRARY □
Charleston, WV
Bailey, E.R., Hd., Circ.
MURRAY STATE UNIVERSITY - LIBRARY □
Murray, KY
Bailey, Edgar C., Jr., Ref.Libn.
PROVIDENCE COLLEGE - PHILLIPS MEMORIAL
LIBRARY □ Providence, RI
Bailey, Elizabeth, Asst.Libn.
ERNST & WHINNEY - NATIONAL OFFICE
LIBRARY □ Cleveland, OH
Bailey, F. Ruth, Asst.Libn./Rd.Serv.
NYACK COLLEGE - LIBRARY □ Nyack, NY
Bailey, Florence, Supv.
MONTGOMERY COUNTY PLANNING
COMMISSION - RESEARCH LIBRARY □
Norristown, PA
Bailey, George M., Assoc.Dir. of Libs.
THE CLAREMONT COLLEGES - LIBRARY □
Claremont, CA
Bailey, Prof. James F., III, Dir., Law Lib.
INDIANA UNIVERSITY, INDIANAPOLIS -
SCHOOL OF LAW LIBRARY □ Indianapolis, IN
Bailey, Jean M., Libn.
GLATFELTER (P.H.) COMPANY - RESEARCH
LIBRARY □ Spring Grove, PA
Bailey, Kay, Libn.
TEXAS EASTERN TRANSMISSION
CORPORATION - LIBRARY □ Houston, TX
Bailey, Linda, Ref.Libn.
KENTON COUNTY PUBLIC LIBRARY -
KENTUCKY & LOCAL HISTORY DEPARTMENT □
Covington, KY
Bailey, Marlene, Libn.
LAFAYETTE JOURNAL AND COURIER - LIBRARY
□ Lafayette, IN
Bailey, Martha J., Life Sci.Libn.
PURDUE UNIVERSITY - BIOCHEMISTRY
LIBRARY □ West Lafayette, IN
Bailey, Martha J., Life Sci.Libn.
PURDUE UNIVERSITY - LIFE SCIENCE LIBRARY
□ West Lafayette, IN
Bailey, Mercedes M., Chf.Libn.
INTER-AMERICAN DEFENSE COLLEGE -
LIBRARY □ Washington, DC
Bailey, Virginia S.
RENSSELAER POLYTECHNIC INSTITUTE -
ARCHITECTURE LIBRARY □ Troy, NY
Bailey, William M., Libn.
HILLSBOROUGH COUNTY LAW LIBRARY □
Tampa, FL
Baillargeon, Danielle, Ref.
CEGEP DE TROIS-RIVIERES - BIBLIOTHEQUE □
Trois-Rivieres, PQ
Baillie, Joan L., Archv./Rec.Mgr.
CANADIAN OPERA COMPANY - ARCHIVES □
Toronto, ON
Baily, Prof. Dee, Music Libn.
BROOKLYN COLLEGE OF THE CITY UNIVERSITY
OF NEW YORK - MUSIC LIBRARY □ Brooklyn, NY
Bain, Christine A., Assoc.Libn.
NEW YORK STATE LIBRARY - SCIENCES/
HEALTH SCIENCES/TECHNOLOGY REFERENCE
SERVICES □ Albany, NY
Bain, Harry, Tax Mgr.
MURPHY OIL USA, INC. - TAX LIBRARY □ El
Dorado, AR

Baird, Dennis, Libn.
UNIVERSITY OF IDAHO - SOCIAL SCIENCE
LIBRARY □ Moscow, ID
Baird, Joanne, Asst.Med.Libn.
MONTREAL CHILDREN'S HOSPITAL - MEDICAL
LIBRARY □ Montreal, PQ
Baird, M., Tech.Serv.
GOLDEY BEACOM COLLEGE - J. WILBUR
HIRONS LIBRARY □ Wilmington, DE
Baird, Marilyn J., Ref.Libn.
DETROIT EDISON COMPANY - REFERENCE
SERVICES □ Detroit, MI
Baird, Nancy, Ref.Libn.
WESTERN KENTUCKY UNIVERSITY - DEPT. OF
SPECIAL COLLECTIONS - KENTUCKY LIBRARY
AND MUSEUM/UNIVERSITY ARCHIVES □
Bowling Green, KY
Baka, George M., Libn.
JAPANESE-AMERICAN SOCIETY FOR
PHILATELY - LIBRARY □ El Cerrito, CA
Bakaian, Sharon, Libn.
DETREX CHEMICAL INDUSTRIES, INC. -
RESEARCH LABORATORIES - LIBRARY □
Detroit, MI
Bakcsy, Gabriel, Dir.
LONG ISLAND COLLEGE HOSPITAL - HOAGLAND
MEDICAL LIBRARY □ Brooklyn, NY
Bake, Maj. A.S.J., Hd., Arts & Spec.Coll.Div
ROYAL MILITARY COLLEGE OF CANADA -
MASSEY LIBRARY & SCIENCE/ENGINEERING
LIBRARY □ Kingston, ON
Baker, A. Albert, Hd.
UNIVERSITY OF SOUTHERN CALIFORNIA -
SCIENCE & ENGINEERING LIBRARY □ Los
Angeles, CA
Baker, Alberta, Law Libn.
CITIES SERVICE OIL & GAS CORPORATION -
LEGAL DIVISION LIBRARY □ Tulsa, OK
Baker, Aurelia S., Libn.
CENTRAL STATE HOSPITAL - MEDICAL
LIBRARY □ Indianapolis, IN
Baker, B. Gene, Dir.
FLORIDA STATE LEGISLATURE - DIVISION OF
LEGISLATIVE LIBRARY SERVICES □
Tallahassee, FL
Baker, Bonnie, Asst.Libn.
HARDING GRADUATE SCHOOL OF RELIGION -
L.M. GRAVES MEMORIAL LIBRARY □ Memphis,
TN
Baker, Bradley, Doc.Libn.
NORTHEASTERN ILLINOIS UNIVERSITY -
LIBRARY □ Chicago, IL
Baker, Carl R., Cat.
LOS ANGELES COUNTY MUSEUM OF ART -
RESEARCH LIBRARY □ Los Angeles, CA
Baker, Carolyn, Asst.Libn.
OKLAHOMA REGIONAL LIBRARY FOR THE
BLIND AND PHYSICALLY HANDICAPPED □
Oklahoma City, OK
Baker, Connie, Chf.Libn.
U.S. VETERANS ADMINISTRATION (CA-San
Diego) - MEDICAL CENTER LIBRARY □ San
Diego, CA
Baker, Consuelo B., Cat.
PANAMA CANAL COMMISSION - LIBRARY □
APO Miami, FL
Baker, David, Bus.Mgr.
INDIANA STATE LIBRARY □ Indianapolis, IN
Baker, Dudley L., Exec.Sec.
SOCIETY OF ST. VINCENT DE PAUL - LIBRARY
□ St. Louis, MO
Baker, Eileen, Libn.
WANG INSTITUTE OF GRADUATE STUDIES -
LIBRARY □ Tyngsboro, MA
Baker, Elizabeth, Libn.
URBAN LAND INSTITUTE - LIBRARY† □
Washington, DC
Baker, Elizabeth B., Cons.
HALIFAX HISTORICAL SOCIETY, INC. -
LIBRARY □ Daytona Beach, FL
Baker, Elizabeth K., Libn.
EASTERN KENTUCKY UNIVERSITY - MUSIC
LIBRARY □ Richmond, KY

Baker, Grace E., Libn.
SOCIETY OF CALIFORNIA PIONEERS - JOSEPH A. MOORE LIBRARY □ San Francisco, CA

Baker, James W., Res.Libn.
PLIMOTH PLANTATION, INC. - LIBRARY □ Plymouth, MA

Baker, Janet, Libn.
BANK OF AMERICA, NT & SA - REFERENCE LIBRARY □ San Francisco, CA

Baker, Joanne T., Law Libn.
LAKE COUNTY LAW LIBRARY □ Waukegan, IL

Baker, Judith, Assoc.Dir.
HAHNEMANN UNIVERSITY - WARREN H. FAKE LIBRARY† □ Philadelphia, PA

Baker, Lynda, Ref.Libn.
MC MASTER UNIVERSITY - HEALTH SCIENCES LIBRARY □ Hamilton, ON

Baker, Martha A., Libn.
HOBART BROTHERS TECHNICAL CENTER - JOHN H. BLANKENBUEHLER MEMORIAL LIBRARY □ Troy, OH

Baker, Maryann, Hd.
FREE LIBRARY OF PHILADELPHIA - LITERATURE DEPARTMENT □ Philadelphia, PA

Baker, Naydean L., Law Libn.
VENTURA COUNTY LAW LIBRARY □ Ventura, CA

Baker, Paula J., Dept.Hd.
TOLEDO-LUCAS COUNTY PUBLIC LIBRARY - FINE ARTS AND AUDIO SERVICE DEPARTMENT □ Toledo, OH

Baker, Russell P., Archv.Supv.
ARKANSAS (State) HISTORY COMMISSION - ARCHIVES □ Little Rock, AR

Baker, Sara W., Dir., Lib.Serv.
HURON ROAD HOSPITAL - LIBRARY AND AUDIOVISUAL CENTER □ Cleveland, OH

Baker, Sylva, Hd.Libn.
ACADEMY OF NATURAL SCIENCES - LIBRARY □ Philadelphia, PA

Baker, Tracey, Asst.Libn.
MINNESOTA HISTORICAL SOCIETY - SPECIAL LIBRARIES □ St. Paul, MN

Baker-Batsel, John. D., Dir.
GRADUATE THEOLOGICAL UNION - LIBRARY □ Berkeley, CA

Baker-Shear, E. Ann, Lib.Mgr.
DIGITAL EQUIPMENT CORPORATION - HUDSON LSI LIBRARY □ Hudson, MA

Bakken, Douglas A., Dir.
HENRY FORD MUSEUM AND GREENFIELD VILLAGE - ARCHIVES & RESEARCH LIBRARY □ Dearborn, MI

Bakos, Dr. Edward, Med.Dir.
CLEVELAND PSYCHIATRIC INSTITUTE - KARNOSH LIBRARY □ Cleveland, OH

Balaban, Ruth, Libn.
DUNHILL - BUSINESS RESEARCH LIBRARY □ Fort Lauderdale, FL

Balaban, Vivian, Asst.Libn.
HUNTER COLLEGE OF THE CITY UNIVERSITY OF NEW YORK - HUNTER COLLEGE SCHOOL OF SOCIAL WORK - LIBRARY □ New York, NY

Balachandran, M., Libn.
UNIVERSITY OF ILLINOIS - COMMERCE LIBRARY □ Urbana, IL

Balamuth, Eva D., Chm., Lib.Comm.
PARRISH ART MUSEUM - LIBRARY □ Southampton, NY

Balanoff, Elizabeth, Dir.
ROOSEVELT UNIVERSITY - ORAL HISTORY PROJECT IN LABOR HISTORY □ Chicago, IL

Balassone, Bro. Gabriel, Lib.Dir.
DUNS SCOTUS LIBRARY □ Southfield, MI

Balazs, Andrew, Dept.Libn.
ALBERTA - DEPARTMENT OF THE ATTORNEY GENERAL - ATTORNEY GENERAL LAW LIBRARY □ Edmonton, AB

Baldini, Bernadette, Tech.Serv.
UNIVERSITY OF KENTUCKY - MEDICAL CENTER LIBRARY □ Lexington, KY

Baldock, Margaret, Libn.
UNIVERSITY OF SASKATCHEWAN - EDUCATION BRANCH LIBRARY □ Saskatoon, SK

Baldridge, Alan, Hd.Libn.
STANFORD UNIVERSITY - HOPKINS MARINE STATION - LIBRARY □ Pacific Grove, CA

Baldridge, Sheila, Libn.
CALIFORNIA STATE UNIVERSITY AND COLLEGES - MOSS LANDING MARINE LABORATORIES - LIBRARY □ Moss Landing, CA

Baldwin, Carol, Ref./Bibliog.
UNIVERSITY OF MINNESOTA - ENGINEERING LIBRARY □ Minneapolis, MN

Baldwin, Jane, Music Ref.Libn.
UNIVERSITY OF WESTERN ONTARIO - MUSIC LIBRARY □ London, ON

Baldwin, Janet E., Libn.
EXPLORERS CLUB - JAMES B. FORD MEMORIAL LIBRARY □ New York, NY

Baldwin, Jerome C., Dir., Lib./Info.Serv.
MINNESOTA STATE DEPARTMENT OF TRANSPORTATION - LIBRARY AND INFORMATION SERVICES SECTION □ St. Paul, MN

Baldwin, Joan K., Libn.
PENNZOIL EXPLORATION AND PRODUCTION COMPANY - TECHNICAL INFORMATION SERVICES □ Houston, TX

Baldwin, Mark F., Mgr., Tech.Info.Ctr.
RAYTHEON COMPANY - SUBMARINE SIGNAL DIVISION - TECHNICAL INFORMATION CENTER □ Portsmouth, RI

Baldwin, Dr. Ruth
UNIVERSITY OF FLORIDA - BALDWIN LIBRARY □ Gainesville, FL

Baldyga, Louise, Asst.Libn.
CONNECTICUT STATE LIBRARY - LAW LIBRARY AT BRIDGEPORT □ Bridgeport, CT

Bale, Marion C., Libn.
BRAUN (C.F.) COMPANY - MURRAY HILL DIVISION - ENGINEERING LIBRARY† □ Murray Hill, NJ

Balester, Vivian S., Hd.Libn.
SQUIRE, SANDERS & DEMPSEY - LAW LIBRARY □ Cleveland, OH

Balius, Sharon, Hd., Ref./Spec.Coll.
UNIVERSITY OF MICHIGAN - ENGINEERING-TRANSPORTATION LIBRARY □ Ann Arbor, MI

Ball, Darlene L., Mgr.
BURLINGTON INDUSTRIES, INC. - LIBRARY INFORMATION SERVICES □ Greensboro, NC

Ball, Evelyn
HARTFORD PUBLIC LIBRARY - BUSINESS, SCIENCE & TECHNOLOGY DEPARTMENT □ Hartford, CT

Ball, Mrs. Frank C., Cur.
CANADIAN COUNTY HISTORICAL MUSEUM - LIBRARY □ El Reno, OK

Ball, Helen, Cur. of Spec.Coll.
MIAMI UNIVERSITY - WALTER HAVIGHURST SPECIAL COLLECTIONS LIBRARY □ Oxford, OH

Ball, Lucile, Libn.
UNIVERSITY OF MIAMI - LOWE ART MUSEUM LIBRARY □ Coral Gables, FL

Ball, Susan Campbell, Libn.
PUGET SOUND POWER AND LIGHT COMPANY LIBRARY □ Bellevue, WA

Ballard, Amy H., Dir., Med.Rec.
CLIFTON SPRINGS HOSPITAL AND CLINIC - MEDICAL LIBRARY □ Clifton Springs, NY

Ballard, Natalie C., Libn.
LAWRENCE LAW LIBRARY □ Lawrence, MA

Ballasch, Sandra S., Libn.
UNIVERSITY OF IOWA - LIBRARY SCIENCE LIBRARY □ Iowa City, IA

Ballen, Marcia, Data Bank Mgr.
CONSERVATION AND RENEWABLE ENERGY INQUIRY AND REFERRAL SERVICE □ Philadelphia, PA

Ballentine, Frances D., Multi-Media Coord.
ORANGEBURG-CALHOUN TECHNICAL COLLEGE - GRESSETTE LEARNING RESOURCE CENTER □ Orangeburg, SC

Ballentine, Rebecca S., Libn.
UNIVERSITY OF NORTH CAROLINA, CHAPEL HILL - INSTITUTE OF GOVERNMENT - LIBRARY □ Chapel Hill, NC

Balliet, Patrice, Children's Serv.
U.S. ARMY POST - FORT LEWIS - LIBRARY SYSTEM □ Ft. Lewis, WA

Ballinger, Barbara, Hd.Libn.
OAK PARK PUBLIC LIBRARY - LOCAL AUTHOR AND LOCAL HISTORY COLLECTIONS □ Oak Park, IL

Ballinger, Dr. Charles E., Exec.Sec.
NATIONAL COUNCIL ON YEAR-ROUND EDUCATION - LIBRARY □ San Diego, CA

Ballou, Raelaine, Libn.
TEMPLE UNIVERSITY - CENTRAL LIBRARY SYSTEM - COLLEGE OF ENGINEERING AND ARCHITECTURE - LIBRARY □ Philadelphia, PA

Balodis, Diane, Assoc.Libn.
ORLANDO REGIONAL MEDICAL CENTER - MEDICAL LIBRARY □ Orlando, FL

Balogh, Cornelia O., Act.Hd.
CALIFORNIA STATE UNIVERSITY, LOS ANGELES - SCIENCE AND TECHNOLOGY REFERENCE ROOM† □ Los Angeles, CA

Balogh, Margie A., Supv.
AMERICAN STOCK EXCHANGE - MARTIN J. KEENA MEMORIAL LIBRARY □ New York, NY

Balpataky, Susanne, Libn.
METROPOLITAN TORONTO LIBRARY - HISTORY DEPARTMENT □ Toronto, ON

Balshone-Becze, Cathy, Music Libn.
HARVARD UNIVERSITY - RADCLIFFE COLLEGE - MORSE MUSIC LIBRARY □ Cambridge, MA

Balsley, Susan, Libn.
VESTIGIA - LIBRARY □ Stanhope, NJ

Baltais, Helen, Libn. 2
METROPOLITAN TORONTO LIBRARY - BOOK INFORMATION AND INTERLOAN DEPARTMENT □ Toronto, ON

Balterman, Andrew M., Libn.
PUBLIC LIBRARY OF CINCINNATI AND HAMILTON COUNTY - ART AND MUSIC DEPARTMENT □ Cincinnati, OH

Baltes, Jack, Dir., Info.Serv.
INTERNATIONAL FOUNDATION OF EMPLOYEE BENEFIT PLANS - INFORMATION CENTER □ Brookfield, WI

Balthazar, Luiza, Hd., ILL
NEW YORK MEDICAL COLLEGE AND THE WESTCHESTER ACADEMY OF MEDICINE - WESTCHESTER MEDICAL CENTER LIBRARY □ Valhalla, NY

Balthrop, Barry, Hd., Foreign Patents
U.S. PATENT & TRADEMARK OFFICE - SCIENTIFIC LIBRARY† □ Arlington, VA

Balzekas, Stanley, Jr., Pres.
BALZEKAS MUSEUM OF LITHUANIAN CULTURE - RESEARCH LIBRARY □ Chicago, IL

Baman, Alfred, Libn.
PENNIE & EDMONDS - LAW LIBRARY □ New York, NY

Bamattre, Robert, Hd., Pub.Serv.
BIOLA UNIVERSITY - LIBRARY □ La Mirada, CA

Banas, Carol, Med.Libn.
GREAT FALLS CLINIC - MEDICAL LIBRARY □ Great Falls, MT

Banash, Maxine Wisner, Dir.
HISTORICAL SOCIETY OF PALM BEACH COUNTY - LIBRARY, ARCHIVES AND MUSEUM† □ Palm Beach, FL

Banayo, Manny, Dir. of Info.Ctr.
SEARS, ROEBUCK AND CO. - ARCHIVES, BUSINESS HISTORY AND INFORMATION CENTER □ Chicago, IL

Bancone, Mary-Lynne, Asst.Libn.
TEACHERS INSURANCE AND ANNUITY ASSOCIATION OF AMERICA - BUSINESS LIBRARY □ New York, NY

Bandachowicz, Krystyna, Info.Spec.
CIGNA CORPORATION - PHILADELPHIA LIBRARY □ Philadelphia, PA

Bandemer, June, Asst.Dir./Hd., Rd.Serv.
UNIVERSITY OF PITTSBURGH - FALK LIBRARY
OF THE HEALTH SCIENCES □ Pittsburgh, PA
Bander, Edward, Law Libn.
SUFFOLK UNIVERSITY - LAW LIBRARY □
Boston, MA
Bandurraga, Peter L., Dir.
NEVADA HISTORICAL SOCIETY - LIBRARY □
Reno, NV
Bandy, Charles, Dir.
UNIVERSITY OF COLORADO HEALTH SCIENCES
CENTER - DENISON MEMORIAL LIBRARY† □
Denver, CO
Bandy, Margaret, Libn.
ST. JOSEPH HOSPITAL - HEALTH SCIENCES
LIBRARY □ Denver, CO
Banek, Barbara Minne, Libn.
INLAND STEEL COMPANY - RESEARCH
LABORATORIES - LIBRARY □ East Chicago, IN
Banfi, Valori, Clinical Libn./Med.
HARTFORD HOSPITAL - HEALTH SCIENCE
LIBRARIES □ Hartford, CT
Banfield, Elizabeth, Coord., Ref.Serv.
NOVA SCOTIA - PROVINCIAL LIBRARY □
Halifax, NS
Bangalore, Nirmala, Cat.Libn.
ILLINOIS INSTITUTE OF TECHNOLOGY -
INFORMATION AND LIBRARY RESOURCES
CENTER† □ Chicago, IL
Bangiolo, Joseph, Dir.
U.S. NATL. INSTITUTES OF HEALTH -
NATIONAL CANCER INSTITUTE - CANCER
INFORMATION CLEARINGHOUSE □ Bethesda,
MD
Bangsberg, Nadine, Adm. Libn.
U.S. NAVY - NAVAL AMPHIBIOUS BASE (CA-
Coronado) - LIBRARY □ San Diego, CA
Banja, John, Dir. of Training
EMORY UNIVERSITY - REHABILITATION
RESEARCH AND TRAINING LIBRARY □ Atlanta,
GA
Banker, Sanford J., Chf., Lib.Serv.
U.S. VETERANS ADMINISTRATION (MN-St.
Cloud) - MEDICAL CENTER LIBRARY □ St. Cloud,
MN
Bankes, Cryder H., III, Mgr., Lib.Serv.
CBS INC. - CBS NEWS REFERENCE LIBRARY □
New York, NY
Bankhead, Jean, Hd., Ref.Serv./ILL
U.S. NATL. OCEANIC & ATMOSPHERIC
ADMINISTRATION - MOUNTAIN
ADMINISTRATIVE SUPPORT CTR. - LIBRARY □
Boulder, CO
Banks, Brenda, Libn.
EDMONTON ART GALLERY - REFERENCE
LIBRARY □ Edmonton, AB
Banks, Elizabeth S., Coll.Mgr.
U.S. NATL. PARK SERVICE - FREDERICK LAW
OLMSTED NATL. HISTORIC SITE - ARCHIVES □
Brookline, MA
Banks, Joyce, Rare Bks./Cons.Libn.
NATIONAL LIBRARY OF CANADA - RARE BOOK
DIVISION □ Ottawa, ON
Banks, Dr. Margaret A., Libn.
UNIVERSITY OF WESTERN ONTARIO - LAW
LIBRARY □ London, ON
Banks, Marie, Hd.Libn.
LORAIN COUNTY PRINTING & PUBLISHING
COMPANY - ELYRIA CHRONICLE-TELEGRAM -
LIBRARY □ Elyria, OH
Banks, Mary Ellen, Lib.Supv.
SCHLUMBERGER-DOLL - RESEARCH LIBRARY □
Ridgefield, CT
Banks, Tom, Dp.Chf.Libn.
ORLANDO SENTINEL NEWSPAPER - LIBRARY □
Orlando, FL
Banman, Michiko, Bibliog.
UNIVERSITY OF OREGON - ORIENTALIA
COLLECTION □ Eugene, OR
Bannen, Carol, Libn.
REINHART, BOERNER, VAN DEUREN, NORRIS &
RIESELBACH - LIBRARY □ Milwaukee, WI

Bannigan, Margaret Mary, Coord. of Serv.
ST. PAUL SEMINARY - JOHN IRELAND
MEMORIAL LIBRARY □ St. Paul, MN
Banov, Elizabeth, Asst.Libn.
FORSYTH DENTAL CENTER - PERCY HOWE
MEMORIAL LIBRARY □ Boston, MA
Bansal, Arlene, Dp.Dir.
ARIZONA STATE DEPARTMENT OF LIBRARY,
ARCHIVES & PUBLIC RECORDS □ Phoenix, AZ
Banta, David A., Exec.Dir.
MARYLAND PHARMACEUTICAL ASSOCIATION -
LIBRARY □ Baltimore, MD
Banta, John J., Chf. Law Libn.
WHITE AND CASE - LIBRARY □ New York, NY
Bantin, Philip C., Assoc.Archv.
MARQUETTE UNIVERSITY - DEPARTMENT OF
SPECIAL COLLECTIONS AND UNIVERSITY
ARCHIVES □ Milwaukee, WI
Bantling, Bro. Cozen P.
INTERNATIONAL BROTHERHOOD OF OLD
BASTARDS, INC. - SIR THOMAS CRAPPER
MEMORIAL ARCHIVES □ St. Louis, MO
Banton, Isabel, Asst.Libn.
DONALDSON, LUFKIN AND JENRETTE, INC. -
CORPORATE INFORMATION CENTER □ New
York, NY
Baptist, Jean, Cons., Lib. Media Serv.
WINNIPEG SCHOOL DIVISION NO. 1 -
TEACHERS LIBRARY AND RESOURCE CENTRE □
Winnipeg, MB
Baptiste, Nancy, Cons.
LAS CRUCES PUBLIC SCHOOL TEACHERS'
CENTER - TOY LENDING LIBRARY & EARLY
CHILDHOOD RESOURCE CENTER □ Las Cruces,
NM
Barad, Morton, Libn.
REID AND PRIEST - LAW LIBRARY □ New York,
NY
Baradi, Edita R., Acq.Libn.
YALE UNIVERSITY - ECONOMIC GROWTH
CENTER COLLECTION □ New Haven, CT
Baradi, Edita R., Acq.Libn.
YALE UNIVERSITY - SOCIAL SCIENCE LIBRARY
□ New Haven, CT
Baranski, L.D., Archv.
LONDON CLUB - ARCHIVES □ Topeka, KS
Barbalas, Louis X., Chf.
U.S. ARMY - TANK-AUTOMOTIVE COMMAND -
TECHNICAL LIBRARY SERVICE BRANCH □
Warren, MI
Barbash, Bronia, Libn.
MIAMI HEART INSTITUTE HOSPITAL -
MEDICAL LIBRARY □ Miami Beach, FL
Barbasiewicz, Kathryn, Libn. I
MILWAUKEE COUNTY LAW LIBRARY □
Milwaukee, WI
Barber, Dr. Cyril J., Acq.Cons.
INTERNATIONAL CHRISTIAN GRADUATE
UNIVERSITY - LIBRARY □ San Bernardino, CA
Barber, Dr. Elinore, Dir., Bach Inst.
BALDWIN-WALLACE COLLEGE -
RIEMENSCHNEIDER BACH INSTITUTE - BACH
LIBRARY □ Berea, OH
Barber, Frank T., Chf., Patent Counsel
GREYHOUND CORPORATION - PATENT LAW
DEPARTMENT LIBRARY □ Scottsdale, AZ
Barber, Mary S., Asst. to Dir.
UNIVERSITY OF LOUISVILLE - KORNHAUSER
HEALTH SCIENCES LIBRARY □ Louisville, KY
Barber, Mildred, Hist.
CLOUD COUNTY HISTORICAL MUSEUM -
LIBRARY □ Concordia, KS
Barber, Raymond R., Libn.
CORNING GLASS WORKS - TECHNICAL
INFORMATION CENTER □ Corning, NY
Barber, Rhonda, Libn.
VARIAN CANADA INC. - TECHNICAL LIBRARY†
□ Georgetown, ON
Barber, Sylvia P., Cur.
SALISBURY HISTORICAL SOCIETY - ARCHIVES
□ Andover, NH

Barbour, David, Photo Ed.
CANADA - NATIONAL FILM BOARD OF CANADA
- PHOTOTHEQUE □ Ottawa, ON
Barbour, Harriet, Hd., Govt.Serv.
OKLAHOMA STATE DEPARTMENT OF
LIBRARIES □ Oklahoma City, OK
Barbour, Jean, Adm.
AMERICAN MIME, INC. - LIBRARY □ New York,
NY
Barbour, Wendell, Assoc.Dir./Rd.Serv.
GEORGIA SOUTHERN COLLEGE - ARCHIVES/
SPECIAL COLLECTIONS† □ Statesboro, GA
Barbour-Talley, Donna, Dir., Med.Lib.
NORTH MEMORIAL MEDICAL CENTER -
MEDICAL LIBRARY □ Robbinsdale, MN
Barbula, P. Marvin, Dir.
SAN DIEGO COUNTY OFFICE OF EDUCATION -
PROFESSIONAL INFORMATION AND RESOURCE
CENTER □ San Diego, CA
Barbuschak, Laurie A., Tech.Serv.Spec.
NATIONAL RESTAURANT ASSOCIATION -
INFORMATION SERVICE AND LIBRARY □
Washington, DC
Barciauskas, Jonas, Hd.Libn.
WADHAMS HALL SEMINARY - COLLEGE
LIBRARY □ Ogdensburg, NY
Barclay, Elizabeth, Ref. & Cat.Libn.
UNIVERSITY OF PITTSBURGH - WESTERN
PSYCHIATRIC INSTITUTE AND CLINIC -
LIBRARY □ Pittsburgh, PA
Barclay, Julius P., Cur. of Rare Bks.
UNIVERSITY OF VIRGINIA - LIBRARY - RARE
BOOK DEPARTMENT □ Charlottesville, VA
Barclay, Susan, Coll.Libn.
DURHAM COLLEGE OF APPLIED ARTS AND
TECHNOLOGY - MAIN LIBRARY & SIMCOE
RESOURCE CENTRE □ Oshawa, ON
Bardenwerper, Fred L., Asst.Res.Dir.
DEFENSE RESEARCH INSTITUTE, INC. - BRIEF
BANK □ Chicago, IL
Bardolph, Anne D., Cat.Libn.
FLORIDA STATE UNIVERSITY - LAW LIBRARY □
Tallahassee, FL
Bardwell, John D., Dir.
UNIVERSITY OF NEW HAMPSHIRE -
DEPARTMENT OF MEDIA SERVICES - FILM
LIBRARY □ Durham, NH
Barefoot, Gary Fenton, Libn.
MOUNT OLIVE COLLEGE - FREE WILL BAPTIST
HISTORICAL COLLECTION □ Mount Olive, NC
Barefoot, Martha, Rd.Serv.
UNIVERSITY OF NORTH CAROLINA, CHAPEL
HILL - LAW LIBRARY □ Chapel Hill, NC
Barge, Silvey W., Tech.Libn.
HANSON ENGINEERS, INC. - TECHNICAL
LIBRARY □ Springfield, IL
Barich, Phyllis, Hd. Film Booking/Ref.Serv
MANITOBA - DEPARTMENT OF EDUCATION -
LIBRARY □ Winnipeg, MB
Barish, Larry, Res.Anl.
WISCONSIN STATE LEGISLATIVE REFERENCE
BUREAU □ Madison, WI
Barkdull, Margery, Supv., Map Lib.
NATIONAL GEOGRAPHIC SOCIETY - LIBRARY □
Washington, DC
Barker, Alonzo M., Pres.
AMERICAN INDIAN REFUGEES - NATIVE
LIBRARY □ Miami, FL
Barker, Gray, Dir.
SPACE AND UNEXPLAINED CELESTIAL EVENTS
RESEARCH SOCIETY - LIBRARY □ Clarksburg,
WV
Barker, Lytton T., Tech.Serv.Libn.
GUILFORD TECHNICAL COMMUNITY COLLEGE -
LEARNING RESOURCE CENTER □ Jamestown,
NC
Barker, Sr. R. Mildred, Cur. of Mss.
UNITED SOCIETY OF BELIEVERS - THE SHAKER
LIBRARY □ Poland Spring, ME
Barker, Richard T., Univ.Libn.
APPALACHIAN STATE UNIVERSITY - BELK
LIBRARY - SPECIAL COLLECTIONS □ Boone, NC

Barker, S.E., Mgr.
BRITISH COLUMBIA - MINISTRY OF FORESTS - LIBRARY □ Victoria, BC

Barkey, Patrick, Dir.
THE CLAREMONT COLLEGES - LIBRARY □ Claremont, CA

Barkley, Marlene, Mgr., Info.Serv.
DANIEL, MANN, JOHNSON AND MENDENHALL - LIBRARY □ Los Angeles, CA

Barkley, T.M., Cur. of Herbarium
KANSAS STATE UNIVERSITY - HERBARIUM LIBRARY □ Manhattan, KS

Barkman, Yvonne, Health Sci.Libn.
HIALEAH HOSPITAL - HEALTH SCIENCE LIBRARY □ Hialeah, FL

Barlas, Julie Sandall, Libn.
HARVARD UNIVERSITY - GORDON MC KAY LIBRARY - DIVISION OF APPLIED SCIENCES □ Cambridge, MA

Barley, Nancy, Tech.Libn.
CONOCO INC. - COAL RESEARCH DIVISION - TECHNICAL LIBRARY □ Library, PA

Barloga, Carolyn, Asst.Libn.
ST. FRANCIS HOSPITAL - HEALTH SCIENCE LEARNING CENTER □ Milwaukee, WI

Barloga, Carolyn J., Libn.
ST. MARY'S HOSPITAL - HEALTH SCIENCES LIBRARY □ Milwaukee, WI

Barlow, George W., Chf.Libn.
MC GRAW-HILL, INC. - LIBRARY □ New York, NY

Barlow, John, Info.Rsrcs.Spec.
MISSISSIPPI STATE DEPARTMENT OF EDUCATION - EDUCATIONAL MEDIA SERVICES □ Jackson, MS

Barmann, Edgar V., Ed.
CATHOLIC UNIVERSE BULLETIN - LIBRARY □ Cleveland, OH

Barmann, Floyd A., Dir.
CLARK COUNTY HISTORICAL SOCIETY - LIBRARY □ Springfield, OH

Barnaba, Eugenia M., Mgr., Tech.Serv.
CORNELL UNIVERSITY - RESOURCE INFORMATION LABORATORY □ Ithaca, NY

Barnard, Henry, Asst.Chf.Libn./Cat.
PORT AUTHORITY OF NEW YORK AND NEW JERSEY - LIBRARY □ New York, NY

Barnard, Kathleen, Ref.Libn.
INDIANA STATE LIBRARY - INDIANA DIVISION □ Indianapolis, IN

Barnard, Mary S., Bus.Libn.
RICE UNIVERSITY - JONES GRADUATE SCHOOL OF ADMINISTRATION - BUSINESS INFORMATION CENTER □ Houston, TX

Barnard, Sarah, Judaica Libn.
HEBREW UNION COLLEGE - JEWISH INSTITUTE OF RELIGION - KLAU LIBRARY □ Cincinnati, OH

Barner, Barry, Libn.
CANADA - CANADIAN FORESTRY SERVICE - MARITIMES FOREST RESEARCH CENTRE - LIBRARY □ Fredericton, NB

Barnes, Andrew, Cat.Libn.
UNIVERSITY OF TEXAS, AUSTIN - SCHOOL OF LAW - TARLTON LAW LIBRARY □ Austin, TX

Barnes, Leonard N., Sr., AV Libn.
FLORIDA STATE UNIVERSITY - SCHOOL OF NURSING - LEARNING RESOURCE CENTER □ Tallahassee, FL

Barnes, Lorna, Libn.
UNITY OF FAIRFAX - LIBRARY □ Oakton, VA

Barnes, Norma, Libn.
PHILIPS ROXANE, INC. - TECHNICAL LIBRARY □ St. Joseph, MO

Barnes, Ocedell, Ref.Libn.
U.S. DEPT. OF THE INTERIOR - DIVISION OF INFORMATION AND LIBRARY SERVICES - LAW BRANCH □ Washington, DC

Barnes, Patricia A., ILL Libn.
U.S. NATL. INSTITUTES OF HEALTH - LIBRARY □ Bethesda, MD

Barnes, Robert, Hd.
ROCHESTER PUBLIC LIBRARY - REYNOLDS AUDIO-VISUAL DEPARTMENT □ Rochester, NY

Barnes, Virginia, Info.Spec.
KERR-MC GEE CORPORATION - MC GEE LIBRARY □ Oklahoma City, OK

Barnett, Cherie P., Cur.
PRINCE GEORGE'S COUNTY MEMORIAL LIBRARY SYSTEM - SOJOURNER TRUTH ROOM □ Oxon Hill, MD

Barnett, Ellen, Asst.Libn.
FRITO-LAY, INC. - TECHNICAL INFORMATION CENTER □ Dallas, TX

Barnett, Gloria, Info.Spec.
REPUBLIC GEOTHERMAL, INC. - INFORMATION RESOURCES CENTER □ Santa Fe Springs, CA

Barnett, Janet K., Dir.
GREY ADVERTISING, INC. - INFORMATION CENTER □ New York, NY

Barnett, Judith B., Asst.Libn.
UNIVERSITY OF RHODE ISLAND, NARRAGANSETT BAY - PELL MARINE SCIENCE LIBRARY† □ Narragansett, RI

Barnett, Karen, Dp.Libn.
HUNTER COLLEGE OF THE CITY UNIVERSITY OF NEW YORK - HEALTH PROFESSIONS LIBRARY □ New York, NY

Barnett, Kathy, Libn.
EG&G, INC. - SANTA BARBARA DIVISION - LIBRARY □ Goleta, CA

Barnett, Lynda, Design Libn.
CANADIAN BROADCASTING CORPORATION - REFERENCE LIBRARY □ Toronto, ON

Barnett, Lynn, Asst.Dir.
ERIC CLEARINGHOUSE ON HIGHER EDUCATION □ Washington, DC

Barnett, Lynn, Cat.Libn.
UNIVERSITY OF KENTUCKY - MEDICAL CENTER LIBRARY □ Lexington, KY

Barnett, Molly C., Plaza Libn.
REYNOLDS (R.J.) INDUSTRIES, INC. - RJR CORPORATE LIBRARY-PLAZA □ Winston-Salem, NC

Barnett, Patricia, Assoc.Musm.Libn.
METROPOLITAN MUSEUM OF ART - THOMAS J. WATSON LIBRARY □ New York, NY

Barnett, Philip, Searcher/Indexer
AYERST LABORATORIES - INFORMATION CENTER □ New York, NY

Barnett, Stanley, Libn.
FIRST BAPTIST CHURCH - LIBRARY □ Booneville, MS

Barnett-Robisheaux, Mason
DUKE UNIVERSITY - ARCHIVES □ Durham, NC

Barnette, Donald C., Jr., Dept.Hd.
TOLEDO-LUCAS COUNTY PUBLIC LIBRARY - HISTORY-TRAVEL-BIOGRAPHY DEPARTMENT □ Toledo, OH

Barney, Alan, Hd., Adm.Serv.Dept.
CENTER FOR RESEARCH LIBRARIES □ Chicago, IL

Barney, Frances J., Libn.
U.S. FOREST SERVICE - ROCKY MOUNTAIN FOREST & RANGE EXPERIMENT STATION - LIBRARY □ Fort Collins, CO

Barnum, Amy, Libn.
NEW YORK STATE HISTORICAL ASSOCIATION - LIBRARY □ Cooperstown, NY

Barnum, Sally J., Mgr.
UNITED WAY OF CHICAGO - LIBRARY □ Chicago, IL

Baron, Ethelnel, Staff Sec.
SHENANGO VALLEY OSTEOPATHIC HOSPITAL - MEDICAL LIBRARY □ Farrell, PA

Baron, Judy, Sr.Libn.
KENTUCKY STATE DEPARTMENT FOR LIBRARIES & ARCHIVES - KENTUCKY TALKING BOOK LIBRARY □ Frankfort, KY

Baron, Krystyna, Libn.
POLISH INSTITUTE OF ARTS AND SCIENCES IN AMERICA, INC. - RESEARCH LIBRARY □ New York, NY

Baron, Lorraine C., Libn.
IONICS, INC. - RESEARCH DEPARTMENT LIBRARY □ Watertown, MA

Barone, Rita, Law Libn.
METROPOLITAN LIFE INSURANCE COMPANY - LAW LIBRARY □ New York, NY

Barr, Douglas R., Sta.Mgr.
MC GILL UNIVERSITY - SUB-ARCTIC RESEARCH STATION LIBRARY □ Schefferville, PQ

Barr, Eleanor M., Archv.
SWARTHMORE COLLEGE - FRIENDS HISTORICAL LIBRARY - PEACE COLLECTION □ Swarthmore, PA

Barr, John, Cat.
MEDICAL COLLEGE OF PENNSYLVANIA - EASTERN PENNSYLVANIA PSYCHIATRIC INST. - MENTAL HEALTH AND NEUROSCIENCES LIB. □ Philadelphia, PA

Barr, Mary P., Hd., Pub.Serv.
UNIVERSITY OF CALIFORNIA, SAN FRANCISCO - LIBRARY □ San Francisco, CA

Barra, Carol H., Hd.Libn.
BREED, ABBOTT & MORGAN - LIBRARY □ New York, NY

Barranco, Mary Seeley, Hd.Libn.
BALTIMORE COUNTY CIRCUIT COURT - LAW LIBRARY □ Towson, MD

Barravecchia, Mary, Hd.Libn.
U.S. NAVY - NAVAL UNDERWATER SYSTEMS CENTER - NEWPORT TECHNICAL LIBRARY† □ Newport, RI

Barre, Louise, Asst.Libn.
WESTCOAST TRANSMISSION COMPANY LIMITED - LIBRARY □ Vancouver, BC

Barrera, Pablo, Ref.Libn.
ILLINOIS INSTITUTE OF TECHNOLOGY - INFORMATION AND LIBRARY RESOURCES CENTER† □ Chicago, IL

Barret, Beth, Libn.
ST. MARY'S MEDICAL CENTER, INC. - SCHOOL OF NURSING LIBRARY □ Knoxville, TN

Barrett, Carol A., Libn.
BELL HELICOPTER TEXTRON - ENGINEERING TECHNICAL LIBRARY □ Fort Worth, TX

Barrett, Darryl, Prof.Asst.
MINNEAPOLIS PUBLIC LIBRARY & INFORMATION CENTER - ART, MUSIC & FILMS DEPARTMENT □ Minneapolis, MN

Barrett, Deborah, Libn.
METROPOLITAN PITTSBURGH PUBLIC BROADCASTING, INC. - WQED LIBRARY □ Pittsburgh, PA

Barrett, Donald J., Asst.Dir., Pub.Serv.
U.S. AIR FORCE ACADEMY - LIBRARY □ Colorado Springs, CO

Barrett, Dorothy, Asst.Libn.
COMPUTER SCIENCES CORPORATION - TECHNICAL LIBRARY □ Falls Church, VA

Barrett, Dorothy L., Chm., Lib.Comm.
UNITED DAUGHTERS OF THE CONFEDERACY - CAROLINE MERIWETHER GOODLETT LIBRARY □ Richmond, VA

Barrett, Jan, Libn.
FRASER AND BEATTY - LIBRARY □ Toronto, ON

Barrett, Jane R., Libn.
CANADIAN INSTITUTE OF INTERNATIONAL AFFAIRS - LIBRARY □ Toronto, ON

Barrett, Jerry E.
U.S. VETERANS ADMINISTRATION (TX-Houston) - MEDICAL CENTER LIBRARY □ Houston, TX

Barrett, Laura, AV Libn.
UNIVERSITY OF MEDICINE AND DENTISTRY OF NEW JERSEY AT NEWARK - GEORGE F. SMITH LIBRARY □ Newark, NJ

Barrett, Michele L., Libn./Dir.
NEW YORK CHIROPRACTIC COLLEGE - LIBRARY □ Glen Head, NY

Barrett, Rosemary, Libn.
FRITO-LAY, INC. - LIBRARY □ Dallas, TX

Barrett, Dr. Stephen
LEHIGH VALLEY COMMITTEE AGAINST HEALTH FRAUD, INC. - LIBRARY □ Allentown, PA
Barrette-Pilon, Nicole, Libn.
AYERST, MC KENNA & HARRISON, INC. - LIBRARY □ Montreal, PQ
Barrick, Susan O., Lib.Dir.
VIRGINIA INSTITUTE OF MARINE SCIENCE LIBRARY □ Gloucester Point, VA
Barringer, George M., Spec.Coll.Libn.
GEORGETOWN UNIVERSITY - SPECIAL COLLECTIONS DIVISION - LAUINGER MEMORIAL LIBRARY □ Washington, DC
Barringer, Nancy Franzen, Libn.
AMERICAN HOECHST CORPORATION - TECHNICAL INFORMATION CENTER □ Leominster, MA
Barrington, David S., Cur.
UNIVERSITY OF VERMONT - PRINGLE HERBARIUM - LIBRARY □ Burlington, VT
Barritt, Marjorie, Asst.Archv.
UNIVERSITY OF MICHIGAN - MICHIGAN HISTORICAL COLLECTIONS - BENTLEY HISTORICAL LIBRARY □ Ann Arbor, MI
Barron, Edwina T., Libn.
PREFORMED LINE PRODUCTS - RESEARCH & ENGINEERING LIBRARY □ Cleveland, OH
Barrow, John, Libn.
AMERICAN ACADEMY OF DRAMATIC ARTS - LIBRARY □ New York, NY
Barrow, Sarilou A., Libn.
ORANGE COUNTY LAW LIBRARY† □ Orlando, FL
Barrows, Allen F., Dir. of Pub.Serv.
UNIVERSITY OF WISCONSIN, STEVENS POINT - JAMES H. ALBERTSON CENTER FOR LEARNING RESOURCES □ Stevens Point, WI
Barrows, Julie B., Dir.
DANBURY SCOTT-FANTON MUSEUM AND HISTORICAL SOCIETY - LIBRARY □ Danbury, CT
Barrows, Richard S., Libn.
U.S. NAVY - OFFICE OF THE JUDGE ADVOCATE GENERAL - LAW LIBRARY □ Alexandria, VA
Barrows, William, Info.Coord.
FAMILY HEALTH INTERNATIONAL - LIBRARY □ Research Triangle Park, NC
Barry, Ann, Dir. of Res.
HANDY ASSOCIATES, INC. - RESEARCH LIBRARY □ New York, NY
Barry, Colette, Libn.
QUEBEC PROVINCE - ARCHIVES NATIONALES DU QUEBEC - BIBLIOTHEQUE □ Ste. Foy, PQ
Barry, Sr. Justin, O.P., Archv.
DOMINICAN SISTERS - CONGREGATION OF THE HOLY NAME - ARCHIVES □ San Rafael, CA
Barry, Kevin, Res.Libn., Mgt.
METROPOLITAN LIFE INSURANCE COMPANY - CORPORATE INFORMATION CENTER AND LIBRARY □ New York, NY
Barry, Marilyn Gibbs, Med.Libn.
DE KALB GENERAL HOSPITAL - MEDICAL LIBRARY □ Decatur, GA
Barry, Sr. Martin, Asst.Archv.
DOMINICAN SISTERS - CONGREGATION OF THE HOLY NAME - ARCHIVES □ San Rafael, CA
Barry, Nancy, Cat.
BROOKINGS INSTITUTION - LIBRARY □ Washington, DC
Barry, Richard A., Engr.-Ref.Libn.
MANHATTAN COLLEGE - GROVER M. HERMANN ENGINEERING LIBRARY □ Bronx, NY
Barss, David S., Mgr.
COMPUTERIZED GENEALOGY LIBRARY □ North Salt Lake, UT
Bart, Hans, Musm.Libn.
UNIVERSITY OF ARIZONA - ARIZONA STATE MUSEUM LIBRARY □ Tucson, AZ
Bartel, Betty, Rec.Mgmt.Asst.
KELLER (J.J.) & ASSOCIATES, INC. - RESEARCH & TECHNICAL LIBRARY □ Neenah, WI
Bartell, Blaine, Newsreel Archv.
UNIVERSITY OF CALIFORNIA, LOS ANGELES - UCLA FILM ARCHIVES □ Los Angeles, CA

Bartelli, Alice, Libn.
HAWAII STATE LIBRARY - EDNA ALLYN ROOM □ Honolulu, HI
Barten, Sharon, Asst.Libn.
CATHOLIC MEDICAL CENTER OF BROOKLYN & QUEENS, INC. - CENTRAL MEDICAL LIBRARY □ Jamaica, NY
Bartenbach, Wilhelm, Exec.Dir.
PUBLIC AFFAIRS INFORMATION SERVICE □ New York, NY
Barth, Dr. Edward W., Supv., Lib. & Media Serv.
PRINCE GEORGE'S COUNTY PUBLIC SCHOOLS - PROFESSIONAL LIBRARY □ Landover, MD
Barth, Joseph M., Coll.Dev.Libn.
U.S. ARMY - MILITARY ACADEMY - LIBRARY □ West Point, NY
Barth, Miles, Cur., Archv. & Coll.
INTERNATIONAL CENTER OF PHOTOGRAPHY - RICHARD A. HILLMAN RESEARCH COLLECTIONS □ New York, NY
Barth, Paul, Dir.
BELLEVUE HOSPITAL - MEDICAL LIBRARY □ New York, NY
Barth, Sherrill, Libn.
DISADA PRODUCTIONS LTD. - WALT DISNEY MEMORIAL LIBRARY □ Montreal, PQ
Bartis, Peter, Folklife Res.
LIBRARY OF CONGRESS - AMERICAN FOLKLIFE CENTER □ Washington, DC
Bartkowski, Patricia, Archv.
WAYNE STATE UNIVERSITY - ARCHIVES OF LABOR AND URBAN AFFAIRS/UNIVERSITY ARCHIVES □ Detroit, MI
Bartl, Richard, Libn./Data Anl.
IIT RESEARCH INSTITUTE - GUIDANCE AND CONTROL INFORMATION ANALYSIS CENTER (GACIAC) □ Chicago, IL
Bartlett, Chris, Dir., LRC
CAMBRIAN COLLEGE OF APPLIED ARTS AND TECHNOLOGY - LEARNING RESOURCES CENTRE □ Sudbury, ON
Bartlett, Eleanor A., Chf.
DISTRICT OF COLUMBIA PUBLIC LIBRARY - HISTORY, TRAVEL AND GEOGRAPHY DIVISION □ Washington, DC
Bartlett, Elinor, SDI Libn.
BELL CANADA - INFORMATION RESOURCE CENTRE □ Montreal, PQ
Bartlett, Helen, Hd.Cat.
YALE UNIVERSITY - JOHN HERRICK JACKSON MUSIC LIBRARY □ New Haven, CT
Bartlett, Maye A., Libn.
IBM CORPORATION - SITE TECHNICAL LIBRARY/INFORMATION CENTER □ Austin, TX
Bartlett, Opal, Libn.
MEDICAL CENTER - SIMON SCHWOB MEDICAL LIBRARY □ Columbus, GA
Bartlett, Vern, Info.Spec.
HONEYWELL, INC. - SYSTEMS & RESEARCH CENTER - LIBRARY □ Minneapolis, MN
Bartlett-Cahill, Leah A., Tech.Info.Supv.
NL INDUSTRIES, INC. - INFORMATION CENTER □ Houston, TX
Bartley, Gertrude N., Libn.
OROVILLE HOSPITAL AND MEDICAL CENTER - EDWARD P. GODDARD, M.D., MEMORIAL LIBRARY □ Oroville, CA
Bartley, Margaret, Asst.Libn.
BOSTON ARCHITECTURAL CENTER - ALFRED SHAW AND EDWARD DURELL STONE LIBRARY □ Boston, MA
Bartman, Marie, Libn.
CONGREGATION AGUDAS ACHIM - BERNARD RUBENSTEIN LIBRARY □ San Antonio, TX
Barto, Stephen C., Res.Assoc.
STATEN ISLAND HISTORICAL SOCIETY - LIBRARY □ Staten Island, NY
Barton, Barbara, Asst.Libn.
CROSBY, HEAFEY, ROACH & MAY - LAW LIBRARY □ Oakland, CA
Barton, Bill, Hd., Hist.Res.Div.
WYOMING STATE ARCHIVES MUSEUMS & HISTORICAL DEPARTMENT □ Cheyenne, WY

Barton, Carol P., Libn.
CANADA - MINISTRY OF STATE FOR ECONOMIC & REGIONAL DEVELOPMENT - LIBRARY □ Ottawa, ON
Barton, Mrs. J. Floyd, Libn.
KENT HISTORICAL SOCIETY - LIBRARY □ Kent, CT
Barton, Jean, Libn.
KANSAS STATE DEPARTMENT OF SOCIAL & REHABILITATION SERVICES - STAFF DEVELOPMENT TRAINING CENTER LIBRARY □ Topeka, KS
Barton, Joan, Hd., Ref.
BRITISH COLUMBIA - LEGISLATIVE LIBRARY □ Victoria, BC
Barton, Ruth, Libn.
DETROIT PUBLIC LIBRARY - FINE ARTS DEPARTMENT □ Detroit, MI
Barton, Ruth Anne, Chm., Lib.Commn.
GREATER LOS ANGELES ZOO ASSOCIATION - LIBRARY □ Los Angeles, CA
Bartosh, Eloise, Asst.Libn.
MERCY HOSPITAL - MEDICAL LIBRARY □ Scranton, PA
Bartoshesky, Florence, Mss. and Archv.
HARVARD UNIVERSITY - HARVARD BUSINESS SCHOOL - BAKER LIBRARY □ Boston, MA
Bartow, Martha M., Hd.Libn.
PUBLIC UTILITY COMMISSION OF TEXAS - LIBRARY □ Austin, TX
Bartram, Robert, Ref.Libn.
JOHNS HOPKINS UNIVERSITY - MILTON S. EISENHOWER LIBRARY - GEORGE PEABODY COLLECTION □ Baltimore, MD
Bartucca, Peter, Libn.
BURKE & BURKE - LAW LIBRARY □ New York, NY
Bartz, Christine, Hd.Libn.
CRANBROOK INSTITUTE OF SCIENCE - LIBRARY □ Bloomfield Hills, MI
Baruth, Christopher M., Map Cat./Ref.Libn.
AMERICAN GEOGRAPHICAL SOCIETY COLLECTION OF THE UNIVERSITY OF WISCONSIN, MILWAUKEE - GOLDA MEIR LIBRARY □ Milwaukee, WI
Basar, Dorothy L., Hd.Libn.
BEAVER COUNTY TIMES - LIBRARY □ Beaver, PA
Basart, Ann P.
UNIVERSITY OF CALIFORNIA, BERKELEY - MUSIC LIBRARY □ Berkeley, CA
Basche, Sr. Elaine, Libn.
ST. LAWRENCE SEMINARY - LIBRARY □ Mount Calvary, WI
Baschnagel, Mrs. Robert, Libn.
GARDEN CENTER OF ROCHESTER - LIBRARY □ Rochester, NY
Basciani, Caroline, Tax Libn.
ARTHUR ANDERSEN & CO. - TAX LIBRARY □ Chicago, IL
Basel, Dona, Libn.
BEDFORD HISTORICAL SOCIETY - LIBRARY □ Bedford, OH
Basford, Terry, Asst.Hum.Libn.
OKLAHOMA STATE UNIVERSITY - HUMANITIES DIVISION □ Stillwater, OK
Bashover, Linda K., Libn.
COLLEGE RETIREMENT EQUITIES FUND - CREF RESEARCH LIBRARY □ New York, NY
Basile, Victor, Asst.Libn., Tech.Proc.
UNIVERSITY OF MEDICINE AND DENTISTRY OF NEW JERSEY AT NEWARK - GEORGE F. SMITH LIBRARY □ Newark, NJ
Baskerville, Frances, Hd.Libn.
BRITISH COLUMBIA - MINISTRY OF CONSUMER AND CORPORATE AFFAIRS - LIBRARY SERVICES □ Victoria, BC
Baskin, Jeffrey, AV Libn.
UNIVERSITY OF ARKANSAS FOR MEDICAL SCIENCES - MEDICAL SCIENCES LIBRARY □ Little Rock, AR

Baskin, Karen
MIAMI-DADE PUBLIC LIBRARY - ART AND
MUSIC DIVISION □ Miami, FL
Basler, Thomas G., Dir. of Libs.
MEDICAL COLLEGE OF GEORGIA - LIBRARY □
Augusta, GA
Basnight, Jane, Libn.
NORTH CAROLINA STATE DEPT. OF NATURAL
RESOURCES & COMMUNITY DEVELOPMENT -
ENVIRONMENTAL MGT. LIBRARY □ Raleigh, NC
Bass, Bohuslawa Z-P., Br.Supv.
DU PONT DE NEMOURS (E.I.) & COMPANY, INC.
- LIBRARY NETWORK □ Wilmington, DE
Bass, Deborah, Ref.
HUGHES AIRCRAFT COMPANY - GROUND
SYSTEMS GROUP - TECHNICAL LIBRARY □
Fullerton, CA
Bass, James, Cat.
ST. MARY'S UNIVERSITY - LAW LIBRARY† □
San Antonio, TX
Bass, Jocelyn C., Asst.Libn.
WILMINGTON AREA HEALTH EDUCATION
CENTER - HEALTH SCIENCES LIBRARY □
Wilmington, NC
Bass, W.H., Dir.
POLK (James K.) ANCESTRAL HOME - LIBRARY
□ Columbia, TN
Bass, Wilma, Hd.Cat.
GEORGETOWN UNIVERSITY - MEDICAL
CENTER - DAHLGREN MEMORIAL LIBRARY □
Washington, DC
Bassett, Barbara C., Libn.
CHURCH OF JESUS CHRIST OF LATTER-DAY
SAINTS - LOVELL, WYOMING BRANCH
GENEALOGICAL LIBRARY □ Lovell, WY
Bassett, Betty A., Mgr., Tech.Info.Ctr.
XEROX RESEARCH CENTRE OF CANADA -
TECHNICAL INFORMATION CENTRE □
Mississauga, ON
Bassett, Pegeen, Docs.Libn.
NORTHWESTERN UNIVERSITY - LAW SCHOOL
LIBRARY □ Chicago, IL
Bassett, Ruth, Libn.
BRANDYWINE RIVER MUSEUM LIBRARY □
Chadds Ford, PA
Bassett, Sandy
AKIN, GUMP, STRAUSS, HAUER & FELD LAW
LIBRARY □ Dallas, TX
Bassist, Norma H., Libn.
BASSIST COLLEGE - LIBRARY □ Portland, OR
Bastien, Carol, Acq.Libn.
SOUTHWESTERN BAPTIST THEOLOGICAL
SEMINARY - A. WEBB ROBERTS LIBRARY □ Fort
Worth, TX
Bastille, Jacqueline, Dir.
MASSACHUSETTS GENERAL HOSPITAL - MGH
HEALTH SCIENCES LIBRARIES □ Boston, MA
Batchelder, Robert, Map/Airphoto Libn.
UNIVERSITY OF CALGARY - ENVIRONMENT-
SCIENCE-TECHNOLOGY LIBRARY† □ Calgary,
AB
Batchelor, Mary Ellen, Ref.Libn.
SOUTHERN METHODIST UNIVERSITY -
SCIENCE/ENGINEERING LIBRARY □ Dallas, TX
Bateman, Audray, Cur.
AUSTIN PUBLIC LIBRARY - AUSTIN HISTORY
CENTER □ Austin, TX
Bateman, Mary Ruth, Mgr., Tech.Info.
ST. REGIS CORPORATION - TECHNICAL
CENTER LIBRARY □ West Nyack, NY
Bateman, Robert, Hd., Tech.Serv.
ALBERTA - DEPARTMENT OF AGRICULTURE -
LIBRARY □ Edmonton, AB
Bater, Richard E., Lrng.Rsrcs.Spec.
PUBLIC SERVICE ELECTRIC AND GAS
COMPANY - NUCLEAR TRAINING CENTER
LIBRARY □ Salem, NJ
Bates, Cathy, Med.Libn.
HOULTON REGIONAL HOSPITAL - LIBRARY □
Houlton, ME

Bates, David, Ref. & Copyright Libn.
GENERAL ELECTRIC COMPANY - CORPORATE
RESEARCH & DEVELOPMENT - WHITNEY
INFORMATION SERVICES □ Schenectady, NY
Bates, Mariette, Resource Ctr.Coord.
ONE TO ONE - RESOURCE CENTER □ New York,
NY
Bates, Peta, Libn.
LAW SOCIETY OF SASKATCHEWAN -
BARRISTERS LIBRARY □ Saskatoon, SK
Bates, Peter J., Info.Spec.
SYNCRUDE CANADA, LTD. - RESEARCH AND
DEVELOPMENT LIBRARY □ Edmonton, AB
Bates, S. Mabell, Spec.Coll.Libn.
BRIDGEWATER STATE COLLEGE - CLEMENT C.
MAXWELL LIBRARY □ Bridgewater, MA
Batey, Deborah G., Med.Libn.
U.S. NAVY - NAVAL HOSPITAL (CA-Camp
Pendleton) - MEDICAL LIBRARY □ Camp
Pendleton, CA
Bathalon, Real, Libn.
CENTRE INTERCULTUREL MONCHANIN -
BIBLIOTHEQUE □ Montreal, PQ
Batiste, Pamela J., Info.Spec.
GULF OIL CORPORATION - LIBRARY AND
INFORMATION CENTER □ Houston, TX
Batliner, Doris J., Chf.Libn.
COURIER-JOURNAL AND LOUISVILLE TIMES -
LIBRARY □ Louisville, KY
Batra, Gretchen, Plan./Coord., Educ.
BOSTON UNIVERSITY - GERONTOLOGY
RESOURCE CENTER □ Boston, MA
Battaglia, Nancy W., Med.Libn.
CHILDREN'S HOSPITAL, INC. - MEDICAL-
NURSING LIBRARY □ St. Paul, MN
Battaile, Constance
SOUTHERN OREGON STATE COLLEGE -
LIBRARY □ Ashland, OR
Batterman, Rene, Libn.
TEMPLE EMANUEL - LIBRARY† □ Cherry Hill, NJ
Battipaglia, Nicholas S., Jr., Math/Sci.Libn.
U.S. ARMY - MILITARY ACADEMY - LIBRARY □
West Point, NY
Battista, Dr. O.A., Pres.
RESEARCH SERVICES CORPORATION - THE
O.A. BATTISTA RESEARCH INSTITUTE -
LIBRARY □ Fort Worth, TX
Battiste, Anita L., Asst.Ref.Libn.
UNIVERSITY OF FLORIDA - HUME LIBRARY □
Gainesville, FL
Battisti, Josephine, Libn.
UNIVERSITY OF WYOMING - GEOLOGY
LIBRARY† □ Laramie, WY
Battle, Thomas C., Cur. of Mss.
HOWARD UNIVERSITY - MOORLAND-SPINGARN
RESEARCH CENTER - MANUSCRIPT DIVISION □
Washington, DC
Batty, Ellen, Circ.Libn.
ATHENAEUM OF PHILADELPHIA □ Philadelphia,
PA
Baty, L.A., Prints & Photographs
MARYLAND HISTORICAL SOCIETY - LIBRARY □
Baltimore, MD
Baucom, Thomas L., Pub.Aff.Off.
U.S. FOREST SERVICE - NORTHEASTERN
FOREST EXPERIMENT STATION LIBRARY □
Broomall, PA
Baudhuin, Margaret G., Libn./Info.Spec.
UNIVERSITY OF WISCONSIN, MADISON -
DEPARTMENT OF PSYCHIATRY - LITHIUM
INFORMATION CENTER □ Madison, WI
Bauer, David C., Libn.
BRAINERD STATE HOSPITAL - LIBRARY □
Brainerd, MN
Bauer, Frederick E., Jr., Assoc.Libn.
AMERICAN ANTIQUARIAN SOCIETY - LIBRARY
□ Worcester, MA
Bauer, Roxy, Libn.
SCIENCE ASSOCIATES/INTERNATIONAL, INC.
- LIBRARY □ New York, NY

Baughman, Charlotte, Lib.Res.Anl.
ROCKWELL INTERNATIONAL - SPACE
BUSINESSES - TECHNICAL INFORMATION
CENTER □ Downey, CA
Baughman, Susan, Assoc.Libn.
HARVARD UNIVERSITY - GRADUATE SCHOOL
OF EDUCATION - GUTMAN LIBRARY □
Cambridge, MA
Baule, John A., Dir.
ST. LAWRENCE COUNTY HISTORICAL
ASSOCIATION - ARCHIVES □ Canton, NY
Baum, Inge, Libn.
SCOTTISH RITE SUPREME COUNCIL - LIBRARY
□ Washington, DC
Baum, Judith, Dir., Info.Serv.
PUBLIC EDUCATION ASSOCIATION - LIBRARY
AND ARCHIVES □ New York, NY
Baum, Mary, Libn.
CLEVELAND MUSEUM OF NATURAL HISTORY -
HAROLD TERRY CLARK LIBRARY □ Cleveland,
OH
Bauman, Nancy, Asst.Cat.
CAPITAL UNIVERSITY - LAW SCHOOL LIBRARY
□ Columbus, OH
Bauman, Dr. Richard, Dir.
UNIVERSITY OF TEXAS, AUSTIN - CENTER FOR
INTERCULTURAL STUDIES IN FOLKLORE AND
ETHNOMUSICOLOGY - LIBRARY □ Austin, TX
Baumann, Anne, Libn.
WOOD GUNDY LTD. - LIBRARY □ Toronto, ON
Baumann, Roland M., Div.Chf.
PENNSYLVANIA STATE HISTORICAL & MUSEUM
COMMISSION - DIVISION OF ARCHIVES AND
MANUSCRIPTS □ Harrisburg, PA
Baumann, Susan, Coord.
ONTARIO - MINISTRY OF NORTHERN AFFAIRS
- LIBRARY AND RECORDS □ Toronto, ON
Baumruk, Robert, Dept.Hd.
CHICAGO PUBLIC LIBRARY CENTRAL LIBRARY -
GOVERNMENT PUBLICATIONS DEPARTMENT □
Chicago, IL
Baun, Barbara F., Libn.
NAVAJO NATION LIBRARY □ Window Rock, AZ
Bauner, Dr. Ruth, Educ. & Psych.Libn.
SOUTHERN ILLINOIS UNIVERSITY,
CARBONDALE - EDUCATION AND PSYCHOLOGY
DIVISION LIBRARY □ Carbondale, IL
Bausch, Donna, Asst.Libn.
SUTHERLAND, ASBILL & BRENNAN - LIBRARY □
Washington, DC
Baut, Donald V., Cur. of Res.
DEARBORN HISTORICAL MUSEUM - RESEARCH
DIVISION - ARCHIVES AND LIBRARY† □
Dearborn, MI
Bautista, Anne T., Libn.
MICHIGAN STATE LEGISLATIVE COUNCIL -
LEGISLATIVE SERVICE BUREAU LIBRARY □
Lansing, MI
Bauza, Emma, Ref.Libn.
PUERTO RICO - SUPREME COURT - LAW
LIBRARY □ San Juan, PR
Baver, Florence, Mgr.
PENNSYLVANIA DUTCH FOLK CULTURE
SOCIETY, INC. - BAVER MEMORIAL LIBRARY □
Lenhartsville, PA
Baxter, Charlene, Cat.Libn.
LA GRANGE COLLEGE - WILLIAM AND EVELYN
BANKS LIBRARY - SPECIAL COLLECTIONS □
LaGrange, GA
Baxter, E., U.N. Doc.
WAYNE STATE UNIVERSITY - G. FLINT PURDY
LIBRARY □ Detroit, MI
Baxter, Marie, Lib.Supv.
U.S. NAVY - NAVAL AIR STATION (FL-
Pensacola) - LIBRARY □ Pensacola, FL
Baxter, Pam, Psych.Libn.
PURDUE UNIVERSITY - PSYCHOLOGICAL
SCIENCES LIBRARY □ West Lafayette, IN
Baxter, Patricia, Libn.
ALBERTA HOSPITAL ASSOCIATION -
RESOURCE CENTRE □ Edmonton, AB

Baxter, Paula, Ref.libn.
MUSEUM OF MODERN ART - LIBRARY □ New York, NY
Baxter, Ruth, Med.Lib.Dir.
SOUTHEAST ALABAMA MEDICAL CENTER - MEDICAL LIBRARY □ Dothan, AL
Baxter, Susanna G., Libn.
SHRINERS HOSPITAL FOR CRIPPLED CHILDREN - ORTHOPEDIC LIBRARY □ Houston, TX
Baxter, William E., Libn.
CACI, INC. - LIBRARY AND TECHNICAL INFORMATION CENTER □ Arlington, VA
Baxtresser, Betty, Chf.
U.S. BUREAU OF THE CENSUS - LIBRARY & INFORMATION SERVICES BRANCH □ Washington, DC
Bay, Sonja, Libn.
GUGGENHEIM (Solomon R.) MUSEUM - LIBRARY □ New York, NY
Bayard, Mary Ivy, Libn.
TEMPLE UNIVERSITY - CENTRAL LIBRARY SYSTEM - TYLER SCHOOL OF FINE ARTS - LIBRARY □ Philadelphia, PA
Bayer, Bernard, Hd.
OHIO STATE UNIVERSITY - MECHANIZED INFORMATION CENTER (MIC) □ Columbus, OH
Bayless, Donna J., Libn.
ST. JOSEPH'S MEDICAL CENTER - MEDICAL LIBRARY □ South Bend, IN
Baylies, Zoe, Res.Dir.
TOBACCO MERCHANTS ASSOCIATION OF THE U.S. - HOWARD S. CULLMAN LIBRARY □ New York, NY
Bayne, Pauline S., Libn.
UNIVERSITY OF TENNESSEE - MUSIC LIBRARY □ Knoxville, TN
Baynes, Randall K., Supt.
U.S. NATL. PARK SERVICE - HOMESTEAD NATL. MONUMENT - RESEARCH LIBRARY □ Beatrice, NE
Bayorgeon, Mary M., Dir., Lib.Serv.
ST. ELIZABETH HOSPITAL - HEALTH SCIENCE LIBRARY □ Appleton, WI
Bayrak, Bettie, Libn.
ALBERTA - DEPARTMENT OF MUNICIPAL AFFAIRS - LIBRARY □ Edmonton, AB
Bayron, Vilma Rivera, Libn.
UNIVERSITY OF PUERTO RICO - GRADUATE SCHOOL OF LIBRARIANSHIPS - LIBRARY □ San Juan, PR
Bays-Coutts, Eileen, Dp.Chf., Tech.Serv.
CANADA - DEPARTMENT OF FINANCE - FINANCE/TREASURY BOARD LIBRARY □ Ottawa, ON
Bazemore, Barbara, Ref.
TENNESSEE VALLEY AUTHORITY - TECHNICAL LIBRARY □ Chattanooga, TN
Bazin, Genevieve, Libn.
UNIVERSITE DE MONTREAL - COLLECTIONS SPECIALES □ Montreal, PQ
Beach, Alta, Sr.Libn.
NEW YORK STATE LIBRARY - SCIENCES/ HEALTH SCIENCES/TECHNOLOGY REFERENCE SERVICES □ Albany, NY
Beach, Annabelle, Asst.Libn.
UNIVERSITY OF MISSOURI, KANSAS CITY - LAW LIBRARY □ Kansas City, MO
Beach, Linda M., Med.Libn.
GRAND VIEW HOSPITAL - EDWARD F. BURROW MEMORIAL LIBRARY □ Sellersville, PA
Beach, R.M., Dir.
GOLDEY BEACOM COLLEGE - J. WILBUR HIRONS LIBRARY □ Wilmington, DE
Beach, Rosemary, Dir.
CEDAR FALLS HISTORICAL SOCIETY - ROWND HISTORICAL LIBRARY □ Cedar Falls, IA
Beacock, Bruce, Archv.Techn.
SIMCOE COUNTY ARCHIVES □ Minesing, ON
Beadle, Carol, Pk.Techn., Interp.
U.S. NATL. PARK SERVICE - HALEAKALA NATL. PARK - LIBRARY □ Makawao, HI

Beal, Gretchen F., Libn.
KNOXVILLE-KNOX COUNTY METROPOLITAN PLANNING COMMISSION - LIBRARY □ Knoxville, TN
Beal, William C., Jr., Archv.
UNITED METHODIST CHURCH - GENERAL COMMISSION ON ARCHIVES AND HISTORY - LIBRARY AND ARCHIVES □ Madison, NJ
Beale, Joel A., Dir.
GULF OIL PRODUCTS COMPANY - CHEMICAL INFORMATION CENTER □ Houston, TX
Beall, R.L., Lib.Dir.
GREENSBORO DAILY NEWS AND RECORD - LIBRARY □ Greensboro, NC
Beals, Sheila, Ser.
KANSAS CITY ART INSTITUTE - LIBRARY □ Kansas City, MO
Beam, Hope, Libn.
LEKOTEK TOY LIBRARY □ Evanston, IL
Beam, Kathryn L., Ms.Libn.
UNIVERSITY OF MICHIGAN - DEPARTMENT OF RARE BOOKS AND SPECIAL COLLECTIONS - LIBRARY □ Ann Arbor, MI
Beaman, Barbara, Supv.
HERCULES, INC. - LIBRARY □ Wilmington, DE
Beaman, Patricia, Libn.
SAN ANTONIO STATE CHEST HOSPITAL - HEALTH SCIENCE LIBRARY □ San Antonio, TX
Bean, Betsy, Asst.Libn.
EAST TENNESSEE BAPTIST HOSPITAL - HEALTH SCIENCES LIBRARY □ Knoxville, TN
Bean, Ethelle, Cat./Asst.Libn.
NATIONAL COLLEGE - THOMAS JEFFERSON LEARNING RESOURCE CENTER □ Rapid City, SD
Bean, Frances, Tech.Info.Spec.
U.S. NATL. HIGHWAY TRAFFIC SAFETY ADMINISTRATION - TECHNICAL REFERENCE DIVISION □ Washington, DC
Bean, Nancy, Libn.
INTERFIRST BANK FORT WORTH, N.A. - LIBRARY □ Fort Worth, TX
Bean, Norma, Assoc.Dir.
TEXAS SOUTHERN UNIVERSITY - PHARMACY LIBRARY □ Houston, TX
Beard, Lucie, Libn.
DETROIT OSTEOPATHIC HOSPITAL - MEDICAL LIBRARY □ Highland Park, MI
Bearden, E. Holmes, Mgr.
MOBIL OIL CORPORATION - PUBLIC AFFAIRS SECRETARIAT □ New York, NY
Bearden, Kayron F., Asst.
KING & SPALDING - LAW LIBRARY† □ Atlanta, GA
Beardsley, Mary Jane, Libn.
UNIVERSITY OF RHODE ISLAND - INTERNATIONAL CENTER FOR MARINE RESOURCE DEVELOPMENT - LIBRARY □ Kingston, RI
Beardsley, Sylvia, Info.Spec.
UNITED STATES GYPSUM COMPANY - GRAHAM J. MORGAN RESEARCH LIBRARY □ Libertyville, IL
Beardwood, B., Asst.Libn.
MORGAN, LEWIS & BOCKIUS - LIBRARY □ Philadelphia, PA
Bears, E., Supv.
STANDARD OIL COMPANY OF INDIANA - LIBRARY/INFORMATION CENTER □ Chicago, IL
Beasley, Carmalita J., Libn.
BADISCHE CORPORATION - LIBRARY □ Williamsburg, VA
Beasley, Lorna L., Libn.
AMERICAN INSURANCE ASSOCIATION - LAW LIBRARY □ New York, NY
Beasley, Noel, Exec.V.P.
DEBS (Eugene V.) FOUNDATION - LIBRARY □ Terre Haute, IN
Beasley, Vivian A., Ref.
KENTUCKY STATE LAW LIBRARY □ Frankfort, KY

Beasman, T., Law Libn.
NEW YORK STATE SUPREME COURT - 9TH JUDICIAL DISTRICT - LAW LIBRARY □ White Plains, NY
Beaton, Joyce H., Legal Serv.Techn.
MASSACHUSETTS MUTUAL LIFE INSURANCE COMPANY - LAW LIBRARY □ Springfield, MA
Beaton, Patricia A., Ref./Govt.Doc.
NEW HAMPSHIRE COLLEGE - SHAPIRO LIBRARY □ Manchester, NH
Beatson, E.H.
PRINCETON UNIVERSITY - DEPARTMENT OF ART & ARCHAEOLOGY - INDEX OF CHRISTIAN ART □ Princeton, NJ
Beattie, Barbara C., Dir., Lib.Serv.
CUMBERLAND COUNTY HOSPITAL SYSTEM, INC. - CAPE FEAR VALLEY HOSPITAL - LIBRARY SERVICES □ Fayetteville, NC
Beattie, Emily L., Hd., Tech.Serv.
BOSTON UNIVERSITY MEDICAL CENTER - ALUMNI MEDICAL LIBRARY □ Boston, MA
Beattie, Janice, Tech.Info.Spec.
POPULATION REFERENCE BUREAU, INC. - LIBRARY/INFORMATION SERVICE □ Washington, DC
Beattie, Judith, Hd., Res. & Ref.
HUDSON'S BAY COMPANY ARCHIVES □ Winnipeg, MB
Beattie, Lorraine, Asst.to the Libn., Adm.
UNIVERSITY OF WATERLOO - DANA PORTER ARTS LIBRARY □ Waterloo, ON
Beatty, Betty, Act.Dir.
WITTENBERG UNIVERSITY - THOMAS LIBRARY □ Springfield, OH
Beatty, Frank, Libn.
U.S. GEOLOGICAL SURVEY - NATIONAL MAPPING DIVISION ASSISTANCE FACILITY - LIBRARY □ NSTL Station, MS
Beatty, Suzanne D., Tech.Libn.
CHICAGO BRIDGE & IRON COMPANY - TECHNICAL LIBRARY □ Oak Brook, IL
Beatty, William K., Archival Assoc.
NORTHWESTERN UNIVERSITY - ARCHIVES □ Evanston, IL
Beaty, M. Paul, Asst.Cat.
EAST STROUDSBURG UNIVERSITY - KENT LIBRARY† □ East Stroudsburg, PA
Beaubien, Anne K., Dir.
UNIVERSITY OF MICHIGAN - MICHIGAN INFORMATION TRANSFER SOURCE (MITS) □ Ann Arbor, MI
Beauchamp, Andrea, Prog.Coord.
UNIVERSITY OF MICHIGAN - HOPWOOD ROOM □ Ann Arbor, MI
Beauchamp, Barbara, Archv.Asst.
FLORIDA STATE DIVISION OF ARCHIVES, HISTORY & REC. MANAGEMENT - BUREAU OF FLORIDA FOLKLIFE PROGRAMS - ARCHIVES □ White Springs, FL
Beauclair, Rene, Hd.Libn.
CINEMATHEQUE QUEBECOISE - CENTRE DE DOCUMENTATION CINEMATOGRAPHIQUE □ Montreal, PQ
Beaudet, Francoise
UNIVERSITE DE MONTREAL - THEOLOGIE-PHILOSOPHIE BIBLIOTHEQUE □ Montreal, PQ
Beaudet, Louise, Hd. of Animation
CINEMATHEQUE QUEBECOISE - ARCHIVES & FILM MUSEUM □ Montreal, PQ
Beaudet, Normand, Bibliotechnicien
INSTITUT PHILIPPE PINEL - LIBRARY† □ Montreal, PQ
Beaudoin, Kathleen, Libn.
CANADIAN MEDICAL ASSOCIATION - LIBRARY □ Ottawa, ON
Beaudoin, Robert A., Chm., Archv.Comm.
ASSOCIATION CANADO-AMERICAINE - INSTITUT CANADO-AMERICAIN □ Manchester, NH
Beaudoin, Yolande, Libn.
UNIVERSITE DE MONTREAL - PSYCHO-EDUCATION-BIBLIOTHEQUE □ Montreal, PQ

Beauford, Fred, Lib.Cons.
INNER CITY CULTURAL CENTER - LANGSTON HUGHES MEMORIAL LIBRARY† □ Los Angeles, CA

Beaumier, Renald, Dir.
UNIVERSITE DU QUEBEC A MONTREAL - BIBLIOTHEQUE DE MUSIQUE □ Montreal, PQ

Beaumont, Mabel, Libn.
WOODWARD GOVERNOR CO. - WOODWARD LIBRARY □ Rockford, IL

Beaumont, Mary, Libn.
NEW JERSEY STATE DEPARTMENT OF LAW AND PUBLIC SAFETY - ATTORNEY GENERAL'S LIBRARY □ Trenton, NJ

Beaumont, Richard
UNIVERSITY OF CALIFORNIA, RIVERSIDE - MAP SECTION - LIBRARY □ Riverside, CA

Beaupre, Louis
MONTREAL URBAN COMMUNITY TRANSIT COMMISSION - LIBRARY □ Montreal, PQ

Beauregard, Christine, Asst.Libn.
NEW YORK STATE LIBRARY - MANUSCRIPTS AND SPECIAL COLLECTIONS □ Albany, NY

Beauregard, John, Dir.
GORDON COLLEGE - WINN LIBRARY □ Wenham, MA

Beaver, H.H., Chm., Dept. of Geol.
BAYLOR UNIVERSITY - DEPARTMENT OF GEOLOGY - FERDINAND ROEMER GEOLOGICAL LIBRARY □ Waco, TX

Beazell, Tuula, Chf., Lib.Serv.
U.S. VETERANS ADMINISTRATION (PA-Pittsburgh) - MEDICAL CENTER LIBRARY SERVICE (142D) □ Pittsburgh, PA

Beazley, Sara Anne, Asst.Libn.
COFFIELD UNGARETTI HARRIS & SLAVIN - LIBRARY □ Chicago, IL

Bebbington, Marguerite, Tech.Info.Spec.
ENGELHARD CORPORATION - TECHNICAL INFORMATION CENTER □ Edison, NJ

Bechtel, Gertrude M., Asst.Libn.
TAMPA BAY REGIONAL PLANNING COUNCIL - RESEARCH & INFORMATION LIBRARY □ St. Petersburg, FL

Bechtel, Robert B., Dir., Env.Psych.
UNIVERSITY OF ARIZONA ENVIRONMENTAL PSYCHOLOGY PROGRAM - LIBRARY □ Tucson, AZ

Beck, Agnes, Coord., Ancillary Serv.
NEW YORK ASSOCIATION FOR THE BLIND - LIGHTHOUSE LIBRARY □ New York, NY

Beck, Armin, Dean
NAES COLLEGE - LIBRARY AND RESOURCE CENTER □ Chicago, IL

Beck, Beatrice M., Libn.
RANCHO SANTA ANA BOTANIC GARDEN - LIBRARY □ Claremont, CA

Beck, Clare, Govt.Doc.Libn.
EASTERN MICHIGAN UNIVERSITY - CENTER OF EDUCATIONAL RESOURCES - GOVERNMENT DOCUMENTS COLLECTION □ Ypsilanti, MI

Beck, Clark L., Jr.
GENEALOGICAL SOCIETY OF NEW JERSEY - MANUSCRIPT COLLECTIONS □ New Brunswick, NJ

Beck, Clark L., Jr., Mss.Cur.
RUTGERS UNIVERSITY, THE STATE UNIVERSITY OF NEW JERSEY - DEPARTMENT OF SPECIAL COLLECTIONS AND ARCHIVES □ New Brunswick, NJ

Beck, James M., Libn.
OHIO POWER COMPANY - LIBRARY □ Canton, OH

Beck, Jocelyne, Chf., Ref.
CANADA - SECRETARY OF STATE - TRANSLATION BUREAU - DOCUMENTATION DIRECTORATE† □ Ottawa, ON

Beck, Kenneth L., Libn.
KENTUCKY CHRISTIAN COLLEGE - MEDIA CENTER □ Grayson, KY

Beck, Miriam R., Sec.
THOMAS COUNTY HISTORICAL SOCIETY - LIBRARY □ Colby, KS

Beck, Patricia, Res.Libn.
DRACKETT COMPANY - RESEARCH AND DEVELOPMENT LIBRARY □ Cincinnati, OH

Beck, Dr. Shirley S., Chm., Div. of Prof.Educ.
TUSCULUM COLLEGE - INSTRUCTIONAL MATERIALS CENTER □ Greeneville, TN

Beckenstein, Gail, Asst.Libn.
PAUL, WEISS, RIFKIND, WHARTON AND GARRISON - LIBRARY □ New York, NY

Becker, Ann, Libn.
LAND O'LAKES, INC. - RESEARCH & DEVELOPMENT LIBRARY □ Minneapolis, MN

Becker, Barbara K., Supv.
WARNER-LAMBERT/PARKE-DAVIS - RESEARCH LIBRARY† □ Ann Arbor, MI

Becker, Carol, Cat.Libn.
NORTHERN KENTUCKY UNIVERSITY - SALMON P. CHASE COLLEGE OF LAW - LIBRARY □ Highland Heights, KY

Becker, Daniel
AMERICAN AMBULANCE ASSOCIATION - INFORMATION CENTER □ Youngstown, OH

Becker, Jacquelyn B., Mgr.
HELENE CURTIS INDUSTRIES, INC. - CORPORATE INFORMATION CENTER □ Chicago, IL

Becker, Jeanne, Med.Libn.
CABRINI MEDICAL CENTER - DR. MASSIMO BAZZINI MEMORIAL LIBRARY □ New York, NY

Becker, Linda, Jnl.Libn.
AMERICAN HOME PRODUCTS CORPORATION - WYETH LABORATORIES DIVISION LIBRARY □ Philadelphia, PA

Becker, Mary J., Law Libn.
CAHILL GORDON & REINDEL - LIBRARY □ Washington, DC

Becker, Nada, Info.Anl.
FOOTE CONE & BELDING - INFORMATION CENTER □ Chicago, IL

Becker, Roger, Sys.Anl.Libn.
UNIVERSITY OF PUGET SOUND - SCHOOL OF LAW LIBRARY □ Tacoma, WA

Becker, Ronald L.
GENEALOGICAL SOCIETY OF NEW JERSEY - MANUSCRIPT COLLECTIONS □ New Brunswick, NJ

Becker, Ronald L.
RUTGERS UNIVERSITY, THE STATE UNIVERSITY OF NEW JERSEY - DEPARTMENT OF SPECIAL COLLECTIONS AND ARCHIVES □ New Brunswick, NJ

Becker, Stephen, Dir.
RIVERSIDE COUNTY HISTORICAL COMMISSION - LIBRARY □ Rubidoux, CA

Becker, Terry, Res.Techn.
WAUKESHA COUNTY HISTORICAL MUSEUM - RESEARCH CENTER □ Waukesha, WI

Becker-Zawadowski, Iris, Libn.
ONTARIO - MINISTRY OF THE SOLICITOR GENERAL - OFFICE OF THE FIRE MARSHAL LIBRARY □ Toronto, ON

Beckman, Gary, Asst.Cur.
YALE UNIVERSITY - BABYLONIAN COLLECTION □ New Haven, CT

Beckman, Margaret L., Chf.Libn.
UNIVERSITY OF GUELPH - LIBRARY □ Guelph, ON

Beckman, Roger, Hd.
INDIANA UNIVERSITY - OPTOMETRY LIBRARY □ Bloomington, IN

Beckner, Barbara, Libn.
FLORIDA HOSPITAL - MEDICAL LIBRARY □ Orlando, FL

Beckner, Carol, Hd., Access Serv.Sect.
BROOKHAVEN NATIONAL LABORATORY - TECHNICAL INFORMATION DIVISION □ Upton, NY

Beckstead, Jean B., Libn.
U.S. BUREAU OF MINES - SALT LAKE CITY RESEARCH CENTER - LIBRARY □ Salt Lake City, UT

Beckwith, Doris, Libn.
SAN JOAQUIN LOCAL HEALTH DISTRICT - LIBRARY □ Stockton, CA

Beckwith, Herbert H., Cat.
NATIONAL MARITIME MUSEUM - J. PORTER SHAW LIBRARY □ San Francisco, CA

Beckwith, Terry, Pub.Serv.Libn.
UNIVERSITY OF UTAH - LAW LIBRARY □ Salt Lake City, UT

Beckwith, Terry Lee, Assoc.Libn.
WASHINGTON & LEE UNIVERSITY - LAW LIBRARY □ Lexington, VA

Becraft, Carolyn, Proj.Dir.
WOMEN'S EQUITY ACTION LEAGUE - NATIONAL INFORMATION CENTER ON WOMEN AND THE MILITARY □ Washington, DC

Bedard, Laura, Spec.Coll.Libn.
GEORGETOWN UNIVERSITY - FRED O. DENNIS LAW LIBRARY □ Washington, DC

Beddoes, Thomas R., Hd., Ref.Sect.
PENNSYLVANIA STATE LIBRARY □ Harrisburg, PA

Bedford, Mary, Rsrcs./Reporting Coord.
NATIONAL 4-H COUNCIL - COMMUNICATIONS DIVISION □ Chevy Chase, MD

Bedikian, Elizabeth O., Div.Hd.
NEW ORLEANS PUBLIC LIBRARY - BUSINESS AND SCIENCE DIVISION □ New Orleans, LA

Bednarz, Monica, Sec.
UNIVERSITY OF NORTH DAKOTA - MATH-PHYSICS LIBRARY □ Grand Forks, ND

Bedrosky, Nannette, Cat.Libn.
CREIGHTON UNIVERSITY - HEALTH SCIENCES LIBRARY □ Omaha, NE

Bedverftig, Paul, Tech.Libn.
GULF SOUTH RESEARCH INSTITUTE - LIBRARY □ New Orleans, LA

Bedwell, Mrs. Moneta, Libn.
GRAHAM HOSPITAL ASSOCIATION - MEDICAL STAFF LIBRARY □ Canton, IL

Bedwell, Mrs. Moneta, Libn.
GRAHAM HOSPITAL ASSOCIATION - SCHOOL OF NURSING LIBRARY □ Canton, IL

Beebe, Allen, Tech.Mgr.
HUDSON RIVER ENVIRONMENTAL SOCIETY - RICHARD W. BARNETT MEMORIAL LIBRARY □ Staatsburg, NY

Beech, Beatrice H., Hd.
WESTERN MICHIGAN UNIVERSITY - INSTITUTE OF CISTERCIAN STUDIES LIBRARY □ Kalamazoo, MI

Beecham, Janis, Lib.Ck.
WINFIELD STATE HOSPITAL AND TRAINING CENTER - PROFESSIONAL AND MEDICAL LIBRARY □ Winfield, KS

Beecher, John, Hd., Pub.Serv.
UNIVERSITY OF MINNESOTA, ST. PAUL - CENTRAL LIBRARY □ St. Paul, MN

Beecher, Raymond, Libn.
GREENE COUNTY HISTORICAL SOCIETY - VEDDER MEMORIAL LIBRARY □ Coxsackie, NY

Beecher, Ms. Sally, Act.Coord.
BOSTON PUBLIC LIBRARY - HUMANITIES REFERENCE □ Boston, MA

Beechert, Edward, Dir.
UNIVERSITY OF HAWAII - DEPARTMENT OF HISTORY - PACIFIC REGIONAL ORAL HISTORY PROGRAM - LIBRARY □ Honolulu, HI

Beeching, Deanna S., Libn.
PATRIOT NEWS COMPANY - NEWS LIBRARY □ Harrisburg, PA

Beede, Marie, Res.Asst.
KELLER (J.J.) & ASSOCIATES, INC. - RESEARCH & TECHNICAL LIBRARY □ Neenah, WI

Beeler, Richard, Bus./Econ.Libn.
COLORADO STATE UNIVERSITY - WILLIAM E. MORGAN LIBRARY □ Fort Collins, CO

Beene, Sophia D., Pres.
DATAQUE INTERNATIONAL INC. - TECHNICAL INFORMATION CENTER □ Chicago, IL

Beer, Florence, Libn.
SUNY - SYRACUSE EDUCATIONAL
OPPORTUNITY CENTER - PAUL ROBESON
LIBRARY □ Syracuse, NY
Beer, Richard L., Dir.
ADAMS-PRATT OAKLAND COUNTY LAW
LIBRARY □ Pontiac, MI
Beers, Vera F., Adm.Off.
INSTITUTE FOR DEVELOPMENT
ANTHROPOLOGY - LIBRARY □ Binghamton, NY
Beeson, Lone C., Hd.Libn.
WORLD AFFAIRS COUNCIL OF NORTHERN
CALIFORNIA - LIBRARY □ San Francisco, CA
Begg, Debra, Libn.
UNIVERSITY OF OTTAWA - MUSIC LIBRARY □
Ottawa, ON
Begg, Robert T., Dir.
UNION UNIVERSITY - ALBANY LAW SCHOOL -
LIBRARY □ Albany, NY
Beggs, Vera H., Tech.Serv.Libn.
MASSACHUSETTS STATE TRANSPORTATION
LIBRARY □ Boston, MA
Behers, Janice, Lib.Techn.
U.S. BUREAU OF MINES - RENO RESEARCH
CENTER - LIBRARY† □ Reno, NV
Behles, Patricia, Govt.Doc.Libn.
UNIVERSITY OF BALTIMORE - LAW LIBRARY □
Baltimore, MD
Behm, Leslie M., Libn.
MICHIGAN STATE UNIVERSITY - CLINICAL
CENTER LIBRARY □ East Lansing, MI
Behm, Leslie M., Libn.
MICHIGAN STATE UNIVERSITY - VETERINARY
CLINICAL CENTER LIBRARY □ East Lansing, MI
Behr, Alice S., Tech.Libn.
UNION CARBIDE CORPORATION - RESEARCH
AND DEVELOPMENT INFORMATION CENTER □
South Charleston, WV
Behrends, Mary, Music Lib.Asst.
GUSTAVUS ADOLPHUS COLLEGE - LUND MUSIC
LIBRARY □ St. Peter, MN
Behrens, Marge, Slavic/Orntl.Libn.
RAND CORPORATION - LIBRARY† □ Santa
Monica, CA
Behringer, Nedra, Mgr., Corp.Lib.
WARNER-LAMBERT COMPANY - CORPORATE
LIBRARY □ Morris Plains, NJ
Beil, Eloise, Archv./Libn.
STATEN ISLAND INSTITUTE OF ARTS AND
SCIENCES - ARCHIVES AND LIBRARY □ Staten
Island, NY
Beilby, Mary, Coll.Dev.Libn.
SUNY - COLLEGE AT CORTLAND - MEMORIAL
LIBRARY □ Cortland, NY
Beiler, Dorthea, Libn.
FIRST PRESBYTERIAN CHURCH - LIBRARY □ De
Land, FL
Beiman, Frances, Prin.Libn.
NEWARK PUBLIC LIBRARY - EDUCATION
DIVISION □ Newark, NJ
Beinbrech, Pauline C., Mgr.
PETROLITE CORPORATION - INFORMATION
CENTER □ St. Louis, MO
Beintema, William J., Law Libn.
OKLAHOMA CITY UNIVERSITY - LAW LIBRARY
□ Oklahoma City, OK
Bejnar, Thaddeus, Legal Res.Libn.
UNIVERSITY OF NEW MEXICO - SCHOOL OF
LAW LIBRARY □ Albuquerque, NM
Bekar, Carol, Sr.Adm., Lib.Serv.
STERLING DRUG, INC. STERLING-WINTHROP
RESEARCH INSTITUTE - LIBRARY □ Rensselaer,
NY
Beker, Janet M., Br.Asst.
SAN DIEGO COUNTY LAW LIBRARY - VISTA
BRANCH □ Vista, CA
Bekiares, Susan, Doc.Libn.
UNIVERSITY OF ILLINOIS - DOCUMENTS
LIBRARY □ Urbana, IL
Beland, Andre, Ref.Libn.
UNIVERSITE DU QUEBEC EN ABITIBI-
TEMISCAMINGUE - BIBLIOTHEQUE □ Rouyn, PQ

Belangar, Brien, Circ.Libn.
MOODY BIBLE INSTITUTE - LIBRARY □ Chicago,
IL
Belanger, Reine, Documentalist
TELE-UNIVERSITE - CENTRE DE
DOCUMENTATION □ Quebec, PQ
Belanger, Roland, Archv.
SOCIETE HISTORIQUE DU SAGUENAY -
BIBLIOTHEQUE □ Chicoutimi, PQ
Belanger, Sandra
SAN JOSE STATE UNIVERSITY - JOHN
STEINBECK RESEARCH CENTER □ San Jose, CA
Belastock, Tjalda, Hd., Rd.Serv.
BENTLEY COLLEGE - SOLOMON R. BAKER
LIBRARY □ Waltham, MA
Belcher, C. Francis, Archv./Cons.
APPALACHIAN MOUNTAIN CLUB - LIBRARY† □
Boston, MA
Belcher, Faye, Assoc.Dir.
MOREHEAD STATE UNIVERSITY - CAMDEN-
CARROLL LIBRARY □ Morehead, KY
Beldan, A. Chris, Libn.
MOUNTAIN VIEW BIBLE COLLEGE - LIBRARY □
Didsbury, AB
Belgum, Katherine, Assoc. Law Libn.
UNIVERSITY OF IOWA - LAW LIBRARY □ Iowa
City, IA
Belina, Aniela, Documentaliste
UNIVERSITE DE MONTREAL - CENTRE
INTERNATIONAL DE CRIMINOLOGIE
COMPAREE - DOCUMENTATION CENTRE □
Montreal, PQ
Beling, Dorothy, Asst.Dir., Database Oper.
ERIC CLEARINGHOUSE ON HANDICAPPED &
GIFTED CHILDREN - CEC INFORMATION
SERVICES □ Reston, VA
Beliveau, Karen D., Coord.
ALBERTA RESEARCH COUNCIL - SOLAR & WIND
ENERGY RESEARCH PROGRAM (SWERP)
INFORMATION CENTRE □ Edmonton, AB
Bell, Anita, Med.Libn.
U.S. VETERANS ADMINISTRATION (GA-
Augusta) - HOSPITAL LIBRARY □ Augusta, GA
Bell, Anne, Libn.
ABILENE REPORTER-NEWS - LIBRARY □
Abilene, TX
Bell, Barbara, Hd.
VANCOUVER PUBLIC LIBRARY - BUSINESS &
ECONOMICS DIVISION □ Vancouver, BC
Bell, Becky, Ser.Libn.
COUNTRY MUSIC FOUNDATION - LIBRARY AND
MEDIA CENTER □ Nashville, TN
Bell, Bonnie, Mgr., Off.Serv.
ACACIA MUTUAL LIFE INSURANCE COMPANY -
LIBRARY □ Washington, DC
Bell, C.M., Info.Anl.
CHEVRON RESEARCH COMPANY - TECHNICAL
INFORMATION CENTER □ Richmond, CA
Bell, Carol A., Hd.Libn.
BECHTEL POWER CORPORATION - LIBRARY □
Gaithersburg, MD
Bell, Charlotte M., Dir., Media Serv.
FIRST BAPTIST CHURCH - LIBRARY □
Greensboro, NC
Bell, Christine L., Dir., Lib.Serv.
NEWTON-WELLESLEY HOSPITAL - PAUL
TALBOT BABSON MEMORIAL LIBRARY □ Newton
Lower Falls, MA
Bell, Elsie, Chf., Main Lib.
OKLAHOMA CITY METROPOLITAN LIBRARY
SYSTEM - BUSINESS-SCIENCE SECTION □
Oklahoma City, OK
Bell, F., Database/Indexing Serv.
XEROX CORPORATION - TECHNICAL
INFORMATION CENTER □ Webster, NY
Bell, Frances, Div.Hd.
DALLAS PUBLIC LIBRARY - HUMANITIES
DIVISION □ Dallas, TX
Bell, Frieda, Libn.
U.S.D.A. - AGRICULTURAL RESEARCH SERVICE
- WATER CONSERVATION LABORATORY
LIBRARY† □ Phoenix, AZ

Bell, Irena L., Asst.Chf.
NATIONAL LIBRARY OF CANADA -
MULTILINGUAL BIBLIOSERVICE □ Ottawa, ON
Bell, JoAnn, Ph.D., Dir.
EAST CAROLINA UNIVERSITY - HEALTH
SCIENCES LIBRARY □ Greenville, NC
Bell, John P., Dir., Info.Serv.
MILLION DOLLAR ROUND TABLE -
INFORMATION SERVICES □ Des Plaines, IL
Bell, Jolene, Docs.Libn.
GENERAL DYNAMICS CORPORATION - FORT
WORTH DIVISION - TECHNICAL LIBRARY □
Fort Worth, TX
Bell, Karen L., Info.Off.
ROLLS-ROYCE INC. - LIBRARY □ Atlanta, GA
Bell, Lois, Rd.Adv.
DISTRICT OF COLUMBIA PUBLIC LIBRARY -
WASHINGTONIANA DIVISION □ Washington,
DC
Bell, Margaret, Coll.Asst.
UNIVERSITY OF NORTH CAROLINA, CHAPEL
HILL - RARE BOOK COLLECTION □ Chapel Hill,
NC
Bell, Marilyn, Libn.
PRINCE EDWARD ISLAND - PLANNING LIBRARY
□ Charlottetown, PE
Bell, Mary, Asst.Libn.
ALBRIGHT-KNOX ART GALLERY - ART
REFERENCE LIBRARY □ Buffalo, NY
Bell, Mary, Asst.Libn.
OAK FOREST HOSPITAL - PROFESSIONAL
LIBRARY† □ Oak Forest, IL
Bell, Marylin, Hd., Ref.
TENNESSEE STATE LIBRARY AND ARCHIVES -
ARCHIVES & MANUSCRIPTS SECTION □
Nashville, TN
Bell, Mertys W., Dean of Lrng.Rsrcs.
GUILFORD TECHNICAL COMMUNITY COLLEGE -
LEARNING RESOURCE CENTER □ Jamestown,
NC
Bell, Rebecca, Tech.Serv.Libn.
SOUTH DAKOTA STATE LIBRARY & ARCHIVES □
Pierre, SD
Bell, Sarah, Libn.
MIDRASHA COLLEGE OF JEWISH STUDIES -
LIBRARY† □ Southfield, MI
Bell, Steven J., Ref.Libn.
PHILADELPHIA CORPORATION FOR AGING -
LIBRARY □ Philadelphia, PA
Bell, Susanne, Music Libn.
WASHINGTON UNIVERSITY - GAYLORD MUSIC
LIBRARY □ St. Louis, MO
Bell, Wanda R., Libn.
PENNSYLVANIA STATE DEPT. OF
ENVIRONMENTAL RESOURCES -
ENVIRONMENTAL PROTECTION TECHNICAL
REFERENCE LIBRARY □ Harrisburg, PA
Bell, Willard
MAASS (Clara) MEDICAL CENTER -
RADIOGRAPHY PROGRAM LIBRARY □ Belleville,
NJ
Bell-Koski, Cheryl, Film Libn.
PORTLAND ART ASSOCIATION - NORTHWEST
FILM STUDY CENTER - CIRCULATING FILM
LIBRARY □ Portland, OR
Bellamy, Jane Young, Libn.
SAN BERNARDINO COUNTY - ENVIRONMENTAL
PUBLIC WORKS AGENCY - RESOURCE CENTER
□ San Bernardino, CA
Bellamy, Shannon G., Libn.
SASKATCHEWAN - DEPARTMENT OF THE
ENVIRONMENT - LIBRARY □ Regina, SK
Bellamy, Dr. Virginia Nelle, Archv.
PROTESTANT EPISCOPAL CHURCH - ARCHIVES
□ Austin, TX
Bellanti, Robert, Hd.
UNIVERSITY OF CALIFORNIA, LOS ANGELES -
MANAGEMENT LIBRARY □ Los Angeles, CA
Bellardo, Dr. Lewis, Dir.
KENTUCKY STATE DEPARTMENT FOR
LIBRARIES & ARCHIVES - ARCHIVES □
Frankfort, KY

Bellefontaine, Edgar J., Libn.
SOCIAL LAW LIBRARY □ Boston, MA

Bellerose, Celine, Lib.Techn.
HYDRO-QUEBEC - V.P. PLANIFICATION
GENERALE - CENTRE DE DOCUMENTATION □
Montreal, PQ

Bellis, Gloria, Libn.
FUGRO INTER, INC. - LIBRARY □ Houston, TX

Bellis, Norma, Libn.
TWENTIETH CENTURY TRENDS INSTITUTE,
INC. - SOURCE LIBRARY □ Darien, CT

Belliveau, Gerard J., Jr., Libn.
RACQUET AND TENNIS CLUB - LIBRARY □ New
York, NY

Bellows, Jacqueline L., Tech.Serv.Libn.
FRANCIS BACON FOUNDATION, INC. -
FRANCIS BACON LIBRARY □ Claremont, CA

Belrose, N., Lib. Co-chm.
CONGREGATION SOLEL - LIBRARY □ Highland
Park, IL

Belsterling, Jean I., Med.Libn.
WEST JERSEY HOSPITAL, EASTERN DIVISION -
STAFF MEDICAL LIBRARY □ Voorhees, NJ

Belt, Jane, Med.Libn.
CENTRAL WASHINGTON HOSPITAL -
HEMINGER HEALTH SCIENCES LIBRARY □
Wenatchee, WA

Belt, Marva, Hd.
ENOCH PRATT FREE LIBRARY - SOCIAL
SCIENCE AND HISTORY DEPARTMENT □
Baltimore, MD

Belton, Jennifer, Dir., Info.Serv.
NATIONAL JOURNAL LIBRARY □ Washington, DC

Beltran, Lucrecia
UNIVERSITY OF PUERTO RICO - SCHOOL OF
PUBLIC ADMINISTRATION - LIBRARY† □ Rio
Piedras, PR

Belyea, Kathy, Ref.Libn.
AT & T BELL LABORATORIES - LIBRARY □
Whippany, NJ

Bemis, Michael F., Law Libn.
WISCONSIN STATE DEPARTMENT OF JUSTICE
- LAW LIBRARY □ Madison, WI

Bemis, Nancy M., Libn.
U.S. AIR FORCE BASE - FAIRCHILD BASE
LIBRARY □ Fairchild AFB, WA

Ben-Shir, Rya, Mgr.
MAC NEAL HOSPITAL - HEALTH SCIENCES
RESOURCE CENTER □ Berwyn, IL

Ben-Zvi, Mrs. Hava, Libn.
JEWISH FEDERATION COUNCIL OF GREATER
LOS ANGELES - PETER M. KAHN JEWISH
COMMUNITY LIBRARY □ Los Angeles, CA

Benally, Elaine, Info.Spec.
ERIC CLEARINGHOUSE ON RURAL EDUCATION
AND SMALL SCHOOLS □ Las Cruces, NM

Benatar, Joy, Tech.Libn.
DIGITAL EQUIPMENT CORPORATION -
MERRIMACK LIBRARY SERVICES □ Merrimack,
NJ

Bendall, Teresa, Asst.Libn.
ALBERTA - DEPARTMENT OF SOCIAL SERVICES
AND COMMUNITY HEALTH - LIBRARY □
Edmonton, AB

Bendell, Beverley, Libn.
MONENCO CONSULTANTS LIMITED - LIBRARY
□ Calgary, AB

Bendell, Beverly, Club Libn.
ALPINE CLUB OF CANADA - LIBRARY □ Banff,
AB

Bender, Jennifer, Hd., Pubns.
INSTITUTE OF CONTEMPORARY ART -
LIBRARY □ Boston, MA

Bender, Suzanne D., Ch.Libn.
BURLINGTON COUNTY LYCEUM OF HISTORY
AND NATURAL SCIENCE - MOUNT HOLLY
LIBRARY □ Mt. Holly, NJ

Bender, Thomas R., Jr., Biologist
PENNSYLVANIA STATE FISH COMMISSION
LIBRARY - BENNER SPRING FISH RESEARCH
STATION □ Bellefonte, PA

Benedetti, Joan M., Musm.Libn.
CRAFT AND FOLK ART MUSEUM - LIBRARY/
MEDIA RESOURCE CENTER □ Los Angeles, CA

Benedetto, Bob, Archv.
BISHOP (Bernice P.) MUSEUM - LIBRARY □
Honolulu, HI

Benedict, Karen, Chf.Libn. & Corp.Archv.
NATIONWIDE MUTUAL INSURANCE COMPANY -
LIBRARY/CORPORATE ARCHIVES □ Columbus,
OH

Benedict, Kay, Cur.
CASA GRANDE VALLEY HISTORICAL SOCIETY -
MUSEUM LIBRARY □ Casa Grande, AZ

Benedict, Sr. Mary, O.S.B., Asst.Libn.
ST. BENEDICT'S ABBEY - BENET LIBRARY □
Benet Lake, WI

Benedict, Mary Jane, Libn.
SPEED (J.B.) ART MUSEUM - LIBRARY □
Louisville, KY

Benedict, William
THEATRE HISTORICAL SOCIETY COLLECTION
□ Chicago, IL

Benefiel, Norma, Off.Serv.Supv.
PHILLIPS PETROLEUM COMPANY -
ENGINEERING LIBRARY □ Bartlesville, OK

Benelisha, Eleanor, Dir., Lib.Serv.
ST. MARY'S HOSPITAL AND MEDICAL CENTER -
MEDICAL LIBRARY □ San Francisco, CA

Benemann, William E., Act.Dir.
GOLDEN GATE UNIVERSITY - SCHOOL OF LAW
LIBRARY □ San Francisco, CA

Benenfeld, Alan R., Coord.
UNIVERSITY OF CALIFORNIA, LOS ANGELES -
PHYSICAL SCIENCES & TECHNOLOGY
LIBRARIES □ Los Angeles, CA

Benet, Rebecca, Asst.Libn.
SUNY - COLLEGE OF OPTOMETRY - HAROLD
KOHN MEMORIAL VISUAL SCIENCE LIBRARY □
New York, NY

Benet, Sandra, Music Libn.
UNIVERSITY OF VICTORIA - MC PHERSON
LIBRARY - MUSIC & AUDIO COLLECTION □
Victoria, BC

Benevich, Lauren A., Ref.Libn.
EMORY UNIVERSITY - SCHOOL OF MEDICINE -
A.W. CALHOUN MEDICAL LIBRARY □ Atlanta,
GA

Benglas, Gitta, Libn.
TECHNICON INSTRUMENTS CORPORATION -
LIBRARY □ Tarrytown, NY

Bengstrom, John
UNIVERSITY OF IOWA - LAW LIBRARY □ Iowa
City, IA

Benguiat, Vance, Exec.Dir.
CITIZENS UNION OF THE CITY OF NEW YORK -
LIBRARY □ New York, NY

Benincasa, Anne, Circ.Supv.
YORK UNIVERSITY - STEACIE SCIENCE
LIBRARY □ Downsview, ON

Benjamin, Azalia, Branch Libn.
CHURCH OF JESUS CHRIST OF LATTER-DAY
SAINTS - LANSING BRANCH GENEALOGICAL
LIBRARY □ East Lansing, MI

Benjamin, Mrs. M., Libn.
CANADIAN MARCONI COMPANY - LIBRARY† □
Montreal, PQ

Benjamin, Marianne, Rsrc.Mgr.
AT & T BELL LABORATORIES - AT & T
RESOURCE MANAGEMENT - CORPORATE
RESEARCH CENTER □ Piscataway, NJ

Benjamin, Marianne V., Rsrc.Mgr.
AT & T - CORPORATE RESEARCH CENTER □
New York, NY

Benjamin, Wilma E., Rec.Coord.
NATIONAL PARENT TEACHER ASSOCIATION -
INFORMATION RESOURCE CENTER □ Chicago,
IL

Bennet, Dr. L.H., Metallurgist
U.S. NATL. BUREAU OF STANDARDS - ALLOY
PHASE DIAGRAM DATA CENTER □ Washington,
DC

Bennett, Alice, Libn.
NEWTOWN HISTORIC ASSOCIATION, INC. -
RESEARCH CENTER OF NEWTOWN AREA
HISTORY □ Newton, PA

Bennett, Arlene R., Adm.Sec.
UNIVERSITY OF MINNESOTA - UNDERGROUND
SPACE CENTER - LIBRARY □ Minneapolis, MN

Bennett, Barbara S., Act.Dir.
GEORGIA HISTORICAL SOCIETY - LIBRARY □
Savannah, GA

Bennett, Christine, Tech.Libn.
KMS FUSION, INC. - FUSION LIBRARY† □ Ann
Arbor, MI

Bennett, Claire, Spec.Coll.Libn.
SOUTHERN CONNECTICUT STATE UNIVERSITY
- H.C. BULEY LIBRARY - SPECIAL COLLECTIONS
□ New Haven, CT

Bennett, Donna, Rd.Serv.Libn.
NORTHERN KENTUCKY UNIVERSITY - SALMON
P. CHASE COLLEGE OF LAW - LIBRARY □
Highland Heights, KY

Bennett, Dorothea E., Chf., Lib.Serv.
U.S. VETERANS ADMINISTRATION (CA-
Martinez) - HOSPITAL LIBRARY □ Martinez, CA

Bennett, Dr. John M., Lib. Media Tech.Asst.
OHIO STATE UNIVERSITY - LATIN AMERICAN
STUDIES READING ROOM AND LIBRARY □
Columbus, OH

Bennett, Julie, Archv.
DISCOVERY HALL MUSEUM - RESEARCH
LIBRARY □ South Bend, IN

Bennett, K. Sharon, Libn.
CHARLESTON MUSEUM - LIBRARY† □
Charleston, SC

Bennett, Laurie, Libn.
SPERRY COMPUTER SYSTEMS - LIBRARY □
Mississauga, ON

Bennett, Mary, Photographs Libn.
STATE HISTORICAL SOCIETY OF IOWA -
LIBRARY □ Iowa City, IA

Bennett, Michael W., Health Sci.Libn.
KAISER-PERMANENTE MEDICAL CENTER -
HEALTH SCIENCES LIBRARY □ Sacramento, CA

Bennett, Michael W., Musm.Dir.
SAN JOAQUIN COUNTY HISTORICAL MUSEUM □
Lodi, CA

Bennett, Patricia G., Asst.Libn.
CHARLESTON LIBRARY SOCIETY □ Charleston,
SC

Bennett, Peggy, Circ.
KING & SPALDING - LAW LIBRARY† □ Atlanta,
GA

Bennett, Peggy, Cat.
SOUTHERN MISSIONARY COLLEGE - MC KEE
LIBRARY - SPECIAL COLLECTIONS □
Collegedale, TN

Bennett, Richard E., Hd.
UNIVERSITY OF MANITOBA - ARCHIVES AND
SPECIAL COLLECTIONS □ Winnipeg, MB

Bennett, Roy V., Ref./Doc. & ILL
WESTERN OREGON STATE COLLEGE - LIBRARY
□ Monmouth, OR

Bennett, Swannee, Cur.
ARKANSAS TERRITORIAL RESTORATION -
LIBRARY □ Little Rock, AR

Bennett, Terry, Info.Spec.
PRICE WATERHOUSE - NATIONAL
INFORMATION CENTER □ New York, NY

Bennin, Cheryl S., Libn.
HAIGHT, GARDNER, POOR AND HAVENS -
LIBRARY □ New York, NY

Benoit, Nicole, Data Dissem.Off.
CANADA - STATISTICS CANADA - ADVISORY
SERVICES - MONTREAL REFERENCE CENTRE □
Montreal, PQ

Benoit, Vance, Engr.Libn.
COLUMBIA GULF TRANSMISSION COMPANY -
ENGINEERING LIBRARY □ Houston, TX

Bensing, Karen M., Asst.Libn.
CLEVELAND METROPOLITAN GENERAL
HOSPITAL - HAROLD H. BRITTINGHAM
MEMORIAL LIBRARY □ Cleveland, OH

Bensinger, Mildred, Med.Ed.
U.S. AIR FORCE - AEROSPACE MEDICAL
DIVISION - SCHOOL OF AEROSPACE MEDICINE
- STRUGHOLD AEROMEDICAL LIBRARY □ Brooks
AFB, TX

Bensman, Dr. Marvin R., Assoc.Prof.
MEMPHIS STATE UNIVERSITY LIBRARIES -
RADIO PROGRAM HISTORY COLLECTION □
Memphis, TN

Benson, Dr. Barbara E., Dir. of Lib.
HISTORICAL SOCIETY OF DELAWARE -
LIBRARY □ Wilmington, DE

Benson, Barbara J., Ref.Spec.
MITRE CORPORATION - BEDFORD
OPERATIONS LIBRARY □ Bedford, MA

Benson, Debra Bedford, Cat.
UNIVERSITY OF MANITOBA - E.K. WILLIAMS
LAW LIBRARY □ Winnipeg, MB

Benson, George R., Dir. of Media Serv.
KENTUCKY SCHOOL FOR THE DEAF - LEARNING
RESOURCE CENTER □ Danville, KY

Benson, Harold W., Libn.
NEW YORK CITY HUMAN RESOURCES
ADMINISTRATION - LIBRARY □ New York, NY

Benson, Hazel B., Asst.Dir.
OHIO STATE UNIVERSITY - HEALTH SCIENCES
LIBRARY □ Columbus, OH

Benson, Isabel, Libn.
STOCKTON-SAN JOAQUIN COUNTY PUBLIC
LIBRARY - CALIFORNIA ROOM □ Stockton, CA

Benson, Jane
CLAY COUNTY ARCHIVES - FRANK HUGHES
LIBRARY □ Liberty, MO

Benson, Joan, Libn.
RANDOLPH CIRCUIT COURT - LAW LIBRARY □
Winchester, IN

Benson, Joseph, Dir., Info.Serv.
CHICAGO TRANSIT AUTHORITY - HAROLD S.
ANTHON MEMORIAL LIBRARY □ Chicago, IL

Benson, Judith, Libn.
MICHENER CENTRE - STAFF LIBRARY □ Red
Deer, AB

Benson, Paula G., Ref.Libn.
UNIVERSITY OF SOUTH CAROLINA - COLEMAN
KARESH LAW LIBRARY □ Columbia, SC

Benson, Shelley, Clghse.Dept.
NATIONAL RESOURCE CENTER FOR
CONSUMERS OF LEGAL SERVICES -
CLEARINGHOUSE □ Washington, DC

Benson, Willis, Reports & ILL
U.S. AIR FORCE - WRIGHT-PATTERSON
TECHNICAL LIBRARY □ Dayton, OH

Bente, June, Mgr.
ORTHO PHARMACEUTICAL CORPORATION -
HARTMAN LIBRARY □ Raritan, NJ

Bente, Dr. Paul F., Jr., Exec.Dir.
BIO-ENERGY COUNCIL - LIBRARY □
Washington, DC

Bentley, Carol, Hd., Mtls.Ctr.
CHICAGO STATE UNIVERSITY - DOUGLAS
LIBRARY - SPECIAL COLLECTIONS† □ Chicago,
IL

Bentley, James R., Act.Dir.
FILSON CLUB - LIBRARY □ Louisville, KY

Bentley, Jane, Libn.
SAN DIEGO MUSEUM OF MAN - SCIENTIFIC
LIBRARY □ San Diego, CA

Bentley, Janice B., Libn.
MAYER, BROWN & PLATT - LIBRARY† □
Chicago, IL

Benton, Mary, Acq.Libn.
WESTMINSTER CHOIR COLLEGE - TALBOTT
LIBRARY □ Princeton, NJ

Benyo, John C., Asst.Libn.
ST. VINCENT COLLEGE AND ARCHABBEY -
LIBRARIES □ Latrobe, PA

Benz, Delsa I., Corp.Libn.
BAUSCH & LOMB, INC. - LIBRARY RESOURCE
CENTER □ Rochester, NY

Benzer, Susan L., Hd., Circ.
U.S. AIR FORCE BASE - HANSCOM BASE
LIBRARY □ Hanscom AFB, MA

Benzie-Youseff, Arta, Ch.Libn.
OAKLAND PUBLIC LIBRARY - LATIN AMERICAN
LIBRARY □ Oakland, CA

Berardinucci, H., Supv., Cat. & Acq.
CANADIAN PACIFIC, LTD. - CORPORATE
LIBRARY/INFORMATION CENTRE □ Montreal,
PQ

Berberian, Kevork, Cat.Libn.
KEAN COLLEGE OF NEW JERSEY - NANCY
THOMPSON LIBRARY† □ Union, NJ

Berch, Victor A., Spec.Coll.Libn.
BRANDEIS UNIVERSITY - SPECIAL
COLLECTIONS □ Waltham, MA

Bercovitch, Sari, Dir. of Info.Serv.
TOWERS, PERRIN, FORSTER & CROSBY LTD. -
INFORMATION CENTRE □ Toronto, ON

Berdahl, James N., Libn.
MINNESOTA ORCHESTRA - MUSIC LIBRARY □
Minneapolis, MN

Berdnikoff, William, Hd.
CANADA - CONSUMER AND CORPORATE
AFFAIRS CANADA - PATENT OFFICE LIBRARY □
Ottawa, ON

Bereday, Patricia, Libn.
HOLLAND SOCIETY OF NEW YORK - LIBRARY □
New York, NY

Berenbaum, Adrienne, Libn.
UNIVERSITY OF MEDICINE AND DENTISTRY OF
NEW JERSEY - RUTGERS MEDICAL SCHOOL -
MEDIA LIBRARY □ Piscataway, NJ

Berg, Christine, Circ.
UNIVERSITY OF WISCONSIN, LA CROSSE -
MURPHY LIBRARY □ La Crosse, WI

Berg, Claudia, Media Prod./Graphics Serv
UNIVERSITY OF MICHIGAN - SCHOOL OF
EDUCATION & SCHOOL OF LIB. SCI. - INSTR.
STRATEGY SERV. □ Ann Arbor, MI

Berg, E.K., Dir. of Pub.Serv.
BISHOP COLLEGE - ZALE LIBRARY - BANKS
AFRO-AMERICAN HERITAGE COLLECTION □
Dallas, TX

Berg, Edith, Coord.
SASKATCHEWAN - DEPARTMENT OF
CONSUMER AND COMMERICAL AFFAIRS -
CONSUMER INFORMATION CENTRE □ Regina,
SK

Berg, Helen I., Circ.Libn.
KUTZTOWN UNIVERSITY - ROHRBACH
LIBRARY □ Kutztown, PA

Berg, Mrs. James, Supv.
BOB JONES UNIVERSITY - CHURCH
MINISTRIES RESOURCE LAB □ Greenville, SC

Berg, Kathy L., Libn.
WORCESTER ART MUSEUM - LIBRARY† □
Worcester, MA

Berg, Rebecca, Asst.Libn.
ASSOCIATION OF OPERATING ROOM NURSES -
LIBRARY □ Denver, CO

Berg, Richard R., Asst.Libn.
UNITED THEOLOGICAL SEMINARY - LIBRARY □
Dayton, OH

Bergamini, Sr. Rita, S.P., Archv.
SISTERS OF PROVIDENCE - SACRED HEART
PROVINCE - ARCHIVES □ Seattle, WA

Bergan, Helen, Chf.
DISTRICT OF COLUMBIA PUBLIC LIBRARY -
BIOGRAPHY DIVISION □ Washington, DC

Berge, Dale L., Dir.
BRIGHAM YOUNG UNIVERSITY - MUSEUM OF
PEOPLES AND CULTURES LIBRARY □ Provo, UT

Berge, Patricia, Asst.Sci.Libn.
MARQUETTE UNIVERSITY - SCIENCE LIBRARY
□ Milwaukee, WI

Berge, William H., Dir.
EASTERN KENTUCKY UNIVERSITY - ORAL
HISTORY CENTER □ Richmond, KY

Bergen, John V., Map Libn.
WESTERN ILLINOIS UNIVERSITY - GEOGRAPHY
& MAP LIBRARY □ Macomb, IL

Berger, Al, Ref.
SOLAR ENERGY RESEARCH INSTITUTE - SERI
TECHNICAL LIBRARY □ Golden, CO

Berger, Alvin C., Act.Dir.
EAST STROUDSBURG UNIVERSITY - KENT
LIBRARY† □ East Stroudsburg, PA

Berger, Carol A., Owner
C. BERGER AND COMPANY - LIBRARY □
Wheaton, IL

Berger, Clyde Cochran, Tech.Libn.
INSTITUTE OF LOGOPEDICS - TECHNICAL
LIBRARY □ Wichita, KS

Berger, Edward, Cur.
RUTGERS UNIVERSITY, THE STATE
UNIVERSITY OF NEW JERSEY - INSTITUTE OF
JAZZ STUDIES □ Newark, NJ

Berger, JoEllen, Asst.Libn.
PEPPER, HAMILTON AND SCHEETZ - LAW
LIBRARY □ Philadelphia, PA

Berger, L.W., Sr.Res.Info.Spec.
UNITED STATES STEEL CORPORATION -
TECHNICAL INFORMATION CENTER □
Monroeville, PA

Berger, Leslie, Ref./ILL Libn.
EAST STROUDSBURG UNIVERSITY - KENT
LIBRARY† □ East Stroudsburg, PA

Berger, Martin J., Mgr.
U.S. NATL. BUREAU OF STANDARDS - PHOTON
AND CHARGED PARTICLE DATA CENTER □
Gaithersburg, MD

Berger, Patricia W., Chf.Info.Rsrcs./Serv.Dir.
U.S. NATL. BUREAU OF STANDARDS - LIBRARY
□ Washington, DC

Berger, Pearl, Hd.Libn.
YESHIVA UNIVERSITY - MENDEL GOTTESMAN
LIBRARY OF HEBRAICA AND JUDAICA □ New
York, NY

Berger, Pearl, Hd.Libn.
YESHIVA UNIVERSITY - POLLACK LIBRARY -
LANDOWNE-BLOOM COLLECTION □ New York,
NY

Berger, Robert, Asst.Libn.
UNIVERSITY OF CALIFORNIA, SAN FRANCISCO
- HASTINGS COLLEGE OF THE LAW - LEGAL
INFORMATION CENTER □ San Francisco, CA

Berger, Roberta, Asst.Libn.
NEW YORK CITY BOARD OF EDUCATION -
DIVISION OF SPECIAL EDUCATION -
MANHATTAN REGIONAL RESOURCE CENTER □
New York, NY

Bergeron, Cheri, Libn.
MONTANA STATE OFFICE OF PUBLIC
INSTRUCTION - RESOURCE CENTER† □ Helena,
MT

Bergeron, Gilles, Rd.Serv.Libn.
UNIVERSITE DU QUEBEC A HULL -
BIBLIOTHEQUE □ Hull, PQ

Berggren, Nancy, Adm.Serv.Supv.
IOWA STATE DEPARTMENT OF WATER, AIR
AND WASTE MANAGEMENT - TECHNICAL
LIBRARY □ Des Moines, IA

Bergin, Dorothy O., Libn.
MOBIL SOLAR ENERGY CORPORATION -
LIBRARY □ Waltham, MA

Bergles, Frances, Dept.Hd.
SASKATOON PUBLIC LIBRARY - FINE AND
PERFORMING ARTS DEPARTMENT □ Saskatoon,
SK

Berglin, Merlin, Off.Supv.
POPE COUNTY HISTORICAL SOCIETY &
MUSEUM - LIBRARY □ Glenwood, MN

Berglund, Earl, Exec.Dir.
U.S. HOCKEY HALL OF FAME - LIBRARY □
Eveleth, MN

Berglund, Edean, Dir., Lib.Serv.
ST. PETER HOSPITAL - PROFESSIONAL
LIBRARY □ Olympia, WA

Berglund, Martha J., Dir. of Lib.
HARBRIDGE HOUSE, INC. - LIBRARY □ Boston,
MA

Bergman, Bruce J., Lib.Dir.
PACE UNIVERSITY - LIBRARY □ New York, NY

Bergman, Emily, Asst.Libn.
CALIFORNIA SCHOOL OF PROFESSIONAL
PSYCHOLOGY - LOS ANGELES LIBRARY □ Los
Angeles, CA

Bergman, Janet L., Libn.
JANUS FOUNDATION - LIBRARY □ San
Francisco, CA
Bergman, Maia I., Archv.Libn.
UNIVERSITY OF MICHIGAN - INST. FOR
SOCIAL RESEARCH - INTER-UNIVERSITY
CONSORTIUM FOR POLITICAL & SOC. RES. □
Ann Arbor, MI
Bergman, Stanley, Assoc.Libn.
YIVO INSTITUTE FOR JEWISH RESEARCH -
LIBRARY AND ARCHIVES □ New York, NY
Bergmann, Emily, Libn.
CONDELL MEMORIAL HOSPITAL - FOHRMAN
LIBRARY □ Libertyville, IL
Bergmann, L. James, Gen. Solicitor
UNION PACIFIC RAILROAD COMPANY - LAW
LIBRARY □ Portland, OR
Bergsten, Bebe, Libn.
LOCARE MOTION PICTURE RESEARCH GROUP -
LIBRARY □ Los Angeles, CA
Berk, Lawrence S., Assoc.Dir., Lib.
HUDSON VALLEY COMMUNITY COLLEGE -
DWIGHT MARVIN LEARNING RESOURCES
CENTER □ Troy, NY
Berkeley, Edmund, Jr., Cur. of Archv.
UNIVERSITY OF VIRGINIA - LIBRARY -
MANUSCRIPTS DEPARTMENT & UNIVERSITY
ARCHIVES □ Charlottesville, VA
Berkey, Irene, Foreign/Intl. Law Libn.
NORTHWESTERN UNIVERSITY - LAW SCHOOL
LIBRARY □ Chicago, IL
Berkey, Mary G., Libn.
U.S. FOOD & DRUG ADMINISTRATION -
BUREAU OF RADIOLOGICAL HEALTH -
LIBRARY† □ Rockville, MD
Berkley, Audrey L., Libn.
ST. LOUIS METROPOLITAN MEDICAL SOCIETY
- ST. LOUIS SOCIETY FOR MEDICAL AND
SCIENTIFIC EDUCATION - LIBRARY □ St. Louis,
MO
Berkman, Frank W., Exec.Dir.
HOTEL SALES AND MARKETING ASSOCIATION
INTERNATIONAL - SALES RESEARCH LIBRARY†
□ Washington, DC
Berkner, Alice, Dir.
INTERNATIONAL BIRD RESCUE RESEARCH
CENTER - LIBRARY □ Berkeley, CA
Berlin, Art, Mgr., Lib.Serv.
SANDERS ASSOCIATES, INC. - LIBRARY
SERVICES □ Nashua, NH
Berlin, Lenka, Libn.
DELOITTE HASKINS & SELLS - LIBRARY □
Philadelphia, PA
Berliner, Donna, Libn.
TEMPLE EMANU-EL - ALEX F. WEISBERG
LIBRARY □ Dallas, TX
Berliner, Mary Ann, Dir., Lib.Serv.
LOS ANGELES COUNTY HARBOR-UCLA MEDICAL
CENTER - A.F. PARLOW LIBRARY OF THE
HEALTH SCIENCES □ Torrance, CA
Berman, Andrea B., Corp.Libn.
CONVERSE CONSULTANTS - CORPORATE
LIBRARY □ Pasadena, CA
Berman, Ellen M., Dir. of Clinical Trng.
MARRIAGE COUNCIL OF PHILADELPHIA -
DIVISION OF FAMILY STUDY AND MARRIAGE
COUNCIL LIBRARY □ Philadelphia, PA
Berman, Howard A., Rabbi
CHICAGO SINAI CONGREGATION - EMIL G.
HIRSCH LIBRARY □ Chicago, IL
Berman, Marsha, Assoc. Music Libn.
UNIVERSITY OF CALIFORNIA, LOS ANGELES -
MUSIC LIBRARY □ Los Angeles, CA
Bernard, Dr.
ST. JOSEPH'S HOSPITAL - MEDICAL LIBRARY □
Stockton, CA
Bernard, B.A., Res.Libn.
EMERY INDUSTRIES - RESEARCH LIBRARY □
Cincinnati, OH
Bernard, David M., Area Dir.
U.S. DEPT. OF LABOR - OSHA - IDAHO AREA
OFFICE - LIBRARY □ Boise, ID

Bernard, Lorna, Jr.Libn.
ONTARIO HYDRO - LIBRARY □ Toronto, ON
Bernard, Marielle, Lib.Techn.
QUEBEC PROVINCE - REGIE DE L'ELECTRICITE
ET DU GAZ - BIBLIOTHEQUE □ Montreal, PQ
Bernard, S.R., Dir.
OAK RIDGE NATIONAL LABORATORY -
INFORMATION CENTER FOR INTERNAL
EXPOSURE □ Oak Ridge, TN
Bernauer, Peter, Res.Libn.
CANADIAN PARAPLEGIC ASSOCIATION -
LIBRARY □ Toronto, ON
Berndt, Fred, Libn.
ST. PAUL TECHNICAL VOCATIONAL LIBRARY □
St. Paul, MN
Berndt, Gertrude, Libn.
NORTH DAKOTA STATE HOSPITAL - HEALTH
SCIENCE LIBRARY □ Jamestown, ND
Berner, Andrew J., Asst.Libn.
UNIVERSITY CLUB LIBRARY □ New York, NY
Berner, Richard, Hd.Libn.
UNIVERSITY OF WASHINGTON - UNIVERSITY
ARCHIVES & MANUSCRIPT DIVISION -
MANUSCRIPT COLLECTION □ Seattle, WA
Berner, Richard C., Univ.Archv.
UNIVERSITY OF WASHINGTON - UNIVERSITY
ARCHIVES & MANUSCRIPT DIVISION -
UNIVERSITY ARCHIVES □ Seattle, WA
Bernhart, Barbara, Libn.
MOBIL LAND DEVELOPMENT CORPORATION -
LIBRARY □ Redwood City, CA
Bernholdt, Jocelyn A., Med.Libn.
ALEXIAN BROTHERS MEDICAL CENTER -
MEDICAL LIBRARY† □ Elk Grove Village, IL
Bernita, Sr. M., S.S.J., Lib.Dir.
BON SECOURS HOSPITAL - HEALTH SCIENCE
LIBRARY □ Grosse Pointe, MI
Bernstein, Bernice G., Asst.Libn.
MARYLAND STATE LAW LIBRARY □ Annapolis,
MD
Bernstein, Beth, Libn.
SEYFARTH, SHAW, FAIRWEATHER &
GERALDSON - LIBRARY □ Los Angeles, CA
Bernstein, Elizabeth, Libn./Pub.Info.Coord.
INSTITUTE FOR DEFENSE AND DISARMAMENT
STUDIES - LIBRARY □ Brookline, MA
Bernstein, Fran, Med.Libn.
U.S. VETERANS ADMINISTRATION (CT-West
Haven) - MEDICAL CENTER LIBRARY □ West
Haven, CT
Bernstein, Gloria S., Mgr., Lib.Info.Serv.
LIPTON (Thomas J.), INC. - RESEARCH LIBRARY
□ Englewood Cliffs, NJ
Bernstein, Joan, Asst.Libn.
UNIVERSITY OF PENNSYLVANIA - ANNENBERG
SCHOOL OF COMMUNICATIONS - LIBRARY† □
Philadelphia, PA
Bernstein, Joan, Staff Res.Spec./Prog.
YALE UNIVERSITY - SOCIAL SCIENCE LIBRARY
□ New Haven, CT
Bernstein, Judith, Bus.Adm.Libn.
UNIVERSITY OF NEW MEXICO - WILLIAM J.
PARISH MEMORIAL LIBRARY □ Albuquerque, NM
Bernstein, Lillian, Libn.
NEWARK BETH ISRAEL MEDICAL CENTER - DR.
VICTOR PARSONNET MEMORIAL LIBRARY □
Newark, NJ
Bernstein, Merle, Libn.
U.S. BUREAU OF MINES - TWIN CITIES
RESEARCH CENTER - LIBRARY □ Minneapolis,
MN
Bernstein, Patricia, Tech.Lib.Asst.
BURNS AND ROE, INC. - TECHNICAL LIBRARY □
Oradell, NJ
Bernthal, Rebecca, Pub.Serv.Libn.
CONCORDIA TEACHERS COLLEGE - LINK
LIBRARY □ Seward, NE
Bernthaler, Jeanette, Act.Archv.
SAN BERNARDINO COUNTY HISTORICAL
ARCHIVES □ San Bernardino, CA
Berntsen, Robert, Res.
CHASE MANHATTAN BANK, N.A. -
INFORMATION CENTER □ New York, NY

Berra, Marilyn, Circ.Supv.
EDEN THEOLOGICAL SEMINARY - LIBRARY □
Webster Groves, MO
Berragry, Mary Ann, Info.Anl.
AMERICAN HOSPITAL SUPPLY CORPORATION -
CORPORATE INFORMATION CENTER □
Evanston, IL
Berrien, Helen, Libn.
NEW ENGLAND FIRE & HISTORY MUSEUM -
LIBRARY AND ARCHIVE □ Brewster, MA
Berring, Robert, Law Libn.
UNIVERSITY OF CALIFORNIA, BERKELEY - LAW
LIBRARY □ Berkeley, CA
Berry, Birdie, Info.Serv.Coord.
EAST-WEST GATEWAY COORDINATING
COUNCIL - REFERENCE AREA □ St. Louis, MO
Berry, Gayle C., Ref.
CLARKSON UNIVERSITY - EDUCATIONAL
RESOURCES CENTER □ Potsdam, NY
Berry, Irwin, Libn.
UNIVERSITY OF COLORADO HEALTH SCIENCES
CENTER - RENE A. SPITZ PSYCHIATRIC
LIBRARY □ Denver, CO
Berry, James, Res.Coord.
HOUSING ASSOCIATION OF DELAWARE VALLEY
- LIBRARY □ Philadelphia, PA
Berry, Joy, Ref.Libn.
CALIFORNIA HISTORICAL SOCIETY -
SCHUBERT HALL LIBRARY □ San Francisco, CA
Berry, Marie, Hd.
SAN ANTONIO PUBLIC LIBRARY AND
INFORMATION CENTER - HISTORY, SOCIAL
SCIENCE & GENERAL REFERENCE DEPT. □ San
Antonio, TX
Berry, Mary Jane, Libn.
PORTERVILLE STATE HOSPITAL - MEDICAL
LIBRARY □ Porterville, CA
Berry, Patrick, Libn.
LADISH CO. - METALLURGICAL DEPARTMENT
LIBRARY† □ Cudahy, WI
Berry, Paul, Libn.
CALVERT MARINE MUSEUM - LIBRARY □
Solomons, MD
Berry, Rachel, Mgr.
PILLSBURY COMPANY - BUSINESS REFERENCE
LIBRARY □ Minneapolis, MN
Berry, Robert H., Tech.Info.Spec.
GENERAL ELECTRIC COMPANY -
TRANSPORTATION TECHNOLOGY CENTER -
TECHNICAL INFORMATION CENTER □ Erie, PA
Berry, Stephen, Lib.Asst.
DISCIPLES OF CHRIST HISTORICAL SOCIETY -
LIBRARY □ Nashville, TN
Berry, Vernice W., Libn.
ADOPTION CENTER OF DELAWARE VALLEY -
LIBRARY □ Philadelphia, PA
Berry, Wayne, Info.Off.
INTERGOVERNMENTAL COMMITTEE ON URBAN
AND REGIONAL RESEARCH (ICURR) -
INFORMATION EXCHANGE SERVICE □ Toronto,
ON
Berson, Bella Z., Act.Med.Libn.
YALE UNIVERSITY - MEDICAL LIBRARY □ New
Haven, CT
Bert, Anne E., Tech.Info.Spec.
U.S. ARMY - INTELLIGENCE AND THREAT
ANALYSIS CENTER - TECHNICAL
INFORMATION CENTER □ Arlington, VA
Bertelli, Frances, Tech.Serv.Libn.
AETNA LIFE & CASUALTY COMPANY - LAW
LIBRARY □ Hartford, CT
Berthelette, Carole, Info.Off.
CANADA - PUBLIC ARCHIVES OF CANADA -
NATL. FILM, TELEVISION & SOUND ARCHIVES -
DOCUMENTATION & PUB. SERV. □ Ottawa, ON
Berthelot, Benoit, Asst.Libn.
COLLEGE DOMINICAIN DE PHILOSOPHIE ET DE
THEOLOGIE - BIBLIOTHEQUE □ Ottawa, ON
Berthelsen, Barbara, Map Libn.
CORNELL UNIVERSITY - MAPS, MICROTEXTS,
NEWSPAPERS DEPARTMENT □ Ithaca, NY

Berthelsen, John F., Spec.Subj.Asst.
DARTMOUTH COLLEGE - MAP SECTION □
Hanover, NH

Berthold, Carol A., Asst.Div.Hd.
CARNEGIE LIBRARY OF PITTSBURGH -
BUSINESS DIVISION □ Pittsburgh, PA

Bertholf, Robert J., Cur.
SUNY AT BUFFALO - POETRY/RARE BOOKS
COLLECTION □ Buffalo, NY

Bertolucci, Katherine, Libn.
TRANS-PACIFIC GEOTHERMAL, INC. - LIBRARY
□ Oakland, CA

Bertolucci, Kathy, Hd.Libn.
WHALE CENTER - EXTINCT SPECIES
MEMORIAL FUND - LIBRARY □ Oakland, CA

Bertolucci, Ysabel R., Health Sci.Libn.
KAISER-PERMANENTE MEDICAL CENTER -
SOUTH SAN FRANCISCO HEALTH SCIENCES
LIBRARY† □ South San Francisco, CA

Bertram, Lee Ann, Ref.Libn.
ELI LILLY AND COMPANY - SCIENTIFIC
LIBRARY □ Indianapolis, IN

Bertsch, Donald A., Jr., Libn.
SOUTHERN MAINE VOCATIONAL TECHNICAL
INSTITUTE - LIBRARY □ South Portland, ME

Bertuccelli, Dr. Angela, Libn.
AMERICAN HYPNOTISTS' ASSOCIATION -
HYPNOSIS TECHNICAL CENTER □ San
Francisco, CA

Berube, Mrs. F., Ref.Techn.
ROYAL CANADIAN MOUNTED POLICE - LAW
ENFORCEMENT REFERENCE CENTRE □ Ottawa,
ON

Berwick, Philip, Asst.Libn., Pub.Serv.
GEORGETOWN UNIVERSITY - FRED O. DENNIS
LAW LIBRARY □ Washington, DC

Besant, Larry X., Dir.
LINDA HALL LIBRARY □ Kansas City, MO

Besemer, Susan, Assoc.Dir.
SUNY - COLLEGE AT BUFFALO - EDWARD H.
BUTLER LIBRARY □ Buffalo, NY

Beskid, Stephan J., Circ.Libn.
ST. VLADIMIR'S ORTHODOX THEOLOGICAL
SEMINARY - FR. GEORGES FLOROVSKY
LIBRARY □ Tuckahoe, NY

Besley, Drucie, Tech.Info.Spec.
NATIONAL INJURY INFORMATION
CLEARINGHOUSE □ Washington, DC

Beson, Carolyn, Supv., Tech.Info.Serv.
AMOCO PRODUCTION COMPANY - RESEARCH
CENTER LIBRARY □ Tulsa, OK

Bessette, Irene, Libn.
QUEEN'S UNIVERSITY AT KINGSTON - LAW
LIBRARY □ Kingston, ON

Best, Donna Jo, Chf., Bus.Off.
WYOMING STATE LIBRARY □ Cheyenne, WY

Best, G. Ronnie, Assoc.Dir.
UNIVERSITY OF FLORIDA - CENTER FOR
WETLANDS REFERENCE LIBRARY □ Gainesville,
FL

Best, Irma, Libn.
CHURCH OF JESUS CHRIST OF LATTER-DAY
SAINTS - EUGENE, OREGON BRANCH
GENEALOGICAL LIBRARY □ Eugene, OR

Best, Lois G., Asst.Libn.
UNIVERSITY OF NORTH CAROLINA, CHAPEL
HILL - INSTITUTE OF GOVERNMENT - LIBRARY
□ Chapel Hill, NC

Best, Margaret, Libn.
EASTERN MICHIGAN UNIVERSITY - CENTER OF
EDUCATIONAL RESOURCES - INSTRUCTIONAL
MATERIALS CENTER □ Ypsilanti, MI

Best, Reba A., Hd., Cat.
UNIVERSITY OF TENNESSEE - COLLEGE OF
LAW LIBRARY □ Knoxville, TN

Best, Rickey D., Asst.Libn.
SAN DIEGO HISTORICAL SOCIETY - RESEARCH
ARCHIVES □ San Diego, CA

Besterman, Elaine, Mgr., Lib.Serv.
DOW CHEMICAL COMPANY - MERRELL DOW
PHARMACEUTICALS, INC. - RESEARCH CENTER
LIBRARY □ Cincinnati, OH

Betancourt, Sylvette, Asst.Libn.
PUERTO RICO - OFFICE OF BUDGET &
MANAGEMENT - LIBRARY □ San Juan, PR

Beth, Dana Lynn, Asst.Libn./Tech.Serv.
ST. LOUIS ART MUSEUM - RICHARDSON
MEMORIAL LIBRARY □ St. Louis, MO

Bethea, Sally, Asst.Dir.Pub.Serv.
UNIVERSITY OF TEXAS HEALTH SCIENCE
CENTER, SAN ANTONIO - LIBRARY □ San
Antonio, TX

Bethel, Gay, Info.Res.Spec.
TEXAS EMPLOYERS INSURANCE ASSOCIATION
- ENGINEERING INFORMATION CENTER □
Dallas, TX

Bettenberg, Julie, Rsrcs.Ed.
AEROSPACE EDUCATION ASSOCIATION □
Reston, VA

Bettendorf, Rev. James B., Dir.
FLINT NEWMAN CENTER - LIBRARY AND
CATHOLIC INFORMATION CENTER □ Flint, MI

Bettez, Jules, Dir.
SEMINAIRE DES TROIS RIVIERES - ARCHIVES
□ Trois-Rivieres, PQ

Bettis, Gary, Archv.
IDAHO STATE HISTORICAL SOCIETY -
LIBRARY AND ARCHIVES □ Boise, ID

Betts, Frances, Libn.
MERCY REGIONAL MEDICAL CENTER LIBRARY
□ Vicksburg, MS

Betts, Renee Allard, Supv.Libn.
PENNSYLVANIA STATE SUPERIOR COURT -
APPELLATE COURTS LIBRARY □ Philadelphia, PA

Betz, Dr. Ellen, Supv. of Lib.
UNIVERSITY OF MINNESOTA - OCCUPATIONAL
INFORMATION LIBRARY □ Minneapolis, MN

Betz, Shirley M., Dir.
NAZARETH HOSPITAL - MEDICAL LIBRARY □
Philadelphia, PA

Bevan, Barbara H., Libn.
YORK HOSPITAL - LIBRARY □ York, PA

Bevan, David, Dir., Info.Serv.Div.
NORTH CAROLINA STATE DEPARTMENT OF
CULTURAL RESOURCES - DIVISION OF THE
STATE LIBRARY □ Raleigh, NC

Bevens, Helen L., Asst.V.P., Supv./Libn.
FIRST HAWAIIAN BANK - RESEARCH DIVISION
LIBRARY† □ Honolulu, HI

Beverage, John, Pub.Serv.Libn.
DALLAS THEOLOGICAL SEMINARY - MOSHER
LIBRARY □ Dallas, TX

Beverly, James E., Info.Dir.
U.S. AGENCY FOR INTERNATIONAL
DEVELOPMENT - WATER & SANITATION FOR
HEALTH PROJECT - INFORMATION CENTER □
Arlington, VA

Beverly, Lendell, Chf., Lib.Serv.
U.S. VETERANS ADMINISTRATION (OH-Dayton)
- CENTER LIBRARY □ Dayton, OH

Beversdorf, Anne, Info. Dissemination Spec.
INDIANA UNIVERSITY - DEVELOPMENTAL
TRAINING CENTER - INFORMATION AND
MATERIALS SYSTEM (IMS) □ Bloomington, IN

Bevilacqua, Ann. F., Doc.Libn.
FRANKLIN AND MARSHALL COLLEGE - SHADEK-
FACKENTHAL LIBRARY - SPECIAL
COLLECTIONS □ Lancaster, PA

Bewick, Brenda, Libn.
MC GILL UNIVERSITY - EXPERIMENTAL
SURGERY LIBRARY □ Montreal, PQ

Bewley, John, Rec.Cat.
RUTGERS UNIVERSITY, THE STATE
UNIVERSITY OF NEW JERSEY - BLANCHE AND
IRVING LAURIE MUSIC LIBRARY □ New
Brunswick, NJ

Beyea, Marion, Prov.Archv.
NEW BRUNSWICK - PROVINCIAL ARCHIVES OF
NEW BRUNSWICK □ Fredericton, NB

Beyer, Ann, Ref.Libn.
UNIVERSITY OF CALIFORNIA - LOS ALAMOS
NATIONAL LABORATORY - LIBRARY □ Los
Alamos, NM

Beyer, Carol, Asst.Libn.
CANADIAN CONSULATE GENERAL - LIBRARY □
New York, NY

Beyer, Robyn L., Dir., Lib.Serv.
PEPPER, HAMILTON AND SCHEETZ - LAW
LIBRARY □ Philadelphia, PA

Beyerlein, Lydia, Res.Libn.
ALCOLAC, INC. - RESEARCH LIBRARY □
Baltimore, MD

Beymer, Charles R., Asst.Dir.
CALIFORNIA POLYTECHNIC STATE
UNIVERSITY - ROBERT E. KENNEDY LIBRARY □
San Luis Obispo, CA

Beynen, G. Koolemans, Slavic Bibliog.
OHIO STATE UNIVERSITY - EAST EUROPEAN
AND SLAVIC READING ROOM □ Columbus, OH

Bezera, Elizabeth, Hd., Pub.Serv.
EMERSON COLLEGE - LIBRARY □ Boston, MA

Bezugloff, Natalia B., Dept.Hd.
CLEVELAND PUBLIC LIBRARY - FOREIGN
LITERATURE DEPARTMENT □ Cleveland, OH

Bhan, Esme E., Mss.Res.Assoc.
HOWARD UNIVERSITY - MOORLAND-SPINGARN
RESEARCH CENTER - MANUSCRIPT DIVISION □
Washington, DC

Bhansali, K.J., Dir.
U.S. NATL. BUREAU OF STANDARDS - ALLOY
PHASE DIAGRAM DATA CENTER □ Washington,
DC

Bhati, Pushpa, Sr.Libn.
CREEDMOOR PSYCHIATRIC CENTER - HEALTH
SCIENCES LIBRARY □ Queens Village, NY

Bhatnagar, M.E., Dept.Libn.
ALBERTA - DEPARTMENT OF AGRICULTURE -
LIBRARY □ Edmonton, AB

Bial, Raymond, Acq.Libn.
PARKLAND COLLEGE - LEARNING RESOURCE
CENTER □ Champaign, IL

Bialecki, Anthony G., Libn.
U.S. AIR FORCE - OFFICE OF SCIENTIFIC
RESEARCH - LIBRARY □ Bolling AFB, DC

Bianchi, Nancy, Clinical Libn.
ST. FRANCIS HOSPITAL AND MEDICAL CENTER
- WILSON C. JAINSEN LIBRARY □ Hartford, CT

Bianchini, Mr. L., Hd.Libn.
MOUNT SAINT VINCENT UNIVERSITY -
LIBRARY □ Halifax, NS

Biasiol, Rev. Virgilio, O.F.M., Dir.
SANTA BARBARA MISSION ARCHIVE-LIBRARY
□ Santa Barbara, CA

Bibbee, Robert, Per.Hd.
CHICAGO PUBLIC LIBRARY CENTRAL LIBRARY -
BUSINESS/SCIENCE/TECHNOLOGY DIVISION
□ Chicago, IL

Bibby, Elizabeth A., Info.Rsrc.Adm.
TECHNICAL ASSOCIATION OF THE PULP AND
PAPER INDUSTRY - LIBRARY □ Atlanta, GA

Biblo, Herbert, Dir.
LONG ISLAND LIBRARY RESOURCES COUNCIL,
INC. (LILRC) □ Bellport, NY

Bice, Mary, Libn.
LIMA STATE HOSPITAL - OAKWOOD FORENSIC
CENTER □ Lima, OH

Bick, Israel, Exec.Dir.
INTERNATIONAL STAMP COLLECTORS
SOCIETY - LIBRARY □ Van Nuys, CA

Bick-Gregoire, Lorraine, Mgr.
RAYTHEON COMPANY - MISSILE SYSTEMS
DIVISION - BEDFORD LABORATORIES -
TECHNICAL INFORMATION CENTER □ Bedford,
MA

Bickel, Vernon P., Cur.
AMERICAN THEATRE ORGAN SOCIETY -
ARCHIVES/LIBRARY □ Chula Vista, CA

Bickerstaff, Elaine K., Libn.
WESTINGHOUSE ELECTRIC CORPORATION -
WIPP TECHNICAL LIBRARY □ Albuquerque, NM

Bickford, Lawrence C., Court Adm.
CENTRE COUNTY LAW LIBRARY □ Bellefonte,
PA

Bickford, Priscilla, Libn.
MAINE STATE DEPARTMENT OF ENVIRONMENTAL PROTECTION & DEPARTMENT OF CONSERVATION - DEP-DOC JOINT LIBRARY □ Augusta, ME

Bickston, Devertt D., Libn.
SOUTHERN METHODIST UNIVERSITY - SCIENCE/ENGINEERING LIBRARY □ Dallas, TX

Biddinger, Nancy, Circ.
OHIO NORTHERN UNIVERSITY - COLLEGE OF LAW - JAY P. TAGGART MEMORIAL LAW LIBRARY □ Ada, OH

Biddle, V., Asst.Libn.
SOUTH DAKOTA STATE SUPREME COURT - LIBRARY† □ Pierre, SD

Bidwell, John, Ref.Libn.
UNIVERSITY OF CALIFORNIA, LOS ANGELES - WILLIAM ANDREWS CLARK MEMORIAL LIBRARY □ Los Angeles, CA

Bidwell, Sharon, Mgr./Lib.Ref.Serv.
COURIER-JOURNAL AND LOUISVILLE TIMES - LIBRARY □ Louisville, KY

Bieber, Doris M., Libn.
VANDERBILT UNIVERSITY - ALYNE QUEENER MASSEY LAW LIBRARY □ Nashville, TN

Bieber, Ralph, Instr.Mtls.Spec.
COLUMBUS TECHNICAL INSTITUTE - EDUCATIONAL RESOURCES CENTER □ Columbus, OH

Bieber, Susan, Law Libn.
CBS INC. - CBS LAW LIBRARY □ New York, NY

Bieble, Ruth, Libn.
CHEMICAL BANK - RESEARCH LIBRARY □ New York, NY

Biefeld, Rebecca, Bibliog.
SYRACUSE UNIVERSITY - E.S. BIRD LIBRARY - HUMANITIES DEPARTMENT □ Syracuse, NY

Biehl, Nancy, Map Rm.
METROPOLITAN TORONTO LIBRARY - HISTORY DEPARTMENT □ Toronto, ON

Bielefield, Arlene F., Hd., Div.Rd.Serv.
CONNECTICUT STATE LIBRARY □ Hartford, CT

Bielmann, Lorraine, Hd.Libn.
CLINICAL RESEARCH INSTITUTE OF MONTREAL - MEDICAL LIBRARY □ Montreal, PQ

Bienenstock, N. I., Cur.
FURNITURE LIBRARY ASSOCIATION □ High Point, NC

Bienkowski, Alexander C., AV Libn.
UNIVERSITY OF TEXAS MEDICAL BRANCH - MOODY MEDICAL LIBRARY □ Galveston, TX

Bier, Robert A., Jr., Chf.Libn.
U.S. GEOLOGICAL SURVEY - DENVER LIBRARY □ Denver, CO

Bierlein, John Francis, Dir., Res.Dev.
DEMOCRATIC NATIONAL COMMITTEE - RESEARCH LIBRARY† □ Washington, DC

Bierschenk, Ruth, Ref.
UNIVERSITY OF TEXAS HEALTH SCIENCE CENTER, SAN ANTONIO - LIBRARY □ San Antonio, TX

Biever, Erik, Lib.Asst.
UNIVERSITY OF MINNESOTA, ST. PAUL - PLANT PATHOLOGY LIBRARY □ St. Paul, MN

Bigas, Juan R.
UNIVERSITY OF PUERTO RICO - PUERTO RICAN COLLECTION† □ Rio Piedras, PR

Bigbee, Jesse E., Dir.
TEXAS BAPTIST HISTORICAL CENTER/ MUSEUM - LIBRARY □ Brenham, TX

Bigeau, Cindy Ives, Distribution Rep.
CANADA - NATIONAL FILM BOARD OF CANADA - FILM LIBRARY □ Saskatoon, SK

Bigelow, Leonard, Mgr. of Lib.Serv.
MEDTRONIC, INC. - LIBRARY† □ Minneapolis, MN

Biggins, Jeanne, Libn.
ONONDAGA COUNTY PUBLIC LIBRARY - BUSINESS AND INDUSTRIAL DEPARTMENT □ Syracuse, NY

Biggio, Eugene, Dir.
KENT MEMORIAL LIBRARY - HISTORICAL ROOM □ Suffield, CT

Biggs, Barbara R., Libn.
EXXON COMPANY, U.S.A. - EXXON RESEARCH & DEVELOPMENT LABORATORIES LIBRARY □ Baton Rouge, LA

Biggs, Catherine, Libn.
HEWLETT-PACKARD COMPANY - CUPERTINO LIBRARY □ Cupertino, CA

Biggs, Donald W., Sr.Libn.
NORTH PRINCETON DEVELOPMENTAL CENTER - PROFESSIONAL LIBRARY □ Princeton, NJ

Biggs, Dorothy, Libn.
MORRIS ANIMAL FOUNDATION - LIBRARY □ Englewood, CO

Bigman, Rita H., Libn.
DETROIT PSYCHIATRIC INSTITUTE - LIBRARY □ Detroit, MI

Bilbrey, Dale E., Libn.
SCARRITT COLLEGE FOR CHRISTIAN WORKERS - VIRGINIA DAVIS LASKEY LIBRARY □ Nashville, TN

Biles, Roberta F., Lib.Dir.
AMERICAN RED CROSS - NATIONAL HEADQUARTERS LIBRARY □ Washington, DC

Bilinski, Rev. Donald, O.F.M., Dir./Libn.
POLISH MUSEUM OF AMERICA - ARCHIVES & LIBRARY □ Chicago, IL

Bill, Ruby, Libn.
LAKELAND COUNSELING CENTER - LIBRARY† □ Elkhorn, WI

Billesbach, Ann E., Cur.
NEBRASKA STATE HISTORICAL SOCIETY - WILLA CATHER HISTORICAL CENTER - ARCHIVES □ Red Cloud, NE

Billiar, Joanne, Hd.Libn.
ST. VINCENT CHARITY HOSPITAL - LIBRARY □ Cleveland, OH

Billick, Pam, Dir.
ST. LUKE'S HOSPITAL - MEDICAL LIBRARY □ Cleveland, OH

Billings, Carol D., Dir.
LAW LIBRARY OF LOUISIANA† □ New Orleans, LA

Billings, Edward S., Law Libn.
U.S.D.A. - OFFICE OF GENERAL COUNSEL - LAW LIBRARY □ Washington, DC

Billings, Pennie, Ref./CML Libn.
SCOTT & WHITE MEMORIAL HOSPITAL - MEDICAL LIBRARY □ Temple, TX

Billings, Robert, Bibliog.
CENTRAL CONNECTICUT STATE UNIVERSITY - ELIHU BURRITT LIBRARY □ New Britain, CT

Billingsley, Robert, Libn.
U.S. DEFENSE TECHNICAL INFORMATION CENTER - TECHNICAL LIBRARY □ Alexandria, VA

Billops, Camille, Exec.Dir.
HATCH-BILLOPS COLLECTION, INC. □ New York, NY

Bills, Melinda, Info.Spec.
EUROPEAN COMMUNITY INFORMATION SERVICE - LIBRARY □ Washington, DC

Bills, Rex E., Owner
GOLDEN AGE RADIO - THE BEST OF OLD TIME RADIO COLLECTION □ Portland, OR

Billy, George J., Libn.
U.S. MERCHANT MARINE ACADEMY - SCHUYLER OTIS BLAND MEMORIAL LIBRARY □ Kings Point, NY

Bilodeau, Francoise, Bibliotechnicienne
QUEBEC PROVINCE - MINISTERE DE LA JUSTICE - BIBLIOTHEQUE □ Ste. Foy, PQ

Bilopavlovich, Sharon, Libn.
ST. RITA'S MEDICAL CENTER - MEDICAL LIBRARY □ Lima, OH

Bilsland, Clare, Supv., Lib.Res. & Tech.
TORONTO BOARD OF EDUCATION - EDUCATION CENTRE LIBRARY □ Toronto, ON

Binau, Myra, Coord., Lib.Serv.
WASHINGTON COUNTY HOSPITAL - WROTH MEMORIAL LIBRARY □ Hagerstown, MD

Bindas, Nancy L., Med.Libn.
WARREN GENERAL HOSPITAL - MEDICAL STAFF LIBRARY □ Warren, OH

Binford, Janet
RHODODENDRON SPECIES FOUNDATION - LAWRENCE J. PIERCE RHODODENDRON LIBRARY □ Federal Way, WA

Bingaman, Joseph W., Cur., Latin Amer.Coll.
STANFORD UNIVERSITY - HOOVER INSTITUTION ON WAR, REVOLUTION AND PEACE - LIBRARY □ Stanford, CA

Bingham, F. Keith, Assoc.Libn.
COLLEGE OF THE VIRGIN ISLANDS - FOUNDATION CENTER REGIONAL COLLECTION □ St. Thomas, VI

Bingham, James, Assoc.Dir./Adm.Aff.
HOUSTON ACADEMY OF MEDICINE - TEXAS MEDICAL CENTER LIBRARY □ Houston, TX

Binion, Francie G., Mgr.
ANSER - TECHNICAL LIBRARY □ Arlington, VA

Binkowski, Laura, Ref.Libn.
COLUMBIA UNIVERSITY - HERBERT H. LEHMAN LIBRARY □ New York, NY

Binns, Mrs. W.G., Adult Lib.
REVEILLE UNITED METHODIST CHURCH - REVEILLE MEMORIAL LIBRARY □ Richmond, VA

Bintliff, Barbara, Ref.Libn.
UNIVERSITY OF DENVER - COLLEGE OF LAW - WESTMINSTER LAW LIBRARY □ Denver, CO

Birch, Paul, Ref.
UNIVERSITY OF ALABAMA - SCHOOL OF LAW LIBRARY □ University, AL

Birch, Tobeylynn, Hd.Libn.
CALIFORNIA SCHOOL OF PROFESSIONAL PSYCHOLOGY - LOS ANGELES LIBRARY □ Los Angeles, CA

Birchard, Jane M., Libn.
FLINT HILLS AREA VOCATIONAL-TECHNICAL SCHOOL - LIBRARY □ Emporia, KS

Birchfield, Martha J., Dir.
LEXINGTON COMMUNITY COLLEGE - LIBRARY □ Lexington, KY

Birchler, Edith, Cur.
PROWERS COUNTY HISTORICAL SOCIETY - BIG TIMBERS MUSEUM - LIBRARY □ Lamar, CO

Bird, Bonnie, Mgr., Rd.Serv.
CANADIAN CENTRE FOR OCCUPATIONAL HEALTH AND SAFETY - DOCUMENTATION SERVICES/SERVICE DE DOCUMENTATION □ Hamilton, ON

Bird, Jacqueline, Chf.Libn.
U.S. VETERANS ADMINISTRATION (MD-Fort Howard) - HOSPITAL LIBRARY □ Fort Howard, MD

Bird, Judi, Hd., Acq.
SUNY - AGRICULTURAL AND TECHNICAL COLLEGE AT FARMINGDALE - THOMAS D. GREENLEY LIBRARY □ Farmingdale, NY

Bird, Nora, Rd.Serv.Libn.
BRANDEIS UNIVERSITY - GERSTENZANG SCIENCE LIBRARY □ Waltham, MA

Bird, Warren, Dir.
DUKE UNIVERSITY - MEDICAL CENTER LIBRARY □ Durham, NC

Birk, Nancy, Assoc.Cur.
KENT STATE UNIVERSITY - DEPARTMENT OF SPECIAL COLLECTIONS □ Kent, OH

Birknes, Margaretha E.H., Law Libn.
NEW BEDFORD LAW LIBRARY □ New Bedford, MA

Birks, Grant, Mgr., Info.Rsrc.Ctr.
BELL-NORTHERN RESEARCH LTD. - INFORMATION RESOURCE CENTRE □ Ottawa, ON

Birladeanu, Ludmila, Supv.
HARVARD UNIVERSITY - CHEMISTRY LIBRARY □ Cambridge, MA

Birnbach, Melanie R., Med.Libn.
CHILDREN'S HOSPITAL - FORBES MEDICAL LIBRARY □ Denver, CO

Birnbaum, Denise, Tech.Libn.
GARRETT CORPORATION - GARRETT TURBINE ENGINE COMPANY - ENGINEERING LIBRARY □ Phoenix, AZ

Birnbaum, Henry, Univ.Libn.
PACE UNIVERSITY - LIBRARY □ New York, NY

Birnbaum, Kerry, Libn.
MERCER MEDICAL CENTER - SCHOOL OF
NURSING - LIBRARY □ Trenton, NJ
Birschel, Dee, Assoc.Dir.
INTERNATIONAL FOUNDATION OF EMPLOYEE
BENEFIT PLANS - INFORMATION CENTER □
Brookfield, WI
Bisaccia, Linda A. Collenberg, Med.Libn.
FREDERICK MEMORIAL HOSPITAL - WALTER F.
PRIOR MEDICAL LIBRARY □ Frederick, MD
Bisaillon, Blaise, Dir.
FORBES LIBRARY □ Northampton, MA
Bisch, Thelma, Libn.
KITCHENER-WATERLOO HOSPITAL - HEALTH
SCIENCES LIBRARY† □ Kitchener, ON
Bischoff, Frances, Media Serv.Coord.
WISHARD (William N.) MEMORIAL HOSPITAL -
PROFESSIONAL LIBRARY/MEDIA SERVICES† □
Indianapolis, IN
Bischoff, Mary, Asst.Dir.
GRADUATE THEOLOGICAL UNION - LIBRARY □
Berkeley, CA
Biscoe, Eleanor, Dir.
NATIONAL REHABILITATION INFORMATION
CENTER □ Washington, DC
Bishop, Betty, Coord., Educ. LRC
UNIVERSITY OF HOUSTON - AUDIOVISUAL
SERVICES □ Houston, TX
Bishop, David, Univ.Libn.
UNIVERSITY OF CALIFORNIA, SAN FRANCISCO
- LIBRARY □ San Francisco, CA
Bishop, Delbert A., Asst.Dir., CPR
U.S. NATL. ARCHIVES & RECORDS SERVICE -
NATL. PERSONNEL RECORDS CENTER □ St.
Louis, MO
Bishop, Elizabeth, Arts & Lit.Libn.
RYERSON POLYTECHNICAL INSTITUTE -
LEARNING RESOURCES CENTRE □ Toronto, ON
Bishop, Francis, Acq.Libn.
TENNESSEE VALLEY AUTHORITY - TECHNICAL
LIBRARY □ Chattanooga, TN
Bishop, Jean, Pub.Serv.
MONTANA COLLEGE OF MINERAL SCIENCE AND
TECHNOLOGY - LIBRARY □ Butte, MT
Bishop, Patricia, Cat.
MORGAN GUARANTY TRUST COMPANY OF NEW
YORK - LIBRARY □ New York, NY
Bismuti, Gene, Chf., Info.Serv.Div.
WASHINGTON STATE LIBRARY □ Olympia, WA
Bissett, John P., Cat.Libn.
WASHINGTON & LEE UNIVERSITY - LAW
LIBRARY □ Lexington, VA
Bistolfi, Dr. Guido, Dir.
ITALIAN CULTURAL SERVICE - LIBRARY □
Montreal, PQ
Bitman, Leslie, Assoc.Libn.
SQUIRE, SANDERS & DEMPSEY - LAW LIBRARY
□ Cleveland, OH
Bitner, Harry, Legal Bibliog.
COLUMBIA UNIVERSITY - LAW LIBRARY □ New
York, NY
Bitter, Diane S., Cat.
UNIVERSITY OF TOLEDO - COLLEGE OF LAW
LIBRARY □ Toledo, OH
Bitter, Jane L., Tech.Libn.
MOBIL RESEARCH & DEVELOPMENT
CORPORATION - PAULSBORO LABORATORY -
TECHNICAL INFORMATION SERVICES □
Paulsboro, NJ
Bittle, Christine, Archv.
OKLAHOMA HISTORICAL SOCIETY - ARCHIVES
AND MANUSCRIPT DIVISION □ Oklahoma City,
OK
Bitzer, June, Acq./Ref.Libn.
DELAWARE VALLEY COLLEGE OF SCIENCE AND
AGRICULTURE - JOSEPH KRAUSKOPF
MEMORIAL LIBRARY □ Doylestown, PA
Bivins, Hulen E., Hd.
ALABAMA REGIONAL LIBRARY FOR THE BLIND
AND PHYSICALLY HANDICAPPED □
Montgomery, AL

Bjerke, Cheryl A., Dir.
NORTHWESTERN COLLEGE OF CHIROPRACTIC
- LIBRARY □ Bloomington, MN
Bjerken, Lisa C., Dir., Lib.Serv.
FAIRVIEW SOUTHDALE HOSPITAL - MARY ANN
KING HEALTH SCIENCES LIBRARY† □ Edina, MN
Bjorge, Gary, Assoc.Libn.
UNIVERSITY OF KANSAS - EAST ASIAN
LIBRARY □ Lawrence, KS
Bjork, Carol, Libn.
MUSEUM OF FINE ARTS - SCHOOL LIBRARY □
Boston, MA
Bjornberg, Linda, Libn.
WILLMAR STATE HOSPITAL - LIBRARY □
Willmar, MN
Black, B.A., Dir.
BRITISH COLUMBIA - MINISTRY OF
EDUCATION - PROVINCIAL EDUCATIONAL
MEDIA CENTRE □ Richmond, BC
Black, Bernice, Chf., Lib.Br.
U.S. ARMY - ENGINEER WATERWAYS
EXPERIMENT STATION - TECHNICAL
INFORMATION CENTER □ Vicksburg, MS
Black, Deanna, Libn.
NCR CORPORATION - SE/SR LIBRARY □ San
Diego, CA
Black, Dorothy M., Asst. to Dir.
PHILADELPHIA COLLEGE OF BIBLE - LIBRARY □
Langhorne, PA
Black, Ernest L., Mgr.
BURGESS INDUSTRIES - ENGINEERING
LIBRARY† □ Dallas, TX
Black, George W., Sci.Libn.
SOUTHERN ILLINOIS UNIVERSITY,
CARBONDALE - SCIENCE DIVISION LIBRARY □
Carbondale, IL
Black, Dr. J., Assoc.Libn.
UNIVERSITY OF GUELPH - LIBRARY □ Guelph,
ON
Black, Rev. J. Bernard, Libn.
UNIVERSITY OF TORONTO - ST. MICHAEL'S
COLLEGE - JOHN M. KELLY LIBRARY □ Toronto,
ON
Black, Lawrence, Sr.Libn.
NEW YORK STATE INSTITUTE FOR BASIC
RESEARCH IN DEVELOPMENTAL DISABILITIES
- LIBRARY □ Staten Island, NY
Black, Lea, Libn.
BUTLER & BINION - LAW LIBRARY □ Houston,
TX
Black, Margaret, Info.Spec.
CONFERENCE BOARD, INC. - INFORMATION
SERVICE □ New York, NY
Black, Sandra M., Chf.Libn.
MOHAWK COLLEGE OF APPLIED ARTS AND
TECHNOLOGY - MOHAWK LIBRARY RESOURCE
CENTRE □ Hamilton, ON
Black, Sophie K., Assoc.Libn., Pub.Serv.
NORTHEASTERN ILLINOIS UNIVERSITY -
LIBRARY □ Chicago, IL
Black, Suzanne W., Libn.
MONTGOMERY MUSEUM OF FINE ARTS -
LIBRARY □ Montgomery, AL
Blackbeard, Bill, Dir.
SAN FRANCISCO ACADEMY OF COMIC ART -
LIBRARY† □ San Francisco, CA
Blackburn, A.S.T., Co-Dir.
MARQUANDIA SOCIETY FOR STUDIES IN
HISTORY AND LITERATURE - LIBRARY □
Williamsburg, VA
Blackburn, Joy M., Libn.
WASHINGTON NATIONAL INSURANCE
COMPANY - INFORMATION RESOURCES
CENTER □ Evanston, IL
Blackburn, Sharon, Automated Res.Coord.
TEXAS TECH UNIVERSITY - SCHOOL OF LAW
LIBRARY □ Lubbock, TX
Blackford, James, Lib.Adm.
EL DORADO COUNTY LAW LIBRARY† □
Placerville, CA
Blackford, M., Libn.
MARITIME MUSEUM OF THE ATLANTIC -
LIBRARY □ Halifax, NS

Blackman, Tim, Libn.
ADLER PLANETARIUM - LIBRARY □ Chicago, IL
Blackstone, M.F., Assoc. Law Libn.
UNIVERSITY OF WYOMING - LAW LIBRARY □
Laramie, WY
Blackwelder, Mary, Coord., User Serv.
MEDICAL COLLEGE OF WISCONSIN -
LIBRARIES □ Milwaukee, WI
Blackwell, Linda, Sec. IV/Hd.Libn.
FLORIDA STATE OFFICE OF THE COMPTROLLER
- DEPARTMENT OF BANKING & FINANCE -
LEGAL LIBRARY □ Tallahassee, FL
Blacquiere, Mrs. F., Sys.Libn.
CANADA - HEALTH AND WELFARE CANADA -
DEPARTMENTAL LIBRARY SERVICES □ Ottawa,
ON
Bladen, Marguerite, Med.Lib.Cons.
DOWNEY COMMUNITY HOSPITAL - HEALTH
SCIENCES LIBRARY □ Downey, CA
Bladstrom, Anne M., Corp.Fin.Libn.
PRUDENTIAL-BACHE SECURITIES INC. -
CORPORATE FINANCE DEPARTMENT LIBRARY
□ New York, NY
Blain, Andre, Gen.Mgr.
WARNOCK HERSEY PROFESSIONAL SERVICES
LTD. - LIBRARY □ LaSalle, PQ
Blain-Juneau, Jocelyne, Chf.Libn.
CENTRE HOSPITALIER COTE-DES-NEIGES -
CENTRE DE DOCUMENTATION □ Montreal, PQ
Blaine, Miles, Lib.Asst.
SAN DIEGO AERO-SPACE MUSEUM - N. PAUL
WHITTIER HISTORICAL AVIATION LIBRARY □
San Diego, CA
Blaine, Susan F., Dir., LRC
BELL & HOWELL EDUCATION GROUP - DE VRY
INSTITUTE OF TECHNOLOGY - LIBRARY □
Columbus, OH
Blair, Holley M., Libn.
JACKSON, KELLY, HOLT & O'FARRELL - LIBRARY
□ Charleston, WV
Blair, John, Sys.Libn.
NORTHEASTERN OHIO UNIVERSITIES COLLEGE
OF MEDICINE - BASIC MEDICAL SCIENCES
LIBRARY □ Rootstown, OH
Blair, Marsha, ILL Libn.
EAST TEXAS STATE UNIVERSITY - JAMES
GILLIAM GEE LIBRARY □ Commerce, TX
Blair, Marva, Asst.Libn.
AMERICAN EXPRESS COMPANY - SYSTEMS
LIBRARY □ Lauderhill, FL
Blair, Ruth, Mss.Cat.
CONNECTICUT HISTORICAL SOCIETY -
LIBRARY □ Hartford, CT
Blais, Diane A., Supv.
SPRINGFIELD NEWSPAPERS - LIBRARY □
Springfield, MA
Blais, Pierre-Paul, Dir.
QUEBEC PROVINCE - MINISTERE DU REVENU -
BIBLIOTHEQUE □ Ste. Foy, PQ
Blaisdell, Dr. Doris, Assoc.Archv.
TEXAS TECH UNIVERSITY - SOUTHWEST
COLLECTION □ Lubbock, TX
Blake, Deloris, Med.Libn.
BAPTIST HOSPITAL OF SOUTHEAST TEXAS -
MEDICAL LIBRARY □ Beaumont, TX
Blake, Joy A., Libn.
CHAPARRAL GENEALOGICAL SOCIETY -
LIBRARY □ Tomball, TX
Blake, Martha A., Libn.
U.S. ARMY - CONSTRUCTION ENGINEERING
RESEARCH LABORATORY - H.B. ZACKRISON
MEMORIAL LIBRARY □ Champaign, IL
Blake, William R., Transl.
PHILLIPS PETROLEUM COMPANY - RESEARCH &
DEVELOPMENT DEPARTMENT - TECHNICAL
INFORMATION BRANCH □ Bartlesville, OK
Blakeley, Phyllis R., Prov.Archv.
NOVA SCOTIA - PUBLIC ARCHIVES OF NOVA
SCOTIA □ Halifax, NS
Blakely, Jan, Pub.Div.
OKLAHOMA STATE DEPARTMENT OF
LIBRARIES □ Oklahoma City, OK

Blalock, Mary Beth, Act.Dir.
VANDERBILT UNIVERSITY - JEAN AND
ALEXANDER HEARD LIBRARY - EDUCATION
LIBRARY □ Nashville, TN
Blanchard, J., Libn.
CANADA - AGRICULTURE CANADA - CANADIAN
GRAIN COMMISSION - LIBRARY □ Winnipeg, MB
Blanchard, Patricia A., Libn.
EDMUNDSON (Jennie) MEMORIAL HOSPITAL -
LIBRARY □ Council Bluffs, IA
Blanco, Jean, Cur./Bibliog.
UNIVERSITY OF PITTSBURGH - SPECIAL
COLLECTIONS DEPARTMENT □ Pittsburgh, PA
Bland, Catherine V., Dir., Lib.Serv.
VIRGINIA STATE UNIVERSITY - JOHNSTON
MEMORIAL LIBRARY - SPECIAL COLLECTIONS
□ Petersburg, VA
Bland, Larry, Ed.
MARSHALL (George C.) RESEARCH
FOUNDATION - GEORGE C. MARSHALL
RESEARCH LIBRARY† □ Lexington, VA
Blandamer, Ann, Libn.
FOSTER ASSOCIATES, INC. - LIBRARY □
Washington, DC
Blandy, Susan, Mtls. Selection
HUDSON VALLEY COMMUNITY COLLEGE -
DWIGHT MARVIN LEARNING RESOURCES
CENTER □ Troy, NY
Blank, Karen, Hd., Circ.Dept.
SOUTH DAKOTA STATE UNIVERSITY - HILTON
M. BRIGGS LIBRARY □ Brookings, SD
Blankenheim, Mary, Info.Anl.
CONTINENTAL ILLINOIS NATIONAL BANK AND
TRUST COMPANY OF CHICAGO -
INFORMATION SERVICES DIVISION □ Chicago,
IL
Blankenship, Edith, Cat.
UTAH STATE LIBRARY □ Salt Lake City, UT
Blarton, Michael M., Health Sci.Libn., LR Div.
U.S. VETERANS ADMINISTRATION (AR-Little
Rock) - HOSPITAL LIBRARIES □ Little Rock, AR
Blaschak, Mary C., Sr.Libn.
ALLIED CORPORATION - ALLIED AUTOMOTIVE
SECTOR LIBRARY □ Southfield, MI
Blase, Nancy G., Hd.
UNIVERSITY OF WASHINGTON - NATURAL
SCIENCES LIBRARY □ Seattle, WA
Blaser, Kathleen, Libn.
ST. NICHOLAS HOSPITAL - HEALTH SCIENCES
LIBRARY† □ Sheboygan, WI
Blatherwick, Mary, Prog.Dir./Art Cons.
SUNBURY SHORES ARTS AND NATURE CENTRE,
INC. - SUNBURY SHORES LIBRARY □ St.
Andrews, NB
Blatt, Jeannette, Asst.Libn.
LATNER (Albert J.) JEWISH PUBLIC LIBRARY □
Willowdale, ON
Blauet, Doris M., Dir.
FLINT OSTEOPATHIC HOSPITAL - DR. E.
HERZOG MEMORIAL MEDICAL LIBRARY □ Flint,
MI
Blauvelt, Thomas, Hd., Ref.Serv.
NORTH COUNTRY REFERENCE & RESEARCH
RESOURCES COUNCIL - LIBRARY □ Canton, NY
Blaylock, James C., Libn.
BAPTIST MISSIONARY ASSOCIATION
THEOLOGICAL SEMINARY - KELLAR LIBRARY □
Jacksonville, TX
Blazer, Shirley C., Patent Coord.
GREYHOUND CORPORATION - PATENT LAW
DEPARTMENT LIBRARY □ Scottsdale, AZ
Blazina, Vesna, Libn.
UNIVERSITE DE MONTREAL - BIOLOGIE-
BIBLIOTHEQUE □ Montreal, PQ
Bleakley, Nancy, Govt.Docs.Libn.
SUFFOLK UNIVERSITY - LAW LIBRARY □
Boston, MA
Blechman, Burton M., Ref.Asst.
NEW YORK UNIVERSITY MEDICAL CENTER -
FREDERICK L. EHRMAN MEDICAL LIBRARY □
New York, NY

Bleecker, Ruth M., Cur. of Music
BOSTON PUBLIC LIBRARY - MUSIC
DEPARTMENT □ Boston, MA
Blenkush, Sharon, Cat.
OHIO NORTHERN UNIVERSITY - HETERICK
MEMORIAL LIBRARY □ Ada, OH
Bless, Donald R., Res.Libn.
UNIVERSITY OF ILLINOIS AT CHICAGO -
ENERGY RESOURCES CENTER - DOCUMENTS
CENTER □ Chicago, IL
Blesse, Robert E., Hd.
UNIVERSITY OF NEVADA, RENO - SPECIAL
COLLECTIONS DEPARTMENT/UNIVERSITY
ARCHIVES □ Reno, NV
Bleuer, Jeanne, Asst.Dir., User Serv.
ERIC CLEARINGHOUSE ON COUNSELING AND
PERSONNEL SERVICES - LEARNING
RESOURCES CENTER □ Ann Arbor, MI
Blevins, Donald L., Libn.
U.S.D.A. - AGRICULTURAL RESEARCH SERVICE
- NORTHERN REGIONAL RESEARCH CENTER
LIBRARY □ Peoria, IL
Blevins, Elliott, Asst.Libn.
GENERAL DYNAMICS CORPORATION - PUBLIC
AFFAIRS LIBRARY □ St. Louis, MO
Blewett, Dan
LOUISIANA STATE UNIVERSITY - REFERENCE
SERVICES □ Baton Rouge, LA
Blinks, Doris, Lib.Supv.
OLMSTED COUNTY HISTORICAL SOCIETY -
LIBRARY AND ARCHIVES □ Rochester, MN
Blittersdorf, Pamela, Audiotape Libn.
CBS INC. - CBS NEWS AUDIO ARCHIVES □ New
York, NY
Blitz, Roberta, Fine Arts
COLUMBIA UNIVERSITY - AVERY
ARCHITECTURAL AND FINE ARTS LIBRARY □
New York, NY
Blixrud, Julia, OCLC Coord.
MINITEX □ Minneapolis, MN
Blocher, Joan, Asst.Libn.
CHICAGO THEOLOGICAL SEMINARY -
HAMMOND LIBRARY □ Chicago, IL
Block, Eleanor, Hd.Libn.
OHIO STATE UNIVERSITY - JOURNALISM
LIBRARY □ Columbus, OH
Block, Phil, Assoc.Dir., Educ.
INTERNATIONAL CENTER OF PHOTOGRAPHY -
LIBRARY RESOURCE CENTER □ New York, NY
Blocker, Martha G., Hd.Libn.
INDIANAPOLIS MUSEUM OF ART - REFERENCE
LIBRARY □ Indianapolis, IN
Blockson, Charles L., Cur.
TEMPLE UNIVERSITY - CENTRAL LIBRARY
SYSTEM - CHARLES L. BLOCKSON AFRO-
AMERICAN HISTORICAL COLL. □ Philadelphia,
PA
Blodgett, Jan, Asst.Archv.
TEXAS TECH UNIVERSITY - SOUTHWEST
COLLECTION □ Lubbock, TX
Bloeme, Allyn Rice, Chf.Libn.
TRAPHAGEN SCHOOL OF FASHION - ETHEL
TRAPHAGEN LEIGH MEMORIAL LIBRARY □ New
York, NY
Bloeth, Kay, Photo.Libn.
NEWSDAY, INC. - LIBRARY □ Melville, NY
Blommel, Henry H., Collector-Dir.
BLOMMEL HISTORIC AUTOMOTIVE DATA
COLLECTION - LIBRARY AND INFORMATION
CENTER □ Connersville, IN
Blomquist, Laura, Hd.Libn.
OHIO STATE UNIVERSITY - EDUCATION/
PSYCHOLOGY LIBRARY □ Columbus, OH
Blomstrann, Lois L., Asst. to Dir.
NEW BRITAIN MUSEUM OF AMERICAN ART -
LIBRARY □ New Britain, CT
Bloom, John Porter, Dir.
UNIVERSITY OF THE PACIFIC - STUART
LIBRARY OF WESTERN AMERICANA □ Stockton,
CA
Bloom, Karl B., Asst.Libn.
VERMONT HISTORICAL SOCIETY - LIBRARY □
Montpelier, VT

Bloom, Vicki D., Med.Libn.
CHICAGO COLLEGE OF OSTEOPATHIC
MEDICINE - ALUMNI MEMORIAL LIBRARY □
Chicago, IL
BloomBecker, Jay J., Dir.
NATIONAL CENTER FOR COMPUTER CRIME
DATA □ Los Angeles, CA
Bloomer, Jerry M., Libn.
NORTON (R.W.) ART GALLERY - REFERENCE-
RESEARCH LIBRARY □ Shreveport, LA
Bloomfield, Mr. Masse, Supv.
HUGHES AIRCRAFT COMPANY - ELECTRO-
OPTICAL & DATA SYSTEMS GROUP -
TECHNICAL LIBRARY □ El Segundo, CA
Blose, Donna D., Libn.
U.S. VETERANS ADMINISTRATION (PA-Butler) -
MEDICAL CENTER LIBRARY □ Butler, PA
Blosser, Patricia, Assoc.Dir., User Serv.
ERIC CLEARINGHOUSE FOR SCIENCE,
MATHEMATICS AND ENVIRONMENTAL
EDUCATION □ Columbus, OH
Blough, Keith, Law Libn.
COLUMBUS LAW LIBRARY ASSOCIATION □
Columbus, OH
Blouin, Francis X., Jr., Dir.
UNIVERSITY OF MICHIGAN - MICHIGAN
HISTORICAL COLLECTIONS - BENTLEY
HISTORICAL LIBRARY □ Ann Arbor, MI
Blouin, Rick, Hd., Official Pubn.Sect.
NATIONAL LIBRARY OF CANADA - CANADIAN
BOOK EXCHANGE CENTRE (CBEC) □ Ottawa, ON
Blount, Monica
SPOTSYLVANIA HISTORICAL ASSOCIATION,
INC. - RESEARCH MUSEUM AND LIBRARY □
Spotsylvania, VA
Blue, Jackalie, Asst.Libn.
KNOXVILLE STATE TECHNICAL INSTITUTE -
EDUCATIONAL RESOURCE CENTER □ Knoxville,
TN
Blue, Jerry, Prof.Asst.
MINNEAPOLIS PUBLIC LIBRARY &
INFORMATION CENTER - SOCIOLOGY
DEPARTMENT □ Minneapolis, MN
Bluestein, Patricia Y., Hd.Libn.
AMERICAN BANKER, INC. - LIBRARY □ New
York, NY
Bluh, Fanny L., Adm.Asst.
UNITED CEREBRAL PALSY OF NEW YORK CITY,
INC. - LIBRARY □ New York, NY
Bluh, Pamela, Asst.Libn., Tech.Serv.
UNIVERSITY OF MARYLAND, BALTIMORE -
SCHOOL OF LAW - MARSHALL LAW LIBRARY □
Baltimore, MD
Blum, John P., Dir.
NEW MEXICO STATE SUPREME COURT - LAW
LIBRARY □ Santa Fe, NM
Blum, Phyllis R., Libn.
U.S. NAVY - NAVAL SCHOOL OF HEALTH
SCIENCES - LIBRARY □ Bethesda, MD
Blumberg, Janet, Chf., Tech.Serv.Div.
WASHINGTON STATE LIBRARY □ Olympia, WA
Blume, Peter F., Dir.
ALLENTOWN ART MUSEUM - RESEARCH
LIBRARY □ Allentown, PA
Blumenfeld, Lea, Sr. Staff Libn.
CARNEGIE LIBRARY OF PITTSBURGH -
CENTRAL CHILDREN'S ROOM HISTORICAL
COLLECTION □ Pittsburgh, PA
Blumenthal, Marcia, Chm., Lib.Comm.
ALL SOULS UNITARIAN CHURCH - E. BURDETTE
BACKUS LIBRARY □ Indianapolis, IN
Blums, Z.B., Transl.
HERCULES, INC. - RESEARCH CENTER -
TECHNICAL INFORMATION DIVISION □
Wilmington, DE
Blunt, Terry, Exec.Dir.
CONNECTICUT RIVER WATERSHED COUNCIL -
LIBRARY □ Easthampton, MA
Blust, Sandra, Libn.
PENNSYLVANIA STATE DEPARTMENT OF
ENVIRONMENTAL RESOURCES - BUREAU OF
TOPOGRAPHIC & GEOLOGIC SURVEY LIB. □
Harrisburg, PA

Bluth, John F., Cur.
BRIGHAM YOUNG UNIVERSITY - ARCHIVES
AND MANUSCRIPTS DIVISION - ARCHIVES OF
RECORDED SOUND □ Provo, UT

Blyskal, Barbara R., Gen.Sec.
POLISH SINGERS ALLIANCE OF AMERICA -
LIBRARY □ New York, NY

Blythe, David, Asst.Libn.
VINSON & ELKINS - LAW LIBRARY □ Houston,
TX

Blythe, Joanne, Ed.
TRANET - LIBRARY □ Rangeley, ME

Blythe, Katherine, Info.Spec.
CORPORATE-TECH PLANNING - RESEARCH
LIBRARY □ Waltham, MA

Boadt, Lawrence E., C.S.P., Libn.
ST. PAUL'S COLLEGE - LIBRARY □ Washington,
DC

Boardman, June M., Supv., Lib./Files
ROSEWOOD CENTER - MIRIAM LODGE
PROFESSIONAL LIBRARY □ Owings Mills, MD

Boardman, Richard C., Map Libn.
FREE LIBRARY OF PHILADELPHIA - SOCIAL
SCIENCE & HISTORY DEPARTMENT - MAP
COLLECTION □ Philadelphia, PA

Boast, Carol, Hd., Ref.
UNIVERSITY OF ILLINOIS - LAW LIBRARY □
Champaign, IL

Bobb, Frank W., Libn. & Cur.
GRAND LODGE OF FREE AND ACCEPTED
MASONS OF PENNSYLVANIA - LIBRARY □
Philadelphia, PA

Bober, Dr. Robert, Asst.Archv.
OHIO STATE UNIVERSITY - ARCHIVES □
Columbus, OH

Bobka, Marlene S., Chf., Lib.Serv.
BIOSPHERICS INC. - LIBRARY □ Rockville, MD

Bobrek, Nancy, Asst.Libn.
PITNEY BOWES - TECHNICAL INFORMATION
CENTER† □ Stamford, CT

Bobrek, Nancy, Ref.Libn.
SACRED HEART UNIVERSITY - LIBRARY □
Bridgeport, CT

Bobrov, Anna, Asst.Libn.
ARTHUR ANDERSEN & CO. - LIBRARY □ Boston,
MA

Boccieri, Kathryn A., Libn.
FRANKLIN GENERAL HOSPITAL - MEDICAL
LIBRARY □ Valley Stream, NY

Bochte, Terry, Libn.
CURATIVE REHABILITATION CENTER -
LEARNING RESOURCE CENTER □ Wauwatosa,
WI

Bock, L., Dir., Info.Serv.
MARTIN/WILLIAMS ADVERTISING AGENCY -
LIBRARY/INFORMATION CENTER □
Minneapolis, MN

Bock, Mary Ann, Res.Assoc.
BILLINGTON, FOX & ELLIS - RESEARCH
DEPARTMENT - LIBRARY □ Chicago, IL

Bock, Rochelle, Sr.Ref.Libn.
UNIVERSITY OF CALIFORNIA, IRVINE -
BIOMEDICAL LIBRARY □ Irvine, CA

Bockelman, Paul, Asst.Dir.
CAMBRIDGE HISTORICAL COMMISSION -
LIBRARY □ Cambridge, MA

Bocking, D.H., Assoc.Prov.Archv.
SASKATCHEWAN ARCHIVES BOARD □ Regina,
SK

Bockman, Marilyn M., V.P.
AMERICAN ASSOCIATION OF ADVERTISING
AGENCIES - MEMBER INFORMATION SERVICE
□ New York, NY

Bockstruck, Lloyd DeWitt, Div.Hd.
DALLAS PUBLIC LIBRARY - GENEALOGY
COLLECTION □ Dallas, TX

Bodapati, R.A., Libn.
SVERDRUP & PARCEL AND ASSOCIATES, INC. -
TECHNICAL LIBRARY □ St. Louis, MO

Bodem, Dennis R., Dir.
BESSER (Jesse) MUSEUM - LIBRARY □ Alpena,
MI

Bodine, Jean, Hd. of Files
TIME, INC. - LIBRARY □ New York, NY

Bodley, Margaret J., Dir.
NATIONAL COUNCIL ON FAMILY RELATIONS -
FAMILY RESOURCE & REFERRAL CENTER □
Minneapolis, MN

Bodnar, John, Dir.
INDIANA UNIVERSITY - ORAL HISTORY
RESEARCH PROJECT - LIBRARY □ Bloomington,
IN

Bodnar, Marta, Libn.
ORTHO PHARMACEUTICAL (Canada), LTD. -
LIBRARY □ Don Mills, ON

Bodnariuk, Stefan, Supv. Film Ed.
AMERICAN CANCER SOCIETY - AUDIO VISUAL
LIBRARIES □ New York, NY

Bodoh, Lois C., Tech.Libn.
U.S. INDUSTRIAL CHEMICALS COMPANY -
TUSCOLA PLANT TECHNICAL LIBRARY AND
INFORMATION CENTER □ Tuscola, IL

Bodre, Robert J., Info.Supv.
MONSANTO FIBERS & INTERMEDIATES
COMPANY - TECHNOLOGY CENTER LIBRARY □
Texas City, TX

Body, Laura C., Libn.
ROYAL CANADIAN MILITARY INSTITUTE -
LIBRARY □ Toronto, ON

Bodziak, Karen, Dir. of Educ.
RIGHT TO LIFE LEAGUE OF SOUTHERN
CALIFORNIA - LIBRARY □ Los Angeles, CA

Boeckel, Olga, Hd.Libn.
SHREWSBURY DAILY-SUNDAY REGISTER -
LIBRARY □ Shrewsbury, NJ

Boede, Carol, Cat.
MORAINE PARK TECHNICAL INSTITUTE -
LEARNING RESOURCE CENTER □ Fond du Lac,
WI

Boeder, Thelma, Archv./Exec.Sec.
UNITED METHODIST COMMN. ON ARCHIVES &
HIST. - MINNESOTA ANNUAL CONFERENCE -
ARCHIVES & HISTORICAL LIB. □ Minneapolis,
MN

Boehle, June, Libn.
REPUBLICAN ASSOCIATES OF LOS ANGELES
COUNTY - RESEARCH LIBRARY □ Glendale, CA

Boehm, Joanne, Libn.
REFORMED BIBLE COLLEGE - LIBRARY □ Grand
Rapids, MI

Boehnlein, Edward, Anl.
SHERWIN-WILLIAMS COMPANY -
INFORMATION CENTER □ Cleveland, OH

Boek, Dr. Jean K., Chm., Lib.Comm.
NATIONAL GRADUATE UNIVERSITY - LIBRARY
□ Arlington, VA

Boemeke, Olga, Asst.Libn.
PRINCETON UNIVERSITY - OFFICE OF
POPULATION RESEARCH - LIBRARY □ Princeton,
NJ

Boen, Daniel K.L., Cat.Libn.
UNIVERSITY OF WINDSOR - PAUL MARTIN
LAW LIBRARY □ Windsor, ON

Boer, Aileen C., Mgr.
FEDERAL RESERVE BANK OF PHILADELPHIA -
LIBRARY □ Philadelphia, PA

Boeringer, James, Dir.
MORAVIAN MUSIC FOUNDATION, INC. - PETER
MEMORIAL LIBRARY □ Winston-Salem, NC

Boerner, Susan C., Asst.Libn.
CAPITOL INSTITUTE OF TECHNOLOGY - JOHN
G. PUENTE LIBRARY □ Kensington, MD

Boettcher, Barry, Chf., Rd.Serv., Logistics
U.S. AIR FORCE INSTITUTE OF TECHNOLOGY -
LIBRARY □ Wright-Patterson AFB, OH

Boettcher, Jolene, Cat.Libn.
OHIO HISTORICAL SOCIETY - ARCHIVES-
LIBRARY □ Columbus, OH

Boettcher, Ursula S., Libn.
MIDDLETOWN HOSPITAL ASSOCIATION - ADA
I. LEONARD MEMORIAL LIBRARY □ Middletown,
OH

Bogan, Mary E., Spec.Coll.Libn.
EMPORIA STATE UNIVERSITY - WILLIAM
ALLEN WHITE LIBRARY - SPECIAL
COLLECTIONS □ Emporia, KS

Bogart, Harold, Assoc. State Libn.
NEW MEXICO STATE LIBRARY □ Santa Fe, NM

Boggess, Jennylind C., Staff Libn.
U.S. NATL. INSTITUTES OF HEALTH - LIBRARY
□ Bethesda, MD

Boggess, John, Dp.Br.Hd.
U.S. NASA - GODDARD SPACE FLIGHT CENTER
- LIBRARY† □ Greenbelt, MD

Boggs, Alice G.
SALEM COUNTY HISTORICAL SOCIETY -
LIBRARY □ Salem, NJ

Boggs, Steven, Prog.Mgr.
OKLAHOMA CORPORATION COMMISSION -
ENERGY CONSERVATION SERVICES DIVISION
- TECHNICAL INFORMATION CENTER □
Oklahoma City, OK

Bogie, Thomas M., Mgr.
DALLAS PUBLIC LIBRARY - HISTORY AND
SOCIAL SCIENCES DIVISION □ Dallas, TX

Bognar, Dorothy McAdoo, Hd.
UNIVERSITY OF CONNECTICUT - MUSIC
LIBRARY □ Storrs, CT

Bogner, Susan, Libn.
MC BRIDE, BAKER, WIENKE - LAW LIBRARY† □
Chicago, IL

Bogosian, Narcisse, Asst.Libn.
ANHEUSER-BUSCH COMPANIES, INC. -
CORPORATE LIBRARY □ St. Louis, MO

Bohack, Marge, Hd.Libn.
WICHITA GENERAL HOSPITAL - MEDICAL
LIBRARY □ Wichita Falls, TX

Bohanan, Robert, Libn.
U.S. PRESIDENTIAL LIBRARIES - CARTER
PRESIDENTIAL MATERIALS PROJECT □ Atlanta,
GA

Bohannon, Paulene, Supv., R&D Rec.
PHILLIPS PETROLEUM COMPANY - RESEARCH &
DEVELOPMENT DEPARTMENT - TECHNICAL
INFORMATION BRANCH □ Bartlesville, OK

Bohem, Hilda, Pub.Serv.Libn.
UNIVERSITY OF CALIFORNIA, LOS ANGELES -
DEPARTMENT OF SPECIAL COLLECTIONS □ Los
Angeles, CA

Bohlen, Jeanne, Dir.
FOUNDATION CENTER - CLEVELAND - KENT H.
SMITH LIBRARY □ Cleveland, OH

Bohley, Ronald, Libn.
UNIVERSITY OF MISSOURI, ROLLA - CURTIS
LAWS WILSON LIBRARY □ Rolla, MO

Bohling, Raymond A., Hd.
UNIVERSITY OF MINNESOTA - ENGINEERING
LIBRARY □ Minneapolis, MN

Bohlmann, Irene, Hd.
CEDARS MEDICAL CENTER - MEDICAL LIBRARY
□ Miami, FL

Bohne, Jean, Libn.
UNIVERSITY OF TORONTO - FACULTY OF
FORESTRY LIBRARY □ Toronto, ON

Bohnert, Kathy, Asst.
CHARLESTON GAZETTE-MAIL - LIBRARY □
Charleston, WV

Bohr, P. Richard, Dir.
MIDWEST CHINA CENTER □ St. Paul, MN

Boilard, David, Dir.
UNIVERSITY OF NORTH DAKOTA - SCHOOL OF
MEDICINE - HARLEY E. FRENCH MEDICAL
LIBRARY □ Grand Forks, ND

Boilesen, Bernice, Cur.
UNITED METHODIST CHURCH - NEBRASKA
CONFERENCE - HISTORICAL CENTER □ Lincoln,
NE

Boisclair, Nicole, Directrice
CONSERVATOIRE DE MUSIQUE DE MONTREAL -
CENTRE DE DOCUMENTATION □ Montreal, PQ

Boisvenue, Ms. M.-J., Libn.
CANADA - AGRICULTURE CANADA - RESEARCH
STATION, VINELAND STATION - LIBRARY □
Vineland Station, ON

Boisvenue, Marie-Josee, Entomology Res.Libn.
CANADA - AGRICULTURE CANADA - ENTOMOLOGY RESEARCH LIBRARY □ Ottawa, ON

Boisvert, Danielle, Ref.Libn.
UNIVERSITE DU QUEBEC A HULL - BIBLIOTHEQUE □ Hull, PQ

Boisvert, Donald J., Libn.
RHODE ISLAND STATE DEPARTMENT OF COMMUNITY AFFAIRS - REFERENCE LIBRARY □ Providence, RI

Boisvert, Michel, Hd. of Ref.Serv.
RADIO QUEBEC - CENTRE DES RESSOURCES DOCUMENTAIRES □ Montreal, PQ

Boite, Mary, Libn.
REGISTERED NURSES' ASSOCIATION OF ONTARIO - LIBRARY □ Toronto, ON

Bojin, Minda, Libn.
CANADA - NATIONAL MUSEUMS OF CANADA - NATIONAL MUSEUM OF SCIENCE AND TECHNOLOGY - LIBRARY □ Ottawa, ON

Boland, Miriam, Lib.Dir.
GEORGIA STATE DEPARTMENT OF HUMAN RESOURCES - LIBRARY □ Atlanta, GA

Bolanos, Marie K., Dir.
ST. JOHN HOSPITAL - MEDICAL LIBRARY □ Detroit, MI

Bolas, Deborah, Libn.
RALSTON PURINA COMPANY - INFORMATION CENTER □ St. Louis, MO

Bolden, C.E., Dir.
WASHINGTON STATE LAW LIBRARY □ Olympia, WA

Bolden, Elizabeth C., Libn.
U.S. ARMY HOSPITALS - MADIGAN ARMY MEDICAL CENTER - MEDICAL LIBRARY □ Tacoma, WA

Bolden, M. Scott, Asst.Libn.
NATIONAL GEOGRAPHIC SOCIETY - ILLUSTRATIONS LIBRARY □ Washington, DC

Boldrick, Sam J., Libn.
MIAMI-DADE PUBLIC LIBRARY - FLORIDA COLLECTION □ Miami, FL

Bolef, Doris, Dir.
RUSH-PRESBYTERIAN-ST. LUKE'S MEDICAL CENTER - LIBRARY OF RUSH UNIVERSITY □ Chicago, IL

Bolen, Val, Ph.D., Ref.Libn.
CAPITAL UNIVERSITY - LAW SCHOOL LIBRARY □ Columbus, OH

Boles, Frank, Asst.Archv.
UNIVERSITY OF MICHIGAN - MICHIGAN HISTORICAL COLLECTIONS - BENTLEY HISTORICAL LIBRARY □ Ann Arbor, MI

Boley, Sue Judith, Libn./Info.Off.
ADMINISTRATIVE CONFERENCE OF THE UNITED STATES (ACUS) - LIBRARY □ Washington, DC

Bolger, Bill, Dir.
NATIONAL RESOURCE CENTER FOR CONSUMERS OF LEGAL SERVICES - CLEARINGHOUSE □ Washington, DC

Bolig, David, Info.Spec.
MICHIGAN STATE UNIVERSITY - INSTITUTE FOR RESEARCH ON TEACHING - INFORMATION CENTER □ East Lansing, MI

Bolin, Carolyn, Libn.
MIAMI COUNTY LAW LIBRARY □ Troy, OH

Boling, Ellen, Pk.Techn.
U.S. NATL. PARK SERVICE - CHACO CANYON NATL. MONUMENT - STUDY LIBRARY □ Bloomfield, NM

Boll, James, Supv.Pk. Ranger
U.S. NATL. PARK SERVICE - TIMPANOGOS CAVE NATL. MONUMENT - LIBRARY □ American Fork, UT

Bolles, Charles, State Libn.
IDAHO STATE LIBRARY □ Boise, ID

Bollier, John, Asst.Libn.
YALE UNIVERSITY - DIVINITY SCHOOL LIBRARY □ New Haven, CT

Bollinger, Laura Ann, Plant Libn.
BURROUGHS WELLCOME COMPANY - PLANT LIBRARY □ Greenville, NC

Bolner, Myrtle S., Act.Hd.
LOUISIANA STATE UNIVERSITY - BUSINESS ADMINISTRATION/GOVERNMENT DOCUMENTS DEPARTMENT □ Baton Rouge, LA

Bolner, Myrtle S., Act.Hd.Bus.Adm./Govt.Doc.
LOUISIANA STATE UNIVERSITY - CENTER FOR ENGINEERING & BUSINESS ADMINISTRATION READING ROOM □ Baton Rouge, LA

Bolshaw, Cynthia, Slide Libn.
WORCESTER ART MUSEUM - LIBRARY† □ Worcester, MA

Bolton, Anita S., Coord., Circ. & ILL
ROSEMONT COLLEGE - GERTRUDE KISTLER MEMORIAL LIBRARY - SPECIAL COLLECTIONS □ Rosemont, PA

Bolton, Barbara G., Libn.
DOMTAR, INC. - RESEARCH CENTRE LIBRARY □ Senneville, PQ

Bolton, Emily, Pub.Info.Asst.
U.S. NATL. PARK SERVICE - MIDWEST REGIONAL OFFICE LIBRARY† □ Omaha, NE

Bolton, Norah, Exec.Adm.
ONTARIO CHORAL FEDERATION - LIBRARY □ Toronto, ON

Bomar, Barbara R., Info.Mgr.
NATIONAL CRIME PREVENTION INSTITUTE - INFORMATION CENTER □ Louisville, KY

Bomgardner, Barbara-Ann, Base Libn.
U.S. AIR FORCE BASE - MC GUIRE BASE LIBRARY □ McGuire AFB, NJ

Bomgardner, Martha, Lib.Dir.
CONGRESSIONAL QUARTERLY, INC. - EDITORIAL REPORTS LIBRARY □ Washington, DC

Bomgardner, Martha, Libn.
U.S. DEPT. OF JUSTICE - UNITED STATES ATTORNEY, DISTRICT OF NEW JERSEY - LAW LIBRARY† □ Newark, NJ

Bommicino, Patricia
U.S. DEPT. OF LABOR - BUREAU OF LABOR STATISTICS - INFORMATION AND ADVISORY SECTION □ New York, NY

Bonacorda, Jim, Asst.Libn.
WHITE AND CASE - LIBRARY □ New York, NY

Bond, Beverly, Cat./Ser.
WEST LIBERTY STATE COLLEGE - ELBIN LIBRARY □ West Liberty, WV

Bond, Janet, Asst.Cat.Libn.
KUTZTOWN UNIVERSITY - ROHRBACH LIBRARY □ Kutztown, PA

Bond, Marvin A., Chf., Lib.Res.Dev.
U.S. NATL. BUREAU OF STANDARDS - LIBRARY □ Washington, DC

Bond, Mary, Libn.
COORS (Adolph) COMPANY - TECHNICAL LIBRARY □ Golden, CO

Bond, Randall, Art Bibliog.
SYRACUSE UNIVERSITY - E.S. BIRD LIBRARY - FINE ARTS DEPARTMENT □ Syracuse, NY

Bondar, Robert, Tech.Info.Spec.
BASF WYANDOTTE CORPORATION - RESEARCH LIBRARY □ Wyandotte, MI

Bondarovich, Mary F., Mgr., Tech.Info.Ctr.
BRISTOL-MYERS PRODUCTS - TECHNICAL INFORMATION CENTER □ Hillside, NJ

Bonds, Evan, Music Libn.
UNIVERSITY OF VIRGINIA - MUSIC LIBRARY □ Charlottesville, VA

Bonds, Jean F., Supv.
HOLY NAME OF JESUS HOSPITAL - LIBRARY □ Gadsden, AL

Boner, M. Christopher, Dir.
CALLAWAY EDUCATIONAL ASSOCIATION - COLEMAN LIBRARY □ LaGrange, GA

Bonetti, Kay, Project Dir.
NEW WAVE CORPORATION - AMERICAN AUDIO PROSE LIBRARY □ Columbia, MO

Bonge, Barbara, Rd.Serv.Libn.
COOLEY (Thomas M.) LAW SCHOOL - LIBRARY □ Lansing, MI

Bongiorno, M., Supv., Spec.Serv.
AIR PRODUCTS AND CHEMICALS, INC. - CRSD INFORMATION SERVICES □ Allentown, PA

Bonham, A. Kathleen, Libn.
JONES (W. Alton) CELL SCIENCE CENTER - GEORGE AND MARGARET GEY LIBRARY □ Lake Placid, NY

Bonham, Miriam, Ref.Libn.
AT & T TECHNOLOGIES, INC. - LIBRARY □ Indianapolis, IN

Bonhomme, Mary S., Mgr., Info./Commun.
CABOT CORPORATION - TECHNICAL INFORMATION CENTER □ Kokomo, IN

Boni-Awotwi, Sekum, Asst.Libn.
HOWARD UNIVERSITY - HEALTH SCIENCES LIBRARY □ Washington, DC

Bonin, Claude-Andre, Info.Mgr.
HYDRO-QUEBEC - BIBLIOTHEQUE □ Montreal, PQ

Bonin, Lionel, Libn.
LAURENTIAN UNIVERSITY - SCHOOL OF EDUCATION - LIBRARY □ Sudbury, ON

Bonis, Eva M., Mgr., Corp.Info.Rsrcs.
DENNISON MANUFACTURING COMPANY - RESEARCH LIBRARY □ Framingham, MA

Bonn, Jane, Ref./Circ.Libn.
U.S. GEOLOGICAL SURVEY - DENVER LIBRARY □ Denver, CO

Bonn, Marie Jean, Supv.Libn.
EASTMAN KODAK COMPANY - U.S. APPARATUS DIVISION - TECHNICAL LIBRARY □ Rochester, NY

Bonn, Thomas, Media Libn.
SUNY - COLLEGE AT CORTLAND - MEMORIAL LIBRARY □ Cortland, NY

Bonnell, Brenda E., Energy Conserv.Libn.
U.S. DEPT. OF ENERGY - BONNEVILLE POWER ADMINISTRATION - LIBRARY □ Portland, OR

Bonnelly, Claude, Dir. Adjoint
UNIVERSITE LAVAL - BIBLIOTHEQUE □ Ste. Foy, PQ

Bonner, Jean, Dir.
COMMUNITY HOSPITAL OF INDIANAPOLIS, INC. - LIBRARY □ Indianapolis, IN

Bonnett, JoAnn, Chf., Lib.Br.
U.S. ARMY - TACOM SUPPORT ACTIVITY-SELFRIDGE - RECREATION SERVICES LIBRARY □ Selfridge Air Natl. Guard Base, MI

Bonney, Ms. Frances, Libn.
CANADA - SCIENCE COUNCIL OF CANADA - LIBRARY† □ Ottawa, ON

Bonniwell, Cora
DELAWARE STATE DEVELOPMENT OFFICE - TECHNICAL LIBRARY □ Dover, DE

Bonoca, Shirley, Ref.Libn.
LAKEHEAD UNIVERSITY - CHANCELLOR PATERSON LIBRARY □ Thunder Bay, ON

Bontrager, Robert, Media Spec.
OREGON STATE SCHOOL FOR THE DEAF - LIBRARY □ Salem, OR

Bonura, Larry S., Dir.
BIKELIBRARY □ Odenton MD

Bonynge, Jeanne R., Libn.
U.S. TAX COURT - LIBRARY □ Washington, DC

Boodis, Maxine, Libn.
BALTIMORE CITY MAYOR'S OFFICE OF MANPOWER RESOURCES - LIBRARY □ Baltimore, MD

Boody, Patricia W., Tech.Libn.
TAMPA ELECTRIC COMPANY - TECHNICAL REFERENCE CENTER □ Tampa, FL

Booher, Craig S., Libn.
INSTITUTE OF PAPER CHEMISTRY - LIBRARY □ Appleton, WI

Booher, Harold H., Libn.
EPISCOPAL THEOLOGICAL SEMINARY OF THE SOUTHWEST - LIBRARY □ Austin, TX

Booher, Patricia M., Circ.Libn.
EPISCOPAL THEOLOGICAL SEMINARY OF THE SOUTHWEST - LIBRARY □ Austin, TX

Booker, Robert C., Supv.
MINNEAPOLIS INSTITUTE OF ARTS - ARTS
RESOURCE AND INFORMATION CENTER □
Minneapolis, MN

Booker, Susan, Tech.Serv.Libn.
MIDWESTERN BAPTIST THEOLOGICAL
SEMINARY - LIBRARY† □ Kansas City, MO

Bookhout, Dr. Theodore A., Unit Leader
OHIO STATE UNIVERSITY - OHIO
COOPERATIVE WILDLIFE RESEARCH UNIT -
LIBRARY □ Columbus, OH

Bookmyer, Jane, Supv.
PPG INDUSTRIES, INC. - GLASS RESEARCH
CENTER - INFORMATION SERVICES □
Pittsburgh, PA

Boone, Beth A., Libn.
UNIVERSITY OF NORTH CAROLINA, CHAPEL
HILL - HIGHWAY SAFETY RESEARCH CENTER -
LIBRARY □ Chapel Hill, NC

Boone, Mrs. Daniel
BOB JONES UNIVERSITY - CHURCH
MINISTRIES RESOURCE LAB □ Greenville, SC

Boone, Edward J., Jr., Archv.
MAC ARTHUR (General Douglas) MEMORIAL -
LIBRARY AND ARCHIVES □ Norfolk, VA

Boone, Dr. Elizabeth, Dir. of Stud.
HARVARD UNIVERSITY - DUMBARTON OAKS
CENTER FOR PRE-COLUMBIAN STUDIES -
LIBRARY □ Washington, DC

Boone, Emory, Libn.
U.S. VETERANS ADMINISTRATION (TN-Johnson
City) - MEDICAL CENTER LIBRARY □ Mountain
Home, TN

Boone, Susan L., Cur.
SMITH COLLEGE - SOPHIA SMITH COLLECTION
- WOMEN'S HISTORY ARCHIVE □ Northampton,
MA

Boorkman, Jo Anne, Hd., Coll.Dev.
UNIVERSITY OF NORTH CAROLINA, CHAPEL
HILL - HEALTH SCIENCES LIBRARY □ Chapel
Hill, NC

Booth, Larry, Cur.
SAN DIEGO HISTORICAL SOCIETY - RESEARCH
ARCHIVES - PHOTOGRAPH COLLECTION □ San
Diego, CA

Booth, Lois, Ref.Libn.
U.S. ARMY POST - FORT BENNING -
RECREATION SERVICES LIBRARY BRANCH† □
Ft. Benning, GA

Boothe, Sabrina, Libn.
CENTER FOR THE STUDY OF THE PRESIDENCY
- LIBRARY □ New York, NY

Boram, Joan, Libn.
ASSOCIATED GENERAL CONTRACTORS OF
AMERICA - INFORMATION CENTER □ Detroit,
MI

Boram, Joan M., Libn.
CONSTRUCTION CONSULTANTS, INC. -
LIBRARY □ Detroit, MI

Borbely, Jack, Mgr.
AT & T COMMUNICATIONS - INFORMATION
RESEARCH CENTER □ Morris Plains, NJ

Borbon, Sharon, Law Lib.Coord.
TULARE COUNTY LAW LIBRARY □ Visalia, CA

Borda, Eva, Coll./Ref.Libn.
UNIVERSITY OF WESTERN ONTARIO -
SCIENCES LIBRARY □ London, ON

Borden, Ann, Exec.V.P.
NATIONAL ENERGY FOUNDATION - ENERGY
REFERENCE AND RESOURCE CENTER □ New
York, NY

Borden, Barbara, Libn.
PACIFIC-UNION CLUB - LIBRARY □ San
Francisco, CA

Borden, Margaret, Libn.
U.S. ARMY - ELECTRONICS R & D COMMAND
(ERADCOM) - TECHNICAL LIBRARY DIVISION □
Ft. Monmouth, NJ

Borders, Florence E., Sr.Archv.
AMISTAD RESEARCH CENTER - LIBRARY/
ARCHIVES □ New Orleans, LA

Borders, Patrick, Ctr.Dir.
U.S. NATL. ARCHIVES & RECORDS SERVICE -
FEDERAL ARCHIVES AND RECORDS CENTER,
REGION 6 □ Kansas City, MO

Bordner, Ken, Dir.
CONSERVATION AND RENEWABLE ENERGY
INQUIRY AND REFERRAL SERVICE □
Philadelphia, PA

Bordonaro, Karen, Info.Spec.
CONFERENCE BOARD, INC. - INFORMATION
SERVICE □ New York, NY

Borg, Anne W., Asst.Dir.
KENT MEMORIAL LIBRARY - HISTORICAL
ROOM □ Suffield, CT

Borgen, Dianne A., Info.Spec.
AMES LABORATORY - DOCUMENT LIBRARY □
Ames, IA

Borgen, Wanda, Med.Libn.
VALLEY HOSPITAL - LIBRARY □ Ridgewood, NJ

Borger, Anna Louise, Libn.
BUTLER COUNTY HISTORICAL SOCIETY -
OLIVE CLIFFORD STONE LIBRARY □ El Dorado,
KS

Borger, Irene, Asst.libn.
JUNG (C.G.) INSTITUTE OF LOS ANGELES, INC.
- MAX AND LORE ZELLER IBRARY □ Los Angeles,
CA

Borgersen, Richard, Lib.Dir.
JEWISH BRAILLE INSTITUTE OF AMERICA,
INC. - LIBRARY □ New York, NY

Borges, Ray, Automotive Res.
HARRAH'S AUTOMOTIVE LIBRARY □ Reno, NV

Borgeson, Earl C., Libn.
SOUTHERN METHODIST UNIVERSITY -
UNDERWOOD LAW LIBRARY □ Dallas, TX

Borglund, Shirley, Hd.Libn.
STORMONT-VAIL REGIONAL MEDICAL CENTER
AND SHAWNEE COUNTY MEDICAL SOCIETY -
HEALTH SCIENCES LIBRARY □ Topeka, KS

Borgman, Betty, Ref.Libn.
WAYNE STATE UNIVERSITY - EDUCATION
LIBRARY □ Detroit, MI

Boris, Charry D., Asst.Libn.
AMAX, INC. - LIBRARY □ Greenwich, CT

Boriss, Diana, Ref.Libn.
CHICAGO SUN-TIMES - EDITORIAL LIBRARY □
Chicago, IL

Borja, Beata C., Br.Lib.Supv.
FLORES (Nieves M.) MEMORIAL LIBRARY □
Agana, GU

Borland, Monica, Libn.
EAI CORPORATION - LIBRARY □ Frederick, MD

Borner, Albert P., Libn.
DONOVAN, LEISURE, NEWTON & IRVINE -
LIBRARY □ New York, NY

Bornfleth, Marcus, Hd., Info.Ctr.
SWIFT AND COMPANY - RESEARCH AND
DEVELOPMENT INFORMATION CENTER† □ Oak
Brook, IL

Borntrager, Rev. Conrad M., O.S.M., Archv.
ORDER OF SERVANTS OF MARY - EASTERN
PROVINCE LIBRARY - MORINI MEMORIAL
COLLECTION □ Berwyn, IL

Borntrager, Rev. Conrad M., O.S.M., Archv.
OUR LADY OF SORROWS BASILICA - ARCHIVES
□ Chicago, IL

Borock, Mrs. Freddie, Med.Libn.
BROOKHAVEN MEMORIAL HOSPITAL MEDICAL
CENTER - MEDICAL LIBRARY □ Patchogue, NY

Borodacz, Marusia, Libn.
ONTARIO - MINISTRY OF NATURAL
RESOURCES - NATURAL RESOURCES LIBRARY □
Toronto, ON

Boroson, Sarah, Info.Sci.
AVON PRODUCTS, INC. - RESEARCH LIBRARY □
Suffern, NY

Borovansky, Vladimir T., Hd.
ARIZONA STATE UNIVERSITY - DANIEL E.
NOBLE SCIENCE AND ENGINEERING LIBRARY □
Tempe, AZ

Borraccino, Jean H., Law Libn.
KINGS COUNTY LAW LIBRARY □ Hanford, CA

Borrhersen, Jane, Ref.
FIDELITY MANAGEMENT & RESEARCH
COMPANY - LIBRARY □ Boston, MA

Borrowman, Gerald L., Chf.Libn.
UNITED STATES SPACE EDUCATION
ASSOCIATION - G.L. BORROWMAN
ASTRONAUTICS LIBRARY □ Weyburn, SK

Borschell, Betty, Libn.
AMERICAN CONCRETE INSTITUTE - LIBRARY □
Detroit, MI

Borsuk, Elaine, Lib.Techn.
BUILT ENVIRONMENT COORDINATORS
LIMITED - BEC INFORMATION SYSTEM (BIS)†
□ Toronto, ON

Borts, Dolly, Hd. of Tech.Serv.
PROVIDENCE ATHENAEUM - LIBRARY □
Providence, RI

Bosa, Real, Dir., Pub.Serv.
QUEBEC PROVINCE - BIBLIOTHEQUE
NATIONALE DU QUEBEC □ Montreal, PQ

Bosca, David T., Div.Chf.
CHICAGO PUBLIC LIBRARY CULTURAL CENTER
- LITERATURE AND LANGUAGE DIVISION □
Chicago, IL

Boscamp, Vaunda, Libn.
WELDER (Rob & Bessie) WILDLIFE
FOUNDATION - LIBRARY □ Sinton, TX

Bosco, Julius C., Dir.
PHILADELPHIA COLLEGE OF BIBLE - LIBRARY □
Langhorne, PA

Bosco, Lillian, Libn.
IBM CORPORATION - DSD SITE LIBRARY □
Kingston, NY

Boski, Marina M., Libn.
MONTREAL NEUROLOGICAL INSTITUTE -
LIBRARY† □ Montreal, PQ

Bosler, Deborah M., Supv., Lib.Serv.
GILBERT/COMMONWEALTH, INC. - LIBRARY
AND INFORMATION SERVICES □ Reading, PA

Bosley, Jane M., Libn.
INSTITUTE FOR CANCER RESEARCH - LIBRARY
□ Philadelphia, PA

Bosma, Elske, Tech.Libn.
BANK OF MONTREAL - TECHNICAL
INFORMATION CENTRE □ Scarborough, ON

Boss, Catherine M., Dir.
ELIZABETH GENERAL MEDICAL CENTER -
CHARLES H. SCHLICHTER, M.D. HEALTH
SCIENCE LIBRARY □ Elizabeth, NJ

Boss, Lillian R., Law Libn.
SUTTER COUNTY LAW LIBRARY □ Yuba City, CA

Bosse, Maurice H., Dir. of Lib.Serv.
MASSACHUSETTS MARITIME ACADEMY -
CAPTAIN CHARLES H. HURLEY LIBRARY □
Buzzards Bay, MA

Bosseau, Don L., Univ.Libn.
SAN DIEGO STATE UNIVERSITY - MALCOLM A.
LOVE LIBRARY - SPECIAL COLLECTIONS† □ San
Diego, CA

Bossler, Kathryn C., Law Libn.
COLUMBIA GAS SYSTEM SERVICE
CORPORATION - LAW LIBRARY □ Wilmington,
DE

Bossong, Ken, Coord.
CITIZENS' ENERGY PROJECT, INC. - LIBRARY
□ Washington, DC

Bossong, Ken, Coord.
CITIZENS' ENERGY PROJECT, INC. - PASSIVE
SOLAR FOUNDATION - LIBRARY □ Washington,
DC

Bostock, Katherine Bruce, Hd.Libn.
UNIVERSITY OF CALIFORNIA, DAVIS -
INSTITUTE OF GOVERNMENTAL AFFAIRS -
LIBRARY □ Davis, CA

Boston, Barry E., Libn.Supv.
BALTIMORE CITY - DEPARTMENT OF
LEGISLATIVE REFERENCE - LIBRARY □
Baltimore, MD

Boswell, Roy V., Cur.
CALIFORNIA STATE UNIVERSITY, FULLERTON -
COLLECTION FOR THE HISTORY OF
CARTOGRAPHY† □ Fullerton, CA

Bosworth, Lilian, Coll.Dev./Circ.
ENVIRONMENTAL PROTECTION AGENCY -
ANDREW W. BREIDENBACH ENVIRONMENTAL
RESEARCH CTR., CINCINNATI - TECH.LIB. □
Cincinnati, OH

Botelho, John, Ref.-Transl.
U.P.E.C. CULTURAL CENTER - J.A. FREITAS
LIBRARY □ San Leandro, CA

Both, Stephanie, Libn.
MC GILL UNIVERSITY - LIBRARY SCIENCE
LIBRARY □ Montreal, PQ

Bothmer, A. James, Hd., HSIN
UNIVERSITY OF WYOMING - SCIENCE AND
TECHNOLOGY LIBRARY □ Laramie, WY

Botkin, Karen, Res.Libn.
NATIONAL BROADCASTING COMPANY, INC. -
REFERENCE LIBRARY □ New York, NY

Bott, Audrey L., Dir. of Lib.Serv.
BUSINESS INTERNATIONAL - RESEARCH
LIBRARY □ New York, NY

Bott, Herbert, Asst. to the Hd.Libn.
COOPER UNION FOR THE ADVANCEMENT OF
SCIENCE AND ART - LIBRARY □ New York, NY

Botta, Gail, Coll.Dev.
UNION UNIVERSITY - ALBANY MEDICAL
COLLEGE - SCHAFFER LIBRARY OF THE HEALTH
SCIENCES □ Albany, NY

Botterill, Rosa, Res.Asst.
TEXAS A & M UNIVERSITY - MEDICAL
SCIENCES LIBRARY □ College Station, TX

Botti, Linda M., Supv., Lib.Serv.
AMERICAN CYANAMID COMPANY -
CONSUMERS PRODUCTS RESEARCH DIVISION -
LIBRARY □ Clifton, NJ

Bottoms, Jane R., Libn.
CHILDREN'S MEDICAL CENTER - LIBRARY† □
Dayton, OH

Bottoms, Rita, Hd., Spec. Coll.
UNIVERSITY OF CALIFORNIA, SANTA CRUZ -
DEAN E. MC HENRY LIBRARY □ Santa Cruz, CA

Botts, Jean, Libn.
NORWALK HOSPITAL - R. GLEN WIGGANS
MEMORIAL LIBRARY □ Norwalk, CT

Bouchard, Charlotte, Bibliotechnicienne
QUEBEC PROVINCE - OFFICE DE
PLANIFICATION ET DE DEVELOPPEMENT DU
QUEBEC - BIBLIOTHEQUE† □ Quebec, PQ

Bouchard, Helene H., Bibliotechnicienne
CENTRE HOSPITALIER COOKE - BIBLIOTHEQUE
MEDICALE ET ADMINISTRATIVE† □ Trois-
Rivieres, PQ

Bouchard, Lucie, Documentaliste
UNIVERSITE DE MONTREAL - CENTRE
D'ETUDES ET DE DOCUMENTATION
EUROPEENNES □ Montreal, PQ

Bouchard, Nancy, Libn.
CHARETTE, FORTIER, HAWEY/TOUCHE, ROSS
- LIBRARY □ Montreal, PQ

Bouche, Nicole, Libn.
LOS ANGELES COUNTY MUSEUM OF NATURAL
HISTORY - RESEARCH LIBRARY □ Los Angeles,
CA

Boucher, Lorna, Ref.Libn.
CONCORDIA UNIVERSITY - LOYOLA CAMPUS -
GEORGES P. VANIER LIBRARY □ Montreal, PQ

Boucher, Sr. Marcelle, Archv.
MONASTERE DES URSULINES - ARCHIVES DES
URSULINES DE QUEBEC □ Quebec, PQ

Boucher, Pauline A., Asst.Sci.Libn.
TUFTS UNIVERSITY - MATHEMATICS-PHYSICS
LIBRARY □ Medford, MA

Boucher, Pauline A., Asst.Sci.Libn.
TUFTS UNIVERSITY - ROCKWELL CHEMISTRY
LIBRARY □ Medford, MA

Boucher, Phyllis Jean, Libn.
SHANNON & WILSON, INC. - TECHNICAL
LIBRARY† □ Seattle, WA

Boucher, Robert, Dir.
SEMINAIRE ST-ALPHONSE - BIBLIOTHEQUE □
Ste. Anne de Beaupre, PQ

Boucher, Shirley, Libn.
MISSOURI STATE CHEST HOSPITAL - MEDICAL
LIBRARY □ Mount Vernon, MO

Boudreau, Allan, Dir. & Cur.
GRAND LODGE OF NEW YORK, F. AND A.M. -
ROBERT R. LIVINGSTON LIBRARY AND
MUSEUM □ New York, NY

Boudreau, Berthe, Dir.
UNIVERSITE DE MONCTON - FACULTE DES
SCIENCES DE L'EDUCATION - CENTRE DE
RESSOURCES PEDAGOGIQUES □ Moncton, NB

Boudreau, Denis, Regional Adviser
CANADA - STATISTICS CANADA - ADVISORY
SERVICES - MONTREAL REFERENCE CENTRE □
Montreal, PQ

Boudreau, Gerald, Chf., Acq.Dept.
ECOLE DES HAUTES ETUDES COMMERCIALES
DE MONTREAL - BIBLIOTHEQUE □ Montreal, PQ

Boudreau, Richard A., Libn.
THOMAS COLLEGE - MARRINER LIBRARY □
Waterville, ME

Bougas, Stanley J., Dir.
U.S. DEPT. OF COMMERCE - LIBRARY □
Washington, DC

Boulby, Christine, Film Depot
METROPOLITAN TORONTO LIBRARY -
REGIONAL AUDIO VISUAL DEPARTMENT □
Toronto, ON

Boulet, Marcel, Hd.Libn.
COLLEGE UNIVERSITAIRE DE ST. BONIFACE -
BIBLIOTHEQUE ALFRED-MONNIN □ Saint-
Boniface, MB

Boulet, Mychelle, Ref.Libn.
UNIVERSITE DU QUEBEC A MONTREAL -
BIBLIOTHEQUE DES SCIENCES □ Montreal, PQ

Boulton, Earl M., Ref.Libn.
CREIGHTON UNIVERSITY - HEALTH SCIENCES
LIBRARY □ Omaha, NE

Bouniol, Eileen Collier, Hd. Law Libn.
UNIVERSITY OF SOUTH DAKOTA - MC KUSICK
LAW LIBRARY □ Vermillion, SD

Bourbonnais, Gabrielle, Hd.
QUEBEC PROVINCE - BIBLIOTHEQUE
NATIONALE DU QUEBEC - SERVICE DES
COLLECTIONS SPECIALES - SECTEUR MUSIQUE
□ Montreal, PQ

Bourdeau, Fernand, Supv., Adm.Serv.
CANADIAN BROADCASTING CORPORATION -
MUSIC SERVICES LIBRARY □ Montreal, PQ

Bourdon, Don, Hd.Archv.
ALPINE CLUB OF CANADA - LIBRARY □ Banff,
AB

Bourdon, Donald, Hd.Archv.
ARCHIVES OF THE CANADIAN ROCKIES □
Banff, AB

Bourg, Elizabeth A., Libn.
ATOMIC INDUSTRIAL FORUM - LIBRARY □
Bethesda, MD

Bourgeois, Miss A.E., Hd., Lib.Serv.
CANADA - GEOLOGICAL SURVEY OF CANADA -
LIBRARY □ Ottawa, ON

Bourgeois, Catherine, Libn.
IBM CANADA, LTD. - EASTERN REGION
REFERENCE LIBRARY† □ Montreal, PQ

Bourget, Mary, Libn.
AKERMAN, SENTERFITT, & EIDSON - LAW
LIBRARY □ Orlando, FL

Bourke, Marion, Supv., Braille Lib.
CALIFORNIA STATE LIBRARY □ Sacramento, CA

Bourke, Thomas, Chf.
NEW YORK PUBLIC LIBRARY - MICROFORMS
DIVISION □ New York, NY

Bourne, Sheila, Libn.
RESEARCH INSTITUTE FOR THE STUDY OF
MAN - LIBRARY □ New York, NY

Bourque, Mureille, Documentaliste
CENTRE D'ETUDES DU TOURISME - TECHNICAL
INFORMATION CENTRE □ Montreal, PQ

Bourque, William A., Tech.Serv.Libn.
HARVARD UNIVERSITY - GODFREY LOWELL
CABOT SCIENCE LIBRARY □ Cambridge, MA

Bousfield, Wendy, Bibliog.
SYRACUSE UNIVERSITY - E.S. BIRD LIBRARY -
HUMANITIES DEPARTMENT □ Syracuse, NY

Bousquet, Ann M., Med.Libn.
FANNY ALLEN HOSPITAL - INFORMATION
CENTER □ Winooski, VT

Boutin, Helen M., Lib.Techn.
SAN FRANCISCO UNIFIED SCHOOL DISTRICT -
TEACHERS PROFESSIONAL LIBRARY □ San
Francisco, CA

Boutin, Jocelyne, Hd., Tech.Serv.
CANADA - PUBLIC SERVICE STAFF RELATIONS
BOARD - LIBRARY □ Ottawa, ON

Boutinon, Elizabeth R., Chf.Libn.
SHEARSON LEHMAN/AMERICAN EXPRESS INC.
- RESEARCH LIBRARY □ New York, NY

Bouton, Ellen N., Libn.
NATIONAL RADIO ASTRONOMY OBSERVATORY
- LIBRARY □ Charlottesville, VA

Boutros, David L., Ms.Spec.
WESTERN HISTORICAL MANUSCRIPT
COLLECTION/STATE HISTORICAL SOCIETY OF
MISSOURI MANUSCRIPTS JOINT COLLECTION
□ Kansas City, MO

Boutwell, Barbara, Libn.
MINE SAFETY APPLIANCES COMPANY -
BUSINESS LIBRARY □ Pittsburgh, PA

Boutwell, Barbara, Supv., Lib.Serv.
MINE SAFETY APPLIANCES COMPANY -
TECHNICAL LIBRARY □ Pittsburgh, PA

Bova, Adrienne M., Ed.
READER'S DIGEST - INDEX □ Pleasantville, NY

Bova, Patrick, Libn.
UNIVERSITY OF CHICAGO - NATIONAL
OPINION RESEARCH CENTER - LIBRARY AND
DATA ARCHIVES □ Chicago, IL

Bovey, John A., Prov.Archv.
BRITISH COLUMBIA - MINISTRY OF
PROVINCIAL SECRETARY & GOVERNMENT
SERVICES - PROVINCIAL ARCHIVES □ Victoria,
BC

Bovie, Chris, Med.Libn.
U.S. VETERANS ADMINISTRATION (ME-Togus)
- MEDICAL & REGIONAL OFFICE CENTER □
Augusta, ME

Bovie, Christopher, Med.Libn.
U.S. VETERANS ADMINISTRATION (ME-
Augusta) - CENTER LIBRARY □ Augusta, ME

Bow, Joan, Libn.
NATHAN (Robert R.) ASSOCIATES, INC. -
LIBRARY □ Washington, DC

Bowar, Jean M., Law Libn.
MONTGOMERY COUNTY LAW LIBRARY □
Montgomery, AL

Bowden, Virginia, Assoc.Dir.
UNIVERSITY OF TEXAS HEALTH SCIENCE
CENTER, SAN ANTONIO - LIBRARY □ San
Antonio, TX

Bowdler, Debbie, Energy Info.Spec.
SOUTH CAROLINA STATE ENERGY EXTENSION
SERVICE - ENERGY INFORMATION CENTER □
Columbia, SC

Bowell, Daniel, Asst., Pub.Serv.
WHEATON COLLEGE - BUSWELL MEMORIAL
LIBRARY □ Wheaton, IL

Bowen, Johanna, Ser./Per.Libn.
SUNY - COLLEGE AT CORTLAND - MEMORIAL
LIBRARY □ Cortland, NY

Bowen, Laurel, Cur. of Mss.
ILLINOIS STATE HISTORICAL LIBRARY □
Springfield, IL

Bowen, Louisa, Mss.
SOUTHERN ILLINOIS UNIVERSITY,
CARBONDALE - SPECIAL COLLECTIONS □
Carbondale, IL

Bowens, Kay, Adult Serv.Libn.
MEMORIAL PRESBYTERIAN CHURCH - LIBRARY
□ Midland, MI

Bower, Barbara A., Dir.
FORT LEWIS MILITARY MUSEUM - MUSEUM
RESEARCH LIBRARY □ Fort Lewis, WA

Bower, Dr. Barton, Sr.Res.Chem.
HERCULES, INC. - RESEARCH CENTER -
TECHNICAL INFORMATION DIVISION □
Wilmington, DE

Bower, Cynthia E., Hd.Doc.Libn.
UNIVERSITY OF ARIZONA - GOVERNMENT
DOCUMENTS DEPARTMENT □ Tucson, AZ
Bower, Donald E., Dir.
NATIONAL WRITERS CLUB - LIBRARY □ Aurora,
CO
Bower, Janice, Info.Sci.
MASSACHUSETTS INSTITUTE OF TECHNOLOGY
- LINCOLN LABORATORY LIBRARY □ Lexington,
MA
Bower, Mary M., Dir.
FERRIS STATE COLLEGE - LIBRARY □ Big
Rapids, MI
Bower, Mary M., Dir., Coll.Lib.
FERRIS STATE COLLEGE - SCHOOL OF
PHARMACY - PHARMACY READING ROOM □ Big
Rapids, MI
Bower, Peter, Prov.Archv.
MANITOBA - PROVINCIAL ARCHIVES OF
MANITOBA □ Winnipeg, MB
Bowers, Ann M., Asst.Dir., Univ.Archv.
BOWLING GREEN STATE UNIVERSITY -
CENTER FOR ARCHIVAL COLLECTIONS □
Bowling Green, OH
Bowers, Kent, Radio Rd.Serv.
OKLAHOMA REGIONAL LIBRARY FOR THE
BLIND AND PHYSICALLY HANDICAPPED □
Oklahoma City, OK
Bowers, Linda, Hd.Cat.
MUHLENBERG COLLEGE - JOHN A.W. HAAS
LIBRARY □ Allentown, PA
Bowers, Sandra, Hd.Ref.Libn.
U.S. BUREAU OF RECLAMATION - LIBRARY† □
Denver, CO
Bowes, Winifred B., Libn.
ALCAN ALUMINUM CORPORATION -
CORPORATE LIBRARY □ Cleveland, OH
Bowie, Claire D., Chf., Rd.Serv.
CUNY - GRADUATE SCHOOL AND UNIVERSITY
CENTER - LIBRARY □ New York, NY
Bowler, Peter, Sr.Info.Spec., Bus.
GOODRICH (B.F.) COMPANY - AKRON
INFORMATION CENTER □ Akron, OH
Bowler, Richard, Assoc.Libn./Ref.Serv.
UNIVERSITY OF NEW MEXICO - SCHOOL OF
LAW LIBRARY □ Albuquerque, NM
Bowles, Garrett, Music Libn.
UNIVERSITY OF CALIFORNIA, SAN DIEGO -
UNIVERSITY LIBRARIES □ La Jolla, CA
Bowles, Larry, Interim Dir.
MUSEUM OF WESTERN COLORADO - ARCHIVES
□ Grand Junction, CO
Bowles, Nancy J., Lib.Dir.
DILLON, READ & COMPANY, INC. - LIBRARY □
New York, NY
Bowlin, Helen R., Health Prof.Coord.
INTERNATIONAL DIABETES CENTER - LIBRARY
□ Minneapolis, MN
Bowling, Mary, Archv.
U.S. NATL. PARK SERVICE - EDISON NATL.
HISTORIC SITE - ARCHIVES □ West Orange, NJ
Bowman, Anne
WOOD GUNDY INC. - LIBRARY □ New York, NY
Bowman, Dona, Med.Libn.
MADISON GENERAL HOSPITAL - MEDICAL
LIBRARY □ Madison, WI
Bowman, F.A., Supv., Ref.Serv.
ATLANTIC-RICHFIELD COMPANY -
INFORMATION RESEARCH CENTER □ Los
Angeles, CA
Bowman, Dr. Inci A., Cur., Hist./Med.
UNIVERSITY OF TEXAS MEDICAL BRANCH -
MOODY MEDICAL LIBRARY □ Galveston, TX
Bowman, Leslie, Hd., Tech.Serv./Cat.
PHILADELPHIA COLLEGE OF PHARMACY AND
SCIENCE - JOSEPH W. ENGLAND LIBRARY □
Philadelphia, PA
Bowman, Lois B., Asst.
EASTERN MENNONITE COLLEGE - MENNO
SIMONS HISTORICAL LIBRARY AND ARCHIVES
□ Harrisonburg, VA

Bowman, Lucille, Asst.Libn.
PIEDMONT BIBLE COLLEGE - GEORGE M.
MANUEL MEMORIAL LIBRARY □ Winston-Salem,
NC
Bowman, M. June, Med.Libn.
JOHN PETER SMITH HOSPITAL - MARIETTA
MEMORIAL MEDICAL LIBRARY □ Fort Worth, TX
Bowman, Mary Jane, Tech.Serv.
AMERICAN COUNCIL OF LIFE INSURANCE -
LIBRARY □ Washington, DC
Bowne, Debra R.A., Res.Cons.
PRUDENTIAL INSURANCE COMPANY OF
AMERICA - FINANCIAL RESEARCH CENTER □
Newark, NJ
Bowser, Mrs. Merle L., Pres.
CAMERON COUNTY HISTORICAL SOCIETY -
LITTLE MUSEUM □ Emporium, PA
Bowsfield, Hartwell, Univ.Archv.
YORK UNIVERSITY - UNIVERSITY ARCHIVES □
Downsview, ON
Bowsher, Rose Marie, Libn.
MOTOROLA, INC. - SYSTEMS DIVISION -
TECHNICAL LIBRARY □ Franklin Park, IL
Bowyer, Dr. Bobbie J., Staff Libn.
PRINCE WILLIAM COUNTY SCHOOLS - STAFF
LIBRARY □ Manassas, VA
Bowyer, Valerie, Pub.Serv. & Info.
CONSULATE-GENERAL OF JAPAN - JAPANESE
CONSULATE LIBRARY† □ Edmonton, AB
Box, Susan C., Hist.Rm.Cur.
BARTLESVILLE PUBLIC LIBRARY - HISTORY
ROOM □ Bartlesville, OK
Boxerman, Yvonne, Libn.
BECKMAN INSTRUMENTS, INC. - SPINCO
DIVISION - TECHNICAL LIBRARY □ Palo Alto,
CA
Boyajian, J.G., Chf.Libn.
GENERAL DYNAMICS CORPORATION - POMONA
DIVISION - DIVISION LIBRARY MZ 4-20 □
Pomona, CA
Boyce, Louise, Libn.
CHARLES RIVER BROADCASTING COMPANY -
WCRB LIBRARY □ Waltham, MA
Boyce, Richard D., Morale Sup.Lib.Coord.
U.S. ARMY POST - FORT STEWART/HUNTER
AAF LIBRARY SYSTEM □ Ft. Stewart, GA
Boyce, Ronald H., Hd., Lib.Serv.
LOYALIST COLLEGE OF APPLIED ARTS &
TECHNOLOGY - ANDERSON RESOURCE
CENTRE† □ Belleville, ON
Boyd, Anita, Libn. A
FEDERAL RESERVE BANK OF ST. LOUIS -
RESEARCH LIBRARY □ St. Louis, MO
Boyd, Barbara J., Spec.Coll.Libn.
GLENDALE PUBLIC LIBRARY - SPECIAL
COLLECTIONS □ Glendale, CA
Boyd, Daniel, Dir., Handicapped Serv.
SOUTH DAKOTA STATE LIBRARY & ARCHIVES □
Pierre, SD
Boyd, Effie W., Tech.Libn., Doc.Div.
ARNOLD ENGINEERING DEVELOPMENT CENTER
TECHNICAL LIBRARY □ Arnold Air Force Sta., TN
Boyd, Kenneth A., Media Serv.
ASBURY THEOLOGICAL SEMINARY - B.L.
FISHER LIBRARY □ Wilmore, KY
Boyd, Louise, Supv.
U.S. NAVY - NAVAL AVIONICS CENTER -
TECHNICAL LIBRARY □ Indianapolis, IN
Boyd, Lynn D., Govt.Doc.Libn.
ALABAMA (State) SUPREME COURT - SUPREME
COURT AND STATE LAW LIBRARY □
Montgomery, AL
Boyd, Marge, Mgr.
INTEL CORPORATION - TECHNICAL
INFORMATION CENTER □ Santa Clara, CA
Boyd, Mary T., Libn.
MADISON BUSINESS COLLEGE - LIBRARY □
Madison, WI
Boyd, Patricia, Law Libn.
BECHTEL POWER CORPORATION - LEGAL
DEPARTMENT LIBRARY □ San Francisco, CA

Boyd, Ronald, First Asst.
DALLAS PUBLIC LIBRARY - HUMANITIES
DIVISION □ Dallas, TX
Boyd, Sandra, Ref.Libn.
WESTON SCHOOL OF THEOLOGY - LIBRARY □
Cambridge, MA
Boyd, Sandra H., Lib.Asst.
EASTMAN KODAK COMPANY - TENNESSEE
EASTMAN COMPANY - BUSINESS LIBRARY □
Kingsport, TN
Boyd, Stephanie, Tech.Serv.Libn.
BELL CANADA - INFORMATION RESOURCE
CENTRE □ Montreal, PQ
Boyd, Sylvia, Libn.
PATIENT CARE COMMUNICATIONS, INC. -
LIBRARY □ Darien, CT
Boyd, Trenton, Libn.
UNIVERSITY OF MISSOURI - VETERINARY
MEDICAL LIBRARY □ Columbia, MO
Boyer, Carol M., Med.Libn.
BOULDER VALLEY MEDICAL LIBRARY □ Boulder,
CO
Boyer, Fay E., Med.Libn.
GEORGIA BAPTIST MEDICAL CENTER -
MEDICAL LIBRARY □ Atlanta, GA
Boyer, Florence Irene, Libn.
SPRINGFIELD ART ASSOCIATION - MICHAEL
VICTOR II ART LIBRARY □ Springfield, IL
Boyer, Ginette, Libn.
HOTEL-DIEU DE MONTREAL - SERVICE DE
DOCUMENTATION □ Montreal, PQ
Boyer, J.S., Hd.Libn.
UNION PACIFIC RAILROAD COMPANY -
LIBRARY □ Omaha, NE
Boyer, Jack K., Dir.
CARSON (Kit) MEMORIAL FOUNDATION -
HISTORICAL RESEARCH LIBRARY AND
ARCHIVES □ Taos, NM
Boyer, Larry, Mgr., Law Lib.
U.S. GENERAL ACCOUNTING OFFICE - OFFICE
OF LIBRARY SERVICES □ Washington, DC
Boyer, Margaret B., Libn.
ARMSTRONG WORLD INDUSTRIES, INC. -
MANAGEMENT REFERENCE SERVICES □
Lancaster, PA
Boyer, Maryse, Lib.Techn.
INSTITUT DE READAPTATION DE MONTREAL -
BIBLIOTHEQUE MEDICALE† □ Montreal, PQ
Boykin, Carol, Asst.Libn.
LUTHERAN HOSPITAL - MEDICAL STAFF
LIBRARY AND SCHOOL FOR NURSES LIBRARY □
Moline, IL
Boykin, Joseph, Dir.
CLEMSON UNIVERSITY - ROBERT MULDROW
COOPER LIBRARY □ Clemson, SC
Boykin, Lucile, Local Hist.Spec.
DALLAS PUBLIC LIBRARY - TEXAS/DALLAS
HISTORY AND ARCHIVES DIVISION □ Dallas, TX
Boykiw, Al, Asst.Libn.
ST. VLADIMIR'S UKRAINIAN ORTHODOX
CULTURAL CENTRE - LIBRARY AND ARCHIVES
□ Calgary, AB
Boylan, Lee, Ref.Libn.
BATTEN, BARTON, DURSTINE, OSBORN, INC. -
INFORMATION RETRIEVAL CENTER† □ New
York, NY
Boylan, Ray, Asst.Dir.
CENTER FOR RESEARCH LIBRARIES □ Chicago,
IL
Boyle, C.S., Dir., Lib.Serv.
CANADA - FISHERIES & OCEANS - LIBRARY† □
Ottawa, ON
Boyle, Cecilia, Cat.Libn.
COOK COUNTY HOSPITAL - TICE MEMORIAL
LIBRARY □ Chicago, IL
Boyle, Eileen, Libn.
SAN DIEGO PUBLIC LIBRARY - LITERATURE &
LANGUAGES SECTION □ San Diego, CA
Boyle, Eileen, Libn.
SAN DIEGO PUBLIC LIBRARY - WANGENHEIM
ROOM □ San Diego, CA

Boyle, James E., Libn.
OVERSEAS DEVELOPMENT COUNCIL - LIBRARY □ Washington, DC
Boyle, John, Dp.Dir.
U.S. DEPT. OF HEALTH AND HUMAN SERVICES - DEPARTMENT LIBRARY† □ Washington, DC
Boyle, Sr. Mary David, C.S.A., Libn.
ST. AGNES HOSPITAL - LIBRARY □ Fond du Lac, WI
Boyle, Mary Lee Ervin, Sr.Archv.
OKLAHOMA HISTORICAL SOCIETY - ARCHIVES AND MANUSCRIPT DIVISION □ Oklahoma City, OK
Boyle, Stephen, Supv., Info.Serv.
NALCO CHEMICAL COMPANY - TECHNICAL CENTER - INFORMATION SERVICES □ Naperville, IL
Boyles, Eleanor J., Doc.Libn.
MICHIGAN STATE UNIVERSITY - DOCUMENTS LIBRARY □ East Lansing, MI
Boysen, Jessica, Staff Libn.
COMMUNITY-GENERAL HOSPITAL OF GREATER SYRACUSE - STAFF LIBRARY □ Syracuse, NY
Boytos, Carol, Asst.Libn.
DAVID LIBRARY OF THE AMERICAN REVOLUTION □ Washington Crossing, PA
Braaten, Mary, Fld.Libn.
NORTH DAKOTA STATE LIBRARY □ Bismarck, ND
Braatz, Karen K., Info.Spec.
SCHREIBER FOODS, INC. - LIBRARY □ Green Bay, WI
Bracey, Maricia, Prts. & Photo Libn.
HOWARD UNIVERSITY - MOORLAND-SPINGARN RESEARCH CENTER - MANUSCRIPT DIVISION □ Washington, DC
Brachen, Mary Jo, Media Serv.Libn.
WAKE FOREST UNIVERSITY - LAW LIBRARY □ Winston-Salem, NC
Brackett, N. Scott, Tech.Libn.
LEAR SIEGLER, INC. - INSTRUMENT DIVISION - ENGINEERING LIBRARY □ Grand Rapids, MI
Brackney, Kathryn S., Arch.Libn.
GEORGIA INSTITUTE OF TECHNOLOGY - PRICE GILBERT MEMORIAL LIBRARY - ARCHITECTURE LIBRARY □ Atlanta, GA
Brackney, William H., Exec.Dir.
AMERICAN BAPTIST CHURCHES IN THE U.S.A. - BOARD OF EDUCATIONAL MINISTRIES - EDITORIAL LIBRARY □ Valley Forge, PA
Brackney, William H., Exec.Dir.
AMERICAN BAPTIST HISTORICAL SOCIETY - SAMUEL COLGATE BAPTIST HISTORICAL LIBRARY □ Rochester, NY
Brackney, William H., Exec.Dir.
DANISH BAPTIST GENERAL CONFERENCE OF AMERICA - ARCHIVES □ Rochester, NY
Bradburd, Nancy M., Libn.
PHILADELPHIA ORCHESTRA ASSOCIATION - LIBRARY □ Philadelphia, PA
Bradbury, Corinne, Tech.Serv.Supv.
CITY OF COMMERCE PUBLIC LIBRARY □ Commerce, CA
Bradbury, John F., Jr., Mss.Spec.
WESTERN HISTORICAL MANUSCRIPT COLLECTION/STATE HISTORICAL SOCIETY OF MISSOURI MANUSCRIPTS JOINT COLLECTION □ Rolla, MO
Braddock, Betty, Dir.
KANSAS HERITAGE CENTER - LIBRARY □ Dodge City, KS
Braddock, Virginia, Hd., MGRC
BOULDER PUBLIC LIBRARY - MUNICIPAL GOVERNMENT REFERENCE CENTER □ Boulder, CO
Braden, Ann, Hd., Client Serv.
CANADA - INDIAN & NORTHERN AFFAIRS CANADA - DEPARTMENTAL LIBRARY □ Ottawa, ON
Braden, Jan, Dir., Lib.Serv.
WESLEY MEDICAL CENTER - H.B. MC KIBBIN HEALTH SCIENCE LIBRARY □ Wichita, KS

Bradfield, Margaret, Lib.Techn.
ALBERTA - DEPARTMENT OF HOSPITALS AND MEDICAL CARE - HOSPITAL SERVICES LIBRARY □ Edmonton, AB
Bradford, Georganne F., First Asst.
PUBLIC LIBRARY OF CINCINNATI AND HAMILTON COUNTY - LITERATURE DEPARTMENT □ Cincinnati, OH
Bradford, Mary K., Med.Lib.Techn.
U.S. ARMY HOSPITALS - BAYNE JONES ARMY COMMUNITY HOSPITAL - MEDICAL LIBRARY □ Ft. Polk, LA
Bradford, Michael, Treas./Libn.
MEDFORD HISTORICAL SOCIETY - LIBRARY □ Medford, MA
Bradford, Rae, Mgr.
CANADA - REGIONAL INDUSTRIAL EXPANSION - CANADIAN GOVERNMENT OFFICE OF TOURISM □ Ottawa, ON
Bradford, Roberta, Asst.Libn.
STOWE-DAY FOUNDATION - LIBRARY □ Hartford, CT
Bradley, Annette, Hd., Ser.
LAURENTIAN UNIVERSITY - MAIN LIBRARY □ Sudbury, ON
Bradley, Barbara, Hd., AV Dept.
SOUTHEAST MICHIGAN REGIONAL FILM LIBRARY □ Monroe, MI
Bradley, Dr. Carol June, Assoc.Dir.
SUNY AT BUFFALO - MUSIC LIBRARY □ Buffalo, NY
Bradley, Catherine, Law Libn.
ILLINOIS STATE - SUPREME COURT LIBRARY □ Springfield, IL
Bradley, Helen, Asst.Chf.
U.S. GENERAL SERVICES ADMINISTRATION - GSA LIBRARY □ Washington, DC
Bradley, Jana, Dir.
WISHARD (William N.) MEMORIAL HOSPITAL - PROFESSIONAL LIBRARY/MEDIA SERVICES† □ Indianapolis, IN
Bradley, Joseph W., Physics Lib.Supv.
UNIVERSITY OF DELAWARE, NEWARK - HUGH M. MORRIS LIBRARY - PHYSICS BRANCH LIBRARY □ Newark, DE
Bradley, M.J., Tech.Serv.Libn.
UNIVERSITY COMMUNITY HOSPITAL - MEDICAL LIBRARY □ Tampa, FL
Bradley, Murray L., Hd., Rd.Serv.
U.S. NAVY - NAVAL WAR COLLEGE - LIBRARY □ Newport, RI
Bradley, Patricia V., Med.Libn.
GALLUP INDIAN MEDICAL CENTER - MEDICAL LIBRARY □ Gallup, NM
Bradley, Verdelle V., Libn.
VIRGINIA UNION UNIVERSITY - WILLIAM J. CLARK LIBRARY - SPECIAL COLLECTIONS □ Richmond, VA
Bradley, William M., Dir.
U.S. DEPT. OF COMMERCE - INTERNATIONAL TRADE ADMINISTRATION - PITTSBURGH DISTRICT OFFICE LIBRARY □ Pittsburgh, PA
Bradshaw, Evelyn, Acq.Techn.
NATIONAL COLLEGE - THOMAS JEFFERSON LEARNING RESOURCE CENTER □ Rapid City, SD
Bradshaw, Janice, Supv.
CHICAGO DEPARTMENT OF HUMAN SERVICES - LIBRARY □ Chicago, IL
Bradshaw, Judith, Asst.Libn.
B.C. HYDRO - ENGINEERING LIBRARY □ Vancouver, BC
Bradt, D.M. Sontag, Mgr.
ECONOMICS LABORATORY, INC. - CORPORATE INFORMATION CENTER □ St. Paul, MN
Bradunas, Elena, Folklife Spec.
LIBRARY OF CONGRESS - AMERICAN FOLKLIFE CENTER □ Washington, DC
Bradwell, David, Pres.
BRADWELL (David) & ASSOCIATES, INC. - LIBRARY □ San Rafael, CA
Brady, Ann, Hd., Bibliog.Serv.
MECHANICS' INSTITUTE LIBRARY □ San Francisco, CA

Brady, Ann, Cons.
NEVADA STATE LIBRARY □ Carson City, NV
Brady, Ann, Hd., Info.Ctr.
NEWSPAPER ADVERTISING BUREAU, INC. - INFORMATION CENTER □ New York, NY
Brady, Bonnie, Law Libn.
INDIANA COUNTY LAW LIBRARY □ Indiana, PA
Brady, Brenda, Supv.Libn.
UNITED STATES INFORMATION SERVICE - LIBRARY SERVICE □ Ottawa, ON
Brady, Dorothy L., Libn.
GEOLOGICAL SURVEY OF ALABAMA - LIBRARY □ University, AL
Brady, Elizabeth Hawkins, Act.Lib.Mgr.
CANADIAN NURSES ASSOCIATION - HELEN K. MUSSALLEM LIBRARY □ Ottawa, ON
Brady, Eugene G., Jr., Libn.
MEMPHIS COMMERCIAL APPEAL - LIBRARY □ Memphis, TN
Brady, Frank B., Exec.Dir.
INSTITUTE OF NAVIGATION - LIBRARY □ Washington, DC
Brady, J.J., Mgr.
GENERAL ELECTRIC COMPANY - AIRCRAFT ENGINE GROUP - TECHNICAL INFORMATION CENTER □ Cincinnati, OH
Brady, Joann, Graphic Designer
UNIVERSITY OF NEW HAMPSHIRE - DEPARTMENT OF MEDIA SERVICES - FILM LIBRARY □ Durham, NH
Brady, John D., Jr., Div.Hd.
QUEENS BOROUGH PUBLIC LIBRARY - SCIENCE & TECHNOLOGY DIVISION □ Jamaica, NY
Brady, Joseph J., Pres.
ACME, INC. - THE ASSOCIATION OF MANAGEMENT CONSULTING FIRMS - LIBRARY □ New York, NY
Brady, Josiah B., Libn.II
MEMPHIS-SHELBY COUNTY PUBLIC LIBRARY AND INFORMATION CENTER - MEMPHIS ROOM COLLECTIONS □ Memphis, TN
Brady, Mary, Telephone Ref.Serv.
NEW YORK PUBLIC LIBRARY - MID-MANHATTAN LIBRARY - GENERAL REFERENCE SERVICE/EDUCATION □ New York, NY
Brady, Mary, Hd., Ser.Dept.
SOUTH DAKOTA STATE UNIVERSITY - HILTON M. BRIGGS LIBRARY □ Brookings, SD
Brady, Mary, Proj.Dir.
UNIVERSITY OF WISCONSIN, MADISON - TRACE R & D CENTER - LIBRARY □ Madison, WI
Brady, Mary Ann, Libn.
UNION CARBIDE CORPORATION - COATINGS SERVICE DEPARTMENT - LIBRARY □ Indianapolis, IN
Brady, Sr. Mary William, Archv.
COLLEGE OF ST. CATHERINE - LIBRARY - RUTH SAWYER COLLECTION □ St. Paul, MN
Brady, Maxine L., Libn.
FOUNDATION FOR BLOOD RESEARCH - LIBRARY □ Scarborough, ME
Brady, Peggy M., Hd., Ref.Dept.
NORTH OLYMPIC LIBRARY SYSTEM - PORT ANGELES BRANCH - PACIFIC NORTHWEST ROOM □ Port Angeles, WA
Brady, Randall, Dir.
TENNESSEE STATE DEPARTMENT OF HEALTH AND ENVIRONMENT - FILM LIBRARY □ Nashville, TN
Brady, Randall, Dir., Resource Ctr.
TENNESSEE STATE DEPARTMENT OF PUBLIC HEALTH - MCH/HWP RESOURCE CENTER† □ Nashville, TN
Brady, Ruth E., Hd.Libn.
OUR LADY QUEEN OF MARTYRS - ST. LUCIAN LIBRARY □ Birmingham, MI
Bragdon, Lynn L., Chf., Lib.Serv.
U.S. VETERANS ADMINISTRATION (CO-Grand Junction) - MEDICAL CENTER MEDICAL LIBRARY □ Grand Junction, CO
Brager, Beverly J., Supv.
MADISON PUBLIC LIBRARY - ART AND MUSIC DIVISION □ Madison, WI

Brahmi, Fran, Med.Ref./Search Anl.
INDIANA UNIVERSITY, INDIANAPOLIS - SCHOOL OF MEDICINE LIBRARY □ Indianapolis, IN

Brahms, Thomas W., Exec.Dir.
INSTITUTE OF TRANSPORTATION ENGINEERS - LIBRARY □ Washington, DC

Braik, Mary Ann, Ref.Libn.
LA GRANGE COLLEGE - WILLIAM AND EVELYN BANKS LIBRARY - SPECIAL COLLECTIONS □ LaGrange, GA

Brajsa, Bogdana, Libn.
UNIVERSITY OF WESTERN ONTARIO - ENGINEERING LIBRARY □ London, ON

Bralower, Paul, Mng.Ed. for Res.
MARQUIS WHO'S WHO, INC. - RESEARCH DEPARTMENT LIBRARY □ Chicago, IL

Braly, Shari, Ref.
MARTIN MARIETTA AEROSPACE - DENVER RESEARCH LIBRARY □ Denver, CO

Bramhall, Nancy, Sec.
SOUTHERN ILLINOIS UNIVERSITY, EDWARDSVILLE - HUMAN SERVICES LIBRARY □ Edwardsville, IL

Bramley, Jeffrey L., Libn.
MEDINA COUNTY LAW LIBRARY ASSOCIATION □ Medina, OH

Brand, Alice, Chf.Libn.
MENNINGER FOUNDATION - PROFESSIONAL LIBRARY □ Topeka, KS

Brand, Dr. Charles, Dir.
UNIVERSITY OF MARYLAND, COLLEGE PARK - M. LUCIA JAMES CURRICULUM LABORATORY □ College Park, MD

Brandak, George, Mss.Cur.
UNIVERSITY OF BRITISH COLUMBIA - SPECIAL COLLECTIONS DIVISION □ Vancouver, BC

Brandeis, Dr. Robert C., Chf.Libn.
UNIVERSITY OF TORONTO - VICTORIA UNIVERSITY - LIBRARY □ Toronto, ON

Brandhorst, Ted, Dir.
ERIC PROCESSING AND REFERENCE FACILITY □ Bethesda, MD

Brandreth, Sr. Elizabeth Anne, Libn.
MERCY HOSPITAL - MEDICAL LIBRARY □ Scranton, PA

Brandstadter, Dianne, Dean, Lrng.Rsrcs.
SUMTER AREA TECHNICAL COLLEGE - LIBRARY □ Sumter, SC

Brandt, Charles A.E., Chf.Consrv.
MANITOBA - PROVINCIAL ARCHIVES OF MANITOBA □ Winnipeg, MB

Brandt, Kandy B., Hd.
SEATTLE PUBLIC LIBRARY - MEDIA & PROGRAM SERVICES† □ Seattle, WA

Brandt, Patricia, Soc.Sci./Hum. & Bus.
OREGON STATE UNIVERSITY - WILLIAM JASPER KERR LIBRARY □ Corvallis, OR

Brandt, Paula O., Coord.
UNIVERSITY OF IOWA - COLLEGE OF EDUCATION - CURRICULUM RESOURCES LABORATORY □ Iowa City, IA

Brandt, Steven, Dir.
MENNONITE BRETHREN BIBLICAL SEMINARY - HIEBERT LIBRARY □ Fresno, CA

Branham, Gloria, Libn.
SOUTHWESTERN PUBLIC SERVICE COMPANY - LIBRARY □ Amarillo, TX

Brann, Andrew R., Hd., Cat.Dept.
OHIO STATE UNIVERSITY - LAW LIBRARY □ Columbus, OH

Brann, Evelyn M., Libn.
EG&G, INC. - MASON RESEARCH INSTITUTE - LIBRARY □ Worcester, MA

Brann, Virginia C., Sr.Archv.Asst.
DE PAUW UNIVERSITY - ARCHIVES OF DE PAUW UNIVERSITY AND INDIANA UNITED METHODISM □ Greencastle, IN

Brann, Virginia C., Sr.Archv.Asst.
PUTNAM COUNTY HISTORICAL SOCIETY - ARCHIVES □ Greencastle, IN

Branson, Jody, Med.Libn.
HUMANA HOSPITAL UNIVERSITY - GRADIE R. ROWNTREE MEDICAL LIBRARY □ Louisville, KY

Branson, Patricia, Libn.
U.S. NATL. MARINE FISHERIES SERVICE - W.F. THOMPSON MEMORIAL LIBRARY □ Kodiak, AK

Brant, Jonathan J., Exec.Dir.
NATIONAL INTERFRATERNITY CONFERENCE - LIBRARY □ Indianapolis, IN

Branton, Sharon, Hd. of Cat.
MC MASTER UNIVERSITY - HEALTH SCIENCES LIBRARY □ Hamilton, ON

Brantz, Malcolm, AV Libn.
UNIVERSITY OF CONNECTICUT - HEALTH CENTER - LYMAN MAYNARD STOWE LIBRARY □ Farmington, CT

Brashear, Jan, Res.Libn.
PUBLIC AFFAIRS RESEARCH COUNCIL OF LOUISIANA - RESEARCH LIBRARY □ Baton Rouge, LA

Brasseaux, Carl A., Asst.Dir.
UNIVERSITY OF SOUTHWESTERN LOUISIANA - CENTER FOR LOUISIANA STUDIES □ Lafayette, LA

Brassil, Ellen, Hd., Info.Mgt.Educ.
UNIVERSITY OF NORTH CAROLINA, CHAPEL HILL - HEALTH SCIENCES LIBRARY □ Chapel Hill, NC

Braswell, Laura, Dir.
COLUMBIA BIBLE COLLEGE - LEARNING RESOURCES CENTER □ Columbia, SC

Bratcher, Diane, Pubn.Mgr.
NATIONAL COUNCIL OF CHURCHES - INTERFAITH CENTER ON CORPORATE RESPONSIBILITY □ New York, NY

Braten, Marlene, Asst.Libn.
ST. LUKE'S HOSPITAL CENTER - RICHARD WALKER BOLLING MEMORIAL MEDICAL LIBRARY† □ New York, NY

Bratton, Barbara, MRI Libn.
FLORIDA INSTITUTE OF TECHNOLOGY - LIBRARY □ Melbourne, FL

Braucher, Jane, Libn.
U.S. FEDERAL AVIATION ADMINISTRATION - LAW LIBRARY □ Washington, DC

Braucht, Karen, Libn.
FOSTER, PEPPER & RIVIERA - LAW LIBRARY □ Seattle, WA

Braude, Robert M., Dir.
UNIVERSITY OF NEBRASKA MEDICAL CENTER - MC GOOGAN LIBRARY OF MEDICINE □ Omaha, NE

Brault, C., Ref.Libn.
UNIVERSITY OF MANITOBA - SCIENCE LIBRARY □ Winnipeg, MB

Brault, M. Jean-Remi, Conservateur en Chef
QUEBEC PROVINCE - BIBLIOTHEQUE NATIONALE DU QUEBEC □ Montreal, PQ

Braun, Beverly, IMC Dir.
FRESNO COUNTY OFFICE OF EDUCATION - IMC-LIBRARY □ Fresno, CA

Braun, Carl, Dept.Hd.
SYRACUSE UNIVERSITY - E.S. BIRD LIBRARY - SOCIAL SCIENCES DEPARTMENT □ Syracuse, NY

Braun, Linda, Sr.Libn.
NEW YORK STATE LIBRARY - HUMANITIES REFERENCE SECTION □ Albany, NY

Braun, Nancy R., Circ.Supv.
VANDERBILT UNIVERSITY - JEAN AND ALEXANDER HEARD LIBRARY - DIVINITY LIBRARY □ Nashville, TN

Braun, Nancy R., Circ.Supv.
VANDERBILT UNIVERSITY - JEAN AND ALEXANDER HEARD LIBRARY - DIVINITY LIBRARY - KESLER CIRCULATING LIBRARY □ Nashville, TN

Braun, Robin, Health Sci.Libn.
TUALITY COMMUNITY HOSPITAL - HEALTH SCIENCES LIBRARY □ Hillsboro, OR

Braun, Susan, Pres.
DANCE FILMS ASSOCIATION, INC. □ New York, NY

Braunger, Bunny, Health Sci.Libn.
BETH ISRAEL HOSPITAL & GERIATRIC CENTER - HEALTH SCIENCE LIBRARY† □ Denver, CO

Braunschweiger, Louise, Dir.
CALIFORNIA HISTORICAL SOCIETY - HISTORY CENTER LIBRARY □ Los Angeles, CA

Braunstein, Mark, Hd., Slide/Photo Dept.
RHODE ISLAND SCHOOL OF DESIGN - LIBRARY □ Providence, RI

Brautigam, Patsy, Ref.Libn.
LAW LIBRARY OF LOUISIANA† □ New Orleans, LA

Bravo, Priscilla B., Archv.
DIOCESE OF SAVANNAH - CHANCERY ARCHIVES & DIOCESAN ARCHIVES □ Savannah, GA

Bravy, Gary, Govt.Docs. & Media
GEORGETOWN UNIVERSITY - FRED O. DENNIS LAW LIBRARY □ Washington, DC

Brawer, Dr. Florence B., Res.Educ.
ERIC CLEARINGHOUSE FOR JUNIOR COLLEGES □ Los Angeles, CA

Braxton, Anne, Fine Arts Libn.
OHIO UNIVERSITY - FINE ARTS COLLECTION □ Athens, OH

Bray, Mary, Libn.
LAKELAND HOSPITAL - MEDICAL LIBRARY □ Elkhorn, WI

Bray, Michael, Law Libn.
ATLANTA LAW SCHOOL - LIBRARY □ Atlanta, GA

Bray, Ora, Libn.
SPERRY ELECTRONIC SYSTEMS - ENGINEERING LIBRARY □ Charlottesville, VA

Bray, Susan, Libn.
PENN (Annie) MEMORIAL HOSPITAL - MEDICAL LIBRARY □ Reidsville, NC

Brayfield, Mary Jane, Libn.
BENDIX CORPORATION - BENDIX ENERGY CONTROLS DIVISION - ENGINEERING LIBRARY □ South Bend, IN

Brazelton, Dr. Frank, Sec.-Tres.
AMERICAN ACADEMY OF OPTOMETRY - LIBRARY □ Washington, DC

Brazil, Lynn, Hd.Libn.
PETTIT & MARTIN - LIBRARY □ San Francisco, CA

Brazin, Lillian, Res.Libn.
JEFFERSON (Thomas) UNIVERSITY - SCOTT MEMORIAL LIBRARY □ Philadelphia, PA

Brazynetz, Helen C., Lib.Asst., Acq.
CASE WESTERN RESERVE UNIVERSITY - LAW SCHOOL LIBRARY† □ Cleveland, OH

Brecht, Albert, Dir.
UNIVERSITY OF SOUTHERN CALIFORNIA - LAW LIBRARY □ Los Angeles, CA

Breck, Evelyn M., Dir.
MIDDLESEX MEMORIAL HOSPITAL - HEALTH SCIENCES LIBRARY □ Middletown, CT

Bredehoft, Thomas H., Pres.
HEISEY COLLECTORS OF AMERICA, INC. - HCA LIBRARY & ARCHIVES □ Newark, OH

Bredemeier, Virginia, Libn.
DU PONT DE NEMOURS (E.I.) & COMPANY, INC. - STINE LABORATORY LIBRARY† □ Newark, DE

Bredemeyer, Carol, Rd.Serv.Libn.
NORTHERN KENTUCKY UNIVERSITY - SALMON P. CHASE COLLEGE OF LAW - LIBRARY □ Highland Heights, KY

Breeden, Rebecca, Asst.Libn.
MENNINGER FOUNDATION - PROFESSIONAL LIBRARY □ Topeka, KS

Breeding, Sharon, Sr.Libn.
KENTUCKY STATE DEPARTMENT FOR LIBRARIES AND ARCHIVES - STATE LIBRARY SERVICES DIVISION □ Frankfort, KY

Breedlove, Elizabeth, Hd., Tech.Serv.
NEW JERSEY STATE LIBRARY □ Trenton, NJ

Breen, Catherine F., Libn.
GASTON SNOW & ELY BARTLETT □ Boston, MA

Breen, Richard F., Jr., Law Libn.
WILLAMETTE UNIVERSITY - LAW LIBRARY □ Salem, OR

Breese, John K., Mgr., RTL
KELLER (J.J.) & ASSOCIATES, INC. - RESEARCH
& TECHNICAL LIBRARY □ Neenah, WI

Breeze, Hope, Asst.Cat.Libn.
DUKE UNIVERSITY - SCHOOL OF LAW LIBRARY
□ Durham, NC

Breeze, Mary, Career Serv.Spec.
GUILFORD TECHNICAL COMMUNITY COLLEGE -
LEARNING RESOURCE CENTER □ Jamestown,
NC

Bregaint, C., Asst.Dir., Field
CANADA - AGRICULTURE CANADA - LIBRARIES
DIVISION □ Ottawa, ON

Bregoli, Marilyn Smith, Libn.
SIMMONS COLLEGE - SCHOOL OF SOCIAL
WORK LIBRARY □ Boston, MA

Bregzis, Ilze, Libn., Tech.Serv.
ONTARIO INSTITUTE FOR STUDIES IN
EDUCATION (OISE) - R.W.B. JACKSON LIBRARY
□ Toronto, ON

Breijer, Johanna H., Lib.Techn. II
ALBERTA - DEPARTMENT OF TREASURY -
CORPORATE TAX ADMINISTRATION LIBRARY □
Edmonton, AB

Breinich, John A., Dir.
HAWAII MEDICAL LIBRARY, INC. □ Honolulu, HI

Breitenstein, Paul R., Libn.
TREXLER (Harry C.) MASONIC LIBRARY □
Allentown, PA

Brement, Gineen, Assoc.Prog.Tech.
U.S. AIR FORCE - ROME AIR DEVELOPMENT
CENTER - DATA & ANALYSIS CENTER FOR
SOFTWARE □ Griffiss AFB, NY

Bremer, Elizabeth, Hd.
MUTUAL OF OMAHA/UNITED OF OMAHA -
LIBRARY† □ Omaha, NE

Bremer, Robert, Asst.Libn.
SOUTHERN CALIFORNIA RAPID TRANSIT
DISTRICT - INFORMATION CENTER LIBRARY □
Los Angeles, CA

Bremer, Suzanne, Asst. to Mgr.
PRICE WATERHOUSE - INFORMATION CENTER
□ Boston, MA

Bremmer, Sally, Res.Lab.Libn.
PETRO-CANADA - LIBRARY SERVICES □
Calgary, AB

Bren, Nancy, Record Cat./Ref.Libn.
SUNY AT BUFFALO - MUSIC LIBRARY □ Buffalo,
NY

Breneau, Don, Ref.Coll.Dev.
WAYNE STATE UNIVERSITY - G. FLINT PURDY
LIBRARY □ Detroit, MI

Brening, Dorothy, Asst.Libn.
BROWARD COUNTY LAW LIBRARY □ Fort
Lauderdale, FL

Brennan, Ann M., Info.Spec.
WORLD DATA CENTER A - GLACIOLOGY
INFORMATION CENTER □ Boulder, CO

Brennan, Christopher, Asst.Libn.
ROCHESTER MUSEUM AND SCIENCE CENTER -
LIBRARY □ Rochester, NY

Brennan, David K., Circuit Libn.
U.S. COURT OF APPEALS, 8TH CIRCUIT -
LIBRARY □ St. Louis, MO

Brennan, Diane, Libn.
MANKATO AREA VOCATIONAL-TECHNICAL
INSTITUTE - LIBRARY □ North Mankato, MN

Brennan, Elizabeth G., Libn.
MC NAMEE, PORTER & SEELEY - MPS
ENGINEERING LIBRARY† □ Ann Arbor, MI

Brennan, Ellen, Libn.
PENNSYLVANIA ECONOMY LEAGUE - EASTERN
DIVISION - LIBRARY □ Philadelphia, PA

Brennan, Helga, Res.Anl.
SRI INTERNATIONAL - STRATEGIC CENTER
LIBRARY □ Arlington, VA

Brennan, Jane, Asst.Libn.
NEW YORK BOTANICAL GARDEN - LIBRARY† □
Bronx, NY

Brennan, Jean, Med.Libn.
SARATOGA GENERAL HOSPITAL - HEALTH
SCIENCE LIBRARY □ Detroit, MI

Brennan, Jeffrey C., Law Lib./Bar Assn.Dir.
KALAMAZOO COUNTY LAW LIBRARY -
RAYMOND W. FOX MEMORIAL LIBRARY □
Kalamazoo, MI

Brennan, Dr. John A., Cur.
UNIVERSITY OF COLORADO, BOULDER -
WESTERN HISTORICAL COLLECTION &
UNIVERSITY ARCHIVES □ Boulder, CO

Brennan, M.E., Ref.Libn.
AT & T LABORATORIES & TECHNOLOGIES -
LIBRARY □ Reading, PA

Brennan, Margaret, Sr.Cat.
ART GALLERY OF ONTARIO - EDWARD P.
TAYLOR AUDIO-VISUAL CENTRE □ Toronto, ON

Brennan, Margaret A., Med.Libn.
U.S. VETERANS ADMINISTRATION (MO-Kansas
City) - MEDICAL CENTER LIBRARY □ Kansas
City, MO

Brennan, Margret, Supv., News Serv.
MOBIL OIL CORPORATION - PUBLIC AFFAIRS
SECRETARIAT □ New York, NY

Brennan, MaryLu, Supv.
SCARBOROUGH BOARD OF EDUCATION - A.B.
PATTERSON PROFESSIONAL LIBRARY □
Scarborough, ON

Brennan, Nola, Libn.
NOVA SCOTIA INSTITUTE OF TECHNOLOGY -
LEARNING RESOURCES CENTER □ Halifax, NS

Brennan, Robert, Pres.
GREATER MADISON CHAMBER OF COMMERCE -
MATERIALS REFERENCE LIBRARY □ Madison,
WI

Brennan, T.G., Libn./Cur.
NEWPORT HISTORICAL SOCIETY - LIBRARY □
Newport, RI

Brennan, T. Patrick, Cur.
OGLEBAY INSTITUTE - MANSION MUSEUM
LIBRARY □ Wheeling, WV

Brennan, Theresa, Mgr., Rec./Off.Sys.
URBAN TRANSPORTATION DEVELOPMENT
CORPORATION - METRO CANADA LIBRARY □
Kingston, ON

Brenneise, Harvey, Assoc.Ref.Libn
ANDREWS UNIVERSITY - JAMES WHITE
LIBRARY† □ Berrien Springs, MI

Brenneman, Betsey, Acq.
WORCESTER STATE COLLEGE - LEARNING
RESOURCES CENTER □ Worcester, MA

Brennen, Dolly M., Off.Mgr.
SWIGART MUSEUM - LIBRARY □ Huntingdon, PA

Brennen, Patrick W., Dir.
MEDICAL COLLEGE OF WISCONSIN -
LIBRARIES □ Milwaukee, WI

Brenner, M. Diane, Musm.Archv.
ANCHORAGE HISTORICAL AND FINE ARTS
MUSEUM - ARCHIVES □ Anchorage, AK

Brenner, Marilyn R., Libn.
TEMPLE BETH EL - PRENTIS MEMORIAL
LIBRARY □ Birmingham, MI

Brenny, Nancy, Libn.
PILLSBURY COMPANY - BUSINESS REFERENCE
LIBRARY □ Minneapolis, MN

Bresinger, Sheindel, Libn.
MAIMONIDES HOSPITAL GERIATRIC CENTRE -
POLLACK LIBRARY □ Montreal, PQ

Breslauer, Lester M., Chf.Libn.
BELL AEROSPACE TEXTRON - LAWRENCE D.
BELL MEMORIAL LIBRARY □ Buffalo, NY

Bresnahan, Alice, Libn.
3M - 209 LIBRARY □ St. Paul, MN

Bresnahan, Patti, Asst.Libn.
STARK COUNTY LAW LIBRARY ASSOCIATION -
LAW LIBRARY □ Canton, OH

Bressler, Nancy, Cur., Pub.Aff./Papers
PRINCETON UNIVERSITY - RARE BOOKS AND
SPECIAL COLLECTIONS □ Princeton, NJ

Bret-Harte, Margaret S., Hd.Libn.
ARIZONA HISTORICAL SOCIETY - LIBRARY □
Tucson, AZ

Brethauer, Jean, Career Libn.
OHIO STATE UNIVERSITY - PERSONNEL AND
CAREER EXPLORATION (PACE) RESOURCE
CENTER □ Columbus, OH

Brethauer, Thomas E., Libn.
INDIANA STATE DEPARTMENT OF HIGHWAYS -
PLANNING DIVISION - TECHNICAL REFERENCE
LIBRARY □ Indianapolis, IN

Brethour, Sherie, Libn.
ONTARIO FILM INSTITUTE - LIBRARY &
INFORMATION CENTRE □ Don Mills, ON

Brett, Lorraine E., Cat.
VIGO COUNTY SCHOOL CORPORATION -
INSTRUCTIONAL MATERIALS CENTER □ Terre
Haute, IN

Brewer, Annie M., Sr.Ed./Libn.
GALE RESEARCH COMPANY - LIBRARY □
Detroit, MI

Brewer, Calvin, Hd.
OKLAHOMA STATE UNIVERSITY - PHYSICAL
SCIENCES AND ENGINEERING DIVISION □
Stillwater, OK

Brewer, Delores, Libn.
ST. LUKE'S MEMORIAL HOSPITAL - A.M.
JOHNSON MEMORIAL MEDICAL LIBRARY □
Spokane, WA

Brewer, Imogene, Cat.Libn.
CARSON-NEWMAN COLLEGE LIBRARY -
SPECIAL COLLECTIONS □ Jefferson City, TN

Brewer, Joan Scherer, Info.Serv.Off.
KINSEY INSTITUTE FOR RESEARCH IN SEX,
GENDER & REPRODUCTION, INC. - LIBRARY
AND INFORMATION SERVICE □ Bloomington, IN

Brewer, John, Lib. Contact
BUREAU OF GOVERNMENTAL RESEARCH -
LIBRARY □ New Orleans, LA

Brewer, Karen, Dir.
NORTHEASTERN OHIO UNIVERSITIES COLLEGE
OF MEDICINE - BASIC MEDICAL SCIENCES
LIBRARY □ Rootstown, OH

Brewer, Martha, Dp.Dir.
LIFE PLANNING/HEALTH SERVICES -
LIBRARY/MEDIA SERVICES □ Dallas, TX

Brewer, Dr. Robert F., Chm., Lib.Comm.
UNIVERSITY OF CALIFORNIA - KEARNEY
AGRICULTURAL CENTER □ Parlier, CA

Brewer, Stanley E., Hd.Libn.
GULF OIL CORPORATION - LIBRARY AND
INFORMATION CENTER □ Houston, TX

Brewster, John W., Economic Libn.
REPUBLICBANK CORPORATION - ECONOMIC
RESEARCH LIBRARY □ Dallas, TX

Brewster, Mary Jane, Hd.
U.S. NAVY - NAVAL SURFACE WEAPONS
CENTER - WHITE OAK LIBRARY† □ Silver
Spring, MD

Brewster, Olive N., Chf., Tech.Proc.
U.S. AIR FORCE - AEROSPACE MEDICAL
DIVISION - SCHOOL OF AEROSPACE MEDICINE
- STRUGHOLD AEROMEDICAL LIBRARY □ Brooks
AFB, TX

Brey, Steven, Mgr., Support Serv.
CHURCH OF JESUS CHRIST OF LATTER-DAY
SAINTS - GENEALOGICAL LIBRARY □ Salt Lake
City, UT

Breyfogle, J.W., III, Libn.
JOHNSON COUNTY LAW LIBRARY □ Olathe, KS

Brian, Ray, Libn.
CALIFORNIA ACADEMY OF SCIENCES - J.W.
MAILLIARD, JR. LIBRARY □ San Francisco, CA

Briand, Margaret, Asst.Libn.
BURROUGHS WELLCOME COMPANY - LIBRARY
□ Research Triangle Park, NC

Brichford, Maynard, Univ.Archv.
UNIVERSITY OF ILLINOIS - UNIVERSITY
ARCHIVES □ Urbana, IL

Bricker, Florence M., Archv.
EVANGELICAL AND REFORMED HISTORICAL
SOCIETY - LANCASTER CENTRAL ARCHIVES
AND LIBRARY □ Lancaster, PA

Bricker, Kathleen, Asst.Libn.
LAFAYETTE JOURNAL AND COURIER - LIBRARY
□ Lafayette, IN

Brickett, Dorothy
HARTFORD PUBLIC LIBRARY - REFERENCE AND
GENERAL READING DEPARTMENT □ Hartford,
CT

Brickley, Richard R., Dir.
RESEARCH & INFORMATION SERVICES FOR EDUCATION - MONTGOMERY COUNTY INTERMEDIATE UNIT LIBRARY □ King of Prussia, PA

Bridge, Deborah, Asst.Libn.
HARBRIDGE HOUSE, INC. - LIBRARY □ Boston, MA

Bridge, Shirley, Acq.Libn./Accounting
UNIVERSITY OF SOUTH DAKOTA - MC KUSICK LAW LIBRARY □ Vermillion, SD

Bridgeforth, Jacqui, Ref.Libn.
ELI LILLY AND COMPANY - SCIENTIFIC LIBRARY □ Indianapolis, IN

Bridges, Barbara, Govt.Doc.Libn.
UNIVERSITY OF TEXAS, AUSTIN - SCHOOL OF LAW - TARLTON LAW LIBRARY □ Austin, TX

Bridges, Laine, Libn.
COMMUNITY HOSPITAL OF BUNNELL - MEDICAL LIBRARY □ Bunnell, FL

Bridges, Marian, ILL Libn.
CENTRAL CAROLINA TECHNICAL COLLEGE - LEARNING RESOURCE CENTER □ Sanford, NC

Bridges, Patricia Gaspari, Asst.Libn./Map Libn.
PRINCETON UNIVERSITY - GEOLOGY LIBRARY □ Princeton, NJ

Bridges, Dr. Roger D., Hd.Libn. & Dir., Res.
ILLINOIS STATE HISTORICAL LIBRARY □ Springfield, IL

Bridgford, M. Ferne, Supv.Mgt.Asst.
U.S. BUREAU OF LAND MANAGEMENT - NEW MEXICO STATE OFFICE LIBRARY □ Santa Fe, NM

Bridgwater, Dorothy W., Asst.Libn.
YALE UNIVERSITY - BENJAMIN FRANKLIN COLLECTION □ New Haven, CT

Bridson, Gavin D.R., Bibliog.
CARNEGIE-MELLON UNIVERSITY - HUNT INSTITUTE FOR BOTANICAL DOCUMENTATION □ Pittsburgh, PA

Bridson, Marie, Libn.
MEMPHIS-SHELBY COUNTY PUBLIC LIBRARY AND INFO. CTR. - SCIENCE/BUSINESS/SOCIAL SCI.DEPT. □ Memphis, TN

Brie-Berard, Marie, Documentaliste
CONFERENCE DES RECTEURS ET DES PRINCIPAUX DES UNIVERSITES DU QUEBEC - CENTRE DE DOCUMENTATION □ Montreal, PQ

Briegleb, Ann, Ethnomusicology Archv.
UNIVERSITY OF CALIFORNIA, LOS ANGELES - MUSIC LIBRARY □ Los Angeles, CA

Brien, Therese, Exec.Sec.
INSTITUTE OF OCCUPATIONAL AND ENVIRONMENTAL HEALTH - ARCHIVES □ Montreal, PQ

Brigandi, Carmen E., Law Libn.
NEW YORK STATE SUPREME COURT - APPELLATE DIVISION, 4TH JUDICIAL DEPARTMENT - LAW LIBRARY □ Syracuse, NY

Briggs, Mary Kay, Libn.
U.S. AIR FORCE BASE - MATHER BASE LIBRARY† □ Mather AFB, CA

Briggs, Shirley A., Exec.Dir.
RACHEL CARSON COUNCIL, INC. - LIBRARY □ Chevy Chase, MD

Briggs, Thomas R., Ph.D., Principal
UNITED CEREBRAL PALSY ASSOCIATION OF THE GREATER WATERBURY AREA - PROFESSIONAL RESOURCE CENTER □ Waterbury, CT

Brigham, Florence C., Cur.
FALL RIVER HISTORICAL SOCIETY - MUSEUM/ LIBRARY □ Fall River, MA

Brigham, Jeffrey L., Asst.Libn./Tech.Serv.
NYACK COLLEGE - LIBRARY □ Nyack, NY

Bright, Brenda B., Libn.
UNIVERSITY OF NORTH CAROLINA - INSTITUTE OF MARINE SCIENCES - LIBRARY □ Morehead City, NC

Bright, Charles D., Supv.
WYOMING STATE HOSPITAL - MEDICAL LIBRARY □ Evanston, WY

Bright, Elizabeth, Libn.
IRON RANGE RESEARCH CENTER □ Chisholm, MN

Brightbill, George D., Print Libn.
TEMPLE UNIVERSITY - CENTRAL LIBRARY SYSTEM - PHOTO-JOURNALISM COLLECTION □ Philadelphia, PA

Brighton, Capt. B.
CANADA - NATIONAL DEFENCE - NORTHERN REGION HEADQUARTERS LIBRARY □ Yellowknife, NT

Brigl, Bob, Asst.Cur., Exhibits
WESTERN KENTUCKY UNIVERSITY - DEPT. OF SPECIAL COLLECTIONS - KENTUCKY LIBRARY AND MUSEUM/UNIVERSITY ARCHIVES □ Bowling Green, KY

Briley, John B., Mgr.
OHIO HISTORICAL SOCIETY - CAMPUS MARTIUS MUSEUM - LIBRARY □ Marietta, OH

Brill, Faye, Mgr., Info. Analysts
FOOTE CONE & BELDING - INFORMATION CENTER □ Chicago, IL

Brill, Wesley A., Act.Adm.
COLT INDUSTRIES - FM ENGINE DIVISION LIBRARY □ Beloit, WI

Brindle, John V., Cur. of Art Emeritus
CARNEGIE-MELLON UNIVERSITY - HUNT INSTITUTE FOR BOTANICAL DOCUMENTATION □ Pittsburgh, PA

Briner, Lisa, Tech.Commun.Spec.
HERSHEY FOODS CORPORATION - COMMUNICATIONS CENTER □ Hershey, PA

Brink, Clarence, Coord., Ref.Serv.
VIGO COUNTY PUBLIC LIBRARY - SPECIAL COLLECTIONS □ Terre Haute, IN

Brinkley, Margaret, Adm.Asst.
UNIVERSITY OF PENNSYLVANIA - JOHN PENMAN WOOD LIBRARY OF NATIONAL DEFENSE □ Philadelphia, PA

Brinkley, Margot, Dir.
FOUNDATION CENTER - WASHINGTON BRANCH LIBRARY □ Washington, DC

Brinkman, Carol S., Dir.
UNIVERSITY OF LOUISVILLE - KERSEY LIBRARY □ Louisville, KY

Brinkmeier, Hermina, Supv., Lib. & Rec.
MONSANTO RESEARCH CORPORATION - MOUND TECHNICAL INFORMATION CENTER □ Miamisburg, OH

Brinkmeyer, Ann, Coll.Libn.
NEVADA STATE LIBRARY □ Carson City, NV

Brinks, Herbert, Cur., Heritage Hall
CALVIN COLLEGE AND SEMINARY - LIBRARY □ Grand Rapids, MI

Brinson, Elizabeth, Assoc.Dir., LRC
FORT VALLEY STATE COLLEGE - HENRY ALEXANDER HUNT MEMORIAL LEARNING RESOURCES CENTER □ Fort Valley, GA

Brinson, Elizabeth, Act.Dir.
FORT VALLEY STATE COLLEGE - HENRY ALEXANDER HUNT MEMORIAL LEARNING RESOURCES CENTER □ Fort Valley, GA

Brinton, Yuki T., Libn.
PENDLE HILL - LIBRARY □ Wallingford, PA

Brisco, Valerie, Res.Asst.
NOVA SCOTIA - DEPARTMENT OF MINES & ENERGY - LIBRARY† □ Halifax, NS

Briscoe, Georgia, Hd., Tech.Serv./Doc.
UNIVERSITY OF SAN DIEGO - MARVIN & LILLIAN KRATTER LAW LIBRARY □ San Diego, CA

Brislin, Jane F., Dir., Info.Serv.
INDUSTRIAL HEALTH FOUNDATION, INC. - LIBRARY □ Pittsburgh, PA

Bristor, Patricia, Libn.
GENERAL MOTORS CORPORATION - RESEARCH LABORATORIES LIBRARY □ Warren, MI

Britain, Karla, Dir.
PORTER MEMORIAL HOSPITAL - HARLEY E. RICE MEMORIAL LIBRARY □ Denver, CO

Britt, Terry, Assoc.Dir. of Libs.
U.S. NAVY - NAVAL POSTGRADUATE SCHOOL - DUDLEY KNOX LIBRARY □ Monterey, CA

Britton, Barbara S., Per.Asst.
BRIDGEWATER STATE COLLEGE - CLEMENT C. MAXWELL LIBRARY □ Bridgewater, MA

Britton, Constance J., Libn.
OHIO (State) AGRICULTURAL RESEARCH AND DEVELOPMENT CENTER - LIBRARY □ Wooster, OH

Britton, J.J., Libn.
CENTRAL PRESBYTERIAN CHURCH - LIBRARY □ Houston, TX

Britton, Ruth, Libn.
UNIVERSITY OF SOUTHERN CALIFORNIA - SOCIAL WORK LIBRARY □ Los Angeles, CA

Britz, Andrew M., Libn.
ST. PETER'S ABBEY & COLLEGE - LIBRARY □ Muenster, SK

Britz, Daniel A., Bibliog. of Africana
NORTHWESTERN UNIVERSITY - MELVILLE J. HERSKOVITS LIBRARY OF AFRICAN STUDIES □ Evanston, IL

Broad, Julia, Libn.
HARRIS-STOWE STATE COLLEGE LIBRARY □ St. Louis, MO

Broad, Martha, Ref.Libn.
BELL COMMUNICATIONS RESEARCH, INC. - INFORMATION RESOURCES SERVICES CENTER □ Morristown, NJ

Broaddus, Billie, Dir.
UNIVERSITY OF CINCINNATI - MEDICAL CENTER LIBRARIES - HISTORY OF HEALTH SCIENCES LIBRARY AND MUSEUM □ Cincinnati, OH

Broadnax, Lavonda, Asst.Libn.
HOWARD UNIVERSITY - HEALTH SCIENCES LIBRARY □ Washington, DC

Broadus, Laurie, Libn.Coord.
ST. MARGARET HOSPITAL - SALLIE M. TYRRELL, M.D. MEMORIAL LIBRARY □ Hammond, IN

Broadway, Martha, Trade Ref.Asst.
U.S. DEPT. OF COMMERCE - INTERNATIONAL TRADE ADMINISTRATION - NASHVILLE DISTRICT OFFICE LIBRARY □ Nashville, TN

Broadwin, John, Asst.Engr.Libn./Oper.
STANFORD UNIVERSITY - ENGINEERING LIBRARY □ Stanford, CA

Broberg, Lisa, Dir.
MIDDLESEX COUNTY HISTORICAL SOCIETY - LIBRARY □ Middletown, CT

Brochu, Lynn, Data Dissemination Off.
CANADA - STATISTICS CANADA - ADVISORY SERVICES - EDMONTON REFERENCE CENTRE □ Edmonton, AB

Brock, Bill, Asst.Cur.
AUSTIN PUBLIC LIBRARY - AUSTIN HISTORY CENTER □ Austin, TX

Brock, Jo Ann, Assoc.Libn.
UNIVERSITY OF CALIFORNIA, BERKELEY - GOVERNMENT DOCUMENTS DEPARTMENT □ Berkeley, CA

Brock, Susan
TEXAS MEDICAL ASSOCIATION - MEMORIAL LIBRARY □ Austin, TX

Brockhurst, S., Lib.Techn.
CANADA - HEALTH AND WELFARE CANADA - HEALTH PROTECTION BRANCH - TORONTO REGIONAL LIBRARY† □ Scarborough, ON

Brockington, Martha W., Law Libn.
BARNSTABLE LAW LIBRARY □ Barnstable, MA

Brockman, Mary, Ref.Libn.
VANDERBILT UNIVERSITY - JEAN AND ALEXANDER HEARD LIBRARY - CENTRAL DIV. - SARA SHANNON STEVENSON SCI. LIB. □ Nashville, TN

Brockway, Duncan, Dir. of Libs.
SCHOOLS OF THEOLOGY IN DUBUQUE - LIBRARIES □ Dubuque, IA

Brodie, Tom S., Acq. & Dist.
SHELL OIL COMPANY - INFORMATION & LIBRARY SERVICES □ Houston, TX

Brodnex, Cynthia, Law Libn.
SAGINAW COUNTY LAW LIBRARY □ Saginaw, MI

Brody, Catherine T., Chf.Libn.
CUNY - NEW YORK CITY TECHNICAL COLLEGE LIBRARY/LEARNING RESOURCE CENTER □ Brooklyn, NY

Brody, Julia J., Chf. & Assoc.Dir.
NEW YORK PUBLIC LIBRARY - MID-MANHATTAN LIBRARY □ New York, NY

Brody, Leon, Ref.Libn.
U.S. OFFICE OF PERSONNEL MANAGEMENT - LIBRARY □ Washington, DC

Broering, Naomi C., Libn.
GEORGETOWN UNIVERSITY - MEDICAL CENTER - DAHLGREN MEMORIAL LIBRARY □ Washington, DC

Brofft, Dottie F., Ref.Libn.
ENVIRONMENTAL PROTECTION AGENCY - ANDREW W. BREIDENBACH ENVIRONMENTAL RESEARCH CTR., CINCINNATI - TECH.LIB. □ Cincinnati, OH

Broida, Patricia, Asst.Libn.
AMERICAN COLLEGE OF OBSTETRICIANS AND GYNECOLOGISTS - RESOURCE CENTER □ Washington, DC

Brokalakis, Melissa, Mgr., Info./Lib.Serv.
HONEYWELL, INC. - HONEYWELL INFORMATION SYSTEMS - INFORMATION AND LIBRARY SERVICES □ Waltham, MA

Bromer, A. Susan, Curric.Mtls.Libn.
EAST STROUDSBURG UNIVERSITY - KENT LIBRARY† □ East Stroudsburg, PA

Bromley, James R., Dir.
NORTHWOOD INSTITUTE OF TEXAS - FREEDOM EDUCATION CENTER □ Cedar Hill, TX

Bromwich, G.R.E., V.P., Res. & Info.Dept.
REED STENHOUSE, LTD. - RESEARCH DEPARTMENT LIBRARY □ Toronto, ON

Brondie, Priscilla, Circ.
WENTWORTH INSTITUTE OF TECHNOLOGY - LIBRARY □ Boston, MA

Brong, Gerald R., Pres.
INFORMATION FUTURES - INFORMATION CENTER □ Pullman, WA

Brongers, Lore, Ref.Libn.
UNIVERSITY OF BRITISH COLUMBIA - MAC MILLAN FORESTRY/AGRICULTURE LIBRARY □ Vancouver, BC

Brongers, Rein J., Hd.
UNIVERSITY OF BRITISH COLUMBIA - MATHEMATICS LIBRARY □ Vancouver, BC

Brongers, Rein J., Hd.
UNIVERSITY OF BRITISH COLUMBIA - SCIENCE DIVISION □ Vancouver, BC

Bronner, Edwin B., Cur.
HAVERFORD COLLEGE - TREASURE ROOM AND QUAKER COLLECTION □ Haverford, PA

Bronson, Barbara, Libn.
WARREN COUNTY LAW LIBRARY† □ Lebanon, OH

Bronstein, Lois H., Tech.Serv.Supv.
DU PONT DE NEMOURS (E.I.) & COMPANY, INC. - LIBRARY NETWORK □ Wilmington, DE

Brook, Dr. Barry S., Dir.
REPERTOIRE INTERNATIONAL D'ICONOGRAPHIE MUSICALE - RESEARCH CENTER FOR MUSICAL ICONOGRAPHY - LIBRARY □ New York, NY

Brooke, Anna, Libn.
SMITHSONIAN INSTITUTION - HIRSHHORN MUSEUM AND SCULPTURE GARDEN - LIBRARY □ Washington, DC

Brooker, Alice, Libn.
SPRINGFIELD ART MUSEUM - ART REFERENCE LIBRARY □ Springfield, MO

Brookes, Betty, AV
EDEN THEOLOGICAL SEMINARY - LIBRARY □ Webster Groves, MO

Brookfield, Margaret A., Law Libn.
GETTY REFINING AND MARKETING COMPANY - LAW LIBRARY □ Tulsa, OK

Brookreson, Frances, Libn.
HENDRICK MEDICAL CENTER - MARY MEEK SCHOOL OF NURSING - MEEK LIBRARY EDUCATIONAL PROGRAMS □ Abilene, TX

Brooks, Barbara, Med.Libn.
FORBES HEALTH SYSTEM - FORBES REGIONAL HEALTH CENTER - MEDICAL LIBRARY □ Monroeville, PA

Brooks, Beverly, Hd.Libn.
TRIDENT TECHNICAL COLLEGE - NORTH CAMPUS LIBRARY □ North Charleston, SC

Brooks, Charles, Educ.Cur.
BUFFALO & ERIE COUNTY HISTORICAL SOCIETY - LIBRARY† □ Buffalo, NY

Brooks, Jerrold Lee, Dir.
HISTORICAL FOUNDATION OF THE PRESBYTERIAN AND REFORMED CHURCHES - LIBRARY AND ARCHIVES □ Montreat, NC

Brooks, Judith, Asst.Libn.
OAKLAND SCHOOLS - EDUCATIONAL RESOURCE CENTER □ Pontiac, MI

Brooks, Lois J., Libn.
BROOKS MINERALS, INC. - LIBRARY □ Lakewood, CO

Brooks, Mary Ellen, Bibliog.
UNIVERSITY OF GEORGIA - RARE BOOKS DEPARTMENT □ Athens, GA

Brooks, Peggy, Lib.Chm.
ANALYTICAL PSYCHOLOGY CLUB OF NEW YORK - KRISTINE MANN LIBRARY □ New York, NY

Brooks, Robert E., Hd.Ref.Libn.
YALE UNIVERSITY - LAW LIBRARY □ New Haven, CT

Brooks, Ruth H., Asst.Libn.
SOUTHWEST FOUNDATION FOR BIOMEDICAL RESEARCH - PRESTON G. NORTHROP MEMORIAL LIBRARY □ San Antonio, TX

Brooks, Violette Y., Ref.Libn.
CHICAGO TRANSIT AUTHORITY - HAROLD S. ANTHON MEMORIAL LIBRARY □ Chicago, IL

Broom, Harriet L., Libn.
MIDSTATE TECHNICAL INSTITUTE - EDUCATIONAL RESOURCE CENTER-LIBRARY □ Wisconsin Rapids, WI

Broome, Douglas, Music Libn.
NEW ORLEANS BAPTIST THEOLOGICAL SEMINARY - JOHN T. CHRISTIAN LIBRARY □ New Orleans, LA

Broomfield, Phyllis, Libn.
FLORIDA STATE UNIVERSITY - CTR. FOR STUDIES IN VOCATIONAL EDUC. - FLORIDA EDUCATIONAL INFO. SERV. □ Tallahassee, FL

Brophy, Cynthia, Project Dir.
CRIME & JUSTICE FOUNDATION - MASCARELLO LIBRARY OF CRIMINAL JUSTICE □ Boston, MA

Brophy, Jill, Adm.Asst.
RAND CORPORATION - LIBRARY† □ Santa Monica, CA

Brophy, K.
HARTFORD PUBLIC LIBRARY - ART, MUSIC AND RECREATION DEPARTMENT □ Hartford, CT

Brosamer, Laura L., Libn.
ST. MARY'S HOSPITAL - HEALTH SCIENCE LIBRARY □ Decatur, IL

Brose, Jean M., Hd.Libn.
ROCHESTER METHODIST HOSPITAL - METHODIST KAHLER LIBRARY □ Rochester, MN

Brosky, Catherine, Hd.
CARNEGIE LIBRARY OF PITTSBURGH - SCIENCE AND TECHNOLOGY DEPARTMENT □ Pittsburgh, PA

Brosman, Geraldine Y., Libn.
U.S. AIR FORCE BASE - MINOT BASE LIBRARY □ Minot AFB, ND

Bross, Mary Louise, Circ.
MORAVIAN COLLEGE - REEVES LIBRARY □ Bethlehem, PA

Broughton, Pansy D., Ref.Libn.
REYNOLDS (R.J.) TOBACCO COMPANY - ENGINEERING - TECHNICAL INFORMATION/ RECORDS SECTION □ Winston-Salem, NC

Broughton, Rita, Supv.
ST. LOUIS PUBLIC LIBRARY - FILM LIBRARY SERVICE □ St. Louis, MO

Brouillette, Connie, Libn.
DALLAS PUBLIC LIBRARY - URBAN INFORMATION CENTER □ Dallas, TX

Broun, Patricia M., Ref.Libn.
AT & T BELL LABORATORIES - LIBRARY □ Short Hills, NJ

Brouwer, Norman J., Ship Hist.
SOUTH STREET SEAPORT MUSEUM - LIBRARY □ New York, NY

Brover, Hilary J., Med.Libn.
ANAHEIM MEMORIAL HOSPITAL - MEDICAL LIBRARY □ Anaheim, CA

Browder, Carol F., Asst.Libn.
HARBOR BRANCH FOUNDATION, INC. - LIBRARY □ Fort Pierce, FL

Brown, A., Jr., Hd., Engr.Serv.
HENRY (J.J.) CO., INC. - ENGINEERING LIBRARY □ Moorestown, NJ

Brown, Adelaide Loretta, Libn.
U.S. DEPT. OF JUSTICE - LAND AND NATURAL RESOURCES DIVISION LIBRARY □ Washington, DC

Brown, Anne, Mgr.
ONTARIO - SUPREME COURT OF ONTARIO - JUDGES' LIBRARY† □ Toronto, ON

Brown, Rev. Arthur E., M.M., Libn.
MARYKNOLL SEMINARY - LIBRARY □ Maryknoll, NY

Brown, Bennie, Jr., Libn.
GUNSTON HALL PLANTATION - HOUSE MUSEUM - LIBRARY □ Lorton, VA

Brown, Betty, Oklahoma Rm.
OKLAHOMA STATE DEPARTMENT OF LIBRARIES □ Oklahoma City, OK

Brown, Beverly, Tech.Serv.Libn.
CANADIAN MEMORIAL CHIROPRACTIC COLLEGE - C.C. CLEMMER LIBRARY □ Toronto, ON

Brown, Beverly, Info.Sci.
SCHERING-PLOUGH CORPORATION - PHARMACEUTICAL RESEARCH DIVISION - LIBRARY INFORMATION CENTER □ Bloomfield, NJ

Brown, Bobby J., Dir.
U.S. ARMY - ENGINEER WATERWAYS EXPERIMENT STATION - HYDRAULIC ENGINEERING INFORMATION ANALYSIS CENTER □ Vicksburg, MS

Brown, Bonnie Jean, Libn.
ROCKWELL INTERNATIONAL - ROCKWELL HANFORD OPERATIONS - LEGAL LIBRARY □ Richland, WA

Brown, Bruce M., Univ.Archv.
COLGATE UNIVERSITY - EVERETT NEEDHAM CASE LIBRARY - ARCHIVES □ Hamilton, NY

Brown, Carmen, Hd., Pub.Serv./Ref.
WORCESTER POLYTECHNIC INSTITUTE - GEORGE C. GORDON LIBRARY □ Worcester, MA

Brown, Carol A., Supv., Info.Serv.
CONSOLIDATED NATURAL GAS SERVICE CO., INC. - RESEARCH DEPARTMENT LIBRARY □ Cleveland, OH

Brown, Carolyn P., Chf.
U.S. NATL. INSTITUTES OF HEALTH - LIBRARY □ Bethesda, Md.

Brown, Cathleen Galloway, Libn.
ENVIRONMENTAL IMPACT PLANNING CORPORATION - LIBRARY □ San Francisco, CA

Brown, Charles A., Dir. of Lib.
MEMORIAL MEDICAL CENTER - HEALTH SCIENCES LIBRARY □ Corpus Christi, TX

Brown, Charlotte B., Archv./Spec.Coll.Libn.
FRANKLIN AND MARSHALL COLLEGE - SHADEK-FACKENTHAL LIBRARY - SPECIAL COLLECTIONS □ Lancaster, PA

Brown, Christine B., Trade Ref.Asst.
U.S. DEPT. OF COMMERCE - INTERNATIONAL TRADE ADMINISTRATION - ATLANTA DISTRICT OFFICE LIBRARY □ Atlanta, GA

Brown, Claire L., Spec.
HARVARD UNIVERSITY - LITTAUER LIBRARY □ Cambridge, MA

Brown, Connis O., Asst. State Archv.
VIRGINIA STATE LIBRARY □ Richmond, VA
Brown, Dale W., Dir., Lib. & Media Serv.
ALEXANDRIA CITY PUBLIC SCHOOLS -
EDUCATIONAL MEDIA CENTER - NICHOLS
PROFESSIONAL LIBRARY □ Alexandria, VA
Brown, Daniel, Hist.
U.S. NATL. PARK SERVICE - STONES RIVER
NATL. BATTLEFIELD - LIBRARY □ Murfreesboro,
TN
Brown, Danielle K., Mgr.
SANDIA NATIONAL LABORATORIES -
TECHNICAL LIBRARY □ Albuquerque, NM
Brown, David
INTERNATIONAL THOMSON EDUCATIONAL
PUBLISHING, INC. - EDITORIAL LIBRARY □
New York, NY
Brown, David, Ref. & Cat.
UNIVERSITY OF CALGARY - EDUCATION
MATERIALS CENTER □ Calgary, AB
Brown, David C., Adm.Libn.
U.S. MARINE CORPS - EDUCATION CENTER -
JAMES CARSON BRECKINRIDGE LIBRARY &
AMPHIBIOUS WARFARE RESEARCH FACILITY □
Quantico, VA
Brown, David W., Libn.
UNIVERSITY OF CALIFORNIA, BERKELEY -
GRADUATE SCHOOL OF JOURNALISM -
LIBRARY† □ Berkeley, CA
Brown, Deborah, Horticulture Ext.Spec.
UNIVERSITY OF MINNESOTA - AGRICULTURAL
EXTENSION SERVICE - DIAL-U INSECT AND
PLANT INFORMATION CLINIC □ St. Paul, MN
Brown, Diana L., Res.Assoc./Coord.
AMERICAN COLLEGE OF HOSPITAL
ADMINISTRATORS - RAY E. BROWN
MANAGEMENT COLLECTION □ Chicago, IL
Brown, Diane, Pub.Serv.Libn.
UNIVERSITY OF CALIFORNIA, BERKELEY -
SEBASTIAN S. KRESGE ENGINEERING LIBRARY
□ Berkeley, CA
Brown, Donald R., Coord., Coll.Mgt.
PENNSYLVANIA STATE LIBRARY □ Harrisburg,
PA
Brown, Dorothy, Sr.Libn.
WILMINGTON NEWS-JOURNAL COMPANY -
LIBRARY □ Wilmington, DE
Brown, Dorothy Eady, Sr.Libn.
UNIVERSITY OF ALABAMA - BUSINESS
LIBRARY □ University, AL
Brown, Dwight, Tax Libn.
MILBANK, TWEED, HADLEY & MC CLOY -
LIBRARY □ New York, NY
Brown, E.S.
UNIVERSITY OF TORONTO - FACULTY OF
ENGINEERING LIBRARY □ Toronto, ON
Brown, Eleanor, Musm.Cur.
SISKIYOU COUNTY HISTORICAL SOCIETY -
LIBRARY □ Yreka, CA
Brown, Eleanor T., Hd.
AMHERST COLLEGE - SCIENCE LIBRARY □
Amherst, MA
Brown, Elisabeth Potts, Quaker Bibliog.
HAVERFORD COLLEGE - TREASURE ROOM AND
QUAKER COLLECTION □ Haverford, PA
Brown, Ellen K., Hd., Archv./Hist.Mss.
BAYLOR UNIVERSITY - TEXAS COLLECTION □
Waco, TX
Brown, Elsie, Ref.Supv.
UNIVERSITY OF WESTERN ONTARIO - SCHOOL
OF BUSINESS ADMINISTRATION - BUSINESS
LIBRARY & INFORMATION CENTRE □ London,
ON
Brown, Esther, Project Asst.
ALBERTA HISTORICAL RESOURCES
FOUNDATION - LIBRARY □ Calgary, AB
Brown, Eve, Rec.Mgt.Supv.
MOTT (Charles Stewart) FOUNDATION -
LIBRARY □ Flint, MI
Brown, Evelyn, Ed.
RILEY COUNTY GENEALOGICAL SOCIETY -
LIBRARY □ Manhattan, KS

Brown, F., Act.Libn.
GEORGIA STATE FORESTRY COMMISSION -
LIBRARY □ Macon, GA
Brown, G.H., Libn.
MONTGOMERY, MC CRACKEN, WALKER &
RHOADS - LIBRARY □ Philadelphia, PA
Brown, George C., Music Dir.
CHARLES RIVER BROADCASTING COMPANY -
WCRB LIBRARY □ Waltham, MA
Brown, Gerald R., Chf.Libn.
WINNIPEG SCHOOL DIVISION NO. 1 -
TEACHERS LIBRARY AND RESOURCE CENTRE □
Winnipeg, MB
Brown, Geraldine McColgan, Hd.Libn.
XEROX CORPORATION - LAW LIBRARY □
Stamford, CT
Brown, Grant, Libn.
ONTARIO GENEALOGICAL SOCIETY - LIBRARY
□ Willowdale, ON
Brown, Helen-Ann, Med.Libn.
NATIONAL JEWISH HOSPITAL & RESEARCH
CTR./NATIONAL ASTHMA CTR. - GERALD
TUCKER MEMORIAL MEDICAL LIBRARY □
Denver, CO
Brown, Helen G., Info.Anl.
GENERAL ELECTRIC COMPANY - AIRCRAFT
ENGINE BUSINESS GROUP - DR. C.W. SMITH
TECHNICAL INFORMATION CTR., 24001 □
Lynn, MA
Brown, Helene, Sr.Libn.
GENERAL MOTORS CORPORATION - RESEARCH
LABORATORIES LIBRARY □ Warren, MI
Brown, Howard C., Archv.
NEWFOUNDLAND - PROVINCIAL ARCHIVES OF
NEWFOUNDLAND AND LABRADOR □ St. John's,
NF
Brown, Ina A., Lib. Group Supv.
AT & T LABORATORIES & TECHNOLOGIES -
LIBRARY □ Reading, PA
Brown, J. Robin, Dept.Libn.
ALBERTA - DEPARTMENT OF TREASURY -
LIBRARY SERVICES □ Edmonton, AB
Brown, Jack Perry, Libn.
CLEVELAND MUSEUM OF ART - INGALLS
LIBRARY □ Cleveland, OH
Brown, James W., Dir.
UNIVERSITY OF ILLINOIS - COMMUNITY
RESEARCH CENTER - INFORMATION
RESOURCE CENTER □ Champaign, IL
Brown, Jan, Doc.Libn.
WASHBURN UNIVERSITY OF TOPEKA - SCHOOL
OF LAW LIBRARY □ Topeka, KS
Brown, Jane, Assoc.Libn.
UNIVERSITY OF SASKATCHEWAN - ST.
THOMAS MORE COLLEGE - SHANNON LIBRARY
□ Saskatoon, SK
Brown, Jane G., Exec.Dir.
INTERNATIONAL TENNIS HALL OF FAME AND
TENNIS MUSEUM - LIBRARY □ Newport, RI
Brown, Janis, LRC Coord.
UNIVERSITY OF SOUTHERN CALIFORNIA -
HEALTH SCIENCES CAMPUS - NORRIS
MEDICAL LIBRARY □ Los Angeles, CA
Brown, Jann Braudis, Cat.Libn.
SETON HALL UNIVERSITY - SCHOOL OF LAW -
LAW LIBRARY □ Newark, NJ
Brown, Jay M.
CONGREGATION MISHKAN ISRAEL - ADULT
LIBRARY □ Hamden, CT
Brown, Jeanine, Chf., Lib.Serv.
U.S. VETERANS ADMINISTRATION (AR-
Fayetteville) - MEDICAL CENTER LIBRARY □
Fayetteville, AR
Brown, Jeanne I., Libn.
PARSONS, BRINCKERHOFF, QUADE & DOUGLAS
- LIBRARY □ New York, NY
Brown, Judith, Hd.Ref.Libn.
AMARILLO GENEALOGICAL SOCIETY - LIBRARY
□ Amarillo, TX
Brown, Judith, Ref.Libn.
AMARILLO PUBLIC LIBRARY - LOCAL HISTORY
COLLECTION □ Amarillo, TX

Brown, Karen, Children's Libn.
TUCSON PUBLIC LIBRARY - STEINHEIMER
COLLECTION OF SOUTHWESTERN CHILDREN'S
LITERATURE □ Tucson, AZ
Brown, Karen, Lib.Tech.Asst.
UNIVERSITY OF FLORIDA - AQUATIC WEED
PROGRAM - INFORMATION AND RETRIEVAL
CENTER □ Gainesville, FL
Brown, Dr. Katharine L., Exec.Dir.
WILSON (Woodrow) BIRTHPLACE
FOUNDATION, INC. - RESEARCH LIBRARY &
ARCHIVES □ Staunton, VA
Brown, Kathryn, Catalog Ed.
U.S. GENERAL SERVICES ADMINISTRATION -
CONSUMER INFORMATION CENTER □
Washington, DC
Brown, Kay, Cat.Libn.
SUNY - COLLEGE AT POTSDAM - FREDERICK W.
CRUMB MEMORIAL LIBRARY □ Potsdam, NY
Brown, Laura Ferris, Chf.Libn.
AMERICAN ARBITRATION ASSOCIATION -
EASTMAN ARBITRATION LIBRARY □ New York,
NY
Brown, Lauren R., Cur.
UNIVERSITY OF MARYLAND, COLLEGE PARK -
LIBRARIES - HISTORICAL MANUSCRIPTS AND
ARCHIVES DEPARTMENT □ College Park, MD
Brown, Linda Gail, Dir. of Lib.Serv.
FLORIDA STATE HOSPITAL - PATIENT/STAFF
LIBRARY □ Chattahoochee, FL
Brown, Lisle G., Cur.
MARSHALL UNIVERSITY - JAMES E. MORROW
LIBRARY - SPECIAL COLLECTIONS □
Huntington, WV
Brown, Lois, Braille Coord.
CANADIAN NATIONAL INSTITUTE FOR THE
BLIND - NATIONAL LIBRARY SERVICES -
SHERMAN SWIFT REFERENCE LIBRARY □
Toronto, ON
Brown, Lorna E., Libn.
ONTARIO PROVINCIAL POLICE
HEADQUARTERS - CAREER MANAGEMENT
BRANCH - LIBRARY □ Toronto, ON
Brown, Lucille, Sr.Info.Anl.
AMERICAN CRITICAL CARE - INFORMATION
CENTER □ McGaw Park, IL
Brown, M., Asst.Cur.
ROYAL CANADIAN ORDNANCE CORPS MUSEUM
- LIBRARY □ Montreal, PQ
Brown, Mabel C., Dir., Lib.Serv.
OTTAWA CIVIC HOSPITAL - DR. GEORGE S.
WILLIAMSON HEALTH SCIENCES LIBRARY □
Ottawa, ON
Brown, Marie, Lib.Asst.
BON SECOURS HOSPITAL - HEALTH SCIENCES
LIBRARY □ Baltimore, MD
Brown, Marion, Libn.
U.S. ARMY SERGEANTS MAJOR ACADEMY -
OTHON O. VALENT LEARNING RESOURCES
CENTER □ Ft. Bliss, TX
Brown, Mark, Pres.
MERCER COUNTY HISTORICAL SOCIETY -
LIBRARY AND ARCHIVES □ Mercer, PA
Brown, Mark N., Cur., Mss.
BROWN UNIVERSITY - SPECIAL COLLECTIONS
□ Providence, RI
Brown, Mary Ann, Assoc.Dir.
DUKE UNIVERSITY - MEDICAL CENTER
LIBRARY □ Durham, NC
Brown, Mary Anne, Asst.
NUCLEAR ASSURANCE CORPORATION -
INFORMATION CENTER □ Norcross, GA
Brown, Sr. Mary Georgia, Med.Libn.
LEILA HOSPITAL AND HEALTH CENTER -
MEDICAL LIBRARY □ Battle Creek, MI
Brown, Mary Grace H., Med.Lib./Media Serv.Dir.
PETERSBURG GENERAL HOSPITAL - MEDICAL
LIBRARY MEDIA SERVICES □ Petersburg, VA
Brown, Milton H., Exec.Sec.
AMERICAN CAMELLIA SOCIETY - LIBRARY □
Fort Valley, GA

Brown, Milton M., Sec.
NATIONAL AERONAUTIC ASSOCIATION - LIBRARY □ Washington, DC
Brown, Morton R., Libn.
SMITH BARNEY, HARRIS UPHAM & COMPANY, INC. - LIBRARY □ New York, NY
Brown, Muriel, Children's Lit.Spec.
DALLAS PUBLIC LIBRARY - HUMANITIES DIVISION □ Dallas, TX
Brown, Myra Suzanne, Act.Chm./Assoc.Libn.
UNIVERSITY OF FLORIDA - EDUCATION LIBRARY □ Gainesville, FL
Brown, Pat, Libn.
SOUTHERN BAPTIST CONVENTION - HISTORICAL COMMISSION - SOUTHERN BAPTIST HISTORICAL LIBRARY & ARCHIVES □ Nashville, TN
Brown, Patricia I., Asst. Law Libn.
SUFFOLK UNIVERSITY - LAW LIBRARY □ Boston, MA
Brown, Patti, Info.Spec.
UNIVERSITY OF SOUTHERN CALIFORNIA - NASA INDUSTRIAL APPLICATION CENTER (NIAC) □ Los Angeles, CA
Brown, Paula, Mgr.
BATTEN, BARTON, DURSTINE, OSBORN, INC. - INFORMATION RETRIEVAL CENTER† □ New York, NY
Brown, Philip, Pub.Serv.Libn.
SOUTH DAKOTA STATE UNIVERSITY - HILTON M. BRIGGS LIBRARY □ Brookings, SD
Brown, Rebecca, Libn.
MEMORIAL HOSPITAL OF ALAMANCE COUNTY, INC. - MEDICAL LIBRARY □ Burlington, NC
Brown, Regina, Hd.Libn.
OHIO STATE UNIVERSITY - ORTON MEMORIAL LIBRARY OF GEOLOGY □ Columbus, OH
Brown, Richard H., Academic V.P.
NEWBERRY LIBRARY □ Chicago, IL
Brown, Richard L., Dir.
ARIZONA STATE UNIVERSITY - COLLEGE OF LAW - LIBRARY □ Tempe, AZ
Brown, Ron, Ref.Libn.
NEW YORK UNIVERSITY - SCHOOL OF LAW LIBRARY □ New York, NY
Brown, Ronald D., Group Supv.
JOHNS HOPKINS UNIVERSITY - APPLIED PHYSICS LABORATORY - CHEMICAL PROPULSION INFORMATION AGENCY □ Laurel, MD
Brown, Ruth, Asst.
ST. LOUIS - COMPTROLLERS OFFICE - MICROFILM DEPARTMENT □ St. Louis, MO
Brown, Sandra, Med.Ref./Search Anl.
INDIANA UNIVERSITY, INDIANAPOLIS - SCHOOL OF MEDICINE LIBRARY □ Indianapolis, IN
Brown, Sharon, Asst.Libn.
NEW YORK SOCIETY LIBRARY □ New York, NY
Brown, Sharon P., Libn.
CONOCO, INC. - MINERALS LIBRARY† □ Denver, CO
Brown, Stanley W., Cur., Rare Books
DARTMOUTH COLLEGE - SPECIAL COLLECTIONS □ Hanover, NH
Brown, Suzanne, Asst.Libn.
COLONIAL WILLIAMSBURG - AUDIO-VISUAL LIBRARY† □ Williamsburg, VA
Brown, Teresa, Libn.
MPR ASSOCIATES, INC. - TECHNICAL LIBRARY □ Washington, DC
Brown, W.S., Hd., Info.Sys.Dept.
AT & T BELL LABORATORIES - LIBRARIES AND INFORMATION SYSTEMS CENTER □ Murray Hill, NJ
Brown, Rev. William J., Asst.Supt., Curric.
METROPOLITAN (Toronto) SEPARATE SCHOOL BOARD - CATHOLIC EDUCATION CENTRE LIBRARY □ Toronto, ON
Brown, Yvonne, Hd., Art Sect.
CHICAGO PUBLIC LIBRARY CULTURAL CENTER - FINE ARTS DIVISION - ART SECTION □ Chicago, IL

Brown-Comment, Anna Mae, Adm.Asst.
COLLEGE OF THE VIRGIN ISLANDS - CARIBBEAN RESEARCH INSTITUTE - LIBRARY □ St. Thomas, VI
Brown-Inz, Pamela Sue, Asst.Libn.-Cat.
LORD, DAY & LORD - LIBRARY □ New York, NY
Brownberger, Mrs. M., Sec./Libn.
LAKE COUNTY HISTORICAL SOCIETY - LIBRARY □ Tavares, FL
Browne, Alice R., Ref.Libn.
RENSSELAER POLYTECHNIC INSTITUTE - FOLSOM LIBRARY □ Troy, NY
Browne, Cynthia E., Cat.
NEW JERSEY HISTORICAL SOCIETY - LIBRARY □ Newark, NJ
Browne, D.A., Pubn.Coord.
HERCULES, INC. - AEROSPACE DIVISION - MC GREGOR TECHNICAL INFORMATION CENTER □ McGregor, TX
Browne, Dr. Gary, Ed.
MARYLAND HISTORICAL SOCIETY - LIBRARY □ Baltimore, MD
Browne, Kelvin, Mgr., Ontario Lib.Serv.
ONTARIO - MINISTRY OF CITIZENSHIP AND CULTURE - LIBRARIES AND COMMUNITY INFORMATION □ Toronto, ON
Browne, Lynda S., Acq./Per.Libn.
BROOKINGS INSTITUTION - LIBRARY □ Washington, DC
Browne, Mamie G., Univ.Archv.
ALABAMA A & M UNIVERSITY - J. F. DRAKE MEMORIAL LEARNING RESOURCES CENTER □ Normal, AL
Browne, Sarah, Ref. & Acq.
NEW YORK STATE LEGISLATIVE LIBRARY □ Albany, NY
Browne, Valerie Gerrard, Asst.Univ.Archv.
LOYOLA UNIVERSITY OF CHICAGO - CUDAHY MEMORIAL LIBRARY - UNIVERSITY ARCHIVES □ Chicago, IL
Browning, Bonnie B., Asst. Staff Supv.
SOUTH CENTRAL BELL TELEPHONE COMPANY - RESOURCE CENTER □ Birmingham, AL
Browning, Donna, Med.Libn.
DEACONESS HOSPITAL - MEDICAL LIBRARY □ Buffalo, NY
Browning, Mark, Mgr.
TEXAS STATE - RAILROAD COMMISSION OF TEXAS - CENTRAL RECORDS □ Austin, TX
Browning, Mary L., Chf., Rd.Serv., Engr.Div.
U.S. AIR FORCE INSTITUTE OF TECHNOLOGY - LIBRARY □ Wright-Patterson AFB, OH
Browning, Phyllis M., Sci.Info.Mgr.
BECKMAN INSTRUMENTS, INC. - SPINCO DIVISION - TECHNICAL LIBRARY □ Palo Alto, CA
Brownlee, Evelyn, Asst.Libn.
DELAWARE LAW SCHOOL OF WIDENER UNIVERSITY - LAW LIBRARY □ Wilmington, DE
Brownlee, Dr. Richard S., Dir.
STATE HISTORICAL SOCIETY OF MISSOURI - LIBRARY □ Columbia, MO
Brownlee, Virginia, Dir., Nursing Educ.
LARNED STATE HOSPITAL - J.T. NARAMORE LIBRARY □ Larned, KS
Brownlow, Frances, Libn. & Cat.
PUBLIC UTILITY COMMISSION OF TEXAS - LIBRARY □ Austin, TX
Brownlow, Judith, Libn.
U.S. NATL. MARINE FISHERIES SERVICE - NORTHEAST FISHERIES CENTER - LIBRARY □ Woods Hole, MA
Browse, Cary Graham, Hd.Libn.
DRAPER (Charles Stark) LABORATORY, INC. - TECHNICAL INFORMATION CENTER □ Cambridge, MA
Brubaker, Maryellen, Lib.Dir.
CORTEZ PUBLIC LIBRARY - SOUTHWEST COLLECTION □ Cortez, CO
Brubaker, Robert L., Cur., Spec.Coll.
CHICAGO HISTORICAL SOCIETY - RESEARCH COLLECTIONS □ Chicago, IL

Bruce, Christine, Lib.Asst.
QUEEN'S UNIVERSITY AT KINGSTON - ELECTRICAL ENGINEERING LIBRARY □ Kingston, ON
Bruce, Helen G., Libn.
BRITISH COLUMBIA - MINISTRY OF INDUSTRY & SMALL BUSINESS DEVELOPMENT - LIBRARY □ Victoria, BC
Bruce, Nancy, Hd., Rare Bks.Serv.
UNIVERSITY OF NORTH CAROLINA, CHAPEL HILL - HEALTH SCIENCES LIBRARY □ Chapel Hill, NC
Bruce, Robert K., Dept.Hd.
MINNEAPOLIS PUBLIC LIBRARY & INFORMATION CENTER - HISTORY DEPARTMENT □ Minneapolis, MN
Bruckman, Jan, Supv., Film Lib.
UNIVERSITY OF UTAH - INSTRUCTIONAL MEDIA SERVICES □ Salt Lake City, UT
Brude, Deborah J., Media Serv.Coord.
ANOKA AREA VOCATIONAL TECHNICAL INSTITUTE - MEDIA CENTER □ Anoka, MN
Brudvig, Glenn L., Dir. of Libs.
CALIFORNIA INSTITUTE OF TECHNOLOGY - MILLIKAN LIBRARY □ Pasadena, CA
Brudvig, Karen L., Libn.
MOUNDS PARK HOSPITAL - HEALTH SCIENCES LIBRARY □ St. Paul, MN
Brue, Donald W., Libn.
LUTHERAN BRETHREN SCHOOLS - BIBLE COLLEGE AND SEMINARY LIBRARY □ Fergus Falls, MN
Brueck, Lora, Spec.Coll.
WORCESTER POLYTECHNIC INSTITUTE - GEORGE C. GORDON LIBRARY □ Worcester, MA
Bruemmer, Bruce, Archv.
UNIVERSITY OF MINNESOTA - CHARLES BABBAGE INSTITUTE COLLECTION □ Minneapolis, MN
Bruemner, Alice, Lib.Serv.Supv.
ALLSTATE INSURANCE COMPANY - LAW LIBRARY □ Northbrook, IL
Bruenjes, Alice, Hd.Libn.
JEWISH HOSPITAL AT WASHINGTON UNIVERSITY MEDICAL CENTER - SCHOOL OF NURSING - MOSES SHOENBERG MEMORIAL LIBRARY □ St. Louis, MO
Bruette, Vernon, Ref.Libn.
MONTEFIORE MEDICAL CENTER - MEDICAL LIBRARY □ Bronx, NY
Brugh, Anne
GENEALOGICAL SOCIETY OF NEW JERSEY - MANUSCRIPT COLLECTIONS □ New Brunswick, NJ
Brugh, Anne
RUTGERS UNIVERSITY, THE STATE UNIVERSITY OF NEW JERSEY - DEPARTMENT OF SPECIAL COLLECTIONS AND ARCHIVES □ New Brunswick, NJ
Bruguier, Leonard, Assoc.Dir.
AMERICAN INDIAN RESEARCH PROJECT - LIBRARY □ Vermillion, SD
Bruhm, Lorna, Inspector
CANADA - NATIONAL FILM BOARD OF CANADA - FILM LIBRARY □ Thunder Bay, ON
Bruland, Rev. Osborne Y., Libn.
FAITH EVANGELICAL LUTHERAN SEMINARY - LIBRARY □ Tacoma, WA
Brumbaugh, Dorothy
LOWELL OBSERVATORY - LIBRARY □ Flagstaff, AZ
Brumbaugh, Tedd S., Dir.
MESA COUNTY VALLEY SCHOOL DISTRICT 51 - DEPARTMENT OF RESOURCES, RESEARCH AND DEVELOPMENT □ Grand Junction, CO
Brumm, Janet, Tech.Serv.
WAYNE STATE COLLEGE - U.S. CONN LIBRARY □ Wayne, NE
Brun, Christian, Dept.Hd.
UNIVERSITY OF CALIFORNIA, SANTA BARBARA - DEPARTMENT OF SPECIAL COLLECTIONS □ Santa Barbara, CA

Bruner, Mrs. James G., Libn.
ST. THOMAS MORE HOSPITAL - MEDICAL
LIBRARY □ Canon City, CO

Brunet, Fran, Hd.Libn.
BECHTEL POWER CORPORATION - SFPD
LIBRARY □ San Francisco, CA

Brunfelt, Pamela A., Libn./Res.
OTTER TAIL COUNTY HISTORICAL SOCIETY -
LIBRARY □ Fergus Falls, MN

Brunka, Veronica, Lib.Supv.
ONTARIO - MINISTRY OF HEALTH - LIBRARY □
Toronto, ON

Brunke, Mrs. Conrad, Libn.
WARREN COUNTY HISTORICAL SOCIETY -
LIBRARY AND ARCHIVES □ Warren, PA

Brunke, Sally, Asst.Libn.
RESURRECTION HOSPITAL - MEDICAL LIBRARY
& ALLIED HEALTH SCIENCES □ Chicago, IL

Brunner, Earl C., Jr., Chf.Libn.
CHURCH OF JESUS CHRIST OF LATTER-DAY
SAINTS - LAS VEGAS BRANCH GENEALOGICAL
LIBRARY □ Las Vegas, NV

Brunner, Karen B., Law Libn.
MORRIS COUNTY LAW LIBRARY □ Morristown,
NJ

Brunnschweiler, Dr. Tamara, Bibliog.Lat.Amer.Stud
MICHIGAN STATE UNIVERSITY -
INTERNATIONAL LIBRARY □ East Lansing, MI

Brunson, Madelon, Archv.
REORGANIZED CHURCH OF JESUS CHRIST OF
LATTER DAY SAINTS - LIBRARY & ARCHIVES □
Independence, MO

Brunson, Ruth H., Dir.
UNIVERSITY OF ARKANSAS AT LITTLE ROCK -
PULASKI COUNTY LAW LIBRARY □ Little Rock,
AR

Brunstad, Mrs. Dera C., Libn.
CEDAR VALE REGIONAL HOSPITAL - LIBRARY □
Cedar Vale, KS

Brunton, Angela, Libn.
CALIFORNIA STATE DIVISION OF MINES AND
GEOLOGY - LIBRARY □ San Francisco, CA

Brunworth, Courtney, Libn.
FIRST PRESBYTERIAN CHURCH - LIBRARY† □
Upland, CA

Brush, Carol, Cat.
DRAPER (Charles Stark) LABORATORY, INC. -
TECHNICAL INFORMATION CENTER □
Cambridge, MA

Brustman, Mary Jane, Ref.
SUNY AT ALBANY - GRADUATE LIBRARY FOR
PUBLIC AFFAIRS AND POLICY □ Albany, NY

Bryan, A.R., Libn.
MARYLAND HISTORICAL SOCIETY - LIBRARY □
Baltimore, MD

Bryan, Betty A., Asst.Dir.
AMERICAN SOCIETY FOR METALS - METALS
INFORMATION □ Metals Park, OH

Bryan, Bruce F., Info.Off. & Res.Engr.
WELDING INSTITUTE OF CANADA - LIBRARY □
Oakville, ON

Bryan, Catherine, Libn.
OLD MANSE LIBRARY □ Newcastle, NB

Bryant, A.L., Engr.Br.Libn.
LOCKHEED MISSILES & SPACE COMPANY, INC.
- TECHNICAL INFORMATION CENTER □ Palo
Alto, CA

Bryant, Bonnie, Asst.Libn.
HINSDALE SANITARIUM AND HOSPITAL - A.C.
LARSON LIBRARY □ Hinsdale, IL

Bryant, Charles R., Cur.
YALE UNIVERSITY - SOUTHEAST ASIA
COLLECTION □ New Haven, CT

Bryant, Darcel, Spec.Serv.
DELAWARE STATE DEPARTMENT OF
COMMUNITY AFFAIRS - DIVISION OF
LIBRARIES □ Dover, DE

Bryant, James, Pres.
MARSHALL HISTORICAL SOCIETY - ARCHIVES
□ Marshall, MI

Bryant, Jean, Lib.Dir.
CITY OF INDUSTRY - RALPH W. MILLER GOLF
LIBRARY □ City of Industry, CA

Bryant, Lillian, Libn.
UNIVERSITY OF PENNSYLVANIA - SCHOOL OF
VETERINARY MEDICINE - C.J. MARSHALL
MEMORIAL LIBRARY □ Philadelphia, PA

Bryant, Nancy J., Dir., Lib. & Archv.
ATLANTA HISTORICAL SOCIETY - ARCHIVES □
Atlanta, GA

Bryant, Paul F., Tech.Libn.
CHAMPION INTERNATIONAL - CHAMPION
PAPERS TECHNICAL LIBRARY □ Hamilton, OH

Bryant, Prudence W., Supv., Ref. & Info.Serv.
ALABAMA A & M UNIVERSITY - J. F. DRAKE
MEMORIAL LEARNING RESOURCES CENTER □
Normal, AL

Bryce, Maria, Hd., Printed Coll.
NATIONAL LIBRARY OF CANADA - MUSIC
DIVISION □ Ottawa, ON

Brysh, Janet F., Libn.
UNIVERSITY OF SOUTHERN MAINE - CENTER
FOR RESEARCH & ADVANCED STUDY -
RESEARCH CENTER LIBRARY □ Portland, ME

Brysh, Janet F., Libn.
UNIVERSITY OF SOUTHERN MAINE - NEW
ENTERPRISE INSTITUTE - ENTERPRISE
INFORMATION SERVICE □ Portland, ME

Brzoska, Ellen, Libn.
YAKIMA VALLEY GENEALOGICAL SOCIETY -
LIBRARY □ Yakima, WA

Bube, Judith, Acq.Libn.
UNIVERSITY OF CALIFORNIA, IRVINE -
BIOMEDICAL LIBRARY □ Irvine, CA

Bucciferro, Rose, Cur.
WILL COUNTY HISTORICAL SOCIETY -
ARCHIVES □ Lockport, IL

Buchan, Robert, Cur.
SHERIDAN COUNTY HISTORICAL SOCIETY,
INC. - AGNES & CLARENCE BENSCHOTER
MEMORIAL LIBRARY □ Rushville, NE

Buchanan, Barbara R., Libn.
DOW CHEMICAL CANADA INC. - LIBRARY □
Sarnia, ON

Buchanan, Gerald, Asst.Dir., Lib.Oper.
MISSISSIPPI STATE LIBRARY COMMISSION □
Jackson, MS

Buchanan, Holly S., Dir.
NKC HOSPITALS, INC. - MEDICAL LIBRARY □
Louisville, KY

Buchanan, J.R., Dir.
OAK RIDGE NATIONAL LABORATORY -
NUCLEAR SAFETY INFORMATION CENTER □
Oak Ridge, TN

Buchanan, Jack T., Res.Libn.
EASTMAN KODAK COMPANY - TEXAS EASTMAN
COMPANY - RESEARCH & DEVELOPMENT
LIBRARY □ Longview, TX

Buchanan, Jean, Lib.Asst.
ONTARIO NURSES ASSOCIATION - ONA
LIBRARY □ Toronto, ON

Buchanan, Jim, Dir.
HOUSING ADVOCATES - LAW AND CONSUMER
AFFAIRS LIBRARY □ Cleveland, OH

Buchberg, Karl, Consrv.
PRINCETON UNIVERSITY - RARE BOOKS AND
SPECIAL COLLECTIONS □ Princeton, NJ

Bucher, Eric, Ref.Libn.
MEDICAL COLLEGE OF WISCONSIN -
LIBRARIES □ Milwaukee, WI

Buchheit, Mary E., Dir., Med.Lib.
KINGSBROOK JEWISH MEDICAL CENTER -
MEDICAL LIBRARY □ Brooklyn, NY

Buchsen, Dolores M., Cur.
PENNSYLVANIA STATE HISTORICAL & MUSEUM
COMMISSION - PENNSYLVANIA LUMBER
MUSEUM - LIBRARY □ Galeton, PA

Buck, A.M., Dist.Mgr.
BELL COMMUNICATIONS RESEARCH, INC. -
INFORMATION RESOURCES & SERVICES
DISTRICT □ Livingston, NJ

Buck, Ivan L., AV Coord.
NORTHWEST HOSPITAL - EFFIE M. STOREY
LEARNING CENTER □ Seattle, WA

Buck, Joan, Lib.Res.Anl.
ROCKWELL INTERNATIONAL - SPACE
BUSINESSES - TECHNICAL INFORMATION
CENTER □ Downey, CA

Buck, Judith L., Cur.
DELAWARE COUNTY HISTORICAL SOCIETY -
LIBRARY □ Chester, PA

Buck, Patricia, Asst.Libn.
PHILADELPHIA BOARD OF EDUCATION -
PEDAGOGICAL LIBRARY† □ Philadelphia, PA

Buck, S.A.
DOW CHEMICAL COMPANY - TECHNICAL
INFORMATION SERVICES - CENTRAL REPORT
INDEX □ Midland, MI

Buck, S.A.
DOW CHEMICAL COMPANY - TECHNICAL
INFORMATION SERVICES - CHEMICAL
LIBRARY □ Midland, MI

Buckardt, Dr. Henry L., Pres.
AMERICAN WORK HORSE MUSEUM - LIBRARY □
Paeonian Springs, VA

Buckel, William, Ref.Libn.
BATTELLE-COLUMBUS LABORATORIES -
LIBRARY □ Columbus, OH

Buckhout, Robert, Prof. of Psychology
BROOKLYN COLLEGE OF THE CITY UNIVERSITY
OF NEW YORK - CENTER FOR RESPONSIVE
PSYCHOLOGY - LIBRARY □ Brooklyn, NY

Buckingham, J., Ref.Libn.
UNIVERSITY OF ALBERTA - JOHN W. SCOTT
HEALTH SCIENCES LIBRARY □ Edmonton, AB

Buckley, C.E., Supv.
NORTHWEST INDUSTRIES LTD. - TECHNICAL
DATA CONTROL CENTRE □ Edmonton, AB

Buckley, Dr. Jay S., Jr., Dir., Tech.Info.
PFIZER, INC. - CENTRAL RESEARCH
TECHNICAL INFORMATION SERVICES □ Groton,
CT

Buckley, Keith, Ref.Libn.
INDIANA UNIVERSITY - LAW LIBRARY □
Bloomington, IN

Buckley, M. Constance, Doc.Ctr.
CORNELL UNIVERSITY - MARTIN P.
CATHERWOOD LIBRARY OF INDUSTRIAL AND
LABOR RELATIONS □ Ithaca, NY

Buckley, Margaret, Libn.
DES MOINES ART CENTER - LIBRARY □ Des
Moines, IA

Buckley, Steven F., Hd. of Tech.Serv.
SUNY - COLLEGE AT BROCKPORT - DRAKE
MEMORIAL LIBRARY □ Brockport, NY

Buckner, Rebecca S., Med.Libn.
BAPTIST MEMORIAL HOSPITAL - MEDICAL
LIBRARY □ Gadsden, AL

Buckwald, Joel, Chf., Archv.Br.
U.S. NATL. ARCHIVES & RECORDS SERVICE -
FEDERAL ARCHIVES AND RECORDS CENTER,
REGION 2 □ Bayonne, NJ

Bucy, Beth, Asst.Archv.
DALLAS HISTORICAL SOCIETY - RESEARCH
CENTER □ Dallas, TX

Budai, Joyce M., Dir.
UNIVERSITY OF MICHIGAN - DEPARTMENT OF
GEOLOGICAL SCIENCES - SUBSURFACE
LABORATORY LIBRARY □ Ann Arbor, MI

Buday, Magda, Bus.Libn.
WASHINGTON UNIVERSITY - BUSINESS
ADMINISTRATION LIBRARY □ St. Louis, MO

Budde, Jacqueline, Libn.
UNIVERSITY OF MINNESOTA - HORMEL
INSTITUTE - LIBRARY □ Austin, MN

Buddenbohm, Coralu D., Libn.
MEMPHIS PINK PALACE MUSEUM - LIBRARY □
Memphis, TN

Budet, Ramon, Ref.Libn.
UNIVERSITY OF PUERTO RICO - HUMACAO
UNIVERSITY COLLEGE - LIBRARY □ Humacao,
PR

Budet, Virginia E., Patients Libn.
U.S. VETERANS ADMINISTRATION (PR-San
Juan) - HOSPITAL LIBRARY □ San Juan, PR

Budge, Amy, Photograph Search Serv.
UNIVERSITY OF NEW MEXICO - TECHNOLOGY
APPLICATION CENTER □ Albuquerque, NM

Buechler, John, Asst.Dir., Spec.Coll.
UNIVERSITY OF VERMONT - WILBUR
COLLECTION OF VERMONTIANA □ Burlington,
VT

Buehler, Fred M., Asst.Ref.Libn.
UNIVERSITY OF WISCONSIN, STEVENS POINT
- JAMES H. ALBERTSON CENTER FOR
LEARNING RESOURCES □ Stevens Point, WI

Buehning, Dr. Peter, Pres.
U.S. TEAM HANDBALL FEDERATION -
ADMINISTRATIVE OFFICE LIBRARY □ Colorado
Springs, CO

Buelna, Joseph L., Base Libn.
U.S. AIR FORCE BASE - VANDENBERG BASE
LIBRARY □ Lompoc, CA

Bueno, Luis, Hd.Libn.
MIAMI HERALD - LIBRARY □ Miami, FL

Buescher, Cynthia L., Libn.
IRISH-AMERICAN CULTURAL ASSOCIATION -
LIBRARY □ Chicago, IL

Bueschlen, Wava, Dir. of the Lib.
FORT WAYNE BIBLE COLLEGE - S.A. LEHMAN
MEMORIAL LIBRARY □ Fort Wayne, IN

Bueter, Rita Van Assche, Libn.
FRUEHAUF CORPORATION - RESEARCH AND
DEVELOPMENT DIVISION - LIBRARY □ Detroit,
MI

Bueter, Rita Van Assche, Libn.
KELSEY-HAYES COMPANY - RESEARCH &
DEVELOPMENT CENTER LIBRARY □ Ann Arbor,
MI

Buff, Iva, Acq.Libn.
UNIVERSITY OF ROCHESTER - EASTMAN
SCHOOL OF MUSIC - SIBLEY MUSIC LIBRARY □
Rochester, NY

Buffa, Bette M., Sr. Law Libn.
MONSANTO COMPANY - LAW LIBRARY □ St.
Louis, MO

Buffalomeat, Nellie, Libn.
SOUTHWESTERN INDIAN POLYTECHNIC
INSTITUTE - INSTRUCTIONAL MATERIALS
CENTER □ Albuquerque, NM

Bugbee, Mrs. A. Newton, Asst.Libn.
LEHIGH COUNTY HISTORICAL SOCIETY -
SCOTT ANDREW TREXLER II MEMORIAL
LIBRARY □ Allentown, PA

Bugbee, Ann Lee S., Cur.
HOLY TRINITY (Old Swedes) CHURCH
FOUNDATION, INC. - HENDRICKSON HOUSE
LIBRARY □ Wilmington, DE

Bugeaud, Danielle, Coord.
ALBERTA - DEPARTMENT OF PUBLIC WORKS,
SUPPLY & SERVICES - LIBRARY □ Edmonton, AB

Bugg, Luci, Dir., Facility Serv.
GENERAL RESEARCH CORPORATION - LIBRARY
□ McLean, VA

Buhman, Lesley A., Pub.Serv.Libn.
LEWIS AND CLARK LAW SCHOOL -
NORTHWESTERN SCHOOL OF LAW - PAUL L.
BOLEY LAW LIBRARY □ Portland, OR

Buhr, L.R., Hd., Info. & Ref.Serv.
ALBERTA - LEGISLATIVE ASSEMBLY OF
ALBERTA - LEGISLATURE LIBRARY □ Edmonton,
AB

Buhr, Rosemary E., Dir. of Lib.Serv.
LOGAN COLLEGE OF CHIROPRACTIC - LIBRARY
□ Chesterfield, MO

Buie, Delinda Stephens, Asst.Cur., Rare Bks.
UNIVERSITY OF LOUISVILLE - DEPARTMENT
OF RARE BOOKS AND SPECIAL COLLECTIONS □
Louisville, KY

Buika, Gina, Ph.D., Dir., Med.Lib.
COLER MEMORIAL HOSPITAL - MEDICAL
LIBRARY† □ New York, NY

Buis, Hildy, Acq.Libn.
ROCKWELL INTERNATIONAL - NORTH
AMERICAN AIRCRAFT OPERATIONS -
TECHNICAL INFORMATION CENTER □ Los
Angeles, CA

Buist, Diane L., Libn.
GRAND RAPIDS PRESS - REFERENCE LIBRARY □
Grand Rapids, MI

Bujak, Janine, Law Libn.
DENVER DISTRICT COURT, 2ND JUDICIAL
DISTRICT - LAW LIBRARY □ Denver, CO

Bulerin, Josefina, Hd., Circ. & Ref.
UNIVERSITY OF PUERTO RICO - LAW SCHOOL
LIBRARY □ Rio Piedras, PR

Bulgarelli, Nancy T., Co-Dir.
CHILDREN'S HOSPITAL OF MICHIGAN -
MEDICAL LIBRARY □ Detroit, MI

Bulger, Janet T., Act.Libn.
AMERICAN ELECTRIC POWER SERVICE CORP.
- LIBRARY† □ New York, NY

Bull, Ellen, Med.Libn.
WESTERN MISSOURI MENTAL HEALTH CENTER
- LIBRARY† □ Kansas City, MO

Bull, Margarita A., Libn.
BOOTHE, PRICHARD & DUDLEY - LAW LIBRARY
□ Fairfax, VA

Bull, Margery, Ref.Libn.
CANADA - REVENUE CANADA - TAXATION
LIBRARY □ Ottawa, ON

Bull, Patty, Bus.Libn.
TANDEM COMPUTERS, INC. - CORPORATE
INFORMATION CENTER □ Cupertino, CA

Bullard, Mrs. Jack, Cur.
JEFFERSON HISTORICAL SOCIETY AND
MUSEUM - ARCHIVES □ Jefferson, TX

Bullard, Kathleen, Hd.
LOUISVILLE FREE PUBLIC LIBRARY -
GOVERNMENT DOCUMENTS DIVISION† □
Louisville, KY

Bullard, Kathleen, Sr.Res.Assoc.
MEIDINGER, INC. - INFORMATION CENTER □
Louisville, KY

Bullen, Ida, Asst.Dir./Adm.Libn.
DU PAGE LIBRARY SYSTEM - SYSTEM CENTER
□ Geneva, IL

Buller, Grace, Mgr., Pub.Lib.Serv.
ONTARIO - MINISTRY OF CITIZENSHIP AND
CULTURE - LIBRARIES AND COMMUNITY
INFORMATION □ Toronto, ON

Bulley, Joan S., Med.Libn.
WASHINGTON (Mary) HOSPITAL - MEDICAL
LIBRARY □ Fredericksburg, VA

Bullington, Neal, Asst.Chf. Ranger
U.S. NATL. PARK SERVICE - FIRE ISLAND NATL.
SEASHORE - HEADQUARTERS LIBRARY □
Patchogue, NY

Bullion, Laura, Sr.Mss.Spec.
WESTERN HISTORICAL MANUSCRIPT
COLLECTION/STATE HISTORICAL SOCIETY OF
MISSOURI MANUSCRIPTS JOINT COLLECTION
□ Columbia, MO

Bullock, Ednita W., Hd.Libn.
BENNETT COLLEGE - THOMAS F. HOLGATE
LIBRARY - SPECIAL COLLECTIONS □
Greensboro, NC

Bullock, Sybil H., Libn.
U.S. ARMY - AEROMEDICAL RESEARCH
LABORATORY - SCIENTIFIC INFORMATION
CENTER □ Ft. Rucker, AL

Bult, Conrad J., Asst.Dir., Ref.
CALVIN COLLEGE AND SEMINARY - LIBRARY □
Grand Rapids, MI

Bunce, Peter W., Chf., Archv.Br.
U.S. NATL. ARCHIVES & RECORDS SERVICE -
FEDERAL ARCHIVES AND RECORDS CENTER,
REGION 5 □ Chicago, IL

Bunce, William C., Dir. & Hd.Libn.
UNIVERSITY OF WISCONSIN, MADISON -
KOHLER ART LIBRARY □ Madison, WI

Bundren, Nancy, Oper. Control Supv.
STANDARD & POOR'S COMPUSTAT SERVICES,
INC. - DATA RESOURCE CENTER □ Engelwood,
CO

Bundy, Linda, Med.Libn.
TRUMBULL MEMORIAL HOSPITAL - WEAN
MEDICAL LIBRARY □ Warren, OH

Bunker, Neil, Bibliog.Spec.
UNIVERSITY OF ROCHESTER - EASTMAN
SCHOOL OF MUSIC - SIBLEY MUSIC LIBRARY □
Rochester, NY

Bunker, Phil, Law Libn.
WASHINGTON STATE ATTORNEY GENERAL'S
LIBRARY □ Olympia, WA

Bunnell, Chet, Pub.Serv.Libn.
UNIVERSITY OF MISSISSIPPI - SCHOOL OF
LAW LIBRARY □ University, MS

Bunnell, Laura, Libn.
U.S. DISTRICT COURT - LAW LIBRARY □
Anchorage, AK

Buntin, Steven Leslie, Bibliothecar
KXE6S VEREIN CHESS SOCIETY - SPECIAL/
RESEARCH LIBRARY - EAST DIVISION □ Chapel
Hill, NC

Bunting, Alison, Act.Hd.Libn.
UNIVERSITY OF CALIFORNIA, LOS ANGELES -
BIOMEDICAL LIBRARY □ Los Angeles, CA

Bunting, Anne Carroll, Hd., Tech.Serv.Dept.
UNIVERSITY OF TENNESSEE - CENTER FOR
THE HEALTH SCIENCES LIBRARY □ Memphis,
TN

Bunting, Helen, Sr.Libn.
WILLARD PSYCHIATRIC CENTER - HATCH
LIBRARY □ Willard, NY

Bunyan, Linda E., Med.Libn.
ST. THOMAS HOSPITAL - MEDICAL LIBRARY □
Akron, OH

Bunyan, Patrick, Libn.
AMERICAN HERITAGE PUBLISHING COMPANY,
INC. - LIBRARY □ New York, NY

Buono, Irene, Ser. & ILL Libn.
RAYTHEON COMPANY - RESEARCH DIVISION -
LIBRARY □ Lexington, MA

Burack, Cathy, Dir.
UNIVERSITY OF MISSOURI, ST. LOUIS -
WOMEN'S CENTER □ St. Louis, MO

Burch, Della C., Tech.Libn., Lib.Div.
ARNOLD ENGINEERING DEVELOPMENT CENTER
TECHNICAL LIBRARY □ Arnold Air Force Sta., TN

Burch, James R., Act.Hd.
UNIVERSITY OF CALIFORNIA, BERKELEY -
ENVIRONMENTAL DESIGN LIBRARY □ Berkeley,
CA

Burch, Marybelle, Ms.Libn.
INDIANA STATE LIBRARY - INDIANA DIVISION
□ Indianapolis, IN

Burcham, Margaret, Lib.Asst.
VIRGINIA MUSEUM OF FINE ARTS - LIBRARY □
Richmond, VA

Burcham, S. Anne, Dir.
WAYNE COUNTY HISTORICAL MUSEUM -
LIBRARY □ Richmond, IN

Burchill, Mary D., Pub.Serv.Libn.
UNIVERSITY OF KANSAS - SCHOOL OF LAW
LIBRARY □ Lawrence, KS

Burckel, Nicholas C., Dir.
UNIVERSITY OF WISCONSIN, PARKSIDE -
UNIVERSITY ARCHIVES AND AREA RESEARCH
CENTER □ Kenosha, WI

Burday, Claire H., Corp.Libn.
SUNKIST GROWERS, INC. - CORPORATE
LIBRARY □ Sherman Oaks, CA

Burden, John, Tech.Pubn.Libn.
GRUMMAN AEROSPACE CORPORATION -
TECHNICAL INFORMATION CENTER □
Bethpage, NY

Burden, Rev. Karl N., Exec.Dir.
ALCOHOL AND DRUG CONCERNS, INC. -
AUDIOVISUAL LIBRARY □ Scarborough, ON

Burdett, Ollie Mae, Rec.Mgt.Supv.
PHILLIPS PETROLEUM COMPANY - GAS & GAS
LIQUIDS GROUP - LIBRARY □ Bartlesville, OK

Burdett, Pamela, Asst.Ref.Libn.
STETSON UNIVERSITY - COLLEGE OF LAW -
CHARLES A. DANA LAW LIBRARY □ St.
Petersburg, FL

Burdett, Thomas B., Cur.
UNIVERSITY OF TEXAS, EL PASO - LIBRARY -
S.L.A. MARSHALL MILITARY HISTORY
COLLECTION □ El Paso, TX

Burdette, Eleanor, Ref.Serv.
U.S. NASA - HEADQUARTERS LIBRARY □
Washington, DC

Burdick, Elizabeth B., Dir.
INTERNATIONAL THEATRE INSTITUTE OF THE
UNITED STATES, INC. - INTERNATIONAL
THEATRE COLLECTION □ New York, NY

Burdick, Vanroy, Asst.Libn.
CALIFORNIA COLLEGE OF ARTS AND CRAFTS -
MEYER LIBRARY □ Oakland, CA

Burg, Roxanne, Archv.
ATLANTIC RICHFIELD COMPANY - CORPORATE
ARCHIVES □ Los Angeles, CA

Burge, Joseph M., Hd., Lib.Div.
U.S. NAVY - NAVAL WEAPONS CENTER -
LIBRARY DIVISION □ China Lake, CA

Burgener, Helen M., Libn.
U.S. NATL. PARK SERVICE - ROCKY MOUNTAIN
NATIONAL PARK - LIBRARY □ Estes Park, CO

Burger, Barbara, Archv.
U.S. NATL. ARCHIVES & RECORDS SERVICE -
STILL PICTURE BRANCH □ Washington, DC

Burger, Janice, Libn.
ZACHRY (H.B.) COMPANY - CENTRAL RECORDS
AND LIBRARY □ San Antonio, TX

Burger, Leslie, Plan.Supv.
CONNECTICUT STATE LIBRARY □ Hartford, CT

Burger, Robert H., Slavic Cat.
UNIVERSITY OF ILLINOIS - SLAVIC AND EAST
EUROPEAN LIBRARY □ Urbana, IL

Burgess, A., Libn.
UNIVERSITY OF TORONTO - KNOX COLLEGE -
CAVEN LIBRARY □ Toronto, ON

Burgess, Dr. Larry E., Cur.
LINCOLN MEMORIAL SHRINE - LIBRARY □
Redlands, CA

Burgman, Elmer, Dir.
SOCIETY OF WIRELESS PIONEERS, INC. -
BRENIMAN NAUTICAL-WIRELESS LIBRARY &
MUSEUM OF COMMUNICATIONS □ Santa Rosa,
CA

Burgmann, Walter S., Dir.
U.S. AIR FORCE ENVIRONMENTAL TECHNICAL
APPLICATIONS CENTER - AIR WEATHER
SERVICE TECHNICAL LIBRARY □ Scott AFB, IL

Burgos, Carmen Gloria, Libn.
OFFICE OF BILINGUAL EDUCATION -
RESOURCE LIBRARY AND INFORMATION UNIT
□ Brooklyn, NY

Burgress, Jim, Cur.
U.S. NATL. PARK SERVICE - MANASSAS NATL.
BATTLEFIELD PARK - LIBRARY □ Manassas, VA

Burhans, Barbara C., Biomed.Libn.
U.S. VETERANS ADMINISTRATION (MI-Battle
Creek) - MEDICAL CENTER LIBRARY □ Battle
Creek, MI

Buri, Maura, Per.Libn.
VILLANOVA UNIVERSITY - PULLING LAW
LIBRARY □ Villanova, PA

Burich, Nancy J., Libn.
UNIVERSITY OF KANSAS REGENTS CENTER -
LIBRARY □ Shawnee Mission, KS

Burich, Paula, Comp. Applications
MAYO FOUNDATION - MAYO CLINIC LIBRARY □
Rochester, MN

Burk, William R., Botany Libn.
UNIVERSITY OF NORTH CAROLINA, CHAPEL
HILL - JOHN N. COUCH LIBRARY □ Chapel Hill,
NC

Burkart, Jeff, AV Dir.
CONCORDIA COLLEGE - BUENGER MEMORIAL
LIBRARY □ St. Paul, MN

Burkart, Martha, Curric.Coord.
CONCORDIA COLLEGE - BUENGER MEMORIAL
LIBRARY □ St. Paul, MN

Burke, Dorothy, Spec.Coll.Libn.
MINNEAPOLIS PUBLIC LIBRARY &
INFORMATION CENTER - HISTORY
DEPARTMENT □ Minneapolis, MN

Burke, Rev. Edward T., S.J., Libn.
CALIFORNIA PROVINCE OF THE SOCIETY OF
JESUS - JESUIT CENTER LIBRARY □ Los Gatos,
CA

Burke, Ellen, Circ.Libn.
STATE HISTORICAL SOCIETY OF WISCONSIN -
LIBRARY □ Madison, WI

Burke, Lois, Libn.
BENTON AND BOWLES, INC. - LIBRARY □ New
York, NY

Burke, Margaret, Libn.
UNIVERSITY OF BRITISH COLUMBIA - SCHOOL
OF LIBRARIANSHIP READING ROOM □
Vancouver, BC

Burke, Mary Jo, Chf., HQ Serv.Sect.
U.S. DEPT. OF TRANSPORTATION - LIBRARY
AND DISTRIBUTION SERVICES DIVISION □
Washington, DC

Burke, Vic, Asst.Libn.
MARION COUNTY SCHOOL BOARD - TEACHERS'
PROFESSIONAL LIBRARY □ Ocala, FL

Burke, Vivienne C., Asst.V.P./Mgr.
RAINIER NATIONAL BANK - INFORMATION
CENTER □ Seattle, WA

Burkert, Teresa, Coll.Spec.
DENVER PUBLIC LIBRARY - BUSINESS,
SCIENCE & TECHNOLOGY DIVISION □ Denver,
CO

Burkett, Joan, ILL & Online Searching
UNIVERSITY OF NEVADA, RENO - SAVITT
MEDICAL LIBRARY □ Reno, NV

Burkey, Rev. Blaine, Archv./Hist.
ELLIS COUNTY HISTORICAL SOCIETY -
ARCHIVES □ Hays, KS

Burkhardt, Sue, Cat.
MERCER UNIVERSITY - LAW SCHOOL -
FURMAN SMITH LAW LIBRARY □ Macon, GA

Burkhart, Elizabeth, Coord., LRC
MEDICAL UNIVERSITY OF SOUTH CAROLINA -
LIBRARY □ Charleston, SC

Burkholder, Sue, Cat.Libn.
WASHINGTON UNIVERSITY - SCHOOL OF LAW
- FREUND LAW LIBRARY □ St. Louis, MO

Burleigh, Joan, Libn.
MENDOCINO ART CENTER - ART LIBRARY □
Mendocino, CA

Burlingham, Merry, South Asian Libn.
UNIVERSITY OF TEXAS, AUSTIN - ASIAN
COLLECTION □ Austin, TX

Burlinson, John, Libn.
TEXAS STATE DEPARTMENT OF HEALTH -
LIBRARY □ Austin, TX

Burman, Marilyn, Asst.Libn., Acq.
HAMLINE UNIVERSITY SCHOOL OF LAW -
LIBRARY □ St. Paul, MN

Burn, Barbara L., Libn.
GRAND VIEW COLLEGE - ARCHIVES □ Des
Moines, IA

Burn, Harry T., Libn.
OAK RIDGE ASSOCIATED UNIVERSITIES -
MANPOWER EDUCATION, RESEARCH, AND
TRAINING DIVISION - LIBRARY □ Oak Ridge,
TN

Burna, George, Mgr.
SCOTT PAPER COMPANY - RESEARCH LIBRARY
& TECHNICAL INFORMATION SERVICE □
Philadelphia, PA

Burndorfer, Hans, Hd.
UNIVERSITY OF BRITISH COLUMBIA - MUSIC
LIBRARY □ Vancouver, BC

Burnes, Aileen V., Libn.
GEORGESON & COMPANY - LIBRARY □ New
York, NY

Burnes, Richard, Supv., Tech.Proc.
MASSACHUSETTS INSTITUTE OF TECHNOLOGY
- LINCOLN LABORATORY LIBRARY □ Lexington,
MA

Burnett, Barbara J., Mgr.
MONTGOMERY WARD AND CO. -
INFORMATION SERVICES† □ Chicago, IL

Burnett, Betty, Supv., Main Lib.
UNIVERSITY OF CALIFORNIA - LOS ALAMOS
NATIONAL LABORATORY - LIBRARY □ Los
Alamos, NM

Burnett, Judy K., Libn.
CHAMPAIGN COUNTY LAW LIBRARY □ Urbana,
OH

Burnett, Kathryn E., Assoc.Libn.
SMITH COLLEGE - WERNER JOSTEN LIBRARY
OF THE PERFORMING ARTS □ Northampton, MA

Burnett, M.N., Info.Anl.
CHEVRON RESEARCH COMPANY - TECHNICAL
INFORMATION CENTER □ Richmond, CA

Burnett, Rosa S., Libn.
STATE TECHNICAL INSTITUTE AT MEMPHIS -
GEORGE E. FREEMAN LIBRARY □ Memphis, TN

Burnett, Stephen L., Dir.
GEORGE MASON UNIVERSITY - SCHOOL OF
LAW - LIBRARY □ Arlington, VA

Burnett, Mrs. T.J., Jr., Chm.
HARRIS COUNTY HERITAGE SOCIETY -
LIBRARY □ Houston, TX

Burnett, Rev. Timothy J., O.S.B., Dir. of Lib.
ST. JOSEPH SEMINARY COLLEGE - PERE
ROUQUETTE LIBRARY □ St. Benedict, LA

Burnett, Torrey, Slides & Media
MASSACHUSETTS COLLEGE OF ART - LIBRARY
□ Boston, MA

Burney, Dorothee, Hd.Libn.
GOETHE INSTITUTE BOSTON - LIBRARY □
Boston, MA

Burnham, Betty L., Libn.
BENDIX CORPORATION - ELECTRICAL
COMPONENTS DIVISION - ENGINEERING
LIBRARY □ Sidney, NY

Burnham, Ernest, Pres.
CLINTON HISTORICAL SOCIETY - LIBRARY □
Clinton, CT

Burnham, John P., Hd.Libn.
UNIVERSITY OF MAINE, FARMINGTON -
MANTOR LIBRARY† □ Farmington, ME

Burnham, Judy, Act.Libn.
UNITED STATES SPORTS ACADEMY - LIBRARY
□ Mobile, AL

Burnham, Phyllis, Mss.Cat.
WESTERN MICHIGAN UNIVERSITY - ARCHIVES
AND REGIONAL HISTORY COLLECTIONS □
Kalamazoo, MI

Burnham, Ruth, Asst.Ref.Libn.
UNIVERSITY OF SOUTHERN COLORADO -
LIBRARY - SPECIAL COLLECTIONS □ Pueblo, CO

Burns, Carol A., Dir.
EMORY UNIVERSITY - SCHOOL OF MEDICINE -
A.W. CALHOUN MEDICAL LIBRARY □ Atlanta,
GA

Burns, Carolyn, Supv., Tech.Serv.
WEYERHAEUSER COMPANY - CORPORATE
LIBRARY □ Tacoma, WA

Burns, Mrs. D.J., Libn.
BIRMINGHAM BOTANICAL GARDENS - HORACE
HAMMOND MEMORIAL LIBRARY □ Birmingham,
AL

Burns, Dean A., Chf.
U.S. ARMY - INTELLIGENCE AND THREAT
ANALYSIS CENTER - TECHNICAL
INFORMATION CENTER □ Arlington, VA

Burns, Dorothy, Ser.Libn.
LOYOLA UNIVERSITY OF CHICAGO - MEDICAL
CENTER LIBRARY □ Maywood, IL

Burns, Elaine, Libn.
SAN GORGONIO PASS MEMORIAL HOSPITAL -
MEDICAL LIBRARY □ Banning, CA

Burns, Elizabeth, Hd.Libn.
COLORADO SPRINGS GAZETTE TELEGRAPH -
LIBRARY □ Colorado Springs, CO

Burns, Ellen J., Music Libn.
RICE UNIVERSITY - MUSIC LIBRARY □ Houston,
TX

Burns, Frances C., Dir., Lib. & Info.Serv.
COUNCIL FOR FINANCIAL AID TO EDUCATION
- FOUNDERS ROOM LIBRARY □ New York, NY

Burns, Germaine, Supv.
NEW BRUNSWICK - DEPARTMENT OF
EDUCATION - LIBRARY □ Fredericton, NB

Burns, Janice, Res.Libn.
WESTRECO, INC. - FOOD RESEARCH AND
DEVELOPMENT - LIBRARY □ Fulton, NY

Burns, Dr. Jeffrey M., Archv.
ARCHDIOCESE OF SAN FRANCISCO -
CHANCERY ARCHIVES □ Colma, CA

Burns, Jerry, Hist.Libn.
CREDIT UNION NATIONAL ASSOCIATION - INFORMATION RESOURCE CENTER □ Madison, WI

Burns, Jimmy, Libn.
IOWA STATE COMMISSION FOR THE BLIND - LIBRARY FOR THE BLIND & PHYSICALLY HANDICAPPED □ Des Moines, IA

Burns, John A., Libn.
CRISWELL CENTER FOR BIBLICAL STUDIES - LIBRARY† □ Dallas, TX

Burns, John F., Chf. of Archv.
CALIFORNIA - STATE ARCHIVES □ Sacramento, CA

Burns, John T., Exec.Dir.
FOUNDATION FOR THE STUDY OF CYCLES INC. - LIBRARY □ Pittsburgh, PA

Burns, Leo D., Mgr.
IBM CORPORATION - INFORMATION PRODUCTS DIVISION - TECHNICAL LIBRARY/IC □ Lexington, KY

Burns, Lorayne R., Libn.
IBM CORPORATION - INFORMATION PRODUCTS DIVISION - TECHNICAL LIBRARY/IC □ Lexington, KY

Burns, Lynn, Cat.
PHILADELPHIA COLLEGE OF TEXTILES AND SCIENCE - PASTORE LIBRARY □ Philadelphia, PA

Burns, Marie T., Libn./Rec.Mgr.
UNITED CHARITIES OF CHICAGO - LIBRARY □ Chicago, IL

Burns, Mary Ada, Sr.Asst.Libn.
SAN DIEGO STATE UNIVERSITY - MEDIA & CURRICULUM CENTER† □ San Diego, CA

Burns, Mary C., Corp. Files Mgr.
STANDARD & POOR'S CORPORATION - RESEARCH LIBRARY □ New York, NY

Burns, Norma, Asst. to Dir.
CANADA - NATIONAL RESEARCH COUNCIL - CANADA INSTITUTE FOR SCIENTIFIC AND TECHNICAL INFORMATION (CISTI) □ Ottawa, ON

Burns, Ruth S., Mgr., Lib.Serv.
FRANKLIN MINT - INFORMATION RESEARCH SERVICES □ Franklin Center, PA

Burns, Violanda O., Info.Anl.
MOBIL CHEMICAL COMPANY - PLASTICS DIVISION - INFORMATION CENTER □ Macedon, NY

Burnside, Mary, Acq.
U.S. AIR FORCE BASE - TINKER BASE LIBRARY □ Tinker AFB, OK

Burr, Irene, Asst.Libn.
DURHAM HERALD-SUN NEWSPAPER - LIBRARY □ Durham, NC

Burr, Irma, Libn. Volunteer Coord.
OKLAHOMA REGIONAL LIBRARY FOR THE BLIND AND PHYSICALLY HANDICAPPED □ Oklahoma City, OK

Burr, Robert L., Dir.
GONZAGA UNIVERSITY - CROSBY LIBRARY □ Spokane, WA

Burr, Dr. Samuel Engle, Jr., Act.Libn.
BURR (Aaron) ASSOCIATION - LIBRARY □ Hightstown, NJ

Burrell, Jon C., Exec.Dir.
MARYLAND MUNICIPAL LEAGUE - LIBRARY □ Annapolis, MD

Burrell, Lois, Chf.
NATIONAL LIBRARY OF CANADA - NEWSPAPER DIVISION □ Ottawa, ON

Burrell, Luchy S., Supv.
MEMPHIS STATE UNIVERSITY - GRADUATE DEPT. OF PLANNING & REGIONAL ECONOMIC DEVELOPMENT CTR. - PLANNING LIBRARY □ Memphis, TN

Burris, Brenda S., Law Libn.
HERCULES, INC. - LAW DEPARTMENT LIBRARY† □ Wilmington, DE

Burroughs, Carol F., Hd., Pub.Serv.
GONZAGA UNIVERSITY - CROSBY LIBRARY □ Spokane, WA

Burroughs, Charles, Cur.
DU SABLE MUSEUM OF AFRICAN AMERICAN HISTORY - LIBRARY □ Chicago, IL

Burroughs, Dr. Margaret, Dir.
DU SABLE MUSEUM OF AFRICAN AMERICAN HISTORY - LIBRARY □ Chicago, IL

Burroughs, Martha, Ref.Libn.
DENVER MEDICAL LIBRARY □ Denver, CO

Burroughs, Richard, Libn.
JOHNSON (Donald) ARCHIVE □ Encino, CA

Burrows, Ann Lewis, Exec.Dir.
MARY BALL WASHINGTON MUSEUM AND LIBRARY, INC. □ Lancaster, VA

Burrows, Suzetta C., Assoc.Dir./Media Prog.
UNIVERSITY OF MIAMI - SCHOOL OF MEDICINE - LOUIS CALDER MEMORIAL LIBRARY □ Miami, FL

Burry, Lynne, Res.-Cat.
ART GALLERY OF ONTARIO - EDWARD P. TAYLOR AUDIO-VISUAL CENTRE □ Toronto, ON

Bursik, Carol J., Chf.
U.S. ARMY - NATICK RESEARCH AND DEVELOPMENT CENTER - TECHNICAL LIBRARY □ Natick, MA

Burstein, Lee, Chf.Acq.Libn.
COOK COUNTY LAW LIBRARY □ Chicago, IL

Burston, Madeline H., Pub. Health Adm.
NASSAU COUNTY DEPARTMENT OF HEALTH - DIVISION OF LABORATORIES & RESEARCH - MEDICAL LIBRARY □ Hempstead, NY

Burt, DeVere, Musm.Dir.
CINCINNATI MUSEUM OF NATURAL HISTORY - LIBRARY □ Cincinnati, OH

Burt, Eleanor J., Libn.
TENNESSEE STATE PLANNING OFFICE - LIBRARY □ Nashville, TN

Burt, Jennifer, Lib.Techn.
U.S. VETERANS ADMINISTRATION (AL-Birmingham) - HOSPITAL MEDICAL LIBRARY □ Birmingham, AL

Burt, Karen, Circ.Libn.
CLEVELAND HEALTH SCIENCES LIBRARY - HEALTH CENTER LIBRARY □ Cleveland, OH

Burt, Sandra, Libn.
CANADA - CANADIAN FORESTRY SERVICE - GREAT LAKES FOREST RESEARCH CENTRE - LIBRARY □ Sault Ste. Marie, ON

Burtnett, I.K., Hd.Libn.
U.S. NAVY - NAVAL AIR STATION - TECHNICAL LIBRARY† □ Point Mugu, CA

Burton, Claudia, Rd.Adv.
ALABAMA REGIONAL LIBRARY FOR THE BLIND AND PHYSICALLY HANDICAPPED □ Montgomery, AL

Burton, Elisabeth, Libn.
NOLAND (Lloyd) HOSPITAL - DAVID KNOX MC KAMY MEDICAL LIBRARY □ Fairfield, AL

Burton, Mrs. F.H., Mgr.
CHURCH OF ENGLAND INSTITUTE - LIBRARY □ Saint John, NB

Burton, Lois, Libn.
INDIANA ACADEMY OF SCIENCE - JOHN SHEPARD WRIGHT MEMORIAL LIBRARY □ Indianapolis, IN

Burton, R. Paul, Cur.
UNIVERSITY OF SOUTHERN CALIFORNIA - LAW LIBRARY □ Los Angeles, CA

Burtschi, Josephine, Archv./Act.Libn.
VANDALIA HISTORICAL SOCIETY - JAMES HALL LIBRARY □ Vandalia, IL

Burtschi, Mary, Dir.
VANDALIA HISTORICAL SOCIETY - JAMES HALL LIBRARY □ Vandalia, IL

Burwell, Marilyn, Libn.
BROWN & CALDWELL - SEATTLE BRANCH OFFICE LIBRARY □ Seattle, WA

Bury, Mary Ann, Supv., Lib.Serv.
CELANESE CORPORATION - SUMMIT RESEARCH LABORATORIES - TECHNICAL INFORMATION CENTER □ Summit, NJ

Burylo, Michelle A., Bus.Libn.
AIR PRODUCTS AND CHEMICALS, INC. - BUSINESS LIBRARY □ Allentown, PA

Busby, Lorraine, Tech.Libn.
3M CANADA - TECHNICAL INFORMATION CENTRE □ London, ON

Busch, Anita, Libn.
CHISHOLM TRAIL MUSEUM - ARCHIVES AND LIBRARY □ Wellington, KS

Busch, B.J., Area Coord.
UNIVERSITY OF ALBERTA - HUMANITIES AND SOCIAL SCIENCES LIBRARY □ Edmonton, AB

Busch, Betty, Libn.
DAYTON LAW LIBRARY ASSOCIATION† □ Dayton, OH

Busch, John R.
UNIVERSITY OF IDAHO - IDAHO WATER RESOURCES RESEARCH INSTITUTE - TECHNICAL INFO. CENTER & READING ROOM □ Moscow, ID

Busch, Kate, Dir., Member Serv.
ALLIANCE OF RESIDENT THEATRES/NEW YORK - LIBRARY □ New York, NY

Busenbark, Beverly V., Mgr., Lib.Serv.
BELL & HOWELL COMPANY - DATATAPE DIVISION - LIBRARY/TECHNICAL INFORMATION SERVICES† □ Pasadena, CA

Busey, Madge J., Lib.Dir.
U.S. ARMY ENGINEER SCHOOL - LIBRARY □ Ft. Belvoir, VA

Busey, Madge J., Dir.
U.S. ARMY POST - FORT BELVOIR - VAN NOY LIBRARY □ Ft. Belvoir, VA

Bush, Alfred L., Cur., W. Americana
PRINCETON UNIVERSITY - RARE BOOKS AND SPECIAL COLLECTIONS □ Princeton, NJ

Bush, Carmel, Hd., Cat.
UNIVERSITY OF TEXAS HEALTH SCIENCE CENTER, DALLAS - LIBRARY □ Dallas, TX

Bush, Donna E., Dir., Lib.Serv.
FOREST INSTITUTE OF PROFESSIONAL PSYCHOLOGY - LIBRARY □ Des Plaines, IL

Bush, Eileen R., Libn.
CAPE COD MUSEUM OF NATURAL HISTORY - LIBRARY AND INFORMATION CENTER □ Brewster, MA

Bush, Geneva, Sr.Hosp.Libn.
UNIVERSITY OF SOUTH ALABAMA - COLLEGE OF MEDICINE - BIOMEDICAL LIBRARY □ Mobile, AL

Bush, Janet E.N., Med.Rec.Adm.
CHILDREN'S HOSPITAL, INC. - MEDICAL LIBRARY □ Baltimore, MD

Bush, Lena M., Media Lib.Dir.
NORTH CENTRAL BAPTIST CHURCH - MEDIA LIBRARY □ Gainesville, FL

Bush, Mary E., Libn.
BROUGHTON HOSPITAL - MEDICAL LIBRARY† □ Morganton, NC

Bush, Phyllis, Asst.Libn.
VETERANS HOME OF CALIFORNIA - LINCOLN MEMORIAL LIBRARY □ Yountville, CA

Bush, R.A., Ref.Spec.
BATTELLE-NORTHWEST - PACIFIC NORTHWEST LABORATORY - HANFORD TECHNICAL LIBRARY □ Richland, WA

Bush, Robert D., Dir.
WYOMING STATE ARCHIVES MUSEUMS & HISTORICAL DEPARTMENT □ Cheyenne, WY

Bushart, Kathy M., Lib.Asst.
EASTMAN KODAK COMPANY - PHOTOGRAPHIC TECHNOLOGY DIVISION - LIBRARY □ Rochester, NY

Bushey, Mary E., Libn.
U.S. AIR FORCE BASE - LORING BASE LIBRARY □ Loring AFB, ME

Bushman, Ted, Libn.
BUSHMAN (Ted) LAW OFFICES - LIBRARY □ Santa Maria, CA

Bushnell, Dr. Amy Turner, Hist.
HISTORIC ST. AUGUSTINE PRESERVATION BOARD - HISPANIC RESEARCH LIBRARY □ St. Augustine, FL

Bushnell, Marietta P., Libn.
PENNSYLVANIA ACADEMY OF THE FINE ARTS - LIBRARY □ Philadelphia, PA

Buske, A.G.
DOW CHEMICAL COMPANY - TECHNICAL
INFORMATION SERVICES - CHEMICAL
LIBRARY □ Midland, MI

Busler, C., Dir., Res.
INTERNATIONAL FABRICARE INSTITUTE -
RESEARCH CENTER LIBRARY □ Silver Spring,
MD

Bussey, Holly J., Mgr. of AIC
AYER (NW) INCORPORATED - AYER
INFORMATION CENTER (AIC) □ New York, NY

Bussey, Margaret, Med.Libn./Dir., Med.Rec.
HIGHLAND HOSPITAL, INC. - MEDICAL
LIBRARY □ Lubbock, TX

Bustamante-Barron, Cecelia, Libn.
CONAC - LIBRARY □ Washington, DC

Bustillos, Vicki, Lib.Asst.
PACIFIC LIGHTING CORPORATION - LAW
LIBRARY □ Los Angeles, CA

Buswell, Christa, Chf., Lib.Serv.
U.S. VETERANS ADMINISTRATION (CA-Los
Angeles) - WADSWORTH MEDICAL LIBRARY
691W/142D □ Los Angeles, CA

Butcher, Nevine, Mgr.
BENHAM GROUP - INFORMATION RESOURCE
CENTER □ Oklahoma City, OK

Butcher, Theresa M., Lib.Mgr.
MACLEAN HUNTER/FINANCIAL POST -
LIBRARY □ Toronto, ON

Buth, Olga, Music
UNIVERSITY OF TEXAS, AUSTIN - FINE ARTS
LIBRARY □ Austin, TX

Buthod, J. Craig, Dept.Hd.
TULSA CITY-COUNTY LIBRARY SYSTEM -
BUSINESS AND TECHNOLOGY DEPARTMENT □
Tulsa, OK

Butisbauch, Vera, Law Libn.
NEVADA COUNTY LAW LIBRARY □ Nevada City,
CA

Butkovic, Margaret, AV Lib.Techn.
CANADIAN MEMORIAL CHIROPRACTIC
COLLEGE - C.C. CLEMMER LIBRARY □ Toronto,
ON

Butkovich, Margaret, Assoc.Dir.
UNIVERSITY OF COLORADO HEALTH SCIENCES
CENTER - DENISON MEMORIAL LIBRARY† □
Denver, CO

Butler, Adios, Libn.
ALAN WOFSY FINE ARTS - REFERENCE
LIBRARY □ San Francisco, CA

Butler, Anne H., Libn.
ALSTON & BIRD - LIBRARY □ Atlanta, GA

Butler, Anthony M., Lib.Dir.
BRIDGETON FREE PUBLIC LIBRARY - SPECIAL
COLLECTIONS □ Bridgeton, NJ

Butler, Barbara S., Libn.
SAN LUIS OBISPO COUNTY LAW LIBRARY □ San
Luis Obispo, CA

Butler, Mr. Beverley, Hd.Libn.
HUNTON & WILLIAMS - LAW LIBRARY† □
Richmond, VA

Butler, Cynthia, Hd., Pub.Serv.
UNIVERSITY OF CALIFORNIA, IRVINE -
BIOMEDICAL LIBRARY □ Irvine, CA

Butler, Dean, Sr.Libn.
IBM CORPORATION - BOULDER LIBRARY □
Boulder, CO

Butler, Eva K., Libn.
SCOTT PAPER COMPANY - MARKETING
LIBRARY □ Philadelphia, PA

Butler, Evelyn, Libn.
UNIVERSITY OF PENNSYLVANIA - SCHOOL OF
SOCIAL WORK - SMALLEY LIBRARY OF SOCIAL
WORK† □ Philadelphia, PA

Butler, Geoffrey J., Law Libn.
UTAH STATE LAW LIBRARY □ Salt Lake City, UT

Butler, Sr. Gertrude, Asst.Libn.
MERCY HOSPITAL - SCHOOL OF NURSING
LIBRARY □ Pittsburgh, PA

Butler, Janice, Hd., Coll.Dev.
UNIVERSITY OF COLORADO HEALTH SCIENCES
CENTER - DENISON MEMORIAL LIBRARY† □
Denver, CO

Butler, Kathy, Inst.Libn.
WASHINGTON STATE LIBRARY - LAKELAND
VILLAGE BRANCH LIBRARY □ Medical Lake, WA

Butler, Margaret, Law Libn.
NEW YORK LIFE INSURANCE COMPANY - LAW
LIBRARY □ New York, NY

Butler, Margaret K., Dir.
ARGONNE NATIONAL LABORATORY -
NATIONAL ENERGY SOFTWARE CENTER □
Argonne, IL

Butler, Marguerite, Acq./Ref.Libn.
TEXAS SOUTHERN UNIVERSITY - LAW
LIBRARY† □ Houston, TX

Butler, Martha, Tech.Asst.
CHICAGO THEOLOGICAL SEMINARY -
HAMMOND LIBRARY □ Chicago, IL

Butler, Mary Ann, Lib.Coord.
PERRY MEMORIAL HOSPITAL - DR. KENNETH O.
NELSON LIBRARY OF THE HEALTH SCIENCES □
Princeton, IL

Butler, Patricia, Assoc.Libn.
CANADA - NATIONAL FILM BOARD OF CANADA
- REFERENCE LIBRARY □ Montreal, PQ

Butler, Richard M., Dir., Medical Rec.
RIVERSIDE GENERAL HOSPITAL - MEDICAL
LIBRARY □ Riverside, CA

Butler, Ruth G., Libn.
HOUGHTON COLLEGE - BUFFALO SUBURBAN
CAMPUS - ADA M. KIDDER MEMORIAL LIBRARY
□ West Seneca, NY

Butler, Sharon K., Sr.Libn., User Serv.
BETH ISRAEL MEDICAL CTR. - HOSPITAL FOR
JOINT DISEASES ORTHOPAEDIC INST. -
SEYMOUR J. PHILLIPS HEALTH SCI.LIB. □ New
York, NY

Butrymowicz, Daniel B., Dir.
U.S. NATL. BUREAU OF STANDARDS -
METALLURGY DIVISION - DIFFUSION IN
METALS DATA CENTER □ Washington, DC

Butske, Carol L., Libn.
NORTHVILLE HISTORICAL SOCIETY - LIBRARY
□ Northville, MI

Butson, Linda, Asst.Dir.
MOUNTAIN AREA HEALTH EDUCATION CENTER
- INFORMATION & MEDIA SERVICES □
Asheville, NC

Buttars, Gerald, Dir.
UTAH STATE LIBRARY - BLIND AND
PHYSICALLY HANDICAPPED PROGRAM -
REGIONAL LIBRARY □ Salt Lake City, UT

Butter, Karen, Pub.Serv.
UNIVERSITY OF UTAH - SPENCER S. ECCLES
HEALTH SCIENCES LIBRARY □ Salt Lake City,
UT

Butterfield, Cliff C., Supv., Tech.Data/Rpt.Serv
LOCKHEED-CALIFORNIA COMPANY -
TECHNICAL INFORMATION CENTER □ Burbank,
CA

Butterill, Mary, Hd., Tech.Serv.
CANADA - REVENUE CANADA - TAXATION
LIBRARY □ Ottawa, ON

Buttermore, Gregg, Archv.
AUBURN-CORD-DUESENBERG MUSEUM - TRI-
KAPPA COLLECTION OF AUBURN AUTOMOTIVE
LITERATURE □ Auburn, IN

Butterworth, Donald A., Asst.Dir.
ASBURY THEOLOGICAL SEMINARY - B.L.
FISHER LIBRARY □ Wilmore, KY

Button, Carol J.
UNIVERSITY OF ALASKA - WILDLIFE LIBRARY
□ Fairbanks, AK

Button, Katherine, MEDLINE Anl.
MASSACHUSETTS GENERAL HOSPITAL - MGH
HEALTH SCIENCES LIBRARIES □ Boston, MA

Butz, Helen S., Rare Bk.Libn.
UNIVERSITY OF MICHIGAN - DEPARTMENT OF
RARE BOOKS AND SPECIAL COLLECTIONS -
LIBRARY □ Ann Arbor, MI

Buus, David B., Libn.
BURR-BROWN RESEARCH CORPORATION -
LIBRARY □ Tucson, AZ

Buyukmihci, Hope Sawyer, Sec.
UNEXPECTED WILDLIFE REFUGE - LIBRARY □
Newfield, NJ

Buzzanga, Joseph, Libn.
LONG ISLAND UNIVERSITY - C.W. POST
CAMPUS - CENTER FOR BUSINESS RESEARCH □
Greenvale, NY

Bycio, Janet, Libn.
CANADA SYSTEMS GROUP - REFERENCE
LIBRARY □ Mississauga, ON

Bye, John E., Archv.
NORTH DAKOTA STATE UNIVERSITY -
INSTITUTE FOR REGIONAL STUDIES □ Fargo,
ND

Byerly, Eleanor, Ref./Bibliog.Instr.Libn.
PONTIFICAL COLLEGE JOSEPHINUM - A.T.
WEHRLE MEMORIAL LIBRARY □ Columbus, OH

Byerly, Jill, AHEC Libn./Coord.
NORTHWEST AREA HEALTH EDUCATION
CENTER - NW AHEC LIBRARY □ Boone, NC

Byers, Bertina, Chf., Doc.Ctr.
U.S. ARMY COMMAND AND GENERAL STAFF
COLLEGE - COMBINED ARMS RESEARCH
LIBRARY □ Ft. Leavenworth, KS

Byers, Deborah T., Libn.
OHIO STATE ATTORNEY GENERAL'S OFFICE -
LAW LIBRARY □ Columbus, OH

Byers, Dorothy F., Hd.
UNIVERSITY OF CINCINNATI - ENGINEERING
LIBRARY □ Cincinnati, OH

Byers, Jane, Res.Libn.
PEAT, MARWICK, MITCHELL & CO. -
INFORMATION SERVICES □ Dallas, TX

Byers, Laura, Libn.
HARVARD UNIVERSITY - DUMBARTON OAKS
GARDEN LIBRARY OF THE CENTER FOR
STUDIES IN LANDSCAPE ARCHITECTURE □
Washington, DC

Byers, Montez, Rd.Serv.Libn.
BENNETT COLLEGE - THOMAS F. HOLGATE
LIBRARY - SPECIAL COLLECTIONS □
Greensboro, NC

Byers, Rosemarie, Lib.Dir.
CITY OF MIDLAND - GRACE A. DOW MEMORIAL
LIBRARY - SPECIAL COLLECTIONS □ Midland,
MI

Byng, Lala, Libn.
COMO ZOO - LIBRARY □ St. Paul, MN

Bynon, George E., Dir.
UNIVERSITY OF OREGON - INSTRUCTIONAL
MEDIA CENTER □ Eugene, OR

Byock, Gayle, Assoc.Dir.
ERIC CLEARINGHOUSE FOR JUNIOR COLLEGES
□ Los Angeles, CA

Byrd, Betty, Libn.
ST. JOSEPH HOSPITAL - INFORMATION
SERVICES □ Alton, IL

Byrd, Caroline, Hd., Pub.Serv.
ST. MARY'S UNIVERSITY - LAW LIBRARY† □
San Antonio, TX

Byrd, Dr. Cecil K., Cons.
INDIANA UNIVERSITY - LILLY LIBRARY □
Bloomington, IN

Byrd, Gary, Assoc.Dir.
UNIVERSITY OF NORTH CAROLINA, CHAPEL
HILL - HEALTH SCIENCES LIBRARY □ Chapel
Hill, NC

Byrd, Harvey C., III, Prog.Dir.
U.S. DEPT. OF JUSTICE - NATIONAL
INSTITUTE OF JUSTICE - NATL. CRIMINAL
JUSTICE REF. SERVICE □ Rockville, MD

Byrd, Jonda, ILL Libn.
ENVIRONMENTAL PROTECTION AGENCY -
ANDREW W. BREIDENBACH ENVIRONMENTAL
RESEARCH CTR., CINCINNATI - TECH.LIB. □
Cincinnati, OH

Byrd, Nancy, Govt.Doc.Spec.
AUSTIN PUBLIC LIBRARY - AUSTIN HISTORY
CENTER □ Austin, TX

Byrd, Robert L., Mss.Libn.
DUKE UNIVERSITY - MANUSCRIPT
DEPARTMENT □ Durham, NC

Byrn, Sandra, Chf., Tech.Serv.Br.
U.S. ARMED FORCES STAFF COLLEGE - LIBRARY □ Norfolk, VA
Byrne, Fr. Basil, Libn.
ST. JOSEPH'S ABBEY - LIBRARY □ Spencer, MA
Byrne, Christine C., Hd.
ATOMIC ENERGY OF CANADA, LTD. - CANDU OPERATIONS LIBRARY □ Mississauga, ON
Byrne, Elizabeth D., Hd.
UNIVERSITY OF CINCINNATI - DESIGN, ARCHITECTURE, ART & PLANNING LIBRARY □ Cincinnati, OH
Byrne, Frank P., Jr., Chf.Libn.
U.S. MARINE CORPS - MARINE BAND LIBRARY □ Washington, DC
Byrne, Frederick, Libn.
COLUMBIA UNIVERSITY - BURGESS-CARPENTER LIBRARY □ New York, NY
Byrne, Frederick, Libn.
COLUMBIA UNIVERSITY - COLUMBIA COLLEGE LIBRARY □ New York, NY
Byrne, Frederick, Libn.
COLUMBIA UNIVERSITY - PHILOSOPHY LIBRARY □ New York, NY
Byrne, Jeraldine, Acq.Libn.
WEST COAST UNIVERSITY - ELCONIN CENTER LIBRARY □ Los Angeles, CA
Byrne, Kathleen, Med.Libn.
GAYLORD HOSPITAL - MEDICAL LIBRARY □ Wallingford, CT
Byrne, Margaret A., Libn.
U.S. AIR FORCE BASE - OFFUTT BASE LIBRARY† □ Offutt AFB, NE
Byrne, Nadene, Dir.
ART INSTITUTE OF CHICAGO - SCHOOL OF THE ART INSTITUTE OF CHICAGO - LIBRARY □ Chicago, IL
Byrnes, Jeanne, Ref.Libn.
OHIO STATE UNIVERSITY - HEALTH SCIENCES LIBRARY □ Columbus, OH
Byrnes, Martha, Asst.Libn.
UNIVERSITY OF UTAH - LAW LIBRARY □ Salt Lake City, UT
Byrnes, Stephanie C., Libn.
AMERICAN INSTITUTE OF ARCHITECTS - LIBRARY □ Washington, DC
Byrum, Lois, Sr.Libn.
MINNESOTA STATE DEPARTMENT OF EDUCATION - INTERAGENCY RESOURCE AND INFORMATION CENTER □ St. Paul, MN
Bystram, Mrs. A.M., Dir., Lib.Serv.Br.
CANADA - ENVIRONMENT CANADA - LIBRARY SERVICES BRANCH □ Ottawa, ON
Bystrom, Marcia M., Ref.Libn.
TENNESSEE VALLEY AUTHORITY - TECHNICAL LIBRARY □ Muscle Shoals, AL
Byun, Il, Libn.
ADLER PLANETARIUM - LIBRARY □ Chicago, IL

C

Caballero, Cesar, Hd.Spec.Coll.Dept.
UNIVERSITY OF TEXAS, EL PASO - LIBRARY - SPECIAL COLLECTIONS □ El Paso, TX
Caballero, Isabel S., Hist. of Med.Libn.
UNIVERSITY OF MIAMI - SCHOOL OF MEDICINE - LOUIS CALDER MEMORIAL LIBRARY □ Miami, FL
Cabeen, Jeannette, Rare Bk.Cat.
JOHNS HOPKINS UNIVERSITY - MILTON S. EISENHOWER LIBRARY - SPECIAL COLLECTIONS DIVISION □ Baltimore, MD
Cabeen, S.K., Dir.
ENGINEERING SOCIETIES LIBRARY □ New York, NY
Cable, Carole, Fine Arts Libn.
UNIVERSITY OF TEXAS, AUSTIN - FINE ARTS LIBRARY □ Austin, TX
Cable, Leslie, Ref.Libn.
OREGON HEALTH SCIENCES UNIVERSITY - LIBRARY □ Portland, OR

Cabrita, Paul M., Hd.Libn.
MARIST COLLEGE - LIBRARY □ Washington, DC
Caccamo, James F., Archv.
HUDSON LIBRARY AND HISTORICAL SOCIETY □ Hudson, OH
Cadam, Ronnie, Libn.
STONE, MARRACCINI & PATTERSON - RESEARCH & DEVELOPMENT LIBRARY □ San Francisco, CA
Cadet, Janine, Libn.
UNIVERSITE DE MONTREAL - PHYSIQUE-BIBLIOTHEQUE □ Montreal, PQ
Cadieux, J., Hd., Tech.Serv.
CANADA - TRANSPORT CANADA - LIBRARY & INFORMATION CENTRE □ Ottawa, ON
Cadieux, Louise, Chf.Libn.
CENTRE HOSPITALIER HOTEL-DIEU DE SHERBROOKE - BIBLIOTHEQUE □ Sherbrooke, PQ
Cady, Jean L., Base Libn.
U.S. AIR FORCE BASE - MYRTLE BEACH BASE LIBRARY □ Myrtle Beach AFB, SC
Caffey, David, Dir.
HARWOOD FOUNDATION LIBRARY OF THE UNIVERSITY OF NEW MEXICO □ Taos, NM
Caffrey, Margaret M., Libn.
ALLENTOWN STATE HOSPITAL - HEIM MEMORIAL LIBRARY □ Allentown, PA
Cagle, William R., Libn.
INDIANA UNIVERSITY - LILLY LIBRARY □ Bloomington, IN
Cahalan, Sally Smith, Dir.
JAMES BUCHANAN FOUNDATION FOR THE PRESERVATION OF WHEATLAND - LIBRARY □ Lancaster, PA
Cahall, Marcia, Libn.
PROCTER & GAMBLE COMPANY - LIBRARY □ Cincinnati, OH
Cahall, Michael, Dir.
CHAMPAIGN COUNTY HISTORICAL MUSEUM - LIBRARY □ Champaign, IL
Cahill, Colleen, Ref.Libn.
INDIANA HISTORICAL SOCIETY - WILLIAM HENRY SMITH MEMORIAL LIBRARY □ Indianapolis, IN
Cahill, George F., Pres.
NATIONAL FLAG FOUNDATION - FLAG PLAZA LIBRARY □ Pittsburgh, PA
Cahill, Jacqueline S., Med.Libn.
U.S. VETERANS ADMINISTRATION (VA-Salem) - MEDICAL CENTER LIBRARY □ Salem, VA
Cahill, Ms. L., Libn.
NESBITT THOMSON BONGARD INC. - RESEARCH LIBRARY □ Montreal, PQ
Cahill, Linda Justus, Mgr.
INSTITUTE OF TEXTILE TECHNOLOGY - TEXTILE INFORMATION SERVICES - ROGER MILLIKEN TEXTILE LIBRARY □ Charlottesville, VA
Cahill, Rosemary, Ed.
GAY ALLIANCE OF GENESEE VALLEY INC. - LIBRARY □ Rochester, NY
Cahoon, Herbert, Cur., Autog.Mss.
PIERPONT MORGAN LIBRARY □ New York, NY
Cahow, Adam, Cur., Geographic Mtls.
UNIVERSITY OF WISCONSIN, EAU CLAIRE - SIMPSON GEOGRAPHIC RESEARCH CENTER - MAP LIBRARY □ Eau Claire, WI
Caiazzo, Ralph
NEW YORK LAW INSTITUTE - LIBRARY □ New York, NY
Caiger, Anne, Univ.Archv.
UNIVERSITY OF CALIFORNIA, LOS ANGELES - DEPARTMENT OF SPECIAL COLLECTIONS □ Los Angeles, CA
Cail, Nada, Cat.
VILLANOVA UNIVERSITY - PULLING LAW LIBRARY □ Villanova, PA
Cain, Anne, Prin.Libn./Ref.Serv.
PASADENA PUBLIC LIBRARY - ALICE COLEMAN BATCHELDER MUSIC LIBRARY □ Pasadena, CA

Cain, Anne, Prin.Libn./Ref.Serv.
PASADENA PUBLIC LIBRARY - BUSINESS-TECHNOLOGY DIVISION □ Pasadena, CA
Cain, Anne, Prin.Libn./Ref.Serv.
PASADENA PUBLIC LIBRARY - FINE ARTS DIVISION □ Pasadena, CA
Cain, Anne, Prin.Libn./Ref.Serv.
PASADENA PUBLIC LIBRARY - REFERENCE DIVISION □ Pasadena, CA
Cain, Anthony, Asst. Mgr., Ref.Serv.
U.S. DEPT. OF JUSTICE - NATIONAL INSTITUTE OF JUSTICE - NATL. CRIMINAL JUSTICE REF. SERVICE □ Rockville, MD
Cain, Charlene C., Archv.
LOUISIANA STATE OFFICE OF THE SECRETARY OF STATE - STATE ARCHIVES AND RECORDS SERVICE - ARCHIVES SECTION □ Baton Rouge, LA
Cain, Irene, Ref.Libn.
AT & T TECHNOLOGIES, INC. - LIBRARY □ Indianapolis, IN
Cain, Katherine, Book Selector/Archv.
BOSTON UNIVERSITY - DEPARTMENT OF SPECIAL COLLECTIONS □ Boston, MA
Cain, Melissa, Libn.
UNIVERSITY OF ILLINOIS - ENGLISH LIBRARY □ Urbana, IL
Cain, Myrna, Info.Spec.
CANADIAN TOBACCO MANUFACTURERS COUNCIL - INFORMATION CENTER □ Montreal, PQ
Cain, Robert, Docs.Libn.
UNIVERSITY OF SOUTHERN COLORADO - LIBRARY - SPECIAL COLLECTIONS □ Pueblo, CO
Cain, Ronald L., Hd., AV Serv.
WITTENBERG UNIVERSITY - THOMAS LIBRARY □ Springfield, OH
Cain, Virginia J.H., Proc.Archv.
EMORY UNIVERSITY - SPECIAL COLLECTIONS DEPARTMENT □ Atlanta, GA
Caine, Irene J., Corp.Libn.
HANSON MATERIALS ENGINEERING (Western) LTD. - CORPORATE LIBRARY □ Edmonton, AB
Cairns, Irene, Libn.
BECHTEL CANADA LIMITED - ENGINEERING CONSULTANTS - LIBRARY □ Toronto, ON
Cairns, Phyllis, Lib.Dir.
BRAILLE INSTITUTE OF AMERICA - LIBRARY □ Los Angeles, CA
Cakste, Anastasija, Libn., Res.Ref.
NORTHEASTERN UNIVERSITY - DANA RESEARCH CENTER - PHYSICS ELECTRICAL ENGINEERING LIBRARY† □ Boston, MA
Calabretta, Nancy, Ref.Libn.
JEFFERSON (Thomas) UNIVERSITY - SCOTT MEMORIAL LIBRARY □ Philadelphia, PA
Calcese, Sarah L., Libn.
UNIVERSITY OF WISCONSIN, MADISON - WATER RESOURCES CENTER - LIBRARY □ Madison, WI
Caldeira, Prof. Greg, Dir.
UNIVERSITY OF IOWA - LABORATORY FOR POLITICAL RESEARCH □ Iowa City, IA
Calder, Ann, Asst.Libn.
VICTORIA CONSERVATORY OF MUSIC - LIBRARY □ Victoria, BC
Caldwell, Alva
GARRETT-EVANGELICAL AND SEABURY-WESTERN THEOLOGICAL SEMINARIES - UNITED LIBRARY □ Evanston, IL
Caldwell, Audrey W., Asst.Libn.
DUKE POWER COMPANY - PRODUCTION DEPARTMENTS - INFORMATION RESOURCE CENTER (IRC) □ Cornelius, NC
Caldwell, Evelyn B., Libn.
AMERICAN ENTERPRISE INSTITUTE FOR PUBLIC POLICY RESEARCH - LIBRARY □ Washington, DC
Caldwell, Iris J., Libn.
UNIVERSITY OF FLORIDA - AGRICULTURAL RESEARCH & EDUCATION CENTER - FORT LAUDERDALE LIBRARY □ Fort Lauderdale, FL

Caldwell, John, Dir.
AUGUSTANA COLLEGE - DENKMANN MEMORIAL
LIBRARY - SPECIAL COLLECTIONS □ Rock
Island, IL

Caldwell, John, Libn.
PHILADELPHIA COLLEGE OF ART - SLIDE
LIBRARY □ Philadelphia, PA

Caldwell, John, Congressional Archv.
UNIVERSITY OF OKLAHOMA - WESTERN
HISTORY COLLECTIONS □ Norman, OK

Caldwell, Rick, Libn.
HISTORICAL SOCIETY OF SEATTLE & KING
COUNTY - SOPHIE FRYE BASS LIBRARY OF
NORTHWEST AMERICANA □ Seattle, WA

Calhoon, William, Sci.Libn.
WESLEYAN UNIVERSITY - SCIENCE LIBRARY □
Middletown, CT

Calhoun, Catherine, Exec.Dir.
TORRINGTON HISTORICAL SOCIETY - LIBRARY
□ Torrington, CT

Calhoun, Clayne, Libn.
ROANOKE LAW LIBRARY □ Roanoke, VA

Calhoun, James, Music Libn.
DALLAS PUBLIC LIBRARY - FINE ARTS
DIVISION □ Dallas, TX

Calhoun, Judith G., Ph.D., Coord., LRC
UNIVERSITY OF MICHIGAN - MEDICAL SCHOOL
- LEARNING RESOURCE CENTER □ Ann Arbor,
MI

Calhoun, Michele, Ref.Libn.
FIELD MUSEUM OF NATURAL HISTORY -
LIBRARY □ Chicago, IL

Caliendo, Lorraine V., Dir.
AMERICAN MARKETING ASSOCIATION -
INFORMATION CENTER □ Chicago, IL

Calkins, Christopher M., Hist./Park Ranger
U.S. NATL. PARK SERVICE - PETERSBURG
NATL. BATTLEFIELD - LIBRARY □ Petersburg,
VA

Call, Edward E., Hd.Libn.
WEST COAST BIBLE COLLEGE - MC BRAYER
LIBRARY - HUGHES MEMORIAL RESEARCH
PENTECOSTAL CENTER □ Fresno, CA

Callaghan, J. Claire, Dir., Lib.Serv.
CANADIAN MEMORIAL CHIROPRACTIC
COLLEGE - C.C. CLEMMER LIBRARY □ Toronto,
ON

Callaghy, Jane, Adm.Asst.
CENTER FOR THE STUDY OF HUMAN RIGHTS -
LIBRARY □ New York, NY

Callaham, Betty E., State Libn.
SOUTH CAROLINA STATE LIBRARY □ Columbia,
SC

Callahan, Barbara A., Libn.
HARVARD UNIVERSITY - ARNOLD ARBORETUM
& GRAY HERBARIUM - LIBRARY □ Cambridge,
MA

Callahan, Daniel, Lib.Supv.
HASTINGS CENTER LIBRARY - INSTITUTE OF
SOCIETY, ETHICS & THE LIFE SCIENCES □
Hastings-on-Hudson, NY

Callahan, Ellen, Hd. of Bk.Serv.
TIME, INC. - LIBRARY □ New York, NY

Callahan, Harriet, Hd., Louisiana Dept.
LOUISIANA STATE LIBRARY □ Baton Rouge, LA

Callahan, Howard, Jr., Institute Mgr.
RESEARCH SERVICES CORPORATION - THE
O.A. BATTISTA RESEARCH INSTITUTE -
LIBRARY □ Fort Worth, TX

Callahan, Isabella M., Med.Libn.
SOUTHWOOD COMMUNITY HOSPITAL -
MEDICAL LIBRARY □ Norfolk, MA

Callahan, John, Ref.Libn.
UNIVERSITY OF LOWELL, SOUTH CAMPUS -
DANIEL H. O'LEARY LIBRARY - SPECIAL
COLLECTIONS □ Lowell, MA

Callahan, Kathleen E., Lib.Asst.
MICHIGAN (State) DEPARTMENT OF
AGRICULTURE - LIBRARY □ East Lansing, MI

Callahan, Linda A., Asst.Libn.
GCA CORPORATION - TECHNOLOGY DIVISION
- LIBRARY □ Bedford, MA

Callahan, Mary Helen, Accounts Adm.
UNIVERSITY OF DELAWARE, NEWARK -
COLLEGE OF URBAN AFFAIRS - LIBRARY □
Newark, DE

Callahan, Nola V., Tech.Libn.
SIECOR CORPORATION - TECHNICAL
INFORMATION CENTER □ Hickory, NC

Callahan, Patricia, Hd.Cat.
UNIVERSITY OF PENNSYLVANIA - BIDDLE LAW
LIBRARY □ Philadelphia, PA

Callahan, Virginia C., Libn.
AMERICAN CETACEAN SOCIETY - NATIONAL
LIBRARY □ San Pedro, CA

Callard, Joanne, General Serv.
UNIVERSITY OF OKLAHOMA - HEALTH
SCIENCES CENTER LIBRARY □ Oklahoma City,
OK

Callarman, Barbara, Dir.
DOWNEY HISTORICAL SOCIETY MUSEUM -
LIBRARY □ Downey, CA

Callen, Rev. Robert V., S.J., Univ. Archv.
MARQUETTE UNIVERSITY - DEPARTMENT OF
SPECIAL COLLECTIONS AND UNIVERSITY
ARCHIVES □ Milwaukee, WI

Callen, Rev. Robert V., S.J., Univ.Archv.
MARQUETTE UNIVERSITY - MEMORIAL
LIBRARY □ Milwaukee, WI

Callery, Bernadette G., Libn.
CARNEGIE-MELLON UNIVERSITY - HUNT
INSTITUTE FOR BOTANICAL DOCUMENTATION
□ Pittsburgh, PA

Calligan, Jacqueline M., Libn. II
NEW MEXICO STATE DEPARTMENT OF HEALTH
& ENVIRONMENT - ENVIRONMENTAL
IMPROVEMENT DIVISION - LIBRARY □ Santa
Fe, NM

Callinan, Mary L., Mgr.
GOLDOME BANK - INFORMATION CENTER □
New York, NY

Callis, Mina, Cat.Libn.
CHRIST THE KING SEMINARY - LIBRARY □ East
Aurora, NY

Callow, Bette R., Slide Libn.
MEMPHIS ACADEMY OF ARTS - G. PILLOW
LEWIS MEMORIAL LIBRARY □ Memphis, TN

Calman, John Douglas, Asst.Hd.
FLORIDA STATE UNIVERSITY - SCIENCE-
TECHNOLOGY DIVISION □ Tallahassee, FL

Calomiris, Ellen, Hist.Cur.
LONG BEACH PUBLIC LIBRARY - RANCHO LOS
CERRITOS MUSEUM - LIBRARY □ Long Beach,
CA

Calvano, Margaret, Med.Info.Spec.
NATIONAL MULTIPLE SCLEROSIS SOCIETY -
MEDICAL LIBRARY □ New York, NY

Calvaresi, Frances, Tech.Libn.
GILBERT/COMMONWEALTH, INC. - LIBRARY
AND INFORMATION SERVICES □ Reading, PA

Calvert, Judy, Libn.
VIGO COUNTY HISTORICAL SOCIETY -
HISTORICAL MUSEUM OF THE WABASH VALLEY
- LIBRARY □ Terre Haute, IN

Calvert, Kerri, Lib.Asst.
UNIVERSITY OF ALBERTA - DEPT. OF
SOCIOLOGY - STANLEY TAYLOR SOCIOLOGY
READING ROOM □ Edmonton, AB

Calvin, Betsy, Libn.
INSTITUTE OF ECOSYSTEM STUDIES -
LIBRARY □ Millbrook, NY

Calvin, Diane, Govt.Doc.
NORTHWESTERN OKLAHOMA STATE
UNIVERSITY - LIBRARY □ Alva, OK

Camacho, Nancy, Libn.
PROCTOR COMMUNITY HOSPITAL - MEDICAL
LIBRARY □ Peoria, IL

Camacho, Perfecto, Libn.
UNIVERSITY OF PUERTO RICO - SCHOOL OF
PUBLIC ADMINISTRATION - LIBRARY† □ Rio
Piedras, PR

Cambridge, J.J., Project Mgr.
IBM CORPORATION - FEDERAL SYSTEMS
DIVISION - AVIONICS SYSTEMS - LIBRARY □
Owego, NY

Camden, Thomas, Mss.Cat.
NEW HAMPSHIRE HISTORICAL SOCIETY -
LIBRARY □ Concord, NH

Cameloford, Rumil of, Libn.
PARMAR ELDALIEVA LIBRARY □ Scranton, PA

Cameron, A.K., Cur.
MARITIME MUSEUM OF BRITISH COLUMBIA -
LIBRARY □ Victoria, BC

Cameron, Connie, Asst.Libn.
BRYANT COLLEGE OF BUSINESS
ADMINISTRATION - EDITH M. HODGSON
MEMORIAL LIBRARY □ Smithfield, RI

Cameron, Dorothy, Ref.Libn.
BRITISH COLUMBIA LAW LIBRARY
FOUNDATION - VANCOUVER COURTHOUSE
LIBRARY □ Vancouver, BC

Cameron, Jane, Asst.Libn.
KNOXVILLE STATE TECHNICAL INSTITUTE -
EDUCATIONAL RESOURCE CENTER □ Knoxville,
TN

Cameron, Jean, Info.Spec.
RAYTHEON SERVICE COMPANY -
INFORMATION CENTER □ Burlington, MA

Cameron, Rev. Kenneth W., Archv./Histographer
PROTESTANT EPISCOPAL CHURCH -
EPISCOPAL DIOCESE OF CONNECTICUT -
DIOCESAN LIBRARY AND ARCHIVES □ Hartford,
CT

Cameron, Linda G., Libn.
CENTRAL VERMONT PUBLIC SERVICE
CORPORATION - CORPORATE LIBRARY □
Rutland, VT

Cameron, Margaret, Libn.
CLARKSON GORDON - BUSINESS LIBRARY □
Montreal, PQ

Cameron, Mary R., Libn.
REYNOLDS METALS COMPANY - TECHNICAL
INFORMATION SERVICES LIBRARY □ Richmond,
VA

Cameron, Mrs. Pat, Libn.
TRINITY MEMORIAL HOSPITAL - LIBRARY □
Cudahy, WI

Cameron, Richard A., Field Dir.
MINNESOTA HISTORICAL SOCIETY - DIVISION
OF ARCHIVES AND MANUSCRIPTS □ St. Paul,
MN

Cameron, Sam, Archv.
MEHARRY MEDICAL COLLEGE - MEDICAL
LIBRARY - LEARNING RESOURCES CENTER □
Nashville, TN

Camfield, Ms. B., Hd., Lib.Info.Serv.
CANADA - EMPLOYMENT & IMMIGRATION
CANADA - LIBRARY □ Ottawa, ON

Caminiti, Benella, Mgr.
UNIVERSITY OF WASHINGTON - REGIONAL
PRIMATE RESEARCH CENTER - PRIMATE
INFORMATION CENTER □ Seattle, WA

Camlioglu, Ergun, Chf.
NATIONAL LIBRARY OF CANADA - CANADIAN
BOOK EXCHANGE CENTRE (CBEC) □ Ottawa, ON

Camp, Kathryn M., Asst.Libn.
NORTHERN TRUST COMPANY - LIBRARY† □
Chicago, IL

Camp, Kathy, Asst.Cat.
ILLINOIS INSTITUTE OF TECHNOLOGY -
CHICAGO KENT LAW SCHOOL - LIBRARY† □
Chicago, IL

Camp, Paul Eugen, Exec.Sec.
FLORIDA HISTORICAL SOCIETY - LIBRARY† □
Tampa, FL

Camp, Paul Eugen, Assoc.Libn.
UNIVERSITY OF SOUTH FLORIDA - LIBRARY -
SPECIAL COLLECTIONS DEPARTMENT □
Tampa, FL

Camp, Thomas E., Libn.
UNIVERSITY OF THE SOUTH - SCHOOL OF
THEOLOGY LIBRARY □ Sewanee, TN

Campbell, A., Libn.
CANADA - PUBLIC SERVICE COMMISSION -
LIBRARY SERVICES DIVISION □ Ottawa, ON

Campbell, Alma B., Mgr.
SPERRY COMPUTER SYSTEMS - INFORMATION
CENTER† □ Blue Bell, PA

Campbell, Ann, Cat./Online
COTTAGE HOSPITAL - DAVID L. REEVES
MEDICAL LIBRARY □ Santa Barbara, CA

Campbell, Barbara, Libn.
NOVA SCOTIA BARRISTERS' SOCIETY -
LIBRARY □ Halifax, NS

Campbell, Billy W., Supv.
HUGHES AIRCRAFT COMPANY - ELECTRO-
OPTICAL & DATA SYSTEMS GROUP - COMPANY
TECHNICAL DOCUMENT CENTER □ El Segundo,
CA

Campbell, Clara, Libn.
ROSICRUCIAN ORDER, AMORC - ROSICRUCIAN
RESEARCH LIBRARY □ San Jose, CA

Campbell, Connie, Libn.
KNOX COUNTY LAW LIBRARY □ Rockland, ME

Campbell, Dan, Libn.
U.S. AGENCY FOR INTERNATIONAL
DEVELOPMENT - WATER & SANITATION FOR
HEALTH PROJECT - INFORMATION CENTER □
Arlington, VA

Campbell, Deirdre, Libn.
UNIVERSITY OF ARIZONA - ARID LANDS
INFORMATION CENTER □ Tucson, AZ

Campbell, Deirdre, Libn.
UNIVERSITY OF ARIZONA - OFFICE OF ARID
LANDS STUDIES - BIORESOURCES RESEARCH
LIBRARY □ Tucson, AZ

Campbell, Doris, Asst.Libn.
NATIONAL ASSOCIATION OF HOME BUILDERS -
NATIONAL HOUSING CENTER LIBRARY □
Washington, DC

Campbell, Dorothy M., Libn.
UNITED STATES TESTING COMPANY, INC. -
LIBRARY† □ Hoboken, NJ

Campbell, Douglas, Dir.
AIR AND SPACE MARKETING - INFORMATION
CENTER □ Alexandria, VA

Campbell, Eliza, Asst.Libn.
ALSTON & BIRD - LIBRARY □ Atlanta, GA

Campbell, Frances D., Libn.
COLORADO STATE SUPREME COURT LIBRARY □
Denver, CO

Campbell, Francis D., Jr., Libn.
AMERICAN NUMISMATIC SOCIETY - LIBRARY
□ New York, NY

Campbell, Frank C., Chf.
NEW YORK PUBLIC LIBRARY - PERFORMING
ARTS RESEARCH CENTER - MUSIC DIVISION □
New York, NY

Campbell, George R., Act.Dir.
U.S. DEPT. OF COMMERCE - INTERNATIONAL
TRADE ADMINISTRATION - DETROIT
DISTRICT OFFICE LIBRARY □ Detroit, MI

Campbell, Helen G., Media Spec.
PINELLAS COUNTY SCHOOL BOARD - MIRROR
LAKE/TOMLINSON EDUCATION CENTER -
LIBRARY/MEDIA CENTER □ St. Petersburg, FL

Campbell, Hugh, Lib.Asst.
AUSTRALIAN INFORMATION SERVICE -
REFERENCE LIBRARY/INFORMATION SERVICE
□ New York, NY

Campbell, Jane, Circ.Dir.
FIRST BAPTIST CHURCH - I.C. ANDERSON
MEMORIAL LIBRARY & MEDIA CENTER □ Waco,
TX

Campbell, Jerry D., Libn.
SOUTHERN METHODIST UNIVERSITY -
PERKINS SCHOOL OF THEOLOGY - LIBRARY □
Dallas, TX

Campbell, Joan E., Mgr.
NATIONAL RESTAURANT ASSOCIATION -
INFORMATION SERVICE AND LIBRARY □
Washington, DC

Campbell, Joanne, Asst.Libn.-Cat.
AVCO CORPORATION - AVCO-EVERETT
RESEARCH LABORATORY - LIBRARY† □ Everett,
MA

Campbell, John, Musm.Dir.
U.S. ARMY - PATTON MUSEUM OF CAVALRY &
ARMOR - EMERT L. DAVIS MEMORIAL LIBRARY
□ Ft. Knox, KY

Campbell, Louisa, Bus.Spec.
FERGUSON LIBRARY - BUSINESS-TECHNOLOGY
DEPARTMENT □ Stamford, CT

Campbell, Margaret, Libn.
CENTRAL SOYA COMPANY, INC. - FOOD
RESEARCH LIBRARY □ Fort Wayne, IN

Campbell, Margaret E., Libn.
COUNCIL OF MARITIME PREMIERS - ATLANTIC
COASTAL RESOURCE INFORMATION CENTRE
LIBRARY □ Amherst, NS

Campbell, Margaret E., Libn.
COUNCIL OF MARITIME PREMIERS -
MARITIME RESOURCE MANAGEMENT SERVICE
- INFORMATION CENTRE □ Amherst, NS

Campbell, Martha, Libn.
COLORADO STATE SUPREME COURT LIBRARY □
Denver, CO

Campbell, Mary Jane, Libn.
FERRO CORPORATION - FERRO CHEMICAL
DIVISION - FERRO CHEMICAL LIBRARY □
Bedford, OH

Campbell, Nancy Berth, Supv., Lib.
THEDA CLARK REGIONAL MEDICAL CENTER -
HEALTH SCIENCES LIBRARY □ Neenah, WI

Campbell, Neil, Asst.Dir./Tech.Serv.
TEXAS TECH UNIVERSITY - HEALTH SCIENCES
CENTER - LIBRARY OF THE HEALTH SCIENCES
□ Lubbock, TX

Campbell, Paul R., Libn.
RHODE ISLAND HISTORICAL SOCIETY -
LIBRARY □ Providence, RI

Campbell, Sally, Info.Mgr.
BANK OF HAWAII - INFORMATION CENTER □
Honolulu, HI

Campbell, Ms. Sammie, Libn.
UNIVERSITY HOSPITAL AND CLINIC -
HERBERT L. BRYANS MEMORIAL LIBRARY □
Pensacola, FL

Campbell, Sandra, Ref.Libn.
UNIVERSITY OF ALBERTA - SCIENCE AND
TECHNOLOGY LIBRARY □ Edmonton, AB

Campbell, Shirley A., Med.Libn.
U.S. VETERANS ADMINISTRATION (TX-Dallas) -
MEDICAL CENTER LIBRARY (142D) □ Dallas, TX

Campbell, Stanley, Dir.
CENTRE COLLEGE - GRACE DOHERTY LIBRARY
- SPECIAL COLLECTIONS □ Danville, KY

Campbell, Susan L., Libn./Res.
VANIER INSTITUTE OF THE FAMILY -
RESOURCE & INFORMATION CENTRE □ Ottawa,
ON

Campbell, Terry, Act.Ref.Libn.
UNIVERSITY OF TENNESSEE - COLLEGE OF
LAW LIBRARY □ Knoxville, TN

Campbell, Vivian L., Asst.Libn., Coll.Dev.
GEORGETOWN UNIVERSITY - FRED O. DENNIS
LAW LIBRARY □ Washington, DC

Campeau, M., Hd., Curatorial Serv.
CANADA - PUBLIC ARCHIVES OF CANADA -
MANUSCRIPT DIVISION □ Ottawa, ON

Campese, Michael A., Lib.Dir.
ST. ELIZABETH'S HOSPITAL - HEALTH SCIENCE
LIBRARY □ Belleville, IL

Campfield, Mary, Dir. of Lib.Serv.
WINNEBAGO MENTAL HEALTH INSTITUTE -
MEDICAL LIBRARY □ Winnebago, WI

Campion, Serge G., Chf.Libn.
CANADA - TRANSPORT CANADA - LIBRARY &
INFORMATION CENTRE □ Ottawa, ON

Campo, Charles A., Hd.Libn.
BANGOR DAILY NEWS - LIBRARY □ Bangor, ME

Campo, L.D.
OLIN CORPORATION - RESEARCH CENTER/
INFORMATION CENTER □ New Haven, CT

Canby, Susan M. Fifer, Dir.
NATIONAL GEOGRAPHIC SOCIETY - LIBRARY □
Washington, DC

Candau, Eugenie, Libn.
SAN FRANCISCO MUSEUM OF MODERN ART -
LOUISE S. ACKERMAN FINE ARTS LIBRARY □
San Francisco, CA

Candelaria, Gary, Chf. Park Ranger
U.S. NATL. PARK SERVICE - SITKA NATL.
HISTORICAL PARK - LIBRARY □ Sitka, AK

Cane, Betsey, Ref.
DIGITAL EQUIPMENT CORPORATION -
MAYNARD AREA INFORMATION SERVICES □
Maynard, MA

Canelake, Audrey, Libn.
MINNEAPOLIS PUBLIC LIBRARY &
INFORMATION CENTER - HISTORY
DEPARTMENT □ Minneapolis, MN

Cangialosi, Ruth, Asst.Libn.
MC GRAW-HILL, INC. - LIBRARY □ New York,
NY

Canick, Maureen, Mgr., Tech.Lib.
U.S. GENERAL ACCOUNTING OFFICE - OFFICE
OF LIBRARY SERVICES □ Washington, DC

Cann, Cheryle J., Health Sci.Libn.
UNIVERSITY OF MISSOURI, ST. LOUIS -
HEALTH SCIENCES LIBRARY □ St. Louis, MO

Cann, Sharon, Libn.
NORTHSIDE HOSPITAL - WOODRUFF HEALTH
SCIENCE LIBRARY □ Atlanta, GA

Cannan, Julia, Supv.
KENT STATE UNIVERSITY - MAP LIBRARY □
Kent, OH

Cannard, Bonnie, Asst.Libn./Tech.Serv.
GEORGETOWN UNIVERSITY - MEDICAL
CENTER - DAHLGREN MEMORIAL LIBRARY □
Washington, DC

CannCasciato, Kathleen, Rsrc.Libn.
U.S. BANCORP - RESOURCE LIBRARY □ Portland,
OR

Canney, Michele R., Libn.
ARIZONA DAILY STAR - LIBRARY □ Tucson, AZ

Canning, Ruby M., Supv.
WEST VIRGINIA UNIVERSITY - CREATIVE
ARTS CENTER - MUSIC LIBRARY □ Morgantown,
WV

Cannings, S., Cur.
UNIVERSITY OF BRITISH COLUMBIA -
SPENCER ENTOMOLOGICAL MUSEUM -
LIBRARY □ Vancouver, BC

Cannizzaro, Mary Jane, Mgr., Black & White Dept.
FPG, INTERNATIONAL CORPORATION □ New
York, NY

Cannon, Anne, Asst.Hd.
YORK UNIVERSITY - GOVERNMENT
DOCUMENTS/ADMINISTRATIVE STUDIES
LIBRARY □ Downsview, ON

Cannon, Earl, Mgr., Res.
MISSOURI STATE DIVISION OF COMMUNITY
AND ECONOMIC DEVELOPMENT - RESEARCH
LIBRARY □ Jefferson City, MO

Cannon, Joan D., Asst.Libn.
FLORIDA STATE SUPREME COURT LIBRARY □
Tallahassee, FL

Cannon, Linda L., Sec.
NEW YORK STATE COLLEGE OF CERAMICS AT
ALFRED UNIVERSITY - SAMUEL R. SCHOLES
LIBRARY OF CERAMICS □ Alfred, NY

Cannon, Maris L., Adm.Asst.
UNIVERSITY OF DETROIT - LIBRARY MEDIA
CENTER □ Detroit, MI

Cannon, Peter, Res.Anl.
WISCONSIN STATE LEGISLATIVE REFERENCE
BUREAU □ Madison, WI

Cannon, Ruth M.E., Libn.
FEDERAL RESERVE BANK OF RICHMOND -
RESEARCH LIBRARY □ Richmond, VA

Cannon, Tyrone H., Soc. Work Libn.
COLUMBIA UNIVERSITY - WHITNEY M. YOUNG,
JR. MEMORIAL LIBRARY OF SOCIAL WORK □
New York, NY

Canose, Joseph A., Lib. Group Supv.
AT & T INFORMATION SYSTEMS - TECHNICAL
LIBRARY □ Lincroft, NJ

Cant, Elaine, Libn.
SANTA ROSA PRESS DEMOCRAT - EDITORIAL
LIBRARY □ Santa Rosa, CA

Canter, Judy Gerritts, Chf.Libn.
SAN FRANCISCO EXAMINER - LIBRARY □ San
Francisco, CA

Canton, Doreen B., Patent Law Libn.
UPJOHN COMPANY - PATENT LAW
DEPARTMENT - LIBRARY □ Kalamazoo, MI
Cantor, Beverly, Br.Libn.
AMERICAN HOME PRODUCTS CORPORATION -
WYETH LABORATORIES DIVISION LIBRARY □
Philadelphia, PA
Cantor, Beverly L., Tech.Libn.
AMERICAN HOME PRODUCTS CORPORATION -
WYETH LABORATORIES DIVISION -
ANTIBIOTICS LABORATORIES LIBRARY □ West
Chester, PA
Cantrell, Gary, Music Libn.
ADELPHI UNIVERSITY - FINE ARTS LIBRARY -
SPECIAL COLLECTIONS - ARCHIVES† □ Garden
City, NY
Cantrell, Jacques, Libn.
M.P.K. OMEGA COMPANY - B.O.T.I. SPECIAL
RESEARCH COLLECTION □ Amarillo, TX
Cantrell, Jacques, Corp.Libn.
M.P.K. OMEGA COMPANY - BIOSCIENCE
LIBRARY □ Amarillo, TX
Cantrell, Marilyn, Dir., Med.Rec.
COMMUNITY HOSPITAL ASSOCIATION -
MEDICAL LIBRARY □ Battle Creek, MI
Capel, Gloria, Adm.
CROWN ZELLERBACH CORPORATION -
CORPORATE INFORMATION CENTER □ San
Francisco, CA
Capel, James E., Comm. of Adm.
NEW YORK STATE DIVISION OF HUMAN
RIGHTS - REFERENCE LIBRARY □ New York, NY
Capelle, Eleanor, Sr.Libn.
CALIFORNIA STATE LIBRARY - SUTRO LIBRARY
□ San Francisco, CA
Capellen, J.M., Asst.Chem.II
IOWA STATE UNIVERSITY - ENERGY AND
MINERAL RESOURCES RESEARCH INSTITUTE -
RARE-EARTH INFORMATION CENTER □ Ames,
IA
Capitani, Cheryl A., Dir., Lib./Media Serv.
HARRISBURG HOSPITAL - LIBRARY/MEDIA
SERVICES □ Harrisburg, PA
Caplan, Bernard, Res.Spec.
ENSANIAN PHYSICOCHEMICAL INSTITUTE -
INFORMATION CENTER FOR GRAVITATION
CHEMISTRY □ Eldred, PA
Caplan, Rayna Lee, Libn.
ANALYTICAL SYSTEMS ENGINEERING
CORPORATION - LIBRARY □ Burlington, MA
Caplette, Francine, Hd.
UNIVERSITE DE MONTREAL - GEOGRAPHIE-
BIBLIOTHEQUE □ Montreal, PQ
Capodagli, James, Ref.Libn.
SUNY - UPSTATE MEDICAL CENTER LIBRARY □
Syracuse, NY
Caponigro, Angelina, Hd.Libn.
ST. AGNES MEDICAL CENTER - HEALTH
SCIENCE LIBRARY □ Philadelphia, PA
Capozzoli, Susan, Doc.Supv.
SALOMON BROTHERS - CORPORATE FINANCE
LIBRARY □ New York, NY
Cappa-Rotunno, MaryAnn, Asst.Libn.
IRELL & MANELLA - LIBRARY □ Los Angeles, CA
Capps, Gene T., Dir., Dept. of Educ.
OLD SALEM, INC. - LIBRARY □ Winston-Salem,
NC
Capps, Marie T., Maps & Mss.Libn.
U.S. ARMY - MILITARY ACADEMY - LIBRARY □
West Point, NY
Cappuccilli, Terry
HONEYWELL, INC. - HONEYWELL
INFORMATION SYSTEMS - INFORMATION AND
LIBRARY SERVICES □ Waltham, MA
Capra, Shari, Supv.
RUST-OLEUM CORPORATION - R & D LIBRARY
□ Evanston, IL
Capraro, Betsey, Res.Anl.
HONEYWELL, INC. - AEROSPACE AND DEFENSE
LIBRARY □ McLean, VA

Capritta, Dianne, Coord., Coll.Dev.
SUNY - COLLEGE OF ENVIRONMENTAL SCIENCE
AND FORESTRY - F. FRANKLIN MOON LIBRARY
□ Syracuse, NY
Capron, Shirley, Pub.Serv.Libn.
EXPERIMENT IN INTERNATIONAL LIVING -
SCHOOL FOR INTERNATIONAL TRAINING -
DONALD B. WATT LIBRARY □ Brattleboro, VT
Capuano, James
NEWARK PUBLIC LIBRARY - SCIENCE AND
TECHNOLOGY DIVISION □ Newark, NJ
Caranci, Anna Maria, Med.Info.Off.
BURROUGHS WELLCOME COMPANY - MEDICAL
INFORMATION CENTER □ Kirkland, PQ
Caravella, Joseph R., Dir., Prof.Serv.
NATIONAL COUNCIL OF TEACHERS OF
MATHEMATICS - TEACHER/LEARNING CENTER
□ Reston, VA
Caraway, Helen B., Libn.
U.S. NATIONAL MINE HEALTH AND SAFETY
ACADEMY - LEARNING RESOURCE CENTER □
Beckley, WV
Carballo, Gladis, Spanish Lang.Serv.Coord.
OAKLAND PUBLIC LIBRARY - LATIN AMERICAN
LIBRARY □ Oakland, CA
Carbonara, Dr. R.S., Assoc.Mgr.
BATTELLE-COLUMBUS LABORATORIES -
RAPIDLY SOLIDIFIED MATERIALS (RaSoMat) -
RESOURCE CENTER □ Columbus, OH
Carbone, Carmela, Dp.Dir.
ENGINEERING SOCIETIES LIBRARY □ New
York, NY
Card, Sandra, Sys.Dev.Off.
CALIFORNIA INSTITUTE OF TECHNOLOGY -
MILLIKAN LIBRARY □ Pasadena, CA
Cardace, Ann, Libn.
NATIONAL ASSOCIATION OF BROADCASTERS -
LIBRARY □ Washington, DC
Cardell, Betty, Acq.
U.S. CENTERS FOR DISEASE CONTROL - CDC
LIBRARY □ Atlanta, GA
Cardell, Victor, Asst.Libn.
YALE UNIVERSITY - JOHN HERRICK JACKSON
MUSIC LIBRARY □ New Haven, CT
Cardello, Patricia, Automated Serv.Libn.
AVCO CORPORATION - AVCO-EVERETT
RESEARCH LABORATORY - LIBRARY† □ Everett,
MA
Carder, Robert W., Libn.
MADISON HISTORICAL SOCIETY, INC. -
LIBRARY □ Madison, CT
Cardew, Cecily, Lib.Dir. & Archv.
MOLESWORTH INSTITUTE - LIBRARY AND
ARCHIVES □ Storrs, CT
Cardillo, Wayne, Tech.Serv.Libn.
SUNY AT BUFFALO - CHARLES B. SEARS LAW
LIBRARY □ Buffalo, NY
Cardinal, J.J., Dir., Adm. & Personnel
CANADA - LIBRARY OF PARLIAMENT □ Ottawa,
ON
Cardinal, L., Chf., Modern Cart.Sect.
CANADA - PUBLIC ARCHIVES OF CANADA -
NATIONAL MAP COLLECTION □ Ottawa, ON
Cardinale, Susan, Coord.
UNIVERSITY OF MARYLAND, COLLEGE PARK -
LIBRARIES - WOMEN'S STUDIES PAMPHLET
COLLECTION □ College Park, MD
Cardoza, Donna, Lib.Ck.
EMANUEL MEDICAL CENTER - MEDICAL
LIBRARY □ Turlock, CA
Cardozo, Carol L., Libn.
MASSACHUSETTS TAXPAYERS FOUNDATION,
INC. - LIBRARY □ Boston, MA
Cardozo, Manoel, Cur.
CATHOLIC UNIVERSITY OF AMERICA -
OLIVEIRA LIMA LIBRARY □ Washington, DC
Cardwell, Diane O., Asst.Dir. of Res.
LAMALIE ASSOCIATES, INC. - RESEARCH
DEPARTMENT □ Tampa, FL
Caren, Loretta, Libn.
UNIVERSITY OF ROCHESTER - LABORATORY
FOR LASER ENERGETICS - LIBRARY □
Rochester, NY

Caren, Loretta, Hd.
UNIVERSITY OF ROCHESTER - PHYSICS-
OPTICS-ASTRONOMY LIBRARY □ Rochester, NY
Carew, Virginia, Ref.Libn.
AMERICAN BIBLE SOCIETY - LIBRARY □ New
York, NY
Carey, Barbara H., Libn.
CONTROL DATA CORPORATION -
GOVERNMENT SYSTEMS LIBRARY □ Alexandria,
VA
Carey, Belinda, Lib.Asst.
TAYLOR (Moses) HOSPITAL - LIBRARY □
Scranton, PA
Carey, Diana K., Mgr.
BOEING COMPANY - SEATTLE SERVICES
DIVISION - TECHNICAL LIBRARIES† □ Seattle,
WA
Carey, John E., Gen.Mgr.
FOI SERVICES, INC. - LIBRARY □ Rockville, MD
Carey, Lois, Ref.Libn. Open Lit.Sect.
U.S. ARMY - BELVOIR RESEARCH &
DEVELOPMENT CENTER - TECHNICAL LIBRARY
□ Ft. Belvoir, VA
Carey, Verda, Libn.
ALASKA STATE DIVISION OF STATE LIBRARIES
& MUSEUMS - HISTORICAL LIBRARY □ Juneau,
AK
Cargill, Jennifer, Assoc.Dir./Tech.Proc.
TEXAS TECH UNIVERSITY - LIBRARY □
Lubbock, TX
Caricone, Paul, Cat.
COLLEGE OF INSURANCE - INSURANCE
SOCIETY OF NEW YORK - LIBRARY □ New York,
NY
Carini, Helen, Supv.Libn.
GAF CORPORATION - TECHNICAL
INFORMATION SERVICES† □ Wayne, NJ
Carkhuff, Roxanne K., Chm., Lib.Comm.
HUNTERDON COUNTY HISTORICAL SOCIETY -
HIRAM E. DEATS MEMORIAL LIBRARY □
Flemington, NJ
Carlburg, C. David, Asst.Libn.
CALIFORNIA STATE DEPARTMENT OF JUSTICE
- ATTORNEY GENERAL'S OFFICE - LAW
LIBRARY □ Los Angeles, CA
Carle, Patricia Miles
UNIVERSITY OF PITTSBURGH - SCHOOL OF
SOCIAL WORK - BUHL LIBRARY □ Pittsburgh, PA
Carleton, Dr. Don E., Hd.Libn./Archv.
UNIVERSITY OF TEXAS, AUSTIN - EUGENE C.
BARKER TEXAS HISTORY CENTER □ Austin, TX
Carlin, Beth, Asst.Libn.
ST. LOUIS COLLEGE OF PHARMACY - O.J.
CLOUGHLY ALUMNI LIBRARY □ St. Louis, MO
Carlin, John, Lib.Asst.
HARVARD UNIVERSITY - STATISTICS LIBRARY
□ Cambridge, MA
Carlisle, Hilda, Lib.Chm.
FIRST UNITED METHODIST CHURCH -
GERTRUDE CALLIHAN MEMORIAL LIBRARY □
San Marcos, TX
Carll, Lindy R., Ref.
WHITTIER COLLEGE - SCHOOL OF LAW -
LIBRARY □ Los Angeles, CA
Carlock, Walter, Libn.
MINNEAPOLIS PUBLIC LIBRARY &
INFORMATION CENTER - TECHNOLOGY AND
SCIENCE DEPARTMENT □ Minneapolis, MN
Carlsen, Robert, Teacher-Libn.
NORTHERN WISCONSIN CENTER FOR THE
DEVELOPMENTALLY DISABLED - LIBRARY/
INSTRUCTIONAL MATERIALS CENTER □
Chippewa Falls, WI
Carlson, Aileen A., Libn.
AMERICAN OPTICAL CORPORATION -
RESEARCH CENTER LIBRARY □ Southbridge, MA
Carlson, Barbara, Cat.
OLD SLAVE MART MUSEUM - LIBRARY □
Sullivan's Island, SC
Carlson, Bruce, Supv.
UNIVERSITY OF MANITOBA - MUSIC LIBRARY
□ Winnipeg, MB

Carlson, C.R., Network Sys.Sup.Mgr.
BELL COMMUNICATIONS RESEARCH, INC. -
INFORMATION RESOURCES & SERVICES
DISTRICT □ Livingston, NJ

Carlson, Cathleen A., Cur. of Mss.
CONFEDERATE MEMORIAL LITERARY SOCIETY
- MUSEUM OF THE CONFEDERACY - ELEANOR
S. BROCKENBROUGH LIBRARY □ Richmond, VA

Carlson, Gordon, Chf.Libn.
U.S. VETERANS ADMINISTRATION (ID-Boise) -
MEDICAL CENTER LIBRARY (142D) □ Boise, ID

Carlson, Jacquelynn, Chf.Libn.
ST. MARY'S HOSPITAL - STAFF LIBRARY □
Minneapolis, MN

Carlson, Linda, Rd.Serv.Libn.
JOHNS HOPKINS UNIVERSITY - SCHOOL OF
ADVANCED INTERNATIONAL STUDIES -
SYDNEY R. & ELSA W. MASON LIBRARY □
Washington, DC

Carlson, Livija, Libn.
UNIVERSITY OF MINNESOTA, ST. PAUL -
VETERINARY MEDICAL LIBRARY □ St. Paul, MN

Carlson, Lois O., Media Coord.
PHOENIX DAY SCHOOL FOR THE DEAF -
LIBRARY/MEDIA CENTER □ Phoenix, AZ

Carlson, Mrs. Pat, Hd.Libn.
SOUTHERN CALIFORNIA COLLEGE OF
OPTOMETRY - M.B. KETCHUM MEMORIAL
LIBRARY □ Fullerton, CA

Carlson, Patricia, Libn.
UNIVERSITY OF MINNESOTA, CROOKSTON -
KIEHLE LIBRARY - MEDIA RESOURCES □
Crookston, MN

Carlsson, Vera R., Hd. of Acq.
UNIVERSITY OF MINNESOTA - LAW LIBRARY □
Minneapolis, MN

Carlsten, Marcia, Hd.
FLINT PUBLIC LIBRARY - CHILDREN'S
DEPARTMENT □ Flint, MI

Carlton, Beverly E., Med.Libn.
HOLLYWOOD COMMUNITY HOSPITAL -
MEDICAL STAFF LIBRARY □ Hollywood, CA

Carlton, Gary, Hd., Circ.
UNIVERSITY OF CALIFORNIA, SANTA CRUZ -
DEAN E. MC HENRY LIBRARY □ Santa Cruz, CA

Carlton, Jerry, Prin.Archv.
KENTUCKY STATE DEPARTMENT FOR
LIBRARIES & ARCHIVES - ARCHIVES □
Frankfort, KY

Carlton, William H., Dir., Adm.Div.
TEXAS STATE LIBRARY □ Austin, TX

Carlucci, Robert, Asst.Cur.
COLUMBIA UNIVERSITY - DEPARTMENT OF
ART HISTORY & ARCHAEOLOGY - PHOTOGRAPH
COLLECTION □ New York, NY

Carman, Carol, Leg.Libn.
MARYLAND STATE DEPARTMENT OF
LEGISLATIVE REFERENCE - LIBRARY □
Annapolis, MD

Carmichael, A.P., Corp.Libn.
CAROLINA POWER & LIGHT COMPANY -
TECHNICAL LIBRARY □ Raleigh, NC

Carmichael, Dr. Ian
UNIVERSITY OF NOTRE DAME - RADIATION
LABORATORY - RADIATION CHEMISTRY DATA
CENTER □ Notre Dame, IN

Carmichael, Kathleen M., Asst.Libn.
HARPER-GRACE HOSPITALS - HARPER
HOSPITAL DIVISION - DEPARTMENT OF
LIBRARIES □ Detroit, MI

Carmichael, Mrs. M.F., Lib.Dir.
WATERBURY HOSPITAL HEALTH CENTER -
HEALTH CENTER LIBRARY □ Waterbury, CT

Carmichael, Mary D., Libn.
FLORIDA CONSERVATION FOUNDATION, INC. -
ENVIRONMENTAL INFORMATION CENTER □
Winter Park, FL

Carnahan, Joan A., Mgr., Lib. & Info.Ctr.
NUODEX, INC. - LIBRARY □ Piscataway, NJ

Carneglia, Anna, Lib.Tech.Asst.
NOVO LABORATORIES INC. - LIBRARY □ Wilton,
CT

Carnell, Helen, Libn.
WILMINGTON NEWS-JOURNAL COMPANY -
LIBRARY □ Wilmington, DE

Carnes, Betty M., Libn.
PUEBLO CHIEFTAIN AND STAR-JOURNAL
PUBLISHING CORPORATION - LIBRARY □
Pueblo, CO

Carnes, Judith O., Ref.Libn. & Coll.Dev.
YALE UNIVERSITY - SOCIAL SCIENCE LIBRARY
□ New Haven, CT

Carnes, Suzanne M., Libn.
COPLEY PRESS, INC. - THE JAMES S. COPLEY
LIBRARY □ La Jolla, CA

Carney, Donald W., Supv. Park Ranger
U.S. NATL. PARK SERVICE - GRAND PORTAGE
NATL. MONUMENT - LIBRARY □ Grand Marais,
MN

Carney, Eileen, Asst.Libn.
BRUNDAGE, STORY & ROSE, INVESTMENT
COUNSEL - LIBRARY □ New York, NY

Carney, Ellen, Res.Libn.
CONSUMERS UNION OF UNITED STATES, INC. -
LIBRARY □ Mount Vernon, NY

Carney, James, Info.Off.
UNITED NATIONS - CENTRE FOR HUMAN
SETTLEMENTS - INFORMATION OFFICE □
Vancouver, BC

Carney, Patrick J., Lib.Dir.
U.S. MARINE CORPS - CAMP PENDLETON
LIBRARY SYSTEM □ Camp Pendleton, CA

Carol, Marcel C., Libn.
BAYLOR UNIVERSITY, DALLAS - LIBRARY □
Dallas, TX

Caroll, Bruce, Circ.Libn.
COMMUNITY COLLEGE OF BALTIMORE -
LIBRARIES/LEARNING RESOURCES CENTERS □
Baltimore, MD

Caron, Kathy, Acq.
JENKINS (Theodore F.) MEMORIAL LAW
LIBRARY COMPANY - LIBRARY □ Philadelphia,
PA

Caron, Theodore, Hd.Cat.
MAYO FOUNDATION - MAYO CLINIC LIBRARY □
Rochester, MN

Carozzi, Mila E., Sr.Libn.
SHELL CANADA RESOURCES LIMITED -
TECHNICAL LIBRARY □ Calgary, AB

Carparelli, Felicia, Rec.Libn.
CHICAGO PUBLIC LIBRARY CULTURAL CENTER
- FINE ARTS DIVISION - MUSIC SECTION □
Chicago, IL

Carpenter, Betty M., Libn.
SUFFOLK COUNTY HISTORICAL SOCIETY -
LIBRARY □ Riverhead, NY

Carpenter, Catherine B., Chf.Cat.
HARVARD UNIVERSITY - LITTAUER LIBRARY □
Cambridge, MA

Carpenter, Dale, Info.Spec.
SINGER COMPANY - LINK FLIGHT SIMULATION
DIVISION - INFORMATION CENTER □
Binghamton, NY

Carpenter, Debbie, Ref.Libn.
U.S. ARMY - ENGINEER WATERWAYS
EXPERIMENT STATION - TECHNICAL
INFORMATION CENTER □ Vicksburg, MS

Carpenter, Deborah, Asst.Libn./Printed Coll.
SOUTHERN METHODIST UNIVERSITY -
DEGOLYER LIBRARY - FIKES HALL OF SPECIAL
COLLECTIONS □ Dallas, TX

Carpenter, Esther M., Archv.
MUSEUM OF MODERN ART - DEPARTMENT OF
RIGHTS AND REPRODUCTIONS -
PHOTOGRAPHIC ARCHIVES □ New York, NY

Carpenter, Mrs. Forrest, Libn.
OAK GROVE LUTHERAN CHURCH - MEMORIAL
LIBRARY† □ Richfield, MN

Carpenter, Karenn, Ref.Libn.
WILLKIE FARR & GALLAGHER - LIBRARY □ New
York, NY

Carpenter, Margot, Cons.
AESTHETIC REALISM FOUNDATION, INC. -
LIBRARY □ New York, NY

Carpenter, Myra A., Soc.Res.Asst.
UNIVERSITY OF NORTH CAROLINA, CHAPEL
HILL - CENTER FOR ALCOHOL STUDIES -
LIBRARY □ Chapel Hill, NC

Carpenter, Tosca N., Hd.Libn.
NEWPORT HOSPITAL - INA MOSHER HEALTH
SCIENCES LIBRARY □ Newport, RI

Carpenter, Wendell, Coord., Rd.Serv.
CHRISTIAN RECORD BRAILLE FOUNDATION,
INC. - LENDING LIBRARY □ Lincoln, NE

Carper, Anna M., Dir.
ELIZABETHTOWN COLLEGE - ZUG MEMORIAL
LIBRARY - ARCHIVES □ Elizabethtown, PA

Carper, Lee, Circ.Hd.
COLORADO SCHOOL OF MINES - ARTHUR
LAKES LIBRARY □ Golden, CO

Carr, Barbara, Ref.Libn.
ST. LAWRENCE COLLEGE SAINT-LAURENT -
LEARNING RESOURCE CENTRE □ Kingston, ON

Carr, Bobbie, Hd., Cat.Div.
U.S. NAVY - NAVAL POSTGRADUATE SCHOOL -
DUDLEY KNOX LIBRARY □ Monterey, CA

Carr, Caryn J., Chf. of Lib.Serv.
ALTOONA HOSPITAL - GLOVER MEMORIAL
MEDICAL AND NURSING LIBRARY □ Altoona, PA

Carr, Elizabeth N., Libn.
FLORIDA A&M UNIVERSITY - SCHOOL OF
BUSINESS & INDUSTRY LIBRARY □ Tallahassee,
FL

Carr, Sr. Frances A., Archv.
UNITED SOCIETY OF BELIEVERS - THE SHAKER
LIBRARY □ Poland Spring, ME

Carr, Jo Ann, Pub.Serv., Instr.Prog.
UNIVERSITY OF WISCONSIN, MADISON -
SCHOOL OF EDUCATION - INSTRUCTIONAL
MATERIALS CENTER □ Madison, WI

Carr, Kathy, Asst.Libn.
UNIVERSITY OF WASHINGTON - FISHERIES-
OCEANOGRAPHY LIBRARY □ Seattle, WA

Carr, Kathy M., Libn.
UNIVERSITY OF WASHINGTON - FRIDAY
HARBOR LABORATORIES - LIBRARY □ Friday
Harbor, WA

Carr, Kris, Asst.Libn.
DISTRICT ONE TECHNICAL INSTITUTE -
LIBRARY - EDUCATIONAL RESOURCE CENTER □
Eau Claire, WI

Carr, Mary M., Hd., Tech.Serv.
GONZAGA UNIVERSITY - CROSBY LIBRARY □
Spokane, WA

Carr, Richard D., Tech.Serv.Libn.
PALMER COLLEGE OF CHIROPRACTIC - DAVID
D. PALMER LIBRARY □ Davenport, IA

Carr, Sarah P., Libn.
ROSENN, JENKINS & GREENWALD, ATTORNEYS
AT LAW - LIBRARY □ Wilkes-Barre, PA

Carr, William, Chf.
PENNSYLVANIA STATE DEPT. OF
ENVIRONMENTAL RESOURCES -
ENVIRONMENTAL PROTECTION TECHNICAL
REFERENCE LIBRARY □ Harrisburg, PA

Carr-Harris, Ian, Dir.
ONTARIO COLLEGE OF ART - LIBRARY/
AUDIOVISUAL CENTRE □ Toronto, ON

Carraro, Sylvia, Tech.Asst.
ACADEMY OF AERONAUTICS - LIBRARY □
Flushing, NY

Carraway, Edward E., Hd.Libn.
JONES, DAY, REAVIS & POGUE - LAW LIBRARY
□ Dallas, TX

Carrick, Barbara J., Libn.
U.S. NATL. OCEANIC & ATMOSPHERIC
ADMINISTRATION - GREAT LAKES
ENVIRONMENTAL RESEARCH LABORATORY
LIBRARY† □ Ann Arbor, MI

Carrier, Lois, Libn.
UNIVERSITY OF BRITISH COLUMBIA -
HUMANITIES AND SOCIAL SCIENCES DIVISION
□ Vancouver, BC

Carrigan, Esther, Ser.Cat.
TEXAS A & M UNIVERSITY - MEDICAL
SCIENCES LIBRARY □ College Station, TX

Carrigan, Jean, Dir.
EQUITABLE LIFE ASSURANCE SOCIETY OF THE U.S. - INFORMATION SERVICES DIVISION □ New York, NY

Carrigan, Jennie L., Libn.
KENTUCKY STATE COUNCIL OF HIGHER EDUCATION - LIBRARY □ Frankfort, KY

Carrigan, John L., Info.Spec.
CITY OF HOPE NATIONAL MEDICAL CENTER - GRAFF MEDICAL AND SCIENTIFIC LIBRARY □ Duarte, CA

Carrington, David K., Hd., Tech.Serv.
LIBRARY OF CONGRESS - GEOGRAPHY & MAP DIVISION □ Washington, DC

Carrison, Dale K., Dean of Lib.
MANKATO STATE UNIVERSITY - LIBRARY - SPECIAL COLLECTIONS □ Mankato, MN

Carro, Jorge L., Hd.Libn.
UNIVERSITY OF CINCINNATI - ROBERT S. MARX LAW LIBRARY □ Cincinnati, OH

Carrol, J.N., Asst.
GULF OIL CHEMICALS COMPANY - POLYMER RESEARCH LIBRARY† □ Houston, TX

Carroll, Angelica, Mgr.
MOODY'S INVESTORS SERVICE, INC. - INFORMATION CENTER □ New York, NY

Carroll, Barbara, Libn.
SAN DIEGO PUBLIC LIBRARY - ART, MUSIC & RECREATION SECTION □ San Diego, CA

Carroll, Bonnie C., Asst.Mgr.
U.S. DEPT. OF ENERGY - OFFICE OF SCIENTIFIC AND TECHNICAL INFORMATION (OSTI) - TECHNICAL INFORMATION CENTER □ Oak Ridge, TN

Carroll, C., Hd., Pub.Aff.Archv.
CANADA - PUBLIC ARCHIVES OF CANADA - MANUSCRIPT DIVISION □ Ottawa, ON

Carroll, Rev. Clifford, S.J., Archv.
SOCIETY OF JESUS - OREGON PROVINCE ARCHIVES □ Spokane, WA

Carroll, Diane, Lib.Dir.
CENTRAL MAINE MEDICAL CENTER - GERRISH-TRUE HEALTH SCIENCE LIBRARY □ Lewiston, ME

Carroll, Elizabeth J., Adm.Asst.
PENNSYLVANIA STATE UNIVERSITY - CENTER FOR AIR ENVIRONMENT STUDIES - CAES INFORMATION SERVICES □ University Park, PA

Carroll, Judith A., Res.Spec.
UNIVERSITY OF WISCONSIN, MADISON - DEPARTMENT OF PSYCHIATRY - LITHIUM INFORMATION CENTER □ Madison, WI

Carroll, Karen, Archv.
GREENSBORO HISTORICAL MUSEUM - ARCHIVES □ Greensboro, NC

Carroll, Larry, Asst.Adm.
INDIANAPOLIS - DEPARTMENT OF METROPOLITAN DEVELOPMENT - DIVISION OF PLANNING - LIBRARY □ Indianapolis, IN

Carroll, Patricia, ILL Libn.
STERLING DRUG, INC. STERLING-WINTHROP RESEARCH INSTITUTE - LIBRARY □ Rensselaer, NY

Carroll, Ruth, Dir. of Libs.
ST. FRANCIS HOSPITAL AND MEDICAL CENTER - WILSON C. JAINSEN LIBRARY □ Hartford, CT

Carroll, Ruth P., Dir.
ST. FRANCIS HOSPITAL AND MEDICAL CENTER - SCHOOL OF NURSING LIBRARY □ Hartford, CT

Carroll, Virginia D., Libn.
CALHOUN COUNTY MUSEUM - ARCHIVES AND LIBRARY □ St. Matthews, SC

Carroll, Virginia L., Libn.
CAMP DRESSER & MC KEE, INC. - HERMAN G. DRESSER LIBRARY □ Boston, MA

Carroon, Robert G., Dir.
LITCHFIELD HISTORICAL SOCIETY - INGRAHAM LIBRARY □ Litchfield, CT

Carruthers, W. Eric, Prin. Planner
SANTA CLARA COUNTY PLANNING AND DEVELOPMENT DEPARTMENT - LIBRARY □ San Jose, CA

Carsch, Judith S., Libn.
WISE (Isaac M.) TEMPLE - RALPH COHEN MEMORIAL LIBRARY □ Cincinnati, OH

Carson, Donald, Chf.Libn.
COLLEGE OF INSURANCE - INSURANCE SOCIETY OF NEW YORK - LIBRARY □ New York, NY

Carson, Roberta, Med.Rec.Libn.
CALIFORNIA STATE MEDICAL FACILITY - STAFF LIBRARY □ Vacaville, CA

Carson-Croes, Judith, Dir., Lib. & Lrng.Serv.
COGSWELL COLLEGE - LIBRARY □ San Francisco, CA

Carstens, Patricia, Libn.
BAIRD HOLM MC EACHEN PEDERSEN & HAMANN LAW OFFICES - LIBRARY □ Omaha, NE

Carstensen, Chris, Libn.
FIRST BAPTIST CHURCH - LIBRARY □ Sioux Falls, SD

Carswell, Mary Alice, Dir.
ACADEMY OF THE NEW CHURCH - LIBRARY □ Bryn Athyn, PA

Carter, Ann Hadley, Res.Asst./Libn.
SOUTHERN REGIONAL EDUCATION BOARD - LIBRARY □ Atlanta, GA

Carter, Ann M., Lib.Mgr.
DORSEY & WHITNEY - LAW LIBRARY □ Minneapolis, MN

Carter, Barbara, Libn.
MUSCATATUCK STATE HOSPITAL & TRAINING CENTER - RESIDENT AND STAFF DEVELOPMENT LIBRARY □ Butlerville, IN

Carter, Bobby R., Dir., Lib.Serv.
TEXAS COLLEGE OF OSTEOPATHIC MEDICINE - HEALTH SCIENCES LIBRARY □ Fort Worth, TX

Carter, Catherine J., Libn.
CHICAGO MERCANTILE EXCHANGE - LIBRARY □ Chicago, IL

Carter, David, Archv.
ANGLICAN CHURCH OF CANADA - DIOCESE OF CALGARY - ANGLICAN ARCHIVES □ Calgary, AB

Carter, Donald, Supv., LRC
U.S. VETERANS ADMINISTRATION (MA-Brockton) - MEDICAL CENTER LIBRARY □ Brockton, MA

Carter, Edward, Asst., Film Study Ctr.
MUSEUM OF MODERN ART - FILM STUDY CENTER □ New York, NY

Carter, Dr. Edward C., II, Libn.
AMERICAN PHILOSOPHICAL SOCIETY - LIBRARY □ Philadelphia, PA

Carter, Eleanor M., Dir.
SUNY - AGRICULTURAL AND TECHNICAL COLLEGE AT COBLESKILL - JARED VAN WAGENEN, JR. LEARNING RESOURCE CENTER† □ Cobleskill, NY

Carter, Fay T., Acq.Libn.
LINCOLN UNIVERSITY OF MISSOURI - INMAN E. PAGE LIBRARY □ Jefferson City, MO

Carter, Georgia Kay, Supv. Chemist
HERCULES, INC. - HATTIESBURG PLANT LABORATORY - LIBRARY □ Hattiesburg, MS

Carter, Henry L., Act.Chf.
U.S. NATL. OCEANIC & ATMOSPHERIC ADM. - NATL. OCEAN SERVICE - PHYSICAL SCIENCE SERVICES SECT. - MAP LIB. □ Riverdale, MD

Carter, Ida, Tech.Libn.
GARD - LIBRARY □ Niles, IL

Carter, James W., Supv.
BABCOCK AND WILCOX COMPANY - RESEARCH CENTER LIBRARY □ Alliance, OH

Carter, Jewell Alexander, Lib.Dir.
BAPTIST MEDICAL CENTERS-SAMFORD UNIVERSITY - IDA V. MOFFETT SCHOOL OF NURSING - L.R. JORDAN LIBRARY† □ Birmingham, AL

Carter, John E., Cur., Photographs
NEBRASKA STATE HISTORICAL SOCIETY - LIBRARY □ Lincoln, NE

Carter, Karen R., Mgr., Info.Rsrc.Dept.
AMERICAN ACADEMY OF FAMILY PHYSICIANS - INFORMATION RESOURCE DEPARTMENT □ Kansas City, MO

Carter, Kent, Chf., Archv.Br.
U.S. NATL. ARCHIVES & RECORDS SERVICE - FEDERAL ARCHIVES AND RECORDS CENTER, REGION 7 □ Fort Worth, TX

Carter, Marva L., Lib.Tech.Asst.Supv.
FLORIDA A&M UNIVERSITY - SCHOOL OF NURSING LIBRARY □ Tallahassee, FL

Carter, Mary, Libn.
FIRST PRESBYTERIAN CHURCH - EWING MEMORIAL LIBRARY □ Houston, TX

Carter, N.G., Ref.Spec.
BATTELLE-NORTHWEST - PACIFIC NORTHWEST LABORATORY - HANFORD TECHNICAL LIBRARY □ Richland, WA

Carter, Nancy Carol, Dir.
GOLDEN GATE UNIVERSITY - SCHOOL OF LAW LIBRARY □ San Francisco, CA

Carter, Rick, Info.Spec.
HOLLINGSWORTH (John D.) ON WHEELS, INC. - INFORMATION SERVICES □ Greenville, SC

Carter, Rita A., Libn.
COMMUNICATIONS SATELLITE CORPORATION - CENTRAL LIBRARY† □ Washington, DC

Carter, Robert Allan, Sr.Libn.
NEW YORK STATE LIBRARY - LEGISLATIVE AND GOVERNMENTAL SERVICES □ Albany, NY

Carter, Robert L., Asst.Libn.
INDIANA STATE UNIVERSITY - DEPARTMENT OF RARE BOOKS AND SPECIAL COLLECTIONS □ Terre Haute, IN

Carter, Sharon, Info.Spec.
ST. PAUL FIRE & MARINE INSURANCE COMPANY - RISK MANAGEMENT SERVICES DIVISION INFORMATION CENTER □ St. Paul, MN

Carter, Sharon C., Libn.
WORCESTER TELEGRAM AND GAZETTE, INC. - LIBRARY □ Worcester, MA

Carter, Sheila, Libn.
BECHTEL POWER CORPORATION - LIBRARY □ Houston, TX

Carter, Susan Miller, Hist.Libn.
PLAINFIELD PUBLIC LIBRARY - GUILFORD TOWNSHIP HISTORICAL COLLECTION □ Plainfield, IN

Carter, Violet L., Adm.Off.
U.S. DEPT. OF HEALTH AND HUMAN SERVICES - DEPARTMENT LIBRARY† □ Washington, DC

Carter, Wendy, Rd.Serv.Spec.
U.S. VETERANS ADMINISTRATION (DC-Washington) - HEADQUARTERS LIBRARY DIVISION (142D) □ Washington, DC

Carter, Wendy N., Rd.Serv.Spec.
U.S. VETERANS ADMINISTRATION (DC-Washington) - HEADQUARTERS CENTRAL OFFICE LIBRARY (142D1) □ Washington, DC

Cartier, Celine R., Dir.
UNIVERSITE LAVAL - BIBLIOTHEQUE □ Ste. Foy, PQ

Cartier, Jacques, Law Libn.
DESJARDINS DUCHARME DESJARDINS & BOURQUE - LAW LIBRARY† □ Montreal, PQ

Cartledge, Ellen, Libn.
CONNECTICUT MUTUAL LIFE INSURANCE COMPANY - BUSINESS INFORMATION SERVICES† □ Hartford, CT

Cartwright, Sarah, Libn.
MARYCREST COLLEGE - CONE LIBRARY □ Davenport, IA

Carty, Kevin J., Libn.
METROPOLITAN PROPERTY & LIABILITY INSURANCE COMPANY - LAW & CORPORATE INFORMATION CENTER □ Warwick, RI

Caruso, Joy Louise, Mgr., Info.Serv.
CPC INTERNATIONAL - MOFFETT TECHNICAL LIBRARY □ Argo, IL

Caruso, Karin, Dir., AV Serv.
NEW HAMPSHIRE COLLEGE - SHAPIRO LIBRARY □ Manchester, NH

Caruso, Naomi, Coord.
JEWISH PUBLIC LIBRARY OF MONTREAL □ Montreal, PQ

Caruso, Nicholas C., Libn.
UNIVERSITY OF PITTSBURGH - GRADUATE
SCHOOL OF PUBLIC & INTERNATIONAL
AFFAIRS LIBRARY □ Pittsburgh, PA

Carvajal, Elena, Libn.
DALLAS PUBLIC LIBRARY - URBAN
INFORMATION CENTER □ Dallas, TX

Carvalho, Eugene, Libn.
UNIVERSITY OF KANSAS - EAST ASIAN
LIBRARY □ Lawrence, KS

Carvalho, Florina, ILL
ROCKWELL INTERNATIONAL - SCIENCE
CENTER LIBRARY □ Thousand Oaks, CA

Carvalho, Joseph, III, Coll.Libn.
SPRINGFIELD CITY LIBRARY - WARTIME
PROPAGANDA COLLECTION† □ Springfield, MA

Carver, Ann, Asst.Libn.
SEATTLE TIMES - LIBRARY† □ Seattle, WA

Carver, Chad, Asst.Libn.
THE ALLENTOWN HOSPITAL - HEALTH
SCIENCES LIBRARY □ Allentown, PA

Carver, Jane Warren, Med.Libn.
ST. JOSEPH HOSPITAL - MEDICAL LIBRARY □
St. Joseph, MO

Carver, Joseph E., Inst.Libn.
BRITISH COLUMBIA INSTITUTE OF
TECHNOLOGY - LIBRARY SERVICES DIVISION
□ Burnaby, BC

Carver, Larry, Dept.Hd.
UNIVERSITY OF CALIFORNIA, SANTA BARBARA
- MAP AND IMAGERY LABORATORY - LIBRARY
□ Santa Barbara, CA

Carver, Richard, Chf., P.R. Off.
NATIONAL LIBRARY OF CANADA/
BIBLIOTHEQUE NATIONALE DU CANADA □
Ottawa, ON

Cary, Howard B., Dir.
HOBART BROTHERS TECHNICAL CENTER -
JOHN H. BLANKENBUEHLER MEMORIAL
LIBRARY □ Troy, OH

Casale, Kathleen, Info.Spec.
AT & T COMMUNICATIONS - INFORMATION
RESEARCH CENTER □ New York, NY

Casciero, Albert J., Dir.
UNIVERSITY OF THE DISTRICT OF COLUMBIA -
LEARNING RESOURCES DIVISION† □
Washington, DC

Cascio, Nina, AV Libn.
SUNY AT BUFFALO - CHARLES B. SEARS LAW
LIBRARY □ Buffalo, NY

Case, Evangeline S., Pubn.Off.
UNIVERSITY OF CALGARY - CANADIAN
INSTITUTE OF RESOURCES LAW - LIBRARY □
Calgary, AB

Case, Frances, Dir., Div. of Blind
SOUTH CAROLINA STATE LIBRARY □ Columbia,
SC

Case, Howard E.
SUSSEX COUNTY HISTORICAL SOCIETY -
LIBRARY† □ Newton, NJ

Case, Josephine Young, Pres.
VAN HORNESVILLE COMMUNITY
CORPORATION - OWEN D. YOUNG COLLECTION
□ Van Hornesville, NY

Case, Julia L., Libn.
UNIVERSITY OF MICHIGAN - BURN CENTER -
LIBRARY □ Ann Arbor, MI

Case, Patricia J., Cur.
TEMPLE UNIVERSITY - CENTRAL LIBRARY
SYSTEM - CONTEMPORARY CULTURE
COLLECTION □ Philadelphia, PA

Case, Susan, Sr. Clinical Med.Libn.
UNIVERSITY OF MISSOURI, KANSAS CITY -
HEALTH SCIENCES LIBRARY □ Kansas City, MO

Casebier, Janet, Hd., Hum.Soc.Sci.Lib.
CALIFORNIA INSTITUTE OF TECHNOLOGY -
MILLIKAN LIBRARY □ Pasadena, CA

Casella, Roberta, Libn., Spec.Serv.
TEXAS TECH UNIVERSITY - LIBRARY □
Lubbock, TX

Casement, Susan, Libn.
UNIVERSITY OF CALIFORNIA, DAVIS -
AGRICULTURAL ECONOMICS BRANCH LIBRARY
□ Davis, CA

Casey, James B., Hd.Libn.
OHIO HISTORICAL SOCIETY - ARCHIVES-
LIBRARY □ Columbus, OH

Casey, Joan A., Dir., Lib./Pubns.
CITIZENS FORUM ON SELF-GOVERNMENT/
NATIONAL MUNICIPAL LEAGUE, INC. -
MURRAY SEASONGOOD LIBRARY □ New York,
NY

Casey, John W., Libn.
BRILEY, WILD AND ASSOCIATES, INC. -
LIBRARY □ Ormond Beach, FL

Casey, Kathleen E., Asst.Libn.
ST. LOUIS UNIVERSITY - DIVINITY LIBRARY □
St. Louis, MO

Casey, Nancy, Sec.
SHERMAN GRINBERG FILM LIBRARIES, INC. □
New York, NY

Casey, Philip M., Chf., Sci./Tech.Info.
U.S. ARMY - ARMAMENT RESEARCH &
DEVELOPMENT CENTER - BENET WEAPONS
LABORATORY - TECHNICAL LIBRARY □
Watervliet, NY

Casey, Sandra, Educ.Libn.
QUEEN'S UNIVERSITY AT KINGSTON -
EDUCATION LIBRARY □ Kingston, ON

Casey, Verna, Libn.
EASTERN KENTUCKY UNIVERSITY - LAW
ENFORCEMENT LIBRARY □ Richmond, KY

Casey, William T., Lib.Dir.
FITCHBURG STATE COLLEGE - LIBRARY □
Fitchburg, MA

Cash, Mary C., Libn.
STAMFORD CATHOLIC LIBRARY, INC.† □
Stamford, CT

Cash, Pamela J., Libn.
JOHNSON PUBLISHING COMPANY, INC. -
LIBRARY □ Chicago, IL

Cash, Susan R., Ref.Libn.
FEDERAL RESERVE BANK OF RICHMOND -
RESEARCH LIBRARY □ Richmond, VA

Cashau, George R., Dir., Tech.Res.
ANPA - TECHNICAL RESEARCH DEPARTMENT -
LIBRARY □ Reston, VA

Cashman, Norine Duncan, Cur.
BROWN UNIVERSITY - ART DEPARTMENT
SLIDE ROOM □ Providence, RI

Casile, Theresa K., Principal Libn.
NEW YORK PUBLIC LIBRARY - BELMONT
REGIONAL LIBRARY - ENRICO FERMI
CULTURAL CENTER □ Bronx, NY

Casino, Joseph J., Archv.
ST. CHARLES BORROMEO SEMINARY - RYAN
MEMORIAL LIBRARY □ Philadelphia, PA

Caskey, Elizabeth, Libn.
UNIVERSITY OF BRITISH COLUMBIA -
HUMANITIES AND SOCIAL SCIENCES DIVISION
□ Vancouver, BC

Caso, Gasper, Act.State Libn.
MASSACHUSETTS STATE LIBRARY □ Boston,
MA

Cason, Cleo S., Law Libn.
MADISON COUNTY - ELBERT H. PARSONS
PUBLIC LAW LIBRARY □ Huntsville, AL

Cason, Maidel, African Doc.Libn.
NORTHWESTERN UNIVERSITY - MELVILLE J.
HERSKOVITS LIBRARY OF AFRICAN STUDIES □
Evanston, IL

Casper, Dale E., Libn.
MICHIGAN STATE UNIVERSITY - C.W. BARR
PLANNING AND DESIGN LIBRARY □ East
Lansing, MI

Casper, Dale E., Libn.
MICHIGAN STATE UNIVERSITY - URBAN
POLICY AND PLANNING LIBRARY □ East
Lansing, MI

Casper, Glenda, Mgr., Info.Ctr.
NUCLEAR ASSURANCE CORPORATION -
INFORMATION CENTER □ Norcross, GA

Casper, Gordon C., Bus.Libn.
BRIGHAM YOUNG UNIVERSITY - TANNER
SCHOOL OF MANAGEMENT - LIBRARY □ Provo,
UT

Casper, Roderick J., Hd., Rd.Serv.
CALIFORNIA INSTITUTE OF TECHNOLOGY -
MILLIKAN LIBRARY □ Pasadena, CA

Cass, D., Archv.
GLENBOW-ALBERTA INSTITUTE - LIBRARY &
ARCHIVES □ Calgary, AB

Cassaro, Jim, Asst.Mus.Libn.
CORNELL UNIVERSITY - MUSIC LIBRARY □
Ithaca, NY

Cassel, Debra, Dir.
MONTEFIORE MEDICAL CENTER - MEDICAL
LIBRARY □ Bronx, NY

Cassell, Jo Anne S., Asst.Libn.
NATIONAL INSTITUTE OF EDUCATION -
EDUCATIONAL RESEARCH LIBRARY □
Washington, DC

Cassell, Judy A., Libn.
COCA-COLA COMPANY - COCA COLA USA -
MARKETING INFORMATION CENTER □ Atlanta,
GA

Cassell, Ollan C., Exec.Dir.
NATIONAL TRACK & FIELD HALL OF FAME -
LIBRARY □ Indianapolis, IN

Cassels, Sheila E., Asst.Libn., Ref.
PUBLIC SERVICE ELECTRIC AND GAS
COMPANY - LIBRARY □ Newark, NJ

Cassidy, Eileen E., Hd.Libn.
PALO ALTO MEDICAL FOUNDATION -
BARNETT-HALL LIBRARY □ Palo Alto, CA

Cassidy, John A., Libn.
SERGENT, HAUSKINS & BECKWITH,
CONSULTING GEOTECHNICAL ENGINEERS -
LIBRARY □ Phoenix, AZ

Cassidy, Joni, Cat.
NEW YORK COUNTY LAWYERS' ASSOCIATION -
LIBRARY □ New York, NY

Cassidy, Phoebe, Res.Libn.
SUN TECH, INC. - LIBRARY & INFORMATION
SERVICE □ Marcus Hook, PA

Cassiet, Maria, Cat.Libn.
BROWN UNIVERSITY - JOHN CARTER BROWN
LIBRARY □ Providence, RI

Cassler, Phyllis S., Libn.
U.S. ARMY - PATTON MUSEUM OF CAVALRY &
ARMOR - EMERT L. DAVIS MEMORIAL LIBRARY
□ Ft. Knox, KY

Cassoni, Brenda L., Asst.Libn.
PENNWALT CORPORATION - LUCIDOL
DIVISION - RESEARCH LIBRARY† □ Buffalo, NY

Castagno, Judith M., Supv., Info.Serv.
CALIFORNIA INSTITUTE OF TECHNOLOGY -
JET PROPULSION LABORATORY - LIBRARY □
Pasadena, CA

Castaldi, Ellena
TEXAS MEDICAL ASSOCIATION - MEMORIAL
LIBRARY □ Austin, TX

Castaneda, Liliana, Health Sci.Lib.Coord.
ST. JOSEPH HOSPITAL - LIBRARY □ Chicago, IL

Castaneda, Rosie
SAN ANTONIO EXPRESS AND NEWS - LIBRARY†
□ San Antonio, TX

Casteel, Kathleen, Hd.Ref.Libn./AV
CLEVELAND HEALTH SCIENCES LIBRARY -
HEALTH CENTER LIBRARY □ Cleveland, OH

Caster, Suzanne, Hd.Libn.
SAN FRANCISCO CHRONICLE - LIBRARY □ San
Francisco, CA

Castillo, Delfa, Lib.Dir.
ST. MATTHEW'S & ST. TIMOTHY'S
NEIGHBORHOOD CENTER, INC. - TUTORIAL
PROGRAM LIBRARY □ New York, NY

Castle, Joseph, Spanish Mss. & Maps
LOUISIANA STATE MUSEUM - LOUISIANA
HISTORICAL CENTER □ New Orleans, LA

Castlen, Peggy, Off.Serv.Supv.
NERCO, INC. - LIBRARY □ Portland, OR

Castricone, Robert, Info.Spec.
U.S. DEPT. OF HEALTH AND HUMAN SERVICES -
REGION I INFORMATION CENTER □ Boston, MA

Castro, Virginia, Lib.Tech.Asst.
CALIFORNIA STATE OFFICE OF LEGISLATIVE
COUNSEL - LIBRARY □ Sacramento, CA
Castronis, Orlean, Archv.Assoc.
UNIVERSITY OF GEORGIA - RICHARD B.
RUSSELL MEMORIAL LIBRARY □ Athens, GA
Caswell, Lucy S., Cur.
OHIO STATE UNIVERSITY - LIBRARY FOR
COMMUNICATION AND GRAPHIC ARTS □
Columbus, OH
Catalano, Kathleen, Cur.
U.S. NATL. PARK SERVICE - LONGFELLOW
NATL. HISTORIC SITE - LIBRARY □ Cambridge,
MA
Catania, Rose, Per.
GEE & JENSON ENGINEERS, ARCHITECTS,
PLANNERS, INC. - LIBRARY □ West Palm Beach,
FL
Cate, L., Asst.Libn
AMERICAN GAS ASSOCIATION - LIBRARY □
Arlington, VA
Catelli, Carmen, Hd.
BIBLIOTHEQUE DE LA VILLE DE MONTREAL -
COLLECTION GAGNON □ Montreal, PQ
Cater, Judy, Acq.
PALOMAR COMMUNITY COLLEGE - LIBRARY -
SPECIAL COLLECTIONS □ San Marcos, CA
Cates, Jane, Rd.Adv.
DISTRICT OF COLUMBIA PUBLIC LIBRARY -
BUSINESS, ECONOMICS & VOCATIONS
DIVISION □ Washington, DC
Cathcart, Cynthia
CONDE NAST PUBLICATIONS, INC. - LIBRARY □
New York, NY
Cathcart, John D., Act.Dir.
BENTLEY COLLEGE - SOLOMON R. BAKER
LIBRARY □ Waltham, MA
Cathey, Eva M., Adm.Libn.
U.S. ARMY MISSILE & MUNITIONS CENTER &
SCHOOL - MMCS TECHNICAL LIBRARY □
Redstone Arsenal, AL
Catlett, Stephen, Mss.Libn.
AMERICAN PHILOSOPHICAL SOCIETY -
LIBRARY □ Philadelphia, PA
Catt, Valery, Unit Sec.
UNIVERSITY OF ARIZONA - ARIZONA
COOPERATIVE WILDLIFE RESEARCH UNIT -
RESEARCH COLLECTION □ Tucson, AZ
Catterall, Susan, Ref./Circ.Libn.
DRAKE UNIVERSITY - LAW LIBRARY □ Des
Moines, IA
Caudill, A. Jeannine, Mgr., Lib.Serv.
GNOSTIC CONCEPTS, INC. - TECHNICAL
LIBRARY □ San Mateo, CA
Caudron, John Armand, Pres.
FIREARMS RESEARCH AND IDENTIFICATION
ASSOCIATION - LIBRARY □ Rowland Heights,
CA
Cauger, Jean, Asst.Sci.Libn.
BUTLER UNIVERSITY - SCIENCE LIBRARY □
Indianapolis, IN
Caughman, Rudolph, Chf.Libn.
BENDER (Matthew) AND COMPANY, INC. -
LIBRARY □ New York, NY
Caulker, Olive S., Asst.Dir./Tech.Serv.
MARQUETTE UNIVERSITY - MEMORIAL
LIBRARY □ Milwaukee, WI
Cavacini, Giovina, Libn.
U.S. NAVY - NAVAL HOSPITAL (PA-Philadelphia)
- MEDICAL LIBRARY □ Philadelphia, PA
Cavalcante, Bernard F., Asst.Hd.
U.S. NAVY - NAVAL HISTORICAL CENTER -
OPERATIONAL ARCHIVES □ Washington, DC
Cavallari, Elfrieda L., Chf., Cat.
U.S. AIR FORCE - AIR FORCE SYSTEMS
COMMAND - AIR FORCE GEOPHYSICS
LABORATORY - RESEARCH LIBRARY □ Bedford,
MA
Cavallo, Barbara, Supv.
RUTGERS UNIVERSITY, THE STATE
UNIVERSITY OF NEW JERSEY - PHYSICS
LIBRARY □ Piscataway, NJ

Cavanaugh, Dr. Jerome, Dir.
FAR EASTERN RESEARCH LIBRARY □
Minneapolis, MN
Cavanaugh, Marianne L., Libn.
KALAMAZOO INSTITUTE OF ARTS - ART
CENTER LIBRARY □ Kalamazoo, MI
Cavano, Joseph X., Info.Spec.
AMSTAR CORPORATION - RESEARCH AND
DEVELOPMENT LIBRARY □ Brooklyn, NY
Caver, Katy, Cur.
TEXARKANA HISTORICAL SOCIETY & MUSEUM
- LIBRARY □ Texarkana, TX
Cavis, Melinda, Libn.
U.S. DEPT. OF JUSTICE - FEDERAL BUREAU OF
INVESTIGATION - F.B.I. ACADEMY - LIBRARY □
Quantico, VA
Cawthon, Kayce, Lib.Sec.
COUNTRY MUSIC FOUNDATION - LIBRARY AND
MEDIA CENTER □ Nashville, TN
Caylor, Lawrence, Acq.Libn.
UNIVERSITY OF LOWELL, SOUTH CAMPUS -
DANIEL H. O'LEARY LIBRARY - SPECIAL
COLLECTIONS □ Lowell, MA
Cebula, Theodore, Coord.Sci./Bus.Div.
MILWAUKEE PUBLIC LIBRARY - SCIENCE &
BUSINESS DIVISION □ Milwaukee, WI
Cecere, Vikki, Libn.
U.S. VETERANS ADMINISTRATION (NY-
Canandaigua) - MEDICAL CENTER LIBRARY
(142D) □ Canandaigua, NY
Cecula, Lorie, Marketing Info.Spec.
UNION CARBIDE CORPORATION - CORPORATE
LIBRARY □ Danbury, CT
Cederholm, Theresa, Cur.
BOSTON PUBLIC LIBRARY - FINE ARTS
DEPARTMENT □ Boston, MA
Ceibert, Mary, Asst.Libn.
UNIVERSITY OF ILLINOIS - RARE BOOK ROOM
□ Urbana, IL
Celle, Deborah, Asst.Libn., Tech.Serv.
U.S. COURT OF APPEALS, 9TH CIRCUIT -
LIBRARY □ San Francisco, CA
Cellini, Nick, Libn.
BEVERLY HILLS PUBLIC LIBRARY - FINE ARTS
DIVISION □ Beverly Hills, CA
Celone, Barbara, Hd.Libn.
STANFORD UNIVERSITY - CUBBERLEY
EDUCATION LIBRARY □ Stanford, CA
Center, Sue L., Asst.Dir.
UNIVERSITY OF WISCONSIN, MADISON - LAW
SCHOOL LIBRARY - CRIMINAL JUSTICE
REFERENCE & INFORMATION CENTER □
Madison, WI
Centing, Richard, Hd.
OHIO STATE UNIVERSITY - ENGLISH, THEATRE
AND COMMUNICATION GRADUATE LIBRARY □
Columbus, OH
Cento, Caroline, Med.Rec.Techn.
MASSACHUSETTS STATE HOSPITAL SCHOOL -
MEDICAL LIBRARY □ Canton, MA
Cepek, Larry, Dir., Media Ctr.
OHIO DOMINICAN COLLEGE - SPANGLER
LIBRARY □ Columbus, OH
Ceravolo, Teresa, Asst.Archv.
LINN-HENLEY LIBRARY FOR SOUTHERN
HISTORICAL RESEARCH - DEPARTMENT OF
ARCHIVES AND MANUSCRIPTS □ Birmingham,
AL
Ceravolo, Teresa A., Archv.
BIRMINGHAM PUBLIC AND JEFFERSON
COUNTY FREE LIBRARY - SOUTHERN WOMEN'S
ARCHIVES □ Birmingham, AL
Ceresa, Mario A., Hd.Libn.
DETROIT COLLEGE OF LAW - LIBRARY □
Detroit, MI
Cerny, Katarina, Cur.
AMERICAN SWEDISH HISTORICAL MUSEUM -
NORD LIBRARY □ Philadelphia, PA
Cerny, Lucretia, Publicist
TRITON MUSEUM OF ART - LIBRARY □ Santa
Clara, CA

Cerny, Nina, Hd.Libn.
WALTER, CONSTON & SCHURTMAN, P.C. - LAW
LIBRARY □ New York, NY
Cerutti, Elsie, Chf., Ref. & Bibliog.Serv
U.S. NATL. INSTITUTES OF HEALTH - LIBRARY
□ Bethesda, MD
Cesanek, Sylvia B., Libn.
SACRED HEART HOSPITAL - WILLIAM A.
HAUSMAN MEDICAL LIBRARY □ Allentown, PA
Cesard, Mary Alice, Libn.
ENGLEWOOD HOSPITAL - SCHOOL OF NURSING
LIBRARY □ Englewood, NJ
Chabot, V., Hd., French Archv.
CANADA - PUBLIC ARCHIVES OF CANADA -
MANUSCRIPT DIVISION □ Ottawa, ON
Chabran, Richard, Assoc.Libn./Coord.
UNIVERSITY OF CALIFORNIA, LOS ANGELES -
CHICANO STUDIES RESEARCH LIBRARY □ Los
Angeles, CA
Chace, Laura L., Libn.
CINCINNATI HISTORICAL SOCIETY - LIBRARY
□ Cincinnati, OH
Chack, Ellen R., Libn.
PENNSYLVANIA STATE - OFFICE OF ATTORNEY
GENERAL - LAW LIBRARY □ Harrisburg, PA
Chadbourn, Erika S., Cur. of Mss.
HARVARD UNIVERSITY - LAW SCHOOL
LIBRARY □ Cambridge, MA
Chadbourne, Janice H., Ref.Libn.
BOSTON PUBLIC LIBRARY - FINE ARTS
DEPARTMENT □ Boston, MA
Chadey, Henry F., Dir.
SWEETWATER COUNTY HISTORICAL MUSEUM
- INFORMATION CENTER □ Green River, WY
Chadwell, Patricia, Unit Mgr., Soc.Sci.Div.
FORT WORTH PUBLIC LIBRARY - GENEALOGY
AND LOCAL HISTORY DEPARTMENT □ Fort
Worth, TX
Chadwick, Alena, Ref.Libn.
UNIVERSITY OF MASSACHUSETTS, AMHERST -
MORRILL BIOLOGICAL & GEOLOGICAL
SCIENCES LIBRARY □ Amherst, MA
Chadwick, Alena, Ref.Libn.
UNIVERSITY OF MASSACHUSETTS, AMHERST -
PHYSICAL SCIENCES LIBRARY □ Amherst, MA
Chadwick, Leroy, Ser.Libn.
UNIVERSITY OF WASHINGTON - HEALTH
SCIENCES LIBRARY □ Seattle, WA
Chaff, Sandra L., Dir., Archv.
MEDICAL COLLEGE OF PENNSYLVANIA -
ARCHIVES AND SPECIAL COLLECTIONS ON
WOMEN IN MEDICINE □ Philadelphia, PA
Chaffee, Joan K., Libn.
NORTON COMPANY - LIBRARY □ Worcester, MA
Chagoya, Janine, Search Serv.
INVESTIGATIVE RESOURCE CENTER - DATA
CENTER □ Oakland, CA
Chagpar, Mrs. N., Ref.Off.
ONTARIO - MINISTRY OF INDUSTRY AND
TRADE - INFORMATION CENTRE □ Toronto, ON
Chai, Julia, Asst.Libn.
AMERICAN CANCER SOCIETY - MEDICAL
LIBRARY □ New York, NY
Chaikin, Mary, Asst.Libn.
CARRIER FOUNDATION - NOLAN D.C. LEWIS
LIBRARY† □ Belle Mead, NJ
Chaikind, Hannah, Archv.
NEW HAVEN COLONY HISTORICAL SOCIETY -
WHITNEY LIBRARY □ New Haven, CT
Chait, Lauri, Asst.Cat.
UNIVERSITY OF MIAMI - SCHOOL OF
MEDICINE - LOUIS CALDER MEMORIAL
LIBRARY □ Miami, FL
Chalik, Barbara, Exec.Dir.
NATIONAL ASSOCIATION OF QUICK PRINTERS
- INTERNATIONAL QUICK PRINTING
FOUNDATION LIBRARY □ Chicago, IL
Challacombe, Elaine M., Libn.
STRONG (Margaret Woodbury) MUSEUM -
LIBRARY □ Rochester, NY
Chalmers, Deborah, Libn.
CANADIAN RED CROSS SOCIETY - LIBRARY □
Toronto, ON

Chalmers, JoAnn, Libn.
UNIVERSITY OF DETROIT - EVENING COLLEGE OF BUSINESS AND ADMINISTRATION - LIBRARY □ Detroit, MI

Chalmers, John, Libn.
UNIVERSITY OF TEXAS, AUSTIN - HARRY RANSOM HUMANITIES RESEARCH CENTER □ Austin, TX

Chalmers, V.J., Lib.Dir.
MANITOBA INDIAN CULTURAL EDUCATION CENTRE - PEOPLES LIBRARY □ Winnipeg, MB

Chamberlain, Donna, Sec.
DOCUMENTATION ASSOCIATES □ Los Angeles, CA

Chamberlain, Ellen, Sec.
UNIVERSITY OF TORONTO - DEPARTMENT OF BOTANY LIBRARY □ Toronto, ON

Chamberlain, Erna, Sci.Ref.Libn.
SUNY AT BINGHAMTON - SCIENCE LIBRARY □ Binghamton, NY

Chamberlain, Ken, Hd.Libn.
CARR (Emily) COLLEGE OF ART - LIBRARY □ Vancouver, BC

Chamberlain, L. Carl, Rare Books Cat.
GEORGETOWN UNIVERSITY - SPECIAL COLLECTIONS DIVISION - LAUINGER MEMORIAL LIBRARY □ Washington, DC

Chamberlain, William R., Asst.Dir., Gen.Lib.
VIRGINIA STATE LIBRARY □ Richmond, VA

Chamberlain, Zella, Assoc.Libn.
BOISE BIBLE COLLEGE - LIBRARY □ Boise, ID

Chamberlin, David R., Hd., Lib. & Maps Sect.
BRITISH COLUMBIA - MINISTRY OF PROVINCIAL SEC. & GOVERNMENT SERV. - PROVINCIAL ARCHIVES - MAP COLLECTION □ Victoria, BC

Chamberlin, Richard, Asst.Libn.
INDIANA UNIVERSITY OF PENNSYLVANIA - UNIVERSITY LIBRARY □ Indiana, PA

Chambers, A., Asst.Tech.Applic.Anl.
KERR INDUSTRIAL APPLICATIONS CENTER □ Durant, OK

Chambers, Clarke, Dir.
UNIVERSITY OF MINNESOTA - SOCIAL WELFARE HISTORY ARCHIVES □ Minneapolis, MN

Chambers, Eugene, Dir., Law Lib.
HARRIS COUNTY LAW LIBRARY □ Houston, TX

Chambers, Frances
CUNY - CITY COLLEGE LIBRARY - SCIENCE/ENGINEERING DIVISION □ New York, NY

Chambers, Harold, Hd., Ref. & Info.Serv.
MONTANA STATE LIBRARY □ Helena, MT

Chambers, Jeanette A., Lib.Techn.
U.S. ARMY HOSPITALS - LYSTER ARMY COMMUNITY HOSPITAL - MEDICAL LIBRARY □ Ft. Rucker, AL

Chambers, Martha, Spec.Coll.Libn.
SUNY - COLLEGE AT ONEONTA - JAMES M. MILNE LIBRARY - SPECIAL COLLECTIONS □ Oneonta, NY

Chambers, Steven, Ref.
NATIONAL CENTER FOR RESEARCH IN VOCATIONAL EDUCATION - RESEARCH LIBRARY □ Columbus, OH

Champagne, Eric A., Libn.
CANADA - AGRICULTURE CANADA - RESEARCH STATION, HARROW - LIBRARY† □ Harrow, ON

Champeau, Louise, Supv., Music/Rec.Lib.
CANADIAN BROADCASTING CORPORATION - MUSIC SERVICES LIBRARY □ Montreal, PQ

Champion, B., Ref.Libn.
UNIVERSITY OF ALBERTA - HUMANITIES AND SOCIAL SCIENCES LIBRARY □ Edmonton, AB

Champion, Walter, Asst.Ref.Libn.
VILLANOVA UNIVERSITY - PULLING LAW LIBRARY □ Villanova, PA

Champlin, Margaret, Sci. & Tech.Libn.
CALIFORNIA STATE UNIVERSITY, LOS ANGELES - SCIENCE AND TECHNOLOGY REFERENCE ROOM† □ Los Angeles, CA

Champoux, Raymond J.
EG&G, INC. - CORPORATE HEADQUARTERS - BUSINESS & FINANCIAL REFERENCE LIBRARY □ Wellesley, MA

Champreys, Weldon B., Libn.
U.S. AIR FORCE BASE - MC CLELLAN BASE LIBRARY □ McClellan AFB, CA

Chan, Charlie, Supv., Tech.Serv.
CHINESE NATIONALIST LEAGUE OF CANADA - LIBRARY† □ Vancouver, BC

Chan, Miss H.M., Libn.
ONTARIO - MINISTRY OF CORRECTIONAL SERVICES - LIBRARY SERVICES □ Toronto, ON

Chan, Julia, Med.Libn.
ST. JOSEPH'S HEALTH CENTRE - GEORGE PENNAL LIBRARY □ Toronto, ON

Chan, Lillian, Sci.Libn.
SAN DIEGO STATE UNIVERSITY - SCIENCE DEPARTMENT† □ San Diego, CA

Chan, M.L., Hd.Cat.
UNIVERSITY OF CALGARY - MEDICAL LIBRARY† □ Calgary, AB

Chan, Margy, Supv., Coll.Dev.
ALCOHOLISM AND DRUG ADDICTION RESEARCH FOUNDATION - LIBRARY □ Toronto, ON

Chan, Margy, Libn.
DOCTORS HOSPITAL - ALEXANDER RAXLER LIBRARY □ Toronto, ON

Chan, Shirley S., Libn.
COLUMBIA HOSPITAL - COLLEGE OF NURSING - LIBRARY □ Milwaukee, WI

Chan, Wing, Info.Libn.
AT & T BELL LABORATORIES - LIBRARY □ West Long Branch, NJ

Chander, Suneeta, Hd., Cat.Sect.
CANADA - REVENUE CANADA - CUSTOMS & EXCISE LIBRARY □ Ottawa, ON

Chandler, Deborah G., Info.Spec.
SCOTT PAPER COMPANY - S.D. WARREN COMPANY - RESEARCH LIBRARY □ Westbrook, ME

Chandler, Harold, Acq.Libn.
MEMPHIS THEOLOGICAL SEMINARY - LIBRARY† □ Memphis, TN

Chandler, Jody, Lib.Supv.
BRIGHAM YOUNG UNIVERSITY - BEAN MUSEUM - RESEARCH LIBRARY □ Provo, UT

Chaney, Virginia, Lib.Dir.
U.S. ARMY POST - FORT RICHARDSON - LIBRARY □ Ft. Richardson, AK

Chang, Chun Chuan, Chf.Libn.
GROLIER INCORPORATED - LIBRARY □ Danbury, CT

Chang, David, Chinese Cat.
PRINCETON UNIVERSITY - GEST ORIENTAL LIBRARY AND EAST ASIAN COLLECTIONS □ Princeton, NJ

Chang, Dr. Henry C., Dir.
VIRGIN ISLANDS - DEPARTMENT OF CONSERVATION & CULTURAL AFFAIRS - BUREAU OF LIBRARIES AND MUSEUMS □ St. Thomas, VI

Chang, Huei-Ju, Sr.Cat.Libn.
YALE UNIVERSITY - EAST ASIAN COLLECTION □ New Haven, CT

Chang, Janice, Mgr.
NORTHROP CORPORATION - CORPORATE LIBRARY □ Los Angeles, CA

Chang, Joseph, Bibliog./Cat. (Japanese)
UNIVERSITY OF PITTSBURGH - EAST ASIAN LIBRARY □ Pittsburgh, PA

Chang, Margaret, Archv.
NEWFOUNDLAND - PROVINCIAL ARCHIVES OF NEWFOUNDLAND AND LABRADOR □ St. John's, NF

Chang, Roy, Cat.Libn.
WESTERN ILLINOIS UNIVERSITY - LIBRARIES □ Macomb, IL

Chang, Sherry, Libn.
SUNY AT STONY BROOK - MATHEMATICS-PHYSICS LIBRARY □ Stony Brook, NY

Chang, Theresa, Hd., Tech.Serv.
GALLAUDET COLLEGE LIBRARY - SPECIAL COLLECTIONS† □ Washington, DC

Chang, Yeen-Mei Wu, China Libn.
UNIVERSITY OF WASHINGTON - EAST ASIA LIBRARY □ Seattle, WA

Chanin, Leah F., Dir., Law Lib.
MERCER UNIVERSITY - LAW SCHOOL - FURMAN SMITH LAW LIBRARY □ Macon, GA

Channon, Geraldine, Dir., Res. & Info.Serv.
CANADIAN TEACHERS' FEDERATION - GEORGE G. CROSKERY MEMORIAL LIBRARY □ Ottawa, ON

Chao, Gloria, Cat.Libn.
RUTGERS UNIVERSITY, THE STATE UNIVERSITY OF NEW JERSEY - SCHOOL OF LAW LIBRARY† □ Camden, NJ

Chao, Paul, Assoc.Libn.
SETON HALL UNIVERSITY - MC LAUGHLIN LIBRARY □ South Orange, NJ

Chao, Theresa, Per.Libn.
UNIVERSITY OF WISCONSIN, STEVENS POINT - JAMES H. ALBERTSON CENTER FOR LEARNING RESOURCES □ Stevens Point, WI

Chao, Mr. Yen-pin, Libn.
ONTARIO POLICE COLLEGE - LIBRARY □ Aylmer West, ON

Chao, Mrs. Yen-Shew Lynn, Cur. of Rubel Coll.
HARVARD UNIVERSITY - FINE ARTS LIBRARY □ Cambridge, MA

Chapel, Ann Elizabeth, Libn.
U.S. BUREAU OF MINES - CHARLES W. HENDERSON MEMORIAL LIBRARY □ Denver, CO

Chapin, Caroline Davis, Cur., Mss. & Bk.
PILGRIM SOCIETY - PILGRIM HALL LIBRARY □ Plymouth, MA

Chapin, Georganne, Proc.Coord.
ERIC CLEARINGHOUSE ON URBAN EDUCATION □ New York, NY

Chapin, Marcie, Ed.
AT & T - EDITORIAL RESEARCH CENTER† □ New York, NY

Chapin, Shirley, Libn.
NEW YORK CITY - PUBLIC HEALTH LABORATORIES - WILLIAM HALLOCK PARK MEMORIAL LIBRARY □ New York, NY

Chapis, Marilyn D., Med. Staff Libn.
POTTSTOWN MEMORIAL MEDICAL CENTER - MEDICAL STAFF LIBRARY □ Pottstown, PA

Chaplan, Margaret A., Libn.
UNIVERSITY OF ILLINOIS - INSTITUTE OF LABOR AND INDUSTRIAL RELATIONS LIBRARY □ Champaign, IL

Chapman, Allan D., Musm.Libn.
METROPOLITAN MUSEUM OF ART - ROBERT GOLDWATER LIBRARY □ New York, NY

Chapman, Christine, Libn.
WOMEN & INFANTS HOSPITAL OF RHODE ISLAND - HEALTH SCIENCES INFORMATION CENTER □ Providence, RI

Chapman, David L., Assoc.Archv.
TEXAS A & M UNIVERSITY - ARCHIVES & MANUSCRIPTS COLLECTIONS □ College Station, TX

Chapman, Dorothy H., Cur.
TEXAS SOUTHERN UNIVERSITY - LIBRARY - HEARTMAN COLLECTION □ Houston, TX

Chapman, Edith B., Sr.Lit.Sci.
WARNER-LAMBERT COMPANY - CORPORATE LIBRARY □ Morris Plains, NJ

Chapman, Janet, Info.Sci.
EXXON CORPORATION - MEDICINE & ENVIRONMENTAL HEALTH DEPT. - RESEARCH & ENVIRONMENTAL HEALTH DIV.LIB. □ East Millstone, NJ

Chapman, Marian L., Dir.
RESEARCH FOR BETTER SCHOOLS, INC. - RESOURCE CENTER □ Philadelphia, PA

Chapman, Mary, Assoc.Libn.,Tech.Serv.
NEW YORK UNIVERSITY - SCHOOL OF LAW LIBRARY □ New York, NY

Chapman, Philip, Pres.
L-5 SOCIETY - LIBRARY □ Tucson, AZ

Chapman, Rene, Hd.Cat.
UNIVERSITY OF IOWA - LAW LIBRARY □ Iowa City, IA

Chapman, Ruby, Ref.Libn.
AT & T BELL LABORATORIES - LIBRARY □ Naperville, IL

Chapman, William, Libn.
CHAPMAN (Bruce) COMPANY - LIBRARY □ Grafton, VT

Chappell, Barbara A., Hd., Ref./Circ.
U.S. GEOLOGICAL SURVEY - LIBRARY □ Reston, VA

Chappell, Gordon, Regional Hist.
U.S. NATL. PARK SERVICE - WESTERN REGIONAL OFFICE - REGIONAL RESOURCES LIBRARY □ San Francisco, CA

Chappell, Kate, Rsrcs.Anl.
SOUTHERN ILLINOIS UNIVERSITY, EDWARDSVILLE - RESEARCH & PROJECTS OFFICE LIBRARY □ Edwardsville, IL

Chappell, Susan, Med.Libn.
GREENVILLE HOSPITAL SYSTEM - HEALTH SCIENCE LIBRARY† □ Greenville, SC

Charan, Dr. Kirti K., Assoc.Prof. & Dir.
MC GILL UNIVERSITY - SCHOOL OF HUMAN COMMUNICATION DISORDERS - LIBRARY □ Montreal, PQ

Charbonneau, Monique, Lib.Dir.
QUEBEC PROVINCE - MINISTERE DES COMMUNICATIONS - BIBLIOTHEQUE ADMINISTRATIVE □ Quebec, PQ

Charbonneau, Ron, Res.Libn.
HOUSE EAR INSTITUTE - GEORGE KELEMEN LIBRARY □ Los Angeles, CA

Charest, Ginette, Audiovideotheque
HOPITAL STE-JUSTINE - CENTRE D'INFORMATION SUR LA SANTE DE L'ENFANT □ Montreal, PQ

Charest, Ms. J., Tech.Serv.Supv.
BEDFORD INSTITUTE OF OCEANOGRAPHY - LIBRARY □ Dartmouth, NS

Charest, Nicole, Dir.
RADIO QUEBEC - CENTRE DES RESSOURCES DOCUMENTAIRES □ Montreal, PQ

Charette, Gail L., Hd.Libn.
TEMPLE UNIVERSITY - CENTER FOR THE STUDY OF FEDERALISM - LIBRARY □ Philadelphia, PA

Charette, Marcel, Ck. in Charge
CANADA - AGRICULTURE CANADA - NEATBY LIBRARY □ Ottawa, ON

Chariton, May, Libn.
SOUTHSIDE HOSPITAL - MEDICAL LIBRARY □ Bay Shore, NY

Charlebois, Joyce C., Chf.Libn.
PRATT AND WHITNEY CANADA, INC. - LIBRARY □ Longueuil, PQ

Charles, John W., Spec.Coll.Libn.
UNIVERSITY OF ALBERTA - BRUCE PEEL SPECIAL COLLECTIONS LIBRARY □ Edmonton, AB

Charles, Kimberly, Chartist/Prog.
BRUNDAGE, STORY & ROSE, INVESTMENT COUNSEL - LIBRARY □ New York, NY

Charles, Sharon, Circuit Libn.
ABBOTT-NORTHWESTERN HOSPITAL CORPORATION - HEALTH SCIENCES RESOURCE CENTER □ Minneapolis, MN

Charlet, Jim, Dist.Dir.
U.S. DEPT. OF COMMERCE - INTERNATIONAL TRADE ADMINISTRATION - NASHVILLE DISTRICT OFFICE LIBRARY □ Nashville, TN

Charlton, Barbara A., Sci./Tech.Ref.Libn.
CALIFORNIA STATE UNIVERSITY, SACRAMENTO - LIBRARY - SCIENCE & TECHNOLOGY REFERENCE DEPARTMENT □ Sacramento, CA

Charlton, Mary Lou, Libn.
HEALTH AND WELFARE PLANNING ASSOCIATION OF ALLEGHENY COUNTY - LIBRARY □ Pittsburgh, PA

Charlton, Dr. Thomas L., Chm.,Texas Coll.Comm.
BAYLOR UNIVERSITY - TEXAS COLLECTION □ Waco, TX

Charnow, Elaine, Libn.
NORTH SHORE SYNAGOGUE - CHARLES COHN MEMORIAL LIBRARY □ Syosset, NY

Charron, Sr. Irene, S.P., Med.Libn.
ST. ELIZABETH MEDICAL CENTER - HEALTH SCIENCES LIBRARY □ Yakima, WA

Charton, Rebecca, Libn.
KEY (Francis Scott) MEDICAL CENTER - HAROLD E. HARRISON LIBRARY □ Baltimore, MD

Chase, Angela, Govt.Doc.Libn.
HARTFORD PUBLIC LIBRARY - BUSINESS, SCIENCE & TECHNOLOGY DEPARTMENT □ Hartford, CT

Chase, Bradley, Tech.Asst.
SUNY AT BUFFALO - HEALTH SCIENCES LIBRARY □ Buffalo, NY

Chase, D. Thompson, Libn.
PUBLIC LIBRARY OF CINCINNATI AND HAMILTON COUNTY - CHILDREN'S DEPARTMENT □ Cincinnati, OH

Chase, Eleanor L., Hd.Libn.
UNIVERSITY OF WASHINGTON - GOVERNMENT PUBLICATIONS DIVISION □ Seattle, WA

Chase, Judith Wragg, Lib.Dir.
OLD SLAVE MART MUSEUM - LIBRARY □ Sullivan's Island, SC

Chase, Karen, Tech.Serv.Libn.
OREGON INSTITUTE OF TECHNOLOGY - LEARNING RESOURCES CENTER □ Klamath Falls, OR

Chase, Marcelle, Ref.Libn.
ARIZONA STATE UNIVERSITY - COLLEGE OF LAW - LIBRARY □ Tempe, AZ

Chase, Michael H., Dir.
UNIVERSITY OF CALIFORNIA, LOS ANGELES - BRAIN INFORMATION SERVICE □ Los Angeles, CA

Chase, Robert, Hd., Doc.Distr.Ctr.
RHODE ISLAND STATE LIBRARY □ Providence, RI

Chase, Rory L., Corp.Libn.
CINCINNATI MILACRON INDUSTRIES, INC. - CORPORATE INFORMATION CENTER □ Cincinnati, OH

Chasen, Larry, Mgr.
GENERAL ELECTRIC COMPANY - SPACE/SYSTEMS DIVISION LIBRARIES □ Philadelphia, PA

Chastain, Christine, Ref.Libn.
NATIONAL INSTITUTE OF ENVIRONMENTAL HEALTH SCIENCES - LIBRARY □ Research Triangle Park, NC

Chatfield, Mary, Libn.
HARVARD UNIVERSITY - HARVARD BUSINESS SCHOOL - BAKER LIBRARY □ Boston, MA

Chauncey, Donald E., Film Libn.
MIAMI-DADE PUBLIC LIBRARY - AUDIO/VISUAL DEPARTMENT □ Miami, FL

Chavez, Alice M., Libn. I
UNIVERSITY OF TEXAS, EL PASO - NURSING/MEDICAL LIBRARY □ El Paso, TX

Chavis, Mr. C., Libn.
AMERICAN STANDARDS TESTING BUREAU, INC. - SAM TOUR LIBRARY □ New York, NY

Chayes, Marion C., Libn.
ABINGTON MEMORIAL HOSPITAL - WILMER MEMORIAL MEDICAL LIBRARY □ Abington, PA

Cheape, Kathleen, Asst. Law Libn.
UNIVERSITY OF NORTH CAROLINA, CHAPEL HILL - LAW LIBRARY □ Chapel Hill, NC

Cheek, Emory, Lib.Assoc.
UNIVERSITY OF GEORGIA - GEORGIA COASTAL PLAIN EXPERIMENT STATION LIBRARY □ Tifton, GA

Cheek, Fern M., Asst.Libn.
HENRY FORD HOSPITAL - FRANK J. SLADEN LIBRARY □ Detroit, MI

Cheff, Christine M., Ref. & Pub.Serv.Libn.
WESTERN STATE UNIVERSITY - COLLEGE OF LAW - LIBRARY □ San Diego, CA

Cheff, Frank, Hd., Acq.
CANADA - CANADIAN INTERNATIONAL DEVELOPMENT AGENCY - DEVELOPMENT INFORMATION CENTRE □ Hull, PQ

Chekouras, E., Ref.Libn.
AKRON CITY HOSPITAL - MEDICAL LIBRARY □ Akron, OH

Chen, Alice S., Supv.
ALBERTA - DEPARTMENT OF ENERGY AND NATURAL RESOURCES - MAP & AIR PHOTO REFERENCE LIBRARY □ Edmonton, AB

Chen, Bess, Asst.Libn.
CALIFORNIA STATE UNIVERSITY, SACRAMENTO - LIBRARY - SCIENCE & TECHNOLOGY REFERENCE DEPARTMENT □ Sacramento, CA

Chen, Catherine, Hd.Libn.
NORTHWOOD INSTITUTE - STROSACKER LIBRARY □ Midland, MI

Chen, Charles K.H., Far Spec. and Cur.
DARTMOUTH COLLEGE - ORIENTAL COLLECTION □ Hanover, NH

Chen, Chi-Ping, Libn.
UNIVERSITY OF CALIFORNIA, BERKELEY - CENTER FOR CHINESE STUDIES - LIBRARY □ Berkeley, CA

Chen, Christina, Tech.Serv.Libn.
LOS ANGELES COUNTY/UNIVERSITY OF SOUTHERN CALIFORNIA MEDICAL CENTER - MEDICAL LIBRARIES □ Los Angeles, CA

Chen, David, Asst.Libn./Tech.Serv.
EMORY UNIVERSITY - PITTS THEOLOGY LIBRARY □ Atlanta, GA

Chen, Faustina, Libn.
DALHOUSIE UNIVERSITY - INSTITUTE OF PUBLIC AFFAIRS - LIBRARY □ Halifax, NS

Chen, Flora, Libn.
CANADA - NATIONAL RESEARCH COUNCIL - PLANT BIOTECHNOLOGY INSTITUTE - LIBRARY □ Saskatoon, SK

Chen, Frances, Libn.
PRINCETON UNIVERSITY - SCHOOL OF ARCHITECTURE LIBRARY □ Princeton, NJ

Chen, Freda, Cat.
OKLAHOMA STATE DEPARTMENT OF LIBRARIES □ Oklahoma City, OK

Chen, Hsiao-Chiang, Prin.Cat.Libn.
YALE UNIVERSITY - EAST ASIAN COLLECTION □ New Haven, CT

Chen, Joanna, Libn.
NATIONAL INSTITUTE ON AGING - GERONTOLOGY RESEARCH CENTER LIBRARY □ Baltimore, MD

Chen, Mrs. Mai, Coord., Tech.Serv.
QUEEN'S UNIVERSITY AT KINGSTON - LAW LIBRARY □ Kingston, ON

Chenan, Margaret
PROVIDENCE PUBLIC LIBRARY - ART AND MUSIC DEPARTMENT □ Providence, RI

Cheney, M. Margaret, Med.Libn.
LEONARD MORSE HOSPITAL - MEDICAL LIBRARY† □ Natick, MA

Cheng, Charmian, Chinese Cat.
PRINCETON UNIVERSITY - GEST ORIENTAL LIBRARY AND EAST ASIAN COLLECTIONS □ Princeton, NJ

Cheng, Mrs.H.J., Cat.
NELSON-ATKINS MUSEUM OF ART - SPENCER ART REFERENCE LIBRARY □ Kansas City, MO

Cheng, James K., Chf.Libn.
CHINESE NATIONALIST LEAGUE OF CANADA - LIBRARY† □ Vancouver, BC

Cheng, James K.M., Cur.
UNIVERSITY OF CHICAGO - FAR EASTERN LIBRARY □ Chicago, IL

Cheng, Juliana, Libn.
DELAWARE STATE DEPARTMENT OF TRANSPORTATION - LIBRARY □ Dover, DE

Cheng, Juliana, Sr.Libn.
LOS ANGELES PUBLIC LIBRARY, CHINATOWN BRANCH - CHINESE COLLECTION □ Los Angeles, CA

Cheng, Mu-chin, Doc.Libn.
UNIVERSITY OF ILLINOIS - COLLEGE OF
ENGINEERING - ENGINEERING DOCUMENTS
CENTER □ Urbana, IL

Cheng, Nancy, Govt.Docs.
UNIVERSITY OF UTAH - LAW LIBRARY □ Salt
Lake City, UT

Cheng, Paul P.W., East Asian Libn.
CORNELL UNIVERSITY - WASON COLLECTION □
Ithaca, NY

Cheng, Dr. W.S., Dir., R & D Lab.
AULT FOODS, LTD. - RESEARCH &
DEVELOPMENT LIBRARY □ London, ON

Chenier, Andre, Directeur
UNIVERSITE DU QUEBEC A HULL -
BIBLIOTHEQUE □ Hull, PQ

Cheong, Ken, Cat.Libn.
O'MELVENY AND MYERS - INFORMATION
SERVICES □ Los Angeles, CA

Cherellia, Peter P., Libn.
CITIZENS LAW LIBRARY† □ Greensburg, PA

Chernega, Ann, Lib.Mgr.
WESTINGHOUSE ELECTRIC CORPORATION -
NUCLEAR ENERGY SYSTEMS - ADVANCED
REACTORS DIVISION - LIBRARY† □ Madison,
PA

Chernis, Ms. Terry, Env. Health
CANADA - HEALTH AND WELFARE CANADA -
LIBRARY SERVICES □ Ottawa, ON

Cherniv, Raisa, Libn.
LUTHERAN HOSPITAL OF FORT WAYNE, INC. -
HEALTH SCIENCES LIBRARY □ Fort Wayne, IN

Chernofsky, Ellen, Libn.
AB BOOKMAN PUBLICATIONS, INC. - LIBRARY
□ Clifton, NJ

Cheron, Theodore, Lit.Res.Anl.
AEROSPACE CORPORATION - CHARLES C.
LAURITSEN LIBRARY □ Los Angeles, CA

Cherry, Cheryl A., Libn.
FISCHER & PORTER CO. - CORPORATE
ENGINEERING LIBRARY □ Warminster, PA

Cherry, Ronald L., Dir.
UNIVERSITY OF ARIZONA - COLLEGE OF LAW
LIBRARY† □ Tucson, AZ

Chertok, Bernard, Pres.
SHERMAN GRINBERG FILM LIBRARIES, INC. □
New York, NY

Chervenak, Joe, Acq.
SOLAR ENERGY RESEARCH INSTITUTE - SERI
TECHNICAL LIBRARY □ Golden, CO

Chervenie, P., Per.Libn.
PACE UNIVERSITY, PLEASANTVILLE/
BRIARCLIFF - EDWARD AND DORIS MORTOLA
LIBRARY □ Pleasantville, NY

Chervin, Shirley, Libn.
POMONA VALLEY COMMUNITY HOSPITAL -
MEDICAL LIBRARY □ Pomona, CA

Cheshier, Robert G., Dir.
CLEVELAND HEALTH SCIENCES LIBRARY □
Cleveland, OH

Cheshire, Victoria, Dir. of Res.
KORN/FERRY INTERNATIONAL - RESEARCH
LIBRARY □ Chicago, IL

Cheski, Richard M., State Libn.
STATE LIBRARY OF OHIO □ Columbus, OH

Chesky, James A., Sec./Archv.
LUTHERAN CHURCH IN AMERICA - NORTH
CAROLINA SYNOD - ARCHIVES □ Salisbury, NC

Chesler, N., Coord.
BELL COMMUNICATIONS RESEARCH, INC. -
INFORMATION RESOURCES SERVICES CENTER
□ Piscataway, NJ

Cheslock, Rosalind P., Mgr., Tech.Info.Serv.
MARTIN MARIETTA LABORATORIES - LIBRARY
□ Baltimore, MD

Chesney, Carolyn E., Libn.
HOUSE BEAUTIFUL - STAFF LIBRARY □ New
York, NY

Chestnut, James D., Div.Libn.
U.S. ARMY - CORPS OF ENGINEERS - SOUTH
ATLANTIC DIVISION - LIBRARY &
INFORMATION CENTER □ Atlanta, GA

Chetner, Sylvia R., Act. Area Coord.
UNIVERSITY OF ALBERTA - JOHN W. SCOTT
HEALTH SCIENCES LIBRARY □ Edmonton, AB

Chettle, Charles, Res.Asst.
U.S. NATL. OCEANIC & ATMOSPHERIC ADM. -
NATL. OCEAN SERVICE - PHYSICAL SCIENCE
SERVICES SECT. - MAP LIB. □ Riverdale, MD

Cheung, Anthony, Chf.Libn.
CANADA - DEFENCE AND CIVIL INSTITUTE OF
ENVIRONMENTAL MEDICINE - SCIENTIFIC
INFORMATION CENTRE □ Downsview, ON

Cheung, G., Acq.Libn.
COLLEGE MILITAIRE ROYAL DE ST-JEAN -
LIBRARY □ St. Jean, PQ

Chiang, Katherine S., Hd.
UNIVERSITY OF MINNESOTA, ST. PAUL -
ENTOMOLOGY, FISHERIES AND WILDLIFE
LIBRARY □ St. Paul, MN

Chiang, Shu-nan T., Tech.Libn.
SINGER COMPANY - LINK DIVISION -
TECHNICAL LIBRARY □ Sunnyvale, CA

Chiang, Win-Shin S., Law Libn.
LOYOLA UNIVERSITY (New Orleans) - LAW
LIBRARY □ New Orleans, LA

Chiasson, Gilles, Mgr.
SPORT INFORMATION RESOURCE CENTRE □
Ottawa, ON

Chibnik, Katharine, Urban Plan.
COLUMBIA UNIVERSITY - AVERY
ARCHITECTURAL AND FINE ARTS LIBRARY □
New York, NY

Chichura, Edward, Chf.Libn.
U.S. COURT OF APPEALS, 9TH CIRCUIT -
LIBRARY □ San Francisco, CA

Chickanzeff, Sharon, Lib.Dir.
PARSONS SCHOOL OF DESIGN - ADAM AND
SOPHIE GIMBEL DESIGN LIBRARY □ New York,
NY

Chiesa, Adele M., Chf., Lrng.Rsrcs.Ctr.
NATIONAL EMERGENCY TRAINING CENTER -
LIBRARY □ Emmitsburg, MD

Child, Margaret, Asst.Dir.
SMITHSONIAN INSTITUTION LIBRARIES □
Washington, DC

Childress, Susan
VIRGINIA STATE DEPARTMENT OF GENERAL
SERVICES - DIVISION OF CONSOLIDATED
LABORATORY SERVICES LIBRARY □ Richmond,
VA

Childs, Beverly, Info. Purchasing
CHASE MANHATTAN BANK, N.A. -
INFORMATION CENTER □ New York, NY

Childs, Martha C., Libn.
UNIVERSITY OF TENNESSEE - MEMORIAL
RESEARCH CENTER AND HOSPITAL - PRESTON
MEDICAL LIBRARY □ Knoxville, TN

Childs, Peter P., Dir.
BOROUGH OF COLLINGSWOOD - FREE PUBLIC
LIBRARY - NEW JERSEY HISTORY ROOM □
Collingswood, NJ

Childs, Suse, Libn.
METROPOLITAN MUSEUM OF ART - CLOISTERS
LIBRARY □ New York, NY

Childs, Ward, Asst.Archv.
PHILADELPHIA - CITY ARCHIVES □ Philadelphia,
PA

Chillingworth, Margaret, Libn.
PRESTON, THORGRIMSON, ELLIS & HOLMAN -
LIBRARY □ Seattle, WA

Chillman, Helen, Slide Libn.
YALE UNIVERSITY - ART AND ARCHITECTURE
LIBRARY □ New Haven, CT

Chilton, Betty H., Staff Lib.Spec.
FAIRFAX COUNTY PUBLIC SCHOOLS -
PROFESSIONAL REFERENCE LIBRARY IN
EDUCATION □ Fairfax, VA

Chilton, Janina, Libn.
UTAH STATE HOSPITAL - LIBRARY □ Provo, UT

Chilton, Joan, Med.Libn.
COMMUNITY HOSPITAL - MEDICAL LIBRARY □
Santa Rosa, CA

Chin, Ann, Client Serv.Supv.
ALCOHOLISM AND DRUG ADDICTION
RESEARCH FOUNDATION - LIBRARY □ Toronto,
ON

Chin, Cecilia, Chf.Libn.
SMITHSONIAN INSTITUTION - NATIONAL
MUSEUM OF AMERICAN ART/NATIONAL
PORTRAIT GALLERY - LIBRARY □ Washington,
DC

Chin, Celeste, Foreign Lang.Spec.
DETROIT PUBLIC LIBRARY - FOREIGN
LANGUAGE COLLECTION □ Detroit, MI

Chin, Elise, Hd., Cat.Sect.
UNIVERSITY OF WASHINGTON - EAST ASIA
LIBRARY □ Seattle, WA

Chin, Dr. Loretta M., Lib./Media Spec.
ALAMEDA COUNTY SUPERINTENDENT OF
SCHOOLS - TEACHERS' PROFESSIONAL AND
CURRICULUM LIBRARY □ Hayward, CA

Chin, Teruko Kyuma, Japan Libn.
UNIVERSITY OF WASHINGTON - EAST ASIA
LIBRARY □ Seattle, WA

Chinea, Idalia, Cat.
UNIVERSITY OF PUERTO RICO - LAW SCHOOL
LIBRARY □ Rio Piedras, PR

Chinkiwsky, Joan, Mgr.
TELECOM CANADA - INFORMATION RESOURCE
CENTRE □ Ottawa, ON

Chinn, Barbara, Ref.Libn.
CANADIAN EMBASSY - LIBRARY □ Washington,
DC

Chinn, Mr. D., Asst.Libn.
ST. THOMAS SEMINARY - LIBRARY □ Denver,
CO

Chinn, Helen, Chm., Coll.Dev.
LOMA LINDA UNIVERSITY - DEL E. WEBB
MEMORIAL LIBRARY □ Loma Linda, CA

Chinn, Lillian, Libn.
FAR WEST LABORATORY FOR EDUCATIONAL
RESEARCH AND DEVELOPMENT - LIBRARY AND
ARCHIVES† □ San Francisco, CA

Chinnici, Lucile, Pres.
OUR LADY OF LIGHT LIBRARY □ Santa Barbara,
CA

Chiong, Anna F., Libn.
PLYMOUTH CONGREGATIONAL CHURCH - VIDA
B. VAREY LIBRARY □ Seattle, WA

Chiorazzi, Michael, Ref.Libn.
DUKE UNIVERSITY - SCHOOL OF LAW LIBRARY
□ Durham, NC

Chipman, Ernestine, Libn.
GRACE (W.R.) AND COMPANY - NATURAL
RESOURCES GROUP - INFORMATION CENTER □
Dallas, TX

Chisholm, Diane, Archv.
YUKON TERRITORY - DEPARTMENT OF
TOURISM, RECREATION AND CULTURE -
YUKON ARCHIVES □ Whitehorse, YT

Chisholm, Margaret, Pub.Serv.Libn.
YALE UNIVERSITY - LAW LIBRARY □ New
Haven, CT

Chisholm, Martha Lee, Libn.
DALLAS COUNTY CIRCUIT COURT - LIBRARY □
Selma, AL

Chisman, Janet, Sr.Libn.
KENTUCKY STATE DEPARTMENT FOR
LIBRARIES AND ARCHIVES - STATE LIBRARY
SERVICES DIVISION □ Frankfort, KY

Chitnis, N., ILL
BELL-NORTHERN RESEARCH LTD. -
INFORMATION RESOURCE CENTRE □ Ottawa,
ON

Chittampalli, Ms. Padma, Med.Libn.
NORTH CENTRAL BRONX HOSPITAL - J.L.
AMSTER HEALTH SCIENCES LIBRARY □ Bronx,
NY

Chittick, Elizabeth L., Dir.
NATIONAL WOMAN'S PARTY - FLORENCE
BAYARD HILLES LIBRARY □ Washington, DC

Chitty, Mary G., Assoc.Libn.
MASSACHUSETTS COLLEGE OF PHARMACY &
ALLIED HEALTH SCIENCES - SHEPPARD
LIBRARY □ Boston, MA

Chiu, Kai-Yun, Law Libn.
LIBRARY COMPANY OF THE BALTIMORE BAR - LIBRARY □ Baltimore, MD
Chiu, Laura, Cat./Ser.Libn.
U.S. NASA - LYNDON B. JOHNSON SPACE CENTER - TECHNICAL LIBRARY □ Houston, TX
Chiu, Liwa, Libn.
PAN AMERICAN WORLD AIRWAYS - CORPORATE LIBRARY □ New York, NY
Chiu, Mr. S., Libn. 1
METROPOLITAN TORONTO LIBRARY - LANGUAGES DEPARTMENT □ Toronto, ON
Choe, Yoon-Whan, Korea Libn.
UNIVERSITY OF WASHINGTON - EAST ASIA LIBRARY □ Seattle, WA
Choe, Young-Hi, Cat.
BALCH INSTITUTE FOR ETHNIC STUDIES - LIBRARY □ Philadelphia, PA
Choi, Eunice, Libn.
ILLINOIS STATE BUREAU OF EMPLOYMENT SECURITY - LABOR MARKET INFORMATION CENTER† □ Chicago, IL
Choi, Jean, Cat.
TEMPLE UNIVERSITY - HEALTH SCIENCES CENTER - LIBRARY □ Philadelphia, PA
Choi, Suja, Cat.Libn.
SYNTEX, U.S.A. - CORPORATE LIBRARY/ INFORMATION SERVICES □ Palo Alto, CA
Chojenski, Peter P., Ref.Libn.
PURDUE UNIVERSITY, CALUMET - LIBRARY □ Hammond, IN
Chojnacki, Stanislaw, Dir. of Lib.
UNIVERSITY OF SUDBURY - LIBRARY □ Sudbury, ON
Choldin, Marianna, Asst.Dir. of Gen.Serv.
UNIVERSITY OF ILLINOIS - SLAVIC AND EAST EUROPEAN LIBRARY □ Urbana, IL
Chong, Nan S., Libn., Panama Coll.
PANAMA CANAL COMMISSION - LIBRARY □ APO Miami, FL
Choppa, John J., Staff Dev.Coord.
BRANDON TRAINING SCHOOL - LIBRARY □ Brandon, VT
Choppe, Elaine, Prin.Ck.
OCEAN COUNTY LAW LIBRARY† □ Toms River, NJ
Chopra, Mrs. Swaran Lata, Adm.Supv./Dir.
CHILDREN'S HOSPITAL OF PHILADELPHIA - MEDICAL LIBRARY □ Philadelphia, PA
Choquette, Diane, Hd., Pub.Serv.
GRADUATE THEOLOGICAL UNION - LIBRARY □ Berkeley, CA
Chorvat, Lillian K., Libn./Musm.Cur.
CZECHOSLOVAK HERITAGE MUSEUM - LIBRARY AND ARCHIVES □ Berwyn, IL
Chosak, Michael S., Chm., Lib.Comm.
TEMPLE EMANUEL - LIBRARY □ Orange, CT
Chou, Min-Chih, Chinese Bibliog.
PRINCETON UNIVERSITY - GEST ORIENTAL LIBRARY AND EAST ASIAN COLLECTIONS □ Princeton, NJ
Chou, Dr. Nelson, Libn.
RUTGERS UNIVERSITY, THE STATE UNIVERSITY OF NEW JERSEY - ALEXANDER LIBRARY - EAST ASIAN LIBRARY □ New Brunswick, NJ
Chouinard, Germain, Dir.
UNIVERSITE DE SHERBROOKE - FACULTE DE MEDECINE - BIBLIOTHEQUE DES SCIENCES DE LA SANTE □ Sherbrooke, PQ
Chouinard, Joseph, Music Libn.
SUNY - COLLEGE AT FREDONIA - MUSIC LIBRARY □ Fredonia, NY
Chovelak, Elissa, Info.Spec.
BANK ADMINISTRATION INSTITUTE - INFORMATION CENTER □ Rolling Meadows, IL
Chow, Mrs. Oi-Yung, Dir., State Lib.
HAWAII STATE LIBRARY - HAWAII AND PACIFIC SECTION I □ Honolulu, HI
Chowdhury, Mr. Manny, Chf.Libn.
HARLEM HOSPITAL MEDICAL CENTER - HEALTH SCIENCES LIBRARY □ New York, NY

Chrisant, Rosemarie, Lib.Dir.
AKRON LAW LIBRARY □ Akron, OH
Chrisman, Barbra
BLACK HILLS STATE COLLEGE - E.Y. BERRY LIBRARY-LEARNING CENTER - SPECIAL COLLECTIONS □ Spearfish, SD
Chrisman, Dawn, Lib.Ck.
HONEYWELL, INC. - PROCESS CONTROLS DIVISION - INFORMATION CENTER, M.S. 221 □ Fort Washington, PA
Christ, Joan E., Libn.
UNIVERSITY OF WASHINGTON - GEOGRAPHY LIBRARY □ Seattle, WA
Christ, Joan E., Libn.
UNIVERSITY OF WASHINGTON - PHILOSOPHY LIBRARY □ Seattle, WA
Christenberry, David, Nat.Hist.Libn.
PHOTO RESEARCHERS, INC. - LIBRARY □ New York, NY
Christensen, Brian, Fisheries Geologist
SASKATCHEWAN - DEPARTMENT OF PARKS AND RENEWABLE RESOURCES - FISH ENHANCEMENT DIVISION LIBRARY† □ Prince Albert, SK
Christensen, Gail M., Dir.
CROW WING COUNTY HISTORICAL SOCIETY - MUSEUM LIBRARY □ Brainerd, MN
Christensen, John E., Dir.
WASHBURN UNIVERSITY OF TOPEKA - SCHOOL OF LAW LIBRARY □ Topeka, KS
Christensen, Karl, Ref.Libn.
ST. JOHN'S UNIVERSITY - LAW LIBRARY □ Jamaica, NY
Christensen, Kate, Libn.
SUNRAE LEARNING RESOURCES CENTER □ Goleta, CA
Christensen, Laura A., Mgr., Info.Serv.
AMAX EXPLORATION, INC. - SCIENCE LIBRARY □ Golden, CO
Christensen, Mary Ellen, Libn.
DOW CHEMICAL U.S.A. - WESTERN DIVISION - LIBRARY □ Pittsburg, CA
Christensen, Pia, Libn.
UNIVERSITY OF BRITISH COLUMBIA - HUMANITIES AND SOCIAL SCIENCES DIVISION □ Vancouver, BC
Christensen, Ruth M., Libn.
SOUTHWEST MUSEUM - RESEARCH LIBRARY† □ Los Angeles, CA
Christensen, Sheryl, Cat.Libn.
NORTH DAKOTA STATE SUPREME COURT LAW LIBRARY □ Bismarck, ND
Christenson, Eugenia, Libn.
SHARON GENERAL HOSPITAL - MEDICAL STAFF LIBRARY □ Sharon, PA
Christenson, Eugenia, Libn.
SHARON GENERAL HOSPITAL - SCHOOL OF NURSING - LIBRARY □ Sharon, PA
Christenson, Phyllis, Dir.
U.S. GENERAL ACCOUNTING OFFICE - OFFICE OF LIBRARY SERVICES □ Washington, DC
Christenson, Virginia, Asst. to Dir.
SMITH COLLEGE - SOPHIA SMITH COLLECTION - WOMEN'S HISTORY ARCHIVE □ Northampton, MA
Christerson, M.F., Coord. LRC
OKLAHOMA STATE UNIVERSITY - SCHOOL OF TECHNICAL TRAINING - OKMULGEE BRANCH LIBRARY □ Okmulgee, OK
Christian, A. Munro, Dir.
H.M.S. BOUNTY SOCIETY, INTERNATIONAL - RESEARCH LIBRARY AND DEPOSITORY □ Tiburon, CA
Christian, Thomas W., Sect.Supv.
JOHNS HOPKINS UNIVERSITY - APPLIED PHYSICS LABORATORY - CHEMICAL PROPULSION INFORMATION AGENCY □ Laurel, MD
Christiani, Linnea, Asst.Libn.
SOHIO PETROLEUM COMPANY - CENTRAL LIBRARY AND INFORMATION SERVICES □ San Francisco, CA

Christiano, David, Libn.
MEIKLEJOHN CIVIL LIBERTIES INSTITUTE - LIBRARY □ Berkeley, CA
Christiansen, Carol, Asst.Libn.
ARTHUR YOUNG & COMPANY - LIBRARY □ New York, NY
Christiansen, Kay, Asst.Libn.
QUARLES & BRADY - LIBRARY □ Milwaukee, WI
Christiansen, Lisa, Asst.Libn.
HEALD COLLEGE TECHNICAL DIVISION - TECHNICAL LIBRARY □ Santa Clara, CA
Christianson, Elin B., Cur.
HOBART HISTORICAL SOCIETY, INC. - MARIAM J. PLEAK MEMORIAL LIBRARY AND ARCHIVE □ Hobart, IN
Christianson, Vicky, Med.Libn.
VALLEY MEDICAL CENTER OF FRESNO - MEDICAL LIBRARY □ Fresno, CA
Christie, Edward F., Mgr., Inquiry Serv.
SRI INTERNATIONAL - BUSINESS INTELLIGENCE PROGRAM - INFORMATION CENTER† □ Menlo Park, CA
Christie, Kathryn, Ref./Res.Libn.
DUKE UNIVERSITY - SCHOOL OF LAW LIBRARY □ Durham, NC
Christie, Lucille, Dir.
LOMPOC MUSEUM - LIBRARY □ Lompoc, CA
Christie, Patricia F., Ed.Libn.
CHURCH OF THE NAZARENE - INTERNATIONAL HEADQUARTERS - EDITORIAL LIBRARY □ Kansas City, MO
Christoph, Peter R., Assoc.Libn.
NEW YORK STATE LIBRARY - MANUSCRIPTS AND SPECIAL COLLECTIONS □ Albany, NY
Christopher, Edna, Cat.
UNIVERSITY OF CHICAGO - MUSIC COLLECTION □ Chicago, IL
Christopher, Irene, Chf.Libn.
BOSTON UNIVERSITY MEDICAL CENTER - ALUMNI MEDICAL LIBRARY □ Boston, MA
Christopher, Rachel, Hd., Per.
MURRAY STATE UNIVERSITY - LIBRARY □ Murray, KY
Christopherson, Frances, Libn.
GREATER VANCOUVER REGIONAL DISTRICT - LIBRARY □ Vancouver, BC
Christy, Mrs. Nicholas P., Exec.Sec.
HUGUENOT SOCIETY OF AMERICA - LIBRARY □ New York, NY
Chronister, Diane, Tech.Asst.
POCONO HOSPITAL - MARSHALL R. METZGAR MEDICAL LIBRARY □ East Stroudsburg, PA
Chronister, Peg, Cur.
MUSEUM OF INDEPENDENT TELEPHONY - ARCHIVES COLLECTION □ Abilene, KS
Chryst, Elizabeth
INTERLOCHEN CENTER FOR THE ARTS - MUSIC LIBRARY □ Interlochen, MI
Chu, B., Libn.
UNIVERSITY OF TORONTO - DEPARTMENT OF PHYSICS LIBRARY □ Toronto, ON
Chu, Ellen M., Libn.
U.S. NATL. INSTITUTES OF HEALTH - DIVISION OF COMPUTER RESEARCH & TECHNOLOGY - LIBRARY □ Bethesda, MD
Chu, Insoo, Sr.Tech.Info.Spec.
STAUFFER CHEMICAL COMPANY - DE GUIGNE TECHNICAL CENTER - RESEARCH LIBRARY □ Richmond, CA
Chu, Dr. Nori, Lib.Adm.
AMERICAN OPTICAL CORPORATION - RESEARCH CENTER LIBRARY □ Southbridge, MA
Chu, Ruby, Hd.Libn.
ZENITH ELECTRONICS CORPORATION - TECHNICAL LIBRARY □ Glenview, IL
Chu, Sally, AV Med.Libn.
UNIVERSITY OF MISSOURI, KANSAS CITY - HEALTH SCIENCES LIBRARY □ Kansas City, MO
Chu, Wendy, Mgr., Lib.Serv.
RCA CORPORATION - DAVID SARNOFF LIBRARY □ Princeton, NJ

Chu, Wendy, Mgr.
RCA CORPORATION - RCA LABORATORIES -
DAVID SARNOFF RESEARCH CENTER - LIBRARY
□ Princeton, NJ

Chuang, Felicia S., Libn.
TEXAS RESEARCH INSTITUTE OF MENTAL
SCIENCES - LIBRARY □ Houston, TX

Chui, Anita, Sr.Libn.
ONTARIO HYDRO - LIBRARY □ Toronto, ON

Chumak, O., Chf., Tech.Serv.
CANADA - AGRICULTURE CANADA - LIBRARIES
DIVISION □ Ottawa, ON

Chumas, Sophie J., NCSCI Supv.
U.S. NATL. BUREAU OF STANDARDS -
NATIONAL CENTER FOR STANDARDS AND
CERTIFICATION INFORMATION □ Washington,
DC

Chumney, Candes, Supv.
FUNDING INFORMATION CENTER □ San
Antonio, TX

Chun, Vivian, Res.Anl.
RAINIER NATIONAL BANK - INFORMATION
CENTER □ Seattle, WA

Chun-Spielberg, Patricia, Libn.
INSTITUTE FOR RESEARCH IN SOCIAL
BEHAVIOR - LIBRARY □ Oakland, CA

Chung, Ann
ALBERTA - WORKERS' HEALTH SAFETY &
COMPENSATION - OCCUPATIONAL HEALTH &
SAFETY LIBRARY □ Edmonton, AB

Chung, Helen, R&D Libn.
REYNOLDS (R.J.) TOBACCO COMPANY - R&D
SCIENTIFIC INFORMATION SERVICES
LIBRARY □ Winston-Salem, NC

Church, Miss C., Supv. of Tech.Serv.
ONTARIO BIBLE COLLEGE/ONTARIO
THEOLOGICAL SEMINARY - J. WILLIAM
HORSEY LIBRARY □ Willowdale, ON

Church, Mrs. C.A., Archv.
SCHENECTADY COUNTY HISTORICAL SOCIETY
- LIBRARY AND ARCHIVES □ Schenectady, NY

Church, James, Asst.Dir.
CITY OF COMMERCE PUBLIC LIBRARY □
Commerce, CA

Church, Linda, Mgr., Community Info.Serv
ONTARIO - MINISTRY OF CITIZENSHIP AND
CULTURE - LIBRARIES AND COMMUNITY
INFORMATION □ Toronto, ON

Church, Virginia, Asst.Dir., Tech.Serv.
ROCHESTER INSTITUTE OF TECHNOLOGY -
WALLACE MEMORIAL LIBRARY □ Rochester, NY

Churchfield, Beth, Info.Spec.
KETCHUM COMMUNICATIONS INC. - LIBRARY
SERVICES □ Pittsburgh, PA

Churchill, Barbara, Per. & Acq.Libn.
MAINE MARITIME ACADEMY - NUTTING
MEMORIAL LIBRARY □ Castine, ME

Churchill, Charles, Ref.Libn./Tech.Serv.
MASSACHUSETTS COLLEGE OF ART - LIBRARY
□ Boston, MA

Churchill, Sauci S., Law Libn.
U.S. NUCLEAR REGULATORY COMMISSION -
LAW LIBRARY □ Washington, DC

Churchland, Norman, Hd.Libn.
INSURANCE CORPORATION OF BRITISH
COLUMBIA - LAW LIBRARY □ North Vancouver,
BC

Churchman, Alice, Coord.
ETOBICOKE BOARD OF EDUCATION -
RESOURCE LIBRARY □ Etobicoke, ON

Churgin, James, Data Serv.
U.S. NATL. OCEANIC & ATMOSPHERIC
ADMINISTRATION - NATIONAL
OCEANOGRAPHIC DATA CENTER □ Washington,
DC

Churgin, James, Dir.
WORLD DATA CENTER A - OCEANOGRAPHY □
Washington, DC

Churgin, Sylvia, Chf., STRI Lib.
SMITHSONIAN INSTITUTION LIBRARIES □
Washington, DC

Churma, Thomas P., Libn.
LEGAL AID SOCIETY OF HAWAII - LIBRARY† □
Honolulu, HI

Churney, Sarah, Cat.
LAW LIBRARY OF LOUISIANA† □ New Orleans,
LA

Chysh, Zola, Asst.Libn.
BEAVER COUNTY TIMES - LIBRARY □ Beaver,
PA

Ciacco, Catherine, Ref.
KUTAK ROCK & HUIE - LAW LIBRARY □ Omaha,
NE

Cianfarini, Margaret, Acq./Cat.Libn.
NORTHEASTERN UNIVERSITY - LAW SCHOOL
LIBRARY □ Boston, MA

Ciaramella, Mary A., Chf.Libn.
LUMMUS CREST, INC. - LUMMUS TECHNICAL
CENTER - TECHNICAL INFORMATION
DEPARTMENT □ Bloomfield, NJ

Ciarkowski, Elaine E., Asst.Libn., Users Serv.
HARVARD UNIVERSITY - SCHOOLS OF
MEDICINE, DENTAL MED. & PUBLIC HEALTH,
BOSTON MED.LIB. - FRANCIS A. COUNTWAY
LIB. □ Boston, MA

Cibulskis, Elizabeth R., Tech.Libn.
WRIGLEY (Wm., Jr.) COMPANY - QUALITY
ASSURANCE BRANCH LIBRARY □ Chicago, IL

Cibulskis, Elizabeth R., Tech.Libn.
WRIGLEY (Wm., Jr.) COMPANY - RESEARCH &
DEVELOPMENT LIBRARY □ Chicago, IL

Ciccone, Amy Navratil, Libn.
CHRYSLER MUSEUM - JEAN OUTLAND
CHRYSLER LIBRARY □ Norfolk, VA

Ciccone, Barbara Gurdon, Marketing Res.Cons.
PRUDENTIAL INSURANCE COMPANY OF
AMERICA - MARKETING RESEARCH CENTER □
Newark, NJ

Ciejka, Patricia A., Clinical Med.Libn.
UNIVERSITY OF TEXAS MEDICAL BRANCH -
MOODY MEDICAL LIBRARY □ Galveston, TX

Ciesielski, Joseph S., Dir.
UNIVERSITY OF SAN DIEGO - MARVIN &
LILLIAN KRATTER LAW LIBRARY □ San Diego,
CA

Ciko, Anthony, Sr.Med.Libn.
ERIE COUNTY MEDICAL CENTER - MEDICAL
LIBRARY† □ Buffalo, NY

Cimino, David, Media Techn.
ELMCREST PSYCHIATRIC INSTITUTE -
PROFESSIONAL LIBRARY □ Portland, CT

Cimon, Florence, Per.
ST. ANSELM'S COLLEGE - GEISEL LIBRARY □
Manchester, NH

Cimpl, Kay, Weston Lib.
UNIVERSITY OF WISCONSIN, MADISON -
CENTER FOR HEALTH SCIENCES LIBRARIES† □
Madison, WI

Cintron, Carmelo Delgado, Law Libn.
UNIVERSITY OF PUERTO RICO - LAW SCHOOL
LIBRARY □ Rio Piedras, PR

Ciochon, Miriam, Lib.Mgr.
FEDERAL RESERVE BANK OF SAN FRANCISCO -
RESEARCH LIBRARY □ San Francisco, CA

Cioppa, Lawrence, Supv. Drama Libn.
NEW YORK PUBLIC LIBRARY - GENERAL
LIBRARY OF THE PERFORMING ARTS □ New
York, NY

Ciosek, Jane P., Libn.
INSTITUTE FOR DEFENSE ANALYSES -
COMMUNICATIONS RESEARCH DIVISION -
LIBRARY □ Princeton, NJ

Circiello, Jean, Chf., Info.Sys.Sect.
ENVIRONMENTAL PROTECTION AGENCY -
REGION IX LIBRARY/INFORMATION CENTER □
San Francisco, CA

Cirocco, Dixie, Dir.
HEMET VALLEY HOSPITAL DISTRICT - DR.
LESLIE J. CLARK MEMORIAL LIBRARY □ Hemet,
CA

Ciskey, Debra J., Libn.
AMERICAN COLLECTORS ASSOCIATION, INC. -
ACA MEMORIAL LIBRARY □ Minneapolis, MN

Citro, Kathleen, Ref.Serv.
EMBRY RIDDLE AERONAUTICAL UNIVERSITY -
LEARNING RESOURCES CENTER □ Daytona
Beach, FL

Citroen, Julie, Libn.
MANUFACTURERS LIFE INSURANCE COMPANY
- BUSINESS LIBRARY □ Toronto, ON

Citron, Dr. Helen R., Assoc.Dir.
GEORGIA INSTITUTE OF TECHNOLOGY - PRICE
GILBERT MEMORIAL LIBRARY □ Atlanta, GA

Ciurczak, Alexis K., Lib.Dir.
PALOMAR COMMUNITY COLLEGE - LIBRARY -
SPECIAL COLLECTIONS □ San Marcos, CA

Civille, Mary, Text Libn.
ATLANTA NEWSPAPERS - REFERENCE LIBRARY
□ Atlanta, GA

Civinskas, Anne Marie, Adm.
GENERAL FOODS CORPORATION - MAXWELL
HOUSE - TECHNICAL INFORMATION CENTER†
□ Hoboken, NJ

Claasen, Lynda, Spec.Coll.Libn.
UNIVERSITY OF CALIFORNIA, SAN DIEGO -
UNIVERSITY LIBRARIES □ La Jolla, CA

Claffey, Joan M., Dir.
MICHIGAN STATE UNIVERSITY - NONFORMAL
EDUCATION INFORMATION CENTER □ East
Lansing, MI

Claflin, Brenda H., Corp.Libn.
CONNECTICUT GENERAL LIFE INSURANCE
COMPANY - CORPORATE LIBRARY† □ Hartford,
CT

Clair, Gina Rabai, Leg.Libn.
MORRISON & FOERSTER - BRANCH LAW
LIBRARY □ Washington, DC

Clancy, Jeanne M., Libn.
SASAKI ASSOCIATES, INC. - LIBRARY □
Watertown, MA

Clancy, Justine V., Dir.
PARSONS SCHOOL OF DESIGN - OTIS ART
INSTITUTE - LIBRARY □ Los Angeles, CA

Clancy, Kathleen, ILL Libn.
PACE UNIVERSITY - LIBRARY □ New York, NY

Clancy, Patricia, Libn.
LONG ISLAND LIGHTING COMPANY -
CORPORATE LIBRARY† □ Hicksville, NY

Clancy, Stephen, Ref.Libn.
UNIVERSITY OF CALIFORNIA, IRVINE -
BIOMEDICAL LIBRARY □ Irvine, CA

Clapp, Mrs. E., Libn.
UNITED CHURCH OF CANADA - CENTRAL
ARCHIVES† □ Toronto, ON

Clapp, Laurel R., Law Libn.
SAMFORD UNIVERSITY - CUMBERLAND
SCHOOL OF LAW - CORDELL HULL LAW
LIBRARY □ Birmingham, AL

Clare, Harvey H., Sec./Treas.
CONSERVATION COUNCIL OF ONTARIO -
LIBRARY □ Toronto, ON

Clare, Sr. Lillian, Libn.
ST. JOHN'S HOSPITAL - MEDICAL LIBRARY □
Springfield, MO

Clare, Nancy, Cat.
CANADIAN INSTITUTE OF INTERNATIONAL
AFFAIRS - LIBRARY □ Toronto, ON

Claridge, J.R., Exec.Dir.
ERIE COUNTY HISTORICAL SOCIETY □ Erie, PA

Clark, Adrienne, Asst.Libn.
COLLEGE OF PHYSICIANS AND SURGEONS OF
BRITISH COLUMBIA - MEDICAL LIBRARY
SERVICE □ Vancouver, BC

Clark, Alfrieda, Chf., Spec. Projects
U.S. ARMY - ENGINEER WATERWAYS
EXPERIMENT STATION - TECHNICAL
INFORMATION CENTER □ Vicksburg, MS

Clark, Alson, Libn.
UNIVERSITY OF SOUTHERN CALIFORNIA -
ARCHITECTURE & FINE ARTS LIBRARY □ Los
Angeles, CA

Clark, Andrea Cantrell, Dir., Lib.Rsrcs.
OKLAHOMA HISTORICAL SOCIETY - DIVISION
OF LIBRARY RESOURCES □ Oklahoma City, OK

Clark, Annetta, Assoc.Dir.
JACKSON METROPOLITAN LIBRARY -
INFORMATION AND REFERENCE DIVISION □
Jackson, MS

Clark, Audrey M., Hd.Libn.
DESERET NEWS PUBLISHING CO. - DESERET
NEWS LIBRARY & INFORMATION □ Salt Lake
City, UT

Clark, Barton M., Libn.
UNIVERSITY OF ILLINOIS - EDUCATION AND
SOCIAL SCIENCE LIBRARY □ Urbana, IL

Clark, Beth, Mgr.
MAC FARLANE & COMPANY, INC. - FRY
CONSULTANTS INCORPORATED -
MANAGEMENT CENTRE, INC. □ Atlanta, GA

Clark, Betty D., Hd. of Media Serv.
BIRMINGHAM PUBLIC AND JEFFERSON
COUNTY FREE LIBRARY - MEDIA SERVICES □
Birmingham, AL

Clark, Betty J., Libn.
PURE CARBON CO., INC. - ENGINEERING
LIBRARY □ St. Marys, PA

Clark, Blanche T., Dept.Hd.
BRONSON (Silas) LIBRARY - BUSINESS,
INDUSTRY, AND TECHNOLOGY DEPARTMENT†
□ Waterbury, CT

Clark, Brenda B., Mgr., Info.Ctr.
TOBACCO INSTITUTE - INFORMATION CENTER
□ Washington, DC

Clark, Charmian
CONCORD ANTIQUARIAN MUSEUM - LIBRARY
OF RALPH WALDO EMERSON □ Concord, MA

Clark, Christine
FIRST UNITED METHODIST CHURCH - ALLEN
LIBRARY □ Kalamazoo, MI

Clark, Collin, Info.Mgr.
CALIFORNIA STATE LIBRARY □ Sacramento, CA

Clark, Dan O., Libn.
OHIO UNIVERSITY - MUSIC/DANCE LIBRARY □
Athens, OH

Clark, Elaine, Asst.Libn.
NEW YORK STATE LIBRARY - LAW/SOCIAL
SCIENCE REFERENCE SERVICES □ Albany, NY

Clark, Ellen McCallister, Libn.
MOUNT VERNON LADIES' ASSOCIATION OF
THE UNION - RESEARCH AND REFERENCE
LIBRARY □ Mount Vernon, VA

Clark, Georgia A., Law Libn.
WAYNE STATE UNIVERSITY - ARTHUR NEEF
LAW LIBRARY □ Detroit, MI

Clark, Glenda, Libn.
ST. MARY'S MEDICAL CENTER, INC. - MEDICAL
LIBRARY □ Knoxville, TN

Clark, Greta, Libn.
PHILADELPHIA STATE HOSPITAL - STAFF
LIBRARY† □ Philadelphia, PA

Clark, Holly B., Clinical Libn./Pediatrics
HARTFORD HOSPITAL - HEALTH SCIENCE
LIBRARIES □ Hartford, CT

Clark, James Lee, Base Libn.
U.S. AIR FORCE BASE - LITTLE ROCK BASE
LIBRARY □ Little Rock AFB, AR

Clark, James M., Libn.
PHILADELPHIA COURT OF COMMON PLEAS -
LAW LIBRARY □ Philadelphia, PA

Clark, James P., Dir.
U.S. ARMY - MISSILE COMMAND & MARSHALL
SPACE FLIGHT CENTER - REDSTONE
SCIENTIFIC INFORMATION CENTER □
Redstone Arsenal, AL

Clark, Jane F., Dir.
SOUTHERN STATES ENERGY BOARD (SSEB) -
SOUTHERN ENERGY/ENVIRONMENTAL
INFORMATION CENTER (SEEIC) □ Atlanta, GA

Clark, Jane L., Dir., Med.Lib.Serv.
TIMKEN MERCY HOSPITAL - MEDICAL LIBRARY
□ Canton, OH

Clark, Jean, Asst.Libn.
U.S. COURT OF APPEALS, 2ND CIRCUIT -
LIBRARY □ New York, NY

Clark, John L.D., Dir.
ERIC CLEARINGHOUSE ON LANGUAGES AND
LINGUISTICS □ Washington, DC

Clark, Kit, Cat.
NOVA SCOTIA COLLEGE OF ART AND DESIGN -
LIBRARY □ Halifax, NS

Clark, Laurel, Libn.
CALIFORNIA STATE DEPARTMENT OF
TRANSPORTATION - TRANSPORTATION
LIBRARY □ Sacramento, CA

Clark, Lois O., Med.Libn.
LONG BEACH COMMUNITY HOSPITAL -
MEDICAL LIBRARY □ Long Beach, CA

Clark, M. Rosemary, Res.Anl.
RAINIER NATIONAL BANK - INFORMATION
CENTER □ Seattle, WA

Clark, Margery M., Chf.Libn.
NATIONAL ASSOCIATION OF HOME BUILDERS -
NATIONAL HOUSING CENTER LIBRARY □
Washington, DC

Clark, Marianna, Hd.Libn.
U.S. MARINE CORPS - EL TORO AIR STATION
LIBRARY □ Santa Ana, CA

Clark, Martha, Circ.Libn.
YALE UNIVERSITY - LAW LIBRARY □ New
Haven, CT

Clark, Mary Ann H., Staff Libn.
MONROE DEVELOPMENTAL CENTER - STAFF/
PARENT LIBRARY □ Rochester, NY

Clark, Mary Ellen, Asst. to Cur.
SWARTHMORE COLLEGE - FRIENDS
HISTORICAL LIBRARY - PEACE COLLECTION □
Swarthmore, PA

Clark, Maryanne, Asst.Libn.
NEW YORK STATE SUPREME COURT -
APPELLATE DIVISION, 4TH JUDICIAL
DEPARTMENT - LAW LIBRARY □ Rochester, NY

Clark, Melba, Libn.
ST. JOSEPH HOSPITAL - MEDICAL LIBRARY □
Albuquerque, NM

Clark, Michael, Hd., Govt.Docs.
MURRAY STATE UNIVERSITY - LIBRARY □
Murray, KY

Clark, Nancy A., Chf., Lib.Serv.
U.S. VETERANS ADMINISTRATION (NC-
Fayetteville) - HOSPITAL LIBRARY □ Fayetteville,
NC

Clark, Newton P., Rec. Retention Ctr.
MARTIN MARIETTA AEROSPACE - DENVER
RESEARCH LIBRARY □ Denver, CO

Clark, Prudence, Coll.Dev.Libn.
VIRGINIA COMMONWEALTH UNIVERSITY -
MEDICAL COLLEGE OF VIRGINIA - TOMPKINS-
MC CAW LIBRARY □ Richmond, VA

Clark, Rae, Sr.Libn., Tech.Serv.
NEW YORK STATE DEPARTMENT OF HEALTH -
CENTER FOR LABORATORIES AND RESEARCH
LIBRARY □ Albany, NY

Clark, Robert, Hd.Libn.
MONTANA HISTORICAL SOCIETY - LIBRARY/
ARCHIVES □ Helena, MT

Clark, Robert L., Jr., Dir.
OKLAHOMA STATE DEPARTMENT OF
LIBRARIES □ Oklahoma City, OK

Clark, Sara, Spec.Coll.
NEW YORK STATE HISTORICAL ASSOCIATION
- LIBRARY □ Cooperstown, NY

Clark, Susan, Libn.
FAIRVIEW DEACONESS HOSPITAL - MEDICAL
LIBRARY† □ Minneapolis, MN

Clark, Susan, Tech.Libn.
ROCHESTER INSTITUTE OF TECHNOLOGY -
TECHNICAL & EDUCATION CENTER FOR THE
GRAPHIC ARTS - GRAPHIC ARTS INFO.SERV. □
Rochester, NY

Clark, Warren S., Jr., Exec.Dir.
AMERICAN DRY MILK INSTITUTE - LIBRARY □
Chicago, IL

Clark, Wendolyn, Ref.Libn.
TENNESSEE VALLEY AUTHORITY - TECHNICAL
LIBRARY □ Muscle Shoals, AL

Clarke, Barbara, Libn., CRC
SUNY - COLLEGE AT GENESEO - COLLEGE
LIBRARIES □ Geneseo, NY

Clarke, Beverley, Sr.Libn.
IBM CORPORATION - RESEARCH LIBRARY □
San Jose, CA

Clarke, Carol B.
MANATEE COUNTY PLANNING AND
DEVELOPMENT DEPARTMENT - TECHNICAL
REFERENCE LIBRARY □ Bradenton, FL

Clarke, Jean B., Libn.
MOBIL RESEARCH & DEVELOPMENT
CORPORATION - CENTRAL RESEARCH
DIVISION LIBRARY □ Princeton, NJ

Clarke, Karen B., Asst.Cur., Ornithology
TRINITY COLLEGE - WATKINSON LIBRARY □
Hartford, CT

Clarke, Bro. Lewis N.
INTERNATIONAL BROTHERHOOD OF OLD
BASTARDS, INC. - SIR THOMAS CRAPPER
MEMORIAL ARCHIVES □ St. Louis, MO

Clarke, Robert F., Ph.D., Dir.
U.S. FOOD & DRUG ADMINISTRATION -
CENTER FOR FOOD SAFETY & APPLIED
NUTRITION - LIBRARY □ Washington, DC

Clarke, Sarah H., Circ./Tchg.Rsrcs.Ctr.
NORTH ADAMS STATE COLLEGE - EUGENE L.
FREEL LIBRARY - SPECIAL COLLECTIONS □
North Adams, MA

Clarke-Hazlett, Janet, Art Libn.
VASSAR COLLEGE - ART LIBRARY □
Poughkeepsie, NY

Clarkson, Dorothy J., Supv.
POLYSAR, LTD. - INFORMATION CENTRE □
Sarnia, ON

Clarkson, Kelly, Photographer
NANAIMO CENTENNIAL MUSEUM - ARCHIVES □
Nanaimo, BC

Clarkson, Sarah B., Libn.
SOUTH CAROLINA STATE COMMISSION ON
ALCOHOL AND DRUG ABUSE - RESOURCE
CENTER □ Columbia, SC

Clarkson, Teresa N., Libn.
DUANE, MORRIS & HECKSCHER - LAW LIBRARY
□ Philadelphia, PA

Clary, Ann Roane, Chf.Libn.
FEDERAL RESERVE SYSTEM - BOARD OF
GOVERNORS - RESEARCH LIBRARY □
Washington, DC

Clary, Kay, Res.Anl.
GREATER EGYPT REGIONAL PLANNING AND
DEVELOPMENT COMMISSION - LIBRARY-
RESEARCH CENTER □ Carbondale, IL

Clasper, James W., Asst.Corp.Libn.
CINCINNATI MILACRON INDUSTRIES, INC. -
CORPORATE INFORMATION CENTER □
Cincinnati, OH

Classen, Joanne E., Coll.Spec.
DENVER PUBLIC LIBRARY - GENEALOGY
DIVISION □ Denver, CO

Clausen, Nancy M., Dir. of Res.
LAMALIE ASSOCIATES, INC. - RESEARCH
DEPARTMENT □ Tampa, FL

Clausman, Gilbert J., Libn.
NEW YORK UNIVERSITY MEDICAL CENTER -
FREDERICK L. EHRMAN MEDICAL LIBRARY □
New York, NY

Claussen, Norma, Engr./Math Libn.
UNIVERSITY OF CALIFORNIA, SANTA BARBARA
- SCIENCES-ENGINEERING LIBRARY □ Santa
Barbara, CA

Clausz, Joan A., Med.Libn.
WEST ALLIS MEMORIAL HOSPITAL - MEDICAL
LIBRARY □ West Allis, WI

Clawson, States, Mgr.
U.S. DEPT. OF COMMERCE - COMMERCE
PRODUCTIVITY CENTER □ Washington, DC

Claxton, Lois, Coord./Info.Serv.
UNIVERSITY OF WATERLOO - DANA PORTER
ARTS LIBRARY □ Waterloo, ON

Clay, Debra J., Supv., Lib.Serv.
GETTY OIL COMPANY, INC. - RESEARCH
CENTER LIBRARY □ Houston, TX

Clay, Donna, Lrng.Assoc.
EL CENTRO JOBS TRAINING CENTER -
LEARNING RESOURCE CENTER □ Dallas, TX

Clay, Donna J., Drug Info. Pharmacist
UNIVERSITY OF CHICAGO HOSPITALS &
CLINICS - PHARMACEUTICAL SERVICES -
DRUG INFORMATION CENTER □ Chicago, IL

Clay, Jason W., Dir. of Res./Ed.
CULTURAL SURVIVAL, INC. - LIBRARY □
Cambridge, MA

Clay, Katherine, Coord., Comp.Serv.
SAN MATEO COUNTY EDUCATIONAL
RESOURCES CENTER □ Redwood City, CA

Clayton, Carla J., Mgr., Tech.Info.Serv.
WATERS ASSOCIATES INC. - INFORMATION
RESOURCE CENTER □ Milford, MA

Clayton, Dr. J. Glen, Spec.Coll.Libn.
FURMAN UNIVERSITY LIBRARY - SPECIAL
COLLECTIONS □ Greenville, SC

Clayton, John M., Jr., Archv./Dir., Rec.Mgt
UNIVERSITY OF DELAWARE, NEWARK -
ARCHIVES □ Newark, DE

Clayton, Mary E., Law Libn.
LANE COUNTY LAW LIBRARY □ Eugene, OR

Clayton, Minnie H., Div.Hd./Archv.
ATLANTA UNIVERSITY CENTER - ROBERT W.
WOODRUFF LIBRARY □ Atlanta, GA

Claytor, Jane B., Med.Libn.
ST. LAWRENCE HOSPITAL - MEDICAL LIBRARY
□ Lansing, MI

Cleaver, Dr. Betty P., Dir.
OHIO STATE UNIVERSITY - EDGAR DALE
EDUCATIONAL MEDIA & INSTRUCTIONAL
MATERIALS LABORATORY □ Columbus, OH

Clegg, Michael B., Mgr., Genealogy Dept.
ALLEN COUNTY PUBLIC LIBRARY - FRED J.
REYNOLDS HISTORICAL GENEALOGY
COLLECTION □ Fort Wayne, IN

Clegg, Nancy, Libn.
VANCOUVER PUBLIC LIBRARY - BUSINESS &
ECONOMICS DIVISION □ Vancouver, BC

Cleland, Carole, Chf.Libn.
U.S. FEDERAL DEPOSIT INSURANCE
CORPORATION - LIBRARY □ Washington, DC

Clemens, Ethel E., Libn.
OHR KODESH CONGREGATION - SISTERHOOD
LIBRARY □ Chevy Chase, MD

Clemens, Joan, Ref.Libn.
GRUMMAN AEROSPACE CORPORATION -
TECHNICAL INFORMATION CENTER □
Bethpage, NY

Clement, Charles, Mgr., Tech.Serv.
CHURCH OF JESUS CHRIST OF LATTER-DAY
SAINTS - GENEALOGICAL LIBRARY □ Salt Lake
City, UT

Clement, Emily, Assoc.Libn.
BAKER & BOTTS - LAW LIBRARY† □ Houston,
TX

Clement, Hope, Assoc.Natl.Libn.
NATIONAL LIBRARY OF CANADA/
BIBLIOTHEQUE NATIONALE DU CANADA □
Ottawa, ON

Clement, R., ILL
CANADA - DEPARTMENT OF FINANCE -
FINANCE/TREASURY BOARD LIBRARY □
Ottawa, ON

Clement, Robert, Lit.Chem.
FERRO CORPORATION - LIBRARY □
Independence, OH

Clement, Susan D., Supv., Ref.Serv.
DETROIT EDISON COMPANY - REFERENCE
SERVICES □ Detroit, MI

Clementine, Sister Mary, Libn.
ST. MARY HOSPITAL - MEDICAL LIBRARY □
Livonia, MI

Clemis, Jack D., M.D., Ed.-Libn.
AMERICAN OTOLOGICAL SOCIETY, INC. -
LIBRARY □ Rochester, MN

Clemmer, Dan O., Chf., Rd.Serv.
U.S. DEPT. OF STATE - LIBRARY □ Washington,
DC

Clemons, A.L.
DOW CHEMICAL COMPANY - TECHNICAL
INFORMATION SERVICES - CENTRAL REPORT
INDEX □ Midland, MI

Clemson, Beverly C., Musm.Dir.
WALNUT CREEK HISTORICAL SOCIETY -
SHADELANDS RANCH HISTORICAL MUSEUM -
HISTORY ROOM □ Walnut Creek, CA

Clendaniel, Estella C., Supv., Lib. & Files
EASTERN SHORE HOSPITAL CENTER -
PROFESSIONAL LIBRARY □ Cambridge, MD

Clermont, Simonne, Law Libn.
UNIVERSITE DE MONCTON - BIBLIOTHEQUE DE
DROIT □ Moncton, NB

Cleveland, Berniece, Act.Libn.
ALASKA STATE COURT SYSTEM - KETCHIKAN
LAW LIBRARY □ Ketchikan, AK

Cleveland, Granville, Asst. Law Libn.
UNIVERSITY OF NOTRE DAME - LAW SCHOOL
LIBRARY □ Notre Dame, IN

Cleveland, Susan, Dir.
UNIVERSITY OF PENNSYLVANIA - UNIVERSITY
HOSPITAL LIBRARY† □ Philadelphia, PA

Cleveland, W.M., Hist.
ELEVENTH BOMBARDMENT GROUP (H)
ASSOCIATION - ARCHIVES □ Portsmouth, NH

Cleveland, Mr. W.M., Hist.
MOSQUITO ASSOCIATION - ARCHIVES □
Portsmouth, NH

Cleveland, Mr. W.M., Hist.
PEARL HARBOR SURVIVORS ASSOCIATION -
ARCHIVES □ Portsmouth, NH

Clever, Elaine, Film Libn.
TEMPLE UNIVERSITY - CENTRAL LIBRARY
SYSTEM - PHOTO-JOURNALISM COLLECTION □
Philadelphia, PA

Clever, Richard E., Pres.
FRIENDS OF THE WESTERN PHILATELIC
LIBRARY □ Sunnyvale, CA

Clever, Shannon J., Sci Libn.
MILES LABORATORIES, INC. - LIBRARY
RESOURCES AND SERVICES □ Elkhart, IN

Clevesy, Sandra, Dir.Lib.Serv.
FRAMINGHAM UNION HOSPITAL - CESARE
GEORGE TEDESCHI LIBRARY □ Framingham, MA

Cliff, Janet M., Archv.
UNIVERSITY OF OREGON - DEPARTMENT OF
ENGLISH - RANDALL V. MILLS ARCHIVES OF
NORTHWEST FOLKLORE □ Eugene, OR

Clifford, Christina, Libn.
SAN DIEGO PUBLIC LIBRARY - ART, MUSIC &
RECREATION SECTION □ San Diego, CA

Clifford, Esther B., Libn.
ORANGE AND ROCKLAND UTILITIES, INC. -
LIBRARY □ Pearl River, NY

Clifford, Naomi, Natl.Off.Libn.
ERNST & WHINNEY - NATIONAL OFFICE
LIBRARY □ Cleveland, OH

Clifford, Susan G., Lib.Supv.
HUGHES AIRCRAFT COMPANY - EL SEGUNDO
LIBRARY □ Los Angeles, CA

Clift, Crystal, Lib.Dir.
CONTROL DATA BUSINESS ADVISORS, INC. -
FACTFINDERS □ Minneapolis, MN

Clift, Evelyn S., Cur.
HENRY COUNTY HISTORICAL SOCIETY -
LIBRARY □ New Castle, IN

Clifton, David L., Mgr., Info.Serv.
ROCKWELL INTERNATIONAL - ELECTRONICS
OPERATIONS - DALLAS INFORMATION CENTER
□ Dallas, TX

Clifton, Dorothy I., Dir.
VALDEZ HISTORICAL SOCIETY, INC. N-P -
VALDEZ HERITAGE ARCHIVES ALIVE □ Valdez,
AK

Clifton, Joe Ann, Mgr., Tech.Libs.
LITTON INDUSTRIES - DATA SYSTEMS
DIVISION - ENGINEERING LIBRARY† □ Van
Nuys, CA

Clifton, Joe Ann, Mgr., Info.Serv.
LITTON INDUSTRIES - GUIDANCE AND
CONTROL SYSTEMS - LIBRARY □ Woodland Hills,
CA

Clifton, Margaret F., Med.Libn.
U.S. VETERANS ADMINISTRATION (NC-Durham)
- MEDICAL CENTER LIBRARY □ Durham, NC

Cline, Daniel, Dir.
UNIVERSITY OF NEVADA, RENO - RESEARCH
AND EDUCATIONAL PLANNING CENTER □ Reno,
NV

Cline, Fred A., Jr., Libn.
ASIAN ART MUSEUM OF SAN FRANCISCO -
LIBRARY □ San Francisco, CA

Cline, Inez E., City/County Hist./Dir.
GARLAND COUNTY HISTORICAL SOCIETY -
ARCHIVES □ Hot Springs, AR

Cline, John R., Med.Libn.
U.S. VETERANS ADMINISTRATION (IL-Chicago)
- WESTSIDE HOSPITAL LIBRARY □ Chicago, IL

Cline, Larry, Doc. Control
ENVIRONMENTAL PROTECTION AGENCY -
ANDREW W. BREIDENBACH ENVIRONMENTAL
RESEARCH CTR., CINCINNATI - TECH.LIB. □
Cincinnati, OH

Clinkscales, C.C., III, Natl.Dir.
NATIONAL ALLIANCE OF SENIOR CITIZENS -
LIBRARY □ Arlington, VA

Clinkscales, Carrie, Exec.Asst.
TRI-COUNTY REGIONAL PLANNING
COMMISSION - INFORMATION RESOURCE
CENTER □ Lansing, MI

Clinkscales, Joyce M., Libn.
UNIVERSITY OF ARKANSAS, FAYETTEVILLE -
FINE ARTS LIBRARY □ Fayetteville, AR

Clinton, Janet, Chf. of Lib.Serv.
MERCY CATHOLIC MEDICAL CENTER - HEALTH
SCIENCES LIBRARY □ Darby, PA

Clinton, Janet C., Chf. of Lib.Serv.
MERCY CATHOLIC MEDICAL CENTER -
MISERICORDIA DIVISION LIBRARY □
Philadelphia, PA

Clinton, Marion, Libn.
U.S. ARMY - COMMUNICATIONS-ELECTRONICS
COMMAND - TECHNICAL LIBRARY □ Ft.
Monmouth, NJ

Clinton, Marshall, Chf.Libn.
LAKEHEAD UNIVERSITY - CHANCELLOR
PATERSON LIBRARY □ Thunder Bay, ON

Clintworth, Bill, Pub.Serv.Libn.
UNIVERSITY OF SOUTHERN CALIFORNIA -
HEALTH SCIENCES CAMPUS - NORRIS
MEDICAL LIBRARY □ Los Angeles, CA

Clisby, Roger D., Cur.
CROCKER ART MUSEUM - RESEARCH LIBRARY
□ Sacramento, CA

Clise, Eleanore R., Chf.Archv.
GENEVA HISTORICAL SOCIETY AND MUSEUM -
JAMES D. LUCKETT MEMORIAL ARCHIVES □
Geneva, NY

Clissold, Penn, Libn.
LEHIGH-NORTHAMPTON COUNTIES JOINT
PLANNING COMMISSION - LIBRARY □ Lehigh
Valley, PA

Clist, Mary, Hd., Access Serv.
SUNY - AGRICULTURAL AND TECHNICAL
COLLEGE AT COBLESKILL - JARED VAN
WAGENEN, JR. LEARNING RESOURCE CENTER†
□ Cobleskill, NY

Clonda, Georges, Libn.
UNIVERSITE DE MONTREAL -
BIBLIOTHECONOMIE-BIBLIOTHEQUE □
Montreal, PQ

Close, Elizabeth G., Tech.Info.Off.
U.S. FOREST SERVICE - INTERMOUNTAIN
FOREST & RANGE EXPERIMENT STATION -
LIBRARY □ Ogden, UT

Closson, Sally, Cat.
KANSAS CITY ART INSTITUTE - LIBRARY □
Kansas City, MO

Closson, Trudy, Rec.Mgr.
U.S. BUREAU OF LAND MANAGEMENT - CASPER
DISTRICT OFFICE - LIBRARY □ Casper, WY

Clotfelter, Barbara, Libn.
BIRMINGHAM PUBLIC AND JEFFERSON
COUNTY FREE LIBRARY - GOVERNMENT
DOCUMENTS DEPARTMENT □ Birmingham, AL

Cloud, Gayla, Sci.Libn.
TEXAS A & M UNIVERSITY - REFERENCE
DIVISION □ College Station, TX

Clough, Jeffory, Asst.Libn.
PORTLAND SCHOOL OF ART - LIBRARY □
Portland, ME
Clougherty, Leo, Assoc.Ref.Libn.
UNIVERSITY OF ARKANSAS FOR MEDICAL
SCIENCES - MEDICAL SCIENCES LIBRARY □
Little Rock, AR
Clouten, Keith H., Lib.Serv.Dir.
CANADIAN UNION COLLEGE - LIBRARY □
College Heights, AB
Cloutier, Denise, Info.Mgr.
STATE STREET CONSULTANTS, INC. -
INFORMATION CENTER □ Boston, MA
Cloutier, Jacques, Acq.
UNIVERSITE DU QUEBEC A HULL -
BIBLIOTHEQUE □ Hull, PQ
Clubb, Warren A., Res.Coord.
SASKATCHEWAN WESTERN DEVELOPMENT
MUSEUM - GEORGE SHEPHERD LIBRARY □
Saskatoon, SK
Cluff, Dr. E. Dale, Dir. of Libs.
TEXAS TECH UNIVERSITY - LIBRARY □
Lubbock, TX
Cluff, Ervin, Libn.
CHURCH OF JESUS CHRIST OF LATTER-DAY
SAINTS - SAFFORD-THATCHER STAKES -
GENEALOGICAL LIBRARY □ Safford, AZ
Clum, Audna T., Libn.
ST. MARY'S HOSPITAL - MEDICAL STAFF
LIBRARY □ Troy, NY
Clyburn, Emily E., Staff Libn.
U.S. VETERANS ADMINISTRATION (SC-
Columbia) - WILLIAM JENNINGS BRYAN-DORN
VETERANS HOSPITAL - LIBRARY □ Columbia, SC
Clyde, Arlene, Asst.Libn.
FREE METHODIST CHURCH OF NORTH
AMERICA - MARSTON MEMORIAL HISTORICAL
LIBRARY □ Winona Lake, IN
Clyne, Barbara A., Asst.Libn.
SULLIVAN AND CROMWELL - LIBRARY† □ New
York, NY
Coakley, Gene, Faculty Serv.Libn.
YALE UNIVERSITY - LAW LIBRARY □ New
Haven, CT
Coalter, Milton J., Jr., Act.Dir.
ILIFF SCHOOL OF THEOLOGY - IRA J. TAYLOR
LIBRARY □ Denver, CO
Coan, Mary L., Dir.
MOUNT VERNON HOSPITAL - LIBRARY AND
INFORMATION SERVICES □ Mount Vernon, NY
Coash, Sally-Ann, Dir.
AMERICAN MERCHANT MARINE LIBRARY
ASSOCIATION - PUBLIC LIBRARY OF THE HIGH
SEAS □ New York, NY
Coates, Mary Jo
SAMBORN, STEKETEE, OTIS & EVANS, INC. -
RESOURCE & INFORMATION CENTER □ Toledo,
OH
Coates, Penny, Libn.
KITCHENER-WATERLOO RECORD - LIBRARY □
Kitchener, ON
Coates, W. Paul, Mss.Libn.
HOWARD UNIVERSITY - MOORLAND-SPINGARN
RESEARCH CENTER - MANUSCRIPT DIVISION □
Washington, DC
Coatsworth, Patricia, Hd.Libn.
MERRIAM CENTER LIBRARY □ Chicago, IL
Cobaugh, Stephen M., Intl.Pres.
UNITED STATES SPACE EDUCATION
ASSOCIATION - USSEA MEDIA CENTER □
Elizabethtown, PA
Cobb, Dana Faye
STILL WATERS FOUNDATION, INC. - STILL
WATERS CENTRE LIBRARY □ Pensacola, FL
Cobb, David A., Libn.
UNIVERSITY OF ILLINOIS - MAP AND
GEOGRAPHY LIBRARY □ Urbana, IL
Cobb, Jean, Ref.Libn.
SCHOOL OF THEOLOGY AT CLAREMONT -
THEOLOGY LIBRARY □ Claremont, CA

Cobb, Kenneth R., Asst.Dir.
NEW YORK CITY - DEPARTMENT OF RECORDS
AND INFORMATION SERVICES - MUNICIPAL
ARCHIVES □ New York, NY
Cobb, Margaret L., Med.Libn.
FORSYTH MEMORIAL HOSPITAL - JOHN C.
WHITAKER LIBRARY □ Winston-Salem, NC
Cobb, Sandra, Music Cat.
CLEVELAND INSTITUTE OF MUSIC - LIBRARY □
Cleveland, OH
Cobbett, Linda, Libn.
FOREST ENGINEERING RESEARCH INSTITUTE
OF CANADA - LIBRARY □ Pointe Claire, PQ
Coberly, Jean, Hd., History Dept.
SEATTLE PUBLIC LIBRARY - HISTORY,
GOVERNMENT AND BIOGRAPHY DEPARTMENT†
□ Seattle, WA
Coble, Kathy, Med.Libn.
MERCY HOSPITAL - MEDICAL LIBRARY □
Bakersfield, CA
Coble, Ruth B., Coord., Tech.Serv.
PENNSYLVANIA STATE LIBRARY □ Harrisburg,
PA
Coburn, Christine S., Libn.
MICROWAVE ASSOCIATES, INC. - M/A COM
LIBRARY □ Burlington, MA
Coburn, Louisa, User Serv.Coord.
ERIC CLEARINGHOUSE ON TESTS,
MEASUREMENT AND EVALUATION □ Princeton,
NJ
Cocci, Mary Lou, Asst.Dir.
INSURANCE LIBRARY ASSOCIATION OF
BOSTON □ Boston, MA
Cochran, Carolyn, Dir., LRC
BELL & HOWELL EDUCATION GROUP - DE VRY
INSTITUTE OF TECHNOLOGY - LEARNING
RESOURCE CENTER □ Irving, TX
Cochran, Catherine F., Libn.
GENERAL MOTORS CORPORATION - PUBLIC
RELATIONS STAFF LIBRARY □ Detroit, MI
Cochran, J. Wesley, Assoc. Law Libn.
UNIVERSITY OF WASHINGTON - MARIAN
GOULD GALLAGHER LAW LIBRARY □ Seattle,
WA
Cochran, Janet O., Mgr., Info.Serv.
CONSUMER EDUCATION RESOURCE NETWORK
(CERN)† □ Rosslyn, VA
Cock, Barbara
PROVIDENCE PUBLIC LIBRARY - ART AND
MUSIC DEPARTMENT □ Providence, RI
Cockcroft, Chris, Asst.Educ.Libn.
UNIVERSITY OF SOUTHERN CALIFORNIA -
EDUCATION & INFORMATION STUDIES
LIBRARY □ Los Angeles, CA
Cocke, John, Libn.
CARPENTER (Guy) & COMPANY, INC. - LIBRARY
AND INFORMATION SERVICES □ New York, NY
Cockhill, Brian, State Archv.
MONTANA HISTORICAL SOCIETY - LIBRARY/
ARCHIVES □ Helena, MT
Cockrell, Diane, Libn.
HERNER AND COMPANY - LIBRARY □ Arlington,
VA
Cockrum, Frances E., AHEC Libn.
TRINITY MEDICAL CENTER - ANGUS L.
CAMERON MEDICAL LIBRARY† □ Minot, ND
Cocks, J. Fraser, III, Cur., Spec.Coll.
COLBY COLLEGE - MILLER LIBRARY - SPECIAL
COLLECTIONS □ Waterville, ME
Coco, Alfred J., Libn.
UNIVERSITY OF DENVER - COLLEGE OF LAW -
WESTMINSTER LAW LIBRARY □ Denver, CO
Coco, Madeline A., Chf.Libn.
U.S. VETERANS ADMINISTRATION (NY-Batavia)
- MEDICAL CENTER LIBRARY □ Batavia, NY
Cocozzoli, Gary R., Dir.
LAWRENCE INSTITUTE OF TECHNOLOGY -
LIBRARY □ Southfield, MI
Cody, Jan R., Music Libn.
RUTGERS UNIVERSITY, THE STATE
UNIVERSITY OF NEW JERSEY - BLANCHE AND
IRVING LAURIE MUSIC LIBRARY □ New
Brunswick, NJ

Cody, Jay, Dir./Cur.
LEACOCK (Stephen) MEMORIAL HOME -
LIBRARY □ Orillia, ON
Cody, Shirley A., Libn.
WALLA WALLA COLLEGE - SCHOOL OF NURSING
PROFESSIONAL LIBRARY □ Portland, OR
Coe, Corrine B., Acq.Libn.
YALE UNIVERSITY - KLINE SCIENCE LIBRARY □
New Haven, CT
Coe, Douglas, Res.Tech.
SAN DIEGO STATE UNIVERSITY - SOCIAL
SCIENCE RESEARCH LABORATORY - LIBRARY □
San Diego, CA
Coe, G., Ref.Libn.
GOLDEY BEACOM COLLEGE - J. WILBUR
HIRONS LIBRARY □ Wilmington, DE
Coe, Richard E., Lib.Dir.
SONS OF THE REVOLUTION IN THE STATE OF
CALIFORNIA SOCIETY - LIBRARY □ Glendale,
CA
Coello, Elizabeth, Ser.Cat.
TEACHERS COLLEGE - MILBANK MEMORIAL
LIBRARY □ New York, NY
Coen, James, Ref.Libn.
COLUMBIA UNIVERSITY - THOMAS J. WATSON
LIBRARY OF BUSINESS AND ECONOMICS □ New
York, NY
Coffee, E. Guy, Hd.Libn.
KANSAS STATE UNIVERSITY - VETERINARY
MEDICAL LIBRARY □ Manhattan, KS
Coffey, Barbara, Assoc.Libn.
WENTWORTH INSTITUTE OF TECHNOLOGY -
LIBRARY □ Boston, MA
Coffey, Patricia, Libn.
OAKLAND PUBLIC LIBRARY - SCIENCE/
SOCIOLOGY DIVISION □ Oakland, CA
Coffin, Mrs. Charles, Libn.
HISTORICAL SOCIETY OF EARLY AMERICAN
DECORATION, INC. - LIBRARY □ Albany, NY
Coffin, Shirley E., Libn.
PUBLIC LIBRARY OF CINCINNATI AND
HAMILTON COUNTY - ART AND MUSIC
DEPARTMENT □ Cincinnati, OH
Coffindaffer, Clarence L., State Libn.
SOUTH DAKOTA STATE LIBRARY & ARCHIVES □
Pierre, SD
Coffman, Andrea G., Libn.
OCEAN AND COASTAL LAW CENTER - LIBRARY
□ Eugene, OR
Coffman, M. Hope, Mgr.
DRAPER (Charles Stark) LABORATORY, INC. -
TECHNICAL INFORMATION CENTER □
Cambridge, MA
Coffman, Mel, Supv.Clas. Loan Ctr.
MARTIN MARIETTA AEROSPACE - DENVER
RESEARCH LIBRARY □ Denver, CO
Coffman, Ralph, Hd., Spec.Coll.
BOSTON COLLEGE - SPECIAL COLLECTIONS
DEPARTMENT □ Chestnut Hill, MA
Coffman, Randall, Libn.
GEARHART INDUSTRIES, INC. - TECHNICAL
LIBRARY □ Fort Worth, TX
Coffroth, Irene, Libn.
SOMERSET COUNTY LAW LIBRARY □ Somerset,
PA
Cofta, Mary Ann, Asst.Libn.
ALCAN ALUMINUM CORPORATION -
CORPORATE LIBRARY □ Cleveland, OH
Cogan, Gale, Dir.
ST. JOHN'S HOSPITAL - HEALTH SCIENCE
LIBRARY □ Lowell, MA
Cogelow, Linda, Coord.
WILLMAR PUBLIC SCHOOLS - COMMUNITY
EDUCATION TOY LIBRARY □ Willmar, MN
Cogelow, Mary Ann, Prog.Dir.
DAYTONS BLUFF AREA EARLY CHILDHOOD &
FAMILY EDUCATION PROGRAM - TOY & BOOK
LIBRARY □ St. Paul, MN
Coggin, Lucy Dos Passos, Prog.Coord.
HISTORIC ANNAPOLIS, INC. - WILLIAM PACA
GARDEN CONSERVATION CENTER □ Annapolis,
MD

Coggins, Timothy, Hd., Rd.Serv.
UNIVERSITY OF NORTH CAROLINA, CHAPEL HILL - LAW LIBRARY □ Chapel Hill, NC

Coghlan, Patricia M., Dir.
MEDICAL CENTER OF BEAVER COUNTY - HEALTH SCIENCES LIBRARY □ Beaver, PA

Cogliano, Betsy F., Supv.
MITRE CORPORATION - BEDFORD OPERATIONS LIBRARY □ Bedford, MA

Cogswell, Robert E., Cat.
EPISCOPAL THEOLOGICAL SEMINARY OF THE SOUTHWEST - LIBRARY □ Austin, TX

Cohan, Lois, Lib.Dir.
KLINE (Nathan S.) INSTITUTE FOR PSYCHIATRIC RESEARCH - ROCKLAND HEALTH SCIENCES LIBRARY □ Orangeburg, NY

Cohan, Michaela M., Libn.
WASHINGTON METROPOLITAN AREA TRANSIT AUTHORITY - OFFICE OF PUBLIC AFFAIRS - LIBRARY □ Washington, DC

Cohen, Anne, Med.Libn.
SISTERS OF CHARITY HOSPITAL - MEDICAL STAFF LIBRARY □ Buffalo, NY

Cohen, Ari, Hd., Cat.Dept.
ENGINEERING SOCIETIES LIBRARY □ New York, NY

Cohen, Arthur M., Dir.
ERIC CLEARINGHOUSE FOR JUNIOR COLLEGES □ Los Angeles, CA

Cohen, Barry L., MAP Libn.
NEW YORK CITY HUMAN RESOURCES ADMINISTRATION - MEDICAL ASSISTANCE PROGRAM - MEDICAID LIBRARY □ New York, NY

Cohen, David, Prog.Dir.
QUEENS COLLEGE OF THE CITY UNIVERSITY OF NEW YORK - ETHNIC MATERIALS INFORMATION CENTER □ Flushing, NY

Cohen, Elaine, Libn.
TEMPLE SINAI - JACK BALABAN MEMORIAL LIBRARY □ Cinnaminson, NJ

Cohen, Elinor, Adm., Tech.Info.Serv.
GENERAL FOODS CORPORATION - TECHNICAL CENTER - TARRYTOWN TECHNICAL INFORMATION CENTER □ White Plains, NY

Cohen, Faya, Asst.Libn.
WINTHROP, STIMSON, PUTNAM AND ROBERTS - LIBRARY □ New York, NY

Cohen, George L., Ph.D., Chm., Lib.Comm.
SOCIETY OF COSMETIC CHEMISTS - LIBRARY □ New York, NY

Cohen, Harriet, Div.Hd.
INDIANAPOLIS-MARION COUNTY PUBLIC LIBRARY - NEWSPAPER AND PERIODICAL DIVISION □ Indianapolis, IN

Cohen, Harriet V., Med.Libn.
U.S. NAVY - NAVAL HOSPITAL (CA-Oakland) - MEDICAL LIBRARY □ Oakland, CA

Cohen, Jackson B., Hd., Sci.Lib.
QUEENS COLLEGE OF THE CITY UNIVERSITY OF NEW YORK - SCIENCE LIBRARY □ Flushing, NY

Cohen, Jane, Ref.Libn.
U.S. ARMY IN EUROPE (USAREUR) - LIBRARY AND RESOURCE CENTER □ APO New York, NY

Cohen, Jane Taubenfield, Prin., Rel.Sch.
TEMPLE SINAI - LIBRARY† □ Brookline, MA

Cohen, Jodi R., Supv., Rec.Ctr.
CALGARY PLANNING DEPARTMENT - INFORMATION SERVICES □ Calgary, AB

Cohen, Joseph S., Chf.
U.S. DEFENSE LOGISTICS AGENCY - DEFENSE CONSTRUCTION SUPPLY CTR. - TECH. DATA PROCESSING BRANCH - LIBRARY □ Columbus, OH

Cohen, Judith H., Dir.
WISCONSIN INFORMATION SERVICE □ Milwaukee, WI

Cohen, Leonard, Hd., Rd.Serv.
SUNY - COLLEGE AT CORTLAND - MEMORIAL LIBRARY □ Cortland, NY

Cohen, Madeline, Mgr., Lib.Serv.
AMERICAN BROADCASTING COMPANIES, INC. - ABC NEWS INFORMATION CENTER □ New York, NY

Cohen, Margery A., Libn.
CONNECTICUT STATE DEPARTMENT OF HEALTH SERVICES - STANLEY H. OSBORN MEDICAL LIBRARY □ Hartford, CT

Cohen, Marsha, Mgr., Info.Serv.
ALLY AND GARGANO, INC. - INFORMATION CENTER □ New York, NY

Cohen, Matalie, Libn.
NORTH SHORE CONGREGATION ISRAEL - ROMANEK LIBRARY □ Glencoe, IL

Cohen, Morris L., Libn.
YALE UNIVERSITY - LAW LIBRARY □ New Haven, CT

Cohen, Nancy, Med.Libn.
GRANT HOSPITAL - MEDICAL LIBRARY □ Columbus, OH

Cohen, Nancy, Asst.Libn.
PAINE WEBBER INC. - PAINE WEBBER BLYTH EASTMAN - LIBRARY □ New York, NY

Cohen, Nancy B., Dir.
MOUNT SINAI HOSPITAL - HEALTH SCIENCES LIBRARY† □ Hartford, CT

Cohen, Philip, Chf. Hydrologist
U.S. GEOLOGICAL SURVEY - WATER RESOURCES DIVISION - NATL. WATER DATA STORAGE & RETRIEVAL SYSTEM □ Reston, VA

Cohen, Rachel, Asst.Libn.
PARSONS, BRINCKERHOFF, QUADE & DOUGLAS - LIBRARY □ New York, NY

Cohen, Ronald D., Co-Dir.
INDIANA UNIVERSITY NORTHWEST - CALUMET REGIONAL ARCHIVES □ Gary, IN

Cohen, Rosemary, Hd., Cat.Sect.
BROOKHAVEN NATIONAL LABORATORY - TECHNICAL INFORMATION DIVISION □ Upton, NY

Cohen, Samuel, Legal Res.Libn.
COLUMBIA UNIVERSITY - LAW LIBRARY □ New York, NY

Cohen, Sharon, Dir. of Lib.Serv.
PROVIDENCE HOSPITAL - PANZNER MEMORIAL LIBRARY □ Southfield, MI

Cohen, Mrs. Shifra, Res.Anl.
BALTIMORE CITY DEPARTMENT OF HOUSING AND COMMUNITY DEVELOPMENT - RESEARCH LIBRARY □ Baltimore, MD

Cohn, Adele, Libn.
TEMPLE EMANU-EL - WILLIAM P. ENGEL LIBRARY □ Birmingham, AL

Cohn, Alan M., Hum.Libn.
SOUTHERN ILLINOIS UNIVERSITY, CARBONDALE - HUMANITIES DIVISION LIBRARY □ Carbondale, IL

Cohn, Gary, Libn.
BECHTEL PETROLEUM INC. - LIBRARY □ San Francisco, CA

Coil, Dorothy, Libn.
UNIVERSITY OF NOTRE DAME - LIFE SCIENCES RESEARCH LIBRARY □ Notre Dame, IN

Colabrese, Elizabeth, Libn.
DATA SYSTEMS ANALYSTS - TECHNICAL LIBRARY □ Pennsauken, NJ

Colas, Elisa, Tech.Info.Spec.
U.S. DEPT. OF COMMERCE - INTERNATIONAL TRADE ADMINISTRATION - NEW YORK DISTRICT OFFICE LIBRARY □ New York, NY

Colavito, Greta, Lib.Hd.
THOMPSON (Boyce) INSTITUTE - LIBRARY □ Ithaca, NY

Colbeck, Lynda, Libn.
UNIVERSITY OF TORONTO - ASTRONOMY LIBRARY □ Toronto, ON

Colbert, Melissa, Libn.
BAKER & BOTTS - LAW LIBRARY† □ Houston, TX

Colburn, C.E., Libn.
GENERAL ELECTRIC COMPANY - APOLLO SYSTEMS - TECHNICAL AND SERVICES SUPPORT LIBRARY □ Houston, TX

Colby, Anita, Doc.Coord.
ERIC CLEARINGHOUSE FOR JUNIOR COLLEGES □ Los Angeles, CA

Colby, Anne, Dir.
RADCLIFFE COLLEGE - HENRY A. MURRAY RESEARCH CENTER □ Cambridge, MA

Colby, Autumn E., Res.Info.Spec.
GULF RESEARCH AND DEVELOPMENT COMPANY - TECHNICAL INFORMATION SERVICES† □ Pittsburgh, PA

Colby, Beverly, Libn.
MASSACHUSETTS INSTITUTE OF TECHNOLOGY - PLASMA FUSION CENTER - DAVID J. ROSE LIBRARY □ Cambridge, MA

Colby, Charles C., III, Assoc.Libn./BML Serv
HARVARD UNIVERSITY - SCHOOLS OF MEDICINE, DENTAL MED. & PUBLIC HEALTH, BOSTON MED.LIB. - FRANCIS A. COUNTWAY LIB. □ Boston, MA

Coldsmith, Elizabeth E., Asst.Libn.
HARRISBURG HOSPITAL - LIBRARY/MEDIA SERVICES □ Harrisburg, PA

Cole, Anna B., Libn.
MILES & STOCKBRIDGE, ATTORNEYS-AT-LAW - LIBRARY □ Baltimore, MD

Cole, Beatrice, Libn.
AKWESASNE LIBRARY CULTURAL CENTER □ Hogansburg, NY

Cole, David C., Cur.
U.S. ARMY - FORT MEADE MUSEUM - LIBRARY □ Ft. George G. Meade, MD

Cole, E., Sec.
NORTHEASTERN UNIVERSITY - MARINE SCIENCE AND MARITIME STUDIES CENTER □ Nahant, MA

Cole, Eileen F., Ref.Libn.
VITRO CORPORATION - LIBRARY □ Silver Spring, MD

Cole, Evelyn, Sec.
UNIVERSITY OF NORTH DAKOTA - CHEMISTRY LIBRARY □ Grand Forks, ND

Cole, Georgia R., Coord.
VIGO COUNTY SCHOOL CORPORATION - INSTRUCTIONAL MATERIALS CENTER □ Terre Haute, IN

Cole, Glenore, Tech.Serv.
ARIZONA STATE REGIONAL LIBRARY FOR THE BLIND AND PHYSICALLY HANDICAPPED □ Phoenix, AZ

Cole, Herman, Jr., Dir.
ROSE-HULMAN INSTITUTE OF TECHNOLOGY - JOHN A. LOGAN LIBRARY □ Terre Haute, IN

Cole, Howson W., Libn.
VIRGINIA HISTORICAL SOCIETY - LIBRARY □ Richmond, VA

Cole, Dr. Jack, Dir.
ERIC CLEARINGHOUSE ON RURAL EDUCATION AND SMALL SCHOOLS □ Las Cruces, NM

Cole, James H., Cur.
CORNELL UNIVERSITY - WASON COLLECTION □ Ithaca, NY

Cole, Jane B., Libn.
DESERT BOTANICAL GARDEN - RICHTER LIBRARY □ Phoenix, AZ

Cole, John, Ref.Libn.
UNIVERSITY OF BRITISH COLUMBIA - WOODWARD BIOMEDICAL LIBRARY □ Vancouver, BC

Cole, L.M., Tech.Info.Serv.Supv.
AT & T BELL LABORATORIES - LIBRARIES AND INFORMATION SYSTEMS CENTER □ Murray Hill, NJ

Cole, Lorna P., Mgr., Info.Serv.
UNIROYAL, LTD. - RESEARCH LABORATORIES LIBRARY □ Guelph, ON

Cole, Marian G., Libn.
NORFOLK BOTANICAL GARDENS - LIBRARY □ Norfolk, VA

Cole, Marsha, Ref.Libn.
MIDWEST RESEARCH INSTITUTE - PATTERSON REFERENCE LIBRARY AND ECONOMICS REFERENCE CENTER □ Kansas City, MO

Cole, Martha F., Med.Libn.
BETH ISRAEL HOSPITAL - LASSOR AGOOS LIBRARY □ Boston, MA

Cole, Orin D., Hd.
PUBLIC LIBRARY OF YOUNGSTOWN AND MAHONING COUNTY - SCIENCE AND INDUSTRY COLLECTION □ Youngstown, OH

Cole, Patricia N., Med.Libn.
WINTER PARK MEMORIAL HOSPITAL - MEDICAL STAFF LIBRARY† □ Winter Park, FL

Cole, Sally M., Libn.
TINLEY PARK MENTAL HEALTH CENTER - INSTRUCTIONAL MEDIA LIBRARY† □ Tinley Park, IL

Cole, Sara Turley, Law Libn.
MEMPHIS STATE UNIVERSITY LIBRARIES - SCHOOL OF LAW LIBRARY □ Memphis, TN

Coleman, Frances N., Act.Hd., Spec.Coll.
MISSISSIPPI STATE UNIVERSITY - MITCHELL MEMORIAL LIBRARY - SPECIAL COLLECTIONS □ Mississippi State, MS

Coleman, James R., Ref.Libn.
SUFFOLK UNIVERSITY - MILDRED F. SAWYER LIBRARY - COLLECTION OF AFRO-AMERICAN LITERATURE □ Boston, MA

Coleman, Merry J., Dir.
BECKER COUNTY HISTORICAL SOCIETY - WALTER D. BIRD MEMORIAL HISTORICAL LIBRARY □ Detroit Lakes, MN

Coleman, Mildred, Libn.
COLLEGE OF PREACHERS - LIBRARY □ Washington, DC

Coleman, Patrick, Hd., Acq.
MINNESOTA HISTORICAL SOCIETY - REFERENCE LIBRARY □ St. Paul, MN

Coleman, Sandra, Dp.Libn.
HARVARD UNIVERSITY - LAW SCHOOL LIBRARY □ Cambridge, MA

Coles, Bernice, Per.Libn.
FEDERAL RESERVE SYSTEM - BOARD OF GOVERNORS - RESEARCH LIBRARY □ Washington, DC

Coles, Fred, Pres.
GARDEN GROVE HISTORICAL SOCIETY - E.G. WARE LIBRARY □ Garden Grove, CA

Coles, Lynne L., Med.Libn.
MOUNT CLEMENS GENERAL HOSPITAL - STUCK MEDICAL LIBRARY □ Mt. Clemens, MI

Coles, Mary, Musm. Registrar
ARKANSAS STATE UNIVERSITY MUSEUM - HISTORICAL LIBRARY □ State University, AR

Coletti, Jeannette D., Libn.
NATIONAL ENDOWMENT FOR THE HUMANITIES - LIBRARY □ Washington, DC

Coletti, Margaret H., Ref.Libn.
U.S. ARMY - NATICK RESEARCH AND DEVELOPMENT CENTER - TECHNICAL LIBRARY □ Natick, MA

Coley, Betty A., Libn.
BAYLOR UNIVERSITY - ARMSTRONG BROWNING LIBRARY □ Waco, TX

Coley, Robert E., Hd., Archv./Spec.Coll.
MILLERSVILLE UNIVERSITY OF PENNSYLVANIA - HELEN A. GANSER LIBRARY - SPECIAL COLLECTIONS □ Millersville, PA

Colfax, Leslie, Libn.
HOMOSEXUAL INFORMATION CENTER - TANGENT GROUP □ Hollywood, CA

Colgan, Dolores, Libn.
NATIONAL ECONOMIC RESEARCH ASSOCIATES, INC. - LIBRARY □ White Plains, NY

Colhoun, Jean, Hd., Circ.
UNIVERSITY OF WESTERN ONTARIO - FACULTY OF EDUCATION LIBRARY □ London, ON

Coll, Judith A., Law Libn.
CLEVELAND ELECTRIC ILLUMINATING COMPANY - LAW LIBRARY □ Cleveland, OH

Collazo, Odila, Asst. to Dir.
INTERAMERICAN UNIVERSITY OF PUERTO RICO - SCHOOL OF LAW - DOMINGO TOLEDO ALAMO LAW LIBRARY† □ Santurce, PR

Collet, CDR Mal J., Dir.
CITADEL - THE MILITARY COLLEGE OF SOUTH CAROLINA - ARCHIVES/MUSEUM □ Charleston, SC

Collet, Lois W., Mgr.
D'ARCY, MAC MANUS, MASIUS - LIBRARY INFORMATION SERVICES □ Bloomfield Hills, MI

Collett, Stewart, Mgr.
FALCONBRIDGE NICKEL MINES, LTD. - FALCONBRIDGE INFORMATION CENTRE† □ Toronto, ON

Collette, Jacklyn, Libn.
SHRIVER (Eunice Kennedy) CENTER FOR MENTAL RETARDATION, INC. - LIBRARY □ Waltham, MA

Collette, Maria D., Libn.
ST. LUKE'S HOSPITAL OF BETHLEHEM, PENNSYLVANIA - W.L. ESTES, JR. MEMORIAL LIBRARY □ Bethlehem, PA

Colley, Dr. Charles C., Dir.
UNIVERSITY OF TEXAS, ARLINGTON - LIBRARY - DIVISION OF SPECIAL COLLECTIONS AND ARCHIVES □ Arlington, TX

Colley, Martha, Patient Libn.
HARRISBURG STATE HOSPITAL - STAFF LIBRARY □ Harrisburg, PA

Collier, Alfred D., Cur.
COLLIER STATE PARK LOGGING MUSEUM - LIBRARY □ Klamath Falls, OR

Collier, Claire, Archv.
ROCKEFELLER UNIVERSITY - ROCKEFELLER ARCHIVE CENTER □ North Tarrytown, NY

Collier, Harry, Libn.
AEROPHILATELIC FEDERATION OF THE AMERICAS - LIBRARY □ Elgin, IL

Collier, Monica, Microforms
WAYNE STATE UNIVERSITY - G. FLINT PURDY LIBRARY □ Detroit, MI

Collier, Virginia, U.S.Govt.Doc.
OKLAHOMA STATE DEPARTMENT OF LIBRARIES □ Oklahoma City, OK

Colligan, Nancy, Info.Spec.
NATIONAL REHABILITATION INFORMATION CENTER □ Washington, DC

Collins, Anita B., Info.Mgr./Libn.
B.E.A. ASSOCIATES, INC. - LIBRARY □ New York, NY

Collins, Betty, Asst.Libn.
WALKER MEMORIAL HOSPITAL - LIBRARY □ Avon Park, FL

Collins, Catherine L., Cat.Libn.
CAPITAL DISTRICT LIBRARY COUNCIL FOR REFERENCE AND RESEARCH RESOURCES - BIBLIOGRAPHIC CENTER □ Latham, NY

Collins, Cheryl, Libn.
RILEY COUNTY HISTORICAL SOCIETY - SEATON MEMORIAL LIBRARY □ Manhattan, KS

Collins, D.L., Subdistrict Chf.
U.S. GEOLOGICAL SURVEY - WATER RESOURCES LIBRARY □ Grand Junction, CO

Collins, Donald N., V.P., Commun.
FERTILIZER INSTITUTE □ Washington, DC

Collins, Mrs. E., Hd., Circ.
UNIVERSITY OF TORONTO - ST. MICHAEL'S COLLEGE - JOHN M. KELLY LIBRARY □ Toronto, ON

Collins, Edward, Libn.
KETTERING COLLEGE OF MEDICAL ARTS - LEARNING RESOURCES CENTER □ Kettering, OH

Collins, Miss Evron, Map Libn.
BOWLING GREEN STATE UNIVERSITY - MAP LIBRARY □ Bowling Green, OH

Collins, Evron, Hd.Libn.
BOWLING GREEN STATE UNIVERSITY - POPULAR CULTURE LIBRARY □ Bowling Green, OH

Collins, Jane, Hd.Cat.
NATIONAL GALLERY OF ART - LIBRARY □ Washington, DC

Collins, Janet, Libn.
ROSS & HARDIES - LAW LIBRARY □ Chicago, IL

Collins, John W., Hd.
BOSTON UNIVERSITY - EDUCATIONAL RESOURCES LIBRARY □ Boston, MA

Collins, Kay, Libn.
U.S. RAILROAD RETIREMENT BOARD - LIBRARY □ Chicago, IL

Collins, L.A., Lib.Asst.
DU PONT CANADA, INC. - CUSTOMER TECHNICAL CENTRE LIBRARY □ Kingston, ON

Collins, Lucie, Co-Dir.
SHARON HOSPITAL - HEALTH SCIENCES LIBRARY □ Sharon, CT

Collins, M., Internal Doc.Serv.Mgr.
BELL COMMUNICATIONS RESEARCH, INC. - INFORMATION RESOURCES & SERVICES DISTRICT □ Livingston, NJ

Collins, M. Eileen, Doc.Libn.
U.S. ARMY - NATICK RESEARCH AND DEVELOPMENT CENTER - TECHNICAL LIBRARY □ Natick, MA

Collins, Marlene F., Off.Mgr.
GEAUGA COUNTY HISTORICAL SOCIETY - LIBRARY □ Burton, OH

Collins, Meredith M., Pres.
BROWN BROTHERS - PHOTOGRAPH COLLECTION □ Sterling, PA

Collins, Molly, Staff Mgr.
BELL COMMUNICATIONS RESEARCH, INC. - INFORMATION RESOURCES SERVICES CENTER □ Red Bank, NJ

Collins, Pat, Lib.Techn.
MANITOBA - DEPT. OF ENVIRONMENTAL & WORKPLACE SAFETY & HEALTH - ENVIRONMENTAL MANAGEMENT LIBRARY □ Winnipeg, MB

Collins, Patti Jill, Doc./Cat.Libn.
UNIVERSITY OF NEW BRUNSWICK - LAW LIBRARY □ Fredericton, NB

Collins, Rosemary, Mgr.
ASSOCIATION OF NATIONAL ADVERTISERS - LIBRARY □ New York, NY

Collins, Sara, Virginiana Libn.
ARLINGTON COUNTY CENTRAL LIBRARY - VIRGINIANA COLLECTION □ Arlington, VA

Collins, Sheila A., Libn./Info.Spec.
DUFF AND PHELPS, INC. - RESEARCH LIBRARY □ Chicago, IL

Collins, Sue, Hist.
STILLWATER PUBLIC LIBRARY - ST. CROIX VALLEY ROOM □ Stillwater, MN

Collins-Williams, Jean, Act.Hd.Libn.
ONTARIO - MINISTRY OF LABOUR - LIBRARY □ Toronto, ON

Collis, Mary, Ch.Lit.Libn.
NATIONAL LIBRARY OF CANADA - CHILDREN'S LITERATURE SERVICE □ Ottawa, ON

Collister, Edward, SDI
QUEBEC PROV. - MIN. DE L'ENERGIE ET DES RESSOURCES - SERVICE DE DOCUMENTATION ET DE RENSEIGNEMENTS □ Quebec, PQ

Collord, Kathryn, Libn.
FIRST UNITED METHODIST CHURCH - LIBRARY □ Glen Ellyn, IL

Collyer, Dolores G., Adm.
AMERICAN SOCIETY FOR TESTING AND MATERIALS - INFORMATION CENTER □ Philadelphia, PA

Colman, Gould, Univ.Archv.
CORNELL UNIVERSITY - DEPARTMENT OF MANUSCRIPTS AND UNIVERSITY ARCHIVES □ Ithaca, NY

Colon, Elsie
UNIVERSITY OF PUERTO RICO - PUERTO RICAN COLLECTION† □ Rio Piedras, PR

Colon, Mirta, Cat.Libn.
PUERTO RICO - SUPREME COURT - LAW LIBRARY □ San Juan, PR

Colon, Roberto, Cat.
PONCE SCHOOL OF MEDICINE - LIBRARY □ Ponce, PR

Colson, Donnie, Ref./Circ.Libn.
HOWARD UNIVERSITY - SCHOOL OF LAW -
ALLEN MERCER DANIEL LAW LIBRARY □
Washington, DC

Colston, Stephen A., Dir.
SAN DIEGO STATE UNIVERSITY - SAN DIEGO
HISTORY RESEARCH CENTER† □ San Diego, CA

Colter, Carole, Health Sci.Libn.
MIDLAND HOSPITAL CENTER - HEALTH
SCIENCES LIBRARY □ Midland, MI

Colton, Margaret, Libn.
PHOENIX MUTUAL LIFE INSURANCE COMPANY
- LIBRARY □ Hartford, CT

Colvig, Richard, Sr.Libn.
OAKLAND PUBLIC LIBRARY - ART, MUSIC,
RECREATION □ Oakland, CA

Colvin, Alison J., Libn.
STRATHY, ARCHIBALD AND SEAGRAM - LAW
LIBRARY □ Toronto, ON

Colvin, Gloria, Assoc.Libn.
DURHAM HERALD-SUN NEWSPAPER - LIBRARY
□ Durham, NC

Colvin, Linda, Asst.
CHARLESTON GAZETTE-MAIL - LIBRARY □
Charleston, WV

Colwell, David, Ref.Libn.
SUSQUEHANNA COUNTY HISTORICAL SOCIETY
AND FREE LIBRARY ASSOCIATION □ Montrose,
PA

Colwell, Judith, Libn.
BAPTIST CONVENTION OF ONTARIO AND
QUEBEC - CANADIAN BAPTIST ARCHIVES □
Hamilton, ON

Colwin, Jane, Libn.
UNIVERSITY OF WISCONSIN, MADISON -
CENTER FOR LIMNOLOGY - LIBRARY □ Madison,
WI

Coman, Patrick, Supv.Dept.Asst.
METROPOLITAN MUSEUM OF ART - THOMAS J.
WATSON LIBRARY □ New York, NY

Combe, David A., Libn.
TULANE UNIVERSITY OF LOUISIANA - LAW
LIBRARY □ New Orleans, LA

Combouzou, Mable T., Assoc.Dir.
LOUISIANA STATE OFFICE OF THE SECRETARY
OF STATE - STATE ARCHIVES AND RECORDS
SERVICE - ARCHIVES SECTION □ Baton Rouge,
LA

Combs, Jim, Chf./Adm.Serv.Sect.
IOWA STATE DEPARTMENT OF WATER, AIR
AND WASTE MANAGEMENT - TECHNICAL
LIBRARY □ Des Moines, IA

Comeaux, Anne, Ref.
UNIVERSITY OF TEXAS HEALTH SCIENCE
CENTER, SAN ANTONIO - LIBRARY □ San
Antonio, TX

Comer, Harriet, Libn.
MACON TELEGRAPH AND NEWS - LIBRARY □
Macon, GA

Commes, Kristy, Chf., Spec.Serv.Div.
WASHINGTON STATE LIBRARY □ Olympia, WA

Commings, Karen, Sr.Info.Spec.
WESTINGHOUSE ELECTRIC CORPORATION -
WATER REACTOR DIVISIONS - INFORMATION
RESOURCE CENTER □ Pittsburgh, PA

Compas, German B., Ref.Libn.
KAYE, SCHOLER, FIERMAN, HAYS & HANDLER -
LAW LIBRARY □ New York, NY

Compean, Keith, Asst. to Dir./Circ.
SUNY - COLLEGE AT POTSDAM - FREDERICK W.
CRUMB MEMORIAL LIBRARY □ Potsdam, NY

Comport, Jean, First Asst.
DETROIT PUBLIC LIBRARY - FINE ARTS
DEPARTMENT □ Detroit, MI

Compton, Lisa A., Dir.
OLD COLONY HISTORICAL SOCIETY - MUSEUM
& LIBRARY □ Taunton, MA

Comptor, Anne, Coord.
JOHNS HOPKINS UNIVERSITY - POPULATION
INFORMATION PROGRAM □ Baltimore, MD

Conahan, J.E., Acq.Libn.
LOCKHEED MISSILES & SPACE COMPANY, INC.
- TECHNICAL INFORMATION CENTER □ Palo
Alto, CA

Conant, Margaret, Hd., Rd.Serv. & ILL
COLLEGE OF ST. CATHERINE - LIBRARY -
WOMAN'S COLLECTION □ St. Paul, MN

Conaway, Sr. Mary Christine, Libn./Dir., Media Ctr.
ST. JOSEPH HOSPITAL - LIBRARY □ Ottumwa,
IA

Conaway, Mary Sue, Libn./Res.Assoc.
DEFENSE SYSTEMS, INC. - LIBRARY □ McLean,
VA

Concert, Carol, Asst.Libn.
CENTER FOR THE STUDY OF THE PRESIDENCY
- LIBRARY □ New York, NY

Concholar, Dan R., Dir.
ART INFORMATION CENTER, INC. □ New York,
NY

Conde, Ana I., Hd.
INTER-AMERICAN DEVELOPMENT BANK -
TECHNICAL INFORMATION CENTER □
Washington, DC

Condon, Erika, Lib.Dir.
MOUNT ST. MARY'S COLLEGE - NEWMAN
SEMINAR □ Los Angeles, CA

Condon, William J., Lib.Mgr.
BLUE CROSS AND BLUE SHIELD OF FLORIDA -
CORPORATE RESEARCH LIBRARY □
Jacksonville, FL

Condron, Barbara J., Libn.
U.S. GEOLOGICAL SURVEY - WATER
RESOURCES DIVISION - COLORADO DISTRICT
LIBRARY □ Denver, CO

Cone, Judy, Libn.
MAC FARLANE & COMPANY, INC. - FRY
CONSULTANTS INCORPORATED -
MANAGEMENT CENTRE, INC. □ Atlanta, GA

Cone, Lind, Ref.Libn.
FITCHBURG STATE COLLEGE - LIBRARY □
Fitchburg, MA

Conelley, Jean M., Asst.Dir., Tech.Serv.
UNIVERSITY OF MASSACHUSETTS MEDICAL
SCHOOL & WORCESTER DISTRICT MEDICAL
SOCIETY - LIBRARY □ Worcester, MA

Congdon, Rodney H., Chf. Law Libn.
FEDERAL RESERVE BANK OF NEW YORK - LAW
LIBRARY DIVISION □ New York, NY

Conger, Job C., IV, Exec.Dir.
AIRCHIVE - HISTORAIR FILE □ Springfield, IL

Congleton, Caryl, Libn.
FLORIDA POWER & LIGHT COMPANY -
CORPORATE LIBRARY □ Miami, FL

Coniglio, Susan, Ref.Libn.
SANDIA NATIONAL LABORATORIES -
TECHNICAL LIBRARY† □ Livermore, CA

Conklin, Annette, Rsrcs.Libn.
NOVATO UNIFIED SCHOOL DISTRICT -
INSTRUCTIONAL MATERIALS CENTER □
Novato, CA

Conklin, Charlotte L., Libn.
MC GEAN-ROHCO, INC. - RESEARCH LIBRARY □
Cleveland, OH

Conklin, Curt, Cat.Libn.
BRIGHAM YOUNG UNIVERSITY - J. REUBEN
CLARK LAW SCHOOL LIBRARY □ Provo, UT

Conklin, Gary, Libn.
ALLEN COUNTY PUBLIC LIBRARY - BUSINESS
AND TECHNOLOGY DEPARTMENT □ Fort Wayne,
IN

Conklin, Susan L., Hist.
GENESEE COUNTY - DEPARTMENT OF HISTORY
- RESEARCH LIBRARY □ Batavia, NY

Conkling, Thomas W., Hd.
PENNSYLVANIA STATE UNIVERSITY -
ENGINEERING LIBRARY □ University Park, PA

Conlan, Ann A., Chf., Lib.Serv.
U.S. VETERANS ADMINISTRATION (FL-Bay
Pines) - CENTER LIBRARY □ Bay Pines, FL

Conlee, Julia, AV Libn.
COLONIAL WILLIAMSBURG - AUDIO-VISUAL
LIBRARY† □ Williamsburg, VA

Conley, John, Media Spec.
PARKLAND COLLEGE - LEARNING RESOURCE
CENTER □ Champaign, IL

Conley, Linda, Libn.
HASSARD, BONNINGTON, ROGERS & HUBER -
LIBRARY □ San Francisco, CA

Conley, Mindi E., Hd. Law Libn.
STANISLAUS COUNTY LAW LIBRARY □
Modesto, CA

Conley, Patricia, Ref.Libn.
MINNESOTA STATE LEGISLATIVE REFERENCE
LIBRARY □ St. Paul, MN

Conley, Philip, Libn.
ASSOCIATED GRANTMAKERS OF
MASSACHUSETTS, INC. - RESOURCE CENTER
FOR PHILANTHROPY □ Boston, MA

Conlon, Diane, Asst. to Exec.Dir.
INTERNATIONAL OMBUDSMAN INSTITUTE -
I.O.I. LIBRARY □ Edmonton, AB

Conlon, Mary, Dir.
ALEXIAN BROTHERS HOSPITAL - MEDICAL
LIBRARY □ Elizabeth, NJ

Conlon, Mary L., Libn.
CEDARCREST REGIONAL HOSPITAL - MEDICAL
LIBRARY □ Newington, CT

Conlon, Rosa K., Sect.Mgr.
AVON PRODUCTS, INC. - RESEARCH LIBRARY □
Suffern, NY

Connaughton, Theresa, Asst.Supv., Tech.Proc.
UNIVERSITY OF CALIFORNIA - LOS ALAMOS
NATIONAL LABORATORY - LIBRARY □ Los
Alamos, NM

Connell, Carol, Asst.Libn.
INDIANA UNIVERSITY OF PENNSYLVANIA -
UNIVERSITY LIBRARY □ Indiana, PA

Connell, Karen, Libn.
MC NEIL LABORATORIES (Canada) LIMITED -
LIBRARY □ Stouffville, ON

Connell, Michael, Dir.
MONTCLAIR PUBLIC LIBRARY - LOCAL
HISTORY FILE □ Montclair, NJ

Connell, Muriel H., Libn.
TENNESSEE BOTANICAL GARDENS & FINE
ARTS CENTER - MINNIE RITCHEY & JOEL
OWSLEY CHEEK LIBRARY □ Nashville, TN

Connell, Robert, Asst.Law Libn./Tech.Serv.
UNIVERSITY OF CONNECTICUT - LAW SCHOOL
LIBRARY □ Hartford, CT

Connell, Sarah G., Hd. Law Libn.
WIDETT, SLATER & GOLDMAN P.C. - LIBRARY □
Boston, MA

Connelley, Melba, Libn.
TEXAS ELECTRIC SERVICE COMPANY -
LIBRARY □ Fort Worth, TX

Connelly, Linda M., Mgr.
JAY (John) HOMESTEAD - LIBRARY □ Katonah,
NY

Connery, Susan E., Dir.
TRENTON TIMES - LIBRARY □ Trenton, NJ

Connolly, Betty F., Chf., Lib.Serv.
U.S. VETERANS ADMINISTRATION (CA-Long
Beach) - MEDICAL CENTER LIBRARY □ Long
Beach, CA

Connolly, Bruce E., Dir.
NEW YORK STATE COLLEGE OF CERAMICS AT
ALFRED UNIVERSITY - SAMUEL R. SCHOLES
LIBRARY OF CERAMICS □ Alfred, NY

Connolly, Bruce E., Hd., Tech.Serv.
NEW YORK STATE COLLEGE OF CERAMICS AT
ALFRED UNIVERSITY - SAMUEL R. SCHOLES
LIBRARY OF CERAMICS □ Alfred, NY

Connolly, Sr. Madeline, Libn.
ST. AUGUSTINE'S SEMINARY - LIBRARY □
Scarborough, ON

Connolly, Mary, Ref.Libn.
EASTMAN KODAK COMPANY - RESEARCH
LIBRARY □ Rochester, NY

Connolly, Patricia, Cur.
PRICE-POTTENGER NUTRITION FOUNDATION -
LIBRARY □ San Diego, CA

Connolly, Robert, Lib.Asst.
COLUMBIA UNIVERSITY - PATERNO LIBRARY □
New York, NY

Connor, A. Christine, Lib.Dir.
ST. BARNABAS MEDICAL CENTER - MEDICAL
LIBRARY □ Livingston, NJ
Connor, Billie M., Dept.Mgr.
LOS ANGELES PUBLIC LIBRARY - SCIENCE &
TECHNOLOGY DEPARTMENT □ Los Angeles, CA
Connor, Christine, Dir. of Pubns./Pub.Info.
HISTORIC LANDMARKS FOUNDATION OF
INDIANA, INC. - INFORMATION CENTER □
Indianapolis, IN
Connor, Lynn S., Libn.
MARION COUNTY LAW LIBRARY □ Indianapolis,
IN
Connor, Paul L., Med.Libn.
U.S. VETERANS ADMINISTRATION (CA-Fresno)
- HOSPITAL MEDICAL LIBRARY □ Fresno, CA
Connors, Jean, Law Libn.
U.S. DEPT. OF ENERGY - BONNEVILLE POWER
ADMINISTRATION - LIBRARY □ Portland, OR
Connors, John F., Adm.Libn.
U.S. VETERANS ADMINISTRATION (NY-Albany)
- MEDICAL CENTER LIBRARY (500/142-D) □
Albany, NY
Connors, Matthew J., Sys.Anl.
SANDIA NATIONAL LABORATORIES -
TECHNICAL LIBRARY† □ Livermore, CA
Conole, Philip, Music Record Cur.
SUNY AT BINGHAMTON - FINE ARTS LIBRARY □
Binghamton, NY
Conole, Philip, Cur., Conole Archv.
SUNY AT BINGHAMTON - SPECIAL
COLLECTIONS □ Binghamton, NY
Conquest, Robert, Cur., Russia & Europe
STANFORD UNIVERSITY - HOOVER
INSTITUTION ON WAR, REVOLUTION AND
PEACE - LIBRARY □ Stanford, CA
Conrad, Elizabeth, Lib.Techn.
MILWAUKEE AREA TECHNICAL COLLEGE -
SOUTH CAMPUS LIBRARY □ Oak Creek, WI
Conrad, Eva, Fed.Doc.Libn.
MIAMI-DADE PUBLIC LIBRARY - FEDERAL
DOCUMENTS DIVISION □ Miami, FL
Conrad, Glenn R., Dir.
UNIVERSITY OF SOUTHWESTERN LOUISIANA -
CENTER FOR LOUISIANA STUDIES □ Lafayette,
LA
Conrad, James, Coord.
EAST TEXAS STATE UNIVERSITY - ORAL
HISTORY PROGRAM □ Commerce, TX
Conrad, LaVerna J., Libn.
WHITE RIVER VALLEY HISTORICAL SOCIETY
MUSEUM - LIBRARY □ Auburn, WA
Conrad, Leigh, Cat.
MARICOPA COUNTY LAW LIBRARY □ Phoenix,
AZ
Conrad, Mary T., Trade Spec.
U.S. DEPT. OF COMMERCE - INTERNATIONAL
TRADE ADMINISTRATION - BALTIMORE
DISTRICT OFFICE LIBRARY □ Baltimore, MD
Conradi, Carol, Libn.
RICE MEMORIAL HOSPITAL - HEALTH SCIENCE
LIBRARY □ Willmar, MN
Conron, Frank, Sr.Libn.
NEW YORK STATE LIBRARY FOR THE BLIND
AND VISUALLY HANDICAPPED □ Albany, NY
Conroy, Audrey, Libn.
CANADA - FISHERIES & OCEANS -
NEWFOUNDLAND REGIONAL LIBRARY □ St.
John's, NF
Conroy, Marcia E., Cur. of Educ.
MASSACHUSETTS INSTITUTE OF TECHNOLOGY
- M.I.T. MUSEUM AND HISTORICAL
COLLECTIONS □ Cambridge, MA
Constance, Joe, Archv.
GEORGIA STATE UNIVERSITY - SPECIAL
COLLECTIONS DEPARTMENT □ Atlanta, GA
Constantine, Marianne, Med.Libn.
MONTREAL CHEST HOSPITAL CENTRE -
MEDICAL LIBRARY □ Montreal, PQ
Constantz, Mark Quinn, Med.Libn.
SAN MATEO COUNTY DEPARTMENT OF HEALTH
SERVICES - LIBRARY □ San Mateo, CA

Conti, Shirley Ann, Adm.Asst.
NATIONAL CENTER FOR STATE COURTS -
NORTHEASTERN REGIONAL OFFICE - DONALD
J. HURLEY LIBRARY □ North Andover, MA
Contini, Janice, Ref.Libn.
UNIVERSITY OF SOUTHERN CALIFORNIA -
HEALTH SCIENCES CAMPUS - NORRIS
MEDICAL LIBRARY □ Los Angeles, CA
Converse, Dr. W.R., Chf.Libn.
UNIVERSITY OF WINNIPEG - LIBRARY -
SPECIAL COLLECTIONS □ Winnipeg, MB
Conway, Eileen, Rsrc.Coord.
U.S. DEPT. OF JUSTICE - NATIONAL
INSTITUTE OF CORRECTIONS - NIC
INFORMATION CENTER □ Boulder, CO
Conway, Jeanne, Hd., Pub.Serv.
GALLAUDET COLLEGE LIBRARY - SPECIAL
COLLECTIONS† □ Washington, DC
Conway, John, Dir.
MONMOUTH MEDICAL CENTER - ALTSCHUL
MEDICAL LIBRARY □ Long Branch, NJ
Conway, Laurie A., Med.Libn.
WYMAN PARK HEALTH SYSTEM, INC. -
MEDICAL LIBRARY □ Baltimore, MD
Conway, Mary, Med.Libn.
U.S. VETERANS ADMINISTRATION (OH-
Brecksville) - HOSPITAL LIBRARY □ Brecksville,
OH
Conway, Mary, Med.Libn.
U.S. VETERANS ADMINISTRATION (OH-
Cleveland) - HOSPITAL LIBRARY □ Cleveland, OH
Conway, Suzanne, Chf.Ref.Libn.
ST. LOUIS UNIVERSITY - MEDICAL CENTER
LIBRARY □ St. Louis, MO
Coogan, Helen M., Supv., Lib.
ROCKWELL INTERNATIONAL - SCIENCE
CENTER LIBRARY □ Thousand Oaks, CA
Cook, Alan D., Sr. Horticulturist
DAWES ARBORETUM - LIBRARY □ Newark, OH
Cook, Alan F., Asst.Libn.
PRINCETON UNIVERSITY - ENGINEERING
LIBRARY □ Princeton, NJ
Cook, Cathy, Pub.Lib.Cons.
OKLAHOMA STATE DEPARTMENT OF
LIBRARIES □ Oklahoma City, OK
Cook, Claudia, Ref.Libn.
O'MELVENY AND MYERS - INFORMATION
SERVICES □ Los Angeles, CA
Cook, D. Louise, Dir.
KING (Martin Luther, Jr.) CENTER FOR SOCIAL
CHANGE - KING LIBRARY AND ARCHIVES □
Atlanta, GA
Cook, Elizabeth C., Park Techn.
U.S. NATL. PARK SERVICE - STONES RIVER
NATL. BATTLEFIELD - LIBRARY □ Murfreesboro,
TN
Cook, Ellen, Chf., Info.Sys.
U.S. DEPT. OF THE INTERIOR - NATURAL
RESOURCES LIBRARY □ Washington, DC
Cook, Esther M., Libn.
WESTMINSTER PRESBYTERIAN CHURCH -
LIBRARY □ Alexandria, VA
Cook, Florence, Cat.
WINEBRENNER THEOLOGICAL SEMINARY -
LIBRARY □ Findlay, OH
Cook, Miss Francis, Libn.
CENTRAL CHRISTIAN CHURCH - LIBRARY □
Lexington, KY
Cook, Guinevere, Asst.Libn.
HINSDALE SANITARIUM AND HOSPITAL - A.C.
LARSON LIBRARY □ Hinsdale, IL
Cook, J. Frank, Dir.
UNIVERSITY OF WISCONSIN, MADISON -
ARCHIVES □ Madison, WI
Cook, Janice L., Tech.Serv.Libn.
KANSAS STATE SUPREME COURT - LAW
LIBRARY □ Topeka, KS
Cook, Joan, Libn.
RAYTHEON COMPANY - LAW LIBRARY† □
Lexington, MA

Cook, Joyce, Libn.
ONONDAGA COUNTY PUBLIC LIBRARY - LOCAL
HISTORY AND GENEALOGY DEPARTMENT □
Syracuse, NY
Cook, Kathleen M., Asst.Libn.
GARRETT CORPORATION - AIRESEARCH
MANUFACTURING COMPANY - TECHNICAL
LIBRARY □ Torrance, CA
Cook, Dr. Kathy, Asst.Libn.
SOUTHERN ILLINOIS UNIVERSITY,
CARBONDALE - EDUCATION AND PSYCHOLOGY
DIVISION LIBRARY □ Carbondale, IL
Cook, Lawrence P., Dir.
U.S. NATL. BUREAU OF STANDARDS - PHASE
DIAGRAMS FOR CERAMISTS - DATA CENTER □
Washington, DC
Cook, Loretta, Libn.
SAMUEL ROBERTS NOBLE FOUNDATION, INC. -
BIOMEDICAL DIVISION LIBRARY □ Ardmore,
OK
Cook, Lucy, Asst.Libn.
PHILIP MORRIS, U.S.A. - RESEARCH CENTER
LIBRARY □ Richmond, VA
Cook, Margaret C., Cur., Mss./Rare Bks.
COLLEGE OF WILLIAM AND MARY - EARL
GREGG SWEM LIBRARY - SPECIAL
COLLECTIONS □ Williamsburg, VA
Cook, Marilyn, Dir.
WASHINGTON HOSPITAL CENTER - MEDICAL
LIBRARY □ Washington, DC
Cook, Marjorie E., Med.Libn.
WEST VOLUSIA MEMORIAL HOSPITAL -
MEDICAL LIBRARY □ De Land, FL
Cook, Mary, Coord., Instr.Sup.Serv.
PHOENIX ELEMENTARY SCHOOLS - DISTRICT
NO. 1 - CURRICULUM MEDIA CENTER □
Phoenix, AZ
Cook, Mary Aline, Libn.
NEW HARMONY WORKINGMEN'S INSTITUTE -
LIBRARY AND MUSEUM □ New Harmony, IN
Cook, Mary E., Dir. of Lib.Serv.
EAST TEXAS STATE UNIVERSITY - JAMES
GILLIAM GEE LIBRARY □ Commerce, TX
Cook, Nedra, Libn.
FORT SANDERS REGIONAL MEDICAL CENTER -
MEDICAL/NURSING LIBRARY □ Knoxville, TN
Cook, Pamela
MARSH AND MC LENNAN, INC. - INFORMATION
CENTER □ New York, NY
Cook, Patricia, Libn.
U.S. NATL. MARINE FISHERIES SERVICE -
NORTHWEST & ALASKA FISHERIES CENTER -
LIBRARY □ Seattle, WA
Cook, Patricia, ILL
U.S. NAVY - NAVAL RESEARCH LABORATORY -
RUTH H. HOOKER TECHNICAL LIBRARY □
Washington, DC
Cook, Paul, Lib.Dir.
PARADE PUBLICATIONS, INC. - LIBRARY □ New
York, NY
Cook, Peggy, Libn.
HILLCREST MEDICAL CENTER - LIBRARY □
Tulsa, OK
Cook, Richard L., Hosp.Libn.
HINSDALE SANITARIUM AND HOSPITAL - A.C.
LARSON LIBRARY □ Hinsdale, IL
Cook, Romilda F., Med.Libn.
BAPTIST MEDICAL CENTER - MEDICAL
LIBRARY □ Birmingham, AL
Cook, Ruth E., Asst. to Dir.
LINCOLN NATIONAL LIFE FOUNDATION - LOUIS
A. WARREN LINCOLN LIBRARY AND MUSEUM □
Fort Wayne, IN
Cook, Sherry, Libn.
BECHTEL - DATA PROCESSING LIBRARY □ San
Francisco, CA
Cook, Sterling, Cur.
MC GUFFEY (William Holmes) HOUSE AND
MUSEUM - LIBRARY □ Oxford, OH
Cook, Sue E., Adm.Off.
DAVIS (J.M.) GUN MUSEUM - RESEARCH
LIBRARY □ Claremore, OK

Cook, T., Chf., Soc. & Nat.Res.Rec.
CANADA - PUBLIC ARCHIVES OF CANADA -
FEDERAL ARCHIVES DIVISION □ Ottawa, ON
Cook, Trudy Katz, Tech.Libn.
NCR CORPORATION - TECHNICAL LIBRARY □
West Columbia, SC
Cook, Virginia I., Med.Libn.
NASSAU HOSPITAL - BENJAMIN WHITE
SEAMAN MEDICAL LIBRARY □ Mineola, NY
Cook, William, Libn.
ONONDAGA COUNTY PUBLIC LIBRARY - LOCAL
HISTORY AND GENEALOGY DEPARTMENT □
Syracuse, NY
Cooke, Mrs. A., Mgr., Coll.Org.
CANADA - HEALTH AND WELFARE CANADA -
DEPARTMENTAL LIBRARY SERVICES □ Ottawa,
ON
Cooke, Mrs. Dudley S., Libn.
ROCKY HILL HISTORICAL SOCIETY - ACADEMY
HALL MUSEUM - LIBRARY □ Rocky Hill, CT
Cooke, Eileen D., Dir.
AMERICAN LIBRARY ASSOCIATION -
WASHINGTON OFFICE □ Washington, DC
Cooke, Mrs. G.A., Libn.
UNIVERSITY OF ALBERTA - BOREAL INSTITUTE
FOR NORTHERN STUDIES - LIBRARY □
Edmonton, AB
Cooke, Marcia Lynn, Libn.
UNIVERSITY OF WISCONSIN, MADISON -
WASHBURN OBSERVATORY - WOODMAN
ASTRONOMICAL LIBRARY □ Madison, WI
Cooke, Melva, Libn.
SOURIS VALLEY REGIONAL CARE CENTER -
MEDICAL & HEALTH SCIENCES LIBRARY □
Weyburn, SK
Cooke, Mr. O.A., Sr. Archival Off.
CANADA - NATIONAL DEFENCE -
DIRECTORATE OF HISTORY LIBRARY □ Ottawa,
ON
Cooke, Sarah E., Archv.
TIPPECANOE COUNTY HISTORICAL
ASSOCIATION - ALAMEDA MC COLLOUGH
RESEARCH & GENEALOGY LIBRARY □ Lafayette,
IN
Cooklock, Richard A., Dir.
UNIVERSITY OF WISCONSIN, RIVER FALLS -
CHALMER DAVEE LIBRARY □ River Falls, WI
Cooksey, Phyllis, Dir. of Educ. & Trng.
PLANNED PARENTHOOD OF MINNESOTA -
POPULATION RESOURCE CENTER □ St. Paul, MN
Cooley, Lillian, Evening Ref.Libn.
MISSISSIPPI COLLEGE SCHOOL OF LAW - LAW
LIBRARY □ Jackson, MS
Coolidge, Alison, Libn.
WALTHAM HOSPITAL - MEDICAL LIBRARY □
Waltham, MA
Coombs, James A., Map Libn.
SOUTHWEST MISSOURI STATE UNIVERSITY -
MAP COLLECTION □ Springfield, MO
Coombs, Leonard, Asst.Archv.
UNIVERSITY OF MICHIGAN - MICHIGAN
HISTORICAL COLLECTIONS - BENTLEY
HISTORICAL LIBRARY □ Ann Arbor, MI
Coombs, Sarah, Mgr.
ONTARIO - MINISTRY OF CONSUMER AND
COMMERCIAL RELATIONS - CONSUMER
INFORMATION CENTRE □ Toronto, ON
Coomes, Rev. J. Eugene, S.J., Libn.
ST. LOUIS UNIVERSITY - COLLEGE OF
PHILOSOPHY AND LETTERS - FUSZ MEMORIAL
LIBRARY □ St. Louis, MO
Coon, Kathy, Asst.Libn., Pub.Serv.
JENKINS (Theodore F.) MEMORIAL LAW
LIBRARY COMPANY - LIBRARY □ Philadelphia,
PA
Cooney, Charles W., Jr., Cur., Res.Coll.
MILWAUKEE COUNTY HISTORICAL SOCIETY -
LIBRARY AND ARCHIVES □ Milwaukee, WI
Cooney, Jane, Chf., Oper.
U.S. ARMY - MISSILE COMMAND & MARSHALL
SPACE FLIGHT CENTER - REDSTONE
SCIENTIFIC INFORMATION CENTER □
Redstone Arsenal, AL

Coonley, Joyce, Tech.Info.Spec.
NATIONAL INJURY INFORMATION
CLEARINGHOUSE □ Washington, DC
Cooper, Alene, Coord., Lib.Dev.
MONTANA STATE LIBRARY □ Helena, MT
Cooper, Amy, Hd., Tech.Serv.
UNIVERSITY OF VERMONT - DIVISION OF
HEALTH SCIENCES - CHARLES A. DANA
MEDICAL LIBRARY □ Burlington, VT
Cooper, Beverly Jane, Libn.
UNIVERSITY OF WASHINGTON - GRADUATE
SCHOOL - JOINT CENTER FOR GRADUATE
STUDY - LIBRARY □ Richland, WA
Cooper, Byron D., Dir.
UNIVERSITY OF DETROIT - SCHOOL OF LAW
LIBRARY □ Detroit, MI
Cooper, Cathy, Assoc.Libn.
KEENELAND ASSOCIATION - LIBRARY □
Lexington, KY
Cooper, Constance, Mss.Libn.
HISTORICAL SOCIETY OF DELAWARE -
LIBRARY □ Wilmington, DE
Cooper, Diana, Fine Arts Ref.Libn.
UNIVERSITY OF BRITISH COLUMBIA - FINE
ARTS DIVISION □ Vancouver, BC
Cooper, Ellen, Libn.
PRESBYTERIAN HOSPITAL - LEARNING
RESOURCE CENTER □ Charlotte, NC
Cooper, Gracie, Libn.
METROPOLITAN JEWISH GERIATRIC CENTER -
MAX B. & LOUISA S. MARKS MEMORIAL
MEDICAL LIBRARY □ Brooklyn, NY
Cooper, Jean L., Tech.Serv.Libn.
UNIVERSITY OF VIRGINIA - SCIENCE &
ENGINEERING LIBRARY □ Charlottesville, VA
Cooper, Jetta J., Libn.
HARVARD UNIVERSITY - CENTER FOR SCIENCE
AND INTERNATIONAL AFFAIRS LIBRARY □
Cambridge, MA
Cooper, Joanne S., Dir.
MERCYHURST COLLEGE - LIBRARY - ARCHIVES
□ Erie, PA
Cooper, Joyce, Libn.
U.S. FISH & WILDLIFE SERVICE - FISH
FARMING EXPERIMENTAL STATION - LIBRARY
□ Stuttgart, AR
Cooper, Katherine A., Res.Spec.
UNIVERSITY OF DETROIT - SCHOOL OF LAW
LIBRARY □ Detroit, MI
Cooper, Marguerite, Med.Libn.
ARIZONA STATE HOSPITAL - MEDICAL
LIBRARY □ Phoenix, AZ
Cooper, Mary Jo, Asst.Cur.
AUSTIN PUBLIC LIBRARY - AUSTIN HISTORY
CENTER □ Austin, TX
Cooper, Mary L., Tech.Serv.Libn.
UNIVERSITY OF VIRGINIA - ARTHUR J.
MORRIS LAW LIBRARY □ Charlottesville, VA
Cooper, Melissa, Circ.libn.
U.S. AIR FORCE BASE - TINKER BASE LIBRARY
□ Tinker AFB, OK
Cooper, Nancy, Dir., Lib./Info.Serv.
GRUY (H.J.) & ASSOCIATES, INC. - LIBRARY □
Irving, TX
Cooper, Norma M., Music Libn.
PACIFIC UNIVERSITY - MUSIC DEPARTMENT -
LIBRARY □ Forest Grove, OR
Cooper, Philip Glenn, Assoc. Law Libn.
THE COCA-COLA COMPANY - LAW LIBRARY □
Atlanta, GA
Cooper, Richard S., Assoc.Univ.Libn.
UNIVERSITY OF CALIFORNIA, SAN FRANCISCO
- LIBRARY □ San Francisco, CA
Cooper, Robert W., Exec.Sec.
AMERICAN FEDERATION OF ASTROLOGERS,
INC. - LIBRARY □ Tempe, AZ
Cooper, S. Jane, Hd.Med.Libn.
OKLAHOMA OSTEOPATHIC HOSPITAL - L.C.
BAXTER MEDICAL LIBRARY □ Tulsa, OK
Cooper, Sara E., Chf.Libn.
AMERICAN FEDERATION OF ASTROLOGERS,
INC. - LIBRARY □ Tempe, AZ

Cooper, Sarah, Dir.
SOUTHERN CALIFORNIA LIBRARY FOR SOCIAL
STUDIES AND RESEARCH □ Los Angeles, CA
Cooper, W., Hd., Docs.
U.S. NASA - JOHN F. KENNEDY SPACE CENTER
- LIBRARY □ Kennedy Space Center, FL
Cooperrider, Shirley, Rsrcs.Coord.
GOLDEN GATE ENERGY CENTER - LIBRARY □
Sausalito, CA
Coorsh, Kathy, Client Serv.
CANADIAN NATIONAL INSTITUTE FOR THE
BLIND - NATIONAL LIBRARY SERVICES -
SHERMAN SWIFT REFERENCE LIBRARY □
Toronto, ON
Coover, Diane, Mgr., Ref.Sys. & Serv.
BIBLIOGRAPHICAL CENTER FOR RESEARCH -
ROCKY MOUNTAIN REGION, INC. □ Denver, CO
Coover, James, Dir.
SUNY AT BUFFALO - MUSIC LIBRARY □ Buffalo,
NY
Copas, James, Act.Chm.,Lib.Serv.
BLACK HAWK COLLEGE - LEARNING
RESOURCES CENTER □ Moline, IL
Cope, Jennifer, Libn.
NORTHWOOD INSTITUTE OF TEXAS - LIBRARY
□ Cedar Hill, TX
Copeland, Cheryl A., Dir., Micropubn.
GENERAL MICROFILM COMPANY - MICROFORM
LIBRARY □ Watertown, MA
Copeland, Julia, Doc.Libn.
MINNEAPOLIS PUBLIC LIBRARY &
INFORMATION CENTER - GOVERNMENT
DOCUMENTS □ Minneapolis, MN
Copeley, William, Assoc.Libn.
NEW HAMPSHIRE HISTORICAL SOCIETY -
LIBRARY □ Concord, NH
Coppage, Kathy, Lib.Assoc.
DALLAS PUBLIC LIBRARY - GOVERNMENT
PUBLICATIONS DIVISION □ Dallas, TX
Coppel, Lynn M., Coord.
CALIFORNIA STATE UNIVERSITY, FULLERTON -
LIBRARY - FREEDOM CENTER† □ Fullerton, CA
Coppenoll, Lee, Prog.Assoc.
BARNARD COLLEGE WOMEN'S CENTER -
BIRDIE GOLDSMITH AST RESOURCE
COLLECTION □ New York, NY
Coppens, Paul, Hd., Media Serv.
UNIVERSITY OF LOWELL, SOUTH CAMPUS -
DANIEL H. O'LEARY LIBRARY - SPECIAL
COLLECTIONS □ Lowell, MA
Coppin, Ann S., Supv.
CHEVRON OIL FIELD RESEARCH COMPANY -
TECHNICAL INFORMATION SERVICES □ La
Habra, CA
Coppola, Judy, Sci.Libn.
MICHIGAN STATE UNIVERSITY - SCIENCE
LIBRARY □ East Lansing, MI
Coraggio, Mary, Hd., Tech.Serv.Br.
U.S. NAVY - NAVAL WEAPONS CENTER -
LIBRARY DIVISION □ China Lake, CA
Coral, Lenore, Music Libn.
CORNELL UNIVERSITY - MUSIC LIBRARY □
Ithaca, NY
Corbett, Anne, Libn.
NORTHWESTERN CONNECTICUT COMMUNITY
COLLEGE - LIBRARY □ Winsted, CT
Corbett, Marilyn, Hd., Lib.Serv.
ALBERTA - DEPARTMENT OF THE
ENVIRONMENT - LIBRARY □ Edmonton, AB
Corbin, Brenda G., Libn.
U.S. NAVY - NAVAL OBSERVATORY - MATTHEW
FONTAINE MAURY MEMORIAL LIBRARY □
Washington, DC
Corbin, Diane, Res.Libn.
NATIONAL BROADCASTING COMPANY, INC. -
REFERENCE LIBRARY □ New York, NY
Corbin, Grace, Tech.Info.Spec.
U.S. ARMY COMPUTER SYSTEMS COMMAND -
TECHNICAL LIBRARY† □ Ft. Belvoir, VA
Corcoran, Nancy, Libn.
MINNEAPOLIS PUBLIC LIBRARY &
INFORMATION CENTER - MUNICIPAL
INFORMATION LIBRARY □ Minneapolis, MN

Corcoran, Virginia, Robinson Libn.
HARTFORD HOSPITAL - HEALTH SCIENCE
LIBRARIES □ Hartford, CT

Corcos, Christine, Acq.Libn.
UNIVERSITY OF OKLAHOMA - LAW LIBRARY □
Norman, OK

Cordasci, Terry, Gen. Color Lib.
PHOTO RESEARCHERS, INC. - LIBRARY □ New
York, NY

Cordeiro, Daniel, Latin Amer.Bibliog.
SYRACUSE UNIVERSITY - E.S. BIRD LIBRARY -
AREA STUDIES DEPARTMENT □ Syracuse, NY

Cordero, Aura S.
UNIVERSITY OF PUERTO RICO - NATURAL
SCIENCE LIBRARY □ Rio Piedras, PR

Corey, D. Steven, Spec.Coll.Libn.
UNIVERSITY OF SAN FRANCISCO - SPECIAL
COLLECTIONS DEPARTMENT/DONOHUE RARE
BOOK ROOM □ San Francisco, CA

Corey, Karen M., Rd.Serv.Libn.
PURDUE UNIVERSITY, CALUMET - LIBRARY □
Hammond, IN

Corey, Marjorie, Libn.
CLAYTON ENVIRONMENTAL CONSULTANTS -
LIBRARY AND INFORMATION CENTER □
Southfield, MI

Corkran, Charles W., Asst.Dir.
U.S. PRESIDENTIAL LIBRARIES - LYNDON B.
JOHNSON LIBRARY □ Austin, TX

Corkum, Myrtle, Mgr., Member Serv.
HALIFAX BOARD OF TRADE - LIBRARY □ Halifax,
NS

Corless, Denise, Libn.
JOSLIN DIABETES CENTER, INC. - MEDICAL
LIBRARY □ Boston, MA

Corley, Dr. Al, Project Dir.
ORTHOPEDIC FOUNDATION FOR ANIMALS -
OFA HIP DYSPLASIA REGISTRY □ Columbia, MO

Corley, Jannis, Law Libn.
SAGINAW COUNTY LAW LIBRARY □ Saginaw,
MI

Corley, Pamela B., Libn.
LOGICON, INC. - INFORMATION CENTER □ San
Pedro, CA

Corliss, Mary, Cur.Asst., Stills
MUSEUM OF MODERN ART - FILM STUDY
CENTER □ New York, NY

Corman, Linda Wilson, Hd.Libn.
UNIVERSITY OF TORONTO - UNIVERSITY OF
TRINITY COLLEGE - LIBRARY □ Toronto, ON

Cormier, George Anne, Asst.Libn.
SAN ANTONIO MUSEUM ASSOCIATION -
LIBRARIES □ San Antonio, TX

Corn, Ruth, Info.Spec.
TECHNOMIC INFORMATION SERVICES □
Chicago, IL

Cornacchia, Rocco, Reg.Libn.
CANADA - PUBLIC WORKS CANADA - ONTARIO
REGIONAL LIBRARY □ Willowdale, ON

Corneil, Charlotte, Pub.Serv.
LOUISIANA STATE UNIVERSITY - LAW
LIBRARY □ Baton Rouge, LA

Corneil, Dorothy, Asst. to Libn.
CANADA - LABOUR CANADA - LIBRARY
SERVICES - OCCUPATIONAL SAFETY AND
HEALTH BRANCH - RESOURCE CENTRE □ Hull,
PQ

Cornelius, John, Cat.Libn.
U.S. NATL. DEFENSE UNIVERSITY - LIBRARY □
Washington, DC

Cornell, Donna, Photo Coll.Mgr.
NATIONAL BASEBALL HALL OF FAME AND
MUSEUM, INC. - NATIONAL BASEBALL LIBRARY
□ Cooperstown, NY

Cornell, Dr. George W., Dir. of Lib.Serv.
SUNY - COLLEGE AT BROCKPORT - DRAKE
MEMORIAL LIBRARY □ Brockport, NY

Cornell, Kim, Libn.
ONTARIO HYDRO - LIBRARY □ Toronto, ON

Cornet, Susan, Info.Spec.
MITRE CORPORATION - TECHNICAL REPORT
CENTER □ Bedford, MA

Cornett, John, Libn.
NATIONAL SOLAR OBSERVATORY - TECHNICAL
LIBRARY □ Sunspot, NM

Cornett, Lloyd H., Jr., Dir.
U.S. AIR FORCE - HISTORICAL RESEARCH
CENTER □ Maxwell AFB, AL

Cornish, Jeanette, Libn.
MERCANTILE GENERAL REINSURANCE
COMPANY - LIBRARY □ Toronto, ON

Cornog, Martha, Spec.Proj.Coord.
NATIONAL FEDERATION OF ABSTRACTING
AND INFORMATION SERVICES □ Philadelphia,
PA

Cornwall, Mrs. W., Pres.
TWENTIETH CENTURY TRENDS INSTITUTE,
INC. - SOURCE LIBRARY □ Darien, CT

Cornwell, Douglas, Corp.Libn.
FLORIDA POWER CORPORATION - CORPORATE
LIBRARY □ St. Petersburg, FL

Cornwell, Gary, Asst.Libn./U.S., Fed.Docs
UNIVERSITY OF FLORIDA - DOCUMENTS
LIBRARY □ Gainesville, FL

Cornwell, Joy, Cat.
MAYO FOUNDATION - MAYO CLINIC LIBRARY □
Rochester, MN

Cornwell, Robena Eng, Asst.Univ.Libn.
UNIVERSITY OF FLORIDA - MUSIC LIBRARY □
Gainesville, FL

Cornwell, Sophy H., Spec.Coll.Libn.
LINCOLN UNIVERSITY - LANGSTON HUGHES
MEMORIAL LIBRARY - SPECIAL COLLECTIONS†
□ Lincoln University, PA

Coronado, Barbara, Med.Libn.
U.S. VETERANS ADMINISTRATION (TX-Temple)
- MEDICAL CENTER MEDICAL LIBRARY □
Temple, TX

Corontzes, Arthur N., Assoc.Dir.
CITADEL - THE MILITARY COLLEGE OF SOUTH
CAROLINA - DANIEL LIBRARY □ Charleston, SC

Corrado, Margaret, Ref.Libn.
HOFFMANN-LA ROCHE, INC. - SCIENTIFIC
LIBRARY □ Nutley, NJ

Corrales, Helen M., Employee Serv.
AT & T TECHNOLOGIES, INC. - LIBRARY □
Phoenix, AZ

Corrin, Nancy, Mgr.
NATIONAL FIRE PROTECTION ASSOCIATION -
CHARLES S. MORGAN TECHNICAL LIBRARY □
Quincy, MA

Corriveau, Conrad, Dir.
UNIVERSITE DU QUEBEC A MONTREAL -
BIBLIOTHEQUE DES SCIENCES □ Montreal, PQ

Corry, Ann Marie, Dental Libn.
UNIVERSITY OF MISSOURI, KANSAS CITY -
SCHOOL OF DENTISTRY LIBRARY □ Kansas City,
MO

Corry, Ruth L., Hd., Ctrl.Res.
GEORGIA STATE DEPARTMENT OF ARCHIVES
AND HISTORY - CENTRAL RESEARCH LIBRARY†
□ Atlanta, GA

Corsaro, James, Sr.Libn.
NEW YORK STATE LIBRARY - MANUSCRIPTS
AND SPECIAL COLLECTIONS □ Albany, NY

Corsello, Doris M.E., Cat.
DUQUESNE UNIVERSITY - LAW LIBRARY □
Pittsburgh, PA

Corso, Johanna M., Ed.
RUTGERS UNIVERSITY, THE STATE
UNIVERSITY OF NEW JERSEY - GOTTSCHO
PACKAGING INFORMATION CENTER □
Piscataway, NJ

Corson, David W., Hist. of Sci.Libn.
CORNELL UNIVERSITY - HISTORY OF SCIENCE
COLLECTIONS □ Ithaca, NY

Corson, Richard, Law Libn.
YAVAPAI COUNTY LAW LIBRARY† □ Prescott,
AZ

Corson, Richard H., Libn.
SUNY - MARITIME COLLEGE - STEPHEN B.
LUCE LIBRARY □ Bronx, NY

Corson, Somers, Act.Cur.
CAPE MAY COUNTY HISTORICAL &
GENEALOGICAL SOCIETY - LIBRARY □ Cape
May Court House, NJ

Cort, Margaret M., Hd.Libn.
SPERRY - SPERRY ELECTRONIC SYSTEMS -
TECHNICAL INFORMATION CENTER □
Clearwater, FL

Cortek, Larry, Asst.Libn., Tech.Serv.
DADE COUNTY LAW LIBRARY □ Miami, FL

Cortelyou, Catherine, Pub.Serv.Libn.
UNIVERSITY OF CALIFORNIA, BERKELEY -
INSTITUTE OF TRANSPORTATION STUDIES
LIBRARY □ Berkeley, CA

Cortez, Gloria, Info. & Referral Coord.
MEXICAN-AMERICAN OPPORTUNITY
FOUNDATION - INFORMATION AND REFERRAL
SERVICE - RESOURCE CENTER □ Monterey
Park, CA

Cory, Salome, Libn.
PARK AVENUE SYNAGOGUE - ROTHSCHILD
LIBRARY □ New York, NY

Coscarelli, Mary, Dir.
AMERICAN ALLIANCE FOR HEALTH, PHYSICAL
EDUCATION, RECREATION & DANCE - UNIT ON
PROGRAMS FOR THE HANDICAPPED □ Reston,
VA

Cose, Patricia, Asst.Chf.Libn./Ref.
PORT AUTHORITY OF NEW YORK AND NEW
JERSEY - LIBRARY □ New York, NY

Cosgrave, Martin, Sect.Hd.
EXXON RESEARCH AND ENGINEERING
COMPANY - FLORHAM PARK INFORMATION
CENTER† □ Florham Park, NJ

Cosgrove, Mary, Libn.
ROBINSON, SILVERMAN, PEARCE, ARONSOHN
& BERMAN - LIBRARY & INFORMATION CENTER
□ New York, NY

Cosimi, Ivan A., Dir.
U.S. DEPT. OF COMMERCE - INTERNATIONAL
TRADE ADMINISTRATION - MIAMI DISTRICT
OFFICE LIBRARY □ Miami, FL

Cosme, Angel, Per.Libn.
HISPANIC SOCIETY OF AMERICA - LIBRARY □
New York, NY

Cossette, Ms. C., Res.Anl.
MC GILL UNIVERSITY - LABOUR AGREEMENTS
DATA BANK □ Montreal, PQ

Cossette, Joseph, S.J., Lib.Dir.
COMPAGNIE DE JESUS - JESUITS LIBRARY □
St. Jerome, PQ

Costa, Helena, Cat./Gen.Ref.Libn.
RHODE ISLAND STATE LIBRARY □ Providence,
RI

Costa, Joseph J., Pres.
AUSTEN (Jane) SOCIETY OF NORTH AMERICA -
ARCHIVES □ Nanuet, NY

Costa, Lerleen, Tech.Serv.Sect.
UNIVERSITY OF CALIFORNIA, LOS ANGELES -
MANAGEMENT LIBRARY □ Los Angeles, CA

Costa, Paulo, Libn.
BRAZILIAN-AMERICAN CULTURAL INSTITUTE,
INC. - HAROLD E. WIBBERLEY, JR. LIBRARY □
Washington, DC

Costa-Ramos, Carmen M., Dir.
CARIBBEAN REGIONAL LIBRARY □ San Juan, PR

Costanza, Susan, Info.Spec.
NATIONAL ASSOCIATION OF PURCHASING
MANAGEMENT, INC. - INFORMATION CENTER
□ Oradell, NJ

Costanzo, Anthony J., Info.Spec.
ATLANTIC-RICHFIELD COMPANY - ARCO
CHEMICAL COMPANY - RESEARCH &
DEVELOPMENT LIBRARY □ Newton Square, PA

Costas, Dr. Aida R. Caro, Dir.
UNIVERSITY OF PUERTO RICO - HISTORICAL
RESEARCH CENTER □ Rio Piedras, PR

Costello, Robert C.
WILLIAM M. MERCER, INC. - LIBRARY
INFORMATION CENTER □ Los Angeles, CA

Costo, Dr. Jeanette Henry, Exec.Sec.
AMERICAN INDIAN HISTORICAL SOCIETY -
LIBRARY □ San Francisco, CA

Cote, Gisele, Acq.
CINEMATHEQUE QUEBECOISE - ARCHIVES &
FILM MUSEUM □ Montreal, PQ

Cote, Lois, Libn.
ST. PETER'S SEMINARY - LIBRARY □ London,
ON

Cote, Michelle, Documentaliste
UNIVERSITE DE MONTREAL - CENTRE DE
RECHERCHES CARAIBES - BIBLIOTHEQUE □
Montreal, PQ

Cote, Monique, Libn.
UNIVERSITE DU QUEBEC A MONTREAL -
CENTRE DE DOCUMENTATION ECONOMIE-
ADMINISTRATION □ Montreal, PQ

Cote, Paul, Asst.Libn.-Ref.
AVCO CORPORATION - AVCO-EVERETT
RESEARCH LABORATORY - LIBRARY† □ Everett,
MA

Cote, Rene, Chf.Libn.
HOPITAL ST-LUC - BIBLIOTHEQUE MEDICALE†
□ Montreal, PQ

Cote-Thibodeau, Donna E., Libn.
CARY MEDICAL CENTER - HEALTH SCIENCE
LIBRARY □ Caribou, ME

Cotham, Steve, Tech.Serv./Ref.Libn.
KNOX COUNTY PUBLIC LIBRARY SYSTEM - MC
CLUNG HISTORICAL COLLECTION □ Knoxville,
TN

Cotilla, Linda, Hd.Libn.
TEMPLE UNIVERSITY - CENTRAL LIBRARY
SYSTEM - ZAHN INSTRUCTIONAL MATERIALS
CTR./SOCIAL ADM. LIB. □ Philadelphia, PA

Cotsoridis, Paul, Hd., Circ. Control
U.S. NAVY - NAVAL EDUCATION AND TRAINING
CENTER - LIBRARY SYSTEM □ Newport, RI

Cotten, Alice R., Asst.Cur.
UNIVERSITY OF NORTH CAROLINA, CHAPEL
HILL - NORTH CAROLINA COLLECTION □ Chapel
Hill, NC

Cotter, Rev. Lawrence E., Archv.
DIOCESE OF OGDENSBURG - ARCHIVES □
Ogdensburg, NY

Cotter, Tom, Libn.
CHATTANOOGA TIMES - LIBRARY □
Chattanooga, TN

Cotton, Karolyn, Libn.
RACINE JOURNAL TIMES - LIBRARY □ Racine,
WI

Cottrell, Linda D., Map Cat.Libn.
UNIVERSITY OF ARIZONA - MAP COLLECTION
□ Tucson, AZ

Couch, Dale, Archv.Asst.
GEORGIA STATE SURVEYOR GENERAL
DEPARTMENT - LIBRARY □ Atlanta, GA

Coughlin, Caroline M., Asst.Dir.
DREW UNIVERSITY - LIBRARY □ Madison, NJ

Coughlin, Douglas, Film Libn.
UNIVERSITY OF CALGARY - MEDIA
UTILIZATION UNIT & FILM LIBRARY □ Calgary,
AB

Coughlin, Janice, Dir.
SIR SANDFORD FLEMING COLLEGE OF APPLIED
ARTS & TECHNOLOGY - EDUCATIONAL
RESOURCE CENTER □ Peterborough, ON

Coughlin, Patricia A., Law Libn.
ILLINOIS STATE LEGISLATIVE REFERENCE
BUREAU □ Springfield, IL

Coulic, Jo-Anne, Asst.Libn.
UNIVERSITY OF SASKATCHEWAN - ST.
ANDREW'S COLLEGE - LIBRARY □ Saskatoon,
SK

Coulombe, Solange, Acq.
CEGEP DE TROIS-RIVIERES - BIBLIOTHEQUE □
Trois-Rivieres, PQ

Coulson, Rafael E., Lib.Dir.
U.S. ARMY SCHOOL OF THE AMERICAS -
LIBRARY/LEARNING CENTER □ APO Miami, FL

Coulter, Cynthia M., Dir.
EAST CENTRAL OKLAHOMA STATE
UNIVERSITY - OKLAHOMA ENVIRONMENTAL
INFORMATION/MEDIA CENTER □ Ada, OK

Coulter, Linda H., Asst.Dir./Med.Rec.
BRYAN MEMORIAL HOSPITAL - MEDICAL
LIBRARY □ Lincoln, NE

Coulter, Shirley, Coord., Sch.Libs.
NOVA SCOTIA - PROVINCIAL LIBRARY □
Halifax, NS

Coupe, Sandra, Libn.
U.S. DEPT. OF JUSTICE - FEDERAL BUREAU OF
INVESTIGATION - F.B.I. ACADEMY - LIBRARY □
Quantico, VA

Cournoyea, Wende, Exec.Sec.
NORTON RESEARCH CORPORATION (Canada)
LTD. - LIBRARY □ Niagara Falls, ON

Courtis, Shirley, Libn.
NORANDA RESEARCH CENTRE - LIBRARY □
Pointe Claire, PQ

Courtney, Grace, Cat.
NEW YORK BOTANICAL GARDEN - LIBRARY† □
Bronx, NY

Courtney, Mary E., Libn.
MEMORIAL HOSPITAL - MEDICAL AND
NURSING LIBRARY □ Cumberland, MD

Courtney, Susan, Lib.Dir.
JONES LANG WOOTTON - INFORMATION
CENTER □ New York, NY

Courtney, Vincent, Tech.Serv.
UNIVERSITY OF MAINE, FARMINGTON -
MANTOR LIBRARY† □ Farmington, ME

Courtright, Martha, Libn.
ONTARIO HYDRO - LIBRARY □ Toronto, ON

Courvoisier, Lois, Cat.
CROCKER ART MUSEUM - RESEARCH LIBRARY
□ Sacramento, CA

Couture, Diane R., Supv.
OTTAWA GENERAL HOSPITAL - MEDICAL
LIBRARY □ Ottawa, ON

Covalesky, Eleanor, Cat.Libn.
UNIVERSITY OF SAN FRANCISCO - SCHOOL OF
LAW LIBRARY □ San Francisco, CA

Covalt, Jeanie, Res.Libn.
KANSAS HERITAGE CENTER - LIBRARY □ Dodge
City, KS

Covarrubias, Donna, Lib.Asst.
CALIFORNIA INSTITUTE OF TECHNOLOGY -
EARTHQUAKE ENGINEERING RESEARCH
LIBRARY □ Pasadena, CA

Cover, Peggy, Ref.Serv.
CLEMSON UNIVERSITY - ROBERT MULDROW
COOPER LIBRARY □ Clemson, SC

Covert, Richard P., Dir.
AMERICAN HOSPITAL ASSOCIATION -
CLEARINGHOUSE FOR HOSPITAL
MANAGEMENT & SYSTEMS □ Chicago, IL

Covey, Carol, Ser.Libn.
WESTERN ILLINOIS UNIVERSITY - LIBRARIES
□ Macomb, IL

Covey, Martha, Hd., Ref.
GEORGIA STATE DEPARTMENT OF EDUCATION
- DIVISION OF PUBLIC LIBRARY SERVICES □
Atlanta, GA

Covington, Mrs. B.A., Lib.Techn.
MONTREAL GENERAL HOSPITAL - NURSES
LIBRARY □ Montreal, PQ

Covington, Carolyn M., Chf., Lib.Br.
U.S. AIR FORCE BASE - ROBINS BASE LIBRARY
□ Robins AFB, GA

Covington, Louise, Tech.Serv.Libn.
TEXAS TECH UNIVERSITY - SCHOOL OF LAW
LIBRARY □ Lubbock, TX

Covington, Mary W., Mgr., Info.Serv.
ZINC INSTITUTE - INFORMATION SERVICE □
New York, NY

Covington, William, Libn.
OPTIKON RESEARCH LABORATORIES -
LIBRARY† □ West Cornwall, CT

Covotsos, Louis J., Hd.Libn.
MC DERMOTT, WILL & EMERY - LIBRARY □
Chicago, IL

Cowan, Anita, Proj.Mgr.
CLEARINGHOUSE ON CHILD ABUSE AND
NEGLECT INFORMATION □ Washington, DC

Cowan, Anita P., Dir.
NATIONAL CLEARINGHOUSE FOR FAMILY
PLANNING INFORMATION □ Rockville, MD

Cowan, Catherine, Libn.
VANCOUVER ART GALLERY - LIBRARY □
Vancouver, BC

Cowan, David G., Instr.Serv. Law Libn.
UNIVERSITY OF MISSOURI - SCHOOL OF LAW
LIBRARY □ Columbia, MO

Cowan, George A., Libn.
LINCOLN COUNTY LAW LIBRARY† □ Wiscasset,
ME

Coward, Robert Y., Hd.Libn.
FRANKLIN COLLEGE - SPECIAL COLLECTIONS □
Franklin, IN

Cowart, Cecilia, Dir., Commun.
AMERICAN BRAHMAN BREEDERS
ASSOCIATION - LIBRARY □ Houston, TX

Cowe, Dorothy B., Sr.Tech.Libn.
ITEK CORPORATION - OPTICAL SYSTEMS
DIVISION - LIBRARY □ Lexington, MA

Cowell, Judy Mehl, Dir.
OHIO COLLEGE OF PODIATRIC MEDICINE -
LIBRARY/MEDIA CENTER □ Cleveland, OH

Cowen, Janet, Media Rsrc.Libn.
MOUNT SINAI SCHOOL OF MEDICINE OF THE
CITY UNIVERSITY OF NEW YORK - GUSTAVE L.
& JANET W. LEVY LIBRARY □ New York, NY

Cowen, Ron, Sci. Correspondent
TRACOR JITCO, INC. - RESEARCH RESOURCES
INFORMATION CENTER □ Rockville, MD

Cowen, Sandra T., Chf., Info.Serv.
UNIVERSITY OF SOUTH CAROLINA - BUREAU
OF GOVERNMENTAL RESEARCH AND SERVICE -
LIBRARY □ Columbia, SC

Cowie, Gloria M., Libn.
CONEMAUGH VALLEY MEMORIAL HOSPITAL -
HEALTH SCIENCES LIBRARY □ Johnstown, PA

Cowper, Mrs. D., Libn.
TORONTO GENERAL HOSPITAL - FUDGER
MEDICAL LIBRARY □ Toronto, ON

Cox, Alice G., Libn.
MISSISSIPPI BAPTIST CONVENTION BOARD -
MISSISSIPPI BAPTIST HISTORICAL
COMMISSION □ Clinton, MS

Cox, Barbara, Map Libn.
UNIVERSITY OF UTAH - MAP LIBRARY □ Salt
Lake City, UT

Cox, Brenda J., Libn.
HOWARD UNIVERSITY - SOCIAL WORK
LIBRARY □ Washington, DC

Cox, Christopher, Libn.
BATON ROUGE STATE-TIMES & MORNING
ADVOCATE NEWSPAPERS - LIBRARY □ Baton
Rouge, LA

Cox, Dorothy, Asst.Libn.
LOYOLA UNIVERSITY OF CHICAGO - LAW
LIBRARY □ Chicago, IL

Cox, Dwayne, Assoc.Univ.Archv.
UNIVERSITY OF LOUISVILLE - UNIVERSITY
ARCHIVES AND RECORDS CENTER □ Louisville,
KY

Cox, Dwayne, Co-Dir.
UNIVERSITY OF LOUISVILLE - UNIVERSITY
ARCHIVES AND RECORDS CENTER - ORAL
HISTORY CENTER □ Louisville, KY

Cox, James C., Chf.Libn.
LOYOLA UNIVERSITY OF CHICAGO - MEDICAL
CENTER LIBRARY □ Maywood, IL

Cox, Joan, Asst.
FALCONBRIDGE NICKEL MINES, LTD. -
FALCONBRIDGE INFORMATION CENTRE† □
Toronto, ON

Cox, Julie P., Asst. State Archv.
VERMONT STATE OFFICE OF THE SECRETARY
OF STATE - VERMONT STATE PAPERS □
Montpelier, VT

Cox, Mahala, Curric.Libn.
EDEN THEOLOGICAL SEMINARY - LIBRARY □
Webster Groves, MO

Cox, Marjorie A.
NOVA SCOTIA HOSPITAL - HEALTH SCIENCE
LIBRARY □ Dartmouth, NS

Cox, Martha M., Dir.
STARK COUNTY LAW LIBRARY ASSOCIATION -
LAW LIBRARY □ Canton, OH
Cox, Mary Lee, Info.Spec.
NEW ENGLAND RESOURCE CENTER FOR
CHILDREN AND FAMILIES □ Boston, MA
Cox, Richard J., Hd., Archv. & Rec.Div.
ALABAMA STATE DEPARTMENT OF ARCHIVES
AND HISTORY - REFERENCE ROOM □
Montgomery, AL
Cox, Shelley, Libn.
SOUTHERN ILLINOIS UNIVERSITY,
CARBONDALE - SPECIAL COLLECTIONS □
Carbondale, IL
Cox, Tina, Mgr.
GENERAL ELECTRIC COMPANY - INDUSTRIAL
ELECTRONICS INFORMATION CENTER □
Charlottesville, VA
Coykendall, Mary, Libn.
MONROE COUNTY DEPARTMENT OF HEALTH -
HEALTH EDUCATION LIBRARY □ Rochester, NY
Coyle, Mary, Ref.Libn.
MITRE CORPORATION - LIBRARY □ McLean, VA
Coyle, Michael P., Hd.
FREE LIBRARY OF PHILADELPHIA - LIBRARY
FOR THE BLIND AND PHYSICALLY
HANDICAPPED □ Philadelphia, PA
Coyle, Rosalie, Asst.Libn.
RAWLE AND HENDERSON - LAW LIBRARY □
Philadelphia, PA
Coyne, Jeffrey, Info.Dir.
EARTHWORM, INC. - RECYCLING
INFORMATION CENTER □ Boston, MA
Coyne, Joyce, Mgr., Adm.Serv.
BIBLIOGRAPHICAL CENTER FOR RESEARCH -
ROCKY MOUNTAIN REGION, INC. □ Denver, CO
Cozzolino, Dorothy A., Chf.Libn.
U.S. COURT OF APPEALS, 3RD CIRCUIT -
LIBRARY □ Philadelphia, PA
Crabtree, Gillian, Law Libn.
FRASER HYNDMAN, BARRISTERS &
SOLICITORS - LAW LIBRARY □ Vancouver, BC
Craft, Darinka, Slavic Cat.
UNIVERSITY OF ILLINOIS - SLAVIC AND EAST
EUROPEAN LIBRARY □ Urbana, IL
Craft, Dolores, Act.Libn.
FEDERAL RESERVE BANK OF CLEVELAND -
PITTSBURGH BRANCH LIBRARY □ Pittsburgh, PA
Craft, Margaret E., Libn.
WYOMING HISTORICAL AND GEOLOGICAL
SOCIETY - BISHOP MEMORIAL LIBRARY □
Wilkes-Barre, PA
Crager, Janet, Biomed.Ref.Libn.
BROWN UNIVERSITY - SCIENCES LIBRARY □
Providence, RI
Crahan, Elizabeth S., Dir., Lib.Serv.
LOS ANGELES COUNTY MEDICAL ASSOCIATION
- LIBRARY† □ Los Angeles, CA
Craig, Helen, Asst.Libn.
UNIVERSITY OF NEW BRUNSWICK -
EDUCATION RESOURCE CENTRE □ Fredericton,
NB
Craig, James, Assoc.Dir., TALON
UNIVERSITY OF TEXAS HEALTH SCIENCE
CENTER, DALLAS - LIBRARY □ Dallas, TX
Craig, James H., Dir.
SYNERGY POWER INSTITUTE - LIBRARY □
Berkeley, CA
Craig, James L., Libn.
UNIVERSITY OF MASSACHUSETTS, AMHERST -
MORRILL BIOLOGICAL & GEOLOGICAL
SCIENCES LIBRARY □ Amherst, MA
Craig, Marge, Co-Dir.
SYNERGY POWER INSTITUTE - LIBRARY □
Berkeley, CA
Craig, Susan V., Art Libn.
UNIVERSITY OF KANSAS - MURPHY LIBRARY
OF ART HISTORY □ Lawrence, KS
Craiglow, James, Assoc. Dean
ANTIOCH/NEW ENGLAND GRADUATE SCHOOL
- PROFESSIONAL RESOURCE CENTER □ Keene,
NH

Crain, Sandra Bonner, Tech.Serv.Mgr.
MORGAN STANLEY & COMPANY, INC. -
LIBRARY SERVICES □ New York, NY
Crain, W.H., Cur., Theater Arts
UNIVERSITY OF TEXAS, AUSTIN - HARRY
RANSOM HUMANITIES RESEARCH CENTER □
Austin, TX
Crain, Dr. William H., Cur.
UNIVERSITY OF TEXAS, AUSTIN - HUMANITIES
RESEARCH CENTER - THEATRE ARTS
COLLECTIONS □ Austin, TX
Crainey, M., Mgr.
STANDARDS COUNCIL OF CANADA -
STANDARDS INFORMATION DIVISION □
Ottawa, ON
Crais, Mina L., Libn.
INTERNATIONAL HOUSE LIBRARY □ New
Orleans, LA
Cram, Barbra J., Curric.Libn.
BLACK HILLS STATE COLLEGE - E.Y. BERRY
LIBRARY-LEARNING CENTER - CURRICULUM
LIBRARY □ Spearfish, SD
Cram, Miss Kendall, Dir.
TENNESSEE STATE LIBRARY - STATE LIBRARY
DIVISION □ Nashville, TN
Cram, Sandra, Asst.Libn.
FEDERAL RESERVE BANK OF BOSTON -
RESEARCH LIBRARY† □ Boston, MA
Cramblitt, Valerie A., Asst.Libn.
BALTIMORE GAS AND ELECTRIC COMPANY -
LIBRARY □ Baltimore, MD
Cramer, Anne, Dir.
EASTERN VIRGINIA MEDICAL SCHOOL -
MOORMAN MEMORIAL LIBRARY □ Norfolk, VA
Cramer, Jane, Libn.
BROOKLYN PUBLIC LIBRARY - SOCIAL SCIENCE
AND PHILOSOPHY DIVISION □ Brooklyn, NY
Cramer, Kenneth C., College Archv.
DARTMOUTH COLLEGE - SPECIAL
COLLECTIONS □ Hanover, NH
Crampon, Jean, Hd.Ref.Libn.
SOUTHERN ILLINOIS UNIVERSITY - SCHOOL OF
MEDICINE - MEDICAL LIBRARY □ Springfield, IL
Crampton, Melanie, Libn.
BOY SCOUTS OF CANADA - NATIONAL LIBRARY
□ Ottawa, ON
Crampton, Melanie E., Cur./Libn.
BOY SCOUTS OF CANADA - MUSEUM &
ARCHIVES OF CANADIAN SCOUTING □ Ottawa,
ON
Crandall, D.H., Dir.
OAK RIDGE NATIONAL LABORATORY -
CONTROLLED FUSION ATOMIC DATA CENTER □
Oak Ridge, TN
Crandall, Dr. Ralph J., Dir./Ed.
NEW ENGLAND HISTORIC GENEALOGICAL
SOCIETY - LIBRARY □ Boston, MA
Crandall, Shirley, Asst.Libn.
REORGANIZED CHURCH OF JESUS CHRIST OF
LATTER DAY SAINTS - LIBRARY & ARCHIVES □
Independence, MO
Crandlemere, R. Wayne, Dir.
BRIGGS ENGINEERING & TESTING COMPANY,
INC. - LIBRARY □ Norwell, MA
Crane, Andrea, Asst.Libn.
RIVERSIDE COMMUNITY MEMORIAL HOSPITAL
- HEALTH SCIENCE LIBRARY □ Waupaca, WI
Crane, Joan S., Cur.Amer.Lit.
UNIVERSITY OF VIRGINIA - CLIFTON WALLER
BARRETT LIBRARY □ Charlottesville, VA
Crane, Joan St.C., Cur., Amer.Lit.Coll.
UNIVERSITY OF VIRGINIA - LIBRARY - RARE
BOOK DEPARTMENT □ Charlottesville, VA
Crane, Kathryn K., Libn.
TEMPLE DE HIRSCH SINAI - LIBRARY □ Seattle,
WA
Crane, Lois F., Libn.
WICHITA ART MUSEUM - LIBRARY □ Wichita,
KS
Crane, Dr. Maurice A., Hd.
MICHIGAN STATE UNIVERSITY - G. ROBERT
VINCENT VOICE LIBRARY □ East Lansing, MI

Cranford, Theodore, Lib.Res.Anl.
ROCKWELL INTERNATIONAL - SPACE
BUSINESSES - TECHNICAL INFORMATION
CENTER □ Downey, CA
Cranor, Alice T., Hd., Info.Serv.Div.
U.S. NAVY - NAVAL INTELLIGENCE SUPPORT
CENTER - INFORMATION SERVICES DIVISION
□ Washington, DC
Cranston, Karen, Ref.
FULLER THEOLOGICAL SEMINARY - MC
ALISTER LIBRARY† □ Pasadena, CA
Crary, Jean K., Rec.Mgt.Adm.
UNIVERSITY OF DELAWARE, NEWARK -
ARCHIVES □ Newark, DE
Craven, James, Consrv.
UNIVERSITY OF MICHIGAN - MICHIGAN
HISTORICAL COLLECTIONS - BENTLEY
HISTORICAL LIBRARY □ Ann Arbor, MI
Craven, Pat, Libn.
WISCONSIN HOSPITAL ASSOCIATION -
MEMORIAL LIBRARY† □ Madison, WI
Craven, R. Jayne, Hd., Art & Music
PUBLIC LIBRARY OF CINCINNATI AND
HAMILTON COUNTY - ART AND MUSIC
DEPARTMENT □ Cincinnati, OH
Craven, Trudy W., Libn.
MILLIKEN RESEARCH CORPORATION -
RESEARCH LIBRARY □ Spartanburg, SC
Cravens, Sally, Libn.
UNIVERSITY OF FLORIDA - DOCUMENTS
LIBRARY □ Gainesville, FL
Cravets, Bertha, Libn.
TEMPLE B'RITH KODESH - LIBRARY □
Rochester, NY
Crawford, Alan, Libn.
CANADA - LABOUR RELATIONS BOARD -
LIBRARY □ Ottawa, ON
Crawford, Anthony R., Univ.Archv.
KANSAS STATE UNIVERSITY - FARRELL
LIBRARY □ Manhattan, KS
Crawford, Anthony R., Univ.Archv.
KANSAS STATE UNIVERSITY - UNIVERSITY
ARCHIVES □ Manhattan, KS
Crawford, Brenda, Libn.
ERNST & WHINNEY - LIBRARY □ Detroit, MI
Crawford, Carter, Libn.
OPPENHEIMER & CO., INC. - LIBRARY □ New
York, NY
Crawford, David S., Asst. Area Libn.
MC GILL UNIVERSITY - MEDICAL LIBRARY □
Montreal, PQ
Crawford, Doris L., Libn.
ST. ELIZABETH HOSPITAL MEDICAL CENTER
SCHOOL OF NURSING - LIBRARY □ Youngstown,
OH
Crawford, Dorothea, Acq.Libn.
CROWN ZELLERBACH CORPORATION -
CENTRAL RESEARCH LIBRARY □ Camas, WA
Crawford, Emmy, Mgr., Info.Serv.
AMERICAN PRODUCTIVITY CENTER -
INFORMATION SERVICES □ Houston, TX
Crawford, Marguerite C., Res.Spec.
CORNELL UNIVERSITY - JOHN M. ECHOLS
COLLECTION ON SOUTHEAST ASIA □ Ithaca, NY
Crawford, Marilyn, Libn.
KAISER FOUNDATION HOSPITAL -
MANAGEMENT EFFECTIVENESS LIBRARY □ Los
Angeles, CA
Crawford, Marilyn, Mgt.Libn.
KAISER-PERMANENTE MEDICAL CENTER -
KAISER FOUNDATION HOSPITAL MEDICAL
LIBRARY □ Los Angeles, CA
Crawford, Marjorie, ILL/Circ.
RUTGERS UNIVERSITY, THE STATE
UNIVERSITY OF NEW JERSEY - JUSTICE
HENRY ACKERSON LIBRARY OF LAW &
CRIMINAL JUSTICE □ Newark, NJ
Crawford, Miriam I., Cur.
TEMPLE UNIVERSITY - CENTRAL LIBRARY
SYSTEM - CONWELLANA-TEMPLANA
COLLECTION □ Philadelphia, PA

Crawford, Paul C., Plan.Dir.
SAN LUIS OBISPO COUNTY PLANNING
DEPARTMENT - TECHNICAL INFORMATION
LIBRARY □ San Luis Obispo, CA

Crawford, Prof. Susan Y., Dir.
WASHINGTON UNIVERSITY - SCHOOL OF
MEDICINE LIBRARY □ St. Louis, MO

Crawford, William, Lib.Techn.
UNIVERSITY OF THE DISTRICT OF COLUMBIA -
HARVARD STREET LIBRARY† □ Washington, DC

Crawshaw, Mrs. E., Group Ldr.
GEORGE BROWN COLLEGE OF APPLIED ARTS &
TECHNOLOGY - LIBRARY □ Toronto, ON

Cray, Katherine, Asst.Mgr.
GOLDMAN, SACHS AND COMPANY - LIBRARY □
New York, NY

Creamer, Robert, Libn.
MORRISON & FOERSTER - LIBRARY □ Los
Angeles, CA

Creech, Heather E., Ref.Libn.
DALHOUSIE UNIVERSITY - LAW LIBRARY □
Halifax, NS

Creech, Mary, Archv.
MORAVIAN CHURCH IN AMERICA - SOUTHERN
PROVINCE - MORAVIAN ARCHIVES □ Winston-
Salem, NC

Creekmore, Cynthia, Asst.Libn.
INDIANA UNIVERSITY OF PENNSYLVANIA -
UNIVERSITY LIBRARY □ Indiana, PA

Creelan, Marilee S., Dir. of Hosp.Libs.
AKRON CITY HOSPITAL - MEDICAL LIBRARY □
Akron, OH

Creesy, Virginia, Cat.Libn.
COUDERT BROTHERS - LIBRARY □ New York,
NY

Creighton, Alice S., Asst.Libn., Spec.Coll.
U.S. NAVY - NAVAL ACADEMY - NIMITZ
LIBRARY □ Annapolis, MD

Creighton, James, Recordings Archv.
UNIVERSITY OF TORONTO - FACULTY OF
MUSIC LIBRARY □ Toronto, ON

Crellin, Paul, Cur.
COUNTRY DOCTOR MUSEUM - LIBRARY □
Bailey, NC

Creme, Francine, Tech.Libn.
BARR ENGINEERING COMPANY - LIBRARY □
Minneapolis, MN

Crenshaw, Tena, Libn.
WESTINGHOUSE ELECTRIC CORPORATION -
STEAM TURBINE GENERATOR DIVISION -
LIBRARY □ Orlando, FL

Cresap, Anne H., Cat.Libn.
UNIVERSITY OF RICHMOND - WILLIAM T.
MUSE MEMORIAL LAW LIBRARY □ Richmond,
VA

Crespin, Christine Yolanda, Supv.Libn.
ST. ANTHONY HOSPITAL SYSTEMS -
MEMORIAL MEDICAL LIBRARY □ Denver, CO

Crespo, Donnie, Archv.
WEYERHAEUSER COMPANY - ARCHIVES □
Tacoma, WA

Cressman, Ruth, Asst.Libn.
UNIVERSITY OF MICHIGAN - DENTISTRY
LIBRARY □ Ann Arbor, MI

Cretecos, Yvonne I., Med.Libn.
HUNT MEMORIAL HOSPITAL - GEORGE B.
PALMER MEMORIAL LIBRARY □ Danvers, MA

Cretini, Blanche, Coord., User Serv.
LOUISIANA STATE LIBRARY □ Baton Rouge, LA

Cretini, Gene, Info.Serv.Dir.
LOUISIANA STATE DEPT. OF COMMERCE -
OFFICE OF COMMERCE & INDUSTRY -
INDUSTRIAL DEVELOPMENT REFERENCE
LIBRARY □ Baton Rouge, LA

Crews, B.C., Hd., Tech.Serv.
NORTH CAROLINA AGRICULTURAL &
TECHNICAL STATE UNIVERSITY - F.D.
BLUFORD LIBRARY □ Greensboro, NC

Crider, Carol, Cat.
ANDREWS UNIVERSITY - JAMES WHITE
LIBRARY† □ Berrien Springs, MI

Crigler, Alberta, Libn.
CALIFORNIA THOROUGHBRED BREEDERS
ASSOCIATION - CARLETON F. BURKE
MEMORIAL LIBRARY □ Arcadia, CA

Crinkerhoff, Jess, Hd.Libn.
CHURCH OF JESUS CHRIST OF LATTER-DAY
SAINTS - TRI-CITIES BRANCH GENEALOGICAL
LIBRARY □ Richland, WA

Crippen, David R., Ref.Archv.
HENRY FORD MUSEUM AND GREENFIELD
VILLAGE - ARCHIVES & RESEARCH LIBRARY □
Dearborn, MI

Crispen, Joanne, Dir. of Lib.Serv.
LUTHERAN GENERAL HOSPITAL - LIBRARY† □
Park Ridge, IL

Crissinger, John D., Geology & Map Libn.
VIRGINIA POLYTECHNIC INSTITUTE AND
STATE UNIVERSITY - GEOLOGY LIBRARY □
Blacksburg, VA

Critchfield, Elizabeth J., Supv.Info.Acq. & Dissem.
LORD CORPORATION - INFORMATION
CENTERS □ Erie, PA

Critchfield, Sue, Hd.Libn.
MUSEUM OF NEW MEXICO - MUSEUM OF FINE
ARTS - LIBRARY □ Santa Fe, NM

Critchley, Alice, Libn.
WESTERN UNION CORPORATION - LIBRARY† □
Upper Saddle River, NJ

Crites, Elaine M., Med.Libn.
ST. ANNE'S HOSPITAL - SULLIVAN MEDICAL
LIBRARY □ Fall River, MA

Crocker, Anne, Law Libn.
UNIVERSITY OF NEW BRUNSWICK - LAW
LIBRARY □ Fredericton, NB

Crocker, Sherry L., Libn.
INTERTECHNOLOGY/SOLAR CORPORATION -
LIBRARY □ Warrenton, VA

Crockett, M.C., Chf.Libn.
UNIVERSITY OF PRINCE EDWARD ISLAND -
ROBERTSON LIBRARY □ Charlottetown, PE

Crockett, Mary S., Chf.Libn.
CHARLESTON EVENING POST/NEWS AND
COURIER - LIBRARY □ Charleston, SC

Croft, Elizabeth, Asst.Adm.
PRICE WATERHOUSE - NEW YORK OFFICE
INFORMATION CENTER □ New York, NY

Croft, Martha, Doc.Libn.
CENTRAL CONNECTICUT STATE UNIVERSITY -
ELIHU BURRITT LIBRARY □ New Britain, CT

Croft, P.H., Pres.
AMERICAN SHORT LINE RAILROAD
ASSOCIATION - LIBRARY □ Washington, DC

Croft, Vicki F., Hd.
WASHINGTON STATE UNIVERSITY -
VETERINARY MEDICAL/PHARMACY LIBRARY □
Pullman, WA

Croix, Jean, Hd.
UNION CARBIDE CORPORATION - SOLVENTS &
INTERMEDIATES DIVISION - PLANT LIBRARY □
Texas City, TX

Crombie, H. David, M.D., Libn.
HARTFORD MEDICAL SOCIETY - WALTER
STEINER MEMORIAL LIBRARY □ Hartford, CT

Crombie, Kenneth C., Tech.Libn.
GENERAL MOTORS CORPORATION - DELCO
SYSTEMS OPERATIONS - TECHNICAL LIBRARY
□ Goleta, CA

Cromie, Mark, Sr.Mgr., Mktg.
UNIVERSITY OF PITTSBURGH - NASA
INDUSTRIAL APPLICATIONS CENTER (NIAC) □
Pittsburgh, PA

Crompton, Dianne, Lib.Techn.
CANADA WIRE AND CABLE, LTD. - TECHNICAL
LIBRARY □ Toronto, ON

Crompton, Mary L., Libn.
UNIVERSITY OF WISCONSIN, MADISON -
GERALD G. SOMERS GRADUATE REFERENCE
ROOM □ Madison, WI

Cromwell, Ann, Leg.Libn.
CAPLIN & DRYSDALE - LIBRARY† □ Washington,
DC

Croneis, Karen S., Libn.
UNIVERSITY OF KENTUCKY - MATHEMATICAL
SCIENCES LIBRARY □ Lexington, KY

Cronenwett, Philip N., Cur. of Mss.
DARTMOUTH COLLEGE - SPECIAL
COLLECTIONS □ Hanover, NH

Cronin, F.J., Res.Info.Spec.
LOCKHEED-GEORGIA COMPANY - TECHNICAL
INFORMATION DEPARTMENT □ Marietta, GA

Cronin, Frances, Libn.
NEWTOWN HISTORIC ASSOCIATION, INC. -
RESEARCH CENTER OF NEWTOWN AREA
HISTORY □ Newton, PA

Cronin, John R., Libn.
NEWS GROUP BOSTON, INC. - BOSTON HERALD
LIBRARY □ Boston, MA

Cronin, Mary J., Asst.Dir., Pub.Serv.
MARQUETTE UNIVERSITY - MEMORIAL
LIBRARY □ Milwaukee, WI

Cronk, Michael Sam, Musm.Dir./Cur.
ONTARIO PUPPETRY ASSOCIATION CENTRE -
RESOURCE LIBRARY □ Willowdale, ON

Crooks, James E., Libn.
UNIVERSITY OF MICHIGAN - LIBRARY
SCIENCE LIBRARY □ Ann Arbor, MI

Crosby, Cynthia J., Libn.
DOW CHEMICAL U.S.A. - HOUSTON DOW
CENTER LIBRARY □ Houston, TX

Crosby, Ramona C.T., Supv.Info./Comp.Serv.
STAUFFER CHEMICAL COMPANY - EASTERN
RESEARCH CENTER INFORMATION SERVICES □
Dobbs Ferry, NY

Crosby, S., Supv.
STANDARD OIL COMPANY OF INDIANA -
LIBRARY/INFORMATION CENTER □ Chicago, IL

Crosier, Oma Jean
U.S. VETERANS ADMINISTRATION (AZ-Phoenix)
- HOSPITAL LIBRARY □ Phoenix, AZ

Croslin, Kenneth, Dir.
TROY STATE UNIVERSITY - LIBRARY -
SPECIAL COLLECTIONS □ Troy, AL

Cross, Dorothy A., Dir.
U.S. ARMY - PENTAGON LIBRARY □ Washington,
DC

Cross, James, Libn.
UNIVERSITY OF GEORGIA - RICHARD B.
RUSSELL MEMORIAL LIBRARY □ Athens, GA

Cross, Jennie B., Asst.Dir.
OAKLAND SCHOOLS - EDUCATIONAL RESOURCE
CENTER □ Pontiac, MI

Cross, Joseph R., Jr., Act.Hd. Law Lib.
UNIVERSITY OF SOUTH CAROLINA - COLEMAN
KARESH LAW LIBRARY □ Columbia, SC

Cross, Linda, Cat.
UNIVERSITY OF ARKANSAS AT LITTLE ROCK -
PULASKI COUNTY LAW LIBRARY □ Little Rock,
AR

Cross, Louise, Cur.
FRONTIER GATEWAY MUSEUM - LIBRARY □
Glendive, MT

Cross, M., ILL
TORONTO BOARD OF EDUCATION -
EDUCATION CENTRE LIBRARY □ Toronto, ON

Cross, Mary, Cat.Libn.
SOUTH CAROLINA STATE LIBRARY □ Columbia,
SC

Cross, Maxine, Libn.
CALIFORNIA MISSIONARY BAPTIST
INSTITUTE & SEMINARY - SCHOOL LIBRARY □
Bellflower, CA

Cross, P., Mgr., Info.Serv.
BELL-NORTHERN RESEARCH LTD. -
INFORMATION RESOURCE CENTRE □ Ottawa,
ON

Cross, Peggy J.
CHAUTAUQUA COUNTY LAW LIBRARY □
Mayville, NY

Crossett, Dave, Libn.
GILA COUNTY LAW LIBRARY □ Globe, AZ

Crossfield, Nancy L., Libn.
UNIVERSITY OF WISCONSIN, MADISON -
GEOLOGY-GEOPHYSICS LIBRARY □ Madison, WI

Crossland, Maynard A., Hd., Ext.Serv.
ILLINOIS STATE HISTORICAL LIBRARY □
Springfield, IL

Crossley, Virginia A., Asst.Med.Libn.
BEAUMONT (William) HOSPITAL - MEDICAL
LIBRARY □ Royal Oak, MI

Crosthwaite, E., Hd., AV Area
KELSEY INSTITUTE OF APPLIED ARTS AND
SCIENCES - LEARNING RESOURCES CENTRE □
Saskatoon, SK

Crouch, Howard E., Pres.
DAMIEN DUTTON SOCIETY FOR LEPROSY AID,
INC. - LIBRARY □ Bellmore, NY

Crouch, James, Libn.
U.S. NAVY - NAVAL SUPPLY SYSTEMS
COMMAND - LIBRARY □ Washington, DC

Crouch, Keith, Chf.Libn.
ROYAL MILITARY COLLEGE OF CANADA -
MASSEY LIBRARY & SCIENCE/ENGINEERING
LIBRARY □ Kingston, ON

Crouse, Moses C., Cur.
AURORA COLLEGE - JENKS MEMORIAL
COLLECTION OF ADVENTUAL MATERIALS □
Aurora, IL

Crow, Linda H., Libn.
BRIDGEWATER COURIER-NEWS - LIBRARY □
Bridgewater, NJ

Crowe, Richard T., Dir.
IRISH-AMERICAN CULTURAL ASSOCIATION -
LIBRARY □ Chicago, IL

Crowe, Susan, Supv., Tech.Serv.
AEROSPACE CORPORATION - CHARLES C.
LAURITSEN LIBRARY □ Los Angeles, CA

Crowe, Virginia, Pub.Serv.
VIRGINIA COMMONWEALTH UNIVERSITY -
MEDICAL COLLEGE OF VIRGINIA - TOMPKINS-
MC CAW LIBRARY □ Richmond, VA

Crowell, Florence, Cur.
WATERTOWN HISTORICAL SOCIETY INC. -
LIBRARY □ Oakville, CT

Crowley, Mary Catherine H., Libn.
HALE AND DORR - LIBRARY □ Boston, MA

Crowley, Mary Jo, Mgr., Lib./Info.Ctr.
PHILADELPHIA NEWSPAPERS, INC. - INQUIRER
AND DAILY NEWS LIBRARY □ Philadelphia, PA

Crowley, Patience L., Dir.
GIFFORD MEMORIAL HOSPITAL - HEALTH
INFORMATION CENTER □ Randolph, VT

Crowley, Sandra, Ref.Libn.
U.S. NASA - LEWIS RESEARCH CENTER -
LIBRARY† □ Cleveland, OH

Crownfield, Alice, Med.Libn.
U.S. NAVY - NAVAL HOSPITAL (FL-Orlando) -
MEDICAL LIBRARY† □ Orlando, FL

Crowther, Janet L., Asst.Libn.
KIRKLAND & ELLIS - LIBRARY □ Chicago, IL

Croxford, Agnes M., Chf.Libn.
FENCO ENGINEERS, INC. - LIBRARY □ Toronto,
ON

Croydon, Monika, Slide Libn.
SOUTHERN ALBERTA INSTITUTE OF
TECHNOLOGY - LEARNING RESOURCES CENTRE
- ALBERTA COLLEGE OF ART BRANCH □ Calgary,
AB

Crozier, Ron, Libn.
SANTA BARBARA MUSEUM OF ART - MUSEUM
LIBRARY AND ARCHIVES □ Santa Barbara, CA

Crozier-Parkinson, Ms. S., Sr.Libn.
GULF CANADA RESOURCES INC. - LIBRARY □
Calgary, AB

Cruikshank, Clara C., Libn.
DOUGLASS BOULEVARD CHRISTIAN CHURCH -
LIBRARY □ Louisville, KY

Crum, Mary, Engr.Libn.
U.S. NAVY - NAVAL FACILITIES ENGINEERING
COMMAND - NORTHERN DIVISION - DESIGN
DIVISION LIBRARY □ Philadelphia, PA

Crum, Norm, Supv., Online Res.
LOCKHEED-CALIFORNIA COMPANY -
TECHNICAL INFORMATION CENTER □ Burbank,
CA

Crumpler, Ann P., Chf., Ref.Sec.
U.S. ARMY - OFFICE OF THE CHIEF OF
ENGINEERS - LIBRARY □ Washington, DC

Crumpler, Yvonne, Libn.
LINN-HENLEY LIBRARY FOR SOUTHERN
HISTORICAL RESEARCH - TUTWILER
COLLECTION OF SOUTHERN HISTORY AND
LITERATURE □ Birmingham, AL

Crutchfield, Benjamin F., Jr., Dir., Lib.Serv.
WEST VIRGINIA WESLEYAN COLLEGE - ANNIE
MERNER PFEIFFER LIBRARY □ Buckhannon, WV

Crutchfield, Mary Jane, Chf., Lib.Serv.
U.S. VETERANS ADMINISTRATION (TN-Johnson
City) - MEDICAL CENTER LIBRARY □ Mountain
Home, TN

Crutchfield, Sharon R., Dir.
DAUGHTERS OF THE REPUBLIC OF TEXAS -
LIBRARY □ San Antonio, TX

Cruys, Mae, Hd.Libn.
HOLY TRINITY LUTHERAN CHURCH - LIBRARY
□ Minneapolis, MN

Cruz, Joanne E., Lib.Coord.
COMPUTER AIDED MANUFACTURING-
INTERNATIONAL, INC. (CAM-I) - LIBRARY □
Arlington, TX

Cruze, Marianne H., Exec.Dir.
INTERNATIONAL VISITORS INFORMATION
SERVICE □ Washington, DC

Cryderman, Sandra A., Dir.
ST. JOSEPH HOSPITAL OF MT. CLEMENS -
MEDICAL LIBRARY □ Mt. Clemens, MI

Csaky, Susan D., Prof./Law Libn.
UNIVERSITY OF MISSOURI - SCHOOL OF LAW
LIBRARY □ Columbia, MO

Cseh, Eugene, Coll.Mgt.Libn.
UNIVERSITY OF CONNECTICUT - HEALTH
CENTER - LYMAN MAYNARD STOWE LIBRARY □
Farmington, CT

Csetalvay, Edmund, Acq.Libn.
U.S. DEPT. OF THE TREASURY - INFORMATION
SERVICES DIVISION - TREASURY DEPT.
LIBRARY □ Washington, DC

Csuros, Dr. Barna, Assoc.Dir.
KEAN COLLEGE OF NEW JERSEY - NANCY
THOMPSON LIBRARY† □ Union, NJ

Cubit, James, Asst.Dir., Tech.Serv.
UNIVERSITY OF MISSOURI, ROLLA - CURTIS
LAWS WILSON LIBRARY □ Rolla, MO

Cucchiara, Anthony M., Archv.
BRYANT LIBRARY - LOCAL HISTORY
COLLECTION □ Roslyn, NY

Cuellar, Susan, Adm.Asst.
TRANSAMERICA OCCIDENTAL LIFE
INSURANCE COMPANY - LAW LIBRARY □ Los
Angeles, CA

Cuenot, Addie Petit, Libn. I
AVCO - LYCOMING DIVISION - LIBRARY &
TECHNICAL INFORMATION CENTER □
Stratford, CT

Cuesta, Emerita M., Res.Libn.
AMERIFIRST FEDERAL SAVINGS & LOAN -
LIBRARY □ Miami, FL

Cuesta, Yolanda J., Chf. of Lib.Dev.
CALIFORNIA STATE LIBRARY □ Sacramento, CA

Cuillard, Doug, Chf. Naturalist
U.S. NATL. PARK SERVICE - DENALI NATL.
PARK - LIBRARY □ McKinley Park, AK

Culbert, Lorraine M., Libn.
SOHIO ALASKA PETROLEUM COMPANY -
INFORMATION RESOURCE CENTER □
Anchorage, AK

Culbertson, Diana, Libn.
DAIRY RESEARCH FOUNDATION - PRODUCT/
PROCESS INFORMATION SERVICES □
Rosemont, IL

Culbertson, Lillian D., Supv., Lib.Serv.
CHICAGO TRANSIT AUTHORITY - HAROLD S.
ANTHON MEMORIAL LIBRARY □ Chicago, IL

Culbertson, Margaret, Libn.
UNIVERSITY OF HOUSTON - FRANZHEIM
ARCHITECTURE LIBRARY □ Houston, TX

Cullen, Art, Asst.Prof.
IDAHO STATE UNIVERSITY - COLLEGE OF
EDUCATION - INSTRUCTIONAL MATERIALS
CENTER □ Pocatello, ID

Cullen, J.B., Chf., Forest Info. & Plan
NEW HAMPSHIRE STATE DIVISION OF
FORESTS AND LANDS - FOX FOREST LIBRARY □
Hillsboro, NH

Cullen, Marygael, Pub.Info.Off.
ILLINOIS STATE HISTORICAL LIBRARY □
Springfield, IL

Cullen, Rosemary L., Cur., Amer. Poetry/Plays
BROWN UNIVERSITY - SPECIAL COLLECTIONS
□ Providence, RI

Culley, Paul T., Hd., Tech.Ref.
NEW YORK STATE COLLEGE OF CERAMICS AT
ALFRED UNIVERSITY - SAMUEL R. SCHOLES
LIBRARY OF CERAMICS □ Alfred, NY

Cullinan, Joan C., Dir., Lib.Dev./Spec.Serv.
MICHIGAN STATE - LIBRARY OF MICHIGAN □
Lansing, MI

Cullison, William R., Cur.
TULANE UNIVERSITY OF LOUISIANA -
SOUTHEASTERN ARCHITECTURAL ARCHIVE □
New Orleans, LA

Culp, Gus B.
3M - PATENT AND TECHNICAL
COMMUNICATIONS SERVICES □ St. Paul, MN

Culp, Robert, ILL Libn.
MOUNT SINAI SCHOOL OF MEDICINE OF THE
CITY UNIVERSITY OF NEW YORK - GUSTAVE L.
& JANET W. LEVY LIBRARY □ New York, NY

Culpepper, Betty M., Bibliog./Hd., Ref.Dept.
HOWARD UNIVERSITY - MOORLAND-SPINGARN
RESEARCH CENTER - LIBRARY DIVISION □
Washington, DC

Culpepper, Jetta, Hd., Acq.
MURRAY STATE UNIVERSITY - LIBRARY □
Murray, KY

Culver, Harriet L., Pres.
CULVER PICTURES, INC. - LIBRARY □ New
York, NY

Culverhouse, Gertrude, Chf., Ref./Pub.Serv.
U.S. SOCIAL SECURITY ADMINISTRATION -
LIBRARY INFORMATION & GRAPHICS
SERVICES BRANCH □ Baltimore, MD

Culwell, Marie, Med.Rec.Mgr.
LAUREL GROVE HOSPITAL - MEDICAL &
DENTAL STAFF LIBRARY □ Castro Valley, CA

Cummin, K.H., Pres.
RADNOR HISTORICAL SOCIETY - RESEARCH
LIBRARY □ Wayne, PA

Cumming, Denise, Info.Spec.
HONEYWELL, INC. - TECHNOLOGY STRATEGY
CENTER - INFORMATION SERVICES □ Roseville,
MN

Cumming, George, Sci.Ref.Libn.
BOSTON PUBLIC LIBRARY - GOVERNMENT
DOCUMENTS, MICROTEXT, NEWSPAPERS □
Boston, MA

Cumming, J., Hd., Soc./Cultural Archv.
CANADA - PUBLIC ARCHIVES OF CANADA -
MANUSCRIPT DIVISION □ Ottawa, ON

Cumming, Robert, Asst.Libn.
XEROX CORPORATION - XEROX EDUCATION
PUBLICATIONS - LIBRARY □ Middletown, CT

Cummings, Abigail, Libn.
FOOTE CONE & BELDING - INFORMATION
CENTER □ Chicago, IL

Cummings, Bettylou, Med. Staff Coord.
LAKE FOREST HOSPITAL - MEDICAL STAFF
LIBRARY □ Lake Forest, IL

Cummings, Charles F., Supv.Libn.
NEWARK PUBLIC LIBRARY - NEW JERSEY
REFERENCE DIVISION □ Newark, NJ

Cummings, Joe, Chf., Res. & Stat.
TENNESSEE STATE DEPARTMENT OF
EMPLOYMENT SECURITY - RESEARCH &
STATISTICS SECTION □ Nashville, TN

Cummings, Assoc.Prof. John P., Assoc.Dir.
U.S. NAVY - NAVAL ACADEMY - NIMITZ
LIBRARY □ Annapolis, MD

Cummings, Judith, Ref.Libn.
PALO ALTO MEDICAL FOUNDATION -
BARNETT-HALL LIBRARY □ Palo Alto, CA

Cummings, Lester, Cur.
MEETING HOUSE GREEN MEMORIAL AND
HISTORICAL ASSOCIATION, INC. - TUCK
MEMORIAL MUSEUM - LIBRARY □ Hampton, NH

Cummings, Roberta S., Asst. Law Libn./Acq.
SOUTHERN UNIVERSITY - LAW SCHOOL
LIBRARY □ Baton Rouge, LA

Cummings, Veronica, Libn.
FEDERAL RESERVE BANK OF NEW YORK -
RESEARCH LIBRARY □ New York, NY

Cummings, Vicki, Act.Dir.
MUSEUM OF INDIAN HERITAGE - LIBRARY □
Indianapolis, IN

Cummins, James, Cur.
UNIVERSITY OF CINCINNATI - GEORGE
ELLISTON POETRY COLLECTION □ Cincinnati,
OH

Cummins, Kathryn, Dir.
MIDLAND COUNTY HISTORICAL SOCIETY -
ARCHIVES □ Midland, MI

Cummins, M. Johnette, Chf., Lib.Serv.
U.S. VETERANS ADMINISTRATION (AL-
Montgomery) - MEDICAL CENTER LIBRARY
(142D) □ Montgomery, AL

Cummins, Maria
MIAMI-DADE PUBLIC LIBRARY - ART AND
MUSIC DIVISION □ Miami, FL

Cummins, Thomas, Patients' Libn.
U.S. VETERANS ADMINISTRATION (FL-Miami) -
MEDICAL CENTER LIBRARY □ Miami, FL

Cundall, Christine, Libn.
UNIVERSITY OF MINNESOTA - NEWMAN
CENTER LIBRARY □ Minneapolis, MN

Cunha, Evano L., Acq.Libn.
U.S. AIR FORCE - AIR FORCE SYSTEMS
COMMAND - AIR FORCE GEOPHYSICS
LABORATORY - RESEARCH LIBRARY □ Bedford,
MA

Cunliffe, William H., Chf.
U.S. NATL. ARCHIVES & RECORDS SERVICE -
NATL. ARCHIVES - CARTOGRAPHIC &
ARCHITECTURAL BRANCH □ Washington, DC

Cunningham, Carolyn, Exec.Dir.
FEDERATED CONSERVATIONISTS OF
WESTCHESTER COUNTY - FCWC OFFICE
RESOURCE LIBRARY □ Purchase, NY

Cunningham, Charles, Asst.Libn.
TULSA WORLD-TULSA TRIBUNE - LIBRARY
DEPARTMENT □ Tulsa, OK

Cunningham, Clifford, Asst.Libn.
KITCHENER-WATERLOO RECORD - LIBRARY □
Kitchener, ON

Cunningham, Elizabeth A., Corp.Libn.
HOLLISTER INCORPORATED - CORPORATE
LIBRARY □ Libertyville, IL

Cunningham, Esther, Guide/Archv.
OLD CATHEDRAL PARISH CHURCH - BRUTE
LIBRARY □ Vincennes, IN

Cunningham, Francis W., Mss.Cat.
ONEIDA HISTORICAL SOCIETY - LIBRARY □
Utica, NY

Cunningham, Jay, Supv., Tech.Serv.
CALIFORNIA STATE LIBRARY □ Sacramento, CA

Cunningham, Joyce, Libn.
HUDSON RIVER PSYCHIATRIC CENTER -
MEDICAL LIBRARY □ Poughkeepsie, NY

Cunningham, Judith, Dir./Cur.
CALAVERAS COUNTY MUSEUM AND ARCHIVES
□ San Andreas, CA

Cunningham, Lynda S., Tech.Serv./Hd.
MARYLAND STATE DEPARTMENT OF
LEGISLATIVE REFERENCE - LIBRARY □
Annapolis, MD

Cunningham, Margaret A., Libn.
HANCOCK COUNTY LAW LIBRARY, INC. □
Ellsworth, ME

Cunningham, Robert, Ref., Cat.
BOSTON CONSERVATORY OF MUSIC - ALBERT
ALPHIN MUSIC LIBRARY □ Boston, MA

Cunningham, Susan C., Libn.
SHANLEY & FISHER - LAW LIBRARY □ Newark,
NJ

Cupelli, Louise, Dir., Info. & Commun.
CHILTON COMPANY - MARKETING &
ADVERTISING INFORMATION CENTER □
Radnor, PA

Cupit, Jane, Ref.Libn.
UNIVERSITY OF BALTIMORE - LAW LIBRARY □
Baltimore, MD

Cupoli, Patricia, Libn.
GENERAL MOTORS CORPORATION -
INFORMATION SYSTEMS & COMMUNICATIONS
ACTIVITY - TECHNICAL INFORMATION
CENTER □ Warren, MI

Cupryk, Robert, Ref.Libn.
UNIVERSITY OF MEDICINE AND DENTISTRY OF
NEW JERSEY AT NEWARK - GEORGE F. SMITH
LIBRARY □ Newark, NJ

Curnes, Janice, Asst.Libn.
MOUNT SINAI MEDICAL CENTER - MEDICAL
LIBRARY □ Milwaukee, WI

Curnoe, W. Glen, Libn.
LONDON PUBLIC LIBRARIES AND MUSEUMS -
LONDON ROOM □ London, ON

Curran, George, Search Anl.
INTERNATIONAL MINERALS & CHEMICALS
CORPORATION - IMC RESEARCH &
DEVELOPMENT LIBRARY □ Terre Haute, IN

Curran, George L., III, Supv./Libn.
BOEHRINGER MANNHEIM CORPORATION - BMC
INFORMATION CENTER □ Indianapolis, IN

Curran, Gertrude, Asst.Libn.
LUTHERAN GENERAL HOSPITAL - LIBRARY† □
Park Ridge, IL

Curran, Helen M., Libn.
ROHM & HAAS COMPANY - RESEARCH
DIVISION - INFORMATION SERVICES
DEPARTMENT □ Spring House, PA

Curran, Rev. Paul F., Dir.
ARCHDIOCESE OF PHILADELPHIA - CATHOLIC
INFORMATION CENTER □ Philadelphia, PA

Curran, Peggy, Supv.Libn.
U.S. NAVY - NAVAL WEAPONS SUPPORT
CENTER - LIBRARY† □ Crane, IN

Curren, J., Chf., Acq.Serv.
CANADA - AGRICULTURE CANADA - LIBRARIES
DIVISION □ Ottawa, ON

Currie, Clifford, Libn.
COLLEGE OF WILLIAM AND MARY - EARL
GREGG SWEM LIBRARY - SPECIAL
COLLECTIONS □ Williamsburg, VA

Currie, Hildegard, Ref. & Rd.Serv.
U.S. ARMY POST - FORT HUACHUCA LIBRARY
DIVISION - TECHNICAL LIBRARY □ Fort
Huachuca, AZ

Currie, John G., Hd., Info.Serv.
CANADA - DEFENCE RESEARCH
ESTABLISHMENT SUFFIELD - INFORMATION
SERVICES† □ Ralston, AB

Currie, June, Libn.
CANADA - FISHERIES & OCEANS - R&D
DIRECTORATE - ARCTIC BIOLOGICAL
STATION LIBRARY □ Ste. Anne-de-Bellevue, PQ

Currie, Kathleen, Acq. & Spec. Coll.
MOUNT SAINT VINCENT UNIVERSITY -
LIBRARY □ Halifax, NS

Currin, Dr. Douglas R., Chm., Lib.Comm.
VALLEY GENERAL HOSPITAL - LIBRARY □
Renton, WA

Curry, Brenda J., Libn.
UNITED HOSPITAL CENTER INC. - MEDICAL
LIBRARY □ Clarksburg, WV

Curry, David R., Dir.
BURROUGHS CORPORATION - CORPORATE
INFORMATION RESEARCH CENTER □ Detroit,
MI

Curry, David S., Libn.
UNIVERSITY OF IOWA - HEALTH SCIENCES
LIBRARY □ Iowa City, IA

Curry, Judy, Libn.
METROPOLITAN TORONTO LIBRARY -
MUNICIPAL REFERENCE DEPARTMENT □
Toronto, ON

Curry, Sr. Marilyn, Libn.
ST. MARTHA'S HOSPITAL - SCHOOL OF
NURSING LIBRARY □ Antigonish, NS

Curry, Rev. Robert, Archv.-Libn.
UNITED METHODIST CHURCH - HISTORICAL
SOCIETY OF THE EASTERN PENNSYLVANIA
CONFERENCE - ARCHIVES ROOM □ Annville, PA

Curteman, Marilyn, Doc.Coord.
NEPTUNE MICROFLOC, INC. - RESEARCH AND
TECHNICAL LIBRARY □ Corvallis, OR

Curtin, Raymond W., Libn.
EASTMAN KODAK COMPANY - ENGINEERING
LIBRARY □ Rochester, NY

Curtin-Stevenson, Mary, Hd.Cat.
EMERSON COLLEGE - LIBRARY □ Boston, MA

Curtis, Dr. George H., Asst.Dir.
U.S. PRESIDENTIAL LIBRARIES - HARRY S
TRUMAN LIBRARY □ Independence, MO

Curtis, Gloria, Info.Spec.
AMDAHL CORPORATION - CORPORATE
LIBRARY □ Sunnyvale, CA

Curtis, Gwen, Hd.
UNIVERSITY OF KENTUCKY - MARGARET I.
KING LIBRARY - GOVERNMENT
PUBLICATIONS/MAP DEPARTMENT - MAP
COLLECTION □ Lexington, KY

Curtis, Helen L., Libn.
ILLINOIS SCHOOL FOR THE VISUALLY
IMPAIRED - LIBRARY □ Jacksonville, IL

Curtis, Jim, AV Libn.
EAST TENNESSEE STATE UNIVERSITY,
QUILLEN-DISHNER COLLEGE OF MEDICINE -
DEPT. OF LEARNING RSRCS. - MEDICAL
LIBRARY† □ Johnson City, TN

Curtis, Judy I., Tech.Serv.Supv.
PERKIN-ELMER CORPORATION - CORPORATE
LIBRARY □ Norwalk, CT

Curtis, Karen, Libn.
TULSA CITY-COUNTY LIBRARY SYSTEM -
BUSINESS AND TECHNOLOGY DEPARTMENT □
Tulsa, OK

Curtis, Marilyn D., Hd., Tech.Serv.
U.S. NAVY - NAVAL WAR COLLEGE - LIBRARY □
Newport, RI

Curtis, Paul J., Dir.
AMERICAN MIME, INC. - LIBRARY □ New York,
NY

Curtis, Peter H., Hd.Libn.
STATE HISTORICAL SOCIETY OF IOWA -
LIBRARY □ Iowa City, IA

Curtis, Peter H., Cur.
UNIVERSITY OF MARYLAND, COLLEGE PARK -
LIBRARIES - MARYLANDIA DEPARTMENT □
College Park, MD

Curtis, Ruth L., Info.Coord.
NORTHWEST POWER PLANNING COUNCIL -
LIBRARY/PUBLIC READING ROOM □ Portland,
OR

Curtis, Sylvia Y., Act.Libn.
UNIVERSITY OF CALIFORNIA, SANTA BARBARA
- BLACK STUDIES LIBRARY UNIT □ Santa
Barbara, CA

Curtis, W. Ronald, Coord.
BLACKHAWK TECHNICAL INSTITUTE,
JANESVILLE - LEARNING MATERIALS CENTER
□ Janesville, WI

Curtis-Kellett, Mary E., Chf., Lib.Serv.
U.S. VETERANS ADMINISTRATION (TX-Temple)
- MEDICAL CENTER MEDICAL LIBRARY □
Temple, TX

Curtiss, Ruth E., Online Search
HERCULES, INC. - RESEARCH CENTER -
TECHNICAL INFORMATION DIVISION □
Wilmington, DE

Cusack, Edythe, Libn.
LONDON FREE PRESS PUBLISHING COMPANY,
LTD. - EDITORIAL LIBRARY □ London, ON

Cuseo, William J., Hd.
ROCHESTER PUBLIC LIBRARY - LITERATURE,
BIOGRAPHY AND SPORTS DIVISION □
Rochester, NY

Cushing, Alexandra, Cur.
STRATFORD SHAKESPEAREAN FESTIVAL
FOUNDATION OF CANADA - STRATFORD
FESTIVAL ARCHIVES □ Stratford, ON

Cushing, John D., Libn.
MASSACHUSETTS HISTORICAL SOCIETY -
RESEARCH LIBRARY □ Boston, MA

Cushing, Marie, Hd., Branches
LAWRENCE LIVERMORE NATIONAL
LABORATORY - TECHNICAL INFORMATION
DEPARTMENT LIBRARY □ Livermore, CA

Cushing, Stanley E., Consrv.
BOSTON ATHENAEUM LIBRARY □ Boston, MA

Cushing, Stanley Ellis, Lib.Chm.
GUILD OF BOOK WORKERS - LIBRARY □ Boston,
MA

Cushman, Helen M.B., Dir.
BAKER (H.M.) ASSOCIATES - RESEARCH
COLLECTION □ Westfield, NJ

Cushman, Robert, Photographic Serv.
ACADEMY OF MOTION PICTURE ARTS AND
SCIENCES - MARGARET HERRICK LIBRARY □
Beverly Hills, CA

Cusimano, Linda, Info.Anl./Rec.Mgt.
ALLERGAN PHARMACEUTICALS, INC. -
MEDICAL & SCIENCE INFORMATION □ Irvine,
CA

Cuskelly, Kathryn J., Ref./ILL Libn.
VITRO CORPORATION - LIBRARY □ Silver
Spring, MD

Cussins, Marcia, Libn.
MISSOURI STATE DIVISION OF GEOLOGY AND
LAND SURVEY - LIBRARY □ Rolla, MO

Custer, Charles D., Exec.Dir.
CAPITAL DISTRICT LIBRARY COUNCIL FOR
REFERENCE AND RESEARCH RESOURCES -
BIBLIOGRAPHIC CENTER □ Latham, NY

Custer, Virginia, Libn.
WESTERN AND SOUTHERN LIFE INSURANCE
CO. - LIBRARY □ Cincinnati, OH

Custon-Feinberg, Barbara, Acq.Libn.
OHIO STATE UNIVERSITY - LAW LIBRARY □
Columbus, OH

Cutler, C.M., Lib. Area Coord.
CANADA - AGRICULTURE CANADA - RESEARCH
STATION, LETHBRIDGE - LIBRARY □ Lethbridge,
AB

Cutler, C.M., Lib. Area Coord.
CANADA - AGRICULTURE CANADA - RESEARCH
STATION, VANCOUVER - LIBRARY □ Vancouver,
BC

Cutler, Millicent, Coord.
INDUSTRIAL HOME FOR THE BLIND - NASSAU-
SUFFOLK BRAILLE LIBRARY □ Hempstead, NY

Cutress, Bertha, Res.Assoc.
UNIVERSITY OF PUERTO RICO - MAYAGUEZ
CAMPUS LIBRARY - MARINE SCIENCES
COLLECTION □ Mayaguez, PR

Cutter, Margaret D., Health Sci.Libn.
LIMA MEMORIAL HOSPITAL - HEALTH
SCIENCES LIBRARY □ Lima, OH

Cutting, Eunice, Lib.Asst.
ALBERTA - DEPARTMENT OF THE SOLICITOR
GENERAL - LIBRARY □ Edmonton, AB

Cvejanovich, Susan H., Cat.Libn.
GETTY OIL COMPANY, INC. - RESEARCH
CENTER LIBRARY □ Houston, TX

Cybruch, Stella J., Supv., Lib./Info.Serv.
AES DATA INC. - ATRIUM LIBRARY □
Mississauga, ON

Cylke, Frank Kurt, Dir.
LIBRARY OF CONGRESS - NATIONAL LIBRARY
SERVICE FOR THE BLIND AND PHYSICALLY
HANDICAPPED □ Washington, DC

Cyr, Donald L., Ed.
STONEHENGE STUDY GROUP - STONEHENGE
VIEWPOINT LIBRARY □ Santa Barbara, CA

Cyr, Helen W., Hd.
ENOCH PRATT FREE LIBRARY - AUDIO-VISUAL
DEPARTMENT □ Baltimore, MD

Cyr, Joan L., Libn.
STONEHENGE STUDY GROUP - STONEHENGE
VIEWPOINT LIBRARY □ Santa Barbara, CA

Cyr, Lucy L., Libn.
CONNECTICUT STATE LIBRARY - LAW LIBRARY
AT WATERBURY† □ Waterbury, CT

Cyr, Paul, Libn.
NEW BEDFORD FREE PUBLIC LIBRARY -
GENEALOGY ROOM† □ New Bedford, MA

Cyr, Paul, Cur.
NEW BEDFORD FREE PUBLIC LIBRARY -
MELVILLE WHALING ROOM† □ New Bedford, MA

Czajkowski, Marian G., Dir. of Lib.Serv.
HOWARD COUNTY GENERAL HOSPITAL -
HEALTH SCIENCES LIBRARY □ Columbia, MD

Czajkowski, Sandra, Rec.Libn.
JUILLIARD SCHOOL - LILA ACHESON WALLACE
LIBRARY □ New York, NY

Czanyo, Mrs. M., Assoc.Dir.
CANADA - ENVIRONMENT CANADA - LIBRARY
SERVICES BRANCH □ Ottawa, ON

Czarnetzky, Lucille L., Cur.
MINER (Alice T.) COLONIAL COLLECTION -
LIBRARY □ Chazy, NY

Czarnota, Les, Info.Spec.
IMPERIAL OIL, LTD. - BUSINESS INFORMATION
CENTRE □ Toronto, ON

Czechowicz, Maria, Dir.
FLUSHING HOSPITAL AND MEDICAL CENTER -
MEDICAL LIBRARY □ Flushing, NY

Cziffra, Lisa, Libn./Archv.
CARNEGIE FOUNDATION FOR THE
ADVANCEMENT OF TEACHING - LIBRARY □
Princeton NJ

Cziffra, Peter, Libn.
PRINCETON UNIVERSITY - ASTRONOMY
LIBRARY □ Princeton, NJ

Cziffra, Peter, Libn.
PRINCETON UNIVERSITY - MATHEMATICS,
PHYSICS AND STATISTICS LIBRARY □
Princeton, NJ

Czike, Stephen F., Exec.Libn.
CHICAGO BAR ASSOCIATION - LIBRARY □
Chicago, IL

Czisny, Julie, Educ.Libn.
UNIVERSITY OF WISCONSIN, MILWAUKEE -
GOLDA MEIR LIBRARY - CURRICULUM
COLLECTION □ Milwaukee, WI

Czujak, Maureen, Hd., Rd.Serv.
NEW YORK MEDICAL COLLEGE AND THE
WESTCHESTER ACADEMY OF MEDICINE -
WESTCHESTER MEDICAL CENTER LIBRARY □
Valhalla, NY

D

D' Souza, Yolande, Libn.
C-I-L INC. - PATENT LIBRARY □ North York, ON

Daane, Wilma A., Ref.Libn.
U.S. AIR FORCE - ACCOUNTING AND FINANCE
CENTER - TECHNICAL LIBRARY □ Denver, CO

Dabbs, Joyce
SOUTHERN WISCONSIN CENTER FOR THE
DEVELOPMENTALLY DISABLED - LIBRARY □
Union Grove, WI

Dablemont, Maria, Libn.
INTERNATIONAL LIBRARY, ARCHIVES &
MUSEUM OF OPTOMETRY □ St. Louis, MO

Dabney, Dan, Ref.Libn.
UNIVERSITY OF TEXAS, AUSTIN - SCHOOL OF
LAW - TARLTON LAW LIBRARY □ Austin, TX

Dabrishus, Michael J., Cur.
UNIVERSITY OF ARKANSAS, FAYETTEVILLE -
SPECIAL COLLECTIONS DIVISION □
Fayetteville, AR

D'Accurzio, Connie, Libn.
CROUSE-IRVING MEMORIAL HOSPITAL -
LIBRARY □ Syracuse, NY

Dacey, Laura, Asst.Libn.
PIERSON, BALL & DOWD - LAW LIBRARY □
Washington, DC

Dacker, Paula, Fld.Serv.Libn.
BRAILLE INSTITUTE OF AMERICA - LIBRARY □
Los Angeles, CA

Dacko, A., Sr.Info.Sci.
ALUMINUM COMPANY OF AMERICA - ALCOA
TECHNICAL CENTER - INFORMATION
DEPARTMENT □ Alcoa Center, PA

D'Adamo, Peggy, Pres.
ALTERNATIVE PRESS CENTER - LIBRARY □
Baltimore, MD

Daebeler, Barbara A., Asst.Libn.
VILLANOVA UNIVERSITY - LIBRARY SCIENCE
LIBRARY □ Villanova, PA

Daffron, Mary Ellen, Libn.
U.S. FEDERAL MARITIME COMMISSION -
LIBRARY □ Washington, DC

Dagenhart, Nancy, Info.Spec.
NATIONAL ACADEMY OF SCIENCES -
NATIONAL RESEARCH COUNCIL - HIGHWAY
RESEARCH INFORMATION SERVICE □
Washington, DC

Daggy, Robert E., Cur.
BELLARMINE COLLEGE - THOMAS MERTON
STUDIES CENTER □ Louisville, KY

Daghita, Joan, Hd., Circ.
U.S. NATL. INSTITUTES OF HEALTH - LIBRARY
□ Bethesda, MD

Dagley, Linda, Med.Libn.
U.S. VETERANS ADMINISTRATION (MO-
Columbia) - HOSPITAL LIBRARY □ Columbia, MO

Dahl, Mr. E., Chf., Early Cart.Sect
CANADA - PUBLIC ARCHIVES OF CANADA -
NATIONAL MAP COLLECTION □ Ottawa, ON

Dahl, Lorraine, Libn.
AVIATION ELECTRIC, LTD. - TECHNICAL DATA
SECTION LIBRARY □ Montreal, PQ

Dahlgren, Dorothy, Cur.
MUSEUM OF NORTH IDAHO, INC. - ARCHIVES □
Coeur d'Alene, ID

Dahlin, Deborah C., Dept.Hd.
BIRMINGHAM PUBLIC AND JEFFERSON
COUNTY FREE LIBRARY - SCIENCE,
TECHNOLOGY & BUSINESS DEPT. - SPECIAL
COLLECTIONS □ Birmingham, AL

Dahlquist, Nancy, Lib.Adm.
MOUNT OLIVET LUTHERAN CHURCH - LIBRARY
□ Minneapolis, MN

Dahm, Mary C., Libn.
ST. LOUIS COUNTY LAW LIBRARY □ Clayton,
MO

Dahm, Minnie Julia, Archv.
DORDT COLLEGE - ARCHIVES AND DUTCH
MEMORIAL COLLECTION □ Sioux Center, IA

Dahnke, Beatrice, Libn.
WESTVIEW CHRISTIAN REFORMED CHURCH -
LIBRARY □ Grand Rapids, MI

D'Aho, Mary Ann, Libn.
INTERNATIONAL COUNCIL OF SHOPPING
CENTERS - LIBRARY □ New York, NY

Dainard, Norma, Asst. in Charge
METROPOLITAN TORONTO LIBRARY -
NEWSPAPER UNIT □ Toronto, ON

Dainauskas, Jonas, Cat. & Ref.Libn.
LIBRARY OF INTERNATIONAL RELATIONS □
Chicago, IL

Dains, Jeffrey, Lib.Asst.
UNIVERSITY OF MINNESOTA, ST. PAUL -
BIOCHEMISTRY LIBRARY □ St. Paul, MN

Dais, Romeo, Libn.
MADISON PUBLIC LIBRARY - BUSINESS AND
SCIENCE DIVISION □ Madison, WI

Daitchman, Norman
ZITTRER, SIBLIN, STEIN, LEVINE - LIBRARY □
Montreal, PQ

Dakan, Tony, Dir., USAF Libs.
U.S. AIR FORCE - AIR FORCE MANPOWER &
PERSONNEL CENTER - MORALE, WELFARE &
RECREATION DIVISION - LIBRARY SERVICES
BR. □ Randolph AFB, TX

Dalbothen, Diana, Libn.
UNIVERSITY OF MINNESOTA - ST. ANTHONY FALLS HYDRAULIC LABORATORY - LORENZ G. STRAUB MEMORIAL LIBRARY □ Minneapolis, MN

Dalby, Barbara M., Hd.Libn.
CHURCH OF JESUS CHRIST OF LATTER-DAY SAINTS - TAMPA BRANCH GENEALOGICAL LIBRARY □ Tampa, FL

Dalcourt, Dawn, Lib.Techn.
EDMONTON CITY ENGINEERING DEPARTMENT - MATERIALS & TESTING LIBRARY □ Edmonton, AB

Dale, David T., Libn.
YALE CLUB OF NEW YORK CITY - LIBRARY □ New York, NY

Dale, John W., Prog.Coord.
U.S. BUREAU OF THE CENSUS - INFORMATION SERVICES PROGRAM - KANSAS CITY REGIONAL OFFICE - LIBRARY □ Kansas City, KS

Dale, Nancy, Libn.
ST. ANTHONY HOSPITAL MEDICAL CENTER - MEDICAL LIBRARY □ Rockford, IL

Dalechek, Marjorie E., Photo Libn.
U.S. GEOLOGICAL SURVEY - DENVER LIBRARY □ Denver, CO

D'Aleo, Ruth P., Ref.Libn.
MORAVIAN COLLEGE - REEVES LIBRARY □ Bethlehem, PA

Dalesandro, Anne, Ref.Libn.
RUTGERS UNIVERSITY, THE STATE UNIVERSITY OF NEW JERSEY - SCHOOL OF LAW LIBRARY† □ Camden, NJ

Daley, Carol, Rsrc.Libn.
U.S. BANCORP - RESOURCE LIBRARY □ Portland, OR

Daley, Marian, Libn.
U.S. VETERANS ADMINISTRATION (IL-Hines) - LIBRARY SERVICES (142D) □ Hines, IL

Daley, Patricia, Res.Libn.
COLUMBIA GAS SYSTEM SERVICE CORPORATION - RESEARCH LIBRARY □ Columbus, OH

Daley, Trudy, Chf.Libn.
UNITED STATES TRUST COMPANY - INVESTMENT LIBRARY □ New York, NY

Dallaire, Danielle, Libn.
BEAUCHEMIN-BEATON-LAPOINTE, INC. - BBL LIBRARY □ Montreal, PQ

Dallas, Shirley, Info.Spec.
WASHINGTON STATE SUPERINTENDENT OF PUBLIC INSTRUCTION - RESOURCE INFORMATION CENTER □ Olympia, WA

Dallavalle, Ann, Lib.Serv.Asst.
YALE UNIVERSITY - OBSERVATORY LIBRARY □ New Haven, CT

Dalligan, Alice C., Chf.
DETROIT PUBLIC LIBRARY - BURTON HISTORICAL COLLECTION □ Detroit, MI

Dalphin, George R., Ref.Supv.
SANDIA NATIONAL LABORATORIES - TECHNICAL LIBRARY □ Albuquerque, NM

Dalrymple, Prudence, Coord., Lib.Serv.
ROCKFORD MEMORIAL HOSPITAL - HEALTH SCIENCE LIBRARY □ Rockford, IL

Dalton, Alice, Hd., Circ.
HARVARD UNIVERSITY - GODFREY LOWELL CABOT SCIENCE LIBRARY □ Cambridge, MA

Daly, Gail M., Hd. of Cat.
UNIVERSITY OF MINNESOTA - LAW LIBRARY □ Minneapolis, MN

Daly, Jerry, Chm., Media Serv.
LOMA LINDA UNIVERSITY - DEL E. WEBB MEMORIAL LIBRARY □ Loma Linda, CA

Daly, John, Dir.
ILLINOIS STATE - OFFICE OF THE SECRETARY OF STATE - STATE ARCHIVES □ Springfield, IL

Daly, Rev. Lowrie J., Microfilm Projects
ST. LOUIS UNIVERSITY - KNIGHTS OF COLUMBUS VATICAN FILM LIBRARY □ St. Louis, MO

Daly, Maria C., Med.Libn.
KENNEDY (John F.) MEDICAL CENTER - LIBRARY □ Edison, NJ

Daly, Rev. Simeon, O.S.B., Libn.
ST. MEINRAD ARCHABBEY - COLLEGE & SCHOOL OF THEOLOGY - LIBRARY □ St. Meinrad, IN

Daly, Susan, Libn.
BULL, HOUSSER AND TUPPER - LIBRARY □ Vancouver, BC

Dam, Tran, Libn.
ONTARIO HYDRO - LIBRARY □ Toronto, ON

Damaskos, James, Libn.
HARVARD UNIVERSITY - LITTAUER LIBRARY □ Cambridge, MA

D'Ambrosio, Ann Marie, Lib.Techn.
U.S. CUSTOMS SERVICE - REGION II - LAW LIBRARY □ New York, NY

D'Ambrosio, Margaret, Assoc.Libn.
AMERICAN NUMISMATIC SOCIETY - LIBRARY □ New York, NY

Dame, Fern Shrewsberry, Illus.Libn.
NATIONAL GEOGRAPHIC SOCIETY - ILLUSTRATIONS LIBRARY □ Washington, DC

Damkoehler, Esther, Libn.
HOPE LUTHERAN CHURCH - LIBRARY □ Milwaukee, WI

Damm, Robert L., Dir.
BUFFALO & ERIE COUNTY HISTORICAL SOCIETY - LIBRARY† □ Buffalo, NY

Damon, Cora M., Libn.
MID-MAINE MEDICAL CENTER - CLARA HODGKINS MEMORIAL HEALTH SCIENCES LIBRARY □ Waterville, ME

Damon, Shirley, Hd.Libn.
COMPTON ADVERTISING INC. - RESEARCH LIBRARY □ New York, NY

Dana, Dale Winslow, Proj.Coord.
SANTA CLARA COUNTY OFFICE OF EDUCATION - CENTRAL CALIFORNIA CENTER FOR EDUCATIONAL IMPROVEMENT - LIBRARY □ San Jose, CA

Danahar, Catherine M., Libn.
HARVARD UNIVERSITY - HARVARD FOREST LIBRARY □ Petersham, MA

Dance, Barbara, Libn.
TOUCHE, ROSS & COMPANY/TOUCHE ROSS & PARTNERS - INFORMATION CENTRE □ Toronto, ON

Dancik, Deborah, Educ.Libn.
UNIVERSITY OF ALBERTA - H.T. COUTTS LIBRARY □ Edmonton, AB

D'Andrea, Julia, Cat.
UNIVERSITY OF PITTSBURGH - FALK LIBRARY OF THE HEALTH SCIENCES □ Pittsburgh, PA

Dandurand, Gary, AV Libn.
UNIVERSITY OF HEALTH SCIENCES/CHICAGO MEDICAL SCHOOL - LIBRARY □ North Chicago, IL

Dane, William J., Supv.
NEWARK PUBLIC LIBRARY - ART AND MUSIC DEPARTMENT □ Newark, NJ

Danforth, Susan, Cur. of Maps & Prints
BROWN UNIVERSITY - JOHN CARTER BROWN LIBRARY □ Providence, RI

Dang, Charlotte, Libn.
LEEWARD COMMUNITY COLLEGE LIBRARY - SPECIAL COLLECTIONS □ Honolulu, HI

Daniel, Dr. David P., Act.Dir., Lib.Serv.
CONCORDIA SEMINARY - LIBRARY □ St. Louis, MO

Daniel, E.L., Cat.
BATTELLE-NORTHWEST - PACIFIC NORTHWEST LABORATORY - HANFORD TECHNICAL LIBRARY □ Richland, WA

Daniel, Eileen, Libn.
NORTHERN TELECOM, LTD. - NT LIBRARY □ Mississauga, ON

Daniel, Eleanor M., Hd.Libn.
OHIO STATE UNIVERSITY - BLACK STUDIES LIBRARY □ Columbus, OH

Daniel, Wayne, Libn./Archv.
FORT CONCHO MUSEUM - REFERENCE LIBRARY □ San Angelo, TX

Daniells, Laurenda, Univ.Archv.
UNIVERSITY OF BRITISH COLUMBIA - SPECIAL COLLECTIONS DIVISION □ Vancouver, BC

Daniells, Lorna M., Bus.Bibliog.
HARVARD UNIVERSITY - HARVARD BUSINESS SCHOOL - BAKER LIBRARY □ Boston, MA

Daniels, Dr. Boyd L., Coord. of Lib.Serv.
AMERICAN BIBLE SOCIETY - LIBRARY □ New York, NY

Daniels, Bruce E., Deputy Dir.
RHODE ISLAND STATE DEPARTMENT OF STATE LIBRARY SERVICES □ Providence, RI

Daniels, Deborah, Info.Cons.
CITE RESOURCE CENTER □ Austin, TX

Daniels, Delores E., Libn.
U.S. COURT OF APPEALS, 9TH CIRCUIT - LIBRARY □ Phoenix, AZ

Daniels, Elizabeth, Br.Asst.
SAN DIEGO COUNTY LAW LIBRARY - SOUTH BAY BRANCH □ Chula Vista, CA

Daniels, Ellen, Mgr., Info.Serv.
WORK IN AMERICA INSTITUTE, INC. - LIBRARY □ Scarsdale, NY

Daniels, Jerome P., Dir.
UNIVERSITY OF WISCONSIN, PLATTEVILLE - KARRMANN LIBRARY - SPECIAL COLLECTIONS □ Platteville, WI

Daniels, John E., Dir.
U.S. DEPT. OF ENERGY - ENERGY INFORMATION ADMINISTRATION - NATIONAL ENERGY INFORMATION CENTER □ Washington, DC

Daniels, Westwell R., Law Libn.
UNIVERSITY OF MIAMI - SCHOOL OF LAW LIBRARY □ Coral Gables, FL

Daniels, William G., Pres.
DELTA COUNTY HISTORICAL SOCIETY MUSEUM LIBRARY □ Escanaba, MI

Dankert, Phillip, Coll.Dev.
CORNELL UNIVERSITY - MARTIN P. CATHERWOOD LIBRARY OF INDUSTRIAL AND LABOR RELATIONS □ Ithaca, NY

Dankewych, Dr. Michael, Libn.
U.S. NAVY - DAVID W. TAYLOR NAVAL SHIP RESEARCH AND DEVELOPMENT CENTER - TECHNICAL INFORMATION CENTER □ Bethesda, MD

Danko, Diana M., Supv., Info.Serv.
PPG INDUSTRIES, INC. - CHEMICAL DIVISION - RESEARCH LIBRARY □ Barberton, OH

Dankow, Marcella, Lib.Techn.
SYNCRUDE CANADA, LTD. - OPERATIONS LIBRARY □ Fort McMurray, AB

Dann, John C., Dir.
UNIVERSITY OF MICHIGAN - WILLIAM L. CLEMENTS LIBRARY □ Ann Arbor, MI

Danner, Mrs. Michael, Libn.
AMERICAN WATCHMAKERS INSTITUTE - LIBRARY □ Cincinnati, OH

Danner, Richard, Dir.
DUKE UNIVERSITY - SCHOOL OF LAW LIBRARY □ Durham, NC

Danner, Susan, Med.Libn.
ARCHBOLD (John D.) MEMORIAL HOSPITAL - RALPH PERKINS MEMORIAL LIBRARY □ Thomasville, GA

Danner, Susan T., Med.Libn.
SOUTH GEORGIA MEDICAL CENTER - MEDICAL LIBRARY □ Valdosta, GA

Dano, Robert W., Tech.Info.Spec.
U.S. FOREST SERVICE - ROCKY MOUNTAIN FOREST & RANGE EXPERIMENT STATION - LIBRARY □ Fort Collins, CO

Dansereau, Heather, Med.Libn.
CIBA-GEIGY (Canada) LTD. - PHARMACEUTICAL LIBRARY □ Mississauga, ON

Dansker, Shirley E., Dir.
LENOX HILL HOSPITAL - HEALTH SCIENCES LIBRARY □ New York, NY

Danskey, Mrs. Kit, Libn.
MASSACHUSETTS FINANCIAL SERVICES, INC. - BUSINESS LIBRARY □ Boston, MA

Dantin, Doris
LOUISIANA STATE UNIVERSITY - REFERENCE
SERVICES □ Baton Rouge, LA
Danziger, Margaret, Dept.Hd.
TOLEDO-LUCAS COUNTY PUBLIC LIBRARY -
BUSINESS DEPARTMENT □ Toledo, OH
Daoust, Richard L., Hd.Libn.
MICHIGAN STATE DEPARTMENT OF LABOR -
MICHIGAN EMPLOYMENT SECURITY
COMMISSION - LIBRARY □ Detroit, MI
Daoust, Dr. Roger, Info.Dir.
MONTREAL CANCER INSTITUTE - LIBRARY □
Montreal, PQ
Daragan, Patricia A., Hd., Tech.Serv.
U.S. COAST GUARD ACADEMY - LIBRARY □ New
London, CT
Darbee, Leigh, Hd., Ref./Bibliog.Serv.
INDIANA HISTORICAL SOCIETY - WILLIAM
HENRY SMITH MEMORIAL LIBRARY □
Indianapolis, IN
Darby, A. K., V.P., Mktg.
FUTURE AVIATION PROFESSIONALS OF
AMERICA (FAPA) - INFORMATION CENTER □
Decatur, GA
Darby, Gail, Lib.Asst.
NEW BRUNSWICK - DEPARTMENT OF THE
ENVIRONMENT - LIBRARY □ Fredericton, NB
Darby, Janet, Libn.
TORY, TORY, DESLAURIERS & BINNINGTON -
LIBRARY □ Toronto, ON
Darby, Dr. William J., Honor.Cur.
VANDERBILT UNIVERSITY - MEDICAL CENTER
LIBRARY □ Nashville, TN
Darcy, Madeleine A., Sr.Libn.
CALIFORNIA STATE RESOURCES AGENCY -
LIBRARY □ Sacramento, CA
Darcy, William, Base Libn.
U.S. AIR FORCE BASE - LAUGHLIN BASE
LIBRARY □ Laughlin AFB, TX
Darcy, William E., Libn.
U.S. AIR FORCE BASE - CHARLESTON BASE
LIBRARY □ Charleston AFB, SC
Dare, Philip N., Hd.Libn.
LEXINGTON THEOLOGICAL SEMINARY -
BOSWORTH MEMORIAL LIBRARY □ Lexington,
KY
Darga, Carol, Cat.
CRANBROOK ACADEMY OF ART - LIBRARY □
Bloomfield Hills, MI
Darknell, Edith, Supv.Libn.
CALIFORNIA STATE DEPARTMENT OF
TRANSPORTATION - TRANSPORTATION
LIBRARY □ Sacramento, CA
Darling, John B., Libn.
UNIVERSITY OF NORTH CAROLINA, CHAPEL
HILL - ZOOLOGY LIBRARY □ Chapel Hill, NC
Darling, Margaret, Ref.Libn.
CANADA - NATIONAL DEFENCE - FORT
FRONTENAC LIBRARY □ Kingston, ON
Darling, Mary, Ref.Libn.
SDS BIOTECH CORPORATION - CORPORATE
LIBRARY □ Painesville, OH
Darling, Mikell C., Dir.
EVANSTON HISTORICAL SOCIETY - CHARLES
GATES DAWES HOME - LIBRARY □ Evanston, IL
Darlington, Gerard, Libn.
QUEBEC PROVINCE - MINISTERE DES
AFFAIRES SOCIALES - SERVICE DE LA
DOCUMENTATION □ Montreal, PQ
Darnell, Linda, Libn.
CONWAY (E.A.) MEMORIAL HOSPITAL -
MEDICAL LIBRARY □ Monroe, LA
Darnell, Polly C., Libn.
SHELDON ART MUSEUM - GOVERNOR JOHN W.
STEWART & MR. & MRS. CHARLES M. SWIFT
RESEARCH CENTER LIBRARY □ Middlebury, VT
Darr, Joyce S., Libn.
U.S.D.A. - AGRICULTURAL RESEARCH SERVICE
- HORTICULTURAL RESEARCH LABORATORY
LIBRARY □ Orlando, FL
Darr, William, Asst.Dir.
GRACE THEOLOGICAL SEMINARY - LIBRARY □
Winona Lake, IN

Darroch, Prof. Gordon
YORK UNIVERSITY - INSTITUTE FOR SOCIAL
RESEARCH - DATA BANK □ Downsview, ON
Dartnell, Anne, Supv.
TCR SERVICE, INC. - COMMON LAW LIBRARY □
Croton-on-Hudson, NY
Darvill, Eunice, Dir.
SKAGIT COUNTY HISTORICAL MUSEUM -
HISTORICAL REFERENCE LIBRARY □ La Conner,
WA
Darwin, Karen Lee, Projects Ed.
ENVIRONMENTAL EDUCATION GROUP -
LIBRARY □ Camarillo, CA
Das Gupta, Krishna, Tech.Serv.
WORCESTER STATE COLLEGE - LEARNING
RESOURCES CENTER □ Worcester, MA
Dashnaw, Susan, Natl.Prog.Dir.
NATIONAL ENERGY FOUNDATION - ENERGY
REFERENCE AND RESOURCE CENTER □ New
York, NY
Dass, Patsy, Slide Cur.
TEMPLE UNIVERSITY - CENTRAL LIBRARY
SYSTEM - TYLER SCHOOL OF FINE ARTS -
SLIDE LIBRARY □ Philadelphia, PA
Dassance, Mary
LANSING COMMUNITY COLLEGE -
PROFESSIONAL RESOURCE CENTER □ Lansing,
MI
Date, Sandra, Sr. Libn.
PILLSBURY COMPANY - BUSINESS REFERENCE
LIBRARY □ Minneapolis, MN
Dater, Lois, Cur.
STAMFORD HISTORICAL SOCIETY - LIBRARY □
Stamford, CT
D'Atri, Bianca G., Acq.Libn.
U.S. ARMY - NATICK RESEARCH AND
DEVELOPMENT CENTER - TECHNICAL LIBRARY
□ Natick, MA
Daub, Peggy E., Music Libn.
UNIVERSITY OF MICHIGAN - MUSIC LIBRARY □
Ann Arbor, MI
Daudelin, Robert, Exec.Dir.
CINEMATHEQUE QUEBECOISE - ARCHIVES &
FILM MUSEUM □ Montreal, PQ
Daughenbaugh, Norman E., Tech.Libn.
HERCULES, INC. - PICCO RESINS DIVISION -
LIBRARY □ Clairton, PA
Daugherty, Betty J., Dir. of Lib.Serv.
BALL MEMORIAL HOSPITAL - HEALTH SCIENCE
LIBRARY □ Muncie, IN
Daugherty, Carolyn M., Libn.
UNION MEMORIAL HOSPITAL - NURSING
LIBRARY □ Baltimore, MD
Daugherty, Norma A., Asst.Libn.
INSTITUTE OF LIVING - MEDICAL LIBRARY □
Hartford, CT
Daughtrey, Margery, Extension Assoc.
LONG ISLAND HORTICULTURAL RESEARCH
LABORATORY - LIBRARY □ Riverhead, NY
Daum, Patricia B., Info.Coord.
THE MC ELHANNEY GROUP LTD. -
INFORMATION CENTRE □ Vancouver, BC
Daum, Dr. Raymond W., Cur.
UNIVERSITY OF TEXAS, AUSTIN - HUMANITIES
RESEARCH CENTER - THEATRE ARTS
COLLECTIONS □ Austin, TX
Dauphinais, Edward, Libn.
UNIVERSITY OF NEW HAMPSHIRE -
CHEMISTRY LIBRARY □ Durham, NH
Dauphinais, Edward, Libn.
UNIVERSITY OF NEW HAMPSHIRE - DAVID G.
CLARK MEMORIAL PHYSICS LIBRARY □ Durham,
NH
Dauphinais, Edward, Libn.
UNIVERSITY OF NEW HAMPSHIRE -
ENGINEERING-MATH LIBRARY □ Durham, NH
Davenport, Barbara, Med.Libn.
CHILDREN'S HOSPITAL MEDICAL CENTER OF
NORTHERN CALIFORNIA - MEDICAL LIBRARY □
Oakland, CA
Davenport, Constance B., Info.Ctr.Supv.
LOGICON, INC. - INFORMATION CENTER □ San
Pedro, CA

Davenport, Diane, Supv.Prog.Libn.
BERKELEY PUBLIC LIBRARY - ART AND MUSIC
DEPARTMENT □ Berkeley, CA
Davenport, Janet, Libn.
OMAHA PUBLIC LIBRARY - BUSINESS, SCIENCE
& TECHNOLOGY DEPARTMENT □ Omaha, NE
Davenport, John B., Spec.Coll.Libn.
COLLEGE OF ST. THOMAS - O'SHAUGHNESSY
LIBRARY - SPECIAL COLLECTIONS □ St. Paul,
MN
Davenport, Margaret J., Libn.
CAHILL GORDON & REINDEL - LAW LIBRARY □
New York, NY
Davenport, Vanny, Libn. & Cur.
NATIONAL BANK OF ALASKA - HERITAGE
LIBRARY AND MUSEUM □ Anchorage, AK
Davern, Maggi, Exec.Dir.
VOLUNTARY ACTION CENTER OF THE ST. PAUL
AREA - LIBRARY □ St. Paul, MN
Daves, Bryan, Res.Assoc.
NATIONAL JOURNAL LIBRARY □ Washington, DC
David, Carol A., Hd.Libn.
CRAIN COMMUNICATIONS, INC. -
INFORMATION CENTER □ Chicago, IL
David, Charlotte, Chf., Legal Info.Serv.
U.S. NUCLEAR REGULATORY COMMISSION -
LAW LIBRARY □ Washington, DC
David, Douglas, Supv., Instr.Serv.
BOCES - ORLEANS-NIAGARA EDUCATIONAL
COMMUNICATIONS CENTER □ Sanborn, NY
David, Mrs. Farilla A., Libn.
FOUNDATION FOR RESEARCH ON THE NATURE
OF MAN - INSTITUTE FOR PARAPSYCHOLOGY -
RESEARCH LIBRARY □ Durham, NC
David, Shirley H., County Law Libn.
SACRAMENTO COUNTY LAW LIBRARY □
Sacramento, CA
David, Zdenek V., Libn.
WILSON (Woodrow) INTERNATIONAL CENTER
FOR SCHOLARS - LIBRARY □ Washington, DC
Davidoff, Donna J., Hd.Libn.
TEMPLE BETH ZION - LIBRARY □ Buffalo, NY
Davidoff, Marcia, Chf.Libn.
U.S. NAVY - NAVAL TRAINING EQUIPMENT
CENTER - TECHNICAL INFORMATION CENTER
□ Orlando, FL
Davidson, B.J., Libn.
U.S. DEPT. OF ENERGY - LARAMIE PROJECTS
LIBRARY □ Laramie, WY
Davidson, Brian, Ref.&Ser.Rec.
CANADIAN BANKERS ASSOCIATION - LIBRARY
□ Toronto, ON
Davidson, Mrs. Elfa M., Libn.
CENTRE FOR CHRISTIAN STUDIES - LIBRARY†
□ Toronto, ON
Davidson, Gwen, Libn.
U.S. NATL. PARK SERVICE - LAKE MEAD NATL.
RECREATION AREA - LIBRARY □ Boulder City,
NV
Davidson, Janet, Relg.Educ.Libn.
MC CORMICK THEOLOGICAL SEMINARY -
LIBRARY† □ Chicago, IL
Davidson, Lloyd, Life Sci.Libn.
NORTHWESTERN UNIVERSITY - SEELEY G.
MUDD LIBRARY FOR SCIENCE AND
ENGINEERING □ Evanston, IL
Davidson, Mary, Libn.
SOCIETY OF FRIENDS - PHILADELPHIA YEARLY
MEETING - LIBRARY □ Philadelphia, PA
Davidson, Mary Wallace, Libn.
UNIVERSITY OF ROCHESTER - EASTMAN
SCHOOL OF MUSIC - SIBLEY MUSIC LIBRARY □
Rochester, NY
Davidson, Nancy, Sr.Res.Assoc.
REYNOLDS (Russell) ASSOCIATES, INC. -
LIBRARY □ Chicago, IL
Davidson, Patricia L., Br.Ref.
IBM CORPORATION - DSD LIBRARY/LEARNING
CENTER □ Poughkeepsie, NY
Davidson, Rosemary, Corp.Libn./Dept.Hd.
NORDSON CORPORATION WORLD
HEADQUARTERS - TECHNICAL INFORMATION
DEPARTMENT □ Westlake, OH

Davidson, Sarah, Info.Coord.
FARMLAND INDUSTRIES, INC. - J.W. CUMMINS
MEMORIAL LIBRARY □ Kansas City, MO

Davidson, Silvia, Libn.
YESHIVA UNIVERSITY - ALBERT EINSTEIN
COLLEGE OF MEDICINE - DEPT. OF
PSYCHIATRY - J. THOMPSON PSYCHIATRY LIB.
□ Bronx, NY

Davidson, Dr. William D., Sr.Res.Info.Sci.
GENERAL MILLS, INC. - JAMES FORD BELL
TECHNICAL CENTER - TECHNICAL
INFORMATION SERVICES □ Minneapolis, MN

Davies, Denise M., Libn.
UNIVERSITY OF HAWAII - WAIKIKI
AQUARIUM - LIBRARY □ Honolulu, HI

Davies, Dennis B., Chf. Naturalist-Dir.
U.S. NATL. PARK SERVICE - DINOSAUR NATL.
MONUMENT - QUARRY VISITOR CENTER -
LIBRARY† □ Jensen, UT

Davies, Lydia P., Lib.Mgr.
SALOMON BROTHERS - CORPORATE FINANCE
LIBRARY □ New York, NY

Davies, Patty, Ref.Libn.
OREGON HEALTH SCIENCES UNIVERSITY -
LIBRARY □ Portland, OR

Davies, Richard L., Exec.Dir.
SILVER INSTITUTE - LIBRARY □ Washington,
DC

Davies, Steven, Project Dir.
PROJECT FOR PUBLIC SPACES - LIBRARY □
New York, NY

Davies, Thelma S., Spec.Serv.Libn.
FRANCIS BACON FOUNDATION, INC. -
FRANCIS BACON LIBRARY □ Claremont, CA

Davignon, Dr. Jean, Cons.
CLINICAL RESEARCH INSTITUTE OF
MONTREAL - MEDICAL LIBRARY □ Montreal, PQ

d'Avignon, Marguerite-Marie, Bibliotechnician
CANADIAN CENTRE FOR ECUMENISM -
LIBRARY □ Montreal, PQ

Davila, Carmen Alicia, Archv.
PUERTO RICO - INSTITUTE OF PUERTO RICAN
CULTURE - ARCHIVO GENERAL DE PUERTO
RICO □ San Juan, PR

Davila, Valida, Libn.
CHILDHOOD SENSUALITY CIRCLE - LIBRARY □
San Diego, CA

Davini, Thurston, Libn.
UNIVERSITY OF WISCONSIN, MADISON -
SCHOOL OF SOCIAL WORK - VIRGINIA L.
FRANKS MEMORIAL LIBRARY □ Madison, WI

Davis, Alta, Automation Libn.
U.S. NATL. DEFENSE UNIVERSITY - LIBRARY □
Washington, DC

Davis, Alyce L., Sr.Libn.
CALIFORNIA STATE DEPARTMENT OF
TRANSPORTATION - DISTRICT 7 LIBRARY □
Los Angeles, CA

Davis, Anne, Hd., Lrng.Rsrc.Ctr.
STANFORD UNIVERSITY - LANE MEDICAL
LIBRARY □ Stanford, CA

Davis, Anne C., Libn.
UNIVERSITY OF MICHIGAN - MENTAL HEALTH
RESEARCH INSTITUTE - LIBRARY □ Ann Arbor,
MI

Davis, Arthur, III, Data & Anl.Spec.
GREENSBORO PLANNING & COMMUNITY
DEVELOPMENT DEPARTMENT - LIBRARY □
Greensboro, NC

Davis, Barbara, Dept.Hd.
LONG BEACH PUBLIC LIBRARY - PERFORMING
ARTS DEPARTMENT □ Long Beach, CA

Davis, Barbara L., Exec.Sec.
GOLF COURSE SUPERINTENDENTS
ASSOCIATION OF AMERICA - GCSAA LIBRARY
□ Lawrence, KS

Davis, Barbara M., Mgr.
CABOT CORPORATION - TECHNICAL
INFORMATION CENTER □ Billerica, MA

Davis, Becky C., Libn.
TYRE, KAMINS, KATZ & GRANOF - LIBRARY □
Los Angeles, CA

Davis, Benjamin, Supt.
U.S. NATL. PARK SERVICE - CARL SANDBURG
HOME NATL. HISTORIC SITE - MUSEUM/
LIBRARY □ Flat Rock, NC

Davis, Betty L., Libn.
OKLAHOMA VETERANS CENTER - TALIHINA
DIVISION - LIBRARY □ Talihina, OK

Davis, Bill, Media Spec. & Coord.
NEW MEXICO SCHOOL FOR THE VISUALLY
HANDICAPPED - LIBRARY AND MEDIA CENTER
□ Alamogordo, NM

Davis, Bonnie D., Adm.Libn.
U.S. NAVY - NAVAL EXPLOSIVE ORDNANCE
DISPOSAL TECHNOLOGY CENTER - TECHNICAL
LIBRARY □ Indian Head, MD

Davis, Prof. Carlos J.R., Dir.
INTERAMERICAN UNIVERSITY OF PUERTO
RICO - SCHOOL OF LAW - DOMINGO TOLEDO
ALAMO LAW LIBRARY† □ Santurce, PR

Davis, Carol J., Libn.
ALABAMA POWER COMPANY - LIBRARY □
Birmingham, AL

Davis, Carol S., Sr.Cat.Libn.
WEST VIRGINIA UNIVERSITY - LAW LIBRARY
□ Morgantown, WV

Davis, Carolyn, Asst. to Div.Hd.
DALLAS PUBLIC LIBRARY - BUSINESS AND
TECHNOLOGY DIVISION □ Dallas, TX

Davis, Carolyn, Archv./Libn.
WAYNE STATE UNIVERSITY - ARCHIVES OF
LABOR AND URBAN AFFAIRS/UNIVERSITY
ARCHIVES □ Detroit, MI

Davis, Carolyn A., Mss.Libn.
SYRACUSE UNIVERSITY - GEORGE ARENTS
RESEARCH LIBRARY FOR SPECIAL
COLLECTIONS □ Syracuse, NY

Davis, Charlene E., Br.Mgr., Tech.Sup.
KENTUCKY STATE DEPARTMENT FOR
LIBRARIES AND ARCHIVES - STATE LIBRARY
SERVICES DIVISION □ Frankfort, KY

Davis, Charlene F., Lib.Techn.
U.S.D.A. - AGRICULTURAL RESEARCH SERVICE
- STORED-PRODUCT INSECTS RESEARCH &
DEVELOPMENT LAB. - LIB. □ Savannah, GA

Davis, Charles E., Dir. of Libs./Archv.
SOUTHERN MISSIONARY COLLEGE - MC KEE
LIBRARY - SPECIAL COLLECTIONS □
Collegedale, TN

Davis, Chester L., Exec.Sec.
MARK TWAIN RESEARCH FOUNDATION -
LIBRARY □ Perry, MO

Davis, Mrs. Clayla, Lib.Dir.
NAPA VALLEY WINE LIBRARY ASSOCIATION -
LIBRARY □ St. Helena, CA

Davis, Clifton, Libn.
BANGOR THEOLOGICAL SEMINARY - MOULTON
LIBRARY □ Bangor, ME

Davis, Corliss C., Asst.Libn.
AKRON - DEPARTMENT OF PLANNING AND
URBAN DEVELOPMENT - LIBRARY □ Akron, OH

Davis, Cullom, Dir.
SANGAMON STATE UNIVERSITY - ORAL
HISTORY OFFICE - LIBRARY □ Springfield, IL

Davis, Dana, Ref.Libn.
UNIVERSITY OF ARKANSAS AT LITTLE ROCK -
PULASKI COUNTY LAW LIBRARY □ Little Rock,
AR

Davis, David J., Prov.Archv.
NEWFOUNDLAND - PROVINCIAL ARCHIVES OF
NEWFOUNDLAND AND LABRADOR □ St. John's,
NF

Davis, Deborah, Asst.Libn.
JUILLIARD SCHOOL - LILA ACHESON WALLACE
LIBRARY □ New York, NY

Davis, Donna L., Med.Libn.
BAPTIST MEMORIAL HOSPITAL - JOHN L. MC
GEHEE LIBRARY □ Memphis, TN

Davis, Elisabeth B., Libn.
UNIVERSITY OF ILLINOIS - BIOLOGY LIBRARY
□ Urbana, IL

Davis, Elizabeth
HARTFORD PUBLIC LIBRARY - REFERENCE AND
GENERAL READING DEPARTMENT □ Hartford,
CT

Davis, Emma, Circ.Libn.
CENTER FOR RESEARCH LIBRARIES □ Chicago,
IL

Davis, Estelle, Dir. of Lib.Serv.
SHARP MEMORIAL HOSPITAL - HEALTH
SCIENCE LIBRARY □ San Diego, CA

Davis, Esther, Dir. of Lib.Serv.
FIRST BAPTIST CHURCH - I.C. ANDERSON
MEMORIAL LIBRARY & MEDIA CENTER □ Waco,
TX

Davis, Fannie M., Libn.
SUMTER AREA TECHNICAL COLLEGE - LIBRARY
□ Sumter, SC

Davis, Frances F., Libn.
TUSKEGEE INSTITUTE - SCHOOL OF
ENGINEERING LIBRARY □ Tuskegee Institute,
AL

Davis, Gail A., Libn.
YORK COUNTY LAW LIBRARY □ York, PA

Davis, Gentry, Supt.
U.S. NATL. PARK SERVICE - GEORGE
WASHINGTON CARVER NATL. MONUMENT -
LIBRARY □ Diamond, MO

Davis, Gerald F., Lib.Dir.
SPRINGFIELD COLLEGE - BABSON LIBRARY -
SPECIAL COLLECTIONS □ Springfield, MA

Davis, Ida E., Adm.Libn.
U.S. ARMY HOSPITALS - BROOKE ARMY
MEDICAL CENTER - MEDICAL LIBRARY □ Ft.
Sam Houston, TX

Davis, Ilse, Lib.Techn.
UNIVERSITY OF OKLAHOMA - SCHOOL OF
ARCHITECTURE LIBRARY □ Norman, OK

Davis, Jack, Asst.Dir./Tech.Serv.
UNIVERSITY OF CONNECTICUT - INSTITUTE
FOR SOCIAL INQUIRY □ Storrs, CT

Davis, Jacquelyn D., Libn.
DELTA ENGINEERING CORPORATION -
LIBRARY† □ Houston, TX

Davis, James, Rare Bks.Libn.
UNIVERSITY OF CALIFORNIA, LOS ANGELES -
DEPARTMENT OF SPECIAL COLLECTIONS □ Los
Angeles, CA

Davis, Jeffrey, Media Spec.
LUTHERAN THEOLOGICAL SEMINARY - KRAUTH
MEMORIAL LIBRARY □ Philadelphia, PA

Davis, Joan, Rsrcs.Ctr.Mgr.
MURRAY PROPERTIES COMPANY - RESOURCE
CENTER† □ Dallas, TX

Davis, John, Ref.Libn.
UNIVERSITY OF MANITOBA - E.K. WILLIAMS
LAW LIBRARY □ Winnipeg, MB

Davis, John R., Chf., Interp.
U.S. NATL. PARK SERVICE - PETERSBURG
NATL. BATTLEFIELD - LIBRARY □ Petersburg,
VA

Davis, Karen
BURGE SCHOOL OF NURSING - LIBRARY □
Springfield, MO

Davis, Karen A., Med.Libn.
WINONA MEMORIAL HOSPITAL - HEALTH
SCIENCES LIBRARY† □ Indianapolis, IN

Davis, Kathryn E., Selection/Acq.Libn.
U.S. ARMY WAR COLLEGE - LIBRARY □ Carlisle
Barracks, PA

Davis, Dr. Kathy, Coord.
GEORGIA COLLEGE - MEDIA SERVICES □
Milledgeville, GA

Davis, Leslie, Libn.
NEW YORK ASSOCIATION FOR THE BLIND -
LIGHTHOUSE LIBRARY □ New York, NY

Davis, Linda, Asst.Cat.
GEORGETOWN UNIVERSITY - FRED O. DENNIS
LAW LIBRARY □ Washington, DC

Davis, Lulie, Sec.-Libn.
WASHINGTON COUNTY HISTORICAL SOCIETY
- LIBRARY □ Salem, IN

Davis, Lynda C., Chf., Lib.Div.
MARYLAND STATE DEPARTMENT OF
LEGISLATIVE REFERENCE - LIBRARY □
Annapolis, MD

Davis, Lynn, Photo Libn.
BISHOP (Bernice P.) MUSEUM - LIBRARY □
Honolulu, HI

Davis, Margaret, Asst.Libn.
AKRON BEACON JOURNAL - REFERENCE
LIBRARY □ Akron, OH

Davis, Marianne, Chf., Med.Lib.
U.S. VETERANS ADMINISTRATION (CA-Los
Angeles) - WADSWORTH MEDICAL LIBRARY
691W/142D □ Los Angeles, CA

Davis, Martha A., Libn.
U.S. ARMY COMMAND AND GENERAL STAFF
COLLEGE - COMBINED ARMS RESEARCH
LIBRARY □ Ft. Leavenworth, KS

Davis, Mary B., Libn.
HUNTINGTON FREE LIBRARY - MUSEUM OF
THE AMERICAN INDIAN - LIBRARY □ Bronx, NY

Davis, Mary M., Lib.Techn.
PIKES PEAK LIBRARY DISTRICT - LOCAL
HISTORY COLLECTION □ Colorado Springs, CO

Davis, Mary R., Supv.
STEPAN COMPANY - TECHNICAL
INFORMATION CENTER □ Northfield, IL

Davis, Nancy, Dir.
FRANKLIN MINT - INFORMATION RESEARCH
SERVICES □ Franklin Center, PA

Davis, Nancy, Asst.Libn.
UNIVERSITY OF ILLINOIS - AGRICULTURE
LIBRARY □ Urbana, IL

Davis, Nini, Info.Res.
ROGERS CORPORATION - LURIE LIBRARY □
Rogers, CT

Davis, Mrs. Ollye G., Res.Libn.
CLARK COLLEGE - SOUTHERN CENTER FOR
STUDIES IN PUBLIC POLICY - RESEARCH
LIBRARY □ Atlanta, GA

Davis, Phyllis, Libn.
BENDIX CORPORATION - COMMUNICATIONS
DIVISION - ENGINEERING LIBRARY† □
Baltimore, MD

Davis, Robert J., Hist.
INTERNATIONAL SOCIETY FOR
PHILOSOPHICAL ENQUIRY - ARCHIVES □
Belmont, MA

Davis, Robert J., Libn.
SEWARD & KISSEL - LIBRARY □ New York, NY

Davis, Russell L., Dir.
UTAH STATE LIBRARY □ Salt Lake City, UT

Davis, Sally, Libn.
UNIVERSITY OF WISCONSIN, MADISON -
LIBRARY SCHOOL LIBRARY □ Madison, WI

Davis, Samuel A., Spec.Coll.Libn.
JEFFERSON (Thomas) UNIVERSITY - SCOTT
MEMORIAL LIBRARY □ Philadelphia, PA

Davis, Sandra, Mgr., Lib.Serv.
LEEDS AND NORTHRUP COMPANY - TECHNICAL
CENTER LIBRARY □ North Wales, PA

Davis, Sara, Libn.
JACOBS ENGINEERING GROUP - TECHNICAL
INFORMATION SERVICES DEPARTMENT □
Houston, TX

Davis, Sharon, Asst.Dir., Info.Serv.
UNIVERSITY OF COLORADO HEALTH SCIENCES
CENTER - DENISON MEMORIAL LIBRARY† □
Denver, CO

Davis, Susan, Ser.Libn.
ILLINOIS INSTITUTE OF TECHNOLOGY -
INFORMATION AND LIBRARY RESOURCES
CENTER† □ Chicago, IL

Davis, Susan E., Cur. of Mss.
NEW YORK PUBLIC LIBRARY - RARE BOOKS &
MANUSCRIPTS DIVISION - MANUSCRIPTS AND
ARCHIVES COLLECTION □ New York, NY

Davis, Thomas H., Libn.
PLUMAS COUNTY LAW LIBRARY □ Quincy, CA

Davis, Trisha L., Mgr., Tech.Serv.Sect.
OCLC, INC. - LIBRARY □ Dublin, OH

Davis, Virginia, Ref.Libn.
CHICAGO SUN-TIMES - EDITORIAL LIBRARY □
Chicago, IL

Davis, Wendy A., Sr.Libn.
GULF CANADA LIMITED - CENTRAL LIBRARY† □
Toronto, ON

Davis, William J., Exec.Dir.
NORFOLK AND PORTSMOUTH BAR
ASSOCIATION - LAW LIBRARY □ Norfolk, VA

Davis, Wylma J., Ref.Libn.
VIRGINIA MILITARY INSTITUTE - PRESTON
LIBRARY □ Lexington, VA

Davis-Millis, Nina, Libn.
MANHATTAN SCHOOL OF MUSIC - FRANCES
HALL BALLARD LIBRARY† □ New York, NY

Davison, Frieda, Hd., Tech.Serv.
EAST TENNESSEE STATE UNIVERSITY,
QUILLEN-DISHNER COLLEGE OF MEDICINE -
DEPT. OF LEARNING RSRCS. - MEDICAL
LIBRARY† □ Johnson City, TN

Davisson, Lori, Res.Spec.
ARIZONA HISTORICAL SOCIETY - LIBRARY □
Tucson, AZ

Davitt, Theresa B., Libn.
ST. VINCENT HOSPITAL - JOHN J. DUMPHY
MEMORIAL LIBRARY □ Worcester, MA

Davoli, Joyce M., Hd.
BUFFALO & ERIE COUNTY PUBLIC LIBRARY -
BUSINESS AND LABOR DEPARTMENT □ Buffalo,
NY

Davy, Edgar W., Dewey Libn.
MASSACHUSETTS INSTITUTE OF TECHNOLOGY
- DEWEY LIBRARY □ Cambridge, MA

Dawkins, Mrs. B.T., Libn.
RAPIDES GENERAL HOSPITAL - MEDICAL
LIBRARY† □ Alexandria, LA

Dawood, Rosemary, Asst.Chf.
CHICAGO PUBLIC LIBRARY CULTURAL CENTER
- LITERATURE AND LANGUAGE DIVISION □
Chicago, IL

Dawson, Alma, Hd.
LOUISIANA STATE UNIVERSITY - LIBRARY
SCHOOL LIBRARY □ Baton Rouge, LA

Dawson, Barbara, Res.Spec.
VIRGINIA STATE OFFICE OF EMERGENCY &
ENERGY SERVICES - ENERGY INFORMATION
AND SERVICES CENTER □ Richmond, VA

Dawson, Bernice M., Lib.Asst.
UNIVERSITY OF TEXAS, AUSTIN - CLASSICS
LIBRARY □ Austin, TX

Dawson, Jane M., Asst.Libn.
AMERICAN COLLEGE - VANE B. LUCAS
MEMORIAL LIBRARY □ Bryn Mawr, PA

Dawson, Lawrence, Supv., Tech.Info.Ctr.
INSTITUTE OF GAS TECHNOLOGY - TECHNICAL
INFORMATION CENTER □ Chicago, IL

Dawson, Therese F., Supv.
ST. LOUIS PUBLIC LIBRARY - APPLIED
SCIENCE DEPARTMENT □ St. Louis, MO

Dawson, Victoria A., Mgr., Res.Lib.
EDUCATIONAL BROADCASTING CORPORATION
- THIRTEEN RESEARCH LIBRARY □ New York,
NY

Day, Deborah, Archv.
UNIVERSITY OF CALIFORNIA, SAN DIEGO -
SCRIPPS INSTITUTION OF OCEANOGRAPHY
LIBRARY □ La Jolla, CA

Day, Elizabeth H., Med.Libn.
GOOD SAMARITAN HOSPITAL - RICHARD S.
BEINECKE MEDICAL LIBRARY □ West Palm
Beach, FL

Day, Frances Bethea, Mgr., Corp.Lib.
UNITED SERVICES AUTOMOBILE ASSOCIATION
- CORPORATE LIBRARY □ San Antonio, TX

Day, Jane, Hd., Ser.
SUNY AT BUFFALO - HEALTH SCIENCES
LIBRARY □ Buffalo, NY

Day, John, Acq.
GEE & JENSON ENGINEERS, ARCHITECTS,
PLANNERS, INC. - LIBRARY □ West Palm Beach,
FL

Day, Judith D., Asst. Congressional Archv
UNIVERSITY OF OKLAHOMA - WESTERN
HISTORY COLLECTIONS □ Norman, OK

Day, Leslie, Libn.
MUTUAL LIFE ASSURANCE COMPANY OF
CANADA - LIBRARY □ Waterloo, ON

Day, Linda, Adm.Asst.
ALTERNATIVE SOURCES OF ENERGY, INC. -
LIBRARY AND REFERRAL SERVICE □ Milaca, MN

Day, Linda, Libn.
NORTH SHORE MEDICAL CENTER - MEDICAL
LIBRARY □ Miami, FL

Day, Margaret, Info.Spec.
BURROUGHS WELLCOME COMPANY - LIBRARY
□ Research Triangle Park, NC

Day, Mario, Responsable
QUEBEC PROVINCE - MINISTERE DE
L'INDUSTRIE, DU COMMERCE ET DU
TOURISME - BIBLIOTHEQUE MINISTERIELLE □
Quebec, PQ

Day, Melisa, Asst.Dir.
BALL MEMORIAL HOSPITAL - HEALTH SCIENCE
LIBRARY □ Muncie, IN

Day, Ronald, Ref.
UNIVERSITY OF PENNSYLVANIA - BIDDLE LAW
LIBRARY □ Philadelphia, PA

Day, Serenna, Sr.Libn.
LOS ANGELES PUBLIC LIBRARY - CHILDREN'S
LITERATURE DEPARTMENT □ Los Angeles, CA

Day, Susan, Asst.Libn.
ROYAL ROADS MILITARY COLLEGE - LIBRARY†
□ Victoria, BC

Day, Virginia M., Libn.
MASSACHUSETTS VOCATIONAL CURRICULUM
RESOURCE CENTER - MVCRC LIBRARY □
Lexington, MA

Day-Feldman, Sharon, Libn.
ONTARIO - MINISTRY OF THE ATTORNEY
GENERAL - LIBRARY □ Toronto, ON

Daydif, Eloise, Co-Libn.
WAUKEGAN HISTORICAL SOCIETY - JOHN
RAYMOND MEMORIAL LIBRARY □ Waukegan, IL

Dayhoff, Judy, Supv., Info.Serv.
BALL AEROSPACE SYSTEMS DIVISION -
TECHNICAL LIBRARY □ Boulder, CO

Daze, Colleen J., Libn.
SCHENECTADY GAZETTE - LIBRARY □
Schenectady, NY

De Arman, Charles, Supv.Libn.
U.S. NATL. ARCHIVES & RECORDS SERVICE -
NATL. ARCHIVES - MOTION PICTURE, SOUND,
& VIDEO BRANCH □ Washington, DC

De Bear, Estelle, Tech.Serv.Libn.
ST. JOHN'S PROVINCIAL SEMINARY - LIBRARY
□ Plymouth, MI

de Bellefeville, Louise, Tech.Libn.
LA LAURENTIENNE COMPAGNIE
D'ASSURANCES GENERALES - LIBRARY† □
Quebec, PQ

De Bellis, Serena, Cur.
SAN FRANCISCO STATE UNIVERSITY - FRANK
V. DE BELLIS COLLECTION □ San Francisco, CA

de Benko, Dr. Eugene, Hd., Intl.Lib.
MICHIGAN STATE UNIVERSITY -
INTERNATIONAL LIBRARY □ East Lansing, MI

de Bruijn, Elsie, Assoc.Libn.
UNIVERSITY OF BRITISH COLUMBIA -
WOODWARD BIOMEDICAL LIBRARY □
Vancouver, BC

De Camp, S., Prog.Dir.
ACADEMY FOR EDUCATIONAL DEVELOPMENT,
INC. - EDUCATIONAL FACILITIES
LABORATORIES DIVISION - LIBRARY □ New
York, NY

de Costa, Serpil, Asst.Libn.
SONNENSCHEIN CARLIN NATH & ROSENTHAL -
LIBRARY □ Chicago, IL

De Crenascol, Joan, Ref.Libn.
KEAN COLLEGE OF NEW JERSEY - NANCY
THOMPSON LIBRARY† □ Union, NJ

de De Leon, Celia
UNIVERSITY OF PUERTO RICO - NATURAL
SCIENCE LIBRARY □ Rio Piedras, PR

De Fato, Elizabeth, Libn.
SEATTLE ART MUSEUM - LIBRARY □ Seattle, WA

de Forest, Kellam, Dir.
DE FOREST RESEARCH, INC. - LIBRARY □ Hollywood, CA

De Georges, Frank, Libn.
INSTITUTES OF RELIGION AND HEALTH - LIBRARY □ New York, NY

De Grace, Paula, Plan.Off.
CANADA - SECRETARY OF STATE - TRANSLATION BUREAU - DOCUMENTATION DIRECTORATE† □ Ottawa, ON

De Gruson, Eugene H., Spec.Coll.Libn.
PITTSBURG STATE UNIVERSITY - LEONARD H. AXE LIBRARY - SPECIAL COLLECTIONS □ Pittsburg, KS

De Himer, Barbara S., Registrar/Conservator
ROME HISTORICAL SOCIETY - ELAINE & WILLIAM E. SCRIPTURE MEMORIAL LIBRARY □ Rome, NY

de Ingrao, Vivian P. Quiroga, Exec.Dir.
PAN AMERICAN SOCIETY OF NEW ENGLAND - SHATTUCK MEMORIAL LIBRARY □ Brookline, MA

de Jesus, A.M., Libn.
UNION CARBIDE CANADA, LTD. - TECHNICAL CENTRE LIBRARY □ Pointe-Aux-Trembles, PQ

de Jong, N.J., Prov.Archv.
PRINCE EDWARD ISLAND - PUBLIC ARCHIVES □ Charlottetown, PE

De Klerk, Peter, Hd., Theological Div.
CALVIN COLLEGE AND SEMINARY - LIBRARY □ Grand Rapids, MI

de la Cruz, Estrella P., Libn.
NORWEGIAN-AMERICAN HOSPITAL, INC. - SEUFERT MEMORIAL LIBRARY† □ Chicago, IL

de la Haye, Larry, Libn.
VICTORIA CONSERVATORY OF MUSIC - LIBRARY □ Victoria, BC

de la Paz, Salvacion S., Coord., Bibliog.Oper.
SUNY - COLLEGE OF ENVIRONMENTAL SCIENCE AND FORESTRY - F. FRANKLIN MOON LIBRARY □ Syracuse, NY

De La Rosa, Luis, Archv.
PUERTO RICO - INSTITUTE OF PUERTO RICAN CULTURE - ARCHIVO GENERAL DE PUERTO RICO □ San Juan, PR

de la Torre, David, Dev.Dir.
TRITON MUSEUM OF ART - LIBRARY □ Santa Clara, CA

de la Vega, Amalia, ILL Coord.
UNIVERSITY OF MIAMI - SCHOOL OF MEDICINE - LOUIS CALDER MEMORIAL LIBRARY □ Miami, FL

De Laforest, Marcel, Hd., Adm.Br.
SASKATCHEWAN - PROVINCIAL LIBRARY □ Regina, SK

De Las Casas, Prof. Manuel Victor, Dir. & Med.Libn.
GORGAS MEMORIAL LABORATORY OF TROPICAL AND PREVENTIVE MEDICINE, INC. - BIO-MEDICAL RESEARCH LIBRARY □ APO Miami, FL

De Las Casas, Prof. Manuel Victor, Dir. & Med.Libn.
GORGAS MEMORIAL LABORATORY OF TROPICAL AND PREVENTIVE MEDICINE, INC. - VIROLOGY UNIT LIBRARY □ APO Miami, FL

De Leo, Michael
BRONSON (Silas) LIBRARY - BUSINESS, INDUSTRY, AND TECHNOLOGY DEPARTMENT† □ Waterbury, CT

de Liesseline, Elizabeth, Info.Spec.
WESTVACO CORPORATION - INFORMATION SERVICES CENTER □ North Charleston, SC

De Long, Kathleen, Asst.Educ.Libn.
UNIVERSITY OF ALBERTA - H.T. COUTTS LIBRARY □ Edmonton, AB

de Mandy, Claire, Asst.Libn.
NEW-YORK HISTORICAL SOCIETY - LIBRARY □ New York, NY

De Mund, Mary, Lib.Dir.
DENVER MEDICAL LIBRARY □ Denver, CO

De Muro, Linda, Pub.Serv.Libn.
UNITED HOSPITALS MEDICAL CENTER OF NEWARK - LIBRARY/INFORMATION SERVICES □ Newark, NJ

De Narvaez, Martha M., Mss./Rare Bks.Cur.
HISPANIC SOCIETY OF AMERICA - LIBRARY □ New York, NY

De Natale, Rose Marie, Libn.
DMS, INC. - TECHNICAL LIBRARY □ Greenwich, CT

de Onis, Johanna, Ref.Libn.
U.S. NATL. DEFENSE UNIVERSITY - LIBRARY □ Washington, DC

de Piolenc, F. Marc, Archv.
ASSOCIATION OF BALLOON & AIRSHIP CONSTRUCTORS - TECHNICAL LIBRARY □ Rosemead, CA

de Reus, M.J., Res.Libn.
BOARD OF TRADE OF METROPOLITAN TORONTO - RESOURCE CENTRE □ Toronto, ON

De-Rouyn, Solange, Chf.
CENTRE HOSPITALIER ST-JOSEPH - BIBLIOTHEQUE MEDICALE ET ADMINISTRATIVE □ Trois-Rivieres, PQ

de Temple, Jean, Asst.Dir.
OTTAWA PUBLIC LIBRARY - OTTAWA ROOM □ Ottawa, ON

de Tonnancour, P. Roger, Chf.Libn.
GENERAL DYNAMICS CORPORATION - FORT WORTH DIVISION - TECHNICAL LIBRARY □ Fort Worth, TX

De Turk, William, Archv.
GUILD OF CARILLONNEURS IN NORTH AMERICA - ARCHIVES □ Ann Arbor, MI

de Vallet, Christine, Libn.
PAIER COLLEGE OF ART, INC. - LIBRARY □ Hamden, CT

De-Vreeze, Beatrice, Hd.Libn.
NATIONAL THEATRE SCHOOL OF CANADA - THEATRICAL LIBRARY □ Montreal, PQ

De Vries, Eileen, Libn.
CULINARY INSTITUTE OF AMERICA - KATHARINE ANGELL LIBRARY □ Hyde Park, NY

De Wall, Lois T., Res.Asst.
SUFFOLK COUNTY HISTORICAL SOCIETY - LIBRARY □ Riverhead, NY

De Wit, Wim, Cur., Arch.Coll.
CHICAGO HISTORICAL SOCIETY - RESEARCH COLLECTIONS □ Chicago, IL

De Witt, Benjamin L., Mgr., Tech.Info.Serv.
GENERAL CABLE COMPANY - RESEARCH CENTER LIBRARY □ Edison, NJ

de Zengotita, Katherine, Ref.Lib./Cat.
UNIVERSITY OF NEW ENGLAND - COLLEGE OF OSTEOPATHIC MEDICINE - NECOM LIBRARY† □ Biddeford, ME

Deahl, Thomas F., Info.Sys.Engr.
MICRODOC - TECHNICAL DOCUMENTATION COLLECTION □ Philadelphia, PA

Deal, Robin L., Doc. Control Adm.
CHEM-NUCLEAR SYSTEMS, INC. - INFORMATION CENTER □ Columbia, SC

DeAlleaume, William, Hd., Coll.Acq.
NEW YORK STATE LIBRARY □ Albany, NY

Deamer, Debra, Res.
TRENTON TIMES - LIBRARY □ Trenton, NJ

Dean, Barbara, Sec.
FRANKLIN INSTITUTE - LIBRARY □ Philadelphia, PA

Dean, Carole, Asst.Dir./Chf.,Tech.Serv.
U.S. CENTERS FOR DISEASE CONTROL - CDC LIBRARY □ Atlanta, GA

Dean, Dr. Frederick C., Supv.
UNIVERSITY OF ALASKA - WILDLIFE LIBRARY □ Fairbanks, AK

Dean, Grant, Assoc.Libn.
CHICAGO HISTORICAL SOCIETY - RESEARCH COLLECTIONS □ Chicago, IL

Dean, Jenny C.
THATCHER GLASS CORPORATION - RESEARCH CENTER LIBRARY □ Elmira, NY

Dean, Kathryn, Cur. of Mss.
UNIVERSITY OF MANITOBA - ARCHIVES AND SPECIAL COLLECTIONS □ Winnipeg, MB

Dean, Laurie Orr, Hd., Ref.Lib.
BIRMINGHAM NEWS - REFERENCE LIBRARY □ Birmingham, AL

Dean, Lee Ann, Mgr.
MELLON BANK EAST - INFORMATION CENTER □ Philadelphia, PA

Dean, Louise M., Libn.
UNIVERSITY OF MAINE, ORONO - IRA C. DARLING CENTER LIBRARY □ Walpole, ME

Dean, Marilyn C., Mgr.
NATIONAL BROADCASTING COMPANY, INC. - RECORDS ADMINISTRATION INFORMATION AND ARCHIVES □ New York, NY

Dean, Marilyn W., Lib.Supv.
AROOSTOOK MEDICAL CENTER - A.R. GOULD DIVISION - HEALTH SCIENCES LIBRARY □ Presque Isle, ME

Deane, Roxanne, Chf.
DISTRICT OF COLUMBIA PUBLIC LIBRARY - WASHINGTONIANA DIVISION □ Washington, DC

Dearborn, David C., Ref.Libn.
NEW ENGLAND HISTORIC GENEALOGICAL SOCIETY - LIBRARY □ Boston, MA

Dearborn, Josephine, Asst.Libn.
VIRGINIA THEOLOGICAL SEMINARY - BISHOP PAYNE LIBRARY □ Alexandria, VA

Deathe, Frances, Acq.Libn.
OKLAHOMA CITY UNIVERSITY - LAW LIBRARY □ Oklahoma City, OK

Deaven, Barbara E., Med.Libn.
U.S. VETERANS ADMINISTRATION (PA-Lebanon) - MEDICAL CENTER LIBRARY □ Lebanon, PA

Deaver, Sarah, Sch.Libn.
ST. LUKE'S HOSPITAL - SCHOOL OF NURSING LIBRARY □ St. Louis, MO

Deavy, Elizabeth, Hd., Pub.Serv.
NATIONAL LIBRARY OF CANADA - OFFICIAL PUBLICATIONS DIVISION □ Ottawa, ON

DeBardeleben, Julie A., Dir./Info., Res., Pubn.
CLUB MANAGERS ASSOCIATION OF AMERICA - INFORMATION, RESEARCH & STATISTICS DEPARTMENT □ Washington, DC

DeBardeleben, Marian Z., Res.Libn.
PHILIP MORRIS, U.S.A. - RESEARCH CENTER LIBRARY □ Richmond, VA

DeBaun, Robert R., Base Libn.
U.S. AIR FORCE BASE - NORTON BASE LIBRARY □ Norton AFB, CA

DeBell, Jeanne K., Cur.
SOMERS HISTORICAL SOCIETY - ARCHIVES □ Somers, CT

Deberry, Katie W., Libn.
U.S. VETERANS ADMINISTRATION (MO-St. Louis) - HOSPITAL LIBRARY □ St. Louis, MO

DeBois, Mildred, Cat.Libn.
STATE TECHNICAL INSTITUTE AT MEMPHIS - GEORGE E. FREEMAN LIBRARY □ Memphis, TN

DeBolt, Dean, Spec.Coll.Libn.
UNIVERSITY OF WEST FLORIDA - JOHN C. PACE LIBRARY - SPECIAL COLLECTIONS □ Pensacola, FL

Debusman, Paul M., Ref./Ser.Libn.
SOUTHERN BAPTIST THEOLOGICAL SEMINARY - JAMES P. BOYCE CENTENNIAL LIBRARY □ Louisville, KY

DeCamps, Alice L., Hd.
RICHMOND PUBLIC LIBRARY - BUSINESS, SCIENCE & TECHNOLOGY DEPARTMENT □ Richmond, VA

DeCarufel, Gertrude S., Hd.Libn.
QUEBEC PROVINCE - CENTRALE DES BIBLIOTHEQUES - CENTRE DOCUMENTAIRE □ Montreal, PQ

Dechow, Eileen M., Dir.
BUTTERWORTH HOSPITAL - HEALTH SCIENCES LIBRARY □ Grand Rapids, MI

Decker, Debra, Instr.Mtls.Ctr.
CLARION UNIVERSITY OF PENNSYLVANIA -
RENA M. CARLSON LIBRARY □ Clarion, PA
Decker, Joanne, Doc.Coord.
AMERICAN CRITICAL CARE - INFORMATION
CENTER □ McGaw Park, IL
Decker, Leon, Cat.
CATERPILLAR TRACTOR COMPANY -
TECHNICAL INFORMATION CENTER □ Peoria,
IL
Decker, Ronnie, Libn.
KENTUCKY STATE DEPARTMENT OF
ECONOMIC DEVELOPMENT - RESEARCH &
PLANNING DIVISION - LIBRARY □ Frankfort, KY
DeCorso, Deborah, Asst.Libn./Pub.Serv.
SACRED HEART UNIVERSITY - LIBRARY □
Bridgeport, CT
DeCoux, Elizabeth A., Adm.Libn.
U.S. AIR FORCE BASE - KEESLER BASE - MC
BRIDE LIBRARY □ Keesler AFB, MS
Dederen, Louise, Cur., Heritage Rm.
ANDREWS UNIVERSITY - JAMES WHITE
LIBRARY† □ Berrien Springs, MI
Dederick, Donald H., Lib.Dir.
BURLINGTON COUNTY LYCEUM OF HISTORY
AND NATURAL SCIENCE - MOUNT HOLLY
LIBRARY □ Mt. Holly, NJ
Dee, Cheryl, Med.Libn.
WATSON CLINIC - MEDICAL LIBRARY □
Lakeland, FL
Dee, Cheryl, Cons.
WINTER HAVEN HOSPITAL - J.G. CONVERSE
MEMORIAL MEDICAL LIBRARY □ Winter Haven,
FL
Dee, Cheryl R., Med.Libn.
LAKELAND GENERAL HOSPITAL - MEDICAL
LIBRARY □ Lakeland, FL
Deegan, Joyce, Libn.
ROCKWELL INTERNATIONAL - ELECTRONICS
OPERATIONS - DALLAS INFORMATION CENTER
□ Dallas, TX
Deel, D.L., Tech. Applications Anl.
KERR INDUSTRIAL APPLICATIONS CENTER □
Durant, OK
Deering, Dr. Ronald F., Libn.
SOUTHERN BAPTIST THEOLOGICAL SEMINARY
- BILLY GRAHAM ROOM □ Louisville, KY
Deering, Dr. Ronald F., Libn.
SOUTHERN BAPTIST THEOLOGICAL SEMINARY
- JAMES P. BOYCE CENTENNIAL LIBRARY □
Louisville, KY
Dees, Anthony R., Dir.
GEORGIA HISTORICAL SOCIETY - LIBRARY □
Savannah, GA
DeFato, Joan, Plant Sci.Libn.
LOS ANGELES COUNTY DEPARTMENT OF
ARBORETA AND BOTANIC GARDENS - PLANT
SCIENCE LIBRARY □ Arcadia, CA
Degani, Edith, Asst.Libn.
JEWISH THEOLOGICAL SEMINARY OF
AMERICA - LIBRARY □ New York, NY
DeGarmo, Judy, Asst.Cat.Libn.
JOHN MARSHALL LAW SCHOOL - LIBRARY □
Chicago, IL
Degen, Marjorie, Libn.
TUSCARAWAS COUNTY GENEALOGICAL
SOCIETY - LIBRARY □ New Philadelphia, OH
Degenhardt, Judith, Asst.Libn.
LUTHERAN GENERAL HOSPITAL - LIBRARY† □
Park Ridge, IL
DeGeus, Marilyn J., Dir. of Libs.
UNIVERSITY OF HEALTH SCIENCES - LIBRARY
□ Kansas City, MO
DeGolyer, Christine, Chem.Libn.
ROCHESTER INSTITUTE OF TECHNOLOGY -
CHEMISTRY GRADUATE RESEARCH LIBRARY □
Rochester, NY
DeGraff, Kathryn, Spec.Coll.Libn.
DE PAUL UNIVERSITY, LINCOLN PARK CAMPUS
LIBRARY - SPECIAL COLLECTIONS
DEPARTMENT □ Chicago, IL

Dehart, Odell, Cat.
BAKER & BOTTS - LAW LIBRARY† □ Houston,
TX
Dehart, Odell, Tech.Serv.Libn.
FRIED FRANK HARRIS SHRIVER & KAMPELMAN
- LIBRARY □ Washington, DC
Deighton, Anne, Acq.Libn.
LAKEHEAD UNIVERSITY - CHANCELLOR
PATERSON LIBRARY □ Thunder Bay, ON
Deiss, Kathryn, Asst.Musm.Libn.
METROPOLITAN MUSEUM OF ART - THOMAS J.
WATSON LIBRARY □ New York, NY
Deitch, Dora, Libn.
DETROIT PUBLIC LIBRARY - FINE ARTS
DEPARTMENT □ Detroit, MI
Deitlen, Joann, Ser.Libn.
GENERAL ELECTRIC COMPANY - CORPORATE
RESEARCH & DEVELOPMENT - WHITNEY
INFORMATION SERVICES □ Schenectady, NY
DeJarnatt, Jim, Dir.
GEORGIA STATE DEPARTMENT OF EDUCATION
- LIBRARY FOR THE BLIND & PHYSICALLY
HANDICAPPED □ Atlanta, GA
DeJohn, William, Dir.
MINITEX □ Minneapolis, MN
deKalands, Carol, Archv.
SLOAN (Alfred P., Jr.) MUSEUM - MERLE G.
PERRY ARCHIVES □ Flint, MI
Deken, Jean Marie, Archv.
ST. LOUIS MERCANTILE LIBRARY
ASSOCIATION - LIBRARY □ St. Louis, MO
Del Bianco, Lesie, Asst.Libn.
UNIVERSITY OF TORONTO - UNIVERSITY OF
TRINITY COLLEGE - LIBRARY □ Toronto, ON
Del Cont, Mary, Libn.
WEST VIRGINIA STATE LEGISLATIVE
REFERENCE LIBRARY □ Charleston, WV
del Fierro, Julie B., Lib.Serv.Supv.
GTE PRODUCTS CORPORATION - SYLVANIA
SYSTEMS GROUP - WESTERN DIVISION -
TECHNICAL LIBRARY □ Mountain View, CA
Del Piccolo, Alberta, Chartist
BRUNDAGE, STORY & ROSE, INVESTMENT
COUNSEL - LIBRARY □ New York, NY
Del Pilar Barber, Giovanna, Hd.
UNIVERSITY OF PUERTO RICO - NATURAL
SCIENCE LIBRARY □ Rio Piedras, PR
del Rosario, Leticia, Inst.Dir.
PUERTO RICAN CULTURE INSTITUTE - LUIS
MUNOZ RIVERA LIBRARY AND MUSEUM □
Barranquitas, PR
del Valle, C.J.
DOW CHEMICAL COMPANY - TECHNICAL
INFORMATION SERVICES - CHEMICAL
LIBRARY □ Midland, MI
DeLa Pena, Rita, Tech.Asst.
IIT RESEARCH INSTITUTE - COMPUTER
SEARCH CENTER† □ Chicago, IL
Delahanty, Hon. Thomas E., Libn.
ANDROSCOGGIN COUNTY LAW LIBRARY □
Auburn, ME
Delak, Carol, Res.Libn.
CAMPBELL-MITHUN, INC. - INFORMATION
SERVICES □ Minneapolis, MN
Delana, Genevieve, Hd.Libn.
LOYOLA UNIVERSITY OF CHICAGO - JULIA
DEAL LEWIS LIBRARY □ Chicago, IL
Delancett, Jeannine, Res.Libn.
ORLANDO SENTINEL NEWSPAPER - LIBRARY □
Orlando, FL
Delaney, Caldwell, Musm.Dir.
MUSEUMS OF THE CITY OF MOBILE - MUSEUM
REFERENCE LIBRARY □ Mobile, AL
DeLaney, Edith, Libn./Archv.
WHALING MUSEUM SOCIETY, INC. - LIBRARY □
Cold Spring Harbor, NY
Delaney, Edward N., Res.Dir.
NATIONAL TAX EQUALITY ASSOCIATION -
LIBRARY □ Washington, DC
Delaney, Esther J., Libn.
SAFECO INSURANCE COMPANY - LIBRARY □
Seattle, WA

Delaney, Jerry, Hd.
CHICAGO PUBLIC LIBRARY CENTRAL LIBRARY -
GENERAL INFORMATION SERVICES DIV. -
NEWSPAPERS & GEN. PERIODICALS CTR. □
Chicago, IL
Delaney, Linda, ILL
AMOCO PRODUCTION COMPANY
INTERNATIONAL - LIBRARY INFORMATION
CENTER □ Houston, TX
Delaney, Oliver, Legislative Ref.
OKLAHOMA STATE DEPARTMENT OF
LIBRARIES □ Oklahoma City, OK
Delaney, Dr. Robert W., Dir.
FORT LEWIS COLLEGE - CENTER OF
SOUTHWEST STUDIES □ Durango, CO
Delaney, Verlean, Chf.Libn.
U.S. VETERANS ADMINISTRATION (OK-
Oklahoma City) - MEDICAL CENTER LIBRARY □
Oklahoma City, OK
DeLap, James H., Chem. Professor
STETSON UNIVERSITY - CHEMISTRY LIBRARY†
□ De Land, FL
DeLape, Carol, Sr.Sci.Info.Coord.
AMERICAN MC GAW - TECHNICAL
INFORMATION CENTER □ Santa Ana, CA
Delargy, Ann, Asst.Libn.
ROSS ROY, INC. - RESEARCH LIBRARY □
Detroit, MI
DeLargy, Margaret, Assoc.Libn.
DILLON, READ & COMPANY, INC. - LIBRARY □
New York, NY
Delaries, Anita K., Cur. of Archv. & Mss.
EMORY UNIVERSITY - PITTS THEOLOGY
LIBRARY □ Atlanta, GA
DeLashmitt, Eleanor, Ref.Libn.
UNIVERSITY OF TEXAS, AUSTIN - SCHOOL OF
LAW - TARLTON LAW LIBRARY □ Austin, TX
Delbaum, Judith, Libn.
BLUE CROSS OF GREATER PHILADELPHIA - E.A.
VAN STEENWYK MEMORIAL LIBRARY □
Philadelphia, PA
Delbene, Marie, Law Libn.
CONTINENTAL ILLINOIS NATIONAL BANK AND
TRUST COMPANY OF CHICAGO -
INFORMATION SERVICES DIVISION □ Chicago,
IL
Delevich, Mrs. Biljana, Design Libn.
GENERAL MOTORS CORPORATION - DESIGN
STAFF LIBRARY □ Warren, MI
DelFrate, Adelaide A., Hd., Lib.Br.
U.S. NASA - GODDARD SPACE FLIGHT CENTER
- LIBRARY† □ Greenbelt, MD
Delgado, Milton, Ref. & Circ.Libn.
CATHOLIC UNIVERSITY OF PUERTO RICO -
MONSIGNOR JUAN FREMIOT TORRES OLIVER
LAW LIBRARY □ Ponce, PR
DeLille, Carolyn, Libn.
UNIVERSITY OF ARKANSAS, FAYETTEVILLE -
CHEMISTRY LIBRARY □ Fayetteville, AR
Deline, Phyllis, Mgr.
HOFFMANN-LA ROCHE, INC. - SCIENTIFIC
LIBRARY □ Nutley, NJ
Dell, Geraldine, Circ.Libn.
CREIGHTON UNIVERSITY - HEALTH SCIENCES
LIBRARY □ Omaha, NE
della Cava, Olha, Libn.
COLUMBIA UNIVERSITY - LIBRARY SERVICE
LIBRARY □ New York, NY
Dellapa, June, Asst.Hd.Libn.
SAN FRANCISCO CHRONICLE - LIBRARY □ San
Francisco, CA
Dellenbach, Marcia, Comp.Ref.Ctr.Hd.
CHICAGO PUBLIC LIBRARY CENTRAL LIBRARY -
BUSINESS/SCIENCE/TECHNOLOGY DIVISION
□ Chicago, IL
Deller, Howard A., Lit.Anl.
AMERICAN GEOGRAPHICAL SOCIETY
COLLECTION OF THE UNIVERSITY OF
WISCONSIN, MILWAUKEE - GOLDA MEIR
LIBRARY □ Milwaukee, WI
Dellovo, Marie C., Info.Spec.
ARTHUR D. LITTLE, INC. - LIFE SCIENCES
LIBRARY □ Cambridge, MA

Delman, Farrell, Exec.Dir.
TOBACCO MERCHANTS ASSOCIATION OF THE U.S. - HOWARD S. CULLMAN LIBRARY □ New York, NY

Delmont, Mary Karen, Asst. to Dir.
SUNY - COLLEGE AT BUFFALO - EDWARD H. BUTLER LIBRARY □ Buffalo, NY

Delmore, Sr. Elizabeth, Lib.Dir.
COLLEGE OF ST. CATHERINE - SAINT CATHERINE LIBRARY □ St. Paul, MN

Delnay, June, Cat.Libn.
BAPTIST BIBLE COLLEGE OF PENNSYLVANIA - RICHARD J. MURPHY MEMORIAL LIBRARY □ Clarks Summit, PA

Delo, James G., Chf./Med.Libn.
U.S. VETERANS ADMINISTRATION (NJ-Lyons) - HOSPITAL LIBRARY □ Lyons, NJ

Delong, Charles J., Dir.
ALABAMA INSTITUTE FOR THE DEAF AND BLIND - LIBRARY FOR THE BLIND AND PHYSICALLY HANDICAPPED □ Talladega, AL

DeLong, Sharon K., Libn.
TRW, INC. - AIRCRAFT COMPONENTS GROUP LIBRARY □ Cleveland, OH

Delorey, Karen, Ref.Libn.
BENTLEY COLLEGE - SOLOMON R. BAKER LIBRARY □ Waltham, MA

DeLorme, Margaret M., Mgr., Res. & Lib.Serv.
ITT CORPORATION - HEADQUARTERS LIBRARY □ New York, NY

Delozier, Mr. Lynn F., Chf.Libn.
U.S. VETERANS ADMINISTRATION (MD-Perry Point) - HOSPITAL MEDICAL LIBRARY □ Perry Point, MD

Delplace, Nicole
NORWICH-EATON - FILM LIBRARY □ Cambridge, ON

Delsey, Tom, Dir., Cat.
NATIONAL LIBRARY OF CANADA/ BIBLIOTHEQUE NATIONALE DU CANADA □ Ottawa, ON

Deltieure, Henri, Pres.
SOCIETE CULINAIRE PHILANTHROPIQUE DE NEW YORK, INC. - LIBRARY □ New York, NY

Delts, Jean, Cat.
ORAL ROBERTS UNIVERSITY - O.W. COBURN LAW LIBRARY† □ Tulsa, OK

Deluca, Joanne, Libn.
DONALDSON, LUFKIN AND JENRETTE, INC. - PERSHING DIVISION - RESEARCH LIBRARY† □ New York, NY

Delveaux, Alex, Chf., Coll.Org.Sect.
CANADA - PUBLIC ARCHIVES OF CANADA - LIBRARY □ Ottawa, ON

Delvin, Robert C., Fine Arts Libn.
ILLINOIS WESLEYAN UNIVERSITY - THORPE MUSIC LIBRARY □ Bloomington, IL

DeMan, Thomas, O.P., Dir.
ST. THOMAS MORE CENTER - TIMOTHY PARKMAN MEMORIAL LIBRARY □ Tucson, AZ

Demaray, Carolyn, Libn.
SAN DIEGO PUBLIC LIBRARY - SCIENCE & INDUSTRY SECTION □ San Diego, CA

DeMarco, Elizabeth, Libn.
ONONDAGA COUNTY PUBLIC LIBRARY - ART AND MUSIC DEPARTMENT □ Syracuse, NY

DeMaria, Paula, Libn.
BATEMAN EICHLER, HILL RICHARDS, INC. - RESEARCH LIBRARY □ Los Angeles, CA

DeMarrais, Margaret F., Asst.Libn.
HOLY NAME HOSPITAL - MEDICAL LIBRARY □ Teaneck, NJ

DeMarrais, Margaret F., Libn.
PASCACK VALLEY HOSPITAL - DAVID GOLDBERG MEMORIAL MEDICAL LIBRARY† □ Westwood, NJ

DeMars, Tina, Info.Spec.-Bus./Tech.
POLYSAR, LTD. - INFORMATION CENTRE □ Sarnia, ON

DeMayo, Rev. John B., Dir. of Libs.
ST. CHARLES BORROMEO SEMINARY - RYAN MEMORIAL LIBRARY □ Philadelphia, PA

Dembek, Barbara, Libn.
COMBUSTION ENGINEERING, INC. - POWER SYSTEMS GROUP LIBRARY SERVICES† □ Windsor, CT

Demchuk, Maggie, Patient Educ.Libn.
U.S. VETERANS ADMINISTRATION (VA-Hampton) - MEDICAL CENTER LIBRARY □ Hampton, VA

Dement, Alice R., Tech.Serv.Libn.
SAN BERNARDINO COUNTY LAW LIBRARY □ San Bernardino, CA

DeMerritt, Lynne, Libn.
MUNICIPAL RESEARCH AND SERVICES CENTER OF WASHINGTON - LIBRARY □ Seattle, WA

Demers, Philippe, Dir.
JARDIN ZOOLOGIQUE DE QUEBEC - BIBLIOTHEQUE □ Charlesbourg, PQ

d'Emery, Else B., Libn.
U.S. ARMY - LANGUAGE TRAINING FACILITY - LIBRARY □ Ft. Hood, TX

Demick, Susan, Off.Mgr.
SUMMER INSTITUTE OF LINGUISTICS - DALLAS/NORMAN LIBRARY □ Dallas, TX

Demos, Shirley, Dir., Info.Rsrcs.
UNIVERSITY OF LOUISVILLE - URBAN STUDIES CENTER - LIBRARY □ Louisville, KY

DeMoss, Lucille G., Law Libn.
MAHONING LAW LIBRARY □ Youngstown, OH

DeMott, Robert, Res.Ctr.Dir.
SAN JOSE STATE UNIVERSITY - JOHN STEINBECK RESEARCH CENTER □ San Jose, CA

Dempsey, Carol, Ref.Libn.
AMERICAN COUNCIL OF LIFE INSURANCE - LIBRARY □ Washington, DC

Dempsey, Jan B., Ref.Libn.
U.S. NAVY - NAVAL HOSPITAL (CA-San Diego) - THOMPSON MEDICAL LIBRARY □ San Diego, CA

Dempsey, Margaret A., Asst.Archv.
PROTESTANT EPISCOPAL CHURCH - EPISCOPAL DIOCESE OF MASSACHUSETTS - DIOCESAN LIBRARY AND ARCHIVES □ Boston, MA

Dempsey, Margie, Sr.Med.Libn.
BOSTON CITY HOSPITAL - MEDICAL LIBRARY† □ Boston, MA

Dempsey, Robert, Hd., Ser.
MEDICAL LIBRARY CENTER OF NEW YORK† □ New York, NY

DeMuth, Phyllis J., Libn.
ALASKA STATE DIVISION OF STATE LIBRARIES & MUSEUMS - HISTORICAL LIBRARY □ Juneau, AK

Denaro, Mary Rose
GREENWOOD PRESS - LIBRARY □ Westport, CT

Dendy, Adele, Hd.
INDIANA UNIVERSITY - EDUCATION LIBRARY □ Bloomington, IN

Denecke, Mildred F., Mgr.
ENVIRONMENTAL RESEARCH INSTITUTE OF MICHIGAN - INFRARED INFORMATION AND ANALYSIS CENTER (IRIA) □ Ann Arbor, MI

Denert, Gloria, Photograph Libn.
XEROX CORPORATION - XEROX EDUCATION PUBLICATIONS - LIBRARY □ Middletown, CT

Denfeld, Kay, Online Coord.
UNIVERSITY OF WASHINGTON - HEALTH SCIENCES LIBRARY □ Seattle, WA

Dengel, Bette Sue, Law Libn.
BEAVER COUNTY LAW LIBRARY □ Beaver, PA

Dengler, Eartha, Ser.
MERRIMACK VALLEY TEXTILE MUSEUM - LIBRARY □ North Andover, MA

Dengler, Thomas P., Med.Libn.
LOS ANGELES COUNTY/LONG BEACH GENERAL HOSPITAL - MEDICAL LIBRARY □ Long Beach, CA

DeNino, Marie, Asst.Libn.
PENNIE & EDMONDS - LAW LIBRARY □ New York, NY

Denison, Cara Dufour, Cur., Draw./Prints
PIERPONT MORGAN LIBRARY □ New York, NY

Denker, Bert, DAPC Libn.
DU PONT (Henry Francis) WINTERTHUR MUSEUM - LIBRARY □ Winterthur, DE

Denman, Monica, Tech.Libn.
ITT ADVANCED TECHNOLOGY CENTER - LIBRARY □ Shelton, CT

Dennett, Stephen, Sys.Anl.
SRI INTERNATIONAL - LIBRARY AND RESEARCH INFORMATION SERVICES DEPARTMENT □ Menlo Park, CA

Denney, Dorothy, Biomed.Libn.
LAWRENCE BERKELEY LABORATORY - LIBRARY □ Berkeley, CA

Dennhardt, Lauren, Hd.Libn.
AMERICAN CONSERVATORY OF MUSIC - LIBRARY □ Chicago, IL

Denning, Catherine, Cur., Incunabula
BROWN UNIVERSITY - SPECIAL COLLECTIONS □ Providence, RI

Dennis, Anne, Dir., Info.Rsrcs.
FIND/SVP - LIBRARY □ New York, NY

Dennis, Nancy K., Dir. of Lib.
WEST COAST UNIVERSITY - ELCONIN CENTER LIBRARY □ Los Angeles, CA

Dennis, Robert J., Recorded Sound Libn.
HARVARD UNIVERSITY - EDA KUHN LOEB MUSIC LIBRARY □ Cambridge, MA

Dennis, Rodney G., Cur. of Mss.
HARVARD UNIVERSITY - HOUGHTON LIBRARY □ Cambridge, MA

Dennis, Sandra, Mgr., Lib.Serv.
INFORONICS, INC. - TECHNICAL LIBRARY □ Littleton, MA

Dennis, Sharon, Ref.Libn.
COOPER HOSPITAL/UNIVERSITY MEDICAL CENTER - REUBEN L. SHARP HEALTH SCIENCE LIBRARY □ Camden, NJ

Dennison, Jacquelyn H., Coll.Dev.Libn.
MEDICAL COLLEGE OF GEORGIA - LIBRARY □ Augusta, GA

Dennison, Sam, Cur.
FREE LIBRARY OF PHILADELPHIA - EDWIN A. FLEISHER COLLECTION OF ORCHESTRAL MUSIC □ Philadelphia, PA

Denniston, Donna, Asst.Libn.
OKLAHOMA STATE UNIVERSITY - OKLAHOMA CITY BRANCH - TECHNICAL INSTITUTE LIBRARY □ Oklahoma City, OK

Denoon, Anne, Loans Cons.
ART GALLERY OF ONTARIO - EDWARD P. TAYLOR AUDIO-VISUAL CENTRE □ Toronto, ON

Denor, Judy, Libn.
MORAINE PARK TECHNICAL INSTITUTE - LEARNING RESOURCE CENTER □ Fond du Lac, WI

Denson, Janeen, Circ.Libn.
DUKE UNIVERSITY - SCHOOL OF LAW LIBRARY □ Durham, NC

Denton, Leslie, Supv.
INDIANA UNIVERSITY - AFRO-AMERICAN LEARNING RESOURCE CENTER □ Bloomington, IN

Denton, Ramona, Rsrcs.Libn.
DARGAN-CARVER LIBRARY □ Nashville, TN

Denton, Richard, Ser.Libn.
SCHOOL OF THEOLOGY AT CLAREMONT - THEOLOGY LIBRARY □ Claremont, CA

DePasquale, Mary S., Hd.Libn.
MORGAN GUARANTY TRUST COMPANY OF NEW YORK - LIBRARY □ New York, NY

Depatie-Bourassa, Lise, Coord., AV Serv.
BIBLIOTHEQUE DE LA VILLE DE MONTREAL - CINEMATHEQUE □ Montreal, PQ

Depatie-Bourassa, Lise, Coord., AV Serv.
BIBLIOTHEQUE DE LA VILLE DE MONTREAL - SONOTHEQUE □ Montreal, PQ

DePiesse, Larry, Hd.
WICHITA PUBLIC LIBRARY - BUSINESS AND TECHNOLOGY DIVISION □ Wichita, KS

Depke, Robert W., II, Mgr., Info.Serv.
TECHNOMIC INFORMATION SERVICES □ Chicago, IL

DePlaen, Jacqueline, Hd., Doc.
UNIVERSITE DE MONTREAL - CENTRE
INTERNATIONAL DE CRIMINOLOGIE
COMPAREE - DOCUMENTATION CENTRE □
Montreal, PQ

Deplazes, Sister Therese, Spec.Coll.Libn.
SAINT MARY COLLEGE - DE PAUL LIBRARY -
SPECIAL COLLECTIONS CENTER □ Leavenworth,
KS

DePopolo, Margaret, Rotch Libn.
MASSACHUSETTS INSTITUTE OF TECHNOLOGY
- ROTCH LIBRARY OF ARCHITECTURE AND
PLANNING □ Cambridge, MA

DePuy, Rolfe, Hd., Tech.Serv.
SUNY - DOWNSTATE MEDICAL CENTER -
MEDICAL RESEARCH LIBRARY OF BROOKLYN†
□ Brooklyn, NY

Der Manuelian, Dr. Lucy, Board Member
ARMENIAN LIBRARY AND MUSEUM OF
AMERICA □ Belmont, MA

Derbyshire, Joseph J., Libn.
BATES COLLEGE - GEORGE AND HELEN LADD
LIBRARY - SPECIAL COLLECTIONS □ Lewiston,
ME

Derfer, Marian M., Mgr., Info.Serv.
SCM CORPORATION - ORGANIC CHEMICALS
DIVISION - TECHNICAL LIBRARY □ Jacksonville,
FL

Derge, Charlene C., Libn.
U.S. SECURITIES AND EXCHANGE
COMMISSION - LIBRARY □ Washington, DC

Derkach, Mary Ann, Lib.Ck.
OAKITE PRODUCTS INC. - CHEMICAL
RESEARCH LIBRARY □ Berkeley Heights, NJ

Derksen, Charlotte R.M., Libn./Bibliog.
STANFORD UNIVERSITY - BRANNER EARTH
SCIENCES LIBRARY □ Stanford, CA

Derrberry, Donna, Libn.
MARYLAND GENERAL HOSPITAL - SCHOOL OF
NURSING LIBRARY □ Baltimore, MD

Dershem, Larry, Asst.Libn.
SAN DIEGO COUNTY LAW LIBRARY □ San Diego,
CA

Derwart, Margaret Rees, Libn.
HISTORICAL AND GENEALOGICAL SOCIETY OF
INDIANA COUNTY - LIBRARY AND ARCHIVES □
Indiana, PA

Dery, Mary A., Asst.Libn.
HARPER-GRACE HOSPITALS - GRACE
HOSPITAL DIVISION - OSCAR LE SEURE
PROFESSIONAL LIBRARY □ Detroit, MI

des Bordes, Mary S., Cat.
LOYOLA UNIVERSITY (New Orleans) - LAW
LIBRARY □ New Orleans, LA

Des Chene, Dorice, Hd.
UNIVERSITY OF CINCINNATI - OESPER
CHEMISTRY-BIOLOGY LIBRARY □ Cincinnati, OH

Des Lauriers, Don, Cur.
KANKAKEE COUNTY HISTORICAL SOCIETY -
LIBRARY □ Kankakee, IL

Desbarats, Aileen, Hd.
UNIVERSITY OF OTTAWA - MAP LIBRARY □
Ottawa, ON

Deschamps, N., Ref.Libn.
CANADIAN BROADCASTING CORPORATION -
HEAD OFFICE LIBRARY □ Ottawa, ON

Deschatelets, Gilles, Chf., Sci.Coll.
UNIVERSITE LAVAL - BIBLIOTHEQUE □ Ste.
Foy, PQ

Deschenes, J.
CANADA - AGRICULTURE CANADA -
EXPERIMENTAL FARM LIBRARY □ La Pocatiere,
PQ

DeSchryver, Victor, Dir.
UNIVERSITY OF DETROIT - SCHOOL OF
DENTISTRY LIBRARY □ Detroit, MI

Desilets, Andree, Pres.
SOCIETE D'HISTOIRE DES CANTONS DE L'EST
- BIBLIOTHEQUE □ Sherbrooke, PQ

DeSimone, Elizabeth A., Act.Supv.
KNOLLS ATOMIC POWER LABORATORY -
LIBRARIES □ Schenectady, NY

DesJardins, Andrea C., Libn.
ART INSTITUTE OF BOSTON - LIBRARY □
Boston, MA

Deslauriers, Pierre, Dir., Bibliog.Serv.
QUEBEC PROVINCE - BIBLIOTHEQUE
NATIONALE DU QUEBEC □ Montreal, PQ

Desmarais, Charles, Dir.
UNIVERSITY OF CALIFORNIA, RIVERSIDE -
CALIFORNIA MUSEUM OF PHOTOGRAPHY □
Riverside, CA

Desmarais, Christiane, Cartothecaire
INSTITUT NATIONAL DE LA RECHERCHE
SCIENTIFIQUE - CARTOTHEQUE □ Montreal, PQ

Desmarais, Norman, Tech.Serv.Libn.
COMMUNITY COLLEGE OF BALTIMORE -
LIBRARIES/LEARNING RESOURCES CENTERS □
Baltimore, MD

Desmond, Bro. Scott, F.O.C., Libn.
NATIONAL ECUMENICAL COALITION, INC. -
LIBRARY □ Washington, DC

Desoer, J.J., Res.Libn.
CHEVRON RESEARCH COMPANY - TECHNICAL
INFORMATION CENTER □ Richmond, CA

Despres, Kathleen, Med.Libn.
CHICAGO COLLEGE OF OSTEOPATHIC
MEDICINE - ALUMNI MEMORIAL LIBRARY □
Chicago, IL

Desrochers, Edmond E., Dir.
MAISON BELLARMIN LIBRARY □ Montreal, PQ

DesRoches, Amy, Libn.
VIRGINIA STATE TRUCK AND ORNAMENTALS
RESEARCH STATION - LIBRARY □ Virginia
Beach, VA

DesRoches, Richard
PROVIDENCE PUBLIC LIBRARY - ART AND
MUSIC DEPARTMENT □ Providence, RI

Desrosiers, Shirley, Libn.
BRITISH COLUMBIA - MINISTRY OF LANDS,
PARKS AND HOUSING - PARKS LIBRARY □
Victoria, BC

Dessouky, Ibtesam, Libn.
ILLINOIS STATE WATER SURVEY - LIBRARY □
Champaign, IL

Dessy, Blane, Pub.Lib.Cons.
OKLAHOMA STATE DEPARTMENT OF
LIBRARIES □ Oklahoma City, OK

DeStefano, Rita A., Cat.Libn.
ST. CHARLES BORROMEO SEMINARY - RYAN
MEMORIAL LIBRARY □ Philadelphia, PA

D'Estout, Marc, Asst.Dir.
TRITON MUSEUM OF ART - LIBRARY □ Santa
Clara, CA

Detjen, Gustav, Jr., Libn.
SOCIETY OF PHILATICIANS - LIBRARY □ St.
Augustine, FL

Detrich, R.D., Abstractor
MC DONNELL DOUGLAS CORPORATION - MC
DONNELL AIRCRAFT LIBRARY □ St. Louis, MO

Detweiler, Gladys, Libn.
UNION NATIONAL BANK AND TRUST COMPANY
- LIBRARY □ Souderton, PA

Detwiler, Doris, Chf.
DETROIT PUBLIC LIBRARY - LABOR
COLLECTION □ Detroit, MI

Detwiler, Doris, Chf.
DETROIT PUBLIC LIBRARY - SOCIOLOGY AND
ECONOMICS DEPARTMENT □ Detroit, MI

Deuss, Jean, Chf.Libn.
FEDERAL RESERVE BANK OF NEW YORK -
RESEARCH LIBRARY □ New York, NY

Deutch, Morton, Hand Binder
MISSOURI BOTANICAL GARDEN - LIBRARY □
St. Louis, MO

Devaney, James M., Dir.
BULOVA (Joseph) SCHOOL - LIBRARY □
Woodside, Queens, NY

Devault, Lillian A., Sr.Info.Spec.
GOODRICH (B.F.) COMPANY - RESEARCH AND
DEVELOPMENT CENTER - BRECKSVILLE
INFORMATION CENTER □ Brecksville, OH

DeVeaux, Ann, Asst.Libn., Pub.Serv.
UNIVERSITY OF BRIDGEPORT - SCHOOL OF
LAW - LAW LIBRARY □ Bridgeport, CT

Deveny, Dan, Per.
NORTHWESTERN UNIVERSITY - DENTAL
SCHOOL LIBRARY □ Chicago, IL

deVergie, Adrienne, Cat.Libn.
UNIVERSITY OF TEXAS, AUSTIN - SCHOOL OF
LAW - TARLTON LAW LIBRARY □ Austin, TX

DeVierno, Alice, Med.Libn.
PIEDMONT HOSPITAL - SAULS MEMORIAL
LIBRARY □ Atlanta, GA

DeVilbiss, Mary Lee, Spec.Coll.Libn.
CALIFORNIA STATE POLYTECHNIC
UNIVERSITY, POMONA - LIBRARY - SPECIAL
COLLECTIONS □ Pomona, CA

DeVille, Gayle A., Elementary Libn.
KENTUCKY SCHOOL FOR THE DEAF - LEARNING
RESOURCE CENTER □ Danville, KY

DeVillier, Pat, Libn.
SPERRY FLIGHT SYSTEMS - ENGINEERING
LIBRARY □ Phoenix, AZ

DeVilliers, G., Hd., Proc. & Sys.
CANADA - PUBLIC SERVICE COMMISSION -
LIBRARY SERVICES DIVISION □ Ottawa, ON

deVincentis, Sarah, Exec.Dir.
LEKOTEK TOY LIBRARY □ Evanston, IL

Devine, Jane, First Asst.
NEW YORK PUBLIC LIBRARY - MID-
MANHATTAN LIBRARY - LITERATURE AND
LANGUAGE DEPARTMENT □ New York, NY

Devine, Judith W., Supv.
ST. PAUL PUBLIC LIBRARY - REFERENCE ROOM
□ St. Paul, MN

Devine, Maureen W., Res.Libn.
VANCOUVER BOARD OF TRADE - RESOURCE
LIBRARY† □ Vancouver, BC

Devlin, Arlene, Chf., Lib.Serv.
U.S. VETERANS ADMINISTRATION (MI-Allen
Park) - MEDICAL CENTER LIBRARY SERVICE
(142D) □ Allen Park, MI

Devlin, Elizabeth, Asst.Dir./Rd.Serv.
VILLANOVA UNIVERSITY - PULLING LAW
LIBRARY □ Villanova, PA

Devlin, Margaret, Circ.Libn.
JEFFERSON (Thomas) UNIVERSITY - SCOTT
MEMORIAL LIBRARY □ Philadelphia, PA

Devlin-Willis, Mary K., Br.Mgr., Lib.Serv.
PORTLAND GENERAL ELECTRIC - CORPORATE
AND TECHNICAL LIBRARIES □ Portland, OR

DeVoe, Michele, Ref.Libn.
UNIVERSITY OF SOUTHERN CALIFORNIA -
HEALTH SCIENCES CAMPUS - NORRIS
MEDICAL LIBRARY □ Los Angeles, CA

DeVoe, Stanley E., Mgr., Lit.Serv.
AMERICAN CYANAMID COMPANY - LEDERLE
LABORATORIES DIVISION - SUBBAROW
MEMORIAL LIBRARY† □ Pearl River, NY

DeVore, Marynelle, Ref./Govt.Doc.
BRIGHAM YOUNG UNIVERSITY, HAWAII
CAMPUS - JOSEPH F. SMITH LIBRARY AND
MEDIA CENTER - SPECIAL COLLECTION □ Laie,
HI

DeVore, Ralph E., Pub.Rel.Dir.
WESTERN MARYLAND PUBLIC LIBRARIES -
REGIONAL LIBRARY □ Hagerstown, MD

DeVroom, Hendrikus D., Hd.
ORGANIZATION FOR ECONOMIC
COOPERATION AND DEVELOPMENT -
PUBLICATIONS AND INFORMATION CENTER □
Washington, DC

Dew, Roderick, Libn.
COLORADO SPRINGS FINE ARTS CENTER -
REFERENCE LIBRARY AND TAYLOR MUSEUM
LIBRARY □ Colorado Springs, CO

DeWaal, Ronald, Hum.Libn.
COLORADO STATE UNIVERSITY - WILLIAM E.
MORGAN LIBRARY □ Fort Collins, CO

Dewald, Elmer J., Law Libn.
NORTH DAKOTA STATE SUPREME COURT LAW
LIBRARY □ Bismarck, ND

Dewberry, Betty B., Assoc.Libn.
JOHNSON & SWANSON - LIBRARY □ Dallas, TX

DeWeerd, Barbara, Libn.
ST. MICHAEL'S HOSPITAL - HEALTH SCIENCES
LIBRARY □ Stevens Point, WI

Deweese, Charles W.
SOUTHERN BAPTIST CONVENTION - HISTORICAL COMMISSION - SOUTHERN BAPTIST HISTORICAL LIBRARY & ARCHIVES □ Nashville, TN

DeWeese, Sharman, Info.Spec.
HIGH BLOOD PRESSURE INFORMATION CENTER □ Bethesda, MD

Dewey, Cecilia, Info.Spec.
CONFERENCE BOARD, INC. - INFORMATION SERVICE □ New York, NY

Dewitt, Beth, Libn.
RCA CORPORATION - PICTURE TUBE DIVISION - LIBRARY □ Marion, IN

DeWitt, Zona, Libn.
MINNESOTA STATE LEGISLATIVE REFERENCE LIBRARY □ St. Paul, MN

DeWolf, Cheryl, Mgr., Lib.Serv.
CLARKSON GORDON/WOODS GORDON - LIBRARY □ Calgary, AB

Dexter, Joan, Libn.
RAYTHEON COMPANY - EQUIPMENT DIVISION - TECHNICAL INFORMATION CENTER □ Sudbury, MA

Dexter, Martha M., Mgr., Info.Serv.
U.S. OFFICE OF TECHNOLOGY ASSESSMENT - INFORMATION CENTER □ Washington, DC

Dexter, Patrick J., Info.Serv.Supv.
GILLETTE MEDICAL EVALUATION LABORATORIES - INFORMATION CENTER □ Rockville, MD

Deyman, Marie, Asst.Libn.
BUTTERWORTH HOSPITAL - SCHOOL OF NURSING LIBRARY □ Grand Rapids, MI

Deyo, Lisa, Lib.Asst.
GEORGE WASHINGTON UNIVERSITY - MELVIN GELMAN LIBRARY - SINO-SOVIET INFORMATION CENTER □ Washington, DC

DeYoung, Marie, Libn.
NOVA SCOTIA - DEPARTMENT OF LABOUR AND MANPOWER - LIBRARY □ Halifax, NS

Di Cesare, Annmaria, Mgr., Info.Serv.
MAGAZINE PUBLISHERS ASSOCIATION - MAGAZINE INFORMATION CENTER □ New York, NY

Di Cuollo, R.A., Group Supv.
AT & T BELL LABORATORIES & TECHNOLOGIES - LIBRARY □ Allentown, PA

Di Giovanni, Joseph C., Adm.
ROME HISTORICAL SOCIETY - ELAINE & WILLIAM E. SCRIPTURE MEMORIAL LIBRARY □ Rome, NY

Di Giulio, Eva Maria, Libn.
AMAX, INC. - CLIMAX MOLYBDENUM COMPANY OF MICHIGAN - AMAX MATERIALS RESEARCH CENTER □ Ann Arbor, MI

di Lisio, Roch-Josef, Act.Dir.
SACRED HEART UNIVERSITY - LIBRARY □ Bridgeport, CT

Di Martino, Diane, Asst.Chf.
BROOKLYN PUBLIC LIBRARY - SOCIAL SCIENCE AND PHILOSOPHY DIVISION □ Brooklyn, NY

Di Muccio, Mary-Jo, Adm.Libn.
SUNNYVALE PATENT INFORMATION CLEARINGHOUSE □ Sunnyvale, CA

Di Nello, Dr. Mario C., Dir.
TEXAS WOMAN'S UNIVERSITY - CENTER FOR THE STUDY OF LEARNING - LIBRARY □ Denton, TX

Di Roma, Edward, Div.Chf.
NEW YORK PUBLIC LIBRARY - ECONOMIC AND PUBLIC AFFAIRS DIVISION □ New York, NY

Di Salvi, Margaret, Libn.
NEWARK MUSEUM - MUSEUM LIBRARY □ Newark, NJ

Di Trolio, Frank, Coll.
UNIVERSITY OF OTTAWA - MORISSET LIBRARY □ Ottawa, ON

Di Trolio, Trudi, Libn.
CANADIAN DENTAL ASSOCIATION - SYDNEY WOOD BRADLEY MEMORIAL LIBRARY □ Ottawa, ON

Diage, Katherine V., Cur.
UNIVERSITY OF CALIFORNIA, RIVERSIDE - CALIFORNIA MUSEUM OF PHOTOGRAPHY □ Riverside, CA

Diakun, Carol M., Mgr., Tech.Info.Serv.
BANK OF MONTREAL - TECHNICAL INFORMATION CENTRE □ Scarborough, ON

Dial, Zona P., Libn.
AMERICAN COLLEGE OF NATURAL THERAPEUTICS & ARIZONA COLLEGE OF NATUROPATHIC MEDICINE - LIBRARY □ Mesa, AZ

Diamond, Ruth Y., Dir.
TEMPLE UNIVERSITY - HEALTH SCIENCES CENTER - LIBRARY □ Philadelphia, PA

Diamond, Shirley E., Corp.Libn.
DEWEY, BALLANTINE, BUSHBY, PALMER & WOOD - LIBRARY □ New York, NY

Diatchun, Barbara, Ref.Libn.
MATHEMATICAL REVIEWS - LIBRARY □ Ann Arbor, MI

Diaz, Carol, Adm.Asst.
PUBLIC EDUCATION ASSOCIATION - LIBRARY AND ARCHIVES □ New York, NY

Diaz, Norka, Div.Hd.
NEW ORLEANS PUBLIC LIBRARY - FOREIGN LANGUAGE DIVISION □ New Orleans, LA

Diaz, Sylvia, Search Anl.
BOEHRINGER INGELHEIM LTD. - SCIENTIFIC INFORMATION SERVICES □ Ridgefield, CT

DiBartolomeis, Elizabeth, Spec.Coll.Cur.
BABSON COLLEGE - HORN LIBRARY - SPECIAL COLLECTIONS† □ Babson Park, MA

DiBattista, Lori, Asst.Libn.
CITY-TV - CITY PULSE LIBRARY □ Toronto, ON

DiBenedetto, Linda, Supv., Circ.
BOSTON UNIVERSITY - SCIENCE AND ENGINEERING LIBRARY □ Boston, MA

Dibner, Dr. Bern, Dir.
BURNDY LIBRARY □ Norwalk, CT

Dicaire, Raymond, Act.Libn.
UNIVERSITY OF OTTAWA - LAW LIBRARY □ Ottawa, ON

DiCarlo, Rachel, Coord.
INSTITUTE FOR RESPONSIVE EDUCATION - NATIONAL CLEARINGHOUSE ON CITIZEN AND YOUTH PARTICIPATION □ Boston, MA

DiCecco, M. Jane, Law Libn.
DU PONT DE NEMOURS (E.I.) & COMPANY, INC. - LEGAL DEPARTMENT LIBRARY □ Wilmington, DE

Dick, Anne C., Libn.
ST. JOSEPH'S HOSPITAL - HEALTH SCIENCE LIBRARY □ Lowell, MA

Dick, Carol, Libn.
FIRST INTERSTATE BANK - LIBRARY □ Portland, OR

Dick, Daniel, Ref.
WORCESTER STATE COLLEGE - LEARNING RESOURCES CENTER □ Worcester, MA

Dickensheet, Dean, Dir.
SAN FRANCISCO ACADEMY OF COMIC ART - LIBRARY† □ San Francisco, CA

Dickensheet, Shirley, Dir.
SAN FRANCISCO ACADEMY OF COMIC ART - LIBRARY† □ San Francisco, CA

Dickerson, Arlette K., Consrv.
LOUISIANA STATE OFFICE OF THE SECRETARY OF STATE - STATE ARCHIVES AND RECORDS SERVICE - ARCHIVES SECTION □ Baton Rouge, LA

Dickerson, Carol, Ref.Libn.
VANDERBILT UNIVERSITY - JEAN AND ALEXANDER HEARD LIBRARY - WALKER MANAGEMENT LIBRARY □ Nashville, TN

Dickerson, Deborah J., Libn.
WEST VIRGINIA STATE ATTORNEY GENERAL - LAW LIBRARY □ Charleston, WV

Dickerson, Jimmy, Chem.Libn.
UNIVERSITY OF NORTH CAROLINA, CHAPEL HILL - KENAN CHEMISTRY LIBRARY □ Chapel Hill, NC

Dickerson, Mary E., Hd., Info. & Ref.Serv.
ONTARIO - LEGISLATIVE ASSEMBLY - LEGISLATIVE LIBRARY RESEARCH AND INFORMATION SERVICES □ Toronto, ON

Dickey, David, Lib.Dir.
TAYLOR UNIVERSITY - AYRES ALUMNI MEMORIAL LIBRARY - SPECIAL COLLECTIONS □ Upland, IN

Dickey, Dr. David S., Tech.Dir.
CHEMINEER, INC. - LIBRARY □ Dayton, OH

Dickey, Jack W., Libn.
UNIVERSITY OF IOWA - PHYSICS LIBRARY □ Iowa City, IA

Dickey, Jack W., Libn.
UNIVERSITY OF IOWA - ZOOLOGY LIBRARY □ Iowa City, IA

Dickey, Loren L., Libn.
OZARK BIBLE COLLEGE - LIBRARY □ Joplin, MO

Dickey, Neysa, Lead Park Techn.
U.S. NATL. PARK SERVICE - GRANT-KOHRS RANCH NATL. HISTORIC SITE □ Deer Lodge, MT

Dickey, Robert, Asst.Libn.
ARENT, FOX, KINTNER, PLOTKIN & KAHN - LIBRARY† □ Washington, DC

Dickinson, Dan, Med.Libn.
INDIO COMMUNITY HOSPITAL - MEDICAL LIBRARY □ Indio, CA

Dickinson, Fidelia, Coll.Dev.Libn.
SAN DIEGO STATE UNIVERSITY - MALCOLM A. LOVE LIBRARY - SPECIAL COLLECTIONS† □ San Diego, CA

Dickinson, Janet, Asst.Dir., Cat.
ILLINOIS STATE LIBRARY □ Springfield, IL

Dickinson, June M., Pres.
SCHUMANN MEMORIAL FOUNDATION, INC. - LIBRARY □ Livonia, NY

Dickinson, Luren E., Dir.
AMBASSADOR COLLEGE - LIBRARY - SPECIAL COLLECTIONS □ Big Sandy, TX

Dickison, R.R., Chf.Libn.
OAK RIDGE NATIONAL LABORATORY - LIBRARIES† □ Oak Ridge, TN

Dickman, Floyd, Prog.Dev.Supv.
STATE LIBRARY OF OHIO □ Columbus, OH

Dickmeyer, John N., Mgr.
ALLEN COUNTY PUBLIC LIBRARY - BUSINESS AND TECHNOLOGY DEPARTMENT □ Fort Wayne, IN

Dickson, Lance E., Dir.
LOUISIANA STATE UNIVERSITY - LAW LIBRARY □ Baton Rouge, LA

Dickson, Margaret A., Libn. & Chm., Cat.
TEXAS TECH UNIVERSITY - LIBRARY □ Lubbock, TX

Didham, Reginald, Hd.Libn.
BOSTON CONSERVATORY OF MUSIC - ALBERT ALPHIN MUSIC LIBRARY □ Boston, MA

Didier, Elaine K., Ph.D., Dir.
UNIVERSITY OF MICHIGAN - SCHOOL OF EDUCATION & SCHOOL OF LIB. SCI. - INSTR. STRATEGY SERV. □ Ann Arbor, MI

Diehl, David J., Dir. of Lib.
TEXAS STATE TECHNICAL INSTITUTE, HARLINGEN CAMPUS - LIBRARY □ Harlingen, TX

Diehl, John A., Libn.
OHIO COVERED BRIDGE COMMITTEE - LIBRARY □ Cincinnati, OH

Diercks, John, Chm.
HOLLINS COLLEGE - MUSIC DEPARTMENT - ERICH RATH LIBRARY - LISTENING CENTER □ Hollins College, VA

Dieter, Martin L., Info.Sys.Anl.
SANDIA NATIONAL LABORATORIES - TECHNICAL LIBRARY □ Albuquerque, NM

Dieterle, Diane, Dir.
GENEALOGICAL CENTER - LIBRARY □ Atlanta, GA

Dietrich, Bruce L., Dir.
READING PUBLIC MUSEUM AND ART GALLERY - REFERENCE LIBRARY† □ Reading, PA

Dietrich, Bruce L., Dir. of Planetarium
READING SCHOOL DISTRICT PLANETARIUM - LIBRARY □ Reading, PA

Dietrich, Lyn, Libn.
MC LEAN HOSPITAL - MAILMAN RESEARCH
CENTER LIBRARY □ Belmont, MA
Dietrich, Peter James, Assoc.Libn.
CONSOLIDATED EDISON COMPANY OF NEW
YORK, INC. - LIBRARY □ New York, NY
Dietrich, Dr. R. Krystyna, Dir.
DIETRICH COLLECTION □ West Canaan, NH
Dietrich, Sherri S., Tech.Serv.Libn.
GORDON COLLEGE - WINN LIBRARY □ Wenham,
MA
Dietzel, Anita, Lib.Techn.
U.S. AIR FORCE BASE - BARKSDALE BASE
LIBRARY □ Barksdale AFB, LA
Diffendal, Anne P., Mss.Cur.
NEBRASKA STATE HISTORICAL SOCIETY -
ARCHIVES □ Lincoln, NE
Differding, Jane, Ref.Libn.
TANDEM COMPUTERS, INC. - CORPORATE
INFORMATION CENTER □ Cupertino, CA
Diffin, E. Marilyn, Asst.Libn.
CALAIS FREE LIBRARY □ Calais, ME
Diggin, Denise B., Germantown Libn.
U.S. DEPT. OF ENERGY - ENERGY LIBRARY □
Washington, DC
DiGiovanna, Josephine A., Libn.
TOWNLEY & UPDIKE - LAW LIBRARY □ New
York, NY
DiGregorio, Marcia, Dept.Hd.
PROVIDENCE PUBLIC LIBRARY - BUSINESS-
INDUSTRY-SCIENCE DEPARTMENT □
Providence, RI
Dilorio, A.A., Corp.Libn.
CANADIAN PACIFIC, LTD. - CORPORATE
LIBRARY/INFORMATION CENTRE □ Montreal,
PQ
Dilorio, Carla, Libn.
MADISON PUBLIC LIBRARY - LITERATURE AND
SOCIAL SCIENCES □ Madison, WI
Dilgard, David, Lib.Spec.
EVERETT PUBLIC LIBRARY - NORTHWEST
HISTORY COLLECTION □ Everett, WA
Dill, Michele, Ref.Libn.
WESTERN NEW ENGLAND COLLEGE - SCHOOL
OF LAW LIBRARY □ Springfield, MA
Dilley, Rick, Act.Dir.
SOUTHERN ILLINOIS UNIVERSITY - SCHOOL OF
MEDICINE - MEDICAL LIBRARY □ Springfield, IL
Dillibe, Anne, Dir.
CITY OF HOPE NATIONAL MEDICAL CENTER -
GRAFF MEDICAL AND SCIENTIFIC LIBRARY □
Duarte, CA
Dillin, Dorothy B., Libn.
CARNEGIE INSTITUTION OF WASHINGTON -
TERRESTRIAL MAGNETISM DEPARTMENT
LIBRARY □ Washington, DC
Dilling, M.L.
DOW CHEMICAL COMPANY - TECHNICAL
INFORMATION SERVICES - CENTRAL REPORT
INDEX □ Midland, MI
Dillingham, Louise, Assoc.Cur.
TEXARKANA HISTORICAL SOCIETY & MUSEUM
- LIBRARY □ Texarkana, TX
Dillon, Dennis, Map Libn.
UNIVERSITY OF TEXAS, AUSTIN - MAP
COLLECTION □ Austin, TX
Dillon, John H., Mgr.
ADISTRA CORPORATION - R & D LIBRARY □
Plymouth, MI
Dillon, Mary P., Assoc.Dir./Lib.Prog.
UNIVERSITY OF MIAMI - SCHOOL OF
MEDICINE - LOUIS CALDER MEMORIAL
LIBRARY □ Miami, FL
Dillon, Rodney, Res.Hist.
FORT LAUDERDALE HISTORICAL SOCIETY -
LIBRARY & ARCHIVES □ Fort Lauderdale, FL
Dillon, William A., Dir.
JERVIS PUBLIC LIBRARY □ Rome, NY
Dilno, Dennis, Hd.Cat.
PRICE WATERHOUSE - NATIONAL
INFORMATION CENTER □ New York, NY

DiLoreto, Ann, Law Libn.
HERRICK AND SMITH - LAW LIBRARY □ Boston,
MA
Dilworth, Kirby, Libn.
CARNEGIE LIBRARY OF PITTSBURGH - MUSIC
AND ART DEPARTMENT □ Pittsburgh, PA
Dimataris, Mary Kluttz, Tech.Libn.
DRESSER INDUSTRIES, INC. - MAGCOBAR
RESEARCH LIBRARY □ Houston, TX
DiMauro, Paul, Coll.Dev.Libn.
RUSH-PRESBYTERIAN-ST. LUKE'S MEDICAL
CENTER - LIBRARY OF RUSH UNIVERSITY □
Chicago, IL
Dimes-Smith, Judy, Dir.
HOWARD UNIVERSITY - SCHOOL OF LAW -
ALLEN MERCER DANIEL LAW LIBRARY □
Washington, DC
Dimit, Robert L., Dir.
DELAWARE MUSEUM OF NATURAL HISTORY -
LIBRARY □ Greenville, DE
Dimitroff, Lucienne Bloch, Supv.
BLOCH (Ernest) SOCIETY - ARCHIVES □ Gualala,
CA
Dimonski, Susan A., Libn.
CARROLL (John) UNIVERSITY -
SEISMOLOGICAL LIBRARY □ Cleveland, OH
Dimsdale, Mrs. C., Mgr., Strategic Info.
BELL-NORTHERN RESEARCH LTD. -
INFORMATION RESOURCE CENTRE □ Ottawa,
ON
Dimunation, Mark, Lib. for Sys. & Oper.
STANFORD UNIVERSITY - DEPARTMENT OF
SPECIAL COLLECTIONS □ Stanford, CA
Din, Munir U., Med.Libn.
HOSPITAL FOR SPECIAL SURGERY - KIM
BARRETT MEMORIAL LIBRARY □ New York, NY
Ding, Shirley T.L., Libn.
TEMPLE UNIVERSITY HOSPITAL - HEALTH
SCIENCES CENTER - DEPARTMENT OF
DIAGNOSTIC IMAGING - LIBRARY □
Philadelphia, PA
Dingeman, Gaye M., Libn.
SAN DIEGO ECOLOGY CENTER - LIBRARY □ San
Diego, CA
Dingley, Doris A., Ref.Libn.
CONTROL DATA CORPORATION - CORPORATE
LIBRARY □ Minneapolis, MN
Dingman, Nancy R., Chf.Libn.
U.S. VETERANS ADMINISTRATION (MI-
Saginaw) - MEDICAL CENTER LIBRARY □
Saginaw, MI
Dinin, Kenneth, Libn.
METROPOLITAN MUSEUM OF ART - THOMAS J.
WATSON LIBRARY □ New York, NY
Dinkelacker, Mark, Circ.
UNIVERSITY OF CINCINNATI - ROBERT S.
MARX LAW LIBRARY □ Cincinnati, OH
Dinniman, Margo, Sr.Info.Spec.
WESTON (Roy F.), INC. - TECHNICAL
INFORMATION CENTER AND LIBRARY† □ West
Chester, PA
Dinsmore, Marianne S., Libn.
LYMAN ALLYN MUSEUM - LIBRARY □ New
London, CT
Dintrone, Charles, Doc.Libn.
SAN DIEGO STATE UNIVERSITY -
GOVERNMENT PUBLICATIONS DEPARTMENT†
□ San Diego, CA
Dinwiddie, Robert, Archv./Asst.Dir.
GEORGIA STATE UNIVERSITY - SPECIAL
COLLECTIONS DEPARTMENT □ Atlanta, GA
Dion, Chantale
TRANS QUEBEC & MARITIMES INC. - CENTRE
DE DOCUMENTATION □ Montreal, PQ
Dion, Gilles, Chf.
SOCIETE QUEBECOISE D'INITIATIVES
PETROLIERES - DOCUMENTATION CENTRE† □
Ste. Foy, PQ
Dion, Kathleen, Asst. Law Libn.
NEVADA STATE SUPREME COURT - LIBRARY □
Carson City, NV

Dion, Nicole, Dir., Serv.Hosp.
HOPITAL ST-FRANCOIS D'ASSISE -
BIBLIOTHEQUE MEDICALE ET
ADMINISTRATIVE† □ Quebec, PQ
Dion, Pierre, Cat.Libn.
BELL CANADA - INFORMATION RESOURCE
CENTRE □ Montreal, PQ
Dionne, Beatrice, Chf.
CENTRE HOSPITALIER DE L'UNIVERSITE
LAVAL - BIBLIOTHEQUE DES SCIENCES DE LA
SANTE† □ Ste. Foy, PQ
Dionne, JoAnn L., Ref.Libn. & Data Archv.
YALE UNIVERSITY - SOCIAL SCIENCE LIBRARY
□ New Haven, CT
Dionne, Richard J., Libn.
YALE UNIVERSITY - ANTHROPOLOGY LIBRARY
□ New Haven, CT
Dionne, Richard J., Sci.Libn.
YALE UNIVERSITY - KLINE SCIENCE LIBRARY □
New Haven, CT
DiPaolo, Joanna, Internal Coord.
ANTIOCH UNIVERSITY - RESOURCE CENTER □
Philadelphia, PA
DiPiazza, Anna, Chf.
DETROIT PUBLIC LIBRARY - HISTORY AND
TRAVEL DEPARTMENT □ Detroit, MI
DiPietro, Loraine, Dir.
GALLAUDET COLLEGE - NATIONAL
INFORMATION CENTER ON DEAFNESS □
Washington, DC
Dirks, Laura E., Libn.
PILOTS INTERNATIONAL ASSOCIATION -
LIBRARY □ Minneapolis, MN
Dirlam, Dona Mary, Libn.
GEMOLOGICAL INSTITUTE OF AMERICA -
RESEARCH LIBRARY □ Santa Monica, CA
Discavage, Carol Lee, Libn.
MC CARTER & ENGLISH - LAW LIBRARY† □
Newark, NJ
Disinger, John, Assoc.Dir., Env.Educ.
ERIC CLEARINGHOUSE FOR SCIENCE,
MATHEMATICS AND ENVIRONMENTAL
EDUCATION □ Columbus, OH
Disrude, Elizabeth E., Supt.
U.S. NATL. PARK SERVICE - HOPEWELL
VILLAGE NATL. HISTORIC SITE - LIBRARY □
Elverson, PA
Ditchey, Linnea, Mgr.
ALLIED CORPORATION - LIBRARY &
INFORMATION SERVICES □ Morristown, NJ
Ditchie, Carole A., Res.Asst./Libn.
PANNELL KERR FORSTER - MANAGEMENT
ADVISORY SERVICES - LIBRARY □ Chicago, IL
Dittenhoffer, Tony, Ref.Coord.
CANADA - SOLICITOR GENERAL CANADA -
MINISTRY LIBRARY & REFERENCE CENTRE □
Ottawa, ON
Ditterline, Susan Y., Libn./Supv.
BUCKS COUNTY COURIER TIMES - LIBRARY □
Levittown, PA
Divilbiss, D.A., Hd.Libn.
MISSOURI STATE SUPREME COURT LIBRARY □
Jefferson City, MO
Divor, Joan C., Mgr.
CIGNA CORPORATION - PHILADELPHIA
LIBRARY □ Philadelphia, PA
Dixon, Anne
MUNICIPAL ASSOCIATION OF SOUTH
CAROLINA - LIBRARY AND REFERENCE CENTER
□ Columbia, SC
Dixon, Enanu, Ref.
HARVARD UNIVERSITY - HARVARD BUSINESS
SCHOOL - BAKER LIBRARY □ Boston, MA
Dixon, G., Dp. Consul-General/Info.
AUSTRALIAN INFORMATION SERVICE -
REFERENCE LIBRARY/INFORMATION SERVICE
□ New York, NY
Dixon, Margaret, ILL
JACKSON METROPOLITAN LIBRARY -
INFORMATION AND REFERENCE DIVISION □
Jackson, MS

Dixon, Oma, Doc.Libn.
NORLAND CORPORATION - TECHNICAL
LIBRARY □ Fort Atkinson, WI

Dixon, Thomas W., Jr., Pres.
CHESAPEAKE & OHIO HISTORICAL SOCIETY,
INC. - C&O ARCHIVAL COLLECTION □ Newport
News VA

Dixon, Yvette, Assoc.Libn.
MARYLAND STATE DEPARTMENT OF HEALTH &
MENTAL HYGIENE - LIBRARY† □ Baltimore, MD

Doak, Wesley A., State Libn.
OREGON STATE LIBRARY □ Salem, OR

Doares, Wade A., Journalism Libn.
COLUMBIA UNIVERSITY - SULZBERGER
JOURNALISM LIBRARY □ New York, NY

Dobb, Linda S., Tech.Serv.Libn.
U.S. CUSTOMS SERVICE - LIBRARY AND
INFORMATION CENTER □ Washington, DC

Dobbert, Irene A., Corp.Libn.
SENTRY INSURANCE COMPANY - LIBRARY† □
Stevens Point, WI

Dobbins, Nancy, Spec.Actv.Coord.
BAYLOR UNIVERSITY - ARMSTRONG
BROWNING LIBRARY □ Waco, TX

Dobbs, George E., Law Libn.
NEW YORK STATE SUPREME COURT - 2ND
JUDICIAL DISTRICT - LAW LIBRARY □
Brooklyn, NY

Dobbs, Sr. M. Kathryn, C.S.F.N., Dir.
HOLY FAMILY COLLEGE - LIBRARY - SPECIAL
COLLECTIONS □ Philadelphia, PA

Dobi, Ellen K., Chf., Ref. & Circ.
U.S. AIR FORCE - AIR FORCE SYSTEMS
COMMAND - AIR FORCE GEOPHYSICS
LABORATORY - RESEARCH LIBRARY □ Bedford,
MA

Dobkin, Mr. J.B., Spec.Coll.Libn.
UNIVERSITY OF SOUTH FLORIDA - LIBRARY -
SPECIAL COLLECTIONS DEPARTMENT □
Tampa, FL

Dobransky, Joseph T., Libn.
IBM CORPORATION - SYSTEMS TECHNOLOGY
DIVISION - LIBRARY □ Endicott, NY

Dobratz, Amy, Asst.Libn.
DONORS FORUM OF CHICAGO - LIBRARY □
Chicago, IL

Dobrosky, Patricia M., Dir.
U.S. CUSTOMS SERVICE - LIBRARY AND
INFORMATION CENTER □ Washington, DC

Dobson, Christine, Corp.Libn./Archv.
AMERICAN AIRLINES, INC. - CORPORATE
LIBRARY □ Dallas-Fort Worth Airport, TX

Dobson, Dawn, Libn.
CANADIAN LABOUR CONGRESS - LIBRARY □
Ottawa, ON

Dobson, John, Spec.Coll.Libn.
UNIVERSITY OF TENNESSEE - SPECIAL
COLLECTIONS □ Knoxville, TN

Dobson, Nancy H., Libn.
AUSTIN STATE HOSPITAL - STAFF LIBRARY □
Austin, TX

Dockstader, Ray, Dp.Dir.
LIBRARY OF CONGRESS - AMERICAN FOLKLIFE
CENTER □ Washington, DC

Doctoroff, Cynthia, Libn.
MASSACHUSETTS MENTAL HEALTH CENTER -
CHARLES MAC FIE CAMPBELL MEMORIAL
LIBRARY □ Boston, MA

Doctorow, Erica, Hd.
ADELPHI UNIVERSITY - FINE ARTS LIBRARY -
SPECIAL COLLECTIONS - ARCHIVES† □ Garden
City, NY

Dodd, J.L., Supv.
TENNESSEE VALLEY AUTHORITY - MAPS AND
SURVEYS BRANCH - MAP INFORMATION AND
RECORDS UNIT □ Chattanooga, TN

Dodd, James B., Hd., User Serv.Div.
GEORGIA INSTITUTE OF TECHNOLOGY - PRICE
GILBERT MEMORIAL LIBRARY □ Atlanta, GA

Dodd, Jane, Sci.Ref.Libn.
TEXAS A & M UNIVERSITY - REFERENCE
DIVISION □ College Station, TX

Dodd, June, Sec.
LOUISIANA STATE UNIVERSITY - MUSEUM OF
GEOSCIENCE - ARCHAEOLOGY & GEOLOGY
BOOK & REPRINT LIBRARIES □ Baton Rouge, LA

Dodd, Lawrence L., Cur. of Mss. & Spec.Coll.
WHITMAN COLLEGE - EELLS NORTHWEST
COLLECTION AND NORTHWEST ARCHIVES □
Walla Walla, WA

Dodd, Phyllis, Supv.
DENVER PUBLIC SCHOOL DISTRICT 1 -
PROFESSIONAL LIBRARY □ Denver, CO

Dodd, Sue A., Libn.
UNIVERSITY OF NORTH CAROLINA, CHAPEL
HILL - INSTITUTE FOR RESEARCH IN SOCIAL
SCIENCE - DATA LIBRARY □ Chapel Hill, NC

Dodd, Virginia, Asst.
FALCONBRIDGE NICKEL MINES, LTD. -
FALCONBRIDGE INFORMATION CENTRE† □
Toronto, ON

Dodds, Gordon, Chf., Govt.Rec.
MANITOBA - PROVINCIAL ARCHIVES OF
MANITOBA □ Winnipeg, MB

Dodge, Alice C., Libn.
ONEIDA HISTORICAL SOCIETY - LIBRARY □
Utica, NY

Dodge, Major Frank
U.S. AIR FORCE ACADEMY - LAW LIBRARY □
Colorado Springs, CO

Dodge, Nancy L., Libn.
NEW HAMPSHIRE VOCATIONAL-TECHNICAL
COLLEGE - LIBRARY □ Stratham, NH

Dodge, Dr. Robert J., Local Govt.Rec.Spec.
KENT STATE UNIVERSITY - AMERICAN
HISTORY RESEARCH CENTER □ Kent, OH

Dodson, Ann T., Mgr.
OCLC, INC. - LIBRARY □ Dublin, OH

Dodson, Brenda, Libn.
LOWNDES COUNTY LAW LIBRARY □ Columbus,
MS

Dodson, Janelle, Libn.
DALLAS PUBLIC LIBRARY - BUSINESS AND
TECHNOLOGY DIVISION □ Dallas, TX

Dodson, Linda, Libn.
BOOZ, ALLEN & HAMILTON, INC. - LIBRARY □
Bethesda, MD

Dodson, Max G., Circuit Libn.
U.S. COURT OF APPEALS, 5TH CIRCUIT -
LIBRARY □ New Orleans, LA

Dodson, Sherry, Libn.
PROVIDENCE MEDICAL CENTER - HORTON
HEALTH SCIENCES LIBRARY □ Seattle, WA

Dodson, Snowdy, Sci.Ref.Libn.
CALIFORNIA STATE UNIVERSITY,
NORTHRIDGE - LIBRARY - HEALTH SCIENCE
COLLECTION □ Northridge, CA

Dodson, Suzanne, Hd.
UNIVERSITY OF BRITISH COLUMBIA -
GOVERNMENT PUBLICATIONS & MICROFORMS
DIVISIONS □ Vancouver, BC

Dodson, Vivian S., Chf., Lrng.Rsrcs.Div.
U.S. ARMY INFANTRY SCHOOL - DONOVAN
TECHNICAL LIBRARY □ Ft. Benning, GA

Doebel, Dr. Karl, Dir.
CIBA-GEIGY CORPORATION -
PHARMACEUTICALS DIVISION - SCIENTIFIC
INFORMATION CENTER† □ Summit, NJ

Doering, Joyce, Tech.Info.Spec.
ATLANTIC RESEARCH CORPORATION -
TECHNICAL INFORMATION CENTER □
Gainesville, VA

Doerksen, J. Ray, Dir. of Lib.Serv.
FOOTHILLS CHRISTIAN COLLEGE - LIBRARY □
Calgary, AB

Doerr, Dean, Pub.Lib.Cons.
OKLAHOMA STATE DEPARTMENT OF
LIBRARIES □ Oklahoma City, OK

Doerr, Deborah K., Cat.
UNION CARBIDE AGRICULTURAL PRODUCTS
COMPANY, INC. - LIBRARY □ Research Triangle
Park, NC

Doerr, Joan L., Supv.
WESTINGHOUSE ELECTRIC CORPORATION -
DEFENSE & ELECTRONIC CENTER - TECHNICAL
INFORMATION CENTER □ Baltimore, MD

Doesburgh, John P., Med.Libn.
ATLANTIC CITY MEDICAL CENTER - ATLANTIC
CITY DIVISION - HEALTH SCIENCE LIBRARY □
Atlantic City, NJ

Doesburgh, John P., Med.Libn.
ATLANTIC CITY MEDICAL CENTER -
MAINLAND DIVISION - HEALTH SCIENCE
LIBRARY □ Pomona, NJ

Doganges, Jacqueline, Ref.Libn.
U.S. COMMITTEE FOR UNICEF - INFORMATION
CENTER ON CHILDREN'S CULTURES □ New
York, NY

Doherty, Amy S., Univ.Archv.Libn.
SYRACUSE UNIVERSITY - GEORGE ARENTS
RESEARCH LIBRARY FOR SPECIAL
COLLECTIONS □ Syracuse, NY

Doherty, Janet, Libn.
LAKEVILLE HOSPITAL - HEALTH SCIENCES
LIBRARY □ Lakeville, MA

Doherty, Joseph H., Dir.
PROVIDENCE COLLEGE - PHILLIPS MEMORIAL
LIBRARY □ Providence, RI

Doherty, Marianne, Hd.Ref.Libn.
RUSH-PRESBYTERIAN-ST. LUKE'S MEDICAL
CENTER - LIBRARY OF RUSH UNIVERSITY □
Chicago, IL

Doherty, Mary F., Assoc.Musm.Libn.
METROPOLITAN MUSEUM OF ART -
PHOTOGRAPH AND SLIDE LIBRARY □ New York,
NY

Doherty, Patricia, Ref.Libn.
RAYTHEON COMPANY - MISSILE SYSTEMS
DIVISION - BEDFORD LABORATORIES -
TECHNICAL INFORMATION CENTER □ Bedford,
MA

Doherty, R. Austin, Libn.
HOGAN & HARTSON - LIBRARY □ Washington,
DC

Doherty, Mrs. S., Libn.
CANADIAN WOOD COUNCIL - LIBRARY □
Ottawa, ON

Doherty, Walter E., Law Libn.
LEWIS & ROCA - LIBRARY □ Phoenix, AZ

Doidge, Florence, Circ.Libn.
UNIVERSITY OF BRITISH COLUMBIA -
WOODWARD BIOMEDICAL LIBRARY □
Vancouver, BC

Doikos, Helen, Libn.
SCUDDER, STEVENS & CLARK - LIBRARY □
Boston, MA

Dojka, John, Univ.Archv.
YALE UNIVERSITY - MANUSCRIPTS AND
ARCHIVES □ New Haven, CT

Doksansky, Florence Kell, Asst.Univ.Libn.
BROWN UNIVERSITY - SCIENCES LIBRARY □
Providence, RI

Dolan, Eileen, Cat.
SHEARMAN & STERLING - LIBRARY □ New York,
NY

Dolan, Janet, Health Info.Spec.
CLARK COUNTY DISTRICT HEALTH
DEPARTMENT - LIBRARY □ Las Vegas, NV

Dolan, Mary, Res.Info.Spec.
MINNESOTA HOSPITAL ASSOCIATION/
MINNESOTA ASSOCIATION OF HOMES FOR
THE AGING - LIBRARY □ Minneapolis, MN

Dolan, Robert J., Lib./Media Spec.
CONNECTICUT STATE BOARD OF EDUCATION -
J.M. WRIGHT TECHNICAL SCHOOL - LIBRARY □
Stamford, CT

Dolce, Judith, Info.Spec.
JIM WALTER RESEARCH CORPORATION -
LIBRARY □ St. Petersburg, FL

Dolin, Susan, Spec.Coll.Libn.
UNIVERSITY OF NEVADA, LAS VEGAS -
GAMING RESEARCH CENTER □ Las Vegas, NV

Dolinar, Mary M., Asst.Libn.
UNIVERSITY OF PITTSBURGH - CIOCCO
LIBRARY □ Pittsburgh, PA

Doman, Shelley C., Chf., Lib.Serv.
U.S. VETERANS ADMINISTRATION (WV-Beckley) - MEDICAL CENTER LIBRARY □ Beckley, WV

Domanico, Angela, Oper.Supv.
UNIVERSITY OF MARYLAND, COLLEGE PARK - LIBRARIES NONPRINT MEDIA SERVICES □ College Park, MD

Dombrowski, Andrea, Lib. Aide
NORTHWESTERN CONNECTICUT COMMUNITY COLLEGE - LIBRARY □ Winsted, CT

Domenech, H., Archv.
WIDENER UNIVERSITY - WOLFGRAM MEMORIAL LIBRARY □ Chester, PA

Domine, Kay J., Coll.Archv.
COLLEGE OF WILLIAM AND MARY - EARL GREGG SWEM LIBRARY - SPECIAL COLLECTIONS □ Williamsburg, VA

Domingo, Araceli, Coll.Dev.
CORNELL UNIVERSITY - MEDICAL COLLEGE - SAMUEL J. WOOD LIBRARY □ New York, NY

Dominguez, Richard B., Adm. Asst.
U.S. NAVY - SUBMARINE BASE - SUBMARINE FORCE LIBRARY AND MUSEUM □ Groton, CT

Dominianni, Beth, Info.Serv.Cons.
AETNA LIFE & CASUALTY COMPANY - CORPORATE INFORMATION CENTER □ Hartford, CT

Dominic, Sister, Cat.Libn.
ST. THOMAS MORE CENTER - TIMOTHY PARKMAN MEMORIAL LIBRARY □ Tucson, AZ

Domit, Moussa M., Dir.
DIXON GALLERY AND GARDENS - LIBRARY □ Memphis, TN

Donaho, Patricia M., Lib.Supv.
MARYLAND CRIMINAL JUSTICE COORDINATING COUNCIL - LIBRARY □ Towson, MD

Donahue, Harold, Mtls. Clerk
TENNESSEE VALLEY AUTHORITY - CONTRACT SERVICES □ Knoxville, TN

Donahue, Katharine E., Musm.Libn.
LOS ANGELES COUNTY MUSEUM OF NATURAL HISTORY - RESEARCH LIBRARY □ Los Angeles, CA

Donald, Alison, Asst.Libn.
MAIN HURDMAN - LIBRARY □ New York, NY

Donaldson, David, Hd.Libn.
LEGAL AID SOCIETY - LIBRARIES □ New York, NY

Donaldson, Eva, Libn.
WILMINGTON NEWS-JOURNAL COMPANY - LIBRARY □ Wilmington, DE

Donaldson, George, Cur.
TEXAS STATE BUREAU OF ECONOMIC GEOLOGY - WELL SAMPLE AND CORE LIBRARY □ Austin, TX

Donaldson, Judith, Libn.
FINANCIAL EXECUTIVES RESEARCH FOUNDATION - LIBRARY □ Morristown, NJ

Donaldson, Patrica B., Libn.
NEW YORK STATE SUPREME COURT - 5TH JUDICIAL DISTRICT - WATERTOWN LAW LIBRARY □ Watertown, NY

Donati, Robert, Dir., Domestic Oper.
DIALOG INFORMATION SERVICES, INC. □ Palo Alto, CA

Donato, Anne, Cur., Waring Lib.
MEDICAL UNIVERSITY OF SOUTH CAROLINA - LIBRARY □ Charleston, SC

Doncevic, Lois A., Dir. of Lib.Serv.
ALLENTOWN CALL-CHRONICLE - NEWSPAPER LIBRARY □ Allentown, PA

Donegan, Nora, Tech.Serv.Libn.
MERCANTILE LIBRARY ASSOCIATION - MERCANTILE LIBRARY □ New York, NY

Donelson, Frances A., Libn.
BACONE COLLEGE - LIBRARY - SPECIAL COLLECTIONS □ Muskogee, OK

Donen, Jerome S., Dir.
EASTERN WASHINGTON UNIVERSITY - INSTRUCTIONAL MEDIA CENTER □ Cheney, WA

Dong, Betty, Supv., Circ.
ARIZONA STATE UNIVERSITY - DANIEL E. NOBLE SCIENCE AND ENGINEERING LIBRARY □ Tempe, AZ

Donica, Wayne, Congressional Rec.Spec.
UNIVERSITY OF OKLAHOMA - WESTERN HISTORY COLLECTIONS □ Norman, OK

Donini, Elizabeth A., Rsrc.Ctr.Mgr.
AIRCRAFT TECHNICAL PUBLISHERS - RESOURCE CENTER □ Brisbane, CA

Donio, Dorothy, Libn. I
MIAMI-DADE PUBLIC LIBRARY - ART AND MUSIC DIVISION □ Miami, FL

Donio, Thomas, Slide Libn.
PHILADELPHIA MUSEUM OF ART - SLIDE LIBRARY □ Philadelphia, PA

Donkin, Kate, Map Cur.
MC MASTER UNIVERSITY - MAP LIBRARY □ Hamilton, ON

Donna, Jim, Gen. Sales Mgr.
WIDE WORLD PHOTOS, INC. □ New York, NY

Donnell, Dr. H. Denny, Jr., Hist./Libn.
CHRISTMAS SEAL AND CHARITY STAMP SOCIETY - LIBRARY □ Chicago, IL

Donnell, Mary Ann, Libn.
PROVIDENCE HOSPITAL & SCHOOL OF NURSING - PROVIDENCE HEALTH SCIENCE LIBRARY □ Mobile, AL

Donnell, Robert, Hd.
UNIVERSITY OF SOUTH ALABAMA - COLLEGE OF MEDICINE - BIOMEDICAL LIBRARY □ Mobile, AL

Donnelly, A.R., Asst.Libn.
UNIVERSITY OF FLORIDA - LAW LIBRARY □ Gainesville, FL

Donnelly, Celia, Info.Serv.Libn.
CANADIAN NATIONAL RAILWAYS - DECHIEF LIBRARY □ Montreal, PQ

Donnelly, Daniel, Act.Hd.
UNIVERSITY OF MINNESOTA - LEARNING RESOURCES CENTER - NON-PRINT LIBRARY □ Minneapolis, MN

Donnelly, Grace, Adm., Tech.Info.Rsrcs.
GENERAL FOODS CORPORATION - CRANBURY TECHNICAL INFORMATION CENTER □ Cranbury, NJ

Donnelly, Kathleen, Asst.Ref., AV/Govt.Doc.
CASE WESTERN RESERVE UNIVERSITY - LAW SCHOOL LIBRARY† □ Cleveland, OH

Donoho, Thomas A., Dept.Hd.
LOUISVILLE FREE PUBLIC LIBRARY - LIBRARY BROADCASTING† □ Louisville, KY

Donohue, Evelyn, Lib.Techn.
ASHLAND CHEMICAL COMPANY - TECHNICAL INFORMATION CENTER □ Columbus, OH

Donohue, Joyce, Law Libn.
U.S. SOCIAL SECURITY ADMINISTRATION - LIBRARY INFORMATION & GRAPHICS SERVICES BRANCH □ Baltimore, MD

Donovan, Aileen M., Mgr.
SOHIO PETROLEUM COMPANY - CENTRAL LIBRARY AND INFORMATION SERVICES □ San Francisco, CA

Donovan, Ann, Curric.Libn.
CENTRAL WASHINGTON UNIVERSITY - LIBRARY - CURRICULUM LABORATORY □ Ellensburg, WA

Donovan, Catherine N., Sec.
PHOENIX PLANNING DEPARTMENT - LONG RANGE PLANNING DIVISION - LIBRARY □ Phoenix, AZ

Donovan, Elisabeth, Online Res.
MIAMI HERALD - LIBRARY □ Miami, FL

Donovan, James, Libn.
HENRY COUNTY LAW LIBRARY □ Napoleon, OH

Donovan, Joanne, Act.Circ.Libn.
UNIVERSITY OF CALIFORNIA, SAN DIEGO - UNIVERSITY LIBRARIES □ La Jolla, CA

Donovan, Judy
HONEYWELL, INC. - HONEYWELL INFORMATION SYSTEMS - INFORMATION AND LIBRARY SERVICES □ Waltham, MA

Donovan, Kathryn M., Mgr.
PENNWALT CORPORATION - INFORMATION SERVICES DEPARTMENT □ King Of Prussia, PA

Donovan, Mary, Pub.Serv.Libn.
TEACHERS COLLEGE - MILBANK MEMORIAL LIBRARY □ New York, NY

Donovan, Maureen H., Japanese Bibliog./Cat.
OHIO STATE UNIVERSITY - EAST ASIAN COLLECTION □ Columbus, OH

Donovan, Mike, Libn.
CORNELL UNIVERSITY - SANFORD V. LENZ LIBRARY □ New York, NY

Doolen, Richard, Assoc.Libn., Rd.Serv.
CHRISTIAN THEOLOGICAL SEMINARY - LIBRARY □ Indianapolis, IN

Dooley, Cynthia, Libn.
LITERARY AND HISTORICAL SOCIETY OF QUEBEC - LIBRARY† □ Quebec, PQ

Dooling, Marie, Libn.
ROCKEFELLER FOUNDATION - LIBRARY □ New York, NY

Doolittle, Carol, AV Coord.
CORNELL UNIVERSITY - AUDIO-VISUAL RESOURCE CENTER □ Ithaca, NY

Dopp, Bonnie Jo, Rd.Adv.
DISTRICT OF COLUMBIA PUBLIC LIBRARY - MUSIC & RECREATION DIVISION □ Washington, DC

Doran, Christine, Libn.
ARCHIVES OF CALIFORNIA ART □ Oakland, CA

Doran, Doris, Asst./Network Dev.
U.S. VETERANS ADMINISTRATION (DC-Washington) - HEADQUARTERS CENTRAL OFFICE LIBRARY (142D1) □ Washington, DC

Doran, Doris, Asst./Network Dev.
U.S. VETERANS ADMINISTRATION (DC-Washington) - HEADQUARTERS LIBRARY DIVISION (142D) □ Washington, DC

Doran, Jennifer, Libn.
SCIENCE APPLICATIONS, INC. - FOREIGN SYSTEMS RESEARCH CENTER - LIBRARY □ Englewood, CO

Dore, Eleanor, Rd.Adv.
DISTRICT OF COLUMBIA PUBLIC LIBRARY - POPULAR LIBRARY □ Washington, DC

Dorfler, Melayn, Ser.Libn.
CLARION UNIVERSITY OF PENNSYLVANIA - RENA M. CARLSON LIBRARY □ Clarion, PA

Dorfman, Andrew, Act.Libn.
KENTUCKY WESLEYAN COLLEGE - LIBRARY LEARNING CENTER - SPECIAL COLLECTIONS □ Owensboro, KY

Dorfman, Marcia, Asst.Libn.
GOOD SAMARITAN HOSPITAL - SHANK MEMORIAL LIBRARY □ Dayton, OH

Dorham, Barbara, Libn.
BROOKSIDE HOSPITAL - MEDICAL STAFF LIBRARY □ San Pablo, CA

Dorigan, M., Supv.
STANDARD OIL COMPANY OF INDIANA - LIBRARY/INFORMATION CENTER □ Chicago, IL

Dorilag, Lourdes (Ludy), Mgr.
AMDAHL CORPORATION - CORPORATE LIBRARY □ Sunnyvale, CA

Dorman, Janise Paulson, Libn.
UNITED HOSPITAL - LIBRARY □ Grand Forks, ND

Dorman, Kay, Archv.
NEW MEXICO STATE COMMISSION OF PUBLIC RECORDS AND ARCHIVES - ARCHIVAL SERVICES DIVISION □ Santa Fe, NM

Dorman, Phae H., Mgr.
DOW CHEMICAL U.S.A. - BUSINESS INFORMATION CENTER □ Midland, MI

Dorman, Shirley, Lib.Asst.
OHIO UNIVERSITY - MUSIC/DANCE LIBRARY □ Athens, OH

Dorn, ElRene A., Libn.
SOUTH CENTRAL MONTANA REGIONAL MENTAL HEALTH CENTER - LIBRARY □ Billings, MT

Dorn, Georgette M., Spec./Hispanic Culture
LIBRARY OF CONGRESS - HISPANIC DIVISION
□ Washington, DC

Dorner, Steven J., Mgr., Lib.Serv.
AMERICAN GAS ASSOCIATION - LIBRARY □
Arlington, VA

Dornseif, Karen, Libn.
GEORGIA STATE DEPARTMENT OF OFFENDER
REHABILITATION - REFERENCE/RESOURCE
CENTER □ Atlanta, GA

Dorr, Rev. E. John, Libn.
CATHOLIC SEMINARY FOUNDATION OF
INDIANAPOLIS - LIBRARY □ Indianapolis, IN

Dorr, Greg, Tech.Spec.
NOVA UNIVERSITY - LAW LIBRARY □ Fort
Lauderdale, FL

Dorris, Daniel, Chf., Ref.Serv.
U.S. ARMY COMMAND AND GENERAL STAFF
COLLEGE - COMBINED ARMS RESEARCH
LIBRARY □ Ft. Leavenworth, KS

Dorris, Olive A., Asst.Libn.
CENTRAL NEW YORK ACADEMY OF MEDICINE -
LIBRARY □ New Hartford, NY

D'Orsay, Peggy, Tech.Serv.Libn.
TECHNICAL UNIVERSITY OF NOVA SCOTIA -
LIBRARY □ Halifax, NS

Dorsett, Lyle, Cur., Wade Coll.
WHEATON COLLEGE - BUSWELL MEMORIAL
LIBRARY □ Wheaton, IL

Dorsey, Gayle J., Libn./Res.
UNIVERSITY OF NEW HAMPSHIRE - NEW
HAMPSHIRE WATER RESOURCE RESEARCH
CENTER - LIBRARY □ Durham, NH

Dorsey, James C., Chf., Tech.Lib.
U.S. ARMY - CORPS OF ENGINEERS -
SAVANNAH DISTRICT - TECHNICAL LIBRARY □
Savannah, GA

Dorsey, Dr. Learthen, Libn. & Ed.
MICHIGAN STATE UNIVERSITY -
INTERNATIONAL LIBRARY - SAHEL
DOCUMENTATION CENTER □ East Lansing, MI

Dorsey, Margaret, Act.Libn.
HOWARD UNIVERSITY - ARCHITECTURE &
PLANNING LIBRARY □ Washington, DC

Dorst, Thomas S., Asst.Univ.Archv.
NORTHWESTERN UNIVERSITY - ARCHIVES □
Evanston, IL

Dort, Donna, Libn.
PENNSYLVANIA STATE - JOINT STATE
GOVERNMENT COMMISSION - LIBRARY □
Harrisburg, PA

Dort, Frances, Libn.
TEXAS INSTRUMENTS, INC. - NORTH BUILDING
LIBRARY □ Dallas, TX

Dorval, Karen A., Supv./Art Libn.
SPRINGFIELD CITY LIBRARY - FINE ARTS
DEPARTMENT □ Springfield, MA

Dote, Grace, Libn.
UNIVERSITY OF CALIFORNIA, BERKELEY -
GIANNINI FOUNDATION OF AGRICULTURAL
ECONOMICS - RESEARCH LIBRARY □ Berkeley,
CA

Dottavio, Joseph, Asst.Hd., Cat.
NEW YORK UNIVERSITY - SCHOOL OF LAW
LIBRARY □ New York, NY

Dotterrer, Ellen C., Acq.
ROHM & HAAS COMPANY - RESEARCH
DIVISION - INFORMATION SERVICES
DEPARTMENT □ Spring House, PA

Doty, Linda G., Lib.Adm.
INCO UNITED STATES, INC. - LIBRARY □ New
York, NY

Doty, Wendy, Hd.
ENI COMPANIES - INFORMATION CENTER □
Bellevue, WA

Doucet, Yves, Ref.Spec.
ALCAN INTERNATIONAL, LTD. - TECHNICAL
INFORMATION CENTRE □ Jonquiere, PQ

Doucette, Betty, Educ.Ext.Coord.
SASKATCHEWAN - DEPARTMENT OF
ADVANCED EDUCATION AND MANPOWER -
WOMEN'S SERVICES - BRANCH RESOURCE
CENTRE □ Regina, SK

Doucette, Joan, Libn./Archv.
NEW ENGLAND BOARD OF HIGHER EDUCATION
- LIBRARY □ Wenham, MA

Doucette, Ruth, Sr.Libn.
IBM CORPORATION - MANASSAS LIBRARY AND
INFORMATION CENTER □ Manassas, VA

Doucette, Sylvia, Lib.Asst.
CANADIAN OLYMPIC ASSOCIATION -
LIBRARY/INFORMATION SERVICES □ Montreal,
PQ

Doud, Jess, Exec.Dir./Archv.
NAPA COUNTY HISTORICAL SOCIETY -
LIBRARY □ Napa, CA

Doudna, Eileen B., Libn.
ST. JOSEPH HOSPITAL - HOSPITAL LIBRARY □
Lancaster, PA

Dougherty, Celeste, Tech.Serv.Cons.
AETNA LIFE & CASUALTY COMPANY -
CORPORATE INFORMATION CENTER □
Hartford, CT

Dougherty, Dorothy, Ref.Libn.
U.S. SOCIAL SECURITY ADMINISTRATION -
LIBRARY INFORMATION & GRAPHICS
SERVICES BRANCH □ Baltimore, MD

Dougherty, Nancy, Libn.
U.S. VETERANS ADMINISTRATION (TN-Johnson
City) - MEDICAL CENTER LIBRARY □ Mountain
Home, TN

Dougherty, Patricia, Libn./Counselor
ENOCH PRATT FREE LIBRARY - JOB AND
CAREER INFORMATION CENTER □ Baltimore,
MD

Doughtery, Nina, Info.Serv.
UNIVERSITY OF UTAH - SPENCER S. ECCLES
HEALTH SCIENCES LIBRARY □ Salt Lake City,
UT

Doughtie, Susan C., Libn.
ACRES AMERICAN INC. - LIBRARY □ Buffalo,
NY

Doughty, Barbara P., Med.Ref.Libn.
UNIVERSITY OF ALABAMA - COLLEGE OF
COMMUNITY HEALTH SCIENCES - HEALTH
SCIENCES LIBRARY □ University, AL

Doughty, Esther C.D., Libn.
UNIVERSITY OF MINNESOTA - FIRE CENTER □
St. Paul, MN

Douglas, Alan, Cur.
WALKER (Hiram) HISTORICAL MUSEUM -
REFERENCE LIBRARY □ Windsor, ON

Douglas, C. Iona, Libn.
TOUCHE, ROSS AND COMPANY - LIBRARY AND
INFORMATION CENTER □ Vancouver, BC

Douglas, Coreen, Libn.
EDMONTON CITY PLANNING DEPARTMENT -
LIBRARY/RESOURCE CENTRE □ Edmonton, AB

Douglas, F. Samuel, Libn.
FASHION INSTITUTE OF DESIGN &
MERCHANDISING - LIBRARY □ San Francisco,
CA

Douglas, Joel M., Dir.
NATIONAL CENTER FOR THE STUDY OF
COLLECTIVE BARGAINING IN HIGHER
EDUCATION AND THE PROFESSIONS □ New
York, NY

Douglas, Kimberly, Dir.
HANCOCK (Allan) FOUNDATION - HANCOCK
LIBRARY OF BIOLOGY & OCEANOGRAPHY □ Los
Angeles, CA

Douglas, Meredith, Libn.
KNOX COUNTY GOVERNMENTAL LIBRARY □
Knoxville, TN

Douglas, Peter, Asst.Libn.
NEW YORK STATE LIBRARY FOR THE BLIND
AND VISUALLY HANDICAPPED □ Albany, NY

Douglas, Dr. W.A.B., Dir.
CANADA - NATIONAL DEFENCE -
DIRECTORATE OF HISTORY LIBRARY □ Ottawa,
ON

Douglas-Hamilton, Lady Malcolm, Pres.
AMERICAN-SCOTTISH FOUNDATION, INC. -
SCOTTISH RESEARCH LIBRARY □ New York, NY

Douglass, Elizabeth, Exec.Dir.
ASSOCIATION FOR GERONTOLOGY IN HIGHER
EDUCATION - RESOURCE LIBRARY □
Washington, DC

Douglass, Larry, Musm.Dir.
BRIGHAM CITY MUSEUM-GALLERY -
RENTMEISTER WESTERN AMERICANA
LIBRARY □ Brigham City, UT

Douglass, Ms. Leslie, Asst.Libn.
ETHICON, INC. - SCIENTIFIC INFORMATION
SERVICES □ Somerville, NJ

Douglass, Rebecca, Dir.
SANGAMON STATE UNIVERSITY - EAST
CENTRAL NETWORK - LIBRARY □ Springfield, IL

Douglass, William A., Coord.
UNIVERSITY OF NEVADA, RENO - BASQUE
STUDIES PROGRAM □ Reno, NV

Doumato, Lamia, Ref.Libn.
NATIONAL GALLERY OF ART - LIBRARY □
Washington, DC

Douthit, Carl A., Libn.
BOISE BIBLE COLLEGE - LIBRARY □ Boise, ID

Doutrelepont, Jean Francois, Dir.
FONDATION QUEBECOISE D'EDUCATION
ECONOMIQUE - CENTRE D'INFORMATION SUR
LES RESSOURCES EN EDUCATION
ECONOMIQUE □ Montreal, PQ

Douville, Judith A., Info.Sci. & Mgr.
TRC ENVIRONMENTAL CONSULTANTS, INC. -
LIBRARY □ East Hartford, CT

Dove, Janet Hill, Dir.
UNIVERSITY OF DELAWARE, NEWARK -
EDUCATION RESOURCE CENTER □ Newark, DE

Dove, Louise E., Wildlife Biologist
NATIONAL INSTITUTE FOR URBAN WILDLIFE -
LIBRARY □ Columbia, MD

Dow, Prof. Maynard Weston, Dir.
PLYMOUTH STATE COLLEGE - GEOGRAPHERS
ON FILM COLLECTION □ Plymouth, NH

Dow, Ronald F., Mgr., Lib.Serv.
SHEARSON LEHMAN/AMERICAN EXPRESS INC.
- LIBRARY □ New York, NY

Dow, Sandra C., Ref.Libn.
UNIVERSITY OF MICHIGAN - ALFRED
TAUBMAN MEDICAL LIBRARY □ Ann Arbor, MI

Dow, Susan, Pub.Serv.Libn.
URBAN INSTITUTE - LIBRARY □ Washington,
DC

Dow, Victoria, Asst.Ref.Libn.
LEHIGH UNIVERSITY - MART SCIENCE AND
ENGINEERING LIBRARY □ Bethlehem, PA

Dowd, Cherie Montonyx, Cur.
COLE COUNTY HISTORICAL SOCIETY -
MUSEUM AND LIBRARY □ Jefferson City, MO

Dowd, Judith A., Dept.Hd.
KAISER-PERMANENTE MEDICAL CENTER -
KAISER FOUNDATION HOSPITAL MEDICAL
LIBRARY □ Los Angeles, CA

Dowd, W. Timothy, Exec.Dir.
INTERSTATE OIL AND GAS COMPACT
COMMISSION - LIBRARY □ Oklahoma City, OK

Dowdell, Marlene S., Dept.Hd., Data Mgt.
TELEDYNE CAE CORPORATION - ENGINEERING
LIBRARY □ Toledo, OH

Dowdy, Mrs. Rae, Med. Staff Coord.
MEDICAL CENTER HOSPITAL - BELL-MARSH
MEMORIAL LIBRARY □ Tyler, TX

Dowell, David R., Dir.
ILLINOIS INSTITUTE OF TECHNOLOGY -
INFORMATION AND LIBRARY RESOURCES
CENTER† □ Chicago, IL

Dowell, Gail E., Cat. & Music Libn.
HUDSON LIBRARY AND HISTORICAL SOCIETY □
Hudson, OH

Dowell, Mary Evelyn, Dir., Med.Lib.
SINGING RIVER HOSPITAL - MEDICAL LIBRARY
□ Pascagoula, MS

Dowell, Wanda S., Cur.
FORT WARD MUSEUM - DOROTHY C.S. STARR
CIVIL WAR RESEARCH LIBRARY □ Alexandria,
VA

Dowgray, John, Dir.
UNIVERSITY OF TULSA - DIVISION OF
INFORMATION SERVICES □ Tulsa, OK
Dowie, Eve, Hd., Lib.Serv.
CANADA CENTRE FOR INLAND WATERS -
LIBRARY† □ Burlington, ON
Dowler, Lawrence R., Assoc.Libn.
HARVARD UNIVERSITY - HOUGHTON LIBRARY
□ Cambridge, MA
Dowling, Jo A., Ref.Libn.
FLORIDA STATE SUPREME COURT LIBRARY □
Tallahassee, FL
Dowling, Karen, Curric.Libn.
MONTGOMERY COUNTY PUBLIC SCHOOLS -
PROFESSIONAL LIBRARY □ Rockville, MD
Dowling, Kathleen, Ref.Supv.
BATTEN, BARTON, DURSTINE, OSBORN, INC. -
INFORMATION RETRIEVAL CENTER† □ New
York, NY
Dowling, Shelley, Hd., Ref.Dept.
GEORGETOWN UNIVERSITY - FRED O. DENNIS
LAW LIBRARY □ Washington, DC
Dowling, Shelley, Asst.Libn.
UNIVERSITY OF MISSOURI, KANSAS CITY -
LAW LIBRARY □ Kansas City, MO
Downen, Madeline E., Dir., Lib.Serv.
ST. CATHERINE HOSPITAL - MC GUIRE
MEMORIAL LIBRARY □ East Chicago, IN
Downey, Barbara, Asst.Libn.
BAYLOR UNIVERSITY, DALLAS - LIBRARY □
Dallas, TX
Downey, Bernard F., Libn.
RUTGERS UNIVERSITY, THE STATE
UNIVERSITY OF NEW JERSEY - INSTITUTE OF
MANAGEMENT/LABOR RELATIONS LIBRARY □
New Brunswick, NJ
Downey, Marcese W., Libn.
AUGUSTINIAN HISTORICAL INSTITUTE -
LIBRARY □ Villanova, PA
Downey, Myrna, Libn.
HARDWOOD PLYWOOD MANUFACTURERS
ASSOCIATION - LIBRARY □ Reston, VA
Downie, Margaret, Assoc.Cur.
SHRINE TO MUSIC MUSEUM □ Vermillion, SD
Downing, Anthea, Chf.Libn.
ROYAL BANK OF CANADA - INFORMATION
RESOURCES □ Montreal, PQ
Downing, Bernas, Supv., Lit.Serv.
ELI LILLY AND COMPANY - GREENFIELD
LABORATORIES - LIBRARY AGRICULTURAL
SERVICE □ Greenfield, IN
Downing, Fran Braden, Libn.
AMERICAN CONTRACT BRIDGE LEAGUE -
ALBERT H. MOREHEAD MEMORIAL LIBRARY □
Memphis, TN
Downing, Jeannette D., Libn.
NEW ORLEANS MUSEUM OF ART - FELIX J.
DREYOUS LIBRARY □ New Orleans, LA
Downing, Virginia, State Libn.
NEW MEXICO STATE LEGISLATIVE COUNCIL
SERVICE - LIBRARY □ Santa Fe, NM
Downing, Virginia, State Libn.
NEW MEXICO STATE LIBRARY □ Santa Fe, NM
Downs, Judy, Campus Libn.
CENTENNIAL COLLEGE OF APPLIED ARTS &
TECHNOLOGY - PROGRESS CAMPUS RESOURCE
CENTRE □ Scarborough, ON
Doxtader, Judith, Libn.
LONG ISLAND UNIVERSITY - C.W. POST
CAMPUS - CENTER FOR BUSINESS RESEARCH □
Greenvale, NY
Doyle, Ann, Sys. & Circ.Libn.
RYERSON POLYTECHNICAL INSTITUTE -
LEARNING RESOURCES CENTRE □ Toronto, ON
Doyle, Ann C., Asst.Libn.
PRINCETON UNIVERSITY - ENGINEERING
LIBRARY □ Princeton, NJ
Doyle, Dennis, Planner
ULSTER COUNTY PLANNING BOARD - LIBRARY
□ Kingston, NY

Doyle, Frances M., Supv.Libn.
U.S. ARMY - HEADQUARTERS TRADOC/FORT
MONROE LIBRARY & INTERN TRAINING
CENTER □ Ft. Monroe, VA
Doyle, Francis R., Law Libn.
LOYOLA UNIVERSITY OF CHICAGO - LAW
LIBRARY □ Chicago, IL
Doyle, Jacqueline D., Dir.
GOOD SAMARITAN MEDICAL CENTER - HEALTH
SCIENCE LIBRARY □ Phoenix, AZ
Doyle, Bro. James J., Libn.
ST. ANTHONY-ON-HUDSON THEOLOGICAL
LIBRARY □ Rensselaer, NY
Doyle, Jim L., Bus.Libn.
HIGHTOWER (Sara) REGIONAL LIBRARY -
BUSINESS LIBRARY† □ Rome, GA
Doyle, John, Rd.Serv.Libn.
COOLEY (Thomas M.) LAW SCHOOL - LIBRARY □
Lansing, MI
Doyle, John T., Libn.
ALTOONA MIRROR - LIBRARY □ Altoona, PA
Doyle, Judith L., Ref.Libn.
JOHNS HOPKINS UNIVERSITY - SCHOOL OF
HYGIENE AND PUBLIC HEALTH -
INTERDEPARTMENTAL LIBRARY □ Baltimore,
MD
Doyle, Kathryn, Asst.Libn.
ST. LUKE'S HOSPITAL OF KANSAS CITY -
MEDICAL LIBRARY □ Kansas City, MO
Doyle, M. Bridget, Med.Libn.
HEPBURN (A. Barton) HOSPITAL - MEDICAL
LIBRARY† □ Ogdensburg, NY
Doyle, Marjorie, Asst.Libn.
PRESTON, THORGRIMSON, ELLIS & HOLMAN -
LIBRARY □ Seattle, WA
Doyle, Pat, Tech.Libn.
COMINCO LTD. - PRODUCT RESEARCH CENTRE
LIBRARY □ Mississauga, ON
Doyle, Patricia C., Adm.Libn.
U.S. NAVY - NAVAL AIR STATION (FL-
Jacksonville) - LIBRARY □ Jacksonville, FL
Drachkovitch, Milorad M., Archv.
STANFORD UNIVERSITY - HOOVER
INSTITUTION ON WAR, REVOLUTION AND
PEACE - LIBRARY □ Stanford, CA
Draganski, Donald, Libn.
ROOSEVELT UNIVERSITY - MUSIC LIBRARY □
Chicago, IL
Dragasevich, Diane, Libn./Supv.
NORTH YORK PUBLIC LIBRARY -
MULTILINGUAL MATERIALS DEPARTMENT □
North York, ON
Draghi, Prof. Paul, Asst.Dir.
INDIANA UNIVERSITY - RESEARCH INSTITUTE
FOR INNER ASIAN STUDIES - LIBRARY □
Bloomington, IN
Drago, Linda, Assoc. Law Libn.
UNIVERSITY OF PITTSBURGH - LAW LIBRARY □
Pittsburgh, PA
Dragotta, L., Supv., Lib.Serv.
AIR PRODUCTS AND CHEMICALS, INC. - CRSD
INFORMATION SERVICES □ Allentown, PA
Drake, Alicia Sabatine, Tech.Libn.
UNIVERSITY OF SOUTHERN CALIFORNIA -
INFORMATION SCIENCES INSTITUTE -
LIBRARY □ Marina Del Rey, CA
Drake, Betty, Libn.
UNIVERSITY OF SOUTHERN MISSISSIPPI - MC
CAIN LIBRARY □ Hattiesburg, MS
Drake, Frank, Info.Spec.
TELEMEDIA, INC. - INFORMATION CENTER □
Chicago, IL
Drake, Fr. Harold, Hd.
UNIVERSITY OF MANITOBA - ST. PAUL'S
COLLEGE - LIBRARY □ Winnipeg, MB
Drake, Jim, Libn.
REED INC. - R&D LIBRARY □ Quebec, PQ
Drake, Jim, Info.Spec.
REED INC. - TECHNICAL INFORMATION
CENTRE □ Toronto, ON

Drake, Mr. Mayo, Libn.
LOUISIANA STATE UNIVERSITY MEDICAL
CENTER - SCHOOL OF MEDICINE IN
SHREVEPORT - LIBRARY □ Shreveport, LA
Drake, Randel Dean, Kpr./Ephemera
ARCANE ORDER - LIBRARY □ Falls Church, VA
Dralle, Dorothy, Libn.
ELLIS HOSPITAL - MAC MILLAN LIBRARY □
Schenectady, NY
Drancsak, Marina, Tech.Info.Spec.
U.S. DEPT. OF TRANSPORTATION - URBAN
MASS TRANSPORTATION ADM. -
TRANSPORTATION RESEARCH INFO. CENTER
(TRIC) □ Washington, DC
Drapeau, Micheline, Dir.
UNIVERSITE DU QUEBEC A MONTREAL -
BIBLIOTHEQUES DES SCIENCES JURIDIQUES □
Montreal, PQ
Draper, Jan, Law Libn.
LEWIS COUNTY LAW LIBRARY □ Chehalis, WA
Draper, Linda, Hd., Tech.Serv.
INTERNATIONAL LIBRARY, ARCHIVES &
MUSEUM OF OPTOMETRY □ St. Louis, MO
Draper, Rosalie S., Ck.
BETHANY COLLEGE - CHEMISTRY LIBRARY □
Bethany, WV
Draper, Suzanne E., Tech.Serv.Libn.
PILLSBURY COMPANY - TECHNICAL
INFORMATION CENTER □ Minneapolis, MN
Dratch, Gladys I., Assoc.Dir./Cat.
HELLENIC COLLEGE AND HOLY CROSS GREEK
ORTHODOX SCHOOL OF THEOLOGY -
COTSIDAS-TONNA LIBRARY □ Brookline, MA
Draughn, Pearlie M., Res.Libn.
AIR FORCE ASSOCIATION - RESEARCH
LIBRARY □ Washington, DC
Draughon, Dr. Ralph, Jr., Libn./Hist.
STRATFORD HALL PLANTATION - JESSIE BALL
DUPONT MEMORIAL LIBRARY □ Stratford, VA
Draves, William A., Natl.Dir.
LEARNING RESOURCES NETWORK -
PUBLICATIONS AND RESOURCES □ Manhattan,
KS
Drayson, Pamela, Dir.
PROVIDENCE-ST. MARGARET HEALTH CENTER
- LIBRARY □ Kansas City, KS
Drayson, Pamela, Libn.
ST. MARY'S HOSPITAL - FAMILY PRACTICE &
PATIENT EDUCATION LIBRARY† □ Kansas City,
MO
Drazba, Mary T., Libn.
BLUE CROSS AND BLUE SHIELD ASSOCIATION -
LIBRARY □ Chicago, IL
Drazniowsky, Roman, Cur.
AMERICAN GEOGRAPHICAL SOCIETY
COLLECTION OF THE UNIVERSITY OF
WISCONSIN, MILWAUKEE - GOLDA MEIR
LIBRARY □ Milwaukee, WI
Drea, Dr. Edward J., Asst.Dir./Hist.Serv.
U.S. ARMY MILITARY HISTORY INSTITUTE □
Carlisle Barracks, PA
Drees, James D., Assoc.Archv./Hist.
ELLIS COUNTY HISTORICAL SOCIETY -
ARCHIVES □ Hays, KS
Dreher, Janet, Acq./Doc.Libn.
VILLANOVA UNIVERSITY - PULLING LAW
LIBRARY □ Villanova, PA
Dreifort, Jean, Libn.
CENTER FOR HEALTH AFFAIRS - LIBRARY □
Cleveland, OH
Drenowatz, Margaret, Sci.Bibliog.
BOEHRINGER INGELHEIM LTD. - SCIENTIFIC
INFORMATION SERVICES □ Ridgefield, CT
Drew, Dorothy, Libn.
CANADA - AGRICULTURE CANADA - LONDON
RESEARCH CENTRE LIBRARY □ London, ON
Drew, Mary, Lib.Mgr.
TRW, INC. - DEFENSE SYSTEMS GROUP - SEAD
TECHNICAL LIBRARY □ McLean, VA
Drew, Sally J., Dir.
WISCONSIN STATE DIVISION FOR LIBRARY
SERVICES - REFERENCE AND LOAN LIBRARY □
Madison, WI

Drew, Stephen E., Cur.
CALIFORNIA STATE RAILROAD MUSEUM -
LIBRARY □ Sacramento, CA

Drewes, Arlene, Supv., Circ.
NATIONAL GEOGRAPHIC SOCIETY - LIBRARY □
Washington, DC

Drews, Margaret A., Libn.
HENKEL CORPORATION - HENNEPIN
TECHNICAL CENTER LIBRARY □ Minneapolis,
MN

Drinkhouse, Bruce, Pres.
NORTHAMPTON COUNTY HISTORICAL AND
GENEALOGICAL SOCIETY - HISTORICAL
MUSEUM AND LIBRARY □ Easton, PA

Driscoll, Kathleen, Mgr.
ERNST & WHINNEY - INFORMATION CENTER □
Boston, MA

Driscoll, Sr. Loretta, C.D.P., Hd.Libn.
ATHENAEUM OF OHIO - MOUNT ST. MARY'S
SEMINARY OF THE WEST - EUGENE H. MALY
MEMORIAL LIBRARY □ Cincinnati, OH

Driscoll, Michael R., Lib. Aide
ENVIRONMENTAL PROTECTION AGENCY -
CENTRAL REGIONAL LABORATORY - LIBRARY □
Annapolis, MD

Driskell, David, Cur., Aaron Douglas Coll.
AMISTAD RESEARCH CENTER - LIBRARY/
ARCHIVES □ New Orleans, LA

Drittler, John B., Libn.
OSSINING HISTORICAL SOCIETY MUSEUM -
LIBRARY □ Ossining, NY

Driver, Marjorie G., Spanish Period Spec.
UNIVERSITY OF GUAM - MICRONESIAN AREA
RESEARCH CENTER - PACIFIC COLLECTION □
Mangilao, GU

Droessler, Judith, Sci.Libn.
TEXAS A & M UNIVERSITY - REFERENCE
DIVISION □ College Station, TX

Droessler, William F., Libn.
UNIVERSITY OF ARKANSAS, MONTICELLO -
LIBRARY - SPECIAL COLLECTIONS □ Monticello,
AR

Drolet, Bernadette, Chf.Libn.
HOPITAL DU ST-SACREMENT - BIBLIOTHEQUE
MEDICALE† □ Quebec, PQ

Drolet, Leon L., Jr., Dir.
NORTH SUBURBAN LIBRARY SYSTEM &
SUBURBAN LIBRARY SYSTEM - SUBURBAN AV
SERVICE □ La Grange Park, IL

Drong, Josephine V., Security & Storage
HUGHES AIRCRAFT COMPANY - ELECTRO-
OPTICAL & DATA SYSTEMS GROUP - COMPANY
TECHNICAL DOCUMENT CENTER □ El Segundo,
CA

Drouin, Fernand, Dir.
LA PRESSE, LTEE. - CENTRE DE
DOCUMENTATION† □ Montreal, PQ

Drouin, Rev. Georges, Archiviste
SEMINAIRE DE QUEBEC - ARCHIVES □ Quebec,
PQ

Drouin, Roger, Ref.Libn.
HYDRO-QUEBEC - INSTITUT DE RECHERCHE -
BIBLIOTHEQUE □ Varennes, PQ

Druck, Kitty, Hd., Transl.Dept.
HOECHST-ROUSSEL PHARMACEUTICALS, INC. -
LIBRARY □ Somerville, NJ

Drucker, Arlene F., Sr.Lit.Sci.
WARNER-LAMBERT COMPANY - CORPORATE
LIBRARY □ Morris Plains, NJ

Drucker, Elsalyn P., Lib.Dir.
JERSEY SHORE MEDICAL CENTER - ANN MAY
SCHOOL OF NURSING LIBRARY & MEDIA
CENTER □ Neptune, NJ

Dructor, Robert, Assoc.Archv.
PENNSYLVANIA STATE HISTORICAL & MUSEUM
COMMISSION - DIVISION OF ARCHIVES AND
MANUSCRIPTS □ Harrisburg, PA

Druesedow, John E., Jr., Dir.
OBERLIN COLLEGE - CONSERVATORY OF
MUSIC LIBRARY □ Oberlin, OH

Drum, Carol, Univ.Libn.
UNIVERSITY OF FLORIDA - CHEMISTRY
LIBRARY □ Gainesville, FL

Drum, Eunice, Dir., Tech.Serv.
NORTH CAROLINA STATE DEPARTMENT OF
CULTURAL RESOURCES - DIVISION OF THE
STATE LIBRARY □ Raleigh, NC

Drummond, Frances M., Supv.
AMOCO CANADA PETROLEUM COMPANY, LTD. -
LIBRARY/INFORMATION CENTER □ Calgary, AB

Drummond, Kathy, Libn.
COURIER - LIBRARY □ Findlay, OH

Drury, George H., Info.Chf.
KALMBACH PUBLISHING COMPANY -
INFORMATION CENTER □ Milwaukee, WI

Dryden, Deana, Libn.
ROYAL ALEXANDRA HOSPITAL - MEDICAL
LIBRARY □ Edmonton, AB

Dryden, Donna, Med.Libn.
CAMSELL (Charles) GENERAL HOSPITAL - PETER
WILCOCK LIBRARY □ Edmonton, AB

Duane, Carol, ILL Chem.Info.
SDS BIOTECH CORPORATION - CORPORATE
LIBRARY □ Painesville, OH

Duba, B.J., Mgr.
NORTHROP CORPORATION - ELECTRO-
MECHANICAL DIVISION - TECHNICAL
INFORMATION CENTER □ Anaheim, CA

Dube, Gilles, Map Div.
SOCIETE QUEBECOISE D'INITIATIVES
PETROLIERES - DOCUMENTATION CENTRE† □
Ste. Foy, PQ

Duboczy, Julia T., Med.Libn.
ALAMEDA-CONTRA COSTA MEDICAL
ASSOCIATION - LIBRARY □ Oakland, CA

Dubord, Grevard, Ref.
CEGEP DU VIEUX-MONTREAL - LIBRARY □
Montreal, PQ

Dubreuil, Lorraine, Map Cur.
MC GILL UNIVERSITY - MAP AND AIR PHOTO
LIBRARY □ Montreal, PQ

Dubson, Nadine A., Libn.
NEW YORK COUNTY SURROGATE'S COURT -
LAW LIBRARY □ New York, NY

Dubuc, Richard, Assoc.Libn.
BARREAU DE MONTREAL - BIBLIOTHEQUE □
Montreal, PQ

Duca, Karen, Economist
UNIVERSITY OF COLORADO, BOULDER -
BUSINESS RESEARCH DIVISION - TRAVEL
REFERENCE CENTER □ Boulder, CO

Ducas, Ada M., Asst.Med.Libn.
ROYAL VICTORIA HOSPITAL - MEDICAL
LIBRARY† □ Montreal, PQ

Ducey, Richard, Asst.Libn./Rd.Serv.
NEW ENGLAND SCHOOL OF LAW - LIBRARY† □
Boston, MA

Duchesne, Guy
CENTRALE DE L'ENSEIGNEMENT DU QUEBEC -
CENTRE DE DOCUMENTATION □ Quebec, PQ

Duchow, Sandra R., Chf.Med.Libn.
ROYAL VICTORIA HOSPITAL - MEDICAL
LIBRARY† □ Montreal, PQ

Duckett, John, Libn.
WOLF, BLOCK, SCHORR & SOLIS-COHEN -
LIBRARY □ Philadelphia, PA

Duckett, Kenneth, Cur.
UNIVERSITY OF OREGON - SPECIAL
COLLECTIONS DIVISION □ Eugene, OR

Duclow, Geraldine, Libn.-In-Charge
FREE LIBRARY OF PHILADELPHIA - THEATRE
COLLECTION □ Philadelphia, PA

Duda, Sophia, Libn.
UNIVERSITY OF TORONTO - PATHOLOGY
LIBRARY □ Toronto, ON

Dudden, Rosalind, Dir. of Lib.Serv.
MERCY MEDICAL CENTER - LIBRARY AND
MEDIA RESOURCES DEPARTMENT □ Denver, CO

Duderwicz, Diana, Asst.Cat.Libn.
UNIVERSITY OF GEORGIA - LAW LIBRARY □
Athens, GA

Dudinyak, John M.
3M - PATENT AND TECHNICAL
COMMUNICATIONS SERVICES □ St. Paul, MN

Dudley, Annie L., Asst.Libn.
U.S. NAVY - NAVAL EXPLOSIVE ORDNANCE
DISPOSAL TECHNOLOGY CENTER - TECHNICAL
LIBRARY □ Indian Head, MD

Dudley, Durand S., Sr. Law Libn.
MARATHON OIL COMPANY - LAW LIBRARY □
Findlay, OH

Dueker, Sarah C., Chf., Lib.Br.
U.S. NASA - AMES RESEARCH CENTER -
LIBRARY □ Mountain View, CA

Dueltgen, Dr. R.R., Dir., Info.Serv.
HENKEL CORPORATION - HENNEPIN
TECHNICAL CENTER LIBRARY □ Minneapolis,
MN

Duensing, Edward E., Jr., Info.Mgr.
RUTGERS UNIVERSITY, THE STATE
UNIVERSITY OF NEW JERSEY - CENTER FOR
URBAN POLICY RESEARCH LIBRARY □
Piscataway, NJ

Duerell, Anne M., Lib.Techn.
U.S. AIR FORCE BASE - HANSCOM BASE
LIBRARY □ Hanscom AFB, MA

Duesterbeck, Florence, Asst.Libn.
WASCANA INSTITUTE OF APPLIED ARTS AND
SCIENCES - RESOURCE & INFORMATION
CENTRE □ Regina, SK

Duff, Ann M., Res.Libn.
DOFASCO INC. - RESEARCH INFORMATION
CENTRE □ Hamilton, ON

Duff, Jeffrey, Prin.Archv./Br.Mgr.
KENTUCKY STATE DEPARTMENT FOR
LIBRARIES & ARCHIVES - ARCHIVES □
Frankfort, KY

Duff, Lucy W., Coll.Mgt.Libn.
BUREAU OF SOCIAL SCIENCE RESEARCH -
LIBRARY □ Washington, DC

Duff, Polly-Ann, Hd. of Res.
ART REFERENCE BUREAU, INC. □ Pittsfield, MA

Duff, Wendy, Libn.
NOVA SCOTIA - PUBLIC ARCHIVES OF NOVA
SCOTIA □ Halifax, NS

Duffie, Judith, Info.Spec.
AMERICAN HOECHST CORPORATION - FILMS
DIVISION - TECHNICAL INFORMATION
CENTER □ Greer, SC

Duffy, Annette, Hd.Libn.
OKLAHOMA STATE UNIVERSITY - OKLAHOMA
CITY BRANCH - TECHNICAL INSTITUTE
LIBRARY □ Oklahoma City, OK

Duffy, Mark J., Archv.
PROTESTANT EPISCOPAL CHURCH -
EPISCOPAL DIOCESE OF MASSACHUSETTS -
DIOCESAN LIBRARY AND ARCHIVES □ Boston,
MA

Duffy, Mary F., Assoc.Libn.
STATE MUTUAL LIFE ASSURANCE COMPANY OF
AMERICA - LIBRARY □ Worcester, MA

Duffy, Richard, Sr.Libn.
IBM CORPORATION - FEDERAL SYSTEMS
DIVISION - AVIONICS SYSTEMS - LIBRARY □
Owego, NY

Dufort, Robert, Ref.Libn.
CEGEP ST-JEAN SUR RICHELIEU -
BIBLIOTHEQUE □ St. Jean, PQ

Dufour, Doris, Online/SDI Serv.
UNIVERSITE LAVAL - BIBLIOTHEQUE □ Ste.
Foy, PQ

Dufour, Lydia, Assoc.Cur., Iconography
HISPANIC SOCIETY OF AMERICA -
DEPARTMENT OF ICONOGRAPHY - GENERAL
REFERENCE FILE □ New York, NY

Dufresne, Danielle
INSTITUT D'HISTOIRE DE L'AMERIQUE
FRANCAISE (1970) - RESEARCH CENTRE
LIBRARY □ Montreal, PQ

Dufresne, Daphne, Chf.Libn.
UNIVERSITE DU QUEBEC A MONTREAL -
BIBLIOTHEQUE DES ARTS □ Montreal, PQ

Dufresne, Pauline, Techn.
ST. AMANT CENTRE INC. - MEDICAL LIBRARY
□ Winnipeg, MB

Dugan, Dee Ann, Ref.
UNIVERSITY OF SANTA CLARA - EDWIN A.
HEAFEY LAW LIBRARY† □ Santa Clara, CA

Dugas, Dee, Word Proc.
LOUISIANA STATE OFFICE OF THE SECRETARY
OF STATE - STATE ARCHIVES AND RECORDS
SERVICE - ARCHIVES SECTION □ Baton Rouge,
LA

Duggan, Ann V., Mgr., Lib.Serv.
AMERICAN FOUNDRYMEN'S SOCIETY -
TECHNICAL INFORMATION CENTER □ Des
Plaines, IL

Duggan, Elizabeth, Med.Libn.
GRACE GENERAL HOSPITAL - CHESLEY A.
PIPPY, JR. MEDICAL LIBRARY □ St. John's, NF

Duggan, Jane
PROVIDENCE PUBLIC LIBRARY - ART AND
MUSIC DEPARTMENT □ Providence, RI

DuGrenier, Susan B., Patients' Libn.
U.S. VETERANS ADMINISTRATION (VA-Salem) -
MEDICAL CENTER LIBRARY □ Salem, VA

Duguay, Diane, Adm.
CANADIAN AMATEUR MUSICIANS-MUSICIENS
AMATEURS DU CANADA (CAMMAC) - MUSIC
LIBRARY □ Montreal, PQ

Duhamel, Marie, Govt.Pubn.
UNIVERSITY OF OTTAWA - MORISSET
LIBRARY □ Ottawa, ON

Duignan, Peter, Cur., Africa Mid East
STANFORD UNIVERSITY - HOOVER
INSTITUTION ON WAR, REVOLUTION AND
PEACE - LIBRARY □ Stanford, CA

Duimstra, Emilie, Training Coord.
CHILD CARE RESOURCE CENTER □ Des Moines,
IA

Duisin, Xenia W., Libn.
INSTITUTE OF PUBLIC ADMINISTRATION -
LIBRARY □ New York, NY

Dujsik, Gerald, Lib.Mgr.
CHRIST HOSPITAL - HOSPITAL LIBRARY □ Oak
Lawn, IL

Dujsik, Gerald, Lib.Mgr.
EVANGELICAL SCHOOL OF NURSING -
WOJNIAK MEMORIAL LIBRARY □ Oak Lawn, IL

Dukakis, Arthur G., Regional Dir.
U.S. BUREAU OF THE CENSUS - INFORMATION
SERVICES PROGRAM - BOSTON REGIONAL
OFFICE - LIBRARY □ Boston, MA

Duke, Barbara, Hd.
UNIVERSITY OF CALIFORNIA, LOS ANGELES -
EDUCATION & PSYCHOLOGY LIBRARY □ Los
Angeles, CA

Duke, Susanna P., Libn.
LAW SOCIETY OF NEWFOUNDLAND - LIBRARY
□ St. John's, NF

Dukes, Morgan, Dir., Gen.Serv.
AMERICANS UNITED FOR SEPARATION OF
CHURCH AND STATE - ARCHIVES □ Silver
Spring, MD

Dukes, William H., Libn.
GIFFELS ASSOCIATES, INC. - LIBRARY □
Southfield, MI

Dula, Doron A., Tech.Libn.
LITTON APPLIED TECHNOLOGY - LIBRARY □
Sunnyvale, CA

Dulaney, H.G., Lib.Dir.
RAYBURN (Sam) FOUNDATION - SAM RAYBURN
LIBRARY □ Bonham, TX

Dulaney, Sandra, Libn.
UNIVERSITY OF VIRGINIA - BIOLOGY/
PSYCHOLOGY LIBRARY □ Charlottesville, VA

Dumaine, Paul R., Law Libn.
ADLER POLLOCK & SHEEHAN, INC. - LAW
LIBRARY □ Providence, RI

Dumais, Madeleine, Responsable
HOPITAL DE L'ENFANT-JESUS - BIBLIOTHEQUE
MEDICALE □ Quebec, PQ

Dumbauld, Betty, Hd.Libn.
THOMPSON (J. Walter) COMPANY -
INFORMATION CENTER □ Chicago, IL

Dumlao, Mercedes, Libn.
BECHTEL - DATA PROCESSING LIBRARY □ San
Francisco, CA

Dumont, Monique, Mgr.
GESTAS INC. - DOCUMENTATION CENTER □
Montreal, PQ

Dumouchel, Bernard, Dir., Tech.Serv.Br.
CANADA - LIBRARY OF PARLIAMENT □ Ottawa,
ON

Dumouchel, Debbie, Hd.
CANADA - NATIONAL RESEARCH COUNCIL -
CISTI - UPLANDS BRANCH □ Ottawa, ON

Dumoulin, Real, Chf.
QUEBEC PROVINCE - MINISTERE DES
AFFAIRES CULTURELLES - CENTRE DE
DOCUMENTATION† □ Quebec, PQ

Dunbar, Barbara, Dir.
MC LEAN COUNTY HISTORICAL SOCIETY -
MUSEUM AND LIBRARY □ Bloomington, IL

Dunbar, Linda, Lib.Techn.
VANCOUVER TEACHERS' PROFESSIONAL
LIBRARY □ Vancouver, BC

Duncan, Anita E., Lib.Techn.
ALBERTA - DEPARTMENT OF FEDERAL AND
INTERGOVERNMENTAL AFFAIRS - LIBRARY □
Edmonton, AB

Duncan, Barbara, Dir. of Info.
INTERNATIONAL SOCIETY FOR
REHABILITATION OF THE DISABLED/
REHABILITATION INTERNATIONAL - LIBRARY
□ New York, NY

Duncan, Ramona, Cons.
INDIANA HISTORICAL SOCIETY - WILLIAM
HENRY SMITH MEMORIAL LIBRARY □
Indianapolis, IN

Duncombe, Sid, Dir.
UNIVERSITY OF IDAHO - BUREAU OF PUBLIC
AFFAIRS RESEARCH - LIBRARY □ Moscow, ID

Dundon, Theresa, Libn.
UNIVERSITY OF CALIFORNIA, BERKELEY -
NAVAL BIOSCIENCES LABORATORY - LIBRARY
□ Oakland, CA

Dunfield, Everett R., Engr.Libn.
UNIVERSITY OF NEW BRUNSWICK -
ENGINEERING LIBRARY □ Fredericton, NB

Dunikowski, Lynn, Libn.
COLLEGE OF FAMILY PHYSICIANS OF CANADA -
CANADIAN LIBRARY OF FAMILY MEDICINE □
London, ON

Dunkel, Lisa M., Libn.
LANGLEY PORTER PSYCHIATRIC INSTITUTE -
PROFESSIONAL LIBRARY □ San Francisco, CA

Dunkle, William, Data Libn.
WOODS HOLE OCEANOGRAPHIC INSTITUTION
- RESEARCH LIBRARY □ Woods Hole, MA

Dunkly, James, Dir.
WESTON SCHOOL OF THEOLOGY - LIBRARY □
Cambridge, MA

Dunlap, Barbara J., Archv.
CUNY - CITY COLLEGE LIBRARY - COLLEGE
ARCHIVES □ New York, NY

Dunlap, Barbara Jane, Chf., Archv. & Spec.Coll.
CUNY - CITY COLLEGE LIBRARY - SPECIAL
COLLECTIONS □ New York, NY

Dunlap, Ellen S., Dir.
ROSENBACH MUSEUM & LIBRARY □ Philadelphia,
PA

Dunlap, Rosemarie, Asst.Ch.Lit.Spec.
DALLAS PUBLIC LIBRARY - HUMANITIES
DIVISION □ Dallas, TX

Dunleavy, Clara, Chf.Ref.Libn.
YESHIVA UNIVERSITY - ALBERT EINSTEIN
COLLEGE OF MEDICINE - D. SAMUEL
GOTTESMAN LIBRARY □ Bronx, NY

Dunlop, Alice W., Libn.
UNITED NATIONS ASSOCIATION OF THE
UNITED STATES OF AMERICA - GREATER ST.
LOUIS CHAPTER - LIBRARY □ St. Louis, MO

Dunlop, Donna V., Coord., Cooperating Coll.
FOUNDATION CENTER - NEW YORK - LIBRARY
□ New York, NY

Dunlop, Dr. John B., Assoc.Dir., Lib./Archv.
STANFORD UNIVERSITY - HOOVER
INSTITUTION ON WAR, REVOLUTION AND
PEACE - LIBRARY □ Stanford, CA

Dunn, Barbara E., Libn.
HAWAIIAN HISTORICAL SOCIETY - MISSION-
HISTORICAL LIBRARY □ Honolulu, HI

Dunn, Prof. David W., Law Libn.
ORAL ROBERTS UNIVERSITY - O.W. COBURN
LAW LIBRARY† □ Tulsa, OK

Dunn, Diane M., Hd., Ref.Dept.
DETROIT NEWS - GEORGE B. CATLIN
MEMORIAL LIBRARY □ Detroit, MI

Dunn, Donald J., Law Libn.
WESTERN NEW ENGLAND COLLEGE - SCHOOL
OF LAW LIBRARY □ Springfield, MA

Dunn, Eugene E., Dir.
LARAMIE PLAINS MUSEUM ASSOCIATION -
LIBRARY □ Laramie, WY

Dunn, George L., Jr., Libn.
MEMPHIS COMMERCIAL APPEAL - LIBRARY □
Memphis, TN

Dunn, Harriet, Asst.Prof.
NASHVILLE STATE TECHNICAL INSTITUTE -
EDUCATIONAL RESOURCE CENTER □ Nashville,
TN

Dunn, Hedy M., Musm.Dir.
LOS ALAMOS COUNTY HISTORICAL MUSEUM -
ARCHIVES □ Los Alamos, NM

Dunn, Dr. Horton, Jr., Supv., Info.Serv.
LUBRIZOL CORPORATION - CHEMICAL LIBRARY
□ Wickliffe, OH

Dunn, Jamie Niss, Asst.Libn.
DORSEY & WHITNEY - LAW LIBRARY □
Minneapolis, MN

Dunn, John F., Dir. of Educ.
PHILATELIC FOUNDATION - ARCHIVES AND
LIBRARY □ New York, NY

Dunn, Lu Ann, Libn.
LEXINGTON HERALD-LEADER - LIBRARY □
Lexington, KY

Dunn, Mary, Libn.
PRINCE GEORGE'S COUNTY PUBLIC SCHOOLS -
PROFESSIONAL LIBRARY □ Landover, MD

Dunn, Mary B., Law Libn.
NEW YORK STATE SUPREME COURT -
APPELLATE DIVISION, 4TH JUDICIAL
DEPARTMENT - LAW LIBRARY □ Syracuse, NY

Dunn, Nancy, Libn.
CHILDREN'S HOSPITAL OF PITTSBURGH -
BLAXTER MEMORIAL LIBRARY† □ Pittsburgh, PA

Dunn, Pat, Ref.Libn.
UNIVERSITY OF BRITISH COLUMBIA -
CURRICULUM LABORATORY □ Vancouver, BC

Dunn, Richard, Lib.Dir.
TECHNOMIC PUBLISHING CO., INC. (TPC) -
BUSINESS LIBRARY □ Lancaster, PA

Dunn, Sandra, Info.Serv.Off.
ONTARIO CRAFTS COUNCIL - CRAFT
RESOURCE CENTRE □ Toronto, ON

Dunn, Susan M., Libn.
WOODBURY COUNTY BAR ASSOCIATION - LAW
LIBRARY □ Sioux City, IA

Dunnigan, Brian Leigh, Exec.Dir.
OLD FORT NIAGARA ASSOCIATION - LIBRARY
□ Youngstown, NY

Dunnigan, Mary C., Libn.
UNIVERSITY OF VIRGINIA - FISKE KIMBALL
FINE ARTS LIBRARY □ Charlottesville, VA

Dunsky-Shnay, Zipporah, Dir.
JEWISH PUBLIC LIBRARY OF MONTREAL □
Montreal, PQ

Dunstan, Richard, City Editor
NANAIMO DAILY FREE PRESS - LIBRARY □
Nanaimo, BC

Dunstan, Sheila, Libn.
UNIVERSITY OF PUERTO RICO - MAYAGUEZ
CAMPUS LIBRARY - MARINE SCIENCES
COLLECTION □ Mayaguez, PR

Duong, Dr. Buu, Acq.
BRIDGEWATER COLLEGE - ALEXANDER MACK
MEMORIAL LIBRARY - SPECIAL COLLECTIONS
□ Bridgewater, VA

Duperreault, Jeanne, Libn.
ONTARIO SCIENCE CENTRE - LIBRARY □ Don
Mills, ON

Duplaix, Sally, Dir.
PROVIDENCE ATHENAEUM - LIBRARY □
Providence, RI

Dupont, Denise, Act.Libn.
ST. FRANCES CABRINI HOSPITAL - MEDICAL
LIBRARY □ Alexandria, LA

Dupont, Elizabeth D., Libn.
MERCER (George, Jr.) SCHOOL OF THEOLOGY -
LIBRARY □ Garden City, NY

DuPont, Ginny, Med.Libn.
U.S. VETERANS ADMINISTRATION (DC-
Washington) - MEDICAL CENTER LIBRARY □
Washington, DC

Duppstadt, Mary Ann, Asst.Chf.Libn.
LTV AEROSPACE AND DEFENSE COMPANY -
VOUGHT MISSILES AND ADVANCED PROGRAMS
DIVISION - LIBRARY 3-58200 □ Dallas, TX

Dupree, Harry K., Dir.
U.S. FISH & WILDLIFE SERVICE - FISH
FARMING EXPERIMENTAL STATION - LIBRARY
□ Stuttgart, AR

Dupuis, Betsy, Libn.
ADDISON-WESLEY PUBLISHING COMPANY -
LIBRARY □ Reading, MA

Dupuis, Michel, Libn.
QUEBEC PROVINCE - REGIE DES RENTES -
CENTRE DE DOCUMENTATION □ Quebec, PQ

Dupuis, Sylvie, Lib.Techn.
HOPITAL DE MONT-JOLI, INC. - BIBLIOTHEQUE
□ Mont-Joli, PQ

Dupuy, E.J., Libn.
HAMMOND, INC. - EDITORIAL DIVISION
LIBRARY □ Maplewood, NJ

Dupuy, Ronald J., Interpretive Ranger
LA PURISIMA MISSION - ARCHIVES □ Lompoc,
CA

Duquette, Diane, Chf.Libn.
TREAD OF PIONEERS MUSEUM - ROUTT
COUNTY COLLECTION □ Steamboat Springs, CO

Duran, Cheryl, Ph.D., Dir.
CALIFORNIA HOSPITAL MEDICAL CENTER -
MEDICAL STAFF LIBRARY □ Los Angeles, CA

Duran, Karin, Dir.
CALIFORNIA STATE UNIVERSITY,
NORTHRIDGE - INSTRUCTIONAL MATERIALS
LABORATORY □ Northridge, CA

Durance, Cynthia, Dir., Off. Network Dev.
NATIONAL LIBRARY OF CANADA/
BIBLIOTHEQUE NATIONALE DU CANADA □
Ottawa, ON

Durand, Joan W., Libn.
MOUNT ST. ALPHONSUS THEOLOGICAL
SEMINARY - LIBRARY† □ Esopus, NY

Durand, Marielle, Libn.
UNIVERSITE DE MONTREAL - EDUCATION/
PSYCHOLOGIE/COMMUNICATION-
BIBLIOTHEQUE □ Montreal, PQ

Durant, Gail D., Dir. of Adm.
AMERICAN PATENT LAW ASSOCIATION -
PATENT LAW LIBRARY □ Arlington, VA

Durant, H. Lawrence, Cat.
BOSTON COLLEGE - SPECIAL COLLECTIONS
DEPARTMENT □ Chestnut Hill, MA

DuRant, Thomas A., Pict.Libn.
U.S. NATL. PARK SERVICE - HARPERS FERRY
CENTER - BRANCH OF GRAPHICS RESEARCH -
PICTURE LIBRARY □ Springfield, VA

Durbin, Hugh A., Dir.
COLUMBUS PUBLIC SCHOOLS - PROFESSIONAL
LIBRARY □ Columbus, OH

Durbrow, Mary C., Libn.
NEW CANAAN HISTORICAL SOCIETY -
LIBRARY □ New Canaan, CT

Durden, Jesse N., Dir.
U.S. DEPT. OF COMMERCE - INTERNATIONAL
TRADE ADMINISTRATION - DES MOINES
DISTRICT OFFICE LIBRARY □ Des Moines, IA

Durham, Eileen C., Libn.
CONTINENTAL PAGE ENGINEERS, INC. -
TECHNICAL LIBRARY □ Vienna, VA

Durham, Vaida, Libn.
HARRIS HOSPITAL - MEDICAL LIBRARY □ Fort
Worth, TX

Durie, Debbie, Info.Off.
CANADIAN MENTAL HEALTH ASSOCIATION -
SUICIDE INFORMATION AND EDUCATION
CENTRE □ Calgary, AB

Durivage, Mary Jo, Med.Libn.
U.S. VETERANS ADMINISTRATION (MI-Allen
Park) - MEDICAL CENTER LIBRARY SERVICE
(142D) □ Allen Park, MI

Durkin, Margaret M.R., Asst.Pub.Serv.Libn.
UNIVERSITY OF GEORGIA - LAW LIBRARY □
Athens, GA

Durkin, Marilyn, Tech.Libn.
XEROX CORPORATION - EL SEGUNDO
TECHNICAL LIBRARY □ El Segundo, CA

Durkin, Virginia, Mgr.,Lib.Serv.
ST. VINCENT'S HOSPITAL - GARCEAU LIBRARY
□ Indianapolis, IN

Durnan, Mary L., Dir.
MARSHALL COUNTY HISTORICAL SOCIETY
MUSEUM - LIBRARY □ Plymouth, IN

Durnbaugh, Hedda, Cat./Spec.Coll.
BETHANY AND NORTHERN BAPTIST
THEOLOGICAL SEMINARIES - LIBRARY □ Oak
Brook, IL

Durnell, Sr. Mary Eileen, Hd.Libn.
MERCY HEALTH CENTER - MEDICAL LIBRARY □
Oklahoma City, OK

Durr, Dr. W. Theodore, Dir.
UNIVERSITY OF BALTIMORE - LANGSDALE
LIBRARY - SPECIAL COLLECTIONS
DEPARTMENT □ Baltimore, MD

Durrett, Parthenia, Circ.
UNIVERSITY OF LOUISVILLE - KORNHAUSER
HEALTH SCIENCES LIBRARY □ Louisville, KY

Durso, Angie, Dir.
CHILDREN'S HOSPITAL OF SAN FRANCISCO -
EMGE MEDICAL LIBRARY □ San Francisco, CA

Durso, Michael P., Libn.
U.S. DEPT. OF ENERGY - ENVIRONMENTAL
MEASUREMENTS LABORATORY LIBRARY □ New
York, NY

Durst, Leslie, Libn.
WEST VIRGINIA SCHOOLS FOR THE DEAF AND
BLIND - WV SCHOOL FOR THE BLIND LIBRARY
□ Romney, WV

Dusch, Margaret C., Asst.Dept.Hd.
CARNEGIE LIBRARY OF PITTSBURGH - MUSIC
AND ART DEPARTMENT □ Pittsburgh, PA

Duskiewicz, Irene A., Dir.
HEMPSTEAD PUBLIC LIBRARY - SPECIAL
COLLECTIONS □ Hempstead, NY

Dusold, Frederick, Sr.Prin.Libn.
NEW YORK PUBLIC LIBRARY - MID-
MANHATTAN LIBRARY - SCIENCE/BUSINESS
DEPARTMENT □ New York, NY

Dusoulier, Nathalie, Chf., Tech.Oper/Pubn.Serv
UNITED NATIONS HEADQUARTERS - DAG
HAMMARSKJOLD LIBRARY □ New York, NY

Dustin, M.J., Ref.Coord.
MINITEX □ Minneapolis, MN

Dutcher, David C., Chf.Pk.Hist.
U.S. NATL. PARK SERVICE - INDEPENDENCE
NATL. HISTORICAL PARK - LIBRARY† □
Philadelphia, PA

Dutcher, Henry, Ref.Libn.
SPRINGFIELD COLLEGE - BABSON LIBRARY -
SPECIAL COLLECTIONS □ Springfield, MA

Dutikow, Irene V., Ref.Libn.
RADIO FREE EUROPE/RADIO LIBERTY INC. -
REFERENCE LIBRARY □ New York, NY

Dutton, Lee, Cur.
NORTHERN ILLINOIS UNIVERSITY -
SOUTHEAST ASIA COLLECTION □ DeKalb, IL

Dutton, Marilyn, Libn.
UNIVERSITY OF BRITISH COLUMBIA -
HUMANITIES AND SOCIAL SCIENCES DIVISION
□ Vancouver, BC

Duval, Barbara, Libn.
MERCY SCHOOL OF NURSING - LIBRARY □
Charlotte, NC

Duval, Linda G., Mgr., Law/Tax Lib.
MAY DEPARTMENT STORES COMPANY -
INFORMATION CENTER □ St. Louis, MO

DuVal, Mary J., Libn.
ORGANIZATION RESOURCES COUNSELORS,
INC. - INFORMATION CENTER □ New York, NY

Duvall, Alice, Coord.
COUNCIL ON QUALITY EDUCATION -
"BRINGING THE SCHOOL TO THE
COMMUNITY" RESOURCE CENTER □ Lewiston,
MN

Duvall, Eloise, Prin.Libn.
KENTUCKY STATE DEPARTMENT FOR
LIBRARIES AND ARCHIVES - STATE LIBRARY
SERVICES DIVISION □ Frankfort, KY

Duvall, John, Cat.
HOGAN & HARTSON - LIBRARY □ Washington,
DC

DuVall, Rev. Justin, O.S.B., Asst.Libn.
ST. MEINRAD ARCHABBEY - COLLEGE &
SCHOOL OF THEOLOGY - LIBRARY □ St.
Meinrad, IN

Duvall, Mary Lou, Ref.Libn.
KING COUNTY LAW LIBRARY □ Seattle, WA

Duvall, Scott, Asst.Cur./Bks.
BRIGHAM YOUNG UNIVERSITY - SPECIAL
COLLECTIONS □ Provo, UT

Duvally, Charlotte, Engr.Libn.
DREXEL UNIVERSITY - SCIENCE AND
TECHNOLOGY LIBRARY □ Philadelphia, PA

Duwel, Lucretia, Ref.Libn.
SACRED HEART UNIVERSITY - LIBRARY □
Bridgeport, CT

Dux-Ideus, Sherrie, Training Off./Libn.
BEATRICE STATE DEVELOPMENTAL CENTER -
MEDIA RESOURCE CENTER □ Beatrice, NE

Duyka, Ann, Hd.Cat.
TEXAS A & M UNIVERSITY - MEDICAL
SCIENCES LIBRARY □ College Station, TX

Duyst, Jo, Acq.
CALVIN COLLEGE AND SEMINARY - LIBRARY □
Grand Rapids, MI

Dvorak, Dr. Anna, Libn.
NORTH CAROLINA MUSEUM OF ART - ART
REFERENCE LIBRARY □ Raleigh, NC

Dvorak, Dana, Hd., Tech.Serv.Dept.
LAW SOCIETY OF UPPER CANADA - GREAT
LIBRARY □ Toronto, ON

Dvorak, Mary Ann, Asst.Info.Spec.
VIRGINIA ELECTRIC AND POWER COMPANY -
LIBRARY AND INFORMATION SERVICES □
Richmond, VA

Dvorin, Nancy, Libn.
BOWKER (R.R.) COMPANY - FREDERIC G.
MELCHER LIBRARY □ New York, NY

Dvorzak, Marie, Hd.
UNIVERSITY OF MINNESOTA - GEOLOGY
LIBRARY □ Minneapolis, MN

Dwelley, Linda J., Media Resource Supv.
MAINE CRIMINAL JUSTICE ACADEMY - MEDIA
RESOURCES □ Waterville, ME

Dworman, Thomas J.
DWORMAN (Thomas J.) - LIBRARY □ Detroit, MI

Dwoskin, Beth, Libn.
TEMPLE LIBRARY □ Cleveland, OH

Dwyer, Bertha R., Libn.
RAYMOND, PARISH, PINE & WEINER, INC. -
LIBRARY □ Tarrytown, NY

Dwyer, Charles L., Hd., Thomason/Spec.Coll.
SAM HOUSTON STATE UNIVERSITY - LIBRARY
- SPECIAL COLLECTIONS □ Huntsville, TX

Dwyer, Diana L., Libn.
U.S. FISH & WILDLIFE SERVICE - WILDLIFE
RESEARCH CENTER LIBRARY □ Denver, CO

Dwyer, Janet C., Libn.
JENSEN ASSOCIATES, INC. - LIBRARY □
Boston, MA

Dwyer, Jo, Lib.Acq.
PORT OF PORTLAND - LIBRARY □ Portland, OR

Dwyer, John, Med.Libn.
ST. FRANCIS HOSPITAL - MEDICAL LIBRARY □
Roslyn, NY

Dwyer, John, Supv., Ref.Serv.
U.S. NATL. ARCHIVES & RECORDS SERVICE -
NATL. ARCHIVES - CARTOGRAPHIC &
ARCHITECTURAL BRANCH □ Washington, DC

Dwyer, Mary, Musm.Serv.
NATIONAL SOARING MUSEUM - LIBRARY &
ARCHIVES □ Elmira, NY
Dwyer, Mary, Hd.Libn.
ST. PAUL RAMSEY MEDICAL CENTER -
MEDICAL LIBRARY □ St. Paul, MN
Dwyer, Melva J., Hd.
UNIVERSITY OF BRITISH COLUMBIA - FINE
ARTS DIVISION □ Vancouver, BC
Dwyer, William E., Dir.
U.S. DEPT. OF COMMERCE - INTERNATIONAL
TRADE ADMINISTRATION - ALBUQUERQUE
DISTRICT OFFICE LIBRARY □ Albuquerque, NM
Dyal, Donald A., Hd., Spec.Coll.Div.
TEXAS A & M UNIVERSITY - SPECIAL
COLLECTIONS DIVISION □ College Station, TX
Dyck, Marilyn, Ref.Libn.
CANADA - PUBLIC WORKS CANADA -
INFORMATION, RESEARCH & LIBRARY
SERVICES □ Ottawa, ON
Dyckman, Lisa M., Prog.Asst./Libn.
GREAT LAKES COLLEGES ASSOCIATION -
PHILADELPHIA URBAN SEMESTER - LIBRARY □
Philadelphia, PA
Dye, Betty, Law Libn.
LINN COUNTY BAR ASSOCIATION - LAW
LIBRARY □ Cedar Rapids, IA
Dye, Glenn W., Sec.-Treas.
NATIONAL ASSOCIATION OF PRECANCEL
COLLECTORS, INC. - CHESTER DAVIS
MEMORIAL LIBRARY □ Wildwood, NJ
Dye, Margarette M., Libn.
POWELL, GOLDSTEIN, FRAZER & MURPHY -
LIBRARY □ Atlanta, GA
Dye, Patricia, Hd.
METROPOLITAN TORONTO LIBRARY -
BUSINESS DEPARTMENT □ Toronto, ON
Dyer, Bruce, Libn.
LABRADOR CITY COLLEGIATE - LIBRARY □
Labrador City, NF
Dyer, Charles R., Law Libn.
UNIVERSITY OF MISSOURI, KANSAS CITY -
LAW LIBRARY □ Kansas City, MO
Dyer, Helen, Res.Libn.
BRISTOL-MYERS PRODUCTS - TECHNICAL
INFORMATION CENTER □ Hillside, NJ
Dyer, Judith C., Libn.
SAN DIEGO SOCIETY OF NATURAL HISTORY -
NATURAL HISTORY MUSEUM LIBRARY □ San
Diego, CA
Dyer, Matthew F., Libn.
KENNEBEC COUNTY LAW LIBRARY □ Augusta,
ME
Dyer, Rosemary, Hd., Tech.Serv.
GEORGIA STATE DEPARTMENT OF EDUCATION
- DIVISION OF PUBLIC LIBRARY SERVICES □
Atlanta, GA
Dyer, Ms. S.M., Libn.
SASKATCHEWAN TEACHERS' FEDERATION -
STEWART RESOURCES CENTRE □ Saskatoon,
SK
Dyer, Susan, Health Sci.Libn.
SALEM HOSPITAL - HEALTH SCIENCES
LIBRARY AND INFORMATION CENTER □ Salem,
OR
Dyess, Dr. Stewart W., Asst.Dir./Lib.Adm.Serv.
TEXAS TECH UNIVERSITY - LIBRARY □
Lubbock, TX
Dyess, William, Dir., Rec.Mgt.Div.
TEXAS STATE LIBRARY □ Austin, TX
Dykas, Lucille, Lib.Mgr.
ST. JOSEPH HEALTH CENTER - HEALTH
SCIENCE LIBRARY □ St. Charles, MO
Dykstra, Stephanie, Ser.Libn.
UNIVERSITY OF BRITISH COLUMBIA -
WOODWARD BIOMEDICAL LIBRARY □
Vancouver, BC
Dyment, Jane, Libn.
CANADA - NATIONAL RESEARCH COUNCIL -
CISTI - ELECTRICAL ENGINEERING BRANCH □
Ottawa, ON

Dyni, Victor P., Rd.Adv.
DISTRICT OF COLUMBIA PUBLIC LIBRARY -
MUSIC & RECREATION DIVISION □ Washington,
DC
Dysart, Jane, Chf.Libn.
ROYAL BANK OF CANADA - INFORMATION
RESOURCES □ Toronto, ON
Dysart, Janice, Research Park Libn.
UNIVERSITY OF MISSOURI - RESEARCH PARK
LIBRARY □ Columbia, MO
Dysenchuk, Paul, Res.Asst./Libn.
UNITED NATIONS - CENTRE ON
TRANSNATIONAL CORPORATIONS - LIBRARY □
New York, NY
Dyson, Allan J., Univ.Libn.
UNIVERSITY OF CALIFORNIA, SANTA CRUZ -
DEAN E. MC HENRY LIBRARY □ Santa Cruz, CA
Dyson-Bonter, Peter, Dir., N.S.F.L.
CANADIAN FILM INSTITUTE - NATIONAL
SCIENCE FILM LIBRARY □ Mississauga, ON
Dytyniak, Olga S., Dir.
HAMILTON HOSPITAL - MEDICAL LIBRARY □
Trenton, NJ
Dziedzic, Donna, Asst. State Libn.
NEW JERSEY STATE LIBRARY □ Trenton, NJ
Dziedzina, Christine, Chf.Libn.
CLEVELAND METROPOLITAN GENERAL
HOSPITAL - HAROLD H. BRITTINGHAM
MEMORIAL LIBRARY □ Cleveland, OH
Dzierzak, Edward, Dir.
MARSHALL UNIVERSITY - SCHOOL OF
MEDICINE - HEALTH SCIENCE LIBRARIES □
Huntington, WV
Dzurinko, Ms. M., Cat.
COVINGTON AND BURLING - LIBRARY □
Washington, DC
Dzwonkoski, Peter, Hd.
UNIVERSITY OF ROCHESTER - DEPARTMENT
OF RARE BOOKS AND SPECIAL COLLECTIONS □
Rochester, NY

E

Eady, Lois A., Cur.
BIRMINGHAM PUBLIC AND JEFFERSON
COUNTY FREE LIBRARY - COLLINS
COLLECTION OF THE DANCE □ Birmingham, AL
Eagan, Joseph, Libn.
ENOCH PRATT FREE LIBRARY - MARYLAND
DEPARTMENT □ Baltimore, MD
Eagen, Marian, Libn.
ALBERTA AND SOUTHERN GAS COMPANY LTD.
- LIBRARY □ Calgary, AB
Eagle, T., Res.Libn.
AVON PRODUCTS, INC. - RESEARCH LIBRARY □
Suffern, NY
Eaglesfield, Jean, Lindgren Libn.
MASSACHUSETTS INSTITUTE OF TECHNOLOGY
- LINDGREN LIBRARY □ Cambridge, MA
Eagleton, Kathy, Dir.
BRANDON GENERAL HOSPITAL - LIBRARY
SERVICES □ Brandon, MB
Eakin, Dottie, Pub.Serv.Coord.
UNIVERSITY OF MICHIGAN - ALFRED
TAUBMAN MEDICAL LIBRARY □ Ann Arbor, MI
Eakin, Laurabelle, Dir.
UNIVERSITY OF PITTSBURGH - FALK LIBRARY
OF THE HEALTH SCIENCES □ Pittsburgh, PA
Eames, Carol, Educ.Cur.
TULSA ZOOLOGICAL PARK - LIBRARY □ Tulsa,
OK
Earhart, Marilyn, Acq.
UNIVERSITY OF SANTA CLARA - EDWIN A.
HEAFEY LAW LIBRARY† □ Santa Clara, CA
Earle, Edward James, Libn.
UNIVERSITY OF TEXAS, DALLAS - CALLIER
CENTER FOR COMMUNICATIONS DISORDERS -
LIBRARY □ Dallas, TX

Earle, Edward W., Cur., Keystone-Mast Coll.
UNIVERSITY OF CALIFORNIA, RIVERSIDE -
CALIFORNIA MUSEUM OF PHOTOGRAPHY □
Riverside, CA
Earley, Jeannine, Musm.Asst.
WESTMORELAND MUSEUM OF ART - ART
REFERENCE LIBRARY □ Greensburg, PA
Earley, Jerome, Lrng.Sys.
SUNY - COLLEGE AT BUFFALO - EDWARD H.
BUTLER LIBRARY □ Buffalo, NY
Earls, Leone, Hd.Libn.
CANADIAN BROADCASTING CORPORATION -
REFERENCE LIBRARY □ Toronto, ON
Early, Charles, Asst.Engr.Libn./Ref.
STANFORD UNIVERSITY - ENGINEERING
LIBRARY □ Stanford, CA
Earnest, Kathryn L., Field Serv.Libn.
U.S. ARMY - OFFICE OF THE ADJUTANT
GENERAL - MORALE SUPPORT DIRECTORATE -
LIBRARY ACTIVITIES DIVISION □ Alexandria,
VA
Earnest, Ola May, Pres.
LINN COUNTY HISTORICAL SOCIETY -
LIBRARY □ Pleasanton, KS
Easley, Jane, Libn.
U.S. NAVY - NAVAL HOSPITAL (WA-Bremerton)
- MEDICAL LIBRARY □ Bremerton, WA
Eason, Catherine, Ref.Libn.
U.S. COURT OF APPEALS, 10TH CIRCUIT -
LIBRARY □ Denver, CO
Eason, Robert, Theater Libn.
DALLAS PUBLIC LIBRARY - FINE ARTS
DIVISION □ Dallas, TX
Easson, Dr. Kay P., Exec.Sec.
AMERICAN BLAKE FOUNDATION - RESEARCH
LIBRARY □ Memphis, TN
Easson, Dr. Roger R., Exec.Dir.
AMERICAN BLAKE FOUNDATION - RESEARCH
LIBRARY □ Memphis, TN
East, Catherine, Info.Serv.Spec.
U.S. POSTAL SERVICE - LIBRARY □ Washington,
DC
East, Dr. Dennis, Hd.
OHIO HISTORICAL SOCIETY - ARCHIVES-
LIBRARY □ Columbus, OH
Easter, Beth, Libn.
MASSACHUSETTS INSTITUTE OF TECHNOLOGY
- AERONAUTICS AND ASTRONAUTICS LIBRARY
□ Cambridge, MA
Easter, Mona Jeanne, Hd., Tech.Serv.
NEBRASKA STATE LIBRARY COMMISSION □
Lincoln, NE
Easter, Ruth H., Libn.
AMERICAN ENKA COMPANY - BUSINESS AND
TECHNICAL LIBRARY† □ Enka, NC
Eastman, Betty-Jean, Med.Libn.
CENTRAL VERMONT HOSPITAL - MEDICAL
LIBRARY □ Barre, VT
Eastman, Esther, Coord.
ATLANTIC-RICHFIELD COMPANY -
GOVERNMENT RESOURCE CENTER† □ Los
Angeles, CA
Eastman, Janice M., Libn.
CENTER FOR EARLY EDUCATION - LAURA M.
ELLIS MEMORIAL LIBRARY □ Los Angeles, CA
Eastwood, Ron, Supv.
MONTEREY COUNTY OFFICE OF EDUCATION -
TEACHERS' RESOURCE CENTER □ Salinas, CA
Eaton, Casindania P., Libn.
AMERICAN ACADEMY AND INSTITUTE OF
ARTS AND LETTERS - LIBRARY □ New York, NY
Eaton, Conrad P., Libn.
U.S. DEPT. OF STATE - LIBRARY □ Washington,
DC
Eaton, Donna, Lib.Techn.
U.S. ARMY - SPECIAL SERVICES DIVISION -
SHARPE ARMY DEPOT - LIBRARY □ Lathrop, CA
Eaton, Elizabeth K., Dir.
TUFTS UNIVERSITY - HEALTH SCIENCES
LIBRARY □ Boston, MA
Eaton, Eugenia, Hd.
UNIVERSITY OF CALIFORNIA, LOS ANGELES -
PUBLIC AFFAIRS SERVICE □ Los Angeles, CA

Eaton, Mrs. James T., Libn.
CARMEL PRESBYTERIAN CHURCH - MEMORIAL LIBRARY □ Glenside, PA

Eaton, Katherine G., Libn.
UNIVERSITY OF OREGON - BUREAU OF GOVERNMENTAL RESEARCH AND SERVICE LIBRARY □ Eugene, OR

Eaton, Sharon, Info.Spec.
LOUISIANA STATE HOUSE OF REPRESENTATIVES LEGISLATIVE SERVICES - RESEARCH LIBRARY □ Baton Rouge, LA

Eaton, Trudy, Asst.Libn.
CERTAINTEED CORPORATION - CORPORATE LIBRARY/INFORMATION CENTER □ Blue Bell, PA

Eatroff, Elaine B., Cur. of Rare Books
U.S. ARMY - MILITARY ACADEMY - LIBRARY □ West Point, NY

Ebanks, Hilma, Info.Spec.
CONFERENCE BOARD, INC. - INFORMATION SERVICE □ New York, NY

Ebanks, Mrs. Jessie B., Archv.Libn.
ATLANTA UNIVERSITY CENTER - ROBERT W. WOODRUFF LIBRARY □ Atlanta, GA

Ebarb, Louis, Video Techn.
BROOKLYN PUBLIC LIBRARY - AUDIO VISUAL DIVISION □ Brooklyn, NY

Ebbinghouse, C., Ref./Media
SOUTHWESTERN UNIVERSITY - SCHOOL OF LAW LIBRARY □ Los Angeles, CA

Ebbott, William, Asst.Dir., Rd.Serv.
UNIVERSITY OF WISCONSIN, MADISON - LAW SCHOOL LIBRARY □ Madison, WI

Eber, Beryl, Supv.Libn.
NEW YORK PUBLIC LIBRARY - DONNELL LIBRARY CENTER - NATHAN STRAUS YOUNG ADULT LIBRARY □ New York, NY

Eberhardt, Claire, Asst.Libn.
NEW YORK STATE LIBRARY - LAW/SOCIAL SCIENCE REFERENCE SERVICES □ Albany, NY

Eberhardt, Rev. N.C., Dir., Lib.Serv.
ST. JOHN'S SEMINARY - EDWARD LAURENCE DOHENY MEMORIAL LIBRARY □ Camarillo, CA

Eberhart, Martha, ILL Libn.
MEDICAL COLLEGE OF WISCONSIN - LIBRARIES □ Milwaukee, WI

Eberhart, Dr. Richard B., Adm.
HARTFORD SEMINARY LIBRARY □ Hartford, CT

Eberle, Dr. Charles F., Med.Dir.
TINGLEY (Carrie) CRIPPLED CHILDREN'S HOSPITAL - MEDICAL LIBRARY □ Albuquerque, NM

Ebersole, Brian, Ref.Libn.
THE CLAREMONT COLLEGES - SEELEY G. MUDD SCIENCE LIBRARY □ Claremont, CA

Ebert, Diane M., Law Ck.
OUTAGAMIE COUNTY LAW LIBRARY □ Appleton, WI

Ebner, William E., Chf.
TELEDYNE RYAN AERONAUTICAL - TECHNICAL INFORMATION SERVICES □ San Diego, CA

Ebro, Diane C.P., Dir.
UNIVERSITY OF MINNESOTA, DULUTH - HEALTH SCIENCE LIBRARY □ Duluth, MN

Eby, Dr. Harold H., Dir., Corp.Serv.Sect.
CONOCO, INC. - RESEARCH AND DEVELOPMENT DEPARTMENT - TECHNICAL INFORMATION SERVICES □ Ponca City, OK

Echols, Susan P., Libn.
BRYAN MEMORIAL HOSPITAL - SCHOOL OF NURSING - LIBRARY □ Lincoln, NE

Echtenkamp, Joan, Hist.Coll.Libn.
UNIVERSITY OF VIRGINIA - MEDICAL CENTER - CLAUDE MOORE HEALTH SCIENCES LIBRARY □ Charlottesville, VA

Eckardt, Allison, Assoc.Ed.
BRANT PUBLICATIONS, INC. - THE ANTIQUES MAGAZINE - LIBRARY □ New York, NY

Eckart, Daniel, Ref.Libn.
PROVIDENCE COLLEGE - PHILLIPS MEMORIAL LIBRARY □ Providence, RI

Eckel, Virginia E., Dir.
U.S. AIR FORCE INSTITUTE OF TECHNOLOGY - LIBRARY □ Wright-Patterson AFB, OH

Eckerman, Nancy, Assoc.Libn., Tech.Serv
CHRISTIAN THEOLOGICAL SEMINARY - LIBRARY □ Indianapolis, IN

Eckersley, Sandy, Med.Libn.
ST. BENEDICT'S HOSPITAL - HEALTH SCIENCES LIBRARY □ Ogden, UT

Eckert, Dan, Libn.
HOLY FAMILY HOSPITAL - HEALTH SCIENCE LIBRARY □ Manitowoc, WI

Eckert, Tim, Regional Archv.
WASHINGTON STATE OFFICE OF SECRETARY OF STATE - DIVISION OF ARCHIVES AND RECORD MANAGEMENT □ Olympia, WA

Eckert, Dr. William G., Dir.
INTERNATIONAL REFERENCE ORGANIZATION IN FORENSIC MEDICINE AND SCIENCES - LIBRARY AND REFERENCE CENTER □ Wichita, KS

Eckes, Mark, Adm.Coord.
MINITEX □ Minneapolis, MN

Eckey, Carol, Libn.
IOWA STATE COMMISSION FOR THE BLIND - LIBRARY FOR THE BLIND & PHYSICALLY HANDICAPPED □ Des Moines, IA

Eckhardt, Barbara R., Sr.Lit.Sci.
WARNER-LAMBERT COMPANY - CORPORATE LIBRARY □ Morris Plains, NJ

Ecklund, L., Tech.Info.Spec.
ATLANTIC-RICHFIELD COMPANY - INFORMATION RESEARCH CENTER □ Los Angeles, CA

Eckman, Charles, Libn.
ALLEN COUNTY PUBLIC LIBRARY - BUSINESS AND TECHNOLOGY DEPARTMENT □ Fort Wayne, IN

Eckman, Phyllis, Libn.
PARKVIEW MEMORIAL HOSPITAL - PARKVIEW-METHODIST SCHOOL OF NURSING - LIBRARY □ Fort Wayne, IN

Economous, Dr. Charles, Dir. of Workshops
CLARION UNIV. OF PENNSYLVANIA - COLL. OF LIBRARY SCIENCE - CTR. FOR THE STUDY OF RURAL LIBRARIANSHIP - LIB. □ Clarion, PA

Edblom, Nancy, Doc.Libn.
SUNY - COLLEGE AT POTSDAM - FREDERICK W. CRUMB MEMORIAL LIBRARY □ Potsdam, NY

Eddison, Elizabeth Bole, Pres.
WARNER-EDDISON ASSOCIATES, INC. - INFORMATION SERVICE □ Cambridge, MA

Eddy, Dolores D., Regional Libn.
ENVIRONMENTAL PROTECTION AGENCY - REGION VIII LIBRARY □ Denver, CO

Eddy, Donald, Libn.
CORNELL UNIVERSITY - RARE BOOKS DEPARTMENT □ Ithaca, NY

Eddy, Holly H., Med.Libn.
SPRINGFIELD HOSPITAL - INFORMATION CENTER LIBRARY □ Springfield, VT

Eddy, Leonard M., Dir.
UNIVERSITY OF LOUISVILLE - KORNHAUSER HEALTH SCIENCES LIBRARY □ Louisville, KY

Edelman, Gayle, Law Libn.
RIVERSIDE COUNTY LAW LIBRARY □ Riverside, CA

Edelman, Gayle S., Hd., Tech.Serv.
UNIVERSITY OF CHICAGO - LAW SCHOOL LIBRARY □ Chicago, IL

Edelstein, Elizabeth, Libn.
GLADMAN (Everett A.) MEMORIAL HOSPITAL - MEDICAL LIBRARY □ Oakland, CA

Edelstein, J.M., Chf.Libn.
NATIONAL GALLERY OF ART - LIBRARY □ Washington, DC

Edge, Karen, Asst. Music Libn.
UNIVERSITY OF VIRGINIA - MUSIC LIBRARY □ Charlottesville, VA

Edgerton, Linda Kate, Libn.
SOCIETY OF THE FOUNDERS OF NORWICH, CONNECTICUT - LEFFINGWELL INN LIBRARY □ Norwich, CT

Edgington, Cindy, Asst.Libn.
LEXINGTON COMMUNITY COLLEGE - LIBRARY □ Lexington, KY

Edick, Vicki L., Health Sci.Libn.
LAKE COUNTY MEMORIAL HOSPITALS - MEDICAL LIBRARIES (East and West) □ Painesville, OH

Edinburg, Gloria L., Hd.Libn.
OXFORD MUSEUM - LIBRARY □ Oxford, MA

Edmonds, Edmund P., Law Libn.
COLLEGE OF WILLIAM AND MARY - MARSHALL-WYTHE LAW LIBRARY □ Williamsburg, VA

Edmonson, James, Cur.
CLEVELAND HEALTH SCIENCES LIBRARY - HISTORICAL DIVISION □ Cleveland, OH

Edmunds, Eileen, Libn.
YUKON TERRITORY - DEPARTMENT OF TOURISM, RECREATION AND CULTURE - YUKON ARCHIVES □ Whitehorse, YT

Edmunds, Rebecca, Acq.
KEMPER GROUP - LIBRARY □ Long Grove, IL

Edmundson, Henry, Mgr., Info.
SCHLUMBERGER-DOLL - RESEARCH LIBRARY □ Ridgefield, CT

Edsall, Shirley, Mgr.
UNITED HEALTH SERVICES/WILSON HOSPITAL - LEARNING RESOURCES DEPARTMENT □ Johnson City, NY

Edson, Wendy B., Asst.Libn.
PHILLIPS, LYTLE, HITCHCOCK, BLAINE AND HUBER - LIBRARY □ Buffalo, NY

Edwards, Alice, Ref.Libn.
UNIVERSITY OF MISSOURI - HEALTH SCIENCES LIBRARY □ Columbia, MO

Edwards, Barry, Libn. 2, Coll. & Ref.
METROPOLITAN TORONTO LIBRARY - LANGUAGES DEPARTMENT □ Toronto, ON

Edwards, Cecilia C., Med.Libn.
U.S. ARMY HOSPITALS - WOMACK ARMY COMMUNITY HOSPITAL - MEDICAL LIBRARY □ Ft. Bragg, NC

Edwards, Elizabeth, Circ.Supv.
WASHINGTON STATE UNIVERSITY - VETERINARY MEDICAL/PHARMACY LIBRARY □ Pullman, WA

Edwards, Fern, College Libn.
GALLAUDET COLLEGE LIBRARY - SPECIAL COLLECTIONS† □ Washington, DC

Edwards, Fran, Lib.Techn.
ALABAMA STATE DEPARTMENT OF PUBLIC HEALTH - REFERENCE LIBRARY □ Montgomery, AL

Edwards, Harford, Jr., Hist.
U.S. ARMY - AVIATION MUSEUM - LIBRARY □ Fort Rucker, AL

Edwards, Jan, Tech.Libn.
LOCKHEED-GEORGIA COMPANY - TECHNICAL INFORMATION DEPARTMENT □ Marietta, GA

Edwards, Jessica, Libn.
AMERICAN CERAMIC SOCIETY - LIBRARY □ Columbus, OH

Edwards, Joan M., Dir.
DUNLAP AND ASSOCIATES EAST, INC. - LIBRARY □ Darien, CT

Edwards, Dr. John Carver, Rec.Off./Archv.
UNIVERSITY OF GEORGIA - DEPARTMENT OF RECORDS MANAGEMENT & UNIVERSITY ARCHIVES □ Athens, GA

Edwards, John D., Assoc.Libn.
UNIVERSITY OF OKLAHOMA - LAW LIBRARY □ Norman, OK

Edwards, Karen J., Law Libn.
LOWELL LAW LIBRARY □ Lowell, MA

Edwards, Margo, Asst.Libn.
CAHILL GORDON & REINDEL - LAW LIBRARY □ New York, NY

Edwards, Mark T., Libn.
CALIFORNIA AIR RESOURCES BOARD - LIBRARY □ Sacramento, CA

Edwards, Melanie G., Mgr., Ref.Pubns.
AMERICAN SOCIETY OF CIVIL ENGINEERS - INFORMATION SERVICES □ New York, NY

Edwards, Norman, Supt.
LITTLE WHITE HOUSE HISTORIC SITE -
ARCHIVES □ Warm Springs, GA
Edwards, Patricia A.
ARTHUR ANDERSEN & CO. - BUSINESS LIBRARY
□ Houston, TX
Edwards, Peggy
GENERAL ELECTRIC COMPANY - AIRCRAFT
ENGINE GROUP - LAW LIBRARY† □ Cincinnati,
OH
Edwards, Peggy, Asst.Ref.Libn.
TEXAS TECH UNIVERSITY - HEALTH SCIENCES
CENTER - LIBRARY OF THE HEALTH SCIENCES
□ Lubbock, TX
Edwards, Philip, Ref.Spec.
SMITHSONIAN INSTITUTION LIBRARIES -
NATIONAL AIR AND SPACE MUSEUM - LIBRARY
□ Washington, DC
Edwards, Rita, Hd.
ADELPHI UNIVERSITY - SOCIAL WORK
LIBRARY† □ Garden City, NY
Edwards, Rita L., Dir./Lib. & AV Serv.
GEORGE BROWN COLLEGE OF APPLIED ARTS &
TECHNOLOGY - LIBRARY □ Toronto, ON
Edwards, Shelia, Lib.Techn.
WAKE COUNTY MEDICAL CENTER - MEDICAL
LIBRARY □ Raleigh, NC
Edwards, Willie M., Hd.Libn.
INSTITUTE OF GERONTOLOGY - LEARNING
RESOURCE CENTER □ Ann Arbor, MI
Egan, Rhonda R., Libn.
SACRAMENTO AREA COUNCIL OF
GOVERNMENTS - LIBRARY □ Sacramento, CA
Egertson, Yvonne L., Libn.
AMERICAN NEWSPAPER PUBLISHERS
ASSOCIATION - LIBRARY □ Reston, VA
Eggert, Charlean, Hd. Law Libn.
DU PAGE COUNTY LAW LIBRARY □ Wheaton, IL
Eggert, Jean, Photo.Libn.
GREEN BAY PRESS-GAZETTE - LIBRARY □
Green Bay, WI
Eggert, Nancy A., Adm.Asst.
ALTERNATIVE SOURCES OF ENERGY, INC. -
LIBRARY AND REFERRAL SERVICE □ Milaca, MN
Eggleston, Gerald R., Acq.Libn.
STATE HISTORICAL SOCIETY OF WISCONSIN -
LIBRARY □ Madison, WI
Eggleston, Tom, Grand Sec./Libn.
GRAND LODGE OF IOWA, A.F. AND A.M. - IOWA
MASONIC LIBRARY □ Cedar Rapids, IA
Ehernberger, Nicolette
ST. LOUIS PUBLIC LIBRARY - HUMANITIES AND
SOCIAL SCIENCES DEPARTMENT □ St. Louis,
MO
Ehlers, William J., Libn.
SIMAT, HELLIESEN AND EICHNER - LIBRARY □
New York, NY
Ehlert, Arnold D., Dir., Lib.
INSTITUTE FOR CREATION RESEARCH -
LIBRARY □ El Cajon, CA
Ehr, Patricia H., Hd.Libn.
NORTHWESTERN MUTUAL LIFE INSURANCE
COMPANY - REFERENCE LIBRARY □ Milwaukee,
WI
Ehrenberg, Ralph E., Asst.Chf.
LIBRARY OF CONGRESS - GEOGRAPHY & MAP
DIVISION □ Washington, DC
Ehret, Judie, Rsrcs. Teacher
SANTA CLARA COUNTY OFFICE OF EDUCATION
- CENTRAL CALIFORNIA CENTER FOR
EDUCATIONAL IMPROVEMENT - LIBRARY □ San
Jose, CA
Ehrhardt, Mr. Allyn, Libn.
FRANKLIN UNIVERSITY - LIBRARY □ Columbus,
OH
Ehrhart, Carl Y., Act.Libn.
UNITED METHODIST CHURCH - HISTORICAL
SOCIETY OF THE EASTERN PENNSYLVANIA
CONFERENCE - ARCHIVES ROOM □ Annville, PA
Ehrig, Ellen, Chf.Ref./ILL Libn.
SUNY - AGRICULTURAL AND TECHNICAL
COLLEGE AT ALFRED - WALTER C. HINKLE
MEMORIAL LIBRARY □ Alfred, NY

Ehrmann, Marie, Res.Libn.
UNITED STATES GYPSUM COMPANY - GRAHAM
J. MORGAN RESEARCH LIBRARY □ Libertyville,
IL
Eiberson, Harold, Chf.Libn.
BARUCH (Bernard M.) COLLEGE OF THE CITY
UNIVERSITY OF NEW YORK - LIBRARY† □ New
York, NY
Eichell, Nanette D., Info.Rsrcs.Coord.
COUNCIL OF STATE GOVERNMENTS - STATES
INFORMATION CENTER □ Lexington, KY
Eicher, Thomas, Ref.
UNIVERSITY OF IOWA - LAW LIBRARY □ Iowa
City, IA
Eichholz, Tanya, Info.Sci.
HOECHST-ROUSSEL PHARMACEUTICALS, INC. -
LIBRARY □ Somerville, NJ
Eichinger, Ann, Ref.Libn.
SOUTH DAKOTA STATE LIBRARY & ARCHIVES □
Pierre, SD
Eichman, Barbara J., Libn.
AMERICAN CIVIL LIBERTIES UNION -
LIBRARY/ARCHIVES □ New York, NY
Eichstadt, John R., Assoc. Law Libn.
NEW MEXICO STATE SUPREME COURT - LAW
LIBRARY □ Santa Fe, NM
Eick, Barbara, Archv.
STANFORD UNIVERSITY - MUSIC LIBRARY □
Stanford, CA
Eickenhorst, Joanna W., Tech.Info.Spec.
STAUFFER CHEMICAL COMPANY - TECHNICAL
INFORMATION CENTER □ Farmington, CT
Eickhoff, B.M., Physics Libn.
WASHINGTON UNIVERSITY - PFEIFFER
PHYSICS LIBRARY □ St. Louis, MO
Eide, Margaret, Soc.Sci.Libn.
EASTERN MICHIGAN UNIVERSITY - CENTER OF
EDUCATIONAL RESOURCES - ARCHIVES/
SPECIAL COLLECTIONS □ Ypsilanti, MI
Eifling, Janice K., Libn.
U.S.D.A. - AGRICULTURAL RESEARCH SERVICE
- NATL. ANIMAL DISEASE CENTER LIBRARY □
Ames, IA
Eifrig, Janice
DIGITAL EQUIPMENT CORPORATION -
MAYNARD AREA INFORMATION SERVICES □
Maynard, MA
Eigner, Selma W., Libn.
WHIDDEN MEMORIAL HOSPITAL - LIBRARY □
Everett, MA
Eikeland, Audrey, Ref.
UNIVERSITY OF ALBERTA - LAW LIBRARY □
Edmonton, AB
Eikens, Kathy, Supv., Circ.
COLUMBIA UNION COLLEGE - THEOFIELD G.
WEIS LIBRARY □ Takoma Park, MD
Eilering, Susan, Ref./Coll.Dev.Libn.
COLUMBIA UNIVERSITY - AMBROSE MONELL
ENGINEERING LIBRARY □ New York, NY
Einowski, Ilona, Archv.
UNIVERSITY OF CALIFORNIA, BERKELEY -
STATE DATA PROGRAM LIBRARY □ Berkeley,
CA
Einstein, Dan, Archv.
UNIVERSITY OF CALIFORNIA, LOS ANGELES -
ACADEMY OF TELEVISION ARTS & SCIENCES -
TELEVISION ARCHIVES □ Los Angeles, CA
Eis, Arlene, Libn.
CRAVATH, SWAINE, & MOORE - LAW LIBRARY
□ New York, NY
Eisemann, Meg, Coll.Supv.
LIBRARY ASSOCIATION OF PORTLAND -
GENERAL INFORMATION DEPARTMENT -
FOUNDATION CENTER □ Portland, OR
Eisen, David J., Dir. of Res. & Info.
NEWSPAPER GUILD - HEYWOOD BROUN
LIBRARY □ Washington, DC
Eisenbeis, Kathleen, Libn.
UNIVERSITY OF TEXAS, AUSTIN - DOCUMENTS
COLLECTION □ Austin, TX

Eisenberg, Ethel, Med.Libn.
ST. VINCENT'S HOSPITAL AND MEDICAL
CENTER OF NEW YORK, WESTCHESTER
BRANCH - MEDICAL LIBRARY □ Harrison, NY
Eisenberg, Gena M., Asst.Libn.
WHITMAN & RANSOM - LIBRARY □ New York,
NY
Eisenberg, Geraldine, Cat.
UNIVERSITY OF TEXAS HEALTH SCIENCE
CENTER, SAN ANTONIO - LIBRARY □ San
Antonio, TX
Eisenberg, Peter L., Libn.
VANDERCOOK COLLEGE OF MUSIC - HARRY
RUPPEL MEMORIAL LIBRARY □ Chicago, IL
Eisenhauer, Jean, Acq.Libn.
WASHINGTON & LEE UNIVERSITY - LAW
LIBRARY □ Lexington, VA
Eisenman, Jean, Asst.Dir., Pub.Serv.
UNIVERSITY OF MISSOURI, ROLLA - CURTIS
LAWS WILSON LIBRARY □ Rolla, MO
Eiser, Mary Jo, Libn.
COMBUSTION ENGINEERING, INC. - TAYLOR
INSTRUMENT TECHNICAL INFORMATION
CENTER □ Rochester, NY
Eisman, Charlotte, Asst.Engr.Libn.
UNIVERSITY OF TEXAS, AUSTIN -
ENGINEERING LIBRARY □ Austin, TX
Eisner, Elyse A., Libn.
CONTRA COSTA TIMES - LIBRARY □ Walnut
Creek, CA
Eiss, Merle I., Mgr.
MC CORMICK & CO. - R & D INFORMATION
CENTER† □ Hunt Valley, MD
Ek, Jacqueline, Div.Hd.
INDIANAPOLIS-MARION COUNTY PUBLIC
LIBRARY - FILM DIVISION □ Indianapolis, IN
Ekdahl, Janis, Asst.Dir.
MUSEUM OF MODERN ART - LIBRARY □ New
York, NY
Ekfelt, Lynn, Cur.
ST. LAWRENCE UNIVERSITY - SPECIAL
COLLECTIONS □ Canton, NY
Ekimov, Roza, Libn.
EXXON COMPANY, U.S.A. - EXPLORATION
LIBRARY □ Houston, TX
Ekins, A. George, Tech.Serv.Libn.
CANADA - TRANSPORT CANADA -
TRANSPORTATION DEVELOPMENT CENTRE -
LIBRARY □ Montreal, PQ
Eklund, Cora Morley, Cat.
WASHINGTON STATE LAW LIBRARY □ Olympia,
WA
Ekman, Sheila, Ref.Libn.
BENTLEY COLLEGE - SOLOMON R. BAKER
LIBRARY □ Waltham, MA
Ekstrand, Nancy, Asst.Dir.
WAKE FOREST UNIVERSITY - BOWMAN GRAY
SCHOOL OF MEDICINE - COY C. CARPENTER
LIBRARY □ Winston-Salem, NC
Elam, Craig, Assoc.Dir., Tech.Serv.
TEXAS COLLEGE OF OSTEOPATHIC MEDICINE -
HEALTH SCIENCES LIBRARY □ Fort Worth, TX
Elam, Joice, Doc.Libn.
EMORY UNIVERSITY - SCHOOL OF LAW
LIBRARY □ Atlanta, GA
Elbert, Dr. E. Duane, Musm.Cur.
COLES COUNTY HISTORICAL SOCIETY -
GREENWOOD SCHOOL MUSEUM - LIBRARY □
Charleston, IL
Elbrecht, Barbara Griffith, Sr.Libn.
CALIFORNIA STATE BOARD OF EQUALIZATION
- LAW LIBRARY □ Sacramento, CA
Elden, Jennifer L., Libn.
GELBERG & ABRAMS - LAW LIBRARY† □ New
York, NY
Elder, Charles W., Hd.Libn.
HUNTER COLLEGE OF THE CITY UNIVERSITY
OF NEW YORK - HUNTER COLLEGE SCHOOL OF
SOCIAL WORK - LIBRARY □ New York, NY
Elder, Kate, Supv.Libn.
FORT LOGAN MENTAL HEALTH CENTER -
MEDICAL LIBRARY □ Denver, CO

Elder, Kathryn, Libn.
YORK UNIVERSITY - FILM LIBRARY □
Downsview, ON

Elder, Margaret, Lib.Techn.
U.S. BUREAU OF RECLAMATION - LIBRARY □
Sacramento, CA

Elder, Nancy, Libn.
UNIVERSITY OF TEXAS, AUSTIN - SCIENCE
LIBRARY □ Austin, TX

Elder, Nelda, ILL
KANSAS STATE UNIVERSITY - FARRELL
LIBRARY □ Manhattan, KS

Elder, Ralph, Pub.Serv.
UNIVERSITY OF TEXAS, AUSTIN - EUGENE C.
BARKER TEXAS HISTORY CENTER □ Austin, TX

Eldevik, Bruce, Asst.Libn.
NORTH AMERICAN BAPTIST SEMINARY -
KAISER-RAMAKER LIBRARY □ Sioux Falls, SD

Eldridge, Robin, Sci.Ref.Libn.
SUNY AT BINGHAMTON - SCIENCE LIBRARY □
Binghamton, NY

Eldridge, Veronica, Co-Dir.
LOWER EAST SIDE FAMILY RESOURCE CENTER
□ New York, NY

Elefante, Marie, Libn.
OREGON STATE DEPARTMENT OF
TRANSPORTATION - LIBRARY □ Salem, OR

Elfman, Sheila, Lib.Spec.
DYNAMICS RESEARCH CORPORATION -
LIBRARY □ Wilmington, MA

Elfner, Margaret, ILL Libn.
HOFFMANN-LA ROCHE, INC. - SCIENTIFIC
LIBRARY □ Nutley, NJ

Elfrank, James, Info.Spec.
AT & T COMMUNICATIONS - INFORMATION
RESEARCH CENTER □ Cincinnati, OH

Elias, D., Lib.Supv.
AME ENGINEERING LTD. - LIBRARY □
Edmonton, AB

Elias, Werner, Libn.
COLLECTORS CLUB - LIBRARY □ New York, NY

Eliasson, Ms. Dale, Chf.Libn.
DISTRICT OF COLUMBIA GENERAL HOSPITAL -
MEDICAL LIBRARY □ Washington, DC

Elijah, Mildred, Index
NEWSDAY, INC. - LIBRARY □ Melville, NY

Elinoff, Linda, Asst.Dir.
MEDICAL GROUP MANAGEMENT ASSOCIATION
- INFORMATION SERVICE □ Denver, CO

Eliot, Valerie J., Libn.
DEACONESS HOSPITAL - SCHOOL OF NURSING
- RICHARD W. ANGERT MEMORIAL LIBRARY □
Cincinnati, OH

Elkins, Elizabeth A., Coord., Pub.Serv.
SUNY - COLLEGE OF ENVIRONMENTAL SCIENCE
AND FORESTRY - F. FRANKLIN MOON LIBRARY
□ Syracuse, NY

Ell, Elizabeth L., Libn.
GREELEY AND HANSEN - LIBRARY† □ Chicago,
IL

Elledge, Dot, Dir., Lib.Serv.
WAYNE COMMUNITY COLLEGE - LEARNING
RESOURCE CENTER □ Goldsboro, NC

Ellefson, Jean, Church Libn.
WOODLAKE LUTHERAN CHURCH - LIBRARY □
Richfield, MN

Ellenberger, Jack S., Libn.
SHEARMAN & STERLING - LIBRARY □ New York,
NY

Ellenwood, Dwight, Rec.Anl.
WASHINGTON STATE OFFICE OF SECRETARY
OF STATE - DIVISION OF ARCHIVES AND
RECORD MANAGEMENT □ Olympia, WA

Ellenwood, Rev. Lee K., Lib.Dir.
FIRST CHURCH OF CHRIST CONGREGATIONAL
- JOHN P. WEBSTER LIBRARY □ West Hartford,
CT

Eller, Barbara A., Chf.Libn.
U.S. ARMY POST - FORT BRAGG - LIBRARY □ Ft.
Bragg, NC

Eller, Dr. William, Dir.
SUNY AT BUFFALO - CENTER FOR CURRICULUM
PLANNING □ Amherst, NY

Ellett, William, Cat.
SOUTH CAROLINA STATE LIBRARY □ Columbia,
SC

Elliker, Calvin, Music Libn.
INDIANA UNIVERSITY OF PENNSYLVANIA -
COGSWELL MUSIC LIBRARY □ Indiana, PA

Elliker, Calvin, Asst.Libn.
INDIANA UNIVERSITY OF PENNSYLVANIA -
UNIVERSITY LIBRARY □ Indiana, PA

Elling, Mary, Bibliog.
SYRACUSE UNIVERSITY - MATHEMATICS
LIBRARY □ Syracuse, NY

Ellingson, Celia S., Info.Serv.Dir.
PEAT, MARWICK, MITCHELL & CO. -
INFORMATION SERVICES □ Dallas, TX

Ellingson, Jo Ann, Asst. State Libn.
STATE LIBRARY OF FLORIDA □ Tallahassee, FL

Ellinwood, Sara B., Libn.
KAMAN-TEMPO - TECHNICAL INFORMATION
CENTER □ Santa Barbara, CA

Elliot, Kimberly, ILL
UNIVERSITY OF SOUTH DAKOTA - CHRISTIAN
P. LOMMEN HEALTH SCIENCES LIBRARY □
Vermillion, SD

Elliot, William T., Libn.
ONONDAGA COUNTY PUBLIC LIBRARY -
BUSINESS AND INDUSTRIAL DEPARTMENT □
Syracuse, NY

Elliott, Barbara, Chf.Libn.
GENERAL DYNAMICS CORPORATION - PUBLIC
AFFAIRS LIBRARY □ St. Louis, MO

Elliott, Beverly, Circ.Supv.
SAN DIEGO STATE UNIVERSITY - MEDIA &
CURRICULUM CENTER† □ San Diego, CA

Elliott, Carol G., Cat.
UNIVERSITY OF ARIZONA - COLLEGE OF LAW
LIBRARY† □ Tucson, AZ

Elliott, Clark A., Assoc.Cur.
HARVARD UNIVERSITY - ARCHIVES □
Cambridge, MA

Elliott, Franki, Tax Libn.
ROYAL BANK OF CANADA - TAXATION
LIBRARY/INTERNATIONAL □ Toronto, ON

Elliott, Hamilton, Asst.Univ.Archv.
UNIVERSITY OF PENNSYLVANIA - ARCHIVES
AND RECORDS CENTER □ Philadelphia, PA

Elliott, James V., Jr., Pub.Rel.Off.
TECHNIC INC. - LIBRARY □ Providence, RI

Elliott, Jill, Libn.
GALLO (E. & J.) WINERY - LIBRARY □ Modesto,
CA

Elliott, Joan M., Spec.Coll.Libn.
WILLARD LIBRARY OF EVANSVILLE - SPECIAL
COLLECTIONS DEPARTMENT □ Evansville, IN

Elliott, Kay M., Chf.Libn.
IOWA STATE DEPARTMENT OF HUMAN
SERVICES - LIBRARY □ Des Moines, IA

Elliott, Ken, Circ.Libn.
REFORMED THEOLOGICAL SEMINARY -
LIBRARY □ Jackson, MS

Elliott, Lois, Libn.
DELLCREST CHILDREN'S CENTRE - LIBRARY □
Downsview, ON

Elliott, Marilyn, Libn.
EDMONTON PUBLIC SCHOOLS - LEARNING
RESOURCES PROFESSIONAL LIBRARY □
Edmonton, AB

Elliott, Mary, Chf.
DISTRICT OF COLUMBIA PUBLIC LIBRARY -
MUSIC & RECREATION DIVISION □ Washington,
DC

Ellis, Brenda M., Libn.
UMSTEAD (John) HOSPITAL - LEARNING
RESOURCE CENTER □ Butner, NC

Ellis, Charlotte, Sr.Asst.
WASHINGTON UNIVERSITY - BIOLOGY
LIBRARY □ St. Louis, MO

Ellis, D., Libn.
AMERICAN INSTITUTE OF MANAGEMENT -
LIBRARY □ Boston, MA

Ellis, Donna Burns, Mss.Libn.
MARYLAND HISTORICAL SOCIETY - LIBRARY □
Baltimore, MD

Ellis, Ellen, Libn.
VANDERBILT UNIVERSITY - JEAN AND
ALEXANDER HEARD LIBRARY - DYER
OBSERVATORY □ Nashville, TN

Ellis, Ethel M., Hd., Tech.Serv.Dept.
HOWARD UNIVERSITY - MOORLAND-SPINGARN
RESEARCH CENTER - LIBRARY DIVISION □
Washington, DC

Ellis, Frances
AMERICAN NATIONAL BUILDING - JOINT
VENTURE LAW LIBRARY □ Denver, CO

Ellis, Georgia, Dir., Lib.Serv.
CANADA - STATISTICS CANADA - LIBRARY □
Ottawa, ON

Ellis, Gloria B., Lib.Dir.
WALSH COLLEGE OF ACCOUNTANCY AND
BUSINESS ADMINISTRATION - LIBRARY □
Troy, MI

Ellis, Dr. Jack D., Dir. of Libs.
MOREHEAD STATE UNIVERSITY - CAMDEN-
CARROLL LIBRARY □ Morehead, KY

Ellis, Joan, Coord.Ref.Serv.
UNIVERSITY OF LOWELL, NORTH CAMPUS -
ALUMNI/LYDON LIBRARY† □ Lowell, MA

Ellis, John C., Dir.
ASSOCIATED GENERAL CONTRACTORS OF
AMERICA - JAMES L. ALLHANDS MEMORIAL
LIBRARY □ Washington, DC

Ellis, Juanita, Pres.
CITIZENS ASSOCIATION FOR SOUND ENERGY
(CASE) - LIBRARY □ Dallas, TX

Ellis, Natalie Paymer, Law Libn.
MARYLAND STATE LAW DEPARTMENT -
ATTORNEY GENERAL'S OFFICE - LIBRARY □
Baltimore, MD

Ellis, Pearl, Asst.Dir.
SOUTHWESTERN ASSEMBLIES OF GOD
COLLEGE - P.C. NELSON MEMORIAL LIBRARY □
Waxahachie, TX

Ellis, Richard, Ref.Libn.
UNIVERSITY OF MANITOBA - D.S. WOODS
EDUCATION LIBRARY □ Winnipeg, MB

Ellis, Robert H., Jr.,Cur.
KENDALL WHALING MUSEUM - LIBRARY □
Sharon, MA

Ellis, William David, Libn.
HEBREW EDUCATIONAL ALLIANCE - LIBRARY □
Denver, CO

Ellis, William N., Exec.Dir.
TRANET - LIBRARY □ Rangeley, ME

Ellis, Y.A., Res.
OAK RIDGE NATIONAL LABORATORY -
NUCLEAR DATA PROJECT □ Oak Ridge, TN

Ellison, Pat, Lib.Assoc.
SINGER (H. Douglas) MENTAL HEALTH CENTER -
LIBRARY □ Rockford, IL

Ellison, Sandra, Pub.Lib.Cons.
OKLAHOMA STATE DEPARTMENT OF
LIBRARIES □ Oklahoma City, OK

Ellison, Shannon-Dean, Lib.Techn., Rec.
CALGARY CITY ELECTRIC SYSTEM - RESOURCE
CENTRE □ Calgary, AB

Ellsworth, Daryl G., Libn.
WARREN STATE HOSPITAL - MEDICAL
LIBRARY □ Warren, PA

Ellsworth, Linda V., Hist.
HISTORIC PENSACOLA PRESERVATION BOARD
- LIBRARY □ Pensacola, FL

Ellsworth, Rudolph C., Libn.
METROPOLITAN SANITARY DISTRICT OF
GREATER CHICAGO - TECHNICAL LIBRARY □
Chicago, IL

Ellwanger, Kendrick J., Supervisory Statistician
U.S. BUREAU OF THE CENSUS - INFORMATION
SERVICES PROGRAM - DENVER REG. OFFICE -
CENSUS PUBLICATION CENTER □ Denver, CO

Ellwood, Katherine B., Search Libn.
GETTY OIL COMPANY, INC. - RESEARCH
CENTER LIBRARY □ Houston, TX

Elman, Stanley A., Mgr.
LOCKHEED-CALIFORNIA COMPANY -
TECHNICAL INFORMATION CENTER □ Burbank,
CA

Elmore, Betty, Ser.Cat.
U.S. DEPT. OF THE TREASURY - INFORMATION SERVICES DIVISION - TREASURY DEPT. LIBRARY □ Washington, DC

Elmore, Faye, Cons., Rd.Serv./GLIN
GEORGIA STATE DEPARTMENT OF EDUCATION - DIVISION OF PUBLIC LIBRARY SERVICES □ Atlanta, GA

Elmstrom, Dr. Gary W., Ctr.Dir.
UNIVERSITY OF FLORIDA - AGRICULTURAL RESEARCH CENTER - LIBRARY □ Leesburg, FL

Elrod, James, Lib.Dir.
CALIFORNIA INSTITUTE OF THE ARTS - LIBRARY □ Valencia, CA

Elsesser, Lionelle, Chf., Lib.Serv.
U.S. VETERANS ADMINISTRATION (MN-Minneapolis) - MEDICAL CENTER LIBRARY SERVICE □ Minneapolis, MN

Elsner, Emily Evans, Libn.
PORTLAND ART MUSEUM - LIBRARY □ Portland, OR

Elston, Charles, Hd., Spec.Coll.
MARQUETTE UNIVERSITY - MEMORIAL LIBRARY □ Milwaukee, WI

Elston, Charles B., Dept.Hd.
MARQUETTE UNIVERSITY - DEPARTMENT OF SPECIAL COLLECTIONS AND UNIVERSITY ARCHIVES □ Milwaukee, WI

Elveson, Leon, Med.Libn.
WOODHULL MEDICAL AND MENTAL HEALTH CENTER - HEALTH SCIENCES LIBRARY □ Brooklyn, NY

Elvidge, Mrs. M., Libn.
OGILVY, RENAULT - LIBRARY† □ Montreal, PQ

Elwell, Pamela M., Libn.
MOUNT CARMEL MEDICAL CENTER - MOTHER M. CONSTANTINE MEMORIAL LIBRARY □ Columbus, OH

Ely, Dr. Donald, Dir.
ERIC CLEARINGHOUSE ON INFORMATION RESOURCES □ Syracuse, NY

Elzy, Dr. Martin I., Supv.Archv.
U.S. PRESIDENTIAL LIBRARIES - CARTER PRESIDENTIAL MATERIALS PROJECT □ Atlanta, GA

Embers, Richard, Map Lib.Assoc.
UNIVERSITY OF KANSAS - MAP LIBRARY □ Lawrence, KS

Emberson, Eileen, Dir., Lib.Serv.
LUTHER HOSPITAL - LIBRARY SERVICES □ Eau Claire, WI

Embrey, Eliza E., Libn.
WAR MEMORIAL MUSEUM OF VIRGINIA - RESEARCH LIBRARY □ Newport News, VA

Embry, Joan, Hd.Libn.
FLORIDA SCHOOL FOR THE DEAF AND BLIND - LIBRARY FOR THE DEAF □ St. Augustine, FL

Emby, Carol, Libn.
ALLENDALE MUTUAL INSURANCE COMPANY - LIBRARY □ Johnston, RI

Emde, Judy, Ref.Libn.
U.S. FOOD & DRUG ADMINISTRATION - NATIONAL CENTER FOR TOXICOLOGICAL RESEARCH - LIBRARY □ Jefferson, AK

Emele, Russell J., Dir. of Lib.
EAST STROUDSBURG UNIVERSITY - KENT LIBRARY† □ East Stroudsburg, PA

Emerick, Kenneth, Cat.
CLARION UNIVERSITY OF PENNSYLVANIA - RENA M. CARLSON LIBRARY □ Clarion, PA

Emerson, Dawn C., Libn.
SENECA FALLS HISTORICAL SOCIETY - LIBRARY □ Seneca Falls, NY

Emerson, John A.
UNIVERSITY OF CALIFORNIA, BERKELEY - MUSIC LIBRARY □ Berkeley, CA

Emerson, Patricia R., Dir., Member Serv.
UNIVERSAL SERIALS & BOOK EXCHANGE, INC. - DUPLICATE EXCHANGE CLEARINGHOUSE & INFORMATION CENTER □ Washington, DC

Emerson, R., Tech.Info.Spec.
U.S. DEFENSE MAPPING AGENCY - AEROSPACE CENTER - TECHNICAL LIBRARY □ St. Louis, MO

Emerson, V., Ref.Serv.
WIDENER UNIVERSITY - WOLFGRAM MEMORIAL LIBRARY □ Chester, PA

Emerson, William R., Dir.
U.S. PRESIDENTIAL LIBRARIES - FRANKLIN D. ROOSEVELT LIBRARY □ Hyde Park, NY

Emery, Arlene, Libn.
FIRST CONGREGATIONAL CHURCH - LIBRARY □ St. Joseph, MI

Emery, C. David, Assoc.Libn./Coll.
UNIVERSITY OF WATERLOO - DANA PORTER ARTS LIBRARY □ Waterloo, ON

Emery, Jean, Asst.Libn.
CHILDREN'S MEMORIAL HOSPITAL - JOSEPH BRENNEMANN LIBRARY □ Chicago, IL

Emery, Jean, Ref.Libn.
NORTHWESTERN UNIVERSITY - HEALTH SCIENCES LIBRARY† □ Chicago, IL

Emery, Mark W., Ref.Libn.
UNIVERSITY OF UTAH - HUMAN RELATIONS AREA FILES □ Salt Lake City, UT

Emery, Mary B., Libn.
UNIVERSITY OF SANTA CLARA - EDWIN A. HEAFEY LAW LIBRARY† □ Santa Clara, CA

Emery, Robert, Ref.Libn.
UNION UNIVERSITY - ALBANY LAW SCHOOL - LIBRARY □ Albany, NY

Emilio, Betty, Lib.Tech.Asst.
SUNY AT STONY BROOK - HEALTH SCIENCES LIBRARY □ East Setauket, NY

Emma, Mary Ann, Info.Spec.
AMERICAN ASSOCIATION OF ADVERTISING AGENCIES - MEMBER INFORMATION SERVICE □ New York, NY

Emmons, Mildred, Hd., Coll.Dev.Div.
GEORGIA INSTITUTE OF TECHNOLOGY - PRICE GILBERT MEMORIAL LIBRARY □ Atlanta, GA

Emmons, Paul, Music Libn.
CENTRAL WASHINGTON UNIVERSITY - MUSIC LIBRARY □ Ellensburg, WA

Emond, Sr. Gemma, Med.Libn.
CENTRE HOSPITALIER DE ST-LAURENT - BIBLIOTHEQUE† □ St. Laurent, PQ

Emory, Bruce B., Dp.Asst.Gen.Mgr.
METROPOLITAN ATLANTA RAPID TRANSIT AUTHORITY - LIBRARY □ Atlanta, GA

Empey, Verla E., Dir.
WELLESLEY HOSPITAL - LIBRARY □ Toronto, ON

Enberg, Henry W., II, Legal Ed.
PRACTISING LAW INSTITUTE - LIBRARY □ New York, NY

Enck, Joe, Presentation Coord.
CARNEGIE-MELLON UNIVERSITY - AUDIO VISUAL SERVICES □ Pittsburgh, PA

Enders, Katy, Asst.Libn.
NEW YORK BOTANICAL GARDEN - LIBRARY† □ Bronx, NY

Enders, Ruth, Lib.Techn.
CANTERRA ENERGY LTD. - LIBRARY □ Calgary, AB

Endicott, Judy G., Chf., Circ.
U.S. AIR FORCE - HISTORICAL RESEARCH CENTER □ Maxwell AFB, AL

Endres, Maureen Doyle
BLOOMSBURG UNIVERSITY OF PENNSYLVANIA - HARVEY A. ANDRUSS LIBRARY - SPECIAL COLLECTIONS □ Bloomsburg, PA

Endsley, Beverly J., Lib.Techn.
U.S. NAVY - NAVAL STATION LIBRARY (Guam) □ FPO San Francisco, CA

Eng, Steve, Cur.
TENNESSEE WESTERN HISTORY AND FOLKLORE SOCIETY - LIBRARY □ Nashville, TN

Engeart, James, Dir.
UNIVERSITY OF ARIZONA - CENTER FOR CREATIVE PHOTOGRAPHY □ Tucson, AZ

Engel, Carl Thomas, Libn.
LAKE COUNTY HISTORICAL SOCIETY - PERCY KENDALL SMITH LIBRARY FOR HISTORICAL RESEARCH □ Mentor, OH

Engel, Catherine T., Ref.Libn.
COLORADO HISTORICAL SOCIETY - STEPHEN H. HART LIBRARY □ Denver, CO

Engel, Cheryl, Libn.
CARNEGIE LIBRARY OF PITTSBURGH - SCIENCE AND TECHNOLOGY DEPARTMENT □ Pittsburgh, PA

Engel, Claire, State Law Libn.
MONTANA STATE LAW LIBRARY □ Helena, MT

Engel, Claire, Chf., Lib.Serv.
NEW YORK STATE DEPARTMENT OF LAW - LIBRARY □ Albany, NY

Engel, Ferd, Archv.
JEWISH FEDERATION OF NASHVILLE AND MIDDLE TENNESSEE - ARCHIVES □ Nashville, TN

Engel, Laura, Libn.
CRANFORD UNITED METHODIST CHURCH - LIBRARY □ Cranford, NJ

Engel, Mary Lou, Tech.Info.Spec.
U.S. NATL. HIGHWAY TRAFFIC SAFETY ADMINISTRATION - TECHNICAL REFERENCE DIVISION □ Washington, DC

Engelhardt, D. LeRoy, Libn.
NEW BRUNSWICK THEOLOGICAL SEMINARY - GARDNER A. SAGE LIBRARY □ New Brunswick, NJ

Engelmann, Hugo O., Ed.
CLEARINGHOUSE FOR SOCIOLOGICAL LITERATURE □ Dekalb, IL

Engeman, Richard H., Asst.Libn.
UNIVERSITY OF WASHINGTON - SPECIAL COLL.DIV. - PACIFIC NORTHWEST COLLECTION - ARCHITECTURAL HISTORY COLL. □ Seattle, WA

Engeman, Richard H., Asst.Libn.
UNIVERSITY OF WASHINGTON - SPECIAL COLL.DIV. - PACIFIC NORTHWEST COLLECTION - HISTORICAL PHOTOGRAPHY COLL. □ Seattle, WA

Engen, Richard B., Dir., Lib. & Musm.Div.
ALASKA STATE DIVISION OF STATE LIBRARIES & MUSEUMS - STATE LIBRARY □ Juneau, AK

Engerman, Jeanne, Asst.Libn.
WASHINGTON STATE HISTORICAL SOCIETY - LIBRARY □ Tacoma, WA

Engfehr, Rev. William, Dir., Educ. Media
CONCORDIA SEMINARY - LIBRARY □ St. Louis, MO

Engfield, R., Dp.Libn.
CANADA - NATIONAL GALLERY OF CANADA - LIBRARY □ Ottawa, ON

England, Angela C., Med.Libn.
HOLSTON VALLEY HOSPITAL AND MEDICAL CENTER - HEALTH SCIENCE LIBRARY □ Kingsport, TN

Englander, Evelyn A., Libn.
U.S. MARINE CORPS - HISTORICAL CENTER LIBRARY† □ Washington, DC

Engle, Helen, Asst.Archv.
MANCHESTER HISTORIC ASSOCIATION - LIBRARY □ Manchester, NH

Engle, Mary F., Libn.
QUEEN ANNE'S COUNTY LAW LIBRARY □ Centreville, MD

Englehardt, Sandra, Pub.Serv.Libn.
ALBERTA - DEPARTMENT OF ENERGY AND NATURAL RESOURCES - LIBRARY □ Edmonton, AB

Englehart, Sherry, Libn.
LEGAL SERVICES ORGANIZATION OF INDIANA, INC. - LIBRARY □ Indianapolis, IN

Engleman, Roberta A., Assoc.Cur./Cat.
UNIVERSITY OF NORTH CAROLINA, CHAPEL HILL - RARE BOOK COLLECTION □ Chapel Hill, NC

Engler, Rose, Law Libn.
TUOLUMNE COUNTY LAW LIBRARY □ Sonora, CA

Engley, Beatrice, Info.Spec.
UNIVERSITY OF MISSOURI - HEALTH CARE TECHNOLOGY CENTER & INFORMATION SCIENCE GROUP - INFORMATION CENTER □ Columbia, MO

English, Cynthia, Hd.Ref.Libn.
BOSTON ATHENAEUM LIBRARY □ Boston, MA

English, David S., Libn.
U.S. AIR FORCE BASE - GRISSOM BASE LIBRARY □ Grissom AFB, IN

English, John, Chm., Lib.Comm.
SELKIRK MENTAL HEALTH CENTRE - CENTRAL LIBRARY □ Selkirk, MB

English, Susan B., Law Libn.
UNIVERSITY OF RICHMOND - WILLIAM T. MUSE MEMORIAL LAW LIBRARY □ Richmond, VA

English, Tom, Libn.
UNIVERSITY OF MINNESOTA - BELL MUSEUM OF NATURAL HISTORY - LIBRARY □ Minneapolis, MN

Englund, Catherine, Ref.Libn.
BRAILLE INSTITUTE OF AMERICA - LIBRARY □ Los Angeles, CA

Engro, Kathe, Dir.
DOCUMENTS PLUS, INC. □ New York, NY

Engst, Elaine, Asst.Archv.
CORNELL UNIVERSITY - DEPARTMENT OF MANUSCRIPTS AND UNIVERSITY ARCHIVES □ Ithaca, NY

Engstrom, Karen, Dir. of Lib.Serv.
ST. FRANCIS HOSPITAL - COMMUNITY HEALTH SCIENCE LIBRARY □ Breckenridge, MN

Enis, Alma, Libn.
ALL SAINTS EPISCOPAL HOSPITAL - F.M. CORSELIUS LIBRARY □ Fort Worth, TX

Ennis, Dr. William B., Jr., Ctr.Dir.
UNIVERSITY OF FLORIDA - AGRICULTURAL RESEARCH & EDUCATION CENTER - FORT LAUDERDALE LIBRARY □ Fort Lauderdale, FL

Enola, John I., Libn.
AUSTINE SCHOOL - LIBRARY □ Brattleboro, VT

Enos, Frances, Res.Libn.
HAWAII STATE - LEGISLATIVE REFERENCE BUREAU LIBRARY □ Honolulu, HI

Enriquez, Sandra A., Asst.Libn.
CENTER FOR ENERGY AND ENVIRONMENT - RESEARCH COLLECTION □ Mayaguez, PR

Ensanian, Armand O., Ref.Libn.
ENSANIAN PHYSICOCHEMICAL INSTITUTE - INFORMATION CENTER FOR GRAVITATION CHEMISTRY □ Eldred, PA

Ensanian, Elizabeth A., Chf.Libn.
ENSANIAN PHYSICOCHEMICAL INSTITUTE - INFORMATION CENTER FOR GRAVITATION CHEMISTRY □ Eldred, PA

Ensanian, Tamara, Res.Spec.
ENSANIAN PHYSICOCHEMICAL INSTITUTE - INFORMATION CENTER FOR GRAVITATION CHEMISTRY □ Eldred, PA

Ensign, David, Asst.Libn.
WASHBURN UNIVERSITY OF TOPEKA - SCHOOL OF LAW LIBRARY □ Topeka, KS

Ensor, Sally U., Libn.
BLUE CROSS AND BLUE SHIELD OF NORTH CAROLINA - INFORMATION CENTER □ Durham, NC

Entorf, Regina, Hd., Instr.Serv./Doc.
WITTENBERG UNIVERSITY - THOMAS LIBRARY □ Springfield, OH

Entze, Jeanne, Libn.
U.S. AIR FORCE ACADEMY - MEDICAL LIBRARY □ Colorado Springs, CO

Enz, Philip I., Adm.Libn.
CARTER (Larue D.) MEMORIAL HOSPITAL - MEDICAL LIBRARY □ Indianapolis, IN

Eorio, Joan, Circ.Supv.
RUTGERS UNIVERSITY, THE STATE UNIVERSITY OF NEW JERSEY - NEW JERSEY VOCATIONAL EDUCATION RESOURCE CENTER □ Old Bridge, NJ

Epelbaum, Marcia, Hd., Circ.
STANFORD UNIVERSITY - LANE MEDICAL LIBRARY □ Stanford, CA

Epstein, B.E., V.P.
FRANKLIN INSTITUTE - FRANKLIN RESEARCH CENTER - INFORMATION MANAGEMENT DEPARTMENT □ Philadelphia, PA

Epstein, Barbara A., Ref.Libn.
UNIVERSITY OF PITTSBURGH - WESTERN PSYCHIATRIC INSTITUTE AND CLINIC - LIBRARY □ Pittsburgh, PA

Epstein, Dena, Asst. Music Libn.
UNIVERSITY OF CHICAGO - MUSIC COLLECTION □ Chicago, IL

Epstein, Elias, Dir. of Res.
NOVOCOL CHEMICAL MANUFACTURING COMPANY, INC. - LIBRARY □ Brooklyn, NY

Epstein, Janet, Circ.Libn.
OHIO STATE SUPREME COURT LAW LIBRARY □ Columbus, OH

Epstein, Michelle, Coord. of Lib.Serv.
WESTERN CENTER ON LAW AND POVERTY, INC. - LIBRARY □ Los Angeles, CA

Epstein, Roni, Bus.Info.Libn.
GULF CANADA LIMITED - CENTRAL LIBRARY† □ Toronto, ON

Epstein, Ruth, Ref.Libn.
UNIVERSITY OF CINCINNATI - MEDICAL CENTER LIBRARIES - HEALTH SCIENCES LIBRARY† □ Cincinnati, OH

Erani, Karen, Assoc.Libn.
PFIZER, INC. - N.Y.O. LIBRARY □ New York, NY

Erbe, Edwin, Per.Libn.
KEAN COLLEGE OF NEW JERSEY - NANCY THOMPSON LIBRARY† □ Union, NJ

Erbeck, Diane, Ref.Libn.
PAINE WEBBER INC. - PAINE WEBBER BLYTH EASTMAN - LIBRARY □ New York, NY

Ercegovac, Zorana, Info.Mgr.
CITICORP/TRANSACTION TECHNOLOGY INC. - TECHNICAL INFORMATION RESEARCH CENTER □ Santa Monica, CA

Erdican, Achilla I., Cat.Libn.
EMORY UNIVERSITY - PITTS THEOLOGY LIBRARY □ Atlanta, GA

Erdmann, Charlotte A., Info.Serv.
SOUTH DAKOTA SCHOOL OF MINES & TECHNOLOGY - DEVEREAUX LIBRARY □ Rapid City, SD

Erganian, Richard, Info.Dir.
THE VINEYARD - REAL ESTATE, SHOPPING CENTER & URBAN DEVELOPMENT INFORMATION CENTER □ Fresno, CA

Ericksen, Paul, Assoc.Archv.
WHEATON COLLEGE - BILLY GRAHAM CENTER - ARCHIVES □ Wheaton, IL

Erickson, Alan E., Sci.Spec.
HARVARD UNIVERSITY - GODFREY LOWELL CABOT SCIENCE LIBRARY □ Cambridge, MA

Erickson, Carolyn A., Libn.
ZOECON CORPORATION - LIBRARY □ Palo Alto, CA

Erickson, Donald, Dir.
ERIC CLEARINGHOUSE ON HANDICAPPED & GIFTED CHILDREN - CEC INFORMATION SERVICES □ Reston, VA

Erickson, James M., Exec.Dir.
SWEDISH PIONEER HISTORICAL SOCIETY - SWEDISH-AMERICAN ARCHIVES OF GREATER CHICAGO □ Chicago, IL

Erickson, Jill, ILL
BOSTON ATHENAEUM LIBRARY □ Boston, MA

Erickson, Jon, Co-Dir.
BIOMEDICAL COMPUTING TECHNOLOGY INFORMATION CENTER □ Nashville, TN

Erickson, Kathy, Supv.
VIRGINIA STATE OFFICE OF EMERGENCY & ENERGY SERVICES - ENERGY INFORMATION AND SERVICES CENTER □ Richmond, VA

Erickson, Linda, Plan.Libn.
SANDIA NATIONAL LABORATORIES - TECHNICAL LIBRARY □ Albuquerque, NM

Erickson, Nancy, Cat.Libn.
MINNESOTA HISTORICAL SOCIETY - SPECIAL LIBRARIES □ St. Paul, MN

Erickson, Pennifer, Chf.
NATIONAL CENTER FOR HEALTH STATISTICS - CLEARINGHOUSE ON HEALTH INDEXES □ Hyattsville, MD

Erickson, Randy, Sys.Spec./PNRHSLS
UNIVERSITY OF WASHINGTON - HEALTH SCIENCES LIBRARY □ Seattle, WA

Erickson, Richard, Dir., IMC
BAPTIST BIBLE COLLEGE OF PENNSYLVANIA - RICHARD J. MURPHY MEMORIAL LIBRARY □ Clarks Summit, PA

Erickson, Rodney, Comm.Chm.
TRINITY LUTHERAN CHURCH - LIBRARY □ Moorhead, MN

Erickson, Shirley K., Ref.Libn.
DUKES COUNTY HISTORICAL SOCIETY - LIBRARY □ Edgartown, MA

Ericson, Christine, Cat.Libn.
COLORADO SCHOOL OF MINES - ARTHUR LAKES LIBRARY □ Golden, CO

Ericson, Margaret, Prof.Asst.
ENOCH PRATT FREE LIBRARY - FINE ARTS AND RECREATION DEPARTMENT □ Baltimore, MD

Ericson, Richard C., Pres.
MINNESOTA CITIZENS COUNCIL ON CRIME AND JUSTICE □ Minneapolis, MN

Ericson, Timothy L., Archv.
UNIVERSITY OF WISCONSIN, RIVER FALLS - CHALMER DAVEE LIBRARY - AREA RESEARCH CENTER □ River Falls, WI

Erlen, Jonathon, Ph.D., Cur., Hist.Coll.
UNIVERSITY OF PITTSBURGH - FALK LIBRARY OF THE HEALTH SCIENCES □ Pittsburgh, PA

Ermatinger, Charles J., Vatican Film Libn.
ST. LOUIS UNIVERSITY - KNIGHTS OF COLUMBUS VATICAN FILM LIBRARY □ St. Louis, MO

Ermili, Nelly E., Hd., Acq.Dept.
YALE UNIVERSITY - LAW LIBRARY □ New Haven, CT

Ernesaks, Sylvia, Sr.Libn.
ONTARIO HYDRO - LIBRARY □ Toronto, ON

Ernst, Dr. Joseph W., Dir.
ROCKEFELLER UNIVERSITY - ROCKEFELLER ARCHIVE CENTER □ North Tarrytown, NY

Erskine, Hilary, Tech.Info.Spec.
CIBA-GEIGY CORPORATION - TECHNICAL INFORMATION SERVICE □ Greensboro, NC

Erskine, Joanne, Lib.Coord.
OAKDALE REGIONAL CENTER FOR DEVELOPMENTAL DISABILITIES - STAFF LIBRARY □ Lapeer, MI

Erslev, A.J., M.D., Found.Dir.
JEFFERSON (Thomas) UNIVERSITY - CARDEZA FOUNDATION - TOCANTINS MEMORIAL LIBRARY □ Philadelphia, PA

Ertel, Monica, Mgr., Info.Rsrcs.
APPLE COMPUTER INC. - LIBRARY AND INFORMATION RESOURCES □ Cupertino, CA

Ertl, Mary, Acq.
UNIVERSITY OF IOWA - LAW LIBRARY □ Iowa City, IA

Ervin, Colleen, Asst.Acq.Libn.
SAN DIEGO COUNTY LAW LIBRARY □ San Diego, CA

Ervin, Linda, Dp.Chf., Client Serv.
CANADA - DEPARTMENT OF FINANCE - FINANCE/TREASURY BOARD LIBRARY □ Ottawa, ON

Ervine, Adele, Libn.
HIGHLAND PARK UNITED METHODIST CHURCH - LIBRARY □ Dallas, TX

Erwin, Clarissa, Sr.Asst.Libn.
SAN DIEGO STATE UNIVERSITY - MEDIA & CURRICULUM CENTER† □ San Diego, CA

Erwin, Jacquelin, Libn.
ST. LUKE HOSPITAL - MEDICAL LIBRARY □ Pasadena, CA

Erwin, Patricia, Ref.Libn.
MAYO FOUNDATION - MAYO CLINIC LIBRARY □ Rochester, MN

Erwin, William R., Jr., Asst.Cur., Cat.
DUKE UNIVERSITY - MANUSCRIPT DEPARTMENT □ Durham, NC

Esau, Eric, Libn.
UNIVERSITY OF MASSACHUSETTS, AMHERST - PHYSICAL SCIENCES LIBRARY □ Amherst, MA

Esbin, Martha, Law Libn.
SHUMAKER, LOOP & KENDRICK - LIBRARY □
Toledo, OH

Escarilla, Jose G., Jr., Corp.Libn.
STAUFFER CHEMICAL COMPANY - CORPORATE
LIBRARY □ Westport, CT

Esch, Harold L., Hist.
AMERICAN LAWN BOWLS ASSOCIATION -
LIBRARY □ Pacific Palisades, CA

Eschenauer, L.A., Sec.
UNIVERSITY OF TORONTO - DEPARTMENT OF
GEOLOGY - COLEMAN LIBRARY □ Toronto, ON

Esckridge, Virginia C., Ref.Libn.
DUQUESNE UNIVERSITY - LAW LIBRARY □
Pittsburgh, PA

Escriu, Maria A., Chf.Libn.
CANADIAN ASSOCIATION - LATIN AMERICA
AND CARIBBEAN - INFORMATION CENTRE □
Toronto, ON

Escudero, Conrado A., U.S. Rep.
ASSOCIATION OF PHILIPPINE COCONUT
DESICCATORS - LIBRARY □ New York, NY

Escudero, Estela, Libn.
COOK COUNTY HOSPITAL - HEALTH SCIENCE
LIBRARY AND ARCHIVES □ Chicago, IL

Esen, Viona, Libn.
BRITISH COLUMBIA RESEARCH COUNCIL -
LIBRARY □ Vancouver, BC

Esen, Viona, Res.Libn.
BRITISH COLUMBIA RESEARCH COUNCIL -
URANIUM INFORMATION CENTRE □ Vancouver,
BC

Eshelman, Ralph, Dir.
CALVERT MARINE MUSEUM - LIBRARY □
Solomons, MD

Eshghi, Fleurin, Electronic Curric.Sys.
TEACHERS COLLEGE - MILBANK MEMORIAL
LIBRARY □ New York, NY

Eskenazi, Howard A., Natl. Sales Mgr.
FPG, INTERNATIONAL CORPORATION □ New
York, NY

Esparza, Arturo, Circ.Sect.
UNIVERSITY OF CALIFORNIA, LOS ANGELES -
MANAGEMENT LIBRARY □ Los Angeles, CA

Espinosa, Silvia
LOUISIANA STATE UNIVERSITY - REFERENCE
SERVICES □ Baton Rouge, LA

Espiritu, Mrs. Trinidad B., Ref.Libn.
SUN LIFE OF CANADA - REFERENCE LIBRARY □
Toronto, ON

Esposito, Michael, Sr.Libn.
NEW YORK STATE LIBRARY - LAW/SOCIAL
SCIENCE REFERENCE SERVICES □ Albany, NY

Espy, Dr. H.H., Mgr.
HERCULES, INC. - RESEARCH CENTER -
TECHNICAL INFORMATION DIVISION □
Wilmington, DE

Esquibel, Sandra, Assoc. State Libn.
NEW MEXICO STATE LIBRARY □ Santa Fe, NM

Esser, Delcina, Mgr., Tech.Info.Ctr.
GORE (W.L.) & ASSOCIATES, INC. - TECHNICAL
INFORMATION CENTER □ Elkton, MD

Essex, Thomas, Asst.Libn.
WARREN COUNTY LAW LIBRARY† □ Lebanon,
OH

Estes, Mark E., Libn.
HOLME ROBERTS & OWEN - LIBRARY □ Denver,
CO

Estes, Pamela, Hd.Ref.Libn.
VANDERBILT UNIVERSITY - JEAN AND
ALEXANDER HEARD LIBRARY - EDUCATION
LIBRARY □ Nashville, TN

Estes, Pamela, Libn.
VANDERBILT UNIVERSITY - JEAN AND
ALEXANDER HEARD LIBRARY - EDUCATION
LIB. - PEABODY COLL. OF BOOKS ON CHILDREN
□ Nashville, TN

Estoppey, Carol, Supv., Tech.Serv.
CONFERENCE BOARD, INC. - INFORMATION
SERVICE □ New York, NY

Estoppey, Joan, Sr.Libn.
COMBUSTION ENGINEERING, INC. - POWER
SYSTEMS GROUP LIBRARY SERVICES† □
Windsor, CT

Estrada, James, Cat.Libn.
UNIVERSITY OF CONNECTICUT - HEALTH
CENTER - LYMAN MAYNARD STOWE LIBRARY □
Farmington, CT

Estry, Douna Seiler, Supv., Tech.Info.Sect.
FORD MOTOR COMPANY - TECHNICAL
INFORMATION SECTION □ Dearborn, MI

Eswein, Dorothy, Med. Staff Libn.
GUADALUPE MEDICAL CENTER - MEDICAL
STAFF LIBRARY □ Carlsbad, NM

Esworthy, Robert S., Dir.
SCHOOL OF THE OZARKS - RALPH FOSTER
MUSEUM - LOIS BROWNELL RESEARCH
LIBRARY □ Point Lookout, MO

Eterovich, Adam S., Dir.
CROATIAN-SLOVENIAN-SERBIAN
GENEALOGICAL SOCIETY - LIBRARY □ San
Carlos, CA

Etheridge, Virginia, Cat.
COUNCIL ON FOREIGN RELATIONS - LIBRARY □
New York, NY

Etherington, Don, Asst.Dir./Consrv.Off.
UNIVERSITY OF TEXAS, AUSTIN - HARRY
RANSOM HUMANITIES RESEARCH CENTER □
Austin, TX

Ethier, Patricia, Asst. to Supv.
ST. PAUL PUBLIC LIBRARY - REFERENCE ROOM
□ St. Paul, MN

Ethridge, Ada C., Med.Libn.
FLORIDA STATE HOSPITAL - HEALTH SCIENCE
LIBRARY □ Chattahoochee, FL

Etler, Selma, Ref.Libn.
GEISINGER MEDICAL CENTER - MEDICAL
LIBRARY □ Danville, PA

Etter, Constance L., Libn.
ILLINOIS STATE - OFFICE OF THE AUDITOR
GENERAL - LIBRARY □ Springfield, IL

Ettl, Lorraine, Pub.Serv.
UNIVERSITY OF NORTH DAKOTA - SCHOOL OF
MEDICINE - HARLEY E. FRENCH MEDICAL
LIBRARY □ Grand Forks, ND

Etzwiler, Nijole, Cur.
SAUK COUNTY HISTORICAL SOCIETY, INC. -
HISTORICAL MUSEUM LIBRARY □ Baraboo, WI

Eubank, Larry, Lib.Info.Spec.
RCA CORPORATION - RCA LABORATORIES -
DAVID SARNOFF RESEARCH CENTER - LIBRARY
□ Princeton, NJ

Eubanks, Marie, Med.Libn.
U.S. VETERANS ADMINISTRATION (TN-
Murfreesboro) - MEDICAL CENTER LIBRARY □
Murfreesboro, TN

Eubanks, Spanola M., Dir., Lib.Serv.
DOROTHEA DIX HOSPITAL - F.T. FULLER STAFF
LIBRARY □ Raleigh, NC

Eudaley, Donna J., Adm.Sec.
DEERE & COMPANY - LAW LIBRARY □ Moline, IL

Eugene, Robert, Cur.
PRINCETON ANTIQUES BOOKFINDERS - ART
MARKETING REFERENCE LIBRARY □ Atlantic
City, NJ

Eugster, Hans P., Chm.
JOHNS HOPKINS UNIVERSITY - DEPARTMENT
OF EARTH AND PLANETARY SCIENCES -
SINGEWALD READING ROOM □ Baltimore, MD

Evalds, Victoria, Libn.
BOSTON UNIVERSITY - AFRICAN STUDIES
LIBRARY □ Boston, MA

Evankow, Lucy, Chf.Libn.
SCHOLASTIC MAGAZINES & BOOK SERVICES -
GENERAL LIBRARY □ New York, NY

Evans, Mrs. Adye Bel, Libn.
UNIVERSITY OF MICHIGAN - INSTITUTE FOR
SOCIAL RESEARCH - LIBRARY □ Ann Arbor, MI

Evans, Anaclare F., Cat./Hd., Tech.Serv.
WAYNE STATE UNIVERSITY - SCHOOL OF
MEDICINE - VERA PARSHALL SHIFFMAN
MEDICAL LIBRARY □ Detroit, MI

Evans, Bruce, Hd.Libn.
OHIO STATE UNIVERSITY - VETERINARY
MEDICINE LIBRARY □ Columbus, OH

Evans, Bruce A., Libn.
MISSISSIPPI STATE UNIVERSITY - COLLEGE
OF VETERINARY MEDICINE - LIBRARY† □
Mississippi State, MS

Evans, Carol, Prof.Asst.
DALLAS PUBLIC LIBRARY - HUMANITIES
DIVISION □ Dallas, TX

Evans, David, Chm., Lib.Comm.
NEW CANAAN HISTORICAL SOCIETY -
LIBRARY □ New Canaan, CT

Evans, Dorothy, Asst.Libn.
CANADA - NATIONAL RESEARCH COUNCIL -
CISTI - ENERGY BRANCH □ Ottawa, ON

Evans, Douglas L., Libn.
WOLFE (Harvey G.) LIBRARY □ Glendale, CA

Evans, Elizabeth
NEW YORK UNIVERSITY - SCHOOL OF LAW
LIBRARY □ New York, NY

Evans, Elizabeth, Ref.Libn.
NEW YORK UNIVERSITY - SCHOOL OF LAW
LIBRARY □ New York, NY

Evans, Elizabeth, Acq.Libn.
TENNESSEE VALLEY AUTHORITY - TECHNICAL
LIBRARY □ Muscle Shoals, AL

Evans, Elizabeth H., Libn.
U.S. NAVY - FLEET ANTI-SUBMARINE
WARFARE TRAINING CENTER, ATLANTIC -
TACTICAL LIBRARY □ Norfolk, VA

Evans, Emrys, Conservator & Binder
UNIVERSITY OF TORONTO - THOMAS FISHER
RARE BOOK LIBRARY □ Toronto, ON

Evans, Everett, Microfilm Supv.
WASHINGTON STATE OFFICE OF SECRETARY
OF STATE - DIVISION OF ARCHIVES AND
RECORD MANAGEMENT □ Olympia, WA

Evans, Gloria B., Ser.Libn.
ALABAMA A & M UNIVERSITY - J. F. DRAKE
MEMORIAL LEARNING RESOURCES CENTER □
Normal, AL

Evans, Grace A., Hist.Spec.
WELLS FARGO BANK - HISTORY DEPARTMENT
921 □ San Francisco, CA

Evans, Jane W., Libn.
CALIFORNIA STATE - COURT OF APPEAL, 1ST
APPELLATE DISTRICT - LAW LIBRARY □ San
Francisco, CA

Evans, Janet, Asst.Libn.
ACADEMY OF NATURAL SCIENCES - LIBRARY □
Philadelphia, PA

Evans, Joanna, Libn.
REPUBLICAN NATIONAL COMMITTEE -
LIBRARY □ Washington, DC

Evans, Linda, Chf., Tech.Lib.
U.S. AIR FORCE - ROME AIR DEVELOPMENT
CENTER - TECHNICAL LIBRARY □ Griffiss AFB,
NY

Evans, Linda J., Assoc.Cur., Archv. & Mss.
CHICAGO HISTORICAL SOCIETY - RESEARCH
COLLECTIONS □ Chicago, IL

Evans, Lois, Adm.Libn.
SDS BIOTECH CORPORATION - CORPORATE
LIBRARY □ Painesville, OH

Evans, M.Rita, Info.Spec.
GULF OIL CORPORATION - BUSINESS
RESEARCH LIBRARY □ Pittsburgh, PA

Evans, Margaret J., Chf.Libn.
U.S. COURT OF APPEALS, 2ND CIRCUIT -
LIBRARY □ New York, NY

Evans, Marilyn L., Br.Supv.
DU PONT DE NEMOURS (E.I.) & COMPANY, INC.
- LIBRARY NETWORK □ Wilmington, DE

Evans, Mark S., Circ.Libn.
FLORIDA STATE UNIVERSITY - LAW LIBRARY □
Tallahassee, FL

Evans, Mary, Libn.
OHIO VALLEY GENERAL HOSPITAL -
PROFESSIONAL LIBRARY □ McKee's Rock, PA

Evans, Max J., Asst.Dir.
STATE HISTORICAL SOCIETY OF WISCONSIN -
ARCHIVES DIVISION □ Madison, WI

Evans, Patricia A., Chr., Lrng.Rsrcs.
U.S. NAVY - NAVAL MEDICAL COMMAND -
NAVAL DENTAL CLINIC - NATIONAL CAPITAL
REGION - WILLIAM L. DARNALL LIBRARY □
Bethesda, MD

Evans, Peter, Ref.Libn.
UNIVERSITY OF CALIFORNIA, BERKELEY -
FORESTRY LIBRARY □ Berkeley, CA

Evans, Peter A., Libn.
UNIVERSITY OF CALIFORNIA, BERKELEY -
FOREST PRODUCTS LIBRARY □ Richmond, CA

Evans, Professor Richard A., Lib.Dir.
U.S. NAVY - NAVAL ACADEMY - NIMITZ
LIBRARY □ Annapolis, MD

Evans, Richard M., Supv., Forestry Sta.
UNIVERSITY OF TENNESSEE - ARBORETUM
SOCIETY - LIBRARY □ Oak Ridge, TN

Evans, Roy B., Exec. V.P.
PROFESSIONAL CONVENTION MANAGEMENT
ASSOCIATION - LIBRARY □ Birmingham, AL

Evans, Shirley, Libn.
FIRESTONE TIRE AND RUBBER COMPANY -
BUSINESS LIBRARY □ Akron, OH

Evans, Shirley A., Ref.Libn.
AT & T BELL LABORATORIES - LIBRARY □
Murray Hill, NJ

Evans, Wayne, Ref.Libn.
OHIO UNIVERSITY - HEALTH SCIENCES
LIBRARY □ Athens, OH

Eveland, Raymond E., Dir.
U.S. DEPT. OF COMMERCE - INTERNATIONAL
TRADE ADMINISTRATION - NEW ORLEANS
DISTRICT OFFICE LIBRARY □ New Orleans, LA

Everett, Dorothy M., Libn.
INDIANA STATE DEPARTMENT OF PUBLIC
INSTRUCTION - PROFESSIONAL LIBRARY □
Indianapolis, IN

Everidge, Barbara T., Sys.Libn.
U.S. ARMY COMMAND AND GENERAL STAFF
COLLEGE - COMBINED ARMS RESEARCH
LIBRARY □ Ft. Leavenworth, KS

Everitt, Janet, Info.Spec.
UPJOHN COMPANY - CORPORATE TECHNICAL
LIBRARY □ Kalamazoo, MI

Evers, Donald J., Chf.Ref.Libn.
U.S. SECURITIES AND EXCHANGE
COMMISSION - PUBLIC REFERENCE LIBRARY □
Chicago, IL

Evers, Irene, Asst.Sci.Libn.
UNIVERSITY OF MONTANA - SCHOOL OF
FORESTRY - OXFORD COLLECTION □ Missoula,
MT

Evers, Jacques J., Mgr.
MOTOR VEHICLE MANUFACTURERS
ASSOCIATION (MVMA) - STATISTICS
INFORMATION CENTER □ Detroit, MI

Everts, Helen L., Libn.
LANCASTER NEWSPAPERS - LIBRARY □
Lancaster, PA

Eves, Bruce, Archv.
INTERNATIONAL GAY INFORMATION CENTER,
INC. □ New York, NY

Eves, Judith A., Libn.
PENNSYLVANIA ECONOMY LEAGUE - WESTERN
DIVISION - LIBRARY □ Pittsburgh, PA

Evetts, Rosemary, Libn.
SOUTH DAKOTA STATE HISTORICAL
RESOURCE CENTER □ Pierre, SD

Evitts, Beth A., Asst.Libn.
YORK HOSPITAL - LIBRARY □ York, PA

Evitts, Virginia, Libn.
AREA COOPERATIVE EDUCATIONAL SERVICES
- TEACHER LIBRARY □ North Haven, CT

Ewald, Katherine, Libn./Res.
GUTHRIE THEATER FOUNDATION - GUTHRIE
THEATER STAFF REFERENCE LIBRARY □
Minneapolis, MN

Ewaskiw, Christine, Tech.Serv./Ref.
UNIVERSITY OF ALBERTA - LAW LIBRARY □
Edmonton, AB

Ewen, Sylvia S., Hd., Ref.
SUNY - AGRICULTURAL AND TECHNICAL
COLLEGE AT FARMINGDALE - THOMAS D.
GREENLEY LIBRARY □ Farmingdale, NY

Ewert, Thomas E., Dir.
UNIVERSITY OF VIRGINIA - BLANDY
EXPERIMENTAL FARM LIBRARY □ Boyce, VA

Ewert, Rev. Wesley C., Archv.
UNITED CHURCH OF CHRIST - CONNECTICUT
CONFERENCE - ARCHIVES □ Hartford, CT

Ewick, C. Ray, Dir.
INDIANA STATE LIBRARY □ Indianapolis, IN

Ewig, Delia, Asst.Libn.
PRC CONSOER, TOWNSEND, INC. - LIBRARY
AND INFORMATION CENTER □ Chicago, IL

Ewing, Alison, Libn.
BROWN & BAIN, P.A. - LIBRARY □ Phoenix, AZ

Ewing, Barbara, Libn.
MEADVILLE CITY HOSPITAL - HUMMER
LIBRARY □ Meadville, PA

Ewing, Florence, Asst.Ref.Libn.
SAN DIEGO COUNTY LAW LIBRARY □ San Diego,
CA

Eyraud, Colbert H., Pres./Cur.
LANDMARK CONSERVATORS - CABOTS OLD
INDIAN PUEBLO MUSEUM LIBRARY □ Desert
Hot Springs, CA

Eyzaguirre, Elena, Asst.Dir.
UNIVERSITY OF UTAH - SPENCER S. ECCLES
HEALTH SCIENCES LIBRARY □ Salt Lake City,
UT

Ezell, Elaine R., Ref.Archv.
BOWLING GREEN STATE UNIVERSITY -
CENTER FOR ARCHIVAL COLLECTIONS □
Bowling Green, OH

Ezell, Miss Francis H., Dir.
TENNESSEE STATE LIBRARY - LIBRARY FOR
THE BLIND AND PHYSICALLY HANDICAPPED □
Nashville, TN

Ezell, John S., Cur.
UNIVERSITY OF OKLAHOMA - WESTERN
HISTORY COLLECTIONS □ Norman, OK

Ezell, John S., Cur.
UNIVERSITY OF OKLAHOMA - WESTERN
HISTORY COLLECTIONS - LIBRARY DIVISION □
Norman, OK

Ezell, Margaret M., Tech.Libn.
GRACE (W.R.) AND COMPANY - CRYOVAC
DIVISION - TECHNICAL LIBRARY† □ Duncan,
SC

Ezera, Mrs. Onuma, Bibliog. Africa Stud.
MICHIGAN STATE UNIVERSITY -
INTERNATIONAL LIBRARY □ East Lansing, MI

Ezquerra, Isabel, Chf.Med.Libn.
MOUNT SINAI MEDICAL CENTER OF GREATER
MIAMI - MEDICAL LIBRARY □ Miami Beach, FL

F

Faber, Katherine, Sr.Info.Spec..
THE BOC GROUP INC. - TECHNICAL CENTER -
INFORMATION CENTER □ Murray Hill, NJ

Fabian, Jaine, Libn.
DELL PUBLISHING COMPANY, INC. - LIBRARY □
New York, NY

Fabian, Ms. Merle G., Libn.
CANADIAN EMBASSY - LIBRARY □ Washington,
DC

Fabian, Sr. Ursula, S.C., Med.Lib.Dir.
HARRISON COMMUNITY HOSPITAL - MEDICAL
LIBRARY □ Mt. Clemens, MI

Fabrizio, Nancy, Assoc.Dir.
SUNY AT BUFFALO - HEALTH SCIENCES
LIBRARY □ Buffalo, NY

Fabro, Andrew, Libn.
CANADA - ENVIRONMENTAL PROTECTION
SERVICE - PACIFIC REGION LIBRARY □ West
Vancouver, BC

Fabugais, Violanda, Asst.Libn.
FULBRIGHT & JAWORSKI - LIBRARY □ Houston,
TX

Faccioli, Ellen, Libn.
CHEM SYSTEMS INC. - INFORMATION CENTER
□ Tarrytown, NY

Fackler, June, Libn.
PAINE WEBBER INC. - PAINE WEBBER
MITCHELL HUTCHINS - LIBRARY □ New York,
NY

Fackler, Ms. Y.O., Mgr.
ROCKWELL INTERNATIONAL - ENERGY
SYSTEMS GROUP - LIBRARY □ Canoga Park, CA

Fackovec, William, S.M., Cat./Bibliog.
UNIVERSITY OF DAYTON - MARIAN LIBRARY □
Dayton, OH

Faesy, Nancy N., Libn.
SAVE THE CHILDREN FOUNDATION, INC. -
LIBRARY □ Westport, CT

Fagan, H. Red, Acq.Libn.
SUNY - AGRICULTURAL AND TECHNICAL
COLLEGE AT MORRISVILLE - LIBRARY □
Morrisville, NY

Fagan, Michele L., Asst.Libn.
LOUISIANA STATE UNIVERSITY - BUSINESS
ADMINISTRATION/GOVERNMENT
DOCUMENTS DEPARTMENT □ Baton Rouge, LA

Fage, Joan E., Libn.
MARITIME TELEGRAPH & TELEPHONE CO. LTD.
- INFORMATION RESOURCE CENTRE □ Halifax,
NS

Fagen, Ernestine H., Volunteer Libn.
HORTICULTURAL ART SOCIETY OF COLORADO
SPRINGS, INC. - LIBRARY □ Colorado Springs,
CO

Fagerlund, M. Liisa, State Archv.
UTAH STATE ARCHIVES □ Salt Lake City, UT

Fagerstrom, David, Libn.
UNIVERSITY OF COLORADO, BOULDER -
SCIENCE LIBRARY □ Boulder, CO

Fagg, Karen, Grants Libn.
DALLAS PUBLIC LIBRARY - URBAN
INFORMATION CENTER □ Dallas, TX

Fahey, Rev. James L., Libn.
POPE JOHN XXIII NATIONAL SEMINARY -
LIBRARY □ Weston, MA

Fahey, Kathy, Asst.Sci.Libn.
SOUTHERN ILLINOIS UNIVERSITY,
CARBONDALE - SCIENCE DIVISION LIBRARY □
Carbondale, IL

Fahey, Nancy, Instr. Media Spec.
WASHINGTON STATE SCHOOL FOR THE DEAF -
LEARNING RESOURCE CENTER □ Vancouver,
WA

Fahnestock, Judi, Ed.
LUTHERAN CHURCH IN AMERICA - BOARD OF
PUBLICATION - LIBRARY □ Philadelphia, PA

Fahnestock, Mimi, Libn.
NEW YORK ROAD RUNNERS CLUB -
INTERNATIONAL RUNNING CENTER LIBRARY □
New York, NY

Faibisy, John, Br.Chf.
U.S. DEFENSE AUDIOVISUAL AGENCY -
DEPOSITORY ACCESSIONS BRANCH (DAVA-N-
OAA) □ Norton AFB, CA

Failor, Maurene, Libn.
GRAIN PROCESSING CORPORATION -
TECHNICAL INFORMATION CENTER, □
Muscatine, IA

Fain, Annie M., Libn.
ST. LUCIE COUNTY - LAW LIBRARY □ Fort
Pierce, FL

Fair, Agnes, Tech.Serv.Libn.
UNITED METHODIST PUBLISHING HOUSE -
LIBRARY □ Nashville, TN

Fairbanks, Aline M., Engr.Ref.Libn.
TRIODYNE INC. CONSULTING ENGINEERS -
INFORMATION CENTER □ Niles, IL

Fairbanks, Dolores, Bibliog., Islamic Arch.
HARVARD UNIVERSITY - FINE ARTS LIBRARY □
Cambridge, MA

Fairbrother, Thomas, Dir., Info.Serv.
MOTOROLA, INC. - MOS INTEGRATED
CIRCUITS GROUP - INFORMATION CENTER □
Austin, TX

Fairfull, Thomas M., Musm.Dir.
U.S. ARMY MUSEUM OF HAWAII - REFERENCE
LIBRARY □ Honolulu, HI

Fairley, Bruce, AV Equip. & Prod.
METROPOLITAN TORONTO LIBRARY -
REGIONAL AUDIO VISUAL DEPARTMENT □
Toronto, ON

Fairley, Craig, Libn.
METROPOLITAN TORONTO LIBRARY - GENERAL
REFERENCE DEPARTMENT □ Toronto, ON

Fairman, Elisabeth R., Cat.Libn.
YALE UNIVERSITY - YALE CENTER FOR
BRITISH ART - RARE BOOK COLLECTION □ New
Haven, CT

Fairweather, Faith, Libn.
NEW BRUNSWICK - DEPARTMENT OF HEALTH -
LIBRARY □ Fredericton, NB

Fait, Rev. Thomas, Archv.
ST. FRANCIS SEMINARY - SALZMANN LIBRARY
□ Milwaukee, WI

Falcione, Carol, Dir.
NEW YORK UNIVERSITY - GRADUATE SCHOOL
OF BUSINESS ADMINISTRATION - LIBRARY □
New York, NY

Falco, Nicholas, Div.Hd.
QUEENS BOROUGH PUBLIC LIBRARY - LONG
ISLAND DIVISION □ Jamaica, NY

Falcon, Guillermo Nanez, Ph.D., Mss.Cat.
TULANE UNIVERSITY OF LOUISIANA - SPECIAL
COLLECTIONS DIVISION - MANUSCRIPTS AND
RARE BOOKS SECTION □ New Orleans, LA

Falcone, Rev. Sebastian A., Dean
ST. BERNARD'S INSTITUTE - LIBRARY □
Rochester, NY

Falconer, Joan O., Music Libn.
APPALACHIAN STATE UNIVERSITY - MUSIC
LIBRARY □ Boone, NC

Faletra, Frances, Ser./Acq.Libn.
TUFTS UNIVERSITY - HEALTH SCIENCES
LIBRARY □ Boston, MA

Falger, David E., Chf., Lib.Serv.
U.S. VETERANS ADMINISTRATION (PA-
Lebanon) - MEDICAL CENTER LIBRARY □
Lebanon, PA

Falgiatore, Dominic R., Info.Sci.
ROHM & HAAS COMPANY - RESEARCH
DIVISION - INFORMATION SERVICES
DEPARTMENT □ Spring House, PA

Falgner, Susan, Evening Ref.Libn.
UNIVERSITY OF CINCINNATI - RAYMOND
WALTERS COLLEGE - LIBRARY □ Cincinnati, OH

Falk, Gretchen, Ref.Libn.
PARK FOREST PUBLIC LIBRARY - ORAL
HISTORY OF PARK FOREST COLLECTION □ Park
Forest, IL

Falkenborg, Donna, Ed.
UTAH WATER RESEARCH LABORATORY -
LIBRARY □ Logan, UT

Fallan, JoAnn, Adm.Serv.
MONTANA STATE LIBRARY □ Helena, MT

Fallis, Margaret Giles, Hd., Pub.Serv.
PHILADELPHIA COLLEGE OF PHARMACY AND
SCIENCE - JOSEPH W. ENGLAND LIBRARY □
Philadelphia, PA

Fallon, Margaret S., Libn.
WHITE & WILLIAMS - LIBRARY □ Philadelphia,
PA

Fallon, Robert P., Libn.
PRUDENTIAL INSURANCE COMPANY OF
AMERICA - DRYDEN BUSINESS LIBRARY □
Newark, NJ

Fallone, Violet, Hist.Archv.Asst.
MONTGOMERY COUNTY - DEPARTMENT OF
HISTORY AND ARCHIVES □ Fonda, NY

Fallucco, Marguerite, Archv.
AMERICAN MEDICAL ASSOCIATION -
DIVISION OF LIBRARY AND ARCHIVAL
SERVICES □ Chicago, IL

Faltermeier, Jann, Law Libn.
FEDERAL RESERVE BANK OF KANSAS CITY -
LAW LIBRARY □ Kansas City, MO

Faltz, Judy, Libn.
NIELSEN ENGINEERING & RESEARCH, INC. -
NEAR TECHNICAL LIBRARY □ Mountain View,
CA

Falvey, Genemary, Libn.
COLD SPRING HARBOR LABORATORY - MAIN
LIBRARY □ Cold Spring Harbor, NY

Famularo, Sabiha, Cat.Libn.
JOHNS HOPKINS UNIVERSITY - SCHOOL OF
ADVANCED INTERNATIONAL STUDIES -
SYDNEY R. & ELSA W. MASON LIBRARY □
Washington, DC

Fancher, Pauline, Cur.
WINCHESTER HISTORICAL SOCIETY -
ARCHIVE □ Winsted, CT

Fancy, Margaret, Spec.Coll.Libn.
MOUNT ALLISON UNIVERSITY - WINTHROP P.
BELL COLLECTION OF ACADIANA □ Sackville, NB

Fanelli, Michelle, Rd.Serv.Libn.
PACE UNIVERSITY - LIBRARY □ New York, NY

Fankhauser, Mary, Cat.
VANCOUVER SCHOOL OF THEOLOGY - LIBRARY
□ Vancouver, BC

Fannin, Kathy, Res.Assoc.
MISSOURI STATE DIVISION OF COMMUNITY
AND ECONOMIC DEVELOPMENT - RESEARCH
LIBRARY □ Jefferson City, MO

Fanslow, Mary, Ref.Libn.
MERCER UNIVERSITY - MEDICAL SCHOOL
LIBRARY □ Macon, GA

Fanson, Jean
UNITED CHURCH OF CANADA - ESSEX
PRESBYTERY - RESOURCE CENTRE □ Windsor,
ON

Fanta, David, Asst.Libn.
CHAPMAN AND CUTLER - LAW LIBRARY □
Chicago, IL

Fantozzi, Anthony J., Archv.
U.S. NATL. ARCHIVES & RECORDS SERVICE -
FEDERAL ARCHIVES AND RECORDS CENTER,
REGION 2 □ Bayonne, NJ

Faraday, Joanna, Dir.
STAMFORD HOSPITAL - HEALTH SCIENCES
LIBRARY □ Stamford, CT

Farah, B.D., Hd., Info.Ctr.
GENERAL TIRE AND RUBBER COMPANY -
RESEARCH DIVISION INFORMATION CENTER □
Akron, OH

Farah, Priscilla, Musm.Libn.
METROPOLITAN MUSEUM OF ART -
PHOTOGRAPH AND SLIDE LIBRARY □ New York,
NY

Farghal, Mahmoud, U.N. Spec.
LEAGUE OF ARAB STATES - ARAB
INFORMATION CENTER □ New York, NY

Fariss, Linda K., Assoc.Dir.
INDIANA UNIVERSITY - LAW LIBRARY □
Bloomington, IN

Fark, Ronald, Hd., Circ.
BROWN UNIVERSITY - SCIENCES LIBRARY □
Providence, RI

Farkas, Susan, Gen.Ref.Libn.
EDISON ELECTRIC INSTITUTE - LIBRARY □
Washington, DC

Farley, Dr. A.L., Assoc.Prof. & Supv.
UNIVERSITY OF BRITISH COLUMBIA -
DEPARTMENT OF GEOGRAPHY - MAP AND AIR
PHOTO CENTRE □ Vancouver, BC

Farley, David J., Asst.Dir. for Adm.
MARQUETTE UNIVERSITY - MEMORIAL
LIBRARY □ Milwaukee, WI

Farley, Earl, Dir.
UNIVERSITY OF KANSAS MEDICAL CTR. -
COLLEGE OF HEALTH SCI. AND HOSPITAL -
ARCHIE R. DYKES LIB. OF THE HEALTH SCI. □
Kansas City, KS

Farley, Joanne E., Mgr., Lib.Serv.
FEDERAL RESERVE BANK OF MINNEAPOLIS -
LIBRARY □ Minneapolis, MN

Farley, Marian, Dir.
ANALYTIC SCIENCES CORPORATION -
LIBRARY □ Reading, MA

Farman, Donna L., Libn.
PHOENIX DAY SCHOOL FOR THE DEAF -
LIBRARY/MEDIA CENTER □ Phoenix, AZ

Farmann, Kathleen, Law Libn.
UNIVERSITY OF NOTRE DAME - LAW SCHOOL
LIBRARY □ Notre Dame, IN

Farmann, Stanley, Assoc. Law Libn.
UNIVERSITY OF NOTRE DAME - LAW SCHOOL
LIBRARY □ Notre Dame, IN

Farmer, Dr. David, Cur. of Spec.Coll.
UNIVERSITY OF HOUSTON - LIBRARIES -
SPECIAL COLLECTIONS □ Houston, TX

Farmer, Dr. David, Dir., Rare Bks./Spec.Coll
UNIVERSITY OF TULSA - MC FARLIN LIBRARY -
RARE BOOKS AND SPECIAL COLLECTIONS □
Tulsa, OK

Farmer, Donna, Libn.
VARIAN ASSOCIATES - TECHNICAL LIBRARY □
Palo Alto, CA

Farmer, Gregory, Dir.
CONNECTICUT VALLEY HISTORICAL MUSEUM -
RESEARCH LIBRARY □ Springfield, MA

Farmer, Linda G., Med.Libn.
JACKSON-MADISON COUNTY GENERAL
HOSPITAL - LEARNING CENTER □ Jackson, TN

Farmer, Mabel, Libn.
COLLEGE OF FISHERIES, NAVIGATION,
MARINE ENGINEERING AND ELECTRONICS -
LIBRARY □ St. John's, NF

Farmer, Mary S., Libn.
ATLANTA FULTON PUBLIC LIBRARY - SPECIAL
COLLECTIONS DEPARTMENT □ Atlanta, GA

Farmer, Maureen, Med.Libn.
U.S. VETERANS ADMINISTRATION (WI-Wood)
- MEDICAL CENTER LIBRARY □ Wood, WI

Farnsworth, Frances J., Supv.
LITERACY VOLUNTEERS OF AMERICA, INC. -
LIBRARY □ Syracuse, NY

Farny, Diane M., Dir. of Lib.Serv.
GRADUATE HOSPITAL - LIBRARY □ Philadelphia,
PA

Farooqui, S.A., Cat.
CANADA - FISHERIES & OCEANS - LIBRARY† □
Ottawa, ON

Farr, Donna, Dir., Field Serv. & Prog.
AMERICAN CANCER SOCIETY - HAWAII
DIVISION - LIBRARY □ Honolulu, HI

Farr, Sue, ILL Serv.
NORTH CAROLINA STATE DEPARTMENT OF
CULTURAL RESOURCES - DIVISION OF THE
STATE LIBRARY □ Raleigh, NC

Farrands, Jane E., Libn.
ORGANON, INC. - MEDICAL LIBRARY □ West
Orange, NJ

Farrar, Jennifer, Libn.
OGILVY & MATHER, INC. - RESEARCH
LIBRARY† □ New York, NY

Farrell, Barbara D., Coord.
MOBIL EXPLORATION AND PRODUCING
SERVICES INC. - MEPSI LIBRARY □ Dallas, TX

Farrell, Barbara E., Map Libn.
CARLETON UNIVERSITY - MACODRUM LIBRARY
- MAP LIBRARY □ Ottawa, ON

Farrell, Edward, Ref.Libn.
SACRED HEART UNIVERSITY - LIBRARY □
Bridgeport, CT

Farrell, Helene S., Dir.
SCHOHARIE COUNTY HISTORICAL SOCIETY -
REFERENCE LIBRARY □ Schoharie, NY

Farrell, Patricia, Rec.Mgr.
DAIRY RESEARCH FOUNDATION - PRODUCT/
PROCESS INFORMATION SERVICES □
Rosemont, IL

Farrell, Timothy, Law Ck./Libn.
SALEM COUNTY LAW LIBRARY □ Salem, NJ

Farrell-Duncan, Howertine, Libn./Supv., Ref.
HOWARD UNIVERSITY - HEALTH SCIENCES
LIBRARY □ Washington, DC

Farren, Donald, Assoc.Dir., Spec.Coll.
UNIVERSITY OF MARYLAND, COLLEGE PARK -
LIBRARIES - KATHERINE ANNE PORTER ROOM
□ College Park, MD

Farrington, Polly-Alida, ILL Libn.
RENSSELAER POLYTECHNIC INSTITUTE -
FOLSOM LIBRARY □ Troy, NY

Farris, Donn Michael, Libn.
DUKE UNIVERSITY - DIVINITY SCHOOL
LIBRARY† □ Durham, NC

Farris, Judith, Info.Spec.
UNIVERSITY OF DENVER AND DENVER
RESEARCH INSTITUTE - INDUSTRIAL
ECONOMICS AND MANAGEMENT DIVISION
LIBRARY □ Denver, CO

Farthing, Pat, Libn.
APPALACHIAN STATE UNIVERSITY - BELK
LIBRARY - JUSTICE-QUERY INSTRUCTIONAL
MATERIALS CENTER □ Boone, NC

Farwell, Robert D., Exec.Dir.
WHALING MUSEUM SOCIETY, INC. - LIBRARY □
Cold Spring Harbor, NY

Fashion, Valerie D., Act.Dir.
U.S. ARMY POST - FORT DIX - LIBRARY □ Fort
Dix, NJ

Fassihian, Ahmad, Resource Spec.
TEACHERS OF ENGLISH TO SPEAKERS OF
OTHER LANGUAGES - TESOL LENDING LIBRARY
□ Washington, DC

Fassler, Bettifae, Assoc.Libn.
HOWARD UNIVERSITY - HEALTH SCIENCES
LIBRARY □ Washington, DC

Fast, Stanley, Adm.
MARK TWAIN BIRTHPLACE MUSEUM -
RESEARCH LIBRARY □ Stoutsville, MO

Faubert, Dr. G.M., Assoc.Prof.
MC GILL UNIVERSITY - MACDONALD CAMPUS -
INSTITUTE OF PARASITOLOGY - LIBRARY □
Ste. Anne de Bellevue, PQ

Faubert, Ghyslaine, Lib.Techn.
CANADIAN TEACHERS' FEDERATION - GEORGE
G. CROSKERY MEMORIAL LIBRARY □ Ottawa,
ON

Faubion, Anita, Libn.
UNIVERSITY OF TEXAS, AUSTIN - HOGG
FOUNDATION FOR MENTAL HEALTH - LIBRARY
□ Austin, TX

Fauchier, Pierre, Info.Off.
INTERGOVERNMENTAL COMMITTEE ON URBAN
AND REGIONAL RESEARCH (ICURR) -
INFORMATION EXCHANGE SERVICE □ Toronto,
ON

Fauhl, Ruth D., Lib.Asst.
UNIVERSITY OF KANSAS - WEALTHY BABCOCK
MATHEMATICS LIBRARY □ Lawrence, KS

Faul, Carol, Map Libn.
UNIVERSITY OF PENNSYLVANIA - GEOLOGY
MAP LIBRARY □ Philadelphia, PA

Faul, Mary A., Libn.
PINAL COUNTY HISTORICAL SOCIETY, INC. -
LIBRARY □ Florence, AZ

Faulders, Rita S., Cur., Spec.Coll.
ST. JOHN'S SEMINARY - EDWARD LAURENCE
DOHENY MEMORIAL LIBRARY □ Camarillo, CA

Faulkner, D.A., Meteorologist
CANADA - ATMOSPHERIC ENVIRONMENT
SERVICE - PACIFIC REGION - LIBRARY □
Vancouver, BC

Faunce, Cynthia, Ref.Libn.
INDIANA STATE LIBRARY - INDIANA DIVISION
□ Indianapolis, IN

Faupel, D. William, Dir., Lib. Serv.
ASBURY THEOLOGICAL SEMINARY - B.L.
FISHER LIBRARY □ Wilmore, KY

Faust, Julia B., Dir. of Lib. & Info.Serv.
WEST SUBURBAN HOSPITAL MEDICAL CENTER
- WALTER LAWRENCE MEMORIAL LIBRARY □
Oak Park, IL

Faust, Kathy, Cat.Libn.
LEWIS AND CLARK LAW SCHOOL -
NORTHWESTERN SCHOOL OF LAW - PAUL L.
BOLEY LAW LIBRARY □ Portland, OR

Fauster, Carl U., Dir.
ANTIQUE AND HISTORIC GLASS FOUNDATION
- LIBRARY □ Toledo, OH

Favata, William, Lib.Sys. Designer
WHEATON COLLEGE - BUSWELL MEMORIAL
LIBRARY □ Wheaton, IL

Faverty, Margaret, Archival Proc.
NORTHWESTERN UNIVERSITY - ARCHIVES □
Evanston, IL

Favorite, Miriam, Libn.
CAMDEN COUNTY HISTORICAL SOCIETY -
LIBRARY □ Camden, NJ

Favorite, Susan L., Dir.
FAIRVIEW GENERAL HOSPITAL - HEALTH
MEDIA CENTER □ Cleveland, OH

Favreau, J.-Etienne, Ref.Libn.
UNIVERSITE DU QUEBEC A MONTREAL -
BIBLIOTHEQUE DES SCIENCES DE
L'EDUCATION □ Montreal, PQ

Fawcett, Braden S., Libn.
NORTHWEST BIBLE COLLEGE - J.C. COOKE
LIBRARY □ Edmonton, AB

Fawcett, Georgene E., Hd., Acq./Ser.
UNIVERSITY OF NEBRASKA MEDICAL CENTER -
MC GOOGAN LIBRARY OF MEDICINE □ Omaha,
NE

Fawcett, Rosalie
HARTFORD PUBLIC LIBRARY - REFERENCE AND
GENERAL READING DEPARTMENT □ Hartford,
CT

Fawcett, W. Peyton, Hd.Libn.
FIELD MUSEUM OF NATURAL HISTORY -
LIBRARY □ Chicago, IL

Fay, Evelyn, Lib.Supv.
COTTAGE HOSPITAL - DAVID L. REEVES
MEDICAL LIBRARY □ Santa Barbara, CA

Fay, Peter J., Hd.Libn.
LIBRARY OF CONGRESS - JOHN F. KENNEDY
CENTER FOR THE PERFORMING ARTS - THE
PERFORMING ARTS LIB. □ Washington, DC

Fazzari, Francis, Asst.Libn.
INTERNATIONAL NUMISMATIC SOCIETY -
LIBRARY □ Washington, DC

Fazzone, Nancy, Dir., Lib.Serv.
SALEM HOSPITAL - MACK MEMORIAL HEALTH
SCIENCES LIBRARY □ Salem, MA

Feall, Alea, Libn.
ATLANTA LESBIAN FEMINIST ALLIANCE -
SOUTHEASTERN LESBIAN ARCHIVES □ Atlanta,
GA

Fears, Joyce, Libn.
GEORGIA REGIONAL HOSPITAL AT AUGUSTA -
HOSPITAL LIBRARY □ Gracewood, GA

Featherstone, Thomas, Archv.
WAYNE STATE UNIVERSITY - ARCHIVES OF
LABOR AND URBAN AFFAIRS/UNIVERSITY
ARCHIVES □ Detroit, MI

Feder, Edith, Law Libn.
FEDERAL RESERVE BANK OF NEW YORK - LAW
LIBRARY DIVISION □ New York, NY

Feder, Helga, Hum.Ref.Libn.
CUNY - GRADUATE SCHOOL AND UNIVERSITY
CENTER - LIBRARY □ New York, NY

Fedorek, Thomas, Asst.Libn.
PATTERSON, BELKNAP, WEBB & TYLER -
LIBRARY □ New York, NY

Fedoriw, Daria, Libn.
GENERAL MOTORS CORPORATION - RESEARCH
LABORATORIES LIBRARY □ Warren, MI

Fedoroff, Nina, Asst.Libn.
BOOTH MEMORIAL MEDICAL CENTER - HEALTH
EDUCATION LIBRARY □ Flushing, NY

Fedors, Carmel, Lib.Mgr.
GREENWICH HOSPITAL ASSOCIATION - GRAY
CARTER LIBRARY □ Greenwich, CT

Fedors, Maurica, Tech.Info.Spec.
ENGELHARD CORPORATION - TECHNICAL
INFORMATION CENTER □ Edison, NJ

Fedorzyn-Edgar, Susan, Asst.Libn.
PROVIDENCE JOURNAL COMPANY - NEWS
LIBRARY □ Providence, RI

Fedunok, Suzanne, Hd., Ref. & Coll.Dev.
COLUMBIA UNIVERSITY - AMBROSE MONELL
ENGINEERING LIBRARY □ New York, NY

Fedunok, Suzanne, Hd., Ref. & Coll.Dev.
COLUMBIA UNIVERSITY - MATHEMATICS/
SCIENCE LIBRARY □ New York, NY

Feeley, Edith
IBM CORPORATION - GENERAL TECHNOLOGY
DIVISION - INFORMATION CENTER/LEARNING
CENTER □ Essex Junction, VT

Feeley, Elise, Ref.Libn.
FORBES LIBRARY □ Northampton, MA

Feeley, James, Dir.
ALGONQUIN COLLEGE OF APPLIED ARTS &
TECHNOLOGY - RESOURCE CENTRES† □
Ottawa, ON

Feeney, Karen, Ref.Libn.
UNIVERSITY OF CALIFORNIA, SAN DIEGO -
SCIENCE & ENGINEERING LIBRARY □ La Jolla,
CA

Feeney, M. Patricia, Tech.Libn.Sr.
BURROUGHS CORPORATION - TECHNICAL
INFORMATION CENTER □ Mission Viejo, CA

Feenker, Cherie, Libn.
BIRMINGHAM PUBLIC AND JEFFERSON
COUNTY FREE LIBRARY - SCIENCE,
TECHNOLOGY & BUSINESS DEPT. - SPECIAL
COLLECTIONS □ Birmingham, AL

Feero, Janet, Tech.Serv.Libn.
PETRO-CANADA - LIBRARY SERVICES □
Calgary, AB

Feferman, Chava, Per.Asst.
SPERTUS COLLEGE OF JUDAICA - NORMAN AND
HELEN ASHER LIBRARY □ Chicago, IL

Feheley, JoAnne, Lib.Techn.
U.S. FOREST SERVICE - INSTITUTE OF
TROPICAL FORESTRY - LIBRARY □ Rio Piedras,
PR

Feher, Mr. L., Libn.
QUEENS CHILDREN'S PSYCHIATRIC CENTER -
LAURETTA BENDER STAFF LIBRARY □ Bellerose,
NY

Fehl, Ken, Chm., Lib.Comm.
CONGREGATION BETH AM - LIBRARY† □ Los
Altos Hills, CA

Fehlman, Sheila, Ser.Cat.
SUNY AT BUFFALO - CHARLES B. SEARS LAW
LIBRARY □ Buffalo, NY

Feibes, Erica, Res.Assoc.
MEIDINGER, INC. - INFORMATION CENTER □
Louisville, KY

Feick, Ellen, Mgr.
IBM CORPORATION - BUSINESS INFORMATION
LIBRARY □ Franklin Lakes, NJ

Feinberg, David, Regional Spec.
CUYAHOGA COUNTY PUBLIC LIBRARY -
FAIRVIEW PARK REGIONAL BRANCH - SPECIAL
COLLECTIONS □ Fairview Park, OH

Feindel, Richard, Br.Mgr.
KENTUCKY STATE DEPARTMENT FOR
LIBRARIES & ARCHIVES - KENTUCKY TALKING
BOOK LIBRARY □ Frankfort, KY

Feininger, Ann, Rd.Adv.
DISTRICT OF COLUMBIA PUBLIC LIBRARY -
CHILDREN'S DIVISION □ Washington, DC

Feinman, Marjorie, Asst.Libn.
DEBEVOISE & PLIMPTON - LAW LIBRARY □
New York, NY

Feinstein, Robert, Archv.
ANTIQUE PHONOGRAPH MONTHLY - APM
LIBRARY OF RECORDED SOUND □ Brooklyn, NY

Feir, Mitchell, Info.Spec.
TEXACO INC. - CORPORATE LIBRARY □ White
Plains, NY

Feir, Susan, Info.Spec.
TEXACO INC. - CORPORATE LIBRARY □ White
Plains, NY

Feist, Linda S., Dir.
MINNESOTA STATE LEGISLATIVE REFERENCE
LIBRARY □ St. Paul, MN

Feiszli, Doris M., Lib.Chm.
UNITED CHURCH OF CHRIST (Evangelical and
Reformed) - CHURCH LIBRARY □ Vermilion, OH

Feitler, Lila, Ref.Libn.
IOWA STATE DEPARTMENT OF HUMAN
SERVICES - LIBRARY □ Des Moines, IA

Felch, Patricia Anne, Libn.
COFFIELD UNGARETTI HARRIS & SLAVIN -
LIBRARY □ Chicago, IL
Felcone, Joseph J., Libn.
DAVID LIBRARY OF THE AMERICAN
REVOLUTION □ Washington Crossing, PA
Feld, Maury D., Ref.Libn.
HARVARD UNIVERSITY - LITTAUER LIBRARY □
Cambridge, MA
Felder, Charletta P., Chf., Lib.Serv.
U.S. VETERANS ADMINISTRATION (SC-
Columbia) - WILLIAM JENNINGS BRYAN-DORN
VETERANS HOSPITAL - LIBRARY □ Columbia, SC
Feldick, Peggy, Ref., ILL & On-line Serv.
MACALESTER COLLEGE - WEYERHAEUSER
LIBRARY □ St. Paul, MN
Feldman, Donald H., Mgr.
PLATT SACO LOWELL CORPORATION -
ENGINEERING LIBRARY □ Greenville, SC
Feldman, Edward S., Assoc.Dir., Info.Serv.
NEW YORK STATE DEPARTMENT OF
ENVIRONMENTAL CONSERVATION - OFFICE OF
PUBLIC AFFAIRS - INFORMATION SERVICE □
Albany, NY
Feldman, Eleanor C., Assoc.Spec.
MARTIN MARIETTA LABORATORIES - LIBRARY
□ Baltimore, MD
Feldman, Ellen, Libn.
ANSER - TECHNICAL LIBRARY □ Arlington, VA
Feldman, Eugene, Dir. of Res. & Pubn.
DU SABLE MUSEUM OF AFRICAN AMERICAN
HISTORY - LIBRARY □ Chicago, IL
Feldman, Fran, Libn.
ANDERSEN LABORATORIES, INC. - LIBRARY □
Bloomfield, CT
Feldman, Laurence, Br.Libn.
UNIVERSITY OF MASSACHUSETTS, AMHERST -
MORRILL BIOLOGICAL & GEOLOGICAL
SCIENCES LIBRARY □ Amherst, MA
Feldman, Marguerite S., Ser. & Circ.
ROSWELL PARK MEMORIAL INSTITUTE -
LIBRARY AND INFORMATION MANAGEMENT
SERVICES □ Buffalo, NY
Feldman, Patricia, ILL
COTTAGE HOSPITAL - DAVID L. REEVES
MEDICAL LIBRARY □ Santa Barbara, CA
Feldman, Rayma, Sr.Info.Spec.
U.S. MARITIME ADMINISTRATION - NATL.
MARITIME RESEARCH CENTER - STUDY
CENTER □ Kings Point, NY
Feldman, Rosalie, Libn.
PLATTE RIVER POWER AUTHORITY - LIBRARY
□ Fort Collins, CO
Feldman, T.K., Dir., Literary Arts Dept.
JEWISH COMMUNITY CENTER OF GREATER
WASHINGTON - KASS JUDAIC LIBRARY □
Rockville, MD
Feldstein, Dr. Arthur, Hd. of Lib.Comm.
SEA VIEW HOSPITAL AND HOME - MEDICAL
LIBRARY □ Staten Island, NY
Feldt, Marna, Info.Off.
SWEDISH CONSULATE GENERAL - SWEDISH
INFORMATION SERVICE □ New York, NY
Felice, Michael, Hd., Ser.
UNIVERSITY OF ILLINOIS AT CHICAGO -
HEALTH SCIENCES CENTER - LIBRARY OF THE
HEALTH SCIENCES □ Chicago, IL
Felician, Bro., S.C., Libn.
UNION SAINT-JEAN-BAPTISTE - MALLET
LIBRARY □ Woonsocket, RI
Feliciano, Francisco
UNIVERSITY OF PUERTO RICO - NATURAL
SCIENCE LIBRARY □ Rio Piedras, PR
Felicie, Ada M., Libn.
UNIVERSITY OF PUERTO RICO - PUERTO
RICAN COLLECTION† □ Rio Piedras, PR
Felker, William A., Hd.
FREE LIBRARY OF PHILADELPHIA -
GOVERNMENT PUBLICATIONS DEPARTMENT □
Philadelphia, PA
Fell-Johnson, Barbara, Law Libn.
HAMPSHIRE LAW LIBRARY □ Northampton, MA

Fellabaum, Martha S., Libn.
EXXON CHEMICAL AMERICAS - TECHNICAL
INFORMATION CENTER □ Baytown, TX
Feller, Amy, Libn./Info.Spec.
HALCON SD GROUP, INC. - HALCON RESEARCH
- LIBRARY □ Montvale, NJ
Feller, Irwin, Dir.
PENNSYLVANIA STATE UNIVERSITY -
INSTITUTE FOR POLICY RESEARCH AND
EVALUATION - LIBRARY □ University Park, PA
Feller, Judith M., Doc.Libn.
EAST STROUDSBURG UNIVERSITY - KENT
LIBRARY† □ East Stroudsburg, PA
Fellows, Paul E., Site Supt.
FORT MASSAC HISTORIC SITE - LIBRARY □
Metropolis, IL
Felsten, Judith, Archv.
BALCH INSTITUTE FOR ETHNIC STUDIES -
LIBRARY □ Philadelphia, PA
Felt, Margie A., Med.Lib.Asst.
SCENIC GENERAL HOSPITAL - STANISLAUS
COUNTY MEDICAL LIBRARY □ Modesto, CA
Feltes, Carol A., Mgr., Lib.Serv.
BATTELLE-COLUMBUS LABORATORIES -
LIBRARY □ Columbus, OH
Felts, Carol, Assoc.Libn.
UNIVERSITY OF FLORIDA - LAW LIBRARY □
Gainesville, FL
Feltz, Ms. E., Law Dept.Adm.
GREYHOUND CORPORATION - LAW
DEPARTMENT LIBRARY □ Phoenix, AZ
Felzer, Larry, Mgr.
FIRST PENNSYLVANIA BANK, N.A. -
MARKETING INFORMATION CENTER □
Philadelphia, PA
Fendelet, Connie, Lib.Asst.
UNIVERSITY OF SASKATCHEWAN -
THORVALDSON LIBRARY □ Saskatoon, SK
Fendry, Marie, Res.Libn.
PHARMACIA P-L BIOCHEMICALS, INC. -
RESEARCH LIBRARY □ Milwaukee, WI
Feng, Cyril C.H., Libn.
UNIVERSITY OF MARYLAND, BALTIMORE -
HEALTH SCIENCES LIBRARY □ Baltimore, MD
Feng, Grace C., Supv.Libn.
U.S. ARMY - TROOP SUPPORT AND AVIATION
MATERIEL READINESS COMMAND - STINFO
AND REFERENCE LIBRARY† □ St. Louis, MO
Fenichel, Carol Hansen, Dir., Lib.Serv.
PHILADELPHIA COLLEGE OF PHARMACY AND
SCIENCE - JOSEPH W. ENGLAND LIBRARY □
Philadelphia, PA
Fenn, Dan H., Jr., Dir.
U.S. PRESIDENTIAL LIBRARIES - JOHN F.
KENNEDY LIBRARY □ Boston, MA
Fenn, Martha J., Libn.
BRATTLEBORO MEMORIAL HOSPITAL -
MEDICAL LIBRARY □ Brattleboro, VT
Fennell, Elma, Libn., Per. & Microforms
TEXAS TECH UNIVERSITY - LIBRARY □
Lubbock, TX
Fennell, Janice C., Lib.Dir.
GEORGIA COLLEGE - INA DILLARD RUSSELL
LIBRARY - SPECIAL COLLECTIONS □
Milledgeville, GA
Fennewald, Connie, Acq. Law Libn.
UNIVERSITY OF MISSOURI - SCHOOL OF LAW
LIBRARY □ Columbia, MO
Fenske, Dr. David, Hd.Libn.
INDIANA UNIVERSITY - MUSIC LIBRARY □
Bloomington, IN
Fenster, Madeleine, Libn.
NEW YORK COUNTY - DISTRICT ATTORNEY'S
OFFICE LIBRARY □ New York, NY
Fenstermann, Duane, Hd., Tech.Serv.
LUTHER COLLEGE - PREUS LIBRARY □ Decorah,
IA
Fenton, Miss E.A., Gen.Sec.
CANADIAN TELEPHONE EMPLOYEES'
ASSOCIATION - LIBRARY □ Montreal, PQ
Fenton, Elaine P., Circuit Libn.
U.S. COURT OF APPEALS, 11TH CIRCUIT -
LIBRARY □ Atlanta, GA

Fenton, Irene, Saltfleet Supv.
MOHAWK COLLEGE OF APPLIED ARTS AND
TECHNOLOGY - MOHAWK LIBRARY RESOURCE
CENTRE □ Hamilton, ON
Fenton, Jacquie, Hd., Info.Serv.
UNDERWOOD MC LELLAN LTD. - INFORMATION
SERVICES □ Edmonton, AB
Fenton, Joan, Libn.
FAMILY SERVICE AMERICA - LIBRARY □ New
York, NY
Fenton, N.A., Asst.Libn.
ECONOMICS LABORATORY, INC. - CORPORATE
INFORMATION CENTER □ St. Paul, MN
Fenton, Pat, Ref.Libn.
MINNESOTA STATE DEPARTMENT OF
EDUCATION - INTERAGENCY RESOURCE AND
INFORMATION CENTER □ St. Paul, MN
Fenton, Tom, Coord., Products & Serv.
INVESTIGATIVE RESOURCE CENTER - DATA
CENTER □ Oakland, CA
Ferdinand-Grant, Mrs. I., Libn.
GEORGE BROWN COLLEGE OF APPLIED ARTS &
TECHNOLOGY - LIBRARY □ Toronto, ON
Ferenczy, Eleanora, Techn.
CANADA - HEALTH AND WELFARE CANADA -
HEALTH PROTECTION BRANCH - REGIONAL
LIBRARY □ Longueuil, PQ
Ferestad, Virginia, Mgr., Info.Serv.
CAMPBELL-MITHUN, INC. - INFORMATION
SERVICES □ Minneapolis, MN
Feret, Ronald E.
POPE, BALLARD, SHEPARD AND FOWLE -
LIBRARY† □ Chicago, IL
Fergason, Dorinda, Fire Info.Spec.
NATIONAL FIRE PROTECTION ASSOCIATION -
CHARLES S. MORGAN TECHNICAL LIBRARY □
Quincy, MA
Fergenson, Ruth, Libn.
WORLD ZIONIST ORGANIZATION - AMERICAN
SECTION - ZIONIST ARCHIVES AND LIBRARY □
New York, NY
Ferger, Audrey, Libn.
UNITED COOPERATIVES OF ONTARIO -
HARMAN LIBRARY □ Mississauga, ON
Fergoda, Joy, Lib.Coord.
UNIVERSITY OF CALIFORNIA, DAVIS -
WOMEN'S RESOURCES & RESEARCH CENTER -
LIBRARY □ Davis, CA
Ferguson, Alana K., Pub.Serv.Libn.
PALMER COLLEGE OF CHIROPRACTIC - DAVID
D. PALMER LIBRARY □ Davenport, IA
Ferguson, Barbara O., Circ.Supv.
CORNELL UNIVERSITY - SCHOOL OF HOTEL
ADMINISTRATION LIBRARY □ Ithaca, NY
Ferguson, Connie, Libn.
BLUE CROSS OF WESTERN PENNSYLVANIA -
IN-HOUSE BUSINESS LIBRARY □ Pittsburgh, PA
Ferguson, Diane A., Libn.
U.S. ARMS CONTROL AND DISARMAMENT
AGENCY - LIBRARY □ Washington, DC
Ferguson, Elizabeth E., Ref.Libn.
YALE UNIVERSITY - KLINE SCIENCE LIBRARY □
New Haven, CT
Ferguson, Emilia, Asst.Libn.
HOFFMANN-LA ROCHE, INC. - BUSINESS
INFORMATION CENTER □ Nutley, NJ
Ferguson, Dr. John L., State Hist.
ARKANSAS (State) HISTORY COMMISSION -
ARCHIVES □ Little Rock, AR
Ferguson, John Philip, Dept.Hd.
CLEVELAND PUBLIC LIBRARY - POPULAR
LIBRARY DEPARTMENT □ Cleveland, OH
Ferguson, Patricia, Libn.
BENDIX CORPORATION - BENDIX AVIONICS
DIVISION - LIBRARY □ Fort Lauderdale, FL
Ferguson, Roberta, Sr.Res.Libn.
DATA GENERAL CORPORATION - CORPORATE
LIBRARY □ Westborough, MA
Ferguson, Shirley, Circ.
NORTHWESTERN OKLAHOMA STATE
UNIVERSITY - LIBRARY □ Alva, OK

Ferguson, Stephen, Cur. of Rare Books
PRINCETON UNIVERSITY - RARE BOOKS AND
SPECIAL COLLECTIONS □ Princeton, NJ

Ferguson, Yvette, Coord.
MARSHALLTOWN AREA COMMUNITY HOSPITAL
- SCHOOL OF NURSING RESOURCE CENTER □
Marshalltown, IA

Ferimer, Suzanne, Dir., Lrng.Rsrcs.
UNIVERSITY OF HOUSTON - COLLEGE OF
OPTOMETRY LIBRARY □ Houston, TX

Ferkull, Marion, Hd., Philosophy/Relg.Sect
CHICAGO PUBLIC LIBRARY CENTRAL LIBRARY -
SOCIAL SCIENCES & HISTORY DIVISION □
Chicago, IL

Ferland, Ronald J., Libn.
U.S. AIR FORCE BASE - BARKSDALE BASE
LIBRARY □ Barksdale AFB, LA

Fernandez, Nenita A., Cat.Libn.
YALE UNIVERSITY - ECONOMIC GROWTH
CENTER COLLECTION □ New Haven, CT

Fernandez, Nenita A., Cat.Libn.
YALE UNIVERSITY - SOCIAL SCIENCE LIBRARY
□ New Haven, CT

Fernandez, Nora, Hd., Cat.
ORGANIZATION OF AMERICAN STATES -
COLUMBUS MEMORIAL LIBRARY □ Washington,
DC

Fernandez, Raul P., Asst.Dir.
U.S. MARINE CORPS - CAMP PENDLETON
LIBRARY SYSTEM □ Camp Pendleton, CA

Ferng, Mr. Hou Ran, Hd.Libn.
ST. JOHN'S UNIVERSITY - ASIAN COLLECTION
- LIBRARY □ Jamaica, NY

Ferrante, B., Sys.Mgr.
AT & T COMMUNICATIONS - INFORMATION
RESEARCH CENTER □ Morris Plains, NJ

Ferrante, Barbara, Tax Libn.
PRICE WATERHOUSE - TAX LIBRARY† □ New
York, NY

Ferrara, Deborah, Ref.Supv.
ASPEN SYSTEMS CORPORATION - PROJECT
SHARE □ Rockville, MD

Ferrara, Mark M., Assoc.Dir.
KEAN COLLEGE OF NEW JERSEY - NANCY
THOMPSON LIBRARY† □ Union, NJ

Ferre, Dick, Adm.
NANAIMO CENTENNIAL MUSEUM - ARCHIVES □
Nanaimo, BC

Ferre, Marie Booth, Asst.Cur.
DICKINSON COLLEGE - LIBRARY - SPECIAL
COLLECTIONS† □ Carlisle, PA

Ferree, G. Donald, Assoc.Dir.
UNIVERSITY OF CONNECTICUT - INSTITUTE
FOR SOCIAL INQUIRY □ Storrs, CT

Ferrell, Mrs. Bernie, Libn.
ST. LOUIS CITY HOSPITAL - ST. LOUIS
MUNICIPAL MEDICAL LIBRARY □ St. Louis, MO

Ferrell, Miss Jan, Ser.Acq.Supv.
FORD FOUNDATION - LIBRARY □ New York, NY

Ferrell, Robert, Techn.
P.T. BOATS, INC. - LIBRARY, ARCHIVES &
TECHNICAL INFORMATION CENTER -
NATIONAL HEADQUARTERS □ Memphis, TN

Ferrer, Aida, Libn.
AMERICAN KENNEL CLUB - LIBRARY □ New
York, NY

Ferri, Maria D., Tech.Libn.
PRC SPEAS - TECHNICAL LIBRARY □ Lake
Success, NY

Ferrier, Douglas, Hd., Tech.Serv.
ST. MARY'S UNIVERSITY - LAW LIBRARY† □
San Antonio, TX

Ferrier, Robert C., AV Spec.
IOWA STATE DEPARTMENT OF HUMAN
SERVICES - LIBRARY □ Des Moines, IA

Ferriero, David S., Libn.
MASSACHUSETTS INSTITUTE OF TECHNOLOGY
- HUMANITIES LIBRARY □ Cambridge, MA

Ferrigno, Helen, Asst.Libn.
DANIEL WEBSTER COLLEGE - LIBRARY □
Nashua, NH

Ferrin, Paul, Libn.
MONSANTO COMPANY - RUBBER CHEMICALS
RESEARCH LIBRARY† □ Akron, OH

Ferris, Bill, Pres.
CENTER FOR SOUTHERN FOLKLORE -
ARCHIVES □ Memphis, TN

Ferris, S.E., Libn.
BRITISH COLUMBIA - MINISTRY OF ENERGY,
MINES AND PETROLEUM RESOURCES -
LIBRARY† □ Victoria, BC

Ferry, Joan, Libn.
MOORE (Walter P.) & ASSOCIATES - LIBRARY □
Houston, TX

Ferry, Sheila
BRITISH COLUMBIA INSTITUTE OF
TECHNOLOGY - LIBRARY SERVICES DIVISION
□ Burnaby, BC

Fesenmaier, Frani, Asst.Hd.
WEST VIRGINIA STATE LIBRARY COMMISSION
- FILM SERVICES DEPARTMENT □ Charleston,
WV

Fesenmaier, Steve, Film Libn.
WEST VIRGINIA STATE LIBRARY COMMISSION
- FILM SERVICES DEPARTMENT □ Charleston,
WV

Fesmire, Denise, Libn.
ST. JOSEPH HOSPITAL - HEALTH SCIENCE
LIBRARY □ Memphis, TN

Fessenden, Ann, Tech.Serv.Libn.
UNIVERSITY OF MISSISSIPPI - SCHOOL OF
LAW LIBRARY □ University, MS

Fessenden, Ellen, Dir.
FENTON HISTORICAL SOCIETY - LIBRARY □
Jamestown, NY

Fessenden, Jane, Libn.
MARINE BIOLOGICAL LABORATORY - LIBRARY
□ Woods Hole, MA

Fetesoff, Barbara, Sr.Libn.
SONOMA STATE HOSPITAL AND
DEVELOPMENTAL CENTER - STAFF LIBRARY □
Eldridge, CA

Fetherston, Lynn, Tech.Serv.
NEW BRUNSWICK THEOLOGICAL SEMINARY -
GARDNER A. SAGE LIBRARY □ New Brunswick,
NJ

Fetkovich, Malinda, Dir.
SHADYSIDE HOSPITAL - JAMES FRAZER
HILLMAN HEALTH SCIENCES LIBRARY □
Pittsburgh, PA

Fett, Helen, Tech.Info.Sci.
PILLSBURY COMPANY - TECHNICAL
INFORMATION CENTER □ Minneapolis, MN

Feuer, Dr. Bernice I., Supv.
CELANESE CORPORATION - SUMMIT
RESEARCH LABORATORIES - TECHNICAL
INFORMATION CENTER □ Summit, NJ

Feuerstein, Robin, Dir., Info.Prog./Anl.
INTERPUBLIC GROUP OF COMPANIES -
CENTER FOR ADVERTISING SERVICES □ New
York, NY

Feurer, Gary A., Coord.
UNIVERSITY OF DELAWARE, NEWARK -
COLLEGE OF EDUCATION - COMPUTER BASED
EDUCATION RESEARCH LIBRARY □ Newark, DE

Fiasconaro, Jane, Libn.
HEWLETT-PACKARD COMPANY - FORT
COLLINS FACILITY LIBRARY □ Fort Collins, CO

Fichtelberg, Doris, Prin.Libn., Mus.
FREE PUBLIC LIBRARY OF ELIZABETH, NJ - ART
AND MUSIC DEPARTMENT □ Elizabeth, NJ

Fichtenau, Lane E., Libn.
ADAMS-PRATT OAKLAND COUNTY LAW
LIBRARY □ Pontiac, MI

Fidelia, Sr. M., Med.Libn.
HOLY CROSS HOSPITAL - MEDICAL LIBRARY □
Salt Lake City, UT

Fidler, Linda M., Hd., Mus.Lib.
BOWLING GREEN STATE UNIVERSITY - MUSIC
LIBRARY □ Bowling Green, OH

Fiedler, Christine, Ref.
MUHLENBERG COLLEGE - JOHN A.W. HAAS
LIBRARY □ Allentown, PA

Fiedler, Grace, Asst.Libn.
ASCENSION LUTHERAN CHURCH - LIBRARY □
Milwaukee, WI

Fiedler, Katherine, Libn.
OWENSBORO MESSENGER-INQUIRER -
LIBRARY □ Owensboro, KY

Field, Charles L., Asst. Law Libn.
NORTHEASTERN UNIVERSITY - LAW SCHOOL
LIBRARY □ Boston, MA

Field, Constance N., Asst. Music Libn.
NORTHWESTERN UNIVERSITY - MUSIC
LIBRARY □ Evanston, IL

Field, Judith J., Hd., Gen.Ref.
FLINT PUBLIC LIBRARY - MICHIGAN ROOM □
Flint, MI

Field, Susan C., Docs.Libn.
UNIVERSITY OF GEORGIA - GOVERNMENT
DOCUMENTS DEPARTMENT □ Athens, GA

Field, Whitney K., Circ.Hd.
UNIVERSITY OF MICHIGAN - ALFRED
TAUBMAN MEDICAL LIBRARY □ Ann Arbor, MI

Fielden, Alma Hall, Adm.Asst., Med. Staff
ST. ANTHONY HOSPITAL - MEDICAL LIBRARY □
Louisville, KY

Fielder, Elizabeth, Lib.Chm.
MONTEREY HISTORY & ART ASSOCIATION -
MAYO HAYES O'DONNELL LIBRARY □ Monterey,
CA

Fielder, Mary V., Libn.
CANDLER GENERAL HOSPITAL - MEDICAL
LIBRARY □ Savannah, GA

Fields, Julie, Asst.Libn., Rd.Serv.
CROWELL & MORING - LIBRARY □ Washington,
DC

Fields, Patti, Cat.Libn.
MEDICAL UNIVERSITY OF SOUTH CAROLINA -
LIBRARY □ Charleston, SC

Fields, Robert, Techn.
ST. LUKE'S HOSPITAL OF BETHLEHEM,
PENNSYLVANIA - AUDIOVISUAL LIBRARY □
Bethlehem, PA

Fien, Kerstin, Lib.Techn.
U.S. MARINE CORPS - KANEOHE AIR STATION
LIBRARY □ Kaneohe Bay, HI

Fierberg, Joan, Dir. of Lib.Serv./Libn.
DU PONT (Alfred I.) INSTITUTE OF THE
NEMOURS FOUNDATION LIBRARY □ Wilmington,
DE

Fiering, Norman, Dir./Libn.
BROWN UNIVERSITY - JOHN CARTER BROWN
LIBRARY □ Providence, RI

Fierke, Susan, Info.Spec.
UPJOHN COMPANY - CORPORATE TECHNICAL
LIBRARY □ Kalamazoo, MI

Fiery, Corleah S., Res.
HISTORICAL SOCIETY OF DAUPHIN COUNTY -
ARCHIVES/LIBRARY □ Harrisburg, PA

Fieweger, Harriet, Libn./Sec.
WASHINGTON UNIVERSITY - EDWARD
MALLINCKRODT INSTITUTE OF RADIOLOGY
LIBRARY □ St. Louis, MO

Fife, Frances, AHEC Lib.Asst.Dir.
ROWAN MEMORIAL HOSPITAL - MC KENZIE
MEMORIAL LIBRARY □ Salisbury, NC

Fife, Dr. Jonathan D., Dir.
ERIC CLEARINGHOUSE ON HIGHER EDUCATION
□ Washington, DC

Figatner, Annette, Per.
KENNEDY-KING COLLEGE - LIBRARY† □
Chicago, IL

Figgatt, Bonnie, Info.Spec.
AT & T COMMUNICATIONS - INFORMATION
RESEARCH CENTER □ Cincinnati, OH

Figueras, Myriam, Hd., Reader Serv.
ORGANIZATION OF AMERICAN STATES -
COLUMBUS MEMORIAL LIBRARY □ Washington,
DC

Figueredo, Olga, Per.Libn.
FLORIDA INSTITUTE OF TECHNOLOGY -
COLLEGE OF APPLIED TECHNOLOGY - LIBRARY
□ Jensen Beach, FL

Fike, Claude E., Dir.
UNIVERSITY OF SOUTHERN MISSISSIPPI - MC
CAIN LIBRARY □ Hattiesburg, MS

Filiatreault, Luc, Lib.Ck.
CANADA - REVENUE CANADA - CUSTOMS &
EXCISE - COLLEGE LIBRARY† □ Rigaud, PQ

Filipak, Grace, Sr.Info.Spec./Ref.
GENERAL FOODS CORPORATION - MARKETING
INFORMATION CENTER □ White Plains, NY

Filipkowski, Mrs. J., Mgr., Tech.Serv.
CANADA - HEALTH AND WELFARE CANADA -
DEPARTMENTAL LIBRARY SERVICES □ Ottawa,
ON

Filis, April W., Info. & Referral Coord.
COMPREHENSIVE HEALTH COUNCIL OF
METROPOLITAN CHICAGO - ALCOHOLISM
CENTER - LIBRARY □ Chicago, IL

Fillos, Debra A., Cur.
LYME HISTORICAL SOCIETY, INC. - ARCHIVES
□ Old Lyme, CT

Filsinger, Elaine G., Libn.
PENNSYLVANIA STATE DEPARTMENT OF
PUBLIC WELFARE - PHILIPSBURG STATE
GENERAL HOSPITAL - LIBRARY □ Philipsburg, PA

Filson, Lauren K., Archv.
OREGON STATE UNIVERSITY - ARCHIVES □
Corvallis, OR

Filstrup, E. Christian, Div.Chf.
NEW YORK PUBLIC LIBRARY - ORIENTAL
DIVISION □ New York, NY

Filupeit, Susan M., Tech.Proc.Libn.
MYSTIC SEAPORT, INC. - G.W. BLUNT WHITE
LIBRARY □ Mystic, CT

Finch, Leroy, Sr. Metallurgist
ESCO CORP. - LIBRARY □ Portland, OR

Finch, Linda D., Chm., Lib.Comm.
FIRST MERIDIAN HEIGHTS PRESBYTERIAN
CHURCH - HUDELSON LIBRARY □ Indianapolis,
IN

Finckenor, George A., Sr., Cur.
SUFFOLK COUNTY WHALING MUSEUM -
LIBRARY □ Sag Harbor, NY

Findlay, Gail, Acq.Libn.
UNIVERSITY OF TENNESSEE - CENTER FOR
THE HEALTH SCIENCES LIBRARY □ Memphis,
TN

Findlay, James A., Dir.
RHODE ISLAND SCHOOL OF DESIGN - LIBRARY
□ Providence, RI

Findlay, Peggy, Info.Serv.Libn.
MC MASTER UNIVERSITY - THODE LIBRARY OF
SCIENCE & ENGINEERING □ Hamilton, ON

Findley, Ms. J., Doc.Asst.
CANADA - METRIC COMMISSION CANADA -
REFERENCE SERVICE □ Ottawa, ON

Fine, Dana, ILL
BALL MEMORIAL HOSPITAL - HEALTH SCIENCE
LIBRARY □ Muncie, IN

Fine, Paula H., Libn.
CONGREGATION EMANU-EL B'NE JESHURUN -
RABBI DUDLEY WEINBERG LIBRARY □
Milwaukee, WI

Fine, Susan L., Libn.
FAMILY INSTITUTE OF CHICAGO - CROWLEY
MEMORIAL LIBRARY □ Chicago, IL

Finerty, Michele, Asst.Libn.
UNIVERSITY OF MISSOURI, KANSAS CITY -
LAW LIBRARY □ Kansas City, MO

Finger, Charles S., Ref.Libn.
LOYOLA UNIVERSITY (New Orleans) - LAW
LIBRARY □ New Orleans, LA

Fingerman, Susan, Mgr., Info.Serv.
TELEDYNE ENGINEERING SERVICES -
INFORMATION CENTER □ Waltham, MA

Fingers, Debi, Info.Ctr.Mgr.
GARDNER ADVERTISING COMPANY -
INFORMATION CENTER □ St. Louis, MO

Fingland, Geoffrey, Libn.
CHRISTIAN SCIENCE MONITOR - RESEARCH
LIBRARY □ Boston, MA

Fingold, Sydney, Libn.
HARVARD UNIVERSITY - NEW ENGLAND
REGIONAL PRIMATE RESEARCH CENTER -
LIBRARY □ Southborough, MA

Fink, Diana, Supv.
NORTH YORK PUBLIC LIBRARY - CANADIANA
COLLECTION □ Willowdale, ON

Fink, Eleanor E., Chf.
SMITHSONIAN INSTITUTION - NATIONAL
MUSEUM OF AMERICAN ART - OFFICE OF
VISUAL RSRCS. - SLIDE/PHOTOGRAPH
ARCHIVE □ Washington, DC

Fink, Myron, Libn.
UNIVERSITY OF NEW MEXICO - SCHOOL OF
LAW LIBRARY □ Albuquerque, NM

Finkbiner, Earle P., Libn.
NATIONAL RAILWAY HISTORICAL SOCIETY -
LIBRARY OF AMERICAN TRANSPORTATION □
Jobstown, NJ

Finkel, Kenneth, Cur., Prints/Photographs
LIBRARY COMPANY OF PHILADELPHIA □
Philadelphia, PA

Finkelpearl, Katherine D., Art Libn.
WELLESLEY COLLEGE - ART LIBRARY □
Wellesley, MA

Finkler, Margaret, Circ., Per.
BOSTON CONSERVATORY OF MUSIC - ALBERT
ALPHIN MUSIC LIBRARY □ Boston, MA

Finlay, Constance, Ref.Libn.
CORNELL UNIVERSITY - MARTIN P.
CATHERWOOD LIBRARY OF INDUSTRIAL AND
LABOR RELATIONS □ Ithaca, NY

Finlay, Rev. D.F., Libn.
UNIVERSITY OF TORONTO - PONTIFICAL
INSTITUTE OF MEDIAEVAL STUDIES - LIBRARY
□ Toronto, ON

Finlay, Mary, Chf.Libn.
CANADA - NATIONAL DEFENCE - MOBILE
COMMAND HQ LIBRARY □ St. Hubert, PQ

Finlayson, Janet, Hd.Libn.
MC GILL UNIVERSITY - MACDONALD COLLEGE
- LIBRARY □ Ste. Anne de Bellevue, PQ

Finlayson, Mary S., Libn.
SCIENCE MUSEUM OF MINNESOTA - LOUIS S.
HEADLEY MEMORIAL LIBRARY □ St. Paul, MN

Finley, Howard J., Dir.
OLD BRUTUS HISTORICAL SOCIETY, INC. -
LIBRARY □ Weedsport, NY

Finley, Judith R., Dir., Oral Hist.Proj.
COLORADO COLLEGE - CHARLES LEAMING
TUTT LIBRARY - SPECIAL COLLECTIONS □
Colorado Springs, CO

Finn, Barbara L., Dir. of Med.Lib.
SINAI HOSPITAL OF DETROIT - SAMUEL FRANK
MEDICAL LIBRARY □ Detroit, MI

Finnan, Anne M., Ref.Libn.
FORDHAM UNIVERSITY - LIBRARY AT LINCOLN
CENTER □ New York, NY

Finnegan, Catherine, Dir., Lib.Serv.
BANCROFT, AVERY AND MC ALISTER - LAW
LIBRARY □ San Francisco, CA

Finnegan, Eileen, Libn.
SYMMERS, FISH AND WARNER - RESEARCH
LIBRARY □ New York, NY

Finnegan, Shonnie, Univ.Archv.
SUNY AT BUFFALO - UNIVERSITY ARCHIVES □
Buffalo, NY

Finnemore, Alison, Libn.
PULP AND PAPER RESEARCH INSTITUTE OF
CANADA - LIBRARY □ Pointe Claire, PQ

Finnerty, James L., Ph.D., Dir., Lib.
COLUMBUS-CUNEO-CABRINI MEDICAL CENTER
- COLUMBUS HOSPITAL MEDICAL LIBRARY □
Chicago, IL

Finney, Ann, Educ.Dir.
MARION COUNTY MEMORIAL HOSPITAL -
LIBRARY □ Marion, SC

Finney, Carol D., Mgr.
U.S. DEFENSE TECHNICAL INFORMATION
CENTER - DTIC ON-LINE SERVICE FACILITY □
Los Angeles, CA

Finsten, Hugh, Dir., Res.Br.
CANADA - LIBRARY OF PARLIAMENT □ Ottawa,
ON

Finster, Eileen E., Libn.
PITTSBURGH PRESS - LIBRARY □ Pittsburgh, PA

Fiore, Jannette, Libn.
MICHIGAN STATE UNIVERSITY - SPECIAL
COLLECTIONS LIBRARY □ East Lansing, MI

Fiore, Jannette, Libn.
MICHIGAN STATE UNIVERSITY - SPECIAL
COLLECTIONS LIBRARY - RUSSEL B. NYE
POPULAR CULTURE COLLECTION □ East
Lansing, MI

Firestone, Sharon, Acq., Ser. & Govt.Doc.
ARIZONA STATE UNIVERSITY - COLLEGE OF
LAW - LIBRARY □ Tempe, AZ

Firm, C. Kay, Libn.
JEFFERSON COUNTY LAW LIBRARY □
Steubenville, OH

Firth, Margaret A., Libn.
BEVERLY HOSPITAL - LIBRARY □ Beverly, MA

Fischel, A.F., Chem.-Libn.
ESSO PETROLEUM CANADA - RESEARCH
TECHNICAL INFORMATION CENTRE □ Sarnia,
ON

Fischer, Catherine, Libn.
COMBUSTION ENGINEERING, INC. - POWER
SYSTEMS GROUP LIBRARY SERVICES† □
Windsor, CT

Fischer, Elizabeth, Libn.
HUMANA HOSPITAL AUDUBON - MEDICAL
LIBRARY □ Louisville, KY

Fischer, Howard E., Dir.
CENTER FOR NONPROFIT ORGANIZATIONS,
INC. - LIBRARY □ New York, NY

Fischer, James H., Sec.-Treas.
AMERICAN SOCIETY OF SUGAR BEET
TECHNOLOGISTS - LIBRARY □ Fort Collins, CO

Fischer, Jimmi, Libn.
DALLAS PUBLIC LIBRARY - BUSINESS AND
TECHNOLOGY DIVISION □ Dallas, TX

Fischer, Jonathan, O.S.B., Field Dir.
ST. JOHN'S ABBEY AND UNIVERSITY - HILL
MONASTIC MANUSCRIPT LIBRARY - BUSH
CENTER □ Collegeville, MN

Fischer, Norma L., Libn.
ST. JOHN UNITED CHURCH OF CHRIST -
LIBRARY □ Collinsville, IL

Fischer, P.A., Res.Libn.
MC DONNELL DOUGLAS CORPORATION - MC
DONNELL AIRCRAFT LIBRARY □ St. Louis, MO

Fischer, Robert A., Sec.-Treas.
AMERICAN SOCIETY OF BAKERY ENGINEERS -
INFORMATION SERVICE AND LIBRARY □
Chicago, IL

Fischer, Thea J., Veterinary Med.Libn.
NORTH CAROLINA STATE UNIVERSITY -
VETERINARY MEDICAL LIBRARY □ Raleigh, NC

Fischer, Wenda Webster, Asst.Dir.
NKC HOSPITALS, INC. - MEDICAL LIBRARY □
Louisville, KY

Fischier, Adrienne G., Libn.
HARVARD LIBRARY IN NEW YORK □ New York,
NY

Fischler, Barbara B., Dir. of Libs.
INDIANA UNIVERSITY/PURDUE UNIVERSITY
AT INDIANAPOLIS - UNIVERSITY LIBRARY □
Indianapolis, IN

Fischman, Joshua, Res.
AMERICAN PSYCHOLOGICAL ASSOCIATION -
PSYCHOLOGY TODAY LIBRARY □ Washington,
DC

Fish, Arthur M., Doc.Libn.
UNIVERSITY OF WISCONSIN, STEVENS POINT
- JAMES H. ALBERTSON CENTER FOR
LEARNING RESOURCES □ Stevens Point, WI

Fish, Candace A., Libn.
ICI AMERICAS INC. - PROCESS TECHNOLOGY
DEPARTMENT LIBRARY □ Dighton, MA

Fish, Kaye M., Asst.Libn.
NORTON GALLERY AND SCHOOL OF ART -
LIBRARY □ West Palm Beach, FL

Flanagan, Margaret, Med.Libn.
EPISCOPAL HOSPITAL - MEDICAL LIBRARY □
Philadelphia, PA

Flanagan, Mary T., Cur. of Hist.
CASCADE COUNTY HISTORICAL SOCIETY -
INFORMATION CENTER □ Great Falls, MT

Flanagan, Rosemary M., Med.Libn.
ST. ELIZABETH HOSPITAL - MEDICAL LIBRARY
□ Danville, IL

Flanary, Barbara, Spec.I
MEMPHIS-SHELBY COUNTY PUBLIC LIBRARY
AND INFORMATION CENTER - MEMPHIS ROOM
COLLECTIONS □ Memphis, TN

Flanner, Deborah, Acq./Abstracting Spec.
ALLIED CORPORATION - LIBRARY &
INFORMATION SERVICES □ Morristown, NJ

Flannery, Louis, Chf.Libn.
OREGON HISTORICAL SOCIETY - LIBRARY □
Portland, OR

Flanzraich, Lisa, Libn.
BARUCH COLLEGE OF THE CITY UNIVERSITY
OF NEW YORK - ELIAS LIEBERMAN HIGHER
EDUC. CONTRACT LIB.† □ New York, NY

Flanzraich, Lisa, Film Info.Spec.
EDUCATIONAL FILM LIBRARY ASSOCIATION -
LIBRARY AND INFORMATION CENTER □ New
York, NY

Flautz, Nan, Acq.
MUHLENBERG COLLEGE - JOHN A.W. HAAS
LIBRARY □ Allentown, PA

Flavin, Linda M., Hd.Cat.
MEDICAL COLLEGE OF GEORGIA - LIBRARY □
Augusta, GA

Flax, Judy, Libn.
TOM BAKER CANCER CENTER - LIBRARY □
Calgary, AB

Flax, Sandra P., Asst. V.P.
BANKERS TRUST COMPANY - CORPORATE
FINANCE DEPARTMENT - INFORMATION
CENTER □ New York, NY

Flaxman, Dr. Erwin, Dir.
ERIC CLEARINGHOUSE ON URBAN EDUCATION
□ New York, NY

Fleagle, James W., Mgr., Info.Serv.
NOVO LABORATORIES INC. - LIBRARY □ Wilton,
CT

Fleckenstein, Marsha, Mgr.
DALLAS PUBLIC LIBRARY - GENERAL
REFERENCE DEPARTMENT □ Dallas, TX

Fleckner, John A., Archv.
SMITHSONIAN INSTITUTION LIBRARIES -
NATIONAL MUSEUM OF AMERICAN HISTORY -
ARCHIVES CENTER □ Washington, DC

Fleckner, Maxine, Film Archv.
UNIVERSITY OF WISCONSIN, MADISON -
WISCONSIN CENTER FOR FILM AND THEATER
RESEARCH □ Madison, WI

Fledderus, Helen, Libn.
READER'S DIGEST - ADVERTISING AND
MARKETING LIBRARY □ New York, NY

Fleenor, Elisabeth J., Chf., Cat.Div.
U.S. AIR FORCE ACADEMY - LIBRARY □
Colorado Springs, CO

Fleharty, Janet L., Media Spec.
COLORADO SCHOOL FOR THE DEAF AND THE
BLIND - MEDIA CENTER □ Colorado Springs, CO

Fleischer, Mary Beth, Asst.Libn.
UNIVERSITY OF TEXAS, AUSTIN - EUGENE C.
BARKER TEXAS HISTORY CENTER □ Austin, TX

Fleischhauer, Carl, Folklife Spec.
LIBRARY OF CONGRESS - AMERICAN FOLKLIFE
CENTER □ Washington, DC

Fleming, Ann, Res.Libn.
INSTITUTE FOR DEFENSE ANALYSES -
TECHNICAL INFORMATION SERVICES □
Alexandria, VA

Fleming, Dan, Pub.Serv.Libn.
ILIFF SCHOOL OF THEOLOGY - IRA J. TAYLOR
LIBRARY □ Denver, CO

Fleming, John, Spec.Coll.Libn.
EDINBORO UNIVERSITY OF PENNSYLVANIA -
BARON-FORNESS LIBRARY □ Edinboro, PA

Fleming, Paula J., Asst.Dir.
SMITHSONIAN INSTITUTION - NATIONAL
ANTHROPOLOGICAL ARCHIVES □ Washington,
DC

Fleming, Peter, Chf., Lib.Serv.
U.S. VETERANS ADMINISTRATION (NY-
Canandaigua) - MEDICAL CENTER LIBRARY
(142D) □ Canandaigua, NY

Fleming, Sharon L., Mss.Spec.
WESTERN HISTORICAL MANUSCRIPT
COLLECTION/STATE HISTORICAL SOCIETY OF
MISSOURI MANUSCRIPTS JOINT COLLECTION
□ Columbia, MO

Fleming, Thomas B., Chf. Law Libn.
U.S. DEPT. OF COMMERCE - LAW LIBRARY □
Washington, DC

Flemming, Tom, Hd., ILL
DALHOUSIE UNIVERSITY - W.K. KELLOGG
HEALTH SCIENCES LIBRARY □ Halifax, NS

Flesher, Lorna J., Supv.Libn.
CALIFORNIA STATE DEPARTMENT OF
TRANSPORTATION - LAW LIBRARY □
Sacramento, CA

Fleshmen, Nancy Acker, Res.Libn.
CRS SIRRINE, INC. - LIBRARY □ Houston, TX

Fletcher, Herb, Libn.
ATOMIC ENERGY OF CANADA, LTD. -
COMMERCIAL PRODUCTS LIBRARY □ Ottawa,
ON

Fletcher, James R., Lib.Ck.
NORTHWEST GEORGIA REGIONAL HOSPITAL
AT ROME - MEDICAL LIBRARY† □ Rome, GA

Fletcher, Karen, Sys./Cat.
ALBERTA RESEARCH COUNCIL - LIBRARY
SERVICES □ Edmonton, AB

Fletcher, Lyle, Archv.
WOOD COUNTY HISTORICAL SOCIETY -
HISTORICAL MUSEUM LIBRARY □ Bowling
Green, OH

Fletcher, Marjorie Amos, Dir.
AMERICAN COLLEGE - VANE B. LUCAS
MEMORIAL LIBRARY - ORAL HISTORY CENTER
& ARCHIVES □ Bryn Mawr, PA

Fletcher, P.A., Libn.
AMERICAN ALPINE CLUB - LIBRARY □ New
York, NY

Fletcher, Stephen J., Asst.Cur. of Photographs
CALIFORNIA HISTORICAL SOCIETY -
SCHUBERT HALL LIBRARY □ San Francisco, CA

Flewellen, Icabod, Dir.
AFRO-AMERICAN CULTURAL AND HISTORICAL
SOCIETY MUSEUM - LIBRARY □ Cleveland, OH

Flickinger, B. Floyd, Pres.
FLICKINGER FOUNDATION FOR AMERICAN
STUDIES, INC. - LIBRARY □ Baltimore, MD

Flickinger, Eugenia, Libn.
YAKIMA VALLEY GENEALOGICAL SOCIETY -
LIBRARY □ Yakima, WA

Fling, M., Ref.Libn.
INDIANA UNIVERSITY - MUSIC LIBRARY □
Bloomington, IN

Flinn, Mary, Soc.Adm.
NORTH ANDOVER HISTORICAL SOCIETY -
LIBRARY □ North Andover, MA

Flint, J.G., Sec./Exec.Off.
MINNESOTA STATE BOARD OF ANIMAL HEALTH
- LIBRARY □ St. Paul, MN

Flint, Katherine, Lib.Ck.
NEW YORK STATE SUPREME COURT - 6TH
JUDICIAL DISTRICT - LAW LIBRARY □ Delhi, NY

Flint, Richard, Cur., Prints/Photographs
PEALE MUSEUM - REFERENCE CENTER □
Baltimore, MD

Flint, Steve, Tech.Dir.
IIT RESEARCH INSTITUTE - RELIABILITY
ANALYSIS CENTER □ Rome, NY

Flitton, Deborah, Libn.
BRITISH COLUMBIA - MINISTRY OF
CONSUMER AND CORPORATE AFFAIRS -
LIBRARY SERVICES □ Victoria, BC

Floerke, Sue, Consortium Coord.
MEMORIAL MEDICAL CENTER - HEALTH
SCIENCES LIBRARY □ Corpus Christi, TX

Flokstra, Gerard J., Jr., Lib.Dir.
CENTRAL BIBLE COLLEGE - LIBRARY □
Springfield, MO

Flood, Brian, Cat.
WILFRID LAURIER UNIVERSITY - LIBRARY □
Waterloo, ON

Flood, Jeff, Info.Spec.
ESSO RESOURCES CANADA LIMITED - LIBRARY
INFORMATION CENTRE □ Calgary, AB

Flood, Tracy, Libn.
ENERGY & ENVIRONMENTAL ANALYSIS, INC. -
LIBRARY □ Arlington, VA

Florance, Valerie, Docs.
UNIVERSITY OF UTAH - SPENCER S. ECCLES
HEALTH SCIENCES LIBRARY □ Salt Lake City,
UT

Flores, Clarita H., Libn.
AMERICAN CHEMICAL SOCIETY, INC. -
LIBRARY □ Washington, DC

Flores, Jose, Archv.
PUERTO RICO - INSTITUTE OF PUERTO RICAN
CULTURE - ARCHIVO GENERAL DE PUERTO
RICO □ San Juan, PR

Flores, Sr. Maria Carolina, C.D.P., Asst.Archv.
OUR LADY OF THE LAKE UNIVERSITY - OLD
SPANISH MISSIONS HISTORICAL RESEARCH
LIBRARY □ San Antonio, TX

Flores, Norman, Circ.Lib.
YESHIVA UNIVERSITY - ALBERT EINSTEIN
COLLEGE OF MEDICINE - D. SAMUEL
GOTTESMAN LIBRARY □ Bronx, NY

Florin, Carol C., Lib.Dir.
RAMSEY COUNTY LAW LIBRARY □ St. Paul, MN

Florio, Joseph, Ref.Libn.
SHEARMAN & STERLING - LIBRARY □ New York,
NY

Florio, R.A., Exec.Dir.
ART STUDENTS LEAGUE OF NEW YORK -
LIBRARY □ New York, NY

Flory, Dan L., Registrar
CINCINNATI COLLEGE OF MORTUARY SCIENCE
- LIBRARY □ Cincinnati, OH

Flory, Tom, Data Libn.
UNIVERSITY OF WISCONSIN, MADISON - DATA
AND PROGRAM LIBRARY SERVICE □ Madison,
WI

Flournoy, Donald B., Chf., Cartography
U.S. AIR FORCE - AIR UNIVERSITY - LIBRARY □
Maxwell AFB, AL

Flower, Eric S., Dept.Hd.
UNIVERSITY OF MAINE, ORONO - RAYMOND H.
FOGLER LIBRARY - SPECIAL COLLECTIONS
DEPARTMENT □ Orono, ME

Flower, Kenneth, Chf., Ref.Serv.
MASSACHUSETTS STATE LIBRARY □ Boston,
MA

Flowers, Kathryn L., Libn./Info.Spec.
ENVIRODYNE ENGINEERS, INC. - LIBRARY □ St.
Louis, MO

Flowers, Loretta, Pub.Lib.Cons.
STATE LIBRARY OF FLORIDA □ Tallahassee, FL

Floyd, Nancy L., Lib.Info.Asst.
AMERICAN ASSOCIATION OF UNIVERSITY
WOMEN - EDUCATIONAL FOUNDATION
LIBRARY AND ARCHIVES □ Washington, DC

Fluchel, Robert W., Dir.
FONTENELLE FOREST NATURE CENTER -
REFERENCE LIBRARY □ Bellevue, NE

Fludd, Marcella, ILL
ST. ELIZABETHS HOSPITAL - HEALTH
SCIENCES LIBRARY □ Washington, DC

Flukinger, Roy, Cur., Photog.
UNIVERSITY OF TEXAS, AUSTIN - HARRY
RANSOM HUMANITIES RESEARCH CENTER □
Austin, TX

Flumiani, Dr. C.M., Dir.
AMERICAN CLASSICAL COLLEGE - LIBRARY □
Albuquerque, NM

Flumiani, Dr. C.M., Dir.
AMERICAN CLASSICAL COLLEGE - STOCK
MARKET LIBRARY □ Albuquerque, NM

Flynn, Barbara L., Hd., AV Center
CHICAGO PUBLIC LIBRARY CULTURAL CENTER
- AUDIOVISUAL CENTER □ Chicago, IL

Flynn, Elizabeth J., Mgr., Tech.Adm.
OLIN CORPORATION - ECUSTA PAPER AND
FILM GROUP - TECHNICAL LIBRARY† □ Pisgah
Forest, NC

Flynn, John C., Libn.
MOOSE LAKE STATE HOSPITAL - STAFF
LIBRARY □ Moose Lake, MN

Flynn, Karen L., Supv.
3M - 201 TECHNICAL LIBRARY □ St. Paul, MN

Flynn, Kathleen M., Law Libn.
HAMPDEN LAW LIBRARY □ Springfield, MA

Flynn, Lauri R., Asst.Libn.
LEWIS AND CLARK LAW SCHOOL -
NORTHWESTERN SCHOOL OF LAW - PAUL L.
BOLEY LAW LIBRARY □ Portland, OR

Flynn, Lawrence E., Ck. of Courts
WISCONSIN STATE - RACINE COUNTY LAW
LIBRARY □ Racine, WI

Flynn, Patti, Patient Libn.
U.S. VETERANS ADMINISTRATION (CA-Long
Beach) - MEDICAL CENTER LIBRARY □ Long
Beach, CA

Flynn, Phyllis, Asst.Libn.
AMERICAN JEWISH COMMITTEE - BLAUSTEIN
LIBRARY □ New York, NY

Flynn, Richard M., Libn.
FOUNDATION OF THE FEDERAL BAR
ASSOCIATION - FEDERAL BAR FOUNDATION
LIBRARY □ Washington, DC

Flynn, Thomas, Dir.
NEW YORK STATE DEPARTMENT OF HEALTH -
CENTER FOR LABORATORIES AND RESEARCH
LIBRARY □ Albany, NY

Fodor, Elza O., Libn.
PUBLIC UTILITIES COMMISSION OF OHIO -
LIBRARY □ Columbus, OH

Fody, Barbara A., Asst. V.P.
PAINE WEBBER INC. - PAINE WEBBER BLYTH
EASTMAN - LIBRARY □ New York, NY

Foell, John F., Sr.Info.Spec.
CONOCO, INC. - RESEARCH AND
DEVELOPMENT DEPARTMENT - TECHNICAL
INFORMATION SERVICES □ Ponca City, OK

Foerstel, Herbert N., Hd.Libn.
UNIVERSITY OF MARYLAND, COLLEGE PARK -
LIBRARIES - ENGINEERING & PHYSICAL
SCIENCES LIBRARY □ College Park, MD

Fogarty, Catharine M., NJ Rm.Libn.
FAIRLEIGH DICKINSON UNIVERSITY -
MESSLER LIBRARY - NEW JERSEY ROOM □
Rutherford, NJ

Fogel, Connie Jean, Dir.
BELL & HOWELL EDUCATION GROUP - DE VRY
INSTITUTE OF TECHNOLOGY - LEARNING
RESOURCE CENTER □ Kansas City, MO

Fogerty, James E., Dp. State Archv.
MINNESOTA HISTORICAL SOCIETY - DIVISION
OF ARCHIVES AND MANUSCRIPTS □ St. Paul,
MN

Fogg, Mrs. Donald, Curator
CHELMSFORD HISTORICAL SOCIETY -
BARRETT-BYAM HOMESTEAD LIBRARY □
Chelmsford, MA

Fogg, Elizabeth C., Dir.
SALEM FREE PUBLIC LIBRARY - SPECIAL
COLLECTIONS □ Salem, NJ

Fogg, Grace, Ref. & Per.Libn.
ASSOCIATION FOR RESEARCH AND
ENLIGHTENMENT - EDGAR CAYCE
FOUNDATION - LIBRARY □ Virginia Beach, VA

Fogo, Eloise, Rd.Adv.
DISTRICT OF COLUMBIA PUBLIC LIBRARY -
SOCIOLOGY, GOVERNMENT & EDUCATION
DIVISION □ Washington, DC

Fohl, Claire M., Asst.Libn.
NATIONAL WATER WELL ASSOCIATION -
NATIONAL GROUND WATER INFORMATION
CENTER □ Worthington, OH

Folen, Doris, Hd., Doc.Sect.
U.S. NAVY - NAVAL RESEARCH LABORATORY -
RUTH H. HOOKER TECHNICAL LIBRARY □
Washington, DC

Foley, Bob, Hd.Libn.
BANFF CENTRE FOR CONTINUING EDUCATION
- LIBRARY □ Banff, AB

Foley, Kathy, Chf.Libn.
HOUSTON POST - LIBRARY/INFORMATION
CENTER □ Houston, TX

Foley, Mary Anne, Tech.Libn.
MOTOROLA, INC. - PORTABLE PRODUCTS
DIVISION - TECHNICAL LIBRARY □ Fort
Lauderdale, FL

Foley, Nancy, Coord, Adult Serv.
SEATTLE PUBLIC LIBRARY - DOUGLASS-TRUTH
BRANCH LIBRARY □ Seattle, WA

Foley, Patricia H., Bus.Libn.
UNIVERSITY OF IOWA - BUSINESS LIBRARY □
Iowa City, IA

Foley, Robert, ILL
FITCHBURG STATE COLLEGE - LIBRARY □
Fitchburg, MA

Foley, Sheila, Libn.
BRITISH COLUMBIA - COUNCIL OF FOREST
INDUSTRIES OF BRITISH COLUMBIA - LIBRARY
□ Vancouver, BC

Folk, Charlotte C., Libn.
ENVIRONMENTAL PROTECTION AGENCY -
ENVIRONMENTAL RESEARCH LABORATORY,
ATHENS - LIBRARY □ Athens, GA

Folke, Carolyn, Search Anl./Libn.
WISCONSIN STATE DEPARTMENT OF PUBLIC
INSTRUCTION - WISCONSIN DISSEMINATION
PROGRAM (WDP) □ Madison, WI

Folkes, Tom, Health Sci.Libn.
MENTAL HEALTH INSTITUTE - HEALTH
SCIENCE LIBRARY □ Cherokee, IA

Folkestad, Patricia, Ser.Libn.
UNIVERSITY OF NORTH DAKOTA - OLAF H.
THORMODSGARD LAW LIBRARY □ Grand Forks,
ND

Folland, Linda, Archv.
HERMAN MILLER, INC. - RESOURCE CENTER □
Zeeland, MI

Folsom, Mrs. Robert, Libn.
LAKEWOOD HISTORICAL SOCIETY - LIBRARY □
Lakewood, OH

Foltz, Faye, Hd., Ser.Sect.
WAKE FOREST UNIVERSITY - BOWMAN GRAY
SCHOOL OF MEDICINE - COY C. CARPENTER
LIBRARY □ Winston-Salem, NC

Foltz, Susan, Libn.
GOOD SAMARITAN HOSPITAL - KROHN
MEMORIAL LIBRARY □ Lebanon, PA

Fones-Wolf, Kenneth, Asst.Cur.
TEMPLE UNIVERSITY - CENTRAL LIBRARY
SYSTEM - URBAN ARCHIVES □ Philadelphia, PA

Fonfa, Lynn, Asst.Archv.
MAGNES (Judah L.) MEMORIAL MUSEUM -
WESTERN JEWISH HISTORY CENTER □
Berkeley, CA

Fong, Florence, Ref.Libn.
LOS ANGELES COUNTY/UNIVERSITY OF
SOUTHERN CALIFORNIA MEDICAL CENTER -
MEDICAL LIBRARIES □ Los Angeles, CA

Fong, Lawrence, Registrar
UNIVERSITY OF ARIZONA - CENTER FOR
CREATIVE PHOTOGRAPHY □ Tucson, AZ

Fonger, Lesley, Asst.Libn.
MIAMI NEWS - LIBRARY □ Miami, FL

Font, Walter, Cur.
ALLEN COUNTY-FORT WAYNE HISTORICAL
SOCIETY - LIBRARY AND MANUSCRIPT
COLLECTIONS □ Fort Wayne, IN

Fontaine, Linda, Libn.
WESTRECO, INC. - TECHNICAL LIBRARY □ New
Milford, CT

Fontaine, Marcel, Conservateur-Adjoint
QUEBEC PROVINCE - BIBLIOTHEQUE
NATIONALE DU QUEBEC □ Montreal, PQ

Fontenette, E.J., Libn.
UNIVERSITY OF ARKANSAS, PINE BLUFF -
JOHN BROWN WATSON MEMORIAL LIBRARY† □
Pine Bluff, AR

Fontenot, LaRue, Libn.
CH2M HILL, INC. - ROCKY MOUNTAIN
REGIONAL OFFICE - LIBRARY □ Denver, CO

Fontes, Geraldine I., Staff Serv.Anl.
CALIFORNIA STATE HEALTH AND WELFARE
AGENCY DATA CENTER - TECHNICAL LIBRARY
UNIT □ Sacramento, CA

Foohey, Mary Ann, Group Supv.
VITRO CORPORATION - LIBRARY □ Silver
Spring, MD

Foos, Donald D., Dir.
UNIVERSITY OF ARKANSAS AT LITTLE ROCK -
CENTER FOR LIBRARY & INFORMATION
SCIENCE EDUCATION & RES. (CLISER) □ Little
Rock, AR

Foote, J. Steven, Ser.Cat.
EMORY UNIVERSITY - SCHOOL OF MEDICINE -
A.W. CALHOUN MEDICAL LIBRARY □ Atlanta,
GA

Footman, Annie B., Libn.
SIBLEY MEMORIAL HOSPITAL - MEDICAL
LIBRARY □ Washington, DC

Forbes, Bonnie, Musm.Cur.
WILSON COUNTY HISTORICAL SOCIETY -
MUSEUM LIBRARY □ Fredonia, KS

Forbes, Charles F., Hd.
UNIVERSITY OF BRITISH COLUMBIA -
HUMANITIES AND SOCIAL SCIENCES DIVISION
□ Vancouver, BC

Forbes, Evelyn H., Libn.
NASHVILLE METROPOLITAN GENERAL
HOSPITAL - HEALTH SCIENCE LIBRARY □
Nashville, TN

Forbes, Dr. John M., Dir. of Libs.
BAKER UNIVERSITY - QUAYLE RARE BIBLE
COLLECTION □ Baldwin City, KS

Forbes, Nancy, Ref.Libn.
UNIVERSITY OF BRITISH COLUMBIA -
BIOMEDICAL BRANCH LIBRARY □ Vancouver,
BC

Forbes, Olive, Hd.Libn.
UNIVERSITY OF TEXAS, AUSTIN - WASSERMAN
PUBLIC AFFAIRS LIBRARY □ Austin, TX

Forbes, Lt.Col. P.A., Hd.Sup.Br.
U.S. MARINE CORPS - HISTORICAL CENTER
LIBRARY† □ Washington, DC

Forbes, Susan, West.Hist.Cat.
KANSAS STATE HISTORICAL SOCIETY -
LIBRARY □ Topeka, KS

Forbes, Suzanne, Libn.
OMAHA PUBLIC POWER DISTRICT -
MANAGEMENT SYSTEMS SERVICES - LIBRARY
□ Omaha, NE

Forbes, Terry, Lib.Techn.
ALBERTA - ENVIRONMENT COUNCIL -
INFORMATION CENTRE □ Edmonton, AB

Forbes, Zona Gale, Archv./Libn.
HISTORICAL SOCIETY OF LONG BEACH -
ARCHIVES □ Long Beach, CA

Forcht, Wanda, Libn.
WASHINGTON STATE SCHOOL FOR THE DEAF -
LEARNING RESOURCE CENTER □ Vancouver,
WA

Forcier, Ben R., Jr., Libn.
WALLA WALLA COUNTY LAW LIBRARY □ Walla
Walla, WA

Forcier, Lise, Chf., Tech.Serv.
CENTRE HOSPITALIER STE. JEANNE D'ARC -
BIBLIOTHEQUE MEDICALE □ Montreal, PQ

Ford, Beverly, Archv./Libn.
ST. JOSEPH HOSPITAL - LIBRARY □ Chicago, IL

Ford, Carolyn, Libn.
TUSKEGEE INSTITUTE - VETERINARY
MEDICINE LIBRARY† □ Tuskegee Institute, AL

Ford, Cathryn, Libn.
IOWA STATE COMMISSION FOR THE BLIND -
LIBRARY FOR THE BLIND & PHYSICALLY
HANDICAPPED □ Des Moines, IA

Ford, Constance, Chf.Libn.
UNION ELECTRIC COMPANY - LIBRARY □ St. Louis, MO

Ford, Heidi, Asst.Libn., Tech.Serv.
LAKE FOREST COLLEGE - THOMAS OSCAR FREEMAN MEMORIAL LIBRARY □ Lake Forest, IL

Ford, James, Libn.
NARCOTICS EDUCATION, INC. - SCHARFFENBERG MEMORIAL LIBRARY □ Washington, DC

Ford, Jennifer, Libn.
ELGIN MENTAL HEALTH CENTER - ANTON BOISEN PROFESSIONAL LIBRARY □ Elgin, IL

Ford, Jim, Rec.Mgr.
SEVENTH-DAY ADVENTISTS - GENERAL CONFERENCE - OFFICE OF ARCHIVES AND STATISTICS □ Washington, DC

Ford, Joann, Cat.
ANTIOCH UNIVERSITY - RESOURCE CENTER □ Philadelphia, PA

Ford, Joseph M., Musm.Dir.
OWENSBORO AREA MUSEUM - LIBRARY □ Owensboro, KY

Ford, Karen, Lib.Asst., Engr.Lib.
ESSO RESOURCES CANADA LIMITED - LIBRARY INFORMATION CENTRE □ Calgary, AB

Ford, Prof. Laura, Supv.
YORK UNIVERSITY - FACULTY OF EDUCATION - EDUCATION CENTRE □ Downsview, ON

Ford, Mrs. M., Supv. of Pub.Serv.
ONTARIO BIBLE COLLEGE/ONTARIO THEOLOGICAL SEMINARY - J. WILLIAM HORSEY LIBRARY □ Willowdale, ON

Ford, Marjorie M., Libn.
MONTGOMERY (James M.), CONSULTING ENGINEERS - LIBRARY □ Pasadena, CA

Ford, Oscar, Asst. State Libn./Plan.
NEVADA STATE LIBRARY □ Carson City, NV

Ford, Patricia D., Acq.Libn.
ALABAMA A & M UNIVERSITY - J. F. DRAKE MEMORIAL LEARNING RESOURCES CENTER □ Normal, AL

Ford, Peggy A., Musm.Coord.
GREELEY MUNICIPAL MUSEUM - LIBRARY □ Greeley, CO

Ford, Peter, Lib.Dir.
ROCHESTER TIMES-UNION AND ROCHESTER DEMOCRAT & CHRONICLE - LIBRARY □ Rochester, NY

Ford, Robert S., Asst.Libn.
CALIFORNIA RAILWAY MUSEUM - LIBRARY □ Suisun City, CA

Ford, Sabrina, Cat.
OLD SLAVE MART MUSEUM - LIBRARY □ Sullivan's Island, SC

Ford, Vicki, Ch.Libn.
GRAND RAPIDS PUBLIC LIBRARY - MAY G. QUIGLEY COLLECTION □ Grand Rapids, MI

Ford, Virginia, Lit.Res.Anl.
AEROSPACE CORPORATION - CHARLES C. LAURITSEN LIBRARY □ Los Angeles, CA

Forde, Jean, Libn. 2
METROPOLITAN TORONTO LIBRARY - BOOK INFORMATION AND INTERLOAN DEPARTMENT □ Toronto, ON

Forde, Keston, Lib.Supv.
MC GILL UNIVERSITY - METEOROLOGY LIBRARY □ Montreal, PQ

Fordham, Joan A., Adm.
INTERNATIONAL CRANE FOUNDATION - LIBRARY □ Baraboo, WI

Foreman, Anne P., Chf.Libn.
U.S. ARMY AVIATION TRAINING LIBRARY □ Ft. Rucker, AL

Foreman, Dorothy, Asst. Law Libn.
U.S. VETERANS ADMINISTRATION (DC-Washington) - GENERAL COUNSEL'S LAW LIBRARY (026H) □ Washington, DC

Foreman, Iona, Textbook Cons.
GEORGIA STATE DEPARTMENT OF EDUCATION - LIBRARY FOR THE BLIND & PHYSICALLY HANDICAPPED □ Atlanta, GA

Foreman, Laura, Pres.
COMPOSERS AND CHOREOGRAPHERS THEATRE, INC. - MASTER TAPE LIBRARY □ New York, NY

Foreman, Robyn, Mgr., Rd.Serv.
SEATTLE PUBLIC LIBRARY - WASHINGTON LIBRARY FOR THE BLIND AND PHYSICALLY HANDICAPPED □ Seattle, WA

Forer, Daniel, Coord.
SAN FRANCISCO LIGHTHOUSE CENTER FOR THE BLIND - LIBRARY □ San Francisco, CA

Foresman, Joyce, Libn.
OGLE PETROLEUM INC. - LIBRARY □ Santa Barbara, CA

Forestell, Peter R., Libn.
PALMER, O'CONNELL, LEGER, TURNBULL & TURNBULL - LAW LIBRARY† □ Saint John, NB

Forgach, L. Violet, Supv., Bus.Info.
SDS BIOTECH CORPORATION - CORPORATE LIBRARY □ Painesville, OH

Forgang, David, Cur.
U.S. NATL. PARK SERVICE - YOSEMITE NATL. PARK - RESEARCH LIBRARY □ Yosemite National Park, CA

Forget, Gerald, AV Libn.
BIBLIOTHEQUE DE LA VILLE DE MONTREAL - SONOTHEQUE □ Montreal, PQ

Forget, Louis, Dir., Lib.Sys.Ctr.
NATIONAL LIBRARY OF CANADA/BIBLIOTHEQUE NATIONALE DU CANADA □ Ottawa, ON

Forish, Linda E., Adm.Sec.
WESTMORELAND COUNTY HISTORICAL SOCIETY - CALVIN E. POLLINS MEMORIAL LIBRARY □ Greensburg, PA

Forman, Mrs. Elmer, Ref.Libn.
CINCINNATI HISTORICAL SOCIETY - LIBRARY □ Cincinnati, OH

Forman, George, Pres.
PIAGET (Jean) SOCIETY - LIBRARY □ Newark, DE

Forman, Dr. John W., Mgr.
IBM CORPORATION - SYSTEMS TECHNOLOGY DIVISION - LIBRARY □ Endicott, NY

Fornof, Dorothy, Supv., Lib.Serv.
LIBERTY MUTUAL INSURANCE COMPANY - BUSINESS REFERENCE LIBRARY □ Pittsburgh, PA

Forrest, Fred H., Libn.
WEBB INSTITUTE OF NAVAL ARCHITECTURE - LIVINGSTON LIBRARY □ Glen Cove, NY

Forrest, Joseph, Assoc.Dir.
HOWARD UNIVERSITY - HEALTH SCIENCES LIBRARY □ Washington, DC

Forsee, Joe B., Dir.
GEORGIA STATE DEPARTMENT OF EDUCATION - DIVISION OF PUBLIC LIBRARY SERVICES □ Atlanta, GA

Forsman, Avis B., Libn.
KUTAK ROCK & HUIE - LAW LIBRARY □ Omaha, NE

Forsman, Rick B., Assoc.Dir./Tech.Serv
UNIVERSITY OF ALABAMA IN BIRMINGHAM - LISTER HILL LIBRARY OF THE HEALTH SCIENCES □ Birmingham, AL

Forssblad, Marianne, Dir./Hd.Libn.
NORDIC HERITAGE MUSEUM - WALTER JOHNSON LIBRARY □ Seattle, WA

Forsstrom, Alice E., Hd. of Children's Serv.
WARWICK PUBLIC LIBRARY - CENTRAL CHILDREN'S LIBRARY □ Warwick, RI

Forstall, Louise D., Hd.Libn.
TIME-LIFE BOOKS INC. - REFERENCE LIBRARY □ Alexandria, VA

Forstall, Philip L., Libn.
RAND MC NALLY AND COMPANY - LIBRARY □ Skokie, IL

Forster, Sr. Charles Marie, Archv.
DIOCESE OF AMARILLO - DIOCESAN ARCHIVES □ Amarillo, TX

Forsyth, Brian, Sr.Arch.Adv.
ONTARIO - MINISTRY OF CITIZENSHIP AND CULTURE - PLANNING AND TECHNICAL SERVICES □ Toronto, ON

Fortado, Robert J., Doc.Libn.
SOUTHERN ILLINOIS UNIVERSITY, EDWARDSVILLE - DOCUMENTS COLLECTION □ Edwardsville, IL

Fortenberry, Bobbie, Libn.
AMARILLO GLOBE-NEWS LIBRARY □ Amarillo, TX

Fortier, Bernard, Cat.
FRANCISCAN FRIARS OF THE ATONEMENT - ATONEMENT SEMINARY LIBRARY □ Washington, DC

Fortier, John W., Archv.
ONTARIO - MINISTRY OF CITIZENSHIP AND CULTURE - MAP LIBRARY □ Toronto, ON

Fortier, Real, Hd., Info. to Citizens
QUEBEC PROV. - MIN. DE L'ENERGIE ET DES RESSOURCES - SERVICE DE DOCUMENTATION ET DE RENSEIGNEMENTS □ Quebec, PQ

Fortin, Jean-Marc, Lib.Techn./Asst.
SEMINAIRE DE CHICOUTIMI - BIBLIOTHEQUE □ Chicoutimi, PQ

Fortin, Patricia, Libn.
TORONTO INSTITUTE OF MEDICAL TECHNOLOGY - LIBRARY □ Toronto, ON

Fortin, Mrs. V., Tech.Serv.Libn.
MC GILL UNIVERSITY - MACDONALD COLLEGE - LIBRARY □ Ste. Anne de Bellevue, PQ

Fortin, V., Cat. & Proc.Libn.
MC GILL UNIVERSITY - MEDICAL LIBRARY □ Montreal, PQ

Fortman, Pamela P., Lib.Dir.
TODAY NEWSPAPER - LIBRARY† □ Cocoa, FL

Fortner, Donald D.
U.S. VETERANS ADMINISTRATION (TX-Big Spring) - HOSPITAL LIBRARY □ Big Spring, TX

Fortner, Roger L., Dir.
U.S. DEPT. OF COMMERCE - INTERNATIONAL TRADE ADMINISTRATION - CHARLESTON DISTRICT OFFICE LIBRARY □ Charleston, WV

Fortney, Lynn M., Assoc.Dir./Pub.Serv.
UNIVERSITY OF ALABAMA IN BIRMINGHAM - LISTER HILL LIBRARY OF THE HEALTH SCIENCES □ Birmingham, AL

Fortney, Mary, Map Libn.
NORTHWESTERN UNIVERSITY - MAP COLLECTION □ Evanston, IL

Fortney, V.J., Hd., Info.Serv.Dept.
AT & T BELL LABORATORIES - LIBRARIES AND INFORMATION SYSTEMS CENTER □ Murray Hill, NJ

Fortune, Mark, Cat.Techn.
ROYAL CANADIAN MOUNTED POLICE - LAW ENFORCEMENT REFERENCE CENTRE □ Ottawa, ON

Fortvaler, Diana
CONSERVATION AND RENEWABLE ENERGY INQUIRY AND REFERRAL SERVICE □ Philadelphia, PA

Forward, Kay, Mgr.
UNIVERSITY OF TEXAS, AUSTIN - BUREAU OF ECONOMIC GEOLOGY READING ROOM/DATA CENTER □ Austin, TX

Forys, John W., Libn.
UNIVERSITY OF IOWA - ENGINEERING LIBRARY □ Iowa City, IA

Fosher, Shirley, Tech.Serv.Libn.
DRAKE UNIVERSITY - LAW LIBRARY □ Des Moines, IA

Fossum, Correne, Asst.Libn.
MINOT DAILY NEWS - LIBRARY □ Minot, ND

Fossum, Dennis, Monograph Libn.
UNIVERSITY OF NORTH DAKOTA - OLAF H. THORMODSGARD LAW LIBRARY □ Grand Forks, ND

Fostel, Donald, Prin.Libn.
NEWARK PUBLIC LIBRARY - SOCIAL SCIENCE DIVISION □ Newark, NJ

Foster, B.R., Assyriologist
YALE UNIVERSITY - BABYLONIAN COLLECTION
□ New Haven, CT

Foster, Christine, Libn./Search Anl.
WISHARD (William N.) MEMORIAL HOSPITAL -
PROFESSIONAL LIBRARY/MEDIA SERVICES† □
Indianapolis, IN

Foster, Dale, Archv./Rec.Mgt.
GEORGE MASON UNIVERSITY - FENWICK
LIBRARY - SPECIAL COLLECTIONS □ Fairfax, VA

Foster, Eileen, Lib.Mgr.
CANADA - TELESAT CANADA - COMPANY
LIBRARY □ Ottawa, ON

Foster, Eloise C., Dir.
AMERICAN HOSPITAL ASSOCIATION - ASA S.
BACON MEMORIAL LIBRARY □ Chicago, IL

Foster, Eugenia, Cur.
UNIVERSITY OF CINCINNATI - JOHN MILLER
BURNAM CLASSICAL LIBRARY □ Cincinnati, OH

Foster, George A., Jr., Supv., Product Lit.
MILES LABORATORIES, INC. - LIBRARY
RESOURCES AND SERVICES □ Elkhart, IN

Foster, Helen M., Lib.Mgr.
GEE & JENSON ENGINEERS, ARCHITECTS,
PLANNERS, INC. - LIBRARY □ West Palm Beach,
FL

Foster, Jacqulyn G., Supv., Circ.Serv.
ALABAMA A & M UNIVERSITY - J. F. DRAKE
MEMORIAL LEARNING RESOURCES CENTER □
Normal, AL

Foster, Jane, Dir.
LENNOX AND ADDINGTON COUNTY MUSEUM -
LIBRARY & ARCHIVES □ Napanee, ON

Foster, Jane N., Lib.Adm.
U.S. NASA - WALLOPS FLIGHT CENTER -
TECHNICAL LIBRARY □ Wallops Island, VA

Foster, Janice, Libn.
ST. JOSEPH HOSPITAL - HEALTH SCIENCE
LIBRARY □ Kansas City, MO

Foster, Jim, Dir., LRC
CENTRAL CAROLINA TECHNICAL COLLEGE -
LEARNING RESOURCE CENTER □ Sanford, NC

Foster, Julia, Ref. & Cat.Libn.
METHODIST THEOLOGICAL SCHOOL IN OHIO -
JOHN W. DICKHAUT LIBRARY □ Delaware, OH

Foster, Leslie A., Res.Assoc.
DALHOUSIE UNIVERSITY - LAW LIBRARY □
Halifax, NS

Foster, Lynn, Dir./Hd.Libn.
OHIO NORTHERN UNIVERSITY - COLLEGE OF
LAW - JAY P. TAGGART MEMORIAL LAW
LIBRARY □ Ada, OH

Foster, Olive S., State Hist.
ILLINOIS STATE HISTORICAL LIBRARY □
Springfield, IL

Foster, Paul H., Cons.
OKLAHOMA GEOLOGICAL SURVEY - OKLAHOMA
GEOPHYSICAL OBSERVATORY LIBRARY □
Leonard, OK

Foster, Saba L., Chf.Libn.
NATIONAL LIFE INSURANCE COMPANY -
LIBRARY □ Montpelier, VT

Foster, Sandra, Asst.Libn.
ARTHUR ANDERSEN & CO. - LIBRARY □ San
Francisco, CA

Foster, Selma V., OCLC Coord.
SUNY - COLLEGE AT POTSDAM - FREDERICK W.
CRUMB MEMORIAL LIBRARY □ Potsdam, NY

Foster, Shirley, Libn.
TORONTO STOCK EXCHANGE - LIBRARY □
Toronto, ON

Foster, Theodore, Map Libn.
OHIO UNIVERSITY - MAP COLLECTION □
Athens, OH

Fotias, Anna, Leg.Spec.
U.S. NUCLEAR REGULATORY COMMISSION -
LAW LIBRARY □ Washington, DC

Foubert, Marietta S., Preparator
UNIVERSITY OF WASHINGTON - ART SLIDE
COLLECTION □ Seattle, WA

Foudray, Rita, Libn.
DALLAS PUBLIC LIBRARY - HUMANITIES
DIVISION □ Dallas, TX

Fourchalk, Joy, Libn.
BRITISH COLUMBIA - MINISTRY OF HEALTH -
MENTAL HEALTH SERVICES LIBRARY □
Burnaby, BC

Fourney, Norah, Hd.Libn.
ST. LAWRENCE COLLEGE SAINT-LAURENT -
LEARNING RESOURCE CENTRE† □ Cornwall, ON

Fournier, Jacques, SDI
QUEBEC PROV. - MIN. DE L'ENERGIE ET DES
RESSOURCES - SERVICE DE DOCUMENTATION
ET DE RENSEIGNEMENTS □ Quebec, PQ

Fournier, Marc, Depository Prog. & Cat.
QUEBEC PROVINCE - MINISTERE DES
COMMUNICATIONS - BIBLIOTHEQUE
ADMINISTRATIVE □ Quebec, PQ

Fouser, Jane G., Res.Supv.
CONTINENTAL ILLINOIS NATIONAL BANK AND
TRUST COMPANY OF CHICAGO -
INFORMATION SERVICES DIVISION □ Chicago,
IL

Foust, Judith M., Dir., Lib.Dev.Div.
PENNSYLVANIA STATE LIBRARY □ Harrisburg,
PA

Foutana, Cecilia, Libn.
MAGNAVOX GOVERNMENT & INDUSTRIAL
ELECTRONICS COMPANY - ADVANCED
PRODUCTS DIVISION - LIBRARY □ Torrance, CA

Foutty, Kitty, Ref.Libn.
U.S. NASA - AMES RESEARCH CENTER -
LIBRARY □ Mountain View, CA

Fow, Mark I., Act.Dir.
U.S. FOOD & DRUG ADMINISTRATION - NATL.
CLEARINGHOUSE FOR POISON CONTROL
CENTERS □ Rockville, MD

Fowler, Albert W., Assoc.Dir.
SWARTHMORE COLLEGE - FRIENDS
HISTORICAL LIBRARY □ Swarthmore, PA

Fowler, Ann, Coord.
NORTH CAROLINA STATE DEPARTMENT OF
PUBLIC INSTRUCTION - EDUCATION
INFORMATION CENTER □ Raleigh, NC

Fowler, Bessie, Cat.
HOWARD UNIVERSITY - MOORLAND-SPINGARN
RESEARCH CENTER - LIBRARY DIVISION □
Washington, DC

Fowler, Cary, Prog.Dir.
NATIONAL SHARECROPPERS FUND/RURAL
ADVANCEMENT FUND - F.P. GRAHAM
RESOURCE CENTER □ Pittsboro, NC

Fowler, Cristina, Ref.Libn.
UNIVERSITY OF CALIFORNIA, BERKELEY -
PUBLIC HEALTH LIBRARY □ Berkeley, CA

Fowler, David J., Res.Assoc.
DAVID LIBRARY OF THE AMERICAN
REVOLUTION □ Washington Crossing, PA

Fowler, M. Michelle, Slide Libn.
CLEVELAND INSTITUTE OF ART - JESSICA R.
GUND MEMORIAL LIBRARY □ Cleveland, OH

Fox, Betty L., Info. Programs Mgr.
U.S. DEFENSE NUCLEAR AGENCY - TECHNICAL
LIBRARY □ Washington, DC

Fox, Carolyn, Ref.Libn.
UNIVERSITY OF VERMONT - DIVISION OF
HEALTH SCIENCES - CHARLES A. DANA
MEDICAL LIBRARY □ Burlington, VT

Fox, Charles H., Chf., Spec.Serv.Sect.
NORTH CAROLINA STATE DEPARTMENT OF
CULTURAL RESOURCES - LIBRARY FOR THE
BLIND AND PHYSICALLY HANDICAPPED □
Raleigh, NC

Fox, Dexter, Chf./Tech.Serv.Sect.
U.S. ARMY - PENTAGON LIBRARY □ Washington,
DC

Fox, Elizabeth, Cat.Libn.
QUEEN'S UNIVERSITY AT KINGSTON - LAW
LIBRARY □ Kingston, ON

Fox, Gertrude L., Libn.
SALEM STATE COLLEGE - PROFESSIONAL
STUDIES RESOURCES CENTER □ Salem, MA

Fox, Howard, Libn.
SEATTLE PUBLIC LIBRARY - GOVERNMENTAL
RESEARCH ASSISTANCE LIBRARY† □ Seattle,
WA

Fox, James, Soc.Stud.Libn.
SOUTHERN ILLINOIS UNIVERSITY,
CARBONDALE - SOCIAL STUDIES DIVISION
LIBRARY □ Carbondale, IL

Fox, James R., Law Libn.
DICKINSON SCHOOL OF LAW - SHEELY-LEE
LAW LIBRARY □ Carlisle, PA

Fox, Jane G., Libn.
FOX RESEARCH AND LIBRARY SERVICE □
Swarthmore, PA

Fox, Janice L., Res.-in-Residence
MISSOURI HISTORICAL SOCIETY - RESEARCH
LIBRARY □ St. Louis, MO

Fox, Janis M., Libn.
PONTIAC OSTEOPATHIC HOSPITAL - MEDICAL
LIBRARY □ Pontiac, MI

Fox, Jennifer B., Libn.
BARTHOLOMEW (Harland) AND ASSOCIATES,
INC. - LIBRARY □ Memphis, TN

Fox, Karin, Microforms Libn.
STATE HISTORICAL SOCIETY OF WISCONSIN -
LIBRARY □ Madison, WI

Fox, Karl M., Info.Cons.
FOX RESEARCH AND LIBRARY SERVICE □
Swarthmore, PA

Fox, Mabert E., Exec.Sec.
WASHINGTON COUNTY MUSEUM OF FINE ARTS
- LIBRARY □ Hagerstown, MD

Fox, Mark, Cat.Libn.
NEVADA STATE LIBRARY □ Carson City, NV

Fox, Peggy, Libn.
HILL JUNIOR COLLEGE - CONFEDERATE
RESEARCH CENTER AND GUN MUSEUM □
Hillsboro, TX

Fox, Priscilla, Reserve Rd.Rm.Libn.
CENTRAL CONNECTICUT STATE UNIVERSITY -
ELIHU BURRITT LIBRARY □ New Britain, CT

Fox, Sandra, Proj.Mgr.
WOMEN'S MOVEMENT ARCHIVES □ Toronto,
ON

Fox, Susan R.
AMERICAN INTERNATIONAL COLLEGE - ORAL
HISTORY CENTER □ Springfield, MA

Fox, Wanda J., Supv.
ROCKWELL INTERNATIONAL - ELECTRONICS
OPERATIONS - DALLAS INFORMATION CENTER
□ Dallas, TX

Foxman, Carole, Med.Libn.
BROOKLINE HOSPITAL - MEDICAL LIBRARY □
Brookline, MA

Foxman, Diane, Hd., AV Serv.
UNIVERSITY OF NORTH CAROLINA, CHAPEL
HILL - HEALTH SCIENCES LIBRARY □ Chapel
Hill, NC

Foy, Mary W., Asst. Law Libn.
JEFFERSON COUNTY LAW LIBRARY □
Birmingham, AL

Fracasso, John, Automated Sys. & Serv.
UNIVERSITY OF WESTERN ONTARIO - SCHOOL
OF LIBRARY & INFORMATION SCIENCE -
LIBRARY □ London, ON

Fracolli, Dena, Ref.Libn.
MONTANA COLLEGE OF MINERAL SCIENCE AND
TECHNOLOGY - LIBRARY □ Butte, MT

Fradin, Sharyn, Asst.Libn.
UNIVERSITY OF HEALTH SCIENCES/CHICAGO
MEDICAL SCHOOL - LIBRARY □ North Chicago,
IL

Fradlein, Louise G.
TRENTON STATE COLLEGE - ROSCOE L. WEST
LIBRARY - SPECIAL COLLECTIONS □ Trenton,
NJ

Fraenkel, Howard A., Supv., Info. & Comp.Serv.
ALLIED CORPORATION - ALLIED CHEMICAL -
SYRACUSE RESEARCH LABORATORY - LIBRARY
□ Solvay, NY

Fragale, John, Adm.Libn.
COMMODITY FUTURES TRADING COMMISSION
- LIBRARY □ Washington, DC

Frahm, Catharine C., Dir.
WASHINGTON COUNTY HISTORICAL
ASSOCIATION - MUSEUM LIBRARY □ Fort
Calhoun, NE

Fraitag, Shelly, Info.Spec.
INTERPUBLIC GROUP OF COMPANIES -
CENTER FOR ADVERTISING SERVICES □ New
York, NY

Frakes, Laura, Libn.
IMODCO - BUSINESS LIBRARY □ Los Angeles,
CA

Fraley, Ruth A., Hd.Libn.
SUNY AT ALBANY - GRADUATE LIBRARY FOR
PUBLIC AFFAIRS AND POLICY □ Albany, NY

Fralick, D., Cat.Serv.
ALBERTA - DEPARTMENT OF THE
ENVIRONMENT - LIBRARY □ Edmonton, AB

France, Jeannette, Asst.Libn.
DENVER CONSERVATIVE BAPTIST SEMINARY -
CAREY S. THOMAS LIBRARY □ Denver, CO

Francis, Carol A., Libn.
BRISTOL LAW LIBRARY □ Taunton, MA

Francis, Mrs. F., Ref.Libn.
UNIVERSITY OF GUELPH - HUMANITIES AND
SOCIAL SCIENCES DIVISION - MAP
COLLECTION† □ Guelph, ON

Francis, Frank, Gen.Mgr.
CRAVEN FOUNDATION - AUTOMOTIVE
REFERENCE LIBRARY† □ Toronto, ON

Francis, Gloria, Chf.
DETROIT PUBLIC LIBRARY - NATIONAL
AUTOMOTIVE HISTORY COLLECTION □ Detroit,
MI

Francis, Mary
OAK RIDGE NATIONAL LABORATORY -
INFORMATION DIVISION - ENVIRONMENTAL
MUTAGEN INFORMATION CENTER □ Oak Ridge,
TN

Francis, Nancy E., Libn.
KITCHENER-WATERLOO ART GALLERY -
ELEANOR CALVERT MEMORIAL LIBRARY □
Kitchener, ON

Franck, Jane P., Dir.
TEACHERS COLLEGE - MILBANK MEMORIAL
LIBRARY □ New York, NY

Frandsen, Rex, Archv.
BRIGHAM YOUNG UNIVERSITY, HAWAII
CAMPUS - JOSEPH F. SMITH LIBRARY AND
MEDIA CENTER - SPECIAL COLLECTION □ Laie,
HI

Frank, Agnes T., Dir.
ST. VINCENT'S HOSPITAL AND MEDICAL
CENTER - MEDICAL LIBRARY □ New York, NY

Frank, Anita, Libn.
ROYAL TRUST CORPORATION OF CANADA -
INVESTMENT RESEARCH LIBRARY □ Toronto,
ON

Frank, Annette, Asst.Libn.
CABRINI MEDICAL CENTER - DR. MASSIMO
BAZZINI MEMORIAL LIBRARY □ New York, NY

Frank, Bernice C., Law Libn.
BURROUGHS CORPORATION - LAW LIBRARY □
Detroit, MI

Frank, Conie J., Libn.
ST. JOSEPH COUNTY LAW LIBRARY □ South
Bend, IN

Frank, Dennis, Ref.Libn.
UNIVERSITY OF MAINE, PRESQUE ISLE -
LIBRARY AND LEARNING RESOURCES CENTER -
SPECIAL COLLECTIONS □ Presque Isle, ME

Frank, Marion, Libn.-in-Charge
INDUSTRIAL ACCIDENT PREVENTION
ASSOCIATION - RESOURCE LIBRARY &
INFORMATION SERVICE □ Toronto, ON

Frank, Maureen Sherr, Lib.Dir.
ATLANTIC CITY FREE PUBLIC LIBRARY -
SPECIAL COLLECTIONS □ Atlantic City, NJ

Frank, Penny, Info.Spec.
CRAVATH, SWAINE, & MOORE - LAW LIBRARY
□ New York, NY

Frank, Robyn, Dir.
U.S.D.A. - NATIONAL AGRICULTURAL LIBRARY
- FOOD AND NUTRITION INFORMATION
CENTER □ Beltsville, MD

Frank, Stuart M., Dir.
KENDALL WHALING MUSEUM - LIBRARY □
Sharon, MA

Franke, Gail, ILL & Ref.Libn.
ROSWELL PARK MEMORIAL INSTITUTE -
LIBRARY AND INFORMATION MANAGEMENT
SERVICES □ Buffalo, NY

Frankel, Jessica, Res.
BOOZ, ALLEN & HAMILTON, INC. - RESEARCH
SERVICE □ New York, NY

Frankel, Norma, Search Anl.
LONG ISLAND JEWISH-HILLSIDE MEDICAL
CENTER - HEALTH SCIENCES LIBRARY □ New
Hyde Park, NY

Frankel, Vivian, Med.Libn.
LONG ISLAND JEWISH-HILLSIDE MEDICAL
CENTER - QUEENS HOSPITAL CENTER -
HEALTH SCIENCE LIBRARY □ Jamaica, NY

Frankenberg, Celestine G., Dir. of Lib.Serv.
YOUNG AND RUBICAM INTERNATIONAL -
LIBRARY □ New York, NY

Frankhouse, Dorothy M., Libn.
STOCKTON NEWSPAPERS INC. - STOCKTON
RECORD LIBRARY □ Stockton, CA

Franklin, Berenice, Mgr./Lib. Photo Serv.
COURIER-JOURNAL AND LOUISVILLE TIMES -
LIBRARY □ Louisville, KY

Franklin, Ms. D., Chf., Govt.Rec.Sect.
CANADA - PUBLIC ARCHIVES OF CANADA -
NATIONAL MAP COLLECTION □ Ottawa, ON

Franklin, George, Jr., Acq.Dir.
INTERNATIONAL RESEARCH & EVALUATION
(IRE) - INFORMATION & TECHNOLOGY
TRANSFER RESOURCE CENTER □ Eagan, MN

Franklin, Josephine, Coord., Info.Serv.
EDUCATIONAL RESEARCH SERVICE - LIBRARY
□ Arlington, VA

Franklin, Madeleine L'Engle, Writer in Residence
CATHEDRAL OF ST. JOHN THE DIVINE -
CATHEDRAL LIBRARY □ New York, NY

Franklin, Sr. Mary Lawrence, Archv.
MERCYHURST COLLEGE - LIBRARY - ARCHIVES
□ Erie, PA

Franklin, Ralph, Dir.
YALE UNIVERSITY - BEINECKE RARE BOOK
AND MANUSCRIPT LIBRARY □ New Haven, CT

Franklin, Robert A., Ph.D., Dir. of Res.
MOTION PICTURE ASSOCIATION OF AMERICA
- LIBRARY □ New York, NY

Franks, Jeffrey, Sci.Libn.
MICHIGAN STATE UNIVERSITY - SCIENCE
LIBRARY □ East Lansing, MI

Fransen, Janet, Med.Libn.
CANBY COMMUNITY HOSPITAL - MEDICAL
LIBRARY □ Canby, MN

Fransiszyn, M., Hd., Pub.Serv.
MC GILL UNIVERSITY - OSLER LIBRARY □
Montreal, PQ

Frantz, Diane, Libn.
ST. LUKE'S HOSPITAL OF BETHLEHEM,
PENNSYLVANIA - SCHOOL OF NURSING -
TREXLER NURSES' LIBRARY □ Bethlehem, PA

Franz, Donald, Exec.Sec.
STUDIO SUPPLIERS ASSOCIATION - BUSINESS
LIBRARY □ Hawthorne, NJ

Franz, Louise, Libn.
PITTSBURGH-DES MOINES CORPORATION -
ENGINEERING LIBRARY □ Coraopolis, PA

Franze, J.P., Info.Ret.
ARMSTRONG WORLD INDUSTRIES, INC. -
TECHNICAL CENTER - TECHNICAL
INFORMATION SERVICES □ Lancaster, PA

Frappier, Francine, Br.Libn.
CANADA - LABOUR CANADA - LIBRARY
SERVICES - OCCUPATIONAL SAFETY AND
HEALTH BRANCH - RESOURCE CENTRE □ Hull,
PQ

Fraser, Alex W., Pres.
GLENGARRY GENEALOGICAL SOCIETY -
HIGHLAND HERITAGE RESEARCH LIBRARY □
Lancaster, ON

Fraser, Bette-Ann, Sr.Lib.Techn.
CENTENNIAL COLLEGE OF APPLIED ARTS &
TECHNOLOGY - ASHTONBEE CAMPUS
RESOURCE CENTRE □ Scarborough, ON

Fraser, C. William, Dir.
COLLEGE OF PHYSICIANS AND SURGEONS OF
BRITISH COLUMBIA - MEDICAL LIBRARY
SERVICE □ Vancouver, BC

Fraser, Carol A., Libn.
INSURANCE INFORMATION INSTITUTE -
LIBRARY □ New York, NY

Fraser, Christine A., Libn.
U.S. DEPT. OF HOUSING AND URBAN
DEVELOPMENT - REGION I - LIBRARY† □
Boston, MA

Fraser, David, Hd.Libn.
HISTORICAL SOCIETY OF PENNSYLVANIA -
LIBRARY □ Philadelphia, PA

Fraser, Gail, Supv.
HOME OIL COMPANY, LTD. - TECHNICAL
INFORMATION CENTER □ Calgary, AB

Fraser, Gwen, Asst. for Pub.Educ.
WESTMINSTER INSTITUTE FOR ETHICS AND
HUMAN VALUES - LIBRARY □ London, ON

Fraser, Judith, Tech.Serv.Libn.
QUEEN'S UNIVERSITY AT KINGSTON -
DOCUMENTS LIBRARY □ Kingston, ON

Fraser, Marjory, Supv., Rd.Rm.
UNIVERSITY OF PENNSYLVANIA - RARE BOOK
COLLECTION† □ Philadelphia, PA

Frattolillo, Pierce, Process Dev.Supt.
NORANDA MINES LTD. - CCR DIVISION -
PROCESS DEVELOPMENT LIBRARY □ Montreal,
PQ

Fraulino, Philip, Libn.
U.S. NATL. OCEANIC & ATMOSPHERIC
ADMINISTRATION - GEOPHYSICAL FLUID
DYNAMICS LABORATORY - LIBRARY □
Princeton, NJ

Frayler, John M., Cur.
U.S. NATL. PARK SERVICE - SALEM MARITIME
NATL. HISTORIC SITE - LIBRARY □ Salem, MA

Frazee, Mary Louise, Libn.
WESTINGHOUSE ELECTRIC CORPORATION -
BETTIS ATOMIC POWER LABORATORY -
LIBRARY† □ West Mifflin, PA

Frazelle, Betty, Lib.Techn.
U.S. NAVY - NAVAL HOSPITAL (NC-Camp
Lejeune) - MEDICAL LIBRARY □ Camp Lejeune,
NC

Frazier, Ken, Hd., Info.Serv.
UNIVERSITY OF WISCONSIN, MADISON -
STEENBOCK MEMORIAL LIBRARY □ Madison,
WI

Frebold, Mrs. E., Hd., Info.Serv.
CANADA - GEOLOGICAL SURVEY OF CANADA -
LIBRARY □ Ottawa, ON

Frechette, Dorothy, Lib.Plan., Dev.Info.Serv.
RHODE ISLAND STATE DEPARTMENT OF STATE
LIBRARY SERVICES □ Providence, RI

Frechtling, Dr. Douglas, Dir.
U.S. TRAVEL DATA CENTER - LIBRARY □
Washington, DC

Frederick, Marsha, Asst.Libn.
U.S. COURT OF APPEALS, 3RD CIRCUIT -
LIBRARY □ Philadelphia, PA

Frederick, Olivia, Cons.Archv.
JEFFERSON COUNTY OFFICE OF HISTORIC
PRESERVATION AND ARCHIVES □ Louisville, KY

Frederick, Tallulah, Tech.Libn.
LITTON INDUSTRIES - DATA SYSTEMS
DIVISION - ENGINEERING LIBRARY† □ Van
Nuys, CA

Fredericksen, Richard B., Dir.
UNIVERSITY OF ALABAMA IN BIRMINGHAM -
LISTER HILL LIBRARY OF THE HEALTH
SCIENCES □ Birmingham, AL

Frederickson, Jeanne, Media Spec.
EMPORIA STATE UNIVERSITY - BUTCHER TOY
LENDING LIBRARY □ Emporia, KS

Frederickson, Joan A., Libn.
HAZELDEN FOUNDATION - STAFF LIBRARY† □
Center City, MN

Frederickson, Karen, Sr.Sec.
UNIVERSITY OF MINNESOTA - DEPARTMENT
OF LINGUISTICS - LINGUISTICS LIBRARY □
Minneapolis, MN

Fredette, Kevin, Docs.Libn.
INDIANA UNIVERSITY - LAW LIBRARY □
Bloomington, IN

Fredrick, Tim, Regional Archv.
WASHINGTON STATE OFFICE OF SECRETARY
OF STATE - DIVISION OF ARCHIVES AND
RECORD MANAGEMENT □ Olympia, WA

Fredrickson, Stephen C., Att.Supv.
FLORIDA STATE DEPT. OF INSURANCE AND
STATE TREASURER - DEPT. OF INSURANCE -
LAW LIBRARY □ Tallahassee, FL

Free, Opal M., Hd.
FLORIDA STATE UNIVERSITY - SPECIAL
COLLECTIONS □ Tallahassee, FL

Freed, J. Arthur, Hd.Libn.
UNIVERSITY OF CALIFORNIA - LOS ALAMOS
NATIONAL LABORATORY - LIBRARY □ Los
Alamos, NM

Freed, Shanon, Circ.Supv.
ASBURY THEOLOGICAL SEMINARY - B.L.
FISHER LIBRARY □ Wilmore, KY

Freedman, Arlene L., Dir. of Lib.Serv.
BETH ISRAEL MEDICAL CTR. - HOSPITAL FOR
JOINT DISEASES ORTHOPAEDIC INST. -
SEYMOUR J. PHILLIPS HEALTH SCI.LIB. □ New
York, NY

Freedman, Henry A., Dir.
CENTER ON SOCIAL WELFARE POLICY AND
LAW - LIBRARY □ New York, NY

Freeh, Mary Beth, Ref.
MUHLENBERG COLLEGE - JOHN A.W. HAAS
LIBRARY □ Allentown, PA

Freehling, Catherine A., State Law Libn.
MAINE STATE LAW AND LEGISLATIVE
REFERENCE LIBRARY □ Augusta, ME

Freehling, Dan J., Law Libn.
UNIVERSITY OF MAINE SCHOOL OF LAW -
DONALD L. GARBRECHT LAW LIBRARY □
Portland, ME

Freehling, Leonore, Libn.
REISS-DAVIS CHILD STUDY CENTER -
RESEARCH LIBRARY □ Los Angeles, CA

Freeland, Alison, Pub.Serv.
BRIDGEWATER COLLEGE - ALEXANDER MACK
MEMORIAL LIBRARY - SPECIAL COLLECTIONS
□ Bridgewater, VA

Freels, Donna, Asst.Libn.
BERNALILLO COUNTY - DISTRICT COURT LAW
LIBRARY □ Albuquerque, NM

Freeman, Adrian, Asst.Libn.
SUNDSTRAND AVIATION - ENGINEERING
LIBRARY □ Rockford, IL

Freeman, Allan, Libn.
GENERAL DRAFTING COMPANY, INC. - MAP
LIBRARY† □ Convent Station, NJ

Freeman, Betty, Asst.Libn.
BAYLOR UNIVERSITY, DALLAS - LIBRARY □
Dallas, TX

Freeman, Corinne A., Soc.Serv.Libn.
FORDHAM UNIVERSITY - LIBRARY AT LINCOLN
CENTER □ New York, NY

Freeman, Douglas K., Hd., Coll.&Serv.
KINSEY INSTITUTE FOR RESEARCH IN SEX,
GENDER & REPRODUCTION, INC. - LIBRARY
AND INFORMATION SERVICE □ Bloomington, IN

Freeman, Frank H., Dir.
CENTER FOR CREATIVE LEADERSHIP -
LIBRARY □ Greensboro, NC

Freeman, George C., Hd., Biomed.Br.
UNIVERSITY OF BRITISH COLUMBIA -
BIOMEDICAL BRANCH LIBRARY □ Vancouver,
BC

Freeman, Homer W., Church Libn.
FIRST UNITED METHODIST CHURCH -
MEMORIAL LIBRARY □ Santa Barbara, CA

Freeman, Jane B., Sr.Libn.
FEDERAL RESERVE BANK OF DALLAS -
RESEARCH LIBRARY □ Dallas, TX

Freeman, Joanne, Libn.
UNITED TECHNOLOGIES CORPORATION -
INMONT - LIBRARY □ Clifton, NJ

Freeman, Dr. John C., Hd.
INSTITUTE FOR STORM RESEARCH - LIBRARY
□ Houston, TX

Freeman, John Crosby, Dir.
AMERICAN LIFE FOUNDATION AND STUDY
INSTITUTE - AMERICANA RESEARCH LIBRARY
□ Watkins Glen, NY

Freeman, Larry, Cur., Dec. Arts Lib.
AMERICAN LIFE FOUNDATION AND STUDY
INSTITUTE - AMERICANA RESEARCH LIBRARY
□ Watkins Glen, NY

Freeman, Mary Ann, Commun.Mgr.
NATIONAL COLLEGE OF DISTRICT ATTORNEYS
- RESOURCE CENTER □ Houston, TX

Freeman, Mary B., Staff Supv.-Lib.
AT & T - GOVERNMENT COMMUNICATIONS
LIBRARY □ Washington, DC

Freeman, Mary Lee, Libn.
MOBIL EXPLORATION AND PRODUCING
SERVICES INC. - MEPSI LIBRARY □ Dallas, TX

Freeman, Nancy, Libn.
SCM CORPORATION - PIGMENTS DIVISION -
LIBRARY □ Baltimore, MD

Freeman, Ruth, Cur., Pict.Bk.Coll.
AMERICAN LIFE FOUNDATION AND STUDY
INSTITUTE - AMERICANA RESEARCH LIBRARY
□ Watkins Glen, NY

Freeman, Sandra, Asst.Libn.
SEATTLE TIMES - LIBRARY† □ Seattle, WA

Freeman, Terry, Ref.Libn.
U.S. PUBLIC HEALTH SERVICE - PARKLAWN
HEALTH LIBRARY □ Rockville, MD

Freese, Catherine, Asst.Libn./Pub.Serv.
VERMONT LAW SCHOOL - LIBRARY □ South
Royalton, VT

Freese, Robert T., Area Libn.
MC GILL UNIVERSITY - PHYSICAL SCIENCES
AND ENGINEERING LIBRARY □ Montreal, PQ

Freeze, Bernice, Pres.
BENTON COUNTY HISTORICAL SOCIETY -
MUSEUM & LIBRARY/ARCHIVES □ Siloam
Springs, AR

Freggiaro, Diane, Libn./Archv.
THE HAGGIN MUSEUM - ALMEDA MAY CASTLE
PETZINGER LIBRARY □ Stockton, CA

Freiherr, Gregory, Asst.Dir.
TRACOR JITCO, INC. - RESEARCH RESOURCES
INFORMATION CENTER □ Rockville, MD

Freiling, Loretta, Prog.Asst.
UNIVERSITY OF WISCONSIN, MADISON -
INSTITUTE FOR RESEARCH IN THE
HUMANITIES - LIBRARY □ Madison, WI

Freitag, Doris, Consrv.
HARVARD UNIVERSITY - DIVINITY SCHOOL -
ANDOVER-HARVARD THEOLOGICAL LIBRARY □
Cambridge, MA

Freitag, Rosalie, Libn.
MADISON PUBLIC LIBRARY - LITERATURE AND
SOCIAL SCIENCES □ Madison, WI

Freitag, Wolfgang, Libn.
HARVARD UNIVERSITY - FINE ARTS LIBRARY □
Cambridge, MA

French, A.F., Info.Sys.Mgr.
BELL COMMUNICATIONS RESEARCH, INC. -
INFORMATION RESOURCES & SERVICES
DISTRICT □ Livingston, NJ

French, Beverlee, Libn.
UNIVERSITY OF CALIFORNIA, SAN DIEGO -
SCIENCE & ENGINEERING LIBRARY □ La Jolla,
CA

French, Curtis M., Libn.
GEORGIA STATE SUPREME COURT LIBRARY □
Atlanta, GA

French, Edward D., Libn.
UNIVERSITY OF MARYLAND - SCHOOL OF
MEDICINE - DEPT. OF PSYCHIATRY - HELEN C.
TINGLEY MEMORIAL LIBRARY □ Catonsville, MD

French, Frances, Libn.
MEMPHIS-SHELBY COUNTY PUBLIC LIBRARY
AND INFO. CTR. - SCIENCE/BUSINESS/SOCIAL
SCI.DEPT. □ Memphis, TN

French, LaWanda, Supv.
PONCA CITY CULTURAL CENTER & MUSEUMS -
LIBRARY □ Ponca City, OK

French, Col. Lawrence R., Commander
U.S. AIR FORCE ENVIRONMENTAL TECHNICAL
APPLICATIONS CENTER - AIR WEATHER
SERVICE TECHNICAL LIBRARY □ Scott AFB, IL

French, Rae, Resource Ctr.Coord.
SASKATCHEWAN - DEPARTMENT OF CO-
OPERATION - LIBRARY □ Regina, SK

French, Robert B., Pres.
LOUISVILLE ACADEMY OF MUSIC - LIBRARY □
Louisville, KY

French, Sharon K., Libn.
BANK OF AMERICA, NT & SA - LAW LIBRARY □
San Francisco, CA

French, Thomas, Tech.Serv.Libn.
NORTHERN KENTUCKY UNIVERSITY - SALMON
P. CHASE COLLEGE OF LAW - LIBRARY □
Highland Heights, KY

French, William D., Exec.Dir.
AMERICAN SOCIETY OF PHOTOGRAMMETRY -
HEINZ GRUNER LIBRARY □ Falls Church, VA

Frenette, Geraldine, Chf.
DETROIT PUBLIC LIBRARY - PHILOSOPHY,
RELIGION AND EDUCATION DEPARTMENT □
Detroit, MI

Frenza, Mary, Asst.Dir., Info.Proc.
ERIC CLEARINGHOUSE ON COUNSELING AND
PERSONNEL SERVICES - LEARNING
RESOURCES CENTER □ Ann Arbor, MI

Freshley, Katherine T., Libn.
TEXTILE MUSEUM - ARTHUR D. JENKINS
LIBRARY □ Washington, DC

Freshwater, Marjorie, Cat.
NATIONAL CENTER FOR RESEARCH IN
VOCATIONAL EDUCATION - RESEARCH
LIBRARY □ Columbus, OH

Fretwell, Jacqueline K., Lib.Dir.
ST. AUGUSTINE HISTORICAL SOCIETY -
LIBRARY □ St. Augustine, FL

Freudenberger, Elsie, Cat.Libn.
SCHOOL OF THEOLOGY AT CLAREMONT -
THEOLOGY LIBRARY □ Claremont, CA

Freund, Clare, Cat.
EASTMAN KODAK COMPANY - RESEARCH
LIBRARY □ Rochester, NY

Frew, Kathleen Pratt, Preservation Techn.
OLD STURBRIDGE VILLAGE - RESEARCH
LIBRARY □ Sturbridge, MA

Frey, Charles, Spec.Coll.Libn.
PEORIA HISTORICAL SOCIETY - HARRY L.
SPOONER MEMORIAL LIBRARY □ Peoria, IL

Frey, Charles J., Spec.Coll.Libn.
BRADLEY UNIVERSITY - VIRGINIUS H. CHASE
SPECIAL COLLECTIONS CENTER - APCO
HISTORICAL COLLECTION □ Peoria, IL

Frey, Charles J., Spec.Coll.Libn.
BRADLEY UNIVERSITY - VIRGINIUS H. CHASE
SPECIAL COLLECTIONS CENTER - CHARLES A.
BENNETT COLLECTION □ Peoria, IL

Frey, Charles J., Spec.Coll.Libn.
BRADLEY UNIVERSITY - VIRGINIUS H. CHASE
SPECIAL COLLECTIONS CENTER - CHASE
COLLECTION □ Peoria, IL

Frey, Charles J., Spec.Coll.Libn.
BRADLEY UNIVERSITY - VIRGINIUS H. CHASE
SPECIAL COLLECTIONS CENTER - LINCOLN
COLLECTIONS □ Peoria, IL

Frey, Emil F., Dir.
UNIVERSITY OF TEXAS MEDICAL BRANCH -
MOODY MEDICAL LIBRARY □ Galveston, TX

Frey, Gail, Med.Libn.
U.S. VETERANS ADMINISTRATION (AL-
Birmingham) - HOSPITAL MEDICAL LIBRARY □
Birmingham, AL

Frey, Luanne, Asst.Info.Sci.
JOHNSON (S.C.) AND SON, INC. - TECHNICAL &
BUSINESS INFORMATION CENTER □ Racine, WI

Frey, Peter A., Asst.Libn.
U.S. COURT OF APPEALS, 4TH CIRCUIT -
LIBRARY □ Richmond, VA

Frey, William, Dir.
MICHIGAN STATE UNIVERSITY - UNIVERSITY
CENTER FOR INTERNATIONAL
REHABILITATION (UCIR) - RESOURCE LIB. □
East Lansing, MI

Freyer, Bryna, Res.Asst.
SMITHSONIAN INSTITUTION LIBRARIES -
NATIONAL MUSEUM OF AFRICAN ART - ELIOT
ELISOFON ARCHIVES □ Washington, DC

Freyman, Marcelle, Asst. Dental Libn.
TEMPLE UNIVERSITY - HEALTH SCIENCES
CENTER - LIBRARY □ Philadelphia, PA

Fricke, Lorraine, Law Libn.
AT & T - LAW LIBRARY □ New York, NY

Frickensmith, William
MGIC INVESTMENT CORPORATION -
CORPORATE LIBRARY □ Milwaukee, WI

Fridenberg, D., Mgr., Lib.Serv.
ALCOHOLISM AND DRUG ADDICTION
RESEARCH FOUNDATION - LIBRARY □ Toronto,
ON

Frideres, Dr. James S., Dir.
CANADIAN ETHNIC STUDIES ASSOCIATION -
RESEARCH CENTRE □ Calgary, AB

Fridley, Bonnie, Chf., Pub.Serv.
U.S. AIR FORCE - AEROSPACE MEDICAL
DIVISION - SCHOOL OF AEROSPACE MEDICINE
- STRUGHOLD AEROMEDICAL LIBRARY □ Brooks
AFB, TX

Frie, George, Engr.Adm.
CRANE COMPANY - HYDRO-AIRE DIVISION -
TECHNICAL LIBRARY □ Burbank, CA

Fried, Ava, Dir.
UNIVERSITY OF CINCINNATI - MEDICAL
CENTER LIBRARIES - COLLEGE OF NURSING &
HEALTH - LEVI MEMORIAL LIBRARY □
Cincinnati, OH

Frieday, Mrs. L.A., Hd., Automated Oper.
CANADA - GEOLOGICAL SURVEY OF CANADA -
LIBRARY □ Ottawa, ON

Friede, John A., Pres.
VIDEO TAPE NETWORK, INC. - LIBRARY □ New
York, NY

Friedeborn, Doris, Corp.Libn.
CODEX CORPORATION - CORPORATE LIBRARY
□ Mansfield, MA

Friedel, Marie, Exec.Dir.
NATIONAL FOUNDATION FOR GIFTED AND
CREATIVE CHILDREN - LIBRARY □ Warwick, RI

Friedman, Arthur L., Media Libn.
NASSAU COMMUNITY COLLEGE - NEW YORK
STATE HEALTH FILM COLLECTION □ Garden
City, NY

Friedman, Esther K., Lib.Dir.
JOHNSON SCHOOL OF TECHNOLOGY - LIBRARY
□ Scranton, PA

Friedman, Heidi S., Libn.
HORTICULTURAL SOCIETY OF NEW YORK -
PUBLIC REFERENCE LIBRARY □ New York, NY

Friedman, Joan, Ref.Libn.
UNIVERSITY OF CALIFORNIA, BERKELEY -
PUBLIC HEALTH LIBRARY □ Berkeley, CA

Friedman, Joan M., Cur. of Rare Bks.
YALE UNIVERSITY - YALE CENTER FOR
BRITISH ART - RARE BOOK COLLECTION □ New
Haven, CT

Friedman, Joel I., Tech.Info.Spec.
NATIONAL INJURY INFORMATION
CLEARINGHOUSE □ Washington, DC

Friedman, Judy, Mgr./Lib. & Ref.Serv.
NATIONAL BROADCASTING COMPANY, INC. -
REFERENCE LIBRARY □ New York, NY

Friedman, Kathleen M., Law Libn.
WAYNE COUNTY CIRCUIT COURT - LAW
LIBRARY† □ Detroit, MI

Friedman, Lydia, Chf.Med.Libn.
MAIMONIDES MEDICAL CENTER - GEORGE A.
DEGENSHEIN, M.D. MEMORIAL LIBRARY □
Brooklyn, NY

Friedman, Martha, Libn.
UNIVERSITY OF ILLINOIS - HISTORY AND
PHILOSOPHY LIBRARY □ Urbana, IL

Friedman, Susan, Tech.Serv.Libn.
BATTEN, BARTON, DURSTINE, OSBORN, INC. -
INFORMATION RETRIEVAL CENTER† □ New
York, NY

Friedmann, Ted, Clinical Libn.
ST. FRANCIS HOSPITAL AND MEDICAL CENTER
- WILSON C. JAINSEN LIBRARY □ Hartford, CT

Fries, James R., Libn.
DARTMOUTH COLLEGE - FELDBERG LIBRARY □
Hanover, NH

Fries, Victoria, Ref.Libn.
U.S. PEACE CORPS - INFORMATION SERVICES
DIVISION □ Washington, DC

Friesen, Eva, Tech.Serv.Libn.
RYERSON POLYTECHNICAL INSTITUTE -
LEARNING RESOURCES CENTRE □ Toronto, ON

Friesen, Karen, Libn.
WINNIPEG BIBLE COLLEGE/WINNIPEG
THEOLOGICAL SEMINARY - LIBRARY □
Otterburne, MB

Friesen, Lillian, Dir., Lib.Serv.
ALDERSGATE COLLEGE - WILSON MEMORIAL
LIBRARY □ Moose Jaw, SK

Friesen, Ralph, Film Rep.
CANADA - NATIONAL FILM BOARD OF CANADA
- FILM LIBRARY† □ Winnipeg, MB

Friesen, Ronald, Libn.
EDMONTON POWER - LIBRARY □ Edmonton, AB

Friesner, Vee, Dir., Lib.Dev.
KANSAS STATE LIBRARY □ Topeka, KS

Friewer, K.A.
DOW CHEMICAL COMPANY - TECHNICAL
INFORMATION SERVICES - CHEMICAL
LIBRARY □ Midland, MI

Frihart, Anne R., Libn.
RESPONSE ANALYSIS CORPORATION -
LIBRARY □ Princeton, NJ

Friis, Harriet, Dept.Hd.
LONG BEACH PUBLIC LIBRARY - LITERATURE
AND HISTORY DEPARTMENT □ Long Beach, CA

Frimer, Baer M., Pres.
PICTORIAL PARADE INC. - LIBRARY □ New
York, NY

Frins, Sarah L., Tech.Serv.Libn.
ALABAMA (State) SUPREME COURT - SUPREME
COURT AND STATE LAW LIBRARY □
Montgomery, AL

Frisby, Wilfred, Ref.Libn.
PHILADELPHIA COLLEGE OF TEXTILES AND
SCIENCE - PASTORE LIBRARY □ Philadelphia, PA

Frisch, Irene, Lib.Dir.
STERLING DRUG, INC. - WINTHROP
LABORATORIES - MEDICAL LIBRARY □ New
York, NY

Frisch, Sylvia, Libn.
MINNEAPOLIS PUBLIC LIBRARY &
INFORMATION CENTER - BUSINESS AND
ECONOMICS DEPARTMENT □ Minneapolis, MN

Fritschel, Linda, Libn.
MINNEAPOLIS PUBLIC LIBRARY &
INFORMATION CENTER - LITERATURE AND
LANGUAGE DEPARTMENT □ Minneapolis, MN

Fritz, Al, Libn.
UNIVERSITY OF WASHINGTON - POLITICAL
SCIENCE LIBRARY □ Seattle, WA

Fritz, Dr. Charles G., Dir.
ETHICON, INC. - SCIENTIFIC INFORMATION
SERVICES □ Somerville, NJ

Fritz, Flora, Libn.
CANADA - GEOLOGICAL SURVEY OF CANADA -
INSTITUTE OF SEDIMENTARY & PETROLEUM
GEOLOGY - LIBRARY □ Calgary, AB

Fritz, Pamela R., Info.Spec.
PPG INDUSTRIES, INC. - SPECIALTY
PRODUCTS UNIT - LIBRARY □ Chicago, IL

Fritz, William Richard, Sr., Libn.
LUTHERAN THEOLOGICAL SOUTHERN
SEMINARY - LINEBERGER MEMORIAL LIBRARY
□ Columbia, SC

Frobom, Jerome B., Chf., Govt.Pubn.
WYOMING STATE LIBRARY □ Cheyenne, WY

Froiland, Sven, Dir.
AUGUSTANA COLLEGE - CENTER FOR
WESTERN STUDIES □ Sioux Falls, SD

Froistad, Carol, Libn.
MADISON PUBLIC LIBRARY - LITERATURE AND
SOCIAL SCIENCES □ Madison, WI

Froman, Barry, Co-Owner
STOVE KING - LIBRARY □ Salt Lake City, UT

Froman, Clarence, Owner
STOVE KING - LIBRARY □ Salt Lake City, UT

Fromkes, Ruth, Hd., Info.Ctr.
CUNNINGHAM AND WALSH, INC. -
INFORMATION CENTER □ New York, NY

Fromm, Esther, Archv./Dir., GPL
GREELEY PUBLIC LIBRARY - SPECIAL
COLLECTIONS □ Greeley, CO

Fromm, Ken, Asst.Dir./Media Ctr.
OHIO DOMINICAN COLLEGE - SPANGLER
LIBRARY □ Columbus, OH

Frommer, Saul I., Sr.Musm.Sci.
UNIVERSITY OF CALIFORNIA, RIVERSIDE -
DEPARTMENT OF ENTOMOLOGY - LIBRARY □
Riverside, CA

Froncek, Memory R., Info.Spec.
WEYERHAEUSER COMPANY - SFRD TECHNICAL
INFORMATION CENTER □ Hot Springs, AR

Frontz, Stephanie, Libn.
UNIVERSITY OF ROCHESTER - CHARLOTTE
WHITNEY ALLEN LIBRARY □ Rochester, NY

Frontz, Stephanie, Libn.
UNIVERSITY OF ROCHESTER - FINE ARTS
LIBRARY □ Rochester, NY

Frosch, Paula, Asst.Musm.Libn.
METROPOLITAN MUSEUM OF ART - THOMAS J.
WATSON LIBRARY □ New York, NY

Frost, Annette K., Mgr., Lib.Serv.
FANSHAWE COLLEGE OF APPLIED ARTS AND
TECHNOLOGY - MAIN LIBRARY □ London, ON

Frost, Bruce, Cat. Law Libn.
UNIVERSITY OF MISSOURI - SCHOOL OF LAW
LIBRARY □ Columbia, MO

Frost, E., Dir.
CANADA - PUBLIC ARCHIVES OF CANADA -
FEDERAL ARCHIVES DIVISION □ Ottawa, ON

Frost, J. William, Dir.
SWARTHMORE COLLEGE - FRIENDS
HISTORICAL LIBRARY □ Swarthmore, PA

Frost, Mary Kay, Info.Spec.
GENERAL ELECTRIC COMPANY - CORPORATE
INFORMATION SYSTEMS LIBRARY □ Bridgeport,
CT

Frost, R.C., Libn.
REYNOLDS, SMITH & HILLS - LIBRARY □
Jacksonville, FL

Frost, Dr. Shimon, Dir.
JEWISH EDUCATION SERVICE OF NORTH
AMERICA, INC. - LIBRARY □ New York, NY

Froud, Miss L., Sec.
GENSTAR CEMENT, LTD. - TECHNICAL
LIBRARY □ Edmonton, AB

Frow, Richard G., Libn.
MIAMI-DADE PUBLIC LIBRARY - URBAN
AFFAIRS LIBRARY □ Miami, FL

Fruehe, Margot, Dir.
MIDWEST COLLEGE OF ENGINEERING -
JOSEPH M. HARRER LIBRARY □ Lombard, IL

Frum, Martin, Hd., Circ.
SUNY - DOWNSTATE MEDICAL CENTER -
MEDICAL RESEARCH LIBRARY OF BROOKLYN†
□ Brooklyn, NY

Frump, John A., Info.Spec.
INTERNATIONAL MINERALS & CHEMICALS
CORPORATION - IMC RESEARCH &
DEVELOPMENT LIBRARY □ Terre Haute, IN

Fry, Donald W., Dir.
U.S. DEPT. OF COMMERCE - INTERNATIONAL
TRADE ADMINISTRATION - PHOENIX
DISTRICT OFFICE LIBRARY □ Phoenix, AZ

Fry, Eileen, Slide Libn.
INDIANA UNIVERSITY - FINE ARTS SLIDE
LIBRARY □ Bloomington, IN

Fry, Hazel, Northern Stud.Libn.
ARCTIC INSTITUTE OF NORTH AMERICA -
LIBRARY† □ Calgary, AB

Fry, Hazel, Area Hd.
UNIVERSITY OF CALGARY - ENVIRONMENT-
SCIENCE-TECHNOLOGY LIBRARY† □ Calgary,
AB

Fry, James W., State Libn.
MICHIGAN STATE - LIBRARY OF MICHIGAN □
Lansing, MI

Fry, Louise T., Libn.
CENTER FOR RELIGION, ETHICS & SOCIAL
POLICY - ANNE CARRY DURLAND MEMORIAL
ALTERNATIVES LIBRARY □ Ithaca, NY

Fry, Margaret, Ref. & Online Serv.
GEORGETOWN UNIVERSITY - FRED O. DENNIS
LAW LIBRARY □ Washington, DC

Fry, Mary Anne C., Libn.
KING & SPALDING - LAW LIBRARY† □ Atlanta,
GA

Fry, Morel, Hd., Adm.Serv.
NEBRASKA STATE LIBRARY COMMISSION □
Lincoln, NE

Fry, Sally, Libn.
UNIVERSITY OF IOWA - BOTANY-CHEMISTRY
LIBRARY □ Iowa City, IA

Fry, Sally, Libn.
UNIVERSITY OF IOWA - MATHEMATICS
LIBRARY □ Iowa City, IA

Fry, Stephen M., Music Libn.
UNIVERSITY OF CALIFORNIA, LOS ANGELES -
MUSIC LIBRARY □ Los Angeles, CA

Fryar, Linda, Libn.
U.S. AIR FORCE BASE - SHEPPARD BASE
LIBRARY □ Sheppard AFB, TX

Frye, Irene S., Asst.Libn.
HISPANIC SOCIETY OF AMERICA - LIBRARY □
New York, NY

Frye, Judith, Hd.
UNIVERSITY OF BRITISH COLUMBIA -
MARJORIE SMITH LIBRARY □ Vancouver, BC

Frye, Margaret, Cat.
NORTHWEST COLLEGE OF THE ASSEMBLIES OF
GOD - HURST LIBRARY† □ Kirkland, WA

Frye, Nanna, Assoc.Libn.
SQUIRE, SANDERS & DEMPSEY - LAW LIBRARY
□ Cleveland, OH

Fryer, Philip, Film Unit Supv.
UNIVERSITY OF MARYLAND, COLLEGE PARK -
LIBRARIES NONPRINT MEDIA SERVICES □
College Park, MD

Fryer, R. Kenny, Hd., Ref.Libn.
YALE UNIVERSITY - MEDICAL LIBRARY □ New
Haven, CT

Fryer, William N., Chf., Psych.Serv.
ABILENE STATE SCHOOL - SPECIAL LIBRARY □
Abilene, TX

Frymark, Kathleen, Circ.Libn.
MARQUETTE UNIVERSITY - MEMORIAL
LIBRARY □ Milwaukee, WI

Fryshdorf, Hannah, Asst.Dir.
YIVO INSTITUTE FOR JEWISH RESEARCH -
LIBRARY AND ARCHIVES □ New York, NY

Fu, Paul S., Law Libn.
OHIO STATE SUPREME COURT LAW LIBRARY □
Columbus, OH

Fu, Theresa, Cat.Libn.
UNIVERSITY OF BRIDGEPORT - SCHOOL OF
LAW - LAW LIBRARY □ Bridgeport, CT

Fuchs, Carl, Libn.
RESEARCH & EDUCATION ASSOCIATION -
LIBRARY □ New York, NY

Fuchs, Joseph H., III, Sr.Libn.
GLENDALE PUBLIC LIBRARY - BRAND LIBRARY
□ Glendale, CA

Fuchs, Joseph L., Chf., Users' Serv.
UNITED NATIONS HEADQUARTERS - DAG
HAMMARSKJOLD LIBRARY □ New York, NY

Fuchs, Suzanne, ILL Libn.
LEBOEUF, LAMB, LEIBY & MAC RAE - LIBRARY □
New York, NY

Fugate, Cynthia, Docs.Ser.Libn.
UNIVERSITY OF WASHINGTON - GOVERNMENT
PUBLICATIONS DIVISION □ Seattle, WA

Fugate, K.O., Pres. & Libn.
PANEL DISPLAYS, INC. - TECHNICAL LIBRARY
□ Inglewood, CA

Fugate, Liz, Libn.
UNIVERSITY OF WASHINGTON - DRAMA
LIBRARY □ Seattle, WA

Fugate, Mary, Libn.
PERKINS AND WILL ARCHITECTS, INC. -
RESOURCE CENTER □ Chicago, IL

Fuge, Heidi A., Dir.
HISTORICAL SOCIETY OF SARATOGA SPRINGS
- MUSEUM AND LIBRARY □ Saratoga Springs, NY

Fugere, Joseph, Evening Supv.
UNIVERSITY OF TOLEDO - COLLEGE OF LAW
LIBRARY □ Toledo, OH

Fugle, Mary, Libn.
LUTHERAN MEDICAL CENTER - MEDICAL
LIBRARY □ Brooklyn, NY

Fuhr, J.R., Physicist
U.S. NATL. BUREAU OF STANDARDS - DATA
CENTER ON ATOMIC TRANSITION
PROBABILITIES □ Washington, DC

Fujimoto, Patricia, Info.Ctr.Dir.
BATTEN, BARTON, DURSTINE & OSBORN
(BBDO) - CHICAGO INFORMATION CENTER □
Chicago, IL

Fujiwara, Susan, Info.Spec.
BNR INC. - INFORMATION RESOURCE CENTER†
□ Mountain View, CA

Fukuji, Delia, Libn.
HAWAII STATE LIBRARY - EDNA ALLYN ROOM
□ Honolulu, HI

Fulcher, Jane M., Law Libn.
WASHINGTON COUNTY LAW LIBRARY □
Washington, PA

Fulda, Pauline, Dir.
SOUTHERN BAPTIST HOSPITAL - LEARNING
RESOURCE CENTER □ New Orleans, LA

Fulkerson, Lynda, Asst.Libn.
MAGNAVOX GOVERNMENT & INDUSTRIAL
ELECTRONICS COMPANY - ENGINEERING
LIBRARY† □ Fort Wayne, IN

Fullam, Alice F., Dept.Hd.
TRENTON FREE PUBLIC LIBRARY - ART &
MUSIC DEPARTMENT □ Trenton, NJ

Fullam, Paul J., Lib.Dir.
ST. JOSEPH'S SEMINARY - ARCHBISHOP
CORRIGAN MEMORIAL LIBRARY □ Yonkers, NY

Fullam, R., Asst.Libn.
MC NEIL LABORATORIES - LIBRARY □ Fort
Washington, PA

Fullen, Jennifer, Ref.
ALBERTA RESEARCH COUNCIL - LIBRARY
SERVICES □ Edmonton, AB

Fuller, Brenda, Prin.Libn.
KENTUCKY STATE DEPARTMENT FOR
LIBRARIES AND ARCHIVES - STATE LIBRARY
SERVICES DIVISION □ Frankfort, KY

Fuller, Dawn, Libn.
U.S. ARMY POST - FORT MC PHERSON -
LIBRARY SYSTEM □ Ft. McPherson, GA

Fuller, Elizabeth G., Libn.
WESTCHESTER COUNTY HISTORICAL SOCIETY
- LIBRARY □ Valhalla, NY

Fuller, Ernest F., Jr., Chm.
PARK COUNTY BAR ASSOCIATION - LAW
LIBRARY □ Cody, WY

Fuller, Jean, Libn.
ST. MARY'S HOSPITAL - FINKELSTEIN LIBRARY
□ Waterbury, CT

Fuller, John W., Dir.
UNIVERSITY OF IOWA - INSTITUTE OF URBAN
AND REGIONAL RESEARCH - LIBRARY □ Iowa
City, IA

Fuller, Kathleen, Hd.Libn.
FERRO CORPORATION - LIBRARY □
Independence, OH

Fuller, Kathryn Wagnild, Sr.Libn.
CALIFORNIA STATE - COURT OF APPEAL, 4TH
APPELLATE DISTRICT, DIVISION ONE - LAW
LIBRARY □ San Diego, CA

Fuller, Linda P., Gen.Serv.Libn.
NORTH CAROLINA STATE UNIVERSITY - D.H.
HILL LIBRARY □ Raleigh, NC

Fuller, Ms. LoRene, Libn.
ENVIRONMENTAL PROTECTION AGENCY -
ROBERT S. KERR ENVIRONMENTAL RESEARCH
CENTER - LIBRARY □ Ada, OK

Fuller, Marnelyn, Ref.Libn.
MEHARRY MEDICAL COLLEGE - MEDICAL
LIBRARY - LEARNING RESOURCES CENTER □
Nashville, TN

Fuller, Mary B., Libn.
WATERBURY AMERICAN-REPUBLICAN -
LIBRARY □ Waterbury, CT

Fuller, Nancy F., Libn.
UNIVERSITY OF MISSISSIPPI - SCHOOL OF
PHARMACY - AUSTIN A. DODGE PHARMACY
LIBRARY □ University, MS

Fuller, Peggy, Med.Libn.
SWEDISH AMERICAN HOSPITAL - HEALTH
CARE LIBRARY† □ Rockford, IL

Fuller, Sherrilynne, Dir.
UNIVERSITY OF MINNESOTA - BIOMEDICAL
LIBRARY □ Minneapolis, MN

Fuller, Sherrilynne, Assoc.Dir.
UNIVERSITY OF SOUTHERN CALIFORNIA -
HEALTH SCIENCES CAMPUS - NORRIS
MEDICAL LIBRARY □ Los Angeles, CA

Fullerton, Sylvia J., Asst.Univ.Libn., Sci.
DALHOUSIE UNIVERSITY - MACDONALD
SCIENCE LIBRARY □ Halifax, NS

Fullshire, Lynn C., Sr. Law Libn.
NEW YORK STATE SUPREME COURT - 10TH
JUDICIAL DISTRICT - LAW LIBRARY □
Riverhead, NY

Fulmer, Dina J., Libn.
PSYCHOLOGICAL SERVICE OF PITTSBURGH -
LIBRARY □ Pittsburgh, PA

Fulmer, Russell, Asst.Dir., Tech.Serv.
COLORADO SCHOOL OF MINES - ARTHUR
LAKES LIBRARY □ Golden, CO

Fulton, Elaine, Exec.Sec.
NATIONAL ASSOCIATION OF
PARLIAMENTARIANS - TECHNICAL
INFORMATION CENTER □ Kansas City, MO

Fulton, Elizabeth W., Sr.Res.Libn.
NATIONAL STEEL CORPORATION - RESEARCH
CENTER LIBRARY □ Weirton, WV

Fulton, June M., Dir., Med.Doc.Serv.
COLLEGE OF PHYSICIANS OF PHILADELPHIA -
LIBRARY AND MEDICAL DOCUMENTATION
SERVICE □ Philadelphia, PA

Fulton, William A., Asst.Chf., Law Br.
U.S. DEPT. OF COMMERCE - LIBRARY □
Washington, DC

Fulton, William Alan, Asst.Chf.
U.S. DEPT. OF COMMERCE - LAW LIBRARY □
Washington, DC

Fultz, Gloria, Lib.Mgr.
CONSERVATION AND RENEWABLE ENERGY
INQUIRY AND REFERRAL SERVICE □
Philadelphia, PA

Funderburg, John B., Dir.
NORTH CAROLINA STATE MUSEUM OF
NATURAL HISTORY - H.H. BRIMLEY MEMORIAL
LIBRARY □ Raleigh, NC

Funk, Carla J., Dir. Automation/Tech.Serv
AMERICAN MEDICAL ASSOCIATION -
DIVISION OF LIBRARY AND ARCHIVAL
SERVICES □ Chicago, IL

Funk, Kendal, Libn.
SUN CHEMICAL CORPORATION - RESEARCH
LIBRARY □ Carlstadt, NJ

Funk, Mark E., Hd., Coll.Dev.
UNIVERSITY OF NEBRASKA MEDICAL CENTER -
MC GOOGAN LIBRARY OF MEDICINE □ Omaha,
NE

Funke, Rory, Hd.
UNIVERSITY OF OREGON - MICROFORMS AND
RECORDINGS DEPARTMENT □ Eugene, OR
Funkhouser, Richard L., Libn.
PURDUE UNIVERSITY - MATHEMATICAL
SCIENCES LIBRARY □ West Lafayette, IN
Funnell, Maureen D., Libn.
SOUTHWEST FOUNDATION FOR BIOMEDICAL
RESEARCH - PRESTON G. NORTHROP
MEMORIAL LIBRARY □ San Antonio, TX
Furbeyre, Mae L., Interim Hd.Libn.
UNIVERSITY OF SOUTHERN CALIFORNIA -
EDUCATION & INFORMATION STUDIES
LIBRARY □ Los Angeles, CA
Furey, Joan, Libn.
TEMPLE ADATH ISRAEL - RUBEN LIBRARY □
Merion, PA
Furlan, Colette, Coord., Doc./Rsrcs.
CANADA - CANADIAN INTERNATIONAL
DEVELOPMENT AGENCY - DEVELOPMENT
INFORMATION CENTRE □ Hull, PQ
Furlan, Nancy J., Info.Serv.Adm.
ALUMINUM COMPANY OF AMERICA -
CORPORATE LIBRARY □ Pittsburgh, PA
Furlong, Robert E., Lib.Group Supv.
AT & T BELL LABORATORIES - LIBRARY □
Naperville, IL
Furlow, Karen L., Corp.Libn.
MC DERMOTT INC. - CORPORATE
INFORMATION CENTER □ New Orleans, LA
Furman, Holly J., Corp.Lib.Adm.
TEXACO INC. - CORPORATE LIBRARY □ White
Plains, NY
Furman, Jean, Tech.Info.Spec.
ALLIED CORPORATION - LIBRARY &
INFORMATION SERVICES □ Morristown, NJ
Furnish, Jean, Ref.Libn.
UNIVERSITY OF CALIFORNIA - LOS ALAMOS
NATIONAL LABORATORY - LIBRARY □ Los
Alamos, NM
Furnstahl, Sr. Mary Leone, Media Cons.
DIOCESE OF ST. CLOUD - BUREAU OF
EDUCATION - MEDIA CENTER □ St. Cloud, MN
Furst, Kenneth W., Libn.
SUNY AT STONY BROOK - ENGINEERING
LIBRARY □ Stony Brook, NY
Furtak, Rosemary, Dir.
WALKER ART CENTER - STAFF REFERENCE
LIBRARY □ Minneapolis, MN
Fusco, Betsy, Libn.
LOURDES HOSPITAL - HEALTH SCIENCES
LIBRARY □ Paducah, KY
Fusco, Margaret, Mss.Spec./Adm.Asst.
UNIVERSITY OF CHICAGO - SPECIAL
COLLECTIONS □ Chicago, IL
Fuscoe, James C., Chf.Libn.
ROHR INDUSTRIES - CORPORATE LIBRARY □
Chula Vista, CA
Futrell, Gene, Curric.Lab.Libn.
EAST TEXAS BAPTIST UNIVERSITY - MAMYE
JARRETT LEARNING CENTER □ Marshall, TX
Futrell, Iva M., Libn.
ENVIRONMENTAL LAW INSTITUTE - LIBRARY □
Washington, DC

G

Gaar, Marcella C., Info.Off.
WASHINGTON MUTUAL SAVINGS BANK -
INFORMATION CENTER & DIETRICH SCHMITZ
MEMORIAL LIBRARY □ Seattle, WA
Gabarry, Suzanne A., Libn.
MERCY HOSPITAL - MEDICAL STAFF LIBRARY†
□ Pittsburgh, PA
Gabbert, Gretchen W., Libn.
JACK G. RAUB COMPANY - LIBRARY □ Mission
Viejo, CA
Gabbert, Roy E., Libn.
ADAMS COUNTY LAW LIBRARY □ West Union,
OH

Gabel, E. Margaret
ELIZABETHTOWN COLLEGE - ZUG MEMORIAL
LIBRARY - ARCHIVES □ Elizabethtown, PA
Gable, June R., Tech.Lib.Br.Hd.
U.S. NAVY - STRATEGIC SYSTEMS PROJECT
OFFICE - TECHNICAL LIBRARY □ Washington,
DC
Gable, Sarah, Ref.Libn.
UNIVERSITY OF SOUTH CAROLINA - SCHOOL
OF MEDICINE LIBRARY □ Columbia, SC
Gabor, Barbara, Pub.Serv.Libn.
O'MELVENY AND MYERS - INFORMATION
SERVICES □ Los Angeles, CA
Gabriel, Andrea, Cat.Libn.
U.S. FOREST SERV. - PACIFIC SOUTHWEST
FOREST & RANGE EXPERIMENT STA. -
WESTFORNET-BERKELEY SERV.CTR. □
Berkeley, CA
Gabriel, Jennifer, Libn.
RECONSTRUCTIONIST RABBINICAL COLLEGE -
MORDECAI M. KAPLAN LIBRARY □ Wyncote, PA
Gabriel, Linda, Supv.
LOCKHEED ELECTRONICS COMPANY, INC. -
TECHNICAL INFORMATION CENTER □ Plainfield,
NJ
Gaddis, Jane L., Libn.
LORD, BISSELL AND BROOK - LAW LIBRARY □
Chicago, IL
Gadke, Candy L., Libn.
PENNZOIL COMPANY - DUVAL RESEARCH &
DEVELOPMENT LIBRARY □ Tucson, AZ
Gadola, Ruth, Libn.
DAIN BOSWORTH, INC. - LIBRARY □
Minneapolis, MN
Gadsden, Alice H., Med.Libn.
U.S. ARMY HOSPITALS - WALSON ARMY
HOSPITAL - MEDICAL LIBRARY □ Ft. Dix, NJ
Gadula, Marie, Supv., Info.Serv.
MC KINSEY & COMPANY, INC. - INFORMATION
CENTRE □ Toronto, ON
Gadzikowski, Claire E., Spec.Proj.Coord., MCRMLP
UNIVERSITY OF NEBRASKA MEDICAL CENTER -
MC GOOGAN LIBRARY OF MEDICINE □ Omaha,
NE
Gaeddert, Kathryn, Cur.
SACRAMENTO - MUSEUM AND HISTORY
DIVISION - LIBRARY □ Sacramento, CA
Gaertner, Courtney
MARSH AND MC LENNAN, INC. - INFORMATION
CENTER □ New York, NY
Gaetano, Darlene, Tech.Serv.
UNIVERSITY OF KANSAS MEDICAL CTR. -
COLLEGE OF HEALTH SCI. AND HOSPITAL -
ARCHIE R. DYKES LIB. OF THE HEALTH SCI. □
Kansas City, KS
Gaffey, Debra, Asst.Libn.
NATIONAL ECONOMIC RESEARCH
ASSOCIATES, INC. - LIBRARY □ White Plains,
NY
Gaffney, Thomas, Cur.
MAINE HISTORICAL SOCIETY - LIBRARY □
Portland, ME
Gafvert, Jane M., Info.Spec.
U.S. FEDERAL JUDICIAL CENTER -
INFORMATION SERVICE† □ Washington, DC
Gage, Dr. J. Fred, Dir.
UNIVERSITY OF PITTSBURGH - UNIVERSITY
CENTER FOR INSTRUCTIONAL RESOURCES □
Pittsburgh, PA
Gage, Kathleen Rosso, Legal Asst.Adm.
FITZGERALD, ABBOTT AND BEARDSLEY - LAW
LIBRARY □ Oakland, CA
Gage, Sandra V., Hd.
FAIRLEIGH DICKINSON UNIVERSITY - WEINER
LIBRARY - REFERENCE/GOVERNMENT
DOCUMENTS DEPARTMENT □ Teaneck, NJ
Gagen, Cynthia, Info.Spec.
TOWERS, PERRIN, FORSTER & CROSBY, INC. -
INFORMATION CENTER □ New York, NY
Gagliardi, Mr. Francis J., Assoc.Dir.
CENTRAL CONNECTICUT STATE UNIVERSITY -
ELIHU BURRITT LIBRARY □ New Britain, CT

Gagne, Joan, Educ.Libn.
MC GILL UNIVERSITY - EDUCATION LIBRARY □
Montreal, PQ
Gagne, Joan, Educ.Libn.
MC GILL UNIVERSITY - EDUCATION LIBRARY -
SAM RABINOVITCH MEMORIAL COLLECTION □
Montreal, PQ
Gagne, Mireille, Regional Dir.
CANADIAN MUSIC CENTRE - LIBRARY □
Montreal, PQ
Gagner, Ron
IBM CORPORATION - GENERAL TECHNOLOGY
DIVISION - INFORMATION CENTER/LEARNING
CENTER □ Essex Junction, VT
Gagnier, Ginette, Libn.
UNIVERSITE DE MONTREAL -
AUDIOVIDEOTHEQUE □ Montreal, PQ
Gagnon, Claude, Hd., Music Serv.
CANADIAN BROADCASTING CORPORATION -
MUSIC SERVICES LIBRARY □ Montreal, PQ
Gagnon, Claudine, Coord.
SOLEIL LIMITEE - CENTRE DE
DOCUMENTATION □ Quebec, PQ
Gagnon, Mr. R., Chf.Libn.
CANADA - PUBLIC WORKS CANADA -
INFORMATION, RESEARCH & LIBRARY
SERVICES □ Ottawa, ON
Gagnon, Richard, Libn.
AMERICAN-CANADIAN GENEALOGICAL
SOCIETY - LIBRARY □ Manchester, NH
Gagnon, Vernon N., Libn.
BOISE CASCADE CORPORATION - PULP &
PAPER RESEARCH LIBRARY □ Vancouver, WA
Gaines, James E., Hd.Libn.
VIRGINIA MILITARY INSTITUTE - PRESTON
LIBRARY □ Lexington, VA
Gaines, Paul G., Proj.Dir.
NATIONAL CLEARING HOUSE OF
REHABILITATION TRAINING MATERIALS -
REFERENCE COLLECTION □ Stillwater, OK
Gaines, Willene J., Chf., Tech.Serv.
U.S. DEPT. OF COMMERCE - LIBRARY □
Washington, DC
Gaines, William C., Pub.Serv.Libn.
PARKLAND COLLEGE - LEARNING RESOURCE
CENTER □ Champaign, IL
Gaiser, Robert, Plan.
NASSAU COUNTY PLANNING COMMISSION -
LIBRARY □ Mineola, NY
Gaiser, Rosemary, Hd.
PUBLIC LIBRARY OF CINCINNATI AND
HAMILTON COUNTY - SCIENCE AND
TECHNOLOGY DEPARTMENT □ Cincinnati, OH
Galante, Evelyn, Asst.Libn.
NEW YORK STATE LIBRARY FOR THE BLIND
AND VISUALLY HANDICAPPED □ Albany, NY
Galarneau, Pierrette, Med.Libn.
HOPITAL JEAN-TALON - BIBLIOTHEQUE
MEDICALE □ Montreal, PQ
Galban, Victoria S., Asst.Cur., Res.
METROPOLITAN MUSEUM OF ART - ROBERT
LEHMAN COLLECTION - LIBRARY □ New York,
NY
Galbraith, Jeanne, Circ.Libn.
SUNY AT STONY BROOK - HEALTH SCIENCES
LIBRARY □ East Setauket, NY
Galbraith, Mr. Leslie R., Libn.
CHRISTIAN THEOLOGICAL SEMINARY -
LIBRARY □ Indianapolis, IN
Galbraith, Marc, Dir., Ref.
KANSAS STATE LIBRARY □ Topeka, KS
Galbraith, Paula, Online Serv., TALON
UNIVERSITY OF TEXAS HEALTH SCIENCE
CENTER, DALLAS - LIBRARY □ Dallas, TX
Gale, Margaret J., Libn.
BRITISH INFORMATION SERVICES - LIBRARY □
New York, NY
Gale, Virginia, Lib.Techn.
ST. JOSEPH HOSPITAL - HEALTH SCIENCE
LIBRARY □ Joliet, IL
Galganski, Carol, Med.Libn.
MC KENNAN HOSPITAL - MEDICAL LIBRARY □
Sioux Falls, SD

Galipault, John B., Pres.
AVIATION SAFETY INSTITUTE - ASI TECHNICAL LABS. - LIBRARY □ Worthington, OH

Galkowski, Patricia, Phys.Sci.Ref.Libn.
BROWN UNIVERSITY - SCIENCES LIBRARY □ Providence, RI

Gall, Dr. Einar
ROCKEFELLER UNIVERSITY - NEUROSCIENCES RESEARCH PROGRAM - LIBRARY □ New York, NY

Gallagher, Sr. Annette, Ref.
MARYCREST COLLEGE - CONE LIBRARY □ Davenport, IA

Gallagher, Barbara A., Hd., Lib.Serv.
AMERICAN CHEMICAL SOCIETY, INC. - LIBRARY □ Washington, DC

Gallagher, Brian
IBM CORPORATION - GENERAL TECHNOLOGY DIVISION - INFORMATION CENTER/LEARNING CENTER □ Essex Junction, VT

Gallagher, Charles F., Supv.Libn.
U.S. NAVY - NAVAL ORDNANCE STATION - TECHNICAL LIBRARY (5246) □ Indian Head, MD

Gallagher, Connell, Mss.
UNIVERSITY OF VERMONT - WILBUR COLLECTION OF VERMONTIANA □ Burlington, VT

Gallagher, Eileen W., Libn.
ALLEGHENY LUDLUM STEEL CORPORATION - RESEARCH CENTER TECHNICAL LIBRARY □ Brackenridge, PA

Gallagher, J.W., Mgr.
UNIVERSITY OF COLORADO, BOULDER - JOINT INSTITUTE FOR LABORATORY ASTROPHYSICS - DATA CENTER □ Boulder, CO

Gallagher, Jeanne, Libn.
UNION OIL COMPANY OF CALIFORNIA - LIBRARY-FILE ROOM □ Ventura, CA

Gallagher, Philip J., Libn.
JOHNSON (Robert Wood) FOUNDATION - LIBRARY □ Princeton, NJ

Gallagher, William T., Mgr.
IBM CORPORATION - RESEARCH LIBRARY □ San Jose, CA

Gallant, Jung, Dir.
ST. JOHN AND WEST SHORE HOSPITAL - MEDIA CENTER □ Westlake, OH

Gallaway, Rae, Dir. of Res.
LEAGUE FOR INTERNATIONAL FOOD EDUCATION - LIBRARY □ Washington, DC

Gallery, Christine, Res.Assoc.
KAMAN-TEMPO - METAL MATRIX COMPOSITES INFORMATION ANALYSIS CENTER □ Santa Barbara, CA

Galli, Marilyn, Res.Lib.Adm.
BROOKHAVEN NATIONAL LABORATORY - TECHNICAL INFORMATION DIVISION □ Upton, NY

Gallicchio, Virginia, Mgr.
GOODRICH (B.F.) COMPANY - AKRON INFORMATION CENTER □ Akron, OH

Galligan, John, Municipal Prog.Spec.
NEW YORK STATE CONFERENCE OF MAYORS AND MUNICIPAL OFFICIALS - LIBRARY □ Albany, NY

Galligan, Regina M., Asst.V.P./Mgr.
FIRST BOSTON CORPORATION - INFORMATION CENTER □ New York, NY

Galligan, Sara, Info.Rsrc.Spec.
MINNESOTA STATE DEPARTMENT OF TRANSPORTATION - LIBRARY AND INFORMATION SERVICES SECTION □ St. Paul, MN

Gallimore, C.R., Chf., Lib.Serv.
U.S. VETERANS ADMINISTRATION (CA-Palo Alto) - MEDICAL CENTER - MEDICAL LIBRARIES □ Palo Alto, CA

Gallimore, Howard, Supv.
DARGAN-CARVER LIBRARY □ Nashville, TN

Gallivan, Barbara A., Libn.
UNIVERSITY OF TORONTO - FACULTY OF PHARMACY - R.O. HURST LIBRARY □ Toronto, ON

Gallivan, Donna M., Dir., Med.Rec.Dept.
GRACE MATERNITY HOSPITAL - MEDICAL LIBRARY □ Halifax, NS

Gallo, Bela, Dir.
STANFORD UNIVERSITY - J. HUGH JACKSON LIBRARY □ Stanford, CA

Gallo, Gary R., Dir.
UNIVERSITY OF MINNESOTA - DRUG INFORMATION SERVICES □ Minneapolis, MN

Galloway, Delfina C., Chf.Libn.
U.S. ARMY AIR DEFENSE SCHOOL - LIBRARY† □ Ft. Bliss, TX

Galloway, Elizabeth, Lib.Dir.
ART CENTER COLLEGE OF DESIGN - JAMES LEMONT FOGG MEMORIAL LIBRARY □ Pasadena, CA

Galloway, Randy J., Info.Rsrcs.Mgr.
ARGOSYSTEMS - INC. - TECHNICAL LIBRARY† □ Sunnyvale, CA

Galloway, Sue, Children's Cons.
OKLAHOMA STATE DEPARTMENT OF LIBRARIES □ Oklahoma City, OK

Gallup, Jane, Libn.
GOLEMBE ASSOCIATES - LIBRARY □ Washington, DC

Galneder, Mary, Map Libn.
UNIVERSITY OF WISCONSIN, MADISON - CARTOGRAPHIC LABORATORY - ARTHUR H. ROBINSON MAP LIBRARY □ Madison, WI

Galpern, Nina F., Libn.
METROPOLITAN HOSPITAL - PARKVIEW DIVISION - MEDICAL LIBRARY □ Philadelphia, PA

Galt, Alfreda S., Sec.
LIFWYNN FOUNDATION, INC. - LIBRARY □ Westport, CT

Galt, Judith A., Mktg.Res.Info.Spec.
GENERAL MILLS, INC. - MARKETING RESEARCH INFORMATION CENTER □ Minneapolis, MN

Galvez, Joan, Libn.
ALAMEDA COUNTY LIBRARY - BUSINESS & GOVERNMENT LIBRARY □ Oakland, CA

Galvin, Dennis, Supv., Serv.Ctr.
U.S. FOREST SERV. - PACIFIC SOUTHWEST FOREST & RANGE EXPERIMENT STA. - WESTFORNET-BERKELEY SERV.CTR. □ Berkeley, CA

Galvin, Joyce, Ser.Supv.
FRANKLIN PIERCE LAW CENTER - LIBRARY □ Concord, NH

Galyon, Betty S., Libn.
WASHINGTON UNIVERSITY - BIOLOGY LIBRARY □ St. Louis, MO

Gamache, Rose Ann, Libn.
ENVIRONMENTAL PROTECTION AGENCY - ENVIRONMENTAL RESEARCH LABORATORY, NARRAGANSETT - LIBRARY† □ Narragansett, RI

Gamache, Virginia M., Lib.Asst.
KRAUSE MILLING COMPANY - TECHNICAL LIBRARY □ Milwaukee, WI

Gamaluddin, Connie, Ref.Libn.
CLARION UNIVERSITY OF PENNSYLVANIA - RENA M. CARLSON LIBRARY □ Clarion, PA

Gambini, Ellen
BRONSON (Silas) LIBRARY - BUSINESS, INDUSTRY, AND TECHNOLOGY DEPARTMENT† □ Waterbury, CT

Gamble, Mary, Steinbeck Libn.
SALINAS PUBLIC LIBRARY - JOHN STEINBECK LIBRARY □ Salinas, CA

Gamble, Robert, Univ.Archv.
UNIVERSITY OF TEXAS, ARLINGTON - LIBRARY - DIVISION OF SPECIAL COLLECTIONS AND ARCHIVES □ Arlington, TX

Gamboa, Dr. Carlos A., Chf.
PAN AMERICAN HEALTH ORGANIZATION - BIBLIOGRAPHIC INFORMATION OFFICE† □ Washington, DC

Gambrell, Drucilla, Ref.Libn.
TENNESSEE VALLEY AUTHORITY - TECHNICAL LIBRARY □ Muscle Shoals, AL

Gamer, Mary Lim, Dir.
KANSAS CITY ART INSTITUTE - LIBRARY □ Kansas City, MO

Gamiero, Helena, Ref.Libn.
CONCORDIA UNIVERSITY - LOYOLA CAMPUS - GEORGES P. VANIER LIBRARY □ Montreal, PQ

Gammon, Donald B., Area Coord. Atlantic
CANADA - AGRICULTURE CANADA - RESEARCH STATION, FREDERICTON - LIBRARY □ Fredericton, NB

Ganahl, Nancy, Bureau Libn.
NEWSWEEK, INC. - WASHINGTON BUREAU LIBRARY □ Washington, DC

Ganas, Irene, Tech.Info.Serv.Mgr.
THERMARK CORPORATION - TECHNICAL INFORMATION SERVICES† □ Schererville, IN

Gandee, Rose M., Asst.Libn.
AMERICAN PUBLIC TRANSIT ASSOCIATION - APTA INFORMATION CENTER □ Washington, DC

Gandy, Dollie, Libn.
MEMPHIS COMMERCIAL APPEAL - LIBRARY □ Memphis, TN

Ganem, Debbie A., Libn.
DU PONT DE NEMOURS (E.I.) & COMPANY, INC. - VICTORIA PLANT LIBRARY □ Victoria, TX

Gangadharan, Geetha, Libn.
GREAT-WEST LIFE ASSURANCE COMPANY - CORPORATE LIBRARY □ Denver, CO

Gangl, Susan, Psych./Lib.Sci.Bibliog.
UNIVERSITY OF MINNESOTA - EDUCATION-PSYCHOLOGY-LIBRARY SCIENCE COLLECTION □ Minneapolis, MN

Gangle, Susan, Libn.
UNIVERSITY OF MINNESOTA - LEARNING RESOURCES CENTER - NON-PRINT LIBRARY □ Minneapolis, MN

Ganguli, Mrs. Partha, Math/Natural Sci.Libn.
INSTITUTE FOR ADVANCED STUDY - LIBRARIES □ Princeton, NJ

Ganley, John V., Hd., Pub.Serv.Sect.
NEW YORK PUBLIC LIBRARY - ECONOMIC AND PUBLIC AFFAIRS DIVISION □ New York, NY

Gann, Daniel, Div.Hd.
INDIANAPOLIS-MARION COUNTY PUBLIC LIBRARY - ARTS DIVISION □ Indianapolis, IN

Gannaway, Paula, Assoc.Dir./Ref.Libn.
LUBBOCK CHRISTIAN COLLEGE - MOODY LIBRARY □ Lubbock, TX

Gannon, Barbara, Ref.
ST. ANSELM'S COLLEGE - GEISEL LIBRARY □ Manchester, NH

Gannon, Carol, Libn.
CHESEBROUGH-POND'S, INC. - RESEARCH LIBRARY □ Trumbull, CT

Gano, Richard, Dir., Exhibits
WRATHER PORT PROPERTIES, LTD. - ARCHIVES AND RESOURCE CENTER □ Long Beach, CA

Gans, Liz, Cat.
DIGITAL EQUIPMENT CORPORATION - MAYNARD AREA INFORMATION SERVICES □ Maynard, MA

Gant, Thomasine C., Coord., Instr.Serv.
GUILFORD TECHNICAL COMMUNITY COLLEGE - LEARNING RESOURCE CENTER □ Jamestown, NC

Gantman, Howard, Acq.
HUGHES AIRCRAFT COMPANY - ELECTRO-OPTICAL & DATA SYSTEMS GROUP - TECHNICAL LIBRARY □ El Segundo, CA

Gantner, Doris, Code
MILWAUKEE - LEGISLATIVE REFERENCE BUREAU - LEGISLATIVE LIBRARY □ Milwaukee, WI

Gantt, Marlene, Libn.
(Moline) DAILY DISPATCH - LIBRARY □ Moline, IL

Gantt, Mary Jane, Info.Sci.
AMERICAN TYPE CULTURE COLLECTION - DONOVICK LIBRARY □ Rockville, MD

Gantz, Joan, Libn.
CARNEGIE INSTITUTION OF WASHINGTON - MOUNT WILSON & LAS CAMPANAS OBSERVATORIES - LIBRARY □ Pasadena, CA

Ganyard, Margaret, Libn.
ST. LOUIS PUBLIC LIBRARY - READERS SERVICES/DOCUMENTS DEPARTMENT □ St. Louis, MO

Gapin, Michael, Prog.Dir.
HERKIMER-ONEIDA COUNTIES COMPREHENSIVE PLANNING PROGRAM - LIBRARY □ Utica, NY

Garafola, Gerald A., Law Libn.
SETON HALL UNIVERSITY - SCHOOL OF LAW - LAW LIBRARY □ Newark, NJ

Garbade, Ernie, Info.Libn.
MONARCH MARKING SYSTEMS - TECHNICAL LIBRARY □ Miamisburg, OH

Garbarino, Mary, Libn.
AMPEX CORPORATION - TECHNICAL INFORMATION SERVICES □ Redwood City, CA

Garber, Kim M., Libn.
HERMAN SMITH (Herman) ASSOCIATES - LIBRARY □ Hinsdale, IL

Garber, Sandra Ducoff, Slide Cur.
UNIVERSITY OF CALIFORNIA, LOS ANGELES - ART DEPARTMENT - VISUAL RESOURCE COLLECTION & SERVICES □ Los Angeles, CA

Garber, Shirley, Med.Libn.
NORTH DETROIT GENERAL HOSPITAL - MEDICAL LIBRARY □ Detroit, MI

Garcia, Ceil, Info.Spec.
GAF CORPORATION - TECHNICAL INFORMATION SERVICES† □ Wayne, NJ

Garcia, Lana Caswell, Law Libn./Res.Spec.
EAST TEXAS LEGAL SERVICES - LIBRARY □ Beaumont, TX

Garcia, Laura C., Pub.Serv.Coord.
UNIVERSITY OF PUERTO RICO - HUMACAO UNIVERSITY COLLEGE - LIBRARY □ Humacao, PR

Garcia, Maritza, Ser.Libn.
UNIVERSITY OF PUERTO RICO - MEDICAL SCIENCES CAMPUS - LIBRARY □ Rio Piedras, PR

Garcia-Ayvens, Francisco, Coord.
UNIVERSITY OF CALIFORNIA, BERKELEY - CHICANO STUDIES LIBRARY† □ Berkeley, CA

Garcia-Godoy, Dr. Christian, Pres.
SAN MARTIN SOCIETY OF WASHINGTON, DC - INFORMATION CENTER □ McLean, VA

Gard, Lynn Yeomans, Libn.
UNIVERSITY OF TENNESSEE - MEMORIAL RESEARCH CENTER AND HOSPITAL - PRESTON MEDICAL LIBRARY □ Knoxville, TN

Gardewing, Rosemary H., Lib.Asst.
NLO, INC. - LIBRARY □ Cincinnati, OH

Gardiner, Elizabeth, Bibliog.
SYRACUSE UNIVERSITY - E.S. BIRD LIBRARY - HUMANITIES DEPARTMENT □ Syracuse, NY

Gardiner, Sr. M. Angelus, Libn.
ST. ANTHONY'S MEMORIAL HOSPITAL - HEALTH SCIENCE LIBRARY □ Effingham, IL

Gardinier, Holly, Music Libn.
MANSFIELD UNIVERSITY - BUTLER CENTER LIBRARY □ Mansfield, PA

Gardiser, Kathleen E., Libn.
CROCKER NATIONAL BANK - LIBRARY □ San Francisco, CA

Gardner, A.E., Libn.
GRAPHIC COMMUNICATIONS WORLD/ TECHNICAL INFORMATION, INC. - LIBRARY □ Tallahassee, FL

Gardner, E. Helen, Libn.
FIRST CHURCH IN ALBANY (Reformed) - LIBRARY □ Albany, NY

Gardner, Fred, Hd., Pub.Serv.
CALIFORNIA INSTITUTE OF THE ARTS - LIBRARY □ Valencia, CA

Gardner, Hugh, Trng.Rep.
GEORGIA POWER COMPANY - LIBRARY SERVICES □ Atlanta, GA

Gardner, Jane, Field Serv.Libn./Ch.
SOUTH CAROLINA STATE LIBRARY □ Columbia, SC

Gardner, Margaret, Bus.Info.Spec.
BAXTER TRAVENOL LABORATORIES, INC. - BUSINESS AND LAW INFORMATION RESOURCE CENTER □ Deerfield, IL

Gardner, Phillip
CUSTER COUNTY HISTORICAL SOCIETY - LIBRARY □ Broken Bow, NE

Gardner, Robert, College Historian
SHORTER COLLEGE - MEMORABILIA ROOM □ Rome, GA

Gardner, Roberta J., Dir., Info.Serv.
HODES (Bernard) ADVERTISING - INFORMATION CENTER □ New York, NY

Gardner, Timothy J., Horticulturist
KINGWOOD CENTER - LIBRARY □ Mansfield, OH

Gardner, Trudy L., Asst.Dir., Info.Serv.
RUSH-PRESBYTERIAN-ST. LUKE'S MEDICAL CENTER - LIBRARY OF RUSH UNIVERSITY □ Chicago, IL

Gardner, William M., Dir. of Libs.
MARQUETTE UNIVERSITY - MEMORIAL LIBRARY □ Milwaukee, WI

Gardner-Flint, Judy, Sr. Rare Bk.Cat.
JOHNS HOPKINS UNIVERSITY - MILTON S. EISENHOWER LIBRARY - SPECIAL COLLECTIONS DIVISION □ Baltimore, MD

Gardos, Susan Jo, Libn.
HARVARD UNIVERSITY - RUSSIAN RESEARCH CENTER - LIBRARY □ Cambridge, MA

Gardy, Thais, Libn.
PENNSYLVANIA PUBLIC UTILITY COMMISSION - LIBRARY □ Harrisburg, PA

Gareau, Andre
INSTITUT D'HISTOIRE DE L'AMERIQUE FRANCAISE (1970) - RESEARCH CENTRE LIBRARY □ Montreal, PQ

Garfin, Molly, Mgr., Lib.
MC ADAMS, WILLIAM DOUGLAS, INC. - MEDICAL LIBRARY □ New York, NY

Garganta, Narciso M., Dir., Med.Lib.
BURBANK COMMUNITY HOSPITAL - MEDICAL LIBRARY □ Burbank, CA

Gargotta, Dr. Maria A., Hd.Libn.
ITALIAN CULTURAL INSTITUTE - LIBRARY □ New York, NY

Gargour, Nadia, Adm.Dir.
CANADIAN PSYCHOANALYTIC SOCIETY - LIBRARY □ Montreal, PQ

Garland, Robert R., Hd.Libn.
CASE WESTERN RESERVE UNIVERSITY - SEARS LIBRARY □ Cleveland, OH

Garlow, Vicki, Info.Spec.
SYNTEX, U.S.A. - CORPORATE LIBRARY/ INFORMATION SERVICES □ Palo Alto, CA

Garm, Mary O., Libn.
SUSQUEHANNA COUNTY HISTORICAL SOCIETY AND FREE LIBRARY ASSOCIATION □ Montrose, PA

Garmany, Mary C., Dir.
ORLANDO REGIONAL MEDICAL CENTER - MEDICAL LIBRARY □ Orlando, FL

Garn, Nancy W., Dir.
UNIVERSITY OF HEALTH SCIENCES/CHICAGO MEDICAL SCHOOL - LIBRARY □ North Chicago, IL

Garneau, E.H.P., Exec.Sec.
ROYAL SOCIETY OF CANADA - LIBRARY □ Ottawa, ON

Garneau, Francine, Bibliothecaire
CENTRE HOSPITALIER REGIONAL DE LANAUDIERE - BIBLIOTHEQUE MEDICALE □ Joliette, PQ

Garneau, Patricia, Libn.
EDMONTON JOURNAL - LIBRARY □ Edmonton, AB

Garner, Eleanor, Act.Libn.
SIMCOE COUNTY LAW ASSOCIATION - LIBRARY† □ Barrie, ON

Garner, Holly W., Mgr., Info.Serv.
WILLIAM M. MERCER, INC. - LIBRARY/ INFORMATION CENTER □ Boston, MA

Garner, Jane, Archv.
UNIVERSITY OF TEXAS, AUSTIN - BENSON LATIN AMERICAN COLLECTION □ Austin, TX

Garner, Sherril, Libn.
METHODIST MEDICAL CENTER - SCHOOL OF NURSING LIBRARY □ St. Joseph, MO

Garnett, Ms. C.R., Libn.
CANADA - FISHERIES & OCEANS - BIOLOGICAL STATION LIBRARY □ St. Andrews, NB

Garnham, David, Coord.
UNIVERSITY OF WISCONSIN, MILWAUKEE - INSTITUTE OF WORLD AFFAIRS - RESOURCE CENTER □ Milwaukee, WI

Garnier, Fay, Asst.
REORGANIZED CHURCH OF JESUS CHRIST OF LATTER DAY SAINTS - SERVICES TO THE BLIND □ Independence, MO

Garon, Agathe, Chf., Circ.
UNIVERSITE LAVAL - BIBLIOTHEQUE □ Ste. Foy, PQ

Garrell, Lillian B., Law Libn.
U.S. DISTRICT COURT - EASTERN DISTRICT OF NEW YORK - LIBRARY □ Brooklyn, NY

Garren, Alice K., Libn.
GRACEWOOD STATE SCHOOL AND HOSPITAL - LIBRARY† □ Gracewood, GA

Garrett, Carolyn A., Cat.Libn.
U.S. ARMY POST - PRESIDIO OF SAN FRANCISCO - POST LIBRARY SYSTEM □ Presidio of San Francisco, CA

Garrett, D.Janean, Hd., Tech.Serv.Br.
U.S. NAVY - NAVAL INTELLIGENCE SUPPORT CENTER - INFORMATION SERVICES DIVISION □ Washington, DC

Garrett, Dean R., Chf.
U.S. NATL. PARK SERVICE - ALLEGHENY PORTAGE RAILROAD NATL. HISTORIC SITE - LIBRARY □ Cresson, PA

Garrett, Laura, Libn.
STATE FARM MUTUAL AUTOMOBILE INSURANCE COMPANY - LAW LIBRARY □ Bloomington, IL

Garrett, Lynda, Libn.
U.S. FISH & WILDLIFE SERVICE - PATUXENT WILDLIFE RESEARCH CENTER LIBRARY □ Laurel, MD

Garrett, Myrta, Ser.Libn.
SOUTHWESTERN BAPTIST THEOLOGICAL SEMINARY - A. WEBB ROBERTS LIBRARY □ Fort Worth, TX

Garrett, Paul D., Libn.
ST. VLADIMIR'S ORTHODOX THEOLOGICAL SEMINARY - FR. GEORGES FLOROVSKY LIBRARY □ Tuckahoe, NY

Garrett, Rose J., Libn.
BRYAN, CAVE, MC PHEETERS & MC ROBERTS - LIBRARY† □ St. Louis, MO

Garrett, Sarah A., Unit Supv.
GULF OIL CORPORATION - EXPLORATION AND PRODUCTION COMPANY - INFORMATION CENTER □ Casper, WY

Garrett-Packer, Joan, Ref.Libn.
CENTRAL CONNECTICUT STATE UNIVERSITY - ELIHU BURRITT LIBRARY □ New Britain, CT

Garrigan, Margaret
ONGWANADA HOSPITAL - PENROSE & HOPKINS DIVISIONS - PENROSE DIVISION LIBRARY† □ Kingston, ON

Garrison, Betty L., Libn.
MAASS (Clara) MEDICAL CENTER - DOCTORS' LIBRARY† □ Belleville, NJ

Garrison, Betty L., Dir., Med.Lib.
ST. MICHAEL MEDICAL CENTER - AQUINAS MEDICAL LIBRARY □ Newark, NJ

Garrison, Dr. Ellen, Dir.
EAST TENNESSEE STATE UNIVERSITY - ARCHIVES OF APPALACHIA □ Johnson City, TN

Garrison, Jeanne, Health Sci.Libn.
BRIDGETON HOSPITAL - HEALTH SCIENCES LIBRARY □ Bridgeton, NJ

Garry, Diana Lim, Libn.
NATIVE AMERICAN RIGHTS FUND - NATIONAL INDIAN LAW LIBRARY □ Boulder, CO

Garside, Barbara, Med.Libn.
ST. JUDE HOSPITAL & REHABILITATION CENTER - MEDICAL LIBRARY □ Fullerton, CA

Gartland, Joan, Cur., Print
HENRY FORD MUSEUM AND GREENFIELD VILLAGE - ARCHIVES & RESEARCH LIBRARY □ Dearborn, MI

Gartrell, Ellen G., Asst.Cur., Rd.Serv.
DUKE UNIVERSITY - MANUSCRIPT DEPARTMENT □ Durham, NC

Garvey, Eleanor M., Cur., Printing
HARVARD UNIVERSITY - HOUGHTON LIBRARY □ Cambridge, MA

Garvey, Helen, Libn.
CRESAP, MC CORMICK, AND PAGET, INC. - LIBRARY† □ New York, NY

Garvey, Jeffrey M., Libn.
MERCY HOSPITAL OF WATERTOWN - HEALTH SCIENCE LIBRARY □ Watertown, NY

Garvey, Nancy G., Libn.
AUTOMATIC SWITCH COMPANY - ASCO LIBRARY† □ Florham Park, NJ

Garvin, David, Mgr.
U.S. NATL. BUREAU OF STANDARDS - CHEMICAL THERMODYNAMICS DATA CENTER □ Washington, DC

Garvin, Virginia, Asst.Dir./Coll.Dev.
CLEVELAND HEALTH SCIENCES LIBRARY - HEALTH CENTER LIBRARY □ Cleveland, OH

Garwig, Paul, Mgr., Tech.Info.Serv.
FMC CORPORATION - CHEMICAL RESEARCH & DEVELOPMENT CENTER - TECHNICAL INFORMATION SERVICES □ Princeton, NJ

Garwood, Darrell D., Mss.Spec.
WESTERN HISTORICAL MANUSCRIPT COLLECTION/STATE HISTORICAL SOCIETY OF MISSOURI MANUSCRIPTS JOINT COLLECTION □ Columbia, MO

Gary, Carlotta, Sr. Orchestra Libn.
NEW YORK PUBLIC LIBRARY - GENERAL LIBRARY OF THE PERFORMING ARTS □ New York, NY

Garza, Lynne, Asst.Libn.
DETROIT INSTITUTE OF ARTS - RESEARCH LIBRARY □ Detroit, MI

Gasaway, Laura N., Dir.
UNIVERSITY OF OKLAHOMA - LAW LIBRARY □ Norman, OK

Gashus, Karin, Lib.Asst., Law Lib.
ESSO RESOURCES CANADA LIMITED - LIBRARY INFORMATION CENTRE □ Calgary, AB

Gaskin, Annette C., Libn.
DESIGN PROFESSIONALS FINANCIAL CORPORATION - LIBRARY† □ San Francisco, CA

Gaspar, N.J., Hd., Info.Serv.
ESSO PETROLEUM CANADA - RESEARCH TECHNICAL INFORMATION CENTRE □ Sarnia, ON

Gaspar, Mr. T.A.
BATTELLE-COLUMBUS LABORATORIES - RAPIDLY SOLIDIFIED MATERIALS (RaSoMat) - RESOURCE CENTER □ Columbus, OH

Gass, A. Beverley, Coord., Lib.Serv.
GUILFORD TECHNICAL COMMUNITY COLLEGE - LEARNING RESOURCE CENTER □ Jamestown, NC

Gasser, James R., Mgr., Doc.Ctr.
UNITED STATES RAILWAY ASSOCIATION - USRA DOCUMENT CENTER □ Washington, DC

Gast, Marie, Libn.
CORNELL UNIVERSITY - MAPS, MICROTEXTS, NEWSPAPERS DEPARTMENT □ Ithaca, NY

Gaston, Judith A., Dir.
UNIVERSITY OF MINNESOTA - AUDIO VISUAL LIBRARY SERVICE □ Minneapolis, MN

Gately, Charles F., Dir.
U.S. DEPT. OF HEALTH AND HUMAN SERVICES - DEPARTMENT LIBRARY† □ Washington, DC

Gately, Frank, Acq.Libn.
NOVA UNIVERSITY - LAW LIBRARY □ Fort Lauderdale, FL

Gates, Dione, Ref.Libn.
JOHNSON & SWANSON - LIBRARY □ Dallas, TX

Gates, Earl, Libn.
UNIVERSITY OF KANSAS - THOMAS GORTON MUSIC LIBRARY □ Lawrence, KS

Gates, Francis, Libn.
SEDGWICK, DETERT, MORAN & ARNOLD - LIBRARY AND INFORMATION CENTER □ San Francisco, CA

Gates, Harry
SOUTHERN OREGON STATE COLLEGE - LIBRARY □ Ashland, OR

Gates, James, Staff Libn.
UNIVERSITY OF NOTRE DAME - LAW SCHOOL LIBRARY □ Notre Dame, IN

Gates, Linda, Asst.Dir., Lib.Dev.
MISSISSIPPI STATE LIBRARY COMMISSION □ Jackson, MS

Gates, M. Jane, Hd.Libn.
STRYBING ARBORETUM SOCIETY - HELEN CROCKER RUSSELL LIBRARY† □ San Francisco, CA

Gates, Thomas, Hist.Spec.
CONTRA COSTA COUNTY - CENTRAL LIBRARY - LOCAL HISTORY COLLECTION □ Pleasant Hill, CA

Gatlin, Nancy, Dir.
SOUTHERN COLLEGE OF OPTOMETRY - WILLIAM P. MAC CRACKEN, JR. MEMORIAL LIBRARY □ Memphis, TN

Gatlin, Patricia F., Supv. of Lib.Serv.
UNION ELECTRIC COMPANY - LIBRARY □ St. Louis, MO

Gattinger, F. Eugene, Coord., Lib.Serv.
TORONTO BOARD OF EDUCATION - EDUCATION CENTRE LIBRARY □ Toronto, ON

Gattis, R. Guy, Asst.Libn.
UNIVERSITY OF MICHIGAN - TRANSPORTATION RESEARCH INSTITUTE - LIBRARY □ Ann Arbor, MI

Gatton, Frank D., Hd., Archival Serv.
NORTH CAROLINA STATE DEPT. OF CULTURAL RESOURCES - DIV. OF ARCHIVES AND HISTORY - ARCHIVES & RECORDS SECTION □ Raleigh, NC

Gattullo, Vincent, Dir.
STATEN ISLAND ZOOLOGICAL SOCIETY - LIBRARY □ Staten Island, NY

Gau, Rev. Wayne W., Abbot
THE CELTIC EVANGELICAL CHURCH - COMMUNITY OF ST. COLUMBA - LIBRARY □ Honolulu, HI

Gauch, M. Lois, Libn.
EASTMAN KODAK COMPANY - BUSINESS INFORMATION CENTER □ Rochester, NY

Gaucher, Elaine M., Libn.
U.S. NAVY - NAVAL SUBMARINE MEDICAL RESEARCH LABORATORY - MEDICAL LIBRARY □ Groton, CT

Gaucher, Monique, Libn.
UNIVERSITE DU QUEBEC A MONTREAL - BIBLIOTHEQUE DES SCIENCES DE L'EDUCATION □ Montreal, PQ

Gaudette, Micheline, Bibliotechnicienne
CENTRE DE SERVICES SOCIAUX DU MONTREAL METROPOLITAIN (CSSMM) - BIBLIOTHEQUE □ Montreal, PQ

Gaudette, Nancy, Worcester Coll.Libn.
WORCESTER PUBLIC LIBRARY - REFERENCE AND READER SERVICES □ Worcester, MA

Gause, Sharon, Libn.
UNIVERSITY OF COLORADO, BOULDER - AUDIOVISUAL/MICROFORMS DEPARTMENT □ Boulder, CO

Gauthier, Ghislaine, Info.Spec.
BELL-NORTHERN RESEARCH LTD. - TECHNICAL INFORMATION CENTRE □ Verdun, PQ

Gauthier, Roland, Dir.
ORATOIRE ST-JOSEPH - CENTRE DE DOCUMENTATION □ Montreal, PQ

Gavin, Christine B., Instr. Media Spec.
ARLINGTON DEVELOPMENTAL CENTER - PROFESSIONAL LIBRARY □ Arlington, TN

Gavin, William, Law Libn.
MASSACHUSETTS STATE DISTRICT COURT - FOURTH EASTERN MIDDLESEX COURT - LAW LIBRARY □ Woburn, MA

Gavora, Eva, Libn.
CANADA - AGRICULTURE CANADA - PLANT RESEARCH LIBRARY □ Ottawa, ON

Gay, Eva, Info.Serv.Spec.
U.S. BUREAU OF THE CENSUS - INFORMATION SERVICES PROGRAM - LOS ANGELES REGIONAL OFFICE - LIBRARY □ Los Angeles, CA

Gay, Ms. Zan, Libn.
UNIVERSITY OF MIAMI - LOWE ART MUSEUM LIBRARY □ Coral Gables, FL

Gaydos, Mary, Ref.Libn.
NEW YORK CITY HUMAN RESOURCES ADMINISTRATION - LIBRARY □ New York, NY

Gazillo, Mark J., Pharmacy Libn.
MASSACHUSETTS COLLEGE OF PHARMACY AND ALLIED HEALTH SCIENCES - LIBRARY □ Springfield, MA

Gazillo, Mark J., Asst.Libn.
MASSACHUSETTS COLLEGE OF PHARMACY & ALLIED HEALTH SCIENCES - SHEPPARD LIBRARY □ Boston, MA

Geahigan, Priscilla C., Asst.Libn.
PURDUE UNIVERSITY - MANAGEMENT AND ECONOMICS LIBRARY □ West Lafayette, IN

Gearhart, Clara, Supv., Tech.Proc.
SANDIA NATIONAL LABORATORIES - TECHNICAL LIBRARY □ Albuquerque, NM

Gearn, Helen VerNooy, Chm. of Lib.Comm.
HISTORICAL SOCIETY OF NEWBURGH BAY AND THE HIGHLANDS - LIBRARY □ Newburgh, NY

Geary, Carolyn, Sec.
INSURANCE INSTITUTE OF SOUTHERN ALBERTA - LIBRARY† □ Calgary, AB

Gebbie, A., Pres.
GEBBIE PRESS, INC. - HOUSE MAGAZINE LIBRARY □ New Paltz, NY

Gebhard, Mr. K.M., Hd., Sound Archv.
SASKATCHEWAN ARCHIVES BOARD □ Regina, SK

Gecas, Judith G., Dir.
DE PAUL UNIVERSITY - LAW SCHOOL LIBRARY □ Chicago, IL

Gecas, Judith G., Hd., Pub.Serv.
UNIVERSITY OF CHICAGO - LAW SCHOOL LIBRARY □ Chicago, IL

Geddert, Jacob, Tech.Serv.Libn.
PRAIRIE BIBLE INSTITUTE - LIBRARY □ Three Hills, AB

Geddes, C.L., Dir.
AMERICAN INSTITUTE OF ISLAMIC STUDIES - MUSLIM BIBLIOGRAPHIC CENTER □ Denver, CO

Geddes, Janice C., Dir. of Tourism
DELAWARE STATE TRAVEL SERVICE □ Dover, DE

Geddes, Marian, Asst.Libn.
SACRAMENTO COUNCIL FOR DELAYED PRESCHOOLERS - DAISY TOY LENDING LIBRARY □ Sacramento, CA

Geddes, Tom, Libn.
BAPTIST UNION OF WESTERN CANADA - BAPTIST LEADERSHIP TRAINING SCHOOL LIBRARY □ Calgary, AB

Gedeika, Danute Muraska, Libn.
U.S. VETERANS ADMINISTRATION (PA-Philadelphia) - MEDICAL CENTER LIBRARY □ Philadelphia, PA

Gee, Betty, Res.Ctr.Coord.
NEW YORK STATE DIVISION OF SUBSTANCE ABUSE SERVICES - BUREAU OF TRAINING & RESOURCE DEVELOPMENT - RESOURCE CENTER □ New York, NY

Gee, Carol, Cat.
EQUITABLE LIFE ASSURANCE SOCIETY OF THE U.S. - INFORMATION SERVICES DIVISION □ New York, NY

Gee, Sharon M., Mgr.
ALBERTA RESEARCH COUNCIL - LIBRARY
SERVICES □ Edmonton, AB

Geer, Beth, Assoc.Libn.
DIGITAL EQUIPMENT CORPORATION -
MERRIMACK LIBRARY SERVICES □ Merrimack,
NJ

Geering, Margaret B., Coord., Med. Staff Serv.
MONTICELLO MEDICAL CENTER - MEDICAL
STAFF LIBRARY □ Longview, WA

Geers, Elmer L., Libn.
CINCINNATI POST - LIBRARY □ Cincinnati, OH

Geesken, Terry, Stills Asst.
MUSEUM OF MODERN ART - FILM STUDY
CENTER □ New York, NY

Gegan, Kathryn M., Libn.
COMMUNITY HOSPITAL AT GLEN COVE -
MEDICAL LIBRARY □ Glen Cove, NY

Gegelys, Mary, Dir., Info.Ctr.
THOMPSON (J. Walter) COMPANY -
INFORMATION CENTER □ New York, NY

Gehani, Taro G., Acq.Libn.
UNIVERSITY OF THE DISTRICT OF COLUMBIA -
HARVARD STREET LIBRARY† □ Washington, DC

Gehres, Eleanor M., Mgr., Western Hist.Dept.
DENVER PUBLIC LIBRARY - SPECIAL
COLLECTIONS ROOM □ Denver, CO

Gehres, Eleanor M., Mgr.
DENVER PUBLIC LIBRARY - WESTERN HISTORY
DEPARTMENT □ Denver, CO

Gehring, Adrian, Lib.Techn.
TORONTO TRANSIT COMMISSION - HEAD
OFFICE LIBRARY† □ Toronto, ON

Geiger, Elizabeth, Info.Spec./Mkt.Res.
CORNING GLASS WORKS/CORNING MEDICAL &
SCIENTIFIC - DAVID R. STEINBERG
INFORMATION CENTER □ Medfield, MA

Geiger, Gene, Spec.Coll.Libn.
AUBURN UNIVERSITY - DEPARTMENT OF
SPECIAL COLLECTIONS □ Auburn, AL

Geiger, Kate, Law Libn.
BUTLER COUNTY LAW LIBRARY □ Butler, PA

Geiger, Richard, Lib.Mgr.
SAN JOSE MERCURY NEWS - LIBRARY □ San
Jose, CA

Geiger, Sharon J., Dir.
CARRIER FOUNDATION - NOLAN D.C. LEWIS
LIBRARY† □ Belle Mead, NJ

Geil, Jean, Assoc. Music Libn.
UNIVERSITY OF ILLINOIS - MUSIC LIBRARY □
Urbana, IL

Geiling, Carolyn S., Law Libn.
MONMOUTH COUNTY LAW LIBRARY □ Freehold,
NJ

Geiser, Cherie, Automation
KANSAS STATE UNIVERSITY - FARRELL
LIBRARY □ Manhattan, KS

Geiser, Marie, Hd. of Film Lib.
RADIO QUEBEC - CENTRE DES RESSOURCES
DOCUMENTAIRES □ Montreal, PQ

Geisler, Mary H., Adm.
HARRISONBURG-ROCKINGHAM HISTORICAL
SOCIETY AND MUSEUM - JOHN W. WAYLAND
LIBRARY □ Harrisonburg, VA

Geisser, Seymour, Dir.
UNIVERSITY OF MINNESOTA - STATISTICS
LIBRARY □ Minneapolis, MN

Geist, Janet, Libn.
INTERNORTH - LAW LIBRARY □ Omaha, NE

Geist, John G., Exec.Dir.
HEALTH AND WELFARE COUNCIL OF CENTRAL
MARYLAND, INC. - STAFF REFERENCE LIBRARY
□ Baltimore, MD

Geith, Patt, Asst.Ed.
INSTITUTE OF GAS TECHNOLOGY - TECHNICAL
INFORMATION CENTER □ Chicago, IL

Gelarden-Cooper, Diane, Med.Libn.
U.S. VETERANS ADMINISTRATION (KY-
Lexington) - MEDICAL CENTER LIBRARY □
Lexington, KY

Gelb, Linda, Rd.Serv.Libn.
BRANDEIS UNIVERSITY - GERSTENZANG
SCIENCE LIBRARY □ Waltham, MA

Gelber, Robert C., Asst.Libn.
NEW YORK STATE SUPREME COURT -
APPELLATE DIVISION, 1ST JUDICIAL
DEPARTMENT - LAW LIBRARY† □ New York, NY

Gelbmann, Elizabeth C., Libn.
MINNESOTA STATE POLLUTION CONTROL
AGENCY - LIBRARY □ Roseville, MN

Geldon, Ruth, Libn.
FAUCETT (Jack) ASSOCIATES - LIBRARY □
Chevy Chase, MD

Gelinas, Gratien, Bibliothecaire
CENTRE HOSPITALIER CHRIST-ROI -
BIBLIOTHEQUE MEDICALE □ Quebec, PQ

Gelinas, Michel, Libn.
UNIVERSITE DU QUEBEC - ECOLE NATIONALE
D'ADMINISTRATION PUBLIQUE - CENTRE DE
DOCUMENTATION □ Ste. Foy, PQ

Gelinas, Yvon-D., O.P., Hd.Libn.
DOMINICAINS DE ST-ALBERT-LE-GRAND,
MONTREAL - INSTITUT D'ETUDES
MEDIEVALES - BIBLIOTHEQUE □ Montreal, PQ

Gelman, Marsha E., Med.Libn.
LATROBE AREA HOSPITAL - MEDICAL &
NURSING LIBRARIES □ Latrobe, PA

Geltz, Elizabeth, Nursing Libn.
UNIVERSITY OF PITTSBURGH - FALK LIBRARY
OF THE HEALTH SCIENCES □ Pittsburgh, PA

Gemeinhart, Ruth, Clerk
KENTUCKY CHRISTIAN COLLEGE - MEDIA
CENTER □ Grayson, KY

Gemind, Joan, Mgr., Tech.Info.Serv.
NABISCO BRANDS, INC. - TECHNICAL
INFORMATION CENTER □ Wilton, CT

Genco, Carol, Coord.Lib./Inquiry Serv.
MICHIGAN MUNICIPAL LEAGUE - LIBRARY □
Ann Arbor, MI

Gendler, Carol, Libn.
DOUGLAS COUNTY LAW LIBRARY □ Omaha, NE

Gendron, Ruth, Libn.
STS. MARY AND ELIZABETH HOSPITAL -
MEDICAL LIBRARY □ Louisville, KY

Generao, Clarita M., Libn.
KNIGHT (Lester B.) & ASSOCIATES, INC. -
MANAGEMENT CONSULTING LIBRARY† □
Chicago, IL

Generoso, James, Ref.Libn.
CUNY - CITY COLLEGE LIBRARY - SCIENCE/
ENGINEERING DIVISION □ New York, NY

Genest, Helene, Online/SDI Serv.
UNIVERSITE LAVAL - BIBLIOTHEQUE □ Ste.
Foy, PQ

Genett, Mary, Asst.Libn.Ref.Serv./Cons.
AMERICAN MUSEUM OF NATURAL HISTORY -
DEPARTMENT OF LIBRARY SERVICES □ New
York, NY

Genetta, Beverly, Info.Ctr.Dir.
RUTGERS UNIVERSITY, THE STATE
UNIVERSITY OF NEW JERSEY - NEW JERSEY
VOCATIONAL EDUCATION RESOURCE CENTER
□ Old Bridge, NJ

Genetti, Raynna, Ref.Libn.
PROVIDENCE COLLEGE - PHILLIPS MEMORIAL
LIBRARY □ Providence, RI

Genna, David E., Libn.
ARNHOLD AND S. BLEICHROEDER, INC. -
LIBRARY □ New York, NY

Genoe, M.W., Corp.Libn.
NOVA - CORPORATE LIBRARY □ Calgary, AB

Genovese, Robert, Asst. for Tech.Serv.
COLGATE ROCHESTER/BEXLEY HALL/CROZER
THEOLOGICAL SEMINARIES - AMBROSE
SWASEY LIBRARY □ Rochester, NY

Genrich, Mrs. Fran, Libn.
SUNDSTRAND AVIATION - ENGINEERING
LIBRARY □ Rockford, IL

Gensel, Susan, Dir., Libs. & Marketing
COLD SPRING HARBOR LABORATORY - MAIN
LIBRARY □ Cold Spring Harbor, NY

Gent-Sandford, Louise, Libn.
SHEARSON LEHMAN/AMERICAN EXPRESS INC.
- LIBRARY □ New York, NY

Genther, Phyllis A., Res.
JAPAN ECONOMIC INSTITUTE OF AMERICA -
LIBRARY □ Washington, DC

Gentry, Cynthia, Tech.Serv.Libn.
CENTRAL BIBLE COLLEGE - LIBRARY □
Springfield, MO

Gentry, James, Dir.
SOUTHERN HIGHLAND HANDICRAFT GUILD -
FOLK ART CENTER LIBRARY □ Asheville, NC

Gentry, Linda F., Libn.
POLYMER INDUSTRIES - LIBRARY □ Greenville,
SC

Gentry, Mark, Ref.Libn.
CENTRAL BIBLE COLLEGE - LIBRARY □
Springfield, MO

Gentry, Susan K., Tech.Libn.
HUGHES AIRCRAFT COMPANY - SANTA
BARBARA RESEARCH CENTER - TECHNICAL
LIBRARY □ Goleta, CA

Gentzler, Lynn Wolf, Asst.Dir.
WESTERN HISTORICAL MANUSCRIPT
COLLECTION/STATE HISTORICAL SOCIETY OF
MISSOURI MANUSCRIPTS JOINT COLLECTION
□ Columbia, MO

Genung, Marie, Hd., Educ.Serv.
UNIVERSITY OF CALIFORNIA, RIVERSIDE -
EDUCATION SERVICES LIBRARY □ Riverside,
CA

Geofroy, Rose, Supv.
CANADIAN BROADCASTING CORPORATION -
RECORD LIBRARY □ Toronto, ON

Georg, Kathleen R., Coord.
U.S. NATL. PARK SERVICE - GETTYSBURG
NATL. MILITARY PARK - CYCLORAMA CENTER
LIBRARY □ Gettysburg, PA

George, Doris, Libn.
FALCONBRIDGE NICKEL MINES, LTD. -
METALLURGICAL LABORATORIES
INFORMATION SERVICES† □ Thornhill, ON

George, Harvey F., Exec. V.P./Res.Dir.
GRAVURE RESEARCH INSTITUTE - LIBRARY □
Port Washington, NY

George, John, Sr.Doc.Libn.
DALLAS PUBLIC LIBRARY - GOVERNMENT
PUBLICATIONS DIVISION □ Dallas, TX

George, Joy, Hd.Libn.
CITY-TV - CITY PULSE LIBRARY □ Toronto, ON

George, Marion D., V.P., Info.Serv/Corp.Rec.
UNITED VIRGINIA BANK - INFORMATION
CENTER □ Richmond, VA

George, Melvin R., Dir.
NORTHEASTERN ILLINOIS UNIVERSITY -
LIBRARY □ Chicago, IL

George, Melvin R., Dir. Of Libs.
OREGON STATE UNIVERSITY - WILLIAM
JASPER KERR LIBRARY □ Corvallis, OR

George, Muriel S., Supv., Lib.Oper.
SQUIBB (E.R.) & SONS, INC. - SQUIBB INST.
FOR MEDICAL RES. - SCIENCE INFO. DEPT. -
NEW BRUNSWICK LIBRARY □ New Brunswick,
NJ

George, Rachel, Libn.
REFORMED PRESBYTERIAN THEOLOGICAL
SEMINARY - LIBRARY □ Pittsburgh, PA

George, Ralph, Asst.Libn.
SOCIETY OF MAYFLOWER DESCENDANTS IN
THE STATE OF CALIFORNIA - LIBRARY □
Oakland, CA

George, Susan C., Libn.
DARTMOUTH COLLEGE - KRESGE PHYSICAL
SCIENCES LIBRARY □ Hanover, NH

George, Twig C., Educ.Coord.
WHALE PROTECTION FUND - ENVIRONMENTAL
EDUCATION RESOURCE LIBRARY □ Washington,
DC

Georgenson, Gail S., Res.Libn.
UNIVERSITY OF ARIZONA - SPACE IMAGERY
CENTER □ Tucson, AZ

Georges, Mary Ann, Staff Libn.
QUEEN STREET MENTAL HEALTH CENTRE -
HEALTH SCIENCES LIBRARY □ Toronto, ON

Georgeson, Jody L., Libn.
MOUNTAIN BELL TELEPHONE COMPANY - LIBRARY □ Denver, CO

Gera, V. Lynn, Adm.Libn.
U.S. ARMY - WALTER REED ARMY INSTITUTE OF RESEARCH - LIBRARY □ Washington, DC

Geraghty, Rev. James F., Archv.
DIOCESE OF LAFAYETTE, LOUISIANA - ARCHIVES □ Lafayette, LA

Gerard, Gary, Mgr.
KAISER ALUMINUM & CHEMICAL CORPORATION - TECHNICAL INFORMATION CENTER □ Pleasanton, CA

Gerard, Gerald B., Libn.
CANADIAN INSTITUTE OF CHARTERED ACCOUNTANTS - RESEARCH DEPARTMENT LIBRARY† □ Toronto, ON

Gerardi, Florence, Libn.
TIMEPLEX, INC. - ENGINEERING LIBRARY □ Rochelle Park, NJ

Gerathowold, Amrei
ALTERNATIVE PRESS CENTER - LIBRARY □ Baltimore, MD

Gerbens, Martin, Hd., Caribbean Coll.
VIRGIN ISLANDS - DEPARTMENT OF CONSERVATION & CULTURAL AFFAIRS - BUREAU OF LIBRARIES AND MUSEUMS □ St. Thomas, VI

Gerber, Judy, Chf.Libn., R & D
MANVILLE SERVICE CORPORATION - RESEARCH AND DEVELOPMENT INFORMATION CENTER □ Denver, CO

Gerberding, Dr. Richard, Mss.Cat.
ST. JOHN'S ABBEY AND UNIVERSITY - HILL MONASTIC MANUSCRIPT LIBRARY - BUSH CENTER □ Collegeville, MN

Gerberg, Dr. Eugene J., Pres.
INSECT CONTROL AND RESEARCH, INC. - LIBRARY □ Baltimore, MD

Gerdes, Rev. Neil W., Libn.
CHICAGO THEOLOGICAL SEMINARY - HAMMOND LIBRARY □ Chicago, IL

Gerdes, Rev. Neil W., Libn.
MEADVILLE/LOMBARD THEOLOGICAL SCHOOL - LIBRARY □ Chicago, IL

Gerdine, Peter C., Acq.Libn.
RENSSELAER POLYTECHNIC INSTITUTE - FOLSOM LIBRARY □ Troy, NY

Gerding, Jean, Tech.Info.Spec.
NATL.INST. OF ENVIRONMENTAL HEALTH SCI. - NATL. TOXICOLOGY PROGRAM - ENVIRONMENTAL TERATOLOGY INFO.CTR. □ Research Triangle Park, NC

Gerdts, Abigail Booth, Archv.
NATIONAL ACADEMY OF DESIGN - LIBRARY AND ARCHIVES □ New York, NY

Gerduk, Nettie, Libn.
TWENTIETH CENTURY FUND - LIBRARY □ New York, NY

Gergely, Emma, Health Sci.Info.Spec.
ALLIED CORPORATION - LIBRARY & INFORMATION SERVICES □ Morristown, NJ

Gerhardt, Edwin L., Cur.
TOWSON STATE UNIVERSITY - GERHARDT LIBRARY OF MUSICAL INFORMATION □ Towson, MD

Gerhardt, Edwin L., Cur.
TOWSON STATE UNIVERSITY - GERHARDT MARIMBA & XYLOPHONE COLLECTION □ Towson, MD

Gericke, Dr. Paul, Dir. of Lib.
NEW ORLEANS BAPTIST THEOLOGICAL SEMINARY - JOHN T. CHRISTIAN LIBRARY □ New Orleans, LA

Gerken, Ann E., Data Archv.
CORNELL INSTITUTE FOR SOCIAL AND ECONOMIC RESEARCH (CISER) - DATA ARCHIVE □ Ithaca, NY

Gerken, C., Info.Spec.
BURROUGHS WELLCOME COMPANY - LIBRARY □ Research Triangle Park, NC

Gerl, Brian Jonathan, Dir.
WISCONSIN CONSERVATORY OF MUSIC - LIBRARY □ Milwaukee, WI

Gerlach, Gary G., Dir.
BIRMINGHAM BOTANICAL GARDENS - HORACE HAMMOND MEMORIAL LIBRARY □ Birmingham, AL

Gerlach, Patricia, Libn.
ST. PAUL PUBLIC LIBRARY - BUSINESS & SCIENCE ROOM □ St. Paul, MN

Gerling, Sally M., Chf.Libn.
GENESEE HOSPITAL - SAMUEL J. STABINS, M.D., HEALTH SCIENCES LIBRARY □ Rochester, NY

Germain, Claire, Hd.Ref.Libn.
DUKE UNIVERSITY - SCHOOL OF LAW LIBRARY □ Durham, NC

Germain, Pierre, Loan & Per.
CEGEP DE TROIS-RIVIERES - BIBLIOTHEQUE □ Trois-Rivieres, PQ

Germann, Malcolm, Libn.
WESLEY MEDICAL CENTER - H.B. MC KIBBIN HEALTH SCIENCE LIBRARY □ Wichita, KS

Gern, Maria
FALKIRK HOSPITAL - LIBRARY □ Central Valley, NY

Geron, Cary Ann, Libn.
SOUTHERN BAPTIST CONVENTION - FOREIGN MISSION BOARD - MISSIONARY LEARNING CENTER LIBRARY □ Richmond, VA

Gerowitz, R., Res.
ELYSIUM ARCHIVES □ Los Angeles, CA

Gerrard, Philip, Prin.Coord.Libn.
NEW YORK PUBLIC LIBRARY - DONNELL LIBRARY CENTER □ New York, NY

Gerstenberg, H.M.
U.S. NATL. BUREAU OF STANDARDS - PHOTON AND CHARGED PARTICLE DATA CENTER □ Gaithersburg, MD

Gerstner, Dr. Patsy A., Chf.Cur.
CLEVELAND HEALTH SCIENCES LIBRARY - HISTORICAL DIVISION □ Cleveland, OH

Gertrude, Sister, S.C., Libn.
ST. MARY'S HOSPITAL - MEDICAL ALLIED HEALTH LIBRARY† □ Passaic, NJ

Gertz, Vivian, Natl.Treas.
DAUGHTERS OF UNION VETERANS OF THE CIVIL WAR - NATIONAL HEADQUARTERS LIBRARY & MUSEUM □ Springfield, IL

Geruntino, Dr.
SOUTHWESTERN UNIVERSITY - A.J. GERUNTINO LIBRARY □ Tucson, AZ

Gervino, Joan, Dir.
AMERICAN BANKERS ASSOCIATION - LIBRARY & INFORMATION SERVICES □ Washington, DC

Gerwing, Howard B., Rare Bks.Libn.
UNIVERSITY OF VICTORIA - MC PHERSON LIBRARY - SPECIAL COLLECTIONS □ Victoria, BC

Geske, Aina, Hd.Libn.
KENYON & ECKHARDT ADVERTISING - INFORMATION CENTER □ New York, NY

Geske, Dulcie, Lib.Techn.
U.S. AIR FORCE BASE - LUKE BASE LIBRARY† □ Luke AFB, AZ

Gess, Catherine, Asst.Libn.
TAMPA TRIBUNE & TAMPA TIMES - LIBRARY □ Tampa, FL

Getz, George F., Jr., Pres.
HALL OF FAME - RICHARD S. FOWLER MEMORIAL LIBRARY □ Phoenix, AZ

Getz, Oscar, Founder
BARTON MUSEUM OF WHISKEY HISTORY - LIBRARY □ Bardstown, KY

Getze, Frederick B., Assoc.Libn.
UNIVERSITY OF DELAWARE, NEWARK - AGRICULTURE LIBRARY □ Newark, DE

Gex, Robert C., Chf.Libn.
STANFORD LINEAR ACCELERATOR CENTER - LIBRARY □ Stanford, CA

Geyer, Barbara, Ref.Libn.
TEXAS TECH UNIVERSITY - LIBRARY - DOCUMENTS DEPARTMENT □ Lubbock, TX

Geyer, Della M., Law Libn.
BAYLOR UNIVERSITY - LAW LIBRARY □ Waco, TX

Geyer, Enid, Tech.Proc.
UNION UNIVERSITY - ALBANY MEDICAL COLLEGE - SCHAFFER LIBRARY OF THE HEALTH SCIENCES □ Albany, NY

Geyger, Alexander, Rd.Adv.
DISTRICT OF COLUMBIA PUBLIC LIBRARY - LANGUAGE, LITERATURE & FOREIGN LANGUAGE DIVISION □ Washington, DC

Geyger, Barbara F., Chf.
DISTRICT OF COLUMBIA PUBLIC LIBRARY - CHILDREN'S DIVISION □ Washington, DC

Ghali, Raouf, Assoc.Libn.
NEW YORK UNIVERSITY - DENTAL CENTER - JOHN & BERTHA E. WALDMANN MEMORIAL LIBRARY □ New York, NY

Ghent, Gretchen, Area Hd.
UNIVERSITY OF CALGARY - SOCIAL SCIENCES LIBRARY† □ Calgary, AB

Ghering, Sr. M. Virgil, O.P., Libn.
ST. THOMAS INSTITUTE - LIBRARY □ Cincinnati, OH

Ghidotti, Pauline, Asst.Dir.
UNIVERSITY OF ARKANSAS AT LITTLE ROCK - PULASKI COUNTY LAW LIBRARY □ Little Rock, AR

Ghikas, Mary W., Exec.Dir.
UNIVERSAL SERIALS & BOOK EXCHANGE, INC. - DUPLICATE EXCHANGE CLEARINGHOUSE & INFORMATION CENTER □ Washington, DC

Ghist, Ann, Libn.
ARTHUR ANDERSEN & CO. - BUSINESS LIBRARY □ Houston, TX

Gholston, H.D., Supv.Tech.Lib.
CHEVRON RESEARCH COMPANY - TECHNICAL INFORMATION CENTER □ Richmond, CA

Giambastiani, Barbara J., Dir.
MADISON COUNTY HISTORICAL SOCIETY - LIBRARY □ Oneida, NY

Giannico, Nicoletta, Prog.Anl.
LOUISIANA STATE UNIVERSITY - COASTAL INFORMATION REPOSITORY □ Baton Rouge, LA

Giannini, Evelyn, Libn.
KEMPER GROUP - LIBRARY □ Long Grove, IL

Giannotti, Marshall J., Adm. of Libs.
NEW YORK COLLEGE OF PODIATRIC MEDICINE - MEDICAL LIBRARY □ New York, NY

Giasi, Marie, Ref.Libn.
BROOKLYN BOTANIC GARDEN - LIBRARY □ Brooklyn, NY

Gibbany, Jack, Prog.Coord.
PALO ALTO UNIFIED SCHOOL DISTRICT - INSTRUCTIONAL MATERIALS CENTER □ Palo Alto, CA

Gibbons, Dr. Barbara H., Res.
UNIVERSITY OF HAWAII - PACIFIC BIO-MEDICAL RESEARCH CENTER - LIBRARY □ Honolulu, HI

Gibbons, Gayle, Info.Spec.
AMERICAN PUBLIC HEALTH ASSOCIATION - INTERNATIONAL HEALTH PROGRAMS - RESOURCE CENTER □ Washington, DC

Gibbons, Katherine, Cat.
NEW YORK MEDICAL COLLEGE AND THE WESTCHESTER ACADEMY OF MEDICINE - WESTCHESTER MEDICAL CENTER LIBRARY □ Valhalla, NY

Gibbons, Susan Jane, Libn.
DECHERT, PRICE AND RHOADS - LIBRARY □ Philadelphia, PA

Gibbs, Andrea, Cat.
NATIONAL GALLERY OF ART - PHOTOGRAPHIC ARCHIVES □ Washington, DC

Gibbs, Donald, Bibliog.
UNIVERSITY OF TEXAS, AUSTIN - BENSON LATIN AMERICAN COLLECTION □ Austin, TX

Gibbs, Dr. Hyatt, Supv.
UNIVERSITY OF ARIZONA - OPTICAL SCIENCES CENTER - READING ROOM† □ Tucson, AZ

Gibbs, John R., Asst.Libn.
UNIVERSITY OF WASHINGTON - MUSIC
LIBRARY □ Seattle, WA

Gibbs, K.L., Act.Dir.
BRITISH COLUMBIA - MINISTRY OF TOURISM -
PHOTOGRAPHIC LIBRARY† □ Victoria, BC

Gibbs, Phyllis A., Med.Libn.
U.S. NAVY - NAVAL HOSPITAL (IL-Great Lakes) -
MEDICAL LIBRARY □ Great Lakes, IL

Gibson, C. Richard, Govt.Docs./Ref.Libn.
GEORGE MASON UNIVERSITY - SCHOOL OF
LAW - LIBRARY □ Arlington, VA

Gibson, Elizabeth, Libn.
SUN LIFE OF CANADA - INVESTMENT LIBRARY
□ Toronto, ON

Gibson, Ellen M., Assoc.Dir.
SUNY AT BUFFALO - CHARLES B. SEARS LAW
LIBRARY □ Buffalo, NY

Gibson, Gladys, Chf.Libn.
ATOMIC ENERGY OF CANADA, LTD. - WNRE
LIBRARY □ Pinawa, MB

Gibson, Harold R., Libn.
GUEDEL MEMORIAL ANESTHESIA CENTER -
LIBRARY □ San Francisco, CA

Gibson, Harold R., Libn.
PACIFIC MEDICAL CENTER & UNIVERSITY OF
THE PACIFIC SCHOOL OF DENTISTRY - HEALTH
SCIENCES LIBRARY □ San Francisco, CA

Gibson, Helen R., Libn.
GREENSFELDER, HEMKER, WIESE, GALE &
CHAPPELOW - LIBRARY □ St. Louis, MO

Gibson, Imogene, Coll.Libn.
AUSTIN COLLEGE - HOPKINS LIBRARY -
SPECIAL COLLECTIONS □ Sherman, TX

Gibson, James, Braille Libn.
ALABAMA REGIONAL LIBRARY FOR THE BLIND
AND PHYSICALLY HANDICAPPED □
Montgomery, AL

Gibson, Jane, Hd.
TELEMEDIA, INC. - INFORMATION CENTER □
Chicago, IL

Gibson, Julie A., Adm.Libn.
U.S. ARMY - TRADOC SYSTEMS ANALYSIS
ACTIVITY - TRASANA TECHNICAL LIBRARY □
White Sands Missile Range, NM

Gibson, Kay, Med.Libn.
ST. MARY'S HOSPITAL - MEDICAL LIBRARY
(6E) □ Huntington, WV

Gibson, Marianne, Libn.
AMERICAN SOYBEAN ASSOCIATION - LIBRARY
□ St. Louis, MO

Gibson, Mignon, Musm.Dir.
SAN JOSE HISTORICAL MUSEUM - ARCHIVES □
San Jose, CA

Gibson, P., Asst.Hd., Pub.Serv.
CANADA - ENERGY, MINES & RESOURCES
CANADA - HEADQUARTERS LIBRARY □ Ottawa,
ON

Gibson, Patricia, Libn.
ST. FRANCIS HOSPITAL - SCHOOL OF NURSING
LIBRARY □ Evanston, IL

Gibson, Robert W., Jr., Dept.Hd.
GENERAL MOTORS CORPORATION - RESEARCH
LABORATORIES LIBRARY □ Warren, MI

Gibson-MacDonald, Norma, Canadiana Acq.Spec.
CANADIAN CENTRE FOR OCCUPATIONAL
HEALTH AND SAFETY - DOCUMENTATION
SERVICES/SERVICE DE DOCUMENTATION □
Hamilton, ON

Giedrys, Ilona, Res.Libn.
MERCK & COMPANY, INC. - MERCK SHARP &
DOHME RESEARCH LABORATORIES -
LITERATURE RESOURCES □ Rahway, NJ

Giefer, Gerald J., Libn.
UNIVERSITY OF CALIFORNIA, BERKELEY -
WATER RESOURCES CENTER ARCHIVES □
Berkeley, CA

Gieger, Geraldine, Res.Libn.
EXXON RESEARCH AND ENGINEERING
COMPANY - LIBRARY □ Baytown, TX

Giehl, Dudley, Pres.
ANIMAL LIBERATION, INC. - LIBRARY □ New
York, NY

Giella, Vicki C., Info.Ctr.Coord.
CARNATION COMPANY - LIBRARY† □ Los
Angeles, CA

Gier, Edwin F., Chf., Tech.Lib.
U.S. ARMY - CHEMICAL RESEARCH &
DEVELOPMENT CENTER - INFORMATION
SERVICES BRANCH - TECHNICAL LIBRARY □
Aberdeen Proving Ground, MD

Gieryic, Michael, Hd.Libn.
SUNY - AGRICULTURAL AND TECHNICAL
COLLEGE AT MORRISVILLE - LIBRARY □
Morrisville, NY

Giesbrecht, Herbert, College Libn.
MENNONITE BRETHREN BIBLE COLLEGE -
LIBRARY □ Winnipeg, MB

Giesbrecht, John W., Asst.Libn.
MANITOBA - DEPARTMENT OF INDUSTRY,
TRADE AND TECHNOLOGY - BUSINESS LIBRARY
□ Winnipeg, MB

Giet, G. Robert, Libn.
MARITIME MUSEUM (Allen Knight) - LIBRARY □
Monterey, CA

Giffen, Linda, Oper.Mgr.
ALBERTA - DEPARTMENT OF CONSUMER AND
CORPORATE AFFAIRS - RESOURCE CENTRE □
Edmonton, AB

Gifford, Curtis, Forestry/Agri.Sci.Libn.
COLORADO STATE UNIVERSITY - WILLIAM E.
MORGAN LIBRARY □ Fort Collins, CO

Gifford, Karlee, Libn.
YALE UNIVERSITY - COWLES FOUNDATION
FOR RESEARCH IN ECONOMICS - LIBRARY □
New Haven, CT

Gifford, R.A., Owner
HARRIS & GIFFORD - LIBRARY □ Arlington, VA

Gifford, Robert V., Asst.Archv.
CHESAPEAKE & OHIO HISTORICAL SOCIETY,
INC. - C&O ARCHIVAL COLLECTION □ Newport
News VA

Gifford, Sanford, M.D., Dir.
BOSTON PSYCHOANALYTIC SOCIETY &
INSTITUTE, INC. - LIBRARY □ Boston, MA

Gift, Kathryn, Libn.
SNYDER COUNTY HISTORICAL SOCIETY, INC. -
LIBRARY □ Middleburg, PA

Gigante, Vickilyn M., Mgr., Lib. & Info.Serv.
ECOLOGICAL ANALYSTS, INC. - LIBRARY □
Sparks, MD

Gignac, Solange G., Libn.
DENVER BOTANIC GARDENS - HELEN FOWLER
LIBRARY □ Denver, CO

Gilbaine, Miss E., Libn.
CRAFT CENTER MUSEUM - CRAFT CENTER
LIBRARY □ Wilton, CT

Gilbard, Sylvia, Tech.Info.Spec.
U.S. NATL. HIGHWAY TRAFFIC SAFETY
ADMINISTRATION - TECHNICAL REFERENCE
DIVISION □ Washington, DC

Gilbert, Alice, Libn.
CONNECTICUT STATE DEPARTMENT ON
AGING - LIBRARY □ Hartford, CT

Gilbert, Carole M., Dir.
METROPOLITAN HOSPITAL - MEDICAL
LIBRARY □ Detroit, MI

Gilbert, Deborah D., Chf.Hosp.Libn.
CHILDREN'S HOSPITAL/NATIONAL MEDICAL
CENTER - HOSPITAL LIBRARY† □ Washington,
DC

Gilbert, Elizabeth X., Sec.-Treas.
GEM VILLAGE MUSEUM - GREEN MEMORIAL
LIBRARY □ Bayfield, CO

Gilbert, Ellen, Libn.
NEW YORK PSYCHOANALYTIC INSTITUTE -
ABRAHAM A. BRILL LIBRARY □ New York, NY

Gilbert, Gail R., Hd., Art Lib.
UNIVERSITY OF LOUISVILLE - ALLEN R. HITE
ART INSTITUTE - MARGARET M. BRIDWELL
ART LIBRARY □ Louisville, KY

Gilbert, Harry, Libn.
UNIVERSITY OF KENTUCKY - HUNTER M.
ADAMS ARCHITECTURE LIBRARY □ Lexington,
KY

Gilbert, Holly, Ref.Libn.
UNIVERSITY OF NORTH DAKOTA - GEOLOGY
LIBRARY □ Grand Forks, ND

Gilbert, Jane C., Law Lib.Ck.
HERKIMER COUNTY LAW LIBRARY □ Herkimer,
NY

Gilbert, Leon, Translator
AMERICAN RED CROSS - NATIONAL
HEADQUARTERS LIBRARY □ Washington, DC

Gilbert, Mary, Libn.
NORTHEAST GEORGIA MEDICAL CENTER AND
HALL SCHOOL OF NURSING/BRENAU COLLEGE -
LIBRARY □ Gainesville, GA

Gilbert, Mattana, Supv., Indexing/Cat.
NATIONAL SAFETY COUNCIL - LIBRARY □
Chicago, IL

Gilbert, Nancy L., Asst.Dir./Lib.Serv.
U.S. ARMY MILITARY HISTORY INSTITUTE □
Carlisle Barracks, PA

Gilbert, Ruth E., Chf., Lib.Serv.
U.S. VETERANS ADMINISTRATION (CO-Denver)
- HOSPITAL LIBRARY □ Denver, CO

Gilbert, Thelma, Acq.Libn.
ANDREWS UNIVERSITY - JAMES WHITE
LIBRARY† □ Berrien Springs, MI

Gilbert, Thomas F., Tech.Serv.Libn.
ANDOVER NEWTON THEOLOGICAL SCHOOL -
TRASK LIBRARY □ Newton Centre, MA

Gilbert, Rev. Thomas F., Dir., LRC
EASTERN BAPTIST THEOLOGICAL SEMINARY -
LIBRARY □ Philadelphia, PA

Gilbert, Thomas F., Cat.Libn.
UNIVERSITY OF THE SOUTH - SCHOOL OF
THEOLOGY LIBRARY □ Sewanee, TN

Gilbertson, Jean, Libn.
UNIVERSITY OF WISCONSIN, MADISON -
COLLEGE OF ENGINEERING - TECHNICAL
REPORTS CENTER □ Madison, WI

Gilbertson, Kathi, Hd., Tech.Serv.
UNIVERSITY OF WISCONSIN, MADISON -
STEENBOCK MEMORIAL LIBRARY □ Madison,
WI

Gilbertson, Mary Edith, Acq.Libn.
WILLAMETTE UNIVERSITY - LAW LIBRARY □
Salem, OR

Gilborn, Craig, Dir.
ADIRONDACK HISTORICAL ASSOCIATION -
ADIRONDACK MUSEUM - RESEARCH LIBRARY □
Blue Mountain Lake, NY

Gilbride, Irene
LITTON INDUSTRIES - GUIDANCE AND
CONTROL SYSTEMS - LIBRARY □ Woodland Hills,
CA

Gildemeister, Glen A., Dir.
NORTHERN ILLINOIS UNIVERSITY - REGIONAL
HISTORY CENTER □ DeKalb, IL

Gildemeister, Glen A., Archv.
NORTHERN ILLINOIS UNIVERSITY -
UNIVERSITY ARCHIVES □ DeKalb, IL

Gilden, Anita, Libn.
BALTIMORE MUSEUM OF ART - REFERENCE
LIBRARY □ Baltimore, MD

Gildzen, Alex, Assoc.Cur.
KENT STATE UNIVERSITY - DEPARTMENT OF
SPECIAL COLLECTIONS □ Kent, OH

Giles, Charles E., Chf.Libn.
GENERAL DYNAMICS CORPORATION -
ELECTRIC BOAT DIVISION - DIVISION
LIBRARY □ Groton, CT

Giles, Esther L., Corp.Libn.
TRANS WORLD AIRLINES, INC. - CORPORATE
LIBRARY □ New York, NY

Giles, Garred, Scientific Serv.
CORNELL UNIVERSITY - ARECIBO
OBSERVATORY - LIBRARY □ Arecibo, PR

Giles, Sondra L., Asst.Libn.
RHODE ISLAND STATE LAW LIBRARY □
Providence, RI

Giles, Sue, Coord., Lib.Serv.
RYERSON POLYTECHNICAL INSTITUTE -
LEARNING RESOURCES CENTRE □ Toronto, ON

Gilheany, Rosary S., Dir./Lib. & Ref.Serv.
UNITED HOSPITALS MEDICAL CENTER OF NEWARK - LIBRARY/INFORMATION SERVICES □ Newark, NJ

Gilkes, Beryl, Supv.
NATIONAL LEAGUE FOR NURSING, INC. - LIBRARY/RECORDS CENTER □ New York, NY

Gill, Barbara, Libn.
HISTORICAL SOCIETY OF BERKS COUNTY - LIBRARY □ Reading, PA

Gill, Carol Winfield, Tech.Libn.
PHILLIPS PETROLEUM COMPANY - RESEARCH & DEVELOPMENT DEPARTMENT - TECHNICAL INFORMATION BRANCH □ Bartlesville, OK

Gill, Elizabeth D., Dir.
SRI INTERNATIONAL - LIBRARY AND RESEARCH INFORMATION SERVICES DEPARTMENT □ Menlo Park, CA

Gill, Gail P., Libn.
DELAWARE ACADEMY OF MEDICINE - LIBRARY □ Wilmington, DE

Gill, Lyn Cooper, Exec.Dir.
PLANNED PARENTHOOD OF CLEVELAND, INC. - LIBRARY □ Cleveland, OH

Gill, Marylile, Teacher/Libn.
VANCOUVER TALMUD TORAH SCHOOL - LIBRARY □ Vancouver, BC

Gill, Molly, Libn.
PINELLAS COUNTY JUVENILE WELFARE BOARD - MAILANDE W. HOLLAND LIBRARY □ St. Petersburg, FL

Gill, Norman N., Exec.Dir.
CITIZENS' GOVERNMENTAL RESEARCH BUREAU, INC. □ Milwaukee, WI

Gill, Sam, Archv.
ACADEMY OF MOTION PICTURE ARTS AND SCIENCES - MARGARET HERRICK LIBRARY □ Beverly Hills, CA

Gill, Victoria, English Lit.Spec.
METROPOLITAN TORONTO LIBRARY - LITERATURE DEPARTMENT □ Toronto, ON

Gillard, Peter McCann, Dir.
SMITHTOWN LIBRARY - SPECIAL COLLECTIONS □ Smithtown, NY

Gillesby, John D., Hd.Ref.Libn.
UNIVERSITY OF WISCONSIN, STEVENS POINT - JAMES H. ALBERTSON CENTER FOR LEARNING RESOURCES □ Stevens Point, WI

Gillespie, Harriet, Res.Libn.
HARBISON-WALKER REFRACTORIES COMPANY - GARBER RESEARCH CENTER LIBRARY □ Pittsburgh, PA

Gillespie, J.C., Libn.
MARTIN MARIETTA ENERGY SYSTEMS INC. - NUCLEAR DIV. - PADUCAH GASEOUS DIFFUSION PLANT INFO. CENTER □ Paducah, KY

Gillespie, Norman, Asst.Libn.
MIAMI-DADE PUBLIC LIBRARY - FLORIDA COLLECTION □ Miami, FL

Gillespie, Stuart P., Pres.
PEMAQUID HISTORICAL ASSOCIATION - HARRINGTON MEETING HOUSE - LIBRARY □ Pemaquid, ME

Gillette, Catherine Hall, Asst.Dir., Pub.Serv.
CLEVELAND STATE UNIVERSITY - JOSEPH W. BARTUNEK III LAW LIBRARY □ Cleveland, OH

Gillette, Doug, Chf.Libn.
SHERMAN GRINBERG FILM LIBRARIES, INC. □ New York, NY

Gillette, Gerald W., Mgr., Res. & Lib.Serv.
PRESBYTERIAN CHURCH (U.S.A.). - PRESBYTERIAN HISTORICAL SOCIETY - LIBRARY □ Philadelphia, PA

Gillette, Michael, Chf., Oral Hist.Sect.
U.S. PRESIDENTIAL LIBRARIES - LYNDON B. JOHNSON LIBRARY □ Austin, TX

Gilliam, Dorothy, Cat.
UNION THEOLOGICAL SEMINARY IN VIRGINIA - LIBRARY □ Richmond, VA

Gilliam, Susanne, Cat.
UNIVERSITY OF CINCINNATI - MEDICAL CENTER LIBRARIES - HISTORY OF HEALTH SCIENCES LIBRARY AND MUSEUM □ Cincinnati, OH

Gilliana, Mr. Zia Solomon, Med.Libn.
RAVENSWOOD HOSPITAL MEDICAL CENTER - MEDICAL-NURSING LIBRARY □ Chicago, IL

Gillie, Margaret Elizabeth, Archv.
STRATFORD HALL PLANTATION - JESSIE BALL DUPONT MEMORIAL LIBRARY □ Stratford, VA

Gillies, Elizabeth W., Libn.
HUEBNER (S.S.) FOUNDATION FOR INSURANCE EDUCATION - LIBRARY □ Philadelphia, PA

Gillikin, Phyllis C., Dir., AHEC Lib.
NORTHWEST AREA HEALTH EDUCATION CENTER - NW AHEC LIBRARY □ Hickory, NC

Gilliland, Donna, Sch.Lib.Cons.
SOUTH DAKOTA STATE LIBRARY & ARCHIVES □ Pierre, SD

Gilliland, Mr. L.P., Libn.
FRANKLIN REGIONAL MEDICAL CENTER - MEDICAL LIBRARY □ Franklin, PA

Gillingham, Cameron
DAWE'S LABORATORIES, LTD. - TECHNICAL AND AGRICULTURAL LIBRARIES □ Lincolnwood, IL

Gillis, Charles, Info.Dir.
I/H INCORPORATED - GAY AND LESBIAN ARCHIVES OF TEXAS† □ Houston, TX

Gillis, Eileen W., Libn.
MERCY HOSPITAL - MC GLANNAN MEMORIAL LIBRARY □ Baltimore, MD

Gillis, Eileen W., Libn.
MERCY HOSPITAL, INC. - NURSING LIBRARY □ Baltimore, MD

Gillis, Jeff, Pres.
DURANT FAMILY REGISTRY - LIBRARY □ Green Bay, WI

Gillispie, James E., Libn.
JOHNS HOPKINS UNIVERSITY - MILTON S. EISENHOWER LIBRARY - GOVERNMENT PUBN./MAPS/LAW LIBRARY □ Baltimore, MD

Gillmar, Dian, Info.Coord.
METROPOLITAN TRANSPORTATION COMMISSION - ASSOCIATION OF BAY AREA GOVERNMENTS (ABAG) - LIBRARY □ Oakland, CA

Gillock, Oliver, Jr., Coord., Plan. & Dev.
NEW JERSEY STATE LIBRARY □ Trenton, NJ

Gilman, Francie, User Serv.Coord.
ERIC CLEARINGHOUSE ON TEACHER EDUCATION □ Washington, DC

Gilman, Naomi P., Info.Dir.
GILMAN MUSEUM - LIBRARY □ Hellertown, PA

Gilman, Nelson J., Libn./Dir.
UNIVERSITY OF SOUTHERN CALIFORNIA - HEALTH SCIENCES CAMPUS - NORRIS MEDICAL LIBRARY □ Los Angeles, CA

Gilman, Susy B., Asst.Libn.
UNIVERSITY OF FLORIDA - LAW LIBRARY □ Gainesville, FL

Gilmer, Ann, Assoc.Dir.
TEXAS TECH UNIVERSITY - HEALTH SCIENCES CENTER - LIBRARY OF THE HEALTH SCIENCES □ Lubbock, TX

Gilmer, Wesley, Jr., State Law Libn.
KENTUCKY STATE LAW LIBRARY □ Frankfort, KY

Gilmor, Sr. Victoria, Libn.
ANGLICAN CHURCH ARMY IN CANADA - COWAN MEMORIAL LIBRARY □ Toronto, ON

Gilmore, Larry D., Cur.
COLUMBIA RIVER MARITIME MUSEUM - LIBRARY □ Astoria, OR

Gilmore, Willard H., Asst.Libn.
MAINE MARITIME ACADEMY - NUTTING MEMORIAL LIBRARY □ Castine, ME

Gilner, David J., Ref./Pub.Serv.Libn.
HEBREW UNION COLLEGE - JEWISH INSTITUTE OF RELIGION - KLAU LIBRARY □ Cincinnati, OH

Gilpin, Risa, Hd. of Pub.Serv.
PROVIDENCE ATHENAEUM - LIBRARY □ Providence, RI

Gilreath, Charles, Hd., Automated Info.Ret.
TEXAS A & M UNIVERSITY - REFERENCE DIVISION □ College Station, TX

Gilroy, Dorothy A., Chf.Res.Libn.
UNIVERSITY AFFILIATED CINCINNATI CENTER FOR DEVELOPMENTAL DISORDERS - RESEARCH LIBRARY □ Cincinnati, OH

Giltinan, Mary J., Rd.Serv.Libn.
ST. CHARLES BORROMEO SEMINARY - RYAN MEMORIAL LIBRARY □ Philadelphia, PA

Gilvin, Marjorie, Libn.
POLK PUBLIC MUSEUM - MEMORIAL LIBRARY □ Lakeland, FL

Gimelson, Deborah, Adm.Dir.
POETRY SOCIETY OF AMERICA - VAN VOORHIS LIBRARY† □ New York, NY

Gimter, Donald W., Cur.
MID-CONTINENT RAILWAY HISTORICAL SOCIETY, INC. - MUSEUM LIBRARY □ North Freedom, WI

Gin, Diana, Libn.
SACRAMENTO PUBLIC LIBRARY - BUSINESS & MUNICIPAL DEPARTMENT† □ Sacramento, CA

Gindlesberger, Thomas D., Law Libn.
HOLMES COUNTY LAW LIBRARY □ Millersburg, OH

Gindra, Janice J., Asst.Libn.
NATIONAL ASSOCIATION OF INSURANCE COMMISSIONERS - NAIC INFORMATION CENTER □ Kansas City, MO

Ginger, Ann Fagan, Pres.
MEIKLEJOHN CIVIL LIBERTIES INSTITUTE - LIBRARY □ Berkeley, CA

Gingery, Jim, Ref.Libn.
SCHOOLS OF THEOLOGY IN DUBUQUE - LIBRARIES □ Dubuque, IA

Ginkel, Elizabeth, Asst. Law Libn.
UNIVERSITY OF MAINE SCHOOL OF LAW - DONALD L. GARBRECHT LAW LIBRARY □ Portland, ME

Ginn, Marjorie, Acq.Libn.
MAYO FOUNDATION - MAYO CLINIC LIBRARY □ Rochester, MN

Gino, John, Prog.Dir.
STATEN ISLAND COOPERATIVE CONTINUUM - EDUCATIONAL RESOURCE CENTER □ Staten Island, NY

Ginsberg, Judy, Hd., Cat.
YORK UNIVERSITY - LAW LIBRARY □ Downsview, ON

Ginsberg, Sally, Ref.Libn.
STETSON UNIVERSITY - COLLEGE OF LAW - CHARLES A. DANA LAW LIBRARY □ St. Petersburg, FL

Ginsburg, Carol L., Asst. V.P./Info.Off.
BANKERS TRUST COMPANY - CORPORATE FINANCE DEPARTMENT - INFORMATION CENTER □ New York, NY

Ginsburgs, Ida G., Map Libn.
TEMPLE UNIVERSITY - CENTRAL LIBRARY SYSTEM - REFERENCE DEPARTMENT MAP UNIT □ Philadelphia, PA

Gionfriddo, Jacqueline, Dir.
ST. JOSEPH'S HOSPITAL - JEROME MEDICAL LIBRARY □ St. Paul, MN

Gionfriddo, Jane, Circ.
BOSTON COLLEGE - LAW SCHOOL LIBRARY† □ Newton Centre, MA

Giordano, Joan, Mgr., Med.Lib.
WHITE PLAINS HOSPITAL - BERTON LATTIN MEMORIAL MEDICAL LIBRARY □ White Plains, NY

Giovanetti, Carolyn, Libn.
POLAR GAS PROJECT - LIBRARY □ Toronto, ON

Giovannini, Kathleen A., Info.Sci.
AMERICAN CAN COMPANY - PRINCETON RESEARCH INFORMATION CENTER □ Princeton, NJ

Giral, Angela, Libn.
COLUMBIA UNIVERSITY - AVERY
ARCHITECTURAL AND FINE ARTS LIBRARY □
New York, NY

Giraldi, Alfred, Supv.Libn.
AT & T INFORMATION SYSTEMS - LIBRARY □
Morristown, NJ

Girard, Louise H., Hd., Tech.Serv.
UNIVERSITY OF TORONTO - ST. MICHAEL'S
COLLEGE - JOHN M. KELLY LIBRARY □ Toronto,
ON

Girard, Peter, Doc.Libn.
QUEEN'S UNIVERSITY AT KINGSTON -
DOCUMENTS LIBRARY □ Kingston, ON

Girard, Rodrigue, Bibliotechnicien
HOPITAL DE CHICOUTIMI INC. -
BIBLIOTHEQUE† □ Chicoutimi, PQ

Girard, Suzanne, Archv.
SEMINAIRE DES TROIS RIVIERES - ARCHIVES
□ Trois-Rivieres, PQ

Girshick, David, Cat.Libn.
MONTANA HISTORICAL SOCIETY - LIBRARY/
ARCHIVES □ Helena, MT

Gish, Elizabeth, Info.Dir.
NEWTOWN HISTORIC ASSOCIATION, INC. -
RESEARCH CENTER OF NEWTOWN AREA
HISTORY □ Newton, PA

Gisondi, Gary G., Libn.
NEW YORK PUBLIC LIBRARY - PERFORMING
ARTS RESEARCH CENTER - RODGERS &
HAMMERSTEIN ARCHIVES OF RECORDED
SOUND □ New York, NY

Gissendanner, Cassandra S., Cat.Libn.
UNIVERSITY OF SOUTH CAROLINA - COLEMAN
KARESH LAW LIBRARY □ Columbia, SC

Gitner, Fred J., Libn.
FRENCH INSTITUTE/ALLIANCE FRANCAISE -
LIBRARY □ New York, NY

Gitt, Joyce, Lib.Techn.
ETOBICOKE GENERAL HOSPITAL - MEDICAL
LIBRARY □ Rexdale, ON

Gitt, Robert, Film Preservation
UNIVERSITY OF CALIFORNIA, LOS ANGELES -
UCLA FILM ARCHIVES □ Los Angeles, CA

Gittelsohn, I. Marc, Undergraduate Libn.
UNIVERSITY OF CALIFORNIA, SAN DIEGO -
UNIVERSITY LIBRARIES □ La Jolla, CA

Gittinger, Mrs. L.J., Chm.
UNITED DAUGHTERS OF THE CONFEDERACY -
TEXAS CONFEDERATE MUSEUM LIBRARY □
Austin, TX

Gittings, Barbara, Coord.
GAY TASK FORCE - INFORMATION CENTER □
Philadelphia, PA

Gittings, Dan, Libn.
U.S. NATL. MARINE FISHERIES SERVICE -
SOUTHWEST FISHERIES CENTER - LIBRARY □
La Jolla, CA

Gittings, Jeanne A., Med.Libn.
LUTHERAN HOSPITAL - MEDICAL STAFF
LIBRARY AND SCHOOL FOR NURSES LIBRARY □
Moline, IL

Gittings, June A., Lib.Coord.
SALK INSTITUTE FOR BIOLOGICAL STUDIES -
LIBRARY □ San Diego, CA

Gittings, Monte V., Cat.Libn.
U.S. DEPT. OF ENERGY - BONNEVILLE POWER
ADMINISTRATION - LIBRARY □ Portland, OR

Giustino, Emily L., Dir.
ST. MARY MEDICAL CENTER - BELLIS MEDICAL
LIBRARY □ Long Beach, CA

Givens, Beth, Coord., Lib.Serv.
MONTANA STATE LIBRARY □ Helena, MT

Givens, Mary K., ILL Libn./Hd.Ref.Libn.
UNIVERSITY OF TENNESSEE - CENTER FOR
THE HEALTH SCIENCES LIBRARY □ Memphis,
TN

Gjellstad, Rolfe, Ser.Libn.
YALE UNIVERSITY - DIVINITY SCHOOL
LIBRARY □ New Haven, CT

Gjelten, Dan, Ref.Libn.
MINNESOTA STATE LEGISLATIVE REFERENCE
LIBRARY □ St. Paul, MN

Gjeruldsen, Carol, Book Acq.Supv.
FORD FOUNDATION - LIBRARY □ New York, NY

Gladis, Pat, Cons.Libn.
UNIVERSITY OF PITTSBURGH - SPECIAL
COLLECTIONS DEPARTMENT □ Pittsburgh, PA

Gladson, Patricia, Lib.Asst.
CALIFORNIA INSTITUTE OF TECHNOLOGY -
COMPUTER SCIENCE LIBRARY □ Pasadena, CA

Glaser, June, Libn.
EASTMAN DENTAL CENTER - BASIL G. BIBBY
LIBRARY □ Rochester, NY

Glasford, G. Richard, Circ.Libn.
JUILLIARD SCHOOL - LILA ACHESON WALLACE
LIBRARY □ New York, NY

Glaskow, Dr. W.G., Cur.
COSSACK LIBRARY IN NEW YORK □ New York,
NY

Glass, Gary B., Dir./State Geologist
GEOLOGICAL SURVEY OF WYOMING - PUBLIC
RECORDS SECTION □ Laramie, WY

Glass, Robert, Asst.Dir./Hd., Spec.Coll.
CENTRE COLLEGE - GRACE DOHERTY LIBRARY
- SPECIAL COLLECTIONS □ Danville, KY

Glasser, Dorothy, Dept.Hd.
HOUSTON PUBLIC LIBRARY - TEXAS AND
LOCAL HISTORY DEPARTMENT □ Houston, TX

Glasser, Leo G., Dir.
MOUNT CUBA ASTRONOMICAL OBSERVATORY
- LAMBERT L. JACKSON MEMORIAL LIBRARY □
Wilmington, DE

Glassman, Roslyn S., Staff Libn.
LONG ISLAND COLLEGE HOSPITAL - HOAGLAND
MEDICAL LIBRARY □ Brooklyn, NY

Glassmeyer, Anita T., Media Libn.
UNIVERSITY OF ARIZONA - ARIZONA HEALTH
SCIENCES CENTER LIBRARY □ Tucson, AZ

Glatfelter, Dr. Charles H., Dir.
ADAMS COUNTY HISTORICAL SOCIETY -
LIBRARY □ Gettysburg, PA

Glatt, Carol R., Dir.
HELENE FULD MEDICAL CENTER - HEALTH
SCIENCES LIBRARY □ Trenton, NJ

Glaxton-Oldfield, Patricia, Libn.
MC LAUGHLIN (Robert) GALLERY - LIBRARY □
Oshawa, ON

Glazener, Shirley R., Hd., Acq.Dept.
VIRGINIA POLYTECHNIC INSTITUTE AND
STATE UNIVERSITY - CAROL M. NEWMAN
LIBRARY □ Blacksburg, VA

Glazier, Joan W., Lib.Off.
MARINE MIDLAND BANK - LIBRARY □ New
York, NY

Gleason, Burton J., Hd., Office of Info.
AMES LABORATORY - DOCUMENT LIBRARY □
Ames, IA

Gleason, James, Asst.Libn.
ST. FRANCIS OF THE WOODS LTD. - EASTERN
ORTHODOX CATHOLIC CHURCH IN AMERICA -
LIBRARY □ Coyle, OK

Gleason, Linda, Acq.Libn.
MEMORIAL SLOAN-KETTERING CANCER
CENTER - LEE COOMBE MEMORIAL LIBRARY □
New York, NY

Gleboff, Nancy, Indexer
AMERICAN CHEMICAL SOCIETY, INC. -
LIBRARY □ Washington, DC

Glencross, L., Asst. to Lib.Supv.
SASKATCHEWAN - DEPARTMENT OF HEALTH -
LIBRARY □ Regina, SK

Glendenning, Burton, Supv., Hist.Div.
NEW BRUNSWICK - PROVINCIAL ARCHIVES OF
NEW BRUNSWICK □ Fredericton, NB

Glendon, Natasha, Ref.Libn.
AT & T BELL LABORATORIES & TECHNOLOGIES
- LIBRARY □ North Andover, MA

Glenister, Peter, Cat.
MOUNT SAINT VINCENT UNIVERSITY -
LIBRARY □ Halifax, NS

Glenn, James R., Sr. Archv.
SMITHSONIAN INSTITUTION - NATIONAL
ANTHROPOLOGICAL ARCHIVES □ Washington,
DC

Glenn, Jerry, Libn.
UPPER SNAKE RIVER VALLEY HISTORICAL
SOCIETY - LIBRARY □ Rexburg, ID

Glenn, Leila S., Cat.
UNIVERSITY OF MIAMI - SCHOOL OF LAW
LIBRARY □ Coral Gables, FL

Glenn, Lucy D., Chf.Med.Libn.
ROANOKE MEMORIAL HOSPITALS - MEDICAL
LIBRARY □ Roanoke, VA

Glenn, Michael D., Ref.Libn.
SPRINGFIELD-GREENE COUNTY PUBLIC
LIBRARIES - EDWARD M. SHEPARD MEMORIAL
ROOM □ Springfield, MO

Glenn, Susan, Cat.
MITRE CORPORATION - BEDFORD
OPERATIONS LIBRARY □ Bedford, MA

Glenney, Karen, Pub.Aff.Dir.
PLANNED PARENTHOOD CENTER OF SAN
ANTONIO - LIBRARY □ San Antonio, TX

Glennon, Mary, Cat.
UNIVERSITY OF CALIFORNIA, SAN FRANCISCO
- HASTINGS COLLEGE OF THE LAW - LEGAL
INFORMATION CENTER □ San Francisco, CA

Glessner, Charles T., Dir.
U.S. NATL. ARCHIVES & RECORDS SERVICE -
FEDERAL ARCHIVES AND RECORDS CENTER,
REGION 3 □ Philadelphia, PA

Glessner, Debra, Libn.
HAWKINS, DELAFIELD & WOOD - LIBRARY □
New York, NY

Glessner, Eileen E., Dir., Lib.Serv.
BETHESDA LUTHERAN MEDICAL CENTER -
MEDICAL-NURSING LIBRARY □ St. Paul, MN

Glessner, Greta, Dir., Med.Rec.
BACHARACH (Betty) REHABILITATION
HOSPITAL - MEDICAL AND CLINICAL STAFF
LIBRARY □ Pomona, NJ

Glick, Jacqueline, Ref.Libn.
MEDICAL COLLEGE OF WISCONSIN -
LIBRARIES □ Milwaukee, WI

Glick, Nansi, Asst.Dir.
NATIONAL YIDDISH BOOK CENTER, INC. -
LIBRARY □ Amherst, MA

Glick, Dr. Robert, Dir. of Dev.
FOLGER SHAKESPEARE LIBRARY □ Washington,
DC

Glick, Ruth I., Dir.
HUNTINGTON HOSPITAL - MEDICAL LIBRARY □
Huntington, NY

Glickman, Linda S., Libn.
SYSTEM PLANNING CORPORATION -
TECHNICAL LIBRARY □ Arlington, VA

Glidden, Joan, Info.Spec.
AT & T COMMUNICATIONS - INFORMATION
RESEARCH CENTER □ Bedminster, NJ

Glinski, Sharon, Med.Libn.
NORTHWEST COMMUNITY HOSPITAL -
MEDICAL LIBRARY □ Arlington Heights, IL

Glock, Diane C., Cat.
GENERAL ELECTRIC COMPANY - MAIN
LIBRARY □ Schenectady, NY

Glock, Jennie, Libn.
ST. MARY'S HOSPITAL - HEALTH SCIENCES
LIBRARY □ West Palm Beach, FL

Glock, Martha, User Serv.Libn.
U.S. CUSTOMS SERVICE - LIBRARY AND
INFORMATION CENTER □ Washington, DC

Glodek, C.J., Dir.
MICHIGAN CANCER FOUNDATION - LEONARD
N. SIMONS RESEARCH LIBRARY □ Detroit, MI

Glodkowski, Susan J., Sr.Info.Anl.
CONTINENTAL ILLINOIS NATIONAL BANK AND
TRUST COMPANY OF CHICAGO -
INFORMATION SERVICES DIVISION □ Chicago,
IL

Gloeckner, Sylvia, Cur. of Educ.
STUDENTS' MUSEUM, INC. - LIBRARY □
Knoxville, TN

Gloede, Yvonne, Info.Spec.
ALLY AND GARGANO, INC. - INFORMATION
CENTER □ New York, NY

Glogowski, Maryruth, Coord., Search Serv.
SUNY - COLLEGE AT BUFFALO - EDWARD H.
BUTLER LIBRARY □ Buffalo, NY

Gloriod, Barbara, Rd.Adv.
DISTRICT OF COLUMBIA PUBLIC LIBRARY -
LANGUAGE, LITERATURE & FOREIGN
LANGUAGE DIVISION □ Washington, DC

Glover, Carol, Mgr.
ROCKWELL INTERNATIONAL - TECHNICAL
INFORMATION CENTER □ Anaheim, CA

Glover, Clara Ann, Dir.
WHEAT RIDGE REGIONAL CENTER -
EMPLOYEE'S LIBRARY □ Wheat Ridge, CO

Glover, Erika, Assoc.Dir.
GRANGER COLLECTION □ New York, NY

Glover, Frank J., Ref.Libn.
CALIFORNIA STATE LIBRARY - SUTRO LIBRARY
□ San Francisco, CA

Glover, Gwen L., Libn.
CENTRAL CAROLINA TECHNICAL COLLEGE -
LEARNING RESOURCE CENTER □ Sanford, NC

Glover, Jack, Owner
SUNSET TRADING POST-OLD WEST MUSEUM -
LIBRARY □ Sunset, TX

Glover, Janice M., Chf., Lib.Serv.Div.
CANADA - ATMOSPHERIC ENVIRONMENT
SERVICE - LIBRARY □ Downsview, ON

Glover, Lisa, Libn.
AMERICAN COUNCIL FOR THE ARTS - LIBRARY
□ New York, NY

Glover, William, Dir.
GRANGER COLLECTION □ New York, NY

Glovin, Robert P., Sales Mgr.
ISOCHEM RESINS COMPANY - TECHNICAL
INFORMATION CENTER† □ Lincoln, RI

Glowacz, John, Med.Ed.
U.S. AIR FORCE - AEROSPACE MEDICAL
DIVISION - SCHOOL OF AEROSPACE MEDICINE
- STRUGHOLD AEROMEDICAL LIBRARY □ Brooks
AFB, TX

Glueckert, John P., Asst.Libn.
UNIVERSITY OF SOUTHERN CALIFORNIA -
HEALTH SCIENCES CAMPUS - DENTISTRY
LIBRARY □ Los Angeles, CA

Glunz, Diane, Ref.Libn.
UNIVERSITY OF SOUTHERN CALIFORNIA -
HEALTH SCIENCES CAMPUS - NORRIS
MEDICAL LIBRARY □ Los Angeles, CA

Glushakow, Mildred, Dir.
SPRING GARDEN COLLEGE - LIBRARY □
Chestnut Hill, PA

Glynn, Cindy, Pub.Serv.Libn.
SALEM STATE COLLEGE - STUDENT
GOVERNMENT ASSOCIATION & LIBRARY -
LIBRARY OF SOCIAL ALTERNATIVES □ Salem,
MA

Glynn, Jeannette E., Mgr.
BANK OF AMERICA - TECHNOLOGY LIBRARY -
3099 B □ San Francisco, CA

Glynn, Joseph M., Jr., Dir./Libn.
INSTITUTE OF FAMILY HISTORY & GENEALOGY
- LIBRARY □ New Bedford, MA

Glynn, Joseph M., Jr., Dir./Libn.
IRISH GENEALOGICAL SOCIETY - LIBRARY □
New Bedford, MA

Glynn, Joseph M., Jr., Dir./Libn.
ITALIAN FAMILY HISTORY SOCIETY - LIBRARY
□ New Bedford, MA

Gnat, Jean M., Hd., Pub.Serv.
INDIANA UNIVERSITY/PURDUE UNIVERSITY
AT INDIANAPOLIS - 38TH STREET CAMPUS
LIBRARY □ Indianapolis, IN

Gnerre, Elizabeth, Res.
DISNEY (Walt) PRODUCTIONS - LIBRARY □
Burbank, CA

Go, Fe Susan, Doc.Libn.
COMMUNITY SYSTEMS FOUNDATION -
NUTRITION PLANNING INFORMATION
SERVICE □ Ann Arbor, MI

Go, Ivonne K., Libn.
GOVERNOR BACON HEALTH CENTER - MEDICAL
LIBRARY □ Delaware City, DE

Gobar, Anne, Musm.Dir.
HEADLEY-WHITNEY MUSEUM - LIBRARY □
Lexington, KY

Gobeille, Jim, Access/Facilities Serv.
GEORGE WASHINGTON UNIVERSITY -
MEDICAL CENTER - PAUL HIMMELFARB
HEALTH SCIENCES LIBRARY □ Washington, DC

Goble, Frank G., Pres.
JEFFERSON (Thomas) RESEARCH CENTER -
LIBRARY □ Pasadena, CA

Godavari, S. Norma, Hd.Libn.
MANITOBA - DEPT. OF ENVIRONMENTAL &
WORKPLACE SAFETY & HEALTH -
ENVIRONMENTAL MANAGEMENT LIBRARY □
Winnipeg, MB

Godbout-Mercure, Micheline, Hd. of Tech.Serv.
RADIO QUEBEC - CENTRE DES RESSOURCES
DOCUMENTAIRES □ Montreal, PQ

Goddard, John, Cat.
CORNELL UNIVERSITY - MARTIN P.
CATHERWOOD LIBRARY OF INDUSTRIAL AND
LABOR RELATIONS □ Ithaca, NY

Goddard, Susan, Faculty Libn.
UNIVERSITY OF TORONTO - FACULTY OF
DENTISTRY LIBRARY □ Toronto, ON

Godding, Martha, Libn.Dir.
ST. JOSEPH STATE HOSPITAL - PROFESSIONAL
LIBRARY† □ St. Joseph, MO

Goderwis, Cherie L., R.N., Dir.
RUTLAND REGIONAL MEDICAL CENTER -
HEALTH SCIENCE LIBRARY □ Rutland, VT

Godfrey, Charles A., Assoc.Dir.
INTERNATIONAL DEVELOPMENT RESEARCH
CENTRE - LIBRARY† □ Ottawa, ON

Godfrey, Eleanor, Media Rsrcs.Dir.
UNION THEOLOGICAL SEMINARY IN VIRGINIA
- LIBRARY □ Richmond, VA

Godfrey, Lois, Asst.Hd.Libn.
UNIVERSITY OF CALIFORNIA - LOS ALAMOS
NATIONAL LABORATORY - LIBRARY □ Los
Alamos, NM

Godfrey, Norma R., Chf., Lib.Serv.
U.S. VETERANS ADMINISTRATION (KS-Topeka)
- DR. KARL A. MENNINGER MEDICAL LIBRARY □
Topeka, KS

Godlewski, Susan Glover, Hd., Rd.Serv. & Spec.Coll
ART INSTITUTE OF CHICAGO - RYERSON AND
BURNHAM LIBRARIES □ Chicago, IL

Godoy, Alicia, Libn. II
MIAMI-DADE PUBLIC LIBRARY - FOREIGN
LANGUAGES DIVISION □ Miami, FL

Godwin, Carol, Libn.
NATIONAL ENQUIRER - RESEARCH
DEPARTMENT LIBRARY □ Lantana, FL

Godwin, Gerrie, Asst.Libn.
MENNONITE HOSPITAL AND COLLEGE OF
NURSING - HEALTH SCIENCES LIBRARY □
Bloomington, IL

Godwin, Bro. Roy, C.F.A., Prov.Archv.
CONGREGATION OF THE ALEXIAN BROTHERS -
PROVINCIAL ARCHIVES □ Elk Grove Village, IL

Goebel, Heather L., Unit Mgr.
FORT WORTH PUBLIC LIBRARY - ARTS
DEPARTMENT □ Fort Worth, TX

Goecke, Wanda M., Libn.
U.S. AIR FORCE BASE - HOLLOMAN BASE
LIBRARY† □ Holloman AFB, NM

Goeckeler, Steve, Asst.Libn.
BURNS AND MC DONNELL ENGINEERING
COMPANY - TECHNICAL LIBRARY □ Kansas
City, MO

Goedde, Gayle, Asst.Libn.
U.S. DISTRICT COURT - NORTHERN
CALIFORNIA DISTRICT - LOUIS E. GOODMAN
MEMORIAL LIBRARY □ San Francisco, CA

Goedecke, Jane L., Libn.
CANTON HISTORICAL SOCIETY - LIBRARY □
Collinsville, CT

Goedeken, Edward, Tech.Proc.Libn.
WILLIAM PENN COLLEGE - WILCOX LIBRARY -
SPECIAL COLLECTIONS □ Oskaloosa, IA

Goedeker, Marianne C., Libn.
JOHNSON (George) ADVERTISING - LIBRARY □
St. Louis, MO

Goehner, Donna, Acq.Libn.
WESTERN ILLINOIS UNIVERSITY - LIBRARIES
□ Macomb, IL

Goekler, Lester A., Asst.Libn.
TEXAS RESEARCH INSTITUTE OF MENTAL
SCIENCES - LIBRARY □ Houston, TX

Goel, Krishan S., Libn.
U.S. ARMY - ENVIRONMENTAL HYGIENE
AGENCY - LIBRARY □ Aberdeen Proving Ground,
MD

Goeldner, C.R., Dir.
UNIVERSITY OF COLORADO, BOULDER -
BUSINESS RESEARCH DIVISION - BUSINESS &
ECONOMIC COLLECTION □ Boulder, CO

Goeldner, C.R., Dir.
UNIVERSITY OF COLORADO, BOULDER -
BUSINESS RESEARCH DIVISION - TRAVEL
REFERENCE CENTER □ Boulder, CO

Goerig, Janet, Dir., Lib.Serv.
ST. VINCENT'S MEDICAL CENTER - DANIEL T.
BANKS HEALTH SCIENCE LIBRARY □ Bridgeport,
CT

Goerler, Dr. Raimund E., Univ.Archv.
OHIO STATE UNIVERSITY - ARCHIVES □
Columbus, OH

Goerner, Richard, Libn.
BERGEN COUNTY HISTORICAL SOCIETY -
JOHNSON LIBRARY □ River Edge, NJ

Goers, Willona Graham, Corp.Libn.
PIONEER HI-BRED INTERNATIONAL, INC. -
CORPORATE LIBRARY □ Des Moines, IA

Goertzen, Norma S., Dir.
NORTH PARK COLLEGE AND THEOLOGICAL
SEMINARY - MELLANDER LIBRARY □ Chicago,
IL

Goertzen, Peter, Mgr.
MENNONITE VILLAGE MUSEUM (Canada) INC. -
LIBRARY □ Steinbach, MB

Goethert, Gay D., Lib.Supv.
ARNOLD ENGINEERING DEVELOPMENT CENTER
TECHNICAL LIBRARY □ Arnold Air Force Sta., TN

Goetsch, Rev. Ronald W., Archv.
LUTHERAN CHURCH - MISSOURI SYNOD -
NORTH WISCONSIN DISTRICT ARCHIVES □
Wausau, WI

Goetz, Phyllis E., Chf., Lib.Serv.
U.S. VETERANS ADMINISTRATION (MI-Iron
Mountain) - MEDICAL CENTER LIBRARY □ Iron
Mountain, MI

Goff, Dewey A., Jr., Chf., Docs.
U.S. AIR FORCE - AEROSPACE MEDICAL
DIVISION - SCHOOL OF AEROSPACE MEDICINE
- STRUGHOLD AEROMEDICAL LIBRARY □ Brooks
AFB, TX

Goff, Fred, Exec.Dir.
INVESTIGATIVE RESOURCE CENTER - DATA
CENTER □ Oakland, CA

Goff, Karen E., Ref.Libn.
WEST VIRGINIA STATE LIBRARY COMMISSION
- REFERENCE LIBRARY □ Charleston, WV

Goff, Linda J., Local Hist.Libn.
FRESNO COUNTY FREE LIBRARY - SPECIAL
COLLECTIONS □ Fresno, CA

Goff, William J., Libn.
UNIVERSITY OF CALIFORNIA, SAN DIEGO -
SCRIPPS INSTITUTION OF OCEANOGRAPHY
LIBRARY □ La Jolla, CA

Gogeen, Patricia A., Dir.
WESTERN ILLINOIS UNIVERSITY - LIBRARIES
□ Macomb, IL

Gohlke, Annette, Libn.
U.S. AIR FORCE BASE - CHANUTE BASE
TECHNICAL BRANCH LIBRARY† □ Chanute AFB,
IL

Gohmann, Rev. Myron, C.P., Hd.Libn.
KENRICK SEMINARY LIBRARY □ St. Louis, MO

Gokhale, Shakuntala, Libn.
FORT WORTH PUBLIC LIBRARY - ARTS
DEPARTMENT □ Fort Worth, TX

Gold, Betty, Libn.
NATIONAL COUNCIL ON ALCOHOLISM, INC. -
YVELIN GARDNER ALCOHOLISM LIBRARY □
New York, NY

Gold, David, Dir. & Archv.
GOLD PARACHUTE LIBRARY, ARCHIVES &
TECHNICAL INFORMATION CENTER □
Ridgecrest, CA

Gold, Ethel, Ref.
NEW YORK INSTITUTE OF TECHNOLOGY -
LIBRARY □ Old Westbury, NY

Gold, James
HARTFORD PUBLIC LIBRARY - REFERENCE AND
GENERAL READING DEPARTMENT □ Hartford,
CT

Gold, Jeffrey, Educ.Off.
EMBASE (Excerpta Medica Online) □ New York,
NY

Gold, Leonard S., Div.Chf.
NEW YORK PUBLIC LIBRARY - JEWISH
DIVISION □ New York, NY

Gold, Suzanne, Libn./Asst.Hd.
UNIVERSITY OF CALIFORNIA, BERKELEY -
GOVERNMENT DOCUMENTS DEPARTMENT □
Berkeley, CA

Gold, Virginia, Libn.
AGUDAS ACHIM CONGREGATION - STEIN
MEMORIAL LIBRARY □ Columbus, OH

Goldbach, Elaine M., Info.Spec.
UNION CARBIDE CORPORATION - BATTERY
PRODUCTS DIVISION - TECHNICAL
INFORMATION CENTER □ Westlake, OH

Goldbeck, Gwendolyn, Asst.Sci.Libn.
MARQUETTE UNIVERSITY - SCIENCE LIBRARY
□ Milwaukee, WI

Goldberg, Barbara B., Chf.Libn.
U.S. VETERANS ADMINISTRATION (NY-
Brooklyn) - MEDICAL CENTER LIBRARY □
Brooklyn, NY

Goldberg, Elizabeth D., Adm.Libn.
CONSUMER PRODUCT SAFETY COMMISSION -
LIBRARY □ Washington, DC

Goldberg, Eve M., Libn.
RHODE ISLAND STATE DEPARTMENT OF
ELDERLY AFFAIRS - LIBRARY □ Providence, RI

Goldberg, Joan E., Tech.Libn.
BETZ LABORATORIES, INC. - RESEARCH
LIBRARY □ Trevose, PA

Goldberg, Kenneth, Res.Libn.
NORTHEAST OHIO AREAWIDE COORDINATING
AGENCY - RESEARCH LIBRARY† □ Cleveland,
OH

Goldberg, Louise, Libn.
CANADIAN BROADCASTING CORPORATION -
REFERENCE LIBRARY □ Toronto, ON

Goldberg, Dr. Louise, Rare Books Libn.
UNIVERSITY OF ROCHESTER - EASTMAN
SCHOOL OF MUSIC - SIBLEY MUSIC LIBRARY □
Rochester, NY

Goldberg, Marcia, Ref.Libn.
U.S. MERCHANT MARINE ACADEMY -
SCHUYLER OTIS BLAND MEMORIAL LIBRARY □
Kings Point, NY

Goldberg, Rebecca, Dir.
LAKE COUNTY MUSEUM - LIBRARY AND
INFORMATION CENTER □ Wauconda, IL

Goldberg, Richard, Media Spec.
ST. JOHN'S UNIVERSITY - COLLEGE OF
PHARMACY & ALLIED HEALTH PROFESSIONS -
HEALTH EDUCATION RESOURCE CENTER □
Jamaica, NY

Goldberg, Ronnie, Search Spec.
SUNY AT BINGHAMTON - SCIENCE LIBRARY □
Binghamton, NY

Goldblatt, Margaret, Ser.Libn.
WASHINGTON UNIVERSITY - SCHOOL OF LAW
- FREUND LAW LIBRARY □ St. Louis, MO

Golden, Barbara, Ref.Libn.
HENNEPIN COUNTY LAW LIBRARY† □
Minneapolis, MN

Golden, Barbara, Coord., County Lib.Proj.
MINNESOTA STATE LAW LIBRARY □ St. Paul,
MN

Golden, Nancy J., Hd., Pub.Serv.
BOSTON UNIVERSITY MEDICAL CENTER -
ALUMNI MEDICAL LIBRARY □ Boston, MA

Golden, Patricia
NEW ZEALAND EMBASSY - LIBRARY □
Washington, DC

Golden, Susan, Libn./Ch.Lit.Spec.
APPALACHIAN STATE UNIVERSITY - BELK
LIBRARY - JUSTICE-QUERY INSTRUCTIONAL
MATERIALS CENTER □ Boone, NC

Goldenberg, Stephen, Video Libn.
SEATTLE PUBLIC LIBRARY - MEDIA &
PROGRAM SERVICES† □ Seattle, WA

Goldfarb, Amy Jo, Art & Arch.Libn.
PRATT INSTITUTE - LIBRARY □ Brooklyn, NY

Goldfarb, Harriet, Cur.
PERELMAN ANTIQUE TOY MUSEUM - LIBRARY
□ Philadelphia, PA

Goldin, Ruth, Ref.Libn.
AT & T BELL LABORATORIES & TECHNOLOGIES
- LIBRARY □ Columbus, OH

Goldman, Arlene, Libn.
AMERICAN ASSOCIATION OF MEDICO-LEGAL
CONSULTANTS - LIBRARY □ Philadelphia, PA

Goldman, Cynthia A., Libn.
U.S. NATL. BUREAU OF STANDARDS - OFFICE
OF STANDARD REFERENCE DATA - REFERENCE
CENTER □ Washington, DC

Goldman, Elaine, Info.Spec.
AMERICAN ASSOCIATION OF ADVERTISING
AGENCIES - MEMBER INFORMATION SERVICE
□ New York, NY

Goldman, Irene, Asst.Libn.
CONNECTICUT GENERAL LIFE INSURANCE
COMPANY - CORPORATE LIBRARY† □ Hartford,
CT

Goldman, Kimberly, ILL Libn.
UNIVERSITY OF ILLINOIS AT CHICAGO -
HEALTH SCIENCES CENTER - LIBRARY OF THE
HEALTH SCIENCES □ Chicago, IL

Goldman, Martha, Libn.
KELLEY, DRYE & WARREN - LAW LIBRARY □
New York, NY

Goldman, Rose, Libn.
LOCH HAVEN ART CENTER, INC. - LIBRARY □
Orlando, FL

Goldman, Viki, Ref.Libn.
BATTEN, BARTON, DURSTINE, OSBORN, INC. -
INFORMATION RETRIEVAL CENTER† □ New
York, NY

Goldman, Wendy, Res.Libn.
CONSUMERS UNION OF UNITED STATES, INC. -
LIBRARY □ Mount Vernon, NY

Goldner, Loren, Libn.
HARVARD UNIVERSITY - CENTER FOR
EUROPEAN STUDIES - LIBRARY □ Cambridge,
MA

Golds, Gaye, Film Libn.
APPALACHIAN STATE UNIVERSITY - BELK
LIBRARY - JUSTICE-QUERY INSTRUCTIONAL
MATERIALS CENTER □ Boone, NC

Goldschmid, Johanna, Spec.Coll.Libn.
SAN FRANCISCO PUBLIC LIBRARY - SPECIAL
COLLECTIONS DEPARTMENT □ San Francisco,
CA

Goldschmidt, Eric N., Sr.Lit.Sci.
WARNER-LAMBERT COMPANY - CORPORATE
LIBRARY □ Morris Plains, NJ

Goldstaub, Curt S., Cat.Libn.
KUTZTOWN UNIVERSITY - ROHRBACH
LIBRARY □ Kutztown, PA

Goldstein, Arthur A.A., Chf.Cat.
KXE6S VEREIN CHESS SOCIETY - SPECIAL/
RESEARCH LIBRARY - EAST DIVISION □ Chapel
Hill, NC

Goldstein, Doris, Dir., Lib. & Info.Serv.
GEORGETOWN UNIVERSITY - KENNEDY
INSTITUTE OF ETHICS - CENTER FOR
BIOETHICS LIBRARY □ Washington, DC

Goldstein, Evelyn M., Dir.
AMERICAN ASSOCIATION OF MEDICO-LEGAL
CONSULTANTS - LIBRARY □ Philadelphia, PA

Goldstein, Florence, Asst.
TEMPLE EMANU-EL - WILLIAM P. ENGEL
LIBRARY □ Birmingham, AL

Goldstein, Harold S., Exec.Dir.
AMERICAN ROSE SOCIETY - LIBRARY □
Shreveport, LA

Goldstein, Dr. Kenneth, Hd.
UNIVERSITY OF PENNSYLVANIA -
DEPARTMENT OF FOLKLORE & FOLKLIFE -
ARCHIVE □ Philadelphia, PA

Goldstein, Norma, Patients' Libn.
U.S. VETERANS ADMINISTRATION (NY-
Montrose) - HOSPITAL LIBRARY □ Montrose, NY

Goldstein, Rachael K., Libn.
COLUMBIA UNIVERSITY - HEALTH SCIENCES
LIBRARY □ New York, NY

Goldstein, Sidney, Dir.
BROWN UNIVERSITY - POPULATION STUDIES
AND TRAINING CENTER - DEMOGRAPHY
LIBRARY □ Providence, RI

Goldstone, Murray A., M.D., Chm., Lib.Comm.
CLEVELAND PSYCHOANALYTIC SOCIETY -
LIBRARY □ Cleveland, OH

Goldzwig, Jeanne B., Libn.
TEMPLE ISRAEL - RABBI LOUIS WITT
MEMORIAL LIBRARY □ Dayton, OH

Gole, Lidwina J., Chf., Preparations Br.
U.S. ARMY WAR COLLEGE - LIBRARY □ Carlisle
Barracks, PA

Golembiewski, Terri M., Chf.Ref.Libn.
CHICAGO SUN-TIMES - EDITORIAL LIBRARY □
Chicago, IL

Golightly, Bonnie, Libn.
SEAMEN'S CHURCH INSTITUTE OF NEW YORK
- JOSEPH CONRAD LIBRARY □ New York, NY

Gollop, Sandra, Ref.Libn.
MC GRAW-HILL, INC. - LIBRARY □ New York,
NY

Gollub, George A., Law Libn.
NORTHAMPTON COUNTY LAW LIBRARY □
Easton, PA

Golob, Mimi, Mgr.
AYERST LABORATORIES - INFORMATION
CENTER □ New York, NY

Golobic, Eleonora, Archv.
JEWISH LABOR BUND - BUND ARCHIVES OF
THE JEWISH LABOR MOVEMENT □ New York,
NY

Golobish, Robert W., Commun.Res.Coord.
INDIANAPOLIS POWER & LIGHT COMPANY -
CORPORATE COMMUNICATIONS REFERENCE
CENTER □ Indianapolis, IN

Golrick, Michael A., Hd.
BRIDGEPORT PUBLIC LIBRARY - TECHNOLOGY
AND BUSINESS DEPARTMENT □ Bridgeport, CT

Golt, Lucille, Abstractor/Indexer
HERCULES, INC. - RESEARCH CENTER -
TECHNICAL INFORMATION DIVISION □
Wilmington, DE

Goltz, Eileen, Pub.Docs.
LAURENTIAN UNIVERSITY - MAIN LIBRARY □
Sudbury, ON

Gomez, Aurora, Libn.
BORICUA COLLEGE - LIBRARY - SPECIAL
COLLECTIONS □ New York, NY

Gomez, Gerardo, Libn.
BRONX-LEBANON HOSPITAL CENTER -
CONCOURSE DIVISION MEDICAL LIBRARY □
Bronx, NY

Gomez, Phillip J., Park Techn.
U.S. NATL. PARK SERVICE - FORT LARAMIE
NATL. HISTORIC SITE - LIBRARY □ Fort
Laramie, WY

Gomez, Rosa, Per.Coord.
UNIVERSITY OF MIAMI - SCHOOL OF
MEDICINE - LOUIS CALDER MEMORIAL
LIBRARY □ Miami, FL

Gomien, Margaret, Libn.
BETHESDA HOSPITAL - INFORMATION
RESOURCE CENTER† □ Cincinnati, OH

Gondy, Allie Wise, Music Libn.
WESTERN ILLINOIS UNIVERSITY - LIBRARIES
□ Macomb, IL

Gong, James G., Ref.Libn.
SEATTLE-FIRST NATIONAL BANK - LIBRARY □ Seattle, WA

Gongoll, Ward E., Hd.Libn.
OBLATES THEOLOGY LIBRARY □ Washington, DC

Gonnami, Tsuneharu, Japanese Ref.Libn.
UNIVERSITY OF BRITISH COLUMBIA - ASIAN STUDIES LIBRARY □ Vancouver, BC

Gonos, Kleanthy, Cons., Lib.Serv.
CONTRA COSTA COUNTY OFFICE OF EDUCATION - ACCESS INFORMATION CENTER & PROFESSIONAL LIBRARY □ Concord, CA

Gontrum, Barbara S., Dir.
UNIVERSITY OF MARYLAND, BALTIMORE - SCHOOL OF LAW - MARSHALL LAW LIBRARY □ Baltimore, MD

Gonyon, Sr. Jeanne M., Libn.
CARMELITE MONASTERY - LIBRARY OF THE IMMACULATE HEART OF MARY □ Barre, VT

Gonyou, James F., Dir., Agri.Res.
GREAT WESTERN SUGAR COMPANY - AGRICULTURAL RESEARCH CENTER - RESEARCH LIBRARY □ Longmont, CO

Gonzales, Andrea, Mktg.Info.Spec.
LEVI STRAUSS & COMPANY - CORPORATE MARKETING INFORMATION CENTER† □ San Francisco, CA

Gonzalez, Carmen A., Libn.
UNIVERSITY OF PUERTO RICO - NATURAL SCIENCE LIBRARY □ Rio Piedras, PR

Gonzalez, Louis, Dir.
KAMAN-TEMPO - METAL MATRIX COMPOSITES INFORMATION ANALYSIS CENTER □ Santa Barbara, CA

Gonzalez, Raphael, Libn.
ROGERS & WELLS - LAW LIBRARY □ New York, NY

Gonzalez, Valentin, Coll.Dev. & Ref.Libn.
INTERAMERICAN UNIVERSITY OF PUERTO RICO - SCHOOL OF LAW - DOMINGO TOLEDO ALAMO LAW LIBRARY† □ Santurce, PR

Gonzalez, Victoria, Med.Libn.
BERGEN PINES COUNTY HOSPITAL - MEDICAL LIBRARY □ Paramus, NJ

Gooch, William D., Asst. State Libn.
TEXAS STATE LIBRARY □ Austin, TX

Good, Julanne M., Supv.
ST. LOUIS PUBLIC LIBRARY - CAROL MC DONALD GARDNER RARE BOOK ROOM □ St. Louis, MO

Good, Julanne M., Supv.
ST. LOUIS PUBLIC LIBRARY - CHILDREN'S LITERATURE ROOM □ St. Louis, MO

Good, Ruth, Hd.Libn.
TOCCOA FALLS COLLEGE - SEBY JONES LIBRARY □ Toccoa Falls, GA

Goodale, Leslie, Dir.
CHILDREN'S MEMORIAL HOSPITAL - JOSEPH BRENNEMANN LIBRARY □ Chicago, IL

Goodale, Leslie J., Lib.Dir.
MEHARRY MEDICAL COLLEGE - MEDICAL LIBRARY - LEARNING RESOURCES CENTER □ Nashville, TN

Goodchild, Eleanor, Biomed.Libn.
UNIVERSITY OF PENNSYLVANIA - BIOMEDICAL LIBRARY □ Philadelphia, PA

Goode, Allan, AV
OKLAHOMA STATE DEPARTMENT OF LIBRARIES □ Oklahoma City, OK

Goode, Robbie, Libn.
CHARLESTON EVENING POST/NEWS AND COURIER - LIBRARY □ Charleston, SC

Goodell, Lela, Asst.Libn.
HAWAIIAN MISSION CHILDREN'S SOCIETY - LIBRARY □ Honolulu, HI

Goodelle, Malcolm, Archv.
CAYUGA COUNTY HISTORICAL RESEARCH CENTER - LIBRARY □ Auburn, NY

Goodemote, Rita L., Assoc.Dir.
SCHERING-PLOUGH CORPORATION - PHARMACEUTICAL RESEARCH DIVISION - LIBRARY INFORMATION CENTER □ Bloomfield, NJ

Gooden, Gerald L., Dir.
BIOLA UNIVERSITY - LIBRARY □ La Mirada, CA

Gooden, Kathryn, Libn.
GREENE COUNTY HISTORICAL SOCIETY - LIBRARY AND MUSEUM □ Waynesburg, PA

Goodhartz, Gerald, Libn.
KAYE, SCHOLER, FIERMAN, HAYS & HANDLER - LAW LIBRARY □ New York, NY

Goodhouse, Barbara A., Libn.
YORK RESEARCH CORPORATION - LIBRARY† □ Stamford, CT

Goodlett, Doris, Hd., Adult Serv.
FERGUSON LIBRARY - BUSINESS-TECHNOLOGY DEPARTMENT □ Stamford, CT

Goodman, Barbara, Libn.
U.S. DEPT. OF LABOR - OSHA - REGION III LIBRARY □ Philadelphia, PA

Goodman, Barbara W., Tech.Sec.-Libn.
THIELE KAOLIN COMPANY - RESEARCH & DEVELOPMENT LIBRARY □ Sandersville, GA

Goodman, David
NATIONAL ACTION/RESEARCH ON THE MILITARY-INDUSTRIAL COMPLEX - LIBRARY □ Philadelphia, PA

Goodman, Dr. David, Libn.
PRINCETON UNIVERSITY - CHEMISTRY & BIOCHEMISTRY LIBRARY □ Princeton, NJ

Goodman, Edward, Educ.Bibliog.
SYRACUSE UNIVERSITY - E.S. BIRD LIBRARY - SOCIAL SCIENCES DEPARTMENT □ Syracuse, NY

Goodman, Eva, Asst.Libn.
LAFAYETTE JOURNAL AND COURIER - LIBRARY □ Lafayette, IN

Goodman, Jerry, Exec.Dir.
NATIONAL CONFERENCE ON SOVIET JEWRY (NCSJ) - RESEARCH BUREAU □ New York, NY

Goodman, Bro. L. Dennis, F.S.C., Archv.
MORAGA HISTORICAL SOCIETY - ARCHIVES □ Moraga, CA

Goodman, L. M., Coord.
AMERICAN LIFE FOUNDATION - PRANG-MARK SOCIETY - LIBRARY □ Watkins Glen, NY

Goodman, Lois A., Asst.Dir., Info.Serv.
ROCHESTER INSTITUTE OF TECHNOLOGY - WALLACE MEMORIAL LIBRARY □ Rochester, NY

Goodman, Marcia M., Libn.
UNIVERSITY OF OKLAHOMA - HISTORY OF SCIENCE COLLECTIONS □ Norman, OK

Goodman, Marcia M., Libn.
UNIVERSITY OF OKLAHOMA - LIMITED ACCESS COLLECTION □ Norman, OK

Goodman, Marion, Libn.
MARYLAND NATIONAL CAPITAL PARK AND PLANNING COMMISSION - MONTGOMERY COUNTY PLANNING DEPARTMENT - LIBRARY □ Silver Spring, MD

Goodman, Roy E., Reading Rm.Libn.
AMERICAN PHILOSOPHICAL SOCIETY - LIBRARY □ Philadelphia, PA

Goodrich, Klara B., Med.Libn.
RESURRECTION HOSPITAL - MEDICAL LIBRARY & ALLIED HEALTH SCIENCES □ Chicago, IL

Goodrich, Margaret, Libn.
DENVER ART MUSEUM - FREDERIC H. DOUGLAS LIBRARY OF ANTHROPOLOGY AND ART □ Denver, CO

Goodridge, Betty, Info.Ctr.Coord.
CELANESE CORPORATION - CELANESE CHEMICAL COMPANY, INC. - TECHNICAL CENTER - LIBRARY† □ Corpus Christi, TX

Goodridge, Kathleen Powers, Cat.Libn.
JOHN MARSHALL LAW SCHOOL - LIBRARY □ Chicago, IL

Goodsell, Joan, Cat.
THOMPSON (J. Walter) COMPANY - INFORMATION CENTER □ New York, NY

Goodstein, Donna, Libn.
MEDICAL LETTER - LIBRARY □ New Rochelle, NY

Goodstein, Dr. Judith, Inst.Archv.
CALIFORNIA INSTITUTE OF TECHNOLOGY - MILLIKAN LIBRARY □ Pasadena, CA

Goodwell, Don A., Curator
WAYNE COUNTY HISTORICAL MUSEUM - LIBRARY □ Richmond, IN

Goodwin, Cheryl M., Libn.
ST. JOSEPH HOSPITAL AND HEALTH CARE CENTER - HOSPITAL LIBRARY □ Tacoma, WA

Goodwin, Conrad M., Libn.
BOSTON UNIVERSITY - CENTER FOR ARCHAEOLOGICAL STUDIES - LIBRARY □ Boston, MA

Goodwin, George H., Jr., Chf.Libn.
U.S. GEOLOGICAL SURVEY - LIBRARY □ Reston, VA

Goodwin, J.H., Libn.
VIRGINIA THEOLOGICAL SEMINARY - BISHOP PAYNE LIBRARY □ Alexandria, VA

Goodwin, Joann, Ref.Libn.
SAN DIEGO STATE UNIVERSITY - GOVERNMENT PUBLICATIONS DEPARTMENT† □ San Diego, CA

Goodwin, Linda M., Photo Libn.
ONTARIO - MINISTRY OF TOURISM AND RECREATION - PHOTO LIBRARY □ Toronto, ON

Goodwin, Marlene, Med.Libn.
SAN BERNARDINO COMMUNITY HOSPITAL - MEDICAL LIBRARY □ San Bernardino, CA

Goodwin, Vania, Act.Hd., Tech.Serv.
INDIANA UNIVERSITY/PURDUE UNIVERSITY AT INDIANAPOLIS - UNIVERSITY LIBRARY □ Indianapolis, IN

Goodwin, Dr. William N., Dir.
YOUNG MEN'S CHRISTIAN ASSOCIATION OF METROPOLITAN HARTFORD, INC. - CAREER COUNSELING CENTER LIBRARY □ Hartford, CT

Goold, Karla P., Libn.
UNIVERSITY OF NOTRE DAME - CHEMISTRY/PHYSICS LIBRARY □ Notre Dame, IN

Goolsby, Peggy B., Lib.Techn.
U.S. DEPT. OF DEFENSE - DEFENSE INDUSTRIAL PLANT EQUIPMENT CENTER - TECHNICAL DATA REPOSITORY & LIBRARY □ Memphis, TN

Goon, Diane, Ref.Libn.
COLUMBIA UNIVERSITY - HERBERT H. LEHMAN LIBRARY □ New York, NY

Goorough, Gary, Coord., Film Lib.
UNIVERSITY OF WISCONSIN, LA CROSSE - AUDIOVISUAL CENTER - FILM LIBRARY □ La Crosse, WI

Goostray, Margaret R., Asst.Dir.
BOSTON UNIVERSITY - DEPARTMENT OF SPECIAL COLLECTIONS □ Boston, MA

Gorchels, Dr. Clarence, Dir.
WESTERN OREGON STATE COLLEGE - LIBRARY □ Monmouth, OR

Gorden, Jan, Lib.Spec.
UNIVERSITY OF WASHINGTON - COMPUTING INFORMATION CENTER □ Seattle, WA

Gordon, Anne M., Dir.
NEW YORK CITY - MUNICIPAL REFERENCE AND RESEARCH CENTER □ New York, NY

Gordon, Anne W., Hd.
UNIVERSITY OF PITTSBURGH - HENRY CLAY FRICK FINE ARTS LIBRARY □ Pittsburgh, PA

Gordon, Barbara B., Hd.
UNIVERSITY OF WASHINGTON - FOREST RESOURCES LIBRARY □ Seattle, WA

Gordon, Charles L., Film Lib.Coord.
UNIVERSITY OF SOUTH FLORIDA - DIVISION OF EDUCATIONAL RESOURCES - FILM LIBRARY □ Tampa, FL

Gordon, Constance G., Rare Book Cat.
CHICAGO PUBLIC LIBRARY CULTURAL CENTER - SPECIAL COLLECTIONS DIVISION □ Chicago, IL

Gordon, Donna M., Libn.
ALBERTA - DEPARTMENT OF ECONOMIC DEVELOPMENT - LIBRARY □ Edmonton, AB

Gordon, Dr. Irving, Supv.
OCCIDENTAL CHEMICAL CORPORATION - TECHNICAL INFORMATION CENTER □ Niagara Falls, NY

Gordon, James, Ref.Libn.
BROOKLYN LAW SCHOOL - LAW LIBRARY □ Brooklyn, NY

Gordon, Jayne, Dir.
ALCOTT (Louisa May) MEMORIAL ASSOCIATION - LIBRARY □ Concord, MA

Gordon, Jean, Archv.Asst.
CHAMPAIGN COUNTY HISTORICAL ARCHIVES □ Urbana, IL

Gordon, Martin, Per.Libn.
FRANKLIN AND MARSHALL COLLEGE - SHADEK-FACKENTHAL LIBRARY - SPECIAL COLLECTIONS □ Lancaster, PA

Gordon, Mary, AIDS Abstractor
FOREST PRODUCTS RESEARCH SOCIETY - FOREST INFORMATION RETRIEVAL SYSTEM □ Madison, WI

Gordon, Miriam, Ref.
CLEVELAND HEALTH SCIENCES LIBRARY - HEALTH CENTER LIBRARY □ Cleveland, OH

Gordon, Myrtle, Libn.
BETH EMET, THE FREE SYNAGOGUE - BRUCE GORDON MEMORIAL LIBRARY □ Evanston, IL

Gordon, Phyllis, Libn.
CUYAHOGA COUNTY REGIONAL PLANNING COMMISSION - LIBRARY □ Cleveland, OH

Gordon, Renita, Libn.
FOOTE CONE & BELDING - INFORMATION CENTER □ Chicago, IL

Gordon, Richard, Lib.Mgr.
UNITED CEREBRAL PALSY OF NEW YORK CITY, INC. - LIBRARY □ New York, NY

Gordon, Mrs. Robert, Sec.
MIDDLEBURY HISTORICAL SOCIETY - MIDDLEBURY ACADEMY MUSEUM LIBRARY □ Wyoming, NY

Gordon, Robert N., Exec.Dir.
BRAILLE CIRCULATING LIBRARY, INC. □ Richmond, VA

Gordon, Sharon L., Tech.Serv.
LANCASTER BIBLE COLLEGE - STOLL MEMORIAL LIBRARY □ Lancaster, PA

Gordon, Tom, Rd.Serv.Libn.
FORSYTH TECHNICAL INSTITUTE - LIBRARY □ Winston-Salem, NC

Gordon, Warren, Hd.Libn.
FRIED FRANK HARRIS SHRIVER JACOBSON - LIBRARY & INFORMATION CENTER □ New York, NY

Gordon, William B., Hd.
COLUMBIA MUSEUMS OF ART & SCIENCE - LIBRARY □ Columbia, SC

Gordy, Dawn, Tech.Info.Spec.
U.S. NATL. HIGHWAY TRAFFIC SAFETY ADMINISTRATION - TECHNICAL REFERENCE DIVISION □ Washington, DC

Gore, LCDR M., Lib.Off.
U.S. NAVY - NAVAL AIR STATION (FL-Key West) - LIBRARY □ Key West, FL

Gorecki, Sr. M. Tiburtia, Dir.
HILBERT COLLEGE - MC GRATH LIBRARY - SPECIAL COLLECTIONS □ Hamburg, NY

Gorecki, Sr. M. Tiburtia, F.S.S.J., Cons.
ST. JOSEPH INTERCOMMUNITY HOSPITAL - MEDICAL STAFF LIBRARY □ Cheektowaga, NY

Goregliad, Sergei, Asst.Libn.
BUSINESS INTERNATIONAL - RESEARCH LIBRARY □ New York, NY

Goren, Morton S., Libn.
U.S. DRUG ENFORCEMENT ADMINISTRATION - LIBRARY □ Washington, DC

Goren, Simon L., Law Libn.
CASE WESTERN RESERVE UNIVERSITY - LAW SCHOOL LIBRARY† □ Cleveland, OH

Gorghan, Ann, Med.Libn.
ST. JOSEPH'S MEDICAL CENTER - MEDICAL LIBRARY □ Yonkers, NY

Gorin, Robert, ILL
STATE LIBRARY OF FLORIDA □ Tallahassee, FL

Gorman, Barbara M., Cur. of Hist.
KANSAS CITY MUSEUM OF HISTORY AND SCIENCE - ARCHIVES □ Kansas City, MO

Gorman, Daria, Cat.
UNIVERSITY OF MEDICINE AND DENTISTRY OF NEW JERSEY AT NEWARK - GEORGE F. SMITH LIBRARY □ Newark, NJ

Gorman, Evelyn S., Dir., Lib.Serv.
ST. JOSEPH'S HOSPITAL - MEDICAL LIBRARY □ Phoenix, AZ

Gorman, J.F., Mgr.
VALLEY NATIONAL BANK - LIBRARY/INFORMATION CENTER □ Phoenix, AZ

Gorman, Kathleen, Ref./Lib.Sci.Bibliog.
UNIVERSITY OF MINNESOTA - EDUCATION-PSYCHOLOGY-LIBRARY SCIENCE COLLECTION □ Minneapolis, MN

Gorman, Patricia, Docs.
PLANNING RESEARCH CORPORATION - TECHNICAL LIBRARY □ McLean, VA

Gormezano, Keith S., Dir./Coord.
LE BEACON PRESSE - SMALL PRESS COLLECTION □ Seattle, WA

Gormley, Eric, Archv.
GLENBOW-ALBERTA INSTITUTE - LIBRARY & ARCHIVES □ Calgary, AB

Gormley, Mary T., Supv.
AMERICAN CAN COMPANY - BARRINGTON TECHNICAL CENTER - TECHNICAL INFORMATION CENTER □ Barrington, IL

Gorrell, Fleeta, Asst.Libn.
BAKER & BOTTS - LAW LIBRARY† □ Houston, TX

Gorrell, Linda Graves, Res.Asst.
OHIO POETRY THERAPY CENTER - WELCH LIBRARY □ Columbus, OH

Gorrell, Lisa, Chf.Libn.
CALIFORNIA RAILWAY MUSEUM - LIBRARY □ Suisun City, CA

Gorski, Susan
UNIVERSITY OF ALASKA, ANCHORAGE - ANCHORAGE URBAN OBSERVATORY - LIBRARY □ Anchorage, AK

Gorsky, Jane, Ref.Libn.
UNIVERSITY OF CINCINNATI - MEDICAL CENTER LIBRARIES - HEALTH SCIENCES LIBRARY† □ Cincinnati, OH

Goshulak, Osyp, European Lit.Spec.
METROPOLITAN TORONTO LIBRARY - LITERATURE DEPARTMENT □ Toronto, ON

Gosier, Doris, Coord.Pub.Serv.
FORT VALLEY STATE COLLEGE - HENRY ALEXANDER HUNT MEMORIAL LEARNING RESOURCES CENTER □ Fort Valley, GA

Goss, Anita B., Res.Libn.
PARADE PUBLICATIONS, INC. - LIBRARY □ New York, NY

Goss, Anne S., Hd.Libn.
OHIO UNIVERSITY - HEALTH SCIENCES LIBRARY □ Athens, OH

Goss, Dorothy K., Chf.Libn.
HUGHES HELICOPTERS - LIBRARY □ Culver City, CA

Goss, Jessica S., Hd.Libn.
WORCESTER HISTORICAL MUSEUM - LIBRARY □ Worcester, MA

Goss, Sue, Libn.
MOTOROLA, INC. - GOVERNMENT ELECTRONICS GROUP - TECHNICAL LIBRARY □ Scottsdale, AZ

Gosselin, Guy, Dir.
MOUNT WASHINGTON OBSERVATORY - LIBRARY □ Gorham, NH

Gosselin, Jean W., Educ.Asst.
UNIVERSITY OF CONNECTICUT - INSTITUTE OF URBAN RESEARCH - LIBRARY □ Storrs, CT

Gosselin, Odette, Lib. & Info.Off.
CANADIAN COUNCIL ON SOCIAL DEVELOPMENT - LIBRARY □ Ottawa, ON

Gossen, Eleanor A., Libn.
NEW YORK STATE MUSEUM AND SCIENCE SERVICE - MUSEUM LIBRARY □ Albany, NY

Gosson, John F., Cur.
MARINE MUSEUM AT FALL RIVER, INC. - LIBRARY □ Fall River, MA

Gothberg, Loren A., Chm., Lib.Comm.
ST. LUKE'S MEMORIAL HOSPITAL - A.M. JOHNSON MEMORIAL MEDICAL LIBRARY □ Spokane, WA

Gotlieb, Dr. Howard B., Dir.
BOSTON UNIVERSITY - DEPARTMENT OF SPECIAL COLLECTIONS □ Boston, MA

Gott, Gary, Assoc.Libn., Tech.Serv.
UNIVERSITY OF TEXAS, AUSTIN - SCHOOL OF LAW - TARLTON LAW LIBRARY □ Austin, TX

Gottesman, Itzek, Archv.
YIVO INSTITUTE FOR JEWISH RESEARCH - LIBRARY AND ARCHIVES □ New York, NY

Gottesman, Natan, Pres.
HASHOMER HATZAIR-ZIONIST YOUTH MOVEMENT - LIBRARY □ New York, NY

Gottesman, Regina E., Lib.Coord.
AVON PRODUCTS, INC. - CENTRAL LIBRARY† □ New York, NY

Gottfried, Mike, Ref.Libn.
WILLKIE FARR & GALLAGHER - LIBRARY □ New York, NY

Gottlieb, Gerald, Cur., Early Ch. Books
PIERPONT MORGAN LIBRARY □ New York, NY

Gottlieb, Jane, Hd.Libn.
MANNES COLLEGE OF MUSIC - HARRY SCHERMAN LIBRARY □ New York, NY

Gottlieb, Naomi, Bus.Mgr.
COMMUNITY SYSTEMS FOUNDATION - NUTRITION PLANNING INFORMATION SERVICE □ Ann Arbor, MI

Gottschalk, Dennis, Pres.
THEOSOPHICAL BOOK ASSOCIATION FOR THE BLIND, INC. □ Ojai, CA

Gottschalk, Libbie, Libn.
FRYE-SILLS, INC. - LIBRARY □ Englewood, CO

Gottselig, Leonard J., Chf.Libn.
GLENBOW-ALBERTA INSTITUTE - LIBRARY & ARCHIVES □ Calgary, AB

Goudy, Allie Wise, Music Libn.
WESTERN ILLINOIS UNIVERSITY - MUSIC LIBRARY □ Macomb, IL

Goudy, Frank, Ref.Libn.
WESTERN ILLINOIS UNIVERSITY - LIBRARIES □ Macomb, IL

Gough, Paul, Libn.
CONNECTICUT AGRICULTURAL EXPERIMENT STATION - OSBORNE LIBRARY □ New Haven, CT

Gouke, Mary, Ref.
OHIO STATE UNIVERSITY - EDUCATION/PSYCHOLOGY LIBRARY □ Columbus, OH

Gould, Alan V., Asst. Professor
UNIVERSITY OF NEBRASKA, LINCOLN - ENGINEERING LIBRARY □ Lincoln, NE

Gould, Belle
INSTITUTE FOR CANCER AND BLOOD RESEARCH - LIBRARY □ Beverly Hills, CA

Gould, Lisa, Lib.Asst.
MASSACHUSETTS INSTITUTE OF TECHNOLOGY - DEPARTMENT OF CHEMICAL ENGINEERING READING ROOM □ Cambridge, MA

Gould, Marian A., Act.Dir., Spec.Coll.
UNIVERSITY OF WISCONSIN, GREEN BAY - AREA RESEARCH CENTER □ Green Bay, WI

Gould, Susan, Chf., Cat.Serv.
U.S. CENTERS FOR DISEASE CONTROL - CDC LIBRARY □ Atlanta, GA

Gould, Terri F., Dir. of Educ.
ACTION-HOUSING, INC. - LIBRARY & HOUSING INFORMATION CENTER □ Pittsburgh, PA

Goulden, Darrell R., Med.Libn.
U.S. FEDERAL AVIATION ADMINISTRATION -
AERONAUTICAL CENTER LIBRARY, AAC-64D □
Oklahoma City, OK

Goulet, Karen, Engr.Libn.
MEMOREX CORPORATION - TECHNICAL
INFORMATION CENTER □ Santa Clara, CA

Goulet, Louise, Chf., Cat.Dept.
ECOLE DES HAUTES ETUDES COMMERCIALES
DE MONTREAL - BIBLIOTHEQUE □ Montreal, PQ

Goulet, Patricia J., Libn.
RED DEER ADVOCATE - NEWSPAPER LIBRARY
□ Red Deer, AB

Goulet, Reginald, S.J., Dir.
CANADIAN CENTRE FOR ECUMENISM -
LIBRARY □ Montreal, PQ

Gour, Pauline Lefebvre, Libn.
QUEBEC PROVINCE - CAISSE DE DEPOT ET
PLACEMENT DU QUEBEC - LIBRARY† □
Montreal, PQ

Gourlay, Una M., Mgr.
KELLOGG (M.W.) - RESEARCH INFORMATION
DIVISION □ Houston, TX

Gouveia, Sara, Med.Libn.
U.S. VETERANS ADMINISTRATION (CA-San
Francisco) - MEDICAL CENTER LIBRARY □ San
Francisco, CA

Govaars, Inga, Libn.
CROCKER NATIONAL BANK - LIBRARY □ San
Francisco, CA

Gove, Carolyn, Coord./Ser.
BAYSTATE MEDICAL CENTER - HEALTH
SCIENCES LIBRARY □ Springfield, MA

Gowan, Christa, Ser.
WHITTIER COLLEGE - SCHOOL OF LAW -
LIBRARY □ Los Angeles, CA

Gower, Dr. Calvin W., Dir.
CENTRAL MINNESOTA HISTORICAL CENTER -
LIBRARY □ St. Cloud, MN

Gower, Wendy, Libn.
QUEEN'S UNIVERSITY AT KINGSTON -
INDUSTRIAL RELATIONS CENTRE - LIBRARY □
Kingston, ON

Gowerluk, Eleanor, Lib.Techn.
MANITOBA ASSOCIATION OF REGISTERED
NURSES - LIBRARY □ Winnipeg, MB

Goyer, Doreen S., Dir., Lib. Core
UNIVERSITY OF TEXAS, AUSTIN - POPULATION
RESEARCH CENTER LIBRARY □ Austin, TX

Goyette, Nicole, Libn.
LAVALIN - CENTRE DE DOCUMENTATION □
Montreal, PQ

Grab, Laura, Asst.Dir.
SINAI HOSPITAL OF DETROIT - SAMUEL FRANK
MEDICAL LIBRARY □ Detroit, MI

Grabach, Kenneth A., Ref.Libn.
U.S. ARMY - LOGISTICS LIBRARY □ Ft. Lee, VA

Graber, Lynne B., Libn.
VALLEY GENERAL HOSPITAL - LIBRARY □
Renton, WA

Grabetz, Joseph M., Libn.
TRAFFIC INJURY RESEARCH FOUNDATION OF
CANADA (TIRF) - TECHNICAL INFORMATION
CENTRE □ Ottawa, ON

Grabowska, Flora
UNIVERSITY OF CALGARY - ENVIRONMENT-
SCIENCE-TECHNOLOGY LIBRARY† □ Calgary,
AB

Graboyes, Betty, Libn.
MAIN LINE REFORM TEMPLE - LIBRARY □
Wynnewood, PA

Grace, Judith, AV Libn.
U.S. VETERANS ADMINISTRATION (NJ-East
Orange) - MEDICAL CENTER LIBRARY □ East
Orange, NJ

Grace, Lorann, Per. & Exch.
SOUTHERN MISSIONARY COLLEGE - MC KEE
LIBRARY - SPECIAL COLLECTIONS □
Collegedale, TN

Grace, Michael J., S.J., Univ.Archv.
LOYOLA UNIVERSITY OF CHICAGO - CUDAHY
MEMORIAL LIBRARY - UNIVERSITY ARCHIVES
□ Chicago, IL

Gracia-Pena, Idilio, Dir.
NEW YORK CITY - DEPARTMENT OF RECORDS
AND INFORMATION SERVICES - MUNICIPAL
ARCHIVES □ New York, NY

Gracie, Helen, Per.
IBM CORPORATION - GENERAL PRODUCTS
DIVISION - STL LIBRARY □ San Jose, CA

Gracy, David B., II, Dir., Archv.
TEXAS STATE LIBRARY □ Austin, TX

Gracy, Dr. David B., II, Dir.
TEXAS STATE LIBRARY - TEXAS ARCHIVES
DIVISION □ Austin, TX

Grad, Marilyn, Assoc.Libn.
TORONTO GLOBE AND MAIL, LTD. - LIBRARY □
Toronto, ON

Grady, Mamie, First Asst.
CHICAGO PUBLIC LIBRARY CULTURAL CENTER
- FINE ARTS DIVISION - ART SECTION □
Chicago, IL

Grady, Marguerite, Asst. Art Libn.
STANFORD UNIVERSITY - ART AND
ARCHITECTURE LIBRARY □ Stanford, CA

Grady, Mary F., Info.Serv.Spec.
U.S. BUREAU OF THE CENSUS - INFORMATION
SERVICES PROGRAM - CHICAGO REGIONAL
OFFICE - REFERENCE CENTER □ Chicago, IL

Grady, William H., Ref.Libn.
UNIVERSITY OF RICHMOND - WILLIAM T.
MUSE MEMORIAL LAW LIBRARY □ Richmond,
VA

Graening, Paige, Libn.
CITIES SERVICE COMPANY - ERG - RESEARCH
LIBRARY □ Tulsa, OK

Graesser, Christine, Asst.Libn.
WEBSTER & SHEFFIELD - LIBRARY □ New York,
NY

Graff, Pam, Tech.Serv.
NORTH DAKOTA STATE SUPREME COURT LAW
LIBRARY □ Bismarck, ND

Graffagnino, J.K., Cur.
UNIVERSITY OF VERMONT - WILBUR
COLLECTION OF VERMONTIANA □ Burlington,
VT

Graham, Amy, Info.Asst.
MC KINSEY & COMPANY, INC. - LIBRARY □
Washington, DC

Graham, Bob, Media Coord.
FLORIDA SCHOOL FOR THE DEAF AND BLIND -
LIBRARY FOR THE DEAF □ St. Augustine, FL

Graham, Catherine, Libn.
CANADA - ENVIRONMENTAL PROTECTION
SERVICE - LIBRARY □ Toronto, ON

Graham, Chibeck, Libn.
UNIVERSITY OF TORONTO - MATHEMATICS
LIBRARY □ Toronto, ON

Graham, Deborah, Dir., Lib.Serv.
SACRED HEART GENERAL HOSPITAL AND
MEDICAL CENTER - LIBRARY SERVICES □
Eugene, OR

Graham, Dorothy M., Sr.Libn.
CALIFORNIA STATE DEPARTMENT OF JUSTICE
- ATTORNEY GENERAL'S LIBRARY □ San
Francisco, CA

Graham, Duncan M., Exec.Dir.
COUNCIL OF GOVERNMENTS OF THE CENTRAL
NAUGATUCK VALLEY - LIBRARY □ Waterbury,
CT

Graham, Elizabeth, Res.Att.
ALABAMA (State) SUPREME COURT - SUPREME
COURT AND STATE LAW LIBRARY □
Montgomery, AL

Graham, F. Pamela, Doc./Tech.Serv.Libn.
GEORGIA STATE LIBRARY □ Atlanta, GA

Graham, Flora O., Cur.
HOUGHTON COUNTY HISTORICAL SOCIETY -
LIBRARY □ Lake Linden, MI

Graham, Gretchen A., Libn.
KANSAS STATE UNIVERSITY -
INTERNATIONAL AGRICULTURAL PROGRAMS -
RESOURCES ON DEVELOPING COUNTRIES □
Manhattan, KS

Graham, J., Libn.
TORONTO PUBLIC LIBRARY - MARGUERITE G.
BAGSHAW COLLECTION† □ Toronto, ON

Graham, John, Dir.
WAGNER FREE INSTITUTE OF SCIENCE -
LIBRARY □ Philadelphia, PA

Graham, Julie, Libn.
UNION OIL COMPANY OF CANADA, LTD. -
LIBRARY □ Calgary, AB

Graham, Ken
BECHTEL - CENTRAL LIBRARY □ San Francisco,
CA

Graham, M., ILL
CANADA - AGRICULTURE CANADA - NEATBY
LIBRARY □ Ottawa, ON

Graham, Margaret H., Mgr.
EXXON RESEARCH AND ENGINEERING
COMPANY - INFORMATION SERVICES □
Annandale, NJ

Graham, Marianna, Libn.
NATIONAL COUNCIL FOR U.S.-CHINA TRADE -
LIBRARY □ Washington, DC

Graham, Mary E., Libn.
HEARD MUSEUM - LIBRARY □ Phoenix, AZ

Graham, Robert W., Field Rep.
NORTHERN ILLINOIS UNIVERSITY - REGIONAL
HISTORY CENTER □ DeKalb, IL

Graham, Sr. Rosalie, Dir.
OHIO DOMINICAN COLLEGE - SPANGLER
LIBRARY □ Columbus, OH

Graham, Selma, Sci.Libn.
MEDI-PHYSICS, INC. - SCIENTIFIC LIBRARY □
Emeryville, CA

Graham, Sylvia, Ref.Libn.
VANDERBILT UNIVERSITY - JEAN AND
ALEXANDER HEARD LIBRARY - WALKER
MANAGEMENT LIBRARY □ Nashville, TN

Graham, William C., Libn.
BENDIX FIELD ENGINEERING CORPORATION -
GRAND JUNCTION OFFICE - TECHNICAL
LIBRARY □ Grand Junction, CO

Grahner, Richard, Mgr.
FLOATING POINT SYSTEMS, INC. -
INFORMATION CENTER/LIBRARY □ Beaverton,
OR

Grainger, Mr. B., Pub.Serv.Libn.
MC GILL UNIVERSITY - MACDONALD COLLEGE
- LIBRARY □ Ste. Anne de Bellevue, PQ

Grainger, Claudia, Ref.Libn.
ST. VINCENT MEDICAL CENTER - HEALTH
SCIENCE LIBRARY □ Toledo, OH

Grainger, Shirley J., Libn.
DARTMOUTH COLLEGE - DANA BIOMEDICAL
LIBRARY □ Hanover, NH

Graley, Jennifer J., Stenographer
WEST VIRGINIA STATE DEPARTMENT OF
HEALTH - STATE HYGIENIC LABORATORY -
LIBRARY □ South Charleston, WV

Gralnick, Sandra Freed, Libn.
TEMPLE BETH EL OF GREATER BUFFALO -
LIBRARY □ Tonawanda, NY

Gram, Carmel M., Dir., Lib.Serv.
LAWRENCE GENERAL HOSPITAL - HEALTH
SCIENCE LIBRARY □ Lawrence, MA

Gramenz, Francis L., Hd.
BOSTON UNIVERSITY - MUSIC LIBRARY □
Boston, MA

Granade, Ray, Libn.
OUACHITA BAPTIST UNIVERSITY - RILEY
LIBRARY □ Arkadelphia, AR

Granados, Rose A., Tech.Libn.
CALIFORNIA STATE OFFICE OF THE STATE
ARCHITECT - ARCHITECTURE/ENGINEERING
LIBRARY □ Sacramento, CA

Granberg, Margaret Daly, Libn.
DRAKE UNIVERSITY - COLLEGE OF PHARMACY
- LIBRARY □ Des Moines, IA

Grandage, Karen K., Dir., Med.Lib.
WAKE COUNTY MEDICAL CENTER - MEDICAL
LIBRARY □ Raleigh, NC

Grande, Anne W., Dir.
HENNEPIN COUNTY LAW LIBRARY† □
Minneapolis, MN

Grande, Professor D., Hd., Tech.Serv.
JOHN JAY COLLEGE OF CRIMINAL JUSTICE OF
THE CITY UNIVERSITY OF NEW YORK -
REISMAN MEMORIAL LIBRARY □ New York, NY
Grande, Sally, Info.Sys.Anl.
HOME OIL COMPANY, LTD. - TECHNICAL
INFORMATION CENTER □ Calgary, AB
Grandy, Maryann M., Mgr., Info.Serv.
CHEM SYSTEMS INC. - INFORMATION CENTER
□ Tarrytown, NY
Granek, Jacqueline, Libn.
BRIGER & ASSOCIATES - LIBRARY† □ New
York, NY
Granese, Mary, Supv./Doc.
MASSACHUSETTS INSTITUTE OF TECHNOLOGY
- LINCOLN LABORATORY LIBRARY □ Lexington,
MA
Granger, Daniel, Dir.
SUNY - EMPIRE STATE COLLEGE - CENTER FOR
DISTANCE LEARNING □ Saratoga Springs, NY
Granger, Ethel M., Libn.
ST. MARY HOSPITAL - HEALTH SCIENCE
LIBRARY □ Port Arthur, TX
Granger, William S., Dept.Hd.
TOLEDO-LUCAS COUNTY PUBLIC LIBRARY -
LITERATURE/FICTION DEPARTMENT □ Toledo,
OH
Granifei, Dinah, Hd.Libn.
UNIVERSITY OF WEST LOS ANGELES - LAW
LIBRARY □ Culver City, CA
Grant, Benjamin, Supv., Lib. Media Ctr.
LEXINGTON SCHOOL FOR THE DEAF - LIBRARY
MEDIA CENTER □ Jackson Heights, NY
Grant, Elizabeth, Chf.Info.Off.
EUROPEAN COMMUNITY INFORMATION
SERVICE - LIBRARY □ New York, NY
Grant, G.E., Lib. Network Sup.Supv.
AT & T BELL LABORATORIES - LIBRARIES AND
INFORMATION SYSTEMS CENTER □ Murray Hill,
NJ
Grant, George, Libn.
METROPOLITAN TORONTO LIBRARY - FINE
ART DEPARTMENT □ Toronto, ON
Grant, Gloria, Libn.
CANADA - PUBLIC ARCHIVES OF CANADA -
NATL. FILM, TELEVISION & SOUND ARCHIVES -
DOCUMENTATION & PUB. SERV. □ Ottawa, ON
Grant, Jason C., III, Dir.
HAMPTON INSTITUTE - COLLIS P.
HUNTINGTON MEMORIAL LIBRARY - SPECIAL
COLLECTIONS† □ Hampton, VA
Grant, Jerry V., Dir.
SHAKER COMMUNITY, INC. - LIBRARY □
Pittsfield, MA
Grant, Joan, Libn.
CYRUS J. LAWRENCE, INC. - LIBRARY† □ New
York, NY
Grant, Linda, Libn.
CENTRAL BAPTIST CHURCH - MEDIA CENTER □
St. Paul, MN
Grant, Madeline, Libn.
CRANE (J.W.) MEMORIAL LIBRARY □ Toronto,
ON
Grant, Marena, Exec.Dir.
LOCH HAVEN ART CENTER, INC. - LIBRARY □
Orlando, FL
Grant, Marion, Libn.
SOLANO COUNTY LAW LIBRARY □ Fairfield, CA
Grant, Mary, ILL
UNIVERSITY OF LOUISVILLE - KORNHAUSER
HEALTH SCIENCES LIBRARY □ Louisville, KY
Grant, Mary A., Dir.
ST. JOHN'S UNIVERSITY - COLLEGE OF
PHARMACY & ALLIED HEALTH PROFESSIONS -
HEALTH EDUCATION RESOURCE CENTER □
Jamaica, NY
Grant, Mary McNierney, Mgr.
LONG ISLAND UNIVERSITY - C.W. POST
CAMPUS - CENTER FOR BUSINESS RESEARCH □
Greenvale, NY

Grant, Mildred P., Libn.
CLEVELAND HEARING AND SPEECH CENTER -
LUCILE DAUBY GRIES MEMORIAL LIBRARY □
Cleveland, OH
Grant, Owen, Libn.
LEE COUNTY LAW LIBRARY □ Fort Myers, FL
Grant, Sharlane, Preservation Libn.
STATE HISTORICAL SOCIETY OF IOWA -
LIBRARY □ Iowa City, IA
Grantham, Gayle, Circ.Supv.
VANDERBILT UNIVERSITY - MEDICAL CENTER
LIBRARY □ Nashville, TN
Grantham, Glenna, ILL
MOHAWK COLLEGE OF APPLIED ARTS AND
TECHNOLOGY - MOHAWK LIBRARY RESOURCE
CENTRE □ Hamilton, ON
Grantham, Walter, Asst.Div.Chf.
CHICAGO PUBLIC LIBRARY CENTRAL LIBRARY -
SOCIAL SCIENCES & HISTORY DIVISION □
Chicago, IL
Grasing, Kathleen, Dp. State Libn.
OREGON STATE LIBRARY □ Salem, OR
Grasmick, Charles, Per.
CARROLL COLLEGE - LIBRARY □ Helena, MT
Grass, Charlene, Cat.
KANSAS STATE UNIVERSITY - FARRELL
LIBRARY □ Manhattan, KS
Grass, Gene
HARTFORD PUBLIC LIBRARY - BUSINESS,
SCIENCE & TECHNOLOGY DEPARTMENT □
Hartford, CT
Grass, Gene
HARTFORD PUBLIC LIBRARY - REFERENCE AND
GENERAL READING DEPARTMENT □ Hartford,
CT
Grassinger, John, Asst.Libn.
INDIANA UNIVERSITY OF PENNSYLVANIA -
UNIVERSITY LIBRARY □ Indiana, PA
Grasso, Mary Ann, Lib.Coord.
BURBANK PUBLIC LIBRARY - WARNER
RESEARCH COLLECTION □ Burbank, CA
Grater, Fred A., Cat.Libn.
EMORY UNIVERSITY - PITTS THEOLOGY
LIBRARY □ Atlanta, GA
Graterole, Nidia Miranda, Dir.
PUERTO RICO - GENERAL COURT OF JUSTICE -
OFFICE OF COURT ADMINISTRATION -
LIBRARY DIVISION □ Hato Rey, PR
Gration, Selby U., Dir. of Libs.
SUNY - COLLEGE AT CORTLAND - MEMORIAL
LIBRARY □ Cortland, NY
Gratz, Delbert L., Libn.
BLUFFTON COLLEGE - MENNONITE
HISTORICAL LIBRARY □ Bluffton, OH
Gravell, Helen E., Asst.Libn.
ST. FRANCIS HOSPITAL, INC. - MEDICAL
LIBRARY □ Wilmington, DE
Graves, Carolyn, Chf., Tech.Serv.
U.S. ARMY POST - FORT BELVOIR - VAN NOY
LIBRARY □ Ft. Belvoir, VA
Graves, Earl G., Dir.
MINORITY BUSINESS INFORMATION
INSTITUTE, INC. - LIBRARY □ New York, NY
Graves, Geraldine N., Dir., Lib.Serv.
SOUTHERN CALIFORNIA PERMANENTE
MEDICAL CENTER - HEALTH SCIENCES
LIBRARY/MEDIA CENTER □ Bellflower, CA
Graves, Karen, Mgr., Info.Serv.
CANADIAN RESTAURANT & FOODSERVICES
ASSOCIATION - RESOURCE CENTRE □ Toronto,
ON
Graves, Karen J., Hd., Educ.Serv.Dept.
UNIVERSITY OF TENNESSEE - CENTER FOR
THE HEALTH SCIENCES LIBRARY □ Memphis,
TN
Graves, Leon
INSTITUTE FOR STORM RESEARCH - LIBRARY
□ Houston, TX
Graves, Roberta
U.S. NAVY - NAVAL AIR ENGINEERING CENTER
- TECHNICAL LIBRARY, CODE 1115 □
Lakehurst, NJ

Graves, Shirley, Chm., Ser.
LOMA LINDA UNIVERSITY - DEL E. WEBB
MEMORIAL LIBRARY □ Loma Linda, CA
Gray, Ann, Libn.
UNIVERSITY OF NORTH CAROLINA, CHAPEL
HILL - INSTITUTE FOR RESEARCH IN SOCIAL
SCIENCE - DATA LIBRARY □ Chapel Hill, NC
Gray, Beverly A., Hd., African Sect.
LIBRARY OF CONGRESS - AFRICAN & MIDDLE
EASTERN DIVISION □ Washington, DC
Gray, Carol J., Doc.Libn.
WASHINGTON UNIVERSITY - SCHOOL OF LAW
- FREUND LAW LIBRARY □ St. Louis, MO
Gray, David, Dp. State Archv.
STATE HISTORICAL SOCIETY OF NORTH
DAKOTA - STATE ARCHIVES AND HISTORICAL
RESEARCH LIBRARY □ Bismarck, ND
Gray, Donald P.
AMERICAN TEILHARD ASSOCIATION FOR THE
FUTURE OF MAN - LIBRARY □ White Plains, NY
Gray, Gary, Coord.
OREGON INSTITUTE OF TECHNOLOGY -
LEARNING RESOURCES CENTER □ Klamath Falls,
OR
Gray, Gary B., Asst.Lib.Mgr./Media Ctr.
METHODIST HOSPITAL OF INDIANA, INC. -
LIBRARY SERVICES □ Indianapolis, IN
Gray, Gayl, Ref.Libn.
NATIONAL CENTER FOR ATMOSPHERIC
RESEARCH - MESA LIBRARY □ Boulder, CO
Gray, Heli, Lib.Asst.
UNIVERSITY CONGREGATIONAL CHURCH -
LIBRARY □ Seattle, WA
Gray, Keir, Libn.Asst.
FLORIDA STATE DEPT. OF NATURAL
RESOURCES - BUREAU OF MARINE RESEARCH -
LIBRARY □ St. Petersburg, FL
Gray, Mary Clare, Chf.
SMITHSONIAN INSTITUTION LIBRARIES -
CENTRAL REFERENCE SERVICES† □
Washington, DC
Gray, Paul, Dir., Lib.Serv.
LE TOURNEAU COLLEGE - MARGARET ESTES
LIBRARY □ Longview, TX
Gray, Paul D., Asst.Dir., MPR
U.S. NATL. ARCHIVES & RECORDS SERVICE -
NATL. PERSONNEL RECORDS CENTER □ St.
Louis, MO
Gray, Paula A., Libn.
SELIGMAN (J. & W.) & CO. INCORPORATED -
RESEARCH LIBRARY □ New York, NY
Gray, Randall J., Dir. of Info.Serv.
ADAMS, DUQUE & HAZELTINE - LIBRARY □ Los
Angeles, CA
Gray, Sharon, Mgr.
NATIONAL ASSOCIATION OF PURCHASING
MANAGEMENT, INC. - INFORMATION CENTER
□ Oradell, NJ
Gray, Walter P., III, Archv.
CALIFORNIA STATE RAILROAD MUSEUM -
LIBRARY □ Sacramento, CA
Gray, Wayne, Mgr.
DALLAS PUBLIC LIBRARY - TEXAS/DALLAS
HISTORY AND ARCHIVES DIVISION □ Dallas, TX
Graydon, Elizabeth, Libn.
PRINCETON UNIVERSITY - PLASMA PHYSICS
LIBRARY □ Princeton, NJ
Grayson, Linda M., Chf., Leg.Res.Serv.
ONTARIO - LEGISLATIVE ASSEMBLY -
LEGISLATIVE LIBRARY RESEARCH AND
INFORMATION SERVICES □ Toronto, ON
Grayson, Virginia S., Libn.
AMAX, INC. - LAW LIBRARY □ Greenwich, CT
Grayson, Virginia S., Libn.
AMAX, INC. - LIBRARY □ Greenwich, CT
Graziano, Patti A., Lib.Dir.
PLAIN DEALER PUBLISHING COMPANY -
LIBRARY □ Cleveland, OH
Grazier, Margaret, Libn.
DETROIT GARDEN CENTER - LIBRARY □
Detroit, MI

Greathouse, Stewart R., Info.Spec.
UNIVERSITY OF SOUTHERN CALIFORNIA -
ETHEL PERCY ANDRUS GERONTOLOGY CENTER
- GERONTOLOGICAL INFO. CENTER □ Los
Angeles, CA

Greathouse, Mrs. W.S., Pres.
FRYE (Charles and Emma) ART MUSEUM -
LIBRARY □ Seattle, WA

Greaves, F. Landon, Jr., Lib.Dir.
SOUTHEASTERN LOUISIANA UNIVERSITY - L.A.
SIMS MEMORIAL LIBRARY □ Hammond, LA

Greaves, H.P., Chf.Libn.
NORTH YORK BOARD OF EDUCATION - F.W.
MINKLER LIBRARY □ North York, ON

Greaves, Jim, Info.Serv.Libn.
STEVENS INSTITUTE OF TECHNOLOGY -
SAMUEL C. WILLIAMS LIBRARY □ Hoboken, NJ

Grech, Anthony P., Libn.
ASSOCIATION OF THE BAR OF THE CITY OF
NEW YORK - LIBRARY □ New York, NY

Greek, Dawn M., Asst.Cur.
CAPE MAY COUNTY HISTORICAL &
GENEALOGICAL SOCIETY - LIBRARY □ Cape
May Court House, NJ

Greeley, Ronald, Professor
ARIZONA STATE UNIVERSITY - SPACE
PHOTOGRAPHY LABORATORY □ Tempe, AZ

Green, Aida R., Libn.
WOODWARD-CLYDE CONSULTANTS, EASTERN
REGION - WCC LIBRARY □ Wayne, NJ

Green, Anna M., Libn.
MILWAUKEE COUNTY MENTAL HEALTH
COMPLEX - MICHAEL KASAK LIBRARY □
Milwaukee, WI

Green, Avi, Chf.
UNITED NATIONS FUND FOR POPULATION
ACTIVITIES - LIBRARY □ New York, NY

Green, Barbara, Cons.
ETOBICOKE BOARD OF EDUCATION -
RESOURCE LIBRARY □ Etobicoke, ON

Green, Barbara, Libn.
O'CONNOR (Lindsay A. & Olive B.) HOSPITAL -
LIBRARY □ Delhi, NY

Green, Carol, Asst.Libn.
UNIVERSITY OF WASHINGTON - ENGINEERING
LIBRARY □ Seattle, WA

Green, Chuck, Dir.
MUSEUM OF CARTOON ART - LIBRARY □ Rye
Brook, NY

Green, David, Lib.Dir.
GENERAL THEOLOGICAL SEMINARY OF THE
PROTESTANT EPISCOPAL CHURCH IN THE
U.S.A. - ST. MARK'S LIBRARY □ New York, NY

Green, Dorothy, Res.Assoc.
SMITH COLLEGE - SOPHIA SMITH COLLECTION
- WOMEN'S HISTORY ARCHIVE □ Northampton,
MA

Green, Ellen Wilson, Dir. of Libs.
CEDARS-SINAI MEDICAL CENTER - HEALTH
SCIENCES INFORMATION CENTER □ Los
Angeles, CA

Green, Florence, Libn.
CARROLL COUNTY BAR ASSOCIATION -
LIBRARY □ Westminster, MD

Green, Frank L., Libn.
WASHINGTON STATE HISTORICAL SOCIETY -
LIBRARY □ Tacoma, WA

Green, Gary, Sci.Libn.
MIAMI UNIVERSITY - BRILL SCIENCE LIBRARY
□ Oxford, OH

Green, H., Info.Sci.
BURROUGHS WELLCOME COMPANY - LIBRARY
□ Research Triangle Park, NC

Green, Hazel, Tech.Serv.Libn.
PPG INDUSTRIES, INC. - GLASS RESEARCH
CENTER - INFORMATION SERVICES □
Pittsburgh, PA

Green, James N., Cur./Printed Books
LIBRARY COMPANY OF PHILADELPHIA □
Philadelphia, PA

Green, Janice, Libn.
WILLIAM M. MERCER, LTD. - INFORMATION
CENTRE □ Toronto, ON

Green, Jeannine, Spec.Coll.libn.
UNIVERSITY OF ALBERTA - BRUCE PEEL
SPECIAL COLLECTIONS LIBRARY □ Edmonton,
AB

Green, Jeff, Res.Tech.
SAN DIEGO STATE UNIVERSITY - SOCIAL
SCIENCE RESEARCH LABORATORY - LIBRARY □
San Diego, CA

Green, Karen, Libn.
ATLANTIC-RICHFIELD COMPANY - ANACONDA
ALUMINUM COMPANY - COLUMBIA FALLS
REDUCTION DIVISION - LIBRARY □ Columbia
Falls, MT

Green, Katherine A., Hd.Libn.
MILLER, CANFIELD, PADDOCK & STONE -
LIBRARY □ Detroit, MI

Green, L., Libn.
INCO LIMITED - J. ROY GORDON RESEARCH
LABORATORY □ Mississauga, ON

Green, LaMerle C., Act.Libn.
INTERNATIONAL PAPER COMPANY - LAND &
TIMBER GROUP - FOREST PRODUCTIVITY &
RESEARCH - FOREST RESEARCH LIBRARY† □
Mobile, AL

Green, Leona, Exec.Sec.
CENTER FOR ULCER RESEARCH AND
EDUCATION FOUNDATION (CURE) - LIBRARY □
Los Angeles, CA

Green, Leslie, Ref.Libn.
SOUTHERN METHODIST UNIVERSITY -
SCIENCE/ENGINEERING LIBRARY □ Dallas, TX

Green, Lynn A., Dir., Lib. & Info.Serv.
PILLSBURY, MADISON AND SUTRO - LIBRARY □
San Francisco, CA

Green, M., Hd., Tech.Serv.
WINNIPEG SCHOOL DIVISION NO. 1 -
TEACHERS LIBRARY AND RESOURCE CENTRE □
Winnipeg, MB

Green, Marion, Chf.Med.Ed.
U.S. AIR FORCE - AEROSPACE MEDICAL
DIVISION - SCHOOL OF AEROSPACE MEDICINE
- STRUGHOLD AEROMEDICAL LIBRARY □ Brooks
AFB, TX

Green, Mary P., Act.Dir.
UNIVERSITY OF TEXAS, AUSTIN - NATURAL
FIBERS INFORMATION CENTER □ Austin, TX

Green, Michael, AV Lib.Techn.
U.S. VETERANS ADMINISTRATION (DC-
Washington) - HEADQUARTERS CENTRAL
OFFICE LIBRARY (142D1) □ Washington, DC

Green, Michael, AV lib.Techn.
U.S. VETERANS ADMINISTRATION (DC-
Washington) - HEADQUARTERS LIBRARY
DIVISION (142D) □ Washington, DC

Green, Nancy, Libn.
AMERICAN NUMISMATIC ASSOCIATION -
LIBRARY □ Colorado Springs, CO

Green, Patricia W., Libn.
AEROSPACE CORPORATION - WASHINGTON
LIBRARY □ Washington, DC

Green, Peggy, Asst.Libn.
UNIVERSITY OF WISCONSIN, MADISON -
LIBRARY SCHOOL LIBRARY □ Madison, WI

Green, Richard, Map Libn.
UNIVERSITY OF IOWA - SPECIAL
COLLECTIONS DEPARTMENT □ Iowa City, IA

Green, Rita C., Libn.
COLORADO (State) DIVISION OF WILDLIFE -
LIBRARY □ Denver, CO

Green, Rosemary, Asst.Libn.
SHENANDOAH COLLEGE & CONSERVATORY OF
MUSIC - HOWE LIBRARY □ Winchester, VA

Green, Ruth A.
U.S. NATL. OCEANIC & ATMOSPHERIC
ADMINISTRATION - ATMOSPHERIC
TURBULENCE & DIFFUSION LABORATORY -
LIBRARY □ Oak Ridge, TN

Green, Willa, Asst.Libn.
SUNY - SYRACUSE EDUCATIONAL
OPPORTUNITY CENTER - PAUL ROBESON
LIBRARY □ Syracuse, NY

Greenawalt, Ruth, Dir.
BRIDGEWATER COLLEGE - ALEXANDER MACK
MEMORIAL LIBRARY - SPECIAL COLLECTIONS
□ Bridgewater, VA

Greenbaum, Rabbi Alan
TEMPLE B'NAI ISRAEL - LASKER MEMORIAL
LIBRARY □ Galveston, TX

Greenbaum, Diane, Chf.Libn.
MIDLAND-ROSS CORPORATION - LIBRARY □
Cleveland, OH

Greenbaum, Leo, Libn.
JEWISH LABOR BUND - BUND ARCHIVES OF
THE JEWISH LABOR MOVEMENT □ New York,
NY

Greenbaum, Marilyn, Br./Ref.
NORTHROP CORPORATION - AIRCRAFT
DIVISION - LIBRARY SERVICES □ Hawthorne,
CA

Greenberg, Adele, Rd.Adv.
NEW YORK PUBLIC LIBRARY - MID-
MANHATTAN LIBRARY - READERS' ADVISER'S
OFFICE □ New York, NY

Greenberg, Arlene, Chf.Med.Libn.
SIR MORTIMER B. DAVIS JEWISH GENERAL
HOSPITAL - LADY DAVIS INSTITUTE FOR
MEDICAL RESEARCH - RESEARCH LIBRARY □
Montreal, PQ

Greenberg, Arlene, Chf.Med.Libn.
SIR MORTIMER B. DAVIS JEWISH GENERAL
HOSPITAL - MEDICAL LIBRARY □ Montreal, PQ

Greenberg, Carolyn, Sys.Libn.
MASSACHUSETTS INSTITUTE OF TECHNOLOGY
- LINCOLN LABORATORY LIBRARY □ Lexington,
MA

Greenberg, Emily R., Dir.
UNIVERSITY OF BALTIMORE - LAW LIBRARY □
Baltimore, MD

Greenberg, Gerald, Chf., Data Acq.
U.S. GEOLOGICAL SURVEY - NATL.
CARTOGRAPHIC INFORMATION CENTER
(NCIC) - WESTERN BRANCH □ Menlo Park, CA

Greenberg, Hinda, Assoc.Libn.
EDUCATIONAL TESTING SERVICE - CARL
CAMPBELL BRIGHAM LIBRARY □ Princeton, NJ

Greenberg, Ida, Asst.Per.
INTERFAITH MEDICAL CENTER - BROOKLYN
JEWISH SITE - MEDICAL & NURSING LIBRARY
□ Brooklyn, NY

Greenberg, Joan, Hd.Libn.
JENKINTOWN LIBRARY - PENNSYLVANIA
COLLECTION □ Jenkintown, PA

Greenberg, Ruth, Libn.
CHICAGO-READ MENTAL HEALTH CENTER -
PROFESSIONAL LIBRARY† □ Chicago, IL

Greenberg, Thomas R., Res.Libn.
FUND FOR PEACE - CENTER FOR DEFENSE
INFORMATION - LIBRARY □ Washington, DC

Greenblatt, Melinda, Chf.Libn.
U.S. COMMITTEE FOR UNICEF - INFORMATION
CENTER ON CHILDREN'S CULTURES □ New
York, NY

Greenblatt, Ruth, Dir.
BETH ISRAEL CONGREGATION - LIBRARY □
Vineland, NJ

Greene, Barbara, Asst.Dir., Tchg.Lrng.Ctr.
UNIVERSITY OF TEXAS HEALTH SCIENCE
CENTER, SAN ANTONIO - LIBRARY □ San
Antonio, TX

Greene, Bill, Hist.
ALLEGANY COUNTY MUSEUM - LIBRARY □
Belmont, NY

Greene, Casey Edward, Dir., Lib./Archv.
DALLAS HISTORICAL SOCIETY - RESEARCH
CENTER □ Dallas, TX

Greene, Catherine, Libn.
GENERAL DATACOMM INDUSTRIES, INC. -
CORPORATE LIBRARY □ Danbury, CT

Greene, Debbie, Libn.
GOOD SAMARITAN HOSPITAL - HEALTH-
SCIENCE LIBRARY □ Mt. Vernon, IL

Greene, Deborah, Music Libn.
BALDWIN-WALLACE COLLEGE -
RIEMENSCHNEIDER BACH INSTITUTE - BACH
LIBRARY □ Berea, OH

Greene, Edward J., Supv.Pk.Ranger
U.S. NATL. PARK SERVICE - BANDELIER NATL.
MONUMENT - LIBRARY □ Los Alamos, NM

Greene, Frances G., Libn.
BAIRD CORPORATION - TECHNICAL LIBRARY†
□ Bedford, MA

Greene, Harlan, Archv.
SOUTH CAROLINA HISTORICAL SOCIETY -
LIBRARY □ Charleston, SC

Greene, Jane F., Dept.Hd.
BIRMINGHAM PUBLIC AND JEFFERSON
COUNTY FREE LIBRARY - ART AND MUSIC
DEPARTMENT □ Birmingham, AL

Greene, Jeremiah, Cat.
FITCHBURG STATE COLLEGE - LIBRARY □
Fitchburg, MA

Greene, Jon S., Libn.
UNIVERSITY OF CALIFORNIA, LOS ANGELES -
ARCHITECTURE & URBAN PLANNING LIBRARY
□ Los Angeles, CA

Greene, Judith, Exec.Sec.
LIZZADRO MUSEUM OF LAPIDARY ART -
LIBRARY □ Elmhurst, IL

Greene, Kingsley W., Hd., Rd.Serv.
RENSSELAER POLYTECHNIC INSTITUTE -
FOLSOM LIBRARY □ Troy, NY

Greene, Lucy R., Asst.Libn.
U.S. ARMY - LOGISTICS LIBRARY □ Ft. Lee, VA

Greene, Mary, Ch.Libn.
PROVIDENCE ATHENAEUM - LIBRARY □
Providence, RI

Greene, Mildred R., Chf.
DISTRICT OF COLUMBIA PUBLIC LIBRARY -
POPULAR LIBRARY □ Washington, DC

Greene, Nancy, Asst.Libn./Tech.Serv.
UNIVERSITY OF WYOMING - LAW LIBRARY □
Laramie, WY

Greene, Richard, Libn.
UNIVERSITE DE MONTREAL - SCIENCES
HUMAINES ET SOCIALES-BIBLIOTHEQUE □
Montreal, PQ

Greene, William T., Mgr.
3M - ENGINEERING INFORMATION SERVICES
□ St. Paul, MN

Greene-Cohen, Mary E., Asst.Libn., Cat.
PUBLIC SERVICE ELECTRIC AND GAS
COMPANY - LIBRARY □ Newark, NJ

Greenfield, Liga, Hd., Tech.Doc.Serv.
UPJOHN COMPANY - CORPORATE TECHNICAL
LIBRARY □ Kalamazoo, MI

Greenfield, Marjorie, Libn.
METROPOLITAN HOSPITAL - CENTRAL
DIVISION - LEVIN MEMORIAL LIBRARY □
Philadelphia, PA

Greenfield, Patricia J., Chf., Hosp.Lib.Serv.
TOURO INFIRMARY - HOSPITAL LIBRARY
SERVICES □ New Orleans, LA

Greenhalgh, James A., Libn.
U.S. DEPT. OF LABOR - MINE SAFETY & HEALTH
ADMINISTRATION - INFORMATIONAL
SERVICES LIBRARY □ Denver, CO

Greenhalgh, Kathleen, Libn.
INDIAN AND COLONIAL RESEARCH CENTER,
INC. - EVA BUTLER LIBRARY □ Old Mystic, CT

Greenholz, Carol, Hd., Tech.Serv./Cat.
SUNY - AGRICULTURAL AND TECHNICAL
COLLEGE AT FARMINGDALE - THOMAS D.
GREENLEY LIBRARY □ Farmingdale, NY

Greeniaus, Barbara, Dir., Lib.Serv.
WINNIPEG HEALTH SCIENCES CENTRE -
LIBRARY SERVICES □ Winnipeg, MB

Greening, Walter, Sr.Libn.
STOCKTON STATE HOSPITAL - PROFESSIONAL
LIBRARY □ Stockton, CA

Greenlaw, Evelyn A., Libn.
ST. MARY'S GENERAL HOSPITAL - HEALTH
SCIENCES LIBRARY □ Lewiston, ME

Greenlee, John W., Libn.
BELMONT COUNTY LAW LIBRARY □ St.
Clairsville, OH

Greenshields, H., Chf.Libn.
ATOMIC ENERGY OF CANADA, LTD. -
TECHNICAL INFORMATION BRANCH - MAIN
LIBRARY □ Chalk River, ON

Greenslit, Ruth, Circ.
WORCESTER STATE COLLEGE - LEARNING
RESOURCES CENTER □ Worcester, MA

Greenstein, David, Dir.
BETTMANN ARCHIVE □ New York, NY

Greenstein, Mrs. Milton, Libn.
CONGREGATION KINS OF WEST ROGERS PARK
- JORDAN E. FEUER LIBRARY □ Chicago, IL

Greenwald, Camille D., Libn.
JOHNS HOPKINS UNIVERSITY-SCHOOL OF
HYGIENE & PUBLIC HEALTH-MATERNAL &
CHILD HEALTH/POPULATION DYNAMICS LIB. □
Baltimore, MD

Greenwald, Diane, Interlib.Coop.Coord.
DELAWARE STATE DEPARTMENT OF
COMMUNITY AFFAIRS - DIVISION OF
LIBRARIES □ Dover, DE

Greenwood, Florine H., Libn.
NATIONAL SOCIETY, DAUGHTERS OF THE
AMERICAN REVOLUTION - ALOHA CHAPTER -
MEMORIAL LIBRARY □ Honolulu, HI

Greenwood, Jan, Libn.
ONTARIO MEDICAL ASSOCIATION - LIBRARY □
Toronto, ON

Greenwood, Larry, Educ.Libn.
UNIVERSITY OF KENTUCKY - EDUCATION
LIBRARY □ Lexington, KY

Greenwood, Michael
UNIVERSITY OF COLORADO, BOULDER -
CENTER FOR ECONOMIC ANALYSIS - LIBRARY
□ Boulder, CO

Greenwood, Paula, Staff Libn.
EASTERN STATE HOSPITAL - STAFF LIBRARY □
Williamsburg, VA

Greenwood, Paula, Circuit Libn.
FISH MEMORIAL HOSPITAL - MEDICAL
LIBRARY □ De Land, FL

Greer, Kathleen M., Asst.Libn.
POLK COUNTY HISTORICAL AND
GENEALOGICAL LIBRARY □ Bartow, FL

Greer, Nancy, Hd., Tech.Serv.
SOLAR ENERGY RESEARCH INSTITUTE - SERI
TECHNICAL LIBRARY □ Golden, CO

Gref, Beverly, Hd.Libn.
PETRO-CANADA - LIBRARY SERVICES □
Calgary, AB

Grefsheim, Suzanne, Assoc.Dir./Chf.Tech Serv.
GEORGE WASHINGTON UNIVERSITY -
MEDICAL CENTER - PAUL HIMMELFARB
HEALTH SCIENCES LIBRARY □ Washington, DC

Gregg, Anne, Info.Anl.
AMERICAN CRITICAL CARE - INFORMATION
CENTER □ McGaw Park, IL

Gregg, Joseph, Hd., Acq.
NORTHEASTERN ILLINOIS UNIVERSITY -
LIBRARY □ Chicago, IL

Gregg, Kimberly, Lib.Adm.
CONTROL DATA CORPORATION - CORPORATE
LIBRARY □ Minneapolis, MN

Gregg, Martha C., Libn.
COMMUNITY SYSTEMS FOUNDATION -
NUTRITION PLANNING INFORMATION
SERVICE □ Ann Arbor, MI

Gregg, Rosalie, Exec.Dir.
WISE COUNTY HISTORICAL COMMISSION
ARCHIVE □ Decatur, TX

Grego, Mrs. Noel R., Hd.
KENNEDY-KING COLLEGE - LIBRARY† □
Chicago, IL

Gregoire, Fleurette, Ref.
UNIVERSITY OF OTTAWA - HEALTH SCIENCES
LIBRARY □ Ottawa, ON

Gregoire, Shirlie, Asst.Libn.
ST. AUGUSTINE'S SEMINARY - LIBRARY □
Scarborough, ON

Gregory, Alan, Music Cat.
UNIVERSITY OF NORTH CAROLINA, CHAPEL
HILL - MUSIC LIBRARY □ Chapel Hill, NC

Gregory, Carla L., Corp.Libn.
REYNOLDS METALS COMPANY - CORPORATE
LIBRARY SERVICES □ Richmond, VA

Gregory, Carol, Libn.
CANADIAN NUMISMATIC ASSOCIATION -
LIBRARY □ Cookstown, ON

Gregory, Edwin, Libn.
BREWERS ASSOCIATION OF CANADA -
LIBRARY □ Ottawa, ON

Gregory, Jean, Chf.Libn.
BECHTEL POWER CORPORATION - LIBRARY □
Los Angeles, CA

Gregory, Martha, Br.Mgr., Pub.Serv.
KENTUCKY STATE DEPARTMENT FOR
LIBRARIES AND ARCHIVES - STATE LIBRARY
SERVICES DIVISION □ Frankfort, KY

Gregory, Martha, Info. II Libn.
TULSA CITY-COUNTY LIBRARY SYSTEM -
BUSINESS AND TECHNOLOGY DEPARTMENT □
Tulsa, OK

Gregory, Pamela J., Law Libn.
PRINCE GEORGE'S COUNTY CIRCUIT COURT -
LAW LIBRARY □ Upper Marlboro, MD

Gregory, Ralph, Pres.
HEARST (Phoebe Apperson) HISTORICAL
SOCIETY, INC. - MUSEUM CENTER □ St. Clair,
MO

Gregory, Virginia, Libn.
SLOAN-KETTERING INSTITUTE FOR CANCER
RESEARCH - DONALD S. WALKER LABORATORY
- C.P. RHOADS MEMORIAL LIBRARY □ Rye, NY

Gregson, Jean, Libn.
LANGLEY SCHOOL DISTRICT - RESOURCE
CENTRE □ Langley, BC

Greig, Jack R., Res.
NAPA COUNTY HISTORICAL SOCIETY -
LIBRARY □ Napa, CA

Greil, Barbara, Ser./Ref.Libn.
SUNY - AGRICULTURAL AND TECHNICAL
COLLEGE AT ALFRED - WALTER C. HINKLE
MEMORIAL LIBRARY □ Alfred, NY

Greismann, Jacqueline, Asst.Libn.
WEINBERG & GREEN, ATTORNEYS-AT-LAW -
LIBRARY □ Baltimore, MD

Greist, John H., M.D., Co-Dir.
UNIVERSITY OF WISCONSIN, MADISON -
DEPARTMENT OF PSYCHIATRY - LITHIUM
INFORMATION CENTER □ Madison, WI

Grele, Ronald J., Dir.
COLUMBIA UNIVERSITY - ORAL HISTORY
COLLECTION □ New York, NY

Gremmels, Gillian S., Ref.Libn.
SCHOOLS OF THEOLOGY IN DUBUQUE -
LIBRARIES □ Dubuque, IA

Grenda, Johanna, Tech.Info.Spec.
RAYTHEON COMPANY - RESEARCH DIVISION -
LIBRARY □ Lexington, MA

Grenier, Patricia, Coord., Info.Serv.
ONTARIO - MINISTRY OF EDUCATION -
INFORMATION CENTRE □ Toronto, ON

Gres, Beverly, Ref.Libn.
MAITLAND PUBLIC LIBRARY - ANDRE SMITH
COLLECTION □ Maitland, FL

Gresack, Barbara, Libn.
CENTRAL SYNAGOGUE OF NASSAU COUNTY -
HELEN BLAU MEMORIAL LIBRARY □ Rockville
Centre, NY

Gresehover, Robert, Dp.Dir.
JOHNS HOPKINS UNIVERSITY - WILLIAM H.
WELCH MEDICAL LIBRARY □ Baltimore, MD

Gresens, Julie, Asst. Audit Libn.
COOPERS & LYBRAND - AUDIT LIBRARY □
Chicago, IL

Gresser, Marylyn E., Chf., Lib.Serv.
U.S. VETERANS ADMINISTRATION (FL-
Gainesville) - HOSPITAL LIBRARY □ Gainesville,
FL

Gresseth, Dale, Ser.
UNIVERSITY OF WISCONSIN, LA CROSSE -
MURPHY LIBRARY □ La Crosse, WI

Gressley, Dr. Gene M., Dir.
UNIVERSITY OF WYOMING - PETROLEUM HISTORY AND RESEARCH CENTER LIBRARY □ Laramie, WY

Gressley, Dr. Gene M., Dir.
UNIVERSITY OF WYOMING - WESTERN HISTORY RESEARCH CENTER LIBRARY □ Laramie, WY

Gretes, Frances C., Mgr., Info.Serv.
SKIDMORE, OWINGS & MERRILL - INFORMATION SERVICES DEPARTMENT □ New York, NY

Greven, Maryanne, Circuit Rider Coord.
CENTRAL MAINE MEDICAL CENTER - GERRISH-TRUE HEALTH SCIENCE LIBRARY □ Lewiston, ME

Grevera, Dorothy, Mgr., Lib.Serv.
FOUR-PHASE SYSTEMS - CORPORATE LIBRARY □ Cupertino, CA

Grewal, Mrs. Harcharan, Libn. 2, Back-up Serv.
METROPOLITAN TORONTO LIBRARY - LANGUAGES DEPARTMENT □ Toronto, ON

Grey, Catherine, Asst.Chf.
BROOKLYN PUBLIC LIBRARY - AUDIO VISUAL DIVISION □ Brooklyn, NY

Grier, Margot E., Per.Libn.
NATIONAL GALLERY OF ART - LIBRARY □ Washington, DC

Griese, Nancy C., Hd.Libn.
TRI-COUNTY TECHNICAL COLLEGE - LEARNING RESOURCE CENTER □ Pendleton, SC

Grieve, Isabel, Libn.
ANTHROPOSOPHICAL SOCIETY IN CANADA - RUDOLPH STEINER LIBRARY† □ Toronto, ON

Griffen, Charles S., Hd.
HARTFORD PUBLIC LIBRARY - BUSINESS, SCIENCE & TECHNOLOGY DEPARTMENT □ Hartford, CT

Griffin, Ann, Adm.Asst.
INDIANA UNIVERSITY/PURDUE UNIVERSITY AT INDIANAPOLIS - UNIVERSITY LIBRARY □ Indianapolis, IN

Griffin, Cynthia A., Libn.
MOTORCYCLE SAFETY FOUNDATION - INFORMATION RESOURCE CENTER □ Chadds Ford, PA

Griffin, Gene C., Dir.
NORTH DAKOTA STATE UNIVERSITY - UPPER GREAT PLAINS TRANSPORTATION INSTITUTE - INFORMATION CENTER □ Fargo, ND

Griffin, Gerald T., Chf., Lib.Br.
U.S. AIR FORCE BASE - HANSCOM BASE LIBRARY □ Hanscom AFB, MA

Griffin, Hillis L., Dir.
ARGONNE NATIONAL LABORATORY - TECHNICAL INFORMATION SERVICES DEPARTMENT† □ Argonne, IL

Griffin, James R., Dept.Hd.
VITRO CORPORATION - LIBRARY □ Silver Spring, MD

Griffin, Janette, Cat. & Per.
NEW ORLEANS BAPTIST THEOLOGICAL SEMINARY - JOHN T. CHRISTIAN LIBRARY □ New Orleans, LA

Griffin, Kathleen, Libn.
SAN DIEGO PUBLIC LIBRARY - SOCIAL SCIENCES SECTION □ San Diego, CA

Griffin, Lila B., Proj.Archv.
ATLANTA UNIVERSITY CENTER - ROBERT W. WOODRUFF LIBRARY □ Atlanta, GA

Griffin, Linda, Libn.
SAN DIEGO PUBLIC LIBRARY - ART, MUSIC & RECREATION SECTION □ San Diego, CA

Griffin, Marianne L., Libn.
SHOOK, HARDY & BACON - LIBRARY □ Kansas City, MO

Griffin, Marie, Libn.
RUTGERS UNIVERSITY, THE STATE UNIVERSITY OF NEW JERSEY - INSTITUTE OF JAZZ STUDIES □ Newark, NJ

Griffin, Olive L., Libn.
MERCER COUNTY LAW LIBRARY □ Mercer, PA

Griffin, Pamela, Asst.Med.Libn.
UNIVERSITY OF CALGARY - MEDICAL LIBRARY† □ Calgary, AB

Griffin, Stephanie, Cat.
BENTLEY COLLEGE - SOLOMON R. BAKER LIBRARY □ Waltham, MA

Griffin, Dr. William, Libn./Archv.
AMERICAN IRISH HISTORICAL SOCIETY - LIBRARY □ New York, NY

Griffis, Miriam, Audio Supv.
BAYLOR UNIVERSITY - CROUCH MUSIC LIBRARY □ Waco, TX

Griffiss, Keating, Libn.
HUNTER MUSEUM OF ART - REFERENCE LIBRARY □ Chattanooga, TN

Griffith, Alice B., Lib.Dir.
MOHAWK VALLEY COMMUNITY COLLEGE LIBRARY - SPECIAL COLLECTIONS □ Utica, NY

Griffith, Jack W., Libn., NLR Div.
U.S. VETERANS ADMINISTRATION (AR-Little Rock) - HOSPITAL LIBRARIES □ Little Rock, AR

Griffith, Jerry, Libn.
U.S. ARMY - ENGINEER WATERWAYS EXPERIMENT STATION - TECHNICAL INFORMATION CENTER □ Vicksburg, MS

Griffith, Karen K., Dir., Lib.
CLEVELAND INSTITUTE OF MUSIC - LIBRARY □ Cleveland, OH

Griffith, Mona C., Chf.Libn.
MARTIN MARIETTA CORPORATION - ORLANDO AEROSPACE DIVISION - INFORMATION CENTER □ Orlando, FL

Griffith, Sheryl, Act.Supv.Libn.
U.S. PRESIDENTIAL LIBRARIES - FRANKLIN D. ROOSEVELT LIBRARY □ Hyde Park, NY

Griffith, Vicki L., Libn.
HANCOCK (Allan) FOUNDATION - HANCOCK LIBRARY OF BIOLOGY & OCEANOGRAPHY □ Los Angeles, CA

Griffiths, June, Asst.Libn.
LEHIGH COUNTY HISTORICAL SOCIETY - SCOTT ANDREW TREXLER II MEMORIAL LIBRARY □ Allentown, PA

Griffiths, Marion, Asst.Dir., Adm. Code
ILLINOIS STATE LIBRARY □ Springfield, IL

Griffiths, Suzanne, Libn.
UNIVERSITY OF ILLINOIS - CLASSICS LIBRARY □ Urbana, IL

Griffitts, Donna K., Adm.Libn.
U.S. ARMY/U.S. AIR FORCE - OFFICES OF THE SURGEONS GENERAL - JOINT MEDICAL LIBRARY □ Washington, DC

Griffitts, Joan K., Libn.
RCA CORPORATION - SELECTAVISION VIDEODISC OPERATIONS - TECHNICAL LIBRARY □ Indianapolis, IN

Grifhorst, James R., Data Archv.Mgr.
UNIVERSITY OF IOWA - LABORATORY FOR POLITICAL RESEARCH □ Iowa City, IA

Grigg, Susan, Cur.
UNIVERSITY OF MINNESOTA - IMMIGRATION HISTORY RESEARCH CENTER COLLECTION □ St. Paul, MN

Grigg, Virginia C., Chf., Bur.Lib.Dev.
STATE LIBRARY OF FLORIDA □ Tallahassee, FL

Griggs, Charlotte, Libn.
PHILLIPS PETROLEUM COMPANY - ENGINEERING LIBRARY □ Bartlesville, OK

Griggs, John B., Libn.
LLOYD LIBRARY AND MUSEUM □ Cincinnati, OH

Grigst, Denise, Asst.Libn.
IRELL & MANELLA - LIBRARY □ Los Angeles, CA

Grilikhes, Sandra B., Hd.Libn.
UNIVERSITY OF PENNSYLVANIA - ANNENBERG SCHOOL OF COMMUNICATIONS - LIBRARY† □ Philadelphia, PA

Grimble, Heather, Lib.Techn.
GCG ENGINEERING PARTNERSHIP - LIBRARY □ Edmonton, AB

Grimes, Deirdre, Libn.
ROYAL BANK OF CANADA - INFORMATION RESOURCES □ Toronto, ON

Grimes, Janice L., Sec./Asst.Libn.
CHARLESTON LIBRARY SOCIETY □ Charleston, SC

Grimes, Julia D., Libn.
LOVELACE BIOMEDICAL & ENVIRONMENTAL RESEARCH INSTITUTE, INC. - INHALATION TOXICOLOGY RESEARCH INST. - LIB.† □ Albuquerque, NM

Grimes, Marie T., Asst.Libn.
GENERAL AMERICAN INVESTORS CO., INC. - LIBRARY □ New York, NY

Grimes, Maxyne M., Act.Dir.
UNIVERSITY OF SOUTH FLORIDA - MEDICAL CENTER LIBRARY □ Tampa, FL

Grimm, Ann C., Libn.
UNIVERSITY OF MICHIGAN - TRANSPORTATION RESEARCH INSTITUTE - LIBRARY □ Ann Arbor, MI

Grimm, Ann C., Libn.
UNIVERSITY OF MICHIGAN - TRANSPORTATION RESEARCH INSTITUTE - PUBLIC INFORMATION MATERIALS CENTER □ Ann Arbor, MI

Grimm, Susan, Music Cat.
VASSAR COLLEGE - GEORGE SHERMAN DICKINSON MUSIC LIBRARY □ Poughkeepsie, NY

Grimshaw, Cynthia A., Law Libn.
NEW YORK STATE SUPREME COURT - 7TH JUDICIAL DISTRICT - LAW LIBRARY □ Bath, NY

Grimshaw, Polly S., Libn./Cur.
INDIANA UNIVERSITY - FOLKLORE COLLECTION □ Bloomington, IN

Grimsley, Judy L., Info.Rsrcs.Supv.
ORLANDO SENTINEL NEWSPAPER - LIBRARY □ Orlando, FL

Grinbergs, Diana
NATIONAL COLLEGE OF EDUCATION - LEARNING RESOURCE CENTERS □ Evanston, IL

Grincevicius, Ceslovas V., Dir.
LITHUANIAN AMERICAN COMMUNITY OF THE U.S.A. - LITHUANIAN WORLD ARCHIVES □ Chicago, IL

Grincewich, P., Mgr., Tech.Info.Ctr.
IBM CORPORATION - GENERAL PRODUCTS DIVISION - TECHNICAL INFORMATION CENTER □ San Jose, CA

Griner, Mrs. Marina, Supv.Libn.
U.S. ARMY SOLDIER SUPPORT CENTER - MAIN LIBRARY† □ Ft. Benjamin Harrison, IN

Grinnell, Margaret Tielke, Act.Dir.
MENDOTA MENTAL HEALTH INSTITUTE - LIBRARY MEDIA CENTER† □ Madison, WI

Grisak, Garry, Coord., Lib.Serv.
OLDS COLLEGE - LEARNING RESOURCES CENTRE - SPECIAL COLLECTIONS □ Olds, AB

Griscom, Richard, Cat.
NORTHWESTERN UNIVERSITY - MUSIC LIBRARY □ Evanston, IL

Griskavich, Marcia, Cat.Libn.
UNIVERSITY OF WISCONSIN, MADISON - LAW SCHOOL LIBRARY □ Madison, WI

Griskavich, Marcia, Libn.
UNIVERSITY OF WISCONSIN, MADISON - LAW SCHOOL LIBRARY - CRIMINAL JUSTICE REFERENCE & INFORMATION CENTER □ Madison, WI

Grissett, Patty P., Tech.Serv.Libn
BAPTIST MEDICAL CENTERS-SAMFORD UNIVERSITY - IDA V. MOFFETT SCHOOL OF NURSING - L.R. JORDAN LIBRARY† □ Birmingham, AL

Griswold, Joan, Libn.
SOUTH CONGREGATIONAL CHURCH - ETHEL L. AUSTIN LIBRARY □ Granby, CT

Griswold, June, Cur.
KOOTENAY LAKE HISTORICAL SOCIETY - LIBRARY □ Kaslo, BC

Gritton, James H., Law Libn.
IOWA STATE LAW LIBRARY □ Des Moines, IA

Gritzmacher, Lucy G., Libn.
PHARMACEUTICAL MANUFACTURERS ASSOCIATION - LIBRARY □ Washington, DC

Grobar, Bonnie, Mgr., Pub.Serv.Dept.
TEXAS STATE LIBRARY - INFORMATION
SERVICES DIVISION □ Austin, TX
Grochowski, Barbara, Chf., Ref.Dept.
U.S. ARMY POST - FORT BELVOIR - VAN NOY
LIBRARY □ Ft. Belvoir, VA
Grodski, Renata, Libn.
ONTARIO - MINISTRY OF CITIZENSHIP AND
CULTURE - MINISTRY OF TOURISM AND
RECREATION - LIBRARY/RESOURCE CENTRE □
Toronto, ON
Grodzicky, Dr. Roman R., Chf.Libn.
MARIANOPOLIS COLLEGE - LIBRARY - SPECIAL
COLLECTIONS □ Montreal, PQ
Groen, Frances, Life Sci. Area Libn.
MC GILL UNIVERSITY - MEDICAL LIBRARY □
Montreal, PQ
Groen, Paulette, Libn.
SOCIETY OF MANUFACTURING ENGINEERS -
SME LIBRARY □ Dearborn, MI
Grof-lanelli, Martie, Asst.Libn.
UNIVERSITY OF WESTERN ONTARIO - SCHOOL
OF LIBRARY & INFORMATION SCIENCE -
LIBRARY □ London, ON
Groft, Mary LaRue, Supv., Info.Serv.
PEAT, MARWICK, MITCHELL & CO. - AUDIT/
MCD LIBRARY □ Chicago, IL
Grogan, Dennis P., Assoc.Med.Dir.
TINGLEY (Carrie) CRIPPLED CHILDREN'S
HOSPITAL - MEDICAL LIBRARY □ Albuquerque,
NM
Grogan, Evelent, Res.Libn.
NORTHROP CORPORATION - CORPORATE
LIBRARY □ Los Angeles, CA
Grondines, Louise, Cat.Libn.
UNIVERSITE DU QUEBEC A HULL -
BIBLIOTHEQUE □ Hull, PQ
Gronski, Alice, Rec.Libn.
WASHINGTON ARCHAEOLOGICAL RESEARCH
CENTER - LIBRARY □ Pullman, WA
Grooms, Carole, Assoc.Libn.
UNIVERSITY OF FLORIDA - LAW LIBRARY □
Gainesville, FL
Groot, Elizabeth H., Mgr., Tech.Info.Serv.
SCHENECTADY CHEMICALS, INC. - W.
HOWARD WRIGHT RESEARCH CENTER -
LIBRARY □ Schenectady, NY
Grosbeck, Alan, Media Spec.
UTAH VALLEY HOSPITAL - MEDICAL LIBRARY □
Provo, UT
Gross, Alice, Mgr., Lib.Serv.
SEAGRAM (Joseph E.) & SONS, INC. -
CORPORATE LIBRARY □ New York, NY
Gross, Edith, Med.Libn.
MONSOUR MEDICAL CENTER - HEALTH
SERVICES LIBRARY □ Jeannette, PA
Gross, Jerianne, Coll.Dev.-Ser.
CLEVELAND HEALTH SCIENCES LIBRARY -
HEALTH CENTER LIBRARY □ Cleveland, OH
Gross, John, Dir.
SALINAS PUBLIC LIBRARY - JOHN STEINBECK
LIBRARY □ Salinas, CA
Gross, Kathleen, Asst.Libn.
RCA CORPORATION - GSD - GOVERNMENT
COMMUNICATIONS SYSTEMS - LIBRARY □
Camden, NJ
Gross, Kenneth L., Lib.Serv.Dir.
NORTHWEST MUNICIPAL CONFERENCE -
GOVERNMENT INFORMATION CENTER □ Mt.
Prospect, IL
Gross, Leonard, Archv.
HISTORICAL COMMITTEE OF THE MENNONITE
CHURCH - ARCHIVES OF THE MENNONITE
CHURCH □ Goshen, IN
Gross, Margaret B., Libn.
SPAR AEROSPACE LTD. - LIBRARY □ Ste. Anne
de Bellevue, PQ
Gross, Margarete K., Pict.Libn.
CHICAGO PUBLIC LIBRARY CULTURAL CENTER
- FINE ARTS DIVISION - ART SECTION □
Chicago, IL

Gross, Sally, Assoc.Cur./Printed Coll.
SOUTHERN METHODIST UNIVERSITY -
DEGOLYER LIBRARY - FIKES HALL OF SPECIAL
COLLECTIONS □ Dallas, TX
Grosse, Mrs. Alfred C., Lib.Chm.
EAST DALLAS CHRISTIAN CHURCH - HAGGARD
MEMORIAL LIBRARY† □ Dallas, TX
Grosse, June, Info.Sci.
AMERICAN CYANAMID COMPANY -
AGRICULTURAL RESEARCH DIVISION -
TECHNICAL INFORMATION SERVICES □
Princeton, NJ
Grosshans, Maxine, Sr.Ref.Libn.
UNIVERSITY OF MARYLAND, BALTIMORE -
SCHOOL OF LAW - MARSHALL LAW LIBRARY □
Baltimore, MD
Grossman, Dr. Burton J., Chf. of Med. Staff
LA RABIDA CHILDREN'S HOSPITAL AND
RESEARCH CENTER - LAWRENCE MERCER
PICK MEMORIAL LIBRARY □ Chicago, IL
Grossman, Charles, Libn.
RAILROAD ENTHUSIASTS NEW YORK
DIVISION, INC. - WILLIAMSON LIBRARY □ New
York, NY
Grossman, George S., Libn.
NORTHWESTERN UNIVERSITY - LAW SCHOOL
LIBRARY □ Chicago, IL
Grossman, Nancy, Sci. & Tech.Libn.
RYERSON POLYTECHNICAL INSTITUTE -
LEARNING RESOURCES CENTRE □ Toronto, ON
Grossman, Robert, Libn.
PHILADELPHIA ORCHESTRA ASSOCIATION -
LIBRARY □ Philadelphia, PA
Grossmann, Maria, Libn.
HARVARD UNIVERSITY - DIVINITY SCHOOL -
ANDOVER-HARVARD THEOLOGICAL LIBRARY □
Cambridge, MA
Grosso, Pete, Automotive Res.
HARRAH'S AUTOMOTIVE LIBRARY □ Reno, NV
Grot-Zakrzewski, Zena C., Mgr.
COMBUSTION ENGINEERING, INC. - POWER
SYSTEMS GROUP LIBRARY SERVICES† □
Windsor, CT
Groth, Paul E., Pres.
PAUL DE HAEN INTERNATIONAL, INC. - DRUG
INFORMATION SYSTEMS AND SERVICES □
Englewood, CO
Groth, Virginia, Libn.
3M - LAW LIBRARY □ St. Paul, MN
Grotsky, Stephen R., Libn.
NEW YORK STATE SUPREME COURT -
APPELLATE DIVISION, 1ST JUDICIAL
DEPARTMENT - LAW LIBRARY† □ New York, NY
Groulx, Denise, Supv.
CANADA - IMMIGRATION APPEAL BOARD -
LIBRARY □ Ottawa, ON
Grout, Barbara, Dir.
MEMORIAL HOSPITAL - LIBRARY □ Belleville, IL
Grove, Donna, Dept.Hd.
HOUSTON PUBLIC LIBRARY - SPECIAL
COLLECTIONS DEPARTMENT □ Houston, TX
Grove, Steven J., Hd.Libn.
HOLZHEIMER INTERIORS - RESEARCH CENTER
□ Cleveland, OH
Grover, Monica, Sect.Hd.
COLGATE PALMOLIVE COMPANY - TECHNICAL
INFORMATION CENTER □ Piscataway, NJ
Grover, Rachel, Mss.Libn.
UNIVERSITY OF TORONTO - THOMAS FISHER
RARE BOOK LIBRARY □ Toronto, ON
Grover, Robert L., Chm.
BLUE SPRINGS HISTORICAL SOCIETY -
LIBRARY □ Independence, MO
Grover, Wilma S., Libn.
ST. FRANCIS HOSPITAL - MEDICAL LIBRARY □
Miami Beach, FL
Groves, Percilla, Spec.Coll.Libn.
SIMON FRASER UNIVERSITY - LIBRARY -
SPECIAL COLLECTIONS □ Burnaby, BC
Grow, William B., Marketing Anl.
BANKERS LIFE & CASUALTY COMPANY -
MARKETING INFORMATION DEPARTMENT -
LIBRARY □ Chicago, IL

Gruben, Karl T., Libn.
VINSON & ELKINS - LAW LIBRARY □ Houston,
TX
Gruber, Dorothy H., Libn.
INSTITUTE FOR MEDICAL RESEARCH -
LIBRARY □ Camden, NJ
Gruenthal, Linda, Libn.
COLORADO STATE SUPREME COURT LIBRARY □
Denver, CO
Gruettner, Ruth, Info.Spec.
AMERICAN CAN COMPANY - BUSINESS
INFORMATION CENTER □ Greenwich, CT
Gruhn, Adolph M., Chm., Lib.Comm.
PSYCHOANALYTIC ASSOCIATION OF SEATTLE
- EDITH BUXBAUM LIBRARY □ Seattle, WA
Grunberger, Michael, Libn.
GRATZ COLLEGE - LIBRARY □ Philadelphia, PA
Grund, Henry J., II, Dir.
LIBRARY OF HENRY J. GRUND† □ Mentor, OH
Grundke, Patricia J., Libn.
COMMUNITY MEMORIAL GENERAL HOSPITAL -
MEDICAL LIBRARY □ La Grange, IL
Grundman, John, Rec.Mgr.
MORGAN STANLEY & COMPANY, INC. -
LIBRARY SERVICES □ New York, NY
Grundset, Eric G., Staff Libn.
NATIONAL SOCIETY, DAUGHTERS OF THE
AMERICAN REVOLUTION - LIBRARY □
Washington, DC
Grundy, Robert S., Law Libn./Att.
CONOCO, INC. - LEGAL INFORMATION CENTER
□ Houston, TX
Grundy, Ruth, Libn.
UNIVERSITY OF TEXAS - PORT ARANSAS
MARINE LABORATORY - LIBRARY □ Port
Aransas, TX
Gruner, Gail, Dir.
NEW ENGLAND INSTITUTE OF APPLIED ARTS
AND SCIENCES - NATIONAL CENTER FOR
DEATH EDUCATION □ Boston, MA
Grunow, Millie H., Med.Libn.
DEACONESS HOSPITAL - HEALTH SCIENCE
LIBRARY □ Evansville, IN
Gruntorad, Lois C., Libn.
U.S. NAVY - NAVAL AIR STATION (CA-Lemoore)
- LIBRARY □ Lemoore, CA
Grunwald, Rabbi Binyomin, Hd.Libn.
TELSHE YESHIVA - RABBI A.N. SCHWARTZ
LIBRARY □ Wickliffe, OH
Gruver, Eileen, Asst. Law Libn.
CAPITAL UNIVERSITY - LAW SCHOOL LIBRARY
□ Columbus, OH
Grygo, Alice B., Ser.Libn.
MINNESOTA HISTORICAL SOCIETY -
REFERENCE LIBRARY □ St. Paul, MN
Gschneidner, Karl A., Jr., Dir.
IOWA STATE UNIVERSITY - ENERGY AND
MINERAL RESOURCES RESEARCH INSTITUTE -
RARE-EARTH INFORMATION CENTER □ Ames,
IA
Guagliardo, Georgeann, Sec./Libn.
U.S. DEPT. OF TRANSPORTATION -
TRANSPORTATION TEST CENTER - TECHNICAL
LIBRARY □ Pueblo, CO
Guano, Bro. Jose "Bat", O.B., Chf., Archv./Kpr.
INTERNATIONAL BROTHERHOOD OF OLD
BASTARDS, INC. - SIR THOMAS CRAPPER
MEMORIAL ARCHIVES □ St. Louis, MO
Guarducci, Elizabeth B., Med.Libn.
ESSEX COUNTY HOSPITAL CENTER -
HAMILTON MEMORIAL LIBRARY □ Cedar Grove,
NJ
Guay, Alice, Hd., Coll. Organization
NATIONAL LIBRARY OF CANADA - OFFICIAL
PUBLICATIONS DIVISION □ Ottawa, ON
Gubert, Betty, Hd., Ref./Coop.Serv.
NEW YORK PUBLIC LIBRARY - SCHOMBURG
CENTER FOR RESEARCH IN BLACK CULTURE □
New York, NY
Gubiotti, Ross A., Project Mgr.
BATTELLE-COLUMBUS LABORATORIES -
COPPER DATA CENTER □ Columbus, OH

Gubman, Nancy, Dir.
NEW YORK UNIVERSITY - COURANT INSTITUTE OF MATHEMATICAL SCIENCES - LIBRARY □ New York, NY

Gucma, Mrs. Mina, Libn.
DOFASCO INC. - MAIN OFFICE LIBRARY □ Hamilton, ON

Gude, Gilbert, Dir.
LIBRARY OF CONGRESS - CONGRESSIONAL RESEARCH SERVICE □ Washington, DC

Gudelis, Louise, Local Hist.Ref.Libn.
GREENWICH LIBRARY - ORAL HISTORY PROJECT □ Greenwich CT

Gudgel, Joan, Dir., Info.Serv.
NATIONAL FEDERATION OF LOCAL CABLE PROGRAMMERS - LIBRARY □ Washington, DC

Gudowitz, Stuart, Ref.Libn.
CORNELL UNIVERSITY - SCHOOL OF HOTEL ADMINISTRATION LIBRARY □ Ithaca, NY

Guelzow, D., Hd., Proc.
U.S. NASA - JOHN F. KENNEDY SPACE CENTER - LIBRARY □ Kennedy Space Center, FL

Guenette, Marie-Marthe, French Film Rep.
CANADA - NATIONAL FILM BOARD OF CANADA - FILM LIBRARY† □ Winnipeg, MB

Guensler, Tammy, Dir.
SACRAMENTO COUNCIL FOR DELAYED PRESCHOOLERS - DAISY TOY LENDING LIBRARY □ Sacramento, CA

Guenter, Doreen A., Chf.
NATIONAL LIBRARY OF CANADA - OFFICIAL PUBLICATIONS DIVISION □ Ottawa, ON

Guenther, Cecile, Circ.Reserve Asst.
WASHINGTON UNIVERSITY - BIOLOGY LIBRARY □ St. Louis, MO

Guerena, Sal, Assoc.Libn./Unit Hd.
UNIVERSITY OF CALIFORNIA, SANTA BARBARA - LIBRARY - CHICANO STUDIES COLLECTION □ Santa Barbara, CA

Guerette, Jacques, RESORS Mgr.
CANADA - CANADA CENTRE FOR REMOTE SENSING - TECHNICAL INFORMATION SERVICE □ Ottawa, ON

Guerette, Normand, Dir.
QUEBEC PROV. - MIN. DE L'ENERGIE ET DES RESSOURCES - SERVICE DE DOCUMENTATION ET DE RENSEIGNEMENTS □ Quebec, PQ

Guerin, Betty B., Supv.Libn.
U.S. OFFICE OF PERSONNEL MANAGEMENT - LIBRARY □ Washington, DC

Guerra, Cara, Mstr.Libn.
SACRED HEART UNIVERSITY - LIBRARY □ Bridgeport, CT

Guerra, Elizabeth, Med.Rec.Dir.
SAN ANTONIO COMMUNITY HOSPITAL - WEBER MEMORIAL LIBRARY □ Upland, CA

Guerrero, Felicito C., Dir.
U.S. DEPT. OF COMMERCE - INTERNATIONAL TRADE ADMINISTRATION - HOUSTON DISTRICT OFFICE LIBRARY† □ Houston, TX

Guerrero, Virginia A. Leon, Children's Libn.
FLORES (Nieves M.) MEMORIAL LIBRARY □ Agana, GU

Guerriero, Donald A., Lib.Dir.
U.S. DEFENSE COMMUNICATIONS AGENCY - TECHNICAL AND MANAGEMENT INFORMATION CENTER □ Washington, DC

Guerriers, Ann B., Tech.Info.Spec.
U.S. ARMY - TROPIC TEST CENTER - TECHNICAL INFORMATION CENTER □ APO Miami, FL

Guest, Rev. Francis F., O.F.M., Archv.-Hist.
SANTA BARBARA MISSION ARCHIVE-LIBRARY □ Santa Barbara, CA

Guffey, Gloria, Libn.
U.S. AIR FORCE BASE - BOLLING BASE LIBRARY □ Washington, DC

Guffy, Gloria, Resource Ctr.Supv.
TEXAS A & M UNIVERSITY - DEPARTMENTS OF OCEANOGRAPHY AND METEOROLOGY - WORKING COLLECTION □ College Station, TX

Gugisberg, Mercedes, Libn.
ST. THOMAS AQUINAS NEWMAN CENTER - LIBRARY □ Albuquerque, NM

Guida, Pat, Pres.
GUIDA (Pat) ASSOCIATES - LIBRARY □ Pine Brook, NJ

Guido, John F., Hd.
WASHINGTON STATE UNIVERSITY - MANUSCRIPTS, ARCHIVES, & SPECIAL COLLECTIONS □ Pullman, WA

Guido, Lucille, Pres.
NATIONAL COUNCIL ON YEAR-ROUND EDUCATION - LIBRARY □ San Diego, CA

Guilbert, Mary C., Libn.
PIMA COUNCIL ON AGING - LIBRARY □ Tucson, AZ

Guilfoil, Elizabeth J., Dir.
SACRED HEART MEDICAL CENTER - HEALTH SCIENCES LIBRARY □ Spokane, WA

Guillermard, Teresita, Ref. & Circ.Dept.Dir.
CATHOLIC UNIVERSITY OF PUERTO RICO - MONSIGNOR JUAN FREMIOT TORRES OLIVER LAW LIBRARY □ Ponce, PR

Guillet, Nancy M., Chf.Libn.
U.S. VETERANS ADMINISTRATION (LA-Alexandria) - MEDICAL CENTER MEDICAL LIBRARY □ Alexandria, LA

Guin, Marilyn, Libn.
OREGON STATE UNIVERSITY - HATFIELD MARINE SCIENCE CENTER - LIBRARY □ Newport, OR

Guinyard, Margie, Libn.
NEW YORK UNIVERSITY - SALOMON BROTHERS CENTER FOR THE STUDY OF FINANCIAL INSTITUTIONS - LIBRARY □ New York, NY

Guion, Dennis, Ref.Libn.
UNIVERSITY OF MARYLAND, BALTIMORE - SCHOOL OF LAW - MARSHALL LAW LIBRARY □ Baltimore, MD

Guiu, Elizabeth, Libn.
NEW ENGLAND BAPTIST HOSPITAL - HELENE FULD LIBRARY □ Boston, MA

Guiu, Rafael, Mgr.
SWEDENBORG LIBRARY AND BOOKSTORE □ Boston, MA

Gulbinowicz, Eva, Libn.
ONTARIO - MINISTRY OF THE SOLICITOR GENERAL - CENTRE OF FORENSIC SCIENCES - H. WARD SMITH LIBRARY □ Toronto, ON

Gulick, Melba, Ref.Libn.
SUNY - COLLEGE AT POTSDAM - FREDERICK W. CRUMB MEMORIAL LIBRARY □ Potsdam, NY

Gulledge, Dr. James L., Dir.
CORNELL UNIVERSITY - LABORATORY OF ORNITHOLOGY - LIBRARY OF NATURAL SOUNDS □ Ithaca, NY

Gulley, Larry, Mss.Libn.
UNIVERSITY OF GEORGIA - MANUSCRIPTS COLLECTION □ Athens, GA

Gulliver, JoAnne, Mgr., Lib.Serv.
MC MILLAN, BINCH - LIBRARY □ Toronto, ON

Gully, W., Libn.
CANADA - NATIONAL RESEARCH COUNCIL - CISTI - DOMINION RADIO ASTROPHYSICAL OBSERVATORY BRANCH □ Penticton, BC

Gulstad, Wilma, Hd., Cat.
UNIVERSITY OF MISSOURI - HEALTH SCIENCES LIBRARY □ Columbia, MO

Gulvezan, Karen M., Asst.Libn.
MICHIGAN CONSOLIDATED GAS COMPANY - CORPORATE LIBRARY □ Detroit, MI

Gunby, Norma, Owner
COWETA COUNTY GENEALOGICAL SOCIETY - LIBRARY □ Newnan, GA

Gunderson, Jeff, Lib.Dir.
COLLEGE OF THE SAN FRANCISCO ART INSTITUTE - ANNE BREMER MEMORIAL LIBRARY □ San Francisco, CA

Gundlach, Alyne R., Chf.
PUBLIC LIBRARY OF NASHVILLE AND DAVIDSON COUNTY - BUSINESS INFORMATION SERVICE □ Nashville, TN

Gundry, L.D., Chf.Med.Libn.
BRYN MAWR HOSPITAL - MEDICAL LIBRARY □ Bryn Mawr, PA

Gundry, L.D., Chf.Med.Libn.
BRYN MAWR HOSPITAL - MEDICAL LIBRARY - NURSING DIVISION □ Bryn Mawr, PA

Gunn, Arthur C., Libn.
UNIVERSITY OF PITTSBURGH - AFRO-AMERICAN LIBRARY □ Pittsburgh, PA

Gunn, Diane, Slide Cur.
CRANBROOK ACADEMY OF ART - LIBRARY □ Bloomfield Hills, MI

Gunn, Leah M., Chf. Order Libn.
UNIVERSITY OF MICHIGAN - LAW LIBRARY □ Ann Arbor, MI

Gunner, Jean, Bookbinder & Consrv.
CARNEGIE-MELLON UNIVERSITY - HUNT INSTITUTE FOR BOTANICAL DOCUMENTATION □ Pittsburgh, PA

Gunning, C., Asst.Libn.
NORTH BAY COLLEGE EDUCATION CENTRE - LIBRARY □ North Bay, ON

Gunning, M.K., Div.Chf.
BROOKLYN PUBLIC LIBRARY - SOCIAL SCIENCE AND PHILOSOPHY DIVISION □ Brooklyn, NY

Gunning, Ruth T., Mgr., Bus.Info.Serv.
ROCKWELL INTERNATIONAL - BUSINESS RESEARCH CENTER □ Pittsburgh, PA

Gunther, Barbara, Libn.
ANTHROPOSOPHICAL SOCIETY IN CANADA - RUDOLPH STEINER LIBRARY† □ Toronto, ON

Gunther, Barbara, Hd.
METROPOLITAN TORONTO LIBRARY - LANGUAGES DEPARTMENT □ Toronto, ON

Gupta, J., Hd., Acq.
CANADA - TRANSPORT CANADA - LIBRARY & INFORMATION CENTRE □ Ottawa, ON

Gupta, Mrs. Pushpa, Libn.
CONSULATE GENERAL OF INDIA - INFORMATION SERVICE OF INDIA LIBRARY □ New York, NY

Guptill, Barbara, Mng.Libn.
SEATTLE PUBLIC LIBRARY - GOVERNMENTAL RESEARCH ASSISTANCE LIBRARY† □ Seattle, WA

Gurewitsch, Bonnie, Res.Libn.
CENTER FOR HOLOCAUST STUDIES - DOCUMENTATION & RESEARCH □ Brooklyn, NY

Gurn, Robert M., Hd.
BUFFALO & ERIE COUNTY PUBLIC LIBRARY - FILM DEPARTMENT □ Buffalo, NY

Gurner, Richard, Lib.Adm.
POLAROID CORPORATION - RESEARCH LIBRARY □ Cambridge, MA

Gurney, Graham, Dist.Mgr.
SPERRY - TECHNICAL LIBRARY □ New York, NY

Gurney, Susan, Ref.Libn.
SMITHSONIAN INSTITUTION - NATIONAL MUSEUM OF AMERICAN ART/NATIONAL PORTRAIT GALLERY - LIBRARY □ Washington, DC

Gusby, Laura, Asst.Mgr.
SOHIO CHEMCIAL COMPANY - INFORMATION CENTER □ Cleveland, OH

Gustafson, Maxine, Lib.Techn.
U.S. AIR FORCE HOSPITAL - SHEPPARD REGIONAL HOSPITAL - MEDICAL LIBRARY □ Sheppard AFB, TX

Gustin, Deborah A., Chf., Lib.Serv.
U.S. VETERANS ADMINISTRATION (MD-Baltimore) - MEDICAL CENTER LIBRARY SERVICE (142D) □ Baltimore, MD

Guston, G. David, Archv.
BAPTIST GENERAL CONFERENCE - ARCHIVES □ St. Paul, MN

Gusts, Lilita, Ref.Libn.
COLUMBIA UNIVERSITY - THOMAS J. WATSON LIBRARY OF BUSINESS AND ECONOMICS □ New York, NY

Gutenburg, U., Lib.Techn.
UNIVERSITY OF TORONTO - INSTITUTE FOR POLICY ANALYSIS - LIBRARY □ Toronto, ON

Guth, Karen, Dir.
ST. LUKE'S HOSPITAL - HEALTH SCIENCES
LIBRARY □ Denver, CO

Guthrie, Isabella, Asst.Libn.
ROYAL ONTARIO MUSEUM - LIBRARY† □
Toronto, ON

Guthrie, Rosalie, Asst.Br.Libn.
ST. PAUL PUBLIC LIBRARY - HIGHLAND PARK
BRANCH - PERRIE JONES MEMORIAL ROOM □
St. Paul, MN

Guthrie, Mrs. William, Cat.
REVEILLE UNITED METHODIST CHURCH -
REVEILLE MEMORIAL LIBRARY □ Richmond, VA

Guthrie, William, Libn.
UNIVERSITY OF WESTERN ONTARIO - MUSIC
LIBRARY □ London, ON

Gutierrez, Aleta, Mgr., Bus.Off.
BIBLIOGRAPHICAL CENTER FOR RESEARCH -
ROCKY MOUNTAIN REGION, INC. □ Denver, CO

Gutierrez-Witt, Laura, Libn.
UNIVERSITY OF TEXAS, AUSTIN - BENSON
LATIN AMERICAN COLLECTION □ Austin, TX

Gutowski-Connell, Jane E., Libn.
FIRST NATIONAL BANK OF BOSTON - LIBRARY†
□ Boston, MA

Gutscher, Dianne M., Cur.
BOWDOIN COLLEGE - LIBRARY - SPECIAL
COLLECTIONS □ Brunswick, ME

Gutshall, Judy H., Libn.
PENNSYLVANIA STATE DEPARTMENT OF
TRANSPORTATION - TRANSPORTATION
INFORMATION CENTER □ Harrisburg, PA

Gutterman, Morton, Info.Off.
METROPOLITAN DADE COUNTY PLANNING
DEPARTMENT - LIBRARY/INFORMATION
CENTER □ Miami, FL

Guttman, Glenda, Libn.
VANCOUVER PUBLIC LIBRARY - BUSINESS &
ECONOMICS DIVISION □ Vancouver, BC

Guttman, Renee
SDS BIOTECH CORPORATION - CORPORATE
LIBRARY □ Painesville, OH

Guttshail, Judith, Med.Libn.
U.S. VETERANS ADMINISTRATION (KS-
Leavenworth) - CENTER MEDICAL LIBRARY □
Leavenworth, KS

Gutz, Robert R., Asst.Libn.
NEW YORK STATE SUPREME COURT -
APPELLATE DIVISION, 4TH JUDICIAL
DEPARTMENT - LAW LIBRARY □ Rochester, NY

Gutzmann, Hilda E., Sec.
CANADA - ATMOSPHERIC ENVIRONMENT
SERVICE - WESTERN REGION HEADQUARTERS
LIBRARY □ Edmonton, AB

Guy, Ann, Libn.
KINNEY (A.M.) INC. - LIBRARY □ Cincinnati, OH

Guy, Nancy A., Law Libn.
HUMBOLDT COUNTY LAW LIBRARY† □ Eureka,
CA

Guyton, Joanne S., Libn.
METHODIST HOSPITAL SCHOOL OF NURSING -
LESLIE M. STRATTON NURSING LIBRARY □
Memphis, TN

Guzicki, Ronald M., Supv. Economist
U.S. DEPT. OF LABOR - BUREAU OF LABOR
STATISTICS - NORTH CENTRAL REGIONAL
OFFICE REFERENCE LIBRARY □ Chicago, IL

Guzman, Alberto, Ref.Libn.
INTERAMERICAN UNIVERSITY OF PUERTO
RICO - SCHOOL OF LAW - DOMINGO TOLEDO
ALAMO LAW LIBRARY† □ Santurce, PR

Guzman, Diane, Libn.
BROOKLYN MUSEUM - WILBOUR LIBRARY OF
EGYPTOLOGY □ Brooklyn, NY

Guzman, Violeta, Per.Libn.
UNIVERSITY OF PUERTO RICO - HUMACAO
UNIVERSITY COLLEGE - LIBRARY □ Humacao,
PR

Guzzo, Diane, Asst.Div.Hd.
QUEENS BOROUGH PUBLIC LIBRARY -
LANGUAGE & LITERATURE DIVISION □
Jamaica, NY

Gwinn, Nancy E., Asst.Dir.
SMITHSONIAN INSTITUTION LIBRARIES □
Washington, DC

Gwirtzman, Lisa L., Registrar/Cur.
CHINA TRADE MUSEUM - ARCHIVES □ Milton,
MA

Gwyn, Ann S., Asst.Dir., Spec.Coll.
JOHNS HOPKINS UNIVERSITY - MILTON S.
EISENHOWER LIBRARY - SPECIAL
COLLECTIONS DIVISION □ Baltimore, MD

Gydesen, S.P., Ref.Spec.
BATTELLE-NORTHWEST - PACIFIC
NORTHWEST LABORATORY - HANFORD
TECHNICAL LIBRARY □ Richland, WA

Gyorgyey, Ferenc A., Med.Hist.Libn.
YALE UNIVERSITY - MEDICAL LIBRARY □ New
Haven, CT

Gyulahazi, Maria, Libn.
WEST VIRGINIA STATE DEPARTMENT OF
AGRICULTURE - PLANT PEST CONTROL &
LABORATORY SERVICES DIVISION LIBRARY □
Charleston, WV

H

Haab, Nancy J., Libn.
WINTHROP, STIMSON, PUTNAM AND ROBERTS
- LIBRARY □ New York, NY

Haaland, Ardis, Med.Libn.
DAKOTA HOSPITAL - FRANCIS J. BUTLER
HEALTH SCIENCE LIBRARY □ Fargo, ND

Haas, Al H., Chf. Judge
COLORADO STATE DISTRICT COURT, 6TH
JUDICIAL DISTRICT - LAW LIBRARY □ Durango,
CO

Haas, Edward F., Dir.
LOUISIANA STATE MUSEUM - LOUISIANA
HISTORICAL CENTER □ New Orleans, LA

Haas, Janice L., Ref.Libn.
HAYES (Rutherford B.) PRESIDENTIAL CENTER -
LIBRARY □ Fremont, OH

Haas, Mary, Geology Coll.Libn.
KERN COUNTY LIBRARY SYSTEM - BEALE
MEMORIAL LIBRARY □ Bakersfield, CA

Haas, Marynell, Libn.
LOUISVILLE DEPARTMENT OF LAW - LIBRARY □
Louisville, KY

Haas, Stephen, Asst.Libn.
LOUISIANA STATE UNIVERSITY - BUSINESS
ADMINISTRATION/GOVERNMENT
DOCUMENTS DEPARTMENT □ Baton Rouge, LA

Haase, Gretchen, Libn.
OPPENHEIMER, WOLFF, FOSTER, SHEPARD &
DONNELLY - LIBRARY □ St. Paul, MN

Haase, Sue, Info.Spec.
GENERAL ELECTRIC COMPANY - LIGHTING
RESEARCH AND TECHNICAL SERVICES
OPERATIONS - LIBRARY □ Cleveland, OH

Habekost, Ulla, Libn.
GOETHE INSTITUTE TORONTO - LIBRARY □
Toronto, ON

Habel, Sue, Asst.Div.Chf.
BROOKLYN PUBLIC LIBRARY - HISTORY,
TRAVEL, RELIGION AND BIOGRAPHY DIVISION
□ Brooklyn, NY

Habelman, Carolyn, Supv.
MONROE COUNTY LOCAL HISTORY ROOM &
LIBRARY □ Sparta, WI

Habelman, Carolyn, Pres.
MONROE, JUNEAU, JACKSON COUNTY,
WISCONSIN GENEALOGY WORKSHOP -
LIBRARY □ Black River Falls, WI

Haber, Barbara, Cur. of Printed Bks.
RADCLIFFE COLLEGE - ARTHUR AND
ELIZABETH SCHLESINGER LIBRARY ON THE
HISTORY OF WOMEN IN AMERICA □
Cambridge, MA

Haber, Elinor, Info.Spec.
U.S. MARITIME ADMINISTRATION - NATL.
MARITIME RESEARCH CENTER - STUDY
CENTER □ Kings Point, NY

Haberman, Linda, Health Educator
NORTH SHORE UNIVERSITY HOSPITAL -
OFFICE OF HEALTH EDUC. - WE CARE ABOUT
SPECIAL CHILDREN MOBIL RESOURCE LIB. □
Manhasset, NY

Haberman, Vera, Archv.
ASPEN HISTORICAL SOCIETY - LIBRARY □
Aspen, CO

Habermann, Margaret J., Cat.Libn.
MINNESOTA HISTORICAL SOCIETY -
REFERENCE LIBRARY □ St. Paul, MN

Habetler, Anna M., Lib.Dir.
MERCY HOSPITAL AND MEDICAL CENTER -
JEAN FARB MEMORIAL MEDICAL LIBRARY □
San Diego, CA

Habousha, Rachline, Asst.Ref.Libn.
YESHIVA UNIVERSITY - ALBERT EINSTEIN
COLLEGE OF MEDICINE - D. SAMUEL
GOTTESMAN LIBRARY □ Bronx, NY

Hache, Michel, Tech.Serv.
CEGEP DU VIEUX-MONTREAL - LIBRARY □
Montreal, PQ

Hacinold, Dr. Alfred, Res.Sci.
OREGON STATE UNIVERSITY - DEPARTMENT
OF CROP SCIENCE - HOP RESEARCH CENTER -
WORKING COLLECTION □ Corvallis, OR

Hack, Carole, Libn.
ILLINOIS SCHOOL FOR THE DEAF - SCHOOL
MEDIA CENTER □ Jacksonville, IL

Hack, Leo M., Libn.
BLACK & VEATCH CONSULTING ENGINEERS -
CENTRAL LIBRARY □ Kansas City, MO

Hack, Rosalinda, Div.Chf.
CHICAGO PUBLIC LIBRARY CULTURAL CENTER
- FINE ARTS DIVISION - ART SECTION □
Chicago, IL

Hack, Rosalinda, Div.Chf.
CHICAGO PUBLIC LIBRARY CULTURAL CENTER
- FINE ARTS DIVISION - MUSIC SECTION □
Chicago, IL

Hackathorn, Merrianne, Geologist
OHIO (State) DIVISION OF GEOLOGICAL
SURVEY - LIBRARY □ Columbus, OH

Hacker, Lois, Chf.Tech.Serv.Libn.
CUNY - GRADUATE SCHOOL AND UNIVERSITY
CENTER - LIBRARY □ New York, NY

Hackett, Gabriel D., Owner, Ed.
HACKETT (G.D.) PHOTO AGENCY AND
ARCHIVES □ New York, NY

Hackleman, Michael A., Res.Dir.
EARTHMIND - LIBRARY □ Mariposa, CA

Hackney, Brian, AV Libn.
AUGSBURG COLLEGE - GEORGE SVERDRUP
LIBRARY AND MEDIA CENTER □ Minneapolis,
MN

Hackney, Katherine, Libn.
EAST LIBERTY PRESBYTERIAN CHURCH -
LIBRARY □ Pittsburgh, PA

Hadala, Paul F., Dir.
U.S. ARMY - ENGINEER WATERWAYS
EXPERIMENT STATION - SOIL MECHANICS
INFORMATION ANALYSIS CENTER □ Vicksburg,
MS

Hadbavny, Joellen A., Info.Techn.
TIMKEN COMPANY - RESEARCH LIBRARY □
Canton, OH

Haddaway, William, Art Libn.
DALLAS PUBLIC LIBRARY - FINE ARTS
DIVISION □ Dallas, TX

Haddick, Vern, Lib.Dir.
CALIFORNIA INSTITUTE OF INTEGRAL
STUDIES - LIBRARY □ San Francisco, CA

Hadidian, Dikran Y., Libn.
PITTSBURGH THEOLOGICAL SEMINARY -
CLIFFORD E. BARBOUR LIBRARY □ Pittsburgh,
PA

Hadley, Rosemary J., Map Libn.
UNIVERSITY OF BRITISH COLUMBIA -
DEPARTMENT OF GEOGRAPHY - MAP AND AIR
PHOTO CENTRE □ Vancouver, BC

Hadlow, Ruth M., Dept.Hd.
CLEVELAND PUBLIC LIBRARY - CHILDREN'S
LITERATURE DEPARTMENT □ Cleveland, OH

Hadman, Karen L., Chf., Lib.Br.
U.S. DEPT. OF ENERGY - BONNEVILLE POWER ADMINISTRATION - LIBRARY □ Portland, OR

Hadsel, Dr. Fred L., Dir.
MARSHALL (George C.) RESEARCH FOUNDATION - GEORGE C. MARSHALL RESEARCH LIBRARY† □ Lexington, VA

Haeberle, Dr. Erwin J., Dir.
INSTITUTE FOR ADVANCED STUDY OF HUMAN SEXUALITY - RESEARCH LIBRARY □ San Francisco, CA

Haefliger, Kathleen, Libn.
COLUMBIA UNIVERSITY - MUSIC LIBRARY □ New York, NY

Haertle, Robert J., Hd., Coll.Dept.
MARQUETTE UNIVERSITY - MEMORIAL LIBRARY □ Milwaukee, WI

Haesler, Helena, Voorhees Br.Libn.
CUNY - NEW YORK CITY TECHNICAL COLLEGE LIBRARY/LEARNING RESOURCE CENTER □ Brooklyn, NY

Hafer, Edna M., Asst.Res.
EVANGELICAL AND REFORMED HISTORICAL SOCIETY - LANCASTER CENTRAL ARCHIVES AND LIBRARY □ Lancaster, PA

Hafer, Mary S., Cur.
BEDFORD HISTORICAL SOCIETY - LIBRARY □ Bedford, MA

Haffner, Jack W., Educ.Coord.
PORTSMOUTH RECEIVING HOSPITAL - MEDICAL LIBRARY □ Portsmouth, OH

Hafner, Arthur W., Ph.D., Dir.
AMERICAN MEDICAL ASSOCIATION - DIVISION OF LIBRARY AND ARCHIVAL SERVICES □ Chicago, IL

Hag, Sylvia
CLARKSON UNIVERSITY - EDUCATIONAL RESOURCES CENTER □ Potsdam, NY

Hagan, Jane, Lib.Serv.Supv.
GLENDALE PUBLIC LIBRARY - BRAND LIBRARY □ Glendale, CA

Hagberg, Betty S., Mgr., Lib.Serv.
DEERE & COMPANY - LIBRARY □ Moline, IL

Hage, Betsy, Asst.Dept.Hd.
MINNEAPOLIS PUBLIC LIBRARY & INFORMATION CENTER - SOCIOLOGY DEPARTMENT □ Minneapolis, MN

Hagen, Carlos B., Hd.
UNIVERSITY OF CALIFORNIA, LOS ANGELES - MAP LIBRARY □ Los Angeles, CA

Hagen, William H., Libn.
U.S. NAVY - REGIONAL DATA AUTOMATION CENTER - TECHNICAL LIBRARY □ Washington, DC

Hagens, A.L. Bennett
PRINCETON UNIVERSITY - DEPARTMENT OF ART & ARCHAEOLOGY - INDEX OF CHRISTIAN ART □ Princeton, NJ

Hagens, Elizabeth, Dir.
OUTLOOK - OUTLOOK ACCESS CENTER □ Park Forest, IL

Hager, Lucille, Dir.
CHRIST SEMINARY - SEMINEX LIBRARY □ Austin, TX

Hager, Mary Ann, Photo/Cart.Spec.
LUNAR AND PLANETARY INSTITUTE - PLANETARY IMAGE CENTER† □ Houston, TX

Haggart, Elizabeth M., Libn.
COLUMBIA HOSPITAL FOR WOMEN - MEDICAL LIBRARY □ Washington, DC

Haggerty, Patrick, Libn.
OAKLAND PUBLIC LIBRARY - LATIN AMERICAN LIBRARY □ Oakland, CA

Haggerty, Diann, Comp.Mgr.
DU PAGE LIBRARY SYSTEM - SYSTEM CENTER □ Geneva, IL

Haggerty, Gary, Asst.Libn.
BERKLEE COLLEGE OF MUSIC - LIBRARY □ Boston, MA

Haggerty, Maxine R., Doc.Acq.Libn.
UNIVERSITY OF UTAH - DOCUMENTS DIVISION □ Salt Lake City, UT

Haggerty, Thomas M., Chf., 10A Serv.Sect.
U.S. DEPT. OF TRANSPORTATION - LIBRARY AND DISTRIBUTION SERVICES DIVISION □ Washington, DC

Haggins, Angela, Chf.
SMITHSONIAN INSTITUTION LIBRARIES - SMITHSONIAN ENVIRONMENTAL RESEARCH CENTER LIBRARY-ROCKVILLE □ Rockville, MD

Haggins, Angela N., Chf.
SMITHSONIAN INSTITUTION LIBRARIES - SMITHSONIAN ENVIRONMENTAL RESEARCH CENTER LIBRARY-EDGEWATER □ Edgewater, MD

Haggstrom, David, AV Libn.
SUNY - AGRICULTURAL AND TECHNICAL COLLEGE AT ALFRED - WALTER C. HINKLE MEMORIAL LIBRARY □ Alfred, NY

Hagloch, Joseph, Circuit Libn.
CLEVELAND HEALTH SCIENCES LIBRARY - ALLEN MEMORIAL LIBRARY □ Cleveland, OH

Haglund, Doris, Base Libn.
U.S. AIR FORCE BASE - TINKER BASE LIBRARY □ Tinker AFB, OK

Hagopian, Alan K.E., Ph.D., Mgr.
MILES LABORATORIES, INC. - LIBRARY RESOURCES AND SERVICES □ Elkhart, IN

Hagopian, Shake, Libn.
CHAIT SALOMON - LIBRARY □ Montreal, PQ

Hague, Amy, Res.Anl.
WISCONSIN STATE LEGISLATIVE REFERENCE BUREAU □ Madison, WI

Hagy, John T., Adm.Off.
NEW YORK STATE LEGISLATIVE LIBRARY □ Albany, NY

Hahn, Bob, Libn.
CINCINNATI POST - LIBRARY □ Cincinnati, OH

Hahn, Boksoon, Hd.Cat.Libn.
YALE UNIVERSITY - EAST ASIAN COLLECTION □ New Haven, CT

Hahn, Bonnie, Tech.Libn.
BOEING VERTOL COMPANY - LYDIA RANKIN TECHNICAL LIBRARY □ Philadelphia, PA

Hahn, Dr. Byungchai Cora, Media Coord.
UNIVERSITY OF CONNECTICUT - SCHOOL OF EDUCATION - I.N. THUT WORLD EDUCATION CENTER □ Storrs, CT

Hahn, Ellen, Chf.
LIBRARY OF CONGRESS - GEN. READING ROOMS DIV. □ Washington, DC

Hahn, Ermina, Hd., Tech.Serv.
RUTGERS UNIVERSITY, THE STATE UNIVERSITY OF NEW JERSEY - JUSTICE HENRY ACKERSON LIBRARY OF LAW & CRIMINAL JUSTICE □ Newark, NJ

Hahn, Madeleine, Libn.
SAI/JRB LIBRARY □ McLean, VA

Hahn, Robert C., Libn.
UNIVERSITY OF MISSOURI - JOURNALISM LIBRARY □ Columbia, MO

Haichert, Colleen, Lib.Techn.
CANADA - CANADIAN WILDLIFE SERVICE - PRAIRIE MIGRATORY BIRD RESEARCH CENTRE - LIBRARY □ Saskatoon, SK

Haider, Ellen, Libn.
OHIO (State) DEPARTMENT OF TRANSPORTATION - LIBRARY □ Columbus, OH

Haight, Larry L., Libn.
ASSEMBLIES OF GOD GRADUATE SCHOOL - CORDAS C. BURNETT LIBRARY† □ Springfield, MO

Hail, Christopher, Asst./Ref.Libn.
HARVARD UNIVERSITY - GRADUATE SCHOOL OF DESIGN - FRANCES LOEB LIBRARY □ Cambridge, MA

Haile, Dr. Getatchew, Mss.Cat.
ST. JOHN'S ABBEY AND UNIVERSITY - HILL MONASTIC MANUSCRIPT LIBRARY - BUSH CENTER □ Collegeville, MN

Haimson, Fima, Transl./Interpretation
PHILLIPS PETROLEUM COMPANY - RESEARCH & DEVELOPMENT DEPARTMENT - TECHNICAL INFORMATION BRANCH □ Bartlesville, OK

Haines, Ann H., Med.Libn.
EASTMORELAND GENERAL HOSPITAL - HEALTH SCIENCES LIBRARY □ Portland, OR

Haines, Ann H., Med.Libn.
KAISER SUNNYSIDE MEDICAL CENTER - LIBRARY □ Clackamas, OR

Haines, Mrs. D. Gale, Libn.
PETERSHAM HISTORICAL SOCIETY, INC. - LIBRARY □ Petersham, MA

Haines, Janice, Acq.Libn.
U.S. NATL. DEFENSE UNIVERSITY - LIBRARY □ Washington, DC

Hainsworth, Melody M., Libn.
ALBERTA - DEPARTMENT OF THE ATTORNEY GENERAL - JUDGES' LAW LIBRARY □ Calgary, AB

Hainsworth, Melody M., Libn.
LAW SOCIETY OF ALBERTA - CALGARY LIBRARY □ Calgary, AB

Hair, Sara J., Libn.
NATIONAL STEEL CORPORATION - RESEARCH CENTER LIBRARY □ Weirton, WV

Haire, Gloria, Hd.Libn.
LAWRENCE BERKELEY LABORATORY - LIBRARY □ Berkeley, CA

Haire, Loretta, Health Rec.Adm.
WAINWRIGHT GENERAL HOSPITAL - MEDICAL LIBRARY □ Wainwright, AB

Haitz, M. Cherie, Dir.
MOUNT AUBURN HOSPITAL - HEALTH SCIENCES LIBRARY □ Cambridge, MA

Hakala, Bettina, Libn.
FASKEN & CALVIN, BARRISTERS AND SOLICITORS - LIBRARY† □ Toronto, ON

Halasz, Marilynn, Mgr., Info.Serv.Sect.
PORTLAND CEMENT ASSOCIATION/ CONSTRUCTION TECHNOLOGY LABORATORIES - INFORMATION SERVICES SECTION □ Skokie, IL

Halberstam, Rabbi N., Libn.
WORLD JEWISH GENEALOGY ORGANIZATION - LIBRARY □ Brooklyn, NY

Halbrook, Anne-Mieke, Libn.
GETTY (J. Paul) CENTER FOR THE HISTORY OF ART AND THE HUMANITIES - LIBRARY □ Santa Monica, CA

Halbrook, Barbara, Assoc.Dir.
WASHINGTON UNIVERSITY - SCHOOL OF MEDICINE LIBRARY □ St. Louis, MO

Halder, Mrs. Gita, Med.Libn.
ST. JOSEPH'S HOSPITAL - MEDICAL LIBRARY □ Tampa, FL

Hale, Barbara, Assoc.Docs.Libn.
UNIVERSITY OF KENTUCKY - MARGARET I. KING LIBRARY - GOVERNMENT PUBLICATIONS/MAP DEPARTMENT □ Lexington, KY

Hale, Dr. Charles E., Lib.Dir.
MILLIKIN UNIVERSITY - STALEY LIBRARY - SPECIAL COLLECTIONS □ Decatur, IL

Hale, Elizabeth F., Libn.Cons.
ST. HELEN'S ISLAND MUSEUM MONTREAL - DAVID M. STEWART LIBRARY† □ Montreal, PQ

Hale, Judy E., Mgr., Info.Serv.
GOODYEAR TIRE AND RUBBER COMPANY - TECHNICAL INFORMATION CENTER □ Akron, OH

Hale, Kay K., Libn.
UNIVERSITY OF MIAMI - DOROTHY & LEWIS ROSENSTIEL SCHOOL OF MARINE & ATMOSPHERIC SCIENCES - LIBRARY □ Miami, FL

Hale, Kaycee, Dir.
FASHION INSTITUTE OF DESIGN & MERCHANDISING - RESOURCE AND RESEARCH CENTER† □ Los Angeles, CA

Hale, Louis J., Standards Engr.
GARRETT MANUFACTURING, LTD. - ENGINEERING LIBRARY □ Rexdale, ON

Hale, Peter P., Pres.
WALLINGFORD HISTORICAL SOCIETY, INC. - LIBRARY □ Wallingford, CT

Hale, Relda D., Libn.
U.S. NAVY - NAVAL AIR STATION (TN-Memphis)
- LIBRARY □ Millington, TN

Hale, Ruth, Hd., Bibliog.Serv.Div.
GEORGIA INSTITUTE OF TECHNOLOGY - PRICE
GILBERT MEMORIAL LIBRARY □ Atlanta, GA

Halevy, Prof. B.J., Libn.
YORK UNIVERSITY - LAW LIBRARY □
Downsview, ON

Haley, Dan, Info.Spec.
UNIVERSITY OF SOUTHERN CALIFORNIA -
NASA INDUSTRIAL APPLICATION CENTER
(NIAC) □ Los Angeles, CA

Haley, Jack D., Assoc.Cur.
UNIVERSITY OF OKLAHOMA - WESTERN
HISTORY COLLECTIONS □ Norman, OK

Haley, Jack D., Assoc.Cur.
UNIVERSITY OF OKLAHOMA - WESTERN
HISTORY COLLECTIONS - LIBRARY DIVISION □
Norman, OK

Haley, June, Libn.
ATLANTIC COUNCIL OF THE UNITED STATES,
INC. - LIBRARY □ Washington, DC

Haley, Roger K., Senate Libn.
U.S. SENATE - LIBRARY □ Washington, DC

Halferdahl, W., Asst.Libn.
CANADIAN INSTITUTE OF INTERNATIONAL
AFFAIRS - LIBRARY □ Toronto, ON

Halfpenny, Lucille S., Libn.
ST. THOMAS SEMINARY LIBRARY - ALUMNI
COLLECTION □ Bloomfield, CT

Halgrimson, Andrea H., Hd.Libn.
FORUM PUBLISHING CO. - LIBRARY □ Fargo, ND

Halicki, Kenneth C., Libn.
SEYFARTH, SHAW, FAIRWEATHER &
GERALDSON - LIBRARY □ Chicago, IL

Halifax, Robert, Dir. of Rec./City Archv.
CITY OF TORONTO ARCHIVES □ Toronto, ON

Halkovic, Prof. Stephen, Dir.
INDIANA UNIVERSITY - RESEARCH INSTITUTE
FOR INNER ASIAN STUDIES - LIBRARY □
Bloomington, IN

Hall, A.E., Asst.Prof.
UNIVERSITY OF BRITISH COLUMBIA - MINING
& METALLURGICAL READING ROOM □
Vancouver, BC

Hall, Ann Bowman, Libn.
U.S. NATL. MARINE FISHERIES SERVICE -
SOUTHEAST FISHERIES CENTER - BEAUFORT
LABORATORY LIBRARY† □ Beaufort, NC

Hall, Benner A., Pres.
CHURCH OF JESUS CHRIST OF LATTER-DAY
SAINTS - MESA BRANCH GENEALOGICAL
LIBRARY □ Mesa, AZ

Hall, Blaine H., Div.Coord.
BRIGHAM YOUNG UNIVERSITY - HUMANITIES
AND ARTS DIVISION LIBRARY □ Provo, UT

Hall, Bonlyn G., Libn.
UNIVERSITY OF RICHMOND - MUSIC LIBRARY
□ Richmond, VA

Hall, Bonnie, Asst.Libn.
ABCOR, INC. - LIBRARY □ Wilmington, MA

Hall, Carolyn, Lib.Techn.
BRITISH COLUMBIA HEALTH ASSOCIATION
(BCHA) - LIBRARY □ Vancouver, BC

Hall, Cathy, Assoc. Law Libn.
GEORGIA STATE UNIVERSITY - COLLEGE OF
LAW LIBRARY □ Atlanta, GA

Hall, David, Libn., Leg.Lib.
MILWAUKEE - LEGISLATIVE REFERENCE
BUREAU - LEGISLATIVE LIBRARY □ Milwaukee,
WI

Hall, Deborah A., Dir.
MOUNT SINAI MEDICAL CENTER - MEDICAL
LIBRARY □ Milwaukee, WI

Hall, Dorothy, Dir.
OKLAHOMA STATE DEPARTMENT OF HEALTH -
INFORMATION & REFERRAL HEALTHLINE† □
Oklahoma City, OK

Hall, Elede Toppy, Libn.
ADDISON-WESLEY PUBLISHING COMPANY -
LIBRARY □ Menlo Park, CA

Hall, Elizabeth, Chf. Photographer
MINNESOTA HISTORICAL SOCIETY - SPECIAL
LIBRARIES □ St. Paul, MN

Hall, Ellen F., Lib.Dir.
PRESENTATION COLLEGE - LIBRARY □
Aberdeen, SD

Hall, Esther, Order Libn.
BATTELLE-COLUMBUS LABORATORIES -
LIBRARY □ Columbus, OH

Hall, Frances H., Libn.
NORTH CAROLINA STATE SUPREME COURT
LIBRARY □ Raleigh, NC

Hall, George, Libn.
SOLAR TURBINES INCORPORATED - LIBRARY □
San Diego, CA

Hall, H. Brent, Ref.Supv. & ILL
MAINE MARITIME ACADEMY - NUTTING
MEMORIAL LIBRARY □ Castine, ME

Hall, Helen, Archv.
YARMOUTH COUNTY HISTORICAL SOCIETY -
RESEARCH LIBRARY AND ARCHIVES □
Yarmouth, NS

Hall, Holly, Hd.
WASHINGTON UNIVERSITY - DEPARTMENT OF
SPECIAL COLLECTIONS □ St. Louis, MO

Hall, J.D., Mgr., R & D
EDDY (E.B.) FOREST PRODUCTS, LTD. -
LIBRARY □ Hull, PQ

Hall, Jack, Med.Libn.
PUTNAM (Henry W.) MEMORIAL HOSPITAL -
MEDICAL LIBRARY □ Bennington, VT

Hall, Jack C., Sr.Musm.Sci.
UNIVERSITY OF CALIFORNIA, RIVERSIDE -
DEPARTMENT OF ENTOMOLOGY - LIBRARY □
Riverside, CA

Hall, James N., Dir.
UP FRONT, INC. - LIBRARY □ Miami, FL

Hall, Jeanette, Asst.Libn.
UNITED WAY OF THE LOWER MAINLAND -
SOCIAL PLANNING AND RESEARCH
DEPARTMENT LIBRARY □ Vancouver, BC

Hall, Joan Ann, Libn.
COLLINS CANADA - TIC LIBRARY □ Toronto, ON

Hall, John B., Libn.
UNION UNIVERSITY - ALBANY COLLEGE OF
PHARMACY - LIBRARY □ Albany, NY

Hall, Dr. Joseph H., Libn.
COVENANT THEOLOGICAL SEMINARY - J.
OLIVER BUSWELL, JR. LIBRARY □ St. Louis, MO

Hall, Juanita, Hd., Tech.Serv.
MOREHEAD STATE UNIVERSITY - CAMDEN-
CARROLL LIBRARY □ Morehead, KY

Hall, Julie A., Dir. of Med.Rec.
MEMORIAL MEDICAL CENTER OF WEST
MICHIGAN - LIBRARY □ Ludington, MI

Hall, Dr. Kenneth R., Dir.
TEXAS A & M UNIVERSITY -
THERMODYNAMICS RESEARCH CENTER □
College Station, TX

Hall, Linda, Libn.
U.S. NATL. PARK SERVICE - INFORMATION
CLEARINGHOUSE □ Atlanta, GA

Hall, Louise P., Dir.
SMITHTOWN HISTORICAL SOCIETY -
LIBRARY† □ Smithtown, NY

Hall, Lynda
UNIVERSITY OF CALGARY - ENVIRONMENT-
SCIENCE-TECHNOLOGY LIBRARY† □ Calgary,
AB

Hall, Lysa, Law Cat.
WILLAMETTE UNIVERSITY - LAW LIBRARY □
Salem, OR

Hall, Margaret, Asst.Libn.
HENNEPIN COUNTY LAW LIBRARY† □
Minneapolis, MN

Hall, Marion, Print Coll.
MERRIMACK VALLEY TEXTILE MUSEUM -
LIBRARY □ North Andover, MA

Hall, Mary C., Hd., Cat.
SUNY - COLLEGE AT BUFFALO - EDWARD H.
BUTLER LIBRARY □ Buffalo, NY

Hall, Mary H., Lib.Techn.
U.S. ARMY - CORPS OF ENGINEERS - LOWER
MISSISSIPPI VALLEY DIV. - MISSISSIPPI
RIVER COMMN. TECHNICAL LIB. □ Vicksburg,
MS

Hall, Milta, Hd., Pub.Serv.
DE PAUL UNIVERSITY - LAW SCHOOL LIBRARY
□ Chicago, IL

Hall, Patrick A., Libn.
KRAMER CHIN AND MAYO INC. - LIBRARY □
Seattle, WA

Hall, R. Cargill, Chf., Res.Div.
U.S. AIR FORCE - HISTORICAL RESEARCH
CENTER □ Maxwell AFB, AL

Hall, Richard B., Cons., Bldg./Films
GEORGIA STATE DEPARTMENT OF EDUCATION
- DIVISION OF PUBLIC LIBRARY SERVICES □
Atlanta, GA

Hall, Russell, Med.Libn.
U.S. VETERANS ADMINISTRATION (NY-Buffalo)
- MEDICAL CENTER LIBRARY SERVICE □
Buffalo, NY

Hall, Verona, Lib./Drug Info.Asst.
CAMP HILL HOSPITAL - HEALTH SCIENCES
LIBRARY □ Halifax, NS

Hall, Virginia, Libn.
TEXAS STATE DEPARTMENT OF AGRICULTURE
- LIBRARY □ Austin, TX

Hall, Virginius C., Jr., Assoc.Dir.,Lib.Serv.
VIRGINIA HISTORICAL SOCIETY - LIBRARY □
Richmond, VA

Hall, Vivian S., Libn.
UNIVERSITY OF KENTUCKY - GEORGE W.
PIRTLE GEOLOGY LIBRARY □ Lexington, KY

Hallblade, Shirley, Dir.
VANDERBILT UNIVERSITY - JEAN AND
ALEXANDER HEARD LIBRARY - WALKER
MANAGEMENT LIBRARY □ Nashville, TN

Haller, Blanche W., Dir. of Lib.Serv.
MONTCLAIR STATE COLLEGE - HARRY A.
SPRAGUE LIBRARY - SPECIAL COLLECTIONS □
Upper Montclair, NJ

Haller, Douglas, Cur. of Photographs
CALIFORNIA HISTORICAL SOCIETY -
SCHUBERT HALL LIBRARY □ San Francisco, CA

Haller, Uli, Asst.Archv.
ROSENBERG LIBRARY - GALVESTON AND
TEXAS HISTORY CENTER □ Galveston, TX

Hallett, B.
CANADA - PUBLIC ARCHIVES OF CANADA -
NATIONAL MAP COLLECTION □ Ottawa, ON

Hallett, Dessie M., Libn.
MOUNT VERNON PLACE UNITED METHODIST
CHURCH - DESSIE M. HALLETT LIBRARY† □
Washington, DC

Hallett, Dudley W., Pres.
FALMOUTH HISTORICAL SOCIETY -
RESOURCES CENTER - HISTORY & GENEALOGY
ARCHIVES □ Falmouth, MA

Hallewell, Dr. Laurence, Bibliog.
OHIO STATE UNIVERSITY - LATIN AMERICAN
STUDIES READING ROOM AND LIBRARY □
Columbus, OH

Halliday, Margaret, Comp.Supv.
INDUSTRIAL HOME FOR THE BLIND - NASSAU-
SUFFOLK BRAILLE LIBRARY □ Hempstead, NY

Hallier, Sara, Libn.
REORGANIZED CHURCH OF JESUS CHRIST OF
LATTER DAY SAINTS - LIBRARY & ARCHIVES □
Independence, MO

Hallingby, Leigh, Libn.
SEX INFORMATION & EDUCATION COUNCIL OF
THE U.S. - SIECUS INFORMATION SERVICE
AND LIBRARY □ New York, NY

Hallman, Clark, Hd., Ref.Dept.
SOUTH DAKOTA STATE UNIVERSITY - HILTON
M. BRIGGS LIBRARY □ Brookings, SD

Hallman, Howard, Jr., Indus.Engr.
AMAX, INC. - CLIMAX MOLYBDENUM COMPANY
- TECHNICAL LIBRARY □ Climax, CO

Hallman, Richard, Ref.Libn.
ATLANTA NEWSPAPERS - REFERENCE LIBRARY
□ Atlanta, GA

Hammargren, Adelaide, Supv. of Lib.Serv.
CIBA-GEIGY CORPORATION -
PHARMACEUTICALS DIVISION - SCIENTIFIC
INFORMATION CENTER† □ Summit, NJ
Hammarskjold, Carolyn, Libn.
MICHIGAN STATE UNIVERSITY - W.K.
KELLOGG BIOLOGICAL STATION - WALTER F.
MOROFSKY MEMORIAL LIBRARY □ Hickory
Corners, MI
Hammell, Kathryn, Hd., Acq.
UNIVERSITY OF ILLINOIS AT CHICAGO -
HEALTH SCIENCES CENTER - LIBRARY OF THE
HEALTH SCIENCES □ Chicago, IL
Hammer, Deborah, Div.Hd.
QUEENS BOROUGH PUBLIC LIBRARY -
HISTORY, TRAVEL & BIOGRAPHY DIVISION □
Jamaica, NY
Hammer, Stanley F., Asst.Libn.
CAMPBELL UNIVERSITY - SCHOOL OF LAW -
LAW LIBRARY □ Buies Creek, NC
Hammersmith, Ruth K., Dir.
NATIONAL SAFETY COUNCIL - LIBRARY □
Chicago, IL
Hammett, S.A., Med.Libn.
MEMORIAL HOSPITALS ASSOCIATION -
MEDICAL LIBRARY □ Modesto, CA
Hammill, Roseann, Music Libn.
MICHIGAN STATE UNIVERSITY - MUSIC
LIBRARY □ East Lansing, MI
Hammond, Anna, Libn.
UNIVERSITY OF ALBERTA - DIVISION OF
EDUCATIONAL RESEARCH - TECHNICAL
LIBRARY □ Edmonton, AB
Hammond, Charles, Dir.
GORE PLACE SOCIETY, INC. - LIBRARY □
Waltham, MA
Hammond, Dorothy S., Dir. of Lib.Serv.
FIRST BAPTIST CHURCH - MEDIA CENTER □
Gainesville, FL
Hammond, J. Samuel, Libn.
DUKE UNIVERSITY - MUSIC LIBRARY □ Durham,
NC
Hammond, Jane L., Law Libn.
CORNELL UNIVERSITY - LAW LIBRARY □
Ithaca, NY
Hammond, Joshua, Dir., Commun.
NATIONAL MENTAL HEALTH ASSOCIATION -
CLIFFORD BEERS MEMORIAL LIBRARY □
Arlington, VA
Hammond, Karen L., Mgr., Info.Rsrcs.
NORANDA SALES CORPORATION, LTD. - SALES
LIBRARY □ Toronto, ON
Hammond, Lois D., Chf.Tech.Libn.
CINCINNATI ELECTRONICS CORPORATION -
TECHNICAL LIBRARY □ Cincinnati, OH
Hammond, Lyman H., Jr., Dir.
MAC ARTHUR (General Douglas) MEMORIAL -
LIBRARY AND ARCHIVES □ Norfolk, VA
Hammond, Ms. Lyn Smith, Med.Libn.
PARKVIEW EPISCOPAL MEDICAL CENTER -
MEDICAL LIBRARY □ Pueblo, CO
Hammond, Margaret, Chf.
DETROIT PUBLIC LIBRARY - BUSINESS AND
FINANCE DEPARTMENT □ Detroit, MI
Hammond, Mary Love, Libn.
SOUTHERN COLLEGE - LIBRARY □ Orlando, FL
Hammond, Sue, Libn.
CAMPBELL TAGGART, INC. - RESEARCH
DIVISION - LIBRARY □ Dallas, TX
Hammond, Theresa M., Dir., Lib.Serv.
NEWPORT NEWS DAILY PRESS, INC. - LIBRARY
□ Newport News, VA
Hammond, Wayne G., Asst.Libn.
WILLIAMS COLLEGE - CHAPIN LIBRARY □
Williamstown, MA
Hampton, Denise, Coord.
MOBIL PRODUCING TEXAS & NEW MEXICO
INC. - INFORMATION RESOURCE CENTER □
Houston, TX
Hampton, Martha N., Law Ser.Libn.
UNIVERSITY OF GEORGIA - LAW LIBRARY □
Athens, GA

Hamrick, Sharon R., Libn.
DYNAPOL - LIBRARY† □ Palo Alto, CA
Hamson, Darryl, Med.Libn.
YORK HOSPITAL - HEALTH SCIENCES LIBRARY
□ York, ME
Han, Chin-Soon, Med.Libn.
BON SECOURS HOSPITAL - MEDICAL STAFF
LIBRARY □ Methuen, MA
Hanafee, Valerie, Libn.
DICKINSON, WRIGHT, MOON, VAN DUSEN &
FREEMAN - LIBRARY □ Detroit, MI
Hanchett, Catherine, Doc.Cat.Libn.
SUNY - COLLEGE AT CORTLAND - MEMORIAL
LIBRARY □ Cortland, NY
Hanchett, Esther, Act.Libn.
MATERNITY CENTER ASSOCIATION -
REFERENCE LIBRARY □ New York, NY
Hanchett, Mildred, Dir./Supv.
WAYNE HISTORICAL MUSEUM - HISTORICAL
COMMISSION ARCHIVES □ Wayne, MI
Hancin, Marianna
ARIZONA STATE DEPARTMENT OF LIBRARY,
ARCHIVES & PUBLIC RECORDS □ Phoenix, AZ
Hancock, Dan, Pub.Serv.Libn.
COMMUNITY COLLEGE OF BALTIMORE -
LIBRARIES/LEARNING RESOURCES CENTERS □
Baltimore, MD
Hancock, Don, Info.Coord.
SOUTHWEST RESEARCH & INFORMATION
CENTER □ Albuquerque, NM
Hancock, Richard, Libn.
TIMES-WORLD CORPORATION - NEWSPAPER
LIBRARY □ Roanoke, VA
Hand, Anne T., Exec.Sec.
REXHAM CORPORATION - PACKAGING
TECHNICAL LIBRARY† □ Flemington, NJ
Hand, Linda M., Libn.
JEFFERSON COUNTY LAW LIBRARY □
Birmingham, AL
Hand, Mark, Libn.
CANADIAN MUSIC CENTRE - LIBRARY □
Toronto, ON
Hand, Russ, Prog.
OHIO STATE UNIVERSITY - MECHANIZED
INFORMATION CENTER (MIC) □ Columbus, OH
Hand, Sally C., Asst.Libn.
U.S. COURT OF APPEALS, 2ND CIRCUIT -
LIBRARY □ New York, NY
Hande, Mr. D., Staff Archv.
SASKATCHEWAN ARCHIVES BOARD □ Regina,
SK
Handfield, F. Gerald, Fld.Libn.
INDIANA HISTORICAL SOCIETY - WILLIAM
HENRY SMITH MEMORIAL LIBRARY □
Indianapolis, IN
Handley, William, Hd.
FREE LIBRARY OF PHILADELPHIA - SOCIAL
SCIENCE & HISTORY DEPARTMENT □
Philadelphia, PA
Handman, Pamela, Info.Spec.
CETUS CORPORATION - RESEARCH LIBRARY □
Emeryville, CA
Handrea, Mihai H., Libn.
PFORZHEIMER (Carl & Lily) FOUNDATION, INC. -
CARL H. PFORZHEIMER LIBRARY □ New York,
NY
Handville, Donna, Libn.
AMERICAN INSURANCE SERVICES GROUP, INC.
- ENGINEERING & SAFETY DEPARTMENT
LIBRARY □ New York, NY
Handy, Harold, Archv.
AMISTAD RESEARCH CENTER - LIBRARY/
ARCHIVES □ New Orleans, LA
Handy, Mary Jane, Libn.
WINDSOR STAR - LIBRARY □ Windsor, ON
Handy, Riley, Hd., Spec.Coll.Dept.
WESTERN KENTUCKY UNIVERSITY - DEPT. OF
SPECIAL COLLECTIONS - KENTUCKY LIBRARY
AND MUSEUM/UNIVERSITY ARCHIVES □
Bowling Green, KY
Hanegraaf, Mary, Libn.
RIVERSIDE COMMUNITY MEMORIAL HOSPITAL
- HEALTH SCIENCE LIBRARY □ Waupaca, WI

Hanel, Mary, Hist.Libn.
KERN COUNTY LIBRARY SYSTEM - BEALE
MEMORIAL LIBRARY □ Bakersfield, CA
Hanes, Fred W., Dir. of Libs.
UNIVERSITY OF TEXAS, EL PASO - LIBRARY -
SPECIAL COLLECTIONS □ El Paso, TX
Haney, Diana D., Libn.
IBM CORPORATION - BUSINESS INFORMATION
LIBRARY □ Franklin Lakes, NJ
Hanf, Betty, Sr.Info.Chem.
CROMPTON & KNOWLES CORPORATION - DYES
AND CHEMICALS DIVISION - GIBRALTAR
RESEARCH LIBRARY □ Reading, PA
Hanford, Sally, Asst.Libn./Tech.Admin.
AMERICAN INSTITUTE OF ARCHITECTS -
LIBRARY □ Washington, DC
Hanft, Margie, Film Libn.
CALIFORNIA INSTITUTE OF THE ARTS -
LIBRARY □ Valencia, CA
Hanif, Ibraham, Asst. Biological Sci.Libn
OKLAHOMA STATE UNIVERSITY - BIOLOGICAL
SCIENCES DIVISION □ Stillwater, OK
Hanig, M.W., Lib. Co-chm.
CONGREGATION SOLEL - LIBRARY □ Highland
Park, IL
Hankamer, Roberta A., Libn.
GRAND LODGE OF MASSACHUSETTS, A.F. AND
A.M. - LIBRARY □ Boston, MA
Hanke, Maxine, Dp.Chf.
U.S. NATL. INSTITUTES OF HEALTH - LIBRARY
□ Bethesda, MD
Hankey, Dr. W.J., Chf.Libn.
UNIVERSITY OF KING'S COLLEGE - KING'S
COLLEGE LIBRARY □ Halifax, NS
Hankison, Jill, Libn.
UPJOHN COMPANY - BUSINESS LIBRARY 88-91
□ Kalamazoo, MI
Hanks, Ellen Todd, Coll.Dev.
UNIVERSITY OF TEXAS HEALTH SCIENCE
CENTER, SAN ANTONIO - LIBRARY □ San
Antonio, TX
Hanks, Janice, Asst.Libn.
UNIVERSITY OF SOUTHERN CALIFORNIA - VON
KLEINSMID LIBRARY □ Los Angeles, CA
Hanks, Mrs. John, Libn.
FIRST METHODIST CHURCH - BLISS MEMORIAL
LIBRARY □ Shreveport, LA
Hanks, Nancy C., Asst.Prof./Libn.
NORTHWEST MISSOURI STATE UNIVERSITY -
HORACE MANN LEARNING CENTER □ Maryville,
MO
Hanley, Mr. Heschel, Hd., Tech.Serv.
CANADA - SOLICITOR GENERAL CANADA -
MINISTRY LIBRARY & REFERENCE CENTRE □
Ottawa, ON
Hanley, Patricia, Med.Libn.
KAISER-PERMANENTE MEDICAL CENTER -
MEDICAL LIBRARY □ Portland, OR
Hanley, Prof. Thomas L., Libn.
UNIVERSITY OF DAYTON - LAW SCHOOL
LIBRARY □ Dayton, OH
Hanley, Timothy J., Asst.Libn.
LORD, DAY & LORD - LIBRARY □ New York, NY
Hanlon, Mary, Libn.
CHRIST HOSPITAL - HOSPITAL LIBRARY □ Oak
Lawn, IL
Hanlon, Mary T., Libn.
ROSELAND COMMUNITY HOSPITAL - HEALTH
SCIENCE LIBRARY □ Chicago, IL
Hanna, Alfreda H., Med.Libn.
U.S. ARMY HOSPITALS - FORT CARSON ARMY
HOSPITAL - MEDICAL LIBRARY □ Ft. Carson, CO
Hanna, David L., Hd.Libn.
U.S. NAVY - NAVAL UNDERWATER SYSTEMS
CENTER - NEW LONDON TECHNICAL LIBRARY†
□ New London, CT
Hanna, Jean, Libn.
UNIVERSITY OF OREGON - OREGON INSTITUTE
OF MARINE BIOLOGY - LIBRARY □ Charleston,
OR
Hanna, Jill C., Chf.Libn.
U.S. NAVY - CENTER FOR NAVAL ANALYSES -
LIBRARY □ Alexandria, VA

Hanna, William, Cur., Spec.Coll.
MISSISSIPPI STATE DEPARTMENT OF ARCHIVES AND HISTORY - ARCHIVES AND LIBRARY DIVISION □ Jackson, MS

Hannan, Joyce, Cat. & Clas.
FEDERAL RESERVE BANK OF BOSTON - RESEARCH LIBRARY† □ Boston, MA

Hannan, Laurianne L., Coll. Botanist
UNIVERSITY OF MICHIGAN - MATTHAEI BOTANICAL GARDENS - LIBRARY □ Ann Arbor, MI

Hanne, Dan
PASADENA PUBLIC LIBRARY - BUSINESS-TECHNOLOGY DIVISION □ Pasadena, CA

Hannigan, Sr. Noeleen, Med.Libn.
INCARNATE WORD HOSPITAL - MEDICAL LIBRARY □ St. Louis, MO

Hannigan, Sallie, Prin.Libn., Ref.
NEWARK PUBLIC LIBRARY - HUMANITIES DIVISION □ Newark, NJ

Hannon, Elizabeth, Libn.
VANCOUVER SCHOOL OF THEOLOGY - LIBRARY □ Vancouver, BC

Hannon, Dr. John P., Dir.
BRYANT COLLEGE OF BUSINESS ADMINISTRATION - EDITH M. HODGSON MEMORIAL LIBRARY □ Smithfield, RI

Hannover, Karol, Bioscience Libn.
ICI AMERICAS INC. - ATLAS LIBRARY □ Wilmington, DE

Hanowski, Laura M., Libn.
SASKATCHEWAN GENEALOGICAL SOCIETY - LIBRARY □ Regina, SK

Hanrahan, Christine, Libn.
UNIVERSITY OF ARIZONA - INSTITUTE OF ATMOSPHERIC PHYSICS LIBRARY □ Tucson, AZ

Hanrath, Linda, Corp.Libn.
WRIGLEY (Wm., Jr.) COMPANY - CORPORATE LIBRARY □ Chicago, IL

Hansard, William, Lib.Dir.
ARKANSAS STATE UNIVERSITY - DEAN B. ELLIS LIBRARY - SPECIAL COLLECTIONS □ State University, AR

Hanscom, Marion, Spec.Coll./Fine Arts Libn
SUNY AT BINGHAMTON - FINE ARTS LIBRARY □ Binghamton, NY

Hanscom, Marion, Spec.Coll.Libn.
SUNY AT BINGHAMTON - SPECIAL COLLECTIONS □ Binghamton, NY

Hansel, Judith, Law Libn.
ALLSTATE INSURANCE COMPANY - COMMERCIAL LAW LIBRARY □ South Barrington, IL

Hansen, Alice, Supv.
SANDERS ASSOCIATES, INC. - LIBRARY SERVICES □ Nashua, NH

Hansen, Asta, Libn.
UNIVERSITY OF WESTERN ONTARIO - CPRI LIBRARY □ London, ON

Hansen, Cheryl A., Engr.Ref.Libn.
TRIODYNE INC. CONSULTING ENGINEERS - INFORMATION CENTER □ Niles, IL

Hansen, Clark Bradley, Libn., Bookdealer
ORPHAN VOYAGE - KAMMANDALE LIBRARY □ St. Paul, MN

Hansen, Eric, Res.Anl.
ALASKA PUBLIC UTILITIES COMMISSION - LIBRARY □ Anchorage, AK

Hansen, Erika M., Med.Libn.
HOLLYWOOD PRESBYTERIAN MEDICAL CENTER - HEALTH SCIENCES LIBRARY □ Los Angeles, CA

Hansen, Gladys, City Archv.
SAN FRANCISCO PUBLIC LIBRARY - SAN FRANCISCO ROOM AND ARCHIVES □ San Francisco, CA

Hansen, James L., Rd.Serv.Libn.
STATE HISTORICAL SOCIETY OF WISCONSIN - LIBRARY □ Madison, WI

Hansen, Jim, Photo Ed.
RELIGIOUS NEWS SERVICE - PHOTOGRAPH LIBRARY □ New York, NY

Hansen, Joanne, Sci. & Tech.Libn.
EASTERN MICHIGAN UNIVERSITY - CENTER OF EDUCATIONAL RESOURCES - MAP LIBRARY □ Ypsilanti, MI

Hansen, Kathleen, Prof./Libn.
UNIVERSITY OF MINNESOTA - ERIC SEVAREID JOURNALISM LIBRARY □ Minneapolis, MN

Hansen, Mary E.
3M - 201 TECHNICAL LIBRARY □ St. Paul, MN

Hansen, Peggy Ann, Archv.
PROTESTANT EPISCOPAL CHURCH OF WESTERN WASHINGTON - DIOCESE OF OLYMPIA - ARCHIVES □ Seattle, WA

Hansen, Rena, Adm.
WOMEN ARTISTS NEWS - ARCHIVES □ New York, NY

Hansen, Roland, Hd. of Rd.Serv.
ART INSTITUTE OF CHICAGO - SCHOOL OF THE ART INSTITUTE OF CHICAGO - LIBRARY □ Chicago, IL

Hansen, Thorvald, Archv.
GRAND VIEW COLLEGE - ARCHIVES □ Des Moines, IA

Hansen, William H., Chf.Libn.
U.S. ARMY ARMOR SCHOOL - LIBRARY □ Ft. Knox, KY

Hanson, Ann, Cur. of Papyrology
PRINCETON UNIVERSITY - RARE BOOKS AND SPECIAL COLLECTIONS □ Princeton, NJ

Hanson, Bruce, Circ./Ref.Libn.
DELAWARE VALLEY COLLEGE OF SCIENCE AND AGRICULTURE - JOSEPH KRAUSKOPF MEMORIAL LIBRARY □ Doylestown, PA

Hanson, Daniel J., Ref.Libn.
DAVIS POLK & WARDWELL - LIBRARY □ New York, NY

Hanson, Diane, Prov. Law Libn.
BARRISTERS' SOCIETY OF NEW BRUNSWICK - LAW LIBRARY† □ Fredericton, NB

Hanson, Donna, Libn.
UNIVERSITY OF IDAHO - SCIENCE AND TECHNOLOGY LIBRARY □ Moscow, ID

Hanson, Gene, Dir., Lib. & Media Serv.
SHIPPENSBURG UNIVERSITY - EZRA LEHMAN LIBRARY □ Shippensburg, PA

Hanson, Grete, Libn.
LUTHERAN BROTHERHOOD INSURANCE SOCIETY - LB LIBRARY □ Minneapolis, MN

Hanson, Kaye, Libn.
TEXAS STATE EMPLOYMENT COMMISSION - TEC LIBRARY □ Austin, TX

Hanson, Margaret, ILL Libn.
NEW ENGLAND NUCLEAR CORPORATION - LIBRARY □ Boston, MA

Hanson, Mary, Libn.
ONTARIO HYDRO - LIBRARY □ Toronto, ON

Hanson, Mary A., Med.Libn.
ST. MARY'S HOSPITAL - LIBRARY □ Grand Rapids, MI

Hanson, Nancy A., Med.Libn.
WUESTHOFF MEMORIAL HOSPITAL - MEDICAL LIBRARY □ Rockledge, FL

Hanson, Paul S., Tech.Info.Spec.
SYVA COMPANY - LIBRARY/INFORMATION CENTER □ Palo Alto, CA

Hanson, Ruth M., Exec.Dir.
VISITING NURSE SERVICE, INC. - LIBRARY □ Madison, WI

Hanssen, Nancy E., Doc. & Env.Stud.Libn.
WILLIAMS COLLEGE - CENTER FOR ENVIRONMENTAL STUDIES - LIBRARY □ Williamstown, MA

Hanton, Rena C., Libn.
TULSA COUNTY LAW LIBRARY† □ Tulsa, OK

Hanus, Otto, Libn./Cur.
SLAVONIC BENEVOLENT ORDER OF THE STATE OF TEXAS - LIBRARY, ARCHIVES, MUSEUM □ Temple, TX

Hape, Geri, Bus.Mgr.
U.S. NATL. PARK SERVICE - YELLOWSTONE LIBRARY AND MUSEUM ASSOCIATION □ Yellowstone National Park, WY

Harader, William H., Dir.
INDIANA STATE UNIVERSITY - CENTER FOR GOVERNMENTAL SERVICES □ Terre Haute, IN

Harahan, Katherine, Libn.
U.S. LEAGUE OF SAVINGS INSTITUTIONS - LIBRARY □ Washington, DC

Harber, P., French Lib.Cons.
TORONTO BOARD OF EDUCATION - EDUCATION CENTRE LIBRARY □ Toronto, ON

Harbert, Cathy, Hd., Ref./ILL
GEORGE WASHINGTON UNIVERSITY - MEDICAL CENTER - PAUL HIMMELFARB HEALTH SCIENCES LIBRARY □ Washington, DC

Harbison, Yung, Search Coord.
MORRISON-KNUDSEN CO., INC. - INFORMATION RESEARCH CENTER □ Boise, ID

Harbour, Nancy, Libn.
MUTUAL LIFE ASSURANCE COMPANY OF CANADA - LIBRARY □ Waterloo, ON

Hardacre, Elizabeth, Lib.Techn.
CANADA - HEALTH AND WELFARE CANADA - HEALTH PROTECTION BRANCH - REGIONAL LIBRARY □ Vancouver, BC

Hardee, Ethel R., Libn.
BALTIMORE ZOO - ARTHUR R. WATSON LIBRARY □ Baltimore, MD

Harden, Helen R., Dept.Supv.
FRITO-LAY, INC. - LIBRARY □ Dallas, TX

Hardin, Al, Chf., Law Sect.
U.S. ARMY - PENTAGON LIBRARY □ Washington, DC

Hardin, Betty, Libn./Info.Spec.
CASTLE & COOKE, INC. - LAW & GOVERNMENT DEPARTMENT INFORMATION CENTER □ San Francisco, CA

Hardin, Karl R., Libn.
KERN COUNTY SUPERINTENDENT OF SCHOOLS OFFICE - INSTRUCTIONAL RESOURCES CENTER □ Bakersfield, CA

Hardin, M.F., Chf.Libn.
U.S. ARMY POST - FORT HOOD - MSA DIVISION - CASEY MEMORIAL LIBRARY □ Ft. Hood, TX

Hardin, Mary, ILL
OKLAHOMA STATE DEPARTMENT OF LIBRARIES □ Oklahoma City, OK

Hardin, Nancy
U.S. DEPT. OF ENERGY - OFFICE OF SCIENTIFIC AND TECHNICAL INFORMATION (OSTI) - TECHNICAL INFORMATION CENTER □ Oak Ridge, TN

Harding, Jean, Supv., Media Lib.
RYERSON POLYTECHNICAL INSTITUTE - LEARNING RESOURCES CENTRE □ Toronto, ON

Harding, Jonathan, Photodup./Archv.
BOSTON ATHENAEUM LIBRARY □ Boston, MA

Harding, Kathy, Sr.Lib.Asst.
QUEEN'S UNIVERSITY AT KINGSTON - MAP AND AIR PHOTO LIBRARY □ Kingston, ON

Harding, Mary, Ref.Libn.
FORD FOUNDATION - LIBRARY □ New York, NY

Harding, Shirley A., Cur./Libn.
U.S. NATL. PARK SERVICE - DEATH VALLEY NATL. MONUMENT - REFERENCE AND RESEARCH LIBRARY □ Death Valley, CA

Hardison, Betty Jo, Chf.Libn.
BECHTEL - CENTRAL LIBRARY □ San Francisco, CA

Hardison, Mary S., Acq.Libn.
U.S. DEPT. OF COMMERCE - LIBRARY □ Washington, DC

Hardnett, Carolyn J., Chf.Libn.
CHICAGO TRIBUNE PRESS SERVICE - WASHINGTON BUREAU - LIBRARY □ Washington, DC

Hardy, Carol J., Libn.
SANTA BARBARA NEWS PRESS - LIBRARY □ Santa Barbara, CA

Hardy, D. Clive, Archv.
UNIVERSITY OF NEW ORLEANS - EARL K. LONG LIBRARY - ARCHIVES & MANUSCRIPTS/ SPECIAL COLLECTIONS DEPT. □ New Orleans, LA

Hardy, Ethel
LOS ANGELES - DEPARTMENT OF WATER AND POWER - LEGAL DIVISION - LAW LIBRARY □ Los Angeles, CA

Hardy, Floyd C., Ph.D., Dir. of Lib.Serv.
CHEYNEY UNIVERSITY OF PENNSYLVANIA - LESLIE PINCKNEY HILL LIBRARY - SPECIAL COLLECTIONS □ Cheyney, PA

Hardy, Mr. J., Archivist
GEORGE BROWN COLLEGE OF APPLIED ARTS & TECHNOLOGY - LIBRARY □ Toronto, ON

Hardy, John L., Archv.
GEORGE BROWN COLLEGE OF APPLIED ARTS & TECHNOLOGY - ARCHIVES □ Toronto, ON

Hardy, Margaret C., Dir.
MIAMI VALLEY HOSPITAL - EDUCATIONAL RESOURCES CENTER - MEDICAL LIBRARY □ Dayton, OH

Hardy, Patricia F., Libn.
COLUMBUS LEDGER-ENQUIRER - LIBRARY □ Columbus, GA

Hardy, Rene, Pres.
INSTITUT D'HISTOIRE DE L'AMERIQUE FRANCAISE (1970) - RESEARCH CENTRE LIBRARY □ Montreal, PQ

Hardy, Susan, Coord., Info.Serv.
U.S. BUREAU OF THE CENSUS - INFORMATION SERVICES PROGRAM - DETROIT REGIONAL OFFICE - INFORMATION CENTER □ Detroit, MI

Hardy, Susanna, Libn.
SAN DIEGO PUBLIC LIBRARY - LITERATURE & LANGUAGES SECTION □ San Diego, CA

Hare, Evelyn, Libn.
STATEN ISLAND INSTITUTE OF ARTS AND SCIENCES - HIGH ROCK PARK CONSERVATION CENTER - LIBRARY □ Staten Island, NY

Hare, Frances A., Archv.
YAKIMA VALLEY MUSEUM AND HISTORICAL ASSOCIATION - ARCHIVES □ Yakima, WA

Hare, John B., Supv.
PFIZER, INC. - CENTRAL RESEARCH TECHNICAL INFORMATION SERVICES □ Groton, CT

Hare, Judy L., Supv., Lib. & Files
BATTELLE-NORTHWEST - PACIFIC NORTHWEST LABORATORY - HANFORD TECHNICAL LIBRARY □ Richland, WA

Hare, Virginia, Pub.Serv.Libn.
UNIVERSITY OF ALABAMA - SCHOOL OF LAW LIBRARY □ University, AL

Haren, V., Ref.Libn.
AKRON CITY HOSPITAL - MEDICAL LIBRARY □ Akron, OH

Hargens, Amy, Assoc.Libn.
FEDERAL RESERVE BANK OF MINNEAPOLIS - LIBRARY □ Minneapolis, MN

Hargis, Patricia L., Asst.Libn.
U.S. COURT OF APPEALS, 4TH CIRCUIT - LIBRARY □ Richmond, VA

Hargrave, Jean, Sr.Libn.
NEW YORK STATE LIBRARY - LEGISLATIVE AND GOVERNMENTAL SERVICES □ Albany, NY

Haring, Gayle, Mgr., Info.Serv.
BURSON-MARSTELLER - INFORMATION SERVICE □ New York, NY

Harkanyi, Katalin, Asst.Sci.Libn.
SAN DIEGO STATE UNIVERSITY - SCIENCE DEPARTMENT† □ San Diego, CA

Harke, Toby, Ref.Libn.
TEMPLE UNIVERSITY - HEALTH SCIENCES CENTER - LIBRARY □ Philadelphia, PA

Harker, Carol, Hd., Database Serv.
UNIVERSITY OF BRIDGEPORT - MAGNUS WAHLSTROM LIBRARY - SPECIAL COLLECTIONS □ Bridgeport, CT

Harker, Susan, Chf., Patient Educ.Lib.
U.S. VETERANS ADMINISTRATION (CA-Los Angeles) - WADSWORTH MEDICAL LIBRARY 691W/142D □ Los Angeles, CA

Harkins, Brian J., Libn.
WARNER & STACKPOLE - LAW LIBRARY □ Boston, MA

Harkins, John, Archv.
MEMPHIS-SHELBY COUNTY PUBLIC LIBRARY AND INFORMATION CENTER - MEMPHIS ROOM COLLECTIONS □ Memphis, TN

Harkins, Dr. John E., Supv.Archv.
WEST TENNESSEE HISTORICAL SOCIETY - LIBRARY □ Memphis, TN

Harkins, William, Cat.
NATIONAL GALLERY OF ART - PHOTOGRAPHIC ARCHIVES □ Washington, DC

Harkonen, Jeanine, Circuit Libn.
CLEVELAND HEALTH SCIENCES LIBRARY - ALLEN MEMORIAL LIBRARY □ Cleveland, OH

Harlan, James H., Libn.
SAN PEDRO PENINSULA HOSPITAL - MEDICAL LIBRARY □ San Pedro, CA

Harlem, Susan, Law Libn.
U.S. GENERAL SERVICES ADMINISTRATION - GSA LIBRARY □ Washington, DC

Harlow, Bonnie, Cur., Coll.
ST. JOSEPH MUSEUM - LIBRARY □ St. Joseph, MO

Harlow, Ethelyn, Libn.
ONTARIO - ARCHIVES OF ONTARIO - LIBRARY □ Toronto, ON

Harlow, Jeanette, Libn.
IIT RESEARCH INSTITUTE - COMPUTER SEARCH CENTER† □ Chicago, IL

Harlow, Jeanette, Tech.Libn.
IIT RESEARCH INSTITUTE - LIBRARY & INFORMATION CENTER □ Chicago, IL

Harman, Susan, Ref. & Circ.Libn.
MEDICAL AND CHIRURGICAL FACULTY OF THE STATE OF MARYLAND - LIBRARY □ Baltimore, MD

Harmatz, B., Res.
OAK RIDGE NATIONAL LABORATORY - NUCLEAR DATA PROJECT □ Oak Ridge, TN

Harmeling, Sr. Deborah, Cat./AV Libn.
ATHENAEUM OF OHIO - MOUNT ST. MARY'S SEMINARY OF THE WEST - EUGENE H. MALY MEMORIAL LIBRARY □ Cincinnati, OH

Harmon, Angelina, Libn.
MEMORIAL SLOAN-KETTERING CANCER CENTER - LEE COOMBE MEMORIAL LIBRARY □ New York, NY

Harmon, Merlynn S., Res.Libn.
BIBLIOGRAPHIC RESEARCH LIBRARY □ San Jose, CA

Harmon, Pamela, Libn.
GREENLEAF (Simon) SCHOOL OF LAW - LIBRARY† □ Orange, CA

Harmon, Patricia Ann, Libn.
UNIROYAL, INC. - UNIROYAL CHEMICAL DIVISION - MANAGEMENT & TECHNICAL INFORMATION SERVICES/LIBRARY □ Naugatuck, CT

Harmon, Robert B., Res.Bibliog.
BIBLIOGRAPHIC RESEARCH LIBRARY □ San Jose, CA

Harmon, Sarah, Network Coord.
UNIVERSITY OF SOUTH FLORIDA - MEDICAL CENTER LIBRARY □ Tampa, FL

Harmony, Stephena, Libn.
UNIVERSITY OF CINCINNATI - MEDICAL CENTER LIBRARIES - HEALTH SCIENCES LIBRARY† □ Cincinnati, OH

Harms, Adele J., Libn.
ALLEN MEMORIAL HOSPITAL - HEALTH SCIENCES LIBRARY □ Waterloo, IA

Harms, Rev. Elvin R., Exec.Asst.
LUTHERAN CHURCH - MISSOURI SYNOD - SOUTHERN ILLINOIS DISTRICT ARCHIVES □ Belleville, IL

Harms, Herbert, Libn.
EMMAUS LUTHERAN CHURCH - LIBRARY □ Denver, CO

Harms, Richard, Spec.
MICHIGAN STATE UNIVERSITY - UNIVERSITY ARCHIVES AND HISTORICAL COLLECTIONS □ East Lansing, MI

Harms, Sally, Dir.
ST. LUKE'S METHODIST HOSPITAL - HEALTH SCIENCE LIBRARY □ Cedar Rapids, IA

Harmsen, Mark S., Res.Dir.
REPUBLICAN ASSOCIATES OF LOS ANGELES COUNTY - RESEARCH LIBRARY □ Glendale, CA

Harnden, Donna J., Hd.Libn.
PEAT, MARWICK, MITCHELL & CO. - LIBRARY □ Minneapolis, MN

Harned, Marilyn, Ref.Libn.
U.S. NAVY - NAVAL AIR SYSTEMS COMMAND - TECHNICAL LIBRARY AIR-7226 □ Washington, DC

Harness, Gregory C., Hd.Ref.Libn.
U.S. SENATE - LIBRARY □ Washington, DC

Harnish, Rita M., Libn.
SPRINGFIELD BAR AND LAW LIBRARY ASSOCIATION - LIBRARY† □ Springfield, OH

Harnois, Helene, Lib.Techn.
MONTREAL CANCER INSTITUTE - LIBRARY □ Montreal, PQ

Harold, Steve, Musm.Dir.
MANISTEE COUNTY HISTORICAL MUSEUM - FORTIER MEMORIAL LIBRARY □ Manistee, MI

Harold, Steve, Dir.
PIONEER STUDY CENTER □ Traverse City, MI

Haroldsen, Karen, Ser.Libn.
BRIGHAM YOUNG UNIVERSITY - J. REUBEN CLARK LAW SCHOOL LIBRARY □ Provo, UT

Harouny, Janet, Med.Libn.
U.S. VETERANS ADMINISTRATION (IN-Indianapolis) - MEDICAL CENTER LIBRARY □ Indianapolis, IN

Harper, Cynthia J., Circ.Libn.
LOYOLA UNIVERSITY (New Orleans) - LAW LIBRARY □ New Orleans, LA

Harper, Deidre, ILL
DREXEL UNIVERSITY - SCIENCE AND TECHNOLOGY LIBRARY □ Philadelphia, PA

Harper, Judith, Hd.
UNIVERSITY OF MANITOBA - AGRICULTURE LIBRARY □ Winnipeg, MB

Harper, Kathryn, Libn.
MEDFORD MAIL TRIBUNE - LIBRARY □ Medford, OR

Harper, Robert L., Hd.Libn.
CALIFORNIA COLLEGE OF ARTS AND CRAFTS - MEYER LIBRARY □ Oakland, CA

Harper, Shirley, Med.Libn.
ST. MARY-CORWIN HOSPITAL - FINNEY MEMORIAL LIBRARY □ Pueblo, CO

Harper, Shirley F., Libn.
CORNELL UNIVERSITY - MARTIN P. CATHERWOOD LIBRARY OF INDUSTRIAL AND LABOR RELATIONS □ Ithaca, NY

Harpole, Patricia C., Chf. of Ref.Lib.
MINNESOTA HISTORICAL SOCIETY - REFERENCE LIBRARY □ St. Paul, MN

Harpster, Robert W., Exec.Dir.
LEAGUE OF IOWA MUNICIPALITIES - LIBRARY □ Des Moines, IA

Harrah, Gerry, Med.Libn.
BINGHAM MEMORIAL HOSPITAL - MEDICAL LIBRARY □ Blackfoot, ID

Harrell, Alfonso, Supv., Rec.Ctr.
PHILADELPHIA - CITY ARCHIVES □ Philadelphia, PA

Harrell, Haywood S., Chf.Hist.
U.S. NATL. PARK SERVICE - MANASSAS NATL. BATTLEFIELD PARK - LIBRARY □ Manassas, VA

Harrell, Helen C., Dir.
HERMANN HOSPITAL - SCHOOL OF VOCATIONAL NURSING LIBRARY □ Houston, TX

Harrell, Virginia, Libn.
DALLAS PUBLIC LIBRARY - BUSINESS AND TECHNOLOGY DIVISION □ Dallas, TX

Harrigan, Anne T., Libn.
WOODWARD-CLYDE CONSULTANTS, WESTERN REGION - INFORMATION CENTER† □ Walnut Creek, CA

Harrington, Anne W., Med. Staff Libn.
CHESTER COUNTY HOSPITAL - MEDICAL STAFF
& SCHOOL OF NURSING LIBRARIES □ West
Chester, PA

Harrington, Charlotte, Asst.Libn.
CHADBOURNE, PARKE, WHITESIDE, & WOLFF -
LIBRARY □ New York, NY

Harrington, Judy, Libn.
UPDATA PUBLICATIONS, INC. - LIBRARY □ Los
Angeles, CA

Harrington, Richard B., Cur., Mil.Coll.
BROWN UNIVERSITY - SPECIAL COLLECTIONS
□ Providence, RI

Harrington, Robert D., Dir.
SAN MATEO COUNTY LAW LIBRARY □ Redwood
City, CA

Harrington, Thomas, Media Libn.
GALLAUDET COLLEGE LIBRARY - SPECIAL
COLLECTIONS† □ Washington, DC

Harris, Alice D., Res.Info.Spec.
EAST-WEST CENTER - EAPI/PI/RSI
RESEARCH MATERIALS COLLECTION □
Honolulu, HI

Harris, Anna L., Libn.
CLEVELAND PSYCHIATRIC INSTITUTE -
KARNOSH LIBRARY □ Cleveland, OH

Harris, Mr. Carol, Cur.
JACKSONVILLE PUBLIC LIBRARY - FLORIDA
COLLECTION □ Jacksonville, FL

Harris, Carol A., Med.Libn.
DEBORAH HEART AND LUNG CENTER -
MEDICAL LIBRARY □ Browns Mills, NJ

Harris, Catherine K., Libn.
TEXAS ADVISORY COMMISSION ON
INTERGOVERNMENTAL RELATIONS -
INFORMATION CENTER □ Austin, TX

Harris, Cheryl, Biomed.Libn.
U.S. AIR FORCE HOSPITAL MEDICAL CENTER -
MEDICAL LIBRARY (OH-Wright-Patterson AFB) □
Wright-Patterson AFB, OH

Harris, Cheryl, Health Sci.Libn.
U.S. VETERANS ADMINISTRATION (OH-Dayton)
- CENTER LIBRARY □ Dayton, OH

Harris, Consuelo W., Dept.Hd.
PUBLIC LIBRARY OF CINCINNATI AND
HAMILTON COUNTY - CHILDREN'S
DEPARTMENT □ Cincinnati, OH

Harris, Dwight, Archv., Govt.Rec.
MISSISSIPPI STATE DEPARTMENT OF
ARCHIVES AND HISTORY - ARCHIVES AND
LIBRARY DIVISION □ Jackson, MS

Harris, Elaine S., Info.Res.Anl.
SPERRY COMPUTER SYSTEMS - INFORMATION
CENTER† □ Blue Bell, PA

Harris, Eleanor, JBC Libn.
FLORIDA INSTITUTE OF TECHNOLOGY -
LIBRARY □ Melbourne, FL

Harris, Eleanor S., Br.Libn.
FLORIDA INSTITUTE OF TECHNOLOGY -
COLLEGE OF APPLIED TECHNOLOGY - LIBRARY
□ Jensen Beach, FL

Harris, Gale, Engr.Libn.
GENERAL DYNAMICS CORPORATION - FORT
WORTH DIVISION - TECHNICAL LIBRARY □
Fort Worth, TX

Harris, Glenda, Libn.
LAS VEGAS REVIEW-JOURNAL - LIBRARY □ Las
Vegas, NV

Harris, Gregory P., Libn.
SHEPARD'S/MC GRAW-HILL - LIBRARY □
Colorado Springs, CO

Harris, Helen Y., Libn.
SEMMES, BOWEN & SEMMES - LAW LIBRARY □
Baltimore, MD

Harris, Dr. Jan L., Supv.
VIRGINIA STATE DEPT. OF EDUCATION -
DIVISION OF MANAGEMENT INFORMATION
SERVICES - DATA UTILIZATION & REPORTING
□ Richmond, VA

Harris, Jane F., Asst.Libn.
SCOTT, FORESMAN & COMPANY, INC. -
EDITORIAL LIBRARY □ Glenview, IL

Harris, Jeanne, Info.Spec.
PEAT, MARWICK, MITCHELL & CO. - LIBRARY □
Houston, TX

Harris, Jerry D., Supv., Tech.Serv.
OKLAHOMA STATE UNIVERSITY - AUDIO
VISUAL CENTER □ Stillwater, OK

Harris, Jewel, Act.Acq./Pub.Serv.Libn.
COMMUNITY COLLEGE OF BALTIMORE -
LIBRARIES/LEARNING RESOURCES CENTERS □
Baltimore, MD

Harris, John C., Coll.Libn.
PENNSYLVANIA COLLEGE OF PODIATRIC
MEDICINE - CHARLES E. KRAUSZ LIBRARY □
Philadelphia, PA

Harris, John M., Dir.
TIPPECANOE COUNTY HISTORICAL
ASSOCIATION - ALAMEDA MC COLLOUGH
RESEARCH & GENEALOGY LIBRARY □ Lafayette,
IN

Harris, Kathryn, User Serv.
SOUTHERN ILLINOIS UNIVERSITY - SCHOOL OF
MEDICINE - MEDICAL LIBRARY □ Springfield, IL

Harris, Laura, Info.Spec.
NEW YORK UNIVERSITY - SCHOOL OF
CONTINUING EDUC. - REAL ESTATE
INSTITUTE - JACK BRAUSE LIBRARY & INFO.
CENTER □ New York, NY

Harris, Lee, Ref.Libn.
CONCORDIA UNIVERSITY - SIR GEORGE
WILLIAMS CAMPUS - SCIENCE &
ENGINEERING LIBRARY □ Montreal, PQ

Harris, Lois, Spec.Coll.Libn.
VIGO COUNTY PUBLIC LIBRARY - SPECIAL
COLLECTIONS □ Terre Haute, IN

Harris, Lois E., Dir., Lib. & AV Serv.
PACIFIC HOSPITAL OF LONG BEACH - MEDICAL
STAFF LIBRARY† □ Long Beach, CA

Harris, M.G., Div.Libn.
MOBIL OIL CORPORATION - E & P DIVISION
LIBRARY □ Denver, CO

Harris, Madlynne, Ref.Libn.
UNIVERSITY OF PITTSBURGH - FALK LIBRARY
OF THE HEALTH SCIENCES □ Pittsburgh, PA

Harris, Margaret J., Asst.Libn.
HOUSTON PUBLIC LIBRARY - CLAYTON
LIBRARY - CENTER FOR GENEALOGICAL
RESEARCH □ Houston, TX

Harris, Marinelle, Ser.Libn.
SOUTHWESTERN OKLAHOMA STATE
UNIVERSITY - AL HARRIS LIBRARY □
Weatherford, OK

Harris, Mark, Hd.
LOUISVILLE FREE PUBLIC LIBRARY -
KENTUCKY DIVISION† □ Louisville, KY

Harris, Mary E., Asst.Sci.Libn.
SAN DIEGO STATE UNIVERSITY - SCIENCE
DEPARTMENT† □ San Diego, CA

Harris, Mary Lou, Asst.Dir./Adm.Serv.
U.S. ARMY MILITARY HISTORY INSTITUTE □
Carlisle Barracks, PA

Harris, Maureen, Pub.Docs.
CLEMSON UNIVERSITY - ROBERT MULDROW
COOPER LIBRARY □ Clemson, SC

Harris, Melanie, Asst.Libn.
QUEEN'S UNIVERSITY AT KINGSTON -
EDUCATION LIBRARY □ Kingston, ON

Harris, Mildred, Libn.
CUMBERLAND COUNTY HISTORICAL SOCIETY -
PIRATE HOUSE LIBRARY □ Greenwich, NJ

Harris, Mollie S., Hd.Libn.
JEWISH COMMUNITY CENTER - SAMUEL &
REBECCA ASTOR JUDAICA LIBRARY □ San
Diego, CA

Harris, N., Asst.Dir. of Instr.
NEWFOUNDLAND - DEPARTMENT OF
EDUCATION - INSTRUCTIONAL MATERIALS
LIBRARY □ St. John's, NF

Harris, Patricia J., Hd., Pub.Serv.
NOVA UNIVERSITY - LAW LIBRARY □ Fort
Lauderdale, FL

Harris, Richard J., Tech.Serv.Coord.
EASTERN VIRGINIA MEDICAL SCHOOL -
MOORMAN MEMORIAL LIBRARY □ Norfolk, VA

Harris, Hon. Richard M., Pres., Lib. Trustees
SOLANO COUNTY LAW LIBRARY □ Fairfield, CA

Harris, Dr. S.J., Cat.
CANADA - NATIONAL DEFENCE -
DIRECTORATE OF HISTORY LIBRARY □ Ottawa,
ON

Harris, Sandra S., Libn.
LIGGETT & MYERS TOBACCO CO. -
INFORMATION SERVICES □ Durham, NC

Harris, Terri A., Supv.
ESSO RESOURCES CANADA LIMITED - LIBRARY
INFORMATION CENTRE □ Calgary, AB

Harris, William, Hd., Genealogy Div.
INDIANA STATE LIBRARY □ Indianapolis, IN

Harris, Dr. Woodfin G., Dir.
OKLAHOMA STATE UNIVERSITY - AUDIO
VISUAL CENTER □ Stillwater, OK

Harrison, Alice W., Libn.
ATLANTIC SCHOOL OF THEOLOGY - LIBRARY†
□ Halifax, NS

Harrison, Amalia, Hd., Info.Serv.
ALABAMA PUBLIC LIBRARY SERVICE -
INFORMATION SERVICE □ Montgomery, AL

Harrison, Annie, Sr.Libn.
KENTUCKY STATE DEPARTMENT FOR
LIBRARIES AND ARCHIVES - STATE LIBRARY
SERVICES DIVISION □ Frankfort, KY

Harrison, Carolyn J., Asst.Libn.
NATIONAL GEOGRAPHIC SOCIETY -
ILLUSTRATIONS LIBRARY □ Washington, DC

Harrison, Dennis I., Cur. of Mss.
WESTERN RESERVE HISTORICAL SOCIETY -
LIBRARY □ Cleveland, OH

Harrison, Elaine, Mss.Libn.
WESTERN KENTUCKY UNIVERSITY - DEPT. OF
SPECIAL COLLECTIONS - KENTUCKY LIBRARY
AND MUSEUM/UNIVERSITY ARCHIVES □
Bowling Green, KY

Harrison, Mrs. George, Chm.
RHODODENDRON SPECIES FOUNDATION -
LAWRENCE J. PIERCE RHODODENDRON
LIBRARY □ Federal Way, WA

Harrison, John, ILL
NEW YORK STATE OFFICE OF MENTAL HEALTH
- NEW YORK STATE PSYCHIATRIC INSTITUTE
- LIBRARY □ New York, NY

Harrison, John P., Hd.Cat.
BOSTON ATHENAEUM LIBRARY □ Boston, MA

Harrison, Kathi, Lib.Asst.
GENERAL DYNAMICS CORPORATION - PUBLIC
AFFAIRS LIBRARY □ St. Louis, MO

Harrison, Marjorie T., Hd.Libn.
MAINE MARITIME ACADEMY - NUTTING
MEMORIAL LIBRARY □ Castine, ME

Harrison, Michael, Dir.
UNIVERSITY OF CALIFORNIA, DAVIS -
MICHAEL AND MARGARET B. HARRISON
WESTERN RESEARCH CENTER □ Davis, CA

Harrison, Pamela, Hd., Per. & Circ.
RAND CORPORATION - LIBRARY† □ Santa
Monica, CA

Harrison, Patti, Circ.Libn.
PHILLIPS UNIVERSITY - GRADUATE SEMINARY
LIBRARY □ Enid, OK

Harrison, Rayma, Assoc.Libn.
CALIFORNIA INSTITUTE OF TECHNOLOGY -
ENVIRONMENTAL ENGINEERING LIBRARY □
Pasadena, CA

Harrison, Russell J., Dir.
U.S. DEPT. OF HOUSING AND URBAN
DEVELOPMENT - REGION III - LIBRARY† □
Philadelphia, PA

Harrison, T., Hd., Print Area
KELSEY INSTITUTE OF APPLIED ARTS AND
SCIENCES - LEARNING RESOURCES CENTRE □
Saskatoon, SK

Harrison, Tom W., Mgr.
KERR-MC GEE CORPORATION - MC GEE
LIBRARY □ Oklahoma City, OK

Harrison, Veronica C., Libn.
MERCY HOSPITAL - SCHOOL OF NURSING
LIBRARY □ Pittsburgh, PA

Harrison, Zelda, Libn.
TEMPLE JUDEA - MEL HARRISON MEMORIAL
LIBRARY □ Coral Gables, FL

Harriss, Charlotte, Supv., Pub.Serv.
CALIFORNIA STATE LIBRARY □ Sacramento, CA

Harriston, Victoria, Asst.Corp.Libn.
WASHINGTON GAS LIGHT COMPANY -
CORPORATE LIBRARY† □ Springfield, VA

Harrover, May, Libn.
ROGERS (Millicent) MUSEUM - LIBRARY □ Taos,
NM

Harrsch, Reid, Acq./Bibliog.Serv.Libn.
WISCONSIN STATE DIVISION FOR LIBRARY
SERVICES - REFERENCE AND LOAN LIBRARY □
Madison, WI

Harstad, Ortha R., Libn.
FIRST LUTHERAN CHURCH - ADULT LIBRARY □
Cedar Rapids, IA

Hart, Anne, Hd.
MEMORIAL UNIVERSITY OF NEWFOUNDLAND -
QUEEN ELIZABETH II LIBRARY - CENTRE FOR
NEWFOUNDLAND STUDIES □ St. John's, NF

Hart, Dorothy, Base Libn.
U.S. AIR FORCE BASE - NELLIS BASE LIBRARY □
Nellis AFB, NV

Hart, Edward J., Dir.
ARCHIVES OF THE CANADIAN ROCKIES □
Banff, AB

Hart, J. Robert, Dir.
HERTY FOUNDATION - LIBRARY □ Savannah, GA

Hart, James D., Dir.
UNIVERSITY OF CALIFORNIA, BERKELEY -
BANCROFT LIBRARY □ Berkeley, CA

Hart, Lenore, Forensic Libn.
FLORIDA STATE HOSPITAL - PATIENT/STAFF
LIBRARY □ Chattahoochee, FL

Hart, Lyn, Libn.
JOHNS HOPKINS UNIVERSITY - MILTON S.
EISENHOWER LIBRARY - GEORGE PEABODY
COLLECTION □ Baltimore, MD

Hart, Merrily F., Libn.
FAIRMOUNT TEMPLE - SAM AND EMMA MILLER
LIBRARY □ Cleveland, OH

Hart, Robert G., Gen.Mgr.
U.S. DEPT. OF THE INTERIOR - INDIAN ARTS
AND CRAFTS BOARD □ Washington, DC

Hart, Winifred M., Libn.
U.S. DEPT. OF JUSTICE - CRIMINAL DIVISION -
LIBRARY □ Washington, DC

Harten, Lucille, Pubn.Ed.
IDAHO STATE UNIVERSITY - IDAHO MUSEUM
OF NATURAL HISTORY - LIBRARY □ Pocatello,
ID

Hartenstein, Jeanne L., Dir., Lib.Serv.
BRONSON METHODIST HOSPITAL - HEALTH
SCIENCES LIBRARY □ Kalamazoo, MI

Harter, Margaret, Lib.Asst.
RICHMOND PUBLIC LIBRARY - ART AND MUSIC
DEPARTMENT □ Richmond, VA

Hartford, Sandra, Legal Info.Spec.
UNION MUTUAL LIFE INSURANCE COMPANY -
CORPORATE INFORMATION CENTER □ Portland,
ME

Hartgen, David T., Hd., Trans.Stat.Anl.Sect.
NEW YORK STATE DEPARTMENT OF
TRANSPORTATION - PUBLIC
TRANSPORTATION - LIBRARY □ Albany, NY

Harthan, Stephen, Tech.Serv.Libn.
DALLAS THEOLOGICAL SEMINARY - MOSHER
LIBRARY □ Dallas, TX

Harthorn, Sandy, Cur./Registrar
BOISE GALLERY OF ART - LIBRARY □ Boise, ID

Hartig, Dr. Linda, Act.Libn.
NASHOTAH HOUSE - LIBRARY □ Nashotah, WI

Hartigan, Barry, Assoc.Libn.
UNIVERSITY OF FLORIDA - ENGINEERING &
PHYSICS LIBRARY □ Gainesville, FL

Hartinger, Bert, Mgr., City Rec.Ctr.
MILWAUKEE - LEGISLATIVE REFERENCE
BUREAU - LEGISLATIVE LIBRARY □ Milwaukee,
WI

Hartje, George N., Dir. of Lib.
NORTHEAST MISSOURI STATE UNIVERSITY -
PICKLER MEMORIAL LIBRARY - SPECIAL
COLLECTIONS □ Kirksville, MO

Hartke, Larry, Info.Spec.
U.S. BUREAU OF THE CENSUS - INFORMATION
SERVICES PROGRAM - SEATTLE REGIONAL
OFFICE - LIBRARY □ Seattle, WA

Hartley, Bette L., Libn.
UNIVERSITY OF WISCONSIN, MADISON -
DEPARTMENT OF PSYCHIATRY - LITHIUM
INFORMATION CENTER □ Madison, WI

Hartley, Debra, Ref.Libn.
LUTHER COLLEGE - PREUS LIBRARY □ Decorah,
IA

Hartley, Gloria R., Tech.Libn.
LUKENS STEEL COMPANY - TECHNICAL
LIBRARY □ Coatesville, PA

Hartley, Patty Y., Dir.
BETHESDA HOSPITAL - LIBRARY AND
EDUCATION SERVICES □ Zanesville, OH

Hartman, Barbara, Med.Libn.
ST. MARGARET MEMORIAL HOSPITAL - PAUL
TITUS MEMORIAL LIBRARY AND SCHOOL OF
NURSING LIBRARY □ Pittsburgh, PA

Hartman, Eleanor C., Musm.Libn.
LOS ANGELES COUNTY MUSEUM OF ART -
RESEARCH LIBRARY □ Los Angeles, CA

Hartman, Gwen, Libn.
DELAVAN INC. - ENGINEERING LIBRARY □
West Des Moines, IA

Hartman, Marie, First Asst./U.S.Doc.Libn.
DALLAS PUBLIC LIBRARY - GOVERNMENT
PUBLICATIONS DIVISION □ Dallas, TX

Hartman, Dr. Richard T., Dir.
UNIVERSITY OF PITTSBURGH - PYMATUNING
LABORATORY OF ECOLOGY - TRYON LIBRARY □
Linesville, PA

Hartman, Rose, Libn.
ST. BERNARD'S PARISH - HAZARDVILLE
CATHOLIC LIBRARY □ Enfield, CT

Hartman, Ruth Dahlgren, Govt.Doc.Libn.
CENTRAL WASHINGTON UNIVERSITY -
LIBRARY DOCUMENTS DEPARTMENT □
Ellensburg, WA

Hartman, Sherry, Ref. & Database
UNION UNIVERSITY - ALBANY MEDICAL
COLLEGE - SCHAFFER LIBRARY OF THE HEALTH
SCIENCES □ Albany, NY

Hartman, Wilma L., Libn., Pub.Serv.
LINDA HALL LIBRARY □ Kansas City, MO

Hartmere, Anne-Marie, Libn.
ARCHITECTS COLLABORATIVE - LIBRARY† □
Cambridge, MA

Hartness-Kane, Ann, Asst.Hd.Libn.
UNIVERSITY OF TEXAS, AUSTIN - BENSON
LATIN AMERICAN COLLECTION □ Austin, TX

Hartsook, Herbert, Mss.Libn.
UNIVERSITY OF SOUTH CAROLINA - SOUTH
CAROLINIANA LIBRARY □ Columbia, SC

Hartung, David D., Libn.
WISCONSIN INDIANHEAD TECHNICAL
INSTITUTE, NEW RICHMOND CAMPUS -
LEARNING RESOURCE CENTER □ New
Richmond, WI

Hartwell, Sarah I., Coord. of Info. & Rsrcs.
WOMEN'S CAREER CENTER - LIBRARY □
Rochester, NY

Hartwig, Deborah, Libn.
WASHINGTON UNIVERSITY - EARTH AND
PLANETARY SCIENCES LIBRARY □ St. Louis, MO

Hartz, Mary K., User Serv.Libn.
BUREAU OF SOCIAL SCIENCE RESEARCH -
LIBRARY □ Washington, DC

Hartzel, Gwen N., Chm., Lib.Comm.
ZION MENNONITE CHURCH - LIBRARY □
Souderton, PA

Hartzler, Mary, Hd., Cat.Div.
INDIANA STATE LIBRARY □ Indianapolis, IN

Harvan, Christine C., Libn.
CHESTER COUNTY LAW AND MISCELLANEOUS
LIBRARY ASSOCIATION □ West Chester, PA

Harvath, John, Dept.Hd.
HOUSTON PUBLIC LIBRARY - FINE ARTS &
RECREATION DEPARTMENT □ Houston, TX

Harvey, Andy
SATELLITE VIDEO EXCHANGE SOCIETY -
VIDEO INN LIBRARY □ Vancouver, BC

Harvey, Avis E., Rsrcs./Info.Off.
PROTESTANT EPISCOPAL CHURCH EXECUTIVE
COUNCIL - HENRY KNOX SHERRILL RESOURCE
CENTER □ New York, NY

Harvey, Charlie, Law Libn.
RUTGERS UNIVERSITY, THE STATE
UNIVERSITY OF NEW JERSEY - JUSTICE
HENRY ACKERSON LIBRARY OF LAW &
CRIMINAL JUSTICE □ Newark, NJ

Harvey, Sr. Coronata, Dir.
DOMINICAN EDUCATION CENTER - LIBRARY □
Sinsinawa, WI

Harvey, Dorothy, Dept.Hd.
SACRAMENTO PUBLIC LIBRARY - BUSINESS &
MUNICIPAL DEPARTMENT† □ Sacramento, CA

Harvey, Elaine, Acq.Libn.
EDEN THEOLOGICAL SEMINARY - LIBRARY □
Webster Groves, MO

Harvey, Karen J., Libn.
SMITH COLLEGE - HILLYER ART LIBRARY □
Northampton, MA

Harvey, Mrs. Kenneth, Hd.
TALBOT COUNTY FREE LIBRARY - MARYLAND
ROOM □ Easton, MD

Harvey, Linda, Hd., Pub.Serv.
DALHOUSIE UNIVERSITY - W.K. KELLOGG
HEALTH SCIENCES LIBRARY □ Halifax, NS

Harvey, Mabel E., Med.Libn.
SOUTH FLORIDA STATE HOSPITAL - MEDICAL
AND PROFESSIONAL LIBRARY† □ Hollywood, FL

Harvey, Mary Alice, Libn.
COOK COUNTY HISTORICAL SOCIETY - GRAND
MARAIS LIBRARY □ Grand Marais, MN

Harvey, Susan M., Corp.Libn.
METCUT RESEARCH ASSOCIATES, INC. -
MACHINABILITY DATA CENTER □ Cincinnati,
OH

Harvey, Suzanne, Cat.Libn.
UNIVERSITY OF PUGET SOUND - SCHOOL OF
LAW LIBRARY □ Tacoma, WA

Harvie, Robert W., Sr., Ref.Libn.
FEDERAL ENERGY REGULATORY COMMISSION -
LIBRARY □ Washington, DC

Harvin, Marie, Res.Med.Libn.
UNIVERSITY OF TEXAS - M.D. ANDERSON
HOSPITAL AND TUMOR INSTITUTE -
RESEARCH MEDICAL LIBRARY □ Houston, TX

Harvison, Sonya
SPOTSYLVANIA HISTORICAL ASSOCIATION,
INC. - RESEARCH MUSEUM AND LIBRARY □
Spotsylvania, VA

Harwood, Dr. Judith Ann, Libn.
SOUTHERN ILLINOIS UNIVERSITY,
CARBONDALE - UNDERGRADUATE LIBRARY □
Carbondale, IL

Harwood, Kay F., Libn.
RICHLAND MEMORIAL HOSPITAL - JOSEY
MEMORIAL MEDICAL LIBRARY □ Columbia, SC

Harwood, Rodene, Supv.
REGIONAL TRANSPORTATION DISTRICT
(Metropolitan Denver Area) - RESEARCH &
RECORDS SERVICES □ Denver, CO

Hasbrouck, Kenneth E., Dir.
HUGUENOT HISTORICAL SOCIETY, NEW PALTZ
- LIBRARY □ New Paltz, NY

Hasbury, Susan, Documentation
CANADA - NATIONAL GALLERY OF CANADA -
LIBRARY □ Ottawa, ON

Hasegawa, Kay, Libn.
SIOUX VALLEY HOSPITAL - MEDICAL LIBRARY
□ Sioux Falls, SD

Hasegawa, Raymond K., Att.
CARLSMITH, CARLSMITH, WICHMAN & CASE -
LIBRARY □ Hilo, HI

Hasfjord, Nellie N., Dir.
ADAMS STATE COLLEGE - LIBRARY - SPECIAL
COLLECTIONS □ Alamosa, CO

Hashim, Elinor M., Ref.Supv.
PERKIN-ELMER CORPORATION - CORPORATE
LIBRARY □ Norwalk, CT

Hasija, Mr. Gian C., Med.Libn.
JERSEY SHORE MEDICAL CENTER - MEDICAL
LIBRARY □ Neptune, NJ

Hasil, Denise, Hd.Libn.
ROSENMAN, COLIN, FREUND, LEWIS & COHEN -
LAW LIBRARY □ New York, NY

Haskel, Peter, Libn.
REGIONAL PLAN ASSOCIATION, INC. -
LIBRARY □ New York, NY

Haskell, Mary B., Cat.
COLONIAL WILLIAMSBURG - RESEARCH
LIBRARY & ARCHIVES† □ Williamsburg, VA

Hasker, Leslie A., Lib.Asst.
SHELBURNE MUSEUM, INC. - RESEARCH
LIBRARY □ Shelburne, VT

Haskin, Peggy, Libn.
FLORIDA STATE UNIVERSITY - CTR. FOR
STUDIES IN VOCATIONAL EDUC. - FLORIDA
EDUCATIONAL INFO. SERV. □ Tallahassee, FL

Haskin, Susan M., Dp. State Libn.
MICHIGAN STATE - LIBRARY OF MICHIGAN □
Lansing, MI

Haskins, Norma W., Chf., Lib.Serv.
U.S. VETERANS ADMINISTRATION (NY-Bath) -
MEDICAL CENTER LIBRARY □ Bath, NY

Hasko, John, Ref.
UNIVERSITY OF SOUTHERN CALIFORNIA - LAW
LIBRARY □ Los Angeles, CA

Haslam, Anne Marie, Libn.
DELAWARE ART MUSEUM - LIBRARY □
Wilmington, DE

Haspiel, Elizabeth, Per. & Mailing Serv.
ST. LOUIS MERCANTILE LIBRARY
ASSOCIATION - LIBRARY □ St. Louis, MO

Hass, Joan, Hd.Libn.
AKIN, GUMP, STRAUSS, HAUER & FELD LAW
LIBRARY □ Dallas, TX

Hass, Louise, Asst.Libn.
ST. VINCENT'S HOSPITAL - GARCEAU LIBRARY
□ Indianapolis, IN

Hassan, Deborah, Lib.Info.Mgr.
NATIONAL EMPLOYMENT LAW PROJECT, INC. -
LIBRARY □ New York, NY

Hassan, Dr. M.U., Libn.
SASKATCHEWAN - DEPARTMENT OF
HIGHWAYS AND TRANSPORTATION -
PLANNING BRANCH LIBRARY □ Regina, SK

Hasse, Henry, Lrng.Rsrcs.Spec.
WINTER HAVEN HOSPITAL - J.G. CONVERSE
MEMORIAL MEDICAL LIBRARY □ Winter Haven,
FL

Hassen, Marjorie, Record Libn.
PRINCETON UNIVERSITY - PHONOGRAPH
RECORD LIBRARY □ Princeton, NJ

Hassert, Judith A., Res.Libn.
CHICOPEE, INC. - RESEARCH DIVISION -
LIBRARY† □ Milltown, NJ

Hassett, Ann, Lib.Ck.
OUR LADY OF VICTORY HOSPITAL - HOSPITAL
LIBRARY □ Lackawanna, NY

Hast, Adele, Editor-in-Chief
MARQUIS WHO'S WHO, INC. - RESEARCH
DEPARTMENT LIBRARY □ Chicago, IL

Hastings, David, Asst. State Archv.
WASHINGTON STATE OFFICE OF SECRETARY
OF STATE - DIVISION OF ARCHIVES AND
RECORD MANAGEMENT □ Olympia, WA

Hastings, Joy, Mgr.
HUNT-WESSON FOODS - INFORMATION
CENTER □ Fullerton, CA

Hastings, Margaret, Asst.Libn.
BRITISH COLUMBIA - LEGISLATIVE LIBRARY □
Victoria, BC

Haswell, Hollee, Libn.
SLEEPY HOLLOW RESTORATIONS, INC. -
SPECIAL LIBRARY & ARCHIVES □ Tarrytown, NY

Hatch, James V.
HATCH-BILLOPS COLLECTION, INC. □ New
York, NY

Hatch, Sherry A., Registrar
SACRAMENTO - MUSEUM AND HISTORY
DIVISION - LIBRARY □ Sacramento, CA

Hatcher, Jan, Lib.Mgr.
U.S. AIR FORCE HOSPITAL - EHRLING
BERGQUIST REGIONAL HOSPITAL - MEDICAL
LIBRARY □ Offutt AFB, NE

Hatcher, Juanita, Libn.
EDITOR & PUBLISHER - LIBRARY □ New York,
NY

Hatcher, Velda E., Ref.Libn.
BOSTON UNIVERSITY MEDICAL CENTER -
ALUMNI MEDICAL LIBRARY □ Boston, MA

Hatfield, Frances, Dir.
BROWARD COUNTY PUBLIC SCHOOLS -
LEARNING RESOURCES - PROFESSIONAL
LIBRARY □ Davie, FL

Hatfield, Dr. Susan
HARPER-GRACE HOSPITALS - DRUG
INFORMATION CENTER □ Detroit, MI

Hatfield, Wendy, Sr.Libn.
KENTUCKY STATE DEPARTMENT FOR
LIBRARIES & ARCHIVES - KENTUCKY TALKING
BOOK LIBRARY □ Frankfort, KY

Hathaway, Gary, Chf., Div. of Interp.
U.S. NATL. PARK SERVICE - LAVA BEDS NATL.
MONUMENT - LIBRARY □ Tulelake, CA

Hathaway, Joyce, Asst.Libn.
CHURCH OF JESUS CHRIST OF LATTER-DAY
SAINTS - UPPER SNAKE RIVER BRANCH
GENEALOGICAL LIBRARY □ Rexburg, ID

Hathaway, Kay E., Asst.Libn.
JHK & ASSOCIATES - TECHNICAL LIBRARY -
EAST □ Alexandria, VA

Hathaway, Richard, Libn.
DALLAS CHRISTIAN COLLEGE - LIBRARY □
Dallas, TX

Hathaway, Richard J., Dir., Info. & Govt.Serv.
MICHIGAN STATE - LIBRARY OF MICHIGAN □
Lansing, MI

Hathaway, Sue, Circuit Libn.
UNITED HEALTH SERVICES/WILSON HOSPITAL
- LEARNING RESOURCES DEPARTMENT □
Johnson City, NY

Hathaway, Teresa M., Adm.Libn.
U.S. AIR FORCE - STRATEGIC AIR COMMAND -
321 CSG/SS - LIBRARY† □ Grand Forks AFB, ND

Hathorn, Isabel V., Libn.
SUFFOLK ACADEMY OF MEDICINE - LIBRARY □
Hauppauge, NY

Hathway, Judith, Cat.
UNIVERSITY OF WISCONSIN, MADISON -
CENTER FOR HEALTH SCIENCES LIBRARIES† □
Madison, WI

Hatmaker, N.A., Info.Spec.
OAK RIDGE NATIONAL LABORATORY -
RADIATION SHIELDING INFORMATION
CENTER □ Oak Ridge, TN

Hatt, Gretchen, Comp. Search Spec.
DORSEY & WHITNEY - LAW LIBRARY □
Minneapolis, MN

Hatten, Bob, Libn.
STANDARD OIL OF CALIFORNIA - CHEVRON
U.S.A., INC. - EASTERN REGION LIBRARY □
New Orleans, LA

Hatten, Valerie, Libn.
MANITOBA MUSEUM OF MAN AND NATURE -
LIBRARY □ Winnipeg, MB

Hauck, Carolyn, Asst.Hd.
ENOCH PRATT FREE LIBRARY - AUDIO-VISUAL
DEPARTMENT □ Baltimore, MD

Hauck, Katy, Eligibility/Equip.Dist.
MINNESOTA STATE SERVICES FOR THE BLIND
AND VISUALLY HANDICAPPED -
COMMUNICATION CENTER □ St. Paul, MN

Hauck, Maeve, Info.Spec.
ESSO RESOURCES CANADA LIMITED - LIBRARY
INFORMATION CENTRE □ Calgary, AB

Hauck, Dr. Philomena, Dir.
UNIVERSITY OF CALGARY - EDUCATION
MATERIALS CENTER □ Calgary, AB

Hauer, Warner, Hd.Libn.
CHURCH OF JESUS CHRIST OF LATTER-DAY
SAINTS - MORRISTOWN, NEW JERSEY BRANCH
GENEALOGICAL LIBRARY □ Morristown, NJ

Hauerstein, Terry, Info.Serv.Mgr.
LEVER RESEARCH AND DEVELOPMENT CENTER
- RESEARCH LIBRARY □ Edgewater, NJ

Hauff, John H., Libn.
SAN FRANCISCO LAW LIBRARY □ San Francisco,
CA

Haug, Barbara, Hist.
SMITH MEMORIAL LIBRARY □ Chautauqua, NY

Haugen, Marsha, Libn.
HEWLETT-PACKARD COMPANY - LOVELAND
FACILITY LIBRARY □ Loveland, CO

Haugen, Ruth D., Tech.Serv.Supv.
LIBERTY MUTUAL INSURANCE COMPANY -
EDUCATION/INFORMATION RESOURCES □
Boston, MA

Haugh, Beth, AV Serv.
WEST VIRGINIA UNIVERSITY - MEDICAL
CENTER LIBRARY □ Morgantown, WV

Haught, Alberta Y., Ref.Libn.
ALTOONA AREA PUBLIC LIBRARY & DISTRICT
CENTER - PENNSYLVANIA ROOM □ Altoona, PA

Haugrud, Jack, Pres.
STANFORD ENVIRONMENTAL LAW SOCIETY -
LIBRARY □ Stanford, CA

Haulk, June H., Libn.
NATIONAL STANDARDS COUNCIL OF
AMERICAN EMBROIDERERS - NSCAE LIBRARY
□ Carnegie, PA

Haumont, Corinne, Libn.
UNIVERSITE DE MONTREAL - CHIMIE-
BIBLIOTHEQUE □ Montreal, PQ

Haun, Barbara, Libn.
ZELLER (George A.) MENTAL HEALTH CENTER -
PROFESSIONAL LIBRARY □ Peoria, IL

Hauner, Dolores, Ck.
NASSAU COUNTY POLICE DEPARTMENT -
POLICE ACADEMY - LIBRARY □ Williston Park,
NY

Haury, David A., Archv.
BETHEL COLLEGE - MENNONITE LIBRARY AND
ARCHIVES □ North Newton, KS

Hausen, Reba, Dir.
ANCHOR FOUNDATION - LIBRARY OF SOCIAL
HISTORY □ New York, NY

Hauser, Betty, Libn.
HARVARD UNIVERSITY - SCHOOL OF PUBLIC
HEALTH - KRESGE CENTER LIBRARY □ Boston,
MA

Hauser, Lori, Cat.
AMERICAN PETROLEUM INSTITUTE - LIBRARY
□ Washington, DC

Hauser, William G., Visual Info.Off.
U.S. FOREST SERVICE - PERMANENT
PHOTOGRAPHIC COLLECTION □ Washington,
DC

Hausler, Donald, Libn.
OAKLAND PUBLIC LIBRARY - HISTORY/
LITERATURE DIVISION □ Oakland, CA

Hauth, Allan C., Pub.Serv.Coord.
JACKSON METROPOLITAN LIBRARY -
INFORMATION AND REFERENCE DIVISION □
Jackson, MS

Haver, Richard, Chf.Libn.
U.S. VETERANS ADMINISTRATION (NC-
Asheville) - MEDICAL CENTER LIBRARY □
Asheville, NC

Haviaras, Stratis, Cur.
HARVARD UNIVERSITY - WOODBERRY POETRY
ROOM □ Cambridge, MA

Havlena, Betty W., Chf.Libn.
DETROIT NEWS - GEORGE B. CATLIN
MEMORIAL LIBRARY □ Detroit, MI

Havlik, Robert J., Engr.Libn.
UNIVERSITY OF NOTRE DAME - ENGINEERING
LIBRARY □ Notre Dame, IN

Haw, Rosalind, Sr.Mgr., Adm.
UNIVERSITY OF PITTSBURGH - NASA
INDUSTRIAL APPLICATIONS CENTER (NIAC) □
Pittsburgh, PA

Hawes, Rena E., Libn.
SOUTHEASTERN PENNSYLVANIA
TRANSPORTATION AUTHORITY - SEPTA
LIBRARY □ Philadelphia, PA

Hawke, Susan, Libn.
CONCORDIA UNIVERSITY - SIR GEORGE
WILLIAMS CAMPUS - GUIDANCE
INFORMATION CENTRE □ Montreal, PQ

Hawkes, Warren G., Assoc.Libn.
NEW YORK STATE NURSES ASSOCIATION -
LIBRARY □ Guilderland, NY

Hawkins, D.T., Info.Ret./Alerting Serv.
AT & T BELL LABORATORIES - LIBRARIES AND
INFORMATION SYSTEMS CENTER □ Murray Hill,
NJ

Hawkins, Dave, Mgr.
SCARBOROUGH RESOURCE CENTRE □
Scarborough, ON

Hawkins, Jan, Libn.
LE BONHEUR CHILDREN'S MEDICAL CENTER -
HEALTH SCIENCES LIBRARY □ Memphis, TN

Hawkins, Mary Ann, Archv.
U.S. NATL. ARCHIVES & RECORDS SERVICE -
FEDERAL ARCHIVES AND RECORDS CENTER,
REGION 4 □ East Point, GA

Hawkins, Mary Diane, Med.Libn.
PENNOCK HOSPITAL - MEDICAL LIBRARY □
Hastings, MI

Hawkshaw, Paul, Artistic Coord.
NATIONAL YOUTH ORCHESTRA ASSOCIATION
OF CANADA - LIBRARY □ Toronto, ON

Hawley, Ann, Res.Libn.
MOLSON BREWERIES OF CANADA, LTD. -
INFORMATION CENTRE □ Montreal, PQ

Hawley, Robert A., Dir.
SIMSBURY HISTORICAL SOCIETY - SIMSBURY
RESEARCH LIBRARY □ Simsbury, CT

Haworth, Cathy, Libn.
GEORGE WASHINGTON UNIVERSITY -
TELECOMMUNICATIONS INFORMATION
CENTER □ Washington, DC

Hawryliuk, D.M., Libn.
SUDBURY GENERAL HOSPITAL - HOSPITAL
LIBRARY □ Sudbury, ON

Hawthorne, Dottie, Ref.Libn.
MAYO FOUNDATION - MAYO CLINIC LIBRARY □
Rochester, MN

Hawver, Nancy, Libn.
SANTA BARBARA BOTANIC GARDEN - LIBRARY
□ Santa Barbara, CA

Hay, Charles C., Dir.
EASTERN KENTUCKY UNIVERSITY -
UNIVERSITY ARCHIVES □ Richmond, KY

Hay, E. Patricia, Exec.Coord.
ONTARIO - LEGISLATIVE ASSEMBLY -
LEGISLATIVE LIBRARY RESEARCH AND
INFORMATION SERVICES □ Toronto, ON

Hay, Gerald M., Libn.
ITT TELECOM NSD - LIBRARY □ Columbus, OH

Hayden, Carla, Lib.Serv.Coord.
MUSEUM OF SCIENCE & INDUSTRY - KRESGE
LIBRARY □ Chicago, IL

Hayden, Henry, Asst.Lib.Dir.
BRAILLE INSTITUTE OF AMERICA - LIBRARY □
Los Angeles, CA

Hayden, K.W. (Bill), Mktg.Dir.
COMMONWEALTH MICROFILM LIBRARY □
Mississauga, ON

Hayden, Lee, Asst.Supv.
MADISON PUBLIC LIBRARY - BUSINESS AND
SCIENCE DIVISION □ Madison, WI

Hayden, Margaret M., Law Libn.
MCI NORFOLK LAW LIBRARY □ Norfolk, MA

Hayden, Nina, Hd.Libn.
KNOXVILLE STATE TECHNICAL INSTITUTE -
EDUCATIONAL RESOURCE CENTER □ Knoxville,
TN

Hayden, Peggy A., Tech.Libn.
SINGER COMPANY - HRB-SINGER, INC. -
TECHNICAL INFORMATION CENTER □ State
College, PA

Hayden, Richard, Clinical Libn.
ROSWELL PARK MEMORIAL INSTITUTE -
LIBRARY AND INFORMATION MANAGEMENT
SERVICES □ Buffalo, NY

Hayden, Sharon A., Libn.
NIXON, HARGRAVE, DEVANS & DOYLE - LAW
LIBRARY □ Rochester, NY

Hayes, Rev. Bonaventure F., O.F.M., Lib.Dir.
CHRIST THE KING SEMINARY - LIBRARY □ East
Aurora, NY

Hayes, Carolyn, Ref.Libn.
DE PAUL UNIVERSITY - LAW SCHOOL LIBRARY
□ Chicago, IL

Hayes, Charles F., III, Res.Dir.
NEW YORK STATE ARCHEOLOGICAL
ASSOCIATION - LIBRARY □ Rochester, NY

Hayes, Cynthia, Libn.
BUFFALO COURIER-EXPRESS - LIBRARY □
Buffalo, NY

Hayes, Denise E., Tech.Info.Spec.
U.S. DEPT. OF LABOR - OSHA - TECHNICAL
DATA CENTER □ Washington, DC

Hayes, Eleanor, Libn.
MOUNT SINAI HOSPITAL - SIDNEY LISWOOD
LIBRARY □ Toronto, ON

Hayes, Elizabeth, Hd.
YALE UNIVERSITY - ENGINEERING AND
APPLIED SCIENCE LIBRARY □ New Haven, CT

Hayes, Grom M., Libn. Emeritus
HARTFORD STATE TECHNICAL COLLEGE -
GROM HAYES LIBRARY □ Hartford, CT

Hayes, Helen M., Lib.Dir./Irish Coll.Libn.
CHESTNUT HILL COLLEGE - LOGUE LIBRARY -
SPECIAL COLLECTIONS □ Philadelphia, PA

Hayes, Joan P., Libn.
UNIVERSITY OF PUERTO RICO -
AGRICULTURAL EXPERIMENT STATION -
LIBRARY □ Rio Piedras, PR

Hayes, Katharine, District Libn.
U.S. ARMY - CORPS OF ENGINEERS - ST. LOUIS
DISTRICT - LIBRARY □ St. Louis, MO

Hayes, L. Susan, Info.Spec.
GOULD, INC. - COMPUTER SYSTEMS DIVISION
- TECHNICAL INFORMATION CENTER □ Fort
Lauderdale, FL

Hayes, Lois F., Med.Libn.
CHICAGO COLLEGE OF OSTEOPATHIC
MEDICINE - OLYMPIA FIELDS OSTEOPATHIC
MEDICAL CENTER LIBRARY □ Olympia Fields, IL

Hayes, Margaret L., Libn.
AMERICAN PLAYERS THEATRE, INC. (APT) -
LIBRARY □ Spring Green, WI

Hayes, Mary Beth, Libn.
PASADENA COLLEGE OF CHIROPRACTIC -
LIBRARY □ Pasadena, CA

Hayes, Mary E., Ref.Libn.
UNIVERSITY OF DETROIT - SCHOOL OF LAW
LIBRARY □ Detroit, MI

Hayes, Susan M., Regional Libn.
U.S. DEPT. OF HOUSING AND URBAN
DEVELOPMENT - REGION VI - LIBRARY □ Fort
Worth, TX

Hayes, Suzanne, Ref.Libn.
BATTEN, BARTON, DURSTINE, OSBORN, INC. -
INFORMATION RETRIEVAL CENTER† □ New
York, NY

Hayes, Toussaint, Training Dir.
U.S. DEPT. OF LABOR - EMPLOYMENT &
TRAINING ADMINISTRATION - REGION IV
RESOURCE CENTER □ Atlanta, GA

Hayes, Vivian, Tech.Proc.Libn.
CARROLL COLLEGE - LIBRARY □ Helena, MT

Hayes, William, Hist.
OREGON ELECTRIC RAILWAY HISTORICAL
SOCIETY, INC. - TROLLEY PARK - LIBRARY □
Forest Grove, OR

Hayes-Clabots, K.J., Libn.
ECONOMICS LABORATORY, INC. - CORPORATE
INFORMATION CENTER □ St. Paul, MN

Hayhurst, Carol, Supv.
PUBLIC SERVICE COMPANY OF OKLAHOMA -
REFERENCE CENTER □ Tulsa, OK

Hayhurst, Ruth I., Libn.
WEST VIRGINIA STATE GEOLOGICAL AND
ECONOMIC SURVEY - LIBRARY □ Morgantown,
WV

Haylock, Harry V., Supv.
VARIAN CANADA INC. - TECHNICAL LIBRARY†
□ Georgetown, ON

Haymond, Jay M., Libn.
UTAH STATE HISTORICAL SOCIETY -
RESEARCH LIBRARY □ Salt Lake City, UT

Haymond, Phillip M., Chf., Info./Lib.Serv.Dir.
U.S. DEPT. OF THE INTERIOR - NATURAL
RESOURCES LIBRARY □ Washington, DC

Haynes, Donald, State Libn.
VIRGINIA STATE LIBRARY □ Richmond, VA

Haynes, Dorothy F., Med.libn.
U.S. AIR FORCE HOSPITAL - MEDICAL LIBRARY
(TX-Reese AFB) □ Reese AFB, TX

Haynes, Gene M., Med.libn.
U.S. VETERANS ADMINISTRATION (KY-
Louisville) - HOSPITAL LIBRARY □ Louisville, KY

Haynes, Judy, Educ.Spec.
AMERICAN FISHING TACKLE MANUFACTURERS
ASSOCIATION - RESOURCE & RESEARCH
LIBRARY □ Arlington Heights, IL

Haynes, Stelma, Lib.Asst.
FERGUSON BAPTIST CHURCH - LIBRARY □
Ferguson, KY

Hays, Susan E., Health Sci.Libn.
NEW MILFORD HOSPITAL - HEALTH SCIENCES
LIBRARY □ New Milford, CT

Hays, Timothy P., Chf., Tech.Lib.
U.S. ARMY - CORPS OF ENGINEERS - NEW
ENGLAND DIVISION - TECHNICAL LIBRARY □
Waltham, MA

Haysley, Mrs. Frances, Base Libn.
U.S. AIR FORCE BASE - GEORGE BASE
LIBRARY† □ George AFB, CA

Hayter, Ursula, Libn.
IMMACULATE HEART OF MARY - PARISH
LIBRARY □ Los Alamos, NM

Haythorn, J. Denny, Dir./Assoc.Prof.
WHITTIER COLLEGE - SCHOOL OF LAW -
LIBRARY □ Los Angeles, CA

Hayward, Diane, Asst.Libn./Midtown Lib.
DEWEY, BALLANTINE, BUSHBY, PALMER &
WOOD - LIBRARY □ New York, NY

Hayward, Fredric, Dir.
MEN'S RIGHTS, INC. - READING CENTER □
Sacramento, CA

Hayward, Miriam, Sci.Info.Coord.
PFIZER CANADA INC. - MEDICAL LIBRARY □
Pointe Claire-Dorval, PQ

Hayward, Oliver S., Libn.
SOCIETY OF MAYFLOWER DESCENDANTS IN
THE STATE OF CALIFORNIA - LIBRARY □
Oakland, CA

Hayward, Sheila, Asst.Libn.
COOPERS & LYBRAND - LIBRARY AND
INFORMATION CENTER □ Boston, MA

Hayward, Zita, Lib.Asst.
NORTHWESTERN UNIVERSITY -
MATHEMATICS LIBRARY □ Evanston, IL

Haywood, Beverly, Legal Adm.
ALASKA STATE DEPARTMENT OF LAW -
ATTORNEY GENERAL'S LIBRARY □ Juneau, AK

Haywood, Henry, Hd., Ref.Serv.
MILBANK, TWEED, HADLEY & MC CLOY -
LIBRARY □ New York, NY

Hazekamp, Phyllis, Libn.
PALMER COLLEGE OF CHIROPRACTIC - WEST -
LIBRARY □ Sunnyvale, CA

Hazelett, Barbara W., Adm.Libn.
U.S. NATL. LABOR RELATIONS BOARD - LAW
LIBRARY □ Washington, DC

Hazelton, Jane, Media Coord.
UNIVERSITY OF TEXAS, AUSTIN - FILM
LIBRARY □ Austin, TX

Hazelton, Penny A., Asst.Libn., Res.
U.S. SUPREME COURT - LIBRARY □ Washington,
DC

Hazen, Natalie, Ser.Libn.
PALO ALTO MEDICAL FOUNDATION -
BARNETT-HALL LIBRARY □ Palo Alto, CA

Hazlett, Florence E., Chm., Lib.Bd.
MEMORIAL PRESBYTERIAN CHURCH - LIBRARY
□ Midland, MI

Haznedari, Ismail, Supv.Libn.
U.S. ARMY - ARMAMENT RESEARCH &
DEVELOPMENT CENTER - SCIENTIFIC AND
TECHNICAL INFORMATION DIVISION □ Dover,
NJ

Head, Anita K., Prof. of Law/Law Libn.
GEORGE WASHINGTON UNIVERSITY -
NATIONAL LAW CENTER - JACOB BURNS LAW
LIBRARY □ Washington, DC

Head, Jeanne M., Acq.Libn.
QUAKER OATS COMPANY - JOHN STUART
RESEARCH LABORATORIES - RESEARCH
LIBRARY □ Barrington, IL

Head, Dr. John, Dir. of Res.
CLARION UNIV. OF PENNSYLVANIA - COLL. OF
LIBRARY SCIENCE - CTR. FOR THE STUDY OF
RURAL LIBRARIANSHIP - LIB. □ Clarion, PA

Head, Judith, Hd.Libn.
UNIVERSITY OF MANITOBA -
ADMINISTRATIVE STUDIES LIBRARY □
Winnipeg, MB

Headley, Ava Dell, Libn.
U.S. ARMY OPERATIONAL TEST & EVALUATION
AGENCY (OTEA) - TECHNICAL LIBRARY □ Falls
Church, VA

Heagy, Jan B., Info. & Res.Libn.
AMOCO PRODUCTION COMPANY
INTERNATIONAL - LIBRARY INFORMATION
CENTER □ Houston, TX

Healy, Sr. Frances, Dir.
PROVIDENCE HOSPITAL - HEALTH SCIENCES
LIBRARY □ Washington, DC

Healy, Helen J., Libn.
WESTERN MICHIGAN UNIVERSITY -
EDUCATIONAL LIBRARY □ Kalamazoo, MI

Healy, Julie
SATELLITE VIDEO EXCHANGE SOCIETY -
VIDEO INN LIBRARY □ Vancouver, BC

Healy, Leigh Watson, Libn.
FEDERAL RESERVE BANK OF ATLANTA -
RESEARCH LIBRARY □ Atlanta, GA

Heaps, Jerry, Entomology Ext. Fellow
UNIVERSITY OF MINNESOTA - AGRICULTURAL
EXTENSION SERVICE - DIAL-U INSECT AND
PLANT INFORMATION CLINIC □ St. Paul, MN

Heard, Donna, Rec.Supv.
MICHIGAN WISCONSIN PIPELINE COMPANY -
LIBRARY □ Houston, TX

Heard, Lt.Col. W.G., Cur.
ROYAL CANADIAN MILITARY INSTITUTE -
LIBRARY □ Toronto, ON

Hearder-Moan, W., Libn.
HAMILTON LAW ASSOCIATION - LAW LIBRARY
□ Hamilton, ON

Hearn, Gerry, Lib.Supv.
DECATUR HERALD AND REVIEW - LIBRARY □
Decatur, IL

Hearn, Helen O., Lib.Mgr.
U.S. ARMY HOSPITALS - MC DONALD USA
COMMUNITY HOSPITAL - MEDICAL LIBRARY† □
Ft. Eustis, VA

Hearst, Nancy, Libn.
HARVARD UNIVERSITY - JOHN K. FAIRBANK
CENTER FOR EAST ASIAN RESEARCH -
LIBRARY □ Cambridge, MA

Heaser, Eileen, Assoc.Ref.Libn.
CALIFORNIA STATE UNIVERSITY,
SACRAMENTO - LIBRARY - SCIENCE &
TECHNOLOGY REFERENCE DEPARTMENT □
Sacramento, CA

Heaslip, Lloyd, Dir., Info. & Ref.Br.
CANADA - LIBRARY OF PARLIAMENT □ Ottawa,
ON

Heath, Dr. Gordon G., Pres.
VISION INFORMATION PROGRAM, INC. □
Bloomington, IN

Heath, John Wright, Dir./Lib. & Info.Serv.
ATLANTA BUREAU OF PLANNING - LIBRARY □
Atlanta, GA

Heather, Joleen, Acq.
PEPPERDINE UNIVERSITY - LAW LIBRARY □
Malibu, CA

Heaton, Ms. G., Hd.
UNIVERSITY OF TORONTO - GENERAL LIBRARY
- SCIENCE AND MEDICINE DEPARTMENT □
Toronto, ON

Heaton, Sandra
NATIONAL CLEARING HOUSE OF
REHABILITATION TRAINING MATERIALS -
REFERENCE COLLECTION □ Stillwater, OK

Hebditch, Suzan, Asst.Govt.Pubns.Libn.
UNIVERSITY OF ALBERTA - HUMANITIES AND
SOCIAL SCIENCES LIBRARY - GOVERNMENT
PUBLICATIONS □ Edmonton, AB

Heberer, Kathy Santilli, Assoc.Libn.
AKERMAN, SENTERFITT, & EIDSON - LAW
LIBRARY □ Orlando, FL

Hebert, Fernande, Med.Libn.
MARICOPA MEDICAL CENTER - MEDICAL
LIBRARY □ Phoenix, AZ

Hebert, Francoise, Exec.Dir.
CANADIAN NATIONAL INSTITUTE FOR THE
BLIND - NATIONAL LIBRARY SERVICES -
SHERMAN SWIFT REFERENCE LIBRARY □
Toronto, ON

Hebert, John R., Act.Chf.
LIBRARY OF CONGRESS - HISPANIC DIVISION
□ Washington, DC

Hebert, Madeline, Ref.
LOUISIANA STATE UNIVERSITY - LAW
LIBRARY □ Baton Rouge, LA

Hebert, Mary, Libn.
BLUE CROSS HOSPITAL SERVICE, INC. -
LIBRARY □ St. Louis, MO

Hebert, R. Vivian, Law Libn.
U.S. ARMY - JUDGE ADVOCATE GENERAL'S
SCHOOL - LIBRARY □ Charlottesville, VA

Hecht, Toby E., Libn.
GPU NUCLEAR - TECHNICAL LIBRARY □
Parsippany, NJ

Heck, Thomas, Hd.Libn.
OHIO STATE UNIVERSITY - MUSIC LIBRARY □
Columbus, OH

Heck, Thomas F., Archv.
GUITAR FOUNDATION OF AMERICA - ARCHIVE
□ Columbus, OH

Heckard, David C., Mgr.
ARMCO, INC. - TECHNICAL INFORMATION
CENTER □ Middletown, OH

Hecker, Frances E., Hd.
TULANE UNIVERSITY OF LOUISIANA -
ARCHITECTURE LIBRARY □ New Orleans, LA

Heckman, Florence E., Ref.Libn.
NATIONAL SCIENCE FOUNDATION - LIBRARY □
Washington, DC

Hedderick, Alice Marie, Libn.
ANGLICAN CHURCH OF CANADA - CHURCH
HOUSE LIBRARY □ Toronto, ON

Hedgecock, Sheila D., Asst.Info.Spec.
VIRGINIA ELECTRIC AND POWER COMPANY -
LIBRARY AND INFORMATION SERVICES □
Richmond, VA

Hedrick, Donine, Asst.Libn.
CALIFORNIA STATE UNIVERSITY,
SACRAMENTO - LIBRARY - SCIENCE &
TECHNOLOGY REFERENCE DEPARTMENT □
Sacramento, CA

Hedrick, Mildred S., Libn.
FIRST UNITED METHODIST CHURCH - ALLEN
LIBRARY □ Kalamazoo, MI

Hedrick, Susan K., Libn.
OKLAHOMA STATE DEPARTMENT OF
VOCATIONAL AND TECHNICAL EDUCATION -
CURRICULUM DIVISION - LIBRARY □ Stillwater,
OK

Heemeryck, Gloria, Libn.
ASSOCIATED ENGINEERING SERVICES, LTD. -
INFORMATION CENTRE □ Edmonton, AB

Heenan, Daniel J., Dir.
NYACK HOSPITAL - MEMORIAL LIBRARY □
Nyack, NY

Heer, Prof. David M., Assoc.Dir.
UNIVERSITY OF SOUTHERN CALIFORNIA -
POPULATION RESEARCH LABORATORY -
LIBRARY □ Los Angeles, CA

Heeter, Judy, Libn.
ST. CLOUD HOSPITAL - HEALTH SCIENCES
LIBRARY □ St. Cloud, MN

Heffernan, Steve, Libn.
CAMPBELL-MITHUN, INC. - RESEARCH
INFORMATION CENTER □ Chicago, IL

Heffernan, T.L., Lab.Supv.
TEXAS STATE PARKS & WILDLIFE
DEPARTMENT - MARINE LABORATORY
LIBRARY □ Rockport, TX

Hefler, Barbara, Pub.Serv.Libn.
NEW ENGLAND CONSERVATORY OF MUSIC -
HARRIET M. SPAULDING LIBRARY □ Boston, MA

Heflin, Shelia E., Supv.
OWENSBORO-DAVIESS COUNTY PUBLIC
LIBRARY - KENTUCKY ROOM □ Owensboro, KY

Hefner, Loretta L., Bur.Archv./Rec.Anl.
UTAH STATE ARCHIVES □ Salt Lake City, UT

Hefner, Sr. M. Xavier, Archv./Libn.
SISTERS OF ST. MARY OF NAMUR - MOUNT ST.
MARY RESEARCH CENTER □ Kenmore, NY

Hefte, Pearl, Archv.
DAKOTA STATE COLLEGE - KARL E. MUNDT
LIBRARY □ Madison, SD

Hegarty, Kevin, Dir.
TACOMA PUBLIC LIBRARY - SPECIAL
COLLECTIONS □ Tacoma, WA

Hegenwald, Shirley B., Chf., Lib.Serv.
U.S. VETERANS ADMINISTRATION (LA-
Shreveport) - MEDICAL CENTER LIBRARY □
Shreveport, LA

Hehl, Walter A., Hd.
CENTRAL CHRISTIAN CHURCH - LIBRARY □
Lexington, KY

Hehman, Jennifer L., Asst.Hd.Libn.
INDIANA UNIVERSITY, INDIANAPOLIS -
UNIVERSITY LIBRARY/HERRON SCHOOL OF
ART □ Indianapolis, IN

Hehr, Pamela L., Libn.
CABOT CORPORATION - READING
TECHNOLOGY LIBRARY □ Reading, PA

Heiberger, Elana, Med.Libn.
PENROSE HOSPITAL - WEBB MEMORIAL
LIBRARY □ Colorado Springs, CO

Heidel, Mary, Lib.Techn.
U.S. ARMY HOSPITALS - BASSETT ARMY
HOSPITAL - MEDICAL LIBRARY □ Ft.
Wainwright, AK

Heideman, Carol, Regional Libn.
PUBLIC LIBRARY OF CINCINNATI AND
HAMILTON COUNTY - LIBRARY FOR THE BLIND
AND PHYSICALLY HANDICAPPED □ Cincinnati,
OH

Heidenreich, Fred, Hd., Ref.Serv.
UNIVERSITY OF ARIZONA - ARIZONA HEALTH
SCIENCES CENTER LIBRARY □ Tucson, AZ

Heidgerd, Lloyd H., Br.Libn.
UNIVERSITY OF NEW HAMPSHIRE -
BIOLOGICAL SCIENCES LIBRARY □ Durham, NH

Heidlage, Robert, Lib.Asst.
UNIVERSITY OF MISSOURI - GEOLOGY
LIBRARY □ Columbia, MO

Heidner, Vivian, Media Serv.Libn.
BRIERCREST BIBLE COLLEGE - ARCHIBALD
LIBRARY □ Caronport, SK

Heigold, William G., Med.Libn.
BLISS (Malcolm) MENTAL HEALTH CENTER -
ROBERT J. BROCKMAN MEMORIAL LIBRARY □
St. Louis, MO

Heikkila, Mrs. E., Dir., Med.Rec.
MINERAL SPRINGS HOSPITAL - MEDICAL
LIBRARY □ Banff, AB

Heil-Zampier, Kathleen, Libn.
UNIVERSITY OF MARYLAND, SOLOMONS - CTR. FOR ENVIRONMENT & ENVIRONMENTAL STUD. - CHESAPEAKE BIOL. LAB. - LIB. □ Solomons, MD

Heilakka, Dr. Edwin, Orchestra Libn.
CURTIS INSTITUTE OF MUSIC - LIBRARY □ Philadelphia, PA

Heileman, Gene, Tech.Libn.
WHIRLPOOL CORPORATION - TECHNICAL INFORMATION CENTER □ Benton Harbor, MI

Heim, Keith M., Interim Dean
MURRAY STATE UNIVERSITY - LIBRARY □ Murray, KY

Heim, Keith M., Hd., Spec.Coll.
MURRAY STATE UNIVERSITY - LIBRARY □ Murray, KY

Hein, Paul G., Sr. Cartographer
NEW YORK STATE DEPARTMENT OF TRANSPORTATION - MAP INFORMATION UNIT □ Albany, NY

Heindselman, Mark, Sr.Res.Libn.
MONSANTO COMPANY - FISHER CONTROLS COMPANY - R.A. ENGEL TECHNICAL LIBRARY □ Marshalltown, IA

Heine, Aalbert, Musm.Dir.
CORPUS CHRISTI MUSEUM - STAFF LIBRARY □ Corpus Christi, TX

Heine, Russel J., Tech.Pub.Anl.
WESTINGHOUSE ELECTRIC CORPORATION - ELECTRICAL SYSTEMS DIVISION - TECHNICAL LIBRARY† □ Lima, OH

Heineke, Mary Lou, Libn.
CAMPBELL-MITHUN, INC. - INFORMATION SERVICES □ Minneapolis, MN

Heinen, Margaret, Rd.Serv.Libn.
WAYNE STATE UNIVERSITY - ARTHUR NEEF LAW LIBRARY □ Detroit, MI

Heinlen, Bethany A., Med.Libn.
LANSING GENERAL HOSPITAL - OSTEOPATHIC - K.M. BAKER MEMORIAL LIBRARY □ Lansing, MI

Heinritz, Mrs. Robert, Hd.Libn.
PRINCE OF PEACE LUTHERAN CHURCH - LIBRARY □ Milwaukee, WI

Heins, Alison S., Libn.
JORDAN COLLEGE ENERGY INSTITUTE - LIBRARY □ Comstock Park, MI

Heintzelman, Susan, Asst.Dir., Coll.
TEACHERS COLLEGE - MILBANK MEMORIAL LIBRARY □ New York, NY

Heinz, Catharine, Dir.
BROADCAST PIONEERS LIBRARY □ Washington, DC

Heinz-Boewe, Karl, Ref.Libn.
UNIVERSITY OF KENTUCKY - MEDICAL CENTER LIBRARY □ Lexington, KY

Heinzeroth, Lynn, Cat.
U.S. AIR FORCE INSTITUTE OF TECHNOLOGY - LIBRARY □ Wright-Patterson AFB, OH

Heise, Dorothy, Tech.Info.Spec.
U.S.D.A. - ECONOMIC RESEARCH SERVICE - ERS REFERENCE CENTER □ Washington, DC

Heise, Marlin L., Hd.Cat.Libn.
MINNESOTA HISTORICAL SOCIETY - REFERENCE LIBRARY □ St. Paul, MN

Heiser, John S., Asst.Hist.
U.S. NATL. PARK SERVICE - GETTYSBURG NATL. MILITARY PARK - CYCLORAMA CENTER LIBRARY □ Gettysburg, PA

Heiser, Lois, Libn.
INDIANA UNIVERSITY - GEOLOGY LIBRARY □ Bloomington, IN

Heiser, Rev. W. Charles, S.J., Libn.
ST. LOUIS UNIVERSITY - DIVINITY LIBRARY □ St. Louis, MO

Heiser, Wilma, Lib.Spec.
PENNSYLVANIA STATE UNIVERSITY - APPLIED RESEARCH LABORATORY - LIBRARY □ State College, PA

Heiserman, Sonya, Libn.
SAN DIEGO COUNTY - DEPARTMENT OF PLANNING AND LAND USE - LIBRARY □ San Diego, CA

Heisey, Terry M., Libn.
EVANGELICAL SCHOOL OF THEOLOGY - ROSTAD LIBRARY □ Myerstown, PA

Heising, Anne S., Libn.
TIME-LIFE BOOKS INC. - REFERENCE LIBRARY □ Alexandria, VA

Heisler, Helen P., Libn.
SARGENT & LUNDY ENGINEERS - TECHNICAL LIBRARY □ Chicago, IL

Heisler, Rosemary, Govt.Docs.Libn.
BROOKLYN LAW SCHOOL - LAW LIBRARY □ Brooklyn, NY

Heisman, Beryl, Lit.Spec.
MOBIL RESEARCH & DEVELOPMENT CORPORATION - ENGINEERING DEPARTMENT - INFORMATION CENTER □ Princeton, NJ

Heiss, Phyllis M., Br.Libn.
CHURCH OF JESUS CHRIST OF LATTER-DAY SAINTS - WEST PALM BEACH FLORIDA STAKE BRANCH GENEALOGICAL LIBRARY □ Boca Raton, FL

Heist, Beverly, Law Libn.
MISSOURI STATE COURT OF APPEALS, SOUTHERN DISTRICT - LAW LIBRARY □ Springfield, MO

Heister, Carla G, Libn.
UNIVERSITY OF ILLINOIS - ILLINOIS STATE NATURAL HISTORY SURVEY - LIBRARY □ Champaign, IL

Heitkamp, Martha, First Asst.
PUBLIC LIBRARY OF CINCINNATI AND HAMILTON COUNTY - GOVERNMENT AND BUSINESS DEPARTMENT □ Cincinnati, OH

Heitman, Roy K.
U.S. DEFENSE AUDIOVISUAL AGENCY - STILL PICTURE LIBRARY □ Washington, DC

Heitz, Thomas R., Libn.
NATIONAL BASEBALL HALL OF FAME AND MUSEUM, INC. - NATIONAL BASEBALL LIBRARY □ Cooperstown, NY

Heitzenrater, Richard, Dir.
SOUTHERN METHODIST UNIVERSITY - BRIDWELL LIBRARY - CENTER FOR METHODIST STUDIES □ Dallas, TX

Helander, Joel, Lib.Comm.Chm.
GUILFORD KEEPING SOCIETY, INC. - LIBRARY □ Guilford, CT

Held, Jon, Video & Sports Libn.
DALLAS PUBLIC LIBRARY - FINE ARTS DIVISION □ Dallas, TX

Helde, Joan, Libn.
GEORGETOWN UNIVERSITY - CENTER FOR POPULATION RESEARCH - LIBRARY □ Washington, DC

Helfter, Clyde, Cur. of Iconography
BUFFALO & ERIE COUNTY HISTORICAL SOCIETY - LIBRARY† □ Buffalo, NY

Helge, Brian, Assoc.Libn.
LUTHERAN SCHOOL OF THEOLOGY AT CHICAGO - KRAUSS LIBRARY† □ Chicago, IL

Helgeson, Stanley, Assoc.Dir., Sci.
ERIC CLEARINGHOUSE FOR SCIENCE, MATHEMATICS AND ENVIRONMENTAL EDUCATION □ Columbus, OH

Helguera, Byrd S., Assoc.Dir.
VANDERBILT UNIVERSITY - MEDICAL CENTER LIBRARY □ Nashville, TN

Helie, Caroline, Phys.Sci.Ref.Libn.
BROWN UNIVERSITY - SCIENCES LIBRARY □ Providence, RI

Helkowski, William, Chf.Tech. Data Mgr.
U.S. DEFENSE LOGISTICS AGENCY - DEFENSE INDUSTRIAL SUPPLY CENTER - TECHNICAL DATA MANAGEMENT OFFICE □ Philadelphia, PA

Heller, Betty, Ser.Libn.
BROWN UNIVERSITY - SCIENCES LIBRARY □ Providence, RI

Heller, James, Libn.
UNIVERSITY OF IDAHO - LAW LIBRARY □ Moscow, ID

Heller, Jonathan, Archv.
U.S. NATL. ARCHIVES & RECORDS SERVICE - STILL PICTURE BRANCH □ Washington, DC

Heller, Sharon, Western Jnl.Acq.Libn.
MATHEMATICAL REVIEWS - LIBRARY □ Ann Arbor, MI

Heller, Susan J., Regional Libn.
U.S. DEPT. OF HOUSING AND URBAN DEVELOPMENT - REGION II - LIBRARY □ New York, NY

Heller, Vonda, Libn./Rec.Coord.
SPRINGHOUSE CORPORATION - CORPORATE LIBRARY □ Spring House, PA

Hellickson, Michele, Interpretation Chf.
U.S. NATL. PARK SERVICE - THEODORE ROOSEVELT NATL. PARK - LIBRARY □ Medora, ND

Helling, James T., Chf., Rd.Serv.
U.S. AIR FORCE INSTITUTE OF TECHNOLOGY - LIBRARY □ Wright-Patterson AFB, OH

Hellmers, Norman D., Supt.
U.S. NATL. PARK SERVICE - LINCOLN BOYHOOD NATL. MEMORIAL - LIBRARY □ Lincoln City, IN

Hellwig, E. Nancy, AV Libn.
U.S. VETERANS ADMINISTRATION (NY-Syracuse) - MEDICAL CENTER LIBRARY □ Syracuse, NY

Helman, Jennifer, Supv.
UNIVERSITY OF NOTRE DAME - MATHEMATICS LIBRARY □ Notre Dame, IN

Helman, Dr. W.P.
UNIVERSITY OF NOTRE DAME - RADIATION LABORATORY - RADIATION CHEMISTRY DATA CENTER □ Notre Dame, IN

Helmberger, Rose, Libn.
MADISON PUBLIC LIBRARY - LITERATURE AND SOCIAL SCIENCES □ Madison, WI

Helmbold, F. Wilbur, Cur.
SAMFORD UNIVERSITY - BAPTIST HISTORICAL COLLECTION □ Birmingham, AL

Helmer, Jody, Libn.
PRESBYTERIAN DENVER HOSPITAL - BRADFORD MEMORIAL LIBRARY □ Denver, CO

Helmich, Stephen G., Hist.
SACRAMENTO - MUSEUM AND HISTORY DIVISION - LIBRARY □ Sacramento, CA

Helmreich, R.F.
DOW CHEMICAL COMPANY - TECHNICAL INFORMATION SERVICES - CHEMICAL LIBRARY □ Midland, MI

Helms, Mary, Hd., Tech.Serv.
UNIVERSITY OF SOUTH DAKOTA - CHRISTIAN P. LOMMEN HEALTH SCIENCES LIBRARY □ Vermillion, SD

Helms, Susan, Asst.Libn.
U.S. VETERANS ADMINISTRATION (AL-Montgomery) - MEDICAL CENTER LIBRARY (142D) □ Montgomery, AL

Helmuth, Ruth, Archv.
CASE WESTERN RESERVE UNIVERSITY - UNIVERSITY ARCHIVES □ Cleveland, OH

Helsabeck, Rosemary E., Libn.
FLORIDA STATE COURT OF APPEAL - 3RD DISTRICT - LAW LIBRARY □ Miami, FL

Helser, Fred, Assoc.Libn.
FRANKLIN UNIVERSITY - LIBRARY □ Columbus, OH

Helser, Tracy, Files Dev. & Maintenance
INVESTIGATIVE RESOURCE CENTER - DATA CENTER □ Oakland, CA

Helton, Helen, Chf., Tech.Serv.
U.S. AIR FORCE INSTITUTE OF TECHNOLOGY - LIBRARY □ Wright-Patterson AFB, OH

Helton, Sharon, ILL Asst.
VANDERBILT UNIVERSITY - MEDICAL CENTER LIBRARY □ Nashville, TN

Heltsley, Mary K., Libn.
FARIBAULT STATE HOSPITAL - LIBRARY □ Faribault, MN

Helyar, L.E.J., Cur. in Graphics
UNIVERSITY OF KANSAS - DEPARTMENT OF
SPECIAL COLLECTIONS □ Lawrence, KS

Helyar, Thelma, Libn.
UNIVERSITY OF KANSAS - CENTER FOR PUBLIC
AFFAIRS □ Lawrence, KS

Hemingway, George, Graphic Artist
OAKLAND SCHOOLS - EDUCATIONAL RESOURCE
CENTER □ Pontiac, MI

Hemming, Charles, Abstractor-Indexer
NATIONAL ACADEMY OF SCIENCES -
NATIONAL RESEARCH COUNCIL - HIGHWAY
RESEARCH INFORMATION SERVICE □
Washington, DC

Hemming, J. Terry, Chf.Libn.
U.S. COURT OF APPEALS, 10TH CIRCUIT -
LIBRARY □ Denver, CO

Hemming, Richard, Prof.Asst.
ST. PAUL PUBLIC LIBRARY - BUSINESS &
SCIENCE ROOM □ St. Paul, MN

Hempel, Ruth, Cat.Libn.
UNIVERSITY OF SOUTH CAROLINA - SCHOOL
OF MEDICINE LIBRARY □ Columbia, SC

Hemperley, Mr. Marion R., Dp. Surveyor Gen.
GEORGIA STATE SURVEYOR GENERAL
DEPARTMENT - LIBRARY □ Atlanta, GA

Hemsley, G., Info.Off.
CANADA - TRANSPORT CANADA - ST.
LAWRENCE SEAWAY AUTHORITY -
INFORMATION OFFICE □ Ottawa, ON

Hench, Joan M., Chf., Coll.Dev.Br.
U.S. ARMY WAR COLLEGE - LIBRARY □ Carlisle
Barracks, PA

Hench, Merrill, Tech. Data Libn.
BAYBANKS DATA SERVICES, INC. - TECHNICAL
DATA LIBRARY □ Waltham, MA

Henderer, Carolyn, Libn.
BAHAI REFERENCE LIBRARY OF PEORIA □
Peoria, IL

Henderer, Edmond, Libn.
NATIONAL CAPITAL HISTORICAL MUSEUM OF
TRANSPORTATION - LIBRARY □ Silver Spring,
MD

Hendershot, Dr. Carl H., Publ.
HENDERSHOT BIBLIOGRAPHY & CONSULTANTS
- LIBRARY □ Bay City, MI

Hendershot, Carol, D.P. Specialist
INFORMATION TECHNOLOGY CENTER -
LIBRARY □ New York, NY

Henderson, Beth, Libn.
LAKE CIRCUIT COURT - LIBRARY □ Crown
Point, IN

Henderson, Carolyn, Mgr.
ALLERGAN PHARMACEUTICALS, INC. -
MEDICAL & SCIENCE INFORMATION □ Irvine,
CA

Henderson, Catherine, Res.Libn.
UNIVERSITY OF TEXAS, AUSTIN - HARRY
RANSOM HUMANITIES RESEARCH CENTER □
Austin, TX

Henderson, Deborah, Jr.Libn.
ONTARIO HYDRO - LIBRARY □ Toronto, ON

Henderson, Diane, Chf.Libn.
UNIVERSITY OF TORONTO - FACULTY OF
LIBRARY SCIENCE LIBRARY □ Toronto, ON

Henderson, E.M., Libn.
LITTON BIONETICS, INC. - SCIENTIFIC
LIBRARY □ Kensington, MD

Henderson, Edith G., Cur./Treasure Rm.
HARVARD UNIVERSITY - LAW SCHOOL
LIBRARY □ Cambridge, MA

Henderson, Floyd L., Libn.
U.S. FOREST SERVICE - NORTH CENTRAL
FOREST EXPERIMENT STATION LIBRARY □ St.
Paul, MN

Henderson, Gail M., Libn.
U.S. ARMY - CORPS OF ENGINEERS -
GALVESTON DISTRICT - LIBRARY □ Galveston,
TX

Henderson, Helen H., Libn.
U.S. VETERANS ADMINISTRATION (MO-St.
Louis) - HOSPITAL LIBRARY □ St. Louis, MO

Henderson, Jim, Ref.Libn.
UNIVERSITY OF BRITISH COLUMBIA -
WOODWARD BIOMEDICAL LIBRARY □
Vancouver, BC

Henderson, Joanne L., Libn.
HERCULES, INC. - LIBRARY □ Wilmington, DE

Henderson, Jon M., Mgr., Lib.Serv.
HALLMARK CARDS, INC. - CREATIVE
RESEARCH LIBRARY □ Kansas City, MO

Henderson, Judy, Tech.Serv.Coord.
LOUISIANA STATE UNIVERSITY - COASTAL
INFORMATION REPOSITORY □ Baton Rouge, LA

Henderson, Katherine, Asst. Law Libn.
MC GEORGE SCHOOL OF LAW - LAW LIBRARY □
Sacramento, CA

Henderson, Linda E., Info.Ctr.Coord.
ASSOCIATION OF GOVERNING BOARDS OF
UNIVERSITIES AND COLLEGES - TRUSTEE
INFORMATION CENTER □ Washington, DC

Henderson, Lois E., Lib.Supv.
FLORENCE CITY SCHOOLS - CENTRAL
RESOURCE CENTER □ Florence, AL

Henderson, Marjorie A., Mgr., Lib.Serv.
XEROX CORPORATION - INFORMATION
PRODUCTS DIVISION - LIBRARY SERVICES □
Dallas, TX

Henderson, Dr. Mary C., Cur.
MUSEUM OF THE CITY OF NEW YORK -
THEATRE COLLECTION □ New York, NY

Henderson, Mary Emma S., Libn.
ABRAHAM BALDWIN AGRICULTURAL COLLEGE
- LIBRARY □ Tifton, GA

Henderson, Phyllis, Assoc.Cur. of Musm.
CITADEL - THE MILITARY COLLEGE OF SOUTH
CAROLINA - ARCHIVES/MUSEUM □ Charleston,
SC

Henderson, Dr. Robbye R., Hd.Libn.
MISSISSIPPI VALLEY STATE UNIVERSITY -
JAMES HERBERT WHITE LIBRARY - SPECIAL
COLLECTIONS □ Itta Bena, MS

Henderson, Ross M., Campus Libn.
VANCOUVER VOCATIONAL INSTITUTE -
LIBRARY □ Vancouver, BC

Henderson, Ruth, Libn.
CUNY - CITY COLLEGE LIBRARY - MUSIC
LIBRARY □ New York, NY

Henderson, Mrs. S.H., Libn.
TRAVIS AVENUE BAPTIST CHURCH - MAURINE
HENDERSON LIBRARY □ Fort Worth, TX

Henderson, Dr. Sourya, Med.Libn.
AMERICAN CANCER SOCIETY - MEDICAL
LIBRARY □ New York, NY

Hendley, David D., Law Libn.
BETHLEHEM STEEL CORPORATION - BERNARD
D. BROEKER LAW LIBRARY □ Bethlehem, PA

Hendrick, Henrietta, Career Info.Asst.
ROCKLAND COUNTY GUIDANCE CENTER -
LIBRARY □ Nyack, NY

Hendrick, Karen, Ref.Libn.
TEXAS TECH UNIVERSITY - LIBRARY -
DOCUMENTS DEPARTMENT □ Lubbock, TX

Hendricks, D.R., Pres.
HAYES (Stanley W.) RESEARCH FOUNDATION -
LIBRARY □ Richmond, IN

Hendricks, Ms. Epsy Y., Lib.Dir.
ALCORN STATE UNIVERSITY - JOHN DEWEY
BOYD LIBRARY† □ Lorman, MS

Hendricks, Dr. William O., Dir.
SHERMAN RESEARCH LIBRARY □ Corona Del
Mar, CA

Hendrickson, F., Spec.Coll.
WEST TEXAS STATE UNIVERSITY - CORNETTE
LIBRARY - SPECIAL COLLECTIONS □ Canyon,
TX

Hendrickson, Gordon O., Assoc.Dir.
WESTERN HISTORICAL MANUSCRIPT
COLLECTION/STATE HISTORICAL SOCIETY OF
MISSOURI MANUSCRIPTS JOINT COLLECTION
□ Kansas City, MO

Hendrickson, Hope Coppage, Exec.Dir.
CLIVEDEN - LIBRARY □ Philadelphia, PA

Hendrie, Lynn
UNIVERSITY OF CALGARY - SOCIAL SCIENCES
LIBRARY† □ Calgary, AB

Hendrix, Kenneth D., Pres.
SPRINGFIELD HISTORICAL SOCIETY - LIBRARY
□ Springfield, NJ

Hendry, Barbara L., Chf., Tech.Serv.Div.
U.S. AIR FORCE - HISTORICAL RESEARCH
CENTER □ Maxwell AFB, AL

Hendry, Helen I., Libn.
NOVA SCOTIA RESEARCH FOUNDATION
CORPORATION - LIBRARY† □ Dartmouth, NS

Hendsey, Susanne B., Lib.Dir.
U.S. FEDERAL TRADE COMMISSION - LIBRARY
□ Washington, DC

Henexson, Fay, Libn.
CALIFORNIA STATE DEPARTMENT OF JUSTICE
- ATTORNEY GENERAL'S OFFICE - LAW
LIBRARY □ San Diego, CA

Heney, James, Asst.Libn.
GENERAL THEOLOGICAL LIBRARY □ Boston, MA

Hengel, Susan L., Cat.
UNIVERSITY OF PENNSYLVANIA - BIDDLE LAW
LIBRARY □ Philadelphia, PA

Henke, Dan F., Dir.
UNIVERSITY OF CALIFORNIA, SAN FRANCISCO
- HASTINGS COLLEGE OF THE LAW - LEGAL
INFORMATION CENTER □ San Francisco, CA

Henley, Brooke, Chf., Cat.Rec.
SMITHSONIAN INSTITUTION LIBRARIES □
Washington, DC

Henley, Carol, Supv., Tech.Serv.
DIGITAL EQUIPMENT CORPORATION -
MAYNARD AREA INFORMATION SERVICES □
Maynard, MA

Henley, Heather D., Lib.Techn.
SASKATCHEWAN - DEPARTMENT OF SUPPLY &
SERVICES - SYSTEMS CENTRE LIBRARY □
Regina, SK

Henley, J.Brian, Libn.
HAMILTON PUBLIC LIBRARY - SPECIAL
COLLECTIONS □ Hamilton, ON

Henley, James E., Exec.Dir.
SACRAMENTO - MUSEUM AND HISTORY
DIVISION - LIBRARY □ Sacramento, CA

Henley, Juliette J., Act.Hd.Libn.
UNIVERSITY OF ALBERTA - FACULTE ST-JEAN
- BIBLIOTHEQUE □ Edmonton, AB

Hennessey, Gregg, Adm.
SAN DIEGO HISTORICAL SOCIETY - RESEARCH
ARCHIVES □ San Diego, CA

Hennessy, Colm, Circ.Libn.
RUSH-PRESBYTERIAN-ST. LUKE'S MEDICAL
CENTER - LIBRARY OF RUSH UNIVERSITY □
Chicago, IL

Hennigar, Lori, Libn.
MC MILLAN, BINCH - LIBRARY □ Toronto, ON

Henning, Coral, Chf.Asst.Libn.
SAN FRANCISCO LAW LIBRARY □ San Francisco,
CA

Henning, Darrell D., Cur.
NORWEGIAN-AMERICAN MUSEUM -
REFERENCE LIBRARY □ Decorah, IA

Henning, Louise, Asst.Libn.
UNIVERSITY OF WISCONSIN, MADISON -
KOHLER ART LIBRARY □ Madison, WI

Henning, Mary, Libn.
CANFIELD MEMORIAL LIBRARY - RUSSELL
VERMONTIANA COLLECTION □ Arlington, VT

Henning, Neva, Libn.
SPOKANE MEDICAL LIBRARY □ Spokane, WA

Henning, Patricia A., Libn.
GERMANTOWN HISTORICAL SOCIETY -
LIBRARY □ Philadelphia, PA

Henning, William T., Jr., Cur. of Coll.
HUNTER MUSEUM OF ART - REFERENCE
LIBRARY □ Chattanooga, TN

Hennip, Susan, ILL
EDINBORO UNIVERSITY OF PENNSYLVANIA -
BARON-FORNESS LIBRARY □ Edinboro, PA

Hennrich, Christine M., Tech.Info.Sci.
ALUMINUM COMPANY OF AMERICA - ALCOA
TECHNICAL CENTER - INFORMATION
DEPARTMENT □ Alcoa Center, PA

Henri, Muriel, Libn.
INDUSTRIAL GRAIN PRODUCTS, LTD. -
RESEARCH & DEVELOPMENT LIBRARY† □
Montreal, PQ

Henrich, Paul C., Sr. Law Libn.
NEW YORK STATE SUPREME COURT - 2ND
JUDICIAL DISTRICT - LAW LIBRARY □
Brooklyn, NY

Henrichs, Virginia, Libn.
CHICAGO BOTANIC GARDEN - LIBRARY □
Glencoe, IL

Henricks, Duane, Govt.Doc.Libn.
ST. MARY'S UNIVERSITY - LAW LIBRARY† □
San Antonio, TX

Henriksen, Astrid, Libn.
CHARLESTON EVENING POST/NEWS AND
COURIER - LIBRARY □ Charleston, SC

Henrikson, Gregor, Prof.Asst.
MINNEAPOLIS PUBLIC LIBRARY &
INFORMATION CENTER - SOCIOLOGY
DEPARTMENT □ Minneapolis, MN

Henry, Alice C., Asst.Dir.
WISCONSIN INFORMATION SERVICE □
Milwaukee, WI

Henry, Carla R., Libn.
CLARION COUNTY HISTORICAL SOCIETY -
LIBRARY/MUSEUM □ Clarion, PA

Henry, Diane, Hd.Libn.
CAMBRIAN COLLEGE OF APPLIED ARTS AND
TECHNOLOGY - LEARNING RESOURCES CENTRE
□ Sudbury, ON

Henry, Diane, Asst.Chf.
DISTRICT OF COLUMBIA PUBLIC LIBRARY -
TECHNOLOGY AND SCIENCE DIVISION □
Washington, DC

Henry, Jean B., Co-Libn.
ALASKA STATE LEGISLATURE/LEGISLATIVE
AFFAIRS AGENCY - REFERENCE LIBRARY □
Juneau, AK

Henry, Judy G., Libn.
ST. JOSEPH'S HOSPITAL - MEDICAL LIBRARY □
Savannah, GA

Henry, Karen, Community Serv.Spec.
U.S. BUREAU OF THE CENSUS - INFORMATION
SERVICES PROGRAM - DETROIT REGIONAL
OFFICE - INFORMATION CENTER □ Detroit, MI

Henry, Dr. M.L., Jr., Exec.Dir.
FUND FOR MODERN COURTS - LIBRARY □ New
York, NY

Henry, Marcia, Libn.
ENVIRONMENTAL RESEARCH & TECHNOLOGY,
INC. - WESTERN REGIONAL OFFICE - LIBRARY
□ Newbury Park, CA

Henry, Nancy J., Hd.Libn.
ROOKS, PITTS, FULLAGAR & POUST - LIBRARY
□ Chicago, IL

Henry, Patricia W., Supv. of Intern Trng.
U.S. ARMY - HEADQUARTERS TRADOC/FORT
MONROE LIBRARY & INTERN TRAINING
CENTER □ Ft. Monroe, VA

Henry, Paula M., Acq.Libn.
SUNY - COLLEGE AT GENESEO - COLLEGE
LIBRARIES □ Geneseo, NY

Henry, Renee, Musm.Dir.
BARTHOLOMEW COUNTY HISTORICAL
SOCIETY LIBRARY □ Columbus, IN

Henry, Ruth, Int.Doc.Coord.
BELL COMMUNICATIONS RESEARCH, INC. -
INFORMATION RESOURCES SERVICES CENTER
□ Morristown, NJ

Henry, Sharon, Dp.Libn.
INTERNATIONAL DEVELOPMENT RESEARCH
CENTRE - LIBRARY† □ Ottawa, ON

Henry, Sr. Teresa Marie, D.C., Asst.Dir.
DE PAUL HEALTH CENTER - MEDICAL LIBRARY
□ Bridgeton, MO

Hensel, Nancy, Hist. of Med.Libn.
MAYO FOUNDATION - MAYO CLINIC LIBRARY □
Rochester, MN

Hensel, Sue, Children's Libn.
CAMBRIA LIBRARY ASSOCIATION -
PRESCHOOL ADVENTURE LIBRARY □
Johnstown, PA

Henshall, Barbara, Cur.
MARTIN AND OSA JOHNSON SAFARI MUSEUM -
STOTT EXPLORERS LIBRARY □ Chanute, KS

Hensley, Paul B., Archv.
DU PONT (Henry Francis) WINTERTHUR
MUSEUM - LIBRARY □ Winterthur, DE

Henson, Clara, Lib.Asst.
PFIZER, INC. - N.Y.O. LIBRARY □ New York, NY

Henson, Mrs. Gena R., Film Libn.
MISSISSIPPI STATE DEPARTMENT OF HEALTH
- AUDIOVISUAL LIBRARY □ Jackson, MS

Henson, Gloria, Dept.Hd.
SPOHN HOSPITAL - MEDICAL LIBRARY □ Corpus
Christi, TX

Henson, Kristin E., Ref.Libn.
ALUMINUM COMPANY OF AMERICA -
CORPORATE LIBRARY □ Pittsburgh, PA

Henson, Llewellyn L., Dir.
FLORIDA INSTITUTE OF TECHNOLOGY -
LIBRARY □ Melbourne, FL

Heppell, Shirley G., Libn.
CORTLAND COUNTY HISTORICAL SOCIETY -
LIBRARY □ Cortland, NY

Herald, Andrew, Sr. Indexer
KENTON COUNTY PUBLIC LIBRARY -
KENTUCKY & LOCAL HISTORY DEPARTMENT □
Covington, KY

Herbert, Faith M., Lib.Techn.
ORANGE COUNTY DEPARTMENT OF
EDUCATION - LIBRARY □ Santa Ana, CA

Herbert, Teri Lynn, Libn.
UNIVERSITY OF GEORGIA - SKIDAWAY
INSTITUTE OF OCEANOGRAPHY - LIBRARY □
Savannah, GA

Herdendorf, Charles E., Dir.
OHIO STATE UNIVERSITY - CENTER FOR LAKE
ERIE AREA RESEARCH - LAKE ERIE PROGRAM
LIBRARY □ Columbus, OH

Herdman, Elena, Supv., Tech.Serv.
STANDARD OIL COMPANY OF CALIFORNIA -
CORPORATE LIBRARY □ San Francisco, CA

Herfurth, Sharon, Grants Libn.
DALLAS PUBLIC LIBRARY - URBAN
INFORMATION CENTER □ Dallas, TX

Heriot, Ruthanne, Spec.Coll.Libn.
U.S. NATL. PARK SERVICE - HARPERS FERRY
CENTER LIBRARY □ Harpers Ferry, WV

Herkes, Norma T., Hd.
HAWAII STATE LIBRARY - FEDERAL
DOCUMENTS SECTION □ Honolulu, HI

Herman, Dorothy W., Libn.
MARLBOROUGH GALLERY - LIBRARY □ New
York, NY

Herman, Georgianna, Libn. & Supv.
UNIVERSITY OF MINNESOTA - INDUSTRIAL
RELATIONS CENTER - REFERENCE ROOM □
Minneapolis, MN

Herman, L., Libn.
TOUCHE ROSS AND COMPANY - LIBRARY □
Calgary, AB

Herman, L., Libn.
TOUCHE ROSS AND COMPANY - LIBRARY □
Calgary, AB

Herman, Linda E., Spec.Coll.Libn.
CALIFORNIA STATE UNIVERSITY, FULLERTON -
COLLECTION FOR THE HISTORY OF
CARTOGRAPHY† □ Fullerton, CA

Herman, Margaret, Asst.Dir., Acq.
ILLINOIS STATE LIBRARY □ Springfield, IL

Herman, Miriam, Lib.Techn.
UNIVERSITY OF TORONTO - INSTITUTE OF
CHILD STUDY - LIBRARY □ Toronto, ON

Hermann, Ann M., Dir.
STAMFORD HISTORICAL SOCIETY - LIBRARY □
Stamford, CT

Hermesch, Monica, Chf.Libn.
TRAVENOL LABORATORIES, INC. - HYLAND
DIVISION - RESEARCH LIBRARY □ Duarte, CA

Hernandez, Alberto H., Hd.Libn.
CONSERVATORIO DE MUSICA DE PUERTO
RICO - BIBLIOTECA □ Hato Rey, PR

Hernandez, Edna, Libn.
CALIFORNIA STATE DEPARTMENT OF HEALTH
SERVICES - VECTOR BIOLOGY AND CONTROL
SECTION - LIBRARY □ Berkeley, CA

Hernandez, Esther Rosario, Libn.
PUERTO RICO - DEPARTMENT OF HEALTH -
MEDICAL LIBRARY □ San Juan, PR

Hernandez, Jo Farb, Dir.
TRITON MUSEUM OF ART - LIBRARY □ Santa
Clara, CA

Hernandez, John, Info.Serv.Spec.
U.S. BUREAU OF THE CENSUS - INFORMATION
SERVICES PROGRAM - LOS ANGELES REGIONAL
OFFICE - LIBRARY □ Los Angeles, CA

Hernandez, Marilyn J., Coord. of Info.Rsrcs.
MANITOBA - DEPARTMENT OF HEALTH -
INFORMATION RESOURCES □ Winnipeg, MB

Hernandez, Tamsen M., Dir.
CONFERENCE BOARD, INC. - INFORMATION
SERVICE □ New York, NY

Heron, Carol, Cat.Libn.
PARSONS SCHOOL OF DESIGN - OTIS ART
INSTITUTE - LIBRARY □ Los Angeles, CA

Heron, Carol, Tech.Serv.
WHITTIER COLLEGE - SCHOOL OF LAW -
LIBRARY □ Los Angeles, CA

Heron, David W., Hd., Rd.Serv.
STANFORD UNIVERSITY - HOOVER
INSTITUTION ON WAR, REVOLUTION AND
PEACE - LIBRARY □ Stanford, CA

Heroux, Genevieve, Lib.Techn.
ABBOTT LABORATORIES, LTD. - COMPANY
LIBRARY □ Montreal, PQ

Heroux, Mr. Rejean, Chf., Tech.Serv.
CANADA - SECRETARY OF STATE -
TRANSLATION BUREAU - DOCUMENTATION
DIRECTORATE† □ Ottawa, ON

Heroux-Bouchard, Helene, Bibliotechnicienne
HOPITAL DU HAUT-RICHELIEU -
BIBLIOTHEQUE MEDICALE □ St-Jean, PQ

Herperger, Mr. D., Staff Archv.
SASKATCHEWAN ARCHIVES BOARD □ Regina,
SK

Herr, Marcianne, Cur. of Educ.
AKRON ART MUSEUM - LIBRARY □ Akron, OH

Herrera, Deborah D., Ref.Libn.
SETON HALL UNIVERSITY - SCHOOL OF LAW -
LAW LIBRARY □ Newark, NJ

Herrgesell, Ron, Libn.
AGWAY, INC. - CORPORATE LIBRARY □
Syracuse, NY

Herring, Rebecca, Asst.Archv.
TEXAS TECH UNIVERSITY - SOUTHWEST
COLLECTION □ Lubbock, TX

Herrling, Ricki, Libn.
AMERICAN ASSOCIATION OF OCCUPATIONAL
HEALTH NURSES - LIBRARY □ Atlanta, GA

Herrmann, Gretchen, Soc.Sci.Ref.-Bibliog.
SUNY - COLLEGE AT CORTLAND - MEMORIAL
LIBRARY □ Cortland, NY

Herrmann, Loretta, Libn.
NEWMONT MINING CORPORATION -
TECHNICAL ENGINEERING LIBRARY □ New
York, NY

Herrmann, Vicki R., Libn.
U.S. BUREAU OF ALCOHOL, TOBACCO AND
FIREARMS - REFERENCE LIBRARY □
Washington, DC

Herron, Carol, Asst. to the Cur.
COPLEY PRESS, INC. - THE JAMES S. COPLEY
LIBRARY □ La Jolla, CA

Herron, Margie E., Dir. of Field Serv.
SOUTH CAROLINA STATE LIBRARY □ Columbia,
SC

Herschman, Judith, Ref.Libn.
UNIVERSITY OF CALIFORNIA, SAN DIEGO -
UNIVERSITY LIBRARIES □ La Jolla, CA

Hershaft, Dr. Alex, Libn.
VEGETARIAN INFORMATION SERVICE, INC. -
INFORMATION CENTER □ Bethesda MD

Hershbell, Prof. Jackson, Libn.
UNIVERSITY OF MINNESOTA - CLASSICS
DEPARTMENT - SEMINAR LIBRARY □
Minneapolis, MN

Hershberger, J. Richard, Assoc. Minister
WESTMINSTER PRESBYTERIAN CHURCH -
LIBRARY □ Oklahoma City, OK

Hershcopf, Marian, Libn.
COLORADO (State) DIVISION OF WILDLIFE -
RESEARCH CENTER LIBRARY □ Fort Collins, CO

Hershey, Robert A., Dir./State Geologist
TENNESSEE STATE DEPARTMENT OF
CONSERVATION - DIVISION OF GEOLOGY -
CONSERVATION RESOURCE CENTER □
Nashville, TN

Hertel, Maureen, Adm.Mgr.
WATER QUALITY ASSOCIATION - RESEARCH
COUNCIL LIBRARY □ Lisle, IL

Hertel, Ute, Rec.Mgr./Libn.
WOODWARD-CLYDE CONSULTANTS -
LIBRARY/INFORMATION CENTER □ Santa Ana,
CA

Hertz, J. Shalom, Cur.
JEWISH LABOR BUND - BUND ARCHIVES OF
THE JEWISH LABOR MOVEMENT □ New York,
NY

Hertzler, Mrs. James, Chm., Lib.Comm.
CUMBERLAND COUNTY HISTORICAL SOCIETY
& HAMILTON LIBRARY □ Carlisle, PA

Hertzsprung, Colleen, Pub.Serv.Libn.
PRAIRIE BIBLE INSTITUTE - LIBRARY □ Three
Hills, AB

Herzberg, Elsie, Chf. of Circ.Dept.
YESHIVA UNIVERSITY - ALBERT EINSTEIN
COLLEGE OF MEDICINE - D. SAMUEL
GOTTESMAN LIBRARY □ Bronx, NY

Herzberg, Lois, Ref.Libn.
YONKERS PUBLIC LIBRARY - FINE ARTS
DEPARTMENT □ Yonkers, NY

Herzceg, C., Sr.Info.Spec.
ALLERGAN PHARMACEUTICALS, INC. -
MEDICAL & SCIENCE INFORMATION □ Irvine,
CA

Herzfeldt, Patricia D., Supv., Med.Rec.
OBICI (Louise) MEMORIAL HOSPITAL - LIBRARY
□ Suffolk, VA

Herzog, Diana E., Vice Pres.
SMYTHE (R.M.) AND COMPANY - OBSOLETE
AND INACTIVE SECURITIES LIBRARY □ New
York, NY

Herzog, Kandace, Libn.
FARM JOURNAL, INC. - MARKETING RESEARCH
LIBRARY □ Philadelphia, PA

Herzog, Susan, Libn.
THOMAS, SNELL, JAMISON, RUSSELL,
WILLIAMSON AND ASPERGER - LIBRARY □
Fresno, CA

Herzstein, Barbara B., Libn.
HABITAT INSTITUTE - NATURAL HISTORY
LIBRARY □ Belmont, MA

Heseltine, Inez, Asst.Dir.
CANADA - NATIONAL RESEARCH COUNCIL -
CANADA INSTITUTE FOR SCIENTIFIC AND
TECHNICAL INFORMATION (CISTI) □ Ottawa,
ON

Heslin, Catherine M., Info.Sci.
WILLIAM H. RORER, INC. - RESEARCH LIBRARY
□ Fort Washington, PA

Hess, Clare Marie, Hd.Libn.
OXFORD UNIVERSITY PRESS, INC. - LIBRARY □
New York, NY

Hess, Gertrude D., Libn.
HISTORICAL SOCIETY OF HADDONFIELD -
LIBRARY □ Haddonfield, NJ

Hess, J. William, Assoc.Dir.
ROCKEFELLER UNIVERSITY - ROCKEFELLER
ARCHIVE CENTER □ North Tarrytown, NY

Hess, Jane S., Hd., Tech.Lib.Br.
U.S. NASA - LANGLEY RESEARCH CENTER -
TECHNICAL LIBRARY MS 185† □ Hampton, VA

Hess, Joyce, Art
UNIVERSITY OF TEXAS, AUSTIN - FINE ARTS
LIBRARY □ Austin, TX

Hess, M. Cathern, Asst.Hd.Libn.
INDIANAPOLIS NEWSPAPERS, INC. -
INDIANAPOLIS STAR AND INDIANAPOLIS
NEWS - REFERENCE LIBRARY □ Indianapolis, IN

Hess, Mary E., Asst.Libn.
TOURO INFIRMARY - HOSPITAL LIBRARY
SERVICES □ New Orleans, LA

Hess, Robert, Info.Off.
CENTER FOR NONPROFIT ORGANIZATIONS,
INC. - LIBRARY □ New York, NY

Hess, Stanley W., Libn.
NELSON-ATKINS MUSEUM OF ART - SPENCER
ART REFERENCE LIBRARY □ Kansas City, MO

Hess, Stephen H., Dir.
UNIVERSITY OF UTAH - INSTRUCTIONAL
MEDIA SERVICES □ Salt Lake City, UT

Hesse, John A., Assoc.Cur.
MEMPHIS STATE UNIVERSITY LIBRARIES -
C.H. NASH MUSEUM LIBRARY □ Memphis, TN

Hesse, Sharon, Off.Mgr.
CENTER FOR SOUTHERN FOLKLORE -
ARCHIVES □ Memphis, TN

Hessel, Carolyn S., Coord.
JEWISH EDUCATION SERVICE OF NORTH
AMERICA, INC. - NATIONAL EDUCATIONAL
RESOURCE CENTER □ New York, NY

Hesselberth, Wanda, Lib.Coord.
MC FARLAND MENTAL HEALTH CENTER -
STAFF LIBRARY □ Springfield, IL

Hested, Elayne
"I LIKE MYSELF" EARLY CHILDHOOD & FAMILY
EDUCATION PROGRAM - TOY LENDING
LIBRARY □ Fairmont, MN

Hester, Helen, Libn.
CENTRAL VIRGINIA TRAINING CENTER -
PROFESSIONAL LIBRARY □ Lynchburg, VA

Hester, Leslie, Ref.Libn.
NEVADA STATE LIBRARY □ Carson City, NV

Hester, Ralph, Tech.Info.Spec.
NATIONAL INSTITUTE OF ENVIRONMENTAL
HEALTH SCIENCES - LIBRARY □ Research
Triangle Park, NC

Hesz, Mrs. Bianka M., Med.Libn.
UNIVERSITY OF PITTSBURGH -
PRESBYTERIAN-UNIVERSITY HOSPITAL -
MEDICAL STAFF LIBRARY □ Pittsburgh, PA

Hettinger, Susan F., Hd.
PUBLIC LIBRARY OF CINCINNATI AND
HAMILTON COUNTY - EDUCATION AND
RELIGION DEPARTMENT □ Cincinnati, OH

Hetu, Sylvie, Libn.
UNIVERSITE DE MONTREAL - CENTRE DE
RECHERCHE SUR LES TRANSPORTS -
DOCUMENTATION CENTRE □ Montreal, PQ

Hetzler, Rosemary, Hist.-Libn.
PIONEERS' MUSEUM - LIBRARY AND ARCHIVES
□ Colorado Springs, CO

Hetzner, Bernice M., Hist. of NE Med.
UNIVERSITY OF NEBRASKA MEDICAL CENTER -
MC GOOGAN LIBRARY OF MEDICINE □ Omaha,
NE

Heuer, Barry, Libn.
NOOTER CORPORATION - TECHNICAL LIBRARY
□ St. Louis, MO

Heureux, Suzanne
QUEBEC PROVINCE - COMMISSION DE LA
SANTE ET DE LA SECURITE DU TRAVAIL -
CENTRE DE DOCUMENTATION □ Montreal, PQ

Heuser, Frederic, Archv.
PRESBYTERIAN CHURCH (U.S.A.) -
PRESBYTERIAN HISTORICAL SOCIETY -
LIBRARY □ Philadelphia, PA

Heusner, Carol, Libn.
STERLING DRUG, INC. - HILTON-DAVIS
CHEMICAL COMPANY DIVISION - LIBRARY □
Cincinnati, OH

Heusser, Dolly, Exec.Sec./Treas.
NATL. ASSN. OF PRIVATE, NONTRADITIONAL
SCHOOLS & COLLEGES - ACCREDITING
COMMN. ON POSTSECONDARY EDUC. - LIB. □
Grand Junction, CO

Heusser, H. Earl, Ed.D., Exec.Dir.
NATL. ASSN. OF PRIVATE, NONTRADITIONAL
SCHOOLS & COLLEGES - ACCREDITING
COMMN. ON POSTSECONDARY EDUC. - LIB. □
Grand Junction, CO

Hevey, Kathleen G., Municipal Ref.Coord.
VIRGINIA BEACH PUBLIC LIBRARY SYSTEM -
MUNICIPAL REFERENCE LIBRARY □ Virginia
Beach, VA

Hewings, Margot, Hd.
METROPOLITAN TORONTO LIBRARY -
MUNICIPAL REFERENCE DEPARTMENT □
Toronto, ON

Hewison, Nancy, Hd.Ref.Libn.
OREGON HEALTH SCIENCES UNIVERSITY -
LIBRARY □ Portland, OR

Hewitt, Fran, ILL
ALBERTA - DEPARTMENT OF AGRICULTURE -
LIBRARY □ Edmonton, AB

Hewitt, Helen, Med.Lib.Tech.
VICTORY MEMORIAL HOSPITAL - MEDICAL
LIBRARY □ Waukegan, IL

Hewitt, Jan, Mktg.Info.Spec.
LEVI STRAUSS & COMPANY - CORPORATE
MARKETING INFORMATION CENTER† □ San
Francisco, CA

Hewitt, Julia F., Mgr.
GENERAL ELECTRIC COMPANY - MAIN
LIBRARY □ Schenectady, NY

Hewitt, Margaret W., Dir.
NORTHWEST CHRISTIAN COLLEGE - LEARNING
RESOURCE CENTER □ Eugene, OR

Hewitt, Raymond G., Dir. of Res.
RHODE ISLAND PUBLIC EXPENDITURE
COUNCIL - LIBRARY □ Providence, RI

Hewlett, Carol C., Libn.
MUNICIPAL TECHNICAL ADVISORY SERVICE -
LIBRARY □ Knoxville, TN

Hewlings, Charlotte H., Libn.
DELAWARE COUNTY LAW LIBRARY □ Media, PA

Heyck, H., SDI Libn.
CANADA - TRANSPORT CANADA - LIBRARY &
INFORMATION CENTRE □ Ottawa, ON

Heyd, Michael, Dir.
WILLIAMSPORT HOSPITAL - LEARNING
RESOURCES CENTER □ Williamsport, PA

Heyer, Mr. Terry L., Lib.Dir.
L.D.S. HOSPITAL - LIBRARY □ Salt Lake City, UT

Heyman, Reba R., Info.Spec.
FOI SERVICES, INC. - LIBRARY □ Rockville, MD

Heyum, Renee, Cur.
UNIVERSITY OF HAWAII - SPECIAL
COLLECTIONS - PACIFIC COLLECTION □
Honolulu, HI

Hiatt, Denise, Sec.
SETON, JOHNSON & ODELL, INC. - TECHNICAL
INFORMATION CENTER □ Portland, OR

Hibbard, R. Ashley, Asst.Libn.
NEW YORK STATE DEPARTMENT OF LABOR -
LIBRARY □ New York, NY

Hibbard, Richard L., Dir.
GLENVIEW AREA HISTORICAL SOCIETY -
LIBRARY □ Glenview, IL

Hibbeler, Sara J., Asst.Libn.
SHOOK, HARDY & BACON - LIBRARY □ Kansas
City, MO

Hibberd, Cynthia, Info.Spec.
ARTHUR D. LITTLE, INC. - MANAGEMENT
LIBRARY† □ Cambridge, MA

Hibbs, A.A., Jr., Mgr.
ADAMS ADVERTISING AGENCY, INC. -
LIBRARY □ Chicago, IL

Hibpshman, Lawrence E., State Archv.
SOUTH DAKOTA STATE LIBRARY & ARCHIVES -
SOUTH DAKOTA STATE ARCHIVES □ Pierre, SD

Hick, Sharon, Assoc.Libn.
ROYAL ONTARIO MUSEUM - LIBRARY† □
Toronto, ON

Hickerson, H. Thomas, Chm.
CORNELL UNIVERSITY - DEPARTMENT OF
MANUSCRIPTS AND UNIVERSITY ARCHIVES □
Ithaca, NY

Hickerson, Joseph C., Hd.
LIBRARY OF CONGRESS - AMERICAN FOLKLIFE
CENTER - ARCHIVE OF FOLK CULTURE □
Washington, DC

Hickey, Colleen M., S.S.J., Assoc.Dir.
UNIVERSITY OF DETROIT - SCHOOL OF LAW
LIBRARY □ Detroit, MI

Hickey, Damon D., Assoc.Lib.Dir./Cur.
GUILFORD COLLEGE - LIBRARY - SPECIAL
COLLECTIONS □ Greensboro, NC

Hickey, James T., Cur., Lincoln Coll.
ILLINOIS STATE HISTORICAL LIBRARY □
Springfield, IL

Hickey, Kate D., Dir., Lib.Serv.
WILLIAMSPORT AREA COMMUNITY COLLEGE -
SLOAN FINE ARTS LIBRARY □ Williamsport, PA

Hickey, Margaret, Libn.
U.S. SMALL BUSINESS ADMINISTRATION -
REFERENCE LIBRARY □ Washington, DC

Hickling, Jeanne, Libn.
INDIANA INSTITUTE OF TECHNOLOGY - MC
MILLEN LIBRARY □ Fort Wayne, IN

Hicks, Anita, Tech.Libn.
HITCO - TECHNICAL LIBRARY □ Gardena, CA

Hicks, Anne, Cat.
WINNIPEG SCHOOL DIVISION NO. 1 -
TEACHERS LIBRARY AND RESOURCE CENTRE □
Winnipeg, MB

Hicks, Audrey K., Staff Archv.
BLUE EARTH COUNTY HISTORICAL SOCIETY -
MUSEUM ARCHIVES □ Mankato, MN

Hicks, Cathy, Libn.
KENTUCKY SCHOOL FOR THE BLIND - LIBRARY
□ Louisville, KY

Hicks, Dorthea, Info.Spec.
HENKEL CORPORATION - HENNEPIN
TECHNICAL CENTER LIBRARY □ Minneapolis,
MN

Hicks, Frances P., Info.Anl.
SOUTHWEST RESEARCH INSTITUTE -
NONDESTRUCTIVE TESTING INFORMATION
ANALYSIS CENTER □ San Antonio, TX

Hicks, Garnet, Assoc.Mgr.
BELL COMMUNICATIONS TECHNICAL
EDUCATION CENTER - LEARNING RESOURCE
CENTER □ Lisle, IL

Hicks, Marilyn, Bus.Libn.
UNIVERSITY OF WISCONSIN, MADISON -
WILLIAM A. SCOTT BUSINESS LIBRARY □
Madison, WI

Hicks, Paul, Asst.Libn.
INDIANA UNIVERSITY OF PENNSYLVANIA -
UNIVERSITY LIBRARY □ Indiana, PA

Hicks, Pauline, Assoc.Univ.Libn.
FLORIDA A&M UNIVERSITY - PHARMACY
LIBRARY □ Tallahassee, FL

Hickson, Charlotte A., Libn. & Chm., Acq.
TEXAS TECH UNIVERSITY - LIBRARY □
Lubbock, TX

Hickson, Irene, Cat.
POWELL, GOLDSTEIN, FRAZER & MURPHY -
LIBRARY □ Atlanta, GA

Hiddinga, Sally A., Br.Lib.Ck.
MICHIGAN STATE UNIVERSITY - MICROFORMS
LIBRARY □ East Lansing, MI

Hidy, Paula, Ref.Libn.
OHIO STATE SUPREME COURT LAW LIBRARY □
Columbus, OH

Hieb, Louis A., Hd.Libn.
UNIVERSITY OF ARIZONA - SPECIAL
COLLECTIONS DEPARTMENT† □ Tucson, AZ

Hieb, Roland D., Exec.Dir.
NATIONAL CABLE TELEVISION INSTITUTE -
LIBRARY □ Denver, CO

Hiestand, John P., Libn.
UNIVERSITY OF CINCINNATI - OMI COLLEGE
OF APPLIED SCIENCE - TIMOTHY C. DAY
TECHNICAL LIBRARY □ Cincinnati, OH

Hifner, William, Libn.
WASHINGTON POST - LIBRARY □ Washington,
DC

Higby, Helen E., Lib.Dev.Off.
WYOMING STATE LIBRARY □ Cheyenne, WY

Higdon, Mary Ann, Libn. & Chm., Doc.
TEXAS TECH UNIVERSITY - LIBRARY □
Lubbock, TX

Higdon, Mary Ann, Doc.Libn.
TEXAS TECH UNIVERSITY - LIBRARY -
DOCUMENTS DEPARTMENT □ Lubbock, TX

Higdon, Thomas D., Libn.
UNIVERSITY OF ARIZONA - ARIZONA HEALTH
SCIENCES CENTER LIBRARY □ Tucson, AZ

Higginbotham, Jay, Local Hist.Spec.
MOBILE PUBLIC LIBRARY - SPECIAL
COLLECTIONS DIVISION □ Mobile, AL

Higginbotham, Susan B., Med.Libn.
LUTHERAN MEDICAL CENTER - MEDICAL
LIBRARY □ Wheat Ridge, CO

Higgins, Bertha, Coord., Tech.Serv.
NOVA SCOTIA - PROVINCIAL LIBRARY □
Halifax, NS

Higgins, Clare, Sci.Libn.
PRATT INSTITUTE - LIBRARY □ Brooklyn, NY

Higgins, James, Ref.Libn.
INSTITUTE FOR DEFENSE ANALYSES -
TECHNICAL INFORMATION SERVICES □
Alexandria, VA

Higgins, Karen, Assoc.Dir.
JOHNS HOPKINS UNIVERSITY - WILLIAM H.
WELCH MEDICAL LIBRARY □ Baltimore, MD

Higgins, Larry H., Mgr., Educ.
MEAD JOHNSON AND COMPANY - MEAD
JOHNSON INSTITUTE - LIBRARY □ Evansville,
IN

Higgins, Matthew J., Asst. State Libn.
NEW HAMPSHIRE STATE LIBRARY □ Concord,
NH

Higgins, Norma, Spec.Coll.Tech.Spec.
ALFRED UNIVERSITY - HERRICK MEMORIAL
LIBRARY - OPENHYM COLLECTION □ Alfred, NY

Higgins, Norma B., Univ.Archv.
ALFRED UNIVERSITY - HERRICK MEMORIAL
LIBRARY - SPECIAL COLLECTIONS □ Alfred, NY

Higgins, Susan, LCDC
CANADA - HEALTH AND WELFARE CANADA -
LIBRARY SERVICES □ Ottawa, ON

Higgins, Vicky L., Dir., Med.Rec.
DEAF SMITH GENERAL HOSPITAL - LIBRARY □
Hereford, TX

Higginson, M., Lib.Asst.
CIP RESEARCH LTD. - LIBRARY □ Hawkesbury,
ON

Higgs, Norman C., Libn.
MACON COUNTY LAW LIBRARY □ Decatur, IL

Higgs, Patricia V., Supv.
INSTITUTE OF EARLY AMERICAN HISTORY
AND CULTURE - KELLOCK LIBRARY □
Williamsburg, VA

High, Walter M., Hd. Monographic Cat.
NORTH CAROLINA STATE UNIVERSITY - D.H.
HILL LIBRARY □ Raleigh, NC

Highfill, Karen, Libn.
INSTITUTE OF AMERICAN INDIAN ARTS -
LIBRARY □ Santa Fe, NM

Hihn, Nerisha, Asst.Libn.
BROWN & CALDWELL - LIBRARY □ Walnut
Creek, CA

Hijek, Barbara, Health Sci.Libn.
BAYFRONT MEDICAL CENTER, INC. - HEALTH
SCIENCES LIBRARY □ St. Petersburg, FL

Hiland, Emelyn L., Lib.Mgr.
PROCTER & GAMBLE COMPANY - MIAMI
VALLEY LABORATORIES - TECHNICAL LIBRARY
□ Cincinnati, OH

Hiland, Rev. Gerard P., Dir.
ARCHDIOCESE OF CINCINNATI - ARCHIVES □
Cincinnati, OH

Hilarius, MiMi, Media Ctr.Coord.
ZOOLOGICAL SOCIETY OF CINCINNATI -
MEDIA CENTER □ Cincinnati, OH

Hildebrand, Janice, Libn.
SHEBOYGAN PRESS LIBRARY □ Sheboygan, WI

Hildebrand, Karen, Libn.
CALIFORNIA SCHOOL OF PROFESSIONAL
PSYCHOLOGY - BERKELEY LIBRARY □ Berkeley,
CA

Hildebrand, N. Louise, Tech.Info.Spec./Acq.
U.S. DEFENSE MAPPING AGENCY - AEROSPACE
CENTER - TECHNICAL LIBRARY □ St. Louis, MO

Hildebrandt, Myers, Mgr.
UNIVERSITY OF WASHINGTON - COMPUTING
INFORMATION CENTER □ Seattle, WA

Hildebrandt, Rudolph, Cartographer
U.S. GEOLOGICAL SURVEY - NATL.
CARTOGRAPHIC INFORMATION CENTER
(NCIC) □ Denver, CO

Hildebrant, Kevin, Chf.Instr.
NATIONAL OUTDOOR LEADERSHIP SCHOOL -
OUTDOOR EDUCATION RESOURCE LIBRARY □
Lander, WY

Hildreth, John L., Supv.Rec.Libn.
NEW YORK PUBLIC LIBRARY - GENERAL
LIBRARY OF THE PERFORMING ARTS □ New
York, NY

Hildreth, Mildred, Ref.Libn.
MARSHALL UNIVERSITY - SCHOOL OF
MEDICINE - HEALTH SCIENCE LIBRARIES □
Huntington, WV

Hilford, Janet, Libn.
ORANGE COUNTY ENVIRONMENTAL
MANAGEMENT AGENCY - EMA LIBRARY □ Santa
Ana, CA

Hilgert, Earle, Coll.Dev.
MC CORMICK THEOLOGICAL SEMINARY -
LIBRARY† □ Chicago, IL

Hilgert, Elvire R., Libn.
MC CORMICK THEOLOGICAL SEMINARY -
LIBRARY† □ Chicago, IL

Hilgert, Dr. W. Earle, Act.Libn.
JESUIT SCHOOL OF THEOLOGY IN CHICAGO -
LIBRARY† □ Chicago, IL

Hilke, Mary, Exec.Sec. & Cur.
KOOCHICHING COUNTY HISTORICAL SOCIETY
- MUSEUM □ International Falls, MN

Hilker, Emerson, Hd.
WAYNE STATE UNIVERSITY - SCIENCE
LIBRARY □ Detroit, MI

Hilkey, Carol L., Info. Data Spec.
ITT CORPORATION - AEROSPACE/OPTICAL
DIVISION - INFORMATION SERVICES CENTER
□ Fort Wayne, IN

Hilkey, Marion, Libn.
U.S. NATL. PARK SERVICE - ZION NATL. PARK -
LIBRARY □ Springdale, UT

Hill, Amelita, User Serv.
ERIC CLEARINGHOUSE ON RURAL EDUCATION
AND SMALL SCHOOLS □ Las Cruces, NM

Hill, Barbara, Dir./Trustee
PROSPEROS - LIBRARY □ El Monte, CA

Hill, Barbara M., Libn.
MASSACHUSETTS COLLEGE OF PHARMACY &
ALLIED HEALTH SCIENCES - SHEPPARD
LIBRARY □ Boston, MA

Hill, Barbarie
UNIVERSITY AFFILIATED CINCINNATI CENTER
FOR DEVELOPMENTAL DISORDERS - RESEARCH
LIBRARY □ Cincinnati, OH

Hill, Betty, Archv.
U.S. NATL. ARCHIVES & RECORDS SERVICE -
STILL PICTURE BRANCH □ Washington, DC

Hill, Brad S., Cur., Lowy Coll.
NATIONAL LIBRARY OF CANADA - RARE BOOK
DIVISION □ Ottawa, ON

Hill, Carolyn F., Med.Libn.
BOCA RATON COMMUNITY HOSPITAL - HEALTH
SCIENCES LIBRARY □ Boca Raton, FL

Hill, Deane W., Dir.
UNIVERSITY OF WISCONSIN, MADISON -
SCHOOL OF EDUCATION - INSTRUCTIONAL
MATERIALS CENTER □ Madison, WI

Hill, Diane E., Media Libn.
SUNY - UPSTATE MEDICAL CENTER LIBRARY □
Syracuse, NY

Hill, Dorothy, Hd., Acq.
MOUNT SINAI SCHOOL OF MEDICINE OF THE
CITY UNIVERSITY OF NEW YORK - GUSTAVE L.
& JANET W. LEVY LIBRARY □ New York, NY

Hill, Edwin L., Spec.Coll.Libn.
UNIVERSITY OF WISCONSIN, LA CROSSE -
CENTER FOR CONTEMPORARY POETRY □ La
Crosse, WI

Hill, Eleanor, ILL Libn.
RUSH-PRESBYTERIAN-ST. LUKE'S MEDICAL
CENTER - LIBRARY OF RUSH UNIVERSITY □
Chicago, IL

Hill, Elizabeth C., Info.Spec.
CELANESE PLASTICS & SPECIALTIES COMPANY
- TECHNICAL CENTER - RESEARCH LIBRARY □
Jeffersontown, KY

Hill, Frances B., Libn.
THE BICKELHAUPT ARBORETUM - EDUCATION
CENTER □ Clinton, IA

Hill, Gary, Ref.Libn.
BRIGHAM YOUNG UNIVERSITY - J. REUBEN
CLARK LAW SCHOOL LIBRARY □ Provo, UT

Hill, Hazel, Acq.
JOHN MARSHALL LAW SCHOOL - LIBRARY □
Chicago, IL

Hill, Helen, Libn.
SOCIETY OF MANAGEMENT ACCOUNTANTS OF
CANADA - RESOURCE CENTRE □ Hamilton, ON

Hill, Howard, Hd.Cat.
WESTERN OREGON STATE COLLEGE - LIBRARY
□ Monmouth, OR

Hill, Judith L., Libn.
AMERICAN COLLEGE - VANE B. LUCAS
MEMORIAL LIBRARY □ Bryn Mawr, PA

Hill, Laurie J., Libn.
ST. JOSEPH'S GENERAL HOSPITAL - MEDICAL
LIBRARY □ Thunder Bay, ON

Hill, Rev. Lawrence H., O.S.B., Ref. & Per.Libn.
ST. VINCENT COLLEGE AND ARCHABBEY -
LIBRARIES □ Latrobe, PA

Hill, Linda L., Mgr.
CITIES SERVICE COMPANY - ERG - RESEARCH
LIBRARY □ Tulsa, OK

Hill, Loren G., Dir.
UNIVERSITY OF OKLAHOMA - BIOLOGICAL
STATION LIBRARY □ Kingston, OK

Hill, M., Libn.
ROSENBERG (Paul) ASSOCIATES - LIBRARY □
Pelham, NY

Hill, Margaret, Ser.Libn.
BALL MEMORIAL HOSPITAL - HEALTH SCIENCE
LIBRARY □ Muncie, IN

Hill, Marjorie, Dir.
LAVENTHOL AND HORWATH - NATIONAL
INFORMATION CENTER □ Philadelphia, PA

Hill, May Davis, Assoc.Archv.
UNIVERSITY OF MICHIGAN - MICHIGAN
HISTORICAL COLLECTIONS - BENTLEY
HISTORICAL LIBRARY □ Ann Arbor, MI

Hill, Nancy I., Lib.Techn.
U.S. DEPT. OF DEFENSE - LANGUAGE
INSTITUTE - ACADEMIC LIBRARY □ Monterey,
CA

Hill, Paul F., Ref.Libn.
CREIGHTON UNIVERSITY - LAW SCHOOL -
KLUTZNICK LIBRARY† □ Omaha, NE

Hill, Richard L., First Asst., Annex
NEW YORK PUBLIC LIBRARY - ANNEX SECTION
- NEWSPAPERS AND OTHER RESEARCH
MATERIALS COLLECTION □ New York, NY

Hill, Richard L., First Asst., Annex
NEW YORK PUBLIC LIBRARY - ANNEX SECTION
- PATENTS COLLECTION □ New York, NY

Hill, Rowena, Bibliog.Spec.
LOUISIANA STATE UNIVERSITY - COASTAL
INFORMATION REPOSITORY □ Baton Rouge, LA

Hill, Ruth E., Oral Hist.Coord.
RADCLIFFE COLLEGE - ARTHUR AND
ELIZABETH SCHLESINGER LIBRARY ON THE
HISTORY OF WOMEN IN AMERICA □
Cambridge, MA

Hill, Susan, ILL Libn.
CLEVELAND HEALTH SCIENCES LIBRARY -
ALLEN MEMORIAL LIBRARY □ Cleveland, OH

Hill, Susan M., Dir.
NATIONAL ASSOCIATION OF BROADCASTERS -
LIBRARY □ Washington, DC

Hill, T.T., Libn.
MARQUETTE COPPERSMITHING COMPANY -
LIBRARY □ Philadelphia, PA

Hill, Vienda, Asst. Law Libn.
HARRIS COUNTY LAW LIBRARY □ Houston, TX

Hill, William F., Regional Dir.
U.S. BUREAU OF THE CENSUS - INFORMATION
SERVICES PROGRAM - NEW YORK REGIONAL
OFFICE - LIBRARY □ New York, NY

Hillam, Johanne, Circ.Libn.
BRIGHAM YOUNG UNIVERSITY - J. REUBEN
CLARK LAW SCHOOL LIBRARY □ Provo, UT

Hilland, Marlene, Adm.Sec.
DUCKS UNLIMITED CANADA - LIBRARY □
Winnipeg, MB

Hillard, James M., Dir. of Libs.
CITADEL - THE MILITARY COLLEGE OF SOUTH
CAROLINA - DANIEL LIBRARY □ Charleston, SC

Hillary, Anthony, Rd.Adv.
DISTRICT OF COLUMBIA PUBLIC LIBRARY -
PHILOSOPHY, PSYCHOLOGY AND RELIGION
DIVISION □ Washington, DC

Hillbruner, Fred, Hd. of Tech.Serv.
ART INSTITUTE OF CHICAGO - SCHOOL OF THE
ART INSTITUTE OF CHICAGO - LIBRARY □
Chicago, IL

Hillegas, James B., Pres.
TALLMADGE HISTORICAL SOCIETY - LIBRARY
& ARCHIVES □ Tallmadge, OH

Hillegas, Sally Ann, Med.Libn.
U.S. VETERANS ADMINISTRATION (NY-Bath) -
MEDICAL CENTER LIBRARY □ Bath, NY

Hillen, Nancy, Lib.Mgr.
BROWN COUNTY MENTAL HEALTH CENTER -
H.H. HUMPHREY MEMORIAL STAFF LIBRARY □
Green Bay, WI

Hillengas, Paul G., Libn.
NEW YORK STATE OFFICE OF MENTAL HEALTH
- RESEARCH RESOURCE CENTER □ Albany, NY

Hiller, Steven Z., Hd.
UNIVERSITY OF WASHINGTON - MAP SECTION
□ Seattle, WA

Hilligoss, Leland
ST. LOUIS PUBLIC LIBRARY - HISTORY AND
GENEALOGY DEPARTMENT □ St. Louis, MO

Hilligoss, Martha, Supv.
ST. LOUIS PUBLIC LIBRARY - ART
DEPARTMENT □ St. Louis, MO

Hillis, Janet B., Lib.Techn.
SMITH, KLINE & FRENCH CANADA, LTD. -
MEDICAL/MARKETING LIBRARY □ Mississauga,
ON

Hillman, Aaron W., Ph.D., Sec.
CONFLUENT EDUCATION DEVELOPMENT AND
RESEARCH CENTER - CEDARC INFORMATION
CENTER □ Santa Barbara, CA

Hillson, Muriel V., Libn.
NORFOLK REGIONAL CENTER - STAFF LIBRARY
□ Norfolk, NE

Hillyer, Lila N., Libn.
WISCONSIN ALUMNI RESEARCH FOUNDATION
- LIBRARY □ Madison, WI

Hilman, Catherine A., Health Sci.Libn.
PERTH AMBOY GENERAL HOSPITAL - HEALTH
SCIENCE LIBRARY □ Perth Amboy, NJ

Hilmoe, DeAnn DeKay, Med.Libn.
ST. MARY'S HOSPITAL - MEDICAL LIBRARY □
Pierre, SD

Hilscher, Arthur, Dir.
CARTER-WALLACE, INC. - LIBRARY □ Cranbury,
NJ

Hilt, Gerri, Dir. of Res.
REYNOLDS (Russell) ASSOCIATES, INC. -
LIBRARY □ Chicago, IL

Hilton, Bev, AV Libn.
UNIVERSITY OF KENTUCKY - MEDICAL
CENTER LIBRARY □ Lexington, KY

Hilton, Pamela M., Libn.
U.S. NAVY - NAVAL AIR TEST CENTER - NAVAL
AIR STATION - PATUXENT RIVER CENTRAL
LIBRARY □ Patuxent River, MD

Hilton, Warren, Libn.
OLD YORK ROAD HISTORICAL SOCIETY -
ARCHIVES □ Jenkintown, PA

Hilton-Ross, Krista, Libn.
JOHNSON COUNTY MENTAL HEALTH CENTER -
JOHN R. KEACH MEMORIAL LIBRARY □ Mission,
KS

Himsl, Susan, Asst.Libn.
FOSTER WHEELER DEVELOPMENT
CORPORATION - JOHN BLIZARD RESEARCH
CENTER - INFORMATION CENTER AND
LIBRARY □ Livingston, NJ

Hinchliffe, Louise M., Lib.Techn.
U.S. NATL. PARK SERVICE - GRAND CANYON
RESEARCH LIBRARY† □ Grand Canyon, AZ

Hindman, Axie, Libn.
U.S. FISH & WILDLIFE SERVICE - COLUMBIA
NATIONAL FISHERIES RESEARCH LABORATORY
LIBRARY □ Columbia, MO

Hindmarsh, Douglas, Ref.Serv.Dir.
UTAH STATE LIBRARY □ Salt Lake City, UT

Hinds, Orlean A., Libn.
WHITTAKER CORPORATION - TASKER
SYSTEMS DIVISION - TECHNICAL LIBRARY □
Simi Valley, CA

Hines, Eugene E., Exec.Dir.
AMERICAN SOCIETY OF NOTARIES - LIBRARY
□ Washington, DC

Hines, Lydia, Staff Sci.
UPJOHN COMPANY - CORPORATE TECHNICAL
LIBRARY □ Kalamazoo, MI

Hines, Susie K., Libn.
U.S. NATL. MARINE FISHERIES SERVICE -
NORTHEAST FISHERIES CENTER - OXFORD
LAB. LIBRARY □ Oxford, MD

Hing, Ng. George, Libn./Archv.
CHILDREN'S MUSEUM OF INDIANAPOLIS -
RAUH MEMORIAL LIBRARY □ Indianapolis, IN

Hinkle, Gina, Corp.Libn.
SONAT INC. - CORPORATE LIBRARY □
Birmingham, AL

Hinkle, John, Act.Hd., Lib.Serv.
OKLAHOMA STATE DEPARTMENT OF
LIBRARIES □ Oklahoma City, OK

Hinkle, Mary R., Hd., Soc.Sci.Dept.
VIRGINIA POLYTECHNIC INSTITUTE AND
STATE UNIVERSITY - CAROL M. NEWMAN
LIBRARY □ Blacksburg, VA

Hinks, Yvonne
UNIVERSITY OF CALGARY - ENVIRONMENT-
SCIENCE-TECHNOLOGY LIBRARY† □ Calgary,
AB

Hinman, Marjory B., Libn.
BROOME COUNTY HISTORICAL SOCIETY -
RESEARCH CENTER - JOSIAH T. NEWCOMB
LIBRARY □ Binghamton, NY

Hinrichs, Donald F., Sr.Libn.
LOS ANGELES PUBLIC LIBRARY - MUNICIPAL
REFERENCE DEPARTMENT - WATER & POWER
LIBRARY □ Los Angeles, CA

Hinrichs, Linda Keir, Rare Bk.Libn.
UNIVERSITY OF DAYTON - ROESCH LIBRARY -
SPECIAL COLLECTIONS/RARE BOOKS □ Dayton,
OH

Hinshaw, Glennis, Libn.
NEW MEXICO STATE ENERGY AND MINERALS
DEPARTMENT - LIBRARY □ Santa Fe, NM

Hinshaw, Janet G., Libn.
WILSON ORNITHOLOGICAL SOCIETY -
JOSSELYN VAN TYNE MEMORIAL LIBRARY □
Ann Arbor, MI

Hinson, Doris M., Cat.Libn.
CAMPBELL UNIVERSITY - SCHOOL OF LAW -
LAW LIBRARY □ Buies Creek, NC

Hinton, Rebekah G., Adm.Libn.
PHOENIX INDIAN MEDICAL CENTER - LIBRARY
□ Phoenix, AZ

Hinton, Theron D., Hist.
LOUISIANA STATE OFFICE OF THE SECRETARY
OF STATE - STATE ARCHIVES AND RECORDS
SERVICE - ARCHIVES SECTION □ Baton Rouge,
LA

Hinz, Julianne P., Doc.Libn.
UNIVERSITY OF UTAH - DOCUMENTS DIVISION
□ Salt Lake City, UT
Hinz, Robert P., Dir.
JACKSONVILLE HEALTH EDUCATION
PROGRAMS, INC. - BORLAND HEALTH
SCIENCES LIBRARY □ Jacksonville, FL
Hipp, Marianne, Cat.
LAWRENCE INSTITUTE OF TECHNOLOGY -
LIBRARY □ Southfield, MI
Hippe, Erwin L., Libn.
KING COUNTY MASONIC LIBRARY
ASSOCIATION - LIBRARY □ Seattle, WA
Hirota, Norma C., Libn./Art & Arch.Spec.
HAWAII STATE LIBRARY - FINE ARTS AND
AUDIOVISUAL SECTION □ Honolulu, HI
Hirsch, Gary
THE INFORMATION SPECIALISTS, INC. - THE
A.F. MEMORIAL LIBRARY □ Cleveland, OH
Hirsch, Miriam, Med.Libn.
SAN FRANCISCO GENERAL HOSPITAL MEDICAL
CENTER - BARNETT-BRIGGS LIBRARY □ San
Francisco, CA
Hirsch, Sarah, Libn.
GILCREASE (Thomas) INSTITUTE OF
AMERICAN HISTORY AND ART - LIBRARY □
Tulsa, OK
Hirschfeld, L.G., Libn.
KAISER-PERMANENTE MENTAL HEALTH
CENTER - LIBRARY □ Los Angeles, CA
Hirschfeld, Robert A., Ed./Publ.
SINGLE DAD'S LIFESTYLE MAGAZINE -
LIBRARY □ Scottsdale, AZ
Hirst, Donna, Tech.Serv.
UNIVERSITY OF IOWA - LAW LIBRARY □ Iowa
City, IA
Hirth, Annetherese, Off./Prog.Mgr.
WENNER-GREN FOUNDATION FOR
ANTHROPOLOGICAL RESEARCH - LIBRARY □
New York, NY
Hirtz, Carrie, Libn.
SKADDEN, ARPS, SLATE, MEAGHER & FLOM -
LIBRARY† □ New York, NY
Hiscock, Philip, Asst.Archv.
MEMORIAL UNIVERSITY OF NEWFOUNDLAND -
FOLKLORE AND LANGUAGE ARCHIVE □ St.
John's, NF
Hitchcock, Gail, Acq.Libn.
SOUTHERN ILLINOIS UNIVERSITY - SCHOOL OF
MEDICINE - MEDICAL LIBRARY □ Springfield, IL
Hitchens, Dennis, Libn.
FLORIDA STATE DEPT. OF COMMERCE -
RESEARCH LIBRARY □ Tallahassee, FL
Hitchings, Gladys, Libn.
DAVENPORT ART GALLERY - ART REFERENCE
LIBRARY □ Davenport, IA
Hitchings, Sinclair H., Kpr. of Prints
BOSTON PUBLIC LIBRARY - PRINTS □ Boston,
MA
Hitt, Raymond W., Dir., Lib.Dev.Div.
TEXAS STATE LIBRARY □ Austin, TX
Hitt, Samuel, Dir.
UNIVERSITY OF NORTH CAROLINA, CHAPEL
HILL - HEALTH SCIENCES LIBRARY □ Chapel
Hill, NC
Hixson, Janice, Animal Mgt.Sec.
WASHINGTON PARK ZOO - LIBRARY □ Portland,
OR
Hlatshwayo, Cecilia, Bus. & Econ.Libn.
U.S. CUSTOMS SERVICE - LIBRARY AND
INFORMATION CENTER □ Washington, DC
Ho, C.Y., Dir.
PURDUE UNIVERSITY - CINDAS - ELECTRONIC
PROPERTIES INFORMATION CENTER □ West
Lafayette, IN
Ho, C.Y., Dir.
PURDUE UNIVERSITY - CINDAS -
THERMOPHYSICAL PROPERTIES RESEARCH
CENTER - LIBRARY □ West Lafayette, IN
Ho, Cora C., Assoc.Libn.
TUFTS UNIVERSITY - HEALTH SCIENCES
LIBRARY □ Boston, MA

Ho, Don T., Lib. Group Supv.
AT & T BELL LABORATORIES - LIBRARY □
Whippany, NJ
Ho, Mr. J., Hd., Cat.Div.
CANADA - ENERGY, MINES & RESOURCES
CANADA - CANMET - LIBRARY† □ Ottawa, ON
Ho, Lucy, Assoc.Musm.Libn.
METROPOLITAN MUSEUM OF ART - THOMAS J.
WATSON LIBRARY □ New York, NY
Ho, Paul J., Dp.Cur.
UNIVERSITY OF PITTSBURGH - EAST ASIAN
LIBRARY □ Pittsburgh, PA
Ho, Susan, Med.Libn.
U.S. AIR FORCE HOSPITAL - MEDICAL LIBRARY
(NY-Rome) □ Rome, NY
Ho, Suzel, Asst.Libn.
VETERANS HOME OF CALIFORNIA - LINCOLN
MEMORIAL LIBRARY □ Yountville, CA
Hoad, Linda, Mss.Libn.
NATIONAL LIBRARY OF CANADA - LITERARY
MANUSCRIPTS COLLECTION □ Ottawa, ON
Hoag, Elizabeth, Info.Sci.
SCHERING-PLOUGH CORPORATION -
PHARMACEUTICAL RESEARCH DIVISION -
LIBRARY INFORMATION CENTER □ Bloomfield,
NJ
Hoagland, Louise C., Libn.
NORFOLK LAW LIBRARY □ Dedham, MA
Hoar, Col. Charles F., Exec.Sec.
ANCIENT AND HONORABLE ARTILLERY
COMPANY OF MASSACHUSETTS - LIBRARY □
Boston, MA
Hoare, Mr. C.G.D., Supv., Sci.Info.
HOFFMANN-LA ROCHE, LTD. - CORPORATE
LIBRARY □ Etobicoke, ON
Hoare, Valerie E., Chf.Libn.
CANADA - ENERGY, MINES & RESOURCES
CANADA - SURVEYS & MAPPING BRANCH -
LIBRARY □ Ottawa, ON
Hobbie, Margaret C., Dir.
DEWITT HISTORICAL SOCIETY OF TOMPKINS
COUNTY - ARCHIVE/LIBRARY/MUSEUM □
Ithaca, NY
Hobbs, Anna, Lib.Asst.
MINNEAPOLIS PUBLIC LIBRARY &
INFORMATION CENTER - HISTORY
DEPARTMENT □ Minneapolis, MN
Hobbs, Barbara H., Chf., Lib.Serv.
U.S. VETERANS ADMINISTRATION (TX-Waco) -
MEDICAL CENTER LIBRARY □ Waco, TX
Hobbs, Irma, Chm., Lib.Comm.
WICHITA ART ASSOCIATION, INC. -
REFERENCE LIBRARY □ Wichita, KS
Hobbs, John, Res.Assoc.
MISSOURI STATE DIVISION OF COMMUNITY
AND ECONOMIC DEVELOPMENT - RESEARCH
LIBRARY □ Jefferson City, MO
Hobbs, Kathleen, Ref.Libn.
CONCORDIA UNIVERSITY - SIR GEORGE
WILLIAMS CAMPUS - SCIENCE &
ENGINEERING LIBRARY □ Montreal, PQ
Hobbs, Mary, Trade Spec.
U.S. DEPT. OF COMMERCE - INTERNATIONAL
TRADE ADMINISTRATION - MINNEAPOLIS
DISTRICT OFFICE LIBRARY □ Minneapolis, MN
Hobby, Daniel T., Exec.Dir.
FORT LAUDERDALE HISTORICAL SOCIETY -
LIBRARY & ARCHIVES □ Fort Lauderdale, FL
Hobrock, Brice G., Dean of Libs.
KANSAS STATE UNIVERSITY - FARRELL
LIBRARY □ Manhattan, KS
Hobson, Kitty A., Archv.
OSHKOSH PUBLIC MUSEUM - LIBRARY &
ARCHIVES □ Oshkosh, WI
Hoch, Sandy, Asst.Libn.
DISTRICT ONE TECHNICAL INSTITUTE -
LIBRARY - EDUCATIONAL RESOURCE CENTER □
Eau Claire, WI
Hochman, M., Cat.Libn.
LOS ANGELES TRADE-TECHNICAL COLLEGE -
LIBRARY □ Los Angeles, CA

Hocker, Sarah H., Botany Libn.
UNIVERSITY OF KANSAS - DEPARTMENT OF
SPECIAL COLLECTIONS □ Lawrence, KS
Hockman, Elaine M., Prog.Anl.
UNIVERSITY OF MICHIGAN - MEDICAL SCHOOL
- LEARNING RESOURCE CENTER □ Ann Arbor,
MI
Hodapp, Gladys, Asst.Libn.
COLLEGE OF INSURANCE - INSURANCE
SOCIETY OF NEW YORK - LIBRARY □ New York,
NY
Hodapp, Lawrence C., Controller
NEWBERRY LIBRARY □ Chicago, IL
Hodder, Alfred A., Pres.
MEDIC ALERT FOUNDATION INTERNATIONAL -
CENTRAL REFERENCE FILE OF MEMBERSHIP □
Turlock, CA
Hodge, Patricia, Group Ldr., Lib./Off.Serv
EXXON CORPORATION - MEDICINE &
ENVIRONMENTAL HEALTH DEPT. - RESEARCH
& ENVIRONMENTAL HEALTH DIV.LIB. □ East
Millstone, NJ
Hodge, W.J., Gen.Mgr.
NAVY LEAGUE OF CANADA - NATIONAL OFFICE
- LIBRARY □ Ottawa, ON
Hodges, Betty J., Lib.Spec.
WASHINGTON PUBLIC POWER SUPPLY SYSTEM
- LIBRARY □ Richland, WA
Hodges, Patricia M., Archv.
WESTERN KENTUCKY UNIVERSITY -
DEPARTMENT OF SPECIAL COLLECTIONS -
FOLKLORE, FOLKLIFE & ORAL HISTORY
ARCHIVES □ Bowling Green, KY
Hodges, Robert, Bus.Mgr.
UNIVERSAL SERIALS & BOOK EXCHANGE, INC.
- DUPLICATE EXCHANGE CLEARINGHOUSE &
INFORMATION CENTER □ Washington, DC
Hodges, Susan, Acq.Libn.
INTERNATIONAL DEVELOPMENT RESEARCH
CENTRE - LIBRARY† □ Ottawa, ON
Hodges, T. Mark, Dir.
VANDERBILT UNIVERSITY - MEDICAL CENTER
LIBRARY □ Nashville, TN
Hodgins, R., Chf., Pub.Serv.
CANADA - AGRICULTURE CANADA - LIBRARIES
DIVISION □ Ottawa, ON
Hodgson, Cynthia A., Mgr.
WESTINGHOUSE ELECTRIC CORPORATION -
WATER REACTOR DIVISIONS - INFORMATION
RESOURCE CENTER □ Pittsburgh, PA
Hodgson, Glenda P., Res.
LAMALIE ASSOCIATES, INC. - RESEARCH
DEPARTMENT □ Tampa, FL
Hodgson, James, Libn.
HARVARD UNIVERSITY - GRADUATE SCHOOL
OF DESIGN - FRANCES LOEB LIBRARY □
Cambridge, MA
Hodgson, John C., Chf.Libn.
NEW YORK DAILY NEWS - LIBRARY† □ New
York, NY
Hodina, Alfred J., Hd.
UNIVERSITY OF CALIFORNIA, SANTA BARBARA
- SCIENCES-ENGINEERING LIBRARY □ Santa
Barbara, CA
Hodock, Irene, Libn.
INDIANA STATE SCHOOL FOR THE DEAF -
LIBRARY □ Indianapolis, IN
Hoehn, Philip, Libn./Map Rm.
UNIVERSITY OF CALIFORNIA, BERKELEY -
GOVERNMENT DOCUMENTS DEPARTMENT □
Berkeley, CA
Hoehn, Philip, Map Libn.
UNIVERSITY OF CALIFORNIA, BERKELEY - MAP
ROOM □ Berkeley, CA
Hoekstra, L.K.
3M - ENGINEERING INFORMATION SERVICES
□ St. Paul, MN
Hoel, Jeanette, Cat.
U.S. ARMY POST - FORT RILEY - LIBRARIES† □
Ft. Riley, KS
Hoelle, Dolores M., Libn.
PRINCETON UNIVERSITY - ENGINEERING
LIBRARY □ Princeton, NJ

Hoelle, Edith, Libn.
GLOUCESTER COUNTY HISTORICAL SOCIETY -
LIBRARY □ Woodbury, NJ

Hoeman, Mary Ann, Asst.Libn., Tech.Serv.
LOGAN COLLEGE OF CHIROPRACTIC - LIBRARY
□ Chesterfield, MO

Hoerman, Heidi, Hd., Tech.Sys. & Bibliog.
TEACHERS COLLEGE - MILBANK MEMORIAL
LIBRARY □ New York, NY

Hoessle, Charles, Dir.
ST. LOUIS ZOOLOGICAL PARK - LIBRARY □ St.
Louis, MO

Hoetzer, Walter G., Sec./Treas.
INTERNATIONAL ASSOCIATION FOR
IDENTIFICATION - LIBRARY □ Columbia, SC

Hoey, Evelyn L., Dir.
SUNY - UPSTATE MEDICAL CENTER LIBRARY □
Syracuse, NY

Hoff, Deborah J., Coord.
BELL COMMUNICATIONS RESEARCH, INC. -
INFORMATION RESOURCES SERVICES CENTER
□ Morristown, NJ

Hoffenberg, Ruth, Asst. Libn.
LENOX HILL HOSPITAL - HEALTH SCIENCES
LIBRARY □ New York, NY

Hoffer, Ann Kramer, Pres.
CUMBERLAND COUNTY HISTORICAL SOCIETY
& HAMILTON LIBRARY □ Carlisle, PA

Hoffman, Barbara, Night Supv.
INDIANAPOLIS NEWSPAPERS, INC. -
INDIANAPOLIS STAR AND INDIANAPOLIS
NEWS - REFERENCE LIBRARY □ Indianapolis, IN

Hoffman, Christine, Cat.
MANHATTAN SCHOOL OF MUSIC - FRANCES
HALL BALLARD LIBRARY† □ New York, NY

Hoffman, David, Chf.Libn.
NEWSDAY, INC. - LIBRARY □ Melville, NY

Hoffman, David R., Dir., Lib.Serv.Div.
PENNSYLVANIA STATE LIBRARY □ Harrisburg,
PA

Hoffman, Donna, Lib.Asst.
UNIVERSITY CONGREGATIONAL CHURCH -
LIBRARY □ Seattle, WA

Hoffman, Donna M., Libn.
U.S. DEPT. OF LABOR - OSHA - REGIONAL
LIBRARY □ Seattle, WA

Hoffman, Elliott W., Dir.
WEBSTER (Noah) FOUNDATION & HISTORICAL
SOCIETY OF WEST HARTFORD - LIBRARY □
West Hartford, CT

Hoffman, Gladys C., Cat.
AMERICAN PHILATELIC RESEARCH LIBRARY □
State College, PA

Hoffman, Helen, Libn.
RUTGERS UNIVERSITY, THE STATE
UNIVERSITY OF NEW JERSEY - WAKSMAN
INSTITUTE OF MICROBIOLOGY LIBRARY □
Piscataway, NJ

Hoffman, J.W., Jr., Mgr.
GIBBS AND COX, INC. - TECHNICAL
INFORMATION CENTER □ New York, NY

Hoffman, Jane, Tax Libn.
DEWEY, BALLANTINE, BUSHBY, PALMER &
WOOD - LIBRARY □ New York, NY

Hoffman, John, Libn.
UNIVERSITY OF ILLINOIS - ILLINOIS
HISTORICAL SURVEY LIBRARY □ Urbana, IL

Hoffman, Kathy, Asst.Dir./Tech.Serv.
HOUSTON ACADEMY OF MEDICINE - TEXAS
MEDICAL CENTER LIBRARY □ Houston, TX

Hoffman, Margaret, Tech.Serv.Libn.
HAHNEMANN UNIVERSITY - WARREN H. FAKE
LIBRARY† □ Philadelphia, PA

Hoffman, Mary, Info.Spec.
FOI SERVICES, INC. - LIBRARY □ Rockville, MD

Hoffman, Mary, Res.Libn., Med.
METROPOLITAN LIFE INSURANCE COMPANY -
CORPORATE INFORMATION CENTER AND
LIBRARY □ New York, NY

Hoffman, Mary Ann, Act. Health Sci.Libn.
WRIGHT STATE UNIVERSITY - HEALTH
SCIENCES LIBRARY □ Dayton, OH

Hoffman, Melia M., Supv.
CRUM AND FORSTER CORPORATION -
BUSINESS INFORMATION CENTER □ Basking
Ridge, NJ

Hoffman, Michael, Dir. of Marketing
INTERNATIONAL FOODSERVICE
MANUFACTURERS ASSOCIATION -
INFORMATION SERVICE □ Chicago, IL

Hoffman, Sharon, Spec.Serv.Libn.
DU PAGE LIBRARY SYSTEM - SYSTEM CENTER
□ Geneva, IL

Hoffman, Shirley W., Hist./Genealogy
ROWAN PUBLIC LIBRARY - EDITH M. CLARK
HISTORY ROOM □ Salisbury, NC

Hoffman, Susan, Ref.Libn.
CLEVELAND HEALTH SCIENCES LIBRARY -
ALLEN MEMORIAL LIBRARY □ Cleveland, OH

Hoffmann, Linda, Hd., Gov.Docs.
UNIVERSITY OF CALIFORNIA, DAVIS -
UNIVERSITY LIBRARIES - SPECIAL
COLLECTIONS □ Davis, CA

Hoffsis, Wallis D., Acq.Libn.
FLORIDA STATE UNIVERSITY - LAW LIBRARY □
Tallahassee, FL

Hofmann, Gwenn, Asst. to Dir.
FEDERAL ELECTION COMMISSION - NATIONAL
CLEARINGHOUSE ON ELECTION
ADMINISTRATION - DOCUMENT CENTER □
Washington, DC

Hofmann, Hannah, Ref.Libn.
BATTEN, BARTON, DURSTINE, OSBORN, INC. -
INFORMATION RETRIEVAL CENTER† □ New
York, NY

Hofmeister, Ms. Tye, MIRS Libn.
NCR CANADA LTD. - MIRS LIBRARY □
Mississauga, ON

Hofstad, Richard, Athenaeum Libn.
MINNEAPOLIS PUBLIC LIBRARY &
INFORMATION CENTER - HUTTNER ABOLITION
AND ANTI-SLAVERY COLLECTION □
Minneapolis, MN

Hofstad, Richard, Athenaeum Libn.
MINNEAPOLIS PUBLIC LIBRARY &
INFORMATION CENTER - KITTLESON WORLD
WAR II COLLECTION □ Minneapolis, MN

Hofstad, Richard, Athenaeum Libn.
MINNEAPOLIS PUBLIC LIBRARY &
INFORMATION CENTER - MINNEAPOLIS
ATHENAEUM LIBRARY □ Minneapolis, MN

Hofstad, Richard, Athenaeum Libn.
MINNEAPOLIS PUBLIC LIBRARY &
INFORMATION CENTER - 19TH CENTURY
AMERICAN STUDIES COLLECTION □
Minneapolis, MN

Hofstadter, Dr. Marc, Libn.
SAN FRANCISCO MUNICIPAL RAILWAY -
LIBRARY □ San Francisco, CA

Hofstetter, Sheila, Staff Libn.
COMMUNITY HOSPITAL OF INDIANAPOLIS,
INC. - LIBRARY □ Indianapolis, IN

Hogan, Curtis J., Gen.Sec.
INTERNATIONAL FEDERATION OF PETROLEUM
AND CHEMICAL WORKERS - LIBRARY □ Denver,
CO

Hogan, Debra K., Libn.
SHEPPARD, MULLIN, RICHTER & HAMPTON -
LAW LIBRARY† □ Los Angeles, CA

Hogan, Ed P., Hist.
INTERNATIONAL SILVER COMPANY -
HISTORICAL LIBRARY† □ Meriden, CT

Hogan, Kristine K., Asst.Archv./Libn.
STATEN ISLAND INSTITUTE OF ARTS AND
SCIENCES - ARCHIVES AND LIBRARY □ Staten
Island, NY

Hogan, Matthew, Cur.
FRANKLIN FURNACE ARCHIVES, INC. -
LIBRARY □ New York, NY

Hogan, Rose, Dir.
UNIVERSITY OF ARKANSAS FOR MEDICAL
SCIENCES - MEDICAL SCIENCES LIBRARY □
Little Rock, AR

Hogans, Mary, Act.Libn.
OUR LADY OF THE WAY HOSPITAL - MEDICAL
LIBRARY □ Martin, KY

Hogenson, Barbara, Dir.
FOOTE CONE & BELDING - CREATIVE
ARCHIVES □ New York, NY

Hogg, Muriel, Sr.Libn.
STAUFFER CHEMICAL COMPANY - EASTERN
RESEARCH CENTER INFORMATION SERVICES □
Dobbs Ferry, NY

Hogg, Rosemary, Libn./Archv.
GEORGE MASON UNIVERSITY - FENWICK
LIBRARY - SPECIAL COLLECTIONS □ Fairfax, VA

Hohl, Robert, Cat.
ST. MARY'S COLLEGE - MUSIC SEMINAR ROOM
□ Notre Dame, IN

Hohmann, Judith, Cat./Ref.Libn.
DELAWARE VALLEY COLLEGE OF SCIENCE AND
AGRICULTURE - JOSEPH KRAUSKOPF
MEMORIAL LIBRARY □ Doylestown, PA

Hohn, Dianne, Chf., Lib.Serv.
U.S. VETERANS ADMINISTRATION (PA-Butler) -
MEDICAL CENTER LIBRARY □ Butler, PA

Hohn, Dr. Richard C., Dir.
NATIONAL ASSOCIATION FOR SPORT &
PHYSICAL EDUCATION (NASPE) - MEDIA
RESOURCE CENTER □ Columbia, SC

Hohner, Vicki, Supv.
WASHINGTON STATE UNIVERSITY -
EDUCATION LIBRARY □ Pullman, WA

Hoke, Sheila Wilder, Lib.Dir.
SOUTHWESTERN OKLAHOMA STATE
UNIVERSITY - AL HARRIS LIBRARY □
Weatherford, OK

Holab-Abelman, Robin, Tech.Libn.
FLUOR ENGINEERS, INC. - FLUOR HOUSTON
LIBRARY □ Sugar Land, TX

Holahan, Jane, Div.Hd.
DALLAS PUBLIC LIBRARY - FINE ARTS
DIVISION □ Dallas, TX

Holava, H., Ctrl.Sci.Rec.
BRISTOL-MYERS COMPANY - SCIENTIFIC
INFORMATION DEPARTMENT □ Syracuse, NY

Holbert, Beulah, Rd.Adv.
DISTRICT OF COLUMBIA PUBLIC LIBRARY -
CHILDREN'S DIVISION □ Washington, DC

Holbert, Sue E., State Archv.
MINNESOTA HISTORICAL SOCIETY - DIVISION
OF ARCHIVES AND MANUSCRIPTS □ St. Paul,
MN

Holbert, Zella J., Curric.Libn.
COLUMBIA UNION COLLEGE - THEOFIELD G.
WEIS LIBRARY □ Takoma Park, MD

Holbrook, Carol, Dir.
UNIVERSITY OF MICHIGAN - KRESGE
BUSINESS ADMINISTRATION LIBRARY □ Ann
Arbor, MI

Holbrook, Jean, Dir., Info.Ctr.
SAN MATEO COUNTY EDUCATIONAL
RESOURCES CENTER □ Redwood City, CA

Holden, Claire A., Supv., Info.Serv.
MOBIL CHEMICAL COMPANY - RESEARCH &
DEVELOPMENT - INFORMATION SERVICES □
Edison, NJ

Holden, Elizabeth, Libn.
FIRST PRESBYTERIAN CHURCH - LIBRARY □
Phoenixville, PA

Holden, Harley P., Cur.
HARVARD UNIVERSITY - ARCHIVES □
Cambridge, MA

Holden, Wendy, Cur.
UNIVERSITY OF MICHIGAN - HISTORY OF ART
DEPARTMENT - ARCHIVES OF ASIAN ART □
Ann Arbor, MI

Holder, Nell T., Libn.
COMBUSTION ENGINEERING, INC. -
METALLURGICAL AND MATERIALS LIBRARY □
Chattanooga, TN

Holdman, L.L., Libn.
MONSANTO COMPANY - CENTRAL
ENGINEERING LIBRARY - CS71 □ St. Louis, MO

Holdorf, Sally, Libn.
ST. ELIZABETH HOSPITAL - HEALTH SCIENCES
LIBRARY □ Elizabeth, NJ
Hole, Robert, Second Sec.
NEW ZEALAND EMBASSY - LIBRARY □
Washington, DC
Holey, George, Pres.
RICE COUNTY HISTORICAL SOCIETY -
ARCHIVES □ Faribault, MN
Holian, Lydia T., Assoc.Dir.
CLEVELAND HEALTH SCIENCES LIBRARY -
ALLEN MEMORIAL LIBRARY □ Cleveland, OH
Holiber, Jerome A., Chf.
U.S. NATL. HIGHWAY TRAFFIC SAFETY
ADMINISTRATION - TECHNICAL REFERENCE
DIVISION □ Washington, DC
Holicky, Bernard H., Dir.
PURDUE UNIVERSITY, CALUMET - LIBRARY □
Hammond, IN
Holifield, Betty, Cat.
GMI ENGINEERING & MANAGEMENT
INSTITUTE - LIBRARY □ Flint, MI
Holl, Deborah G., Rd.Serv.Libn.
ROSEMONT COLLEGE - GERTRUDE KISTLER
MEMORIAL LIBRARY - SPECIAL COLLECTIONS
□ Rosemont, PA
Holland, Connie, Asst.Dir./Ref. & Instr.
TEXAS TECH UNIVERSITY - LIBRARY □
Lubbock, TX
Holland, Harold, Hd., Consrv.Div.
NEW BRUNSWICK - PROVINCIAL ARCHIVES OF
NEW BRUNSWICK □ Fredericton, NB
Holland, Dr. Harold, Dir.
PEPPERDINE UNIVERSITY - LIBRARY -
SPECIAL COLLECTIONS □ Malibu, CA
Holland, Jane D., Libn.
FULBRIGHT & JAWORSKI - LIBRARY □ Houston,
TX
Holland, Maurita P., Libn.
UNIVERSITY OF MICHIGAN - ENGINEERING-
TRANSPORTATION LIBRARY □ Ann Arbor, MI
Holland, Maurita Petersen, Hd.
UNIVERSITY OF MICHIGAN - NORTH
ENGINEERING LIBRARY □ Ann Arbor, MI
Holland, Nancy J., Hd.Libn.
PEAT, MARWICK, MITCHELL & CO. - LIBRARY □
Washington, DC
Holland, Patsy, Tech.Libn.
DU PONT DE NEMOURS (E.I.) & COMPANY, INC.
- POLYMER PRODUCTS DEPARTMENT -
TECHNICAL LIBRARY □ Orange, TX
Holland, Robert, Anl.
SHERWIN-WILLIAMS COMPANY -
INFORMATION CENTER □ Cleveland, OH
Holland, Robert P., Supv.
GOODYEAR TIRE AND RUBBER COMPANY -
GOODYEAR ATOMIC CORPORATION -
TECHNICAL LIBRARY □ Piketon, OH
Hollands, Nora, Libn.
AMERICAN STANDARD - ENGINEERING
LIBRARY □ Toronto, ON
Hollar, Robyn, Hd., Circ.
GEORGIA STATE DEPARTMENT OF EDUCATION
- DIVISION OF PUBLIC LIBRARY SERVICES □
Atlanta, GA
Hollenback, Frank, Sci.Anl.
KELLER (J.J.) & ASSOCIATES, INC. - RESEARCH
& TECHNICAL LIBRARY □ Neenah, WI
Hollenbeck, Leo, Ref.Libn.
U.S. SOCIAL SECURITY ADMINISTRATION -
LIBRARY INFORMATION & GRAPHICS
SERVICES BRANCH □ Baltimore, MD
Hollenhorts, Sr. Bernice, CSC, Lib.Dir.
SAINT MARY'S COLLEGE - CUSHWA-LEIGHTON
LIBRARY - SPECIAL COLLECTIONS □ Notre
Dame, IN
Hollens, Deborah
SOUTHERN OREGON STATE COLLEGE -
LIBRARY □ Ashland, OR
Holles, Jean Marie, Mgr.
CONWED CORPORATION - BUSINESS
INFORMATION CENTER □ St. Paul, MN

Holley, Donald H., Assoc. Attorney
NEW YORK STATE DEPARTMENT OF LABOR -
WORKERS' COMPENSATION BOARD -
LIBRARY† □ New York, NY
Holliday, Charles, Asst.Soc.Stud.Libn.
SOUTHERN ILLINOIS UNIVERSITY,
CARBONDALE - SOCIAL STUDIES DIVISION
LIBRARY □ Carbondale, IL
Holliday, Judith E., Libn.
CORNELL UNIVERSITY - FINE ARTS LIBRARY □
Ithaca, NY
Holliday, Loretta, Dir.
TAMPA GENERAL HOSPITAL - MEDICAL
LIBRARY □ Tampa, FL
Hollifield, John H., Asst.Dir.
JOHNS HOPKINS UNIVERSITY - RESEARCH &
DEVELOPMENT CENTER - CENTER FOR SOCIAL
ORGANIZATION OF SCHOOLS □ Baltimore, MD
Hollingshead, Diane, Libn.
CAMDEN COUNTY BAR ASSOCIATION - LAW
LIBRARY† □ Camden, NJ
Hollingsworth, Daysi, Libn.
U.S. NAVY - FLEET ANALYSIS CENTER (FLTAC)
- LIBRARY □ Corona, CA
Hollis, Betty S., Tech.Libn.
CABOT CORPORATION - TECHNICAL
INFORMATION CENTER □ Kokomo, IN
Hollman, Edward G., Hd.
OKLAHOMA STATE UNIVERSITY - SOCIAL
SCIENCE DIVISION □ Stillwater, OK
Hollowak, Thomas, Res. Herald
POLISH NOBILITY ASSOCIATION - VILLA
ANNESLIE ARCHIVES □ Anneslie, MD
Holloway, Doris, Doc.Libn.
NORTH CAROLINA STATE DEPARTMENT OF
CULTURAL RESOURCES - DIVISION OF THE
STATE LIBRARY □ Raleigh, NC
Holloway, Dorothy, Dir.
FERGUSON BAPTIST CHURCH - LIBRARY □
Ferguson, KY
Holloway, Lisabeth M., Dir.
PENNSYLVANIA COLLEGE OF PODIATRIC
MEDICINE - CENTER FOR THE HISTORY OF
FOOT CARE AND FOOT WEAR □ Philadelphia, PA
Hollowell, S.G., Rec.Adm.
HAMILTON CITY HALL - LIBRARY □ Hamilton,
ON
Hollrah, Warren M., Musm.Mgr./Coll.Archv.
WESTMINSTER COLLEGE - WINSTON
CHURCHILL MEMORIAL AND LIBRARY □ Fulton,
MO
Holly, Janet S., Assoc.Libn.
UNITED ENGINEERS & CONSTRUCTORS INC. -
LIBRARY □ Philadelphia, PA
Hollyer, Cameron, Doyle/Am.Lit.Spec.
METROPOLITAN TORONTO LIBRARY -
LITERATURE DEPARTMENT □ Toronto, ON
Holm, Carl B., Prin. Planner
CUMBERLAND COUNTY DEPT. OF PLANNING &
DEVELOPMENT - TECHNICAL REFERENCE
LIBRARY □ Bridgeton, NJ
Holman, Anna, Libn.
UNIVERSITY OF WESTERN ONTARIO -
FACULTY OF EDUCATION LIBRARY □ London,
ON
Holmberg, James, Ms.Asst.
FILSON CLUB - LIBRARY □ Louisville, KY
Holmen, Ginny, Law Libn.
MENDOCINO COUNTY LAW LIBRARY □ Ukiah,
CA
Holmer, Eileen, Tech.Serv.Libn.
DEERE & COMPANY - LIBRARY □ Moline, IL
Holmes, Bettie S., Libn.
BALTIMORE COUNTY GENERAL HOSPITAL -
HEALTH SCIENCES LIBRARY □ Randallstown,
MD
Holmes, Bonnie M., Supv., Law Lib.Serv.
TENNESSEE VALLEY AUTHORITY - LAW
LIBRARY □ Knoxville, TN
Holmes, Diane Morton, Lib.Dir.
MIND SCIENCE FOUNDATION - LIBRARY □ San
Antonio, TX

Holmes, Elizabeth H., Libn.
RICHMOND PUBLIC LIBRARY - BUSINESS,
SCIENCE & TECHNOLOGY DEPARTMENT □
Richmond, VA
Holmes, Ethel T., Attendant
WILDWOOD HISTORICAL COMMISSION -
WILDWOOD LIBRARY OF NEW JERSEY
HISTORY □ Wildwood, NJ
Holmes, Grace, Dir. Homework Assist.Prog
QUEENS BOROUGH PUBLIC LIBRARY -
LANGSTON HUGHES COMMUNITY LIBRARY AND
CULTURAL CENTER □ Corona, NY
Holmes, Janet, Cur.Asst.
ROYAL ONTARIO MUSEUM - CANADIANA
GALLERY LIBRARY† □ Toronto, ON
Holmes, Jill, Educ.Libn.
OKLAHOMA STATE UNIVERSITY - SOCIAL
SCIENCE DIVISION □ Stillwater, OK
Holmes, Linda, Assoc.Libn.
BROOKLYN LAW SCHOOL - LAW LIBRARY □
Brooklyn, NY
Holmes, Lois A., Supv., Info.Serv.
BATTELLE-NORTHWEST - PACIFIC
NORTHWEST LABORATORY - HANFORD
TECHNICAL LIBRARY □ Richland, WA
Holmes, Marion C., Archv.
SAN MATEO COUNTY HISTORICAL
ASSOCIATION - LIBRARY □ San Mateo, CA
Holmes, Sue
UTAH STATE LIBRARY □ Salt Lake City, UT
Holmes, Susan B., Mgt.Info.Spec.
COMMERCE UNION BANK - LIBRARY □ Nashville,
TN
Holmes, W., Lib.Techn.
BRITISH COLUMBIA ALCOHOL AND DRUG
PROGRAMS - LIBRARY† □ Vancouver, BC
Holmlund, Jan, Dir.
EDWARD-DEAN MUSEUM ART REFERENCE
LIBRARY □ Cherry Valley, CA
Holmquist, Carolyn J., Hd.
SEATTLE PUBLIC LIBRARY - ART AND MUSIC
DEPARTMENT† □ Seattle, WA
Holmquist, Jane E., Asst.Libn.
PRINCETON UNIVERSITY - PLASMA PHYSICS
LIBRARY □ Princeton, NJ
Holobeck, Noel C., Supv.
ST. LOUIS PUBLIC LIBRARY - HISTORY AND
GENEALOGY DEPARTMENT □ St. Louis, MO
Holoch, Alan, Dir./Asst.Prof.
VILLANOVA UNIVERSITY - PULLING LAW
LIBRARY □ Villanova, PA
Holowitz, Esther, Libn.
CANADA - NATIONAL FILM BOARD OF CANADA
- FILM LIBRARY □ Thunder Bay, ON
Holsinger, Katherine, Mgr.
UNIVERSITY OF ARIZONA - DIVISION OF
MEDIA & INSTRUCTIONAL SERVICES - FILM
LIBRARY □ Tucson, AZ
Holst, Ruth, Dir., Lib.Serv.
COLUMBIA HOSPITAL - MEDICAL LIBRARY □
Milwaukee, WI
Holston, Kim, Libn.
AMERICAN INSTITUTE FOR PROPERTY &
LIABILITY UNDERWRITERS - INSURANCE
INSTITUTE OF AMERICA - LIBRARY □ Malvern,
PA
Holt, Agnes M., Libn.
LOS ANGELES BAPTIST COLLEGE - ROBERT L.
POWELL MEMORIAL LIBRARY □ Newhall, CA
Holt, Alison, Asst.Libn./Cat.
ART CENTER COLLEGE OF DESIGN - JAMES
LEMONT FOGG MEMORIAL LIBRARY □
Pasadena, CA
Holt, Barbara Cornwell, Libn.
KARR, TUTTLE, KOCH, CAMPBELL, MAWER &
MORROW - LAW LIBRARY □ Seattle, WA
Holt, Daniel D., Acq.
ILLINOIS STATE HISTORICAL LIBRARY □
Springfield, IL

Holt, Janice C., Hd.Libn.
MARYLAND NATIONAL CAPITAL PARK AND
PLANNING COMMISSION - MONTGOMERY
COUNTY PLANNING DEPARTMENT - LIBRARY □
Silver Spring, MD

Holt, June C., Libn.
MASSACHUSETTS REHABILITATION
COMMISSION - LIBRARY □ Boston, MA

Holt, Laura J., Libn.
MUSEUM OF NEW MEXICO - LABORATORY OF
ANTHROPOLOGY - LIBRARY† □ Santa Fe, NM

Holt, Mae L., Dir. of Lib.Serv.
WINSTON-SALEM STATE UNIVERSITY -
O'KELLY LIBRARY - SPECIAL COLLECTIONS □
Winston-Salem, NC

Holt, Marian, Rd.Adv.
DISTRICT OF COLUMBIA PUBLIC LIBRARY -
BIOGRAPHY DIVISION □ Washington, DC

Holt, Suzy, Info.Spec.
SHODAIR CHILDREN'S HOSPITAL - MEDICAL
REFERENCE LIBRARY □ Helena, MT

Holt, Wendy M., Libn.
CARPENTER TECHNOLOGY CORPORATION -
RESEARCH AND DEVELOPMENT CENTER
LIBRARY □ Reading, PA

Holterhoff, Sally, Doc.Libn.
VALPARAISO UNIVERSITY - LAW LIBRARY □
Valparaiso, IN

Holton, Alice K., Lib.Serv.Asst.
UNIVERSITY OF PENNSYLVANIA - NEW
BOLTON CENTER - JEAN AUSTIN DU PONT
LIBRARY □ Kennett Square, PA

Holton, Charlotte, Libn.
AMERICAN MUSEUM OF NATURAL HISTORY -
OSBORN LIBRARY OF VERTEBRATE
PALEONTOLOGY □ New York, NY

Holtz, Jerome E., Mgr.
MERCK & COMPANY, INC. - MERCK SHARP &
DOHME RESEARCH LABORATORIES -
LITERATURE RESOURCES □ Rahway, NJ

Holtz, Virginia, Dir.
UNIVERSITY OF WISCONSIN, MADISON -
CENTER FOR HEALTH SCIENCES LIBRARIES† □
Madison, WI

Holum, Katharine, Music Libn.
UNIVERSITY OF MINNESOTA - MUSIC LIBRARY
□ Minneapolis, MN

Holz, Gloria, Circ./Reserve Libn.
UNIVERSITY OF WISCONSIN, MADISON - LAW
SCHOOL LIBRARY □ Madison, WI

Holzbauer, H., Chief Libn.
U.S. DEFENSE INTELLIGENCE AGENCY -
LIBRARY RTS-2A □ Washington, DC

Holzer, Francine, Hd.Libn.
METROMEDIA INC. - CORPORATE RESEARCH
LIBRARY† □ New York, NY

Holzhausen, Richard, Supv.Archv., AV
U.S. PRESIDENTIAL LIBRARIES - GERALD R.
FORD LIBRARY □ Ann Arbor, MI

Holzmann, Thomas, Libn.
PRINCETON UNIVERSITY - OFFICE OF
POPULATION RESEARCH - LIBRARY □ Princeton,
NJ

Hom, Kimiyo T., Libn.
UNIVERSITY OF CALIFORNIA, BERKELEY -
ASTRONOMY-MATHEMATICS-STATISTICS-
COMPUTER SCIENCES LIBRARY □ Berkeley, CA

Hom, Lily W., Tech.Info.Spec.
U.S. VETERANS ADMINISTRATION (NY-New
York) - OFFICE OF TECHNOLOGY TRANSFER -
REFERENCE COLLECTION □ New York, NY

Homan, Joyce, Lib.Techn.
U.S. VETERANS ADMINISTRATION (MO-
Columbia) - HOSPITAL LIBRARY □ Columbia, MO

Homan, Michael, Hd., Info.Serv.
UPJOHN COMPANY - CORPORATE TECHNICAL
LIBRARY □ Kalamazoo, MI

Homer, Merlin, ESL Coord.
YORK UNIVERSITY - FACULTY OF ARTS -
PROGRAMME IN ENGLISH AS A SECOND
LANGUAGE - ESL RESOURCE COLLECTION □
Downsview, ON

Homer, Ruth, Cat., ILL
PHILADELPHIA COLLEGE OF BIBLE - LIBRARY □
Langhorne, PA

Homewood, Donna, Chf., Lib.Serv.
U.S. VETERANS ADMINISTRATION (WY-
Sheridan) - MEDICAL CENTER LIBRARY □
Sheridan, WY

Homrighausen, Carol L., Libn.
WOODSIDE RECEIVING HOSPITAL - STAFF
RESOURCE LIBRARY/PATIENTS' LIBRARY □
Youngstown, OH

Honchul, Quava, Hd., Legal Rsrcs.
MURRAY STATE UNIVERSITY - LIBRARY □
Murray, KY

Hondrodemos, Cleopatra, Asst.Libn.
UNITED ENGINEERS & CONSTRUCTORS INC. -
BOSTON OFFICE - LIBRARY □ Boston, MA

Honebrink, Andrea C., Mgr.Lib./Info.Serv.
GENERAL MILLS, INC. - MGO LIBRARY/
INFORMATION CENTER □ Minneapolis, MN

Honeychurch, Deborah, Hd.
LOUISIANA STATE UNIVERSITY - MICROFORM
ROOM □ Baton Rouge, LA

Honeychurch, Sallie, Libn.
BATON ROUGE STATE-TIMES & MORNING
ADVOCATE NEWSPAPERS - LIBRARY □ Baton
Rouge, LA

Honeywell, Joan L., Courthouse Libn.
BRITISH COLUMBIA LAW LIBRARY
FOUNDATION - VANCOUVER COURTHOUSE
LIBRARY □ Vancouver, BC

Honhart, Dr. Frederick L., Dir.
MICHIGAN STATE UNIVERSITY - UNIVERSITY
ARCHIVES AND HISTORICAL COLLECTIONS □
East Lansing, MI

Honjo, Miss Tatsuko, Dir. of Info.
CHAMBER OF COMMERCE OF HAWAII -
INFORMATION OFFICE □ Honolulu, HI

Honor, Naomi Goldberg, Libn.
ADATH JESHURUN CONGREGATION - JENNY
GROSS MEMORIAL LIBRARY □ Minneapolis, MN

Honsowitz, Aletha, Rd.Serv.Libn.
COOLEY (Thomas M.) LAW SCHOOL - LIBRARY □
Lansing, MI

Hood, Elizabeth, Circ.
LAWRENCE INSTITUTE OF TECHNOLOGY -
LIBRARY □ Southfield, MI

Hood, Howard A., Legal Info.Spec.
VANDERBILT UNIVERSITY - ALYNE QUEENER
MASSEY LAW LIBRARY □ Nashville, TN

Hood, Katherine, Bibliog.Instr.
BENTLEY COLLEGE - SOLOMON R. BAKER
LIBRARY □ Waltham, MA

Hood, Larry, Law Libn.
DALLAS COUNTY LAW LIBRARY - RICHARDSON
BRANCH □ Richardson, TX

Hood, Lawrence E., Dir.
DALLAS COUNTY LAW LIBRARY □ Dallas, TX

Hood, Mary D., Hd., Pub.Serv.
UNIVERSITY OF SANTA CLARA - EDWIN A.
HEAFEY LAW LIBRARY† □ Santa Clara, CA

Hood, Sandi, Cat.
DAUGHTERS OF THE REPUBLIC OF TEXAS -
LIBRARY □ San Antonio, TX

Hooft, Vicki C., Ref.Libn.
DETROIT EDISON COMPANY - REFERENCE
SERVICES □ Detroit, MI

Hoogakker, David, Cat.
GENERAL THEOLOGICAL SEMINARY OF THE
PROTESTANT EPISCOPAL CHURCH IN THE
U.S.A. - ST. MARK'S LIBRARY □ New York, NY

Hoogerwerf, Sharon, Libn.
GOETHE INSTITUTE ATLANTA - GERMAN
CULTURAL CENTER - LIBRARY □ Atlanta, GA

Hook, Carolyn, Ref./Coll.Dev.Libn.
WASHINGTON STATE UNIVERSITY -
EDUCATION LIBRARY □ Pullman, WA

Hook, Sara, Pub.Serv.Libn.
INDIANA UNIVERSITY, INDIANAPOLIS -
SCHOOL OF DENTISTRY LIBRARY □ Indianapolis,
IN

Hook, William, Ref.Libn.
VANDERBILT UNIVERSITY - JEAN AND
ALEXANDER HEARD LIBRARY - DIVINITY
LIBRARY □ Nashville, TN

Hooker, Alicia Randisi, Hd.Libn.
SETTLEMENT MUSIC SCHOOL - BLANCHE WOLF
KOHN LIBRARY □ Philadelphia, PA

Hooker, Catherine J. Lenix, Interim Adm.
NEW YORK PUBLIC LIBRARY - SCHOMBURG
CENTER FOR RESEARCH IN BLACK CULTURE □
New York, NY

Hooker, Claude, Dir., Oper.
UNIVERSAL SERIALS & BOOK EXCHANGE, INC.
- DUPLICATE EXCHANGE CLEARINGHOUSE &
INFORMATION CENTER □ Washington, DC

Hooker, Lloyd W., Libn.
U.S. DEPT. OF JUSTICE - FEDERAL PRISON
SYSTEM - LIBRARY □ Washington, DC

Hooks, James, Asst.Libn.
INDIANA UNIVERSITY OF PENNSYLVANIA -
UNIVERSITY LIBRARY □ Indiana, PA

Hoolihan, Christopher, Rare Bk.Libn.
WASHINGTON UNIVERSITY - SCHOOL OF
MEDICINE LIBRARY □ St. Louis, MO

Hoonicki, Joseph, Ref.
SEYFARTH, SHAW, FAIRWEATHER &
GERALDSON - LIBRARY □ Chicago, IL

Hooper, Dorothy L., Chm., Lib.Comm.
FIRST UNITED METHODIST CHURCH OF
ALHAMBRA - LIBRARY □ Alhambra, CA

Hooper, Jimmie, Asst.Dept.Hd.
WICHITA PUBLIC LIBRARY - BUSINESS AND
TECHNOLOGY DIVISION □ Wichita, KS

Hooper, Judge Perry O., Dir.
MONTGOMERY COUNTY LAW LIBRARY □
Montgomery, AL

Hoopes, Mary Anne, Libn.
CLOROX COMPANY - TECHNICAL CENTER
LIBRARY □ Pleasanton, CA

Hooser, D.R., Cur.
SURREY MUSEUM - ARCHIVES □ Surrey, BC

Hooten, Rebecca, Doc. Examiner
ARKANSAS STATE DEPARTMENT OF
POLLUTION CONTROL - BUSINESS LIBRARY □
Little Rock, AR

Hoover, Audrey, Libn.
EASTMAN KODAK COMPANY - COLORADO
DIVISION - ENGINEERING AND INFORMATION
SERVICES LIBRARY □ Windsor, CO

Hoover, Danise, Per.Libn.
BROOKLYN PUBLIC LIBRARY - SOCIAL SCIENCE
AND PHILOSOPHY DIVISION □ Brooklyn, NY

Hoover, J.C., Libn.
STEARNS-ROGER ENGINEERING
CORPORATION - TECHNICAL LIBRARY □
Denver, CO

Hoover, James L., Law Libn.
COLUMBIA UNIVERSITY - LAW LIBRARY □ New
York, NY

Hoover, John Neal, Fine Arts Libn.
SOUTHERN ILLINOIS UNIVERSITY,
EDWARDSVILLE - HUMANITIES & FINE ARTS
LIBRARY □ Edwardsville, IL

Hoover, Nancy, Asst.Libn.
U.S. COURT OF APPEALS, 9TH CIRCUIT -
LIBRARY □ Portland, OR

Hoover, Nancy, Asst.Libn.
U.S. DISTRICT COURT - DISTRICT OF OREGON
- LIBRARY □ Portland, OR

Hoover, Peter R., Dir.
PALEONTOLOGICAL RESEARCH INSTITUTION -
LIBRARY □ Ithaca, NY

Hoover, Priscilla W., Libn.
DURHAM COUNTY HOSPITAL CORPORATION -
WATTS SCHOOL OF NURSING - LIBRARY □
Durham, NC

Hoover, Rebecca, Info.Sys.Proj.
MINNESOTA STATE LEGISLATIVE REFERENCE
LIBRARY □ St. Paul, MN

Hope, Monica, Doc.
INTERGOVERNMENTAL COMMITTEE ON URBAN
AND REGIONAL RESEARCH (ICURR) -
INFORMATION EXCHANGE SERVICE □ Toronto,
ON
Hope, Dr. Nelson W., Tech.Res.Libn.
GARRETT CORPORATION - GARRETT TURBINE
ENGINE COMPANY - ENGINEERING LIBRARY □
Phoenix, AZ
Hopfinger, Jeannine, Film Off.
CANADA - NATIONAL FILM BOARD OF CANADA
- FILM PREVIEW LIBRARY □ Montreal, PQ
Hopgood, Heather, Asst.Libn.
HAMILTON SPECTATOR - REFERENCE
LIBRARY† □ Hamilton, ON
Hopkins, B., U.S. Doc.
WAYNE STATE UNIVERSITY - G. FLINT PURDY
LIBRARY □ Detroit, MI
Hopkins, Benjamin, Hd.Libn.
MASSACHUSETTS COLLEGE OF ART - LIBRARY
□ Boston, MA
Hopkins, Charles, Film Archv.
UNIVERSITY OF CALIFORNIA, LOS ANGELES -
UCLA FILM ARCHIVES □ Los Angeles, CA
Hopkins, Dianne, Dir.
WISCONSIN STATE DEPARTMENT OF PUBLIC
INSTRUCTION - WISCONSIN DISSEMINATION
PROGRAM (WDP) □ Madison, WI
Hopkins, Dorothy, Libn.
PITTSBURGH BOARD OF EDUCATION -
PROFESSIONAL LIBRARY □ Pittsburgh, PA
Hopkins, Frank Joy, Chf.Libn.
AMERICAN WORK HORSE MUSEUM - LIBRARY □
Paeonian Springs, VA
Hopkins, Helen G., Ref.Libn.
U.S. ARMY POST - FORT CLAYTON - MORALE
SUPPORT ACTIVITIES - LIBRARY □ APO Miami,
FL
Hopkins, Jan, Cat.Libn.
CROWN ZELLERBACH CORPORATION -
CENTRAL RESEARCH LIBRARY □ Camas, WA
Hopkins, Joan M., Pub.Serv.Libn.
ILLINOIS BENEDICTINE COLLEGE - THEODORE
LOWNIK LIBRARY □ Lisle, IL
Hopkins, Linda Mitro, Mgr.
ROSS LABORATORIES - LIBRARY □ Columbus,
OH
Hopkins, M., Chf., Ref. & Info.Proc.
CANADA - PUBLIC ARCHIVES OF CANADA -
FEDERAL ARCHIVES DIVISION □ Ottawa, ON
Hopkins, Mary C., Libn.
WOODLAND PARK ZOOLOGICAL GARDENS -
LIBRARY □ Seattle, WA
Hopkins, Pat, Res.Archv.
WASHINGTON STATE OFFICE OF SECRETARY
OF STATE - DIVISION OF ARCHIVES AND
RECORD MANAGEMENT □ Olympia, WA
Hopkins, Phyl A., Engr.Libn.
GOODYEAR TIRE AND RUBBER COMPANY -
GOODYEAR ATOMIC CORPORATION -
TECHNICAL LIBRARY □ Piketon, OH
Hopkins, R. Bruce, Cur.
FIREFIGHTERS' MUSEUM OF NOVA SCOTIA -
LIBRARY & INFORMATION CENTER □ Yarmouth,
NS
Hopper, Jean G., Libn.
GRAY PANTHERS - NATIONAL OFFICE LIBRARY
□ Philadelphia, PA
Hopper, Johanne, Libn.
UNIVERSITE DE MONTREAL - BIBLIOTHEQUE
PARA-MEDICALE □ Montreal, PQ
Hoppes, Muriel, Law Libn.
CALIFORNIA STATE LIBRARY □ Sacramento, CA
Hopson, Dallas C., Med.Libn.
INTERFAITH MEDICAL CENTER - ST. JOHN'S
EPISCOPAL HOSPITAL - NURSING AND
MEDICAL LIBRARY □ Brooklyn, NY
Hopson, Emily, Archv.
KENT HISTORICAL SOCIETY - LIBRARY □ Kent,
CT

Hopson, Jean B., Lib.Dir.
WAKE FOREST UNIVERSITY - BABCOCK
GRADUATE SCHOOL OF MANAGEMENT -
LIBRARY □ Winston-Salem, NC
Hopwood, Susan, Found.Coll.Libn.
MARQUETTE UNIVERSITY - FOUNDATION
CENTER REGIONAL REFERENCE COLLECTION □
Milwaukee, WI
Hopwood, Susan, Coord., Ref. & Info.Serv.
MARQUETTE UNIVERSITY - MEMORIAL
LIBRARY □ Milwaukee, WI
Horacek, Margot, Ref.Libn.
UNIVERSITY OF SOUTH FLORIDA - MEDICAL
CENTER LIBRARY □ Tampa, FL
Horan, Nancy, Asst.Libn.
NEW YORK STATE LIBRARY - LAW/SOCIAL
SCIENCE REFERENCE SERVICES □ Albany, NY
Horgan, Maureen, Personnel/Fin.Coord.
TEACHERS COLLEGE - MILBANK MEMORIAL
LIBRARY □ New York, NY
Horie, Ruth, Jr. RMC Spec.
INSTITUTE OF CULTURE AND
COMMUNICATION - CCPC - RESOURCE
MATERIALS COLLECTION □ Honolulu, HI
Horikawa, Emi K., Libn.
SWARTHMORE COLLEGE - CORNELL LIBRARY
OF SCIENCE AND ENGINEERING □ Swarthmore,
PA
Horikawa, Emi K., Libn.
SWARTHMORE COLLEGE - SPROUL
OBSERVATORY LIBRARY □ Swarthmore, PA
Horn, Betty L., Base Libn.
U.S. AIR FORCE BASE - LUKE BASE LIBRARY† □
Luke AFB, AZ
Horn, Eileen, Chem.Libn.
WASHINGTON UNIVERSITY - CHEMISTRY
LIBRARY □ St. Louis, MO
Horn, Harold E., Pres.
CABLE TELEVISION INFORMATION CENTER □
Alexandria, VA
Horn, Janice, Hd.Cat.
CLARION UNIVERSITY OF PENNSYLVANIA -
RENA M. CARLSON LIBRARY □ Clarion, PA
Horn, Karen, Cat.
NATIONAL GALLERY OF ART - PHOTOGRAPHIC
ARCHIVES □ Washington, DC
Horn, Larry, Libn.
ANTAEUS RESEARCH INSTITUTE - LIBRARY □
Fayetteville, AR
Horn, Margaret, Cat./Ref.Libn.
CONCORDIA COLLEGE - BUENGER MEMORIAL
LIBRARY □ St. Paul, MN
Horn, Roger, Coll.Libn.
CLARION UNIVERSITY OF PENNSYLVANIA -
RENA M. CARLSON LIBRARY □ Clarion, PA
Horn, W. Richard, Libn.
U.S. NATL. PARK SERVICE - WESTERN
ARCHEOLOGICAL AND CONSERVATION CENTER
- LIBRARY □ Tucson, AZ
Hornbach, Ruth, Hd.Libn.
KENDALL SCHOOL OF DESIGN - LEARNING
RESOURCE CENTER □ Grand Rapids, MI
Hornby, C., Res.Libn.
EDMONTON SEPARATE SCHOOL BOARD -
PROFESSIONAL LIBRARY □ Edmonton, AB
Horne, Ernest L., Sr.Libn.
GENERAL MOTORS CORPORATION - RESEARCH
LABORATORIES LIBRARY □ Warren, MI
Horner, William C., Systems Libn.
NORTH CAROLINA STATE UNIVERSITY - D.H.
HILL LIBRARY □ Raleigh, NC
Horney, Joyce, ILL Libn.
SOUTHERN ILLINOIS UNIVERSITY - SCHOOL OF
MEDICINE - MEDICAL LIBRARY □ Springfield, IL
Hornickle, Robert, Tech.Info.Spec.
U.S. NATL. HIGHWAY TRAFFIC SAFETY
ADMINISTRATION - TECHNICAL REFERENCE
DIVISION □ Washington, DC
Horning, Kathleen, Spec.Coll.Coord.
UNIVERSITY OF WISCONSIN, MADISON -
COOPERATIVE CHILDREN'S BOOK CENTER
(CCBC) □ Madison, WI

Hornsby, Penelope, Asst. Regional Libn.
NORTH CAROLINA STATE DEPARTMENT OF
CULTURAL RESOURCES - LIBRARY FOR THE
BLIND AND PHYSICALLY HANDICAPPED □
Raleigh, NC
Horowitz, Cyma M., Lib.Dir.
AMERICAN JEWISH COMMITTEE - BLAUSTEIN
LIBRARY □ New York, NY
Horowitz, Harvey P., Libn.
HEBREW UNION COLLEGE - JEWISH
INSTITUTE OF RELIGION - FRANCES-HENRY
LIBRARY □ Los Angeles, CA
Horowitz, Marc, AV Libn.
U.S. VETERANS ADMINISTRATION (NY-
Northport) - HEALTH SCIENCE LIBRARY □
Northport, NY
Horowitz, R., Info.Spec.
ALLERGAN PHARMACEUTICALS, INC. -
MEDICAL & SCIENCE INFORMATION □ Irvine,
CA
Horrell, Jeffrey L., Libn.
DARTMOUTH COLLEGE - SHERMAN ART
LIBRARY □ Hanover, NH
Horres, Mary, Libn.
UNIVERSITY OF CALIFORNIA, SAN DIEGO -
BIOMEDICAL LIBRARY □ La Jolla, CA
Horrocks, David A., Supv.Archv.
U.S. PRESIDENTIAL LIBRARIES - GERALD R.
FORD LIBRARY □ Ann Arbor, MI
Horsbrugh, Patrick, Chm.
ENVIRONIC FOUNDATION INTERNATIONAL,
INC. - LIBRARY AND FILES □ Notre Dame, IN
Horst, Karen, Dir. of Lib.Serv.
ST. LUKE'S HOSPITAL OF KANSAS CITY -
MEDICAL LIBRARY □ Kansas City, MO
Hort, Jean L., Base Libn.
U.S. AIR FORCE BASE - POPE BASE LIBRARY □
Pope AFB, NC
Hortin, Judith, Libn.
AMERICAN INSTITUTE OF BAKING - LIBRARY □
Manhattan, KS
Horton, Dorothy, Libn.
CLARINDA MENTAL HEALTH INSTITUTION -
RESIDENTS AND STAFF LIBRARY □ Clarinda, IA
Horton, Geraldine R., Mgr., Lib.
QUAKER OATS COMPANY - JOHN STUART
RESEARCH LABORATORIES - RESEARCH
LIBRARY □ Barrington, IL
Horton, Sung In, Asst.Libn.
UNIVERSITY OF CALIFORNIA, SANTA BARBARA
- ORIENTAL COLLECTION □ Santa Barbara, CA
Horvat, Kathleen L., Tech.Libn.
WESTINGHOUSE ELECTRIC CORPORATION -
NUCLEAR ENERGY SYSTEMS - ADVANCED
REACTORS DIVISION - LIBRARY† □ Madison,
PA
Horvath, David, Asst.Cur./Cat.
UNIVERSITY OF LOUISVILLE - PHOTOGRAPHIC
ARCHIVES □ Louisville, KY
Horvath, Dr. Janos, Pres.
KOSSUTH FOUNDATION - HUNGARIAN
RESEARCH LIBRARY □ Indianapolis, IN
Horvath, Patricia, Asst. Law Libn.
UNIVERSITY OF PITTSBURGH - LAW LIBRARY □
Pittsburgh, PA
Horvitz, Eleanor F., Libn./Archv.
RHODE ISLAND JEWISH HISTORICAL
ASSOCIATION - LIBRARY □ Providence, RI
Horwitz, Ruth, Media Spec.
BENTLEY COLLEGE - SOLOMON R. BAKER
LIBRARY □ Waltham, MA
Hoshaw, Judy A., Libn.
U.S. NAVY - NAVAL AIR STATION (ME-
Brunswick) - LIBRARY □ Brunswick, ME
Hosken, Fran P., Ed.
WOMEN'S INTERNATIONAL NETWORK □
Lexington, MA
Hoskin, Adele, Chf.Libn.
ELI LILLY AND COMPANY - SCIENTIFIC
LIBRARY □ Indianapolis, IN
Hoskins, Becky, Cur.
HISTORIC BETHLEHEM INC. - LIBRARY/
ARCHIVES □ Bethlehem, PA

Hoskins, Charles R., Info.Dir.
INTERNATIONAL NUMISMATIC SOCIETY -
LIBRARY □ Washington, DC

Hoskins, Mrs. Pat S., Hd.Libn.
CONOCO, INC. - RESEARCH AND
DEVELOPMENT DEPARTMENT - TECHNICAL
INFORMATION SERVICES □ Ponca City, OK

Hosler, Dr. Robert M.
GREAT LAKES HISTORICAL SOCIETY -
CLARENCE METCALF RESEARCH LIBRARY □
Vermilion, OH

Hoslett, Andrea, Hd., Children's Serv.
OWATONNA PUBLIC LIBRARY - TOY LIBRARY □
Owatonna, MN

Hospodka, Vera, Hd.Libn.
PENNSYLVANIA STATE UNIVERSITY - KING OF
PRUSSIA CENTER - LIBRARY □ King Of Prussia,
PA

Hossler, Roy, Asst. Planner/Lib.
FORT WAYNE DEPARTMENT OF COMMUNITY
DEVELOPMENT & PLANNING - PLANNING
LIBRARY □ Fort Wayne, IN

Hostetter, Sandra F., Bus.Libn./Info.Spec.
ROHM & HAAS COMPANY - HOME OFFICE
LIBRARY □ Philadelphia, PA

Hotard, Sandra, Archv.
LOUISIANA STATE OFFICE OF THE SECRETARY
OF STATE - STATE ARCHIVES AND RECORDS
SERVICE - ARCHIVES SECTION □ Baton Rouge,
LA

Hotchkiss, Deborah, Ref.Libn.
SOUTH CAROLINA STATE LIBRARY □ Columbia,
SC

Hotton, Julia, Hd., Art, Prints & Photo.
NEW YORK PUBLIC LIBRARY - SCHOMBURG
CENTER FOR RESEARCH IN BLACK CULTURE □
New York, NY

Hotton, Kevin, Cur./Astronomy
KINGMAN MUSEUM OF NATURAL HISTORY -
LIBRARY □ Battle Creek, MI

Houck, Michael, Libn.
GREATER BALTIMORE MEDICAL CENTER - DR.
JOHN E. SAVAGE MEDICAL STAFF LIBRARY □
Baltimore, MD

Houck, Tammy A., Libn.
SPERRY - NEW HOLLAND ENGINEERING
LIBRARY □ New Holland, PA

Houdek, Frank, Assoc.Dir.
UNIVERSITY OF SOUTHERN CALIFORNIA - LAW
LIBRARY □ Los Angeles, CA

Hough, Bonnie Rose, Coord.
YOUNG WOMEN'S CHRISTIAN ASSOCIATION
OF MARIN - RESOURCE CENTER □ San Anselmo,
CA

Hough, Carolyn A., Mgr., Lib.Serv.
MICHIGAN OSTEOPATHIC MEDICAL CENTER,
INC. - HEALTH SCIENCE LIBRARY □ Detroit, MI

Hough, Leslie S., Dir.
GEORGIA STATE UNIVERSITY - SPECIAL
COLLECTIONS DEPARTMENT □ Atlanta, GA

Houkom, Susan, Acq.Libn.
MEDICAL COLLEGE OF WISCONSIN -
LIBRARIES □ Milwaukee, WI

Houmes, Ms. Chris, Exec.Dir.
MUSEUM OF YORK COUNTY - EDUCATIONAL
LIBRARY □ Rock Hill, SC

House, Dorothy A., Libn.
MUSEUM OF NORTHERN ARIZONA - HAROLD S.
COLTON MEMORIAL LIBRARY† □ Flagstaff, AZ

House, Katherine, Cat.
FILSON CLUB - LIBRARY □ Louisville, KY

House, Myron W., Spec.Coll.Libn.
WEST GEORGIA COLLEGE - IRVINE SULLIVAN
INGRAM LIBRARY - ANNIE BELLE WEAVER
SPECIAL COLLECTIONS □ Carrollton, GA

Householder, B., Bk.Cat./Ref.
U.S. NAVY - NAVAL COASTAL SYSTEMS
CENTER - TECHNICAL INFORMATION
SERVICES BRANCH† □ Panama City, FL

Householder, Carolyn, Hd.
NASHVILLE STATE TECHNICAL INSTITUTE -
EDUCATIONAL RESOURCE CENTER □ Nashville,
TN

Houser, Ed, Mgr., Product Info.Serv.
ALLERGAN PHARMACEUTICALS, INC. -
MEDICAL & SCIENCE INFORMATION □ Irvine,
CA

Houser, Gloria W., Hd., Ser.Dept.
NORTH CAROLINA STATE UNIVERSITY - D.H.
HILL LIBRARY □ Raleigh, NC

Housewright, Stephen, Libn.
DALLAS PUBLIC LIBRARY - HUMANITIES
DIVISION □ Dallas, TX

Houston, Diana Boardman, Libn.
TEXAS STATE DEPARTMENT OF HUMAN
RESOURCES - LIBRARY □ Austin, TX

Houston, Jeanne E., Libn.
BEAUMONT ENTERPRISE & JOURNAL - LIBRARY
□ Beaumont, TX

Houyoux, Philippe, Chf., Soc.Sci./Hum.Coll.
UNIVERSITE LAVAL - BIBLIOTHEQUE □ Ste.
Foy, PQ

Hovde, Roberta, Libn.
MINNESOTA STATE DEPARTMENT OF ENERGY
AND ECONOMIC DEVELOPMENT - ENERGY
LIBRARY □ St. Paul, MN

Hoveland, Lori
SASKATOON STAR-PHOENIX - LIBRARY □
Saskatoon, SK

Hover, Leila M., Dir.
HOLY NAME HOSPITAL - MEDICAL LIBRARY □
Teaneck, NJ

Hovorka, Diana, Asst.Ref.Libn.
SUNY - AGRICULTURAL AND TECHNICAL
COLLEGE AT ALFRED - WALTER C. HINKLE
MEMORIAL LIBRARY □ Alfred, NY

How, Janet, Dir., Info.Serv.
ERNST & WHINNEY - INFORMATION CENTER □
New York, NY

How, Sarah E., Hd.
UNIVERSITY OF CALIFORNIA, LOS ANGELES -
GEOLOGY-GEOPHYSICS LIBRARY □ Los Angeles,
CA

Howard, Alison, Hd.
UNIVERSITY OF CALIFORNIA, BERKELEY -
OPTOMETRY LIBRARY □ Berkeley, CA

Howard, Bill, Chf.
KENTUCKY STATE DEPARTMENT OF
COMMERCE - DIVISION OF RESEARCH - MAP
LIBRARY □ Frankfort, KY

Howard, Bill, Exec.Dir.
NORTHWEST ALABAMA COUNCIL OF LOCAL
GOVERNMENTS - LIBRARY □ Muscle Shoals, AL

Howard, Charles H., Libn.
PENOBSCOT MARINE MUSEUM - STEPHEN
PHILLIPS MEMORIAL LIBRARY □ Searsport, ME

Howard, Donald H., Div.Coord.
BRIGHAM YOUNG UNIVERSITY - RELIGION AND
HISTORY DIVISION LIBRARY □ Provo, UT

Howard, Donald H., Div.Coord.
BRIGHAM YOUNG UNIVERSITY - UTAH VALLEY
BRANCH GENEALOGICAL LIBRARY □ Provo, UT

Howard, Doris, Asst. Law Libn.
HARRIS COUNTY LAW LIBRARY □ Houston, TX

Howard, Eleanor, Med.Libn.
HAVERHILL MUNICIPAL (Hale) HOSPITAL -
MEDICAL LIBRARY □ Haverhill, MA

Howard, Elizabeth M., Libn.
AVCO CORPORATION - SYSTEMS DIVISION -
RESEARCH LIBRARY □ Wilmington, MA

Howard, Ellen, Ref.Coord.
UNIVERSITY OF WASHINGTON - HEALTH
SCIENCES LIBRARY □ Seattle, WA

Howard, Jeanne, Libn.
UNIVERSITY OF OKLAHOMA - PHYSICS-
ASTRONOMY LIBRARY □ Norman, OK

Howard, Jeanne G., Libn.
UNIVERSITY OF OKLAHOMA - CHEMISTRY-
MATHEMATICS LIBRARY □ Norman, OK

Howard, John, Assoc.Libn.
ROYAL ONTARIO MUSEUM - FAR EASTERN
LIBRARY □ Toronto, ON

Howard, Joseph H., Dir.
U.S.D.A. - NATIONAL AGRICULTURAL LIBRARY
□ Beltsville, MD

Howard, L. Dianne, Supv., Info. Retrieval
LORD CORPORATION - INFORMATION
CENTERS □ Erie, PA

Howard, Marjorie, Coord.
ONTARIO - MINISTRY OF CITIZENSHIP AND
CULTURE - MINISTRY OF TOURISM AND
RECREATION - LIBRARY/RESOURCE CENTRE □
Toronto, ON

Howard, Norma K., User.Serv.
ERIC CLEARINGHOUSE ON ELEMENTARY AND
EARLY CHILDHOOD EDUCATION □ Champaign,
IL

Howard, Patricia, Libn.
SISKIYOU COUNTY LAW LIBRARY □ Yreka, CA

Howard, Richard C., Asst.Chf.
LIBRARY OF CONGRESS - ASIAN DIVISION □
Washington, DC

Howard, Roberta L., Tech.Libn.
DU PONT DE NEMOURS (E.I.) & COMPANY, INC.
- POLYMER PRODUCTS LIBRARY □ Beaumont,
TX

Howard, Sallie M., Staff Att.
KENTUCKY STATE LAW LIBRARY □ Frankfort,
KY

Howard, Sally J., Asst.Libn.
KIRKLAND & ELLIS - LIBRARY □ Chicago, IL

Howard, Stephen R., Assoc.Archv.
FIRST CHURCH OF CHRIST SCIENTIST -
ARCHIVES AND LIBRARY □ Boston, MA

Howarth, Joe, Info.Serv.Supv.
LOS ANGELES COUNTY - SANITATION
DISTRICTS TECHNICAL LIBRARY □ Whittier, CA

Howarth, Marna, Libn.
HASTINGS CENTER LIBRARY - INSTITUTE OF
SOCIETY, ETHICS & THE LIFE SCIENCES □
Hastings-on-Hudson, NY

Howatt, Pauline, Dept.Libn.
ALBERTA - DEPARTMENT OF SOCIAL SERVICES
AND COMMUNITY HEALTH - LIBRARY □
Edmonton, AB

Howden, Norman, Prog.Dir.
LOUISIANA STATE UNIVERSITY - COASTAL
INFORMATION REPOSITORY □ Baton Rouge, LA

Howe, E. Jane, Asst.Libn.
ROYAL BANK OF CANADA - LIBRARY □ Calgary,
AB

Howe, Elizabeth, Libn.
PASADENA PRESBYTERIAN CHURCH - LIBRARY
□ St. Petersburg, FL

Howe, Helen E., Hd.Libn.
PHILADELPHIA BOARD OF EDUCATION -
PEDAGOGICAL LIBRARY† □ Philadelphia, PA

Howe, Jane, Asst.Libn.
CANTERRA ENERGY LTD. - LIBRARY □ Calgary,
AB

Howe, Robert W., Dir.
ERIC CLEARINGHOUSE FOR SCIENCE,
MATHEMATICS AND ENVIRONMENTAL
EDUCATION □ Columbus, OH

Howell, Alan, Acq.Libn.
BRIDGEWATER STATE COLLEGE - CLEMENT C.
MAXWELL LIBRARY □ Bridgewater, MA

Howell, Glen W., Chf.Libn.
LAW SOCIETY OF UPPER CANADA - GREAT
LIBRARY □ Toronto, ON

Howell, Mrs. Joseph, Libn.
ZANESVILLE ART CENTER - LIBRARY □
Zanesville, OH

Howell, Dr. M.G., Hd., Tech.Info.Serv.
AMERICAN CYANAMID COMPANY - LEDERLE
LABORATORIES DIVISION - SUBBAROW
MEMORIAL LIBRARY† □ Pearl River, NY

Howell, Patricia, Pub.Serv.Libn.
YALE UNIVERSITY - BEINECKE RARE BOOK
AND MANUSCRIPT LIBRARY □ New Haven, CT

Howell, Sandra, Law Libn.
FULTON COUNTY LAW LIBRARY □ Atlanta, GA

Howell, Virginia B., Law Libn.
ALLEN COUNTY LAW LIBRARY ASSOCIATION,
INC. □ Fort Wayne, IN

Howenstine, Barbara, Ref.Libn.
U.S. DEPT. OF COMMERCE - LIBRARY □
Washington, DC

Howerton, Betty J., Hd.Libn.
WADDELL AND REED, INC. - RESEARCH
LIBRARY □ Kansas City, MO

Howes, Barbara, Sci.Libn.
BUTLER UNIVERSITY - SCIENCE LIBRARY □
Indianapolis, IN

Howey, Marion L., Doc.Libn.
UNIVERSITY OF KANSAS - DOCUMENTS
COLLECTION □ Lawrence, KS

Howie, Dr. Ed, Res.Assoc.
UNIVERSITY OF ARKANSAS AT LITTLE ROCK -
CENTER FOR LIBRARY & INFORMATION
SCIENCE EDUCATION & RES. (CLISER) □ Little
Rock, AR

Howitson, Brenda, Chf., Spec.Coll.
MASSACHUSETTS STATE LIBRARY □ Boston,
MA

Howk, Cynthia, Res.Coord.
LANDMARK SOCIETY OF WESTERN NEW YORK
- WENRICH MEMORIAL LIBRARY □ Rochester,
NY

Howland, Joan, Assoc.Libn., Pub.Serv.
HARVARD UNIVERSITY - LAW SCHOOL
LIBRARY □ Cambridge, MA

Howland, Margaret E.C., Cur.
GREENFIELD COMMUNITY COLLEGE
FOUNDATION - ARCHIBALD MAC LEISH
COLLECTION □ Greenfield, MA

Howrey, Mary M., Lib.Dir.
AURORA COLLEGE - JENKS MEMORIAL
COLLECTION OF ADVENTUAL MATERIALS □
Aurora, IL

Howse, Beth M., Spec.Coll.Libn.
FISK UNIVERSITY - SPECIAL COLLECTIONS
DEPARTMENT □ Nashville, TN

Hoxit, Dr. L. Ray, Act.Dir.
WORLD DATA CENTER A - METEOROLOGY □
Asheville, NC

Hoyle, Karen Nelson, Cur.
UNIVERSITY OF MINNESOTA - CHILDREN'S
LITERATURE RESEARCH COLLECTIONS □
Minneapolis, MN

Hoyt, Dr. William D., Cur.
SANDY BAY HISTORICAL SOCIETY AND
MUSEUM - LIBRARY □ Rockport, MA

Hruby, Rev. B.S., Exec.Dir.
RESEARCH CENTER FOR RELIGION & HUMAN
RIGHTS IN CLOSED SOCIETIES -
INFORMATION CENTER □ New York, NY

Hruska, Dorothy, Co-Dir. & Cur.
LE SUEUR COUNTY HISTORICAL SOCIETY
MUSEUM - LIBRARY □ Elysian, MN

Hruska, James E., Dir.
LE SUEUR COUNTY HISTORICAL SOCIETY
MUSEUM - LIBRARY □ Elysian, MN

Hrycyna, Patricia, Per.Libn.
GULF CANADA LIMITED - CENTRAL LIBRARY† □
Toronto, ON

Hsia, Tao-Tai, Chf.
LIBRARY OF CONGRESS - LAW LIBRARY - FAR
EASTERN LAW DIVISION □ Washington, DC

Hsiao, Gene, Cat.Libn.
UNIVERSITY OF ARIZONA - ORIENTAL
STUDIES COLLECTION □ Tucson, AZ

Hsieh, Lucia, Ref.Libn.
MORGAN GUARANTY TRUST COMPANY OF NEW
YORK - LIBRARY □ New York, NY

Hsieh, Teresa, Instr.-Libn.
UNIVERSITY OF TORONTO - EAST ASIAN
LIBRARY □ Toronto, ON

Hsu, Bonnie C., Libn.
TOBEY HOSPITAL - STILLMAN LIBRARY □
Wareham, MA

Hsu, Veronica, Tech.Libn.
RCA CORPORATION - G & CS - AUTOMATED
SYSTEMS - ENGINEERING LIBRARY □
Burlington, MA

Hu, Chia-Yaung, Asst.Libn./Chinese Sect.
HARVARD UNIVERSITY - HARVARD-YENCHING
LIBRARY □ Cambridge, MA

Hu, David Y., Bibliog.
OHIO STATE UNIVERSITY - EAST ASIAN
COLLECTION □ Columbus, OH

Hu, Evelyn, Cat.Libn.
STANFORD UNIVERSITY - J. HUGH JACKSON
LIBRARY □ Stanford, CA

Hu, Lucia, Cat.
TUCSON MUSEUM OF ART - LIBRARY □ Tucson,
AZ

Hu, Shih-Sheng, Chf.Prov. Law Libn.
LAW SOCIETY OF ALBERTA - EDMONTON
LIBRARY □ Edmonton, AB

Hu, Shih-Sheng, Chf.Prov. Law Libn.
QUEEN'S BENCH - COURT OF APPEAL JUDGES'
LIBRARY □ Edmonton, AB

Huang, Anson, Asst.Libn.
U.S. COAST GUARD - SUPPORT CENTER
LIBRARY □ New York, NY

Huang, Becky, Tech.Serv.Libn.
MICHIGAN OSTEOPATHIC MEDICAL CENTER,
INC. - HEALTH SCIENCE LIBRARY □ Detroit, MI

Huang, Mr. C.K., Dir.
SUNY AT BUFFALO - HEALTH SCIENCES
LIBRARY □ Buffalo, NY

Huang, Dora, Br.Hd.Libn.
U.S. NAVY - NAVAL AIR DEVELOPMENT
CENTER - TECHNICAL INFORMATION BRANCH
□ Warminster, PA

Huang, Sam, Legal Ref.Libn.
UNIVERSITY OF SOUTH DAKOTA - MC KUSICK
LAW LIBRARY □ Vermillion, SD

Huang, Steve, Assoc. Law Libn.
UNIVERSITY OF SOUTH CAROLINA - COLEMAN
KARESH LAW LIBRARY □ Columbia, SC

Hubbard, Bruce, Libn.
BROWN & CALDWELL - LIBRARY □ Walnut
Creek, CA

Hubbard, Edwina M., Libn.
U.S. VETERANS ADMINISTRATION (WY-
Cheyenne) - CENTER LIBRARY □ Cheyenne, WY

Hubbard, Elizabeth, Lib.Assoc.
UNIVERSITY OF PITTSBURGH - ECONOMICS/
COLLECTION IN REGIONAL ECONOMICS □
Pittsburgh, PA

Hubbard, Kathy, Lib.Mgr.
BROWN & ROOT, INC. - TECHNICAL LIBRARY □
Houston, TX

Hubbard, Marguerite B., Musm.Cur.
U.S. PRESIDENTIAL LIBRARIES - FRANKLIN D.
ROOSEVELT LIBRARY □ Hyde Park, NY

Hubbard, Marlis, Libn.
CONCORDIA UNIVERSITY - SIR GEORGE
WILLIAMS CAMPUS - GUIDANCE
INFORMATION CENTRE □ Montreal, PQ

Hubbard, Mary B., Dept.Hd.
TOLEDO-LUCAS COUNTY PUBLIC LIBRARY -
SCIENCE AND TECHNOLOGY DEPARTMENT □
Toledo, OH

Hubbard, Mary Lou, Libn. (West Site)
ST. JOSEPH HOSPITAL OF MT. CLEMENS -
MEDICAL LIBRARY □ Mt. Clemens, MI

Hubbard, Russell G., Libn.
MADISON COUNTY HISTORICAL SOCIETY -
LIBRARY □ Oneida, NY

Hubbard, Terry, Soc.Sci.Libn.
COLORADO STATE UNIVERSITY - WILLIAM E.
MORGAN LIBRARY □ Fort Collins, CO

Hubbard, William J., Dir., Lib.Serv.
VIRGINIA STATE LIBRARY □ Richmond, VA

Hubbard, Willis M., Coll.Libn.
GETTYSBURG COLLEGE - MUSSELMAN LIBRARY
- SPECIAL COLLECTIONS □ Gettysburg, PA

Hubbell, J.H.
U.S. NATL. BUREAU OF STANDARDS - PHOTON
AND CHARGED PARTICLE DATA CENTER □
Gaithersburg, MD

Hubbs, Catherine, Asst.Libn.
UNIVERSITY OF OKLAHOMA - BIOLOGICAL
STATION LIBRARY □ Kingston, OK

Huber, Bertha, Ref.Libn.
U.S. ARMY - ACADEMY OF HEALTH SCIENCES -
STIMSON LIBRARY □ Ft. Sam Houston, TX

Huber, Celia R., Libn.
TEMPLE BETH SHOLOM - LIBRARY □ Miami
Beach, FL

Huber, Donald L., Libn.
TRINITY LUTHERAN SEMINARY - HAMMA
LIBRARY □ Columbus, OH

Huber, George K., Music Libn.
SWARTHMORE COLLEGE - DANIEL UNDERHILL
MUSIC LIBRARY □ Swarthmore, PA

Huberdeau, Arsene, Dir.
MANITOBA - DEPT. OF EDUCATION - BUREAU
DE L'EDUCATION FRANCAISE - DIRECTION
DES RESSOURCES EDUCATIVES FRANCAISES □
Saint-Boniface, MB

Hubert, J.M., Mgr., Tech.Info.Ctr.
CHEVRON RESEARCH COMPANY - TECHNICAL
INFORMATION CENTER □ Richmond, CA

Hubscher, Elenore, Libn.
MCMASTER MEIGHEN - LAW LIBRARY □
Montreal, PQ

Huckins, Barbara W., Chf., Lib.Serv.
U.S. VETERANS ADMINISTRATION (TX-Dallas) -
MEDICAL CENTER LIBRARY (142D) □ Dallas, TX

Hucks, Herbert, Jr., Cur.
UNITED METHODIST COMMN. ON ARCHIVES &
HISTORY - SOUTH CAROLINA CONFERENCE -
HISTORICAL LIBRARY □ Spartanburg, SC

Hucks, Herbert, Jr., Archv.
WOFFORD COLLEGE - SANDOR TESZLER
LIBRARY - ARCHIVES □ Spartanburg, SC

Hudder, Jean A., Info.Coord.
NATIONAL CLEARING HOUSE OF
REHABILITATION TRAINING MATERIALS -
REFERENCE COLLECTION □ Stillwater, OK

Huddleson, Sue, Sci. & Tech.Libn.
CALIFORNIA STATE UNIVERSITY, LOS
ANGELES - SCIENCE AND TECHNOLOGY
REFERENCE ROOM† □ Los Angeles, CA

Huddleston, Joann, Libn.
JOHN HANCOCK MUTUAL LIFE INSURANCE
COMPANY - COMPANY LIBRARY □ Boston, MA

Huddleston, Marsha, Libn.
CHICAGO PUBLIC LIBRARY CULTURAL CENTER
- THOMAS HUGHES CHILDREN'S LIBRARY □
Chicago, IL

Hudman, Betty, Libn.
UNIVERSITY OF TEXAS, AUSTIN - CENTER FOR
TRANSPORTATION RESEARCH □ Austin, TX

Hudson, Alice C., Div.Chf.
NEW YORK PUBLIC LIBRARY - MAP DIVISION □
New York, NY

Hudson, Avon L., Libn.
VIRGINIA STATE DEPARTMENT OF
CONSERVATION & ECONOMIC DEVELOPMENT -
NATIONAL CARTOGRAPHIC INFORMATION
CENTER □ Charlottesville, VA

Hudson, Calvin, Act.Libn.
INSTITUTE OF JUDICIAL ADMINISTRATION -
LIBRARY □ New York, NY

Hudson, Crystal M., Info.Serv.Spec.
U.S. BUREAU OF THE CENSUS - INFORMATION
SERVICES PROGRAM - CHICAGO REGIONAL
OFFICE - REFERENCE CENTER □ Chicago, IL

Hudson, Dale L., Music Libn.
FLORIDA STATE UNIVERSITY - WARREN D.
ALLEN MUSIC LIBRARY □ Tallahassee, FL

Hudson, Donna M., Libn.
WEST VIRGINIA SCHOOL OF OSTEOPATHIC
MEDICINE - WVSOM LIBRARY □ Lewisburg, WV

Hudson, Garnett, Cur.
WYANDOT COUNTY HISTORICAL SOCIETY -
WYANDOT MUSEUM - LIBRARY □ Upper
Sandusky, OH

Hudson, Gary, Hd., Acq.Dept.
SOUTH DAKOTA STATE UNIVERSITY - HILTON
M. BRIGGS LIBRARY □ Brookings, SD

Hudson, J. William, Exec.Dir.
REFRIGERATION RESEARCH FOUNDATION -
LIBRARY □ Bethesda, MD

Hudson, Jean, Supv., Tech.Serv.
SCHERING-PLOUGH CORPORATION -
PHARMACEUTICAL RESEARCH DIVISION -
LIBRARY INFORMATION CENTER □ Bloomfield,
NJ

Hudson, Joan, Libn.
FRASER AND BEATTY - LIBRARY □ Toronto, ON

Hudson, Kathy, Adm.Asst.
MAINE MARITIME MUSEUM - LIBRARY/
ARCHIVES □ Bath, ME

Hudson, N.J., Mgr., Tech.Serv.
AMERICAN SOCIETY OF SAFETY ENGINEERS -
TECHNICAL INFORMATION CENTER □ Park
Ridge, IL

Hudson, Patricia, Spec.
MICHIGAN STATE UNIVERSITY - UNIVERSITY
ARCHIVES AND HISTORICAL COLLECTIONS □
East Lansing, MI

Hudson, Roberta L., Libn.
HAYES (Rutherford B.) PRESIDENTIAL CENTER -
LIBRARY □ Fremont, OH

Hudson, Saundra H., Dir.
ST. JOHN'S MERCY MEDICAL CENTER - JOHN
YOUNG BROWN MEMORIAL LIBRARY □ St.
Louis, MO

Hudson, Thomas G., Dir.
U.S. NATL. ARCHIVES & RECORDS SERVICE -
FEDERAL ARCHIVES AND RECORDS CENTER,
REGION 4 □ East Point, GA

Hudzik, Robert, Hd.
PUBLIC LIBRARY OF CINCINNATI AND
HAMILTON COUNTY - FILMS AND RECORDINGS
CENTER □ Cincinnati, OH

Huecker, Celeste, Cat.Libn.
U.S. SOCIAL SECURITY ADMINISTRATION -
LIBRARY INFORMATION & GRAPHICS
SERVICES BRANCH □ Baltimore, MD

Huelsbeck, Charles, Libn.
U.S. VETERANS ADMINISTRATION (IA-Des
Moines) - HOSPITAL LIBRARY □ Des Moines, IA

Huemer, Christina, Hd., Access & Sup.Serv.
COLUMBIA UNIVERSITY - AVERY
ARCHITECTURAL AND FINE ARTS LIBRARY □
New York, NY

Huertas, G.
SPERRY - LAW LIBRARY □ New York, NY

Huesing, Steven A., HCIB Secretariat
HEALTH COMPUTER INFORMATION BUREAU □
Edmonton, AB

Huey, Dorothy, Libn.
IBM CORPORATION - COMMUNICATION
PRODUCTS DIVISION - LIBRARY □ Research
Triangle Park, NC

Huff, Margaret F., Dean, LRC
ORANGEBURG-CALHOUN TECHNICAL COLLEGE
- GRESSETTE LEARNING RESOURCE CENTER □
Orangeburg, SC

Huff, Rose Marie, Acq.Libn.
TRIDENT TECHNICAL COLLEGE - NORTH
CAMPUS LIBRARY □ North Charleston, SC

Huff, Susan, Spec.Res.Libn.
GOLDEN GATE UNIVERSITY - SCHOOL OF LAW
LIBRARY □ San Francisco, CA

Huff, Susan, Asst.Libn.
UNIVERSITY OF CALIFORNIA, BERKELEY -
GOVERNMENT DOCUMENTS DEPARTMENT □
Berkeley, CA

Huff-Duff, Barbara, Acq.Libn.
LOYOLA LAW SCHOOL - LIBRARY □ Los Angeles,
CA

Huffaker, Christine R., Rec.Mgr.
U.S. DEPT. OF THE INTERIOR - MINERALS
MANAGEMENT SERVICE - ALASKA OUTER
CONTINENTAL SHELF REGIONAL LIBRARY □
Anchorage, AK

Huffman, George E., Dir.
AMARILLO COLLEGE - LEARNING RESOURCE
CENTER - SPECIAL COLLECTIONS† □ Amarillo,
TX

Hufford, Laurel, Children's Libn.
UNIVERSITY CONGREGATIONAL CHURCH -
LIBRARY □ Seattle, WA

Hufford, Mary, Folklife Spec.
LIBRARY OF CONGRESS - AMERICAN FOLKLIFE
CENTER □ Washington, DC

Hug, Dr. Gordon
UNIVERSITY OF NOTRE DAME - RADIATION
LABORATORY - RADIATION CHEMISTRY DATA
CENTER □ Notre Dame, IN

Huge, Sharon
PUBLIC LIBRARY OF CINCINNATI AND
HAMILTON COUNTY - MUNICIPAL REFERENCE
LIBRARY □ Cincinnati, OH

Huge, Sharon A., Libn.
DINSMORE & SHOHL - LIBRARY □ Cincinnati, OH

Huggins, Una D., Chf.Acq.Libn.
U.S. ARMY - OFFICE OF THE ADJUTANT
GENERAL - MORALE SUPPORT DIRECTORATE -
LIBRARY ACTIVITIES DIVISION □ Alexandria,
VA

Hughes, Rev. Canon M.A., Adm.Off.
ANGLICAN CHURCH OF CANADA - DIOCESE OF
MONTREAL - ARCHIVES □ Montreal, PQ

Hughes, Catherine, ILL Libn.
SUNY - COLLEGE AT GENESEO - COLLEGE
LIBRARIES □ Geneseo, NY

Hughes, Charles Z., Libn.
BROADLAWNS MEDICAL CENTER - HEALTH
SCIENCES LIBRARY □ Des Moines, IA

Hughes, Donald, Pub.Serv./Ref.Libn.
UNIVERSITY OF NORTH DAKOTA - OLAF H.
THORMODSGARD LAW LIBRARY □ Grand Forks,
ND

Hughes, Dorothy, Lib.Asst.
FERGUSON BAPTIST CHURCH - LIBRARY □
Ferguson, KY

Hughes, Dorothy S., Libn.
SEATTLE TRUST & SAVINGS BANK - LIBRARY □
Seattle, WA

Hughes, Gay, Doc.Supv.
CURRY COLLEGE - LOUIS R. LEVIN MEMORIAL
LIBRARY - SPECIAL COLLECTIONS† □ Milton,
MA

Hughes, Inez H., Musm.Dir.
HARRISON COUNTY HISTORICAL MUSEUM -
INEZ HATLEY HUGHES RESEARCH CENTER □
Marshall, TX

Hughes, Rev. Ivan W., O.S.B., Dir., Lib.Serv.
CATHOLIC SEMINARY FOUNDATION OF
INDIANAPOLIS - LIBRARY □ Indianapolis, IN

Hughes, Dr. J. Marshal, II, Ctr.Libn.
U.S. NAVY - NAVAL SURFACE WEAPONS
CENTER - CENTER LIBRARY □ Dahlgren, VA

Hughes, J. Michael, Asst.Ref.Libn.
YALE UNIVERSITY - LAW LIBRARY □ New
Haven, CT

Hughes, Jean, Sr.Libn.
SAN DIEGO PUBLIC LIBRARY - HISTORY &
WORLD AFFAIRS SECTION □ San Diego, CA

Hughes, Jean, Sr.Libn.
SAN DIEGO PUBLIC LIBRARY - INFORMATION/
DIRECTORY SERVICE SECTION □ San Diego, CA

Hughes, Judy L., Libn.
FIRST BAPTIST CHURCH OF LAKEWOOD -
CHURCH LIBRARY □ Long Beach, CA

Hughes, Karen, Media Spec.
JEWISH HOSPITAL - MEDICAL LIBRARY
SERVICES □ Louisville, KY

Hughes, Mrs. Lealer M., Libn.
U.S. ARMY - RESEARCH AND TECHNOLOGY
LABS (AVRADCOM) - APPLIED TECH.
LABORATORY - TECHNICAL LIB. □ Ft. Eustis, VA

Hughes, Norma, Dir.
MOHAVE MUSEUM OF HISTORY AND ARTS -
LIBRARY □ Kingman, AZ

Hughes, Raymond, Mus.Cur.
BUFFALO & ERIE COUNTY HISTORICAL
SOCIETY - LIBRARY† □ Buffalo, NY

Hughes, Rita A., Chf. Libn.
MERRILL LYNCH PIERCE FENNER & SMITH,
INC. - LIBRARY† □ New York, NY

Hughes, Susan K., Corp.Libn.
DATAPOINT CORPORATION - INFORMATION
RESOURCE CENTER □ San Antonio, TX

Hughes, Suzanne, Adm.
LOUISIANA STATE HOUSE OF
REPRESENTATIVES LEGISLATIVE SERVICES -
RESEARCH LIBRARY □ Baton Rouge, LA

Hughes, Virginia, Ed., In The News
SCHERING-PLOUGH CORPORATION - BUSINESS
INFORMATION CENTER - LIBRARY □
Kenilworth, NJ

Hughes, Virginia C., Libn.
U.S. FEDERAL AVIATION ADMINISTRATION -
AERONAUTICAL CENTER LIBRARY, AAC-64D □
Oklahoma City, OK

Hughston, Milan, Assoc.Libn.
CARTER (Amon) MUSEUM - LIBRARY □ Fort
Worth, TX

Hugs, Theo D., Park Techn.
U.S. NATL. PARK SERVICE - BIGHORN CANYON
NATL. RECREATION AREA - LIBRARY □ Fort
Smith, MT

Hui, Timothy, Ser.Libn.
DALLAS THEOLOGICAL SEMINARY - MOSHER
LIBRARY □ Dallas, TX

Huijgen, Diane, Libn.
RAND INFORMATION SYSTEMS, INC. -
LIBRARY □ San Francisco, CA

Huisman, Lois K., Asst.Libn.
BLODGETT MEMORIAL MEDICAL CENTER -
RICHARD ROOT SMITH LIBRARY □ Grand
Rapids, MI

Huitfeldt, J., Mgr., Info.Res.
CARRIER CORPORATION - LOGAN LEWIS
LIBRARY □ Syracuse, NY

Huizar, Lois, Instr.Mtls.Ctr.Libn.
UNIVERSITY OF WISCONSIN, STEVENS POINT
- JAMES H. ALBERTSON CENTER FOR
LEARNING RESOURCES □ Stevens Point, WI

Huizer-Rivera, Diana, Map Libn.
MICHIGAN STATE UNIVERSITY - ART/MAPS
LIBRARY □ East Lansing, MI

Hulbert, Linda, Assoc.Libn., Coll.Dev.
SUNY - UPSTATE MEDICAL CENTER LIBRARY □
Syracuse, NY

Hulcher, Leigh S., Lib.Cons.
ST. PAUL'S EPISCOPAL CHURCH - LIBRARY □
Richmond, VA

Hulkonen, David A., Dir.
UNIVERSITY OF SOUTH DAKOTA - CHRISTIAN
P. LOMMEN HEALTH SCIENCES LIBRARY □
Vermillion, SD

Hull, Cheryl, Tech.Ref.Asst.
ROCKWELL INTERNATIONAL - HEAVY
VEHICLES COMPONENTS OPERATION -
REFERENCE CENTER □ Troy, MI

Hull, David, Prin.Libn.
NATIONAL MARITIME MUSEUM - J. PORTER
SHAW LIBRARY □ San Francisco, CA

Hull, Doris M., Ref.Libn.
HOWARD UNIVERSITY - MOORLAND-SPINGARN
RESEARCH CENTER - LIBRARY DIVISION □
Washington, DC

Hull, Marcelle, Archival Libn.
DALLAS PUBLIC LIBRARY - TEXAS/DALLAS
HISTORY AND ARCHIVES DIVISION □ Dallas, TX

Hull, Nancy, Libn.
AMERICAN INSTITUTES FOR RESEARCH -
LIBRARY □ Palo Alto, CA

Hull, Nina M., Health Sci.Libn.
HOLY CROSS HOSPITAL - HEALTH SCIENCES
LIBRARY □ Mission Hills, CA

Hull, Sharon, Acq.Libn.
MEHARRY MEDICAL COLLEGE - MEDICAL
LIBRARY - LEARNING RESOURCES CENTER □
Nashville, TN

Hull, Thomas V., Dir.
AMERICAN LEGION - NATIONAL
HEADQUARTERS - LIBRARY □ Indianapolis, IN

Hull, Yvonne C., Libn.
XAVIER UNIVERSITY OF LOUISIANA - COLLEGE
OF PHARMACY - LIBRARY† □ New Orleans, LA

Hulse, Granvyl, Libn.
NUMISMATICS INTERNATIONAL - LIBRARY □
Colebrook, NH

Hulse, Phyllis, Libn.
DALLAS PUBLIC LIBRARY - BUSINESS AND
TECHNOLOGY DIVISION □ Dallas, TX

Hulser, Richard P., Sr.Libn.
IBM CORPORATION - GENERAL TECHNOLOGY
DIVISION - EAST FISHKILL FACILITY -
LIBRARY □ Hopewell Junction, NY

Hulsizer, Bernice Lord, Libn.
UNIVERSITY OF ILLINOIS - PHYSICS/
ASTRONOMY LIBRARY □ Urbana, IL
Hulsker, W., Found.Ctr.Coll.
WAYNE STATE UNIVERSITY - G. FLINT PURDY
LIBRARY □ Detroit, MI
Hulsker, William, Ref.Libn.
WAYNE STATE UNIVERSITY - SCIENCE
LIBRARY □ Detroit, MI
Hume, Howard, Dp.Dir.
U.S. NATL. DEFENSE UNIVERSITY - LIBRARY □
Washington, DC
Humes, Aileen W., Libn.
NEW BRUNSWICK ELECTRIC POWER
COMMISSION - REFERENCE CENTER† □
Fredericton, NB
Hummel, Muriel H., Libn.
CALTEX PETROLEUM CORPORATION -
CORPORATE LIBRARY† □ Dallas, TX
Hummer, Kathryn, Res.Libn.
PERSONAL PRODUCTS COMPANY - RESEARCH
& DEVELOPMENT LIBRARY □ Milltown, NJ
Humphreville, Joanne, Libn.
FOOTE CONE & BELDING - INFORMATION
CENTER □ Chicago, IL
Humphrey, Jean, Asst.Libn., Tech.Serv.
UNIVERSITY OF ARIZONA - COLLEGE OF LAW
LIBRARY† □ Tucson, AZ
Humphrey, Louise, Libn.
TRUE VINE MISSIONARY BAPTIST CHURCH -
LIBRARY† □ Alexandria, LA
Humphrey, Ms. M. Moss, Sr.Med.Libn.
LOS ANGELES COUNTY/KING/DREW MEDICAL
CENTER - HEALTH SCIENCES LIBRARY □ Los
Angeles, CA
Humphrey, Margaret Long, Libn.
COLORADO STATE DEPARTMENT OF SOCIAL
SERVICE - LIBRARY □ Denver, CO
Humphreys, Glenn E., Ref.Libn.
CALIFORNIA HISTORICAL SOCIETY -
SCHUBERT HALL LIBRARY □ San Francisco, CA
Humphreys, Jo Ann, Pub.Serv. Law Libn.
UNIVERSITY OF MISSOURI - SCHOOL OF LAW
LIBRARY □ Columbia, MO
Humphreys, Kenneth K., Exec.Dir.
AMERICAN ASSOCIATION OF COST
ENGINEERS - LIBRARY □ Morgantown, WV
Humphreys, Richard H., Libn.
DELAWARE LAW SCHOOL OF WIDENER
UNIVERSITY - LAW LIBRARY □ Wilmington, DE
Humphries, Donna I., Libn.
CANADIAN UTILITIES LIMITED - LIBRARY □
Edmonton, AB
Hund, June, Tech.Serv.Libn.
MICHIGAN OSTEOPATHIC MEDICAL CENTER,
INC. - HEALTH SCIENCE LIBRARY □ Detroit, MI
Hundt, Lindsey, Asst.Info.Spec.
U.S. FEDERAL JUDICIAL CENTER -
INFORMATION SERVICE† □ Washington, DC
Hungate, Robert H., Act.Dir.
SAN DIEGO STATE UNIVERSITY - BUREAU OF
BUSINESS & ECONOMIC RESEARCH LIBRARY □
San Diego, CA
Hunger, Charles, Dir., AV Serv.
KENT STATE UNIVERSITY - AUDIOVISUAL
SERVICES □ Kent, OH
Hungerford, Anthos, Dir.
HURLEY MEDICAL CENTER - HAMADY HEALTH
SCIENCES LIBRARY □ Flint, MI
Hunisak, Peter, Cartographic Techn.
NEW YORK STATE DEPARTMENT OF
TRANSPORTATION - MAP INFORMATION UNIT
□ Albany, NY
Hunka, Dr. Steve, Coord.
UNIVERSITY OF ALBERTA - DIVISION OF
EDUCATIONAL RESEARCH - TECHNICAL
LIBRARY □ Edmonton, AB
Hunn, Marvin, Ref.Libn.
DALLAS THEOLOGICAL SEMINARY - MOSHER
LIBRARY □ Dallas, TX

Hunnewell, John J., Exec.Dir.
INTERNATIONAL INSTITUTE OF MUNICIPAL
CLERKS - MANAGEMENT INFORMATION
CENTER □ Pasadena, CA
Hunsicker, Marya, Lib. for the Blind
NEW JERSEY STATE LIBRARY □ Trenton, NJ
Hunsicker, Susan
PENNWALT CORPORATION - INFORMATION
SERVICES DEPARTMENT □ King Of Prussia, PA
Hunsucker, Alice E., Asst.V.P./Mgr.
WELLS FARGO BANK - LIBRARY 888 □ San
Francisco, CA
Hunsucker, Miss Coy K., Hd.
PUBLIC LIBRARY OF CINCINNATI AND
HAMILTON COUNTY - EXCEPTIONAL
CHILDREN'S DIVISION □ Cincinnati, OH
Hunt, Alta N., Libn.
U.S. AIR FORCE BASE - GUNTER BASE LIBRARY
□ Gunter AFS, AL
Hunt, Ann C., Libn.
TRANSAMERICA DE LAVAL INC. - TECHNICAL
LIBRARY □ Trenton, NJ
Hunt, Barbara, Asst.Libn., Adm.
DADE COUNTY LAW LIBRARY □ Miami, FL
Hunt, Carol, Cur., Hist.Coll.
PUTNAM MUSEUM - LIBRARY □ Davenport, IA
Hunt, Cathy S., Music Libn.
UNIVERSITY OF KENTUCKY - MUSIC LIBRARY/
LISTENING CENTER □ Lexington, KY
Hunt, Charles, Law Libn.
LYCOMING COUNTY LAW LIBRARY† □
Williamsport, PA
Hunt, Cheryl R., Ref.Asst./Patent Libn.
PROVIDENCE PUBLIC LIBRARY - BUSINESS-
INDUSTRY-SCIENCE DEPARTMENT □
Providence, RI
Hunt, Deborah, Asst.Libn./Circ.
LANCASTER BIBLE COLLEGE - STOLL
MEMORIAL LIBRARY □ Lancaster, PA
Hunt, Diana E., Libn.
RUSSELL AND DUMOULIN - LIBRARY □
Vancouver, BC
Hunt, Florine E., Corp.Libn.
PUBLIC SERVICE ELECTRIC AND GAS
COMPANY - LIBRARY □ Newark, NJ
Hunt, Gary A., Hd.
OHIO UNIVERSITY - DEPARTMENT OF
ARCHIVES AND SPECIAL COLLECTIONS □
Athens, OH
Hunt, Janet, Asst.Libn.
UNIVERSITY OF KING'S COLLEGE - KING'S
COLLEGE LIBRARY □ Halifax, NS
Hunt, Judith Lin, Univ.Libn.
UNIVERSITY OF BRIDGEPORT - MAGNUS
WAHLSTROM LIBRARY - SPECIAL
COLLECTIONS □ Bridgeport, CT
Hunter, Ann, Corp.Libn.
ANHEUSER-BUSCH COMPANIES, INC. -
CORPORATE LIBRARY □ St. Louis, MO
Hunter, Beryl M., Libn.
CANADA - OFFICE OF THE COMMISSIONER OF
OFFICIAL LANGUAGES - LIBRARY □ Ottawa, ON
Hunter, Debbie, Pub.Serv.Libn.
ALBERTA - DEPARTMENT OF LABOUR -
LIBRARY SERVICES □ Edmonton, AB
Hunter, Diane C., Mgr., Lib.Serv.
ATLANTA NEWSPAPERS - REFERENCE LIBRARY
□ Atlanta, GA
Hunter, Glen, Libn.
METROPOLITAN TORONTO LIBRARY -
THEATRE DEPARTMENT □ Toronto, ON
Hunter, Gregory S., Dir. of Archv.Prog.
UNITED NEGRO COLLEGE FUND, INC. -
DEPARTMENT OF ARCHIVES AND HISTORY □
New York, NY
Hunter, Isabel, Dir.
BAYSTATE MEDICAL CENTER - HEALTH
SCIENCES LIBRARY □ Springfield, MA
Hunter, J.A., Libn.
UNIVERSITY OF PENNSYLVANIA - WISTAR
INSTITUTE OF ANATOMY & BIOLOGY -
LIBRARY □ Philadelphia, PA

Hunter, J.E.B., Chf.Libn.
CANADA - NATIONAL GALLERY OF CANADA -
LIBRARY □ Ottawa, ON
Hunter, James, Libn.
COLUMBUS DISPATCH - EDITORIAL LIBRARY □
Columbus, OH
Hunter, Janice, Lib.Supv.
ARIZONA-SONORA DESERT MUSEUM - LIBRARY
□ Tucson, AZ
Hunter, JoAnn, Dir. of Musm.
CARROLL COUNTY FARM MUSEUM - LANDON
BURNS MEMORIAL LIBRARY □ Westminster, MD
Hunter, Josephine R., Libn.
HUMAN RESOURCES RESEARCH
ORGANIZATION - VAN EVERA LIBRARY □
Alexandria, VA
Hunter, Joy W., Chf., Lib.Serv.
U.S. VETERANS ADMINISTRATION (TN-
Murfreesboro) - MEDICAL CENTER LIBRARY □
Murfreesboro, TN
Hunter, Julie V., Act.Dir.
ATLANTA UNIVERSITY CENTER - ROBERT W.
WOODRUFF LIBRARY □ Atlanta, GA
Hunter, M. Edward, Libn.
METHODIST THEOLOGICAL SCHOOL IN OHIO -
JOHN W. DICKHAUT LIBRARY □ Delaware, OH
Hunter, Steve, Libn.
MEMORIAL HOSPITAL - HOMER GAGE LIBRARY
□ Worcester, MA
Huntington, Claire A., Libn.
GEISINGER MEDICAL CENTER - SCHOOL OF
NURSING LIBRARY □ Danville, PA
Huot, Madeleine, Ref.Spec.
ALCAN INTERNATIONAL, LTD. - TECHNICAL
INFORMATION CENTRE □ Jonquiere, PQ
Hupfer, Holly, Info.Coord.
NATIONAL CAR RENTAL SYSTEM, INC. -
BUSINESS INFORMATION CENTER □
Minneapolis, MN
Huppert, Ramona, Libn.
3M - 251 LIBRARY □ St. Paul, MN
Hurd, Christian P., District Libn.
U.S. ARMY - CORPS OF ENGINEERS -
PORTLAND DISTRICT - LIBRARY □ Portland, OR
Hurd, Douglas P., Pub.Serv.Libn.
UNIVERSITY OF VIRGINIA - SCIENCE &
ENGINEERING LIBRARY □ Charlottesville, VA
Hurd, Sr. Naomi, S.P., Libn.
ST. JOSEPH MEDICAL CENTER - HEALTH
SCIENCE LIBRARY □ Burbank, CA
Hurkett, Jack, Hd., Agency Oper.
IOWA STATE LIBRARY COMMISSION □ Des
Moines, IA
Hurlbert, Betty E., Libn.
ASARCO INC. - LIBRARY □ South Plainfield, NJ
Hurlebaus, Alice, Acq.Libn.
UNIVERSITY OF CINCINNATI - MEDICAL
CENTER LIBRARIES - HEALTH SCIENCES
LIBRARY† □ Cincinnati, OH
Hurley, Carolyn
CRAIN COMMUNICATIONS, INC. -
INFORMATION CENTER □ Chicago, IL
Hurley, Hazel, Libn.
NEW MEXICO STATE DEPARTMENT OF
HOSPITALS - STATE HOSPITAL - ELLA P. KIEF
MEMORIAL LIBRARY □ Las Vegas, NM
Hurley, Marianne, Hd. of Branches
CANADA - NATIONAL RESEARCH COUNCIL -
CANADA INSTITUTE FOR SCIENTIFIC AND
TECHNICAL INFORMATION (CISTI) □ Ottawa,
ON
Hurley, Maureen, Adv.
BOSTON UNIVERSITY - WOMEN'S CENTER -
LIBRARY □ Boston, MA
Hurley, Richard N., Photographer
BROWN UNIVERSITY - JOHN CARTER BROWN
LIBRARY □ Providence, RI
Hurley, Tom
INSTITUTE OF NOETIC SCIENCES - LIBRARY □
Sausalito, CA
Hurn, Doris P., Libn.
MARION GENERAL HOSPITAL - MEDICAL
LIBRARY □ Marion, OH

Hurn, Doris P., Libn.
SMITH (Frederick C.) CLINIC - MEDICAL
LIBRARY □ Marion, OH
Hurnard, Shirley A., Libn.
SASKATCHEWAN - DEPARTMENT OF THE
ATTORNEY GENERAL - COURT OF APPEAL
LIBRARY □ Regina, SK
Hurst, Earlene, Ser.Libn.
STETSON UNIVERSITY - COLLEGE OF LAW -
CHARLES A. DANA LAW LIBRARY □ St.
Petersburg, FL
Hurst, Louann, Educ.Serv.Libn.
UNIVERSITY OF TENNESSEE - CENTER FOR
THE HEALTH SCIENCES LIBRARY □ Memphis,
TN
Hurst, Martha, Libn.
PLOUGH, INC. - RESEARCH LIBRARY □
Memphis, TN
Hurt, Anne, Asst. to Dir.
ST. JOHN'S UNIVERSITY - COLLEGE OF
PHARMACY & ALLIED HEALTH PROFESSIONS -
HEALTH EDUCATION RESOURCE CENTER □
Jamaica, NY
Hurt, Byrnice R., Tech.Libn.
KIMBERLY-CLARK CORPORATION - TECHNICAL
LIBRARY □ Roswell, GA
Hurt, Howard, Hd.
UNIVERSITY OF BRITISH COLUMBIA -
CURRICULUM LABORATORY □ Vancouver, BC
Hurtado, Louisa, Doc.Libn.
BRIGHAM YOUNG UNIVERSITY - J. REUBEN
CLARK LAW SCHOOL LIBRARY □ Provo, UT
Hurtes, Reva, Libn.
UNIVERSITY OF MIAMI - SCHOOL OF
MEDICINE - BASCOM PALMER EYE INSTITUTE
- LIBRARY □ Miami, FL
Hurtt, James, Circ./ILL Libn.
ATHENAEUM OF OHIO - MOUNT ST. MARY'S
SEMINARY OF THE WEST - EUGENE H. MALY
MEMORIAL LIBRARY □ Cincinnati, OH
Huschen, Mary, Asst.Mgr.
CHICAGO TRIBUNE - EDITORIAL
INFORMATION CENTER □ Chicago, IL
Huseman, Howard W., Assoc.Univ.Libn.
UNIVERSITY OF FLORIDA - ARCHITECTURE &
FINE ARTS LIBRARY □ Gainesville, FL
Huseth, Layne, Hd., Shipyard Tech.Lib.
U.S. NAVY - NAVAL SHIPYARD (CA-Mare Island)
- TECHNICAL LIBRARY □ Vallejo, CA
Husman, Susan, Libn.
SOUTH CAROLINA STATE ATTORNEY
GENERAL'S OFFICE - LEGAL LIBRARY □
Columbia, SC
Hussain, Mohammad Riaz, Libn.
TECHNICAL UNIVERSITY OF NOVA SCOTIA -
LIBRARY □ Halifax, NS
Hussain, Tahira, Sr.Libn.
TECHNICAL UNIVERSITY OF NOVA SCOTIA -
LIBRARY □ Halifax, NS
Hussey, Rev. M. Edmund, Archv.Cons.
ARCHDIOCESE OF CINCINNATI - ARCHIVES □
Cincinnati, OH
Husted, Shirley C., County Hist.
MONROE COUNTY HISTORIAN'S DEPARTMENT
- LIBRARY □ Rochester, NY
Hustein, Joseph, Pres.
AMERICAN INTERNATIONAL DATASEARCH □
Sacramento, CA
Huston, Jane, Branch Libn.
SHEARMAN & STERLING - LIBRARY □ New York,
NY
Hustvedt, Lloyd, Exec.Sec.
NORWEGIAN-AMERICAN HISTORICAL
ASSOCIATION - ARCHIVES □ Northfield, MN
Hutchason, Clark, Supv.
COEN COMPANY, INC. - TECHNICAL LIBRARY†
□ Burlingame, CA
Hutchens, Shirley, Archv.
SAMFORD UNIVERSITY - BAPTIST HISTORICAL
COLLECTION □ Birmingham, AL

Hutchens, Shirley, Baptist Archv.
SAMFORD UNIVERSITY - HARWELL GOODWIN
DAVIS LIBRARY - SPECIAL COLLECTION □
Birmingham, AL
Hutchins, Andrea, Dp.Mgr.
ANSER - TECHNICAL LIBRARY □ Arlington, VA
Hutchins, Barbara M., Exec.Sec.
RELIGIOUS ARTS GUILD - MUSIC LIBRARY □
Boston, MA
Hutchins, Betsy, Info.Off.
AMERICAN DONKEY AND MULE SOCIETY -
INFORMATION OFFICE □ Denton, TX
Hutchins, Carol, Hd.
INDIANA UNIVERSITY - SWAIN HALL LIBRARY
□ Bloomington, IN
Hutchins, Richard G., Dir.
SETON HALL UNIVERSITY - SCHOOL OF LAW -
LAW LIBRARY □ Newark, NJ
Hutchinson, Ann P., Lib.Dir.
ROSWELL PARK MEMORIAL INSTITUTE -
LIBRARY AND INFORMATION MANAGEMENT
SERVICES □ Buffalo, NY
Hutchinson, Mary, Libn.
ST. LOUIS PUBLIC LIBRARY - READERS
SERVICES/DOCUMENTS DEPARTMENT □ St.
Louis, MO
Hutchinson, Neville, Microfilm Supv.
AMERICAN STOCK EXCHANGE - MARTIN J.
KEENA MEMORIAL LIBRARY □ New York, NY
Hutchison, Jill, Res.Off.
AUSTRALIAN INFORMATION SERVICE -
REFERENCE LIBRARY/INFORMATION SERVICE
□ New York, NY
Hutchison, Margaret, Staff Archv.
SASKATCHEWAN ARCHIVES BOARD □ Regina,
SK
Hutchison, Omega, Supv.
MORGAN COUNTY HISTORICAL SOCIETY -
LIBRARY □ Versailles, MO
Hutchison, Mrs. R.L., Libn.
WESTMINSTER PRESBYTERIAN CHURCH -
LIBRARY □ Pittsburgh, PA
Hutchison, Ron, Proc.
ERIC CLEARINGHOUSE ON ELEMENTARY AND
EARLY CHILDHOOD EDUCATION □ Champaign,
IL
Huth, Mary, Asst.Hd.
UNIVERSITY OF ROCHESTER - DEPARTMENT
OF RARE BOOKS AND SPECIAL COLLECTIONS □
Rochester, NY
Huthnance, John R., Dir.
UNIVERSITY OF ALABAMA - JONES LAW
INSTITUTE - LIBRARY □ Montgomery, AL
Hutslar, Dr. Jack, Exec.Dir.
NORTH AMERICAN YOUTH SPORT INSTITUTE -
INFORMATION CENTER □ Kernersville, NC
Hutson, Dorothy, Mgr., Tech.Serv.
GENERAL ELECTRIC COMPANY - ADVANCED
REACTOR SYSTEMS DEPT. - LIBRARY □
Sunnyvale, CA
Hutson, J.P., Info.Ctr.Asst.
OAK RIDGE NATIONAL LABORATORY -
TOXICOLOGY INFORMATION RESPONSE
CENTER □ Oak Ridge, TN
Hutson, James H., Chf.
LIBRARY OF CONGRESS - MANUSCRIPT
DIVISION □ Washington, DC
Hutto, Rebecca, Cat.Libn.
SAMFORD UNIVERSITY - CUMBERLAND
SCHOOL OF LAW - CORDELL HULL LAW
LIBRARY □ Birmingham, AL
Hutton, Mary Ann, Coord., Libs.
NATIONAL INSTITUTE ON MENTAL
RETARDATION - NATIONAL REFERENCE
SERVICE LIBRARY □ Downsview, ON
Hutton, Richard, Cat.
NATIONAL GALLERY OF ART - PHOTOGRAPHIC
ARCHIVES □ Washington, DC
Hyam, G., Hd., British Archv.
CANADA - PUBLIC ARCHIVES OF CANADA -
MANUSCRIPT DIVISION □ Ottawa, ON

Hyatt, Dennis R., Libn.
UNIVERSITY OF OREGON - LAW LIBRARY □
Eugene, OR
Hyatt, Mrs. Robert
FIRST BAPTIST CHURCH - MEDIA CENTER □
Gainesville, FL
Hycnar, Barbara J., Assoc.Libn./Tech.Serv.
NORTHWESTERN UNIVERSITY - LAW SCHOOL
LIBRARY □ Chicago, IL
Hyde, Ann, Mss.Libn.
UNIVERSITY OF KANSAS - DEPARTMENT OF
SPECIAL COLLECTIONS □ Lawrence, KS
Hyde, Mary Lynn, Govt.Doc./ILL
UNIVERSITY OF SAN DIEGO - MARVIN &
LILLIAN KRATTER LAW LIBRARY □ San Diego,
CA
Hyde, Samuel R., Libn.
UNIVERSITY OF HOUSTON - MUSIC LIBRARY □
Houston, TX
Hyde, W.F.L., Grand Libn.
GRAND LODGE OF MANITOBA, A.F. AND A.M. -
MASONIC LIBRARY† □ Winnipeg, MB
Hyer, David C., Exec.Dir.
BUCK (Pearl S.) BIRTHPLACE FOUNDATION -
LIBRARY □ Hillsboro, WV
Hyer, Susan, Asst.Libn.
NEWSPAPER ADVERTISING BUREAU, INC. -
INFORMATION CENTER □ New York, NY
Hyland, Sr. John Bosco, Cat.
DOMINICAN EDUCATION CENTER - LIBRARY □
Sinsinawa, WI
Hyland, Maureen, Res.Libn.
LAW SOCIETY OF UPPER CANADA - GREAT
LIBRARY □ Toronto, ON
Hylton, Ramona, Info.Spec.
AMERICAN ASSOCIATION OF ADVERTISING
AGENCIES - MEMBER INFORMATION SERVICE
□ New York, NY
Hyman, Barry E., Asst.Prov.Archv.
MANITOBA - PROVINCIAL ARCHIVES OF
MANITOBA □ Winnipeg, MB
Hyman, Edith T., Libn.
HALL (Lydia E.) HOSPITAL - MEDICAL LIBRARY
□ Freeport, NY
Hyman, Irwin A., Dir.
NATIONAL CENTER FOR THE STUDY OF
CORPORAL PUNISHMENT & ALTERNATIVES IN
THE SCHOOLS - LIBRARY □ Philadelphia, PA
Hyman, Laura, Asst.Libn.
COLD SPRING HARBOR LABORATORY - MAIN
LIBRARY □ Cold Spring Harbor, NY
Hyzy, Laura, Ser.Mgr.
JOHN MARSHALL LAW SCHOOL - LIBRARY □
Chicago, IL

I

Iacono, Frank
RHODE ISLAND STATE DEPARTMENT OF STATE
LIBRARY SERVICES □ Providence, RI
Iamele, Richard T., Lib.Dir.
LOS ANGELES COUNTY LAW LIBRARY □ Los
Angeles, CA
Iannucci, Patricia J., Mkt.Res.Mgr.
PALL CORPORATION - LIBRARY □ Glen Cove, NY
Ibach, Robert, Dir.
GRACE THEOLOGICAL SEMINARY - LIBRARY □
Winona Lake, IN
Ichinose, Mitsuko, Prin.Cat./Ref.Libn.
YALE UNIVERSITY - EAST ASIAN COLLECTION
□ New Haven, CT
Ickes, Clark F., Hd.Libn.
BALTIMORE NEWS AMERICAN - REFERENCE
LIBRARY □ Baltimore, MD
Idland, Myrtle, Libn.
PHOENIX GENERAL HOSPITAL - MEDICAL
LIBRARY □ Phoenix, AZ
Iemma, John A., Asst.Dir., DED
RHODE ISLAND STATE DEPARTMENT OF
ECONOMIC DEVELOPMENT - RESEARCH
DIVISION LIBRARY □ Providence, RI

Ikehara, Mr. Chris R., Mgr., Info.Rsrcs.
SPECIAL LIBRARIES ASSOCIATION -
INFORMATION RESOURCES CENTER □ New
York, NY
Iliff, Warren J., Dir.
WASHINGTON PARK ZOO - LIBRARY □ Portland,
OR
Ilisevich, Robert, Libn.
CRAWFORD COUNTY HISTORICAL SOCIETY -
LIBRARY AND ARCHIVES □ Meadville, PA
Illman, Harry R., Libn.
PRESS CLUB OF SAN FRANCISCO - WILL
AUBREY MEMORIAL LIBRARY □ San Francisco,
CA
Ilnicki, Henry, Hd., Gift Sect.
NEW YORK STATE LIBRARY □ Albany, NY
Iltis, H.H., Dir. of Herbarium
UNIVERSITY OF WISCONSIN, MADISON -
BOTANY DEPARTMENT - HERBARIUM LIBRARY
□ Madison, WI
Im, Nam-Hee, Sr.Info.Spec.
SYNTEX, U.S.A. - CORPORATE LIBRARY/
INFORMATION SERVICES □ Palo Alto, CA
Imamoto, Jean, Res.Libn.
HAWAII STATE - LEGISLATIVE REFERENCE
BUREAU LIBRARY □ Honolulu, HI
Imel, Susan, Asst.Dir.
ERIC CLEARINGHOUSE ON ADULT, CAREER
AND VOCATIONAL EDUCATION - NATL. CTR.
FOR RESEARCH IN VOCATIONAL EDUC. □
Columbus, OH
Imhof, Peter H., Libn.
U.S. NAVY - NAVAL RESEARCH LABORATORY -
RUTH H. HOOKER TECHNICAL LIBRARY □
Washington, DC
Immel, Jean L., Archv.
ARMSTRONG WORLD INDUSTRIES, INC. -
MANAGEMENT REFERENCE SERVICES □
Lancaster, PA
Ingalls, Bruce, Ref.Sect.
ENVIRONMENTAL PROTECTION AGENCY -
HEADQUARTERS LIBRARY† □ Washington, DC
Ingalls, Joan V., Libn.
WINE INSTITUTE - LIBRARY □ San Francisco,
CA
Ingalls, Nell, Asst.Libn.
WINSTON & STRAWN - LIBRARY □ Chicago, IL
Inge, Barclay, Leg.Spec.
WILMER, CUTLER & PICKERING - LAW
LIBRARY □ Washington, DC
Ingersoll, Hilde, Asst.Libn., ILL
RIVERSIDE HOSPITAL - MEDICAL LIBRARY □
Wilmington, DE
Ingersoll, Joan, Hd.
U.S. NAVY - NAVAL OCEAN SYSTEMS CENTER -
TECHNICAL LIBRARY □ San Diego, CA
Ingibergsson, Asgeir, Hd.Libn.
CAMROSE LUTHERAN COLLEGE - LIBRARY □
Camrose, AB
Inglis, Catherine, Libn.
SEYFARTH, SHAW, FAIRWEATHER &
GERALDSON - LIBRARY □ New York, NY
Inglis, Mike, Assoc.Dir.
UNIVERSITY OF NEW MEXICO - TECHNOLOGY
APPLICATION CENTER □ Albuquerque, NM
Ingmire, Mary, Libn.
SILVER CROSS HOSPITAL - MEDICAL LIBRARY
□ Joliet, IL
Ingraham, Alice L., Ref./Info.Serv.
PENNSYLVANIA STATE LIBRARY □ Harrisburg,
PA
Ingraham, Kathleen A., Libn.
WIGGIN AND DANA - LIBRARY □ New Haven,
CT
Ingram, Arlyn, Techn.
CORNELL UNIVERSITY - RESOURCE
INFORMATION LABORATORY □ Ithaca, NY
Ingram, Barbara, Hd., Circ.
LAWRENCE LIVERMORE NATIONAL
LABORATORY - TECHNICAL INFORMATION
DEPARTMENT LIBRARY □ Livermore, CA

Ingram, C., Tech.Serv.Supv.
ALBERTA - DEPARTMENT OF ENERGY AND
NATURAL RESOURCES - LIBRARY □ Edmonton,
AB
Ingram, Charles, Acq./Pharmacy Libn.
SOUTHWESTERN OKLAHOMA STATE
UNIVERSITY - AL HARRIS LIBRARY □
Weatherford, OK
Ingram, John E., Archv.
COLONIAL WILLIAMSBURG - RESEARCH
LIBRARY & ARCHIVES† □ Williamsburg, VA
Ingram, L. Marie, Law Libn.
MANATEE COUNTY BAR ASSOCIATION - LAW
LIBRARY □ Bradenton, FL
Ingram, Mark A., Med.Libn.
HOPKINS COUNTY - REGIONAL MEDICAL
CENTER - LIBRARY □ Madisonville, KY
Ingram, Sara, Mgr.
CONSUMERS UNION OF UNITED STATES, INC. -
LIBRARY □ Mount Vernon, NY
Injejikian, Susan, Libn.
GRIFFITH OBSERVATORY - LIBRARY □ Los
Angeles, CA
Inkster, Al, Printed Mtls.Libn.
NORTH AMERICAN RADIO ARCHIVES (NARA) -
TAPE AND PRINTED MATERIALS LIBRARIES □
Flagstaff, AZ
Innerst, Betty, Libn.
ST. THOMAS AQUINAS NEWMAN CENTER -
LIBRARY □ Albuquerque, NM
Innis, Janet, Lib.Asst.
QUEEN'S UNIVERSITY AT KINGSTON -
CHEMISTRY LIBRARY □ Kingston, ON
Inskeep, Lois J., Chf., Lib.Serv.
U.S. VETERANS ADMINISTRATION (NE-Omaha)
- HOSPITAL LIBRARY □ Omaha, NE
Insler, Linda, Libn.
TEMPLE BETH-EL OF GREAT NECK - ARNOLD &
MARIE SCHWARTZ LIBRARY □ Great Neck, NY
Insler, Prof. Stanley, Chm.
YALE UNIVERSITY - INDOLOGICAL AND
LINGUISTIC SEMINAR - LIBRARY □ New Haven,
CT
Intal, Rita, Libn.
FRITZSCHE, DODGE AND OLCOTT, INC. -
RESEARCH LIBRARY □ New York, NY
Iobst, Barbara J., Dir. of Lib.Serv.
THE ALLENTOWN HOSPITAL - HEALTH
SCIENCES LIBRARY □ Allentown, PA
Ipolito, Dorry, Ref.Libn.
ENOCH PRATT FREE LIBRARY - AUDIO-VISUAL
DEPARTMENT □ Baltimore, MD
Ippolito, Andrew V., Dir. of Lib. & Res.
NEWSDAY, INC. - LIBRARY □ Melville, NY
Ippolito, Elizabeth, Lib.Asst.
C.I.T. FINANCIAL CORPORATION - BUSINESS/
LEGAL INFORMATION CENTER □ Livingston, NJ
Ireland, J., Libn.
PRUDENTIAL LIFE INSURANCE COMPANY OF
AMERICA - BUSINESS LIBRARY† □ Toronto, ON
Ireland, Tessa J., Sec.
UNIVERSITY OF TORONTO - ANTHROPOLOGY
READING ROOM □ Toronto, ON
Irene, Sr. M., O.S.F., Libn.
DIOCESE OF ALLENTOWN - PRO-LIFE LIBRARY
□ Bethlehem, PA
Irish, Ned, Chm., Pubn.Comm.
AMERICAN HEMEROCALLIS SOCIETY -
ARCHIVES □ DeQueen, AR
Irvine, Betty Jo, Hd.
INDIANA UNIVERSITY - FINE ARTS LIBRARY □
Bloomington, IN
Irvine, Cynthia E., Pres./Adm.
MONTEREY INSTITUTE FOR RESEARCH IN
ASTRONOMY - PRISCILLA FAIRFIELD BOK
LIBRARY □ Monterey, CA
Irvine, Dr. James S., Asst.Libn., Pub.Serv.
PRINCETON THEOLOGICAL SEMINARY - SPEER
LIBRARY □ Princeton, NJ
Irvine, Kay, Hd.Libn.
WESTERN STATES CHIROPRACTIC COLLEGE -
W.A. BUDDEN MEMORIAL LIBRARY □ Portland,
OR

Irvine, Terry, Lib.Techn.
SASKATCHEWAN - DEPARTMENT OF
ADVANCED EDUCATION AND MANPOWER -
WOMEN'S SERVICES - BRANCH RESOURCE
CENTRE □ Regina, SK
Irving, Ophelia M., Asst.Dir., Info.Serv.
NORTH CAROLINA STATE DEPARTMENT OF
CULTURAL RESOURCES - DIVISION OF THE
STATE LIBRARY □ Raleigh, NC
Irving, Richard, Bibliog.
SUNY AT ALBANY - GRADUATE LIBRARY FOR
PUBLIC AFFAIRS AND POLICY □ Albany, NY
Irwin, Ann, Libn.
CANADIAN BROADCASTING CORPORATION -
REFERENCE LIBRARY □ Toronto, ON
Irwin, Barbara Smith, Lib.Dir.
NEW JERSEY HISTORICAL SOCIETY - LIBRARY
□ Newark, NJ
Irwin, Ruth, Cons.
RIVERSIDE HOSPITAL - MEDICAL LIBRARY □
Wilmington, DE
Irwin, Ruth A., Libn.
DELAWARE STATE HOSPITAL - MEDICAL
LIBRARY □ New Castle, DE
Isa, Jacqueline, Acq.Libn.
CENTRAL CONNECTICUT STATE UNIVERSITY -
ELIHU BURRITT LIBRARY □ New Britain, CT
Isaac, Mrs. Torrey, Libn.
SMITH MEMORIAL LIBRARY □ Chautauqua, NY
Isaacs, Ann Fabe, Hd.
NATIONAL ASSOCIATION FOR CREATIVE
CHILDREN AND ADULTS (NACCA) - LIBRARY □
Cincinnati, OH
Isaacson, Richard T., Libn.
GARDEN CENTER OF GREATER CLEVELAND -
ELEANOR SQUIRE LIBRARY □ Cleveland, OH
Isabel, Yvon, Directeur
UNIVERSITE DU QUEBEC - MEDIATHEQUE† □
Ste. Foy, PQ
Isadore, Harold, Asst. Law Libn./Ref./Res.
SOUTHERN UNIVERSITY - LAW SCHOOL
LIBRARY □ Baton Rouge, LA
Isbell, Anne, Bus.Res.Supv.
LAMB-WESTON - BUSINESS RESEARCH
CENTER □ Portland, OR
Isbell, Mary, Asst.Libn.
SOUTHERN ILLINOIS UNIVERSITY,
CARBONDALE - EDUCATION AND PSYCHOLOGY
DIVISION LIBRARY □ Carbondale, IL
Ische, John P., Dir.
LOUISIANA STATE UNIVERSITY MEDICAL
CENTER - LIBRARY □ New Orleans, LA
Isenberg, Helena, Libn.
LATNER (Albert J.) JEWISH PUBLIC LIBRARY □
Willowdale, ON
Isenstein, Ellen, Ref.Libn.
HARVARD UNIVERSITY - JOHN FITZGERALD
KENNEDY SCHOOL OF GOVERNMENT - LIBRARY
□ Cambridge, MA
Ishee, Charles E., Libn.
PUBLIC LIBRARY OF CINCINNATI AND
HAMILTON COUNTY - ART AND MUSIC
DEPARTMENT □ Cincinnati, OH
Isherwood, Doreen, Lib.Asst.
VICTORIA GENERAL HOSPITAL (North) -
HEALTH SCIENCES LIBRARY □ Victoria, BC
Isherwood, Helen C., Libn.
NEW YORK INSTITUTE FOR THE EDUCATION
OF THE BLIND - WALTER BROOKS LIBRARY □
Bronx, NY
Isley, Natelle, Mgr.
MISSISSIPPI (State) RESEARCH AND
DEVELOPMENT CENTER - INFORMATION
SERVICES DIVISION □ Jackson, MS
Ismail, Mrs. Fathia, Libn.
INTERNATIONAL CIVIL AVIATION
ORGANIZATION - LIBRARY □ Montreal, PQ
Ismarin, Corazon O'S., Libn.
ST. LUKE'S HOSPITAL - MEDICAL LIBRARY □
San Francisco, CA

Isom, Patricia B., Libn.
AMERICAN HEALTH FOUNDATION - NAYLOR DANA INSTITUTE FOR DISEASE PREVENTION - LIBRARY □ Valhalla, NY

Israel, Mrs. Kilja, Libn.
ST. FRANCIS MEDICAL CENTER - CAPE COUNTY MEMORIAL MEDICAL LIBRARY, INC. □ Cape Girardeau, MO

Itesco, Victor, Hd.Libn.
MONTREAL URBAN COMMUNITY TRANSIT COMMISSION - LIBRARY □ Montreal, PQ

Itina, Irene, Hd., Govt.Doc.Sect.
NEW YORK PUBLIC LIBRARY - ECONOMIC AND PUBLIC AFFAIRS DIVISION □ New York, NY

Itoga, Mary Ann T., Libn.
YALE UNIVERSITY - AMERICAN ORIENTAL SOCIETY LIBRARY □ New Haven, CT

Ittner, Dwight, Libn.
UNIVERSITY OF ALASKA - BIO-MEDICAL LIBRARY □ Fairbanks, AK

Iula, Jeff, Asst.Gen.Mgr.
INTERNATIONAL SOAP BOX DERBY - LIBRARY □ Akron, OH

Ivain, Denise, Lib.Asst.
WATERBURY STATE TECHNICAL COLLEGE - HELEN HAHLO LIBRARY □ Waterbury, CT

Ivanisevic, Vlatka, Libn.
CASE WESTERN RESERVE UNIVERSITY - APPLIED SOCIAL SCIENCES LIBRARY □ Cleveland, OH

Ivanus, Theodore B., Hd.
UNIVERSITY OF NOTRE DAME - INTERNATIONAL DOCUMENTATION CENTER □ Notre Dame, IN

Iverson, John, Musm.Dir.
EARLHAM COLLEGE - JOSEPH MOORE MUSEUM - HADLEY LIBRARY □ Richmond, IN

Iverson, Theresa, Proc.Libn.
UNIVERSITY OF BRITISH COLUMBIA - GOVERNMENT PUBLICATIONS & MICROFORMS DIVISIONS □ Vancouver, BC

Ives, Mrs. A., Adm. & Info.Serv.
MC GILL UNIVERSITY - MACDONALD CAMPUS - BRACE RESEARCH INSTITUTE LIBRARY □ Ste. Anne de Bellevue, PQ

Ives, Colta, Cur.
METROPOLITAN MUSEUM OF ART - DEPARTMENT OF PRINTS AND PHOTOGRAPHS □ New York, NY

Ives, Edward D., Dir.
UNIVERSITY OF MAINE, ORONO - NORTHEAST ARCHIVES OF FOLKLORE AND ORAL HISTORY □ Orono, ME

Ives, Jackie A., Libn.
ASSOCIATED SPRING BARNES GROUP, INC. - CORPORATE LIBRARY □ Bristol, CT

Ives, Sidney, Libn.
UNIVERSITY OF FLORIDA - BELKNAP COLLECTION FOR THE PERFORMING ARTS □ Gainesville, FL

Ives, Sidney, Libn.
UNIVERSITY OF FLORIDA - RARE BOOKS & MANUSCRIPTS □ Gainesville, FL

Ivey, Donna M., Supv., Lib.Serv.
CONSUMERS' GAS COMPANY - LIBRARY SERVICES† □ Scarborough, ON

Ivey, Robert, Libn.
GAINESVILLE SUN - LIBRARY □ Gainesville, FL

Ivey-Clark, Mary, Libn.
COCA-COLA COMPANY - FOODS DIVISION - CITRUS RESEARCH & DEVELOPMENT TECHNICAL LIBRARY □ Plymouth, FL

Ivie, Sharlene, Libn.
TERRA TEK RESEARCH - TECHNICAL LIBRARY □ Salt Lake City, UT

Ivins, Melody, Libn.
CAROLINA LIBRARY SERVICES, INC. - WOMEN'S BOOK EXCHANGE □ Chapel Hill, NC

Ivory, Paul W., Dir. of Chesterwood
CHESTERWOOD - LIBRARY □ Stockbridge, MA

Ivy, Karen E., Libn.
COOPERS & LYBRAND - LIBRARY □ San Francisco, CA

Iwami, Russell, Pub.Serv.Libn.
NATIONAL COLLEGE OF CHIROPRACTIC - LEARNING RESOURCE CENTER □ Lombard, IL

Izbicki, Donna R., Libn.
CONNECTICUT STATE LIBRARY - LAW LIBRARY AT PUTNAM □ Putnam, CT

Izmirlian, Christine, Lib.Asst.
MC GILL UNIVERSITY - DENTISTRY LIBRARY □ Montreal, PQ

Izzo, Kathleen A., Libn.
ST. JOSEPH HOSPITAL - HEALTH SCIENCES LIBRARY □ Reading, PA

J

Jaansoo-Boudreau, T., Hd., User Serv.
CANADA - PUBLIC SERVICE COMMISSION - LIBRARY SERVICES DIVISION □ Ottawa, ON

Jabbour, Alan, Dir.
LIBRARY OF CONGRESS - AMERICAN FOLKLIFE CENTER □ Washington, DC

Jablonowski, Christina, Libn.
CHANDLER EVANS, INC. - COMPANY LIBRARY† □ West Hartford, CT

Jackanicz, Donald W., Pres.
BERTRAND RUSSELL SOCIETY, INC. - LIBRARY □ San Francisco, CA

Jacke, Edith, Libn.
MURRAY (Warren G.) DEVELOPMENTAL CENTER - LIBRARY □ Centralia, IL

Jacklin, Kathleen, Archv.
CORNELL UNIVERSITY - DEPARTMENT OF MANUSCRIPTS AND UNIVERSITY ARCHIVES □ Ithaca, NY

Jackonen, Felix V., Pres.
FINNISH AMERICAN HISTORICAL SOCIETY OF MICHIGAN □ Southfield, MI

Jackson, Andrew P., Exec.Dir.
QUEENS BOROUGH PUBLIC LIBRARY - LANGSTON HUGHES COMMUNITY LIBRARY AND CULTURAL CENTER □ Corona, NY

Jackson, Audrey M., Lib. Group Supv.
AT & T TECHNOLOGIES, INC. - LIBRARY □ Indianapolis, IN

Jackson, Beverly J., Lib.Ck.
HOLZER MEDICAL CENTER - MEDICAL LIBRARY □ Gallipolis, OH

Jackson, Brinton, Libn.
JUILLIARD SCHOOL - LILA ACHESON WALLACE LIBRARY □ New York, NY

Jackson, Carolyn, Cat.
EAST TEXAS BAPTIST UNIVERSITY - MAMYE JARRETT LEARNING CENTER □ Marshall, TX

Jackson, Cathi, Libn.
ESPEY MFG. & ELECTRONICS CORP. - COMPONENT SPECIFICATIONS LIBRARY □ Saratoga Springs, NY

Jackson, Douglas M., Libn.
U.S. AIR FORCE HOSPITAL - MEDICAL LIBRARY (FL-Patrick AFB) □ Patrick AFB, FL

Jackson, E., Libn.
WESTINGHOUSE CANADA LTD. - ELECTRONICS DIVISION LIBRARY† □ Burlington, ON

Jackson, Elizabeth Christian, Lib.Dir.
MERCER UNIVERSITY - SOUTHERN COLLEGE OF PHARMACY - H. CUSTER NAYLOR LIBRARY □ Atlanta, GA

Jackson, Elizabeth S., Assoc.Libn.
GEORGETOWN UNIVERSITY - FRED O. DENNIS LAW LIBRARY □ Washington, DC

Jackson, Ella J., Libn.
TETRA TECH, INC. - LIBRARY† □ Pasadena, CA

Jackson, Gale, Lib.Adv.-Black Heritage
QUEENS BOROUGH PUBLIC LIBRARY - LANGSTON HUGHES COMMUNITY LIBRARY AND CULTURAL CENTER □ Corona, NY

Jackson, Gloria M., Asst.Libn.
MUSEUM OF OUR NATIONAL HERITAGE - VAN GORDEN-WILLIAMS LIBRARY □ Lexington, MA

Jackson, Jack, Art Res.
BOSTON ATHENAEUM LIBRARY □ Boston, MA

Jackson, James, Dept.Libn.
LONG BEACH PUBLIC LIBRARY - CALIFORNIA PETROLEUM INDUSTRY COLLECTION □ Long Beach, CA

Jackson, James E., Asstl.Libn., ILL
CALIFORNIA ACADEMY OF SCIENCES - J.W. MAILLIARD, JR. LIBRARY □ San Francisco, CA

Jackson, James H., Libn.
AMERICAN MEDICAL ASSOCIATION - WASHINGTON OFFICE LIBRARY □ Washington, DC

Jackson, Judith, Rsrc.Ctr.Dir.
CANADIAN FOUNDATION FOR ECONOMIC EDUCATION - RESOURCE CENTRE □ Toronto, ON

Jackson, Katherine M., Hd., Ref.Div.
TEXAS A & M UNIVERSITY - REFERENCE DIVISION □ College Station, TX

Jackson, Lauren, Cat.Libn.
PACE UNIVERSITY, PLEASANTVILLE/ BRIARCLIFF - EDWARD AND DORIS MORTOLA LIBRARY □ Pleasantville, NY

Jackson, Lillian S., Chem. Faculty
GETTYSBURG COLLEGE - DEPARTMENT OF CHEMISTRY - LIBRARY □ Gettysburg, PA

Jackson, M.E., Lit. Searcher
AT & T BELL LABORATORIES & TECHNOLOGIES - ENGINEERING RESEARCH CENTER - TECHNICAL LIBRARY □ Princeton, NJ

Jackson, M.W., Sr.Libn.
MILES LABORATORIES, INC. - DELBAY PHARMACEUTICALS - RESEARCH LIBRARY □ West Haven, CT

Jackson, Margot, Archv.
PENINSULA LIBRARY AND HISTORICAL SOCIETY† □ Peninsula, OH

Jackson, Martin F., Info.Dir.
NOSTALGIA PRESS, INC. - ARCHIVES AND ART LIBRARY □ Franklin Square, NY

Jackson, Meliza, Patients' Libn.
UNIVERSITY OF PITTSBURGH - WESTERN PSYCHIATRIC INSTITUTE AND CLINIC - LIBRARY □ Pittsburgh, PA

Jackson, Patience K., Lib.Dir.
DANIEL WEBSTER COLLEGE - LIBRARY □ Nashua, NH

Jackson, Shirley A., Libn.
OKLAHOMA GEOLOGICAL SURVEY - OKLAHOMA GEOPHYSICAL OBSERVATORY LIBRARY □ Leonard, OK

Jackson, Sue, Asst.Archv.
MONTANA HISTORICAL SOCIETY - LIBRARY/ ARCHIVES □ Helena, MT

Jackson, Susan, Dir., Lib.Serv.
CANADA - DEPARTMENT OF JUSTICE - LIBRARY □ Ottawa, ON

Jackson, Susan, Asst.Libn.
MC DERMOTT, WILL & EMERY - LIBRARY □ Chicago, IL

Jackson, Susan, Libn.
PACIFIC POWER AND LIGHT COMPANY - LIBRARY □ Portland, OR

Jacob, John, Archv.
MARSHALL (George C.) RESEARCH FOUNDATION - GEORGE C. MARSHALL RESEARCH LIBRARY† □ Lexington, VA

Jacob, Louis A., Hd., Southern Asia Sect.
LIBRARY OF CONGRESS - ASIAN DIVISION □ Washington, DC

Jacob, Rosamond T., Libn.
ST. PAUL PUBLIC LIBRARY - GOVERNMENT PUBLICATIONS OFFICE □ St. Paul, MN

Jacobs, Eric L., Dir.
NORTH AMERICAN JEWISH STUDENTS' NETWORK - LIBRARY □ New York, NY

Jacobs, James A., Doc./Ref.Libn.
TEXAS TECH UNIVERSITY - LIBRARY - DOCUMENTS DEPARTMENT □ Lubbock, TX

Jacobs, Leslie R., Info.Spec.
MILLIPORE CORPORATION - INFORMATION CENTER □ Bedford, MA

Jacobs, Margaret M., Dir.
AKWESASNE LIBRARY CULTURAL CENTER □ Hogansburg, NY

Jacobs, Mary C., Ref.Libn.
BELL COMMUNICATIONS RESEARCH, INC. - INFORMATION RESOURCES SERVICES CENTER □ Piscataway, NJ

Jacobs, Naomi, Res.Libn.
NATIONAL CENTER FOR RESEARCH IN VOCATIONAL EDUCATION - RESEARCH LIBRARY □ Columbus, OH

Jacobs, Nina, Libn.
U.S. AIR FORCE BASE - TRAVIS BASE LIBRARY □ Travis AFB, CA

Jacobs, Roger F., Libn.
U.S. SUPREME COURT - LIBRARY □ Washington, DC

Jacobs, Susan, Asst.Dir.
TOLEDO HOSPITAL - LIBRARY □ Toledo, OH

Jacobs, William, Med.Libn.
CEDARS-SINAI MEDICAL CENTER - HEALTH SCIENCES INFORMATION CENTER □ Los Angeles, CA

Jacobs, Zena, Hd., Ref.Dept.
POLYTECHNIC INSTITUTE OF NEW YORK - SPICER LIBRARY □ Brooklyn, NY

Jacobsen, Brent N., Lib.Adm.
EG&G, INC. - IDAHO NATIONAL ENGINEERING LABORATORY - INEL TECHNICAL LIBRARY □ Idaho Falls, ID

Jacobsen, Elizabeth, Hd., Domestic Res.
SALOMON BROTHERS - CORPORATE FINANCE LIBRARY □ New York, NY

Jacobsen, Lawrence, Hd.Libn.
UNIVERSITY OF WISCONSIN, MADISON - WISCONSIN REGIONAL PRIMATE RESEARCH CENTER - PRIMATE CENTER LIBRARY □ Madison, WI

Jacobsen, T.D., Asst.Dir.
CARNEGIE-MELLON UNIVERSITY - HUNT INSTITUTE FOR BOTANICAL DOCUMENTATION □ Pittsburgh, PA

Jacobson, Betty, Libn.
FOUNDATION OF THE WALL & CEILING INDUSTRY - JOHN H. HAMPSHIRE REFERENCE & RESEARCH LIBRARY □ Washington, DC

Jacobson, Charlotte, Cur. of Archv.
NORWEGIAN-AMERICAN HISTORICAL ASSOCIATION - ARCHIVES □ Northfield, MN

Jacobson, Frances B., Libn.
NATIONAL ENQUIRER - RESEARCH DEPARTMENT LIBRARY □ Lantana, FL

Jacobson, Helen, Lib.Techn.
U.S. BUREAU OF MINES - ALASKA FIELD OPERATIONS CENTER LIBRARY □ Juneau, AK

Jacobson, Janet A., Libn.
RIDER, BENNETT, EGAN & ARUNDEL - LIBRARY □ Minneapolis, MN

Jacobson, Jeanette, Asst.Libn./Cat.
WESTMINSTER CHOIR COLLEGE - TALBOTT LIBRARY □ Princeton, NJ

Jacobson, June B., Libn.
FLORIDA STATE DEPT. OF AGRICULTURE AND CONSUMER SERVICES - DIVISION OF PLANT INDUSTRY - LIBRARY □ Gainesville, FL

Jacobson, Maria B., Tech.Libn.
AMF, INC. - TECHNICAL INFORMATION CENTER □ Stamford, CT

Jacobson, Naomi, Co-Chm.
LAND, INC. - LIBRARY □ Rudolph, WI

Jacobson, Sabina, Asst.Libn., Tech.Proc.
U.S. DEPT. OF LABOR - LIBRARY† □ Washington, DC

Jacobstein, Prof. J. Myron, Law Libn.
STANFORD UNIVERSITY - LAW LIBRARY □ Stanford, CA

Jacoby, Dr. Barbara, Dir.
UNIVERSITY OF MARYLAND, COLLEGE PARK - NATIONAL CLEARINGHOUSE FOR COMMUTER PROGRAMS □ College Park, MD

Jacolev, Leon, Lib.Dir.
ASSOCIATED TECHNICAL SERVICES, INC. - RESEARCH LIBRARY □ Glen Ridge, NJ

Jacome, Winifred M., Lib.Techn.
U.S. NAVY - NAVAL HOSPITAL (RI-Newport) - MEDICAL LIBRARY □ Newport, RI

Jacox, Elizabeth P., Libn.
IDAHO STATE HISTORICAL SOCIETY - LIBRARY AND ARCHIVES □ Boise, ID

Jacques, E. Lynne, Libn.
CIBA-GEIGY CORPORATION - TECHNICAL INFORMATION SERVICE □ Greensboro, NC

Jacques, Michelle, Documentalist
MONTREAL ASSOCIATION FOR THE MENTALLY RETARDED - DOCUMENTATION CENTRE† □ Montreal, PQ

Jacquette, Janet, Libn.
GEERS GROSS ADV. INC. - LIBRARY □ New York, NY

Jacquin, Mary Louise, Libn.
PEORIA COUNTY LAW LIBRARY □ Peoria, IL

Jacyna, Raymond, Libn.
CANADA - NATIONAL RESEARCH COUNCIL - CISTI - PHYSICS BRANCH □ Ottawa, ON

Jaeger, Doris, Ser.Libn.
MOUNT SINAI SCHOOL OF MEDICINE OF THE CITY UNIVERSITY OF NEW YORK - GUSTAVE L. & JANET W. LEVY LIBRARY □ New York, NY

Jaffe, Robin, Res.
BOOZ, ALLEN & HAMILTON, INC. - RESEARCH SERVICE □ New York, NY

Jaffe, Steven, Libn.
CONSOLIDATED EDISON COMPANY OF NEW YORK, INC. - LIBRARY □ New York, NY

Jafri, Nuzhat, Coord., Current Awareness
ONTARIO - MINISTRY OF EDUCATION - INFORMATION CENTRE □ Toronto, ON

Jagels, Suellen, Libn.
EASTERN MAINE MEDICAL CENTER - HEALTH SCIENCES LIBRARY □ Bangor, ME

Jagiellowicz, Jadzia, Asst.Libn.
MANUFACTURERS LIFE INSURANCE COMPANY - BUSINESS LIBRARY □ Toronto, ON

Jagusch, Sybille, Chf.
LIBRARY OF CONGRESS - CHILDREN'S LITERATURE CENTER □ Washington, DC

Jahnke, Ruth, Libn.
HYSTER COMPANY - ENGINEERING LIBRARY □ Portland, OR

Jaimes, Mr. Rene, Hd.
INTERNATIONAL PLANNED PARENTHOOD FEDERATION - WESTERN HEMISPHERE REGION - DOCUMENTATION & PUBLICATIONS CTR. □ New York, NY

Jain, Dr. Nirmal K., Hd., Sci.Lib.
ACADIA UNIVERSITY - SCIENCE LIBRARY □ Wolfville, NS

Jajko, Edward A., Near East Bibliog.
YALE UNIVERSITY - SEMITIC REFERENCE LIBRARY† □ New Haven, CT

Jakel, Kathleen, Libn.
AMERICAN PLAYERS THEATRE, INC. (APT) - LIBRARY □ Spring Green, WI

Jakeman, Jeff, Asst.Archv.
AUBURN UNIVERSITY - ARCHIVES □ Auburn, AL

Jakowiski, Rabbi, Libn.
NER ISRAEL RABBINICAL COLLEGE - LIBRARY □ Baltimore, MD

Jakubczak, Dorothy K., Tech.Libn.
DURO-TEST CORPORATION - TECHNICAL LIBRARY† □ North Bergen, NJ

Jakus, Florence I., Ed.D., Med.Libn.
HUMANA HOSPITAL SUNRISE - MEDICAL LIBRARY □ Las Vegas, NV

Jamar, Lucy, Asst.Libn.
U.S. AIR FORCE BASE - TINKER BASE LIBRARY □ Tinker AFB, OK

James, Ann, Libn.
EXPORT DEVELOPMENT CORPORATION - LIBRARY □ Ottawa, ON

James, Cecilia, Libn.
WILMINGTON NEWS-JOURNAL COMPANY - LIBRARY □ Wilmington, DE

James, Charles, Libn.
CANADA SAFETY COUNCIL (CSC) - LIBRARY □ Ottawa, ON

James, Charles, Tech.Info.Off.
ROADS AND TRANSPORTATION ASSOCIATION OF CANADA - TECHNICAL INFORMATION SERVICE □ Ottawa, ON

James, Craig, Docs.Libn.
SASKATCHEWAN - LEGISLATIVE LIBRARY† □ Regina, SK

James, Geraldine R., Libn.
PQ CORPORATION - RESEARCH LIBRARY □ Lafayette Hill, PA

James, Gloria R., Chf., Tech.Lib.Div.
U.S. ARMY - BELVOIR RESEARCH & DEVELOPMENT CENTER - TECHNICAL LIBRARY □ Ft. Belvoir, VA

James, John K., Dir. of Coll.Dev.
DARTMOUTH COLLEGE - ORIENTAL COLLECTION □ Hanover, NH

James, John V., Libn.
UNIVERSITY OF SASKATCHEWAN - WESTERN COLLEGE OF VETERINARY MEDICINE - LIBRARY □ Saskatoon, SK

James, Karin, Libn.
SCHUYLKILL VALLEY NATURE CENTER - LIBRARY □ Philadelphia, PA

James, Kathleen, Assoc.Cur.
BROWN UNIVERSITY - ART DEPARTMENT SLIDE ROOM □ Providence, RI

James, Leslie, Libn.
WESLEY MEDICAL CENTER - H.B. MC KIBBIN HEALTH SCIENCE LIBRARY □ Wichita, KS

James, Linda L., Asst.Libn.
MINNEAPOLIS STAR AND TRIBUNE - LIBRARY □ Minneapolis, MN

James, Mary, Libn.
EASTON HOSPITAL - MEDICAL LIBRARY □ Easton, PA

James, Mary Lou, Libn.
COOPERS & LYBRAND - LIBRARY □ Washington, DC

James, Marylin, Act.Hd.Cat.Libn.
UNIVERSITY OF VIRGINIA - MEDICAL CENTER - CLAUDE MOORE HEALTH SCIENCES LIBRARY □ Charlottesville, VA

James, Nancy B., Lib.Mgr.
DIGITAL EQUIPMENT CORPORATION - MERRIMACK LIBRARY SERVICES □ Merrimack, NJ

James, Olive C., Chf.
LIBRARY OF CONGRESS - LOAN DIVISION □ Washington, DC

James, William, Dir.
UNIVERSITY OF KENTUCKY - LAW LIBRARY □ Lexington, KY

James, Zoe S., Exec.Dir.
AMERICAN TRUCK HISTORICAL SOCIETY - LIBRARY □ Birmingham, AL

Jameson, Betty, Libn.
ALTON MEMORIAL HOSPITAL - HEALTH SCIENCES LIBRARY □ Alton, IL

Jameson, Martha, Libn.
ARTHUR YOUNG & COMPANY - LIBRARY □ Chicago, IL

Jameson, V. Lloyd, Div.Coord.
BOSTON PUBLIC LIBRARY - GOVERNMENT DOCUMENTS, MICROTEXT, NEWSPAPERS □ Boston, MA

Jamieson, Marianne, Ref.Libn.
UNIVERSITY OF ALBERTA - SCIENCE AND TECHNOLOGY LIBRARY □ Edmonton, AB

Jamison, Leila, Asst.Archv.
UNIVERSITY OF PITTSBURGH - ARCHIVES □ Pittsburgh, PA

Jamriska, Gerald J., Dir. of Plan.
GLENDALE CITY - PLANNING DIVISION - TECHNICAL LIBRARY □ Glendale, CA

Jandl, Nancy, Tech.Info.Mgr.
CHARLES RIVER ASSOCIATES, INC. - LIBRARY □ Boston, MA

Jane, Alberta, Cat.
OCTAMERON ASSOCIATES, INC. - RESEARCH LIBRARY □ Alexandria, VA

Janes, Janina, Per.Libn.
UNIVERSITY OF SOUTHERN COLORADO -
LIBRARY - SPECIAL COLLECTIONS □ Pueblo, CO

Janes, Jodith, Circuit Libn.
CLEVELAND HEALTH SCIENCES LIBRARY -
ALLEN MEMORIAL LIBRARY □ Cleveland, OH

Janes, Judy C., Asst. Law Libn.
UNIVERSITY OF CALIFORNIA, DAVIS - SCHOOL
OF LAW - LAW LIBRARY □ Davis, CA

Jang, Stephanie, Libn.
SIGNETICS CORPORATION - LIBRARY □
Sunnyvale, CA

Janiak, Jane M., Chf.Libn.
PORT AUTHORITY OF NEW YORK AND NEW
JERSEY - LIBRARY □ New York, NY

Janicki, Sandra, Libn.
CARNEGIE LIBRARY OF PITTSBURGH -
SCIENCE AND TECHNOLOGY DEPARTMENT □
Pittsburgh, PA

Janik, Toni, Hosp.Libn.
HOTEL-DIEU OF ST. JOSEPH HOSPITAL -
MEDICAL LIBRARY □ Windsor, ON

Janjua, Mrs. Zaytoon, Libn./Info.Off.
CENTRE FOR RESEARCH AND DEVELOPMENT
IN MASONRY (CRDM) - LIBRARY □ Calgary, AB

Jankos, William, Cur.
UNIVERSITY OF SOUTHERN CALIFORNIA -
LIBRARY - DEPARTMENT OF SPECIAL
COLLECTIONS - AMERICAN LITERATURE
COLLECTION □ Los Angeles, CA

Jankovics, Esther M., Supv.
SCHERING-PLOUGH CORPORATION - BUSINESS
INFORMATION CENTER - LIBRARY □
Kenilworth, NJ

Jankowski, Dorothy A., Supv., Tech.Info.Serv.
STANDARD OIL COMPANY OF OHIO -
CORPORATE ENGINEERING LIBRARY □
Cleveland, OH

Jankowski, Susan H., Libn.
QUARLES & BRADY - LIBRARY □ Milwaukee, WI

Jann, Adele, Hd.Cat.
PACE UNIVERSITY - LIBRARY □ New York, NY

Jannusch, Celeste, Asst.Libn.
STEIN ROE AND FARNHAM - LIBRARY □
Chicago, IL

Janofsky, Stephen, Med.Libn.
CUNY - CITY COLLEGE LIBRARY - SCIENCE/
ENGINEERING DIVISION □ New York, NY

Jansen, Ann C., Per.Libn.
ATHENAEUM OF OHIO - MOUNT ST. MARY'S
SEMINARY OF THE WEST - EUGENE H. MALY
MEMORIAL LIBRARY □ Cincinnati, OH

Jansen, Bernadette, Lib.Techn.
PRAIRIE AGRICULTURAL MACHINERY
INSTITUTE - LIBRARY □ Humboldt, SK

Jansen, Robert H., Hd.Libn.
MINNEAPOLIS STAR AND TRIBUNE - LIBRARY □
Minneapolis, MN

Janss, Mary H., Res.Assoc.
WORLD VISION INTERNATIONAL -
INFORMATION RESOURCE CENTER □ Monrovia,
CA

Janssen, Ruth S., Libn.
U.S. ARMY MEDICAL RESEARCH INSTITUTE OF
INFECTIOUS DISEASES - MEDICAL LIBRARY □
Frederick, MD

Janssens, Soudabeh, Mss.Div.
IOWA (State) HISTORICAL DEPARTMENT
LIBRARY □ Des Moines, IA

Janto, Joyce Manna, Acq.Libn.
UNIVERSITY OF RICHMOND - WILLIAM T.
MUSE MEMORIAL LAW LIBRARY □ Richmond,
VA

Jantzi, Naomi, Asst.Libn.
PIGEON DISTRICT LIBRARY - SPECIAL
COLLECTIONS □ Pigeon, MI

Jaques, Thomas F., State Libn.
LOUISIANA STATE LIBRARY □ Baton Rouge, LA

Jarabek, Leona, Ref.Libn.
U.S. NASA - LEWIS RESEARCH CENTER -
LIBRARY† □ Cleveland, OH

Jarasitis, Ute, ILL
U.S. ARMY POST - FORT LEWIS - LIBRARY
SYSTEM □ Ft. Lewis, WA

Jardine, Barbara, Rsrc.Ctr.Coord.
CONFERENCE BOARD OF CANADA -
INFORMATION RESOURCE CENTER □ Ottawa,
ON

Jarett, Nella L., Libn.
LOEB AND LOEB - LAW LIBRARY □ Los Angeles,
CA

Jarman, James, Act.Dir. of Libs.
POLYTECHNIC INSTITUTE OF NEW YORK -
SPICER LIBRARY □ Brooklyn, NY

Jarocha-Ernst, Christopher P., Coord.
RUTGERS UNIVERSITY, THE STATE
UNIVERSITY OF NEW JERSEY - CENTER FOR
COMPUTER AND INFORMATION SERVICES □
Piscataway, NJ

Jaros, John R., Cur.
AURORA HISTORICAL SOCIETY - MUSEUM
LIBRARY □ Aurora, IL

Jarrell, Randall, Dir.
UNIVERSITY OF CALIFORNIA, SANTA CRUZ -
REGIONAL HISTORY PROJECT □ Santa Cruz, CA

Jarrett, Paula, Sec./Libn.
CENTER FOR MENTAL HEALTH - LIBRARY □
Anderson, IN

Jarsoz, Jean, Ref.Libn.
NORTHEASTERN OHIO UNIVERSITIES COLLEGE
OF MEDICINE - BASIC MEDICAL SCIENCES
LIBRARY □ Rootstown, OH

Jarvis, Katherine S., Tech.Info.Spec.
XEROX CORPORATION - PALO ALTO RESEARCH
CENTER - TECHNICAL INFORMATION CENTER
□ Palo Alto, CA

Jarvis, Mary J., Med.Libn.
METHODIST HOSPITALS OF DALLAS - MEDICAL
LIBRARY □ Dallas, TX

Jarvis, Melissa, Lib.Asst.
CITICORP/TRANSACTION TECHNOLOGY INC. -
TECHNICAL INFORMATION RESEARCH CENTER
□ Santa Monica, CA

Jarvis, William, Asst.Ref.Libn.
LEHIGH UNIVERSITY - MART SCIENCE AND
ENGINEERING LIBRARY □ Bethlehem, PA

Jasek, Paul, Res.Asst.
CENTRAL NEW YORK REGIONAL PLANNING
BOARD - LIBRARY & INFORMATION CENTER □
Syracuse, NY

Jasen, Arnold, AV Libn.
U.S. VETERANS ADMINISTRATION (FL-Bay
Pines) - CENTER LIBRARY □ Bay Pines, FL

Jasken, Eloise M., Libn.
3M - 270 LIBRARY □ St. Paul, MN

Jasko, Sr. Agnese, P.H.J.C., Libn.
SACRED HEART MONASTERY - LEO DEHON
LIBRARY† □ Hales Corners, WI

Jaskula, Gary, Assoc.Libn.
CURTIS, MALLET-PREVOST, COLT AND MOSLE -
LIBRARY □ New York, NY

Jasnich, Adrienne, Sr.Info.Sci.
QUAKER OATS COMPANY - JOHN STUART
RESEARCH LABORATORIES - RESEARCH
LIBRARY □ Barrington, IL

Jason, Nora H., Project Ldr.
U.S. NATL. BUREAU OF STANDARDS - FIRE
RESEARCH INFORMATION SERVICES □
Washington, DC

Jaspal, Lelita, Ref.Libn.
BANK STREET COLLEGE OF EDUCATION -
LIBRARY □ New York, NY

Jassmann, Sherrida
AUBURN UNIVERSITY - VETERINARY MEDICAL
LIBRARY □ Auburn University, AL

Jaster, Gloria, Off.Supv.
WINEDALE HISTORICAL CENTER - LIBRARY □
Round Top, TX

Jastrab, Kathy, Lib.Asst.
SACRED HEART MONASTERY - LEO DEHON
LIBRARY† □ Hales Corners, WI

Jaworski, Teresa M., Libn.
J.P. STEVENS AND CO., INC. - TECHNICAL
LIBRARY □ Greenville, SC

Jayaraman, H.R., Info.Spec.
PHILLIPS PETROLEUM COMPANY - RESEARCH &
DEVELOPMENT DEPARTMENT - TECHNICAL
INFORMATION BRANCH □ Bartlesville, OK

Jayes, Linda, Cat.
MAINE HISTORICAL SOCIETY - LIBRARY □
Portland, ME

Jayne, JoAnn, Hd.Libn.
ACADEMY OF AERONAUTICS - LIBRARY □
Flushing, NY

Jaynes, Phyllis E., Dir. of Lib. User Serv.
DARTMOUTH COLLEGE - ORIENTAL
COLLECTION □ Hanover, NH

Jazwinski, Wanda, Pres.
POLISH AMERICAN CONGRESS - SOUTHERN
CALIFORNIA-ARIZONA DIVISION - POLAND'S
MILLENIUM LIBRARY □ Los Angeles, CA

Jedlicka, Janet, Libn./Res.Ck.
SOCIETY OF AUTOMOTIVE ENGINEERS - SAE
LIBRARY □ Warrendale, PA

Jedrey, Micheline E., Assoc.Libn.
MASSACHUSETTS INSTITUTE OF TECHNOLOGY
- ROTCH LIBRARY OF ARCHITECTURE AND
PLANNING □ Cambridge, MA

Jeffcott, Janet B., Tech.Libn.
MADISON AREA TECHNICAL COLLEGE -
TECHNICAL CENTER LIBRARY □ Madison, WI

Jefferies, Rev. William Bowler, Dir. of Archv.
UNITED METHODIST CHURCH - NORTHERN
CALIFORNIA-NEVADA CONFERENCE - J.A.B.
FRY RESEARCH LIBRARY □ Stockton, CA

Jefferson, Jacqueline, Jay St.Br.Libn.
CUNY - NEW YORK CITY TECHNICAL COLLEGE
LIBRARY/LEARNING RESOURCE CENTER □
Brooklyn, NY

Jefferson, James W., M.D., Co-Dir.
UNIVERSITY OF WISCONSIN, MADISON -
DEPARTMENT OF PSYCHIATRY - LITHIUM
INFORMATION CENTER □ Madison, WI

Jefferson, Karen L., Sr.Mss.Libn.
HOWARD UNIVERSITY - MOORLAND-SPINGARN
RESEARCH CENTER - MANUSCRIPT DIVISION □
Washington, DC

Jeffrey, Joanne
UNIVERSITY AFFILIATED CINCINNATI CENTER
FOR DEVELOPMENTAL DISORDERS - RESEARCH
LIBRARY □ Cincinnati, OH

Jeffries, Mary, Cat.
LORAIN COUNTY HISTORICAL SOCIETY -
GERALD HICKS MEMORIAL LIBRARY □ Elyria,
OH

Jehle, Clara, Hd., Tech.Serv.Div.
ALABAMA STATE DEPARTMENT OF ARCHIVES
AND HISTORY - REFERENCE ROOM □
Montgomery, AL

Jelich, Carol, Mgr., Lib.
NATIONAL CLEARINGHOUSE FOR ALCOHOL
INFORMATION - LIBRARY† □ Rockville, MD

Jelks, Joyce, Libn.
ATLANTA FULTON PUBLIC LIBRARY - SPECIAL
COLLECTIONS DEPARTMENT □ Atlanta, GA

Jelley, David R., Hd.Libn.
GTE LABORATORIES - LIBRARY □ Waltham, MA

Jen, Albert, Hd., Cat.
NORTHEASTERN ILLINOIS UNIVERSITY -
LIBRARY □ Chicago, IL

Jen, Rosa, Asst.Libn.
INDIANA UNIVERSITY OF PENNSYLVANIA -
UNIVERSITY LIBRARY □ Indiana, PA

Jendryk, Elizabeth, Asst.Libn.
UNIVERSITY OF PENNSYLVANIA - SCHOOL OF
DENTAL MEDICINE - LEON LEVY LIBRARY □
Philadelphia, PA

Jeng, Helene W., Libn.
MARYLAND STATE DEPARTMENT OF STATE
PLANNING - LIBRARY □ Baltimore, MD

Jenkins, Ann A., Mgr.
MERCK & COMPANY, INC. - KELCO DIVISION -
LITERATURE AND INFORMATION SERVICES □
San Diego, CA

Jenkins, Glen, Rare Bk.Libn./Archv.
CLEVELAND HEALTH SCIENCES LIBRARY -
HISTORICAL DIVISION □ Cleveland, OH

Jenkins, Harriet, Asst.Hd.
ENOCH PRATT FREE LIBRARY - SOCIAL
SCIENCE AND HISTORY DEPARTMENT □
Baltimore, MD
Jenkins, Janice, Music Libn.
STETSON UNIVERSITY - SCHOOL OF MUSIC
LIBRARY □ De Land, FL
Jenkins, Kathy K., Acq.Libn.
HOWARD UNIVERSITY - MOORLAND-SPINGARN
RESEARCH CENTER - LIBRARY DIVISION □
Washington, DC
Jenkins, Leola H., Chf.Libn.
U.S. VETERANS ADMINISTRATION (NC-Durham)
- MEDICAL CENTER LIBRARY □ Durham, NC
Jenkins, Mary M., Hd.Libn.
WEST VIRGINIA STATE DEPARTMENT OF
CULTURE AND HISTORY - ARCHIVES AND
HISTORY LIBRARY □ Charleston, WV
Jenkins, Norma P.H., Libn.
CORNING MUSEUM OF GLASS - LIBRARY □
Corning, NY
Jenkins, Pamela U., Asst. to Coord.
SMITHSONIAN INSTITUTION - NATL. MUSEUM
OF AMERICAN ART - INVENTORY OF
AMERICAN PAINTINGS EXECUTED BEFORE
1914 □ Washington, DC
Jenkins, Patricia, Ref.Libn.
NORTH YORK PUBLIC LIBRARY - CANADIANA
COLLECTION □ Willowdale, ON
Jenkins, Phyllis A., Lib.Techn.
U.S. VETERANS ADMINISTRATION (TN-
Murfreesboro) - MEDICAL CENTER LIBRARY □
Murfreesboro, TN
Jenkins, Robert, Tech.Rpt.Libn.
GRUMMAN AEROSPACE CORPORATION -
TECHNICAL INFORMATION CENTER □
Bethpage, NY
Jenks, George M., Coll.Dev.Libn.
BUCKNELL UNIVERSITY - ELLEN CLARKE
BERTRAND LIBRARY □ Lewisburg, PA
Jenks, Linda N., Sr.Libn./Info.Mgr.
POPULATION CRISIS COMMITTEE/DRAPER
FUND - LIBRARY □ Washington, DC
Jenneman, Eugene A., Asst.Dir.
BESSER (Jesse) MUSEUM - LIBRARY □ Alpena,
MI
Jennerich, Elaine Z., Info.Spec.
AETNA LIFE & CASUALTY COMPANY -
FINANCIAL LIBRARY □ Hartford, CT
Jennings, David, Asst.Libn.
BOSTON GLOBE NEWSPAPER COMPANY -
LIBRARY □ Boston, MA
Jennings, Bro.Ed, S.J., Asst.Archv.
SOCIETY OF JESUS - OREGON PROVINCE
ARCHIVES □ Spokane, WA
Jennings, Gary, First Asst.
DALLAS PUBLIC LIBRARY - TEXAS/DALLAS
HISTORY AND ARCHIVES DIVISION □ Dallas, TX
Jennings, Jan, Mgr./Libn.
OKLAHOMA WELL LOG LIBRARY, INC. □ Tulsa,
OK
Jennings, Jill, Ref.Libn.
COLUMBIA UNIVERSITY - THOMAS J. WATSON
LIBRARY OF BUSINESS AND ECONOMICS □ New
York, NY
Jennings, Kelly, Libn.
TULSA CITY-COUNTY LIBRARY SYSTEM -
BUSINESS AND TECHNOLOGY DEPARTMENT □
Tulsa, OK
Jennings, Lucile H., Proj.Dir.
AMERICAN HARP SOCIETY REPOSITORY □
Hollywood, CA
Jennings, Marie D., Adm.Libn.
U.S. AIR FORCE BASE - PATRICK BASE
LIBRARY† □ Patrick AFB, FL
Jennings, Ruth Dougherty, Libn.
SUFFOLK MARINE MUSEUM - HERVEY GARRETT
SMITH RESEARCH LIBRARY □ West Sayville, NY
Jensen, Bro. Aaron, Asst.Libn.
ASSUMPTION ABBEY - LIBRARY □ Richardton,
ND

Jensen, Ann M., Libn.
UNIVERSITY OF CALIFORNIA, BERKELEY -
SCIENCE & MATHEMATICS EDUCATION
LIBRARY □ Berkeley, CA
Jensen, Barbara, Adm.Off.
U.S. PRESIDENTIAL LIBRARIES - LYNDON B.
JOHNSON LIBRARY □ Austin, TX
Jensen, Becky, Mgr., Info.Serv.
UNIVERSITY OF SOUTHERN CALIFORNIA -
NASA INDUSTRIAL APPLICATION CENTER
(NIAC) □ Los Angeles, CA
Jensen, Betty Jo, Med.Libn.
WHATCOM/ISLAND HEALTH SERVICES -
LIBRARY □ Bellingham, WA
Jensen, Charla, Sys.Libn.
BRIGHAM YOUNG UNIVERSITY - J. REUBEN
CLARK LAW SCHOOL LIBRARY □ Provo, UT
Jensen, Dennis F., Lib.Mgr.
STANDARD & POOR'S CORPORATION -
RESEARCH LIBRARY □ New York, NY
Jensen, Gary, Hd., Main Reading Rm.
LIBRARY OF CONGRESS - GEN. READING
ROOMS DIV. □ Washington, DC
Jensen, Gunvor, Asst.Libn.
WAGNER COLLEGE - HORRMANN LIBRARY □
Staten Island, NY
Jensen, Jess, Libn.
DALLAS PUBLIC LIBRARY - HUMANITIES
DIVISION □ Dallas, TX
Jensen, Joseph E., Libn.
MEDICAL AND CHIRURGICAL FACULTY OF THE
STATE OF MARYLAND - LIBRARY □ Baltimore,
MD
Jensen, L.B., Act.Hd., Info.Serv.
CANADA - DEFENCE RESEARCH
ESTABLISHMENT PACIFIC - LIBRARY □
Victoria, BC
Jensen, Dr. Louis R., Asst. Dean
INDIANA STATE UNIVERSITY - CONTINUING
EDUCATION AND EXTENDED SERVICES -
LIBRARY □ Terre Haute, IN
Jensen, M. Wayne, Jr., Dir.
TILLAMOOK COUNTY PIONEER MUSEUM -
LIBRARY □ Tillamook, OR
Jensen, Margaret P., Hd.
UNIVERSITY OF MICHIGAN - FINE ARTS
LIBRARY □ Ann Arbor, MI
Jensen, Mary Ann, Cur. of Theatre Coll.
PRINCETON UNIVERSITY - RARE BOOKS AND
SPECIAL COLLECTIONS □ Princeton, NJ
Jensen, Mary Ann, Cur.
PRINCETON UNIVERSITY - WILLIAM SEYMOUR
THEATRE COLLECTION □ Princeton, NJ
Jensen, Richard, Div.Coord.
BRIGHAM YOUNG UNIVERSITY - SCIENCE
DIVISION LIBRARY □ Provo, UT
Jensen, Sharon, Libn.
DANA COLLEGE - C.A. DANA-LIFE LIBRARY □
Blair, NE
Jensen, Yvette M., Libn.
MASSACHUSETTS MUTUAL LIFE INSURANCE
COMPANY - LIBRARY† □ Springfield, MA
Jenson, Annette, Libn.
GRAY, PLANT, MOOTY, MOOTY, AND BENNETT
- LAW LIBRARY† □ Minneapolis, MN
Jenson, David L., Libn.
MINNEAPOLIS TECHNICAL INSTITUTE/
MINNEAPOLIS COMMUNITY COLLEGE -
LIBRARY† □ Minneapolis, MN
Jerashen, A.J., Mgr.
GRANDMET USA, INC. - CORPORATE LIBRARY
□ Montvale, NJ
Jerde, Curtis D., Cur.
TULANE UNIVERSITY OF LOUISIANA -
WILLIAM RANSOM HOGAN JAZZ ARCHIVE □
New Orleans, LA
Jergens, Clare M., Chf., Lib.Serv.
U.S. VETERANS ADMINISTRATION (IA-Des
Moines) - HOSPITAL LIBRARY □ Des Moines, IA
Jerkovich, George, Dir./Cur.
UNIVERSITY OF KANSAS - SLAVIC
COLLECTION □ Lawrence, KS

Jernigan, Thomas, M.D., Med.Dir.
NEW YORK LIFE INSURANCE COMPANY -
MEDICAL DEPARTMENT LIBRARY □ New York,
NY
Jernigan, Dr. W.W., Dir.
ORAL ROBERTS UNIVERSITY - LIBRARY - HOLY
SPIRIT RESEARCH CENTER □ Tulsa, OK
Jernigan, Dr. William W., Dir.
ORAL ROBERTS UNIVERSITY - GRADUATE
THEOLOGY LIBRARY - JOHN MESSICK
LEARNING RESOURCE CENTER □ Tulsa, OK
Jerousek, William, Libn.
OAK PARK PUBLIC LIBRARY - LOCAL AUTHOR
AND LOCAL HISTORY COLLECTIONS □ Oak Park,
IL
Jerrido, Margaret, Asst.Archv.
MEDICAL COLLEGE OF PENNSYLVANIA -
ARCHIVES AND SPECIAL COLLECTIONS ON
WOMEN IN MEDICINE □ Philadelphia, PA
Jerscheid, Mary Teresa, Law Libn.
FIDELITY & DEPOSIT COMPANY OF MARYLAND
- LAW LIBRARY† □ Baltimore, MD
Jersey, Patricia J., Ref./ILL Libn.
EAST STROUDSBURG UNIVERSITY - KENT
LIBRARY† □ East Stroudsburg, PA
Jervis, Pam, Cat.Libn.
BETHEL THEOLOGICAL SEMINARY - RESOURCE
CENTER □ St. Paul, MN
Jeryn, Irene, Libn.
HOSPITAL FOR SICK CHILDREN - HOSPITAL
LIBRARY □ Toronto, ON
Jeschke, Channing R., Libn.
EMORY UNIVERSITY - PITTS THEOLOGY
LIBRARY □ Atlanta, GA
Jeschke, Freya, Libn.
GOETHE HOUSE NEW YORK - LIBRARY □ New
York, NY
Jesse, William
NATIONAL COLLEGE OF EDUCATION -
LEARNING RESOURCE CENTERS □ Evanston, IL
Jessup, Helen C., Libn.
POTOMAC ELECTRIC POWER COMPANY -
LIBRARY □ Washington, DC
Jestes, Edward, Libn.
UNIVERSITY OF CALIFORNIA, DAVIS -
PHYSICAL SCIENCES LIBRARY □ Davis, CA
Jestin, Catherine, Libn.
YALE UNIVERSITY - LEWIS WALPOLE LIBRARY
□ Farmington, CT
Jesudawson, Ben, Libn.
EAST CENTRAL LEGAL SERVICES - LIBRARY □
Anderson, IN
Jeter, Ann, Libn.
HUGHES & HILL - LIBRARY □ Dallas, TX
Jeter, Edie, Libn.
VALENTINE MUSEUM - LIBRARY □ Richmond,
VA
Jett, Don, Libn.
UNIVERSITY OF TENNESSEE - AGRICULTURE-
VETERINARY MEDICINE LIBRARY □ Knoxville,
TN
Jett, John H., Dir.
ARIZONA STATE DEPARTMENT OF MINERAL
RESOURCES - LIBRARY □ Phoenix, AZ
Jette, Jean-Paul, Dir.
UNIVERSITE DE MONTREAL - MEDECINE
VETERINAIRE-BIBLIOTHEQUE □ St-Hyacinthe,
PQ
Jevnikar, Jana, Info.Coord.
CLEARINGHOUSE FOR ARTS INFORMATION -
CENTER FOR ARTS INFORMATION □ New York,
NY
Jewell, M.D., Mgr., Engr.Doc.
INGERSOLL-RAND COMPANY - ENGINEERING
LIBRARY □ Nashua, NH
Jewell, Mary Ellen, Asst.Libn.
HURON ROAD HOSPITAL - LIBRARY AND
AUDIOVISUAL CENTER □ Cleveland, OH
Jewett, Christine C., Libn.
FULLER THEOLOGICAL SEMINARY - MC
ALISTER LIBRARY† □ Pasadena, CA

Jhass, Jasveer, Lib.Techn.
ALBERTA - PERSONNEL ADMINISTRATION
OFFICE - LIBRARY □ Edmonton, AB

Jilbert, Louise, Libn.
ROCK COUNTY HEALTH CARE CENTER - STAFF
LIBRARY □ Janesville, WI

Jimenez, Manuel, Mgr., Spec.Proj.
ATLANTIC RICHFIELD COMPANY - CORPORATE
ARCHIVES □ Los Angeles, CA

Jimenez, Margarita, ILL Libn.
UNIVERSITY OF PUERTO RICO - MEDICAL
SCIENCES CAMPUS - LIBRARY □ Rio Piedras, PR

Jirkovsky, Z., Hd., Sci. & Engr.Lib.
CONCORDIA UNIVERSITY - SIR GEORGE
WILLIAMS CAMPUS - SCIENCE &
ENGINEERING LIBRARY □ Montreal, PQ

Jivraj, Mumtaz, Hd.Libn.
HOLY CROSS HOSPITAL OF CALGARY -
DEPARTMENT OF LIBRARY SERVICES □ Calgary,
AB

Jo, Julitta, Ser.Libn.
SUNY AT STONY BROOK - HEALTH SCIENCES
LIBRARY □ East Setauket, NY

Jo, Yong Cha, Hd.
UNIVERSITY OF MANITOBA - SCIENCE
LIBRARY □ Winnipeg, MB

Joachim, Linda, Hd.
INDIANA UNIVERSITY - HEALTH, PHYSICAL
EDUCATION & RECREATION LIBRARY □
Bloomington, IN

Joanisse, Marcel, Cat.
UNIVERSITY OF OTTAWA - LAW LIBRARY □
Ottawa, ON

Joba, Judith, Info.Spec.
C.I. POWER SERVICES - INFORMATION
CENTRE □ Montreal, PQ

Jobe, Shirley A., Lib.Dir.
BOSTON GLOBE NEWSPAPER COMPANY -
LIBRARY □ Boston, MA

Jocz, E. Anne, Hd.Cat.
UNIVERSITY OF TORONTO - THOMAS FISHER
RARE BOOK LIBRARY □ Toronto, ON

Johannessen, Joanne, Libn.
WERTHEIM AND COMPANY, INC. - RESEARCH
LIBRARY† □ New York, NY

Johansen, Priscilla, Map Libn.
AMOCO PRODUCTION COMPANY
INTERNATIONAL - LIBRARY INFORMATION
CENTER □ Houston, TX

Johmann, Nancy, Hd., Ref./Info.
BRIDGEPORT PUBLIC LIBRARY - TECHNOLOGY
AND BUSINESS DEPARTMENT □ Bridgeport, CT

John, Stephanie, Dir.
SAGINAW HEALTH SCIENCES LIBRARY □
Saginaw, MI

Johnle, Herbert A., Mgr.
BUDD COMPANY TECHNICAL LIBRARY □ Fort
Washington, PA

Johns, Alan B., Libn.
UNIVERSITY OF TENNESSEE - ENERGY,
ENVIRONMENT & RESOURCES CENTER - JOINT
RESEARCH CENTERS' LIBRARY □ Knoxville, TN

Johns, Bernice, Hd.
OMAHA PUBLIC LIBRARY - BUSINESS, SCIENCE
& TECHNOLOGY DEPARTMENT □ Omaha, NE

Johns, Frank, Libn.
BLUE CROSS AND BLUE SHIELD OF VIRGINIA -
PLANS LIBRARY □ Richmond, VA

Johns, Gerald, Asst.Sci.Libn.
SAN DIEGO STATE UNIVERSITY - SCIENCE
DEPARTMENT† □ San Diego, CA

Johns, Gloria F.L., Libn.
CANADA LIFE ASSURANCE COMPANY -
LIBRARY □ Toronto, ON

Johns, John E., First Asst.
PUBLIC LIBRARY OF CINCINNATI AND
HAMILTON COUNTY - SCIENCE AND
TECHNOLOGY DEPARTMENT □ Cincinnati, OH

Johns, Michele, Br.Libn.
UNIVERSITY OF ILLINOIS AT CHICAGO -
HEALTH SCIENCES CENTER - LIBRARY OF THE
HEALTH SCIENCES □ Peoria, IL

Johns, Michelle, Asst.Libn.
NORTH CENTRAL BIBLE COLLEGE - T.J. JONES
MEMORIAL LIBRARY† □ Minneapolis, MN

Johns, Nellie, Libn.
EMORY UNIVERSITY - YERKES REGIONAL
PRIMATE CENTER - LIBRARY □ Atlanta, GA

Johnson, A. Kristine, Hd.
UNIVERSITY OF MINNESOTA - ARCHITECTURE
LIBRARY □ Minneapolis, MN

Johnson, Adele, Acq.Libn.
NEW YORK STATE HISTORICAL ASSOCIATION
- LIBRARY □ Cooperstown, NY

Johnson, Alice K., Libn.
PPG INDUSTRIES, INC. - CHEMICAL DIVISION
- NATRIUM RESEARCH AND DEVELOPMENT
LIBRARY □ New Martinsville, WV

Johnson, Allan R., Lib.Dir.
BRIERCREST BIBLE COLLEGE - ARCHIBALD
LIBRARY □ Caronport, SK

Johnson, Andrew, Cat.
MARYLAND INSTITUTE, COLLEGE OF ART -
DECKER LIBRARY □ Baltimore, MD

Johnson, Andrew F., State/Local Docs.Libn.
UNIVERSITY OF WASHINGTON - GOVERNMENT
PUBLICATIONS DIVISION □ Seattle, WA

Johnson, Anita k., Dir.
ST. FRANCIS MEDICAL CENTER - HEALTH
SCIENCES LIBRARY □ Trenton, NJ

Johnson, Ann Kinken, Hd.Libn.
VIRGINIAN-PILOT & LEDGER-STAR - LIBRARY
□ Norfolk, VA

Johnson, Anne, Asst.Libn.
ALSTON & BIRD - LIBRARY □ Atlanta, GA

Johnson, Audrey, Act. County Hist.
MONROE COUNTY LOCAL HISTORY ROOM &
LIBRARY □ Sparta, WI

Johnson, B.G.H., Biologist
CANADA - FISHERIES & OCEANS - SEA
LAMPREY CONTROL CENTRE - LIBRARY □ Sault
Ste. Marie, ON

Johnson, Barbara Coe, Dir. of Libs.
HARPER-GRACE HOSPITALS - HARPER
HOSPITAL DIVISION - DEPARTMENT OF
LIBRARIES □ Detroit, MI

Johnson, Bernice W., Hd.Libn.
BROCKTON DAILY ENTERPRISE AND
BROCKTON TIMES-ENTERPRISE - LIBRARY □
Brockton, MA

Johnson, Bethey J., Libn.
U.S. AIR FORCE BASE - BLYTHEVILLE BASE
LIBRARY □ Blytheville AFB, AR

Johnson, Bobbie, Hd.Libn.
PAUL, HASTINGS, JANOFSKY AND WALKER -
LAW LIBRARY† □ Los Angeles, CA

Johnson, Br. James G., C.P., Libn.
PASSIONIST MONASTIC SEMINARY - LIBRARY
□ Jamaica, NY

Johnson, Bruce L., Lib.Dir.
CALIFORNIA HISTORICAL SOCIETY -
SCHUBERT HALL LIBRARY □ San Francisco, CA

Johnson, Bruce S., Chf.Ref.Libn.
UNIVERSITY OF MICHIGAN - LAW LIBRARY □
Ann Arbor, MI

Johnson, Candice M., Libn.
STANDARD OIL COMPANY OF OHIO - THE
PFAUDLER COMPANY - TECHNICAL LIBRARY □
Rochester, NY

Johnson, Carol A., Proj.Mgr.
U.S. DEPT. OF HOUSING AND URBAN
DEVELOPMENT - LIBRARY □ Washington, DC

Johnson, Carolyn, Hd.
ROCHESTER PUBLIC LIBRARY - BUSINESS,
ECONOMICS AND LEGISLATION DIVISION □
Rochester, NY

Johnson, Cassandra K., Libn.
CHURCH OF JESUS CHRIST OF LATTER-DAY
SAINTS - LAIE, HAWAII STAKE BRANCH
GENEALOGICAL LIBRARY □ Laie, HI

Johnson, Catherine, Lib.Asst.
QUEEN'S UNIVERSITY AT KINGSTON -
PHYSICS LIBRARY □ Kingston, ON

Johnson, Cathy, Microfilm Coord.
TRIANGLE PUBLICATIONS, INC. - TV GUIDE
MICROFILM LIBRARY □ Radnor, PA

Johnson, Rev. Charles B., Dir.
ST. THOMAS SEMINARY LIBRARY - ALUMNI
COLLECTION □ Bloomfield, CT

Johnson, Charles H., Supv. of Lib.
SPRING GROVE HOSPITAL CENTER -
SULZBACHER MEMORIAL LIBRARY† □
Baltimore, MD

Johnson, Charlotte, Sci.Libn.
SOUTHERN ILLINOIS UNIVERSITY,
EDWARDSVILLE - SCIENCE LIBRARY □
Edwardsville, IL

Johnson, Dr. Clifton H., Exec.Dir.
AMISTAD RESEARCH CENTER - LIBRARY/
ARCHIVES □ New Orleans, LA

Johnson, D. Thomas
KINGMAN MUSEUM OF NATURAL HISTORY -
LIBRARY □ Battle Creek, MI

Johnson, Dale L., Archv.
UNIVERSITY OF MONTANA - MAUREEN & MIKE
MANSFIELD LIBRARY - K. ROSS TOOLE
ARCHIVES □ Missoula, MT

Johnson, David J., Libn./Archv.
ARICA INSTITUTE, INC. - LIBRARY AND
ARCHIVES □ New York, NY

Johnson, David J., State Archv.
MICHIGAN STATE HISTORY DIVISION -
ARCHIVES □ Lansing, MI

Johnson, David L., Dir.
PARKLAND COLLEGE - LEARNING RESOURCE
CENTER □ Champaign, IL

Johnson, Dr. David P.
AMERICAN COLLEGE OF HERALDRY - LIBRARY
□ University, AL

Johnson, Dennis
U.S. BUREAU OF THE CENSUS - INFORMATION
SERVICES PROGRAM - KANSAS CITY
REGIONAL OFFICE - LIBRARY □ Kansas City, KS

Johnson, Diana, Dir.
WHEATON COMMUNITY HOSPITAL - MEDICAL
LIBRARY □ Wheaton, MN

Johnson, Diana, Ref./ILL
WORCESTER POLYTECHNIC INSTITUTE -
GEORGE C. GORDON LIBRARY □ Worcester, MA

Johnson, Diane, Ser.Libn.
SUNY - COLLEGE AT GENESEO - COLLEGE
LIBRARIES □ Geneseo, NY

Johnson, Diane, Hd., ILL
UNIVERSITY OF MISSOURI - HEALTH
SCIENCES LIBRARY □ Columbia, MO

Johnson, Donna, Dir, Rsrc.Ctr.
ABBOTT-NORTHWESTERN HOSPITAL
CORPORATION - HEALTH SCIENCES RESOURCE
CENTER □ Minneapolis, MN

Johnson, Duane A., Command Libn.
U.S. AIR FORCE - AIR TRAINING COMMAND -
LIBRARY PROGRAM □ Randolph AFB, TX

Johnson, Duane F., State Libn.
KANSAS STATE LIBRARY □ Topeka, KS

Johnson, E. William, Chf.Archv.
U.S. PRESIDENTIAL LIBRARIES - JOHN F.
KENNEDY LIBRARY □ Boston, MA

Johnson, Elaine B., Libn.
BALTIMORE POLICE DEPARTMENT -
EDUCATION AND TRAINING DIVISION -
LIBRARY □ Baltimore, MD

Johnson, Elaine C., Tech.Info.Spec.
U.S. DEPT. OF LABOR - OSHA - TECHNICAL
DATA CENTER □ Washington, DC

Johnson, Eleanor, Asst.Libn.
WISCONSIN INDIANHEAD TECHNICAL
INSTITUTE, SUPERIOR CAMPUS - LIBRARY† □
Superior, WI

Johnson, Elizabeth, Sr.Archv.
GEORGIA STATE SURVEYOR GENERAL
DEPARTMENT - LIBRARY □ Atlanta, GA

Johnson, Elizabeth, Cat.
INDIANA UNIVERSITY - LILLY LIBRARY □
Bloomington, IN

Johnson, Ellen, Assoc.Libn.
UNIVERSITY OF KANSAS - THOMAS GORTON
MUSIC LIBRARY □ Lawrence, KS

Johnson, Ellen M., Libn.
FEDERAL RESERVE BANK OF KANSAS CITY -
RESEARCH LIBRARY □ Kansas City, MO

Johnson, Elly, Music Cat.
UNIVERSITY OF WISCONSIN, MILWAUKEE -
MUSIC COLLECTION □ Milwaukee, WI

Johnson, Esther, Libn.
UNIVERSITY OF CALIFORNIA, BERKELEY -
FORESTRY LIBRARY □ Berkeley, CA

Johnson, Eunice Bisbee, Sr.Lib.Asst.
UNIVERSITY OF MINNESOTA - PUBLIC
ADMINISTRATION LIBRARY □ Minneapolis, MN

Johnson, F.T., Rec.Mgr.
UNIVERSITY OF UTAH - SPECIAL COLLECTIONS
DEPARTMENT □ Salt Lake City, UT

Johnson, Fran, Ref.Libn.
MARICOPA TECHNICAL COMMUNITY COLLEGE
- LIBRARY RESOURCE CENTER □ Phoenix, AZ

Johnson, Garry, Dir., Lib.Serv.
LOUISVILLE BAPTIST HOSPITALS - HAGAN
LIBRARY □ Louisville, KY

Johnson, Gertrude D., Archv.
ST. CHARLES COUNTY HISTORICAL SOCIETY -
ARCHIVES □ St. Charles, MO

Johnson, Glenderlyn, Ed., Journal
NEW YORK PUBLIC LIBRARY - SCHOMBURG
CENTER FOR RESEARCH IN BLACK CULTURE □
New York, NY

Johnson, Guela G., Libn.
UNIVERSITY OF WASHINGTON - SOCIAL WORK
LIBRARY □ Seattle, WA

Johnson, H. Christine, Mgr., Law Lib. & Rec.Ctr.
THE COCA-COLA COMPANY - LAW LIBRARY □
Atlanta, GA

Johnson, Harvey G., Info.Sci.
GENERAL MILLS, INC. - JAMES FORD BELL
TECHNICAL CENTER - TECHNICAL
INFORMATION SERVICES □ Minneapolis, MN

Johnson, Harvey J., Dir.
CATHOLIC CENTRAL UNION OF AMERICA -
CENTRAL BUREAU LIBRARY □ St. Louis, MO

Johnson, Herb, Dir., Media Ctr.
MC PHERSON COLLEGE - MILLER LIBRARY □
McPherson, KS

Johnson, Jackie, Leg.Ref.Libn.
EDISON ELECTRIC INSTITUTE - LIBRARY □
Washington, DC

Johnson, James, Libn.
ONTARIO BIBLE COLLEGE/ONTARIO
THEOLOGICAL SEMINARY - J. WILLIAM
HORSEY LIBRARY □ Willowdale, ON

Johnson, James, Assoc.Dir.
SLOAN (Alfred P., Jr.) MUSEUM - MERLE G.
PERRY ARCHIVES □ Flint, MI

Johnson, James, Jr., Dp. State Libn.
SOUTH CAROLINA STATE LIBRARY □ Columbia,
SC

Johnson, James P., Chf.Libn.
HOWARD UNIVERSITY - MOORLAND-SPINGARN
RESEARCH CENTER - LIBRARY DIVISION □
Washington, DC

Johnson, James R., Hd., Hist. & Travel
MEMPHIS-SHELBY COUNTY PUBLIC LIBRARY
AND INFORMATION CENTER - MEMPHIS ROOM
COLLECTIONS □ Memphis, TN

Johnson, Janet, Lib.Asst.
OTTER TAIL POWER COMPANY - LIBRARY □
Fergus Falls, MN

Johnson, Janice, Libn.
AMERICAN VETERINARY MEDICAL
ASSOCIATION - LIBRARY □ Schaumburg, IL

Johnson, Janice, Libn.
KOKOMO TRIBUNE - LIBRARY □ Kokomo, IN

Johnson, Jeffrey, Supv., Pub.Serv.
QUEEN'S UNIVERSITY AT KINGSTON - LAW
LIBRARY □ Kingston, ON

Johnson, Dr. Jerry, Dir.
UNIVERSITY OF SOUTH DAKOTA - BUSINESS
RESEARCH BUREAU □ Vermillion, SD

Johnson, Joan, Asst.Libn.
MC PHERSON COLLEGE - MILLER LIBRARY □
McPherson, KS

Johnson, JoAnn, Chf., Lib.Serv.
ENVIRONMENTAL PROTECTION AGENCY -
ANDREW W. BREIDENBACH ENVIRONMENTAL
RESEARCH CTR., CINCINNATI - TECH.LIB. □
Cincinnati, OH

Johnson, Johanna, Patent Libn.
DALLAS PUBLIC LIBRARY - GOVERNMENT
PUBLICATIONS DIVISION □ Dallas, TX

Johnson, John, Doc.
KANSAS STATE UNIVERSITY - FARRELL
LIBRARY □ Manhattan, KS

Johnson, Joyce H., Adm.Off.
TRANSPORTATION INSTITUTE - RESEARCH
DOCUMENTATION CENTER □ Greensboro, NC

Johnson, Judith, Archv.
SALVATION ARMY - ARCHIVES AND RESEARCH
CENTER □ New York, NY

Johnson, June, Libn.
REDMOND (J.W.) COMPANY - LIBRARY □
Washington, DC

Johnson, Kathleen, Ref.
HARVARD UNIVERSITY - HARVARD BUSINESS
SCHOOL - BAKER LIBRARY □ Boston, MA

Johnson, Kathleen A., Assoc.Prof.
UNIVERSITY OF NEBRASKA, LINCOLN -
ARCHITECTURE LIBRARY □ Lincoln, NE

Johnson, Laura, Hd., Ext.Div.
INDIANA STATE LIBRARY □ Indianapolis, IN

Johnson, Laura M., Mgr.
BOZELL & JACOBS, INC. - CORPORATE
INFORMATION CENTER □ Chicago, IL

Johnson, Leanne, Libn.
CONNAUGHT LABORATORIES, LTD. - BALMER
NEILLY LIBRARY □ Willowdale, ON

Johnson, Lee Z., Archv.
FIRST CHURCH OF CHRIST SCIENTIST -
ARCHIVES AND LIBRARY □ Boston, MA

Johnson, Leith, Archv.
AETNA LIFE & CASUALTY COMPANY -
CORPORATE INFORMATION CENTER □
Hartford, CT

Johnson, Lenora I., Musm.Dir.
NORMAN COUNTY HISTORICAL SOCIETY -
MEMORIAL MUSEUM LIBRARY □ Ada, MN

Johnson, Leone, Libn.
MINNEAPOLIS PUBLIC LIBRARY &
INFORMATION CENTER - GOVERNMENT
DOCUMENTS □ Minneapolis, MN

Johnson, Linda, Res.Assoc.
FOUNDATION FOR PUBLIC AFFAIRS -
RESOURCE CENTER □ Washington, DC

Johnson, Lisa F., Exec.Dir.
SENECA FALLS HISTORICAL SOCIETY -
LIBRARY □ Seneca Falls, NY

Johnson, Liz, Libn.
ALBERTA - ENERGY RESOURCES
CONSERVATION BOARD - LIBRARY □ Calgary,
AB

Johnson, Lori, Per.Libn.
MOODY BIBLE INSTITUTE - LIBRARY □ Chicago,
IL

Johnson, Ms. M.A., Engr.Libn.
GENERAL DYNAMICS CORPORATION -
DATAGRAPHIX, INC. - ENGINEERING LIBRARY
□ San Diego, CA

Johnson, M.L., Asst.Libn.
NEW YORK STATE DEPARTMENT OF STATE -
INFORMATION RESOURCE CENTER □ Albany,
NY

Johnson, M. Malinda, Post Libn.
U.S. ARMY POST - FORT STEWART/HUNTER
AAF LIBRARY SYSTEM □ Ft. Stewart, GA

Johnson, Margaret, Hd., Tech.Serv.
UNIVERSITY OF MINNESOTA, ST. PAUL -
CENTRAL LIBRARY □ St. Paul, MN

Johnson, Margaret Ann, ILL Libn.
UNIVERSITY OF ARKANSAS FOR MEDICAL
SCIENCES - MEDICAL SCIENCES LIBRARY □
Little Rock, AR

Johnson, Marguerite H., Law Libn.
PALM BEACH COUNTY - LAW LIBRARY □ West
Palm Beach, FL

Johnson, Marion, Dir., Pub.Lib.Dev.
NORTH CAROLINA STATE DEPARTMENT OF
CULTURAL RESOURCES - DIVISION OF THE
STATE LIBRARY □ Raleigh, NC

Johnson, Mrs. Marion E., Hd., Info.Rsrcs.
FORINTEK CANADA CORPORATION - WESTERN
LABORATORY - LIBRARY □ Vancouver, BC

Johnson, Marlys J., Tech.Libn.
FLUIDYNE ENGINEERING CORPORATION -
TECHNICAL LIBRARY □ Minneapolis, MN

Johnson, Mary E., Libn.
FOREST HISTORY SOCIETY, INC. - LIBRARY
AND ARCHIVES □ Durham, NC

Johnson, Mary E., Libn.
MISSOURI INSTITUTE OF PSYCHIATRY
LIBRARY □ St. Louis, MO

Johnson, Mary E., Asst.Libn.
U.S. ARMY - CORPS OF ENGINEERS - SEATTLE
DISTRICT - LIBRARY □ Seattle, WA

Johnson, Mary H., Libn.
MENTAL HEALTH ASSOCIATION OF
WESTCHESTER COUNTY - LIBRARY □ White
Plains, NY

Johnson, Mary Jane, Sec.
PENNSYLVANIA STATE UNIVERSITY -
INSTITUTE FOR POLICY RESEARCH AND
EVALUATION - LIBRARY □ University Park, PA

Johnson, Mary K., Libn.
BASF WYANDOTTE CORPORATION - PIGMENTS
LIBRARY □ Holland, MI

Johnson, Mel, Hist.Site Asst.
NEW YORK STATE BUREAU OF HISTORIC
SITES - WASHINGTON'S HEADQUARTERS
STATE HISTORIC SITE - LIBRARY □ Newburgh,
NY

Johnson, Michelle, Lib.Mgr.
DIGITAL EQUIPMENT CORPORATION -
MARLBORO LIBRARY □ Marlboro, MA

Johnson, Millard F., Jr., Res.Assoc.
WASHINGTON UNIVERSITY - SCHOOL OF
MEDICINE LIBRARY □ St. Louis, MO

Johnson, Nancy, Assoc. Law Libn.
GEORGIA STATE UNIVERSITY - COLLEGE OF
LAW LIBRARY □ Atlanta, GA

Johnson, Norma, Adm.Spec.
KENTUCKY STATE FINANCE AND
ADMINISTRATION CABINET - GOVERNMENT
SERVICES CENTER LIBRARY □ Frankfort, KY

Johnson, P.G., Libn.
BATTELLE MEMORIAL INSTITUTE - LIBRARY □
Columbus, OH

Johnson, Pam, Acq.
OHIO NORTHERN UNIVERSITY - COLLEGE OF
LAW - JAY P. TAGGART MEMORIAL LAW
LIBRARY □ Ada, OH

Johnson, Pat M., Dir., Libs./Rec.
MC CLELLAND ENGINEERS, INC. - CORPORATE
TECHNICAL LIBRARY □ Houston, TX

Johnson, Patty, Info.Spec.
MC KINSEY & COMPANY, INC. - INFORMATION
CENTER □ Los Angeles, CA

Johnson, Paul H., Hd.Libn.
U.S. COAST GUARD ACADEMY - LIBRARY □ New
London, CT

Johnson, Paula, Libn.
U.S. NATL. MARINE FISHERIES SERVICE -
AUKE BAY FISHERIES LABORATORY -
FISHERIES RESEARCH LIBRARY □ Auke Bay, AK

Johnson, Peggy B., Exec.Sec.
CLINTON RIVER WATERSHED COUNCIL -
LIBRARY □ Utica, MI

Johnson, Penelope B., Hd.
WORCESTER PUBLIC LIBRARY - REFERENCE
AND READER SERVICES □ Worcester, MA

Johnson, Peter, Index
NEWSDAY, INC. - LIBRARY □ Melville, NY

Johnson, Rachael H., Cur.
NEW HAMPSHIRE ANTIQUARIAN SOCIETY -
LIBRARY □ Hopkinton Village, NH

Johnson, Ressie, Prin.Libn., KENCLIP
KENTUCKY STATE DEPARTMENT FOR
LIBRARIES AND ARCHIVES - STATE LIBRARY
SERVICES DIVISION □ Frankfort, KY

Johnson, Reta, Dp.Libn.
NEBRASKA STATE LIBRARY □ Lincoln, NE

Johnson, Dr. Robert N., Dir.
OAKLAND SCHOOLS - EDUCATIONAL RESOURCE
CENTER □ Pontiac, MI

Johnson, Robert O., Hd.
UNIVERSITY OF CINCINNATI - COLLEGE
CONSERVATORY OF MUSIC - GORNO
MEMORIAL MUSIC LIBRARY □ Cincinnati, OH

Johnson, Roy C., Libn.
NEW YORK UNIVERSITY - DENTAL CENTER -
JOHN & BERTHA E. WALDMANN MEMORIAL
LIBRARY □ New York, NY

Johnson, Ruth H., Hd.Libn.
BABCOCK AND WILCOX COMPANY - UTILITY
POWER GENERATION DIVISION - LIBRARY □
Lynchburg, VA

Johnson, Samuel V., Hd., Automation Serv.
RENSSELAER POLYTECHNIC INSTITUTE -
FOLSOM LIBRARY □ Troy, NY

Johnson, Sandra, Asst.Cur.
PENSACOLA HISTORICAL SOCIETY - LELIA
ABERCROMBIE HISTORICAL LIBRARY □
Pensacola, FL

Johnson, Sharon, Adm.Libn.
U.S. ARMY HOSPITALS - FITZSIMONS ARMY
MEDICAL CENTER - MEDICAL-TECHNICAL
LIBRARY □ Aurora, CO

Johnson, Sheila G., Hd.
OKLAHOMA STATE UNIVERSITY - BIOLOGICAL
SCIENCES DIVISION □ Stillwater, OK

Johnson, Shirley, Ref.Libn.
CLARION UNIVERSITY OF PENNSYLVANIA -
RENA M. CARLSON LIBRARY □ Clarion, PA

Johnson, Sigrid, Icelandic Libn.
UNIVERSITY OF MANITOBA - ARCHIVES AND
SPECIAL COLLECTIONS □ Winnipeg, MB

Johnson, Stephen C., Dir., Lib.Serv.
ST. ALEXIS HOSPITAL - HEALTH SCIENCES
LIBRARY □ Cleveland, OH

Johnson, Steven P., Archv.-Libn.
NEW YORK ZOOLOGICAL SOCIETY - LIBRARY □
Bronx, NY

Johnson, Sue Ann M., Hd.Libn.
UNIVERSITY OF CALIFORNIA, SAN DIEGO -
MEDICAL CENTER LIBRARY □ San Diego, CA

Johnson, Sue H., Libn.
CARRINGTON, COLEMAN, SLOMAN &
BLUMENTHAL - LIBRARY □ Dallas, TX

Johnson, Susan, Libn.
SASKATCHEWAN - DEPARTMENT OF LABOUR -
OCCUPATIONAL HEALTH AND SAFETY
DIVISION - LIBRARY □ Regina, SK

Johnson, Susan E., Asst.Libn.
MULTNOMAH SCHOOL OF THE BIBLE - JOHN
AND MARY MITCHELL LIBRARY □ Portland, OR

Johnson, Suzanne, Biomed.Sci.Libn.
COLORADO STATE UNIVERSITY - WILLIAM E.
MORGAN LIBRARY □ Fort Collins, CO

Johnson, Bro. Theodore E., Dir.
UNITED SOCIETY OF BELIEVERS - THE SHAKER
LIBRARY □ Poland Spring, ME

Johnson, Thomas L., Asst.Libn.
UNIVERSITY OF SOUTH CAROLINA - SOUTH
CAROLINIANA LIBRARY □ Columbia, SC

Johnson, Wallace, Hd.Libn.
CHURCH OF JESUS CHRIST OF LATTER-DAY
SAINTS - TACOMA BRANCH GENEALOGY
LIBRARY □ Tacoma, WA

Johnson, Wayne H., State Libn.
WYOMING STATE LIBRARY □ Cheyenne, WY

Johnson, Willa H., Libn.
CHURCH OF THE INCARNATION - MARMION
LIBRARY □ Dallas, TX

Johnson, William E., Dir., AT/AV Lab.
TUSKEGEE INSTITUTE - VETERINARY
MEDICINE LIBRARY† □ Tuskegee Institute, AL

Johnson, William E., Law Libn./Professor
WEST VIRGINIA UNIVERSITY - LAW LIBRARY
□ Morgantown, WV

Johnson, William G., Div.Hd.
AKRON-SUMMIT COUNTY PUBLIC LIBRARY -
BUSINESS, LABOR AND GOVERNMENT
DIVISION □ Akron, OH

Johnson, William J., Chf., NCIC - W.
U.S. GEOLOGICAL SURVEY - NATL.
CARTOGRAPHIC INFORMATION CENTER
(NCIC) - WESTERN BRANCH □ Menlo Park, CA

Johnson-Champ, D., Ref.
SOUTHWESTERN UNIVERSITY - SCHOOL OF
LAW LIBRARY □ Los Angeles, CA

Johnsrud, Thomas, Ref.Libn.
SAN DIEGO COUNTY LAW LIBRARY □ San Diego,
CA

Johnston, Bruce, Med.Libn.
EYE AND EAR HOSPITAL OF PITTSBURGH -
BLAIR-LIPPINCOTT LIBRARY □ Pittsburgh, PA

Johnston, D.L., Hd.
UNIVERSITY OF PITTSBURGH - BIOLOGICAL
SCIENCES AND PSYCHOLOGY LIBRARY □
Pittsburgh, PA

Johnston, Dinnie K., Med.Libn.
VICKSBURG HOSPITAL, INC. - MEDICAL
LIBRARY □ Vicksburg, MS

Johnston, Ellen A., Chf.Libn.
ALCAN ALUMINUM, LTD. - INFORMATION
CENTRE □ Montreal, PQ

Johnston, Ezelyn S., Cat.
EAST CHICAGO HISTORICAL SOCIETY -
LIBRARY □ East Chicago, IN

Johnston, Francena, Med.Libn.
SAN ANTONIO COMMUNITY HOSPITAL -
WEBER MEMORIAL LIBRARY □ Upland, CA

Johnston, George F., Asst.Libn.
COVENANT THEOLOGICAL SEMINARY - J.
OLIVER BUSWELL, JR. LIBRARY □ St. Louis, MO

Johnston, Janelle D., Clerk
SASKATCHEWAN - DEPARTMENT OF PARKS
AND RENEWABLE RESOURCES - FORESTRY
DIVISION LIBRARY □ Prince Albert, SK

Johnston, Janis, Ser.Libn.
INDIANA UNIVERSITY - LAW LIBRARY □
Bloomington, IN

Johnston, John W., Dir.
ASSOCIATION OF INTERNATIONAL COLLEGES
& UNIVERSITIES - AICU INTERNATIONAL
EDUCATION LIBRARY □ Independence, MO

Johnston, Judy, Coord., Online Searches
UNIVERSITY OF SOUTH ALABAMA - COLLEGE
OF MEDICINE - BIOMEDICAL LIBRARY □
Mobile, AL

Johnston, June, Med.Rec.Dir.
ST. FRANCIS MEDICAL CENTER - CAPE
COUNTY MEMORIAL MEDICAL LIBRARY, INC. □
Cape Girardeau, MO

Johnston, Margaret E., Cur.
HAVERFORD TOWNSHIP HISTORICAL SOCIETY
- LIBRARY □ Havertown, PA

Johnston, Midge, Bus.Mgr.
U.S. NATL. PARK SERVICE - BADLANDS NATL.
PARK - LIBRARY □ Interior, SD

Johnston, Nancy S., Dir.
NATIONAL INJURY INFORMATION
CLEARINGHOUSE □ Washington, DC

Johnston, Norma, Libn.
MC GILL UNIVERSITY - ISLAMIC STUDIES
LIBRARY □ Montreal, PQ

Johnston, Norma, Hd.Libn.
MC GILL UNIVERSITY - RELIGIOUS STUDIES
LIBRARY □ Montreal, PQ

Johnston, Patricia A., Cat. Lead
BOEING COMPANY - SEATTLE SERVICES
DIVISION - TECHNICAL LIBRARIES† □ Seattle,
WA

Johnston, Rebecca, Hd.Cat.
WAKE FOREST UNIVERSITY - BOWMAN GRAY
SCHOOL OF MEDICINE - COY C. CARPENTER
LIBRARY □ Winston-Salem, NC

Johnston, Stanley, Exec.Sec.
ILLINOIS STATE LEGISLATIVE REFERENCE
BUREAU □ Springfield, IL

Johnston, Stephanie, Libn.
UNIVERSITY OF TORONTO - DEPARTMENT OF
COMPUTER SCIENCE LIBRARY □ Toronto, ON

Johnstone, Betty Lu, Rd.Serv.Libn.
WESTERN CONSERVATIVE BAPTIST SEMINARY
- CLINE-TUNNELL LIBRARY □ Portland, OR

Johnstone, Ellen, Health Sci.Libn.
BATH MEMORIAL HOSPITAL - HEALTH
SCIENCES LIBRARY □ Bath, ME

Johnstone, Jay, Dir.
NATIONAL INFORMATION CENTER FOR
EDUCATIONAL MEDIA (NICEM) □ Albuquerque,
NM

Johnstone, Lydia O., Hd.Libn.
WILLIAMS INTERNATIONAL - LIBRARY □
Walled Lake, MI

Johnting, Wendell E., Tech.Serv.Libn.
INDIANA UNIVERSITY, INDIANAPOLIS -
SCHOOL OF LAW LIBRARY □ Indianapolis, IN

Joiner, E. Earl, Cur.
STETSON UNIVERSITY - FLORIDA BAPTIST
HISTORICAL COLLECTION □ De Land, FL

Joines, Vann, Pres.
SOUTHEAST INSTITUTE - LIBRARY □ Chapel
Hill, NC

Jolin, Louise, Libn.
HOPITAL STE-JUSTINE - CENTRE
D'INFORMATION SUR LA SANTE DE L'ENFANT □
Montreal, PQ

Jolley, Kea, Depository
MONTANA COLLEGE OF MINERAL SCIENCE AND
TECHNOLOGY - LIBRARY □ Butte, MT

Jollie, Edward S., Jr., Supv., Tech.Serv.
CALIFORNIA INSTITUTE OF TECHNOLOGY -
JET PROPULSION LABORATORY - LIBRARY □
Pasadena, CA

Jolliff, Edna Lee, Assoc.Libn.
HARPER-GRACE HOSPITALS - HARPER
HOSPITAL DIVISION - DEPARTMENT OF
LIBRARIES □ Detroit, MI

Jolly, Wanda, Libn.
ATLANTA FULTON PUBLIC LIBRARY - IVAN
ALLEN, JR. DEPARTMENT OF SCIENCE,
INDUSTRY AND GOVERNMENT □ Atlanta, GA

Jonas, Mrs. Bill, Dir. of Lib.Serv.
CRESCENT HEIGHTS BAPTIST CHURCH -
LIBRARY† □ Abilene, TX

Jonas, Eva, Libn.
HARVARD UNIVERSITY - MUSEUM OF
COMPARATIVE ZOOLOGY - LIBRARY □
Cambridge, MA

Jonasson, Catherine, Hd.
ART GALLERY OF ONTARIO - EDWARD P.
TAYLOR AUDIO-VISUAL CENTRE □ Toronto, ON

Jones, Albert, Asst.Libn.
BECHTEL PETROLEUM INC. - LIBRARY □ San
Francisco, CA

Jones, Alfred H., Libn.
UNIVERSITY OF MISSOURI - ENGINEERING
LIBRARY □ Columbia, MO

Jones, Alfred H., Libn.
UNIVERSITY OF MISSOURI - MATH SCIENCES
LIBRARY □ Columbia, MO

Jones, Dr. Allen W., Archv.
AUBURN UNIVERSITY - ARCHIVES □ Auburn, AL

Jones, Andrea, Libn.
CARNEGIE LIBRARY OF PITTSBURGH -
CENTRAL CHILDREN'S ROOM HISTORICAL
COLLECTION □ Pittsburgh, PA

Jones, Ann, Law Libn.
SOUTHERN UNIVERSITY - LAW SCHOOL
LIBRARY □ Baton Rouge, LA

Jones, Anne, Libn.
AMERICAN MANAGEMENT ASSOCIATIONS -
LIBRARY □ New York, NY

Jones, Dr. Arthur E., Jr., Dir.
DREW UNIVERSITY - LIBRARY □ Madison, NJ

Jones, Barbara A., Libn.
BETHANY UNITED METHODIST CHURCH -
LIBRARY □ Wauwatosa, WI

Jones, Beverly, Chf.Plan.Off.
OKLAHOMA STATE DEPARTMENT OF
LIBRARIES □ Oklahoma City, OK

Jones, C.H., Lib.Supv.
BOEING MILITARY AIRPLANE COMPANY -
LIBRARY □ Wichita, KS

Jones, Mr. Carol D., Sci.Libn.
MICHIGAN STATE UNIVERSITY - SCIENCE
LIBRARY □ East Lansing, MI

Jones, Carol Y., Libn.
NORTHWESTERN COLLEGE OF CHIROPRACTIC
- LIBRARY □ Bloomington, MN

Jones, Carolyn G., Dir., Lib.Serv.
U.S. NAVY - NAVAL AMPHIBIOUS SCHOOL -
JOHN SIDNEY MC CAIN AMPHIBIOUS
WARFARE LIBRARY □ Norfolk, VA

Jones, Charles E., Res.Archv.
UNIVERSITY OF CHICAGO - ORIENTAL
INSTITUTE - DIRECTOR'S LIBRARY □ Chicago,
IL

Jones, Charlotte, Mng.Ed./Libn.
UNITED STATES TRADEMARK ASSOCIATION -
LAW LIBRARY □ New York, NY

Jones, Cheryl, Pub.Serv.Libn.
UNIVERSITY OF KENTUCKY - LAW LIBRARY □
Lexington, KY

Jones, Clarita, Asst.Libn.
FORBES, INC. - LIBRARY† □ New York, NY

Jones, Clifton H., Dir.
SOUTHERN METHODIST UNIVERSITY -
DEGOLYER LIBRARY - FIKES HALL OF SPECIAL
COLLECTIONS □ Dallas, TX

Jones, Clydia, Pict.Libn.
PLAYBOY ENTERPRISES, INC. - PHOTO
LIBRARY† □ Chicago, IL

Jones, Daniel, ILL
UNIVERSITY OF TEXAS HEALTH SCIENCE
CENTER, SAN ANTONIO - LIBRARY □ San
Antonio, TX

Jones, Darlene, Dir.
WASCANA HOSPITAL - HEALTH SCIENCES
LIBRARY □ Regina, SK

Jones, David, Chm., Lib.Comm.
MIGRAINE FOUNDATION - LIBRARY† □
Toronto, ON

Jones, David, Coll.Coord.
UNIVERSITY OF ALBERTA - SCIENCE AND
TECHNOLOGY LIBRARY □ Edmonton, AB

Jones, DeAnna, Acq.Sect.Supv.
JOHNS HOPKINS UNIVERSITY - APPLIED
PHYSICS LABORATORY - R.E. GIBSON LIBRARY
AND INFORMATION CENTER □ Laurel, MD

Jones, Deborah, Libn./Mgr.
MARYLAND STATE ENERGY OFFICE - LIBRARY
□ Baltimore, MD

Jones, Debra, Reader Serv.
DICKINSON SCHOOL OF LAW - SHEELY-LEE
LAW LIBRARY □ Carlisle, PA

Jones, Delores, Libn.
UNIVERSITY OF SOUTHERN MISSISSIPPI - MC
CAIN LIBRARY □ Hattiesburg, MS

Jones, Donald, Dept.Hd.
COMMUNITY COLLEGE OF PHILADELPHIA -
EDUCATION RESOURCES CENTER† □
Philadelphia, PA

Jones, Donald Bemis, Libn.
COLLEGE OF ST. CATHERINE - PERFORMING
ARTS LIBRARY □ St. Paul, MN

Jones, Dora Ann, Spec.Coll.Libn.
BLACK HILLS STATE COLLEGE - E.Y. BERRY
LIBRARY-LEARNING CENTER - SPECIAL
COLLECTIONS □ Spearfish, SD

Jones, Dorothy K., Chf., Lib.Serv.
U.S. VETERANS ADMINISTRATION (GA-
Augusta) - HOSPITAL LIBRARY □ Augusta, GA

Jones, Douglas E., Sci.Engr.Ref.Libn.
UNIVERSITY OF ARIZONA - SCIENCE-
ENGINEERING LIBRARY □ Tucson, AZ

Jones, Eleanor, Hd., Proc. Unit
UNIVERSITY OF WESTERN ONTARIO - LAW
LIBRARY □ London, ON

Jones, Ellen, Supv., Info.Serv.
AMAX, INC. - CLIMAX MOLYBDENUM COMPANY
- TECHNICAL INFORMATION DEPARTMENT† □
Greenwich, CT

Jones, Esther, Pub.Serv.Libn.
UNIVERSITY OF FLORIDA - J. HILLIS MILLER
HEALTH CENTER LIBRARY □ Gainesville, FL

Jones, Mrs. Everette M., Asst.Libn.
TRINITY LUTHERAN CHURCH - LIBRARY □
Madison, WI

Jones, Florence, Order Libn.
UNIVERSITY OF KENTUCKY - MEDICAL
CENTER LIBRARY □ Lexington, KY

Jones, Mrs. G.B., Libn.
HILLSBOROUGH COUNTY HISTORICAL
COMMISSION - LIBRARY □ Tampa, FL

Jones, H.G., Cur.
UNIVERSITY OF NORTH CAROLINA, CHAPEL
HILL - NORTH CAROLINA COLLECTION □ Chapel
Hill, NC

Jones, J. Elias, Bibliog./Archv.
DRAKE UNIVERSITY - COWLES LIBRARY -
SPECIAL COLLECTIONS □ Des Moines, IA

Jones, Janie S., Libn.
U.S. GEOLOGICAL SURVEY - WATER
RESOURCES DIVISION - READING ROOM □
Albuquerque, NM

Jones, Jennifer, Libn.
GENERAL AMERICAN INVESTORS CO., INC. -
LIBRARY □ New York, NY

Jones, Jo, Libn.
ODESSA AMERICAN - EDITORIAL LIBRARY □
Odessa, TX

Jones, John B., Ser.Libn.
BARUCH (Bernard M.) COLLEGE OF THE CITY
UNIVERSITY OF NEW YORK - LIBRARY† □ New
York, NY

Jones, Joseph, Libn.
UNIVERSITY OF BRITISH COLUMBIA -
HUMANITIES AND SOCIAL SCIENCES DIVISION
□ Vancouver, BC

Jones, Joy
WILSON FOODS, INC. - RESEARCH LIBRARY† □
Oklahoma City, OK

Jones, June D., Music Libn.
BRANDON UNIVERSITY - MUSIC LIBRARY □
Brandon, MB

Jones, Kathy, Personnel Ck.
SECURITY BENEFIT LIFE INSURANCE
COMPANY - LIBRARY □ Topeka, KS

Jones, Kevin, AV Libn.
U.S. ARMY - MILITARY ACADEMY - LIBRARY □
West Point, NY

Jones, Larry, Hist.
IDAHO STATE HISTORICAL SOCIETY -
LIBRARY AND ARCHIVES □ Boise, ID

Jones, LaVerne K., Libn.
OKLAHOMA STATE UNIVERSITY - VETERINARY
MEDICINE LIBRARY □ Stillwater, OK

Jones, Leigh R., Historic Site Mgr.
SENATE HOUSE STATE HISTORIC SITE -
LIBRARY & ARCHIVES □ Kingston, NY

Jones, Leslie, Mgr.
CANADA - MORTGAGE AND HOUSING
CORPORATION - CANADIAN HOUSING
INFORMATION CENTRE □ Ottawa, ON

Jones, Lesya, Libn.
METROPOLITAN TORONTO LIBRARY - GENERAL
REFERENCE DEPARTMENT □ Toronto, ON

Jones, Linda, Libn.
OPEN BIBLE COLLEGE - CARRIE HARDY
MEMORIAL LIBRARY □ Des Moines, IA

Jones, Linda, Acq.Libn.
SAMFORD UNIVERSITY - CUMBERLAND
SCHOOL OF LAW - CORDELL HULL LAW
LIBRARY □ Birmingham, AL

Jones, Lois W., Dir. of Lib.
BERKSHIRE CHRISTIAN COLLEGE - DR. LINDEN
J. CARTER LIBRARY □ Lenox, MA

Jones, Marianna C., Libn.
SAN ANTONIO CONSERVATION SOCIETY -
FOUNDATION LIBRARY □ San Antonio, TX

Jones, Mark, Archv.
CONNECTICUT STATE LIBRARY □ Hartford, CT

Jones, Sr. Martin Joseph, Hd.Archv./Spec.Coll.
SUNY - COLLEGE AT BUFFALO - EDWARD H.
BUTLER LIBRARY □ Buffalo, NY

Jones, Mary-Jo, Libn.
AT & T TECHNOLOGIES, INC. - HEADQUARTERS
LIBRARY† □ New York, NY

Jones, Mary Virginia Currie, Mgr., Rec.Mgt.Sect.
SOUTHERN BAPTIST CONVENTION - FOREIGN
MISSION BOARD - ARCHIVES CENTER □
Richmond, VA

Jones, Mary Virginia Currie, Mgr.
SOUTHERN BAPTIST CONVENTION - FOREIGN
MISSION BOARD - JENKINS RESEARCH
CENTER □ Richmond, VA

Jones, Maureen, Bk./ILL Libn.
SCHLUMBERGER-DOLL - RESEARCH LIBRARY □
Ridgefield, CT

Jones, Michelle, Asst.Mgr./AV
AMERICAN INSTITUTE OF ARCHITECTS -
LIBRARY □ Washington, DC

Jones, Millie, Tech.Libn.
LOS ANGELES COUNTY - DEPARTMENT OF
DATA PROCESSING - TECHNICAL LIBRARY □
Downey, CA

Jones, Miriam C., Hd., Pub.Serv.Div.
ALABAMA STATE DEPARTMENT OF ARCHIVES
AND HISTORY - REFERENCE ROOM □
Montgomery, AL

Jones, Miss Orlo, Prov.Geneal.
PRINCE EDWARD ISLAND MUSEUM AND
HERITAGE FOUNDATION - GENEALOGICAL
COLLECTION □ Charlottetown, PE

Jones, Patricia B., Corp.Libn.
LIBBEY-OWENS-FORD COMPANY - CORPORATE
LIBRARY† □ Toledo, OH

Jones, Paul, Volunteer Coord.
ALABAMA REGIONAL LIBRARY FOR THE BLIND
AND PHYSICALLY HANDICAPPED □
Montgomery, AL

Jones, Rebecca, Libn.
ROYAL BANK OF CANADA - INFORMATION
RESOURCES □ Toronto, ON

Jones, Richard E., Music Libn.
UNIVERSITY OF WISCONSIN, MILWAUKEE -
MUSIC COLLECTION □ Milwaukee, WI

Jones, Robert B., Hd., Microfilm Lab.
OHIO HISTORICAL SOCIETY - ARCHIVES-
LIBRARY □ Columbus, OH

Jones, Robert E., Pres.
VESTIGIA - LIBRARY □ Stanhope, NJ

Jones, Roger C., Hd., Tech.Serv.Br.
NORTH CAROLINA STATE DEPT. OF CULTURAL
RESOURCES - DIV. OF ARCHIVES AND HISTORY
- ARCHIVES & RECORDS SECTION □ Raleigh, NC

Jones, Royden R., Med.Libn.
U.S. AIR FORCE HOSPITAL - WILFORD HALL
U.S.A.F. MEDICAL CENTER - MEDICAL LIBRARY
(SGEL) □ San Antonio, TX

Jones, Ruth A., Chf.Libn.
U.S. VETERANS ADMINISTRATION (WA-
Spokane) - MEDICAL CENTER LIBRARY □
Spokane, WA

Jones, Sarah C., Dir., Lib.Serv.
MORGAN STANLEY & COMPANY, INC. -
LIBRARY SERVICES □ New York, NY

Jones, Dr. Shirley T., LRC Dean
WAYNE COMMUNITY COLLEGE - LEARNING
RESOURCE CENTER □ Goldsboro, NC

Jones, Stephanie, Info.Spec.
AT & T COMMUNICATIONS - INFORMATION
RESEARCH CENTER □ Piscataway, NJ

Jones, Suad, Med.Libn.
U.S. NAVY - NAVAL HOSPITAL (VA-Portsmouth)
- MEDICAL LIBRARY □ Portsmouth, VA

Jones, Terrance, Cat.
UNIVERSITY OF WISCONSIN, MADISON -
CENTER FOR HEALTH SCIENCES LIBRARIES† □
Madison, WI

Jones, Varena, Docs.
HUGHES AIRCRAFT COMPANY - GROUND
SYSTEMS GROUP - TECHNICAL LIBRARY □
Fullerton, CA

Jones, Venola, Cat.
AMISTAD RESEARCH CENTER - LIBRARY/
ARCHIVES □ New Orleans, LA

Jones, Verdelle B., Asst.Lib., Tech.Proc.
WARNER-LAMBERT COMPANY - CORPORATE
LIBRARY □ Morris Plains, NJ

Jones, Virgil L., Ref.Libn.
UNIVERSITY OF OKLAHOMA - HEALTH
SCIENCES CENTER LIBRARY □ Oklahoma City,
OK

Jones, Virginia Purefoy, Asst.Libn.
NORTH CAROLINA CENTRAL UNIVERSITY -
SCHOOL OF LIBRARY SCIENCE - LIBRARY □
Durham, NC

Jones, W. Marshall, Dir.
BILLINGS PUBLIC SCHOOLS - INSTRUCTIONAL
MATERIALS CENTER □ Billings, MT

Jones, Walter, Libn.
UNIVERSITY OF UTAH - SPECIAL COLLECTIONS
DEPARTMENT □ Salt Lake City, UT

Jones, William A., Spec.Coll.Libn.
CALIFORNIA STATE UNIVERSITY, CHICO -
MERIAM LIBRARY - SPECIAL COLLECTIONS □
Chico, CA

Jones, Prof. William D,, Libn.
BAPTIST BIBLE INSTITUTE - IDA J. MC MILLAN
LIBRARY □ Graceville, FL

Jonsen, Larry, Hd., BDS
UNIVERSITY OF WYOMING - SCIENCE AND
TECHNOLOGY LIBRARY □ Laramie, WY

Jonson, Joanne, Dir.
MINNESOTA STATE SERVICES FOR THE BLIND
AND VISUALLY HANDICAPPED -
COMMUNICATION CENTER □ St. Paul, MN

Jonynas, Alexandre, Asst.Dir.
UNIVERSITE DE MONTREAL - SCIENCES
HUMAINES ET SOCIALES-BIBLIOTHEQUE □
Montreal, PQ

Joorfetz, Clara, Libn.
ST. DOMINIC-JACKSON MEMORIAL HOSPITAL -
LUTHER MANSHIP MEDICAL LIBRARY† □
Jackson, MS

Joost, Laura R., Chm., Lib.Comm.
CUMMER GALLERY OF ART - LIBRARY □
Jacksonville, FL

Joplin, James, Asst.Dir., Prod.Serv.
UNIVERSITY OF HOUSTON - AUDIOVISUAL
SERVICES □ Houston, TX

Joplin, Peggy J., Supv.
DU PONT DE NEMOURS (E.I.) & COMPANY, INC.
- PHOTO PRODUCTS DEPARTMENT -
INFORMATION CENTER □ Parlin, NJ

Jordahl, Kristine, Off.Mgr.
SWEDENBORG FOUNDATION - LIBRARY □ New
York, NY

Jordahl, Leigh D., Hd.Libn.
LUTHER COLLEGE - PREUS LIBRARY □ Decorah,
IA

Jordahl, Ron, Libn.
PRAIRIE BIBLE INSTITUTE - LIBRARY □ Three
Hills, AB

Jordan, Anne, Rare Bks.Libn.
UNIVERSITY OF TEXAS, AUSTIN - BENSON
LATIN AMERICAN COLLECTION □ Austin, TX

Jordan, B., Lib.Techn.
SYNCRUDE CANADA, LTD. - RESEARCH AND
DEVELOPMENT LIBRARY □ Edmonton, AB

Jordan, Christiana E., Asst.Med.Libn.
WAKE COUNTY MEDICAL CENTER - MEDICAL
LIBRARY □ Raleigh, NC

Jordan, Flo, Lib.Assoc.
MARION LABORATORIES, INC. - R & D LIBRARY
□ Kansas City, MO

Jordan, Florence E., Proj.Off./Tech.Info.Spec.
NATL.INST. OF ENVIRONMENTAL HEALTH SCI.
- NATL. TOXICOLOGY PROGRAM -
ENVIRONMENTAL TERATOLOGY INFO.CTR. □
Research Triangle Park, NC

Jordan, Isabel, Circ.Mgr.
CATHOLIC THEOLOGICAL UNION AT CHICAGO
- LIBRARY □ Chicago, IL

Jordan, Joyce, Tech.Libn.
SANGAMO WESTON GROUP - EMR
PHOTOELECTRIC DIVISION - INFORMATION
CENTER □ Princeton, NJ

Jordan, Judy C., Lib.Techn.
U.S. BUREAU OF MINES - BRANCH OF
OPERATIONS & SUPPORT - LIBRARY □
Washington, DC

Jordan, June, Assoc.Dir.
ERIC CLEARINGHOUSE ON HANDICAPPED &
GIFTED CHILDREN - CEC INFORMATION
SERVICES □ Reston, VA

Jordan, K.C., Libn.
GETTY REFINING AND MARKETING COMPANY -
TECHNICAL LIBRARY □ Delaware City, DE

Jordan, Katherine C., Sci.Ed.
FARNHAM (Frank C.) COMPANY, INC. -
LIBRARY† □ Philadelphia, PA

Jordan, Kathy, Law Libn.
SANTA BARBARA COUNTY LAW LIBRARY □
Santa Barbara, CA

Jordan, Dr. Louis, Hd.
UNIVERSITY OF NOTRE DAME - MEDIEVAL
INSTITUTE LIBRARY □ Notre Dame, IN

Jordan, Marie, Slide Libn.
ART CENTER COLLEGE OF DESIGN - JAMES
LEMONT FOGG MEMORIAL LIBRARY □
Pasadena, CA

Jordan, Pamela C., Libn.
YALE UNIVERSITY - SCHOOL OF DRAMA
LIBRARY □ New Haven, CT

Jordan, Patti Lee, Supv.
TRW, INC. - OPERATIONS & SUPPORT GROUP -
ELECTRONICS & DEFENSE SECTOR - TECH.
INFORMATION CENTER □ Redondo Beach, CA

Jordan, Peter A., Regional Libn.
CANADA - CANADIAN WILDLIFE SERVICE -
WESTERN AND NORTHERN REGION LIBRARY □
Edmonton, AB

Jordan, Robert R., State Geologist
DELAWARE STATE GEOLOGICAL SURVEY -
LIBRARY □ Newark, DE

Jordan, Sharon, Libn.
SAN DIEGO PUBLIC LIBRARY - SOCIAL
SCIENCES SECTION □ San Diego, CA

Jordan, Stephen, Lib.Dir.
ASSOCIATION FOR RESEARCH AND
ENLIGHTENMENT - EDGAR CAYCE
FOUNDATION - LIBRARY □ Virginia Beach, VA

Jordan, Vernon, Asst.Div.Chf.
BROOKLYN PUBLIC LIBRARY - LANGUAGE AND
LITERATURE DIVISION □ Brooklyn, NY

Jordanowski, Stanislaw, Pres.
PILSUDSKI (Jozef) INSTITUTE OF AMERICA
FOR RESEARCH IN THE MODERN HISTORY OF
POLAND - LIBRARY □ New York, NY

Jorgens, Dorothy, Dir.
LAKEWOOD HOSPITAL - MEDICAL LIBRARY □
Lakewood, OH

Jorgensen, Julie A., Dir.
UNIVERSITY OF WISCONSIN, MILWAUKEE -
FEMINIST CENTER - LIBRARY □ Milwaukee, WI

Jorgensen, Loell R., Musm.Dir.
DODGE COUNTY HISTORICAL SOCIETY - LOUIS
E. MAY MUSEUM □ Fremont, NE

Jorgenson, Delores, Cat./ILL Libn.
UNIVERSITY OF SOUTH DAKOTA - MC KUSICK
LAW LIBRARY □ Vermillion, SD

Jose, Jean, Asst.Dir.
INDIANA STATE LIBRARY □ Indianapolis, IN

Jose, Phyllis, Dir.
OAKLAND COUNTY REFERENCE LIBRARY □
Pontiac, MI

Joseph, Claire, Dir.
SOUTH NASSAU COMMUNITIES HOSPITAL -
JULES REDISH MEMORIAL MEDICAL LIBRARY □
Oceanside, NY

Joseph, Hildegard M., Assoc.Libn.
HENRY FORD HOSPITAL - FRANK J. SLADEN
LIBRARY □ Detroit, MI

Joseph, Marjorie, Libn.
UNIVERSITY OF TENNESSEE - SPACE
INSTITUTE LIBRARY □ Tullahoma, TN

Joseph, Nancy G., Asst.Libn.
NEW YORK LAW INSTITUTE - LIBRARY □ New
York, NY

Joseph, Thomas, Libn.
EASTERN CHRISTIAN COLLEGE - LIBRARY □ Bel
Air, MD

Josephs, Elmer, Libn.
NATIONAL PUBLICATIONS LIBRARY □
Minneapolis, MN

Josiek, Julianne, Hd.Libn.
U.S. NATL. MARINE FISHERIES SERVICE -
SOUTHEAST FISHERIES CENTER - MIAMI LAB.
LIBRARY □ Miami, FL

Joslyn, David D., Libn.
VERMONT STATE DEPARTMENT OF
EDUCATION - VERMONT EDUCATIONAL
RESOURCE CENTER (VERC) □ Montpelier, VT

Joss, Charles, Supv.
BOB JONES UNIVERSITY - SCHOOL OF
EDUCATION - MEDIA CENTER □ Greenville, SC

Joullian, R., Dir.
LAMBDA, INC. - BARNES LIBRARY □
Birmingham, AL

Journot, Jane, Genealogy Cat.
KANSAS STATE HISTORICAL SOCIETY -
LIBRARY □ Topeka, KS

Joy, Elizabeth, Hd.Med.Libn.
CLEVELAND CLINIC EDUCATION FOUNDATION
- MEDICAL LIBRARY/AUDIOVISUAL CENTER† □
Cleveland, OH

Joyce, Margaret, Chairwoman
SHELTER ISLAND HISTORICAL SOCIETY -
ARCHIVES □ Shelter Island, NY

Joyes, Dennis, The Americas
METROPOLITAN TORONTO LIBRARY - HISTORY
DEPARTMENT □ Toronto, ON

Joyner, Lorna K., Adm.
REYNOLDS METALS COMPANY - PACKAGING
DIVISION - TECHNOLOGY LIBRARY† □
Richmond, VA

Joyner, Marjorie, Arch.Libn.
BALL STATE UNIVERSITY - COLLEGE OF
ARCHITECTURE & PLANNING - LIBRARY □
Muncie, IN

Juchimek, Mr. V., Hd.Libn.
ST. JOSEPH'S HOSPITAL HEALTH CENTER -
MEDICAL AND SCHOOL OF NURSING LIBRARIES
□ Syracuse, NY

Judah, Marjorie, Libn.
MC GILL UNIVERSITY - HOWARD ROSS
LIBRARY OF MANAGEMENT □ Montreal, PQ

Judd, Donna, Libn./Dir.
LAKEVIEW MEDICAL CENTER - LEARNING
RESOURCE CENTER □ Danville, IL

Judd, Dorothy, Supv.
BECHTEL - AUDIO-VISUAL LIBRARY □ San
Francisco, CA

Judd, Inge M., Div.Hd.
QUEENS BOROUGH PUBLIC LIBRARY -
LANGUAGE & LITERATURE DIVISION □
Jamaica, NY

Judd, J. Vanderveer, Hd., Coll.Mgmt.
NEW YORK STATE LIBRARY □ Albany, NY

Judd, William J., Dir., Univ.Lib.Serv.
VIRGINIA COMMONWEALTH UNIVERSITY -
MEDICAL COLLEGE OF VIRGINIA - TOMPKINS-
MC CAW LIBRARY □ Richmond, VA

Judge, Harriet E., Indexer/Sys.Libn.
ALBERTA RESEARCH COUNCIL - SOLAR & WIND
ENERGY RESEARCH PROGRAM (SWERP)
INFORMATION CENTRE □ Edmonton, AB

Judge, Dr. Joseph M., Mgr.
ARMSTRONG WORLD INDUSTRIES, INC. -
TECHNICAL CENTER - TECHNICAL
INFORMATION SERVICES □ Lancaster, PA

Judge, Sara, Doc.Cat.
KANSAS STATE HISTORICAL SOCIETY -
LIBRARY □ Topeka, KS

Judkins, Dolores, Dental Libn.
OREGON HEALTH SCIENCES UNIVERSITY -
DENTAL BRANCH LIBRARY □ Portland, OR
Judkins, Timothy C., Asst.Dir.
ORAL ROBERTS UNIVERSITY - HEALTH
SCIENCES LIBRARY □ Tulsa, OK
Judman, Mark, Info.Sci.
COLGATE PALMOLIVE COMPANY - TECHNICAL
INFORMATION CENTER □ Piscataway, NJ
Judson, Janet, Med.Libn.
RANCHO LOS AMIGOS HOSPITAL - MEDICAL
LIBRARY □ Downey, CA
Juengling, Pamela, Mus.Libn.
UNIVERSITY OF MASSACHUSETTS, AMHERST -
MUSIC LIBRARY □ Amherst, MA
Juggins, Warren, Asst.Libn.
BAR ASSOCIATION OF THE DISTRICT OF
COLUMBIA - LIBRARY† □ Washington, DC
Juknis, Ann, Libn.
ALTOBELLO (Henry D.) CHILDREN AND YOUTH
CENTER - PROFESSIONAL LIBRARY □ Meriden,
CT
Julian, Julie L., Libn./Res.Asst.
UPPER ROOM DEVOTIONAL LIBRARY, MUSEUM
AND ARCHIVES □ Nashville, TN
Julias, Sandi, Ref.Libn.
UNIVERSITY OF COLORADO HEALTH SCIENCES
CENTER - DENISON MEMORIAL LIBRARY† □
Denver, CO
Julien, Heidi, Sec.
UNIVERSITY OF ALBERTA - CENTRE FOR THE
STUDY OF MENTAL RETARDATION - LIBRARY □
Edmonton, AB
Julien, Patricia A., Libn.
UNITED STATES GYPSUM COMPANY -
CORPORATE LIBRARY □ Chicago, IL
Julkes, Willie M., Libn.
LAKE COUNTY SUPERIOR COURT LIBRARY† □
Gary, IN
Jumonville, Florence M., Hd.Libn.
HISTORIC NEW ORLEANS COLLECTION -
LIBRARY □ New Orleans, LA
Junaid, Iqbal, Hd., Cat.Dept.
SOUTH DAKOTA STATE UNIVERSITY - HILTON
M. BRIGGS LIBRARY □ Brookings, SD
June, Mary, Asst.Libn.
MICHAEL, BEST & FRIEDRICH - LAW LIBRARY □
Milwaukee, WI
Juneau, Gerard, Libn.
OBLATE FATHERS - BIBLIOTHEQUE
DESCHATELETS □ Ottawa, ON
Juneau, Jean, Ref.Libn.
UNIVERSITE DU QUEBEC A MONTREAL -
BIBLIOTHEQUE DES SCIENCES □ Montreal, PQ
Jung, Ursula, ILL
AYERST LABORATORIES - INFORMATION
CENTER □ New York, NY
Jung, Zing, Dir.
AMERICAN PSYCHIATRIC ASSOCIATION -
LIBRARY AND ARCHIVES □ Washington, DC
Jungwirth, Theresa M., Ck.
ST. PAUL CITY COUNCIL - RESEARCH LIBRARY
□ St. Paul, MN
Juni, Kathleen, Cur.
BROWN COUNTY HISTORICAL SOCIETY -
MUSEUM LIBRARY □ New Ulm, MN
Junier, Artemisia J., Chf., Lib.Serv.
U.S. VETERANS ADMINISTRATION (AL-
Tuskegee) - MEDICAL CENTER LIBRARY □
Tuskegee, AL
Jurkins, Jacquelyn J., Law Libn.
MULTNOMAH LAW LIBRARY □ Portland, OR
Jurries, Elaine, ILL Libn.
UNIVERSITY OF SOUTHERN COLORADO -
LIBRARY - SPECIAL COLLECTIONS □ Pueblo, CO
Jursik, Kathy
3M - PATENT AND TECHNICAL
COMMUNICATIONS SERVICES □ St. Paul, MN
Juska, Philip, Asst.Dir.
PENNSYLVANIA RESOURCES AND
INFORMATION CENTER FOR SPECIAL
EDUCATION □ King Of Prussia, PA

Justice, Joyce, Archv.
U.S. NATL. ARCHIVES & RECORDS SERVICE -
FEDERAL ARCHIVES AND RECORDS CENTER,
REGION 10 □ Seattle, WA
Justice, Sylvia, Asst.Libn.
STATE FARM MUTUAL AUTOMOBILE
INSURANCE COMPANY - LAW LIBRARY □
Bloomington, IL
Jutzi, Alan, Cur., Rare Books
HUNTINGTON (Henry E.) LIBRARY, ART
GALLERY AND BOTANICAL GARDENS □ San
Marino, CA
Jwaideh, Zuhair E., Chf.
LIBRARY OF CONGRESS - LAW LIBRARY - NEAR
EASTERN AND AFRICAN LAW DIVISION □
Washington, DC

K

Kaar, David R.
3M - PATENT AND TECHNICAL
COMMUNICATIONS SERVICES □ St. Paul, MN
Kaaret, Meeri, Hd., Tech.Serv.
CORNELL UNIVERSITY - ALBERT R. MANN
LIBRARY □ Ithaca, NY
Kabakeris, Dorothy, Assoc.Libn.
STERLING DRUG, INC. - WINTHROP
LABORATORIES - MEDICAL LIBRARY □ New
York, NY
Kabelac, Karl S., Mss.Libn.
UNIVERSITY OF ROCHESTER - DEPARTMENT
OF RARE BOOKS AND SPECIAL COLLECTIONS □
Rochester, NY
Kabler, Anne W., Assoc.Dir. of Libs.
MEDICAL UNIVERSITY OF SOUTH CAROLINA -
LIBRARY □ Charleston, SC
Kacer, Karen Faye, Res.Libn.
ST. LOUIS MERCANTILE LIBRARY
ASSOCIATION - LIBRARY □ St. Louis, MO
Kach, Claire, Asst.Div.Hd.
QUEENS BOROUGH PUBLIC LIBRARY - ART AND
MUSIC DIVISION □ Jamaica, NY
Kachel, Dr. Harold S., Cur.
PANHANDLE STATE UNIVERSITY - NO MAN'S
LAND HISTORICAL MUSEUM - LIBRARY □
Goodwell, OK
Kachkowski, Albert, Dir.
UKRAINIAN MUSEUM OF CANADA - LIBRARY □
Saskatoon, SK
Kaczmarek, Mary F., Libn.
JOHNSON CONTROLS, INC. - CORPORATE INFO.
CTR./LIBRARY M47 □ Milwaukee, WI
Kaczor, Lynn, Oper.Mgr.
STANFORD UNIVERSITY - SWAIN LIBRARY OF
CHEMISTRY AND CHEMICAL ENGINEERING □
Stanford, CA
Kaczor, Sue, Tech.Libn.
REFLECTONE, INC. - ENGINEERING LIBRARY □
Tampa, FL
Kadavy, Rhonda, Dir.
CONTACT LITERACY CENTER - AAAA CONTACT
CENTER □ Lincoln, NE
Kadish, Elisa F., Libn.
SMITH, CURRIE & HANCOCK - LAW LIBRARY □
Atlanta, GA
Kadoyama, Margaret, Asst.Cur.
ART MUSEUM OF SOUTH TEXAS - LIBRARY □
Corpus Christi, TX
Kafes, Fred, Dir.
OUR LADY OF LOURDES MEDICAL CENTER -
MEDICAL LIBRARY □ Camden, NJ
Kafka, Miriam, Act.Libn.
LOS ANGELES COUNTY/OLIVE VIEW MEDICAL
CENTER - HEALTH SCIENCES LIBRARY □ Van
Nuys, CA
Kaganoff, Nathan M., Libn.
AMERICAN JEWISH HISTORICAL SOCIETY -
LIBRARY □ Waltham, MA

Kagehiro, Phyllis, Jr.Lib.Spec.
EAST-WEST CENTER - EAPI/PI/RSI
RESEARCH MATERIALS COLLECTION □
Honolulu, HI
Kager, Jeff, Med.Libn.
U.S. VETERANS ADMINISTRATION (FL-Miami) -
MEDICAL CENTER LIBRARY □ Miami, FL
Kahan, D.J., Metallurgist
U.S. NATL. BUREAU OF STANDARDS - ALLOY
PHASE DIAGRAM DATA CENTER □ Washington,
DC
Kahin, Audrey
CORNELL UNIVERSITY - SOUTHEAST ASIA
PROGRAM - CORNELL MODERN INDONESIA
PROJECT □ Ithaca, NY
Kahl, Barbara J., Dept.Hd.
LIBRARY ASSOCIATION OF PORTLAND -
LITERATURE AND HISTORY DEPARTMENT □
Portland, OR
Kahl, Barbara J.
LIBRARY ASSOCIATION OF PORTLAND -
OREGON COLLECTION □ Portland, OR
Kahl, Julie, Libn.
MARIN GENERAL HOSPITAL - LIBRARY □ San
Rafael, CA
Kahles, John F., Dir.
METCUT RESEARCH ASSOCIATES, INC. -
MACHINABILITY DATA CENTER □ Cincinnati,
OH
Kahlich, Nancy, Archv.
SWEDISH PIONEER HISTORICAL SOCIETY -
SWEDISH-AMERICAN ARCHIVES OF GREATER
CHICAGO □ Chicago, IL
Kahn, Joy, Sr.Bibliog.
GEORGETOWN UNIVERSITY - KENNEDY
INSTITUTE OF ETHICS - CENTER FOR
BIOETHICS LIBRARY □ Washington, DC
Kahn, Leybl, Libn.
LEAGUE FOR YIDDISH - LIBRARY □ New York,
NY
Kahn, Nina, Law Libn.
U.S. VETERANS ADMINISTRATION (DC-
Washington) - GENERAL COUNSEL'S LAW
LIBRARY (026H) □ Washington, DC
Kahn-Ruben, Karen, ILL, Ref.Libn.
BENTLEY COLLEGE - SOLOMON R. BAKER
LIBRARY □ Waltham, MA
Kahwa, Henne, Hd., Rd.Serv.
CANADA - ENVIRONMENT CANADA - LIBRARY
SERVICES BRANCH □ Ottawa, ON
Kaige, Alice, Libn.
ILLINOIS STATE DEPARTMENT OF COMMERCE
& COMMUNITY AFFAIRS - DCCA LIBRARY □
Springfield, IL
Kaige, Alice, Libn.
ILLINOIS STATE DEPARTMENT OF COMMERCE
& COMMUNITY AFFAIRS - LIBRARY □
Springfield, IL
Kaighn, Anna Lee, Libn.
EG&G, INC. - TECHNICAL LIBRARY □ Las Vegas,
NV
Kaimowitz, Dr. Jeffrey H., Cur.
TRINITY COLLEGE - WATKINSON LIBRARY □
Hartford, CT
Kaiser, Barbara J., Coll.Dev.
STATE HISTORICAL SOCIETY OF WISCONSIN -
ARCHIVES DIVISION □ Madison, WI
Kaiser, Clara, Libn./Genealogist
AUDRAIN COUNTY HISTORICAL SOCIETY -
ROSS HOUSE LIBRARY/AMERICAN SADDLE
HORSE MUSEUM LIBRARY □ Mexico, MO
Kaiser, Dorothy, Tech.Serv./Archv.
KENRICK SEMINARY LIBRARY □ St. Louis, MO
Kaiser, Margaret, AV Serv.Libn.
GEORGETOWN UNIVERSITY - MEDICAL
CENTER - DAHLGREN MEMORIAL LIBRARY □
Washington, DC
Kaiser, Michael N., Exec.Dir.
LEHIGH-NORTHAMPTON COUNTIES JOINT
PLANNING COMMISSION - LIBRARY □ Lehigh
Valley, PA

Kaiser, Nancy E., Res.Libn.
SOUTHERN STATES ENERGY BOARD (SSEB) -
SOUTHERN ENERGY/ENVIRONMENTAL
INFORMATION CENTER (SEEIC) □ Atlanta, GA

Kakish, William J., Chf.Libn.
SARGENT & LUNDY ENGINEERS - COMPUTER
SOFTWARE LIBRARY □ Chicago, IL

Kaklamanos, Ann C., Libn.
FLORIDA STATE DEPT. OF LEGAL AFFAIRS -
ATTORNEY GENERAL'S LIBRARY □ Tallahassee,
FL

Kakoschke, Mona, Med.Libn.
YORK-FINCH GENERAL HOSPITAL - DR.
THOMAS J. MALCHO MEMORIAL LIBRARY □
Downsview, ON

Kalanyos, Imre, Rd.Rm.Supv.
UNIVERSITY OF NORTH CAROLINA, CHAPEL
HILL - RARE BOOK COLLECTION □ Chapel Hill,
NC

Kalb, Mary, Urban Doc.Prog.
GREENWOOD PRESS - LIBRARY □ Westport, CT

Kaleem, Ata Ullah, Info.Dir.
AHMADIYYA MOVEMENT IN ISLAM - MUSLIM
LIBRARY □ Washington, DC

Kalinin, Tatiana, Act.Libn.
TOLSTOY FOUNDATION INC. - ALEXANDRA
TOLSTOY MEMORIAL LIBRARY □ Valley Cottage,
NY

Kalkanis, Agatha Pfeiffer, Chf.
DETROIT PUBLIC LIBRARY - MUSIC AND
PERFORMING ARTS DEPARTMENT □ Detroit, MI

Kalkus, Stanley, Dir.
U.S. NAVY - DEPARTMENT LIBRARY □
Washington, DC

Kallaway, William D., Tech.Libn.
DORR-OLIVER INC. - CENTRAL TECHNOLOGY
LIBRARY† □ Stamford, CT

Kallmann, Dr. Helmut, Chf.
NATIONAL LIBRARY OF CANADA - MUSIC
DIVISION □ Ottawa, ON

Kalloch, Phillip C., Jr., Supv., Info.Serv.
UNION MUTUAL LIFE INSURANCE COMPANY -
CORPORATE INFORMATION CENTER □ Portland,
ME

Kallop, Sharon M., Libn.
BIGHAM, ENGLAR, JONES AND HOUSTON -
LIBRARY† □ New York, NY

Kalman, Georgia, Libn.
TEMPLE ISRAEL - LIBRARY □ Minneapolis, MN

Kalsch, Alvina, Assoc.Libn.Tech.Serv.
SUNY - MARITIME COLLEGE - STEPHEN B.
LUCE LIBRARY □ Bronx, NY

Kalvonjian, Araxie, Tech.Proc./Acq.Libn.
GATEWAY VOCATIONAL TECHNICAL & ADULT
EDUCATION DISTRICT - LEARNING
RESOURCES CENTER □ Kenosha, WI

Kalyoncu, Aydan, Sr.Libn.
UNIVERSITY OF ALABAMA - ENGINEERING
LIBRARY □ University, AL

Kamaka, A., Lib.Spec.
ALLERGAN PHARMACEUTICALS, INC. -
MEDICAL & SCIENCE INFORMATION □ Irvine,
CA

Kamenoff, Lovisa, Mgr., Lib.Serv.
BROCKTON HOSPITAL - LIBRARY □ Brockton,
MA

Kamichaitis, Penelope H., Libn.
MONTREAL ENGINEERING COMPANY, LTD. -
LIBRARY □ Montreal, PQ

Kaminsky, Laura
GREENWOOD PRESS - LIBRARY □ Westport, CT

Kamm, Keith A., Bibliog.
ATHENAEUM OF PHILADELPHIA □ Philadelphia,
PA

Kamman, Jeanette G., Dir.
ORPHAN VOYAGE - KAMMANDALE LIBRARY □
St. Paul, MN

Kammer, Jean, Libn.
D'ARCY, MAC MANUS, MASIUS - LIBRARY† □
St. Louis, MO

Kammerer, Kay, Health Sci.Libn.
ALTA BATES HOSPITAL - STUART MEMORIAL
LIBRARY □ Berkeley, CA

Kamosa, Cathy, Libn.
GENERAL REFRACTORIES COMPANY - U.S.
REFRACTORIES DIVISION - RESEARCH
CENTER LIBRARY □ Baltimore, MD

Kampel, Ellen, Info.Dir.
U.S. DEPT. OF LABOR - EMPLOYMENT &
TRAINING ADMINISTRATION - REGION X
RESOURCE CENTER □ Seattle, WA

Kamra, Mr. S.K., Chf.Libn.
CANADA - NATIONAL DEFENCE - FORT
FRONTENAC LIBRARY □ Kingston, ON

Kamrud, Sylvia, Libn.
AMERICAN HARDWARE MUTUAL INSURANCE
COMPANY - LIBRARY □ Minneapolis, MN

Kan, Halina, Libn.
NL INDUSTRIES, INC. - MARKETING &
TECHNICAL INFORMATION SERVICE† □
Hightstown, NJ

Kan, Halina S., Libn.
RCA CORPORATION - SOLID STATE DIVISION -
LIBRARY □ Somerville, NJ

Kanabrodzki, Christina C., Commun.Libn.
MOTOR VEHICLE MANUFACTURERS
ASSOCIATION (MVMA) - COMMUNICATIONS
LIBRARY □ Detroit, MI

Kanafani, Marwan, Info.Off.
LEAGUE OF ARAB STATES - ARAB
INFORMATION CENTER □ New York, NY

Kancel, Rita Hollecker, Law Libn.
WYANDOTTE COUNTY LAW LIBRARY □ Kansas
City, KS

Kandoian, Nancy A., Map Cat.
NEW YORK PUBLIC LIBRARY - MAP DIVISION □
New York, NY

Kane, Angelika, Libn.
PITTSBURGH POST-GAZETTE PUBLISHING
COMPANY - LIBRARY □ Pittsburgh, PA

Kane, Casey, Libn.
RAND CORPORATION - LIBRARY □ Washington,
DC

Kane, Edward M., Libn.
MADISON COUNTY LAW LIBRARY □ Wampsville,
NY

Kane, Ellen, Res.
BOSTON UNIVERSITY - GERONTOLOGY
RESOURCE CENTER □ Boston, MA

Kane, John F., Sr.Info.Sci.
ALUMINUM COMPANY OF AMERICA - ALCOA
TECHNICAL CENTER - INFORMATION
DEPARTMENT □ Alcoa Center, PA

Kane, Katherine, Hd., Pub.Serv. & Access
COLORADO HISTORICAL SOCIETY - STEPHEN
H. HART LIBRARY □ Denver, CO

Kane, Sr. Mary Edith, Curric.Libn.
MARYCREST COLLEGE - CONE LIBRARY □
Davenport, IA

Kane, Nancy J., Libn.
GENERAL ELECTRIC COMPANY - PLASTICS
BUSINESS GROUP - INFORMATION RESOURCE
CENTER □ Pittsfield, MA

Kane, William E., Chf., Lib.Serv.
U.S. VETERANS ADMINISTRATION (NY-Castle
Point) - MEDICAL CENTER LIBRARY □ Castle
Point, NY

Kaneko, Hideo, Cur.
YALE UNIVERSITY - EAST ASIAN COLLECTION
□ New Haven, CT

Kanekuni, Phyllis, Tech. Writer/Libn.
DALY (Leo A.) COMPANY - YEE DIVISION -
LIBRARY □ Honolulu, HI

Kanemura, Marilyn May, Libn.
HEALD COLLEGE TECHNICAL DIVISION -
TECHNICAL LIBRARY □ Santa Clara, CA

Kang, Nam-Hee, Supv., Tech.Info.Serv.
OCCIDENTAL RESEARCH CORPORATION -
TECHNICAL INFORMATION CENTER† □ Irvine,
CA

Kangas, James, Hd.
FLINT PUBLIC LIBRARY - ART, MUSIC & DRAMA
DEPARTMENT □ Flint, MI

Kangas, Jill, Musm.Dir.
LEWIS COUNTY HISTORICAL MUSEUM -
LIBRARY □ Chehalis, WA

Kannel, Selma, Med.Libn.
HARRISON MEMORIAL HOSPITAL - HEALTH
SCIENCES LIBRARY □ Bremerton, WA

Kanner, Dr. Elliott E., Rsrcs.Coord./Info.Libn.
NORTH SUBURBAN LIBRARY SYSTEM -
PROFESSIONAL INFORMATION CENTER □
Wheeling, IL

Kanocz, Otto, Chf.Libn.
FEDERATION EMPLOYMENT & GUIDANCE
SERVICE - RICHARD J. BERNHARD MEMORIAL
LIBRARY □ New York, NY

Kansfield, Norman J., Dir. of Lib.Serv.
COLGATE ROCHESTER/BEXLEY HALL/CROZER
THEOLOGICAL SEMINARIES - AMBROSE
SWASEY LIBRARY □ Rochester, NY

Kanter, Dorothy, Coll.Dev.
UNIVERSITY OF WISCONSIN, MADISON -
CENTER FOR HEALTH SCIENCES LIBRARIES† □
Madison, WI

Kantor, Judith, Hd.Libn.
UNIVERSITY OF CALIFORNIA, LOS ANGELES -
UNIVERSITY ELEMENTARY SCHOOL LIBRARY □
Los Angeles, CA

Kanu, Ahmed H., AV & Doc.Libn.
OHIO STATE SUPREME COURT LAW LIBRARY □
Columbus, OH

Kao, Angela H., Orientalia Libn.
U.S. ARMY - MILITARY ACADEMY - LIBRARY □
West Point, NY

Kao, Bernice C., Pres.
INFOTEK CONSULTANTS - LIBRARY □ Arlington
Heights, IL

Kao, Joyce, Ser.Cat.
MAYO FOUNDATION - MAYO CLINIC LIBRARY □
Rochester, MN

Kapadia, Sushila, Info.Sys.Libn.
UNIVERSITY OF MEDICINE AND DENTISTRY OF
NEW JERSEY AT NEWARK - GEORGE F. SMITH
LIBRARY □ Newark, NJ

Kapecky, Michele Ann, Chief Libn.
DETROIT FREE PRESS - LIBRARY □ Detroit, MI

Kaplan, Alice D., Assoc.Libn.
PLANNED PARENTHOOD FEDERATION OF
AMERICA, INC. - KATHARINE DEXTER MC
CORMICK LIBRARY □ New York, NY

Kaplan, Bess D., Materials Coord.
FOUNDATION FOR BLIND CHILDREN - LIBRARY
□ Scottsdale, AZ

Kaplan, Isabel, Libn.
UNIVERSITY OF ROCHESTER - ENGINEERING
LIBRARY □ Rochester, NY

Kaplan, Janine J., Hd.Libn.
DELOITTE HASKINS & SELLS - LIBRARY □ New
York, NY

Kaplan, Judith M., Hd.Libn.
AMERICAN FOUNDATION FOR THE BLIND -
M.C. MIGEL MEMORIAL LIBRARY □ New York,
NY

Kaplan, Karen, Info.Dir.
BLUEFIELD DAILY TELEGRAPH - LIBRARY □
Bluefield, WV

Kaplan, Leslie, Media Serv.
UNIVERSITY OF LOWELL, NORTH CAMPUS -
ALUMNI/LYDON LIBRARY† □ Lowell, MA

Kaplan, Leslie, Media Prod.Libn.
UNIVERSITY OF LOWELL, SOUTH CAMPUS -
DANIEL H. O'LEARY LIBRARY - SPECIAL
COLLECTIONS □ Lowell, MA

Kaplan, Renee, Asst.Div.Hd.
QUEENS BOROUGH PUBLIC LIBRARY - SOCIAL
SCIENCES DIVISION □ Jamaica, NY

Kaplan, Richard, Info.Serv.Libn.
SUNY AT BUFFALO - HEALTH SCIENCES
LIBRARY □ Buffalo, NY

Kaplan, Temma, Dir., Women's Ctr.
BARNARD COLLEGE WOMEN'S CENTER -
BIRDIE GOLDSMITH AST RESOURCE
COLLECTION □ New York, NY

Kapnick, Laura B., Dir.
CBS INC. - CBS NEWS REFERENCE LIBRARY □
New York, NY

Kappenberg, Alice W., Archv.-Kpr.
SUFFOLK COUNTY HISTORICAL SOCIETY -
LIBRARY □ Riverhead, NY

Kappesser, Russell E., Chf., Tech.Lib.
U.S. DEFENSE MAPPING AGENCY - AEROSPACE
CENTER - TECHNICAL LIBRARY □ St. Louis, MO

Kapur, Umesh, Asst.Dir., Tech.Serv.
UNIVERSITY OF HOUSTON - AUDIOVISUAL
SERVICES □ Houston, TX

Kapust, Karen, Libn.
HELENE FULD SCHOOL OF NURSING - LIBRARY†
□ Camden, NJ

Karan, Audette, Supv., Spec.Coll.
BELL & HOWELL COMPANY - MICRO PHOTO
DIVISION - MICROFORMS ARCHIVE† □
Wooster, OH

Karasick, Alice, Circuit-Rider Libn.
UNIVERSITY OF SOUTHERN CALIFORNIA -
HEALTH SCIENCES CAMPUS - NORRIS
MEDICAL LIBRARY □ Los Angeles, CA

Karbo, Karen, Regional Serv.
PORTLAND ART ASSOCIATION - NORTHWEST
FILM STUDY CENTER - CIRCULATING FILM
LIBRARY □ Portland, OR

Karch, Linda S., Libn.
MERCY HOSPITAL - MEDICAL LIBRARY □
Buffalo, NY

Karcheski, Walter J., Jr., Assoc.Cur.
HIGGINS ARMORY MUSEUM - MEMORIAL
LIBRARY □ Worcester, MA

Karchewski, Barbara, Libn.
SASKATCHEWAN CANCER FOUNDATION -
ALLAN BLAIR MEMORIAL CLINIC - LIBRARY □
Regina, SK

Karchmer, Norman T., Libn.
ANCORA PSYCHIATRIC HOSPITAL - HEALTH
SCIENCES LIBRARY □ Hammonton, NJ

Karcz, JoAnn, AV Coord.
ST. PETER'S MEDICAL CENTER - LIBRARY† □
New Brunswick, NJ

Kardell, May, Libn.
CHEVY CHASE BAPTIST CHURCH - SEBRING
MEMORIAL LIBRARY □ Washington, DC

Kare, Carol A., Cat.
VILLANOVA UNIVERSITY - LIBRARY SCIENCE
LIBRARY □ Villanova, PA

Karesh, Jane, Info.Spec.
INTERPUBLIC GROUP OF COMPANIES -
CENTER FOR ADVERTISING SERVICES □ New
York, NY

Karg, Anita L., Asst.Archv.
CARNEGIE-MELLON UNIVERSITY - HUNT
INSTITUTE FOR BOTANICAL DOCUMENTATION
□ Pittsburgh, PA

Kargacin, Kevin, Asst. Economist
UNIVERSITY OF NEW MEXICO - BUREAU OF
BUSINESS & ECONOMIC RESEARCH DATA BANK
□ Albuquerque, NM

Karhoff, Brenton, Pres.
KNOX COUNTY HISTORICAL SOCIETY -
LIBRARY □ Edina, MO

Karic, Seid, Cat.
INDIANA UNIVERSITY - NEAR EASTERN
COLLECTION □ Bloomington, IN

Karklins, Vija L., Assoc.Dir.
SMITHSONIAN INSTITUTION LIBRARIES □
Washington, DC

Karlen, Ann, Libn.
WASHINGTON COUNTY LAW LIBRARY† □
Hillsboro, OR

Karlin, Estelle, Libn.
HARVARD UNIVERSITY - OBSERVATORY
LIBRARY □ Cambridge, MA

Karlin, Martin, Chf.
U.S. DEPT. OF LABOR - BUREAU OF LABOR
STATISTICS - INFORMATION AND ADVISORY
SECTION □ New York, NY

Karn, Jane B., Med.Libn.
LEWISTOWN HOSPITAL - MEDICAL LIBRARY†
□ Lewistown, PA

Karnani, Achla B., Media Consultant
UNIVERSITY OF MICHIGAN - MEDICAL SCHOOL
- LEARNING RESOURCE CENTER □ Ann Arbor,
MI

Karnath, Lori T., Supv., Tech.Lib.
DOW CORNING CORPORATION -
INFORMATION CENTER - TECHNICAL LIBRARY
(022) □ Midland, MI

Karnig, Jack J., Forest Mgr.
HARVARD UNIVERSITY - HARVARD BLACK
ROCK FOREST LIBRARY □ Cornwall, NY

Karow, Betty, Libn.
MILWAUKEE ART MUSEUM - LIBRARY □
Milwaukee, WI

Karp, Margot, Lib.Sci.Libn.
PRATT INSTITUTE - LIBRARY □ Brooklyn, NY

Karpevych, Christine, Info.Mgr./Libn.
JOURNAL OF COMMERCE - EDITORIAL LIBRARY
□ New York, NY

Karpinski, Leszek M., Libn.
UNIVERSITY OF BRITISH COLUMBIA -
HUMANITIES AND SOCIAL SCIENCES DIVISION
□ Vancouver, BC

Karpisek, Marian, Hd.
SALT LAKE CITY SCHOOLS - DISTRICT
LEARNING CENTER □ Salt Lake City, UT

Karr, Diane, Tech.Libn.
INTEL CORPORATION - TECHNICAL
INFORMATION CENTER □ Phoenix, AZ

Karr, Diane, Info.Spec.
INTEL CORPORATION - TECHNICAL
INFORMATION CENTER □ Santa Clara, CA

Karr, Roger N., Libn.
U.S. DEPT. OF JUSTICE - ANTITRUST DIVISION
LIBRARY □ Washington, DC

Karr, Ronald, Pub.Serv.Libn.
NORTHWESTERN UNIVERSITY -
TRANSPORTATION LIBRARY □ Evanston, IL

Karras, Thomas, Libn.
SAN DIEGO PUBLIC LIBRARY - SCIENCE &
INDUSTRY SECTION □ San Diego, CA

Kars, Marge, Dir.
HOLLAND COMMUNITY HOSPITAL - HOSPITAL
AND MEDICAL STAFF LIBRARY □ Holland, MI

Karson, William V., Spec.Proj.
NEW YORK STATE CONFERENCE OF MAYORS
AND MUNICIPAL OFFICIALS - LIBRARY □
Albany, NY

Karukin, Mildred, Assoc.Libn.
MOUNT SINAI MEDICAL CENTER OF GREATER
MIAMI - MEDICAL LIBRARY □ Miami Beach, FL

Kasakaitis, Jurgis, Hd.Libn.
BALZEKAS MUSEUM OF LITHUANIAN CULTURE
- RESEARCH LIBRARY □ Chicago, IL

Kasalko, Sally, Ref.Libn.
UNIVERSITY OF ARKANSAS FOR MEDICAL
SCIENCES - MEDICAL SCIENCES LIBRARY □
Little Rock, AR

Kaschsins, Elizabeth, Hd.Ref.Libn.
LUTHER COLLEGE - PREUS LIBRARY □ Decorah,
IA

Kascus, Marie, Ser.Libn.
CENTRAL CONNECTICUT STATE UNIVERSITY -
ELIHU BURRITT LIBRARY □ New Britain, CT

Kase, Arlene, Libn.
BETH EL SYNAGOGUE - MAX SHAPIRO LIBRARY
□ St. Louis Park, MN

Kashyap, Ms. Meera, Asst. Law Libn.
HOWARD UNIVERSITY - SCHOOL OF LAW -
ALLEN MERCER DANIEL LAW LIBRARY □
Washington, DC

Kasinec, Edward, Div.Chf.
NEW YORK PUBLIC LIBRARY - SLAVONIC
DIVISION □ New York, NY

Kaskey, Sid, Libn.
SMATHERS & THOMPSON - LAW LIBRARY □
Miami, FL

Kasman, Dorothy, Chf.Libn.
COOPERS & LYBRAND - NATIONAL LIBRARY† □
New York, NY

Kasner, Betsie, Hd., Info.Serv.
UNIVERSITY OF NEW MEXICO - BUREAU OF
BUSINESS & ECONOMIC RESEARCH DATA BANK
□ Albuquerque, NM

Kasner, Sr. M. Dolores, O.P., Dir.
TEXAS CATHOLIC HISTORICAL SOCIETY -
CATHOLIC ARCHIVES OF TEXAS □ Austin, TX

Kasner, Merrialyce, Adm., Tech.Serv.
OREGON STATE LIBRARY □ Salem, OR

Kasow, Nadine, Ref.Libn.
THOMPSON (J. Walter) COMPANY -
INFORMATION CENTER □ New York, NY

Kasper, Barbara, Field Serv.Libn.
SOUTH CAROLINA STATE LIBRARY □ Columbia,
SC

Kasprowicz, Margo, Info.Spec.
LOUISIANA STATE HOUSE OF
REPRESENTATIVES LEGISLATIVE SERVICES -
RESEARCH LIBRARY □ Baton Rouge, LA

Kass, Adelaide, Sr.Lit. Searcher
SIGNAL UOP RESEARCH CENTER - TECHNICAL
INFORMATION CENTER □ Des Plaines, IL

Kass, Kenneth J., Pres.
CONTINENTAL CHEMISTE CORPORATION -
LIBRARY □ Chicago, IL

Kassam, Shamim, Libn.
TRANSALTA UTILITIES CORPORATION -
LIBRARY □ Calgary, AB

Kasten, Cleo, Libn.
CENTRAL BAPTIST CHURCH - MEDIA CENTER □
St. Paul, MN

Kasten, Lloyd, Prof.
UNIVERSITY OF WISCONSIN, MADISON -
SEMINARY OF MEDIEVAL SPANISH STUDIES -
LIBRARY □ Madison, WI

Kasten, Ulla, Musm.Ed.
YALE UNIVERSITY - BABYLONIAN COLLECTION
□ New Haven, CT

Kastner, James F., Chf.Libn.
U.S. VETERANS ADMINISTRATION (KY-
Louisville) - HOSPITAL LIBRARY □ Louisville, KY

Kastner, Margaret N., Hd. of Index
TIME, INC. - LIBRARY □ New York, NY

Katayama, Jane H., Lib.Mgr.
MASSACHUSETTS INSTITUTE OF TECHNOLOGY
- LINCOLN LABORATORY LIBRARY □ Lexington,
MA

Kates, Jacqueline R., Corp.Libn.
ALLIED CORPORATION - ALLIED ANALYTICAL
SYSTEMS - LIBRARY □ Andover, MA

Kates, Jacqueline R., Mgr., Lib.Serv.
ALLIED CORPORATION - INSTRUMENTATION
LABORATORY - LIBRARY □ Lexington, MA

Katherman, Agnete V., Libn.
IBM CORPORATION - NATIONAL ACCOUNTS
DIVISION - LIBRARY □ Houston, TX

Katre, Helen, Acq.Libn.
HELLENIC COLLEGE AND HOLY CROSS GREEK
ORTHODOX SCHOOL OF THEOLOGY -
COTSIDAS-TONNA LIBRARY □ Brookline, MA

Kats, Natasha, Exec.Sec.
BAY AREA COUNCIL ON SOVIET JEWRY -
ARCHIVES □ San Francisco, CA

Katsh, Sara, Libn.
ASSOCIATION OF OPERATING ROOM NURSES -
LIBRARY □ Denver, CO

Katucki, June P., Hd.Libn.
EMERGENCY CARE RESEARCH INSTITUTE -
LIBRARY □ Plymouth Meeting, PA

Katz, Annelise, Libn.
HARVARD UNIVERSITY - PSYCHOLOGY
RESEARCH LIBRARY □ Cambridge, MA

Katz, Annelise, Libn.
HARVARD UNIVERSITY - SOCIAL RELATIONS/
SOCIOLOGY LIBRARY □ Cambridge, MA

Katz, Mrs. Barry
TEMPLE ISRAEL - PAUL PELTASON LIBRARY □
Creve Coeur, MO

Katz, Doris B., Mgr.
NATIONAL BROADCASTING COMPANY, INC. -
INFORMATION SERVICES - RESEARCH
DEPARTMENT □ New York, NY

Katz, Helen, Asst.Mgr.
CANADIAN IMPERIAL BANK OF COMMERCE -
INFORMATION CENTRE □ Toronto, ON
Katz, Jane, Libn.
JOHNS HOPKINS UNIVERSITY - JOHN WORK
GARRETT LIBRARY □ Baltimore, MD
Katz, Janet Rocklin, Indexing Libn.
R & D ASSOCIATES - TECHNICAL
INFORMATION SERVICES □ Marina Del Rey, CA
Katz, Lilian G., Ph.D., Dir.
ERIC CLEARINGHOUSE ON ELEMENTARY AND
EARLY CHILDHOOD EDUCATION □ Champaign,
IL
Katz, Marilyn, Libn.
CHILD WELFARE LEAGUE OF AMERICA, INC. -
INFORMATIONAL RESOURCE SERVICES -
DOROTHY L. BERNHARD LIBRARY □ New York,
NY
Katz, Susan, Law Libn.
FEDERAL RESERVE BANK OF NEW YORK - LAW
LIBRARY DIVISION □ New York, NY
Katzer, Ellen, Libn.
UNIVERSITY OF MICHIGAN - SCHOOL OF
PUBLIC HEALTH - CENTER FOR POPULATION
PLANNING - REFERENCE COLLECTION □ Ann
Arbor, MI
Katzmann, Betty, Ch.Serv.Supv.
CITY OF COMMERCE PUBLIC LIBRARY □
Commerce, CA
Katzung, Alice C., Libn.
MARIN WILDLIFE CENTER - LIBRARY □ San
Rafael, CA
Katzung, Judith, Hd.Libn.
ST. PAUL DISPATCH-PIONEER PRESS -
LIBRARY □ St. Paul, MN
Kaubris-Kowalzyk, S.A., Asst.Libn.
BANGOR THEOLOGICAL SEMINARY - MOULTON
LIBRARY □ Bangor, ME
Kauer, Erminia U., Info.Spec.
SAVANNAH RIVER PLANT - TECHNICAL
LIBRARY □ Aiken, SC
Kaufenberg, Jane, Acq.Asst.
HONEYWELL, INC. - TECHNOLOGY STRATEGY
CENTER - INFORMATION SERVICES □ Roseville,
MN
Kauff, Joan L., Chf.Med.Libn.
LONG ISLAND JEWISH-HILLSIDE MEDICAL
CENTER - HILLSIDE DIVISION - HEALTH
SCIENCES LIBRARY† □ Glen Oaks, NY
Kauffman, Inge, Dir.
CALIFORNIA SCHOOL OF PROFESSIONAL
PSYCHOLOGY - FRESNO LIBRARY □ Fresno, CA
Kauffman, Phyllis, Cat.
UNIVERSITY OF WISCONSIN, MADISON -
CENTER FOR HEALTH SCIENCES LIBRARIES† □
Madison, WI
Kaufman, David, Asst.Libn.
INDIANA UNIVERSITY OF PENNSYLVANIA -
UNIVERSITY LIBRARY □ Indiana, PA
Kaufman, Debra, Supv.
CONTINENTAL GROUP, INC. - INFORMATION
RESOURCE CENTER □ Stamford, CT
Kaufman, Judith, Libn.
SUNY AT STONY BROOK - MUSIC LIBRARY □
Stony Brook, NY
Kaufman, Marianna, Libn.
ATLANTA FULTON PUBLIC LIBRARY - IVAN
ALLEN, JR. DEPARTMENT OF SCIENCE,
INDUSTRY AND GOVERNMENT □ Atlanta, GA
Kaufman, Sonya, Hd., Ref.Serv.
UNIVERSITY OF CALIFORNIA, BERKELEY -
EDUCATION/PSYCHOLOGY LIBRARY □
Berkeley, CA
Kaul, Judith, Media Libn.
CLEVELAND STATE UNIVERSITY - JOSEPH W.
BARTUNEK III LAW LIBRARY □ Cleveland, OH
Kaul, K.L., Hd.
WAYNE STATE UNIVERSITY - G. FLINT PURDY
LIBRARY □ Detroit, MI
Kaupa, Joyce, Libn.
U.S. VETERANS ADMINISTRATION (NY-Buffalo)
- MEDICAL CENTER LIBRARY SERVICE □
Buffalo, NY

Kausar, Inamul Haq, Asst.
AHMADIYYA MOVEMENT IN ISLAM - MUSLIM
LIBRARY □ Washington, DC
Kaushagen, Beverly A., Lib. Group Supv.
AT & T BELL LABORATORIES & TECHNOLOGIES
- LIBRARY □ Columbus, OH
Kavanagh, Janette L., Tech.Info.Spec. II
AMERICAN WATER WORKS ASSOCIATION -
INFORMATION SERVICES DEPARTMENT □
Denver, CO
Kavanagh, Judy, Dir., Rsrc.Ctr.
TOYS 'N THINGS, TRAINING & RESOURCE
CENTER, INC. □ St. Paul, MN
Kavass, Igor I., Dir.
VANDERBILT UNIVERSITY - ALYNE QUEENER
MASSEY LAW LIBRARY □ Nashville, TN
Kawakami, Toyo S., Asst.Hd.
OHIO STATE UNIVERSITY - EDUCATION/
PSYCHOLOGY LIBRARY □ Columbus, OH
Kawakami, Mrs. Toyo S., Hd.Libn.
OHIO STATE UNIVERSITY - SOCIAL WORK
LIBRARY □ Columbus, OH
Kawata, Jean, Libn., Leg.Lib.
MILWAUKEE - LEGISLATIVE REFERENCE
BUREAU - LEGISLATIVE LIBRARY □ Milwaukee,
WI
Kawula, John
POINT OF PURCHASE ADVERTISING
INSTITUTE - INFORMATION CENTER □ New
York, NY
Kay, Deniston J., Ph.D., Lib.Dir.
CLARK COUNTY LAW LIBRARY □ Las Vegas, NV
Kay, Janice
DALHOUSIE UNIVERSITY - INSTITUTE OF
PUBLIC AFFAIRS - LIBRARY □ Halifax, NS
Kay, Mary, Ref./Coll.Dev.Libn.
COLUMBIA UNIVERSITY - CHEMISTRY
LIBRARY □ New York, NY
Kay, Mary, Ref./Coll.Dev.Libn.
COLUMBIA UNIVERSITY - PHYSICS LIBRARY □
New York, NY
Kay, Patricia, Libn.
AUSTRALIAN EMBASSY - LIBRARY □
Washington, DC
Kay, Mrs. Sidney R.
TEMPLE B'NAI ISRAEL - LASKER MEMORIAL
LIBRARY □ Galveston, TX
Kaya, Beatrice S., Chf.Libn.
HAWAII NEWSPAPER AGENCY - LIBRARY □
Honolulu, HI
Kayaian, Mary, Hd., Lib.Serv.
WORLD BOOK INC.- RESEARCH LIBRARY □
Chicago, IL
Kaye, Barbara, Cat.
CANADA - PUBLIC WORKS CANADA -
INFORMATION, RESEARCH & LIBRARY
SERVICES □ Ottawa, ON
Kaye, Doug, Hd.
UNIVERSITY OF BRITISH COLUMBIA - WILSON
RECORDINGS COLLECTION □ Vancouver, BC
Kaye, Geraldine C., Libn.
HARVARD UNIVERSITY - FARLOW REFERENCE
LIBRARY □ Cambridge, MA
Kaye, Margit E., Sr.Lib.Spec.
YALE UNIVERSITY - MAP COLLECTION □ New
Haven, CT
Kayes, Mary Jane, Libn.
RESIDUALS MANAGEMENT TECHNOLOGY, INC.
- LIBRARY □ Madison, WI
Kays, Maureen, Circ./Ref.Libn.
UNIVERSITY OF MAINE SCHOOL OF LAW -
DONALD L. GARBRECHT LAW LIBRARY □
Portland, ME
Kazan, Caryl, Asst.Chf
U.S. VETERANS ADMINISTRATION (NY-
Northport) - HEALTH SCIENCE LIBRARY □
Northport, NY
Kazlauskas, Edward J., Sr. Partner
PACIFIC INFORMATION INC. - INFORMATION
SERVICES □ Studio City, CA
Kazymyra-Dzioba, Ms. N.
CANADA - PUBLIC ARCHIVES OF CANADA -
NATIONAL MAP COLLECTION □ Ottawa, ON

Keadle, Robert L., Unit Chf.
U.S. DEPT. OF JUSTICE - FEDERAL BUREAU OF
INVESTIGATION - F.B.I. ACADEMY - LIBRARY □
Quantico, VA
Kealey, Cathy, Tech.Res.Libn.
BANK OF NOVA SCOTIA - TECHNICAL
LIBRARY/RESEARCH CENTRE □ Scarborough,
ON
Kealey, Dorothy, Asst.Archv.
ANGLICAN CHURCH OF CANADA - GENERAL
SYNOD ARCHIVES □ Toronto, ON
Kealty, Diane, Pres.
HISTORIC WALKER'S POINT, INC. - LIBRARY □
Milwaukee, WI
Kean, Manuel, Owner
KEAN ARCHIVES □ Philadelphia, PA
Kean, Randolph, Archv.
CHESAPEAKE & OHIO HISTORICAL SOCIETY,
INC. - C&O ARCHIVAL COLLECTION □ Newport
News VA
Keane, Theresa, Asst.Libn.
HUNT MEMORIAL HOSPITAL - GEORGE B.
PALMER MEMORIAL LIBRARY □ Danvers, MA
Kear, Becky, Libn.
DAMES & MOORE - LIBRARY □ Atlanta, GA
Kearley, Timothy, Foreign Law Libn.
UNIVERSITY OF ILLINOIS - LAW LIBRARY □
Champaign, IL
Kearney, Eileen, Tech.Proc.Libn.
ST. CHARLES BORROMEO SEMINARY - RYAN
MEMORIAL LIBRARY □ Philadelphia, PA
Kearney, Joan A., Dir.
ASSOCIATED PRESS - NEWSPHOTO LIBRARY □
New York, NY
Kearney, Kate, Dir.
MC KEESPORT HOSPITAL - HEALTH SERVICES
LIBRARY □ McKeesport, PA
Kearney, Lorraine, Coord., Lib.Serv.
DISTRICT ONE TECHNICAL INSTITUTE -
LIBRARY - EDUCATIONAL RESOURCE CENTER □
Eau Claire, WI
Kearns, Susan, Libn.
METROPOLITAN TORONTO LIBRARY - HISTORY
DEPARTMENT □ Toronto, ON
Keating, Cynthia, Libn.
CENTRAL MAINE POWER COMPANY - LIBRARY
SERVICES □ Augusta, ME
Keating, John, Cat.
MASSACHUSETTS COLLEGE OF ART - LIBRARY
□ Boston, MA
Keating, Mary, Asst.Med.Libn.
BRYN MAWR HOSPITAL - MEDICAL LIBRARY -
NURSING DIVISION □ Bryn Mawr, PA
Keating, Michael, Sr. Market Anl.
PENTON/IPC - MARKETING INFORMATION
CENTER □ Cleveland, OH
Keating, Shirley, Asst.Dir.
MC GRAW-HILL PUBLICATIONS COMPANY -
MARKETING INFORMATION CENTER □ New
York, NY
Keaveney, Sydney, Art & Arch.Libn.
PRATT INSTITUTE - LIBRARY □ Brooklyn, NY
Keays, H. Thomas, Chem.Bibliog.
SYRACUSE UNIVERSITY - SCIENCE AND
TECHNOLOGY LIBRARY □ Syracuse, NY
Keck, Bruce, Libn.
U.S. NATL. OCEANIC & ATMOSPHERIC
ADMINISTRATION - SEATTLE CENTER □
Seattle, WA
Keck, Dr. C. William, Dir. of Health
AKRON CITY HEALTH DEPARTMENT - PUBLIC
HEALTH LIBRARY □ Akron, OH
Keddle, David G., Dir., Med.Lib.
INGHAM MEDICAL CENTER - JOHN W. CHI
MEMORIAL MEDICAL LIBRARY □ Lansing, MI
Kee, Ruth, Nursing Educ.Libn.
ERLANGER MEDICAL CENTER - SCHOOL OF
NURSING - SARAH C. BARTON LIBRARY □
Chattanooga, TN
Keebaugh, Karen, Alpine County Ck.
ALPINE COUNTY LAW LIBRARY □ Markleeville,
CA

Keefe, Margaret, Libn.
METROPOLITAN TORONTO LIBRARY - SOCIAL SCIENCES DEPARTMENT □ Toronto, ON
Keefer, Elaine, Ref.Libn.
EMORY UNIVERSITY - SCHOOL OF MEDICINE - A.W. CALHOUN MEDICAL LIBRARY □ Atlanta, GA
Keefer, Ruth L., Lit.Spec.
MOBIL RESEARCH & DEVELOPMENT CORPORATION - DALLAS RESEARCH DIVISION - LIBRARY □ Dallas, TX
Keegan, M., Info.Spec.
SOUTH FLORIDA REGIONAL PLANNING COUNCIL - LIBRARY □ Hollywood, FL
Keeler, Elizabeth, Asst.Engr.Libn.
PURDUE UNIVERSITY - ENGINEERING LIBRARY □ West Lafayette, IN
Keeler, Dr. Robert W., Cur. of Coll.
WASHINGTON COUNTY MUSEUM - LIBRARY □ Portland, OR
Keeley, Kurt M., Dir., Info.Serv.
AMERICAN WATER WORKS ASSOCIATION - INFORMATION SERVICES DEPARTMENT □ Denver, CO
Keeling, Alfreida, Libn.
U.S. VETERANS ADMINISTRATION (MO-St. Louis) - HOSPITAL LIBRARY □ St. Louis, MO
Keely, Veronica, Off.Mgr.
CANADIAN BOOK PUBLISHERS' COUNCIL - LIBRARY □ Toronto, ON
Keem, Lida, Ser.Libn.
WAYNE STATE UNIVERSITY - ARTHUR NEEF LAW LIBRARY □ Detroit, MI
Keen, Barbara, Sci. & Govt.Proj.Libn.
BATTELLE MEMORIAL INSTITUTE - HUMAN AFFAIRS RESEARCH CENTER - SEATTLE RESEARCH CENTERS LIBRARY □ Seattle, WA
Keena, Katherine, Prog.Spec.
GIRL SCOUTS OF THE USA - JULIETTE GORDON LOW GIRL SCOUT NATIONAL CENTER □ Savannah, GA
Keenan, Eleanor M., Libn.
WEST VIRGINIA STATE COMMISSION ON AGING - LIBRARY □ Charleston, WV
Keenan, Grace G., Asst.Libn.
JOSLYN ART MUSEUM - ART REFERENCE LIBRARY □ Omaha, NE
Keenan, Mary T., Pub.Serv.Libn.
ILLINOIS COLLEGE OF OPTOMETRY - CARL F. SHEPARD MEMORIAL LIBRARY □ Chicago, IL
Keene, Catherine, Dir.
PASSAIC COUNTY HISTORICAL SOCIETY - LIBRARY □ Paterson, NJ
Keener, Donald S., Asst.Dir.Gen.Serv.
NORTH CAROLINA STATE UNIVERSITY - D.H. HILL LIBRARY □ Raleigh, NC
Keener, Edison W., Att.
PEOPLES NATURAL GAS COMPANY - LAW LIBRARY □ Pittsburgh, PA
Keesee, R. Eugene, Owner
PHOTO TRENDS - LIBRARY □ Freeport, NY
Keeth, Kent, Dir.
BAYLOR UNIVERSITY - TEXAS COLLECTION □ Waco, TX
Kegg, Janet, Libn.
AMERICAN ASSOCIATION FOR THE ADVANCEMENT OF SCIENCE - LIBRARY □ Washington, DC
Kehde, Edward, Archv.
UNIVERSITY OF KANSAS - UNIVERSITY ARCHIVES □ Lawrence, KS
Kehoe, Patrick E., Dir.
AMERICAN UNIVERSITY - WASHINGTON COLLEGE OF LAW - LIBRARY □ Washington, DC
Kehrein, James E., Libn.
ILLINOIS RAILWAY MUSEUM - TECHNICAL LIBRARY □ Union, IL
Kehrer, Ms. Shelby J., Asst.Libn.
CINCINNATI ELECTRONICS CORPORATION - TECHNICAL LIBRARY □ Cincinnati, OH
Keighley, David, Media Spec.
UNIVERSITY OF CONNECTICUT - PHARMACY LIBRARY AND LEARNING CENTER □ Storrs, CT

Keim, Julia, Lit. Search
ROCKWELL INTERNATIONAL - ROCKETDYNE DIVISION - TECHNICAL INFORMATION CENTER □ Canoga Park, CA
Keiner, Harry, Archv.
TRAVELERS INSURANCE COMPANIES - CORPORATE LIBRARY □ Hartford, CT
Keister, Martha W., Hd., Pub.Serv.
PACE UNIVERSITY - SCHOOL OF LAW LIBRARY □ White Plains, NY
Keiswetter, Kim, Archv./Educ.Dir.
FORT LARNED HISTORICAL SOCIETY, INC. - SANTA FE TRAIL CENTER LIBRARY □ Larned, KS
Keiter, Linda S., Asst. Dir., Sci.Libs.
UNIVERSITY OF WYOMING - SCIENCE AND TECHNOLOGY LIBRARY □ Laramie, WY
Keith, Donald, Exec.Dir.
CENTER FOR STUDY OF MULTIPLE BIRTH - RESOURCE LIBRARY □ Chicago, IL
Keith, Marie C., Assoc.Libn.
FRICK ART REFERENCE LIBRARY □ New York, NY
Keith, Susan, Info.Spec.
PRIME COMPUTER, INC. - INFORMATION CENTER† □ Framingham, MA
Keitzer, Geri K., Libn.
UNITED TECHNOLOGIES CORPORATION - ELLIOTT COMPANY - LIBRARY □ Jeannette, PA
Keizur, Berta, Hd., Info.Proc.
LAWRENCE LIVERMORE NATIONAL LABORATORY - TECHNICAL INFORMATION DEPARTMENT LIBRARY □ Livermore, CA
Keklock, Donna, Chf.Libn.
CHARLOTTE MEMORIAL HOSPITAL AND MEDICAL CENTER - MEDICAL LIBRARY OF MECKLENBURG COUNTY/LRC OF CHARLOTTE AHEC □ Charlotte, NC
Keleher, Hugh, Tech.Info.Spec.
KAISER ALUMINUM & CHEMICAL CORPORATION - TECHNICAL INFORMATION CENTER □ Pleasanton, CA
Kelien, Becky Lacefield, Med.Libn.
CLARK COUNTY MEMORIAL HOSPITAL - MEDICAL LIBRARY □ Jeffersonville, IN
Kell, Mary Kate, Asst. Law Libn.
CONOCO, INC. - LEGAL INFORMATION CENTER □ Houston, TX
Kelleher, Kathleen, Libn.
TEACHERS INSURANCE AND ANNUITY ASSOCIATION OF AMERICA - BUSINESS LIBRARY □ New York, NY
Kellen, Erin, Libn.
BALCH, BINGHAM, BAKER, WARD, SMITH, BOWMAN & THAGARD - LIBRARY □ Birmingham, AL
Kellen, James D., Cat.
COLLEGE OF ST. THOMAS - O'SHAUGHNESSY LIBRARY - SPECIAL COLLECTIONS □ St. Paul, MN
Keller, Alfred, Libn.
GERMAN SOCIETY OF PENNSYLVANIA - JOSEPH HORNER MEMORIAL LIBRARY □ Philadelphia, PA
Keller, Dean H., Cur.
KENT STATE UNIVERSITY - DEPARTMENT OF SPECIAL COLLECTIONS □ Kent, OH
Keller, George, Sci.Ref.Libn.
UNIVERSITY OF CALIFORNIA, SANTA CRUZ - SCIENCE LIBRARY □ Santa Cruz, CA
Keller, Joan R., Ext.Serv.Libn.
U.S. ARMY POST - PRESIDIO OF SAN FRANCISCO - POST LIBRARY SYSTEM □ Presidio of San Francisco, CA
Keller, Madeline, Ref.Libn.
MANUFACTURERS HANOVER TRUST COMPANY - CORPORATE LIBRARY/INVESTMENT LIBRARY DIVISION† □ New York, NY
Keller, Michael A., Hd.
UNIVERSITY OF CALIFORNIA, BERKELEY - MUSIC LIBRARY □ Berkeley, CA
Keller, Mildred, Mgr., Tech.Info.Serv.
DURACELL INC. - TECHNICAL INFORMATION CENTER □ Burlington, MA

Keller, Pat, Acq.
UNIVERSITY OF CINCINNATI - ROBERT S. MARX LAW LIBRARY □ Cincinnati, OH
Keller, Wanda, Libn.
ALLEGANY COUNTY CIRCUIT COURT - LIBRARY† □ Cumberland, MD
Keller, William B., Hd.Libn.
MARYLAND HISTORICAL SOCIETY - LIBRARY □ Baltimore, MD
Keller, William E., Hd., Adm.Asst.
ILLINOIS STATE HISTORICAL LIBRARY □ Springfield, IL
Kellerman, Frank, Biology/Psych.Ref.Libn.
BROWN UNIVERSITY - SCIENCES LIBRARY □ Providence, RI
Kellerstrass, Amy, Asst.Dir., Info.Serv.
ILLINOIS STATE LIBRARY □ Springfield, IL
Kellet, Patricia G., Law Libn.
SCHUYLKILL COUNTY LAW LIBRARY □ Pottsville, PA
Kelley, Mrs., Genealogist
LEBANON COUNTY HISTORICAL SOCIETY - LIBRARY □ Lebanon, PA
Kelley, Bruce, Dir./Cur.
ANTIQUE WIRELESS ASSOCIATION, INC. - LIBRARY □ Holcomb, NY
Kelley, Donald, Art Gallery
BOSTON ATHENAEUM LIBRARY □ Boston, MA
Kelley, Evelyn C., Pres.
PEN AND BRUSH INC. - LIBRARY □ New York, NY
Kelley, John F., Dir.
BRANDYWINE HOSPITAL - HEALTH SCIENCES LIBRARY AND INFORMATION RESOURCE CENTER □ Caln Township, PA
Kelley, John F., Dir.
BRANDYWINE HOSPITAL - SCHOOL OF NURSING - LIBRARY □ Coatesville, PA
Kelley, Lorain M., Libn.
CHAMPION INTERNATIONAL - CORPORATE INFORMATION CENTER† □ Stamford, CT
Kelley, Marianne, Mgr., Info.Serv.
ABBOTT-NORTHWESTERN HOSPITAL CORPORATION - HEALTH SCIENCES RESOURCE CENTER □ Minneapolis, MN
Kelley, Marilyn, Asst.Libn.
STURGIS LIBRARY† □ Barnstable, MA
Kelley, Neil, Coord., Pub.Serv.
UNIVERSITY OF ARKANSAS FOR MEDICAL SCIENCES - MEDICAL SCIENCES LIBRARY □ Little Rock, AR
Kelley, Rosemary G., Med.Libn.
UNIVERSITY OF NEW ENGLAND - COLLEGE OF OSTEOPATHIC MEDICINE - NECOM LIBRARY† □ Biddeford, ME
Kelley, Ruth, Med.Libn.
HAMPTON GENERAL HOSPITAL - MEDICAL LIBRARY □ Hampton, VA
Kelley, Stephanie, Supv.
REORGANIZED CHURCH OF JESUS CHRIST OF LATTER DAY SAINTS - SERVICES TO THE BLIND □ Independence, MO
Kelley, Tina, Legal Ref.Libn.
U.S. DEPT. OF THE TREASURY - INFORMATION SERVICES DIVISION - TREASURY DEPT. LIBRARY □ Washington, DC
Kellie, Mary, Inservice Coord.
NOTRE DAME HOSPITAL - LIBRARY □ Hearst, ON
Kelliher, Rev. Alexander, S.A., Mgr.
FRIARS OF THE ATONEMENT - CARDINAL SPELLMAN LIBRARY □ Garrison, NY
Kellman, Amy, Hd., Ch.Dept.
CARNEGIE LIBRARY OF PITTSBURGH - CENTRAL CHILDREN'S ROOM HISTORICAL COLLECTION □ Pittsburgh, PA
Kellogg, Eleanore, Asst.Libn.
CRANBROOK INSTITUTE OF SCIENCE - LIBRARY □ Bloomfield Hills, MI
Kellogg, Pat, Prog.Archv./Mus.Lib.Serv.
CANADIAN BROADCASTING CORPORATION - MUSIC LIBRARY □ Toronto, ON

Kelly, Ann, Libn./Archv.
SHAKER MUSEUM FOUNDATION - EMMA B. KING LIBRARY □ Old Chatham, NY

Kelly, Ann, Libn./Archv.
SHAKER MUSEUM FOUNDATION - EMMA B. KING LIBRARY □ Old Chatham, NY

Kelly, Ann M., Libn.
ST. ELIZABETH'S HOSPITAL - NURSING SCHOOL LIBRARY □ Utica, NY

Kelly, Ardie L., Libn.
MARINERS MUSEUM - LIBRARY □ Newport News, VA

Kelly, Barbara, Prog.Asst./Supv.
UNIVERSITY OF WISCONSIN, MADISON - THEORETICAL CHEMISTRY INSTITUTE - LIBRARY □ Madison, WI

Kelly, Barbara R., Libn.
COMMONWEALTH EDISON COMPANY - LIBRARY □ Chicago, IL

Kelly, Callista, Libn.
CANADA - DEPARTMENT OF COMMUNICATIONS - COMMUNICATIONS RESEARCH CENTRE LIBRARY □ Ottawa, ON

Kelly, Claire B., Res.Libn.
MERCK FROSST CANADA INC. - RESEARCH LIBRARY □ Pointe Claire-Dorval, PQ

Kelly, Clara, Act.Libn.
NATIONAL JUDICIAL COLLEGE - LAW LIBRARY □ Reno, NV

Kelly, Deborah M., Corp.Libn.
BRINCO LIMITED - LIBRARY† □ Toronto, ON

Kelly, Eleanor M., Libn.
OUR LADY OF LOURDES MEDICAL CENTER - SCHOOL OF NURSING - LIBRARY □ Camden, NJ

Kelly, Elizabeth, Hd., Access Serv.
WASHINGTON UNIVERSITY - SCHOOL OF MEDICINE LIBRARY □ St. Louis, MO

Kelly, Elizabeth C., Assoc.Dir.
CREIGHTON UNIVERSITY - LAW SCHOOL - KLUTZNICK LIBRARY† □ Omaha, NE

Kelly, Elizabeth C., Dir., Med.Lib.
U.S. FOOD & DRUG ADMINISTRATION - NATIONAL CENTER FOR DRUGS AND BIOLOGIES - MEDICAL LIBRARY/HFN-630 □ Rockville, MD

Kelly, Elizabeth S., Libn.
UNIVERSITY OF PENNSYLVANIA - BIDDLE LAW LIBRARY □ Philadelphia, PA

Kelly, Elizabeth Slusser, Law Lib.Dir.
SOUTHERN ILLINOIS UNIVERSITY, CARBONDALE - SCHOOL OF LAW LIBRARY □ Carbondale, IL

Kelly, Genevieve, Libn.
CONGRESSIONAL QUARTERLY, INC. - EDITORIAL REPORTS LIBRARY □ Washington, DC

Kelly, Glen, Hd., Acq.
LAURENTIAN UNIVERSITY - MAIN LIBRARY □ Sudbury, ON

Kelly, James W., Cur.
HIGHLAND PARK HERBARIUM - LIBRARY □ Rochester, NY

Kelly, Joanne, Co-Dir.
VIDEO FREE AMERICA - LIBRARY □ San Francisco, CA

Kelly, John, Cur.
UNIVERSITY OF SOUTHERN MISSISSIPPI - MC CAIN LIBRARY □ Hattiesburg, MS

Kelly, Judy, Doc.Libn.
LOYOLA UNIVERSITY (New Orleans) - LAW LIBRARY □ New Orleans, LA

Kelly, Karon M., Dir.
WESTERN INTERSTATE COMMISSION FOR HIGHER EDUCATION - LIBRARY □ Boulder, CO

Kelly, Kay, Med.Libn.
BURNS (Dean C.) HEALTH SCIENCES LIBRARY □ Petoskey, MI

Kelly, Michael T., Cur.
WICHITA STATE UNIVERSITY - SPECIAL COLLECTIONS □ Wichita, KS

Kelly, N., Info.Spec.
STANDARD OIL COMPANY OF INDIANA - LIBRARY/INFORMATION CENTER □ Chicago, IL

Kelly, Nancy P., Libn.
INSTITUTE FOR THE STUDY OF LABOR AND ECONOMIC CRISIS - LIBRARY AND DATABANK □ San Francisco, CA

Kelly, Patrick, Asst.Libn.
BRYANT COLLEGE OF BUSINESS ADMINISTRATION - EDITH M. HODGSON MEMORIAL LIBRARY □ Smithfield, RI

Kelly, Peggy, Libn.
PIERCE/GOODWIN/ALEXANDER - LIBRARY/RESOURCE CENTER □ Houston, TX

Kelly, Rhona S., Assoc.Libn.
ST. VINCENT'S HOSPITAL AND MEDICAL CENTER - MEDICAL LIBRARY □ New York, NY

Kelly, Richard, Tech.Serv.Libn.
WARNER-PACIFIC COLLEGE - OTTO F. LINN LIBRARY □ Portland, OR

Kelly, Robert Q., Dir.
CREIGHTON UNIVERSITY - LAW SCHOOL - KLUTZNICK LIBRARY† □ Omaha, NE

Kelly, Ruth, Libn.
JEWISH HOSPITAL AT WASHINGTON UNIVERSITY MEDICAL CENTER - ROTHSCHILD MEDICAL LIBRARY □ St. Louis, MO

Kelly, Susan, Ref.Dept.Hd.
NEW BEDFORD FREE PUBLIC LIBRARY - GENEALOGY ROOM† □ New Bedford, MA

Kelsay, Susan M., Asst.Dir.
MORRIS (Robert) ASSOCIATES - LIBRARY □ Philadelphia, PA

Kelsey, Mary Jane, Adm.Serv.Libn.
YALE UNIVERSITY - LAW LIBRARY □ New Haven, CT

Kelsh, Virginia, Law Libn./Assoc.Prof.
UNIVERSITY OF SAN FRANCISCO - SCHOOL OF LAW LIBRARY □ San Francisco, CA

Kelso, Mark A., First Asst.
PUBLIC LIBRARY OF CINCINNATI AND HAMILTON COUNTY - EXCEPTIONAL CHILDREN'S DIVISION □ Cincinnati, OH

Kelty, Linda, Libn.
INDIANA UNIVERSITY - SOCIAL STUDIES DEVELOPMENT CENTER - CURRICULUM RESOURCE CENTER □ Bloomington, IN

Kemble, Harold E., Mss.Cur.
RHODE ISLAND HISTORICAL SOCIETY - LIBRARY □ Providence, RI

Kemp, Barbara, Hd., Hum./Soc.Pub.Serv.
WASHINGTON STATE UNIVERSITY - EDUCATION LIBRARY □ Pullman, WA

Kemp, Carla, Pub.Rec.Supv.
FLORIDA STATE DIVISION OF ARCHIVES, HISTORY & RECORDS MANAGEMENT - FLORIDA STATE ARCHIVES □ Tallahassee, FL

Kemp, Carla, Univ.Archv.
UNIVERSITY OF FLORIDA - UNIVERSITY ARCHIVES AND UNIVERSITY COLLECTION □ Gainesville, FL

Kemp, Charles H., Dir.
OREGON INSTITUTE OF TECHNOLOGY - LEARNING RESOURCES CENTER □ Klamath Falls, OR

Kemp, Dana, Med.Libn.
ST. JOSEPH MEMORIAL HOSPITAL - HEALTH SCIENCE LIBRARY □ Kokomo, IN

Kemp, Harry, Mgr.
U.S. FEDERAL AVIATION ADMINISTRATION - TECHNICAL INFORMATION RESEARCH FACILITY (ACT 624) □ Atlantic City Airport, NJ

Kemp, Jane, Circ.Libn.
LUTHER COLLEGE - PREUS LIBRARY □ Decorah, IA

Kemp, Jeanne, Asst.Dir.
CENTRAL OPERA SERVICE - INFORMATION CENTER AND LIBRARY □ New York, NY

Kemp, Leatrice M., Libn.
ROCHESTER MUSEUM AND SCIENCE CENTER - LIBRARY □ Rochester, NY

Kemp, Leora, Tech.Proc.Libn.
TEXAS STATE TECHNICAL INSTITUTE, WACO CAMPUS - LIBRARY □ Waco, TX

Kemp, Linda, Libn.
TEXAS EDUCATION AGENCY - RESOURCE CENTER LIBRARY □ Austin, TX

Kemp, Virginia, Libn.
SPRAGUE ELECTRIC COMPANY - RESEARCH LIBRARY □ North Adams, MA

Kemp, W. Daunine, Libn.
SWAN WOOSTER CONSULTANTS LIMITED - LIBRARY □ Calgary, AB

Kempel, Peter M., Dir., Res.Serv.
COOLEY (Thomas M.) LAW SCHOOL - LIBRARY □ Lansing, MI

Kemper, Lyle, Chf., User Serv.Br.
U.S. GEOLOGICAL SURVEY - NATL. CARTOGRAPHIC INFORMATION CENTER (NCIC) □ Reston, VA

Kemper, Robert E., Dir.
NORTHERN ARIZONA UNIVERSITY - LIBRARIES† □ Flagstaff, AZ

Kemper, Suzanne, Libn.
ONTARIO LOTTERY CORPORATION - LIBRARY □ Toronto, ON

Kemper, Suzanne W., Coll.Dev./Ref./ILL
NORTH ADAMS STATE COLLEGE - EUGENE L. FREEL LIBRARY - SPECIAL COLLECTIONS □ North Adams, MA

Kenamore, Jane A., Archv.
ROSENBERG LIBRARY - GALVESTON AND TEXAS HISTORY CENTER □ Galveston, TX

Kenan, Charlotte, Libn.
TUCSON CITIZEN - LIBRARY □ Tucson, AZ

Kendall, B., ILL
ALBERTA - DEPARTMENT OF THE ENVIRONMENT - LIBRARY □ Edmonton, AB

Kendall, Charles T., Libn.
ANDERSON COLLEGE - SCHOOL OF THEOLOGY - BYRD MEMORIAL LIBRARY □ Anderson, IN

Kendall, John, Act.Archv.
UNIVERSITY OF MASSACHUSETTS, AMHERST - LIBRARY - DEPARTMENT OF ARCHIVES □ Amherst, MA

Kendall, John D., Hd.
UNIVERSITY OF MASSACHUSETTS, AMHERST - LIBRARY - SPECIAL COLLECTIONS AND RARE BOOKS □ Amherst, MA

Kendall, Nellie, Libn.
DALLAS PUBLIC LIBRARY - HISTORY AND SOCIAL SCIENCES DIVISION □ Dallas, TX

Kendig, Bobbi, Info.Spec.
WESTINGHOUSE ELECTRIC CORPORATION - WATER REACTOR DIVISIONS - INFORMATION RESOURCE CENTER □ Pittsburgh, PA

Kendra, William, Libn.
OMAHA PUBLIC LIBRARY - BUSINESS, SCIENCE & TECHNOLOGY DEPARTMENT □ Omaha, NE

Kendrick, Alice M., Dir.
LUTHERAN COUNCIL IN THE U.S.A. - RECORDS AND INFORMATION CENTER - REFERENCE LIBRARY □ New York, NY

Kendris, Yolanda, Libn.
NEW YORK STATE OFFICE OF MENTAL RETARDATION AND DEVELOPMENTAL DISABILITIES - REFERENCE CENTER □ Albany, NY

Keng, Mr. Hsiu-Yun, Dir.
SOUTH CAROLINA STATE DEPARTMENT OF MENTAL RETARDATION - WHITTEN CENTER LIBRARY & MEDIA RESOURCE SERVICES □ Clinton, SC

Kenna, Diane, Asst.Libn.
UNIVERSITY OF WISCONSIN, MADISON - NIEMAN-GRANT JOURNALISM READING ROOM □ Madison, WI

Kenneally, Louise M., Archv.
STONEHILL COLLEGE - ARNOLD B. TOFIAS INDUSTRIAL ARCHIVES □ North Easton, MA

Kennedy, Ann, Tech.Libn.
ABAM ENGINEERS, INC. - TECHNICAL LIBRARY □ Tacoma, WA

Kennedy, Doris Autrey, Libn.
CHRISTIAN CHURCH (Disciples of Christ), INC. - LIBRARY □ Indianapolis, IN

Kennedy, Eleanor, Curric.Libn.
LOYOLA UNIVERSITY OF CHICAGO - JULIA
DEAL LEWIS LIBRARY □ Chicago, IL

Kennedy, Elizabeth, Libn.
FRASER INC. - CENTRAL TECHNICAL
DEPARTMENT LIBRARY □ Edmundston, NB

Kennedy, Helen, Dir.
PACIFICA RADIO NETWORK - PACIFICA RADIO
ARCHIVE □ Los Angeles, CA

Kennedy, James R., Libn.
ST. ANSELM'S COLLEGE - GEISEL LIBRARY □
Manchester, NH

Kennedy, Jane F., Gen.Mgr.
U.S. POSTAL SERVICE - LIBRARY □ Washington,
DC

Kennedy, Jean A., Chf.Libn.
U.S. VETERANS ADMINISTRATION (VA-Salem) -
MEDICAL CENTER LIBRARY □ Salem, VA

Kennedy, Joan
PASADENA PUBLIC LIBRARY - BUSINESS-
TECHNOLOGY DIVISION □ Pasadena, CA

Kennedy, Joan
PASADENA PUBLIC LIBRARY - REFERENCE
DIVISION □ Pasadena, CA

Kennedy, Joanne, Libn.
ST. JOHN'S MEDICAL CENTER - HEALTH
SCIENCE LIBRARY† □ Oxnard, CA

Kennedy, Katherine, Tech.Info.Spec.
U.S. ARMY - ENGINEER WATERWAYS
EXPERIMENT STATION - TECHNICAL
INFORMATION CENTER □ Vicksburg, MS

Kennedy, Kathleen, Asst.Dir./Bibliog./Ref.
GLASSBORO STATE COLLEGE - SAVITZ
LIBRARY - LLOYD V. MANWILLER CURRICULUM
LABORATORY □ Glassboro, NJ

Kennedy, Kevin, Asst. Physical Sci.Libn.
OKLAHOMA STATE UNIVERSITY - PHYSICAL
SCIENCES AND ENGINEERING DIVISION □
Stillwater, OK

Kennedy, Marcia, Regional Libn. (South)
ALBERTA - DEPARTMENT OF THE SOLICITOR
GENERAL - LIBRARY □ Edmonton, AB

Kennedy, Marcia G., Regional Libn./South
ALBERTA - DEPARTMENT OF THE SOLICITOR
GENERAL - CALGARY CORRECTIONAL CENTRE
- STAFF LIBRARY □ Calgary, AB

Kennedy, Marsha, Coord., Film Distr.
UNIVERSITY OF NEW HAMPSHIRE -
DEPARTMENT OF MEDIA SERVICES - FILM
LIBRARY □ Durham, NH

Kennedy, P., Preconfederation Archv.
CANADA - PUBLIC ARCHIVES OF CANADA -
MANUSCRIPT DIVISION □ Ottawa, ON

Kennedy, P.N., Libn.
BENNINGTON MUSEUM - GENEALOGICAL
LIBRARY □ Bennington, VT

Kennedy, Pat, Asst.Libn.
MIDDLESEX COUNTY LAW LIBRARY □ New
Brunswick, NJ

Kennedy, Theodore C., Supv.Libn.
U.S. AIR FORCE SCHOOL OF HEALTH CARE
SCIENCES - ACADEMIC LIBRARY □ Sheppard
AFB, TX

Kennedy, Win, Regional Mgr.
CANADA - EMPLOYMENT & IMMIGRATION
CANADA - PUBLIC AFFAIRS - MANITOBA
REGIONAL OFFICE LIBRARY □ Winnipeg, MB

Kennet, Elsie, Ref./Info.Serv.Libn.
KUTZTOWN UNIVERSITY - ROHRBACH
LIBRARY □ Kutztown, PA

Kenney, Anne R., Assoc.Dir.
WESTERN HISTORICAL MANUSCRIPT
COLLECTION/STATE HISTORICAL SOCIETY OF
MISSOURI MANUSCRIPTS JOINT COLL. □ St.
Louis, MO

Kenney, Bernard, Br.Libn.
U.S. BUREAU OF MINES - BOEING SERVICES
INTERNATIONAL - LIBRARY □ Pittsburgh, PA

Kenney, Donald J., Hd., Gen.Ref.Dept.
VIRGINIA POLYTECHNIC INSTITUTE AND
STATE UNIVERSITY - CAROL M. NEWMAN
LIBRARY □ Blacksburg, VA

Kenney, Evelyn, Libn.
RIVERSIDE HOSPITAL - HEALTH SCIENCES
LIBRARY □ Newport News, VA

Kenney, Noreen M., Regional Staff Libn.
NORTHEAST OHIO DEVELOPMENTAL CENTER-
BROADVIEW CAMPUS - REGIONAL STAFF
LIBRARY □ Broadview Heights, OH

Kenney, W.J., Law Ck.
CANADA - NATIONAL DEFENCE - OFFICE OF
THE JUDGE ADVOCATE GENERAL - LIBRARY □
Ottawa, ON

Kennington, Candice Cortes, Libn.
SMALL, CRAIG & WERKENTHIN - LIBRARY □
Austin, TX

Kenny, Ann, Asst.Libn.
ERNST & WHINNEY - INFORMATION CENTER □
Boston, MA

Keno, Sandy, Lib.Techn.
SACRED HEART MEDICAL CENTER - HEALTH
SCIENCES LIBRARY □ Spokane, WA

Kensinger, Colleen, Tech.Serv.Libn.
ALAMEDA COUNTY LAW LIBRARY □ Oakland, CA

Kent, Beverley, Chf.Libn.
BANK OF NOVA SCOTIA - LIBRARY □ Toronto,
ON

Kent, Carrie, Ref.Libn.
HARVARD UNIVERSITY - GODFREY LOWELL
CABOT SCIENCE LIBRARY □ Cambridge, MA

Kent, Charles Robert, Archv.
LOCK HAVEN STATE COLLEGE - GEORGE B.
STEVENSON LIBRARY - ARCHIVES □ Lock
Haven, PA

Kent, Diana, Ref.Libn.
UNIVERSITY OF BRITISH COLUMBIA -
WOODWARD BIOMEDICAL LIBRARY □
Vancouver, BC

Kent, Frederick J., Hd.
FREE LIBRARY OF PHILADELPHIA - MUSIC
DEPARTMENT □ Philadelphia, PA

Kent, Frederick J., Hd.
FREE LIBRARY OF PHILADELPHIA - MUSIC
DEPARTMENT - DRINKER LIBRARY OF CHORAL
MUSIC □ Philadelphia, PA

Kent, Mary, Spec.Coll.Libn.
CONNECTICUT COLLEGE - LIBRARY - SPECIAL
COLLECTIONS □ New London, CT

Kent, Peter, Sys.Libn.
ATLANTA NEWSPAPERS - REFERENCE LIBRARY
□ Atlanta, GA

Kenworthy, Eleanora M., Dir.
HAHNEMANN UNIVERSITY - WARREN H. FAKE
LIBRARY† □ Philadelphia, PA

Kenworthy, Katherine, Hd., Tech.Serv.
CRAVATH, SWAINE, & MOORE - LAW LIBRARY
□ New York, NY

Kenyon, Carleton W., Law Libn.
LIBRARY OF CONGRESS - LAW LIBRARY □
Washington, DC

Kenyon, Cynthia, Dir.
U.S.D.A. - ECONOMIC RESEARCH SERVICE -
ERS REFERENCE CENTER □ Washington, DC

Kenyon, Kay A., Chf.Libn.
SMITHSONIAN INSTITUTION LIBRARIES -
NATIONAL ZOOLOGICAL PARK - LIBRARY □
Washington, DC

Kenyon, Kenneth, Hd. of Res.Dept.
TWENTIETH CENTURY FOX FILM
CORPORATION - RESEARCH LIBRARY □ Beverly
Hills, CA

Kenyon, Lowell Anson, Dir.
INTERNATIONAL MILITARY ARCHIVES □
Washington, DC

Kenyon, Sharon, Libn.
TRINITY LUTHERAN CHURCH - LIBRARY □
Madison, WI

Kenyon, Xena, Libn.
U.S. VETERANS ADMINISTRATION (WI-Tomah)
- HOSPITAL LIBRARY □ Tomah, WI

Keogh, Jeanne M., Tech.Libn.
LIBBEY-OWENS-FORD COMPANY - TECHNICAL
CENTER LIBRARY □ Toledo, OH

Keough, Doreen B., Libn.
ST. VINCENT MEDICAL CENTER - HEALTH
SCIENCES LIBRARY □ Los Angeles, CA

Keough, Kristin, Act.Chf./Interp.
BUFFALO & ERIE COUNTY HISTORICAL
SOCIETY - LIBRARY† □ Buffalo, NY

Kepes, Katherine, Libn.
CARNEGIE LIBRARY OF PITTSBURGH - MUSIC
AND ART DEPARTMENT □ Pittsburgh, PA

Kepes, Mary Lois, Libn.
UNIVERSITY OF PITTSBURGH - GRADUATE
SCHOOL OF PUBLIC & INTERNATIONAL
AFFAIRS LIBRARY □ Pittsburgh, PA

Kepner, Frances, Cat.
INDIANA STATE UNIVERSITY - DEPARTMENT
OF RARE BOOKS AND SPECIAL COLLECTIONS □
Terre Haute, IN

Keppel, Betty Jo, Ser./Acq.Libn.
OREGON HEALTH SCIENCES UNIVERSITY -
LIBRARY □ Portland, OR

Kepple, Robert J., Libn.
WESTMINSTER THEOLOGICAL SEMINARY -
MONTGOMERY LIBRARY† □ Philadelphia, PA

Kerbel, Sandra S., Libn.
UNIVERSITY OF PITTSBURGH - BEVIER
ENGINEERING LIBRARY □ Pittsburgh, PA

Kerbel, Sandra S., Hd.
UNIVERSITY OF PITTSBURGH - MATHEMATICS
LIBRARY □ Pittsburgh, PA

Keresztesy, Frances, Mgr., Res.Info.
MERCK & COMPANY, INC. - MERCK SHARP &
DOHME RESEARCH LABORATORIES -
RESEARCH INFORMATION SYSTEMS □ Rahway,
NJ

Kerka, Sandra, Acq.Coord.
ERIC CLEARINGHOUSE ON ADULT, CAREER
AND VOCATIONAL EDUCATION - NATL. CTR.
FOR RESEARCH IN VOCATIONAL EDUC. □
Columbus, OH

Kern, Betty, Acq. & Ser.
LAW LIBRARY OF LOUISIANA† □ New Orleans,
LA

Kern, Wilma, Pres.
HENRY COUNTY HISTORICAL SOCIETY -
LIBRARY □ New Castle, IN

Kern-Simirenko, Cheryl, Slavic Bibliog.
SYRACUSE UNIVERSITY - E.S. BIRD LIBRARY -
AREA STUDIES DEPARTMENT □ Syracuse, NY

Kern-Simirenko, Cheryl, Bibliog.
SYRACUSE UNIVERSITY - E.S. BIRD LIBRARY -
SOCIAL SCIENCES DEPARTMENT □ Syracuse,
NY

Kerndt, Miriam E., Geog.Libn.
UNIVERSITY OF WISCONSIN, MADISON -
GEOGRAPHY LIBRARY □ Madison, WI

Kerns, J. Thomas, Supv., Tech.Info.Serv.
CHEVRON ENVIRONMENTAL HEALTH CENTER,
INC. - TECHNICAL INFORMATION CENTER† □
Richmond, CA

Kerns, Ruth, Pub.Serv.Libn/Archv.
GEORGE MASON UNIVERSITY - FENWICK
LIBRARY - SPECIAL COLLECTIONS □ Fairfax, VA

Kerr, Audrey M., Hd.Med.Libn.
UNIVERSITY OF MANITOBA - MEDICAL
LIBRARY □ Winnipeg, MB

Kerr, Donald R., Assoc.Dir.
EAST TEXAS STATE UNIVERSITY - JAMES
GILLIAM GEE LIBRARY □ Commerce, TX

Kerr, Mr. G., Hd., Pub.Serv.
ALBERTA ENVIRONMENTAL CENTRE - LIBRARY
□ Vegreville, AB

Kerr, Judith, Acq.
CALVARY BAPTIST THEOLOGICAL SEMINARY -
LIBRARY □ Lansdale, PA

Kerr, Ken, Asst.Libn.
UNIVERSITY OF CONNECTICUT - SCHOOL OF
BUSINESS ADMINISTRATION LIBRARY □
Hartford, CT

Kerridge, Dr. Kenneth A., Hd., Lit.Sect.
BRISTOL-MYERS COMPANY - SCIENTIFIC
INFORMATION DEPARTMENT □ Syracuse, NY

Kerrigan, J., Lib.Cons.
TORONTO BOARD OF EDUCATION -
EDUCATION CENTRE LIBRARY □ Toronto, ON
Kerschner, Joan G., Asst. State Libn/Pub.Serv
NEVADA STATE LIBRARY □ Carson City, NV
Kersey, Jamie, Libn.
ASHLAND OIL, INC. - TECHNICAL
INFORMATION CENTER □ Ashland, KY
Kersey, Marion C., Lib.Mgr.
PLANNING RESEARCH CORPORATION -
TECHNICAL LIBRARY □ McLean, VA
Kerstetter, John P., Supv., Acq./Cat.
KENT STATE UNIVERSITY - AUDIOVISUAL
SERVICES □ Kent, OH
Kerwin, Maryann, Libn.
MIXING EQUIPMENT COMPANY, INC. - MIXCO
R&D LIBRARY† □ Rochester, NY
Keshin, Jesse G., Dir./Cont.Med.Educ.
NORTH SHORE MEDICAL CENTER - MEDICAL
LIBRARY □ Miami, FL
Kesler, Cynthia J., Libn.
MAC KENZIE, SMITH, LEWIS, MICHELL &
HUGHES - LAW LIBRARY □ Syracuse, NY
Kesling, Patricia, Act.Adm.
SONS OF THE REVOLUTION IN THE STATE OF
NEW YORK - LIBRARY □ New York, NY
Kessel, Shirley, Libn.
AMERICAN MINING CONGRESS - AMC LIBRARY
□ Washington, DC
Kessenich, Judy, Ref.Libn.
U.S. FOREST SERVICE - FOREST PRODUCTS
LABORATORY LIBRARY □ Madison, WI
Kessler, Barbara R., Ref.Libn.
COLUMBIA UNIVERSITY - LAW LIBRARY □ New
York, NY
Kessler, Beverly, Libn.
OHIO STATE SCHOOL FOR THE BLIND -
LIBRARY □ Columbus, OH
Kessler, Carl, Chf.
U.S. DEPT. OF THE INTERIOR - DIVISION OF
INFORMATION AND LIBRARY SERVICES - LAW
BRANCH □ Washington, DC
Kessler, Debbie, Libn.
FIRST BAPTIST CHURCH - LIBRARY □ St. Paul,
MN
Kessler, Deborah, Libn.
U.S. VETERANS ADMINISTRATION (KY-
Lexington) - MEDICAL CENTER LIBRARY □
Lexington, KY
Kessler, Ruth, Act.Dir.
OHIO STATE UNIVERSITY - LAW LIBRARY □
Columbus, OH
Kessler-Post, Nancy, Libn.
MUSEUM OF THE CITY OF NEW YORK -
LIBRARY □ New York, NY
Kester, Gary, Mgr., Res.Info.
MERCK & COMPANY, INC. - MERCK SHARP &
DOHME RESEARCH LABORATORIES -
RESEARCH INFORMATION SYSTEMS □ Rahway,
NJ
Ketchell, Debbie, Outreach Libn.
UNIVERSITY OF NEVADA, RENO - SAVITT
MEDICAL LIBRARY □ Reno, NV
Kethley, Sue, Libn.
WACO-MC LENNAN COUNTY LIBRARY -
SPECIAL COLLECTIONS DEPARTMENT □ Waco,
TX
Kettner, Judith, Sys.Libn.
AMERICAN EXPRESS COMPANY - CARD
DIVISION - WESTERN REGION OPERATIONS
CENTER - SYSTEMS LIBRARY □ Phoenix, AZ
Key, G.R.F., Rd.Adv.
DISTRICT OF COLUMBIA PUBLIC LIBRARY -
WASHINGTONIANA DIVISION □ Washington,
DC
Key, Jack D., Libn.
MAYO FOUNDATION - MAYO CLINIC LIBRARY □
Rochester, MN
Key, Mary P., Hd.Libn.
OHIO STATE UNIVERSITY - AGRICULTURE
LIBRARY □ Columbus, OH

Keys, Dr. Marshall, Dir.
CURRY COLLEGE - LOUIS R. LEVIN MEMORIAL
LIBRARY - SPECIAL COLLECTIONS† □ Milton,
MA
Keys, Sylvia A., Libn.
VINNELL CORPORATION - CORPORATE/
PROGRAM DEVELOPMENT LIBRARY □ Fairfax,
VA
Keyser, Meredith J., Dir., Lib.Serv.
COOPER INSTITUTE - KNOXVILLE
BUSINESS COLLEGE - LIBRARY □ Knoxville, TN
Keyserling, Leon H., Pres./Dir. of Staff
CONFERENCE ON ECONOMIC PROGRESS -
LIBRARY □ Washington, DC
Khan, A.R., Mgr., Tech.Info.Serv.
HENKEL CORPORATION - HENNEPIN
TECHNICAL CENTER LIBRARY □ Minneapolis,
MN
Khan, Erwyn, Dir.
RADIO ADVERTISING BUREAU - MARKETING
INFORMATION CENTER □ New York, NY
Khan, Syed, Asst. Life Sci.Libn.
PURDUE UNIVERSITY - LIFE SCIENCE LIBRARY
□ West Lafayette, IN
Kharbas, Datta, Libn.
UNIVERSITY OF ROCHESTER - MANAGEMENT
LIBRARY □ Rochester, NY
Kharbas, Datta S., Libn.
UNIVERSITY OF ROCHESTER - ASIA LIBRARY □
Rochester, NY
Khavari, Sue, Hd., Cat.
MARQUETTE UNIVERSITY - LEGAL RESEARCH
CENTER □ Milwaukee, WI
Kho, Miss Lian Tie, Libn.
YALE UNIVERSITY - SOUTHEAST ASIA
COLLECTION □ New Haven, CT
Khoo, Oon-Chor, Theol.Libn.
ORAL ROBERTS UNIVERSITY - GRADUATE
THEOLOGY LIBRARY - JOHN MESSICK
LEARNING RESOURCE CENTER □ Tulsa, OK
Khoury, George, Dir., Info.Serv.
CONFERENCE BOARD OF CANADA -
INFORMATION RESOURCE CENTER □ Ottawa,
ON
Kibbey, Ray Anne
SOUTHERN OREGON STATE COLLEGE -
LIBRARY □ Ashland, OR
Kibildis, Melba, Libn.
UNITED AUTOMOBILE, AEROSPACE &
AGRICULTURAL IMPLEMENT WORKERS OF
AMERICA - RESEARCH LIBRARY □ Detroit, MI
Kichuk, Diana, Libn.
CANADA - AGRICULTURE CANADA - RESEARCH
STATION, SASKATOON - LIBRARY □ Saskatoon,
SK
Kiczek, Steven A., Libn.
ST. MARY SEMINARY - JOSEPH M. BRUENING
LIBRARY □ Cleveland, OH
Kidd, Betty, Dir.
CANADA - PUBLIC ARCHIVES OF CANADA -
NATIONAL MAP COLLECTION □ Ottawa, ON
Kidd, Claren M., Libn.
UNIVERSITY OF OKLAHOMA - GEOLOGY
LIBRARY □ Norman, OK
Kidney, Ann, Asst.Libn.
POPE JOHN XXIII NATIONAL SEMINARY -
LIBRARY □ Weston, MA
Kiefer, Karen, Info.Spec.
UTAH INTERNATIONAL, INC. - INFORMATION
SERVICES/LIBRARY □ San Francisco, CA
Kiefer, Rosemary Milner, Info.Rsrcs.Mgr.
REICHHOLD CHEMICALS, INC. - RESEARCH
LIBRARY □ Pensacola, FL
Kiefer, Shirley
HARTFORD PUBLIC LIBRARY - REFERENCE AND
GENERAL READING DEPARTMENT □ Hartford,
CT
Kiefer, Susan, Hd. of Pub.Serv.
HAMLINE UNIVERSITY SCHOOL OF LAW -
LIBRARY □ St. Paul, MN
Kiehnle, Nancy, Libn.
GENERAL FOODS CORPORATION - FINANCIAL
INFORMATION CENTER □ White Plains, NY

Kielty, J., Mgr., Tech.Pubn.
AMERICAN SOCIETY OF SAFETY ENGINEERS -
TECHNICAL INFORMATION CENTER □ Park
Ridge, IL
Kiene, Andrea, Libn.
JENSEN (Rolf) & ASSOCIATES - LIBRARY □
Deerfield, IL
Kiernan, John, Jr., Hd.Libn.
WATERBURY STATE TECHNICAL COLLEGE -
HELEN HAHLO LIBRARY □ Waterbury, CT
Kiersky, Loretta J., Mgr.
THE BOC GROUP INC. - TECHNICAL CENTER -
INFORMATION CENTER □ Murray Hill, NJ
Kigar, Lorraine, Libn.
GRAND RAPIDS BAPTIST COLLEGE &
SEMINARY - MILLER LIBRARY □ Grand Rapids,
MI
Kiger, Robert W., Dir.
CARNEGIE-MELLON UNIVERSITY - HUNT
INSTITUTE FOR BOTANICAL DOCUMENTATION
□ Pittsburgh, PA
Kightlinger, Margret, Libn./Techn.
U.S. ARMY - LANGUAGE TRAINING FACILITY -
LIBRARY □ Ft. George G. Meade, MD
Kihl, Marilyn, Curric.Lab.
SUNY - COLLEGE AT BUFFALO - EDWARD H.
BUTLER LIBRARY □ Buffalo, NY
Kikta, Christine, Mgr., Info.Serv.
SOHIO CHEMCIAL COMPANY - INFORMATION
CENTER □ Cleveland, OH
Kikta, Stepan, Pres.
UKRAINIAN MUSEUM - ARCHIVES, INC. □
Cleveland, OH
Kilbourn, Richard C., Dir.
U.S. DEPT. OF COMMERCE - INTERNATIONAL
TRADE ADMINISTRATION - HARTFORD
DISTRICT OFFICE LIBRARY □ Hartford, CT
Kilbourne, John D., Dir.
SOCIETY OF THE CINCINNATI - ANDERSON
HOUSE LIBRARY AND MUSEUM □ Washington,
DC
Kilburn, Gudrun, Lit.Cat./Ref.Libn.
SUNY AT BUFFALO - MUSIC LIBRARY □ Buffalo,
NY
Kildegard, Arne, Mng.Ed.
MERRIAM CENTER LIBRARY □ Chicago, IL
Kile, Barbara, Hd.
RICE UNIVERSITY - GOVERNMENT
DOCUMENTS AND MICROFORMS DEPARTMENT
□ Houston, TX
Kilfoyle, Marjorie J., Ref.Libn.
POLAROID CORPORATION - RESEARCH
LIBRARY □ Cambridge, MA
Kilgore, Robert B., Info.Spec.
BURROUGHS WELLCOME COMPANY - LIBRARY
□ Research Triangle Park, NC
Kilkenny, Angela, Asst.Libn.
CANADIAN EMBASSY - LIBRARY □ Washington,
DC
Killen, Genevieve R., Dir., Med.Rec.
BRADFORD HOSPITAL - HUFF MEMORIAL
LIBRARY □ Bradford, PA
Killian, Sandra L., Supv., Lib.Serv.
MC DONNELL DOUGLAS CORPORATION - MC
DONNELL DOUGLAS ASTRONAUTICS COMPANY
- TECHNICAL LIBRARY SERVICES □ Huntington
Beach, CA
Killingsworth, Letty E., Lib.Tech.
FLUOR ENGINEERS, INC. - OCEAN SERVICES
DIVISION - LIBRARY □ Houston, TX
Killion, Vicki, Sci.Libn.
MIAMI UNIVERSITY - BRILL SCIENCE LIBRARY
□ Oxford, OH
Kilpatrick, Norman, Dir.
SURFACE MINING RESEARCH LIBRARY □
Charleston, WV
Kilrain, John J., Libn.
NEW YORK STATE DEPARTMENT OF
COMMERCE - LIBRARY □ Albany, NY
Kim, Bang, Hd., Doc.
SOUTH DAKOTA STATE UNIVERSITY - HILTON
M. BRIGGS LIBRARY □ Brookings, SD

Kim, Chin, Lib.Dir.
CALIFORNIA WESTERN SCHOOL OF LAW -
LIBRARY □ San Diego, CA

Kim, Chung N., Cat.Libn.
CORNELL UNIVERSITY - MARTIN P.
CATHERWOOD LIBRARY OF INDUSTRIAL AND
LABOR RELATIONS □ Ithaca, NY

Kim, Helen, Libn.
MUNGER, TOLLES & RICKERSHAUSER -
LIBRARY □ Los Angeles, CA

Kim, Helen K., Tech.Libn./Res.Chem.
WITCO CHEMICAL CORPORATION - LIBRARY □
Houston, TX

Kim, Mr. Ik-Sam, Hd.
UNIVERSITY OF CALIFORNIA, LOS ANGELES -
ORIENTAL LIBRARY □ Los Angeles, CA

Kim, Jeannie, Acq.Libn.
ILLINOIS INSTITUTE OF TECHNOLOGY -
INFORMATION AND LIBRARY RESOURCES
CENTER† □ Chicago, IL

Kim, Mr. Jei Whan, Libn.
HOWARD UNIVERSITY - HEALTH SCIENCES
LIBRARY - ANNEX (Pharmacy) □ Washington, DC

Kim, K.J., Pub.Serv.
WIDENER UNIVERSITY - WOLFGRAM
MEMORIAL LIBRARY □ Chester, PA

Kim, Kay, Sr.Lit. Searcher
SIGNAL UOP RESEARCH CENTER - TECHNICAL
INFORMATION CENTER □ Des Plaines, IL

Kim, Ke Chung, Cur.
PENNSYLVANIA STATE UNIVERSITY - FROST
ENTOMOLOGICAL MUSEUM - TAXONOMIC
RESEARCH LIBRARY □ University Park, PA

Kim, Moon H., Libn.
NISSAN MOTOR CORPORATION - CORPORATE
LIBRARY† □ Carson, CA

Kim, Mrs. Myung-Jha, AV Libn.
HOWARD UNIVERSITY - SCHOOL OF LAW -
ALLEN MERCER DANIEL LAW LIBRARY □
Washington, DC

Kim, Mrs. San Oak, Asst.Hd.
UNIVERSITY OF CALIFORNIA, LOS ANGELES -
EDUCATION & PSYCHOLOGY LIBRARY □ Los
Angeles, CA

Kim, Soon Duck, Cat.
SOLAR ENERGY RESEARCH INSTITUTE - SERI
TECHNICAL LIBRARY □ Golden, CO

Kim, Soowan Y., Hd., Japanese/Korean Sect
PRINCETON UNIVERSITY - GEST ORIENTAL
LIBRARY AND EAST ASIAN COLLECTIONS □
Princeton, NJ

Kim, Stella P., Hd., Tech.Proc.
BIOLA UNIVERSITY - LIBRARY □ La Mirada, CA

Kim, Sungha, Asst.Libn./Korean Sect.
HARVARD UNIVERSITY - HARVARD-YENCHING
LIBRARY □ Cambridge, MA

Kim, Won H., Libn.
U.S. NATL. PARK SERVICE - STATUE OF
LIBERTY NATL. MONUMENT - AMERICAN
MUSEUM OF IMMIGRATION - LIBRARY □ New
York, NY

Kimball, Dorothy R., Chf.
U.S. ARMY - LANGUAGE TRAINING FACILITY -
LIBRARY □ Ft. George G. Meade, MD

Kimball, Richard H., Exec.Dir.
NORTH COUNTRY REFERENCE & RESEARCH
RESOURCES COUNCIL - LIBRARY □ Canton, NY

Kimberlin, Robert, Act.Hd.
CATHOLIC UNIVERSITY OF AMERICA -
ENGINEERING/ARCHITECTURE/
MATHEMATICS LIBRARY □ Washington, DC

Kimberlin, Robert F., III, Chf.
FEDERAL ENERGY REGULATORY COMMISSION -
LIBRARY □ Washington, DC

Kimberly, Laura, Asst.Libn. for Tech.Serv.
U.S. COURT OF APPEALS, DISTRICT OF
COLUMBIA CIRCUIT - LIBRARY □ Washington,
DC

Kimble, Kathleen R., Libn.
MISSOULIAN NEWSPAPER - LIBRARY □
Missoula, MT

Kimbro, L.W., Tech.Libn.
LOCKHEED-GEORGIA COMPANY - TECHNICAL
INFORMATION DEPARTMENT □ Marietta, GA

Kimzey, M. Virginia, Coord., Health Sci.Lib.
TEXAS WOMAN'S UNIVERSITY, DALLAS
CENTER - F.W. AND BESSIE DYE MEMORIAL
LIBRARY □ Dallas, TX

Kinch, Michael, Agriculture-Forestry
OREGON STATE UNIVERSITY - WILLIAM
JASPER KERR LIBRARY □ Corvallis, OR

Kindlin, Jean, Dir., Lib. & Media Serv.
UNIVERSITY OF PITTSBURGH - SCHOOL OF
LIBRARY & INFORMATION SCIENCE -
INTERNATIONAL LIB. INFO. CTR. □ Pittsburgh,
PA

Kindlin, Jean, Dir., Lib. & Media Serv.
UNIVERSITY OF PITTSBURGH - SCHOOL OF
LIBRARY & INFORMATION SCIENCE -
LIBRARY† □ Pittsburgh, PA

Kindness, Faith Dickhaut, Fine Arts Libn.
WHEATON COLLEGE - LIBRARY - FINE ARTS
COLLECTION □ Norton, MA

Kinevan, Col. M.E., Prof. of Law
U.S. AIR FORCE ACADEMY - LAW LIBRARY □
Colorado Springs, CO

King, Albert
GENEALOGICAL SOCIETY OF NEW JERSEY -
MANUSCRIPT COLLECTIONS □ New Brunswick,
NJ

King, Ann H., Asst.Ref.Libn.
UNIVERSITY OF FLORIDA - HUME LIBRARY □
Gainesville, FL

King, Annie G., Hd.Libn.
TUSKEGEE INSTITUTE - HOLLIS BURKE
FRISSELL LIBRARY-ARCHIVES □ Tuskegee
Institute, AL

King, Betsy, Libn.
HONEYWELL, INC. - ENGINEERING LIBRARY □
Tampa, FL

King, Betty Claire, Hd.
SAN ANTONIO PUBLIC LIBRARY AND
INFORMATION CENTER - HARRY HERTZBERG
CIRCUS COLLECTION □ San Antonio, TX

King, Betty Jeanne, Anl.Libn.Res.
ROCKWELL INTERNATIONAL - ROCKWELL
HANFORD OPERATIONS - BASALT WASTE
ISOLATION PROJECT - LIBRARY □ Richland, WA

King, Carol, Ref.Libn.
PUBLIC UTILITY COMMISSION OF TEXAS -
LIBRARY □ Austin, TX

King, Carole, Prof.Asst.
ST. PAUL PUBLIC LIBRARY - ART AND MUSIC □
St. Paul, MN

King, Charles H., Jr., Cat.
SMITHSONIAN INSTITUTION - NATIONAL
MUSEUM OF AMERICAN ART/NATIONAL
PORTRAIT GALLERY - LIBRARY □ Washington,
DC

King, Christee, Mgr., Lib.Serv.
TUCSON MEDICAL CENTER - MEDICAL
LIBRARY □ Tucson, AZ

King, Cornelia, Rare Book Bibliog.
TEMPLE UNIVERSITY - CENTRAL LIBRARY
SYSTEM - RARE BOOK & MANUSCRIPT
COLLECTION □ Philadelphia, PA

King, Cyrus B., Asst.Dir.Coll.Dev.
NORTH CAROLINA STATE UNIVERSITY - D.H.
HILL LIBRARY □ Raleigh, NC

King, David E., Libn.
STANDARD EDUCATIONAL CORPORATION -
EDITORIAL LIBRARY □ Chicago, IL

King, Dorothy T., Libn.
EAST HAMPTON FREE LIBRARY - LONG ISLAND
COLLECTION □ East Hampton, NY

King, Duane, Exec.Dir.
CHEROKEE NATIONAL HISTORICAL SOCIETY,
INC. - CHEROKEE NATIONAL ARCHIVES □
Tahlequah, OK

King, Dwight, Ref.Libn.
UNIVERSITY OF BALTIMORE - LAW LIBRARY □
Baltimore, MD

King, F. Wayne, Dir.
UNIVERSITY OF FLORIDA - FLORIDA STATE
MUSEUM LIBRARY □ Gainesville, FL

King, Helen, Oper.Mgr.
HARRAH'S AUTOMOTIVE LIBRARY □ Reno, NV

King, Jae Luree, Educ.Mtls.Coord.
CHICAGO URBAN SKILLS INSTITUTE -
DAWSON SKILL CENTER LIBRARY □ Chicago, IL

King, James W., Info.Spec.
NITROGEN FIXATION BY TROPICAL
AGRICULTURAL LEGUMES - NIFTAL
INFORMATION CENTER □ Paia, HI

King, Jane E., Chf.Libn.
BANK OF CANADA - LIBRARY □ Ottawa, ON

King, Jean E., Doc.Libn.
GTE - COMMUNICATION SYSTEMS DIVISION -
MAIN LIBRARY □ Needham Heights, MA

King, Jean T., Acq.Libn.
GTE - COMMUNICATION SYSTEMS DIVISION -
MAIN LIBRARY □ Needham Heights, MA

King, Johnny L., Libn.
THE (Shreveport) TIMES - LIBRARY □
Shreveport, LA

King, Joseph A. Cutshall, Dir.
GLENS FALLS-QUEENSBURY HISTORICAL
ASSN., INC. - CHAPMAN HISTORICAL MUSM. -
RUSSELL M.L. CARSON MEMORIAL LIB. □ Glens
Falls, NY

King, Karen P., Libn.
SASKATCHEWAN ALCOHOLISM COMMISSION -
LIBRARY □ Regina, SK

King, Katherine, Fed.Leg.Libn.
ARENT, FOX, KINTNER, PLOTKIN & KAHN -
LIBRARY† □ Washington, DC

King, Luci, Lib.Chm.
GRAND RAPIDS ART MUSEUM - MC BRIDE
LIBRARY □ Grand Rapids, MI

King, Lynn, Libn.
LEWISTON TRIBUNE LIBRARY □ Lewiston, ID

King, Dr. Margot, Libn.
UNIVERSITY OF SASKATCHEWAN - ST.
THOMAS MORE COLLEGE - SHANNON LIBRARY
□ Saskatoon, SK

King, Maryde Fahey, Mgr.
GENERAL ELECTRIC COMPANY - CORPORATE
RESEARCH & DEVELOPMENT - WHITNEY
INFORMATION SERVICES □ Schenectady, NY

King, Olive, Bus. & Mgt.Libn.
RYERSON POLYTECHNICAL INSTITUTE -
LEARNING RESOURCES CENTRE □ Toronto, ON

King, Dr. Patricia M., Dir.
RADCLIFFE COLLEGE - ARTHUR AND
ELIZABETH SCHLESINGER LIBRARY ON THE
HISTORY OF WOMEN IN AMERICA □
Cambridge, MA

King, Peggy D., Leg.Libn.
KENTUCKY STATE LEGISLATIVE RESEARCH
COMMISSION - LIBRARY □ Frankfort, KY

King, Peter, Hd., Ed.Serv.
DALHOUSIE UNIVERSITY - W.K. KELLOGG
HEALTH SCIENCES LIBRARY □ Halifax, NS

King, Radford G., Dir.
UNIVERSITY OF SOUTHERN CALIFORNIA -
NASA INDUSTRIAL APPLICATION CENTER
(NIAC) □ Los Angeles, CA

King, Samuel, Ref.Libn.
NOVA SCOTIA AGRICULTURAL COLLEGE -
LIBRARY □ Truro, NS

King, Virginia, Rpt.Cat.
U.S. AIR FORCE WEAPONS LABORATORY -
TECHNICAL LIBRARY □ Kirtland AFB, NM

King, Wanda W., Med.Libn.
HINDS GENERAL HOSPITAL - WILLIAM M.
SUTTLE MEDICAL LIBRARY □ Jackson, MS

King, William E., Univ.Archv.
DUKE UNIVERSITY - ARCHIVES □ Durham, NC

Kingman, Elizabeth Y., Libn.
SCHOOL OF AMERICAN RESEARCH - LIBRARY □
Santa Fe, NM

Kingman, Winifred, Libn.
JACK LONDON RESEARCH CENTER AND
LIBRARY □ Glen Ellen, CA

Kingsbury, Mildred E., Lib.Dir.
MARQUETTE GENERAL HOSPITAL - KEVIN F.
O'BRIEN HEALTH SCIENCES LIBRARY □
Marquette, MI

Kingshill, Mary, Libn.
HELLMUTH, OBATA & KASSABAUM, INC. -
LIBRARY/ARCHIVES □ San Francisco, CA

Kingsley, Thomas C., Libn.
SYRACUSE UNIVERSITY - LAW LIBRARY □
Syracuse, NY

Kinkaid, Yvonne A., Chf.
U.S. AIR FORCE - AIR FORCE SYSTEMS
COMMAND - TECHNICAL INFORMATION
CENTER □ Washington, DC

Kinnaird, Helga, Chf.Libn.
NORTHERN ALBERTA INSTITUTE OF
TECHNOLOGY - LEARNING RESOURCE CENTRE
□ Edmonton, AB

Kinne, Abby, Founder
CENTER FOR HUMANE OPTIONS IN
CHILDBIRTH EXPERIENCES (CHOICE) -
LIBRARY □ Columbus, OH

Kinne, Jane S., Pres.
PHOTO RESEARCHERS, INC. - LIBRARY □ New
York, NY

Kinnett, David, Mss.Libn.
STATE HISTORICAL SOCIETY OF IOWA -
LIBRARY □ Iowa City, IA

Kinney, John M., State Archv.
ALASKA STATE DEPARTMENT OF
ADMINISTRATION - STATE ARCHIVES □
Juneau, AK

Kinney, Margaret M., Chf.Libn.
U.S. VETERANS ADMINISTRATION (NY-Bronx) -
MEDICAL CENTER LIBRARY □ Bronx, NY

Kinney, Mary, Tech.Serv.Libn.
MAITLAND PUBLIC LIBRARY - ANDRE SMITH
COLLECTION □ Maitland, FL

Kinney, Nancy S., Dir. of Res.
WESTERN COSTUME COMPANY - RESEARCH
LIBRARY □ Los Angeles, CA

Kinney, Paul J., Musm.Cur.
U.S. NATL. PARK SERVICE - STATUE OF
LIBERTY NATL. MONUMENT - AMERICAN
MUSEUM OF IMMIGRATION - LIBRARY □ New
York, NY

Kinney, Therese C., Rsrcs.Coord.
UTICA MUTUAL INSURANCE COMPANY -
RESOURCE CENTER □ New Hartford, NY

Kinsedahl, Bob, Libn.
U.S. NAVY - NAVAL SUPPORT ACTIVITY -
LIBRARY □ Seattle, WA

Kinsella, Wendy, Hd.Libn.
ALBERTA - DEPARTMENT OF LABOUR -
LIBRARY SERVICES □ Edmonton, AB

Kinsey, Carol, Bus.Libn.
EASTMAN KODAK COMPANY - TEXAS EASTMAN
COMPANY - BUSINESS LIBRARY □ Longview, TX

Kinsey, Carol, Circ./ILL
NEW BRUNSWICK THEOLOGICAL SEMINARY -
GARDNER A. SAGE LIBRARY □ New Brunswick,
NJ

Kinslow, Barbara A., Libn.
KAMAN SCIENCES CORPORATION - LIBRARY □
Colorado Springs, CO

Kinsman, Mary Jean, Res.
JEFFERSON COUNTY OFFICE OF HISTORIC
PRESERVATION AND ARCHIVES □ Louisville, KY

Kinzy, Louise, Libn.
APPALACHIA EDUCATIONAL LABORATORY -
RESEARCH & INFORMATION CENTER □
Charleston, WV

Kipel, Vitaut, Act.Chf.
NEW YORK PUBLIC LIBRARY - SCIENCE AND
TECHNOLOGY RESEARCH CENTER □ New York,
NY

Kipel, Zora, Libn.
BYELORUSSIAN INSTITUTE OF ARTS AND
SCIENCES, INC. - LIBRARY □ Rutherford, NJ

Kipilii, Mary Lu, Libn./AV Spec.
HAWAII STATE LIBRARY - FINE ARTS AND
AUDIOVISUAL SECTION □ Honolulu, HI

Kirby, Chris, Chf., Photograph Ret.
CANADA - NATIONAL MUSEUMS OF CANADA -
LIBRARY SERVICES DIRECTORATE □ Ottawa,
ON

Kirby, Connie, Asst.Doc.Libn.
OKLAHOMA STATE UNIVERSITY - DOCUMENTS
DEPARTMENT □ Stillwater, OK

Kirby, Don, Chf., Ref.Sect.
U.S. ARMY - ENGINEER WATERWAYS
EXPERIMENT STATION - TECHNICAL
INFORMATION CENTER □ Vicksburg, MS

Kirby, Paul, Info.Sys.Anl.
SANDIA NATIONAL LABORATORIES -
TECHNICAL LIBRARY □ Albuquerque, NM

Kirby, Robert, Asst.Libn.
INDIANA UNIVERSITY OF PENNSYLVANIA -
UNIVERSITY LIBRARY □ Indiana, PA

Kircher, Roland E., Dir.
UNITED METHODIST CHURCH - WESLEY
THEOLOGICAL SEMINARY - LIBRARY □
Washington, DC

Kirchfeld, Friedhelm, Libn.
NATIONAL COLLEGE OF NATUROPATHIC
MEDICINE - LIBRARY □ Portland, OR

Kirchner, Andras, Med.Libn.
UNIVERSITY OF CALGARY - MEDICAL
LIBRARY† □ Calgary, AB

Kirchner, Elizabeth, Chf.Med.Libn.
CALGARY GENERAL HOSPITAL - LIBRARY
SERVICES □ Calgary, AB

Kirchner, Elizabeth, Dir./Libn.
ST. LOUIS MERCANTILE LIBRARY
ASSOCIATION - LIBRARY □ St. Louis, MO

Kiriazis, Judy, Exec.Dir.
LAKE MICHIGAN FEDERATION -
ENVIRONMENTAL LIBRARY □ Chicago, IL

Kirk, Cheryl, Info.Spec.
STANDARD OIL COMPANY OF INDIANA -
CENTRAL RESEARCH LIBRARY □ Naperville, IL

Kirk, Darcy, Tech.Serv.
BOSTON COLLEGE - LAW SCHOOL LIBRARY† □
Newton Centre, MA

Kirk, Denise L., Dir., Libs.
MISERICORDIA HOSPITAL - MEDICAL
LIBRARY† □ Bronx, NY

Kirk, Eliza, Acq.Libn.
MEMPHIS STATE UNIVERSITY LIBRARIES -
SCHOOL OF LAW LIBRARY □ Memphis, TN

Kirk, James H., Libn.
ST. CLARE'S HOSPITAL & HEALTH CENTER -
MEDICAL LIBRARY □ New York, NY

Kirk, Jay H., Hd., Sci.Lib.
MARQUETTE UNIVERSITY - SCIENCE LIBRARY
□ Milwaukee, WI

Kirk, Muriel S., Coord. for Lib.
MUSEUM OF FINE ARTS - ART REFERENCE
LIBRARY □ St. Petersburg, FL

Kirk, Tom L., Chf.Libn.
U.S. AIR FORCE BASE - VANCE BASE LIBRARY □
Vance AFB, OK

Kirkbride, Becky, Libn.
OKLAHOMA STATE UNIVERSITY - SCHOOL OF
TECHNICAL TRAINING - OKMULGEE BRANCH
LIBRARY □ Okmulgee, OK

Kirkbride, Pamela, Res.
BOSTON CONSULTING GROUP - WEST COAST
INFORMATION CENTER □ Menlo Park, CA

Kirkbride, Susan, Ref.Libn.
UNIVERSITY OF WISCONSIN, MADISON -
CENTER FOR HEALTH SCIENCES LIBRARIES† □
Madison, WI

Kirking, Clayton C., Libn.
PHOENIX ART MUSEUM - LIBRARY □ Phoenix,
AZ

Kirkland, James A., Libn.
TEXAS BAPTIST INSTITUTE/SEMINARY -
LIBRARY □ Henderson, TX

Kirkland, Talley, Hist.
U.S. NATL. PARK SERVICE - FORT PULASKI
NATL. MONUMENT - LIBRARY □ Tybee Island,
GA

Kirklin, Linda, Jr.Libn.
IBM CORPORATION - BOULDER LIBRARY □
Boulder, CO

Kirkman, Jacqueline N., Tech.Libn.
MARTIN MARIETTA CHEMICALS - SODYECO
DIVISION - TECHNICAL LIBRARY □ Charlotte,
NC

Kirkman, Penny, Dir., Lib.Serv.
YPSILANTI REGIONAL PSYCHIATRIC HOSPITAL
- STAFF LIBRARY □ Ypsilanti, MI

Kirkpatrick, Brett A., Libn.
NEW YORK ACADEMY OF MEDICINE - LIBRARY
□ New York, NY

Kirkpatrick, Carol, Lib.Ck.
MOUNTAIN STATES ENERGY, INC. - CDIF
TECHNICAL LIBRARY □ Butte, MT

Kirkpatrick, Mrs. Gabriel W., Med.Libn.
KENNEBEC VALLEY MEDICAL CENTER -
MEDICAL LIBRARY □ Augusta, ME

Kirkpatrick, Josephine, Chm.
INDIAN RIVER MEMORIAL HOSPITAL -
PROFESSIONAL LIBRARY □ Vero Beach, FL

Kirkpatrick, Mel, Libn.
IDS/AMERICAN EXPRESS, INC. - INVESTMENT
LIBRARY □ Minneapolis, MN

Kirkpatrick, Nancy, Hd., Slide Dept.
ART INSTITUTE OF CHICAGO - RYERSON AND
BURNHAM LIBRARIES □ Chicago, IL

Kirkwood, Chris, Act.Dir.
VALPARAISO UNIVERSITY - LAW LIBRARY □
Valparaiso, IN

Kirkwood, Isabell, Tech.Serv.Supv.
FLORIDA STATE DIVISION OF ARCHIVES,
HISTORY & RECORDS MANAGEMENT - FLORIDA
STATE ARCHIVES □ Tallahassee, FL

Kirkwood, Dr. K., Chf.Res.Off.
PEEL COUNTY BOARD OF EDUCATION - J.A.
TURNER PROFESSIONAL LIBRARY □
Mississauga, ON

Kirkwood, Patricia, Ref.Libn.
BELL COMMUNICATIONS RESEARCH, INC. -
INFORMATION RESOURCES SERVICES CENTER
□ Livingston, NJ

Kirkwood, Patricia E., Libn.
CLARK DIETZ ENGINEERS - LIBRARY □ Urbana,
IL

Kirlin, George B., Libn.
KIRKLAND & ELLIS - LIBRARY □ Washington, DC

Kirn, Judith, Asst.Libn.
ST. MARY'S SEMINARY - ST. MARY'S OF THE
BARRENS LIBRARY □ Perryville, MO

Kirner, Clara M., Spec.Coll.Libn.
GLASSBORO STATE COLLEGE - SAVITZ
LIBRARY - STEWART ROOM □ Glassboro, NJ

Kirsch, Anne, Med.Libn.
CENTRAL SUFFOLK HOSPITAL - MEDICAL
LIBRARY† □ Riverhead, NY

Kirsch, Gerald B., ILL Libn.
SUNY - AGRICULTURAL AND TECHNICAL
COLLEGE AT COBLESKILL - JARED VAN
WAGENEN, JR. LEARNING RESOURCE CENTER†
□ Cobleskill, NY

Kirsch, John A.W., Dir.
UNIVERSITY OF WISCONSIN, MADISON -
ZOOLOGICAL MUSEUM LIBRARY □ Madison, WI

Kirsch, Judith L., Tech.Info.Spec.
U.S. NATL. INSTITUTES OF HEALTH - NATL.
INST. OF NEUROLOGICAL & COMMUNICATIVE
DISORDERS & STROKE - EPILEPSY LIB. □
Bethesda, MD

Kirsch, Mary, Circ./ILL
HUDSON VALLEY COMMUNITY COLLEGE -
DWIGHT MARVIN LEARNING RESOURCES
CENTER □ Troy, NY

Kirsh, Julie, Chf.Libn.
TORONTO SUN - LIBRARY □ Toronto, ON

Kirshenbaum, Anne, Libn.
TEMPLE BETH EL - LIBRARY □ Rochester, NY

Kirven, Marian, Libn.
SWEDENBORG SCHOOL OF RELIGION -
LIBRARY □ Newton, MA

Kiser, Dr. Donald L., Supv.
GRAIN PROCESSING CORPORATION -
TECHNICAL INFORMATION CENTER, □
Muscatine, IA

Kishinsky, Amy J., Therapeutic Rec.Spec.
BETH ABRAHAM HOSPITAL - PATIENT LIBRARY
□ Bronx, NY

Kiss, Terri, Chf.Libn.
U.S. ARMY POST - FORT MC PHERSON -
LIBRARY SYSTEM □ Ft. McPherson, GA

Kiss, Terry, Ref.Libn.
U.S. ARMY - ENGINEER WATERWAYS
EXPERIMENT STATION - TECHNICAL
INFORMATION CENTER □ Vicksburg, MS

Kissel, Elaine Lynette, Med.Libn.
HOLY CROSS HOSPITAL - HEALTH SCIENCE
LIBRARY □ Detroit, MI

Kissoore, Mr. D., Hd., Tech.Serv. & Sys.
ROYAL MILITARY COLLEGE OF CANADA -
MASSEY LIBRARY & SCIENCE/ENGINEERING
LIBRARY □ Kingston, ON

Kisthardt, James, Hd., Cat.Dept.
TRENTON FREE PUBLIC LIBRARY -
GOVERNMENT DOCUMENTS COLLECTION □
Trenton, NJ

Kistler, Robert, Dir.
U.S. DEPT. OF COMMERCE - INTERNATIONAL
TRADE ADMINISTRATION - PHILADELPHIA
DISTRICT OFFICE LIBRARY □ Philadelphia, PA

Kistler, Winifred E., Pub.Serv.Libn.
UNIVERSITY OF CALIFORNIA, DAVIS - HEALTH
SCIENCES LIBRARY □ Davis, CA

Kistner, Glen, Hd., Circ.
NORTHEASTERN ILLINOIS UNIVERSITY -
LIBRARY □ Chicago, IL

Kitchen, Nancy J., Dir.
PEPPERDINE UNIVERSITY - LAW LIBRARY □
Malibu, CA

Kitchens, Caroline, Pub.Info.Off.
ATLANTA BUREAU OF PLANNING - LIBRARY □
Atlanta, GA

Kitcher, Philip, Dir.
UNIVERSITY OF MINNESOTA - MINNESOTA
CENTER FOR PHILOSOPHY OF SCIENCE -
DEPARTMENTAL LIBRARY □ Minneapolis, MN

Kitt, Sandra, Libn.
AMERICAN MUSEUM OF NATURAL HISTORY -
HAYDEN PLANETARIUM - RICHARD S. PERKIN
LIBRARY □ New York, NY

Kittelson, David, Assoc.Lib.Spec.
UNIVERSITY OF HAWAII - SPECIAL
COLLECTIONS - ARCHIVES □ Honolulu, HI

Kittrell, Kay, Mgr.
WILLIAMS BROTHERS ENGINEERING COMPANY
- TECHNICAL INFORMATION CENTER† □ Tulsa,
OK

Kivel, Andy, Search Serv.
INVESTIGATIVE RESOURCE CENTER - DATA
CENTER □ Oakland, CA

Kjellberg, Judith, Info.Off.
UNIVERSITY OF TORONTO - CENTRE FOR
URBAN AND COMMUNITY STUDIES -
RESOURCE ROOM □ Toronto, ON

Klaassen, David, Cur.
UNIVERSITY OF MINNESOTA - SOCIAL
WELFARE HISTORY ARCHIVES □ Minneapolis,
MN

Kladko, Joseph, Asst.Dir., Tech.Oper.
STANFORD UNIVERSITY - HOOVER
INSTITUTION ON WAR, REVOLUTION AND
PEACE - LIBRARY □ Stanford, CA

Klahn, Tanemi, Law Libn.
PLACER COUNTY LAW LIBRARY □ Auburn, CA

Klammer, Paul, Musm.Dir.
BROWN COUNTY HISTORICAL SOCIETY -
MUSEUM LIBRARY □ New Ulm, MN

Klammer, Werner, Coord., AV Serv.
CONCORDIA TEACHERS COLLEGE - LINK
LIBRARY □ Seward, NE

Klamner, Lori, Libn.
ENVIRONMENTAL ACTION COALITION -
LIBRARY/RESOURCE CENTER □ New York, NY

Klasey, Glory, Hd.Libn.
KANKAKEE DAILY JOURNAL - LIBRARY □
Kankakee, IL

Klasing, Jane P., Educ.Spec., Media
BROWARD COUNTY PUBLIC SCHOOLS -
LEARNING RESOURCES - PROFESSIONAL
LIBRARY □ Davie, FL

Klass, Lionel, Ed. & Libn.
BROOKLYN DAILY LIBRARY □ Brooklyn, NY

Klassen, Bonnie M., Libn.
SALT RIVER PROJECT - LIBRARY □ Phoenix, AZ

Klassen, Georgeen, Asst.Chf.Archv.
GLENBOW-ALBERTA INSTITUTE - LIBRARY &
ARCHIVES □ Calgary, AB

Klassen, Krys, Supv., Info.Sys.
IMPERIAL OIL, LTD. - BUSINESS INFORMATION
CENTRE □ Toronto, ON

Klassen, Laura, Tech.Serv.Libn.
BRIERCREST BIBLE COLLEGE - ARCHIBALD
LIBRARY □ Caronport, SK

Klatt, Mary, Coll.Libn.
LOYOLA UNIVERSITY OF CHICAGO - MEDICAL
CENTER LIBRARY □ Maywood, IL

Klaw, Paula, Pres.
MOVIE STAR NEWS - PHOTOGRAPH
COLLECTION □ New York, NY

Klayman, Cesira, Info.Spec.
EUROPEAN COMMUNITY INFORMATION
SERVICE - LIBRARY □ Washington, DC

Klecker, Anita N., Dir. of Lib.Serv.
TORRANCE MEMORIAL HOSPITAL MEDICAL
CENTER - HEALTH SCIENCES LIBRARY □
Torrance, CA

Kleczewski, Bro. Eugene, Dir.
FRANCISCAN MONASTERY LIBRARY □
Washington, DC

Kleedorfer, Marsha L., Cur.
PENNSYLVANIA CANAL SOCIETY - CANAL
MUSEUM - RESEARCH LIBRARY □ Easton, PA

Kleiber, Michael C., Hd.Libn.
UNIVERSITY OF CALIFORNIA, BERKELEY -
INSTITUTE OF TRANSPORTATION STUDIES
LIBRARY □ Berkeley, CA

Klein, Agnes, Adm.
YESHIVA UNIVERSITY - ALBERT EINSTEIN
COLLEGE OF MEDICINE - DEPARTMENT OF
ANESTHESIOLOGY - LIBRARY □ Bronx, NY

Klein, Elizabeth, Libn.
HOLY FAMILY HOSPITAL - HEALTH SCIENCES
LIBRARY □ Des Plaines, IL

Klein, Francine R., Off.Mgr.
FOI SERVICES, INC. - LIBRARY □ Rockville, MD

Klein, Francis, Pres.
CARVER COUNTY HISTORICAL SOCIETY, INC. -
LIBRARY □ Waconia, MN

Klein, Henry, Libn.
AMERICAN INSTITUTE FOR MARXIST STUDIES
- LIBRARY □ New York, NY

Klein, Jeffrey, Audiotape Libn.
CBS INC. - CBS NEWS AUDIO ARCHIVES □ New
York, NY

Klein, Joanne S., Tech.Libn.
JONES AND LAUGHLIN STEEL CORPORATION -
GRAHAM LIBRARY □ Pittsburgh, PA

Klein, Larry, Mss.Cur.
TEACHERS COLLEGE - MILBANK MEMORIAL
LIBRARY □ New York, NY

Klein, Leanne A., Assoc.Cur., Coll.Mgt.
MINNESOTA MUSEUM OF ART - LIBRARY □ St.
Paul, MN

Klein, Lori, Med.Ref./Search Anl.
INDIANA UNIVERSITY, INDIANAPOLIS -
SCHOOL OF MEDICINE LIBRARY □ Indianapolis,
IN

Klein, Lori, Chf., Lib.Serv.
U.S. VETERANS ADMINISTRATION (SD-Sioux
Falls) - HOSPITAL LIBRARY □ Sioux Falls, SD

Klein, Michele S., Dir., Lib.Serv.
CHILDREN'S HOSPITAL OF MICHIGAN -
MEDICAL LIBRARY □ Detroit, MI

Klein, Regina, Bus.Libn.
MONSANTO COMPANY - INFORMATION
CENTER □ St. Louis, MO

Klein, Richard S., Dir., Lib.Serv.
SCHOLL (Dr. William M.) COLLEGE OF
PODIATRIC MEDICINE - LIBRARY □ Chicago, IL

Klein, Robert, Libn.
U.S. VETERANS ADMINISTRATION (MO-St.
Louis) - HOSPITAL LIBRARY □ St. Louis, MO

Klein, Sami, Chf.
ENVIRONMENTAL PROTECTION AGENCY -
HEADQUARTERS LIBRARY† □ Washington, DC

Klein, Sami, Chf., Lib.Info.Serv.
U.S. NATL. BUREAU OF STANDARDS - LIBRARY
□ Washington, DC

Klein, Stephanie, Libn./Archv.
MISSOURI HISTORICAL SOCIETY - ARCHIVES
AND MANUSCRIPTS □ St. Louis, MO

Klein, Stephanie A., Libn./Archv.
MISSOURI HISTORICAL SOCIETY - RESEARCH
LIBRARY □ St. Louis, MO

Klein, Susan, Lib.Instr.
UNIVERSITY OF WISCONSIN, LA CROSSE -
MURPHY LIBRARY □ La Crosse, WI

Klein, Susan R., Hd.Libn.
STURGIS LIBRARY† □ Barnstable, MA

Klein, Wells C., Exec.Dir.
AMERICAN COUNCIL FOR NATIONALITIES
SERVICE - LIBRARY AND INFORMATION
CENTER □ New York, NY

Kleinbaum, Sharon, Asst.Dir.
NATIONAL YIDDISH BOOK CENTER, INC. -
LIBRARY □ Amherst, MA

Kleindienst, John, Sr.Res.Assoc.
MISSOURI STATE DIVISION OF COMMUNITY
AND ECONOMIC DEVELOPMENT - RESEARCH
LIBRARY □ Jefferson City, MO

Kleiner, Donna, Sr.Info.Spec.
SRI INTERNATIONAL - LIBRARY AND
RESEARCH INFORMATION SERVICES
DEPARTMENT □ Menlo Park, CA

Kleiner, Jane
LOUISIANA STATE UNIVERSITY - REFERENCE
SERVICES □ Baton Rouge, LA

Kleinhesselink, Don, Cur. of Hist.
RIVERSIDE COUNTY HISTORICAL
COMMISSION - LIBRARY □ Rubidoux, CA

Kleinman, Elsa C., Libn.
CALIFORNIA STATE DEPARTMENT OF
EDUCATION - SCHOOL FOR THE DEAF LIBRARY
□ Fremont, CA

Kleinmuntz, Dalia S., Lib.Dir.
GRANT HOSPITAL OF CHICAGO - LINDON SEED
LIBRARY □ Chicago, IL

Kleinschmidt, Betty, Asst.Libn
BETHEL THEOLOGICAL SEMINARY - RESOURCE
CENTER □ St. Paul, MN

Klekner, Paul M., Libn.
HONEYWELL, INC. - COMMERCIAL DIVISION -
LIBRARY □ Arlington Heights, IL

Kleman, Eleanor, Med.Libn.
PRINCE GEORGE'S GENERAL HOSPITAL &
MEDICAL CENTER - SAUL SCHWARTZBACH
MEMORIAL LIBRARY □ Cheverly, MD

Klemarczyk, Laurice, Libn.
HARTFORD INSURANCE GROUP - LOSS
CONTROL DEPARTMENT LIBRARY □ Hartford,
CT

Klembara, D., Supv., Internal Info.Sys.
SCM CORPORATION - GLIDDEN COATINGS &
RESINS DIVISION/DURKEE FOODS DIVISION -
TECHNICAL INFORMATION SERVICES □
Strongsville, OH

Klemm, Carol B., Staff Coord.
UNION CARBIDE CORPORATION - TECHNICAL
INFORMATION SERVICE □ Bound Brook, NJ

Klemmer, Sara Gesler, Hd.Libn.
CHARLOTTE OBSERVER AND THE CHARLOTTE
NEWS - LIBRARY □ Charlotte, NC

Klemt, Calvin, Libn.
AUSTIN PRESBYTERIAN THEOLOGICAL
SEMINARY - STITT LIBRARY □ Austin, TX

Klepfisz, Rose, Dir., Archv.
AMERICAN JEWISH JOINT DISTRIBUTION
COMMITTEE - ARCHIVES □ New York, NY

Klepich, David P., Hd., Tech.Serv.
EG&G, INC. - IDAHO NATIONAL ENGINEERING LABORATORY - INEL TECHNICAL LIBRARY □ Idaho Falls, ID

Klepper, Michael, Media Serv.Libn.
UNIVERSITY OF VIRGINIA - ARTHUR J. MORRIS LAW LIBRARY □ Charlottesville, VA

Kleptach, Sharon M., Tech.Serv.Libn.
SHENANDOAH COLLEGE & CONSERVATORY OF MUSIC - HOWE LIBRARY □ Winchester, VA

Klesney, S.P.
DOW CHEMICAL COMPANY - TECHNICAL INFORMATION SERVICES - CENTRAL REPORT INDEX □ Midland, MI

Klesney, S.P.
DOW CHEMICAL COMPANY - TECHNICAL INFORMATION SERVICES - CHEMICAL LIBRARY □ Midland, MI

Kley, Ronald J., Musm. Registrar/Cur.
MAINE STATE MUSEUM - RESOURCE CENTER □ Augusta, ME

Klieman, Janet S., Med.Libn.
ST. MARY OF NAZARETH HOSPITAL - SISTER STELLA LOUISE HEALTH SCIENCE LIBRARY† □ Chicago, IL

Klika, Mary, Film Libn.
UNIVERSITY OF NEBRASKA, LINCOLN - INSTRUCTIONAL MEDIA CENTER □ Lincoln, NE

Klimiades, Mario N., Libn.
AMERIND FOUNDATION, INC. - FULTON-HAYDEN MEMORIAL LIBRARY □ Dragoon, AZ

Kliminski, Diane M., Tech.Libn.
INGERSOLL-RAND RESEARCH, INC. - TECHNICAL LIBRARY □ Princeton, NJ

Klimley, Susan, Libn.
COLUMBIA UNIVERSITY - GEOLOGY LIBRARY □ New York, NY

Klimley, Susan, Libn.
COLUMBIA UNIVERSITY - LAMONT-DOHERTY GEOLOGICAL OBSERVATORY - GEOSCIENCE LIBRARY □ Palisades, NY

Klinck, Patricia E., State Libn.
VERMONT STATE DEPARTMENT OF LIBRARIES □ Montpelier, VT

Kline, Doris, Libn.
BORG-WARNER CORPORATION - YORK DIVISION - ENGINEERING LIBRARY □ York, PA

Kline, Eve, Libn./Dir.
PENNSYLVANIA STATE DEPARTMENT OF PUBLIC WELFARE - SOMERSET STATE HOSPITAL - LIBRARY □ Somerset, PA

Kline, Ken, Libn.
UNIVERSITY OF SOUTHERN CALIFORNIA - VON KLEINSMID LIBRARY - ORIENTALIA COLLECTION □ Los Angeles, CA

Kline, Laura, Spec.Coll.Libn.
IOWA STATE UNIVERSITY - LIBRARY - DEPARTMENT OF SPECIAL COLLECTIONS □ Ames, IA

Kline, Dr. Milton V., Dir. of Institute
INSTITUTE FOR RESEARCH IN HYPNOSIS - BERNARD B. RAGINSKY RESEARCH LIBRARY □ New York, NY

Kling, Allan, Dir., Comp. & Law
CANADIAN LAW INFORMATION COUNCIL - RESOURCE CENTRE FOR COMPUTERS AND LAW □ Ottawa, ON

Kling, Harriet, Med.Libn.
QUAIN AND RAMSTAD CLINIC - MEDICAL LIBRARY □ Bismarck, ND

Kling, Susan, Hd., Ref./Info.Serv.
NEBRASKA STATE LIBRARY COMMISSION □ Lincoln, NE

Klingensmith, Kathryn, Libn.
MONTANA STATE UNIVERSITY - VETERINARY RESEARCH LABORATORY - HUIDEKOPER LIBRARY □ Bozeman, MT

Klinger, Robert A., Grand Libn.
GRAND LODGE OF FREE AND ACCEPTED MASONS OF CALIFORNIA - LIBRARY AND MUSEUM □ San Francisco, CA

Klingle, Philip A., Sr. Law Libn.
NEW YORK STATE SUPREME COURT - 2ND JUDICIAL DISTRICT - LAW LIBRARY □ Staten Island, NY

Klingler, Evelyn L., Ref.Libn.
MORRIS COUNTY FREE LIBRARY - NEW JERSEY COLLECTION □ Whippany, NJ

Klingman, Fred E., Pres.
CHURCH OF JESUS CHRIST OF LATTER-DAY SAINTS - SOUTHERN CALIFORNIA AREA GENEALOGICAL LIBRARY □ Los Angeles, CA

Klivcks, Walter, Libn.
METROPOLITAN HOSPITAL CENTER - DRAPER HALL LIBRARY □ New York, NY

Kloberdanz, Timothy J., Hd.Archv.
INDIANA UNIVERSITY - FOLKLORE ARCHIVES □ Bloomington, IN

Kloc, Stanley J., Act.Dir.
WEST VIRGINIA UNIVERSITY - COLLEGE OF BUSINESS AND ECONOMICS - BUREAU OF BUSINESS RESEARCH □ Morgantown, WV

Klos, Ann, Ref.Libn.
U.S. AIR FORCE WEAPONS LABORATORY - TECHNICAL LIBRARY □ Kirtland AFB, NM

Klose, Fred W., Archv.
U.S. NATL. ARCHIVES & RECORDS SERVICE - FEDERAL ARCHIVES AND RECORDS CENTER, REGION 9 □ Laguna Niguel, CA

Klosky, Patricia W., Libn.
INTERNATIONAL FOOD POLICY RESEARCH INSTITUTE - LIBRARY □ Washington, DC

Kluever, Connie L., Libn.
BROWN, WOOD, IVEY, MITCHELL & PETTY - LIBRARY □ New York, NY

Klupping, Mary Ellen, Med.libn.
U.S. VETERANS ADMINISTRATION (IL-Hines) - LIBRARY SERVICES (142D) □ Hines, IL

Kluss, Esther, Ref.Libn.
QUEENS BOROUGH PUBLIC LIBRARY - HISTORY, TRAVEL & BIOGRAPHY DIVISION □ Jamaica, NY

Kluttz, Arletta M., Libn.
CONE MILLS CORPORATION - LIBRARY □ Greensboro, NC

Klyve, Cordell, Libn.
WISCONSIN STATE DEPARTMENT OF TRANSPORTATION - LIBRARY □ Madison, WI

Knaap, Marjory, Libn.
CENTRAL BAPTIST SEMINARY - DR. W. GORDON BROWN MEMORIAL LIBRARY □ Toronto, ON

Knachel, Dr. Philip A., Act.Dir.
FOLGER SHAKESPEARE LIBRARY □ Washington, DC

Knap, Marie S., Hd.Libn.
UNITED ENGINEERS & CONSTRUCTORS INC. - LIBRARY □ Philadelphia, PA

Knapik, Robert, Ref.Libn.
SACRED HEART UNIVERSITY - LIBRARY □ Bridgeport, CT

Knapik, Robert M., Lib.Supv.
UNITED TECHNOLOGIES CORPORATION - SIKORSKY AIRCRAFT DIVISION - DIVISION LIBRARY □ Stratford, CT

Knapke, Beth J., Asst.Libn.
CACI, INC. - LIBRARY AND TECHNICAL INFORMATION CENTER □ Arlington, VA

Knapp, Catherine C., Asst.Libn.
WADSWORTH ATHENEUM - AUERBACH ART LIBRARY □ Hartford, CT

Knapp, David, Libn., Tech.Serv.
OBERLIN COLLEGE - CONSERVATORY OF MUSIC LIBRARY □ Oberlin, OH

Knapp, Sharon E., Cat./Subj.Spec.
DUKE UNIVERSITY - MANUSCRIPT DEPARTMENT □ Durham, NC

Knapp, Vertie, Cur./Libn.
MONROE COUNTY HISTORICAL SOCIETY - LIBRARY AND MUSEUM □ Stroudsburg, PA

Knasiak, Theresa J., Adm.Libn.
U.S. AIR FORCE BASE - WRIGHT-PATTERSON GENERAL LIBRARY □ Wright-Patterson AFB, OH

Knauer, Kathleen M., Res.Libn.
HONEYWELL, INC. - SOLID STATE ELECTRONICS DIVISION LIBRARY □ Plymouth, MN

Knauff, Elisabeth S., Mgr., Info.Serv.Div.
U.S. DEPT. OF THE TREASURY - INFORMATION SERVICES DIVISION - TREASURY DEPT. LIBRARY □ Washington, DC

Knauth, Michael G., Chf.Libn.
SUNY - AGRICULTURAL AND TECHNICAL COLLEGE AT FARMINGDALE - THOMAS D. GREENLEY LIBRARY □ Farmingdale, NY

Knecht, Fred W., Law Libn.
KANSAS STATE SUPREME COURT - LAW LIBRARY □ Topeka, KS

Knecht, Paula, Cat.
PEPPERDINE UNIVERSITY - LAW LIBRARY □ Malibu, CA

Knect, Margaret, Asst.Libn.
KANSAS STATE HISTORICAL SOCIETY - LIBRARY □ Topeka, KS

Knefel, Mary Anne, Ref.Libn.
SCHOOLS OF THEOLOGY IN DUBUQUE - LIBRARIES □ Dubuque, IA

Kneil, Gertrude M., Asst.Libn./Cat.
MELLON BANK, N.A. - LIBRARY† □ Pittsburgh, PA

Knerr, Linda J., Med.Libn.
U.S. VETERANS ADMINISTRATION (TX-Dallas) - MEDICAL CENTER LIBRARY (142D) □ Dallas, TX

Kniesner, John T., Libn.
CENTRAL OHIO TRANSIT AUTHORITY - LIBRARY □ Columbus, OH

Knight, Alice E., Libn.
WEST VIRGINIA STATE ATTORNEY GENERAL - LAW LIBRARY □ Charleston, WV

Knight, Anne, Libn.
LINN-HENLEY LIBRARY FOR SOUTHERN HISTORICAL RESEARCH - TUTWILER COLLECTION OF SOUTHERN HISTORY AND LITERATURE □ Birmingham, AL

Knight, Barbara, Lib.-Media Coord.
ST. LUKE'S REGIONAL MEDICAL CENTER - LIBRARY-MEDIA CENTER □ Sioux City, IA

Knight, Dorothy H., Libn.
PASSAVANT MEMORIAL AREA HOSPITAL ASSOCIATION - SIBERT LIBRARY □ Jacksonville, IL

Knight, Helen, Univ.Archv.
WESTERN KENTUCKY UNIVERSITY - DEPT. OF SPECIAL COLLECTIONS - KENTUCKY LIBRARY AND MUSEUM/UNIVERSITY ARCHIVES □ Bowling Green, KY

Knight, John, Comp.Prog.Techn.
ENVIRONMENTAL PROTECTION AGENCY - LIBRARY SERVICES □ Research Triangle Park, NC

Knight, Marie, Sr.Tech.Libn.
LOCKHEED ELECTRONICS COMPANY, INC. - TECHNICAL INFORMATION CENTER □ Plainfield, NJ

Knight, Mary Ann, Dept.Hd.
BERKSHIRE ATHENAEUM - MUSIC AND ARTS DEPARTMENT □ Pittsfield, MA

Knight, Mary Jane, Libn.
HAWAIIAN MISSION CHILDREN'S SOCIETY - LIBRARY □ Honolulu, HI

Knight, Nancy, Ref.Libn.
GEORGETOWN UNIVERSITY - MEDICAL CENTER - DAHLGREN MEMORIAL LIBRARY □ Washington, DC

Knight, Olga, Dir.
UNIVERSITY OF CALIFORNIA, BERKELEY - EXTENSION MEDIA CENTER □ Berkeley, CA

Knight, Regina L., Info.Res.Spec.
AMERICAN DADE - AMERICAN HOSPITAL SUPPLY CORPORATION - LIBRARY □ Miami, FL

Knihnicki, Edwin, Asst.Libn.
U.S. ARMY - RESEARCH AND TECHNOLOGY LABS (AVRADCOM) - APPLIED TECH. LABORATORY - TECHNICAL LIB. □ Ft. Eustis, VA

Knihnicki, Marion H., Supv.Libn.
U.S. ARMY TRANSPORTATION - TECHNICAL
INFORMATION AND RESEARCH CENTER □ Ft.
Eustis, VA

Knipe, Laura F., Exec.Sec.
AMERICAN SOCIETY FOR PSYCHICAL
RESEARCH - LIBRARY □ New York, NY

Knitter, Judy, Pres.
DEL NORTE COUNTY HISTORICAL SOCIETY -
LIBRARY □ Crescent City, CA

Knobil, Carole W., Assoc.Libn., Spec.Coll.
UNIVERSITY OF TEXAS, AUSTIN - SCHOOL OF
LAW - TARLTON LAW LIBRARY □ Austin, TX

Knobloch, Shirley, Asst.Libn.
CHILDREN'S HOSPITAL/NATIONAL MEDICAL
CENTER - HOSPITAL LIBRARY† □ Washington,
DC

Knodel, Karyl, Ser.Libn.
UNIVERSITY OF SOUTH DAKOTA - MC KUSICK
LAW LIBRARY □ Vermillion, SD

Knoeppel, Helga K., Libn.
INTERNATIONAL MILITARY ARCHIVES □
Washington, DC

Knop, Judy, Cat.
MC CORMICK THEOLOGICAL SEMINARY -
LIBRARY† □ Chicago, IL

Knopf, Carol L., Libn.
BROWN UNIVERSITY - POPULATION STUDIES
AND TRAINING CENTER - DEMOGRAPHY
LIBRARY □ Providence, RI

Knopf, Vicki, Asst.Libn.
GREY ADVERTISING, INC. - INFORMATION
CENTER □ New York, NY

Knopp, Mary, Cat.
ST. PAUL SEMINARY - JOHN IRELAND
MEMORIAL LIBRARY □ St. Paul, MN

Knor, Frank
BRITISH COLUMBIA INSTITUTE OF
TECHNOLOGY - LIBRARY SERVICES DIVISION
□ Burnaby, BC

Knorr, Martin, Dir.
HARRIS-STOWE STATE COLLEGE LIBRARY □ St.
Louis, MO

Knott, Judith, Asst.Libn.
AMERICAN HOME PRODUCTS CORPORATION -
WYETH LABORATORIES DIVISION LIBRARY □
Philadelphia, PA

Knott, Marie A., Libn.
SOUTHERN OHIO GENEALOGICAL SOCIETY -
REFERENCE LIBRARY □ Hillsboro, OH

Knott, Martha, Tchg.Lrng.Ctr.
UNIVERSITY OF TEXAS HEALTH SCIENCE
CENTER, SAN ANTONIO - LIBRARY □ San
Antonio, TX

Knotts, Mary Ann, Chf., Lib.Serv.
U.S. VETERANS ADMINISTRATION (AL-
Birmingham) - HOSPITAL MEDICAL LIBRARY □
Birmingham, AL

Knowlton, David L., Exec.Dir.
NEW JERSEY OPTOMETRIC ASSOCIATION -
DR. E.C. NUROCK LIBRARY† □ Trenton, NJ

Knowlton, Deborah, Corp.Libn.
HAWAIIAN ELECTRIC CO., INC. - CORPORATE
LIBRARY □ Honolulu, HI

Knowlton, Deborah, Corp.Libn.
HAWAIIAN ELECTRIC CO., INC. -
ENGINEERING LIBRARY □ Honolulu, HI

Knowlton, Ruth, Cat.
NEW HAVEN COLONY HISTORICAL SOCIETY -
WHITNEY LIBRARY □ New Haven, CT

Knox, Elizabeth B., Sec./Libn./Cur.
NEW LONDON COUNTY HISTORICAL SOCIETY -
LIBRARY □ New London, CT

Knox, Penny
ARTHUR ANDERSEN & CO. - BUSINESS LIBRARY
□ Houston, TX

Knubel, Helen, Archv.Cons.
LUTHERAN COUNCIL IN THE U.S.A. - RECORDS
AND INFORMATION CENTER - REFERENCE
LIBRARY □ New York, NY

Knuds, Monica, Ref.Libn.
SMITHSONIAN INSTITUTION LIBRARIES -
NATIONAL AIR AND SPACE MUSEUM - LIBRARY
□ Washington, DC

Knudsen, Helen Z., Libn.
CALIFORNIA INSTITUTE OF TECHNOLOGY -
ASTROPHYSICS LIBRARY □ Pasadena, CA

Knudsen, Patricia, Dp.Dir.
UNIVERSITY OF MARYLAND, BALTIMORE -
HEALTH SCIENCES LIBRARY □ Baltimore, MD

Knudtson, Gail, Ref.
U.S. AIR FORCE - WRIGHT-PATTERSON
TECHNICAL LIBRARY □ Dayton, OH

Knupp, Valerie, Supv., Info.Serv.
MC KINSEY & COMPANY, INC. - INFORMATION
SERVICES □ New York, NY

Knutson, Maurice C., Chf., Lib.Serv.
U.S. VETERANS ADMINISTRATION (MT-Fort
Harrison) - MEDICAL CENTER LIBRARY □ Fort
Harrison, MT

Knutson, Robert, Hd., Dept.Spec.Coll.
UNIVERSITY OF SOUTHERN CALIFORNIA -
LIBRARY - CINEMA LIBRARY □ Los Angeles, CA

Knutson, Robert, Hd.
UNIVERSITY OF SOUTHERN CALIFORNIA -
LIBRARY - DEPARTMENT OF SPECIAL
COLLECTIONS □ Los Angeles, CA

Knutt, Teresa, Asst.Ref.Libn.
TEXAS TECH UNIVERSITY - HEALTH SCIENCES
CENTER - LIBRARY OF THE HEALTH SCIENCES
□ Lubbock, TX

Knuttunen, Jane, Hd., Tech.Serv.
HARVARD UNIVERSITY - FINE ARTS LIBRARY □
Cambridge, MA

Kobayashi, Hanako, Res.Libn.
HAWAII STATE - LEGISLATIVE REFERENCE
BUREAU LIBRARY □ Honolulu, HI

Kobelski, Pamela G., Tech.Info.Supv.
TEXTRON, INC. - SPENCER KELLOGG DIVISION
- RESEARCH CENTER LIBRARY □ Buffalo, NY

Kober, Gary Lee, Asst.Libn.
MONTREAL GENERAL HOSPITAL - MEDICAL
LIBRARY □ Montreal, PQ

Kober, Mary J., Dir.
STEARNS CATALYTIC CORPORATION -
PHILADELPHIA LIBRARY □ Philadelphia, PA

Kobialka, Nancy, Music Libn.
UNIVERSITY OF MIAMI - SCHOOL OF MUSIC -
ALBERT PICK MUSIC LIBRARY □ Coral Gables,
FL

Kobrynska, Anna, Acq.
SHEVCHENKO SCIENTIFIC SOCIETY, INC. -
LIBRARY AND ARCHIVES □ New York, NY

Kobulnicky, Paul, Libn.
UNIVERSITY OF PITTSBURGH - COMPUTER
SCIENCE LIBRARY □ Pittsburgh, PA

Kobulnicky, Paul J., Libn.
UNIVERSITY OF PITTSBURGH - CHEMISTRY
LIBRARY □ Pittsburgh, PA

Kobulnicky, Paul J., Libn.
UNIVERSITY OF PITTSBURGH - PHYSICS
LIBRARY □ Pittsburgh, PA

Kobus, Julia, Docs.
SOUTHERN CONNECTICUT STATE UNIVERSITY
- H.C. BULEY LIBRARY - SPECIAL COLLECTIONS
□ New Haven, CT

Kobylecky, Ruth, Libn.
NEEDHAM, HARPER & STEERS ADVERTISING,
INC. - INFORMATION SERVICES □ Chicago, IL

Kobzina, Norma, Hd.
UNIVERSITY OF CALIFORNIA, BERKELEY -
NATURAL RESOURCES LIBRARY □ Berkeley, CA

Koch, Charles W., Dir., Lrng.Rsrcs.
NORTHWEST MISSOURI STATE UNIVERSITY -
OWENS LIBRARY - SPECIAL COLLECTIONS □
Maryville, MO

Koch, David V., Cur./Archv.
SOUTHERN ILLINOIS UNIVERSITY,
CARBONDALE - SPECIAL COLLECTIONS □
Carbondale, IL

Koch, Dr. Erwin T., Treas.
SCHUMANN MEMORIAL FOUNDATION, INC. -
LIBRARY □ Livonia, NY

Koch, Janet W., Conservator
NEW JERSEY HISTORICAL SOCIETY - LIBRARY
□ Newark, NJ

Koch, Jean E., Dir.
URBANA FREE LIBRARY - URBANA MUNICIPAL
DOCUMENTS PROJECT □ Urbana, IL

Koch, Kathy, Asst.Libn., Cat.
FMC CORPORATION - ORDNANCE DIVISION -
OD TECHNICAL LIBRARY □ San Jose, CA

Koch, Kathy, Acq.
NORTHWESTERN OKLAHOMA STATE
UNIVERSITY - LIBRARY □ Alva, OK

Koch, Patricia A., Libn.
U.S. ADVISORY COMMISSION ON
INTERGOVERNMENTAL RELATIONS - LIBRARY
□ Washington, DC

Koch, Rev. R. David, Assoc.Libn./Tech.Serv.
EASTERN BAPTIST THEOLOGICAL SEMINARY -
LIBRARY □ Philadelphia, PA

Koch, William, Adm.Libn.
U.S. ARMY HOSPITALS - LETTERMAN ARMY
MEDICAL CENTER - MEDICAL LIBRARY □
Presidio of San Francisco, CA

Kochevar, Carole, Hd., ILL
UNIVERSITY OF CALIFORNIA, LOS ANGELES -
PHYSICAL SCIENCES & TECHNOLOGY
LIBRARIES □ Los Angeles, CA

Koda, Paul S., Cur.
UNIVERSITY OF NORTH CAROLINA, CHAPEL
HILL - RARE BOOK COLLECTION □ Chapel Hill,
NC

Koder, Sr. Alma, Libn.
LANKENAU HOSPITAL - SCHOOL OF NURSING
LIBRARY □ Philadelphia, PA

Koedel, Barbara E., Libn.
ATLANTIC COUNTY HISTORICAL SOCIETY -
LIBRARY □ Somers Point, NJ

Koehl, Mr. B.G.
BATTELLE-COLUMBUS LABORATORIES -
RAPIDLY SOLIDIFIED MATERIALS (RaSoMat) -
RESOURCE CENTER □ Columbus, OH

Koehler, Boyd, Rd.Serv. & Ref.Libn.
AUGSBURG COLLEGE - GEORGE SVERDRUP
LIBRARY AND MEDIA CENTER □ Minneapolis,
MN

Koehler, Joyce, Info.sci.
SCHERING-PLOUGH CORPORATION -
PHARMACEUTICAL RESEARCH DIVISION -
LIBRARY INFORMATION CENTER □ Bloomfield,
NJ

Koehler, Sue, Libn.
MADISON PUBLIC LIBRARY - LITERATURE AND
SOCIAL SCIENCES □ Madison, WI

Koehler, Thea, Ref.Libn.
U.S. SENATE - LIBRARY □ Washington, DC

Koehler, Rev. Theodore, S.M., Dir.
UNIVERSITY OF DAYTON - MARIAN LIBRARY □
Dayton, OH

Koek, Eva B., Info.Spec.
SEARLE (G.D.) & CO. - RESEARCH LIBRARY □
Skokie, IL

Koel, Ottilia, Libn. & Cur. of Mss.
NEW HAVEN COLONY HISTORICAL SOCIETY -
WHITNEY LIBRARY □ New Haven, CT

Koelle, Joyce G., Mgr.
SANDOZ PHARMACEUTICALS - INFORMATION
SERVICES □ East Hanover, NJ

Koenderink, Ms. Myrla J., Libn.
ROYAL BANK OF CANADA - LIBRARY □ Calgary,
AB

Koenig, Daniel D., Dir., Lrng.Rscs.
PIEDMONT TECHNICAL COLLEGE - LIBRARY □
Greenwood, SC

Koenig, Dorothy A., Libn.
UNIVERSITY OF CALIFORNIA, BERKELEY -
ANTHROPOLOGY LIBRARY □ Berkeley, CA

Koenig, Laura, Libn.
TEXAS STATE INDUSTRIAL COMMISSION -
RESEARCH LIBRARY □ Austin, TX

Koenig, Susan L., Libn.
NEW SCHOOL OF MUSIC, INC. - ALICE TULLY
LIBRARY □ Philadelphia, PA

Koenig, Terry R., Dir. of Musm.
ARTESIA HISTORICAL MUSEUM AND ART
CENTER - LIBRARY □ Artesia, NM

Koenigsberg, Allen, Dir.
ANTIQUE PHONOGRAPH MONTHLY - APM
LIBRARY OF RECORDED SOUND □ Brooklyn, NY

Koenke, Karl, Assoc.Dir.
ERIC CLEARINGHOUSE ON READING AND
COMMUNICATIONS SKILLS □ Urbana, IL

Koepf, Linda S., Dir., Lib.
TEXAS STATE TECHNICAL INSTITUTE, WACO
CAMPUS - LIBRARY □ Waco, TX

Koepp, Donna, Map Spec.
DENVER PUBLIC LIBRARY - MAP COLLECTION □
Denver, CO

Koester, Darwin, Gen.Ref.Libn.
U.S. GENERAL SERVICES ADMINISTRATION -
GSA LIBRARY □ Washington, DC

Koester, Kristin L., Libn.
OREGON SCHOOL OF ARTS AND CRAFTS -
LIBRARY □ Portland, OR

Koester, Robert J., Dir.
BALL STATE UNIVERSITY - CENTER FOR
ENERGY RESEARCH/EDUCATION/SERVICE
(CERES) □ Muncie, IN

Koetitz, Edward A., Ref.Libn.
BETHANY BIBLE COLLEGE - LIBRARY □ Scotts
Valley, CA

Koff, Manuel J.
BAKER & MC KENZIE - LIBRARY □ San
Francisco, CA

Kohl, Arlene F., Tech.Libn.
FAIRCHILD-WESTON SYSTEMS INC. - WESTON
CONTROLS DIVISION - TECHNICAL LIBRARY □
Archbald, PA

Kohl, Michael, Spec.Coll.Libn.
CLEMSON UNIVERSITY - ROBERT MULDROW
COOPER LIBRARY □ Clemson, SC

Kohlhorst, Gail L., Chf.
U.S. GENERAL SERVICES ADMINISTRATION -
GSA LIBRARY □ Washington, DC

Kohli, Kathi, Res.Libn.
CARGILL, INC. - INFORMATION CENTER □
Minneapolis, MN

Kohlrieser, Lillian
U.S. DEPT. OF LABOR - BUREAU OF LABOR
STATISTICS - INFORMATION AND ADVISORY
SECTION □ New York, NY

Kohn, Vicky, Asst.Cur. of Educ.
WESTERN KENTUCKY UNIVERSITY - DEPT. OF
SPECIAL COLLECTIONS - KENTUCKY LIBRARY
AND MUSEUM/UNIVERSITY ARCHIVES □
Bowling Green, KY

Kohout, Joan G., Libn.
IMMANUEL MEDICAL CENTER - PROFESSIONAL
LIBRARY □ Omaha, NE

Kohrs, Charlotte, Supv., Info.Serv.
PEAT, MARWICK, MITCHELL & CO. - LIBRARY □
Houston, TX

Kohut, Dr. J.J., Sci.Libn.
PORTLAND STATE UNIVERSITY - SCIENCE
LIBRARY □ Portland, OR

Kohutiak, Bohdan I., Chf., Serv.Br.
U.S. ARMY WAR COLLEGE - LIBRARY □ Carlisle
Barracks, PA

Kok, Fr. Bede, O.C.S.O., Libn.
GETHSEMANI ABBEY - LIBRARY □ Trappist, KY

Kok, John, Dir.
FOOTE CONE & BELDING - INFORMATION
CENTER □ Chicago, IL

Kokott, Angie, Libn.
U.S. FISH & WILDLIFE SERVICE - NORTHERN
PRAIRIE WILDLIFE RESEARCH CENTER
LIBRARY □ Jamestown, ND

Kolaczek, Jan, Libn.
UNIVERSITY OF OTTAWA - TEACHER
EDUCATION LIBRARY □ Ottawa, ON

Kolb, C. Haven, Sec.
NATURAL HISTORY SOCIETY OF MARYLAND -
LIBRARY □ Baltimore, MD

Kolb, Lawrence P., Hd.
CALIFORNIA STATE REGIONAL WATER
QUALITY CONTROL BOARD, SAN FRANCISCO
BAY REGION - LIBRARY □ Oakland, CA

Kolbre, Kaarin, Supv.
AMERICAN CYANAMID COMPANY -
ENVIRONMENTAL HEALTH LIBRARY† □ Wayne,
NJ

Kolby, Shirley, Coord./Acq.
BAYSTATE MEDICAL CENTER - HEALTH
SCIENCES LIBRARY □ Springfield, MA

Kolesnyk, Petro, Slavic Cat.
UNIVERSITY OF ILLINOIS - SLAVIC AND EAST
EUROPEAN LIBRARY □ Urbana, IL

Kollegger, James G., Pres. & Pub.
EIC/INTELLIGENCE, INC. □ New York, NY

Kollmorgan, M. Ann, Asst. Law Libn.
MC GEORGE SCHOOL OF LAW - LAW LIBRARY □
Sacramento, CA

Kolloge, Sandra, Act.Hd.
HAWAII STATE LIBRARY - LANGUAGE,
LITERATURE AND HISTORY SECTION □
Honolulu, HI

Kolmes, Bea, Info.Sci.
AMERICAN CYANAMID COMPANY -
AGRICULTURAL RESEARCH DIVISION -
TECHNICAL INFORMATION SERVICES □
Princeton, NJ

Kolner, Stuart J., Br.Libn.
UNIVERSITY OF ILLINOIS - COLLEGE OF
MEDICINE AT ROCKFORD - LIBRARY OF THE
HEALTH SCIENCES □ Rockford, IL

Kolomeychuk, Terry, Film Rep.
CANADA - NATIONAL FILM BOARD OF CANADA
- FILM LIBRARY† □ Winnipeg, MB

Kolp, John, Prog.Assoc.
UNIVERSITY OF IOWA - LABORATORY FOR
POLITICAL RESEARCH □ Iowa City, IA

Komai, Lois, Ref.Libn.
UNIVERSITY OF WISCONSIN, MADISON -
STEENBOCK MEMORIAL LIBRARY □ Madison,
WI

Komarjanski, Dzwinka, Circuit Libn.
CLEVELAND HEALTH SCIENCES LIBRARY -
ALLEN MEMORIAL LIBRARY □ Cleveland, OH

Komarjanski, Dzwinka, Circuit Libn.
WOMAN'S GENERAL HOSPITAL - MEDICAL
LIBRARY □ Cleveland, OH

Kommer, Joen B., Mgr., Lib.Serv.
WED ENTERPRISES - RESEARCH LIBRARY □
Glendale, CA

Komoto, David T., Database Dev.Coord.
UNIVERSITY OF SOUTHERN CALIFORNIA -
NASA INDUSTRIAL APPLICATION CENTER
(NIAC) □ Los Angeles, CA

Komp, Joel T., Sr.Res.Info.Sci.
GENERAL MILLS, INC. - JAMES FORD BELL
TECHNICAL CENTER - TECHNICAL
INFORMATION SERVICES □ Minneapolis, MN

Kondo, Gail, Asst.Libn.
PEAT, MARWICK, MITCHELL & CO. - LIBRARY □
Washington, DC

Kondraske, Linda, Search Anl.
UNIVERSITY OF TEXAS HEALTH SCIENCE
CENTER, DALLAS - LIBRARY □ Dallas, TX

Konjevich, M., Lib.Mgr.
U.S. NASA - JOHN F. KENNEDY SPACE CENTER
- LIBRARY □ Kennedy Space Center, FL

Konop, Arthur J., Dir.-Archv.
ST. FRANCIS COLLEGE - JAMES A. KELLY
INSTITUTE FOR LOCAL HISTORICAL STUDIES -
LIBRARY □ Brooklyn, NY

Konop, Bonnie, Asst.Libn./State Docs.
UNIVERSITY OF FLORIDA - DOCUMENTS
LIBRARY □ Gainesville, FL

Konoshima, Sumiye, Res.Info.Spec.
INSTITUTE OF CULTURE AND
COMMUNICATION - CCPC - RESOURCE
MATERIALS COLLECTION □ Honolulu, HI

Konrath, Rose, Pub.Serv.Libn.
HUGHES AIRCRAFT COMPANY - ELECTRO-
OPTICAL & DATA SYSTEMS GROUP -
TECHNICAL LIBRARY □ El Segundo, CA

Konstantinow, George, Sr.Lit.Sci.
REYNOLDS (R.J.) TOBACCO COMPANY - R&D
SCIENTIFIC INFORMATION SERVICES
LIBRARY □ Winston-Salem, NC

Koo, S., Sr.Res.Libn.
FIRESTONE TIRE AND RUBBER COMPANY -
CENTRAL RESEARCH LIBRARY □ Akron, OH

Koob, Marian, Tech.Serv.
HOFFMANN-LA ROCHE, INC. - SCIENTIFIC
LIBRARY □ Nutley, NJ

Koons, Jane Baker, Dir., Prog.Dev.
MIDWEST CHINA CENTER - MIDWEST CHINA
ORAL HISTORY ARCHIVES AND MUSEUM
COLLECTION □ St. Paul, MN

Kooperman, Evelyn, Libn.
SAN DIEGO PUBLIC LIBRARY - ART, MUSIC &
RECREATION SECTION □ San Diego, CA

Kooy, Dianne Vander, Libn.
WARNER, NORCROSS & JUDD - LIBRARY □
Grand Rapids, MI

Koozer, Donald, Hd.
ARIZONA STATE UNIVERSITY - HOWE
ARCHITECTURE LIBRARY □ Tempe, AZ

Koozer, Donald E., Supv.
UNIVERSITY OF OKLAHOMA - ART LIBRARY† □
Norman, OK

Kopelke, Harold, Cons.
COPLEY PRESS, INC. - THE JAMES S. COPLEY
LIBRARY □ La Jolla, CA

Kopezynski, Rita
UNIVERSITY OF NOTRE DAME - CENTER FOR
THE STUDY OF HUMAN RIGHTS - READING
ROOM □ Notre Dame, IN

Kopischke, John, Dir.
NEBRASKA STATE LIBRARY COMMISSION □
Lincoln, NE

Kopkin, T.J., Res.Info.Spec.
LOCKHEED-GEORGIA COMPANY - TECHNICAL
INFORMATION DEPARTMENT □ Marietta, GA

Koplan, Margarette D., Chf.Libn.
ERLANGER MEDICAL CENTER - MEDICAL
LIBRARY† □ Chattanooga, TN

Koplan, Margarette D., Chf.Libn.
ERLANGER MEDICAL CENTER - SCHOOL OF
NURSING - SARAH C. BARTON LIBRARY □
Chattanooga, TN

Koplan, Stephen M., Libn.
GEORGIA STATE DEPARTMENT OF HUMAN
RESOURCES - GEORGIA MENTAL HEALTH
INSTITUTE - ADDISON M. DUVAL LIBRARY† □
Atlanta, GA

Koplowitz, Brad, State Archv.
OKLAHOMA STATE DEPARTMENT OF
LIBRARIES □ Oklahoma City, OK

Kopp, James, Gen.Ed.
COLUMBIA UNIVERSITY - AVERY
ARCHITECTURAL AND FINE ARTS LIBRARY □
New York, NY

Kopp, Marilyn G., Libn.
WABCO - CONSTRUCTION AND MINING
EQUIPMENT - ENGINEERING TECHNICAL
LIBRARY □ Peoria, IL

Kopper, Carolyn, Med.Libn.
ESKATON AMERICAN RIVER HOSPITAL - ERLE
M. BLUNDEN, M.D. MEMORIAL LIBRARY □
Carmichael, CA

Kopper, Carolyn S., Asst.Libn., UCDMC
UNIVERSITY OF CALIFORNIA, DAVIS - HEALTH
SCIENCES LIBRARY □ Davis, CA

Kopper, John, Hd., Tech.Proc.
MAYO FOUNDATION - MAYO CLINIC LIBRARY □
Rochester, MN

Koppie, Craig A., Visual Info.Spec.
U.S. FISH & WILDLIFE SERVICE - OFFICE OF
AUDIO-VISUAL - LIBRARY □ Washington, DC

Kopron, Eileen, Circ.
DICKINSON STATE COLLEGE - STOXEN
LIBRARY □ Dickinson, ND

Kopycinski, Joseph V., Dir.
UNIVERSITY OF LOWELL, NORTH CAMPUS -
ALUMNI/LYDON LIBRARY† □ Lowell, MA

Korb, Linda A., Libn.
U.S. FOREST SERVICE - SOUTHERN FOREST
EXPERIMENT STATION LIBRARY □ New
Orleans, LA

Korda, Marion, Libn.
UNIVERSITY OF LOUISVILLE - DWIGHT
ANDERSON MEMORIAL MUSIC LIBRARY† □
Louisville, KY

Korenic, Lynn, Libn.
INDIANA UNIVERSITY - FINE ARTS LIBRARY □
Bloomington, IN

Korevaar, Jacob, Assoc.Libn.
HARVARD UNIVERSITY - LAW SCHOOL
LIBRARY □ Cambridge, MA

Korey, Marie, Rare Book Libn.
FREE LIBRARY OF PHILADELPHIA - RARE BOOK
DEPARTMENT □ Philadelphia, PA

Korf, Harold E., Dir.
GOLDEN GATE UNIVERSITY - LIBRARIES □ San
Francisco, CA

Korman, Adrienne, Libn.
NEW ENGLAND MUTUAL LIFE INSURANCE
COMPANY - BUSINESS LIBRARY □ Boston, MA

Korman, Amy, LRC Assoc.
UNIVERSITY OF PITTSBURGH - FALK LIBRARY
OF THE HEALTH SCIENCES □ Pittsburgh, PA

Kormanak, Steven, Tech.Libn.
CAI - TECHNICAL LIBRARY □ Barrington, IL

Kormann, Jeff, Res.Assoc.
MISSOURI STATE DIVISION OF COMMUNITY
AND ECONOMIC DEVELOPMENT - RESEARCH
LIBRARY □ Jefferson City, MO

Kormelink, Barbara, Med.Libn.
BAY MEDICAL CENTER - HEALTH SCIENCES
LIBRARY □ Bay City, MI

Kornfeld, Carol, Lib.Info.Spec.
LIPTON (Thomas J.), INC. - RESEARCH LIBRARY
□ Englewood Cliffs, NJ

Kornstein, Barbara, Hd., Lib.
UNIVERSITY OF CALIFORNIA, BERKELEY -
EDUCATION/PSYCHOLOGY LIBRARY □
Berkeley, CA

Korobaylo, Lesia, Asst.Libn.
CLARKSON, GORDON/WOODS, GORDON -
LIBRARY □ Toronto, ON

Korth, Rev. Eugene H., S.J., Asst.Univ.Archv.
MARQUETTE UNIVERSITY - DEPARTMENT OF
SPECIAL COLLECTIONS AND UNIVERSITY
ARCHIVES □ Milwaukee, WI

Kos, Lorraine D., Libn.
WRIGHT INSTITUTE - GRADUATE DIVISION
LIBRARY □ Berkeley, CA

Kosack, Charlene, Hd., Lib.Sect.
CANADA - PRAIRIE FARM REHABILITATION
ADMINISTRATION - LIBRARY □ Regina, SK

Kosaka, Emi, Med.Libn.
MEMORIAL HOSPITAL MEDICAL CENTER OF
LONG BEACH - MEDICAL LIBRARY† □ Long
Beach, CA

Kosanovic, Virginia M., Hd.Libn.
STANFORD UNIVERSITY - PHYSICS LIBRARY □
Stanford, CA

Kosche, Mr. L., Libn.
CANADA - NATIONAL MUSEUMS OF CANADA -
CANADIAN WAR MUSEUM - LIBRARY □ Ottawa,
ON

Kosciusko, Adrienne, Dir., Lib. & Info.Serv.
U.S. EXECUTIVE OFFICE OF THE PRESIDENT -
LIBRARY □ Washington, DC

Kosek, Reynold, Assoc.Libn.
MERCER UNIVERSITY - LAW SCHOOL -
FURMAN SMITH LAW LIBRARY □ Macon, GA

Koshar, Marion, Corp.Libn.
MUTUAL OF NEW YORK (MONY) - CORPORATE
LIBRARY/INFORMATION SERVICE □ New York,
NY

Koshar, Marion, Libn.
MUTUAL OF NEW YORK (MONY) - LAW LIBRARY
□ New York, NY

Koshy, P.J., AV Libn.
SUNY AT BUFFALO - SCIENCE AND
ENGINEERING LIBRARY □ Buffalo, NY

Kosiba, Brenda, Libn.
UNIVERSITY OF SOUTHWESTERN LOUISIANA -
ORNAMENTAL HORTICULTURE LIBRARY □
Lafayette, LA

Koslov, Marcia J., State Law Libn.
WISCONSIN STATE SUPREME COURT -
WISCONSIN STATE LAW LIBRARY □ Madison,
WI

Koslow, Donald M., Assoc.Libn.
U.S. ARMY - MILITARY ACADEMY - LIBRARY □
West Point, NY

Kosmin, Linda J., Dir.
JOHNS HOPKINS UNIVERSITY - APPLIED
PHYSICS LABORATORY - R.E. GIBSON LIBRARY
AND INFORMATION CENTER □ Laurel, MD

Kosowski, Helen, Supv., Lib.Oper.
SQUIBB (E.R.) AND SONS, INC. - SQUIBB
INSTITUTE FOR MEDICAL RESEARCH -
SCIENCE INFORMATION DEPARTMENT □
Princeton, NJ

Kossowsky, Irene H., Mgr., Info.Ctr.
DANCER FITZGERALD SAMPLE, INC. -
INFORMATION CENTER □ New York, NY

Koste, Jodi, Archv.
VIRGINIA COMMONWEALTH UNIVERSITY -
MEDICAL COLLEGE OF VIRGINIA - TOMPKINS-
MC CAW LIBRARY □ Richmond, VA

Kostecky, John S., Asst.Libn.
KAYE, SCHOLER, FIERMAN, HAYS & HANDLER -
LAW LIBRARY □ New York, NY

Kostel, Mary Lou, Libn.
SOUTH DAKOTA HUMAN SERVICES CENTER -
MEDICAL LIBRARY □ Yankton, SD

Koster, Desmond, Ref.Libn.
MEDICAL UNIVERSITY OF SOUTH CAROLINA -
LIBRARY □ Charleston, SC

Koster, Lewis, Chf., Lib.Serv.
U.S. VETERANS ADMINISTRATION (TX-Marlin) -
MEDICAL CENTER LIBRARY SERVICE (142D) □
Marlin, TX

Kotcher, Betty, AV Libn.
NATIONAL GEOGRAPHIC SOCIETY -
AUDIOVISUAL LIBRARY □ Washington, DC

Kotecha, Sudi, Ref.Libn..
RUSH-PRESBYTERIAN-ST. LUKE'S MEDICAL
CENTER - LIBRARY OF RUSH UNIVERSITY □
Chicago, IL

Kotin, David B., Hd.
METROPOLITAN TORONTO LIBRARY -
CANADIAN HISTORY DEPARTMENT □ Toronto,
ON

Koto, Ann S., Asst. Law Libn.
HAWAII STATE SUPREME COURT - LAW
LIBRARY □ Honolulu, HI

Kotow, Nickolas C., Info.Spec.
GULF RESEARCH AND DEVELOPMENT
COMPANY - TECHNICAL INFORMATION
SERVICES† □ Pittsburgh, PA

Kotseas, Cosette M., Info.Spec.
RILEY STOKER CORPORATION - LIBRARY □
Worcester, MA

Kott, Kathy, Hd., Tech.Serv.
DUKE UNIVERSITY - SCHOOL OF LAW LIBRARY
□ Durham, NC

Kouo, Lily, Sr.Libn.
NEW YORK STATE DEPARTMENT OF LAW -
LIBRARY □ Albany, NY

Kouril, Gail M., Asst.Mgr., Info.Serv.
U.S. OFFICE OF TECHNOLOGY ASSESSMENT -
INFORMATION CENTER □ Washington, DC

Kourre, Olga C., Libn.
YONKERS HISTORICAL SOCIETY - LIBRARY □
Yonkers, NY

Kovac, R.J., Media Ref.Libn.
PURDUE UNIVERSITY - FILM LIBRARY □ West
Lafayette, IN

Kovacic, Ellen S., Cat.Libn.
HEBREW UNION COLLEGE - JEWISH
INSTITUTE OF RELIGION - KLAU LIBRARY □
Cincinnati, OH

Kovacs, Katherine Maras, Archv.
CORCORAN GALLERY OF ART - CORCORAN
ARCHIVES □ Washington, DC

Kovacs, Laszlo L., Hum.Libn.
PURDUE UNIVERSITY - HUMANITIES, SOCIAL
SCIENCE AND EDUCATION LIBRARY □ West
Lafayette, IN

Koval, Susan, AV Techn.
U.S. VETERANS ADMINISTRATION (IL-Chicago)
- WESTSIDE HOSPITAL LIBRARY □ Chicago, IL

Kovalik, Gustave T., Assoc.Ref.Libn.
UNIVERSITY OF FLORIDA - HUME LIBRARY □
Gainesville, FL

Kovan, Allan, Cur.
UNIVERSITY OF WISCONSIN, MILWAUKEE -
AREA RESEARCH CENTER □ Milwaukee, WI

Kovats, Jabor, Intl. Law/Doc.Libn.
RUTGERS UNIVERSITY, THE STATE
UNIVERSITY OF NEW JERSEY - SCHOOL OF
LAW LIBRARY† □ Camden, NJ

Koved, Ruth, Libn.
CARDINAL SPELLMAN PHILATELIC MUSEUM,
INC. - LIBRARY □ Weston, MA

Kovel-Jarboe, Patricia, Census Info.Spec.
UNIVERSITY OF MINNESOTA - AGRICULTURAL
EXTENSION SERVICE - MINNESOTA ANALYSIS
& PLANNING SYSTEM □ St. Paul, MN

Kovitz, Nancy R., Res.Libn.
FRANKEL & COMPANY - RESEARCH LIBRARY □
Chicago, IL

Kovnat, Steven, Asst.Libn., Media Rsrcs.
SUNY AT BUFFALO - HEALTH SCIENCES
LIBRARY □ Buffalo, NY

Kovtun, Emil, Libn.
PHYSICS INTERNATIONAL COMPANY -
LIBRARY □ San Leandro, CA

Kowal, Bohdan, Cat.
SHEVCHENKO SCIENTIFIC SOCIETY, INC. -
LIBRARY AND ARCHIVES □ New York, NY

Kowalewski, Denis S., Libn.
CHAPMAN AND CUTLER - LAW LIBRARY □
Chicago, IL

Kowalewski, Rosanna, Act.Dir. of Univ.Libs.
UNIVERSITY OF LOWELL, SOUTH CAMPUS -
DANIEL H. O'LEARY LIBRARY - SPECIAL
COLLECTIONS □ Lowell, MA

Kowalkowski, Carolyn, Dir.
ST. JOSEPH'S HOSPITAL - HEALTH SCIENCE
LIBRARY □ Chippewa Falls, WI

Kowalski, Barbara, Libn.
DALLAS PUBLIC LIBRARY - BUSINESS AND
TECHNOLOGY DIVISION □ Dallas, TX

Kowitz, Aletha A., Dir.
AMERICAN DENTAL ASSOCIATION - BUREAU
OF LIBRARY SERVICES □ Chicago, IL

Kowrach, Rev. Edward J., Archv.
DIOCESE OF SPOKANE - DIOCESAN CHANCERY
ARCHIVES □ Spokane, WA

Kozaczka, Stanley J., Hd.Libn.
ALLIANCE COLLEGE - LIBRARY - SPECIAL
COLLECTIONS □ Cambridge Springs, PA

Kozak, Marlene Galante, Mgr., Info.Serv.
AMERICAN CRITICAL CARE - INFORMATION
CENTER □ McGaw Park, IL

Kozak, Reka, Asst.Dir.
LOGAN COLLEGE OF CHIROPRACTIC - LIBRARY
□ Chesterfield, MO

Kozelka, Cathy Collins, Mgr.
DE SOTO, INC. - INFORMATION CENTER □ Des
Plaines, IL

Koziol, Scott, Non-print cat.
UNIVERSITY OF PITTSBURGH - UNIVERSITY
CENTER FOR INSTRUCTIONAL RESOURCES □
Pittsburgh, PA

Kozlowski, Anne, Coord.
CATHOLIC SOCIAL SERVICES - LIBRARY □
Milwaukee, WI

Kozlowski, Celeste F., Libn.
SOMERVILLE HOSPITAL - CARR HEALTH
SCIENCES LIBRARY □ Somerville, MA

Kraemer, Linda L., Mgr., Info.Serv.
MC KINSEY & COMPANY, INC. - LIBRARY □ San
Francisco, CA

Krafchow, Edward, Libn.
AMERICAN UNIVERSITY OF ORIENTAL
STUDIES - LIBRARY □ Los Angeles, CA

Kraft, Joan E., Chm., Lib.Comm.
ARCHAEOLOGICAL SOCIETY OF NEW JERSEY -
LIBRARY† □ South Orange, NJ
Kraft, Mary E., C.S.J., Archv.
SISTERS OF ST. JOSEPH OF CARONDELET - ST.
PAUL PROVINCE - ARCHIVES □ St. Paul, MN
Kraft, Nancy, Cat.Libn.
STATE HISTORICAL SOCIETY OF IOWA -
LIBRARY □ Iowa City, IA
Kraft, Sandra, Libn.
YOUNG RADIATOR COMPANY - LIBRARY† □
Racine, WI
Krahn, Allan, Automation Libn.
LUTHER NORTHWESTERN SEMINARY -
LIBRARY □ St. Paul, MN
Krajnak, Patricia, Info.Spec.
MILLER BREWING COMPANY - SCIENTIFIC
TECHNICAL INFORMATION FACILITY □
Milwaukee, WI
Krakauer, Eleanor, Libn.
AMC CANCER RESEARCH CENTER AND
HOSPITAL - GRACE & PHILIP LICHTENSTEIN
SCIENTIFIC LIBRARY □ Lakewood, CO
Kralicek, Mary, Ser. & Ref.Libn.
UNIVERSITY OF HEALTH SCIENCES - LIBRARY
□ Kansas City, MO
Kralisz, Victor F., Adm.Mgr.
DALLAS PUBLIC LIBRARY - FILM SERVICE □
Dallas, TX
Kramer, Cecile E., Dir.
NORTHWESTERN UNIVERSITY - HEALTH
SCIENCES LIBRARY† □ Chicago, IL
Kramer, Gretchen G., Libn.
CALIFORNIA JOCKEY CLUB AT BAY MEADOWS
- WILLIAM P. KYNE MEMORIAL LIBRARY □ San
Mateo, CA
Kramer, Helen, Libn.
SANTA FE DRILLING COMPANY - LIBRARY □
Orange, CA
Kramer, Ilse, Asst.Chf., Cat.
BROWN UNIVERSITY - JOHN CARTER BROWN
LIBRARY □ Providence, RI
Kramer, Joseph, Assoc.Ref.Libn.
CALIFORNIA STATE UNIVERSITY,
SACRAMENTO - LIBRARY - SCIENCE &
TECHNOLOGY REFERENCE DEPARTMENT □
Sacramento, CA
Kramer, Kathryn, Cur.
COLUMBIA UNIVERSITY - DEPARTMENT OF
ART HISTORY & ARCHAEOLOGY - PHOTOGRAPH
COLLECTION □ New York, NY
Kramer, Kyle, Libn.
U.S. DEPT. OF JUSTICE - NATIONAL
INSTITUTE OF JUSTICE - LIBRARY □
Washington, DC
Kramer, Linda, Ref.
OHIO STATE UNIVERSITY - EDUCATION/
PSYCHOLOGY LIBRARY □ Columbus, OH
Kramer, Marcella, Asst. Law Libn.
NORTH DAKOTA STATE SUPREME COURT LAW
LIBRARY □ Bismarck, ND
Kramer, Margy L., Libn.
HOCKING TECHNICAL COLLEGE - LIBRARY □
Nelsonville, OH
Kramer, Mary, Libn.
INDIANAPOLIS BAR ASSOCIATION - LIBRARY†
□ Indianapolis, IN
Kramer, Raymond J., Asst.Libn.
U.S. SECURITIES AND EXCHANGE
COMMISSION - LIBRARY □ Washington, DC
Kramer, Susan, Libn.
HARRIS (Louis) & ASSOCIATES, INC. -
INFORMATION SERVICES □ New York, NY
Kramer, Wendy H., Adm.Libn.
U.S.D.A. - AGRICULTURAL RESEARCH SERVICE
- EASTERN REGIONAL RESEARCH CENTER
LIBRARY □ Philadelphia, PA
Kramp, Robert, Libn.
OAKLAND SCHOOLS - EDUCATIONAL RESOURCE
CENTER □ Pontiac, MI
Kranish, Arthur, Hd.
SCIENCE TRENDS - LIBRARY □ Washington, DC

Krantz, Gordon, Libn.
EDGEWATER BAPTIST CHURCH - LIBRARY □
Minneapolis, MN
Kranz, Ralph E., AV Libn.
UNIVERSITY OF UTAH - AUDIO-VISUAL
SERVICES □ Salt Lake City, UT
Krash, Ron, Dir.
UNIVERSITY OF MISSOURI, ST. LOUIS -
THOMAS JEFFERSON LIBRARY - SPECIAL
COLLECTIONS □ St. Louis, MO
Kratz, Barbara, ILL Libn.
NATIONAL ACADEMY OF SCIENCES -
NATIONAL ACADEMY OF ENGINEERING -
LIBRARY □ Washington, DC
Kratz, Eva, Dir. of Lib.Serv.
ST. FRANCIS MEDICAL CENTER - MOTHER
MACARIA HEALTH SCIENCE LIBRARY □
Lynwood, CA
Kratz, Kathryn C., Br.Libn.
U.S. COURT OF APPEALS, 8TH CIRCUIT -
RESEARCH LIBRARY □ St. Paul, MN
Kraus, David H., Act.Chf.
LIBRARY OF CONGRESS - EUROPEAN DIVISION
□ Washington, DC
Kraus, Elizabeth W., Info.Assoc./Lib.Mgr.
EASTMAN KODAK COMPANY - RESEARCH
LIBRARY □ Rochester, NY
Kraus, Marilyn J., Med.Libn.
U.S. VETERANS ADMINISTRATION (IA-Iowa
City) - HOSPITAL LIBRARY □ Iowa City, IA
Kraus, Richard, Spec.Proj.Libn.
LILLICK MC HOSE & CHARLES, ATTORNEYS AT
LAW - LAW LIBRARY □ Los Angeles, CA
Krauss, Barbara L., Libn.
COMMUNITY LEGAL SERVICES, INC. - LAW
LIBRARY □ Philadelphia, PA
Krauss, Barbara L., Libn.
PHILADELPHIA COMMUNITY LEGAL SERVICES,
INC. - LAW LIBRARY □ Philadelphia, PA
Krauss, Sharon, Libn./Asst.Prof.
ST. JOHN'S UNIVERSITY - INSTRUCTIONAL
MATERIALS CENTER □ Jamaica, NY
Kravchenko, Dmitri P., Mgr.
COSSACK LIBRARY IN NEW YORK □ New York,
NY
Kravitz, Rhonda Rios, Ref.Libn.
MASSACHUSETTS GENERAL HOSPITAL - MGH
HEALTH SCIENCES LIBRARIES □ Boston, MA
Krayewski, Fran, Supv.
IMPERIAL OIL, LTD. - ESSO PETROLEUM
INFORMATION CENTRE □ Toronto, ON
Kredel, Olivia, Mgr.
NATIONAL LEAGUE OF CITIES - MUNICIPAL
REFERENCE SERVICE □ Washington, DC
Kregel, Charles E., Jr., Info.Serv.Mgr.
KIRKLAND & ELLIS - LIBRARY □ Chicago, IL
Kregstein, Phyllis L., Biomed.Libn.
U.S. VETERANS ADMINISTRATION (NM-
Albuquerque) - MEDICAL CENTER LIBRARY □
Albuquerque, NM
Kreh, David, Dir.Tchg.Mtls.Ctr.
SUNY - COLLEGE AT CORTLAND - MEMORIAL
LIBRARY □ Cortland, NY
Kreider, Robert, Dir.
BETHEL COLLEGE - MENNONITE LIBRARY AND
ARCHIVES □ North Newton, KS
Kreie, Kati, Libn.
NORTHRIDGE HOSPITAL MEDICAL CENTER -
ATCHERLEY MEDICAL LIBRARY □ Northridge,
CA
Kreinbring, Mary G., Tech.Serv.Libn.
CONTINENTAL ILLINOIS NATIONAL BANK AND
TRUST COMPANY OF CHICAGO -
INFORMATION SERVICES DIVISION □ Chicago,
IL
Kreiter, Marion A., Libn.
UNIVERSITY OF PENNSYLVANIA -
MATHEMATICS-PHYSICS-ASTRONOMY
LIBRARY □ Philadelphia, PA
Krekemeyer, Lynn, Libn.
ISI CORPORATION - RESEARCH LIBRARY □
Oakland, CA

Krell, H. Barbara, Dir. of Libs.
STRAYER COLLEGE - WILKES LIBRARY □
Washington, DC
Kremer, Jill L., Libn.
COHEN, SHAPIRO, POLISHER, SHIEKMAN AND
COHEN - LIBRARY □ Philadelphia, PA
Kremer, Susan, Corp.Libn./Anl.
MEAD CORPORATION - CORPORATE LIBRARY □
Dayton, OH
Kremer, Teresa, Libn.
JEWISH BOARD OF FAMILY & CHILDREN
SERVICES - MARY & LOUIS ROBINSON LIBRARY
□ New York, NY
Krenta, Alicja, Hd.Acq.Libn.
YALE UNIVERSITY - MEDICAL LIBRARY □ New
Haven, CT
Krents, Irma Kopp, Dir.
AMERICAN JEWISH COMMITTEE - WILLIAM E.
WIENER ORAL HISTORY LIBRARY □ New York,
NY
Krents, Milton E., Sr.Cons.
AMERICAN JEWISH COMMITTEE - WILLIAM E.
WIENER ORAL HISTORY LIBRARY □ New York,
NY
Kreps, Stephanie, Res.
AT & T BELL LABORATORIES - AT & T
RESOURCE MANAGEMENT - CORPORATE
RESEARCH CENTER □ Piscataway, NJ
Kreslins, Janis, Ref.Asst.
COUNCIL ON FOREIGN RELATIONS - LIBRARY □
New York, NY
Kresse, Jill A., Lib.Mgr.
ST. JAMES HOSPITAL - MEDICAL LIBRARY □
Pontiac, IL
Kressel, Marilyn, Dir.
AMERICAN ASSOCIATION OF HIGHER
EDUCATION - THE CENTER FOR LEARNING AND
TELECOMMUNICATIONS □ Washington, DC
Kreta, Rev.Fr. Joseph P., Dean
ST. HERMAN'S ORTHODOX THEOLOGICAL
SEMINARY - LIBRARY □ Kodiak, AK
Kretschmann, Kate, AV Libn.
CLEVELAND CLINIC EDUCATION FOUNDATION
- MEDICAL LIBRARY/AUDIOVISUAL CENTER† □
Cleveland, OH
Kreuger, Miles M., Cur.
INSTITUTE OF THE AMERICAN MUSICAL, INC.
- LIBRARY □ Los Angeles, CA
Krichbaum, Mary, Asst.Libn.
HURON ROAD HOSPITAL - LIBRARY AND
AUDIOVISUAL CENTER □ Cleveland, OH
Krichmar, Albert, Linguistics/Commun.Libn.
UNIVERSITY OF CALIFORNIA, SANTA BARBARA
- SCIENCES-ENGINEERING LIBRARY □ Santa
Barbara, CA
Krick, Mary, Libn.
ILLINOIS STATE GEOLOGICAL SURVEY -
LIBRARY □ Champaign, IL
Krick, Robert K., Chf.Hist.
U.S. NATL. PARK SERVICE - FREDERICKSBURG
& SPOTSYLVANIA NATL. MILITARY PARK -
LIBRARY □ Fredericksburg, VA
Krieger, Michael, Hd., Cat.Dept.
UNIVERSITY OF DAYTON - LAW SCHOOL
LIBRARY □ Dayton, OH
Krieger, Nava, Ref.Libn./Spec.Educ.
BOARD OF COOPERATIVE EDUCATIONAL
SERVICES OF NASSAU COUNTY (BOCES) -
NASSAU EDUC. RSRCS. CTR. (NERC) □ Carle
Place, NY
Kriete, Dorothy S., Ref.Libn.
U.S. ARMY WAR COLLEGE - LIBRARY □ Carlisle
Barracks, PA
Krigge, Linda Will, Assoc.Libn.
BRACEWELL & PATTERSON - LAW LIBRARY □
Houston, TX
Kriigel, Barbara, Doc.Libn.
OCLC, INC. - LIBRARY □ Dublin, OH
Krikorian, Rosanne, Asst.Dir.
WHITTIER COLLEGE - SCHOOL OF LAW -
LIBRARY □ Los Angeles, CA

Kriman, Dr. Marianne, Lit. Searcher
ALLIED CORPORATION - LIBRARY &
INFORMATION SERVICES □ Morristown, NJ
Krimmel, Dean, Musm.Ref.Ctr.Supv.
PEALE MUSEUM - REFERENCE CENTER □
Baltimore, MD
Krisciunas, Kathy P., Tech.Serv.Libn.
UNIVERSITY OF DETROIT - SCHOOL OF LAW
LIBRARY □ Detroit, MI
Krismann, Carol, Bus.Libn.
UNIVERSITY OF COLORADO, BOULDER -
WILLIAM M. WHITE BUSINESS LIBRARY □
Boulder, CO
Kristofferson, Eric, Ref./Info.Spec.
UNITED TECHNOLOGIES CORPORATION -
CHEMICAL SYSTEMS DIVISION - LIBRARY □
San Jose, CA
Kritzman, Janie, Assoc.Dir.
BARNARD COLLEGE WOMEN'S CENTER -
BIRDIE GOLDSMITH AST RESOURCE
COLLECTION □ New York, NY
Krivanek, Judy M., Med.Libn.
U.S. ARMY HOSPITALS - D.D. EISENHOWER
ARMY MEDICAL CENTER - MEDICAL LIBRARY†
□ Ft. Gordon, GA
Krivatsy, Dr. Nati H., Ref.Libn.
FOLGER SHAKESPEARE LIBRARY □ Washington,
DC
Krivda, Marita J., Lib.Dir.
PENNSYLVANIA COLLEGE OF OPTOMETRY -
ALBERT FITCH MEMORIAL LIBRARY □
Philadelphia, PA
Kriz, Harry M., Hd., Sci./Tech.Dept.
VIRGINIA POLYTECHNIC INSTITUTE AND
STATE UNIVERSITY - CAROL M. NEWMAN
LIBRARY □ Blacksburg, VA
Kroah, Larry, Libn.
WILMINGTON COLLEGE - CURRICULUM
MATERIALS CENTER □ Wilmington, OH
Krodshen, Breta M., Law Libn.
UNITED BANK OF DENVER, N.A. - UNITED BANK
CENTER - LAW LIBRARY □ Denver, CO
Kroeger, Karl, Music Libn.
UNIVERSITY OF COLORADO, BOULDER - MUSIC
LIBRARY □ Boulder, CO
Kroft, Robin A., Libn.
JOHNS HOPKINS UNIVERSITY - SCHOOL OF
MEDICINE - JOSEPH L. LILIENTHAL LIBRARY □
Baltimore, MD
Krogstad, Roland J., Dir.
WISCONSIN STATE BOARD OF VOCATIONAL,
TECHNICAL & ADULT EDUCATION - RESEARCH
COORDINATING UNIT RESOURCE CTR. □
Madison, WI
Krohn, Alan, Ph.D., Chm., Lib.Comm.
MICHIGAN PSYCHOANALYTIC INSTITUTE -
IRA MILLER MEMORIAL LIBRARY □ Southfield,
MI
Krois, Jerry, Chf., Lib. Automation
WYOMING STATE LIBRARY □ Cheyenne, WY
Kroll, Mark, Tech.Serv.Libn.
ILLINOIS BENEDICTINE COLLEGE - THEODORE
LOWNIK LIBRARY □ Lisle, IL
Kroll, Susan, Ref.Libn.
OHIO STATE UNIVERSITY - HEALTH SCIENCES
LIBRARY □ Columbus, OH
Kromminga, Arlene, Libn.
MINNESOTA STATE INFORMATION SYSTEMS
DIVISION - LIBRARY □ St. Paul, MN
Kronauer, Margaret L., Info.Spec.
UNIVERSITY OF SOUTHERN CALIFORNIA -
ETHEL PERCY ANDRUS GERONTOLOGY CENTER
- GERONTOLOGICAL INFO. CENTER □ Los
Angeles, CA
Kronenfeld, Michael, Dir.
SOUTH CAROLINA STATE DEPARTMENT OF
HEALTH & ENVIRONMENTAL CONTROL -
EDUCATIONAL RESOURCE CENTER □ Columbia,
SC
Kronick, Dr. David A., Libn.
UNIVERSITY OF TEXAS HEALTH SCIENCE
CENTER, SAN ANTONIO - LIBRARY □ San
Antonio, TX

Kronk, Janet C., Libn.
MADISON COUNTY LAW LIBRARY □ London, OH
Kronstedt, Richard, Hd.Libn.
MINNEAPOLIS COLLEGE OF ART AND DESIGN -
LIBRARY AND MEDIA CENTER □ Minneapolis,
MN
Kronzek, Andrea, Info.Spec.
FOI SERVICES, INC. - LIBRARY □ Rockville, MD
Krouse, Philip E., Chf.
U.S. ARMY - ARMAMENT, MUNITIONS AND
CHEMICAL COMMAND - TECHNICAL LIBRARY □
Rock Island, IL
Krueger, Geraldine L., Sr.Res.Assoc.
UNIVERSITY OF CINCINNATI - DEPARTMENT
OF ENVIRONMENTAL HEALTH LIBRARY □
Cincinnati, OH
Krueger, Kathleen, Cur. of Coll.
BAY COUNTY HISTORICAL SOCIETY - LIBRARY
□ Bay City, MI
Krueger, Linda C., Libn.
LUTHERAN CHURCH - MISSOURI SYNOD -
CENTRAL LIBRARY □ St. Louis, MO
Krueger, Richard L., Lib.Spec.
DELAWARE STATE DEPARTMENT OF PUBLIC
INSTRUCTION - LIBRARY INFORMATION
CENTER □ Dover, DE
Kruger, Debora, Cur.
LATAH COUNTY HISTORICAL SOCIETY -
LIBRARY □ Moscow, ID
Krugman, Marian, Patients' Libn.
U.S. VETERANS ADMINISTRATION (NJ-Lyons) -
HOSPITAL LIBRARY □ Lyons, NJ
Kruk, Pauline A., Libn.
FAIRFIELD HILLS HOSPITAL - HEALTH
SCIENCES LIBRARY □ Newtown, CT
Kruk, Valerie K., Libn.
COOK COUNTY STATE'S ATTORNEY'S OFFICE
LIBRARY □ Chicago, IL
Krull, Dr. Charles F., V.P., Corn Res.
DE KALB-PFIZER GENETICS - RESEARCH
LIBRARY □ DeKalb, IL
Krull, Lisa, Cur.
JACKSON HOMESTEAD - LIBRARY &
MANUSCRIPT COLLECTION □ Newton, MA
Krumm, Roger V., Libn.
UNIVERSITY OF FLORIDA - ENGINEERING &
PHYSICS LIBRARY □ Gainesville, FL
Krummes, Daniel, Tech.Serv.Libn.
UNIVERSITY OF CALIFORNIA, BERKELEY -
INSTITUTE OF TRANSPORTATION STUDIES
LIBRARY □ Berkeley, CA
Krupp, Dr. E.C., Dir.
GRIFFITH OBSERVATORY - LIBRARY □ Los
Angeles, CA
Krupp, Mary, Adm., Corp.Lib.
GETTY OIL COMPANY, INC. - CORPORATE
LIBRARY† □ Los Angeles, CA
Krupp, R.A., Lib.Dir.
WESTERN CONSERVATIVE BAPTIST SEMINARY
- CLINE-TUNNELL LIBRARY □ Portland, OR
Kruse, Carol M., Unit Mgr.
U.S. NATL. PARK SERVICE - FORT UNION NATL.
MONUMENT - LIBRARY □ Watrous, NM
Kruse, Gerald R., Dir.
RESEARCH MEDICAL CENTER - LOCKWOOD
MEMORIAL LIBRARY □ Kansas City, MO
Kruse, Ginny Moore, Dir.
UNIVERSITY OF WISCONSIN, MADISON -
COOPERATIVE CHILDREN'S BOOK CENTER
(CCBC) □ Madison, WI
Kruse, Harriet, Libn./Circ.
UNITED THEOLOGICAL SEMINARY OF THE
TWIN CITIES - LIBRARY □ New Brighton, MN
Kruse, Rhoda E., Sr.Libn.
SAN DIEGO PUBLIC LIBRARY - CALIFORNIA
ROOM □ San Diego, CA
Kruse, Rhoda E., Sr.Libn.
SAN DIEGO PUBLIC LIBRARY - GENEALOGY
ROOM □ San Diego, CA
Krush, Elizabeth, Info.Spec.
LAVENTHOL AND HORWATH - NATIONAL
INFORMATION CENTER □ Philadelphia, PA

Kruyer, Sheri, Hd., Ref.
LOS ANGELES COUNTY MEDICAL ASSOCIATION
- LIBRARY† □ Los Angeles, CA
Krymkowski, Joseph, O.F.M., Libn.
FRANCISCAN FRIARS - ASSUMPTION FRIARY
LIBRARY □ Pulaski, WI
Krynicki, Marguerite J., Hd.Libn.
ILLINOIS BELL TELEPHONE COMPANY -
LIBRARY □ Chicago, IL
Kryszak, Wayne D., Chf.
DISTRICT OF COLUMBIA PUBLIC LIBRARY -
BUSINESS, ECONOMICS & VOCATIONS
DIVISION □ Washington, DC
Kryztski, Michael, Ref.Libn.
AT & T BELL LABORATORIES - LIBRARY □
Murray Hill, NJ
Krzys, Dr. Richard, Dir.
UNIVERSITY OF PITTSBURGH - SCHOOL OF
LIBRARY & INFORMATION SCIENCE -
INTERNATIONAL LIB. INFO. CTR. □ Pittsburgh,
PA
Krzysiak, Patricia B., Libn.
DAMES & MOORE - CHICAGO LIBRARY □ Park
Ridge, IL
Kubal, Gene, Chf., Gen.Ref.Sect.
U.S. ARMY - PENTAGON LIBRARY □ Washington,
DC
Kubiak, Richard, Hist.
MERCYHURST COLLEGE - LIBRARY - ARCHIVES
□ Erie, PA
Kubic, J. Craig, Rd.Serv.Libn.
GOLDEN GATE BAPTIST THEOLOGICAL
SEMINARY - LIBRARY □ Mill Valley, CA
Kubik, Kim, Tech.Info.Spec.
SYVA COMPANY - LIBRARY/INFORMATION
CENTER □ Palo Alto, CA
Kubilius, Ramune, Ref. & Ser.Libn.
UNIVERSITY OF HEALTH SCIENCES/CHICAGO
MEDICAL SCHOOL - LIBRARY □ North Chicago,
IL
Kubiniec, Sr. Joyce, Asst.Libn.
HILBERT COLLEGE - MC GRATH LIBRARY -
SPECIAL COLLECTIONS □ Hamburg, NY
Kubisiak, Michael J., Hd., Acq.Sect.
U.S. GEOLOGICAL SURVEY - LIBRARY □ Reston,
VA
Kubjas, Anne, Health Sci.Libn.
SCARBOROUGH GENERAL HOSPITAL - HEALTH
SCIENCES LIBRARY □ Scarborough, ON
Kublin, Joyce A., Libn.
VICTORIA GENERAL HOSPITAL - HEALTH
SCIENCES LIBRARY □ Halifax, NS
Kubota, Charleen, Ref.Libn.
UNIVERSITY OF CALIFORNIA, BERKELEY -
PUBLIC HEALTH LIBRARY □ Berkeley, CA
Kubrin, Francine, Libn.
VALLEY PRESBYTERIAN HOSPITAL - LIBRARY
FOR MEDICAL AND HEALTH SCIENCES □ Van
Nuys, CA
Kucharski, Chris, Libn.
DETROIT FREE PRESS - LIBRARY □ Detroit, MI
Kuchinsky, Brenda, Hd. of Tech.Serv.
HARVARD UNIVERSITY - JOHN FITZGERALD
KENNEDY SCHOOL OF GOVERNMENT - LIBRARY
□ Cambridge, MA
Kuchinsky, Saul, Libn.
BROOKLYN HOSPITAL - MEDICAL LIBRARY □
Brooklyn, NY
Kuchler, LaVerne, Act.Libn.
CONTEMPORARY CRAFTS ASSOCIATION -
LIBRARY □ Portland, OR
Kuchta, Irene, Central Info. Files Libn.
CARPENTER (Guy) & COMPANY, INC. - LIBRARY
AND INFORMATION SERVICES □ New York, NY
Kuchta, Linda, Cat.Libn.
PRATT AND WHITNEY CANADA, INC. -
LIBRARY □ Longueuil, PQ
Kuck, Mary S., Libn.
U.S. COURT OF MILITARY APPEALS - LIBRARY
□ Washington, DC
Kucsma, Susan, Mgr.
MARSH AND MC LENNAN, INC. - INFORMATION
CENTER □ New York, NY

Kuczborski, Jackie, Sec./Libn.
UNIVERSITY OF MICHIGAN - AEROSPACE ENGINEERING DEPARTMENTAL LIBRARY □ Ann Arbor, MI

Kuczynski, Kathleen, Lib.Dir.
HELEN HAYES HOSPITAL - LIBRARY □ West Haverstraw, NY

Kudej, Blan Ka, Spec.Coll.
NEW YORK UNIVERSITY - SCHOOL OF LAW LIBRARY □ New York, NY

Kudiesy, Norma M., Pub.Serv.Libn.
U.S. ARMY AIR DEFENSE SCHOOL - LIBRARY† □ Ft. Bliss, TX

Kudlaty, Ruth, Libn.
ORPHAN VOYAGE - KAMMANDALE LIBRARY □ St. Paul, MN

Kudo, Kathleen S., Libn.
HONOLULU (City and County) - MUNICIPAL REFERENCE AND RECORDS CENTER □ Honolulu, HI

Kuehl, Warren F., Dir.
UNIVERSITY OF AKRON - CENTER FOR PEACE STUDIES - LIBRARY □ Akron, OH

Kuehling, Mary Alice, Libn.
METHODIST HOSPITAL - LIBRARY □ Madison, WI

Kuehn, Claire R., Archv./Libn.
PANHANDLE-PLAINS HISTORICAL MUSEUM - RESEARCH CENTER □ Canyon, TX

Kuehn, Jennifer, Info.Spec.
OHIO STATE UNIVERSITY - MECHANIZED INFORMATION CENTER (MIC) □ Columbus, OH

Kuehne, Patricia, Asst.Dir.
WESTERN EVANGELICAL SEMINARY - GEORGE HALLAUER MEMORIAL LIBRARY □ Milwaukie, OR

Kufahl, Catherine, Libn.
OLD AMERICAN INSURANCE COMPANY - LIBRARY □ Kansas City, MO

Kuhfeld, Albert, Cur. of Instruments
BAKKEN FOUNDATION - BAKKEN LIBRARY OF ELECTRICITY IN LIFE □ Minneapolis, MN

Kuhl, Danuta, Acq.Libn.
AMERICAN PETROLEUM INSTITUTE - LIBRARY □ Washington, DC

Kuhlmey-Williams, Karlan, Tech.Libn.
HONEYWELL, INC. - RESIDENTIAL ENGINEERING RESOURCE AND LEARNING CENTER □ Golden Valley, MN

Kuhn, Hannah R., Spec.Libn.
BRANDEIS-BARDIN INSTITUTE - HOUSE OF THE BOOK □ Brandeis, CA

Kuhner, David, Asst.Dir., Sci.
THE CLAREMONT COLLEGES - LIBRARY □ Claremont, CA

Kuhner, David, Libn.
THE CLAREMONT COLLEGES - NORMAN F. SPRAGUE MEMORIAL LIBRARY □ Claremont, CA

Kuhner, David, Libn.
THE CLAREMONT COLLEGES - SEELEY G. MUDD SCIENCE LIBRARY □ Claremont, CA

Kuhnlein, Sharon S., IRC Supv.
U.S. GEOLOGICAL SURVEY - WATER RESOURCES DIVISION - INFORMATION RESOURCE CENTER □ Indianapolis, IN

Kuhr, Charmain, Circ.Asst.
MC CORMICK THEOLOGICAL SEMINARY - LIBRARY† □ Chicago, IL

Kuhta, Candace, Coord., Pub.Serv./Dir.
FOUNDATION CENTER - NEW YORK - LIBRARY □ New York, NY

Kuhta, R., Rd.Serv.Libn.
PACE UNIVERSITY, PLEASANTVILLE/ BRIARCLIFF - EDWARD AND DORIS MORTOLA LIBRARY □ Pleasantville, NY

Kukla, Dr. Jon K., Asst.Dir., Pubn.
VIRGINIA STATE LIBRARY □ Richmond, VA

Kuklin, Susan B., County Law Libn.
SANTA CLARA COUNTY LAW LIBRARY □ San Jose, CA

Kulawiec, Barbara T., Mgr.
HIGH BLOOD PRESSURE INFORMATION CENTER □ Bethesda, MD

Kulberg, Lenore, Libn.
BUREAU OF JEWISH EDUCATION - COMMUNITY LIBRARY □ Getzville, NY

Kulchar, Alexander, Med.Libn.
BRYN MAWR HOSPITAL - MEDICAL LIBRARY □ Bryn Mawr, PA

Kulchar, Alexander, Med.Libn.
BRYN MAWR HOSPITAL - MEDICAL LIBRARY - NURSING DIVISION □ Bryn Mawr, PA

Kulenkamp, Dorothy, Lib.Asst.
ST. ANTHONY'S HOSPITAL - LIBRARY □ Alton, IL

Kull, Christine L., Archv.
MONROE COUNTY HISTORICAL MUSEUM - ARCHIVES □ Monroe, MI

Kuller, Alice B., Dir.
HARMARVILLE REHABILITATION CENTER - STAFF LIBRARY □ Pittsburgh, PA

Kulleseid, Eleanor, Lib.Dir.
BANK STREET COLLEGE OF EDUCATION - LIBRARY □ New York, NY

Kulys, Alfred, Cat.Libn.
COOK COUNTY LAW LIBRARY □ Chicago, IL

Kumar, Shireen, Labor Libn.
PROSKAUER, ROSE, GOETZ & MENDELSOHN - LIBRARY □ New York, NY

Kumar, Vijay, Hd., Proc.Serv.
UNIVERSITY OF WESTERN ONTARIO - SCIENCES LIBRARY □ London, ON

Kumatz, Cynthia C., Libn.
NORWICH EATON PHARMACEUTICALS, INC. - RESEARCH AND DEVELOPMENT LIBRARY □ Norwich, NY

Kumatz, Tad G., Asst.Dir.
PRATT INSTITUTE - LIBRARY □ Brooklyn, NY

Kunda, Vera, Ref.Coord.
UNIVERSITY OF ALBERTA - SCIENCE AND TECHNOLOGY LIBRARY □ Edmonton, AB

Kunde, Nancy, Archv./Rec.Mgr.
UNIVERSITY OF WISCONSIN, MADISON - ARCHIVES □ Madison, WI

Kunen, Eleanor, Libn.
MARLBOROUGH HOSPITAL - HEALTH SCIENCE LIBRARY □ Marlborough, MA

Kunes, Ella R., Libn.-Cat.
GENERAL ELECTRIC COMPANY - CORPORATE RESEARCH & DEVELOPMENT - WHITNEY INFORMATION SERVICES □ Schenectady, NY

Kung, Wen-Kai, Bibliog.
UNIVERSITY OF OREGON - ORIENTALIA COLLECTION □ Eugene, OR

Kunitz, Donald, Hd., Spec.Coll.
UNIVERSITY OF CALIFORNIA, DAVIS - UNIVERSITY LIBRARIES - SPECIAL COLLECTIONS □ Davis, CA

Kunkel, Barbara, Techn.
U.S. VETERANS ADMINISTRATION (NY-Buffalo) - MEDICAL CENTER LIBRARY SERVICE □ Buffalo, NY

Kunkel, Barbara K., Sr.Libn.
GENERAL MOTORS CORPORATION - RESEARCH LABORATORIES LIBRARY □ Warren, MI

Kunkel, Rita, Asst.Tech.Libn.
INSTITUTE OF LOGOPEDICS - TECHNICAL LIBRARY □ Wichita, KS

Kuntz, Helen H., Libn.
UNIVERSITY OF WISCONSIN, MADISON - PLANT PATHOLOGY MEMORIAL LIBRARY □ Madison, WI

Kuo, Andrew, Bible Cat.
AMERICAN BIBLE SOCIETY - LIBRARY □ New York, NY

Kuo, Frank F., Dir.
PORTLAND STATE UNIVERSITY - AUDIO-VISUAL SERVICES □ Portland, OR

Kuo, Margaret, Engr.Libn.
SCHLUMBERGER WELL SERVICES - ENGINEERING LIBRARY □ Houston, TX

Kuo, Mon-hua Mona, Chf., Cat.Sect.
U.S. DEPT. OF TRANSPORTATION - LIBRARY AND DISTRIBUTION SERVICES DIVISION □ Washington, DC

Kuo, Dr. Thomas, Cur.
UNIVERSITY OF PITTSBURGH - EAST ASIAN LIBRARY □ Pittsburgh, PA

Kupferberg, Natalie, Asst.Ref.
CORNELL UNIVERSITY - MEDICAL COLLEGE - SAMUEL J. WOOD LIBRARY □ New York, NY

Kupstas, Cassie, Libn.
MORTGAGE BANKERS ASSOCIATION OF AMERICA - LIBRARY □ Washington, DC

Kupstas, Kathryn, Hd., Tech.Serv.
AMERICAN BANKERS ASSOCIATION - LIBRARY & INFORMATION SERVICES □ Washington, DC

Kuramoto, Mary I., Res.Libn.
FIRST HAWAIIAN BANK - RESEARCH DIVISION LIBRARY† □ Honolulu, HI

Kurceba, Kathy, Libn.
BURNET, DUCKWORTH & PALMER, BARRISTERS & SOLICITORS - LIBRARY □ Calgary, AB

Kurka, Adele R., Asst.Mgr.-Libn.
OHIO BELL - CORPORATE LIBRARY □ Cleveland, OH

Kurland, Mildred, Libn.
CONGREGATION RODEPH SHALOM - LIBRARY □ Philadelphia, PA

Kurland, Roslyn, Libn.
TEMPLE BETH EL - BILLIE DAVIS RODENBERG MEMORIAL LIBRARY □ Hollywood, FL

Kurtik, Frank, Proj.Archv.
UNIVERSITY OF PITTSBURGH - ARCHIVES OF INDUSTRIAL SOCIETY □ Pittsburgh, PA

Kurtz, Diana, Assoc.
INSTITUTE FOR THEOLOGICAL & PHILOSOPHICAL STUDIES - LIBRARY □ Bloomington, IL

Kurtz, Dr. James, Dir.
INSTITUTE FOR THEOLOGICAL & PHILOSOPHICAL STUDIES - LIBRARY □ Bloomington, IL

Kurtz, Joan, Assoc.
INSTITUTE FOR THEOLOGICAL & PHILOSOPHICAL STUDIES - LIBRARY □ Bloomington, IL

Kurtz, Kathy, Info.Ctr.Coord.
PLANNED PARENTHOOD ASSOCIATION OF ST. LOUIS - FAMILY PLANNING LIBRARY □ St. Louis, MO

Kurtz, Martha, AV Room
REVEILLE UNITED METHODIST CHURCH - REVEILLE MEMORIAL LIBRARY □ Richmond, VA

Kurtz, Mike, Classified Info.Serv.
RAND CORPORATION - LIBRARY† □ Santa Monica, CA

Kurutz, Gary, Supv., Spec.Coll.
CALIFORNIA STATE LIBRARY □ Sacramento, CA

Kurutz, K.D., Cur., Educ.
CROCKER ART MUSEUM - RESEARCH LIBRARY □ Sacramento, CA

Kusada, Haruyoshi, Dir.
INSTITUTE OF BUDDHIST STUDIES - LIBRARY □ Berkeley, CA

Kusche, Genevieve, Libn.
KANKAKEE COUNTY HISTORICAL SOCIETY - LIBRARY □ Kankakee, IL

Kushner, Ricki, Co-Dir.
NATIONAL PUBLIC RADIO - BROADCAST LIBRARY □ Washington, DC

Kuskowski, Rev. Jerome, S.A.C., Libn.
PALLOTTINE PROVINCIALATE LIBRARY □ Milwaukee, WI

Kusmik, Cornell J., Acq.Libn.
CONCORDIA COLLEGE - KLINCK MEMORIAL LIBRARY □ River Forest, IL

Kusnerz, Peggy Ann, Libn.
UNIVERSITY OF MICHIGAN - ART & ARCHITECTURE LIBRARY □ Ann Arbor, MI

Kussow, Zolitta, Libn.
MADISON PUBLIC LIBRARY - LITERATURE AND SOCIAL SCIENCES □ Madison, WI

Kustelski, Jeanette, Libn.
CHAMPION INTERNATIONAL - TECHNICAL CENTER LIBRARY □ St. Paul, MN

Kutaka-Barkley, Aileen, Info.Spec.
WED ENTERPRISES - RESEARCH LIBRARY □
Glendale, CA
Kuther, Patricia A., Med.Lib.Techn.
U.S. AIR FORCE HOSPITAL - MEDICAL LIBRARY
(AL-Montgomery) □ Montgomery, AL
Kutzner, Dr. Patricia L., Exec.Dir.
WORLD HUNGER EDUCATION SERVICE -
LIBRARY □ Washington, DC
Kuzma, Pamela J., Anl./Libn.
SHERWIN-WILLIAMS COMPANY -
INFORMATION CENTER □ Cleveland, OH
Kwan, Patrick, Supv., Pub.Serv.
CHINESE NATIONALIST LEAGUE OF CANADA -
LIBRARY† □ Vancouver, BC
Kwiatek, Gary W., Archv.
EVANGELICAL AND REFORMED HISTORICAL
SOCIETY - EDEN ARCHIVES □ Webster Groves,
MO
Kwiatkowski, Phillip C., Dir.
SLOAN (Alfred P., Jr.) MUSEUM - MERLE G.
PERRY ARCHIVES □ Flint, MI
Kwong, Bella, Women's Hosp.Libn.
LOS ANGELES COUNTY/UNIVERSITY OF
SOUTHERN CALIFORNIA MEDICAL CENTER -
MEDICAL LIBRARIES □ Los Angeles, CA
Kyed, James M., Hd., Engr.Libs.
MASSACHUSETTS INSTITUTE OF TECHNOLOGY
- BARKER ENGINEERING LIBRARY □ Cambridge,
MA
Kyed, James M., Act.Hd., Sci.Libs.
MASSACHUSETTS INSTITUTE OF TECHNOLOGY
- SCIENCE LIBRARY □ Cambridge, MA
Kyle, Jacque, Ref.Libn.
MOBIL RESEARCH & DEVELOPMENT
CORPORATION - DALLAS RESEARCH DIVISION
- LIBRARY □ Dallas, TX
Kysely, Elizabeth, Chf., Ref.Div.
U.S. AIR FORCE ACADEMY - LIBRARY □
Colorado Springs, CO
Kyser, Jack, Chamber Econ.
LOS ANGELES CHAMBER OF COMMERCE -
ECONOMIC INFORMATION & RESEARCH
DEPARTMENT LIBRARY □ Los Angeles, CA

L

La Count, Louise W., Chf.Libn.
CHURCH OF JESUS CHRIST OF LATTER-DAY
SAINTS - VENTURA BRANCH GENEALOGICAL
LIBRARY □ Ventura, CA
La Grange, Charlene, Circ. & ILL
UNION UNIVERSITY - ALBANY MEDICAL
COLLEGE - SCHAFFER LIBRARY OF THE HEALTH
SCIENCES □ Albany, NY
La Haye, Claude, Documentaliste
LA SOCIETE LA HAYE OUELLET - LIBRAIRIE □
Montreal, PQ
La Manna, Joan, Libn.
MC KESSON - R & D CENTER LIBRARY □ Dublin,
CA
La Pointe, Madeleine, Lib.Techn.
SHERIDAN COLLEGE OF APPLIED ARTS AND
TECHNOLOGY - SCHOOL OF DESIGN - LIBRARY
□ Mississauga, ON
La Rocco, August, Spec. Projects Libn.
UNIVERSITY OF MIAMI - SCHOOL OF
MEDICINE - LOUIS CALDER MEMORIAL
LIBRARY □ Miami, FL
La Rose, Al, Hd.Ref.Libn.
WITTENBERG UNIVERSITY - THOMAS LIBRARY
□ Springfield, OH
Laats, Armilda, Cat.
PORT AUTHORITY OF NEW YORK AND NEW
JERSEY - LIBRARY □ New York, NY
LaBarbera, Diane, Libn.
KANSAS STATE UNIVERSITY - GRAIN SCIENCE
AND INDUSTRY - SWANSON MEMORIAL
LIBRARY □ Manhattan, KS

LaBau, Anthony F., Dir.
XAVIER SOCIETY FOR THE BLIND - NATIONAL
CATHOLIC PRESS AND LIBRARY FOR THE
VISUALLY HANDICAPPED □ New York, NY
Labault, Fernando
HARTFORD PUBLIC LIBRARY - REFERENCE AND
GENERAL READING DEPARTMENT □ Hartford,
CT
Labedz, Elizabeth K., Hd.Libn.
HINCKLEY & ALLEN - LAW LIBRARY □
Providence, RI
LaBerge, Ann, Asst.Dir.
VIRGINIA POLYTECHNIC INSTITUTE AND
STATE UNIVERSITY - CENTER FOR THE STUDY
OF SCIENCE IN SOCIETY - LIBRARY □
Blacksburg, VA
Laberge, Leo, Dir.
OBLATE FATHERS - BIBLIOTHEQUE
DESCHATELETS □ Ottawa, ON
Labille, Lucien, Dir.
QUEBEC PROVINCE - OFFICE DES
COMMUNICATIONS SOCIALES - BIBLIOTHEQUE
ET CENTRE DE DOCUMENTATION □ Montreal,
PQ
LaBissoniere, William, Libn.
UNIVERSITY OF MINNESOTA - GOVERNMENT
PUBLICATIONS LIBRARY □ Minneapolis, MN
Labonte, Ronald, Hd., Per. Unit
NATIONAL LIBRARY OF CANADA - CANADIAN
BOOK EXCHANGE CENTRE (CBEC) □ Ottawa, ON
Laborie, Tim, Hd.
DREXEL UNIVERSITY - W.W. HAGERTY
LIBRARY - SPECIAL COLLECTIONS □
Philadelphia, PA
Labovitz, Judy, Mgr.
CETUS CORPORATION - RESEARCH LIBRARY □
Emeryville, CA
Labree, Rosanne, Dir.
MC LEAN HOSPITAL - MENTAL HEALTH
SCIENCES LIBRARY □ Belmont, MA
Labrie, Jean-Marc, Libn., Online Serv.
QUEBEC PROVINCE - MINISTERE DES
COMMUNICATIONS - BIBLIOTHEQUE
ADMINISTRATIVE □ Quebec, PQ
Labun, Lynn, Sci.Info.Spec.
CARNEGIE-MELLON UNIVERSITY -
ENGINEERING & SCIENCE LIBRARY □
Pittsburgh, PA
Lacayo, Carmela G., Natl.Exec.Dir.
ASOCIACION NACIONAL PRO PERSONAS
MAYORES - LIBRARY □ Los Angeles, CA
Lachance, Lise, Documentaliste
CHAMBRE DES NOTAIRES DU QUEBEC -
CENTRE DE DOCUMENTATION □ Montreal, PQ
Lacher, Pam, Lib.Mgr.
MERCY HOSPITAL - MEDICAL LIBRARY □ Valley
City, ND
LaChine, Guy L., Supv. Park Ranger
U.S. NATL. PARK SERVICE - DE SOTO NATL.
MEMORIAL - LIBRARY □ Bradenton, FL
Lachowicz, Audrey D., Med.Libn.
LEWIS-GALE HOSPITAL CORPORATION -
LEWIS-GALE MEDICAL LIBRARY □ Salem, VA
Lackner, Irene, Libn.
CANADA - ECONOMIC COUNCIL OF CANADA -
LIBRARY □ Ottawa, ON
Lacoste, Marie, Lib.Techn.
CANADA - SECRETARY OF STATE -
TRANSLATION BUREAU - LIBRARY □ Montreal,
PQ
Lacourte, Carol, Libn.
SHAWINIGAN CONSULTANTS INC. - LIBRARY □
Montreal, PQ
LaCroix, Carla, Libn.
DALLAS PUBLIC LIBRARY - BUSINESS AND
TECHNOLOGY DIVISION □ Dallas, TX
Lacroix, Denise, Libn.
UNIVERSITE DE MONTREAL - OPTOMETRIE-
BIBLIOTHEQUE □ Montreal, PQ
Lacy, Margaret A., Med.Serv.Sec.
BISSELL (Emily P.) HOSPITAL - MEDICAL
LIBRARY □ Wilmington, DE

Ladd, Anna, Asst.Libn.
TRINITY LUTHERAN CHURCH - LIBRARY □
Madison, WI
Ladd, Everett C., Jr., Exec.Dir.
UNIVERSITY OF CONNECTICUT - INSTITUTE
FOR SOCIAL INQUIRY □ Storrs, CT
Ladd, Everett C., Exec.Dir.
UNIVERSITY OF CONNECTICUT - ROPER
CENTER □ Storrs, CT
Ladeau, Beth, Pk.Libn.
U.S. NATL. PARK SERVICE - GLACIER NATL.
PARK - GEORGE C. RUHLE LIBRARY □ West
Glacier, MT
Ladeira, Caroline, Procurement Ref.Libn.
U.S. GENERAL SERVICES ADMINISTRATION -
GSA LIBRARY □ Washington, DC
Ladell, Daniel W., Archv.
STRATFORD SHAKESPEAREAN FESTIVAL
FOUNDATION OF CANADA - STRATFORD
FESTIVAL ARCHIVES □ Stratford, ON
Ladion, Gertrudes J., Law Libn.
SAN JOAQUIN COUNTY LAW LIBRARY □
Stockton, CA
Ladley, Barbara, Res.Libn.
NATIONAL BROADCASTING COMPANY, INC. -
REFERENCE LIBRARY □ New York, NY
Ladner, Betty, Clinical Res.Libn.
WAKE FOREST UNIVERSITY - BOWMAN GRAY
SCHOOL OF MEDICINE - COY C. CARPENTER
LIBRARY □ Winston-Salem, NC
Ladner, Mary H., Libn.
HARRISON COUNTY LAW LIBRARY □ Gulfport,
MS
Ladner, Robert, Sr.Res.Assoc.
BEHAVIORAL SCIENCE RESEARCH
CORPORATION - INFORMATION CENTER □
Coral Gables, FL
Ladner, Sharon, Adm., Lib.Serv.
CORDIS CORPORATION - LIBRARY □ Miami, FL
Ladner, Terry T., Hd.Libn.
ITT CORPORATION - ITT AVIONICS/DEFENSE
COMMUNICATIONS DIVISION - TECHNICAL
LIBRARY □ Nutley, NJ
Laduke, M. J. Cockerline, Archv.
MISSISQUOI HISTORICAL SOCIETY - CORNELL
MILL MUSEUM - REFERENCE LIBRARY &
ARCHIVES □ Stanbridge East, PQ
Lady, Lynn, Sr.Archv.
KENTUCKY STATE DEPARTMENT FOR
LIBRARIES & ARCHIVES - ARCHIVES □
Frankfort, KY
Laes, Diane L., Libn.
GREEN BAY PRESS-GAZETTE - LIBRARY □
Green Bay, WI
Lafferty, LaVedi, Libn.
PHILOSOPHICAL HERITAGE INSTITUTE -
LIBRARY OF ESOTERIC STUDIES □ Fairbanks,
AK
Lafleur, Sr. Germaine, Hd. of Dept.
ST. VINCENT HOSPITAL - MEDICAL LIBRARY □
Ottawa, ON
LaFleur, Leslie, Curric.Libn.
UNIVERSITY OF ALBERTA - H.T. COUTTS
LIBRARY □ Edmonton, AB
LaFollette, Rosemarie B., Libn.
COMBS COLLEGE OF MUSIC - LIBRARY □ Bryn
Mawr, PA
LaFon-Horstmann, Zantha, Coord.
WASHINGTON COUNTY TOY LENDING LIBRARY
□ Stillwater, MN
Lafortune, Francois, Chf.Libn.
MUSEE DU QUEBEC - BIBLIOTHEQUE □ Quebec,
PQ
Lafrance, Claude, Dir.
CENTRE DE RECHERCHE INDUSTRIELLE DU
QUEBEC - DIRECTION DE L'INFORMATION
TECHNOLOGIQUE □ Ste. Foy, PQ
Lafranchi, William E., Dir., Libs./Media Rsrcs.
INDIANA UNIVERSITY OF PENNSYLVANIA -
UNIVERSITY LIBRARY □ Indiana, PA

LaFrank, Kathleen, Prog.Anl.
NEW YORK STATE PARKS AND RECREATION - DIVISION FOR HISTORIC PRESERVATION - FIELD SERVICES BUREAU - LIBRARY □ Albany, NY

Lagano, Vincent, Med.Libn.
KAISER-PERMANENTE MEDICAL CENTER - HEALTH SCIENCES LIBRARY □ San Francisco, CA

Lagarec, Catherine, Hd., Monographs Unit
NATIONAL LIBRARY OF CANADA - CANADIAN BOOK EXCHANGE CENTRE (CBEC) □ Ottawa, ON

Lagasse, Carol T., Cat.Libn.
RENSSELAER POLYTECHNIC INSTITUTE - FOLSOM LIBRARY □ Troy, NY

LaGasse, Robert C., Exec.Dir.
INTERNATIONAL MICROWAVE POWER INSTITUTE - REFERENCE LIBRARY □ Vienna, VA

Lagroue, Mary, Med.Libn.
OUR LADY OF LOURDES REGIONAL MEDICAL & EDUCATION CENTER - LEARNING RESOURCE CENTER† □ Lafayette, LA

LaGrutta, Charles, Info./Rec.Mgr..
URBAN INVESTMENT AND DEVELOPMENT COMPANY - INFORMATION CENTER □ Chicago, IL

Lahey, Joanne I., Libn.
BATTELLE NEW ENGLAND MARINE RESEARCH LABORATORIES - LIBRARY □ Duxbury, MA

Lahey, Michelle, Ser.Libn.
ST. LUKE'S HOSPITAL OF KANSAS CITY - MEDICAL LIBRARY □ Kansas City, MO

Lai, Grace, Asst.Libn.
SUNY - SYRACUSE EDUCATIONAL OPPORTUNITY CENTER - PAUL ROBESON LIBRARY □ Syracuse, NY

Lai, John Yung-Hsiang, Assoc.Libn./Cat.
HARVARD UNIVERSITY - HARVARD-YENCHING LIBRARY □ Cambridge, MA

Lai, Kum Pui, Res.
HAWAII CHINESE HISTORY CENTER - LIBRARY □ Honolulu, HI

Lai, Violet L., Hd.Libn.
HAWAII CHINESE HISTORY CENTER - LIBRARY □ Honolulu, HI

Lain, Christine R., Libn.
U.S. AIR FORCE BASE - CARSWELL BASE LIBRARY □ Carswell AFB, TX

Lain, Mildred, Hist.
COLUMBIA COUNTY HISTORICAL SOCIETY - MUSEUM □ St. Helens, OR

Laing, Gregory H., Cur./Genealogist
HAVERHILL PUBLIC LIBRARY - SPECIAL COLLECTIONS DIVISION □ Haverhill, MA

Laing, Michele, Ref.Libn.
UNIVERSITY OF MANITOBA - ARCHITECTURE & FINE ARTS LIBRARY □ Winnipeg, MB

Laird, Marilyn Poe, Hd.Libn.
SOUTH SUBURBAN GENEALOGICAL & HISTORICAL SOCIETY - LIBRARY □ South Holland, IL

Laird, Mary Susan, Mgr., Lib.Serv.
ALZA CORPORATION - RESEARCH LIBRARY □ Palo Alto, CA

Laite, Berkley, Ctr.Libn.
SHIPPENSBURG UNIVERSITY - EZRA LEHMAN LIBRARY □ Shippensburg, PA

Lajara, Luz M., Libn.
UNIVERSITY OF PUERTO RICO - PUERTO RICAN COLLECTION† □ Rio Piedras, PR

Lake, Carlton, Exec.Cur., French Coll.
UNIVERSITY OF TEXAS, AUSTIN - HARRY RANSOM HUMANITIES RESEARCH CENTER □ Austin, TX

Lake, David
INTERLOCHEN CENTER FOR THE ARTS - MUSIC LIBRARY □ Interlochen, MI

Lake, Jeff, Microcomputer Cons.
SANGAMON STATE UNIVERSITY - EAST CENTRAL NETWORK - LIBRARY □ Springfield, IL

Lake, Nora, Exec.Dir.
MIAMI VALLEY REGIONAL PLANNING COMMISSION - LIBRARY □ Dayton, OH

Laki, Georgette, Bibliothecaire
CONSERVATOIRE D'ART DRAMATIQUE DE QUEBEC - BIBLIOTHEQUE □ Quebec, PQ

Lalande, Christine, Asst.Mgr.
SPORT INFORMATION RESOURCE CENTRE □ Ottawa, ON

Lalley, John B., Hd., Acq.
EAST STROUDSBURG UNIVERSITY - KENT LIBRARY† □ East Stroudsburg, PA

Lalonde, Jules, Pub. Search Rm.
CANADA - CONSUMER AND CORPORATE AFFAIRS CANADA - PATENT OFFICE LIBRARY □ Ottawa, ON

Lalonde, Vivian, ILL
WADHAMS HALL SEMINARY - COLLEGE LIBRARY □ Ogdensburg, NY

Lam, Annie S., Libn.
NATIONAL ECONOMIC RESEARCH ASSOCIATES, INC. - LIBRARY □ Los Angeles, CA

Lam, Judy, Libn.
DE SOTO, INC. - INFORMATION CENTER □ Des Plaines, IL

Lamar, Christine, Ref.Libn.
RHODE ISLAND HISTORICAL SOCIETY - LIBRARY □ Providence, RI

Lamarche, Roland P., Sec.
INSTITUT CANADIEN-FRANCAIS D'OTTAWA - LIBRARY □ Ottawa, ON

Lamb, Alma, Asst.Libn.
SAN DIEGO STATE UNIVERSITY - MEDIA & CURRICULUM CENTER† □ San Diego, CA

Lamb, Cheryl, Info.Sci.
JAMES RIVER CORPORATION - NEENAH TECHNICAL CENTER - TECHNICAL INFORMATION CENTER □ Neenah, WI

Lamb, Gertrude, Ph.D., Dir.
HARTFORD HOSPITAL - HEALTH SCIENCE LIBRARIES □ Hartford, CT

Lamb, John M., Info.Dir.
LEWIS UNIVERSITY - CANAL ARCHIVES AND SPECIAL COLLECTION OF HISTORY □ Romeoville, IL

Lamb, Jolaine, Br.Libn.
U.S. AIR FORCE - FLIGHT TEST CENTER - TECHNICAL LIBRARY □ Edwards AFB, CA

Lamb, Ms. Lebby B., Bus.Libn.
GREENSBORO PUBLIC LIBRARY - BUSINESS LIBRARY □ Greensboro, NC

Lamb, Norma Jean, Hd.
BUFFALO & ERIE COUNTY PUBLIC LIBRARY - MUSIC DEPARTMENT □ Buffalo, NY

Lamb, Patricia, Law Libn.
DEL NORTE COUNTY LAW LIBRARY □ Crescent City, CA

Lamb, Seonaid, Libn.
UNIVERSITY OF BRITISH COLUMBIA - HUMANITIES AND SOCIAL SCIENCES DIVISION □ Vancouver, BC

Lamb, Sheila, Asst.Tech.Serv./Ref.Libn.
U.S. COAST GUARD ACADEMY - LIBRARY □ New London, CT

Lamb, Una, Asst. to Libn.
GOLDEN VALLEY LUTHERAN COLLEGE - LIBRARY† □ Minneapolis, MN

Lambers, Stephen, Govt.Doc./Info.Serv.
CALVIN COLLEGE AND SEMINARY - LIBRARY □ Grand Rapids, MI

Lamberson, Margaret A., Supv., Rec.Mgt.
MERIDIAN LAND & MINERAL COMPANY - TECHNICAL SERVICES □ Billings, MT

Lambert, Asst.Prof.Robert A.
U.S. NAVY - NAVAL ACADEMY - NIMITZ LIBRARY □ Annapolis, MD

Lambert, Barbara, Adm.Asst.
COMPREHENSIVE HEALTH PLANNING OF NORTHWEST ILLINOIS - LIBRARY □ Rockford, IL

Lambert, Dennis, Libn.
UNIVERSITY OF PITTSBURGH - DARLINGTON MEMORIAL LIBRARY □ Pittsburgh, PA

Lambert, Helene D., Med.Libn.
NEW ROCHELLE HOSPITAL MEDICAL CENTER - J. MARSHALL PERLEY HEALTH SCIENCE LIBRARY □ New Rochelle, NY

Lambert, Jeffrey M., Libn.
ERNST & WHINNEY - LIBRARY □ Los Angeles, CA

Lambert, Maureen, Ref.Libn.
UNIVERSITY OF PITTSBURGH - GRADUATE SCHOOL OF BUSINESS LIBRARY □ Pittsburgh, PA

Lambert, Michael P., Asst.Dir.
NATIONAL HOME STUDY COUNCIL - LIBRARY □ Washington, DC

Lambert, Nancy E.
3M - PATENT AND TECHNICAL COMMUNICATIONS SERVICES □ St. Paul, MN

Lambert, Nancy S., Libn.
YALE UNIVERSITY - ART AND ARCHITECTURE LIBRARY □ New Haven, CT

Lambert, P., Cat.
SOUTHWESTERN UNIVERSITY - SCHOOL OF LAW LIBRARY □ Los Angeles, CA

Lambert, Peggy B., Libn.
DUKE POWER COMPANY - DAVID NABOW LIBRARY □ Charlotte, NC

Lambert, Raymond, Owner
LAMBERT (Harold M.) STUDIOS - LIBRARY □ Philadelphia, PA

Lambert, Rose, Libn.
LOUISIANA STATE MUSEUM - LOUISIANA HISTORICAL CENTER □ New Orleans, LA

Lambkin, Claire A., Chf.Libn.
AMERICAN MANAGEMENT ASSOCIATIONS - LIBRARY □ New York, NY

LaMere, Sheena
MONTANA STATE LIBRARY □ Helena, MT

Lamers, Carl, Foreign Law Libn.
YALE UNIVERSITY - LAW LIBRARY □ New Haven, CT

Lamers, Claire, Asst.Libn.
LONG ISLAND HISTORICAL SOCIETY - LIBRARY □ Brooklyn, NY

Lamirande, Armand, Chf.Libn.
COLLEGE MILITAIRE ROYAL DE ST-JEAN - LIBRARY □ St. Jean, PQ

Lamkin, Shirley, Clerk
HEWLETT-PACKARD COMPANY - AVONDALE DIVISION LIBRARY □ Avondale, PA

Lamont, Bridget L., Dir.
ILLINOIS STATE LIBRARY □ Springfield, IL

Lamont, Joyce H., Cur.
UNIVERSITY OF ALABAMA - WILLIAM STANLEY HOOLE SPECIAL COLLECTIONS LIBRARY □ University, AL

Lamont, Martha, Slide Libn.
TUCSON MUSEUM OF ART - LIBRARY □ Tucson, AZ

Lamont, Sylvia
LOS ANGELES HARBOR COLLEGE - LIBRARY - ARCHIVES □ Wilmington, CA

Lamoreux, Carole, Data Dissem.Off.
CANADA - STATISTICS CANADA - ADVISORY SERVICES - MONTREAL REFERENCE CENTRE □ Montreal, PQ

Lamoureux, Florence, Med.Libn.
BACKUS (William W.) HOSPITAL - MEDICAL/ NURSING LIBRARY □ Norwich, CT

Lamoureux, Lorraine, Doc.
INSTITUT CANADIEN D'EDUCATION DES ADULTES ET RELAIS-FEMMES DE MONTREAL - CENTRE DE DOCUMENTATION □ Montreal, PQ

Lamphear, Alberta E., Libn.
OCEAN CITY HISTORICAL MUSEUM - LIBRARY □ Ocean City, NJ

Lampman, Wilma, Asst.Libn.
SOUTHERN ILLINOIS UNIVERSITY, CARBONDALE - UNDERGRADUATE LIBRARY □ Carbondale, IL

Lampson, Virginia, Dental Libn.
TEMPLE UNIVERSITY - HEALTH SCIENCES CENTER - LIBRARY □ Philadelphia, PA

Lamrey, Helen, Supv., Info.Serv.
   PPG INDUSTRIES, INC. - C & R GROUP -
   RESEARCH CENTER LIBRARY □ Allison Park, PA
Lancaster, Herman, Dir., Res.
   GLENDALE UNIVERSITY - COLLEGE OF LAW
   LIBRARY □ Glendale, CA
Lancaster, John, Hd., Spec.Coll./Archv.
   AMHERST COLLEGE - SPECIAL COLLECTIONS
   DEPARTMENT AND ARCHIVES □ Amherst, MA
Lancaster, Kathryn, Tech.Serv.
   JOHNSON & SWANSON - LIBRARY □ Dallas, TX
Lancaster, Kevin, Asst. Law Libn.
   NEW MEXICO STATE SUPREME COURT - LAW
   LIBRARY □ Santa Fe, NM
Lancaster, Olive V., Chm., LRC
   FAIRVIEW COLLEGE - LEARNING RESOURCES
   CENTRE □ Fairview, AB
Lance, Gary L., Info.Serv.Mgr.
   BOSTON CONSULTING GROUP - WEST COAST
   INFORMATION CENTER □ Menlo Park, CA
Land, Iris L., Mgr., Lib.Serv.
   AIR CANADA - LIBRARY □ Montreal, PQ
Land, R. Brian, Dir.
   ONTARIO - LEGISLATIVE ASSEMBLY -
   LEGISLATIVE LIBRARY RESEARCH AND
   INFORMATION SERVICES □ Toronto, ON
Landau, Cynthia, Pub.Serv.Libn.
   FRANKLIN PIERCE LAW CENTER - LIBRARY □
   Concord, NH
Landau, Zuki, Chf.Libn.
   SCHOOL OF VISUAL ARTS - LIBRARY □ New
   York, NY
Landeck, Mary E., Pub.Serv.Libn.
   MILWAUKEE AREA TECHNICAL COLLEGE -
   RASCHE MEMORIAL LIBRARY □ Milwaukee, WI
Landenberger, Sally, Supv., Tech.Proc.
   SANDIA NATIONAL LABORATORIES -
   TECHNICAL LIBRARY □ Albuquerque, NM
Lander, James H., Lib.Mgr.
   MERCY HEALTH CENTER - ANTHONY C. PFOHL
   HEALTH SCIENCE LIBRARY □ Dubuque, IA
Landers, Katherine, Libn.
   EPISCOPAL CHURCH OF THE HOLY FAITH -
   PARISH LIBRARY □ Santa Fe, NM
Landfield, Jean, Chf.Libn.
   U.S. VETERANS ADMINISTRATION (NE-Lincoln)
   - MEDICAL CENTER LIBRARY □ Lincoln, NE
Landgraff, Sue, Cat.
   HONEYWELL, INC. - SYSTEMS & RESEARCH
   CENTER - LIBRARY □ Minneapolis, MN
Landis, Kay, Lit.Chem.
   ASHLAND CHEMICAL COMPANY - TECHNICAL
   INFORMATION CENTER □ Columbus, OH
Landis, Linda, Dir., ERC
   COLUMBUS TECHNICAL INSTITUTE -
   EDUCATIONAL RESOURCES CENTER □
   Columbus, OH
Landkamer, Mary, Cur.
   CUSTER COUNTY HISTORICAL SOCIETY -
   LIBRARY □ Broken Bow, NE
Landon, Richard G., Dept.Hd.
   UNIVERSITY OF TORONTO - THOMAS FISHER
   RARE BOOK LIBRARY □ Toronto, ON
Landon, Rosemary, Found.Ctr.Coll.
   JACKSON METROPOLITAN LIBRARY -
   INFORMATION AND REFERENCE DIVISION □
   Jackson, MS
Landress, Sylvia, Dir. & Libn.
   WORLD ZIONIST ORGANIZATION - AMERICAN
   SECTION - ZIONIST ARCHIVES AND LIBRARY □
   New York, NY
Landrum, Cathy, Tech.Serv.
   KAISER-PERMANENTE MEDICAL CENTER -
   HEALTH SCIENCES LIBRARY □ Sacramento, CA
Landrum, Hollis, Chf., Tech.Proc.Sect.
   U.S. ARMY - ENGINEER WATERWAYS
   EXPERIMENT STATION - TECHNICAL
   INFORMATION CENTER □ Vicksburg, MS
Landrum, John H., Dir. of Rd.Serv.
   SOUTH CAROLINA STATE LIBRARY □ Columbia,
   SC

Landry, Mr. Berthold, Adm.Asst.
   SOLEIL LIMITEE - CENTRE DE
   DOCUMENTATION □ Quebec, PQ
Lands, Rosemary J., Libn.
   CHARLOTTE AND MECKLENBURG COUNTY
   PUBLIC LIBRARY - CAROLINA ROOM □
   Charlotte, NC
Landsiedel, Diane, Ser. Control Libn.
   WAYNE STATE UNIVERSITY - SCHOOL OF
   MEDICINE - VERA PARSHALL SHIFFMAN
   MEDICAL LIBRARY □ Detroit, MI
Landstreet, Peter, Dp.Dir., CERLAC.
   YORK UNIVERSITY - CENTRE FOR RESEARCH
   ON LATIN AMERICA AND THE CARIBBEAN -
   CERLAC-LARU DOCUMENTATION CENTRE □
   Downsview, ON
Landwirth, Trudy, Dir.
   METHODIST MEDICAL CENTER OF ILLINOIS -
   MEDICAL LIBRARY □ Peoria, IL
Lane, Alice I., Lib.Assoc.
   ILLINOIS STATE DEPARTMENT OF ENERGY
   AND NATURAL RESOURCES - CHICAGO ENERGY
   OPERATIONS LIBRARY □ Chicago, IL
Lane, Beulah R., Media Dir.
   FIRST BAPTIST CHURCH - MATTIE D. HALL
   LIBRARY □ Rosedale, MS
Lane, Carl, Keeper of Mss.
   NEW JERSEY HISTORICAL SOCIETY - LIBRARY
   □ Newark, NJ
Lane, David L., Supt.
   U.S. NATL. PARK SERVICE - PIPESTONE NATL.
   MONUMENT - LIBRARY & ARCHIVES □
   Pipestone, MN
Lane, David T., Adm.Asst./Info.Spec.
   NEW YORK STATE OFFICE OF MENTAL HEALTH
   - NEW YORK STATE PSYCHIATRIC INSTITUTE
   - LIBRARY □ New York, NY
Lane, Diana, Ref.Libn.
   UNIVERSITY OF CALIFORNIA, SAN DIEGO -
   SCRIPPS INSTITUTION OF OCEANOGRAPHY
   LIBRARY □ La Jolla, CA
Lane, Eileen L., Libn.
   GENERAL MOTORS CORPORATION - AC SPARK
   PLUG DIVISION - ENGINEERING LIBRARY □
   Flint, MI
Lane, James B., Co-Dir.
   INDIANA UNIVERSITY NORTHWEST -
   CALUMET REGIONAL ARCHIVES □ Gary, IN
Lane, Joyce A., Libn.
   U.S. NAVY - NAVAL MILITARY PERSONNEL
   COMMAND - TECHNICAL LIBRARY □
   Washington, DC
Lane, M.K., Media Supv.
   RUTGERS UNIVERSITY, THE STATE
   UNIVERSITY OF NEW JERSEY - BLANCHE AND
   IRVING LAURIE MUSIC LIBRARY □ New
   Brunswick, NJ
Lane, Mary G., Sr.Libn.
   HISTORICAL FOUNDATION OF THE
   PRESBYTERIAN AND REFORMED CHURCHES -
   LIBRARY AND ARCHIVES □ Montreat, NC
Lane, Nina M., Lib.Dir.
   GROUP HEALTH ASSOCIATION OF AMERICA,
   INC. - GERTRUDE STURGES MEMORIAL
   LIBRARY □ Washington, DC
Lane, Robert B., Dir.
   U.S. AIR FORCE - AIR UNIVERSITY - LIBRARY □
   Maxwell AFB, AL
Lane, Sandra G., Sr.Libn.
   BROOKHAVEN NATIONAL LABORATORY -
   NUCLEAR WASTE MANAGEMENT LIBRARY □
   Upton, NY
Lane, Suzette, Cur.Asst.
   CORNELL UNIVERSITY - HERBERT F. JOHNSON
   MUSEUM OF ART - REFERENCE LIBRARY □
   Ithaca, NY
Lane, William T., Hd., Info.Serv.
   SUNY - COLLEGE AT GENESEO - COLLEGE
   LIBRARIES □ Geneseo, NY
Lane-Lopez, Rose, Libn.
   COMBUSTION ENGINEERING, INC. - POWER
   SYSTEMS GROUP LIBRARY SERVICES† □
   Windsor, CT

Laneman, Joan, Lib.Dir.
   DE PAUL HEALTH CENTER - MEDICAL LIBRARY
   □ Bridgeton, MO
Laney-Sheehan, Susan, Supv.Libn.
   U.S. FOOD & DRUG ADMINISTRATION -
   NATIONAL CENTER FOR TOXICOLOGICAL
   RESEARCH - LIBRARY □ Jefferson, AK
Lang, Anita, Asst.Libn.
   SOUTHWEST RESEARCH INSTITUTE - THOMAS
   BAKER SLICK MEMORIAL LIBRARY □ San
   Antonio, TX
Lang, Elizabeth, Hd.
   UNIVERSITY OF CALIFORNIA, RIVERSIDE -
   ENGLISH DEPARTMENT LIBRARY □ Riverside,
   CA
Lang, Elizabeth, Archv.
   UNIVERSITY OF SOUTH DAKOTA - I.D. WEEKS
   LIBRARY - RICHARDSON ARCHIVES □
   Vermillion, SD
Lang, George W., Lib.Adm.
   NORTH AMERICAN BAPTIST SEMINARY -
   KAISER-RAMAKER LIBRARY □ Sioux Falls, SD
Lang, Gyorgy, Ref.Libn.
   BOSTON COLLEGE - LAW SCHOOL LIBRARY† □
   Newton Centre, MA
Lang, Isa, Lawyer Libn.
   UNIVERSITY OF MAINE SCHOOL OF LAW -
   DONALD L. GARBRECHT LAW LIBRARY □
   Portland, ME
Lang, Janice, Tech.Serv.Supv.
   WISCONSIN STATE DIVISION FOR LIBRARY
   SERVICES - REFERENCE AND LOAN LIBRARY □
   Madison, WI
Lang, Leona, Dir.
   PASQUA HOSPITAL - HEALTH SCIENCES
   LIBRARY† □ Regina, SK
Lang, Patricia, Lib.Tech.
   BRONSON METHODIST HOSPITAL - HEALTH
   SCIENCES LIBRARY □ Kalamazoo, MI
Lang, R., Info.Spec.
   NORTH CAROLINA STATE SCIENCE AND
   TECHNOLOGY RESEARCH CENTER □ Research
   Triangle Park, NC
Lang, Rev. Ron, Chm.
   UNITED METHODIST CHURCH - YELLOWSTONE
   ANNUAL CONFERENCE - ARCHIVES □ St.
   Ignatius, MT
Lang, Saundra K., Lib.Techn.
   PRO FOOTBALL HALL OF FAME - LIBRARY/
   RESEARCH CENTER □ Canton, OH
Lang, Rev. Walter, Exec.Dir.
   BIBLE SCIENCE ASSOCIATION - RESEARCH
   CENTER □ Minneapolis, MN
Langdon, Joseph, Corp.Libn.
   OAO CORPORATION - INFORMATION CENTER □
   Greenbelt, MD
Lange, Angie, Asst.Libn./Tech.Serv.
   KUTAK ROCK & HUIE - LAW LIBRARY □ Omaha,
   NE
Lange, Carla, Asst.Libn.
   MISSOURI BOTANICAL GARDEN - LIBRARY □
   St. Louis, MO
Lange, Carol R., Libn.
   WASHINGTON THEOLOGICAL UNION - LIBRARY
   □ Silver Spring, MD
Lange, Clifford E., Lib.Dir.
   CARLSBAD CITY LIBRARY - SPECIAL
   COLLECTIONS DEPARTMENT □ Carlsbad, CA
Lange, Naomi, Med.Libn.
   UNIVERSITY OF WYOMING - COLLEGE OF
   HUMAN MEDICINE - FAMILY PRACTICE
   RESIDENCY PROGRAM - LEARNING RESOURCES
   CENTER □ Casper, WY
Lange, R. Thomas, Chf.Med.Libn.
   UNIVERSITY OF SOUTH CAROLINA - SCHOOL
   OF MEDICINE LIBRARY □ Columbia, SC
Langelier, G., Chf., Serv.Sect.
   CANADA - PUBLIC ARCHIVES OF CANADA -
   NATIONAL MAP COLLECTION □ Ottawa, ON
Langen, John S., Sr.Libn.
   UNIVERSITY OF ALABAMA - SCIENCE LIBRARY
   □ University, AL

Langer, Mrs. E., Libn.
WINNIPEG FREE PRESS - LIBRARY □ Winnipeg, MB

Langford, Lynda, Musm.Prog.Spec.
ARKANSAS TERRITORIAL RESTORATION - LIBRARY □ Little Rock, AR

Langhammer, E. Birgit, Libn.
HAMILTON BOARD OF EDUCATION - EDUCATION CENTRE LIBRARY† □ Hamilton, ON

Langkau, Claire Marie, Mgr., Tech.Info.
UNION CARBIDE CORPORATION - BATTERY PRODUCTS DIVISION - TECHNICAL INFORMATION CENTER □ Westlake, OH

Langley, Clarence, Jr., Libn.
NATIONAL RAILWAY HISTORICAL SOCIETY - MOHAWK AND HUDSON CHAPTER - LAWRENCE R. LEE MEMORIAL LIBRARY □ Schenectady, NY

Langlois, Janet L., Dir.
WAYNE STATE UNIVERSITY - FOLKLORE ARCHIVE □ Detroit, MI

Langlois, Rene-Daniel, Libn.
INSTITUT DE TECHNOLOGIE AGRICOLE - RESEARCH LIBRARY† □ La Pocatiere, PQ

Langmo, James, Ref.Libn.
GRAND RAPIDS PUBLIC LIBRARY - FOUNDATION CENTER REGIONAL COLLECTION □ Grand Rapids, MI

Lango, Serilda (Sam), Circ./ILL
DOMINICAN COLLEGE LIBRARY □ Washington, DC

Langston, Gay, Hd., Circ.
UNIVERSITY OF TEXAS HEALTH SCIENCE CENTER, DALLAS - LIBRARY □ Dallas, TX

Lania, Margaret E., Asst.Libn.
MASSACHUSETTS INSTITUTE OF TECHNOLOGY - CENTER FOR SPACE RESEARCH - READING ROOM □ Cambridge, MA

Lanigan, Janet M., Libn.
FLORIDA STATE LEGISLATURE - DIVISION OF LEGISLATIVE LIBRARY SERVICES □ Tallahassee, FL

Lanigan, Karne, Doc./Rpts.Libn.
SCHLUMBERGER-DOLL - RESEARCH LIBRARY □ Ridgefield, CT

Lank, Karen, Acq.
MARICOPA COUNTY LAW LIBRARY □ Phoenix, AZ

Lankford, Nancy, Assoc.Dir.
WESTERN HISTORICAL MANUSCRIPT COLLECTION/STATE HISTORICAL SOCIETY OF MISSOURI MANUSCRIPTS JOINT COLLECTION □ Columbia, MO

Lannin, Sue, Ref.Libn.
MERRIAM CENTER LIBRARY □ Chicago, IL

Lannon, John, Hd., Acq.
BOSTON ATHENAEUM LIBRARY □ Boston, MA

Lansberg, Helen R., Dir.
INSTITUTE OF LIVING - MEDICAL LIBRARY □ Hartford, CT

Lansdale, Metta T., Jr., Mgr., Lib.Serv.
MC CAULEY (CATHERINE) HEALTH CENTER - RIECKER MEMORIAL LIBRARY □ Ann Arbor, MI

Lansdowne, Len, Cur.
PERHAM FOUNDATION - FOOTHILL ELECTRONICS MUSEUM - DE FOREST MEMORIAL ARCHIVES □ Los Altos Hills, CA

Lansing, Elizabeth, Cat.
UNIVERSITY OF NORTH CAROLINA, CHAPEL HILL - RARE BOOK COLLECTION □ Chapel Hill, NC

Lansing, Phyllis, Ref.Serv.
UNIVERSITY OF OKLAHOMA - HEALTH SCIENCES CENTER LIBRARY □ Oklahoma City, OK

Lansing, Rachel, Adm.Oper.Asst.
U.S. GEOLOGICAL SURVEY - WATER RESOURCES DIVISION - LIBRARY □ Madison, WI

Lansky, Aaron, Exec.Dir.
NATIONAL YIDDISH BOOK CENTER, INC. - LIBRARY □ Amherst, MA

Lantz, Bonnie, Libn.
ALTOONA HOSPITAL - GLOVER MEMORIAL MEDICAL AND NURSING LIBRARY □ Altoona, PA

Lantzy, Louise, Assoc.Libn./Acq.
SYRACUSE UNIVERSITY - LAW LIBRARY □ Syracuse, NY

Lao, Mary, Libn.
DOW CHEMICAL U.S.A. - WESTERN DIVISION RESEARCH LABORATORIES - LIBRARY □ Walnut Creek, CA

Lao, Niann, Asst.Libn. & Cat.
OHIO STATE SUPREME COURT LAW LIBRARY □ Columbus, OH

Lape, Jane M., Cur.-Libn.
FORT TICONDEROGA ASSOCIATION, INC. - LIBRARY □ Ticonderoga, NY

LaPerla, Susan, Libn.
U.S. DEPT. OF JUSTICE - NATIONAL INSTITUTE OF JUSTICE - NATL. CRIMINAL JUSTICE REF. SERVICE □ Rockville, MD

Laperle, Isabelle, Documentaliste
UNIVERSITE DE MONTREAL - DEPARTEMENT DE DEMOGRAPHIE - SERVICE DE LA RECHERCHE DOCUMENTATION □ Montreal, PQ

Lapidus, Marshall A., Asst.Libn.
CLARK (Sterling and Francine) ART INSTITUTE - LIBRARY □ Williamstown, MA

Lapierre, Rhona, Corp.Libn.
MANITOBA HYDRO - LIBRARY □ Winnipeg, MB

Laplante, Carole, Libn.
CANADA - REGIONAL INDUSTRIAL EXPANSION - GOVERNMENT DOCUMENTATION CENTRE □ Montreal, PQ

LaPlante, Mrs. Leroy H., Chm.
FIRST CONGREGATIONAL CHURCH OF AUBURN - LIBRARY □ Auburn, MA

Lapointe, Francine, Dir., Lib.Serv.
MISERICORDIA HOSPITAL - WEINLOS MEDICAL LIBRARY □ Edmonton, AB

Lapointe, JoAnne D., Cur.
CENTRE D'HERITAGE FRANCO-AMERICAIN - LIBRARY □ Auburn, ME

Laponce, Iza, Libn.
UNIVERSITY OF BRITISH COLUMBIA - HUMANITIES AND SOCIAL SCIENCES DIVISION □ Vancouver, BC

LaPorte, Sr. Margaret, Dir.
COLUMBUS HOSPITAL - HEALTH SCIENCES LIBRARY □ Great Falls, MT

Lapp, Marilyn, Lib.Asst.
UNIVERSITY OF SASKATCHEWAN - GEOLOGY BRANCH LIBRARY □ Saskatoon, SK

Lapsansky, Phillip, Ref.Libn.
LIBRARY COMPANY OF PHILADELPHIA □ Philadelphia, PA

LaRaia, Barbara B., Archv.
ERICKSON (Milton) FOUNDATION, INC. - ARCHIVES □ Phoenix, AZ

Larche, Thelma B., Hd.Libn.
UNIVERSITY OF FLORIDA - P.K. YONGE LABORATORY SCHOOL - MEAD LIBRARY □ Gainesville, FL

Large, Deborah S., Dir.Lib.Serv.
UNIVERSITY OF TEXAS - INSTITUTE OF TEXAN CULTURES AT SAN ANTONIO - LIBRARY □ San Antonio, TX

Largen, Elsa, Proc.Ctr.
U.S. ARMY POST - FORT LEWIS - LIBRARY SYSTEM □ Ft. Lewis, WA

Lariccia, Louise, Libn.
GOODYEAR AEROSPACE CORPORATION - LIBRARY □ Akron, OH

Larimer, Lawrence M., Chf., Lib.Serv.
U.S. VETERANS ADMINISTRATION (TX-Kerrville) - HEALTH SCIENCES LIBRARY □ Kerrville, TX

Larison, Brenda, Corp.Libn.
ADP NETWORK SERVICES - MARKETING SERVICES LIBRARY □ Ann Arbor, MI

Larison, Ruth A., Libn.
U.S. NATL. PARK SERVICE - LIBRARY □ Denver, CO

Lariviere, Gemma, Libn.
MANITOBA - DEPT. OF EDUCATION - BUREAU DE L'EDUCATION FRANCAISE - DIRECTION DES RESSOURCES EDUCATIVES FRANCAISES □ Saint-Boniface, MB

Larkin, Dorothy, Libn./Exec.Sec.
VESTIGIA - LIBRARY □ Stanhope, NJ

Larkin, Marti, Asst.Libn.
U.S. GEOLOGICAL SURVEY - NATIONAL MAPPING DIVISION ASSISTANCE FACILITY - LIBRARY □ NSTL Station, MS

Larkins, Rosemary, Libn.
OHIO STATE INDUSTRIAL COMMISSION - DIVISION OF SAFETY AND HYGIENE - RESOURCE CENTER □ Columbus, OH

LaRoche, Christian, Musm.Dir.
HISTORICAL SOCIETY OF OKALOOSA & WALTON COUNTIES, INC. - MUSEUM LIBRARY □ Valparaiso, FL

LaRose, Helen, Supv., Archv.
EDMONTON CITY ARCHIVES □ Edmonton, AB

Larose, Luanne, Lib.Techn.
CANADA - DEPARTMENT OF INSURANCE - LIBRARY □ Ottawa, ON

Laroussini, Donna H., Rd.Serv.Libn.
WAKE FOREST UNIVERSITY - LAW LIBRARY □ Winston-Salem, NC

Larragoite, Philip, Libn.
U.S. DEPT. OF ENERGY - ALBUQUERQUE OPERATIONS OFFICE - LIBRARY AND PUBLIC DOCUMENT ROOM □ Albuquerque, NM

Larsen, Christine E., Dir./Adm.Libn.
U.S. NAVY - NAVAL STATION LIBRARY (CA-San Diego) □ San Diego, CA

Larsen, Helen, Musm.Dir.
WESTON COUNTY HISTORICAL SOCIETY - ANNA MILLER MUSEUM - LIBRARY □ Newcastle, WY

Larsen, K.
OAK RIDGE NATIONAL LABORATORY - INFORMATION DIVISION - ENVIRONMENTAL MUTAGEN INFORMATION CENTER □ Oak Ridge, TN

Larsen, Karen, Asst.Libn.
ROCHESTER METHODIST HOSPITAL - METHODIST KAHLER LIBRARY □ Rochester, MN

Larsen, Lida Lou, Libn.
PRINCE GEORGE'S COUNTY PUBLIC SCHOOLS - PROFESSIONAL LIBRARY □ Landover, MD

Larsen, Linda, Mgr., Info.Ctr.
KEARNEY (A.T.), INC. - INFORMATION CENTER □ Chicago, IL

Larsen, Lotte, Hd., Ref. & Lib.Instr.
WESTERN OREGON STATE COLLEGE - LIBRARY □ Monmouth, OR

Larsen, Mary, Libn.
FERNBANK SCIENCE CENTER - LIBRARY □ Atlanta, GA

Larsen, Patricia
SOUTHERN OREGON STATE COLLEGE - LIBRARY □ Ashland, OR

Larsen, Sherman J., Pres.
NATIONAL INVESTIGATIONS COMMITTEE ON AERIAL PHENOMENA - INFORMATION CENTER □ Glenview, IL

Larsgaard, Mary L., Asst.Dir., Spec.Coll.
COLORADO SCHOOL OF MINES - ARTHUR LAKES LIBRARY □ Golden, CO

Larson, Andre P., Dir.
SHRINE TO MUSIC MUSEUM □ Vermillion, SD

Larson, Anne, Libn.
KMG/MAIN HURDMAN - LIBRARY □ San Francisco, CA

Larson, Arne B., Res.Cons.
SHRINE TO MUSIC MUSEUM □ Vermillion, SD

Larson, Donald A., Rec.Mgr.
ALLIED CORPORATION - BUNKER-RAMO ELECTRONIC SYSTEMS DIVISION - MAIN LIBRARY □ Westlake, CA

Larson, Donald F., Counsel
NEW YORK STATE CONFERENCE OF MAYORS AND MUNICIPAL OFFICIALS - LIBRARY □ Albany, NY

Larson, E. Joseph, Chf., AV Br.
U.S. SOIL CONSERVATION SERVICE -
NATIONAL PHOTOGRAPHIC LIBRARY □
Washington, DC

Larson, Mrs. Einar M., Libn.
STRATFORD HISTORICAL SOCIETY - LIBRARY
□ Stratford, CT

Larson, Evva L., Asst.State Libn.
IDAHO STATE LIBRARY - REGIONAL LIBRARY
FOR THE BLIND AND PHYSICALLY
HANDICAPPED □ Boise, ID

Larson, Gretchen S., Asst.Libn.
CASE WESTERN RESERVE UNIVERSITY -
MATTHEW A. BAXTER SCHOOL OF LIBRARY &
INFORMATION SCIENCE □ Cleveland, OH

Larson, Jean, Exec. V.P.
ROA FILMS - LIBRARY □ Milwaukee, WI

Larson, Jeanne M., Med.Libn.
MEMORIAL HOSPITAL OF SOUTH BEND -
MEDICAL LIBRARY □ South Bend, IN

Larson, Joel D., Coord., Film Lib.Serv.
UNIVERSITY OF WISCONSIN, MADISON -
BUREAU OF AUDIOVISUAL INSTRUCTION -
LIBRARY □ Madison, WI

Larson, John A., Archv.
UNIVERSITY OF CHICAGO - ORIENTAL
INSTITUTE - ARCHIVES □ Chicago, IL

Larson, Julian, Libn.
OHIO STATE UNIVERSITY - CENTER FOR
HUMAN RESOURCE RESEARCH - LIBRARY □
Worthington, OH

Larson, Kathleen T., Libn.
U.S. DEPT. OF JUSTICE - CIVIL RIGHTS
DIVISION - LIBRARY □ Washington, DC

Larson, Michelle M., Ref.Libn.
TEXAS CHIROPRACTIC COLLEGE - MAE HILTY
MEMORIAL LIBRARY □ Pasadena, TX

Larson, Patricia Butzer, Dir., Resource Ctr.
MEALS FOR MILLIONS/FREEDOM FROM
HUNGER FOUNDATION - LIBRARY □ Davis, CA

Larson, Pauline, Asst.Archv.
WEYERHAEUSER COMPANY - ARCHIVES □
Tacoma, WA

Larson, Recca A., Agency Libn.
NEBRASKA STATE GAME AND PARKS
COMMISSION - LIBRARY □ Lincoln, NE

Larson, Robert K., Hd., Lib.Serv.
BURROUGHS WELLCOME COMPANY - LIBRARY
□ Research Triangle Park, NC

Larson, Ronald J., Hd.Libn.
WISCONSIN STATE JOURNAL - LIBRARY □
Madison, WI

Larson, Sandra M., Archv.
CALIFORNIA HISTORICAL SOCIETY -
SCHUBERT HALL LIBRARY □ San Francisco, CA

Larson, Stanley, Ref.Libn.
AEROSPACE CORPORATION - CHARLES C.
LAURITSEN LIBRARY □ Los Angeles, CA

Larson, Victor J., Info.Spec.
UNIVERSITY OF WISCONSIN, MILWAUKEE -
GRADUATE SCHOOL - OFFICE OF RESEARCH -
INFORMATION LIBRARY □ Milwaukee, WI

Larter, Cynthia, Asst. Law Libn.
UNIVERSITY OF PITTSBURGH - LAW LIBRARY □
Pittsburgh, PA

LaRue, Robert, Libn.
UNIVERSITY OF VIRGINIA - CHEMISTRY
LIBRARY □ Charlottesville, VA

LaRue, Suzanne, Clinical Libn., Surgery
HARTFORD HOSPITAL - HEALTH SCIENCE
LIBRARIES □ Hartford, CT

Larzelere, David W., Chf.Libn.
FLINT JOURNAL - EDITORIAL LIBRARY □ Flint,
MI

Lasalle, D., ILL
CANADA - FISHERIES & OCEANS - LIBRARY† □
Ottawa, ON

Lasater, Mary Charles, Monographs Libn.
VANDERBILT UNIVERSITY - MEDICAL CENTER
LIBRARY □ Nashville, TN

Lash, Barry, Hd.Libn.
SUNY - AGRICULTURAL AND TECHNICAL
COLLEGE AT ALFRED - WALTER C. HINKLE
MEMORIAL LIBRARY □ Alfred, NY

Lashley, Mark W., Med.Libn.
FLOYD MEDICAL CENTER - LIBRARY† □ Rome,
GA

Laskowitz, Roberta F., Asst.Chf. Law Libn.
FEDERAL RESERVE BANK OF NEW YORK - LAW
LIBRARY DIVISION □ New York, NY

Lason, Karen, Lib.Cons.
WESTERN MICHIGAN UNIVERSITY - CENTER
FOR WOMEN'S SERVICES - LIBRARY □
Kalamazoo, MI

Lass, Dr. William E., Dir.
SOUTHERN MINNESOTA HISTORICAL CENTER -
LIBRARY □ Mankato, MN

Lassanske, Vivian, Libn.
SAN LUIS OBISPO COUNTY PLANNING
DEPARTMENT - TECHNICAL INFORMATION
LIBRARY □ San Luis Obispo, CA

Lasslo, Wilma R., Circ.Libn.
UNIVERSITY OF TENNESSEE - CENTER FOR
THE HEALTH SCIENCES LIBRARY □ Memphis,
TN

Lassonde, Barbara, Asst.Libn.
MINNEAPOLIS INSTITUTE OF ARTS - LIBRARY
□ Minneapolis, MN

Lasworth, M. Louise, Ser.Supv.
SEARLE (G.D.) & CO. - RESEARCH LIBRARY □
Skokie, IL

Lataniotis, Dolores, Libn.
FORBES, INC. - LIBRARY† □ New York, NY

Latendresse, Raymond, Sr.Lit.Chem.
INTERNATIONAL FLAVORS AND FRAGRANCES,
INC. - TECHNICAL INFORMATION CENTER □
Union Beach, NJ

Latham, Cheryl A., Chf., Lib.Serv.
U.S. VETERANS ADMINISTRATION (TX-
Amarillo) - HOSPITAL LIBRARY □ Amarillo, TX

Latham, Mary, Libn.
ITEK CORPORATION - OPTICAL SYSTEMS
DIVISION - LIBRARY □ Lexington, MA

Latham, Pencie, Cat./Circ.Libn.
UNIVERSITY OF MISSISSIPPI - SCHOOL OF
LAW LIBRARY □ University, MS

Latham, Ronald B., Dir.
EDWARDS (Jacob) LIBRARY - SPECIAL
COLLECTIONS □ Southbridge, MA

Lathey, Campbell, Asst.Libn.
NEW YORK STATE LIBRARY - SCIENCES/
HEALTH SCIENCES/TECHNOLOGY REFERENCE
SERVICES □ Albany, NY

Lathrop, Alan K., Cur.
UNIVERSITY OF MINNESOTA - MANUSCRIPTS
DIVISION □ St. Paul, MN

Lathrop, Ann, Coord., Lib.Serv.
SAN MATEO COUNTY EDUCATIONAL
RESOURCES CENTER □ Redwood City, CA

Lathrop, Irene, Dir. of Lib.Serv.
RHODE ISLAND HOSPITAL - PETERS HEALTH
SCIENCES LIBRARY □ Providence, RI

Lathrop, Norman, Mgr.
LATHROP (Norman) ENTERPRISES - LIBRARY □
Wooster, OH

Latimer, Ira H., Exec. V.P.
AMERICAN FEDERATION OF SMALL BUSINESS -
INFORMATION CENTER □ Chicago, IL

Latos, Diane, Info.Anl.
UNIVERSITY OF WYOMING - WYOMING
CAREER INFORMATION SYSTEM □ Laramie, WY

Latour, Terry, Cur.
UNIVERSITY OF SOUTHERN MISSISSIPPI - MC
CAIN LIBRARY □ Hattiesburg, MS

Latta, Dr. B.M., Dir.
J.P. STEVENS AND CO., INC. - TECHNICAL
LIBRARY □ Greenville, SC

Latta, Barbara K., Dir.
PARK-NICOLLET MEDICAL FOUNDATION -
ARNESON LIBRARY □ Minneapolis, MN

Latta, Joan E., Ref.
UNIVERSITY OF NEBRASKA MEDICAL CENTER -
MC GOOGAN LIBRARY OF MEDICINE □ Omaha,
NE

Lattimore, Jack, Nonprint Libn.
UNIVERSITY OF MARYLAND, COLLEGE PARK -
LIBRARIES NONPRINT MEDIA SERVICES □
College Park, MD

Latus, Jane Keating, Hd.Libn.
BOSTON CITY HOSPITAL - NURSING - MORSE-
SLANGER LIBRARY □ Boston, MA

Latus, Sheila E., Med.Libn.
KAISER-PERMANENTE MEDICAL CENTER -
HEALTH SCIENCES LIBRARY □ San Diego, CA

Latyszewskyj, Maria, Hd., Tech.Proc.
CANADA - NATIONAL RESEARCH COUNCIL -
CISTI - AERONAUTICAL & MECHANICAL
ENGINEERING BRANCH □ Ottawa, ON

Latzke, Henry R., Dir., Lib.Serv.
CONCORDIA COLLEGE - KLINCK MEMORIAL
LIBRARY □ River Forest, IL

Lau, Anna, Coord., Info.Rsrcs.
ONTARIO - MINISTRY OF EDUCATION -
INFORMATION CENTRE □ Toronto, ON

Lau, Ray D., Lib.Dir.
NORTHWESTERN OKLAHOMA STATE
UNIVERSITY - LIBRARY □ Alva, OK

Laub, Barbara, Info.Serv.Libn.
STEVENS INSTITUTE OF TECHNOLOGY -
SAMUEL C. WILLIAMS LIBRARY □ Hoboken, NJ

Laube, Lois, Div.Hd.
INDIANAPOLIS-MARION COUNTY PUBLIC
LIBRARY - SOCIAL SCIENCE DIVISION □
Indianapolis, IN

Laubental, Min-Ja, Dir., Lib.Serv.
RIVERVIEW HOSPITAL - STAFF REFERENCE
LIBRARY □ Port Coquitlam, BC

Lauber, John, Exec.Dir.
NEW YORK STATE CONFERENCE OF MAYORS
AND MUNICIPAL OFFICIALS - LIBRARY □
Albany, NY

Laudahn, Ruth, Act.Libn.
ALLEN COUNTY LAW LIBRARY □ Lima, OH

Laudati, Geraldine, Music Libn.
EAST CAROLINA UNIVERSITY - MUSIC
LIBRARY □ Greenville, NC

Laude, Walter, Asst.Libn.
INDIANA UNIVERSITY OF PENNSYLVANIA -
UNIVERSITY LIBRARY □ Indiana, PA

Lauderdale, Kenneth, Hd., Res. Reports Div.
U.S. NAVY - NAVAL POSTGRADUATE SCHOOL -
DUDLEY KNOX LIBRARY □ Monterey, CA

Laue, Stephen, Info.Serv.Spec.
U.S. BUREAU OF THE CENSUS - INFORMATION
SERVICES PROGRAM - CHICAGO REGIONAL
OFFICE - REFERENCE CENTER □ Chicago, IL

Lauer, C.F., Ref.
MC DONNELL DOUGLAS CORPORATION - MC
DONNELL AIRCRAFT LIBRARY □ St. Louis, MO

Lauer, Carol Ann, Coord.
REHABILITATION INSTITUTE OF CHICAGO -
LEARNING RESOURCES CENTER □ Chicago, IL

Lauer, Jonathan, Hd., Pub.Serv.
WHEATON COLLEGE - BUSWELL MEMORIAL
LIBRARY □ Wheaton, IL

Lauer, Judy A., Law Libn.
NEW YORK STATE SUPREME COURT - 6TH
JUDICIAL DISTRICT - LAW LIBRARY □
Binghamton, NY

Lauer, Marjorie, Libn.
IBM CANADA, LTD. - MARKETING LIBRARY □
Don Mills, ON

Laufer, Marilyn, Educ.Cur.
SIOUX CITY ART CENTER ASSOCIATION -
LIBRARY □ Sioux City, IA

Laufer, Samuel, Asst.Libn.
YESHIVA TORAH VODAATH AND MESIFTA -
TORAH VODAATH LIBRARY □ Brooklyn, NY

Laughlin, Karen, Ref.Libn.
STATE HISTORICAL SOCIETY OF IOWA -
LIBRARY □ Iowa City, IA

Laughlin, Patricia, Libn.
MILWAUKEE PUBLIC MUSEUM - REFERENCE
LIBRARY □ Milwaukee, WI

Laughlin, Paul, Pub.Serv.Libn.
MISSISSIPPI COLLEGE SCHOOL OF LAW - LAW
LIBRARY □ Jackson, MS

Laughlin, Sarah B., Dir.
VERMONT INSTITUTE OF NATURAL SCIENCES
- LIBRARY □ Woodstock, VT

Laughlin, Dr. Winston M., Soil Sci.
UNIVERSITY OF ALASKA - ALASKA
AGRICULTURAL EXPERIMENT STATION -
LIBRARY □ Palmer, AK

Laughon, Barbara J., Lib.Adm.
OHIO STATE LEGISLATIVE SERVICE
COMMISSION - RESEARCH LIBRARY □
Columbus, OH

Laun, Carol, Asst.Cur.
SALMON BROOK HISTORICAL SOCIETY -
REFERENCE AND EDUCATIONAL CENTER □
Granby, CT

Laurent, Elizabeth A., Corp.Libn.
SOUTHLAND CORPORATION - CORPORATE
BUSINESS RESEARCH CENTER □ Dallas, TX

Laurin, Michele, Tech.Libn.
GESTAS INC. - DOCUMENTATION CENTER □
Montreal, PQ

Laurinaitis, Bro. Bernard, S.M., Archv.
SOCIETY OF MARY - CINCINNATI PROVINCE -
ARCHIVES □ Dayton, OH

Laursen, Irene S., Science Libn.
WELLESLEY COLLEGE - SCIENCE LIBRARY □
Wellesley, MA

Lautenschlager, Aldona, Dir., Lib.Serv.
SOUTHERN NEVADA MEMORIAL HOSPITAL -
MEDICAL LIBRARY □ Las Vegas, NV

Lauterman, Frieda, Libn.
AGUDATH ISRAEL CONGREGATION - MALCA
PASS MEMORIAL LIBRARY □ Ottawa, ON

Lautzenheiser, Fred, Asst.Archv.
CASE WESTERN RESERVE UNIVERSITY -
UNIVERSITY ARCHIVES □ Cleveland, OH

Lauver, Marvin E., Hd.Libn.
INTERNORTH - TECHNICAL INFORMATION
CENTER □ Omaha, NE

Lauzon, Helene, Hd.Libn.
HOPITAL MAISONNEUVE-ROSEMONT -
SERVICE DES BIBLIOTHEQUES □ Montreal, PQ

Lauzon, Maurice G., Libn.
NEW BEDFORD STANDARD-TIMES LIBRARY □
New Bedford, MA

Lavayna-Portugal, Carmelita, Dir.
UNIVERSITY OF PITTSBURGH - SCHOOL OF
EDUCATION - INTERNATIONAL &
DEVELOPMENT EDUCATION PROGRAM
CLEARINGHOUSE □ Pittsburgh, PA

Lavendel, Giuliana A., Mgr.
XEROX CORPORATION - PALO ALTO RESEARCH
CENTER - TECHNICAL INFORMATION CENTER
□ Palo Alto, CA

Lavender, Jean, Asst.Libn.
UNIVERSITY OF TORONTO - FACULTY OF
MUSIC LIBRARY □ Toronto, ON

Lavender, Dr. Kenneth, Univ.Bibliog.
NORTH TEXAS STATE UNIVERSITY LIBRARIES
- RARE BOOK ROOM □ Denton, TX

LaVerdi, Adelaide L., Hd.Cat.
SUNY - COLLEGE AT GENESEO - COLLEGE
LIBRARIES □ Geneseo, NY

Laverdiere, Sylvie, Libn.
INSTITUTION DES SOURDS DE MONTREAL -
CENTRE DE RESSOURCES MULTI-MEDIA □
Montreal, PQ

Lavergne, Rodolphe, Chf.Libn.
ECOLE DES HAUTES ETUDES COMMERCIALES
DE MONTREAL - BIBLIOTHEQUE □ Montreal, PQ

Lavich, Norma, Music Libn.
CANADIAN BROADCASTING CORPORATION -
MUSIC & RECORD LIBRARY □ Winnipeg, MB

Lavigne, Leo, Cur.
ROYAL CANADIAN ORDNANCE CORPS MUSEUM
- LIBRARY □ Montreal, PQ

LaVigne, Norma, Asst.Libn.
NATIONAL ECUMENICAL COALITION, INC. -
LIBRARY □ Washington, DC

Lavigueur, Elisabeth, Libn.
S.E.R.U. NUCLEAIRE (Canada) LTEE. - LIBRARY
□ Montreal, PQ

Lavigueur, Lucile, Libn.
ST. MARY'S HOSPITAL - MEDICAL LIBRARY □
Montreal, PQ

Lavilla, Sonia, ILL
HAHNEMANN UNIVERSITY - WARREN H. FAKE
LIBRARY† □ Philadelphia, PA

Lavine, Judith, Asst.Libn.
U.S. COURT OF APPEALS, 1ST CIRCUIT -
LIBRARY □ Boston, MA

Laviolette, James A., Ref.Libn.
RENSSELAER POLYTECHNIC INSTITUTE -
FOLSOM LIBRARY □ Troy, NY

LaViolette, Karen L., Info. & Pub.Asst.
AMERICAN ACADEMY OF PHYSICIAN
ASSISTANTS - INFORMATION CENTER □
Arlington, VA

Lavoie, Claire, ILL
CANADA - REGIONAL INDUSTRIAL EXPANSION
- GOVERNMENT DOCUMENTATION CENTRE □
Montreal, PQ

Lavoy, Constance J., Lib.Serv.Supv.
UNION CARBIDE AGRICULTURAL PRODUCTS
COMPANY, INC. - LIBRARY □ Research Triangle
Park, NC

Law, Gordon, Libn.
PURDUE UNIVERSITY - MANAGEMENT AND
ECONOMICS LIBRARY □ West Lafayette, IN

Law, Jane, Info.Off.
CANADIAN INSTITUTE OF GUIDED GROUND
TRANSPORT - INFORMATION CENTRE □
Kingston, ON

Law, John W., Libn.
DECATUR MEMORIAL HOSPITAL - HEALTH
SCIENCE LIBRARY □ Decatur, IL

Law, L., Sr.Info.Spec.
ALLERGAN PHARMACEUTICALS, INC. -
MEDICAL & SCIENCE INFORMATION □ Irvine,
CA

Law, Libby, Field Serv.Libn.
SOUTH CAROLINA STATE LIBRARY □ Columbia,
SC

Law, Phoebe, Hd.Libn.
PHILADELPHIA COLLEGE OF THE PERFORMING
ARTS - LIBRARY □ Philadelphia, PA

Law, Vickie, Asst.Libn.
CAMP DRESSER & MC KEE, INC. - HERMAN G.
DRESSER LIBRARY □ Boston, MA

Lawless, Deborah, Asst.Dir.
SOUTHERN COLLEGE OF OPTOMETRY -
WILLIAM P. MAC CRACKEN, JR. MEMORIAL
LIBRARY □ Memphis, TN

Lawlor-Fennell, Catherine, Libn.
PENNSYLVANIA SCHOOL FOR THE DEAF -
LIBRARY □ Philadelphia, PA

Lawrance, D., Regional Adv.
CANADA - STATISTICS CANADA - ADVISORY
SERVICES - REGINA REFERENCE CENTRE □
Regina, SK

Lawrance, Margaret W., Law Libn.
MERCED COUNTY LAW LIBRARY □ Merced, CA

Lawrence, B., Adm.
AMERICAN INSTITUTE OF AERONAUTICS AND
ASTRONAUTICS - TECHNICAL INFORMATION
SERVICE □ New York, NY

Lawrence, Deirdre E., Prin.Libn.
BROOKLYN MUSEUM - ART REFERENCE
LIBRARY □ Brooklyn, NY

Lawrence, Duncan, Tech.Libn.
M.P.K. OMEGA COMPANY - BIOSCIENCE
LIBRARY □ Amarillo, TX

Lawrence, Ellspath, Libn.
FOREIGN SERVICES RESEARCH INSTITUTE -
WHITEFORD MEMORIAL LIBRARY □
Washington, DC

Lawrence, Jan R., Commun.Mgr.
UNIVERSITY OF MARYLAND, COLLEGE PARK -
MARYLAND CENTER FOR PRODUCTIVITY AND
QUALITY OF WORKING LIFE - LIB. □ College
Park, MD

Lawrence, John P., Coord., Music Lib.
CANADIAN BROADCASTING CORPORATION -
MUSIC LIBRARY □ Toronto, ON

Lawrence, John P., Coord., Prog.Archv.
CANADIAN BROADCASTING CORPORATION -
PROGRAM ARCHIVES (Sound) □ Toronto, ON

Lawrence, John P., Coord.
CANADIAN BROADCASTING CORPORATION -
RECORD LIBRARY □ Toronto, ON

Lawrence, Kathy, Info.Serv.Supv.
DENVER PUBLIC LIBRARY - FOUNDATION
CENTER COLLECTION □ Denver, CO

Lawrence, Patricia A., Dir.
PACIFIC GAS AND ELECTRIC COMPANY -
CORPORATE LIBRARY □ San Francisco, CA

Lawrence, Philip D., Jr., Supv., Info.Serv.
WESTPOINT PEPPERELL - RESEARCH CENTER -
INFORMATION SERVICES LIBRARY □ Valley, AL

Lawrence, Robert, Sci.-Tech.Ref.Libn.
OREGON STATE UNIVERSITY - WILLIAM
JASPER KERR LIBRARY □ Corvallis, OR

Lawrence, Virginia, Sr.Tech.Sec.
CONTEL LABORATORIES - TECHNICAL LIBRARY
□ Norcross, GA

Lawrenz-Miller, Dr. Susanne, Assoc.Dir.
LOS ANGELES - DEPARTMENT OF RECREATION
AND PARKS - CABRILLO MARINE MUSEUM -
LIBRARY □ San Pedro, CA

Lawsine, Mary, Circ.Libn.
ASSOCIATION FOR RESEARCH AND
ENLIGHTENMENT - EDGAR CAYCE
FOUNDATION - LIBRARY □ Virginia Beach, VA

Lawson, Bennett F., Chf., Lib.Serv.
U.S. VETERANS ADMINISTRATION (KS-
Leavenworth) - CENTER MEDICAL LIBRARY □
Leavenworth, KS

Lawson, Christina, Supv., Archv.
U.S. PRESIDENTIAL LIBRARIES - LYNDON B.
JOHNSON LIBRARY □ Austin, TX

Lawson, Constance, Res.Libn.
LONE STAR GAS COMPANY - RESEARCH
LIBRARY† □ Dallas, TX

Lawson, J.E., Chf. Geophysicist
OKLAHOMA GEOLOGICAL SURVEY - OKLAHOMA
GEOPHYSICAL OBSERVATORY LIBRARY □
Leonard, OK

Lawson, Jacqueline, Ref.Libn.
DUN AND BRADSTREET CORP. - BUSINESS
LIBRARY □ New York, NY

Lawson, Judith, Asst.Libn.
CONGREGATION BETH ACHIM - JOSEPH
KATKOWSKY LIBRARY □ Southfield, MI

Lawson, Linda G., Libn.
METROPOLITAN MUSEUM OF ART -
PHOTOGRAPH AND SLIDE LIBRARY □ New York,
NY

Lawson, Mary, Dept.Hd.
MINNEAPOLIS PUBLIC LIBRARY &
INFORMATION CENTER - BUSINESS AND
ECONOMICS DEPARTMENT □ Minneapolis, MN

Lawson, Roger, Cat.
NATIONAL GALLERY OF ART - LIBRARY □
Washington, DC

Lawson, Dr. Terry, Prof., Mathematics
TULANE UNIVERSITY OF LOUISIANA -
MATHEMATICS RESEARCH LIBRARY □ New
Orleans, LA

Lawson, Wayne, Rec.Ctr.Mgr.
WASHINGTON STATE OFFICE OF SECRETARY
OF STATE - DIVISION OF ARCHIVES AND
RECORD MANAGEMENT □ Olympia, WA

Lawton, J., Corp.Libn.
BONNER & MOORE ASSOCIATES, INC. -
LIBRARY □ Houston, TX

Lawton, Natalie V., Libn.
WESTERLY HOSPITAL - MEDICAL LIBRARY □
Westerly, RI

Lay, Douglas H., Dir., Lib.Serv.
WAUSAU INSURANCE COMPANIES - LIBRARY □ Wausau, WI

Lay, Lynn B., Libn.
OHIO STATE UNIVERSITY - INSTITUTE OF POLAR STUDIES - GOLDTHWAIT POLAR LIBRARY □ Columbus, OH

Lay, William, Jr., Musm.Cur.
TIOGA COUNTY HISTORICAL SOCIETY MUSEUM - LIBRARY □ Owego, NY

Layaou, Cora, Govt.Doc.Libn.
OHIO NORTHERN UNIVERSITY - HETERICK MEMORIAL LIBRARY □ Ada, OH

Laycock, Dr. Anitra, Libn.
HALIFAX INFIRMARY - HEALTH SERVICES LIBRARY† □ Halifax, NS

Layman, Velma, Circ.Libn.
WITTENBERG UNIVERSITY - THOMAS LIBRARY □ Springfield, OH

Layne, Cathy, Libn.
TELEDYNE ENERGY SYSTEMS - LIBRARY □ Timonium, MD

Layne, G.S., Res.Assoc.
DOW CHEMICAL U.S.A. - TEXAS DIVISION - LIBRARY □ Freeport, TX

Laynor, Barbara, Hd., Ref.
JEFFERSON (Thomas) UNIVERSITY - SCOTT MEMORIAL LIBRARY □ Philadelphia, PA

Layton, Beth A., Libn.
WINCHESTER MEMORIAL HOSPITAL - HEALTH SCIENCES LIBRARY □ Winchester, VA

Layton, Mrs. S.A., Libn.
PEAT, MARWICK & PARTNERS - LIBRARY □ Toronto, ON

Layvas, Sue D., Chf.Med.Libn.
KAISER FOUNDATION HOSPITAL - MEDICAL LIBRARY □ Fontana, CA

Lazar, Kathy, Asst.Libn./Ref.
STRONG (Margaret Woodbury) MUSEUM - LIBRARY □ Rochester, NY

Lazar, Nancy, Circuit Libn.
U.S. COURT OF APPEALS, DISTRICT OF COLUMBIA CIRCUIT - LIBRARY □ Washington, DC

Lazar, Pamela L., Libn.
SOUTHEAST MICHIGAN COUNCIL OF GOVERNMENTS - SEMCOG LIBRARY □ Detroit, MI

Lazarevic, Martha, Tech.Serv.Libn.
FORD FOUNDATION - LIBRARY □ New York, NY

Lazarus, Simone Rollin, Libn.
PORTER MEDICAL CENTER - MEDICAL LIBRARY AND INFORMATION SERVICE □ Middlebury, VT

Lazor, Gloria J., Pub.Info.Off.
NEW JERSEY STATE MUSEUM - LIBRARY □ Trenton, NJ

Lazore, Elizabeth A., Libn.
SPECIAL METALS CORPORATION - TECHNICAL LIBRARY/INFORMATION CENTER □ New Hartford, NY

Lazouskas, Lorraine, Hd., Circ.
UNIVERSITY OF ILLINOIS AT CHICAGO - HEALTH SCIENCES CENTER - LIBRARY OF THE HEALTH SCIENCES □ Chicago, IL

Le, Vinh P., Ref.Libn.
SENECA COLLEGE OF APPLIED ARTS AND TECHNOLOGY - LESLIE CAMPUS RESOURCE CENTRE □ Willowdale, ON

Le Blanc, F.U., Hd., Rec.Mgt.Div.
NEW BRUNSWICK - PROVINCIAL ARCHIVES OF NEW BRUNSWICK □ Fredericton, NB

Le Blanc, J.-M., Hd., Res./Inquiry Serv.
CANADA - PUBLIC ARCHIVES OF CANADA - MANUSCRIPT DIVISION □ Ottawa, ON

Le Blanc, Therese, Bibliothecaire
INSTITUT CANADIEN D'EDUCATION DES ADULTES ET RELAIS-FEMMES DE MONTREAL - CENTRE DE DOCUMENTATION □ Montreal, PQ

Le Blance, Michel, Prod.Coord.
MANITOBA - DEPT. OF EDUCATION - BUREAU DE L'EDUCATION FRANCAISE - DIRECTION DES RESSOURCES EDUCATIVES FRANCAISES □ Saint-Boniface, MB

Lea, Keith F., Dir., Tech.Serv.
UNIVERSITY OF WISCONSIN, STEVENS POINT - JAMES H. ALBERTSON CENTER FOR LEARNING RESOURCES □ Stevens Point, WI

Lea, Shirley, Lib.Techn.
ALBERTA MENTAL HEALTH SERVICES - CLINIC LIBRARY □ Edmonton, AB

Leach, Sally, Asst. to the Dir.
UNIVERSITY OF TEXAS, AUSTIN - HARRY RANSOM HUMANITIES RESEARCH CENTER □ Austin, TX

Leadbeater, David S., Sr.Rec.Libn.
CANADIAN BROADCASTING CORPORATION - MUSIC & RECORD LIBRARY □ Halifax, NS

Leadbetter, Dorothy, Hd.Libn.
HALIFAX HERALD LTD. - LIBRARY □ Halifax, NS

Leaf, Donald, Dir., Bus. & Tech.Serv.
MICHIGAN STATE - LIBRARY OF MICHIGAN □ Lansing, MI

League, Linda, Libn.
SOUTHWIRE COMPANY - R & D TECHNICAL LIBRARY □ Carrollton, GA

Leahy, Elizabeth, Coord.
PRISON FELLOWSHIP - RESOURCE CENTER □ Washington, DC

Leahy, Germaine, Ref.Libn.
AMERICAN BANKERS ASSOCIATION - LIBRARY & INFORMATION SERVICES □ Washington, DC

Leahy, Mary Ann, Libn.
LATHROP, KOONTZ, RIGHTER, CLAGETT & NORQUIST - LIBRARY □ Kansas City, MO

Leake, Joan, Info.Spec.
INTERPUBLIC GROUP OF COMPANIES - CENTER FOR ADVERTISING SERVICES □ New York, NY

Leamen, Jane, Libn.
CANADIAN BANKERS ASSOCIATION - LIBRARY □ Toronto, ON

Leamon, Christine P., Res.Dir.
WHITNEY COMMUNICATIONS CORPORATION - RESEARCH LIBRARY □ New York, NY

Learn, Darnell, Adm., Policy & Plan.
OREGON STATE WATER RESOURCES DEPARTMENT - LIBRARY & INFORMATION CENTER □ Salem, OR

Leary, Joanne, Circ. Reserve Supv.
CORNELL UNIVERSITY - ENGINEERING LIBRARY □ Ithaca, NY

Leary, Margaret A., Assoc.Dir.
UNIVERSITY OF MICHIGAN - LAW LIBRARY □ Ann Arbor, MI

Leary, Nancy, Sr.Libn.
TRENTON FREE PUBLIC LIBRARY - BUSINESS AND TECHNOLOGY DEPARTMENT □ Trenton, NJ

Leary, Nancy, Sr.Libn.
TRENTON FREE PUBLIC LIBRARY - GOVERNMENT DOCUMENTS COLLECTION □ Trenton, NJ

Leary, T.E., Cur.
SLATER MILL HISTORIC SITE - RESEARCH LIBRARY □ Pawtucket, RI

Leavens, Bill, Chf.Libn.
U.S. VETERANS ADMINISTRATION (IL-Hines) - LIBRARY SERVICES (142D) □ Hines, IL

Leavitt, Charles, AV Spec.
BOSTON ARCHITECTURAL CENTER - ALFRED SHAW AND EDWARD DURELL STONE LIBRARY □ Boston, MA

Leavitt, Donald L., Chf.
LIBRARY OF CONGRESS - MUSIC DIVISION □ Washington, DC

Leavitt, Helen W., Law Libn.
SOMERSET COUNTY LAW LIBRARY □ Somerville, NJ

Leavitt, Judith A., Supv., Info.Ctr.
ROCKWELL INTERNATIONAL - COLLINS DIVISIONS - INFORMATION CENTER □ Cedar Rapids, IA

Lebans, Mrs. A.R., Archv.
ANGLICAN CHURCH OF CANADA - DIOCESE OF MONTREAL - ARCHIVES □ Montreal, PQ

LeBarron, Suzanne, Dir.
KENTUCKY STATE DEPARTMENT FOR LIBRARIES AND ARCHIVES - STATE LIBRARY SERVICES DIVISION □ Frankfort, KY

Lebbin, Lee J., Dir.
MICHIGAN TECHNOLOGICAL UNIVERSITY - LIBRARY □ Houghton, MI

LeBeau, Constance J., Libn.
XEROX CORPORATION - GINN AND COMPANY LIBRARY □ Lexington, MA

Lebeau, Nicole, Tech.Serv.
FLORIDA INSTITUTE OF TECHNOLOGY - COLLEGE OF APPLIED TECHNOLOGY - LIBRARY □ Jensen Beach, FL

LeBel, Grace, Libn.
UNIVERSITY OF CALGARY - KANANASKIS ENVIRONMENTAL SCIENCES CENTRE - LIBRARY □ Seebe, AB

LeBel, Jocelyn, Dir.
NEW BRUNSWICK - LEGISLATIVE LIBRARY □ Fredericton, NB

LeBel, Jocelyne, Act.Dir.
NEW BRUNSWICK - DEPARTMENT OF HISTORICAL AND CULTURAL RESOURCES - NEW BRUNSWICK LIBRARY SERVICE □ Fredericton, NB

Leber, Dolores, Asst. to Cur.
INTERNATIONAL COLLEGE OF SURGEONS HALL OF FAME - DR. JOSEPH MONTAGUE PROCTOLOGIC LIBRARY □ Chicago, IL

Leber, Terese, Jr.Lib.Spec.
EAST-WEST CENTER - EAPI/PI/RSI RESEARCH MATERIALS COLLECTION □ Honolulu, HI

Lebish, Allan, Acq.Libn.
NEW JERSEY INSTITUTE OF TECHNOLOGY - ROBERT W. VAN HOUTEN LIBRARY □ Newark, NJ

Lebl, Carolyn A., Hd. Law Libn.
UNION CARBIDE CORPORATION - LAW DEPARTMENT LIBRARY □ Danbury, CT

LeBlanc, Eric S., Libn.
CANADA - NATIONAL RESEARCH COUNCIL - CISTI - DOMINION ASTROPHYSICAL OBSERVATORY BRANCH □ Victoria, BC

LeBlanc, J., Hd., Rd.Serv.Sect.
CANADA - NATIONAL DEFENCE - NDHQ LIBRARY □ Ottawa, ON

LeBlanc, Janice, Asst.Libn.
CANADA - NATIONAL DEFENCE - CANADIAN FORCES COLLEGE - KEITH HODSON MEMORIAL LIBRARY† □ Toronto, ON

LeBlanc, Jean, Dir.
UNIVERSITY OF OTTAWA - MORISSET LIBRARY □ Ottawa, ON

LeBlanc, Michelle, Ref.
UNIVERSITY OF OTTAWA - HEALTH SCIENCES LIBRARY □ Ottawa, ON

Leblanc, Ronald, Libn.
UNIVERSITE DE MONCTON - CENTRE D'ETUDES ACADIENNES □ Moncton, NB

LeBorgne, Louis, Documentaliste
UNIVERSITE DU QUEBEC A MONTREAL - CENTRE DE DOCUMENTATION EN SCIENCES HUMAINES □ Montreal, PQ

Lebrocoguy, Paula M., Lib.Asst.
NEW HAMPSHIRE PUBLIC UTILITIES COMMISSION - LIBRARY □ Concord, NH

Lecavalier, Monique, Libn.
UNIVERSITE DE MONTREAL - MUSIQUE-BIBLIOTHEQUE □ Montreal, PQ

Lechelt, Alice R., Lib.Techn.
HARDY ASSOCIATES (1978) LTD. - LIBRARY† □ Edmonton, AB

Lechicky, Maria
BLAKE, CASSELS & GRAYDON - LIBRARY □ Toronto, ON

Lechner, Judith, Libn.
AUBURN UNIVERSITY - LEARNING RESOURCES CENTER □ Auburn, AL

LeClair, Daniel P., Dp.Dir.
MASSACHUSETTS STATE DEPARTMENT OF
CORRECTION - CENTRAL OFFICE STAFF
LIBRARY □ Boston, MA

LeClair, Micheline, Lib.Techn.
HOTEL-DIEU D'ARTHABASKA - MEDICAL
LIBRARY-DOCUMENTATION SERVICE† □
Arthabaska, PQ

LeClaire, Ann, Dir., Lib.Serv.
MIRIAM HOSPITAL - MEDICAL LIBRARY □
Providence, RI

Leclerc, Helene
MONTREAL URBAN COMMUNITY TRANSIT
COMMISSION - LIBRARY □ Montreal, PQ

Leclerc, Ms. P., Chf.Libn.
ALCAN INTERNATIONAL, LTD. - TECHNICAL
INFORMATION CENTRE □ Jonquiere, PQ

Lecompte, Louis-Lue, Hd.
HOPITAL STE-JUSTINE - CENTRE
D'INFORMATION SUR LA SANTE DE L'ENFANT □
Montreal, PQ

Lecture, Anne, Dir.
SAN FRANCISCO ACADEMY OF COMIC ART -
LIBRARY† □ San Francisco, CA

Ledbetter, Barbara A., Asst.Archv.
FORT BELKNAP ARCHIVES, INC. - LIBRARY □
Newcastle, TX

Ledbetter, Sherry, Dept.Hd.
ENOCH PRATT FREE LIBRARY - BUSINESS,
SCIENCE AND TECHNOLOGY DEPARTMENT □
Baltimore, MD

LeDell, Betty W., Libn.
GRACE LUTHERAN CHURCH - LIBRARY □
Wayzata, MN

Lederer, Frances, Hd., Gifts & Exchange
NATIONAL GALLERY OF ART - LIBRARY □
Washington, DC

Ledford, Carole L., Libn.
UNIVERSITY OF GEORGIA - GEORGIA
AGRICULTURAL EXPERIMENT STATION
LIBRARY □ Experiment, GA

Ledford, Elizabeth F., Libn.
CHARLOTTE LAW BUILDING ASSN. -
CHARLOTTE LAW LIBRARY □ Charlotte, NC

LeDuc, Carol, Sr.Libn.
HENNEPIN COUNTY LIBRARY SYSTEM -
GOVERNMENT CENTER INFORMATION
LIBRARY □ Minneapolis, MN

Leduc, Lise, Renseignements
HOPITAL STE-JUSTINE - CENTRE
D'INFORMATION SUR LA SANTE DE L'ENFANT □
Montreal, PQ

Ledwell, Bill, Chf. of Educ. Media
PRINCE EDWARD ISLAND - DEPARTMENT OF
EDUCATION - MEDIA CENTRE □ Charlottetown,
PE

Lee, Alice T., Libn.
U.S. AIR FORCE HOSPITAL - MEDICAL LIBRARY
(NM-Kirtland AFB) □ Kirtland AFB, NM

Lee, Alma, Libn.
KANSAS CITY - CITY DEVELOPMENT
DEPARTMENT - LIBRARY □ Kansas City, MO

Lee, Beverly A., Libn.
UNIVERSITY OF MINNESOTA - CHEMISTRY
LIBRARY □ Minneapolis, MN

Lee, Carolyn T., Cur.
CATHOLIC UNIVERSITY OF AMERICA -
CLEMENTINE LIBRARY □ Washington, DC

Lee, Carolyn T., Cur.
CATHOLIC UNIVERSITY OF AMERICA -
SEMITICS - INSTITUTE OF CHRISTIAN
ORIENTAL RESEARCH (ICOR) LIBRARY □
Washington, DC

Lee, Charles E., Dir.
SOUTH CAROLINA STATE DEPARTMENT OF
ARCHIVES & HISTORY - ARCHIVES SEARCH
ROOM □ Columbia, SC

Lee, Chung, Asst.Cat.
PRICE WATERHOUSE - NATIONAL
INFORMATION CENTER □ New York, NY

Lee, Claire, Asst.Libn., Cat.
HAMLINE UNIVERSITY SCHOOL OF LAW -
LIBRARY □ St. Paul, MN

Lee, Dennis, ILL
NORTHWEST COLLEGE OF THE ASSEMBLIES OF
GOD - HURST LIBRARY† □ Kirkland, WA

Lee, Diana, Hd., Info.Serv.
ALBERTA ENVIRONMENTAL CENTRE - LIBRARY
□ Vegreville, AB

Lee, Frank, Mgr.
DALLAS PUBLIC LIBRARY - GOVERNMENT
PUBLICATIONS DIVISION □ Dallas, TX

Lee, Fred, Supv.
DOW CORNING CORPORATION - CORPORATE
SITE INFORMATION CENTER □ Midland, MI

Lee, Grace, Doc.Libn.
TEXAS TECH UNIVERSITY - SCHOOL OF LAW
LIBRARY □ Lubbock, TX

Lee, Helen, Libn.
UNION CAMP CORP. - R & D DIVISION
LIBRARY† □ Princeton, NJ

Lee, Hyosoo, Tech.Serv.Libn.
CLEVELAND INSTITUTE OF ART - JESSICA R.
GUND MEMORIAL LIBRARY □ Cleveland, OH

Lee, J., Evening Libn.
PACE UNIVERSITY, PLEASANTVILLE/
BRIARCLIFF - EDWARD AND DORIS MORTOLA
LIBRARY □ Pleasantville, NY

Lee, Jane Yu, Libn.
GTE COMMUNICATION SYSTEMS - LIBRARY □
Northlake, IL

Lee, Jennifer B., Rd.Serv.
BROWN UNIVERSITY - SPECIAL COLLECTIONS
□ Providence, RI

Lee, Joanne, Libn.
U.S. DEPT. OF HOUSING AND URBAN
DEVELOPMENT - REGION IX - LIBRARY □ San
Francisco, CA

Lee, Joel M., Libn.
AMERICAN LIBRARY ASSOCIATION -
HEADQUARTERS LIBRARY □ Chicago, IL

Lee, Joyce C., Hd., Pub.Serv.
NEVADA STATE LIBRARY □ Carson City, NV

Lee, Judith C., Info.Rsrcs.Mgr.
HYDRO RESEARCH SCIENCE - LIBRARY† □
Santa Clara, CA

Lee, Julia T., Libn.
MICHIGAN MOLECULAR INSTITUTE - LIBRARY
□ Midland, MI

Lee, Kathryn, Libn.
INSURANCE EDUCATIONAL ASSOCIATION -
THE INSURANCE LIBRARY OF LOS ANGELES □
Los Angeles, CA

Lee, L., Specifications
U.S. NASA - JOHN F. KENNEDY SPACE CENTER
- LIBRARY □ Kennedy Space Center, FL

Lee, Lila J., Libn.
HELD-POAGE MEMORIAL HOME & RESEARCH
LIBRARY □ Ukiah, CA

Lee, Marianne S., Hd.Libn.
NORTHERN TRUST COMPANY - LIBRARY† □
Chicago, IL

Lee, Marilyn M., Law Libn.
FRANKLIN LAW LIBRARY □ Greenfield, MA

Lee, Marjorie, Libn.
FLORIDA STATE LEGISLATURE - DIVISION OF
LEGISLATIVE LIBRARY SERVICES □
Tallahassee, FL

Lee, Marjorie, Coord.
UNIVERSITY OF CALIFORNIA, LOS ANGELES -
ASIAN AMERICAN STUDIES CENTER READING
ROOM □ Los Angeles, CA

Lee, Martha Ann, Mgr., Tech.Proc.
MISSISSIPPI (State) RESEARCH AND
DEVELOPMENT CENTER - INFORMATION
SERVICES DIVISION □ Jackson, MS

Lee, Minja, Tech.Serv.Libn.
BARUCH (Bernard M.) COLLEGE OF THE CITY
UNIVERSITY OF NEW YORK - LIBRARY† □ New
York, NY

Lee, Nancy Craig, Hd., Tech.Serv.
UNIVERSITY OF LOUISVILLE - KORNHAUSER
HEALTH SCIENCES LIBRARY □ Louisville, KY

Lee, On-Sook, Asst.Libn.
ALEXIAN BROTHERS MEDICAL CENTER -
MEDICAL LIBRARY† □ Elk Grove Village, IL

Lee, Patricia, Ref.Libn.
UNIVERSITY OF TEXAS MEDICAL BRANCH -
MOODY MEDICAL LIBRARY □ Galveston, TX

Lee, Paul J., Libn.
CINCINNATI PUBLIC SCHOOLS -
PROFESSIONAL LIBRARY† □ Cincinnati, OH

Lee, Penni, Act.Libn.
ONTARIO - MINISTRY OF REVENUE - LIBRARY
□ Oshawa, ON

Lee, Dr. Richard, Libn.
COLUMBIA CHRISTIAN COLLEGE - LIBRARY -
SPECIAL COLLECTIONS □ Portland, OR

Lee, Rita, ILL Coord.
NEW YORK MEDICAL COLLEGE AND THE
WESTCHESTER ACADEMY OF MEDICINE -
WESTCHESTER MEDICAL CENTER LIBRARY □
Valhalla, NY

Lee, Robert, Asst.Libn.
JEFFERSON (Thomas) UNIVERSITY - SCOTT
MEMORIAL LIBRARY □ Philadelphia, PA

Lee, Robert A., Hd., Res.Dept.
UNIVERSAL CITY STUDIOS - RESEARCH
DEPARTMENT LIBRARY □ Universal City, CA

Lee, Robert D., Jr.
PENNSYLVANIA STATE UNIVERSITY -
INSTITUTE OF PUBLIC ADMINISTRATION -
LIBRARY □ University Park, PA

Lee, Rodney, Cur., Black Heritage Ctr.
QUEENS BOROUGH PUBLIC LIBRARY -
LANGSTON HUGHES COMMUNITY LIBRARY AND
CULTURAL CENTER □ Corona, NY

Lee, Sara Jane, Libn.
TRACOR, INC. - TECHNICAL LIBRARY □ Austin,
TX

Lee, Shirley, Unclassified Lib.Supv.
R & D ASSOCIATES - TECHNICAL
INFORMATION SERVICES □ Marina Del Rey, CA

Lee, Soon-Ho, Libn.
AMERICAN HOSPITAL SUPPLY CORPORATION -
CORPORATE INFORMATION CENTER □
Evanston, IL

Lee, Stephen, Bagshaw Comm.Chm.
TORONTO PUBLIC LIBRARY - MARGUERITE G.
BAGSHAW COLLECTION† □ Toronto, ON

Lee, Sue T., Asst.Libn.
U.S. COURT OF APPEALS, 11TH CIRCUIT -
LIBRARY □ Atlanta, GA

Lee, Takika, Comparative Law Libn
UNIVERSITY OF WASHINGTON - MARIAN
GOULD GALLAGHER LAW LIBRARY □ Seattle,
WA

Lee, Mr. Wynn, Dir.
MARK TWAIN MEMORIAL - LIBRARY □ Hartford,
CT

Leech, Sara, Assoc.
UNIVERSITY OF KENTUCKY - MEDICAL
CENTER LIBRARY □ Lexington, KY

Leedale, Joan E., Libn.
DU PONT CANADA, INC. - PATENT DIVISION
LIBRARY □ Mississauga, ON

Leeds, Doris M., Adm./Libn.
NCR CORPORATION - E&M DIVISION LIBRARY
□ San Diego, CA

Leeds, Pauline R., Libn.
NEW ENGLAND NUCLEAR CORPORATION -
LIBRARY □ Boston, MA

Leen, Mary, Libn.
BOSTONIAN SOCIETY - LIBRARY □ Boston, MA

Leeper, Mrs. John P., Libn.
MC NAY (Marion Koogler) ART MUSEUM -
LIBRARY □ San Antonio, TX

Leerhoff, Ruth, Asst.Univ.Libn.
SAN DIEGO STATE UNIVERSITY - MALCOLM A.
LOVE LIBRARY - SPECIAL COLLECTIONS† □ San
Diego, CA

Leese, Laura, Med.Libn.
HORTON MEMORIAL HOSPITAL - MEDICAL
LIBRARY □ Middletown, NY

Leesment, Helgi, Cons.Libn.
STOCKMEN'S MEMORIAL FOUNDATION -
LIBRARY □ Calgary, AB

Lefebvre, Diane, Dir.
SOCIETE DE DEVELOPPEMENT DE LA BAIE JAMES - DOCUMENTATION CENTRE □ Montreal, PQ

Lefebvre, Marie, Cartothecaire
UNIVERSITE DU QUEBEC A TROIS-RIVIERES - CARTOTHEQUE □ Trois-Rivieres, PQ

Lefebvre, Ulric, Chief
HOPITAL ST-FRANCOIS D'ASSISE - BIBLIOTHEQUE MEDICALE ET ADMINISTRATIVE† □ Quebec, PQ

Leffingwell, Janna, Cat.Libn.
STANFORD UNIVERSITY - J. HUGH JACKSON LIBRARY □ Stanford, CA

Leffler, Carolyn, Law Libn.
MERCER COUNTY LAW LIBRARY □ Celina, OH

Leffler, Nelle, Univ.Libn.
FLORIDA STATE UNIVERSITY - SCIENCE-TECHNOLOGY DIVISION □ Tallahassee, FL

Leffler, Ruth E., Tech.Libn.
ASSOCIATED TECHNICAL SERVICES, INC. - RESEARCH LIBRARY □ Glen Ridge, NJ

Lefkowitz, Robert J., Dir.
ST. ANTHONY HOSPITAL - O'DONOGHUE MEDICAL LIBRARY □ Oklahoma City, OK

Lefkowski, Mary E., Govt.Doc.Libn.
DICKINSON SCHOOL OF LAW - SHEELY-LEE LAW LIBRARY □ Carlisle, PA

LeGendre, Elaine V., Health Sci.Libn.
LAWRENCE MEMORIAL HOSPITAL OF MEDFORD - HEALTH SCIENCES LIBRARY □ Medford, MA

Legendre, Sally, Sr.Libn.
NEW YORK STATE LIBRARY - LAW/SOCIAL SCIENCE REFERENCE SERVICES □ Albany, NY

Legere, Clarisse, Med.Rec.
ANDROSCOGGIN VALLEY HOSPITAL - MEDICAL LIBRARY □ Berlin, NH

Legere, Fr. Germain, C.P., Libn.
CONGREGATION OF THE PASSION - HOLY CROSS PROVINCE - PROVINCIAL LIBRARY □ Louisville, KY

Legett, Anne, Asst.Lib.Dir.
BATON ROUGE STATE-TIMES & MORNING ADVOCATE NEWSPAPERS - LIBRARY □ Baton Rouge, LA

LeGette, Louise N., Chf.Libn.
TAMPA TRIBUNE & TAMPA TIMES - LIBRARY □ Tampa, FL

Legg, Ardelle F., Hd.
BOSTON UNIVERSITY - SCIENCE AND ENGINEERING LIBRARY □ Boston, MA

Legg, Patricia A., First Asst.
FLINT PUBLIC LIBRARY - ART, MUSIC & DRAMA DEPARTMENT □ Flint, MI

Leggett, Lois, Spec.Coll.Libn.
WINSTON-SALEM STATE UNIVERSITY - O'KELLY LIBRARY - SPECIAL COLLECTIONS □ Winston-Salem, NC

Leggett, Mark, Div.Hd.
INDIANAPOLIS-MARION COUNTY PUBLIC LIBRARY - BUSINESS, SCIENCE AND TECHNOLOGY DIVISION □ Indianapolis, IN

Legry, Mary, Data Coord.
CLARK COUNTY REGIONAL PLANNING COUNCIL - LIBRARY □ Vancouver, WA

LeGuern, Charles A., Tech.Serv.Libn.
MILES LABORATORIES, INC. - LIBRARY RESOURCES AND SERVICES □ Elkhart, IN

Leh, Carol S., Tech.Libn.
SANDERS & THOMAS, INC. - LIBRARY □ Pottstown, PA

Lehman, Carol A., Libn.
GENERAL MOTORS CORPORATION - PUBLIC RELATIONS STAFF LIBRARY □ Detroit, MI

Lehman, Lois J., Libn.
PENNSYLVANIA STATE UNIVERSITY - COLLEGE OF MEDICINE - GEORGE T. HARRELL LIBRARY □ Hershey, PA

Lehman, Melissa, Libn./Educ.Rep.
MEMPHIS STATE UNIVERSITY LIBRARIES - C.H. NASH MUSEUM LIBRARY □ Memphis, TN

Lehman, Sharon, Supv., Lit.Serv.
WARNER-LAMBERT/PARKE-DAVIS - RESEARCH LIBRARY† □ Ann Arbor, MI

Lehmann, Lucile, Archv.
UNIVERSITY OF FLORIDA - COASTAL & OCEANOGRAPHIC ENGINEERING DEPARTMENT - COASTAL ENGINEERING ARCHIVES □ Gainesville, FL

Lehnig, Katharine P., Law Libn.
BUCKS COUNTY LAW LIBRARY □ Doylestown, PA

Lehrer, Susan Frisch, Cur.
CHESTERWOOD - LIBRARY □ Stockbridge, MA

Lehwaldt, Marliese, Hd.Libn.
LABATT BREWING COMPANY LIMITED - CENTRAL RESEARCH LIBRARY □ London, ON

Lei, Polin, Med.Libn.
ST. JOSEPH'S HOSPITAL - BRUCE COLE MEMORIAL LIBRARY □ Tucson, AZ

Leibiger, I., Hd.
LEIBIGER (O.W.) RESEARCH LABORATORIES, INC. - TECHNICAL INFORMATION CENTER □ Hoosick Falls, NY

Leibovici, Martin M., Lib.Dir.
GOLDWATER MEMORIAL HOSPITAL - HEALTH SCIENCES LIBRARY □ Franklin D. Roosevelt Island, NY

Leibowitz, Gerald, Media Libn.
NASSAU COMMUNITY COLLEGE - NEW YORK STATE HEALTH FILM COLLECTION □ Garden City, NY

Leibowitz, Margaret, Dp.Dir.
ALASKA STATE DIVISION OF STATE LIBRARIES & MUSEUMS - STATE LIBRARY □ Juneau, AK

Leibowitz, Martin, Asst.Chf.
BROOKLYN PUBLIC LIBRARY - SCIENCE AND INDUSTRY DIVISION □ Brooklyn, NY

Leich, Harold M., Slavic Acq.
UNIVERSITY OF ILLINOIS - SLAVIC AND EAST EUROPEAN LIBRARY □ Urbana, IL

Leichman, Laurie, Supv., Ref.Serv.
MC KINSEY & COMPANY, INC. - INFORMATION SERVICES □ New York, NY

Leichter, Janice, Libn.
MOUNT ZION HEBREW CONGREGATION - TEMPLE LIBRARY □ St. Paul, MN

Leiderman, Rosalyn, Info.Serv.Libn.
NATIONAL ACADEMY OF SCIENCES - NATIONAL ACADEMY OF ENGINEERING - LIBRARY □ Washington, DC

Leif, Mary D., Libn.
WASHINGTON HOSPITAL - HEALTH SCIENCES LIBRARY □ Washington, PA

Leifer, Claire, Libn.
ANSER - TECHNICAL LIBRARY □ Arlington, VA

Leigh, Kathleen A., Libn.
GERMANTOWN HOSPITAL AND MEDICAL CENTER - LIBRARY □ Philadelphia, PA

Leigh, Ken, Mgr.
LA PURISIMA MISSION - ARCHIVES □ Lompoc, CA

Leigh, Robert, Libn.
ALBERTA - DEPARTMENT OF THE ATTORNEY GENERAL - LAW SOCIETY LIBRARY □ Lethbridge, AB

Leightly, Virginia, Acq.
UNIVERSITY OF LOUISVILLE - KORNHAUSER HEALTH SCIENCES LIBRARY □ Louisville, KY

Leighton, Helene, Hd., Comp.Serv.
MASSACHUSETTS GENERAL HOSPITAL - MGH HEALTH SCIENCES LIBRARIES □ Boston, MA

Leighton, Lee W., Asst.Libn., Cat.Serv.
HARVARD UNIVERSITY - LAW SCHOOL LIBRARY □ Cambridge, MA

Leiman, Bob, Exec.Dir.
AMERICAN INSTITUTE OF PARLIAMENTARIANS - LIBRARY □ Fort Wayne, IN

Lein, Jonella B., Tech.Info.Spec.
U.S. ARMY HOSPITALS - DARNALL ARMY HOSPITAL - MEDICAL LIBRARY □ Ft. Hood, TX

Leiphart, Patricia P., Hist. Site Mgr.
PENNSYLVANIA STATE HISTORICAL & MUSEUM COMMISSION - FORT LE BOEUF MUSEUM - LIBRARY □ Waterford, PA

Leishman, Joan L., Libn.
C-I-L INC. - CHEMICALS RESEARCH LABORATORY LIBRARY □ Mississauga, ON

Leishman, Sara, Cur.
CAMBRIA COUNTY HISTORICAL SOCIETY - MUSEUM & LIBRARY □ Ebensburg, PA

Leishman, Wes, Interpretation Chf.
U.S. NATL. PARK SERVICE - CUMBERLAND GAP NATL. HISTORICAL PARK - LIBRARY □ Middlesboro, KY

Leisner, Edward, Med.Libn.
ERIE COUNTY MEDICAL CENTER - MEDICAL LIBRARY† □ Buffalo, NY

Leister, Jack, Hd.Libn.
UNIVERSITY OF CALIFORNIA, BERKELEY - INSTITUTE OF GOVERNMENTAL STUDIES - LIBRARY □ Berkeley, CA

Leitch, Russell H., Dir.
U.S. DEPT. OF COMMERCE - INTERNATIONAL TRADE ADMINISTRATION - MILWAUKEE DISTRICT OFFICE LIBRARY □ Milwaukee, WI

Leith, Anna R., Hd.
UNIVERSITY OF BRITISH COLUMBIA - WOODWARD BIOMEDICAL LIBRARY □ Vancouver, BC

Leith, David A., Dir.
U.S. FISH & WILDLIFE SERVICE - ABERNATHY SALMON CULTURAL DEVELOPMENT CENTER - RESEARCH & INFO. CENTER □ Longview, WA

Leitner, Gene, Co-Founder
GOLDEN RADIO BUFFS OF MARYLAND, INC. - TAPE LIBRARY □ Baltimore, MD

Leive, Cynthia, Music Cat.
UNIVERSITY OF WESTERN ONTARIO - MUSIC LIBRARY □ London, ON

Leja, Ilga, Legislative Libn.
NOVA SCOTIA - LEGISLATIVE LIBRARY □ Halifax, NS

Lekisch, Barbara, Rsrcs.Libn.
SIERRA CLUB - WILLIAM E. COLBY MEMORIAL LIBRARY □ San Francisco, CA

Lem, Nancy E., Libn.
HEWLETT-PACKARD COMPANY - HP LABORATORIES - DEER CREEK LIBRARY □ Palo Alto, CA

LeMacher, Claire N., Asst.Cur.
PENSACOLA HISTORICAL SOCIETY - LELIA ABERCROMBIE HISTORICAL LIBRARY □ Pensacola, FL

Leman, Amy, Info.Spec.
AT & T COMMUNICATIONS - INFORMATION RESEARCH CENTER □ Basking Ridge, NJ

Leman, Lois A., Lib.Asst.III
NORTHERN ARIZONA UNIVERSITY - SPECIAL COLLECTIONS LIBRARY □ Flagstaff, AZ

Lemaster, Gloria S., Libn.
ALABAMA INSTITUTE FOR THE DEAF AND BLIND - LIBRARY FOR THE BLIND AND PHYSICALLY HANDICAPPED □ Talladega, AL

Lemaster, Regina K., Microfilm Spec.
BOWLING GREEN STATE UNIVERSITY - CENTER FOR ARCHIVAL COLLECTIONS □ Bowling Green, OH

LeMay, Bro. Alan, Libn.
FRANCISCAN FRIARS OF THE ATONEMENT - ATONEMENT SEMINARY LIBRARY □ Washington, DC

Lemay, Louise, Chf.Libn.
CENTRE HOSPITALIER STE. JEANNE D'ARC - BIBLIOTHEQUE MEDICALE □ Montreal, PQ

Lemelin, Evelina E., Libn.
CONNECTICUT STATE LIBRARY - LAW LIBRARY AT LITCHFIELD □ Litchfield, CT

Lemieux, Francine, Ref., Edifice H.
QUEBEC PROVINCE - MINISTERE DES COMMUNICATIONS - BIBLIOTHEQUE ADMINISTRATIVE □ Quebec, PQ

Lemieux, Marcel, Tech.Serv.
COLLEGE UNIVERSITAIRE DE ST. BONIFACE -
BIBLIOTHEQUE ALFRED-MONNIN □ Saint-
Boniface, MB

Lemire, Camil, Med.Libn.
HOPITAL LOUIS H. LAFONTAINE -
BIBLIOTHEQUE □ Montreal, PQ

Lemire, Diane, Aid Libn.
SOCIETE QUEBECOISE D'INITIATIVES
PETROLIERES - DOCUMENTATION CENTRE† □
Ste. Foy, PQ

Lemkau, Henry L., Jr., Dir.
UNIVERSITY OF MIAMI - SCHOOL OF
MEDICINE - LOUIS CALDER MEMORIAL
LIBRARY □ Miami, FL

Lemke, Susan, Chf., Spec.Coll.
U.S. NATL. DEFENSE UNIVERSITY - LIBRARY □
Washington, DC

Lemmon, Helen E., Libn.
JOHNSON BIBLE COLLEGE - GLASS MEMORIAL
LIBRARY □ Knoxville, TN

Lemmon, Virginia, Ref.
RUTGERS UNIVERSITY, THE STATE
UNIVERSITY OF NEW JERSEY - JUSTICE
HENRY ACKERSON LIBRARY OF LAW &
CRIMINAL JUSTICE □ Newark, NJ

LeMoine, Claude, Cur.
NATIONAL LIBRARY OF CANADA - LITERARY
MANUSCRIPTS COLLECTION □ Ottawa, ON

Lemoine, Doris, Lib.Coord
MANITOBA - DEPT. OF EDUCATION - BUREAU
DE L'EDUCATION FRANCAISE - DIRECTION
DES RESSOURCES EDUCATIVES FRANCAISES □
Saint-Boniface, MB

Lemon, Kate, Info.Spec.
LOUISIANA STATE HOUSE OF
REPRESENTATIVES LEGISLATIVE SERVICES -
RESEARCH LIBRARY □ Baton Rouge, LA

Lemon, Pamela R., Tech.Info.Spec.
NATL.INST. OF ENVIRONMENTAL HEALTH SCI.
- NATL. TOXICOLOGY PROGRAM -
ENVIRONMENTAL TERATOLOGY INFO.CTR. □
Research Triangle Park, NC

LeMonde-McIntyre, Michelle, Res.Spec.
HONEYWELL, INC. - HONEYWELL
INFORMATION SYSTEMS - INFORMATION AND
LIBRARY SERVICES □ Waltham, MA

Lempel, Joyce, Resource Coord.
NORTH AMERICAN JEWISH STUDENTS'
NETWORK - LIBRARY □ New York, NY

Lenahan, Richard M., Act.Dir.
U.S. DEPT. OF COMMERCE - INTERNATIONAL
TRADE ADMINISTRATION - ANCHORAGE
DISTRICT OFFICE LIBRARY □ Anchorage, AK

Lenburg, Joanne, Educ.Ref.Libn.
MADISON METROPOLITAN SCHOOL DISTRICT -
EDUCATION REFERENCE LIBRARY □ Madison,
WI

Lenk, P.A., Spec.Coll.Asst.
COLBY COLLEGE - MILLER LIBRARY - SPECIAL
COLLECTIONS □ Waterville, ME

Lennartz, David C., Ph.D., Res.Anl.
MEDICAL PLANNING ASSOCIATES - LIBRARY □
Malibu, CA

Lenneberg, Hans, Art Libn.
UNIVERSITY OF CHICAGO - ART LIBRARY □
Chicago, IL

Lenneberg, Hans, Music Libn.
UNIVERSITY OF CHICAGO - MUSIC
COLLECTION □ Chicago, IL

Lennes, Gregory, Archv.
INTERNATIONAL HARVESTER COMPANY -
CORPORATE ARCHIVES □ Chicago, IL

Lennon, Donald R., Coll.Dir.
EAST CAROLINA UNIVERSITY - EAST
CAROLINA MANUSCRIPT COLLECTION □
Greenville, NC

Lennon, Suzanne, Tech.Libn.
GTE NETWORK SYSTEMS - TECHNICAL
LIBRARY □ Phoenix, AZ

Lenoski, C.G., Asst. Regional Dir.
CANADA - STATISTICS CANADA - ADVISORY
SERVICES - VANCOUVER REFERENCE CENTRE
□ Vancouver, BC

Lensenmayer, Nancy F., Mgr., Pub.Serv.Sect.
OCLC, INC. - LIBRARY □ Dublin, OH

Lent, Judith A., Libn.-Ref. & ILL
GENERAL ELECTRIC COMPANY - CORPORATE
RESEARCH & DEVELOPMENT - WHITNEY
INFORMATION SERVICES □ Schenectady, NY

Lenthall, Franklyn, Cur.
BOOTHBAY THEATRE MUSEUM □ Boothbay, ME

Lentocha, Pat
ASSOCIATION OF NORTH AMERICAN
DIRECTORY PUBLISHERS - PRICE & LEE
COMPANY DIRECTORY LIBRARY □ Bellows Falls,
VT

Lentz, Joyce, Libn.
ELWYN INSTITUTES - LIBRARY □ Elwyn, PA

Lentz, Robert T., Archv.
JEFFERSON (Thomas) UNIVERSITY - SCOTT
MEMORIAL LIBRARY □ Philadelphia, PA

Lenz, Ann
CONNECTICUT STATE LIBRARY - LAW LIBRARY
AT NEW HAVEN □ New Haven, CT

Leo, May K., Libn.
NYACK COLLEGE - LIBRARY □ Nyack, NY

Leon, Eduardo, Archv.
PUERTO RICO - INSTITUTE OF PUERTO RICAN
CULTURE - ARCHIVO GENERAL DE PUERTO
RICO □ San Juan, PR

Leonard, Bill, Hd., Graphic Arts Serv.
UNIVERSITY OF OREGON - INSTRUCTIONAL
MEDIA CENTER □ Eugene, OR

Leonard, Diane, Supv., Cat.Serv.
CANADIAN BROADCASTING CORPORATION -
MUSIC SERVICES LIBRARY □ Montreal, PQ

Leonard, Elsie A., Sect.Chf.
MARYLAND STATE DEPARTMENT OF
EDUCATION - DIVISION OF LIBRARY
DEVELOPMENT & SERVICES - MEDIA SERVICES
CENTER† □ Baltimore, MD

Leonard, Gigi, AV Supv.
MAINE MARITIME ACADEMY - NUTTING
MEMORIAL LIBRARY □ Castine, ME

Leonard, Harriet, Ref.Libn.
DUKE UNIVERSITY - DIVINITY SCHOOL
LIBRARY† □ Durham, NC

Leonard, J.W., Mgr.
IBM CORPORATION - THOMAS J. WATSON
RESEARCH CENTER LIBRARY □ Yorktown
Heights, NY

Leonard, Jean, Med.Libn.
MERCY HOSPITAL OF NEW ORLEANS -
MEDICAL LIBRARY □ New Orleans, LA

Leonard, Jean, Clinical Libn.
U.S. VETERANS ADMINISTRATION (CA-Loma
Linda) - HOSPITAL LIBRARY SERVICE □ Loma
Linda, CA

Leonard, Kevin B., Assoc.Univ.Archv.
NORTHWESTERN UNIVERSITY - ARCHIVES □
Evanston, IL

Leonard, Lawrence E., Lib.Dir.
U.S. DEPT. OF TRANSPORTATION - LIBRARY
AND DISTRIBUTION SERVICES DIVISION □
Washington, DC

Leonard, Lucinda E., V.P.
INFORMATICS GENERAL CORPORATION -
LIBRARY SERVICES DIVISION □ Rockville, MD

Leonard, Nathalie B., Town Hist./Cur.
EDEN HISTORICAL SOCIETY - TOWN
HISTORIAN'S OFFICE AND HISTORICAL
SOCIETY LIBRARY □ Eden, NY

Leonard, Peter H., Dir.
METCO INC. - ENGINEERING LIBRARY □
Westbury, NY

Leonard, Rosalita J., Libn.
NATIONAL WOMAN'S CHRISTIAN
TEMPERANCE UNION - FRANCES E. WILLARD
MEMORIAL LIBRARY □ Evanston, IL

Leonard, Ruth S., Lib.Cons.
PROTESTANT EPISCOPAL CHURCH -
EPISCOPAL DIOCESE OF MASSACHUSETTS -
DIOCESAN LIBRARY AND ARCHIVES □ Boston,
MA

Leonard, Sharen, Asst.Libn., Tech.Serv.
U.S. COURT OF APPEALS, 1ST CIRCUIT -
LIBRARY □ Boston, MA

Leonard, Dr. W. Patrick, Dean
CHICAGO STATE UNIVERSITY - DOUGLAS
LIBRARY - SPECIAL COLLECTIONS† □ Chicago,
IL

Leonard, Rev. William, S.J., Liturgical Coll.Cur
BOSTON COLLEGE - SPECIAL COLLECTIONS
DEPARTMENT □ Chestnut Hill, MA

Leonardo, Joan, Hd., Info.Serv.
CANADA - NATIONAL RESEARCH COUNCIL -
CISTI - AERONAUTICAL & MECHANICAL
ENGINEERING BRANCH □ Ottawa, ON

Leondar, Judith C., Mgr.
AMERICAN CYANAMID COMPANY -
AGRICULTURAL RESEARCH DIVISION -
TECHNICAL INFORMATION SERVICES □
Princeton, NJ

Leone, Dolores, Educ.Dir.
BETHESDA HOSPITAL - PROFESSIONAL
LIBRARY □ Denver, CO

Leone, Lisa A., Ck.
U.S. FOOD AND DRUG ADMINISTRATION -
WINCHESTER ENGINEERING & ANALYTICAL
CENTER - LIBRARY □ Winchester, MA

Leong, E.B., Palo Alto Libn.
LOCKHEED MISSILES & SPACE COMPANY, INC.
- TECHNICAL INFORMATION CENTER □ Palo
Alto, CA

Leong, Molly, Bilingual Res.Libn.
EVALUATION, DISSEMINATION & ASSESSMENT
CENTER - EDAC RESEARCH LIBRARY □
Cambridge, MA

Leonhardt, Ronald D., Dir.
MILWAUKEE - LEGISLATIVE REFERENCE
BUREAU - LEGISLATIVE LIBRARY □ Milwaukee,
WI

Leopold, Lee B., Archv.
PHILADELPHIA JEWISH ARCHIVES CENTER □
Philadelphia, PA

Lepkowski, Frank, Cat.Libn.
SUNY - COLLEGE AT POTSDAM - FREDERICK W.
CRUMB MEMORIAL LIBRARY □ Potsdam, NY

Lepper, Maurice
UNIVERSITY OF CALGARY - SOCIAL SCIENCES
LIBRARY† □ Calgary, AB

Lerch, Barbara, Act.Libn.
ST. ANSELM'S COLLEGE - GEISEL LIBRARY □
Manchester, NH

Lerch, Miriam S., Div.Hd.
CARNEGIE LIBRARY OF PITTSBURGH -
BUSINESS DIVISION □ Pittsburgh, PA

Leredu, Martha, Chf., Lib.Serv.
U.S. VETERANS ADMINISTRATION (WA-
Seattle) - HOSPITAL MEDICAL LIBRARY □
Seattle, WA

Lerew, Ann, Ref.Libn.
COLORADO SCHOOL OF MINES - ARTHUR
LAKES LIBRARY □ Golden, CO

Lergier, Clara S., Chf.Libn.
PUERTO RICO - ATENEO PUERTORRIQUENO -
BIBLIOTECA □ San Juan, PR

Lergier, Marlene, Asst.Libn.
PUERTO RICO - ATENEO PUERTORRIQUENO -
BIBLIOTECA □ San Juan, PR

Lerner, Adele A., Archv.
NEW YORK HOSPITAL-CORNELL MEDICAL
CENTER - MEDICAL ARCHIVES □ New York, NY

Lerner, Dr. Israel, Judaic Spec.
BOARD OF JEWISH EDUCATION OF GREATER
NEW YORK - EDUCATIONAL RESOURCE
LIBRARY □ New York, NY

Lerner, Ron, Faculty/Graphics
GEORGIA COLLEGE - MEDIA SERVICES □
Milledgeville, GA

LeRoy, E.C., M.D., Dir.
MEDICAL UNIVERSITY OF SOUTH CAROLINA -
ARTHRITIS CENTER LIBRARY □ Charleston, SC
Lescay, Monica, Dir., Med.Rec./Libn.
WALKER MEMORIAL HOSPITAL - LIBRARY □
Avon Park, FL
LeSieur, B., Acq. & Coll.Libn.
MC GILL UNIVERSITY - MEDICAL LIBRARY □
Montreal, PQ
Lesiga, Nina, Info.Chem.
LEVER RESEARCH AND DEVELOPMENT CENTER
- RESEARCH LIBRARY □ Edgewater, NJ
Lesniak, Benjamin A., Libn.
CARBON COUNTY LAW LIBRARY† □ Jim Thorpe,
PA
Leson, Henry, Rector
MOHYLA INSTITUTE - LIBRARY AND ARCHIVES
□ Saskatoon, SK
LeSourd, Jill, Libn.
GREENE COUNTY LAW LIBRARY† □ Xenia, OH
LeSourd, Margaret S., Assoc.Univ.Libn.
UNIVERSITY OF FLORIDA - URBAN AND
REGIONAL PLANNING DOCUMENTS
COLLECTION □ Gainesville, FL
L'Esperance, Marcelle, Chf.Libn.
HOPITAL NOTRE DAME - MEDICAL LIBRARY □
Montreal, PQ
Lessard, Elizabeth, Libn.
MANCHESTER HISTORIC ASSOCIATION -
LIBRARY □ Manchester, NH
Lesser, Anita L., Libn.
IBM CORPORATION - SITE TECHNICAL
LIBRARY/INFORMATION CENTER □ Austin, TX
Lesser, Ann, Dir.
WARREN LIBRARY ASSOCIATION - LIBRARY □
Warren, PA
Lesser, Charles H., Asst.Dir./Archv. & Pubn.
SOUTH CAROLINA STATE DEPARTMENT OF
ARCHIVES & HISTORY - ARCHIVES SEARCH
ROOM □ Columbia, SC
Lessing, Joan C., Cur., Oral Hist.Coll.
RESEARCH FOUNDATION FOR JEWISH
IMMIGRATION, INC. - ARCHIVES □ New York,
NY
Lessner, Stephen
NOVA UNIVERSITY - OCEANOGRAPHIC
CENTER LIBRARY □ Dania, FL
Lestage, Micheline, Dir.
SOCIETE NATIONALE DE DIFFUSION
EDUCATIVE ET CULTURELLE - SERVICE
D'INFORMATION SONDEC □ St. Leonard, PQ
Lester, Lillian, Spec.Coll.Libn.
BROOKLYN COLLEGE OF THE CITY UNIVERSITY
OF NEW YORK - HARRY D. GIDEONSE LIBRARY
- SPECIAL COLLECTIONS □ Brooklyn, NY
Lester, Lorraine, Sys. & Mgt.Libn.
UNIVERSITY OF NEW MEXICO - SCHOOL OF
LAW LIBRARY □ Albuquerque, NM
Lester, Marilyn A., Dir. of Lrng.Rsrcs.
NATIONAL COLLEGE OF EDUCATION -
LEARNING RESOURCE CENTERS □ Evanston, IL
LeStourgeon, Zethyl T., Dir.
PROTESTANT EPISCOPAL CHURCH -
EPISCOPAL DIOCESE OF WEST TEXAS -
CATHEDRAL HOUSE ARCHIVES □ San Antonio,
TX
LeSueur, C. Robin, Libn.
HARVARD UNIVERSITY - SCHOOLS OF
MEDICINE, DENTAL MED. & PUBLIC HEALTH,
BOSTON MED.LIB. - FRANCIS A. COUNTWAY
LIB. □ Boston, MA
Lethbridge, Sheila M., Libn.
ORTHOPAEDIC AND ARTHRITIC HOSPITAL -
LIBRARY □ Toronto, ON
Letson, Carol G., Libn.
GREENFIELD COMMUNITY COLLEGE
FOUNDATION - ARCHIBALD MAC LEISH
COLLECTION □ Greenfield, MA
Letson, Carol G., Libn.
GREENFIELD COMMUNITY COLLEGE - PIONEER
VALLEY RESOURCE CENTER □ Greenfield, MA

Letson, Dawn, Mss.Cur.
SOUTHERN METHODIST UNIVERSITY -
DEGOLYER LIBRARY - FIKES HALL OF SPECIAL
COLLECTIONS □ Dallas, TX
Letson, Ruth S., Libn.
TENNESSEE STATE DEPARTMENT OF
TRANSPORTATION - LIBRARY □ Nashville, TN
Lett, Marla, Asst.Libn.
YAVAPAI COUNTY LAW LIBRARY† □ Prescott,
AZ
Lettofsky, Jean Loeb, Dir., Lib.Serv.
CLEVELAND COLLEGE OF JEWISH STUDIES -
AARON GARBER LIBRARY □ Beachwood, OH
Leubbert, Karen M., Dir.
EDEN THEOLOGICAL SEMINARY - LIBRARY □
Webster Groves, MO
Leung, Joyce, Ref.Libn.
BRIDGEWATER STATE COLLEGE - CLEMENT C.
MAXWELL LIBRARY □ Bridgewater, MA
Leutenegger, Fr. Benedict, Archv.
OUR LADY OF THE LAKE UNIVERSITY - OLD
SPANISH MISSIONS HISTORICAL RESEARCH
LIBRARY □ San Antonio, TX
Leuzinger, Nancy J., Libn.
DRAVO ENGINEERS INC. - LIBRARY □
Pittsburgh, PA
Levan, Pat, Lit.Rsrcs.Assoc.
MERCK & COMPANY, INC. - MERCK SHARP &
DOHME RESEARCH LABORATORIES -
LITERATURE RESOURCES □ Rahway, NJ
LeVaseur, Charlotte, Hd., Tech.Serv.
MONTANA STATE LIBRARY □ Helena, MT
Levasseur, Ann, Support Staff
LOS ANGELES COUNTY SUPERINTENDENT OF
SCHOOLS - SOUTHERN CALIFORNIA CENTER
FOR EDUCATIONAL IMPROVEMENT □ Downey,
CA
Leve, L. Arless, Mgr.
UNION CARBIDE CORPORATION - CORPORATE
LIBRARY □ Danbury, CT
LeVeille, Linda L., Info.Spec.
REXNORD INC. - TECHNICAL LIBRARY† □
Milwaukee, WI
Levenson, Joseph, Libn.
SALMAGUNDI CLUB - LIBRARY □ New York, NY
Leventhal, Lou, Asst.Libn.
AMERICAN BANKER, INC. - LIBRARY □ New
York, NY
Levering, Philip, AV Cons.
SUFFOLK COOPERATIVE LIBRARY SYSTEM -
AUDIOVISUAL DEPARTMENT □ Bellport, NY
Levesque, J. C., Asst.Libn.
CANADA - ENERGY, MINES & RESOURCES
CANADA - EARTH PHYSICS BRANCH LIBRARY □
Ottawa, ON
Levesque, M., Hd.Libn.
COMPLEXE SCIENTIFIQUE DU QUEBEC -
SERVICE DE DOCUMENTATION ET DE
BIBLIOTHEQUE □ Ste. Foy, PQ
Levesque, Mrs. M.L., Fire Res.Off.
CANADA - PUBLIC WORKS CANADA - OFFICE
OF THE FIRE COMMISSIONER OF CANADA -
RESOURCE CENTRE □ Ottawa, ON
Levesque, Margaret
CANADAIR, LTD. - COMPANY LIBRARY† □
Montreal, PQ
Levesque, Raymond, Ref.
CEGEP DE TROIS-RIVIERES - BIBLIOTHEQUE □
Trois-Rivieres, PQ
Levi, Alla F., Dir. of Lib.Serv.
LINCOLN FIRST BANK, NA, INC. - LINCOLN
FIRST LIBRARY† □ Rochester, NY
Levi, Dennis L., Chf., Lib.Serv.
U.S. VETERANS ADMINISTRATION (WA-
Tacoma) - MEDICAL CENTER LIBRARY □
Tacoma, WA
Levi, Penny G., Libn.
ST. MARY'S OF THE LAKE HOSPITAL - GIBSON
MEDICAL RESOURCE CENTRE □ Kingston, ON
Levie, Jane H., Chf.Libn.
U.S. VETERANS ADMINISTRATION (CA-
Livermore) - MEDICAL LIBRARY □ Livermore, CA

Levin, Amy, Ref.Libn.
SMITHSONIAN INSTITUTION LIBRARIES -
NATIONAL AIR AND SPACE MUSEUM - LIBRARY
□ Washington, DC
Levin, Ann, Libn.
PENINSULA TEMPLE BETH EL - LIBRARY □ San
Mateo, CA
Levin, Arthur, Dir.
CENTER FOR MEDICAL CONSUMERS AND
HEALTH INFORMATION - LIBRARY □ New York,
NY
Levin, Elizabeth O., Lib.Film Oper.Supv.
FREE LIBRARY OF PHILADELPHIA - FILMS
DEPARTMENT □ Philadelphia, PA
Levin, Ellen, Libn.
ATLANTIC RESEARCH CORPORATION -
LIBRARY† □ Alexandria, VA
Levin, Sylvia, Dir.
MANHASSET PUBLIC LIBRARY - SPECIAL
COLLECTIONS □ Manhasset, NY
Levine, David, Act. State Archv.
OHIO HISTORICAL SOCIETY - ARCHIVES-
LIBRARY □ Columbus, OH
Levine, Janice R., Interim Libn.
LAUBACH LITERACY INTERNATIONAL, INC. -
LIBRARY □ Syracuse, NY
Levine, Joseph, Exec.Sec.
INDIANA JEWISH HISTORICAL SOCIETY -
LIBRARY □ Fort Wayne, IN
Levine, L., Sr.Tech.Info.Spec.
DOW CHEMICAL U.S.A. - TEXAS DIVISION -
LIBRARY □ Freeport, TX
Levine, Lillian, Extramural Coord.
CLEVELAND HEALTH SCIENCES LIBRARY -
ALLEN MEMORIAL LIBRARY □ Cleveland, OH
Levine, Marguerite L., Archv.
AMERICAN FOUNDATION FOR THE BLIND -
HELEN KELLER ARCHIVES □ New York, NY
Levine, Marion, Asst.Dir.
UNIVERSITY OF CONNECTICUT - HEALTH
CENTER - LYMAN MAYNARD STOWE LIBRARY □
Farmington, CT
Levine, Ruth, Patients Libn.
U.S. VETERANS ADMINISTRATION (NY-
Brooklyn) - MEDICAL CENTER LIBRARY □
Brooklyn, NY
Levinson, Debra, Mgr./Info.Ret.Serv.
NATIONAL BROADCASTING COMPANY, INC. -
REFERENCE LIBRARY □ New York, NY
Levinson, Margie, Pub.Serv.Libn.
MERCANTILE LIBRARY ASSOCIATION -
MERCANTILE LIBRARY □ New York, NY
Levinson, Marilyn I., Cat.
BOWLING GREEN STATE UNIVERSITY -
CENTER FOR ARCHIVAL COLLECTIONS □
Bowling Green, OH
Levinton, Juliette, Libn.
SCHRODER (J. Henry) BANK & TRUST COMPANY
- LIBRARY □ New York, NY
Levitas, Irving, Libn.
TEMPLE EMANU-EL OF YONKERS - LEVITAS
LIBRARY □ Yonkers, NY
Leviton, Elsie, Chm., Lib.Comm.
TEMPLE ISRAEL - LIBRARY □ West Palm Beach,
FL
Levkovitz, Susan, Chf.Cat.Libn.
CUNY - GRADUATE SCHOOL AND UNIVERSITY
CENTER - LIBRARY □ New York, NY
Levstik, Joseph, Foreign Law Libn.
UNIVERSITY OF MINNESOTA - LAW LIBRARY □
Minneapolis, MN
Levy, Annette R., Libn.
JEWISH COMMUNITY CENTER - LIBRARY □
Nashville, TN
Levy, Annette R., Dir.
JEWISH FEDERATION OF NASHVILLE AND
MIDDLE TENNESSEE - ARCHIVES □ Nashville,
TN
Levy, Annette R., Libn.
TEMPLE OHABAI SHALOM - LIBRARY □
Nashville, TN

Levy, Annette R., Dir.
WEST END SYNAGOGUE - LIBRARY □ Nashville, TN

Levy, Arlene, Libn.
GOODMAN AND CARR - LIBRARY □ Toronto, ON

Levy, Brooks, Cur. of Numismatics
PRINCETON UNIVERSITY - RARE BOOKS AND SPECIAL COLLECTIONS □ Princeton, NJ

Levy, Charlotte L., Libn.
BROOKLYN LAW SCHOOL - LAW LIBRARY □ Brooklyn, NY

Levy, Jane, Libn./Archv.
MAGNES (Judah L.) MEMORIAL MUSEUM - MORRIS GOLDSTEIN LIBRARY □ Berkeley, CA

Levy, Sarah N., Lib.Dir.
DROPSIE COLLEGE - LIBRARY □ Merion, PA

Levy, Sharon, Libn.
NATIONAL WILDLIFE FEDERATION - FRAZIER MEMORIAL LIBRARY □ Washington, DC

Levy, Susan M., Libn.
DONORS FORUM OF CHICAGO - LIBRARY □ Chicago, IL

Levy, Suzanne S., Libn.
FAIRFAX COUNTY PUBLIC LIBRARY - FAIRFAX CITY REGIONAL LIBRARY - VIRGINIA ROOM □ Fairfax, VA

Lewallen, David, Mgr.
ALAMEDA COUNTY LIBRARY - BUSINESS & GOVERNMENT LIBRARY □ Oakland, CA

Lewandowski, Virginia, Libn.
HARLEM VALLEY PSYCHIATRIC CENTER - INTERDISCIPLINARY LIBRARY □ Wingdale, NY

Lewars, James A., Act.Adm.
PENNSYLVANIA STATE HISTORICAL & MUSEUM COMMISSION - EPHRATA CLOISTER - LIBRARY □ Ephrata, PA

Lewek, Deborah, Chf., Lib.Serv.
U.S. VETERANS ADMINISTRATION (NY-Northport) - HEALTH SCIENCE LIBRARY □ Northport, NY

Lewek, Edward, Asst.Libn.
ROCHESTER GENERAL HOSPITAL - LILLIE B. WERNER HEALTH SCIENCES LIBRARY □ Rochester, NY

Lewin, Jackie, Cur., Hist.
ST. JOSEPH MUSEUM - LIBRARY □ St. Joseph, MO

Lewis, Alan, Asst.Dir.
MINNESOTA STATE DEPARTMENT OF EDUCATION - OFFICE OF PUBLIC LIBRARIES AND INTERLIBRARY COOPERATION - LIBRARY □ St. Paul, MN

Lewis, Alan M., Hd., Lib.Doc.Br.
U.S. NAVY - NAVAL SEA SYSTEMS COMMAND - LIBRARY DOCUMENTATION BRANCH (SEA 09B31) □ Washington, DC

Lewis, Alfred J., Assoc. Law Libn.
UNIVERSITY OF CALIFORNIA, DAVIS - SCHOOL OF LAW - LAW LIBRARY □ Davis, CA

Lewis, Alison M., Libn.
FLORIDA STATE DEPT. OF NATURAL RESOURCES - BUREAU OF GEOLOGY LIBRARY □ Tallahassee, FL

Lewis, Ann L., Med.Libn.
ST. ELIZABETH MEDICAL CENTER - HEALTH SCIENCES LIBRARY† □ Dayton, OH

Lewis, Anthony, Managing Dir.
HOUSING ASSOCIATION OF DELAWARE VALLEY - LIBRARY □ Philadelphia, PA

Lewis, Miss Arel T., Asst.Libn./ILL Libn.
CENTRAL BAPTIST THEOLOGICAL SEMINARY - LIBRARY □ Kansas City, KS

Lewis, Betty K., Libn.
U.S. ARMY HOSPITALS - KENNER ARMY HOSPITAL - MEDICAL LIBRARY □ Ft. Lee, VA

Lewis, Betty Mae, Cur.
FOUNDATION HISTORICAL ASSOCIATION - SEWARD HOUSE □ Auburn, NY

Lewis, Blanche A., Libn.
SAN BERNARDINO SUN-TELEGRAM - LIBRARY □ San Bernardino, CA

Lewis, Brenda, Chf.Libn.
GREATER SOUTHEAST COMMUNITY HOSPITAL - LURA HEALTH SCIENCES LIBRARY† □ Washington, DC

Lewis, Carol E., Ref.Libn.
VANDERBILT UNIVERSITY - MEDICAL CENTER LIBRARY □ Nashville, TN

Lewis, Clementine, Supv.
QUEENS BOROUGH PUBLIC LIBRARY - LANGSTON HUGHES COMMUNITY LIBRARY AND CULTURAL CENTER □ Corona, NY

Lewis, David B., Libn.
COLUMBIA UNIVERSITY - HERBERT H. LEHMAN LIBRARY □ New York, NY

Lewis, David C., Chf.
U.S. BUREAU OF THE CENSUS - INFORMATION SERVICES PROGRAM - PHILADELPHIA REGIONAL OFFICE - LIBRARY □ Philadelphia, PA

Lewis, E. Raymond, Libn.
U.S. HOUSE OF REPRESENTATIVES - LIBRARY □ Washington, DC

Lewis, Edith, Libn.
DISTRICT OF COLUMBIA PUBLIC LIBRARY - LIBRARY FOR THE BLIND AND PHYSICALLY HANDICAPPED □ Washington, DC

Lewis, Eleanor, Res.Assoc.
SMITH COLLEGE - SOPHIA SMITH COLLECTION - WOMEN'S HISTORY ARCHIVE □ Northampton, MA

Lewis, Elizabeth, Rare Book Libn.
MC GILL UNIVERSITY - DEPARTMENT OF RARE BOOKS & SPECIAL COLLECTIONS □ Montreal, PQ

Lewis, Eloise, Libn.
ROSS ROY, INC. - RESEARCH LIBRARY □ Detroit, MI

Lewis, Ethelene, Tech.Info.Spec.
U.S. NATL. BUREAU OF STANDARDS - NATIONAL CENTER FOR STANDARDS AND CERTIFICATION INFORMATION □ Washington, DC

Lewis, Florence E., Libn.
HANCOCK (Allan) FOUNDATION - HANCOCK LIBRARY OF BIOLOGY & OCEANOGRAPHY □ Los Angeles, CA

Lewis, Frank, Libn.
LA GRANGE COLLEGE - WILLIAM AND EVELYN BANKS LIBRARY - SPECIAL COLLECTIONS □ LaGrange, GA

Lewis, Mrs. G., Coll.Coord.
UNIVERSITY OF ALBERTA - HUMANITIES AND SOCIAL SCIENCES LIBRARY □ Edmonton, AB

Lewis, George, Libn.
ADAMS ADVERTISING AGENCY, INC. - LIBRARY □ Chicago, IL

Lewis, Gwendolyn I., Supv.Libn.
U.S. ARMY POST - FORT BENNING - RECREATION SERVICES LIBRARY BRANCH† □ Ft. Benning, GA

Lewis, Hal, Libn.
SCRANTON TRIBUNE AND SCRANTONIAN - LIBRARY □ Scranton, PA

Lewis, Ida
U.S. NATL. OCEANIC & ATMOSPHERIC ADMINISTRATION - GEORGETOWN CENTER □ Washington, DC

Lewis, James, Ref.Libn.
CAROLINA POPULATION CENTER - LIBRARY □ Chapel Hill, NC

Lewis, Jean, Ref./Circ.Libn.
KIRKSVILLE COLLEGE OF OSTEOPATHIC MEDICINE - A.T. STILL MEMORIAL LIBRARY □ Kirksville, MO

Lewis, Joe, Rd.Adv.
DISTRICT OF COLUMBIA PUBLIC LIBRARY - BLACK STUDIES DIVISION □ Washington, DC

Lewis, Dr. Ken, Dir.
CHILD CUSTODY EVALUATION SERVICES, INC. - RESOURCE CENTER □ Glenside, PA

Lewis, Krista, Asst.Dir.
AUSTRIAN PRESS AND INFORMATION SERVICE □ New York, NY

Lewis, Larry C., Sci.Libn.
UNIVERSITY OF WESTERN ONTARIO - SCIENCES LIBRARY □ London, ON

Lewis, Louise, Chf., Pub.Serv.
U.S. CENTERS FOR DISEASE CONTROL - CDC LIBRARY □ Atlanta, GA

Lewis, Margaret, Libn.
SUNY - COLLEGE OF OPTOMETRY - HAROLD KOHN MEMORIAL VISUAL SCIENCE LIBRARY □ New York, NY

Lewis, Marilyn L., Marine Rsrcs.Libn.
SOUTH CAROLINA STATE WILDLIFE AND MARINE RESOURCES DEPARTMENT - LIBRARY □ Charleston, SC

Lewis, Melba H., Libn.
NEW YORK STATE ELECTRIC AND GAS CORPORATION - CORPORATE LIBRARY □ Binghamton, NY

Lewis, Nancy C., Libn.
ARKANSAS STATE ENERGY OFFICE LIBRARY □ Little Rock, AR

Lewis, Nancy J., Libn.
COOLEY, GODWARD, CASTRO, HUDDLESON & TATUM - LIBRARY □ San Francisco, CA

Lewis, Pamela K., Law Libn.
DAVIS, GRAHAM & STUBBS/COLORADO NATIONAL BUILDING - CNB LAW LIBRARY □ Denver, CO

Lewis, Ralph W., Mgr.
LOCKHEED MISSILES & SPACE COMPANY, INC. - TECHNICAL INFORMATION CENTER □ Palo Alto, CA

Lewis, Robert G., Lib.Supv.
COMINCO LTD. - CENTRAL TECHNICAL LIBRARY □ Trail, BC

Lewis, Roberta, Libn.
PFIZER, INC. - CENTRAL RESEARCH TECHNICAL INFORMATION SERVICES □ Groton, CT

Lewis, Ronald A., Univ.Libn.
ST. MARY'S UNIVERSITY - PATRICK POWER LIBRARY □ Halifax, NS

Lewis, Rosalyn, Libn.
UNITED METHODIST PUBLISHING HOUSE - LIBRARY □ Nashville, TN

Lewis, Sharon, Libn.
PRATT INSTITUTE - PRATT/PHOENIX SCHOOL OF DESIGN LIBRARY □ New York, NY

Lewis, Shirley C., Dir., Lib.Serv.
PROVIDENCE HOSPITAL, EVERETT - HEALTH INFORMATION NETWORK SERVICES (HINS) □ Everett, WA

Lewis, Susan, Hd.Libn.
BOSTON ARCHITECTURAL CENTER - ALFRED SHAW AND EDWARD DURELL STONE LIBRARY □ Boston, MA

Lewis, Virginia Anne, Ref.Libn.
BARRETT SMITH SCHAPIRO SIMON & ARMSTRONG - LIBRARY □ New York, NY

Lewis, W.H.
ATASCADERO HISTORICAL SOCIETY - MUSEUM □ Atascadero, CA

Lewis, William P., Exec.Dir.
LACKAWANNA HISTORICAL SOCIETY - LIBRARY AND ARCHIVES □ Scranton, PA

Lewis-Lurin, Eileen, Asst.Libn.
GEORGESON & COMPANY - LIBRARY □ New York, NY

Lex, Katherine V., Libn.
U.S. AIR FORCE BASE - MALMSTROM BASE LIBRARY □ Malmstrom AFB, MT

Ley, Jean, Cat.
CALVARY BAPTIST THEOLOGICAL SEMINARY - LIBRARY □ Lansdale, PA

Leyda, Mabel, Libn.
BEAUMONT PUBLIC LIBRARY SYSTEM - TYRRELL HISTORICAL LIBRARY □ Beaumont, TX

Leyerzapf, James W., Supv.Archv.
U.S. PRESIDENTIAL LIBRARIES - DWIGHT D. EISENHOWER LIBRARY □ Abilene, KS

Leyshon, Frank C., Libn.
GUERNSEY COUNTY LAW LIBRARY □ Cambridge, OH

Leyte-Vidal, Jesus, Cat.
DUKE UNIVERSITY - MANUSCRIPT
DEPARTMENT □ Durham, NC
Leyva, Judith Runyon, Law Libn.
LITTON INDUSTRIES - LAW LIBRARY □ Beverly
Hills, CA
Leyva, Judith Runyon
WESTERN STATE UNIVERSITY - COLLEGE OF
LAW - LIBRARY† □ Fullerton, CA
Lhotka, Jana, Libn.
BECHTEL - DATA PROCESSING LIBRARY □ San
Francisco, CA
Li, Dorothy In-Lan Wang, Hd., Tech Serv.
JOHN MARSHALL LAW SCHOOL - LIBRARY □
Chicago, IL
Li, Marjorie
GENEALOGICAL SOCIETY OF NEW JERSEY -
MANUSCRIPT COLLECTIONS □ New Brunswick,
NJ
Li, Marjorie
RUTGERS UNIVERSITY, THE STATE
UNIVERSITY OF NEW JERSEY - DEPARTMENT
OF SPECIAL COLLECTIONS AND ARCHIVES □
New Brunswick, NJ
Li, Dr. Ming-Yu, Doc.Spec.
UNIVERSITY OF CALIFORNIA, DAVIS -
ENVIRONMENTAL TOXICOLOGY LIBRARY □
Davis, CA
Li, Rose, Assoc.Libn.
NEW YORK BOTANICAL GARDEN - LIBRARY† □
Bronx, NY
Li, Ruth H., Cat.
HOWARD UNIVERSITY - MOORLAND-SPINGARN
RESEARCH CENTER - LIBRARY DIVISION □
Washington, DC
Liang, Marie, Res.Libn.
WESTVACO CORPORATION - LAUREL
RESEARCH LIBRARY □ Laurel, MD
Lianzi, Terry, Sci.Libn.
MIAMI-DADE PUBLIC LIBRARY - BUSINESS,
SCIENCE AND TECHNOLOGY DEPARTMENT □
Miami, FL
Liardon, Carol, Asst.Libn.
ORAL ROBERTS UNIVERSITY - HEALTH
SCIENCES LIBRARY □ Tulsa, OK
Lias, Dr. Sharon G., Dir.
U.S. NATL. BUREAU OF STANDARDS - ION
KINETICS AND ENERGETICS DATA CENTER □
Washington, DC
Libbey, Elizabeth M., Music Libn.
CATHOLIC UNIVERSITY OF AMERICA - MUSIC
LIBRARY □ Washington, DC
Libbey, Frances T., Sci./Engr.Libn.
UNIVERSITY OF HARTFORD - DANA SCIENCE &
ENGINEERING LIBRARY □ West Hartford, CT
Libby, Eileen, Libn.
UNIVERSITY OF CHICAGO - SOCIAL SERVICES
ADMINISTRATION LIBRARY □ Chicago, IL
Libby, Mary Anne Spindler, Libn.
MEDICAL CARE DEVELOPMENT, INC. - LIBRARY
□ Augusta, ME
Libby, Ruth R., Chf.Libn.
BAPTIST MEMORIAL HOSPITAL SYSTEM -
BRUCE A. GARRETT MEMORIAL LIBRARY &
MEDIA CENTER □ San Antonio, TX
Libby, Ms. S., Info.Serv.Libn.
BEDFORD INSTITUTE OF OCEANOGRAPHY -
LIBRARY □ Dartmouth, NS
Libby, Shirley E., Lib.Sec.
BRIDGEWATER STATE COLLEGE - CLEMENT C.
MAXWELL LIBRARY □ Bridgewater, MA
Libby, Susan P., Hosp.Libn.
MONCTON HOSPITAL - HEALTH SCIENCES
LIBRARY □ Moncton, NB
Libertini, Arleen, Libn.
ALBANY GENERAL HOSPITAL - HEALTH
SCIENCES LIBRARY □ Albany, OR
Liberty, Eileen J., Chf., Lib.Serv.
U.S. VETERANS ADMINISTRATION (NY-
Montrose) - HOSPITAL LIBRARY □ Montrose, NY
Libhart, Myles, Dir. of Pubn.
U.S. DEPT. OF THE INTERIOR - INDIAN ARTS
AND CRAFTS BOARD □ Washington, DC

Licht, Juanita, Resident Staff Libn.
SHAPIRO (Samuel H.) DEVELOPMENTAL CENTER
- PROFESSIONAL LIBRARY □ Kankakee, IL
Lichten, Susan A., Libn.
LOO MERIDETH & MC MILLAN - LAW LIBRARY □
Los Angeles, CA
Lichtenfels, Lynn L., Cur.
NEY (Elisabet) MUSEUM - LIBRARY □ Austin, TX
Lichtenstein, Aniela, Hd.Libn.
FILLMORE (Millard) HOSPITAL - KIDENEY
HEALTH SCIENCES LIBRARY □ Buffalo, NY
Lichtenstein, Michela, Asst.Libn.
NEW YORK PUBLIC LIBRARY - BELMONT
REGIONAL LIBRARY - ENRICO FERMI
CULTURAL CENTER □ Bronx, NY
Lichtman, Jacqueline, Rd.Serv.Libn.
UNIVERSITY OF VIRGINIA - ARTHUR J.
MORRIS LAW LIBRARY □ Charlottesville, VA
Lichtman, Marie, Libn.
BIRMINGHAM MUSEUM OF ART - REFERENCE
LIBRARY □ Birmingham, AL
Licitis, Margot B., Transl.
ROHM & HAAS COMPANY - RESEARCH
DIVISION - INFORMATION SERVICES
DEPARTMENT □ Spring House, PA
Liddiard, Karen, Chf.Libn.
CALGARY HERALD - LIBRARY □ Calgary, AB
Lidell, Nora, Asst.Libn.
CHEMICAL BANK - RESEARCH LIBRARY □ New
York, NY
Lidtke, Thomas, Exec.Dir.
WEST BEND GALLERY OF FINE ARTS - LIBRARY
□ West Bend, WI
Lieb, Louise Laughlin, Lib.Adm.
IRELL & MANELLA - LIBRARY □ Los Angeles, CA
Lieber, Winifred, Libn.
ROOSEVELT HOSPITAL - MEDICAL LIBRARY □
New York, NY
Lieberman, E. James, Dir.
ESPERANTIC STUDIES FOUNDATION - LIBRARY
□ Washington, DC
Lieberman, Jan, Libn.
CONGREGATION BETH AM - LIBRARY† □ Los
Altos Hills, CA
Lieberman, Louise, Libn.
CONGREGATION MISHKAN TEFILA - HARRY
AND ANNA FEINBERG LIBRARY □ Chestnut Hill,
MA
Lieberman, Lucille, Dir.
ST. JOSEPH HOSPITAL - HEALTH SCIENCES
LIBRARY □ Stamford, CT
Lieberman, Sherri, Ref.Libn.
MITRE CORPORATION - LIBRARY □ McLean, VA
Liebig, James, Archv./Assoc.Dir.
UNIVERSITY OF WISCONSIN, MADISON -
ARCHIVES □ Madison, WI
Liebler, Rita V., Med.Libn.
BUTLER MEMORIAL HOSPITAL - RUTH
ARMSTRONG MEMORIAL MEDICAL LIBRARY □
Butler, PA
Liebman, Bruce, Asst.Libn.
U.S. COURT OF INTERNATIONAL TRADE - LAW
LIBRARY □ New York, NY
Liegl, Dorothy, Dp. State Libn.
SOUTH DAKOTA STATE LIBRARY & ARCHIVES □
Pierre, SD
Liem, Frieda, ILL
MEDICAL COLLEGE OF PENNSYLVANIA -
EASTERN PENNSYLVANIA PSYCHIATRIC INST.
- MENTAL HEALTH AND NEUROSCIENCES LIB. □
Philadelphia, PA
Lien, Dennis, Contact Person
MINNESOTA SCIENCE FICTION SOCIETY -
LIBRARY □ Minneapolis, MN
Lieser, Robert, Libn.
TULSA CITY-COUNTY LIBRARY SYSTEM -
BUSINESS AND TECHNOLOGY DEPARTMENT □
Tulsa, OK
Lievsay, Lilly, Hd.Cat. & Cur.
FOLGER SHAKESPEARE LIBRARY □ Washington,
DC
Lifland, Donna Z., Libn.
TEMPLE ISRAEL - LIBRARY □ Lawrence, NY

Lifschitz, Edward, Archv.
SMITHSONIAN INSTITUTION LIBRARIES -
NATIONAL MUSEUM OF AFRICAN ART - ELIOT
ELISOFON ARCHIVES □ Washington, DC
Lifschitz, Susan, Cat.
DONALDSON, LUFKIN AND JENRETTE, INC. -
CORPORATE INFORMATION CENTER □ New
York, NY
Lifsey, J., V.P.
FRANKLIN INSTITUTE - FRANKLIN RESEARCH
CENTER - INFORMATION MANAGEMENT
DEPARTMENT □ Philadelphia, PA
Lightfoot, Barbara Arie, Mgr.
AMERICAN HEART ASSOCIATION - LIBRARY/
RECORDS CENTER □ Dallas, TX
Lightman, Benjamin, Chf.Libn.
TIME, INC. - LIBRARY □ New York, NY
Lightman, Ryla Snider, Libn.
CANADIAN FEDERATION OF INDEPENDENT
BUSINESS (CFIB) - RESEARCH LIBRARY □
Toronto, ON
Lightwood, Martha, Asst.Libn.
UNIVERSITY OF PENNSYLVANIA - LIPPINCOTT
LIBRARY □ Philadelphia, PA
Liguori, Nicholas L., Libn.
WESTERN CENTER - LIBRARY □ Canonsburg, PA
Liivak, Arno, Law Libn.
RUTGERS UNIVERSITY, THE STATE
UNIVERSITY OF NEW JERSEY - SCHOOL OF
LAW LIBRARY† □ Camden, NJ
Liles, Martha, Libn.
SYSTEMS CONTROL GROUP - TECHNICAL
LIBRARY □ Palo Alto, CA
Liljequist, Orval, Coord. of Hum.
MILWAUKEE PUBLIC LIBRARY - HUMANITIES
DIVISION - LOCAL HISTORY AND MARINE
ROOM □ Milwaukee, WI
Lilley, D.A., Hist.
U.S. NATL. PARK SERVICE - FREDERICKSBURG
& SPOTSYLVANIA NATL. MILITARY PARK -
LIBRARY □ Fredericksburg, VA
Lilly, Elise, Tech.Serv.Libn.
ROSENMAN, COLIN, FREUND, LEWIS & COHEN -
LAW LIBRARY □ New York, NY
Lim, Elsie, Libn.
CHEMISTS' CLUB LIBRARY - CHEMICAL
INTERNATIONAL INFORMATION CENTER □
New York, NY
Lim, Mr. Hoong, Libn.
BURNABY GENERAL HOSPITAL - DR. H.H.W.
BROOKE MEMORIAL LIBRARY □ Burnaby, BC
Lim, Josefina, Hd., Tech.Serv.
CORNELL UNIVERSITY - MEDICAL COLLEGE -
SAMUEL J. WOOD LIBRARY □ New York, NY
Lim, Lourdes P., Libn.
GENERAL MOTORS CORPORATION -
ECONOMICS STAFF LIBRARY □ New York, NY
Lim, Mary, Libn.
MASSACHUSETTS STATE DEPARTMENT OF
LABOR & INDUSTRIES - DIV. OF
OCCUPATIONAL HYGIENE - SPECIAL
TECHNICAL LIBRARY □ West Newton, MA
Lima, Constance M., Med.Libn.
EXXON CORPORATION - MEDICAL LIBRARY† □
New York, NY
Limbach, Letty, Asst.Libn.
DISTRICT OF COLUMBIA SUPERIOR COURT -
LIBRARY □ Washington, DC
Limke, Marge, Res.Asst.
GREATER CINCINNATI CHAMBER OF
COMMERCE - RESEARCH LIBRARY □ Cincinnati,
OH
Limper, Susan, Staff Futurist
THE STRATEGIC CORPORATION - STRATEGIC
MOVES LIBRARY □ Portland, OR
Lin, Betty A., Libn.
DELAWARE RIVER BASIN COMMISSION -
TECHNICAL LIBRARY □ Trenton, NJ
Lin, Kevin, Libn.
UNIVERSITY OF TEXAS, AUSTIN - ASIAN
COLLECTION □ Austin, TX

Lin, Louise, Coord., Lib.Serv.
ST. JOSEPH'S HOSPITAL - MEDICAL LIBRARY □
London, ON
Lin, Mei-Ying, Chinese Cat.
UNIVERSITY OF MICHIGAN - ASIA LIBRARY □
Ann Arbor, MI
Lin, Raymond, Cat.
SPRINGFIELD COLLEGE - BABSON LIBRARY -
SPECIAL COLLECTIONS □ Springfield, MA
Lin, Shu-fang, Libn./Assoc.Prof.
ST. JOHN'S UNIVERSITY - GOVERNMENT
DOCUMENTS DEPARTMENT □ Jamaica, NY
Lin, Tung-Fen, Asst.Libn.
DELOITTE HASKINS & SELLS - LIBRARY □ New
York, NY
Linard, James L., Libn./Pub.Info.Off.
FAIRFAX COUNTY - COMPREHENSIVE
PLANNING LIBRARY □ Fairfax, VA
Linard, Laura, Cur.
CHICAGO PUBLIC LIBRARY CULTURAL CENTER
- SPECIAL COLLECTIONS DIVISION □ Chicago,
IL
Lincks, Linda S., Mgr.
RALSTON PURINA COMPANY - INFORMATION
CENTER □ St. Louis, MO
Lincoln, Bob, Cur. of Educ.
WESTERN MUSEUM OF MINING & INDUSTRY -
LIBRARY □ Colorado Springs, CO
Lincoln, Carol S., Res.Libn.
BROWN AND WILLIAMSON TOBACCO
CORPORATION - RESEARCH LIBRARY □
Louisville, KY
Lincoln, Christine L., Classified Doc.Supv.
R & D ASSOCIATES - TECHNICAL
INFORMATION SERVICES □ Marina Del Rey, CA
Lincourt, Ghislaine, Adm.
FEDERATION DES MEDECINS
OMNIPRACTICIENS DU QUEBEC -
DOCUMENTATION CENTRE □ Montreal, PQ
Lind, Donna, Exec.Dir.
HENNEPIN COUNTY HISTORICAL SOCIETY -
ARCHIVES □ Minneapolis, MN
Lindahl, Ann, Info.Spec.
ALUMAX INC. - RESEARCH LIBRARY □ San
Mateo, CA
Lindahl, Charles, Assoc.Libn.
UNIVERSITY OF ROCHESTER - EASTMAN
SCHOOL OF MUSIC - SIBLEY MUSIC LIBRARY □
Rochester, NY
Lindahl, John, Cur./Libn.
NEBRASKA STATE HISTORICAL SOCIETY -
JOHN G. NEIHARDT CENTER - RESEARCH
LIBRARY □ Bancroft, NE
Lindberg, Lottie, Libn.
DOW JONES & CO. - LIBRARY □ New York, NY
Lindberg, Lottie, Libn.
WALL STREET JOURNAL - LIBRARY □ New York,
NY
Lindberg, Martha, Libn.
WORLD ASSOCIATION OF DOCUMENT
EXAMINERS - WADE LIBRARY □ Chicago, IL
Lindberg, Mary, Asst.Libn.
PRESBYTERIAN DENVER HOSPITAL -
BRADFORD MEMORIAL LIBRARY □ Denver, CO
Lindeken, Carl, Hist.Res.
WALNUT CREEK HISTORICAL SOCIETY -
SHADELANDS RANCH HISTORICAL MUSEUM -
HISTORY ROOM □ Walnut Creek, CA
Lindemann, Richard H.F., Ref.Archv.
EMORY UNIVERSITY - SPECIAL COLLECTIONS
DEPARTMENT □ Atlanta, GA
Lindemon, Agnes M., Libn.
BALTIMORE GAS AND ELECTRIC COMPANY -
LIBRARY □ Baltimore, MD
Linden, Barbara, Adm.Asst.
MASSACHUSETTS INSTITUTE OF TECHNOLOGY
- M.I.T. MUSEUM AND HISTORICAL
COLLECTIONS □ Cambridge, MA
Linden, Margaret J., Mgr.
STANDARD OIL COMPANY OF CALIFORNIA -
CORPORATE LIBRARY □ San Francisco, CA

Lindenbaum, Ellen, Hd.Libn.
LUTHERAN HOSPITAL OF MARYLAND -
CHARLES G. REIGNER MEDICAL LIBRARY □
Baltimore, MD
Linder, Gloria, Hd., Ref.
STANFORD UNIVERSITY - LANE MEDICAL
LIBRARY □ Stanford, CA
Linder, L.H., Mgr., Tech.Info.Serv.
FORD AEROSPACE & COMMUNICATIONS CORP.
- AERONUTRONIC DIVISION - TECHNICAL
INFORMATION SERVICES □ Newport Beach, CA
Linder, Robert A., Sr.Libn.
UNIVERSITY OF MISSISSIPPI - ARCHIVES &
SPECIAL COLLECTIONS/MISSISSIPPIANA □
University, MS
Lindey, Paula L., Libn.
MINE SAFETY APPLIANCES COMPANY - MSA
RESEARCH CORPORATION - CALLERY
CHEMICAL COMPANY - LIBRARY □ Evans City,
PA
Lindgren, Dallas R., Hd., Ref.Serv.
MINNESOTA HISTORICAL SOCIETY - DIVISION
OF ARCHIVES AND MANUSCRIPTS □ St. Paul,
MN
Lindgren, Mary, Libn.
COURAGE CENTER LIBRARY □ Golden Valley, MN
Lindheimer, Sandi, Lib.Dir.
MIDDLESEX LAW LIBRARY □ Cambridge, MA
Lindloff, Kay, Info.Sci.
THE INSTITUTE FOR REHABILITATION AND
RESEARCH (TIRR) - INFORMATION SERVICES
CENTER □ Houston, TX
Lindner, Charlotte K., Dir. of Lib.
YESHIVA UNIVERSITY - ALBERT EINSTEIN
COLLEGE OF MEDICINE - D. SAMUEL
GOTTESMAN LIBRARY □ Bronx, NY
Lindner, Katherine L., Dir.
ENGLEWOOD HOSPITAL - MEDICAL LIBRARY □
Englewood, NJ
Lindner, Scott-Eric, Cat.
OTTAWA INSTITUTE - IRENE HOLM MEMORIAL
LIBRARY □ Columbus, OH
Lindquist, Charles N., Cur.
LENAWEE COUNTY HISTORICAL MUSEUM -
LIBRARY □ Adrian, MI
Lindqvist, June A.V., Cur., Von Scholton Coll.
VIRGIN ISLANDS - DEPARTMENT OF
CONSERVATION & CULTURAL AFFAIRS -
BUREAU OF LIBRARIES AND MUSEUMS □ St.
Thomas, VI
Lindsay, Carol, Chf.Libn.
TORONTO STAR NEWSPAPERS LTD. - LIBRARY
□ Toronto, ON
Lindsay, Lorin, Asst. Law Libn.
ORAL ROBERTS UNIVERSITY - O.W. COBURN
LAW LIBRARY† □ Tulsa, OK
Lindsay, Louise, Ref.Libn., Edifice G.
QUEBEC PROVINCE - MINISTERE DES
COMMUNICATIONS - BIBLIOTHEQUE
ADMINISTRATIVE □ Quebec, PQ
Lindsay, Merrill K., Pres.
WHITNEY (Eli) MUSEUM - LIBRARY □ North
Branford, CT
Lindsay, Muriel, Libn.
AUTO CLUB OF MISSOURI - INFORMATION
RESOURCE CENTER □ St. Louis, MO
Lindsay, Rosemary, Info.Serv.Spec.
TOWERS, PERRIN, FORSTER & CROSBY LTD. -
INFORMATION CENTRE □ Toronto, ON
Lindsey, John M., Law Prof./Law Libn.
TEMPLE UNIVERSITY - LAW LIBRARY □
Philadelphia, PA
Lindsey, Linda, ILL Techn.
U.S. VETERANS ADMINISTRATION (MN-
Minneapolis) - MEDICAL CENTER LIBRARY
SERVICE □ Minneapolis, MN
Lindsey, Marjorie, Cons., Multitype Lib.Serv
NORTH CAROLINA STATE DEPARTMENT OF
CULTURAL RESOURCES - DIVISION OF THE
STATE LIBRARY □ Raleigh, NC
Lindsey, Thomas K., Ref.Libn.
TEXAS TECH UNIVERSITY - LIBRARY -
DOCUMENTS DEPARTMENT □ Lubbock, TX

Lindstrand, Margaret A., Libn.
ST. JAMES HOSPITAL - HUGO LONG LIBRARY □
Chicago Heights, IL
Lindstrom, Janet, Assoc. Law Libn.
MORRISON & FOERSTER - LAW LIBRARY □ San
Francisco, CA
Lindt, Theodora L.D., Dir.
JEWISH MEMORIAL HOSPITAL - IRVING
DORFMAN MEMORIAL MEDICAL LIBRARY† □
New York, NY
Linehan, Daniel, Libn.
WALTON LANTAFF SCHROEDER & CARSON -
LAW LIBRARY □ Miami, FL
Linehan, Nancy, Asst.Libn.
DIGITAL EQUIPMENT CORPORATION -
TEWKSBURY LIBRARY □ Tewksbury, MA
Liner, Charlotte, Libn.
ADAMS-PRATT OAKLAND COUNTY LAW
LIBRARY □ Pontiac, MI
Linfield, Hadassah, Dir.
U.S. DEPT. OF TRANSPORTATION -
TRANSPORTATION SYSTEMS CENTER -
TECHNICAL REFERENCE CENTER □ Cambridge,
MA
Ling, Evelyn R., Libn.
HIGH STREET CHRISTIAN CHURCH - H.A.
VALENTINE MEMORIAL LIBRARY □ Akron, OH
Lingelbach, Lorene, Libn.
BERLEX LABORATORIES, INC. - RESEARCH AND
DEVELOPMENT DIVISION LIBRARY □ Cedar
Knolls, NJ
Linger, Paul, Asst.Dir.
DENVER ZOOLOGICAL GARDEN - LIBRARY □
Denver, CO
Link, Noreen, Libn.
FOLEY & LARDNER - LIBRARY □ Milwaukee, WI
Linke, Frances Baur, Hd.Libn.
BLUE CROSS OF CALIFORNIA - LIBRARY □ Van
Nuys, CA
Linke, Larry, Info.Serv.Coord.
U.S. DEPT. OF JUSTICE - NATIONAL
INSTITUTE OF CORRECTIONS - NIC
INFORMATION CENTER □ Boulder, CO
Linkins, Germaine C., Bibliog.Serv.Libn.
VIRGINIA POLYTECHNIC INSTITUTE AND
STATE UNIVERSITY - CAROL M. NEWMAN
LIBRARY □ Blacksburg, VA
Linkletter, Esther C., Hd.
SUNY AT STONY BROOK - CHEMISTRY LIBRARY
□ Stony Brook, NY
Linn, Dorothea C., Chf., Lib.Serv.
U.S. VETERANS ADMINISTRATION (TX-
Bonham) - SAM RAYBURN MEMORIAL
VETERANS CENTER MEDICAL LIBRARY □
Bonham, TX
Linn, Mary Jane, Chf., Original Indexing
SMITHSONIAN INSTITUTION LIBRARIES □
Washington, DC
Linnane, Mary Lu, Hd., Tech.Serv.
DE PAUL UNIVERSITY - LAW SCHOOL LIBRARY
□ Chicago, IL
Linquist, Ann, Libn.
KIRKE VAN ORSDEL INC. - LIBRARY □ Des
Moines, IA
Lintner, Mary Kaye, Health Sci.Libn.
MEMORIAL HOSPITAL AT OCONOMOWOC -
HEALTH SCIENCES LIBRARY □ Oconomowoc,
WI
Linton, Anne, Ref.Libn.
GEORGETOWN UNIVERSITY - MEDICAL
CENTER - DAHLGREN MEMORIAL LIBRARY □
Washington, DC
Linton, Helen, Libn.
RIGGS (Austen) CENTER, INC. - AUSTEN FOX
RIGGS LIBRARY □ Stockbridge, MA
Linton, Rebecca, Hd., Ref. & Doc. Unit
TEXAS STATE LIBRARY - INFORMATION
SERVICES DIVISION □ Austin, TX
Linville, Herbert, Hd.
UNIVERSITY OF CALIFORNIA, SANTA BARBARA
- GOVERNMENT PUBLICATIONS DEPARTMENT
□ Santa Barbara, CA

Lioce, Carol A., Mgr., Info.Ctr.
GOODRICH (B.F.) COMPANY - RESEARCH AND
DEVELOPMENT CENTER - BRECKSVILLE
INFORMATION CENTER □ Brecksville, OH

Lioce, Carol Ann, Mgr., Info.Ctr.
GOODRICH (B.F.) COMPANY - GOODRICH
CHEMICAL DIVISION TECHNICAL CENTER -
INFORMATION CENTER □ Avon Lake, OH

Lipa, Jiri (George), Ph.D., Libn.
SEMINARY OF THE IMMACULATE CONCEPTION
- LIBRARY □ Huntington, NY

Lipfert, Nathan, Asst.Cur.Res.
MAINE MARITIME MUSEUM - LIBRARY/
ARCHIVES □ Bath, ME

Lipinsky de Orlov, Lino S., Dir.
GARIBALDI AND MEUCCI MEMORIAL MUSEUM
- LIBRARY OF THE ITALIAN RISORGIMENTO □
Katonah, NY

Lipkin, Hilda, Dir.
TEANECK PUBLIC LIBRARY - ORAL AND LOCAL
HISTORY PROJECT □ Teaneck, NJ

Lipman, Paula, Asst.Libn.
U.S. DEPT. OF ENERGY - OFFICE OF GENERAL
COUNSEL LAW LIBRARY □ Washington, DC

Lipman, Penny, Libn.
RIO ALGOM, LTD. - LIBRARY □ Toronto, ON

Lippencott, Harvey, Archv.
CONNECTICUT AERONAUTICAL HISTORICAL
ASSOCIATION - NEW ENGLAND AIR MUSEUM
REFERENCE LIBRARY □ Windsor Locks, CT

Lippincott, Joan, Hd., Pub.Serv.
CORNELL UNIVERSITY - ALBERT R. MANN
LIBRARY □ Ithaca, NY

Lipscomb, Anne, Libn.
MISSISSIPPI STATE DEPARTMENT OF
ARCHIVES AND HISTORY - ARCHIVES AND
LIBRARY DIVISION □ Jackson, MS

Lipscomb, Carolyn, Coord., Staff Dev./Pubn.
UNIVERSITY OF NORTH CAROLINA, CHAPEL
HILL - HEALTH SCIENCES LIBRARY □ Chapel
Hill, NC

Lipscomb, Cheryl, Ser./Circ.Libn.
NORTH CAROLINA CENTRAL UNIVERSITY -
LAW LIBRARY □ Durham, NC

Lipscombe, Joan M., Libn.
CANADA - PARKS CANADA, ONTARIO REGION -
LIBRARY □ Cornwall, ON

Liptak, Dolores, R.S.M., Spec.Libn./Archv.
CENTER FOR APPLIED RESEARCH IN THE
APOSTOLATE - ARCHIVES AND RESEARCH
LIBRARY □ Washington, DC

Lipton, Saundra
UNIVERSITY OF CALGARY - ARTS AND
HUMANITIES LIBRARY† □ Calgary, AB

Lisca, Dorothy Patterson, Supv./Lib.Tech.Asst.
UNIVERSITY OF FLORIDA - PHYSICS AND
ASTRONOMY READING ROOM □ Gainesville, FL

Lishan, Merrill H., Libn.
BESSEMER TRUST COMPANY, N.A. -
INVESTMENT LIBRARY □ New York, NY

Liskow, Charles, Libn.
HUDSON ESSEX TERRAPLANE CLUB, INC. -
LIBRARY □ Ypsilanti, MI

Liss, Lois, Libn.
PUTNEY, TWOMBLY, HALL & HIRSON - LAW
LIBRARY □ New York, NY

List, Barbara, Ref./Coll.Dev.Libn.
COLUMBIA UNIVERSITY - BIOLOGICAL
SCIENCES LIBRARY □ New York, NY

List, Barbara, Ref./Coll.Dev.Libn.
COLUMBIA UNIVERSITY - PSYCHOLOGY
LIBRARY □ New York, NY

Lister, Judy, Group Ldr.
GEORGE BROWN COLLEGE OF APPLIED ARTS &
TECHNOLOGY - LIBRARY □ Toronto, ON

Liston, Nancy, Supv., Pubn.
COMMUNITY INFORMATION CENTRE OF
METROPOLITAN TORONTO □ Toronto, ON

Liston, Nancy C., Libn.
U.S. ARMY - COLD REGIONS RESEARCH &
ENGINEERING LABORATORY - LIBRARY □
Hanover, NH

Liszewski, Edward H., Asst.Chf.Libn.
U.S. GEOLOGICAL SURVEY - LIBRARY □ Reston,
VA

Litchfield, Meredith, Microforms/AV
KANSAS STATE UNIVERSITY - FARRELL
LIBRARY □ Manhattan, KS

Litten, Georgene, Libn.
TOUCHE ROSS AND COMPANY - LIBRARY □ Los
Angeles, CA

Little, Ann, Libn.
MANUFACTURERS HANOVER TRUST COMPANY
- CORPORATE LIBRARY/FINANCIAL LIBRARY
DIVISION† □ New York, NY

Little, Ann, Libn.
MANUFACTURERS HANOVER TRUST COMPANY
- CORPORATE LIBRARY/INVESTMENT LIBRARY
DIVISION† □ New York, NY

Little, Doris P., Libn.
U.S. FEDERAL AVIATION ADMINISTRATION -
SOUTHERN REGION LIBRARY† □ East Point, GA

Little, Erika, Info.Anl.
FOOTE CONE & BELDING - INFORMATION
CENTER □ Chicago, IL

Little, Grace, Libn.
LUTHERAN CHURCH IN AMERICA - FLORIDA
SYNOD - MULTI-MEDIA LIBRARY □ Tampa, FL

Little, Jennifer L., Asst.Libn.
NATIONAL COUNCIL FOR U.S.-CHINA TRADE -
LIBRARY □ Washington, DC

Little, Katherine, Info.Coord.
DNAX RESEARCH INSTITUTE - LIBRARY □ Palo
Alto, CA

Little, Marion, Asst.Libn.
MICHIGAN BELL TELEPHONE COMPANY -
CORPORATE REFERENCE CENTER □ Detroit, MI

Little, Nancy C., Libn.
KNOEDLER (M.) AND COMPANY, INC. - LIBRARY
□ New York, NY

Little, Peter D., Res.Assoc.
INSTITUTE FOR DEVELOPMENT
ANTHROPOLOGY - LIBRARY □ Binghamton, NY

Little, Rosemary Allen, Libn.
PRINCETON UNIVERSITY - PUBLIC
ADMINISTRATION COLLECTION† □ Princeton,
NJ

Littlefield, Frederick, TV Producer-Dir.
UNIVERSITY OF NEW HAMPSHIRE -
DEPARTMENT OF MEDIA SERVICES - FILM
LIBRARY □ Durham, NH

Littlefield, Judy, Supv.Lib.Techn.
U.S. VETERANS ADMINISTRATION (ME-
Augusta) - CENTER LIBRARY □ Augusta, ME

Littlefield, Kinney, Asst.Mgr./Photo.Libn.
DALLAS PUBLIC LIBRARY - FINE ARTS
DIVISION □ Dallas, TX

Littlefield, Mary L., Sec., Lib.Comm.
LUTHERAN HOSPITALS AND HOMES SOCIETY
OF AMERICA - LIBRARY □ Fargo, ND

Littlemeyer, Mary H., Archv.
ASSOCIATION OF AMERICAN MEDICAL
COLLEGES - ARCHIVES □ Washington, DC

Littlepage, Sue E., Mgr.
ENSCO, INC. - TECHNICAL LIBRARY □
Springfield, VA

Littler, Thomas, Libn.
ASSOCIATION OF JUNIOR LEAGUES, INC. -
RESOURCE CENTER □ New York, NY

Littleton, Harold J., Pres./Cur.
LOMBARDY HALL FOUNDATION - LIBRARY □
Wilmington, DE

Littleton, Isaac T., Dir.
NORTH CAROLINA STATE UNIVERSITY - D.H.
HILL LIBRARY □ Raleigh, NC

Littlewood, John, Doc.Libn.
UNIVERSITY OF ILLINOIS - DOCUMENTS
LIBRARY □ Urbana, IL

Littman, Rosette, Cat.
VILLANOVA UNIVERSITY - PULLING LAW
LIBRARY □ Villanova, PA

Litvinoff, Ana, Acq.
LOUISIANA STATE UNIVERSITY - LAW
LIBRARY □ Baton Rouge, LA

Litzenberger, Margaret, Asst.Libn.
BUFFALO PSYCHIATRIC CENTER - BPC
LIBRARY □ Buffalo, NY

Liu, Frank Yining, Law Libn.
DUQUESNE UNIVERSITY - LAW LIBRARY □
Pittsburgh, PA

Liu, John B., Oriental Stud.Libn.
UNIVERSITY OF ARIZONA - ORIENTAL
STUDIES COLLECTION □ Tucson, AZ

Liu, Judy, Hd., Ref.Sect.
BROOKHAVEN NATIONAL LABORATORY -
TECHNICAL INFORMATION DIVISION □ Upton,
NY

Liu, Shari Y., Libn.
BALLARD, SPAHR, ANDREWS AND INGERSOLL -
LAW LIBRARY □ Philadelphia, PA

Liu, Wentsing, Dir.
BUFFALO GENERAL HOSPITAL, INC. - A.H.
AARON MEDICAL LIBRARY† □ Buffalo, NY

Lively, Eileen T., Libn.
SOUTHWEST TEXAS METHODIST HOSPITAL -
LIBRARY □ San Antonio, TX

Lively, Irene, Archv.
UNITED METHODIST CHURCH - KANSAS WEST
CONFERENCE - ARCHIVES AND HISTORY
DEPOSITORY □ Winfield, KS

Lively, Mildred L., Dir. of Lib.Serv.
FIRST BAPTIST CHURCH OF DALLAS - FIRST
BAPTIST ACADEMY - GEORGE W. TRUETT
MEMORIAL LIBRARY† □ Dallas, TX

Lively, William O., Libn.
ARINC RESEARCH CORPORATION - TECHNICAL
LIBRARY □ Annapolis, MD

Livengood, Shirley, Tech. Data Libn.
STANFORD LINEAR ACCELERATOR CENTER -
LIBRARY □ Stanford, CA

Livermore, Jane M., Libn.
SCIENCE SERVICE, INC. - LIBRARY □
Washington, DC

Livingston, J., Ref.Libn.
LOS ANGELES TRADE-TECHNICAL COLLEGE -
LIBRARY □ Los Angeles, CA

Livingston, Kay D., Tech.Serv.
U.S. ARMY - ACADEMY OF HEALTH SCIENCES -
STIMSON LIBRARY □ Ft. Sam Houston, TX

Livingston, Lisa M., Dir.
LONG ISLAND UNIV. - ARNOLD & MARIE
SCHWARTZ COLLEGE OF PHARMACY & HEALTH
SCIENCES - PHARMACEUTICAL STUDY CENTER
□ Brooklyn, NY

Livingston, Marilyn, Off.Mgr.
PSYNETICS FOUNDATION - LIBRARY □
Anaheim, CA

Livingstone, Bertha, Libn.
DUKE UNIVERSITY - BIOLOGY-FORESTRY
LIBRARY □ Durham, NC

Livingstone, Hilary, Res.Asst.
NEEDHAM, HARPER & STEERS OF CANADA,
LTD. - INFORMATION SERVICES CENTRE □
Toronto, ON

Livingstone, John, Dir.
CHURCH OF JESUS CHRIST OF LATTER-DAY
SAINTS - CALGARY INSTITUTE OF RELIGION -
LIBRARY □ Calgary, AB

Liwag, Crisencia, Sr.Lit. Searcher
SIGNAL UOP RESEARCH CENTER - TECHNICAL
INFORMATION CENTER □ Des Plaines, IL

Lizotte, Jeanette S., Libn.
LANDELS, RIPLEY & DIAMOND - LIBRARY □ San
Francisco, CA

Ljungberg, Betty, Libn.
ECUMENICAL LIBRARY □ New York, NY

Llewellyn, Teresa, Dp.Dir.
WILMER, CUTLER & PICKERING - LAW
LIBRARY □ Washington, DC

Lloyd, Eleanor, Libn.
LANCASTER COUNTY LAW LIBRARY □
Lancaster, PA

Lloyd, Heather M., Hd., Gen.Ref.Dept.
OKLAHOMA STATE UNIVERSITY - SPECIAL
COLLECTIONS AND MAPS □ Stillwater, OK

Lloyd, James B., Cur. of Spec.Coll.
WESTERN CAROLINA UNIVERSITY - HUNTER
MEMORIAL LIBRARY - SPECIAL COLLECTIONS
□ Cullowhee, NC

Lloyd, Janice L., Libn.
GRAPHIC ARTS TECHNICAL FOUNDATION -
E.H. WADEWITZ MEMORIAL LIBRARY □
Pittsburgh, PA

Lloyd, Leah R., Libn.
AULTMAN HOSPITAL - MEDICAL LIBRARY □
Canton, OH

Lloyd, Lynn A., Chf., Lib.Serv.
U.S. VETERANS ADMINISTRATION (RI-
Providence) - HEALTH SCIENCES LIBRARY □
Providence, RI

Lloyd, Mark Frazier, Univ.Archv.
UNIVERSITY OF PENNSYLVANIA - ARCHIVES
AND RECORDS CENTER □ Philadelphia, PA

Lloyd, Priscilla, Med.Libn.
NORTHEAST ALABAMA REGIONAL MEDICAL
CENTER - MEDICAL LIBRARY □ Anniston, AL

Llull, Harry P., Hd.Libn./Bibliog.
STANFORD UNIVERSITY - MATHEMATICAL
AND COMPUTER SCIENCES LIBRARY □
Stanford, CA

Lo, Cecilia, Hd., Tech.Serv.
CANADA - DEPARTMENT OF JUSTICE -
LIBRARY □ Ottawa, ON

Lo, Karl, Hd.
UNIVERSITY OF WASHINGTON - EAST ASIA
LIBRARY □ Seattle, WA

Lo, Mary, Libn.
UNIVERSITY OF TENNESSEE - SPACE
INSTITUTE LIBRARY □ Tullahoma, TN

Lo, Maryanne, Libn.
MEDTRONIC, INC. - LIBRARY† □ Minneapolis,
MN

Lo, Sara de Mundo, Libn.
UNIVERSITY OF ILLINOIS - MODERN
LANGUAGES AND LINGUISTICS LIBRARY □
Urbana, IL

Lo, Suzanne, Hd.Libn.
OAKLAND PUBLIC LIBRARY - ASIAN LIBRARY □
Oakland, CA

Loar, Frances E., Chf., Tech.Serv.Br.
U.S. DEPT. OF TRANSPORTATION - LIBRARY
AND DISTRIBUTION SERVICES DIVISION □
Washington, DC

Loar, Leslie, Ref./Doc.Libn.
COLLEGE OF WILLIAM AND MARY - MARSHALL-
WYTHE LAW LIBRARY □ Williamsburg, VA

Lobe, Anne, Cat.
CHRYSLER MUSEUM - JEAN OUTLAND
CHRYSLER LIBRARY □ Norfolk, VA

Lobenstine, Joy, Adm.Asst.
ASSOCIATION FOR GERONTOLOGY IN HIGHER
EDUCATION - RESOURCE LIBRARY □
Washington, DC

Lober, Robin L., Dir.
LOS ANGELES COLLEGE OF CHIROPRACTIC -
HENRY G. HIGHLY LIBRARY □ Whittier, CA

Lobingier, Christopher, Sound Recordings Libn.
PEABODY CONSERVATORY OF MUSIC -
LIBRARY □ Baltimore, MD

LoBosco, Maryellen, Mng.Ed.
ERIC CLEARINGHOUSE ON URBAN EDUCATION
□ New York, NY

Locas, Lise, Doc. Recherchiste
ASSOCIATION PARITAIRE DE PREVENTION
POUR LA SANTE ET LA SECURITE DU TRAVAIL
DU QUEBEC - TECH.INFO. CENTER □ Montreal,
PQ

Locascio, Aline, Asst.Libn.
FRENCH INSTITUTE/ALLIANCE FRANCAISE -
LIBRARY □ New York, NY

Locatelli, Janet, ILL
MICHIGAN TECHNOLOGICAL UNIVERSITY -
LIBRARY □ Houghton, MI

Lochner, Pamela J., Libn.
YARDNEY ELECTRIC CORPORATION -
TECHNICAL INFORMATION CENTER† □
Pawcatuck, CT

Locker, Frank J., Supv.
BAXTER TRAVENOL LABORATORIES, INC. -
BUSINESS AND LAW INFORMATION RESOURCE
CENTER □ Deerfield, IL

Lockerby, Robert L., Engr.Libn.
PORTLAND STATE UNIVERSITY - SCIENCE
LIBRARY □ Portland, OR

Lockett, Sandra, Docs.
UNIVERSITY OF IOWA - LAW LIBRARY □ Iowa
City, IA

Lockhart, Deborah, Rd.Adv.
DISTRICT OF COLUMBIA PUBLIC LIBRARY -
BLACK STUDIES DIVISION □ Washington, DC

Lockrem, Jane, Libn.
SOUTHERN ILLINOIS UNIVERSITY,
CARBONDALE - SPECIAL COLLECTIONS □
Carbondale, IL

Lockstedt, Barbara, Mgr.
INTERNATIONAL OIL SCOUTS ASSOCIATION -
LIBRARY □ Austin, TX

Lockwood, A.W., Info.Spec.
NORTH CAROLINA STATE SCIENCE AND
TECHNOLOGY RESEARCH CENTER □ Research
Triangle Park, NC

Lockwood, David J., Asst.Libn.
U.S. COURT OF APPEALS FOR THE FEDERAL
CIRCUIT - NATIONAL COURTS' LIBRARY □
Washington, DC

Lockwood, Evelyn M., Cat. & Res.Libn.
KENTUCKY STATE LAW LIBRARY □ Frankfort,
KY

Lockwood, Lillie A., Libn.
U.S. VETERANS ADMINISTRATION (GA-
Augusta) - HOSPITAL LIBRARY □ Augusta, GA

Lockwood, Linda, Libn.
AVERY, HODES, COSTELLO & BURMAN -
LIBRARY □ Chicago, IL

Lockwood, Phil, Cur.
SANTA YNEZ VALLEY HISTORICAL SOCIETY -
ELLEN GLEASON LIBRARY □ Santa Ynez, CA

Lodato, James J., Prin. Law Libn.
NASSAU COUNTY SUPREME COURT - LAW
LIBRARY □ Mineola, NY

Lodde, P.A., Libn.
HARLEY-DAVIDSON MOTOR CO., INC. -
ENGINEERING LIBRARY □ Milwaukee, WI

Loeffler, Mildred, Libn.
RILEY COUNTY GENEALOGICAL SOCIETY -
LIBRARY □ Manhattan, KS

Loeffler, Mildred
RILEY COUNTY HISTORICAL SOCIETY -
SEATON MEMORIAL LIBRARY □ Manhattan, KS

Loeppky, Martha, Lib.Techn.
WINNIPEG BIBLE COLLEGE/WINNIPEG
THEOLOGICAL SEMINARY - LIBRARY □
Otterburne, MB

Loeppky, S., Libn.
WINNIPEG CLINIC - LIBRARY □ Winnipeg, MB

Loepprich, Joyce, Ser.Libn.
UNIVERSITY OF CALIFORNIA, IRVINE -
BIOMEDICAL LIBRARY □ Irvine, CA

Loerke, Jean Penn, Musm.Dir./Hist.
WAUKESHA COUNTY HISTORICAL MUSEUM -
RESEARCH CENTER □ Waukesha, WI

Loesel, Louise, Libn.
FIRST UNITED PRESBYTERIAN CHURCH OF
THE COVENANT - BRITTAIN LIBRARY □ Erie,
PA

Loewenberg, Nancy, Ref.Libn.
NEWSWEEK, INC. - LIBRARY □ New York, NY

Lofaro, Susan, Pres.
HALIFAX HISTORICAL SOCIETY, INC. -
LIBRARY □ Daytona Beach, FL

Lofas, Jeannette, Exec.Dir.
STEP FAMILY FOUNDATION, INC. - LIBRARY □
New York, NY

Lofchie, Dr. Michael, Dir.
UNIVERSITY OF CALIFORNIA, LOS ANGELES -
AFRICAN STUDIES CENTER - LIBRARY □ Los
Angeles, CA

Lofthouse, Norma, Libn.
BRITISH COLUMBIA - MINISTRY OF
EDUCATION - LIBRARY □ Victoria, BC

Loftis, Lynnea, Dir., Educ.
SHARP (Ella) MUSEUM - LIBRARY/ARCHIVES □
Jackson, MI

Loftus, Helen E., Dept.Hd.
ELI LILLY AND COMPANY - BUSINESS LIBRARY
□ Indianapolis, IN

Loftus, Joan D., Asst.Libn.
HOWARD RICE NEMEROVSKI CANADY
ROBERTSON & FALK - LIBRARY □ San Francisco,
CA

Logan, Dr. Anne-Marie, Libn./Photo Archv.
YALE UNIVERSITY - YALE CENTER FOR
BRITISH ART - PHOTO ARCHIVE □ New Haven,
CT

Logan, Dr. Anne-Marie, Libn./Photo Archv.
YALE UNIVERSITY - YALE CENTER FOR
BRITISH ART - REFERENCE LIBRARY □ New
Haven, CT

Logan, Charles, Cat.
U.S. NAVY - NAVAL UNDERWATER SYSTEMS
CENTER - NEW LONDON TECHNICAL LIBRARY†
□ New London, CT

Logan, Darryl, Med.Libn.
ST. FRANCIS HOSPITAL - HEALTH SCIENCES
LIBRARY† □ Tulsa, OK

Logan, Kathryn P., Asst. Music Libn.
UNIVERSITY OF NORTH CAROLINA, CHAPEL
HILL - MUSIC LIBRARY □ Chapel Hill, NC

Logan, Kenneth R., Asst.Hd.
UNIVERSITY OF CALIFORNIA, BERKELEY -
SOUTH/SOUTHEAST ASIA LIBRARY SERVICE □
Berkeley, CA

Logan, Marie V., Sr.Libn.
ATASCADERO STATE HOSPITAL -
PROFESSIONAL LIBRARY □ Atascadero, CA

Logan, Michael, Tech.Serv.Libn.
WENTWORTH INSTITUTE OF TECHNOLOGY -
LIBRARY □ Boston, MA

Logsden, Patricia, Libn.
FRESNO GENEALOGICAL SOCIETY - LIBRARY □
Fresno, CA

Logsdon, Paul, Ref.Libn.
OHIO NORTHERN UNIVERSITY - HETERICK
MEMORIAL LIBRARY □ Ada, OH

Logsdon, Robert, Hd., Ref. & Loan/IN Div.
INDIANA STATE LIBRARY □ Indianapolis, IN

Logsdon, Robert, Act.Hd.
INDIANA STATE LIBRARY - INDIANA DIVISION
□ Indianapolis, IN

Loh, Eudora, Foreign Docs.Libn.
UNIVERSITY OF CALIFORNIA, LOS ANGELES -
PUBLIC AFFAIRS SERVICE □ Los Angeles, CA

Lohf, Kenneth A., Libn.
COLUMBIA UNIVERSITY - RARE BOOK AND
MANUSCRIPT LIBRARY □ New York, NY

Lohman, Kathleen, Assoc.Dir.
ILLINOIS STATE LIBRARY □ Springfield, IL

Lohman, William E., Mgr.
ILLINOIS STATE BOARD OF EDUCATION -
MEDIA RESOURCES CENTER □ Springfield, IL

Lohr, Linda, Adm.Asst.
SUNY AT BUFFALO - HEALTH SCIENCES
LIBRARY □ Buffalo, NY

Lohr, Louise, Mgr.
SYVA COMPANY - LIBRARY/INFORMATION
CENTER □ Palo Alto, CA

Lohrer, Fred E., Libn.
ARCHBOLD BIOLOGICAL STATION - LIBRARY □
Lake Placid, FL

Lohse, Maria I.M., Tech.Info.Spec./Patents
UNION CARBIDE CORPORATION - TECHNICAL
INFORMATION SERVICE □ Bound Brook, NJ

Loidolt, Marcus, Asst. to Dir.
CATHOLIC SEMINARY FOUNDATION OF
INDIANAPOLIS - LIBRARY □ Indianapolis, IN

Lola, J.A., Asst. in Chg.
UNIVERSITY OF CHICAGO - YERKES
OBSERVATORY LIBRARY □ Williams Bay, WI

Lolley, Dr. John L., Dir., Lib.Serv.
CENTRAL STATE UNIVERSITY - LIBRARY -
MICROFORMS RESEARCH CENTER □ Edmond,
OK

Loman, Scott S., Health Sci.Libn.
ST. JOHN'S MEDICAL CENTER - HEALTH
SCIENCES LIBRARY □ Anderson, IN
Lomatuway, Michael W., Lib.Asst.II
NORTHERN ARIZONA UNIVERSITY - SPECIAL
COLLECTIONS LIBRARY □ Flagstaff, AZ
Lomax, Helen, Libn.
INDUSTRIAL HOME FOR THE BLIND - NASSAU-
SUFFOLK BRAILLE LIBRARY □ Hempstead, NY
Lomax, Ronald C., Ref.Libn.
ALAMEDA COUNTY LAW LIBRARY □ Oakland, CA
Lombard, Janet S., Asst.Libn.
ZOOLOGICAL SOCIETY OF SAN DIEGO - ERNST
SCHWARZ LIBRARY □ San Diego, CA
Lombardi, Ralph G., Assoc.Libn.
SHEARMAN & STERLING - LIBRARY □ New York,
NY
Lombardo, Daniel J., Cur. of Spec.Coll.
JONES LIBRARY, INC. - SPECIAL COLLECTIONS
□ Amherst, MA
Lombardo, Dr. Thomas, Dir., Staff Dev.
MADDEN (John J.) MENTAL HEALTH CENTER -
PROFESSIONAL LIBRARY □ Hines, IL
Lonabaugh, Helen, Asst.Med.Libn.
BRYN MAWR HOSPITAL - MEDICAL LIBRARY □
Bryn Mawr, PA
Lonabaugh, Helen, Asst.Med.Libn.
BRYN MAWR HOSPITAL - MEDICAL LIBRARY -
NURSING DIVISION □ Bryn Mawr, PA
Loncaric, Inge, Supv.
ATLANTIC-RICHFIELD COMPANY - ARCO OIL
AND GAS COMPANY - RESEARCH &
DEVELOPMENT TECHNICAL INFORMATION
CENTER □ Dallas, TX
London, Frank M., Supv.Libn.
U.S. ARMY - JFK SPECIAL WARFARE CENTER -
MARQUAT MEMORIAL LIBRARY □ Ft. Bragg, NC
London, Glenn, Res.Libn., Med./Archv.
METROPOLITAN LIFE INSURANCE COMPANY -
CORPORATE INFORMATION CENTER AND
LIBRARY □ New York, NY
Lone, Rita J., Instr., Educ.Serv.
MARION GENERAL HOSPITAL - MEDICAL
LIBRARY† □ Marion, IN
Long, Adrienne, Asst.Dir., Tech.Serv.
THE CLAREMONT COLLEGES - LIBRARY □
Claremont, CA
Long, Aram, Staff Libn.
THE VINEYARD - REAL ESTATE, SHOPPING
CENTER & URBAN DEVELOPMENT
INFORMATION CENTER □ Fresno, CA
Long, Caroline C., Health Sci.Bibliog.
SYRACUSE UNIVERSITY - SCIENCE AND
TECHNOLOGY LIBRARY □ Syracuse, NY
Long, Catherine, Act.Libn.
LINCOLN UNIVERSITY OF MISSOURI - INMAN
E. PAGE LIBRARY □ Jefferson City, MO
Long, Charles R., Adm.Libn.
INSTITUTE OF ECOSYSTEM STUDIES -
LIBRARY □ Millbrook, NY
Long, Charles R., Dir.
NEW YORK BOTANICAL GARDEN - LIBRARY† □
Bronx, NY
Long, Elizabeth, Sr. Children's Libn.
NEW YORK PUBLIC LIBRARY - GENERAL
LIBRARY OF THE PERFORMING ARTS □ New
York, NY
Long, Elmer, Doc.Libn.
U.S. NATL. DEFENSE UNIVERSITY - LIBRARY □
Washington, DC
Long, F. Raymond, Asst.Univ.Libn.
UNIVERSITY OF CALIFORNIA, IRVINE -
BIOMEDICAL LIBRARY □ Irvine, CA
Long, Irma R., Lib.Asst.
NEW BRUNSWICK - DEPARTMENT OF NATURAL
RESOURCES - FORESTS BRANCH LIBRARY □
Fredericton, NB
Long, Jean, Dir., Prof.Lib.
NEWINGTON CHILDREN'S HOSPITAL -
PROFESSIONAL LIBRARY □ Newington, CT

Long, Joan C., Mgr.
UNION CARBIDE CORPORATION - PARMA
TECHNICAL CENTER - TECHNICAL
INFORMATION SERVICE □ Cleveland, OH
Long, Kathleen A., Mgr., Tech.Info.Serv.
HONEYWELL, INC. - ELECTRO-OPTICS
DIVISION - TECHNICAL LIBRARY □ Lexington,
MA
Long, Kenneth, Mgr.
PENTON/IPC - MARKETING INFORMATION
CENTER □ Cleveland, OH
Long, Margery, Archv.
WAYNE STATE UNIVERSITY - ARCHIVES OF
LABOR AND URBAN AFFAIRS/UNIVERSITY
ARCHIVES □ Detroit, MI
Long, Nina, Circuit Libn.
CLEVELAND HEALTH SCIENCES LIBRARY -
ALLEN MEMORIAL LIBRARY □ Cleveland, OH
Long, Rosalee, Assoc. Law Libn.
STANFORD UNIVERSITY - LAW LIBRARY □
Stanford, CA
Long, Ruth A., Asst. Law Libn.
HANCOCK COUNTY LAW LIBRARY
ASSOCIATION □ Findlay, OH
Long, Sandra, Acq.
UTAH STATE LIBRARY □ Salt Lake City, UT
Long, Susan, Med.Libn.
KALISPELL REGIONAL HOSPITAL - MEDICAL
LIBRARY □ Kalispell, MT
Long, Tyrone, Media Spec.
ANTIOCH UNIVERSITY - RESOURCE CENTER □
Philadelphia, PA
Long, Prof. Walter K., Dir.
CAYUGA MUSEUM OF HISTORY AND ART -
LIBRARY & ARCHIVES □ Auburn, NY
Longan, Louise, Libn.
TULARE PUBLIC LIBRARY - INEZ L. HYDE
MEMORIAL COLLECTION □ Tulare, CA
Longard, Sharon
DALHOUSIE UNIVERSITY - MACDONALD
SCIENCE LIBRARY □ Halifax, NS
Longenecker, Lois, Asst.Libn.
ASSOCIATED MENNONITE BIBLICAL
SEMINARIES - MENNONITE BIBLICAL
SEMINARY - LIBRARY □ Elkhart, IN
Longland, Jean R., Cur.
HISPANIC SOCIETY OF AMERICA - LIBRARY □
New York, NY
Longley, Charles, Cur. Microtext
BOSTON PUBLIC LIBRARY - GOVERNMENT
DOCUMENTS, MICROTEXT, NEWSPAPERS □
Boston, MA
Longley, Fred, Asst.Dir./Hd., Ref.
CANADA - LABOUR CANADA - LIBRARY
SERVICES† □ Ottawa, ON
Longo, Joy, Libn.
KEY BANK N.A. - INFORMATION CENTER □
Albany, NY
Longstreth, Ronald L., Exec.Sec.
INTERNATIONAL THESPIAN SOCIETY -
LIBRARY □ Cincinnati, OH
Longworth, J. George, Asst.Commnr.
NEW YORK STATE DIVISION OF HUMAN
RIGHTS - REFERENCE LIBRARY □ New York, NY
Longyear, Douglas, Engr.Dir.
CRANE COMPANY - HYDRO-AIRE DIVISION -
TECHNICAL LIBRARY □ Burbank, CA
Lonnberg, Julia, Libn.
COLLEGE LIBRARY OF THE FINGER LAKES -
LIBRARY† □ Corning, NY
Lonning, Roger D., Trustee
FREEBORN COUNTY HISTORICAL SOCIETY -
NELSON LIBRARY □ Albert Lea, MN
Lonsak, John, Regional Mgr.
CUYAHOGA COUNTY PUBLIC LIBRARY -
FAIRVIEW PARK REGIONAL BRANCH - SPECIAL
COLLECTIONS □ Fairview Park, OH
Loomer, Robert F., Mgr.
BEIHOFF MUSIC CORPORATION - SHEET
MUSIC DEPARTMENT □ Milwaukee, WI
Loomis, Ann, Libn.
U.S. NAVY - NAVAL OCEANOGRAPHIC OFFICE -
NAVY LIBRARY □ Bay St. Louis, MS

Loomis, K., Libn.
INTERNATIONAL BIRD RESCUE RESEARCH
CENTER - LIBRARY □ Berkeley, CA
Loomis, M.J., Libn.
SCHOOL OF LIVING - RALPH BORSODI
MEMORIAL LIBRARY □ York, PA
Loomis, R., Ref.Libn.
PACE UNIVERSITY, PLEASANTVILLE/
BRIARCLIFF - EDWARD AND DORIS MORTOLA
LIBRARY □ Pleasantville, NY
Looney, Pat, Libn.
MERCHANTS NATIONAL BANK OF MOBILE -
EMPLOYEES LIBRARY □ Mobile, AL
Looney, Robert F., Cur.
FREE LIBRARY OF PHILADELPHIA - PRINT AND
PICTURE COLLECTION □ Philadelphia, PA
Loop, Jacqueline, Libn.
ENERGY, INC. - TECHNICAL INFORMATION
SERVICES □ Idaho Falls, ID
Loos, Patricia R., Chf.Libn.
LINCOLN JOURNAL-STAR - LIBRARY □ Lincoln,
NE
Loos, William H., Cur.
BUFFALO & ERIE COUNTY PUBLIC LIBRARY -
RARE BOOK ROOM □ Buffalo, NY
Lopez, Eugene V., Libn.
U.S. NAVY - NAVAL AIR STATION (TX-Corpus
Christi) - LIBRARY □ Corpus Christi, TX
Lopez, Frank, Assoc.Libn.
STAUFFER CHEMICAL COMPANY - DE GUIGNE
TECHNICAL CENTER - RESEARCH LIBRARY □
Richmond, CA
Lopez, Juanita, Asst.Libn.
ITT CORPORATION - GILFILLAN ENGINEERING
LIBRARY† □ Van Nuys, CA
LoPresti, George, Hd., Circ. & Reserve
SUNY - AGRICULTURAL AND TECHNICAL
COLLEGE AT FARMINGDALE - THOMAS D.
GREENLEY LIBRARY □ Farmingdale, NY
LoPresti, Maryellen, Libn.
NORTH CAROLINA STATE UNIVERSITY -
HARRYE LYONS DESIGN LIBRARY □ Raleigh, NC
Lopresti, Robert, Docs./Spec.Coll.Libn.
WILLIAM PATERSON COLLEGE OF NEW JERSEY
- SARAH BYRD ASKEW LIBRARY - SPECIAL
COLLECTIONS □ Wayne, NJ
Loranger, Maria, Libn.
ALBERTA TEACHERS' ASSOCIATION - LIBRARY
□ Edmonton, AB
Loranth, Alice N., Dept.Hd.
CLEVELAND PUBLIC LIBRARY - FINE ARTS AND
SPECIAL COLLECTIONS DEPARTMENT - FINE
ARTS SECTION □ Cleveland, OH
Loranth, Alice N., Dept.Hd.
CLEVELAND PUBLIC LIBRARY - JOHN G. WHITE
COLLECTION OF FOLKLORE, ORIENTALIA, &
CHESS □ Cleveland, OH
Lord, Carl, Lib.Off.
U.S. AIR FORCE HOSPITAL - MEDICAL LIBRARY
(CA-Mather AFB) □ Mather AFB, CA
Lord, Catherine, Asst.Libn.
TACOMA NEWS TRIBUNE - LIBRARY □ Tacoma,
WA
Lord, Jonathan, Clinical Libn.
ST. FRANCIS HOSPITAL AND MEDICAL CENTER
- WILSON C. JAINSEN LIBRARY □ Hartford, CT
Lord, Marjorie, ILL
SUNY - COLLEGE AT BUFFALO - EDWARD H.
BUTLER LIBRARY □ Buffalo, NY
Lordi, Joseph A., Dir.
TAYLOR (Bayard) MEMORIAL LIBRARY □ Kennett
Square, PA
Lordi, Michael, Lib.Dir.
NEW SCHOOL FOR SOCIAL RESEARCH -
RAYMOND FOGELMAN LIBRARY □ New York, NY
Lore, Janice, Res.Assoc.
MC KINNON, ALLEN & ASSOCIATES (Western),
LTD. - RESEARCH LIBRARY □ Calgary, AB
Loree, Grace C., Libn.
KENMORE MERCY HOSPITAL - HEALTH
SCIENCES RESOURCE CENTER □ Kenmore, NY

Lorena, Sr. Rose, S.S.J., Circ.Libn.
ST. CHARLES BORROMEO SEMINARY - RYAN
MEMORIAL LIBRARY □ Philadelphia, PA

Lorenz, Stella, Libn.
AMERICAN APPRAISAL COMPANY - LIBRARY □
Milwaukee, WI

Lorenzen, Carol, Libn.
AERIAL PHENOMENA RESEARCH
ORGANIZATION, INC. - LIBRARY
INFORMATION SERVICES □ Tucson, AZ

Lorette, Moureau
BELGIAN CONSULATE GENERAL - LIBRARY □
New York, NY

Loria, Joan, Cur. of Exhibits
MASSACHUSETTS INSTITUTE OF TECHNOLOGY
- M.I.T. MUSEUM AND HISTORICAL
COLLECTIONS □ Cambridge, MA

Lorimer, Joan R., Info.Sci.
NORWICH EATON PHARMACEUTICALS, INC. -
RESEARCH AND DEVELOPMENT LIBRARY □
Norwich, NY

Lorimer, Nicholas, Info. Officer
NEW ZEALAND CONSULATE GENERAL -
LIBRARY □ New York, NY

Loring, Laura, Tech.Serv.Libn.
O'MELVENY AND MYERS - INFORMATION
SERVICES □ Los Angeles, CA

Loring, Lynn, Acq., Ed.
BOSTON CONSERVATORY OF MUSIC - ALBERT
ALPHIN MUSIC LIBRARY □ Boston, MA

Lormand, Robert, Staff Asst., Lib.Oper.
LAWRENCE LIVERMORE NATIONAL
LABORATORY - TECHNICAL INFORMATION
DEPARTMENT LIBRARY □ Livermore, CA

Lormand, Saundra, Online Serv.Libn.
UNIVERSITY OF CALIFORNIA, BERKELEY -
SEBASTIAN S. KRESGE ENGINEERING LIBRARY
□ Berkeley, CA

Lorne, Lorraine K., Assoc.Libn.
DETROIT COLLEGE OF LAW - LIBRARY □
Detroit, MI

Lorrig, Judith, Mayo Med.Sch.Libn.
MAYO FOUNDATION - MAYO CLINIC LIBRARY □
Rochester, MN

Lorz, Kathy, Staff Libn.
WOMEN'S RESOURCE AND ACTION CENTER -
SOJOURNER TRUTH WOMEN'S RESOURCE
LIBRARY □ Iowa City, IA

Loscalzo, Anita, Med.Libn.
GLOVER MEMORIAL HOSPITAL - MEDICAL
LIBRARY □ Needham, MA

Lose, Mary Louise, Res.Libn.
CARGILL, INC. - INFORMATION CENTER □
Minneapolis, MN

Losi, Jan J., Cur.
NIAGARA COUNTY HISTORICAL SOCIETY -
LIBRARY AND ARCHIVES □ Lockport, NY

Losick, Merill, Ref.Libn.
DEAN WITTER REYNOLDS, INC. - LIBRARY □
New York, NY

Lossin, Olga, Co-Cur.
COLEBROOK HISTORICAL SOCIETY - LIBRARY
AND ARCHIVES □ Colebrook, CT

Lothian, Christina R.N., Archv./Libn.
LYMAN HOUSE MEMORIAL MUSEUM - KATHRYN
E. LYLE MEMORIAL LIBRARY □ Hilo, HI

Lott, Linda, Libn.
MUNSON-WILLIAMS-PROCTOR INSTITUTE -
ART REFERENCE AND MUSIC LIBRARY □ Utica,
NY

Lotze, Sr. Louise Therese, Lib.Supv.
ST. FRANCIS MEDICAL CENTER - HEALTH
SCIENCES LIBRARY □ La Crosse, WI

Loubiere, Sue, Libn.
LOUISIANA STATE UNIVERSITY - SCHOOL OF
VETERINARY MEDICINE - LIBRARY □ Baton
Rouge, LA

Loucka, Patricia A., Libn.
GENERAL ELECTRIC COMPANY - REFRACTORY
METAL PRODUCTS DEPARTMENT - LIBRARY □
Cleveland, OH

Loucks, Cami L., Dir.
TRINITY LUTHERAN HOSPITAL - FLORENCE L.
NELSON MEMORIAL LIBRARY □ Kansas City, MO

Loucks, Donna, Libn.
WEYERHAEUSER COMPANY - WESTERN
FORESTRY RESEARCH CENTER - LIBRARY □
Centralia, WA

Loud, Robert L., Libn.
ST. ELIZABETH'S HOSPITAL - SCHOOL OF
NURSING - LIBRARY □ Brighton, MA

Louden, Kristin, Hd., Circ.
UNIVERSITY OF COLORADO HEALTH SCIENCES
CENTER - DENISON MEMORIAL LIBRARY† □
Denver, CO

Louderback, Patricia A., Chf.Libn.
U.S. ARMY POST - FORT LEWIS - LIBRARY
SYSTEM □ Ft. Lewis, WA

Loudon, Betty, Res.Assoc.
NEBRASKA STATE HISTORICAL SOCIETY -
LIBRARY □ Lincoln, NE

Louet, Sandra, Mgr.
ONTARIO - MINISTRY OF NATURAL
RESOURCES - NATURAL RESOURCES LIBRARY □
Toronto, ON

Louet, Sandra, Mgr.
ONTARIO - MINISTRY OF NATURAL
RESOURCES - NATURAL RESOURCES LIBRARY -
MAPLE† □ Maple, ON

Loughlin, Beverly, Adm.Asst.
HARTFORD PUBLIC LIBRARY - REFERENCE AND
GENERAL READING DEPARTMENT □ Hartford,
CT

Loughridge, Nancy, Libn.
CUMBERLAND COUNTY HISTORICAL SOCIETY
& HAMILTON LIBRARY □ Carlisle, PA

Louie, Thelma, Subject Anl.
AEROSPACE CORPORATION - CHARLES C.
LAURITSEN LIBRARY □ Los Angeles, CA

Lounberg, Joyce, Tech.Serv.
UNIVERSITY OF UTAH - SPENCER S. ECCLES
HEALTH SCIENCES LIBRARY □ Salt Lake City,
UT

Lounsbury, Loretta, Act.Libn.
STIEFEL LABORATORIES, INC. - RESEARCH
INSTITUTE LIBRARY □ Oak Hill, NY

Louton, Arlene, Supv., Info.Serv.
DONALDSON COMPANY, INC. - INFORMATION
CENTER □ Minneapolis, MN

Louzin, Brenna, Libn.
BATTELLE MEMORIAL INSTITUTE - HUMAN
AFFAIRS RESEARCH CENTER - SEATTLE
RESEARCH CENTERS LIBRARY □ Seattle, WA

Lovari, John, Libn.
ADVERTISING RESEARCH FOUNDATION -
LIBRARY □ New York, NY

Lovas, Irene, AV Libn.
U.S. VETERANS ADMINISTRATION (CA-Long
Beach) - MEDICAL CENTER LIBRARY □ Long
Beach, CA

Lovas, Irene, Med.Libn.
U.S. VETERANS ADMINISTRATION (NY-New
York) - MEDICAL LIBRARY □ New York, NY

Lovas, Paula M., Hd.
AMERICAN ASSOCIATION OF RETIRED
PERSONS - NATIONAL GERONTOLOGY
RESOURCE CENTER† □ Washington, DC

Love, Barbara, Asst.Libn.
HOBE SOUND BIBLE COLLEGE - LIBRARY □ Hobe
Sound, FL

Love, Barbara, Ref.Libn.
ST. LAWRENCE COLLEGE SAINT-LAURENT -
LEARNING RESOURCE CENTRE □ Kingston, ON

Love, Erika, Dir.
UNIVERSITY OF NEW MEXICO - MEDICAL
CENTER LIBRARY □ Albuquerque, NM

Love, M.J., Libn.
BRITISH COLUMBIA - MINISTRY OF HUMAN
RESOURCES - LIBRARY □ Vancouver, BC

Love, Marilyn, Ref.Libn.
SACRED HEART UNIVERSITY - LIBRARY □
Bridgeport, CT

Lovelace, Robert F., Dir.
BOCKUS RESEARCH INSTITUTE - LIBRARY □
Philadelphia, PA

Loveland, Sandra, Dir., Instr. Media Ctr.
WESTERN STATES CHIROPRACTIC COLLEGE -
W.A. BUDDEN MEMORIAL LIBRARY □ Portland,
OR

Lovell, Bonnie, Text Libn.
DALLAS MORNING NEWS - REFERENCE
DEPARTMENT □ Dallas, TX

Lovelock, Marty H., Libn.
CANADA - CANADIAN TRANSPORT
COMMISSION - LIBRARY □ Ottawa, ON

Lovett, Carol B., Archv.
MARSHALL HISTORICAL SOCIETY - ARCHIVES
□ Marshall, MI

Lovett, Lovell K., Asst.Libn.
CHURCH OF JESUS CHRIST OF LATTER-DAY
SAINTS - EL PASO BRANCH GENEALOGICAL
LIBRARY □ El Paso, TX

Loving, Lloyd, Libn.
DALLAS PUBLIC LIBRARY - BUSINESS AND
TECHNOLOGY DIVISION □ Dallas, TX

Lovitz, Morris Note, M.D., Dir.
UNIVERSITY OF FLORIDA - CENTER FOR
CLIMACTERIC STUDIES - ROBERT B.
GREENBLATT LIBRARY □ Gainesville, FL

Low, Betty P., Res. & Ref.Libn.
HAGLEY MUSEUM AND LIBRARY □ Wilmington,
DE

Low, Erick Baker, Libn.
NATIONAL CENTER FOR STATE COURTS -
LIBRARY □ Williamsburg, VA

Lowden, Arlene M., Libn.
SIEMENS GAMMASONICS, INC. - NUCLEAR
MEDICAL DIVISION - RESEARCH LIBRARY □
Des Plaines, IL

Lowe, C., Res.Mgr.
BELL CANADA - TELEPHONE HISTORICAL
COLLECTION □ Montreal, PQ

Lowe, David, Computer Serv./Docs.
UNIVERSITY OF ALABAMA - SCHOOL OF LAW
LIBRARY □ University, AL

Lowe, James L., Dir.
DELTIOLOGISTS OF AMERICA - LIBRARY □
Ridley Park, PA

Lowe, May, Libn.
MOBILE COUNTY PUBLIC LAW LIBRARY □
Mobile, AL

Lowe, Peggy, Sec.Asst.
EL MONTE HISTORICAL SOCIETY - MUSEUM
LIBRARY □ El Monte, CA

Lowe, Ruthanne, Med. Libn.
COMMUNITY HOSPITAL OF THE MONTEREY
PENINSULA - MEDICAL STAFF LIBRARY □
Monterey, CA

Lowe, William C., Asst.Dir.Ref.Serv.
NORTH CAROLINA STATE UNIVERSITY - D.H.
HILL LIBRARY □ Raleigh, NC

Lowell, Howard, Oklahoma Rsrcs.
OKLAHOMA STATE DEPARTMENT OF
LIBRARIES □ Oklahoma City, OK

Lowell, Waverly, Cur. of Mss.
CALIFORNIA HISTORICAL SOCIETY -
SCHUBERT HALL LIBRARY □ San Francisco, CA

Lowis, Jean Anne, Libn.
BRITISH COLUMBIA SYSTEMS CORPORATION -
LIBRARY □ Victoria, BC

Lowman, Sandra, Archv./Libn.
SEAGRAM MUSEUM - ARCHIVES AND LIBRARY
□ Waterloo, ON

Lowrey, Carol, Tech.Serv.Libn.
ART GALLERY OF ONTARIO - EDWARD P.
TAYLOR REFERENCE LIBRARY □ Toronto, ON

Lowrie, A. Lucille, Libn.
U.S. AIR FORCE BASE - ALTUS BASE LIBRARY†
□ Altus AFB, OK

Lowry, Andree, Libn.
ENVIRONMENTAL PROTECTION AGENCY -
ENVIRONMENTAL RESEARCH LABORATORY,
GULF BREEZE - LIBRARY □ Gulf Breeze, FL

Lowry, Barbara, Hd., Ref.
PHILADELPHIA COLLEGE OF TEXTILES AND
SCIENCE - PASTORE LIBRARY □ Philadelphia, PA
Lowry, Glenn, Sys.Libn.
VIRGINIA POLYTECHNIC INSTITUTE AND
STATE UNIVERSITY - CAROL M. NEWMAN
LIBRARY □ Blacksburg, VA
Lowry, H. Maynard, Dir.
LOMA LINDA UNIVERSITY - DEL E. WEBB
MEMORIAL LIBRARY □ Loma Linda, CA
Lowry, Kim, Supv., Lib.Serv.
AMERICAN COUNCIL OF LIFE INSURANCE -
LIBRARY □ Washington, DC
Lowry, Lisa, Sr.Libn.
KENTUCKY STATE DEPARTMENT FOR
LIBRARIES & ARCHIVES - KENTUCKY TALKING
BOOK LIBRARY □ Frankfort, KY
Lowry, Viola, Asst.Cur.
MERCER COUNTY HISTORICAL SOCIETY -
LIBRARY AND ARCHIVES □ Mercer, PA
Lowy, George, Dean of Libs.
PRATT INSTITUTE - LIBRARY □ Brooklyn, NY
Loyd, Ann M., Ref.Libn.
CARNEGIE LIBRARY OF PITTSBURGH -
PENNSYLVANIA DIVISION □ Pittsburgh, PA
Loyd, Rev. Roger L., Assoc.Libn.
SOUTHERN METHODIST UNIVERSITY -
BRIDWELL LIBRARY - CENTER FOR
METHODIST STUDIES □ Dallas, TX
Loyd, Roger L., Assoc.Libn.
SOUTHERN METHODIST UNIVERSITY -
PERKINS SCHOOL OF THEOLOGY - LIBRARY □
Dallas, TX
Lozano, Eduardo, Bibliog.
UNIVERSITY OF PITTSBURGH - LATIN
AMERICAN COLLECTION □ Pittsburgh, PA
Lozupone, Frank, Chf., Sup.Div.
U.S. DEFENSE MAPPING AGENCY -
HYDROGRAPHIC/TOPOGRAPHIC CENTER-
SUPPORT DIVISION - SCIENTIFIC DATA
DEPARTMENT □ Washington, DC
Lu, C.H., Tech.Dir.
UNIVERSITY OF IOWA - LABORATORY FOR
POLITICAL RESEARCH □ Iowa City, IA
Lu, Dr. Po-Yung, Dir.
NATIONAL LIBRARY OF MEDICINE -
TOXICOLOGY DATA BANK □ Oak Ridge, TN
Lu, Teresa Y., Libn.
VALLEY GENERAL HOSPITAL - LIBRARY □
Renton, WA
Lubetski, Edith, Hd.Libn.
YESHIVA UNIVERSITY - HEDI STEINBERG
LIBRARY □ New York, NY
Luby, Barbara, Archv.Ck.
BUTTERICK COMPANY, INC. - ARCHIVES □ New
York, NY
Lucas, Ann, Ser.Libn.
COOLEY (Thomas M.) LAW SCHOOL - LIBRARY □
Lansing, MI
Lucas, Barb, Med.Libn.
JEWISH HOSPITAL OF CINCINNATI - MEDICAL
LIBRARY □ Cincinnati, OH
Lucas, Dan, Slide Libn.
PORTLAND ART MUSEUM - LIBRARY □ Portland,
OR
Lucas, Dorothy B., Libn.
AMERICAN BAPTIST THEOLOGICAL SEMINARY
- T.L. HOLCOMB LIBRARY □ Nashville, TN
Lucas, Rev. Glenn, Archv./Hist.
UNITED CHURCH OF CANADA - CENTRAL
ARCHIVES† □ Toronto, ON
Lucas, Jean M., Libn.
ATE MANAGEMENT AND SERVICE COMPANY,
INC. - RESOURCE CENTER □ Cincinnati, OH
Lucas, John, Hd., Tech.Serv.
MEDICAL COLLEGE OF OHIO AT TOLEDO -
RAYMON H. MULFORD LIBRARY □ Toledo, OH
Lucas, Leonard, Hd., Soc.Sci. & Hist.
WORCESTER PUBLIC LIBRARY - REFERENCE
AND READER SERVICES □ Worcester, MA

Lucas, Lydia, Hd., Tech.Serv.
MINNESOTA HISTORICAL SOCIETY - DIVISION
OF ARCHIVES AND MANUSCRIPTS □ St. Paul,
MN
Lucas, Lynn, Asst.Libn.
INDIANA UNIVERSITY OF PENNSYLVANIA -
UNIVERSITY LIBRARY □ Indiana, PA
Lucas, R.M., Med.Libn.
U.S. AIR FORCE HOSPITAL - MEDICAL LIBRARY
(IL-Rantoul) □ Rantoul, IL
Lucas, Rosemary, Libn.
WISCONSIN STATE LEGISLATIVE REFERENCE
BUREAU □ Madison, WI
Lucas, Sandra, Community Serv.Spec.
U.S. BUREAU OF THE CENSUS - INFORMATION
SERVICES PROGRAM - DETROIT REGIONAL
OFFICE - INFORMATION CENTER □ Detroit, MI
Lucas, Valeeta, Cat.Libn.
BURNS AND MC DONNELL ENGINEERING
COMPANY - TECHNICAL LIBRARY □ Kansas
City, MO
Lucas-Ford, Betty, Asst. Law Libn.
GEORGIA STATE UNIVERSITY - COLLEGE OF
LAW LIBRARY □ Atlanta, GA
Lucero, Peggy, Tech.Libn.
SUNDSTRAND DATA CONTROL, INC. - LIBRARY
□ Redmond, WA
Lucey, Jean E., Dir.
INSURANCE LIBRARY ASSOCIATION OF
BOSTON □ Boston, MA
Luchinsky, Ellen, Asst.Hd.
ENOCH PRATT FREE LIBRARY - FINE ARTS AND
RECREATION DEPARTMENT □ Baltimore, MD
Luchsinger, Arlene E., Hd.
UNIVERSITY OF GEORGIA - SCIENCE LIBRARY
□ Athens, GA
Lucier, Richard, Dir., Media/Lib.Serv.
UNIVERSITY OF CINCINNATI - MEDICAL
CENTER LIBRARIES - HEALTH SCIENCES
LIBRARY† □ Cincinnati, OH
Lucier, Suzanne, Asst.Libn.
COUNTY OF CARLETON LAW ASSOCIATION -
LAW LIBRARY □ Ottawa, ON
Luciw, Dr. W.O., Dir.
SLAVIA LIBRARY □ State College, PA
Luck, William, Assoc.Libn.
LANCASTER COUNTY HISTORICAL SOCIETY -
LIBRARY □ Lancaster, PA
Lucow, Nancy, Cat.
ALBRIGHT-KNOX ART GALLERY - ART
REFERENCE LIBRARY □ Buffalo, NY
Luddy, Evangeline, Libn.
CONNECTICUT STATE LIBRARY - HARTFORD
LAW BRANCH □ Hartford, CT
Ludmer, Joyce, Art Libn./Dir.
UNIVERSITY OF CALIFORNIA, LOS ANGELES -
ART LIBRARY - ELMER BELT LIBRARY OF
VINCIANA □ Los Angeles, CA
Ludmer, Joyce P., Art Libn.
UNIVERSITY OF CALIFORNIA, LOS ANGELES -
ART LIBRARY □ Los Angeles, CA
Ludovici, Ann, Ref.Libn.
TEMPLE UNIVERSITY - HEALTH SCIENCES
CENTER - LIBRARY □ Philadelphia, PA
Ludt, Bonnie, Hd., Acq.Dept.
CALIFORNIA INSTITUTE OF TECHNOLOGY -
MILLIKAN LIBRARY □ Pasadena, CA
Ludwig, Deborah, Libn.
WASHINGTON STATE UNIVERSITY -
VETERINARY MEDICAL/PHARMACY LIBRARY □
Pullman, WA
Ludwig, Logan, Dir.
ST. LOUIS UNIVERSITY - MEDICAL CENTER
LIBRARY □ St. Louis, MO
Ludwig, Richard M., Asst.Libn.
PRINCETON UNIVERSITY - RARE BOOKS AND
SPECIAL COLLECTIONS □ Princeton, NJ
Ludwikowski, Stella E., Adm.Libn.
U.S. AIR FORCE BASE - EIELSON BASE LIBRARY
□ Eielson AFB, AK
Ludwin, Vivien, Pub.Serv.Libn.
QUEEN'S UNIVERSITY AT KINGSTON -
BRACKEN LIBRARY □ Kingston, ON

Luebbe, Mary, Ref.Libn.
UNIVERSITY OF BRITISH COLUMBIA -
GOVERNMENT PUBLICATIONS & MICROFORMS
DIVISIONS □ Vancouver, BC
Luebke, Margaret F., Med.Libn.
DOCTORS' MEDICAL CENTER - PROFESSIONAL
LIBRARY □ Modesto, CA
Lueck, Antoinette, Physical Sci.Libn.
COLORADO STATE UNIVERSITY - WILLIAM E.
MORGAN LIBRARY □ Fort Collins, CO
Lueders, Julie A., Chf., Lib.Serv.
U.S. VETERANS ADMINISTRATION (CT-
Newington) - HOSPITAL HEALTH SCIENCES
LIBRARY □ Newington, CT
Luhde, Jutta, Libn.
BERKSHIRE MEDICAL CENTER - MEDICAL
LIBRARY □ Pittsfield, MA
Luidens, Dr. John P., Archv.
NETHERLANDS MUSEUM - ARCHIVES AND
LIBRARY □ Holland, MI
Luik, Asta, Libn.
UNIVERSITY OF TORONTO - INSTITUTE FOR
AEROSPACE STUDIES - LIBRARY □ Downsview,
ON
Lukan, Shirley, Asst.Libn.
ST. JOSEPH HOSPITAL - HOSPITAL HEALTH
SCIENCE LIBRARY □ Houston, TX
Lukas, Carla M., Libn.
YALE UNIVERSITY - CLASSICS LIBRARY □ New
Haven, CT
Lukas, Marilyn M., Mgr.
AMERICAN CYANAMID COMPANY - BUSINESS
INFORMATION CENTER □ Wayne, NJ
Lukas, Peter, Mgr., Info. Resource Dev.
CANADIAN CENTRE FOR OCCUPATIONAL
HEALTH AND SAFETY - DOCUMENTATION
SERVICES/SERVICE DE DOCUMENTATION □
Hamilton, ON
Lukasiewich, Halina, Coord., Bibliog. Control
CANADA - CANADIAN INTERNATIONAL
DEVELOPMENT AGENCY - DEVELOPMENT
INFORMATION CENTRE □ Hull, PQ
Lukasiewicz, Paul J., Mathematics Libn.
YALE UNIVERSITY - MATHEMATICS LIBRARY □
New Haven, CT
Luke, Keye L., Libn.
FMC CORPORATION - CENTRAL ENGINEERING
LABORATORIES - LIBRARY □ Santa Clara, CA
Luke, Lisbeth L., Libn.
NATIONAL ACADEMY OF SCIENCES -
NATIONAL RESEARCH COUNCIL -
TRANSPORTATION RESEARCH BOARD LIBRARY
□ Washington, DC
Lukes, Frank, Law Libn.
BAKER & MC KENZIE - LIBRARY □ Chicago, IL
Luks, Lewis F., Cons.
MARIST COLLEGE - LIBRARY □ Washington, DC
Luksik, Joan C., Dir.
MOUNT CARMEL MERCY HOSPITAL - MEDICAL
LIBRARY □ Detroit, MI
Lum, Raymond D., Asst.Libn./Western Sect.
HARVARD UNIVERSITY - HARVARD-YENCHING
LIBRARY □ Cambridge, MA
Lummer, Florence, Libn.
ANTI-DEFAMATION LEAGUE OF B'NAI B'RITH -
JACOB ALSON MEMORIAL LIBRARY □ New York,
NY
Lummis, G.H., Exec.V.P.
HALIFAX BOARD OF TRADE - LIBRARY □ Halifax,
NS
Lumpkin, Hazel, Acq.Libn.
NORTH CAROLINA CENTRAL UNIVERSITY -
LAW LIBRARY □ Durham, NC
Lumpkins, Charles, Asst.Libn.
MAINE MARITIME ACADEMY - NUTTING
MEMORIAL LIBRARY □ Castine, ME
Lumpkins, Charles, Chf., Tech.Serv.
MASSACHUSETTS STATE LIBRARY □ Boston,
MA
Lumsden, Mary, Libn.
GROUP HEALTH COOPERATIVE OF PUGET
SOUND - MEDICAL LIBRARY □ Seattle, WA

Lumsden, Sharmyn, Photo Cur.
AUSTIN PUBLIC LIBRARY - AUSTIN HISTORY
CENTER □ Austin, TX

Lunak, Louise, Libn.
CHICAGO ACADEMY OF SCIENCES - MATTHEW
LAUGHLIN MEMORIAL LIBRARY □ Chicago, IL

Lunan, CWO, Chf.Libn.
ROYAL CANADIAN ARTILLERY MUSEUM -
LIBRARY □ Shilo, MB

Lund, Ann, Libn.
CAPITAL TIMES NEWSPAPER - LIBRARY □
Madison, WI

Lund, Robert, Owner
AMERICAN MUSEUM OF MAGIC - LIBRARY □
Marshall, MI

Lund, Ruth, Supv.Ck.
SONOMA COUNTY PLANNING DEPARTMENT -
LIBRARY □ Santa Rosa, CA

Lunde, Daniel, Hd., Pub.Serv.
MINNESOTA STATE LAW LIBRARY □ St. Paul,
MN

Lundeen, Joel W., Act.Dir.
SWENSON SWEDISH IMMIGRATION RESEARCH
CENTER □ Rock Island, IL

Lundell, Susan, Music Cat.
UNIVERSITY OF CINCINNATI - COLLEGE
CONSERVATORY OF MUSIC - GORNO
MEMORIAL MUSIC LIBRARY □ Cincinnati, OH

Lundgren, Barbara, Rsrc.Coord.
PLANNED PARENTHOOD OF MINNESOTA -
POPULATION RESOURCE CENTER □ St. Paul, MN

Lundgren, Janet, Tech.Serv./Ref.Libn.
UNIVERSITY OF SOUTHERN CALIFORNIA -
CROCKER BUSINESS LIBRARY □ Los Angeles,
CA

Lundquist, Barbara, Chf.
DISTRICT OF COLUMBIA PUBLIC LIBRARY -
TECHNOLOGY AND SCIENCE DIVISION □
Washington, DC

Lundstrom, Lynn, Libn.
U.S. DISTRICT COURT - NORTHERN
CALIFORNIA DISTRICT - LOUIS E. GOODMAN
MEMORIAL LIBRARY □ San Francisco, CA

Lundy, Mack, III, AV Libn.
TRIDENT TECHNICAL COLLEGE - NORTH
CAMPUS LIBRARY □ North Charleston, SC

Lung, Chan-Shen, Asst.Libn.
CAHILL GORDON & REINDEL - LAW LIBRARY □
New York, NY

Lung, Mon Yin, Cat.Libn.
UNIVERSITY OF KANSAS - SCHOOL OF LAW
LIBRARY □ Lawrence, KS

Lung, Vivian, Libn.
BELL CANADA - O.R. INFORMATION RESOURCE
CENTRE □ Toronto, ON

Lunin, Lois, Project Dir.
ARTHRITIS INFORMATION CLEARINGHOUSE □
Arlington, VA

Lunk, William A., Chm. of Lib.Comm.
WILSON ORNITHOLOGICAL SOCIETY -
JOSSELYN VAN TYNE MEMORIAL LIBRARY □
Ann Arbor, MI

Lunn, Deborah E., V.P., Pub.Rel.
AIRPORT OPERATORS COUNCIL
INTERNATIONAL - LIBRARY □ Washington, DC

Lunt, Wilhelmina V., Cur.
HISTORICAL SOCIETY OF OLD NEWBURY -
LIBRARY □ Newburyport, MA

Luostari, Kenneth P., Libn.-Res.
NATIONAL SKI HALL OF FAME AND MUSEUM -
ROLAND PALMEDO NATIONAL SKI LIBRARY □
Ishpeming, MI

Lupo, Mona C., Env.Sci.Tech.Libn.
REYNOLDS ELECTRICAL AND ENGINEERING
COMPANY, INC. - TECHNICAL LIBRARY □ Las
Vegas, NV

Lurie, Maxine
GENEALOGICAL SOCIETY OF NEW JERSEY -
MANUSCRIPT COLLECTIONS □ New Brunswick,
NJ

Lurie, Maxine
RUTGERS UNIVERSITY, THE STATE
UNIVERSITY OF NEW JERSEY - DEPARTMENT
OF SPECIAL COLLECTIONS AND ARCHIVES □
New Brunswick, NJ

Lurye, Joan B., Mgr.
AMERICAN EXPRESS COMPANY - CARD
INFORMATION CENTER □ New York, NY

Lusardi, Frank, Asst.Libn.
TOBACCO MERCHANTS ASSOCIATION OF THE
U.S. - HOWARD S. CULLMAN LIBRARY □ New
York, NY

Lusis, Dr. Peter, Hd.
ONTARIO - MINISTRY OF AGRICULTURE AND
FOOD - VETERINARY SERVICES LABORATORY
LIBRARY □ Kemptville, ON

Lusk, Cathy, Act.Dir.
PERHAM FOUNDATION - FOOTHILL
ELECTRONICS MUSEUM - DE FOREST
MEMORIAL ARCHIVES □ Los Altos Hills, CA

Lussier, Claudine, Libn.
CANADA - CANADIAN FORESTRY SERVICE -
LAURENTIAN FOREST RESEARCH CENTRE -
LIBRARY □ Ste. Foy, PQ

Lussier, Claudine, Libn.
CANADA - EMPLOYMENT & IMMIGRATION
CANADA - QUEBEC REGIONAL LIBRARY† □
Montreal, PQ

Lustig, Joanne, Mgr., Med./Sci.Info.
KNOLL PHARMACEUTICAL COMPANY -
SCIENCE INFORMATION CENTER □ Whippany,
NJ

Luszczynska, Barbara, Lib.Assoc.
WASHINGTON UNIVERSITY - CENTER FOR THE
STUDY OF DATA PROCESSING - CSDP LIBRARY
□ St. Louis, MO

Luszczynska, Barbara, Lib.Assoc.
WASHINGTON UNIVERSITY - MATHEMATICS
LIBRARY □ St. Louis, MO

Lutgen, Tom, Ref./Res.
LOS ANGELES TIMES - EDITORIAL LIBRARY □
Los Angeles, CA

Luther, M. Judy, Dir., Lrng.Rsrcs.
EMBRY RIDDLE AERONAUTICAL UNIVERSITY -
LEARNING RESOURCES CENTER □ Daytona
Beach, FL

Lutz, Maija, Cat.
HARVARD UNIVERSITY - TOZZER LIBRARY □
Cambridge, MA

Lutz, Susan E., Libn.
OKLAHOMA WATER RESOURCES BOARD -
LIBRARY □ Oklahoma City, OK

Lutzker, Professor M., Hd., Rd.Serv.
JOHN JAY COLLEGE OF CRIMINAL JUSTICE OF
THE CITY UNIVERSITY OF NEW YORK -
REISMAN MEMORIAL LIBRARY □ New York, NY

Lutzky, Doris, Kpr.
HONOLULU ACADEMY OF ARTS - SLIDE
COLLECTION □ Honolulu, HI

LuValle, Jean L., Asst.Libn.
ZOECON CORPORATION - LIBRARY □ Palo Alto,
CA

Luzader, JoAnn, Libn., Pub.Serv.
COLUMBUS TECHNICAL INSTITUTE -
EDUCATIONAL RESOURCES CENTER □
Columbus, OH

Lybeck, Marti, Prof.Asst.
ST. PAUL PUBLIC LIBRARY - SOCIAL SCIENCES
& LITERATURE □ St. Paul, MN

Lycamanenko, Olga, Libn.
U.S. VETERANS ADMINISTRATION (MA-Boston)
- OUTPATIENT CLINIC LIBRARY SERVICE
(142D) □ Boston, MA

Lyders, Richard, Exec.Dir.
HOUSTON ACADEMY OF MEDICINE - TEXAS
MEDICAL CENTER LIBRARY □ Houston, TX

Lydia, Sr. M., Libn.
MADONNA COLLEGE - CURRICULUM LIBRARY □
Livonia, MI

Lydon, Mary E., Corp.Libn.
METCALF & EDDY, INC. - LIBRARY □ Boston,
MA

Lyerla, Gloria, Libn., ILL
TEXAS TECH UNIVERSITY - LIBRARY □
Lubbock, TX

Lyle, Martha, Libn.
CARNEGIE LIBRARY OF PITTSBURGH -
SCIENCE AND TECHNOLOGY DEPARTMENT □
Pittsburgh, PA

Lyle, Robert S., Chf., Lib.Serv.
U.S. VETERANS ADMINISTRATION (PA-
Philadelphia) - MEDICAL CENTER LIBRARY □
Philadelphia, PA

Lyle, Royster, Cur. of Coll.
MARSHALL (George C.) RESEARCH
FOUNDATION - GEORGE C. MARSHALL
RESEARCH LIBRARY† □ Lexington, VA

Lyles, Gloria, Adm.
JOHNS HOPKINS UNIVERSITY - WILLIAM H.
WELCH MEDICAL LIBRARY □ Baltimore, MD

Lyman, Norma Jane, Asst. Law Libn.
NEW HAMPSHIRE STATE LIBRARY - LAW
LIBRARY □ Concord, NH

Lynagh, Patricia, Ref.Libn.
UNIVERSITY OF MARYLAND, COLLEGE PARK -
LIBRARIES - ART LIBRARY □ College Park, MD

Lynas, Lothian, Assoc.Libn.
NEW YORK BOTANICAL GARDEN - LIBRARY† □
Bronx, NY

Lynch, Barbara, Ref.Libn.
U.S. NAVY - DEPARTMENT LIBRARY □
Washington, DC

Lynch, Cheryl, Libn.
LAWRENCE EAGLE TRIBUNE - LIBRARY □
Lawrence, MA

Lynch, Donna, Libn.
METROPOLITAN TORONTO LIBRARY -
MUNICIPAL REFERENCE DEPARTMENT □
Toronto, ON

Lynch, Eiko, Ser.Libn.
BISHOP (Bernice P.) MUSEUM - LIBRARY □
Honolulu, HI

Lynch, Evangeline M., Libn./Hd.
LOUISIANA STATE UNIVERSITY - RARE BOOK
COLLECTION □ Baton Rouge, LA

Lynch, Evangeline Mills, Libn./Hd.
LOUISIANA STATE UNIVERSITY - LOUISIANA
ROOM □ Baton Rouge, LA

Lynch, Florence, Cat.
HARVARD UNIVERSITY - EDA KUHN LOEB
MUSIC LIBRARY □ Cambridge, MA

Lynch, Frances H., Asst.Dir., Tech.Serv.
VANDERBILT UNIVERSITY - MEDICAL CENTER
LIBRARY □ Nashville, TN

Lynch, Gina, Ref.Libn.
GASTON SNOW & ELY BARTLETT □ Boston, MA

Lynch, James R., Archv.
CHURCH OF THE BRETHREN GENERAL BOARD -
BRETHREN HISTORICAL LIBRARY AND
ARCHIVES □ Elgin, IL

Lynch, Lawrence D., Pub.Info.Coord.
LOUISIANA STATE OFFICE OF THE SECRETARY
OF STATE - STATE ARCHIVES AND RECORDS
SERVICE - ARCHIVES SECTION □ Baton Rouge,
LA

Lynch, Sr. M. Dennis, S.H.C.J., Lib.Dir.
ROSEMONT COLLEGE - GERTRUDE KISTLER
MEMORIAL LIBRARY - SPECIAL COLLECTIONS
□ Rosemont, PA

Lynch, Marie
THE WORLD INSTITUTE FOR ADVANCED
PHENOMENOLOGICAL RESEARCH AND
LEARNING - LIBRARY AND ARCHIVES □
Belmont, MA

Lynch, Martha E., Dir. of Libs.
METHODIST HOSPITAL - HEALTH SCIENCES
LIBRARY □ Brooklyn, NY

Lynch, Mollie S., Lib.Mgr.
ST. JOSEPH MERCY HOSPITAL - EDUCATIONAL
RESOURCES □ Pontiac, MI

Lynch, Terry R., Ref.Libn.
SAN BERNARDINO COUNTY LAW LIBRARY □
San Bernardino, CA

Lynn, Carol, Med.Libn.
ANCLOTE PSYCHIATRIC CENTER - MEDICAL
LIBRARY □ Tarpon Springs, FL
Lynn, Deanna C., Asst.Libn.
ENVIRONMENTAL RESEARCH & TECHNOLOGY,
INC. - INFORMATION CENTER □ Concord, MA
Lynn, Edna, Exec.Dir.
COLUMBIA COUNTY HISTORICAL SOCIETY -
LIBRARY □ Orangeville, PA
Lynn, Kenneth C., Data Off.
NATIONAL INSTITUTE OF DENTAL RESEARCH -
DENTAL RESEARCH DATA OFFICE □ Bethesda,
MD
Lynn, Mary Evelyn, Libn.
EAST TENNESSEE BAPTIST HOSPITAL -
HEALTH SCIENCES LIBRARY □ Knoxville, TN
Lynn, Ms. Michael Anne, Musm.Dir.
HISTORIC LEXINGTON FOUNDATION -
GARLAND GRAY RESEARCH CENTER & LIBRARY
□ Lexington, VA
Lynott, Nancy B., Libn.
PERKIN-ELMER DATA SYSTEMS GROUP -
LIBRARY □ Tinton Falls, NJ
Lyon, Cathryn C., Mgr., Tech.Info.Serv.
INSTITUTE FOR DEFENSE ANALYSES -
TECHNICAL INFORMATION SERVICES □
Alexandria, VA
Lyon, Frances, Dir. of Lib.Serv.
MEMORIAL HOSPITAL MEDICAL CENTER OF
LONG BEACH - MEDICAL LIBRARY† □ Long
Beach, CA
Lyon, Grace, Hd.Libn.
LYON'S SCHOOL OF BUSINESS - LIBRARY† □
New Castle, PA
Lyon, Maureen, Libn.
PERGAMON INSTITUTE - LIBRARY □ Elmsford,
NY
Lyon, R. Donald, Coord.
BURNABY AND NEW WESTMINSTER SCHOOL
BOARDS - REGIONAL FILM LIBRARY SERVICES
□ Burnaby, BC
Lyon, R. Donald, Coord.
BURNABY SCHOOL BOARD - MEDIA LOANS □
Burnaby, BC
Lyons, Amy, Hd., Circ.
SUNY AT BUFFALO - HEALTH SCIENCES
LIBRARY □ Buffalo, NY
Lyons, Clare, Libn.
ONTARIO - MINISTRY OF LABOUR - ONTARIO
LABOUR RELATIONS BOARD - LIBRARY □
Toronto, ON
Lyons, Grace, Chf.
DISTRICT OF COLUMBIA PUBLIC LIBRARY -
LIBRARY FOR THE BLIND AND PHYSICALLY
HANDICAPPED □ Washington, DC
Lyons, Melinda L., Hd.Libn.
SUMMER INSTITUTE OF LINGUISTICS -
DALLAS/NORMAN LIBRARY □ Dallas, TX
Lyons, Sr. Rita Claire, C.S.C., Dir.
ST. MARY'S COLLEGE - MUSIC SEMINAR ROOM
□ Notre Dame, IN
Lyons, Sarah, Libn.
DENVER CONSERVATIVE BAPTIST SEMINARY -
CAREY S. THOMAS LIBRARY □ Denver, CO
Lyons, Valerie, Photo Libn.
ATLANTA NEWSPAPERS - REFERENCE LIBRARY
□ Atlanta, GA
Lyons, Virginia, ILL Libn.
BATTELLE-COLUMBUS LABORATORIES -
LIBRARY □ Columbus, OH
Lysiuk, Alina, Med.Libn.
HOECHST-ROUSSEL PHARMACEUTICALS, INC. -
LIBRARY □ Somerville, NJ
Lysyk, Pat, Ref.Libn.
UNIVERSITY OF BRITISH COLUMBIA -
WOODWARD BIOMEDICAL LIBRARY □
Vancouver, BC
Lytle, Steve, Archv.
HARTFORD HOSPITAL - HEALTH SCIENCE
LIBRARIES □ Hartford, CT

M

Ma, Margaret C., Libn.
QUADREX CORPORATION - LIBRARY □
Campbell, CA
Ma, Tai-loi, Hd., Cat.
UNIVERSITY OF CHICAGO - FAR EASTERN
LIBRARY □ Chicago, IL
Ma, Vilia, Tech.Libn.
IBM CORPORATION - RESEARCH LIBRARY □
San Jose, CA
Ma, Wei-Yi, Chinese Bibliog.
UNIVERSITY OF MICHIGAN - ASIA LIBRARY □
Ann Arbor, MI
Maack, David, Intl./Foreign Docs.Libn.
UNIVERSITY OF WASHINGTON - GOVERNMENT
PUBLICATIONS DIVISION □ Seattle, WA
Maag, Albert F., Univ.Libn.
CAPITAL UNIVERSITY - CHEMISTRY LIBRARY
□ Columbus, OH
Maass, Dr. Eleanor, Act.Asst.Dir.
UNIVERSITY OF PENNSYLVANIA - CENTER FOR
THE HISTORY OF CHEMISTRY □ Philadelphia, PA
Maberly, Linda, Temporary Libn.
CRANBROOK ACADEMY OF ART - LIBRARY □
Bloomfield Hills, MI
Mabry, Raymond, Libn.
RICHMOND PUBLIC LIBRARY - ART AND MUSIC
DEPARTMENT □ Richmond, VA
Mabry, Shirley, Chf., Lib.Serv.
U.S. VETERANS ADMINISTRATION (FL-Lake
City) - MEDICAL CENTER - LEARNING
RESOURCE CENTER □ Lake City, FL
McAdam, Eileen, Libn.
KAISER-PERMANENTE MEDICAL CENTER -
HEALTH LIBRARY □ Oakland, CA
MacAdam, Jeanette, Tech.Proc.Asst.
NORTHEASTERN UNIVERSITY - LAW SCHOOL
LIBRARY □ Boston, MA
McAdams, B.A., Tech.Libn.
LOCKHEED-GEORGIA COMPANY - TECHNICAL
INFORMATION DEPARTMENT □ Marietta, GA
McAlister, Charles D., Tech.Dir.
INSTRUMENT SOCIETY OF AMERICA - LIBRARY
□ Research Triangle Park, NC
McAlister, George L., Assoc.Dir.
LOMA LINDA UNIVERSITY - DEL E. WEBB
MEMORIAL LIBRARY □ Loma Linda, CA
McAllister, Lowell, Dir.
MASSACHUSETTS AUDUBON SOCIETY -
BERKSHIRE SANCTUARIES - LIBRARY □ Lenox,
MA
McAllister, Sharon L., Sci.Libn.
ALCON LABORATORIES, INC. - RESEARCH &
DEVELOPMENT LIBRARY □ Fort Worth, TX
McAlpin, Sidney, State Archv.
WASHINGTON STATE OFFICE OF SECRETARY
OF STATE - DIVISION OF ARCHIVES AND
RECORD MANAGEMENT □ Olympia, WA
McAlpine, Pearlie, Libn.
WESTERN RESERVE PSYCHIATRIC
HABILITATION CENTER - STAFF LIBRARY □
Northfield, OH
McAnallen, Deborah K., Asst.Libn.
UNIVERSITY OF ARKANSAS, FAYETTEVILLE -
SPECIAL COLLECTIONS DIVISION □
Fayetteville, AR
McAndrew, Marie, Libn.
MERCY HOSPITAL - SCHOOL OF NURSING -
LIBRARY† □ Scranton, PA
McAnich, Sandra, Hd., Govt.Pubns.
UNIVERSITY OF KENTUCKY - MARGARET I.
KING LIBRARY - GOVERNMENT
PUBLICATIONS/MAP DEPARTMENT □
Lexington, KY
McArdle, James J., Libn.
KING COUNTY LAW LIBRARY □ Seattle, WA

Macaree, Mary W., Hd.
UNIVERSITY OF BRITISH COLUMBIA - MAC
MILLAN FORESTRY/AGRICULTURE LIBRARY □
Vancouver, BC
McArthur, JoAnn, Lib.Supv.
HERCULES, INC. - RESEARCH CENTER -
TECHNICAL INFORMATION DIVISION □
Wilmington, DE
MacArthur, Roberta, Hd., Pers./Microform Ctr.
TEACHERS COLLEGE - MILBANK MEMORIAL
LIBRARY □ New York, NY
MacArthur, William J., Jr., Hd.
KNOX COUNTY PUBLIC LIBRARY SYSTEM - MC
CLUNG HISTORICAL COLLECTION □ Knoxville,
TN
McAulay, Louise, Asst.Libn.
NORTHWESTERN MUTUAL LIFE INSURANCE
COMPANY - REFERENCE LIBRARY □ Milwaukee,
WI
McAuliffe, James R., Hd.Libn.
PEIRCE JUNIOR COLLEGE - LIBRARY - SPECIAL
COLLECTIONS □ Philadelphia, PA
McAvity, Margaret, Libn.
PEARSON (Lester B.) COLLEGE OF THE PACIFIC
- LIBRARY □ Victoria, BC
McAvoy, Kathleen C., Libn.
ST. JOSEPH HOSPITAL - HEALTH SCIENCE
LIBRARY □ North Providence, RI
MacAyeal, Bettina R., Libn.
CASE WESTERN RESERVE UNIVERSITY -
MATTHEW A. BAXTER SCHOOL OF LIBRARY &
INFORMATION SCIENCE □ Cleveland, OH
Macbeth, Douglas, Asst.Libn.
EASTERN MAINE MEDICAL CENTER - HEALTH
SCIENCES LIBRARY □ Bangor, ME
McBirney, Constance, Mss.Libn.
INDIANA HISTORICAL SOCIETY - WILLIAM
HENRY SMITH MEMORIAL LIBRARY □
Indianapolis, IN
McBride, Barbara L., Mgr., Info.Serv.
FOOD MARKETING INSTITUTE - INFORMATION
SERVICE □ Washington, DC
McBride, Calista, Libn.
KANSAS STATE UNIVERSITY - PHYSICS
LIBRARY □ Manhattan, KS
McBride, Donna J., Hd.Libn.
NAIAD PRESS, INC. - LESBIAN AND GAY
ARCHIVES □ Tallahassee, FL
McBride, Elizabeth A., Hd., Doc.Dept.
EMORY UNIVERSITY - DOCUMENTS
DEPARTMENT □ Atlanta, GA
McBride, Jerry, Act.Archv.
ARNOLD SCHOENBERG INSTITUTE - ARCHIVES
□ Los Angeles, CA
McBride, JoAnne, Info.Serv.Supv.
DENVER PUBLIC LIBRARY - ARCHERY
COLLECTION □ Denver, CO
McBride, JoAnne, Info.Serv.Supv.
DENVER PUBLIC LIBRARY - FOLK MUSIC
COLLECTION, FRIENDS OF MUSIC □ Denver, CO
McBride, Margaret, Lib.Dir.
PACIFIC GROVE PUBLIC LIBRARY - ALVIN
SEALE SOUTH SEAS COLLECTION □ Pacific
Grove, CA
McBride, Marjorie, Res.Libn.
DATA GENERAL CORPORATION - CORPORATE
LIBRARY □ Westborough, MA
McBride, Mark, Adm.Asst., Pub.Aff.
TENNESSEE STATE DEPARTMENT OF
AGRICULTURE - LOU WALLACE LIBRARY □
Nashville, TN
McBride, Peggy, Planning Ref.Libn.
UNIVERSITY OF BRITISH COLUMBIA - FINE
ARTS DIVISION □ Vancouver, BC
McBride, Regina, Cat.
EDEN THEOLOGICAL SEMINARY - LIBRARY □
Webster Groves, MO
McBroom, Kathleen, ILL
LAWRENCE INSTITUTE OF TECHNOLOGY -
LIBRARY □ Southfield, MI
McBroom, Linda, Bus.Libn.
WEYERHAEUSER COMPANY - CORPORATE
LIBRARY □ Tacoma, WA

McBryde, Sarah E., Rd.Adv.
DISTRICT OF COLUMBIA PUBLIC LIBRARY - ART DIVISION □ Washington, DC

McCabe, C. Russell, Archv.
DELAWARE STATE DIVISION OF HISTORICAL & CULTURAL AFFAIRS - DELAWARE STATE ARCHIVES □ Dover, DE

McCabe, Charles, Libn.
ONONDAGA COUNTY PUBLIC LIBRARY - BUSINESS AND INDUSTRIAL DEPARTMENT □ Syracuse, NY

McCabe, Gerard B., Dir. of Libs.
CLARION UNIVERSITY OF PENNSYLVANIA - RENA M. CARLSON LIBRARY □ Clarion, PA

McCabe, Linda, Lib.Mgr.
LAKESHORE TECHNICAL INSTITUTE - EDUCATIONAL RESOURCE CENTER □ Cleveland, WI

McCabe, Richard E., Dir.Pubns.
WILDLIFE MANAGEMENT INSTITUTE - LIBRARY □ Washington, DC

McCain, Diana, Book Cat.
CONNECTICUT HISTORICAL SOCIETY - LIBRARY □ Hartford, CT

McCain, Margaret J., Libn.
MAINE HISTORICAL SOCIETY - LIBRARY □ Portland, ME

McCall, Mr. Beauford, Ser.Libn.
FRANKLIN UNIVERSITY - LIBRARY □ Columbus, OH

McCall, Jean, Chf.
U.S. ARMY - YUMA PROVING GROUND - FOREIGN INTELLIGENCE, SCIENTIFIC & TECHNICAL INFO.DIV. - TECHNICAL LIB. □ Yuma, AZ

McCall, Kevin, Libn.
PATTON BOGGS AND BLOW - LAW LIBRARY □ Washington, DC

McCall, William J., Sr.Tech.Libn.
NEW ENGLAND POWER COMPANY - TECHNICAL INFORMATION CENTER □ Westborough, MA

MacCallum, Barbara, Info.Spec.
BURSON-MARSTELLER - INFORMATION SERVICE □ New York, NY

McCallum, Dorothy T., Libn.
REX HOSPITAL - LIBRARY □ Raleigh, NC

McCallum, Heather, Hd.
METROPOLITAN TORONTO LIBRARY - THEATRE DEPARTMENT □ Toronto, ON

McCallum, John, Ref./Coll.Libn.
WILFRID LAURIER UNIVERSITY - LIBRARY □ Waterloo, ON

MacCampbell, James C., Dir.
SMITH (Margaret Chase) LIBRARY CENTER □ Skowhegan, ME

McCandless, Patricia, Libn.
UNIVERSITY OF ILLINOIS - APPLIED LIFE STUDIES LIBRARY □ Urbana, IL

McCann, Claire, Mss.Libn.
UNIVERSITY OF KENTUCKY - MARGARET I. KING LIBRARY - SPECIAL COLLECTIONS AND ARCHIVES □ Lexington, KY

McCann, Gary, Assoc.Dir., Rd.Serv.
AMERICAN UNIVERSITY - WASHINGTON COLLEGE OF LAW - LIBRARY □ Washington, DC

McCann, Judy, Libn.
METROPOLITAN TORONTO LIBRARY - SOCIAL SCIENCES DEPARTMENT □ Toronto, ON

McCanna, Charlotte S., Branch Lib.Adm.Asst.
DARTMOUTH COLLEGE - SANBORN HOUSE ENGLISH LIBRARY □ Hanover, NH

McCanna, Phyllis, Lib.Supv.
GULF OIL CORPORATION - BUSINESS RESEARCH LIBRARY □ Pittsburgh, PA

McCardy, Trish, Asst.Libn.
PETTIT & MARTIN - LIBRARY □ San Francisco, CA

McCarley, Marian, Asst.Libn.
UNIVERSITY OF OKLAHOMA - BIOLOGICAL STATION LIBRARY □ Kingston, OK

McCarroll, Colleen L., Libn.
SONNENSCHEIN CARLIN NATH & ROSENTHAL - LIBRARY □ Chicago, IL

McCarron, Edward T., Dir.
ST. LUCIE COUNTY HISTORICAL MUSEUM - LIBRARY □ Fort Pierce, FL

McCarron, Judith B., Music Lib.Supv.
KENT STATE UNIVERSITY - MUSIC LIBRARY □ Kent, OH

McCarron, Mary M., Libn.
SEARS, ROEBUCK AND CO. - MERCHANDISE DEVELOPMENT AND TESTING LABORATORY - LIBRARY, DEPARTMENT 817 □ Chicago, IL

McCarter, Ed, Archv.
U.S. NATL. ARCHIVES & RECORDS SERVICE - STILL PICTURE BRANCH □ Washington, DC

McCarthy, Catherine R., Hd.
MASSACHUSETTS STATE BOARD OF LIBRARY COMMISSIONERS - PROFESSIONAL AND REFERENCE LIBRARY □ Boston, MA

McCarthy, Dan, Pres.
NEBRASKA TESTING LABORATORIES - LIBRARY □ Omaha, NE

McCarthy, Jack, County Archv.
CHESTER COUNTY HISTORICAL SOCIETY - LIBRARY □ West Chester, PA

McCarthy, Jane, Libn.
MUHLENBERG HOSPITAL - E. GORDON GLASS, M.D., MEMORIAL LIBRARY □ Plainfield, NJ

McCarthy, Juanita, Corp.Libn.
MALLINCKRODT, INC. - LIBRARY □ St. Louis, MO

McCarthy, Marcy, Libn.
ANSER - TECHNICAL LIBRARY □ Arlington, VA

McCarthy, Pat
BOLT BERANEK AND NEWMAN, INC. - LIBRARY □ Cambridge, MA

McCarthy, Paul H., Archv./Hd.
UNIVERSITY OF ALASKA - ALASKA AND POLAR REGIONS DEPARTMENT □ Fairbanks, AK

McCarthy, Susan, Ref.Libn.
UNIVERSITY OF COLORADO HEALTH SCIENCES CENTER - DENISON MEMORIAL LIBRARY† □ Denver, CO

McCarthy, Thomas R., Asst.Dir.
IRISH-AMERICAN CULTURAL ASSOCIATION - LIBRARY □ Chicago, IL

McCarthy, Thomas R., Dir.
NATIONAL YOUTH WORK ALLIANCE, INC. - CLEARINGHOUSE/LIBRARY □ Washington, DC

McCarthy, Virginia, Libn.
NEW YORK STATE DEPARTMENT OF CIVIL SERVICE - LIBRARY □ Albany, NY

McCartney, Julie, Tech.Serv.Libn.
U.S. NATL. LABOR RELATIONS BOARD - LAW LIBRARY □ Washington, DC

McCarty, K., Med. Staff Sec.
GILLETTE CHILDREN'S HOSPITAL - PROFESSIONAL LIBRARY □ St. Paul, MN

McCaslin, Michael, Coll.Dev./Tech.Serv.Libn.
DU PAGE LIBRARY SYSTEM - SYSTEM CENTER □ Geneva, IL

McCauley, Betty M., Libn.
ENVIRONMENTAL PROTECTION AGENCY - ENVIRONMENTAL RESEARCH LABORATORY, CORVALLIS - LIBRARY □ Corvallis, OR

McCauley, Carolyn S., Dir. of Lrng.Rsrcs.
OKLAHOMA COLLEGE OF BUSINESS AND TECHNOLOGY - LEARNING RESOURCE CENTER □ Tulsa, OK

McCauley, Cynthia, Libn.
U.S. FISH & WILDLIFE SERVICE - JOHN VAN OOSTEN GREAT LAKES FISHERY RESEARCH LIBRARY □ Ann Arbor, MI

McCauley, Philip F., Cur./Archv.
SOUTH DAKOTA SCHOOL OF MINES & TECHNOLOGY - DEVEREAUX LIBRARY □ Rapid City, SD

McChristian, Douglas C., Supt.
U.S. NATL. PARK SERVICE - FORT DAVIS NATL. HISTORIC SITE - LIBRARY □ Fort Davis, TX

McClain, Ardina M., Lib.Techn.
U.S. NAVY - NAVAL AIR STATION (FL-Key West) - LIBRARY □ Key West, FL

McClain, Clark, News Libn.
ORLANDO SENTINEL NEWSPAPER - LIBRARY □ Orlando, FL

McClain, David C., Hd.Libn.
BAPTIST BIBLE COLLEGE OF PENNSYLVANIA - RICHARD J. MURPHY MEMORIAL LIBRARY □ Clarks Summit, PA

McClain, Gail, Cat.
INTERNATIONAL MUSEUM OF PHOTOGRAPHY AT GEORGE EASTMAN HOUSE - LIBRARY □ Rochester, NY

McClain, Gerald M., Libn.
CITIZENS LAW LIBRARY† □ Greensburg, PA

McClamma, C., Doc.Libn.
SOUTHWESTERN UNIVERSITY - SCHOOL OF LAW LIBRARY □ Los Angeles, CA

McClary, Maryon, Cat.
UNIVERSITY OF ALBERTA - H.T. COUTTS LIBRARY □ Edmonton, AB

McClaughry, Helen C., Base Libn.
U.S. AIR FORCE BASE - LOWRY BASE LIBRARY† □ Lowry AFB, CO

McClean, Ann, Law Lib.Ck.
NEW YORK STATE SUPREME COURT - 9TH JUDICIAL DISTRICT - LAW LIBRARY □ Newburgh, NY

McCleary, G. Louise, Lib. Unit Hd.
GULF RESEARCH AND DEVELOPMENT COMPANY - TECHNICAL INFORMATION SERVICES† □ Pittsburgh, PA

McCleary, Hunter, Lit.Sci.
COLLAGEN CORPORATION - LIBRARY □ Palo Alto, CA

McCleary, Sr. Joan Ignatius, O.S.F., Libn.
ST. FRANCIS HOSPITAL, INC. - MEDICAL LIBRARY □ Wilmington, DE

McClellan, Jane, Asst.Dir.
ERIC CLEARINGHOUSE ON READING AND COMMUNICATIONS SKILLS □ Urbana, IL

McClellan, Michael, Libn.
HONEYWELL, INC. - PHYSICAL SCIENCES CENTER LIBRARY □ Bloomington, MN

McClellan, William M., Music Libn.
UNIVERSITY OF ILLINOIS - MUSIC LIBRARY □ Urbana, IL

McClelland, Margo, Libn.
ILLINOIS STATE PSYCHIATRIC INSTITUTE - JACK WEINBERG LIBRARY □ Chicago, IL

McClenaghan, Norma, Hd., Acq.Dept.
WILFRID LAURIER UNIVERSITY - LIBRARY □ Waterloo, ON

McCloat, Elizabeth, Libn.
METROPOLITAN LIFE INSURANCE COMPANY - CORPORATE INFORMATION CENTER AND LIBRARY □ New York, NY

McClory, Eugene, Pres.
ADLER (Alfred) INSTITUTE - SOL AND ELAINE MOSAK LIBRARY □ Chicago, IL

McCloskey, Brian, Adm.
UNITED METHODIST CHURCH - PHILADELPHIA ANNUAL CONFERENCE - HISTORICAL SOCIETY LIBRARY □ Philadelphia, PA

McCloskey, Richard G., Dir.
HAKLUYT MINOR - LIBRARY □ Bothell, WA

McCloud, Darlene, Dir.
MUNICIPAL ART SOCIETY OF NEW YORK - INFORMATION EXCHANGE □ New York, NY

McCloud, Mabry R., Libn.
AMERICAN TEXTILE MANUFACTURERS INSTITUTE (ATMI) - LIBRARY □ Washington, DC

McCloy, William B., Hd., Tech.Serv.
INDIANA UNIVERSITY - LAW LIBRARY □ Bloomington, IN

McClure, Lola W., Tech.Libn.
HUNTINGTON ALLOYS, INC. - TECHNOLOGY LIBRARY □ Huntington, WV

McClure, Lucretia, Med.Libn.
UNIVERSITY OF ROCHESTER - SCHOOL OF MEDICINE & DENTISTRY - EDWARD G. MINER LIBRARY □ Rochester, NY

McClure, Margaret, Automated Lib.Sys.Coord.
LTV AEROSPACE AND DEFENSE COMPANY -
VOUGHT MISSILES AND ADVANCED PROGRAMS
DIVISION - LIBRARY 3-58200 □ Dallas, TX

McClymont, I., Hd., Prime Min.Archv.
CANADA - PUBLIC ARCHIVES OF CANADA -
MANUSCRIPT DIVISION □ Ottawa, ON

Maccoll, Agathe, ILL
CANADA - CANADIAN TRANSPORT
COMMISSION - LIBRARY □ Ottawa, ON

McColley, Verna L., Lib.Techn.
GENESEE-LAPEER-SHIAWASSEE REGION V
PLANNING & DEVELOPMENT COMMISSION -
LIBRARY □ Flint, MI

McColloch, Dona, Ref.Libn.
TOBACCO INSTITUTE - INFORMATION CENTER
□ Washington, DC

McColloch, Mark, Archv.
UNIVERSITY OF PITTSBURGH - ARCHIVES OF
INDUSTRIAL SOCIETY □ Pittsburgh, PA

McColm, Dene, Hd.
CANADA - NATIONAL RESEARCH COUNCIL -
CISTI - ADMINISTRATION BRANCH □ Ottawa,
ON

McComb, JoEllen, Circ./Ref.Libn.
UNIVERSITY OF KENTUCKY - LAW LIBRARY □
Lexington, KY

McComb, Lola M., Sr.Libn.
NEW YORK LIFE INSURANCE COMPANY - NEW
YORK LIFE LIBRARY □ New York, NY

McComb, Ronald G., Hd.Libn.
CORNISH INSTITUTE - LIBRARY □ Seattle, WA

McConahey, Thomas M., Dir. of Training
ALTON MENTAL HEALTH CENTER -
PROFESSIONAL LIBRARY □ Alton, IL

McConnaughey, W. Cary, Chm.
AMELIA HISTORICAL LIBRARY - JACKSON
MEMORIAL LIBRARY □ Amelia, VA

McConnel, J. Patrick, Dp.Libn.
U.S. NAVY - NAVAL RESEARCH LABORATORY -
RUTH H. HOOKER TECHNICAL LIBRARY □
Washington, DC

McConnell, Dorothy D., Libn.
LOUISIANA STATE DEPARTMENT OF
TRANSPORTATION DEVELOPMENT - OFFICE OF
PUBLIC WORKS - TECHNICAL LIBRARY □ Baton
Rouge, LA

McConnell, Karen S., Corp.Libn.
GULF STATES UTILITIES COMPANY -
CORPORATE LIBRARY □ Beaumont, TX

McConnell, Loretta U., Libn.
AMERICAN LAW INSTITUTE - LIBRARY □
Philadelphia, PA

McConnell, Ms. Merle, Banting Res. Centre
CANADA - HEALTH AND WELFARE CANADA -
LIBRARY SERVICES □ Ottawa, ON

McConnell, Pamela, Tech.Info.Spec.
STANDARD OIL COMPANY OF OHIO -
CORPORATE ENGINEERING LIBRARY □
Cleveland, OH

McConnell, Sharon, Cur.
EASTERN KENTUCKY UNIVERSITY - JOHN
GRANT CRABBE LIBRARY - JOHN WILSON
TOWNSEND ROOM □ Richmond, KY

McConnell, Sherrill, Archv.
UNIVERSITY OF LOUISVILLE - KORNHAUSER
HEALTH SCIENCES LIBRARY □ Louisville, KY

McConnell, Sherrill, Dir., Hist.Coll.
UNIVERSITY OF LOUISVILLE - UNIVERSITY
ARCHIVES AND RECORDS CENTER □ Louisville,
KY

McConnville, Richard, Res.Libn.
MELLON BANK, N.A. - LIBRARY† □ Pittsburgh,
PA

MacConomy, Edward N., Chf.
LIBRARY OF CONGRESS - NATIONAL REFERRAL
CENTER □ Washington, DC

McCook, Katherine, Hd.
METROPOLITAN TORONTO LIBRARY -
LITERATURE DEPARTMENT □ Toronto, ON

McCool, Gary A., Educ.Ctr.Libn.
PLYMOUTH STATE COLLEGE - HERBERT H.
LAMSON LIBRARY - SPECIAL COLLECTIONS □
Plymouth, NH

McCord, Duane H., Legal Lit.Libn.
KANSAS STATE SUPREME COURT - LAW
LIBRARY □ Topeka, KS

McCord, Dr. S. Joe, Lib.Dir.
VICTORIA COLLEGE/UNIVERSITY OF
HOUSTON, VICTORIA - LIBRARY - SPECIAL
COLLECTIONS □ Victoria, TX

McCorison, Marcus A., Dir.
AMERICAN ANTIQUARIAN SOCIETY - LIBRARY
□ Worcester, MA

McCorkle, Barbara B., Cur. of Maps
YALE UNIVERSITY - MAP COLLECTION □ New
Haven, CT

McCormick, B. Jack
WICHITA STATE UNIVERSITY - DEPARTMENT
OF CHEMISTRY - LLOYD MC KINLEY MEMORIAL
CHEMISTRY LIBRARY □ Wichita, KS

McCormick, Dennis, Asst.Libn.
CAPITAL TIMES NEWSPAPER - LIBRARY □
Madison, WI

McCormick, Donald, First Asst.
NEW YORK PUBLIC LIBRARY - PERFORMING
ARTS RESEARCH CENTER - RODGERS &
HAMMERSTEIN ARCHIVES OF RECORDED
SOUND □ New York, NY

McCormick, Dorcas M.C., Div.Hd.
NORTHWESTERN STATE UNIVERSITY OF
LOUISIANA - EUGENE P. WATSON LIBRARY -
SHREVEPORT DIVISION □ Shreveport, LA

MacCormick, Kristina, Cat.Libn.
RENSSELAER POLYTECHNIC INSTITUTE -
FOLSOM LIBRARY □ Troy, NY

McCormick, Lisa L., Res.Libn.
GAMBLE (James N.) INSTITUTE OF MEDICAL
RESEARCH - LIBRARY □ Cincinnati, OH

McCormick, Maureen B., Exec.Dir.
BRITISH COLUMBIA LAW LIBRARY
FOUNDATION - VANCOUVER COURTHOUSE
LIBRARY □ Vancouver, BC

McCormick, Nancy, Circ.
UNIVERSITY OF MINNESOTA - LAW LIBRARY □
Minneapolis, MN

McCorrister, Connie, Lib.Ck.
MANITOBA - DEPARTMENT OF COMMUNITY
SERVICES & CORRECTIONS - MANITOBA
SCHOOL - MEMORIAL LIBRARY □ Portage La
Prairie, MB

McCown, Julie J., Leg.Libn.
TENNESSEE STATE LEGISLATIVE LIBRARY □
Nashville, TN

McCown, Robert A., Mss.Libn.
UNIVERSITY OF IOWA - SPECIAL
COLLECTIONS DEPARTMENT □ Iowa City, IA

McCoy, Evelyn, Libn.
ARKANSAS ARTS CENTER - ELIZABETH
PREWITT TAYLOR MEMORIAL LIBRARY □ Little
Rock, AR

McCoy, James F., Dir.
HUDSON VALLEY COMMUNITY COLLEGE -
DWIGHT MARVIN LEARNING RESOURCES
CENTER □ Troy, NY

McCoy, Laureen, Res.
DISNEY (Walt) PRODUCTIONS - LIBRARY □
Burbank, CA

McCoy, Pamela, Tech.Libn.
ADVANCED MICRO DEVICES, INC. -
TECHNICAL LIBRARY □ Sunnyvale, CA

McCracken, Beverly, Ref.Libn.
THE CLAREMONT COLLEGES - NORMAN F.
SPRAGUE MEMORIAL LIBRARY □ Claremont, CA

McCracken, John, Sect.Mgr.
FORT WORTH PUBLIC LIBRARY - BUSINESS
AND TECHNOLOGY DEPARTMENT □ Fort Worth,
TX

McCracken, John, Sect.Mgr.
FORT WORTH PUBLIC LIBRARY - BUSINESS
AND TECHNOLOGY DEPARTMENT - EARTH
SCIENCE LIBRARY □ Fort Worth, TX

McCracken, M.B., Libn.
INTERNATIONAL GAME FISH ASSOCIATION -
INTERNATIONAL LIBRARY OF FISHES □ Fort
Lauderdale, FL

McCrae, Jocelyn, Bibliog.Asst.
TEMPLE UNIVERSITY - CENTRAL LIBRARY
SYSTEM - BIOLOGY LIBRARY □ Philadelphia, PA

McCrae, Sally, Coll.Libn.
UNIVERSITY OF WESTERN ONTARIO -
FACULTY OF EDUCATION LIBRARY □ London,
ON

McCrank, Dr. Lawrence J.
INDIANA STATE UNIVERSITY - DEPARTMENT
OF RARE BOOKS AND SPECIAL COLLECTIONS □
Terre Haute, IN

McCray, Jeanette C., Assoc.Libn/Hd., Pub.Serv.
UNIVERSITY OF ARIZONA - ARIZONA HEALTH
SCIENCES CENTER LIBRARY □ Tucson, AZ

McCray, Maceo, Assoc.Libn.
HOWARD UNIVERSITY - HEALTH SCIENCES
LIBRARY □ Washington, DC

McCray, Winn, Hd.
ROCHESTER PUBLIC LIBRARY - HISTORY,
GOVERNMENT AND TRAVEL DIVISION □
Rochester, NY

McCray, Yvonne, Educ.Libn.
KEAN COLLEGE OF NEW JERSEY - NANCY
THOMPSON LIBRARY† □ Union, NJ

McCrea, Graydon, Distribution Rep.
CANADA - NATIONAL FILM BOARD OF CANADA
- EDMONTON DISTRICT OFFICE - FILM
LIBRARY □ Edmonton, AB

McCrea, Katherine L., Libn.
NESBITT MEMORIAL HOSPITAL - LIBRARY □
Kingston, PA

McCreadie, Mary, Cat.
NORTHWESTERN UNIVERSITY -
TRANSPORTATION LIBRARY □ Evanston, IL

McCready, Rayburn R., Hd.Libn.
UNIVERSITY OF OREGON - ARCHITECTURE
AND ALLIED ARTS BRANCH LIBRARY □ Eugene,
OR

McCreary, Diane M., Libn.
ENVIRONMENTAL PROTECTION AGENCY -
REGION III LIBRARY □ Philadelphia, PA

Maccubbin, Patricia G., Chf.Libn.
COLONIAL WILLIAMSBURG - AUDIO-VISUAL
LIBRARY† □ Williamsburg, VA

McCulley, Geraldine E., Asst.Libn., Tech.Proc.
UNIVERSITY OF PENNSYLVANIA - LIPPINCOTT
LIBRARY □ Philadelphia, PA

McCulley, Patricia, Asst.Dir.
BRIDGETON FREE PUBLIC LIBRARY - SPECIAL
COLLECTIONS □ Bridgeton, NJ

McCulloch, William L., Exec.Dir.
AMERICAN ORTHOTIC AND PROSTHETIC
ASSOCIATION - LIBRARY □ Alexandria, VA

McCullough, Barbara, Health Educ.
ESCAMBIA COUNTY HEALTH DEPARTMENT -
LIBRARY □ Pensacola, FL

McCullough, Beth, Pub.Serv.Libn.
SCOTT & WHITE MEMORIAL HOSPITAL -
MEDICAL LIBRARY □ Temple, TX

McCullough, Coyla, Hd., Res.Lit.Sect.
BURROUGHS WELLCOME COMPANY - LIBRARY
□ Research Triangle Park, NC

McCullough, Frances, Libn.
MERCY NORTH HOSPITAL - HEALTH SCIENCES
LIBRARY □ Hamilton, OH

McCullough, Kathleen, Hum.Bibliog.
PURDUE UNIVERSITY - HUMANITIES, SOCIAL
SCIENCE AND EDUCATION LIBRARY □ West
Lafayette, IN

McCullough, Mireille, Hd., Ref. & Rd.Serv.
CANADA - DEPARTMENT OF JUSTICE -
LIBRARY □ Ottawa, ON

McCullum, Anne, Circ.Hd.
VANCOUVER SCHOOL OF THEOLOGY - LIBRARY
□ Vancouver, BC

McCully, Nancy B., Libn.
CATERPILLAR TRACTOR COMPANY - BUSINESS
LIBRARY† □ Peoria, IL

McCurdy, Scott, Libn.
U.S. DISTRICT COURT - DISTRICT OF OREGON - LIBRARY □ Portland, OR
McCurdy, Scott M., Libn.
U.S. COURT OF APPEALS, 9TH CIRCUIT - LIBRARY □ Portland, OR
McCutcheon, Dianne, Med.Libn.
KAISER FOUNDATION HOSPITALS - MEDICAL LIBRARY □ Parma, OH
McDade, Portia, Libn.
OHIO STATE DEPARTMENT OF MENTAL HEALTH - EDUCATIONAL MEDIA CENTER □ Columbus, OH
McDaniel, George, Dir. of Res.
CENTER FOR SOUTHERN FOLKLORE - ARCHIVES □ Memphis, TN
McDaniel, James, Instr.Mtls.Cat.
CLARION UNIVERSITY OF PENNSYLVANIA - RENA M. CARLSON LIBRARY □ Clarion, PA
McDaniel, Jean, Med.Libn.
ST. MARY'S HOSPITAL - MEDICAL LIBRARY □ Enid, OK
McDaniel, Karen C., Law Libn.
KENTUCKY STATE DEPARTMENT OF PUBLIC ADVOCACY - LAW LIBRARY □ Frankfort, KY
McDavid, Michael, Mgr.
EQUIFAX, INC. - CORPORATE INFORMATION RESOURCES □ Atlanta, GA
McDermott, Anne, Libn.
LEVER RESEARCH AND DEVELOPMENT CENTER - RESEARCH LIBRARY □ Edgewater, NJ
McDermott, Margaret, Ref./Rd.Serv.Libn.
WASHINGTON UNIVERSITY - SCHOOL OF LAW - FREUND LAW LIBRARY □ St. Louis, MO
McDermott, Marilyn, Ref. & Circ.Libn.
MOHAWK COLLEGE OF APPLIED ARTS AND TECHNOLOGY - MOHAWK LIBRARY RESOURCE CENTRE □ Hamilton, ON
McDermott, Marjorie, Dir., Lrng.Rsrcs.
BELMONT ABBEY COLLEGE - ABBOT VINCENT TAYLOR LIBRARY - SPECIAL COLLECTIONS □ Belmont, NC
McDermott, Patricia M., Libn.
U.S. COURT OF APPEALS FOR THE FEDERAL CIRCUIT - NATIONAL COURTS' LIBRARY □ Washington, DC
McDevitt-Parks, Katherine, Ref.Libn.
MECHANICS' INSTITUTE LIBRARY □ San Francisco, CA
McDole, Julie A., Libn.
AVCO CORPORATION - AEROSTRUCTURES DIVISION - ENGINEERING LIBRARY □ Nashville, TN
McDonald, Ann, Bus.Libn.
C.I.T. FINANCIAL CORPORATION - BUSINESS/ LEGAL INFORMATION CENTER □ Livingston, NJ
McDonald, Ann M., Mgr.
LIBERTY MUTUAL INSURANCE COMPANY - EDUCATION/INFORMATION RESOURCES □ Boston, MA
McDonald, Arlys L., Hd., Music Lib.
ARIZONA STATE UNIVERSITY - MUSIC LIBRARY □ Tempe, AZ
McDonald, Barbara, Info.Spec.
WESTVACO CORPORATION - INFORMATION SERVICES CENTER □ North Charleston, SC
McDonald, Brenda, Hd.
UNIVERSITY OF TEXAS, EL PASO - LIBRARY - DOCUMENTS/MAPS LIBRARY □ El Paso, TX
McDonald, C., Coord./User Serv.
UNIVERSITY OF WATERLOO - ENGINEERING, MATHEMATICS & SCIENCE DIVISIONAL LIBRARY □ Waterloo, ON
Macdonald, Cameron D., Supv.
CANADIAN STANDARDS ASSOCIATION - INFORMATION CENTRE □ Rexdale, ON
MacDonald, Carol, Coord., Info.Serv.
UNIVERSITY OF REGINA - CANADIAN PLAINS RESEARCH CENTER INFORMATION SYSTEM □ Regina, SK
McDonald, Charity, Assoc.Libn.
PHILIP MORRIS, U.S.A. - RESEARCH CENTER LIBRARY □ Richmond, VA

Macdonald, Christine, Mgr., Plan. & Res.
CITADEL GENERAL ASSURANCE COMPANY - INFORMATION CENTRE □ Toronto, ON
MacDonald, Christine, Legislative Libn.
SASKATCHEWAN - LEGISLATIVE LIBRARY† □ Regina, SK
McDonald, Dana, Dir.
INDIANA UNIVERSITY, INDIANAPOLIS - SCHOOL OF MEDICINE LIBRARY □ Indianapolis, IN
McDonald, Edward, Libn.
CHARITY HOSPITAL - SCHOOL OF NURSING - LIBRARY □ New Orleans, LA
MacDonald, Elizabeth, Coord., Pub.Libs.
NOVA SCOTIA - PROVINCIAL LIBRARY □ Halifax, NS
McDonald, Eloise E., Arch. & Plan.Libn.
UNIVERSITY OF TEXAS, AUSTIN - ARCHITECTURE & PLANNING LIBRARY □ Austin, TX
McDonald, Gloria, Hd., Intl.Res.
SALOMON BROTHERS - CORPORATE FINANCE LIBRARY □ New York, NY
McDonald, Isabel, Libn.
OREGON REGIONAL PRIMATE RESEARCH CENTER - LIBRARY □ Beaverton, OR
McDonald, JoAnn, Libn.
PACIFIC COAST BANKING SCHOOL - LIBRARY □ Seattle, WA
McDonald, Lany W., Libn.
NEWS AND OBSERVER PUBLISHING COMPANY - LIBRARY □ Raleigh, NC
McDonald, Linda, Info.Spec.
AT & T COMMUNICATIONS - INFORMATION RESEARCH CENTER □ Piscataway, NJ
McDonald, Lois E., Asst.Cur.
EUGENE O'NEILL MEMORIAL THEATER CENTER, INC. - MONTE CRISTO COTTAGE LIBRARY □ New London, CT
Macdonald, Lorna, Libn.
METROPOLITAN HOSPITAL CENTER - PSYCHIATRY LIBRARY □ New York, NY
McDonald, Marie, Libn.
PROCUREMENT ASSOCIATES - LIBRARY† □ Covina, CA
McDonald, Rev. Mark, M.S.C., Dir.
MSC CENTER LIBRARY □ Shelby, OH
McDonald, Mary A., Adm., Info.Serv.
LINCOLN NATIONAL CORPORATION - LAW LIBRARY □ Fort Wayne, IN
McDonald, Mike, Asst.Libn.
VERNER, LIIPFERT, BERNHARD & MC PHERSON - LIBRARY† □ Washington, DC
McDonald, Sekiko, Prin.Cat.Libn.
YALE UNIVERSITY - EAST ASIAN COLLECTION □ New Haven, CT
MacDonald, W. James, Ref.Libn.
CONNECTICUT COLLEGE - LIBRARY - SPECIAL COLLECTIONS □ New London, CT
McDonald, William H., Exec.Dir.
INDIANA LIMESTONE INSTITUTE OF AMERICA, INC. - LIBRARY AND INFORMATION CENTER □ Bedford, IN
McDonell, Ellen, Ref.Libn.
UNIVERSITY OF TENNESSEE - CENTER FOR THE HEALTH SCIENCES LIBRARY □ Memphis, TN
McDonnell, Anne, Lib.Mgr.
KENTUCKY HISTORICAL SOCIETY - LIBRARY □ Frankfort, KY
McDonnell, Janice P., Libn.
TENNESSEE VALLEY AUTHORITY - DIVISION OF LAND AND FOREST RESOURCES - NATURAL RESOURCES LIBRARY† □ Norris, TN
McDonnell, Michael, Ref.Libn., Maps & Docs.
WESTERN MICHIGAN UNIVERSITY - DOCUMENTS LIBRARY □ Kalamazoo, MI
McDonnell, Michael, Ref.Libn., Maps & Docs.
WESTERN MICHIGAN UNIVERSITY - MAP LIBRARY □ Kalamazoo, MI

McDonnell, Robert W., Cur. of Archv.
MASSACHUSETTS STATE OFFICE OF THE SECRETARY OF STATE - ARCHIVES DIVISION □ Boston, MA
McDonough, J.E., Dir., Leg.Ref.Serv.
ALBERTA - LEGISLATIVE ASSEMBLY OF ALBERTA - LEGISLATURE LIBRARY □ Edmonton, AB
McDonough, M., Asst.Libn.
GILLETTE COMPANY - PERSONAL CARE DIVISION - INFORMATION CENTER† □ Boston, MA
McDonough, Martin P., Lead Libn.
U.S. NASA - LYNDON B. JOHNSON SPACE CENTER - TECHNICAL LIBRARY □ Houston, TX
McDonough, Mary Ellen, Corp.Libn.
DAVIS POLK & WARDWELL - LIBRARY □ New York, NY
McDonough, Richard, Career Counselor
UNIVERSITY OF MONTANA - OFFICE OF CAREER SERVICES - CAREER PLANNING & RESOURCE CENTER □ Missoula, MT
MacDougall, Alan R., Asst.Libn.
BROBECK, PHLEGER & HARRISON - LIBRARY □ San Francisco, CA
McDougall, D.B., Leg.Libn.
ALBERTA - LEGISLATIVE ASSEMBLY OF ALBERTA - LEGISLATURE LIBRARY □ Edmonton, AB
MacDougall, Frank C., Libn.
MICHIGAN STATE UNIVERSITY - EXTERNAL COURSES AND PROGRAMS LIBRARY □ East Lansing, MI
MacDougall, Frank C., Libn.
MICHIGAN STATE UNIVERSITY - HIGHWAY TRAFFIC SAFETY AND COMMUNITY DEVELOPMENT - LIBRARY □ East Lansing, MI
McDougall, Mary
CRESCENT AVENUE PRESBYTERIAN CHURCH - LIBRARY □ Plainfield, NJ
McDowell, Agnes, Selection
UNIVERSITY OF KENTUCKY - AGRICULTURE LIBRARY □ Lexington, KY
McDowell, Jane E., Tech.Libn.
RADIAN CORPORATION - LIBRARY □ Austin, TX
McDowell, Julie H., Libn.
NEW YORK STATE SUPREME COURT - 6TH JUDICIAL DISTRICT - LAW LIBRARY □ Elmira, NY
McDowell, Marie D., Libn.
U.S. NAVY - NAVY PERSONNEL RESEARCH & DEVELOPMENT CENTER - TECHNICAL LIBRARY □ San Diego, CA
McDowell, William L., Jr., Dp.Dir.
SOUTH CAROLINA STATE DEPARTMENT OF ARCHIVES & HISTORY - ARCHIVES SEARCH ROOM □ Columbia, SC
McDuffee, Diana, Dir.
UNIVERSITY OF NORTH CAROLINA, CHAPEL HILL - INSTITUTE FOR RESEARCH IN SOCIAL SCIENCE - DATA LIBRARY □ Chapel Hill, NC
McDugle, Marcia B., Per.Libn.
EASTMAN KODAK COMPANY - RESEARCH LIBRARY □ Rochester, NY
McEachern, Virginia S., Libn.
BRYAN (G. Werber) PSYCHIATRIC HOSPITAL - PROFESSIONAL LIBRARY □ Columbia, SC
Macek, Rosanne, Tech.Libn.
APPLE COMPUTER INC. - LIBRARY AND INFORMATION RESOURCES □ Cupertino, CA
McElfresh, Melvin P., Libn.
U.S. AIR FORCE BASE - KELLY BASE - SPECIAL SERVICES LIBRARY □ Kelly AFB, TX
McElgunn, J.D., Dir.
CANADA - AGRICULTURE CANADA - RESEARCH STATION, KAMLOOPS - LIBRARY† □ Kamloops, BC
McElligott, Mary Ellen, Supv., Ed.Sect.
ILLINOIS STATE HISTORICAL LIBRARY □ Springfield, IL
MacEllven, Douglass T., Dir.
LAW SOCIETY OF SASKATCHEWAN - LIBRARY† □ Regina, SK

McElrath, Andrea, Res.Libn., Med.
METROPOLITAN LIFE INSURANCE COMPANY -
CORPORATE INFORMATION CENTER AND
LIBRARY □ New York, NY

McElrath, Douglas P., Archv./Libn.
MARYLAND STATE HALL OF RECORDS
COMMISSION - LIBRARY □ Annapolis, MD

McElroy, Adriennea, Corp.Libn.
DAVIS POLK & WARDWELL - LIBRARY □ New
York, NY

McElroy, Elizabeth W., Libn.
UNIVERSITY OF MARYLAND, COLLEGE PARK -
LIBRARIES - CHARLES E. WHITE MEMORIAL
LIBRARY □ College Park, MD

McElroy, F. Clifford, Sci.Libn.
BOSTON COLLEGE - WESTON OBSERVATORY -
CATHERINE B. O'CONNOR LIBRARY† □ Weston,
MA

McElroy, Shirley, Subject Anl.
AEROSPACE CORPORATION - CHARLES C.
LAURITSEN LIBRARY □ Los Angeles, CA

McEvers, Samuel L., Res. Preservation Tech.
LOUISIANA STATE OFFICE OF THE SECRETARY
OF STATE - STATE ARCHIVES AND RECORDS
SERVICE - ARCHIVES SECTION □ Baton Rouge,
LA

McEwan, C.R., Mgr.
CANADIAN THOROUGHBRED HORSE SOCIETY -
LIBRARY □ Rexdale, ON

McEwen, Barney, Hd., Div. For Blind
INDIANA STATE LIBRARY □ Indianapolis, IN

MacEwen, G., Field Serv.
CANADA - TRANSPORT CANADA - LIBRARY &
INFORMATION CENTRE □ Ottawa, ON

McEwen, Mrs. H.E., Libn.
FIRST CHRISTIAN CHURCH - LIBRARY □ New
Castle, PA

McEwen, Mrs. Scotty A., Tech.Libn.
GENERAL ELECTRIC COMPANY - NUCLEAR
ENERGY GROUP - LIBRARY □ San Jose, CA

Macey, Barbara, Sr.Libn.
FEDERAL RESERVE BANK OF NEW YORK -
RESEARCH LIBRARY □ New York, NY

Macey, Dr. John F., Hd.Cat.
ST. VINCENT COLLEGE AND ARCHABBEY -
LIBRARIES □ Latrobe, PA

McFadden, Charles, Acq.Libn.
KUTZTOWN UNIVERSITY - ROHRBACH
LIBRARY □ Kutztown, PA

McFadden, Marilyn, Hd., Cat.
MURRAY STATE UNIVERSITY - LIBRARY □
Murray, KY

McFall, Jane, Assoc.Libn
PENNSYLVANIA STATE UNIVERSITY - LIFE
SCIENCES LIBRARY □ University Park, PA

McFarland, Mrs. George, Law Libn.
BREVARD COUNTY - A. MAX BREWER
MEMORIAL LAW LIBRARY □ Titusville, FL

McFarland, Marjorie, Libn.
SANTA ROSA MEDICAL CENTER - HEALTH
SCIENCE LIBRARY □ San Antonio, TX

McFarland, Sharon, Hd., Lib.Serv.
NATIONAL REHABILITATION INFORMATION
CENTER □ Washington, DC

McFarlane, Agnes, Libn.
MONTREAL GAZETTE - LIBRARY □ Montreal, PQ

McFarlane, Donna, Asst. Slide Libn.
YORK UNIVERSITY - DEPARTMENT OF VISUAL
ARTS - SLIDE LIBRARY □ Toronto, ON

Macfarlane, Judy, Mgr.
PEAT, MARWICK, MITCHELL & CO. -
INFORMATION RESOURCES/CENTRE DE
DOCUMENTAION □ Montreal, PQ

McFarlane, Linda, Health Sci.Libn.
SUNNYBROOK MEDICAL CENTRE - HEALTH
SCIENCES LIBRARY □ Toronto, ON

McFarlane, Reva, Res.Asst.
SHERMAN RESEARCH LIBRARY □ Corona Del
Mar, CA

McFee, Michael, Libn.
DUKE UNIVERSITY - CENTER FOR
DEMOGRAPHIC STUDIES - REFERENCE
LIBRARY □ Durham, NC

McGann, Margot, Co-Dir.
NATIONAL PUBLIC RADIO - BROADCAST
LIBRARY □ Washington, DC

McGarry, Dorothy, Hd.Cat.
UNIVERSITY OF CALIFORNIA, LOS ANGELES -
PHYSICAL SCIENCES & TECHNOLOGY
LIBRARIES □ Los Angeles, CA

McGarty, Jean, Libn.
ST. JOHN'S PROVINCIAL SEMINARY - LIBRARY
□ Plymouth, MI

McGarvin, Thomas G., Res.Asst.
UNIVERSITY OF ARIZONA - ARIZONA BUREAU
OF GEOLOGY & MINERAL TECHNOLOGY
LIBRARY □ Tucson, AZ

McGaugh, Lea Ann, Med.Libn.
MC LAREN GENERAL HOSPITAL - MEDICAL
LIBRARY □ Flint, MI

McGaw, Roberta S., Libn.
WINNEBAGO COUNTY LAW LIBRARY □
Rockford, IL

McGeachy, Jack, Docs.Libn.
NORTH CAROLINA STATE UNIVERSITY - D.H.
HILL LIBRARY - DOCUMENTS DEPARTMENT □
Raleigh, NC

McGee, Benton Carol, Med.Libn.
CENTRAL LOUISIANA STATE HOSPITAL -
MEDICAL AND PROFESSIONAL LIBRARY □
Pineville, LA

McGee, Elaine P., Libn.
U.S. VETERANS ADMINISTRATION (AL-
Tuskegee) - MEDICAL CENTER LIBRARY □
Tuskegee, AL

McGee, Joyce
RHODE ISLAND STATE DEPARTMENT OF
SOCIAL AND REHABILITATIVE SERVICES -
STAFF DEVELOPMENT LIBRARY □ Cranston, RI

McGee, Noreen, Libn.
MATTHEWS & BRANSCOMB - LAW LIBRARY □
San Antonio, TX

Mc Gee, Rosa Lee, Cur.
CLARK COUNTY HISTORICAL SOCIETY -
PIONEER MUSEUM - LIBRARY □ Ashland, KS

McGee, Sherry A., Dir., Med.Lib.
WASHOE MEDICAL CENTER - MEDICAL
LIBRARY □ Reno, NV

McGehee, Jettye, Circ.Libn.
TELEDYNE BROWN ENGINEERING - TECHNICAL
LIBRARY □ Huntsville, AL

McGeoch, Mrs. Nelson
BOB JONES UNIVERSITY - CHURCH
MINISTRIES RESOURCE LAB □ Greenville, SC

McGhee, I.
HARTFORD PUBLIC LIBRARY - ART, MUSIC AND
RECREATION DEPARTMENT □ Hartford, CT

McGhee, Ruth D., Libn.
IOWA STATE LEGISLATIVE SERVICE BUREAU -
LIBRARY □ Des Moines, IA

McGill, B.L., Mathematician
OAK RIDGE NATIONAL LABORATORY -
RADIATION SHIELDING INFORMATION
CENTER □ Oak Ridge, TN

McGill, Forrest, Dir. of Musm.
UNIVERSITY OF MISSOURI - MUSEUM LIBRARY
□ Columbia, MO

McGill, Priscilla, Lib.Techn.
U.S. AIR FORCE BASE - GEORGE BASE
LIBRARY† □ George AFB, CA

McGill, R. Bruce, Pres.
EDUCATIONAL RECORDS BUREAU - LIBRARY □
Wellesley, MA

McGill, Theodora, Libn.
EXPORT-IMPORT BANK OF THE UNITED
STATES - LIBRARY □ Washington, DC

MacGillivray, Christine, Adm.Asst.
ST. MARY'S UNIVERSITY - PATRICK POWER
LIBRARY □ Halifax, NS

McGillvray, Virginia, Dir.
TONGASS HISTORICAL SOCIETY, INC. -
ROBBIE BARTHOLOMEW MEMORIAL LIBRARY □
Ketchikan, AK

McGinn, Clint, Tech.Pubn.Spec.
GENERAL ELECTRIC COMPANY - TECHNICAL
INFORMATION CENTER □ St. Petersburg, FL

McGinn, Judy, Staff Libn.
ATHENS MENTAL HEALTH CENTER - STAFF
LIBRARY □ Athens, OH

McGinnis, H. Fran, Slide Cur.
MOORE COLLEGE OF ART - LIBRARY □
Philadelphia, PA

McGinnis, Joan, Chf.Libn.
U.S. VETERANS ADMINISTRATION (NH-
Manchester) - MEDICAL CENTER LIBRARY □
Manchester, NH

McGinnis, Kay W., Adm. & Info.Rsrcs.Spec.
LOUISIANA STATE PLANNING OFFICE -
LIBRARY - INFORMATION RESOURCES CENTER
□ Baton Rouge, LA

McGinnis, Kim, Night Supv.
MERCER UNIVERSITY - MEDICAL SCHOOL
LIBRARY □ Macon, GA

McGinty, John, Circ./ILL Libn.
UNIVERSITY OF CONNECTICUT - HEALTH
CENTER - LYMAN MAYNARD STOWE LIBRARY □
Farmington, CT

McGinty, T.P., Chf.Libn.
LTV AEROSPACE AND DEFENSE COMPANY -
VOUGHT MISSILES AND ADVANCED PROGRAMS
DIVISION - LIBRARY 3-58200 □ Dallas, TX

McGiverin, Rolland H., Hd.
INDIANA STATE UNIVERSITY - TEACHING
MATERIALS AND SPECIAL SERVICES DIVISION
□ Terre Haute, IN

McGlamery, Thornton P., Map Libn.
UNIVERSITY OF CONNECTICUT - MAP LIBRARY
□ Storrs, CT

McGorray, John, Tech.Info.Spec.
INTEL CORPORATION - TECHNICAL
INFORMATION CENTER □ Chandler, AZ

McGorty, Jacqueline W., Libn.
FLORIDA STATE DEPT. OF ENVIRONMENTAL
REGULATION - LIBRARY □ Tallahassee, FL

McGowan, Anne W., Lib.Mgr.
WYOMING STATE DEPARTMENT OF ECONOMIC
PLANNING AND DEVELOPMENT - LIBRARY □
Cheyenne, WY

McGowan, Julie Johnson, Assoc.Med.Libn.
UNIVERSITY OF SOUTH CAROLINA - SCHOOL
OF MEDICINE LIBRARY □ Columbia, SC

McGowan, Kathleen, Ref.Libn.
UNIVERSITY OF ROCHESTER - EDUCATION
LIBRARY □ Rochester, NY

McGowan, Owen T.P., Ph.D., Lib.Dir.
BRIDGEWATER STATE COLLEGE - CLEMENT C.
MAXWELL LIBRARY □ Bridgewater, MA

MacGown, Madge, Hd.
UNIVERSITY OF ALBERTA - H.T. COUTTS
LIBRARY □ Edmonton, AB

McGrane, Arlene M., Libn.
MASSACHUSETTS COMPUTER ASSOCIATES,
INC. - LIBRARY □ Wakefield, MA

McGrane, Jeannine, Ref.
JENKINS (Theodore F.) MEMORIAL LAW
LIBRARY COMPANY - LIBRARY □ Philadelphia,
PA

McGrath, Anna, Tech.Serv.Libn.
UNIVERSITY OF MAINE, PRESQUE ISLE -
LIBRARY AND LEARNING RESOURCES CENTER -
SPECIAL COLLECTIONS □ Presque Isle, ME

McGrath, Anne, Cur.
THOREAU LYCEUM - LIBRARY □ Concord, MA

McGrath, J., Lib.Cons.
TORONTO BOARD OF EDUCATION -
EDUCATION CENTRE LIBRARY □ Toronto, ON

McGrath, John R., Libn.
ASSUMPTION SEMINARY - LIBRARY† □ San
Antonio, TX

McGrath, Kathleen, Asst.Libn.
ARTHUR ANDERSEN & CO. - GENERAL LIBRARY
□ Chicago, IL

McGrath, Rev. L.W., Hd.
ST. JOHN'S SEMINARY - LIBRARY □ Brighton,
MA

McGrath, Mrs. M., Hd., Ref.
UNIVERSITY OF TORONTO - ST. MICHAEL'S
COLLEGE - JOHN M. KELLY LIBRARY □ Toronto,
ON

McGrath, Mary, Circ.Mgr.
SUNY - COLLEGE AT GENESEO - COLLEGE LIBRARIES □ Geneseo, NY

McGrath, MaryJean, Act.Libn.
UNIVERSITY OF WISCONSIN, MADISON - UNIVERSITY CENTER FOR COOPERATIVES - COOPERATIVE LIBRARY □ Madison, WI

McGrath, Patricia J., Chf., Lib.Serv.
U.S. VETERANS ADMINISTRATION (MA-Boston) - HOSPITAL MEDICAL LIBRARY □ Boston, MA

McGrath, Richard, Dir.
CROSIER SEMINARY - LIBRARY □ Onamia, MN

McGrath, Susan, Ref.Libn.
BROOKINGS INSTITUTION - LIBRARY □ Washington, DC

McGreevy, Susan, Dir.
WHEELRIGHT MUSEUM - LIBRARY† □ Santa Fe, NM

MacGregor, Douglas, Dir.
INTERGALACTIC CORP. - LIBRARY □ Salt Lake City, UT

McGregor, George, Sr.Info.Spec.
CETUS CORPORATION - RESEARCH LIBRARY □ Emeryville, CA

McGregor, Howard, Pres.
ENGINEERING DYNAMICS, INC. - LIBRARY† □ Englewood, CO

McGregor, James Wilson, Assoc.Libn., Tech.Serv.
NORTHEASTERN ILLINOIS UNIVERSITY - LIBRARY □ Chicago, IL

MacGregor, Katherine R., Libn.
VARIAN ASSOCIATES - TECHNICAL LIBRARY† □ Beverly, MA

MacGregor, Margaret E., Chf., Course Coord./Circ.
U.S. ARMY WAR COLLEGE - LIBRARY □ Carlisle Barracks, PA

McGriff, Marilyn, Dir.
ISANTI COUNTY HISTORICAL SOCIETY - RESOURCE CENTER □ Cambridge, MN

McGuigan, Milena, Libn.
METROPOLITAN TORONTO LIBRARY - FINE ART DEPARTMENT □ Toronto, ON

McGuinnes, Joyce, Dir.
NEW YORK UNIVERSITY - FILM LIBRARY □ New York, NY

McGuire, Sr. Dominica, Archv.
HOSPITAL SISTERS OF THIRD ORDER OF ST. FRANCIS - ARCHIVES □ Springfield, IL

McGuire, Michael, Ref.Libn./Comp.Serv.Coord
UNIVERSITY OF NEW BRUNSWICK - LAW LIBRARY □ Fredericton, NB

McGuirl, Marlene C., Chf.
LIBRARY OF CONGRESS - LAW LIBRARY - AMERICAN-BRITISH LAW DIVISION □ Washington, DC

McGurrin, Brian, Hd.
CANADA - CANADA CENTRE FOR REMOTE SENSING - TECHNICAL INFORMATION SERVICE □ Ottawa, ON

McHale, Jean L., Gold Info.Coord.
GOLD INFORMATION CENTER □ New York, NY

McHale, Magda Cordell, Dir.
SUNY AT BUFFALO - CENTER FOR INTEGRATIVE STUDIES - LIBRARY □ Buffalo, NY

Machalica, Sr. M. Methodia, Dir.
SLOVAK CATHOLIC CHARITABLE ORGANIZATION - SLOVAK CULTURAL CENTER - LIBRARY □ Oak Forest, IL

McHenry, Janice, Res.Libn.
AMERICAN AUTOMOBILE ASSOCIATION - LIBRARY □ Falls Church, VA

McHenry, Wendie A., Coord., Lib.Serv.
BRITISH COLUMBIA SYSTEMS CORPORATION - LIBRARY □ Victoria, BC

McHollin, Mattie, Ser.Libn.
MEHARRY MEDICAL COLLEGE - MEDICAL LIBRARY - LEARNING RESOURCES CENTER □ Nashville, TN

Machovec, George, Coord.Computer Ref.Serv.
ARIZONA STATE UNIVERSITY - DANIEL E. NOBLE SCIENCE AND ENGINEERING LIBRARY □ Tempe, AZ

Machowski, Edward J., Supv.
ST. LOUIS - COMPTROLLERS OFFICE - MICROFILM DEPARTMENT □ St. Louis, MO

McHugo, Ann, Assoc.Libn./Tech.Serv.
VERMONT LAW SCHOOL - LIBRARY □ South Royalton, VT

McHugo, Roberta, Self-paced Lrng.Coord.
AETNA LIFE & CASUALTY COMPANY - CORPORATE INFORMATION CENTER □ Hartford, CT

Macica, Linda E., Sr. Law Lib.Ck.
NEW YORK STATE SUPREME COURT - 4TH JUDICIAL DISTRICT - LAW LIBRARY □ Saratoga Springs, NY

Maciejewski, Richard, Chf.
DETROIT PUBLIC LIBRARY - MUNICIPAL REFERENCE LIBRARY □ Detroit, MI

McIlroy, N.J., Libn.
ONTARIO - MINISTRY OF THE ENVIRONMENT - LIBRARY† □ Toronto, ON

McIlvain, Bill, Adm.Libn.
OKLAHOMA REGIONAL LIBRARY FOR THE BLIND AND PHYSICALLY HANDICAPPED □ Oklahoma City, OK

McIlvaine, Betsy, Hd.Libn.
NORTH AMERICAN PHILIPS CORPORATION - PHILIPS LABORATORIES RESEARCH LIBRARY □ Briarcliff Manor, NY

McIlvaine, Paul M., Libn.
CIBA-GEIGY CORPORATION - CORPORATE LIBRARY □ Ardsley, NY

McIlveen, Carol J., Libn.
MEDICAL ASSOCIATES - HEALTH CENTER - LIBRARY □ Menomonee Falls, WI

McIlwain, William, Hd., Foreign Lang.Sect.
CHICAGO PUBLIC LIBRARY CULTURAL CENTER - LITERATURE AND LANGUAGE DIVISION □ Chicago, IL

McInerney, Gay, Musm.Dir.
BAY COUNTY HISTORICAL SOCIETY - LIBRARY □ Bay City, MI

Macinick, James W., Sr.Libn.
KINGS PARK PSYCHIATRIC CENTER - LIBRARY □ Kings Park, NY

McInnis, Lisa, Libn.
ST. THOMAS PSYCHIATRIC HOSPITAL - LIBRARY SERVICES □ St. Thomas, ON

McInroy-Hocevar, Moira, AV Libn.
TEXAS COLLEGE OF OSTEOPATHIC MEDICINE - HEALTH SCIENCES LIBRARY □ Fort Worth, TX

McIntire, James W., Dir.
U.S. DEPT. OF COMMERCE - INTERNATIONAL TRADE ADMINISTRATION - SAVANNAH DISTRICT OFFICE LIBRARY □ Savannah, GA

McIntosh, Cam, Info.Spec.
PUGET SOUND COUNCIL OF GOVERNMENTS - INFORMATION CENTER □ Seattle, WA

McIntosh, Jack, Ref.Libn.
UNIVERSITY OF BRITISH COLUMBIA - SCIENCE DIVISION □ Vancouver, BC

McIntosh, Julia E., Hd.Libn.
FEDERAL BUSINESS DEVELOPMENT BANK - DOCUMENTATION CENTRE □ Montreal, PQ

McIntosh, Letitia A., Res.Libn.
PACIFIC-SIERRA RESEARCH CORPORATION - LIBRARY □ Los Angeles, CA

McIntosh, Linda, Dir.
FAIRVIEW COMMUNITY HOSPITALS - HEALTH SCIENCES LIBRARY □ Minneapolis, MN

MacIntosh, M.J., Asst.Dir., Hdq.
CANADA - AGRICULTURE CANADA - LIBRARIES DIVISION □ Ottawa, ON

McIntosh, Nadia, Tech.Serv.Libn.
RHODE ISLAND HISTORICAL SOCIETY - LIBRARY □ Providence, RI

McInturff, Mary Jane, Med.Libn.
SCHICK SHADEL HOSPITAL - MEDICAL LIBRARY □ Seattle, WA

McIntyre, Ann H., Libn.
PLANNED PARENTHOOD OF WISCONSIN - MAURICE RITZ RESOURCE CENTER □ Milwaukee, WI

McIntyre, Ron, Film Serv.Libn.
SOUTH DAKOTA STATE LIBRARY & ARCHIVES □ Pierre, SD

McIntyre, Sandra, Hd., Inquiries
CANADA - STATISTICS CANADA - ADVISORY SERVICES - TORONTO REFERENCE CENTRE □ Toronto, ON

McIntyre, Sharon R., Libn.
JONES, DAY, REAVIS & POGUE - LIBRARY □ Cleveland, OH

McIntyre, Solange V., Renton Lib.Res. Lead
BOEING COMPANY - SEATTLE SERVICES DIVISION - TECHNICAL LIBRARIES† □ Seattle, WA

McIntyre, Susan J., Med.Libn.
MOUNT SINAI HOSPITAL - MEDICAL LIBRARY □ Minneapolis, MN

McIntyre, William A., Ed.D., Dir. of Lrng.Rsrcs
NEW HAMPSHIRE VOCATIONAL-TECHNICAL COLLEGE - LIBRARY □ Nashua, NH

McIsaac, Charles A., Dir., Lib.Serv.
NORTH ADAMS STATE COLLEGE - EUGENE L. FREEL LIBRARY - SPECIAL COLLECTIONS □ North Adams, MA

McIsaac, John, Asst.Archv.
EDMONTON CITY ARCHIVES □ Edmonton, AB

MacIver, Anna M., Libn./Adm.
COUNTY OF YORK LAW ASSOCIATION - COURT HOUSE LIBRARY† □ Toronto, ON

Mack, Anne, Hd.
METROPOLITAN TORONTO LIBRARY - GENERAL REFERENCE DEPARTMENT □ Toronto, ON

Mack, Barbara A., Acq.Libn.
SYSTEM PLANNING CORPORATION - TECHNICAL LIBRARY □ Arlington, VA

Mack, Bonnie R., Dept.Mgr./Lib.Serv.
RUSHMORE NATIONAL HEALTH SYSTEM - HEALTH SCIENCES LIBRARY □ Rapid City, SD

Mack, Debora, Asst.Hd.
ATLANTA FULTON PUBLIC LIBRARY - IVAN ALLEN, JR. DEPARTMENT OF SCIENCE, INDUSTRY AND GOVERNMENT □ Atlanta, GA

Mack, Marilyn, Supv., Info.Serv.
NEEDHAM, HARPER & STEERS ADVERTISING, INC. - INFORMATION SERVICES □ Chicago, IL

Mack, Theodore D., Libn.
PAUL SMITH'S COLLEGE OF ARTS AND SCIENCES - FRANK L. CUBLEY LIBRARY □ Paul Smiths, NY

Mackaman, Frank H., II, Exec.Dir.
DIRKSEN (Everett McKinley) CONGRESSIONAL LEADERSHIP RESEARCH CENTER - LIBRARY □ Pekin, IL

McKann, Michael R., Assoc. State Libn.
LOUISIANA STATE LIBRARY □ Baton Rouge, LA

Mackars, J., Info.Spec.
BURROUGHS WELLCOME COMPANY - LIBRARY □ Research Triangle Park, NC

McKay, Mrs. A., Libn.
ACRES CONSULTING SERVICES, LTD. - LIBRARY □ Niagara Falls, ON

Mc Kay, Ann, Staff Libn./Tech.Serv.
CENTRAL MAINE MEDICAL CENTER - GERRISH-TRUE HEALTH SCIENCE LIBRARY □ Lewiston, ME

McKay, David N., Dir./State Libn.
NORTH CAROLINA STATE DEPARTMENT OF CULTURAL RESOURCES - DIVISION OF THE STATE LIBRARY □ Raleigh, NC

McKay, Elizabeth, Dir.
NORTHERN ILLINOIS UNIVERSITY - TAFT FIELD CAMPUS - INSTRUCTIONAL MATERIALS CENTER □ Oregon, IL

Mackay, Jane, Doc.Libn.
TRINITY UNIVERSITY - ELIZABETH COATES MADDUX LIBRARY - SPECIAL COLLECTIONS □ San Antonio, TX

McKay, Kate, Copyright
NEW YORK UNIVERSITY - SCHOOL OF LAW LIBRARY □ New York, NY

Mackay, Kathy, AV Libn.
U.S. VETERANS ADMINISTRATION (MN-Minneapolis) - MEDICAL CENTER LIBRARY SERVICE □ Minneapolis, MN

McKay, Margaret, Libn.
UNIVERSITY OF TORONTO - FACULTY OF MANAGEMENT STUDIES LIBRARY □ Toronto, ON

McKay, Marion, Libn.
HAWAII STATE LIBRARY - SOCIAL SCIENCE AND PHILOSOPHY SECTION □ Honolulu, HI

MacKay, Pamela, Chf.Libn.
HURON COLLEGE - SILCOX MEMORIAL LIBRARY □ London, ON

McKay, Pamela, Per.
WORCESTER STATE COLLEGE - LEARNING RESOURCES CENTER □ Worcester, MA

McKay, Rosalie, Libn.
UNIVERSITY OF CALIFORNIA, BERKELEY - NATIVE AMERICAN STUDIES LIBRARY □ Berkeley, CA

Mackay-Smith, A., Cur. & Chm. of Bd.
NATIONAL SPORTING LIBRARY, INC. □ Middleburg, VA

McKean, Joan Maier, Chf., Lib.Serv.
U.S. NATL. OCEANIC & ATMOSPHERIC ADMINISTRATION - MOUNTAIN ADMINISTRATIVE SUPPORT CTR. - LIBRARY □ Boulder, CO

McKee, Anna Marie, Health Info.Spec.
GENERAL FOODS CORPORATION - CRANBURY TECHNICAL INFORMATION CENTER □ Cranbury, NJ

McKee, David H., Hd.Libn.
WESTERN MICHIGAN UNIVERSITY - BUSINESS LIBRARY □ Kalamazoo, MI

McKee, George, Bibliog./Ref.Libn.
SUNY AT BINGHAMTON - FINE ARTS LIBRARY □ Binghamton, NY

McKee, James E., Lib.Techn.
ALBERTA - PUBLIC UTILITIES BOARD - LIBRARY □ Edmonton, AB

McKee, Jay R., Chf.Libn.
MARTIN MARIETTA AEROSPACE - DENVER RESEARCH LIBRARY □ Denver, CO

McKee, Jean Allyson, Tech.Serv.
WEST VIRGINIA UNIVERSITY - MEDICAL CENTER LIBRARY □ Morgantown, WV

McKee, Margo, Chm., Lib.Comm.
AMERICAN ALPINE CLUB - LIBRARY □ New York, NY

McKee, Marshall, Libn./Cur. Designer
MASSACHUSETTS SOCIETY FOR THE PREVENTION OF CRUELTY TO ANIMALS (SPCA) - HUMANE EDUCATION LIBRARY □ Framingham, MA

McKee, Nancy, Hd.Ref.Libn.
CLARION UNIVERSITY OF PENNSYLVANIA - RENA M. CARLSON LIBRARY □ Clarion, PA

McKee, Ross, Dir.
MUSIC AND ARTS INSTITUTE OF SAN FRANCISCO - COLLEGE LIBRARY □ San Francisco, CA

McKee, William C., Chf.Archv.
GLENBOW-ALBERTA INSTITUTE - LIBRARY & ARCHIVES □ Calgary, AB

McKeehan, Nancy, Coord., Tech.Serv.
MEDICAL UNIVERSITY OF SOUTH CAROLINA - LIBRARY □ Charleston, SC

McKeever, Kent, Hd., Tech.Serv.
COLUMBIA UNIVERSITY - LAW LIBRARY □ New York, NY

McKeever, Virginia, Libn.
SAN RAFAEL INDEPENDENT JOURNAL - NEWSPAPER LIBRARY □ Novato, CA

McKegney, Michael, Cat.
COLLEGE OF INSURANCE - INSURANCE SOCIETY OF NEW YORK - LIBRARY □ New York, NY

MacKelvie, V.S., Dir., Lib.Serv.
CANADA - LABOUR CANADA - LIBRARY SERVICES† □ Ottawa, ON

McKendry, Brian, Supv., Tech.Info. & Rec.
HOME OIL COMPANY, LTD. - TECHNICAL INFORMATION CENTER □ Calgary, AB

McKenna, Dee, Libn.
NOME LIBRARY/KEGOAYAH KOZGA LIBRARY □ Nome, AK

McKenna, Jan, Slide Libn.
NELSON-ATKINS MUSEUM OF ART - SLIDE LIBRARY □ Kansas City, MO

McKenna, Louise, Lib.Techn./Pub.Serv.
CANADA - TRANSPORT CANADA - CANADIAN COAST GUARD COLLEGE - LIBRARY □ Sydney, NS

McKenna, Mildred A., Libn.
GTE SYLVANIA - ENGINEERING LIBRARY □ Danvers, MA

McKenney, Katherine, Libn.
BISHOP & MC KENZIE, BARRISTERS & SOLICITORS - LIBRARY □ Edmonton, AB

McKenney, Kathryn K., Slide Libn.
DU PONT (Henry Francis) WINTERTHUR MUSEUM - LIBRARY □ Winterthur, DE

McKenzie, Alice, Libn.
BROBECK, PHLEGER & HARRISON - LIBRARY □ San Francisco, CA

MacKenzie, Barbara N., Libn.
NOVA SCOTIA POWER CORPORATION - CORPORATE RESEARCH AND INFORMATION CENTRE □ Halifax, NS

Mackenzie, Cameron A., Dir.
CONCORDIA THEOLOGICAL SEMINARY - LIBRARY □ Fort Wayne, IN

McKenzie, Cheryl L., Libn.
SOUTHERN BELL TELEPHONE AND TELEGRAPH COMPANY - LAW LIBRARY □ Atlanta, GA

McKenzie, Cindy, Libn.
FLORIDA STATE DEPT. OF INSURANCE AND STATE TREASURER - DEPT. OF INSURANCE - LAW LIBRARY □ Tallahassee, FL

McKenzie, Connie, Libn.
ENVIRONMENTAL PROTECTION AGENCY - REGION VII LIBRARY □ Kansas City, MO

McKenzie, Jean, Info.Spec.
BANK MARKETING ASSOCIATION - INFORMATION CENTER □ Chicago, IL

McKenzie, Joanne V., Assoc.Ed.
INSTITUTE OF GAS TECHNOLOGY - TECHNICAL INFORMATION CENTER □ Chicago, IL

McKenzie, Karen, Chf.Libn.
ART GALLERY OF ONTARIO - EDWARD P. TAYLOR REFERENCE LIBRARY □ Toronto, ON

McKenzie, Mary A., Hd., Pub.Serv.
U.S. COAST GUARD ACADEMY - LIBRARY □ New London, CT

MacKenzie, Pamela, Libn.
CIVIC GARDEN CENTRE - LIBRARY □ Don Mills, ON

MacKenzie, Rev. Vincent, S.J., Chf.Libn.
REGIS COLLEGE - LIBRARY† □ Toronto, ON

McKeown, Patricia, Hd., Comp.Ref.
UNIVERSITY OF TEXAS HEALTH SCIENCE CENTER, DALLAS - LIBRARY □ Dallas, TX

McKerlie, Rose
BORG-WARNER CORPORATION - ROY C. INGERSOLL RESEARCH CENTER - TECHNICAL INFORMATION SERVICES □ Des Plaines, IL

McKernon, Mary L., Libn.
HUNTINGTON ART GALLERIES - LIBRARY □ Huntington, WV

Mackesy, Eileen M., Dir./Mng.Ed.
MODERN LANGUAGE ASSOCIATION - CENTER FOR BIBLIOGRAPHICAL SERVICES □ New York, NY

McKevitt, Gerald, S.J., Dir.
UNIVERSITY OF SANTA CLARA - ARCHIVES □ Santa Clara, CA

McKewen, Bill, Libn.
CAPITAL DISTRICT PSYCHIATRIC CENTER - LIBRARY □ Albany, NY

Mackey, Sr. Berthold, Chf.Libn.
ST. FRANCIS XAVIER UNIVERSITY - COADY INTERNATIONAL INSTITUTE - MARIE MICHAEL LIBRARY† □ Antigonish, NS

Mackey, Christine, Tech.Libn.
HONEYWELL, INC. - HONEYWELL MARINE SYSTEMS OPERATIONS - TECHNICAL INFORMATION CENTER □ Seattle, WA

Mackey, Rev. James M., Exec.Dir.
NATIONAL CATHOLIC STEWARDSHIP COUNCIL - INFORMATION CENTER □ Albany, NY

Mackey, Lois M., Libn.
AMERICAN BIO-SCIENCE LABORATORIES - LIBRARY □ Van Nuys, CA

Mackey, Neosha, Hd.Libn.
OHIO STATE UNIVERSITY - HOME ECONOMICS LIBRARY □ Columbus, OH

MacKianon, Merilee
BRITISH COLUMBIA INSTITUTE OF TECHNOLOGY - LIBRARY SERVICES DIVISION □ Burnaby, BC

McKibben, Bernice E., Dir.
SOUTH DAKOTA SCHOOL OF MINES & TECHNOLOGY - DEVEREAUX LIBRARY □ Rapid City, SD

McKibben, Kay, Coord., Consortium
BALL MEMORIAL HOSPITAL - HEALTH SCIENCE LIBRARY □ Muncie, IN

McKiernan, Gerard, Libn.
CARNEGIE MUSEUM OF NATURAL HISTORY - LIBRARY □ Pittsburgh, PA

McKiernan, Gerard, Asst.Libn.
NEW YORK BOTANICAL GARDEN - LIBRARY† □ Bronx, NY

McKim, L., Libn.
CANADA - NATIONAL DEFENCE - NDHQ TECHNICAL LIBRARY □ Ottawa, ON

McKinin, Emma Jean, Hd., Pub.Serv.
UNIVERSITY OF MISSOURI - HEALTH SCIENCES LIBRARY □ Columbia, MO

McKinlay, Bessie J., Med.Libn.
HAMILTON ACADEMY OF MEDICINE - LIBRARY □ Hamilton, ON

McKinlay, Bruce, Dir.
UNIVERSITY OF OREGON - CAREER INFORMATION SYSTEM □ Eugene, OR

McKinley, Alice E., Exec.Dir.
DU PAGE LIBRARY SYSTEM - SYSTEM CENTER □ Geneva, IL

McKinley, Ed
BROCKWAY GLASS COMPANY, INC. - ENGINEERING AND RESEARCH CENTER LIBRARY □ Brockway, PA

McKinley, Juanita, Asst.Hd.Libn.
STANFORD UNIVERSITY - CUBBERLEY EDUCATION LIBRARY □ Stanford, CA

McKinley, Stacey, Libn.
QUEST RESEARCH CORPORATION - LIBRARY □ McLean, VA

McKinney, Georgann, Libn.
ARKANSAS TERRITORIAL RESTORATION - LIBRARY □ Little Rock, AR

McKinney, Joanne, Info.Spec.
AVERY INTERNATIONAL CORPORATION - RESEARCH CENTER LIBRARY □ Pasadena, CA

McKinney, Keith, Libn.
INTERNATIONAL GAY INFORMATION CENTER, INC. □ New York, NY

McKinney, Margaret
BARRISTERS' SOCIETY OF NEW BRUNSWICK - LAW LIBRARY† □ Fredericton, NB

McKinney, Richard, Leg.Libn.
FEDERAL RESERVE SYSTEM - BOARD OF GOVERNORS - LAW LIBRARY □ Washington, DC

McKinney, Richard J., Resource Ctr.Mgr.
AMERICAN PUBLIC WELFARE ASSOCIATION - RESOURCE CENTER □ Washington, DC

McKinney, Shirley M., Libn.
OREGON STATE DEPARTMENT OF FISH AND WILDLIFE - LIBRARY □ Clackamas, OR

McKinney, Susan, Archv.
BALCH INSTITUTE FOR ETHNIC STUDIES - LIBRARY □ Philadelphia, PA

MacKinnon, C., Hd., Econ./Sci.Archv.
CANADA - PUBLIC ARCHIVES OF CANADA - MANUSCRIPT DIVISION □ Ottawa, ON

MacKinnon, Lila, Info.Sci./Libn.
AMERICAN CYANAMID COMPANY -
AGRICULTURAL RESEARCH DIVISION -
TECHNICAL INFORMATION SERVICES □
Princeton, NJ

MacKinnon, Marci, Libn.
METROPOLITAN TORONTO LIBRARY - SOCIAL
SCIENCES DEPARTMENT □ Toronto, ON

McKinnon, Marjorie G., Lib.Techn.
BRANDON MENTAL HEALTH CENTRE -
REFERENCE AND LENDING LIBRARY □ Brandon,
MB

MacKinnon, Mary
DOMGLAS INC. - CORPORATE LIBRARY □
Mississauga, ON

McKinstry, Donald, Sci. Adviser
TRACOR JITCO, INC. - RESEARCH RESOURCES
INFORMATION CENTER □ Rockville, MD

McKinstry, Richard, Asst.Libn., Print Bk.
DU PONT (Henry Francis) WINTERTHUR
MUSEUM - LIBRARY □ Winterthur, DE

McKissack, Connie, Circ./Media Libn.
MEHARRY MEDICAL COLLEGE - MEDICAL
LIBRARY - LEARNING RESOURCES CENTER □
Nashville, TN

McKitterick, Mrs. John
DARIEN HISTORICAL SOCIETY - LIBRARY □
Darien, CT

Mackler, Mrs. Lee, Dir., Lib. & Info.Serv.
POSTGRADUATE CENTER FOR MENTAL HEALTH
- EMIL A. GUTHEIL MEMORIAL LIBRARY □ New
York, NY

Mackler, Leslie G., Dir., Med.Lib.
CONE (Moses H.) MEMORIAL HOSPITAL -
MEDICAL LIBRARY □ Greensboro, NC

McKnight, Joyce A., Div.Hd.
AKRON-SUMMIT COUNTY PUBLIC LIBRARY -
SCIENCE AND TECHNOLOGY DIVISION □ Akron,
OH

McKnight, Michelyn, Libn.
NORMAN MUNICIPAL HOSPITAL - HEALTH
SCIENCE LIBRARY □ Norman, OK

Mackov, Alice O., Ref.Libn.
JEFFERSON (Thomas) UNIVERSITY - SCOTT
MEMORIAL LIBRARY □ Philadelphia, PA

McKown, C.J., Hd.
PENNSYLVANIA STATE UNIVERSITY -
PHYSICAL SCIENCES LIBRARY □ University
Park, PA

Mackowski, Dennis, Asst.Dir., Media Serv.
COMMUNITY COLLEGE OF BALTIMORE -
LIBRARIES/LEARNING RESOURCES CENTERS □
Baltimore, MD

Macksey, Julie, Info.Sci.
UPJOHN COMPANY - CORPORATE TECHNICAL
LIBRARY □ Kalamazoo, MI

Macksey, Susan A., Libn.
U.S. ARMY - MATERIALS & MECHANICS
RESEARCH CENTER - TECHNICAL LIBRARY □
Watertown, MA

McKula, Kathleen, News Libn.
HARTFORD COURANT - NEWS LIBRARY □
Hartford, CT

McKune, Muriel, Asst.Libn.
BEATRICE FOODS CO. - RESEARCH LIBRARY □
Chicago, IL

McLain, Donna, Lib.Cons.
PARKVIEW OSTEOPATHIC HOSPITAL -
LIBRARY □ Toledo, OH

McLain, Joyce D., Law Libn.
ALPENA COUNTY LAW LIBRARY □ Alpena, MI

McLaird, Ms. Lee N., Cur. of Collections
SIOUXLAND HERITAGE MUSEUMS -
PETTIGREW MUSEUM - LIBRARY □ Sioux Falls,
SD

McLallen, Ruth S., Tech.Info.Mgr.
PROCTER & GAMBLE COMPANY - BUCKEYE
CELLULOSE CORPORATION - CELLULOSE &
SPECIALTIES DIV. TECH. INFO.SERV. □
Memphis, TN

McLanahan, Dr. John W., Dir.
FLORIDA STATE UNIVERSITY -
INSTRUCTIONAL SUPPORT CENTER - FILM
LIBRARY □ Tallahassee, FL

McLaren, Don R., Sr.Libn.
CANADIAN BROADCASTING CORPORATION -
MUSIC & RECORD LIBRARY □ Winnipeg, MB

McLaren, Elizabeth, Libn.
B.C. HYDRO - LIBRARY □ Vancouver, BC

McLaren, Norah J., Libn.
VANCOUVER MUSEUMS & PLANETARIUM
ASSOCIATION - LIBRARY AND RESOURCE
CENTRE □ Vancouver, BC

McLaren, Phyllis H., AMA Sci.Jnls. Indexing
AMERICAN MEDICAL ASSOCIATION -
DIVISION OF LIBRARY AND ARCHIVAL
SERVICES □ Chicago, IL

McLaughlin, Barbara L., Chf.
U.S. ARMY - ELECTRONICS R & D COMMAND
(ERADCOM) - HARRY DIAMOND LABORATORIES
- TECHNICAL INFORMATION BRANCH □
Adelphi, MD

McLaughlin, Dorothy, Dir.
ARIZONA PHOTOGRAPHIC ASSOCIATES, INC. -
LIBRARY □ Phoenix, AZ

McLaughlin, Dorothy, Tech.Libn.
MOBIL RESEARCH & DEVELOPMENT
CORPORATION - ENGINEERING DEPARTMENT -
INFORMATION CENTER □ Princeton, NJ

McLaughlin, Kathleen A., Finance Libn.
BECHTEL - FINANCE LIBRARY □ San Francisco,
CA

McLaughlin, Ms. Lee R., Acq.Div.
U.S. AIR FORCE ACADEMY - LIBRARY □
Colorado Springs, CO

McLaughlin, Mary Pat, Libn. & Dir.
RAILROAD AND PIONEER MUSEUM, INC. -
LIBRARY □ Temple, TX

McLaughlin, Nancy, Pub.Info.Off.
BALTIMORE CITY DEPARTMENT OF PLANNING
- LIBRARY □ Baltimore, MD

McLaughlin, Pamela, User Serv.Coord.
ERIC CLEARINGHOUSE ON INFORMATION
RESOURCES □ Syracuse, NY

McLaughlin, Vivian C., Dir.
RESOURCE & RESEARCH CENTER FOR BEAVER
COUNTY & LOCAL HISTORY □ Beaver Falls, PA

McLaughlin, W. Keith, Hd.Libn.
ALBERTA - WORKERS' HEALTH SAFETY &
COMPENSATION - OCCUPATIONAL HEALTH &
SAFETY LIBRARY □ Edmonton, AB

MacLaurin, Corinne K., Chf.Libn.
CANADA - CONSUMER AND CORPORATE
AFFAIRS CANADA - DEPARTMENTAL LIBRARY □
Ottawa, ON

Maclay, Eleanor, Libn.
DEGOLYER AND MAC NAUGHTON - LIBRARY □
Dallas, TX

Maclay, Veronica, Govt.Doc.Libn.
UNIVERSITY OF CALIFORNIA, SAN FRANCISCO
- HASTINGS COLLEGE OF THE LAW - LEGAL
INFORMATION CENTER □ San Francisco, CA

McLean, Austin J., Cur., Spec.Coll.
UNIVERSITY OF MINNESOTA - SPECIAL
COLLECTIONS AND RARE BOOKS LIBRARY □
Minneapolis, MN

McLean, Carla B., Asst.Dir.
HUMAN RESOURCES NETWORK -
INFORMATION CENTER† □ Philadelphia, PA

McLean, Rev. Edward J., Exec.Dir.
ARCHDIOCESE OF HARTFORD - CATHOLIC
LIBRARY & INFORMATION CENTER □ Hartford,
CT

MacLean, Eleanor, Libn.
MC GILL UNIVERSITY - BLACKER/WOOD
LIBRARY OF ZOOLOGY AND ORNITHOLOGY □
Montreal, PQ

McLean, John, Dir.
U.S. NATL. ARCHIVES & RECORDS SERVICE -
NATL. AUDIOVISUAL CENTER - INFORMATION
SERVICES SECTION □ Washington, DC

MacLean, Kay, Supv., Sch.Serv.
ILLINOIS STATE HISTORICAL LIBRARY □
Springfield, IL

McLean, Lisa, Asst.Libn.
WOLF, BLOCK, SCHORR & SOLIS-COHEN -
LIBRARY □ Philadelphia, PA

McLean, Loche, Chf., ADP Sect.
U.S. ARMY - PENTAGON LIBRARY □ Washington,
DC

McLean, Dr. Malcolm D., Dir., Robertson Coll.
UNIVERSITY OF TEXAS, ARLINGTON - LIBRARY
- DIVISION OF SPECIAL COLLECTIONS AND
ARCHIVES □ Arlington, TX

McLean, Marilyn, Sci.Ref.Libn.
BOSTON PUBLIC LIBRARY - GOVERNMENT
DOCUMENTS, MICROTEXT, NEWSPAPERS □
Boston, MA

MacLean, Paul, Mng.Libn., Fraser Lib.
SUNY - COLLEGE AT GENESEO - COLLEGE
LIBRARIES □ Geneseo, NY

McLean, Mrs. S.M., Spec., Purchasing
CANADA - REGIONAL INDUSTRIAL EXPANSION
- LIBRARY □ Ottawa, ON

McLellan, Arnold, Hd.Libn.
BETHANY BIBLE COLLEGE - LIBRARY □ Scotts
Valley, CA

MacLellan, Audrey, Chf.Libn.
HUMBER COLLEGE OF APPLIED ARTS &
TECHNOLOGY - LIBRARY - SPECIAL
COLLECTIONS □ Rexdale, ON

McLellan, Mary, Legislative Ref.
MASSACHUSETTS STATE LIBRARY □ Boston,
MA

McLemare, Cindy, Asst.Libn.
MISSISSIPPI STATE DEPARTMENT OF PUBLIC
WELFARE - JEAN GUNTER SOCIAL WELFARE
LIBRARY □ Jackson, MS

McLendon, Wallace, Hd., Circ.Serv.
UNIVERSITY OF NORTH CAROLINA, CHAPEL
HILL - HEALTH SCIENCES LIBRARY □ Chapel
Hill, NC

McLenna, Evelyn K., Supv.
ATLANTIC-RICHFIELD COMPANY - ANACONDA
MINERALS COMPANY - TECHNICAL
INFORMATION CENTER □ Tucson, AZ

McLeod, A.D., Res.Dir.
SASKATCHEWAN WHEAT POOL - REFERENCE
LIBRARY □ Regina, SK

Mac Leod, June F., Law Libn.
GRAY, CARY, AMES & FRYE - LAW LIBRARY □
San Diego, CA

MacLeod, Linda, Libn.
DALHOUSIE UNIVERSITY - MARITIME SCHOOL
OF SOCIAL WORK - LIBRARY □ Halifax, NS

McLeod, Marj
BRITISH COLUMBIA INSTITUTE OF
TECHNOLOGY - LIBRARY SERVICES DIVISION
□ Burnaby, BC

Macleod, Dr. Mary K., Asst.Dir.
UNIVERSITY OF CAPE BRETON - BEATON
INSTITUTE ARCHIVES □ Sydney, NS

MacLeod, Rev. Neil A., Archv.
UNITED CHURCH OF CANADA - MARITIME
CONFERENCE ARCHIVES □ Halifax, NS

McLeod, Roger, Faculty/Photography
GEORGIA COLLEGE - MEDIA SERVICES □
Milledgeville, GA

MacLowick, F.B. "Rick", Hd., Info.Serv.
MANITOBA - LEGISLATIVE LIBRARY □
Winnipeg, MB

McMahon, Beverly A., Asst.Libn.
HARMARVILLE REHABILITATION CENTER -
STAFF LIBRARY □ Pittsburgh, PA

McMahon, Carolyn H., Libn.
NATIONAL COUNCIL OF TEACHERS OF ENGLISH
- LIBRARY □ Urbana, IL

McMahon, James P., Exec.Asst.Gen. Counsel
NEW YORK CITY TRANSIT AUTHORITY - LAW
LIBRARY □ Brooklyn, NY

McMahon, Rosemary, Cat.Libn.
COLUMBUS TECHNICAL INSTITUTE -
EDUCATIONAL RESOURCES CENTER □
Columbus, OH

McMahon, Suzanne, Info. Agent
LIVESTOCK FEED BOARD OF CANADA -
LIBRARY □ Montreal, PQ

McManimon, M. Frances, Med.Libn.
ST. JOSEPH'S HOSPITAL - SAMUEL ROSENTHAL
MEMORIAL LIBRARY □ Milwaukee, WI

McManus, Mary, Libn.
HAMILTON PSYCHIATRIC HOSPITAL - LIBRARY
RESOURCE CENTRE □ Hamilton, ON

McMaster, Deborah, Drug Lit.Spec.
WAKE FOREST UNIVERSITY - BOWMAN GRAY
SCHOOL OF MEDICINE - COY C. CARPENTER
LIBRARY □ Winston-Salem, NC

McMaster, Jane, Ref.Libn.
OHIO STATE UNIVERSITY - ENGINEERING
LIBRARY □ Columbus, OH

McMaster, Nina, Libn.
HARVARD UNIVERSITY - PHYSICS RESEARCH
LIBRARY □ Cambridge, MA

McMillan, Carnette, Acq.Libn.
MISSISSIPPI COLLEGE SCHOOL OF LAW - LAW
LIBRARY □ Jackson, MS

McMillan, Elizabeth, Med.Libn.
U.S. VETERANS ADMINISTRATION (MD-Perry
Point) - HOSPITAL MEDICAL LIBRARY □ Perry
Point, MD

McMillan, Janice, Hosp.Libn.
BRANT (Joseph) MEMORIAL HOSPITAL -
HOSPITAL LIBRARY† □ Burlington, ON

McMillan, Judith L., Ref.Libn.
HISTORIC NEW ORLEANS COLLECTION -
LIBRARY □ New Orleans, LA

MacMillan, Kitty, Libn.
NORTH AMERICAN LIFE ASSURANCE COMPANY
- LIBRARY □ Toronto, ON

McMillan, Lenora W., Chf.Libn.
U.S. COMMISSION ON CIVIL RIGHTS - NATL.
CLEARINGHOUSE LIBRARY □ Washington, DC

MacMillan, Martha C., Libn.
UNITED CHURCH OF LOS ALAMOS - LIBRARY □
Los Alamos, NM

McMillin, Carol, Ref.Libn.
U.S. ARMY - ENGINEER WATERWAYS
EXPERIMENT STATION - TECHNICAL
INFORMATION CENTER □ Vicksburg, MS

McMonigal, Elizabeth, Br.Libn.
ST. PAUL PUBLIC LIBRARY - HIGHLAND PARK
BRANCH - PERRIE JONES MEMORIAL ROOM □
St. Paul, MN

McMorrow, Kathleen, Libn.
UNIVERSITY OF TORONTO - FACULTY OF
MUSIC LIBRARY □ Toronto, ON

McMullen, Elizabeth, Mgr., Lib.Serv.
ST. PETER'S MEDICAL CENTER - LIBRARY† □
New Brunswick, NJ

McMullen, Rev. John David, O.S.B., Hd.Libn.
BLUE CLOUD ABBEY - LIBRARY† □ Marvin, SD

MacMullen, Kenneth E., Libn.
PLYMOUTH LAW LIBRARY† □ Brockton, MA

McMullen, Patricia, Sec.
SPORTS RESEARCH INSTITUTE - LIBRARY □
University Park, PA

MacMullin, Susan, Proj.Mgr.
INFORMATICS GENERAL CORPORATION - FISH
AND WILDLIFE REFERENCE □ Rockville, MD

MacMurray, A. Christine, Ed./Libn.
ANIMAL MEDICAL CENTER - LIBRARY □ New
York, NY

MacMurray, Gwen, Per.Supv.
HAHNEMANN UNIVERSITY - WARREN H. FAKE
LIBRARY† □ Philadelphia, PA

McMurrin, Jean Ann, Law Libn.
SALT LAKE COUNTY LAW LIBRARY □ Salt Lake
City, UT

McMurrough, Barbara L., Libn.
KENNEDY (Joseph P., Jr.) MEMORIAL HOSPITAL
FOR CHILDREN - MEDICAL LIBRARY □ Brighton,
MA

McNabb, Michele, Archv.Asst.
CHAMPAIGN COUNTY HISTORICAL ARCHIVES
□ Urbana, IL

McNair, Marian B., Libn.
WESTWOOD FIRST PRESBYTERIAN CHURCH -
WALTER LORENZ MEMORIAL LIBRARY □
Cincinnati, OH

McNamara, Alice P., Libn.
MPR ASSOCIATES, INC. - TECHNICAL LIBRARY
□ Washington, DC

McNamara, Charles B., Assoc.Libn.
CORNELL UNIVERSITY - RARE BOOKS
DEPARTMENT □ Ithaca, NY

McNamara, Darrell, Dir., Lib.Serv.
NORTH DAKOTA STATE LIBRARY □ Bismarck,
ND

McNamara, G.A., Libn.
MEMORIAL HOSPITAL - MEDICAL LIBRARY □
Albany, NY

McNamara, Julia I., Law Libn.
VENANGO COUNTY LAW LIBRARY □ Franklin, PA

McNamara, Kathleen, Asst.Libn.
NEW YORK STATE DEPARTMENT OF HEALTH -
CENTER FOR LABORATORIES AND RESEARCH
LIBRARY □ Albany, NY

McNamara, Martha, Ref.Libn.
SUFFOLK UNIVERSITY - MILDRED F. SAWYER
LIBRARY - COLLECTION OF AFRO-AMERICAN
LITERATURE □ Boston, MA

McNamee, Donald W., Chf.Cat.
CALIFORNIA INSTITUTE OF TECHNOLOGY -
MILLIKAN LIBRARY □ Pasadena, CA

McNamee, G.M., Bibliog. Searcher
DOW CHEMICAL U.S.A. - TEXAS DIVISION -
LIBRARY □ Freeport, TX

McNamee, Gilbert, Prin.Libn.
SAN FRANCISCO PUBLIC LIBRARY - BUSINESS
LIBRARY □ San Francisco, CA

McNeal, Kathy A., Libn.
STANLEY CONSULTANTS - TECHNICAL
LIBRARY □ Muscatine, IA

McNealy, Terry A., Lib.Dir.
BUCKS COUNTY HISTORICAL SOCIETY -
SPRUANCE LIBRARY □ Doylestown, PA

McNealy, Terry A., Libn.
EARLY AMERICAN INDUSTRIES ASSOCIATION
- LIBRARY □ Doylestown, PA

MacNeil, Bruce, Assoc.Libn./Pub.Serv.
UNIVERSITY OF WATERLOO - DANA PORTER
ARTS LIBRARY □ Waterloo, ON

McNeil, Don W., Libn.
LEEWARD COMMUNITY COLLEGE LIBRARY -
SPECIAL COLLECTIONS □ Honolulu, HI

MacNeil, Kathrine, Hd., Pub.Serv.
TEXAS A & M UNIVERSITY - MEDICAL
SCIENCES LIBRARY □ College Station, TX

MacNeil, Patricia, Libn.
NOVA SCOTIA COMMISSION ON DRUG
DEPENDENCY - LIBRARY AND INFORMATION
CENTRE □ Halifax, NS

McNeil, Stephen, Ck.
SOCIETY OF FRIENDS - FRIENDS MEETING OF
WASHINGTON - LIBRARY □ Washington, DC

McNeil, W.K., Folklorist
OZARK FOLK CENTER - LIBRARY □ Mt. View, AR

McNeill, Anne, Cur. of Educ.
CARSON COUNTY SQUARE HOUSE MUSEUM -
INFORMATION CENTER □ Panhandle, TX

McNeill, Elizabeth, Co-Cur.
COLEBROOK HISTORICAL SOCIETY - LIBRARY
AND ARCHIVES □ Colebrook, CT

McNeill, Janice, Libn.
CHICAGO HISTORICAL SOCIETY - RESEARCH
COLLECTIONS □ Chicago, IL

MacNeill, Margery, Med.Libn.
U.S. VETERANS ADMINISTRATION (MN-
Minneapolis) - MEDICAL CENTER LIBRARY
SERVICE □ Minneapolis, MN

McNemar, Dr. Donald W., Act.Dir.
PEABODY (Robert S.) FOUNDATION FOR
ARCHEOLOGY - LIBRARY □ Andover, MA

McNerlin, Elizabeth A., Asst.Libn.
DECHERT, PRICE AND RHOADS - LIBRARY □
Philadelphia, PA

McNicoll, Lise
INSTITUT D'HISTOIRE DE L'AMERIQUE
FRANCAISE (1970) - RESEARCH CENTRE
LIBRARY □ Montreal, PQ

MacNintch, Dr. John E., Dir.
BRISTOL-MYERS COMPANY - SCIENTIFIC
INFORMATION DEPARTMENT □ Syracuse, NY

McNitt, Helen, Libn.
MIFFLIN COUNTY HISTORICAL SOCIETY -
LIBRARY AND MUSEUM† □ Lewistown, PA

McNulty, Pamela A., Ref. & Docs.Libn.
U.S. COAST GUARD ACADEMY - LIBRARY □ New
London, CT

McNulty, Patricia J., Supv.
MITRE CORPORATION - TECHNICAL REPORT
CENTER □ Bedford, MA

McNutt, Eleanor, Assoc.Libn.
UNION UNIVERSITY - ALBANY MEDICAL
COLLEGE - SCHAFFER LIBRARY OF THE HEALTH
SCIENCES □ Albany, NY

Macnutt, Glenn, Lib.Archv.
SALEM STATE COLLEGE - LIBRARY - SPECIAL
COLLECTIONS □ Salem, MA

Macomber, Ann Hodge, Libn.
LOUISIANA STATE UNIVERSITY MEDICAL
CENTER - LIBRARY □ New Orleans, LA

Macomber, Sandra, Asst.Libn.
OREGONIAN LIBRARY □ Portland, OR

Macon, Mrs. James, Children's Libn.
REVEILLE UNITED METHODIST CHURCH -
REVEILLE MEMORIAL LIBRARY □ Richmond, VA

MacPhail, Ian, Libn.
MORTON ARBORETUM - STERLING MORTON
LIBRARY □ Lisle, IL

MacPhee, Duncan, Chf.Libn.
METROPOLITAN (Toronto) SEPARATE SCHOOL
BOARD - CATHOLIC EDUCATION CENTRE
LIBRARY □ Toronto, ON

McPhee, James, Search Anl.
SYRACUSE UNIVERSITY - E.S. BIRD LIBRARY -
MEDIA SERVICES DEPARTMENT □ Syracuse, NY

MacPherson, Lillian, Law Libn.
UNIVERSITY OF ALBERTA - LAW LIBRARY □
Edmonton, AB

MacPherson, Lillian, Law Libn.
UNIVERSITY OF ALBERTA - LAW LIBRARY □
Edmonton, AB

McPherson, M., Libn.
METROPOLITAN TORONTO ASSOCIATION FOR
THE MENTALLY RETARDED - HOWARD E.
BACON MEMORIAL LIBRARY □ Toronto, ON

McPherson, Marion White, Assoc.Dir.
UNIVERSITY OF AKRON - ARCHIVES OF THE
HISTORY OF AMERICAN PSYCHOLOGY □ Akron,
OH

McPherson, Mary, Ref.Libn.
UNION CARBIDE CORPORATION - CORPORATE
LIBRARY □ Danbury, CT

MacPherson, Walter S., Libn.
WESTERN MEMORIAL REGIONAL HOSPITAL -
HEALTH SCIENCE LIBRARY† □ Corner Brook, NF

McQuarie, Robert J., Dir.
LITTLETON AREA HISTORICAL MUSEUM -
LIBRARY □ Littleton, CO

McQuillan, David C., Map Libn.
UNIVERSITY OF SOUTH CAROLINA - MAP
LIBRARY □ Columbia, SC

McRae, Anne, Libn.
CONNECTICUT NEWSPAPERS INC. -
ADVOCATE & GREENWICH TIME LIBRARY □
Stamford, CT

Macrae, Georgia, Law Libn.
UNIVERSITY OF CALGARY - LAW LIBRARY† □
Calgary, AB

MacRae, Ruth, Coord.
FOOTHILLS HOSPITAL EDUCATIONAL
SERVICES CENTER □ Calgary, AB

McRaith, Sr. M. Padraig, O.P., Libn. Emeritus
CARROLL COLLEGE - LIBRARY □ Helena, MT

McRorey, Dr. Tom J., Dir.
KERR INDUSTRIAL APPLICATIONS CENTER □
Durant, OK

McRory, Mary, Florida Libn.
STATE LIBRARY OF FLORIDA □ Tallahassee, FL

Macsali, Franceska, Site Libn./Park Ranger
U.S. NATL. PARK SERVICE - ROOSEVELT-VANDERBILT NATL. HISTORIC SITES - MUSEUMS □ Hyde Park, NY

McShane, Carol Brown, Libn./Archv.
SATURDAY EVENING POST SOCIETY - ARCHIVES □ Indianapolis, IN

McShane, Stephen, Archv./Cur.
INDIANA UNIVERSITY NORTHWEST - CALUMET REGIONAL ARCHIVES □ Gary, IN

McSheehey, Bruce, Ref.Libn.
FITCHBURG STATE COLLEGE - LIBRARY □ Fitchburg, MA

McSorley, Rev. Aidan, Hd.Libn.
CONCEPTION ABBEY AND SEMINARY - LIBRARY □ Conception, MO

McSorley, Mary Jo, Mgr.
INTERNATIONAL DATA CORPORATION - INFORMATION CENTER □ Framingham, MA

McSorley, R.T., Act.Dir.
UNIVERSITY OF FLORIDA - TROPICAL RESEARCH & EDUCATION CENTER - HOMESTEAD LIBRARY □ Homestead, FL

McSpedon, Frances M., Libn.
WHITE HAVEN CENTER - STAFF LIBRARY □ White Haven, PA

McSpiritt, Margaret L., Lib.Supv.
AT & T BELL LABORATORIES - LIBRARY □ Short Hills, NJ

MacSween, David N., Libn.
CANADA - TRANSPORT CANADA - CANADIAN COAST GUARD COLLEGE - LIBRARY □ Sydney, NS

McSweeney, Audrey, Libn.
NOVA SCOTIA - DEPARTMENT OF EDUCATION - EDUCATION MEDIA SERVICES □ Halifax, NS

McSweeney, Josephine, Ref.Libn.
PRATT INSTITUTE - LIBRARY □ Brooklyn, NY

McTiernan, Miriam, Territorial Archv.
YUKON TERRITORY - DEPARTMENT OF TOURISM, RECREATION AND CULTURE - YUKON ARCHIVES □ Whitehorse, YT

McTigue, Bernard, Cur., Arents Coll.
NEW YORK PUBLIC LIBRARY - ARENTS COLLECTION OF BOOKS IN PARTS □ New York, NY

McTigue, Bernard, Cur., Arents Coll.
NEW YORK PUBLIC LIBRARY - ARENTS TOBACCO COLLECTION □ New York, NY

McTyre, Jean, Asst. Dean, LRC
LOS ANGELES TRADE-TECHNICAL COLLEGE - LIBRARY □ Los Angeles, CA

MacVean, Donald, Ref.Libn.
WESTERN ILLINOIS UNIVERSITY - LIBRARIES □ Macomb, IL

McVeigh, Roberta, Libn.
AMERICAN PODIATRY ASSOCIATION - WILLIAM J. STICKEL MEMORIAL LIBRARY □ Washington, DC

McVey, Diane Gallagher, Asst.Reg.Dir.
CANADA - STATISTICS CANADA - ADVISORY SERVICES - EDMONTON REFERENCE CENTRE □ Edmonton, AB

McVey, K., Info.Spec.
ALLERGAN PHARMACEUTICALS, INC. - MEDICAL & SCIENCE INFORMATION □ Irvine, CA

McVey, Linda, Lib.Tech.
U.S. ARMY AND AIR FORCE EXCHANGE SERVICE - CENTRAL LIBRARY AD-M □ Dallas, TX

McVicar, Ann L., Libn.
BOY SCOUTS OF AMERICA - LIBRARY □ Irving, TX

McVoy, Jean, Rsrcs.Coord./Spec.
U.S. VETERANS ADMINISTRATION (DC-Washington) - HEADQUARTERS CENTRAL OFFICE LIBRARY (142D1) □ Washington, DC

McVoy, Jean, Rsrcs.Coord./Spec.
U.S. VETERANS ADMINISTRATION (DC-Washington) - HEADQUARTERS LIBRARY DIVISION (142D) □ Washington, DC

McWhirter, David I., Dir. of Lib./Archv.
DISCIPLES OF CHRIST HISTORICAL SOCIETY - LIBRARY □ Nashville, TN

McWhorter, George T., Cur.
UNIVERSITY OF LOUISVILLE - DEPARTMENT OF RARE BOOKS AND SPECIAL COLLECTIONS □ Louisville, KY

McWhorter, Mary J., Act.Hd.Libn.
UNIVERSITY OF ARIZONA - ORIENTAL STUDIES COLLECTION □ Tucson, AZ

McWilliams, David Jackson, Dir.
PUERTO RICO - INSTITUTE OF PUERTO RICAN CULTURE - LA CASA DEL LIBRO □ San Juan, PR

McWilliams, Emilie T., Hd.
PENNSYLVANIA STATE UNIVERSITY - EARTH AND MINERAL SCIENCES LIBRARY □ University Park, PA

McWilliams, Jerry, Mgr.
UTAH INTERNATIONAL, INC. - INFORMATION SERVICES/LIBRARY □ San Francisco, CA

McWilliams, Norma, Hd.Libn.
GRACE COLLEGE OF THE BIBLE - LIBRARY □ Omaha, NE

McWilliams, Paul A., Exec.Dir.
UNIVERSITY OF PITTSBURGH - NASA INDUSTRIAL APPLICATIONS CENTER (NIAC) □ Pittsburgh, PA

MacWilliams, Sylvia E., Lib.Coord.
ST. JOSEPH COMMUNITY HOSPITAL - LIBRARY □ Vancouver, WA

MacWilliams, Sylvia E., Lib.Coord.
VANCOUVER MEMORIAL HOSPITAL - R.D. WISWALL MEMORIAL LIBRARY □ Vancouver, WA

Macy, Sharon, Libn.
ATLANTA FULTON PUBLIC LIBRARY - IVAN ALLEN, JR. DEPARTMENT OF SCIENCE, INDUSTRY AND GOVERNMENT □ Atlanta, GA

Madaire, Patricia, Hd., Pub.Serv.
CANADA - PUBLIC WORKS CANADA - INFORMATION, RESEARCH & LIBRARY SERVICES □ Ottawa, ON

Madaus, Dr. J. Richard, Dir.
NORTHEASTERN OKLAHOMA STATE UNIVERSITY - JOHN VAUGHAN LIBRARY/LRC - SPECIAL COLLECTIONS □ Tahlequah, OK

Maddalena, Betty, Med.Libn.
MERCED COMMUNITY MEDICAL CENTER - MEDICAL LIBRARY □ Merced, CA

Madden, David, Med.Libn.
U.S. VETERANS ADMINISTRATION (NJ-East Orange) - MEDICAL CENTER LIBRARY □ East Orange, NJ

Madden, Florice T., Libn.
FACTORY MUTUAL SYSTEM - FACTORY MUTUAL RESEARCH CORPORATION - LIBRARY □ Norwood, MA

Madden, Margaret E., Reports Libn.
MONSANTO COMPANY - INFORMATION CENTER □ St. Louis, MO

Madden, Sheila, Music Libn.
TEXAS CHRISTIAN UNIVERSITY - MARY COUTS BURNETT LIBRARY - MUSIC LIBRARY AND AUDIO CENTER □ Fort Worth, TX

Maddock, Jerome T., Br.Chf.
SOLAR ENERGY RESEARCH INSTITUTE - SERI TECHNICAL LIBRARY □ Golden, CO

Maddocks, Patty M., Dir.
U.S. NAVY - NAVAL INSTITUTE - REFERENCE & PHOTOGRAPHIC LIBRARY □ Annapolis, MD

Maddox, Bennie F., Chf., Lib.Br.
U.S. ARMY - CORPS OF ENGINEERS - HUMPHREY'S ENGINEERING CENTER - TECHNICAL LIBRARY □ Ft. Belvoir, VA

Maddox, Nova C., Chf.Libn.
U.S. AIR FORCE BASE - RANDOLPH BASE LIBRARY □ Randolph AFB, TX

Maddry, Josephine, Lib.Techn.
MEMPHIS MENTAL HEALTH INSTITUTE - JAMES A. WALLACE LIBRARY □ Memphis, TN

Mader, Sr. Marianne, Staff Libn.
COMMUNITY HOSPITAL OF INDIANAPOLIS, INC. - LIBRARY □ Indianapolis, IN

Madisso, Leida, Act.Libn.
CANADIAN GENERAL ELECTRIC COMPANY, LTD. - ENGINEERING LIBRARY □ Peterborough, ON

Madsen, Debora, Acq.
KANSAS STATE UNIVERSITY - FARRELL LIBRARY □ Manhattan, KS

Madsen, Maureen, Adm.Supv.
ALAMEDA COUNTY LIBRARY - BUSINESS & GOVERNMENT LIBRARY □ Oakland, CA

Madson, Judy I., Dir.
ST. JOSEPH MERCY HOSPITAL - MEDICAL LIBRARY □ Mason City, IA

Madumba, Consuelo R., Act.Dir., Educ. & Trng.
ELMIRA PSYCHIATRIC CENTER - PROFESSIONAL LIBRARY □ Elmira, NY

Mady, Johan, Libn.
CURRIE, COOPERS & LYBRAND, LTD. - INFORMATION CENTRE □ Montreal, PQ

Madyvn, Theodore, Rd.Adv.
DISTRICT OF COLUMBIA PUBLIC LIBRARY - BUSINESS, ECONOMICS & VOCATIONS DIVISION □ Washington, DC

Maes, William, Hd., Pub.Serv.
UNIVERSITY OF CALGARY - MEDICAL LIBRARY† □ Calgary, AB

Maffei, Lisa A., Health Info.Coord.
FAIR ACRES GERIATRIC CENTER - MEDICAL LIBRARY □ Glen Riddle-Lima, PA

Magavero, Filomena, Assoc.Libn.Rd.Serv.
SUNY - MARITIME COLLEGE - STEPHEN B. LUCE LIBRARY □ Bronx, NY

Magee, Donald E., Pk.Supt.
U.S. NATL. PARK SERVICE - STONES RIVER NATL. BATTLEFIELD - LIBRARY □ Murfreesboro, TN

Magee, Edith, Assignment Supv.
INDUSTRIAL HOME FOR THE BLIND - NASSAU-SUFFOLK BRAILLE LIBRARY □ Hempstead, NY

Magee, Eileen, Prog.Coord.
ATHENAEUM OF PHILADELPHIA □ Philadelphia, PA

Magee, Jane, Tech.Serv.
UNIVERSITY OF WISCONSIN, MADISON - SCHOOL OF EDUCATION - INSTRUCTIONAL MATERIALS CENTER □ Madison, WI

Magee, Patricia, Ref.Libn.
GOLDMAN, SACHS AND COMPANY - LIBRARY □ New York, NY

Magee, Robert F., Dir.
U.S. DEPT. OF COMMERCE - INTERNATIONAL TRADE ADMINISTRATION - BUFFALO DISTRICT OFFICE LIBRARY □ Buffalo, NY

Mager, John, Ref.
CLARION UNIVERSITY OF PENNSYLVANIA - RENA M. CARLSON LIBRARY □ Clarion, PA

Maggal, Rabbi Moshe M., Founder & Pres.
NATIONAL JEWISH INFORMATION SERVICE FOR THE PROPAGATION OF JUDAISM - RESEARCH LIBRARY AND ARCHIVES □ Los Angeles, CA

Maggal, Rachel D., P.R. Dir.
NATIONAL JEWISH INFORMATION SERVICE FOR THE PROPAGATION OF JUDAISM - RESEARCH LIBRARY AND ARCHIVES □ Los Angeles, CA

Maggio, Maria Tama, Dept.Libn.
JOHNS HOPKINS UNIVERSITY - WILMER OPHTHALMOLOGICAL INSTITUTE - JONAS S. FRIEDENWALD LIBRARY □ Baltimore, MD

Maghrabi, Syed A., Med.Ref.Libn.
JACKSON PARK HOSPITAL - MEDICAL LIBRARY† □ Chicago, IL

Maginnis, Ann, Lib.Dir.
CORCORAN MUSEUM AND SCHOOL OF ART - LIBRARY □ Washington, DC

Magistrale, Lynda, Educ.Serv.Off.
ONTARIO - MINISTRY OF GOVERNMENT
SERVICES - TECHNICAL REFERENCE LIBRARY
□ Toronto, ON

Magistrate, L.A., Mgr., Bus.Onfo.
OLIN CORPORATION - BUSINESS
INFORMATION CENTER □ Stamford, CT

Magleby, James H., Dir.
AMERICAN ACADEMY OF PSYCHOTHERAPISTS
- TAPE LIBRARY □ Salt Lake City, UT

Maglione, Louise, Dir.
MASSACHUSETTS AUDUBON SOCIETY -
HATHEWAY RESOURCE CENTER □ Lincoln, MA

Magliozzi, Ronald S., Asst. to Supv.
MUSEUM OF MODERN ART - FILM STUDY
CENTER □ New York, NY

Magnaghi, Dr. Russell, Archv.
NATIONAL SKI HALL OF FAME AND MUSEUM -
ROLAND PALMEDO NATIONAL SKI LIBRARY □
Ishpeming, MI

Magnuson, Norris, Dir.
BETHEL THEOLOGICAL SEMINARY - RESOURCE
CENTER □ St. Paul, MN

Magnusson, Jan, Corp.Libn.
WASHINGTON GAS LIGHT COMPANY -
CORPORATE LIBRARY† □ Springfield, VA

Magoon, Charles, Dir. of Res.
UNITED FRESH FRUIT AND VEGETABLE
ASSOCIATION - LIBRARY □ Alexandria, VA

Magoun, Faith, Archv./Dir.
LYNN HISTORICAL SOCIETY/MUSEUM -
LIBRARY □ Lynn, MA

Maguire, Maureen, Libn.
HURONIA REGIONAL CENTRE - LIBRARY □
Orillia, ON

Maguire, Patricia, Spec.
UNIVERSITY OF WISCONSIN, GREEN BAY -
WOMEN'S EDUCATIONAL PROGRAMS -
WOMEN'S STUDIES RESOURCE LIBRARY □
Green Bay, WI

Maguire, Shirley, Div.Libn.
GENERAL DYNAMICS CORPORATION - LAND
SYSTEMS DIVISION - TECHNICAL LIBRARY □
Warren, MI

Mah, Jeffery, Asst.Chf.Libn.
BECHTEL - CENTRAL LIBRARY □ San Francisco,
CA

Mahaffey, Fred T., Exec.Dir.
NATIONAL ASSOCIATION OF BOARDS OF
PHARMACY - LIBRARY □ Chicago, IL

Mahalingam, Mr. V., Tech.Serv.Libn.
QUEEN'S UNIVERSITY AT KINGSTON -
BRACKEN LIBRARY □ Kingston, ON

Mahan, Ruth, State Libn.
NORTH DAKOTA STATE LIBRARY □ Bismarck,
ND

Mahanand, Marilyn E., Cur.
HOWARD UNIVERSITY - CHANNING POLLOCK
THEATRE COLLECTION □ Washington, DC

Mahaney, Pamela A., Libn.
SUN LIFE ASSURANCE COMPANY OF CANADA -
REFERENCE LIBRARY □ Wellesley Hills, MA

Mahant, Sarika, Supv., Info.Sys.Adm.
AMERICAN EXPRESS COMPANY - PSD
TECHNICAL INFORMATION CENTER □ New
York, NY

Mahar, Brenda, Hd., ILL
UNIVERSITY OF TEXAS HEALTH SCIENCE
CENTER, DALLAS - LIBRARY □ Dallas, TX

Mahar, Ellen P., Libn.
COVINGTON AND BURLING - LIBRARY □
Washington, DC

Mahard, Martha R., Assoc.Cur.
HARVARD UNIVERSITY - THEATRE
COLLECTION □ Cambridge, MA

Mahe, Jean Claude, Distribution Rep.
CANADA - NATIONAL FILM BOARD OF CANADA
- EDMONTON DISTRICT OFFICE - FILM
LIBRARY □ Edmonton, AB

Maher, Beth, Tech. Indexer
STANDARD OIL COMPANY OF OHIO -
CORPORATE ENGINEERING LIBRARY □
Cleveland, OH

Maher, Catherine A., Sr. Law Lib.Ck.
NEW YORK STATE SUPREME COURT - 9TH
JUDICIAL DISTRICT - JOSEPH F. BARNARD
MEMORIAL LAW LIBRARY ASSOCIATION □
Poughkeepsie, NY

Maher, James B., Libn.
BROOKS INSTITUTE OF PHOTOGRAPHY -
LIBRARY □ Santa Barbara, CA

Maher, James F., Libn.
U.S. NASA - AMES RESEARCH CENTER -
DRYDEN FLIGHT RESEARCH FACILITY -
LIBRARY □ Edwards, CA

Maher, Marianne, Acq.Libn.
WAYNE STATE UNIVERSITY - ARTHUR NEEF
LAW LIBRARY □ Detroit, MI

Maher, Priscilla, Asst.Libn.
AMERICAN SOCIETY OF ABDOMINAL
SURGEONS - DONALD COLLINS MEMORIAL
LIBRARY □ Melrose, MA

Mahon, Cornelia E., Law Libn.
NEW YORK TELEPHONE COMPANY - LEGAL
DEPARTMENT LIBRARY □ New York, NY

Mahoney, Katherine L., Libn.
CANADA - CANADIAN WILDLIFE SERVICE -
ONTARIO REGION LIBRARY† □ Ottawa, ON

Mahoney, Margaret, Libn.
MASSACHUSETTS INSTITUTE OF TECHNOLOGY
- ENVIRONMENTAL MEDICAL SERVICE -
LIBRARY □ Cambridge, MA

Mahoney, Ronald J., Hd.
CALIFORNIA STATE UNIVERSITY, FRESNO -
HENRY MADDEN LIBRARY - DEPARTMENT OF
SPECIAL COLLECTIONS □ Fresno, CA

Mahony, Doris M., Ref.Libn.
UNIVERSITY OF MICHIGAN - ALFRED
TAUBMAN MEDICAL LIBRARY □ Ann Arbor, MI

Mahony-Plummer, Jill, Ref.Libn.
DALHOUSIE UNIVERSITY - LAW LIBRARY □
Halifax, NS

Maiara, Ann L., Libn.
INTERNATIONAL UNION OF OPERATING
ENGINEERS TRAINING CENTER - LOCAL 68,
68A, 68B - LIBRARY □ West Caldwell, NJ

Maier, Charles, Archv.
YUKON TERRITORY - DEPARTMENT OF
TOURISM, RECREATION AND CULTURE -
YUKON ARCHIVES □ Whitehorse, YT

Maier, Martha S., Lib.Dir.
SWAIN SCHOOL OF DESIGN - LIBRARY □ New
Bedford, MA

Maier, Rita S., Lib.Dir.
BOOTH MEMORIAL MEDICAL CENTER - HEALTH
EDUCATION LIBRARY □ Flushing, NY

Maier, Virginia L., Libn.
DU PONT DE NEMOURS (E.I.) & COMPANY, INC.
- MARSHALL LABORATORY LIBRARY □
Philadelphia, PA

Mailhot, Denise, Libn.
ORDRE DES INFIRMIERES ET DES INFIRMIERS
DU QUEBEC - CENTRE DE DOCUMENTATION† □
Montreal, PQ

Mailloux, Elizabeth N., Mgr.
MOBIL RESEARCH & DEVELOPMENT
CORPORATION - ENGINEERING DEPARTMENT -
INFORMATION CENTER □ Princeton, NJ

Mailloux, Noel, Dir./Prof. Emeritus
CENTRE DE RECHERCHES EN RELATIONS
HUMAINES - BIBLIOTHEQUE □ Montreal, PQ

Main, Mrs. Carl, Libn.
OHIO GENEALOGICAL SOCIETY - LIBRARY □
Mansfield, OH

Main, Mrs. Gale, Libn.
PARKER MEMORIAL BAPTIST CHURCH -
LIBRARY† □ Anniston, AL

Main, Julia, Libn.
MC GILL UNIVERSITY - ALLAN MEMORIAL
INSTITUTE OF PSYCHIATRY - LIBRARY □
Montreal, PQ

Maina, William, Asst.Dir., Pub.Serv.
UNIVERSITY OF TEXAS HEALTH SCIENCE
CENTER, DALLAS - LIBRARY □ Dallas, TX

Mains, Brian, Slide/Media Cur.
PARSONS SCHOOL OF DESIGN - OTIS ART
INSTITUTE - LIBRARY □ Los Angeles, CA

Mains, Cheryl M. Ronning, Libn.
CANADA - AGRICULTURE CANADA - RESEARCH
STATION, LETHBRIDGE - LIBRARY □ Lethbridge,
AB

Maisch, Ursula, Libn.
GOETHE INSTITUTE - LIBRARY □ San Francisco,
CA

Majcher, Michael D., Mgr., Tech.Info.Ctr.
XEROX CORPORATION - TECHNICAL
INFORMATION CENTER □ Webster, NY

Mak, Loretta, Libn.
HELLER, EHRMAN, WHITE & MC AULIFFE -
LIBRARY† □ San Francisco, CA

Makar, Ragai N., Libn.
UNIVERSITY OF UTAH - MIDDLE EAST LIBRARY
□ Salt Lake City, UT

Makela, Helen M., Info.Rsrcs.Coord.
THE AUSTIN COMPANY - LIBRARY □ Cleveland,
OH

Makepeace, Peggy H., Libn.
MURPHY OIL USA, INC. - LIBRARY □ El Dorado,
AR

Maki, G.W., Hd.Libn.
CONFEDERATION COLLEGE OF APPLIED ARTS &
TECHNOLOGY - RESOURCE CENTRE □ Thunder
Bay, ON

Makino, Yasuko, East Asian Cat.
UNIVERSITY OF ILLINOIS - ASIAN LIBRARY □
Urbana, IL

Maksymonko, Philip, Ref.Libn.
ILLINOIS INSTITUTE OF TECHNOLOGY -
CHICAGO KENT LAW SCHOOL - LIBRARY† □
Chicago, IL

Maksymowych, Anna, Spec.Coll.Libn.
MANOR JUNIOR COLLEGE - BASILEIAD
LIBRARY - SPECIAL COLLECTIONS □
Jenkintown, PA

Malach, Mrs. J., Hd., Tech.Proc.
CANADA - NATIONAL DEFENCE - FORT
FRONTENAC LIBRARY □ Kingston, ON

Malakoff, Diane, Info.Spec.
CPC INTERNATIONAL - BEST FOODS
RESEARCH CENTER - INFORMATION CENTER □
Union, NJ

Malamud, Edith, Circ.Libn.
WORLD AFFAIRS COUNCIL OF NORTHERN
CALIFORNIA - LIBRARY □ San Francisco, CA

Malamud, Judie, Asst.Libn., Pub.Serv.
UNIVERSITY OF PENNSYLVANIA - BIOMEDICAL
LIBRARY □ Philadelphia, PA

Malcolm, Carol, Libn.
AIRD & BERLIS - LAW LIBRARY □ Toronto, ON

Malden, Joyce, Libn.
CHICAGO MUNICIPAL REFERENCE LIBRARY □
Chicago, IL

Malec, Paul, Electronic Media Sys.Mgr.
UNIVERSITY OF MARYLAND, COLLEGE PARK -
LIBRARIES NONPRINT MEDIA SERVICES □
College Park, MD

Malecki, Virginia, Libn.
UTICA OBSERVER DISPATCH & UTICA DAILY
PRESS - LIBRARY† □ Utica, NY

Malik, Jane, Ref.Libn.
FOUNDATION CENTER - NEW YORK - LIBRARY
□ New York, NY

Malisheski, Linda M., Libn./Sec.
CONTINENTAL CARBON COMPANY -
TECHNICAL LIBRARY† □ Houston, TX

Malison, Louise, AV Techn.
CONESTOGA COLLEGE OF APPLIED ARTS &
TECHNOLOGY, GUELPH CENTRE - HEALTH
SCIENCES DIV. LEARNING RESOURCE CENTRE
□ Guelph, ON

Malkin, Mrs. Audree, Libn.
UNIVERSITY OF CALIFORNIA, LOS ANGELES -
THEATER ARTS LIBRARY □ Los Angeles, CA

Malkowski, Eugene, Acq.Libn.
U.S. SOCIAL SECURITY ADMINISTRATION -
LIBRARY INFORMATION & GRAPHICS
SERVICES BRANCH □ Baltimore, MD

Mallach, Stanley, Bibliog.
UNIVERSITY OF WISCONSIN, MILWAUKEE -
MORRIS FROMKIN MEMORIAL COLLECTION □
Milwaukee, WI

Mallery, Eula, Hd., Tech.Serv.
U.S. ARMY SOLDIER SUPPORT CENTER - MAIN
LIBRARY† □ Ft. Benjamin Harrison, IN

Mallery, Mary S., Regional Libn.
WESTERN MARYLAND PUBLIC LIBRARIES -
REGIONAL LIBRARY □ Hagerstown, MD

Mallett, Dana D., Corp.Libn.
BDM CORPORATION - CORPORATE LIBRARY □
McLean, VA

Mallette, Danielle, Ref.Libn.
UNIVERSITE DU QUEBEC A MONTREAL -
BIBLIOTHEQUE DES SCIENCES DE
L'EDUCATION □ Montreal, PQ

Mallick, Jerry, Cat./Adm.
NATIONAL GALLERY OF ART - PHOTOGRAPHIC
ARCHIVES □ Washington, DC

Mallison, Irene K., Hd., Sci.Dept.
EMORY UNIVERSITY - SCIENCE LIBRARY† □
Atlanta, GA

Mallon, Connie, Asst.Libn.
MARINE ENVIRONMENTAL SCIENCES
CONSORTIUM - LIBRARY □ Dauphin Island, AL

Mallon, Capt. N.F., Hon.Libn.
ROYAL CANADIAN MILITARY INSTITUTE -
LIBRARY □ Toronto, ON

Mallory, Carlyle, Ref.Libn.
MARSHALL UNIVERSITY - SCHOOL OF
MEDICINE - HEALTH SCIENCE LIBRARIES □
Huntington, WV

Mallos, Diane, Slide Libn.
SMITHSONIAN INSTITUTION - NATIONAL
MUSEUM OF AMERICAN ART - OFFICE OF
VISUAL RSRCS. - SLIDE/PHOTOGRAPH
ARCHIVE □ Washington, DC

Malloy, Lois
UNIVERSITY OF CALIFORNIA, RIVERSIDE -
EDUCATION SERVICES LIBRARY □ Riverside,
CA

Malmgren, Terri L., Libn., UCDMC
UNIVERSITY OF CALIFORNIA, DAVIS - HEALTH
SCIENCES LIBRARY □ Davis, CA

Malmgren, Terri L., Libn.
UNIVERSITY OF CALIFORNIA, DAVIS -
MEDICAL CENTER LIBRARY □ Sacramento, CA

Malone, Jacqueline, Asst.Libn.
E.F. HUTTON & COMPANY, INC. - RESEARCH
LIBRARY □ New York, NY

Malone, Kyle, Ref.Libn.
UNITED STATES INFORMATION SERVICE -
LIBRARY SERVICE □ Ottawa, ON

Malone, Robert, Libn.
U.S. NAVY - NAVAL AIR PROPULSION CENTER -
TECHNICAL LIBRARY □ Trenton, NJ

Maloney, Edmund P., Circ.Libn.
FORDHAM UNIVERSITY - MULCAHY SCIENCE
LIBRARY □ Bronx, NY

Maloney, Joe, Info.Sys.Anl.
SANDIA NATIONAL LABORATORIES -
TECHNICAL LIBRARY □ Albuquerque, NM

Maloney, Juanita, Lib.Asst.
OREGON STATE DEPARTMENT OF EDUCATION
- RESOURCE/DISSEMINATION CENTER □
Salem, OR

Maloney, Margaret Crawford, Hd.
TORONTO PUBLIC LIBRARY - CANADIANA
COLLECTION OF CHILDREN'S BOOKS □ Toronto,
ON

Maloney, Margaret Crawford, Hd.
TORONTO PUBLIC LIBRARY - LILLIAN H. SMITH
COLLECTION OF CHILDREN'S BOOKS □ Toronto,
ON

Maloney, Margaret Crawford, Hd.
TORONTO PUBLIC LIBRARY - OSBORNE
COLLECTION OF EARLY CHILDREN'S BOOKS □
Toronto, ON

Maloney, Sean, Ref.Coord.
FROSTBURG STATE COLLEGE - LIBRARY □
Frostburg, MD

Maloy, Robert, Dir.
SMITHSONIAN INSTITUTION LIBRARIES □
Washington, DC

Malson, Grace H., Asst.Libn.
UNIVERSITY OF WASHINGTON - BUSINESS
ADMINISTRATION LIBRARY □ Seattle, WA

Maltby, Dr. William, Exec.Dir.
CENTER FOR REFORMATION RESEARCH -
LIBRARY □ St. Louis, MO

Maluchnik, Kathryn, Libn.
RIVERSIDE HOSPITAL - SARAH AND JULIUS
STEINBERG MEMORIAL LIBRARY □ Toledo, OH

Malumphy, Sharon M., Corp.Libn.
OHIO EDISON COMPANY - CORPORATE
LIBRARY □ Akron, OH

Malyk, M., Libn.
CANADA - AGRICULTURE CANADA - RESEARCH
STATION, WINNIPEG - LIBRARY† □ Winnipeg,
MB

Mamchur, Natalie J., Mgr., Lib.Res.
RCA CORPORATION - ENGINEERING LIBRARY†
□ Moorestown, NJ

Mamdani, Zenny, Engr.Adm.Asst.
TRICO-KOBE, INC. - ENGINEERING LIBRARY □
Huntington Park, CA

Mamos, Dorothy, Assoc.Libn.
DIGITAL EQUIPMENT CORPORATION - SPIT
BROOK LIBRARY □ Nashua, NH

Mamoulides, Aphrodite, Lib.Supv.
SHELL DEVELOPMENT COMPANY - BELLAIRE
RESEARCH CENTER LIBRARY □ Houston, TX

Managhan, Peter, Staff Libn.
ALBERTA HOSPITAL PONOKA - AHP LIBRARY □
Ponoka, AB

Manahan, Roger S., Libn.
WORCESTER HAHNEMANN HOSPITAL -
MEDICAL LIBRARY □ Worcester, MA

Manahan, Roger S., Libn.
WORCESTER HAHNEMANN HOSPITAL - SCHOOL
OF NURSING LIBRARY □ Worcester, MA

Manaley, Shirley K., Libn.
IBM CORPORATION - SYSTEMS TECHNOLOGY
DIVISION - LIBRARY □ Endicott, NY

Manarin, Dr. Louis H., State Archv.
VIRGINIA STATE LIBRARY □ Richmond, VA

Manbeck, John B., Archv.
KINGSBOROUGH COMMUNITY COLLEGE -
KINGSBOROUGH HISTORICAL SOCIETY† □
Brooklyn, NY

Mancevice, Mark F., Dir., Resource Ctr.
NEW ENGLAND TELEPHONE LEARNING CENTER
- RESOURCE CENTER† □ Marlborough, MA

Manchesi, John, Corp.Info.Spec.
CRAVATH, SWAINE, & MOORE - LAW LIBRARY
□ New York, NY

Mancina, Elaine, Chf.Libn.
DOUGLAS HOSPITAL CENTRE - STAFF LIBRARY
□ Montreal, PQ

Mancini, John F., Exec.Dir.
FOUNDATION FOR PUBLIC AFFAIRS -
RESOURCE CENTER □ Washington, DC

Mandel, Audrey S., Res.
LAMALIE ASSOCIATES, INC. - RESEARCH
DEPARTMENT □ Tampa, FL

Mandel, Carol A., Asst.Univ.Libn.
UNIVERSITY OF CALIFORNIA, SAN DIEGO -
UNIVERSITY LIBRARIES □ La Jolla, CA

Mandel, Ruth B., Dir.
CENTER FOR THE AMERICAN WOMAN &
POLITICS - LIBRARY □ New Brunswick, NJ

Mandel, Tobyann, Libn.
HUGHES AIRCRAFT COMPANY - HUGHES
RESEARCH LABORATORIES LIBRARY □ Malibu,
CA

Mandelman, Ellen, Libn.
CONGREGATION SHALOM - SHERMAN PASTOR
MEMORIAL LIBRARY □ Milwaukee, WI

Manderscheid, Dorothy, Sci.Libn.
MICHIGAN STATE UNIVERSITY - SCIENCE
LIBRARY □ East Lansing, MI

Mandeville, Mrs. Andree N., Libn.
CENTRE HOSPITALIER DE VERDUN -
BIBLIOTHEQUE MEDICALE □ Verdun, PQ

Mandeville, Joanne, Libn.
CRANE COMPANY - HYDRO-AIRE DIVISION -
TECHNICAL LIBRARY □ Burbank, CA

Mandikos, George J., Tech.Dir.
AMERICAN ASSOCIATION OF TEXTILE
CHEMISTS AND COLORISTS - LIBRARY □
Research Triangle Park, NC

Mandracchia, James, Libn.
AKIN HALL ASSOCIATION - AKIN FREE
LIBRARY □ Pawling, NY

Maney, James, Lib.Dir.
OBLATE SCHOOL OF THEOLOGY - LIBRARY □
San Antonio, TX

Maney, Marilyn E., Hd.Libn.
WILLKIE FARR & GALLAGHER - LIBRARY □ New
York, NY

Mang, Jeff, Leg.Libn.
HOGAN & HARTSON - LIBRARY □ Washington,
DC

Mangibuyat, Lydia, Sr.Res.Asst.
BANK OF AMERICA - TECHNOLOGY LIBRARY -
3099 B □ San Francisco, CA

Mangieri, C.N., Dir.
SOUTH MOUNTAIN LABORATORIES, INC. -
LIBRARY □ South Orange, NJ

Mangimeli, John A., Park Techn.
U.S. NATL. PARK SERVICE - MOUND CITY
GROUP NATL. MONUMENT - LIBRARY □
Chillicothe, OH

Mangion, Barbara E., Libn.
BIRD MACHINE COMPANY, INC. - LIBRARY □
South Walpole, MA

Mangravite, Mary Ann, Mgr., Jrnl. Liaison
INSTITUTE FOR SCIENTIFIC INFORMATION □
Philadelphia, PA

Mangum, Neil C., Park Hist.
U.S. NATL. PARK SERVICE - CUSTER
BATTLEFIELD NATL. MONUMENT - LIBRARY □
Crow Agency, MT

Mangus, Anne, Libn.
PRO FOOTBALL HALL OF FAME - LIBRARY/
RESEARCH CENTER □ Canton, OH

Manheim, Theodore, Hd.
WAYNE STATE UNIVERSITY - EDUCATION
LIBRARY □ Detroit, MI

Maniece, Olivia S., Chf.Libn.
U.S. VETERANS ADMINISTRATION (AL-
Tuscaloosa) - HOSPITAL MEDICAL LIBRARY □
Tuscaloosa, AL

Manilla, Dr. George T.
ELKO MEDICAL CLINIC - LIBRARY □ Elko, NV

Manion, Martha L., Libn.
STAUFFER CHEMICAL COMPANY - MOUNTAIN
VIEW RESEARCH CENTER LIBRARY □ Mountain
View, CA

Manjula, Yaramakala, Libn.
ATLANTA FULTON PUBLIC LIBRARY - IVAN
ALLEN, JR. DEPARTMENT OF SCIENCE,
INDUSTRY AND GOVERNMENT □ Atlanta, GA

Mankin, Carole, Res. Project Libn.
MASSACHUSETTS GENERAL HOSPITAL - MGH
HEALTH SCIENCES LIBRARIES □ Boston, MA

Mankin, Charles J., Dir.
OKLAHOMA GEOLOGICAL SURVEY - OKLAHOMA
GEOPHYSICAL OBSERVATORY LIBRARY □
Leonard, OK

Mankowitz, Gloria, Assoc.Dir.
MOTION PICTURE SERVICES □ Livingston, NJ

Mankowitz, Murray, Dir.
MOTION PICTURE SERVICES □ Livingston, NJ

Manley, Cynthia G., Asst.Libn.
UNIVERSITY OF MICHIGAN - CENTER FOR
RESEARCH ON ECONOMIC DEVELOPMENT □
Ann Arbor, MI

Manley, Irwin G., Adm., Info.Serv.
GIBSON, DUNN & CRUTCHER - LAW LIBRARY □
Los Angeles, CA

Manley, Dr. Robert, Sr.Hist.
HALL COUNTY MUSEUM BOARD - STUHR
MUSEUM - LIBRARY AND ARCHIVES □ Grand
Island, NE

Manlove, Patricia A., Libn.
WESTERN MONTANA CLINIC - LIBRARY □
Missoula, MT

Mann, Brenda, Tech.Libn.
U.S. ARMY RESEARCH OFFICE - TECHNICAL
LIBRARY □ Research Triangle Park, NC

Mann, Darlene, Ref.Libn.
WESTERN MARYLAND PUBLIC LIBRARIES -
REGIONAL LIBRARY □ Hagerstown, MD

Mann, David, Hd.
UTAH STATE LIBRARY - FILM PROGRAM □ Salt
Lake City, UT

Mann, Deborah, Assoc.Law Libn.
EMORY UNIVERSITY - SCHOOL OF LAW
LIBRARY □ Atlanta, GA

Mann, I., Res.Libn.
FORD AEROSPACE & COMMUNICATIONS CORP.
- AERONUTRONIC DIVISION - TECHNICAL
INFORMATION SERVICES □ Newport Beach, CA

Mann, Ian, ILL
ONTARIO - MINISTRY OF TRANSPORTATION
AND COMMUNICATIONS - LIBRARY AND
INFORMATION CENTRE □ Downsview, ON

Mann, John B., Coord., AV Serv.
GUILFORD TECHNICAL COMMUNITY COLLEGE -
LEARNING RESOURCE CENTER □ Jamestown,
NC

Mann, Lori, Educ.Dir.
COYOTE POINT MUSEUM - RESOURCE CENTER
□ San Mateo, CA

Mann, Wayne C., Dir.
WESTERN MICHIGAN UNIVERSITY - ARCHIVES
AND REGIONAL HISTORY COLLECTIONS □
Kalamazoo, MI

Mann-Grim, Joyce A., Tech.Info.Off.
U.S. FISH & WILDLIFE SERVICE - NATIONAL
FISHERIES CENTER - TECHNICAL
INFORMATION SERVICES □ Kearneysville, WV

Manning, Ann, Health Sci.Libn.
DALHOUSIE UNIVERSITY - W.K. KELLOGG
HEALTH SCIENCES LIBRARY □ Halifax, NS

Manning, Helen, Libn.
TEXAS INSTRUMENTS, INC. - HOUSTON SITE
LIBRARY □ Houston, TX

Manning, John, Media Serv.Coord.
COLUMBUS TECHNICAL INSTITUTE -
EDUCATIONAL RESOURCES CENTER □
Columbus, OH

Manning, John R., Task Leader
U.S. NATL. BUREAU OF STANDARDS -
METALLURGY DIVISION - DIFFUSION IN
METALS DATA CENTER □ Washington, DC

Manning, Katherine J., Libn.
GEORGIA POWER COMPANY - LIBRARY
SERVICES □ Atlanta, GA

Manning, Kathryn, Libn.
WADLEY INSTITUTES OF MOLECULAR
MEDICINE - RESEARCH INSTITUTE LIBRARY†
□ Dallas, TX

Manning, Leo W., Exec.Dir./Libn.
SOCIETY FOR ACADEMIC ACHIEVEMENT -
LIBRARY □ Quincy, IL

Manning, Leslie A., Assoc. Dean, Tech.Serv.
KANSAS STATE UNIVERSITY - FARRELL
LIBRARY □ Manhattan, KS

Manning, Lucinda, Libn.
LONG ISLAND HISTORICAL SOCIETY - LIBRARY
□ Brooklyn, NY

Manning, Martha, Hd., Info.Serv.
SUNY AT BUFFALO - HEALTH SCIENCES
LIBRARY □ Buffalo, NY

Manning, T.M.
OLIN CORPORATION - RESEARCH CENTER/
INFORMATION CENTER □ New Haven, CT

Mannion, Lynette, Film Libn.
UNIVERSITY OF TORONTO - AUDIO-VISUAL
LIBRARY □ Toronto, ON

Mannion, Mary, Asst.Libn.
MANUFACTURERS HANOVER TRUST COMPANY
- CORPORATE LIBRARY/FINANCIAL LIBRARY
DIVISION† □ New York, NY

Manoogian, Sylva N., Prin.Libn.
LOS ANGELES PUBLIC LIBRARY - FOREIGN
LANGUAGES DEPARTMENT □ Los Angeles, CA

Mansbach, Carolyn, Dir.
JAMAICA HOSPITAL - MEDICAL LIBRARY □
Jamaica, NY

Mansfield, Fred, Bibliog.
UNIVERSITY OF ILLINOIS - LAW LIBRARY □
Champaign, IL

Mansfield, Jerry, Asst.Engr.Libn.
PURDUE UNIVERSITY - ENGINEERING LIBRARY
□ West Lafayette, IN

Mansfield, Juliet I., Libn.
STURDY MEMORIAL HOSPITAL - HEALTH
SCIENCES LIBRARY □ Attleboro, MA

Mansheim, Renee E., Med.Libn.
VIRGINIA CENTER FOR PSYCHIATRY -
MEDICAL LIBRARY □ Portsmouth, VA

Manson, Connie J., Sr.Libn.
WASHINGTON STATE DEPARTMENT OF
NATURAL RESOURCES - DIVISION OF GEOLOGY
AND EARTH RESOURCES - LIBRARY □ Lacey,
WA

Manson, Martha, Cur.
SAN JOSE MUSEUM OF ART - LIBRARY □ San
Jose, CA

Manson-Smith, Pamela, Libn.
UNIVERSITY OF TORONTO - SCHOOL OF
ARCHITECTURE AND PLANNING LIBRARY □
Toronto, ON

Manss, Jacqualin, Hd., Circ.
UNIVERSITY OF CALIFORNIA, SANTA CRUZ -
SCIENCE LIBRARY □ Santa Cruz, CA

Mansur, Jeannell M., Pharm.D., Dir.
UNIVERSITY OF CHICAGO HOSPITALS &
CLINICS - PHARMACEUTICAL SERVICES -
DRUG INFORMATION CENTER □ Chicago, IL

Mantel, Melissa, Asst.Libn.
HOUSTON CHRONICLE - EDITORIAL LIBRARY □
Houston, TX

Manthey, Teresa M., Libn.
BURNHAM HOSPITAL - LIBRARY □ Champaign,
IL

Manton, Kenneth G., Asst.Dir.
DUKE UNIVERSITY - CENTER FOR
DEMOGRAPHIC STUDIES - REFERENCE
LIBRARY □ Durham, NC

Mantzoros, Tessie, Libn.
MC GRAW-HILL, INC. - BUSINESS WEEK
MAGAZINE LIBRARY† □ New York, NY

Manuel, Melbarose, Act.Libn.
SOUTHERN UNIVERSITY - LAW SCHOOL
LIBRARY □ Baton Rouge, LA

Manuel, Robin, Sr.Lib.Asst.
WASHINGTON NATIONAL INSURANCE
COMPANY - INFORMATION RESOURCES
CENTER □ Evanston, IL

Manville, Hope, Info.Spec.
INTERPUBLIC GROUP OF COMPANIES -
CENTER FOR ADVERTISING SERVICES □ New
York, NY

Manwaring, Sally, Hd., Govt.Pubn.Lib.
UNIVERSITY OF ALBERTA - HUMANITIES AND
SOCIAL SCIENCES LIBRARY - GOVERNMENT
PUBLICATIONS □ Edmonton, AB

Manwell, Linda M., Asst.Libn.
INSTITUTE OF PAPER CHEMISTRY - LIBRARY □
Appleton, WI

Mao, Shelley G., Dir.
ST. JOSEPH HOSPITAL - HOSPITAL HEALTH
SCIENCE LIBRARY □ Houston, TX

Maonnis, John, Photo Libn.
NATIONAL MARITIME MUSEUM - J. PORTER
SHAW LIBRARY □ San Francisco, CA

Mapes, Martha, Libn.
TULSA CITY-COUNTY LIBRARY SYSTEM -
BUSINESS AND TECHNOLOGY DEPARTMENT □
Tulsa, OK

Maples, Carol, Chf., Tech.Lib.
U.S. AIR FORCE - FLIGHT TEST CENTER -
TECHNICAL LIBRARY □ Edwards AFB, CA

Maracek, Robert, Coord., ILL
NATIONAL SAFETY COUNCIL - LIBRARY □
Chicago, IL

Marafioti, Mrs. Armida M., Libn.
NEW YORK STATE SUPREME COURT - 3RD
JUDICIAL DISTRICT - EMORY A. CHASE
MEMORIAL LIBRARY □ Catskill, NY

Marano, Nancy, Libn.
STEIN ROE AND FARNHAM - LIBRARY □
Chicago, IL

Marano, Ray, Br.Libn.
WHITE AND CASE - LIBRARY □ New York, NY

Marasco, Bernadette, Sr.Tech.Info.Spec.
INTERNATIONAL PAPER COMPANY -
CORPORATE RESEARCH & DEVELOPMENT
DIVISION - TECHNICAL INFORMATION
CENTER □ Tuxedo, NY

Marble, Beatrice N., Dept.Hd.
ONONDAGA COUNTY PUBLIC LIBRARY - ART
AND MUSIC DEPARTMENT □ Syracuse, NY

Marcano, Enriqueta, Hd.Cat.
UNIVERSITY OF PUERTO RICO - LAW SCHOOL
LIBRARY □ Rio Piedras, PR

Marcello, Dr. Ronald E., Coord.
NORTH TEXAS STATE UNIVERSITY LIBRARIES
- ORAL HISTORY COLLECTION □ Denton, TX

March, Frieda O., Libn.
IDAHO STATE HISTORICAL SOCIETY -
GENEALOGICAL LIBRARY □ Boise, ID

Marchand, L., Hd., Branch Lib.
CANADA - NATIONAL DEFENCE - NDHQ
LIBRARY □ Ottawa, ON

Marchese, Marie-Ann, Lib.Coord.
LEXINGTON SCHOOL FOR THE DEAF - LIBRARY
MEDIA CENTER □ Jackson Heights, NY

Marchetti, Honey, Info.Spec.
WESTINGHOUSE ELECTRIC CORPORATION -
WATER REACTOR DIVISIONS - INFORMATION
RESOURCE CENTER □ Pittsburgh, PA

Marchfield, R.L., Pres.
VOLTAIRE SOCIETY - LIBRARY □ Okeechobee,
FL

Marchi, Gary, Creative Dir.
SPIRIT OF THE FUTURE CREATIVE INSTITUTE
- CENTRAL LIBRARY ARCHIVES □ San
Francisco, CA

Marchiafava, Dr. Louis J., Archv.
HOUSTON PUBLIC LIBRARY - ARCHIVES AND
MANUSCRIPT DEPARTMENT □ Houston, TX

Marchok, Catherine W., Lib.Dir.
MERCER MEDICAL CENTER - DAVID B. ACKLEY
MEDICAL LIBRARY □ Trenton, NJ

Marcolina, Ruth, Dir.
SUNY AT STONY BROOK - HEALTH SCIENCES
LIBRARY □ East Setauket, NY

Marcotte, J., Media Supv.
HAYHURST ADVERTISING, LTD. - MEDIA
RESEARCH LIBRARY □ Toronto, ON

Marcotte, Joan M., Med.Libn.
ALTON OCHSNER MEDICAL FOUNDATION -
MEDICAL LIBRARY □ New Orleans, LA

Marcoux, Catherine L., Libn.
SPERRY - SPERRY ELECTRONIC SYSTEMS -
TECHNICAL INFORMATION CENTER □ Great
Neck, NY

Marcoux, Yves, Chf., Ref.Serv.Sect.
CANADA - PUBLIC ARCHIVES OF CANADA -
LIBRARY □ Ottawa, ON

Marcuccio, Phyllis, Chf.Libn.
NATIONAL SCIENCE TEACHERS ASSOCIATION
- GLENN O. BLOUGH LIBRARY □ Washington, DC

Marcus, Frances, Asst.Libn.
ANDOVER COLLEGE - LIBRARY □ Portland, ME

Marcus, Prof. Jacob R., Dir.
HEBREW UNION COLLEGE - JEWISH
INSTITUTE OF RELIGION - AMERICAN JEWISH
ARCHIVES □ Cincinnati, OH

Marcus, Jacob R., Dir.
HEBREW UNION COLLEGE - JEWISH
INSTITUTE OF RELIGION - AMERICAN JEWISH
PERIODICAL CENTER □ Cincinnati, OH

Marcus, Joyce, Ref.Asst.
BRIDGEWATER STATE COLLEGE - CLEMENT C.
MAXWELL LIBRARY □ Bridgewater, MA

Marcus, Richard W., Dir.
SPERTUS COLLEGE OF JUDAICA - NORMAN AND
HELEN ASHER LIBRARY □ Chicago, IL

Marcus, Ronald, Libn.
STAMFORD HISTORICAL SOCIETY - LIBRARY □
Stamford, CT

Marcus, Sharon, Libn.
UNIVERSITY OF CALIFORNIA, LOS ANGELES -
MATHEMATICS READING ROOM □ Los Angeles,
CA

Marcus, Terry, Libn.
MILWAUKEE INSTITUTE OF ART & DESIGN -
LIBRARY □ Milwaukee, WI

Marcus, Tybe, Ref./ILL
CANADA - ECONOMIC COUNCIL OF CANADA -
LIBRARY □ Ottawa, ON

Marcy, Suzanne, Ref.Libn.
CLEVELAND HEALTH SCIENCES LIBRARY -
ALLEN MEMORIAL LIBRARY □ Cleveland, OH

Marcy, Dr. Willard, Chm., Lib.Comm.
CHEMISTS' CLUB LIBRARY - CHEMICAL
INTERNATIONAL INFORMATION CENTER □
New York, NY

Mardikian, Jackie, Dir.
BORGESS MEDICAL CENTER - HEALTH
INFORMATION LIBRARY □ Kalamazoo, MI

Mardney, Patrick, Media Serv.Spec.
OAKLAND SCHOOLS - EDUCATIONAL RESOURCE
CENTER □ Pontiac, MI

Marenbach, Nicole, Adm.Mgr.
MONSANTO CORPORATION - FABRICATED
PRODUCTS DIVISION - TECHNICAL
INFORMATION CENTER □ Bloomfield, CT

Mares, Claire, Ed.
EASTERN NEBRASKA GENEALOGICAL SOCIETY
- LIBRARY □ Fremont, NE

Marforio, Janet, Tax Libn.
WHITE AND CASE - LIBRARY □ New York, NY

Margeton, Stephen G., Libn.
STEPTOE AND JOHNSON - LIBRARY □
Washington, DC

Margolis, Bernard, Dir., Lib.Sys.
MONROE COUNTY LIBRARY SYSTEM - GENERAL
GEORGE ARMSTRONG CUSTER COLLECTION □
Monroe, MI

Margolis, Bernard A., Dir.
SOUTHEAST MICHIGAN REGIONAL FILM
LIBRARY □ Monroe, MI

Marics, Joseph, Hd. of Circ.
ASSEMBLIES OF GOD GRADUATE SCHOOL -
CORDAS C. BURNETT LIBRARY† □ Springfield,
MO

Marie, Sr. Francis, Libn.
ST. JOSEPH HOSPITAL - OTTO C. BRANTIGAN
MEDICAL LIBRARY □ Towson, MD

Marier, Donald, Dir.
ALTERNATIVE SOURCES OF ENERGY, INC. -
LIBRARY AND REFERRAL SERVICE □ Milaca, MN

Marifke, Linda, Sr.Asst.Libn.
QUARLES & BRADY - LIBRARY □ Milwaukee, WI

Marin, Carmen M., Dir.
NORTH CAROLINA STATE UNIVERSITY -
TOBACCO LITERATURE SERVICE □ Raleigh, NC

Marin, Christine N., Chicano Bibliog.
ARIZONA STATE UNIVERSITY - CHICANO
STUDIES COLLECTION† □ Tempe, AZ

Marion, Donald, Libn.
UNIVERSITY OF MINNESOTA - PHYSICS
LIBRARY □ Minneapolis, MN

Marion, Leon O., Exec.Dir.
AMERICAN COUNCIL OF VOLUNTARY
AGENCIES FOR FOREIGN SERVICE, INC. -
TECH. ASSISTANCE INFO. CLEARING HOUSE □
New York, NY

Marion, Phyllis, Asst. Dir.
UNIVERSITY OF MINNESOTA - LAW LIBRARY □
Minneapolis, MN

Maris, Cheryl K., Tech.Libn.
GENERAL MOTORS CORPORATION - DELCO
ELECTRONICS DIVISION - TECHNICAL
LIBRARY □ Kokomo, IN

Mark, Karen J., Tech.Info.Off.
INTERNATIONAL LABOR OFFICE -
WASHINGTON BRANCH LIBRARY □ Washington,
DC

Mark, Lillian, Med.Libn.
CLEVELAND CLINIC EDUCATION FOUNDATION
- MEDICAL LIBRARY/AUDIOVISUAL CENTER† □
Cleveland, OH

Mark, Ronnie Joan, Dir.
CONEY ISLAND HOSPITAL - HAROLD FINK
MEMORIAL LIBRARY □ Brooklyn, NY

Mark, Ruth, Res.Anl.
CALIFORNIA STATE DEPARTMENT OF
INDUSTRIAL RELATIONS - DIVISION OF LABOR
STATISTICS AND RESEARCH LIBRARY □ San
Francisco, CA

Marke, Julius, Dir.
ST. JOHN'S UNIVERSITY - LAW LIBRARY □
Jamaica, NY

Marker, Rhonda, Cat.
PORT AUTHORITY OF NEW YORK AND NEW
JERSEY - LIBRARY □ New York, NY

Markey, Patricia, Cat.
MERRIMACK VALLEY TEXTILE MUSEUM -
LIBRARY □ North Andover, MA

Markham, Ann, Lrng.Rsrc.Coord.
ILLINOIS MASONIC MEDICAL CENTER -
SCHOOL OF NURSING - DR. JOSEPH DEUTSCH
MEMORIAL LIBRARY □ Chicago, IL

Markham, Dr. Robert P., Coord. of Archv.
UNIVERSITY OF NORTHERN COLORADO -
UNIVERSITY ARCHIVES □ Greeley, CO

Markham, Susan D., Lib.Techn.
U.S. BUREAU OF MINES - TUSCALOOSA
RESEARCH CENTER - REFERENCE LIBRARY □
University, AL

Markoff, Marjorie, Cat., Spec.Coll.
MILLERSVILLE UNIVERSITY OF PENNSYLVANIA
- HELEN A. GANSER LIBRARY - SPECIAL
COLLECTIONS □ Millersville, PA

Markowitz, Gail, Libn.
SKIDMORE, OWINGS & MERRILL - LIBRARY □
Washington, DC

Markowitz, Susan, Engr.Libn.
CORNELL UNIVERSITY - ENGINEERING
LIBRARY □ Ithaca, NY

Markowski, Benedict, Fld.Archv.
DETROIT PUBLIC LIBRARY - BURTON
HISTORICAL COLLECTION □ Detroit, MI

Marks, Cicely, Tech.Serv.Spec.
U.S. VETERANS ADMINISTRATION (DC-
Washington) - HEADQUARTERS LIBRARY
DIVISION (142D) □ Washington, DC

Marks, Cicely P., Tech.Serv.Spec.
U.S. VETERANS ADMINISTRATION (DC-
Washington) - HEADQUARTERS CENTRAL
OFFICE LIBRARY (142D1) □ Washington, DC

Marks, Coralyn, Lib.Dir.
NORTHWEST GENERAL HOSPITAL - MEDICAL
LIBRARY □ Milwaukee, WI

Marks, Deirdre, Info.Spec.
PRICE WATERHOUSE - NEW YORK OFFICE
INFORMATION CENTER □ New York, NY

Marks, Larry M., Dir.
INFO/SEARCH - LIBRARY □ Berkeley, CA

Marks, Lucy, Cat.Libn.
ART INSTITUTE OF CHICAGO - RYERSON AND
BURNHAM LIBRARIES □ Chicago, IL

Marks, Paul J., Pres.
YOUTH RESOURCES, INC. - LIBRARY □ Cabazon,
CA

Marks, Ruth, Harmony Found.Adm.
SOCIETY FOR THE PRESERVATION AND
ENCOURAGEMENT OF BARBER SHOP QUARTET
SINGING IN AMERICA - OLD SONGS LIBRARY □
Kenosha, WI

Marks, Susan, Libn.
ENGINEERS' CLUB OF DAYTON - LIBRARY □
Dayton, OH

Markson, Elizabeth, Dir. for Soc.Res.
BOSTON UNIVERSITY - GERONTOLOGY
RESOURCE CENTER □ Boston, MA

Markus, Mary Beth, Libn.
FOOTE CONE & BELDING - INFORMATION
CENTER □ Chicago, IL

Markwell, Linda Garr, Grady Br.Libn.
EMORY UNIVERSITY - SCHOOL OF MEDICINE -
A.W. CALHOUN MEDICAL LIBRARY □ Atlanta,
GA

Markwiese, Catherine, Ref.Libn.
MILWAUKEE SCHOOL OF ENGINEERING -
WALTER SCHROEDER LIBRARY □ Milwaukee,
WI

Markwood, Carolyn K., Supv., Jackson Lab.Lib.
DU PONT DE NEMOURS (E.I.) & COMPANY, INC.
- LIBRARY NETWORK □ Wilmington, DE

Markworth, Larry, Tech.Libn.
VETCO OFFSHORE, INC. - TECHNICAL LIBRARY
□ Ventura, CA

Marler, Maxine, Coll.Spec.
DENVER PUBLIC LIBRARY - BUSINESS,
SCIENCE & TECHNOLOGY DIVISION □ Denver,
CO

Marley, Carol, Map Cur.-Libn.
MC GILL UNIVERSITY - DEPARTMENT OF RARE
BOOKS & SPECIAL COLLECTIONS ⊔ Montreal,
PQ

Marlow, Kathryn E., Libn.
NUS CORPORATION - TECHNICAL LIBRARY □
Pittsburgh, PA

Marlowe, Constance, Dir., Media Ctr.
METHODIST COLLEGE, INC. - DAVIS
MEMORIAL LIBRARY - SPECIAL COLLECTIONS
□ Fayetteville, NC

Maroney, Mary, Asst.Libn./Tech.Serv.
BRYANT COLLEGE OF BUSINESS
ADMINISTRATION - EDITH M. HODGSON
MEMORIAL LIBRARY □ Smithfield, RI

Marose, Doris, Dir., Med.Lib.
MEMORIAL HOSPITAL - MEDICAL LIBRARY □
Sarasota, FL

Marousek, Kathy, Dental Libn.
FAIRLEIGH DICKINSON UNIVERSITY - SCHOOL
OF DENTISTRY LIBRARY □ Hackensack, NJ

Marquardt, Jennifer, Instr.Rsrcs.
UNIVERSITY OF MICHIGAN - SCHOOL OF
EDUCATION & SCHOOL OF LIB. SCI. - INSTR.
STRATEGY SERV. □ Ann Arbor, MI

Marquette, Carl G., Jr., Hd.
PUBLIC LIBRARY OF CINCINNATI AND
HAMILTON COUNTY - GOVERNMENT AND
BUSINESS DEPARTMENT □ Cincinnati, OH

Marquette, Margaret, Coord.
LOS ANGELES COUNTY SUPERINTENDENT OF
SCHOOLS - PROFESSIONAL REFERENCE
CENTER† □ Downey, CA

Marquez-Sterling, Carlos, Asst.Soc.Stud.Libn.
SOUTHERN ILLINOIS UNIVERSITY,
CARBONDALE - SOCIAL STUDIES DIVISION
LIBRARY □ Carbondale, IL

Marquis, Kay, Tech.Lib.Supv.
NASHUA CORPORATION - TECHNICAL
LIBRARY† □ Nashua, NH

Marr, Antony, Assoc.Cur.
YALE UNIVERSITY - EAST ASIAN COLLECTION
□ New Haven, CT

Marram, Michele, Ref.
HARVARD UNIVERSITY - HARVARD BUSINESS
SCHOOL - BAKER LIBRARY □ Boston, MA

Mars, Maline, Sec./Libn.
SOUTH SHORE HOSPITAL - MEDICAL STAFF
LIBRARY □ Chicago, IL

Marsala, Kathryn, Ref.Libn.
EQUITABLE LIFE ASSURANCE SOCIETY OF THE
U.S. - INFORMATION SERVICES DIVISION □
New York, NY

Marsala, Kathryn, Mgr., Tech.Info.Ctr.
EQUITABLE LIFE ASSURANCE SOCIETY OF THE
U.S. - TECHNICAL INFORMATION CENTER □
New York, NY

Marsala, Rita, Cat.Libn.
COOLEY (Thomas M.) LAW SCHOOL - LIBRARY □
Lansing, MI

Marsden, Dorothy E., Libn.
VALLEJO NAVAL AND HISTORICAL MUSEUM -
LIBRARY □ Vallejo, CA

Marsh, Corrie, Acq.Libn.
GEORGETOWN UNIVERSITY - FRED O. DENNIS
LAW LIBRARY □ Washington, DC

Marsh, Dorothy, Asst.Cur.
HOLY LAND MUSEUM & LIBRARY □ New York,
NY

Marsh, Dorothy, Unit Mgr.
U.S. NATL. PARK SERVICE - RUSSELL CAVE
NATL. MONUMENT - LIBRARY □ Bridgeport, AL

Marsh, John S., Libn.
SIMPSON, THACHER & BARTLETT - LIBRARY† □
New York, NY

Marsh, Josephine, Data. Proc.
UNIVERSITY OF NORTH CAROLINA, CHAPEL
HILL - INSTITUTE FOR RESEARCH IN SOCIAL
SCIENCE - DATA LIBRARY □ Chapel Hill, NC

Marsh, Sheila J., Media Libn.
CALIFORNIA STATE UNIVERSITY,
SACRAMENTO - LIBRARY - MEDIA SERVICES
CENTER □ Sacramento, CA

Marshall, Debra H., Mgr.
SOUTHLAND CORPORATION - CORPORATE
BUSINESS RESEARCH CENTER □ Dallas, TX

Marshall, Denis, Hd.Libn.
UNIVERSITY OF MANITOBA - E.K. WILLIAMS
LAW LIBRARY □ Winnipeg, MB

Marshall, Gordon M., Asst.Libn.
LIBRARY COMPANY OF PHILADELPHIA □
Philadelphia, PA

Marshall, James, Dept.Hd.
TOLEDO-LUCAS COUNTY PUBLIC LIBRARY -
LOCAL HISTORY & GENEALOGY DEPARTMENT □
Toledo, OH

Marshall, Jane, Law Libn.
NORTHWESTERN MUTUAL LIFE INSURANCE
COMPANY - LAW LIBRARY □ Milwaukee, WI

Marshall, Jane, Hd., Tech.Serv.
PACE UNIVERSITY - SCHOOL OF LAW LIBRARY
□ White Plains, NY

Marshall, Jane, Res.Spec.
UNIVERSAL CITY STUDIOS - RESEARCH
DEPARTMENT LIBRARY □ Universal City, CA

Marshall, K. Eric, Hd., Lib.Serv.
CANADA - FISHERIES & OCEANS -
FRESHWATER INSTITUTE LIBRARY □ Winnipeg,
MB

Marshall, Kathryn E., Chf., Lib.Serv.Sect.
U.S. AIR FORCE ENVIRONMENTAL TECHNICAL
APPLICATIONS CENTER - AIR WEATHER
SERVICE TECHNICAL LIBRARY □ Scott AFB, IL

Marshall, Marion, Libn.
TAX FOUNDATION - LIBRARY □ Washington, DC

Marshall, Patricia, Dir., Lib.Rsrcs.
AMERICAN INSTITUTE OF AERONAUTICS AND
ASTRONAUTICS - TECHNICAL INFORMATION
SERVICE □ New York, NY

Marshall, Patricia, Dir., Lib.Rsrcs.
AMERICAN INSTITUTE OF AERONAUTICS AND
ASTRONAUTICS - TECHNICAL INFORMATION
SERVICE □ New York, NY

Marshall, Patricia K., Mgr., Res.Serv.
MOBIL OIL CORPORATION - PUBLIC AFFAIRS
SECRETARIAT □ New York, NY

Marshall, Robert G., Archival Spec.
CHICAGO PUBLIC LIBRARY CULTURAL CENTER
- SPECIAL COLLECTIONS DIVISION □ Chicago,
IL

Marshall, Shirley, Tech.Info.Spec.
U.S. DEPT. OF LABOR - OSHA - TECHNICAL
DATA CENTER □ Washington, DC

Marshall, Thelma L., Libn.
GREAT FALLS GENEALOGY SOCIETY - LIBRARY
□ Great Falls, MT

Marshall, Thomas A., S.J., Libn.
WOODSTOCK THEOLOGICAL CENTER -
LIBRARY □ Washington, DC

Marshall, Warren, Reprographics
FRANKLIN INSTITUTE - LIBRARY □ Philadelphia,
PA

Marshburn, Lawrance, Graduate Ref.Libn.
BIOLA UNIVERSITY - LIBRARY □ La Mirada, CA

Marshment, Pat, Info.Spec.
INTEL CORPORATION - TECHNICAL
INFORMATION CENTER □ Santa Clara, CA

Marsick, Daniel, Tech.Info.Spec.
U.S. DEPT. OF LABOR - OSHA - TECHNICAL
DATA CENTER □ Washington, DC

Marson, Joyce, Dir.
WHITE MEMORIAL MEDICAL CENTER -
COURVILLE-ABBOTT MEMORIAL LIBRARY □ Los
Angeles, CA

Marsteller, Ann L., Libn.
HAWAIIAN SUGAR PLANTERS' ASSOCIATION
EXPERIMENT STATION - LIBRARY □ Aiea, HI

Marston, Claire, Lib.Asst.
UNIVERSITY CONGREGATIONAL CHURCH -
LIBRARY □ Seattle, WA

Martam, Marilyn, Hd., Loan Serv.
UNIVERSITY OF ARIZONA - ARIZONA HEALTH
SCIENCES CENTER LIBRARY □ Tucson, AZ

Martel, Christian, Lib.Techn.
HOTEL-DIEU DU SACRE-COEUR DE JESUS -
BIBLIOTHEQUE MEDICALE □ Quebec, PQ

Martel, Elizabeth, Libn.
DUNHAM TAVERN MUSEUM - LIBRARY □
Cleveland, OH

Martens, Suzi, AV Techn.
NATIONAL COLLEGE - THOMAS JEFFERSON
LEARNING RESOURCE CENTER □ Rapid City, SD

Martha, Sr., Libn.
SACRED HEART HOSPITAL - HEALTH SCIENCE
LIBRARY □ Cumberland, MD

Marti, Hanna, Spec.Coll.Libn.
UNIVERSITY OF WESTERN ONTARIO - SCHOOL
OF LIBRARY & INFORMATION SCIENCE -
LIBRARY □ London, ON

Marti, Norma, Info.Serv.Spec.
U.S. BUREAU OF THE CENSUS - INFORMATION
SERVICES PROGRAM - CHICAGO REGIONAL
OFFICE - REFERENCE CENTER □ Chicago, IL

Martin, Alvia D., Cur.
MADISON TOWNSHIP HISTORICAL SOCIETY -
THOMAS WARNE HISTORICAL MUSEUM AND
LIBRARY □ Matawan, NJ

Martin, Anita, Archv.
ELI LILLY AND COMPANY - LILLY ARCHIVES □
Indianapolis, IN

Martin, Anne F., Libn.
IBM CANADA, LTD. - HEADQUARTERS LIBRARY
□ Markham, ON

Martin, Archie, AV Libn.
EMORY UNIVERSITY - SCHOOL OF MEDICINE -
A.W. CALHOUN MEDICAL LIBRARY □ Atlanta,
GA

Martin, Barbara H.S., Asst.Dir.
MOREHOUSE SCHOOL OF MEDICINE - MULTI-
MEDIA CENTER □ Atlanta, GA

Martin, Bennie E., Chf.Libn.
COOK COUNTY LAW LIBRARY - CRIMINAL
COURT BRANCH □ Chicago, IL

Martin, Boyd A., Dir.
UNIVERSITY OF IDAHO - THE BOYD AND
GRACE MARTIN INSTITUTE OF HUMAN
BEHAVIOR - LIBRARY □ Moscow, ID

Martin, Carol, Asst.Libn.
UNIVERSITY OF ARKANSAS FOR MEDICAL
SCIENCES - NORTHWEST ARKANSAS HEALTH
EDUCATION CENTER - LIBRARY □ Fayetteville,
AR

Martin, Cindy, Asst.Archv.
TEXAS TECH UNIVERSITY - SOUTHWEST
COLLECTION □ Lubbock, TX

Martin, Daniel, Asst.Adm.Libn.
UNIVERSITY OF TEXAS, AUSTIN - SCHOOL OF
LAW - TARLTON LAW LIBRARY □ Austin, TX

Martin, Dannie, P.R.
PORTMAN (John) & ASSOCIATES - LIBRARY □
Atlanta, GA

Martin, Debra, Asst.Libn.
COOLEY, GODWARD, CASTRO, HUDDLESON &
TATUM - LIBRARY □ San Francisco, CA

Martin, Delores, Libn./Off.Mgr.
CABOT CORPORATION - RESEARCH &
DEVELOPMENT LIBRARY† □ Pampa, TX

Martin, Dianne, Asst.
KANSAS STATE UNIVERSITY - PAUL WEIGEL
LIBRARY OF ARCHITECTURE AND DESIGN □
Manhattan, KS

Martin, Dolores M., Ed.
LIBRARY OF CONGRESS - HISPANIC DIVISION
□ Washington, DC

Martin, Donald L., Law Libn.
U.S. DEPT. OF LABOR - LIBRARY - LAW
LIBRARY DIVISION □ Washington, DC

Martin, Dorothy, Libn.
UNIVERSITY OF BRITISH COLUMBIA -
HUMANITIES AND SOCIAL SCIENCES DIVISION
□ Vancouver, BC

Martin, Douglas W., Law Libn.
NORTH CAROLINA CENTRAL UNIVERSITY -
LAW LIBRARY □ Durham, NC

Martin, Miss E.J.V., Chf., Info.Serv.
CANADA - REGIONAL INDUSTRIAL EXPANSION
- LIBRARY □ Ottawa, ON

Martin, G.A., Physicist
U.S. NATL. BUREAU OF STANDARDS - DATA
CENTER ON ATOMIC TRANSITION
PROBABILITIES □ Washington, DC

Martin, Gordon P., Dir., Res.Lib.
CROCKER ART MUSEUM - RESEARCH LIBRARY
□ Sacramento, CA

Martin, Sr. Helen, Ref.Libn.
WADHAMS HALL SEMINARY - COLLEGE
LIBRARY □ Ogdensburg, NY

Martin, I. Margareta, Info.Sci.
COCA-COLA COMPANY - TECHNICAL
INFORMATION SERVICES □ Atlanta, GA

Martin, Irmgarde, Libn.
ANDERSON CLAYTON FOODS - W.L. CLAYTON
RESEARCH CENTER □ Richardson, TX

Martin, J., Dir.
HUNTSVILLE MEMORIAL HOSPITAL - SCHOOL
OF VOCATIONAL NURSING - EARNESTINE
CANNON MEMORIAL LIBRARY† □ Huntsville, TX

Martin, Jack L., Dir.
INDIANAPOLIS MOTOR SPEEDWAY HALL OF
FAME MUSEUM - LIBRARY □ Indianapolis, IN

Martin, Jana, Med.Libn.
JOINT DISEASES/NORTH GENERAL HOSPITAL -
MEDICAL LIBRARY □ New York, NY

Martin, Jean K., Lib.Mgr.
MOLYCORP, INC. - LIBRARY □ Los Angeles, CA

Martin, Jess A., Dir.
UNIVERSITY OF TENNESSEE - CENTER FOR
THE HEALTH SCIENCES LIBRARY □ Memphis,
TN

Martin, John, Pres.
WOODSTOCK HISTORICAL SOCIETY, INC. -
JOHN COTTON DANA LIBRARY □ Woodstock,
VT

Martin, Dr. John H., Dir.
CORNING MUSEUM OF GLASS - LIBRARY □
Corning, NY

Martin, Jorette, Lib.Dir.
BINGHAMTON PRESS AND SUN BULLETIN -
LIBRARY □ Binghamton, NY

Martin, Judith R., Cat.
WEST VIRGINIA WESLEYAN COLLEGE - ANNIE
MERNER PFEIFFER LIBRARY □ Buckhannon, WV

Martin, Katherine Rosser, Dir.
LLOYD (Alice) COLLEGE - APPALACHIAN ORAL
HISTORY PROJECT □ Pippa Passes, KY

Martin, Kathleen M., Lib.Asst.
LICKING MEMORIAL HOSPITAL - MEDICAL
LIBRARY □ Newark, OH

Martin, Kathleen S., Libn.
COHEN AND URETZ - LAW LIBRARY □
Washington, DC

Martin, Kathleen S., Libn.
GINSBURG, FELDMAN, & BRESS - LAW LIBRARY
□ Washington, DC

Martin, Linda, Libn.
PLACER DEVELOPMENT, LTD. - LIBRARY □
Vancouver, BC

Martin, M.J., Dir.
OAK RIDGE NATIONAL LABORATORY -
NUCLEAR DATA PROJECT □ Oak Ridge, TN

Martin, Margaret J., Libn.
U.S. ARMED FORCES STAFF COLLEGE -
LIBRARY □ Norfolk, VA

Martin, Marjorie, Libn.
MIDDLESEX LAW ASSOCIATION - LIBRARY □
London, ON

Martin, Mary Dell, Chf., Pub.Distr.Sect.
U.S. ARMY - ENGINEER WATERWAYS
EXPERIMENT STATION - TECHNICAL
INFORMATION CENTER □ Vicksburg, MS

Martin, MaryLou T., Libn.
OAKLAND PUBLIC LIBRARY - CITYLINE
INFORMATION SERVICE □ Oakland, CA

Martin, Michael G., Jr., Asst.Cur./Archv.
UNIVERSITY OF NORTH CAROLINA, CHAPEL
HILL - SOUTHERN HISTORICAL COLLECTION &
MANUSCRIPTS DEPARTMENT □ Chapel Hill, NC

Martin, Miriam, Asst.Mgr.
DALLAS PUBLIC LIBRARY - GENERAL
REFERENCE DEPARTMENT □ Dallas, TX

Martin, Mona, Asst.Mgr..
WED ENTERPRISES - RESEARCH LIBRARY □
Glendale, CA

Martin, Pamela, Tech.Info.Spec.
U.S. CENTERS FOR DISEASE CONTROL -
CHAMBLEE FACILITY LIBRARY □ Atlanta, GA

Martin, Patricia W., AV Consultant
UNIVERSITY OF MICHIGAN - MEDICAL SCHOOL
- LEARNING RESOURCE CENTER □ Ann Arbor,
MI

Martin, Peggy, Libn.
KILPATRICK & CODY - LIBRARY □ Atlanta, GA

Martin, Peggy, Libn.
MUDGE, ROSE, GUTHRIE, ALEXANDER &
FERDON - LIBRARY □ New York, NY

Martin, Peggy, Dir. of Educ.
ST. GABRIEL'S HOSPITAL - LIBRARY □ Little
Falls, MN

Martin, Mrs. Penny, Med.Libn.
CAPITOL HILL HOSPITAL - WILLIAM MERCER
SPRIGG MEMORIAL LIBRARY □ Washington, DC

Martin, Philippe
QUEBEC PROVINCE - BIBLIOTHEQUE
NATIONALE DU QUEBEC □ Montreal, PQ

Martin, R. Lawrence, Archv.
FERRIS STATE COLLEGE - LIBRARY □ Big
Rapids, MI

Martin, Rebecca, Hd.Libn.
UNIVERSITY OF CALIFORNIA, BERKELEY -
BIOCHEMISTRY LIBRARY □ Berkeley, CA

Martin, Rebecca, Hd.Libn.
UNIVERSITY OF CALIFORNIA, BERKELEY -
BIOLOGY LIBRARY □ Berkeley, CA

Martin, Roger, Hd., Rd.Serv.Div.
U.S. NAVY - NAVAL POSTGRADUATE SCHOOL -
DUDLEY KNOX LIBRARY □ Monterey, CA

Martin, Ruth, Asst.Libn.
SHEARSON LEHMAN/AMERICAN EXPRESS INC.
- RESEARCH LIBRARY □ New York, NY

Martin, Sandra I., Asst.Libn.
HARPER-GRACE HOSPITALS - HARPER
HOSPITAL DIVISION - DEPARTMENT OF
LIBRARIES □ Detroit, MI

Martin, Sara E., Hd.Libn.
TENNECO MINERALS COMPANY - LIBRARY □
Lakewood, CO

Martin, Shirley A., Ref.Libn.
UNIVERSITY OF MAINE, FARMINGTON -
MANTOR LIBRARY† □ Farmington, ME

Martin, Terry, Dir.
HARVARD UNIVERSITY - LAW SCHOOL
LIBRARY □ Cambridge, MA

Martin, Thomasa J., Lib.Off.
U.S. ARMY HOSPITALS - BLISS ARMY HOSPITAL
- MEDICAL LIBRARY □ Ft. Huachuca, AZ

Martin, Vernon, Hd.
HARTFORD PUBLIC LIBRARY - ART, MUSIC AND
RECREATION DEPARTMENT □ Hartford, CT

Martin, Dr. William C., Physicist
U.S. NATL. BUREAU OF STANDARDS - ATOMIC
ENERGY LEVELS DATA CENTER □ Washington,
DC

Martin, Wilma, Per.Libn.
TEXAS STATE TECHNICAL INSTITUTE, WACO
CAMPUS - LIBRARY □ Waco, TX

Martin, Z.C., ILL
GEORGIA STATE DEPARTMENT OF HUMAN
RESOURCES - GEORGIA MENTAL HEALTH
INSTITUTE - ADDISON M. DUVAL LIBRARY† □
Atlanta, GA

Martina, Sr. M., Ph.D., Dir.
MADONNA COLLEGE - CURRICULUM LIBRARY □
Livonia, MI

Martinello, Gilda, Sr.Sys.Libn.
CANADIAN NATIONAL RAILWAYS - DECHIEF
LIBRARY □ Montreal, PQ

Martinez, Eloise F., Supv.
AMOCO PRODUCTION COMPANY
INTERNATIONAL - LIBRARY INFORMATION
CENTER □ Houston, TX

Martinez, Ileana D., Dir.
UNIVERSITY OF PUERTO RICO - HUMACAO
UNIVERSITY COLLEGE - LIBRARY □ Humacao,
PR

Martinez, Katharine, Chf.Libn.
SMITHSONIAN INSTITUTION LIBRARIES -
COOPER-HEWITT MUSEUM OF DESIGN - DORIS
& HENRY DREYFUSS MEMORIAL STUDY
CENTER □ New York, NY

Martinez, L.W., Mgr.
WEYERHAEUSER COMPANY - TECHNICAL
INFORMATION CENTER □ Tacoma, WA

Martinez, Lou Ellen, Archv.
NEW MEXICO STATE COMMISSION OF PUBLIC
RECORDS AND ARCHIVES - ARCHIVAL
SERVICES DIVISION □ Santa Fe, NM

Martinez, Martha, Cat.
INTERAMERICAN UNIVERSITY OF PUERTO
RICO - SCHOOL OF LAW - DOMINGO TOLEDO
ALAMO LAW LIBRARY† □ Santurce, PR

Martinook, Mrs. D., Sec.
CANADA - AGRICULTURE CANADA - RESEARCH
STATION, MORDEN - LIBRARY □ Morden, MB

Martins, Marie A., Adm.Supv.
BROWN UNIVERSITY - JOHN CARTER BROWN
LIBRARY □ Providence, RI

Martinsek, Catherine, Asst.Soc.Stud.Libn.
SOUTHERN ILLINOIS UNIVERSITY,
CARBONDALE - SOCIAL STUDIES DIVISION
LIBRARY □ Carbondale, IL

Martison, Jennifer, Libn.
BENNETT JONES - LIBRARY □ Calgary, AB

Marton, Victor, Supv., Info. Unit
LIBRARY OF CONGRESS - COPYRIGHT PUBLIC
INFORMATION OFFICE □ Washington, DC

Marty, Yvonne B., Legal Info.Sys.Adm.
LEVI STRAUSS & COMPANY - CORPORATE LAW
LIBRARY □ San Francisco, CA

Martyn, Dorian, Hd.Tech.Serv.
UNIVERSITY OF MIAMI - SCHOOL OF
MEDICINE - LOUIS CALDER MEMORIAL
LIBRARY □ Miami, FL

Martyn, Katharine, Asst.Hd.
UNIVERSITY OF TORONTO - THOMAS FISHER
RARE BOOK LIBRARY □ Toronto, ON

Martz, David J., Jr., Dir.
UNIVERSITY OF TOLEDO - WARD M. CANADAY
CENTER □ Toledo, OH

Martz, James, Acq.Libn.
DICKINSON STATE COLLEGE - STOXEN
LIBRARY □ Dickinson, ND

Maru, Olavi, Libn.
AMERICAN BAR FOUNDATION - THE
CROMWELL LIBRARY □ Chicago, IL

Marvel, Dorothy, Libn.
ADAMS EXPRESS COMPANY - LIBRARY □
Baltimore, MD

Marwood, Alice, Libn.
BRITISH COLUMBIA GENEALOGICAL SOCIETY -
REFERENCE LIBRARY □ Richmond, BC

Marx, C., Cat.
UNIVERSITY OF WISCONSIN, LA CROSSE -
MURPHY LIBRARY □ La Crosse, WI

Marx, Lillian, Index
NEWSDAY, INC. - LIBRARY □ Melville, NY

Mary, Sr. Genevieve, Archv.
SERVANTS OF THE IMMACULATE HEART OF
MARY - ARCHIVES □ Immaculata, PA

Maryanow, Maurice, Jr., Chf., Oral Hist.Div.
U.S. AIR FORCE - HISTORICAL RESEARCH
CENTER □ Maxwell AFB, AL

Marz, Sandra, Law Lib.Dir.
WASHOE COUNTY LAW LIBRARY □ Reno, NV

Masak, Phyllis, Cat. & Ref.Libn.
CONCORDIA COLLEGE - KLINCK MEMORIAL
LIBRARY □ River Forest, IL

Masar, Steve, Archv./Processor
UNIVERSITY OF WISCONSIN, MADISON -
ARCHIVES □ Madison, WI

Mascher, Jane, Asst.Libn.
TRANSCONTINENTAL GAS PIPE LINE
CORPORATION - LIBRARY □ Houston, TX

Mascio, Clemente, Libn.
FASHION INSTITUTE OF DESIGN &
MERCHANDISING - RESOURCE AND RESEARCH
CENTER† □ Los Angeles, CA

Masek, Linda, Hd.Libn.
ELYRIA MEMORIAL HOSPITAL - LIBRARY† □
Elyria, OH

Mashbaum, Dr. Jesse, Dir.
BALTIMORE HEBREW COLLEGE - JOSEPH
MEYERHOFF LIBRARY □ Baltimore, MD

Mashburn, Martha, Ref./Rd.Serv.Libn.
GEORGIA STATE LIBRARY □ Atlanta, GA

Masin, Anton, Libn.
UNIVERSITY OF NOTRE DAME -
ARCHITECTURE LIBRARY □ Notre Dame, IN

Maskewitz, Betty F., Dir.
OAK RIDGE NATIONAL LABORATORY -
RADIATION SHIELDING INFORMATION
CENTER □ Oak Ridge, TN

Maslansky, Hannah V., Asst.Libn.
UNION CARBIDE CORPORATION - LIBRARY &
TECHNICAL INFORMATION SERVICE □
Tarrytown, NY

Masling, Annette, Libn.
ALBRIGHT-KNOX ART GALLERY - ART
REFERENCE LIBRARY □ Buffalo, NY

Masling, Charles, Coord.
HOUSTON PUBLIC LIBRARY - COMMUNITY
INFORMATION SERVICE □ Houston, TX

Maslowski, Renata J., Asst.Libn.
RESURRECTION HOSPITAL - MEDICAL LIBRARY
& ALLIED HEALTH SCIENCES □ Chicago, IL

Maslyn, David C., Hd., Spec.Coll.
UNIVERSITY OF RHODE ISLAND - RHODE
ISLAND ORAL HISTORY PROJECT □ Kingston, RI

Maslyn, David C., Hd.
UNIVERSITY OF RHODE ISLAND - SPECIAL
COLLECTIONS □ Kingston, RI

Masner, Virginia C., Libn.
U.S. NAVY - NAVAL HOSPITAL (TN-Memphis) -
GENERAL AND MEDICAL LIBRARY □ Millington,
TN

Mason, Alexandra, Spencer Libn.
UNIVERSITY OF KANSAS - DEPARTMENT OF
SPECIAL COLLECTIONS □ Lawrence, KS

Mason, Charlotte F., Asst.
AMF, INC. - TECHNICAL INFORMATION
CENTER □ Stamford, CT

Mason, David B., Chf.Archv. & Lib.Prog.
BRITISH COLUMBIA - MINISTRY OF
PROVINCIAL SECRETARY & GOVERNMENT
SERVICES - PROVINCIAL ARCHIVES □ Victoria,
BC

Mason, Dorothy, Hd.Libn.
NEW PROVIDENCE HISTORICAL SOCIETY -
LIBRARY □ New Providence, NJ

Mason, Elizabeth B., Assoc.Dir.
COLUMBIA UNIVERSITY - ORAL HISTORY
COLLECTION □ New York, NY
Mason, Elsbeth
LITTON INDUSTRIES - GUIDANCE AND
CONTROL SYSTEMS - LIBRARY □ Woodland Hills,
CA
Mason, Francis S., Jr., Asst.Dir.
PIERPONT MORGAN LIBRARY □ New York, NY
Mason, Frank O., Libn.
UNIVERSITY OF SOUTHERN CALIFORNIA -
HEALTH SCIENCES CAMPUS - DENTISTRY
LIBRARY □ Los Angeles, CA
Mason, Hayden, Libn.
THE C.T. MAIN CORPORATION - LIBRARY □
Boston, MA
Mason, Helen B., Libn.
UNIVERSITY OF TENNESSEE - SPACE
INSTITUTE LIBRARY □ Tullahoma, TN
Mason, Helen F., Adult Serv.Libn.
WARREN LIBRARY ASSOCIATION - LIBRARY □
Warren, PA
Mason, Joy, Lib.Chm.
VIZCAYA GUIDES LIBRARY □ Miami, FL
Mason, Dr. Lee F., Resident Dir.
LOUISIANA STATE UNIVERSITY - SOUTHEAST
RESEARCH STATION - LIBRARY □ Franklinton,
LA
Mason, Margaret E., Corp.Libn.
HEIDRICK & STRUGGLES, INC. - LIBRARY
RESEARCH CENTER □ Chicago, IL
Mason, Marianne, Law Libn.
WOOD COUNTY LAW LIBRARY □ Bowling Green,
OH
Mason, Martha A., Sr.Libn.
BINGHAMTON PSYCHIATRIC CENTER -
PROFESSIONAL LIBRARY □ Binghamton, NY
Mason, Mildred, Dir.
BUREAU OF NATIONAL AFFAIRS, INC. -
LIBRARY AND INFORMATION CENTER □
Washington, DC
Mason, Pauline M., Chf., Lib.Serv.
U.S. VETERANS ADMINISTRATION (PA-
Pittsburgh) - HOSPITAL LIBRARY □ Pittsburgh,
PA
Mason, Philip P., Dir.
WAYNE STATE UNIVERSITY - ARCHIVES OF
LABOR AND URBAN AFFAIRS/UNIVERSITY
ARCHIVES □ Detroit, MI
Mason, Sandra, Med.Libn.
U.S. VETERANS ADMINISTRATION (PA-
Pittsburgh) - MEDICAL CENTER LIBRARY
SERVICE (142D) □ Pittsburgh, PA
Mason, Timothy, Cat.Libn.
TEXAS COLLEGE OF OSTEOPATHIC MEDICINE -
HEALTH SCIENCES LIBRARY □ Fort Worth, TX
Massa, Paul P., Pres.
CONGRESSIONAL INFORMATION SERVICE,
INC. □ Bethesda MD
Massabny, Judy T., Exec.Dir.
GRANGE-FARM FILM FOUNDATION - LIBRARY □
Washington, DC
Massari, Loretta, Bus.Info.Spec.
ALLIED CORPORATION - LIBRARY &
INFORMATION SERVICES □ Morristown, NJ
Masseau, D., Info.Spec.
BELL-NORTHERN RESEARCH LTD. - TECHNICAL
INFORMATION CENTRE □ Toronto, ON
Massengale, R.G., Conference Archv./Hist.
HUNTINGDON COLLEGE - HOUGHTON
MEMORIAL LIBRARY - DEPOSITORY OF
ARCHIVAL AND HISTORICAL MATERIALS □
Montgomery, AL
Massie, Juanita J., Med.Rec.Adm./Libn.
EVANSVILLE PSYCHIATRIC CHILDREN'S
CENTER - STAFF LIBRARY □ Evansville, IN
Massis, Bruce E., Dir.
JEWISH GUILD FOR THE BLIND - YOUNG MEN'S
PHILANTHROPIC LEAGUE - CASSETTE LIBRARY
□ New York, NY
Massman, Virgil F., Exec.Dir.
HILL (James Jerome) REFERENCE LIBRARY □ St.
Paul, MN

Masson, Sandra, Libn.
CNA LIBRARY □ Chicago, IL
Massong, M. Neil, Info.Assoc.
MOTOR VEHICLE MANUFACTURERS
ASSOCIATION (MVMA) - TECHNICAL LIBRARY†
□ Detroit, MI
Masters, Fred N., Jr., Mgr.Tech.Info.Rsrcs.
DEXTER CORPORATION - C.H. DEXTER
DIVISION - TECHNICAL LIBRARY □ Windsor
Locks, CT
Masters, Linda J., Lib.Tech.Asst.
MINER CENTER LIBRARY □ Chazy, NY
Masters, Ray, Res.Techn.
SUNY - COLLEGE OF ENVIRONMENTAL SCIENCE
& FORESTRY - HUNTINGTON WILDLIFE FOREST
LIBRARY □ Newcomb, NY
Masters, Robin J., Rsrc.Spec.
ORANGE COUNTY TRANSIT DISTRICT -
RESOURCE CENTER □ Garden Grove, CA
Masterson, Lynne, Cat.
AMERICAN ASSOCIATION OF RETIRED
PERSONS - NATIONAL GERONTOLOGY
RESOURCE CENTER† □ Washington, DC
Mastriani, Evangeline, Libn.
U.S. DEPT. OF JUSTICE - CIVIL DIVISION
LIBRARY □ Washington, DC
Mastro, Cherie J., Staff Libn.
WASHINGTON STATE DEPARTMENT OF
VETERANS AFFAIRS - STAFF & MEMBER
LIBRARY □ Retsil, WA
Mastropierro, Rae, Law Libn.
VOLUSIA COUNTY LAW LIBRARY □ Daytona
Beach, FL
Mastrovita, Frank, Ref.
MITRE CORPORATION - TECHNICAL REPORT
CENTER □ Bedford, MA
Masur, Harold Q., Exec. V.P.
MYSTERY WRITERS OF AMERICA, INC. -
MYSTERY LIBRARY □ New York, NY
Matcher, Rita, Dir., Lib.Serv.
SINAI HOSPITAL OF BALTIMORE, INC. -
EISENBERG MEDICAL STAFF LIBRARY □
Baltimore, MD
Matchinski, William L., Inst.Prog.Lib.Spec.
WYOMING STATE HOSPITAL - MEDICAL
LIBRARY □ Evanston, WY
Mate, Mrs. Rudolph
RHODODENDRON SPECIES FOUNDATION -
LAWRENCE J. PIERCE RHODODENDRON
LIBRARY □ Federal Way, WA
Matejic, Dr. Predrag, Cur.
OHIO STATE UNIVERSITY - HILANDAR ROOM □
Columbus, OH
Matera, L., Info.Spec.
STANDARD OIL COMPANY OF INDIANA -
LIBRARY/INFORMATION CENTER □ Chicago, IL
Matesic, Kathleen, Asst.Dir., Media Serv.
UNIVERSITY OF PITTSBURGH - UNIVERSITY
CENTER FOR INSTRUCTIONAL RESOURCES □
Pittsburgh, PA
Math, Sandra, Libn.
ASSOCIATION OF AMERICAN PUBLISHERS -
STEPHEN GREENE MEMORIAL LIBRARY AND
INFORMATION CENTER □ New York, NY
Mather, Bryant, Dir.
U.S. ARMY - ENGINEER WATERWAYS
EXPERIMENT STATION - CONCRETE
TECHNOLOGY INFORMATION ANALYSIS
CENTER □ Vicksburg, MS
Mather, Leonard J., Kpr./Memorabilia
ARCANE ORDER - LIBRARY □ Falls Church, VA
Mather, Mildred, Archv.-Libn.
U.S. PRESIDENTIAL LIBRARIES - HERBERT
HOOVER LIBRARY □ West Branch, IA
Mathes, Carolyn B., Chf., Lib.Serv.
U.S. VETERANS ADMINISTRATION (MA-Boston)
- OUTPATIENT CLINIC LIBRARY SERVICE
(142D) □ Boston, MA
Mathes, Karan, Engr.Sec.
JET RESEARCH CENTER, INC. - TECHNICAL
INFORMATION AND SCIENCE LIBRARY □
Arlington, TX

Matheson, Joyce, Dir., Lib.Serv.
HAVERFORD STATE HOSPITAL - HEALTH
SCIENCES LIBRARY† □ Haverford, PA
Matheson, Margaret, Music Libn.
CANADIAN NATIONAL INSTITUTE FOR THE
BLIND - NATIONAL LIBRARY SERVICES -
SHERMAN SWIFT REFERENCE LIBRARY □
Toronto, ON
Matheson, William, Chf.
LIBRARY OF CONGRESS - RARE BOOK &
SPECIAL COLLECTIONS DIVISION □
Washington, DC
Mathew, Susan, Ref.Libn.
UNIVERSITY OF BRITISH COLUMBIA -
GOVERNMENT PUBLICATIONS & MICROFORMS
DIVISIONS □ Vancouver, BC
Mathews, Kathleen, Coord.
HAMILTON PUBLIC LIBRARY - SPECIAL
COLLECTIONS □ Hamilton, ON
Mathews, Marilyn, Libn.
ST. MARY'S HOSPITAL - MEDICAL LIBRARY† □
Kitchener, ON
Mathews, Robert C., Ref.Libn.
U.S. AIR FORCE BASE - KIRTLAND BASE
LIBRARY □ Kirtland AFB, NM
Mathezer, Pauline
UNIVERSITY OF CALGARY - SOCIAL SCIENCES
LIBRARY† □ Calgary, AB
Mathieson, Terry R., Law Lib.Assoc.
VIRGINIA BEACH PUBLIC LIBRARY SYSTEM -
ROBERT S. WAHAB, JR. PUBLIC LAW LIBRARY
□ Virginia Beach, VA
Mathieu, Richard, Chf.Libn.
QUEBEC PROVINCE - MINISTERE DU LOISIR,
DE LA CHASSE ET DE LA PECHE -
BIBLIOTHEQUE DE LA FAUNE □ Montreal, PQ
Mathis, Meyer, Dir., Off.Gen.Adm.
AMERICAN RED CROSS - NATIONAL
HEADQUARTERS LIBRARY □ Washington, DC
Mathis, Wes, Lib.Dir.
NATIONAL LIBRARY OF SPORTS □ San Jose, CA
Mathis, Yvonne, Asst.Libn.
ST. MARY'S HOSPITAL - LIBRARY □ Grand
Rapids, MI
Matiisen, Tina, Hd., Info.Serv.
CANADA - DEFENCE RESEARCH
ESTABLISHMENT OTTAWA - LIBRARY† □
Ottawa, ON
Matkovic, Patricia, Ref.Libn.
INDIANA STATE LIBRARY - INDIANA DIVISION
□ Indianapolis, IN
Matlack, Robert, Libn.
CARNEGIE LIBRARY OF PITTSBURGH -
SCIENCE AND TECHNOLOGY DEPARTMENT □
Pittsburgh, PA
Matlin, Helen, Libn.
GOOD SAMARITAN HOSPITAL - MEDICAL
LIBRARY □ West Islip, NY
Matlock, Teresa A., Info.Coord.
ASHLAND EXPLORATION, INC. - INFORMATION
CENTER □ Houston, TX
Matosian, Marilyn, Sr.Res.
CONTRA COSTA COUNTY OFFICE OF
EDUCATION - ACCESS INFORMATION CENTER
& PROFESSIONAL LIBRARY □ Concord, CA
Matous, Naomi L., Libn.
RESEARCH SERVICES CORPORATION - THE
O.A. BATTISTA RESEARCH INSTITUTE -
LIBRARY □ Fort Worth, TX
Matson, JoAnne, Sec.
RANGE MENTAL HEALTH CENTER - LIBRARY □
Virginia, MN
Matson, Ms. M., Chf., Trade & Commun.Rec.
CANADA - PUBLIC ARCHIVES OF CANADA -
FEDERAL ARCHIVES DIVISION □ Ottawa, ON
Matson, Sheldon, Libn.
PATERSON NEWS - LIBRARY/NEWSPAPER
MORGUE □ Paterson, NJ
Matsuda, Pegi, Community Rel.Rep.
GENERAL TELEPHONE OF CALIFORNIA - FILM
LIBRARY □ Santa Monica, CA

Matsuda, Shizue, Libn.
INDIANA UNIVERSITY - EAST ASIAN
COLLECTION □ Bloomington, IN

Matsui, Masato, Hd., E. Asia Vernacular
UNIVERSITY OF HAWAII - ASIA COLLECTION □
Honolulu, HI

Matsumiya, Don H., Libn.
HUGHES AIRCRAFT COMPANY - GROUND
SYSTEMS GROUP - TECHNICAL LIBRARY □
Fullerton, CA

Matsumoto, Hisao, Hd., Japanese Sect.
LIBRARY OF CONGRESS - ASIAN DIVISION □
Washington, DC

Matt, Salinda M., Chf.Libn.
LANCASTER COUNTY HISTORICAL SOCIETY -
LIBRARY □ Lancaster, PA

Matta, Paula, Libn.
PRINCETON LIBRARY IN NEW YORK □ New
York, NY

Mattei, Janet A., Dir.
AMERICAN ASSOCIATION OF VARIABLE STAR
OBSERVERS - MC ATEER LIBRARY □ Cambridge,
MA

Mattei, Louis, Supv.Plan.
MIDDLESEX COUNTY PLANNING BOARD - DATA
MANAGEMENT & TECHNICAL SERVICES
SECTION - LIBRARY □ New Brunswick, NJ

Mattei-Mejia, Ali, Coord.
TEXAS WOMAN'S UNIVERSITY - LIBRARY
SCIENCE LIBRARY - PROYECTO LEER □ Denton,
TX

Mattern, Joanne A., Archv.Br.Supv.
DELAWARE STATE DIVISION OF HISTORICAL &
CULTURAL AFFAIRS - DELAWARE STATE
ARCHIVES □ Dover, DE

Matteucci, Emily, Map Libn.
DALLAS PUBLIC LIBRARY - GOVERNMENT
PUBLICATIONS DIVISION □ Dallas, TX

Matthes, Dolly, Rec.Coord.
DAIRYLAND POWER COOPERATIVE - LIBRARY
□ La Crosse, WI

Matthew, Jeannette, Archv.
INDIANA UNIVERSITY/PURDUE UNIVERSITY
AT INDIANAPOLIS - UNIVERSITY LIBRARY □
Indianapolis, IN

Matthew, Mildred, Pres.
YADKIN COUNTY HISTORICAL SOCIETY -
LIBRARY □ Yadkinville, NC

Matthewman, Anne, Libn.
ESSEX LAW ASSOCIATION - LIBRARY □
Windsor, ON

Matthews, Mrs. A., Supv.
ALBERTA - OFFICE OF THE OMBUDSMAN -
OMBUDSMAN'S LIBRARY □ Edmonton, AB

Matthews, Ann M., Historic Site Adm.
WATKINS WOOLEN MILL STATE HISTORIC
SITE - RESEARCH LIBRARY □ Lawson, MO

Matthews, Catherine J., Libn.
UNIVERSITY OF TORONTO - CENTRE OF
CRIMINOLOGY - LIBRARY □ Toronto, ON

Matthews, Charles E., Tech.Libn.
DIGITAL EQUIPMENT CORPORATION - SPIT
BROOK LIBRARY □ Nashua, NH

Matthews, Christine, Hd., On-line Serv.
GEORGE WASHINGTON UNIVERSITY -
MEDICAL CENTER - PAUL HIMMELFARB
HEALTH SCIENCES LIBRARY □ Washington, DC

Matthews, Donald N., Libn.
LUTHERAN THEOLOGICAL SEMINARY - A.R.
WENTZ LIBRARY □ Gettysburg, PA

Matthews, Elizabeth W., Cat.Libn.
SOUTHERN ILLINOIS UNIVERSITY,
CARBONDALE - SCHOOL OF LAW LIBRARY □
Carbondale, IL

Matthews, Janice Drumm, Law Lib.Ck.
NEW YORK STATE SUPREME COURT - 4TH
JUDICIAL DISTRICT - LAW LIBRARY □ Oswego,
NY

Matthews, Jaxon K., Libn.
CONTROL DATA CORPORATION - SUNNYVALE
OPERATIONS LIBRARY □ Sunnyvale, CA

Matthews, Jessie, Night Ref.Libn.
RUTGERS UNIVERSITY, THE STATE
UNIVERSITY OF NEW JERSEY - SCHOOL OF
LAW LIBRARY† □ Camden, NJ

Matthews, Linda M., Hd.
EMORY UNIVERSITY - SPECIAL COLLECTIONS
DEPARTMENT □ Atlanta, GA

Matthews, Mrs. Raymond, Libn.
FIRST BAPTIST CHURCH - E.F. WALKER
MEMORIAL LIBRARY □ Luling, TX

Matthews, Richard P., Spec.Coll.Libn.
TRENTON STATE COLLEGE - ROSCOE L. WEST
LIBRARY - SPECIAL COLLECTIONS □ Trenton,
NJ

Matthews, Sandra S., Ref.
U.S. ARMED FORCES RADIOBIOLOGY
RESEARCH INSTITUTE (AFRRI) - LIBRARY
SERVICES □ Bethesda, MD

Mattimore, Maryanne, Med.Libn.
BINGHAMTON GENERAL HOSPITAL - STUART B.
BLAKELY MEMORIAL LIBRARY □ Binghamton, NY

Mattingly, John F., Dir.
ST. PATRICK'S SEMINARY - MC KEON
MEMORIAL LIBRARY □ Menlo Park, CA

Mattingly, Marilyn, Sr.Libn., KENCLIP
KENTUCKY STATE DEPARTMENT FOR
LIBRARIES AND ARCHIVES - STATE LIBRARY
SERVICES DIVISION □ Frankfort, KY

Mattis, Kelly, Libn.
BROWN BROTHERS HARRIMAN & CO. -
RESEARCH LIBRARY □ New York, NY

Mattocks, Geoffrey L., Adm.Dir.
FARMINGDALE PUBLIC SCHOOLS -
PROFESSIONAL LIBRARY □ Farmingdale, NY

Mattocks, Yvonne, Lib.Supv.
MC GILL UNIVERSITY - OCEANOGRAPHY
LIBRARY □ Montreal, PQ

Mattoon, Bruce P., V.P.
FACTORY MUTUAL SYSTEM - FACTORY
MUTUAL RESEARCH CORPORATION - LIBRARY
□ Norwood, MA

Mattrey, Deborah C., Dir., Tech.Serv.
CALIFORNIA WESTERN SCHOOL OF LAW -
LIBRARY □ San Diego, CA

Matts, Constance, Readers Serv.Libn.
INDIANA UNIVERSITY, INDIANAPOLIS -
SCHOOL OF LAW LIBRARY □ Indianapolis, IN

Mattscheck, Barbara, Res.Libn.
HAY ASSOCIATES - RESEARCH LIBRARY □
Philadelphia, PA

Mattson, Bonnie, Libn.
MUNICIPALITY OF METROPOLITAN SEATTLE -
METRO LIBRARY □ Seattle, WA

Mattson, Francis O., Cur. of Rare Bks.
NEW YORK PUBLIC LIBRARY - RARE BOOKS &
MANUSCRIPTS DIVISION - RARE BOOK
COLLECTION □ New York, NY

Mattson, Gerri, Int.Pubns.
IBM CORPORATION - GENERAL PRODUCTS
DIVISION - STL LIBRARY □ San Jose, CA

Mattson, Pamela A., Libn.
MOORE, GARDNER & ASSOCIATES, INC.,
CONSULTING ENGINEERS - LIBRARY □
Asheboro, NC

Mattson, Virginia, Circuit Libn.
CLEVELAND HEALTH SCIENCES LIBRARY -
ALLEN MEMORIAL LIBRARY □ Cleveland, OH

Matturro, Richard C., Libn.
ALBANY BUSINESS COLLEGE - LIBRARY† □
Albany, NY

Matty, Paul, Libn.
PIMA COUNTY PLANNING DEPARTMENT -
LIBRARY □ Tucson, AZ

Matulka, Carol, Med.Libn.
ST. JOSEPH MEDICAL CENTER - HOSPITAL
LIBRARY □ Wichita, KS

Matusak, Susan, Hd.Libn.
SHERMAN COLLEGE OF STRAIGHT
CHIROPRACTIC - TOM AND MAE BAHAN
LIBRARY □ Spartanburg, SC

Matz, Ruth G., Chf.Libn.
MASSACHUSETTS STATE DEPARTMENT OF THE
ATTORNEY GENERAL - LIBRARY □ Boston, MA

Matzek, Richard A., Dir.
NAZARETH COLLEGE OF ROCHESTER -
LORETTE WILMOT LIBRARY - SPECIAL
COLLECTIONS □ Rochester, NY

Matzen, Constance M., Libn.
SMITH, ANDERSON, BLOUNT, DORSETT,
MITCHELL & JERNIGAN - LIBRARY □ Raleigh, NC

Matzka, Liselotte, Hd., Sci.Lib.
ADELPHI UNIVERSITY - SCIENCE LIBRARY† □
Garden City, NY

Matzkanin, George A., Dir.
SOUTHWEST RESEARCH INSTITUTE -
NONDESTRUCTIVE TESTING INFORMATION
ANALYSIS CENTER □ San Antonio, TX

Mau, Evelyn, Libn.
U.S. MARINE CORPS - CAMP H.M. SMITH
LIBRARY □ Honolulu, HI

Maucione, Dorothy M., Med.Libn.
CALVARY HOSPITAL - MEDICAL LIBRARY □
Bronx, NY

Mauck, Virginia, Asst.Cur. of Mss.
INDIANA UNIVERSITY - LILLY LIBRARY □
Bloomington, IN

Maughan, LeRoy R., Lib.Sys.Spec.
GSG, INC. - CTI LIBRARY SYSTEMS, INC. □
Orem, UT

Maughan, Patricia Davitt, Libn.
UNIVERSITY OF CALIFORNIA, BERKELEY -
SEBASTIAN S. KRESGE ENGINEERING LIBRARY
□ Berkeley, CA

Maura, Mariano, Libn.
UNIVERSITY OF PUERTO RICO - NATURAL
SCIENCE LIBRARY □ Rio Piedras, PR

Maurer, Esther J., Hd.
FREE LIBRARY OF PHILADELPHIA -
EDUCATION, PHILOSOPHY, RELIGION
DEPARTMENT □ Philadelphia, PA

Maurin, Raissa, Chf.Libn.
U.S. VETERANS ADMINISTRATION (FL-Miami) -
MEDICAL CENTER LIBRARY □ Miami, FL

Maus, Carol, Ref.Libn.
TEACHERS COLLEGE - MILBANK MEMORIAL
LIBRARY □ New York, NY

Maus, Pat, Adm.
NORTHEAST MINNESOTA HISTORICAL CENTER
- LIBRARY □ Duluth, MN

Mauter, George A., Supv.
FAIRCHILD INDUSTRIES - FAIRCHILD
REPUBLIC COMPANY - TECHNICAL
INFORMATION CENTER □ Farmingdale, NY

Mautner, Robert W., Sci.Engr.Ref.Libn.
UNIVERSITY OF ARIZONA - SCIENCE-
ENGINEERING LIBRARY □ Tucson, AZ

Mawn, Dr. Geoffrey P., Cur.
ARIZONA STATE UNIVERSITY - ARIZONA
COLLECTIONS† □ Tempe, AZ

Max, Lin, Libn.
COGSWELL COLLEGE - LIBRARY □ San
Francisco, CA

Max, Stanley M., Cat.
CENTRAL MICHIGAN UNIVERSITY - CLARKE
HISTORICAL LIBRARY □ Mt. Pleasant, MI

Maxant, Vicary, Libn.
RAYTHEON DATA SYSTEMS COMPANY -
LIBRARY □ Norwood, MA

Maxey, Barbara J., Sr.Libn.
RADIAN CORPORATION - LIBRARY □ Austin, TX

Maxfield, Richard, Ref.
DIGITAL EQUIPMENT CORPORATION -
MAYNARD AREA INFORMATION SERVICES □
Maynard, MA

Maxham, Mrs. Donald G., Libn.
BRAINTREE HISTORICAL SOCIETY, INC. -
LIBRARY □ Braintree, MA

Maxham, Judith, Ref., ILL
MERCYHURST COLLEGE - LIBRARY - ARCHIVES
□ Erie, PA

Maximena, Delores E., Sr.Libn.
GENERAL MOTORS CORPORATION - RESEARCH
LABORATORIES LIBRARY □ Warren, MI

Maxin, Jacqueline A., Supv., Info.Serv.
PPG INDUSTRIES, INC. - FIBER GLASS
RESEARCH CENTER - LIBRARY □ Pittsburgh, PA

Maxon, Bill, Ref.Libn.
GEORGETOWN UNIVERSITY - FRED O. DENNIS
LAW LIBRARY □ Washington, DC
Maxon-Dadd, Josephine, Hd., Info. & Res.
LAWRENCE BERKELEY LABORATORY - LIBRARY
□ Berkeley, CA
Maxstadt, John
LOUISIANA STATE UNIVERSITY - REFERENCE
SERVICES □ Baton Rouge, LA
Maxwell, Miss B., Asst.Libn.
FALCONBRIDGE NICKEL MINES, LTD. -
METALLURGICAL LABORATORIES
INFORMATION SERVICES† □ Thornhill, ON
Maxwell, Claude S., Supv., Photo Serv.
OKLAHOMA STATE UNIVERSITY - AUDIO
VISUAL CENTER □ Stillwater, OK
Maxwell, Daisy D., Libn.
FAYETTEVILLE PUBLISHING COMPANY -
NEWSPAPER LIBRARY □ Fayetteville, NC
Maxwell, Dolores M., Bibliog.
TEXAS TECH UNIVERSITY - LIBRARY □
Lubbock, TX
Maxwell, Faye, Asst.Curric.Libn.
UNIVERSITY OF ALBERTA - H.T. COUTTS
LIBRARY □ Edmonton, AB
Maxwell, Joann M., Lib.Ck.
PORT HURON TIMES HERALD - LIBRARY □ Port
Huron, MI
Maxwell, Littleton M., Libn.
UNIVERSITY OF RICHMOND - E. CLAIBORNE
ROBINS SCHOOL OF BUSINESS LIBRARY □
Richmond, VA
Maxwell, Sara, Testing Techn.
NASHVILLE STATE TECHNICAL INSTITUTE -
EDUCATIONAL RESOURCE CENTER □ Nashville,
TN
May, Arlee, Asst.Dir./Pub.Serv.
SUNY AT STONY BROOK - HEALTH SCIENCES
LIBRARY □ East Setauket, NY
May, Charles, Assoc.Prof./Libn.
NASHVILLE STATE TECHNICAL INSTITUTE -
EDUCATIONAL RESOURCE CENTER □ Nashville,
TN
May, Cindy, Cat.Libn.
UNIVERSITY OF WISCONSIN, MADISON - LAW
SCHOOL LIBRARY □ Madison, WI
May, Dr. Curtis, Adm., Media & Lib.Serv.
SAN MATEO COUNTY EDUCATIONAL
RESOURCES CENTER □ Redwood City, CA
May, J. Bryan, Hd., Doc.Serv.Ctr.
COLUMBIA UNIVERSITY - HERBERT H. LEHMAN
LIBRARY □ New York, NY
May, Joanne M., Libn.
U.S. NAVY - NAVAL ENVIRONMENTAL
PREDICTION RESEARCH FACILITY -
TECHNICAL LIBRARY □ Monterey, CA
May, Maija B., Libn.
ERIKSON INSTITUTE - LIBRARY □ Chicago, IL
May, Nadene N., Secondary Libn.
KENTUCKY SCHOOL FOR THE DEAF - LEARNING
RESOURCE CENTER □ Danville, KY
May, Patricia, Lib.Serv.
ST. JOSEPH'S HOSPITAL AND MEDICAL
CENTER - HEALTH SCIENCES LIBRARY □
Paterson, NJ
May, Ruby S., Assoc.Dir.
UNIVERSITY OF ILLINOIS AT CHICAGO -
HEALTH SCIENCES CENTER - LIBRARY OF THE
HEALTH SCIENCES □ Chicago, IL
May, Sallie, Cat.Supv.
OUR LADY OF LIGHT LIBRARY □ Santa Barbara,
CA
Maycock, Susan E., Survey Dir.
CAMBRIDGE HISTORICAL COMMISSION -
LIBRARY □ Cambridge, MA
Mayden, Priscilla M., Dir.
UNIVERSITY OF UTAH - SPENCER S. ECCLES
HEALTH SCIENCES LIBRARY □ Salt Lake City,
UT
Mayer, Barbara, Dp.Libn.
FEDERAL RESERVE BANK OF CHICAGO -
LIBRARY □ Chicago, IL

Mayer, George L., Coord.
NEW YORK PUBLIC LIBRARY - GENERAL
LIBRARY OF THE PERFORMING ARTS □ New
York, NY
Mayer, Harriet, Libn.
PUBLIC SERVICE ELECTRIC AND GAS
COMPANY - LIBRARY □ Newark, NJ
Mayer, Robert, Asst.Dir./Hd., Tech.Serv.
STANFORD UNIVERSITY - J. HUGH JACKSON
LIBRARY □ Stanford, CA
Mayer, Vera, V.P., Info. & Archv.
NATIONAL BROADCASTING COMPANY, INC. -
RECORDS ADMINISTRATION INFORMATION
AND ARCHIVES □ New York, NY
Mayer, Vera, V.P., Info. & Archv.
NATIONAL BROADCASTING COMPANY, INC. -
REFERENCE LIBRARY □ New York, NY
Mayer, Yisrael, Sec.
FOUNDATION FOR DISABILITY INTERCHANGE
- LIBRARY □ Easton, PA
Mayers, Bernard J., Supv.
INTERNATIONAL FLAVORS AND FRAGRANCES,
INC. - TECHNICAL INFORMATION CENTER □
Union Beach, NJ
Mayers, Karen A., Libn.
PEAT, MARWICK, MITCHELL & CO. - LIBRARY □
San Francisco, CA
Mayeski, John, Dir. of Lib.
KEARNEY STATE COLLEGE - CALVIN T. RYAN
LIBRARY - SPECIAL COLLECTIONS □ Kearney,
NE
Mayfield, David M., Dir.
CHURCH OF JESUS CHRIST OF LATTER-DAY
SAINTS - GENEALOGICAL LIBRARY □ Salt Lake
City, UT
Mayfield, Lloyd D., Dir.
COMMUNITY COLLEGE OF BALTIMORE -
LIBRARIES/LEARNING RESOURCES CENTERS □
Baltimore, MD
Mayfield, Mike, Hd., Musm.Div.
WYOMING STATE ARCHIVES MUSEUMS &
HISTORICAL DEPARTMENT □ Cheyenne, WY
Mayfield, Vada, Music Libn.
MADISON PUBLIC LIBRARY - ART AND MUSIC
DIVISION □ Madison, WI
Mayhall, Pauline, Lib.Mgr.
U.S. ARMY HOSPITALS - NOBLE ARMY
HOSPITAL - MEDICAL LIBRARY □ Ft. McClellan,
AL
Maykuth, Daniel J., Mgr.
TIN RESEARCH INSTITUTE, INC. - LIBRARY &
INFORMATION CENTER □ Columbus, OH
Maylone, Theresa, Lib.Serv.Spec.
GENERAL FOODS CORPORATION -
INFORMATION MANAGEMENT DEPARTMENT -
INFORMATION CENTER □ White Plains, NY
Maynard, Elizabeth, Libn.
FEDERAL RESERVE BANK OF CLEVELAND -
RESEARCH LIBRARY □ Cleveland, OH
Maynard, Judge John, Sr. District Judge
NEZ PERCE COUNTY LAW LIBRARY □ Lewiston,
ID
Maynard, Priscilla, Exec.Sec.
ARABIAN HORSE OWNERS FOUNDATION - W.R.
BROWN MEMORIAL LIBRARY □ Tucson, AZ
Maynerd, J. Edmund, Circ.Libn.
CITADEL - THE MILITARY COLLEGE OF SOUTH
CAROLINA - DANIEL LIBRARY □ Charleston, SC
Mayo, Harriett E., Asst.Libn.
ABRAHAM BALDWIN AGRICULTURAL COLLEGE
- LIBRARY □ Tifton, GA
Mayo, Helen, Hd., Ref.
UNIVERSITY OF TEXAS HEALTH SCIENCE
CENTER, DALLAS - LIBRARY □ Dallas, TX
Mayo, Julia, Chf., Ref.Serv.
U.S. NATL. DEFENSE UNIVERSITY - LIBRARY □
Washington, DC
Mayo, Kathleen, Inst.Cons.
STATE LIBRARY OF FLORIDA □ Tallahassee, FL
Mayo, Martha, Spec.Coll.Libn.
UNIVERSITY OF LOWELL, NORTH CAMPUS -
ALUMNI/LYDON LIBRARY† □ Lowell, MA

Mayo, Martha, Hd., Spec.Coll.
UNIVERSITY OF LOWELL, NORTH CAMPUS -
UNIVERSITY LIBRARIES - SPECIAL
COLLECTIONS □ Lowell, MA
Mayoh, Helen, Ref.Libn.
UNIVERSITY OF BRITISH COLUMBIA - SCIENCE
DIVISION □ Vancouver, BC
Mayor, Carol, Libn.
ST. FRANCIS-ST. GEORGE HOSPITAL - HEALTH
SCIENCES LIBRARY □ Cincinnati, OH
Mayr, Ingrid C.D., Libn.
DITTBERNER ASSOCIATES, INC. - LIBRARY □
Bethesda, MD
Mayrand, F., Asst.Hd., Tech.Serv.
CANADA - ENERGY, MINES & RESOURCES
CANADA - HEADQUARTERS LIBRARY □ Ottawa,
ON
Mayrand, Lise, Libn.
UNIVERSITE DE MONTREAL - EDUCATION
PHYSIQUE-BIBLIOTHEQUE □ Montreal, PQ
Mays, David, Libn.
MEMPHIS-SHELBY COUNTY PUBLIC LIBRARY
AND INFO. CTR. - SCIENCE/BUSINESS/SOCIAL
SCI.DEPT. □ Memphis, TN
Mays, G.T., Asst.Dir.
OAK RIDGE NATIONAL LABORATORY -
NUCLEAR SAFETY INFORMATION CENTER □
Oak Ridge, TN
Mayson, Mary, Sr.Lib.Techn.
QUEEN'S UNIVERSITY AT KINGSTON -
GEOLOGICAL SCIENCES LIBRARY □ Kingston,
ON
Mayti, Peggy, Hd. of Info. Bureau
MARYKNOLL SEMINARY - LIBRARY □ Maryknoll,
NY
Mayton, Regina A., Chf., Sys.Div.
U.S. AIR FORCE - AIR UNIVERSITY - LIBRARY □
Maxwell AFB, AL
Maywood, Susan, Chf.Libn.
VERMONT STATE HOSPITAL - AGENCY OF
HUMAN SERVICES LIBRARY □ Waterbury, VT
Maza, Bernardo, Supv.
REYNOLDS ELECTRICAL AND ENGINEERING
COMPANY, INC. - COORDINATION AND
INFORMATION CENTER □ Las Vegas, NV
Mazareas, Helen, Libn.
BANK OF NEW ENGLAND - CORPORATION
LIBRARY AND INFORMATION SERVICE† □
Boston, MA
Maze, Marilyn, Dir.
EUREKA (The California Career Information
System) □ Richmond, CA
Maze, Terry E., Interp.Spec.
U.S. NATL. PARK SERVICE - PETRIFIED
FOREST NATL. PARK - LIBRARY □ Petrified
Forest Natl. Park, AZ
Mazella, Angela, Sr.Info.Sci.
SCHERING-PLOUGH CORPORATION -
PHARMACEUTICAL RESEARCH DIVISION -
LIBRARY INFORMATION CENTER □ Bloomfield,
NJ
Mazeral, Ms. A., Lib.Info.Off.
BEDFORD INSTITUTE OF OCEANOGRAPHY -
LIBRARY □ Dartmouth, NS
Mazsick, Bro. Frank J., C.F.X., Lib.Dir.
ST. VINCENT DE PAUL REGIONAL SEMINARY -
LIBRARY □ Boynton Beach, FL
Mazur, Diane, Cat.
BAYSTATE MEDICAL CENTER - HEALTH
SCIENCES LIBRARY □ Springfield, MA
Mazur, Marjorie, Dir. of Tech.Serv.
SOUTH CAROLINA STATE LIBRARY □ Columbia,
SC
Mazza, Joanne, Libn.
U.S. COURT OF APPEALS, 9TH CIRCUIT -
LIBRARY □ Los Angeles, CA
Mazzeo, Carole, Libn.
MUHLENBERG MEDICAL CENTER - MEDICAL
LIBRARY □ Bethlehem, PA
Mead, Catherine, Hd., Ref. & Info.Serv.
STATE LIBRARY OF OHIO □ Columbus, OH

Mead, Clifford S., Spec.Coll.Libn.
KEENE STATE COLLEGE - WALLACE E. MASON LIBRARY □ Keene, NH

Mead, John H., Musm.Dir.
BEAR MOUNTAIN TRAILSIDE MUSEUMS - LIBRARY □ Bear Mountain, NY

Mead, Ken, Dir., Med.Lib.
HALIFAX HOSPITAL MEDICAL CENTER - MEDICAL LIBRARY □ Daytona Beach, FL

Mead, Thomas, Tech.Serv.Libn.
BROWN & BAIN, P.A. - LIBRARY □ Phoenix, AZ

Meade, B.R., Supv.
SINGER COMPANY - KEARFOTT DIVISION - TECHNICAL INFORMATION CENTER □ Wayne, NJ

Meade, Robert G., Bus.Libn.
MILES LABORATORIES, INC. - LIBRARY RESOURCES AND SERVICES □ Elkhart, IN

Meade, Sylvia, Adm.Sec.
YORK UNIVERSITY - FACULTY OF ARTS - WRITING WORKSHOP LIBRARY □ Downsview, ON

Meader, Robert F.W., Libn.
SHAKER COMMUNITY, INC. - LIBRARY □ Pittsfield, MA

Meadow, C.Z., Dir.
CENTER FOR MODERN PSYCHOANALYTIC STUDIES - LIBRARY □ New York, NY

Meadows, Barbara A., Chf., Lib.Serv.
U.S. VETERANS ADMINISTRATION (TN-Nashville) - MEDICAL CENTER LIBRARY SERVICE □ Nashville, TN

Meadows, Donna, Med.Libn.
U.S. VETERANS ADMINISTRATION (TX-Temple) - MEDICAL CENTER MEDICAL LIBRARY □ Temple, TX

Meadows, Dorothy, ILL
EAST TEXAS BAPTIST UNIVERSITY - MAMYE JARRETT LEARNING CENTER □ Marshall, TX

Meadows, Janice, Cat./ILL
VIRGINIA INSTITUTE OF MARINE SCIENCE LIBRARY □ Gloucester Point, VA

Meadows, Judith A., Law Libn.
FAIRFAX LAW LIBRARY □ Fairfax, VA

Meadows, Judy, Info.Mgr.
ASPEN SYSTEMS CORPORATION - LAW LIBRARY & INFORMATION CENTER† □ Rockville, MD

Meagher, Dixie, Libn.
U.S. ARMY HOSPITALS - LETTERMAN ARMY MEDICAL CENTER - MEDICAL LIBRARY □ Presidio of San Francisco, CA

Meagher, Marian, Supv.Circ.
QUEEN'S UNIVERSITY AT KINGSTON - EDUCATION LIBRARY □ Kingston, ON

Meagher, Roseann, Libn.
FOOTE CONE & BELDING - INFORMATION CENTER □ Chicago, IL

Meagher, Roseann, Libn.
FOOTE CONE & BELDING - INFORMATION CENTER □ Chicago, IL

Mealey, Catherine, Law Libn./Prof.
UNIVERSITY OF WYOMING - LAW LIBRARY □ Laramie, WY

Meanley, Carolyn A., Mgr., Tech.Info.
JACOBS ENGINEERING GROUP - TECHNICAL INFORMATION SERVICES DEPARTMENT □ Houston, TX

Means, Dr. John B., Exec.Dir.
NATIONAL ASSOCIATION OF SELF-INSTRUCTIONAL LANGUAGE PROGRAMS - NASILP INFORMATION CENTER & ARCHIVES □ Philadelphia, PA

Means, Ray B., Lib.Dir.
CREIGHTON UNIVERSITY - REINERT/ALUMNI MEMORIAL LIBRARY □ Omaha, NE

Meares, Carol Ann, Asst.Mgr./Info.Spec.
U.S. DEPT. OF COMMERCE - COMMERCE PRODUCTIVITY CENTER □ Washington, DC

Measell, John, Asst. AV Dir.
NEW HAMPSHIRE COLLEGE - SHAPIRO LIBRARY □ Manchester, NH

Mebrahtu, Mewail, Asst.Ref.Libn.
SAN DIEGO COUNTY LAW LIBRARY □ San Diego, CA

Mecca, Greg, Asst.Dir.
STAMFORD HISTORICAL SOCIETY - LIBRARY □ Stamford, CT

Mechanic, Margaret A., Ref.Libn.
U.S. DEFENSE MAPPING AGENCY - AEROSPACE CENTER - TECHNICAL LIBRARY □ St. Louis, MO

Mechanic, Sylvia, Bus.Libn.
BROOKLYN PUBLIC LIBRARY - BUSINESS LIBRARY □ Brooklyn, NY

Mecher, Mrs. N.C.
CANADA - TAX COURT OF CANADA - TAX LIBRARY □ Ottawa, ON

Meckly, Eugene P., Libn.
KOPPERS COMPANY, INC. - TECHNICAL INFORMATION GROUP □ Monroeville, PA

Meconitas, Beth, Ref.libn.
U.S. AIR FORCE BASE - KEESLER BASE - MC BRIDE LIBRARY □ Keesler AFB, MS

Mecray, Frieda S., Info.Spec.
PHILADELPHIA QUARTZ COMPANY - BUSINESS/CHEMISTRY INFORMATION CENTER □ Valley Forge, PA

Medearis, Mary, Dir.
SOUTHWEST ARKANSAS REGIONAL ARCHIVES (SARA) □ Washington, AR

Meder, Rev. Stephen A., S.J., Libn.
COLOMBIERE COLLEGE - LIBRARY □ Clarkston, MI

Mederos, Amelia, Libn. I
MIAMI-DADE PUBLIC LIBRARY - FOREIGN LANGUAGES DIVISION □ Miami, FL

Medford, Roberta, State Docs.Libn.
UNIVERSITY OF CALIFORNIA, LOS ANGELES - PUBLIC AFFAIRS SERVICE □ Los Angeles, CA

Medici, Marie C., Libn.
ST. VINCENT'S HOSPITAL - SCHOOL OF NURSING LIBRARY □ New York, NY

Medina, Rubens, Chf.
LIBRARY OF CONGRESS - LAW LIBRARY - HISPANIC LAW DIVISION □ Washington, DC

Medley, Larry, Libn.
SMITH (A.O.) CORPORATION - TECHNICAL LIBRARY □ Milwaukee, WI

Medley, Steven P., Libn.
JOSEPHINE COUNTY LAW LIBRARY □ Grants Pass, OR

Medlicott, Mary Alice, Cur.
FRANKLIN COLLEGE - SPECIAL COLLECTIONS □ Franklin, IN

Medlin, Violet, Res.Libn.
DARGAN-CARVER LIBRARY □ Nashville, TN

Medzie, D., Acq.
WIDENER UNIVERSITY - WOLFGRAM MEMORIAL LIBRARY □ Chester, PA

Meehan, Miriam A., Libn.
AMERICAN PAPER INSTITUTE - LIBRARY □ New York, NY

Meehan, Thomas J., Libn.
HOME MISSIONERS OF AMERICA - GLENMARY NOVITIATE LIBRARY □ Cincinnati, OH

Meehan, Vivian, Adm.Dir.
NATIONAL ASSOCIATION OF ANOREXIA NERVOSA AND ASSOCIATED DISORDERS, INC. (ANAD) - LIBRARY □ Highland Park, IL

Meek, LeRoy, Sr.Lit.Sci.
REYNOLDS (R.J.) TOBACCO COMPANY - R&D SCIENTIFIC INFORMATION SERVICES LIBRARY □ Winston-Salem, NC

Meek, Meredith, Off.Mgr.
SOUTHEAST ASIA RESOURCE CENTER □ Berkeley, CA

Meeks, Marilyn A., Libn.
MEMPHIS-SHELBY COUNTY OFFICE OF PLANNING AND DEVELOPMENT - LIBRARY □ Memphis, TN

Meeks, Tom, Dir. of Plan.Serv.
GREENVILLE COUNTY PLANNING COMMISSION - PLANNING TECHNICAL LIBRARY □ Greenville, SC

Meerdink, Richard E., District Libn.
MILWAUKEE AREA TECHNICAL COLLEGE - RASCHE MEMORIAL LIBRARY □ Milwaukee, WI

Meernik, Mary, Libn.
ANN ARBOR NEWS - LIBRARY □ Ann Arbor, MI

Meerveld, Bert, Music Libn.
MOUNT ALLISON UNIVERSITY - ALFRED WHITEHEAD MEMORIAL MUSIC LIBRARY □ Sackville, NB

Meese, Frances, Dir. of Libs.
MEMORIAL HOSPITAL - MEDICAL-NURSING LIBRARY □ Colorado Springs, CO

Meglis, Anne L., Libn.
DISTRICT OF COLUMBIA DEPARTMENT OF HOUSING AND COMMUNITY DEVELOPMENT LIBRARY □ Washington, DC

Mehalick, Joann, Mgr. of Lib.Serv.
EAST ORANGE GENERAL HOSPITAL - HEALTH SERVICES LIBRARY □ East Orange, NJ

Mehegan, Doris, Hd.
TORONTO PUBLIC LIBRARY - SPACED-OUT LIBRARY □ Toronto, ON

Mehle, Jean, Pubn.Mgr.
LEAGUE OF MINNESOTA CITIES - LIBRARY □ St. Paul, MN

Mehr, Joseph O., Libn.
PROVIDENCE JOURNAL COMPANY - NEWS LIBRARY □ Providence, RI

Mehr, Linda Harris, Lib.Adm.
ACADEMY OF MOTION PICTURE ARTS AND SCIENCES - MARGARET HERRICK LIBRARY □ Beverly Hills, CA

Mei, Chiang C., Prof. Civil Engr.
MASSACHUSETTS INSTITUTE OF TECHNOLOGY - CIVIL ENGINEERING DEPT. - RALPH M. PARSONS LABORATORY - REF. RM. □ Cambridge, MA

Meiboom, Esther, Hosp.Libn.
UNIVERSITY OF MEDICINE AND DENTISTRY OF NEW JERSEY AT NEWARK - GEORGE F. SMITH LIBRARY □ Newark, NJ

Meier, Irene, Engr.Libn.
GENERAL INSTRUMENT CORPORATION, GOVERNMENT SYSTEMS DIVISION - ENGINEERING LIBRARY □ Hicksville, NY

Meier, Kathleen, Libn.
BAPTIST MEMORIAL HOSPITAL - SCHOOL OF NURSING - LIBRARY □ Memphis, TN

Meighen, Mary, Chf.Libn.
U.S. NASA - NATL. SPACE TECHNOLOGY LABORATORIES - RESEARCH LIBRARY □ NSTL Station, MS

Meijer, J., Asst.Res.Chem.
INTERNATIONAL FABRICARE INSTITUTE - RESEARCH CENTER LIBRARY □ Silver Spring, MD

Meikle, Alison, Libn.
KEMPTVILLE COLLEGE OF AGRICULTURAL TECHNOLOGY - PURVIS LIBRARY □ Kemptville, ON

Meinhardt, Cynthia, Libn.
OUTBOARD MARINE CORPORATION - RESEARCH CENTER LIBRARY† □ Milwaukee, WI

Meinwald, Dan, Registrar/Cur.
UNIVERSITY OF CALIFORNIA, RIVERSIDE - CALIFORNIA MUSEUM OF PHOTOGRAPHY □ Riverside, CA

Meiser, Barbara, Corp.Info.Rsrcs.Mgr.
FLUKE (John) MANUFACTURING CO., INC. - LIBRARY □ Everett, WA

Meisner, Cynthia I., Libn.
CINCINNATI PSYCHOANALYTIC INSTITUTE - FREDERIC T. KAPP MEMORIAL LIBRARY □ Cincinnati, OH

Meiss, Harriet, Computer Search Libn.
MOUNT SINAI SCHOOL OF MEDICINE OF THE CITY UNIVERSITY OF NEW YORK - GUSTAVE L. & JANET W. LEVY LIBRARY □ New York, NY

Meister, Anabel, Lib.Chf.
CUNY - CITY COLLEGE LIBRARY - SCIENCE/ ENGINEERING DIVISION □ New York, NY

Meizner, Karen L., Hd. of Cat.
NELSON-ATKINS MUSEUM OF ART - SPENCER ART REFERENCE LIBRARY □ Kansas City, MO

Mejill, Gregorio, Cat.Dept.Dir.
CATHOLIC UNIVERSITY OF PUERTO RICO - MONSIGNOR JUAN FREMIOT TORRES OLIVER LAW LIBRARY □ Ponce, PR

Mekos, Katherine F., Med.Libn.
ARNOT-OGDEN MEMORIAL HOSPITAL - WEY MEMORIAL LIBRARY □ Elmira, NY

Mela, Doris K., Libn.
NATIONAL BIOMEDICAL RESEARCH FOUNDATION - LIBRARY □ Washington, DC

Melamed, Dorothy, Libn.
CARNEGIE LIBRARY OF PITTSBURGH - SCIENCE AND TECHNOLOGY DEPARTMENT □ Pittsburgh, PA

Melanson, Lloyd J., Tech.Serv.Libn.
ATLANTIC SCHOOL OF THEOLOGY - LIBRARY† □ Halifax, NS

Melcher, Marlene
HARTFORD PUBLIC LIBRARY - BUSINESS, SCIENCE & TECHNOLOGY DEPARTMENT □ Hartford, CT

Melde, F.B., Libn.
SHELL DEVELOPMENT COMPANY - BELLAIRE RESEARCH CENTER LIBRARY □ Houston, TX

Meldrum, Lawrie G., Archv.
INDIANA STATE COMMISSION ON PUBLIC RECORDS - ARCHIVES DIVISION □ Indianapolis, IN

Meldrum, Mark, Lib.Dir.
MC KAY DEE HOSPITAL CENTER - LIBRARY □ Ogden, UT

Melendez, Carmen M., Circ.
UNIVERSITY OF PUERTO RICO - LAW SCHOOL LIBRARY □ Rio Piedras, PR

Melendez, Rafael, Libn.
UNIVERSITY OF PUERTO RICO - COLLEGE OF EDUCATION - SELLES SOLA MEMORIAL COLLECTION† □ Rio Piedras, PR

Melican, Robert L., Exec.Dir.
JOCKEY CLUB - LIBRARY □ New York, NY

Melick, Pamela, Tech. Indexer
STANDARD OIL COMPANY OF OHIO - CORPORATE ENGINEERING LIBRARY □ Cleveland, OH

Melillo, David D., Law Libn.
TEXAS SOUTHERN UNIVERSITY - LAW LIBRARY† □ Houston, TX

Melin, Mari Lyn, MEDLINE Libn.
U.S. VETERANS ADMINISTRATION (TN-Memphis) - MEDICAL CENTER LIBRARY □ Memphis, TN

Melito, Joyce, Ref.Libn.
COMPTON ADVERTISING INC. - RESEARCH LIBRARY □ New York, NY

Melius, Charlotte, Circ.
LOUISIANA STATE UNIVERSITY - LAW LIBRARY □ Baton Rouge, LA

Melleney, Herbert C., Exec.V.P./Mng.Dir.
INTERNATIONAL FESTIVALS ASSOCIATION - LIBRARY □ St. Petersburg, FL

Mellichamp, Freddie Ann, Chf., Lib.Sup.Serv.
STATE LIBRARY OF FLORIDA □ Tallahassee, FL

Mellinger, Selma, Libn.
CARNEGIE LIBRARY OF PITTSBURGH - BUSINESS DIVISION □ Pittsburgh, PA

Mellon, Jeanne F., Libn.
ARTHUR YOUNG & COMPANY - LIBRARY □ New York, NY

Mellott, Denise M., Tech.Libn.
CONDIESEL MOBILE EQUIPMENT - ENGINEERING LIBRARY □ Waterbury, CT

Melnick, Dr. Ralph, Hd., Spec.Coll.
COLLEGE OF CHARLESTON - ROBERT SCOTT SMALL LIBRARY - SPECIAL COLLECTIONS □ Charleston, SC

Melnizek, William, Jr., Res.Lit.Chem.
MOBIL CHEMICAL COMPANY - RESEARCH & DEVELOPMENT - INFORMATION SERVICES □ Edison, NJ

Melnychuk, Dianne, Ser.
MUHLENBERG COLLEGE - JOHN A.W. HAAS LIBRARY □ Allentown, PA

Melroy, Virginia, Cat.
UNIVERSITY OF IOWA - LAW LIBRARY □ Iowa City, IA

Melski, Diane, Cat.
CANADA - ECONOMIC COUNCIL OF CANADA - LIBRARY □ Ottawa, ON

Melson, Ruth Ann, Libn.
DELAWARE STATE GENERAL ASSEMBLY - LEGISLATIVE LIBRARY □ Dover, DE

Melton, Becky, Med.Libn.
DRISCOLL FOUNDATION CHILDREN'S HOSPITAL - MEDICAL LIBRARY □ Corpus Christi, TX

Melton, Janet, Libn.
MASONIC GRAND LODGE LIBRARY AND MUSEUM OF TEXAS □ Waco, TX

Meltzer, Morton, Mgr.
MARTIN MARIETTA CORPORATION - ORLANDO AEROSPACE DIVISION - INFORMATION CENTER □ Orlando, FL

Melville, Karen, Libn.
CLARKSON, GORDON/WOODS, GORDON - LIBRARY □ Toronto, ON

Melville, Dr. S. Donald, Dir.
ERIC CLEARINGHOUSE ON TESTS, MEASUREMENT AND EVALUATION □ Princeton, NJ

Melville, Suzanne, Ref.Libn.
PRATT AND WHITNEY CANADA, INC. - LIBRARY □ Longueuil, PQ

Melzak, R.
PRINCETON UNIVERSITY - DEPARTMENT OF ART & ARCHAEOLOGY - INDEX OF CHRISTIAN ART □ Princeton, NJ

Memeriz, William, Libn.
SHERMAN GRINBERG FILM LIBRARIES, INC. □ New York, NY

Memming, Ingrid, Bus.Info.Anl./Mgr.
BASF WYANDOTTE CORPORATION - BUSINESS INFORMATION CENTER □ Parsippany, NJ

Mena, Hector R., Libn.
SOCIETY OF COSTA RICA COLLECTORS (SOCORICO) - EARL FOSSOM MEMORIAL LIBRARY □ Baton Rouge LA

Menan, Nancy V., Chf.
U.S. NATL. ARCHIVES & RECORDS SERVICE - LIBRARY AND PRINTED ARCHIVES BRANCH □ Washington, DC

Menanteaux, Bob, Ref.Libn.
UNIVERSITY OF PUGET SOUND - SCHOOL OF LAW LIBRARY □ Tacoma, WA

Menard, Real, Chf.Libn.
CANADA - DEFENCE RESEARCH ESTABLISHMENT VALCARTIER - LIBRARY □ Courcelette, PQ

Menashi, Ann V., Libn.
BOSTON PSYCHOANALYTIC SOCIETY & INSTITUTE, INC. - LIBRARY □ Boston, MA

Menashian, Ms. L.S., Mgr.
BNR INC. - INFORMATION RESOURCE CENTER† □ Mountain View, CA

Mendelsohn, H., Bibliog.
SUNY AT ALBANY - GRADUATE LIBRARY FOR PUBLIC AFFAIRS AND POLICY □ Albany, NY

Mendenhall, Bethany, Assoc.Libn.
GETTY (J. Paul) CENTER FOR THE HISTORY OF ART AND THE HUMANITIES - LIBRARY □ Santa Monica, CA

Mendenhall, Donna M., Supv., Tech.Info.
ATLANTIC-RICHFIELD COMPANY - ARCO METALS COMPANY - TECHNICAL INFORMATION CENTER† □ Arlington Heights, IL

Mendenhall, Donna M., Mgr.
TRW, INC. - OPERATIONS & SUPPORT GROUP - ELECTRONICS & DEFENSE SECTOR - TECH. INFORMATION CENTER □ Redondo Beach, CA

Mendenhall, Elton. B., Dir.
NEBRASKA RESEARCH COORDINATING UNIT FOR VOCATIONAL EDUCATION □ Lincoln, NE

Mendenhall, Kathryn, Hd., Sys. & Res.
UNIVERSITY OF NORTH CAROLINA, CHAPEL HILL - HEALTH SCIENCES LIBRARY □ Chapel Hill, NC

Mendes, Abel, Mgr., Gen.Serv.
SAVIN CORPORATION - ENGINEERING AND MANUFACTURING DIVISION - SAVIN TECHNICAL INFORMATION CENTER □ Binghamton, NY

Mendez, Gloria, Cat.
INTERAMERICAN UNIVERSITY OF PUERTO RICO - SCHOOL OF LAW - DOMINGO TOLEDO ALAMO LAW LIBRARY† □ Santurce, PR

Mendl, Dido, Selection & Res.Off.
CANADIAN BROADCASTING CORPORATION - PROGRAM ARCHIVES (Sound) □ Toronto, ON

Mendola, Frank, Libn.
ORANGE COUNTY HISTORICAL COMMISSION - MUSEUM LIBRARY □ Orlando, FL

Mendola, James, Med.Libn.
U.S. VETERANS ADMINISTRATION (NY-Buffalo) - MEDICAL CENTER LIBRARY SERVICE □ Buffalo, NY

Mendonca, Francisco J., Supreme Sec.-Libn.
PORTUGUESE CONTINENTAL UNION OF THE U.S.A. - LIBRARY □ Boston, MA

Mendro, Donna, Recordings Libn.
DALLAS PUBLIC LIBRARY - FINE ARTS DIVISION □ Dallas, TX

Menegaux, Sandra, Supv., Ref.Serv.
STANDARD OIL COMPANY OF CALIFORNIA - CORPORATE LIBRARY □ San Francisco, CA

Meneray, Wilbur E., Ph.D., Hd.,Mss./Rare Bks.
TULANE UNIVERSITY OF LOUISIANA - SPECIAL COLLECTIONS DIVISION - MANUSCRIPTS AND RARE BOOKS SECTION □ New Orleans, LA

Menewitch, Myron E., Tech.Libn.
MALCOLM PIRNIE, INC. - TECHNICAL LIBRARY □ White Plains, NY

Meng, Robin, Libn.
CONGREGATION EMANU-EL - IVAN M. STETTENHEIM LIBRARY □ New York, NY

Menke, Mary, Ser.Libn.
UNIVERSITY OF TEXAS, AUSTIN - SCHOOL OF LAW - TARLTON LAW LIBRARY □ Austin, TX

Mennella, Dona, Libn.
BOOZ, ALLEN & HAMILTON, INC. - LIBRARY □ Bethesda, MD

Mennicke, Patricia L., Libn.
SIROTE, PERMUTT, FRIEND, FRIEDMAN, HELD & APOLINSKY, P.C. - LAW LIBRARY □ Birmingham, AL

Mennie, Elizabeth, Ref.Libn.
MC GILL UNIVERSITY - EDUCATION LIBRARY □ Montreal, PQ

Menninger, Margaret, Cat.
ROCKWELL INTERNATIONAL - NORTH AMERICAN AIRCRAFT OPERATIONS - TECHNICAL INFORMATION CENTER □ Los Angeles, CA

Menninger, Dr. Robert G., Dir. of Musm.
MENNINGER FOUNDATION - ARCHIVES □ Topeka, KS

Menocal, Maria Matilde, Libn.
DELAWARE MUSEUM OF NATURAL HISTORY - LIBRARY □ Greenville, DE

Menon, Sizeekumar, Libn.
SHEARSON LEHMAN/AMERICAN EXPRESS INC. - LIBRARY □ New York, NY

Mensch, H.L., Assoc.Dir.
INSTITUTE OF GAS TECHNOLOGY - TECHNICAL INFORMATION CENTER □ Chicago, IL

Mensinger, James, Mgr./Microsystems & Serv.
BIBLIOGRAPHICAL CENTER FOR RESEARCH - ROCKY MOUNTAIN REGION, INC. □ Denver, CO

Ment, David, Hd., Spec.Coll.
TEACHERS COLLEGE - MILBANK MEMORIAL LIBRARY □ New York, NY

Menta, Vishakha, Lib.Dir.
LINDEMANN (Erich) MENTAL HEALTH CENTER - LIBRARY □ Boston, MA

Menthe, Steve, Lib. Coord.
HUXLEY COLLEGE OF ENVIRONMENTAL STUDIES - ENVIRONMENTAL RESOURCE LIBRARY □ Bellingham, WA

Menzies, Robert, Plan.Coord.
DECATUR DEPARTMENT OF COMMUNITY DEVELOPMENT - PLANNING LIBRARY □ Decatur, IL

Merala, Marjan, Libn.
UNIVERSITY OF CALIFORNIA, DAVIS - HEALTH SCIENCES LIBRARY □ Davis, CA

Meranda, Helen F., Rare Bks.Coord.
UNIVERSITY OF MICHIGAN - ALFRED TAUBMAN MEDICAL LIBRARY □ Ann Arbor, MI

Meranda, Mary Ann, Br.Libn.
CHURCH OF JESUS CHRIST OF LATTER-DAY SAINTS - ELKO BRANCH GENEALOGICAL LIBRARY □ Elko, NV

Meranze, Joan, Dir.
HOSPITAL OF THE UNIVERSITY OF PENNSYLVANIA - ROBERT DUNNING DRIPPS LIBRARY OF ANESTHESIA □ Philadelphia, PA

Mercado, Awilda, Auxiliar de Biblioteca
PUERTO RICO - DEPARTMENT OF HEALTH - RAMON EMETERIO BETANCES MEDICAL LIBRARY □ Mayaguez, PR

Mercado, Gloria M.
EVANGELICAL SEMINARY OF PUERTO RICO - JUAN DE VALDES LIBRARY □ Hato Rey, PR

Mercado, Heidi
UNIVERSITY OF WASHINGTON - CHEMISTRY-PHARMACY LIBRARY □ Seattle, WA

Mercado, Violetta, Libn.
UNIVERSITY OF VIRGINIA - PHYSICS LIBRARY □ Charlottesville, VA

Mercer, Elizabeth D., Libn.
SPRINGFIELD HOSPITAL CENTER - MEDICAL LIBRARY □ Sykesville, MD

Mercer, Kristi, Asst.Libn.
ILLINOIS STATE GEOLOGICAL SURVEY - LIBRARY □ Champaign, IL

Merchant, Jacqueline M., Libn.
BALTIMORE CITY PUBLIC SCHOOLS - PROFESSIONAL MEDIA CENTER □ Baltimore, MD

Merchant, Jo Ann, Hd.Libn.
NUS CORPORATION - LIBRARY □ Gaithersburg, MD

Mercieca, Dr. Charles, Exec. V.P.
INTERNATIONAL ASSOCIATION OF EDUCATORS FOR WORLD PEACE - IAEWP CENTER OF INTERCULTURAL INFORMATION □ Huntsville, AL

Mercier, Diane, Libn.
ASSELIN, BENOIT, BOUCHER, DUCHARME, LAPOINTE, INC. - LIBRARY DEPARTMENT □ Montreal, PQ

Mercier, Laurie, Oral Hist.
MONTANA HISTORICAL SOCIETY - LIBRARY/ ARCHIVES □ Helena, MT

Mercier, Pierre, Libn.
METROPOLITAN TORONTO LIBRARY - SOCIAL SCIENCES DEPARTMENT □ Toronto, ON

Mercure, Anne-Marie, Mgr./Archv.
UNIVERSITY OF CONNECTICUT - INSTITUTE FOR SOCIAL INQUIRY □ Storrs, CT

Mercury, Jill, Doc.Libn.
TRW, INC. - DEFENSE SYSTEMS GROUP - SEAD TECHNICAL LIBRARY □ McLean, VA

Mercury, Nicholas E., Mgr.
SYSTEM PLANNING CORPORATION - TECHNICAL LIBRARY □ Arlington, VA

Merdzinski, Marilyn, Registrar
GRAND RAPIDS PUBLIC MUSEUM - PICTORIAL MATERIALS COLLECTION □ Grand Rapids, MI

Meredith, Don L., Libn.
HARDING GRADUATE SCHOOL OF RELIGION - L.M. GRAVES MEMORIAL LIBRARY □ Memphis, TN

Meredith, M.H., Bus.Libn.
CUMMINS ENGINE CO., INC. - LIBRARIES □ Columbus, IN

Meredith, Pamela, Tech.Sys.
GEORGE WASHINGTON UNIVERSITY - MEDICAL CENTER - PAUL HIMMELFARB HEALTH SCIENCES LIBRARY □ Washington, DC

Meredith, Ruth, Supv.Libn.
U.S. ARMY - ARMAMENT RESEARCH & DEVELOPMENT CENTER - SCIENTIFIC AND TECHNICAL INFORMATION DIVISION □ Dover, NJ

Meredith, Sydney J., Asst.Dir., ERIC Oper.
ERIC CLEARINGHOUSE FOR SOCIAL STUDIES/ SOCIAL SCIENCE EDUCATION - RESOURCE & DEMONSTRATION CENTER □ Boulder, CO

Mericle, Kim, Libn.
TEXAS (State) FOREST SERVICE - TEXAS FOREST PRODUCTS LABORATORY - LIBRARY □ Lufkin, TX

Meringolo, Joseph, Asst.Libn.
COHEN AND URETZ - LAW LIBRARY □ Washington, DC

Merkel, Florence V., Lib.Supv.
KETCHUM COMMUNICATIONS INC. - LIBRARY SERVICES □ Pittsburgh, PA

Merkl, Jeanette, Libn.
HOSPITAL CENTER AT ORANGE - WILLIAM PIERSON MEDICAL LIBRARY □ Orange, NJ

Merklin, Sharon R., Libn.
PARK SYNAGOGUE LIBRARY - KRAVITZ MEMORIAL LIBRARY □ Cleveland Heights, OH

Merlo, Vincent V., Dir., Media & Tech.
KEAN COLLEGE OF NEW JERSEY - INSTRUCTIONAL RESOURCE CENTER □ Union, NJ

Merrell, Max J., Chf.Libn.
U.S. VETERANS ADMINISTRATION (WA-Walla Walla) - HOSPITAL LIBRARY □ Walla Walla, WA

Merriam, Louise A., Res.Libn.
COLONIAL WILLIAMSBURG - RESEARCH LIBRARY & ARCHIVES† □ Williamsburg, VA

Merriam, Robert W., Dir.
NEW ENGLAND WIRELESS & STEAM MUSEUM, INC. - LIBRARY □ East Greenwich, RI

Merrigan, Paul G., Lib.Dir.
NASSAU COUNTY MEDICAL CENTER - HEALTH SCIENCES LIBRARY □ East Meadow, NY

Merrill, Andrew, Chf.Libn.
LOS ANGELES DAILY NEWS - EDITORIAL LIBRARY □ Van Nuys, CA

Merrill, Arthur L., Dir.
UNITED THEOLOGICAL SEMINARY OF THE TWIN CITIES - LIBRARY □ New Brighton, MN

Merrill, Dr. Leo, Dir.
HIGH PRESSURE DATA CENTER □ Provo, UT

Merrill-Oldham, Janice, Preservation Spec.
MOLESWORTH INSTITUTE - LIBRARY AND ARCHIVES □ Storrs, CT

Merritt, Betty A., Asst. Law Libn.
PACIFIC GAS AND ELECTRIC COMPANY - LAW LIBRARY □ San Francisco, CA

Merritt, Clinton E., Hd.
HUGHES AIRCRAFT COMPANY - ELECTRO-OPTICAL & DATA SYSTEMS GROUP - INFORMATION RESOURCES SECTION □ El Segundo, CA

Merritt, Ms. D. Easton, Asst.Libn.
HURON COLLEGE - SILCOX MEMORIAL LIBRARY □ London, ON

Merritt, Pat, Libn.
U.S. NAVY - NAVAL SUPERVISOR OF SHIPBUILDING, CONVERSION AND REPAIR - TECHNICAL LIBRARY □ San Diego, CA

Merritt, Paula, Tech.Serv.Libn.
AMERICAN ARBITRATION ASSOCIATION - EASTMAN ARBITRATION LIBRARY □ New York, NY

Merritt, Russell, Dir.
UNIVERSITY OF WISCONSIN, MADISON - WISCONSIN CENTER FOR FILM AND THEATER RESEARCH □ Madison, WI

Merry, Susan A., Mgr./Chf.Libn.
CANADIAN IMPERIAL BANK OF COMMERCE - INFORMATION CENTRE □ Toronto, ON

Merryman, Virginia, Libn.
CH2M HILL, INC. - INFORMATION CENTER □ Redding, CA

Mersky, Roy M., Dir. of Res.
UNIVERSITY OF TEXAS, AUSTIN - SCHOOL OF LAW - TARLTON LAW LIBRARY □ Austin, TX

Merte, Otto, Sr.Res.Supv.
MOTOR VEHICLE MANUFACTURERS ASSOCIATION (MVMA) - PATENT RESEARCH LIBRARY □ Detroit, MI

Mertens, Julia, Tech.Libn.
BALL CORPORATION - RESEARCH LIBRARY □ Muncie, IN

Meryman, Beth, Supv., Tech.Info.
MERYMAN ENVIRONMENTAL ENTERPRISES, INC. - MERYMAN LIBRARY OF AQUATIC RESEARCH □ Riverview, FL

Meryman, Dr. Charles Dale, Pres.
MERYMAN ENVIRONMENTAL ENTERPRISES, INC. - MERYMAN LIBRARY OF AQUATIC RESEARCH □ Riverview, FL

Meryman, Pat, Supv., Lib.Serv.
MERYMAN ENVIRONMENTAL ENTERPRISES, INC. - MERYMAN LIBRARY OF AQUATIC RESEARCH □ Riverview, FL

Mesa, Dr. Rosa Q., Dir.
UNIVERSITY OF FLORIDA - LATIN AMERICAN COLLECTION □ Gainesville, FL

Meserve, Leslie, Libn.
MILLER, NASH, WIENER, HAGER & CARLSEN - LIBRARY □ Portland, OR

Mesh, Rosemary, Foreign Lang.Spec.
BROOKLYN PUBLIC LIBRARY - LANGUAGE AND LITERATURE DIVISION □ Brooklyn, NY

Mesimer, Barbara, Libn.
NCNB - LIBRARY □ Charlotte, NC

Meskin, Amy, Asst.Libn.
DIAMOND SHAMROCK CORPORATION - PROCESS CHEMICALS DIVISION - LIBRARY† □ Morristown, NJ

Mesner, Lillian, Cat.
UNIVERSITY OF KENTUCKY - AGRICULTURE LIBRARY □ Lexington, KY

Mesrobian, Karen, Cur.
NICOLLET COUNTY HISTORICAL SOCIETY - MUSEUM □ St. Peter, MN

Messer, Dr. Wayne, Sr.Res.Chem.
HERCULES, INC. - RESEARCH CENTER - TECHNICAL INFORMATION DIVISION □ Wilmington, DE

Messerle, Judith, Dir.Educ.Rsrcs.
ST. JOSEPH HOSPITAL - INFORMATION SERVICES □ Alton, IL

Messerli, Susan, Music Libn.
UNIVERSITY OF NEBRASKA, LINCOLN - MUSIC LIBRARY† □ Lincoln, NE

Messick, Karen J., Supv.
MERCK & COMPANY, INC. - MERCK SHARP & DOHME RESEARCH LABORATORIES - LITERATURE RESOURCES □ West Point, PA

Messier, Elaine, Libn.
MISSION RESEARCH CORPORATION - INFORMATION CENTER □ Santa Barbara, CA

Messimer, Jean D., Libn.
UNIVERSITY OF COLORADO, BOULDER - ENGINEERING LIBRARY □ Boulder, CO

Messmer, Jamie, Asst.Libn.
NEW YORK STATE LIBRARY - MANUSCRIPTS AND SPECIAL COLLECTIONS □ Albany, NY

Mest, Belle, Mgr., Info.Serv.
NEEDHAM, HARPER & STEERS ADVERTISING, INC. - INFORMATION SERVICES □ Chicago, IL

Meszaros, Gary A., Libn.
BELL & HOWELL EDUCATION GROUP - DE VRY INSTITUTE OF TECHNOLOGY - LEARNING RESOURCE CENTER† □ Chicago, IL

Meszaros, Imre, Hd., Hum.Serv.
WASHINGTON UNIVERSITY - ART & ARCHITECTURE LIBRARY □ St. Louis, MO

Metcalf, Gina, Res.
INTERNATIONAL CENTER OF PHOTOGRAPHY - RICHARD A. HILLMAN RESEARCH COLLECTIONS □ New York, NY

Metcalf, Judy, Ref.Ed.
DALLAS MORNING NEWS - REFERENCE
DEPARTMENT □ Dallas, TX

Metcalf, Marjorie, Libn.
GRACE (W.R.) AND COMPANY - INDUSTRIAL
CHEMICALS GROUP - LIBRARY □ Cambridge, MA

Metcalf, Mary, Libn.
ILLINOIS SCHOOL FOR THE DEAF - SCHOOL
MEDIA CENTER □ Jacksonville, IL

Metcalf, Patricia, Libn.
BOISE CASCADE CORPORATION - CORPORATE
LIBRARY SERVICES □ Boise, ID

Metcalfe, Carole, Libn.
CALGARY BOARD OF EDUCATION -
PROFESSIONAL LIBRARY □ Calgary, AB

Metcalfe, R.E., Info. Chemist
GULF CANADA LIMITED - RESEARCH &
DEVELOPMENT DEPARTMENT - LIBRARY† □
Mississauga, ON

Metcoff, Donald, Libn.
AMERICAN SOCIETY OF ARTISTS, INC. -
RESOURCE CENTER □ Palatine, IL

Metras, Claire, Libn.
CANADIAN MUSIC CENTRE - LIBRARY □
Montreal, PQ

Metraux, Michele, Coord.
YORK UNIVERSITY - DEPARTMENT OF VISUAL
ARTS - SLIDE LIBRARY □ Toronto, ON

Mettle, James, Ref.Libn.
ELI LILLY AND COMPANY - SCIENTIFIC
LIBRARY □ Indianapolis, IN

Metts, Dena, Libn.
SOUTH HIGHLANDS HOSPITAL - MEDICAL
LIBRARY □ Birmingham, AL

Metyer, Joan, Lib.Asst.
SACRED HEART MONASTERY - LEO DEHON
LIBRARY† □ Hales Corners, WI

Metz, Allan, Libn.
TEMPLE BETH-EL - WILLIAM G. BRAUDE
LIBRARY □ Providence, RI

Metz, Betty, Libn.
COHEN, SHAPIRO, POLISHER, SHIEKMAN AND
COHEN - LIBRARY □ Philadelphia, PA

Metz, Carolyn J., Dir., Vis.Rsrcs. & Serv.
INDIANAPOLIS MUSEUM OF ART - SLIDE
COLLECTION □ Indianapolis, IN

Metz, Paul D., Hd., User Serv.Dept.
VIRGINIA POLYTECHNIC INSTITUTE AND
STATE UNIVERSITY - CAROL M. NEWMAN
LIBRARY □ Blacksburg, VA

Metzenbacher, Gary, Dir. of Lib.
WESTERN EVANGELICAL SEMINARY - GEORGE
HALLAUER MEMORIAL LIBRARY □ Milwaukie, OR

Metzer, Laren, Archv. I
CALIFORNIA - STATE ARCHIVES □ Sacramento,
CA

Metzger, Eva, Libn.
CAROLINA LIBRARY SERVICES, INC. -
WOMEN'S BOOK EXCHANGE □ Chapel Hill, NC

Metzger, Eva C., Dir.
CAROLINA LIBRARY SERVICES, INC. □ Chapel
Hill, NC

Metzger, Kristen L., Libn.
HARBOR BRANCH FOUNDATION, INC. -
LIBRARY □ Fort Pierce, FL

Metzger, Kurt, Info.Serv.Spec.
U.S. BUREAU OF THE CENSUS - INFORMATION
SERVICES PROGRAM - DETROIT REGIONAL
OFFICE - INFORMATION CENTER □ Detroit, MI

Metzger, Philip, Spec.Coll.Libn.
SOUTHERN ILLINOIS UNIVERSITY - SCHOOL OF
MEDICINE - MEDICAL LIBRARY □ Springfield, IL

Metzger, Suzanne, Act.Cat.Libn.
UNIVERSITY OF CALIFORNIA, SAN DIEGO -
UNIVERSITY LIBRARIES □ La Jolla, CA

Metzinger, Sylvia V., Rare Books Cat.Archv.
TULANE UNIVERSITY OF LOUISIANA - SPECIAL
COLLECTIONS DIVISION - MANUSCRIPTS AND
RARE BOOKS SECTION □ New Orleans, LA

Metzner, Nancy J., Libn.
EPISCOPAL THEOLOGICAL SEMINARY IN
KENTUCKY - BROWNING MEMORIAL LIBRARY □
Lexington, KY

Meucci, Joyce E., Lib.Assoc.
PRINCE GEORGE'S COUNTY PUBLIC SCHOOLS -
PROFESSIONAL LIBRARY □ Landover, MD

Meurer, Sonia D., Libn.
NABISCO BRANDS, INC. - FAIR LAWN
TECHNICAL CENTER LIBRARY □ Fair Lawn, NJ

Mevers, Frank C., State Archv./Dir.
NEW HAMPSHIRE STATE DEPARTMENT OF
STATE - DIVISION OF RECORDS MANAGEMENT
& ARCHIVES □ Concord, NH

Mewes, Mary, Ref.Libn.
ST. LOUIS MERCANTILE LIBRARY
ASSOCIATION - LIBRARY □ St. Louis, MO

Meyer, Anita R., Act.Libn.
DENVER THEOLOGICAL SEMINARY/BIBLE
INSTITUTE - SAMUEL JAMES BRADFORD
MEMORIAL LIBRARY □ Broomfield, CO

Meyer, Barbara, Pub.Serv.Libn.
UNIVERSITY OF WISCONSIN, MADISON - LAW
SCHOOL LIBRARY □ Madison, WI

Meyer, Barbara, Libn.
UNIVERSITY OF WISCONSIN, MADISON - LAW
SCHOOL LIBRARY - CRIMINAL JUSTICE
REFERENCE & INFORMATION CENTER □
Madison, WI

Meyer, Carol E., Law Libn.
CINCINNATI LAW LIBRARY ASSOCIATION □
Cincinnati, OH

Meyer, Cynthia K., Chf., Lib.Serv.
U.S. VETERANS ADMINISTRATION (CA-Fresno)
- HOSPITAL MEDICAL LIBRARY □ Fresno, CA

Meyer, Daniel, Asst.Univ.Archv.
UNIVERSITY OF CHICAGO - SPECIAL
COLLECTIONS □ Chicago, IL

Meyer, Francis, Asst.Ref.Libn.
TRINITY LUTHERAN CHURCH - LIBRARY □
Madison, WI

Meyer, Gene, Inst.Lib.Cons.
SOUTH DAKOTA STATE LIBRARY & ARCHIVES □
Pierre, SD

Meyer, Geraldine, Med.Lib.Techn.
U.S. VETERANS ADMINISTRATION (WV-
Martinsburg) - CENTER MEDICAL LIBRARY □
Martinsburg, WV

Meyer, Henry R., Sr.Res.Sci.-Info.Off.
DU PONT CANADA, INC. - RESEARCH CENTRE
LIBRARY □ Kingston, ON

Meyer, Jerry, Adm.Libn.
U.S. NAVY - EDWARD RHODES STITT LIBRARY
□ Bethesda, MD

Meyer, Karen M., Law Libn.
CAPLIN & DRYSDALE - LIBRARY† □ Washington,
DC

Meyer, Leo M., Jr.
IDEAL BASIC INDUSTRIES - CEMENT DIVISION
- RESEARCH DEPARTMENT - LIBRARY □ Fort
Collins, CO

Meyer, Marge, Subject Spec.
SANDIA NATIONAL LABORATORIES -
TECHNICAL LIBRARY □ Albuquerque, NM

Meyer, R.W., Assoc.Dir.
CLEMSON UNIVERSITY - ROBERT MULDROW
COOPER LIBRARY □ Clemson, SC

Meyer, Robert, Res.Libn.
NATIONAL BROADCASTING COMPANY, INC. -
REFERENCE LIBRARY □ New York, NY

Meyer, Roger L., Mgr., Tech.Info.Serv.
ENGELHARD CORPORATION - TECHNICAL
INFORMATION CENTER □ Edison, NJ

Meyer, Ruth K., Dir.
TAFT MUSEUM - LIBRARY □ Cincinnati, OH

Meyer, Sharon I., Mgr.
AMERICAN HOSPITAL SUPPLY CORPORATION -
CORPORATE INFORMATION CENTER □
Evanston, IL

Meyer, Steven E., Supv. of Educ.
LAKE COUNTY FOREST PRESERVE DISTRICT -
RYERSON NATURE LIBRARY □ Libertyville, IL

Meyer, W.W.
DOW CHEMICAL COMPANY - TECHNICAL
INFORMATION SERVICES - CHEMICAL
LIBRARY □ Midland, MI

Meyerend, Maude H., Libn.
CHESTNUT HILL HOSPITAL - SCHOOL OF
NURSING LIBRARY □ Philadelphia, PA

Meyerhoff, Erich, Libn.
CORNELL UNIVERSITY - MEDICAL COLLEGE -
SAMUEL J. WOOD LIBRARY □ New York, NY

Meyerhoff, Laurel D., Libn.
EATON CORPORATION - AIL DIVISION -
RESEARCH LIBRARY □ Melville, NY

Meyers, Patricia, Asst.Libn.
STOCKTON NEWSPAPERS INC. - STOCKTON
RECORD LIBRARY □ Stockton, CA

Mezellin, Charlene, Sec.
PENNSYLVANIA BLUE SHIELD - RESEARCH
LIBRARY □ Camp Hill, PA

Micas, Ina, Libn.
U.S. PUBLIC HEALTH SERVICE - NATL.
INSTITUTE OF MENTAL HEALTH - MENTAL
HEALTH STUDY CENTER LIBRARY† □ Adelphi,
MD

Michael, Ann B., Mgr., Lib.Serv.
GAS RESEARCH INSTITUTE - LIBRARY
SERVICES □ Chicago, IL

Michael, Anna M., Libn.
SACRAMENTO BEE - REFERENCE LIBRARY □
Sacramento, CA

Michael, Mrs. H., Libn.
UNITED CHURCH OF CANADA - CENTRAL
ARCHIVES† □ Toronto, ON

Michael, Dr. James Robert, Dir., Bus.Res.
LOUISIANA TECH UNIVERSITY - RESEARCH
DIVISION/COLLEGE OF ADMINISTRATION AND
BUSINESS - LIBRARY □ Ruston, LA

Michael, Nancy B., Tech.Serv.Libn.
U.S. ARMY TRANSPORTATION - TECHNICAL
INFORMATION AND RESEARCH CENTER □ Ft.
Eustis, VA

Michael, Shirley, Prin.Libn.
TRENTON FREE PUBLIC LIBRARY - ART &
MUSIC DEPARTMENT □ Trenton, NJ

Michaelieu, Janet, Libn.
CENTRAL ARIZONA MUSEUM - LIBRARY &
ARCHIVES □ Phoenix, AZ

Michaels, Bess, Hd., Access Serv.
COLUMBIA UNIVERSITY - LAW LIBRARY □ New
York, NY

Michaelson, Robert, Hd.Libn.
NORTHWESTERN UNIVERSITY - SEELEY G.
MUDD LIBRARY FOR SCIENCE AND
ENGINEERING □ Evanston, IL

Michaelson, Susan
TEXAS MEDICAL ASSOCIATION - MEMORIAL
LIBRARY □ Austin, TX

Michalak, Dolores, Bibliog.Asst.
TEMPLE UNIVERSITY - CENTRAL LIBRARY
SYSTEM - CHEMISTRY LIBRARY □ Philadelphia,
PA

Michalak, Naomi, Patients' Libn.
U.S. VETERANS ADMINISTRATION (MA-Boston)
- HOSPITAL MEDICAL LIBRARY □ Boston, MA

Michalova, Dagmar, Assoc.Libn./Br.Lib.Supv.
NEW YORK STATE DEPARTMENT OF HEALTH -
CENTER FOR LABORATORIES AND RESEARCH
LIBRARY □ Albany, NY

Michalowski, Daniel R., Zoological Pk.Dir.
SENECA ZOOLOGICAL SOCIETY - LIBRARY □
Rochester, NY

Michals, Mary, Iconographer
ILLINOIS STATE HISTORICAL LIBRARY □
Springfield, IL

Michalski, Ann, AV Libn.
MADISON PUBLIC LIBRARY - ART AND MUSIC
DIVISION □ Madison, WI

Michaud, Margaret, Coll.Org.Libn.
MASSACHUSETTS GENERAL HOSPITAL - MGH
HEALTH SCIENCES LIBRARIES □ Boston, MA

Michaud, Robert, Libn.
MAINE STATE OFFICE OF ENERGY RESOURCES
- LIBRARY □ Augusta, ME

Michaud, Robert H., Assoc.Libn.
MAINE STATE LAW AND LEGISLATIVE
REFERENCE LIBRARY □ Augusta, ME

Michaud, Yves, Map Libn.
UNIVERSITE DU QUEBEC A RIMOUSKI -
CARTOTHEQUE □ Rimouski, PQ

Michel, Maurice M., Libn.
UNIVERSITY OF MONTANA - SCHOOL OF LAW -
LAW LIBRARY □ Missoula, MT

Michel, Patricia, Coord., Hosp.Lib.Prog.
NORTH COUNTRY REFERENCE & RESEARCH
RESOURCES COUNCIL - LIBRARY □ Canton, NY

Michel, Peter, Cur., Mss.
MISSOURI HISTORICAL SOCIETY - ARCHIVES
AND MANUSCRIPTS □ St. Louis, MO

Michelfelder, Joyce E., Dp.Dir.
U.S. INTERAGENCY ADVANCED POWER GROUP
- POWER INFORMATION CENTER □ Philadelphia,
PA

Michelizzi, Lana, Libn.
(Duluth) NEWS-TRIBUNE & HERALD - LIBRARY □
Duluth, MN

Michels, Dr. Frederick A., Dir.
LAKE SUPERIOR STATE COLLEGE - KENNETH J.
SHOULDICE LIBRARY - MICHIGAN & MARINE
COLLECTIONS □ Sault Ste. Marie, MI

Michelson, Donald, Exec.Dir.
AMERICAN SOCIETY OF MILITARY HISTORY -
LIBRARY □ Los Angeles, CA

Michielsen, Peggy, Ref.Libn.
ALASKA (State) COURT SYSTEM - ALASKA
COURT LIBRARIES □ Anchorage, AK

Michigami, Christine, Libn.
CHAMPION INTERNATIONAL - CORPORATE
INFORMATION CENTER† □ Stamford, CT

Michniewski, Henry J., Hd., Lib.Dev.
NEW JERSEY STATE LIBRARY □ Trenton, NJ

Mick, Minnie, Libn.
SAN JOSE BIBLE COLLEGE - MEMORIAL
LIBRARY □ San Jose, CA

Mickel, E., Off.Mgr.
UNIVERSITY OF NEW MEXICO - DEPARTMENT
OF ANTHROPOLOGY - CLARK FIELD ARCHIVES
AND LIBRARY □ Albuquerque, NM

Micuda, Martha, Asst.Libn., Pub.Serv.
AMERICAN PHILATELIC RESEARCH LIBRARY □
State College, PA

Miczkowski, Ann, Libn.
DETROIT FREE PRESS - LIBRARY □ Detroit, MI

Middendorf, Gertrude, Libn.
WILSON (Woodrow) BIRTHPLACE
FOUNDATION, INC. - RESEARCH LIBRARY &
ARCHIVES □ Staunton, VA

Middendorf, Dr. Jack, Dir.
WAYNE STATE COLLEGE - U.S. CONN LIBRARY
□ Wayne, NE

Middlebrook, Barbara, Ref.Libn.
U.S. NASA - LYNDON B. JOHNSON SPACE
CENTER - TECHNICAL LIBRARY □ Houston, TX

Middlekauff, Robert, Dir.
HUNTINGTON (Henry E.) LIBRARY, ART
GALLERY AND BOTANICAL GARDENS □ San
Marino, CA

Middleton, Anne K., Ref.Libn.
SOUTH CAROLINA STATE LIBRARY □ Columbia,
SC

Middleton, Dale, Assoc.Dir., PNRHSLS
UNIVERSITY OF WASHINGTON - HEALTH
SCIENCES LIBRARY □ Seattle, WA

Middleton, Harry J., Dir.
U.S. PRESIDENTIAL LIBRARIES - LYNDON B.
JOHNSON LIBRARY □ Austin, TX

Middleton, Joseph, Ref.Libn.
SUFFOLK UNIVERSITY - MILDRED F. SAWYER
LIBRARY - COLLECTION OF AFRO-AMERICAN
LITERATURE □ Boston, MA

Middleton, Lily, Hd., Circ.Dept.
POLYTECHNIC INSTITUTE OF NEW YORK -
SPICER LIBRARY □ Brooklyn, NY

Midgley, John D., Asst.Libn.
ARTHUR YOUNG & COMPANY - LIBRARY □ New
York, NY

Midson, Anthony, Asst.Dir.
PORTLAND STATE UNIVERSITY - AUDIO-
VISUAL SERVICES □ Portland, OR

Midson, Anthony J., Dir.
PORTLAND STATE UNIVERSITY - CONTINUING
EDUCATION FILM LIBRARY □ Portland, OR

Midwinter, Christine, Musm. of Man Libn.
CANADA - NATIONAL MUSEUMS OF CANADA -
LIBRARY SERVICES DIRECTORATE □ Ottawa,
ON

Miech, Rev. Lawrence K., Lib.Dir.
ST. FRANCIS SEMINARY - SALZMANN LIBRARY
□ Milwaukee, WI

Miedzinska, Krystyna, Ser.
UNIVERSITY OF OTTAWA - MORISSET
LIBRARY □ Ottawa, ON

Miele, Anthony W., Dir.
ALABAMA PUBLIC LIBRARY SERVICE -
INFORMATION SERVICE □ Montgomery, AL

Miele, Frank, Archv.
AMISTAD RESEARCH CENTER - LIBRARY/
ARCHIVES □ New Orleans, LA

Mielke, Frances, Asst.Curric.Libn.
UNIVERSITY OF ALBERTA - H.T. COUTTS
LIBRARY □ Edmonton, AB

Mielniewski, Jolanta, Lib.Asst.
FLUOR ENGINEERING INC. - FLUOR POWER
SERVICES, INC. - LIBRARY† □ Chicago, IL

Migliacci, Jeanne, Sr.Libn.
MEDFIELD STATE HOSPITAL - MEDICAL
LIBRARY □ Medfield, MA

Mignault, Marcel, Hd.
COLLEGE DE STE-ANNE-DE-LA-POCATIERE -
BIBLIOTHEQUE □ La Pocatiere, PQ

Mignery, Gertrude, Univ.Archv.
UNIVERSITY OF THE SOUTH - ARCHIVES □
Sewanee, TN

Migrala, John, Treas.-Libn.
RADIO HISTORICAL ASSOCIATION OF
COLORADO, INC. - RENTAL TAPE LIBRARY □
Littleton, CO

Mihalik, Ginny Pityo, Dir.
CEDAR CREST COLLEGE - WOMEN'S CENTER†
□ Allentown, PA

Mihalisin, Rhea, Bibliog.Asst.
TEMPLE UNIVERSITY - CENTRAL LIBRARY
SYSTEM - PHYSICS LIBRARY □ Philadelphia, PA

Mihalyko, Jane, Res.Off.
SASKATCHEWAN - DEPARTMENT OF TOURISM
& SMALL BUSINESS - BUSINESS INFORMATION
CENTRE □ Regina, SK

Mikel, Sarah A., Chf., Tech.Info.Div.
U.S. ARMY - OFFICE OF THE CHIEF OF
ENGINEERS - LIBRARY □ Washington, DC

Mikell, William T., Sr. Clerk
NEW YORK STATE DIVISION OF HOUSING AND
COMMUNITY RENEWAL - REFERENCE ROOM† □
New York, NY

Mikita, Elizabeth, Cat.Libn.
JEFFERSON (Thomas) UNIVERSITY - SCOTT
MEMORIAL LIBRARY □ Philadelphia, PA

Mikkelson, Dwight, Pres.
BLACKFORD COUNTY HISTORICAL SOCIETY -
MUSEUM AND BEESON LIBRARY □ Hartford City,
IN

Miklas, Josephine, Tech.Serv.Libn.
ORANGE COUNTY LAW LIBRARY □ Santa Ana,
CA

Miklus, Kathy, Rec.Spec.
FLORIDA STATE DEPT. OF NATURAL
RESOURCES - DIV. OF STATE LANDS - BUREAU
OF STATE LAND MANAGEMENT - TITLE
SECTION □ Tallahassee, FL

Mikulak, Shelagh, Asst. Area Hd.
UNIVERSITY OF CALGARY - SOCIAL SCIENCES
LIBRARY† □ Calgary, AB

Milac, Metod M., Act.Hd.
SYRACUSE UNIVERSITY - GEORGE ARENTS
RESEARCH LIBRARY FOR SPECIAL
COLLECTIONS □ Syracuse, NY

Milam, Margaret M., Assoc.Dir., Tech.Serv.
AMERICAN UNIVERSITY - WASHINGTON
COLLEGE OF LAW - LIBRARY □ Washington, DC

Milam, Vicki, Hd., Acq.
UNIVERSITY OF COLORADO HEALTH SCIENCES
CENTER - DENISON MEMORIAL LIBRARY† □
Denver, CO

Milam, Virginia, Res.Asst.
ANTA CORPORATION - LIBRARY □ Oklahoma
City, OK

Milan, Irene M., Cat.Libn.
CLEVELAND STATE UNIVERSITY - JOSEPH W.
BARTUNEK III LAW LIBRARY □ Cleveland, OH

Milanich, Melanie, Libn.
METROPOLITAN TORONTO LIBRARY - SOCIAL
SCIENCES DEPARTMENT □ Toronto, ON

Milburn, Richard, Hd., Pub.Serv.
ONTARIO COLLEGE OF ART - LIBRARY/
AUDIOVISUAL CENTRE □ Toronto, ON

Miles, Carole W., Med.Libn.
U.S. VETERANS ADMINISTRATION (SD-Hot
Springs) - CENTER LIBRARY □ Hot Springs, SD

Miles, Colin, Regional Dir.
CANADIAN MUSIC CENTRE - BRITISH
COLUMBIA REGIONAL OFFICE - LIBRARY □
Vancouver, BC

Miles, Dione, Archv.
WAYNE STATE UNIVERSITY - ARCHIVES OF
LABOR AND URBAN AFFAIRS/UNIVERSITY
ARCHIVES □ Detroit, MI

Miles, Don, Lib.Dir.
MILLIKEN RESEARCH CORPORATION -
RESEARCH LIBRARY □ Spartanburg, SC

Miles, Elizabeth T., Lib.Techn.
U.S. NAVY - NAVAL ORDNANCE STATION -
TECHNICAL LIBRARY □ Louisville, KY

Miles, George, Cur./W.Amer.
YALE UNIVERSITY - BEINECKE RARE BOOK
AND MANUSCRIPT LIBRARY □ New Haven, CT

Miles, Michele L., Libn.
GOODMAN AND GOODMAN - LIBRARY □
Toronto, ON

Miles, Sally J., Libn.
WEINBERG & GREEN, ATTORNEYS-AT-LAW -
LIBRARY □ Baltimore, MD

Miles, William, Bibliog.
CENTRAL MICHIGAN UNIVERSITY - CLARKE
HISTORICAL LIBRARY □ Mt. Pleasant, MI

Miletich, John, Ref.Libn.
UNIVERSITY OF ALBERTA - SCIENCE AND
TECHNOLOGY LIBRARY □ Edmonton, AB

Miley, Rachel, Acq. & Ser.
LE TOURNEAU COLLEGE - MARGARET ESTES
LIBRARY □ Longview, TX

Milford, Charles C., Libn.
STANFORD UNIVERSITY - FOOD RESEARCH
INSTITUTE - LIBRARY □ Stanford, CA

Milgrom, Linda, Ref./PNRHSLS
UNIVERSITY OF WASHINGTON - HEALTH
SCIENCES LIBRARY □ Seattle, WA

Milholland, Elizabeth, Libn.
HIGHLAND UNITED PRESBYTERIAN CHURCH -
LIBRARY □ New Castle, PA

Milinovich, Michele, Law Libn.
ST. LOUIS COUNTY LAW LIBRARY □ Duluth, MN

Miljenovic, Susan, Asst.Libn.
BAKER AND HOSTETLER - LIBRARY □ Cleveland,
OH

Milkins, Ronald J.
NEW YORK STATE SUPREME COURT -
APPELLATE DIVISION, 3RD JUDICIAL
DEPARTMENT - LAW LIBRARY □ Albany, NY

Millan, Serge
UNIVERSITY OF CALIFORNIA, BERKELEY -
INSTITUTE OF INTERNATIONAL STUDIES
LIBRARY □ Berkeley, CA

Millar, Barbara, Assoc.Univ.Libn.Tech.Serv
UNIVERSITY OF ILLINOIS AT CHICAGO -
HEALTH SCIENCES CENTER - LIBRARY OF THE
HEALTH SCIENCES □ Chicago, IL

Millar, Cynthia
ST. LOUIS PUBLIC LIBRARY - HISTORY AND
GENEALOGY DEPARTMENT □ St. Louis, MO

Millar, Diana, Law Ck.
CANADA - REVENUE CANADA - CUSTOMS & EXCISE - LEGAL SERVICES LIBRARY† □ Ottawa, ON

Millard, Kate, Libn.
CAROLINA LIBRARY SERVICES, INC. - WOMEN'S BOOK EXCHANGE □ Chapel Hill, NC

Millard, Margaret, Libn.
CAROLINA LIBRARY SERVICES, INC. - WOMEN'S BOOK EXCHANGE □ Chapel Hill, NC

Millard, Margot
UNIVERSITY OF CALGARY - SOCIAL SCIENCES LIBRARY† □ Calgary, AB

Millard, Sandra, Hd.Ref.Libn.
UNIVERSITY OF CONNECTICUT - HEALTH CENTER - LYMAN MAYNARD STOWE LIBRARY □ Farmington, CT

Mille, Martha, Circ.
UNIVERSITY OF SANTA CLARA - EDWIN A. HEAFEY LAW LIBRARY† □ Santa Clara, CA

Miller, Alan C., Libn./Archv.
SOUTHERN OREGON HISTORICAL SOCIETY - RESEARCH LIBRARY □ Jacksonville, OR

Miller, Alan V., Collective Member
CANADIAN GAY ARCHIVES - LIBRARY □ Toronto, ON

Miller, Ann, Lib.Asst.
ST. JOSEPH MEDICAL CENTER - HEALTH SCIENCE LIBRARY □ Burbank, CA

Miller, Ann P., Hd.
BUFFALO & ERIE COUNTY PUBLIC LIBRARY - EDUCATION, SOCIOLOGY, PHILOSOPHY & RELIGION DEPARTMENT □ Buffalo, NY

Miller, Ann P., Hd.
BUFFALO & ERIE COUNTY PUBLIC LIBRARY - LANGUAGE, LITERATURE AND ARTS DEPARTMENT □ Buffalo, NY

Miller, Annie, Asst.Libn.
BLUE CROSS AND BLUE SHIELD OF GREATER NEW YORK - CORPORATE REFERENCE INFORMATION SERVICES □ New York, NY

Miller, Arlene, Hd., Circ.
NEW YORK MEDICAL COLLEGE AND THE WESTCHESTER ACADEMY OF MEDICINE - WESTCHESTER MEDICAL CENTER LIBRARY □ Valhalla, NY

Miller, Arthur H., Jr., Coll.Libn.
LAKE FOREST COLLEGE - DONNELLEY LIBRARY - SPECIAL COLLECTIONS □ Lake Forest, IL

Miller, Arthur H., Jr., Coll.Libn.
LAKE FOREST COLLEGE - THOMAS OSCAR FREEMAN MEMORIAL LIBRARY □ Lake Forest, IL

Miller, Barbara, Doc.Asst.
COUNCIL ON FOREIGN RELATIONS - LIBRARY □ New York, NY

Miller, Barbara J., Dir.
ST. PAUL HOSPITAL - C.B. SACHER LIBRARY □ Dallas, TX

Miller, Barry K., Corp.Libn.
REYNOLDS (R.J.) INDUSTRIES, INC. - RJR WORLD HEADQUARTERS CORPORATE LIBRARY □ Winston-Salem, NC

Miller, Beatrice, Lib.Ck.
MANITOBA - DEPARTMENT OF FINANCE - FEDERAL-PROVINCIAL RELATIONS AND RESEARCH DIVISION LIBRARY □ Winnipeg, MB

Miller, Benjamin, Chf.Libn.
BOARD OF JEWISH EDUCATION OF GREATER NEW YORK - EDUCATIONAL RESOURCE LIBRARY □ New York, NY

Miller, Beth, Libn.
UNIVERSITY OF WESTERN ONTARIO - D.B. WELDON LIBRARY - DEPARTMENT OF SPECIAL COLLECTIONS □ London, ON

Miller, Betty, Supv.
CALSPAN CORPORATION - TECHNICAL INFORMATION CENTER □ Buffalo, NY

Miller, Betty, Pub.Lib.Cons.
STATE LIBRARY OF FLORIDA □ Tallahassee, FL

Miller, Brent, Asst.Libn.
CALIFORNIA STATE UNIVERSITY, SACRAMENTO - LIBRARY - SCIENCE & TECHNOLOGY REFERENCE DEPARTMENT □ Sacramento, CA

Miller, Bruce, Coord.
CATHOLIC UNIVERSITY OF AMERICA - RELIGIOUS STUDIES/PHILOSOPHY/ HUMANITIES DIVISION LIBRARY □ Washington, DC

Miller, Carol, Libn.
HEWLETT-PACKARD COMPANY - ANDOVER DIVISION LIBRARY □ Andover, MA

Miller, Carolyn, Sci.Libn.
UNIVERSITY OF CALIFORNIA, SANTA CRUZ - SCIENCE LIBRARY □ Santa Cruz, CA

Miller, Clarine, Spec. Control
SINGER COMPANY - LIBRASCOPE DIVISION - TECHNICAL INFORMATION CENTER □ Glendale, CA

Miller, Dana, Dir.
IRON RANGE RESEARCH CENTER □ Chisholm, MN

Miller, David, Res.Libn.
NATIONAL BROADCASTING COMPANY, INC. - REFERENCE LIBRARY □ New York, NY

Miller, David, Asst.Libn.
OHIO UNIVERSITY - SOUTHEAST ASIA COLLECTION □ Athens, OH

Miller, Diane, Lib.Dir.
BLOOMINGTON-NORMAL DAILY PANTAGRAPH - NEWSPAPER LIBRARY □ Bloomington, IL

Miller, Dick, Hd., Tech.Serv.
STANFORD UNIVERSITY - LANE MEDICAL LIBRARY □ Stanford, CA

Miller, Donald, Libn.
ELIZABETH GENERAL MEDICAL CENTER - CHARLES H. SCHLICHTER, M.D. HEALTH SCIENCE LIBRARY □ Elizabeth, NJ

Miller, Elaine, Asst.Libn.
DELOITTE HASKINS & SELLS - EXECUTIVE OFFICE LIBRARY □ New York, NY

Miller, Elizabeth Jane, Cur.
COLUMBIA HISTORICAL SOCIETY - LIBRARY □ Washington, DC

Miller, Elizabeth R., Hd.Libn.
PENINSULA TIMES TRIBUNE - LIBRARY □ Palo Alto, CA

Miller, Ellen L., Mgr., Res.Serv.
BOOZ, ALLEN & HAMILTON, INC. - RESEARCH SERVICE □ New York, NY

Miller, Elsa A., Acq./Circ.Libn.
SOUTHERN BAPTIST THEOLOGICAL SEMINARY - JAMES P. BOYCE CENTENNIAL LIBRARY □ Louisville, KY

Miller, Dr. Elwood E., Dir.
UNIVERSITY OF COLORADO, BOULDER - ACADEMIC MEDIA SERVICES □ Boulder, CO

Miller, F.M., Res.Dir.
IDEAL BASIC INDUSTRIES - CEMENT DIVISION - RESEARCH DEPARTMENT - LIBRARY □ Fort Collins, CO

Miller, Frances A., Sr.Libn.
NEW YORK STATE DEPARTMENT OF MOTOR VEHICLES - RESEARCH LIBRARY □ Albany, NY

Miller, Dr. Fredric, Cur.
TEMPLE UNIVERSITY - CENTRAL LIBRARY SYSTEM - URBAN ARCHIVES □ Philadelphia, PA

Miller, G., Hd., Lib.Serv.
CANADA - FISHERIES & OCEANS - PACIFIC BIOLOGICAL STATION - LIBRARY □ Nanaimo, BC

Miller, Gail, Circ.Hd.
BROOKS INSTITUTE OF PHOTOGRAPHY - LIBRARY □ Santa Barbara, CA

Miller, George H., Cur.
RIPON HISTORICAL SOCIETY - LIBRARY □ Ripon, WI

Miller, Gerald, Sr.Libn., KENCLIP
KENTUCKY STATE DEPARTMENT FOR LIBRARIES AND ARCHIVES - STATE LIBRARY SERVICES DIVISION □ Frankfort, KY

Miller, Glen
TOMENSON SAUNDERS WHITEHEAD LTD./TA ASSOCIATES - RESOURCE CENTRE □ Toronto, ON

Miller, Glenn E., Libn.
CHICAGO INSTITUTE FOR PSYCHOANALYSIS - MC LEAN LIBRARY □ Chicago, IL

Miller, Glenn Wayne, Staff Libn.
HARRISBURG STATE HOSPITAL - STAFF LIBRARY □ Harrisburg, PA

Miller, Dr. H. Eugene, Info. Res./Sec.Ldr.
GENERAL MILLS, INC. - JAMES FORD BELL TECHNICAL CENTER - TECHNICAL INFORMATION SERVICES □ Minneapolis, MN

Miller, Harold W., Mgr., Info.Serv.
TOUCHE ROSS AND COMPANY - INFORMATION CENTER □ New York, NY

Miller, Harry, Ref.Archv.
STATE HISTORICAL SOCIETY OF WISCONSIN - ARCHIVES DIVISION □ Madison, WI

Miller, Helga, Chm.
CRAFTS GUILD OF MANITOBA - LIBRARY □ Winnipeg, MB

Miller, Herbert A., Jr., Mgr.
MEIDINGER, INC. - INFORMATION CENTER □ Louisville, KY

Miller, Howard, Asst.Mgr.
SWEDENBORG LIBRARY AND BOOKSTORE □ Boston, MA

Miller, I.C.
OAK RIDGE NATIONAL LABORATORY - INFORMATION DIVISION - ENVIRONMENTAL MUTAGEN INFORMATION CENTER □ Oak Ridge, TN

Miller, Inabeth, Libn.
HARVARD UNIVERSITY - GRADUATE SCHOOL OF EDUCATION - GUTMAN LIBRARY □ Cambridge, MA

Miller, Irene K., Libn.
FAIRFIELD HISTORICAL SOCIETY - REFERENCE AND RESEARCH LIBRARY □ Fairfield, CT

Miller, Jack, Cur.
WABASH COUNTY HISTORICAL MUSEUM - HISTORICAL LIBRARY □ Wabash, IN

Miller, Jan P., Sr.Mgr., Sys. & Oper.
UNIVERSITY OF PITTSBURGH - NASA INDUSTRIAL APPLICATIONS CENTER (NIAC) □ Pittsburgh, PA

Miller, Jane G., Libn.
KUTAK ROCK & HUIE, ATTORNEYS AT LAW - LAW LIBRARY □ Atlanta, GA

Miller, Janet, Med.Libn.
NORTH COUNTRY HOSPITAL - MEDICAL LIBRARY □ Newport, VT

Miller, Jean J., Libn.
UNIVERSITY OF HARTFORD - ANNE BUNCE CHENEY LIBRARY □ West Hartford, CT

Miller, Jean K., Dir.
UNIVERSITY OF TEXAS HEALTH SCIENCE CENTER, DALLAS - LIBRARY □ Dallas, TX

Miller, Jean R., Chf.Libn.
BECKMAN INSTRUMENTS, INC. - RESEARCH LIBRARY □ Fullerton, CA

Miller, Jeanne, Asst.Libn.
INSTITUTE OF GERONTOLOGY - LEARNING RESOURCE CENTER □ Ann Arbor, MI

Miller, Jewell, Assoc. Law Libn.
SAMFORD UNIVERSITY - CUMBERLAND SCHOOL OF LAW - CORDELL HULL LAW LIBRARY □ Birmingham, AL

Miller, Jill, Libn.
ARINC RESEARCH CORPORATION - TECHNICAL LIBRARY □ San Diego, CA

Miller, Jill, Lib.Ck.
TEHAMA COUNTY LAW LIBRARY □ Red Bluff, CA

Miller, Jo Ann, Assoc.Libn.
DICK (A.B.) COMPANY - LIBRARY† □ Chicago, IL

Miller, John A., Exec.Dir.
CANADIAN MUSIC CENTRE - LIBRARY □ Toronto, ON

Miller, Joseph A., Libn.
YALE UNIVERSITY - FORESTRY LIBRARY† □
New Haven, CT

Miller, Joseph S., Adm.
MENNONITE HISTORICAL LIBRARY OF
EASTERN PENNSYLVANIA □ Lansdale, PA

Miller, Julia E., Libn.
INTERNATIONAL FOUNDATION OF EMPLOYEE
BENEFIT PLANS - INFORMATION CENTER □
Brookfield, WI

Miller, Juliet V., Dir.
ERIC CLEARINGHOUSE ON ADULT, CAREER
AND VOCATIONAL EDUCATION - NATL. CTR.
FOR RESEARCH IN VOCATIONAL EDUC. □
Columbus, OH

Miller, Karen, Info.Serv./Libn.
SUNY AT BUFFALO - HEALTH SCIENCES
LIBRARY □ Buffalo, NY

Miller, Karl F., AV Libn.
UNIVERSITY OF TEXAS, AUSTIN - FINE ARTS
LIBRARY □ Austin, TX

Miller, Kathleen, Res.Assoc.
MOBIL OIL CORPORATION - PUBLIC AFFAIRS
SECRETARIAT □ New York, NY

Miller, Kathleen, Cat.
U.S. ARMY WAR COLLEGE - LIBRARY □ Carlisle
Barracks, PA

Miller, Kathleen A., Libn.
REED, SMITH, SHAW AND MC CLAY - LAW
LIBRARY □ Pittsburgh, PA

Miller, Kathy, Asst.Libn.
WINTER HAVEN HOSPITAL - J.G. CONVERSE
MEMORIAL MEDICAL LIBRARY □ Winter Haven,
FL

Miller, Kathy, Libn.
WORLD MODELING ASSOCIATION - WMA
LIBRARY □ Croton-on-Hudson, NY

Miller, Kim M., Libn.
AACA LIBRARY & RESEARCH CENTER, INC. □
Hershey, PA

Miller, L. Jeannine, Dir., Lib.Serv.
FIRST BAPTIST CHURCH - MEDIA LIBRARY □
Roswell, NM

Miller, Laura B., Libn.
INDIANA UNIVERSITY - WORKSHOP IN
POLITICAL THEORY & POLICY ANALYSIS -
WORKSHOP LIBRARY □ Bloomington, IN

Miller, Lester L., Jr., Supv.Libn.
U.S. ARMY FIELD ARTILLERY SCHOOL - MORRIS
SWETT TECHNICAL LIBRARY □ Ft. Sill, OK

Miller, Lidie, Libn.
GHOST RANCH CONFERENCE CENTER - GHOST
RANCH LIBRARY □ Abiquiu, NM

Miller, Linda, Libn.
MERCY HOSPITAL - HEALTH SERVICES
LIBRARY □ Cedar Rapids, IA

Miller, Linda D., Dir.
JEFFERSON COUNTY PUBLIC LAW LIBRARY □
Louisville, KY

Miller, Lorraine K., Hd.Libn.
BRODSKY (Saul) JEWISH COMMUNITY LIBRARY
□ St. Louis, MO

Miller, Lynn A., Libn.
UNIVERSITY OF ILLINOIS - HIGHWAY TRAFFIC
SAFETY CENTER - LIBRARY □ Urbana, IL

Miller, M. Stone, Jr., Hd.
LOUISIANA STATE UNIVERSITY -
DEPARTMENT OF ARCHIVES AND
MANUSCRIPTS □ Baton Rouge, LA

Miller, Marcia A., Asst.Libn.
NEW YORK HOSPITAL-CORNELL MEDICAL
CENTER, WESTCHESTER DIVISION - MEDICAL
LIBRARY □ White Plains, NY

Miller, Margaret A., Dir.
ARTHUR D. LITTLE, INC. - LIFE SCIENCES
LIBRARY □ Cambridge, MA

Miller, Marilyn, Ref.Libn.
LOUISIANA STATE UNIVERSITY MEDICAL
CENTER - SCHOOL OF MEDICINE IN
SHREVEPORT - LIBRARY □ Shreveport, LA

Miller, Marjorie, Ref.Libn.
FASHION INSTITUTE OF TECHNOLOGY -
LIBRARY† □ New York, NY

Miller, Marjorie M., Doc.Libn.
PRINCE GEORGE'S COUNTY MEMORIAL
LIBRARY SYSTEM - PUBLIC DOCUMENTS
REFERENCE LIBRARY □ Upper Marlboro, MD

Miller, Mary, Asst.Libn.
MINNEAPOLIS COLLEGE OF ART AND DESIGN -
LIBRARY AND MEDIA CENTER □ Minneapolis,
MN

Miller, Mary, Ser./Acq.Libn.
SUNY AT BUFFALO - CHARLES B. SEARS LAW
LIBRARY □ Buffalo, NY

Miller, Mary B., Archv.
GROUT MUSEUM OF HISTORY AND SCIENCE -
GENEALOGY, ARCHIVES AND REFERENCE
LIBRARY □ Waterloo, IA

Miller, Mary Jane, Lib. Group Supv.
AT & T BELL LABORATORIES - LIBRARY □
Holmdel, NJ

Miller, Mary Lee, Hd.
ROCHESTER PUBLIC LIBRARY - ART DIVISION
□ Rochester, NY

Miller, Mary McG., Chm. of Lib.Comm.
SPRINGFIELD ART CENTER - LIBRARY □
Springfield, OH

Miller, Matthew T., Rd.Serv.Libn.
MEMPHIS STATE UNIVERSITY LIBRARIES -
SCHOOL OF LAW LIBRARY □ Memphis, TN

Miller, Maureen, Subject Anl.
AEROSPACE CORPORATION - CHARLES C.
LAURITSEN LIBRARY □ Los Angeles, CA

Miller, Maxine, Lib.Assoc.
NORTH OLYMPIC LIBRARY SYSTEM - PORT
ANGELES BRANCH - PACIFIC NORTHWEST
ROOM □ Port Angeles, WA

Miller, Michael S., Dir.
MARYLAND STATE LAW LIBRARY □ Annapolis,
MD

Miller, Nancy, Ref.Libn.
CAPITAL UNIVERSITY - LAW SCHOOL LIBRARY
□ Columbus, OH

Miller, Nancy E., Asst.Dir.
OHIO STATE UNIVERSITY - LAW LIBRARY □
Columbus, OH

Miller, Oscar J., Law Libn.
UNIVERSITY OF COLORADO, BOULDER - LAW
LIBRARY □ Boulder, CO

Miller, P., Cat.Libn.
OHIO DOMINICAN COLLEGE - SPANGLER
LIBRARY □ Columbus, OH

Miller, Patricia, Sr.Info.Spec./Tech.Serv.
GENERAL FOODS CORPORATION - MARKETING
INFORMATION CENTER □ White Plains, NY

Miller, Patty, Libn.
NEW HAMPSHIRE VOCATIONAL-TECHNICAL
COLLEGE - LIBRARY □ Laconia, NH

Miller, Pauline M., Hd., Sci. & Tech.Dept.
SYRACUSE UNIVERSITY - SCIENCE AND
TECHNOLOGY LIBRARY □ Syracuse, NY

Miller, Philip E., Libn.
HEBREW UNION COLLEGE - JEWISH
INSTITUTE OF RELIGION - KLAU LIBRARY □
New York, NY

Miller, Richard, Proj.Dir.
MISSOURI STATE LIBRARY □ Jefferson City,
MO

Miller, Rita, Libn.
SHELBY COUNTY LAW LIBRARY □ Sidney, OH

Miller, Robert L., Libn.
UNIVERSITY CITY PUBLIC LIBRARY - RECORD
COLLECTION □ University City, MO

Miller, Robert P., Jr., Law Lib.Coord.
VIRGINIA BEACH PUBLIC LIBRARY SYSTEM -
ROBERT S. WAHAB, JR. PUBLIC LAW LIBRARY
□ Virginia Beach, VA

Miller, Robin, Res.Assoc.
ALLIANCE TO SAVE ENERGY - LIBRARY □
Washington, DC

Miller, Roger, Bus.Info.Assoc.
UNION CARBIDE CORPORATION - CORPORATE
LIBRARY □ Danbury, CT

Miller, Roger M., Lib.Dir.
U.S. ARMY POST - FORT CARSON - LIBRARY □
Ft. Carson, CO

Miller, Ron, Att.
AUGLAIZE COUNTY LAW LIBRARY □
Wapakoneta, OH

Miller, Ron, Hd.Libn.
CHARLESTON GAZETTE-MAIL - LIBRARY □
Charleston, WV

Miller, Ron, Dir.
WORLD ARCHEOLOGICAL SOCIETY -
INFORMATION CENTER □ Hollister, MO

Miller, Rosanna, Hd., Map Coll.
ARIZONA STATE UNIVERSITY - DANIEL E.
NOBLE SCIENCE AND ENGINEERING LIBRARY □
Tempe, AZ

Miller, Rosanna, Hd.
ARIZONA STATE UNIVERSITY - DANIEL E.
NOBLE SCIENCE AND ENGINEERING LIBRARY -
MAP COLLECTION □ Tempe, AZ

Miller, Rose M., Libn.
RETINA FOUNDATION - JOINT RESEARCH
LIBRARY □ Boston, MA

Miller, Mrs. Seymour, Libn.
K.K. BENE ISRAEL/ROCKDALE TEMPLE -
SIDNEY G. ROSE MEMORIAL LIBRARY □
Cincinnati, OH

Miller, Sheldon T., Supv., Lib.Serv.
MEAD CORPORATION - LIBRARY □ Chillicothe,
OH

Miller, Mrs. Steve, Asst.Dir.
WORLD ARCHEOLOGICAL SOCIETY -
INFORMATION CENTER □ Hollister, MO

Miller, Stuart W., Libn.
INTERNATIONAL ASSOCIATION OF ASSESSING
OFFICERS - RESEARCH AND TECHNICAL
SERVICES DEPT. - LIBRARY □ Chicago, IL

Miller, Sue, ILL
U.S. NASA - LANGLEY RESEARCH CENTER -
TECHNICAL LIBRARY MS 185† □ Hampton, VA

Miller, Susan, Dir.
DALLAS CIVIC GARDEN CENTER -
HORTICULTURE LIBRARY □ Dallas, TX

Miller, Suzanne, Law Libn.
UNIVERSITY OF LA VERNE - COLLEGE OF LAW -
LIBRARY □ La Verne, CA

Miller, Terry, Hd.Libn.
ENCYCLOPAEDIA BRITANNICA, INC. -
EDITORIAL LIBRARY □ Chicago, IL

Miller, Thomas, Cat.
CAPE BRETON MINERS' MUSEUM - LIBRARY □
Glace Bay, NS

Miller, Mrs. Tony
BOB JONES UNIVERSITY - CHURCH
MINISTRIES RESOURCE LAB □ Greenville, SC

Miller, Tracey, Coll.Dev./Ref.
UNIVERSITY OF CALIFORNIA, LOS ANGELES -
MANAGEMENT LIBRARY □ Los Angeles, CA

Miller, Veronica, Asst.Libn./Rsrcs.
TEMPLE UNIVERSITY - CENTRAL LIBRARY
SYSTEM - AMBLER CAMPUS LIBRARY □ Ambler,
PA

Miller, Virginia, Computerized Serv.
MEDICAL UNIVERSITY OF SOUTH CAROLINA -
LIBRARY □ Charleston, SC

Miller, Wayne, Libn.
NEW YORK STATE OFFICE OF MENTAL HEALTH
- ST. LAWRENCE PSYCHIATRIC CENTER -
LIBRARY □ Ogdensburg, NY

Miller, William
GENEALOGICAL SOCIETY OF NEW JERSEY -
MANUSCRIPT COLLECTIONS □ New Brunswick,
NJ

Miller, William
RUTGERS UNIVERSITY, THE STATE
UNIVERSITY OF NEW JERSEY - DEPARTMENT
OF SPECIAL COLLECTIONS AND ARCHIVES □
New Brunswick, NJ

Miller, William B., Dir.
PRESBYTERIAN CHURCH (U.S.A.) -
PRESBYTERIAN HISTORICAL SOCIETY -
LIBRARY □ Philadelphia, PA

Miller, William C., Libn.
NAZARENE THEOLOGICAL SEMINARY -
WILLIAM BROADHURST LIBRARY □ Kansas City,
MO

Millican, Beatrice, Spec.Coll.Libn.
HIGHTOWER (Sara) REGIONAL LIBRARY -
HENDERSON ROOM □ Rome, GA

Millican, Rita, Tech.Serv.
LOUISIANA STATE UNIVERSITY - LAW
LIBRARY □ Baton Rouge, LA

Millich, E., ILL
UNIVERSITY OF WISCONSIN, LA CROSSE -
MURPHY LIBRARY □ La Crosse, WI

Milligan, Patricia M., Sr.Cat.
UNIVERSITY OF MAINE SCHOOL OF LAW -
DONALD L. GARBRECHT LAW LIBRARY □
Portland, ME

Milligan, Stuart, Circ.Libn.
UNIVERSITY OF ROCHESTER - EASTMAN
SCHOOL OF MUSIC - SIBLEY MUSIC LIBRARY □
Rochester, NY

Milliken, Christine, Libn.
WESTERN CANADIAN UNIVERSITIES - MARINE
BIOLOGICAL SOCIETY - DEVONIAN LIBRARY □
Bamfield, BC

Milliken, Edna M., Asst.St.Archv.
KENTUCKY STATE DEPARTMENT FOR
LIBRARIES & ARCHIVES - ARCHIVES □
Frankfort, KY

Millington, Kathleen, Asst.Libn.
BERLEX LABORATORIES, INC. - RESEARCH AND
DEVELOPMENT DIVISION LIBRARY □ Cedar
Knolls, NJ

Mills, Amy, Libn.
SCHERING-PLOUGH CORPORATION - BUSINESS
INFORMATION CENTER - LIBRARY □
Kenilworth, NJ

Mills, Betty M., Exec.Dir.
HIGHLAND PARK HISTORICAL SOCIETY -
LIBRARY □ Highland Park, IL

Mills, Carol, Coord., LRC
ERIC CLEARINGHOUSE ON COUNSELING AND
PERSONNEL SERVICES - LEARNING
RESOURCES CENTER □ Ann Arbor, MI

Mills, Carol, Chf., Lib.Serv.
U.S. VETERANS ADMINISTRATION (AZ-
Prescott) - HEALTH SCIENCES LIBRARY □
Prescott, AZ

Mills, Constance A., Ref.Libn.
WESTERN KENTUCKY UNIVERSITY - DEPT. OF
SPECIAL COLLECTIONS - KENTUCKY LIBRARY
AND MUSEUM/UNIVERSITY ARCHIVES □
Bowling Green, KY

Mills, Elaine L., Ed.
SMITHSONIAN INSTITUTION - NATIONAL
ANTHROPOLOGICAL ARCHIVES □ Washington,
DC

Mills, Emilie, Spec.Coll.Libn.
UNIVERSITY OF NORTH CAROLINA,
GREENSBORO - DANCE COLLECTION □
Greensboro, NC

Mills, Emilie, Spec.Coll.Libn.
UNIVERSITY OF NORTH CAROLINA,
GREENSBORO - GIRLS BOOKS IN SERIES □
Greensboro, NC

Mills, Jesse C., Chf.Libn.
TENNESSEE VALLEY AUTHORITY - TECHNICAL
LIBRARY □ Knoxville, TN

Mills, Mary Alice, Dir.
U.S. CENTERS FOR DISEASE CONTROL - CDC
LIBRARY □ Atlanta, GA

Mills, Mary B., Lib.Techn.
U.S. AIR FORCE HOSPITAL - MEDICAL LIBRARY
(OK-Tinker AFB) □ Tinker AFB, OK

Mills, Rich, Cat.
VALPARAISO UNIVERSITY - LAW LIBRARY □
Valparaiso, IN

Mills, Robin K., Law Libn.
EMORY UNIVERSITY - SCHOOL OF LAW
LIBRARY □ Atlanta, GA

Mills, Ruth, Dir.
ART ASSOCIATION OF RICHMOND - LIBRARY □
Richmond, IN

Mills, T. Michael, Energy Educ.Coord.
REDWOOD COMMUNITY ACTION AGENCY -
ENERGY DEMONSTRATION CENTER -
APPROPRIATE TECHNOLOGY LIBRARY □
Eureka, CA

Mills, Theresa, Inst.Cons.
SOUTH CAROLINA STATE LIBRARY □ Columbia,
SC

Mills, Thora, Chm., Archv.Comm.
CANADIAN DIABETES ASSOCIATION -
NATIONAL OFFICE ARCHIVES □ Toronto, ON

Mills, William, Libn.
U.S. DEFENSE COMMUNICATIONS AGENCY -
TECHNICAL AND MANAGEMENT INFORMATION
CENTER □ Washington, DC

Mills, William, Chf., Acq.Sect.
U.S. DEPT. OF TRANSPORTATION - LIBRARY
AND DISTRIBUTION SERVICES DIVISION □
Washington, DC

Mills, William T., Pres.
MADISON HISTORICAL SOCIETY, INC. -
LIBRARY □ Madison, CT

Milne, Richard, Hd., Canadian Pubn. Unit
NATIONAL LIBRARY OF CANADA - CANADIAN
BOOK EXCHANGE CENTRE (CBEC) □ Ottawa, ON

Milne, Ronald L., Libn.
BAROQUE STRINGS OF VANCOUVER - LIBRARY
□ West Vancouver, BC

Milner, Zelda W., Dir.
U.S. DEPT. OF COMMERCE - INTERNATIONAL
TRADE ADMINISTRATION - CLEVELAND
DISTRICT OFFICE LIBRARY □ Cleveland, OH

Milnes, Vicki, Hd., Tech.Serv.
CANADA - LABOUR CANADA - LIBRARY
SERVICES† □ Ottawa, ON

Milsk, Fran
NATIONAL COLLEGE OF EDUCATION -
LEARNING RESOURCE CENTERS □ Evanston, IL

Milszyn, N., Libn.
COLUMBUS HOSPITAL - MEDICAL LIBRARY □
Newark, NJ

Milton, Ardyce, Asst.Libn.
ALLEN-BRADLEY COMPANY - CORPORATE
LIBRARY □ Milwaukee, WI

Milton, Sybil, Chf.Archv.
BAECK (Leo) INSTITUTE - LIBRARY □ New York,
NY

Milton, Vela M., Br. Genealogy Libn.
CHURCH OF JESUS CHRIST OF LATTER-DAY
SAINTS - JACKSONVILLE, FLORIDA BRANCH
GENEALOGICAL LIBRARY □ Jacksonville, FL

Mimeault, Alice, Documentaliste
LE DROIT - CENTRE DE DOCUMENTATION □
Ottawa, ON

Mims, C.C., Int.Tech.Doc.Serv.Supv.
AT & T BELL LABORATORIES - LIBRARIES AND
INFORMATION SYSTEMS CENTER □ Murray Hill,
NJ

Mims, Dorothy H., Spec.Coll.Libn.
MEDICAL COLLEGE OF GEORGIA - LIBRARY □
Augusta, GA

Mims, Gloria J., Spec.Coll.Libn.
ATLANTA UNIVERSITY CENTER - ROBERT W.
WOODRUFF LIBRARY □ Atlanta, GA

Mims, Henrietta, Med.Libn.
U.S. VETERANS ADMINISTRATION (AL-
Birmingham) - HOSPITAL MEDICAL LIBRARY □
Birmingham, AL

Mims, Mary E., Libn.
WASHINGTON STATE LIBRARY - EASTERN
STATE HOSPITAL LIBRARY □ Medical Lake, WA

Mims, Nancy C., Archv./Cur.
TOMPKINS (D.A.) MEMORIAL LIBRARY □
Edgefield, SC

Minailo, Christine, Lib.Techn.
ALBERTA - DEPARTMENT OF TREASURY -
BUREAU OF STATISTICS LIBRARY □ Edmonton,
AB

Mindeman, George A., Dir.
INTERNATIONAL CHRISTIAN GRADUATE
UNIVERSITY - LIBRARY □ San Bernardino, CA

Mindlin, Harold, Prog.Mgr.
BATTELLE-COLUMBUS LABORATORIES -
METALS AND CERAMICS INFORMATION
CENTER □ Columbus, OH

Miner, Aftar, Div.Coord.
BRIGHAM YOUNG UNIVERSITY - SOCIAL
SCIENCE DIVISION LIBRARY □ Provo, UT

Miner, Irene, Chf., Per.Sect.
U.S. ARMY - PENTAGON LIBRARY □ Washington,
DC

Miner, Jerry, Libn.
CANADA - AGRICULTURE CANADA - RESEARCH
STATION, KENTVILLE - LIBRARY □ Kentville, NS

Minesinger, Joan, Chf.Libn.
RIVERSIDE PRESS-ENTERPRISE COMPANY -
EDITORIAL LIBRARY □ Riverside, CA

Ming, Virginia H., Hd., Ser. & Pub.Serv.
BAYLOR UNIVERSITY - TEXAS COLLECTION □
Waco, TX

Ming, William L., Hd., Acq. & Bibliog.
BAYLOR UNIVERSITY - TEXAS COLLECTION □
Waco, TX

Minhoto, Fr. Walter, Libn.
FRESNO DIOCESAN LIBRARY □ Fresno, CA

Mininni, Linda, Supv. .
MERCK & COMPANY, INC. - MERCK SHARP &
DOHME RESEARCH LABORATORIES -
LITERATURE RESOURCES □ Rahway, NJ

Minion, Robin, Asst.Libn.
UNIVERSITY OF ALBERTA - BOREAL INSTITUTE
FOR NORTHERN STUDIES - LIBRARY □
Edmonton, AB

Minjiras, Andrew, Post Libn.
U.S. ARMY POST - PRESIDIO OF SAN
FRANCISCO - POST LIBRARY SYSTEM □
Presidio of San Francisco, CA

Minkel, Vera, Mgr., Lib.Serv.
HONEYWELL, INC. - HONEYWELL
INFORMATION SYSTEMS - TECHNICAL
INFORMATION CENTER □ Phoenix, AZ

Minnerath, Janet, Hd.Libn.
UNIVERSITY OF OKLAHOMA - TULSA MEDICAL
COLLEGE - LIBRARY □ Tulsa, OK

Minnick, Albert C., Libn./Archv.
BUFFALO BILL HISTORICAL CENTER - HAROLD
MC CRACKEN RESEARCH LIBRARY □ Cody, WY

Minns, Edith M., Libn.
PENINSULA LIBRARY AND HISTORICAL
SOCIETY† □ Peninsula, OH

Minor, Barbara, Pubn.Coord.
ERIC CLEARINGHOUSE ON INFORMATION
RESOURCES □ Syracuse, NY

Minor, Carol, Cat.
U.S. COURT OF APPEALS, 10TH CIRCUIT -
LIBRARY □ Denver, CO

Minor, Dorothy, Tech.Serv./Ref.Libn.
FLORIDA STATE DIVISION OF BLIND SERVICES
- FLORIDA REGIONAL LIB. FOR THE BLIND &
PHYSICALLY HANDICAPPED □ Daytona Beach,
FL

Minor, Dr. John T., Sr.Info.Spec.
CONOCO, INC. - RESEARCH AND
DEVELOPMENT DEPARTMENT - TECHNICAL
INFORMATION SERVICES □ Ponca City, OK

Minsky, Norman, Sec./Tres.
PENOBSCOT BAR LIBRARY ASSOCIATION -
LIBRARY† □ Bangor, ME

Mintel, Richard H., Asst.Libn.
TRINITY LUTHERAN SEMINARY - HAMMA
LIBRARY □ Columbus, OH

Minter, Nancy, Ed.
NATIONAL LEAGUE OF CITIES - MUNICIPAL
REFERENCE SERVICE □ Washington, DC

Minton, James, Hd. Map Libn.
UNIVERSITY OF ARIZONA - MAP COLLECTION
□ Tucson, AZ

Mintz, Anne, Mgr., Lib.Serv.
LAZARD FRERES & COMPANY - FINANCIAL
LIBRARY □ New York, NY

Mintz, Edith B., Hd.Libn.
ARTHUR D. LITTLE, INC. - MANAGEMENT
LIBRARY† □ Cambridge, MA

Mirabal, Alfonso, Info.Serv.Spec.
U.S. BUREAU OF THE CENSUS - INFORMATION
SERVICES PROGRAM - DALLAS REGIONAL
OFFICE - LIBRARY □ Dallas, TX

Miracle, Laura J., Libn.
CHICAGO BOARD OF TRADE - LIBRARY† □
Chicago, IL

Miranda, Altagracia, Hd., Ref.
UNIVERSITY OF PUERTO RICO - LAW SCHOOL
LIBRARY □ Rio Piedras, PR

Mirell, Sandee, Libn.
LOS ANGELES CITY ATTORNEY - LAW
LIBRARY† □ Los Angeles, CA

Mirly, Joann, Asst.Dir.
CONCORDIA SEMINARY - LIBRARY □ St. Louis,
MO

Miron, Jacques, Off.-in-Charge
CANADA - ATMOSPHERIC ENVIRONMENT
SERVICE - QUEBEC REGION - BIBLIOTHEQUE
REGIONALE† □ St. Laurent, PQ

Mironenko, Rimma, Tech.Libn.
AEROJET-CHEMICAL CORPORATION -
AEROJET SOLID PROPULSION COMPANY -
TECHNICAL INFORMATION CENTER† □
Sacramento, CA

Mirsky, Phyllis S., Asst.Univ.Libn.
UNIVERSITY OF CALIFORNIA, SAN DIEGO -
UNIVERSITY LIBRARIES □ La Jolla, CA

Mirsky, Sonya Wohl, Univ.Libn./Spec.Coll.Cur.
ROCKEFELLER UNIVERSITY - LIBRARY □ New
York, NY

Mirth, Karlo J., Mgr.
FOSTER WHEELER DEVELOPMENT
CORPORATION - JOHN BLIZARD RESEARCH
CENTER - INFORMATION CENTER AND
LIBRARY □ Livingston, NJ

Mirucki, Emily, Adm.Spec.
BURROUGHS WELLCOME COMPANY - MEDICAL
INFORMATION CENTER □ Kirkland, PQ

Misaghi, Patricia, Acq.
UNIVERSITY OF ARIZONA - COLLEGE OF LAW
LIBRARY† □ Tucson, AZ

Mischo, William, Engr.Libn.
UNIVERSITY OF ILLINOIS - ENGINEERING
LIBRARY □ Urbana, IL

Mishkin, Leah, Hd.Libn. & Cur.
HEBREW THEOLOGICAL COLLEGE - SAUL
SILBER MEMORIAL LIBRARY □ Skokie, IL

Miskin, Rose, Libn.
LATNER (Albert J.) JEWISH PUBLIC LIBRARY □
Willowdale, ON

Missar, Charles D., Supv.Libn.
NATIONAL INSTITUTE OF EDUCATION -
EDUCATIONAL RESEARCH LIBRARY □
Washington, DC

Missfeldt, Ruth, Pub.Serv.Libn./ILL
LUTHERAN THEOLOGICAL SEMINARY - KRAUTH
MEMORIAL LIBRARY □ Philadelphia, PA

Mistaras, Evangeline, Hd., Ref.
NORTHEASTERN ILLINOIS UNIVERSITY -
LIBRARY □ Chicago, IL

Misticabelli, Judith, Sr.Libn.
GEORGETOWN UNIVERSITY - KENNEDY
INSTITUTE OF ETHICS - CENTER FOR
BIOETHICS LIBRARY □ Washington, DC

Mistrik, Mrs. Marion, Libn.
AIR TRANSPORT ASSOCIATION OF AMERICA -
LIBRARY □ Washington, DC

Mitcham, Janet, Assoc. Monographs Libn.
UNIVERSITY OF ARKANSAS FOR MEDICAL
SCIENCES - MEDICAL SCIENCES LIBRARY □
Little Rock, AR

Mitchel, Nonie, Libn.
TEXAS STATE AERONAUTICS COMMISSION -
LIBRARY & INFORMATION CENTER □ Austin, TX

Mitchell, Barbara A., Libn.
HARVARD UNIVERSITY - CENTER FOR
INTERNATIONAL AFFAIRS - LIBRARY □
Cambridge, MA

Mitchell, Barbara A., Libn.
HARVARD UNIVERSITY - CENTER FOR MIDDLE
EASTERN STUDIES - LIBRARY □ Cambridge, MA

Mitchell, Barbara A., Libn.
HARVARD UNIVERSITY - INSTITUTE FOR
INTERNATIONAL DEVELOPMENT - LIBRARY □
Cambridge, MA

Mitchell, Carolyn W., Hd.Libn.
ENVIRONMENTAL PROTECTION AGENCY -
REGION IV LIBRARY □ Atlanta, GA

Mitchell, Christie, Libn.
FEDERAL RESERVE BANK OF NEW YORK -
RESEARCH LIBRARY □ New York, NY

Mitchell, David, Asst.Libn.
CALIFORNIA RAILWAY MUSEUM - LIBRARY □
Suisun City, CA

Mitchell, Elaine, Dir. of Info.Serv.
WILMER, CUTLER & PICKERING - LAW
LIBRARY □ Washington, DC

Mitchell, Eleanor, Dir.
HUMAN RESOURCES NETWORK -
INFORMATION CENTER† □ Philadelphia, PA

Mitchell, Elosia, Chf.
U.S. VETERANS ADMINISTRATION (TX-San
Antonio) - MEDICAL CENTER LIBRARY SERVICE
(142D) □ San Antonio, TX

Mitchell, Gail
ST. LOUIS PUBLIC LIBRARY - ART
DEPARTMENT □ St. Louis, MO

Mitchell, George D., III, Media Lib.Dir.
NORTH TEXAS STATE UNIVERSITY LIBRARIES
- MEDIA LIBRARY □ Denton, TX

Mitchell, Herbert, Arch.
COLUMBIA UNIVERSITY - AVERY
ARCHITECTURAL AND FINE ARTS LIBRARY □
New York, NY

Mitchell, Mrs. Horace, Libn.
PORTSMOUTH ATHENAEUM - LIBRARY &
MUSEUM □ Portsmouth, NH

Mitchell, J.B., Hd.Libn.
FRANKLIN COUNTY HISTORICAL SOCIETY -
STANLEY LIBRARY† □ Ferrum, VA

Mitchell, J. Marcus, Pub.Rel.Dir.
METROPOLITAN COUNCIL FOR EDUCATIONAL
OPPORTUNITY - LIBRARY □ Roxbury, MA

Mitchell, Joan, Adm.
NATIONAL BROADCASTING COMPANY, INC. -
RECORDS ADMINISTRATION INFORMATION
AND ARCHIVES □ New York, NY

Mitchell, Joan, Bibliog.
WILFRID LAURIER UNIVERSITY - LIBRARY □
Waterloo, ON

Mitchell, Judy, Hd.Libn.
MESSENGER COLLEGE - LIBRARY □ Joplin, MO

Mitchell, June M., Chf., Lib./LRC Serv.
U.S. VETERANS ADMINISTRATION (NY-
Syracuse) - MEDICAL CENTER LIBRARY □
Syracuse, NY

Mitchell, Larry G., Cur.
CLASSIC AMX CLUB, INTERNATIONAL - AMX
LIBRARY □ Arvada, CO

Mitchell, Laurie, Info.Serv.Anl.
TOWERS, PERRIN, FORSTER & CROSBY LTD. -
INFORMATION CENTRE □ Toronto, ON

Mitchell, Lynn M., Lib.Techn.
U.S. NATL. PARK SERVICE - MIDWEST
ARCHEOLOGICAL CENTER - RESEARCH
LIBRARY □ Lincoln, NE

Mitchell, Lynn M., Asst.Libn.
U.S. NATL. PARK SERVICE - WESTERN
ARCHEOLOGICAL AND CONSERVATION CENTER
- LIBRARY □ Tucson, AZ

Mitchell, Martha L., Univ.Archv.
BROWN UNIVERSITY - SPECIAL COLLECTIONS
□ Providence, RI

Mitchell, Martha M., Libn.
GRACE (W.R.) AND COMPANY - DEARBORN
CHEMICAL (U.S.) LIBRARY □ Lake Zurich, IL

Mitchell, Mary, Libn.
CANADA - CANADIAN FORESTRY SERVICE -
PETAWAWA NATIONAL FORESTRY INSTITUTE
- LIBRARY □ Chalk River, ON

Mitchell, Mary, Libn.
UNIVERSITY OF SASKATCHEWAN - LUTHERAN
THEOLOGICAL SEMINARY - OTTO OLSON
MEMORIAL LIBRARY □ Saskatoon, SK

Mitchell, Mary E., Ref.Libn.
UNIVERSITY OF BRITISH COLUMBIA - LAW
LIBRARY □ Vancouver, BC

Mitchell, Meredith, Med.Libn.
U.S. VETERANS ADMINISTRATION (CA-Long
Beach) - MEDICAL CENTER LIBRARY □ Long
Beach, CA

Mitchell, Mildred, Libn.
MARSCHALK COMPANY, INC. - LIBRARY† □
Cleveland, OH

Mitchell, Nelly, Ethnic Coord.
NASHUA PUBLIC LIBRARY - CHANDLER
MEMORIAL LIBRARY AND ETHNIC CENTER □
Nashua, NH

Mitchell, Robert P., Intl.Doc.Libn.
UNIVERSITY OF ARIZONA - GOVERNMENT
DOCUMENTS DEPARTMENT □ Tucson, AZ

Mitchell, Sylvia C., Young Adult Libn.
HAWAII STATE LIBRARY - YOUNG ADULT
SECTION □ Honolulu, HI

Mitchell, William L., Consrv.Libn.
UNIVERSITY OF KANSAS - DEPARTMENT OF
SPECIAL COLLECTIONS □ Lawrence, KS

Mithen, Jeanne, Asst.Libn.
RILEY COUNTY HISTORICAL SOCIETY -
SEATON MEMORIAL LIBRARY □ Manhattan, KS

Mittelbach, Frank G., Dir./Prof.
UNIVERSITY OF CALIFORNIA, LOS ANGELES -
HOUSING, REAL ESTATE & URBAN LAND
STUDIES PROGRAM COLLECTION □ Los
Angeles, CA

Mitten, Lisa, Cat./Info.Sci.
FRANKLIN PIERCE LAW CENTER - LIBRARY □
Concord, NH

Mittleman, Ferne E., Asst.Libn.
TEMPLE SHAAREY ZEDEK - LIBRARY □ Amherst,
NY

Miura, Verna K., Libn.
HONOLULU (City and County) - MUNICIPAL
REFERENCE AND RECORDS CENTER □ Honolulu,
HI

Mixer, Robert, Asst.Dir.
UNIVERSITY OF SOUTHERN CALIFORNIA -
NASA INDUSTRIAL APPLICATION CENTER
(NIAC) □ Los Angeles, CA

Mixter, Janet K., Coord., Bibliog.Serv.
LOYOLA UNIVERSITY OF CHICAGO - MEDICAL
CENTER LIBRARY □ Maywood, IL

Miya, Mary Ann, Asst.Libn.
KIRKLAND & ELLIS - LIBRARY □ Chicago, IL

Miyashiro, Fusako, Inst.Libn.
HAWAII STATE LIBRARY - STATE LIBRARY FOR
THE BLIND AND PHYSICALLY HANDICAPPED □
Honolulu, HI

Mize, Marilyn E., Adm.Libn.
U.S. ARMY POST - FORT JACKSON - LIBRARY □
Ft. Jackson, SC

Mize, Virginia G., Libn.
DU PONT DE NEMOURS (E.I.) & COMPANY, INC.
- BENGER LABORATORY - LIBRARY □
Waynesboro, VA

Mizik, Judy G., Dir., Lib.Serv.
PITTSBURGH BOARD OF EDUCATION -
PROFESSIONAL LIBRARY □ Pittsburgh, PA

Mlotek, Eleanor, Archv.
YIVO INSTITUTE FOR JEWISH RESEARCH -
LIBRARY AND ARCHIVES □ New York, NY

Mobley, Arthur B., HRIS Mgr.
NATIONAL ACADEMY OF SCIENCES -
NATIONAL RESEARCH COUNCIL - HIGHWAY
RESEARCH INFORMATION SERVICE □
Washington, DC

Mobley, Beth, Asst.Libn., Tech.Serv.
UNIVERSITY OF BRIDGEPORT - SCHOOL OF
LAW - LAW LIBRARY □ Bridgeport, CT

Mobley, Emily R., Dir.
GMI ENGINEERING & MANAGEMENT
INSTITUTE - LIBRARY □ Flint, MI

Mobley, Fredrick, Training Dir.
ARIZONA STATE DEPARTMENT OF ECONOMIC
SECURITY - ARIZONA TRAINING PROGRAM AT
COOLIDGE - STAFF LIBRARY □ Coolidge, AZ

Mobley, Ree, Local Hist.Libn.
PIKES PEAK LIBRARY DISTRICT - LOCAL
HISTORY COLLECTION □ Colorado Springs, CO

Mobley, Sara, Asst.Libn./Pub.Serv.
EMORY UNIVERSITY - PITTS THEOLOGY
LIBRARY □ Atlanta, GA

Mochedlover, Helene G., Dept.Mgr.
LOS ANGELES PUBLIC LIBRARY - FICTION
DEPARTMENT □ Los Angeles, CA

Mochedlover, Helene G., Dept.Mgr.
LOS ANGELES PUBLIC LIBRARY - LITERATURE
& PHILOLOGY DEPARTMENT □ Los Angeles, CA

Mochizuki, Tomie, Libn.
JAPAN SOCIETY, INC. - LIBRARY □ New York,
NY

Mock, Julie, Info.Spec.
BENHAM GROUP - INFORMATION RESOURCE
CENTER □ Oklahoma City, OK

Mockovak, Holly E., Pub.Serv.Supv.
HARVARD UNIVERSITY - EDA KUHN LOEB
MUSIC LIBRARY □ Cambridge, MA

Modak, Susan Branzell, Libn.
BROWN (Earle Palmer) COMPANIES - THE
SOURCE - LIBRARY □ Bethesda, MD

Modeen, James H., Mgr.
DOW CHEMICAL U.S.A. - LOUISIANA DIVISION
- LIBRARY □ Plaquemine, LA

Moeckel, Nancy, Sci.Libn.
MIAMI UNIVERSITY - BRILL SCIENCE LIBRARY
□ Oxford, OH

Moedritzer, Anne, Ref.Libn.
EDEN THEOLOGICAL SEMINARY - LIBRARY □
Webster Groves, MO

Moeller, Helen Morgan, Pub.Lib.Cons.
STATE LIBRARY OF FLORIDA □ Tallahassee, FL

Moeller, Dr. Henry R., Libn.
CENTRAL BAPTIST THEOLOGICAL SEMINARY -
LIBRARY □ Kansas City, KS

Moeller, Kathleen A., Dir., Lib.Serv.
OVERLOOK HOSPITAL - HEALTH SCIENCES
LIBRARY □ Summit, NJ

Moeller, Dr. Roger, Dir. of Res.
AMERICAN INDIAN ARCHAEOLOGICAL
INSTITUTE, INC. - LIBRARY □ Washington, CT

Moenster, Janet, Tech.Serv.
KENRICK SEMINARY LIBRARY □ St. Louis, MO

Moeny, Christine, Spec.Coll.
ADAMS STATE COLLEGE - LIBRARY - SPECIAL
COLLECTIONS □ Alamosa, CO

Moerschel, Neal, Dir., Info.Ref.Serv.
U.S. DEPT. OF ENERGY - ENERGY
INFORMATION ADMINISTRATION - NATIONAL
ENERGY INFORMATION CENTER □ Washington,
DC

Moffa, Monica, District Libn.
U.S. ARMY - CORPS OF ENGINEERS - DETROIT
DISTRICT - TECHNICAL LIBRARY □ Detroit, MI

Moffat, L., Per./Microforms Libn.
UNIVERSITY OF ALBERTA - HUMANITIES AND
SOCIAL SCIENCES LIBRARY □ Edmonton, AB

Moffat, Patricia A., Libn.
BENEFICIAL MANAGEMENT CORPORATION -
LIBRARY† □ Morristown, NJ

Moffatt, Laurie Norton, Cur.
NORMAN ROCKWELL MUSEUM AT THE OLD
CORNER HOUSE - REFERENCE DEPARTMENT □
Stockbridge, MA

Moffeit, Tony, Hd., Pub. & Tech.Serv.
UNIVERSITY OF SOUTHERN COLORADO -
LIBRARY - SPECIAL COLLECTIONS □ Pueblo, CO

Moffett, Maggie, Asst.Libn.
HONEYWELL, INC. - PHYSICAL SCIENCES
CENTER LIBRARY □ Bloomington, MN

Moffett, Martha, Res.Libn.
NATIONAL ENQUIRER - RESEARCH
DEPARTMENT LIBRARY □ Lantana, FL

Moffitt, Mary, Libn.
WASHINGTON STATE SCHOOL FOR THE DEAF -
LEARNING RESOURCE CENTER □ Vancouver,
WA

Mofjeld, Pamela A., Asst.Libn.
UNIVERSITY OF WASHINGTON - NATURAL
SCIENCES LIBRARY □ Seattle, WA

Moger, Elizabeth Haas, Kpr.
SOCIETY OF FRIENDS - NEW YORK YEARLY
MEETING - RECORDS COMMITTEE - HAVILAND
RECORDS ROOM □ New York, NY

Moggia, Paulette, Libn.
HUMAN FACTORS RESEARCH, INC. -
TECHNICAL LIBRARY □ Goleta, CA

Mohead, Doll, Slide Cur.
SCHOOL OF VISUAL ARTS - LIBRARY □ New
York, NY

Mohlenrich, John S., Chf. Park Interp.
U.S. NATL. PARK SERVICE - LAKE MEAD NATL.
RECREATION AREA - LIBRARY □ Boulder City,
NV

Mohler, Bonnie, Asst.Libn.
HOLLAND & HART - LIBRARY □ Denver, CO

Mohlke, Catherine M., Dir., Lib.Serv.
WESTVILLE CORRECTIONAL CENTER - STAFF
LIBRARY □ Westville, IN

Mohme, Sharon, Pub.Serv.Supv.
UNIVERSITY OF MISSOURI, ST. LOUIS -
EDUCATION LIBRARY □ St. Louis, MO

Mohn, Doris, Cat.
BRYN MAWR HOSPITAL - MEDICAL LIBRARY □
Bryn Mawr, PA

Mohn, Marcia, Tech.Serv.Libn.
U.S. ARMY POST - FORT CARSON - LIBRARY □
Ft. Carson, CO

Mohr, Elizabeth, Libn.
U.S. AIR FORCE - AIR FORCE SYSTEMS
COMMAND - TECHNICAL INFORMATION
CENTER† □ Holloman AFB, NM

Mohrer, Fruma, Archv.
YIVO INSTITUTE FOR JEWISH RESEARCH -
LIBRARY AND ARCHIVES □ New York, NY

Mohrman, Betty J., Libn.
AMERICAN CAPITAL ASSET MANAGEMENT,
INC. - RESEARCH LIBRARY □ Houston, TX

Mohrman, Robert, Med.Libn.
U.S. VETERANS ADMINISTRATION (NY-
Montrose) - HOSPITAL LIBRARY □ Montrose, NY

Mohundro, Jenny, AV Libn.
TEXAS STATE TECHNICAL INSTITUTE, WACO
CAMPUS - LIBRARY □ Waco, TX

Moir, Lindsay, Asst.Libn.
GLENBOW-ALBERTA INSTITUTE - LIBRARY &
ARCHIVES □ Calgary, AB

Moirai, Catherine R., Coord.
OKRA RIDGE FARM - TENNESSEE LESBIAN
ARCHIVES □ Luttrell, TN

Moisant, Janice, Res. & Info.Supv.
PACIFIC LIGHTING GAS SUPPLY COMPANY -
REFERENCE CENTER □ Los Angeles, CA

Moise, C., Ref.
CANADA - FISHERIES & OCEANS - LIBRARY† □
Ottawa, ON

Mojer, Linda L., Cur.
ROLLINS COLLEGE - BEAL-MALTBIE SHELL
MUSEUM - LIBRARY □ Winter Park, FL

Mok, Vicky, Tech.Serv.Libn.
FANSHAWE COLLEGE OF APPLIED ARTS AND
TECHNOLOGY - MAIN LIBRARY □ London, ON

Mokry, Frantisek, Cat.
COLUMBIA UNIVERSITY - LAW LIBRARY □ New
York, NY

Moldenhauer, Dr. Hans, Dir.
MOLDENHAUER ARCHIVES □ Spokane, WA

Moles, Jean Ann, Ser.Libn.
UNIVERSITY OF ARKANSAS FOR MEDICAL
SCIENCES - MEDICAL SCIENCES LIBRARY □
Little Rock, AR

Molgat, Lucie, Lib.Mgr.
CANADA - PUBLIC SERVICE STAFF RELATIONS
BOARD - LIBRARY □ Ottawa, ON

Molholt, Pat, Assoc.Dir.
RENSSELAER POLYTECHNIC INSTITUTE -
FOLSOM LIBRARY □ Troy, NY

Molieri, Loren, Sr.Libn.
IBM CORPORATION - GENERAL PRODUCTS
DIVISION - TECHNICAL INFORMATION
CENTER □ San Jose, CA

Molina, Jose A. Fonseca, Libn.
PUERTO RICO - CENTRAL OFFICE OF
PERSONNEL ADMINISTRATION - INSTITUTE
OF PERSONNEL DEVELOPMENT - LIBRARY □
Santurce, PR

Moline, Sandra, Libn.
UNIVERSITY OF WISCONSIN, MADISON -
PHYSICS LIBRARY □ Madison, WI

Moll, Marita, Prog.Asst.
CANADIAN TEACHERS' FEDERATION - GEORGE
G. CROSKERY MEMORIAL LIBRARY □ Ottawa,
ON

Moll, Sheila, Libn.
YORK BOROUGH BOARD OF EDUCATION -
PROFESSIONAL LIBRARY □ Toronto, ON

Moll, Virginia, Nursing Sch.Libn.
CHESTER COUNTY HOSPITAL - MEDICAL STAFF
& SCHOOL OF NURSING LIBRARIES □ West
Chester, PA

Molloy, Bridget, Libn.
UNIVERSITY OF SOUTHERN CALIFORNIA -
PHILOSOPHY LIBRARY □ Los Angeles, CA

Molloy, Patricia, Libn. I
COLUMBUS COLLEGE OF ART AND DESIGN -
PACKARD LIBRARY □ Columbus, OH

Molod, Samuel E., Dp. State Libn.
CONNECTICUT STATE LIBRARY □ Hartford, CT

Mols, Kathy, Asst.Libn.
BLODGETT MEMORIAL MEDICAL CENTER -
RICHARD ROOT SMITH LIBRARY □ Grand
Rapids, MI

Molter, Maureen, Libn.
MEMORIAL HOSPITAL - HEALTH SCIENCES
LIBRARY □ Easton, MD

Moltke-Hansen, David, Assoc.Dir.
SOUTH CAROLINA HISTORICAL SOCIETY -
LIBRARY □ Charleston, SC

Moltz, Sandra S., Supv.
GENERAL ELECTRIC COMPANY - AIRCRAFT
ENGINE BUSINESS GROUP - DR. C.W. SMITH
TECHNICAL INFORMATION CTR., 24001 □
Lynn, MA

Monaco, Annette M., Spec.Coll.Libn.
LE MOYNE COLLEGE - LIBRARY - SPECIAL
COLLECTIONS □ Syracuse, NY

Monaco, Ralph, Assoc. Law Libn.
ST. JOHN'S UNIVERSITY - LAW LIBRARY □
Jamaica, NY

Monahon, Ruth, Ref.Libn.
UNIVERSITY OF SOUTHERN CALIFORNIA -
HEALTH SCIENCES CAMPUS - NORRIS
MEDICAL LIBRARY □ Los Angeles, CA

Mondou, Cecile, Hd.Libn.
CANADA - SECRETARY OF STATE -
TRANSLATION BUREAU - LIBRARY □ Montreal,
PQ

Mondschein, Henri, Asst.Libn.
LOS ANGELES DAILY NEWS - EDITORIAL
LIBRARY □ Van Nuys, CA

Monette, Gerard, Asst. to Dir.
LA PRESSE, LTEE. - CENTRE DE
DOCUMENTATION† □ Montreal, PQ

Money, David, Asst.Libn.
OKLAHOMA COLLEGE OF OSTEOPATHIC
MEDICINE & SURGERY - LIBRARY □ Tulsa, OK

Money, R.L., Chf., User Serv.Br.
U.S. NATL. OCEANIC & ATMOSPHERIC
ADMINISTRATION - NATIONAL CLIMATIC
DATA CENTER LIBRARY □ Asheville, NC

Mongeon, Jane, Hd., Acq.
UNIVERSITY OF MISSOURI - HEALTH
SCIENCES LIBRARY □ Columbia, MO

Mongold, Alice, Per.
SOUTHERN METHODIST UNIVERSITY -
PERKINS SCHOOL OF THEOLOGY - LIBRARY □
Dallas, TX

Monical, Ruth, Act.Lib.Dir.
SOUTHERN OREGON STATE COLLEGE -
LIBRARY □ Ashland, OR

Monighetti, Kathleen, Asst.Libn.
COMBUSTION ENGINEERING, INC. - POWER
SYSTEMS GROUP LIBRARY SERVICES† □
Windsor, CT

Monk, Janet F., Chf., Lib.Serv.
U.S. VETERANS ADMINISTRATION (NV-Reno) - MEDICAL CENTER - LEARNING CENTER □ Reno, NV

Monkhouse, R.E., Educ. Media Cons.
WELLINGTON COUNTY BOARD OF EDUCATION - EDUCATION LIBRARY □ Guelph, ON

Monkhouse, Valerie, Dir.
CANADA - NATIONAL MUSEUMS OF CANADA - LIBRARY SERVICES DIRECTORATE □ Ottawa, ON

Monkmeyer, Hilde R.
MONKMEYER PRESS PHOTO SERVICE □ New York, NY

Monnig, Donna S., Hd.
PUBLIC LIBRARY OF CINCINNATI AND HAMILTON COUNTY - LITERATURE DEPARTMENT □ Cincinnati, OH

Monroe, Alden N., Mss.Supv.
CINCINNATI HISTORICAL SOCIETY - LIBRARY □ Cincinnati, OH

Monroe, Dawn, Chf., Coll.Dev.Serv.
CANADA - PUBLIC ARCHIVES OF CANADA - LIBRARY □ Ottawa, ON

Monroe, Jean, Ref.Libn.
WAYNE STATE UNIVERSITY - SCIENCE LIBRARY □ Detroit, MI

Monroe, Judy
3M - 270 LIBRARY □ St. Paul, MN

Monroe, Mrs. Lee, Ref.Libn.
NEW HAMPSHIRE STATE LIBRARY - LAW LIBRARY □ Concord, NH

Monroe, Linda, Info.Spec.
ARMOUR RESEARCH CENTER - LIBRARY □ Scottsdale, AZ

Monsivais, Jean, Sec.
LUTHERAN MEDICAL CENTER - MEDICAL LIBRARY □ St. Louis, MO

Monsma, Marvin E., Dir.
CALVIN COLLEGE AND SEMINARY - LIBRARY □ Grand Rapids, MI

Monson, Cleo, Cur.
HOLY LAND MUSEUM & LIBRARY □ New York, NY

Monstad-Ozolins, D.S.L., Libn.
KLOCKNER STADLER HURTER LTD. - LIBRARY □ Montreal, PQ

Montador, Gordon, Natl.Mgr.
CANADIAN BOOK INFORMATION CENTRE - NATIONAL OFFICE □ Toronto, ON

Montag, Hermina, Asst.Div.Hd.
QUEENS BOROUGH PUBLIC LIBRARY - SCIENCE & TECHNOLOGY DIVISION □ Jamaica, NY

Montague, M.E., Lib.Techn.
PROTESTANT SCHOOL BOARD OF GREATER MONTREAL - PROFESSIONAL LIBRARY □ Montreal, PQ

Montalbano, James, Asst.Libn.
SPERRY - SPERRY ELECTRONIC SYSTEMS - TECHNICAL INFORMATION CENTER □ Great Neck, NY

Montanary, Barbara, Hd.Libn.
UNIVERSITY OF CALIFORNIA, RIVERSIDE - BIO-AGRICULTURAL LIBRARY □ Riverside, CA

Montanez, Kathyrn L., Adm.Asst.
UNIVERSITY OF CALIFORNIA - KEARNEY AGRICULTURAL CENTER □ Parlier, CA

Monteith, Margo, Hd., Pub.Serv.
INTERNATIONAL DEVELOPMENT RESEARCH CENTRE - LIBRARY† □ Ottawa, ON

Montekio, Abraham, Libn.
U.S. COURT OF INTERNATIONAL TRADE - LAW LIBRARY □ New York, NY

Monteleone, Natalie, Info.Spec.
AMERICAN PETROLEUM INSTITUTE - LIBRARY □ Washington, DC

Montesinos, Mary Jane, Sr.Info.Sci.
COCA-COLA COMPANY - TECHNICAL INFORMATION SERVICES □ Atlanta, GA

Montgomery, Catherine J., Law Lib.Ck.
AMADOR COUNTY LAW LIBRARY □ Jackson, CA

Montgomery, Chris, Music Libn.
WESLEYAN UNIVERSITY - LIBRARY - WORLD MUSIC ARCHIVES □ Middletown, CT

Montgomery, Dale, Dir.
UNIVERSITY OF WISCONSIN, LA CROSSE - AUDIOVISUAL CENTER - FILM LIBRARY □ La Crosse, WI

Montgomery, Dale, Dir., Instr.Serv.
UNIVERSITY OF WISCONSIN, LA CROSSE - MURPHY LIBRARY □ La Crosse, WI

Montgomery, Dianne, Adm. Aide
FLINT DEPARTMENT OF COMMUNITY DEVELOPMENT - LIBRARY □ Flint, MI

Montgomery, Dorothy, Circ.Libn.
WESTERN ILLINOIS UNIVERSITY - LIBRARIES □ Macomb, IL

Montgomery, Dr. John Warwick, Esq., Dir.
GREENLEAF (Simon) SCHOOL OF LAW - LIBRARY† □ Orange, CA

Montgomery, Jon, Supt.
U.S. NATL. PARK SERVICE - APPOMATTOX COURT HOUSE NATL. HISTORICAL PARK - LIBRARY □ Appomattox, VA

Montgomery, Marie, Hd.Libn.
UNION CARBIDE CORPORATION - LINDE DIVISION - COMMUNICATIONS LIBRARY □ Danbury, CT

Montgomery, Mary E., Res.Libn.
EATON CORPORATION - ENGINEERING & RESEARCH CENTER LIBRARY □ Southfield, MI

Montgomery, Maurice J., Archv.
ROCK COUNTY HISTORICAL SOCIETY - ARCHIVES OF ROCK COUNTY HISTORY □ Janesville, WI

Montgomery, Sherry, Hd., AV Dept.
PHILADELPHIA COLLEGE OF PHARMACY AND SCIENCE - JOSEPH W. ENGLAND LIBRARY □ Philadelphia, PA

Montgomery, Susan, Info.Spec.
AT & T COMMUNICATIONS - INFORMATION RESEARCH CENTER □ Basking Ridge, NJ

Montgomery, Susan J., Mgr.
CONTINENTAL ILLINOIS NATIONAL BANK AND TRUST COMPANY OF CHICAGO - INFORMATION SERVICES DIVISION □ Chicago, IL

Monti, Dr. Laura V., Kpr.
BOSTON PUBLIC LIBRARY - RARE BOOKS AND MANUSCRIPTS □ Boston, MA

Montijo, Maria E., Tech.Serv.Dir.
PUERTO RICO - SUPREME COURT - LAW LIBRARY □ San Juan, PR

Montplaisir, Isabelle, Libn.
MUSEE D'ART CONTEMPORAIN - CENTRE DE DOCUMENTATION† □ Montreal, PQ

Monty, Vivienne, Libn.
YORK UNIVERSITY - GOVERNMENT DOCUMENTS/ADMINISTRATIVE STUDIES LIBRARY □ Downsview, ON

Monuk, Mr. L., Hd.
CANADA - NATIONAL DEFENCE - NDHQ CHIEF CONSTRUCTION AND PROPERTIES LIBRARY □ Ottawa, ON

Moody, Eric, Cur. of Mss.
NEVADA HISTORICAL SOCIETY - LIBRARY □ Reno, NV

Moody, Kenneth E., Dir.
SUNY - DOWNSTATE MEDICAL CENTER - MEDICAL RESEARCH LIBRARY OF BROOKLYN† □ Brooklyn, NY

Moody, Roland H., Dean
NORTHEASTERN UNIVERSITY - ROBERT GRAY DODGE LIBRARY† □ Boston, MA

Moon, Kathryn, Res.Libn.
FEDERAL RESERVE BANK OF CHICAGO - LIBRARY □ Chicago, IL

Moon, Margaret, Libn.
MUSKEGON BUSINESS COLLEGE - LIBRARY □ Muskegon, MI

Moon, Phyllis, Libn.
SYSTEM PLANNING CORPORATION - TECHNICAL LIBRARY □ Arlington, VA

Mooney, Aidan, Chf. Indexer
NEWSWEEK, INC. - LIBRARY □ New York, NY

Mooney, Margaret, Asst.Libn.
UNIVERSITY OF CALIFORNIA, RIVERSIDE - GOVERNMENT PUBLICATIONS DEPARTMENT - LIBRARY □ Riverside, CA

Mooney, Sandra
LOUISIANA STATE UNIVERSITY - REFERENCE SERVICES □ Baton Rouge, LA

Mooney, Shirley E., Libn.
PACIFIC PRESS, LTD. - PRESS LIBRARY □ Vancouver, BC

Moore, Aletta, Supv.
3M - BUSINESS INFORMATION SERVICE □ St. Paul, MN

Moore, Barbara F., Law Libn.
MEMPHIS-SHELBY COUNTY BAR ASSOCIATION - LAW LIBRARY □ Memphis, TN

Moore, Beth, Lib.Asst.
COLORADO STATE DIVISION OF HIGHWAYS - TECHNICAL LIBRARY □ Denver, CO

Moore, Betty Rose, Lib.Serv.Coord.
COLUMBIA UNIVERSITY CANCER CENTER - INSTITUTE OF CANCER RESEARCH □ New York, NY

Moore, Beverly A., Dir.
UNIVERSITY OF SOUTHERN COLORADO - LIBRARY - SPECIAL COLLECTIONS □ Pueblo, CO

Moore, Bevette, Registrar
NORTHEASTERN NEVADA MUSEUM - LIBRARY □ Elko, NV

Moore, Bonnie C., Info.Mgr.
SOUTHWESTERN ILLINOIS METROPOLITAN AND REGIONAL PLANNING COMMISSION - TECHNICAL LIBRARY □ Collinsville, IL

Moore, Carleton B., Dir.
ARIZONA STATE UNIVERSITY - CENTER FOR METEORITE STUDIES - LIBRARY □ Tempe, AZ

Moore, Carol, Doc.Libn.
OREGON INSTITUTE OF TECHNOLOGY - LEARNING RESOURCES CENTER □ Klamath Falls, OR

Moore, Catherine, Libn.
MASSACHUSETTS STATE DEPARTMENT OF PUBLIC HEALTH - CENTRAL LIBRARY □ Boston, MA

Moore, D., Chf., Pub.Serv.
CANADA - PUBLIC ARCHIVES OF CANADA - FEDERAL ARCHIVES DIVISION □ Ottawa, ON

Moore, Dale, Libn.
METROPOLITAN TORONTO LIBRARY - MUNICIPAL REFERENCE DEPARTMENT □ Toronto, ON

Moore, Dallas, Libn.
HONIGMAN MILLER SCHWARTZ & COHN - LAW LIBRARY □ Detroit, MI

Moore, David G., Libn.
ONE, INC. - BLANCHE M. BAKER MEMORIAL LIBRARY □ Los Angeles, CA

Moore, Debbie, Info.Spec.
ARIZONA STATE ENERGY INFORMATION CENTER □ Phoenix, AZ

Moore, Debra, Cur.
WHITTIER HOME ASSOCIATION - LIBRARY □ Amesbury, MA

Moore, Edythe, Mgr., Lib.Serv.
AEROSPACE CORPORATION - CHARLES C. LAURITSEN LIBRARY □ Los Angeles, CA

Moore, Elaine, Lrng.Rsrcs.
CLARION UNIVERSITY OF PENNSYLVANIA - RENA M. CARLSON LIBRARY □ Clarion, PA

Moore, Eleanor, Co-Libn.
WAUKEGAN HISTORICAL SOCIETY - JOHN RAYMOND MEMORIAL LIBRARY □ Waukegan, IL

Moore, Dr. Everett L., Dir., Lib.Serv.
WOODBURY UNIVERSITY - LIBRARY □ Los Angeles, CA

Moore, Gregory, Pres.
UNITED STATES STUDENT ASSOCIATION - INFORMATION SERVICES □ Washington, DC

Moore, Harrison D., Pres.
WOLFEBORO HISTORICAL SOCIETY -
PLEASANT VALLEY SCHOOLHOUSE - LIBRARY &
FIRE ENGINE MUSEUM □ Wolfeboro, NH
Moore, Heather, Chf.
CANADA - SOLICITOR GENERAL CANADA -
MINISTRY LIBRARY & REFERENCE CENTRE □
Ottawa, ON
Moore, Henrietta, Circ.Supv.
TUFTS UNIVERSITY - FLETCHER SCHOOL OF
LAW & DIPLOMACY - EDWIN GINN LIBRARY □
Medford, MA
Moore, J.D., Sec.
CANADIAN EXPORT ASSOCIATION - LIBRARY □
Ottawa, ON
Moore, James, Regional Archv.
WASHINGTON STATE OFFICE OF SECRETARY
OF STATE - DIVISION OF ARCHIVES AND
RECORD MANAGEMENT □ Olympia, WA
Moore, James C., Dir.
ALBUQUERQUE MUSEUM OF ART, HISTORY &
SCIENCE - LIBRARY† □ Albuquerque, NM
Moore, Jane R., Chf.Libn.
CUNY - GRADUATE SCHOOL AND UNIVERSITY
CENTER - LIBRARY □ New York, NY
Moore, Janet E., Hd., Docs. & Pubns.
MASSACHUSETTS INSTITUTE OF TECHNOLOGY
- RESEARCH LABORATORY OF ELECTRONICS -
DOCUMENT ROOM □ Cambridge, MA
Moore, Jean, Libn./Co-Dir.
SHARON HOSPITAL - HEALTH SCIENCES
LIBRARY □ Sharon, CT
Moore, Jim, Ref.Libn.
U.S. ARMY - JFK SPECIAL WARFARE CENTER -
MARQUAT MEMORIAL LIBRARY □ Ft. Bragg, NC
Moore, John M., Br.Libn.
SAN FRANCISCO LAW LIBRARY □ San Francisco,
CA
Moore, Joleta, Supv.
E-SYSTEMS, INC. - DIVISION LIBRARY □
Greenville, TX
Moore, Julie L., Bibliog.
MOORE (Julie) & ASSOCIATES - LIBRARY □
Riverside, CA
Moore, Lennis, Adm.
MIDWEST OLD SETTLERS AND THRESHERS
ASSOCIATION - OLD THRESHERS OFFICE -
LIBRARY □ Mount Pleasant, IA
Moore, Lou Ann, Med.Libn.
U.S. VETERANS ADMINISTRATION (IL-North
Chicago) - HOSPITAL LIBRARY □ North Chicago,
IL
Moore, Mae Frances, Libn.
WESTERN HIGHWAY INSTITUTE - RESEARCH
LIBRARY □ San Bruno, CA
Moore, Marilyn, Dir.
CANADIAN CENTRE FOR OCCUPATIONAL
HEALTH AND SAFETY - DOCUMENTATION
SERVICES/SERVICE DE DOCUMENTATION □
Hamilton, ON
Moore, Marilyn, Coord., Ref.Serv.
MISSISSIPPI (State) RESEARCH AND
DEVELOPMENT CENTER - INFORMATION
SERVICES DIVISION □ Jackson, MS
Moore, Martha, Assoc.Libn.
DIGITAL EQUIPMENT CORPORATION - HUDSON
LSI LIBRARY □ Hudson, MA
Moore, Mary, Sr.Info.Spec., Mgt.
CONFERENCE BOARD, INC. - INFORMATION
SERVICE □ New York, NY
Moore, Mary, Media Libn.
TEXAS TECH UNIVERSITY - HEALTH SCIENCES
CENTER - LIBRARY OF THE HEALTH SCIENCES
□ Lubbock, TX
Moore, Mary, Chf., Lib.Plan.& Dev.Div.
WASHINGTON STATE LIBRARY □ Olympia, WA
Moore, Maureen M., Libn.
INTERNATIONAL MONETARY FUND/WORLD
BANK - JOINT BANK-FUND LIBRARY □
Washington, DC
Moore, Mildred A., Biological Sci.Libn.
UNIVERSITY OF KENTUCKY - BIOLOGICAL
SCIENCES LIBRARY □ Lexington, KY

Moore, Monica, Asst.Cur.
COLUMBIA UNIVERSITY - DEPARTMENT OF
ART HISTORY & ARCHAEOLOGY - PHOTOGRAPH
COLLECTION □ New York, NY
Moore, Nancy H., Dir.
SHENANDOAH COLLEGE & CONSERVATORY OF
MUSIC - HOWE LIBRARY □ Winchester, VA
Moore, Patricia, Ref.Libn.
SAN DIEGO STATE UNIVERSITY -
GOVERNMENT PUBLICATIONS DEPARTMENT†
□ San Diego, CA
Moore, Patricia, Hd., Tech.Serv./Acq.
UNIVERSITY OF CALIFORNIA, LOS ANGELES -
ART LIBRARY □ Los Angeles, CA
Moore, Penelope F., Lib.Techn.
U.S. NATL. DEFENSE UNIVERSITY -
DEPARTMENT OF DEFENSE COMPUTER
INSTITUTE - DODCI TECHNICAL LIBRARY □
Washington, DC
Moore, Ramona L., Ser.Libn.
UNIVERSITY OF MAINE SCHOOL OF LAW -
DONALD L. GARBRECHT LAW LIBRARY □
Portland, ME
Moore, Richard
SOUTHERN OREGON STATE COLLEGE -
LIBRARY □ Ashland, OR
Moore, Rita M., Asst.Libn.
CHESTER COUNTY HISTORICAL SOCIETY -
LIBRARY □ West Chester, PA
Moore, Robert W., Sr.Libn.
AMERICAN INDIAN BIBLE COLLEGE - DOROTHY
CUMMINGS MEMORIAL LIBRARY □ Phoenix, AZ
Moore, Sara L., Asst.Chf.Libn.
DISTRICT OF COLUMBIA GENERAL HOSPITAL -
MEDICAL LIBRARY □ Washington, DC
Moore, Sharon, Asst.Res.Libn.
OHIO STATE LEGISLATIVE SERVICE
COMMISSION - RESEARCH LIBRARY □
Columbus, OH
Moore, Shirley A., Libn.
WILMINGTON STAR-NEWS NEWSPAPERS, INC.
- LIBRARY □ Wilmington, NC
Moore, Stanley D., Reg.Dir.
U.S. BUREAU OF THE CENSUS - INFORMATION
SERVICES PROGRAM - CHICAGO REGIONAL
OFFICE - REFERENCE CENTER □ Chicago, IL
Moore, Susan, P.R. Asst.
CANADA - FARM CREDIT CORPORATION
CANADA - LIBRARY □ Ottawa, ON
Moore, Wanda Lucia, Libn. I
NASHVILLE AND DAVIDSON COUNTY
METROPOLITAN PLANNING COMMISSION -
LIBRARY □ Nashville, TN
Moore, William, Asst.Libn.
SAN ANTONIO SYMPHONY ORCHESTRA -
SYMPHONY LIBRARY □ San Antonio, TX
Moores, Gail, Hd., Tech.Serv.
MEMORIAL UNIVERSITY OF NEWFOUNDLAND -
HEALTH SCIENCES LIBRARY □ St. John's, NF
Moorhead, Katharine, Res.Libn.
MADISON COUNTY HISTORICAL SOCIETY -
MUSEUM LIBRARY □ Edwardsville, IL
Moorhead, Wendy, Ref.Libn.
ROOSEVELT UNIVERSITY - ARCHIVES □
Chicago, IL
Moquin, Henri, Regional Dir.
CANADA - NATIONAL FILM BOARD OF CANADA
- FILM LIBRARY† □ Winnipeg, MB
Morain, Stanley A., Dir.
UNIVERSITY OF NEW MEXICO - TECHNOLOGY
APPLICATION CENTER □ Albuquerque, NM
Morales, Lina B., Hd.Libn.
UNIVERSITY OF PUERTO RICO - COLLEGE OF
EDUCATION - SELLES SOLA MEMORIAL
COLLECTION† □ Rio Piedras, PR
Morales, Susan, Info.Spec.
UNIVERSITY OF ARIZONA - ENVIRONMENTAL
RESEARCH LABORATORY - LIBRARY □ Tucson,
AZ
Moran, Dick, Hd., Data Serv.
CINCINNATI CITY PLANNING COMMISSION -
OFFICE OF PLANNING AND MANAGEMENT
SUPPORT - LIBRARY □ Cincinnati, OH

Moran, Genel F., Libn.
ARNOLD, WHITE & DURKEE - LIBRARY □
Houston, TX
Moran, Joanna
CRAIN COMMUNICATIONS, INC. -
INFORMATION CENTER □ Chicago, IL
Moran, John, Asst.Div.Hd.
QUEENS BOROUGH PUBLIC LIBRARY -
HISTORY, TRAVEL & BIOGRAPHY DIVISION □
Jamaica, NY
Moran, John C., Dir.
CRAWFORD (F. Marion) MEMORIAL SOCIETY -
BIBLIOTHECA CRAWFORDIANA □ Nashville, TN
Moran, Marguerite K., V.P. & Dir.
M AND T CHEMICALS, INC. - TECHNICAL &
BUSINESS INFORMATION CENTER □ Rahway,
NJ
Moran, Marian C., Med.Libn.
DELAWARE VALLEY MEDICAL CENTER - JOHN
A. WHYTE MEDICAL LIBRARY† □ Bristol, PA
Moran, Mary, Supv., Newspaper Dept.
OKLAHOMA HISTORICAL SOCIETY - DIVISION
OF LIBRARY RESOURCES □ Oklahoma City, OK
Moran, Paul F., Libn.
U.S. BUREAU OF MINES - AVONDALE RESEARCH
CENTER LIBRARY □ Avondale, MD
Moran, Peter P., Archv.
SIMCOE COUNTY ARCHIVES □ Minesing, ON
Moran, Robert
INDIANA UNIVERSITY NORTHWEST -
CALUMET REGIONAL ARCHIVES □ Gary, IN
Moran, Sally P., Libn.
NASHVILLE BANNER - LIBRARY □ Nashville, TN
Moran, Sherrie L., Libn.
U.S. ARMY - CORPS OF ENGINEERS - LOWER
MISSISSIPPI VALLEY DIV. - MISSISSIPPI
RIVER COMMN. TECHNICAL LIB. □ Vicksburg,
MS
Moran, Terry, Assoc.Libn.
HOUGHTON MIFFLIN COMPANY - LIBRARY □
Boston, MA
Moravec, Georgina, Libn.
TORONTO CITY PLANNING AND DEVELOPMENT
DEPARTMENT - LIBRARY □ Toronto, ON
Morawetz, Dorina, Adm.
BAKKEN FOUNDATION - BAKKEN LIBRARY OF
ELECTRICITY IN LIFE □ Minneapolis, MN
Morchower, Gail M., Supv.
MASSACHUSETTS INSTITUTE OF TECHNOLOGY
- PHYSICS READING ROOM □ Cambridge, MA
Morden, Lanette, Lib.Techn.
CALGARY CITY ELECTRIC SYSTEM - RESOURCE
CENTRE □ Calgary, AB
More, Hazel M., Tech.Libn.
FAIRCHILD INDUSTRIES - TECHNICAL
INFORMATION SERVICES LIBRARY† □
Germantown, MD
More, Susan L., Acq.Libn.
UNIVERSITY OF TEXAS, AUSTIN - SCHOOL OF
LAW - TARLTON LAW LIBRARY □ Austin, TX
Moreau, Evelyn N., Sec.
NEWTON PUBLIC SCHOOLS - TEACHERS'
PROFESSIONAL LIBRARY □ Newton, MA
Moreau, Vivian, Ref.Libn.
BOSTON COLLEGE - GRADUATE SCHOOL OF
SOCIAL WORK LIBRARY □ Chestnut Hill, MA
Moreland, C. R., Hd.Libn.
U.S. NAVY - NAVAL AIR STATION (FL-
Pensacola) - LIBRARY □ Pensacola, FL
Moreland, Pat, Asst.Med.Libn.
MC LAREN GENERAL HOSPITAL - MEDICAL
LIBRARY □ Flint, MI
Moreland, Rachel, Circ.
KANSAS STATE UNIVERSITY - FARRELL
LIBRARY □ Manhattan, KS
Morency, Anita, Asst.Libn.
LIFE INSURANCE MARKETING AND RESEARCH
ASSOCIATION - LIBRARY □ Hartford, CT
Moreno, Esperanza A., Hd.Libn.
UNIVERSITY OF TEXAS, EL PASO - NURSING/
MEDICAL LIBRARY □ El Paso, TX

Personnel Index

Moreno, Pierrette, Circ.
UNIVERSITY OF TEXAS, AUSTIN - SCHOOL OF LAW - TARLTON LAW LIBRARY □ Austin, TX

Moreth, Susan, Med.Libn.
MESA LUTHERAN HOSPITAL - MEDICAL LIBRARY □ Mesa, AZ

Moretz, James, Dir.
AMERICAN FLORAL ART SCHOOL - FLORAL LIBRARY □ Chicago, IL

Morey, T.J., Mgr., Tech.Serv.
XEROX CORPORATION - TECHNICAL INFORMATION CENTER □ Webster, NY

Morf, Elisabeth, Libn.
GOETHE INSTITUTE MONTREAL - GERMAN CULTURAL CENTRE - LIBRARY □ Montreal, PQ

Morford, Martha, Coord.
COLUMBUS MUSEUM OF ART - RESOURCE CENTER □ Columbus, OH

Morgan, Almarine, Libn.
MORGAN (J. Harris) LAW OFFICE - LAW LIBRARY □ Greenville, TX

Morgan, Anne, Br.Libn.
BRITISH COLUMBIA - MINISTRY OF PROVINCIAL SEC. & GOVERNMENT SERV. - HERITAGE CONSRV. BR. - RESOURCE INFO. CTR. □ Victoria, BC

Morgan, Carol, Ref.Libn.
MEDICAL COLLEGE OF WISCONSIN - LIBRARIES □ Milwaukee, WI

Morgan, Chris, Info.Sys.Anl.
SANDIA NATIONAL LABORATORIES - TECHNICAL LIBRARY □ Albuquerque, NM

Morgan, David, Archv.Techn.
JEFFERSON COUNTY OFFICE OF HISTORIC PRESERVATION AND ARCHIVES □ Louisville, KY

Morgan, Dorothy C., Dir.
MARIN COUNTY HISTORICAL SOCIETY - LIBRARY □ San Rafael, CA

Morgan, Mr. E.C., Staff Archv.
SASKATCHEWAN ARCHIVES BOARD □ Regina, SK

Morgan, Elois, Coll.Mgmt.Libn.
U.S. VETERANS ADMINISTRATION (VA-Hampton) - MEDICAL CENTER LIBRARY □ Hampton, VA

Morgan, F.P., Chf., Lib.Br.
U.S. AIR FORCE BASE - EGLIN BASE LIBRARY □ Eglin AFB, FL

Morgan, George, Circ.
MASSACHUSETTS COLLEGE OF ART - LIBRARY □ Boston, MA

Morgan, Harriette, Ser.
U.S. CENTERS FOR DISEASE CONTROL - CDC LIBRARY □ Atlanta, GA

Morgan, James E., Dir.
OREGON HEALTH SCIENCES UNIVERSITY - LIBRARY □ Portland, OR

Morgan, Jane, Exec.Dir.
COMMUNITY SERVICE, INC. - LIBRARY □ Yellow Springs, OH

Morgan, Judith, Asst.Dir.
OKLAHOMA CITY UNIVERSITY - LAW LIBRARY □ Oklahoma City, OK

Morgan, Julia B., Archv.
JOHNS HOPKINS UNIVERSITY - FERDINAND HAMBURGER, JR. ARCHIVES □ Baltimore, MD

Morgan, Kathryn, Cur.
LOUISIANA STATE UNIVERSITY - E.A. MC ILHENNY NATURAL HISTORY COLLECTION □ Baton Rouge, LA

Morgan, Keithel C., Chf.Interp.
U.S. NATL. PARK SERVICE - RICHMOND NATL. BATTLEFIELD PARK - LIBRARY □ Richmond, VA

Morgan, Lauren, Info.Spec.
STANDARD OIL COMPANY OF OHIO - CORPORATE ENGINEERING LIBRARY □ Cleveland, OH

Morgan, Lynn Kasner, Dir.
MOUNT SINAI SCHOOL OF MEDICINE OF THE CITY UNIVERSITY OF NEW YORK - GUSTAVE L. & JANET W. LEVY LIBRARY □ New York, NY

Morgan, Mrs. Madel J., Dir., Archv. & Lib.Div.
MISSISSIPPI STATE DEPARTMENT OF ARCHIVES AND HISTORY - ARCHIVES AND LIBRARY DIVISION □ Jackson, MS

Morgan, Mary, Archv.
BOSTON COLLEGE - SPECIAL COLLECTIONS DEPARTMENT □ Chestnut Hill, MA

Morgan, Mildred A., Libn.
TRINITY MEDICAL CENTER - SCHOOL OF NURSING LIBRARY† □ Minot, ND

Morgan, Nigel, Act.Dir.
PRINCETON UNIVERSITY - DEPARTMENT OF ART & ARCHAEOLOGY - INDEX OF CHRISTIAN ART □ Princeton, NJ

Morgan, Patricia, Lib.Asst.
U.S. MARINE CORPS - HISTORICAL CENTER LIBRARY† □ Washington, DC

Morgan, Paula, Music Libn.
PRINCETON UNIVERSITY - MUSIC COLLECTION† □ Princeton, NJ

Morgan, Dr. R.J., Dir.
UNIVERSITY OF CAPE BRETON - BEATON INSTITUTE ARCHIVES □ Sydney, NS

Morgan, R.P., Libn.
CANADA - PARKS CANADA, WESTERN REGION - LIBRARY □ Calgary, AB

Morgan, Sherry, Ref.Libn.
HARTFORD HOSPITAL - HEALTH SCIENCE LIBRARIES □ Hartford, CT

Morgan, Vivian, Sect.Chf.
U.S. NATL. INSTITUTE FOR OCCUPATIONAL SAFETY & HEALTH - TECHNICAL INFORMATION BRANCH □ Cincinnati, OH

Morganti, Deena H., Hd., Pub.Serv.
PENNSYLVANIA STATE UNIVERSITY, BERKS CAMPUS - MEMORIAL LIBRARY □ Reading, PA

Morgenstern, Dan, Dir.
RUTGERS UNIVERSITY, THE STATE UNIVERSITY OF NEW JERSEY - INSTITUTE OF JAZZ STUDIES □ Newark, NJ

Moriarity, Wendy, Asst.Dir.
CANADIAN CENTRE FOR OCCUPATIONAL HEALTH AND SAFETY - DOCUMENTATION SERVICES/SERVICE DE DOCUMENTATION □ Hamilton, ON

Morin, Denise Paquet, Tech. en Doc.
HOPITAL ST-FRANCOIS D'ASSISE - BIBLIOTHEQUE MEDICALE ET ADMINISTRATIVE† □ Quebec, PQ

Morin, Sr. Gabrielle, SNJM, Coord. of Rsrcs.
WINDSOR COALITION FOR DEVELOPMENT - THIRD WORLD RESOURCE CENTRE □ Windsor, ON

Morin, Jeannine, Tech.Serv.
QUEBEC PROVINCE - MINISTERE DES AFFAIRES CULTURELLES - CENTRE DE DOCUMENTATION† □ Quebec, PQ

Morin, Shirley, Doc.Supv.
NATIONAL ACADEMY OF SCIENCES - NATIONAL RESEARCH COUNCIL - HIGHWAY RESEARCH INFORMATION SERVICE □ Washington, DC

Morison, William J., Dir./Univ.Archv.
UNIVERSITY OF LOUISVILLE - UNIVERSITY ARCHIVES AND RECORDS CENTER □ Louisville, KY

Morita, Kimiko, Cat.Libn.
POINT LOMA NAZARENE COLLEGE - RYAN LIBRARY □ San Diego, CA

Moritz, Thomas D., Hd.Libn.
UNIVERSITY OF WASHINGTON - FISHERIES-OCEANOGRAPHY LIBRARY □ Seattle, WA

Morlan, Phil, Libn./Acq.Spec.
GENERAL RESEARCH CORPORATION - LIBRARY □ Santa Barbara, CA

Morley, Mae, Libn.
KINGSTON PSYCHIATRIC HOSPITAL - STAFF LIBRARY □ Kingston, ON

Morley, Sarah Knox, Libn.
LOS LUNAS HOSPITAL AND TRAINING SCHOOL - LIBRARY AND RESOURCE CENTER† □ Los Lunas, NM

Morley, William F.E., Cur., Spec.Coll.
QUEEN'S UNIVERSITY AT KINGSTON - SPECIAL COLLECTIONS □ Kingston, ON

Morningstar, Melody M., Div.Libn.
HUGHES TOOL COMPANY - BUSINESS AND TECHNICAL LIBRARY □ Houston, TX

Moroshok, Sharri, Libn.
TALL TIMBERS RESEARCH STATION - LIBRARY □ Tallahassee, FL

Morotte, Anne Marie, Exec.Dir.
FRENCH AMERICAN CULTURAL SERVICES AND EDUCATIONAL AID (FACSEA) □ New York, NY

Morphet, Norman D., Sect.Chf.
SUN TECH, INC. - LIBRARY & INFORMATION SERVICE □ Marcus Hook, PA

Morphy, Majrory L., Hosp.Libn.
NORTH YORK GENERAL HOSPITAL - W. KEITH WELSH LIBRARY □ Willowdale, ON

Morr, Lynell A., Art Libn.
RINGLING (John and Mable) MUSEUM OF ART - ART RESEARCH LIBRARY □ Sarasota, FL

Morrell, Sachiko, Libn.
WASHINGTON UNIVERSITY - EAST ASIAN LIBRARY □ St. Louis, MO

Morrell, Stephanie, Corp.Tech.Libn.
AMERICAN EXPRESS COMPANY - CORPORATE SYSTEMS & TELECOMMUNICATIONS INFORMATION CENTER □ New York, NY

Morrill, Juanita H., Libn.
EASTERN STATE HOSPITAL - RESOURCE LIBRARY □ Lexington, KY

Morrill, Katherine, Asst.Libn.
NEW HAMPSHIRE HISTORICAL SOCIETY - LIBRARY □ Concord, NH

Morris, Annette
INFORMATICS GENERAL CORPORATION - FISH AND WILDLIFE REFERENCE □ Rockville, MD

Morris, Caroline, Libn.-Archv.
PENNSYLVANIA HOSPITAL - DEPARTMENT FOR SICK AND INJURED - HISTORICAL LIBRARY □ Philadelphia, PA

Morris, Caroline, Libn.-Archv.
PENNSYLVANIA HOSPITAL - DEPARTMENT FOR SICK AND INJURED - MEDICAL LIBRARY □ Philadelphia, PA

Morris, Charlene, Tech.Libn.
E-SYSTEMS, INC. - GARLAND DIVISION - TECHNICAL LIBRARY □ Dallas, TX

Morris, Dr. David R., Libn.
CHURCH OF JESUS CHRIST OF LATTER-DAY SAINTS - ST. GEORGE BRANCH GENEALOGICAL LIBRARY □ St. George, UT

Morris, Dorothy, Chf., Lib.
U.S. NASA - LEWIS RESEARCH CENTER - LIBRARY† □ Cleveland, OH

Morris, Dorothy G., Libn.
FRESNO COUNTY LAW LIBRARY† □ Fresno, CA

Morris, Gerald E., Libn.
MYSTIC SEAPORT, INC. - G.W. BLUNT WHITE LIBRARY □ Mystic, CT

Morris, Janice, ILL
D'ARCY, MAC MANUS, MASIUS - LIBRARY INFORMATION SERVICES □ Bloomfield Hills, MI

Morris, Jeanne, Asst.
DE PAUL HOSPITAL - DR. HENRY BOONE MEMORIAL LIBRARY □ Norfolk, VA

Morris, Joan, Ref.Libn.
OPPENHEIMER & CO., INC. - LIBRARY □ New York, NY

Morris, Joan L., Archv.Supv.
FLORIDA STATE DIVISION OF ARCHIVES, HISTORY & RECORDS MANAGEMENT - FLORIDA PHOTOGRAPHIC COLLECTION □ Tallahassee, FL

Morris, Joann, Libn.
HALIFAX REGIONAL VOCATIONAL SCHOOL - LIBRARY □ Halifax, NS

Morris, Karen, Asst.Leg.Ref.Libn.
RHODE ISLAND STATE LIBRARY □ Providence, RI

Morris, Lewis M., Jr., Oral Hist.
LOUISIANA STATE OFFICE OF THE SECRETARY
OF STATE - STATE ARCHIVES AND RECORDS
SERVICE - ARCHIVES SECTION □ Baton Rouge,
LA

Morris, Louis M., Ref./Circ.Sect.Ldr.
VITRO CORPORATION - LIBRARY □ Silver
Spring, MD

Morris, Louise A., Libn.
AKRON - DEPARTMENT OF PLANNING AND
URBAN DEVELOPMENT - LIBRARY □ Akron, OH

Morris, Lynne D., Chf., Lib.Serv.
U.S. VETERANS ADMINISTRATION (IL-Chicago)
- WESTSIDE HOSPITAL LIBRARY □ Chicago, IL

Morris, Marge, Asst.Mgr.
AMERICAN ASSOCIATION OF ADVERTISING
AGENCIES - MEMBER INFORMATION SERVICE
□ New York, NY

Morris, Mary, ILL & Ref.Libn.
CANADA - CONSUMER AND CORPORATE
AFFAIRS CANADA - PATENT OFFICE LIBRARY □
Ottawa, ON

Morris, P. Craig, Libn.
AUGUSTA CHRONICLE-HERALD NEWS -
LIBRARY □ Augusta, GA

Morris, Randy, Ill
UNIVERSITY OF MISSOURI, KANSAS CITY -
HEALTH SCIENCES LIBRARY □ Kansas City, MO

Morris, Robert C., Hd. Rare Bks./Mss./Archv.
NEW YORK PUBLIC LIBRARY - SCHOMBURG
CENTER FOR RESEARCH IN BLACK CULTURE □
New York, NY

Morris, Ruth, Tech.Serv.Libn.
UPJOHN COMPANY - CORPORATE TECHNICAL
LIBRARY □ Kalamazoo, MI

Morris, Sandra V., Libn.
U.S. ARMY - CORPS OF ENGINEERS -
HUNTINGTON DISTRICT - LIBRARY □
Huntington, WV

Morris, Sharee, Mgr., Info.Serv.
VOLUNTEER - THE NATIONAL CENTER FOR
CITIZEN INVOLVEMENT - LIBRARY □ Arlington,
VA

Morris, Sharon, Hd.Libn.
LUTHERAN HOSPITAL OF MARYLAND -
CHARLES G. REIGNER MEDICAL LIBRARY □
Baltimore, MD

Morris, Stephanie A., Cur.
TEMPLE UNIVERSITY - CENTRAL LIBRARY
SYSTEM - NATIONAL IMMIGRATION ARCHIVES
□ Philadelphia, PA

Morris, Thelma J., Dept.Hd.
CLEVELAND PUBLIC LIBRARY - SOCIAL
SCIENCES DEPARTMENT □ Cleveland, OH

Morris, Theodore A., Sr.Lib.Assoc./Spec.
UNIVERSITY OF CINCINNATI - DEPARTMENT
OF ENVIRONMENTAL HEALTH LIBRARY □
Cincinnati, OH

Morrison, Alan E., Libn.
UNIVERSITY OF PENNSYLVANIA - FINE ARTS
LIBRARY □ Philadelphia, PA

Morrison, Annette, Hd.Libn.
TENNESSEAN NEWSPAPER - LIBRARY □
Nashville, TN

Morrison, Carol, Info. Network Libn.
DU PAGE LIBRARY SYSTEM - SYSTEM CENTER
□ Geneva, IL

Morrison, Carol A., Libn.
ONTARIO CANCER INSTITUTE - LIBRARY □
Toronto, ON

Morrison, Daryl, Libn.
UNIVERSITY OF OKLAHOMA - WESTERN
HISTORY COLLECTIONS □ Norman, OK

Morrison, Daryl, Libn.
UNIVERSITY OF OKLAHOMA - WESTERN
HISTORY COLLECTIONS - LIBRARY DIVISION □
Norman, OK

Morrison, Janet, Hd.
UNIVERSITY OF HAWAII - PUBLIC SERVICES -
GOVERNMENT DOCUMENTS, MAPS &
MICROFORMS □ Honolulu, HI

Morrison, Linda, Libn.
BRITISH COLUMBIA LAW LIBRARY
FOUNDATION - VANCOUVER COURTHOUSE
LIBRARY □ Vancouver, BC

Morrison, M. Christine, Hd.
NATIONAL ENDOWMENT FOR THE ARTS - ARTS
LIBRARY/INFORMATION CENTER □
Washington, DC

Morrison, Marcia, Libn.
BUFFALO SOCIETY OF NATURAL SCIENCES -
RESEARCH LIBRARY □ Buffalo, NY

Morrison, Mary, Cat.
BROOKLYN LAW SCHOOL - LAW LIBRARY □
Brooklyn, NY

Morrison, Mary, Ref.Libn.
HARVARD UNIVERSITY - GODFREY LOWELL
CABOT SCIENCE LIBRARY □ Cambridge, MA

Morrison, Mrs. Pat, Pub.Serv. & ILL
SOUTHERN MISSIONARY COLLEGE - MC KEE
LIBRARY - SPECIAL COLLECTIONS □
Collegedale, TN

Morrison, Ralph, Tech.Libn.
M.P.K. OMEGA COMPANY - BIOSCIENCE
LIBRARY □ Amarillo, TX

Morrison, Sandra, Libn.
UNIVERSITY OF MINNESOTA - LITZENBERG-
LUND LIBRARY □ Minneapolis, MN

Morrison, Sarah P., Corp.Libn.
AVANTEK, INC. - TECHNICAL INFORMATION
SERVICE □ Santa Clara, CA

Morrison, Shirley A., Libn.
DUNLOP RESEARCH CENTRE - LIBRARY □
Mississauga, ON

Morrison, Shirley R., Assoc.Libn.
SANTA BARBARA MUSEUM OF NATURAL
HISTORY - LIBRARY □ Santa Barbara, CA

Morrison, Shirley V., Media Spec.
OHIO STATE UNIVERSITY - EDGAR DALE
EDUCATIONAL MEDIA & INSTRUCTIONAL
MATERIALS LABORATORY □ Columbus, OH

Morrison, William C., Libn.
ATLAS TRAVEL, INC. - LIBRARY □ Houston, TX

Morrissett, Elizabeth, Hd.Libn.
MONTANA COLLEGE OF MINERAL SCIENCE AND
TECHNOLOGY - LIBRARY □ Butte, MT

Morrissey, Dorothy M., Assoc.Tech.Libn.
POLAROID CORPORATION - RESEARCH
LIBRARY □ Cambridge, MA

Morrissey, Jennifer, Print Coll.Libn.
FANSHAWE COLLEGE OF APPLIED ARTS AND
TECHNOLOGY - MAIN LIBRARY □ London, ON

Morrow, Darrell R., Dir.
RUTGERS UNIVERSITY, THE STATE
UNIVERSITY OF NEW JERSEY - GOTTSCHO
PACKAGING INFORMATION CENTER □
Piscataway, NJ

Morrow, Deborah, Hd.
BURNETT (Leo) COMPANY, INC. -
INFORMATION CENTER □ Chicago, IL

Morrow, Ellen B., Mgr.
QUAKER CHEMICAL CORPORATION -
INFORMATION RESOURCES CENTER □
Conshohocken, PA

Morrow, Helene T., Serv.Libn.
U.S. ARMY - ACADEMY OF HEALTH SCIENCES -
STIMSON LIBRARY □ Ft. Sam Houston, TX

Morrow, Jean, Libn.
NEW ENGLAND CONSERVATORY OF MUSIC -
HARRIET M. SPAULDING LIBRARY □ Boston, MA

Morrow, Kathe, Cat.Libn.
MOORE COLLEGE OF ART - LIBRARY □
Philadelphia, PA

Morrow, Lory, Photo Archv.
MONTANA HISTORICAL SOCIETY - LIBRARY/
ARCHIVES □ Helena, MT

Morrow, Nancy, Libn.
UPPER SAVANNAH AREA HEALTH EDUCATION
CONSORTIUM - LIBRARY □ Greenwood, SC

Morse, Anita, Dir.
UNIVERSITY OF WISCONSIN, MADISON - LAW
SCHOOL LIBRARY □ Madison, WI

Morse, Carol F., Libn.
PUTNAM COUNTY HISTORICAL SOCIETY -
FOUNDRY SCHOOL MUSEUM - REFERENCE
LIBRARY □ Cold Spring, NY

Morse, Charlene B., Sci.Engr.Ref.Libn.
UNIVERSITY OF ARIZONA - SCIENCE-
ENGINEERING LIBRARY □ Tucson, AZ

Morse, David, Libn.
DOHENY (Estelle) EYE FOUNDATION - KENNETH
T. NORRIS, JR. VISUAL SCIENCE LIBRARY □ Los
Angeles, CA

Morse, David, Tech.Serv.Libn.
UNIVERSITY OF SOUTHERN CALIFORNIA -
HEALTH SCIENCES CAMPUS - NORRIS
MEDICAL LIBRARY □ Los Angeles, CA

Morse, Kenneth T., Chf.Libn.
UNIVERSITY OF RHODE ISLAND,
NARRAGANSETT BAY - PELL MARINE SCIENCE
LIBRARY† □ Narragansett, RI

Morse, Dr. Richard E., Chf., Ref.Div.
U.S. AIR FORCE - HISTORICAL RESEARCH
CENTER □ Maxwell AFB, AL

Morse, Robert, Libn.
FLORIDA STATE DEPT. OF TRANSPORTATION -
CENTRAL REFERENCE LIBRARY □ Tallahassee,
FL

Morse, Tenna, Mgr.
COMPUTER SCIENCES CORPORATION -
SYSTEMS SCIENCES DIVISION - TECHNICAL
INFORMATION CENTER □ Silver Spring, MD

Morse, Terry Lee, Libn.
TEXAS MEMORIAL MUSEUM - LIBRARY† □
Austin, TX

Morse, Yvonne, Dir.
RINGLING SCHOOL OF ART AND DESIGN -
LIBRARY □ Sarasota, FL

Morshead, Sheila, Libn./Media Spec.
CAMBRIDGE SCHOOL DEPARTMENT -
TEACHERS' RESOURCE CENTER □ Cambridge,
MA

Mort, Mary-Ellen, Libn.
OAKLAND PUBLIC LIBRARY - SCIENCE/
SOCIOLOGY DIVISION □ Oakland, CA

Mortensen, Debora K., Libn./Dir.
NEW BRITAIN GENERAL HOSPITAL - HEALTH
SCIENCE LIBRARY □ New Britain, CT

Mortensen, M. Lee, Res.Libn.
NEVADA HISTORICAL SOCIETY - LIBRARY □
Reno, NV

Mortensen, Ruth V., Libn.
LEBOEUF, LAMB, LEIBY & MAC RAE - LIBRARY □
New York, NY

Mortenson, Susan, Map & Photo.Libn.
UTAH STATE HISTORICAL SOCIETY -
RESEARCH LIBRARY □ Salt Lake City, UT

Mortimer, Dorothy, Libn.
METHODIST MEDICAL CENTER OF ILLINOIS -
LEARNING RESOURCE CENTER □ Peoria, IL

Mortimer, Roger, Hd., Spec.Coll.
UNIVERSITY OF SOUTH CAROLINA - THOMAS
COOPER LIBRARY - RARE BOOKS & SPECIAL
COLLECTIONS DEPARTMENT □ Columbia, SC

Mortimer, Ruth, Cur.
SMITH COLLEGE - RARE BOOK ROOM □
Northampton, MA

Mortimer, William J., Mgr., Lib./Ref.Serv.
LIFE INSURANCE MARKETING AND RESEARCH
ASSOCIATION - LIBRARY □ Hartford, CT

Morton, Ann W., Libn.
EMORY UNIVERSITY - DIVISION OF LIBRARY
AND INFORMATION MANAGEMENT LIBRARY □
Atlanta, GA

Morton, Barbara G., Libn.
INLAND STEEL COMPANY - INDUSTRIAL
RELATIONS LIBRARY □ Chicago, IL

Morton, D., Coord., Online Ref.
UNIVERSITY OF WATERLOO - ENGINEERING,
MATHEMATICS & SCIENCE DIVISIONAL
LIBRARY □ Waterloo, ON

Morton, Diane, Pub.Serv.
WEST VIRGINIA UNIVERSITY - MEDICAL
CENTER LIBRARY □ Morgantown, WV

Morton, Donald J., Dir.
UNIVERSITY OF MASSACHUSETTS MEDICAL
SCHOOL & WORCESTER DISTRICT MEDICAL
SOCIETY - LIBRARY □ Worcester, MA

Morton, Dr. Julia F., Dir.
UNIVERSITY OF MIAMI - MORTON
COLLECTANEA □ Coral Gables, FL

Morton, Katharine, Hd.Libn.
YALE UNIVERSITY - MANUSCRIPTS AND
ARCHIVES □ New Haven, CT

Morton, Linda, Dir.
OWYHEE COUNTY HISTORICAL COMPLEX
MUSEUM - LIBRARY □ Murphy, ID

Morton, M.L., Dir., Lib.Div.
CANADA - AGRICULTURE CANADA - LIBRARIES
DIVISION □ Ottawa, ON

Morton, Natalie G., Asst.Libn., Rd.Serv.
U.S. DEPT. OF LABOR - LIBRARY† □ Washington,
DC

Morton, P.W., Mgr., Info.Dept.
ALUMINUM COMPANY OF AMERICA - ALCOA
TECHNICAL CENTER - INFORMATION
DEPARTMENT □ Alcoa Center, PA

Morton, Stephen C., Archv.
KENT STATE UNIVERSITY - AMERICAN
HISTORY RESEARCH CENTER □ Kent, OH

Morton, Stephen C., Univ.Archv.
KENT STATE UNIVERSITY - ARCHIVES □ Kent,
OH

Morton, Thomas, Hd., Tech.Serv.
UNIVERSITY OF CALIFORNIA, SAN DIEGO -
BIOMEDICAL LIBRARY □ La Jolla, CA

Morton, Walter, Cat.Libn.
LOUISIANA STATE UNIVERSITY MEDICAL
CENTER - SCHOOL OF MEDICINE IN
SHREVEPORT - LIBRARY □ Shreveport, LA

Morwood, Shari, Dir.
HEWLETT-PACKARD COMPANY - PORTABLE
COMPUTER DIVISION - TECHNICAL
INFORMATION CENTER □ Corvallis, OR

Moryto, Thomas, Dir. of Educ.
CANADIAN WOOD COUNCIL - LIBRARY □
Ottawa, ON

Mosca, Carlo A., Corp.Dir., Educ.
SEA WORLD, INC. - LIBRARY □ San Diego, CA

Moscatt, Angeline, Supv.Libn.
NEW YORK PUBLIC LIBRARY - DONNELL
LIBRARY CENTER - CENTRAL CHILDREN'S
ROOM □ New York, NY

Moscoso, Ana, Ref.Dept.
UNIVERSITY OF PUERTO RICO - MEDICAL
SCIENCES CAMPUS - LIBRARY □ Rio Piedras, PR

Moscowitz, Beth, Libn.
TEMPLE EMANU-EL - LIBRARY □ Long Beach, NY

Moseley, Eva, Cur. of Mss.
RADCLIFFE COLLEGE - ARTHUR AND
ELIZABETH SCHLESINGER LIBRARY ON THE
HISTORY OF WOMEN IN AMERICA □
Cambridge, MA

Moseley, Mrs. F.A., Lib.Chm.
BLACKHAWK GENEALOGICAL SOCIETY -
LIBRARY □ Rock Island, IL

Moseley, Sally, Hd., Microfilm Lib.
GEORGIA STATE DEPARTMENT OF ARCHIVES
AND HISTORY - CENTRAL RESEARCH LIBRARY†
□ Atlanta, GA

Moser, Margaret L., Libn.
ALLEGHENY COLLEGE - WALTER M. SMALL
GEOLOGY LIBRARY† □ Meadville, PA

Moser, Max L., Dir., Res. & Spec.Proj.
INDIANA STATE CHAMBER OF COMMERCE -
RESEARCH LIBRARY □ Indianapolis, IN

Moser, Maxine, Mgr.
CUBIC CORPORATION - TECHNICAL LIBRARY □
San Diego, CA

Moses, Eva W., Asst.Libn.
NORTON (R.W.) ART GALLERY - REFERENCE-
RESEARCH LIBRARY □ Shreveport, LA

Moses, Paula B., Mgr.
DOW CHEMICAL COMPANY - TECHNICAL
INFORMATION SERVICES - CENTRAL REPORT
INDEX □ Midland, MI

Moses, Paula B., Mgr.
DOW CHEMICAL COMPANY - TECHNICAL
INFORMATION SERVICES - CHEMICAL
LIBRARY □ Midland, MI

Mosher, Jeanette, Med.Libn.
MANATEE MEMORIAL HOSPITAL - WENTZEL
MEDICAL LIBRARY □ Bradenton, FL

Mosher, Lisa, Asst.Libn.
ACADEMY OF MOTION PICTURE ARTS AND
SCIENCES - MARGARET HERRICK LIBRARY □
Beverly Hills, CA

Mosigien, Rose, Circ./Ref.Libn.
UNIVERSITY OF WISCONSIN, MADISON -
CENTER FOR HEALTH SCIENCES LIBRARIES† □
Madison, WI

Mosimann, Elizabeth, Asst.Libn.
CARNEGIE-MELLON UNIVERSITY - HUNT
INSTITUTE FOR BOTANICAL DOCUMENTATION
□ Pittsburgh, PA

Mosiniak, Judith, Lib.Asst.
MINNEAPOLIS PUBLIC LIBRARY &
INFORMATION CENTER - HISTORY
DEPARTMENT □ Minneapolis, MN

Moskal, Fredereike A., Lib.Dir.
LEWIS UNIVERSITY - LIBRARY □ Romeoville, IL

Moske, Marjorie, Libn.
OKLAHOMA SCHOOL FOR THE BLIND -
PARKVIEW LIBRARY □ Muskogee, OK

Moskel, Fredrica, Hd.Libn.
LEWIS UNIVERSITY - CANAL ARCHIVES AND
SPECIAL COLLECTION OF HISTORY □
Romeoville, IL

Moskowitz, Helen S., Asst. to Dir.
PLANTING FIELDS ARBORETUM -
HORTICULTURAL LIBRARY □ Oyster Bay, NY

Moskowitz, Mickey, Dir.
EMERSON COLLEGE - LIBRARY □ Boston, MA

Moskowitz, Nancy, Ref.Libn.
WILLKIE FARR & GALLAGHER - LIBRARY □ New
York, NY

Mosley, Doris R., Chf., Tech.Serv.Br.
U.S. DEPT. OF STATE - LIBRARY □ Washington,
DC

Mosner, Mary K., ILL
MEDICAL COLLEGE OF GEORGIA - LIBRARY □
Augusta, GA

Moss, D., Lib.Spec.
ALLERGAN PHARMACEUTICALS, INC. -
MEDICAL & SCIENCE INFORMATION □ Irvine,
CA

Moss, George H., Jr.
MOSS ARCHIVES □ Sea Bright, NJ

Moss, Hibbert W., Hd.Libn.
COLLEGE FOR HUMAN SERVICES - LIBRARY □
New York, NY

Moss, Dr. Jerome, Dir.
UNIVERSITY OF MINNESOTA, ST. PAUL -
DEPARTMENT OF VOCATIONAL & TECHNICAL
EDUCATION - LEARNING RESOURCE CENTER □
St. Paul, MN

Moss, Karen M., Circuit Libn.
U.S. COURT OF APPEALS, 1ST CIRCUIT -
LIBRARY □ Boston, MA

Moss, Lucille R., Mgr., Health Sci.Lib.
HOLY CROSS HOSPITAL - HEALTH SCIENCES
LIBRARY □ Mission Hills, CA

Moss, Maxey Mixey, Postcard Cur.
MOLESWORTH INSTITUTE - LIBRARY AND
ARCHIVES □ Storrs, CT

Moss, Dr. Roger W., Jr., Exec.Dir.
ATHENAEUM OF PHILADELPHIA □ Philadelphia,
PA

Most, Marguerite, Assoc. Law Libn.
UNIVERSITY OF SAN DIEGO - MARVIN &
LILLIAN KRATTER LAW LIBRARY □ San Diego,
CA

Moten, Inga S., Info.Spec.
NATIONAL EPILEPSY LIBRARY AND RESOURCE
CENTER □ Landover, MD

Mothersell, Patricia, Libn.
LIVINGSTON COUNTY LAW LIBRARY □
Geneseo, NY

Motley, Archie, Cur., Archv. & Mss.
CHICAGO HISTORICAL SOCIETY - RESEARCH
COLLECTIONS □ Chicago, IL

Mott, Dorothy Williams, Libn./Cur.
MOTT RESEARCH GROUP - LIBRARY □
Washington, DC

Motta, Camille A., Dir. of Lib./Archv.
URBAN INSTITUTE - LIBRARY □ Washington,
DC

Motteler, Lee, Geog.
BISHOP (Bernice P.) MUSEUM - LIBRARY □
Honolulu, HI

Mottu, Susan, Rare Bk.Cat.
JOHNS HOPKINS UNIVERSITY - MILTON S.
EISENHOWER LIBRARY - SPECIAL
COLLECTIONS DIVISION □ Baltimore, MD

Mottweiler, Evelyn, Libn./Exec.Dir.
FREE METHODIST CHURCH OF NORTH
AMERICA - MARSTON MEMORIAL HISTORICAL
LIBRARY □ Winona Lake, IN

Motz, Josephine, Libn.
MADISON COUNTY HISTORICAL SOCIETY -
MUSEUM LIBRARY □ Edwardsville, IL

Motzkus, Gisela, Libn.
ILLINOIS STATE DEPARTMENT OF
TRANSPORTATION - TECHNICAL REFERENCE
LIBRARY □ Springfield, IL

Moul, Bonnie, Info.Spec.
UNIVERSITY OF DENVER AND DENVER
RESEARCH INSTITUTE - SOCIAL SYSTEMS
RESEARCH AND EVALUATION LIBRARY □
Denver, CO

Moulder, Cathy, Documentalist
MC MASTER UNIVERSITY - URBAN
DOCUMENTATION CENTRE □ Hamilton, ON

Moules, Mary, Hd.Tech.Serv.
AMERICAN MEDICAL ASSOCIATION -
DIVISION OF LIBRARY AND ARCHIVAL
SERVICES □ Chicago, IL

Moulton, David A., Dir.
STRAYER COLLEGE - LEARNING RESOURCES
CENTER □ Arlington, VA

Moulton, Elizabeth, Per.Supv.
GORDON COLLEGE - WINN LIBRARY □ Wenham,
MA

Moulton, Francis A., Asst.
HARTFORD STATE TECHNICAL COLLEGE -
GROM HAYES LIBRARY □ Hartford, CT

Moulton, James C., Info.Spec.
CONTINENTAL ILLINOIS NATIONAL BANK AND
TRUST COMPANY OF CHICAGO -
INFORMATION SERVICES DIVISION □ Chicago,
IL

Mounce, Carolyn, Libn.
BLUE MOUNTAIN COLLEGE - MUSIC LIBRARY □
Blue Mountain, MS

Mounce, Marvin, Pub.Lib.Cons.
STATE LIBRARY OF FLORIDA □ Tallahassee, FL

Mount, Albertina F., Lib.Supv.
HARKNESS (Edward S.) EYE INSTITUTE - JOHN
M. WHEELER LIBRARY □ New York, NY

Mounts, Earl, Comp.Sci.Libn.
CARNEGIE-MELLON UNIVERSITY -
ENGINEERING & SCIENCE LIBRARY □
Pittsburgh, PA

Mourey, Deborah, Libn.
EASTMAN KODAK COMPANY - MANAGEMENT
SERVICES - LIBRARY □ Rochester, NY

Moushey, Eugene, Ref.Libn.
WESTERN ILLINOIS UNIVERSITY - LIBRARIES
□ Macomb, IL

Moutseous, Margaret L., Lib.Dir.
CHILDREN'S HOSPITAL RESEARCH
FOUNDATION - RESEARCH LIBRARY □
Cincinnati, OH

Mowat, Vaila S., Libn.
HERMES ELECTRONICS LTD. - LIBRARY □
Dartmouth, NS

Mowers, Larry G., Assoc.Libn.
HARVARD UNIVERSITY - EDA KUHN LOEB
MUSIC LIBRARY □ Cambridge, MA

Moy, Gene P., Docs./Circ.Libn.
UNIVERSITY OF DETROIT - SCHOOL OF LAW
LIBRARY □ Detroit, MI
Moyal, Marjorie, Libn.
MAIN HURDMAN - LIBRARY □ New York, NY
Moye, Mary, AV Libn.
STATE LIBRARY OF FLORIDA □ Tallahassee, FL
Moyer, D.K., Dir.
SCHWENKFELDER LIBRARY □ Pennsburg, PA
Moyer, Esther H., Circ.
CALVARY BAPTIST THEOLOGICAL SEMINARY -
LIBRARY □ Lansdale, PA
Moyer, Jane, Libn.
NORTHAMPTON COUNTY HISTORICAL AND
GENEALOGICAL SOCIETY - HISTORICAL
MUSEUM AND LIBRARY □ Easton, PA
Moyer, Jennifer, Dir.
COORDINATING COUNCIL OF LITERARY
MAGAZINES - LIBRARY □ New York, NY
Moyer, Orin M., Libn.
U.S. AIR FORCE BASE - EDWARDS BASE
LIBRARY† □ Edwards AFB, CA
Moyle, Albert, Pres.
OGLESBY HISTORICAL SOCIETY - LIBRARY □
Oglesby, IL
Moyle, D.J., Hd.
CANADA - NATIONAL DEFENCE - NDHQ LAND
TECHNICAL LIBRARY □ Ottawa, ON
Moynihan, Mary K., Libn.
EXXON CORPORATION - LAW-TAX LIBRARY □
New York, NY
Moysa, Susan, Ref.Libn.
UNIVERSITY OF ALBERTA - SCIENCE AND
TECHNOLOGY LIBRARY □ Edmonton, AB
Mozel, Phil, Libn.
ROYAL ASTRONOMICAL SOCIETY OF CANADA -
NATIONAL LIBRARY □ Toronto, ON
Mozes, Dr. George, Dir.
MICHAEL REESE HOSPITAL & MEDICAL
CENTER - DEPARTMENT OF LIBRARY & MEDIA
RESOURCES □ Chicago, IL
Mozorosky, Terry, Mgr.
LORAL ELECTRONIC SYSTEMS - TECHNICAL
INFORMATION CENTER □ Yonkers, NY
Mraz, Svatava, Libn. 1
METROPOLITAN TORONTO LIBRARY - BOOK
INFORMATION AND INTERLOAN DEPARTMENT
□ Toronto, ON
Mroczkowski, Dennis P., Dir.
U.S. ARMY - ARMY TRANSPORTATION MUSEUM
- LIBRARY □ Fort Eustis, VA
Mrozewski, Andrzej H., Chf.Libn.
LAURENTIAN UNIVERSITY - MAIN LIBRARY □
Sudbury, ON
Mubirumusoke, Margaret, Info.Spec.
MASSACHUSETTS INSTITUTE OF TECHNOLOGY
- DEPARTMENT OF NUTRITION AND FOOD
SCIENCE - READING ROOM □ Cambridge, MA
Mudd, Isabelle, Adm.Libn.
U.S. ARMY POST - FORT WAINWRIGHT -
LIBRARY □ Ft. Wainwright, AK
Mudge, Alden, Circ.
NEW YORK UNIVERSITY - GRADUATE SCHOOL
OF BUSINESS ADMINISTRATION - LIBRARY □
New York, NY
Mudloff, Cherrie M., Libn.
DETROIT RECEIVING HOSPITAL & UNIVERSITY
HEALTH CENTER - LIBRARY □ Detroit, MI
Mueckler, Rev. Edwin A., Archv.
LUTHERAN CHURCH - MISSOURI SYNOD -
MICHIGAN DISTRICT ARCHIVES □ Ann Arbor,
MI
Mueller, Bonita, Mgr., Tech.Serv.
U.S. GENERAL ACCOUNTING OFFICE - OFFICE
OF LIBRARY SERVICES □ Washington, DC
Mueller, Dorothy H., Libn.
PHILADELPHIA MARITIME MUSEUM - LIBRARY
□ Philadelphia, PA
Mueller, Heinz Peter, Assoc. Law Libn.
BRIGHAM YOUNG UNIVERSITY - J. REUBEN
CLARK LAW SCHOOL LIBRARY □ Provo, UT

Mueller, Jean E., Libn.
UNIVERSITY OF SOUTHERN CALIFORNIA -
ETHEL PERCY ANDRUS GERONTOLOGY CENTER
- GERONTOLOGICAL INFO. CENTER □ Los
Angeles, CA
Mueller, Jeanette, Ref./Online Serv.
UNIVERSITY OF MINNESOTA, DULUTH -
HEALTH SCIENCE LIBRARY □ Duluth, MN
Mueller, Jeanne G., Dir., Tech.Serv.
INDIANA UNIVERSITY, INDIANAPOLIS -
SCHOOL OF MEDICINE LIBRARY □ Indianapolis,
IN
Mueller, Laura, Chf.Libn.
AUGUSTANA HOSPITAL AND HEALTH CARE
CENTER - CARL A. HEDBERG HEALTH SCIENCE
LIBRARY □ Chicago, IL
Mueller, Lothar, Facilities Mgr.
UNIVERSAL SERIALS & BOOK EXCHANGE, INC.
- DUPLICATE EXCHANGE CLEARINGHOUSE &
INFORMATION CENTER □ Washington, DC
Mueller, Lynne, Ref.Libn.
MISSISSIPPI STATE UNIVERSITY - MITCHELL
MEMORIAL LIBRARY - SPECIAL COLLECTIONS
□ Mississippi State, MS
Mueller, Martha A., Hd., Rd.Serv./ILL
NEW YORK STATE COLLEGE OF CERAMICS AT
ALFRED UNIVERSITY - SAMUEL R. SCHOLES
LIBRARY OF CERAMICS □ Alfred, NY
Mueth, Elizabeth, Asst.Libn.
ST. LOUIS METROPOLITAN MEDICAL SOCIETY
- ST. LOUIS SOCIETY FOR MEDICAL AND
SCIENTIFIC EDUCATION - LIBRARY □ St. Louis,
MO
Muether, John R., Libn.
WESTERN THEOLOGICAL SEMINARY -
BEARDSLEE LIBRARY □ Holland, MI
Muffs, Lauren, Ref.Libn.
BENTLEY COLLEGE - SOLOMON R. BAKER
LIBRARY □ Waltham, MA
Mugglestone, Thomas, Libn.
WILSON, IHRIG & ASSOCIATES - LIBRARY □
Oakland, CA
Muhlberger, Richard, Dir.
SMITH (George Walter Vincent) ART MUSEUM -
LIBRARY □ Springfield, MA
Muir, Daniel T., Cur. Pictorial Coll.
HAGLEY MUSEUM AND LIBRARY □ Wilmington,
DE
Muir, Rodney A., Coord.
HOME OIL COMPANY, LTD. - TECHNICAL
INFORMATION CENTER □ Calgary, AB
Muir, Scott, Libn.
GEORGIA POWER COMPANY - LIBRARY
SERVICES □ Atlanta, GA
Muirhead, Phyllis, Ref.Libn.
TEXAS COLLEGE OF OSTEOPATHIC MEDICINE -
HEALTH SCIENCES LIBRARY □ Fort Worth, TX
Muise, Charmaine, Teacher/Libn.
ALBERTA SCHOOL FOR THE DEAF - L.A.
BROUGHTON LIBRARY □ Edmonton, AB
Mukerji, Jatindra N., Prin. Law Libn.
NEW YORK STATE SUPREME COURT - 2ND
JUDICIAL DISTRICT - LAW LIBRARY □
Brooklyn, NY
Mukherjee, Yolande, Corp.Libn.
IMPERIAL TOBACCO LTD. - CORPORATE
LIBRARY □ Montreal, PQ
Mulcahy, Brian J., Ref.Libn.
ROGERS & WELLS - LAW LIBRARY □ New York,
NY
Mulcahy, Jerry, Libn.
UNIVERSITY OF WESTERN ONTARIO - SCHOOL
OF BUSINESS ADMINISTRATION - BUSINESS
LIBRARY & INFORMATION CENTRE □ London,
ON
Mulder, Marjorie, Libn.
GILFORD INSTRUMENT LABORATORIES, INC. -
TECHNICAL LIBRARY □ Oberlin, OH
Mulhern, Jean, Chf.Libn.
WILBERFORCE UNIVERSITY - REMBERT-
STOKES LEARNING CENTER - ARCHIVES AND
SPECIAL COLLECTIONS □ Wilberforce, OH

Mulholland, Joan, Libn.
DAVIS & COMPANY - LAW LIBRARY □
Vancouver, BC
Mulkey, Jack, Dir.
JACKSON METROPOLITAN LIBRARY -
INFORMATION AND REFERENCE DIVISION □
Jackson, MS
Mull, Brenda, Libn.
DAUPHIN COUNTY LAW LIBRARY □ Harrisburg,
PA
Mull, Suzanne, Doc.Ret.Libn.
UNIVERSITY OF SOUTHERN CALIFORNIA -
NASA INDUSTRIAL APPLICATION CENTER
(NIAC) □ Los Angeles, CA
Mullaly, Sr. Columba, Ph.D., Archv.
TRINITY COLLEGE - ARCHIVES □ Washington,
DC
Mullan, Carolie R., Assoc.Libn.
TEXAS TECH UNIVERSITY - SCHOOL OF LAW
LIBRARY □ Lubbock, TX
Mullan, Ms. S.L., Lib.Techn.
HOPITAL REINE ELIZABETH - A. HOLLIS
MARDEN BIBLIOTHEQUE □ Montreal, PQ
Mullane, Ruth, Chf., Info.Serv.Br.
U.S. ARMY - PENTAGON LIBRARY □ Washington,
DC
Mullane, William H., Spec.Coll.Libn.
NORTHERN ARIZONA UNIVERSITY - SPECIAL
COLLECTIONS LIBRARY □ Flagstaff, AZ
Mullen, Grace, Archv./Pub.Serv.
WESTMINSTER THEOLOGICAL SEMINARY -
MONTGOMERY LIBRARY† □ Philadelphia, PA
Mullen, Kathy, Libn.
ST. LUKE'S HOSPITAL - LIBRARY □ St. Louis,
MO
Mullen, Robert, Pres.
UNIONTOWN HOSPITAL ASSOCIATION -
MEDICAL LIBRARY □ Uniontown, PA
Mullen, Ruth, Libn.
REYNOLDA HOUSE, INC. - LIBRARY □ Winston-
Salem, NC
Mullendore, Betty
HARTFORD PUBLIC LIBRARY - REFERENCE AND
GENERAL READING DEPARTMENT □ Hartford,
CT
Muller, Beverly, Lib.Mgr.
BRAUN (C.F.) COMPANY - REFERENCE LIBRARY
□ Alhambra, CA
Muller, Claudya B., State Libn.
IOWA STATE LIBRARY COMMISSION □ Des
Moines, IA
Muller, Janice Powell, Hd., Tech.Serv.
U.S. UNIFORMED SERVICES UNIVERSITY OF
THE HEALTH SCIENCES - LEARNING RESOURCE
CENTER □ Bethesda, MD
Muller, Robert Donald, Dir.
ONTARIO COUNTY HISTORICAL SOCIETY, INC.
- ARCHIVES □ Canandaigua, NY
Mullett, Philip I., Info.Spec.
NEWFOUNDLAND - DEPARTMENT OF RURAL
DEVELOPMENT - RESOURCE CENTRE □ St.
John's, NF
Mulligan, Kathleen, Cat.
ST. LOUIS MERCANTILE LIBRARY
ASSOCIATION - LIBRARY □ St. Louis, MO
Mulligan, Margaret, Asst.Supv., Lib.Serv.
CIBA-GEIGY CORPORATION -
PHARMACEUTICALS DIVISION - SCIENTIFIC
INFORMATION CENTER† □ Summit, NJ
Mulligan, William H., Jr., Dir.
CENTRAL MICHIGAN UNIVERSITY - CLARKE
HISTORICAL LIBRARY □ Mt. Pleasant, MI
Mullin, Marsha, Chf., Coll.
DISCOVERY HALL MUSEUM - RESEARCH
LIBRARY □ South Bend, IN
Mullin, Mary Frances, Libn.
FRENCH (R.T.) COMPANY - TECHNICAL
LIBRARY □ Rochester, NY
Mullin, Patrick, Anl./Educ.Coord.
SHERWIN-WILLIAMS COMPANY -
INFORMATION CENTER □ Cleveland, OH

Mullin, Viola Day, Hd., Tech.Serv.
YALE UNIVERSITY - DIVINITY SCHOOL LIBRARY □ New Haven, CT

Mullinix, Charlotte, Libn.
U.S. NAVY - NAVAL SURFACE WEAPONS CENTER - WHITE OAK LIBRARY† □ Silver Spring, MD

Mullins, Agnes D., Cur.
U.S. NATL. PARK SERVICE - ARLINGTON HOUSE, THE ROBERT E. LEE MEMORIAL - LIBRARY □ McLean, VA

Mullins, Ethel F., Chf., Lib.Serv.
U.S. VETERANS ADMINISTRATION (KY-Lexington) - MEDICAL CENTER LIBRARY □ Lexington, KY

Mullins, Linda, Mgr., Tech.Proc.
HEWLETT-PACKARD COMPANY - CORPORATE LIBRARY □ Palo Alto, CA

Mulloney, Paul F., Chf., Lib.Br.
U.S. BUREAU OF RECLAMATION - LIBRARY† □ Denver, CO

Mullooly, Elnora E., Libn.
FAYETTE COUNTY LAW LIBRARY □ Uniontown, PA

Mulloy, Betty, Libn.
LAUREN ROGERS MUSEUM OF ART □ Laurel, MS

Multer, Ell-Piret, Tech.Info.Spec.
U.S. FISH & WILDLIFE SERVICE - COLUMBIA NATIONAL FISHERIES RESEARCH LABORATORY LIBRARY □ Columbia, MO

Mulvaney, Carol E., Tech.Libn.
CATERPILLAR TRACTOR COMPANY - TECHNICAL INFORMATION CENTER □ Peoria, IL

Mulvie, Nancy, Cat.
CANADA - PUBLIC ARCHIVES OF CANADA - NATL. FILM, TELEVISION & SOUND ARCHIVES - DOCUMENTATION & PUB. SERV. □ Ottawa, ON

Mulvihill, John, Dir.
AMERICAN GEOLOGICAL INSTITUTE - GEOREF INFORMATION SYSTEM □ Alexandria, VA

Mundeen, Patsy, Info.Spec.
HOSPITAL CORPORATION OF AMERICA - RESEARCH/INFORMATION SERVICES □ Nashville, TN

Munden, Gail, Ref.Libn.
MAYER, BROWN & PLATT - LIBRARY† □ Chicago, IL

Mundie, Carol, Act.Libn.
ST. STEPHEN'S COLLEGE - LIBRARY □ Edmonton, AB

Mundstock, Aileen, Tech.Info.Spec.
UNIVERSAL FOODS CORPORATION - TECHNICAL INFORMATION CENTER □ Milwaukee, WI

Mundy, Angus, Coll.Dev.
KANSAS STATE UNIVERSITY - FARRELL LIBRARY □ Manhattan, KS

Mundy, James G., Jr., Libn.
UNION LEAGUE OF PHILADELPHIA - LIBRARY □ Philadelphia, PA

Munford, Norva, Ser.Libn.
SUNY - AGRICULTURAL AND TECHNICAL COLLEGE AT COBLESKILL - JARED VAN WAGENEN, JR. LEARNING RESOURCE CENTER† □ Cobleskill, NY

Munger, Dr. Edwin S., Dir.
CALIFORNIA INSTITUTE OF TECHNOLOGY - MUNGER AFRICANA LIBRARY □ Pasadena, CA

Munger, Nancy Terry, Mgr., Info.Serv.
THOMPSON (J. Walter) COMPANY - INFORMATION CENTER □ New York, NY

Mungro, Shirley, Doc.Anl.
MOBIL RESEARCH & DEVELOPMENT CORPORATION - ENGINEERING DEPARTMENT - INFORMATION CENTER □ Princeton, NJ

Munke, Margaret Pittman, Libn.
OUR LADY OF THE LAKE UNIVERSITY - WORDEN SCHOOL OF SOCIAL SERVICE - LIBRARY □ San Antonio, TX

Munoz, Patricia, Cat. & Acq.Libn.
MEDICAL AND CHIRURGICAL FACULTY OF THE STATE OF MARYLAND - LIBRARY □ Baltimore, MD

Munro, Jean, Reports Libn.
NATIONAL ACADEMY OF SCIENCES - NATIONAL ACADEMY OF ENGINEERING - LIBRARY □ Washington, DC

Munro, Pat, Libn.
MOBIL OIL CANADA, LTD. - LIBRARY □ Calgary, AB

Munro, Robert, Law Libn.
UNIVERSITY OF FLORIDA - LAW LIBRARY □ Gainesville, FL

Munro, William, Hd.
ATLANTA FULTON PUBLIC LIBRARY - IVAN ALLEN, JR. DEPARTMENT OF SCIENCE, INDUSTRY AND GOVERNMENT □ Atlanta, GA

Munsch, Mary Ann, Lib.Cons.
ALLEGHENY COUNTY - DEPARTMENT OF PLANNING - LIBRARY □ Pittsburgh, PA

Munsey, Joyce, Supv. of Lib. & Files
CROWNSVILLE HOSPITAL CENTER - PROFESSIONAL LIBRARY □ Crownsville, MD

Munson, Harold E., Supv., Project Engr.
TRW, INC. - BEARINGS DIVISION - RESEARCH & DEVELOPMENT TECHNICAL LIBRARY □ Jamestown, NY

Munson, Thomas A., Supt.
U.S. NATL. PARK SERVICE - EFFIGY MOUNDS NATL. MONUMENT - LIBRARY □ McGregor, IA

Muntner, Gail, Stud. & Doc.Adm.
AIR FRANCE - PUBLIC RELATIONS DEPARTMENT - LIBRARY □ New York, NY

Munyer, Marianna, Cur., Hist. Sites
ILLINOIS STATE HISTORICAL LIBRARY □ Springfield, IL

Murata, Louise R., Libn.
INDUSTRIAL INDEMNITY COMPANY - LIBRARY □ San Francisco, CA

Muratori, Robin A., Ck.
ERIE COUNTY LAW LIBRARY □ Sandusky, OH

Murch, Luella, Asst. Program Libn.
UNIVERSITY OF MARYLAND, COLLEGE PARK - COMPUTER SCIENCE CENTER - PROGRAM LIBRARY □ College Park, MD

Murchie, John, Lib.Dir.
NOVA SCOTIA COLLEGE OF ART AND DESIGN - LIBRARY □ Halifax, NS

Murchie, Kevin B., Libn.
ATLANTIC SALMON FEDERATION - J. KENNETH STALLMAN MEMORIAL LIBRARY □ St. Andrews, NB

Murdoch, A.W., Asst.Prov.Archv.
ONTARIO - ARCHIVES OF ONTARIO - LIBRARY □ Toronto, ON

Murdoch, Laurel, Leg.Libn.
TORY, TORY, DESLAURIERS & BINNINGTON - LIBRARY □ Toronto, ON

Murdoch, Martha Tucker, Hd.
UNIVERSITY OF WASHINGTON - MATHEMATICS RESEARCH LIBRARY □ Seattle, WA

Murdoch, S.K., Base Libn.
U.S. AIR FORCE BASE - HOWARD BASE LIBRARY □ APO Miami, FL

Murdock, David, Sr.Libn.
CARNEGIE LIBRARY OF PITTSBURGH - SCIENCE AND TECHNOLOGY DEPARTMENT □ Pittsburgh, PA

Murdock, David A., Visual Info.Spec.
U.S. DEPT. OF HOUSING & URBAN DEVELOPMENT - PHOTOGRAPHY LIBRARY □ Washington, DC

Murdock, Lynn, Libn.
BERKELEY PUBLIC LIBRARY - ART AND MUSIC DEPARTMENT □ Berkeley, CA

Murdock, William J., Lib.Dir.
PACE UNIVERSITY, PLEASANTVILLE/BRIARCLIFF - EDWARD AND DORIS MORTOLA LIBRARY □ Pleasantville, NY

Murdough, Wess-John, Libn.
DEGENKOLB (H.J.) ASSOCIATES, ENGINEERS - LIBRARY □ San Francisco, CA

Muren, C. Kamil, Dir.
TURKISH TOURISM AND INFORMATION OFFICE □ New York, NY

Murley, Karen A., Mgr.
IBM CORPORATION - GENERAL TECHNOLOGY DIVISION - EAST FISHKILL FACILITY - LIBRARY □ Hopewell Junction, NY

Muroga, Prof. S., Chm., Lib.Comm.
UNIVERSITY OF ILLINOIS - DEPARTMENT OF COMPUTER SCIENCE LIBRARY □ Urbana, IL

Murphey, Jane C., Asst.Libn.
UNITED AUTOMOBILE, AEROSPACE & AGRICULTURAL IMPLEMENT WORKERS OF AMERICA - RESEARCH LIBRARY □ Detroit, MI

Murphy, Alice, Spec.Coll.Libn.
CENTRAL BIBLE COLLEGE - LIBRARY □ Springfield, MO

Murphy, Anthony P., Archv.Techn.
NEWFOUNDLAND - PROVINCIAL ARCHIVES OF NEWFOUNDLAND AND LABRADOR □ St. John's, NF

Murphy, Barbara G., Assoc. Law Libn.
UNIVERSITY OF VIRGINIA - ARTHUR J. MORRIS LAW LIBRARY □ Charlottesville, VA

Murphy, Bernard F., Dir.
BALTIMORE CITY - DEPARTMENT OF LEGISLATIVE REFERENCE - LIBRARY □ Baltimore, MD

Murphy, Beth, Mgr., Lib.
HARPER & ROW, PUBLISHERS, INC. - SCHOOL DIVISION LIBRARY □ New York, NY

Murphy, Charles G., Sr.Asst.Libn.
PENNSYLVANIA STATE UNIVERSITY - APPLIED RESEARCH LABORATORY - LIBRARY □ State College, PA

Murphy, Charles J., Pub.Info.Off.
DUTCHESS COUNTY DEPARTMENT OF PLANNING - INFORMATION CENTER □ Poughkeepsie, NY

Murphy, Colleen, Hd., Media Serv.
BENTLEY COLLEGE - SOLOMON R. BAKER LIBRARY □ Waltham, MA

Murphy, Ellen M., Map/Gift Cat.
AMERICAN GEOGRAPHICAL SOCIETY COLLECTION OF THE UNIVERSITY OF WISCONSIN, MILWAUKEE - GOLDA MEIR LIBRARY □ Milwaukee, WI

Murphy, Ellen Rosenberg, Libn.
TEMPLE SINAI - LIBRARY □ Washington, DC

Murphy, Geneva, Hd., Pub.Serv.
U.S. ARMY SOLDIER SUPPORT CENTER - MAIN LIBRARY† □ Ft. Benjamin Harrison, IN

Murphy, H. Frank, Coord., Data Serv.
MISSISSIPPI (State) RESEARCH AND DEVELOPMENT CENTER - INFORMATION SERVICES DIVISION □ Jackson, MS

Murphy, Helen King, Dir.
HIGHLAND HOSPITAL - JOHN R. WILLIAMS, SR., HEALTH SCIENCES LIBRARY □ Rochester, NY

Murphy, Henry, Coll.Dev.Libn.
CORNELL UNIVERSITY - ALBERT R. MANN LIBRARY □ Ithaca, NY

Murphy, Joan, Mgr., Lib.Serv.
VARIAN ASSOCIATES - TECHNICAL LIBRARY □ Palo Alto, CA

Murphy, Kathleen, Hd., Access Serv.
TEACHERS COLLEGE - MILBANK MEMORIAL LIBRARY □ New York, NY

Murphy, Margaret, Libn.
NOVA SCOTIA - ATTORNEY GENERAL'S LIBRARY □ Halifax, NS

Murphy, Margaret M., Chf., Tech.Lib.
U.S. ARMY - MATERIALS & MECHANICS RESEARCH CENTER - TECHNICAL LIBRARY □ Watertown, MA

Murphy, Marilyn, Libn.
NEW ENGLAND AQUARIUM - LIBRARY □ Boston, MA

Murphy, Marilyn L., Libn.
INDIANA UNIVERSITY/PURDUE UNIVERSITY
AT FORT WAYNE - FINE ARTS LIBRARY† □ Fort
Wayne, IN

Murphy, Martha, Res.Libn.
JOSEPHINE COUNTY HISTORICAL SOCIETY -
RESEARCH LIBRARY □ Grants Pass, OR

Murphy, Martha E., Lib. Custodian
JACKSON COUNTY LAW LIBRARY □ Jackson, OH

Murphy, Mary A., Open Lit.Libn.
U.S. AIR FORCE - ARMAMENT DIVISION, AIR
FORCE ARMAMENT LABORATORY - TECHNICAL
LIBRARY □ Eglin AFB, FL

Murphy, Patrick, Libn.
MEDICAL RESEARCH LABORATORIES -
LIBRARY □ Niles, IL

Murphy, Paul, Ref.Libn.
VANDERBILT UNIVERSITY - JEAN AND
ALEXANDER HEARD LIBRARY - CENTRAL DIV. -
SARA SHANNON STEVENSON SCI. LIB. □
Nashville, TN

Murphy, Paul T., Law Libn.
UNIVERSITY OF WINDSOR - PAUL MARTIN
LAW LIBRARY □ Windsor, ON

Murphy, Mrs. R.P., Libn.
ALLIED CORPORATION - FIBERS & PLASTICS
COMPANY - TECHNICAL CENTER LIBRARY □
Petersburg, VA

Murphy, Robert, Dir.
U.S. INFORMATION AGENCY - LIBRARY
PROGRAM DIVISION □ Washington, DC

Murphy, Robert, Dir.
WEST VIRGINIA UNIVERSITY - MEDICAL
CENTER LIBRARY □ Morgantown, WV

Murphy, Robert D., Hd.
ROCHESTER PUBLIC LIBRARY - EDUCATION,
SOCIOLOGY AND RELIGION DIVISION □
Rochester, NY

Murphy, Rosemary, Libn.
ST. CLARE'S HOSPITAL - HEALTH SCIENCES
LIBRARY □ Denville, NJ

Murphy, Sara L., Sr.Libn.
BENDIX FIELD ENGINEERING CORPORATION -
GRAND JUNCTION OFFICE - TECHNICAL
LIBRARY □ Grand Junction, CO

Murphy, Teresa M., Libn.
BRITISH COLUMBIA TEACHERS' FEDERATION -
RESOURCES CENTRE □ Vancouver, BC

Murphy, Terry, Mgr.
GOULD INC. - GOULD INFORMATION CENTER □
Rolling Meadows, IL

Murphy, Virginia, Med.Libn.
NORTHWESTERN MUTUAL LIFE INSURANCE
COMPANY - MEDICAL LIBRARY □ Milwaukee,
WI

Murphy, Wayne, Acq.
VANCOUVER SCHOOL OF THEOLOGY - LIBRARY
□ Vancouver, BC

Murphy, William, Film Off.
CANADA - NATIONAL FILM BOARD OF CANADA
- FILM LIBRARY □ Thunder Bay, ON

Murphy, William, Br.Chf.
U.S. NATL. ARCHIVES & RECORDS SERVICE -
NATL. ARCHIVES - MOTION PICTURE, SOUND,
& VIDEO BRANCH □ Washington, DC

Murphy, Zita, Soc. & Political Sci.Libn.
RYERSON POLYTECHNICAL INSTITUTE -
LEARNING RESOURCES CENTRE □ Toronto, ON

Murrah, Dr. David, Dir.
TEXAS TECH UNIVERSITY - SOUTHWEST
COLLECTION □ Lubbock, TX

Murray, Alice J., Dir.
MC GEORGE SCHOOL OF LAW - LAW LIBRARY □
Sacramento, CA

Murray, Alice R., Dir.
U.S. NAVY - NAVAL SHIPYARD (PA-Philadelphia)
- TECHNICAL LIBRARY □ Philadelphia, PA

Murray, Bill, Dir.
AURORA PUBLIC SCHOOLS - PROFESSIONAL
LIBRARY □ Aurora, CO

Murray, Carol, Libn.
WASHINGTON UNIVERSITY - DENTISTRY
LIBRARY □ St. Louis, MO

Murray, Clare, Libn.
CANADA - DEFENCE RESEARCH
ESTABLISHMENT SUFFIELD - INFORMATION
SERVICES† □ Ralston, AB

Murray, Deborah M., Law Libn.
DISTRICT OF COLUMBIA - CORPORATION
COUNSEL LAW LIBRARY □ Washington, DC

Murray, Elizabeth B., Libn.
BRITISH COLUMBIA TELEPHONE COMPANY -
BUSINESS LIBRARY □ Burnaby, BC

Murray, Frances, Doc.Libn.
NEW YORK STATE LEGISLATIVE LIBRARY □
Albany, NY

Murray, George, Mgr.
CHAMBER OF MINES OF EASTERN BRITISH
COLUMBIA - BUREAU OF INFORMATION □
Nelson, BC

Murray, Georgette, Asst.
SOCIETE NATIONALE DE DIFFUSION
EDUCATIVE ET CULTURELLE - SERVICE
D'INFORMATION SONDEC □ St. Leonard, PQ

Murray, Gloria, Lib.Chm.
PETERBOROUGH HISTORICAL SOCIETY -
LIBRARY □ Peterborough, NH

Murray, Irena, Libn.
MC GILL UNIVERSITY - BLACKADER LIBRARY
OF ARCHITECTURE/LAUTERMAN LIBRARY OF
ART □ Montreal, PQ

Murray, James B., Hd., AV
NEW YORK PUBLIC LIBRARY - SCHOMBURG
CENTER FOR RESEARCH IN BLACK CULTURE □
New York, NY

Murray, James M., Law Libn.
GONZAGA UNIVERSITY SCHOOL OF LAW -
LIBRARY □ Spokane, WA

Murray, James M., Assoc. Law Libn.
WASHINGTON UNIVERSITY - SCHOOL OF LAW
- FREUND LAW LIBRARY □ St. Louis, MO

Murray, Dr. Joanne L., Metallurgist
U.S. NATL. BUREAU OF STANDARDS - ALLOY
PHASE DIAGRAM DATA CENTER □ Washington,
DC

Murray, Johnny F., Chf., Lib.
U.S. DEPT. OF DEFENSE - DEFENSE
INDUSTRIAL PLANT EQUIPMENT CENTER -
TECHNICAL DATA REPOSITORY & LIBRARY □
Memphis, TN

Murray, Kathleen, Dir., Lib.Serv.
PROVIDENCE MEDICAL CENTER - HORTON
HEALTH SCIENCES LIBRARY □ Seattle, WA

Murray, Laura, Hd.
METROPOLITAN TORONTO LIBRARY -
REGIONAL AUDIO VISUAL DEPARTMENT □
Toronto, ON

Murray, Lee M., Pub.Serv.Libn.
SYRACUSE UNIVERSITY - SCIENCE AND
TECHNOLOGY LIBRARY □ Syracuse, NY

Murray, Mrs. M., Libn.
NORTHERN MINER - LIBRARY □ Toronto, ON

Murray, Marijean, Supv.Libn.
U.S. ARMY SERGEANTS MAJOR ACADEMY -
OTHON O. VALENT LEARNING RESOURCES
CENTER □ Ft. Bliss, TX

Murray, Marilyn R., Libn.
ARTHUR ANDERSEN & CO. - GENERAL LIBRARY
□ Chicago, IL

Murray, Mary P., Libn.
MERCY CENTER FOR HEALTH CARE SERVICES -
MEDICAL LIBRARY □ Aurora, IL

Murray, Patricia, Libn./Tech.Ed.
INTERNATIONAL JOINT COMMISSION - GREAT
LAKES REGIONAL OFFICE LIBRARY □ Windsor,
ON

Murray, Paula, Lib.Techn.
BRITISH COLUMBIA CENTRAL CREDIT UNION -
RESOURCE CENTRE □ Vancouver, BC

Murray, Richard N., Dir.
ARCHIVES OF AMERICAN ART/SMITHSONIAN
INSTITUTION - NATIONAL HEADQUARTERS □
New York, NY

Murray, Ruth, Info.Spec.
AMERICAN CHEMICAL SOCIETY, INC. -
RUBBER DIVISION - JOHN H. GIFFORD
MEMORIAL LIBRARY & INFORMATION CTR. □
Akron, OH

Murray, Saundra, Libn.
SINGER COMPANY - LIBRASCOPE DIVISION -
TECHNICAL INFORMATION CENTER □ Glendale,
CA

Murray, Susan, Libn.
UNIVERSITY OF TORONTO - FACULTY OF
DENTISTRY LIBRARY □ Toronto, ON

Murray, Suzanne, Assoc.Dir.
SUNY - UPSTATE MEDICAL CENTER LIBRARY □
Syracuse, NY

Murray, Timothy, Cur., Mss.
WASHINGTON UNIVERSITY - DEPARTMENT OF
SPECIAL COLLECTIONS □ St. Louis, MO

Murray, Toby, Archv.
UNIVERSITY OF TULSA - MC FARLIN LIBRARY -
RARE BOOKS AND SPECIAL COLLECTIONS □
Tulsa, OK

Murray-Lachapelle, Rosemary
CANADA - SUPREME COURT OF CANADA -
LIBRARY □ Ottawa, ON

Murray-O'Hair, R., Dir.
SOCIETY OF SEPARATIONISTS - CHARLES E.
STEVENS AMERICAN ATHEIST LIBRARY AND
ARCHIVES INC. □ Austin, TX

Murrell, Irvin, Circ.-Ref.Libn. & ILL
NEW ORLEANS BAPTIST THEOLOGICAL
SEMINARY - JOHN T. CHRISTIAN LIBRARY □
New Orleans, LA

Murrell, Jeanette, Med.Libn.
MEMORIAL HOSPITAL OF NATRONA COUNTY -
MEDICAL LIBRARY □ Casper, WY

Murry, Joye, Dir.
FIRST ASSEMBLY OF GOD - CHURCH LIBRARY □
North Little Rock, AR

Mursec, Ljudmila, Asst.Sci.Libn.
MARQUETTE UNIVERSITY - SCIENCE LIBRARY
□ Milwaukee, WI

Murstein, Denis, Adm.Dir.
YOUTH NETWORK COUNCIL, INC. -
CLEARINGHOUSE □ Chicago, IL

Musa, Dr. Byron, Chm., Lib.Comm.
EUGENE HOSPITAL AND CLINIC - DOCTORS'
LIBRARY □ Eugene, OR

Muscat, Dr. Ann M., Asst.Dir.
UNIVERSITY OF SOUTHERN CALIFORNIA -
CATALINA MARINE SCIENCE CENTER -
LIBRARY □ Avalon, CA

Muse, Clifford L., Jr., Act.Dir. of Ctr.
HOWARD UNIVERSITY - MOORLAND-SPINGARN
RESEARCH CENTER - MANUSCRIPT DIVISION □
Washington, DC

Muse, Winnie, Tech.Info.Spec.
U.S. DEPT. OF TRANSPORTATION - URBAN
MASS TRANSPORTATION ADM. -
TRANSPORTATION RESEARCH INFO. CENTER
(TRIC) □ Washington, DC

Musgrave, Myles T., Asst. to V.P.
ACHESON INDUSTRIES, INC. - CORPORATE
INFORMATION CENTER □ Port Huron, MI

Musgrove, Arlene F., Tech.Info.Spec.
U.S. NATL. BUREAU OF STANDARDS - ATOMIC
ENERGY LEVELS DATA CENTER □ Washington,
DC

Mushenheim, Cecilia, Archv./Spec.Coll.Libn.
UNIVERSITY OF DAYTON - ROESCH LIBRARY -
SPECIAL COLLECTIONS/RARE BOOKS □ Dayton,
OH

Musher, Evelyn, Dir., Community Rel.
CONSULATE GENERAL OF ISRAEL - LT. DAVID
TAMIR LIBRARY AND READING ROOM □ New
York, NY

Musick, Judith L., Ph.D., Res.Dir.
INSTITUTE FOR THE STUDY OF SEXUAL
ASSAULT - INFORMATION CENTER □ San
Francisco, CA

Muskat, Beatrice T., Libn.
TEMPLE ISRAEL OF GREATER MIAMI - LIBRARY
□ Miami, FL

Musker, Gale, Res.
DISNEY (Walt) PRODUCTIONS - LIBRARY □
Burbank, CA

Muskus, Elizabeth A., Mgr., Info./Res.Serv.
REDDY COMMUNICATIONS, INC. -
INFORMATION/RESEARCH SERVICES □
Greenwich, CT

Musselman, Barbara, Regional Spec.
CUYAHOGA COUNTY PUBLIC LIBRARY -
FAIRVIEW PARK REGIONAL BRANCH - SPECIAL
COLLECTIONS □ Fairview Park, OH

Musser, Geraldyne J., Asst.Libn.
GENERAL MOTORS CORPORATION - TAX STAFF
LIBRARY □ Detroit, MI

Musser, Joyce, Asst.Chf.Libn.
CHURCH OF JESUS CHRIST OF LATTER-DAY
SAINTS - LAS VEGAS BRANCH GENEALOGICAL
LIBRARY □ Las Vegas, NV

Mussett, Marianne, Asst.Libn.
MEMPHIS STATE UNIVERSITY LIBRARIES -
SCHOOL OF LAW LIBRARY □ Memphis, TN

Mustain, Anne, Cat.Libn.
UNIVERSITY OF VIRGINIA - ARTHUR J.
MORRIS LAW LIBRARY □ Charlottesville, VA

Mutale, Elaine, Ref.Libn.
ANDREWS UNIVERSITY - JAMES WHITE
LIBRARY† □ Berrien Springs, MI

Mutch, A. Douglas
LIVESTOCK FEED BOARD OF CANADA -
LIBRARY □ Montreal, PQ

Mutchler, Peter K., Chf.Libn.
ALBERTA - DEPARTMENT OF ENERGY AND
NATURAL RESOURCES - LIBRARY □ Edmonton,
AB

Muth, Allan, Ph.D., Resident Dir.
UNIVERSITY OF CALIFORNIA, RIVERSIDE -
DEEP CANYON DESERT RESEARCH CENTER -
LIBRARY □ Palm Desert, CA

Muth, Ross E., Municipal Prog.Spec.
NEW YORK STATE CONFERENCE OF MAYORS
AND MUNICIPAL OFFICIALS - LIBRARY □
Albany, NY

Mutter, Michael A., Sr.Res.Assoc.
BOSTON MUNICIPAL RESEARCH BUREAU -
LIBRARY □ Boston, MA

Mutton, Judy, Ref. & ILL
CANADA - REGIONAL INDUSTRIAL EXPANSION
- CANADIAN GOVERNMENT OFFICE OF
TOURISM □ Ottawa, ON

Mutty, Stephanie S., Libn.
TEXAS INSTRUMENTS, INC. - LEWISVILLE
TECHNICAL LIBRARY □ Lewisville, TX

Muzzo, Joseph, Dir.
DOCTORS HOSPITAL - W.S. KONOLD
MEMORIAL LIBRARY □ Columbus, OH

Mwalilino, Valerie S., Hd., Acq.
NEW YORK PUBLIC LIBRARY - SCHOMBURG
CENTER FOR RESEARCH IN BLACK CULTURE □
New York, NY

Mycio, Luba, Pub.Aff.
CANADIAN WILDLIFE FEDERATION -
REFERENCE LIBRARY & INFORMATION CENTRE
□ Ottawa, ON

Myer, Nancy, Chf., Lib.Serv.
U.S. VETERANS ADMINISTRATION (NM-
Albuquerque) - MEDICAL CENTER LIBRARY □
Albuquerque, NM

Myers, Dr., Lib.Comm.Chm.
UNIVERSITY OF FLORIDA - AGRICULTURAL
RESEARCH & EDUCATION CENTER - BELLE
GLADE LIBRARY □ Belle Glade, FL

Myers, Anna J., Libn.
PUBLIC LIBRARY OF CINCINNATI AND
HAMILTON COUNTY - ART AND MUSIC
DEPARTMENT □ Cincinnati, OH

Myers, Charles J., Libn.
UNIVERSITY OF PENNSYLVANIA - SCHOOL OF
ENGINEERING AND APPLIED SCIENCE - MOORE
LIBRARY □ Philadelphia, PA

Myers, Charles J., Libn.
UNIVERSITY OF PENNSYLVANIA - SCHOOL OF
ENGINEERING AND APPLIED SCIENCE -
TOWNE LIBRARY □ Philadelphia, PA

Myers, Claryse D., Libn.
U.S. NATL. PARK SERVICE - GREAT SMOKY
MOUNTAINS NATL. PARK - SUGARLANDS
VISITOR CENTER □ Gatlinburg, TN

Myers, Diana, Hd., Tech.Serv.
ONTARIO COLLEGE OF ART - LIBRARY/
AUDIOVISUAL CENTRE □ Toronto, ON

Myers, Elissa Matulis, Dir., Member Serv.
AMERICAN SOCIETY OF ASSOCIATION
EXECUTIVES - INFORMATION CENTRAL □
Washington, DC

Myers, Elizabeth, Hd.
UNIVERSITY OF CALIFORNIA, BERKELEY -
GOVERNMENT DOCUMENTS DEPARTMENT □
Berkeley, CA

Myers, G. Richard, Libn.
GENERAL DYNAMICS CORPORATION - QUINCY
SHIPBUILDING DIVISION LIBRARY† □ Quincy,
MA

Myers, George C., Dir. of Ctr.
DUKE UNIVERSITY - CENTER FOR
DEMOGRAPHIC STUDIES - REFERENCE
LIBRARY □ Durham, NC

Myers, Harriet J., Lib.Techn.
ENVIRONMENTAL PROTECTION AGENCY -
LIBRARY SERVICES □ Research Triangle Park,
NC

Myers, Harry C., Supt.
U.S. NATL. PARK SERVICE - PERRY'S VICTORY
& INTERNATIONAL PEACE MEMORIAL -
LIBRARY □ Put-In-Bay, OH

Myers, Irene L., Sect.Hd.
PROCTER & GAMBLE COMPANY - WINTON HILL
TECHNICAL CENTER - TECHNICAL LIBRARY □
Cincinnati, OH

Myers, James C., Hd.
FLORIDA STATE UNIVERSITY - SCIENCE-
TECHNOLOGY DIVISION □ Tallahassee, FL

Myers, Joan B., Dir.
PHILADELPHIA BOARD OF EDUCATION -
PEDAGOGICAL LIBRARY† □ Philadelphia, PA

Myers, Joan R., Asst.Libn.
HEINZ (H.J.) COMPANY - LIBRARY □ Pittsburgh,
PA

Myers, Joe I., Archv.
STETSON UNIVERSITY - ARCHIVES □ DeLand,
FL

Myers, Judith, Acq.
NEW YORK MEDICAL COLLEGE AND THE
WESTCHESTER ACADEMY OF MEDICINE -
WESTCHESTER MEDICAL CENTER LIBRARY □
Valhalla, NY

Myers, Karen, Ref.Libn.
U.S. PUBLIC HEALTH SERVICE - PARKLAWN
HEALTH LIBRARY □ Rockville, MD

Myers, Linda, Hd., Tech.Serv.
SUNY - AGRICULTURAL AND TECHNICAL
COLLEGE AT COBLESKILL - JARED VAN
WAGENEN, JR. LEARNING RESOURCE CENTER†
□ Cobleskill, NY

Myers, Marcia, South Reg.Libn.
SEATTLE PUBLIC LIBRARY - DOUGLASS-TRUTH
BRANCH LIBRARY □ Seattle, WA

Myers, Mary, Per.Libn.
BRIDGEWATER STATE COLLEGE - CLEMENT C.
MAXWELL LIBRARY □ Bridgewater, MA

Myers, Mindy J., Asst.Libn.
WILLKIE FARR & GALLAGHER - LIBRARY □ New
York, NY

Myers, Nancy Jane, Libn.
WILLIAMS-KUEBELBECK & ASSOCIATES, INC. -
LIBRARY □ Redwood City, CA

Myers, Pam, Advertising
BELL & HOWELL COMPANY - MICRO PHOTO
DIVISION - MICROFORMS ARCHIVE† □
Wooster, OH

Myers, Peggy J., Corp.Libn.
ANCHOR HOCKING CORPORATION -
CORPORATE LIBRARY† □ Lancaster, OH

Myers, Ramon H., Cur., E. Asia Coll.
STANFORD UNIVERSITY - HOOVER
INSTITUTION ON WAR, REVOLUTION AND
PEACE - LIBRARY □ Stanford, CA

Myers, Susan Moore, Exec.Dir.
RAINBOW FLEET, INC. - LIBRARY □ Oklahoma
City, OK

Myers, William, Hd., Mss. & AV
OHIO HISTORICAL SOCIETY - ARCHIVES-
LIBRARY □ Columbus, OH

Myhre, Char, Libn./Educ.Coord.
ST. ANSGAR HOSPITAL - HEALTH SCIENCE
LIBRARY □ Moorhead, MN

Mykrantz, Barbara, Archv.
MISSOURI BOTANICAL GARDEN - LIBRARY □
St. Louis, MO

Mylenki, Mary, Sr.Asst.Libn.
NEW YORK HOSPITAL-CORNELL MEDICAL
CENTER - OSKAR DIETHELM HISTORICAL
LIBRARY □ New York, NY

Mylenki, Mary, Sr.Asst.Libn.
PAYNE WHITNEY PSYCHIATRIC CLINIC
LIBRARY □ New York, NY

Myles, Colette G., Hd.
UNIVERSITY OF CALIFORNIA, BERKELEY -
INSTITUTE OF INTERNATIONAL STUDIES
LIBRARY □ Berkeley, CA

Myles, Margo S., Dir.
NATURE CONSERVANCY - LONG ISLAND
CHAPTER - UPLANDS FARM ENVIRONMENTAL
CENTER □ Cold Spring Harbor, NY

Myong, Jae Hwi, Cat.Libn.
UNIVERSITY OF CALIFORNIA, IRVINE -
BIOMEDICAL LIBRARY □ Irvine, CA

Myrick, Rick, Gen.Mgr.
IFI/PLENUM DATA COMPANY - LIBRARY □
Alexandria, VA

N

Nacchio, Rita, Lit.Rsrcs.Assoc.
MERCK & COMPANY, INC. - MERCK SHARP &
DOHME RESEARCH LABORATORIES -
LITERATURE RESOURCES □ Rahway, NJ

Nacheman, Elinor, Hd., Cat.Dept.
RHODE ISLAND SCHOOL OF DESIGN - LIBRARY
□ Providence, RI

Nachlas-Gabin, Irva B., Libn.
REGIONAL PLANNING COUNCIL - LIBRARY □
Baltimore, MD

Nachod, Katherine, Govt.Doc.Libn.
NEW ORLEANS PUBLIC LIBRARY - BUSINESS
AND SCIENCE DIVISION □ New Orleans, LA

Nadal, Antonio, Hd. Law Libn.
PUERTO RICO - DEPARTMENT OF JUSTICE -
LIBRARY □ San Juan, PR

Nadasdi, Dr. M., Med.Dir.
GLAXO CANADA, LTD. - LIBRARY □ Toronto, ON

Nadeau, Claude-Roger, S.J., Dir.
COMPAGNIE DE JESUS - BIBLIOTHEQUE DE
THEOLOGIE □ Montreal, PQ

Nadeau, Lucienne, Dir.
COLLEGE DE MUSIQUE SAINTE-CROIX -
BIBLIOTHEQUE □ St. Laurent, PQ

Nadeau, Sylvie, Bibliotechnicienne
QUEBEC PROVINCE - L'INSPECTEUR GENERAL
DES INSTITUTIONS FINANCIERES -
BIBLIOTHEQUE □ Quebec, PQ

Nadel, Dr. Benjamin, Exec.Dir.
JEWISH LABOR BUND - BUND ARCHIVES OF
THE JEWISH LABOR MOVEMENT □ New York,
NY

Nador, Robert G., Act.Dir.
ST. LOUIS PUBLIC SCHOOLS - LIBRARY
SERVICES CENTER □ St. Louis, MO

Naeem, Shaukat A., Res.Anl.
INDIANA STATE DEPARTMENT OF COMMERCE
- ENERGY LIBRARY □ Indianapolis, IN

Naese, Ann, Map Cur.
UNIVERSITY OF WATERLOO - UNIVERSITY
MAP AND DESIGN LIBRARY □ Waterloo, ON

Naeseth, Gerhard B., Libn.
VESTERHEIM GENEALOGICAL CENTER/
NORWEGIAN-AMERICAN MUSEUM - LIBRARY □
Madison, WI

Nagata, K. Martha, Libn.
UNION CARBIDE CANADA, LTD. - REFERENCE
LIBRARY □ Toronto, ON
Nagel, Gail, Libn.
COLUMBIA MEMORIAL HOSPITAL - SCHOOL OF
NURSING LIBRARY □ Hudson, NY
Nagel, Mary Kay, Libn.
UNIVERSITY OF WISCONSIN, MADISON -
NIEMAN-GRANT JOURNALISM READING ROOM
□ Madison, WI
Nagel, Paul C., Dir.
VIRGINIA HISTORICAL SOCIETY - LIBRARY □
Richmond, VA
Nager, Emily, Archv.
ROCKEFELLER UNIVERSITY - ROCKEFELLER
ARCHIVE CENTER □ North Tarrytown, NY
Nagg, Shirley, Lib.Aide
ROCHESTER BUSINESS INSTITUTE - BETTY
CRONK MEMORIAL LIBRARY □ Rochester, NY
Nagle, Ellen, Med.Libn.
UNIVERSITY OF VERMONT - DIVISION OF
HEALTH SCIENCES - CHARLES A. DANA
MEDICAL LIBRARY □ Burlington, VT
Nagolski, Donald J., Assoc.Dir.
SCHOLL (Dr. William M.) COLLEGE OF
PODIATRIC MEDICINE - LIBRARY □ Chicago, IL
Nagy, Bernice L., Libn.
KENOSHA NEWS - NEWSPAPER LIBRARY □
Kenosha, WI
Nagy, Jeanette W., Dir.
UNIVERSITY HOSPITALS OF CLEVELAND &
CASE WESTERN RESERVE UNIVERSITY - DEPT.
OF PATHOLOGY - LIBRARY □ Cleveland, OH
Nagy, Mrs. K., Hd., Rd.Serv.
CANADA - ENERGY, MINES & RESOURCES
CANADA - CANMET - LIBRARY† □ Ottawa, ON
Nagy, Karen N., Asst. Music Libn.
NORTHWESTERN UNIVERSITY - MUSIC
LIBRARY □ Evanston, IL
Nagy, Dr. Louis N., Dir.
KEAN COLLEGE OF NEW JERSEY - NANCY
THOMPSON LIBRARY† □ Union, NJ
Nagy, Robert, Cat.
ST. JOHN'S UNIVERSITY - LAW LIBRARY □
Jamaica, NY
Nagy, T.
CANADA - PUBLIC ARCHIVES OF CANADA -
NATIONAL MAP COLLECTION □ Ottawa, ON
Nahley, Duane G., Supv.Libn.
U.S. ARMY IN EUROPE (USAREUR) - LIBRARY
AND RESOURCE CENTER □ APO New York, NY
Nail, K., Archv.
U.S. NASA - JOHN F. KENNEDY SPACE CENTER
- LIBRARY □ Kennedy Space Center, FL
Naimoli, Gail, Instr.Dev.
GUILFORD TECHNICAL COMMUNITY COLLEGE -
LEARNING RESOURCE CENTER □ Jamestown,
NC
Nair, Lola, Cat.
ORAL ROBERTS UNIVERSITY - HEALTH
SCIENCES LIBRARY □ Tulsa, OK
Nairn, Charles E., Ref.Libn.
LAKE SUPERIOR STATE COLLEGE - KENNETH J.
SHOULDICE LIBRARY - MICHIGAN & MARINE
COLLECTIONS □ Sault Ste. Marie, MI
Naisawald, Gretchen, Hd. of Ref.
JOHNS HOPKINS UNIVERSITY - WILLIAM H.
WELCH MEDICAL LIBRARY □ Baltimore, MD
Naisbitt, Jane, Libn.
SASKATCHEWAN - DEPARTMENT OF
EDUCATION - RESOURCE CENTRE □ Regina, SK
Naish, Mary, First Asst.
PUBLIC LIBRARY OF CINCINNATI AND
HAMILTON COUNTY - ART AND MUSIC
DEPARTMENT □ Cincinnati, OH
Naish, Nancy, Asst.Libn.
FIRST UNITED METHODIST CHURCH - JENNIE
E. WEAVER MEMORIAL LIBRARY □ Gloversville,
NY
Naito, Shirley S., Oahu Ch.Coord.
HAWAII STATE LIBRARY - EDNA ALLYN ROOM
□ Honolulu, HI

Nakada, Ayako, Res.Assoc.
METROPOLITAN MUSEUM OF ART - THOMAS J.
WATSON LIBRARY □ New York, NY
Nakagawara, Janice Varner, Med.Libn.
KAISER MEDICAL CENTER - MEDICAL LIBRARY
□ Honolulu, HI
Nakamura, Hanako S., Hd.
HAWAII STATE LIBRARY - BUSINESS,
SCIENCE, TECHNOLOGY UNIT □ Honolulu, HI
Nakao, Julie
BECHTEL - CENTRAL LIBRARY □ San Francisco,
CA
Nalin, Jan, Dir., Med.Rec.Dept.
RICHLAND MEMORIAL HOSPITAL - STAFF
LIBRARY □ Olney, IL
Nall, A., Doc.Libn.
WEST TEXAS STATE UNIVERSITY - CORNETTE
LIBRARY - SPECIAL COLLECTIONS □ Canyon,
TX
Nalls, Clarence T., Asst. Law Libn./Circ.
SOUTHERN UNIVERSITY - LAW SCHOOL
LIBRARY □ Baton Rouge, LA
Nam Yoon, Choong, Hd., Cat.Dept.
NORTHWESTERN UNIVERSITY - LAW SCHOOL
LIBRARY □ Chicago, IL
Namaa, Mari Lin, Tech.Serv./Cat.Libn.
KAYE, SCHOLER, FIERMAN, HAYS & HANDLER -
LAW LIBRARY □ New York, NY
Namath, Nardina L., Dir., Lib.Serv.
HENRY FORD HOSPITAL - FRANK J. SLADEN
LIBRARY □ Detroit, MI
Nanayakkara, D., Libn.
NEWFOUNDLAND - DEPARTMENT OF
EDUCATION - INSTRUCTIONAL MATERIALS
LIBRARY □ St. John's, NF
Nance, Donna, Ref.Libn.
PORT AUTHORITY OF NEW YORK AND NEW
JERSEY - LIBRARY □ New York, NY
Nance, Nancy H., Libn.
DRINKER, BIDDLE & REATH - LAW LIBRARY □
Philadelphia, PA
Nance, Vernice, Asst.Libn.
TENNESSEAN NEWSPAPER - LIBRARY □
Nashville, TN
Nangle, Karen, Black/White Lib.
PHOTO RESEARCHERS, INC. - LIBRARY □ New
York, NY
Nanstiel, Barbara, Dir. of Lib.Serv.
MERCY HOSPITAL - MEDICAL LIBRARY □
Wilkes-Barre, PA
Napert, Faye, Asst.Libn.
DIGITAL EQUIPMENT CORPORATION -
TEWKSBURY LIBRARY □ Tewksbury, MA
Napier, Jill, Mil.Pubn./Cat.Libn.
NORTHROP CORPORATION - AIRCRAFT
DIVISION - LIBRARY SERVICES □ Hawthorne,
CA
Napoli, Gloria, Chf.Libn.
VALUE LINE INC. - BUSINESS LIBRARY □ New
York, NY
Napolitano, Joan, Asst.Libn.
NORTH SHORE UNIVERSITY HOSPITAL -
DANIEL CARROLL PAYSON MEDICAL LIBRARY □
Manhasset, NY
Naraine, Mrs. I., Libn.
DALLAS POWER AND LIGHT COMPANY -
RESEARCH LIBRARY† □ Dallas, TX
Naranjo, Antonio, Foreign Law Libn.
COOK COUNTY LAW LIBRARY □ Chicago, IL
Naranjo, Elaine, Libn.
CHEVRON USA INC. - CENTRAL REGION -
TECHNICAL LIBRARY □ Denver, CO
Naraynsingh, Miss T., Map Libn.
CANADA - GEOLOGICAL SURVEY OF CANADA -
LIBRARY □ Ottawa, ON
Nardin, Doris, Asst.Libn.
PENN MUTUAL LIFE INSURANCE COMPANY -
LAW LIBRARY □ Philadelphia, PA
Nardini, Hannah, Libn.
CARLSMITH, CARLSMITH, WICHMAN & CASE -
LIBRARY □ Hilo, HI

Nardo, Mr. Helio, Asst.Cat.Libn.
WESTERN ILLINOIS UNIVERSITY - LIBRARIES
□ Macomb, IL
Nardone, Ernest, Ref.
RUTGERS UNIVERSITY, THE STATE
UNIVERSITY OF NEW JERSEY - JUSTICE
HENRY ACKERSON LIBRARY OF LAW &
CRIMINAL JUSTICE □ Newark, NJ
Narducci, Fran, Res.
BOOZ, ALLEN & HAMILTON, INC. - RESEARCH
SERVICE □ New York, NY
Nareff, Margaret W., Cur.Assoc.
CRANDALL (Prudence) MEMORIAL MUSEUM -
LIBRARY □ Canterbury, CT
Narvaez, Peter, Archv.
MEMORIAL UNIVERSITY OF NEWFOUNDLAND -
FOLKLORE AND LANGUAGE ARCHIVE □ St.
John's, NF
Narver, Lindy, Slide Cur.
UNIVERSITY OF SOUTHERN CALIFORNIA -
ARCHITECTURE & FINE ARTS LIBRARY □ Los
Angeles, CA
Nase, Lois M., Asst.Libn.
PRINCETON UNIVERSITY - ENGINEERING
LIBRARY □ Princeton, NJ
Nash, Karen, Lib.Coord.
INCO UNITED STATES, INC. - BUSINESS
LIBRARY □ New York, NY
Nash, Michael H., Cur. of Mss.
HAGLEY MUSEUM AND LIBRARY □ Wilmington,
DE
Nash, N. Frederick, Libn.
UNIVERSITY OF ILLINOIS - RARE BOOK ROOM
□ Urbana, IL
Nash, Peggy, Lib.Techn.
ELDORADO RESOURCES LTD. - RESEARCH &
DEVELOPMENT LIBRARY □ Ottawa, ON
Nash, Richard M., Assoc. Law Libn.
ARIZONA STATE UNIVERSITY - COLLEGE OF
LAW - LIBRARY □ Tempe, AZ
Nashu, A. Munim, EPA Coord./Libn.
UPJOHN COMPANY - D.S. GILMORE RESEARCH
LABORATORIES - LIBRARY† □ North Haven, CT
Nasif, Teresa, Director
U.S. GENERAL SERVICES ADMINISTRATION -
CONSUMER INFORMATION CENTER □
Washington, DC
Naslund, Jeanne, Ref.Libn.
UNIVERSITY OF BRITISH COLUMBIA -
CURRICULUM LABORATORY □ Vancouver, BC
Nasser, J., Info.Spec.
AMOCO CANADA PETROLEUM COMPANY, LTD. -
LIBRARY/INFORMATION CENTER □ Calgary, AB
Nath, Herbert T., Ref.Libn.
CITADEL - THE MILITARY COLLEGE OF SOUTH
CAROLINA - DANIEL LIBRARY □ Charleston, SC
Nathanson, David, Chf.Libn.
U.S. NATL. PARK SERVICE - HARPERS FERRY
CENTER LIBRARY □ Harpers Ferry, WV
Nathanson, Esther, Sr.Info.Spec.
WESTINGHOUSE ELECTRIC CORPORATION -
WATER REACTOR DIVISIONS - INFORMATION
RESOURCE CENTER □ Pittsburgh, PA
Nation, James R., Libn.
U.S. GEOLOGICAL SURVEY - FLAGSTAFF FIELD
CENTER - BRANCH LIBRARY □ Flagstaff, AZ
Naulty, Deborah, Ref.Libn.
FEDERAL RESERVE BANK OF PHILADELPHIA -
LIBRARY □ Philadelphia, PA
Nauman, Linda, Natl.Libn.
LEVENTHAL (Kenneth) & COMPANY - LIBRARY □
Los Angeles, CA
Navaretta, Cynthia, Exec.Dir.
WOMEN ARTISTS NEWS - ARCHIVES □ New
York, NY
Nawyn, John P., Libn.
BUCKS COUNTY PLANNING COMMISSION
STAFF LIBRARY □ Doylestown, PA
Naylor, Annajean, Exec.Sec.
SAN DIEGO HALL OF SCIENCE - BERNICE
HARDING LIBRARY □ San Diego, CA

Naylor, Beverly, Supv.
CONNECTICUT STATE LIBRARY - FILM
SERVICE □ Middletown, CT

Naylor, David L., Assoc.Libn./Pub.Serv.
SYRACUSE UNIVERSITY - LAW LIBRARY □
Syracuse, NY

Naylor, Eleanor R., Libn.
BARIUM AND CHEMICALS, INC. - RESEARCH
LIBRARY† □ Steubenville, OH

Nazarro, B., Cat.
SOUTHWESTERN UNIVERSITY - SCHOOL OF
LAW LIBRARY □ Los Angeles, CA

Naznitsky, Ira, Mgr.
GAF CORPORATION - TECHNICAL
INFORMATION SERVICES† □ Wayne, NJ

Nazzaro, Lorraine T., Libn.
AVCO CORPORATION - AVCO-EVERETT
RESEARCH LABORATORY - LIBRARY† □ Everett,
MA

Ndinyah-Quartey, Josephine, Info.Sci.
MERCK & COMPANY, INC. - CALGON
CORPORATION - INFORMATION CENTER □
Pittsburgh, PA

Neafus, S., Libn.
ICI AMERICAS INC. - DARCO EXPERIMENTAL
LABORATORY LIBRARY† □ Marshall, TX

Neal, Anna, Libn.
MEMPHIS STATE UNIVERSITY LIBRARIES -
MUSIC LIBRARY □ Memphis, TN

Neal, Berna E., Libn.
UNIVERSITY OF MARYLAND, COLLEGE PARK -
LIBRARIES - ARCHITECTURE LIBRARY □
College Park, MD

Neal, Christina W., Hd.
UNIVERSITY OF MICHIGAN - SOCIAL WORK
LIBRARY □ Ann Arbor, MI

Neal, Kathryn B., Govt.Doc.Libn.
ALABAMA A & M UNIVERSITY - J. F. DRAKE
MEMORIAL LEARNING RESOURCES CENTER □
Normal, AL

Neal, Larry L., Dir.
UNIVERSITY OF OREGON - INSTITUTE OF
RECREATION RESEARCH AND SERVICE □
Eugene, OR

Neal, Margaret, Coord. & Info.Spec.
CANADIAN TROTTING ASSOCIATION -
STANDARDBRED CANADA LIBRARY □ Toronto,
ON

Neargardner-Shake, Linda, Med.Libn.
SPOHN HOSPITAL - MEDICAL LIBRARY □ Corpus
Christi, TX

Nearon, Mrs. Tish, Hd., Adm.Serv.
JOHNSON (Lawrence) & ASSOCIATES, INC. -
LIBRARY □ Washington, DC

Nearpass, Kate, Cur.Asst.
INTERNATIONAL CENTER OF PHOTOGRAPHY -
RICHARD A. HILLMAN RESEARCH
COLLECTIONS □ New York, NY

Neary, Mary Ann, Doc.Libn.
MASSACHUSETTS STATE LIBRARY □ Boston,
MA

Neary, Sharon
UNIVERSITY OF CALGARY - ENVIRONMENT-
SCIENCE-TECHNOLOGY LIBRARY† □ Calgary,
AB

Neaves, James R., Mgr., Site Lib.
TEXAS INSTRUMENTS, INC. - DATA SYSTEMS
GROUP - SITE LIBRARY† □ Austin, TX

Neaves, Teresa, Libn.
JONES, WALKER, WAECHTER, POITEVENT,
CARRERE & DENEGRE - LAW LIBRARY □ New
Orleans, LA

Nee, Louise A., Info.Spec.
BANK MARKETING ASSOCIATION -
INFORMATION CENTER □ Chicago, IL

Nee, Paul, Sr.Libn.
ATLANTIC CITY FREE PUBLIC LIBRARY -
SPECIAL COLLECTIONS □ Atlantic City, NJ

Needham, Paul, Cur., Printed Bks.
PIERPONT MORGAN LIBRARY □ New York, NY

Neel, Suzanne Pickering, Dir., Prof.Prog./Serv.
ALEXANDER GRAHAM BELL ASSOCIATION FOR
THE DEAF - VOLTA BUREAU LIBRARY □
Washington, DC

Neeley, Kathleen, Asst.Sci.Libn.
UNIVERSITY OF KANSAS - SCIENCE LIBRARY □
Lawrence, KS

Neely, Ann, Ref.Libn.
PARKLAND COLLEGE - LEARNING RESOURCE
CENTER □ Champaign, IL

Neely, Gardner, Map Libn.
PUBLIC LIBRARY OF CINCINNATI AND
HAMILTON COUNTY - HISTORY DEPARTMENT -
MAP UNIT □ Cincinnati, OH

Neely, Jesse G., Med.Libn.
SCRIPPS CLINIC & RESEARCH FOUNDATION -
KRESGE MEDICAL LIBRARY □ La Jolla, CA

Neely, Mark E., Jr., Dir.
LINCOLN NATIONAL LIFE FOUNDATION - LOUIS
A. WARREN LINCOLN LIBRARY AND MUSEUM □
Fort Wayne, IN

Neer, Kathleen, Libn.
CANADA - AGRICULTURE CANADA - RESEARCH
STATION, SUMMERLAND - LIBRARY □
Summerland, BC

Neese, Janet A., Hd., Coll.Dev.
SUNY - COLLEGE AT GENESEO - COLLEGE
LIBRARIES □ Geneseo, NY

Neff, Barbara, Hd., ILL
RAND CORPORATION - LIBRARY† □ Santa
Monica, CA

Neff, Jerry W., Exec.Dir.
WAGNALLS MEMORIAL LIBRARY □ Lithopolis,
OH

Nefsky, Judith, Archv.
CANADIAN JEWISH CONGRESS - NATIONAL
ARCHIVES □ Montreal, PQ

Negaard, Chere, Dir., Lib.Serv.
NORTHROP UNIVERSITY - ALUMNI LIBRARY -
SPECIAL COLLECTIONS† □ Inglewood, CA

Negaard, Gordon R., Dir.
U.S. AIR FORCE - WRIGHT AERONAUTICAL
LABORATORIES - AEROSPACE STRUCTURES
INFORMATION & ANALYSIS CENTER □ Wright-
Patterson AFB, OH

Negin, Arthur W., Libn./V.P.
RICHLAND COUNTY LAW LIBRARY† □
Mansfield, OH

Negrych, Love, Cat.
UNIVERSITY OF MANITOBA - MEDICAL
LIBRARY □ Winnipeg, MB

Neiderkorn, Annette, Ref.Libn.
WESTERN WISCONSIN TECHNICAL INSTITUTE
- LIBRARY □ La Crosse, WI

Neiger, James I., Adm./Coll.Dev.Libn.
HEBREW UNION COLLEGE - JEWISH
INSTITUTE OF RELIGION - KLAU LIBRARY □
Cincinnati, OH

Neighbours, K.F., Archv.
FORT BELKNAP ARCHIVES, INC. - LIBRARY □
Newcastle, TX

Neikirk, Jody, Info.Asst.
UNIVERSITY OF MISSOURI - HEALTH CARE
TECHNOLOGY CENTER & INFORMATION
SCIENCE GROUP - INFORMATION CENTER □
Columbia, MO

Neill, Charlotte, Hd., Tech.Serv.
TEXAS A & M UNIVERSITY - MEDICAL
SCIENCES LIBRARY □ College Station, TX

Neill, Desmond G., Libn.
MASSEY COLLEGE - ROBERTSON DAVIES
LIBRARY □ Toronto, ON

Neilon, Barbara L., Spec.Coll.Libn.
COLORADO COLLEGE - CHARLES LEAMING
TUTT LIBRARY - SPECIAL COLLECTIONS □
Colorado Springs, CO

Neilson, Ann, Libn.
GULF CANADA LIMITED - RESEARCH &
DEVELOPMENT DEPARTMENT - LIBRARY† □
Mississauga, ON

Neilson, Marjorie, Documentalist
MC GILL UNIVERSITY - CENTRE FOR
DEVELOPING AREA STUDIES -
DOCUMENTATION CENTRE □ Montreal, PQ

Neistein, Dr. Jose, Exec.Dir.
BRAZILIAN-AMERICAN CULTURAL INSTITUTE,
INC. - HAROLD E. WIBBERLEY, JR. LIBRARY □
Washington, DC

Neiswender, Yan A., Bur.Archv./Tech.Serv.
UTAH STATE ARCHIVES □ Salt Lake City, UT

Nelhybel, D., Libn.
BURNDY LIBRARY □ Norwalk, CT

Nellis, Martha A., Libn.
NATIONAL SOCIETY OF THE SONS OF THE
AMERICAN REVOLUTION - GENEALOGY
LIBRARY □ Louisville, KY

Nelms, Rosemary, Libn.
MEMPHIS-SHELBY COUNTY PUBLIC LIBRARY
AND INFO. CTR. - SCIENCE/BUSINESS/SOCIAL
SCI.DEPT. □ Memphis, TN

Nelson, Ann M.A., Libn.
UNIVERSITY OF BRITISH COLUMBIA - ERIC W.
HAMBER LIBRARY □ Vancouver, BC

Nelson, April, Tech.Proc.Serv.Libn.
ROSEMONT COLLEGE - GERTRUDE KISTLER
MEMORIAL LIBRARY - SPECIAL COLLECTIONS
□ Rosemont, PA

Nelson, Mr. Armour, Spec.Coll. & Rare Books
CALIFORNIA LUTHERAN COLLEGE - LIBRARY -
SPECIAL COLLECTIONS† □ Thousand Oaks, CA

Nelson, Berneil C., Sr.Lib.Asst.
UNIVERSITY OF MINNESOTA, CROOKSTON -
KIEHLE LIBRARY - MEDIA RESOURCES □
Crookston, MN

Nelson, Brent A., Libn.
UNIVERSITY OF ARKANSAS, FAYETTEVILLE -
TECHNOLOGY CAMPUS LIBRARY □ Little Rock,
AR

Nelson, Carolyn, Libn.
WESTERNERS INTERNATIONAL, A
FOUNDATION - LIBRARY □ Tucson, AZ

Nelson, Carolyn M., Libn.
U.S. BUREAU OF LAND MANAGEMENT -
MONTANA STATE OFFICE LIBRARY □ Billings,
MT

Nelson, Cecilia, Rec.Ck.
IOWA STATE DEPARTMENT OF WATER, AIR
AND WASTE MANAGEMENT - TECHNICAL
LIBRARY □ Des Moines, IA

Nelson, Charles L., Sr.Libn.
ARIZONA STATE DEPARTMENT OF HEALTH
SERVICES - PUBLIC HEALTH LIBRARY □
Phoenix, AZ

Nelson, Cheryl S., Lib.Dir.
NICHOLS COLLEGE - CONANT LIBRARY □
Dudley, MA

Nelson, Clark, ILL Libn.
MAYO FOUNDATION - MAYO CLINIC LIBRARY □
Rochester, MN

Nelson, David M., Dir.
UNIVERSITY OF MINNESOTA - AGRICULTURAL
EXTENSION SERVICE - MINNESOTA ANALYSIS
& PLANNING SYSTEM □ St. Paul, MN

Nelson, Dwayne, Info.Spec.
MARSTELLER, INC. - INFORMATION
SERVICES† □ Chicago, IL

Nelson, Esther, Ref.Libn.
WESTERN ILLINOIS UNIVERSITY - LIBRARIES
□ Macomb, IL

Nelson, Gabrielle S., Mgr.
IBM CORPORATION - DSD LIBRARY/LEARNING
CENTER □ Poughkeepsie, NY

Nelson, Dr. Gareth, Cur.
AMERICAN MUSEUM OF NATURAL HISTORY -
DEPARTMENT OF ICHTHYOLOGY - DEAN
MEMORIAL LIBRARY □ New York, NY

Nelson, Gerald O., Libn.
CALIFORNIA STATE REHABILITATION CENTER
- RESIDENT LIBRARY† □ Norco, CA

Nelson, Glade, Mgr., Ext.Serv.
CHURCH OF JESUS CHRIST OF LATTER-DAY
SAINTS - GENEALOGICAL LIBRARY □ Salt Lake
City, UT

Nelson, Helene W., Mgr., Files/Lib.
PARKER, CHAPIN, FLATTAU AND KLIMPL -
LIBRARY □ New York, NY

Nelson, Hildegard, Per.Libn.
FULLER THEOLOGICAL SEMINARY - MC
ALISTER LIBRARY† □ Pasadena, CA

Nelson, Irene, Libn.
HKM ASSOCIATES ENGINEERS/PLANNERS -
LIBRARY □ Billings, MT

Nelson, Jane Gray, Musm.Libn.
FINE ARTS MUSEUMS OF SAN FRANCISCO -
LIBRARY □ San Francisco, CA

Nelson, Jeannette H., Mgr.
COMPUTER SCIENCES CORPORATION -
TECHNICAL LIBRARY □ El Segundo, CA

Nelson, Ms. Joey, Doc.Libn.
CALIFORNIA LUTHERAN COLLEGE - LIBRARY -
SPECIAL COLLECTIONS† □ Thousand Oaks, CA

Nelson, John D., Law Libn.
UNIVERSITY OF NEBRASKA, LINCOLN -
COLLEGE OF LAW LIBRARY □ Lincoln, NE

Nelson, Jon, Cur.
UNIVERSITY OF NEBRASKA, LINCOLN -
CENTER FOR GREAT PLAINS STUDIES □ Lincoln,
NE

Nelson, Joyce, Map Cur.
LOUISIANA STATE UNIVERSITY -
CARTOGRAPHIC INFORMATION CENTER □
Baton Rouge, LA

Nelson, L.E.
DOW CHEMICAL COMPANY - TECHNICAL
INFORMATION SERVICES - CENTRAL REPORT
INDEX □ Midland, MI

Nelson, Marcia E., Hd.Libn.
ILLINOIS STATE WATER SURVEY - LIBRARY □
Champaign, IL

Nelson, Mariann, Ref.Anl.
UNIVERSITY OF MINNESOTA - INDUSTRIAL
RELATIONS CENTER - REFERENCE ROOM □
Minneapolis, MN

Nelson, Marie, Libn., Patient Educ.Ctr.
U.S. VETERANS ADMINISTRATION (MN-
Minneapolis) - MEDICAL CENTER LIBRARY
SERVICE □ Minneapolis, MN

Nelson, Mary Ann, Ref.
UNIVERSITY OF MINNESOTA - LAW LIBRARY □
Minneapolis, MN

Nelson, Melanie, Acq.
UNIVERSITY OF ARKANSAS AT LITTLE ROCK -
PULASKI COUNTY LAW LIBRARY □ Little Rock,
AR

Nelson, Mona R., Prog.Dir.
KANDIYOHI COUNTY HISTORICAL SOCIETY -
VICTOR E. LAWSON RESEARCH LIBRARY □
Willmar, MN

Nelson, Norma, Asst.Ref.Libn.
YESHIVA UNIVERSITY - ALBERT EINSTEIN
COLLEGE OF MEDICINE - D. SAMUEL
GOTTESMAN LIBRARY □ Bronx, NY

Nelson, P.J., Regional Libn.
CANADA - TRANSPORT CANADA - CANADIAN
AIR TRANSPORTATION ADMINISTRATION -
WESTERN REGIONAL LIBRARY □ Edmonton, AB

Nelson, Paula, Hd.Libn.
LANDAUER ASSOCIATES, INC. - INFORMATION
CENTER □ New York, NY

Nelson, Peg, Libn.
ENVIRONMENTAL PROTECTION AGENCY -
REGION I LIBRARY □ Boston, MA

Nelson, Ron, Pres.
PINE COUNTY HISTORICAL SOCIETY -
LIBRARY □ Askov, MN

Nelson, Sharon, Adm.Libn.
U.S. NAVY - NAVAL AIR STATION (CA-North
Island) - LIBRARY □ San Diego, CA

Nelson, Vance E., Cur.
NEBRASKA STATE HISTORICAL SOCIETY -
FORT ROBINSON MUSEUM - RESEARCH
LIBRARY □ Crawford, NE

Nelson, Veneese, Acq.Libn.
BRIGHAM YOUNG UNIVERSITY - J. REUBEN
CLARK LAW SCHOOL LIBRARY □ Provo, UT

Nelson, Vernon H., Archv.
MORAVIAN CHURCH IN AMERICA - NORTHERN
PROVINCE - MORAVIAN ARCHIVES □
Bethlehem, PA

Nelson, Dr. William N., Dir.
CARSON-NEWMAN COLLEGE LIBRARY -
SPECIAL COLLECTIONS □ Jefferson City, TN

Nelton, Bill, Libn.
MICHIGAN STATE DEPARTMENT OF PUBLIC
HEALTH - LIBRARY □ Lansing, MI

Nemec, Dolores, Libn.
UNIVERSITY OF WISCONSIN, MADISON - F.B.
POWER PHARMACEUTICAL LIBRARY □ Madison,
WI

Nemeth, Martha C., Tech.Libn.
SUNKIST GROWERS, INC. - RESEARCH
LIBRARY □ Ontario, CA

Nemiccolo, Harriet, Chf.Libn.
BOSTON COLLEGE - GRADUATE SCHOOL OF
SOCIAL WORK LIBRARY □ Chestnut Hill, MA

Neri, Rita, Cat.
NEW YORK UNIVERSITY - SCHOOL OF LAW
LIBRARY □ New York, NY

Neroda, Ed, Dir., Lib.Serv.
EASTERN MONTANA COLLEGE - LIBRARY -
SPECIAL COLLECTIONS† □ Billings, MT

Nesbit, Doug, Pub.Info.Off.
WESTERN KENTUCKY UNIVERSITY - DEPT. OF
SPECIAL COLLECTIONS - KENTUCKY LIBRARY
AND MUSEUM/UNIVERSITY ARCHIVES □
Bowling Green, KY

Nesbit, Jennifer, Hd., Educ.Sect.
CHICAGO PUBLIC LIBRARY CENTRAL LIBRARY -
SOCIAL SCIENCES & HISTORY DIVISION □
Chicago, IL

Nesbitt, Ina L., Med.Libn.
U.S. ARMY HOSPITALS - BLANCHFIELD ARMY
COMMUNITY HOSPITAL - MEDICAL LIBRARY □
Ft. Campbell, KY

Nesmith, John Larry, Libn.
U.S. MARINE CORPS - LOGISTICS BASE,
ALBANY, GA - TECHNICAL LIBRARY □ Albany,
GA

Nesper, Mary, Libn.
THE ANDERSONS - MARKET RESEARCH
LIBRARY □ Maumee, OH

Nespor, Robert, Archv.
OKLAHOMA HISTORICAL SOCIETY - ARCHIVES
AND MANUSCRIPT DIVISION □ Oklahoma City,
OK

Ness, DiAnn, Lib.Mgr.
DOUGLAS COUNTY HOSPITAL - HEALTH
SCIENCES LIBRARY □ Alexandria, MN

Nestell, Clifford L., Dir. of Lib.Serv.
SHAWNEE MISSION MEDICAL CENTER -
MEDICAL LIBRARY □ Shawnee Mission, KS

Nesthus, Marie, Principal Libn.
NEW YORK PUBLIC LIBRARY - DONNELL
LIBRARY CENTER - MEDIA CENTER - FILM/
VIDEO COLLECTION □ New York, NY

Nesvig, Lorraine, Libn.
ARMOUR RESEARCH CENTER - LIBRARY □
Scottsdale, AZ

Neswick, Robert A., Mgr.
SPOKANE SPOKESMAN-REVIEW AND SPOKANE
CHRONICLE - NEWSPAPER REFERENCE
LIBRARY† □ Spokane, WA

Nethers, Betty, Mgr.
OWENS-CORNING FIBERGLAS CORPORATION -
TECHNICAL DATA CENTER □ Granville, OH

Nettleton, Lavonne, Asst.Libn.
REFORMED BIBLE COLLEGE - LIBRARY □ Grand
Rapids, MI

Netz, David, Hd.Libn.
WESTERN MICHIGAN UNIVERSITY -
EDUCATIONAL LIBRARY □ Kalamazoo, MI

Netzley, Barbara L., Asst.Libn.
SOUTHERN CALIFORNIA EDISON COMPANY -
LIBRARY □ Rosemead, CA

Netzow, Mary, Chf.Libn.
U.S. VETERANS ADMINISTRATION (DC-
Washington) - MEDICAL CENTER LIBRARY □
Washington, DC

Neu, Margaret J., Hd.Libn.
CORPUS CHRISTI CALLER-TIMES - LIBRARY □
Corpus Christi, TX

Neu, Marilyn, Circ.Libn.
WARNER-PACIFIC COLLEGE - OTTO F. LINN
LIBRARY □ Portland, OR

Neubacher, Mary, Libn.
ADAMS-PRATT OAKLAND COUNTY LAW
LIBRARY □ Pontiac, MI

Neubauer, Carol J., Circ.Libn.
BRIDGEWATER STATE COLLEGE - CLEMENT C.
MAXWELL LIBRARY □ Bridgewater, MA

Neuberg, Joel, Exec.Dir.
HOLOCAUST LIBRARY AND RESEARCH CENTER
OF SAN FRANCISCO □ San Francisco, CA

Neubig, P., Ref.Sys.Supv.
EXXON CORPORATION - COMMUNICATIONS
AND COMPUTER SCIENCE DEPARTMENT-
TECHNICAL LIBRARY† □ Florham Park, NJ

Neuburger, D.A., Chem.Info.Spec.
ECONOMICS LABORATORY, INC. - CORPORATE
INFORMATION CENTER □ St. Paul, MN

Neuendorf, Klaus, Ed./Libn.
OREGON STATE DEPARTMENT OF GEOLOGY
AND MINERAL INDUSTRIES - LIBRARY □
Portland, OR

Neuendorffer, Ruth, Libn.
HISTORICAL SOCIETY OF THE TARRYTOWNS -
HEADQUARTERS LIBRARY □ Tarrytown, NY

Neufeld, Irving H., Chf., UTC Lib.Sys.
UNITED TECHNOLOGIES CORPORATION -
LIBRARY □ East Hartford, CT

Neufeld, Judith, Asst. to the Dir.
LONG ISLAND LIBRARY RESOURCES COUNCIL,
INC. (LILRC) □ Bellport, NY

Neufeld, M. Lynne, Exec.Dir.
NATIONAL FEDERATION OF ABSTRACTING
AND INFORMATION SERVICES □ Philadelphia,
PA

Neugebauer, Janet, Asst.Archv.
TEXAS TECH UNIVERSITY - SOUTHWEST
COLLECTION □ Lubbock, TX

Neuman, Susan, Dir.
UNIVERSITY OF PITTSBURGH - GRADUATE
SCHOOL OF BUSINESS LIBRARY □ Pittsburgh, PA

Neumann, Barbara, Tech.Serv.Libn.
BANK OF NOVA SCOTIA - LIBRARY □ Toronto,
ON

Neumann, D., Data Anl.
U.S. NATL. BUREAU OF STANDARDS -
CHEMICAL THERMODYNAMICS DATA CENTER
□ Washington, DC

Neumann, Evelyn, Lib.Adm.
LIBRARY ASSOCIATION OF LA JOLLA -
ATHENAEUM MUSIC AND ARTS LIBRARY □ La
Jolla, CA

Neushaefer, Jeannette, Asst.Libn.
SOUTHEASTERN COLLEGE OF OSTEOPATHIC
MEDICINE - MEDICAL LIBRARY □ North Miami
Beach, FL

Neutel, W., Natl. Ethnic Archv.
CANADA - PUBLIC ARCHIVES OF CANADA -
MANUSCRIPT DIVISION □ Ottawa, ON

Nevai, Maria, Tech.Serv.Libn.
COOLEY (Thomas M.) LAW SCHOOL - LIBRARY □
Lansing, MI

Neve, Lois, Circ.Libn.
WESTON SCHOOL OF THEOLOGY - LIBRARY □
Cambridge, MA

Neves, Donna, Asst.Libn.
KAISER-PERMANENTE MEDICAL CENTER -
PANORAMA CITY HEALTH SCIENCE LIBRARY†
□ Panorama City, CA

Neveu, Alfred J., Hd., Procedures Dev.
NEW YORK STATE DEPARTMENT OF
TRANSPORTATION - PUBLIC
TRANSPORTATION - LIBRARY □ Albany, NY

Neveu, Ann, Adm.Off.
ONTARIO INSTITUTE FOR STUDIES IN
EDUCATION (OISE) - R.W.B. JACKSON LIBRARY
□ Toronto, ON

Neveu, Wilma B., Chf., Lib.Serv.
U.S. VETERANS ADMINISTRATION (LA-New Orleans) - MEDICAL CENTER LIBRARY □ New Orleans, LA

Neville, Ms. M.J., Hd., Ref.Serv.
ALBERTA ENVIRONMENTAL CENTRE - LIBRARY □ Vegreville, AB

Neville, Maureen, Indexer
HUMAN RESOURCES NETWORK - INFORMATION CENTER† □ Philadelphia, PA

Nevin, Susanne, Cat.
UNIVERSITY OF MINNESOTA - LAW LIBRARY □ Minneapolis, MN

Nevins, Joyce, Bus.Info.Spec.
SEARLE (G.D.) & CO. - RESEARCH LIBRARY □ Skokie, IL

New, Lillian R., Hd.
CHICAGO PUBLIC LIBRARY CULTURAL CENTER - THOMAS HUGHES CHILDREN'S LIBRARY □ Chicago, IL

Newberry, J.M. "Boats", Founder & Dir.
P.T. BOATS, INC. - LIBRARY, ARCHIVES & TECHNICAL INFORMATION CENTER - NATIONAL HEADQUARTERS □ Memphis, TN

Newborg, Gerald, State Archv.
STATE HISTORICAL SOCIETY OF NORTH DAKOTA - STATE ARCHIVES AND HISTORICAL RESEARCH LIBRARY □ Bismarck, ND

Newburg, James D., Act.Dir.
POINT LOMA NAZARENE COLLEGE - RYAN LIBRARY □ San Diego, CA

Newburger, Adele, Archv.
UNIVERSITY OF BALTIMORE - LANGSDALE LIBRARY - SPECIAL COLLECTIONS DEPARTMENT □ Baltimore, MD

Newbury, Susan, Ref.Libn.
BROWN UNIVERSITY - JOHN CARTER BROWN LIBRARY □ Providence, RI

Newby, Bob, Libn.
SPEARS, LUBERSKY, CAMPBELL, BLEDSOE, ANDERSON & YOUNG - LIBRARY □ Portland, OR

Newby, Nella, Ser.Libn.
CATHOLIC MEDICAL CENTER OF BROOKLYN & QUEENS, INC. - CENTRAL MEDICAL LIBRARY □ Jamaica, NY

Newcombe, Barbara T., Mgr.
CHICAGO TRIBUNE - EDITORIAL INFORMATION CENTER □ Chicago, IL

Newcomer, Susan, Corp.Libn.
LAWRY'S FOODS, INC. - LIBRARY □ Los Angeles, CA

Newell, Anita, Mgr.
WESTINGHOUSE ELECTRIC CORPORATION - RESEARCH AND DEVELOPMENT CENTER - RESEARCH LIBRARY □ Pittsburgh, PA

Newell, Elizabeth
NEW PROVIDENCE HISTORICAL SOCIETY - LIBRARY □ New Providence, NJ

Newell, Lynne N., Tech.Proc.
CONNECTICUT STATE LIBRARY □ Hartford, CT

Newgaard, JoAlyce, Ref.Libn.
FOUNDATION CENTER - NEW YORK - LIBRARY □ New York, NY

Newhall, George, Film Libn.
SANDY CORPORATION - LIBRARY □ Troy, MI

Newhams, Susan, Libn.
STONE AND WEBSTER ENGINEERING CORPORATION - TECHNICAL INFORMATION CENTER □ Denver, CO

Newhouse, Frances F., Libn.
SEBASTIAN COUNTY LAW LIBRARY† □ Fort Smith, AR

Newhouse, Professor Wade J., Dir.
SUNY AT BUFFALO - CHARLES B. SEARS LAW LIBRARY □ Buffalo, NY

Newland, Jean, Libn.
ARCHER & GREINER - LIBRARY □ Haddonfield, NJ

Newlin, Deborah L., Info.Spec.
CHEVRON ENVIRONMENTAL HEALTH CENTER, INC. - TECHNICAL INFORMATION CENTER† □ Richmond, CA

Newlin, Jeanne, Cur., Theater Coll.
HARVARD UNIVERSITY - HOUGHTON LIBRARY □ Cambridge, MA

Newlin, Jeanne T., Cur.
HARVARD UNIVERSITY - THEATRE COLLECTION □ Cambridge, MA

Newlon, Kent, First Asst.
PUBLIC LIBRARY OF CINCINNATI AND HAMILTON COUNTY - FILMS AND RECORDINGS CENTER □ Cincinnati, OH

Newman, Anita J., Libn.
PENSION BENEFIT GUARANTY CORPORATION - OFFICE OF THE GENERAL COUNSEL - LIBRARY □ Washington, DC

Newman, Bobbie, Sys.Libn.
OAK RIDGE ASSOCIATED UNIVERSITIES - MANPOWER EDUCATION, RESEARCH, AND TRAINING DIVISION - LIBRARY □ Oak Ridge, TN

Newman, Carol, Libn.
BOULDER VALLEY PUBLIC SCHOOLS, REGION 2 - PROFESSIONAL LIBRARY □ Boulder, CO

Newman, Cheryl, Med.Libn.
RIVERVIEW HOSPITAL - MEDICAL LIBRARY □ Red Bank, NJ

Newman, David, Res.Assoc.
MOBIL OIL CORPORATION - PUBLIC AFFAIRS SECRETARIAT □ New York, NY

Newman, Fletcher C., Hd.
UNIVERSITY OF TEXAS, EL PASO - SCIENCE/ENGINEERING/MATHEMATICS LIBRARY □ El Paso, TX

Newman, Dr. George C., Dir.
SUNY - COLLEGE AT BUFFALO - EDWARD H. BUTLER LIBRARY □ Buffalo, NY

Newman, Janice, Asst.Dir.
UNIVERSITY OF MARYLAND, COLLEGE PARK - M. LUCIA JAMES CURRICULUM LABORATORY □ College Park, MD

Newman, John, Mgr., Info.Serv.
AMERICAN NEWSPAPER PUBLISHERS ASSOCIATION - LIBRARY □ Reston, VA

Newman, John, Proj.Archv.
COLORADO STATE UNIVERSITY - GERMANS FROM RUSSIA PROJECT LIBRARY □ Fort Collins, CO

Newman, John, Spec.Coll.Libn.
COLORADO STATE UNIVERSITY - VIETNAM WAR LITERATURE COLLECTION □ Fort Collins, CO

Newman, John J., Dp.Dir./Archv.
INDIANA STATE COMMISSION ON PUBLIC RECORDS - ARCHIVES DIVISION □ Indianapolis, IN

Newman, Linda P., Asst. Mines & Map Libn.
UNIVERSITY OF NEVADA, RENO - MACKAY SCHOOL OF MINES LIBRARY □ Reno, NV

Newman, Lisa A., Docs.Libn.
NORTH CAROLINA STATE UNIVERSITY - D.H. HILL LIBRARY - DOCUMENTS DEPARTMENT □ Raleigh, NC

Newman, Mark J., Libn.
DORR, COOPER & HAYS - LAW LIBRARY □ San Francisco, CA

Newman, Patricia, Transl.
SANDIA NATIONAL LABORATORIES - TECHNICAL LIBRARY □ Albuquerque, NM

Newman, Susan T., Libn.
FORD FOUNDATION - LIBRARY □ New York, NY

Newman, William, Ph.D., Asst. Law Libn.
CAPITAL UNIVERSITY - LAW SCHOOL LIBRARY □ Columbus, OH

Newman, William, Lib.Dir.
UNIVERSITY OF BALTIMORE - LANGSDALE LIBRARY □ Baltimore, MD

Newnham, Rita, Leg.Libn.
MARYLAND STATE DEPARTMENT OF LEGISLATIVE REFERENCE - LIBRARY □ Annapolis, MD

Newsom, Keith R., Supv.Libn., Open Lit.
U.S. AIR FORCE WEAPONS LABORATORY - TECHNICAL LIBRARY □ Kirtland AFB, NM

Newsom, Mary Margaret, Coord. of Educ.Serv.
U.S. OLYMPIC COMMITTEE - SPORTS MEDICINE INFORMATION CENTER □ Colorado Springs, CO

Newsome, Carla S., Libn.
BENDIX CORPORATION - AUTOMATION GROUP - RESEARCH DIVISION LIBRARY □ Solon, OH

Newsum, Diane, Libn.
MEMPHIS-SHELBY COUNTY PUBLIC LIBRARY AND INFO. CTR. - SCIENCE/BUSINESS/SOCIAL SCI.DEPT. □ Memphis, TN

Newton, Barbara, Supv.Libn., Rpt.
U.S. AIR FORCE WEAPONS LABORATORY - TECHNICAL LIBRARY □ Kirtland AFB, NM

Newton, Deborah A., District Libn.
U.S. ARMY - CORPS OF ENGINEERS - SACRAMENTO DISTRICT - TECHNICAL INFORMATION CENTER □ Sacramento, CA

Newton, Earle W., Dir.
MUSEUM OF THE AMERICAS - LIBRARY □ Brookfield, VT

Newton, Ellen, Libn.
UNITED FOOD AND COMMERCIAL WORKERS INTERNATIONAL UNION - LIBRARY† □ Washington, DC

Newton, Joan, Libn.
WINROCK INTERNATIONAL - LIBRARY† □ Morrilton, AR

Newton, Judy, Mgt.Anl.
U.S. ARCHITECTURAL AND TRANSPORTATION BARRIERS COMPLIANCE BOARD (ATBCB) - TECHNICAL RESOURCES LIBRARY □ Washington, DC

Newton, Mark, Educ.Coord./Cur.
U.S.S. MASSACHUSETTS MEMORIAL COMMITTEE, INC. - ARCHIVES & TECHNICAL LIBRARY □ Fall River, MA

Newton, Pam Wells, Libn.
PANNELL KERR FORSTER - LIBRARY □ New York, NY

Newton, Stephannie K., Libn.
SULLIVAN & CROMWELL - WASHINGTON D.C. LIBRARY □ Washington, DC

Newton, Stephen O., Cat.
ST. ELIZABETHS HOSPITAL - HEALTH SCIENCES LIBRARY □ Washington, DC

Newton, Terra, Libn.
LOGANSPORT STATE HOSPITAL - MEDICAL LIBRARY □ Logansport, IN

Ney, Neal, Adm.Libn.
PARK FOREST PUBLIC LIBRARY - ORAL HISTORY OF PARK FOREST COLLECTION □ Park Forest, IL

Neyland, Cynthia K., Libn.
U.S. NAVY - NAVAL FACILITIES ENGINEERING COMMAND - TECHNICAL LIBRARY □ Alexandria, VA

Ng, Bok, Asst.Libn.
BECHTEL POWER CORPORATION - SFPD LIBRARY □ San Francisco, CA

Ng, Frank, Cat.
LAW SOCIETY OF UPPER CANADA - GREAT LIBRARY □ Toronto, ON

Ng, Hwei Wen, Libn.
CUTTER LABORATORIES - LIBRARY □ Berkeley, CA

Ng, Pauline, Dir.
ELMHURST MEMORIAL HOSPITAL - MARQUARDT MEMORIAL LIBRARY □ Elmhurst, IL

Ng, Tung-King, Hd.
UNIVERSITY OF BRITISH COLUMBIA - ASIAN STUDIES LIBRARY □ Vancouver, BC

Nguyen, Lana, Libn.
BROOKLYN PUBLIC LIBRARY - SOCIAL SCIENCE AND PHILOSOPHY DIVISION □ Brooklyn, NY

Niblick, Patricia, Med.Libn.
CAYLOR-NICKEL CLINIC AND HOSPITAL - MEDICAL LIBRARY □ Bluffton, IN

Nicely, Marilyn K., Tech.Serv.Libn.
UNIVERSITY OF OKLAHOMA - LAW LIBRARY □ Norman, OK

Nicewarner, Metta, Spec.Coll.Libn.
TEXAS WOMAN'S UNIVERSITY - SPECIAL
COLLECTIONS □ Denton, TX
Nicholas, Jeff, Staff Libn.
U.S. ARMY ADMINISTRATION (NY-
Brooklyn) - MEDICAL CENTER LIBRARY □
Brooklyn, NY
Nicholls, Dr. R.V.V., Archv./Libn.
CANADIAN RAILROAD HISTORICAL
ASSOCIATION - LIBRARY □ Montreal, PQ
Nichols, Ann E., Libn.
U.S. ARMY HOSPITALS - BLISS ARMY HOSPITAL
- MEDICAL LIBRARY □ Ft. Huachuca, AZ
Nichols, Carol, Libn.
RICHMOND PUBLIC LIBRARY - BUSINESS,
SCIENCE & TECHNOLOGY DEPARTMENT □
Richmond, VA
Nichols, Diane, Ref.Libn.
UNIVERSITY OF LOUISVILLE - KORNHAUSER
HEALTH SCIENCES LIBRARY □ Louisville, KY
Nichols, Emmet A., Chf. Interpreter
U.S. NATL. PARK SERVICE - KENNESAW
MOUNTAIN NATL. BATTLEFIELD PARK -
LIBRARY □ Marietta, GA
Nichols, Gail, Libn.
UNIVERSITY OF CALIFORNIA, BERKELEY -
GOVERNMENT DOCUMENTS DEPARTMENT □
Berkeley, CA
Nichols, J. Gary, State Libn.
MAINE STATE LIBRARY □ Augusta, ME
Nichols, Jacquelyn, Libn.
HEWLETT-PACKARD COMPANY - COLORADO
SPRINGS DIVISION - ENGINEERING RESOURCE
CENTER □ Colorado Springs, CO
Nichols, Mrs. M., Libn.
BRANDON UNIVERSITY - CHRISTIE
EDUCATION LIBRARY □ Brandon, MB
Nichols, Marian, Supv.
OAKLAND PUBLIC LIBRARY - AMERICAN
INDIAN LIBRARY PROJECT □ Oakland, CA
Nichols, Ruby H., Patients' Libn.
U.S. VETERANS ADMINISTRATION (TN-
Murfreesboro) - MEDICAL CENTER LIBRARY □
Murfreesboro, TN
Nichols, Shirley G., Supv.Libn.
TENNESSEE VALLEY AUTHORITY - TECHNICAL
LIBRARY □ Muscle Shoals, AL
Nichols, William J., Libn.
ASTOR HOME FOR CHILDREN - PROFESSIONAL
LIBRARY □ Rhinebeck, NY
Nicholsen, Margaret, Libn.
EVANSTON HISTORICAL SOCIETY - CHARLES
GATES DAWES HOME - LIBRARY □ Evanston, IL
Nicholson, Doris, Cur.
ERIE COUNTY HISTORICAL SOCIETY □ Erie, PA
Nicholson, Elizabeth S., Libn.
MC CUTCHEN, DOYLE, BROWN & ENERSEN -
LAW LIBRARY □ San Francisco, CA
Nicholson, Jean, Ref.
KING & SPALDING - LAW LIBRARY† □ Atlanta,
GA
Nicholson, Joe, Park Ranger
U.S. NATL. PARK SERVICE - ALLEGHENY
PORTAGE RAILROAD NATL. HISTORIC SITE -
LIBRARY □ Cresson, PA
Nicholson, Lillian, Libn.
SHRINERS HOSPITAL FOR CRIPPLED CHILDREN
- ORTHOPEDIC LIBRARY □ Houston, TX
Nicholson, Marion, V.P.-Lib.
HISTORICAL SOCIETY OF THE TOWN OF
GREENWICH, INC. - LIBRARY □ Cos Cob, CT
Nicholson, Maurice, Cat.
SYSTEM DEVELOPMENT CORPORATION -
LIBRARY □ Santa Monica, CA
Nicholson, Millie, Libn.
MARTIN (Albert C.) & ASSOCIATES -
INFORMATION RESEARCH CENTER □ Los
Angeles, CA
Nicholson, Ruth, Ref.Libn.
PIEDMONT TECHNICAL COLLEGE - LIBRARY □
Greenwood, SC

Nickell, Marla E., Libn.
TENNECO, INC. - CORPORATE LIBRARY □
Houston, TX
Nickerson, Donna L., Spec.Coll.Libn.
MANHATTANVILLE COLLEGE - LIBRARY -
SPECIAL COLLECTIONS AND ARCHIVES □
Purchase, NY
Nickerson, Louann, Ref.Coord.
KERN COUNTY LIBRARY SYSTEM - BEALE
MEMORIAL LIBRARY □ Bakersfield, CA
Nickie, Edna, Libn.
ONTARIO - MINISTRY OF NATURAL
RESOURCES - NATURAL RESOURCES LIBRARY □
Toronto, ON
Nicklas, Linda Cheves, Spec.Coll.Libn.
STEPHEN F. AUSTIN STATE UNIVERSITY -
STEEN LIBRARY - SPECIAL COLLECTIONS
DEPARTMENT □ Nacogdoches, TX
Nicole, Andree, Lib.Supv.
SNC GROUP - LIBRARY □ Montreal, PQ
Nicula, Gail, Chf., Rd.Serv.Br.
U.S. ARMED FORCES STAFF COLLEGE -
LIBRARY □ Norfolk, VA
Nieber, Laura A. N., Libn.
FULTON COUNTY LAW LIBRARY ASSOCIATION
- LAW LIBRARY □ Wauseon, OH
Niebuhr, Mary M., Assoc.Dir.
ERIC CLEARINGHOUSE ON LANGUAGES AND
LINGUISTICS □ Washington, DC
Niehaus, Thomas, Dir.
TULANE UNIVERSITY OF LOUISIANA - LATIN
AMERICAN LIBRARY □ New Orleans, LA
Niekamp, Dorothy, Libn.
NINETY-NINES, INC. - LIBRARY □ Oklahoma
City, OK
Nield, Barbara L., Libn.
BRITISH COLUMBIA - WORKER'S
COMPENSATION BOARD - LIBRARY □ Richmond,
BC
Nielsen, Marian, Abstractor
KUTAK ROCK & HUIE - LAW LIBRARY □ Omaha,
NE
Nielsen, Sonja M., Corp.Libn.
PAYETTE ASSOCIATES - LIBRARY† □ Boston,
MA
Nielsen, William E., Chf., Lib.Serv.
U.S. VETERANS ADMINISTRATION (WI-Tomah)
- HOSPITAL LIBRARY □ Tomah, WI
Nielson, Carol, Ref.Libn.
UNIVERSITY OF CALIFORNIA - LOS ALAMOS
NATIONAL LABORATORY - LIBRARY □ Los
Alamos, NM
Niemann, John M., Dir.
INDIANA VOCATIONAL-TECHNICAL COLLEGE -
RESOURCE CENTER □ Gary, IN
Niemeyer, Dan, Prod.Supv.
UNIVERSITY OF COLORADO, BOULDER -
ACADEMIC MEDIA SERVICES □ Boulder, CO
Niemi, Kenneth E., Archv.Libn.
FINNISH-AMERICAN HISTORICAL ARCHIVES □
Hancock, MI
Niemi, Paula G., Libn.
HANCOCK & ESTABROOK - LAW LIBRARY □
Syracuse, NY
Niemyer, Elizabeth, Acq.Libn.
FOLGER SHAKESPEARE LIBRARY □ Washington,
DC
Nies, Elizabeth A., Info.Sci.
NORWICH EATON PHARMACEUTICALS, INC. -
RESEARCH AND DEVELOPMENT LIBRARY □
Norwich, NY
Nietzschmann, Henry, Libn.
U.S. VETERANS ADMINISTRATION (NY-
Northport) - HEALTH SCIENCE LIBRARY □
Northport, NY
Nieves, Miguel Angel, Dir.
PUERTO RICO - INSTITUTE OF PUERTO RICAN
CULTURE - ARCHIVO GENERAL DE PUERTO
RICO □ San Juan, PR
Nieweg, Clinton F., Principal Libn.
PHILADELPHIA ORCHESTRA ASSOCIATION -
LIBRARY □ Philadelphia, PA

Nikirk, Robert, Libn.
GROLIER CLUB OF NEW YORK - LIBRARY □ New
York, NY
Nikkanen-Hoch, Eeva, Asst.Libn.
GREY ADVERTISING, INC. - INFORMATION
CENTER □ New York, NY
Nilan, Roxanne-Louise, Univ.Archv.
STANFORD UNIVERSITY - UNIVERSITY
ARCHIVES □ Stanford, CA
Niles, Joyce, Children's Libn.
BUREAU OF JEWISH EDUCATION - JEWISH
COMMUNITY LIBRARY □ San Francisco, CA
Niles, Roger, Res.Libn.
PARADE PUBLICATIONS, INC. - LIBRARY □ New
York, NY
Nilsen, Micheline, Circ.Supv./ILL
YALE UNIVERSITY - DIVINITY SCHOOL
LIBRARY □ New Haven, CT
Nimer, Gilda, Libn.
AMERICAN UNIVERSITY - FOREIGN AREA
STUDIES LIBRARY □ Washington, DC
Nims, Chris, Libn.
HARVARD UNIVERSITY - SCHOOL OF
MEDICINE - LUCIEN HOWE LIBRARY OF
OPHTHALMOLOGY □ Boston, MA
Ning, Mary Jane, Corp.Libn.
BECTON, DICKINSON & COMPANY -
CORPORATE INFORMATION CENTER □
Paramus, NJ
Nippert, Carolyn C., Dir.
LEHIGH VALLEY HOSPITAL CENTER - HEALTH
SCIENCES LIBRARY □ Allentown, PA
Nirmel, Kari, Circ./Tech.Serv.Assoc.
INDIANA UNIVERSITY/PURDUE UNIVERSITY
AT INDIANAPOLIS - 38TH STREET CAMPUS
LIBRARY □ Indianapolis, IN
Nisenholt, Esther, Archv.
CANADIAN JEWISH CONGRESS - JEWISH
HISTORICAL SOCIETY OF WESTERN CANADA -
ARCHIVES □ Winnipeg, MB
Nisenoff, Sylvia, Prof.Info.Spec.
AMERICAN ASSOCIATION FOR COUNSELING
AND DEVELOPMENT - PROFESSIONAL
INFORMATION SERVICE □ Alexandria, VA
Nish, Susan, Techn.
ATOMIC ENERGY OF CANADA, LTD. -
ENGINEERING COMPANY LIBRARY □ Montreal,
PQ
Nishimura, Hazel S., Libn.
U.S. NATL. MARINE FISHERIES SERVICE -
HONOLULU LABORATORY - LIBRARY □ Honolulu,
HI
Nishizaki, Colette, Libn.
READER'S DIGEST MAGAZINES LIMITED -
EDITORIAL LIBRARY □ Montreal, PQ
Niss, Barbara, Asst.Archv.
NEW YORK HOSPITAL-CORNELL MEDICAL
CENTER - MEDICAL ARCHIVES □ New York, NY
Nissen, Susan, Libn.
THE MONTANA POWER COMPANY - LAW
LIBRARY □ Butte, MT
Nissen, W.I., Tech.Supv.
U.S. BUREAU OF MINES - SALT LAKE CITY
RESEARCH CENTER - LIBRARY □ Salt Lake City,
UT
Nita, Mania, Ref.Libn.
PANAMA CANAL COMMISSION - LIBRARY □
APO Miami, FL
Nitz, C., Archv.
LUTHERAN CHURCH - MISSOURI SYNOD -
NORTHWEST DISTRICT ARCHIVES □ Portland,
OR
Niven, Garth, Chf.Libn.
LAW SOCIETY OF MANITOBA - LIBRARY† □
Winnipeg, MB
Nix, Frances, Assoc.Dir.
ARKANSAS STATE LIBRARY† □ Little Rock, AR
Nix, James R., Chm., Archv./Res.
LOMA LINDA UNIVERSITY - DEL E. WEBB
MEMORIAL LIBRARY □ Loma Linda, CA
Nixdorff, John S., Libn.
VENABLE BAETJER & HOWARD - LIBRARY □
Baltimore, MD

Nixon, Judith, Libn.
PURDUE UNIVERSITY - CONSUMER AND FAMILY SCIENCES LIBRARY □ West Lafayette, IN

Nixon, Nadine, Tech.Serv.Libn.
CENTRAL VIRGINIA COMMUNITY COLLEGE - LIBRARY - SPECIAL COLLECTIONS □ Lynchburg, VA

Nixon, Nancy, Libn.
FIRST PRESBYTERIAN CHURCH - LIBRARY† □ Roseburg, OR

Nixon, Neal, Cat.
UNIVERSITY OF LOUISVILLE - KORNHAUSER HEALTH SCIENCES LIBRARY □ Louisville, KY

Nixon, Stuart, Gen.Mgr.
REDWOOD EMPIRE ASSOCIATION - LIBRARY □ San Francisco, CA

Nixon, Walter, Ref.Libn.
STANDARD & POOR'S CORPORATION - RESEARCH LIBRARY □ New York, NY

Nizinkevitch, Lori, Lib.Asst.
UNIVERSITY OF SASKATCHEWAN - PHYSICS BRANCH LIBRARY □ Saskatoon, SK

Nobari, Nuchine, Chf.Libn.
DAVIS POLK & WARDWELL - LIBRARY □ New York, NY

Nobbe, Nancy, Libn.
ST. LOUIS UNIVERSITY - PARKS COLLEGE OF AERONAUTICAL TECHNOLOGY - LIBRARY† □ Cahokia, IL

Nobbs, Karen, Cat.
UNIVERSITY OF IOWA - LAW LIBRARY □ Iowa City, IA

Noble, David, Libn.
CANCER CONTROL AGENCY OF BRITISH COLUMBIA - LIBRARY □ Vancouver, BC

Noble, Doris E., Ed.
TENNESSEE STATE DEPARTMENT OF CONSERVATION - DIVISION OF GEOLOGY - CONSERVATION RESOURCE CENTER □ Nashville, TN

Noble, Jean C., Ed.Libn.
PARADE PUBLICATIONS, INC. - LIBRARY □ New York, NY

Noble, Valerie, Hd.
UPJOHN COMPANY - BUSINESS LIBRARY 88-91 □ Kalamazoo, MI

Noblet, Chloris, Libn.
SACRAMENTO PUBLIC LIBRARY - BUSINESS & MUNICIPAL DEPARTMENT† □ Sacramento, CA

Nocera, Jean, Govt.Doc.Libn.
RHODE ISLAND STATE LIBRARY □ Providence, RI

Nocka, Jean, Info.Sci.
SCHERING-PLOUGH CORPORATION - PHARMACEUTICAL RESEARCH DIVISION - LIBRARY INFORMATION CENTER □ Bloomfield, NJ

Noe, Bertha M., Cur.
LAKEWOOD HISTORICAL SOCIETY - LIBRARY □ Lakewood, OH

Noe, Christopher J., Ref./Instr.Serv.Libn.
SOUTHERN ILLINOIS UNIVERSITY, CARBONDALE - SCHOOL OF LAW LIBRARY □ Carbondale, IL

Noe Field, Rev. William, Cur., Spec.Coll.
SETON HALL UNIVERSITY - MAC MANUS COLLECTION □ South Orange, NJ

Noejuru, Rosalie, Bibliothecaire
INSTITUT CANADIEN D'EDUCATION DES ADULTES ET RELAIS-FEMMES DE MONTREAL - CENTRE DE DOCUMENTATION □ Montreal, PQ

Noel, Dr. Nancy L., Cur.
BOSTON UNIVERSITY - DEPARTMENT OF SPECIAL COLLECTIONS - NURSING ARCHIVES □ Boston, MA

Nogrady, Judith, Hd.
CANADA - TRANSPORT CANADA - TRANSPORTATION DEVELOPMENT CENTRE - LIBRARY □ Montreal, PQ

Nolan, Catherine, Libn.
ENGLISH-SPEAKING UNION OF THE U.S.A. - BOOKS ACROSS THE SEA LIBRARY □ New York, NY

Nolan, E., Archv.
EASTERN WASHINGTON STATE HISTORICAL SOCIETY - LIBRARY □ Spokane, WA

Nolan, Elaine, Hd., Ser. & Cat.
CURRY COLLEGE - LOUIS R. LEVIN MEMORIAL LIBRARY - SPECIAL COLLECTIONS† □ Milton, MA

Nolan, Liesel, Libn.
UNIVERSITY OF COLORADO, BOULDER - ART AND ARCHITECTURE LIBRARY □ Boulder, CO

Nolan, Margaret P., Chf.Libn.
METROPOLITAN MUSEUM OF ART - PHOTOGRAPH AND SLIDE LIBRARY □ New York, NY

Nolan, Martha D., Hd.
HARTFORD PUBLIC LIBRARY - REFERENCE AND GENERAL READING DEPARTMENT □ Hartford, CT

Nolan, Dr. Patrick B., Hd. of Archv.
WRIGHT STATE UNIVERSITY - ARCHIVES & SPECIAL COLLECTIONS □ Dayton, OH

Nolan, Richard, Cur.
UNIVERSITY OF PITTSBURGH - SPECIAL COLLECTIONS DEPARTMENT □ Pittsburgh, PA

Nolf, Richard A., Dir.
ST. JOSEPH MUSEUM - LIBRARY □ St. Joseph, MO

Nolin, Loretta, Asst.Libn.
U.S. COURT OF APPEALS, 10TH CIRCUIT - LIBRARY □ Denver, CO

Noll, Mary K., Libn.
RCA CORPORATION - LIBRARY □ Lancaster, PA

Noller, David C., Tech.Info.Spec.
PENNWALT CORPORATION - LUCIDOL DIVISION - RESEARCH LIBRARY† □ Buffalo, NY

Nollman, Ellen A., Hd.Libn.
SMITHSONIAN INSTITUTION - FREER GALLERY OF ART - LIBRARY □ Washington, DC

Nolte, Alice I., Field Serv.Libn.
SOUTH CAROLINA STATE LIBRARY □ Columbia, SC

Nook, Cathy, Hd., Tech.Serv.
OAK RIDGE NATIONAL LABORATORY - LIBRARIES† □ Oak Ridge, TN

Noonan, F. Thomas, Assoc.Rd.Serv.Libn.
HARVARD UNIVERSITY - HOUGHTON LIBRARY □ Cambridge, MA

Norberg, Arthur, Dir.
UNIVERSITY OF MINNESOTA - CHARLES BABBAGE INSTITUTE COLLECTION □ Minneapolis, MN

Norbie, Dorothy, Law Libn.
ROATH & BREGA, P.C. - LAW LIBRARY □ Denver, CO

Norcia, Hope, Dental Cat.
TEMPLE UNIVERSITY - HEALTH SCIENCES CENTER - LIBRARY □ Philadelphia, PA

Norcross, Judith G., Law Libn./Asst.Prof.
FRANKLIN PIERCE LAW CENTER - LIBRARY □ Concord, NH

Nord, W., V.P., Oper.
NORTHERN PIGMENT LIMITED - TECHNICAL LIBRARY† □ Etobicoke, ON

Nordby, Carol, Lib.Ck.
GOLDEN VALLEY HEALTH CENTER - MEDICAL LIBRARY □ Golden Valley, MN

Nordby, Kenneth E., Lay Asst.
OUR SAVIOR'S LUTHERAN CHURCH - LIBRARY □ Milwaukee, WI

Nordee, Robin, Ref.
LONG BEACH CITY COLLEGE - PACIFIC COAST CAMPUS LIBRARY □ Long Beach, CA

Norden, Margaret, Ref.Libn.
UNIVERSITY OF PITTSBURGH - FALK LIBRARY OF THE HEALTH SCIENCES □ Pittsburgh, PA

Nordeng, Diane, Libn.
NEUROPSYCHIATRIC INSTITUTE - LIBRARY □ Fargo, ND

Nordeng, Diane, Libn.
SOUTHEAST HUMAN SERVICES CENTER - LIBRARY □ Fargo, ND

Nordgren, Debra L., Libn.
HOWARD YOUNG MEDICAL CENTER - HEALTH SCIENCE LIBRARY □ Woodruff, WI

Nordhaus, Kathy L., Libn.
TEXAS INSTRUMENTS, INC. - SEMICONDUCTOR BUILDING LIBRARY □ Dallas, TX

Nordin, Paula H., Libn.
MOLLOY, JONES, DONAHUE, TRACHTA, CHILDERS & MALLAMO - LIBRARY† □ Tucson, AZ

Noreau, Patricia, Per.Libn.
UNIVERSITY OF LOWELL, NORTH CAMPUS - ALUMNI/LYDON LIBRARY† □ Lowell, MA

Norell, Angie, Libn.
MINNESOTA ZOOLOGICAL GARDEN - LIBRARY □ Apple Valley, MN

Norelli, Barbara, Hd., Pub.Serv.
UNION UNIVERSITY - ALBANY LAW SCHOOL - LIBRARY □ Albany, NY

Norfleet, Barbara P., Cur.
HARVARD UNIVERSITY - CARPENTER CENTER FOR THE VISUAL ARTS - PHOTOGRAPH COLLECTION □ Cambridge, MA

Norich, Samuel, Exec.Dir.
YIVO INSTITUTE FOR JEWISH RESEARCH - LIBRARY AND ARCHIVES □ New York, NY

Norman, Margaret, Mgr., Sci.Info.Serv.
BOEHRINGER INGELHEIM LTD. - SCIENTIFIC INFORMATION SERVICES □ Ridgefield, CT

Norman, Ranulph F., Dir.
MC GRAW-HILL PUBLICATIONS COMPANY - MARKETING INFORMATION CENTER □ New York, NY

Norman, Wayne, Libn.
PARAPSYCHOLOGY FOUNDATION - EILEEN J. GARRETT LIBRARY □ New York, NY

Normandin, Judy, Supv., Braille Sect.
MINNESOTA STATE SERVICES FOR THE BLIND AND VISUALLY HANDICAPPED - COMMUNICATION CENTER □ St. Paul, MN

Norris, Barry A., Libn.
HOWE (C.D.) INSTITUTE - LIBRARY □ Toronto, ON

Norris, Edmond J., Dir.
U.S. ARMY - COMMUNICATIONS SYSTEMS CENTER - ELECTRONICS MUSEUM† □ Ft. Monmouth, NJ

Norris, Elizabeth D., Libn./Hist.
YOUNG WOMEN'S CHRISTIAN ASSOCIATION - NATIONAL BOARD - LIBRARY □ New York, NY

Norris, Kelli R., Co.Libn.
ESTERLINE ANGUS INSTRUMENT CORPORATION - COMPANY LIBRARY □ Indianapolis, IN

Norris, Leon M., Exec.Sec. & Cur.
ANDROSCOGGIN HISTORICAL SOCIETY - CLARENCE E. MARCH LIBRARY □ Auburn, ME

Norris, Loretta A., Chf., Law Serv.Sect.
U.S. DEPT. OF TRANSPORTATION - LIBRARY AND DISTRIBUTION SERVICES DIVISION □ Washington, DC

Norris, Sally, Libn.
TACOMA ART MUSEUM - LIBRARY □ Tacoma, WA

Norris, Susan K., Libn.
PUBLIC SERVICE COMPANY OF OKLAHOMA - REFERENCE CENTER □ Tulsa, OK

Norris, Thomas D., Mss.Spec.
WESTERN HISTORICAL MANUSCRIPT COLLECTION/STATE HISTORICAL SOCIETY OF MISSOURI MANUSCRIPTS JOINT COLLECTION □ Columbia, MO

Norris, Vernal, Chf.Lib.Asst.
UNIVERSITY OF CALIFORNIA, RIVERSIDE - PHYSICAL SCIENCES LIBRARY □ Riverside, CA

Norstedt, Marilyn, Hd., Hum.Dept.
VIRGINIA POLYTECHNIC INSTITUTE AND STATE UNIVERSITY - CAROL M. NEWMAN LIBRARY □ Blacksburg, VA

North, David, Dir.
NEW TRANSCENTURY FOUNDATION -
DOCUMENTATION CENTER □ Washington, DC
North, Jan, Monographs Libn.
UNIVERSITY OF ARKANSAS FOR MEDICAL
SCIENCES - MEDICAL SCIENCES LIBRARY □
Little Rock, AR
North, John, Dir.
RYERSON POLYTECHNICAL INSTITUTE -
LEARNING RESOURCES CENTRE □ Toronto, ON
North, Patricia L., Law Libn.
NEW YORK STATE SUPREME COURT - 4TH
JUDICIAL DISTRICT - LAW LIBRARY □
Schenectady, NY
North, Paul, Tech.Serv./Ref.
WELLS FARGO BANK - LIBRARY 888 □ San
Francisco, CA
Northcott, Dr. J., Supv.
ALLIED CORPORATION - ALLIED CHEMICAL -
LIBRARY □ Buffalo, NY
Northington, Elizabeth, Med.Libn.
U.S. VETERANS ADMINISTRATION (GA-
Augusta) - HOSPITAL LIBRARY □ Augusta, GA
Northrop, Ruth B., Oral Hist.
NAPA COUNTY HISTORICAL SOCIETY -
LIBRARY □ Napa, CA
Norton, Catherine, Asst.Libn.
MARINE BIOLOGICAL LABORATORY - LIBRARY
□ Woods Hole, MA
Norton, Deborah, Health Rec.Adm.
PRINCE EDWARD HEIGHTS - RESIDENT
RECORDS LIBRARY □ Picton, ON
Norton, Evelyn L., Act.Libn.
U.S. COAST GUARD/AIR STATION - BASE
LIBRARY □ Cape Cod, MA
Norton, Frank M., Adm.Libn.
U.S. ARMY HOSPITALS - DARNALL ARMY
HOSPITAL - MEDICAL LIBRARY □ Ft. Hood, TX
Norton, Linda M., Libn.
U.S. AIR FORCE HOSPITAL - MEDICAL LIBRARY
(WA - Fairchild AFB) □ Fairchild AFB, WA
Norton, Marie A., Med.Libn.
LANKENAU HOSPITAL - MEDICAL LIBRARY □
Philadelphia, PA
Norton, Mary J., Libn.
J&HWF INC. - EMPLOYEE BENEFIT PLAN
DEPARTMENT LIBRARY □ Montreal, PQ
Norton, Maryanne C., Libn.
MARATHON COUNTY HISTORICAL MUSEUM -
LIBRARY □ Wausau, WI
Norton, Myra, Libn.
OVERSEAS PRIVATE INVESTMENT
CORPORATION - LIBRARY □ Washington, DC
Norton, Nancy, Hd., User Serv.
OAK RIDGE NATIONAL LABORATORY -
LIBRARIES† □ Oak Ridge, TN
Norton, R.M., Supv., Info.Serv.
NEWPORT NEWS SHIPBUILDING AND DRY
DOCK COMPANY - LIBRARY SERVICES
DEPARTMENT □ Newport News, VA
Norton, Robert P., V.P.
FIRST FEDERAL SAVINGS AND LOAN
ASSOCIATION OF FORT WAYNE - LIBRARY □
Fort Wayne, IN
Norton, Thomas E., Dir.
DUKES COUNTY HISTORICAL SOCIETY -
LIBRARY □ Edgartown, MA
Norvell, Geneva N., Libn.
ST. JOHN MEDICAL CENTER - HEALTH
SCIENCES LIBRARY† □ Tulsa, OK
Norville, Marla, Media Spec.
MOUNTAIN AREA HEALTH EDUCATION CENTER
- INFORMATION & MEDIA SERVICES □
Asheville, NC
Norwood, Claudia, Ref.Sect.
ENVIRONMENTAL PROTECTION AGENCY -
HEADQUARTERS LIBRARY† □ Washington, DC
Norwood, Terrence, Archv.
COOK COUNTY HOSPITAL - HEALTH SCIENCE
LIBRARY AND ARCHIVES □ Chicago, IL
Noskowitz, Laura, Ref.Libn.
PRATT INSTITUTE - LIBRARY □ Brooklyn, NY

Nossal, Angela M., Libn.
MARKETING INFORMATION INSTITUTE -
SELECTED INFORMATION LIBRARY CENTER □
San Diego, CA
Nossaman, Allen, Dir.
SAN JUAN COUNTY HISTORICAL SOCIETY -
ARCHIVE □ Silverton, CO
Nosseir, Susan, Ref./ILL Libn.
PACE UNIVERSITY - SCHOOL OF LAW LIBRARY
□ White Plains, NY
Nothelfer, Eleanor S., Libn.
LEHIGH UNIVERSITY - FRITZ ENGINEERING
LABORATORY LIBRARY □ Bethlehem, PA
Nourse, Constance, Ref.Libn.
SETON HALL UNIVERSITY - SCHOOL OF LAW -
LAW LIBRARY □ Newark, NJ
Nourse, Mary, Med.Libn.
U.S. VETERANS ADMINISTRATION (OH-
Cleveland) - HOSPITAL LIBRARY □ Cleveland, OH
Novacich, Ann, Libn.
U.S. VETERANS ADMINISTRATION (IL-Hines) -
LIBRARY SERVICES (142D) □ Hines, IL
Novack, Allen R., AV Libn.
RINGLING SCHOOL OF ART AND DESIGN -
LIBRARY □ Sarasota, FL
Novack, D., Info.Spec.
ALLERGAN PHARMACEUTICALS, INC. -
MEDICAL & SCIENCE INFORMATION □ Irvine,
CA
Novak, Gregory M., Attorney/Libn.
ALLEN COUNTY LAW LIBRARY □ Lima, OH
Novak, Jan Ryan, Libn.
CLEVELAND DEPARTMENT OF LAW LIBRARY □
Cleveland, OH
Novak, Jan Ryan, Dept.Hd.
CLEVELAND PUBLIC LIBRARY - PUBLIC
ADMINISTRATION LIBRARY □ Cleveland, OH
Novak, Maryanne, Env./Regulatory Info.Spec
ALLIED CORPORATION - LIBRARY &
INFORMATION SERVICES □ Morristown, NJ
Novak, Susan, Res.Asst.
NEW HAMPSHIRE STATE DEPARTMENT OF
HEALTH & WELFARE - OFFICE OF ALCOHOL &
DRUG ABUSE PREVENTION - LIBRARY □
Concord, NH
Novick, Ruth, Asst.Libn.
BREED, ABBOTT & MORGAN - LIBRARY □ New
York, NY
Novil, Rose, Pub.Serv.Libn.
NATIONAL COLLEGE OF EDUCATION - URBAN
CAMPUS LEARNING RESOURCE CENTER □
Chicago, IL
Novinger, Margaret H., Adm.Libn.
U.S. ARMY SIGNAL CENTER & FORT GORDON -
CONRAD TECHNICAL LIBRARY □ Ft. Gordon, GA
Nowak, Frances A., Supv.
CONOCO, INC. - INTERNATIONAL
PRODUCTION - CENTRAL FILES/LIBRARY □
Houston, TX
Nowakowski, Jane, Choral Libn.
WESTMINSTER CHOIR COLLEGE - TALBOTT
LIBRARY □ Princeton, NJ
Nowlan, Henri, Documentalist
UNIVERSITE DE MONCTON - FACULTE DES
SCIENCES DE L'EDUCATION - CENTRE DE
RESSOURCES PEDAGOGIQUES □ Moncton, NB
Nowosielski, Mrs. M., Hd., Tech.Serv.
CANADA - EMPLOYMENT & IMMIGRATION
CANADA - LIBRARY □ Ottawa, ON
Noxon, Dr. Charles J., Cur.
JOHNSTOWN HISTORICAL SOCIETY - LIBRARY
REFERENCE CENTER □ Johnstown, NY
Noyes, Dan, Mng.Ed.
CENTER FOR INVESTIGATIVE REPORTING -
LIBRARY □ San Francisco, CA
Noyes, Suzanne, Chf., Lib.Serv.
U.S. VETERANS ADMINISTRATION (MA-
Brockton) - MEDICAL CENTER LIBRARY □
Brockton, MA
Nuechterlein, Mary, Registrar
FRANKENMUTH HISTORICAL ASSOCIATION
MUSEUM - LIBRARY □ Frankenmuth, MI

Nuernberg, Donna S., Ref.Libn.
WAUSAU INSURANCE COMPANIES - LIBRARY □
Wausau, WI
Nuffer, R., Ref.
WAYNE STATE UNIVERSITY - G. FLINT PURDY
LIBRARY □ Detroit, MI
Nuffer, Stan, Supv.
PORTLAND STATE UNIVERSITY - AUDIO-
VISUAL SERVICES □ Portland, OR
Nugent, Alice, Lib.Asst.
UNIVERSITY CONGREGATIONAL CHURCH -
LIBRARY □ Seattle, WA
Nugent, Barbara, Regional Br.Libn.
NEW YORK PUBLIC LIBRARY - REGIONAL
LIBRARY FOR THE BLIND AND PHYSICALLY
HANDICAPPED □ New York, NY
Nugent, James
FOREST PRODUCTS ACCIDENT PREVENTION
ASSOCIATION - LIBRARY □ North Bay, ON
Nugent, John M., Univ.Archv.
UNIVERSITY OF KANSAS - UNIVERSITY
ARCHIVES □ Lawrence, KS
Nugent, L., Libn.
MC KINNON (I.N.) MEMORIAL LIBRARY □
Calgary, AB
Nugent, Martha
PRICE WATERHOUSE - LIBRARY □ Montreal, PQ
Nugent, Robert S., Dir.
JERSEY CITY STATE COLLEGE - FORREST A.
IRWIN LIBRARY - SPECIAL COLLECTIONS □
Jersey City, NJ
Nugent, Roberta F., Chf.Libn.
GIVAUDAN CORPORATION - LIBRARY □ Clifton,
NJ
Nulle, Patricia A., Libn.
JOHNS HOPKINS UNIVERSITY - SCHOOL OF
MEDICINE - DEPARTMENT OF PEDIATRICS -
BAETJER MEMORIAL LIBRARY □ Baltimore, MD
Nullmeyer, Vernalee, Lib.Techn.
CALIFORNIA SCHOOL FOR THE BLIND -
LIBRARY MEDIA CENTER □ Fremont, CA
Nunes, Martha, Lib.Techn.
ONTARIO - MINISTRY OF HEALTH - PUBLIC
HEALTH LABORATORIES - LIBRARY □ Toronto,
ON
Nunn, Jeri, Adm.Asst.
COLUMBIA UNIVERSITY - ORAL HISTORY
COLLECTION □ New York, NY
Nunn, Theodore J., Jr., Hd.
DAYTON AND MONTGOMERY COUNTY PUBLIC
LIBRARY - NON-PRINT MEDIA CENTER □
Dayton, OH
Nuquist, Mrs. Reidun D., Libn.
VERMONT HISTORICAL SOCIETY - LIBRARY □
Montpelier, VT
Nurmela, Lillian, Libn.
ALAMEDA COUNTY LIBRARY - BUSINESS &
GOVERNMENT LIBRARY □ Oakland, CA
Nurmi, Anne M., Libn.
VIRGINIA BAPTIST HOSPITAL - BARKSDALE
MEDICAL LIBRARY □ Lynchburg, VA
Nurse, Lori, Info.Ctr.Libn.
RYERSON POLYTECHNICAL INSTITUTE -
LEARNING RESOURCES CENTRE □ Toronto, ON
Nurse, Pamela, Asst.Libn.
ST. PATRICK'S SEMINARY - MC KEON
MEMORIAL LIBRARY □ Menlo Park, CA
Nussbaum, Dr. Raymond O., Lib.Asst. II
UNIVERSITY OF NEW ORLEANS - EARL K. LONG
LIBRARY - ARCHIVES & MANUSCRIPTS/
SPECIAL COLLECTIONS DEPT. □ New Orleans,
LA
Nussenblatt, Sophie
TEMPLE B'NAI ISRAEL - LASKER MEMORIAL
LIBRARY □ Galveston, TX
Nutley, Richard V., Logistics Mgt.Spec.
REYNOLDS ELECTRICAL AND ENGINEERING
COMPANY, INC. - COORDINATION AND
INFORMATION CENTER □ Las Vegas, NV
Nuttall, Mrs. D., Lib.Asst.
QUEEN'S UNIVERSITY AT KINGSTON -
MATHEMATICS LIBRARY □ Kingston, ON

Nuttall, Deborah, Libn.
AMERICAN PUBLIC POWER ASSOCIATION - LIBRARY □ Washington, DC

Nuttall, R.L., Data Anl.
U.S. NATL. BUREAU OF STANDARDS - CHEMICAL THERMODYNAMICS DATA CENTER □ Washington, DC

Nutting, Rebecca F., Libn.
JORDAN (Edward C.) CO., INC. - LIBRARY □ Portland, ME

Nutty, D., AV
WIDENER UNIVERSITY - WOLFGRAM MEMORIAL LIBRARY □ Chester, PA

Nyang'ani, Jean O., Asst.Libn.
ABELL (A.S.) PUBLISHING COMPANY INC. -THE BALTIMORE SUN - LIBRARY □ Baltimore, MD

Nyberg, Cheryl, Docs./Ref.Libn.
UNIVERSITY OF ILLINOIS - LAW LIBRARY □ Champaign, IL

Nyberg, Nancy, Libn.
NYBERG CARTOGRAPHIC COLLECTION □ Shorewood, MN

Nycum, Professor Peter S., Law Libn.
LEWIS AND CLARK LAW SCHOOL - NORTHWESTERN SCHOOL OF LAW - PAUL L. BOLEY LAW LIBRARY □ Portland, OR

Nydegger, Marion, Assoc.Libn.
TRINITY EPISCOPAL CHURCH - LIBRARY □ Santa Barbara, CA

Nye, Phyllis J., Libn.
SPERRY COMPUTER SYSTEMS - LIBRARY/ TECHNICAL INFORMATION CENTER □ Salt Lake City, UT

Nykolyshyn, Helen, Cat.
UNIVERSITY OF DAYTON - MARIAN LIBRARY □ Dayton, OH

Nylander, Robert H., Arch.Hist.
CAMBRIDGE HISTORICAL COMMISSION - LIBRARY □ Cambridge, MA

Nylen, Robert A., Registrar
NEVADA STATE MUSEUM - LIBRARY □ Carson City, NV

Nyquist, Bro. Paul, Hd.Libn.
ASSUMPTION ABBEY - LIBRARY □ Richardton, ND

O

Oakes, Bessie, Braille Libn.
UTAH STATE LIBRARY - BLIND AND PHYSICALLY HANDICAPPED PROGRAM - REGIONAL LIBRARY □ Salt Lake City, UT

Oakes, Karen S., Hd., Circ.
MACALESTER COLLEGE - WEYERHAEUSER LIBRARY □ St. Paul, MN

Oakes, Mary Grace, Libn.
SNELL & WILMER - LAW LIBRARY □ Phoenix, AZ

Oakhill, Harold, Archv.
ROCKEFELLER UNIVERSITY - ROCKEFELLER ARCHIVE CENTER □ North Tarrytown, NY

Oakley, Edna M., Libn.
BERGEN COUNTY LAW LIBRARY† □ Hackensack, NJ

Oakley, Yvonne H., Ctr.Libn.
U.S. DEFENSE LOGISTICS AGENCY - DEFENSE GENERAL SUPPLY CENTER - CENTER LIBRARY □ Richmond, VA

Oakly, Robert L., Law Libn.
GEORGETOWN UNIVERSITY - FRED O. DENNIS LAW LIBRARY □ Washington, DC

Oaksford, Margaret J., Libn.
CORNELL UNIVERSITY - SCHOOL OF HOTEL ADMINISTRATION LIBRARY □ Ithaca, NY

Oates, Coby, Techn.-in-Charge
CANADA - NATIONAL DEFENCE - CANADIAN FORCES COLLEGE - STAFF SCHOOL LIBRARY† □ Toronto, ON

Oatway, Mrs. A., Libn.
SASKATOON CANCER CLINIC - LIBRARY □ Saskatoon, SK

O'Bannon, Paul W., Sr.Libn.
CALIFORNIA MARITIME ACADEMY LIBRARY □ Vallejo, CA

Obecny, Nancy C., Law Libn.
OHIO COUNTY LAW LIBRARY □ Wheeling, WV

Oberc, Susanne, Ref.Libn.
U.S. NASA - LEWIS RESEARCH CENTER - LIBRARY† □ Cleveland, OH

Oberg, Richard, Lib.Spec.
UNIVERSITY OF WASHINGTON - COMPUTING INFORMATION CENTER □ Seattle, WA

Oberhamer, Douglas R., Exec.Dir.
WATER QUALITY ASSOCIATION - RESEARCH COUNCIL LIBRARY □ Lisle, IL

Oberhausen, Judy, Act.Dir./Cur.
ART CENTER, INC. - LIBRARY† □ South Bend, IN

Oberlander, Barbara, Law Libn.
NASSAU COUNTY SUPREME COURT - LAW LIBRARY □ Mineola, NY

Oberle, Holly, Music Cat.
UNIVERSITY OF MIAMI - SCHOOL OF MUSIC - ALBERT PICK MUSIC LIBRARY □ Coral Gables, FL

O'Blennis, Marjorie, Asst.Libn.
LEGAL SERVICES OF EASTERN MISSOURI, INC. - LIBRARY □ St. Louis, MO

Oboruns, Valerie, Lib.Supv.
MC GILL UNIVERSITY - RUTHERFORD PHYSICS LIBRARY □ Montreal, PQ

O'Boyce, Edward J., Res.Assoc.
LOUISIANA TECH UNIVERSITY - RESEARCH DIVISION/COLLEGE OF ADMINISTRATION AND BUSINESS - LIBRARY □ Ruston, LA

O'Brien, Adela, Ref.Libn.
TEXAS COLLEGE OF OSTEOPATHIC MEDICINE - HEALTH SCIENCES LIBRARY □ Fort Worth, TX

O'Brien, Alberta T., Med.Libn.
MONTGOMERY HOSPITAL - MEDICAL LIBRARY □ Norristown, PA

O'Brien, Elizabeth, Libn.
MALDEN HOSPITAL - SCHOOL OF NURSING LIBRARY □ Malden, MA

O'Brien, Elizabeth J., Libn.
MALDEN HOSPITAL - MEDICAL LIBRARY □ Malden, MA

O'Brien, Elmer J., Libn.
UNITED THEOLOGICAL SEMINARY - LIBRARY □ Dayton, OH

O'Brien, Frances E., Med.Libn.
CARNEY HOSPITAL - MEDICAL LIBRARY □ Dorchester, MA

O'Brien, J.W., Chf., State & Mil.Rec.
CANADA - PUBLIC ARCHIVES OF CANADA - FEDERAL ARCHIVES DIVISION □ Ottawa, ON

O'Brien, Joan, Tech.Serv.Libn.
DIGITAL EQUIPMENT CORPORATION - MARLBORO LIBRARY □ Marlboro, MA

O'Brien, Joan, Info.Spec.
PHILLIPS PETROLEUM COMPANY - RESEARCH & DEVELOPMENT DEPARTMENT - TECHNICAL INFORMATION BRANCH □ Bartlesville, OK

O'Brien, Sr. Judith, Cat.
PRESENTATION COLLEGE - LIBRARY □ Aberdeen, SD

O'Brien, Kerry A., Cur.
OLD YORK HISTORICAL SOCIETY - LIBRARY □ York, ME

O'Brien, Lyn, Med.Libn.
DOCTORS' HOSPITAL - MEDICAL LIBRARY □ Miami, FL

O'Brien, Maggie, Res.Libn.
ROSENBERG CAPITAL MANAGEMENT - LIBRARY □ San Francisco, CA

O'Brien, Mary, Libn.
CH2M HILL, INC. - CORVALLIS REGIONAL OFFICE LIBRARY □ Corvallis, OR

O'Brien, Mary Frances, Libn.
NORTHERN RESEARCH & ENGINEERING CORPORATION - LIBRARY □ Woburn, MA

O'Brien, Mary J., Libn.
LINCOLN INSTITUTE OF LAND POLICY - LIBRARY □ Cambridge, MA

O'Brien, Nancy, Libn.
HASKINS LABORATORIES - LIBRARY □ New Haven, CT

O'Brien, Nancy, Libn.
IOWA METHODIST SCHOOL OF NURSING - MARJORIE GERTRUDE MORROW LIBRARY □ Des Moines, IA

Obrig, Kathy S., Libn.
BRONSON METHODIST HOSPITAL - HEALTH SCIENCES LIBRARY □ Kalamazoo, MI

O'Brine, Mrs. Rodney, Asst.Libn.
GRAND LODGE OF IOWA, A.F. AND A.M. - IOWA MASONIC LIBRARY □ Cedar Rapids, IA

Obrochta, Gerald, Hd., Soc.Sci.Sect.
CHICAGO PUBLIC LIBRARY CENTRAL LIBRARY - SOCIAL SCIENCES & HISTORY DIVISION □ Chicago, IL

Obrokta, Carole, Dir.
DIOCESE OF PITTSBURGH - LEARNING MEDIA CENTER □ Pittsburgh, PA

O'Bryant, J.F., Sci.Bibliog.
UNIVERSITY OF VIRGINIA - SCIENCE & ENGINEERING LIBRARY □ Charlottesville, VA

Obrzut, Lorraine, Asst.Libn.
OAKWOOD HOSPITAL - MC LOUTH MEMORIAL HEALTH SCIENCE LIBRARY† □ Dearborn, MI

Obus, Harriett, Ref.
EDUCATIONAL BROADCASTING CORPORATION - THIRTEEN RESEARCH LIBRARY □ New York, NY

O'Callaghan, Linda J., Med.Libn./Online Anl.
GOOD SAMARITAN HOSPITAL - RICHARD S. BEINECKE MEDICAL LIBRARY □ West Palm Beach, FL

Ocampo, Jean, Assoc.Libn.
CLEVELAND ELECTRIC ILLUMINATING COMPANY - LIBRARY □ Cleveland, OH

Occhialini, Nancy E., Lib.Cat.
MASSACHUSETTS COLLEGE OF PHARMACY & ALLIED HEALTH SCIENCES - SHEPPARD LIBRARY □ Boston, MA

Ochal, Bethany J., Dir.
ORANGE COUNTY LAW LIBRARY □ Santa Ana, CA

Ochoa, James J., Hd., Tech.Proc.
LOS ANGELES COUNTY MEDICAL ASSOCIATION - LIBRARY† □ Los Angeles, CA

Ocholik, Teresa, Asst.Libn.
DETROIT MACOMB HOSPITAL CORPORATION - HOSPITAL LIBRARY □ Detroit, MI

Ocholik, Teresa, Asst.Libn.
DETROIT MACOMB HOSPITAL CORPORATION - SOUTH MACOMB HOSPITAL LIBRARY □ Warren, MI

Ochs, Mrs. Merle W., Med.Libn.
DOMINICAN SANTA CRUZ HOSPITAL - HEALTH INFORMATION LIBRARY □ Santa Cruz, CA

Ochs, Michael, Libn.
HARVARD UNIVERSITY - EDA KUHN LOEB MUSIC LIBRARY □ Cambridge, MA

Ockert, Dr. Karl F., Adm.Asst.
ROHM & HAAS COMPANY - RESEARCH DIVISION - INFORMATION SERVICES DEPARTMENT □ Spring House, PA

O'Connell, Colette, Ref.Libn.
RENSSELAER POLYTECHNIC INSTITUTE - FOLSOM LIBRARY □ Troy, NY

O'Connell, Edward M., Law Libn.
NEW YORK COUNTY LAWYERS' ASSOCIATION - LIBRARY □ New York, NY

O'Connell, George E., Dir.
UNIVERSITY OF CONNECTICUT - LABOR EDUCATION CENTER - INFORMATION CENTER □ Storrs, CT

O'Connell, James J., III, Cur.
UNCAP INTERNATIONAL, INC. - PROJECT COLLECTORS RESEARCH LIBRARY □ Los Angeles, CA

O'Connell, Michael T., Asst.Libn.
INSTITUTE OF LIVING - MEDICAL LIBRARY □ Hartford, CT

O'Connell, Monica, Rd.Adv.
DISTRICT OF COLUMBIA PUBLIC LIBRARY -
SOCIOLOGY, GOVERNMENT & EDUCATION
DIVISION □ Washington, DC
O'Conner, Margaret, Cat.
ICI AMERICAS INC. - ATLAS LIBRARY □
Wilmington, DE
O'Connor, Alice, Dir.
JEFFERSON FOUNDATION - LIBRARY □
Washington, DC
O'Connor, Ann E., Law Libn.
FITCHBURG LAW LIBRARY □ Fitchburg, MA
O'Connor, Beth, Libn.
NORTHWESTERN NATIONAL LIFE INSURANCE
COMPANY - LIBRARY □ Minneapolis, MN
O'Connor, Betsy, Libn.
MEMORIAL HOSPITAL OF BURLINGTON
COUNTY - HEALTH SCIENCES LIBRARY □ Mt.
Holly, NJ
O'Connor, Carol A., Law Libn.
CLERMONT COUNTY LAW LIBRARY
ASSOCIATION □ Batavia, OH
O'Connor, Cheryl A., Asst.Libn./Rd.Serv.
WISCONSIN STATE SUPREME COURT -
WISCONSIN STATE LAW LIBRARY □ Madison,
WI
O'Connor, Denis R., Libn.
DEBEVOISE & PLIMPTON - LAW LIBRARY □
New York, NY
O'Connor, Elaine P., Dir.
LONG (Earl K.) MEMORIAL HOSPITAL - MEDICAL
LIBRARY □ Baton Rouge, LA
O'Connor, Frank J., Dir.
U.S. DEPT. OF COMMERCE - INTERNATIONAL
TRADE ADMINISTRATION - BOSTON DISTRICT
OFFICE LIBRARY □ Boston, MA
O'Connor, Marihelen, Med.Libn.
SCOTTSDALE MEMORIAL HOSPITAL - DR.
ROBERT C. FOREMAN HEALTH SCIENCES
LIBRARY □ Scottsdale, AZ
O'Connor, Sylvia, Acq.
ERIC CLEARINGHOUSE ON ELEMENTARY AND
EARLY CHILDHOOD EDUCATION □ Champaign,
IL
Oda, Phyllis, Mgr.
RAYCHEM CORPORATION - CORPORATE
LIBRARY† □ Menlo Park, CA
Oddan, Linda, Med.Libn.
WAUKESHA MEMORIAL HOSPITAL - MEDICAL
LIBRARY □ Waukesha, WI
O'Dell, Charles A., Libn.
ELLIS FISCHEL STATE CANCER CENTER -
LIBRARY & INFORMATION CENTER □ Columbia,
MO
Odell, Joan, Law Libn.
SHASTA COUNTY LAW LIBRARY □ Redding, CA
O'Dell, Shannon, Cur.
HINCKLEY FOUNDATION MUSEUM - LIBRARY □
Ithaca, NY
Odell, Tobe, Coord., Lib.Oper.
ESSO RESOURCES CANADA LIMITED - LIBRARY
INFORMATION CENTRE □ Calgary, AB
Oderberg, I. Manuel, Res.Libn.
THEOSOPHICAL UNIVERSITY - LIBRARY □
Altadena, CA
Odermann, Anita, Dir., Christian Educ.
FIRST UNITED PRESBYTERIAN CHURCH -
LIBRARY □ Albuquerque, NM
Oderwald, S.M., Ref.Libn.
AT & T TECHNOLOGIES, INC. - CORPORATE
EDUCATION CENTER - LIBRARY □ Hopewell, NJ
Odien, Jean, Libn.
ST. MARY'S SCHOOL FOR THE DEAF -
INFORMATION CENTER □ Buffalo, NY
Od'Neal, Mary, Libn.
INTERNATIONAL CITY MANAGEMENT
ASSOCIATION - LIBRARY □ Washington, DC
Odom, Florence, Musm.Cur.
UNITED DAUGHTERS OF THE CONFEDERACY -
TEXAS CONFEDERATE MUSEUM LIBRARY □
Austin, TX

Odom, Katherine C., Clinical Med.Libn.
UNIVERSITY OF TEXAS MEDICAL BRANCH -
MOODY MEDICAL LIBRARY □ Galveston, TX
O'Donnell, Ellen, Ref.Libn.
ST. JOHN HOSPITAL - MEDICAL LIBRARY □
Detroit, MI
O'Donnell, Gerald, Info.Serv.
U.S. BUREAU OF THE CENSUS - INFORMATION
SERVICES PROGRAM - DENVER REG. OFFICE -
CENSUS PUBLICATION CENTER □ Denver, CO
O'Donnell, Kathleen, Supv. Indexer
HUMAN RESOURCES NETWORK -
INFORMATION CENTER† □ Philadelphia, PA
O'Donnell, Kathleen Healy, Libn.
COOPERS & LYBRAND - LIBRARY AND
INFORMATION CENTER □ Boston, MA
O'Donnell, Linda, Instr. TV Coord.
OAKLAND SCHOOLS - EDUCATIONAL RESOURCE
CENTER □ Pontiac, MI
O'Donnell, Sr. Mary Julia, Hd.Libn.
ST. JOHN VIANNEY COLLEGE SEMINARY -
MARY LOUISE MAYTAG MEMORIAL LIBRARY □
Miami, FL
O'Donnell, Maryann, Cat.
WILLKIE FARR & GALLAGHER - LIBRARY □ New
York, NY
O'Donnell, Maureen, Asst.Libn.
CHEMICAL BANK - RESEARCH LIBRARY □ New
York, NY
O'Donnell, Rosemary, Info.Spec.-Tech.
POLYSAR, LTD. - INFORMATION CENTRE □
Sarnia, ON
O'Donoghue, Sharon, Libn.
GAGE & TUCKER - LIBRARY □ Kansas City, MO
O'Donovan, Phyllis H., Libn.
CTB/MC GRAW-HILL - LIBRARY □ Monterey, CA
O'Dowd, Joann T., Mgr.
NATIONAL BROADCASTING COMPANY, INC. -
NEWS ARCHIVAL OPERATIONS □ New York, NY
O'Drobinak, Margaret, Hd., Info.Serv.Br.
U.S. NAVY - NAVAL WEAPONS CENTER -
LIBRARY DIVISION □ China Lake, CA
Odsen, Beth, Tech.Serv.Libn.
ALASKA (State) COURT SYSTEM - ALASKA
COURT LIBRARIES □ Anchorage, AK
Odum, Mark, Info.Off.
NATIONAL REHABILITATION INFORMATION
CENTER □ Washington, DC
O'Dwyer, Edward T., Jr., Media Serv.Coord.
MASSACHUSETTS COLLEGE OF PHARMACY &
ALLIED HEALTH SCIENCES - SHEPPARD
LIBRARY □ Boston, MA
Odyniec, Mary T., Assoc.Ref.Libn.
CONNECTICUT COLLEGE - LIBRARY - SPECIAL
COLLECTIONS □ New London, CT
Oertli, Dave, Hd.Lib. Blind/Phys.Hand.
NEBRASKA STATE LIBRARY COMMISSION □
Lincoln, NE
Oesch, Martha, Libn.
PUBLIC CITIZEN - CONGRESS WATCH -
LIBRARY □ Washington, DC
Oetting, Edward, Cur.
ARIZONA HISTORICAL FOUNDATION - HAYDEN
LIBRARY □ Tempe, AZ
Oetting, Frieda R., Libn.
CHEMPLEX COMPANY - LIBRARY □ Rolling
Meadows, IL
Oey, Giok Po, Cur.
CORNELL UNIVERSITY - JOHN M. ECHOLS
COLLECTION ON SOUTHEAST ASIA □ Ithaca, NY
Offe, Hans Laf, Ref.Libn.
KXE6S VEREIN CHESS SOCIETY - SPECIAL/
RESEARCH LIBRARY - EAST DIVISION □ Chapel
Hill, NC
Offenbeck, John, Pub.Serv.Libn.
QUEEN'S UNIVERSITY AT KINGSTON -
DOCUMENTS LIBRARY □ Kingston, ON
Offermann, Glenn W., Hd.Libn.
CONCORDIA COLLEGE - BUENGER MEMORIAL
LIBRARY □ St. Paul, MN

Ogden, Dale T., Libn.
U.S. AIR FORCE - ELECTRONIC SECURITY
COMMAND - GENERAL LIBRARY □ San Antonio,
TX
Ogden, Grace, Tech.Info.Spec.
U.S. NATL. HIGHWAY TRAFFIC SAFETY
ADMINISTRATION - TECHNICAL REFERENCE
DIVISION □ Washington, DC
Ogden, Helen M., Hd.
RICHMOND PUBLIC LIBRARY - ART AND MUSIC
DEPARTMENT □ Richmond, VA
Ogden, Nina, Libn.
FRANK, BERNSTEIN, CONAWAY & GOLDMAN -
LIBRARY □ Baltimore, MD
Ogden, Suzanne M., Tech.Libn.
FRITO-LAY, INC. - TECHNICAL INFORMATION
CENTER □ Dallas, TX
Ogilvie, Dolores, Libn.
ALBERTA - DEPARTMENT OF HOUSING AND
PUBLIC WORKS - HOUSING LIBRARY □
Edmonton, AB
O'Grady, Jean, Asst.Libn.
PROSKAUER, ROSE, GOETZ & MENDELSOHN -
LIBRARY □ New York, NY
O'Grady, R., Sec.
UNIVERSITY OF TORONTO - DEPARTMENT OF
ZOOLOGY LIBRARY □ Toronto, ON
O'Grady, Susan, Supv.
EG&G, INC. - WASHINGTON ANALYTICAL
SERVICES CENTER - INFORMATION CENTER □
Rockville, MD
Ogura, Irene, Hd.Cat.Libn.
UNIVERSITY OF COLORADO HEALTH SCIENCES
CENTER - DENISON MEMORIAL LIBRARY† □
Denver, CO
Oh, Song Ja, Dir.
STATEN ISLAND HOSPITAL - MEDICAL STAFF
LIBRARY □ Staten Island, NY
Oh, Timothy T., Dir. of Lib.
MERCY HOSPITAL & MEDICAL CENTER -
MEDICAL LIBRARY □ Chicago, IL
O'Halloran, Charles, State Libn.
MISSOURI STATE LIBRARY □ Jefferson City,
MO
O'Hara, Rev. Francis C., Dir., Lib.Serv.
HOLY APOSTLES COLLEGE - LIBRARY □
Cromwell, CT
O'Hara, Kathy Bennett, Lib.Techn.
ONTARIO NURSES ASSOCIATION - ONA
LIBRARY □ Toronto, ON
O'Hara, Kerry, Ser. & Ref.Libn.
ST. PETER'S MEDICAL CENTER - LIBRARY† □
New Brunswick, NJ
Ohlmann, Glenn, Tech.Serv.Libn.
CONCORDIA TEACHERS COLLEGE - LINK
LIBRARY □ Seward, NE
Ohlsen, Joyce, Libn.
FIRST PRESBYTERIAN CHURCH - LIBRARY □
Hastings, NE
Ohst, Alice M., Libn.
DAMES & MOORE - LIBRARY □ Los Angeles, CA
Oh'Uiginn, Hon. Sean, Consul Gen.
IRELAND CONSULATE GENERAL - LIBRARY □
New York, NY
Oihus, Colleen, Asst.Cur.
UNIVERSITY OF NORTH DAKOTA -
DEPARTMENT OF SPECIAL COLLECTIONS □
Grand Forks, ND
Oitzinger, Harvada, Med.Libn.
ELMBROOK MEMORIAL HOSPITAL - MARY BETH
CURTIS HEALTH SCIENCE LIBRARY □
Brookfield, WI
Oiye, Fumiko G., Supv.
TRW, INC. - OPERATIONS & SUPPORT GROUP -
ELECTRONICS & DEFENSE SECTOR - TECH.
INFORMATION CENTER □ Redondo Beach, CA
Oiye, Julie Ann, Libn.
KING COUNTY YOUTH SERVICE CENTER -
LIBRARY □ Seattle, WA
Ojala, Marydee, Lib.Mgr.
BANK OF AMERICA, NT & SA - REFERENCE
LIBRARY □ San Francisco, CA

Ojamaa, Dr. Koit, Dir.
HOME NEWS PUBLISHING COMPANY - LIBRARY □ New Brunswick, NJ

Oka, Susan, Asst.Libn.
ACADEMY OF MOTION PICTURE ARTS AND SCIENCES - MARGARET HERRICK LIBRARY □ Beverly Hills, CA

Okada, Connie T., Libn.
UNIVERSITY OF WASHINGTON - ART LIBRARY □ Seattle, WA

Okajima, Michael, Mgr., Info.Serv.
HEWLETT-PACKARD COMPANY - CORPORATE LIBRARY □ Palo Alto, CA

Okasako-Oshiro, Gloria, Info.Chem.
UNION OIL COMPANY OF CALIFORNIA - TECHNICAL INFORMATION CENTER □ Placentia, CA

O'Keefe, Julie, Asst.Archv.
UNIVERSITY OF SANTA CLARA - ARCHIVES □ Santa Clara, CA

Okell, Robert
U.S. DEPT. OF LABOR - BUREAU OF LABOR STATISTICS - INFORMATION AND ADVISORY SECTION □ New York, NY

Okey, R. Anne, Labadie Coll.Libn.
UNIVERSITY OF MICHIGAN - DEPARTMENT OF RARE BOOKS AND SPECIAL COLLECTIONS - LIBRARY □ Ann Arbor, MI

Okey, S. Paul, Pk.Hist.
U.S. NATL. PARK SERVICE - SARATOGA NATL. HISTORICAL PARK - LIBRARY □ Stillwater, NY

Oko, Andrew J., Cur.
ART GALLERY OF HAMILTON - MURIEL ISABEL BOSTWICK LIBRARY □ Hamilton, ON

Oksner, Claire, Dir.
JUNG (C.G.) INSTITUTE OF LOS ANGELES, INC. - MAX AND LORE ZELLER IBRARY □ Los Angeles, CA

Okuizumi, Eizaburo, Japanese Libn.
UNIVERSITY OF CHICAGO - FAR EASTERN LIBRARY □ Chicago, IL

Okuma, Joanne M., Asst.Libn.
U.S. AIR FORCE BASE - HICKAM BASE LIBRARY □ Hickam AFB, HI

Okur, Rob, Ed.
NATIONAL YIDDISH BOOK CENTER, INC. - LIBRARY □ Amherst, MA

Oldani, Genevieve, Mgr., Info. Liaison
BURROUGHS CORPORATION - CORPORATE INFORMATION RESEARCH CENTER □ Detroit, MI

Oldenberg, Joseph, Mss.Spec.
DETROIT PUBLIC LIBRARY - BURTON HISTORICAL COLLECTION □ Detroit, MI

Oldenquist, Riek A., Libn.
OHIO STATE DEPARTMENT OF DEVELOPMENT - DIVISION OF ENERGY - ENERGY LIBRARY □ Columbus, OH

Oldham, Ellen, Asst.Kpr./Rare Books
BOSTON PUBLIC LIBRARY - RARE BOOKS AND MANUSCRIPTS □ Boston, MA

Oldham, Linda, Non-Print Coll.Libn.
FANSHAWE COLLEGE OF APPLIED ARTS AND TECHNOLOGY - MAIN LIBRARY □ London, ON

Oldham, Mary E., Res.Serv.Anl.
MOBIL OIL CORPORATION - LIBRARY/SECRETARIAT □ Fairfax, VA

Oldman, Vera, Pres., Musm.Corp.
GRAND ENCAMPMENT MUSEUM, INC. - LIBRARY □ Encampment, WY

Olds, Karen, Ref.Libn.
AEROSPACE CORPORATION - CHARLES C. LAURITSEN LIBRARY □ Los Angeles, CA

Oldsen, Diana, Lib.Techn.
UNIVERSITY OF COLORADO, BOULDER - INSTITUTE OF BEHAVIORAL SCIENCE - IBS RESEARCH LIBRARY □ Boulder, CO

O'Leary, Patrick, Libn.
CROSBY, HEAFEY, ROACH & MAY - LAW LIBRARY □ Oakland, CA

O'Leary, Timothy J., Dir., File Res.
HUMAN RELATIONS AREA FILES, INC. □ New Haven, CT

Olechno, Gillian, Dir.
DANIEL FREEMAN MEMORIAL HOSPITAL - MEDICAL LIBRARY & RESOURCE CENTER □ Los Angeles, CA

Olechno, Jill, Lib.Dir.
DANIEL FREEMAN MARINA HOSPITAL MEDICAL LIBRARY & RESOURCE CENTER □ Marina del Rey, CA

Oleksy, Mary, Libn.
REAL ESTATE RESEARCH CORPORATION - LIBRARY □ Chicago, IL

Olenick, Monte, Div.Chf.
BROOKLYN PUBLIC LIBRARY - LANGUAGE AND LITERATURE DIVISION □ Brooklyn, NY

Oler, Christine, Ref.Libn.
METHODIST HOSPITAL OF INDIANA, INC. - LIBRARY SERVICES □ Indianapolis, IN

Oleszkiewicz, Wanda, Libn.
HUSKY OIL OPERATIONS LTD. - LIBRARY/RECORDS MANAGEMENT □ Calgary, AB

O'Lexa, Elizabeth
ALTERNATIVE PRESS CENTER - LIBRARY □ Baltimore, MD

Olian, Irving, Libn.
TEMPLE BETH EL - LIBRARY† □ Plainfield, NJ

Olin, Ferris, Art Libn.
RUTGERS UNIVERSITY, THE STATE UNIVERSITY OF NEW JERSEY - ART LIBRARY □ New Brunswick, NJ

Olin, Joyce, Govt.Docs./Ref.Libn.
DE PAUL UNIVERSITY - LAW SCHOOL LIBRARY □ Chicago, IL

Olinger, Elizabeth B., Libr.Dir.
GREENVILLE TECHNICAL COLLEGE - LEARNING RESOURCES CENTER □ Greenville, SC

Olivares, Jose, Ser.
LAWRENCE BERKELEY LABORATORY - LIBRARY □ Berkeley, CA

Olivas, Arthur L., Photographic Archv.
MUSEUM OF NEW MEXICO - PHOTOGRAPHIC ARCHIVES □ Santa Fe, NM

Olive, Betsy Ann, Libn.
CORNELL UNIVERSITY - GRADUATE SCHOOL OF MANAGEMENT - LIBRARY □ Ithaca, NY

Oliver, Anthony M., Libn.
HAWAII STATE DEPARTMENT OF PLANNING & ECONOMIC DEVELOPMENT - LIBRARY □ Honolulu, HI

Oliver, Bobbie E., Adm.Libn.
MEMPHIS THEOLOGICAL SEMINARY - LIBRARY† □ Memphis, TN

Oliver, Carolyn, Libn.
NORTH OAKLAND GENEALOGICAL SOCIETY - LIBRARY □ Lake Orion, MI

Oliver, Diane, Act.Libn.
FLINT INSTITUTE OF ARTS - LIBRARY □ Flint, MI

Oliver, Florence S., Archv.
SOMERS HISTORICAL SOCIETY - LIBRARY AND ARCHIVES □ Somers, NY

Oliver, Frances M., Tech.Libn.
TECHNOLOGY APPLICATIONS, INC. - TECHNICAL LIBRARY □ Falls Church, VA

Oliver, Helen R., Libn.
CALAIS FREE LIBRARY □ Calais, ME

Oliver, Jessie, Asst., Tchg.Mtls.Ctr.
ANDREWS UNIVERSITY - JAMES WHITE LIBRARY† □ Berrien Springs, MI

Oliver, Lon, AV
NORTHWEST CHRISTIAN COLLEGE - LEARNING RESOURCE CENTER □ Eugene, OR

Oliver, Mary W., Law Libn.
UNIVERSITY OF NORTH CAROLINA, CHAPEL HILL - LAW LIBRARY □ Chapel Hill, NC

Oliver, P.A., Mgr.
GENERAL ELECTRIC COMPANY - TECHNICAL INFORMATION EXCHANGE □ Schenectady, NY

Oliver, Patricia A., Libn.
LOUISIANA STATE DEPARTMENT OF JUSTICE - OFFICE OF THE ATTORNEY GENERAL - HUEY P. LONG MEMORIAL LAW LIBRARY □ Baton Rouge, LA

Olivera, Ruth, Asst.Mss.Cat.
TULANE UNIVERSITY OF LOUISIANA - LATIN AMERICAN LIBRARY □ New Orleans, LA

Olivetti, Trudy, Cat.
NATIONAL GALLERY OF ART - LIBRARY □ Washington, DC

Olivier, Daniel, Dept.Hd.
BIBLIOTHEQUE DE LA VILLE DE MONTREAL - COLLECTION GAGNON □ Montreal, PQ

Olivier, Evelyn, Spec.Proj.
UNIVERSITY OF TEXAS HEALTH SCIENCE CENTER, SAN ANTONIO - LIBRARY □ San Antonio, TX

Olivier, Suzanne, Chief
INSTITUT NAZARETH ET LOUIS-BRAILLE - BIBLIOTHEQUE PUBLIQUE □ Longueuil, PQ

Olm, Jane G., Dir.
TEXAS TECH UNIVERSITY - SCHOOL OF LAW LIBRARY □ Lubbock, TX

Olmstead, Marcia, Asst.Libn.
GTE PRODUCTS CORPORATION - SYLVANIA SYSTEMS GROUP - WESTERN DIVISION - TECHNICAL LIBRARY □ Mountain View, CA

Olmsted, Wilma, Lib.Techn.
SASKATCHEWAN - DEPARTMENT OF EDUCATION - RESOURCE CENTRE □ Regina, SK

Olney, Elaine, Asst.Libn.
RILEY COUNTY GENEALOGICAL SOCIETY - LIBRARY □ Manhattan, KS

Oloizia, Richard
ALTERNATIVE PRESS CENTER - LIBRARY □ Baltimore, MD

Olsen, C., Res.Libn.
CANADIAN PACIFIC, LTD. - CORPORATE LIBRARY/INFORMATION CENTRE □ Montreal, PQ

Olsen, James L., Jr., Libn.
NATIONAL ACADEMY OF SCIENCES - NATIONAL ACADEMY OF ENGINEERING - LIBRARY □ Washington, DC

Olsen, Jan, Libn.
CORNELL UNIVERSITY - ALBERT R. MANN LIBRARY □ Ithaca, NY

Olsen, Robert A., Jr., Libn.
TEXAS CHRISTIAN UNIVERSITY - MARY COUTS BURNETT LIBRARY - BRITE DIVINITY SCHOOL COLLECTION □ Fort Worth, TX

Olsen, Rowena, Libn.
MC PHERSON COLLEGE - MILLER LIBRARY □ McPherson, KS

Olsen, Thomas M., Pres.
UFO INFORMATION RETRIEVAL CENTER, INC. □ Phoenix, AZ

Olsgaard, Jane K., Mgr., Lib.Serv.
CARLE FOUNDATION HOSPITAL - LIBRARY □ Urbana, IL

Olshan, Laura, Libn.
TEMPLE BETH SHOLOM - HERBERT GOLDBERG MEMORIAL LIBRARY† □ Haddon Heights, NJ

Olson, Anton, Asst.Cat.
NORTHWESTERN UNIVERSITY - HEALTH SCIENCES LIBRARY† □ Chicago, IL

Olson, April, Lib.Asst.
CALIFORNIA INSTITUTE OF TECHNOLOGY - CHEMICAL ENGINEERING LIBRARY □ Pasadena, CA

Olson, Carol, Order Libn.
LUTHER NORTHWESTERN SEMINARY - LIBRARY □ St. Paul, MN

Olson, Carol R., Asst.Libn.
NEW YORK STATE DEPARTMENT OF TRANSPORTATION - PUBLIC TRANSPORTATION - LIBRARY □ Albany, NY

Olson, David, Asst.Libn.
DISTRICT ONE TECHNICAL INSTITUTE - LIBRARY - EDUCATIONAL RESOURCE CENTER □ Eau Claire, WI

Olson, David, Ref.Libn.
UNIVERSITY OF MIAMI - SCHOOL OF MEDICINE - LOUIS CALDER MEMORIAL LIBRARY □ Miami, FL

Olson, David J., State Archv.
NORTH CAROLINA STATE DEPT. OF CULTURAL
RESOURCES - DIV. OF ARCHIVES AND HISTORY
- ARCHIVES & RECORDS SECTION □ Raleigh, NC
Olson, Dianne, Cat./Acq.Libn.
LOYOLA UNIVERSITY OF CHICAGO - MEDICAL
CENTER LIBRARY □ Maywood, IL
Olson, Donald D., Tech.Serv.Libn.
UNIVERSITY OF NORTH DAKOTA - OLAF H.
THORMODSGARD LAW LIBRARY □ Grand Forks,
ND
Olson, Douglas A., Libn.
EASTERN WASHINGTON STATE HISTORICAL
SOCIETY - LIBRARY □ Spokane, WA
Olson, Eric, Dir. of Lib.Serv.
REID AND PRIEST - LAW LIBRARY □ New York,
NY
Olson, G., Ref.Libn.
UNIVERSITY OF ALBERTA - HUMANITIES AND
SOCIAL SCIENCES LIBRARY □ Edmonton, AB
Olson, Gordon, Hd.
GRAND RAPIDS PUBLIC LIBRARY - MICHIGAN
ROOM □ Grand Rapids, MI
Olson, Guni, Hd.Libn.
GRACE BIBLE COLLEGE - BULTEMA MEMORIAL
LIBRARY □ Grand Rapids, MI
Olson, Joann, Hum.Libn.
MIAMI UNIVERSITY - ART AND
ARCHITECTURE LIBRARY □ Oxford, OH
Olson, Karen, Libn.
EASTERN WASHINGTON UNIVERSITY - MUSIC
LIBRARY □ Cheney, WA
Olson, Leona, Lib.Supv.
CO-OPERATIVE COLLEGE OF CANADA -
LIBRARY SERVICES □ Saskatoon, SK
Olson, N.J., Hd.Libn.
GREAT LAKES BIBLE COLLEGE - LOUIS M.
DETRO MEMORIAL LIBRARY □ Lansing, MI
Olson, Nancy S., Libn.
PENINSULA CONSERVATION FOUNDATION -
LIBRARY OF THE ENVIRONMENT □ Palo Alto, CA
Olson, Neil B., Dir. of Libs.
SALEM STATE COLLEGE - LIBRARY - SPECIAL
COLLECTIONS □ Salem, MA
Olson, Orville K., Cur. of Musm.
GOODHUE COUNTY HISTORICAL SOCIETY -
LIBRARY □ Red Wing, MN
Olson, Paula, Asst.Libn.
AMERICAN COLLEGE OF OBSTETRICIANS AND
GYNECOLOGISTS - RESOURCE CENTER □
Washington, DC
Olson, Ray A., Ref.Libn.
LUTHER NORTHWESTERN SEMINARY -
LIBRARY □ St. Paul, MN
Olson, Robert, Mgr.
UTAH STATE BOARD OF EDUCATION - UTAH
INFORMATION TECHNICAL DEMONSTRATION
CENTER □ Salt Lake City, UT
Olson, Roxie, Med.Libn.
SACRED HEART HOSPITAL - MEDICAL LIBRARY
□ Yankton, SD
Olson, Rue E., Libn.
ILLINOIS AGRICULTURAL ASSOCIATION - IAA
AND AFFILIATED COMPANIES LIBRARY □
Bloomington, IL
Olson, Sally, Cat.
PILLSBURY COMPANY - TECHNICAL
INFORMATION CENTER □ Minneapolis, MN
Olson-Bullis, Barbara, Med.Libn.
GALESBURG COTTAGE HOSPITAL - HEALTH
SERVICES LIBRARY □ Galesburg, IL
Olsson, Diane T., Ref.Libn.
AMERICAN ARBITRATION ASSOCIATION -
EASTMAN ARBITRATION LIBRARY □ New York,
NY
Olstead, Patricia B., Chf., Lib.Serv.
U.S. ARMY - NATICK RESEARCH AND
DEVELOPMENT CENTER - TECHNICAL LIBRARY
□ Natick, MA
Olver, Meredith, Ref.Libn.
THOMPSON (J. Walter) COMPANY -
INFORMATION CENTER □ New York, NY

O'Mahoney, Elizabeth, V.P.
GOLDMAN, SACHS AND COMPANY - LIBRARY □
New York, NY
O'Malley, Rev. Kenneth, C.P., Lib.Dir.
CATHOLIC THEOLOGICAL UNION AT CHICAGO
- LIBRARY □ Chicago, IL
O'Malley, Nora, AV Libn.
DELAWARE VALLEY COLLEGE OF SCIENCE AND
AGRICULTURE - JOSEPH KRAUSKOPF
MEMORIAL LIBRARY □ Doylestown, PA
O'Malley, William, Arch.
COLUMBIA UNIVERSITY - AVERY
ARCHITECTURAL AND FINE ARTS LIBRARY □
New York, NY
Omar, Eric
UNIVERSITY OF PUERTO RICO - PUERTO
RICAN COLLECTION† □ Rio Piedras, PR
O'Meara, Kathleen C., Hd.
CHICAGO PUBLIC LIBRARY CENTRAL LIBRARY -
GENERAL INFORMATION SERVICES DIVISION-
BIBLIOGRAPHIC & ILL CENTER □ Chicago, IL
O'Neal, Carroll, Dir.
CALVARY BAPTIST CHURCH - LIBRARY □
Kansas City, MO
O'Neal, Ellis E., Jr., Libn.
ANDOVER NEWTON THEOLOGICAL SCHOOL -
TRASK LIBRARY □ Newton Centre, MA
O'Neal, Pat, Circ.Libn.
MERCER UNIVERSITY - LAW SCHOOL -
FURMAN SMITH LAW LIBRARY □ Macon, GA
O'Neal, Terrie, Lib.Techn.
UNIVERSITY OF COLORADO, BOULDER - EARTH
SCIENCES LIBRARY □ Boulder, CO
O'Neil, Cynthia, Libn.
MANCHESTER CITY LIBRARY - NEW
HAMPSHIRE ROOM □ Manchester, NH
O'Neil, Gary, Dir. of Res.
WASHINGTON STATE DEPARTMENT OF
REVENUE - RESEARCH AND INFORMATION
DIVISION □ Olympia, WA
O'Neill, Jennifer E., Cur.
ARCANE ORDER - LIBRARY □ Falls Church, VA
O'Neill, Mary, Libn.
ARTHUR ANDERSEN & CO. - LIBRARY† □
Toronto, ON
O'Neill, Mary E., Res.Libn.
SYRACUSE RESEARCH CORPORATION -
LIBRARY □ Syracuse, NY
O'Neill, Nancy, Hd., Rd.Serv.
SANTA MONICA PUBLIC LIBRARY -
CALIFORNIA SPECIAL COLLECTION □ Santa
Monica, CA
O'Neill, P., Ref.
WIDENER UNIVERSITY - WOLFGRAM
MEMORIAL LIBRARY □ Chester, PA
O'Neill, Robert K., Dir.
INDIANA HISTORICAL SOCIETY - WILLIAM
HENRY SMITH MEMORIAL LIBRARY □
Indianapolis, IN
O'Neill, Susan, Cat.Libn.
MEDICAL COLLEGE OF WISCONSIN -
LIBRARIES □ Milwaukee, WI
O'Neill, Suzanne, Pub.Serv.Libn.
FANSHAWE COLLEGE OF APPLIED ARTS AND
TECHNOLOGY - MAIN LIBRARY □ London, ON
Onesto, Dr. Serene, Coord., Lrng.Rsrcs.
CHICAGO STATE UNIVERSITY - DOUGLAS
LIBRARY - SPECIAL COLLECTIONS† □ Chicago,
IL
Oniewski, Rose, Doc.Libn.
SOUTH DAKOTA STATE LIBRARY & ARCHIVES □
Pierre, SD
Ono, Margaret, Base Libn.
U.S. AIR FORCE BASE - MC CHORD BASE
LIBRARY □ McChord AFB, WA
Onsager, Lawrence W., Lib.Dir.
UNION COLLEGE - ELLA JOHNSON CRANDALL
MEMORIAL LIBRARY - SPECIAL COLLECTIONS
□ Lincoln, NE
Onsi, Patricia, Assoc.Libn., Tech.Serv
SUNY - UPSTATE MEDICAL CENTER LIBRARY □
Syracuse, NY

Ooi, Grace, Cat.
COLUMBIA UNIVERSITY - LAW LIBRARY □ New
York, NY
Opar, Barbara, Arch.Bibliog.
SYRACUSE UNIVERSITY - E.S. BIRD LIBRARY -
FINE ARTS DEPARTMENT □ Syracuse, NY
Opas, Margaret, Asst.Libn.
THOMPSON (J. Walter) COMPANY -
INFORMATION CENTER □ Chicago, IL
Opgrand, Harold J., Dir., Media Rsrcs.
UNIVERSITY OF MINNESOTA, CROOKSTON -
KIEHLE LIBRARY - MEDIA RESOURCES □
Crookston, MN
Oppedal, Teresa, Assoc. Law Libn.
MORRISON & FOERSTER - LAW LIBRARY □ San
Francisco, CA
Oppenheim, Linda, Libn.
PRINCETON UNIVERSITY - WOODROW
WILSON SCHOOL OF PUBLIC AND
INTERNATIONAL AFFAIRS - LIBRARY □
Princeton, NJ
Oppenheim, Micha F., Libn.
AMERICAN JEWISH JOINT DISTRIBUTION
COMMITTEE - LIBRARY □ New York, NY
Oppenheim, Roberta, Libn.
FORSYTH DENTAL CENTER - PERCY HOWE
MEMORIAL LIBRARY □ Boston, MA
Oppenheimer, Gerald J., Dir.
UNIVERSITY OF WASHINGTON - HEALTH
SCIENCES LIBRARY □ Seattle, WA
Oquita, Paula, Libn.
LOGICON, INC. - TACTICAL & TRAINING
SYSTEMS DIVISION LIBRARY □ San Diego, CA
Oraha, O. Paul, Libn.
BECHTEL CIVIL & MINERALS, INC. - MINING &
METALS BUSINESS DEVELOPMENT LIBRARY □
San Francisco, CA
Orbach, Marvin, Ref.Libn.
CONCORDIA UNIVERSITY - LOYOLA CAMPUS -
GEORGES P. VANIER LIBRARY □ Montreal, PQ
Orcutt, Roberta K., D.R.I. Libn.
UNIVERSITY OF NEVADA, RENO - DESERT
RESEARCH INSTITUTE - DANDINI PARK
LIBRARY □ Reno, NV
Orcutt, Roberta K., D.R.I./Phys.Sci.Libn.
UNIVERSITY OF NEVADA, RENO - DESERT
RESEARCH INSTITUTE - LIBRARY □ Reno, NV
Orcutt, Roberta K., Physical Sci.Libn.
UNIVERSITY OF NEVADA, RENO - PHYSICAL
SCIENCES LIBRARY □ Reno, NV
Ordonez, Maria E., Libn.
UNIVERSITY OF PUERTO RICO - PUERTO
RICAN COLLECTION† □ Rio Piedras, PR
Ordway, Jane, Info.Serv.Coord.
WOMEN'S ACTION ALLIANCE, INC. - LIBRARY
□ New York, NY
O'Rear, Pat, Info.Spec.
WESTINGHOUSE ELECTRIC CORPORATION -
WESTINGHOUSE NUCLEAR TRAINING CENTER
- INFORMATION RSRC. CENTER† □ Zion, IL
Orfanos, Minnie, Hd.Libn.
NORTHWESTERN UNIVERSITY - DENTAL
SCHOOL LIBRARY □ Chicago, IL
Orfirer, Lenore F., Librarian
SANTA MONICA HOSPITAL MEDICAL CENTER -
LIBRARY □ Santa Monica, CA
Origlio, Marjorie, Children's Libn.
HUDSON LIBRARY AND HISTORICAL SOCIETY □
Hudson, OH
Orion, Carol, Bus.Libn.
WEYERHAEUSER COMPANY - CORPORATE
LIBRARY □ Tacoma, WA
O'Riordan, Georgeanne, Hd., Access Serv.
COLUMBIA UNIVERSITY - AMBROSE MONELL
ENGINEERING LIBRARY □ New York, NY
Orlando, Richard, Supv.
BANK OF MONTREAL - BUSINESS
INFORMATION CENTRE □ Montreal, PQ
Orlino, Demetrio, Evening Pub.Serv.
LOYOLA LAW SCHOOL - LIBRARY □ Los Angeles,
CA

Orloske, Margaret Q., Corp.Libn. & Hist.
TRAVELERS INSURANCE COMPANIES -
CORPORATE LIBRARY □ Hartford, CT

Orlov, Vladimir, Dir.
UNITED NATIONS HEADQUARTERS - DAG
HAMMARSKJOLD LIBRARY □ New York, NY

Orlowski, Bronnie, Hd., BNL Rpts.Sect.
BROOKHAVEN NATIONAL LABORATORY -
TECHNICAL INFORMATION DIVISION □ Upton,
NY

Orman, Margaret, Ref.Libn.
U.S. VETERANS ADMINISTRATION (MD-Perry
Point) - HOSPITAL MEDICAL LIBRARY □ Perry
Point, MD

Orman, Reba, First Asst.
MEMPHIS-SHELBY COUNTY PUBLIC LIBRARY
AND INFO. CTR. - SCIENCE/BUSINESS/SOCIAL
SCI.DEPT. □ Memphis, TN

Ormerod, Barbara, Res./Data Mgt.Mgr.
MORGAN STANLEY & COMPANY, INC. -
LIBRARY SERVICES □ New York, NY

Ormond, Linda, Libn.
KALAMAZOO NATURE CENTER - REFERENCE
LIBRARY □ Kalamazoo, MI

Ormsby, Eric, Cur.
PRINCETON UNIVERSITY - NEAR EAST
COLLECTIONS† □ Princeton, NJ

Orosz, Barbara J., Hd.Libn.
UNION OIL COMPANY OF CALIFORNIA -
TECHNICAL INFORMATION CENTER □
Placentia, CA

O'Rourke, Kerry, Ref.Libn.
UNIV. OF MEDICINE & DENTISTRY OF NJ -
RUTGERS MED. SCHOOL - MIDDLESEX
GENERAL-UNIV. HOSPITAL - HEALTH SCI.LIB. □
New Brunswick, NJ

O'Rourke, Linda R., Med.Libn.
UNIVERSITY OF OKLAHOMA - HEALTH
SCIENCES CENTER - DEPARTMENT OF
SURGERY LIBRARY □ Oklahoma City, OK

O'Rourke, Margaret M., Libn.
REES-STEALY MEDICAL GROUP - LIBRARY □
San Diego, CA

O'Rourke, Peg
GEORGETOWN UNIVERSITY - BLOMMER
SCIENCE LIBRARY □ Washington, DC

O'Rourke, Sean, Dir.
NATIONAL CLEARINGHOUSE FOR ALCOHOL
INFORMATION - LIBRARY† □ Rockville, MD

O'Rourke, Terrie, Info.Spec.
INFORMATION HANDLING SERVICES - LIBRARY
□ Englewood, CO

Orr, Carolyn B., Libn.
U.S. NAVY - NAVAL SHIPYARD (VA-Norfolk) -
TECHNICAL LIBRARY† □ Portsmouth, VA

Orr, Jay, Hd., Tech.Serv.
COUNTRY MUSIC FOUNDATION - LIBRARY AND
MEDIA CENTER □ Nashville, TN

Orr, Judy, Hd.Libn., Ref. & Res.Serv
VANDERBILT UNIVERSITY - MEDICAL CENTER
LIBRARY □ Nashville, TN

Orr, Margaret, Govt.Libn.
NORTHWEST TERRITORIES - GOVERNMENT
LIBRARY □ Yellowknife, NT

Orr, Marty, Libn.
OREGON STATE DEPARTMENT OF REVENUE -
RESEARCH LIBRARY □ Salem, OR

Orr, Valerie J., Info.Dir.
NATIONAL WATER WELL ASSOCIATION -
NATIONAL GROUND WATER INFORMATION
CENTER □ Worthington, OH

Orr, Valorie, Asst. Area Hd.
UNIVERSITY OF CALGARY - ENVIRONMENT-
SCIENCE-TECHNOLOGY LIBRARY† □ Calgary,
AB

Orr, Dr. William M., Gen.Lib.Adm.
WARNER-PACIFIC COLLEGE - OTTO F. LINN
LIBRARY □ Portland, OR

Orraca, Sadako, Acq.
ICI AMERICAS INC. - ATLAS LIBRARY □
Wilmington, DE

Orser, Lawan, Cat.Libn.
UNIVERSITY OF FLORIDA - HUME LIBRARY □
Gainesville, FL

Orth, Kathy, Racine & Elkhorn Libn.
GATEWAY VOCATIONAL TECHNICAL & ADULT
EDUCATION DISTRICT - LEARNING
RESOURCES CENTER □ Kenosha, WI

Ortiz, Angie, Lib.Ck.
TAUB (Ben) GENERAL HOSPITAL - DOCTOR'S
MEDICAL LIBRARY □ Houston, TX

Ortiz, Cynthia, Libn.
U.S. DEPT. OF ENERGY - NEVADA OPERATIONS
OFFICE - TECHNICAL LIBRARY □ Las Vegas, NV

Ortiz, Daniel
UNIVERSITY OF PUERTO RICO - SCHOOL OF
PUBLIC ADMINISTRATION - LIBRARY† □ Rio
Piedras, PR

Ortiz, Diane, Mgt.Anl./Rec.Mgt.Coord.
LAS VEGAS - CITY MANAGER'S LIBRARY □ Las
Vegas, NV

Ortiz, Maria, Archv.
FRESNO CITY AND COUNTY HISTORICAL
SOCIETY - ARCHIVES □ Fresno, CA

Ortutay, Phyllis, Chf.
U.S. ARMY - MATERIEL DEVELOPMENT &
READINESS COMMAND - HEADQUARTERS -
TECHNICAL LIBRARY □ Alexandria, VA

Osbaldiston, Diana, Cat.Libn.
UNIVERSITY OF SOUTH CAROLINA - COLEMAN
KARESH LAW LIBRARY □ Columbia, SC

Osborn, Linda, Libn.
SCUDDER, STEVENS & CLARK - LIBRARY □ New
York, NY

Osborn, Nicole, Libn.
STRAWBERY BANKE, INC. - THAYER CUMINGS
HISTORICAL REFERENCE LIBRARY □
Portsmouth, NH

Osborn, Russell, Chf. Ranger
U.S. NATL. PARK SERVICE - SCOTTS BLUFF
NATL. MONUMENT - LIBRARY □ Gerling, NE

Osborn, Walter, Ref.Libn.
MOODY BIBLE INSTITUTE - LIBRARY □ Chicago,
IL

Osborn, Walter, Ref.Libn.
MOODY BIBLE INSTITUTE - MOODYANA
COLLECTION □ Chicago, IL

Osborne, Cecil, Lib.Cons.
PUEBLO CHIEFTAIN AND STAR-JOURNAL
PUBLISHING CORPORATION - LIBRARY □
Pueblo, CO

Osborne, James W., Libn.
NORTHEASTERN HOSPITAL - SCHOOL OF
NURSING LIBRARY □ Philadelphia, PA

Osborne, Nancy, Co-Coord.
SUNY - COLLEGE AT OSWEGO - PENFIELD
LIBRARY - SPECIAL COLLECTIONS □ Oswego,
NY

Osborne, Peter, III, Exec.Dir.
MINISINK VALLEY HISTORICAL SOCIETY -
LIBRARY □ Port Jervis, NY

Osborne, Robin A., Libn.
U.S. ARMY - CORPS OF ENGINEERS - FORT
WORTH DISTRICT - TECHNICAL LIBRARY† □
Fort Worth, TX

Osburn, Harriet S., Hd.Libn.
XEROX CORPORATION - XEROX EDUCATION
PUBLICATIONS - LIBRARY □ Middletown, CT

Osburn, Joan, Libn.
ST. PETER'S HOSPITAL - PROFESSIONAL
LIBRARY □ Hamilton, ON

Osburn, Ken, Info.Sys.Anl.
SANDIA NATIONAL LABORATORIES -
TECHNICAL LIBRARY □ Albuquerque, NM

Osenga, Annette, Media Libn.
LIFE CHIROPRACTIC COLLEGE-WEST -
LIBRARY □ San Lorenzo, CA

Oser, Charlotte, Adm.Off.
UNIVERSITY OF HAWAII - CENTER FOR
KOREAN STUDIES - LIBRARY □ Honolulu, HI

Osgood, James B., Asst.Hd./Cat.
KENNEDY-KING COLLEGE - LIBRARY† □
Chicago, IL

Osgood, William E., Libn.
CENTER FOR NORTHERN STUDIES - LIBRARY □
Wolcott, VT

O'Shaughnessy, John, Libn.
ROYAL BANK OF CANADA - INFORMATION
RESOURCES □ Montreal, PQ

O'Shea, Patricia R., Corp.Libn.
TEXASGULF, INC. - RESEARCH LIBRARY† □
Stamford, CT

Oshinsky, Carole, Ref.Libn.
COLUMBIA UNIVERSITY - CENTER FOR
POPULATION & FAMILY HEALTH - LIBRARY/
INFORMATION PROGRAM □ New York, NY

Oshiro, Ruby, Supv., User Serv.
AEROSPACE CORPORATION - CHARLES C.
LAURITSEN LIBRARY □ Los Angeles, CA

Osler, R., Coord., Boys & Girls Serv
TORONTO PUBLIC LIBRARY - MARGUERITE G.
BAGSHAW COLLECTION† □ Toronto, ON

Osmanson, Fleur C., Libn.
HILL, FARRER & BURRILL - LAW LIBRARY □ Los
Angeles, CA

Osorio, Nestor L., Sci.Libn.
NORTHERN ILLINOIS UNIVERSITY - FARADAY
LIBRARY □ DeKalb, IL

Osredker, Marty, Libn.
ST. JOHN'S HOSPITAL - SCHOOL OF NURSING
LIBRARY □ Springfield, MO

Ossenkop, David, Assoc.Libn.
SUNY - COLLEGE AT POTSDAM - CRANE MUSIC
LIBRARY □ Potsdam, NY

Ostergaard, Doris, Libn.
CANADA - NATIONAL FILM BOARD OF CANADA
- FILM LIBRARY □ Calgary, AB

Osterholm, Claire, Assoc.Libn.
GLENWOOD STATE HOSPITAL-SCHOOL - STAFF
LIBRARY □ Glenwood, IA

Ostertag, Ina, Dir.
LORETTO HOSPITAL - HEALTH SCIENCES
LIBRARY □ Chicago, IL

Ostraco, Delores, Chf., Circ.Serv.
U.S. ARMY POST - FORT BELVOIR - VAN NOY
LIBRARY □ Ft. Belvoir, VA

Ostrander, Dona, Curric.Libn.
CENTRAL CONNECTICUT STATE UNIVERSITY -
ELIHU BURRITT LIBRARY □ New Britain, CT

Ostrander, Sheila, Sr.Libn.
NEW YORK STATE LIBRARY - HUMANITIES
REFERENCE SECTION □ Albany, NY

Ostrem, Walter M., Libn.
ST. PAUL PUBLIC SCHOOLS INDEPENDENT
SCHOOL DISTRICT 625 - DISTRICT
PROFESSIONAL LIBRARY □ St. Paul, MN

Ostrove, Geraldine, Lib.Dir.
NEW ENGLAND CONSERVATORY OF MUSIC -
HARRIET M. SPAULDING LIBRARY □ Boston, MA

Ostrow, Julie, Tech.Libn.
STALEY (A.E.) MANUFACTURING COMPANY -
TECHNICAL INFORMATION CENTER □ Decatur,
IL

Ostrow, Stephen Edward, Chf.
LIBRARY OF CONGRESS - PRINTS &
PHOTOGRAPHS DIVISION □ Washington, DC

O'Sullivan, Jane C., Adm.Libn.
U.S. NAVY - NAVAL HOSPITAL (CA-Oakland) -
MEDICAL LIBRARY □ Oakland, CA

Osvald, Karen, Archv.Asst.
GEORGIA HISTORICAL SOCIETY - LIBRARY □
Savannah, GA

Oswald, Edward, Bus.Libn.
MIAMI-DADE PUBLIC LIBRARY - BUSINESS,
SCIENCE AND TECHNOLOGY DEPARTMENT □
Miami, FL

Oswald, Genevieve, Cur.
NEW YORK PUBLIC LIBRARY - PERFORMING
ARTS RESEARCH CENTER - DANCE
COLLECTION □ New York, NY

Oswald, Rev. Robert M., Tech.Serv.
WISCONSIN LUTHERAN SEMINARY - LIBRARY
□ Mequon, WI

Oswalt, Paul, Libn.
DALLAS PUBLIC LIBRARY - HISTORY AND
SOCIAL SCIENCES DIVISION □ Dallas, TX

Oswley, Beatrice R., Lib.Asst. I
UNIVERSITY OF NEW ORLEANS - EARL K. LONG
LIBRARY - ARCHIVES & MANUSCRIPTS/
SPECIAL COLLECTIONS DEPT. □ New Orleans,
LA

Osysko, Halina, Libn.
MANUFACTURERS HANOVER TRUST COMPANY
- INTERNATIONAL ECONOMICS DEPARTMENT -
LIBRARY □ New York, NY

Ota, Diane, First Asst.
BOSTON PUBLIC LIBRARY - MUSIC
DEPARTMENT □ Boston, MA

Otero, Diana, Tariff Libn.
ATLAS TRAFFIC CONSULTANTS CORPORATION
- TARIFF DEPARTMENT LIBRARY □ Flushing, NY

Otis, Peg, Libn.
POLYCHROME CORPORATION - RESEARCH &
DEVELOPMENT LIBRARY† □ Yonkers, NY

Otness, Harold
SOUTHERN OREGON STATE COLLEGE -
LIBRARY □ Ashland, OR

O'Toole, James M., Archv.
ARCHDIOCESE OF BOSTON - ARCHIVES □
Brighton, MA

O'Toole, Susan, Ref.Libn.
FOLEY & LARDNER - LIBRARY □ Milwaukee, WI

Ott, John, Dir.
ATLANTA HISTORICAL SOCIETY - ARCHIVES □
Atlanta, GA

Ott, Kathleen Galiher, Mgr.
TRW, INC. - INFORMATION CENTER/
GOVERNMENT RELATIONS □ Arlington, VA

Ott, Linda, Hd., Ref.Dept.
MORRIS COUNTY FREE LIBRARY - NEW JERSEY
COLLECTION □ Whippany, NJ

Ott, Vera, Libn.
MANITOBA - HEALTH SERVICES COMMISSION
- LIBRARY □ Winnipeg, MB

Ott, Wendell, Dir.
ROSWELL MUSEUM AND ART CENTER - ART
LIBRARY □ Roswell, NM

Otten, Mallory, Audit Libn.
COOPERS & LYBRAND - AUDIT LIBRARY □
Chicago, IL

Ottenheimer, Carole, Libn.
LONG ISLAND UNIVERSITY - C.W. POST
CAMPUS - CENTER FOR BUSINESS RESEARCH □
Greenvale, NY

Ottesen, Carol, Libn.
ALASKA STATE DEPARTMENT OF
TRANSPORTATION & PUBLIC FACILITIES -
TECHNICAL LIBRARY □ Juneau, AK

Otting, Martha F., Libn.
PINELLAS COUNTY LAW LIBRARY - ST.
PETERSBURG BRANCH □ St. Petersburg, FL

Otto, A. Stuart, Dir.
INVISIBLE MINISTRY - LIBRARY □ San Marcos,
CA

Otto, Betty J., Libn./Cur.
U.S. NATL. PARK SERVICE - ANTIETAM NATL.
BATTLEFIELD - VISITOR CENTER LIBRARY □
Sharpsburg, MD

Otto, Kathie, Newspaper Cat.
MONTANA HISTORICAL SOCIETY - LIBRARY/
ARCHIVES □ Helena, MT

Otto, Dr. Theophil, Asst.Libn.
SOUTHERN ILLINOIS UNIVERSITY,
CARBONDALE - HUMANITIES DIVISION
LIBRARY □ Carbondale, IL

Otwaska, Dennis, Supv., Adm.Serv.
WALKER MANUFACTURING CO. - LIBRARY □
Racine, WI

Oubraham, Ourida, Info.Serv.Libn.
STEVENS INSTITUTE OF TECHNOLOGY -
SAMUEL C. WILLIAMS LIBRARY □ Hoboken, NJ

Ouellet, Angelo, Asst.Libn.
COLLEGE DOMINICAIN DE PHILOSOPHIE ET DE
THEOLOGIE - BIBLIOTHEQUE □ Ottawa, ON

Ouellette, Billie Jean, Assoc.Dir.
FLORIDA STATE DIVISION OF BLIND SERVICES
- FLORIDA REGIONAL LIB. FOR THE BLIND &
PHYSICALLY HANDICAPPED □ Daytona Beach,
FL

Ounan, Francis X., Per.Libn.
ST. CHARLES BORROMEO SEMINARY - RYAN
MEMORIAL LIBRARY □ Philadelphia, PA

Oussoren, Mary-Jane, Asst.Libn.
MC CARTHY AND MC CARTHY - LIBRARY □
Toronto, ON

Outhouse, Carole, Res.Tech.
SAN DIEGO STATE UNIVERSITY - SOCIAL
SCIENCE RESEARCH LABORATORY - LIBRARY □
San Diego, CA

Ouyang, Ellen, Tech.Serv.Libn.
UNIVERSITY OF UTAH - LAW LIBRARY □ Salt
Lake City, UT

Ouzts, Philip A., Dir.
U.S. DEPT. OF COMMERCE - INTERNATIONAL
TRADE ADMINISTRATION - RICHMOND
DISTRICT OFFICE LIBRARY □ Richmond, VA

Overbay, Kathleen G., Dir., Lib.Serv.
SOUTHWESTERN STATE HOSPITAL -
PROFESSIONAL LIBRARY □ Marion, VA

Overbeck, Dr. James A., Lib.Dir.
COLUMBIA THEOLOGICAL SEMINARY - JOHN
BULOW CAMPBELL LIBRARY □ Decatur, GA

Overby, Mary E., Cur., Spec.Coll.
GEORGIA BAPTIST HISTORICAL SOCIETY -
LIBRARY □ Macon, GA

Overstad, Elizabeth, Toy Lib.Dir.
TOYS 'N THINGS, TRAINING & RESOURCE
CENTER, INC. □ St. Paul, MN

Overstreet, Sue, Libn.
AMERICAN STATES INSURANCE COMPANY -
LIBRARY □ Indianapolis, IN

Overstreet, Vickie A., Med.Libn.
BAPTIST HOSPITAL - LIBRARY† □ Nashville, TN

Overton, Julie M., Coord., Local Hist.
GREENE COUNTY DISTRICT LIBRARY - GREENE
COUNTY ROOM □ Xenia, OH

Overwein, Martha A., Div.Hd.
DAYTON AND MONTGOMERY COUNTY PUBLIC
LIBRARY - INDUSTRY AND SCIENCE DIVISION
□ Dayton, OH

Ovitsky, Margaret, Hd., Info.Serv.
UNIVERSITY OF ILLINOIS AT CHICAGO -
HEALTH SCIENCES CENTER - LIBRARY OF THE
HEALTH SCIENCES □ Chicago, IL

Owaki, Stephanie, Cat.
UNIVERSITY OF SOUTHERN CALIFORNIA - LAW
LIBRARY □ Los Angeles, CA

Owaroff, Jessica S., Libn.
WOMEN'S CENTER OF SOUTHEASTERN
CONNECTICUT - LIBRARY □ New London, CT

Owen, Alice G., Libn.
NEIGHBORHOOD PLAYHOUSE SCHOOL OF THE
THEATRE - IRENE LEWISOHN LIBRARY† □ New
York, NY

Owen, Allison C.V., Libn.
CORE LABORATORIES, INC. - LIBRARY □ Dallas,
TX

Owen, Amy, Deputy Dir.
UTAH STATE LIBRARY □ Salt Lake City, UT

Owen, Avia, Info.Spec.
CRAVATH, SWAINE, & MOORE - LAW LIBRARY
□ New York, NY

Owen, Barbara L., Libn.
UNITED WAY OF AMERICA - INFORMATION
CENTER □ Alexandria, VA

Owen, Bernice, Cat.Libn.
GONZAGA UNIVERSITY SCHOOL OF LAW -
LIBRARY □ Spokane, WA

Owen, Beth Charnley, Libn.
BENDIX CORPORATION - ENGINEERING
LIBRARY □ Teterboro, NJ

Owen, Eleen M., Libn.
KANSAS TECHNICAL INSTITUTE - TULLIS
RESOURCE CENTER □ Salina, KS

Owen, Katherine, Mgr.
WARNER-LAMBERT/PARKE-DAVIS -
RESEARCH LIBRARY† □ Ann Arbor, MI

Owen, Myra, Dir.
UNIVERSITY OF OTTAWA - HEALTH SCIENCES
LIBRARY □ Ottawa, ON

Owen, Thomas, Asst.Dir.
UNIVERSITY OF LOUISVILLE - UNIVERSITY
ARCHIVES AND RECORDS CENTER □ Louisville,
KY

Owen, Tom, Audio Engr.
NEW YORK PUBLIC LIBRARY - PERFORMING
ARTS RESEARCH CENTER - RODGERS &
HAMMERSTEIN ARCHIVES OF RECORDED
SOUND □ New York, NY

Owen, Valerie, Lib.Supv.
NEW BRUNSWICK RESEARCH AND
PRODUCTIVITY COUNCIL - LIBRARY □
Fredericton, NB

Owens, Beth, Med.libn.
U.S. VETERANS ADMINISTRATION (AL-
Birmingham) - HOSPITAL MEDICAL LIBRARY □
Birmingham, AL

Owens, Betty J., Libn.
U.S. BUREAU OF THE CENSUS - INFORMATION
SERVICES PROGRAM - SEATTLE REGIONAL
OFFICE - LIBRARY □ Seattle, WA

Owens, Bob, Ref.Libn.
ALAMEDA COUNTY LAW LIBRARY □ Oakland, CA

Owens, Carla W., Mgr.
BOOZ, ALLEN & HAMILTON, INC. - LIBRARY □
Chicago, IL

Owens, David, Dp. State Archv.
WASHINGTON STATE OFFICE OF SECRETARY
OF STATE - DIVISION OF ARCHIVES AND
RECORD MANAGEMENT □ Olympia, WA

Owens, Debra, Dir., Tech.Serv.
AMERICAN SOCIETY FOR QUALITY CONTROL -
LIBRARY □ Milwaukee, WI

Owens, Dr. Frederick H., Mgr., Info.Serv.
ROHM & HAAS COMPANY - RESEARCH
DIVISION - INFORMATION SERVICES
DEPARTMENT □ Spring House, PA

Owens, H. Jean, Dir.
INSTITUTE OF GERONTOLOGY - GERONTOLOGY
LEARNING RESOURCES CENTER □ Detroit, MI

Owens, Irene, Libn.
HOWARD UNIVERSITY - SCHOOL OF DIVINITY
LIBRARY □ Washington, DC

Owens, James K., Chf.Archv.
U.S. NATL. ARCHIVES & RECORDS SERVICE -
FEDERAL ARCHIVES AND RECORDS CENTER,
REGION 1 □ Waltham, MA

Owens, Marillyn
MICHIGAN STATE UNIVERSITY - DOCUMENTS
LIBRARY □ East Lansing, MI

Owens, Noel
UNIVERSITY OF CALGARY - SOCIAL SCIENCES
LIBRARY† □ Calgary, AB

Owens, Patricia, Div.Hd.
CONNECTICUT STATE LIBRARY □ Hartford, CT

Owens-Smith, William T., Dir.
HUMAN RIGHTS INTERNET - LIBRARY □
Washington, DC

Owings, Erma, Dir.
BITTER ROOT VALLEY HISTORICAL SOCIETY -
RAVALLI COUNTY MUSEUM □ Hamilton, MT

Ownby, Joanna, Asst.Cur.
CROCKER ART MUSEUM - RESEARCH LIBRARY
□ Sacramento, CA

Ownby, Margaret, Cat./Asst.Libn.
COMMODITY FUTURES TRADING COMMISSION
- LIBRARY □ Washington, DC

Owsley, Lucile, Libn.
U.S. VETERANS ADMINISTRATION (NC-
Salisbury) - MEDICAL CENTER LIBRARY □
Salisbury, NC

Oxley, Anna, Regional Libn.
CANADA - FISHERIES & OCEANS - SCOTIA-
FUNDY REGIONAL LIBRARY □ Halifax, NS

Oxley, Claire, Res.Libn.
TEXAS RESEARCH LEAGUE - LIBRARY □ Austin,
TX

Oxley, Joseph H., Mgr.
BATTELLE-COLUMBUS LABORATORIES - STACK
GAS EMISSION CONTROL COORDINATION
CENTER - LIBRARY □ Columbus, OH

Oxman, Jim, Info.Serv.
SASKATCHEWAN - PROVINCIAL LIBRARY □
Regina, SK
Oxtoby, Lowell, AV Libn.
WESTERN ILLINOIS UNIVERSITY - LIBRARIES
□ Macomb, IL
Oyer, John S., Dir.
MENNONITE HISTORICAL LIBRARY □ Goshen,
IN
Oyer, Ken, Libn.
BERGAN MERCY HOSPITAL - MEDICAL LIBRARY
□ Omaha, NE
Oysler, Cory, Conservation
UNIVERSITY OF CINCINNATI - MEDICAL
CENTER LIBRARIES - HISTORY OF HEALTH
SCIENCES LIBRARY AND MUSEUM □ Cincinnati,
OH
Ozawa, Ritsuko T., Asst.Cur.
SMITH COLLEGE - RARE BOOK ROOM □
Northampton, MA
Ozeroff, Carole G., Libn.
CONGREGATION ADATH JESHURUN -
GOTTLIEB MEMORIAL LIBRARY □ Elkins Park,
PA
Ozment, Judith, Libn.
NATIONAL SPORTING LIBRARY, INC. □
Middleburg, VA
Ozolins, Ilga I., Coord.
OWENS-ILLINOIS - INFORMATION RESEARCH
DEPARTMENT □ Toledo, OH
Ozolins, Sulamit, Cat.Libn.
LUTHER NORTHWESTERN SEMINARY -
LIBRARY □ St. Paul, MN

P

Pabst, Kathleen T., Lib.Dir.
MECHANICS' INSTITUTE LIBRARY □ San
Francisco, CA
Pace, Marjorie, Libn.
BLUE CROSS AND BLUE SHIELD OF FLORIDA -
CORPORATE RESEARCH LIBRARY □
Jacksonville, FL
Pace, Mary, Ref.Libn.
NORTHWESTERN UNIVERSITY - DENTAL
SCHOOL LIBRARY □ Chicago, IL
Pacetti, Karen, Asst.Libn.
AKZO CHEMIE AMERICA - RESEARCH LIBRARY
□ McCook, IL
Pacey, Margaret, Ref. & Ser.Libn.
NEW BRUNSWICK - LEGISLATIVE LIBRARY □
Fredericton, NB
Pachefsky, Reva, Libn.
TREE OF LIFE PRESS - LIBRARY AND ARCHIVES
□ Gainesville, FL
Pachoca, Erlinda, Asst.Libn.
LIBRARY COMPANY OF THE BALTIMORE BAR -
LIBRARY □ Baltimore, MD
Pachter, Fern, Libn.
ATLANTA FULTON PUBLIC LIBRARY - IVAN
ALLEN, JR. DEPARTMENT OF SCIENCE,
INDUSTRY AND GOVERNMENT □ Atlanta, GA
Pachuta, June E., Slavic Bibliog.
UNIVERSITY OF ILLINOIS - SLAVIC AND EAST
EUROPEAN LIBRARY □ Urbana, IL
Package, John A., Chf.Libn.
U.S. VETERANS ADMINISTRATION (VT-White
River Junction) - ALLIED HEALTH SCIENCES
LIBRARY □ White River Junction, VT
Packard, Barbara, Chf.Cat.
UNIVERSITY OF MEDICINE AND DENTISTRY OF
NEW JERSEY AT NEWARK - GEORGE F. SMITH
LIBRARY □ Newark, NJ
Packer, June, Rec.Mgr.
AMERICAN PLYWOOD ASSOCIATION -
INFORMATION CENTER □ Tacoma, WA
Padala, Patricia, Libn.
UNIVERSITY OF MICHIGAN - CENTER FOR
CONTINUING EDUCATION OF WOMEN -
LIBRARY □ Ann Arbor, MI

Padden, Barbara K., Hd.
LIBRARY ASSOCIATION OF PORTLAND - ART
AND MUSIC DEPARTMENT □ Portland, OR
Padgett, Charles, Libn.
DIXON DEVELOPMENTAL CENTER -
PROFESSIONAL LIBRARY □ Dixon, IL
Padgett, LaCona Raines, Hd.Libn.
POLK COUNTY HISTORICAL AND
GENEALOGICAL LIBRARY □ Bartow, FL
Padgett, Mary
MC LENNAN COUNTY LAW LIBRARY† □ Waco,
TX
Padilla, Donald, Archv.
NEW MEXICO STATE COMMISSION OF PUBLIC
RECORDS AND ARCHIVES - ARCHIVAL
SERVICES DIVISION □ Santa Fe, NM
Padilla, Wanda L., Park Lib.Techn.
U.S. NATL. PARK SERVICE - MESA VERDE
NATL. PARK - MUSEUM LIBRARY □ Mesa Verde
Natl. Park, CO
Padnos, Mark, Libn.
MC GRAW-HILL, INC. - AVIATION WEEK &
SPACE TECHNOLOGY LIBRARY □ New York, NY
Padua, Noelia, Dir.
CATHOLIC UNIVERSITY OF PUERTO RICO -
MONSIGNOR JUAN FREMIOT TORRES OLIVER
LAW LIBRARY □ Ponce, PR
Padusis, Miriam D., Libn.
FRANKLIN INSTITUTE - LIBRARY □ Philadelphia,
PA
Paesani, Judith B., Asst.Dir.
UNIVERSITY OF CONNECTICUT - CENTER FOR
REAL ESTATE & URBAN ECONOMIC STUDIES -
REFERENCE & DOCUMENTS ROOM □ Storrs, CT
Paeth, Jean, Supv.Libn.
OAKLAND PUBLIC LIBRARY - HANDICAPPED
SERVICES □ Oakland, CA
Paeth, Ms. Zillah, Hd.Acq.Libn.
WESTERN OREGON STATE COLLEGE - LIBRARY
□ Monmouth, OR
Paff, Mr. Toby
PRINCETON UNIVERSITY - NEAR EAST
COLLECTIONS† □ Princeton, NJ
Page, Carol, Med.Libn.
ST. FRANCIS HOSPITAL - HEALTH SCIENCE
LIBRARY □ Poughkeepsie, NY
Page, E.J., Chf. Chemist
BELDING HEMINWAY COMPANY - BELDING
CORTICELLI RESEARCH CENTER - LIBRARY □
Putnam, CT
Page, Evelyn, Asst.Libn.
LUTHERAN HOSPITAL - MEDICAL STAFF
LIBRARY AND SCHOOL FOR NURSES LIBRARY □
Moline, IL
Page, G. Wilson, Asst.Rec.Off.
UNIVERSITY OF GEORGIA - DEPARTMENT OF
RECORDS MANAGEMENT & UNIVERSITY
ARCHIVES □ Athens, GA
Page, Joyce, Libn.
NATIONAL GENEALOGICAL SOCIETY - LIBRARY
□ Washington, DC
Page, Margareth, Techn., Docs.
HOPITAL DU SACRE COEUR - PAVILLON
ALBERT-PREVOST - MEDICAL LIBRARY† □
Montreal, PQ
Page, Mary, ILL Libn.
NEW JERSEY INSTITUTE OF TECHNOLOGY -
ROBERT W. VAN HOUTEN LIBRARY □ Newark,
NJ
Page, Melda W., Chf.Libn.
U.S. VETERANS ADMINISTRATION (ME-
Augusta) - CENTER LIBRARY □ Augusta, ME
Page, Melda W., Chf.Libn.
U.S. VETERANS ADMINISTRATION (ME-Togus)
- MEDICAL & REGIONAL OFFICE CENTER □
Augusta, ME
Page, Penny B., Libn.
RUTGERS UNIVERSITY, THE STATE
UNIVERSITY OF NEW JERSEY - RUTGERS
CENTER OF ALCOHOL STUDIES - LIBRARY □
Piscataway, NJ

Page, Vera, Foreign Law Libn.
UNIVERSITY OF WISCONSIN, MADISON - LAW
SCHOOL LIBRARY □ Madison, WI
Page, William, Hd., Sci. & Tech.Lib.
DREXEL UNIVERSITY - SCIENCE AND
TECHNOLOGY LIBRARY □ Philadelphia, PA
Pagel, Scott B., Pub.Serv.Libn.
GOLDEN GATE UNIVERSITY - SCHOOL OF LAW
LIBRARY □ San Francisco, CA
Pages, Jose R., Acq.Libn.
UNIVERSITY OF GEORGIA - LAW LIBRARY □
Athens, GA
Paghis, Miriam, Libn.
JEWISH COMMUNITY CENTRE - LIBRARY □
Ottawa, ON
Pahl, Denise, Libn.
NORTH DAKOTA STATE HOSPITAL - HEALTH
SCIENCE LIBRARY □ Jamestown, ND
Paige, Jean, Libn.
ART GALLERY OF GREATER VICTORIA -
LIBRARY □ Victoria, BC
Paik, Nan H., Supv.
ROCKWELL INTERNATIONAL - SPACE
BUSINESSES - TECHNICAL INFORMATION
CENTER □ Downey, CA
Paine, F. Helen, Libn.
MANITOBA - DEPARTMENT OF INDUSTRY,
TRADE AND TECHNOLOGY - BUSINESS LIBRARY
□ Winnipeg, MB
Paine, Jennie, Mgr.
UNIVERSITY OF CALGARY - MEDIA
UTILIZATION UNIT & FILM LIBRARY □ Calgary,
AB
Paine, Joan, Med.Libn.
MUNRO (Dr. E.H.) MEDICAL LIBRARY □ Grand
Junction, CO
Paine, Roberta M., Musm. Educator
METROPOLITAN MUSEUM OF ART - URIS
LIBRARY AND RESOURCE CENTER □ New York,
NY
Painter, Jacqueline M., Libn.
NUTRILITE PRODUCTS, INC. - RESEARCH
LIBRARY □ Buena Park, CA
Painter, Jacqueline S., Doc.Libn./Univ.Archv.
NORWICH UNIVERSITY - CHAPLIN MEMORIAL
LIBRARY - SPECIAL COLLECTIONS □ Northfield,
VT
Painter, Maxine, Cat.
FIRST UNITED METHODIST CHURCH - ALLEN
LIBRARY □ Kalamazoo, MI
Painter, Patricia, Archv.
WAYNE STATE UNIVERSITY - ARCHIVES OF
LABOR AND URBAN AFFAIRS/UNIVERSITY
ARCHIVES □ Detroit, MI
Pairo, Jane M., Asst. State Archv.
VIRGINIA STATE LIBRARY □ Richmond, VA
Pak, Usok, Info.Rsrcs.Coord.
MOBIL RESEARCH & DEVELOPMENT
CORPORATION - ENGINEERING DEPARTMENT -
INFORMATION CENTER □ Princeton, NJ
Pakala, Denise M., Tech.Serv.Libn.
BIBLICAL THEOLOGICAL SEMINARY - LIBRARY
□ Hatfield, PA
Pakala, Dennis, Cat.
WESTMINSTER THEOLOGICAL SEMINARY -
MONTGOMERY LIBRARY† □ Philadelphia, PA
Pakala, James C., Libn.
BIBLICAL THEOLOGICAL SEMINARY - LIBRARY
□ Hatfield, PA
Pakaluk, Michael, Hd.Libn.
HARVARD UNIVERSITY - ROBBINS LIBRARY □
Cambridge, MA
Palant, Celia A., Libn.
GATEWAYS HOSPITAL AND COMMUNITY
MENTAL HEALTH CENTER - PROFESSIONAL
LIBRARY □ Los Angeles, CA
Palatsky, Celine, Assoc.Musm.Libn.
METROPOLITAN MUSEUM OF ART - THOMAS J.
WATSON LIBRARY □ New York, NY
Palazzo, Albert, Proc.Archv.
UNITED NEGRO COLLEGE FUND, INC. -
DEPARTMENT OF ARCHIVES AND HISTORY □
New York, NY

Palazzolo, Janice, Asst.Libn.
GREY ADVERTISING, INC. - INFORMATION
CENTER □ New York, NY

Palen, Roberta, Bibliog.
SYRACUSE UNIVERSITY - E.S. BIRD LIBRARY -
SOCIAL SCIENCES DEPARTMENT □ Syracuse,
NY

Palestrant, Zelma, Br.Libn., Columbus
SQUIRE, SANDERS & DEMPSEY - LAW LIBRARY
□ Cleveland, OH

Palfalvi, Betty, Libn.
ANOKA STATE HOSPITAL - LIBRARY □ Anoka,
MN

Palfenier, Peter, Info.Off.
CANADA - STATISTICS CANADA - ADVISORY
SERVICES - EDMONTON REFERENCE CENTRE □
Edmonton, AB

Paliani, Mary Ann, Lib.Mgr.
ROCKWELL INTERNATIONAL - ENERGY
SYSTEMS GROUP - ROCKY FLATS PLANT -
TECHNICAL LIBRARY† □ Golden, CO

Palincsar, Stephen, Ref.Libn.
U.S. OFFICE OF PERSONNEL MANAGEMENT -
LIBRARY □ Washington, DC

Palkovic, Mark, Rec.Libn.
UNIVERSITY OF CINCINNATI - COLLEGE
CONSERVATORY OF MUSIC - GORNO
MEMORIAL MUSIC LIBRARY □ Cincinnati, OH

Pallay, Steven, Cat.Libn.
UNIVERSITY OF TORONTO - FACULTY OF
MUSIC LIBRARY □ Toronto, ON

Palling, Dr. Barbara R., Hd.Libn.
BUENA VISTA COLLEGE - L.E. & E.L. BALLOU
LIBRARY - SPECIAL COLLECTIONS □ Storm
Lake, IA

Pallitto, Kathryn, Info.Spec.
AT & T COMMUNICATIONS - INFORMATION
RESEARCH CENTER □ Bedminster, NJ

Pallman, Loma, Dir.
GRANDVIEW HOSPITAL - MEDICAL LIBRARY □
Dayton, OH

Pallowick, Richard, Asst.Libn., Cat.
CALIFORNIA ACADEMY OF SCIENCES - J.W.
MAILLIARD, JR. LIBRARY □ San Francisco, CA

Palm, Charles, Act.Archv.
STANFORD UNIVERSITY - HOOVER
INSTITUTION ON WAR, REVOLUTION AND
PEACE - LIBRARY □ Stanford, CA

Palme, Natalie, Libn.
HARVARD MUSICAL ASSOCIATION - LIBRARY □
Boston, MA

Palmer, Barbara, Libn.
U.S. NASA - GODDARD INSTITUTE FOR SPACE
STUDIES - LIBRARY □ New York, NY

Palmer, Beverly, Curric.Rsrc.Cons.
OAKLAND SCHOOLS - EDUCATIONAL RESOURCE
CENTER □ Pontiac, MI

Palmer, Bruce, Cat.
UNIVERSITY OF ARIZONA - COLLEGE OF LAW
LIBRARY† □ Tucson, AZ

Palmer, C.M., Libn.
LAWLER, FELIX & HALL - LAW LIBRARY □ Los
Angeles, CA

Palmer, Cathy, Lib.Supv.
SINAI HOSPITAL OF DETROIT - SAMUEL FRANK
MEDICAL LIBRARY □ Detroit, MI

Palmer, Charlotte, Cat.Libn.
DE PAUL UNIVERSITY - LAW SCHOOL LIBRARY
□ Chicago, IL

Palmer, David C., Mgr.
IBM CORPORATION - GENERAL TECHNOLOGY
DIVISION - INFORMATION CENTER/LEARNING
CENTER □ Essex Junction, VT

Palmer, E. Susan, Tech.Info.Spec.
CHEVRON OIL FIELD RESEARCH COMPANY -
TECHNICAL INFORMATION SERVICES □ La
Habra, CA

Palmer, Edith, Info.Spec.
TEXACO INC. - CORPORATE LIBRARY □ White
Plains, NY

Palmer, Hanna, Rd.Serv.Libn.
ORANGEBURG-CALHOUN TECHNICAL COLLEGE
- GRESSETTE LEARNING RESOURCE CENTER □
Orangeburg, SC

Palmer, Jim, User Serv.Spec.
ERIC CLEARINGHOUSE FOR JUNIOR COLLEGES
□ Los Angeles, CA

Palmer, Marg, Ministry Libn.
BRITISH COLUMBIA - MINISTRY OF
ENVIRONMENT - LIBRARY □ Victoria, BC

Palmer, Miriam, Med.Libn.
PROVIDENCE MEDICAL CENTER - MEDICAL
LIBRARY □ Portland, OR

Palmer, Paul R., Cur.
COLUMBIA UNIVERSITY - COLUMBIANA □ New
York, NY

Palmer, Raymond M., Tech.Libn.
GENERAL ELECTRIC COMPANY - AIRCRAFT
EQUIPMENT DIV. - ARMAMENT & ELECTRICAL
SYSTEMS DEPT. ENGINEERING LIBRARY □
Burlington, VT

Palmer, Richard J., Libn.
MACOMB INTERMEDIATE SCHOOL DISTRICT -
BEAL LIBRARY □ Mt. Clemens, MI

Palmer, Shirley, Res.Libn.
PROGRESSIVE GROCER - RESEARCH LIBRARY □
Stamford, CT

Palmer, Sue, Supv.Int.Tech.Info.Serv.
AT & T BELL LABORATORIES - LIBRARY □
Naperville, IL

Palmieri, Dr. Lucien E., Hd., Coll.Dev.
SUNY - COLLEGE AT BUFFALO - EDWARD H.
BUTLER LIBRARY □ Buffalo, NY

Palmisano, Sharon, Libn.
U.S. FISH & WILDLIFE SERVICE - LIBRARY □
Anchorage, AK

Palmlund, Loring, Libn.
DALLAS PUBLIC LIBRARY - BUSINESS AND
TECHNOLOGY DIVISION □ Dallas, TX

Palmquist, David W., City Archv.
BRIDGEPORT CITY ARCHIVES, RECORDS AND
INFORMATION SERVICES DEPARTMENT □
Bridgeport, CT

Palmquist, David W., Hd., Hist.Coll.
BRIDGEPORT PUBLIC LIBRARY - HISTORICAL
COLLECTIONS □ Bridgeport, CT

Palms, Rev. Roger C., Ed.
GRAHAM (Billy) EVANGELISTIC ASSOCIATION -
LIBRARY □ Minneapolis, MN

Paloma, Karen, Libn.
IOWA STATE COMMISSION FOR THE BLIND -
LIBRARY FOR THE BLIND & PHYSICALLY
HANDICAPPED □ Des Moines, IA

Palsson, Gerald, Asst.Univ.Libn.
SAN DIEGO STATE UNIVERSITY - MALCOLM A.
LOVE LIBRARY - SPECIAL COLLECTIONS† □ San
Diego, CA

Paluka, Frank, Hd.
UNIVERSITY OF IOWA - SPECIAL
COLLECTIONS DEPARTMENT □ Iowa City, IA

Palumbo, Richard, Ref.Libn.
WAGNER COLLEGE - HORRMANN LIBRARY □
Staten Island, NY

Palyvoda, Larissa, Info.Spec.
MC GRAW-EDISON COMPANY - WORTHINGTON
DIVISION - INFORMATION CENTER □
Mountainside, NJ

Pamperin, David, Dir.
MANITOWOC MARITIME MUSEUM - LIBRARY □
Manitowoc, WI

Pan, Chi-Wei, Cat.
FIELD MUSEUM OF NATURAL HISTORY -
LIBRARY □ Chicago, IL

Pana, Lucy M., Dept.Libn.
ALBERTA - DEPARTMENT OF CULTURE -
DEPARTMENTAL LIBRARY □ Edmonton, AB

Pancake, Edwina H., Dir.
UNIVERSITY OF VIRGINIA - SCIENCE &
ENGINEERING LIBRARY □ Charlottesville, VA

Panczyszyn, Dr. Marian, Sec.
UKRAINIAN MEDICAL ASSOCIATION OF NORTH
AMERICA - UKRAINIAN MEDICAL ARCHIVES
AND LIBRARY □ Chicago, IL

Pandelakis, Helene S., Info.Sci.
DCA FOOD INDUSTRIES, INC. - RESEARCH &
DEVELOPMENT DIVISION - SCIENTIFIC
INFORMATION CENTER □ New York, NY

Pandolfi, Rosemary, Cat.
SCHOOL OF VISUAL ARTS - LIBRARY □ New
York, NY

Panek, Robert, Ref.Libn.
ROCKWELL INTERNATIONAL - NORTH
AMERICAN AIRCRAFT OPERATIONS -
TECHNICAL INFORMATION CENTER □ Los
Angeles, CA

Panella, Deborah S., Chf.Libn.
PAUL, WEISS, RIFKIND, WHARTON AND
GARRISON - LIBRARY □ New York, NY

Panella, Nancy Mary, Libn.
ST. LUKE'S HOSPITAL CENTER - RICHARD
WALKER BOLLING MEMORIAL MEDICAL
LIBRARY† □ New York, NY

Panepinto, Aura J., Dir.
UNIVERSITY OF PUERTO RICO - MEDICAL
SCIENCES CAMPUS - LIBRARY □ Rio Piedras, PR

Pankey, Marilyn R., Dir., Med.Rec.
SIERRA VIEW DISTRICT HOSPITAL - MEDICAL
LIBRARY □ Porterville, CA

Pankiewicz, Janet B., Libn.
HALL-BROOKE HOSPITAL - PROFESSIONAL
LIBRARY □ Westport, CT

Pankow, David, Libn.
ROCHESTER INSTITUTE OF TECHNOLOGY -
MELBERT B. CARY, JR. GRAPHIC ARTS
COLLECTION† □ Rochester, NY

Panneton, Jacques, Consrv.
BIBLIOTHEQUE DE LA VILLE DE MONTREAL -
COLLECTION GAGNON □ Montreal, PQ

Panofsky, Hans E., Cur. of Africana
NORTHWESTERN UNIVERSITY - MELVILLE J.
HERSKOVITS LIBRARY OF AFRICAN STUDIES □
Evanston, IL

Pantano, Richard, Dir.
NEW HAMPSHIRE COLLEGE - SHAPIRO
LIBRARY □ Manchester, NH

Pantazis, Fotoula, Asst.Libn.
HAMILTON BOARD OF EDUCATION -
EDUCATION CENTRE LIBRARY† □ Hamilton, ON

Pantell, Brenda E., Law Libn.
NEW YORK STATE SUPREME COURT - 10TH
JUDICIAL DISTRICT - LAW LIBRARY □
Riverhead, NY

Panton, Linda, Hosp.Lib.Coord.
MC MASTER UNIVERSITY - HEALTH SCIENCES
LIBRARY □ Hamilton, ON

Pantridge, Barbara B., Libn.
DUTCHESS COUNTY MENTAL HEALTH LIBRARY
□ Poughkeepsie, NY

Panzarella, Meg, Ref.Libn.
NORTHWESTERN UNIVERSITY - HEALTH
SCIENCES LIBRARY† □ Chicago, IL

Paolillo, Deborah, Hd.
YALE UNIVERSITY - STERLING CHEMISTRY
LIBRARY □ New Haven, CT

Paolino, Eileen F., Asst. Law Libn.
ADLER POLLOCK & SHEEHAN, INC. - LAW
LIBRARY □ Providence, RI

Paolucci, Anne, Pres./Exec.Dir.
COUNCIL ON NATIONAL LITERATURES -
INFORMATION CENTER □ Whitestone, NY

Papa, Angelo R., Lib.Techn.
NEW JERSEY STATE DEPARTMENT OF
ENVIRONMENTAL PROTECTION - DIVISION OF
WATER RESOURCES - LIBRARY □ Trenton, NJ

Papademetriou, Rev. George. C., Ph.D., Dir. of Lib.
HELLENIC COLLEGE AND HOLY CROSS GREEK
ORTHODOX SCHOOL OF THEOLOGY -
COTSIDAS-TONNA LIBRARY □ Brookline, MA

Papakhian, A. Ralph, Tech.Serv.Libn.
INDIANA UNIVERSITY - MUSIC LIBRARY □
Bloomington, IN

Papalambros, Rita, Tech.Serv.Libn.
HONEYWELL, INC. - HONEYWELL
INFORMATION SYSTEMS - INFORMATION AND
LIBRARY SERVICES □ Waltham, MA

Paparelli, Marita E., Law Libn.
LACKAWANNA BAR ASSOCIATION - LAW
LIBRARY □ Scranton, PA

Pape, Ruth Pestalozzi, Med.Libn.
ST. ELIZABETH HOSPITAL MEDICAL CENTER -
BANNON HEALTH SCIENCE LIBRARY □
Lafayette, IN

Papenfuse, Dr. Edward C., Archv.
MARYLAND STATE HALL OF RECORDS
COMMISSION - LIBRARY □ Annapolis, MD

Papermaster, Cynthia, Law Libn.
ORRICK, HERRINGTON, ROWLEY & SUTCLIFFE
- LIBRARY □ San Francisco, CA

Papile-Miller, Louise, AV Spec.
U.S. VETERANS ADMINISTRATION (NV-Reno) -
MEDICAL CENTER - LEARNING CENTER □ Reno,
NV

Papillon, Yvon, Hd.Libn.
QUEBEC PROVINCE - MINISTERE DES
AFFAIRES SOCIALES - SERVICE DE LA
DOCUMENTATION □ Quebec, PQ

Paplinski, William E., Chf., Bur.Lib.Serv.
STATE LIBRARY OF FLORIDA □ Tallahassee, FL

Pappas, Margaret, Dir.
CALIFORNIA FAMILY STUDY CENTER -
LEARNING RESOURCE CENTER □ Burbank, CA

Paprocki, Sharon, Tech.Info.Spec.
ROCHESTER GAS AND ELECTRIC
CORPORATION - TECHNICAL INFORMATION
CENTER □ Rochester, NY

Paquette, Juliette, Libn.
CANADA - NATIONAL FILM BOARD OF CANADA
- EDMONTON DISTRICT OFFICE - FILM
LIBRARY □ Edmonton, AB

Paquette, Melinda Robinson, Med.Libn.
READING HOSPITAL & MEDICAL CENTER -
MEDICAL LIBRARY □ Reading, PA

Paquette, Rita, Libn.
UNIVERSITE DE MONTREAL -
MATHEMATIQUES-BIBLIOTHEQUE □ Montreal,
PQ

Paradis, Olga, Libn.
TEXAS INSTRUMENTS, INC. - RESEARCH
BUILDING LIBRARY □ Dallas, TX

Paradis, Olivier, Dir.
ECOLE POLYTECHNIQUE - BIBLIOTHEQUE □
Montreal, PQ

Paraipan, Aurelian, Dir.
ROMANIAN LIBRARY □ New York, NY

Paraipan, Elena, Exec.Sec.
ROMANIAN LIBRARY □ New York, NY

Pararas-Carayannis, Dr. George, Dir.
INTERNATIONAL TSUNAMI INFORMATION
CENTER □ Honolulu, HI

Pare, Gilles, Libn.
LE DEVOIR - CENTRE DE DOCUMENTATION □
Montreal, PQ

Pare, Richard, Assoc.Libn.
CANADA - LIBRARY OF PARLIAMENT □ Ottawa,
ON

Paredes, Miss Milagros M., Med.Libn.
LINCOLN HOSPITAL - MEDICAL LIBRARY □
Bronx, NY

Parhad, Bronwyn, Hd.
CHICAGO PUBLIC LIBRARY CENTRAL LIBRARY -
GENERAL INFORMATION SERVICES DIVISION -
INFORMATION CENTER □ Chicago, IL

Parhad, Bryan, Patients' Libn.
U.S. VETERANS ADMINISTRATION (IL-Chicago)
- WESTSIDE HOSPITAL LIBRARY □ Chicago, IL

Parham, Ann, Ref.Libn.
U.S. ARMY IN EUROPE (USAREUR) - LIBRARY
AND RESOURCE CENTER □ APO New York, NY

Parham, Sandra H., Libn.
ST. MARY'S HOSPITAL - HEALTH SCIENCES
LIBRARY □ Richmond, VA

Parins, Anita, Asst.Acq.Libn.
U.S. ARMY - OFFICE OF THE ADJUTANT
GENERAL - MORALE SUPPORT DIRECTORATE -
LIBRARY ACTIVITIES DIVISION □ Alexandria,
VA

Paris, Shirley, Chf.Libn.
NEW YORK CITY - MUNICIPAL REFERENCE
AND RESEARCH CENTER - HAVEN EMERSON
PUBLIC HEALTH LIBRARY □ New York, NY

Paris, Terry, Circ. & Ref.
MOUNT SAINT VINCENT UNIVERSITY -
LIBRARY □ Halifax, NS

Parish, David W., Govt.Doc.Libn.
SUNY - COLLEGE AT GENESEO - COLLEGE
LIBRARIES □ Geneseo, NY

Parish, Marisa, Children's Libn.
NEW YORK PUBLIC LIBRARY - BELMONT
REGIONAL LIBRARY - ENRICO FERMI
CULTURAL CENTER □ Bronx, NY

Parisky, Helen, Assoc.Libn. & Cat.
CALIFORNIA LUTHERAN COLLEGE - LIBRARY -
SPECIAL COLLECTIONS† □ Thousand Oaks, CA

Parisot, Beverly, Lib.Mgr.
OMAHA WORLD-HERALD - LIBRARY □ Omaha,
NE

Park, Mrs. A. Belva, Med.Libn.
REGINA GENERAL HOSPITAL - HEALTH
SCIENCES LIBRARY □ Regina, SK

Park, Helen, Cat.Libn.
SUNY AT STONY BROOK - HEALTH SCIENCES
LIBRARY □ East Setauket, NY

Park, Heo, Sr.Libn.
BERKELEY PUBLIC LIBRARY - ART AND MUSIC
DEPARTMENT □ Berkeley, CA

Park, Ms. N.R., Mgr.
CANADA - NATIONAL ENERGY BOARD -
LIBRARY □ Ottawa, ON

Park, Robert C., Dir. of Lib.Serv.
ST. LUKE'S EPISCOPAL & TEXAS CHILDREN'S
HOSPITALS - MEDICAL LIBRARY □ Houston, TX

Park, Yoon S., Cat.
LIBRARY OF INTERNATIONAL RELATIONS □
Chicago, IL

Parker, C. Gerald, Hd., Sound Coll.
NATIONAL LIBRARY OF CANADA - MUSIC
DIVISION □ Ottawa, ON

Parker, Carolyn, AV/Acq.Libn.
WAKE FOREST UNIVERSITY - BOWMAN GRAY
SCHOOL OF MEDICINE - COY C. CARPENTER
LIBRARY □ Winston-Salem, NC

Parker, Carroll T., State Libn.
GEORGIA STATE LIBRARY □ Atlanta, GA

Parker, Cut, Libn.
INVESTMENT COMPANY INSTITUTE - LIBRARY
□ Washington, DC

Parker, Diane C., Dir.
SUNY AT BUFFALO - SCIENCE AND
ENGINEERING LIBRARY □ Buffalo, NY

Parker, Elizabeth L., Libn.
COASTAL ECOSYSTEMS MANAGEMENT, INC. -
LIBRARY □ Fort Worth, TX

Parker, Evelyn, New Bks.Libn.
LTV AEROSPACE AND DEFENSE COMPANY -
VOUGHT MISSILES AND ADVANCED PROGRAMS
DIVISION - LIBRARY 3-58200 □ Dallas, TX

Parker, Evelyn, Libn.
RIVERSIDE PRESBYTERIAN CHURCH - JEAN
MILLER LIBRARY □ Jacksonville, FL

Parker, Evelyn K., Legal Info.Spec.
COMMODITY FUTURES TRADING COMMISSION
- LIBRARY □ Washington, DC

Parker, J. Carlyle, Act.Dir.
CALIFORNIA STATE COLLEGE, STANISLAUS -
LIBRARY - SPECIAL COLLECTIONS □ Turlock,
CA

Parker, Jean, Libn.
MERCY HOSPITAL - HEALTH SCIENCES
LIBRARY □ Muskegon, MI

Parker, Jeanne
GENERAL ELECTRIC COMPANY - LAMP GLASS &
COMPONENTS LIBRARY □ Richmond Heights, OH

Parker, John, Cur.
UNIVERSITY OF MINNESOTA - JAMES FORD
BELL LIBRARY □ Minneapolis, MN

Parker, John A., Hd.Cur.
NORFOLK PUBLIC LIBRARY - SARGEANT
MEMORIAL ROOM □ Norfolk, VA

Parker, M., Info.Spec.
BURROUGHS WELLCOME COMPANY - LIBRARY
□ Research Triangle Park, NC

Parker, Marian, Dir./Asst.Prof.
UNIVERSITY OF TULSA - COLLEGE OF LAW
LIBRARY □ Tulsa, OK

Parker, Mary Ann, Law Libn.
SAN JOAQUIN COLLEGE OF LAW - LIBRARY† □
Fresno, CA

Parker, Mary L., Corp.Libn.
SOUTHERN CALIFORNIA EDISON COMPANY -
LIBRARY □ Rosemead, CA

Parker, Nancy Boothe, Dir.
RICE UNIVERSITY - WOODSON RESEARCH
CENTER □ Houston, TX

Parker, Peter J., Act.Dir.
HISTORICAL SOCIETY OF PENNSYLVANIA -
LIBRARY □ Philadelphia, PA

Parker, Rosemarie, Sr.Info.Sci.
EXXON CORPORATION - MEDICINE &
ENVIRONMENTAL HEALTH DEPT. - RESEARCH
& ENVIRONMENTAL HEALTH DIV.LIB. □ East
Millstone, NJ

Parker, Sandra, Dir., Lib.Serv.
SWEDISH MEDICAL CENTER - LIBRARY □
Englewood, CO

Parker, Sara, State Libn.
MONTANA STATE LIBRARY □ Helena, MT

Parker, Sheila, Asst.Libn.
ROSENMAN, COLIN, FREUND, LEWIS & COHEN -
LAW LIBRARY □ New York, NY

Parker, Stephen B., Libn.
ELECTRIC POWER RESEARCH INSTITUTE -
TECHNICAL LIBRARY □ Palo Alto, CA

Parker, Sybil P., Supv.Libn.
U.S. ARMY MILITARY POLICE SCHOOL -
LIBRARY □ Ft. McClellan, AL

Parker, Thomas W., Dir.
BOSTONIAN SOCIETY - LIBRARY □ Boston, MA

Parker, V., Archv.
AQUATIC RESEARCH INSTITUTE - AQUATIC
SCIENCES & TECHNOLOGY ARCHIVE □
Hayward, CA

Parker, Ms. V.
CANADA - PUBLIC ARCHIVES OF CANADA -
NATIONAL MAP COLLECTION □ Ottawa, ON

Parker, Vivian B., Sr. Data Anl.
U.S. NATL. BUREAU OF STANDARDS -
CHEMICAL THERMODYNAMICS DATA CENTER
□ Washington, DC

Parker, William, Ref.Libn.
UNIVERSITY OF BRITISH COLUMBIA -
WOODWARD BIOMEDICAL LIBRARY □
Vancouver, BC

Parkes, Katherine, Libn.
NATIONAL HOUSING LAW PROJECT/NATIONAL
ECONOMIC DEVELOPMENT AND LAW CENTER -
LIBRARY □ Berkeley, CA

Parkin, Derral, Libn.
UNIVERSITY OF HOUSTON - COLLEGE OF
PHARMACY LIBRARY □ Houston, TX

Parkinson, George, Cur.
WEST VIRGINIA UNIVERSITY - WEST
VIRGINIA AND REGIONAL COLLECTION □
Morgantown, WV

Parkinson, Howard, Circ.Libn.
WILFRID LAURIER UNIVERSITY - LIBRARY □
Waterloo, ON

Parkinson, Janet A., Libn.
PRICE WATERHOUSE - AUDIT LIBRARY □
Vancouver, BC

Parkinson, Robert L., Chf.Libn. & Hist.
CIRCUS WORLD MUSEUM - LIBRARY □ Baraboo,
WI

Parkison, Anne H., Dir. of Lib.Serv.
RECORDING FOR THE BLIND, INC. - MASTER
TAPE LIBRARY □ Princeton, NJ

Parkman, Helen, Cur.
STEELE COUNTY HISTORICAL SOCIETY -
ARCHIVES □ Hope, ND

Parkman, John F., Dir.
MAINE EDUCATIONAL RESOURCES, INC. - MID
COAST TEACHERS' CENTER □ Camden, ME

Parkman, Sally L., Day Supv.
INDIANAPOLIS NEWSPAPERS, INC. -
INDIANAPOLIS STAR AND INDIANAPOLIS
NEWS - REFERENCE LIBRARY □ Indianapolis, IN

Parks, Ann B., Asst.Dir.
LANDMARK SOCIETY OF WESTERN NEW YORK
- WENRICH MEMORIAL LIBRARY □ Rochester,
NY

Parks, Betty, Libn.
CESSNA AIRCRAFT COMPANY - WALLACE
DIVISION - ENGINEERING LIBRARY □ Wichita,
KS

Parks, Crystal M., Libn.
ASBURY UNITED METHODIST CHURCH -
LIBRARY □ Tacoma, WA

Parks, Dennis H., Libn.
PURDUE UNIVERSITY - AVIATION
TECHNOLOGY LIBRARY □ West Lafayette, IN

Parks, Dennis H., Libn.
PURDUE UNIVERSITY - GEOSCIENCES LIBRARY
□ West Lafayette, IN

Parks, Dennis H., Libn.
PURDUE UNIVERSITY - PHYSICS LIBRARY □
West Lafayette, IN

Parks, Dorothy Ruth, Dir.
VANDERBILT UNIVERSITY - JEAN AND
ALEXANDER HEARD LIBRARY - DIVINITY
LIBRARY □ Nashville, TN

Parks, Dorothy Ruth, Dir.
VANDERBILT UNIVERSITY - JEAN AND
ALEXANDER HEARD LIBRARY - DIVINITY
LIBRARY - KESLER CIRCULATING LIBRARY □
Nashville, TN

Parks, James F., Hd.Libn.
CAIN (J.B.) ARCHIVES OF MISSISSIPPI
METHODISM AND MILLSAPS COLLEGE □
Jackson, MS

Parks, Janet, Drawings Cur.
COLUMBIA UNIVERSITY - AVERY
ARCHITECTURAL AND FINE ARTS LIBRARY □
New York, NY

Parks, Mary A., Libn.
MOTE MARINE LABORATORY - DAVIS LIBRARY
□ Sarasota, FL

Parks, Stephen, Cur./Osborn Coll./Mss.
YALE UNIVERSITY - BEINECKE RARE BOOK
AND MANUSCRIPT LIBRARY □ New Haven, CT

Parks, Stephen R., Libn.
YALE UNIVERSITY - ELIZABETHAN CLUB
COLLECTION □ New Haven, CT

Parks, T.
UNIVERSITY OF ILLINOIS - COMMERCE
LIBRARY □ Urbana, IL

Parnell, Pat, Ref.Libn.
UNIVERSITY OF SASKATCHEWAN -
EDUCATION BRANCH LIBRARY □ Saskatoon, SK

Parnes, Carole D., Mgr., Indus.Info.
CBS INC. - CBS NEWS REFERENCE LIBRARY □
New York, NY

Parodi, Jean G., Res.Spec.
WESTERN MONTANA SCIENTISTS'
COMMITTEE FOR PUBLIC INFORMATION -
MONTANA ENVIRONMENTAL LIBRARY □
Missoula, MT

Parr, Mary Anne, Med.Libn.
ST. FRANCIS HOSPITAL - MEDICAL CENTER -
MEDICAL LIBRARY □ Peoria, IL

Parratt, Pat, Libn.
CARNEGIE INSTITUTION OF WASHINGTON -
LIBRARY† □ Washington, DC

Parratt, Ruth W., Libn.
MC KEE (Arthur) CORPORATION -
INFORMATION RESOURCE CENTER† □
Cleveland, OH

Parris, Pat, Libn.
KANSAS STATE UNIVERSITY - CHEMISTRY
LIBRARY □ Manhattan, KS

Parrish, James, Extramural Prog.
UNIVERSITY OF ILLINOIS AT CHICAGO -
HEALTH SCIENCES CENTER - LIBRARY OF THE
HEALTH SCIENCES □ Chicago, IL

Parrish, Jenni, Dir.
UNIVERSITY OF PITTSBURGH - LAW LIBRARY □
Pittsburgh, PA

Parrish, Michael, Hd.
INDIANA UNIVERSITY - BUSINESS/SPEA
LIBRARY □ Bloomington, IN

Parrish, Octavia, Lib.Asst.
PORTSMOUTH PUBLIC LIBRARY - LOCAL
HISTORY ROOM □ Portsmouth, VA

Parrish, Ramona C., Libn.
DE PAUL HOSPITAL - DR. HENRY BOONE
MEMORIAL LIBRARY □ Norfolk, VA

Parrish, Sandra, Libn.
PIERSON, BALL & DOWD - LAW LIBRARY □
Washington, DC

Parrott, Mrs. D., Lib.Techn.
COLLEGE OF TRADES AND TECHNOLOGY -
MEDICAL LIBRARY □ St. John's, NF

Parrott, Mary, Libn.
NORTHEAST WISCONSIN TECHNICAL
INSTITUTE - LEARNING RESOURCE CENTER □
Green Bay, WI

Parry, David R., Dir.
LAKE COUNTY PUBLIC LIBRARY - SPECIAL
COLLECTIONS □ Leadville, CO

Parry, Gladys, Ref.Libn.
MEMPHIS STATE UNIVERSITY LIBRARIES -
SCHOOL OF LAW LIBRARY □ Memphis, TN

Parry, Karnell, Multi-State Libn.
UTAH STATE LIBRARY - BLIND AND
PHYSICALLY HANDICAPPED PROGRAM -
REGIONAL LIBRARY □ Salt Lake City, UT

Parry, Robert, Dp.Dir.
CUYAHOGA COUNTY REGIONAL PLANNING
COMMISSION - LIBRARY □ Cleveland, OH

Parsonage, Dianne L., Dept.Libn.
CANADA - REVENUE CANADA - CUSTOMS &
EXCISE LIBRARY □ Ottawa, ON

Parsons, Catherine, Libn.
DE HAVILLAND AIRCRAFT OF CANADA, LTD. -
ENGINEERING LIBRARY □ Downsview, ON

Parsons, Charles, Govt.Doc.
UNIVERSITY OF CINCINNATI - ROBERT S.
MARX LAW LIBRARY □ Cincinnati, OH

Parsons, Sr. Charles Marie, Asst.Supv., Lib.Serv.
ST. JOHN VIANNEY COLLEGE SEMINARY -
MARY LOUISE MAYTAG MEMORIAL LIBRARY □
Miami, FL

Parsons, Donna, Dir.
COLLEGE OF IDAHO - REGIONAL STUDIES
CENTER - LIBRARY □ Caldwell, ID

Parsons, Frances E., Lib.Supv.
DU PONT DE NEMOURS (E.I.) & COMPANY, INC.
- LAVOISIER LIBRARY □ Wilmington, DE

Parsons, Gerald J., Dept.Hd.
ONONDAGA COUNTY PUBLIC LIBRARY - LOCAL
HISTORY AND GENEALOGY DEPARTMENT □
Syracuse, NY

Parsons, Joan, Hum.Libn.
RYERSON POLYTECHNICAL INSTITUTE -
LEARNING RESOURCES CENTRE □ Toronto, ON

Parsons, Karen, Libn.
SAGAMORE HILLS CHILDREN'S PSYCHIATRIC
HOSPITAL - STAFF MEDICAL LIBRARY □
Northfield, OH

Parsons, Kevin, Dir.
JUSTICE SYSTEM TRAINING ASSOCIATION -
PSYCHO-MOTOR SKILL DESIGN ARCHIVE □
Appleton, WI

Parsons, Patricia, Dept.Libn.
WISCONSIN STATE DEPARTMENT OF NATURAL
RESOURCES - LIBRARY □ Madison, WI

Partington, William M., Jr., Dir.
FLORIDA CONSERVATION FOUNDATION, INC. -
ENVIRONMENTAL INFORMATION CENTER □
Winter Park, FL

Partlow, Richard V., Dept.Mgr.
LOS ANGELES PUBLIC LIBRARY - AUDIO-
VISUAL DEPARTMENT □ Los Angeles, CA

Parton, Bill, Assoc.Dir.
WACO-MC LENNAN COUNTY LIBRARY -
SPECIAL COLLECTIONS DEPARTMENT □ Waco,
TX

Partridge, Cathleen F., Lib.Supv.
HERCULES, INC. - AEROSPACE DIVISION -
BACCHUS WORKS LIBRARY INFORMATION
CENTER □ Magna, UT

Partridge, Charles V., Libn.
DETROIT PUBLIC SCHOOLS - PROFESSIONAL
LIBRARY □ Detroit, MI

Partridge, Lucelia F., Asst.Libn.
KUTAK ROCK & HUIE, ATTORNEYS AT LAW -
LAW LIBRARY □ Atlanta, GA

Pascarelli, Anne M., Assoc.Libn.
NEW YORK ACADEMY OF MEDICINE - LIBRARY
□ New York, NY

Pascavage, Barbara Ann, Libn.
U.S. VETERANS ADMINISTRATION (TX-Waco) -
MEDICAL CENTER LIBRARY □ Waco, TX

Paschal, Curtis, Libn.
MINNEAPOLIS PUBLIC LIBRARY &
INFORMATION CENTER - HISTORY
DEPARTMENT □ Minneapolis, MN

Paschall, Jo Anne, Hd.Libn.
ATLANTA COLLEGE OF ART - LIBRARY □
Atlanta, GA

Pascoe, Frank, Ref. & Loan
MISSOURI STATE LIBRARY □ Jefferson City,
MO

Pascual, S., Info.Spec.
AMOCO CANADA PETROLEUM COMPANY, LTD. -
LIBRARY/INFORMATION CENTER □ Calgary, AB

Pascucci, Joseph T., Libn.
NEW YORK STATE SUPREME COURT -
APPELLATE DIVISION, 4TH JUDICIAL
DEPARTMENT - LAW LIBRARY □ Rochester, NY

Pashley, Anne, Mgr.
CANADIAN GENERAL ELECTRIC COMPANY,
LTD. - CORPORATE INFORMATION CENTRE □
Toronto, ON

Pasini, S. Elaine, Libn.
U.S. DEPT. OF ENERGY - MORGANTOWN
ENERGY TECHNOLOGY CENTER LIBRARY† □
Morgantown, WV

Paskar, Joanne M., Hd.
U.S. AGENCY FOR INTERNATIONAL
DEVELOPMENT - DEVELOPMENT INFORMATION
CENTER □ Washington, DC

Paskowsky, Carol, Libn.
ABINGTON MEMORIAL HOSPITAL - SCHOOL OF
NURSING LIBRARY □ Abington, PA

Pasmik, Eleonor E., Assoc.Libn., Hd.Ref.
NEW YORK UNIVERSITY MEDICAL CENTER -
FREDERICK L. EHRMAN MEDICAL LIBRARY □
New York, NY

Pasqualini, Bernard F., Hd.
FREE LIBRARY OF PHILADELPHIA -
MICROFORMS AND NEWSPAPERS
DEPARTMENT □ Philadelphia, PA

Pasquarella, Kathie, Med.Libn.
OHIO VALLEY HOSPITAL - HEALTH SCIENCES
LIBRARY □ Steubenville, OH

Pasquariella, Susan K., Pres.
ASSOCIATION FOR POPULATION/FAMILY
PLANNING LIBRARIES & INFORMATION
CENTERS INTERNATIONAL □ Chapel Hill, NC

Pasquariella, Susan K., Hd.Libn.
COLUMBIA UNIVERSITY - CENTER FOR
POPULATION & FAMILY HEALTH - LIBRARY/
INFORMATION PROGRAM □ New York, NY

Pasquis-Audant, Colette, Libn.
HOTEL-DIEU DE LEVIS - BIBLIOTHEQUE
MEDICALE† □ Levis, PQ

Pass, E., Libn.
ROYAL ALEXANDRA HOSPITAL - SCHOOL OF
NURSING LIBRARY □ Edmonton, AB

Passarelli, Anne B., Hd.Libn.
UNIVERSITY OF WASHINGTON - BUSINESS
ADMINISTRATION LIBRARY □ Seattle, WA

Passidomo, Donald A., Chf.Libn.
U.S. VETERANS ADMINISTRATION (DE-
Wilmington) - CENTER MEDICAL LIBRARY □
Wilmington, DE

Pastan, Barbara P., Lib.Dir.
FAULKNER HOSPITAL - INGERSOLL BOWDITCH
LIBRARY □ Jamaica Plain, MA

Pastan, Herbert M., Libn.
U.S. ARMY - THE INSTITUTE OF HERALDRY - LIBRARY □ Alexandria, VA

Patail, George, Ref.Libn.
U.S. ARMY IN EUROPE (USAREUR) - LIBRARY AND RESOURCE CENTER □ APO New York, NY

Patchett, Dr. J.E., Asst.Dir. of Res.
NORTON RESEARCH CORPORATION (Canada) LTD. - LIBRARY □ Niagara Falls, ON

Patel, Patricia, Resource Serv.Libn.
GEORGETOWN UNIVERSITY - MEDICAL CENTER - DAHLGREN MEMORIAL LIBRARY □ Washington, DC

Patelke, Elizabeth, ISLA
INVESTIGATIVE RESOURCE CENTER - DATA CENTER □ Oakland, CA

Patermann, H. Maria, Dir. of Libs.
SUNNYVALE PATENT INFORMATION CLEARINGHOUSE □ Sunnyvale, CA

Paterson, Ellen, Sci.Ref.-Bibliog.
SUNY - COLLEGE AT CORTLAND - MEMORIAL LIBRARY □ Cortland, NY

Patience, Alice, Lib.Mgr.
DRAVO ENGINEERS INC. - LIBRARY □ Pittsburgh, PA

Patmon, Marian, Hd., Lib.Rsrcs.
OKLAHOMA STATE DEPARTMENT OF LIBRARIES □ Oklahoma City, OK

Paton, Chris, Archv.
GEORGIA STATE UNIVERSITY - SPECIAL COLLECTIONS DEPARTMENT □ Atlanta, GA

Paton, Jean
ORPHAN VOYAGE - MUSEUM OF ORPHANHOOD - LIBRARY □ Cedaredge, CO

Patricius, Sister Mary, Dir.
ST. MARY HOSPITAL - HEALTH SCIENCE LIBRARY □ Port Arthur, TX

Patrick, Carolyn, Assoc.Dir., Amarillo
TEXAS TECH UNIVERSITY - HEALTH SCIENCES CENTER - LIBRARY OF THE HEALTH SCIENCES □ Lubbock, TX

Patrick, Mrs. Dovie T., Archv.Libn.
ATLANTA UNIVERSITY CENTER - ROBERT W. WOODRUFF LIBRARY □ Atlanta, GA

Patrick, Susan M., Coord., User Serv.
CANADA - CANADIAN RADIO-TELEVISION AND TELECOMMUNICATIONS COMMISSION - LIBRARY □ Ottawa, ON

Patrick, Wendy, Hd.Libn.
MC GILL UNIVERSITY - NURSING/SOCIAL WORK LIBRARY □ Montreal, PQ

Patruno, John, Jr., Assoc.Dir.
UNIVERSITY OF VIRGINIA - MEDICAL CENTER - CLAUDE MOORE HEALTH SCIENCES LIBRARY □ Charlottesville, VA

Patsy, Janet E., Law Libn.
GENESEE COUNTY CIRCUIT COURT - LAW LIBRARY □ Flint, MI

Patten, Frederick W., Cat.Libn.
HUGHES AIRCRAFT COMPANY - ELECTRO-OPTICAL & DATA SYSTEMS GROUP - COMPANY TECHNICAL DOCUMENT CENTER □ El Segundo, CA

Patterson, Ann, Ref.Libn.
EASTERN VIRGINIA MEDICAL SCHOOL - MOORMAN MEMORIAL LIBRARY □ Norfolk, VA

Patterson, Ann, Pub.Serv.libn.
LIFE CHIROPRACTIC COLLEGE-WEST - LIBRARY □ San Lorenzo, CA

Patterson, Belinda C., Slide Cur.
MEMPHIS STATE UNIVERSITY LIBRARIES - ART SLIDE LIBRARY □ Memphis, TN

Patterson, Betty H., Tech.Libn.
MONSANTO FIBERS & INTERMEDIATES COMPANY - TECHNICAL CENTER LIBRARY □ Decatur, AL

Patterson, Mrs. Bobbie J., Coord.
WASHINGTON STATE SUPERINTENDENT OF PUBLIC INSTRUCTION - RESOURCE INFORMATION CENTER □ Olympia, WA

Patterson, Charlean, Libn.
SOLDIERS AND SAILORS MEMORIAL HOSPITAL - HEALTH SCIENCE LIBRARY □ Wellsboro, PA

Patterson, D.J., Engr.Libn.
GENERAL DYNAMICS CORPORATION - POMONA DIVISION - DIVISION LIBRARY MZ 4-20 □ Pomona, CA

Patterson, D.K., Tech.Libn.
LOCKHEED-GEORGIA COMPANY - TECHNICAL INFORMATION DEPARTMENT □ Marietta, GA

Patterson, Dewey F., Lib.Dir.
VERMONT TECHNICAL COLLEGE - HARTNESS LIBRARY □ Randolph Center, VT

Patterson, Flora E., Dir., Pub.Serv.
NATIONAL LIBRARY OF CANADA/ BIBLIOTHEQUE NATIONALE DU CANADA □ Ottawa, ON

Patterson, Gregory R., Dir., Med.Lib.
UTAH VALLEY HOSPITAL - MEDICAL LIBRARY □ Provo, UT

Patterson, Irma Jean, Lib.Assoc.
CHICAGO PUBLIC LIBRARY CULTURAL CENTER - THOMAS HUGHES CHILDREN'S LIBRARY □ Chicago, IL

Patterson, Jack M., Mgr.
BRITISH COLUMBIA AND YUKON CHAMBER OF MINES - LIBRARY □ Vancouver, BC

Patterson, Jacque, Libn.
U.S. ARMY - CORPS OF ENGINEERS - MEMPHIS DISTRICT - LIBRARY □ Memphis, TN

Patterson, Jenny, Libn.
NASHVILLE - METROPOLITAN DEPARTMENT OF PUBLIC HEALTH - LENTZ HEALTH CENTER LIBRARY □ Nashville, TN

Patterson, John, Dir.
CHARLTON PARK HISTORIC VILLAGE & MUSEUM - LIBRARY □ Hastings, MI

Patterson, Judy, Libn.
CAMBRIA COUNTY FREE LAW LIBRARY □ Ebensburg, PA

Patterson, Kim, AV Supv.
OUACHITA BAPTIST UNIVERSITY - RILEY LIBRARY □ Arkadelphia, AR

Patterson, Laura, AV/Per.Libn.
LEWIS UNIVERSITY - LIBRARY □ Romeoville, IL

Patterson, Maureen L.P., Bibliog./Hd.
UNIVERSITY OF CHICAGO - SOUTH ASIA COLLECTION □ Chicago, IL

Patterson, Myron B., Lib.Res.
BRITISH COLUMBIA TELEPHONE COMPANY - BUSINESS LIBRARY □ Burnaby, BC

Patterson, Robert, Hd., Pub.Serv.
MICHIGAN TECHNOLOGICAL UNIVERSITY - LIBRARY □ Houghton, MI

Patterson, Vanessa, Supv., Res.Serv.
HOLIDAY INNS, INC. - CORPORATE RESOURCE CENTER □ Memphis, TN

Patterson, Virginia, Libn.
FIRST BAPTIST CHURCH - LIBRARY □ San Antonio, TX

Patterson, William C., Dir.
SPERRY - BUSINESS PLANNING LIBRARY □ New York, NY

Pattillo, John W., Dir.
SOUTHERN TECHNICAL INSTITUTE - LIBRARY □ Marietta, GA

Pattison, Frederick W., Libn.
AMERICAN JOURNAL OF NURSING COMPANY - SOPHIA F. PALMER LIBRARY □ New York, NY

Pattison, Jane, Sr.Res.Libn.
OCCIDENTAL CHEMICAL CORPORATION - TECHNICAL INFORMATION CENTER □ Niagara Falls, NY

Patton, Bob, Coord., Curric.Div.
OKLAHOMA STATE DEPARTMENT OF VOCATIONAL AND TECHNICAL EDUCATION - CURRICULUM DIVISION - LIBRARY □ Stillwater, OK

Patton, Bruce M., Assoc.Dir./Lib.Hd.
HARVARD UNIVERSITY - PROGRAM ON NEGOTIATION: SPECIALIZED COLLECTION IN DISPUTE RESOLUTION AND NEGOTIATION □ Cambridge, MA

Patton, Joanne S., Res.Assoc.
AUBURN UNIVERSITY - OFFICE OF PUBLIC SERVICE & RESEARCH - RESOURCE CENTER □ Auburn, AL

Patton, L.K., Exec.Dir.
KENTUCKY COVERED BRIDGE ASSOCIATION - LIBRARY □ Fort Thomas, KY

Patton, Nicholas W., Prin.Libn.
NEWARK PUBLIC LIBRARY - SCIENCE AND TECHNOLOGY DIVISION □ Newark, NJ

Patton, Rich, Info.Serv.Supv.
DENVER PUBLIC LIBRARY - BUSINESS, SCIENCE & TECHNOLOGY DIVISION □ Denver, CO

Patton, Robert, Interp.Spec.
U.S. NATL. PARK SERVICE - CAPE LOOKOUT NATL. SEASHORE - LIBRARY □ Beaufort, NC

Patton, Ruth, Coord.
SANGAMON STATE UNIVERSITY - EAST CENTRAL NETWORK - LIBRARY □ Springfield, IL

Patton, Sandy, Media Supv.
COLORADO SPRINGS PUBLIC SCHOOLS - DISTRICT NO. 11 - TEACHERS' PROFESSIONAL LIBRARY □ Colorado Springs, CO

Patton, Trudy, Libn./Res.Assoc.
UNIVERSITY OF ILLINOIS - HOUSING RESEARCH & DEVELOPMENT PROGRAM - LIBRARY □ Urbana, IL

Patzwald, Gari-Anne, Libn.
NATIONAL COLLEGE OF CHIROPRACTIC - LEARNING RESOURCE CENTER □ Lombard, IL

Paul, Andrea I., Mss.Cur.
NEBRASKA STATE HISTORICAL SOCIETY - ARCHIVES □ Lincoln, NE

Paul, Donald C., Libn.
HUGHES AIRCRAFT COMPANY - CANOGA PARK LIBRARY □ Canoga Park, CA

Paul, Donald T., Hd.
DAYTON AND MONTGOMERY COUNTY PUBLIC LIBRARY - LITERATURE AND FINE ARTS DIVISION □ Dayton, OH

Paul, Elizabeth, Ref.Libn.
SACRED HEART UNIVERSITY - LIBRARY □ Bridgeport, CT

Paul, Gary, Hd., Pub.Serv.
FROSTBURG STATE COLLEGE - LIBRARY □ Frostburg, MD

Paul, George P., Ref.Libn.
UNIVERSITY OF VIRGINIA - MEDICAL CENTER - CLAUDE MOORE HEALTH SCIENCES LIBRARY □ Charlottesville, VA

Paul, Jacquelin, Asst.Libn.
DELAWARE LAW SCHOOL OF WIDENER UNIVERSITY - LAW LIBRARY □ Wilmington, DE

Paul,, Jeff, Coord.
SAN JOSE STATE UNIVERSITY - WAHLQUIST LIBRARY - CHICANO LIBRARY RESOURCE CENTER □ San Jose, CA

Paul, Nancy, Asst.Dir., Tech.Serv.
UNIVERSITY OF WISCONSIN, MADISON - LAW SCHOOL LIBRARY □ Madison, WI

Paul, Nora, Lib.Dir.
MIAMI HERALD - LIBRARY □ Miami, FL

Paul, Patricia, Hd.Cat.
UNIVERSITY OF WISCONSIN, STEVENS POINT - JAMES H. ALBERTSON CENTER FOR LEARNING RESOURCES □ Stevens Point, WI

Paul, Patty, Doc.Libn.
STATE LIBRARY OF FLORIDA □ Tallahassee, FL

Paul, Sara, Asst. Law Libn.
WISCONSIN STATE DEPARTMENT OF JUSTICE - LAW LIBRARY □ Madison, WI

Paul, Sherri
SLEEPY HOLLOW RESTORATIONS, INC. - SPECIAL LIBRARY & ARCHIVES □ Tarrytown, NY

Paul, Suzanne O., Dir.
UNIVERSITY OF PITTSBURGH - CIOCCO LIBRARY □ Pittsburgh, PA

Paul, William G., Univ.Archv.
UNIVERSITY OF WISCONSIN, STEVENS POINT - UNIVERSITY ARCHIVES & PORTAGE COUNTY HISTORICAL SOCIETY COLLECTION □ Stevens Point, WI

Pauli, Dan, Info.Spec.
ESSO RESOURCES CANADA LIMITED - LIBRARY
INFORMATION CENTRE □ Calgary, AB
Paull, Frank O., Jr., Dir.
MARQUETTE COUNTY HISTORICAL SOCIETY -
J.M. LONGYEAR RESEARCH LIBRARY □
Marquette, MI
Paulos, Christiane, Resource Coll.Coord.
INTERAMERICA RESEARCH ASSOCIATES, INC.
- NATIONAL CLEARINGHOUSE FOR BILINGUAL
EDUCATION □ Arlington, VA
Paulsen, Clarence, Hist.
CLOUD COUNTY HISTORICAL MUSEUM -
LIBRARY □ Concordia, KS
Paulsen, Sharon R., Libn.
OREGON STATE HOSPITAL - MEDICAL LIBRARY
□ Salem, OR
Paulson, Gale, Dir.
SAN FRANCISCO ACADEMY OF COMIC ART -
LIBRARY† □ San Francisco, CA
Paulson, Peter, Dir.
NEW YORK STATE LIBRARY □ Albany, NY
Paulson, Roger C., Dir.
ARCHIVES OF THE AIRWAVES □ Needham, MA
Paulukonis, Joseph T., Dir.
DAKOTA STATE COLLEGE - KARL E. MUNDT
LIBRARY □ Madison, SD
Pauth, Patricia R., Adm.
PRICE WATERHOUSE - NEW YORK OFFICE
INFORMATION CENTER □ New York, NY
Pauwels, Colleen K., Dir.
INDIANA UNIVERSITY - LAW LIBRARY □
Bloomington, IN
Pavetti, Sally Thomas, Cur.
EUGENE O'NEILL MEMORIAL THEATER
CENTER, INC. - MONTE CRISTO COTTAGE
LIBRARY □ New London, CT
Pavlich, Josephine, Asst.Libn.
MUSKEGON BUSINESS COLLEGE - LIBRARY □
Muskegon, MI
Pavlin, Stefanie A., Hd., Lib.Serv.
ONTARIO - MINISTRY OF TRANSPORTATION
AND COMMUNICATIONS - LIBRARY AND
INFORMATION CENTRE □ Downsview, ON
Pawling, Diane L., Libn.
METROPOLITAN EDISON COMPANY - SYSTEM
LIBRARY □ Reading, PA
Pawloski, Barbara, Hd., Ref.
MARQUETTE UNIVERSITY - LEGAL RESEARCH
CENTER □ Milwaukee, WI
Pawluk, Mr. W.S., Asst. Regional Dir.
CANADA - STATISTICS CANADA - ADVISORY
SERVICES - WINNIPEG REFERENCE CENTRE □
Winnipeg, MB
Payant, France, Libn.
SUN LIFE OF CANADA - REFERENCE LIBRARY □
Montreal, PQ
Payne, Ben, Libn.
PENN VIRGINIA CORPORATION - LIBRARY □
Philadelphia, PA
Payne, Bernetta, Libn.
HOLY CROSS HOSPITAL OF SILVER SPRING -
MEDICAL LIBRARY □ Silver Spring, MD
Payne, JoAnn H., Cat.
U.S. MARINE CORPS - EDUCATION CENTER -
JAMES CARSON BRECKINRIDGE LIBRARY &
AMPHIBIOUS WARFARE RESEARCH FACILITY □
Quantico, VA
Payne, Judith, Cur.
WASHINGTON COUNTY MUSEUM LIBRARY □
Stillwater, MN
Payne, Linda, Cent. Inquiry Libn.
STANDARD & POOR'S CORPORATION -
RESEARCH LIBRARY □ New York, NY
Payne, Lou D., Info.Spec.
PHILLIPS PETROLEUM COMPANY - RESEARCH &
DEVELOPMENT DEPARTMENT - TECHNICAL
INFORMATION BRANCH □ Bartlesville, OK
Payne, Ron G., Mgr., AV Serv.
OKLAHOMA STATE UNIVERSITY - AUDIO
VISUAL CENTER □ Stillwater, OK

Payne, Sherry, Libn.
ASHLAND OIL, INC. - TECHNICAL
INFORMATION CENTER □ Ashland, KY
Payson, Patricia, Libn.
SOUTHWEST WISCONSIN VOCATIONAL-
TECHNICAL INSTITUTE - LEARNING
RESOURCES CENTER □ Fennimore, WI
Paysse, James L., Ed.Asst.
TULANE UNIVERSITY OF LOUISIANA - DELTA
REGIONAL PRIMATE RESEARCH CENTER -
SCIENCE INFORMATION SERVICE □ Covington,
LA
Payton, Patricia, Libn.
NASHOBA COMMUNITY HOSPITAL - MEDICAL
LIBRARY □ Ayer, MA
Pazen, Dick, Res.Anl.
WISCONSIN STATE LEGISLATIVE REFERENCE
BUREAU □ Madison, WI
Pazienza, Lois, Libn.
METASCIENCE FOUNDATION - LIBRARY □
Kingston, RI
Pazmino, John, Libn.
AMATEUR ASTRONOMERS ASSOCIATION -
JANE H. DOUGLAS MEMORIAL LIBRARY □ New
York, NY
Peabody, Elaine, Ref.Libn.
SAN DIEGO COUNTY LAW LIBRARY □ San Diego,
CA
Peach, Tamara, Asst.Libn.
NORTHWESTERN STATE UNIVERSITY OF
LOUISIANA - EUGENE P. WATSON LIBRARY -
SHREVEPORT DIVISION □ Shreveport, LA
Peacock, Dr. Edward, Exec.Dir.
AMERICAN INSTITUTE OF FAMILY RELATIONS
- ROSWELL H. JOHNSON RESEARCH LIBRARY □
North Hollywood, CA
Peacock, Joyce F., Libn.
AAI CORPORATION - TECHNICAL LIBRARY □
Baltimore, MD
Pearce, Dwain H., V.P., Gen.Mgr.
BELL & HOWELL COMPANY - MICRO PHOTO
DIVISION - MICROFORMS ARCHIVE† □
Wooster, OH
Pearce, Edward D., Libn.
MUSEUM OF SCIENCE - LIBRARY □ Boston, MA
Pearce, Kathleen, Libn.
CALIFORNIA STATE - COURT OF APPEAL, 5TH
APPELLATE DISTRICT - LAW LIBRARY □
Fresno, CA
Pearce, Louise O., Asst.Libn.
ETHYL CORPORATION - INFORMATION &
LIBRARY SERVICES LIBRARY □ Baton Rouge, LA
Pearce, Margaret Tranne, Libn.
U.S. COURT OF APPEALS, 8TH CIRCUIT -
LIBRARY □ Kansas City, MO
Pearce, Mona B., Libn.
NEWFOUNDLAND - DEPARTMENT OF JUSTICE -
LAW LIBRARY □ St. John's, NF
Pearce, Stanley, Dir., Info.Serv.
O'MELVENY AND MYERS - INFORMATION
SERVICES □ Los Angeles, CA
Pearlman, Nancy, Exec.Dir.
ECOLOGY CENTER OF SOUTHERN CALIFORNIA
□ Los Angeles, CA
Pearlman, Sandy, Mng.Ed.
CRC PRESS, INC. - LIBRARY† □ Boca Raton, FL
Pearlstein, Sol, Dir.
BROOKHAVEN NATIONAL LABORATORY -
NATIONAL NUCLEAR DATA CENTER □ Upton,
NY
Pearlstein, Ms. Toby, Chf.Libn. & Archv.
MASSACHUSETTS STATE TRANSPORTATION
LIBRARY □ Boston, MA
Pearson, Deborah, Cat.
SEYFARTH, SHAW, FAIRWEATHER &
GERALDSON - LIBRARY □ Chicago, IL
Pearson, Ellen M., Asst.Libn.
UNIVERSITY OF GUELPH - LIBRARY □ Guelph,
ON
Pearson, Frances, Libn.
CALIFORNIA STATE DEPARTMENT OF WATER
RESOURCES - LAW LIBRARY □ Sacramento, CA

Pearson, Fred W., Ref.Libn.
LANCASTER BIBLE COLLEGE - STOLL
MEMORIAL LIBRARY □ Lancaster, PA
Pearson, Frederic C., Circ.Libn.
COOK COUNTY LAW LIBRARY □ Chicago, IL
Pearson, Louise, Cat.
DICKINSON STATE COLLEGE - STOXEN
LIBRARY □ Dickinson, ND
Pearson, Michael, Hd.
METROPOLITAN TORONTO LIBRARY - HISTORY
DEPARTMENT □ Toronto, ON
Pearson, Richard C., Dir.
BRIGHAM YOUNG UNIVERSITY, HAWAII
CAMPUS - JOSEPH F. SMITH LIBRARY AND
MEDIA CENTER - SPECIAL COLLECTION □ Laie,
HI
Pearson, Sherry, Tech.Info.Spec.
U.S. NATL. MARINE FISHERIES SERVICE -
NATIONAL MARINE MAMMAL LABORATORY -
LIBRARY □ Seattle, WA
Pearson, Virginia, Ref.Libn.
WESTERN KENTUCKY UNIVERSITY - DEPT. OF
SPECIAL COLLECTIONS - KENTUCKY LIBRARY
AND MUSEUM/UNIVERSITY ARCHIVES □
Bowling Green, KY
Pease, Mina, Dir.
LEGAL AID SOCIETY OF WESTCHESTER -
LIBRARY □ White Plains, NY
Pease, William, Cat.Dept.
SAN DIEGO STATE UNIVERSITY - MALCOLM A.
LOVE LIBRARY - SPECIAL COLLECTIONS† □ San
Diego, CA
Peaster, Max C., Libn.
ERIE COUNTY LAW LIBRARY □ Erie, PA
Peat, W. Leslie, Law Libn.
VERMONT LAW SCHOOL - LIBRARY □ South
Royalton, VT
Peatross, Elizabeth, Requisitions Libn.
LOUISIANA STATE UNIVERSITY MEDICAL
CENTER - SCHOOL OF MEDICINE IN
SHREVEPORT - LIBRARY □ Shreveport, LA
Peay, Wayne, Computer & Media Serv.
UNIVERSITY OF UTAH - SPENCER S. ECCLES
HEALTH SCIENCES LIBRARY □ Salt Lake City,
UT
Peck, Dr. Abraham J., Assoc.Dir.
HEBREW UNION COLLEGE - JEWISH
INSTITUTE OF RELIGION - AMERICAN JEWISH
ARCHIVES □ Cincinnati, OH
Peck, Betty A., Adm.Asst.
UNIVERSITY OF MICHIGAN - ALFRED
TAUBMAN MEDICAL LIBRARY □ Ann Arbor, MI
Peck, Charles M., Dir./Libn.
MARISKA ALDRICH MEMORIAL FOUNDATION,
INC. - ALDRICH LIBRARY OF MUSIC □
Wrightwood, CA
Peck, David A., Personnel
CONNECTICUT STATE LIBRARY □ Hartford, CT
Peck, Elsie, Sr. Dance Libn.
NEW YORK PUBLIC LIBRARY - GENERAL
LIBRARY OF THE PERFORMING ARTS □ New
York, NY
Peck, Jane, Hd., Hum. & Fine Arts
WORCESTER PUBLIC LIBRARY - REFERENCE
AND READER SERVICES □ Worcester, MA
Peck, Mary J., AHEC Lib.Dir.
ROWAN MEMORIAL HOSPITAL - MC KENZIE
MEMORIAL LIBRARY □ Salisbury, NC
Peck, Thomas D., Educ.Cons.
CALIFORNIA STATE DEPARTMENT OF ALCOHOL
AND DRUG PROGRAMS - INFORMATION
CLEARINGHOUSE □ Sacramento, CA
Peckham, Gloria M., Chf.Libn.
CANADA - ENERGY, MINES & RESOURCES
CANADA - CANMET - LIBRARY† □ Ottawa, ON
Peckham, Harry, Asst.
TIME, INC. - SPORTS LIBRARY □ New York, NY
Pedersen, Dennis, Tech.Info.Sci.
PILLSBURY COMPANY - TECHNICAL
INFORMATION CENTER □ Minneapolis, MN

Pedersen, Lila, Asst.Dir./Coll.Dev.
UNIVERSITY OF NORTH DAKOTA - SCHOOL OF MEDICINE - HARLEY E. FRENCH MEDICAL LIBRARY □ Grand Forks, ND

Pedersen, Naomi, ILL
EG&G, INC. - IDAHO NATIONAL ENGINEERING LABORATORY - INEL TECHNICAL LIBRARY □ Idaho Falls, ID

Pedersen, Wayne A., Dir., Educ. Media
IOWA LUTHERAN HOSPITAL - DEPARTMENT OF EDUCATIONAL MEDIA □ Des Moines, IA

Peel, Richard C., Adm.Libn.
ARIZONA STATE REGIONAL LIBRARY FOR THE BLIND AND PHYSICALLY HANDICAPPED □ Phoenix, AZ

Peele, Bonnie, Spec. Projects Libn.
NORTH CAROLINA STATE DEPARTMENT OF CULTURAL RESOURCES - LIBRARY FOR THE BLIND AND PHYSICALLY HANDICAPPED □ Raleigh, NC

Peele, Linda F., Plan.Div.Asst.
U.S. DEPT. OF ENERGY - ALASKA POWER ADMINISTRATION - LIBRARY □ Juneau, AK

Peeling, Mary Alice, Asst.Libn.
DELAWARE LAW SCHOOL OF WIDENER UNIVERSITY - LAW LIBRARY □ Wilmington, DE

Peelman, Marie A., Hd.Libn.
SAN DIEGO GAS AND ELECTRIC COMPANY - LIBRARY □ San Diego, CA

Peery, Karen, Libn.
STEVENS CLINIC HOSPITAL - LIBRARY □ Welch, WV

Peete, Gary, Foreign Doc.Libn.
UNIVERSITY OF CALIFORNIA, SANTA BARBARA - GOVERNMENT PUBLICATIONS DEPARTMENT □ Santa Barbara, CA

Peffer, Margery, Asst.Hd.
CARNEGIE LIBRARY OF PITTSBURGH - SCIENCE AND TECHNOLOGY DEPARTMENT □ Pittsburgh, PA

Pefley, Lynn M.
OMI INTERNATIONAL CORP. - LIBRARY □ Warren, MI

Pegram, J. Wally, Libn.
UNIVERSITY OF CALIFORNIA, LOS ANGELES - PHYSICS LIBRARY □ Los Angeles, CA

Peirce, Jane, Ref. & ILL
UNIVERSITY OF WISCONSIN, RIVER FALLS - CHALMER DAVEE LIBRARY □ River Falls, WI

Peischl, Dr. Thomas M., Dir. of Libs.
SUNY - COLLEGE AT POTSDAM - FREDERICK W. CRUMB MEMORIAL LIBRARY □ Potsdam, NY

Peiser, Judy, Dir.
CENTER FOR SOUTHERN FOLKLORE - ARCHIVES □ Memphis, TN

Peiser, Richard H., Cat./Libn.
NORTHWEST EDUCATIONAL COOPERATIVE - LIBRARY □ Arlington Heights, IL

Peladeau, Marius B., Dir.
FARNSWORTH (William A.) - LIBRARY AND ART MUSEUM □ Rockland, ME

Pelchat, Eugene, Hd., Tech.Serv.
DALHOUSIE UNIVERSITY - W.K. KELLOGG HEALTH SCIENCES LIBRARY □ Halifax, NS

Peles, Gloria W., Law Libn.
HUNTERDON COUNTY LAW LIBRARY □ Flemington, NJ

Pellan, Laurence, Libn.
WILLIAM M. MERCER, LTD. - INFORMATION CENTRE □ Toronto, ON

Pelland, Joan, Hd., Tech.Serv.
LOYOLA UNIVERSITY (New Orleans) - LAW LIBRARY □ New Orleans, LA

Pellegrino, Clementine, Spec.Coll.Libn.
GEORGETOWN UNIVERSITY - MEDICAL CENTER - DAHLGREN MEMORIAL LIBRARY □ Washington, DC

Pellegrino, Jane, Community Prog.Coord.
EASTERN VIRGINIA MEDICAL SCHOOL - MOORMAN MEMORIAL LIBRARY □ Norfolk, VA

Pellegrino, M., Chf.Libn.
GIBBS & HILL, INC. - LIBRARY □ New York, NY

Pellerin, Darlene
SASKATCHEWAN PIPING INDUSTRY JOINT TRAINING BOARD - LIBRARY □ Regina, SK

Pellerin, Jean L., Assoc.Libn.
ACADIAN GENEALOGICAL & HISTORICAL ASSOCIATION - LIBRARY □ Manchester, NH

Pelletier, Claire, Acq.Libn.
ECOLE POLYTECHNIQUE - BIBLIOTHEQUE □ Montreal, PQ

Pelletier, Flavius, Media Ctr.Dir.
CEGEP DU VIEUX-MONTREAL - LIBRARY □ Montreal, PQ

Pelletier, Gary, ILL Techn.
U.S. VETERANS ADMINISTRATION (ME-Augusta) - CENTER LIBRARY □ Augusta, ME

Pelletier, Jacqueline, Libn.
UNIVERSITE DE MONTREAL - AMENAGEMENT-BIBLIOTHEQUE □ Montreal, PQ

Pelletier, Louise, Hd.
HYDRO-QUEBEC - INSTITUT DE RECHERCHE - BIBLIOTHEQUE □ Varennes, PQ

Pelletier, Paul, Hd., Bus., Sci. & Tech.
WORCESTER PUBLIC LIBRARY - REFERENCE AND READER SERVICES □ Worcester, MA

Pellini, Nancy M., Div.Mgr.
STONE AND WEBSTER ENGINEERING CORPORATION - TECHNICAL INFORMATION CENTER □ Boston, MA

Pellitier, Suzanne I., Acq.Libn.
UNIVERSITY OF MAINE SCHOOL OF LAW - DONALD L. GARBRECHT LAW LIBRARY □ Portland, ME

Peloquin, Margaret, Med.Libn.
AUSTIN COMMUNITY COLLEGE - HEALTH SCIENCES LIBRARY □ Austin, TX

Pelote, Vincent, Asst.Cur.
RUTGERS UNIVERSITY, THE STATE UNIVERSITY OF NEW JERSEY - INSTITUTE OF JAZZ STUDIES □ Newark, NJ

Pelter, Madelaine, Circ.Supv.
ART CENTER COLLEGE OF DESIGN - JAMES LEMONT FOGG MEMORIAL LIBRARY □ Pasadena, CA

Peltier, Valerie, AV Techn.
WISCONSIN INDIANHEAD TECHNICAL INSTITUTE, NEW RICHMOND CAMPUS - LEARNING RESOURCE CENTER □ New Richmond, WI

Pelz, Bruce E., Coll.Mgt.Libn.
UNIVERSITY OF CALIFORNIA, LOS ANGELES - ENGINEERING & MATHEMATICAL SCIENCES LIBRARY □ Los Angeles, CA

Pemberton, Gale, Libn.
DIOCESAN SEMINARY OF THE IMMACULATE CONCEPTION - LIBRARY □ Springfield, IL

Pembroke, Christine, Asst.Libn.
U.S. COURT OF APPEALS, DISTRICT OF COLUMBIA CIRCUIT - LIBRARY □ Washington, DC

Pen, Emma F.C., Lib.Prog.Dir.
FELETI PACIFIC LIBRARY □ Pago Pago, AS

Pena, Mary Jo
ARTHUR ANDERSEN & CO. - BUSINESS LIBRARY □ Houston, TX

Penasack, Sharron B., Tech.Libn.
DIGITAL EQUIPMENT CORPORATION - MERRIMACK LIBRARY SERVICES □ Merrimack, NJ

Penberthy, Catherine, Circ.Libn.
UNIVERSITY OF KENTUCKY - LAW LIBRARY □ Lexington, KY

Pendleton, Dr. Eldridge H., Dir., Coll. & Prog.
OLD YORK HISTORICAL SOCIETY - LIBRARY □ York, ME

Peng, Lily, Info./Circ.Libn.
BAYSTATE MEDICAL CENTER - HEALTH SCIENCES LIBRARY □ Springfield, MA

Pengilly, Linda M., Rsrc.Info.Ctr.Coord.
COLLEGE PLACEMENT COUNCIL, INC. - RESOURCE INFORMATION CENTER □ Bethlehem, PA

Penich, Sonia, Sr. Law Libn.
NEW YORK STATE SUPREME COURT - 1ST JUDICIAL DISTRICT - CRIMINAL BRANCH - LAW LIBRARY □ New York, NY

Penix, Cindy, Libn.
ROCKY MOUNT HISTORICAL ASSOCIATION - LIBRARY □ Piney Flats, TN

Penix, Holly A., Lib.Asst.
UNIVERSITY OF ARIZONA - DIVISION OF ECONOMIC AND BUSINESS RESEARCH - LIBRARY □ Tucson, AZ

Penman, Elizabeth H., Libn.
MERCK & COMPANY, INC. - LAW LIBRARY □ Rahway, NJ

Penne, Carol, Asst.Dir.
AMERICAN BANKERS ASSOCIATION - LIBRARY & INFORMATION SERVICES □ Washington, DC

Pennell, Peggy, Libn.
CHEMICAL BANK - RESEARCH LIBRARY □ New York, NY

Penner, Elaine C., Libn.
U.S. AIR FORCE BASE - GOODFELLOW BASE LIBRARY† □ Goodfellow AFB, TX

Penney, Pearce J., Chf.Prov.Libn.
NEWFOUNDLAND - PUBLIC LIBRARY SERVICES □ St. John's, NF

Penniman, W.D., Dir.
AT & T BELL LABORATORIES - LIBRARIES AND INFORMATION SYSTEMS CENTER □ Murray Hill, NJ

Pennington, Bill, Libn.
MIDWEST HISTORICAL & GENEALOGICAL SOCIETY, INC. - LIBRARY □ Wichita, KS

Pennington, Catherine, Law Libn.
JOHNSON & SWANSON - LIBRARY □ Dallas, TX

Penny, Jennifer, Libn.
UNIVERSITY OF ALBERTA - COMPUTING SCIENCE READING ROOM □ Edmonton, AB

Penny, Laura, Asst.Libn.
PIKES PEAK LIBRARY DISTRICT - LOCAL HISTORY COLLECTION □ Colorado Springs, CO

Penprase, Catherine J., Dir.
CITY OF COMMERCE PUBLIC LIBRARY □ Commerce, CA

Penrose, Anna Mae, Libn.
ST. JOSEPH'S UNIVERSITY - ACADEMY OF FOOD MARKETING - CAMPBELL LIBRARY □ Philadelphia, PA

Penry, Barbara, Legal Asst.
GULF STATES UTILITIES COMPANY - LAW LIBRARY □ Beaumont, TX

Penson, Andrew, Asst.Ref.Libn.
GEORGIA SOUTHERN COLLEGE - ARCHIVES/SPECIAL COLLECTIONS† □ Statesboro, GA

Pensyl, Janeth L., Libn.
MONROE COUNTY LAW LIBRARY □ Stroudsburg, PA

Pensyl, Ornella L., Chf.
U.S. ARMY INTELLIGENCE SCHOOL, DEVENS - LIBRARY† □ Ft. Devens, MA

Pentecost, Peggy, Info.Coord.
AUTOMOTIVE INFORMATION COUNCIL - LIBRARY □ Southfield, MI

Pentland, Michelle, Program Coord.
HEALTH RESEARCH AND EDUCATIONAL TRUST OF NEW JERSEY - LEARNING CENTER† □ Princeton, NJ

Penwell, Donna, Musm.Mgr.
COLTON HALL MUSEUM - LIBRARY □ Monterey, CA

Pepin, Milagros, Archv.
PUERTO RICO - INSTITUTE OF PUERTO RICAN CULTURE - ARCHIVO GENERAL DE PUERTO RICO □ San Juan, PR

Pepin, Patricia M., Chf., Lib.Br.
U.S. ARMY MEDICAL RESEARCH INSTITUTE OF CHEMICAL DEFENSE - WOOD TECHNICAL LIBRARY □ Aberdeen Proving Ground, MD

Pepin, Robert, Hd.
COLUMBIA UNIVERSITY - BUTLER LIBRARY CIRCULATION DEPARTMENT □ New York, NY

Pepper, Alice, Libn.
DETROIT FREE PRESS - LIBRARY □ Detroit, MI

Pepper, Janice, Ref.Libn., Doc.Sect.
U.S. ARMY - BELVOIR RESEARCH &
DEVELOPMENT CENTER - TECHNICAL LIBRARY
□ Ft. Belvoir, VA
Pepper, Jerold, Libn.
ADIRONDACK HISTORICAL ASSOCIATION -
ADIRONDACK MUSEUM - RESEARCH LIBRARY □
Blue Mountain Lake, NY
Pepper, Sheila, Bus.Libn.
MC MASTER UNIVERSITY - BUSINESS LIBRARY
□ Hamilton, ON
Peralta, Lydia, Libn.
MAGNAVOX GOVERNMENT & INDUSTRIAL
ELECTRONICS COMPANY - ENGINEERING
LIBRARY† □ Fort Wayne, IN
Peraza, R.P., Mgr.
OLIN CORPORATION - RESEARCH CENTER/
INFORMATION CENTER □ New Haven, CT
Percaccia, Carol, Adm.Aid
NEW YORK UNIVERSITY - SCHOOL OF LAW
LIBRARY □ New York, NY
Perch, Dr. Robert, Lib.Chm.
MONTGOMERY HOSPITAL - MEDICAL LIBRARY
□ Norristown, PA
Percival, Marjorie, Hd.Libn.
INDIANAPOLIS PUBLIC SCHOOLS - KARL R.
KALP LIBRARY □ Indianapolis, IN
Percival, Mary, Libn.
MC CARTHY AND MC CARTHY - LIBRARY □
Toronto, ON
Percy, Nancy W., Asst. State Libn.
CALIFORNIA STATE LIBRARY □ Sacramento, CA
Percy, Theresa Rini, Libn.
OLD STURBRIDGE VILLAGE - RESEARCH
LIBRARY □ Sturbridge, MA
Perdick, Kathy, Supv.
AT & T BELL LABORATORIES & TECHNOLOGIES
- LIBRARY □ Allentown, PA
Pere, Mildred, Prin.Lib.Asst.
BERGEN COUNTY OFFICE ON AGING -
REFERENCE LIBRARY OF GERONTOLOGY □
Hackensack, NJ
Pereny, Evelyn, Libn.
AULLWOOD AUDUBON CENTER AND FARM -
LIBRARY □ Dayton, OH
Peresich, Sr. Mary Giles, Cat.Libn.
UNIVERSITY OF SOUTH ALABAMA - COLLEGE
OF MEDICINE - BIOMEDICAL LIBRARY □
Mobile, AL
Perez, Carlos, CPR Libn.
UNIVERSITY OF PUERTO RICO - HUMACAO
UNIVERSITY COLLEGE - LIBRARY □ Humacao,
PR
Perez, Denise
UNIVERSITY OF PUERTO RICO - PUERTO
RICAN COLLECTION† □ Rio Piedras, PR
Perez, Ernest, Chf.Libn.
CHICAGO SUN-TIMES - EDITORIAL LIBRARY □
Chicago, IL
Perez, Ida, Asst.Libn., Ref.
HOFFMANN-LA ROCHE, INC. - BUSINESS
INFORMATION CENTER □ Nutley, NJ
Perez, Madeline, Archv.
WAKE FOREST UNIVERSITY - BOWMAN GRAY
SCHOOL OF MEDICINE - COY C. CARPENTER
LIBRARY □ Winston-Salem, NC
Perez, Marjory Allen, County Hist.
WAYNE COUNTY HISTORICAL SOCIETY
MUSEUM - LIBRARY □ Lyons, NY
Perez, Marta E., Hd., Doc.Dept.
UNIVERSITY OF PUERTO RICO - LAW SCHOOL
LIBRARY □ Rio Piedras, PR
Perez, Maureen, Talking Bks.Serv.
METROPOLITAN TORONTO LIBRARY -
REGIONAL AUDIO VISUAL DEPARTMENT □
Toronto, ON
Perez, Nelida, Libn.
CUNY - CENTRO DE ESTUDIOS
PUERTORRIQUENOS □ New York, NY
Perez, Patti
NESTE, BRUDIN & STONE, INC. - CORPORATE
LIBRARY □ San Diego, CA

Perham, Constance B., Owner-Dir.
NEW ALMADEN MERCURY MINING MUSEUM -
LIBRARY □ New Almaden, CA
Peritore, Laura, Ser./Ref.Libn.
UNIVERSITY OF CALIFORNIA, SAN FRANCISCO
- HASTINGS COLLEGE OF THE LAW - LEGAL
INFORMATION CENTER □ San Francisco, CA
Perkins, Angela, Coord.
NORFOLK STATE COLLEGE - W.K. KELLOGG
SOCIAL SCIENCE RESEARCH CENTER -
LIBRARY □ Norfolk, VA
Perkins, Evlyn, Libn.
VOLTARC TUBES INC. - LIBRARY □ Fairfield, CT
Perkins, James A., Pres.
CHATFIELD BRASS BAND INC. - FREE MUSIC
LENDING LIBRARY □ Chatfield, MN
Perkins, Kiva, Cur.
HIVE PUBLISHING COMPANY - MANAGEMENT
HISTORY LIBRARY □ Easton, PA
Perkins, Lee F., Chf.Libn.
FORD AEROSPACE & COMMUNICATIONS CORP.
- WESTERN DEVELOPMENT LABORATORIES
(WDL) - TECHNICAL LIBRARY □ Palo Alto, CA
Perkins, Rev. Louis L.
PROTESTANT EPISCOPAL CHURCH -
EPISCOPAL DIOCESE OF EASTERN OREGON -
ARCHIVES □ LaGrande, OR
Perkins, Shirley, Hd.
UNIVERSITY OF SASKATCHEWAN - SPECIAL
COLLECTIONS - SHORTT LIBRARY OF
CANADIANA □ Saskatoon, SK
Perkins, Steve, Act.Ref.Libn.
UNIVERSITY OF CINCINNATI - ROBERT S.
MARX LAW LIBRARY □ Cincinnati, OH
Perkins, Susan, Dir., Educ.Rsrcs.
FIRST PRESBYTERIAN CHURCH OF
CHARLESTON - LIBRARY □ Charleston, WV
Perkins, Timothy, Media Ctr.Dir.
MINNEAPOLIS COLLEGE OF ART AND DESIGN -
LIBRARY AND MEDIA CENTER □ Minneapolis,
MN
Perkons, Caroline, Info.Serv.Spec.
BEECHAM PRODUCTS - WESTERN HEMISPHERE
RESEARCH - LIBRARY □ Parsippany, NJ
Perl, Ruth
ACKERMAN INSTITUTE FOR FAMILY THERAPY,
INC. - LIBRARY □ New York, NY
Perla, Carole, Asst.Libn.
SUN LIFE ASSURANCE COMPANY OF CANADA -
REFERENCE LIBRARY □ Wellesley Hills, MA
Perlin, Janet, Libn.
TEMPLE ISRAEL - LEONARD M. SANDHAUS
MEMORIAL LIBRARY □ Sharon, MA
Perlin, Ruth R., Cur.-in-Charge
NATIONAL GALLERY OF ART - DEPARTMENT OF
EXTENSION PROGRAMS □ Washington, DC
Perlman, Michael, Ref.Libn.
CHICAGO SUN-TIMES - EDITORIAL LIBRARY □
Chicago, IL
Perlman, Stephen, Libn.
U.S.D.A. - AGRICULTURAL RESEARCH SERVICE
- PLUM ISLAND ANIMAL DISEASE CENTER
LIBRARY □ Greenport, NY
Perlman, Vicky A., Mgr.
STANDARD OIL COMPANY OF INDIANA -
LIBRARY/INFORMATION CENTER □ Chicago, IL
Perlmutter, Jane, Libn.
U.S. DEPT. OF JUSTICE - NATIONAL
INSTITUTE OF CORRECTIONS - NIC
INFORMATION CENTER □ Boulder, CO
Perlmutter, Mary Jeanne, Asst.Libn.
BROOME DEVELOPMENTAL SERVICES - STAFF
LIBRARY □ Binghamton, NY
Perlroth, Irving, Data Preparation
U.S. NATL. OCEANIC & ATMOSPHERIC
ADMINISTRATION - NATIONAL
OCEANOGRAPHIC DATA CENTER □ Washington,
DC
Perman, Karen A., Libn.
ARCHER DANIELS MIDLAND COMPANY -
LIBRARY □ Decatur, IL

Perona, Gerald F., District Libn.
GATEWAY VOCATIONAL TECHNICAL & ADULT
EDUCATION DISTRICT - LEARNING
RESOURCES CENTER □ Kenosha, WI
Perot, Monica, Hd., Circ.
YORK UNIVERSITY - LAW LIBRARY □
Downsview, ON
Perrault, Arthur, Libn.
BARREAU DE MONTREAL - BIBLIOTHEQUE □
Montreal, PQ
Perrault, Robert, ILL
U.S. DEPT. OF TRANSPORTATION -
TRANSPORTATION SYSTEMS CENTER -
TECHNICAL REFERENCE CENTER □ Cambridge,
MA
Perreault, Mrs. C., ILL
SHAWINIGAN CONSULTANTS INC. - LIBRARY □
Montreal, PQ
Perrier, Monique, Act.Chf.Libn.
CANADA - DEPARTMENT OF
COMMUNICATIONS - INFORMATION SERVICES
□ Ottawa, ON
Perrin, Mrs. Lloyd W., Lib.Asst.
HISTORIC DEERFIELD, INC. - HENRY N. FLYNT
LIBRARY - POCUMTUCK VALLEY MEMORIAL
ASSOCIATION □ Deerfield, MA
Perrin, Rosemarie, Film Lib.Mgr.
INSTITUTE OF INDUSTRIAL ENGINEERS, INC. -
FILM LIBRARY □ Norcross, GA
Perrin, Rosemarie, Lib.Mgr.
INSTITUTE OF INDUSTRIAL ENGINEERS, INC. -
FRANK & LILIAN GILBRETH MEMORIAL
LIBRARY □ Norcross, GA
Perrine, Dr. Richard L., Prof.
UNIVERSITY OF CALIFORNIA, LOS ANGELES -
ENVIRONMENTAL SCIENCE AND ENGINEERING
- LIBRARY □ Los Angeles, CA
Perrine, Susan, Libn.
SHEA & GARDNER - LIBRARY □ Washington, DC
Perron, Howard, Ref.Libn.
CONCORDIA UNIVERSITY - LOYOLA CAMPUS -
GEORGES P. VANIER LIBRARY □ Montreal, PQ
Perron, L., Mgr., Info.Sys.
BELL-NORTHERN RESEARCH LTD. -
INFORMATION RESOURCE CENTRE □ Ottawa,
ON
Perron, Sylvie, Analyste
HYDRO-QUEBEC - V.P. PLANIFICATION
GENERALE - CENTRE DE DOCUMENTATION □
Montreal, PQ
Perron-Croteau, Lise, Chf., Pub.Serv.Sect.
CANADA - PUBLIC ARCHIVES OF CANADA -
LIBRARY □ Ottawa, ON
Perrott, H.M., Libn.
DU PONT CANADA, INC. - MAITLAND WORKS
LIBRARY □ Maitland, ON
Perrussel, Jeanette, Hd., Cat. Maintenance
TEACHERS COLLEGE - MILBANK MEMORIAL
LIBRARY □ New York, NY
Perry, Beth I., State Libn.
RHODE ISLAND STATE LIBRARY □ Providence,
RI
Perry, Mrs. Billie Ann, Libn.
AEROSPACE INDUSTRIES ASSOCIATION OF
AMERICA - LIBRARY □ Washington, DC
Perry, Ceil, ILL Libn.
MOUNT ST. ALPHONSUS THEOLOGICAL
SEMINARY - LIBRARY† □ Esopus, NY
Perry, Elizabeth, Libn.
UNIVERSITY OF TORONTO - CENTRE FOR
INDUSTRIAL RELATIONS - INFORMATION
SERVICE □ Toronto, ON
Perry, Ellen, Info.Spec.
BANK ADMINISTRATION INSTITUTE -
INFORMATION CENTER □ Rolling Meadows, IL
Perry, Frances, Law Libn.
TARRANT COUNTY LAW LIBRARY □ Fort Worth,
TX
Perry, Glenda, Ser.Libn.
UNIVERSITY OF TENNESSEE - CENTER FOR
THE HEALTH SCIENCES LIBRARY □ Memphis,
TN

Perry, Guest, Dir.
HOUGHTON MIFFLIN COMPANY - LIBRARY □ Boston, MA

Perry, Helen, Assoc.Dir.
CANADIAN NATIONAL INSTITUTE FOR THE BLIND - NATIONAL LIBRARY SERVICES - SHERMAN SWIFT REFERENCE LIBRARY □ Toronto, ON

Perry, Irene, Sr.Asst.Libn., Engr./ILL
COOPER UNION FOR THE ADVANCEMENT OF SCIENCE AND ART - LIBRARY □ New York, NY

Perry, Lee, Historical Coll.
UNIVERSITY OF BRITISH COLUMBIA - WOODWARD BIOMEDICAL LIBRARY □ Vancouver, BC

Perry, Maxine, Cat.Libn.
PASADENA PRESBYTERIAN CHURCH - LIBRARY □ St. Petersburg, FL

Perry, Molly, Dir.
MASON COUNTY HISTORICAL SOCIETY - ROSE HAWLEY MUSEUM AND HISTORICAL LIBRARY □ Ludington, MI

Perry, Nena K., Ref.Libn.
EMORY UNIVERSITY - SCHOOL OF MEDICINE - A.W. CALHOUN MEDICAL LIBRARY □ Atlanta, GA

Perry, Pat J., District Libn.
U.S. ARMY - CORPS OF ENGINEERS - SEATTLE DISTRICT - LIBRARY □ Seattle, WA

Perry, Patricia, Libn.
ROCKY MOUNTAIN HOSPITAL - C. LLOYD PETERSON MEMORIAL LIBRARY □ Denver, CO

Perry, Paula J., Tech.Serv.Libn.
DAVIS POLK & WARDWELL - LIBRARY □ New York, NY

Perry, Randall A., Archv.
LOUISIANA STATE OFFICE OF THE SECRETARY OF STATE - STATE ARCHIVES AND RECORDS SERVICE - ARCHIVES SECTION □ Baton Rouge, LA

Persaud, Seeta, Asst.Libn.
MUTUAL OF OMAHA/UNITED OF OMAHA - LIBRARY† □ Omaha, NE

Persempere, Dominic A., Pub.Rec.Adm.
CONNECTICUT STATE LIBRARY □ Hartford, CT

Pershing, Gwen, Hd.
INDIANA UNIVERSITY - MEDICAL SCIENCES LIBRARY □ Bloomington, IN

Pershing, Laura M., Law Libn.
IDAHO STATE LAW LIBRARY □ Boise, ID

Persiani, Damon, Libn.
ST. MARY'S HOSPITAL - HEALTH SCIENCES LIBRARY □ Richmond, VA

Person, Roland, Asst.Libn.
SOUTHERN ILLINOIS UNIVERSITY, CARBONDALE - UNDERGRADUATE LIBRARY □ Carbondale, IL

Persons, Jerry, Hd.Libn.
STANFORD UNIVERSITY - MUSIC LIBRARY □ Stanford, CA

Persson, Dorothy M., Libn.
UNIVERSITY OF IOWA - PSYCHOLOGY LIBRARY □ Iowa City, IA

Pertell, Grace M., Asst.Libn.
COMMONWEALTH EDISON COMPANY - LIBRARY □ Chicago, IL

Perton, David, Pres.
LEWIS (Frederic) INC. - PHOTOGRAPHIC LIBRARY □ New York, NY

Pertzog, Betsy S., Med.Libn.
U.S. VETERANS ADMINISTRATION (AL-Tuscaloosa) - HOSPITAL MEDICAL LIBRARY □ Tuscaloosa, AL

Perushek, Diane, Cur.
PRINCETON UNIVERSITY - GEST ORIENTAL LIBRARY AND EAST ASIAN COLLECTIONS □ Princeton, NJ

Perussina, Mary Ann, Ref.Libn.
UNIVERSITY OF TEXAS MEDICAL BRANCH - MOODY MEDICAL LIBRARY □ Galveston, TX

Perwien, Sharon, Lib.Coord.
JEWISH COMMUNITY CENTER OF GREATER MINNEAPOLIS - LIBRARY □ Minneapolis, MN

Peschel, Susan Ewart, Cat./Ref.Libn.
AMERICAN GEOGRAPHICAL SOCIETY COLLECTION OF THE UNIVERSITY OF WISCONSIN, MILWAUKEE - GOLDA MEIR LIBRARY □ Milwaukee, WI

Peshel, Barbara B., Monograph Serv.
UNIVERSITY OF OKLAHOMA - HEALTH SCIENCES CENTER LIBRARY □ Oklahoma City, OK

Pestel, Helen, Mgr., MCIC Info.Serv.
BATTELLE-COLUMBUS LABORATORIES - METALS AND CERAMICS INFORMATION CENTER □ Columbus, OH

Peterman, A.L., Registrar
CANADIAN CREDIT INSTITUTE - CREDIT RESEARCH AND LENDING LIBRARY □ Toronto, ON

Peternell, Therese, Libn.
UNIVERSITE DE MONTREAL - BIBLIOTHEQUE DE LA SANTE □ Montreal, PQ

Peters, Carole, Mgr., Info.Serv.
MONTREAL BOARD OF TRADE - INFORMATION CENTRE □ Montreal, PQ

Peters, Caroline S., Libn.
SAGA CORPORATION - MARKETING LIBRARY □ Menlo Park, CA

Peters, Diane, Ref./Coll.Libn.
WILFRID LAURIER UNIVERSITY - LIBRARY □ Waterloo, ON

Peters, Douglas E., Hist./Libn.
RAILWAYS TO YESTERDAY, INC. - LEHIGH VALLEY TRANSPORTATION RESEARCH CENTER □ Allentown, PA

Peters, Edell M., Libn.
SOUTHEASTERN WISCONSIN REGIONAL PLANNING COMMISSION - REFERENCE LIBRARY □ Waukesha, WI

Peters, Frances E., Libn.
PENNSYLVANIA COLLEGE OF PODIATRIC MEDICINE - CHARLES E. KRAUSZ LIBRARY □ Philadelphia, PA

Peters, Gayle P., Regional Archv.
U.S. NATL. ARCHIVES & RECORDS SERVICE - FEDERAL ARCHIVES AND RECORDS CENTER, REGION 4 □ East Point, GA

Peters, John A., Govt.Pubn.Libn.
STATE HISTORICAL SOCIETY OF WISCONSIN - LIBRARY □ Madison, WI

Peters, K. Scott, Acq.Libn.
ROCKWELL INTERNATIONAL - ROCKETDYNE DIVISION - TECHNICAL INFORMATION CENTER □ Canoga Park, CA

Peters, Margery, Libn.
GENERAL SOCIETY OF MECHANICS AND TRADESMEN OF THE CITY OF NEW YORK - LIBRARY □ New York, NY

Peters, Marion C., Libn.
UNIVERSITY OF CALIFORNIA, LOS ANGELES - CHEMISTRY LIBRARY □ Los Angeles, CA

Peters, Mary, Med.Libn.
TEXAS SCOTTISH RITE HOSPITAL FOR CRIPPLED CHILDREN - BRANDON CARRELL, M.D., MEDICAL LIBRARY □ Dallas, TX

Peters, R.F., Hd., LRC
SOUTHERN ALBERTA INSTITUTE OF TECHNOLOGY - LEARNING RESOURCES CENTRE □ Calgary, AB

Peters, Robert W., Interp.Spec.
U.S. NATL. PARK SERVICE - CARLSBAD CAVERNS NATL. PARK - LIBRARY □ Carlsbad, NM

Peters, Scott M., Cur. of Coll.
SLOAN (Alfred P., Jr.) MUSEUM - MERLE G. PERRY ARCHIVES □ Flint, MI

Peters, William T., Lit.Coord.
SOCIETY OF FRIENDS - OHIO YEARLY MEETING - WESTGATE FRIENDS LIBRARY □ Columbus, OH

Petersen, Barbara, Info.Spec.
TRAVENOL LABORATORIES, INC. - INFORMATION RESOURCE CENTER □ Round Lake, IL

Petersen, Karla D., Hd., Cat.Dept.
CENTER FOR RESEARCH LIBRARIES □ Chicago, IL

Petersen, Marsha C., Dir.
HONOLULU (City and County) - MUNICIPAL REFERENCE AND RECORDS CENTER □ Honolulu, HI

Petersen, Philip V., Dir, Info./Member Serv.
SOCIETY OF AMERICAN FORESTERS - LIBRARY □ Bethesda, MD

Petersen, Phyllis, Hd. of Tech.Serv.
SUNY - AGRICULTURAL AND TECHNICAL COLLEGE AT MORRISVILLE - LIBRARY □ Morrisville, NY

Peterson, Agnes, Cur., W. Europe Coll.
STANFORD UNIVERSITY - HOOVER INSTITUTION ON WAR, REVOLUTION AND PEACE - LIBRARY □ Stanford, CA

Peterson, Arlene C., Asst.Dir., Res.Info.Sys.
MERCK & COMPANY, INC. - MERCK SHARP & DOHME RESEARCH LABORATORIES - RESEARCH INFORMATION SYSTEMS □ Rahway, NJ

Peterson, Betty L., Exec.Dir.
INSTITUTE OF ENVIRONMENTAL SCIENCES - LIBRARY □ Mt. Prospect, IL

Peterson, Charles H., Bk.Chm.
UNIVERSITY OF NORTH CAROLINA - INSTITUTE OF MARINE SCIENCES - LIBRARY □ Morehead City, NC

Peterson, David, Dept.Adm.
MEDICAL COLLEGE OF WISCONSIN - LIBRARIES □ Milwaukee, WI

Peterson, Dennis R., Interim Dir.
PALMER COLLEGE OF CHIROPRACTIC - DAVID D. PALMER LIBRARY □ Davenport, IA

Peterson, Elizabeth, Hd., Tech.Serv.
MINNESOTA STATE LAW LIBRARY □ St. Paul, MN

Peterson, Evelyn, Hd.Libn.
FLORIDA STATE UNIVERSITY - INSTITUTE OF SOCIAL RESEARCH - CENTER FOR THE STUDY OF POPULATION □ Tallahassee, FL

Peterson, Faye V., Supv.
SPERRY COMPUTER SYSTEMS - DEFENSE SYSTEMS DIVISION - INFORMATION SERVICE CENTER □ St. Paul, MN

Peterson, Fred M., Univ.Libn.
ILLINOIS STATE UNIVERSITY - MILNER LIBRARY - SPECIAL COLLECTIONS □ Normal, IL

Peterson, Gale E., Dir.
CINCINNATI HISTORICAL SOCIETY - LIBRARY □ Cincinnati, OH

Peterson, Gerald L., Spec.Coll.Libn.
UNIVERSITY OF NORTHERN IOWA - LIBRARY - SPECIAL COLLECTIONS □ Cedar Falls, IA

Peterson, Gretchen, Tech.Info.Spec.
STAUFFER CHEMICAL COMPANY - DE GUIGNE TECHNICAL CENTER - RESEARCH LIBRARY □ Richmond, CA

Peterson, Harold, Libn.
MINNEAPOLIS INSTITUTE OF ARTS - LIBRARY □ Minneapolis, MN

Peterson, Jean, Libn.
CAMBRIDGE STATE HOSPITAL - LIBRARY □ Cambridge, MN

Peterson, John, Cur. of the Archv.
LUTHERAN THEOLOGICAL SEMINARY - KRAUTH MEMORIAL LIBRARY □ Philadelphia, PA

Peterson, Julia, Mgr.
CARGILL, INC. - INFORMATION CENTER □ Minneapolis, MN

Peterson, Karen, Cat.Libn.
WESTERN CONSERVATIVE BAPTIST SEMINARY - CLINE-TUNNELL LIBRARY □ Portland, OR

Peterson, Linda E., Dir., Lib.Serv.
LIBERTY MUTUAL INSURANCE COMPANY - EDUCATION/INFORMATION RESOURCES □ Boston, MA

Peterson, M.L.
ARMED FORCES COMMUNICATIONS AND ELECTRONICS ASSOCIATION - C3I LIBRARY □ Burke, VA

Peterson, Mark, Chf., Lib.Serv.
U.S. VETERANS ADMINISTRATION (AZ-Tucson) - MEDICAL CENTER LIBRARY □ Tucson, AZ

Peterson, Melva, Chf., Music Lib.
CUNY - CITY COLLEGE LIBRARY - MUSIC LIBRARY □ New York, NY

Peterson, Mildred, Libn.
FOREST PARK COVENANT CHURCH - LIBRARY □ Muskegon, MI

Peterson, Paul, Ref. & Exchange Libn.
LINDA HALL LIBRARY □ Kansas City, MO

Peterson, Peg, Corp.Libn.
MGIC INVESTMENT CORPORATION - CORPORATE LIBRARY □ Milwaukee, WI

Peterson, Pennie D., Coord.
MISSOURI STATE LIBRARY - WOLFNER MEMORIAL LIBRARY FOR THE BLIND & PHYSICALLY HANDICAPPED □ St. Louis, MO

Peterson, Randall T., Dir.
JOHN MARSHALL LAW SCHOOL - LIBRARY □ Chicago, IL

Peterson, Richard A., Ref.Libn.
UNIVERSITY OF VIRGINIA - MEDICAL CENTER - CLAUDE MOORE HEALTH SCIENCES LIBRARY □ Charlottesville, VA

Peterson, Ruth, Libn.
UNIVERSITY OF NORTH DAKOTA - ENGINEERING LIBRARY □ Grand Forks, ND

Peterson, Sara, Hd.Libn.
IOWA STATE UNIVERSITY - VETERINARY MEDICAL LIBRARY □ Ames, IA

Peterson, Sharon R., Med.Libn.
INTERFAITH MEDICAL CENTER - BROOKLYN JEWISH SITE - MEDICAL & NURSING LIBRARY □ Brooklyn, NY

Peterson, Stephen L., Divinity Libn.
YALE UNIVERSITY - DIVINITY SCHOOL LIBRARY □ New Haven, CT

Peterson, Tim, Hd., Photographic Coll.
INDIANA HISTORICAL SOCIETY - WILLIAM HENRY SMITH MEMORIAL LIBRARY □ Indianapolis, IN

Peterson, Vivian A., Dir., Lib.Serv.
CONCORDIA TEACHERS COLLEGE - LINK LIBRARY □ Seward, NE

Petesch, John H., Cat.Libn.
UNIVERSITY OF TEXAS, AUSTIN - SCHOOL OF LAW - TARLTON LAW LIBRARY □ Austin, TX

Pethybridge, Arthur, Dir. of Lib.Serv.
NORTHWESTERN CONNECTICUT COMMUNITY COLLEGE - LIBRARY □ Winsted, CT

Petit, Michael J., Asst.Libn./Tech.Serv.
GEORGE MASON UNIVERSITY - SCHOOL OF LAW - LIBRARY □ Arlington, VA

Petit, Patrick, Assoc. Law Libn.
CATHOLIC UNIVERSITY OF AMERICA - SCHOOL OF LAW - ROBERT J. WHITE LAW LIBRARY □ Washington, DC

Petitmermet, Jane, Ref.Libn.
U.S. NATL. DEFENSE UNIVERSITY - LIBRARY □ Washington, DC

Petko, Charles M., Supv., Spec.Serv.
ENVIRONMENTAL PROTECTION AGENCY - EASTERN ENVIRONMENTAL RADIATION LAB - LIBRARY □ Montgomery, AL

Petrak, Janet C., Libn.
WESTMORELAND HOSPITAL - LIBRARY AND HEALTH RESOURCE CENTER □ Greensburg, PA

Petrauskas, Julia, Supv., Med.Commun.
ALLERGAN PHARMACEUTICALS, INC. - MEDICAL & SCIENCE INFORMATION □ Irvine, CA

Petre, Suzanne M., Libn.
GENERAL MOTORS CORPORATION - PUBLIC RELATIONS STAFF LIBRARY □ Detroit, MI

Petree, David L., Dir.
U.S. NATL. ARCHIVES & RECORDS SERVICE - NATL. PERSONNEL RECORDS CENTER □ St. Louis, MO

Petrelli, Evelyn, Asst.Libn.
EDWARDS (Jacob) LIBRARY - SPECIAL COLLECTIONS □ Southbridge, MA

Petrello, JoAnn, Dept.Hd.
CLEVELAND PUBLIC LIBRARY - HISTORY AND GEOGRAPHY DEPARTMENT □ Cleveland, OH

Petrie, Claire, Ref./Tech.Serv.Libn.
PARSONS SCHOOL OF DESIGN - ADAM AND SOPHIE GIMBEL DESIGN LIBRARY □ New York, NY

Petring, Patricia M., Mgr., Tech.Info.Serv.
OCCIDENTAL RESEARCH CORPORATION - TECHNICAL INFORMATION CENTER† □ Irvine, CA

Petrites, Seyem Deus, Libn.
MANALYTICS, INC. - LIBRARY □ San Francisco, CA

Petroff, Tatiana, Standards Libn.
BECHTEL PETROLEUM INC. - LIBRARY □ San Francisco, CA

Petrone, Anthony, Mgr.
SEARLE (G.D.) & CO. - RESEARCH LIBRARY □ Skokie, IL

Petrov, Jane, Libn.
CENTRE DE READAPTATION CONSTANCE-LETHBRIDGE - MEDICAL LIBRARY □ Montreal, PQ

Petrovics, Gabriella, Libn.
OHIO DOMINICAN COLLEGE - SPANGLER LIBRARY □ Columbus, OH

Petrowski, Carol, Ser.
LOYOLA LAW SCHOOL - LIBRARY □ Los Angeles, CA

Petru, William C., Mgr. of Libs.
HEWLETT-PACKARD COMPANY - CORPORATE LIBRARY □ Palo Alto, CA

Petruga, Patricia L., Libn.
MC KIM ADVERTISING, LTD. - INFORMATION CENTRE □ Toronto, ON

Petry, Dolores M., Libn.
CARNEGIE INSTITUTION OF WASHINGTON - GEOPHYSICAL LABORATORY LIBRARY □ Washington, DC

Petry, John R., Res.Assoc./Assoc.Prof.
MEMPHIS STATE UNIVERSITY LIBRARIES - BUREAU OF EDUCATIONAL RESEARCH AND SERVICES - LIBRARY □ Memphis, TN

Petry, Robyn, Hd.Libn.
AKZO CHEMIE AMERICA - RESEARCH LIBRARY □ McCook, IL

Petry, Sherry, Libn.
ATLANTA FULTON PUBLIC LIBRARY - IVAN ALLEN, JR. DEPARTMENT OF SCIENCE, INDUSTRY AND GOVERNMENT □ Atlanta, GA

Petschaft, Jane I., Libn.
DYNATECH RESEARCH DEVELOPMENT COMPANY - CORPORATION LIBRARY† □ Cambridge, MA

Pett, A. William, Libn.
RHODE ISLAND STATE DEPARTMENT OF HEALTH - GERTRUDE E. STURGES MEMORIAL LIBRARY □ Providence, RI

Pettengill, Helen M., Musm.Dir.
GRAFTON HISTORICAL MUSEUM □ Grafton, VT

Pettengill, Irene R., Med.Libn.
FRANKLIN MEMORIAL HOSPITAL - TURNER MEMORIAL LIBRARY □ Farmington, ME

Pettengill, Sharron L., Hd. Law Libn.
O'CONNOR, CAVANAGH, ANDERSON, WESTOVER, KILLINGSWORTH, BESHEARS - LAW LIBRARY □ Phoenix, AZ

Petter, Christopher, Archv.
UNIVERSITY OF VICTORIA - MC PHERSON LIBRARY - SPECIAL COLLECTIONS □ Victoria, BC

Petterchak, Janice, Supv., Local Hist.
ILLINOIS STATE HISTORICAL LIBRARY □ Springfield, IL

Petticoffer, Dennis, Libn.
CALIFORNIA INSTITUTE OF TECHNOLOGY - INDUSTRIAL RELATIONS CENTER - MANAGEMENT LIBRARY □ Pasadena, CA

Pettinato, Anthony J., Asst.Libn.
WHALE CENTER - EXTINCT SPECIES MEMORIAL FUND - LIBRARY □ Oakland, CA

Pettipas, Sue, Adm.Asst.
INFORMATION SYSTEMS CONSULTANTS INC. - LIBRARY □ Bethesda, MD

Pettit, Charlene, Cat.
MORAINE PARK TECHNICAL INSTITUTE - LEARNING RESOURCE CENTER □ Fond du Lac, WI

Pettit, Katherine D., Spec.Coll.Libn.
TRINITY UNIVERSITY - ELIZABETH COATES MADDUX LIBRARY - SPECIAL COLLECTIONS □ San Antonio, TX

Pettit, Martha, Libn.
DU PONT CANADA, INC. - CENTRAL LIBRARY □ Mississauga, ON

Pettway, Helen, Libn.
KRAFT, INC. - RESEARCH & DEVELOPMENT LIBRARY □ Glenview, IL

Petty, Ruth, Libn.
NORTHWEST COLLEGE OF THE ASSEMBLIES OF GOD - HURST LIBRARY† □ Kirkland, WA

Petty, Timothy, Asst.Libn.
JONES, DAY, REAVIS & POGUE - LIBRARY □ Cleveland, OH

Peyrat, Jean, Libn.
CENTER FOR CREATIVE STUDIES/COLLEGE OF ART & DESIGN - LIBRARY □ Detroit, MI

Peyton, Gail, Inner City Stud.Libn
NORTHEASTERN ILLINOIS UNIVERSITY - LIBRARY □ Chicago, IL

Peyton, Madeleine A., Libn.
U.S. AIR FORCE BASE - MOODY BASE LIBRARY □ Moody AFB, GA

Pezzullo, Diane, Ref./Circ.Libn.
UNIVERSITY OF CALIFORNIA, LOS ANGELES - EDUCATION & PSYCHOLOGY LIBRARY □ Los Angeles, CA

Pfaff, Larry, Dp.Libn./Ref.Libn.
ART GALLERY OF ONTARIO - EDWARD P. TAYLOR REFERENCE LIBRARY □ Toronto, ON

Pfaffenberger, Ann, Ref.Libn.
TEXAS COLLEGE OF OSTEOPATHIC MEDICINE - HEALTH SCIENCES LIBRARY □ Fort Worth, TX

Pfander, Jeanne J., Sci.Engr.Ref.Libn.
UNIVERSITY OF ARIZONA - SCIENCE-ENGINEERING LIBRARY □ Tucson, AZ

Pfann, Mary L., Libn.
RCA CORPORATION - ASTRO-ELECTRONICS-GOVERNMENT SYSTEMS DIVISION - LIBRARY □ Princeton, NJ

Pfarrer, T.R., Asst.Libn.
U.S. NAVY - NAVAL TRAINING EQUIPMENT CENTER - TECHNICAL INFORMATION CENTER □ Orlando, FL

Pfau, Dr. Richard H., Coord.
UNIVERSITY OF CONNECTICUT - SCHOOL OF EDUCATION - I.N. THUT WORLD EDUCATION CENTER □ Storrs, CT

Pfeifer, Barbara, Leg.Libn.
MARYLAND STATE DEPARTMENT OF LEGISLATIVE REFERENCE - LIBRARY □ Annapolis, MD

Pfeifer, Cheryl, Ref.
GMI ENGINEERING & MANAGEMENT INSTITUTE - LIBRARY □ Flint, MI

Pfeiffer, Judith A., Dir.
AMERICAN COUNCIL ON EDUCATION - LIBRARY AND INFORMATION SERVICES □ Washington, DC

Pfeiffer, Katherine N., Licensing Anl./Libn.
GULF STATES UTILITIES COMPANY - NUCLEAR LIBRARY □ Beaumont, TX

Pfeiffer, Mary, Libn.
NATIONAL INSTITUTE ON DRUG ABUSE - ADDICTION RESEARCH CENTER LIBRARY □ Baltimore, MD

Pfeil, Pamela, Libn.
JACKSON COUNTY LAW LIBRARY □ Medford, OR

Pfening, Fred D., Jr.
CIRCUS HISTORICAL SOCIETY - LIBRARY □ Columbus, OH

Pfister, Susan, Cat.Libn.
BRIDGEWATER STATE COLLEGE - CLEMENT C. MAXWELL LIBRARY □ Bridgewater, MA

Pflueger, Kenneth E., Dir., Lib.Serv.
CALIFORNIA LUTHERAN COLLEGE - LIBRARY - SPECIAL COLLECTIONS† □ Thousand Oaks, CA

Pflug, Warner, Asst.Dir.
WAYNE STATE UNIVERSITY - ARCHIVES OF LABOR AND URBAN AFFAIRS/UNIVERSITY ARCHIVES □ Detroit, MI

Pflug-Felder, Kay M., Rec.Mgt.Supv.
CH2M HILL, INC. - TECHNICAL INFORMATION CENTER □ Bellevue, WA

Pfremmer, Patricia J., Law Libn.
SANTA CRUZ COUNTY LAW LIBRARY □ Santa Cruz, CA

Pfund, Leona, Automated Sys.Coord.
U.S. SENATE - LIBRARY □ Washington, DC

Phair, Mr. Arden, Dir.
ST. CATHARINES HISTORICAL MUSEUM - LIBRARY □ St. Catharines, ON

Phelan, Dorcas, Ser.Libn.
FLOATING POINT SYSTEMS, INC. - INFORMATION CENTER/LIBRARY □ Beaverton, OR

Phelps, Edward, Libn.
UNIVERSITY OF WESTERN ONTARIO - D.B. WELDON LIBRARY - REGIONAL COLLECTION □ London, ON

Phelps, Erin, Res.Assoc.
RADCLIFFE COLLEGE - HENRY A. MURRAY RESEARCH CENTER □ Cambridge, MA

Phelps, Evelyn B., Dept.Hd.
ONONDAGA COUNTY PUBLIC LIBRARY - BUSINESS AND INDUSTRIAL DEPARTMENT □ Syracuse, NY

Phelps, Havilah, Libn.
KNOX COMMUNITY HOSPITAL - MEDICAL LIBRARY □ Mount Vernon, OH

Phelps, Marion L., Cur. & Archv.
BROME COUNTY HISTORICAL SOCIETY - ARCHIVES □ Knowlton, PQ

Phelps, Robert L., Ref.Libn.
U.S. NASA - LYNDON B. JOHNSON SPACE CENTER - TECHNICAL LIBRARY □ Houston, TX

Phelps, Mrs. Willard, Dir. & Cur.
MAYVILLE HISTORICAL MUSEUM - LIBRARY □ Mayville, MI

Philbin, Paul P., Ref.Libn.
OCLC, INC. - LIBRARY □ Dublin, OH

Philbrick, Ruth R., Cur.
NATIONAL GALLERY OF ART - PHOTOGRAPHIC ARCHIVES □ Washington, DC

Philip, John, Hd., Field Oper.
STATE LIBRARY OF OHIO □ Columbus, OH

Philips, Rosemary B., Libn.
CHESTER COUNTY HISTORICAL SOCIETY - LIBRARY □ West Chester, PA

Philley, H., Lib.Ck.
SASKATCHEWAN POWER CORPORATION - LIBRARY† □ Regina, SK

Phillips, Beverly R., Libn.
UNIVERSITY OF WISCONSIN, MADISON - LAND TENURE CENTER - LIBRARY □ Madison, WI

Phillips, Carol B., Chf.Ref.Libn.
UNIVERSITY OF TEXAS MEDICAL BRANCH - MOODY MEDICAL LIBRARY □ Galveston, TX

Phillips, Carroll R., Coll.Libn.
ARMSTRONG COLLEGE - LIBRARY □ Berkeley, CA

Phillips, Dee, Mgr.
ONTARIO - MINISTRY OF INDUSTRY AND TRADE - INFORMATION CENTRE □ Toronto, ON

Phillips, Dennis J., Pub.Serv.
MUHLENBERG COLLEGE - JOHN A.W. HAAS LIBRARY □ Allentown, PA

Phillips, Don E., Ck. of Court
MARINETTE COUNTY LAW LIBRARY □ Marinette, WI

Phillips, Dorothy, Adm.
FEDERAL RESERVE BANK OF CHICAGO - LIBRARY □ Chicago, IL

Phillips, Frances M., Dir., Lib. & AV Serv.
HARPER-GRACE HOSPITALS - GRACE HOSPITAL DIVISION - OSCAR LE SEURE PROFESSIONAL LIBRARY □ Detroit, MI

Phillips, Frank, Univ.Libn.
WESTERN STATE UNIVERSITY - COLLEGE OF LAW - LIBRARY† □ Fullerton, CA

Phillips, Ira, Spec.Proj.Prog.Dev.
STATE LIBRARY OF OHIO □ Columbus, OH

Phillips, Jacob, Base Libn.
U.S. AIR FORCE BASE - MAC DILL BASE LIBRARY □ MacDill AFB, FL

Phillips, James W., Sr.Bibliog.
SOUTHERN METHODIST UNIVERSITY - DEGOLYER LIBRARY - FIKES HALL OF SPECIAL COLLECTIONS □ Dallas, TX

Phillips, Jane, Supv.
NEW BRUNSWICK - DEPARTMENT OF COMMERCE & DEVELOPMENT - CENTRAL FILES & LIBRARY □ Fredericton, NB

Phillips, Jane, Libn.
NOVA SCOTIA - DEPARTMENT OF SOCIAL SERVICES - LIBRARY □ Halifax, NS

Phillips, Jerry C., Asst.Tech.Serv.Libn.
UNIVERSITY OF NEW MEXICO - SCHOOL OF LAW LIBRARY □ Albuquerque, NM

Phillips, John, Asst.Doc.Libn.
OKLAHOMA STATE UNIVERSITY - DOCUMENTS DEPARTMENT □ Stillwater, OK

Phillips, John T., Mgr.
MARTIN MARIETTA ENERGY SYSTEMS INC. - ORGDP INFORMATION RESOURCE CENTER □ Oak Ridge, TN

Phillips, Julia, Kent Lib.Res. Lead
BOEING COMPANY - SEATTLE SERVICES DIVISION - TECHNICAL LIBRARIES† □ Seattle, WA

Phillips, Lawrence H., II, Chm., Lib.Comm.
UNIVERSITY OF VIRGINIA - MEDICAL CENTER - DEPARTMENT OF NEUROLOGY - ELIZABETH J. OHRSTROM LIBRARY □ Charlottesville, VA

Phillips, Linda L., Supv., Off.Serv./Doc.Ctr.
ROCHESTER GAS AND ELECTRIC CORPORATION - TECHNICAL INFORMATION CENTER □ Rochester, NY

Phillips, Linda R., Ph.D., Info.Dir.
INFORMATION CONNECTION □ Santa Barbara, CA

Phillips, Marie, Hd.
ROCKFORD PUBLIC LIBRARY - BUSINESS, SCIENCE AND TECHNOLOGY DIVISION† □ Rockford, IL

Phillips, Mary Louise, Local Hist.Libn.
CHARLOTTE AND MECKLENBURG COUNTY PUBLIC LIBRARY - CAROLINA ROOM □ Charlotte, NC

Phillips, Michele, Documentarian
UNIVERSITY OF ARIZONA - OPTICAL SCIENCES CENTER - READING ROOM† □ Tucson, AZ

Phillips, Molly A., Libn. Media Tech.Asst.
OHIO STATE UNIVERSITY - TOPAZ MEMORIAL LIBRARY □ Columbus, OH

Phillips, Phoebe F., Hd.Libn.
OHIO STATE UNIVERSITY - AGRICULTURAL TECHNICAL INSTITUTE - LIBRARY □ Wooster, OH

Phillips, R. Cody, Musm.Cur.
CASEMATE MUSEUM - LIBRARY □ Ft. Monroe, VA

Phillips, R.W., Asst.Libn.
U.S. VETERANS ADMINISTRATION (CA-Martinez) - HOSPITAL LIBRARY □ Martinez, CA

Phillips, Robert, Asst.Libn./Pub.Serv.
SOUTHWESTERN BAPTIST THEOLOGICAL SEMINARY - A. WEBB ROBERTS LIBRARY □ Fort Worth, TX

Phillips, Rodney, Chf.
NEW YORK PUBLIC LIBRARY - GENERAL RESEARCH DIVISION □ New York, NY

Phillips, Ruth M., Chm.
HUGUENOT-THOMAS PAINE HISTORICAL ASSOCIATION OF NEW ROCHELLE - HUFELAND MEMORIAL LIBRARY □ New Rochelle, NY

Phillips, Sandra, Libn.
FLETCHER, MAYO, ASSOCIATES, INC. - LIBRARY □ St. Joseph, MO

Phillips, Sharon A., Dir.
OAKWOOD HOSPITAL - MC LOUTH MEMORIAL HEALTH SCIENCE LIBRARY† □ Dearborn, MI

Phillips, Shelley, Coord., Adm.Dept.
ST. LUKE'S HOSPITAL - SCHOOL OF NURSING LIBRARY □ St. Louis, MO

Phillips, Vicki W., Hd.
OKLAHOMA STATE UNIVERSITY - DOCUMENTS DEPARTMENT □ Stillwater, OK

Phillips, Violet R., Hd.Libn.
LONG BEACH PRESS-TELEGRAM - LIBRARY □ Long Beach, CA

Phillips, William F., Lit.Chem.
INTERNATIONAL MINERALS & CHEMICALS CORPORATION - IMC RESEARCH & DEVELOPMENT LIBRARY □ Terre Haute, IN

Phillpot, Clive, Dir.
MUSEUM OF MODERN ART - LIBRARY □ New York, NY

Philos, Helen S., Libn.
AMERICAN SOCIETY OF INTERNATIONAL LAW - LIBRARY □ Washington, DC

Philpott, Catherine E., Libn.
CANADA - CANADIAN FORESTRY SERVICE - NEWFOUNDLAND FOREST RESEARCH CENTRE - LIBRARY □ St. John's, NF

Phinney, Chad T., Musm.Asst.
PUEBLO GRANDE MUSEUM - RESEARCH LIBRARY □ Phoenix, AZ

Phinney, Hartley K., Jr., Dir.
COLORADO SCHOOL OF MINES - ARTHUR LAKES LIBRARY □ Golden, CO

Phinney, Jeannette, Ref.
DAUGHTERS OF THE REPUBLIC OF TEXAS - LIBRARY □ San Antonio, TX

Phipps, Shelley E., Hd.Libn.
UNIVERSITY OF ARIZONA - SCIENCE-ENGINEERING LIBRARY □ Tucson, AZ

Piatt, Frances A., Libn.
XEROX SPECIAL INFORMATION SYSTEMS - TECHNICAL LIBRARY □ Pasadena, CA

Piazza, Mark, Ref.Libn.
JOHN MARSHALL LAW SCHOOL - LIBRARY □ Chicago, IL

Piazza, Rita, Lib.Mgr.
ONTARIO ENERGY BOARD - LIBRARY □ Toronto, ON

Picard, Bethany, Libn.
EXXON COMPANY, U.S.A. - REFINERY LIBRARY □ Baytown, TX

Picard, June, Staff Libn.
LARNED STATE HOSPITAL - J.T. NARAMORE LIBRARY □ Larned, KS

Picardo, Kathryn, Asst.Prof./Cat.Libn.
PHILADELPHIA COLLEGE OF OSTEOPATHIC MEDICINE - O.J. SNYDER MEMORIAL MEDICAL LIBRARY □ Philadelphia, PA

Picciano, Jacqueline, Circ. & ILL
CORNELL UNIVERSITY - MEDICAL COLLEGE - SAMUEL J. WOOD LIBRARY □ New York, NY

Piccinino, Rocco, Jr., Libn.
UNITED ENGINEERS & CONSTRUCTORS INC. - BOSTON OFFICE - LIBRARY □ Boston, MA

Piccoli, Roberta, Info.Spec.
THOMPSON (J. Walter) COMPANY - INFORMATION CENTER □ Chicago, IL

Piccolotti, Laurie, Libn.
LANTERMAN (Frank D.) STATE HOSPITAL AND DEVELOPMENT CENTER - STAFF LIBRARY □ Pomona, CA

Pichet, Louise, Lib.Techn.
CULINAR FOODS INC. - LIBRARY □ Montreal, PQ

Pick, Paula
BRITISH COLUMBIA INSTITUTE OF TECHNOLOGY - LIBRARY SERVICES DIVISION □ Burnaby, BC

Pickard, Cathy, Supv.
CANADA - TRANSPORT CANADA - TRAINING
INSTITUTE - TECHNICAL INFORMATION
CENTRE □ Cornwall, ON

Pickenpaugh, Eileen, Res.Cons.
U.S. NAVY - NAVAL RESEARCH LABORATORY -
RUTH H. HOOKER TECHNICAL LIBRARY □
Washington, DC

Pickens, Pamela E., Chem.Libn.
EMORY UNIVERSITY - JAMES SAMUEL GUY
LIBRARY □ Atlanta, GA

Pickett, Barbara, Mgr.
LOUISVILLE FREE PUBLIC LIBRARY - FILM
SERVICES† □ Louisville, KY

Pickett, Karen, Coord.
ECOLOGY CENTER - LIBRARY □ Berkeley, CA

Pickett, Thomas E., Assoc.Dir.
DELAWARE STATE GEOLOGICAL SURVEY -
LIBRARY □ Newark, DE

Picott, John B., Libn.
BOSTON STATE HOSPITAL - MEDICAL LIBRARY
□ Boston, MA

Picquet, D. Cheryl, Act.Dir.
UNIVERSITY OF TENNESSEE - COLLEGE OF
LAW LIBRARY □ Knoxville, TN

Pidala, Veronica C., Lib./Rec.Adm.
EBASCO SERVICES, INC. - CORPORATE
LIBRARY □ New York, NY

Pidgeon, Alice, Acq.Libn.
PACE UNIVERSITY - SCHOOL OF LAW LIBRARY
□ White Plains, NY

Piechocki, Virginia, Acq.Libn.
SAN DIEGO COUNTY LAW LIBRARY □ San Diego,
CA

Piel, Mark, Libn.
NEW YORK SOCIETY LIBRARY □ New York, NY

Piele, Dr. Philip K., Prof./Dir.
ERIC CLEARINGHOUSE ON EDUCATIONAL
MANAGEMENT □ Eugene, OR

Pien, Arlene C., Libn.
ST. JOSEPH'S HOSPITAL - HELENE FULD
LEARNING RESOURCE CENTER □ Elmira, NY

Pienitz, Eleanor, Libn./Info.Spec.
HARRIS CORPORATION - GOVERNMENT
SUPPORT SYSTEMS DIVISION - INFORMATION
CENTER □ Syosset, NY

Pieprzyk, Julie, Info.Spec.
SYNTEX, U.S.A. - CORPORATE LIBRARY/
INFORMATION SERVICES □ Palo Alto, CA

Pierce, Barbara, Market Anl.
PENTON/IPC - MARKETING INFORMATION
CENTER □ Cleveland, OH

Pierce, Charlotte G., Libn.
MISSISSIPPI STATE AGRICULTURAL &
FORESTRY EXPERIMENT STATION - DELTA BR.
EXPERIMENT STA. LIBRARY □ Stoneville, MS

Pierce, Deborah L., Music Cat.
UNIVERSITY OF WASHINGTON - MUSIC
LIBRARY □ Seattle, WA

Pierce, Helen V., Libn.
GREENVILLE LAW LIBRARY □ Greenville, OH

Pierce, Irene R., Mgr., News Serv.
MOBIL OIL CORPORATION - PUBLIC AFFAIRS
SECRETARIAT □ New York, NY

Pierce, Karen, Circ.
CALAIS FREE LIBRARY □ Calais, ME

Pierce, Linda, Index Ed.
AMERICAN INSTITUTE OF CERTIFIED PUBLIC
ACCOUNTANTS - LIBRARY SERVICES □ New
York, NY

Pierce, M. Edith, Libn.
U.S. AIR FORCE BASE - CANNON BASE LIBRARY
□ Cannon AFB, NM

Pierce, Mary Lou, Libn.
ARTHUR ANDERSEN & CO. - LIBRARY □ San
Francisco, CA

Pierce, Melissa, Libn.
AETNA LIFE & CASUALTY COMPANY -
ENGINEERING LIBRARY □ Hartford, CT

Pierce, Miriam, Hd.
PENNSYLVANIA STATE UNIVERSITY -
MATHEMATICS LIBRARY □ University Park, PA

Pierce, Pauline D., Cur.
STOCKBRIDGE LIBRARY ASSOCIATION -
HISTORICAL ROOM □ Stockbridge, MA

Pierce, Ruth, Sr.,Libn., KENCLIP
KENTUCKY STATE DEPARTMENT FOR
LIBRARIES AND ARCHIVES - STATE LIBRARY
SERVICES DIVISION □ Frankfort, KY

Pierce, Sally, Cur., Prints/Photographs
BOSTON ATHENAEUM LIBRARY □ Boston, MA

Pierobon, Nancy, Hd.Libn.
ONTARIO - MINISTRY OF ENERGY - LIBRARY □
Toronto, ON

Pierrard, Jesse, Libn.
ST. JOSEPH HOSPITAL - MEDICAL AND
NURSING LIBRARY □ Fort Worth, TX

Pierre, Margaret, Med.Lib.Techn.
ALBERTA HOSPITAL - LIBRARY □ Edmonton, AB

Pierson, Cheryl, Group Leader
MERCK & COMPANY, INC. - MERCK SHARP &
DOHME RESEARCH LABORATORIES -
RESEARCH INFORMATION SYSTEMS □ Rahway,
NJ

Pieschel, Terri, Supv., Lib.
CHEVRON CANADA RESOURCES LTD. - LIBRARY
□ Calgary, AB

Pietropaoli, Frank A., Libn.
SMITHSONIAN INSTITUTION LIBRARIES -
NATIONAL AIR AND SPACE MUSEUM - LIBRARY
□ Washington, DC

Piety, Jean Z., Hd.
CLEVELAND PUBLIC LIBRARY - SCIENCE AND
TECHNOLOGY DEPARTMENT □ Cleveland, OH

Pifer, Richard L., Archv.
UNIVERSITY OF WISCONSIN, EAU CLAIRE -
AREA RESEARCH CENTER AND UNIVERSITY
ARCHIVES □ Eau Claire, WI

Piff, David, Chf., Archv.Br.
U.S. NATL. ARCHIVES & RECORDS SERVICE -
FEDERAL ARCHIVES AND RECORDS CENTER,
REGION 10 □ Seattle, WA

Pigg, B.J., Exec.Dir.
ASBESTOS INFORMATION ASSOCIATION/
NORTH AMERICA - TECHNICAL AND MEDICAL
FILES □ Arlington, VA

Piggott, Mary, Mgr., Search-Law
LAW SOCIETY OF UPPER CANADA - GREAT
LIBRARY □ Toronto, ON

Piggott, Sylvia, Tech.Libn.
BANK OF MONTREAL - TECHNICAL
INFORMATION CENTRE □ Scarborough, ON

Piggott, Sylvia E.A., Tech.Libn.
BANK OF MONTREAL - TECHNICAL
INFORMATION CENTRE □ Montreal, PQ

Pigno, Antonia, Spec.Coll./Archv.
KANSAS STATE UNIVERSITY - FARRELL
LIBRARY □ Manhattan, KS

Pigno, Antonia, Coord., Spec.Coll./Archv.
KANSAS STATE UNIVERSITY - UNIVERSITY
ARCHIVES □ Manhattan, KS

Pigot, F.L., Ref./Libn.
UNIVERSITY OF PRINCE EDWARD ISLAND -
ROBERTSON LIBRARY □ Charlottetown, PE

Pigott, Louis I., Jr., Libn.
INTERNATIONAL ENGINEERING COMPANY,
INC. - LIBRARY □ San Francisco, CA

Pike, B., Technologist
ALBERTA - DEPARTMENT OF ENERGY AND
NATURAL RESOURCES - MAP & AIR PHOTO
REFERENCE LIBRARY □ Edmonton, AB

Pike, Esther, Acq.Libn.
STANFORD UNIVERSITY - J. HUGH JACKSON
LIBRARY □ Stanford, CA

Pike, John R., Mng.Dir.
WISCONSIN ALUMNI RESEARCH FOUNDATION
- LIBRARY □ Madison, WI

Pike, Kermit J., Dir.
WESTERN RESERVE HISTORICAL SOCIETY -
LIBRARY □ Cleveland, OH

Pike, Lorraine H., Libn.
ASCENSION LUTHERAN CHURCH - LIBRARY □
Milwaukee, WI

Pike, Marti, Res.Libn.
TWENTIETH CENTURY FOX FILM
CORPORATION - RESEARCH LIBRARY □ Beverly
Hills, CA

Pilgrim, Auriel J., Dir., Info.Rsrcs.
JOINT CENTER FOR POLITICAL STUDIES, INC.
- OFFICE OF INFORMATION RESOURCES □
Washington, DC

Pilgrim, Laura, Libn.
FOSTER WHEELER ENERGY CORPORATION -
HOUSTON ENGINEERING CENTER LIBRARY □
Houston, TX

Pilikian, Helen M., Chf.Med.Libn.
LONG ISLAND JEWISH-HILLSIDE MEDICAL
CENTER - QUEENS HOSPITAL CENTER -
HEALTH SCIENCE LIBRARY □ Jamaica, NY

Pilkington, James P., Adm.
VANDERBILT UNIVERSITY - JEAN AND
ALEXANDER HEARD LIBRARY - TELEVISION
NEWS ARCHIVES □ Nashville, TN

Pillai, Karlye Ann Gill, Law Libn.
NEW YORK STATE SUPREME COURT - 3RD
JUDICIAL DISTRICT - LAW LIBRARY □ Troy, NY

Pillis, John F., Pres.
WATERTOWN HISTORICAL SOCIETY INC. -
LIBRARY □ Oakville, CT

Pillsbury, Elizabeth, Genealogist
FENTON HISTORICAL SOCIETY - LIBRARY □
Jamestown, NY

Pilmes, Irmine, Res.Libn.
CIBA-GEIGY CORPORATION - CHEMICAL
LIBRARY □ Toms River, NJ

Pinaglia, Kathleen, Law Libn.
NEVADA COUNTY LAW LIBRARY □ Nevada City,
CA

Pinckard, Deane, Tech.Info.Spec.
U.S. ARMY - INTELLIGENCE AND THREAT
ANALYSIS CENTER - TECHNICAL
INFORMATION CENTER □ Arlington, VA

Pinckard, Mara, Hd., Sci.Ref.
ARIZONA STATE UNIVERSITY - DANIEL E.
NOBLE SCIENCE AND ENGINEERING LIBRARY □
Tempe, AZ

Pinckney, Cathey L., Libn.
ST. JOHN'S HOSPITAL AND HEALTH CENTER -
HOSPITAL LIBRARY □ Santa Monica, CA

Pinckney, Mary M., Asst. County Hist.
CAYUGA COUNTY HISTORICAL RESEARCH
CENTER - LIBRARY □ Auburn, NY

Pincus, Lena, Libn.
SOUTHERN CALIFORNIA PSYCHOANALYTIC
INSTITUTE - FRANZ ALEXANDER LIBRARY □
Beverly Hills, CA

Pindar, Maia, Tech.Info.Spec.
XEROX CORPORATION - PALO ALTO RESEARCH
CENTER - TECHNICAL INFORMATION CENTER
□ Palo Alto, CA

Pineda, Conchita J., Mgr.
CITIBANK, N.A. LIBRARY □ New York, NY

Pines, Doralynn, Assoc.Musm.Libn.
METROPOLITAN MUSEUM OF ART - THOMAS J.
WATSON LIBRARY □ New York, NY

Pines, Philip A., Dir.
TROTTING HORSE MUSEUM - PETER D.
HAUGHTON MEMORIAL LIBRARY □ Goshen, NY

Ping, Sr. Harriett, Acq.
MARYCREST COLLEGE - CONE LIBRARY □
Davenport, IA

Pingo, Mary, Cat.Libn.
SCHERING-PLOUGH CORPORATION -
PHARMACEUTICAL RESEARCH DIVISION -
LIBRARY INFORMATION CENTER □ Bloomfield,
NJ

Pinizzotto, Dana, Mgr.
CHURCH OF THE INCARNATION - MARMION
LIBRARY □ Dallas, TX

Pinkard, Inez C., Med.Libn.
U.S. VETERANS ADMINISTRATION (AL-
Tuskegee) - MEDICAL CENTER LIBRARY □
Tuskegee, AL

Pinkerton, Robert L., Exec.Dir.
TRI-COUNTY REGIONAL PLANNING
COMMISSION - LIBRARY □ East Peoria, IL

Pinkham, Eleanor H., Coll.Libn.
KALAMAZOO COLLEGE - UPJOHN LIBRARY - SPECIAL COLLECTIONS □ Kalamazoo, MI

Pinkney, Elaine, Libn.
JOHNS HOPKINS HOSPITAL - DEPARTMENT OF RADIOLOGY - LIBRARY □ Baltimore, MD

Pinkney, Helen L., Libn.
DAYTON ART INSTITUTE - LIBRARY □ Dayton, OH

Pinkowski, Patricia, Prog.Coord.
UNIVERSITY OF ILLINOIS AT CHICAGO - HEALTH SCIENCES CENTER - LIBRARY OF THE HEALTH SCIENCES □ Chicago, IL

Pinnel, Frances B., Med.Libn.
ST. CHRISTOPHER'S HOSPITAL FOR CHILDREN - MEDICAL LIBRARY □ Philadelphia, PA

Pinnell, Elizabeth, Tech.Serv.Libn.
MITRE CORPORATION - LIBRARY □ McLean, VA

Pinnell, Jonalou M., Libn.
SEDGWICK COUNTY LAW LIBRARY† □ Wichita, KS

Pinnell, Richard Hugh, Map Libn.
UNIVERSITY OF WATERLOO - UNIVERSITY MAP AND DESIGN LIBRARY □ Waterloo, ON

Pinney, Martine, Libn.
U.S. ARMY - LANGUAGE TRAINING FACILITY - LIBRARY □ Ft. Hood, TX

Pinnix, Robert A., Cur.
GREENSBORO MASONIC MUSEUM LIBRARY □ Greensboro, NC

Pinseley, Lauren, Asst.Cat.
UNION UNIVERSITY - ALBANY LAW SCHOOL - LIBRARY □ Albany, NY

Pinson, Bob, Principal Res.
COUNTRY MUSIC FOUNDATION - LIBRARY AND MEDIA CENTER □ Nashville, TN

Pintozzi, Chestalene, Libn.
UNIVERSITY OF TEXAS, AUSTIN - GEOLOGY LIBRARY □ Austin, TX

Pinzelik, Barbara, Assoc.Hum.Libn.
PURDUE UNIVERSITY - HUMANITIES, SOCIAL SCIENCE AND EDUCATION LIBRARY □ West Lafayette, IN

Pinzelik, John, Chem.Libn.
PURDUE UNIVERSITY - CHEMISTRY LIBRARY □ West Lafayette, IN

Piotrow, Dr. Phyllis T., Dir.
JOHNS HOPKINS UNIVERSITY - POPULATION INFORMATION PROGRAM □ Baltimore, MD

Pipe, Rebecca, Registrar
OVER (W.H.) MUSEUM - LIBRARY □ Vermillion, SD

Piper, Larry W., Libn.
STOEL, RIVES, BOLEY, ET AL - LIBRARY □ Portland, OR

Piper, Mrs. Pat B., Assoc. Law Libn.
UNIVERSITY OF CALIFORNIA, DAVIS - SCHOOL OF LAW - LAW LIBRARY □ Davis, CA

Pipes, Alice, Med.Libn.
KAISER-PERMANENTE MEDICAL CENTER - HEALTH SCIENCES LIBRARY† □ Hayward, CA

Pirie, Joan, Cat.
NEW YORK UNIVERSITY - SCHOOL OF LAW LIBRARY □ New York, NY

Pirino, Karen, Asst.Libn.
MEMORIAL HOSPITAL - LIBRARY □ Belleville, IL

Piron, Alice, Libn.
MUSEUM OF CONTEMPORARY ART - LIBRARY □ Chicago, IL

Pirosko, Connie M., Libn.
HOLLAND & HART - LIBRARY □ Denver, CO

Piscadlo, Bruce S., Asst. Law Libn.
MONTGOMERY COUNTY LAW LIBRARY† □ Norristown, PA

Pisciotta, Robert A., Hd., Cat.
UNIVERSITY OF NEBRASKA MEDICAL CENTER - MC GOOGAN LIBRARY OF MEDICINE □ Omaha, NE

Pistone, F.J., Pres.
HISTORICAL SOCIETY OF THE TOWN OF NORTH HEMPSTEAD - LIBRARY □ Manhasset, NY

Pistorius, Nancy, Asst.Libn.
UNIVERSITY OF NEW MEXICO - FINE ARTS LIBRARY □ Albuquerque, NM

Pitcher, Deborah J., Lib.Asst.
LOUISIANA STATE UNIVERSITY - BUSINESS ADMINISTRATION/GOVERNMENT DOCUMENTS DEPARTMENT □ Baton Rouge, LA

Pitchford, Harriet, Cat.
U.S. ARMY POST - FORT BENNING - RECREATION SERVICES LIBRARY BRANCH† □ Ft. Benning, GA

Pitchon, Cindy A., Asst.Libn.
PROVIDENT MUTUAL LIFE INSURANCE COMPANY OF PHILADELPHIA - LIBRARY† □ Philadelphia, PA

Pitcock, Allison, Libn.
U.S. COURT OF APPEALS, 8TH CIRCUIT - BRANCH LIBRARY □ Little Rock, AR

Pitkin, Patricia A., Dir.
ROCHESTER INSTITUTE OF TECHNOLOGY - WALLACE MEMORIAL LIBRARY □ Rochester, NY

Pitney, Mrs. James C.
MORRIS MUSEUM OF ARTS AND SCIENCE - REFERENCE LIBRARY □ Morristown, NJ

Pitoniak, Karen, Libn.
ONONDAGA COUNTY PUBLIC LIBRARY - BUSINESS AND INDUSTRIAL DEPARTMENT □ Syracuse, NY

Pitschel, Barbara, Asst.Libn.
STRYBING ARBORETUM SOCIETY - HELEN CROCKER RUSSELL LIBRARY† □ San Francisco, CA

Pitschmann, Louis A., Libn.
CORNELL UNIVERSITY - ICELANDIC COLLECTION □ Ithaca, NY

Pitt, William B., Assoc.Libn.
UNIVERSITY OF MARYLAND, COLLEGE PARK - COLLEGE OF LIBRARY & INFORMATION SERVICES - LIBRARY □ College Park, MD

Pittman, Donna, Libn.
OHIO STATE ENVIRONMENTAL PROTECTION AGENCY - ENVIRONMENTAL TECHNICAL INFORMATION CENTER □ Columbus, OH

Pittman, Julee, Hd.Cat.
CAPITAL UNIVERSITY - LAW SCHOOL LIBRARY □ Columbus, OH

Pitts, J.
OLIN CORPORATION - RESEARCH CENTER/ INFORMATION CENTER □ New Haven, CT

Pitts, Loretta, Cat.
VINSON & ELKINS - LAW LIBRARY □ Houston, TX

Pitts, Terence, Cur., Photo Archv.
UNIVERSITY OF ARIZONA - CENTER FOR CREATIVE PHOTOGRAPHY □ Tucson, AZ

Pitts, V.
OLIN CORPORATION - RESEARCH CENTER/ INFORMATION CENTER □ New Haven, CT

Pitzer, Laura F., Libn.
GREENVILLE MENTAL HEALTH CENTER - LIBRARY □ Greenville, SC

Pivorun, Phyllis, Slide Cur.
CLEMSON UNIVERSITY - EMERY A. GUNNIN ARCHITECTURAL LIBRARY □ Clemson, SC

Piwonka, Ruth, Exec.Dir.
COLUMBIA COUNTY HISTORICAL SOCIETY - HOUSE OF HISTORY LIBRARY □ Kinderhook, NY

Pixley, Lorene, Asst.Libn.
SOUTHERN ILLINOIS UNIVERSITY, CARBONDALE - EDUCATION AND PSYCHOLOGY DIVISION LIBRARY □ Carbondale, IL

Pizer, Irwin H., Univ.Libn.
UNIVERSITY OF ILLINOIS AT CHICAGO - HEALTH SCIENCES CENTER - LIBRARY OF THE HEALTH SCIENCES □ Chicago, IL

Pizer, Laurence R., Dir.
PILGRIM SOCIETY - PILGRIM HALL LIBRARY □ Plymouth, MA

Pizzo, Anthony P., Chm.
HILLSBOROUGH COUNTY HISTORICAL COMMISSION - LIBRARY □ Tampa, FL

Place, Patricia, Libn.
UNIVERSITY RESEARCH CORPORATION - LIBRARY □ Chevy Chase, MD

Place, Dr. Walter, Sr.Archv.
KENTUCKY STATE DEPARTMENT FOR LIBRARIES & ARCHIVES - ARCHIVES □ Frankfort, KY

Place-Beary, Elizabeth, Ref.Libn.
GUILFORD COLLEGE - LIBRARY - SPECIAL COLLECTIONS □ Greensboro, NC

Plainfeather, Mardell Irene, Park Techn./Hist.
U.S. NATL. PARK SERVICE - CUSTER BATTLEFIELD NATL. MONUMENT - LIBRARY □ Crow Agency, MT

Plaisance, Gilbert, Ref.
QUEBEC PROVINCE - MINISTERE DE L'INDUSTRIE, DU COMMERCE ET DU TOURISME - BIBLIOTHEQUE MINISTERIELLE □ Quebec, PQ

Plaiss, Mark, Ref.Libn.
UNIVERSITY OF LOUISVILLE - KORNHAUSER HEALTH SCIENCES LIBRARY □ Louisville, KY

Plamann, Paul E., Hist.
U.S. NATL. PARK SERVICE - FORT MC HENRY NATL. MONUMENT - LIBRARY □ Baltimore, MD

Plambeck, Susan, Libn.
TEMPLE BETH EL - MAX & ANN GOLDBERG LIBRARY □ Fargo, ND

Plamondon, Yolande, Techn.
CENTRE HOSPITALIER ROBERT-GIFFARD - BIBLIOTHEQUE PROFESSIONNELLE □ Beauport, PQ

Plane, Daphne, Geology Libn.
CALIFORNIA INSTITUTE OF TECHNOLOGY - GEOLOGY LIBRARY □ Pasadena, CA

Planetta, Elizabeth, Cur.
UNIVERSITY OF CAPE BRETON - BEATON INSTITUTE ARCHIVES □ Sydney, NS

Plante, Dr. Julian G., Dir.
ST. JOHN'S ABBEY AND UNIVERSITY - HILL MONASTIC MANUSCRIPT LIBRARY - BUSH CENTER □ Collegeville, MN

Plante-Garneau, Suzanne
QUEBEC PROVINCE - OFFICE DE PLANIFICATION ET DE DEVELOPPEMENT DU QUEBEC - BIBLIOTHEQUE† □ Quebec, PQ

Plaskacz, Mrs. Truus, Hd., Cat. Unit
NATIONAL LIBRARY OF CANADA - MULTILINGUAL BIBLIOSERVICE □ Ottawa, ON

Plaso, Kathy, Libn.
PENNSYLVANIA STATE DEPARTMENT OF PUBLIC WELFARE - SOMERSET STATE HOSPITAL - LIBRARY □ Somerset, PA

Plaster, Joyce, Chf., Rd.Serv.
U.S. ARMY - MISSILE COMMAND & MARSHALL SPACE FLIGHT CENTER - REDSTONE SCIENTIFIC INFORMATION CENTER □ Redstone Arsenal, AL

Plasterer, F.R., Asst.Libn.
BABCOCK AND WILCOX COMPANY - UTILITY POWER GENERATION DIVISION - LIBRARY □ Lynchburg, VA

Plate, Kenneth H., Sr. Partner
PACIFIC INFORMATION INC. - INFORMATION SERVICES □ Studio City, CA

Platou, J.S., Dir. of Info.
SULPHUR INSTITUTE - LIBRARY □ Washington, DC

Platt, Gretchen, Supv.
ATLANTIC-RICHFIELD COMPANY - ANACONDA MINERALS COMPANY - INFORMATION CENTER □ Denver, CO

Platt, Janice, Cat.
UNIVERSITY OF CINCINNATI - ROBERT S. MARX LAW LIBRARY □ Cincinnati, OH

Platt, John H., Jr., Asst.Libn. & Cur.
GRAND LODGE OF FREE AND ACCEPTED MASONS OF PENNSYLVANIA - LIBRARY □ Philadelphia, PA

Platt-Brown, Jane, Libn.
NATIONAL ECONOMIC RESEARCH ASSOCIATES, INC. - LIBRARY □ Washington, DC

Platte, James P., Dean/Div.Lrng.Rsrcs.
LANSING COMMUNITY COLLEGE - PROFESSIONAL RESOURCE CENTER □ Lansing, MI

Platthy, Jeno, Ph.D., Libn.
HARVARD UNIVERSITY - CENTER FOR HELLENIC STUDIES - LIBRARY □ Washington, DC

Plattner, Steven, Photo Cur.
CINCINNATI HISTORICAL SOCIETY - LIBRARY □ Cincinnati, OH

Player, Jewell, Tech.Serv.Libn.
U.S. ARMY IN EUROPE (USAREUR) - LIBRARY AND RESOURCE CENTER □ APO New York, NY

Player, Julia, Assoc.Libn.
HOWARD UNIVERSITY - HEALTH SCIENCES LIBRARY □ Washington, DC

Plehaty, Phyllis, Cur.
BOULDER HISTORICAL SOCIETY AND MUSEUM - DOCUMENTARY COLLECTIONS DEPARTMENT □ Boulder, CO

Plese, Pat, Libn.
INTERGALACTIC CORP. - LIBRARY □ Salt Lake City, UT

Plesko, Patricia A., Med.Libn.
ALASKA AIR NATIONAL GUARD - 176TH TACTICAL CLINIC MEDICAL LIBRARY □ Anchorage, AK

Plessinger, Suzanne, Libn.
PAUL, HASTINGS, JANOFSKY AND WALKER - LAW LIBRARY† □ Los Angeles, CA

Plewa, Michele M., Adm.Asst.
MARQUETTE UNIVERSITY - MEMORIAL LIBRARY □ Milwaukee, WI

Pleztke, Chester J., Assoc.Prof. & Dir.
U.S. UNIFORMED SERVICES UNIVERSITY OF THE HEALTH SCIENCES - LEARNING RESOURCE CENTER □ Bethesda, MD

Plitt, Jeanne G., Dir.
ALEXANDRIA LIBRARY - LLOYD HOUSE □ Alexandria, VA

Ploch, Carol S., Med.Libn.
BETHESDA MEMORIAL HOSPITAL - MEDICAL LIBRARY† □ Boynton Beach, FL

Plockelman, Cynthia H., Ref.Libn.
FLORIDA STATE - SOUTH FLORIDA WATER MANAGEMENT DISTRICT - REFERENCE CENTER □ West Palm Beach, FL

Plotnick, Robert Nathan, Libn.
CONNECTICUT STATE LIBRARY - LAW LIBRARY AT BRIDGEPORT □ Bridgeport, CT

Plowden, Arlington A.
NEW YORK LAW INSTITUTE - LIBRARY □ New York, NY

Plowman, Dr. Robert J., Regional Archv.
U.S. NATL. ARCHIVES & RECORDS SERVICE - FEDERAL ARCHIVES AND RECORDS CENTER, REGION 3 □ Philadelphia, PA

Plucinski, Veronica, Chf.Libn.
PFIZER, INC. - N.Y.O. LIBRARY □ New York, NY

Plum, Dorothy A., Libn.
ESSEX COUNTY HISTORICAL SOCIETY - LIBRARY □ Elizabethtown, NY

Plummer, Bill, III, Commun.Dir.
AMATEUR SOFTBALL ASSOCIATION - ASA RESEARCH CENTER AND LIBRARY □ Oklahoma City, OK

Plummer, Bruce, Dir.
WORCESTER STATE COLLEGE - LEARNING RESOURCES CENTER □ Worcester, MA

Plummer, John, Co-Cur., Medv. & Ren.Mss.
PIERPONT MORGAN LIBRARY □ New York, NY

Plunket, Joy, Libn.
CHOATE, HALL AND STEWART - LAW LIBRARY† □ Boston, MA

Pluscauskas, Martha, Coord.
EAST YORK BOARD OF EDUCATION - PROFESSIONAL LIBRARY† □ Toronto, ON

Pober, Susan J., Libn.
BROOKLYN CHILDREN'S MUSEUM - CHILDREN'S RESOURCE LIBRARY □ Brooklyn, NY

Poburko, Mary Jo, Hd.Libn.
GOODWIN, PROCTER & HOAR - LAW LIBRARY □ Boston, MA

Pochert, Marjorie, Children's Libn.
MEMORIAL PRESBYTERIAN CHURCH - LIBRARY □ Midland, MI

Pockrose, Sheryl R., Libn.
PUBLIC LIBRARY OF CINCINNATI AND HAMILTON COUNTY - ART AND MUSIC DEPARTMENT □ Cincinnati, OH

Pocock, Bryna, Libn.
UNIVERSITY OF UTAH - CENTER FOR PUBLIC AFFAIRS AND ADMINISTRATION - RESEARCH LIBRARY □ Salt Lake City, UT

Podboy, Alvin M., Libn.
BAKER AND HOSTETLER - LIBRARY □ Cleveland, OH

Podgajny, Stephen J., Exec.Dir.
DYER-YORK LIBRARY AND MUSEUM □ Saco, ME

Podojil, Merry, Docs.
OHIO NORTHERN UNIVERSITY - COLLEGE OF LAW - JAY P. TAGGART MEMORIAL LAW LIBRARY □ Ada, OH

Podolak, Barbara, Asst.Libn.
INDUSTRIAL HOME FOR THE BLIND - NASSAU-SUFFOLK BRAILLE LIBRARY □ Hempstead, NY

Poe, Celia D., Map Libn.
UNIVERSITY OF NORTH CAROLINA, CHAPEL HILL - MAPS COLLECTION □ Chapel Hill, NC

Poehlman, Dorothy, Chf., Info.Serv.Br.
U.S. DEPT. OF TRANSPORTATION - LIBRARY AND DISTRIBUTION SERVICES DIVISION □ Washington, DC

Poeschl, Peg, Asst.
ORTHODOX CHURCH IN AMERICA - DEPARTMENT OF HISTORY AND ARCHIVES □ Syosset, NY

Poesnecker, Gerald E., Pres.
ROSICRUCIAN FRATERNITY - LIBRARY □ Quakertown, PA

Poff, D., Ref.Coord.
UNIVERSITY OF ALBERTA - HUMANITIES AND SOCIAL SCIENCES LIBRARY □ Edmonton, AB

Poff, J.G., Hd.Libn.
NORTH BAY COLLEGE EDUCATION CENTRE - LIBRARY □ North Bay, ON

Poffenroth, J., Lib.Asst., Ref.
ESSO RESOURCES CANADA LIMITED - LIBRARY INFORMATION CENTRE □ Calgary, AB

Pogacar, Peter, Circ./Ref.Libn.
OHIO NORTHERN UNIVERSITY - COLLEGE OF LAW - JAY P. TAGGART MEMORIAL LAW LIBRARY □ Ada, OH

Pogue, Basil G., Corp.Libn.
SASKATCHEWAN TELECOMMUNICATIONS - CORPORATE LIBRARY □ Regina, SK

Pogue, Laura, Ref.Libn.
SASKATCHEWAN - LEGISLATIVE LIBRARY† □ Regina, SK

Pohl, Gunther, Libn.
NEW YORK GENEALOGICAL AND BIOGRAPHICAL SOCIETY - GENEALOGICAL RESEARCH LIBRARY □ New York, NY

Pohl, Gunther E., Div.Chf.
NEW YORK PUBLIC LIBRARY - UNITED STATES HISTORY, LOCAL HISTORY AND GENEALOGY DIVISION □ New York, NY

Pohorecky, Natalia, Ref.Libn.
UNIVERSITY OF MANITOBA - MEDICAL LIBRARY □ Winnipeg, MB

Poi, Sharie, Circ.
HUGHES AIRCRAFT COMPANY - GROUND SYSTEMS GROUP - TECHNICAL LIBRARY □ Fullerton, CA

Poindexter, Joann, Off.Mgr.
KETRON, INC. - LIBRARY □ Arlington, VA

Pointer, Jan, ILL Libn.
MIDWEST RESEARCH INSTITUTE - PATTERSON REFERENCE LIBRARY AND ECONOMICS REFERENCE CENTER □ Kansas City, MO

Points, Larry G., Chf., Interp.
U.S. NATL. PARK SERVICE - ASSATEAGUE ISLAND NATL. SEASHORE - LIBRARY □ Berlin, MD

Poirier, Linda, Cur. of Coll./Exhibitions
BATTLE CREEK ART CENTER - MICHIGAN ART ARCHIVES □ Battle Creek, MI

Poison, Ellen, Hd., Ref.
CORNELL UNIVERSITY - MEDICAL COLLEGE - SAMUEL J. WOOD LIBRARY □ New York, NY

Poisson, Beth C., Libn.
SHATTUCK (Lemuel) HOSPITAL - MEDICAL LIBRARY □ Jamaica Plain, MA

Poje, Mary Elizabeth, Ref.Libn.
GOLDMAN, SACHS AND COMPANY - LIBRARY □ New York, NY

Pokorny, George, Libn.
CHICAGO MOUNTAINEERING CLUB - JOHN SPECK MEMORIAL LIBRARY □ Glen Ellyn, IL

Pokorny, Jill, Plant Pathology Fellow
UNIVERSITY OF MINNESOTA - AGRICULTURAL EXTENSION SERVICE - DIAL-U INSECT AND PLANT INFORMATION CLINIC □ St. Paul, MN

Polach, Dr. Frank, Dir.
RUTGERS UNIVERSITY, THE STATE UNIVERSITY OF NEW JERSEY - LIBRARY OF SCIENCE & MEDICINE □ Piscataway, NJ

Polacsek, John F., Cur.
GREAT LAKES MARITIME INSTITUTE - DOSSIN GREAT LAKES MUSEUM INFORMATION CENTER □ Detroit, MI

Polacsek, Richard A., M.D., Dir./Libn.
JOHNS HOPKINS UNIVERSITY - WILLIAM H. WELCH MEDICAL LIBRARY □ Baltimore, MD

Polak, Virginia, Libn.
UNIVERSITY OF CALIFORNIA, BERKELEY - UNIVERSITY EXTENSION - CONTINUING EDUCATION OF THE BAR - LIBRARY □ Berkeley, CA

Poland, Jean, Libn.
UNIVERSITY OF OKLAHOMA - ENGINEERING LIBRARY □ Norman, OK

Poland, Ursula H., Libn.
UNION UNIVERSITY - ALBANY MEDICAL COLLEGE - SCHAFFER LIBRARY OF THE HEALTH SCIENCES □ Albany, NY

Poldoian, Jean, Supv.
NEW ENGLAND MUTUAL LIFE INSURANCE COMPANY - BUSINESS LIBRARY □ Boston, MA

Poletti, Edward J., Chf., Lib.Serv.
U.S. VETERANS ADMINISTRATION (WV-Clarksburg) - MEDICAL CENTER LIBRARY SERVICE □ Clarksburg, WV

Polhill, Ruth B., Libn.
VAN WYCK HOMESTEAD MUSEUM - LIBRARY □ Fishkill, NY

Poli, Ross, Info.Spec.
OHIO STATE UNIVERSITY - MECHANIZED INFORMATION CENTER (MIC) □ Columbus, OH

Polinsky, Helga Brink, Exec.Ed.
AUTHENTICATED NEWS INTERNATIONAL - PHOTO LIBRARY □ Katonah, NY

Polinsky, Sidney, Mng.Ed.
AUTHENTICATED NEWS INTERNATIONAL - PHOTO LIBRARY □ Katonah, NY

Polk, Diana, Sr.Ref.Libn.
DEERE & COMPANY - LIBRARY □ Moline, IL

Pollack, Beth, Libn.
OGILVY & MATHER, INC. - RESEARCH LIBRARY† □ New York, NY

Pollack, Carol, Asst. V.P./Mgr.
COMERICA INCORPORATED - RESEARCH LIBRARY† □ Detroit, MI

Pollak, Simona, Circ. & ILL
HEBREW UNION COLLEGE - JEWISH INSTITUTE OF RELIGION - KLAU LIBRARY □ New York, NY

Pollard, Mrs. G.E., Libn.
GEORGE (Henry) SCHOOL OF LOS ANGELES - RESEARCH LIBRARY □ Tujunga, CA

Pollard, Louise, Sys.Libn.
AMERICAN EXPRESS COMPANY - TRAVELERS
CHEQUE DIVISION - T/C SYSTEMS LIBRARY □
Salt Lake City, UT

Pollard, Russell, Tech.Serv.
HARVARD UNIVERSITY - DIVINITY SCHOOL -
ANDOVER-HARVARD THEOLOGICAL LIBRARY □
Cambridge, MA

Pollard, Stewart M.L., Exec.Sec.
MASONIC SERVICE ASSOCIATION OF THE
UNITED STATES - LIBRARY □ Silver Spring, MD

Pollard, W. Robert, Hd., Ref.Dept.
NORTH CAROLINA STATE UNIVERSITY - D.H.
HILL LIBRARY □ Raleigh, NC

Polley, Brian S., Libn.
FLORIDA STATE SUPREME COURT LIBRARY □
Tallahassee, FL

Pollis, Angela R., Staff Supv.
UNITED STATES STEEL CORPORATION -
TECHNICAL INFORMATION CENTER □
Monroeville, PA

Pollock, Ethel, Ref.Libn.
EASTERN VIRGINIA MEDICAL SCHOOL -
MOORMAN MEMORIAL LIBRARY □ Norfolk, VA

Pollock, Ida C., Libn.
TEMPLE BETH-EL - ZISKIND MEMORIAL
LIBRARY □ Fall River, MA

Pollock, James A., Ref.Libn.
CENTRAL VIRGINIA COMMUNITY COLLEGE -
LIBRARY - SPECIAL COLLECTIONS □ Lynchburg,
VA

Pollock, James W., Libn./Cat.
INDIANA UNIVERSITY - NEAR EASTERN
COLLECTION □ Bloomington, IN

Pollock, Miss M.Y., Mgr.
NORTHERN TELECOM CANADA, LTD. - LIBRARY
& TECHNICAL INFORMATION CENTRE □
Montreal, PQ

Polonsky, Howard E., Hd., Rd.Serv.
WESTERN NEW ENGLAND COLLEGE - SCHOOL
OF LAW LIBRARY □ Springfield, MA

Polster, Joanne, Libn.
AMERICAN CRAFT COUNCIL - LIBRARY □ New
York, NY

Polvi, Kim
ALBERTA - WORKERS' HEALTH SAFETY &
COMPENSATION - OCCUPATIONAL HEALTH &
SAFETY LIBRARY □ Edmonton, AB

Polzoni, Sue, Lib.Mgr.
FLUOR ENGINEERS, INC. - MINING & METALS
DIVISION - TECHNICAL LIBRARY □ Redwood
City, CA

Pomager, Carla J., Libn.
U.S. ARMY CHEMICAL SCHOOL - FISHER
LIBRARY □ Fort McClellan, AL

Pomerance, Deborah S., Libn.
DATA USE AND ACCESS LABORATORIES
(DUALABS) - LIBRARY† □ Arlington, VA

Pomerantz, Barbara, Asst.Libn.
KENYON & ECKHARDT ADVERTISING -
INFORMATION CENTER □ New York, NY

Pomerantz, Julius M., Libn.
CARTER, LEDYARD AND MILBURN - LIBRARY† □
New York, NY

Pomeroy, Cornelia, Circ.
WORCESTER POLYTECHNIC INSTITUTE -
GEORGE C. GORDON LIBRARY □ Worcester, MA

Pommer, Michelle A., Libn.
HAWAIIAN TELEPHONE COMPANY - LIBRARY □
Honolulu, HI

Pomponio, Jay, Govt.Doc.Libn.
MAINE MARITIME ACADEMY - NUTTING
MEMORIAL LIBRARY □ Castine, ME

Pond, Frederick, Circuit Libn.
ROCHESTER GENERAL HOSPITAL - LILLIE B.
WERNER HEALTH SCIENCES LIBRARY □
Rochester, NY

Pond, William
UNIVERSITY OF WINNIPEG - LIBRARY -
SPECIAL COLLECTIONS □ Winnipeg, MB

Ponis, Roberta, Rsrc.Spec.
JEFFERSON COUNTY PUBLIC SCHOOLS R1 -
PROFESSIONAL LIBRARY MEDIA CENTER □
Lakewood, CO

Ponomarenko, Ella, Western Bk.Acq.Libn.
MATHEMATICAL REVIEWS - LIBRARY □ Ann
Arbor, MI

Pons, Joyce, Hd.
UNIVERSITY OF CINCINNATI - MATHEMATICS
LIBRARY □ Cincinnati, OH

Pontbriand, Bob
IBM CORPORATION - GENERAL TECHNOLOGY
DIVISION - INFORMATION CENTER/LEARNING
CENTER □ Essex Junction, VT

Pool, Rose, Tech.Serv.Libn.
NATIONAL JOURNAL LIBRARY □ Washington, DC

Poole, Dr. Herbert, Dir.
GUILFORD COLLEGE - LIBRARY - SPECIAL
COLLECTIONS □ Greensboro, NC

Poole, Judy, Census Cons.
UNIVERSITY OF NORTH CAROLINA, CHAPEL
HILL - INSTITUTE FOR RESEARCH IN SOCIAL
SCIENCE - DATA LIBRARY □ Chapel Hill, NC

Poole, Katherine, Lrng.Rsrcs.Libn.
HARVARD UNIVERSITY - GRADUATE SCHOOL
OF DESIGN - FRANCES LOEB LIBRARY □
Cambridge, MA

Poole-Kober, Evelyn M., Tech.Info.Ck.
ENVIRONMENTAL PROTECTION AGENCY -
DIVISION OF METEOROLOGY - INFORMATION
SERVICE CENTER □ Research Triangle Park, NC

Pooler, Margaret, Cat.Libn.
MATHEMATICAL REVIEWS - LIBRARY □ Ann
Arbor, MI

Pooley, Beverley J., Dir.
UNIVERSITY OF MICHIGAN - LAW LIBRARY □
Ann Arbor, MI

Poon, Mrs. Wei Chi, Hd.Libn.
UNIVERSITY OF CALIFORNIA, BERKELEY -
ASIAN AMERICAN STUDIES LIBRARY □
Berkeley, CA

Poor, W.E., Lib.Serv.Mgr.
CUMMINS ENGINE CO., INC. - LIBRARIES □
Columbus, IN

Popa, Peggy L., Staff Info.Anl.
CONTINENTAL ILLINOIS NATIONAL BANK AND
TRUST COMPANY OF CHICAGO -
INFORMATION SERVICES DIVISION □ Chicago,
IL

Pope, Andrew, Educ.Libn.
UNIVERSITY OF NEW BRUNSWICK -
EDUCATION RESOURCE CENTRE □ Fredericton,
NB

Pope, Darrel, Asst. Media Libn.
NORTH TEXAS STATE UNIVERSITY LIBRARIES
- MEDIA LIBRARY □ Denton, TX

Pope, Janice T., Supv.
INTERNATIONAL PAPER COMPANY - ERLING
RIIS RESEARCH LABORATORY - INFORMATION
SERVICES □ Mobile, AL

Pope, Lurrie V., Supv. Park Ranger
U.S. NATL. PARK SERVICE - NATL. CAPITAL
REGION - ROCK CREEK NATURE CENTER
LIBRARY □ Washington, DC

Pope, Mary, Chf., Tech.Serv.Br.
U.S. DEPT. OF THE TREASURY - INFORMATION
SERVICES DIVISION - TREASURY DEPT.
LIBRARY □ Washington, DC

Pope, Nannette M., Hd., Lib.Serv.
U.S. ARMED FORCES RADIOBIOLOGY
RESEARCH INSTITUTE (AFRRI) - LIBRARY
SERVICES □ Bethesda, MD

Pope, W. Nicholas, Asst.Prof./Law Libn.
CLEVELAND STATE UNIVERSITY - JOSEPH W.
BARTUNEK III LAW LIBRARY □ Cleveland, OH

Pope, Wiley R., Ref.Libn.
MINNESOTA HISTORICAL SOCIETY -
REFERENCE LIBRARY □ St. Paul, MN

Popenoe, John, Dir.
FAIRCHILD TROPICAL GARDEN -
MONTGOMERY LIBRARY □ Miami, FL

Popescu, Dr. Constantin, Assoc.Libn.
MILWAUKEE SCHOOL OF ENGINEERING -
WALTER SCHROEDER LIBRARY □ Milwaukee,
WI

Popik, Judith, Asst.Libn.
COUDERT BROTHERS - LIBRARY □ New York,
NY

Popik, Marilyn L., Med.Libn.
ST. BERNARDINE HOSPITAL - NORMAN F.
FELDHEYM LIBRARY □ San Bernardino, CA

Poplawska, Halina, Slide Cur.
KENDALL SCHOOL OF DESIGN - LEARNING
RESOURCE CENTER □ Grand Rapids, MI

Popoff, Ed, Ref./Indexing/Microfilms
CANADA - LABOUR CANADA - LIBRARY
SERVICES† □ Ottawa, ON

Popovich, Charles, Hd.Libn.
OHIO STATE UNIVERSITY - COMMERCE
LIBRARY □ Columbus, OH

Popp, Richard H., Mgr., Corp. Training
WESTERN PUBLISHING COMPANY, INC. -
CORPORATE TRAINING CENTER LIBRARY □
Racine, WI

Popplestone, John A., Dir.
UNIVERSITY OF AKRON - ARCHIVES OF THE
HISTORY OF AMERICAN PSYCHOLOGY □ Akron,
OH

Poray-Wybranowski, Dr. Anna, Chf.Libn.
POLISH INSTITUTE OF ARTS AND SCIENCES IN
CANADA - POLISH LIBRARY □ Montreal, PQ

Porcella, Dr. Brewster, Libn.
TRINITY EVANGELICAL DIVINITY SCHOOL -
ROLFING MEMORIAL LIBRARY □ Deerfield, IL

Porciello, Nancy, Hd.Libn.
AMERICAN SOCIETY OF APPRAISERS -
INTERNATIONAL VALUATION SCIENCES
CENTRE LIBRARY □ Washington, DC

Porpiglia, Johanna, Br.Libn.
FLORIDA STATE SUPREME COURT - 11TH
JUDICIAL CIRCUIT - DADE COUNTY AUXILIARY
LAW LIBRARY □ Miami Beach, FL

Port, Toby G., Adm.Libn.
ST. ELIZABETHS HOSPITAL - HEALTH
SCIENCES LIBRARY □ Washington, DC

Porta, Maria, Circ./Ref.Libn.
UNIVERSITY OF ILLINOIS - LAW LIBRARY □
Champaign, IL

Porte, Masha R., Film Spec.
DALLAS PUBLIC LIBRARY - FILM SERVICE □
Dallas, TX

Porter, Catherine, Supv.
ST. MARY'S HOSPITAL - MEDICAL LIBRARY
(6E) □ Huntington, WV

Porter, Ms. D.
CANADA - PUBLIC ARCHIVES OF CANADA -
NATIONAL MAP COLLECTION □ Ottawa, ON

Porter, Donna J., Owner
STAGECOACH LIBRARY FOR GENEALOGICAL
RESEARCH □ Denver, CO

Porter, Eve, Ref.Libn.Supv.
BRITISH COLUMBIA LAW LIBRARY
FOUNDATION - VANCOUVER COURTHOUSE
LIBRARY □ Vancouver, BC

Porter, G.W., Adm.
UNIVERSITY HEALTH CENTER OF PITTSBURGH
- CENTER FOR EMERGENCY MEDICINE -
LIBRARY □ Pittsburgh, PA

Porter, Helen, Libn.
MUSKINGUM LAW LIBRARY □ Zanesville, OH

Porter, Helen, Libn.
OSAWATOMIE STATE HOSPITAL - RAPAPORT
PROFESSIONAL LIBRARY - MENTAL HEALTH
LIBRARY □ Osawatomie, KS

Porter, J.
HARTFORD PUBLIC LIBRARY - ART, MUSIC AND
RECREATION DEPARTMENT □ Hartford, CT

Porter, Jean, Docs.Libn./Dept.Hd.
NORTH CAROLINA STATE UNIVERSITY - D.H.
HILL LIBRARY - DOCUMENTS DEPARTMENT □
Raleigh, NC

Porter, Jean M., Hd., Doc.Dept.
NORTH CAROLINA STATE UNIVERSITY - D.H.
HILL LIBRARY □ Raleigh, NC

Porter, Kathryn W., Adm.
AETNA LIFE & CASUALTY COMPANY -
CORPORATE INFORMATION CENTER □
Hartford, CT
Porter, Kitty, Libn.
DUKE UNIVERSITY - CHEMISTRY LIBRARY □
Durham, NC
Porter, Mr. L., Asst.Libn.
UNIVERSITY OF GUELPH - LIBRARY □ Guelph,
ON
Porter, Marguerite E., Dir., Lib.Serv.
CANADIAN BIBLE COLLEGE/CANADIAN
THEOLOGICAL SEMINARY - ARCHIBALD
FOUNDATION LIBRARY □ Regina, SK
Porter, Mary E., Hd.Libn.
LUTHERAN BIBLE INSTITUTE - LIBRARY □
Issaquah, WA
Porter, Mary J., Ref.Libn.
U.S. MARINE CORPS - EDUCATION CENTER -
JAMES CARSON BRECKINRIDGE LIBRARY &
AMPHIBIOUS WARFARE RESEARCH FACILITY □
Quantico, VA
Porter, Robert, Mgr., Info.Serv.
AMERICAN COUNCIL FOR THE ARTS - LIBRARY
□ New York, NY
Porter, Sandra L., Adm.Asst.
OHIO VALLEY HEALTH SERVICES FOUNDATION,
INC. - LIBRARY □ Athens, OH
Porter, Sherry, Ser.
UNIVERSITY OF TEXAS HEALTH SCIENCE
CENTER, DALLAS - LIBRARY □ Dallas, TX
Porter-Roth, Anne, Mgr.
ATARI INC. - CORPORATE LIBRARY/
INFORMATION CENTER □ Sunnyvale, CA
Porter-Zadera, Suzanne, Dir.
PARK CITY HOSPITAL - CARLSON FOUNDATION
MEMORIAL LIBRARY □ Bridgeport, CT
Portillo, Christine, Sr.Libn.
CALIFORNIA STATE DEPARTMENT OF
TRANSPORTATION - LABORATORY LIBRARY □
Sacramento, CA
Portlock, Lucile B., Cur., Rm.
NORFOLK PUBLIC LIBRARY - SARGEANT
MEMORIAL ROOM □ Norfolk, VA
Portmann, Douglas A., Tech.Libn.
MOBAY CHEMICAL CORPORATION - RESEARCH
LIBRARY □ New Martinsville, WV
Portolese, Margaret, Libn.
ALLEN COUNTY PUBLIC LIBRARY - BUSINESS
AND TECHNOLOGY DEPARTMENT □ Fort Wayne,
IN
Portsch, Joanne, Libn.
RAYTHEON COMPANY - EQUIPMENT DIVISION
- TECHNICAL INFORMATION CENTER □
Wayland, MA
Portwood, Pamela, Lib.Asst.
UNIVERSITY OF ARIZONA - OFFICE OF ARID
LANDS STUDIES - BIORESOURCES RESEARCH
LIBRARY □ Tucson, AZ
Poses, June A., Asst.Libn.
COLLEGE OF PHYSICIANS OF PHILADELPHIA -
LIBRARY AND MEDICAL DOCUMENTATION
SERVICE □ Philadelphia, PA
Posey, Edwin D., Engr.Libn.
PURDUE UNIVERSITY - ENGINEERING LIBRARY
□ West Lafayette, IN
Posey, George M., III, V.P., Res.
NEWPORT AERONAUTICAL SALES (NAS) -
LIBRARY† □ Costa Mesa, CA
Posey, Jewell, Archv.
UNITED METHODIST COMMISSION ON
ARCHIVES & HISTORY - NORTHWEST TEXAS
ANNUAL CONFERENCE - ARCHIVES □ Abilene,
TX
Posey, Linda L., Asst.Hd.Libn.
KNOX COUNTY PUBLIC LIBRARY SYSTEM - MC
CLUNG HISTORICAL COLLECTION □ Knoxville,
TN
Posik, Jarka, Asst.Libn.
BASSIST COLLEGE - LIBRARY □ Portland, OR

Posner, Cindi S., Res.Bibliog.
UNIVERSITY OF PENNSYLVANIA - POPULATION
STUDIES CENTER - DEMOGRAPHY LIBRARY □
Philadelphia, PA
Posner, Shirley, Hd., Acq.
SUNY - COLLEGE AT BUFFALO - EDWARD H.
BUTLER LIBRARY □ Buffalo, NY
Posner, Walter, Ref.Libn.
SAN DIEGO STATE UNIVERSITY -
GOVERNMENT PUBLICATIONS DEPARTMENT†
□ San Diego, CA
Posniak, John R., Asst.Libn.
EXPORT-IMPORT BANK OF THE UNITED
STATES - LIBRARY □ Washington, DC
Post, Doris, Dir.
GODFREY MEMORIAL LIBRARY □ Middletown,
CT
Post, Edward, Dir.
TRACOR JITCO, INC. - RESEARCH RESOURCES
INFORMATION CENTER □ Rockville, MD
Post, Helen, Med.Libn.
U.S. VETERANS ADMINISTRATION (DE-
Wilmington) - CENTER MEDICAL LIBRARY □
Wilmington, DE
Post, JoAnn J., Libn.
NEW JERSEY STATE DEPARTMENT OF
ENVIRONMENTAL PROTECTION - OFFICE OF
SCIENCE & RESEARCH - INFO. RESEARCH CTR.
□ Trenton, NJ
Post, Linda, Info.Spec.
INTEL CORPORATION - TECHNICAL
INFORMATION CENTER □ Santa Clara, CA
Post, Marilyn, Energy Info.Cons.
NORTHERN STATES POWER COMPANY -
COMMUNICATIONS DEPARTMENT - "ASK NSP"
TAPE LIBRARY □ Minneapolis, MN
Post, Stephen, Dir. of Educ.
AMERICAN INDIAN ARCHAEOLOGICAL
INSTITUTE, INC. - LIBRARY □ Washington, CT
Postell, M.J., Tech.Data Libn.
LOCKHEED MISSILES & SPACE COMPANY, INC.
- TECHNICAL INFORMATION CENTER □ Palo
Alto, CA
Postell, William D., Jr., Med.Libn.
TULANE UNIVERSITY OF LOUISIANA - SCHOOL
OF MEDICINE - RUDOLPH MATAS MEDICAL
LIBRARY† □ New Orleans, LA
Posten, Robin, Libn.
SYSTEMATICS GENERAL CORPORATION -
LIBRARY □ Sterling, VA
Postlewait, Cheryl A., Libn.
ST. MARY'S HOSPITAL - LIBRARY □ Kansas
City, MO
Postrel, Rhonda, Libn.
JOHNSON (Carol R.) & ASSOCIATES, INC. -
LIBRARY □ Cambridge, MA
Potash, Loree E., Assoc.Libn., Pub.Serv.
CASE WESTERN RESERVE UNIVERSITY - LAW
SCHOOL LIBRARY† □ Cleveland, OH
Poteat, James, Mgr., Res.Serv.
TELEVISION INFORMATION OFFICE OF THE
NATIONAL ASSOCIATION OF BROADCASTERS -
RESEARCH SERVICES† □ New York, NY
Poth, Lynn, Cat./Libn.
METROPOLITAN (Toronto) SEPARATE SCHOOL
BOARD - CATHOLIC EDUCATION CENTRE
LIBRARY □ Toronto, ON
Potter, Clare J., Res.Libn.
CALIFORNIA MEDICAL ASSOCIATION -
LIBRARY □ San Francisco, CA
Potter, George E., Pub.Serv.Libn.
HARVARD UNIVERSITY - HARVARD-YENCHING
LIBRARY □ Cambridge, MA
Potter, James E., State Archv.
NEBRASKA STATE HISTORICAL SOCIETY -
ARCHIVES □ Lincoln, NE
Potter, Jean
NORTH CAROLINA MARITIME MUSEUM -
LIBRARY □ Beaufort, NC
Potter, Joyce A., Libn.
U.S. FEDERAL HOME LOAN BANK BOARD - LAW
LIBRARY □ Washington, DC

Potter, Lynne
NATIONAL UNIVERSITY - LAW LIBRARY □ San
Diego, CA
Potter, Marilyn, Asst.Dir./User Serv.
UNIVERSITY OF CONNECTICUT - INSTITUTE
FOR SOCIAL INQUIRY □ Storrs, CT
Potter, Pamela A., Slide Libn.
MARYLAND INSTITUTE, COLLEGE OF ART -
DECKER LIBRARY □ Baltimore, MD
Potter, Sue, Dir., Directed Stud.
WAYNE COMMUNITY COLLEGE - LEARNING
RESOURCE CENTER □ Goldsboro, NC
Potter, T.R., Mgr., Info.Serv.
NORTH CAROLINA STATE SCIENCE AND
TECHNOLOGY RESEARCH CENTER □ Research
Triangle Park, NC
Potter, Theodore A., Acq.
UNIVERSITY OF TOLEDO - COLLEGE OF LAW
LIBRARY □ Toledo, OH
Potter, Virginia, Ref.Supv.
WISCONSIN STATE DIVISION FOR LIBRARY
SERVICES - REFERENCE AND LOAN LIBRARY □
Madison, WI
Potthast, Cheryl, Med.Libn.
U.S. VETERANS ADMINISTRATION (IL-Chicago)
- LAKESIDE HOSPITAL MEDICAL LIBRARY □
Chicago, IL
Potts, Barbara E., Ref.Libn.
EISENHOWER MEDICAL CENTER - DEL E. WEBB
MEMORIAL MEDICAL INFORMATION CENTER □
Rancho Mirage, CA
Potts, Don, Hd., Automation Serv.
MEDICAL LIBRARY CENTER OF NEW YORK† □
New York, NY
Potts, Eleanor, Dir.
FIRST SOUTHERN BAPTIST CHURCH - LIBRARY
□ Tucson, AZ
Potts, Ken, Libn.
MEMPHIS-SHELBY COUNTY PUBLIC LIBRARY
AND INFO. CTR. - SCIENCE/BUSINESS/SOCIAL
SCI.DEPT. □ Memphis, TN
Potts, Nancy, Lib.Techn.
U.S. NATL. PARK SERVICE - HARPERS FERRY
CENTER LIBRARY □ Harpers Ferry, WV
Potvin, Danielle, Sec./Archv.
SOCIETE D'HISTOIRE DES CANTONS DE L'EST
- BIBLIOTHEQUE □ Sherbrooke, PQ
Poulin, Michael, Libn.
UNIVERSITY OF ROCHESTER - CARLSON
LIBRARY □ Rochester, NY
Pouliot, Karen, Per.
NORTHWESTERN UNIVERSITY - DENTAL
SCHOOL LIBRARY □ Chicago, IL
Pouliott, Marianne K., Libn.
GENERAL ELECTRIC COMPANY - SILICONE
PRODUCTS DIVISION - LIBRARY □ Waterford,
NY
Poulis, Andrew D., Chf.Tech.Libn.
U.S. AIR FORCE ENGINEERING AND SERVICES
CENTER - TECHNICAL LIBRARY □ Tyndall AFB,
FL
Pound, M.A., Supv.
SANDIA NATIONAL LABORATORIES -
TECHNICAL LIBRARY† □ Livermore, CA
Povey, Cherryi M., Chf., Lib.Serv.
U.S. VETERANS ADMINISTRATION (UT-Salt
Lake City) - HOSPITAL MEDICAL LIBRARY □ Salt
Lake City, UT
Powdferly, Audrey A., Assoc.Dir., Tech.Serv.
UNIVERSITY OF NEBRASKA MEDICAL CENTER -
MC GOOGAN LIBRARY OF MEDICINE □ Omaha,
NE
Powell, Anita, Lib.Serv. & Tech.Info.
NATIONAL CENTER FOR HEALTH STATISTICS -
CLEARINGHOUSE ON HEALTH INDEXES □
Hyattsville, MD
Powell, Antoinette P., Libn.
UNIVERSITY OF KENTUCKY - AGRICULTURE
LIBRARY □ Lexington, KY
Powell, Bescye, Libn.
FASHION INSTITUTE OF DESIGN &
MERCHANDISING - RESOURCE AND RESEARCH
CENTER† □ Los Angeles, CA

Powell, Bobbie Jean, Circ.Libn.
BATTELLE-COLUMBUS LABORATORIES -
LIBRARY □ Columbus, OH
Powell, Mrs. Bobby H., Med.Libn.
CARRAWAY METHODIST MEDICAL CENTER -
MEDICAL LIBRARY □ Birmingham, AL
Powell, Claudia Lane, Doc.Consrv.Spec.
WESTERN HISTORICAL MANUSCRIPT
COLLECTION/STATE HISTORICAL SOCIETY OF
MISSOURI MANUSCRIPTS JOINT COLLECTION
□ Columbia, MO
Powell, Donald, Bibliog.
TUCSON MUSEUM OF ART - LIBRARY □ Tucson,
AZ
Powell, Evelyn Constance, Ref.Libn.
OHIO UNIVERSITY - HEALTH SCIENCES
LIBRARY □ Athens, OH
Powell, Rev. Gary, O.F.M.Cap., Libn.
ST. CYRIL AND METHODIUS BYZANTINE
CATHOLIC SEMINARY - LIBRARY □ Pittsburgh,
PA
Powell, James, Info.Sci.
UPJOHN COMPANY - CORPORATE TECHNICAL
LIBRARY □ Kalamazoo, MI
Powell, K.L., Coord., Coop.Govt.Serv.
ALBERTA - LEGISLATIVE ASSEMBLY OF
ALBERTA - LEGISLATURE LIBRARY □ Edmonton,
AB
Powell, Kris, Dir., Educ.Serv.
ANNE ARUNDEL GENERAL HOSPITAL -
MEMORIAL LIBRARY □ Annapolis, MD
Powell, Martha C., Church Music Libn.
SOUTHERN BAPTIST THEOLOGICAL SEMINARY
- CHURCH MUSIC LIBRARY □ Louisville, KY
Powell, Michael E., Dir.
WASHINGTON UNIVERSITY - GEORGE WARREN
BROWN SCHOOL OF SOCIAL WORK - LIBRARY &
LEARNING RESOURCES CENTER □ St. Louis, MO
Powell, N.L., Coord., Campus Libs.
CATHOLIC UNIVERSITY OF AMERICA -
CHEMISTRY LIBRARY □ Washington, DC
Powell, N.L., Libn.
CATHOLIC UNIVERSITY OF AMERICA -
NURSING/BIOLOGY LIBRARY □ Washington, DC
Powell, N.L., Coord., Campus Libs.
CATHOLIC UNIVERSITY OF AMERICA -
PHYSICS LIBRARY □ Washington, DC
Powell, Patricia, Libn.
WEST VIRGINIA UNIVERSITY MEDICAL
CENTER - CHARLESTON DIVISION - LEARNING
RESOURCES CENTER □ Charleston, WV
Powell, Richard, Supv., Tchg.Mtls.Ctr.
ANDREWS UNIVERSITY - JAMES WHITE
LIBRARY† □ Berrien Springs, MI
Powell, Russell H., Libn.
UNIVERSITY OF KENTUCKY - ROBERT E.
SHAVER LIBRARY OF ENGINEERING □
Lexington, KY
Powell, Sharon, Asst.Libn.
AEROSPACE INDUSTRIES ASSOCIATION OF
AMERICA - LIBRARY □ Washington, DC
Powell, Mr. T.D., Dir., Rec. & Tech.Serv.
SASKATCHEWAN ARCHIVES BOARD □ Regina,
SK
Powell, Virginia, Music/Educ./AV Libn.
WHEATON COLLEGE - BUSWELL MEMORIAL
LIBRARY □ Wheaton, IL
Powell, Wayne B., Sci./Engr.Libn.
TUFTS UNIVERSITY - RICHARD H. LUFKIN
LIBRARY □ Medford, MA
Power, Genie, Lib.Techn.
NEWFOUNDLAND - DEPARTMENT OF MINES
AND ENERGY - MINERAL DEVELOPMENT
DIVISION - LIBRARY □ St. John's, NF
Power, Hattie, Dir.
CHICAGO PUBLIC LIBRARY CULTURAL CENTER
- VIVIAN G. HARSH COLLECTION OF AFRO-
AMERICAN HISTORY & LIT.† □ Chicago, IL
Power, Mary, Coord., Ref.Serv.
AMERICAN ASSOCIATION OF RETIRED
PERSONS - NATIONAL GERONTOLOGY
RESOURCE CENTER† □ Washington, DC

Power, Pauline V., Asst.Dir., Tech.Serv.
UNIVERSITY OF TEXAS MEDICAL BRANCH -
MOODY MEDICAL LIBRARY □ Galveston, TX
Power, Richard, Libn.
SAN FRANCISCO THEOSOPHICAL SOCIETY -
LIBRARY □ San Francisco, CA
Powers, Audrey, Asst.Libn.
PENNSYLVANIA STATE UNIVERSITY -
ENGINEERING LIBRARY □ University Park, PA
Powers, Carol Ann, Instr./Asst.Libn., Ser.
PHILADELPHIA COLLEGE OF OSTEOPATHIC
MEDICINE - O.J. SNYDER MEMORIAL MEDICAL
LIBRARY □ Philadelphia, PA
Powers, David F., Musm.Cur.
U.S. PRESIDENTIAL LIBRARIES - JOHN F.
KENNEDY LIBRARY □ Boston, MA
Powers, Janet E., Libn.
SHEDD (John G.) AQUARIUM - LIBRARY □
Chicago, IL
Powers, Mrs. Louis L., Libn.
CONGREGATION BETH AM - DOROTHY G.
FELDMAN LIBRARY □ Cleveland Heights, OH
Powers, Nancy A., Hd.
ATLANTA FULTON PUBLIC LIBRARY - IVAN
ALLEN, JR. DEPT. OF SCIENCE, INDUSTRY &
GOVERNMENT - FOUNDATION COLL. □ Atlanta,
GA
Powers, Ruth, Libn.
FIRST PRESBYTERIAN CHURCH - THOMAS E.
BOSWELL MEMORIAL LIBRARY □ Evanston, IL
Powers, Sally, Res.Assoc.
RADCLIFFE COLLEGE - HENRY A. MURRAY
RESEARCH CENTER □ Cambridge, MA
Powers, Thomas, Archv.
UNIVERSITY OF MICHIGAN - MICHIGAN
HISTORICAL COLLECTIONS - BENTLEY
HISTORICAL LIBRARY □ Ann Arbor, MI
Powers, William J., Jr., Exec. Law Libn.
COOK COUNTY LAW LIBRARY □ Chicago, IL
Poyer, Robert, Coord., Pub.Serv.
MEDICAL UNIVERSITY OF SOUTH CAROLINA -
LIBRARY □ Charleston, SC
Pragnell, Ruth, Libn.
GENERAL THEOLOGICAL LIBRARY □ Boston, MA
Pragnell, Terence, Law Libn.
PACIFIC LIGHTING CORPORATION - LAW
LIBRARY □ Los Angeles, CA
Prakash, Judith Middlebrook, Section Hd.
HAWAII STATE LIBRARY - SOCIAL SCIENCE
AND PHILOSOPHY SECTION □ Honolulu, HI
Pralle, Marilee, Pub.Serv.Libn.
PHILLIPS UNIVERSITY - GRADUATE SEMINARY
LIBRARY □ Enid, OK
Pramberger, Ronald, Leg.Libn.
SUTHERLAND, ASBILL & BRENNAN - LIBRARY □
Washington, DC
Prasada-Kole, Usha, Cat.
UNIVERSITY OF ALBERTA - FACULTE ST-JEAN
- BIBLIOTHEQUE □ Edmonton, AB
Prata, Alicia, Chf., Tech.Serv.
CANADA - NATIONAL MUSEUMS OF CANADA -
LIBRARY SERVICES DIRECTORATE □ Ottawa,
ON
Prather-Forbis, Leslie, Ref.Libn.
UNIVERSITY OF TEXAS, AUSTIN - SCHOOL OF
LAW - TARLTON LAW LIBRARY □ Austin, TX
Pratt, Annabelle, Jr.Libn.
OAKLAND PUBLIC LIBRARY - ART, MUSIC,
RECREATION □ Oakland, CA
Pratt, Darnell, Acq.Libn.
STATE LIBRARY OF FLORIDA □ Tallahassee, FL
Pratt, Kathleen L., Libn.
ST. MARY'S HOSPITAL - MAX C. FLEISCHMANN
MEDICAL LIBRARY □ Reno, NV
Pratt, Laura C., Libn.
MARYLAND COLLEGE OF ART & DESIGN -
LIBRARY □ Silver Spring, MD
Pratt, Leoma, Libn.
TYLER COURIER-TIMES-TELEGRAPH - LIBRARY
□ Tyler, TX
Pratt, M., Ill Libn.
BURROUGHS WELLCOME COMPANY - LIBRARY
□ Research Triangle Park, NC

Pratt, Mary S., Dept.Mgr.
LOS ANGELES PUBLIC LIBRARY - HISTORY
DEPARTMENT □ Los Angeles, CA
Pratt, Virginia, Libn.
UNIVERSITY OF CALIFORNIA, BERKELEY -
LIBRARY SCHOOL LIBRARY □ Berkeley, CA
Praver, Robin I., Libn.
EDO CORPORATION - ENGINEERING LIBRARY □
College Point, NY
Pray, Edna, Pharmacy Libn.
UNIVERSITY OF KENTUCKY - MEDICAL
CENTER LIBRARY □ Lexington, KY
Pray, Roberta, Res.Libn.
KANSAS STATE HISTORICAL SOCIETY -
LIBRARY □ Topeka, KS
Prchal, Dolly, Photo Serv./Tech.Serv.
NAPA COUNTY HISTORICAL SOCIETY -
LIBRARY □ Napa, CA
Prebisch, Eliana D., Libn.
INTERNATIONAL MONETARY FUND - LAW
LIBRARY □ Washington, DC
Preble, Leverett L., III, J.D., Hd. Law Libn.
CAPITAL UNIVERSITY - LAW SCHOOL LIBRARY
□ Columbus, OH
Preece, Bonnie, Hd., Acq.
YORK UNIVERSITY - LAW LIBRARY □
Downsview, ON
Preibish, Andre, Dir., Coll.Dev.
NATIONAL LIBRARY OF CANADA/
BIBLIOTHEQUE NATIONALE DU CANADA □
Ottawa, ON
Prelec, Antonija, Assoc.Dir./Coll.Dev.
SUNY AT STONY BROOK - HEALTH SCIENCES
LIBRARY □ East Setauket, NY
Premont, Jacques, Dir.
QUEBEC PROVINCE - BIBLIOTHEQUE DE
L'ASSEMBLEE NATIONALE □ Quebec, PQ
Prendeville, Jet Marie, Art Libn.
RICE UNIVERSITY - ART LIBRARY □ Houston,
TX
Prentice, Catherine T., Libn.
NEWSPAPER COMICS COUNCIL - LIBRARY
INFORMATION CENTER □ Port Chester, NY
Prentice, Janet, Libn.
UNIVERSITY OF ROCHESTER - MANAGEMENT
LIBRARY □ Rochester, NY
Prepond, Leslie, Asst.Libn.,Pub.Serv.
NEW YORK UNIVERSITY - SCHOOL OF LAW
LIBRARY □ New York, NY
Presby, Richard, Dir.
JHK & ASSOCIATES - TECHNICAL LIBRARY -
EAST □ Alexandria, VA
Presby, Richard, Dir. of Libs.
JHK & ASSOCIATES - TECHNICAL LIBRARY -
WEST □ Emeryville, CA
Prescott, Gail, Libn.
HEWLETT PACKARD COMPANY - BOISE SITE
SCIENCE/TECHNICAL LIBRARY □ Boise, ID
Prescott, Margaret, Asst.Libn.
BALTIMORE MUSEUM OF ART - REFERENCE
LIBRARY □ Baltimore, MD
Presho, Barbara, Libn.
CONSUMERS GLASS COMPANY LIMITED -
LIBRARY □ Etobicoke, ON
Preslar, M. Gail, Asst.Res.Libn.
EASTMAN KODAK COMPANY - EASTMAN
CHEMICALS DIVISION - RESEARCH LIBRARY □
Kingsport, TN
Preslock, Karen, Chf.Libn.
SMITHSONIAN INSTITUTION LIBRARIES -
MUSEUM SUPPORT CENTER LIBRARY □
Washington, DC
Press, Marian, Assoc.Libn.
ROYAL ONTARIO MUSEUM - LIBRARY† □
Toronto, ON
Press, Nancy, Educ.Coord./PNRHSLS
UNIVERSITY OF WASHINGTON - HEALTH
SCIENCES LIBRARY □ Seattle, WA
Presser, Carolynne, Assoc.Libn./Plan. & Sys.
UNIVERSITY OF WATERLOO - DANA PORTER
ARTS LIBRARY □ Waterloo, ON

Presser, Richard, Ref.Libn.
MANHATTAN SCHOOL OF MUSIC - FRANCES
HALL BALLARD LIBRARY† □ New York, NY
Pressman, Nancy, Leader, Cat. Team
PRINCETON UNIVERSITY - NEAR EAST
COLLECTIONS† □ Princeton, NJ
Prest, Charles M., Libn.
SEMMES-MURPHEY CLINIC - LIBRARY □
Memphis, TN
Preston, Alfred, Libn.
U.S. ARMY POST - FORT WAINWRIGHT -
LIBRARY □ Ft. Wainwright, AK
Preston, Ann, Spec.Coll.Libn.
DREXEL UNIVERSITY - W.W. HAGERTY
LIBRARY - SPECIAL COLLECTIONS □
Philadelphia, PA
Preston, Carol, Libn.
HUDSON'S BAY COMPANY - LIBRARY □
Winnipeg, MB
Preston, Catherine, Dir.
LEBER KATZ, INC. - MARKETING
INFORMATION CENTER LIBRARY □ New York,
NY
Preston, Cecilia M., Asst.Libn.
FMC CORPORATION - CENTRAL ENGINEERING
LABORATORIES - LIBRARY □ Santa Clara, CA
Preston, Deirdre R., Info. Resource Spec.
REICHHOLD CHEMICALS, INC. - TECHNICAL
LIBRARY □ Tacoma, WA
Preston, Douglas M., Dir., Hist.Soc.
ONEIDA HISTORICAL SOCIETY - LIBRARY □
Utica, NY
Preston, Jean F., Cur. of Mss.
PRINCETON UNIVERSITY - RARE BOOKS AND
SPECIAL COLLECTIONS □ Princeton, NJ
Preston, Jenny, Sect.Mgr.
MC DONNELL DOUGLAS AUTOMATION
COMPANY - MC AUTO CAMPUS LIBRARY □ St.
Louis, MO
Preston, John D., Libn.
NEW YORK CITY POLICE DEPARTMENT -
POLICE ACADEMY LIBRARY □ New York, NY
Preston, K.H., Mgr.
ROCKWELL INTERNATIONAL - NEWPORT
BEACH INFORMATION CENTER □ Newport
Beach, CA
Preston, Larry, Info.Spec.
BALL AEROSPACE SYSTEMS DIVISION -
TECHNICAL LIBRARY □ Boulder, CO
Preston, Linda D., Libn.
U.S. NATL. OCEANIC & ATMOSPHERIC
ADMINISTRATION - NATIONAL CLIMATIC
DATA CENTER LIBRARY □ Asheville, NC
Preston, Margaret, Tech.Res.Assoc.
COMMERCIAL UNION INSURANCE COMPANIES
- RISK CONTROL TECHNICAL RESOURCE
CENTER □ Boston, MA
Preston, William J., Chf., Lib.Serv.
U.S. VETERANS ADMINISTRATION (CT-West
Haven) - MEDICAL CENTER LIBRARY □ West
Haven, CT
Pretlow, Delores Z., Coord., Media Serv.
RICHMOND PUBLIC SCHOOLS - CURRICULUM
MATERIALS CENTER □ Richmond, VA
Prever, Phil, Libn.
NEW HAMPSHIRE VOCATIONAL-TECHNICAL
COLLEGE - LIBRARY □ Claremont, NH
Prevratil, Judith, Hd.
ROCHESTER PUBLIC LIBRARY - SCIENCE AND
TECHNOLOGY DIVISION □ Rochester, NY
Prewitt, Barbara G., Res.Lib.Mgr.
ROHM & HAAS COMPANY - RESEARCH
DIVISION - INFORMATION SERVICES
DEPARTMENT - LIBRARY □ Bristol, PA
Prewitt, Myra, Sr.Libn.
KENTUCKY STATE DEPARTMENT FOR
LIBRARIES AND ARCHIVES - STATE LIBRARY
SERVICES DIVISION □ Frankfort, KY
Prezlock, Colleen, Info.Serv.Libn.
STEVENS INSTITUTE OF TECHNOLOGY -
SAMUEL C. WILLIAMS LIBRARY □ Hoboken, NJ

Prial, Jack, Libn.
MARYLAND REHABILITATION CENTER - R.C.
THOMPSON LIBRARY □ Baltimore, MD
Price, Alvis, Ref.Libn.
UNIVERSITY OF CALIFORNIA, LOS ANGELES -
MANAGEMENT LIBRARY □ Los Angeles, CA
Price, Charlotte S., Archv.
FALMOUTH HISTORICAL SOCIETY -
RESOURCES CENTER - HISTORY & GENEALOGY
ARCHIVES □ Falmouth, MA
Price, David, Info.Spec.
BURROUGHS WELLCOME COMPANY - LIBRARY
□ Research Triangle Park, NC
Price, George W., Supv.Doc.Ctr.
INSTITUTE OF GAS TECHNOLOGY - TECHNICAL
INFORMATION CENTER □ Chicago, IL
Price, Jan, Libn.
HENNEPIN COUNTY LIBRARY SYSTEM -
GOVERNMENT CENTER INFORMATION
LIBRARY □ Minneapolis, MN
Price, Jean
AMERICAN HOIST & DERRICK CO. -
ENGINEERING STANDARDS LIBRARY □ St. Paul,
MN
Price, Joseph W., Chf.
LIBRARY OF CONGRESS - SCIENCE &
TECHNOLOGY DIVISION □ Washington, DC
Price, Kathleen, Dir.
UNIVERSITY OF MINNESOTA - LAW LIBRARY □
Minneapolis, MN
Price, Margaret, Ref.Libn.
UNIVERSITY OF BRITISH COLUMBIA -
WOODWARD BIOMEDICAL LIBRARY □
Vancouver, BC
Price, Dr. Marianne, Dir.
PENNSYLVANIA RESOURCES AND
INFORMATION CENTER FOR SPECIAL
EDUCATION □ King Of Prussia, PA
Price, Marjorie, Asst. Law Libn.
WEST VIRGINIA STATE SUPREME COURT OF
APPEALS - STATE LAW LIBRARY □ Charleston,
WV
Price, May E., Cat.
UNIVERSITY OF CALIFORNIA, DAVIS - HEALTH
SCIENCES LIBRARY □ Davis, CA
Price, Nancy P., Libn.
OAKLAWN PSYCHIATRIC CENTER -
PROFESSIONAL LIBRARY □ Elkhart, IN
Price, Patricia E., Libn.
HAWAII INSTITUTE OF GEOPHYSICS -
LIBRARY □ Honolulu, HI
Price, Peggy A., Libn.
SCIENTIFIC-ATLANTA, INC. - LIBRARY □
Atlanta, GA
Price, Ramon B., Asst.Dir.
DU SABLE MUSEUM OF AFRICAN AMERICAN
HISTORY - LIBRARY □ Chicago, IL
Price, Ronald R., Co-Dir.
BIOMEDICAL COMPUTING TECHNOLOGY
INFORMATION CENTER □ Nashville, TN
Price, Rose M., Libn.
BRAKELEY, JOHN PRICE JONES, INC. - LIBRARY
□ Stamford, CT
Price, Samuel W., Exec.Dir.
NATIONAL TOBACCO-TEXTILE MUSEUM -
LIBRARY AND INFORMATION CENTER □
Danville, VA
Price, Sophie, Hd., Cat.Sect.
NORTHWESTERN UNIVERSITY - HEALTH
SCIENCES LIBRARY† □ Chicago, IL
Price, Whit, Supv., Doc. Delivery
CAROLINA LIBRARY SERVICES, INC. □ Chapel
Hill, NC
Price, Wilma, Acq.Libn.
HUGHES AIRCRAFT COMPANY - GROUND
SYSTEMS GROUP - TECHNICAL LIBRARY □
Fullerton, CA
Prichard, Bro. Leo, Asst.Libn.
CONCEPTION ABBEY AND SEMINARY -
LIBRARY □ Conception, MO
Pride, Dick, Dir.
GROUP HEALTH COOPERATIVE OF PUGET
SOUND - MEDICAL LIBRARY □ Seattle, WA

Prieditis, Dagnia, Libn./Info.Off.
OMAHA-COUNCIL BLUFFS METROPOLITAN
AREA PLANNING AGENCY (MAPA) - LIBRARY □
Omaha, NE
Priest, William G., Mss.Spec.
WESTERN HISTORICAL MANUSCRIPT
COLLECTION/STATE HISTORICAL SOCIETY OF
MISSOURI MANUSCRIPTS JOINT COLLECTION
□ Columbia, MO
Priestly, Diana M., Law Libn.
UNIVERSITY OF VICTORIA - LAW LIBRARY □
Victoria, BC
Prilop, Iona, Libn.
BLUE CROSS AND BLUE SHIELD OF GREATER
NEW YORK - CORPORATE REFERENCE
INFORMATION SERVICES □ New York, NY
Primack, Alice, Assoc.Libn.
UNIVERSITY OF FLORIDA - ENGINEERING &
PHYSICS LIBRARY □ Gainesville, FL
Prime, Eugenie, Lib.Dir.
GLENDALE ADVENTIST MEDICAL CENTER -
LIBRARY □ Glendale, CA
Primer, Benjamin, Archv.
JOHNS HOPKINS UNIVERSITY - MILTON S.
EISENHOWER LIBRARY - SPECIAL
COLLECTIONS DIVISION □ Baltimore, MD
Primov, Karen, Dir., Med.Lib.Serv.
ILLINOIS MASONIC MEDICAL CENTER - NOAH
VAN CLEEF MEDICAL MEMORIAL LIBRARY □
Chicago IL
Prince, Jack, Coord., Instr.Rsrcs.
WYOMING (State) DEPARTMENT OF
EDUCATION - INSTRUCTIONAL RESOURCE
CENTER □ Cheyenne, WY
Prince, Phyllis, Mgr.
CHAMPION INTERNATIONAL - CORPORATE
INFORMATION CENTER† □ Stamford, CT
Prince, Wynona, Supv., Day Circ.
LE TOURNEAU COLLEGE - MARGARET ESTES
LIBRARY □ Longview, TX
Principe, Helen, Res.Libn./Adm.Asst.
TELEDYNE ISOTOPES - BUSINESS LIBRARY □
Westwood, NJ
Pringle, Anne, Hd., Sci. & Psych.Libs.
BRYN MAWR COLLEGE - GEOLOGY LIBRARY □
Bryn Mawr, PA
Pringle, Robert M., Jr., Hd.Libn.
INTERCOLLEGIATE CENTER FOR NURSING
EDUCATION - LIBRARY □ Spokane, WA
Pringle, Yvonne, Info.Spec.
PPG INDUSTRIES, INC. - CHEMICAL DIVISION
- RESEARCH LIBRARY □ Barberton, OH
Prins, Johanna, Slide Cur.
SYRACUSE UNIVERSITY - E.S. BIRD LIBRARY -
FINE ARTS DEPARTMENT □ Syracuse, NY
Prisco, Enzo, Libn.
IMMACULATE CONCEPTION SEMINARY -
LIBRARY □ Mahwah, NJ
Pristash, Kenneth, Audio Libn.
NEW ENGLAND CONSERVATORY OF MUSIC -
HARRIET M. SPAULDING LIBRARY □ Boston, MA
Pritchard, Colleen, Libn.
AMERICAN PHARMACEUTICAL ASSOCIATION -
FOUNDATION LIBRARY □ Washington, DC
Pritchard, Doris, Hd.Libn.
UNIVERSITY OF MANITOBA - DENTAL LIBRARY
□ Winnipeg, MB
Pritchard, Mary Hanson, Prof. & Cur.
UNIVERSITY OF NEBRASKA, LINCOLN - STATE
MUSEUM - HAROLD W. MANTER LABORATORY -
LIBRARY □ Lincoln, NE
Pritchard, Russ A., Dir.
MILITARY ORDER OF THE LOYAL LEGION OF
THE UNITED STATES - WAR LIBRARY AND
MUSEUM □ Philadelphia, PA
Pritkin, Joel M., Cur.
MUSIC CENTER OPERATING COMPANY -
ARCHIVES □ Los Angeles, CA
Privat, Jeannette M., A.V.P. & Mgr.
SEATTLE-FIRST NATIONAL BANK - LIBRARY □
Seattle, WA

Prochovnik, Ammiel, Asst.Libn.
UNIVERSITY OF CHICAGO - JOHN CRERAR LIBRARY □ Chicago, IL

Procopio, C.E., Dir. of Law Libs.
LIBERTY MUTUAL INSURANCE COMPANY - LAW LIBRARY □ Boston, MA

Proctor, Esther W., Libn.
MANCHESTER HISTORICAL SOCIETY - LIBRARY □ Manchester, MA

Proctor, Letitia B., Libn.
MEMPHIS BROOKS MUSEUM OF ART - LIBRARY □ Memphis, TN

Proctor, M. Willette, Mgt.Asst.
U.S. BUREAU OF LAND MANAGEMENT - EASTERN STATES OFFICE LIBRARY □ Alexandria, VA

Proehl, Karl H., Map Libn.
PENNSYLVANIA STATE UNIVERSITY - MAPS SECTION □ University Park, PA

Proffit, Kathleen D., Libn.
SACRAMENTO-EL DORADO MEDICAL SOCIETY - PAUL H. GUTTMAN LIBRARY □ Sacramento, CA

Proffitt, Kevin, Asst.Archv.
HEBREW UNION COLLEGE - JEWISH INSTITUTE OF RELIGION - AMERICAN JEWISH ARCHIVES □ Cincinnati, OH

Progar, Dorothy, Dir., Libs.
WACO-MC LENNAN COUNTY LIBRARY - SPECIAL COLLECTIONS DEPARTMENT □ Waco, TX

Progar, James S., Asst.Dir., Adm.
MISSISSIPPI STATE LIBRARY COMMISSION □ Jackson, MS

Promen, Peter J., Libn.
JOHNS HOPKINS UNIVERSITY - SCHOOL OF ADVANCED INTERNATIONAL STUDIES - SYDNEY R. & ELSA W. MASON LIBRARY □ Washington, DC

Promos, Marianne, Hd.
FREE LIBRARY OF PHILADELPHIA - ART DEPARTMENT □ Philadelphia, PA

Pronger, P.J., III, Dir.
CARSON COUNTY SQUARE HOUSE MUSEUM - INFORMATION CENTER □ Panhandle, TX

Pronin, Monica, V.P., Ed.Prod.
EIC/INTELLIGENCE, INC. □ New York, NY

Pront, Marsha, Hd.Libn.
PROSKAUER, ROSE, GOETZ & MENDELSOHN - LIBRARY □ New York, NY

Proper, David R., Libn.
HISTORIC DEERFIELD, INC. - HENRY N. FLYNT LIBRARY - POCUMTUCK VALLEY MEMORIAL ASSOCIATION □ Deerfield, MA

Propp, Dale W., Dir., Blind Div.
TEXAS STATE LIBRARY □ Austin, TX

Proscino, Patricia, Ref./Acq.
BALCH INSTITUTE FOR ETHNIC STUDIES - LIBRARY □ Philadelphia, PA

Prosser, Judy, Archv./Registrar
MUSEUM OF WESTERN COLORADO - ARCHIVES □ Grand Junction, CO

Protzman, Lois, Libn.
FORT HAMILTON-HUGHES MEMORIAL HOSPITAL CENTER - SOHN MEMORIAL HEALTH SERVICES LIBRARY □ Hamilton, OH

Proudfit, Elisabeth R., Mgr., Info.Ctr.
ADVERTISING RESEARCH FOUNDATION - LIBRARY □ New York, NY

Proudfoot, Mary, Coord., Info.Serv.
CANTERRA ENERGY LTD. - LIBRARY □ Calgary, AB

Proulx, Nicole, Libn.
CANADA - CANADIAN ADVISORY COUNCIL ON THE STATUS OF WOMEN - DOCUMENTATION CENTRE □ Ottawa, ON

Proulx, Steven, Chf.Libn.
OTTAWA CITIZEN - LIBRARY □ Ottawa, ON

Prout, Wilson, Asst. to Dir.
SUNY AT BUFFALO - HEALTH SCIENCES LIBRARY □ Buffalo, NY

Provencher, Raynald, Sec.
GRAND SEMINAIRE DES SAINTS APOTRES - BIBLIOTHEQUE □ Sherbrooke, PQ

Pruc, Anya, Info.Spec.
AMERICAN ASSOCIATION OF ADVERTISING AGENCIES - MEMBER INFORMATION SERVICE □ New York, NY

Prudhomme, Bernard, Mgr.
COCA-COLA COMPANY - TECHNICAL INFORMATION SERVICES □ Atlanta, GA

Prue, Holly, Asst. Campus Libn.
CENTENNIAL COLLEGE OF APPLIED ARTS & TECHNOLOGY - WARDEN WOODS CAMPUS RESOURCE CENTRE □ Scarborough, ON

Pruett, Barbara J., Chf., Lib.Div.
U.S. INTERNATIONAL TRADE COMMISSION - LIBRARY □ Washington, DC

Pruett, Nancy, Subject Spec.
SANDIA NATIONAL LABORATORIES - TECHNICAL LIBRARY □ Albuquerque, NM

Prugh, Daniel F., Dir., Hist./Pub.Rel.
FRANKLIN COUNTY HISTORICAL SOCIETY - CENTER OF SCIENCE & INDUSTRY - CLEMENTS HISTORY MEMORIAL LIBRARY □ Columbus, OH

Pruhs, Sharon, Med.Libn.
LOS ANGELES COUNTY DEPT. OF HEALTH SERVICES-PREVENTIVE PUBLIC HEALTH - HEALTH ADMINISTRATION/MANAGEMENT LIBRARY □ Los Angeles, CA

Pruitt, John E., Jr.
SPOTSYLVANIA HISTORICAL ASSOCIATION, INC. - RESEARCH MUSEUM AND LIBRARY □ Spotsylvania, VA

Prussiano, Naomi E., Hd.Med.Libn.
SOUTHEASTERN COLLEGE OF OSTEOPATHIC MEDICINE - MEDICAL LIBRARY □ North Miami Beach, FL

Pruzin, Christine A., Libn.
INSURANCE INSTITUTE FOR HIGHWAY SAFETY - LIBRARY □ Washington, DC

Pryor, Brandt W., Res.Assoc.
UNIVERSITY OF ILLINOIS - COMMUNITY RESEARCH CENTER - INFORMATION RESOURCE CENTER □ Champaign, IL

Pryor, Mary Patricia, Libn.
ST. ANTHONY HOSPITAL MEDICAL CENTER - SCHOOL OF NURSING - BISHOP LANE LIBRARY □ Rockford, IL

Psomiades, Prof. Harry J., Dir.
QUEENS COLLEGE OF THE CITY UNIVERSITY OF NEW YORK - CTR. FOR BYZANTINE & MODERN GREEK STUD. - LIB. □ Flushing, NY

Ptak, T.M., Supv., External Info.Sys.
SCM CORPORATION - GLIDDEN COATINGS & RESINS DIVISION/DURKEE FOODS DIVISION - TECHNICAL INFORMATION SERVICES □ Strongsville, OH

Puckett, Ann, Assoc.Libn./Pub.Serv.
NORTHWESTERN UNIVERSITY - LAW SCHOOL LIBRARY □ Chicago, IL

Puckett, Linda B., Asst.Libn.
LUTHERAN THEOLOGICAL SOUTHERN SEMINARY - LINEBERGER MEMORIAL LIBRARY □ Columbia, SC

Puckett, Marianne, Circ.Libn.
LOUISIANA STATE UNIVERSITY MEDICAL CENTER - SCHOOL OF MEDICINE IN SHREVEPORT - LIBRARY □ Shreveport, LA

Puckett, Patricia A., Tech.Libn.
TITANIUM METALS CORPORATION OF AMERICA - HENDERSON TECHNICAL LIBRARY □ Henderson, NV

Puckett, Robert A., Dir.
WICHITA-SEDGWICK COUNTY HISTORICAL MUSEUM - LIBRARY & ARCHIVES □ Wichita, KS

Puffer, Kathleen M., Chf.
U.S. VETERANS ADMINISTRATION (CA-Loma Linda) - HOSPITAL LIBRARY SERVICE □ Loma Linda, CA

Pugh, Janet D., Libn.
WISCONSIN STATE DEPARTMENT OF INDUSTRY, LABOR & HUMAN RELATIONS - JOB SERVICE LIBRARY □ Madison, WI

Pugh, Mary-Jane, Info.Spec.
BURROUGHS WELLCOME COMPANY - LIBRARY □ Research Triangle Park, NC

Pugh, Mary Jo, Ref.Archv.
UNIVERSITY OF MICHIGAN - MICHIGAN HISTORICAL COLLECTIONS - BENTLEY HISTORICAL LIBRARY □ Ann Arbor, MI

Pugh, Ronnie, Ref.Libn.
COUNTRY MUSIC FOUNDATION - LIBRARY AND MEDIA CENTER □ Nashville, TN

Pughslen, Fran, Libn.
HANSELL & POST - LIBRARY □ Atlanta, GA

Puhek, Esther L., Libn.
KENOSHA MEMORIAL HOSPITAL - HEALTH SCIENCES LIBRARY □ Kenosha, WI

Pujat, Duressa, Libn.
HACKENSACK MEDICAL CENTER - MEDICAL LIBRARY □ Hackensack, NJ

Pulcini, Theodore, Pub.Serv.
HARVARD UNIVERSITY - DIVINITY SCHOOL - ANDOVER-HARVARD THEOLOGICAL LIBRARY □ Cambridge, MA

Pullen, Mary L., Lib.Mgr.
SOUTHERN RESEARCH INSTITUTE - THOMAS W. MARTIN MEMORIAL LIBRARY □ Birmingham, AL

Pulley, Virginia, Supv., IMC
TUSCULUM COLLEGE - INSTRUCTIONAL MATERIALS CENTER □ Greeneville, TN

Pulleyblank, Miss M., Libn.
GEORGE BROWN COLLEGE OF APPLIED ARTS & TECHNOLOGY - LIBRARY □ Toronto, ON

Pulliam, Wayne, Dir.
CENTER FOR URBAN ENVIRONMENTAL STUDIES, INC. - LIBRARY □ Baltimore, MD

Pulling, Barbara, Project Coord.
ASSOCIATION OF BOOK PUBLISHERS OF BRITISH COLUMBIA - LIBRARY □ Vancouver, BC

Pullum, Thomas W., Dir.
UNIVERSITY OF WASHINGTON - CENTER FOR STUDIES IN DEMOGRAPHY AND ECOLOGY - LIBRARY □ Seattle, WA

Pulsipher, Susan, Assoc.Dir.
FAYETTEVILLE AREA HEALTH EDUCATION CENTER - LIBRARY □ Fayetteville, NC

Pumplin, Paula L., Asst.Libn.
FRICK ART REFERENCE LIBRARY □ New York, NY

Pumroy, Eric, Hd., Mss.
INDIANA HISTORICAL SOCIETY - WILLIAM HENRY SMITH MEMORIAL LIBRARY □ Indianapolis, IN

Pun, Philomena, Sr.Info.Spec.
CANADIAN IMPERIAL BANK OF COMMERCE - INFORMATION CENTRE □ Toronto, ON

Pundy, Paul, M.D., Dir.
UKRAINIAN MEDICAL ASSOCIATION OF NORTH AMERICA - UKRAINIAN MEDICAL ARCHIVES AND LIBRARY □ Chicago, IL

Pupius, Mrs. Nijole K., Tech.Libn.
UNION CARBIDE CORPORATION - FILMS-PACKAGING DIVISION - TECHNICAL LIBRARY □ Chicago, IL

Purcell, Donald, Libn.
NOVA SCOTIA - DEPARTMENT OF DEVELOPMENT - LIBRARY □ Halifax, NS

Purcell, Judith E., Corp.Libn.
FMC CORPORATION - CORPORATE LIBRARY □ Chicago, IL

Purdie, Diane, Libn.
INFORMETRICA LTD. - BUSINESS LIBRARY □ Ottawa, ON

Purpur, Geri, Tech.Serv.Libn.
BANK MARKETING ASSOCIATION - INFORMATION CENTER □ Chicago, IL

Purse, Sheila, Hd.Libn.
CANADIAN CONSULATE GENERAL - LIBRARY □ New York, NY

Pursell, Joan, Local Doc.Libn.
UNIVERSITY OF CALIFORNIA, SANTA BARBARA - GOVERNMENT PUBLICATIONS DEPARTMENT □ Santa Barbara, CA

Pursley, Jim, Coord., Proj.Oper.
UNITED WAY, INC., LOS ANGELES - LIBRARY □ Los Angeles, CA

Purtill, Diane, Div.Chf.
CHICAGO PUBLIC LIBRARY CENTRAL LIBRARY -
SOCIAL SCIENCES & HISTORY DIVISION □
Chicago, IL

Purvis, Harry, First Asst.
CHICAGO PUBLIC LIBRARY CULTURAL CENTER
- FINE ARTS DIVISION - MUSIC SECTION □
Chicago, IL

Purvis, Patsy C.
U.S. FOOD & DRUG ADMINISTRATION -
FISHERY RESEARCH BRANCH - LIBRARY □
Dauphin Island, AL

Puryear, Pamela E., Hd.
NORTH CAROLINA STATE UNIVERSITY -
FOREST RESOURCES LIBRARY □ Raleigh, NC

Purzycki, Marianne V., Circ.Supv.
AT & T BELL LABORATORIES - LIBRARY □
Murray Hill, NJ

Pustay, Marilyn, Libn.
GULF PUBLISHING CO., INC. - EDITORIAL
LIBRARY □ Biloxi, MS

Putman, Bonnie, Libn./Sec.
OREGON STATE DEPARTMENT OF LAND
CONSERVATION AND DEVELOPMENT -
LIBRARY □ Salem, OR

Putney, R. Taylor, Coord., Pub.Serv.
WRIGHT STATE UNIVERSITY - HEALTH
SCIENCES LIBRARY □ Dayton, OH

Pyatt, Sherman E., Docs. & Ser.
CITADEL - THE MILITARY COLLEGE OF SOUTH
CAROLINA - DANIEL LIBRARY □ Charleston, SC

Pyle, Susan, Ref.Libn.
COLUMBUS TECHNICAL INSTITUTE -
EDUCATIONAL RESOURCES CENTER □
Columbus, OH

Pyles, Rodney A., Dir.
WEST VIRGINIA STATE DEPARTMENT OF
CULTURE AND HISTORY - ARCHIVES AND
HISTORY LIBRARY □ Charleston, WV

Pyles, Thomas, Jr., Chf., Lib.Serv.
U.S. VETERANS ADMINISTRATION (MI-Battle
Creek) - MEDICAL CENTER LIBRARY □ Battle
Creek, MI

Pym, Brenda, Chf.Libn.
MECHANICS' INSTITUTE OF MONTREAL -
ATWATER LIBRARY □ Montreal, PQ

Pyne, Charlynn S., Ref.Libn.
HOWARD UNIVERSITY - MOORLAND-SPINGARN
RESEARCH CENTER - LIBRARY DIVISION □
Washington, DC

Q

Quah, Swee-Lan, Cat.
OHIO UNIVERSITY - SOUTHEAST ASIA
COLLECTION □ Athens, OH

Quam, Kirsten, Tech.Serv.Coord.
WISHARD (William N.) MEMORIAL HOSPITAL -
PROFESSIONAL LIBRARY/MEDIA SERVICES† □
Indianapolis, IN

Quan, Alvina M., Ser.Libn.
FLORES (Nieves M.) MEMORIAL LIBRARY □
Agana, GU

Quashen, Anne J., Exec.Dir.
NEW YORK STATE TRIAL LAWYERS
ASSOCIATION - LIBRARY □ New York, NY

Quay, Caren K., Regional Cons.
KAISER-PERMANENTE MEDICAL CENTERS,
NORTHERN CALIFORNIA REGION - REGIONAL
HEALTH LIBRARY SERVICES □ Oakland, CA

Quealey, Mrs. M., Supv., Lib.Serv.
HURONIA HISTORICAL PARKS - RESOURCE
CENTRE □ Midland, ON

Queen, Gertrude, Libn.
HELEN KELLER NATIONAL CENTER -
REFERENCE LIBRARY □ Sands Point, NY

Queen, Margaret E., Supv.Libn.
SAN DIEGO PUBLIC LIBRARY - SOCIAL
SCIENCES SECTION □ San Diego, CA

Quental, Nancy, Tech.Serv.Libn.
UNIVERSITY OF BALTIMORE - LAW LIBRARY □
Baltimore, MD

Queripel, June, Libn.
CUMBERLAND COUNTY HISTORICAL SOCIETY -
PIRATE HOUSE LIBRARY □ Greenwich, NJ

Quezada, Armida, Circ.Supv.
CITY OF COMMERCE PUBLIC LIBRARY □
Commerce, CA

Quezada-Aragon, Manuela, Info.Spec.
ERIC CLEARINGHOUSE ON RURAL EDUCATION
AND SMALL SCHOOLS □ Las Cruces, NM

Quick, Richard C., Dir. of Coll.Libs.
SUNY - COLLEGE AT GENESEO - COLLEGE
LIBRARIES □ Geneseo, NY

Quick, Young Hi, Corp.Archv.
AT & T TECHNOLOGIES, INC. - HEADQUARTERS
LIBRARY† □ New York, NY

Quimby, Harriet B., Recorder
FALMOUTH HISTORICAL SOCIETY -
RESOURCES CENTER - HISTORY & GENEALOGY
ARCHIVES □ Falmouth, MA

Quinlan, Catherine, Libn.
MEMORIAL UNIVERSITY OF NEWFOUNDLAND -
HEALTH SCIENCES LIBRARY □ St. John's, NF

Quinlan, Nora, Hd.
UNIVERSITY OF COLORADO, BOULDER -
SPECIAL COLLECTIONS DEPARTMENT □
Boulder, CO

Quinlivan, Mary, Libn.
ENVIRONMENTAL PROTECTION AGENCY -
NATIONAL ENFORCEMENT INVESTIGATIONS -
LIBRARY □ Denver, CO

Quinn, Alicia B., Supv.
HOUSTON LIGHTING & POWER COMPANY -
LIBRARY □ Houston, TX

Quinn, Allan, Dir., Info.Serv.Div.
TEXAS STATE LIBRARY □ Austin, TX

Quinn, Allan S., Div.Dir.
TEXAS STATE LIBRARY - INFORMATION
SERVICES DIVISION □ Austin, TX

Quinn, Catherine, Cat.
NATIONAL GALLERY OF ART - LIBRARY □
Washington, DC

Quinn, Delores I., Libn.
OAK FOREST HOSPITAL - PROFESSIONAL
LIBRARY† □ Oak Forest, IL

Quinn, Elizabeth A., Ref.Libn.
FRIED FRANK HARRIS SHRIVER & KAMPELMAN
- LIBRARY □ Washington, DC

Quinn, Frances M., Dir., Command Libs.
U.S. AIR FORCE - AIR FORCE SYSTEMS
COMMAND - LIBRARY DIVISION □ Washington,
DC

Quinn, Jane Taggart, Libn.
DELAWARE COUNTY PLANNING COMMISSION -
LIBRARY AND DATA SECTION† □ Lima, PA

Quinn, Linda Sue, Asst.Cat.
UNION THEOLOGICAL SEMINARY IN VIRGINIA
- LIBRARY □ Richmond, VA

Quinn, Marilyn, Media Libn.
WESTMINSTER CHOIR COLLEGE - TALBOTT
LIBRARY □ Princeton, NJ

Quinn, Noreen M., Dir., Info.Serv.
COMPUTER PROCESSING INSTITUTE -
INFORMATION CENTER† □ East Hartford, CT

Quinn, Patrick M., Univ.Archv.
NORTHWESTERN UNIVERSITY - ARCHIVES □
Evanston, IL

Quinones, Grace, Spec.Coll.Libn.
UNIVERSITY OF PUERTO RICO - MAYAGUEZ
CAMPUS LIBRARY - SPECIAL COLLECTIONS □
Mayaguez, PR

Quint, Barbara, Hd., Ref.Serv.
RAND CORPORATION - LIBRARY† □ Santa
Monica, CA

Quintal, Cecile C., Assoc.Dir.
UNIVERSITY OF NEW MEXICO - MEDICAL
CENTER LIBRARY □ Albuquerque, NM

Quintana, Emmanuel, Lib.Acq.
PAN AMERICAN HEALTH ORGANIZATION -
BIBLIOGRAPHIC INFORMATION OFFICE† □
Washington, DC

Quintanales, Mirtha, Info.Dir.
THIRD WORLD WOMEN'S EDUCATIONAL
RESOURCES, INC. - THIRD WORLD WOMEN'S
ARCHIVES □ Brooklyn, NY

Quinton, Raymond F., Asst.Libn.
CHEVRON USA INC. - CENTRAL REGION -
TECHNICAL LIBRARY □ Denver, CO

Quiring, Virginia M., Assoc. Dean, Pub.Serv.
KANSAS STATE UNIVERSITY - FARRELL
LIBRARY □ Manhattan, KS

Quirk, Paula, Mss.Spec.
WESTERN HISTORICAL MANUSCRIPT
COLLECTION/STATE HISTORICAL SOCIETY OF
MISSOURI MANUSCRIPTS JOINT COLLECTION
□ Columbia, MO

Quirk, Ruth
PASADENA PUBLIC LIBRARY - ALICE COLEMAN
BATCHELDER MUSIC LIBRARY □ Pasadena, CA

Quist, Edwin A., Libn.
PEABODY CONSERVATORY OF MUSIC -
LIBRARY □ Baltimore, MD

Quoika-Stanka, W., Ref.Libn.
UNIVERSITY OF ALBERTA - HUMANITIES AND
SOCIAL SCIENCES LIBRARY □ Edmonton, AB

Quy, Le Duy, Cat. & Clas.
CEGEP DE TROIS-RIVIERES - BIBLIOTHEQUE □
Trois-Rivieres, PQ

R

Raabe, Paula, Libn.
ST. PAUL LUTHERAN CHURCH AND SCHOOL -
PARISH LIBRARY □ Skokie, IL

Rabai, Terezia, Libn.
ISHAM, LINCOLN & BEALE - LIBRARY □ Chicago,
IL

Rabasca, David L., Pub.Serv.Coord.
MAINE STATE LAW AND LEGISLATIVE
REFERENCE LIBRARY □ Augusta, ME

Rabb, Mary, Libn.
CHICAGO ZOOLOGICAL PARK - BROOKFIELD
ZOO - LIBRARY □ Brookfield, IL

Rabenstein, Bernard H., Judaica Libn.
HEBREW UNION COLLEGE - JEWISH
INSTITUTE OF RELIGION - KLAU LIBRARY □
Cincinnati, OH

Rabin, Rose Marie, Libn.
SOUTHERN CALIFORNIA INSTITUTE OF
ARCHITECTURE - ARCHITECTURE AND URBAN
PLANNING LIBRARY □ Santa Monica, CA

Rabinowitz, Paula S., Libn.
FRANKLIN COUNTY LAW LIBRARY □
Chambersburg, PA

Rabins, Joan, Archv.
WAYNE STATE UNIVERSITY - ARCHIVES OF
LABOR AND URBAN AFFAIRS/UNIVERSITY
ARCHIVES □ Detroit, MI

Rabjohns, Ann, Chf.
DETROIT PUBLIC LIBRARY - LANGUAGE AND
LITERATURE DEPARTMENT □ Detroit, MI

Rabson, Carolyn, Libn., Rd.Serv.
OBERLIN COLLEGE - CONSERVATORY OF
MUSIC LIBRARY □ Oberlin, OH

Rac, Karola, Chf.Libn.
CERTAINTEED CORPORATION - CORPORATE
LIBRARY/INFORMATION CENTER □ Blue Bell,
PA

Racca, Claudia F., Rec.Mgt.Off.
LOUISIANA STATE OFFICE OF THE SECRETARY
OF STATE - STATE ARCHIVES AND RECORDS
SERVICE - ARCHIVES SECTION □ Baton Rouge,
LA

Rachow, Louis A., Cur.Libn.
HAMPDEN-BOOTH THEATRE LIBRARY □ New
York, NY

Racicot, L., Asst. & Cat.
COLLEGE MILITAIRE ROYAL DE ST-JEAN -
LIBRARY □ St. Jean, PQ

Racine, Rose, Libn.
CHAMBER OF COMMERCE OF THE UNITED STATES OF AMERICA - NATIONAL CHAMBER FOUNDATION LIBRARY □ Washington, DC

Rackemann, Adelaide C., Libn.
CYLBURN ARBORETUM - LIBRARY □ Baltimore, MD

Radatz, Clark, Res.Anl.
WISCONSIN STATE LEGISLATIVE REFERENCE BUREAU □ Madison, WI

Rader, Jennette S., Bus./Econ.Libn.
UNIVERSITY OF CHICAGO - BUSINESS/ ECONOMICS LIBRARY □ Chicago, IL

Rader, Margaret, Act.Dir.
OREGON STATE LIBRARY - SERVICES FOR THE BLIND AND PHYSICALLY HANDICAPPED □ Salem, OR

Rader, Robin, Geneal. Unit
TEXAS STATE LIBRARY - INFORMATION SERVICES DIVISION □ Austin, TX

Rader, Ronald, Lib.Serv.
BIOSPHERICS INC. - LIBRARY □ Rockville, MD

Radin, Ruth Y., Lib. Chairperson
CONGREGATION KENESETH ISRAEL - LIBRARY† □ Allentown, PA

Rado, Stuart Alan, Exec.Dir.
NATIONAL NETWORK OF YOUTH ADVISORY BOARDS, INC. - TECHNICAL ASSISTANCE LIBRARY □ Miami Beach, FL

Radovich, Rena, Mgr., Info.Serv.
REVLON HEALTH CARE GROUP - INFORMATION SERVICES □ Tuckahoe, NY

Radvanyi, Helga, Mgr.
ALBERTA RESEARCH COUNCIL - ALBERTA OIL SANDS INFORMATION CENTRE □ Edmonton, AB

Radwan, Eleanor, Sr.Prin.Libn.
NEW YORK PUBLIC LIBRARY - MID-MANHATTAN LIBRARY - GENERAL REFERENCE SERVICE/EDUCATION □ New York, NY

Radway, Gerry, Libn.
GENERAL ELECTRIC COMPANY - INFORMATION RESOURCES CENTER □ Syracuse, NY

Radzialowski, Thaddeus, Dir.
SOUTHWEST MINNESOTA HISTORICAL CENTER - LIBRARY □ Marshall, MN

Rae, Jay, Regional Archv.
WASHINGTON STATE OFFICE OF SECRETARY OF STATE - DIVISION OF ARCHIVES AND RECORD MANAGEMENT □ Olympia, WA

Raeder, Aggi, Lib.Mgr.
ATLANTIC-RICHFIELD COMPANY - ARCO SOLAR INC. - RESEARCH LIBRARY □ Woodland Hills, CA

Raehse, Susan L., Asst.Libn.
INSURANCE INFORMATION INSTITUTE - LIBRARY □ New York, NY

Rafael, Ruth K., Archv./Libn.
MAGNES (Judah L.) MEMORIAL MUSEUM - WESTERN JEWISH HISTORY CENTER □ Berkeley, CA

Rafail, Patrice, Online Search
ST. ANSELM'S COLLEGE - GEISEL LIBRARY □ Manchester, NH

Rafferty, Eve, Acq.Libn.
AMERICAN ASSOCIATION OF RETIRED PERSONS - NATIONAL GERONTOLOGY RESOURCE CENTER† □ Washington, DC

Rafferty, Josephine, Tech.Libn.
U.S. NAVY - NAVAL SHIPYARD (NH-Portsmouth) - TECHNICAL LIBRARY □ Portsmouth, NH

Rafferty, William L., Ref.Libn.
MINNEAPOLIS STAR AND TRIBUNE - LIBRARY □ Minneapolis, MN

Ragle, Mr. J.L., Lab.Dir.
ORANGE COUNTY SHERIFF/CORONER - FORENSIC SCIENCE SERVICES LIBRARY □ Santa Ana, CA

Ragsdale, Jack, Libn.
BERTRAND RUSSELL SOCIETY, INC. - LIBRARY □ San Francisco, CA

Ragsdale, Richard, Sr.Libn.
OAKLAND PUBLIC LIBRARY - SCIENCE/ SOCIOLOGY DIVISION □ Oakland, CA

Rahal, Patricia, Libn.
COLLEGE OF TRADES AND TECHNOLOGY - LIBRARY □ St. John's, NF

Rahal, Patricia, Libn.
COLLEGE OF TRADES AND TECHNOLOGY - MEDICAL LIBRARY □ St. John's, NF

Rahe, Emily, Lit. Searcher
DOW CHEMICAL COMPANY - MERRELL DOW PHARMACEUTICALS, INC. - RESEARCH CENTER LIBRARY □ Cincinnati, OH

Rahill, Michael, Libn.
U.S. DEPT. OF JUSTICE - TAX DIVISION LIBRARY □ Washington, DC

Rahman, Jacqueline, PHE Libn.
U.S. VETERANS ADMINISTRATION (FL-Bay Pines) - CENTER LIBRARY □ Bay Pines, FL

Rai, Priya, Chf., Tech.Proc.
CENTRAL CONNECTICUT STATE UNIVERSITY - ELIHU BURRITT LIBRARY □ New Britain, CT

Raiche, Steven J., Dir.
NEW YORK STATE PARKS AND RECREATION - DIVISION FOR HISTORIC PRESERVATION - FIELD SERVICES BUREAU - LIBRARY □ Albany, NY

Raichman, Sherwin, Hd.
ST. LAWRENCE COLLEGE SAINT-LAURENT - LEARNING RESOURCE CENTRE □ Kingston, ON

Raida, Dean, Info.Anl.
FOOTE CONE & BELDING - INFORMATION CENTER □ Chicago, IL

Raidford, Drusilla, Info.Serv.Libn.
TUFTS UNIVERSITY - HEALTH SCIENCES LIBRARY □ Boston, MA

Raidt, Mrs. Jack, Dir. of Lib.Serv.
NORTH PARK BAPTIST CHURCH - LIBRARY □ Sherman, TX

Raiford, Drusilla, Asst.Libn
ENERGY RESOURCES COMPANY - LIBRARY† □ Cambridge, MA

Raines, Elaine Y., Chf.Libn.
ARIZONA DAILY STAR - LIBRARY □ Tucson, AZ

Raines, Mark, Educ.Prog.Coord.
NANAIMO CENTENNIAL MUSEUM - ARCHIVES □ Nanaimo, BC

Raines, Sally, Libn.
U.S. DEPT. OF THE INTERIOR - OFFICE OF REGIONAL SOLICITOR - LAW LIBRARY □ Denver, CO

Rainey, Laura J., Mgr.
ROCKWELL INTERNATIONAL - ROCKETDYNE DIVISION - TECHNICAL INFORMATION CENTER □ Canoga Park, CA

Rainey, Nancy, Ref.Libn./Search Anl.
PHILADELPHIA COLLEGE OF PHARMACY AND SCIENCE - JOSEPH W. ENGLAND LIBRARY □ Philadelphia, PA

Rainey, Susan, Spec.Coll.Cat.
BRANDEIS UNIVERSITY - SPECIAL COLLECTIONS □ Waltham, MA

Rainey, Susan, Libn.
NORTHERN TELECOM, INC. - BUSINESS INFORMATION CENTER □ Dallas, TX

Rains, Lisa, Chf.Med.Libn.
UNIVERSITY OF ALABAMA - COLLEGE OF COMMUNITY HEALTH SCIENCES - HEALTH SCIENCES LIBRARY □ University, AL

Rains, Marion E., Libn.
WILLIAM PENN COLLEGE - WILCOX LIBRARY - SPECIAL COLLECTIONS □ Oskaloosa, IA

Rainwater, Barbara C., Law Libn.
EL PASO COUNTY LAW LIBRARY □ Colorado Springs, CO

Rainwater, Kathleen, Res.Libn.
GATES CORPORATION - TECHNICAL INFORMATION CENTER □ Denver, CO

Rainwater, Robert, Kpr. of Prints
NEW YORK PUBLIC LIBRARY - ART, PRINTS & PHOTOGRAPHS DIVISION - PRINTS & PHOTOGRAPHS ROOM □ New York, NY

Raisor, Douglas, Supv./Acq./ILL
KENTUCKY STATE DEPARTMENT FOR HUMAN RESOURCES - LIBRARY □ Frankfort, KY

Rait, Ann, Libn.
BURNS FRY LIMITED - RESEARCH LIBRARY □ Toronto, ON

Raitt, Mildred, Chf., Acq.Serv.
SMITHSONIAN INSTITUTION LIBRARIES □ Washington, DC

Rajguru, Nalini, Libn.
SUTHERLAND, ASBILL & BRENNAN - LIBRARY □ Washington, DC

Rajotte, Colette
TRANS QUEBEC & MARITIMES INC. - CENTRE DE DOCUMENTATION □ Montreal, PQ

Ralls, Robert, Asst.Dir./Sys. & Res.
HOUSTON ACADEMY OF MEDICINE - TEXAS MEDICAL CENTER LIBRARY □ Houston, TX

Ralph, Randy D., Sr.Lit.Sci., R&D
REYNOLDS (R.J.) TOBACCO COMPANY - R&D SCIENTIFIC INFORMATION SERVICES LIBRARY □ Winston-Salem, NC

Ralston, Barbara, Chf.Libn.
U.S. DEFENSE LOGISTICS AGENCY - HEADQUARTERS LIBRARY □ Alexandria, VA

Ralston, Charles A., Tech.Serv.Libn.
U.S. ARMY - MILITARY ACADEMY - LIBRARY □ West Point, NY

Ramage, Patricia, Ser.Libn.
UNIVERSITY OF SOUTH ALABAMA - COLLEGE OF MEDICINE - BIOMEDICAL LIBRARY □ Mobile, AL

Raman, Arsella, Ser.Libn.
STANFORD LINEAR ACCELERATOR CENTER - LIBRARY □ Stanford, CA

Ramavataram, S., Lit. Scanner
OAK RIDGE NATIONAL LABORATORY - NUCLEAR DATA PROJECT □ Oak Ridge, TN

Rambo, Crystal K., Law Libn.
RICHARDS, LAYTON & FINGER - LAW LIBRARY □ Wilmington, DE

Ramer, Ruby, Rd.Adv.
DISTRICT OF COLUMBIA PUBLIC LIBRARY - TECHNOLOGY AND SCIENCE DIVISION □ Washington, DC

Ramey, D., Per.Libn.
LOS ANGELES TRADE-TECHNICAL COLLEGE - LIBRARY □ Los Angeles, CA

Ramey, Victor, Info.Spec.
UNIVERSITY OF FLORIDA - AQUATIC WEED PROGRAM - INFORMATION AND RETRIEVAL CENTER □ Gainesville, FL

Ramirez, Eriana, Acq.
ROCKWELL INTERNATIONAL - ENERGY SYSTEMS GROUP - LIBRARY □ Canoga Park, CA

Ramirez, John, Info.Serv.Spec.
U.S. BUREAU OF THE CENSUS - INFORMATION SERVICES PROGRAM - LOS ANGELES REGIONAL OFFICE - LIBRARY □ Los Angeles, CA

Ramirez, Myrna Y., Libn.
PUERTO RICO - DEPARTMENT OF HEALTH - RAMON EMETERIO BETANCES MEDICAL LIBRARY □ Mayaguez, PR

Ramm, Dorothy, Per./Ref.Libn.
NORTHWESTERN UNIVERSITY - TRANSPORTATION LIBRARY □ Evanston, IL

Ramma, Kamra, Hd.Libn.
CANADA - INDIAN & NORTHERN AFFAIRS CANADA - DEPARTMENTAL LIBRARY □ Ottawa, ON

Ramond, Sue, Ref.
UNIVERSITY OF TEXAS HEALTH SCIENCE CENTER, DALLAS - LIBRARY □ Dallas, TX

Ramos, Anne, Libn.
TEXAS STATE LIBRARY - LIBRARY SCIENCE COLLECTION □ Austin, TX

Rampton, Suzanne, Assoc.Dir. of Res.
THOMPSON (J. Walter) COMPANY - RESEARCH LIBRARY □ Los Angeles, CA

Ramsay, Jane, Rec.Res.
PRESBYTERIAN CHURCH (U.S.A.). - PRESBYTERIAN HISTORICAL SOCIETY - LIBRARY □ Philadelphia, PA

Ramsay, John W., Dir., Hist. & Info.
CONNECTICUT AERONAUTICAL HISTORICAL
ASSOCIATION - NEW ENGLAND AIR MUSEUM
REFERENCE LIBRARY □ Windsor Locks, CT
Ramsbotham, Capt. Robert J., Pres.
STONINGTON HISTORICAL SOCIETY -
WHITEHALL LIBRARY □ Stonington, CT
Ramsden, Diann, Tech.Serv.
EMBRY RIDDLE AERONAUTICAL UNIVERSITY -
LEARNING RESOURCES CENTER □ Daytona
Beach, FL
Ramseur, Jackie, Registrar/Libn.
SCHIELE MUSEUM OF NATURAL HISTORY AND
PLANETARIUM - LIBRARY □ Gastonia, NC
Ramsey, Carol, Cat.Libn.
UNIVERSITY OF GEORGIA - LAW LIBRARY □
Athens, GA
Ramsey, Sally, Adm.
ENVIRONMENTAL RESEARCH & TECHNOLOGY,
INC. - ENVIRONMENTAL CONTRACTING
CENTER LIBRARY □ Fort Collins, CO
Ranadive, Ujwal, Libn.
LEHN & FINK PRODUCTS GROUP - LIBRARY □
Montvale, NJ
Rand, Jane, Dir. of Lib.Serv.
BRATTLEBORO RETREAT - MEDICAL LIBRARY □
Brattleboro, VT
Rand, Robin M., Dir., Lib.Serv.
MAINE MEDICAL CENTER - LIBRARY □ Portland,
ME
Randall, Harriet, Circ.Libn.
GTE - COMMUNICATION SYSTEMS DIVISION -
MAIN LIBRARY □ Needham Heights, MA
Randall, James, Dir.
WASHINGTON STATE SCHOOL FOR THE DEAF -
LEARNING RESOURCE CENTER □ Vancouver,
WA
Randall, Larry, Sys.Libn.
U.S. ARMY - MILITARY ACADEMY - LIBRARY □
West Point, NY
Randall, Laura, Cat.
SOUTHERN METHODIST UNIVERSITY -
PERKINS SCHOOL OF THEOLOGY - LIBRARY □
Dallas, TX
Randall, Lilian M.C., Kpr. of Mss.
WALTERS ART GALLERY - LIBRARY □ Baltimore,
MD
Randall, Linnae, Lekotek Leader
LEKOTEK TOY LIBRARY □ Evanston, IL
Randall, Lynn E., Dp. Law Libn.
MAINE STATE LAW AND LEGISLATIVE
REFERENCE LIBRARY □ Augusta, ME
Randall, Phoebe, Circ.Libn.
MARSHALL UNIVERSITY - SCHOOL OF
MEDICINE - HEALTH SCIENCE LIBRARIES □
Huntington, WV
Randich, Karla M., Asst.Prof./Libn.
WESTERN STATE UNIVERSITY - COLLEGE OF
LAW - LIBRARY □ San Diego, CA
Randle, Jeanne B., Chf.Libn.
FRASER-HICKSON INSTITUTE, MONTREAL -
FREE LIBRARY - SPECIAL COLLECTIONS □
Montreal, PQ
Randlett, Alice L., Acq.Libn.
UNIVERSITY OF WISCONSIN, STEVENS POINT
- JAMES H. ALBERTSON CENTER FOR
LEARNING RESOURCES □ Stevens Point, WI
Randolph, Adrijana Panoska, Dir./Libn.
MACEDONIAN ETHNIC LIBRARY □ Grosse
Pointe Woods, MI
Randolph, Irene, Field Note Spec.
FLORIDA STATE DEPT. OF NATURAL
RESOURCES - DIV. OF STATE LANDS - BUREAU
OF STATE LAND MANAGEMENT - TITLE
SECTION □ Tallahassee, FL
Randolph, Jonathan, Asst.Dir.
INSURANCE LIBRARY ASSOCIATION OF
BOSTON □ Boston, MA
Randolph, Virginia, Spec.Coll.Libn.
PEPPERDINE UNIVERSITY - LIBRARY -
SPECIAL COLLECTIONS □ Malibu, CA

Raney, Allan, Asst.Libn.
NEW YORK STATE LIBRARY - SCIENCES/
HEALTH SCIENCES/TECHNOLOGY REFERENCE
SERVICES □ Albany, NY
Raney, Dr. Leon, Dean of Lib.
SOUTH DAKOTA STATE UNIVERSITY - HILTON
M. BRIGGS LIBRARY □ Brookings, SD
Ranger, Lydia S., Hd.Libn.
HAWAII STATE LIBRARY - STATE LIBRARY FOR
THE BLIND AND PHYSICALLY HANDICAPPED □
Honolulu, HI
Ranger, Paquerette, Libn.
UNIVERSITE DE MONTREAL - DROIT-
BIBLIOTHEQUE □ Montreal, PQ
Rangus, Linda, Lib.Mgr.
OREGON RESEARCH INSTITUTE - LIBRARY □
Eugene, OR
Rank, Inkeri, Libn.
UNIVERSITY OF CALIFORNIA, LOS ANGELES -
WAYLAND D. HAND LIBRARY OF FOLKLORE AND
MYTHOLOGY □ Los Angeles, CA
Rankey, Bro. Edward, S.A., Libn.
FRANCISCAN FRIARS OF THE ATONEMENT -
ATONEMENT SEMINARY LIBRARY □
Washington, DC
Rankin, Jocelyn, Dir., Med.Lib.
MERCER UNIVERSITY - MEDICAL SCHOOL
LIBRARY □ Macon, GA
Rannit, Tatiana, Cur.
YALE UNIVERSITY - SLAVIC & EAST EUROPEAN
COLLECTIONS □ New Haven, CT
Ransier, Nancy, Mktg.Res.Anl.
UNITED BANK OF DENVER, N.A. -
INFORMATION CENTER LIBRARY □ Denver, CO
Ransom, Christina, Mgr.Info.Ctr.
AYERST LABORATORIES, INC. - INFORMATION
CENTER □ Rouses Point, NY
Ransom, Lowell, Cat.
UNIVERSITY OF WISCONSIN, MADISON -
CENTER FOR HEALTH SCIENCES LIBRARIES† □
Madison, WI
Ransom, Margueritte D., Lib.Techn.
MISSISSIPPI STATE DEPARTMENT OF MENTAL
HEALTH - LIBRARY □ Jackson, MS
Ransom, Mary Louise, Supv.libn.
U.S. CIVIL AERONAUTICS BOARD - LIBRARY □
Washington, DC
Ransom, Shirley P., Asst.Dir.
CAMDEN DISTRICT HERITAGE FOUNDATION -
HISTORIC CAMDEN □ Camden, SC
Rantala, Donald, LRC Spec.
WISCONSIN INDIANHEAD TECHNICAL
INSTITUTE, SUPERIOR CAMPUS - LIBRARY† □
Superior, WI
Rao, Angelo, Hd., AV Serv.
ONTARIO COLLEGE OF ART - LIBRARY/
AUDIOVISUAL CENTRE □ Toronto, ON
Raper, James E., Jr., Tech.Serv.Libn.
MOUNT SINAI SCHOOL OF MEDICINE OF THE
CITY UNIVERSITY OF NEW YORK - GUSTAVE L.
& JANET W. LEVY LIBRARY □ New York, NY
Rapetti, V.A., Chf.Libn.
U.S. NASA - JOHN F. KENNEDY SPACE CENTER
- LIBRARY □ Kennedy Space Center, FL
Raphael, Dana, Dir.
HUMAN LACTATION CENTER, LTD. - LIBRARY □
Westport, CT
Raphelson, J., Tech.Serv.Libn.
HURLEY MEDICAL CENTER - HAMADY HEALTH
SCIENCES LIBRARY □ Flint, MI
Rapino, J.R., Dir.
CONFEDERATION COLLEGE OF APPLIED ARTS &
TECHNOLOGY - RESOURCE CENTRE □ Thunder
Bay, ON
Rapp, Jean, Lib.Chm.
CUSHMAN (Charlotte) CLUB - THEATRE
RESEARCH LIBRARY □ Philadelphia, PA
Rapp, William F., Libn.
J-B PUBLISHING COMPANY - RESEARCH
LIBRARY □ Crete, NE
Rappaport, Gersten, Asst.Libn.
FORDHAM UNIVERSITY - SCHOOL OF LAW
LIBRARY □ New York, NY

Rapske, Arnold, Libn.
NORTH AMERICAN BAPTIST COLLEGE AND
DIVINITY SCHOOL - LIBRARY □ Edmonton, AB
Rasche, Richard R., Cat.,Hist.
UNIVERSITY OF TEXAS MEDICAL BRANCH -
MOODY MEDICAL LIBRARY □ Galveston, TX
Rash, Stephen J., Health Planner
MARYLAND STATE DIVISION OF LABOR AND
INDUSTRY - OCCUPATIONAL SAFETY AND
HEALTH LIBRARY □ Baltimore, MD
Raskin, Rosa S., Info.Spec.
GOODRICH (B.F.) COMPANY - RESEARCH AND
DEVELOPMENT CENTER - BRECKSVILLE
INFORMATION CENTER □ Brecksville, OH
Rasmussen, Gary C., Assoc.Dir., Auto.Serv.
UNIVERSITY OF TEXAS MEDICAL BRANCH -
MOODY MEDICAL LIBRARY □ Galveston, TX
Rasmussen, Lise, Libn.
LONG ISLAND UNIVERSITY - C.W. POST
CAMPUS - CENTER FOR BUSINESS RESEARCH □
Greenvale, NY
Rasmussen, Ruth J., Act.Lib.Dir.
DANA COLLEGE - C.A. DANA-LIFE LIBRARY □
Blair, NE
Rasmussen, Steve, Lit. Searcher
MEDTRONIC, INC. - LIBRARY† □ Minneapolis,
MN
Rassam, Dr. G.N., Chf.Ed.
AMERICAN GEOLOGICAL INSTITUTE - GEOREF
INFORMATION SYSTEM □ Alexandria, VA
Ratesh, Ioana, Cat.
FEDERAL RESERVE SYSTEM - BOARD OF
GOVERNORS - RESEARCH LIBRARY □
Washington, DC
Rathbun, Amanda, Acq.Tech.
MARICOPA TECHNICAL COMMUNITY COLLEGE
- LIBRARY RESOURCE CENTER □ Phoenix, AZ
Ratliff, Neil, Fine Arts Libn.
UNIVERSITY OF MARYLAND, COLLEGE PARK -
LIBRARIES - MUSIC LIBRARY □ College Park,
MD
Ratliff, Neil, Fine Arts Lib.
UNIVERSITY OF MARYLAND, COLLEGE PARK -
LIBRARIES - MUSIC LIBRARY -
INTERNATIONAL PIANO ARCHIVES AT
MARYLAND □ College Park, MD
Ratliff, Priscilla, Supv.
ASHLAND CHEMICAL COMPANY - TECHNICAL
INFORMATION CENTER □ Columbus, OH
Ratner, Rhoda, Chf.Libn.
SMITHSONIAN INSTITUTION LIBRARIES -
NATIONAL MUSEUM OF AMERICAN HISTORY -
LIBRARY □ Washington, DC
Rau, Wendy, Asst.Libn.
ANDROSCOGGIN COUNTY LAW LIBRARY □
Auburn, ME
Rauch, Ann B., Tech.Libn.
GENERAL ELECTRIC COMPANY - ORDNANCE
SYSTEMS DIVISION - ENGINEERING LIBRARY □
Pittsfield, MA
Rauch, Marcella, Circ.Libn.
OUACHITA BAPTIST UNIVERSITY - RILEY
LIBRARY □ Arkadelphia, AR
Rauch, Marian, Tech.Libn.
JOHNSON CONTROLS, INC. - CORPORATE AND
TECHNICAL LIBRARY □ Milwaukee, WI
Raup, E. Ann, Libn.
PRICE WATERHOUSE - LIBRARY† □ Chicago, IL
Raus, E.J., Hist.
U.S. NATL. PARK SERVICE - FREDERICKSBURG
& SPOTSYLVANIA NATL. MILITARY PARK -
LIBRARY □ Fredericksburg, VA
Rausch, Carol-Ann, Med.Libn.
PAWTUCKET MEMORIAL HOSPITAL - HEALTH
SCIENCES LIBRARY □ Pawtucket, RI
Rauschenberg, Bradford L.
OLD SALEM, INC. - MUSEUM OF EARLY
SOUTHERN DECORATIVE ARTS (MESDA) -
LIBRARY □ Winston-Salem, NC
Rauschenberg, Dale E., Coord.
TOWSON STATE UNIVERSITY - GERHARDT
LIBRARY OF MUSICAL INFORMATION □
Towson, MD

Rauschenberg, Dale E., Assoc.Prof., Music/Coord.
TOWSON STATE UNIVERSITY - GERHARDT
MARIMBA & XYLOPHONE COLLECTION □
Towson, MD

Ravdin, Susan B., Asst. to Cur.
BOWDOIN COLLEGE - LIBRARY - SPECIAL
COLLECTIONS □ Brunswick, ME

Ravenhall, Mary D., Libn.
UNIVERSITY OF ILLINOIS - CITY PLANNING
AND LANDSCAPE ARCHITECTURE LIBRARY □
Urbana, IL

Raviola, Edith M., Libn.
GENERAL ELECTRIC COMPANY - CORPORATE
RESEARCH & DEVELOPMENT - WHITNEY
INFORMATION SERVICES □ Schenectady, NY

Rawlings, Gloria "Jo", Sr.Libn.
KENTUCKY STATE DEPARTMENT FOR
LIBRARIES AND ARCHIVES - STATE LIBRARY
SERVICES DIVISION □ Frankfort, KY

Rawlins, Lionel, Community Serv.Spec.
U.S. BUREAU OF THE CENSUS - INFORMATION
SERVICES PROGRAM - DALLAS REGIONAL
OFFICE - LIBRARY □ Dallas, TX

Rawls, Andrew B., AV Libn.
SOUTHERN BAPTIST THEOLOGICAL SEMINARY
- AUDIOVISUAL CENTER □ Louisville, KY

Rawls, M., Hd., Rd./Ref.Serv.
U.S. NASA - JOHN F. KENNEDY SPACE CENTER
- LIBRARY □ Kennedy Space Center, FL

Ray, Eleanor, Caretaker
WHITMAN (Walt) HOUSE - LIBRARY □ Camden,
NJ

Ray, Glenn, Exec.Dir.
MINNESOTA STATE HORTICULTURAL SOCIETY
- LIBRARY □ St. Paul, MN

Ray, Jean, Asst.Sci./Map Libn.
SOUTHERN ILLINOIS UNIVERSITY,
CARBONDALE - SCIENCE DIVISION LIBRARY □
Carbondale, IL

Ray, Joyce, Spec.Coll.
UNIVERSITY OF TEXAS HEALTH SCIENCE
CENTER, SAN ANTONIO - LIBRARY □ San
Antonio, TX

Ray, Kathryn, Asst.Chf.
DISTRICT OF COLUMBIA PUBLIC LIBRARY -
WASHINGTONIANA DIVISION □ Washington,
DC

Ray, Katie, Rd.Adv.
ALABAMA REGIONAL LIBRARY FOR THE BLIND
AND PHYSICALLY HANDICAPPED □
Montgomery, AL

Ray, Sr. Mary Dominic, Founder-Dir.
AMERICAN MUSIC RESEARCH CENTER -
LIBRARY □ San Rafael, CA

Ray, Shelley
ALBERTA - WORKERS' HEALTH SAFETY &
COMPENSATION - OCCUPATIONAL HEALTH &
SAFETY LIBRARY □ Edmonton, AB

Raybon, Jean, Hd., Tech.Proc.
OUACHITA BAPTIST UNIVERSITY - RILEY
LIBRARY □ Arkadelphia, AR

Raybourn, J.S., Staff V.P., Commun.
PRODUCE MARKETING ASSOCIATION - PMA
INFORMATION CENTER □ Newark, DE

Rayburn, June, Libn.
METHODIST HOSPITAL AND SCHOOL OF
NURSING - LIBRARY □ Lubbock, TX

Rayman, Ronald, Ref.Libn.
WESTERN ILLINOIS UNIVERSITY - LIBRARIES
□ Macomb, IL

Raymond, Larry, Hd., Microform Lab.
UNIVERSITY OF LOUISVILLE - UNIVERSITY
ARCHIVES AND RECORDS CENTER □ Louisville,
KY

Raymond, Lorraine, Pub.Serv.Libn.
UNIVERSITY OF WASHINGTON - HEALTH
SCIENCES LIBRARY □ Seattle, WA

Raynard, Shirley M., Ref.Libn.
NEW ENGLAND GOVERNORS' CONFERENCE,
INC. - REFERENCE LIBRARY □ Boston, MA

Raynor, E.
HARTFORD PUBLIC LIBRARY - ART, MUSIC AND
RECREATION DEPARTMENT □ Hartford, CT

Razo, Richard, Interp.Spec.
U.S. NATL. PARK SERVICE - CHAMIZAL NATL.
MEMORIAL - LIBRARY □ El Paso, TX

Rea, Ann, Libn.
BEAL COLLEGE - LIBRARY □ Bangor, ME

Rea, Donald, Dir.
COLORADO STATE DEPARTMENT OF
EDUCATION - COLORADO CAREER
INFORMATION SYSTEM □ Longmont, CO

Read, Cynthia, Asst.Cur., Graphics
HENRY FORD MUSEUM AND GREENFIELD
VILLAGE - ARCHIVES & RESEARCH LIBRARY □
Dearborn, MI

Read, Donald L., Spec.Coll.Libn.
CALIFORNIA STATE UNIVERSITY,
NORTHRIDGE - OVIATT LIBRARY - SPECIAL
COLLECTIONS DEPARTMENT □ Northridge, CA

Read, Linda D., Supv., Plan.Info.Ctr.
CALGARY PLANNING DEPARTMENT -
INFORMATION SERVICES □ Calgary, AB

Read, M.E., Metallurgist
U.S. NATL. BUREAU OF STANDARDS - ALLOY
PHASE DIAGRAM DATA CENTER □ Washington,
DC

Read, Mary Margaret M., Sec.
AMERICAN SUFFOLK HORSE ASSOCIATION
(ASHA) - LIBRARY □ Ledbetter, TX

Reade, J.G., Libn.
DALHOUSIE UNIVERSITY - INSTITUTE FOR
RESOURCE AND ENVIRONMENTAL STUDIES -
LIBRARY □ Halifax, NS

Reade, Judy, Libn.
DALHOUSIE OCEAN STUDIES PROGRAMME -
LIBRARY □ Halifax, NS

Reade, Rita, Chf.Libn.
CBS INC. - CBS TECHNOLOGY CENTER† □
Stamford, CT

Reader, Elizabeth, Ref.Libn.
PRATT AND WHITNEY CANADA, INC. -
LIBRARY □ Longueuil, PQ

Ready, Michael J., Hd.Libn.
PEAT, MARWICK, MITCHELL & CO. -
INFORMATION AND RESEARCH CENTER □ New
York, NY

Ready, Dr. Milton, Dir.
UNIVERSITY OF NORTH CAROLINA, ASHEVILLE
- SOUTHERN HIGHLANDS RESEARCH CENTER □
Asheville, NC

Ream, Diane F., Dir.,Health Sci.Lib.Serv.
BAPTIST HOSPITAL OF MIAMI - HEALTH
SCIENCES LIBRARY □ Miami, FL

Ream, Judith K., Assoc.Dir.
NATIONAL COLLEGE OF EDUCATION -
LEARNING RESOURCE CENTERS □ Evanston, IL

Ream, Milton, Cat.
NORTHWESTERN OKLAHOMA STATE
UNIVERSITY - LIBRARY □ Alva, OK

Reams, Bernard D., Jr., Law Libn.
WASHINGTON UNIVERSITY - SCHOOL OF LAW
- FREUND LAW LIBRARY □ St. Louis, MO

Reams, P., Lrng.Rsrc.Ctr.
HURLEY MEDICAL CENTER - HAMADY HEALTH
SCIENCES LIBRARY □ Flint, MI

Reardon, Theodora J., Libn.
CLAIROL, INC. - RESEARCH LIBRARY □
Stamford, CT

Reardon-Anderson, James, Libn.
COLUMBIA UNIVERSITY - C.V. STARR EAST
ASIAN LIBRARY □ New York, NY

Reaves, Alice Cameron, Asst.Libn.
NORTH CAROLINA STATE SUPREME COURT
LIBRARY □ Raleigh, NC

Reaves, Deborah, Asst. in Engr.
UNIVERSITY OF FLORIDA - TRANSPORTATION
RESEARCH CENTER □ Gainesville, FL

Reaves, George A., Chf.Interp. & Rsrcs.Mgt.
U.S. NATL. PARK SERVICE - SHILOH NATL.
MILITARY PARK - LIBRARY □ Shiloh, TN

Reavis, Patricia, AV Libn.
UNIVERSITY OF PITTSBURGH - WESTERN
PSYCHIATRIC INSTITUTE AND CLINIC -
LIBRARY □ Pittsburgh, PA

Rebecca, Richard D., Dept.Hd.
TRENTON FREE PUBLIC LIBRARY - BUSINESS
AND TECHNOLOGY DEPARTMENT □ Trenton, NJ

Reber, Susan V., Libn.
FORBES HEALTH SYSTEM - CORPORATE
OFFICE LIBRARY □ Pittsburgh, PA

Reber, Susan V., Libn.
FORBES HEALTH SYSTEM - FORBES CENTER
FOR GERONTOLOGY - LIBRARY □ Pittsburgh, PA

Reber, Susan V., Libn.
FORBES HEALTH SYSTEM - FORBES
METROPOLITAN HEALTH CENTER LIBRARY □
Pittsburgh, PA

Reble, Jane, Rsrc.Coord.
KITCHENER-WATERLOO OVERSEAS AID INC. -
GLOBAL COMMUNITY CENTRE - LIBRARY □
Kitchener, ON

Recino, R. Margarita, Libn.
MEXICAN AMERICAN LEGAL DEFENSE AND
EDUCATIONAL FUND - LIBRARY □ San
Francisco, CA

Rector, A., Libn.
BRITISH COLUMBIA - JUDGES' LIBRARY -
SUPERIOR & COUNTY COURTS □ Vancouver, BC

Red, Lynn, Module Supv.
WASHINGTON STATE LIBRARY - RAINIER
SCHOOL STAFF LIBRARY □ Buckley, WA

Redalje, Susanne, Sci.Engr.Ref.Libn.
UNIVERSITY OF ARIZONA - SCIENCE-
ENGINEERING LIBRARY □ Tucson, AZ

Redding, Heather M., Ref.Libn.
EG&G, INC. - IDAHO NATIONAL ENGINEERING
LABORATORY - INEL TECHNICAL LIBRARY □
Idaho Falls, ID

Redding, Helene, Libn.
UNIVERSITY OF BRITISH COLUMBIA -
HUMANITIES AND SOCIAL SCIENCES DIVISION
□ Vancouver, BC

Redding, Julie, Asst.Cur. of Educ.
BEAUMONT ART MUSEUM - LIBRARY† □
Beaumont, TX

Redding, O.F., Mgr., Engr.Tech.Serv.
AMERICAN AIRLINES, INC. - ENGINEERING
LIBRARY □ Tulsa, OK

Reddington, Mary E., Hd.Libn.
TOLEDO BLADE - LIBRARY □ Toledo, OH

Reddy, Anna, Tech.Serv.
BROOKLYN BOTANIC GARDEN - LIBRARY □
Brooklyn, NY

Reddy, Arjun, Hd.
UNIVERSITY OF MISSOURI - HEALTH CARE
TECHNOLOGY CENTER & INFORMATION
SCIENCE GROUP - INFORMATION CENTER □
Columbia, MO

Redegeld, Diana, Lib.Techn.
CANADIAN BROADCASTING CORPORATION -
TV CURRENT AFFAIRS LIBRARY† □ Toronto, ON

Redfield, Gretchen, Tech.Info.Spec. I
AMERICAN WATER WORKS ASSOCIATION -
INFORMATION SERVICES DEPARTMENT □
Denver, CO

Reding, Emily, Co-Libn.
GENEALOGICAL FORUM OF PORTLAND,
OREGON, INC. - LIBRARY □ Portland, OR

Redinger, Sarah, Libn.
VISITING NURSE ASSOCIATION OF CHICAGO -
LIBRARY □ Chicago, IL

Redl, Vera, Ref.Libn.
TEACHERS COLLEGE - MILBANK MEMORIAL
LIBRARY □ New York, NY

Redmon, Michael, Hd.Libn.
SANTA BARBARA HISTORICAL SOCIETY -
GLEDHILL LIBRARY □ Santa Barbara, CA

Redmond, Brian, Chm.
WILKES COLLEGE - EARTH AND
ENVIRONMENTAL SCIENCES READING ROOM □
Wilkes-Barre, PA

Redmond, Joan, Nursing Lib.Supv.
MOHAWK COLLEGE OF APPLIED ARTS AND
TECHNOLOGY - MOHAWK LIBRARY RESOURCE
CENTRE □ Hamilton, ON

Redmond, Mary, Hd., Leg./Govt.Serv.
NEW YORK STATE LIBRARY □ Albany, NY

Redmond, Mary, Principal Libn.
NEW YORK STATE LIBRARY - LEGISLATIVE
AND GOVERNMENTAL SERVICES □ Albany, NY

Redrick, Miriam J., Mgr., Lib.Serv.
NATIONAL ASSOCIATION OF ACCOUNTANTS -
LIBRARY □ New York, NY

Redus, Mary H., Res.
HISTORICAL SOCIETY OF DAUPHIN COUNTY -
ARCHIVES/LIBRARY □ Harrisburg, PA

Reed, Bobby M., Hd., Cat.Sect.
U.S. GEOLOGICAL SURVEY - LIBRARY □ Reston,
VA

Reed, David, Dir., Lib.Serv.
LEXINGTON HERALD-LEADER - LIBRARY □
Lexington, KY

Reed, Diane, Libn.
AT & T BELL LABORATORIES & TECHNOLOGIES
- TELETYPE LIBRARY □ Little Rock, AR

Reed, Donna, Health Educ.
PLANNED PARENTHOOD OF SOUTHWESTERN
INDIANA, INC. - LIBRARY □ Evansville, IN

Reed, Duane, Spec.Coll.Libn.
U.S. AIR FORCE ACADEMY - LIBRARY □
Colorado Springs, CO

Reed, Edith, Act.Libn.
SCHOOL OF FINE ARTS - LIBRARY □ Willoughby,
OH

Reed, Howard B., Act. Co-Dir., Musm.Coll.
FAIRBANKS MUSEUM AND PLANETARIUM -
LIBRARY □ St. Johnsbury, VT

Reed, Ida, Dept.Hd.
CARNEGIE LIBRARY OF PITTSBURGH - MUSIC
AND ART DEPARTMENT □ Pittsburgh, PA

Reed, Jane, Libn.
UNION LEAGUE CLUB LIBRARY □ New York, NY

Reed, Janet S., Asst.Mgr.
CONTINENTAL ILLINOIS NATIONAL BANK AND
TRUST COMPANY OF CHICAGO -
INFORMATION SERVICES DIVISION □ Chicago,
IL

Reed, Joanne, Prod.Info.Coord.
HOECHST-ROUSSEL PHARMACEUTICALS, INC. -
LIBRARY □ Somerville, NJ

Reed, John F., Cur., Doc.
VALLEY FORGE HISTORICAL SOCIETY -
LIBRARY □ Valley Forge, PA

Reed, Mabel, Sec. in Charge
HEARST (Phoebe Apperson) HISTORICAL
SOCIETY, INC. - MUSEUM CENTER □ St. Clair,
MO

Reed, Marcia, Assoc.Libn.
GETTY (J. Paul) CENTER FOR THE HISTORY OF
ART AND THE HUMANITIES - LIBRARY □ Santa
Monica, CA

Reed, Margaret S., Libn.
NEW YORK STATE SUPREME COURT - 6TH
JUDICIAL DISTRICT - LAW LIBRARY □ Norwich,
NY

Reed, Mary E., Dir.
LATAH COUNTY HISTORICAL SOCIETY -
LIBRARY □ Moscow, ID

Reed, Renee, Libn.
MINNEAPOLIS PUBLIC LIBRARY &
INFORMATION CENTER - BUSINESS AND
ECONOMICS DEPARTMENT □ Minneapolis, MN

Reed, Richard S., Musm.Dir.
FRUITLANDS MUSEUMS - LIBRARY □ Harvard,
MA

Reed, Roma, Libn.
UNIVERSITY OF VIRGINIA - MATHEMATICS-
ASTRONOMY LIBRARY □ Charlottesville, VA

Reed, Ruth S., Archv.
WESTERN PENNSYLVANIA GENEALOGICAL
SOCIETY - LIBRARY □ Pittsburgh, PA

Reed, Stewart E., D.P.M.
REED LIBRARY OF FOOT & ANKLE □ Des Moines,
IA

Reed, Virginia, Hd., Ser.Serv.
NORTHEASTERN ILLINOIS UNIVERSITY -
LIBRARY □ Chicago, IL

Reedy, Judith El, Med.Libn.
CHAMPLAIN VALLEY - PHYSICIANS HOSPITAL
MEDICAL CENTER - MEDICAL LIBRARY □
Plattsburgh, NY

Reel, Jonathan, Archv.Techn.
SMITHSONIAN INSTITUTION LIBRARIES -
NATIONAL MUSEUM OF AFRICAN ART - ELIOT
ELISOFON ARCHIVES □ Washington, DC

Reel, Linda B., Dir.
JEWISH HOSPITAL - MEDICAL LIBRARY
SERVICES □ Louisville, KY

Reen, Ellen M., Libn.
PHILLIPS, LYTLE, HITCHCOCK, BLAINE AND
HUBER - LIBRARY □ Buffalo, NY

Reenstjerna, Hope, Dir.
COLLEGE OF HEALTH SCIENCES - LEARNING
RESOURCES CENTER □ Roanoke, VA

Reepmeyer, Tina, Asst.Libn.
NEW YORK STATE DEPARTMENT OF LAW -
LIBRARY □ Albany, NY

Rees, Clint, Libn.
CALIFORNIA STATE - COURT OF APPEAL, 4TH
APPELLATE DISTRICT, DIVISION TWO - LAW
LIBRARY □ San Bernardino, CA

Rees, Marian J., Dir.
STANFORD UNIVERSITY - INSTITUTE FOR
ENERGY STUDIES - ENERGY INFORMATION
CENTER □ Stanford, CA

Rees, Pamela, Hd., Info.Serv.
IOWA STATE LIBRARY COMMISSION □ Des
Moines, IA

Rees, Philip A., Art Libn.
UNIVERSITY OF NORTH CAROLINA, CHAPEL
HILL - ART LIBRARY □ Chapel Hill, NC

Rees, Thomas, Ref.Libn.
GRUMMAN AEROSPACE CORPORATION -
TECHNICAL INFORMATION CENTER □
Bethpage, NY

Rees-Potter, Lorna K., Dir. of Res.
CANADIAN LAW INFORMATION COUNCIL -
RESOURCE CENTRE FOR COMPUTERS AND LAW
□ Ottawa, ON

Reese, Anne O., Hd.Libn.
TOLEDO MUSEUM OF ART - ART REFERENCE
LIBRARY† □ Toledo, OH

Reese, Carolyn J., Libn.
U.S. NASA - AMES RESEARCH CENTER -
DRYDEN FLIGHT RESEARCH FACILITY -
LIBRARY □ Edwards, CA

Reese, Faye L., Libn.
PIERCE COUNTY LAW LIBRARY† □ Tacoma, WA

Reese, Gareth L., Libn.
CENTRAL CHRISTIAN COLLEGE OF THE BIBLE -
LIBRARY □ Moberly, MO

Reese, Gary Fuller, Mng.Libn.
TACOMA PUBLIC LIBRARY - SPECIAL
COLLECTIONS □ Tacoma, WA

Reese, Gwynne H., Per.Libn.
EAST STROUDSBURG UNIVERSITY - KENT
LIBRARY† □ East Stroudsburg, PA

Reese, Mary E., Sr.Res.Libn.
TEXACO CHEMICAL COMPANY, INC. -
TECHNICAL LITERATURE SECTION □ Austin, TX

Reeves, Charles R., Archv.
U.S. NATL. ARCHIVES & RECORDS SERVICE -
FEDERAL ARCHIVES AND RECORDS CENTER,
REGION 4 □ East Point, GA

Reeves, Emma, Libn.
WESTMINSTER PRESBYTERIAN CHURCH -
JOHN H. HOLMES LIBRARY □ Cincinnati, OH

Reeves, Marjorie A., Assoc.Dir., Tech.Serv.
OREGON STATE UNIVERSITY - WILLIAM
JASPER KERR LIBRARY □ Corvallis, OR

Reeves, Mary Anna, Info.Sci.
AMERICAN CYANAMID COMPANY -
AGRICULTURAL RESEARCH DIVISION -
TECHNICAL INFORMATION SERVICES □
Princeton, NJ

Reeves, Richard, Sr.Asst.Libn.
TRENTON FREE PUBLIC LIBRARY -
TRENTONIANA COLLECTION □ Trenton, NJ

Reeves, Sharon Stewart, Dir., Lib.Serv.
SAN DIEGO UNION-TRIBUNE PUBLISHING
COMPANY - LIBRARY □ San Diego, CA

Reeves, Sherrill, Libn.
OAKLAND PUBLIC LIBRARY - HISTORY/
LITERATURE DIVISION □ Oakland, CA

Reeves, T.C., Pres.
MERRICK COUNTY HISTORICAL MUSEUM -
ARCHIVES □ Central City, NE

Regan, Helen, Libn.
PEPSICO TECHNICAL CENTER - INFORMATION
CENTER □ Valhalla, NY

Regan, Marguerite, Asst. to Dean
HOFSTRA UNIVERSITY - LIBRARY - SPECIAL
COLLECTIONS □ Hempstead, NY

Regenberg, Patricia, Dir.
MOUNTAINSIDE HOSPITAL - ASSMANN HEALTH
SCIENCES LIBRARY □ Montclair, NJ

Regenstreif, Gene, Libn.
UNIVERSITY OF MICHIGAN - COOPERATIVE
INFORMATION CENTER FOR HOSPITAL
MANAGEMENT STUDIES □ Ann Arbor, MI

Regina, Sr. Maria, Educ.Mtls.Libn.
CHESTNUT HILL COLLEGE - LOGUE LIBRARY -
SPECIAL COLLECTIONS □ Philadelphia, PA

Regis, June, Staff Libn.
NEW BERLIN MEMORIAL HOSPITAL - LIBRARY
□ New Berlin, WI

Regner, Anne L., Libn.
SAN FRANCISCO PSYCHOANALYTIC INSTITUTE
- LIBRARY □ San Francisco, CA

Regnier, Flora D., Hd., Tech.Serv.
RENSSELAER POLYTECHNIC INSTITUTE -
FOLSOM LIBRARY □ Troy, NY

Rehberg, Jeanne, Ref.
UNIVERSITY OF TULSA - COLLEGE OF LAW
LIBRARY □ Tulsa, OK

Rehkopf, Charles F., Archv./Registrar
PROTESTANT EPISCOPAL CHURCH - MISSOURI
DIOCESE - DIOCESAN ARCHIVES □ St. Louis,
MO

Rehmar, Marie, Asst.Dir., Tech.Serv.
CLEVELAND STATE UNIVERSITY - JOSEPH W.
BARTUNEK III LAW LIBRARY □ Cleveland, OH

Reibach, Lois, Cat.Libn.
MINNESOTA STATE LEGISLATIVE REFERENCE
LIBRARY □ St. Paul, MN

Reibman, Jean, Hd., Cat.
CORNELL UNIVERSITY - MEDICAL COLLEGE -
SAMUEL J. WOOD LIBRARY □ New York, NY

Reich, C., Supv.
BRITISH COLUMBIA - MINISTRY OF
ENVIRONMENT - MAPS-B.C. □ Victoria, BC

Reich, Marijane, Patients' Libn.
MENDOTA MENTAL HEALTH INSTITUTE -
LIBRARY MEDIA CENTER† □ Madison, WI

Reich, R.E., Cat.
GRACE BIBLE COLLEGE - BULTEMA MEMORIAL
LIBRARY □ Grand Rapids, MI

Reichenstein, Dorothy, Med.Libn.
U.S. NAVY - NAVAL HOSPITAL (TX-Corpus
Christi) - MEDICAL LIBRARY □ Corpus Christi, TX

Reicherter, Joan M., Libn.
ADAMS & RINEHART, INC. - LIBRARY □ New
York, NY

Reichlin, Elinor, Libn.
SOCIETY FOR THE PRESERVATION OF NEW
ENGLAND ANTIQUITIES - LIBRARY □ Boston,
MA

Reichner, Carol, Libn.
ESL/SUBSIDIARY OF TRW - RESEARCH
LIBRARY □ Sunnyvale, CA

Reichwald, Prof. G.E., Act.Libn.
BETHANY LUTHERAN THEOLOGICAL SEMINARY
- LIBRARY □ Mankato, MN

Reid, Angea S., Libn.
CABOT CORPORATION - TECHNICAL
INFORMATION CENTER □ Billerica, MA

Reid, Bruce D., Chf., Lib.Serv.
U.S. VETERANS ADMINISTRATION (PA-Wilkes-
Barre) - MEDICAL CENTER LIBRARY □ Wilkes-
Barre, PA

Reid, Carol L., Med./Nursing Libn.
MERCY HOSPITAL - MEDICAL/NURSING
LIBRARY □ Rockville Centre, NY

Reid, Carolyn A., Assoc.Dir., MCRMLP
UNIVERSITY OF NEBRASKA MEDICAL CENTER -
MC GOOGAN LIBRARY OF MEDICINE □ Omaha,
NE

Reid, Mrs. D., Group Ldr.
GEORGE BROWN COLLEGE OF APPLIED ARTS &
TECHNOLOGY - LIBRARY □ Toronto, ON

Reid, Douglas G., Hd.Libn.
BRIDGEPORT PUBLIC LIBRARY - TECHNOLOGY
AND BUSINESS DEPARTMENT □ Bridgeport, CT

Reid, Edge R., Volunteer Libn.
COLUMBUS MUSEUM OF ARTS AND SCIENCES -
RESEARCH LIBRARY □ Columbus, GA

Reid, Elizabeth A., Dir.
TORONTO WESTERN HOSPITAL - R.C. LAIRD
HEALTH SCIENCES LIBRARY □ Toronto, ON

Reid, Gare B., Mgr.
KENDALL WHALING MUSEUM - LIBRARY □
Sharon, MA

Reid, Gwen, Ct.Libn.
PIMA COUNTY JUVENILE COURT CENTER -
LIBRARY □ Tucson, AZ

Reid, Henry, Br.Mgr.
UNIVERSAL SERIALS & BOOK EXCHANGE, INC.
- DUPLICATE EXCHANGE CLEARINGHOUSE &
INFORMATION CENTER □ Washington, DC

Reid, J.E.T., Chf.Libn.
CANADA - DEPARTMENT OF FINANCE -
FINANCE/TREASURY BOARD LIBRARY □
Ottawa, ON

Reid, Jean-Paul, Ref.Libn.
UNIVERSITE DU QUEBEC A MONTREAL -
BIBLIOTHEQUES DES SCIENCES JURIDIQUES □
Montreal, PQ

Reid, JoAnne, Ref.Libn.
MITRE CORPORATION - LIBRARY □ McLean, VA

Reid, Linda L., Mgr., Checklist/Cat.Serv.
ONTARIO - LEGISLATIVE ASSEMBLY -
LEGISLATIVE LIBRARY RESEARCH AND
INFORMATION SERVICES □ Toronto, ON

Reid, M.H. (Lefty), Dir. & Cur.
HOCKEY HALL OF FAME AND MUSEUM -
LIBRARY □ Toronto, ON

Reid, Pamela M., Ref.Libn.
GUILFORD TECHNICAL COMMUNITY COLLEGE -
LEARNING RESOURCE CENTER □ Jamestown,
NC

Reid, Richard
ERNST & WHINNEY - INFORMATION CENTER □
New York, NY

Reid, Ruth S., Archv./Rare Bk.Cur.
HISTORICAL SOCIETY OF WESTERN
PENNSYLVANIA - LIBRARY □ Pittsburgh, PA

Reid, Susan, Mgr.
IMPERIAL OIL, LTD. - BUSINESS INFORMATION
CENTRE □ Toronto, ON

Reid, Vicki, Libn.
TEXAS A & M UNIVERSITY - NAUTICAL
ARCHAEOLOGY LIBRARY □ College Station, TX

Reid, William K., Libn.
CRAWFORD COUNTY BAR ASSOCIATION - LAW
LIBRARY† □ Meadville, PA

Reidelbach, Marie A., Hd., Ref.
UNIVERSITY OF NEBRASKA MEDICAL CENTER -
MC GOOGAN LIBRARY OF MEDICINE □ Omaha,
NE

Reider, Mary Winn, Film Serv.Supv.
LOUISVILLE FREE PUBLIC LIBRARY - FILM
SERVICES† □ Louisville, KY

Reidinger, Betsy, Cat.
RUTGERS UNIVERSITY, THE STATE
UNIVERSITY OF NEW JERSEY - JUSTICE
HENRY ACKERSON LIBRARY OF LAW &
CRIMINAL JUSTICE □ Newark, NJ

Reidy, Robin E., Libn.
SACRAMENTO UNION - EDITORIAL LIBRARY □
Sacramento, CA

Reidy, Stephanie, Media & Pub.Serv.libn.
COMMUNITY COLLEGE OF BALTIMORE -
LIBRARIES/LEARNING RESOURCES CENTERS □
Baltimore, MD

Reiger, John, Exec.Dir.
CONNECTICUT AUDUBON CENTER - LIBRARY □
Fairfield, CT

Reikowski, David, Hd. of Circ.
HARVARD UNIVERSITY - JOHN FITZGERALD
KENNEDY SCHOOL OF GOVERNMENT - LIBRARY
□ Cambridge, MA

Reilley, Elaine R., Lib.Assoc.
MANUFACTURERS ASSOCIATION OF CENTRAL
NEW YORK - LIBRARY □ Syracuse, NY

Reilley, Elizabeth K., Dir.
PLANTING FIELDS ARBORETUM -
HORTICULTURAL LIBRARY □ Oyster Bay, NY

Reilly, Catherine R., 2nd V.P., Mgr.
CHASE MANHATTAN BANK, N.A. -
INFORMATION CENTER □ New York, NY

Reilly, Cathy H., Libn.
ST. LOUIS - POLICE LIBRARY □ St. Louis, MO

Reilly, Dayle, Mgr.
RAYTHEON COMPANY - BUSINESS
INFORMATION CENTER □ Lexington, MA

Reilly, Deb, Asst.Cur.
UNIVERSITY OF WISCONSIN, MADISON -
MEMORIAL LIBRARY - DEPARTMENT OF RARE
BOOKS & SPECIAL COLLECTIONS □ Madison, WI

Reilly, Joseph T., Data User Serv.Off.
U.S. BUREAU OF THE CENSUS - INFORMATION
SERVICES PROGRAM - ATLANTA REGIONAL
OFFICE □ Atlanta, GA

Reilly, Michael M., Dir.
REILLY TRANSLATIONS - LIBRARY □ Carson, CA

Reilly, Richard, Cur.
COPLEY PRESS, INC. - THE JAMES S. COPLEY
LIBRARY □ La Jolla, CA

Reilly, Richard, Hum.Libn.
SOUTHERN ILLINOIS UNIVERSITY,
EDWARDSVILLE - HUMANITIES & FINE ARTS
LIBRARY □ Edwardsville, IL

Reilly, S. Kathleen, Mgr., Lib.Serv.
CAPITAL RESEARCH COMPANY - RESEARCH
LIBRARY □ Los Angeles, CA

Reiman, Diane, Circuit Libn.
ROCHESTER GENERAL HOSPITAL - LILLIE B.
WERNER HEALTH SCIENCES LIBRARY □
Rochester, NY

Reiman, Donald H., Ed., Shelley Project
PFORZHEIMER (Carl & Lily) FOUNDATION, INC. -
CARL H. PFORZHEIMER LIBRARY □ New York,
NY

Reiman, E., Ref.Libn.
PACE UNIVERSITY, PLEASANTVILLE/
BRIARCLIFF - EDWARD AND DORIS MORTOLA
LIBRARY □ Pleasantville, NY

Reiman, Julie, Libn.
UNIVERSITY OF NORTH DAKOTA - MUSIC
LIBRARY □ Grand Forks, ND

Reimer, Bette, Libn.
ALBERTA ALCOHOLISM AND DRUG ABUSE
COMMISSION - LIBRARY □ Edmonton, AB

Reimer, Mary, Chm., Pub.Serv.
GREENVILLE TECHNICAL COLLEGE - LEARNING
RESOURCES CENTER □ Greenville, SC

Reimers, Ron, Photographer
UNIVERSITY OF CALIFORNIA, LOS ANGELES -
ART DEPARTMENT - VISUAL RESOURCE
COLLECTION & SERVICES □ Los Angeles, CA

Reinard, John R., Law Libn.
CUMBERLAND COUNTY LAW LIBRARY □
Bridgeton, NJ

Reinarts, Deborah, Info.Sys.Anl.
SANDIA NATIONAL LABORATORIES -
TECHNICAL LIBRARY □ Albuquerque, NM

Reiners, Margaret, Ser. & AV Libn.
NEW ENGLAND SCHOOL OF LAW - LIBRARY† □
Boston, MA

Reinert, Ann, Libn.
NEBRASKA STATE HISTORICAL SOCIETY -
LIBRARY □ Lincoln, NE

Reinertsen, Gail G., Asst.Dir.
FLORIDA STATE UNIVERSITY - LAW LIBRARY □
Tallahassee, FL

Reinhardt, Alice, Chf., Lib.Serv.
LOS ANGELES COUNTY/UNIVERSITY OF
SOUTHERN CALIFORNIA MEDICAL CENTER -
MEDICAL LIBRARIES □ Los Angeles, CA

Reinhardt, Steven, French Mss.
LOUISIANA STATE MUSEUM - LOUISIANA
HISTORICAL CENTER □ New Orleans, LA

Reinhold, Edna J., Supv.
ST. LOUIS PUBLIC LIBRARY - HUMANITIES AND
SOCIAL SCIENCES DEPARTMENT □ St. Louis,
MO

Reinhold, Rachelle, Sr. Staff Res.
INDIANA UNIVERSITY - INSTITUTE FOR
URBAN TRANSPORTATION - RESOURCE
CENTER □ Bloomington, IN

Reinig, Ellen T., Ext.Libn.
MEDICAL UNIVERSITY OF SOUTH CAROLINA -
LIBRARY □ Charleston, SC

Reinke, Bernnett, Lib.Dir.
DICKINSON STATE COLLEGE - STOXEN
LIBRARY □ Dickinson, ND

Reinke, Susan, Act.Dir.
NATIONAL INFORMATION CENTER FOR
SPECIAL EDUCATION MATERIALS (NICSEM) □
Albuquerque, NM

Reinl, Cynthia, Health Sci.Libn.
BELLIN MEMORIAL HOSPITAL - HEALTH
SCIENCES LIBRARY □ Green Bay, WI

Reis, Joseph J., Prog.Dev.Spec.
NATIONAL GALLERY OF ART - DEPARTMENT OF
EXTENSION PROGRAMS □ Washington, DC

Reis, Maria A., Asst.Libn.
PORTUGUESE CONTINENTAL UNION OF THE
U.S.A. - LIBRARY □ Boston, MA

Reisinger, Landon C., Libn.
HISTORICAL SOCIETY OF YORK COUNTY -
LIBRARY AND ARCHIVES □ York, PA

Reisman, Rita C., Asst.Libn.
LEBOEUF, LAMB, LEIBY & MAC RAE - LIBRARY □
New York, NY

Reiss, Dr. Abby P., Dir., Quality Assurance
KINGSBORO PSYCHIATRIC CENTER - MEDICAL
LIBRARY □ Brooklyn, NY

Reiss, Nellie, Lande Libn.
MC GILL UNIVERSITY - DEPARTMENT OF RARE
BOOKS & SPECIAL COLLECTIONS □ Montreal,
PQ

Reist, Paul, Coll.Dev.Libn.
BANK OF AMERICA - TECHNOLOGY LIBRARY -
3099 B □ San Francisco, CA

Reiter, Berle, Libn.
MICHIGAN STATE UNIVERSITY - V.G. GROVE
RESEARCH LIBRARY OF MATHEMATICS-
STATISTICS □ East Lansing, MI

Reiter, Ellie, Libn.
DAMES & MOORE - ENGINEERING LIBRARY† □
Golden, CO

Reiter, Helmut, Hd.Cat.
ILLINOIS INSTITUTE OF TECHNOLOGY -
CHICAGO KENT LAW SCHOOL - LIBRARY† □
Chicago, IL

Reiter, Martha, Mgr.
AMERICAN CYANAMID COMPANY - TECHNICAL
INFORMATION SERVICES □ Stamford, CT

Reith, Dr. Louis J., Rare Book Libn.
FRANCISCAN INSTITUTE - LIBRARY □ St.
Bonaventure, NY

Reitman, Jo, Libn.
NEWSPAPERS, INC. - EDITORIAL LIBRARY □
Milwaukee, WI

Reitnauer, Larilyn, Libn.
SWEDISH EMBASSY - LIBRARY-INFORMATION
CENTER □ Washington, DC

Reitz, Thomas, Archv.
ROCKEFELLER UNIVERSITY - ROCKEFELLER
ARCHIVE CENTER □ North Tarrytown, NY

Relph, Matha H.C., Libn.
U.S. ARMY FIELD ARTILLERY SCHOOL - MORRIS
SWETT TECHNICAL LIBRARY □ Ft. Sill, OK

Relyes, Donald P., Hd.
HOFFREL INSTRUMENTS, INC. - LIBRARY □
Norwalk, CT

Rem, Leona, Info.Sci.
SCHERING-PLOUGH CORPORATION -
PHARMACEUTICAL RESEARCH DIVISION -
LIBRARY INFORMATION CENTER □ Bloomfield,
NJ

Remeikis, Lois A., Dir.
BANK MARKETING ASSOCIATION -
INFORMATION CENTER □ Chicago, IL

Remelts, Glenn, Hd., Pub.Serv./Br.Lib.
BELOIT COLLEGE - HERBERT V. KOHLER
SCIENCE LIBRARY □ Beloit, WI

Remelts, Glenn, Online Search Serv.
KANSAS STATE UNIVERSITY - FARRELL
LIBRARY □ Manhattan, KS

Remillard, Juliette
INSTITUT D'HISTOIRE DE L'AMERIQUE
FRANCAISE (1970) - RESEARCH CENTRE
LIBRARY □ Montreal, PQ

Rempel, S. Patricia, Ref.
UNIVERSITY OF ALBERTA - LAW LIBRARY □
Edmonton, AB

Remy, Richard, Info.Sci.
SOUTHERN RESEARCH INSTITUTE - THOMAS
W. MARTIN MEMORIAL LIBRARY □ Birmingham,
AL

Remy, Ronald E., Dir.
MANSFIELD UNIVERSITY - AUDIO VISUAL
CENTER □ Mansfield, PA

Renaud-Frigon, Claire, Chf.Libn.
CANADA - SECRETARY OF STATE - LIBRARY □
Hull, PQ

Renfrew, Stewart, Lib.Techn.
QUEEN'S UNIVERSITY AT KINGSTON - CIVIL
ENGINEERING LIBRARY □ Kingston, ON

Renfro, Becky S., Libn.
TEXAS STATE DEPARTMENT OF MENTAL
HEALTH & MENTAL RETARDATION - CENTRAL
OFFICE LIBRARY □ Austin, TX

Renfro, Betty, Learning Lab.Coord.
NASHVILLE STATE TECHNICAL INSTITUTE -
EDUCATIONAL RESOURCE CENTER □ Nashville,
TN

Renick, Katherine, Hd.Med.Libn.
MARIN GENERAL HOSPITAL - LIBRARY □ San
Rafael, CA

Renn, Maryellen, Photograph Libn.
XEROX CORPORATION - XEROX EDUCATION
PUBLICATIONS - LIBRARY □ Middletown, CT

Renner, Iris A., Chf., Lib.Serv.
U.S. VETERANS ADMINISTRATION (FL-Tampa)
- MEDICAL LIBRARY □ Tampa, FL

Renner, Virginia J., Rd.Serv.Libn.
HUNTINGTON (Henry E.) LIBRARY, ART
GALLERY AND BOTANICAL GARDENS □ San
Marino, CA

Rennhack, Sharon, Info.Spec.
INTERPUBLIC GROUP OF COMPANIES -
CENTER FOR ADVERTISING SERVICES □ New
York, NY

Rennie, Harold, Info.Off.
CANADA - NATIONAL FILM BOARD OF CANADA
- ATLANTIC FILM & VIDEO CENTER -
REFERENCE LIBRARY □ Halifax, NS

Renninger, Karen, Chf., Lib.Div.
U.S. VETERANS ADMINISTRATION (DC-
Washington) - HEADQUARTERS CENTRAL
OFFICE LIBRARY (142D1) □ Washington, DC

Renninger, Karen, Chf., Lib.Div.
U.S. VETERANS ADMINISTRATION (DC-
Washington) - HEADQUARTERS LIBRARY
DIVISION (142D) □ Washington, DC

Renovitch, Mark, AV Archv.
U.S. PRESIDENTIAL LIBRARIES - FRANKLIN D.
ROOSEVELT LIBRARY □ Hyde Park, NY

Renshaw, Edyth, Cur.
SOUTHERN METHODIST UNIVERSITY - MC
CORD THEATER COLLECTION □ Dallas, TX

Renshawe, Michael, Area Libn., Law
MC GILL UNIVERSITY - LAW LIBRARY □
Montreal, PQ

Renter, Lois, Hd.Libn.
AMERICAN COLLEGE TESTING PROGRAM -
LIBRARY □ Iowa City, IA

Rentof, Beryl, Ref.Libn.
FASHION INSTITUTE OF TECHNOLOGY -
LIBRARY† □ New York, NY

Renz, Rev. Francis J., S.J., Mgr.
ARCHDIOCESE OF PHILADELPHIA - CATHOLIC
INFORMATION CENTER □ Philadelphia, PA

Renzetti, V., Tech.Libn.
MICROTEL PACIFIC RESEARCH LTD. -
TECHNICAL LIBRARY □ Burnaby, BC

Repetto, Ann M., Asst.Dir.
ST. JOHN'S MERCY MEDICAL CENTER - JOHN
YOUNG BROWN MEMORIAL LIBRARY □ St.
Louis, MO

Rephann, Richard, Dir.
YALE UNIVERSITY - COLLECTION OF MUSICAL
INSTRUMENTS - LIBRARY □ New Haven, CT

Repp, Bill, Tech.Libn.
MC KEE (Davy) CORPORATION - LIBRARY
CENTER □ San Ramon, CA

Reppucci, Esther A., Supv., Lib./Rec.Ctr.
COM/ENERGY SERVICES CO. - LIBRARY† □
Cambridge, MA

Reppy, Charlotte, Rsrc.Ctr.Coord.
NATIONAL ASSOCIATION OF SOCIAL
WORKERS - RESOURCE CENTER □ Silver Spring,
MD

ReQua, Eloise, Dir.
LIBRARY OF INTERNATIONAL RELATIONS □
Chicago, IL

Requardt, Cynthia H., Archv.
JEWISH HISTORICAL SOCIETY OF MARYLAND,
INC. - ARCHIVES □ Baltimore, MD

Requena, Linda, Chf., Med.Lib.
U.S. ARMY HOSPITALS - TRIPLER ARMY
MEDICAL CENTER - MEDICAL LIBRARY □ Tripler
AMC, HI

Resch, Ann, ILL
MEDICAL UNIVERSITY OF SOUTH CAROLINA -
LIBRARY □ Charleston, SC

Resco, Carol, Ref.Libn./Comp. Searching
UNIVERSITY OF CALIFORNIA, RIVERSIDE -
PHYSICAL SCIENCES LIBRARY □ Riverside, CA

Reser, Christine M., Chf.Libn.
U.S. ARMY POST - FORT LEONARD WOOD -
MAIN POST LIBRARY □ Ft. Leonard Wood, MO

Resnick, Gina, Libn.
MILBANK, TWEED, HADLEY & MC CLOY -
LIBRARY □ New York, NY

Resnik, Mary, Libn.
FOUNDATION CENTER - WASHINGTON
BRANCH LIBRARY □ Washington, DC

Ressler, Martin E., Owner
RESSLER (Martin E.) - PRIVATE MUSIC LIBRARY
□ Quarryville, PA

Restino, Gloria, Media Libn.
UNITED HEALTH SERVICES/WILSON HOSPITAL
- LEARNING RESOURCES DEPARTMENT □
Johnson City, NY

Reszczynski, Amy, Sec.
UNIVERSITY OF TORONTO - A.E. MAC DONALD
OPHTHALMIC LIBRARY □ Toronto, ON

Retfalvi, Andrea, Libn.
UNIVERSITY OF TORONTO - FINE ARTS
LIBRARY □ Toronto, ON

Rettenmaier, Fred, Ref.Libn.
U.S. NAVY - NAVAL RESEARCH LABORATORY -
RUTH H. HOOKER TECHNICAL LIBRARY □
Washington, DC

Rettew, Gayle A., Cur.
GLENS FALLS-QUEENSBURY HISTORICAL
ASSN., INC. - CHAPMAN HISTORICAL MUSM. -
RUSSELL M.L. CARSON MEMORIAL LIB. □ Glens
Falls, NY

Rettino, Janice, Mgr., Lib.Dev.
UNIVERSITY OF MEDICINE AND DENTISTRY OF
NEW JERSEY AT NEWARK - GEORGE F. SMITH
LIBRARY □ Newark, NJ

Reuby, Cheryl, Hd., Tech.Serv.
WASHINGTON UNIVERSITY - SCHOOL OF
MEDICINE LIBRARY □ St. Louis, MO

Reusch, Rita T., Dir.
UNIVERSITY OF NORTH DAKOTA - OLAF H.
THORMODSGARD LAW LIBRARY □ Grand Forks,
ND

Revilla, Eugenio, Asst.Libn., Foreign
UNIVERSITY OF ARIZONA - COLLEGE OF LAW
LIBRARY† □ Tucson, AZ

Reville, Irene
ALTERNATIVE PRESS CENTER - LIBRARY □
Baltimore, MD

Rexroat, Richard, Hd., Ser.Sect.
UNIVERSITY OF MISSOURI - HEALTH
SCIENCES LIBRARY □ Columbia, MO

Rey, Joyce, Libn.
SMITHSONIAN INSTITUTION LIBRARIES -
ASTROPHYSICAL OBSERVATORY - LIBRARY† □
Cambridge, MA

Reyes, Helen M., Libn.
JOHN MUIR MEMORIAL HOSPITAL - HEALTH
SCIENCES LIBRARY □ Walnut Creek, CA

Reyes, Norma A., Libn.
PARADISE VALLEY HOSPITAL - MEDICAL
LIBRARY □ National City, CA

Reyes, Ruperta, Asst.Libn.
CALIFORNIA STATE - COURT OF APPEAL, 2ND
APPELLATE DISTRICT - LAW LIBRARY □ Los
Angeles, CA

Reynard, Judy, Libn.
MASON, MAC LEOD, LYLE, SMITH -
BARRISTERS AND SOLICITORS - LIBRARY □
Calgary, AB

Reynen, Richard G., Libn.
DELOITTE HASKINS & SELLS - LIBRARY □
Minneapolis, MN

Reynolds, Betty, Dir.
NEW MEXICO INSTITUTE OF MINING AND
TECHNOLOGY - MARTIN SPEARE MEMORIAL
LIBRARY □ Socorro, NM

Reynolds, Brewster C., Archv.
SAN DIEGO AERO-SPACE MUSEUM - N. PAUL
WHITTIER HISTORICAL AVIATION LIBRARY □
San Diego, CA

Reynolds, Catharine J., Hd., Govt.Pubn.
UNIVERSITY OF COLORADO, BOULDER -
GOVERNMENT PUBLICATIONS DIVISION □
Boulder, CO

Reynolds, Daisy, Lib.Tech.
MEMORIAL HOSPITAL - SCHOOL OF
PROFESSIONAL NURSING - LIBRARY □ Danville,
VA

Reynolds, Dennis, Mgr./Bibliog.Sys. & Serv.
BIBLIOGRAPHICAL CENTER FOR RESEARCH -
ROCKY MOUNTAIN REGION, INC. □ Denver, CO

Reynolds, Don L., Cur., Pony Express
ST. JOSEPH MUSEUM - LIBRARY □ St. Joseph,
MO

Reynolds, Dorsey, Libn.
VALLEY FORGE CHRISTIAN COLLEGE - LIBRARY
□ Phoenixville, PA

Reynolds, Elinor, Lib.Dir.
MONROE COMMUNITY HOSPITAL - T.F.
WILLIAMS HEALTH SCIENCES LIBRARY □
Rochester, NY

Reynolds, Janice, Tech.Libn.
BANK OF MONTREAL - TECHNICAL
INFORMATION CENTRE □ Scarborough, ON

Reynolds, Janice, Tech.Libn.
BANK OF MONTREAL - TECHNICAL
INFORMATION CENTRE □ Willowdale, ON

Reynolds, Janice, Libn.
UNIVERSITY OF VIRGINIA - MEDICAL CENTER
- DEPARTMENT OF NEUROLOGY - ELIZABETH J.
OHRSTROM LIBRARY □ Charlottesville, VA

Reynolds, Joan, Libn.
LYNN HISTORICAL SOCIETY/MUSEUM -
LIBRARY □ Lynn, MA

Reynolds, John E., Lib.Mgr.
NORTHROP CORPORATION - AIRCRAFT
DIVISION - LIBRARY SERVICES □ Hawthorne,
CA

Reynolds, Jon K., Univ.Archv.
GEORGETOWN UNIVERSITY - SPECIAL
COLLECTIONS DIVISION - LAUINGER
MEMORIAL LIBRARY □ Washington, DC
Reynolds, Madeline, Dir.
NATIONAL CHAMBER OF COMMERCE FOR
WOMEN - ELIZABETH LEWIN BUSINESS
LIBRARY & INFORMATION CENTER □ New York,
NY
Reynolds, Malcolm, Sr.Libn.
NAPA STATE HOSPITAL - WRENSHALL A.
OLIVER PROFESSIONAL LIBRARY □ Imola, CA
Reynolds, Norman, Supv., Campus Serv.
KENT STATE UNIVERSITY - AUDIOVISUAL
SERVICES □ Kent, OH
Reynolds, Sheila, Ser.
SCOTT & WHITE MEMORIAL HOSPITAL -
MEDICAL LIBRARY □ Temple, TX
Reynolds, Stanley G., Cur.
REYNOLDS MUSEUM - LIBRARY □ Wetaskiwin,
AB
Reynolds, Wanetca, Libn.
HUBER (J.M.) CORPORATION - RESEARCH
LIBRARY □ Borger, TX
Reza, Ernesto, Coord.
FARM LABOR ORGANIZING COMMITTEE -
LIBRARY □ Toledo, OH
Rezab, Gordana, Archv./Spec.Coll.
WESTERN ILLINOIS UNIVERSITY - LIBRARIES
□ Macomb, IL
Rezak, Sheila A., Teacher Educ.Rsrcs.
PURDUE UNIVERSITY, CALUMET - LIBRARY □
Hammond, IN
Rezetka, Mary
HONEYWELL, INC. - HONEYWELL
INFORMATION SYSTEMS - INFORMATION AND
LIBRARY SERVICES □ Waltham, MA
Rheaume, Paul, Cur./Prog.
KINGMAN MUSEUM OF NATURAL HISTORY -
LIBRARY □ Battle Creek, MI
Rhee, Sue M., Tech.Serv.
NORTHWEST CHRISTIAN COLLEGE - LEARNING
RESOURCE CENTER □ Eugene, OR
Rhee, YangHoon, Libn.
JOHN DEERE PRODUCT ENGINEERING CENTER
- LIBRARY □ Waterloo, IA
Rhein, Donna E., Dir.
DALLAS MUSEUM OF ARTS - REFERENCE
LIBRARY □ Dallas, TX
Rhew, David, Libn.
LUTHER RICE SEMINARY - BERTHA SMITH
LIBRARY □ Jacksonville, FL
Rhie, Schi-Zhin, Cat.Libn.
KEAN COLLEGE OF NEW JERSEY - NANCY
THOMPSON LIBRARY† □ Union, NJ
Rhine, Leonard, Tech.Serv.Libn.
UNIVERSITY OF FLORIDA - J. HILLIS MILLER
HEALTH CENTER LIBRARY □ Gainesville, FL
Rhoades, Marjorie, Asst.Engr.Sci.Libn.
COLORADO STATE UNIVERSITY -
ENGINEERING SCIENCES BRANCH LIBRARY □
Fort Collins, CO
Rhoades, Marjorie, Engr.Sci.Libn.
COLORADO STATE UNIVERSITY - WILLIAM E.
MORGAN LIBRARY □ Fort Collins, CO
Rhoads, Ann F., Asst.Dir., Botany
UNIVERSITY OF PENNSYLVANIA - MORRIS
ARBORETUM LIBRARY □ Philadelphia, PA
Rhoads, Donald, Ref.Libn.
P.T. BOATS, INC. - LIBRARY, ARCHIVES &
TECHNICAL INFORMATION CENTER -
NATIONAL HEADQUARTERS □ Memphis, TN
Rhode, Jim, Pres.
SEMANTODONTICS, INC. - LIBRARY □ Phoenix,
AZ
Rhodehamel, John, Archv.
MOUNT VERNON LADIES' ASSOCIATION OF
THE UNION - RESEARCH AND REFERENCE
LIBRARY □ Mount Vernon, VA
Rhodes, Anne, Libn.
BAPTIST MEDICAL CENTER - MEDICAL
LIBRARY □ Montgomery, AL

Rhodes, Dallas D., Dir.
WHITTIER COLLEGE - DEPARTMENT OF
GEOLOGY - FAIRCHILD AERIAL PHOTOGRAPH
COLLECTION† □ Whittier, CA
Rhodes, Rev. Dennis R., Archv.
ORTHODOX CHURCH IN AMERICA -
DEPARTMENT OF HISTORY AND ARCHIVES □
Syosset, NY
Rhodes, Erroll, Sr.Res.
AMERICAN BIBLE SOCIETY - LIBRARY □ New
York, NY
Rhodes, Frieda, Libn.
TEXAS GAS TRANSMISSION CORPORATION -
LIBRARY □ Owensboro, KY
Rhodes, Jean, Govt.Doc.Libn.
FEDERAL RESERVE SYSTEM - BOARD OF
GOVERNORS - RESEARCH LIBRARY □
Washington, DC
Rhodes, Myrtle J., Supv.Libn.
U.S. NAVY - NAVAL COASTAL SYSTEMS
CENTER - TECHNICAL INFORMATION
SERVICES BRANCH† □ Panama City, FL
Rhone, Marilynn, Asst.Libn.
KERR-MC GEE CORPORATION - MC GEE
LIBRARY □ Oklahoma City, OK
Rhyne, Charles S., Gen.Couns.
NATIONAL INSTITUTE OF MUNICIPAL LAW
OFFICES - LIBRARY □ Washington, DC
Ribeiro, Kathryn, Regional Libn. (North)
ALBERTA - DEPARTMENT OF THE SOLICITOR
GENERAL - LIBRARY □ Edmonton, AB
Ribera De Cambre, Iris, Dir., Tech.Serv.
UNIVERSITY OF PUERTO RICO - MEDICAL
SCIENCES CAMPUS - LIBRARY □ Rio Piedras, PR
Ribuoli, Amy A., Libn.
SHAWMUT BANK OF BOSTON, N.A. - LIBRARY □
Boston, MA
Ricard, Michel, Agent de Recherche
QUEBEC PROVINCE - MINISTERE DE LA
JUSTICE - BIBLIOTHEQUE □ Ste. Foy, PQ
Ricards, Philip, Libn.
CENTER FOR PROCESS STUDIES - LIBRARY □
Claremont, CA
Riccardo-Markot, Vickie, Law Libn.
PRUDENTIAL INSURANCE COMPANY OF
AMERICA - LAW LIBRARY □ Newark, NJ
Ricci, Mark, Mgr.
MEMORY SHOP, INC. - MOVIE MEMORABILIA
STILLS □ New York, NY
Rice, Agnes G., Libn.
ALLEN-BRADLEY COMPANY - CORPORATE
LIBRARY □ Milwaukee, WI
Rice, Barbara, Hd., Ref.
NEW YORK STATE LIBRARY □ Albany, NY
Rice, Cecelia E., Pub.Serv.
XEROX CORPORATION - TECHNICAL
INFORMATION CENTER □ Webster, NY
Rice, Chuck, Lib.Serv.Spec.
NATIONAL RURAL ELECTRIC COOPERATIVE
ASSOCIATION - NORRIS MEMORIAL LIBRARY □
Washington, DC
Rice, Cynthia J., Ref.Libn.
UNIVERSITY OF SOUTHWESTERN LOUISIANA -
JEFFERSON CAFFERY LOUISIANA ROOM □
Lafayette, LA
Rice, Dorothy, Libn.
POTTSVILLE HOSPITAL AND WARNE CLINIC -
MEDICAL LIBRARY □ Pottsville, PA
Rice, Eleanor M., Libn.
RAYTHEON COMPANY - BADGER AMERICA,
INC. - LIBRARY □ Cambridge, MA
Rice, Gerald W., Libn.
KOLLSMAN INSTRUMENT COMPANY - KIC
LIBRARY □ Merrimack, NH
Rice, Gwen, Chf., Ref. & ILL
WYOMING STATE LIBRARY □ Cheyenne, WY
Rice, Marvin L., Tech.Libn.
GOODYEAR TIRE AND RUBBER COMPANY -
GOODYEAR ATOMIC CORPORATION -
TECHNICAL LIBRARY □ Piketon, OH
Rice, Patricia A., Libn.
DALTON-DALTON-NEWPORT - RESOURCE
CENTER □ Cleveland, OH

Rice, Ruth, Law Libn.
KLAMATH COUNTY - LOYD DELAP LAW
LIBRARY □ Klamath Falls, OR
Rice, Wendy E., Med.Libn.
BASSETT (Mary Imogene) HOSPITAL - MEDICAL
LIBRARY □ Cooperstown, NY
Rich, Denise A., Info.Sys.Libn.
GENERAL ELECTRIC COMPANY - SPACE/
SYSTEMS DIVISION LIBRARIES □ Philadelphia,
PA
Rich, Maria F., Exec.Dir.
CENTRAL OPERA SERVICE - INFORMATION
CENTER AND LIBRARY □ New York, NY
Rich, Patricia U., Hd. of Ref.
TIME, INC. - LIBRARY □ New York, NY
Richan, Don, Staff Archv.
SASKATCHEWAN ARCHIVES BOARD □ Regina,
SK
Richard, Jerry, Book Ordering
IBM CORPORATION - GENERAL PRODUCTS
DIVISION - STL LIBRARY □ San Jose, CA
Richard, Sheila A., Libn.
AMERICAN OCCUPATIONAL THERAPY
ASSOCIATION - REFERENCE LIBRARY □
Rockville, MD
Richards, Carol, Hd., Ref.
SUNY - COLLEGE AT BUFFALO - EDWARD H.
BUTLER LIBRARY □ Buffalo, NY
Richards, Daniel, Asst.Libn./Rsrcs. & Ref.
COLUMBIA UNIVERSITY - HEALTH SCIENCES
LIBRARY □ New York, NY
Richards, Katherine, Assoc.Libn.
NEW-YORK HISTORICAL SOCIETY - LIBRARY □
New York, NY
Richards, Marilyn
NEW TRANSCENTURY FOUNDATION -
DOCUMENTATION CENTER □ Washington, DC
Richards, Maureen, Act.Libn.
SALVATION ARMY GRACE HOSPITAL - LIBRARY
□ Windsor, ON
Richards, N.J., Legislative Libn.
NEWFOUNDLAND - LEGISLATIVE LIBRARY □ St.
John's, NF
Richards, Robert B., Hd. of Academics
U.S. NAVY - NAVAL TEST PILOT SCHOOL -
RESEARCH LIBRARY □ Patuxent River, MD
Richardson, A. Zelda, Dir.
UNIVERSITY OF NEW MEXICO - BUNTING
MEMORIAL SLIDE LIBRARY □ Albuquerque, NM
Richardson, Beverly, Wake AHEC Libn.
WAKE COUNTY MEDICAL CENTER - MEDICAL
LIBRARY □ Raleigh, NC
Richardson, Carol, Libn.
LOMA LINDA UNIVERSITY - NIELS BJORN
JORGENSEN MEMORIAL LIBRARY† □ Loma
Linda, CA
Richardson, Christine, Libn.
GERMAN SOCIETY OF PENNSYLVANIA -
JOSEPH HORNER MEMORIAL LIBRARY □
Philadelphia, PA
Richardson, Deborah
INFORMATICS GENERAL CORPORATION - FISH
AND WILDLIFE REFERENCE □ Rockville, MD
Richardson, Deborra A., Music Libn.
HOWARD UNIVERSITY - MOORLAND-SPINGARN
RESEARCH CENTER - MANUSCRIPT DIVISION □
Washington, DC
Richardson, Donald, Tech. Reports
WORCESTER POLYTECHNIC INSTITUTE -
GEORGE C. GORDON LIBRARY □ Worcester, MA
Richardson, Donna I., Hd.Info.Serv. Group
CANADA - DEFENCE RESEARCH
ESTABLISHMENT ATLANTIC - LIBRARY □
Dartmouth, NS
Richardson, Donna L., Info.Serv.Mgr.
FATHER FLANAGAN'S BOYS' HOME -
INFORMATION SERVICES □ Boys Town, NE
Richardson, Eleanor, Ref.Libn.
UNIVERSITY OF SOUTH CAROLINA - SOUTH
CAROLINIANA LIBRARY □ Columbia, SC
Richardson, Elizabeth J., Info.Serv.Libn.
TUFTS UNIVERSITY - HEALTH SCIENCES
LIBRARY □ Boston, MA

Richardson, Gail, Libn.
LA JOLLA MUSEUM OF CONTEMPORARY ART -
HELEN PALMER GEISEL LIBRARY □ La Jolla, CA
Richardson, Harry
CUSTER COUNTY HISTORICAL SOCIETY -
LIBRARY □ Broken Bow, NE
Richardson, Hilary, Lib.Asst.
QUEEN'S UNIVERSITY AT KINGSTON -
MECHANICAL ENGINEERING LIBRARY □
Kingston, ON
Richardson, Iris W., Post Libn.
U.S. ARMY POST - FORT JACKSON - LIBRARY □
Ft. Jackson, SC
Richardson, J.A., Res.Libn.
UNITED STATES STEEL CORPORATION -
TECHNICAL INFORMATION CENTER □
Monroeville, PA
Richardson, Jeanne, Sci.Libn.
UNIVERSITY OF KANSAS - SCIENCE LIBRARY □
Lawrence, KS
Richardson, Jo-Anne, Med.Lib.Asst.
CATHOLIC MEDICAL CENTER OF BROOKLYN &
QUEENS, INC. - ST. MARY'S HOSPITAL -
MEDICAL ADMINISTRATIVE LIBRARY □
Brooklyn, NY
Richardson, Karin, Lib.Dir.
FIRST BAPTIST CHURCH - MEDIA LIBRARY □
Abilene, TX
Richardson, Lynn, Search Anl.
CAROLINA POPULATION CENTER - LIBRARY □
Chapel Hill, NC
Richardson, Marie S., Libn.
UNITED ILLUMINATING COMPANY - LIBRARY □
New Haven, CT
Richardson, Mary, Libn.
CARNEGIE LIBRARY OF PITTSBURGH -
CENTRAL CHILDREN'S ROOM HISTORICAL
COLLECTION □ Pittsburgh, PA
Richardson, Mary Elizabeth, Ref.Libn.
WARREN LIBRARY ASSOCIATION - LIBRARY □
Warren, PA
Richardson, Rhonda, Media Equipment Spec.
INDIANA UNIVERSITY - DEVELOPMENTAL
TRAINING CENTER - INFORMATION AND
MATERIALS SYSTEM (IMS) □ Bloomington, IN
Richardson, Robert W., Exec.Dir.
COLORADO RAILROAD HISTORICAL
FOUNDATION - LIBRARY □ Golden, CO
Richardson, Ruth, Libn.
FIRST BAPTIST CHURCH - LIBRARY □ Melrose,
MA
Richardson, Sara J., Libn.
METHODIST HOSPITAL - LIBRARY □
Philadelphia, PA
Richardson, W.H., Libn.
GENERAL MOTORS CORPORATION - ALLISON
GAS TURBINE DIVISION - LIBRARY □
Indianapolis, IN
Richardson, William C., Asst.Ref.Libn.
OKLAHOMA STATE UNIVERSITY - SPECIAL
COLLECTIONS AND MAPS □ Stillwater, OK
Richbourg, Ellen, Libn.
BAPTIST HOSPITAL - MEDICAL LIBRARY □
Pensacola, FL
Richer, Suzanne, Dir.
CANADA - SECRETARY OF STATE -
TRANSLATION BUREAU - DOCUMENTATION
DIRECTORATE† □ Ottawa, ON
Richer, Yvon, Univ.Chf.Libn.
UNIVERSITY OF OTTAWA - MORISSET
LIBRARY □ Ottawa, ON
Richert, Paul, Law Libn.
UNIVERSITY OF AKRON - SCHOOL OF LAW - C.
BLAKE MC DOWELL LAW LIBRARY □ Akron, OH
Richman, Mr. Clare, Regional Dir.
CANADIAN MUSIC CENTRE - PRAIRIE REGION
LIBRARY □ Calgary, AB
Richman, Gratia, Libn.
EASTMINSTER PRESBYTERIAN CHURCH -
LIBRARY† □ Indialantic, FL

Richman, Natalie, Asst.Libn.
ST. JOSEPH'S HOSPITAL AND MEDICAL
CENTER - HEALTH SCIENCES LIBRARY □
Paterson, NJ
Richmond, Alice S., Libn.
NORTH CAROLINA CENTRAL UNIVERSITY -
SCHOOL OF LIBRARY SCIENCE - LIBRARY □
Durham, NC
Richmond, Eero, Hd.Libn.
AMERICAN MUSIC CENTER - LIBRARY □ New
York, NY
Richmond, Joyce, Libn.
ANNE ARUNDEL GENERAL HOSPITAL -
MEMORIAL LIBRARY □ Annapolis, MD
Richmond, Roberta J., Libn.
PIGEON DISTRICT LIBRARY - SPECIAL
COLLECTIONS □ Pigeon, MI
Richter, Adelaide, Sr.Libn.
ROYAL BANK OF CANADA - INFORMATION
RESOURCES □ Montreal, PQ
Richter, Adrienne, Assoc.Libn.
EDUCATIONAL TESTING SERVICE - CARL
CAMPBELL BRIGHAM LIBRARY □ Princeton, NJ
Richter, Glenn, Natl.Coord.
CENTER FOR RUSSIAN & EAST EUROPEAN
JEWRY/STUDENTS STRUGGLE FOR SOVIET
JEWRY - ARCHIVES □ New York, NY
Richter, Heddy A., Imprints Libn.
HAGLEY MUSEUM AND LIBRARY □ Wilmington,
DE
Richter, Peggy A., Staff Dir.
AMERICAN BAR ASSOCIATION - WASHINGTON
OFFICE - INFORMATION SERVICES □
Washington, DC
Richter, Richard, Dir., Television
CONCORDIA COLLEGE - KLINCK MEMORIAL
LIBRARY □ River Forest, IL
Richter, Wendy, Archv.
GARLAND COUNTY HISTORICAL SOCIETY -
ARCHIVES □ Hot Springs, AR
Rickard, Ted, Mgr.
ONTARIO CRAFTS COUNCIL - CRAFT
RESOURCE CENTRE □ Toronto, ON
Rickards, Doris J., Med.Libn.
PAOLI MEMORIAL HOSPITAL - ROBERT M.
WHITE MEMORIAL LIBRARY □ Paoli, PA
Ricker, Alison, Sci.Libn.
OBERLIN COLLEGE - SCIENCE LIBRARY □
Oberlin, OH
Rickerson, Carla, Hd.
UNIVERSITY OF WASHINGTON - SPECIAL
COLLECTIONS DIVISION - PACIFIC
NORTHWEST COLLECTION □ Seattle, WA
Rickerson, Connie, Libn.
HOLMES & NARVER, INC. - TECHNICAL
LIBRARY □ Orange, CA
Ricketts, Faye, Clipping
LOS ANGELES TIMES - EDITORIAL LIBRARY □
Los Angeles, CA
Rickling, Iraida B., Libn.
FLORIDA SOLAR ENERGY CENTER - LIBRARY □
Cape Canaveral, FL
Ricks, Bonnie, Lib.Dir.
U.S. ARMY POST - FORT GREELY - LIBRARY □
APO Seattle, WA
Riddle, Margaret, Lib.Spec.
EVERETT PUBLIC LIBRARY - NORTHWEST
HISTORY COLLECTION □ Everett, WA
Rider, Mary M., Ref.Libn.
CINCINNATI HISTORICAL SOCIETY - LIBRARY
□ Cincinnati, OH
Ridge, Fran, Libn.
ATHENS COUNTY LAW LIBRARY □ Athens, OH
Ridge, Geraldine, Libn.
GOOD SAMARITAN SOCIETY - LIBRARY □
Edmonton, AB
Ridge, Hope S., Libn.
RAWLE AND HENDERSON - LAW LIBRARY □
Philadelphia, PA
Ridgway, Ann, Lib.Assoc.
UNIVERSITY OF CINCINNATI - ENGINEERING
LIBRARY □ Cincinnati, OH

Ridgway, Isabelle, Libn.
ONTARIO PAPER COMPANY, LTD. - LIBRARY □
Thorold, ON
Ridgway, Michelle, Sys.Info.Spec.
LEVI STRAUSS & COMPANY - CORPORATE
MARKETING INFORMATION CENTER† □ San
Francisco, CA
Ridley, Edward L., Dir.
U.S. NATL. OCEANIC & ATMOSPHERIC
ADMINISTRATION - NATIONAL
OCEANOGRAPHIC DATA CENTER □ Washington,
DC
Ridley, Kathy, Libn.
CENTRAL STATE HOSPITAL - MENTAL HEALTH
LIBRARY □ Milledgeville, GA
Ridolphi, Audrey, Mgr.
IRON COUNTY MUSEUM - ARCHIVES □ Caspian,
MI
Riebel, Ellis F., Asst.Circ.Libn.
EAST STROUDSBURG UNIVERSITY - KENT
LIBRARY† □ East Stroudsburg, PA
Riebel, Lynn, Acq.Libn.
FLOATING POINT SYSTEMS, INC. -
INFORMATION CENTER/LIBRARY □ Beaverton,
OR
Ried, Dalene, Lib.Mgr.
ANATEC LABORATORIES, INC. - LIBRARY □
Santa Rosa, CA
Riedel, Louise D., Libn.
SOUTHWEST REGIONAL LABORATORY FOR
EDUCATIONAL RESEARCH AND DEVELOPMENT
- LIBRARY □ Los Alamitos, CA
Rieder, Monica, Tech.Supv.
IFI/PLENUM DATA COMPANY - LIBRARY □
Alexandria, VA
Riegel, Mrs. Jo, Hd.Libn.
WAGNALLS MEMORIAL LIBRARY □ Lithopolis,
OH
Riehle, Dr. Hal F., Dir.
UNIVERSITY OF WISCONSIN, MADISON -
BUREAU OF AUDIOVISUAL INSTRUCTION -
LIBRARY □ Madison, WI
Rieke, Judy, Map Libn.
TEXAS A & M UNIVERSITY - MAP DEPARTMENT
□ College Station, TX
Rieke, Kenneth F., Chf., Rec.Ctr.
CONNECTICUT STATE LIBRARY □ Hartford, CT
Rieken, Marietta K., Libn.
LUTHERAN MUTUAL LIFE INSURANCE
COMPANY - LIBRARY □ Waverly, IA
Riemann, Frederick A., Law Libn.
GULF COMPANIES - LAW LIBRARY □ Houston,
TX
Riemer, Janet
GENEALOGICAL SOCIETY OF NEW JERSEY -
MANUSCRIPT COLLECTIONS □ New Brunswick,
NJ
Riemer, Janet
RUTGERS UNIVERSITY, THE STATE
UNIVERSITY OF NEW JERSEY - DEPARTMENT
OF SPECIAL COLLECTIONS AND ARCHIVES □
New Brunswick, NJ
Riese, Patricia, Libn.
HAZELTON LABS AMERICA, INC. - LIBRARY □
Madison, WI
Riess, Al, Microforms
SUNY - COLLEGE AT BUFFALO - EDWARD H.
BUTLER LIBRARY □ Buffalo, NY
Riess, Rita, Asst.Libn.
DURACELL INC. - TECHNICAL INFORMATION
CENTER □ Burlington, MA
Rife, C. David, Mgr.
LOCKHEED-GEORGIA COMPANY - TECHNICAL
INFORMATION DEPARTMENT □ Marietta, GA
Rife, Wanda, Co-Libn.
HISTORICAL AND GENEALOGICAL SOCIETY OF
INDIANA COUNTY - LIBRARY AND ARCHIVES □
Indiana, PA
Rife, Wanda, Asst.Libn.
INDIANA UNIVERSITY OF PENNSYLVANIA -
UNIVERSITY LIBRARY □ Indiana, PA

Riff, Dr. Michael, Ref.Libn.
BAECK (Leo) INSTITUTE - LIBRARY □ New York, NY

Riffle, Linda, Asst.Mgr.
UNION CARBIDE CORPORATION - PARMA TECHNICAL CENTER - TECHNICAL INFORMATION SERVICE □ Cleveland, OH

Rigaud, Jeanne, Coord.
CANADIAN INSTITUTE OF HYPNOTISM - LIBRARY □ Ste. Anne de Bellevue, PQ

Rigby, Elaine P., Health Sci.Libn.
LYNN HOSPITAL - HEALTH SCIENCES LIBRARY □ Lynn, MA

Rigelman, Mrs. Delma, Libn.
FIRST LUTHERAN CHURCH OF THE LUTHERAN CHURCH IN AMERICA - SCHENDEL MEMORIAL LIBRARY □ Red Wing, MN

Riggle, Cretha L., Lib.Techn.
U.S. BUREAU OF RECLAMATION - TECHNICAL LIBRARY □ Boulder City, NV

Riggle, Keven, Operational Serv.Supv.
MARQUETTE UNIVERSITY - SCIENCE LIBRARY □ Milwaukee, WI

Riggle, Viola P., Sr.Res.Info.Sci.
GENERAL MILLS, INC. - JAMES FORD BELL TECHNICAL CENTER - TECHNICAL INFORMATION SERVICES □ Minneapolis, MN

Riggs, David F., Musm.Cur.
U.S. NATL. PARK SERVICE - VICKSBURG NATL. MILITARY PARK - LIBRARY □ Vicksburg, MS

Riggs, Jane, Libn.
AMAX EXTRACTIVE RESEARCH & DEVELOPMENT, INC. - TECHNICAL INFORMATION CENTER □ Golden, CO

Rights, Edith A., Libn.
MONTCLAIR ART MUSEUM - LE BRUN LIBRARY □ Montclair, NJ

Rigia, Violet, Dir. of Lib.Serv.
BRIDGEPORT HOSPITAL - REEVES MEMORIAL LIBRARY† □ Bridgeport, CT

Rigney, Janet, Libn.
COUNCIL ON FOREIGN RELATIONS - LIBRARY □ New York, NY

Rigney, Shirley A., Tech.Info.Libn.
ST. REGIS CORPORATION - TECHNICAL CENTER LIBRARY □ West Nyack, NY

Riha, Otokar J., Transl.
PHILLIPS PETROLEUM COMPANY - RESEARCH & DEVELOPMENT DEPARTMENT - TECHNICAL INFORMATION BRANCH □ Bartlesville, OK

Riley, Anne, Lib.Asst.
FULLERTON COLLEGE - WILLIAM T. BOYCE LIBRARY - ARCHIVES □ Fullerton, CA

Riley, C.L., Info.Anl.
CHEVRON RESEARCH COMPANY - TECHNICAL INFORMATION CENTER □ Richmond, CA

Riley, Camille, Hd.Ref.Libn.
UNIVERSITY OF CHICAGO - LAW SCHOOL LIBRARY □ Chicago, IL

Riley, Edith M., Libn.
MAINE CHARITABLE MECHANIC ASSOCIATION - LIBRARY □ Portland, ME

Riley, Eleanor D., Asst.Libn.
LOS ANGELES COUNTY MUSEUM OF ART - RESEARCH LIBRARY □ Los Angeles, CA

Riley, Esta Lou, Archv./Spec.Coll.
FORT HAYS STATE UNIVERSITY - FORSYTH LIBRARY - SPECIAL COLLECTIONS □ Hays, KS

Riley, Ivy, Libn.
SOUTHERN FOREST PRODUCTS ASSOCIATION - LIBRARY □ New Orleans, LA

Riley, Louise, Libn.
TUSKEGEE INSTITUTE - DIVISION OF BEHAVIORAL SCIENCE RESEARCH - RURAL DEVELOPMENT RESOURCE CENTER □ Tuskegee Institute, AL

Riley, Lyman W., Asst.Dir. of Libs.
UNIVERSITY OF PENNSYLVANIA - RARE BOOK COLLECTION† □ Philadelphia, PA

Riley, Margaret Crim, Libn.
WESTERN STATE HOSPITAL - PROFESSIONAL LIBRARY □ Hopkinsville, KY

Riley, Martha, Libn.
ST. LOUIS PUBLIC LIBRARY - CAROL MC DONALD GARDNER RARE BOOK ROOM □ St. Louis, MO

Riley, Mary, Spec.Coll.Libn.
BATES COLLEGE - GEORGE AND HELEN LADD LIBRARY - SPECIAL COLLECTIONS □ Lewiston, ME

Riley, Mary, Chf.Ref.Libn.
FORDHAM UNIVERSITY - SPECIAL COLLECTIONS □ Bronx, NY

Riley, Patricia, Ref.
UNIVERSITY OF TEXAS HEALTH SCIENCE CENTER, SAN ANTONIO - LIBRARY □ San Antonio, TX

Riley, Sara J., Libn.
VENTURA COUNTY STAR-FREE PRESS - LIBRARY □ Ventura, CA

Riley, William M., Jr., Exec.Dir.
ARABIAN HORSE TRUST - LIBRARY □ Denver, CO

Rill, Linda L., Dir.
PHOTOPHILE - LIBRARY □ San Diego, CA

Rimer, Dr. J. Thomas, Chf.
LIBRARY OF CONGRESS - ASIAN DIVISION □ Washington, DC

Rinaldi, Julie, Act.Hd.
UNIVERSITY OF CALIFORNIA, BERKELEY - EARTH SCIENCES LIBRARY □ Berkeley, CA

Rinas, Mary E., Libn.
U.S. AIR FORCE BASE - MC CONNELL BASE LIBRARY □ McConnell AFB, KS

Rinden, Constance T., Law Libn.
NEW HAMPSHIRE STATE LIBRARY - LAW LIBRARY □ Concord, NH

Rinehart, Michael, Libn.
CLARK (Sterling and Francine) ART INSTITUTE - LIBRARY □ Williamstown, MA

Rinehart, Ward, Ed.
JOHNS HOPKINS UNIVERSITY - POPULATION INFORMATION PROGRAM □ Baltimore, MD

Rinesmith, Mary E., Libn.
MC NEES, WALLACE AND NURICK - LIBRARY □ Harrisburg, PA

Ring, Joan, Acq./Cat.Libn.
STORMONT-VAIL REGIONAL MEDICAL CENTER AND SHAWNEE COUNTY MEDICAL SOCIETY - HEALTH SCIENCES LIBRARY □ Topeka, KS

Ringdal, June C., Law Libn.
BLAIR COUNTY LAW LIBRARY† □ Hollidaysburg, PA

Ringstrom, Diana, Libn.
ALCOHOLISM FOUNDATION OF MANITOBA - WILLIAM POTOROKA MEMORIAL LIBRARY □ Winnipeg, MB

Ringwelski, Eurdine, Res.
BAY COUNTY HISTORICAL SOCIETY - LIBRARY □ Bay City, MI

Ringwood, Marilyn, Libn.
CROUSE-IRVING MEMORIAL HOSPITAL - LIBRARY □ Syracuse, NY

Riordan, Margaret B., Libn.
EMPLOYEE BENEFIT RESEARCH INSTITUTE - LIBRARY □ Washington, DC

Riordan, Patricia H., Libn.
MELLON BANK, N.A. - LIBRARY† □ Pittsburgh, PA

Rios, Betty Rose, Asst.Dir.
ERIC CLEARINGHOUSE ON RURAL EDUCATION AND SMALL SCHOOLS □ Las Cruces, NM

Rios, Ino, Dir.
UNIVERSITY OF CONNECTICUT - PUERTO RICAN CENTER - ROBERTO CLEMENTE LIBRARY □ Storrs, CT

Rioux, Gaston, O.M.I., Chf.Libn.
UNIVERSITE ST-PAUL - BIBLIOTHEQUE □ Ottawa, ON

Ripatti, Sally K., Spec.Mtls.Libn.
KNOX COUNTY PUBLIC LIBRARY SYSTEM - MC CLUNG HISTORICAL COLLECTION □ Knoxville, TN

Ripin, Laura G., Lib.Dir.
DREXEL BURNHAM LAMBERT INC. - RESEARCH LIBRARY □ New York, NY

Ripley, Ann, Asst.
MURPHY OIL USA, INC. - LAW DEPARTMENT LIBRARY □ El Dorado, AR

Ripley, G. Birch, Libn.
ELRICK AND LAVIDGE, INC. - LIBRARY □ Chicago, IL

Ripley, Victoria, Academic Sup.Serv.Coord.
UNIVERSITY OF WESTERN ONTARIO - SCHOOL OF LIBRARY & INFORMATION SCIENCE - LIBRARY □ London, ON

Ripp, Patrick
MINERAL POINT HISTORICAL SOCIETY - ARCHIVES □ Mineral Point, WI

Rippeon, Janet D., Law Libn.
FREDERICK COUNTY LAW LIBRARY □ Frederick, MD

Ripy, Minnie Sue, Res.Libn.
U.S. EQUAL EMPLOYMENT OPPORTUNITY COMMISSION - LIBRARY □ Washington, DC

Riquier, Myrna D., Corp.Libn.
ROGERS CORPORATION - LURIE LIBRARY □ Rogers, CT

Risbrough, Ned, Exec.Dir.
EUGENE HEARING AND SPEECH CENTER - LIBRARY □ Eugene, OR

Risk, James C., Mgr., Tech.Oper.
STACK'S RARE COIN COMPANY OF NEW YORK - TECHNICAL INFORMATION CENTER □ New York, NY

Ristic, Jovanka, Map Cat./Ref.Libn.
AMERICAN GEOGRAPHICAL SOCIETY COLLECTION OF THE UNIVERSITY OF WISCONSIN, MILWAUKEE - GOLDA MEIR LIBRARY □ Milwaukee, WI

Ritchey, Dennis, Asst.Dir.
SOUTHERN CALIFORNIA PERMANENTE MEDICAL CENTER - HEALTH SCIENCES LIBRARY/MEDIA CENTER □ Bellflower, CA

Ritchie, David, Cat.Libn.
SUNY - COLLEGE AT CORTLAND - MEMORIAL LIBRARY □ Cortland, NY

Ritchie, Mrs. Gaylan, Regional Libn.
CANADA - TRANSPORT CANADA - CANADIAN COAST GUARD, MARITIMES REGION - REGIONAL LIBRARY □ Dartmouth, NS

Ritchie, Mark
EARTHWORK - CENTER FOR RURAL STUDIES □ Minneapolis, MN

Ritchie, Mary M., Act.Libn.
ESSEX INSTITUTE - JAMES DUNCAN PHILLIPS LIBRARY □ Salem, MA

Ritenour, Sharon, Asst.Ed.
MARSHALL (George C.) RESEARCH FOUNDATION - GEORGE C. MARSHALL RESEARCH LIBRARY† □ Lexington, VA

Rittenhouse, Robert J., Tech.Info.Spec. & Mgr.
GOULD, INC. - OCEAN SYSTEMS INFORMATION CENTER □ Cleveland, OH

Rittenhouse, Shirley A., Ref.Libn.
MARYLAND STATE LAW LIBRARY □ Annapolis, MD

Ritter, Audrey, Rsrcs.Spec.
ROCHESTER INSTITUTE OF TECHNOLOGY - NATIONAL TECHNICAL INSTITUTE FOR THE DEAF - STAFF RESOURCE CENTER □ Rochester, NY

Ritter, Darlyne, Libn.
MILWAUKEE PSYCHIATRIC HOSPITAL - LIBRARY □ Wauwatosa, WI

Ritter, Linda, Asst.Libn.
SAN DIEGO UNION-TRIBUNE PUBLISHING COMPANY - LIBRARY □ San Diego, CA

Rivard, Timothy D., Med.Libn.
WORCESTER CITY HOSPITAL - MEDICAL LIBRARY □ Worcester, MA

Rivas, Guillermo, Asst.Libn.
MOUNT SINAI HOSPITAL SERVICES - CITY HOSPITAL CENTER AT ELMHURST - MEDICAL LIBRARY □ Elmhurst, NY

Rivera, Agnes, Cat.
EVANGELICAL SEMINARY OF PUERTO RICO -
JUAN DE VALDES LIBRARY □ Hato Rey, PR
Rivera, Felix, Lib.Asst.
CUNY - CENTRO DE ESTUDIOS
PUERTORRIQUENOS □ New York, NY
Rivera, Israel, Libn.
PUERTO RICO - STATE DEPARTMENT OF
CONSUMER AFFAIRS - LIBRARY □ Santurce, PR
Rivera, Mary, Hd., Bibliog.Rec.Sect.
TEACHERS COLLEGE - MILBANK MEMORIAL
LIBRARY □ New York, NY
Rivera, Miguel A., Circ.
UNIVERSITY OF PUERTO RICO - LAW SCHOOL
LIBRARY □ Rio Piedras, PR
Rivers, Richard D., Mgr. of Res.
ALLIS-CHALMERS CORPORATION - AMERICAN
AIR FILTER DIVISION - TECHNICAL LIBRARY □
Louisville, KY
Rivest, Denis
QUEBEC PROVINCE - BIBLIOTHEQUE
NATIONALE DU QUEBEC - SERVICE DES
COLLECTIONS SPECIALES - SECTEUR MUSIQUE
□ Montreal, PQ
Rix, Dolores, Tech.Libn.
INSTITUTE OF GAS TECHNOLOGY - TECHNICAL
INFORMATION CENTER □ Chicago, IL
Rizzo, L.L., Health Sci.Libn.
KERN MEDICAL CENTER - KERN HEALTH
SCIENCES LIBRARY □ Bakersfield, CA
Roach, Linda C., Libn.
MORGAN, LEWIS & BOCKIUS - LIBRARY □
Philadelphia, PA
Roach, Sue, Hd., Ref./Tech.Serv.
U.S. NAVY - OFFICE OF THE JUDGE ADVOCATE
GENERAL - LAW LIBRARY □ Alexandria, VA
Road, Rachel, Cur. of Photographs
TIPPECANOE COUNTY HISTORICAL
ASSOCIATION - ALAMEDA MC COLLOUGH
RESEARCH & GENEALOGY LIBRARY □ Lafayette,
IN
Roadhouse, Mrs. I.R., Libn.
RIDGETOWN COLLEGE OF AGRICULTURAL
TECHNOLOGY - LIBRARY □ Ridgetown, ON
Roake, JoAnne, Ref.Libn.
PALOMAR COMMUNITY COLLEGE - LIBRARY -
SPECIAL COLLECTIONS □ San Marcos, CA
Robb, Debbie, Sr.Libn.
KENTUCKY STATE DEPARTMENT FOR
LIBRARIES AND ARCHIVES - STATE LIBRARY
SERVICES DIVISION □ Frankfort, KY
Robb, Capt. James A., Exec.Off.
U.S. AIR FORCE ACADEMY - LIBRARY □
Colorado Springs, CO
Robb, Janet, Lib.Mtls.Coord.
ROSEVILLE EARLY CHILDHOOD/FAMILY
PROGRAMS - PLAY 'N' LEARN LIBRARY □ Falcon
Heights, MN
Robba, Diana, Lib.Spec.
HEWLETT-PACKARD COMPANY - SANTA CLARA
DIVISION LIBRARY† □ Santa Clara, CA
Robben, Dorothy D., Supv., Lib. & Rec.
AMERICAN BRANDS, INC. - AMERICAN
TOBACCO COMPANY - DEPARTMENT OF
RESEARCH & DEVELOPMENT LIBRARY □
Hopewell, VA
Robbie, Jorene, Ref.Libn.
COLUMBIA UNIVERSITY - LAW LIBRARY □ New
York, NY
Robbin, Alice, Hd.
UNIVERSITY OF WISCONSIN, MADISON - DATA
AND PROGRAM LIBRARY SERVICE □ Madison,
WI
Robbins, Allan W., Hd.Libn.
ALEXANDRIA LIBRARY - LLOYD HOUSE □
Alexandria, VA
Robbins, Carol, Acq.
MARTIN MARIETTA AEROSPACE - DENVER
RESEARCH LIBRARY □ Denver, CO
Robbins, Irving, Libn.
MINNEAPOLIS PUBLIC LIBRARY &
INFORMATION CENTER - BUSINESS AND
ECONOMICS DEPARTMENT □ Minneapolis, MN

Robbins, Jean, Mgr.
BURROUGHS CORPORATION - COMPUTER
SYSTEMS GROUP - TECHNICAL INFORMATION
RESOURCES CENTER □ Pasadena, CA
Robbins, Jean, Med.Libn.
U.S. AIR FORCE HOSPITAL - MEDICAL LIBRARY
(TX-Carswell AFB) □ Carswell AFB, TX
Robbins, Lynne C., Dir.
PHILLIPS ACADEMY - OLIVER WENDELL
HOLMES LIBRARY - SPECIAL COLLECTIONS □
Andover, MA
Robbins, Nora, Hum.Libn.
UNIVERSITY OF CALGARY - ARTS AND
HUMANITIES LIBRARY† □ Calgary, AB
Robbins, Ortha D., Supv.
ST. PAUL PUBLIC LIBRARY - SOCIAL SCIENCES
& LITERATURE □ St. Paul, MN
Robbins, Patricia V., Dir. of Ref. & Lib.
WISCONSIN STATE LEGISLATIVE REFERENCE
BUREAU □ Madison, WI
Robbins, Rintha, Libn.
MADERA COUNTY HISTORICAL SOCIETY -
MUSEUM/LIBRARY □ Madera, CA
Robbins, Thomas, DACS Prog.Mgr.
U.S. AIR FORCE - ROME AIR DEVELOPMENT
CENTER - DATA & ANALYSIS CENTER FOR
SOFTWARE □ Griffiss AFB, NY
Robbins, William R.
BRANT COUNTY MUSEUM - LIBRARY □
Brantford, ON
Roberge, Monique, Audiovideotheque
CEGEP DE TROIS-RIVIERES - BIBLIOTHEQUE □
Trois-Rivieres, PQ
Roberson, Bernadine C., Libn.
U.S. DEPT. OF COMMERCE - INTERNATIONAL
TRADE ADMINISTRATION - CHICAGO
DISTRICT OFFICE LIBRARY □ Chicago, IL
Roberson, Suzanne, Asst.Libn.
ALBANY INSTITUTE OF HISTORY AND ART -
MC KINNEY LIBRARY □ Albany, NY
Robert, Michel, Chf.Libn.
CEGEP ST-JEAN SUR RICHELIEU -
BIBLIOTHEQUE □ St. Jean, PQ
Roberts, Ammarette, Mgr., Tech.Info.Serv.
MOBIL RESEARCH & DEVELOPMENT
CORPORATION - DALLAS RESEARCH DIVISION
- LIBRARY □ Dallas, TX
Roberts, Andrea, Hd.Cat.
RAND CORPORATION - LIBRARY† □ Santa
Monica, CA
Roberts, Ann B., Mgr.
MC GUIRE, WOODS AND BATTLE -
INFORMATION CENTER □ Richmond, VA
Roberts, Anna Ray, Coord., Lib.Serv.
WYTHEVILLE COMMUNITY COLLEGE - KEGLEY
LIBRARY - SPECIAL COLLECTIONS □ Wytheville,
VA
Roberts, Audrey, Per. & Curric.Libn.
CONCORDIA COLLEGE - KLINCK MEMORIAL
LIBRARY □ River Forest, IL
Roberts, Barbara L., Dir.
CHAMPAIGN COUNTY HISTORICAL ARCHIVES
□ Urbana, IL
Roberts, Cathleen, Res.Asst.
AMERICAN ELECTRIC POWER SERVICE CORP.
- LIBRARY† □ New York, NY
Roberts, Christine, Asst.Libn./Rd.Serv.
PEABODY CONSERVATORY OF MUSIC -
LIBRARY □ Baltimore, MD
Roberts, Dolores M., Dir. of Med.Rec.
CHILDREN'S HOSPITAL OF THE KING'S
DAUGHTERS - MEDICAL LIBRARY □ Norfolk, VA
Roberts, Don L., Hd.
NORTHWESTERN UNIVERSITY - MUSIC
LIBRARY □ Evanston, IL
Roberts, Dr. Edward Graham, Dir.
GEORGIA INSTITUTE OF TECHNOLOGY - PRICE
GILBERT MEMORIAL LIBRARY □ Atlanta, GA
Roberts, Elaine H., Libn.
PISCATAQUIS COUNTY LAW LIBRARY □ Dover-
Foxcroft, ME

Roberts, Elizabeth P., Hd.
WASHINGTON STATE UNIVERSITY - OWEN
SCIENCE AND ENGINEERING LIBRARY □
Pullman, WA
Roberts, Gary B., Res.Libn.
NEW ENGLAND HISTORIC GENEALOGICAL
SOCIETY - LIBRARY □ Boston, MA
Roberts, Gerald F., Spec.Coll.Libn.
BEREA COLLEGE - HUTCHINS LIBRARY -
SPECIAL COLLECTIONS □ Berea, KY
Roberts, Gloria A., Hd.Libn.
PLANNED PARENTHOOD FEDERATION OF
AMERICA, INC. - KATHARINE DEXTER MC
CORMICK LIBRARY □ New York, NY
Roberts, H. Armstrong, III, Pres.
ROBERTS (H. Armstrong) INC. - STOCK
PHOTOGRAPHY LIBRARY □ Philadelphia, PA
Roberts, Helene, Cur. of Visual Coll.
HARVARD UNIVERSITY - FINE ARTS LIBRARY □
Cambridge, MA
Roberts, J. D., Libn.
SALES AND MARKETING MANAGEMENT -
LIBRARY □ New York, NY
Roberts, Jean, Ed./Libn.
THORNDIKE LIBRARY □ Boston, MA
Roberts, Sr. Jean B., S.C.N., Med.Libn.
ST. VINCENT INFIRMARY - MEDICAL LIBRARY†
□ Little Rock, AR
Roberts, Joe, Ed.
NATIONAL RIFLE ASSOCIATION - TECHNICAL
LIBRARY □ Washington, DC
Roberts, Dr. John P., Sec.
NATIONAL MUSEUM OF TRANSPORT -
TRANSPORTATION REFERENCE LIBRARY □ St.
Louis, MO
Roberts, Juanita, Libn.
DARTNELL CORPORATION - PUBLISHING-
RESEARCH LIBRARY □ Chicago, IL
Roberts, Karen, Libn.
ST. ANDREWS HOSPITAL - MEDICAL LIBRARY □
Boothbay Harbor, ME
Roberts, Katherine L., Dir., Med.Rec.
TINGLEY (Carrie) CRIPPLED CHILDREN'S
HOSPITAL - MEDICAL LIBRARY □ Albuquerque,
NM
Roberts, Kathleen, Pub.Serv.Libn.
TEXAS A & M UNIVERSITY AT GALVESTON -
LIBRARY □ Galveston, TX
Roberts, Linda L., Coll.Libn.
OKLAHOMA COLLEGE OF OSTEOPATHIC
MEDICINE & SURGERY - LIBRARY □ Tulsa, OK
Roberts, Linda R., Supv.
ROCKWELL INTERNATIONAL - NORTH
AMERICAN AIRCRAFT OPERATIONS -
TECHNICAL INFORMATION CENTER □ Los
Angeles, CA
Roberts, Lloyd, Libn.
MADISON STATE HOSPITAL - CRAGMONT
MEDICAL LIBRARY □ Madison, IN
Roberts, Patricia A.B., Prog.Mgr.
MONTANA STATE DEPARTMENT OF
COMMERCE - CENSUS & ECONOMIC
INFORMATION CENTER □ Helena, MT
Roberts, Randy, Mss.Spec.
WESTERN HISTORICAL MANUSCRIPT
COLLECTION/STATE HISTORICAL SOCIETY OF
MISSOURI MANUSCRIPTS JOINT COLLECTION
□ Columbia, MO
Roberts, Rebecca, Supv.
UNIVERSITY OF WISCONSIN, MADISON -
SCHOOL OF SOCIAL WORK - VIDEO RESOURCE
LIBRARY □ Madison, WI
Roberts, Richard, Ref.Supv.
FLORIDA STATE DIVISION OF ARCHIVES,
HISTORY & RECORDS MANAGEMENT - FLORIDA
STATE ARCHIVES □ Tallahassee, FL
Roberts, S. Helen, Archv.
RILEY COUNTY HISTORICAL SOCIETY -
SEATON MEMORIAL LIBRARY □ Manhattan, KS
Roberts, Sue, Sec.
BOONE COUNTY GENEALOGICAL SOCIETY -
LIBRARY □ Hewett, WV

Robertson, Ann, Med.Libn.
FRESNO COMMUNITY HOSPITAL - MEDICAL
LIBRARY □ Fresno, CA
Robertson, Ann, Mgr., Info. & Anl.Serv.
MC KINSEY & COMPANY, INC. - LIBRARY □
Washington, DC
Robertson, Betty G., Info.Sec.
LEIGH INSTRUMENTS, LTD. - ENGINEERING &
AEROSPACE DIVISION - TECHNICAL LIBRARY
□ Carleton Place, ON
Robertson, Beverly, Lib.Asst.
METROPOLITAN MUSEUM OF ART - URIS
LIBRARY AND RESOURCE CENTER □ New York,
NY
Robertson, Billy O., Coord.
MIDLAND PUBLIC SCHOOLS - INSTRUCTIONAL
MEDIA CENTER □ Midland, MI
Robertson, Carolyn, Libn.
NATIONAL COTTON COUNCIL OF AMERICA -
LIBRARY □ Memphis, TN
Robertson, Craig A., Chem./Physics Libn.
UNIVERSITY OF VERMONT - CHEMISTRY/
PHYSICS LIBRARY □ Burlington, VT
Robertson, D.F., Dir.
KELSEY INSTITUTE OF APPLIED ARTS AND
SCIENCES - LEARNING RESOURCES CENTRE □
Saskatoon, SK
Robertson, Gail J., Libn.
DURACELL INC. - RESEARCH LIBRARY □
Mississauga, ON
Robertson, Jack, Cat.
BOEING MILITARY AIRPLANE COMPANY -
LIBRARY □ Wichita, KS
Robertson, Jack, Arts Libn.
VANDERBILT UNIVERSITY - JEAN AND
ALEXANDER HEARD LIBRARY - CENTRAL
DIVISION - ARTS LIBRARY □ Nashville, TN
Robertson, Jean, Dir., Info.Ctr.
NATIONAL SOCIETY OF PROFESSIONAL
ENGINEERS - INFORMATION CENTER □
Washington, DC
Robertson, Jean, Ser.Libn.
STANFORD UNIVERSITY - J. HUGH JACKSON
LIBRARY □ Stanford, CA
Robertson, Kathleen, Libn.
PCL-BRAUN-SIMONS LTD. - PBS LIBRARY† □
Calgary, AB
Robertson, Kevin, Circ. & ILL Libn.
UNIVERSITY OF HEALTH SCIENCES/CHICAGO
MEDICAL SCHOOL - LIBRARY □ North Chicago,
IL
Robertson, Lavonne D., Hd.Libn.
SALVATION ARMY SCHOOL FOR OFFICERS
TRAINING - ELFTMAN MEMORIAL LIBRARY □
Rancho Palos Verdes, CA
Robertson, Lori, Circ.Libn.
SOUTHWESTERN BAPTIST THEOLOGICAL
SEMINARY - A. WEBB ROBERTS LIBRARY □ Fort
Worth, TX
Robertson, Mary, Asst.Dir.
CHEROKEE REGIONAL LIBRARY - GEORGIA
HISTORY & GENEALOGICAL ROOM† □
LaFayette, GA
Robertson, Mary, Cur., Mss.
HUNTINGTON (Henry E.) LIBRARY, ART
GALLERY AND BOTANICAL GARDENS □ San
Marino, CA
Robertson, Mary Ruth, Libn.
CHESAPEAKE BAY MARITIME MUSEUM -
HOWARD I. CHAPELLE MEMORIAL LIBRARY □
St. Michaels, MD
Robertson, Renee, Info.Chem.
UNION OIL COMPANY OF CALIFORNIA -
TECHNICAL INFORMATION CENTER □
Placentia, CA
Robertson, Retha, Libn.
HTB, INC. - TECHNICAL INFORMATION
CENTER □ Oklahoma City, OK
Robertson, S., Info.Spec.
STANDARD OIL COMPANY OF INDIANA -
LIBRARY/INFORMATION CENTER □ Chicago, IL

Robertson, S. Donald, Hd.Libn.
SCOTT, FORESMAN & COMPANY, INC. -
EDITORIAL LIBRARY □ Glenview, IL
Robertson, Sharon M., Libn.
LIONS GATE HOSPITAL - DR. H. CARSON
GRAHAM MEMORIAL LIBRARY □ North
Vancouver, BC
Robertson, W. Davenport, Hd.Libn.
NATIONAL INSTITUTE OF ENVIRONMENTAL
HEALTH SCIENCES - LIBRARY □ Research
Triangle Park, NC
Robichaud, M., Sec.
INDUSTRIAL GENERAL INSURANCE COMPANY -
LIBRARY □ Quebec, PQ
Robillard, Jean-Jacques, Chf.Libn./Info.Dir.
COLLEGE DOMINICAIN DE PHILOSOPHIE ET DE
THEOLOGIE - BIBLIOTHEQUE □ Ottawa, ON
Robin, Annabeth, Mgr.
PHILLIPS PETROLEUM COMPANY -
EXPLORATION & PRODUCTION GROUP -
LIBRARY □ Bartlesville, OK
Robins, Mrs. Brooky, Asst. to Dir.
CANADIAN JEWISH CONGRESS - TORONTO
JEWISH CONGRESS - ONTARIO REGION
ARCHIVES □ Willowdale, ON
Robins, Margaret, Med.Libn.
WOMEN'S COLLEGE HOSPITAL - MEDICAL
LIBRARY □ Toronto, ON
Robinson, Agnes F., Asst. Law Libn.
DUQUESNE UNIVERSITY - LAW LIBRARY □
Pittsburgh, PA
Robinson, Alice B., Chf.
DISTRICT OF COLUMBIA PUBLIC LIBRARY -
BLACK STUDIES DIVISION □ Washington, DC
Robinson, Ann, Ref.
DRAPER (Charles Stark) LABORATORY, INC. -
TECHNICAL INFORMATION CENTER □
Cambridge, MA
Robinson, Anne, Media Serv.Libn.
UNIVERSITY OF THE DISTRICT OF COLUMBIA -
HARVARD STREET LIBRARY† □ Washington, DC
Robinson, Chantal, Assoc.Dir.
QUEBEC PROVINCE - DIRECTION GENERALE
DES MOYENS D'ENSEIGNEMENT - CENTRE DE
DOCUMENTATION □ Montreal, PQ
Robinson, Chris, Libn.
ONTARIO HYDRO - LIBRARY □ Toronto, ON
Robinson, D., Libn.
CANADA - CANADIAN FORESTRY SERVICE -
NORTHERN FOREST RESEARCH CENTRE -
LIBRARY □ Edmonton, AB
Robinson, Dean, Supv., Lib.Serv.
TENNESSEE VALLEY AUTHORITY - TECHNICAL
LIBRARY □ Chattanooga, TN
Robinson, Doris, Ref.Libn.
GENERAL ELECTRIC COMPANY - ADVANCED
REACTOR SYSTEMS DEPT. - LIBRARY □
Sunnyvale, CA
Robinson, Elizabeth A., Libn.
GOOD SAMARITAN HOSPITAL - SHANK
MEMORIAL LIBRARY □ Dayton, OH
Robinson, Erika, Coord.
DISTRICT OF COLUMBIA PUBLIC SCHOOLS -
DIVISION OF QUALITY ASSURANCE -
RESEARCH INFORMATION CENTER □
Washington, DC
Robinson, Fay, Br.Libn.
U.S. ARMY POST - FORT LEWIS - LIBRARY
SYSTEM □ Ft. Lewis, WA
Robinson, Hank, Info.Sys.Spec.
MITRE CORPORATION - TECHNICAL REPORT
CENTER □ Bedford, MA
Robinson, Hannah G., Libn., S. Asia Coll.
INSTITUTE FOR ADVANCED STUDIES OF
WORLD RELIGIONS - LIBRARY □ Stony Brook,
NY
Robinson, Jeannette, Sec.
LOUISIANA TECH UNIVERSITY - COLLEGE OF
EDUCATION - EDUCATIONAL RESEARCH
LIBRARY □ Ruston, LA
Robinson, Judy, Hd.Libn.
SAN ANTONIO EXPRESS AND NEWS - LIBRARY†
□ San Antonio, TX

Robinson, Judy, ILL
VIRGINIA COMMONWEALTH UNIVERSITY -
MEDICAL COLLEGE OF VIRGINIA - TOMPKINS-
MC CAW LIBRARY □ Richmond, VA
Robinson, Julie L., Mng.Libn.
CLAREMONT GRADUATE SCHOOL -
EDUCATIONAL RESOURCE & INFORMATION
CENTER □ Claremont, CA
Robinson, Julie L., Mng.Libn.
CLAREMONT GRADUATE SCHOOL - GEORGE G.
STONE CENTER FOR CHILDREN'S BOOKS □
Claremont, CA
Robinson, Juliet, Libn.
MC CRONE (Walter C.) ASSOCIATES - LIBRARY
□ Chicago, IL
Robinson, Karen, Libn.
ORAL ROBERTS UNIVERSITY - LIBRARY - HOLY
SPIRIT RESEARCH CENTER □ Tulsa, OK
Robinson, Kathleen, Asst.Archv.
CORCORAN GALLERY OF ART - CORCORAN
ARCHIVES □ Washington, DC
Robinson, Louise, Supv., Clippings
NATIONAL GEOGRAPHIC SOCIETY - LIBRARY □
Washington, DC
Robinson, Lynn, Libn.
WENTWORTH INSTITUTE OF TECHNOLOGY -
LIBRARY □ Boston, MA
Robinson, Margaret, Hd., Ref.
UNIVERSITY OF CALIFORNIA, SANTA CRUZ -
DEAN E. MC HENRY LIBRARY □ Santa Cruz, CA
Robinson, Marilyn, Acq.Libn.
AMOCO PRODUCTION COMPANY
INTERNATIONAL - LIBRARY INFORMATION
CENTER □ Houston, TX
Robinson, Marjorie, Libn.
CANADIAN TAX FOUNDATION - LIBRARY □
Toronto, ON
Robinson, Mary Lou, Asst.Libn.
FIRST UNITED METHODIST CHURCH - ALLEN
LIBRARY □ Kalamazoo, MI
Robinson, Michaele M., Libn.
ZOOLOGICAL SOCIETY OF SAN DIEGO - ERNST
SCHWARZ LIBRARY □ San Diego, CA
Robinson, Morris, Mgr., Dist.
NATIONAL GALLERY OF ART - DEPARTMENT OF
EXTENSION PROGRAMS □ Washington, DC
Robinson, Nancy, Cat.
SOUTHERN BAPTIST THEOLOGICAL SEMINARY
- JAMES P. BOYCE CENTENNIAL LIBRARY □
Louisville, KY
Robinson, Orvetta, Libn.
ILLINOIS STATE MUSEUM OF NATURAL
HISTORY AND ART - TECHNICAL LIBRARY □
Springfield, IL
Robinson, Paul, Exec.Dir.
SOUTHWEST RESEARCH & INFORMATION
CENTER □ Albuquerque, NM
Robinson, Pearl O., Libn.
U.S. NAVY - NAVAL SHIP SYSTEMS
ENGINEERING STATION HEADQUARTERS -
TECHNICAL LIBRARY □ Philadelphia, PA
Robinson, Miss R., Libn.
HORNER (Frank W.), LTD. - RESEARCH LIBRARY
□ Montreal, PQ
Robinson, Rich, AV Coord.
NATIONAL COLLEGE OF CHIROPRACTIC -
LEARNING RESOURCE CENTER □ Lombard, IL
Robinson, Richard, Ref.Libn.
LAWRENCE BERKELEY LABORATORY - LIBRARY
□ Berkeley, CA
Robinson, Russell, Media Spec./Libn.
BAXTER (Governor) SCHOOL FOR THE DEAF -
LIBRARY □ Portland, ME
Robinson, Sharon, Asst.Dir.
HISTORICAL SOCIETY OF SARATOGA SPRINGS
- MUSEUM AND LIBRARY □ Saratoga Springs, NY
Robinson, Thomas J., Educ.Libn.
UNIVERSITY OF WINDSOR - FACULTY OF
EDUCATION LIBRARY □ Windsor, ON
Robinson, Vera L., Cat.
SCHOOLS OF THEOLOGY IN DUBUQUE -
LIBRARIES □ Dubuque, IA

Robkoff, Irena, Lib.Asst.
NASSAU COUNTY DEPARTMENT OF HEALTH -
OFFICE OF PUBLIC HEALTH - LIBRARY □
Mineola, NY

Robles, Ester, Libn.
U.S. VETERANS ADMINISTRATION (NV-Reno) -
MEDICAL CENTER - LEARNING CENTER □ Reno,
NV

Robson, Betty J., Res.Libn.
UNITED STATES BORAX RESEARCH
CORPORATION - RESEARCH LIBRARY □
Anaheim, CA

Robson, Elizabeth A., Libn.
VIRGINIA STATE DEPARTMENT OF
CORRECTIONS - ACADEMY FOR STAFF
DEVELOPMENT - LIBRARY □ Waynesboro, VA

Robson, John M., Asst.Ref.Libn.
VIRGINIA MILITARY INSTITUTE - PRESTON
LIBRARY □ Lexington, VA

Robson, Timothy D., Music Libn.
CASE WESTERN RESERVE UNIVERSITY -
KULAS MUSIC LIBRARY □ Cleveland, OH

Rocamora, Joel, Dir.
SOUTHEAST ASIA RESOURCE CENTER □
Berkeley, CA

Rocha, Guy L., State Archv.
NEVADA STATE LIBRARY - DIVISION OF
ARCHIVES □ Carson City, NV

Roche, Mary, Adm.Asst.
UNIVERSITY OF CONNECTICUT - INSTITUTE
OF MATERIALS SCIENCE - READING ROOM □
Storrs, CT

Rock, Casey, Libn.
CANADIAN BROADCASTING CORPORATION -
REFERENCE LIBRARY □ Toronto, ON

Rock, Catherine, Adm.
LEVI STRAUSS & COMPANY - CORPORATE
MARKETING INFORMATION CENTER† □ San
Francisco, CA

Rock, Dale, Naturalist
HENNEPIN COUNTY PARK RESERVE DISTRICT -
LOWRY NATURE CENTER - LIBRARY □ Excelsior,
MN

Rock, Susan, Ref.
KUTAK ROCK & HUIE - LAW LIBRARY □ Omaha,
NE

Rockefeller, Shirley J., Tech.Libn.
GENERAL ELECTRIC COMPANY - SPACE/
SYSTEMS DIVISION LIBRARIES □ Philadelphia,
PA

Rocker, Willard L., Chf. of Genealogy
MIDDLE GEORGIA REGIONAL LIBRARY -
WASHINGTON MEMORIAL LIBRARY -
GENEALOGICAL & HISTORICAL ROOM □ Macon,
GA

Rockey, Steven W., Supv.
CORNELL UNIVERSITY - MATHEMATICS
LIBRARY □ Ithaca, NY

Rockwell, Susan P., Lib.Techn.
U.S. NATL. MARINE FISHERIES SERVICE -
NORTHEAST FISHERIES CENTER - LIBRARY □
Woods Hole, MA

Rocky, Helen K., Sec./Treas.
INTERNATIONAL ACADEMY AT SANTA
BARBARA - LIBRARY □ Santa Barbara, CA

Rodawalt, Valarie, Ref.Libn.
DALLAS COUNTY LAW LIBRARY □ Dallas, TX

Rodeffer, Georgia H., Textiles Libn.
NORTH CAROLINA STATE UNIVERSITY -
BURLINGTON TEXTILES LIBRARY □ Raleigh, NC

Roden, Jeanyce, Med.Libn.
U.S. VETERANS ADMINISTRATION (WA-
Seattle) - HOSPITAL MEDICAL LIBRARY □
Seattle, WA

Rodenhauser, Paul C., Grand Recorder
RED CROSS OF CONSTANTINE - UNITED
GRAND IMPERIAL COUNCIL - EDWARD A. GLAD
MEMORIAL LIBRARY □ Chicago, IL

Rodenhaver, Dale, Bus.Libn.
SUN TECH, INC. - LIBRARY & INFORMATION
SERVICE □ Marcus Hook, PA

Rodes, Barbara K., Libn.
CONSERVATION FOUNDATION - LIBRARY □
Washington, DC

Rodgers, Elizabeth L., Exec.Sec.
ASSOCIATION OF STUDENT INTERNATIONAL
LAW SOCIETIES - INFORMATION CENTER □
Washington, DC

Rodgers, Jane C., Supv.
SHELL OIL COMPANY - INFORMATION &
LIBRARY SERVICES □ Houston, TX

Rodgers, Patricia, Coord., Tech.Serv.
UNIVERSITY OF SOUTH ALABAMA - COLLEGE
OF MEDICINE - BIOMEDICAL LIBRARY □
Mobile, AL

Rodney, Mrs. Jamesie, Mgr.
PEABODY (George) COLLEGE FOR TEACHERS OF
VANDERBILT UNIVERSITY - KENNEDY CENTER
- MATERIALS LIBRARY □ Nashville, TN

Rodriguez, Ana Milagros, Libn.
U.S. DISTRICT COURT - LEGAL LIBRARY □ San
Juan, PR

Rodriguez, Cesar, Acq.Libn.
YALE UNIVERSITY - SOCIAL SCIENCE LIBRARY
□ New Haven, CT

Rodriguez, Delma, AV Media Dir.
UNIVERSITY OF SOUTH FLORIDA - DIVISION
OF EDUCATIONAL RESOURCES - FILM LIBRARY
□ Tampa, FL

Rodriguez, Jose F., Circ. & Ref.Libn.
UNIVERSITY OF GEORGIA - LAW LIBRARY □
Athens, GA

Rodriguez, Juanita, Info.Anl.
UNIVERSITY OF WYOMING - WYOMING
CAREER INFORMATION SYSTEM □ Laramie, WY

Rodriguez, Narciso, Hd., Circ.
MEDICAL LIBRARY CENTER OF NEW YORK† □
New York, NY

Rodriquez, Diana, Cat.Dept.Hd.
NEW JERSEY INSTITUTE OF TECHNOLOGY -
ROBERT W. VAN HOUTEN LIBRARY □ Newark,
NJ

Rodwell, Mr. L.W., Staff Archv.
SASKATCHEWAN ARCHIVES BOARD □ Regina,
SK

Roe, Eunice, Info.Anl.
PENNSYLVANIA STATE UNIVERSITY -
INSTITUTE FOR RESEARCH ON LAND AND
WATER RESOURCES - LIBRARY □ University
Park, PA

Roe, Keith, Hd.
PENNSYLVANIA STATE UNIVERSITY - LIFE
SCIENCES LIBRARY □ University Park, PA

Roe, Nancy, Cat.
UNIVERSITY OF MAINE, PRESQUE ISLE -
LIBRARY AND LEARNING RESOURCES CENTER -
SPECIAL COLLECTIONS □ Presque Isle, ME

Roe, Richard, Res.Anl.
WISCONSIN STATE LEGISLATIVE REFERENCE
BUREAU □ Madison, WI

Roe, Ruth E., Libn.
NEWPORT HARBOR ART MUSEUM - LIBRARY □
Newport Beach, CA

Roebuck, Edith V., Libn.
U.S. AIR FORCE BASE - DYESS BASE LIBRARY □
Dyess AFB, TX

Roedell, Raymond Frank, Jr., Dir.
PENNSYLVANIA STATE DEPARTMENT OF
PUBLIC WELFARE - NORRISTOWN STATE
HOSPITAL - PROFESSIONAL/STAFF SERVICES
LIBRARY □ Norristown, PA

Roeder, Christine S., Supv., Health Sci.Lib.
YOUNGSTOWN HOSPITAL ASSOCIATION -
HEALTH SCIENCES LIBRARY □ Youngstown, OH

Roeder, Peggy H., Libn.
PRINCE GEORGE'S COUNTY HEALTH
DEPARTMENT - PUBLIC HEALTH RESOURCE
CENTER □ Cheverly, MD

Roehrenbeck, Carole, Dir.
NOVA UNIVERSITY - LAW LIBRARY □ Fort
Lauderdale, FL

Roehrich, James, Engr. Standards Supv.
SPECTROL ELECTRONICS CORPORATION -
LIBRARY □ Industry, CA

Roeper, Susan, Cat.
CLARK (Sterling and Francine) ART INSTITUTE -
LIBRARY □ Williamstown, MA

Roeske, Betty, Ser.Libn.
OHIO NORTHERN UNIVERSITY - COLLEGE OF
LAW - JAY P. TAGGART MEMORIAL LAW
LIBRARY □ Ada, OH

Roess, Anne C., Mgr., Tech.Info.Ctr.
INSTITUTE OF GAS TECHNOLOGY - TECHNICAL
INFORMATION CENTER □ Chicago, IL

Roess, Anne C., Chf.Libn.
PEOPLES GAS LIGHT AND COKE COMPANY -
LIBRARY □ Chicago, IL

Roessler, Caroline, Asst.Cur.
LE SUEUR COUNTY HISTORICAL SOCIETY
MUSEUM - LIBRARY □ Elysian, MN

Rogachevsky, Linda, Hd.Libn.
PROCTOR & REDFERN, CONSULTING
ENGINEERS - LIBRARY □ Don Mills, ON

Rogal, Patricia, Pict.Coll.
METROPOLITAN TORONTO LIBRARY - FINE
ART DEPARTMENT □ Toronto, ON

Rogalski, Leonore, Mgr.
SIGNAL UOP RESEARCH CENTER - TECHNICAL
INFORMATION CENTER □ Des Plaines, IL

Rogenmoser, Debra, Libn.
FARMERS INSURANCE GROUP, INC. - LIBRARY
□ Los Angeles, CA

Rogers, Barbara, Libn.
OCCIDENTAL EXPLORATION & PRODUCTION
COMPANY - LIBRARY □ Bakersfield, CA

Rogers, Ben, Archv.
SOUTHWESTERN BAPTIST THEOLOGICAL
SEMINARY - A. WEBB ROBERTS LIBRARY □ Fort
Worth, TX

Rogers, Betty, Libn.
HACKLEY HOSPITAL - EDUCATION LIBRARY □
Muskegon, MI

Rogers, Bonnie L., Dean, Instr.Rsrcs.
PALOMAR COMMUNITY COLLEGE - LIBRARY -
SPECIAL COLLECTIONS □ San Marcos, CA

Rogers, Brian D., Coll.Libn.
CONNECTICUT COLLEGE - LIBRARY - SPECIAL
COLLECTIONS □ New London, CT

Rogers, Carl, Lib.Adv.
QUEENS BOROUGH PUBLIC LIBRARY -
LANGSTON HUGHES COMMUNITY LIBRARY AND
CULTURAL CENTER □ Corona, NY

Rogers, Carole, Libn.
UNITED GRAIN GROWERS LTD. - LIBRARY □
Winnipeg, MB

Rogers, Catherine, Tech.Info.Spec.
INTERMEDICS, INC. - LIBRARY □ Freeport, TX

Rogers, Mrs. Clyde, Hostess
DREW COUNTY HISTORICAL SOCIETY -
MUSEUM AND ARCHIVES □ Monticello, AR

Rogers, David H., Gen.Couns.
FOREIGN CLAIMS SETTLEMENT COMMISSION
OF THE UNITED STATES - LIBRARY □
Washington, DC

Rogers, Deborah, Ref.Libn.
MOUNT SINAI SCHOOL OF MEDICINE OF THE
CITY UNIVERSITY OF NEW YORK - GUSTAVE L.
& JANET W. LEVY LIBRARY □ New York, NY

Rogers, Dee, Libn.
AMERICAN CYANAMID COMPANY - SANTA
ROSA PLANT - LIBRARY □ Milton, FL

Rogers, Earl M., Cur. of Archv.
UNIVERSITY OF IOWA - SPECIAL
COLLECTIONS DEPARTMENT □ Iowa City, IA

Rogers, Mr. G.V., Jr., Supv.
TENNESSEE VALLEY AUTHORITY - CONTRACT
SERVICES □ Knoxville, TN

Rogers, Helen M., Ref.
UNIVERSITY OF MIAMI - SCHOOL OF LAW
LIBRARY □ Coral Gables, FL

Rogers, Janet, Libn.
METROPOLITAN TORONTO LIBRARY - SOCIAL
SCIENCES DEPARTMENT □ Toronto, ON

Rogers, Judith, Libn. I
MTS SYSTEMS CORPORATION - INFORMATION
SERVICES □ Eden Prairie, MN

Rogers, Linda, Res.Libn.
WYLE LABORATORIES - TECHNICAL
INFORMATION LIBRARY □ El Segundo, CA

Rogers, M. Margaret, Dir.Info.Serv.
NORTHWEST REGIONAL EDUCATIONAL
LABORATORY - INFORMATION CENTER/
LIBRARY □ Portland, OR

Rogers, Marian, Libn.
WISCONSIN STATE LEGISLATIVE REFERENCE
BUREAU □ Madison, WI

Rogers, Marianne, Ref.Libn.
YORK UNIVERSITY - LAW LIBRARY □
Downsview, ON

Rogers, Marilyn, Ser.Libn.
LOUISIANA STATE UNIVERSITY MEDICAL
CENTER - SCHOOL OF MEDICINE IN
SHREVEPORT - LIBRARY □ Shreveport, LA

Rogers, Marlin, Mgr., Info. & Supply Serv
ALCON LABORATORIES, INC. - RESEARCH &
DEVELOPMENT LIBRARY □ Fort Worth, TX

Rogers, NancyAnn, Res.Libn.
HASTINGS & SONS PUBLISHERS - DAILY
EVENING ITEM - NEWSPAPER MORGUE □ Lynn,
MA

Rogers, Patricia, Bk.Coll.Libn.
HARVARD UNIVERSITY - FINE ARTS LIBRARY □
Cambridge, MA

Rogers, Peggy, Libn.
RIVERSIDE HOSPITAL - HEALTH SCIENCES
LIBRARY □ Newport News, VA

Rogers, Peggy W., Cat.
NATIONAL CENTER FOR STATE COURTS -
LIBRARY □ Williamsburg, VA

Rogers, Raymond J., Educ.Supv.
AMERICAN HORTICULTURAL SOCIETY -
LIBRARY □ Mount Vernon, VA

Rogers, Ruth Reinstein, Kress Lib.
HARVARD UNIVERSITY - HARVARD BUSINESS
SCHOOL - BAKER LIBRARY □ Boston, MA

Rogers, Ruth T., Adm.Libn.
U.S. NAVY - NAVAL AEROSPACE MEDICAL
INSTITUTE - LIBRARY □ Pensacola, FL

Rogers, Mrs. S.L., Hosp.Libn.
ST. JOSEPH'S HOSPITAL - HOSPITAL LIBRARY
□ Hamilton, ON

Rogers, Sally, Asst.Dir./Cur.
TEXAS STATE LIBRARY - LOCAL RECORDS
DIVISION - SAM HOUSTON REGIONAL LIBRARY
AND RESEARCH CENTER □ Liberty, TX

Rogers, Susan, Asst.Libn.
MANITOBA - DEPARTMENT OF HEALTH -
INFORMATION RESOURCES □ Winnipeg, MB

Rogers, Susan, Acq.Libn.
STATE HISTORICAL SOCIETY OF IOWA -
LIBRARY □ Iowa City, IA

Rogers, Vicky, Chf.
DISTRICT OF COLUMBIA PUBLIC LIBRARY -
PHILOSOPHY, PSYCHOLOGY AND RELIGION
DIVISION □ Washington, DC

Rogerson, Mary F., Ref.Libn.
U.S. ARMY POST - FORT HOOD - MSA DIVISION
- CASEY MEMORIAL LIBRARY □ Ft. Hood, TX

Rogge, Rena, Ref.Libn.
KEAN COLLEGE OF NEW JERSEY - NANCY
THOMPSON LIBRARY† □ Union, NJ

Rogier, June, Libn.
UNIVERSITY OF MINNESOTA - LANDSCAPE
ARBORETUM - ELMER L. & ELEANOR J.
ANDERSEN HORTICULTURAL LIBRARY □
Chaska, MN

Rogowski, Alfreda, Acq.Libn.
FIELD MUSEUM OF NATURAL HISTORY -
LIBRARY □ Chicago, IL

Rogozinska, Grace E., Info.Anl.
COMINCO LTD. - INFORMATION SERVICES □
Vancouver, BC

Rogstad, Betty, Libn.
MINOT DAILY NEWS - LIBRARY □ Minot, ND

Rogusz, Rev. Joseph A., C.S.C., Libn.
MOREAU SEMINARY - LIBRARY □ Notre Dame,
IN

Rohira, Dr. L., Chm., Med.Lib.Comm.
CLEVELAND PSYCHIATRIC INSTITUTE -
KARNOSH LIBRARY □ Cleveland, OH

Rohles, Dr. F.H.
KANSAS STATE UNIVERSITY - INSTITUTE FOR
ENVIRONMENTAL RESEARCH - LIBRARY □
Manhattan, KS

Rohlf, Mark A., Asst.Libn.
COMMUNICATIONS SATELLITE CORPORATION
- CENTRAL LIBRARY† □ Washington, DC

Rohm, Yvonne, Asst.Libn.
AID ASSOCIATION FOR LUTHERANS -
CORPORATE LIBRARY □ Appleton, WI

Rohmann, Gloria, Libn.
MINNEAPOLIS PUBLIC LIBRARY &
INFORMATION CENTER - LITERATURE AND
LANGUAGE DEPARTMENT □ Minneapolis, MN

Rohn, Dorcas, Doc.Coord.
ERIC CLEARINGHOUSE ON READING AND
COMMUNICATIONS SKILLS □ Urbana, IL

Rohrer, Ralph, Ref.Libn.
UNIVERSITY OF CHICAGO - BUSINESS/
ECONOMICS LIBRARY □ Chicago, IL

Rohrer, Richard L., Dir.
UNIVERSITY OF MINNESOTA, ST. PAUL -
CENTRAL LIBRARY □ St. Paul, MN

Rohrer, Valera L., Lib.Mgr.
ONAN CORPORATION - LIBRARY □ Minneapolis,
MN

Rohrig, Thomas T., Ref.Libn.
TEXAS TECH UNIVERSITY - LIBRARY -
DOCUMENTS DEPARTMENT □ Lubbock, TX

Rohrlick, Paula, Rsrc.Dir.
ACTION FOR CHILDREN'S TELEVISION - ACT
RESOURCE LIBRARY □ Newtonville, MA

Roizman, Betty, Libn.
CHADWELL & KAYSER, LTD. - LAW LIBRARY □
Chicago, IL

Roldan, Maria Antonia, Archv.
ORGANIZATION OF AMERICAN STATES -
COLUMBUS MEMORIAL LIBRARY □ Washington,
DC

Rolen, Helen, Supv., Tech.Serv.
SRI INTERNATIONAL - LIBRARY AND
RESEARCH INFORMATION SERVICES
DEPARTMENT □ Menlo Park, CA

Rolfs, Rodney D., Music Libn.
UNIVERSITY OF SOUTHERN CALIFORNIA -
MUSIC LIBRARY □ Los Angeles, CA

Roll, Kempton H., Exec.Dir.
METAL POWDER INDUSTRIES FEDERATION -
TECHNICAL INFORMATION CENTER □
Princeton, NJ

Roll, Shirley, Libn.
VANDERBURGH COUNTY LAW LIBRARY □
Evansville, IN

Rolland, Hazel D., Hd.
CANADA - NATIONAL DEFENCE - NDHQ
COMPUTER CENTRE LIBRARY □ Ottawa, ON

Rollefson, John, Acq.Libn.
LAWRENCE BERKELEY LABORATORY - LIBRARY
□ Berkeley, CA

Roller, Duane H.D., Cur.
UNIVERSITY OF OKLAHOMA - HISTORY OF
SCIENCE COLLECTIONS □ Norman, OK

Roller, Duane H.D., Cur.
UNIVERSITY OF OKLAHOMA - LIMITED ACCESS
COLLECTION □ Norman, OK

Rollheiser, Sandra K., Res.Mgr.
HAYES/HILL INCORPORATED - LIBRARY □
Chicago, IL

Rollins, Alden, Gov.Docs.Libn.
UNIVERSITY OF ALASKA, ANCHORAGE -
LIBRARY - GOVERNMENT DOCUMENTS □
Anchorage, AK

Rollins, Betty A., Program Asst.
NATIONAL COUNCIL OF TEACHERS OF
MATHEMATICS - TEACHER/LEARNING CENTER
□ Reston, VA

Rollins, Eleanor, Chf., Lib.Serv.
U.S. VETERANS ADMINISTRATION (VA-
Richmond) - HOSPITAL LIBRARY □ Richmond, VA

Rollins, Fred H., Dir.
WAYNE COUNTY HISTORICAL SOCIETY
MUSEUM - LIBRARY □ Lyons, NY

Rollins, Ken, Dir.
POLK PUBLIC MUSEUM - MEMORIAL LIBRARY □
Lakeland, FL

Rollins, Marilyn H., Ref.Dept.Mgr.
WINSTON-SALEM JOURNAL AND SENTINEL -
REFERENCE DEPARTMENT □ Winston-Salem,
NC

Rollins, William L., Pub.Info.
NEW HAMPSHIRE STATE DEPARTMENT OF
PUBLIC WORKS AND HIGHWAYS - LIBRARY □
Concord, NH

Rollison, Jeffrey, Asst.Archv.
CASE WESTERN RESERVE UNIVERSITY -
UNIVERSITY ARCHIVES □ Cleveland, OH

Rolloff, C.A., Sec.
ROLLOFF (C.A.) FOUR COUNTY LAW LIBRARY □
Montevideo, MN

Rolnicki, Tom, Exec.Dir.
ASSOCIATED COLLEGIATE PRESS/NATIONAL
SCHOLASTIC PRESS ASSOCIATION -
INFORMATION CENTER □ Minneapolis, MN

Roloff, Daphne C., Dir.
ART INSTITUTE OF CHICAGO - RYERSON AND
BURNHAM LIBRARIES □ Chicago, IL

Rolontz, Linda, Law Libn.
GENERAL MILLS, INC. - LAW LIBRARY □
Minneapolis, MN

Rom, Christine, Spec.Coll.Libn.
CLEVELAND INSTITUTE OF ART - JESSICA R.
GUND MEMORIAL LIBRARY □ Cleveland, OH

Romaine, Cynthia, Ref.Libn.
LEWIS AND CLARK LAW SCHOOL -
NORTHWESTERN SCHOOL OF LAW - PAUL L.
BOLEY LAW LIBRARY □ Portland, OR

Roman, Mary Ann, Libn.
BARNES & THORNBURG - LIBRARY □
Indianapolis, IN

Romani, Connie, Photo Libn.
CANADIAN NATIONAL RAILWAYS -
PHOTOGRAPHIC LIBRARY □ Montreal, PQ

Romano, Kathy, Ref.Libn.
AT & T BELL LABORATORIES - LIBRARY □
Naperville, IL

Romanoff, Julius S., Exec.Dir.
B'NAI B'RITH CAREER & COUNSELING
SERVICES - LIBRARY □ Philadelphia, PA

Romard, Judith-Marie, Archv./Lib.Techn.
FORTRESS OF LOUISBOURG NATIONAL
HISTORIC PARK - LIBRARY† □ Louisbourg, NS

Rombough, Dianne, Hd.
CANADA - ENERGY, MINES & RESOURCES
CANADA - SURVEYS & MAPPING BRANCH -
NATIONAL AIR PHOTO LIBRARY □ Ottawa, ON

Romeo, Jean, Asst.Libn.
UNIVERSITY OF FLORIDA - LATIN AMERICAN
COLLECTION □ Gainesville, FL

Romeo, Louis J., Law Libn.
NEW YORK STATE SUPREME COURT - 2ND
JUDICIAL DISTRICT - LAW LIBRARY □
Brooklyn, NY

Romeo, Sheryl, Asst.Libn./AV
AMERICAN INSTITUTE OF ARCHITECTS -
LIBRARY □ Washington, DC

Romero, Fr. Anthony E., O.P., Dir.
ST. THOMAS AQUINAS NEWMAN CENTER -
LIBRARY □ Albuquerque, NM

Romero, Consuelo Serrano, Libn.
PUERTO RICO - DEPARTMENT OF HEALTH -
MENTAL HEALTH LIBRARY □ San Juan, PR

Romero, Dorothy D., Libn.
OUR LADY OF THE LAKE REGIONAL MEDICAL
CENTER - SCHOOL OF NURSING LIBRARY □
Baton Rouge, LA

Romero, Orlando, Res.Libn.
MUSEUM OF NEW MEXICO - HISTORY LIBRARY
□ Santa Fe, NM

Rommelmeyer, Alberta, Archv.
CHIPPEWA VALLEY MUSEUM, INC. - LIBRARY □
Eau Claire, WI

Romoser, Winnifred, Libn.
SOCIETY OF THE FOUR ARTS - LIBRARY □ Palm
Beach, FL

Rondelli, Marilyn H., Mgr.
JOHNSON AND JOHNSON BABY PRODUCTS
COMPANY - RESEARCH INFORMATION CENTER
□ Skillman, NJ

Ronnermann, Gail, Sci.Libn.
QUEENS COLLEGE OF THE CITY UNIVERSITY
OF NEW YORK - SCIENCE LIBRARY □ Flushing,
NY

Ronsheim, Patricia, Cur.
HARRISON (Benjamin) MEMORIAL HOME -
LIBRARY □ Indianapolis, IN

Rood R, Negina, Ref.Libn.
MARINE MIDLAND BANK - LIBRARY □ New
York, NY

Rooks, Ann, Asst. Law Libn.
SANDUSKY COUNTY LAW LIBRARY □ Fremont,
OH

Rooney, Marsha, Dir./Cur.
ANDOVER HISTORICAL SOCIETY - CAROLINE
M. UNDERHILL RESEARCH LIBRARY □ Andover,
MA

Rooney, Mary T., Libn.
NEW YORK STATE OFFICE OF COURT
ADMINISTRATION - BRONX CRIMINAL-FAMILY
COURT - LIBRARY □ Bronx, NY

Rooney, Marylynn, Lib.Asst.
SOUTHERN BAPTIST HOSPITAL - LEARNING
RESOURCE CENTER □ New Orleans, LA

Rooney, Paul, Hd., AV Serv.
ST. MARY'S UNIVERSITY - PATRICK POWER
LIBRARY □ Halifax, NS

Rooney, Robert, Circ.Libn.
TEMPLE UNIVERSITY - HEALTH SCIENCES
CENTER - LIBRARY □ Philadelphia, PA

Roose, Walter R., Subject Spec.
SANDIA NATIONAL LABORATORIES -
TECHNICAL LIBRARY □ Albuquerque, NM

Rooshan, Gertrude I., Info.Spec./lib.Mgr.
KAISER ALUMINUM & CHEMICAL
CORPORATION - BUSINESS LIBRARY □ Oakland,
CA

Root, Beth, Tech.Serv.
U.S. INTERNATIONAL TRADE COMMISSION -
LIBRARY □ Washington, DC

Root, Christine, Spec.Proj.
HUDSON VALLEY COMMUNITY COLLEGE -
DWIGHT MARVIN LEARNING RESOURCES
CENTER □ Troy, NY

Root, Clyde R., Hd.Libn.
NORTHWEST BIBLE COLLEGE - LIBRARY† □
Minot, ND

Root, Dr. Deane L., Cur.
UNIVERSITY OF PITTSBURGH - FOSTER HALL
COLLECTION □ Pittsburgh, PA

Root, Kay A.W., Med.Libn.
U.S. VETERANS ADMINISTRATION (NY-
Syracuse) - MEDICAL CENTER LIBRARY □
Syracuse, NY

Root, Nina J., Chairperson
AMERICAN MUSEUM OF NATURAL HISTORY -
DEPARTMENT OF LIBRARY SERVICES □ New
York, NY

Roper, Donna, Res.Coord.
PENDLETON DISTRICT HISTORICAL AND
RECREATIONAL COMMISSION - REFERENCE
LIBRARY □ Pendleton, SC

Rorabaugh, Francine, Libn.
CHEVRON GEOSCIENCES COMPANY -
LIBRARY† □ Houston, TX

Rosales, Emmanuel N., Cur.
LOS ANGELES - DEPARTMENT OF RECREATION
AND PARKS - CABRILLO MARINE MUSEUM -
LIBRARY □ San Pedro, CA

Rosborough, Brian, Pres.
EARTHWATCH - LIBRARY □ Belmont, MA

Roscher, James T., Libn.
OLWINE, CONNELLY, CHASE, O'DONNELL &
WEYHER - LAW LIBRARY □ New York, NY

Rose, Carol, Sec.
TRINITY COUNTY LAW LIBRARY □ Weaverville,
CA

Rose, David P., Tech.Serv.Libn.
UNITED NATIONS FUND FOR POPULATION
ACTIVITIES - LIBRARY □ New York, NY

Rose, Dianne, Med.Libn.
FRANKFORD HOSPITAL - SCHOOL OF NURSING
- STUDENT LIBRARY □ Philadelphia, PA

Rose, Dianne E., Med.Libn.
FRANKFORD HOSPITAL - HOSPITAL LIBRARIES
□ Philadelphia, PA

Rose, Donald, Hd., Cat.
TEXAS TECH UNIVERSITY - HEALTH SCIENCES
CENTER - LIBRARY OF THE HEALTH SCIENCES
□ Lubbock, TX

Rose, Emily C., Libn.
PARKER, CHAPIN, FLATTAU AND KLIMPL -
LIBRARY □ New York, NY

Rose, Isabel, Hd.
METROPOLITAN TORONTO LIBRARY - MUSIC
DEPARTMENT □ Toronto, ON

Rose, Linda, Libn.
ALLEN COUNTY PUBLIC LIBRARY - BUSINESS
AND TECHNOLOGY DEPARTMENT □ Fort Wayne,
IN

Rose, Margaret, Acq.Libn.
ART CENTER COLLEGE OF DESIGN - JAMES
LEMONT FOGG MEMORIAL LIBRARY □
Pasadena, CA

Rose, William, Dir., Lib./Media Serv.
SOUTH HILLS HEALTH SYSTEM - BEHAN
HEALTH SCIENCE LIBRARY □ Pittsburgh, PA

Roseboro, Dagny, Circuit Libn.
CLEVELAND HEALTH SCIENCES LIBRARY -
ALLEN MEMORIAL LIBRARY □ Cleveland, OH

Rosemeier, Libby, AV Spec.
MAINE MARITIME ACADEMY - NUTTING
MEMORIAL LIBRARY □ Castine, ME

Rosen, Bettylou, Libn.
U.S. AIR FORCE BASE - HOMESTEAD BASE
LIBRARY† □ Homestead AFB, FL

Rosen, Corey, Exec.Dir.
NATIONAL CENTER FOR EMPLOYEE
OWNERSHIP - LIBRARY □ Arlington, VA

Rosen, Jocelyn, Supv., Tech.Info.Serv.
ITT CONTINENTAL BAKING COMPANY -
RESEARCH LABORATORIES LIBRARY □ Rye, NY

Rosen, Judy, Libn.
MINTZ, LEVIN, COHN, FERRIS, GLOVSKY AND
POPEO, P.C. - LAW LIBRARY □ Boston, MA

Rosen, Leslie, Res.Libn.
CONSUMERS UNION OF UNITED STATES, INC. -
LIBRARY □ Mount Vernon, NY

Rosen, Linda, Ref.Libn.
THOMPSON (J. Walter) COMPANY -
INFORMATION CENTER □ New York, NY

Rosen, Mary R., Libn.
TEMPLE OHABEI SHALOM - SISTERHOOD
LIBRARY □ Brookline, MA

Rosen, R., Hd.Libn.
HALCON SD GROUP, INC. - TECHNICAL
INFORMATION CENTER □ New York, NY

Rosen, Robert, Mus.Libn.
BANFF CENTRE FOR CONTINUING EDUCATION
- LIBRARY □ Banff, AB

Rosen, Robert, Dir.
UNIVERSITY OF CALIFORNIA, LOS ANGELES -
ACADEMY OF TELEVISION ARTS & SCIENCES -
TELEVISION ARCHIVES □ Los Angeles, CA

Rosen, Robert, Dir.
UNIVERSITY OF CALIFORNIA, LOS ANGELES -
UCLA FILM ARCHIVES □ Los Angeles, CA

Rosen, Robert, Dir.
UNIVERSITY OF CALIFORNIA, LOS ANGELES -
UCLA RADIO ARCHIVES □ Los Angeles, CA

Rosen, Rochelle, Ref.Libn.
NICHOLS COLLEGE - CONANT LIBRARY □
Dudley, MA

Rosenbaum, David, Ref.Libn.
WAYNE STATE UNIVERSITY - EDUCATION
LIBRARY □ Detroit, MI

Rosenbaum, Don, Libn.
HEBREW THEOLOGICAL COLLEGE - SAUL
SILBER MEMORIAL LIBRARY □ Skokie, IL

Rosenbaum, Thomas, Archv.
ROCKEFELLER UNIVERSITY - ROCKEFELLER
ARCHIVE CENTER □ North Tarrytown, NY

Rosenbaum-Cooper, Judith, Second Asst.
CHICAGO PUBLIC LIBRARY CULTURAL CENTER
- FINE ARTS DIVISION - ART SECTION □
Chicago, IL

Rosenberg, E.H., Pres.
RETORT, INC. - LIBRARY □ Franklin, MA

Rosenberg, Goldie, Mgr.
HOFFMANN-LA ROCHE, INC. - BUSINESS
INFORMATION CENTER □ Nutley, NJ

Rosenberg, Linda S., Pres.
DOCUMENTS PLUS, INC. □ New York, NY

Rosenberg, Lucille, Hosp.Libn.
LINCOLN GENERAL HOSPITAL - HOSPITAL
LIBRARY □ Lincoln, NE

Rosenberg, Melvin H., Prin.Libn.
LOS ANGELES PUBLIC LIBRARY - ART, MUSIC &
RECREATION DEPARTMENT □ Los Angeles, CA

Rosenberg, Neil V., Dir.
MEMORIAL UNIVERSITY OF NEWFOUNDLAND -
FOLKLORE AND LANGUAGE ARCHIVE □ St.
John's, NF

Rosenberger, Stephen, Evening Ref.Libn.
FASHION INSTITUTE OF TECHNOLOGY -
LIBRARY† □ New York, NY

Rosenblatt, Baru, ILL
PLANNING RESEARCH CORPORATION -
TECHNICAL LIBRARY □ McLean, VA

Rosenblatt, David J., Rec.Mgr.
AUBURN UNIVERSITY - ARCHIVES □ Auburn, AL

Rosenbloom, Dolores, Libn.
STROMBERG-CARLSON - TECHNICAL LIBRARY
□ Longwood, FL

Rosendorf, Alvin, Asst.Libn.
VINNELL CORPORATION - CORPORATE/
PROGRAM DEVELOPMENT LIBRARY □ Fairfax,
VA

Roseneder, Jan, Bibliog.
UNIVERSITY OF CALGARY - SPECIAL
COLLECTIONS DIVISION† □ Calgary, AB

Rosenender, Jan
UNIVERSITY OF CALGARY - ARTS AND
HUMANITIES LIBRARY† □ Calgary, AB

Rosenfeld, Anne H., Chf.
U.S. PUBLIC HEALTH SERVICE - NATL.
INSTITUTE OF MENTAL HEALTH - SCIENCE
COMMUNICATION BRANCH - MENTAL HEALTH
LIB. □ Rockville, MD

Rosenfeld, Joseph, Cat.Libn.
NOVA UNIVERSITY - LAW LIBRARY □ Fort
Lauderdale, FL

Rosenfeld, Lillian, Ref.Libn.
AMERICAN INSTITUTE OF CERTIFIED PUBLIC
ACCOUNTANTS - LIBRARY SERVICES □ New
York, NY

Rosenfeld, Mary Augusta, Adm.Libn.
SMITHSONIAN INSTITUTION LIBRARIES □
Washington, DC

Rosenfeld, Susan, Asst. Slide Curator
UNIVERSITY OF CALIFORNIA, LOS ANGELES -
ART DEPARTMENT - VISUAL RESOURCE
COLLECTION & SERVICES □ Los Angeles, CA

Rosenfield, James, V.P.
CAMBRIDGE ENERGY RESEARCH ASSOCIATES -
LIBRARY □ Cambridge, MA

Rosenkrantz, Barbara G.
HARVARD UNIVERSITY - HISTORY OF SCIENCE
LIBRARY □ Cambridge, MA

Rosenplot, David, Libn.
STELCO INC. - RESEARCH AND DEVELOPMENT
LIBRARY □ Hamilton, ON

Rosenstein, Dr. Leon, Dir.
SAN DIEGO STATE UNIVERSITY - EUROPEAN
STUDIES CENTER - LIBRARY □ San Diego, CA

Rosenstein, Linda, Asst.Libn., Tech.Serv.
UNIVERSITY OF PENNSYLVANIA - BIOMEDICAL
LIBRARY □ Philadelphia, PA

Rosenstein, Miriam, Libn.
FAIR OAKS HOSPITAL - MEDICAL LIBRARY □ Summit, NJ

Rosenstein, Philip, Dir. of Libs.
UNIVERSITY OF MEDICINE AND DENTISTRY OF NEW JERSEY AT NEWARK - GEORGE F. SMITH LIBRARY □ Newark, NJ

Rosenstein, Shelley, Libn.
MASSACHUSETTS INSTITUTE OF TECHNOLOGY - ENERGY LABORATORY INFORMATION CENTER □ Cambridge, MA

Rosensweig, Larry, Cur.
MORIKAMI MUSEUM OF JAPANESE CULTURE - DONALD B. GORDON MEMORIAL LIBRARY □ Delray Beach, FL

Rosenthal, Barbara G., Med.Libn.
ST. ELIZABETH HOSPITAL MEDICAL CENTER - MEDICAL LIBRARY† □ Youngstown, OH

Rosenthal, Prof. Jane, Rep.
COLUMBIA UNIVERSITY - DEPARTMENT OF ART HISTORY & ARCHAEOLOGY - PHOTOGRAPH COLLECTION □ New York, NY

Rosenthal, Judith, Info.Spec.
PEAT, MARWICK, MITCHELL & CO. - LIBRARY □ Houston, TX

Rosenthal, Judith, Clin.Med.Libn.
UNIVERSITY OF TEXAS MEDICAL BRANCH - MOODY MEDICAL LIBRARY □ Galveston, TX

Rosenthal, R., Libn.
WESLEYAN WOMEN'S CENTER - LIBRARY □ Middletown, CT

Rosenthal, Robert, Cur.
UNIVERSITY OF CHICAGO - SPECIAL COLLECTIONS □ Chicago, IL

Rosenwasser-Skalak, Diane, Archv.
MEMORIAL SLOAN-KETTERING CANCER CENTER - LEE COOMBE MEMORIAL LIBRARY □ New York, NY

Rosenwinkel, Heather, Coll.Dev.Libn.
OREGON HEALTH SCIENCES UNIVERSITY - LIBRARY □ Portland, OR

Rosenzweig, Nancy J., Reserve Supv.
UNIVERSITY OF MICHIGAN - ALFRED TAUBMAN MEDICAL LIBRARY □ Ann Arbor, MI

Rosenzweig, Susan, Info.Mgr.
UNIVERSITY OF NORTH CAROLINA, CHAPEL HILL - CENTER FOR EARLY ADOLESCENCE - INFORMATION SERVICES DIVISION □ Carrboro, NC

Rosevear, Carol, Hd.
NEW BRUNSWICK MUSEUM - LIBRARY AND ARCHIVES DEPARTMENT □ Saint John, NB

Rosevear, Joanne E., Dir.
CARLETON MEMORIAL HOSPITAL - HEALTH SCIENCES LIBRARY □ Woodstock, NB

Rosicky, Henry, Prog.Mgr.
U.S. PATENT & TRADEMARK OFFICE - SCIENTIFIC LIBRARY† □ Arlington, VA

Rosignolo, Beverly, Assoc.Libn.
COLLEGE OF INSURANCE - INSURANCE SOCIETY OF NEW YORK - LIBRARY □ New York, NY

Rosnagle, Barbara M., Lib.Asst.
HOSPITAL OF ST. RAPHAEL - HEALTH SCIENCES LIBRARY □ New Haven, CT

Rosow, Stella M., Libn.
CARLSON COMPANIES - LIBRARY □ Minneapolis, MN

Ross, Dr. Alberta B., Supv.
UNIVERSITY OF NOTRE DAME - RADIATION LABORATORY - RADIATION CHEMISTRY DATA CENTER □ Notre Dame, IN

Ross, Alexander D., Hd.Libn.
STANFORD UNIVERSITY - ART AND ARCHITECTURE LIBRARY □ Stanford, CA

Ross, Ann K., Chf.
DISTRICT OF COLUMBIA PUBLIC LIBRARY - SOCIOLOGY, GOVERNMENT & EDUCATION DIVISION □ Washington, DC

Ross, Berinda J., Asst.Mgr., Tech.Serv.
WATER POLLUTION CONTROL FEDERATION - LIBRARY □ Washington, DC

Ross, Carol, Libn.
INGALLS MEMORIAL HOSPITAL - MEDICAL LIBRARY □ Harvey, IL

Ross, Deborah, Tech.Serv.Libn.
NEW HAMPSHIRE COLLEGE - SHAPIRO LIBRARY □ Manchester, NH

Ross, Delanie, First Asst.
MEMPHIS-SHELBY COUNTY PUBLIC LIBRARY AND INFORMATION CENTER - MEMPHIS ROOM COLLECTIONS □ Memphis, TN

Ross, Dorothy M., Pres.
AUTOMOTIVE HALL OF FAME, INC. - LIBRARY □ Midland, MI

Ross, I.C., Sys. Design Prog.Supv.
AT & T BELL LABORATORIES - LIBRARIES AND INFORMATION SYSTEMS CENTER □ Murray Hill, NJ

Ross, Ian, Hd.
NORTH YORK PUBLIC LIBRARY - CANADIANA COLLECTION □ Willowdale, ON

Ross, Jeanne
BOLT BERANEK AND NEWMAN, INC. - LIBRARY □ Cambridge, MA

Ross, Johanna, Libn.
UNIVERSITY OF CALIFORNIA, DAVIS - PHYSICAL SCIENCES LIBRARY □ Davis, CA

Ross, Joseph G., Jr., Hd., Info./Pubn.
LIBRARY OF CONGRESS - COPYRIGHT PUBLIC INFORMATION OFFICE □ Washington, DC

Ross, Laureen, ILL
UNIVERSITY OF MINNESOTA, DULUTH - HEALTH SCIENCE LIBRARY □ Duluth, MN

Ross, Leslie, Film Libn.
CANADA - NATIONAL FILM BOARD OF CANADA - FILM LIBRARY □ Saskatoon, SK

Ross, Lillian, Community Serv.Dir.
CENTRAL AGENCY FOR JEWISH EDUCATION - EDUCATIONAL RESOURCE CENTER/LIBRARY† □ Miami, FL

Ross, Margaret, Res.Spec.
UNIVERSAL CITY STUDIOS - RESEARCH DEPARTMENT LIBRARY □ Universal City, CA

Ross, Mary, Pub.Serv.Libn.
SEATTLE PUBLIC LIBRARY - DOUGLASS-TRUTH BRANCH LIBRARY □ Seattle, WA

Ross, Mary Ann, Ref.Libn.
CHICAGO BOARD OF EDUCATION - LIBRARY □ Chicago, IL

Ross, Nancy, Libn.
CANADA - NATIONAL RESEARCH COUNCIL - CISTI - CHEMISTRY BRANCH □ Ottawa, ON

Ross, Peggy, AV Libn.
HAMILTON PSYCHIATRIC HOSPITAL - LIBRARY RESOURCE CENTRE □ Hamilton, ON

Ross, Peggy, Libn.
MONTGOMERY ADVERTISER AND ALABAMA JOURNAL - LIBRARY □ Montgomery, AL

Ross, Philip, Acq.Libn.
WEST LIBERTY STATE COLLEGE - ELBIN LIBRARY □ West Liberty, WV

Ross, Phyllis M., Libn.
BANCROFT-WHITNEY COMPANY - EDITORIAL LIBRARY □ San Francisco, CA

Ross, Rhoda, V.P.
GLENGARRY GENEALOGICAL SOCIETY - HIGHLAND HERITAGE RESEARCH LIBRARY □ Lancaster, ON

Ross, Rosalinda, Online Ref.Libn.
JEFFERSON (Thomas) UNIVERSITY - SCOTT MEMORIAL LIBRARY □ Philadelphia, PA

Ross, Sidnie, Res.Libn.
CARGILL, INC. - INFORMATION CENTER □ Minneapolis, MN

Ross, Susan L., Libn.
MC LAWS & COMPANY - LIBRARY □ Calgary, AB

Ross, Susan L., Libn.
WALSH YOUNG - LIBRARY □ Calgary, AB

Ross, Tina B., Dir., Tech.Info.Serv.
GULF RESEARCH AND DEVELOPMENT COMPANY - TECHNICAL INFORMATION SERVICES† □ Pittsburgh, PA

Ross-Carter, Sheila, ILL Libn.
UNIVERSITY OF TEXAS MEDICAL BRANCH - MOODY MEDICAL LIBRARY □ Galveston, TX

Rosse, Rosanna H., Hd., Ref.Serv.
CLARKSON UNIVERSITY - EDUCATIONAL RESOURCES CENTER □ Potsdam, NY

Rosser, Helen, Libn.
BURLINGTON COUNTY TIMES - LIBRARY □ Willingboro, NJ

Rossi, Carlotta, Libn.
NEW YORK STATE METROPOLITAN TRANSPORTATION AUTHORITY - LIBRARY □ New York, NY

Rossman, Kenneth F., Dir.
U.S. NATL. ARCHIVES & RECORDS SERVICE - FEDERAL ARCHIVES AND RECORDS CENTER, REGION 9 □ Laguna Niguel, CA

Rossman, Seth, Photographer
INDIANA HISTORICAL SOCIETY - WILLIAM HENRY SMITH MEMORIAL LIBRARY □ Indianapolis, IN

Rosswurm, Richard, Supreme Court Law Libn.
WEST VIRGINIA STATE SUPREME COURT OF APPEALS - STATE LAW LIBRARY □ Charleston, WV

Rost, Grace A., Libn.
WEBER COUNTY LAW LIBRARY □ Ogden, UT

Rostad, Barbara, Res.Libn.
PILLSBURY COMPANY - BUSINESS REFERENCE LIBRARY □ Minneapolis, MN

Rostock, Margit, Libn.
GOETHE INSTITUTE ATLANTA - GERMAN CULTURAL CENTER - LIBRARY □ Atlanta, GA

Rosum, Judith T., Libn.
FINANCIAL ACCOUNTING STANDARDS BOARD (FASB) - LIBRARY □ Stamford, CT

Roten, Paul, Libn.
ASSOCIATED MENNONITE BIBLICAL SEMINARIES - MENNONITE BIBLICAL SEMINARY - LIBRARY □ Elkhart, IN

Roth, Britain G., Mgr., Lrng.Rsrcs.
GEISINGER MEDICAL CENTER - MEDICAL LIBRARY □ Danville, PA

Roth, Claire J., Lib.Dir.
MERCANTILE LIBRARY ASSOCIATION - MERCANTILE LIBRARY □ New York, NY

Roth, Dana L., Hd., Sci. & Engr.Lib.
CALIFORNIA INSTITUTE OF TECHNOLOGY - MILLIKAN LIBRARY □ Pasadena, CA

Roth, Dr. David M., Dir.
EASTERN CONNECTICUT STATE UNIVERSITY - CENTER FOR CONNECTICUT STUDIES □ Willimantic, CT

Roth, Eris, Chf., Tech.Serv.
U.S. SOCIAL SECURITY ADMINISTRATION - LIBRARY INFORMATION & GRAPHICS SERVICES BRANCH □ Baltimore, MD

Roth, Theresa, Hd., Ref.Dept.
LAW SOCIETY OF UPPER CANADA - GREAT LIBRARY □ Toronto, ON

Rothbart, Bonnie, Mgr.
METRO-GOLDWYN-MAYER, INC. - PICTURE RESEARCH LIBRARY □ Culver City, CA

Rothbart, Linda, Dir., Lib.Serv.
AMERICAN TRUCKING ASSOCIATIONS, INC. - LIBRARY □ Alexandria, VA

Rothberg, Marjorie, Govt.Doc.Libn.
DREXEL UNIVERSITY - W.W. HAGERTY LIBRARY - SPECIAL COLLECTIONS □ Philadelphia, PA

Rothe, Dorothy L., Cur.
MALDEN HISTORICAL SOCIETY - LIBRARY □ Malden, MA

Rothe, Else, Libn.
CONSULATE GENERAL OF DENMARK - DANISH INFORMATION OFFICE □ New York, NY

Rothenberg, Dianne, Assoc.Dir.
ERIC CLEARINGHOUSE ON ELEMENTARY AND EARLY CHILDHOOD EDUCATION □ Champaign, IL

Rothenberger, James, Dept.Hd.
UNIVERSITY OF CALIFORNIA, RIVERSIDE -
GOVERNMENT PUBLICATIONS DEPARTMENT -
LIBRARY □ Riverside, CA

Rothenberger, James, Dept.Hd.
UNIVERSITY OF CALIFORNIA, RIVERSIDE -
MAP SECTION - LIBRARY □ Riverside, CA

Rothman, Dee, Asst.Libn.
ALSTON & BIRD - LIBRARY □ Atlanta, GA

Rothman, Marie, Law Libn.
FEDERAL RESERVE BANK OF NEW YORK - LAW
LIBRARY DIVISION □ New York, NY

Rothschild, Sieglinde H., Libn.
NEW YORK LAW INSTITUTE - LIBRARY □ New
York, NY

Rothstein, Pauline M., Dir., Info.Serv.
RUSSELL SAGE FOUNDATION - LIBRARY □ New
York, NY

Rothwell, Dr. A., Chm., Lib.Comm.
SALVATION ARMY GRACE HOSPITAL -
MEDICAL STAFF LIBRARY† □ Calgary, AB

Rotman, Elaine C., Dir., Lib.Serv.
HOSPITAL EDUCATIONAL AND RESEARCH
FUND - LILLIAN R. HAYT MEMORIAL LIBRARY □
Albany, NY

Rotman, Laurie D., Asst.Libn.
DRAPER (Charles Stark) LABORATORY, INC. -
TECHNICAL INFORMATION CENTER □
Cambridge, MA

Rott, Richard, Libn./Sys.Anl.
CHICAGO TRIBUNE - EDITORIAL
INFORMATION CENTER □ Chicago, IL

Rotte, Marge, Mgr., Res.Info.
GREATER CINCINNATI CHAMBER OF
COMMERCE - RESEARCH LIBRARY □ Cincinnati,
OH

Rotter, Harriet, Libn.
DISTRICT OF COLUMBIA SUPERIOR COURT -
LIBRARY □ Washington, DC

Rottman, Anne, Libn.
MISSOURI STATE LEGISLATIVE LIBRARY □
Jefferson City, MO

Roudette, Michael, Archv.
WENTWORTH INSTITUTE OF TECHNOLOGY -
LIBRARY □ Boston, MA

Rouen, Edward H., Lib.Asst.
SAN DIEGO AERO-SPACE MUSEUM - N. PAUL
WHITTIER HISTORICAL AVIATION LIBRARY □
San Diego, CA

Rough, Allan C., Hd., Nonprint Media Serv.
UNIVERSITY OF MARYLAND, COLLEGE PARK -
LIBRARIES NONPRINT MEDIA SERVICES □
College Park, MD

Roughley, Jill, Dir.
BUILT ENVIRONMENT COORDINATORS
LIMITED - BEC INFORMATION SYSTEM (BIS)†
□ Toronto, ON

Roullard, June, AV Libn.
U.S. VETERANS ADMINISTRATION (ME-
Augusta) - CENTER LIBRARY □ Augusta, ME

Roullard, June C., Med.Sci.Libn.
U.S. VETERANS ADMINISTRATION (ME-Togus)
- MEDICAL & REGIONAL OFFICE CENTER □
Augusta, ME

Roulston, Patricia, Coord.
MACKENZIE (Norman) ART GALLERY -
RESOURCE CENTRE □ Regina, SK

Roumfort, Susan, Hd.
NEW JERSEY STATE LIBRARY - BUREAU OF
LAW AND REFERENCE □ Trenton, NJ

Rounds, Linn, Pub.Info.Off.
WYOMING STATE LIBRARY □ Cheyenne, WY

Roundtree, Elizabeth S., Coord., Tech.Serv.
LOUISIANA STATE LIBRARY □ Baton Rouge, LA

Roundtree, Ernestiene, Cur.
LOUISIANA STATE DEPT. OF CULTURE,
RECREATION & TOURISM - MANSFIELD STATE
COMMEMORATIVE AREA - MUSEUM & LIB. □
Mansfield, LA

Rountree, Beth M., Hd., Media Spec.
CHARLOTTE-MECKLENBURG SCHOOLS -
CURRICULUM RESEARCH CENTER □ Charlotte,
NC

Rountree, M.E., Hd.Libn.
MC NEIL LABORATORIES - LIBRARY □ Fort
Washington, PA

Rourke, Eileen Elizabeth, Res.Libn.
DEAN WITTER REYNOLDS, INC. - RESEARCH
DEPARTMENT LIBRARY □ New York, NY

Rouse, David, Bus.Info.Ctr.Hd.
CHICAGO PUBLIC LIBRARY CENTRAL LIBRARY -
BUSINESS/SCIENCE/TECHNOLOGY DIVISION
□ Chicago, IL

Rouse, Kendall, Chem.Libn.
UNIVERSITY OF WISCONSIN, MADISON -
CHEMISTRY LIBRARY □ Madison, WI

Rouse, M. Jean, Cat.
LOUISIANA STATE UNIVERSITY MEDICAL
CENTER - LIBRARY □ New Orleans, LA

Rouse, Myra J., Libn.
U.S. NAVY - NAVAL DENTAL RESEARCH
INSTITUTE - LIBRARY □ Great Lakes, IL

Roush, Dona, Assoc.Dir., El Paso
TEXAS TECH UNIVERSITY - HEALTH SCIENCES
CENTER - LIBRARY OF THE HEALTH SCIENCES
□ Lubbock, TX

Roush, Dona, Assoc.Dir.
TEXAS TECH UNIVERSITY - HEALTH SCIENCES
CENTER - REGIONAL ACADEMIC HEALTH
CENTER LIBRARY □ El Paso, TX

Rousseau, Denis, Dir.
UNIVERSITE DU QUEBEC A MONTREAL -
BIBLIOTHEQUE DES SCIENCES DE
L'EDUCATION □ Montreal, PQ

Roussin, R.W., Nuclear Engr.
OAK RIDGE NATIONAL LABORATORY -
RADIATION SHIELDING INFORMATION
CENTER □ Oak Ridge, TN

Routledge, Patricia, Act.Hd.
UNIVERSITY OF MANITOBA - ENGINEERING
LIBRARY □ Winnipeg, MB

Roux, Helen M., Dir.
NEW CASTLE PUBLIC LIBRARY -
PENNSYLVANIA HISTORY ROOM □ New Castle,
PA

Rouzie, Katherine W., Dir., Lib.Serv.
EMANUEL HOSPITAL - LIBRARY SERVICES □
Portland, OR

Rovati, A., ILL Libn.
PAN AMERICAN HEALTH ORGANIZATION -
BIBLIOGRAPHIC INFORMATION OFFICE† □
Washington, DC

Rovig, Lorraine, Libn.
IOWA STATE COMMISSION FOR THE BLIND -
LIBRARY FOR THE BLIND & PHYSICALLY
HANDICAPPED □ Des Moines, IA

Rovner, Mr. J.
PRINCETON UNIVERSITY - NEAR EAST
COLLECTIONS† □ Princeton, NJ

Row, Frances D., Info.Spec.
INTERNATIONAL PAPER COMPANY - ERLING
RIIS RESEARCH LABORATORY - INFORMATION
SERVICES □ Mobile, AL

Rowan, Marilyn G., Sr.Libn.
OAKLAND PUBLIC LIBRARY - HISTORY/
LITERATURE DIVISION □ Oakland, CA

Rowe, David G., Cat.Libn.
FEDERAL BUSINESS DEVELOPMENT BANK -
DOCUMENTATION CENTRE □ Montreal, PQ

Rowe, Dorothy B., Libn.
CENTRAL DU PAGE HOSPITAL - MEDICAL
LIBRARY □ Winfield, IL

Rowe, Gladys E., Subject Spec.
SANDIA NATIONAL LABORATORIES -
TECHNICAL LIBRARY □ Albuquerque, NM

Rowe, Glenn N., Mgr., Pub.Serv.
CHURCH OF JESUS CHRIST OF LATTER-DAY
SAINTS - HISTORICAL DEPARTMENT - CHURCH
LIBRARY-ARCHIVES □ Salt Lake City, UT

Rowe, Joyce, Info.Spec.
MARSTELLER, INC. - INFORMATION
SERVICES† □ Chicago, IL

Rowe, Kenneth E., Methodist Libn.
DREW UNIVERSITY - LIBRARY □ Madison, NJ

Rowe, Kenneth E., Libn.
UNITED METHODIST CHURCH - GENERAL
COMMISSION ON ARCHIVES AND HISTORY -
LIBRARY AND ARCHIVES □ Madison, NJ

Rowe, LaDonna L., Libn.
S-CUBED - TECHNICAL LIBRARY □ La Jolla, CA

Rowe, Linda Jo, Libn.
ST. ANTHONY'S HOSPITAL, INC. - MEDICAL
LIBRARY† □ St. Petersburg, FL

Rowe, Mason, Res.Anl.
TENNESSEE STATE COMMISSION ON AGING -
LIBRARY □ Nashville, TN

Rowe, Paola, Educ.Libn.
WELLINGTON COUNTY BOARD OF EDUCATION
- EDUCATION LIBRARY □ Guelph, ON

Rowe, W.C., Tech.Info.Prog.Engr.
GENERAL ELECTRIC COMPANY - AIRCRAFT
ENGINE GROUP - TECHNICAL INFORMATION
CENTER □ Cincinnati, OH

Rowell, Lois, Cat. & Ref.Libn.
OHIO STATE UNIVERSITY - MUSIC LIBRARY □
Columbus, OH

Rowen, Deborah F., Field Rec.Libn.
U.S. GEOLOGICAL SURVEY - DENVER LIBRARY
□ Denver, CO

Rowland, Anne, Cat.
LANCASTER THEOLOGICAL SEMINARY OF THE
UNITED CHURCH OF CHRIST - PHILIP SCHAFF
LIBRARY □ Lancaster, PA

Rowland, Barbara, Libn.
CLARK COUNTY LAW LIBRARY □ Vancouver, WA

Rowland, Professor Eileen, Chf.Libn.
JOHN JAY COLLEGE OF CRIMINAL JUSTICE OF
THE CITY UNIVERSITY OF NEW YORK -
REISMAN MEMORIAL LIBRARY □ New York, NY

Rowland, Helen M., Supv., Lib.Serv.
ASSOCIATION OF AMERICAN RAILROADS -
ECONOMICS AND FINANCE DEPARTMENT -
RAIL INFORMATION CENTER □ Washington, DC

Rowland, Shirley R., Media Supv.
BRYANT AND STRATTON BUSINESS INSTITUTE
- LIBRARY □ Buffalo, NY

Rowley, Dennis, Asst.Cur./Mss. & Archv.
BRIGHAM YOUNG UNIVERSITY - SPECIAL
COLLECTIONS □ Provo, UT

Rowley, Dennis, Sys.Supv.
SANDIA NATIONAL LABORATORIES -
TECHNICAL LIBRARY □ Albuquerque, NM

Rowley, Gordon S., Music Libn.
NORTHERN ILLINOIS UNIVERSITY - MUSIC
LIBRARY □ DeKalb, IL

Rowling, D.W., LRC Spec.
NORTHEAST WISCONSIN TECHNICAL
INSTITUTE - LEARNING RESOURCE CENTER □
Green Bay, WI

Roy, Alice R., Chf.Libn.
U.S. AIR FORCE BASE - KIRTLAND BASE
LIBRARY □ Kirtland AFB, NM

Roy, Barbara, Cat.Libn.
PRESBYTERIAN CHURCH (U.S.A.). -
PRESBYTERIAN HISTORICAL SOCIETY -
LIBRARY □ Philadelphia, PA

Roy, Sr. Bibiane, O.P., Coord.
DIOCESE OF TUCSON - REGINA CLERI
RESOURCE LIBRARY □ Tucson, AZ

Roy,, Christine, Libn.
CANADA - FISHERIES & OCEANS - LIBRARY □
Quebec City, PQ

Roy, Claudette, Hd., Automated Sys.
QUEBEC PROV. - MIN. DE L'ENERGIE ET DES
RESSOURCES - SERVICE DE DOCUMENTATION
ET DE RENSEIGNEMENTS □ Quebec, PQ

Roy, Donald E., Dir.
NEW YORK MEDICAL COLLEGE AND THE
WESTCHESTER ACADEMY OF MEDICINE -
WESTCHESTER MEDICAL CENTER LIBRARY □
Valhalla, NY

Roy, Ernest Bertrand, Responsable
QUEBEC PROVINCE - MINISTERE DES
AFFAIRES MUNICIPALES - CENTRE DE
DOCUMENTATION □ Quebec, PQ

Roy, Jean-Luc, Libn.
CENTRE D'ANIMATION, DE DEVELOPPEMENT
ET DE RECHERCHE EN EDUCATION -
BIBLIOTHEQUE □ Montreal, PQ

Roy, Jean-Pierre, Libn.
UNIVERSITE DU QUEBEC - MEDIATHEQUE† □
Ste. Foy, PQ

Roy, Lucie, Libn.
CANADIAN AMATEUR MUSICIANS-MUSICIENS
AMATEURS DU CANADA (CAMMAC) - MUSIC
LIBRARY □ Montreal, PQ

Roy, Mary, Hd.Libn.
NORTHWESTERN UNIVERSITY -
TRANSPORTATION LIBRARY □ Evanston, IL

Roy, Muriel, Dir.
UNIVERSITE DE MONCTON - CENTRE
D'ETUDES ACADIENNES □ Moncton, NB

Roy, Robert, Asst.Libn.
BRITISH COLUMBIA INSTITUTE OF
TECHNOLOGY - LIBRARY SERVICES DIVISION
□ Burnaby, BC

Royal, Linda G., Assoc.Info.Spec.
VIRGINIA ELECTRIC AND POWER COMPANY -
LIBRARY AND INFORMATION SERVICES □
Richmond, VA

Royce, Diana, Libn.
STOWE-DAY FOUNDATION - LIBRARY □
Hartford, CT

Roylance, Dale, Cur., Graphic Arts
PRINCETON UNIVERSITY - RARE BOOKS AND
SPECIAL COLLECTIONS □ Princeton, NJ

Royster, Judith, Libn.
WISCONSIN (State) DEPARTMENT OF
DEVELOPMENT - LIBRARY □ Madison, WI

Rozek, Dr. Sue
SUNY - SCHOOL OF PHARMACY - DRUG
INFORMATION SERVICE - LIBRARY □ Buffalo,
NY

Rozen, Nineta, Rd.Adv.
DISTRICT OF COLUMBIA PUBLIC LIBRARY -
HISTORY, TRAVEL AND GEOGRAPHY DIVISION
□ Washington, DC

Rozniatowski, David W., Libn.
WINNIPEG ART GALLERY - CLARA LANDER
LIBRARY □ Winnipeg, MB

Rozofsky, Marlene, Libn.
HERRICK HOSPITAL AND HEALTH CENTER -
PSYCHIATRIC LIBRARY □ Berkeley, CA

Rozsypal, Hana, Acq.
FRANKLIN INSTITUTE - LIBRARY □ Philadelphia,
PA

Rubaloff, Marijoy, Libn.
REGISTER-GUARD - LIBRARY □ Eugene, OR

Ruben, Janis M., Info.Spec.
AMERICAN STERILIZER COMPANY - LIBRARY □
Erie, PA

Rubens, Jane C., Libn.
COUDERT BROTHERS - LIBRARY □ New York,
NY

Rubens, Larry, Mgr./Photography
KENT STATE UNIVERSITY - AUDIOVISUAL
SERVICES □ Kent, OH

Rubenstein, Beverly., Ref./Cat.Libn.
UNIVERSITY OF MARYLAND, BALTIMORE -
SCHOOL OF LAW - MARSHALL LAW LIBRARY □
Baltimore, MD

Rubenstein, Natalie, Supv.Libn./Sci.Coll.
NEW YORK PUBLIC LIBRARY - MID-
MANHATTAN LIBRARY - SCIENCE/BUSINESS
DEPARTMENT □ New York, NY

Rubenstone, Jessie, Hd.Libn.
HAR ZION TEMPLE - IDA AND MATTHEW
RUDOFKER LIBRARY □ Penn Valley, PA

Rubery, Charlene, Indexer
OTTAWA CITIZEN - LIBRARY □ Ottawa, ON

Rubin, Angela, Asst.Libn.
SOUTHERN ILLINOIS UNIVERSITY,
CARBONDALE - HUMANITIES DIVISION
LIBRARY □ Carbondale, IL

Rubin, Ellen, Corp.Libn.
RELIANCE GROUP HOLDINGS, INC. -
CORPORATE LIBRARY □ New York, NY

Rubin, Judith, Libn.
CANADA - LAW REFORM COMMISSION OF
CANADA - LIBRARY □ Ottawa, ON

Rubin, Karen, Libn.
ROOSEVELT HOSPITAL - HEALTH SCIENCE
LIBRARY □ Metuchen, NJ

Rubin, Mehrnoz, Dir. of Oper.
BUSINESS COMMUNICATIONS CO., INC. -
LIBRARY □ Stamford, CT

Rubin, Dr. Samuel, Chm.
NEW ORLEANS PSYCHOANALYTIC INSTITUTE,
INC. - LIBRARY □ New Orleans, LA

Rubino, Beth, Mgr., Color Res.Dept.
FPG, INTERNATIONAL CORPORATION □ New
York, NY

Rubino, Cynthia, Libn.
WORK IN AMERICA INSTITUTE, INC. -
LIBRARY □ Scarsdale, NY

Rubinstein, Edith, Lib.Dir.
PENINSULA HOSPITAL CENTER - MEDICAL
LIBRARY □ Far Rockaway, NY

Rubinton, Phyllis, Libn.
NEW YORK HOSPITAL-CORNELL MEDICAL
CENTER - OSKAR DIETHELM HISTORICAL
LIBRARY □ New York, NY

Rubinton, Phyllis, Libn.
PAYNE WHITNEY PSYCHIATRIC CLINIC
LIBRARY □ New York, NY

Ruby, Carolyn M., Asst. Dental Libn.
UNIVERSITY OF MISSOURI, KANSAS CITY -
SCHOOL OF DENTISTRY LIBRARY □ Kansas City,
MO

Ruby, Florence V., Hosp.Libn.
SACRED HEART HOSPITAL - MEDICAL LIBRARY
□ Pensacola, FL

Rucker, Banny P., Asst.Libn.
PARSONS STATE HOSPITAL AND TRAINING
CENTER - RESEARCH LIBRARY □ Parsons, KS

Rucker, James S., Chf.Med.Libn.
ST. ANTHONY HOSPITAL - PHILIP B.
HARDYMON LIBRARY □ Columbus, OH

Rudavsky, Arnona, Judaica Libn.
HEBREW UNION COLLEGE - JEWISH
INSTITUTE OF RELIGION - KLAU LIBRARY □
Cincinnati, OH

Rudawski, Christina, Lib.Dir.
ST. ANNE'S HOSPITAL - PRESIDENTS HEALTH
SCIENCES LIBRARY □ Chicago, IL

Rudawski, Christina, Lib.Dir.
ST. ELIZABETH'S HOSPITAL - LUKEN HEALTH
SCIENCES LIBRARY □ Chicago, IL

Rudberg, Peggy, Slide Libn.
MINNEAPOLIS COLLEGE OF ART AND DESIGN -
LIBRARY AND MEDIA CENTER □ Minneapolis,
MN

Rudd, Hynda L., Archv.
LOS ANGELES CITY CLERK'S OFFICE - LOS
ANGELES CITY ARCHIVES □ Los Angeles, CA

Ruddle, R.M., Mgr., Traffic Res.
CHESSIE SYSTEM RAILROADS - TRAFFIC
RESEARCH DEPARTMENT - LIBRARY □
Baltimore, MD

Rudeen, Marly, Tech.Serv.Libn.
CATHOLIC THEOLOGICAL UNION AT CHICAGO
- LIBRARY □ Chicago, IL

Rudin, Pearly, Med.Libn.
METHODIST HOSPITAL - MEDICAL LIBRARY □
St. Louis Park, MN

Rudisell, Carol, Mss.Libn.
STANFORD UNIVERSITY - DEPARTMENT OF
SPECIAL COLLECTIONS □ Stanford, CA

Rudisill, Horace Fraser, Hist.
DARLINGTON COUNTY HISTORICAL
COMMISSION - DARLINGTON COUNTY
ARCHIVES □ Darlington, SC

Rudisill, Richard, Hist.
MUSEUM OF NEW MEXICO - PHOTOGRAPHIC
ARCHIVES □ Santa Fe, NM

Rudnicki, Christine, Coord.
SHERBURNE COUNTY SOCIAL SERVICES - THE
BORROWING CORNER, INC. □ Becker, MN

Rudolph, Sr. Catherine, O.S.F., Dir.
UNIVERSITY OF DAYTON - SCHOOL OF
EDUCATION - CURRICULUM MATERIALS
CENTER □ Dayton, OH

Rudolph, Dr. L.C., Cur. of Books
INDIANA UNIVERSITY - LILLY LIBRARY □
Bloomington, IN

Rudolph, Mary Jane, Acq.
KENNEDY-KING COLLEGE - LIBRARY† □
Chicago, IL

Rudser, Ronald J., Dir.
MINOT STATE COLLEGE - MEMORIAL LIBRARY
- SPECIAL COLLECTIONS □ Minot, ND

Rudy, Christine R., Chf., Rd.Serv.Br.
U.S. DEPT. OF THE TREASURY - INFORMATION
SERVICES DIVISION - TREASURY DEPT.
LIBRARY □ Washington, DC

Rudy, Michelle M., Tech.Libn.
U.S. INDUSTRIAL CHEMICALS COMPANY -
RESEARCH DEPARTMENT LIBRARY □ Cincinnati,
OH

Ruege, Ruth, Coord., Fine Arts
MILWAUKEE PUBLIC LIBRARY - ART, MUSIC
AND RECREATION SECTION □ Milwaukee, WI

Ruege, Ruth, Coord., Fine Arts
MILWAUKEE PUBLIC LIBRARY - WISCONSIN
ARCHITECTURAL ARCHIVE □ Milwaukee, WI

Rueger, Brenda, Rare Bk.Libn.
STANFORD UNIVERSITY - DEPARTMENT OF
SPECIAL COLLECTIONS □ Stanford, CA

Ruel, Ginette, Cat.Libn.
QUEBEC PROVINCE - MINISTERE DES
AFFAIRES SOCIALES - SERVICE DE LA
DOCUMENTATION □ Quebec, PQ

Rueth, Catherine M., Sec./Libn.
COUNTRYSIDE HOME - STAFF LIBRARY □
Jefferson, WI

Ruffier, Arthur J., Ref.
WASHINGTON STATE LAW LIBRARY □ Olympia,
WA

Ruffner, Dr. James R., Ref.Libn.
WAYNE STATE UNIVERSITY - SCIENCE
LIBRARY □ Detroit, MI

Ruffolo, Robert E., II, Pres.
PRINCETON ANTIQUES BOOKFINDERS - ART
MARKETING REFERENCE LIBRARY □ Atlantic
City, NJ

Ruge, Audrey L., Libn.
U.S. COMPTROLLER OF THE CURRENCY -
LIBRARY □ Washington, DC

Ruggere, Christine, Cur., Hist.Coll.
COLLEGE OF PHYSICIANS OF PHILADELPHIA -
LIBRARY AND MEDICAL DOCUMENTATION
SERVICE □ Philadelphia, PA

Ruggieri, G.D., Ph.D., Dir.
OSBORN LABORATORIES OF MARINE SCIENCES
- NEW YORK AQUARIUM LIBRARY □ Brooklyn,
NY

Ruggieri, M. Catherine, Rd.Serv.Libn.
MEMORIAL SLOAN-KETTERING CANCER
CENTER - LEE COOMBE MEMORIAL LIBRARY □
New York, NY

Ruggles, Sharon
AKIN, GUMP, STRAUSS, HAUER & FELD LAW
LIBRARY □ Dallas, TX

Ruhl, Darrell, Exec.Dir.
SWEDENBORG FOUNDATION - LIBRARY □ New
York, NY

Ruiz, Carlos C., Exec.Dir.
PUERTO RICAN CONGRESS OF MUSIC & ART -
LIBRARY □ Chicago, IL

Ruiz, Oralia R., Assoc.Libn.
SOUTHWEST RESEARCH INSTITUTE - THOMAS
BAKER SLICK MEMORIAL LIBRARY □ San
Antonio, TX

Ruiz, Rebecca H., Law Libn.
COCONINO COUNTY LAW LIBRARY □ Flagstaff,
AZ

Ruiz, Roxana
UNIVERSITY OF PUERTO RICO - SCHOOL OF
PUBLIC ADMINISTRATION - LIBRARY† □ Rio
Piedras, PR

Ruiz, Vicki L., Ph.D., Dir.
UNIVERSITY OF TEXAS, EL PASO - INSTITUTE
OF ORAL HISTORY □ El Paso, TX
Ruiz de Nieves, Angela M., Cat.
UNIVERSITY OF PUERTO RICO - HUMACAO
UNIVERSITY COLLEGE - LIBRARY □ Humacao,
PR
Rukuts, Velga B., Libn.
ICI AMERICAS INC. - ATLAS LIBRARY □
Wilmington, DE
Ruland, Mary, Leg.Libn.
MARYLAND STATE DEPARTMENT OF
LEGISLATIVE REFERENCE - LIBRARY □
Annapolis, MD
Rumage, Tim, Libn.
AUDUBON SOCIETY OF RHODE ISLAND - HARRY
S. HATHAWAY LIBRARY OF NATURAL HISTORY
AND CONSERVATION □ Providence, RI
Rumble, John, Oral Hist.
COUNTRY MUSIC FOUNDATION - LIBRARY AND
MEDIA CENTER □ Nashville, TN
Rumbyrt, Sandra, Asst.Libn.
TRI BROOK GROUP, INC. - LIBRARY □ Oak
Brook, IL
Rumer, Tom, Libn.
GIRLS CLUBS OF AMERICA - NATIONAL
RESOURCE CENTER □ Indianapolis, IN
Rumsey, Gary L., Dir.
U.S. FISH & WILDLIFE SERVICE - TUNISON
LABORATORY OF FISH NUTRITION - LIBRARY □
Cortland, NY
Rumsey, Nancy S., Info.Spec.
ALADDIN INDUSTRIES INC. - LIBRARY □
Nashville, TN
Runge, William H., Cur., McGregor Lib.
UNIVERSITY OF VIRGINIA - LIBRARY - RARE
BOOK DEPARTMENT □ Charlottesville, VA
Runge, William H., Cur.
UNIVERSITY OF VIRGINIA - TRACY W. MC
GREGOR LIBRARY □ Charlottesville, VA
Runis, Alice, Tech.Serv.Libn.
ILIFF SCHOOL OF THEOLOGY - IRA J. TAYLOR
LIBRARY □ Denver, CO
Runkel, Phillip M., Asst.Archv.
MARQUETTE UNIVERSITY - DEPARTMENT OF
SPECIAL COLLECTIONS AND UNIVERSITY
ARCHIVES □ Milwaukee, WI
Runyon, Cynthia G., Per.Libn.
EMORY UNIVERSITY - PITTS THEOLOGY
LIBRARY □ Atlanta, GA
Ruocco, Patti, Libn.
AT & T BELL LABORATORIES & TECHNOLOGIES
- INFORMATION RESOURCE CENTER □ Lisle, IL
Rupp, Fr. N. Daniel, Archv.
BISHOP BARAGA ASSOCIATION - ARCHIVES □
Marquette, MI
Ruppert, Ann, Ref./Ser.Libn.
POINT LOMA NAZARENE COLLEGE - RYAN
LIBRARY □ San Diego, CA
Rupprecht, Leslie P., Supv.
NEWARK PUBLIC LIBRARY - BUSINESS
LIBRARY □ Newark, NJ
Rupprecht, T.A., Supv., Lib.Serv.
ALLIED CORPORATION - BENDIX AEROSPACE
TECHNOLOGY CENTER LIBRARY □ Columbia, MD
Rups, Anna, Virginia Coll.Libn.
STYLES (Mary Riley) PUBLIC LIBRARY - LOCAL
HISTORY COLLECTION □ Falls Church, VA
Rusak, Halina, Assoc.Art Libn.
RUTGERS UNIVERSITY, THE STATE
UNIVERSITY OF NEW JERSEY - ART LIBRARY □
New Brunswick, NJ
Rusche, Linda, Libn.
MADISON PUBLIC LIBRARY - LITERATURE AND
SOCIAL SCIENCES □ Madison, WI
Ruschin, Siegfried, Libn., Coll.Dev.
LINDA HALL LIBRARY □ Kansas City, MO
Ruschival, Adam, Regional Libn.
KENTUCKY STATE DEPARTMENT FOR
LIBRARIES & ARCHIVES - KENTUCKY TALKING
BOOK LIBRARY □ Frankfort, KY

Rush, Barbara, Program Libn.
UNIVERSITY OF MARYLAND, COLLEGE PARK -
COMPUTER SCIENCE CENTER - PROGRAM
LIBRARY □ College Park, MD
Rush, David E., Assoc.Libn.
MASSACHUSETTS COLLEGE OF PHARMACY &
ALLIED HEALTH SCIENCES - SHEPPARD
LIBRARY □ Boston, MA
Rush, Dorothy C., Libn.
FILSON CLUB - LIBRARY □ Louisville, KY
Rush, John, Libn.
EMMAUS BIBLE SCHOOL - LIBRARY □ Oak Park,
IL
Rush, Martha, Assoc. Law Libn.
COLLEGE OF WILLIAM AND MARY - MARSHALL-
WYTHE LAW LIBRARY □ Williamsburg, VA
Rush, Milagros R., Hd. of Ser.
UNIVERSITY OF MINNESOTA - LAW LIBRARY □
Minneapolis, MN
Rush, Stephan, Mgr., Dept.Lib.
CANADA - REGIONAL INDUSTRIAL EXPANSION
- LIBRARY □ Ottawa, ON
Rushbrook, C. David, Libn.
JOHNSON (Bernard) INC. - TECHNICAL LIBRARY
□ Houston, TX
Rushing, Kathryn K., Ed.
AUDUBON NATURALIST SOCIETY OF THE
CENTRAL ATLANTIC STATES, INC. - LIBRARY □
Chevy Chase, MD
Rushton, David, Hd., Tech.Serv.
ALBERTA - DEPARTMENT OF EDUCATION -
LIBRARY SERVICES □ Edmonton, AB
Rusin, Harriet, Lit. Searcher
ENVIRONMENTAL PROTECTION AGENCY -
ANDREW W. BREIDENBACH ENVIRONMENTAL
RESEARCH CTR., CINCINNATI - TECH.LIB. □
Cincinnati, OH
Ruskin, Jane, Doc.Libn.
BROOKLYN PUBLIC LIBRARY - SOCIAL SCIENCE
AND PHILOSOPHY DIVISION □ Brooklyn, NY
Rusnak, Michael, Activity Chf.
U.S. DEFENSE AUDIOVISUAL AGENCY - STILL
PICTURE LIBRARY □ Washington, DC
Russ, Bonnie, Tech.Libn.
CRAWFORD AND RUSSELL, INC.-JOHN BROWN
- TECHNICAL LIBRARY □ Stamford, CT
Russ, Pamela K., Assoc.Univ.Libn.
UNIVERSITY OF FLORIDA - AGRICULTURAL
RESEARCH & EDUCATION CENTER - LAKE
ALFRED LIBRARY □ Lake Alfred, FL
Russell, Amy J., Asst.Libn.
CABOT CORPORATION - TECHNICAL
INFORMATION CENTER □ Kokomo, IN
Russell, Barbara, Cat.Libn.
SOUTHWESTERN BAPTIST THEOLOGICAL
SEMINARY - A. WEBB ROBERTS LIBRARY □ Fort
Worth, TX
Russell, Beverly, Libn.
SEATTLE TIMES - LIBRARY† □ Seattle, WA
Russell, Carol N., Law Libn.
DELAWARE STATE LAW LIBRARY IN KENT
COUNTY □ Dover, DE
Russell, Dan, Pres.
ST. JOSEPH HOSPITAL AND HEALTH CARE
CENTER - HOSPITAL LIBRARY □ Tacoma, WA
Russell, David
SOUTHERN OREGON STATE COLLEGE -
LIBRARY □ Ashland, OR
Russell, Fraser, Libn.
SASKATCHEWAN - DEPARTMENT OF LABOUR -
LIBRARY □ Regina, SK
Russell, Gay R., Libn.
MONTGOMERY TECHNICAL COLLEGE -
LEARNING RESOURCES CENTER □ Troy, NC
Russell, George Ely, Genealogist
GENEALOGICAL PERIODICALS LIBRARY □
Middletown, MD
Russell, J. Thomas, Lib.Dir.
U.S. NATL. DEFENSE UNIVERSITY - LIBRARY □
Washington, DC

Russell, Jamie B., Info.Spec.
RESEARCH INSTITUTE OF AMERICA -
INFORMATION SERVICES CENTER □ New York,
NY
Russell, Lee G., Hd.Libn.
AVCO - LYCOMING DIVISION - LIBRARY &
TECHNICAL INFORMATION CENTER □
Stratford, CT
Russell, Lockhart, Engr.Bibliog.
SYRACUSE UNIVERSITY - SCIENCE AND
TECHNOLOGY LIBRARY □ Syracuse, NY
Russell, Mattie Underwood, Cur. of Mss.
DUKE UNIVERSITY - MANUSCRIPT
DEPARTMENT □ Durham, NC
Russell, Phyllis, Libn.
MINT MUSEUM OF HISTORY - LASSITER
LIBRARY □ Charlotte, NC
Russell, R.L., Info.Spec.
PPG INDUSTRIES, INC. - CHEMICAL DIVISION
- RESEARCH LIBRARY □ Barberton, OH
Russell, Reba, Cur. of Educ.
DIXON GALLERY AND GARDENS - LIBRARY □
Memphis, TN
Russell, Ruth, Hd., Ctrl.Lib.
CONTRA COSTA COUNTY - CENTRAL LIBRARY -
LOCAL HISTORY COLLECTION □ Pleasant Hill,
CA
Russell, Susan, Hd.Libn.
UNIVERSITY OF CALIFORNIA, IRVINE -
MEDICAL CENTER LIBRARY □ Orange, CA
Russell, Susan L., Mgr.
SAN JOSE HEALTH CENTER - HEALTH SCIENCE
LIBRARY □ San Jose, CA
Russell, Vernon, Libn.
CAMPBELL, GODFREY & LEWTAS - LIBRARY □
Toronto, ON
Russell, Victor L., Archv.Mgr.
CITY OF TORONTO ARCHIVES □ Toronto, ON
Russell, Violet E., Libn.
AULTMAN HOSPITAL - SCHOOL OF NURSING
LIBRARY □ Canton, OH
Russell, Volante H., Dir.
GRACELAND COLLEGE - FREDERICK MADISON
SMITH LIBRARY □ Lamoni, IA
Russo, Barbara, Libn.
WASHINGTON STATE DEPARTMENT OF
TRANSPORTATION - LIBRARY □ Olympia, WA
Russo, Christina, Asst.Libn.
STAMFORD HOSPITAL - HEALTH SCIENCES
LIBRARY □ Stamford, CT
Russo, Edward J., Hd.
LINCOLN LIBRARY - SANGAMON VALLEY
COLLECTION □ Springfield, IL
Russo, Dr. Jean, Dir. of Res.
HISTORIC ANNAPOLIS, INC. - LIBRARY □
Annapolis, MD
Russo, Mary T., Cur., Broadsides
BROWN UNIVERSITY - SPECIAL COLLECTIONS
□ Providence, RI
Russo, RoseMary, Med.Libn.
ST. JOSEPH HOSPITAL - HEALTH SCIENCES
LIBRARY □ Flint, MI
Rusten, Eric P., Staff Assoc.
WASHINGTON UNIVERSITY - DEPARTMENT OF
TECHNOLOGY AND HUMAN AFFAIRS - LIBRARY
□ St. Louis, MO
Ruszkowski, Joan, Asst.Libn.
WATERBURY HOSPITAL HEALTH CENTER -
HEALTH CENTER LIBRARY □ Waterbury, CT
Ruth, David R., Hist.
U.S. NATL. PARK SERVICE - FORT SUMTER
NATL. MONUMENT - LIBRARY □ Sullivan's
Island, SC
Ruth, Olivia, Hd., Comp.Serv.
FULLER THEOLOGICAL SEMINARY - MC
ALISTER LIBRARY† □ Pasadena, CA
Ruthenberg, Donnell
IOWA (State) HISTORICAL DEPARTMENT
LIBRARY □ Des Moines, IA
Rutigliano, James P., Asst.Ct.Adm.
OCEAN COUNTY LAW LIBRARY† □ Toms River,
NJ

Rutledge, Aurora, Libn.
HIDALGO COUNTY LAW LIBRARY† □ Edinburg, TX

Rutledge, Patricia P., Libn.
CINCINNATI ART MUSEUM - LIBRARY □ Cincinnati, OH

Rutledge, Shirley, Libn.
DELTA WATERFOWL RESEARCH STATION - DAVID WINTON BELL MEMORIAL LIBRARY □ Portage La Prairie, MB

Rutsis, Peggy, Med.Libn.
BEECHAM, INC. - BEECHAM LABORATORIES - MEDICAL LIBRARY □ Bristol, TN

Ruttenberg, Shirley W., Info.Anl.
TRIODYNE INC. CONSULTING ENGINEERS - INFORMATION CENTER □ Niles, IL

Rutter, Deborah, Tech.Info.Mgr.
WIRE ASSOCIATION INTERNATIONAL - TECHNICAL INFORMATION CENTER □ Guilford, CT

Rutter, Kim Uden, Libn.
BARNES HOSPITAL - SCHOOL OF NURSING - LIBRARY & INSTRUCTIONAL RESOURCE LABORATORY □ St. Louis, MO

Rutter, Suzanne, Tech.Serv.Libn.
YALE UNIVERSITY - BEINECKE RARE BOOK AND MANUSCRIPT LIBRARY □ New Haven, CT

Ruus, Ms. Laine, Hd., Data Lib.
UNIVERSITY OF BRITISH COLUMBIA - DATA LIBRARY □ Vancouver, BC

Ruxin, Mrs. Olyn, Hd.Cat.Libn.
CLEVELAND HEALTH SCIENCES LIBRARY - HEALTH CENTER LIBRARY □ Cleveland, OH

Ruzicka, Aimee, State Law Libn.
ALASKA (State) COURT SYSTEM - ALASKA COURT LIBRARIES □ Anchorage, AK

Ruzicka, Aimee
ALASKA STATE COURT SYSTEM - VALDEZ LAW LIBRARY □ Valdez, AK

Ryan, Bruce G., Supv.
NEW HAMPSHIRE STATE DEPARTMENT OF EDUCATION - COMPUTER & STATISTICAL SERVICES □ Concord, NH

Ryan, Catherine, Libn.
GRACE GENERAL HOSPITAL - SCHOOL OF NURSING LIBRARY □ St. John's, NF

Ryan, Cynthia K., Hd.Libn.
ALBERTA - DEPARTMENT OF ADVANCED EDUCATION - LIBRARY □ Edmonton, AB

Ryan, David, Dir.
FORT WORTH ART MUSEUM - LIBRARY □ Fort Worth, TX

Ryan, Donald F., Tech.Supt.
ATLANTIC-RICHFIELD COMPANY - ANACONDA ALUMINUM COMPANY - COLUMBIA FALLS REDUCTION DIVISION - LIBRARY □ Columbia Falls, MT

Ryan, Elizabeth C., Asst.Libn.
FEDERAL RESERVE BANK OF CHICAGO - LIBRARY □ Chicago, IL

Ryan, James, Site Mgr.
OLANA STATE HISTORIC SITE - LIBRARY □ Hudson, NY

Ryan, Jan S., Park Techn./Libn.
U.S. NATL. PARK SERVICE - WUPATKI-SUNSET CRATER LIBRARY □ Flagstaff, AZ

Ryan, Jenny L., Libn.
LAUBACH LITERACY INTERNATIONAL, INC. - LIBRARY □ Syracuse, NY

Ryan, Mrs. Jeri A., Libn.
AMERICAN COLLEGE OF SURGEONS - LIBRARY† □ Chicago, IL

Ryan, Joan I., Med.Rec.Libn.
VICTORIA UNION HOSPITAL - MEDICAL LIBRARY □ Prince Albert, SK

Ryan, Karen J., Jr., Data Base Anl.
NORTHERN TELECOM CANADA, LTD. - BUSINESS SYSTEMS LIBRARY □ Islington, ON

Ryan, Ken, Mgr., Tech.Info.Div.
BROOKHAVEN NATIONAL LABORATORY - TECHNICAL INFORMATION DIVISION □ Upton, NY

Ryan, Margot, Libn.
CANADA - PRIVY COUNCIL OFFICE - LIBRARY □ Ottawa, ON

Ryan, Mary, Rd.Serv.Libn.
CURRY COLLEGE - LOUIS R. LEVIN MEMORIAL LIBRARY - SPECIAL COLLECTIONS† □ Milton, MA

Ryan, Mary, Coord., Tech.Serv.
UNIVERSITY OF ARKANSAS FOR MEDICAL SCIENCES - MEDICAL SCIENCES LIBRARY □ Little Rock, AR

Ryan, Michael, Chf.
STANFORD UNIVERSITY - DEPARTMENT OF SPECIAL COLLECTIONS □ Stanford, CA

Ryan, Pat, Libn.
SKAGIT COUNTY LAW LIBRARY □ Mount Vernon, WA

Ryan, Patricia, Hd., Lib.Cons.Serv.
MASSACHUSETTS GENERAL HOSPITAL - MGH HEALTH SCIENCES LIBRARIES □ Boston, MA

Ryan, Richard W., Cur. of Bks.
UNIVERSITY OF MICHIGAN - WILLIAM L. CLEMENTS LIBRARY □ Ann Arbor, MI

Ryan, Rosemary, Mgr.
CHILD CUSTODY EVALUATION SERVICES, INC. - RESOURCE CENTER □ Glenside, PA

Ryan, William V., Dir., Lib.Serv.
BLOOMSBURG UNIVERSITY OF PENNSYLVANIA - HARVEY A. ANDRUSS LIBRARY - SPECIAL COLLECTIONS □ Bloomsburg, PA

Ryan-McIntyre, Colleen, Libn.
LOWENSTEIN (M.) CORPORATION - DESIGN RESEARCH LIBRARY □ New York, NY

Ryans, Kathryn, Supv., Info.Serv.
IMPERIAL OIL, LTD. - BUSINESS INFORMATION CENTRE □ Toronto, ON

Ryant, Carl G., Co-Dir.
UNIVERSITY OF LOUISVILLE - UNIVERSITY ARCHIVES AND RECORDS CENTER - ORAL HISTORY CENTER □ Louisville, KY

Rybicki,, Catherine S., Lib.Spec.
SAVIN CORPORATION - ENGINEERING AND MANUFACTURING DIVISION - SAVIN TECHNICAL INFORMATION CENTER □ Binghamton, NY

Rycroft, Barbara, Sr.Libn.
FAIRVIEW STATE HOSPITAL - STAFF LIBRARY □ Costa Mesa, CA

Ryd, E., Ref.Libn.
AT & T - CORPORATE RESEARCH CENTER □ New York, NY

Ryden, John, Libn.
LEGAL ASSISTANCE FOUNDATION OF CHICAGO - LIBRARY □ Chicago, IL

Ryder, Carolyn
UNIVERSITY OF CALGARY - ARTS AND HUMANITIES LIBRARY† □ Calgary, AB

Ryder, Carolyn
UNIVERSITY OF CALGARY - SPECIAL COLLECTIONS DIVISION† □ Calgary, AB

Ryder, Herboth S., Judge
FLORIDA STATE COURT OF APPEAL - 2ND DISTRICT - LAW LIBRARY □ Lakeland, FL

Ryder, Richard D., Cur.
TACKAPAUSHA MUSEUM - LIBRARY □ Seaford, NY

Ryder, Suzanne M., Dir.
U.S. NAVY - NAVAL AIR TEST CENTER - NAVAL AIR STATION - PATUXENT RIVER CENTRAL LIBRARY □ Patuxent River, MD

Rydesky, Mary, Hd., LRC
UNIVERSITY OF TEXAS HEALTH SCIENCE CENTER, DALLAS - LIBRARY □ Dallas, TX

Rykoskey, Mary S., Libn.
CUMBERLAND COUNTY LAW LIBRARY† □ Carlisle, PA

Rylance, Dan, Coord. of Spec.Coll.
UNIVERSITY OF NORTH DAKOTA - DEPARTMENT OF SPECIAL COLLECTIONS □ Grand Forks, ND

Rynders, Kathryn, Ref.Libn.
UNIVERSITY OF MINNESOTA TECHNICAL COLLEGE, WASECA - LEARNING RESOURCES □ Waseca, MN

Rynning, Cynthia Lowe, Hd. Law Libn.
FRIEDMAN & KOVEN - LAW LIBRARY □ Chicago, IL

Ryoo, Heija B., Acq./Ser.Libn.
SOUTHERN ILLINOIS UNIVERSITY, CARBONDALE - SCHOOL OF LAW LIBRARY □ Carbondale, IL

Ryskamp, Charles A., Dir.
PIERPONT MORGAN LIBRARY □ New York, NY

Ryweck, Morton W., Dir.
JEWISH COMMUNITY RELATIONS COUNCIL - ANTI-DEFAMATION LEAGUE OF MINNESOTA-DAKOTAS - LIBRARY □ Minneapolis, MN

Rzeczkowski, E. Matthew, O.P., Asst.Libn.
DOMINICAN COLLEGE LIBRARY □ Washington, DC

Rzeczkowski, Matthew, O.P., Theology Libn.
PONTIFICAL COLLEGE JOSEPHINUM - A.T. WEHRLE MEMORIAL LIBRARY □ Columbus, OH

Rzepecki, Arnold M., Libn.
SACRED HEART SEMINARY - WARD MEMORIAL LIBRARY □ Detroit, MI

S

Saar, Amanda, Circ.Libn.
UNIVERSITY OF ARKANSAS FOR MEDICAL SCIENCES - MEDICAL SCIENCES LIBRARY □ Little Rock, AR

Saari, David S., Info.Sci.
MILES LABORATORIES, INC. - LIBRARY RESOURCES AND SERVICES □ Elkhart, IN

Sabbag, Connie, Libn.
MEDFIELD HISTORICAL SOCIETY - LIBRARY □ Medfield, MA

Sabella, Marion, Libn.
RHODE ISLAND MEDICAL SOCIETY - LIBRARY □ Providence, RI

Sabin, Christine A., Libn.
CONVALESCENT HOSPITAL FOR CHILDREN - LIBRARY □ Rochester, NY

Sable, Barbara, Asst.Libn.
U.S. DEFENSE LOGISTICS AGENCY - HEADQUARTERS LIBRARY □ Alexandria, VA

Sable, Rev. Thomas F., S.J., Dir.
JOHN XXIII ECUMENICAL CENTER, INC. - CENTER FOR EASTERN CHRISTIAN STUDIES □ Bronx, NY

Sabo, Eleanor A., Legal Libn.
PENNEY (J.C.) COMPANY, INC. - LAW LIBRARY □ New York, NY

Saboe, Michael S., Dir.
INFORMATION/DOCUMENTATION □ Washington, DC

Sabonjian, Aznive, Libn.
AMERICAN HOECHST CORPORATION - BEHRING DIAGNOSTICS - LIBRARY □ La Jolla, CA

Sabourin, Conrad, Delegate
CANADIAN BROADCASTING CORPORATION - MUSIC SERVICES LIBRARY □ Montreal, PQ

Sabowitz, N.C., Systems Libn.
BEDFORD INSTITUTE OF OCEANOGRAPHY - LIBRARY □ Dartmouth, NS

Sachs, Iris, Med.Libn.
WEISS (Louis A.) MEMORIAL HOSPITAL - L. LEWIS COHEN MEMORIAL MEDICAL LIBRARY □ Chicago, IL

Sachse, Renate, Cat.Libn.
FRANKLIN AND MARSHALL COLLEGE - SHADEK-FACKENTHAL LIBRARY - SPECIAL COLLECTIONS □ Lancaster, PA

Sacks, Patricia Ann, Dir. of Libs.
MUHLENBERG COLLEGE - JOHN A.W. HAAS LIBRARY □ Allentown, PA

Saddington, Neil, Lib.Asst.
SAN DIEGO AERO-SPACE MUSEUM - N. PAUL WHITTIER HISTORICAL AVIATION LIBRARY □ San Diego, CA

Sadecki, Win, Corp.Libn.
HOUSEHOLD INTERNATIONAL - CORPORATE LIBRARY □ Prospect Heights, IL

Sadler, Catherine E., Libn.
CHARLESTON LIBRARY SOCIETY □ Charleston, SC

Sadler, Cynthia, Hd.Libn.
TEXAS STATE TECHNICAL INSTITUTE, MID-CONTINENT CAMPUS - LIBRARY □ Amarillo, TX

Sadler, Rowena S., Chf., Lib.Info. & Br.
U.S. SOCIAL SECURITY ADMINISTRATION - LIBRARY INFORMATION & GRAPHICS SERVICES BRANCH □ Baltimore, MD

Sadowski, Edmund R., Libn.
MASONIC HISTORICAL LIBRARY COLLECTION □ Elmwood Park, IL

Sadwith, Lucille, Dir.
CENTER FOR FARM AND FOOD RESEARCH, INC. - LIBRARY □ Falls Village, CT

Saeed, Mr. Munawwar, Mgr.
AHMADIYYA MOVEMENT IN ISLAM - MUSLIM LIBRARY □ Washington, DC

Saenger, Walt, Chf., Visitor Serv.
U.S. NATL. PARK SERVICE - FLORISSANT FOSSIL BEDS NATIONAL MONUMENT - LIBRARY □ Florissant, CO

Saffer, Melinda, Lib.Dir.
WORCESTER FOUNDATION FOR EXPERIMENTAL BIOLOGY - GEORGE F. FULLER LIBRARY □ Shrewsbury, MA

Safley, Ann, Libn.
CARNEGIE LIBRARY OF PITTSBURGH - MUSIC AND ART DEPARTMENT □ Pittsburgh, PA

Sagar, Mary, Libn.
KALSEC, INC. - LIBRARY □ Kalamazoo, MI

Sager, Cindy, Lib.Assoc.
ALLEGHENY GENERAL HOSPITAL - HEALTH SCIENCES LIBRARY □ Pittsburgh, PA

Sager, Roberta K., Supv.
KRUPP WILPUTTE CORPORATION - LIBRARY† □ Murray Hill, NJ

Saggar, Dev, Adm./Economist
CINCINNATI CITY PLANNING COMMISSION - OFFICE OF PLANNING AND MANAGEMENT SUPPORT - LIBRARY □ Cincinnati, OH

Sahak, Judy Harvey, Libn.
THE CLAREMONT COLLEGES - ELLA STRONG DENISON LIBRARY □ Claremont, CA

Sahak, Judy Harvey, Asst.Dir.
THE CLAREMONT COLLEGES - LIBRARY □ Claremont, CA

Sahlem, James R., Principal Law Libn.
NEW YORK STATE SUPREME COURT - 8TH JUDICIAL DISTRICT - LAW LIBRARY† □ Buffalo, NY

Sahu, Mrs. Krishna, Dir.
UNIVERSITY OF OSTEOPATHIC MEDICINE AND HEALTH SCIENCES - LIBRARY† □ Des Moines, IA

Sahyoun, Naim K., Dir. of Libs.
PONTIAC GENERAL HOSPITAL - LIBRARY† □ Pontiac, MI

Saiet, Ronald, Assoc.Dir., Lrng.Serv.
NORTHEASTERN ILLINOIS UNIVERSITY - LIBRARY □ Chicago, IL

Saint, Barbara J., Hd.
UNIVERSITY OF BRITISH COLUMBIA - ST. PAUL'S HOSPITAL HEALTH SCIENCES LIBRARY □ Vancouver, BC

St. Amand, Sylvia, Mus.Libn.
SPRINGFIELD CITY LIBRARY - FINE ARTS DEPARTMENT □ Springfield, MA

St.Clair, Albert W., Law Libn.
WYOMING STATE LAW LIBRARY □ Cheyenne, WY

St. Clair, Craig, Asst.Archv.
ATLANTIC RICHFIELD COMPANY - CORPORATE ARCHIVES □ Los Angeles, CA

St.Clair, Geneva, Acq. Lead
BOEING COMPANY - SEATTLE SERVICES DIVISION - TECHNICAL LIBRARIES† □ Seattle, WA

St. Clair, Guy, Dir.
UNIVERSITY CLUB LIBRARY □ New York, NY

St. Clair, Helen, Med.Libn.
WILMINGTON MEDICAL CENTER (Delaware Division) - MEDICAL STAFF LIBRARY □ Wilmington, DE

St. Clair, Jeffrey W., Med.Libn.
ST. MARY'S HOSPITAL & HEALTH CENTER - RALPH FULLER MEDICAL LIBRARY □ Tucson, AZ

St-Jacques, Suzanne, Hd., Ref.Serv.
UNIVERSITY OF OTTAWA - MORISSET LIBRARY □ Ottawa, ON

St. John, Esther L., Hd.Libn.
FIRST BAPTIST CHURCH - LIBRARY □ North Kansas City, MO

St. John, Louise, Base Libn.
U.S. AIR FORCE BASE - BERGSTROM BASE LIBRARY □ Bergstrom AFB, TX

St-Laurent, Lysanne, Lib.Techn.
CANADIAN BROADCASTING CORPORATION - ENGINEERING HEADQUARTERS LIBRARY □ Montreal, PQ

St. Leger, John B., Coord.
CENTRAL VIRGINIA COMMUNITY COLLEGE - LIBRARY - SPECIAL COLLECTIONS □ Lynchburg, VA

St. Onge, Merle, Ck. Stenographer II
PSYCHIATRIC CENTRE - STAFF LIBRARY □ Weyburn, SK

St-Pierre, Line, Libn.
TA ASSOCIATES - INFORMATION CENTER □ Montreal, PQ

St-Pierre, Nelson, Libn., Coll.Dev.
QUEBEC PROVINCE - MINISTERE DES COMMUNICATIONS - BIBLIOTHEQUE ADMINISTRATIVE □ Quebec, PQ

St. Pierre, Normand, Dir.
CANADA - PUBLIC ARCHIVES OF CANADA - LIBRARY □ Ottawa, ON

Saintcross, Eva M., Stat.Libn.
MARINE MIDLAND BANK - TECHNICAL INFORMATION CENTER □ Buffalo, NY

Saito, Masaei, Asst.Hd.
UNIVERSITY OF MICHIGAN - ASIA LIBRARY □ Ann Arbor, MI

Sakamoto, Louise Y., Libn.
PUREX CORPORATION - TECHNICAL LIBRARY □ Carson, CA

Sakoian, Mary Ann, Libn.
BITUMINOUS COAL RESEARCH, INC. - LIBRARY† □ Monroeville, PA

Sakon, Marie, Hd., Rd.Serv.
SASKATCHEWAN - PROVINCIAL LIBRARY □ Regina, SK

Salabiye, Velma S., Libn.
UNIVERSITY OF CALIFORNIA, LOS ANGELES - AMERICAN INDIAN STUDIES CENTER - LIBRARY □ Los Angeles, CA

Salam, Abdus, Hd.
METROPOLITAN TORONTO LIBRARY - SOCIAL SCIENCES DEPARTMENT □ Toronto, ON

Salaman, David J., Libn.
BETH SHOLOM CONGREGATION - JOSEPH & ELIZABETH SCHWARTZ LIBRARY □ Elkins Park, PA

Salandy, Mrs. Pat, Libn.
EBERSTADT (F.) AND COMPANY - BUSINESS LIBRARY □ New York, NY

Salazar, Viola, Asst.Supv., Main Lib.
UNIVERSITY OF CALIFORNIA - LOS ALAMOS NATIONAL LABORATORY - LIBRARY □ Los Alamos, NM

Salber, Peter, Asst.Lib.Dir.
NEWSWEEK, INC. - LIBRARY □ New York, NY

Salchert, Patricia, Acq.
U.S. MARINE CORPS - EDUCATION CENTER - JAMES CARSON BRECKINRIDGE LIBRARY & AMPHIBIOUS WARFARE RESEARCH FACILITY □ Quantico, VA

Saldinger, J.P., Libn.
EXXON RESEARCH AND ENGINEERING COMPANY - FLORHAM PARK INFORMATION CENTER† □ Florham Park, NJ

Sale, E.T., Exec.Dir.
WINNIPEG SOCIAL PLANNING COUNCIL - LIBRARY □ Winnipeg, MB

Salem, Zoe, Bus.Ref.Libn.
FORDHAM UNIVERSITY - LIBRARY AT LINCOLN CENTER □ New York, NY

Sales, Patricia, Res.Libn.
VENTURA COUNTY HISTORICAL SOCIETY - LIBRARY & ARCHIVES □ Ventura, CA

Saletta, Gerry, Libn.
U.S. COURT OF APPEALS, 3RD CIRCUIT - BRANCH LIBRARY □ Newark, NJ

Saley, Stacey, Chf.Med.Libn.
MOUNT SINAI HOSPITAL SERVICES - CITY HOSPITAL CENTER AT ELMHURST - MEDICAL LIBRARY □ Elmhurst, NY

Salgat, Anne-Marie, Dir. of Lib.Serv.
LANCASTER THEOLOGICAL SEMINARY OF THE UNITED CHURCH OF CHRIST - PHILIP SCHAFF LIBRARY □ Lancaster, PA

Salisbury, Susan, Staff Libn.
UNIVERSITY OF CALIFORNIA, BERKELEY - INST. OF INDUSTRIAL RELATIONS - LABOR OCCUPATIONAL HEALTH PROGRAM LIB. □ Berkeley, CA

Sall, Judy, Asst.Ref.Ed.
DALLAS MORNING NEWS - REFERENCE DEPARTMENT □ Dallas, TX

Sallwasser, Carrie L., Libn.
MERCANTILE TRUST COMPANY - INTERNATIONAL LIBRARY □ St. Louis, MO

Sally, Dana M., Math/Physics Libn.
UNIVERSITY OF NORTH CAROLINA, CHAPEL HILL - ALFRED T. BRAVER LIBRARY □ Chapel Hill, NC

Salmon, Lois, Coord., Main Lib.
NOVA - CORPORATE LIBRARY □ Calgary, AB

Salmon, R.R., Archv.
BROOKGREEN GARDENS - LIBRARY □ Murrells Inlet, SC

Salmond, Jasper, Info.Dir.
WILBUR SMITH AND ASSOCIATES - LIBRARY □ Columbia, SC

Salo, Anna B.
MANCHESTER MEMORIAL HOSPITAL - LIBRARY† □ Manchester, CT

Salo, Annette, Supv.
ST. PAUL PUBLIC LIBRARY - FILM & VIDEO CENTER □ St. Paul, MN

Salo, L.E., Engr.Libn.
GENERAL DYNAMICS CORPORATION - POMONA DIVISION - DIVISION LIBRARY MZ 4-20 □ Pomona, CA

Salome, Sr., Libn.
ST. JOSEPH'S HOSPITAL AND HEALTH CENTER - MEDICAL LIBRARY □ Dickinson, ND

Salomon, Alice, Info.Spec.
U.S. BUREAU OF THE CENSUS - INFORMATION SERVICES PROGRAM - SEATTLE REGIONAL OFFICE - LIBRARY □ Seattle, WA

Salonen, Ethel M., Hd.
ARTHUR D. LITTLE, INC. - RESEARCH LIBRARY □ Cambridge, MA

Salopek, Dianne, Libn.
CENTER FOR GOVERNMENTAL RESEARCH, INC. - LIBRARY □ Rochester, NY

Salovaara, Mary K., Hd., Spec.Proj.
NORTHWESTERN UNIVERSITY - LAW SCHOOL LIBRARY □ Chicago, IL

Salscheider, Rosemary, Supv.
MACALESTER COLLEGE - OLIN SCIENCE LIBRARY □ St. Paul, MN

Salt, David, Engr. & Sci.Libn.
UNIVERSITY OF SASKATCHEWAN - ENGINEERING BRANCH LIBRARY □ Saskatoon, SK

Saltalamachia, Joyce D., Lib.Dir.
NEW YORK LAW SCHOOL - LIBRARY □ New York, NY

Salter, Billie I., Libn. for Social Sci.
YALE UNIVERSITY - ECONOMIC GROWTH
CENTER COLLECTION □ New Haven, CT

Salter, Billie I., Libn. for Social Sci.
YALE UNIVERSITY - SOCIAL SCIENCE LIBRARY
□ New Haven, CT

Salter, Glen, Med.Libn.
MADISON GENERAL HOSPITAL - MEDICAL
LIBRARY □ Madison, WI

Saltzman, Jane E., Dir.
ST. MARY'S MEDICAL CENTER - HERMAN M.
BAKER, M.D. MEMORIAL LIBRARY □ Evansville,
IN

Saltzman, Robbin, Libn.
SPERTUS COLLEGE OF JUDAICA - NORMAN AND
HELEN ASHER LIBRARY □ Chicago, IL

Salumbides, Juliana C., Med.Libn.
GUAM MEMORIAL HOSPITAL AUTHORITY -
MEDICAL LIBRARY □ Tamuning, GU

Salvail, Marthe Dumont, Hd.Libn.
CORPORATION PROFESSIONNELLE DES
MEDECINS DU QUEBEC - INFORMATHEQUE □
Montreal, PQ

Salyers, Connie, Libn.
URBANA COLLEGE - SWEDENBORG MEMORIAL
LIBRARY - SPECIAL COLLECTIONS □ Urbana, OH

Salzman, Edie, Libn.
NORTH SUBURBAN SYNAGOGUE BETH EL -
MAXWELL ABBELL LIBRARY □ Highland Park, IL

Samard, Emiko, Ref.Libn.
UNIVERSITY OF CALIFORNIA, IRVINE -
MEDICAL CENTER LIBRARY □ Orange, CA

Samazan, Paula C., Sr.Lib.Asst.
CALIFORNIA INSTITUTE OF TECHNOLOGY -
APPLIED PHYSICS/ELECTRICAL ENGINEERING
LIBRARY □ Pasadena, CA

Samb, LaVerne, Libn.
LA CROSSE LUTHERAN HOSPITAL - HEALTH
SCIENCES LIBRARY □ La Crosse, WI

Samek, Lois J., Med.Libn.
INDEPENDENCE MENTAL HEALTH INSTITUTE -
MEDICAL LIBRARY □ Independence, IA

Samer, Marcia G., Info.Sci.
NORWICH EATON PHARMACEUTICALS, INC. -
RESEARCH AND DEVELOPMENT LIBRARY □
Norwich, NY

Samet, Janet, Per.Libn.
NEW JERSEY INSTITUTE OF TECHNOLOGY -
ROBERT W. VAN HOUTEN LIBRARY □ Newark,
NJ

Sameth, Marian, Assoc.Dir.
CITIZENS HOUSING AND PLANNING COUNCIL
OF NEW YORK - LIBRARY □ New York, NY

Sammarco, Anthony Mitchell, Vice Pres.
DORCHESTER HISTORICAL SOCIETY -
ROBINSON-LEHANE LIBRARY □ Dorchester, MA

Sammis, Stuart, Archv.
UNIVERSITY OF MEDICINE AND DENTISTRY OF
NEW JERSEY AT NEWARK - GEORGE F. SMITH
LIBRARY □ Newark, NJ

Sammon, Christine E., Libn.
SOUTHERN ALBERTA INSTITUTE OF
TECHNOLOGY - LEARNING RESOURCES CENTRE
- ALBERTA COLLEGE OF ART BRANCH □ Calgary,
AB

Sammons, Christa, Cur./German Coll.
YALE UNIVERSITY - BEINECKE RARE BOOK
AND MANUSCRIPT LIBRARY □ New Haven, CT

Samms, Margaret, Info.Ctr.Mgr.
SASKATCHEWAN RESEARCH COUNCIL -
INFORMATION CENTRE □ Saskatoon, SK

Samora, Joseph, Archv. I
CALIFORNIA - STATE ARCHIVES □ Sacramento,
CA

Samowitz, Arlene, Libn.
NATIONAL COUNCIL OF SAVINGS
INSTITUTIONS - LIBRARY □ Washington, DC

Sample, C.A., Ref.Spec.
BATTELLE-NORTHWEST - PACIFIC
NORTHWEST LABORATORY - HANFORD
TECHNICAL LIBRARY □ Richland, WA

Sample, Elizabeth, AV Serv.Libn.
CREIGHTON UNIVERSITY - HEALTH SCIENCES
LIBRARY □ Omaha, NE

Sample, Rick A., Hd.Libn.
AMERICAN PSYCHOLOGICAL ASSOCIATION -
ARTHUR W. MELTON LIBRARY □ Arlington, VA

Sampson, Dee, Chf., Rd.Serv.
U.S. DEPT. OF JUSTICE - MAIN LIBRARY □
Washington, DC

Sampson, Kathleen M., Libn.
AMERICAN JUDICATURE SOCIETY - RESEARCH
LIBRARY □ Chicago, IL

Sams, Cheryl, Lib.Supv.
MONCTON HOSPITAL - HEALTH SCIENCES
LIBRARY □ Moncton, NB

Samson, Gary, Filmmaker
UNIVERSITY OF NEW HAMPSHIRE -
DEPARTMENT OF MEDIA SERVICES - FILM
LIBRARY □ Durham, NH

Samson, Lucila R., Med.Libn.
YONKERS GENERAL HOSPITAL - MEDICAL
LIBRARY □ Yonkers, NY

Samuda, Madeleine, Ref.
COLLEGE UNIVERSITAIRE DE ST. BONIFACE -
BIBLIOTHEQUE ALFRED-MONNIN □ Saint-
Boniface, MB

Samuel, Evelyn, Hd.Libn.
NEW YORK UNIVERSITY - STEPHEN CHAN
LIBRARY OF FINE ARTS† □ New York, NY

Samuel, Harold E., Libn.
YALE UNIVERSITY - JOHN HERRICK JACKSON
MUSIC LIBRARY □ New Haven, CT

Samuel, Parkash, Chm., Lib.Comm.
NATIONAL PRESBYTERIAN CHURCH - WILLIAM
S. CULBERTSON LIBRARY □ Washington, DC

Samuel, Roma P., Libn.
NATIONAL PRESBYTERIAN CHURCH - WILLIAM
S. CULBERTSON LIBRARY □ Washington, DC

Samuels, Joel L., Adm.V.P., Dp.Libn.
NEWBERRY LIBRARY □ Chicago, IL

Samuels, Lois A., Libn.
NABISCO BRANDS, INC. - TECHNICAL
INFORMATION CENTER □ Wilton, CT

Samuels, Marion J., Libn.
MICHIE COMPANY - LIBRARY □ Charlottesville,
VA

Samuels, William M., Exec.Dir.
NATIONAL SOCIETY FOR MEDICAL RESEARCH -
NSMR DATA BANK □ Washington, DC

Samuelson, Beth, Co-Libn.
OXFORD UNITED METHODIST CHURCH -
OSCAR G. COOK MEMORIAL LIBRARY □ Oxford,
MA

Samuelson, Eileen L., Dir.
GRATZ COLLEGE - ELSIE AND WILLIAM
CHOMSKY EDUCATIONAL RESOURCE CENTER
(CERC) □ Philadelphia, PA

Samuelson, Rick, Res.Info.Sci.
GENERAL MILLS, INC. - JAMES FORD BELL
TECHNICAL CENTER - TECHNICAL
INFORMATION SERVICES □ Minneapolis, MN

San Pedro, Jose, Libn. 1
METROPOLITAN TORONTO LIBRARY -
LANGUAGES DEPARTMENT □ Toronto, ON

Sanborn, George, Ref.Libn.
MASSACHUSETTS STATE TRANSPORTATION
LIBRARY □ Boston, MA

Sanborn, Helen W., Supv., Info.Serv.
CONSOLIDATED PAPERS, INC. - RESEARCH
AND DEVELOPMENT LIBRARY □ Wisconsin
Rapids, WI

Sanborn, Richard, Libn.
CALIFORNIA SCHOOL OF PROFESSIONAL
PSYCHOLOGY - SAN DIEGO LIBRARY □ San
Diego, CA

Sanchez, Hector Ruben, Lib.Dir.
EVANGELICAL SEMINARY OF PUERTO RICO -
JUAN DE VALDES LIBRARY □ Hato Rey, PR

Sanchez, Margarita M., Doc.Libn.
UNIVERSITY OF PUERTO RICO - MAYAGUEZ
CAMPUS LIBRARY - SPECIAL COLLECTIONS □
Mayaguez, PR

Sanchez, Mary Gusse, Libn.
WISCONSIN STATE DEPARTMENT OF HEALTH
& SOCIAL SERVICES - LIBRARY □ Madison, WI

Sand, Nanette O., Libn.
UNIVERSITY OF CALIFORNIA, BERKELEY -
INSTITUTE OF INDUSTRIAL RELATIONS
LIBRARY □ Berkeley, CA

Sand-Steinhouse, Janet, Libn.
VILLE MARIE SOCIAL SERVICE CENTRE -
LIBRARY □ Montreal, PQ

Sandberg, Wanda H., Libn.
WORCESTER COUNTY HORTICULTURAL
SOCIETY - LIBRARY □ Worcester, MA

Sande, Betty, Lib.Spec.Proj.Coord.
MAYO FOUNDATION - MAYO CLINIC LIBRARY □
Rochester, MN

Sandefur, Kristin, Asst.Libn.
FORT WORTH STAR-TELEGRAM - LIBRARY □
Fort Worth, TX

Sandel, Jean, Libn.
DEUTSCH, KERRIGAN AND STILES - LAW
LIBRARY □ New Orleans, LA

Sanden, Michael, Dir.
OKLAHOMA ART CENTER - LIBRARY □ Oklahoma
City, OK

Sanderford, Marianna, Mgr.
MOTOROLA, INC. - COMMUNICATIONS SECTOR
LIBRARY □ Schaumburg, IL

Sanderlin, Otha, Libn.
PORTSMOUTH BAR AND LAW LIBRARY† □
Portsmouth, OH

Sanders, Aimee Devine, Lib.Cons.
HISTORICAL SOCIETY OF BERKS COUNTY -
LIBRARY □ Reading, PA

Sanders, Arthur H., Cur.
MUSICAL MUSEUM - RESEARCH LIBRARY □
Deansboro, NY

Sanders, Don
UNIVERSITY OF CALGARY - LAW LIBRARY† □
Calgary, AB

Sanders, Eleanor, Cat.
UNIVERSITY OF HEALTH SCIENCES - LIBRARY
□ Kansas City, MO

Sanders, Elizabeth, Res.
EVANGELICAL AND REFORMED HISTORICAL
SOCIETY - LANCASTER CENTRAL ARCHIVES
AND LIBRARY □ Lancaster, PA

Sanders, James L., Asst.Ed.
SOIL CONSERVATION SOCIETY OF AMERICA -
H. WAYNE PRITCHARD LIBRARY □ Ankeny, IA

Sanders, James R., Dir.
TEXAS STATE LEGISLATIVE REFERENCE
LIBRARY □ Austin, TX

Sanders, Jean E., Assoc.Dir.
MERRIMACK EDUCATION CENTER □
Chelmsford, MA

Sanders, John, Libn.
OAK HILLS BIBLE INSTITUTE - LIBRARY □
Bemidji, MN

Sanders, Renee, Libn.
JOHNSON & HIGGINS - EBP RESEARCH
LIBRARY† □ New York, NY

Sanders, Samuel, Jr., Dir.
DETROIT JAZZ CENTER - JAZZ ARCHIVE □
Detroit, MI

Sanders, Steven M., Hd., Instr.Rsrcs.
UNIVERSITY OF VIRGINIA - MEDICAL CENTER
- CLAUDE MOORE HEALTH SCIENCES LIBRARY
□ Charlottesville, VA

Sanders, William, Exhibits & Arts Libn.
WESTERN ILLINOIS UNIVERSITY - LIBRARIES
□ Macomb, IL

Sanderson, D., Cat.
CANADA - ATMOSPHERIC ENVIRONMENT
SERVICE - LIBRARY □ Downsview, ON

Sanderson, Harlan, AV Libn.
LUTHER COLLEGE - PREUS LIBRARY □ Decorah,
IA

Sanderson, Sandra, Law Libn.
OWENS-CORNING FIBERGLAS CORPORATION -
LAW DEPARTMENT LIBRARY □ Toledo, OH

Sanderson, William, Non-Print
UNIVERSITY OF UTAH - LAW LIBRARY □ Salt Lake City, UT

Sandford, G. Diane, Hd.Libn.
FRIED FRANK HARRIS SHRIVER & KAMPELMAN - LIBRARY □ Washington, DC

Sandine, Margaret, Tech.Serv.
SOUTH DAKOTA SCHOOL OF MINES & TECHNOLOGY - DEVEREAUX LIBRARY □ Rapid City, SD

Sandler, Bella, Libn.
CHICAGO SINAI CONGREGATION - EMIL G. HIRSCH LIBRARY □ Chicago, IL

Sandler, Claire, AV
UNIVERSITY OF MICHIGAN - SCHOOL OF EDUCATION & SCHOOL OF LIB. SCI. - INSTR. STRATEGY SERV. □ Ann Arbor, MI

Sandlin, Karen, Cat.Supv.
ACADEMY OF NATURAL SCIENCES - LIBRARY □ Philadelphia, PA

Sandor, Ruth, Libn.
UNIVERSITY OF WISCONSIN, MADISON - CENTER FOR DEMOGRAPHY - LIBRARY □ Madison, WI

Sandoval, Juan A., Hd. Chicano Serv.
UNIVERSITY OF TEXAS, EL PASO - LIBRARY - SPECIAL COLLECTIONS □ El Paso, TX

Sandoval, Penny Ann, Photo Libn.
MARYKNOLL FATHERS - PHOTO LIBRARY □ Maryknoll, NY

Sands, Dorothy, Libn.
TYMSHARE, INC. - TECHNICAL LIBRARY □ Cupertino, CA

Sands, Margaret, Circ.Libn.
SUNY - AGRICULTURAL AND TECHNICAL COLLEGE AT ALFRED - WALTER C. HINKLE MEMORIAL LIBRARY □ Alfred, NY

Sands, Nathan J., Mgr.
SINGER COMPANY - LIBRASCOPE DIVISION - TECHNICAL INFORMATION CENTER □ Glendale, CA

Sandula, Margaretta, Chf.
DETROIT PUBLIC LIBRARY - GENERAL INFORMATION DEPARTMENT □ Detroit, MI

Sanduleak, Barbara, Mgr.
IMPERIAL CLEVITE INC. - IC INFORMATION CENTER □ Cleveland, OH

Sandvik, Karin, Acq.
UNIVERSITY OF WISCONSIN, LA CROSSE - MURPHY LIBRARY □ La Crosse, WI

Sandviken, Gordon L., Info.Ctr.Spec.
SOUTHERN CALIFORNIA GAS COMPANY - ENGINEERING INFORMATION CENTER □ Los Angeles, CA

Sandy, John H., Libn.
UNIVERSITY OF TEXAS, AUSTIN - PHYSICS-MATHEMATICS-ASTRONOMY LIBRARY □ Austin, TX

Sandy, Will, Lib.Coord.
AMERICAN JEWISH COMMITTEE - WILLIAM E. WIENER ORAL HISTORY LIBRARY □ New York, NY

Sanford, D. Gregory, State Archv.
VERMONT STATE OFFICE OF THE SECRETARY OF STATE - VERMONT STATE PAPERS □ Montpelier, VT

Sanford, Ed, Coord.
BOSTON PUBLIC LIBRARY - SOCIAL SCIENCES □ Boston, MA

Sanford, Judith, Ed.
HOFFMANN-LA ROCHE, INC. - BUSINESS INFORMATION CENTER □ Nutley, NJ

Sanford, Lynda, Sci./Tech.Info.Hd.
CHICAGO PUBLIC LIBRARY CENTRAL LIBRARY - BUSINESS/SCIENCE/TECHNOLOGY DIVISION □ Chicago, IL

Sanford, Muriel A., Spec.Coll.Libn.
UNIVERSITY OF MAINE, ORONO - RAYMOND H. FOGLER LIBRARY - SPECIAL COLLECTIONS DEPARTMENT □ Orono, ME

Sanger, Helen, Libn.
FRICK ART REFERENCE LIBRARY □ New York, NY

Sangiamo, Irma, Ref.
MARYLAND INSTITUTE, COLLEGE OF ART - DECKER LIBRARY □ Baltimore, MD

Sangster, Collette, Dir.
ST. MARY'S SCHOOL FOR THE DEAF - INFORMATION CENTER □ Buffalo, NY

Sankowski, Andrew, Hd., Rsrc.Ctr.
TEACHERS COLLEGE - MILBANK MEMORIAL LIBRARY □ New York, NY

Sano, Tony, P.R.Supv.
AT & T - EDITORIAL RESEARCH CENTER† □ New York, NY

Sansbury, Michele M., Mgr.
U.S. NATL. INSTITUTES OF HEALTH - NATIONAL CANCER INSTITUTE - FREDERICK CANCER RES. FACILITY - SCIENTIFIC LIB. □ Frederick, MD

Sansobrino, Jean C., Libn.
KENNEDY/JENKS ENGINEERS, INC. - LIBRARY □ San Francisco, CA

Sansone, Antoinette, Supv.
GORE (W.L.) & ASSOCIATES, INC. - TECHNICAL INFORMATION CENTER □ Elkton, MD

Santana, Cdr. Fred J., MSC, Hd.
U.S. ARMY - ARMED FORCES PEST MANAGEMENT BOARD - DEFENSE PEST MANAGEMENT INFORMATION ANALYSIS CENTER □ Washington, DC

Santelano, Mary, Cat.
NORTHWESTERN UNIVERSITY - DENTAL SCHOOL LIBRARY □ Chicago, IL

Santella, Theresa, Dp. Circuit Libn.
U.S. COURT OF APPEALS, DISTRICT OF COLUMBIA CIRCUIT - LIBRARY □ Washington, DC

Santiago, Gladys, Hd.Libn.
PUERTO RICO - OFFICE OF BUDGET & MANAGEMENT - LIBRARY □ San Juan, PR

Santiago, Maria, Acq.Dept.Dir.
CATHOLIC UNIVERSITY OF PUERTO RICO - MONSIGNOR JUAN FREMIOT TORRES OLIVER LAW LIBRARY □ Ponce, PR

Santiago, Miriam J.
UNIVERSITY OF PUERTO RICO - NATURAL SCIENCE LIBRARY □ Rio Piedras, PR

Santoro, Corrado, Ref.Archv.
UNIVERSITY OF MANITOBA - ARCHIVES AND SPECIAL COLLECTIONS □ Winnipeg, MB

Santoro, Louise, Asst.Libn.
WAGNER COLLEGE - HORRMANN LIBRARY □ Staten Island, NY

Sapienza, Diane G., Law Libn.
KADISON, PFAELZER, WOODARD, QUINN & ROSSI - LAW LIBRARY □ Los Angeles, CA

Sapolsky, Dr. Barry S., Dir.
FLORIDA STATE UNIVERSITY - COMMUNICATION RESEARCH CENTER - LIBRARY □ Tallahassee, FL

Sapowith, Marcia K., Ref.Libn.
VILLANOVA UNIVERSITY - PULLING LAW LIBRARY □ Villanova, PA

Sapp, Blossom, Libn.
U.S. NATL. PARK SERVICE - PU'UHONUA O HONAUNAU NATL. HISTORICAL PARK - LIBRARY □ Honaunau, HI

Sapp, V.J., Info.Ctr.Supv.
ALUMINUM COMPANY OF AMERICA - ALCOA TECHNICAL CENTER - INFORMATION DEPARTMENT □ Alcoa Center, PA

Sappers, Vernon J., Cur.
CALIFORNIA RAILWAY MUSEUM - LIBRARY □ Suisun City, CA

Saraidaridis, Susan, Lib.Mgr.
HEWLETT-PACKARD COMPANY - MEDICAL PRODUCTS GROUP - LIBRARY □ Waltham, MA

Saramak, Mary, Asst.Ref.Libn.
NEW YORK UNIVERSITY MEDICAL CENTER - FREDERICK L. EHRMAN MEDICAL LIBRARY □ New York, NY

Sarber, Mary A., Hd., S.W. Coll.
EL PASO PUBLIC LIBRARY - SOUTHWEST RESEARCH COLLECTION □ El Paso, TX

Sargent, Charles W., Ph.D., Dir.
TEXAS TECH UNIVERSITY - HEALTH SCIENCES CENTER - LIBRARY OF THE HEALTH SCIENCES □ Lubbock, TX

Sark, Sue, Coll.Dev.
UNIVERSITY OF TULSA - COLLEGE OF LAW LIBRARY □ Tulsa, OK

Sarkis, Jeanne, Sr. Clinical Med.Libn.
UNIVERSITY OF MISSOURI, KANSAS CITY - HEALTH SCIENCES LIBRARY □ Kansas City, MO

Sarles, Ann, Ref.Libn.
INSTITUTE FOR DEFENSE ANALYSES - TECHNICAL INFORMATION SERVICES □ Alexandria, VA

Sarna, Helen, Asst.Libn.
HEBREW COLLEGE - JACOB AND ROSE GROSSMAN LIBRARY □ Brookline, MA

Sarophim, Tahani, Lib.Ck.
CALGARY SOCIAL SERVICE DEPARTMENT - LIBRARY □ Calgary, AB

Saros, Gust A., Jr., Musm. & Lib.Dir.
DISCOVERY HALL MUSEUM - RESEARCH LIBRARY □ South Bend, IN

Sarr, John T., Pubn.Off.
AFRICAN-AMERICAN LABOR CENTER (AALC) - LIBRARY □ Washington, DC

Sarraga, Raquel, Hd., Spec.Coll.
UNIVERSITY OF PUERTO RICO - GENERAL LIBRARY - SPECIAL COLLECTIONS† □ San Juan, PR

Sarrasin, Louis, Libn.
UNIVERSITE DE MONTREAL - INFORMATIQUE-BIBLIOTHEQUE □ Montreal, PQ

Sartorius, R.C., Info.Anl.
GULF OIL CHEMICALS COMPANY - POLYMER RESEARCH LIBRARY† □ Houston, TX

Saseen, Rosella M., Med.Libn.
WHEELING HOSPITAL, INC. - HENRY G. JEPSON MEMORIAL LIBRARY □ Wheeling, WV

Sass, Dr. Herman, Ref.Libn.
BUFFALO & ERIE COUNTY HISTORICAL SOCIETY - LIBRARY† □ Buffalo, NY

Sassa, Reiko, Asst.Libn.
JAPAN SOCIETY, INC. - LIBRARY □ New York, NY

Sassaman, Richard, AV Coord.
PHILADELPHIA COLLEGE OF ART - AUDIOVISIUAL DEPARTMENT - FILM LIBRARY □ Philadelphia, PA

Sasse, Gary S., Exec.Dir.
RHODE ISLAND PUBLIC EXPENDITURE COUNCIL - LIBRARY □ Providence, RI

Sasser, Ann B., Med.Libn.
MEMORIAL HOSPITAL - MEDICAL LIBRARY □ Danville, VA

Sasser, Caroline A., Supv. of Lib.
GRACE (W.R.) AND COMPANY - RESEARCH DIVISION LIBRARY □ Columbia, MD

Sasso, Mary Beth, Libn./Info.Spec.
AMERICAN PUBLIC WORKS ASSOCIATION - INFORMATION SERVICE □ Chicago, IL

Sasso, Patricia, Libn.
INDUSTRIAL RISK INSURERS - LIBRARY □ Hartford, CT

Sastri, Madugula, Circ.Mgr.
JOHN MARSHALL LAW SCHOOL - LIBRARY □ Chicago, IL

Satin, Allan, Judaica Libn.
HEBREW UNION COLLEGE - JEWISH INSTITUTE OF RELIGION - KLAU LIBRARY □ Cincinnati, OH

Sato, Ellyn, Tech.Serv.Libn.
PEAT, MARWICK, MITCHELL & CO. - CENTRAL LIBRARY† □ Los Angeles, CA

Sato, Mrs. Fumi, Libn.
INTERNATIONAL PACIFIC SALMON FISHERIES COMMISSION - LIBRARY □ New Westminster, BC

Sato, Scarlett, Health Planner
SANTA CLARA COUNTY HEALTH SYSTEMS AGENCY - LIBRARY □ San Jose, CA

Satta, Carol A., Dir., Lib.Serv.
WASHINGTON BIBLE COLLEGE/CAPITAL BIBLE SEMINARY - OYER MEMORIAL LIBRARY □ Lanham, MD

Sattler, Alan H., Supv.Libn.
NEW YORK PUBLIC LIBRARY - GENERAL LIBRARY OF THE PERFORMING ARTS □ New York, NY

Sauceda, Gloria, Academic Bus.Adm.
TEXAS A & M UNIVERSITY - MEDICAL SCIENCES LIBRARY □ College Station, TX

Saucier, Diane, Hd., Ref.Dept.
EAST TEXAS STATE UNIVERSITY - JAMES GILLIAM GEE LIBRARY □ Commerce, TX

Saudek, Robert, Chf.
LIBRARY OF CONGRESS - MOTION PICTURE, BROADCASTING & RECORDED SOUND DIVISION □ Washington, DC

Sauer, David, Bibliog.
BOSTON UNIVERSITY - SCIENCE AND ENGINEERING LIBRARY □ Boston, MA

Sauer, Joan Casson, Libn.
GREENVALE EDITORIAL SERVICES, INC. - LIBRARY □ Port Washington, NY

Sauer, Serge A., Map Cur.
UNIVERSITY OF WESTERN ONTARIO - DEPARTMENT OF GEOGRAPHY - MAP LIBRARY □ London, ON

Saul, Marlene, Med.Libn.
KAISER FOUNDATION HOSPITALS - MEDICAL LIBRARY □ Cleveland, OH

Saul, Philippa, Hd., Tech.Serv.
MANITOBA - LEGISLATIVE LIBRARY □ Winnipeg, MB

Saunders, Charles D., Libn.
RICHMOND NEWSPAPERS, INC. - LIBRARY □ Richmond, VA

Saunders, Dorothy, Supv., Per./Microforms
ARIZONA STATE UNIVERSITY - DANIEL E. NOBLE SCIENCE AND ENGINEERING LIBRARY □ Tempe, AZ

Saunders, Ed, AV
UNIVERSITY OF MICHIGAN - SCHOOL OF EDUCATION & SCHOOL OF LIB. SCI. - INSTR. STRATEGY SERV. □ Ann Arbor, MI

Saunders, J.L., Lib.Dir.
DEER LODGE CENTRE - LIBRARY □ Winnipeg, MB

Saunders, Juliet T., Asst.Dir.
PROVIDENCE ATHENAEUM - LIBRARY □ Providence, RI

Saunders, Larry N., Supv., Media Serv.
ALABAMA A & M UNIVERSITY - J. F. DRAKE MEMORIAL LEARNING RESOURCES CENTER □ Normal, AL

Saunders, Laurel B., Chf.
U.S. ARMY - WHITE SANDS MISSILE RANGE - TECHNICAL LIBRARY DIVISION □ White Sands Missile Range, NM

Saunders, Marjorie, Assoc.Dir.
CLEVELAND HEALTH SCIENCES LIBRARY - HEALTH CENTER LIBRARY □ Cleveland, OH

Saunders, Michael, Local Rec.
WASHINGTON STATE OFFICE OF SECRETARY OF STATE - DIVISION OF ARCHIVES AND RECORD MANAGEMENT □ Olympia, WA

Saunders, Myra, Pub.Serv.
UNIVERSITY OF CALIFORNIA, LOS ANGELES - LAW LIBRARY □ Los Angeles, CA

Saunders, Richard, Chf.Interp. & Rsrcs.Mgt.
U.S. NATL. PARK SERVICE - BOOKER T. WASHINGTON NATL. MONUMENT - LIBRARY □ Hardy, VA

Saunders, Stuart, Ref.Coll.Dev.
PURDUE UNIVERSITY - HUMANITIES, SOCIAL SCIENCE AND EDUCATION LIBRARY □ West Lafayette, IN

Saunders, William B., Libn./External Coord.
ANTIOCH UNIVERSITY - RESOURCE CENTER □ Philadelphia, PA

Sausedo, Ann E., Lib.Dir.
LOS ANGELES HERALD-EXAMINER - NEWSPAPER LIBRARY □ Los Angeles, CA

Sauter, Anne, Ref./Doc.Libn.
PACE UNIVERSITY - SCHOOL OF LAW LIBRARY □ White Plains, NY

Sauter, Hubert E., Adm.
U.S. DEFENSE TECHNICAL INFORMATION CENTER □ Alexandria, VA

Sauter, Lyn F., Libn.
DAMES & MOORE - SEATTLE OFFICE LIBRARY □ Seattle, WA

Sauve, Deborah, Info.Serv.Mgr.
INTERAMERICA RESEARCH ASSOCIATES, INC. - NATIONAL CLEARINGHOUSE FOR BILINGUAL EDUCATION □ Arlington, VA

Savage, Blanche A., Health Sci.Libn.
U.S. AIR FORCE HOSPITAL MEDICAL CENTER - MEDICAL LIBRARY (IL-Scott AFB) □ Scott AFB, IL

Savage, Colin
UNIVERSITY OF TORONTO - DEPARTMENT OF MEDICAL RESEARCH LIBRARY □ Toronto, ON

Savage, Janice, Spec.Coll.
OUACHITA BAPTIST UNIVERSITY - RILEY LIBRARY □ Arkadelphia, AR

Savage, Linda, Circ.
MASSACHUSETTS COLLEGE OF ART - LIBRARY □ Boston, MA

Savage, Rosalind, Cur.
LANGSTON UNIVERSITY - MELVIN B. TOLSON BLACK HERITAGE CENTER† □ Langston, OK

Savard, Madeleine, Lib.Techn.
FEDERATION DES MEDECINS OMNIPRACTICIENS DU QUEBEC - DOCUMENTATION CENTRE □ Montreal, PQ

Savard, Robert, Dir.Gen.
FEDERATION DES ADMINISTRATEURS DES SERVICES DE SANTE ET DES SERVICES SOCIAUX DU QUEBEC - BIBLIOTHEQUE □ Montreal, PQ

Savell, Mrs. John K.
FIRST BAPTIST CHURCH - LIBRARY □ Gulfport, MS

Savitzky, Evelyn R., Br.Supv.
PERKIN-ELMER CORPORATION - CORPORATE LIBRARY □ Norwalk, CT

Savon, Brian, Res.Assoc.
FLORIDA STATE UNIVERSITY - CTR. FOR STUDIES IN VOCATIONAL EDUC. - FLORIDA EDUCATIONAL INFO. SERV. □ Tallahassee, FL

Savoy, Kathleen M., Asst.Libn.
ALTON OCHSNER MEDICAL FOUNDATION - MEDICAL LIBRARY □ New Orleans, LA

Savoy, Marie, Adm.Mgr.
NATIONAL SCIENCE FOUNDATION - LIBRARY □ Washington, DC

Sawaryn, Miss R.M., Libn.
AT & T TECHNOLOGIES, INC. - TECHNICAL LIBRARY □ Baltimore, MD

Sawycky, Roman A., Supv.Libn.
FREE PUBLIC LIBRARY OF ELIZABETH, NJ - ART AND MUSIC DEPARTMENT □ Elizabeth, NJ

Sawyer, Alfred D., Chm., Lib.Comm.
SCOTTISH RITE BODIES, SAN DIEGO - SCOTTISH RITE MASONIC LIBRARY □ San Diego, CA

Sawyer, Ardis C., Libn.
MINNESOTA BIBLE COLLEGE - LIBRARY □ Rochester, MN

Sawyer, Jean, Asst.Libn.
NOVA SCOTIA - LEGISLATIVE LIBRARY □ Halifax, NS

Sawyer, Joanne M., Archv.
HIRAM COLLEGE - TEACHOUT-PRICE MEMORIAL LIBRARY □ Hiram, OH

Sawyer, Marcy, News Libn.
ROCHESTER POST-BULLETIN - NEWS LIBRARY □ Rochester, MN

Sawyer, Marian, Asst. Law Libn.
MC GEORGE SCHOOL OF LAW - LAW LIBRARY □ Sacramento, CA

Sawyer, Rod, Libn.
METROPOLITAN TORONTO LIBRARY - SOCIAL SCIENCES DEPARTMENT □ Toronto, ON

Sawyer, Warren A., Dir.
MEDICAL UNIVERSITY OF SOUTH CAROLINA - LIBRARY □ Charleston, SC

Sawyers, Elizabeth J., Dir.
OHIO STATE UNIVERSITY - HEALTH SCIENCES LIBRARY □ Columbus, OH

Sax, Margaret F., Assoc.Cur.
TRINITY COLLEGE - WATKINSON LIBRARY □ Hartford, CT

Saxe, C., Sr.Tech.Adv.
RAY-O-VAC CORP. - TECHNOLOGY CENTER LIBRARY □ Madison, WI

Saxe, Minna C., Chf.Ser.Libn.
CUNY - GRADUATE SCHOOL AND UNIVERSITY CENTER - LIBRARY □ New York, NY

Saxon, Gerald, Oral Hist.Libn.
DALLAS PUBLIC LIBRARY - TEXAS/DALLAS HISTORY AND ARCHIVES DIVISION □ Dallas, TX

Saxon, Nancy Berry, Dir.
WASHINGTON COUNTY HISTORICAL AND MUSEUM SOCIETY - LE MOYNE HOUSE LIBRARY □ Washington, PA

Sayler, Rod, Dir.
UNIVERSITY OF NORTH DAKOTA - INSTITUTE FOR ECOLOGICAL STUDIES - ENVIRONMENTAL RESOURCE CENTER - LIBRARY □ Grand Forks, ND

Sayles, Adele, Libn.
TEMPLE ISRAEL - LIBRARY □ West Palm Beach, FL

Sayles, Eleanor G., Libn.
EDUCOM, INTERUNIVERSITY COMMUNICATIONS COUNCIL, INC. - LIBRARY† □ Princeton, NJ

Saylik, Halim, Mgr.
AMERICAN ASSOCIATION OF CRIMEAN TURKS, INC. - ISMAIL GASPIRALI LIBRARY □ Brooklyn, NY

Saylor, Helen, Med.Libn.
PRESBYTERIAN HOSPITAL - MEDICAL LIBRARY □ Albuquerque, NM

Saylor, John, Bibliog./Ref.Libn.
CORNELL UNIVERSITY - ENGINEERING LIBRARY □ Ithaca, NY

Saylor, Linda, Lib.Supv.
STAUFFER CHEMICAL COMPANY - DE GUIGNE TECHNICAL CENTER - RESEARCH LIBRARY □ Richmond, CA

Sayre, John L., Dir.
PHILLIPS UNIVERSITY - GRADUATE SEMINARY LIBRARY □ Enid, OK

Sayrs, Judith, Ref.Libn.
CREDIT UNION NATIONAL ASSOCIATION - INFORMATION RESOURCE CENTER □ Madison, WI

Sayus, Teresita D., Circ.Libn.
UNIVERSITY OF MIAMI - SCHOOL OF MEDICINE - LOUIS CALDER MEMORIAL LIBRARY □ Miami, FL

Sayward, Nick, Investment Serv.Libn.
FORD FOUNDATION - INVESTMENT RESEARCH LIBRARY □ New York, NY

Scaccio, Ethel D., Hd., Cat. and Clas.
U.S. DEFENSE NUCLEAR AGENCY - TECHNICAL LIBRARY □ Washington, DC

Scales, Bill, Media Serv.Supv.
AUBURN UNIVERSITY - LEARNING RESOURCES CENTER □ Auburn, AL

Scalley, Paula, Assoc.Libn.
CLEVELAND ELECTRIC ILLUMINATING COMPANY - LIBRARY □ Cleveland, OH

Scalzo, Geraldine, Hd.
UNIVERSITY OF CALIFORNIA, BERKELEY - SOCIAL SCIENCE LIBRARY □ Berkeley, CA

Scalzo, Geraldine, Hd.
UNIVERSITY OF CALIFORNIA, BERKELEY - SOCIAL WELFARE LIBRARY □ Berkeley, CA

Scammell, Harry D., Libn.
YALE UNIVERSITY - GEOLOGY LIBRARY □ New Haven, CT

Scanlan, Jean M., Mgr.
PRICE WATERHOUSE - INFORMATION CENTER □ Boston, MA

Scanlon, Betty, Libn.
LOCKHEED CORPORATION - INTERNATIONAL
MARKETING LIBRARY 07-50 □ Burbank, CA

Scanlon, Mary R., Libn.
UNIV. OF MEDICINE & DENTISTRY OF NJ -
RUTGERS MED. SCHOOL - MIDDLESEX
GENERAL-UNIV. HOSPITAL - HEALTH SCI.LIB. □
New Brunswick, NJ

Scanlon, Virginia, Libn.
CONNECTICUT STATE LIBRARY - LAW LIBRARY
AT ROCKVILLE □ Rockville, CT

Scannell, Elizabeth F., Adm.Libn.
BOSTON SCHOOL COMMITTEE OF THE CITY OF
BOSTON - ADMINISTRATION LIBRARY† □
Boston, MA

Scannell, Kristine M., Med.Libn.
SOUTH BALTIMORE GENERAL HOSPITAL -
MEDICAL LIBRARY □ Baltimore, MD

Scantland, Jean-Marie, Chf., Spec.Coll.
UNIVERSITE LAVAL - BIBLIOTHEQUE □ Ste.
Foy, PQ

Scantlebury, Jane, Libn.
CENTER FOR THE STUDY, EDUCATION &
ADVANCEMENT OF WOMEN - CSEAW LIBRARY
□ Berkeley, CA

Scarborough, Ella Butler, Supv., IRC
DUKE POWER COMPANY - PRODUCTION
DEPARTMENTS - INFORMATION RESOURCE
CENTER (IRC) □ Cornelius, NC

Scarborough, Rebecca, Hd., Govt.Doc.Dept.
BIRMINGHAM PUBLIC AND JEFFERSON
COUNTY FREE LIBRARY - GOVERNMENT
DOCUMENTS DEPARTMENT □ Birmingham, AL

Scarfia, Angela, Libn.
PENNWALT CORPORATION - PENNWALT
PHARMACEUTICAL DIVISION - RESEARCH
LIBRARY □ Rochester, NY

Scarlett, Robert M., Libn.
MEMPHIS ACADEMY OF ARTS - G. PILLOW
LEWIS MEMORIAL LIBRARY □ Memphis, TN

Schaadt, Robert L., Dir./Archv.
TEXAS STATE LIBRARY - LOCAL RECORDS
DIVISION - SAM HOUSTON REGIONAL LIBRARY
AND RESEARCH CENTER □ Liberty, TX

Schaaf, Ray, Pub.Aff.Off.
U.S. FOREST SERVICE - INYO NATL. FOREST -
INFORMATION CENTER □ Bishop, CA

Schaberl, Dorothy, Libn.
DANA CORPORATION - WEATHERHEAD
DIVISION - LIBRARY AND TECHNICAL
INFORMATION CENTER† □ Cleveland, OH

Schachter, Ms. Bert, Mgr./V.P.
BATES (Ted) ADVERTISING - INFORMATION
CENTER □ New York, NY

Schachter, Dr. R., Dir.
WOMEN'S COLLEGE HOSPITAL - PSORIASIS
EDUCATION AND RESEARCH CENTRE □
Toronto, ON

Schachter, Ruth, Commun.Coord.
FOOTWEAR INDUSTRIES OF AMERICA, INC. -
LIBRARY □ Philadelphia, PA

Schackman, Dulcie L., Sr.Info.Adm.
INSTITUTE OF INTERNATIONAL EDUCATION -
LIBRARY/COMMUNICATIONS □ New York, NY

Schade, Margaret, Libn.
CANADA - NATIONAL RESEARCH COUNCIL -
CISTI - SUSSEX BRANCH □ Ottawa, ON

Schaefer, Dr. J.P., Dir.
PRINCE COUNTY HOSPITAL - MEDICAL
LIBRARY □ Summerside, PE

Schaefer, Lyle, District Archv.
LUTHERAN CHURCH - MISSOURI SYNOD -
COLORADO DISTRICT ARCHIVES □ Aurora, CO

Schaefer, Thomas L., Archv.
HISTORICAL SOCIETY OF DAUPHIN COUNTY -
ARCHIVES/LIBRARY □ Harrisburg, PA

Schaeffer, John L., Ed., Gas Abstracts
INSTITUTE OF GAS TECHNOLOGY - TECHNICAL
INFORMATION CENTER □ Chicago, IL

Schaeffer, Judith E., Libn.
EINSTEIN (Albert) MEDICAL CENTER - SCHOOL
OF NURSING LIBRARY □ Philadelphia, PA

Schaeffer, Madeline, Libn.
EASTCHESTER HISTORICAL SOCIETY -
LIBRARY □ Eastchester, NY

Schaeffer, Lt.Col. Reiner H., Dir. of Libs.
U.S. AIR FORCE ACADEMY - LIBRARY □
Colorado Springs, CO

Schafer, Jay, Libn.
SKIDMORE, OWINGS & MERRILL - LIBRARY □
Denver, CO

Schafer, Laura E., Libn.
TOPEKA STATE HOSPITAL - STAFF LIBRARY □
Topeka, KS

Schafer, Robert L., Dir.
U.S.D.A. - AGRICULTURAL RESEARCH SERVICE
- NATL. TILLAGE MACHINERY LABORATORY
LIBRARY □ Auburn, AL

Schafer, Susan, Libn.
KANSAS ENERGY EXTENSION SERVICE □
Manhattan, KS

Schafer, Susan, Cat.
ST. VINCENT MEDICAL CENTER - HEALTH
SCIENCE LIBRARY □ Toledo, OH

Schaffer, Deborah A., Libn.
SHAND, MORAHAN & COMPANY, INC. -
LIBRARY □ Evanston, IL

Schaffer, Ellen, Intl. Law Libn.
GEORGETOWN UNIVERSITY - FRED O. DENNIS
LAW LIBRARY □ Washington, DC

Schaffer, Monica, Libn.
METASCIENCE FOUNDATION - LIBRARY □
Kingston, RI

Schaffer, Rita, Libn.
MERRILL LYNCH WHITE WELD - CAPITAL
MARKETS GROUP - LIBRARY† □ New York, NY

Schalit, Michael, Ref.Libn.
SANDIA NATIONAL LABORATORIES -
TECHNICAL LIBRARY† □ Livermore, CA

Schalk-Greene, Katherine, Dir.
SOUTH JERSEY REGIONAL FILM LIBRARY □
Voorhees, NJ

Schall, Mary Catherine, Hd., Spec.Coll.
CARNEGIE-MELLON UNIVERSITY - SPECIAL
COLLECTIONS □ Pittsburgh, PA

Schaller, Alice, Asst.Supv.
MONROE COUNTY LOCAL HISTORY ROOM &
LIBRARY □ Sparta, WI

Schallert, Ruth, Libn.
SMITHSONIAN INSTITUTION LIBRARIES -
NATIONAL MUSEUM OF NATURAL HISTORY -
BOTANY BRANCH LIBRARY □ Washington, DC

Schallert, Ruth, Libn.
SMITHSONIAN INSTITUTION LIBRARIES -
NATIONAL MUSEUM OF NATURAL HISTORY -
ENTOMOLOGY BRANCH LIBRARY □ Washington,
DC

Schallert, Ruth, Act.Nat.Hist.Libn.
SMITHSONIAN INSTITUTION LIBRARIES -
NATIONAL MUSEUM OF NATURAL HISTORY -
LIBRARY □ Washington, DC

Schalow, Gertrude E., Asst.Libn.
U.S. BUREAU OF RECLAMATION - LIBRARY† □
Denver, CO

Schanck, Peter C., Dir.
UNIVERSITY OF KANSAS - SCHOOL OF LAW
LIBRARY □ Lawrence, KS

Schaner, Marian E., Lib.Dir.
EINSTEIN (Albert) MEDICAL CENTER - MT.
SINAI-DAROFF DIVISION - MEDICAL LIBRARY
□ Philadelphia, PA

Schanzer, Barbara J., Libn.
UNITED SERVICES AUTOMOBILE ASSOCIATION
- CORPORATE LIBRARY □ San Antonio, TX

Schapiro, Benjamin Hall, Coord.
NATIONAL COLLEGE OF EDUCATION - URBAN
CAMPUS LEARNING RESOURCE CENTER □
Chicago, IL

Schapiro, Sue, Govt.Docs.
SUNY - AGRICULTURAL AND TECHNICAL
COLLEGE AT FARMINGDALE - THOMAS D.
GREENLEY LIBRARY □ Farmingdale, NY

Schara, Rita, Libn.
NORWALK STATE TECHNICAL COLLEGE -
LIBRARY □ Norwalk, CT

Scharf, Mary E., Law Libn.
WISCONSIN STATE - FOND DU LAC COUNTY
LAW LIBRARY □ Fond du Lac, WI

Scharlock, Nidia, Hd., Info.Serv.
UNIVERSITY OF NORTH CAROLINA, CHAPEL
HILL - HEALTH SCIENCES LIBRARY □ Chapel
Hill, NC

Scharmer, Roger, Libn.
U.S. FOREST SERVICE - FOREST PRODUCTS
LABORATORY LIBRARY □ Madison, WI

Schart, Charlotte, Hd., Ser.
SUNY - AGRICULTURAL AND TECHNICAL
COLLEGE AT FARMINGDALE - THOMAS D.
GREENLEY LIBRARY □ Farmingdale, NY

Schatz, Natalie, Libn.
TUFTS UNIVERSITY - FLETCHER SCHOOL OF
LAW & DIPLOMACY - EDWIN GINN LIBRARY □
Medford, MA

Schauer, Diane, Asst.Libn.
U.S. DISTRICT COURT - DISTRICT OF OREGON
- LIBRARY □ Portland, OR

Schauer, Dianne, Asst.Libn.
U.S. COURT OF APPEALS, 9TH CIRCUIT -
LIBRARY □ Portland, OR

Schechter, Sue F., Exec.Dir.
PASADENA HISTORICAL SOCIETY - LIBRARY □
Pasadena, CA

Schechtman, Joan, Mgr.
UNION CARBIDE CORPORATION - I.S.
INFORMATION CENTER □ Tarrytown, NY

Schechtman, Joan, Mgr.
UNION CARBIDE CORPORATION - LIBRARY &
TECHNICAL INFORMATION SERVICE □
Tarrytown, NY

Scheele, William E., Dir.
COLUMBUS MUSEUM OF ARTS AND SCIENCES -
RESEARCH LIBRARY □ Columbus, GA

Scheer, Anne B., Libn.
U.S. INTERNAL REVENUE SERVICE - LAW
LIBRARY† □ Washington, DC

Scheeren, Martha, Asst.Libn.
INDIANA UNIVERSITY OF PENNSYLVANIA -
UNIVERSITY LIBRARY □ Indiana, PA

Scheetz, Nicholas B., Mss.Libn.
GEORGETOWN UNIVERSITY - SPECIAL
COLLECTIONS DIVISION - LAUINGER
MEMORIAL LIBRARY □ Washington, DC

Scheffel, Kenneth, Assoc.Archv.
UNIVERSITY OF MICHIGAN - MICHIGAN
HISTORICAL COLLECTIONS - BENTLEY
HISTORICAL LIBRARY □ Ann Arbor, MI

Scheffler, Hannah Nuba, Dir.
NEW YORK PUBLIC LIBRARY - EARLY
CHILDHOOD RESOURCE AND INFORMATION
CENTER □ New York, NY

Scheibner, Irene, Founder
HARTFORD WOMEN'S CENTER - HARTFORD
FEMINIST LIBRARY □ Hartford, CT

Scheier, Francine, Libn.
MONMOUTH COUNTY SOCIAL SERVICES -
LIBRARY □ Freehold, NJ

Scheiman, Royal, Cat.
GRUMMAN AEROSPACE CORPORATION -
TECHNICAL INFORMATION CENTER □
Bethpage, NY

Schein, Lorraine, Br.Libn.
POLYTECHNIC INSTITUTE OF NEW YORK -
LONG ISLAND CENTER LIBRARY □ Long Island,
NY

Schelkopf, Nancy, Tech.Serv.
WHEATON COLLEGE - BILLY GRAHAM CENTER -
LIBRARY □ Wheaton, IL

Schell, Rev. Edwin, Exec.Sec./Libn.
UNITED METHODIST HISTORICAL SOCIETY -
BALTIMORE ANNUAL CONFERENCE - LOVELY
LANE MUSEUM LIBRARY □ Baltimore, MD

Schell, Fran, Ref.Libn.
TENNESSEE STATE LIBRARY - STATE LIBRARY
DIVISION □ Nashville, TN

Schell, Rosalie, Dir., Rd.Serv.
CENTRAL MISSOURI STATE UNIVERSITY -
WARD EDWARDS LIBRARY - SPECIAL
COLLECTIONS □ Warrensburg, MO

Schenck-Hamlin, Donna, Libn.
KANSAS STATE UNIVERSITY - FOOD AND FEED GRAIN INSTITUTE - POST-HARVEST DOCUMENTATION SERVICE □ Manhattan, KS

Schenk, Margaret, Hd., Coll.Dev.
SUNY AT BUFFALO - SCIENCE AND ENGINEERING LIBRARY □ Buffalo, NY

Schenk, Margot, Hd., Pub.Serv.
ST. MARY'S UNIVERSITY - PATRICK POWER LIBRARY □ Halifax, NS

Schepis, Sandra, Libn.
MARCH OF DIMES BIRTH DEFECTS FOUNDATION - REFERENCE ROOM □ White Plains, NY

Schepper, Josee, Ref.Libn.
ECOLE POLYTECHNIQUE - BIBLIOTHEQUE □ Montreal, PQ

Scherer, Alice, Libn.
MERRILL LYNCH WHITE WELD - CAPITAL MARKETS GROUP - LIBRARY† □ New York, NY

Scherer, Herbert, Art Libn.
UNIVERSITY OF MINNESOTA - ART COLLECTION □ Minneapolis, MN

Schermeister, John, Exec.Dir.
CLAY COUNTY HISTORICAL SOCIETY - ARCHIVES □ Moorhead, MN

Schermetzler, Bernard, Archv./Iconographer
UNIVERSITY OF WISCONSIN, MADISON - ARCHIVES □ Madison, WI

Scheuer, Caryl L., Dir., Lib.Serv.
HUTZEL HOSPITAL - MEDICAL LIBRARY □ Detroit, MI

Scheuerer, Elaine, Lib.Coord.
TRENTON PSYCHIATRIC HOSPITAL - MEDICAL LIBRARY □ West Trenton, NJ

Scheuermann, Alyssa N., Libn.
ZOOLOGICAL SOCIETY OF PHILADELPHIA - LIBRARY □ Philadelphia, PA

Scheufele, Iola, Dir.
NATICK HISTORICAL SOCIETY - LIBRARY □ South Natick, MA

Scheufele, Iola, Cat., Proc.
NEW ENGLAND WILD FLOWER SOCIETY, INC. - LAWRENCE NEWCOMB LIBRARY □ Framingham, MA

Schewe, Dr. Donald B., Dir.
U.S. PRESIDENTIAL LIBRARIES - CARTER PRESIDENTIAL MATERIALS PROJECT □ Atlanta, GA

Schifano-Nista, Ann, Asst.Libn.
INSTITUTE FOR CANCER RESEARCH - LIBRARY □ Philadelphia, PA

Schiff, Arthur, Staff V.P.
AMERICAN SOCIETY OF TRAVEL AGENTS - LIBRARY □ Washington, DC

Schiff, Dorothy, Libn.
ST. MARGARET MEMORIAL HOSPITAL - PAUL TITUS MEMORIAL LIBRARY AND SCHOOL OF NURSING LIBRARY □ Pittsburgh, PA

Schiff, Judith A., Chf.Res.Archv.
YALE UNIVERSITY - MANUSCRIPTS AND ARCHIVES □ New Haven, CT

Schiff, Judy, Ref.Libn.
HEBREW COLLEGE - JACOB AND ROSE GROSSMAN LIBRARY □ Brookline, MA

Schiff, Katharine, Libn.
BOOZ, ALLEN & HAMILTON, INC. - LIBRARY □ Bethesda, MD

Schiffman, Leonard, Co-Cur.
CANADIAN COUNTY HISTORICAL MUSEUM - LIBRARY □ El Reno, OK

Schilke, John, AV Coord.
HOSPITAL OF ST. RAPHAEL - HEALTH SCIENCES LIBRARY □ New Haven, CT

Schiller, Timothy, Supv., Ref.
FEDERAL RESERVE BANK OF PHILADELPHIA - LIBRARY □ Philadelphia, PA

Schilling, Irene, Cat.Libn.
AUGSBURG COLLEGE - GEORGE SVERDRUP LIBRARY AND MEDIA CENTER □ Minneapolis, MN

Schilling, Lorraine, Mgr.
MUSEUM OF CARTOON ART - LIBRARY □ Rye Brook, NY

Schimansky, Dobrila-Donya, Musm.Libn.
METROPOLITAN MUSEUM OF ART - THOMAS J. WATSON LIBRARY □ New York, NY

Schimmelbusch, Johannes S., Engr.Libn.
U.S. DEPT. OF ENERGY - BONNEVILLE POWER ADMINISTRATION - LIBRARY □ Portland, OR

Schimmelpfeng, Richard, Libn.
MANSFIELD HISTORICAL SOCIETY - EDITH MASON LIBRARY □ Storrs, CT

Schimmelpfeng, Richard H., Dir., Spec.Coll.
UNIVERSITY OF CONNECTICUT - HOMER BABBIDGE LIBRARY - SPECIAL COLLECTIONS □ Storrs, CT

Schindler, Merril, Sys.Coord.
MOUNT SINAI SCHOOL OF MEDICINE OF THE CITY UNIVERSITY OF NEW YORK - GUSTAVE L. & JANET W. LEVY LIBRARY □ New York, NY

Schipf, Robert, Sci.Libn.
UNIVERSITY OF MONTANA - SCHOOL OF FORESTRY - OXFORD COLLECTION □ Missoula, MT

Schipper, Dr. Edgar, Lit.Sci.
ETHICON, INC. - SCIENTIFIC INFORMATION SERVICES □ Somerville, NJ

Schipper, Joan, Ref.
OKLAHOMA CITY UNIVERSITY - LAW LIBRARY □ Oklahoma City, OK

Schlaerth, Sally G., Hd.Libn.
BUFFALO NEWS - LIBRARY □ Buffalo, NY

Schlage, Jean, Libn.
GENERAL MOTORS CORPORATION - ADVANCED PRODUCT AND MANUFACTURING ENGINEERING STAFF - LIBRARY □ Warren, MI

Schlatter, M. Warren, Hd., Media Ctr.
MEDICAL COLLEGE OF GEORGIA - LIBRARY □ Augusta, GA

Schlee, Marilyn J., Lib.Serv.Off.
NORWEST CORPORATION - LIBRARY □ Minneapolis, MN

Schleg, M., Pub.Serv.Libn.
HURLEY MEDICAL CENTER - HAMADY HEALTH SCIENCES LIBRARY □ Flint, MI

Schleicher, Ben, Adm.Serv.Supv.
WOODWARD GOVERNOR CO. - WOODWARD LIBRARY □ Rockford, IL

Schleif, Julia Woodward, Libn.
GOOD SAMARITAN MEDICAL CENTER - DEACONESS HOSPITAL CAMPUS - HEALTH SCIENCE LIBRARY† □ Milwaukee, WI

Schlenk, Pamela, Record Libn.
CLEVELAND INSTITUTE OF MUSIC - LIBRARY □ Cleveland, OH

Schlereth, Dr. Wendy Clauson, Univ.Archv.
UNIVERSITY OF NOTRE DAME - ARCHIVES □ Notre Dame, IN

Schlesinger, Keith R., Dir., P.R. & Info.
AMERICAN SOCIETY OF AGRONOMY - INFORMATION CENTER □ Madison, WI

Schlimgen, Joan, Libn.
COOPERS & LYBRAND - LIBRARY □ Los Angeles, CA

Schlimm, Rev. Chrysostom V., O.S.B., Dir.
ST. VINCENT COLLEGE AND ARCHABBEY - LIBRARIES □ Latrobe, PA

Schlingman, Dorothy
WILKES COLLEGE - INSTITUTE OF REGIONAL AFFAIRS - LIBRARY □ Wilkes-Barre, PA

Schlosser, Anne G., Lib.Dir.
AMERICAN FILM INSTITUTE - LOUIS B. MAYER LIBRARY □ Los Angeles, CA

Schlossman, Glad, Dir.
TEL-MED HEALTH INFORMATION SERVICE □ Minneapolis, MN

Schlueter, Kay, Docs.Libn.
TEXAS STATE LAW LIBRARY □ Austin, TX

Schlueter, R.A., Libn.
ALLIS-CHALMERS CORPORATION - ADVANCED TECHNOLOGY CENTER - LIBRARY □ Milwaukee, WI

Schluge, Vicki, Instr.Rsrcs.Mgr.
EDGEWOOD COLLEGE - MAUDE WEBSTER MIDDLETON NURSING LIBRARY □ Madison, WI

Schmalz, Rochelle Perrine, Med.Libn.
PROGRAM PLANETREE - HEALTH RESOURCE CENTER □ San Francisco, CA

Schmelz, Gary W., Ph.D., Educ.Dir.
THE CONSERVANCY, INC. - CONSERVANCY NATURE CENTER LIBRARY □ Naples, FL

Schmelzer, Dr. Menahem, Libn.
JEWISH THEOLOGICAL SEMINARY OF AMERICA - LIBRARY □ New York, NY

Schmid, Josef, Jr., Libn.
MIDREX CORPORATION - LIBRARY □ Charlotte, NC

Schmid, Robert, Assoc.Dir.
UNIVERSITY OF HEALTH SCIENCES/CHICAGO MEDICAL SCHOOL - LIBRARY □ North Chicago, IL

Schmid, Wilfried
HARVARD UNIVERSITY - MATHEMATICAL LIBRARY □ Cambridge, MA

Schmidt, Barbara, ILL
OHIO STATE UNIVERSITY - HEALTH SCIENCES LIBRARY □ Columbus, OH

Schmidt, Barbara E., Libn.
LAWYERS' JOINT LAW LIBRARY† □ Minneapolis, MN

Schmidt, Carole, Instr.Rsrcs.
WAYNE STATE COLLEGE - U.S. CONN LIBRARY □ Wayne, NE

Schmidt, Christiane, Libn.
GOETHE INSTITUT CHICAGO - GERMAN CULTURAL CENTER - LIBRARY □ Chicago, IL

Schmidt, David, Mechanical Techn.
MARICOPA TECHNICAL COMMUNITY COLLEGE - LIBRARY RESOURCE CENTER □ Phoenix, AZ

Schmidt, Dean, Libn.
UNIVERSITY OF MISSOURI - HEALTH SCIENCES LIBRARY □ Columbia, MO

Schmidt, Donald T., Dir., Lib.Archv.
CHURCH OF JESUS CHRIST OF LATTER-DAY SAINTS - HISTORICAL DEPARTMENT - CHURCH LIBRARY-ARCHIVES □ Salt Lake City, UT

Schmidt, Dorothy, Coord.
KRAFT, INC. - BUSINESS RESEARCH CENTER □ Glenview, IL

Schmidt, Douglas, Info.Ctr.Coord.
DAYTON HUDSON CORPORATION - INFORMATION CENTER □ Minneapolis, MN

Schmidt, Erika, Libn.
BUTLER HOSPITAL - ISAAC RAY MEDICAL LIBRARY □ Providence, RI

Schmidt, Jan, Libn., Pub.Serv.
ONTARIO INSTITUTE FOR STUDIES IN EDUCATION (OISE) - R.W.B. JACKSON LIBRARY □ Toronto, ON

Schmidt, Jean, Archv.
MONTANA STATE UNIVERSITY - UNIVERSITY ARCHIVES □ Bozeman, MT

Schmidt, Jean Marie, Libn.
U.S. ARMY - CORPS OF ENGINEERS - ST. PAUL DISTRICT - TECHNICAL LIBRARY □ St. Paul, MN

Schmidt, Kathleen, Ser.Supv.
WASHINGTON STATE UNIVERSITY - VETERINARY MEDICAL/PHARMACY LIBRARY □ Pullman, WA

Schmidt, Margaret, Instr.Rsrcs.
UNIVERSITY OF MICHIGAN - SCHOOL OF EDUCATION & SCHOOL OF LIB. SCI. - INSTR. STRATEGY SERV. □ Ann Arbor, MI

Schmidt, Mary Ann, Lib.Dir.
MILWAUKEE SCHOOL OF ENGINEERING - WALTER SCHROEDER LIBRARY □ Milwaukee, WI

Schmidt, Mary Anne, Libn.
FIRST BAPTIST CHURCH OF DALLAS - FIRST BAPTIST ACADEMY - GEORGE W. TRUETT MEMORIAL LIBRARY† □ Dallas, TX

Schmidt, Mary M., Libn.
PRINCETON UNIVERSITY - MARQUAND LIBRARY† □ Princeton, NJ

Schmidt, May, Sr. Staff Libn.
AUSTIN PUBLIC LIBRARY - AUSTIN HISTORY
CENTER □ Austin, TX
Schmidt, Nancy J., Libn.
HARVARD UNIVERSITY - TOZZER LIBRARY □
Cambridge, MA
Schmidt, Paula, Libn.
BAKER & DANIELS - LAW LIBRARY □
Indianapolis, IN
Schmidt, Peter, Faculty Assoc.
WESTERN MICHIGAN UNIVERSITY - ARCHIVES
AND REGIONAL HISTORY COLLECTIONS □
Kalamazoo, MI
Schmidt, Rebecca, First Asst.
PUBLIC LIBRARY OF CINCINNATI AND
HAMILTON COUNTY - CHILDREN'S
DEPARTMENT □ Cincinnati, OH
Schmidt, Robert R., Libn.
HALL OF JUSTICE LIBRARY† □ San Francisco,
CA
Schmidt, Sandra L., Asst.Lib.
MAC NEAL HOSPITAL - HEALTH SCIENCES
RESOURCE CENTER □ Berwyn, IL
Schmidt, Steven, Circ./ILL Assoc.
INDIANA UNIVERSITY/PURDUE UNIVERSITY
AT INDIANAPOLIS - UNIVERSITY LIBRARY □
Indianapolis, IN
Schmidt, Vincent P., Dp.Dir.
ILLINOIS STATE LIBRARY □ Springfield, IL
Schmiechen, Barbara, Ref./Ext.Libn.
UNIVERSITY OF WISCONSIN, MADISON -
CENTER FOR HEALTH SCIENCES LIBRARIES† □
Madison, WI
Schmith, Linda
U.S. NATL. WEATHER SERVICE - WEATHER
SERVICE NUCLEAR SUPPORT OFFICE -
LIBRARY □ Las Vegas, NV
Schmitt, Carol, Libn.
ALLEGHENY COUNTY HEALTH DEPARTMENT -
LIBRARY □ Pittsburgh, PA
Schmitt, Frederick P., Asst.Dir.
THOUSAND ISLANDS MUSEUM, INC. - LIBRARY
□ Clayton, NY
Schmitt, Kaye, Act.Libn.
CAMARILLO STATE HOSPITAL - PROFESSIONAL
LIBRARY □ Camarillo, CA
Schmitt, Laurence A., Libn.
ST. JOSEPH'S SEMINARY - LIBRARY □
Washington, DC
Schmitt, Marilyn, Libn.
IOWA GENEALOGICAL SOCIETY - LIBRARY □
Des Moines, IA
Schmitt, Patricia D., Tech.Libn.
HAMMERMILL PAPER COMPANY - CORPORATE
RESEARCH TECHNICAL LIBRARY □ Erie, PA
Schmitz, Ruth W., Chf.Med.Libn.
NEW YORK COLLEGE OF OSTEOPATHIC
MEDICINE - MEDICAL LIBRARY □ Old Westbury,
NY
Schmock, Fr. Hilarion, O.C.S.O., Libn.
GETHSEMANI ABBEY - LIBRARY □ Trappist, KY
Schmorak, M.R., Res.
OAK RIDGE NATIONAL LABORATORY -
NUCLEAR DATA PROJECT □ Oak Ridge, TN
Schmottlach, Shirley, Lib.Asst.
WESLEYAN UNIVERSITY - PSYCHOLOGY
DEPARTMENT LIBRARY □ Middletown, CT
Schnall, Janet, Consulting Libn.
WALDO GENERAL HOSPITAL - MEDICAL
LIBRARY □ Seattle, WA
Schnare, Robert E., Spec.Coll.Libn.
U.S. ARMY - MILITARY ACADEMY - LIBRARY □
West Point, NY
Schnaubelt, Rev. Joseph C., O.S.A., Dir.
AUGUSTINIAN HISTORICAL INSTITUTE -
LIBRARY □ Villanova, PA
Schneberg, Ben, Law Libn.
BISHOP, LIBERMAN & COOK - LAW LIBRARY □
New York, NY
Schneck, Mildred, Libn.
HUDSON INSTITUTE - LIBRARY □ Croton-On-
Hudson, NY

Schnedeker, Donald, Assoc.Libn.
CORNELL UNIVERSITY - GRADUATE SCHOOL OF
MANAGEMENT - LIBRARY □ Ithaca, NY
Schnee, Hope, Libn.
NEWSDAY, INC. - LIBRARY □ Melville, NY
Schneer, Valerie, Ref.Libn.
YONKERS PUBLIC LIBRARY - FINE ARTS
DEPARTMENT □ Yonkers, NY
Schneider, Anne, Musm.Dir.
MONDAK HERITAGE CENTER - WILLO RALSTON
MEMORIAL LIBRARY FOR HISTORICAL
RESEARCH □ Sidney, MT
Schneider, Carole, Sec./Libn.
SQUIBB CANADA INC. - MEDICAL LIBRARY □
Montreal, PQ
Schneider, Cary A., Libn.
NATIONAL TRUST FOR HISTORIC
PRESERVATION - INFORMATION SERVICES □
Washington, DC
Schneider, Elizabeth, Hd., Tech.Serv.
MASSACHUSETTS GENERAL HOSPITAL - MGH
HEALTH SCIENCES LIBRARIES □ Boston, MA
Schneider, Helen, Ref.Libn.
AYERST LABORATORIES - INFORMATION
CENTER □ New York, NY
Schneider, Hennie R., Ref.Libn.
U.S. INTERNATIONAL TRADE COMMISSION -
LIBRARY □ Washington, DC
Schneider, Janet L., Libn.
U.S. AIR FORCE COMMUNICATIONS COMMAND
- TECHNICAL INFORMATION CENTER □ Scott
AFB, IL
Schneider, Karen, Libn.
THE PHILLIPS COLLECTION - LIBRARY □
Washington, DC
Schneider, Kelley, Dir.
MARICOPA COUNTY LAW LIBRARY □ Phoenix,
AZ
Schneider, L.C., Staff Mgr.
BELL COMMUNICATIONS RESEARCH, INC. -
INFORMATION RESOURCES SERVICES CENTER
□ Livingston, NJ
Schneider, Linda, Libn.
U.S. COURT OF APPEALS, 3RD CIRCUIT -
PITTSBURGH BRANCH LIBRARY □ Pittsburgh, PA
Schneider, Mary, Libn.
HONEYWELL, INC. - MICRO SWITCH
RESOURCE CENTER □ Freeport, IL
Schneider, Mary Jo, Lib.Hd.
THEOSOPHICAL SOCIETY IN AMERICA -
OLCOTT LIBRARY & RESEARCH CENTER □
Wheaton, IL
Schneider, Miriam, Libn.
MAINE AUDUBON SOCIETY - ENVIRONMENTAL
INFORMATION SERVICE □ Falmouth, ME
Schneider, Ralph, Hd., Hist.Sect.
CHICAGO PUBLIC LIBRARY CENTRAL LIBRARY -
SOCIAL SCIENCES & HISTORY DIVISION □
Chicago, IL
Schneidwind, Sarah
BORG-WARNER CORPORATION - ROY C.
INGERSOLL RESEARCH CENTER - TECHNICAL
INFORMATION SERVICES □ Des Plaines, IL
Schnepper, Mary McNamee, Cur. of Coll.
EVANSVILLE MUSEUM OF ARTS AND SCIENCE -
LIBRARY □ Evansville, IN
Schnick, Robert, Med.Libn.
U.S. VETERANS ADMINISTRATION (TX-San
Antonio) - MEDICAL CENTER LIBRARY SERVICE
(142D) □ San Antonio, TX
Schnick, Rosalie A., Tech.Info.Spec.
U.S. FISH & WILDLIFE SERVICE - NATIONAL
FISHERY RESEARCH LABORATORY LIBRARY □
La Crosse, WI
Schnieder, Tom, Asst.Libn.
ILLINOIS RAILWAY MUSEUM - TECHNICAL
LIBRARY □ Union, IL
Schnurrer, Darla, Musm.Asst.
BROWN COUNTY HISTORICAL SOCIETY -
MUSEUM LIBRARY □ New Ulm, MN
Schock, Richard G., Dir.
MOODY BIBLE INSTITUTE - LIBRARY □ Chicago,
IL

Schock, Richard G., Dir.
MOODY BIBLE INSTITUTE - MOODYANA
COLLECTION □ Chicago, IL
Schoelkopf, R. Gerald, Spec.Coll.Libn./Archv.
WEST CHESTER UNIVERSITY - FRANCIS
HARVEY GREEN LIBRARY - SPECIAL
COLLECTIONS □ West Chester, PA
Schoellkopf, Catharine, Hd.Libn.
FIDELITY MANAGEMENT & RESEARCH
COMPANY - LIBRARY □ Boston, MA
Schoen, Charlotte, Tech.Serv.
ASSOCIATION FOR RESEARCH AND
ENLIGHTENMENT - EDGAR CAYCE
FOUNDATION - LIBRARY □ Virginia Beach, VA
Schoen, Myron E., Dir.
UNION OF AMERICAN HEBREW
CONGREGATIONS - SYNAGOGUE
ARCHITECTURAL AND ART LIBRARY† □ New
York, NY
Schoenborn, Mrs. Rougean, Corp.Libn.
THERMO KING CORPORATION - LIBRARY □
Minneapolis, MN
Schoenbrun, Cyndi, Libn./Cons.
HAR ZION TEMPLE - IDA AND MATTHEW
RUDOFKER LIBRARY □ Penn Valley, PA
Schoenthaler, Jean A., Hd., Tech.Serv.
DREW UNIVERSITY - LIBRARY □ Madison, NJ
Schoenung, Dr. James G., Exec.Dir.
PENNSYLVANIA AREA LIBRARY NETWORK AND
UNION LIBRARY CATALOGUE OF
PENNSYLVANIA □ Philadelphia, PA
Schofer, Jane E., Libn.
AKIBA HEBREW ACADEMY - JOSEPH M. FIRST
LIBRARY □ Merion, PA
Schofield-Bodt, Cindy, Staff Libn.
BROOKLYN CHILDREN'S MUSEUM - STAFF
RESEARCH LIBRARY □ Brooklyn, NY
Scholberg, Henry, Libn.
UNIVERSITY OF MINNESOTA - AMES LIBRARY
OF SOUTH ASIA □ Minneapolis, MN
Scholten, Frances, Libn.
AMERICAN CYANAMID COMPANY -
ENVIRONMENTAL HEALTH LIBRARY† □ Wayne,
NJ
Scholtes, Hilda B., Univ.Archv.
MISSISSIPPI STATE UNIVERSITY - MITCHELL
MEMORIAL LIBRARY - SPECIAL COLLECTIONS
□ Mississippi State, MS
Scholz, John, Dir.
FIELD (Eugene) HOUSE AND TOY MUSEUM -
LIBRARY □ St. Louis, MO
Schonbrun, Rena, Libn.
U.S.D.A. - AGRICULTURAL RESEARCH SERVICE
- WESTERN REGIONAL RESEARCH CENTER
LIBRARY □ Berkeley, CA
Schonlaw, Sandra, Med.Libn.
U.S. VETERANS ADMINISTRATION (CA-Los
Angeles) - WADSWORTH MEDICAL LIBRARY
691W/142D □ Los Angeles, CA
Schooler, Helen, Libn.
MIAMI VALLEY REGIONAL PLANNING
COMMISSION - LIBRARY □ Dayton, OH
Schoolfield, Dudley B., Cat.
MOBIL RESEARCH & DEVELOPMENT
CORPORATION - DALLAS RESEARCH DIVISION
- LIBRARY □ Dallas, TX
Schoolman, Harold M., M.D., Act.Dir.
NATIONAL LIBRARY OF MEDICINE □ Bethesda,
MD
Schoon, Margaret S., Tech.Serv.Libn.
PURDUE UNIVERSITY, CALUMET - LIBRARY □
Hammond, IN
Schoonover, David E., Cur./Amer.Lit.
YALE UNIVERSITY - BEINECKE RARE BOOK
AND MANUSCRIPT LIBRARY □ New Haven, CT
Schoonover, Phyllis J., Music Libn.
BUTLER UNIVERSITY - JORDAN COLLEGE OF
FINE ARTS MUSIC LIBRARY □ Indianapolis, IN
Schop, Edith, Libn.
NEW YORK STATE SUPREME COURT - 3RD
JUDICIAL DISTRICT - HAMILTON ODELL
LIBRARY □ Monticello, NY

Schopmeier, Lee, Libn.
FRANKLIN (H.H.) CLUB - LIBRARY □ Cazenovia,
NY

Schorr, Jeanne, Libn.
DALLAS PUBLIC LIBRARY - HUMANITIES
DIVISION □ Dallas, TX

Schortman, Doris, Res.Libn.
PARADE PUBLICATIONS, INC. - LIBRARY □ New
York, NY

Schott, Evelyn, Libn.
OHEV SHALOM SYNAGOGUE - RAY DOBLITZ
MEMORIAL LIBRARY □ Wallingford, PA

Schrader, Jane Marie, Hd.Libn.
SILVER BURDETT COMPANY - EDITORIAL
LIBRARY □ Morristown, NJ

Schrag, Dwayne, Ref./Info.Serv.
KANSAS STATE UNIVERSITY - FARRELL
LIBRARY □ Manhattan, KS

Schram, Judy, AV Coord.
MICHIGAN OSTEOPATHIC MEDICAL CENTER,
INC. - HEALTH SCIENCE LIBRARY □ Detroit, MI

Schram, W., Lib.Instr.
WAYNE STATE UNIVERSITY - G. FLINT PURDY
LIBRARY □ Detroit, MI

Schramm, Jeanne, Ref.Libn.
WEST LIBERTY STATE COLLEGE - ELBIN
LIBRARY □ West Liberty, WV

Schramm, Mary T., Libn./Mgr., Info.Ctr.
PRC CONSOER, TOWNSEND, INC. - LIBRARY
AND INFORMATION CENTER □ Chicago, IL

Schreck, Kathleen A., Asst.Libn.
REPUBLIC STEEL CORPORATION - RESEARCH
CENTER LIBRARY □ Cleveland, OH

Schreiber, Ronnye, Ref.Libn.
AT & T INFORMATION SYSTEMS - LIBRARY □
Morristown, NJ

Schreibstein, Florence, Asst.Libn./Chf.Per.Libn.
YESHIVA UNIVERSITY - ALBERT EINSTEIN
COLLEGE OF MEDICINE - D. SAMUEL
GOTTESMAN LIBRARY □ Bronx, NY

Schreiner, Lyle, Professor
UNIVERSITY OF NEBRASKA, LINCOLN - C.Y.
THOMPSON LIBRARY □ Lincoln, NE

Schreiner, Lyle, Professor
UNIVERSITY OF NEBRASKA, LINCOLN -
DENTISTRY LIBRARY □ Lincoln, NE

Schriefer, Suzanne S., Mgr., Lib.Serv.
DYKEMA, GOSSETT, SPENCER, GOODNOW &
TRIGG - LAW LIBRARY □ Detroit, MI

Schrimpe, Janice, Res.Mgr.
AT & T COMMUNICATIONS - INFORMATION
RESEARCH CENTER □ Morris Plains, NJ

Schroader, Vanessa R.L., Mgr.
EG&G, INC. - WASHINGTON ANALYTICAL
SERVICES CENTER - INFORMATION CENTER □
Rockville, MD

Schroeder, D.
NORTH CAROLINA STATE SCIENCE AND
TECHNOLOGY RESEARCH CENTER □ Research
Triangle Park, NC

Schroeder, Edwin M., Dir.
FLORIDA STATE UNIVERSITY - LAW LIBRARY □
Tallahassee, FL

Schroeder, Eileen E., Hd.
UNIVERSITY OF NEW MEXICO - TIREMAN
LEARNING MATERIALS LIBRARY □ Albuquerque,
NM

Schroeder, Joseph R., Dir.
UNIVERSITY OF HOUSTON - AUDIOVISUAL
SERVICES □ Houston, TX

Schroeder, Leslie P., Libn.
CHRISTIAN CHURCH (Disciples of Christ), INC. -
DIVISION OF HIGHER EDUCATION - LIBRARY □
St. Louis, MO

Schroeder, Mary E., Archv./Hist.Libn.
UNITED METHODIST CHURCH - WISCONSIN
CONFERENCE - ARCHIVES □ Sun Prairie, WI

Schroeder, W.R. Bill, Mng.Dir.
FIRST INTERSTATE BANK ATHLETIC
FOUNDATION - LIBRARY □ Los Angeles, CA

Schroeder, William, Ref.
RUTGERS UNIVERSITY, THE STATE
UNIVERSITY OF NEW JERSEY - JUSTICE
HENRY ACKERSON LIBRARY OF LAW &
CRIMINAL JUSTICE □ Newark, NJ

Schroeppel, Harold S., Exec.Sec.
INSTITUTE FOR ADVANCED PERCEPTION -
LIBRARY □ Oak Park, IL

Schroeter, George, Assoc.Libn.
MOBILE PUBLIC LIBRARY - SPECIAL
COLLECTIONS DIVISION □ Mobile, AL

Schrotberger, W. Buck, Sr.Cons.
COLORADO STATE DEPARTMENT OF
EDUCATION - INSTRUCTIONAL MATERIALS
CENTER FOR THE VISUALLY HANDICAPPED □
Denver, CO

Schroth, Thelma, Cur.
CLOUD COUNTY HISTORICAL MUSEUM -
LIBRARY □ Concordia, KS

Schroyer, Helen, Govt.Doc.Libn.
PURDUE UNIVERSITY - HUMANITIES, SOCIAL
SCIENCE AND EDUCATION LIBRARY □ West
Lafayette, IN

Schryer, Michel, Fed.Lib. Liaison Off.
NATIONAL LIBRARY OF CANADA/
BIBLIOTHEQUE NATIONALE DU CANADA □
Ottawa, ON

Schuback, Judith, Libn.
UNIV. OF MEDICINE AND DENTISTRY OF NEW
JERSEY - SCHOOL OF OSTEOPATHIC MED. - DR.
JERROLD S. SCHWARTZ MEM. LIB. □ Stratford,
NJ

Schuberg, Delphie, Media Coord.
OREGON STATE SCHOOL FOR THE BLIND -
MEDIA CENTER □ Salem, OR

Schubert, Bettye, Ref.Libn.
INSTITUTE FOR DEFENSE ANALYSES -
TECHNICAL INFORMATION SERVICES □
Alexandria, VA

Schueller, Janette H., Info.Spec.
UNIVERSITY OF WASHINGTON - CENTER FOR
LAW & JUSTICE - CLJ/NCADBIP INFORMATION
SERVICE □ Seattle, WA

Schuermann, Lois J., Asst.Libn
AMERICAN PETROLEUM INSTITUTE - LIBRARY
□ Washington, DC

Schuffels, Zenaida, Cat.
LUNDEBERG MARYLAND SEAMANSHIP SCHOOL
- PAUL HALL LIBRARY AND MARITIME MUSEUM
□ Piney Point, MD

Schuh, Walter, Asst.Mgr.
ROA FILMS - LIBRARY □ Milwaukee, WI

Schuhle, Jacob, Educ.Ref.-Bibliog.
SUNY - COLLEGE AT CORTLAND - MEMORIAL
LIBRARY □ Cortland, NY

Schuld, Harry, Libn.
ALBERTA - DEPARTMENT OF PUBLIC WORKS,
SUPPLY & SERVICES - LIBRARY □ Edmonton, AB

Schuldt, Marcia, ILL Libn.
U.S. VETERANS ADMINISTRATION (TN-
Memphis) - MEDICAL CENTER LIBRARY □
Memphis, TN

Schulenberg, Patsy, Res.Spec.,Lib.Serv.
STERLING DRUG, INC. STERLING-WINTHROP
RESEARCH INSTITUTE - LIBRARY □ Rensselaer,
NY

Schuler, Betty K., Libn.
WAYNE COUNTY LAW LIBRARY ASSOCIATION
□ Wooster, OH

Schuler, Gail, Lib.Dir.
NAROPA INSTITUTE - LIBRARY □ Boulder, CO

Schuler, Linette, Lib.Instr.
UNIVERSITY OF WISCONSIN, STEVENS POINT
- JAMES H. ALBERTSON CENTER FOR
LEARNING RESOURCES □ Stevens Point, WI

Schulik, Barbara, Libn.
UNIDYNAMICS/ST. LOUIS, INC. - LIBRARY □
St. Louis, MO

Schulkin, Susan, Assoc.Libn.
PERKINS, COIE, STONE, OLSEN & WILLIAMS -
LAW LIBRARY □ Seattle, WA

Schuller, Dolores I., Asst.Tech.Libn.
BURROUGHS CORPORATION - TECHNICAL
INFORMATION CENTER □ Plymouth, MI

Schulmeyer, Alfred W., Supt.
U.S. NATL. PARK SERVICE - BIG HOLE NATL.
BATTLEFIELD - LIBRARY □ Wisdom, MT

Schulstadt, Chris, Libn.
LAC QUI PARLE COUNTY HISTORICAL SOCIETY
- MUSEUM LIBRARY □ Madison, MN

Schulte, Lorraine, Mgr.
UPJOHN COMPANY - CORPORATE TECHNICAL
LIBRARY □ Kalamazoo, MI

Schultz, Barbara A., Chf., Lib.Serv.
U.S. VETERANS ADMINISTRATION (OH-
Chillicothe) - HOSPITAL LIBRARY □ Chillicothe,
OH

Schultz, C.W., Dir.
MICHIGAN TECHNOLOGICAL UNIVERSITY -
INSTITUTE OF MINERAL RESEARCH □
Houghton, MI

Schultz, Dr. Charles R., Univ.Archv.
TEXAS A & M UNIVERSITY - ARCHIVES &
MANUSCRIPTS COLLECTIONS □ College Station,
TX

Schultz, Diane, Volunteer Coord.
FLORIDA STATE DIVISION OF BLIND SERVICES
- FLORIDA REGIONAL LIB. FOR THE BLIND &
PHYSICALLY HANDICAPPED □ Daytona Beach,
FL

Schultz, Elaine, Info.Spec.
BANK OF HAWAII - INFORMATION CENTER □
Honolulu, HI

Schultz, Erich, Pres.
WATERLOO HISTORICAL SOCIETY - LIBRARY □
Kitchener, ON

Schultz, Erich R.W., Univ.Libn.
WILFRID LAURIER UNIVERSITY - LIBRARY □
Waterloo, ON

Schultz, Henrietta, Libn.
CONGREGATION RODFEI ZEDEK - J.S.
HOFFMAN MEMORIAL LIBRARY □ Chicago, IL

Schultz, Jeffrey R., Dir.
RACINE COUNTY HISTORICAL SOCIETY AND
MUSEUM, INC. - LOCAL HISTORY AND
GENEALOGICAL REFERENCE LIBRARY □ Racine,
WI

Schultz, Jon S., Dir.
UNIVERSITY OF HOUSTON - LAW LIBRARY □
Houston, TX

Schultz, Kathleen, Libn.
WISCONSIN STATE DEPARTMENT OF NATURAL
RESOURCES - SOUTHEAST DISTRICT LIBRARY
□ Milwaukee, WI

Schultz, Linda, Supv.
NORTH DAKOTA STATE UNIVERSITY -
CHEMISTRY RESOURCE CENTER □ Fargo, ND

Schultz, Linda, Supv.
NORTH DAKOTA STATE UNIVERSITY -
PHARMACY RESOURCE CENTER □ Fargo, ND

Schultz, Marion E., Med.Libn.
SALEM COUNTY MEMORIAL HOSPITAL - DAVID
W. GREEN MEDICAL LIBRARY† □ Salem, NJ

Schultz, Mary Agnes, Asst.Libn.
ABELL (A.S.) PUBLISHING COMPANY INC. -THE
BALTIMORE SUN - LIBRARY □ Baltimore, MD

Schultz, Oscar C., Jr., Hd.Libn.
WINEBRENNER THEOLOGICAL SEMINARY -
LIBRARY □ Findlay, OH

Schultz, Ronald, Asst.Dir.
CALIFORNIA COLLEGE OF PODIATRIC
MEDICINE - SCHMIDT MEDICAL LIBRARY □ San
Francisco, CA

Schultz, Ruth, Asst.Dir.
AMERICAN DENTAL ASSOCIATION - BUREAU
OF LIBRARY SERVICES □ Chicago, IL

Schultze, Phyllis A., Libn.
RUTGERS UNIVERSITY, THE STATE
UNIVERSITY OF NEW JERSEY - CRIMINAL
JUSTICE/NCCD COLLECTION □ Newark, NJ

Schulz, Kathleen, Ref. & Per.Libn.
WITTENBERG UNIVERSITY - THOMAS LIBRARY
□ Springfield, OH

Schulz, Marilyn, Mgr., Acq. & Cat.
CANADIAN NATIONAL INSTITUTE FOR THE
BLIND - NATIONAL LIBRARY SERVICES -
SHERMAN SWIFT REFERENCE LIBRARY □
Toronto, ON

Schulze, Richard, Lib.Assoc.
IOWA STATE LAW LIBRARY □ Des Moines, IA

Schumacher, Roger, Dir.
HUNTERDON DEVELOPMENTAL CENTER -
ADAPTIVE LEARNING CENTER - LIBRARY □
Clinton, NJ

Schumaker, Donald, Bus.Anl.
MICHIGAN CONSOLIDATED GAS COMPANY -
CORPORATE LIBRARY □ Detroit, MI

Schumm, R.H., Data Anl.
U.S. NATL. BUREAU OF STANDARDS -
CHEMICAL THERMODYNAMICS DATA CENTER
□ Washington, DC

Schupmann, Mildred, Med.Libn.
MISSOURI BAPTIST HOSPITAL - MEDICAL
LIBRARY □ St. Louis, MO

Schur, Barbara S., Dir. of Lib.Serv.
BRENTWOOD HOSPITAL - LIBRARY □ Cleveland,
OH

Schurk, William L., Recording Archv.
BOWLING GREEN STATE UNIVERSITY - MUSIC
LIBRARY □ Bowling Green, OH

Schuster, Adeline, Hd.Libn.
HARRINGTON INSTITUTE OF INTERIOR
DESIGN - DESIGN LIBRARY □ Chicago, IL

Schutten, Marguerite, Info.Spec.
KRAFT, INC. - RESEARCH & DEVELOPMENT
LIBRARY □ Glenview, IL

Schutter, Daniel W., Supv., Analytical Group
CONGOLEUM CORPORATION - RESILIENT
FLOORING DIVISION - TECHNICAL RESEARCH
LIBRARY □ Trenton, NJ

Schutter, Tom, Corp.Libn.
U-HAUL INTERNATIONAL, INC. - CORPORATE
LIBRARY □ Phoenix, AZ

Schutz, Robert, Transl.
DOW CHEMICAL COMPANY - MERRELL DOW
PHARMACEUTICALS, INC. - RESEARCH CENTER
LIBRARY □ Cincinnati, OH

Schutzberg, Frances, Tech.Libn.
VERBEX CORPORATION - LIBRARY □ Bedford,
MA

Schutzer, Cynthia, Assoc.Libn.
HACKENSACK MEDICAL CENTER - MEDICAL
LIBRARY □ Hackensack, NJ

Schwamb, Don F., Corp.Libn.
VALUATION RESEARCH CORPORATION -
CORPORATE RESEARCH AND REFERENCE
LIBRARY □ Milwaukee, WI

Schwappach, Pat, Musm.Dir.
ANOKA COUNTY HISTORICAL GENEALOGICAL
SOCIETY - LIBRARY □ Anoka, MN

Schwark, Bryan L.
UNIVERSITY OF WISCONSIN, PLATTEVILLE -
KARRMANN LIBRARY - SPECIAL COLLECTIONS
□ Platteville, WI

Schwartz, Amelia, Dir., Lib.Serv.
ZIFF-DAVIS PUBLISHING COMPANY -
TRANSPORTATION DIVISION - LIBRARY □ New
York, NY

Schwartz, Carol, Libn.
INTERNATIONAL LONGSHOREMEN'S AND
WAREHOUSEMEN'S UNION - ANNE RAND
RESEARCH LIBRARY □ San Francisco, CA

Schwartz, Carole, Asst.Libn., Archv.
CINCINNATI ART MUSEUM - LIBRARY □
Cincinnati, OH

Schwartz, Diane G., Ref.Hd.
UNIVERSITY OF MICHIGAN - ALFRED
TAUBMAN MEDICAL LIBRARY □ Ann Arbor, MI

Schwartz, Ellen, Libn.
CALIFORNIA STATE RAILROAD MUSEUM -
LIBRARY □ Sacramento, CA

Schwartz, Heidi, Asst.Libn.
AMERICAN PUBLIC POWER ASSOCIATION -
LIBRARY □ Washington, DC

Schwartz, Herbert, Res.Coord.
BIOVIVAN RESEARCH INSTITUTE - LIBRARY □
Vineland, NJ

Schwartz, Herbert, Sys.
WILFRID LAURIER UNIVERSITY - LIBRARY □
Waterloo, ON

Schwartz, Julie, Libn.
SQUARE D COMPANY - LIBRARY □ Milwaukee,
WI

Schwartz, Lillian, Libn.
TEMPLE EMANU-EL - CONGREGATIONAL
LIBRARY □ Providence, RI

Schwartz, Marla, Tech.Serv.Libn.
URBAN INSTITUTE - LIBRARY □ Washington,
DC

Schwartz, Mortimer D., Law Libn.
UNIVERSITY OF CALIFORNIA, DAVIS - SCHOOL
OF LAW - LAW LIBRARY □ Davis, CA

Schwartz, Pincus, Asst.Libn.
YESHIVA TORAH VODAATH AND MESIFTA -
TORAH VODAATH LIBRARY □ Brooklyn, NY

Schwartz, Rosaline, Dir., Pub.Prog.
YIVO INSTITUTE FOR JEWISH RESEARCH -
LIBRARY AND ARCHIVES □ New York, NY

Schwartz, Ruth, Asst.Libn.
POSTGRADUATE CENTER FOR MENTAL HEALTH
- EMIL A. GUTHEIL MEMORIAL LIBRARY □ New
York, NY

Schwartzbauer, Eileen, Dept.Hd.
MINNEAPOLIS PUBLIC LIBRARY &
INFORMATION CENTER - SOCIOLOGY
DEPARTMENT □ Minneapolis, MN

Schwarz, Betty P., Mgr.
MERCK & COMPANY, INC. - CALGON
CORPORATION - INFORMATION CENTER □
Pittsburgh, PA

Schwarz, Gayle, Libn.
NORTH OAKLAND GENEALOGICAL SOCIETY -
LIBRARY □ Lake Orion, MI

Schwarz, Joanne L., Ldr.
MILLER BREWING COMPANY - SCIENTIFIC
TECHNICAL INFORMATION FACILITY □
Milwaukee, WI

Schwarz, Marta, Dept.Hd.
YONKERS PUBLIC LIBRARY - INFORMATION
SERVICES - TECHNICAL & BUSINESS DIVISION
□ Yonkers, NY

Schwass, Earl R., Dir.
U.S. NAVY - NAVAL WAR COLLEGE - LIBRARY □
Newport, RI

Schwegel, Richard, Hd., Music Sect.
CHICAGO PUBLIC LIBRARY CULTURAL CENTER
- FINE ARTS DIVISION - MUSIC SECTION □
Chicago, IL

Schweitzer, Leland R., Mgr. of Res.Lab.
ASGROW SEED COMPANY - RESEARCH CENTER
□ Twin Falls, ID

Schweitzer, Margaret C., Libn.
HOUGHTON (E.F.) TECHNICAL CENTER -
LIBRARY □ Valley Forge, PA

Schwellenbach, Sue, Asst.Libn.
ROCKY MOUNTAIN NEWS - LIBRARY □ Denver,
CO

Schwenke, Eszter L.K., Hd.
UNIVERSITY OF NEW BRUNSWICK - SCIENCE
LIBRARY □ Fredericton, NB

Schwerzel, Sharon, Hd., Ref.Serv.
FLORIDA INSTITUTE OF TECHNOLOGY -
LIBRARY □ Melbourne, FL

Schwetzer, Ellen, Rd.Serv.
CONCORDIA THEOLOGICAL SEMINARY -
LIBRARY □ Fort Wayne, IN

Schwichtenberg, Cheryl, Libn.
MEDTRONIC, INC. - LIBRARY† □ Minneapolis,
MN

Schwind, Jean, Asst.Libn.
MICHIGAN MOLECULAR INSTITUTE - LIBRARY
□ Midland, MI

Schwinn, Sr. De Paul, S.S.N.D., Hd.
ST. MARY'S SEMINARY - ST. MARY'S OF THE
BARRENS LIBRARY □ Perryville, MO

Sciamma, Leon-Pierre, Responsable
UNIVERSITE DU QUEBEC A MONTREAL -
CARTOTHEQUE □ Montreal, PQ

Sciattara, Diane, Ref.Libn.
PORT AUTHORITY OF NEW YORK AND NEW
JERSEY - LIBRARY □ New York, NY

Sciotti, Angela M., Art & Mus.Libn.
FORBES LIBRARY □ Northampton, MA

Scirica, Rosemarie, Lib.Adm.
SPERRY - LAW LIBRARY □ New York, NY

Scism, Nancy, Cat.Libn.
GUILFORD COLLEGE - LIBRARY - SPECIAL
COLLECTIONS □ Greensboro, NC

Sciuridae, Bro. Solomon, O.B.
INTERNATIONAL BROTHERHOOD OF OLD
BASTARDS, INC. - SIR THOMAS CRAPPER
MEMORIAL ARCHIVES □ St. Louis, MO

Scofield, Constance, Interlib.Coop.Libn.
SOUTH DAKOTA STATE LIBRARY & ARCHIVES □
Pierre, SD

Scofield, James S., Chf.Libn.
ST. PETERSBURG TIMES AND EVENING
INDEPENDENT - LIBRARY □ St. Petersburg, FL

Scoggins, Lillian, Asst.Libn., Tech.Serv.
LUTHERAN THEOLOGICAL SEMINARY - KRAUTH
MEMORIAL LIBRARY □ Philadelphia, PA

Scollie, F.B., Chf.Libn.
CANADA - ENERGY, MINES & RESOURCES
CANADA - HEADQUARTERS LIBRARY □ Ottawa,
ON

Scollin, Ruth B., Libn.
SANTA BARBARA COUNTY GENEALOGICAL
SOCIETY - LIBRARY □ Goleta, CA

Scoones, Lori, Asst.Libn.
GENERAL ELECTRIC COMPANY - AIRCRAFT
EQUIPMENT DIV. - AEROSPACE ELECTRONIC
SYSTEMS DEPT. - INFO.RSRCS. CENTER □
Utica, NY

Scott, Adella B., Dir. of LRC
WASHTENAW COMMUNITY COLLEGE -
LEARNING RESOURCE CENTER - SPECIAL
COLLECTIONS □ Ann Arbor, MI

Scott, Aletris, Lib.Asst.
MEMPHIS STATE UNIVERSITY LIBRARIES -
CHEMISTRY LIBRARY □ Memphis, TN

Scott, Alfredia A., Libn.
GEORGIA STATE DEPARTMENT OF
TRANSPORTATION - RESEARCH LIBRARY □
Atlanta, GA

Scott, Ann, Asst.Dir., Adm.
KANSAS STATE UNIVERSITY - FARRELL
LIBRARY □ Manhattan, KS

Scott, Barbara G., Dir.
BIRMINGHAM-SOUTHERN COLLEGE - CHARLES
ANDREW RUSH LEARNING CENTER/LIBRARY -
SPECIAL COLLECTIONS □ Birmingham, AL

Scott, Betty Ann, Pub.Lib.Cons.
STATE LIBRARY OF FLORIDA □ Tallahassee, FL

Scott, Betty Z., Libn.
SNOHOMISH COUNTY LAW LIBRARY □ Everett
WA

Scott, Brenda, Dir. of Libs.
GEORGIA STATE DEPARTMENT OF HUMAN
RESOURCES - GEORGIA MENTAL HEALTH
INSTITUTE - ADDISON M. DUVAL LIBRARY† □
Atlanta, GA

Scott, Brenda, Supv., Lib. & Files
MARYLAND STATE DEPARTMENT OF HEALTH &
MENTAL HYGIENE - LIBRARY† □ Baltimore, MD

Scott, Carolyn, Libn.
FAEGRE & BENSON - LAW LIBRARY □
Minneapolis, MN

Scott, Catherine D., Libn.
SMITHSONIAN INSTITUTION LIBRARIES -
MUSEUM REFERENCE CENTER □ Washington,
DC

Scott, Sr. Consuela, Per.Libn./ILL
CHRIST THE KING SEMINARY - LIBRARY □ East
Aurora, NY

Scott, Duscha S., Dir.
JACKSON HOMESTEAD - LIBRARY &
MANUSCRIPT COLLECTION □ Newton, MA

Scott, Edward A., Hd.Libn.
KEENE STATE COLLEGE - WALLACE E. MASON
LIBRARY □ Keene, NH

Scott, Enid M., Libn.
KINGSTON GENERAL HOSPITAL - HOSPITAL
LIBRARY □ Kingston, ON

Scott, Gloria, Preservation Coord.
BOWLING GREEN STATE UNIVERSITY -
CENTER FOR ARCHIVAL COLLECTIONS □
Bowling Green, OH

Scott, Gregory M., Pres.
TRIGOM - RESEARCH LIBRARY □ North
Windham, ME

Scott, Hilda, Libn.
NORTON GALLERY AND SCHOOL OF ART -
LIBRARY □ West Palm Beach, FL

Scott, Ingrid
LAKEHEAD UNIVERSITY - CHANCELLOR
PATERSON LIBRARY □ Thunder Bay, ON

Scott, James F., Lib.Dir.
MULTNOMAH SCHOOL OF THE BIBLE - JOHN
AND MARY MITCHELL LIBRARY □ Portland, OR

Scott, Dr. James W., Dir.
WESTERN WASHINGTON UNIVERSITY -
CENTER FOR PACIFIC NORTHWEST STUDIES □
Bellingham, WA

Scott, Jean M., Acq./Doc.Libn.
SETON HALL UNIVERSITY - SCHOOL OF LAW -
LAW LIBRARY □ Newark, NJ

Scott, Joseph
UNIVERSITY OF CONNECTICUT - MUSIC
LIBRARY □ Storrs, CT

Scott, Karen P., Dir.
UNIVERSITY OF WYOMING - WYOMING
CAREER INFORMATION SYSTEM □ Laramie, WY

Scott, Kathryn, Chf.Cat.
NATIONAL SOCIETY, DAUGHTERS OF THE
AMERICAN REVOLUTION - LIBRARY □
Washington, DC

Scott, Linda, Libn.
ALBERTA ALCOHOLISM AND DRUG ABUSE
COMMISSION - LIBRARY □ Calgary, AB

Scott, Linda, Hd.Libn.
GRANT (Alexander) & COMPANY - CHICAGO
OFFICE LIBRARY □ Chicago, IL

Scott, Linda, Lib.Techn.
IMPERIAL OIL, LTD. - AUDIO-VISUAL
RESOURCE CENTRE □ Toronto, ON

Scott, Marianne, Natl.Libn.
NATIONAL LIBRARY OF CANADA/
BIBLIOTHEQUE NATIONALE DU CANADA □
Ottawa, ON

Scott, Mary Ellen, Cat./Archv.
PITTSBURGH THEOLOGICAL SEMINARY -
CLIFFORD E. BARBOUR LIBRARY □ Pittsburgh,
PA

Scott, Mary T., Asst.Corp.Libn.
TRAVELERS INSURANCE COMPANIES -
CORPORATE LIBRARY □ Hartford, CT

Scott, Mary W., Libn.
UNIVERSITY OF NORTH DAKOTA - ENERGY
RESEARCH CENTER - ENERGY LIBRARY □ Grand
Forks, ND

Scott, Melissa, Ref.Libn.
BELL COMMUNICATIONS RESEARCH, INC. -
INFORMATION RESOURCES SERVICES CENTER
□ Piscataway, NJ

Scott, Melvia A., Libn.
FULLER & HENRY - LIBRARY □ Toledo, OH

Scott, Michael D., Exec.Dir.
CENTER FOR COMPUTER/LAW - LIBRARY □ Los
Angeles, CA

Scott, Nancy, Spec.Coll.Libn./Archv.
GETTYSBURG COLLEGE - MUSSELMAN LIBRARY
- SPECIAL COLLECTIONS □ Gettysburg, PA

Scott, Richard D., Mgr.
MASSACHUSETTS INSTITUTE OF TECHNOLOGY
- INFORMATION PROCESSING SERVICES -
READING ROOM □ Cambridge, MA

Scott, Richard P., Cat.
NATIONAL SCIENCE FOUNDATION - LIBRARY □
Washington, DC

Scott, Sandra, Pub.Serv.
TECHNICAL UNIVERSITY OF NOVA SCOTIA -
LIBRARY □ Halifax, NS

Scott, Sarah, Lib.Mgr.
U.S. NASA - GODDARD INSTITUTE FOR SPACE
STUDIES - LIBRARY □ New York, NY

Scott, Sharon, Asst.Cur.
CHICAGO PUBLIC LIBRARY CULTURAL CENTER
- VIVIAN G. HARSH COLLECTION OF AFRO-
AMERICAN HISTORY & LIT.† □ Chicago, IL

Scott, Shirley, Asst.Hd.
MICHIGAN STATE UNIVERSITY - SCIENCE
LIBRARY □ East Lansing, MI

Scott, Sue, Circ.Libn.
NORTH CAROLINA STATE DEPARTMENT OF
CULTURAL RESOURCES - LIBRARY FOR THE
BLIND AND PHYSICALLY HANDICAPPED □
Raleigh, NC

Scott, Ursula, Info.Serv.
TEXAS TECH UNIVERSITY - HEALTH SCIENCES
CENTER - LIBRARY OF THE HEALTH SCIENCES
□ Lubbock, TX

Scott, Virginia, Hd.Libn.
LINN-HENLEY LIBRARY FOR SOUTHERN
HISTORICAL RESEARCH - TUTWILER
COLLECTION OF SOUTHERN HISTORY AND
LITERATURE □ Birmingham, AL

Scott, Wendy, Campus Libn.
CENTENNIAL COLLEGE OF APPLIED ARTS &
TECHNOLOGY - ASHTONBEE CAMPUS
RESOURCE CENTRE □ Scarborough, ON

Scott, Wendy, Sect.Hd.
NATIONAL LIBRARY OF CANADA - REFERENCE
SERVICES SECTION □ Ottawa, ON

Scott, Willie, Asst.Libn.
SOUTHERN ILLINOIS UNIVERSITY,
CARBONDALE - UNDERGRADUATE LIBRARY □
Carbondale, IL

Scotti, Cecelia B., Hd.Libn.
LORD, DAY & LORD - LIBRARY □ New York, NY

Scowcroft, Deborah, Adm.Asst.
AMERICAN JUSTICE INSTITUTE - LIBRARY □
Sacramento, CA

Scowen, Amy L., Info.Serv.Spec.
TOWERS, PERRIN, FORSTER & CROSBY -
INFORMATION CENTRE □ Montreal, PQ

Scrofani, Robert, Exec. V.P.
GEORGE (Henry) SCHOOL OF SOCIAL SCIENCE -
RESEARCH LIBRARY □ San Francisco, CA

Scroggins, Mary B., Libn.
OREGON STATE UNIVERSITY - SCHOOL OF
FORESTRY - FRL LIBRARY □ Corvallis, OR

Scroggs, Marie, Adm.Asst.
U.S. DEPT. OF COMMERCE - LIBRARY □
Washington, DC

Scroggs, W.B., Tech.Info.Coord.
SURGIKOS - TECHNICAL INFORMATION
CENTER □ Arlington, TX

Scudder, G.G.E., Dir.
UNIVERSITY OF BRITISH COLUMBIA -
SPENCER ENTOMOLOGICAL MUSEUM -
LIBRARY □ Vancouver, BC

Scull, Roberta A., Libn.
LOUISIANA STATE UNIVERSITY - BUSINESS
ADMINISTRATION/GOVERNMENT
DOCUMENTS DEPARTMENT □ Baton Rouge, LA

Scully, Mariwayne, Info.Ctr.Mgr.
MOUNTAIN STATES EMPLOYERS COUNCIL -
INFORMATION CENTER □ Denver, CO

Scully, Mary Carol, Info.Anl.
MERCK & COMPANY, INC. - MERCK SHARP &
DOHME RESEARCH LABORATORIES -
RESEARCH INFORMATION SYSTEMS □ Rahway,
NJ

Scura, Georgia, Dir.
UNIVERSITY OF CONNECTICUT - PHARMACY
LIBRARY AND LEARNING CENTER □ Storrs, CT

Seaba, Hazel H., Dir.
UNIVERSITY OF IOWA - COLLEGE OF
PHARMACY - IOWA DRUG INFORMATION
SERVICE □ Iowa City, IA

Seaberg, Eileen J., Hd.Libn.
FLUOR ENGINEERING INC. - FLUOR POWER
SERVICES, INC. - LIBRARY† □ Chicago, IL

Seaberry, Ivy, Lib.Techn.
U.S. NAVY - NAVAL SUPPLY CENTER -
TECHNICAL DIVISION - TECHNICAL LIBRARY □
San Diego, CA

Seabrooks, Nettie H., Mgr.
GENERAL MOTORS CORPORATION - PUBLIC
RELATIONS STAFF LIBRARY □ Detroit, MI

Seaburg, Alan, Mss. and Archv.
HARVARD UNIVERSITY - DIVINITY SCHOOL -
ANDOVER-HARVARD THEOLOGICAL LIBRARY □
Cambridge, MA

Seaburg, Carl, Info.Off./Archv.
UNITARIAN-UNIVERSALIST ASSOCIATION -
ARCHIVES □ Boston, MA

Seabury, Doris, Cur.
MADERA COUNTY HISTORICAL SOCIETY -
MUSEUM/LIBRARY □ Madera, CA

Seagle, Janet, Libn./Musm.Cur.
UNITED STATES GOLF ASSOCIATION - GOLF
HOUSE LIBRARY □ Far Hills, NJ

Seagrave, Gerald, Staff Libn.
CONNECTICUT STATE DEPARTMENT OF
CHILDREN & YOUTH SERVICES - STAFF
LIBRARY □ Hartford, CT

Sealy, Jean, Libn.
CANADA - CANADIAN WILDLIFE SERVICE -
ATLANTIC REGION LIBRARY □ Sackville, NB

Seaman, Anne T., Libn.
HONOLULU ACADEMY OF ARTS - ROBERT
ALLERTON LIBRARY □ Honolulu, HI

Seaman, Mary, Libn.
KWASHA LIPTON - LIBRARY □ Fort Lee, NJ

Seaman, Maureen G., Libn.
OREGON GRADUATE CENTER FOR STUDY AND
RESEARCH - LIBRARY □ Beaverton, OR

Seaman, Sara, Tech.Libn.
WILLIAMS BROTHERS ENGINEERING COMPANY
- TECHNICAL INFORMATION CENTER† □ Tulsa,
OK

Seamans, Nancy H., Libn.
HAYES, SEAY, MATTERN & MATTERN -
TECHNICAL LIBRARY □ Roanoke, VA

Seamans, Warren A., Dir.
MASSACHUSETTS INSTITUTE OF TECHNOLOGY
- M.I.T. MUSEUM AND HISTORICAL
COLLECTIONS □ Cambridge, MA

Seamon, Judy, Assoc.Dir., Media
HUDSON VALLEY COMMUNITY COLLEGE -
DWIGHT MARVIN LEARNING RESOURCES
CENTER □ Troy, NY

Searle, JoAnne M., Dir.
MORRISTOWN MEMORIAL HOSPITAL -
LATHROPE HEALTH SCIENCES LIBRARY □
Morristown, NJ

Searls, Eileen H., Law Libn.
ST. LOUIS UNIVERSITY - SCHOOL OF LAW -
LIBRARY □ St. Louis, MO

Searls, Keith A., Libn.
ASSOCIATION OF TRIAL LAWYERS OF
AMERICA - ATLA LIBRARY □ Washington, DC

Sears, Julienne, Regional Libn.
ENVIRONMENTAL PROTECTION AGENCY -
REGION X LIBRARY □ Seattle, WA

Sears, Linda A., Libn., Sr.
WEST CENTRAL GEORGIA REGIONAL
HOSPITAL - THE LIBRARY □ Columbus, GA

Sears, Patsy Sweeney, Libn.
BIRMINGHAM PUBLIC AND JEFFERSON
COUNTY FREE LIBRARY - ART AND MUSIC
DEPARTMENT □ Birmingham, AL

Sears, Phyllis J., Supv.
CHRYSLER CORPORATION - ENGINEERING
DIVISION - ENGINEERING LIBRARY □ Detroit,
MI

Sears, Russell L., Acq.Libn.
AMERICAN GRADUATE SCHOOL OF
INTERNATIONAL MANAGEMENT - LIBRARY† □
Glendale, AZ

Seath, William B., Info.Mgr.
YAMAHA MOTOR CORPORATION USA -
YAMAHA R&D MINNESOTA - RESEARCH
LIBRARY □ Coon Rapids, MN

Seaton, Helen J., Libn.
MISSOURI BAPTIST HOSPITAL - SCHOOL OF
NURSING LIBRARY □ St. Louis, MO

Seaver, Barry W., Libn.
NEW YORK CITY - OFFICE OF CHIEF MEDICAL
EXAMINER - MILTON HELPERN LIBRARY OF
LEGAL MEDICINE □ New York, NY

Seawell, Karen, AHEC Libn.
CONE (Moses H.) MEMORIAL HOSPITAL -
MEDICAL LIBRARY □ Greensboro, NC

Seboek, L.
CANADA - PUBLIC ARCHIVES OF CANADA -
NATIONAL MAP COLLECTION □ Ottawa, ON

Sechrest, S., Doc.
UNIVERSITY OF WISCONSIN, LA CROSSE -
MURPHY LIBRARY □ La Crosse, WI

Sechrist, Patricia, Law Libn.
AETNA LIFE & CASUALTY COMPANY - LAW
LIBRARY □ Hartford, CT

Secunda, Jeannette L., Libn.
HOME LIFE INSURANCE COMPANY - LIBRARY □
New York, NY

Sederstrom, Gene, Tech.Serv.Libn.
UNIVERSITY OF SOUTH DAKOTA - CHRISTIAN
P. LOMMEN HEALTH SCIENCES LIBRARY □
Vermillion, SD

Sedgwick, Dorothy L., Hd.Libn.
PRICE WATERHOUSE - NATIONAL/TORONTO
OFFICE LIBRARY □ Toronto, ON

Sedgwick, Frederica M., Dir.
LOYOLA LAW SCHOOL - LIBRARY □ Los Angeles,
CA

Sedgwick, Gregory B., Tech.Libn.
LEEDSHILL-HERKENHOFF, INC.- LIBRARY □ San
Francisco, CA

Sedgwick, Kent, Libn.
PRINCE GEORGE CITY PLANNING
DEPARTMENT - PLANNING LIBRARY □ Prince
George, BC

Sedgwick, Shirley, Chf., Acq.
WYOMING STATE LIBRARY □ Cheyenne, WY

Sedlacek, Marie, Cat.
JOSLYN ART MUSEUM - ART REFERENCE
LIBRARY □ Omaha, NE

See, Donna, Libn.
WEST VIRGINIA SCHOOLS FOR THE DEAF AND
BLIND - WV SCHOOL FOR THE BLIND LIBRARY
□ Romney, WV

Seebaum, Carol, Med.Libn.
FAMILY PRACTICE RESIDENCY PROGRAM AT
CHEYENNE - FAMILY PRACTICE LIBRARY AT
CHEYENNE □ Cheyenne, WY

Seeber, Frances M., Sr.Supv.Archv.
U.S. PRESIDENTIAL LIBRARIES - FRANKLIN D.
ROOSEVELT LIBRARY □ Hyde Park, NY

Seeds, Robert, Health Sci.Libn.
PENNSYLVANIA STATE UNIVERSITY - LIFE
SCIENCES LIBRARY □ University Park, PA

Seefeldt, Roberta B., Mgr., Info.Serv.
BORG-WARNER CORPORATION - ROY C.
INGERSOLL RESEARCH CENTER - TECHNICAL
INFORMATION SERVICES □ Des Plaines, IL

Seeger, Anthony, Dir.
INDIANA UNIVERSITY - ARCHIVES OF
TRADITIONAL MUSIC □ Bloomington, IN

Seeger, Lei, Assoc. Law Libn.
UNIVERSITY OF PUGET SOUND - SCHOOL OF
LAW LIBRARY □ Tacoma, WA

Seeger, Marcia K., Libn.
LUTHERAN CHURCH - MISSOURI SYNOD -
LUTHERAN LIBRARY FOR THE BLIND □ St. Louis,
MO

Seegmiller, David W., Libn.
CHURCH OF JESUS CHRIST OF LATTER-DAY
SAINTS - ALBUQUERQUE BRANCH
GENEALOGICAL LIBRARY □ Albuquerque, NM

Seegraber, Frank J., Libn.
BOSTON COLLEGE - SPECIAL COLLECTIONS
DEPARTMENT □ Chestnut Hill, MA

Seeley, Catherine, Ref.Libn.
SUNY - UPSTATE MEDICAL CENTER LIBRARY □
Syracuse, NY

Seeley, Joan, Hd., Circ.Serv.
LAKEHEAD UNIVERSITY - CHANCELLOR
PATERSON LIBRARY □ Thunder Bay, ON

Seeley, Marianna M., Tech.Libn.
BURROUGHS CORPORATION - RANCHO
BERNARDO TECHNICAL INFORMATION CENTER
□ San Diego, CA

Seelick, Beth, Asst.Libn.
DEWEY, BALLANTINE, BUSHBY, PALMER &
WOOD - LIBRARY □ New York, NY

Seeling, Sherri, Res.Spec.
UNIVERSAL CITY STUDIOS - RESEARCH
DEPARTMENT LIBRARY □ Universal City, CA

Seeman, Ann M., Act.Dir.
UNION COLLEGE - SCHAFFER LIBRARY -
SPECIAL COLLECTIONS □ Schenectady, NY

Seemann, Charlie, Dp.Dir., Coll. & Res.
COUNTRY MUSIC FOUNDATION - LIBRARY AND
MEDIA CENTER □ Nashville, TN

Seer, Gitelle, Libn.
DEWEY, BALLANTINE, BUSHBY, PALMER &
WOOD - LIBRARY □ New York, NY

Seery, John A., Pub.Serv.
ASBURY THEOLOGICAL SEMINARY - B.L.
FISHER LIBRARY □ Wilmore, KY

Seevaratnam, Mrs. Rukmini, Supv. Abstractor
NATIONAL ACADEMY OF SCIENCES -
NATIONAL RESEARCH COUNCIL - HIGHWAY
RESEARCH INFORMATION SERVICE □
Washington, DC

Seevers, James, Astronomer
ADLER PLANETARIUM - LIBRARY □ Chicago, IL

Sefcik, Sylvia J., Base Libn.
U.S. AIR FORCE BASE - BEALE BASE LIBRARY □
Beale AFB, CA

Sefton, Amelia K., Libn. I
U.S. ARMY POST - FORT HAMILTON - LIBRARY
□ Brooklyn, NY

Segal, JoAn S., Exec.Dir.
BIBLIOGRAPHICAL CENTER FOR RESEARCH -
ROCKY MOUNTAIN REGION, INC. □ Denver, CO

Segal, Norma, Hd.
SUNY AT BUFFALO - ARCHITECTURE &
ENVIRONMENTAL DESIGN LIBRARY □ Buffalo,
NY

Segal, Sheryl A., Lib.Dir.
U.S. FEDERAL COMMUNICATIONS
COMMISSION - LIBRARY† □ Washington, DC

Segall, Andrea, Law Libn.
LINCOLN UNIVERSITY - LAW LIBRARY† □ San
Francisco, CA

Segall, Michella, Libn.
HEBREW INSTITUTE OF PITTSBURGH - SOL
ROSENBLOOM LIBRARY □ Pittsburgh, PA

Segarra, Carmen G., Libn.
CORNELL UNIVERSITY - ARECIBO
OBSERVATORY - LIBRARY □ Arecibo, PR

Segel, James, Exec.Dir.
MASSACHUSETTS MUNICIPAL ASSOCIATION -
RESEARCH LIBRARY □ Boston, MA

Seger, Susan I., Hd.Libn.
UNIVERSITY OF MICHIGAN - DENTISTRY
LIBRARY □ Ann Arbor, MI

Segger, Martin, Cur.
UNIVERSITY OF VICTORIA - KATHARINE
MALTWOOD COLLECTION □ Victoria, BC

Seglin, Adelia P., Dir., Med.Lib.
ST. JOSEPH'S HOSPITAL - MEDICAL LIBRARY □
Tampa, FL

Seguin, Diane, Lib.Techn.
HOPITAL SANTA CABRINI - BIBLIOTHEQUE
MEDICALE □ Montreal, PQ

Seguin, JoAnn, Registrar
NORTHWOOD INSTITUTE OF TEXAS -
ROSALIND KRESS HALEY LIBRARY □ Cedar Hill,
TX

Seguin, L., Coord.
SIDBEC-DOSCO INC. - CENTRE DE
DOCUMENTATION □ Contrecoeur, PQ

Seibels, Cynthia, Libn.
KENNEDY GALLERIES - ART LIBRARY □ New
York, NY

Seibert, Donald, Dept.Hd./Music Bibliog.
SYRACUSE UNIVERSITY - E.S. BIRD LIBRARY -
FINE ARTS DEPARTMENT □ Syracuse, NY

Seidel, Elizabeth, Cat.
INTERNATIONAL MUSEUM OF PHOTOGRAPHY
AT GEORGE EASTMAN HOUSE - LIBRARY □
Rochester, NY

Seidel, Mrs. Leslie R., Med.Libn.
U.S. ARMY HOSPITALS - CUTLER ARMY
HOSPITAL - MEDICAL LIBRARY □ Ft. Devens,
MA

Seidel, Robert C., Libn.
U.S. ARMY - MATERIALS & MECHANICS
RESEARCH CENTER - TECHNICAL LIBRARY □
Watertown, MA

Seider, Diana L., Asst.Dir.
KERN COUNTY MUSEUM - LIBRARY □
Bakersfield, CA

Seidler, Janice, Hd.Libn.
MATHEMATICAL REVIEWS - LIBRARY □ Ann
Arbor, MI

Seidler, Louise M., Supv.
AMOCO PRODUCTION COMPANY - NEW
ORLEANS REGION -.LIBRARY INFORMATION
CENTER □ New Orleans, LA

Seidman, Ann M., Mgr.
STALEY (A.E.) MANUFACTURING COMPANY -
TECHNICAL INFORMATION CENTER □ Decatur,
IL

Seidman, Ruth K., Dir.
U.S. AIR FORCE - AIR FORCE SYSTEMS
COMMAND - AIR FORCE GEOPHYSICS
LABORATORY - RESEARCH LIBRARY □ Bedford,
MA

Seifer, Marc, Dir.
METASCIENCE FOUNDATION - LIBRARY □
Kingston, RI

Seifert, Jan, Fine Arts Libn.
UNIVERSITY OF OKLAHOMA - MUSIC LIBRARY
□ Norman, OK

Seiffer, Lynn, Ref.Libn.
NEWSWEEK, INC. - LIBRARY □ New York, NY

Seiglar, Barbara, Dir.
BAPTIST MEDICAL CENTER - LIBRARY □
Kansas City, MO

Seigle, Jeanne C., Law Libn.
ALLIED CORPORATION - LAW LIBRARY □
Morristown, NJ

Seilhamer, Larry, Cat.
BRIDGEWATER COLLEGE - ALEXANDER MACK
MEMORIAL LIBRARY - SPECIAL COLLECTIONS
□ Bridgewater, VA

Sein, Jacqueline J., Asst.Chf.
DISTRICT OF COLUMBIA PUBLIC LIBRARY -
POPULAR LIBRARY □ Washington, DC

Seinfeld, Evelyn, Libn.
AMERICAN FEDERATION OF STATE, COUNTY
AND MUNICIPAL EMPLOYEES, AFL-CIO
(AFSCME) - DC37 RESEARCH LIBRARY □ New
York, NY

Seitz, Betty, Supv., Info.Serv.
SCOTT (O.M.) AND SONS - INFORMATION
SERVICES □ Marysville, OH

Sekerak, Bob, Plan.Off.
UNIVERSITY OF VERMONT - DIVISION OF
HEALTH SCIENCES - CHARLES A. DANA
MEDICAL LIBRARY □ Burlington, VT

Seki, Gayle A., Supv.
TRW, INC. - OPERATIONS & SUPPORT GROUP -
ELECTRONICS & DEFENSE SECTOR - TECH.
INFORMATION CENTER □ Redondo Beach, CA

Sekine, Gail, Braneida Supv.
MOHAWK COLLEGE OF APPLIED ARTS AND
TECHNOLOGY - MOHAWK LIBRARY RESOURCE
CENTRE □ Hamilton, ON

Sekscenski, Paul
U.S. DEPT. OF LABOR - BUREAU OF LABOR
STATISTICS - INFORMATION AND ADVISORY
SECTION □ New York, NY

Selakoff, Judith, Libn.
RESEARCH INSTITUTE FOR THE STUDY OF MAN - LIBRARY □ New York, NY

Selavan, Ida Cohen, Judaica Libn.
HEBREW UNION COLLEGE - JEWISH INSTITUTE OF RELIGION - KLAU LIBRARY □ Cincinnati, OH

Selb, Robert, Museum Cur.
CANTON HISTORICAL SOCIETY - LIBRARY □ Collinsville, CT

Selby, Dane R., Info.Dev.Mgr.
HORIZONS (The Illinois Career Information System) □ Springfield, IL

Selby, Joan, Colbeck Libn.
UNIVERSITY OF BRITISH COLUMBIA - SPECIAL COLLECTIONS DIVISION □ Vancouver, BC

Selby, Vickie, Libn.
MISSOURI STATE COURT OF APPEALS, WESTERN DISTRICT - LIBRARY □ Kansas City, MO

Selch, John, Newspaper Libn.
INDIANA STATE LIBRARY - INDIANA DIVISION □ Indianapolis, IN

Seldin, Daniel, Hd.
INDIANA UNIVERSITY - GEOGRAPHY AND MAP LIBRARY □ Bloomington, IN

Seldman, Neil, Dir.
INSTITUTE FOR LOCAL SELF-RELIANCE - LIBRARY □ Washington, DC

Self, David, Libn.
UNIVERSITY OF ILLINOIS - VETERINARY MEDICINE LIBRARY □ Urbana, IL

Self, George Anah, Circ.Libn.
CARSON-NEWMAN COLLEGE LIBRARY - SPECIAL COLLECTIONS □ Jefferson City, TN

Self, Phyllis C., Health Sci.Libn.
UNIVERSITY OF ILLINOIS AT CHICAGO - HEALTH SCIENCES CENTER - LIBRARY OF THE HEALTH SCIENCES □ Urbana, IL

Selfridge, Anna B., Asst.Cur./Mss., Archv.
ALLEN COUNTY HISTORICAL SOCIETY - ELIZABETH M. MAC DONELL MEMORIAL LIBRARY □ Lima, OH

Selgestad, Marcel, Asst.Libn., Acq./Cat.
DAKOTA STATE COLLEGE - KARL E. MUNDT LIBRARY □ Madison, SD

Selig, Edith G., Adm.Asst.
NATIONAL CONFERENCE OF CHRISTIANS AND JEWS - PAULA K. LAZRUS LIBRARY OF INTERGROUP RELATIONS □ New York, NY

Selig, Susan, Br.Libn.
UNIVERSITY OF TENNESSEE - CENTER FOR THE HEALTH SCIENCES LIBRARY □ Memphis, TN

Selix, Harold, Mgr. of Lib.Serv.
EAGLEVILLE HOSPITAL - HENRY S. LOUCHHEIM LIBRARY □ Eagleville, PA

Sellars, Judith, Libn.
MUSEUM OF NEW MEXICO - MUSEUM OF INTERNATIONAL FOLK ART - LIBRARY □ Santa Fe, NM

Sellers, Brenda A., Asst.Libn.
ABRAHAM BALDWIN AGRICULTURAL COLLEGE - LIBRARY □ Tifton, GA

Sellers, Martha M., Tech.Libn.
OLIN CORPORATION - ECUSTA PAPER AND FILM GROUP - TECHNICAL LIBRARY† □ Pisgah Forest, NC

Sellers, Mary Ann, Rare Bk.Libn.
UNIVERSITY OF MICHIGAN - DEPARTMENT OF RARE BOOKS AND SPECIAL COLLECTIONS - LIBRARY □ Ann Arbor, MI

Sellers, Norma L., Chf.Libn.
U.S. ARMY - ACADEMY OF HEALTH SCIENCES - STIMSON LIBRARY □ Ft. Sam Houston, TX

Sellers, Sr. Sue, Circ.
MARYCREST COLLEGE - CONE LIBRARY □ Davenport, IA

Sellin, Fred B., Grand Libn.
GRAND LODGE OF ANCIENT FREE AND ACCEPTED MASONS OF WYOMING - GRAND LODGE LIBRARY □ Cheyenne, WY

Selmer, Marsha L., Map Libn.
UNIVERSITY OF ILLINOIS AT CHICAGO - UNIVERSITY LIBRARY - MAP SECTION □ Chicago, IL

Selph, Jana, Libn.
GENSTAR CORP. - LIBRARY □ San Francisco, CA

Seltzer, Ada M., Asst.Dir., Pub.Serv.
UNIVERSITY OF SOUTH FLORIDA - MEDICAL CENTER LIBRARY □ Tampa, FL

Seltzer, Evelyn
HARTFORD PUBLIC LIBRARY - REFERENCE AND GENERAL READING DEPARTMENT □ Hartford, CT

Seltzer, S.M.
U.S. NATL. BUREAU OF STANDARDS - PHOTON AND CHARGED PARTICLE DATA CENTER □ Gaithersburg, MD

Selwyn, Bobby, Mgr., Circ./AV
UNIVERSITY OF ALABAMA - COLLEGE OF COMMUNITY HEALTH SCIENCES - HEALTH SCIENCES LIBRARY □ University, AL

Selya, Herman C., Pres.
ISOCHEM RESINS COMPANY - TECHNICAL INFORMATION CENTER† □ Lincoln, RI

Selz, Julia, Slide Libn.
BOSTON ARCHITECTURAL CENTER - ALFRED SHAW AND EDWARD DURELL STONE LIBRARY □ Boston, MA

Selzer, Nancy S., Libn.
DU PONT DE NEMOURS (E.I.) & COMPANY, INC. - HASKELL LABORATORY FOR TOXICOLOGY & INDUSTRIAL MEDICINE - LIBRARY □ Newark, DE

Semeleer, Brenda, Asst.Libn.
PHARMACEUTICAL MANUFACTURERS ASSOCIATION - LIBRARY □ Washington, DC

Semenuk, Dr. Nick, Sec.Hd., Lit. Search
SQUIBB (E.R.) AND SONS, INC. - SQUIBB INSTITUTE FOR MEDICAL RESEARCH - SCIENCE INFORMATION DEPARTMENT □ Princeton, NJ

Semkow, Julie, Hd., AV
SUNY - DOWNSTATE MEDICAL CENTER - MEDICAL RESEARCH LIBRARY OF BROOKLYN† □ Brooklyn, NY

Semonche, Barbara P., Chf.Libn.
DURHAM HERALD-SUN NEWSPAPER - LIBRARY □ Durham, NC

Semple, Dr. N.E., Asst.Archv.
UNITED CHURCH OF CANADA - CENTRAL ARCHIVES† □ Toronto, ON

Sendek, Irene, Hd., Loyola Libs.
CONCORDIA UNIVERSITY - LOYOLA CAMPUS - GEORGES P. VANIER LIBRARY □ Montreal, PQ

Senezak, Christina, State Doc.Libn.
RUTGERS UNIVERSITY, THE STATE UNIVERSITY OF NEW JERSEY - JUSTICE HENRY ACKERSON LIBRARY OF LAW & CRIMINAL JUSTICE □ Newark, NJ

Sengstacken, R. Robert, Dir., Info.Serv.
TOBACCO MERCHANTS ASSOCIATION OF THE U.S. - HOWARD S. CULLMAN LIBRARY □ New York, NY

Senior, John, Dir.
BAKKEN FOUNDATION - BAKKEN LIBRARY OF ELECTRICITY IN LIFE □ Minneapolis, MN

Senkus, Linda, Libn.
HERALD PUBLISHING COMPANY - HERALD LIBRARY □ New Britain, CT

Senn, Mary S., Info.Spec.
PACKAGING CORPORATION OF AMERICA - INFORMATION SERVICES DEPARTMENT □ Skokie, IL

Sennett, Paula, Asst.Libn.
LOYOLA UNIVERSITY OF CHICAGO - LAW LIBRARY □ Chicago, IL

Sensale, Maria, Lib.Asst.
MASSACHUSETTS INSTITUTE OF TECHNOLOGY - LABORATORY FOR COMPUTER SCIENCE - READING ROOM □ Cambridge, MA

Sentz, Lilli, Hist. of Med.Libn.
SUNY AT BUFFALO - HEALTH SCIENCES LIBRARY □ Buffalo, NY

Seo, Sr. Lucille, D.C., Bibliotherapist
DE PAUL HEALTH CENTER - MEDICAL LIBRARY □ Bridgeton, MO

Sepehri, Abazar, Libn.
UNIVERSITY OF TEXAS, AUSTIN - MIDDLE EAST COLLECTION □ Austin, TX

Sepessy, Joan L., Asst.Libn.
TOLEDO MUSEUM OF ART - ART REFERENCE LIBRARY† □ Toledo, OH

Sepner, Dr. Dal, Planner
NEW MEXICO ENERGY RESEARCH AND DEVELOPMENT INSTITUTE - LIBRARY □ Santa Fe, NM

Serbu, Rose Marie, Adm.Libn.
U.S. ARMY POST - ABERDEEN PROVING GROUND - MORALE SUPPORT ACTIVITIES DIVISION - POST LIBRARY □ Aberdeen Proving Ground, MD

Serdehely, Rebecca, Libn.
MONTEREY COUNTY LAW LIBRARY □ Salinas, CA

Serebrin, Ray, Prog.Libn.
SEATTLE PUBLIC LIBRARY - MEDIA & PROGRAM SERVICES† □ Seattle, WA

Serena, Richard, Libn.
GOLDEN VALLEY LUTHERAN COLLEGE - LIBRARY† □ Minneapolis, MN

Serenyi, Agnes K., Asst.
KALBA BOWEN ASSOCIATES - LIBRARY □ Cambridge, MA

Sergeant, Barbara E., Sr.Env.Spec.
NEW JERSEY STATE DEPARTMENT OF ENVIRONMENTAL PROTECTION - OFFICE OF SCIENCE & RESEARCH - INFO. RESEARCH CTR. □ Trenton, NJ

Serguison, John, Reports Indexer
CATERPILLAR TRACTOR COMPANY - TECHNICAL INFORMATION CENTER □ Peoria, IL

Sermat-Harding, Kaili, Asst.Libn.
FENCO ENGINEERS, INC. - LIBRARY □ Toronto, ON

Serota, Barbara J., Assoc.Libn.
TEXAS STATE LAW LIBRARY □ Austin, TX

Seruya, Flora, Cat.
AMERICAN CANCER SOCIETY - MEDICAL LIBRARY □ New York, NY

Servis, Willie M., Subject Spec.
SANDIA NATIONAL LABORATORIES - TECHNICAL LIBRARY □ Albuquerque, NM

Servos, Ruth, Dir.
SHAVER HOSPITAL FOR CHEST DISEASES - HEALTH SCIENCES LIBRARY □ St. Catharines, ON

Serzan, Sharon, Hd., Acq.Div.
U.S. NAVY - NAVAL POSTGRADUATE SCHOOL - DUDLEY KNOX LIBRARY □ Monterey, CA

Seskus, Mr. A., Res.Off.
UNIVERSITY OF TORONTO - FACULTY OF APPLIED SCIENCE AND ENGINEERING - CENTRE FOR BUILDING SCIENCE - LIBRARY □ Toronto, ON

Sessa, Jane T., Libn.
CONGRESSIONAL BUDGET OFFICE - LIBRARY □ Washington, DC

Sessions, Marcia, Asst.Libn.
BARRINGTON COLLEGE - LIBRARY □ Barrington, RI

Sessions, Robert, Ref.Libn./Vet.Med.
UNIVERSITY OF WISCONSIN, MADISON - STEENBOCK MEMORIAL LIBRARY □ Madison, WI

Sethna, Mr. Nari, Exec.Mgr.
REFRIGERATION SERVICE ENGINEERS SOCIETY - LIBRARY □ Des Plaines, IL

Setnick, Sandra, Ref.Libn.
SOUTHERN METHODIST UNIVERSITY - SCIENCE/ENGINEERING LIBRARY □ Dallas, TX

Seudy, Ellie, Supv., Tape Textbook Sect
MINNESOTA STATE SERVICES FOR THE BLIND AND VISUALLY HANDICAPPED - COMMUNICATION CENTER □ St. Paul, MN

Seulowitz, Lois, Mgr.
GENERAL FOODS CORPORATION - MARKETING
INFORMATION CENTER □ White Plains, NY

Seuss, Herbert J., Libn.
EATON CORPORATION - CUTLER-HAMMER
LIBRARY □ Milwaukee, WI

Severens, Martha, Cur. of Coll.
CAROLINA ART ASSOCIATION - LIBRARY □
Charleston, SC

Severson, Daryl J., Act.Libn.
ALBANY INSTITUTE OF HISTORY AND ART -
MC KINNEY LIBRARY □ Albany, NY

Sevier, Jeffrey A., Tech.Proc.Libn.
HUGHES AIRCRAFT COMPANY - ELECTRO-
OPTICAL & DATA SYSTEMS GROUP - COMPANY
TECHNICAL DOCUMENT CENTER □ El Segundo,
CA

Sevigny, Paul J., Pres.
AMERICAN SOCIETY OF DOWSERS, INC. -
LIBRARY □ Danville, VT

Sevy, Barbara, Libn.
PHILADELPHIA MUSEUM OF ART - LIBRARY □
Philadelphia, PA

Sewald, Beatrice R., Asst.Libn.
NASSAU COUNTY DEPARTMENT OF HEALTH -
DIVISION OF LABORATORIES & RESEARCH -
MEDICAL LIBRARY □ Hempstead, NY

Seward, Gerry, Mgr.
SYNTEX, U.S.A. - CORPORATE LIBRARY/
INFORMATION SERVICES □ Palo Alto, CA

Seward, Sue, Hd., Ref.
U.S. NASA - LANGLEY RESEARCH CENTER -
TECHNICAL LIBRARY MS 185† □ Hampton, VA

Sewell, Kermit R., Exchange Lib.
UNIVERSITY OF KANSAS - SLAVIC
COLLECTION □ Lawrence, KS

Sewell, Mary B., Adm.
ROCKWELL INTERNATIONAL - TECHNICAL
INFORMATION CENTER □ Tulsa, OK

Sewell, P.L., Hd.Libn.
GENERAL ELECTRIC COMPANY - AIRCRAFT
ENGINE GROUP - TECHNICAL INFORMATION
CENTER □ Cincinnati, OH

Sewell, Robert G., Japanese Bibliog.
UNIVERSITY OF ILLINOIS - ASIAN LIBRARY □
Urbana, IL

Sexton, Ebba Jo, Tech.Serv.Libn.
UNIVERSITY OF KENTUCKY - LAW LIBRARY □
Lexington, KY

Sexton, Marie, Asst. Law Libn./Pub.Serv.
CATHOLIC UNIVERSITY OF AMERICA - SCHOOL
OF LAW - ROBERT J. WHITE LAW LIBRARY □
Washington, DC

Sexton, Mary, Ref.Libn.
TEXAS STATE TECHNICAL INSTITUTE, WACO
CAMPUS - LIBRARY □ Waco, TX

Sexton, Mary E., Lib. Group Supv.
AT & T BELL LABORATORIES & TECHNOLOGIES
- LIBRARY □ North Andover, MA

Sexton, Ms. Spencer Kearns, Libn.
WILMINGTON AREA HEALTH EDUCATION
CENTER - HEALTH SCIENCES LIBRARY □
Wilmington, NC

Seyffarth, Jeanne, Sr.Ref.Libn.
OPPENHEIMER & CO., INC. - LIBRARY □ New
York, NY

Seymour, Bessie, Libn.
U.S. COAST GUARD - SUPPORT CENTER
LIBRARY □ New York, NY

Seymour, Jill, Asst.Libn.
GRACELAND COLLEGE - FREDERICK MADISON
SMITH LIBRARY □ Lamoni, IA

Seymour, Marilyn M., Dir.
MAITLAND PUBLIC LIBRARY - ANDRE SMITH
COLLECTION □ Maitland, FL

Sezak, Nancy, Med.Libn.
CARDINAL CUSHING GENERAL HOSPITAL -
STAFF LIBRARY □ Brockton, MA

Shaak, Graig D., Assoc.Dir.
UNIVERSITY OF FLORIDA - FLORIDA STATE
MUSEUM LIBRARY □ Gainesville, FL

Shackelford, Bruce M., Cur./Dir.
CREEK INDIAN MEMORIAL ASSOCIATION -
CREEK COUNCIL HOUSE MUSEUM - LIBRARY □
Okmulgee, OK

Shackelford, Daria, Med.Libn./Dir.
REHABILITATION INSTITUTE, INC. -
LEARNING RESOURCES CENTER □ Detroit, MI

Shackle, Linda, Chem./Geology Ref.Libn.
ARIZONA STATE UNIVERSITY - DANIEL E.
NOBLE SCIENCE AND ENGINEERING LIBRARY □
Tempe, AZ

Shackleton, Susie, Libn.
SANGAMON STATE UNIVERSITY - EAST
CENTRAL NETWORK - LIBRARY □ Springfield, IL

Shaefer, E.F., Archv.
LUTHERAN CHURCH - MISSOURI SYNOD -
SOUTH DAKOTA DISTRICT ARCHIVES □ Sioux
Falls, SD

Shaeffer, Margaret W.M., Dir.
JEFFERSON COUNTY HISTORICAL SOCIETY -
LIBRARY □ Watertown, NY

Shafer, Wade H., Asst.Dir.
PURDUE UNIVERSITY - CINDAS - ELECTRONIC
PROPERTIES INFORMATION CENTER □ West
Lafayette, IN

Shafer, Wade H., Asst.Dir.
PURDUE UNIVERSITY - CINDAS -
THERMOPHYSICAL PROPERTIES RESEARCH
CENTER - LIBRARY □ West Lafayette, IN

Shaffer, Carol, Rd.Serv.Spec.
LAKESHORE TECHNICAL INSTITUTE -
EDUCATIONAL RESOURCE CENTER □ Cleveland,
WI

Shaffer, Dale E., Lib.Cons. & Dir.
JENNINGS LIBRARY □ Salem, OH

Shaffer, Ellen, Cur.
SILVERADO MUSEUM □ St. Helena, CA

Shaffer, Ethel V., Cat.Libn.
LUTHERAN THEOLOGICAL SEMINARY - A.R.
WENTZ LIBRARY □ Gettysburg, PA

Shaffer, Harold, Docs.Libn.
INDIANA UNIVERSITY, INDIANAPOLIS -
SCHOOL OF MEDICINE LIBRARY □ Indianapolis,
IN

Shaffer, Jack W., Dir.
ST. VINCENT MEDICAL CENTER - HEALTH
SCIENCE LIBRARY □ Toledo, OH

Shaffer, Kenneth M., Jr., Asst.Libn.
BETHANY AND NORTHERN BAPTIST
THEOLOGICAL SEMINARIES - LIBRARY □ Oak
Brook, IL

Shaffer, Marian S., Tech.Libn.
EMERSON ELECTRIC COMPANY - SPACE AND
ELECTRONICS DIVISION - ENGINEERING
LIBRARY □ St. Louis, MO

Shah, Mrs. Neeta N., Chf.Med.Libn.
HALL (William S.) PSYCHIATRIC INSTITUTE -
PROFESSIONAL LIBRARY □ Columbia, SC

Shah, Sushila, Cat.
MACALESTER COLLEGE - WEYERHAEUSER
LIBRARY □ St. Paul, MN

Shaikh, Sunja, Libn.
COMMUNITY MEMORIAL HOSPITAL OF
MENOMONEE FALLS - MC KAY MEMORIAL
LIBRARY □ Menomonee Falls, WI

Shains, Karen, Clinical Libn.
GEORGETOWN UNIVERSITY - MEDICAL
CENTER - DAHLGREN MEMORIAL LIBRARY □
Washington, DC

Shakelton, Mary A., Pub.Serv.Libn.
GORDON COLLEGE - WINN LIBRARY □ Wenham,
MA

Shamble, Helen, Lib.Tech.Asst.
ARGOSYSTEMS - INC. - TECHNICAL LIBRARY†
□ Sunnyvale, CA

Shanahan, Elizabeth, Ref.Libn.
INDIANA STATE LIBRARY - INDIANA DIVISION
□ Indianapolis, IN

Shand, Hope, Res.Dir.
NATIONAL SHARECROPPERS FUND/RURAL
ADVANCEMENT FUND - F.P. GRAHAM
RESOURCE CENTER □ Pittsboro, NC

Shane, Martha P., Archv.
SWARTHMORE COLLEGE - FRIENDS
HISTORICAL LIBRARY - PEACE COLLECTION □
Swarthmore, PA

Shane, Mr. T.C., Jr., Dir., Info.Serv.
INTERNATIONAL MINERALS & CHEMICALS
CORPORATION - IMC RESEARCH &
DEVELOPMENT LIBRARY □ Terre Haute, IN

Shanea, Evan
HOUZE, SHOURDS & MONTGOMERY, INC. -
RESEARCH LIBRARY □ Rolling Hills Estates, CA

Shanefield, Irene Deborah, Med.Libn.
JEWISH CONVALESCENT HOSPITAL CENTRE -
HEALTH SCIENCES INFORMATION CENTRE □
Chomedey, Laval, PQ

Shanfield, Joy, Libn.
THISTLETOWN REGIONAL CENTRE - LIBRARY □
Rexdale, ON

Shangkuan, Jessie, Info.Spec.
AMDAHL CORPORATION - CORPORATE
LIBRARY □ Sunnyvale, CA

Shanholtz, Brenda W., Libn.
U.S. ARMY - ELECTRONICS R & D COMMAND
(ERADCOM) - TECHNICAL LIBRARY DIVISION □
Ft. Monmouth, NJ

Shank, William, Music Libn.
CUNY - GRADUATE SCHOOL AND UNIVERSITY
CENTER - LIBRARY □ New York, NY

Shanks, Doreen, Hd.Libn.
UNIVERSITY OF MANITOBA - D.S. WOODS
EDUCATION LIBRARY □ Winnipeg, MB

Shanks, Kathy, Libn.
AMERICAN ASSOCIATION OF PETROLEUM
GEOLOGISTS - LIBRARY □ Tulsa, OK

Shanks, Polly, Mgr., S.D.I.
MISSISSIPPI (State) RESEARCH AND
DEVELOPMENT CENTER - INFORMATION
SERVICES DIVISION □ Jackson, MS

Shanks, W. Kenneth, Archv.
U.S. NATL. ARCHIVES & RECORDS SERVICE -
FEDERAL ARCHIVES AND RECORDS CENTER,
REGION 5 □ Chicago, IL

Shanley, Elaine, Hd.Cat.
PROVIDENCE COLLEGE - PHILLIPS MEMORIAL
LIBRARY □ Providence, RI

Shannon, Barbara, Med.Libn.
BETHANY MEDICAL CENTER - W.W.
SUMMERVILLE MEDICAL LIBRARY □ Kansas
City, KS

Shannon, John, Tech.Instr.
MASSACHUSETTS INSTITUTE OF TECHNOLOGY
- TRI-SERVICE LIBRARY □ Cambridge, MA

Shannon, Lyle W., Dir.
UNIVERSITY OF IOWA - IOWA URBAN
COMMUNITY RESEARCH CENTER - REFERENCE
LIBRARY □ Iowa City, IA

Shannon, Robert, Educ.Serv.Off., Supv.
U.S. NAVY - NAVAL AIR STATION (CA-Alameda)
- LIBRARY □ Alameda, CA

Shapiro, Barbara, First Asst.
NEW YORK PUBLIC LIBRARY - MID-
MANHATTAN LIBRARY - GENERAL REFERENCE
SERVICE/EDUCATION □ New York, NY

Shapiro, Barbara, Prin.Libn.
NEW YORK PUBLIC LIBRARY - MID-
MANHATTAN LIBRARY - JOB INFORMATION
CENTER □ New York, NY

Shapiro, Barbara, Prin.Libn.
NEW YORK PUBLIC LIBRARY - MID-
MANHATTAN LIBRARY - LEARNER'S ADVISORY
SERVICE □ New York, NY

Shapiro, Fred R., Hist.
NORTH AMERICAN TIDDLYWINKS
ASSOCIATION - ARCHIVES □ Silver Spring, MD

Shapiro, Lea L., Teacher/Libn.
BETH ISRAEL CONGREGATION - LIBRARY □
Vineland, NJ

Shapiro, Leonard P., Dir.
CALIFORNIA COLLEGE OF PODIATRIC
MEDICINE - SCHMIDT MEDICAL LIBRARY □ San
Francisco, CA

Shapiro, Marjorie, Tech.Serv.Div.
NEW YORK INSTITUTE OF TECHNOLOGY -
LIBRARY □ Old Westbury, NY
Shapley, Ellen, Mgr., Info.Serv.
TRACY-LOCKE/BBDO ADVERTISING -
INFORMATION SERVICES DEPARTMENT □
Dallas, TX
Shargorodskaya, Eleanor, Info.Sci.
SCHERING-PLOUGH CORPORATION -
PHARMACEUTICAL RESEARCH DIVISION -
LIBRARY INFORMATION CENTER □ Bloomfield,
NJ
Sharke, Ingrid, Libn.
TROY TIMES RECORD - LIBRARY □ Troy, NY
Sharlach, Duffy, AV Media Spec.
TEXAS CHIROPRACTIC COLLEGE - MAE HILTY
MEMORIAL LIBRARY □ Pasadena, TX
Sharma, Katherine, Libn.
CROSS CANCER INSTITUTE - LIBRARY □
Edmonton, AB
Sharma, Sue, Div.Chf.
BROOKLYN PUBLIC LIBRARY - ART AND MUSIC
DIVISION □ Brooklyn, NY
Sharma, Ved P., Dir.
MANKATO STATE UNIVERSITY - BUREAU OF
BUSINESS AND ECONOMIC RESEARCH -
LIBRARY □ Mankato, MN
Sharman, Roberta, Asst.Ref.Libn.
RAND CORPORATION - LIBRARY† □ Santa
Monica, CA
Sharnas, Timothy C., Supv.
OHIO BELL - CORPORATE LIBRARY □ Cleveland,
OH
Sharon, Dan, Libn.
SPERTUS COLLEGE OF JUDAICA - NORMAN AND
HELEN ASHER LIBRARY □ Chicago, IL
Sharp, Alice L., Cat.
COLORADO HISTORICAL SOCIETY - STEPHEN
H. HART LIBRARY □ Denver, CO
Sharp, Dr. Avery T., Music Libn.
BAYLOR UNIVERSITY - CROUCH MUSIC
LIBRARY □ Waco, TX
Sharp, Don, Tech.Serv.Libn.
LAKEHEAD UNIVERSITY - CHANCELLOR
PATERSON LIBRARY □ Thunder Bay, ON
Sharp, Rev. James C., Univ.Libn.
SETON HALL UNIVERSITY - MC LAUGHLIN
LIBRARY □ South Orange, NJ
Sharp, Larry, Res.Tech.
SAN DIEGO STATE UNIVERSITY - SOCIAL
SCIENCE RESEARCH LABORATORY - LIBRARY □
San Diego, CA
Sharp, Linda Carlson, Hd., Tech.Serv.
INDIANA HISTORICAL SOCIETY - WILLIAM
HENRY SMITH MEMORIAL LIBRARY □
Indianapolis, IN
Sharp, Linda F., Tech.Info.Spec.
U.S. GENERAL ACCOUNTING OFFICE - SAN
FRANCISCO REGIONAL OFFICE - LIBRARY □
San Francisco, CA
Sharp, Lola, Libn.
MOOSE JAW LAW SOCIETY - LIBRARY □ Moose
Jaw, SK
Sharp, M. Elaine, Asst.Libn./Tech.Serv.
WISCONSIN STATE SUPREME COURT -
WISCONSIN STATE LAW LIBRARY □ Madison,
WI
Sharp, Mrs. Marjorie
SALVATION ARMY - EDUCATION DEPARTMENT
LIBRARY □ New York, NY
Sharp, Valetta, Libn.
U.S. ARMY - CORPS OF ENGINEERS - OMAHA
DISTRICT - LIBRARY □ Omaha, NE
Sharpe, Ellen, Libn.
CAE ELECTRONICS, LTD. - ENGINEERING
REFERENCE LIBRARY □ St. Laurent, PQ
Sharpless, Mercedes Benitez, Libn.
LAFAYETTE COLLEGE - KIRBY LIBRARY OF
GOVERNMENT AND LAW† □ Easton, PA
Sharplin, D., Ref.Libn.
UNIVERSITY OF ALBERTA - HUMANITIES AND
SOCIAL SCIENCES LIBRARY □ Edmonton, AB

Shasho, Glenda, Dir., Info. & Res.
DIRECT MARKETING ASSOCIATION, INC. -
INFORMATION CENTER □ New York, NY
Shatkin, Leon, Hd., ILL Ctr.
CONNECTICUT STATE LIBRARY □ Hartford, CT
Shatkin, Robert, Asst.Div.Chf.
BROOKLYN PUBLIC LIBRARY - ART AND MUSIC
DIVISION □ Brooklyn, NY
Shattuck, Beverly, Asst.Dir., Pub.Serv.
UNIVERSITY OF MASSACHUSETTS MEDICAL
SCHOOL & WORCESTER DISTRICT MEDICAL
SOCIETY - LIBRARY □ Worcester, MA
Shatz, Norma, Lib.Coord.
SUNY AT BUFFALO - CENTER FOR CURRICULUM
PLANNING □ Amherst, NY
Shaunesey, Phyllis
KEAN COLLEGE OF NEW JERSEY - EVE ADULT
ADVISORY SERVICES □ Union, NJ
Shaver, D., Hd.
CANADA - NATIONAL DEFENCE - NDHQ
MARITIME TECHNICAL LIBRARY □ Ottawa, ON
Shaver, Donna B., Tech.Libn.
PORTLAND GENERAL ELECTRIC - CORPORATE
AND TECHNICAL LIBRARIES □ Portland, OR
Shaver, Helen, Resource Ctr.Supv.
MOHAWK COLLEGE OF APPLIED ARTS AND
TECHNOLOGY - MOHAWK LIBRARY RESOURCE
CENTRE □ Hamilton, ON
Shaw, Dr. Andrew, Jr., Dir.
WILKES COLLEGE - INSTITUTE OF REGIONAL
AFFAIRS - LIBRARY □ Wilkes-Barre, PA
Shaw, Bill, Hist. Site Mgr.
LOUISIANA STATE DEPT. OF CULTURE,
RECREATION & TOURISM - MANSFIELD STATE
COMMEMORATIVE AREA - MUSEUM & LIB. □
Mansfield, LA
Shaw, C.H., Dir.
MARITIME MUSEUM OF BRITISH COLUMBIA -
LIBRARY □ Victoria, BC
Shaw, Courtney A., Hd.
UNIVERSITY OF MARYLAND, COLLEGE PARK -
LIBRARIES - ART LIBRARY □ College Park, MD
Shaw, Darline, Circ.
BOEING MILITARY AIRPLANE COMPANY -
LIBRARY □ Wichita, KS
Shaw, Debora, Hd., Data Serv.Div.
INDIANA STATE LIBRARY □ Indianapolis, IN
Shaw, Donald C., Libn.
WESTERN NEW YORK GENEALOGICAL
SOCIETY, INC. - LIBRARY □ Hamburg, NY
Shaw, Col. Donald P., Dir.
U.S. ARMY MILITARY HISTORY INSTITUTE □
Carlisle Barracks, PA
Shaw, Elizabeth, Libn.
FLORENCE CITY PLANNING AND
DEVELOPMENT LIBRARY □ Florence, SC
Shaw, Ena, Med.Ed.
U.S. AIR FORCE - AEROSPACE MEDICAL
DIVISION - SCHOOL OF AEROSPACE MEDICINE
- STRUGHOLD AEROMEDICAL LIBRARY □ Brooks
AFB, TX
Shaw, J. Ned, Libn.
U.S. NAVY - NAVAL UNDERWATER SYSTEMS
CENTER - NEW LONDON TECHNICAL LIBRARY†
□ New London, CT
Shaw, John Bennett, Owner
BROTHERS THREE OF MORIARTY - LIBRARY □
Santa Fe, NM
Shaw, John T., Lib. Group Supv.
AT & T BELL LABORATORIES & TECHNOLOGIES
- LIBRARY □ Norcross, GA
Shaw, Joyce M., Libn.
LINCOLN PARK ZOOLOGICAL GARDENS -
LIBRARY □ Chicago, IL
Shaw, Judith E., Assoc.Libn.
CIBA-GEIGY CORPORATION - CORPORATE
LIBRARY □ Ardsley, NY
Shaw, Kerrie S., Pub.Serv.Coord.
EASTERN VIRGINIA MEDICAL SCHOOL -
MOORMAN MEMORIAL LIBRARY □ Norfolk, VA
Shaw, Mark P., Libn.
ARENT, FOX, KINTNER, PLOTKIN & KAHN -
LIBRARY† □ Washington, DC

Shaw, Meg, Art Libn.
UNIVERSITY OF KENTUCKY - MARGARET I.
KING LIBRARY - ART LIBRARY □ Lexington, KY
Shaw, Priscilla B., Libn.
AMERICAN BAPTIST CHURCHES IN THE U.S.A.
- BOARD OF INTERNATIONAL MINISTRIES -
LIBRARY AND CENTRAL FILES □ Valley Forge,
PA
Shaw, Vivian, Libn.
JACKSON COUNTY LAW LIBRARY □ Kansas City,
MO
Shaye, Marc K., General Counsel
SPILL CONTROL ASSOCIATION OF AMERICA -
LIBRARY □ Southfield, MI
Shayne, Mette, Francophone Africa
NORTHWESTERN UNIVERSITY - MELVILLE J.
HERSKOVITS LIBRARY OF AFRICAN STUDIES □
Evanston, IL
Shea, John D., Hd.Libn.
UNION BANK - LIBRARY □ Los Angeles, CA
Shea, Karen A., Libn.
WENDER, MURASE & WHITE - LIBRARY □ New
York, NY
Shea, Larry L., Chf., Lib.Serv.
U.S. VETERANS ADMINISTRATION (OK-
Muskogee) - MEDICAL CENTER LIBRARY □
Muskogee, OK
Shea, Linda Loring, Corp.Libn.
PRIME COMPUTER, INC. - INFORMATION
CENTER† □ Framingham, MA
Shear, Dorothy, Br.Ref.
IBM CORPORATION - DSD LIBRARY/LEARNING
CENTER □ Poughkeepsie, NY
Sheard, Shirley, Libn.
U.S. FEDERAL AVIATION ADMINISTRATION -
EASTERN REGION LIBRARY □ Jamaica, NY
Shearer, Gary, Cur.
PACIFIC UNION COLLEGE - PITCAIRN ISLANDS
STUDY CENTER - LIBRARY □ Angwin, CA
Shearer, John Allen, Jr., Hd.
CAPITOL REGION EDUCATION COUNCIL - ED
SEARCH □ New Britain CT
Shearer, Linda, Exec.Dir.
ARTISTS SPACE - COMMITTEE FOR THE
VISUAL ARTS - UNAFFILIATED ARTISTS FILE □
New York, NY
Shearer, Marilyn, Dir.
ST. FRANCIS HOSPITAL - MEDICAL LIBRARY □
Santa Barbara, CA
Shearer, Susan, Info.Serv.Coord.
NATIONAL TRUST FOR HISTORIC
PRESERVATION - INFORMATION SERVICES □
Washington, DC
Shearin, Malcalm, Dir., Media Prod.
WAYNE COMMUNITY COLLEGE - LEARNING
RESOURCE CENTER □ Goldsboro, NC
Shearouse, Linda Nelson, Libn.
MUSEUM OF FINE ARTS, HOUSTON - HIRSCH
LIBRARY □ Houston, TX
Sheaves, David, Libn.
UNIVERSITY OF NORTH CAROLINA, CHAPEL
HILL - INSTITUTE FOR RESEARCH IN SOCIAL
SCIENCE - DATA LIBRARY □ Chapel Hill, NC
Sheaves, Miriam L., Libn.
UNIVERSITY OF NORTH CAROLINA, CHAPEL
HILL - GEOLOGY LIBRARY □ Chapel Hill, NC
Shediac, Margaret, Libn.
HOWARD RICE NEMEROVSKI CANADY
ROBERTSON & FALK - LIBRARY □ San Francisco,
CA
Shedlarz, Ellen, Mgr.
MC KINSEY & COMPANY, INC. - INFORMATION
SERVICES □ New York, NY
Shedlock, James, Coord. Online Search
UNIVERSITY OF NORTH CAROLINA, CHAPEL
HILL - HEALTH SCIENCES LIBRARY □ Chapel
Hill, NC
Sheehan, Catherine, Ref.Libn.
MEMORIAL UNIVERSITY OF NEWFOUNDLAND -
HEALTH SCIENCES LIBRARY □ St. John's, NF

Sheehan, Joseph J., Archv.
U.S. NATL. ARCHIVES & RECORDS SERVICE -
FEDERAL ARCHIVES AND RECORDS CENTER,
REGION 3 □ Philadelphia, PA
Sheehan, Robert C., Sr. Principal Libn.
NEW YORK PUBLIC LIBRARY - MID-
MANHATTAN LIBRARY - HISTORY AND SOCIAL
SCIENCES DEPARTMENT □ New York, NY
Sheehan, William J., C.S.B., Asst.Libn.
WOODSTOCK THEOLOGICAL CENTER -
LIBRARY □ Washington, DC
Sheehy, Timothy, Libn.
GLENDALE UNIVERSITY - COLLEGE OF LAW
LIBRARY □ Glendale, CA
Sheeley, Lawrence, Acq.
NATIONAL CENTER FOR RESEARCH IN
VOCATIONAL EDUCATION - RESEARCH
LIBRARY □ Columbus, OH
Sheets, Elizabeth, Libn.
IOWA STATE COMMISSION FOR THE BLIND -
LIBRARY FOR THE BLIND & PHYSICALLY
HANDICAPPED □ Des Moines, IA
Sheets, Lorinda, Health Educ.Coord.
KAISER-PERMANENTE MEDICAL CENTER -
HEALTH EDUCATION CENTER □ Hayward, CA
Sheets, Michael, Dir., Med.Lib.
ST. JOSEPH'S HOSPITAL - MEDICAL LIBRARY†
□ Fort Wayne, IN
Sheffler, Victoria, Archv.Spec.
NORTHEASTERN OKLAHOMA STATE
UNIVERSITY - JOHN VAUGHAN LIBRARY/LRC -
SPECIAL COLLECTIONS □ Tahlequah, OK
Shefrin, Jill, Libn.
TORONTO PUBLIC LIBRARY - CANADIANA
COLLECTION OF CHILDREN'S BOOKS □ Toronto,
ON
Shefrin, Jill, Libn.
TORONTO PUBLIC LIBRARY - LILLIAN H. SMITH
COLLECTION OF CHILDREN'S BOOKS □ Toronto,
ON
Shefrin, Jill, Libn.
TORONTO PUBLIC LIBRARY - OSBORNE
COLLECTION OF EARLY CHILDREN'S BOOKS □
Toronto, ON
Sheftel, Ramona, Mgr.Tech.Lib.
COMPUTER SCIENCES CORPORATION -
TECHNICAL LIBRARY □ Falls Church, VA
Sheible, Doris A., Asst.Libn.
U.S. ARMY POST - FORT RICHARDSON -
LIBRARY □ Ft. Richardson, AK
Sheil, Sr. Joan, Dir., Lib.Serv.
MARYCREST COLLEGE - CONE LIBRARY □
Davenport, IA
Sheinwald, Fran, Sr.Libn.
NEW YORK STATE DEPARTMENT OF LAW -
NEW YORK CITY LIBRARY □ New York, NY
Shelander, Frances, Hd.
CROUSE-IRVING MEMORIAL HOSPITAL -
LIBRARY □ Syracuse, NY
Shelar, James W., Libn.
ARNOLD AND PORTER - LIBRARY □ Washington,
DC
Sheldon, Judy, Ref.Libn.
CALIFORNIA HISTORICAL SOCIETY -
SCHUBERT HALL LIBRARY □ San Francisco, CA
Sheldon, Marie A., Med.Lib.Asst.
BAYLEY SETON HOSPITAL - CHARLES
FERGUSON MEDICAL LIBRARY □ Staten Island,
NY
Shelkrot, Elliot L., State Libn.
PENNSYLVANIA STATE LIBRARY □ Harrisburg,
PA
Shell, Dr. E.W., Dir.
AUBURN UNIVERSITY - INTERNATIONAL
CENTER FOR AQUACULTURE - LIBRARY □
Auburn University, AL
Shell, Freeman E., Jr., Ref.Libn.
U.S. ARMY ARMOR SCHOOL - LIBRARY □ Ft.
Knox, KY
Shell, Leslee, Dir.
ST. ELIZABETH COMMUNITY HEALTH CENTER -
MEDICAL LIBRARY □ Lincoln, NE

Shelley, Dr. Harry S., Honor.Cur.
VANDERBILT UNIVERSITY - MEDICAL CENTER
LIBRARY □ Nashville, TN
Shellhammer, Karen, Educ.Coord.
TRITON MUSEUM OF ART - LIBRARY □ Santa
Clara, CA
Shelly, Elaine, Art Libn.
SPRINGHOUSE CORPORATION - CORPORATE
LIBRARY □ Spring House, PA
Shelstad, Kirsten, Libn.
ST. LUKE'S HOSPITAL - MEDICAL LIBRARY† □
Duluth, MN
Shelton, Diana, Hd., Ref.
UNIVERSITY OF WYOMING - SCIENCE AND
TECHNOLOGY LIBRARY □ Laramie, WY
Shelton, Gayle C., Jr., Dir.
U.S. DEPT. OF COMMERCE - INTERNATIONAL
TRADE ADMINISTRATION - BIRMINGHAM
DISTRICT OFFICE LIBRARY □ Birmingham, AL
Shelton, J. Walter, Assoc.Libn.
UNIVERSITY OF CHICAGO - JOHN CRERAR
LIBRARY □ Chicago, IL
Shelton, Kathryn H., Co-Libn.
ALASKA STATE LEGISLATURE/LEGISLATIVE
AFFAIRS AGENCY - REFERENCE LIBRARY □
Juneau, AK
Shelton, Lois, Dir.
UNIVERSITY OF ARIZONA - POETRY CENTER □
Tucson, AZ
Shelton, Pam, Cat.
U.S. ARMY POST - FORT HOOD - MSA DIVISION
- CASEY MEMORIAL LIBRARY □ Ft. Hood, TX
Shelton, Pamela A., Post Libn.
U.S. ARMY POST - FORT CLAYTON - MORALE
SUPPORT ACTIVITIES - LIBRARY □ APO Miami,
FL
Shelton, Peggy, Chf.Libn.
TELEDYNE BROWN ENGINEERING - TECHNICAL
LIBRARY □ Huntsville, AL
Shen, C.T., Pres.
INSTITUTE FOR ADVANCED STUDIES OF
WORLD RELIGIONS - LIBRARY □ Stony Brook,
NY
Shen, Chung-Tai, Chf.Libn.
TRANSPORTATION INSTITUTE - LIBRARY □
Camp Springs, MD
Shende, Sumedha, Asst.Libn., Ref.
FMC CORPORATION - ORDNANCE DIVISION -
OD TECHNICAL LIBRARY □ San Jose, CA
Sheng, Jack T., Law Libn.
DUVAL COUNTY LAW LIBRARY □ Jacksonville,
FL
Sheng, Katherine, Ref.Libn.
TEACHERS COLLEGE - MILBANK MEMORIAL
LIBRARY □ New York, NY
Shenk, Elizabeth, Lib.Anl.
UNIVERSITY OF DELAWARE, NEWARK -
AGRICULTURE LIBRARY □ Newark, DE
Shepard, Elizabeth F., Rec.Ctr.Supv.
CPC INTERNATIONAL - MOFFETT TECHNICAL
LIBRARY □ Argo, IL
Shepard, Eve, Mgr., Info.Serv.
NATIONAL SCHOOL BOARDS ASSOCIATION -
RESOURCE CENTER □ Washington, DC
Shepard, Mrs. Finley, Cur.
CASTLETON HISTORICAL SOCIETY - MUSEUM
LIBRARY □ Castleton, VT
Shepard, Margaret E., Libn.
GENERAL MOTORS CORPORATION - RESEARCH
LABORATORIES LIBRARY □ Warren, MI
Shepard, Martha L., Libn.
U.S. DEPT. OF THE INTERIOR - ALASKA
RESOURCES LIBRARY □ Anchorage, AK
Shepard, Stanley A., Libn.
UNIVERSITY OF IDAHO - SPECIAL
COLLECTIONS LIBRARY □ Moscow, ID
Shephard-Lupo, Pamela, Libn.
MAINE STATE DEPARTMENT OF MARINE
RESOURCES - FISHERIES RESEARCH STATION
- LIBRARY □ West Boothbay Harbor, ME
Shepherd, G. Frederick, Dir.
GEOLOGICAL INFORMATION LIBRARY OF
DALLAS (GILD) □ Dallas, TX

Shepherd, Murray C., Univ.Libn.
UNIVERSITY OF WATERLOO - DANA PORTER
ARTS LIBRARY □ Waterloo, ON
Shepherd, Raymond V., Jr., Dir.
PENNSYLVANIA STATE HISTORICAL & MUSEUM
COMMISSION - OLD ECONOMY VILLAGE -
LIBRARY □ Ambridge, PA
Shepherd, Roger, Mgr.
GREAT PLAINS ZOO & MUSEUM - REFERENCE
LIBRARY □ Sioux Falls, SD
Shepherd, Susan J., Adm.
MERCK & COMPANY, INC. - KELCO DIVISION -
LITERATURE AND INFORMATION SERVICES □
San Diego, CA
Shepherd, Suzanne, Bk.Cat.
U.S. BUREAU OF RECLAMATION - LIBRARY† □
Denver, CO
Shepherd-Schlechter, Rae, Cat.Libn.
SUNY - COLLEGE AT CORTLAND - MEMORIAL
LIBRARY □ Cortland, NY
Shepley, Jean, Supv., Tech.Serv.
ORTHO PHARMACEUTICAL CORPORATION -
HARTMAN LIBRARY □ Raritan, NJ
Shere, Ken, U.S. Gen.Mgr.
NATIONAL FILM BOARD OF CANADA - FILM
LIBRARY □ New York, NY
Sheridan, Alice J., Dir.
FAIRFAX HOSPITAL - JACOB D. ZYLMAN
MEMORIAL LIBRARY □ Falls Church, VA
Sheridan, Clare M., Libn.
MERRIMACK VALLEY TEXTILE MUSEUM -
LIBRARY □ North Andover, MA
Sheridan, Connie, Supv., Tech.Proc.
UNIVERSITY OF CALIFORNIA - LOS ALAMOS
NATIONAL LABORATORY - LIBRARY □ Los
Alamos, NM
Sheridan, Helen, Hd.Libn.
KALAMAZOO INSTITUTE OF ARTS - ART
CENTER LIBRARY □ Kalamazoo, MI
Sheridan, Jean A., Acq.Libn.
PROVIDENCE COLLEGE - PHILLIPS MEMORIAL
LIBRARY □ Providence, RI
Sheridan, JoAnna, Registrar
AMERICAN MUSEUM OF FLY FISHING, INC. -
LIBRARY □ Manchester, VT
Sheridan, John, Hd.Libn.
COLORADO COLLEGE - CHARLES LEAMING
TUTT LIBRARY □ Colorado Springs, CO
Sheridan, Nancy, Ref.Libn.
KIDDER, PEABODY AND COMPANY, INC. -
LIBRARY □ New York, NY
Sheridan, Patricia L., Libn.
U.S.D.A. - AGRICULTURAL RESEARCH SERVICE
- MEAT ANIMAL RESEARCH CENTER □ Clay
Center, NE
Sheridan, Sheila
MONKMEYER PRESS PHOTO SERVICE □ New
York, NY
Sherk, Virginia, Archv.Spec.
DEARBORN HISTORICAL MUSEUM - RESEARCH
DIVISION - ARCHIVES AND LIBRARY† □
Dearborn, MI
Sherlock, Al, Chf., Tech.Info.Ctr.
U.S. ARMY - ENGINEER WATERWAYS
EXPERIMENT STATION - TECHNICAL
INFORMATION CENTER □ Vicksburg, MS
Sherman, Dottie, Dir., Lib./Info.Ctr.
AMERICAN NUCLEAR INSURERS -
INFORMATION RECORDS CENTER □
Farmington, CT
Sherman, James G., Lib.Dir.
SAN FERNANDO VALLEY COLLEGE OF LAW -
LAW LIBRARY† □ Sepulveda, CA
Sherman, Marion, Libn.
ST. LOUIS CONSERVATORY AND SCHOOLS FOR
THE ARTS (CASA) - MAE M. WHITAKER
LIBRARY □ St. Louis, MO
Sherman, Paul T., Adm.Serv.Libn.
CUNY - NEW YORK CITY TECHNICAL COLLEGE
LIBRARY/LEARNING RESOURCE CENTER □
Brooklyn, NY

Sherman, Robert, Acq.Libn.
UNIVERSITY OF PITTSBURGH - FALK LIBRARY
OF THE HEALTH SCIENCES □ Pittsburgh, PA

Sherman, Sarah, Women's Coll.Libn.
NORTHWESTERN UNIVERSITY - SPECIAL
COLLECTIONS DEPARTMENT - WOMEN'S
COLLECTION □ Evanston, IL

Sherman, Sr. Sarah M., RSM, Exec.Dir.
NATIONAL SISTERS VOCATION CONFERENCE -
LIBRARY □ Chicago, IL

Sherman, William F., Weekend Libn.
ILLINOIS BENEDICTINE COLLEGE - THEODORE
LOWNIK LIBRARY □ Lisle, IL

Sherr, Merrill F., Hd.Libn.
NEW YORK POST - LIBRARY □ New York, NY

Sherr, Mrs. Rubby, Soc.Sci.Libn.
INSTITUTE FOR ADVANCED STUDY -
LIBRARIES □ Princeton, NJ

Sherrard, Mary Alice, Libn.
MEMORIAL HOSPITAL OF MARTINSVILLE -
MEDICAL LIBRARY □ Martinsville, VA

Sherratt, Christine, Sci.Engr.Ref.Libn.
UNIVERSITY OF ARIZONA - SCIENCE-
ENGINEERING LIBRARY □ Tucson, AZ

Sherrill, Charles, Hd.Ref.Libn.
WESTERN RESERVE HISTORICAL SOCIETY -
LIBRARY □ Cleveland, OH

Sherrill, Nancy, Geneal.Libn.
VIGO COUNTY PUBLIC LIBRARY - SPECIAL
COLLECTIONS □ Terre Haute, IN

Sherrow, Linda L., Br.Mgr., Network Dev.
KENTUCKY STATE DEPARTMENT FOR
LIBRARIES AND ARCHIVES - STATE LIBRARY
SERVICES DIVISION □ Frankfort, KY

Sherry, Diane H., Mgr., Info.Rsrc.Ctr.
TRAVENOL LABORATORIES, INC. -
INFORMATION RESOURCE CENTER □ Morton
Grove, IL

Sherry, Joseph E., Libn.
VINELAND HISTORICAL AND ANTIQUARIAN
SOCIETY - LIBRARY □ Vineland, NJ

Sherson, Elizabeth, Med.Libn.
HOSPITAL OF THE GOOD SAMARITAN -
MEDICAL LIBRARY □ Los Angeles, CA

Sherstone, D.A., Scientist-in-Charge
CANADA - INDIAN & NORTHERN AFFAIRS
CANADA - INUVIK SCIENTIFIC RESOURCE
CENTRE - LIBRARY† □ Inuvik, NT

Shervey, George M., Cur.
GRANT COUNTY HISTORICAL SOCIETY -
LIBRARY □ Elbow Lake, MN

Sherwin, Helen, Archv.
BOSTON UNIVERSITY - DEPARTMENT OF
SPECIAL COLLECTIONS - NURSING ARCHIVES
□ Boston, MA

Sherwin, Rosalie, Asst.Libn., Tech.Serv.
U.S. SUPREME COURT - LIBRARY □ Washington,
DC

Sherwood, Betty, Libn.
BUTTERWORTH HOSPITAL - SCHOOL OF
NURSING LIBRARY □ Grand Rapids, MI

Sherwood, Betty, ILL Libn./Bibliog.
U.S. NASA - AMES RESEARCH CENTER -
LIBRARY □ Mountain View, CA

Sherwood, Gertrude, Info.Spec.
U.S. NATL. BUREAU OF STANDARDS - OFFICE
OF STANDARD REFERENCE DATA - REFERENCE
CENTER □ Washington, DC

Sherwood, Larry, Assoc.Dir.
NEW ENGLAND SOLAR ENERGY ASSOCIATION -
LIBRARY □ Brattleboro, VT

Sherwood, William F., Systems Anl.
UNIVERSITY OF TEXAS MEDICAL BRANCH -
MOODY MEDICAL LIBRARY □ Galveston, TX

Shetron, Stephen, Sr.Res.Sci.
MICHIGAN TECHNOLOGICAL UNIVERSITY -
FORD FORESTRY CENTER - LIBRARY □ L'Anse,
MI

Shevack, Hilda N., Logistics/Data Mgr.
GENERAL INSTRUMENT CORPORATION,
GOVERNMENT SYSTEMS DIVISION -
ENGINEERING LIBRARY □ Hicksville, NY

Sheviak, Jean K., Ser.Libn.
RENSSELAER POLYTECHNIC INSTITUTE -
FOLSOM LIBRARY □ Troy, NY

Shew, Anita K., Law Libn.
BUTLER COUNTY LAW LIBRARY ASSOCIATION
□ Hamilton, OH

Shew, Anne, Med.Libn.
DAVIES (Ralph K.) MEDICAL CENTER -
FRANKLIN HOSPITAL MEDICAL LIBRARY □ San
Francisco, CA

Shewan, Elizabeth, Libn.
CANADIAN PRESS - LIBRARY □ Toronto, ON

Sheward, Helen C., Libn.
KAISER-PERMANENTE MEDICAL CENTER -
MEDICAL LIBRARY □ Oakland, CA

Shewbridge, Anna M., Libn.
OLD CHARLES TOWN LIBRARY, INC. □ Charles
Town, WV

Shewell, Margaret, Libn.
PINELLAS COUNTY LAW LIBRARY -
CLEARWATER BRANCH □ Clearwater, FL

Shewmaker, Amy Asbury, Pres.
HARRODSBURG HISTORICAL SOCIETY -
MORGAN ROW LIBRARY □ Harrodsburg, KY

Shieh, Monica, Res.Libn.
WASHINGTON UNIVERSITY - COMPUTER
LABORATORIES REFERENCE ROOM □ St. Louis,
MO

Shiel, Diana, Mgr.
GOLD INFORMATION CENTER □ New York, NY

Shields, Andrew T., Lib.Coord.
SOUTHERN CALIFORNIA SOCIETY FOR
PSYCHICAL RESEARCH, INC. - LIBRARY □
Thousand Oaks, CA

Shields, Brigid, Newspaper Ref.Libn.
MINNESOTA HISTORICAL SOCIETY -
REFERENCE LIBRARY □ St. Paul, MN

Shields, Caryl L., ILL Libn.
U.S. GEOLOGICAL SURVEY - DENVER LIBRARY
□ Denver, CO

Shields, Dorothy, Asst.Libn.
UNIVERSITY OF MICHIGAN - ART &
ARCHITECTURE LIBRARY □ Ann Arbor, MI

Shields, Ingrid, Sr.Archv.
GEORGIA STATE SURVEYOR GENERAL
DEPARTMENT - LIBRARY □ Atlanta, GA

Shields, Joyce, Lit. Searcher
LOCKHEED-CALIFORNIA COMPANY -
TECHNICAL INFORMATION CENTER □ Burbank,
CA

shields, larry, Exec.Dir.
THE NATIONAL RAILROAD CONSTRUCTION
AND MAINTENANCE ASSOCIATION, INC. -
TECHNICAL REFERENCE LIBRARY □ Highland,
IN

Shields, Sarah, Cur.
VALENTINE MUSEUM - LIBRARY □ Richmond,
VA

Shiff, Linda Solomon, Chf.Libn.
CANADIAN NURSES ASSOCIATION - HELEN K.
MUSSALLEM LIBRARY □ Ottawa, ON

Shiff, Robert A., Chm.
NATIONAL RECORDS MANAGEMENT COUNCIL -
LIBRARY □ New York, NY

Shiflet, Robert J., Exec. V.P.
PALOMINO HORSE BREEDERS OF AMERICA -
LIBRARY □ Mineral Wells, TX

Shifrin, Judy, Chf., Lib.Serv.
U.S. FEDERAL AVIATION ADMINISTRATION -
CENTRAL REGION LIBRARY □ Kansas City, MO

Shih, Chia-Chun, Asst.Cat.
KIMBELL ART MUSEUM - LIBRARY □ Fort Worth,
TX

Shih, Maria, Supv.
EG&G, INC. - WASHINGTON ANALYTICAL
SERVICES CENTER - INFORMATION CENTER □
Rockville, MD

Shilts, Dorothy, Libn.
OIL INFORMATION LIBRARY OF WICHITA
FALLS □ Wichita Falls, TX

Shimek, Ursula, Sr.Libn.
IBM CORPORATION - INFORMATION CENTER/
LIBRARY □ Rochester, MN

Shimomura, Mariko, Asst.Hd., Japanese Sect.
PRINCETON UNIVERSITY - GEST ORIENTAL
LIBRARY AND EAST ASIAN COLLECTIONS □
Princeton, NJ

Shin, Sun, Rd.Adv.
DISTRICT OF COLUMBIA PUBLIC LIBRARY -
BUSINESS, ECONOMICS & VOCATIONS
DIVISION □ Washington, DC

Shinbaum, Myrna, Assoc.Dir.
NATIONAL CONFERENCE ON SOVIET JEWRY
(NCSJ) - RESEARCH BUREAU □ New York, NY

Shiner, Sharon L., Libn.
INGERSOLL-RAND COMPANY - TECHNICAL
LIBRARY □ Phillipsburg, NJ

Shinomiya, Yae, Libn.
THE (Oakland) TRIBUNE - LIBRARY □ Oakland,
CA

Shipe, Belle B., Libn.
BARNES ENGINEERING COMPANY - LIBRARY □
Stamford, CT

Shipley, Mary K., Staff Sec.
WARREN HOSPITAL - MEDICAL LIBRARY □
Phillipsburg, NJ

Shipley, Michele, Info.Ctr.Mgr.
SEAR-BROWN ASSOCIATES, P.C. -
INFORMATION CENTER □ Rochester, NY

Shipley, Rebecca K., Bus.Res.Asst.
BALL CORPORATION - CORPORATE
INFORMATION CENTER AND LAW LIBRARY □
Muncie, IN

Shipley, Sally, Libn.
AMOCO PRODUCTION COMPANY - LAW
DEPARTMENT LIBRARY □ Tulsa, OK

Shipman, Barbara L., Database Coord.
UNIVERSITY OF MICHIGAN - ALFRED
TAUBMAN MEDICAL LIBRARY □ Ann Arbor, MI

Shipman, Natalie W., Lib.Dir.
TEXAS A & M UNIVERSITY AT GALVESTON -
LIBRARY □ Galveston, TX

Shipman, Patricia E., Hd.Libn.
CAROLINA POPULATION CENTER - LIBRARY □
Chapel Hill, NC

Shipton, Nathaniel S., Cur. of Mss.
NEW ENGLAND HISTORIC GENEALOGICAL
SOCIETY - LIBRARY □ Boston, MA

Shires, Nancy, Music Cat./Asst.Libn.
EAST CAROLINA UNIVERSITY - MUSIC
LIBRARY □ Greenville, NC

Shirk, Gertrude F., Ed.
FOUNDATION FOR THE STUDY OF CYCLES INC.
- LIBRARY □ Pittsburgh, PA

Shirk, Virginia B., Libn.
MINNEGASCO, INC. - LIBRARY □ Minneapolis,
MN

Shirley, Eileen P., Libn.
PARK RIDGE HOSPITAL - LIBRARY □ Rochester,
NY

Shirley, Iris, Handicapped Serv.
SOUTH CAROLINA STATE LIBRARY □ Columbia,
SC

Shirley, Patricia, Libn.
MERCY HOSPITAL - SCHOOL OF NURSING
LIBRARY □ Altoona, PA

Shively, Daniel, Asst.Libn.
INDIANA UNIVERSITY OF PENNSYLVANIA -
UNIVERSITY LIBRARY □ Indiana, PA

Shively, Donald H., Hd.
UNIVERSITY OF CALIFORNIA, BERKELEY -
EAST ASIATIC LIBRARY □ Berkeley, CA

Shoap, Marjorie, Ctr.Lib.Techn.
SHIPPENSBURG UNIVERSITY - EZRA LEHMAN
LIBRARY □ Shippensburg, PA

Shocket, Phyllis B., Ref./Leg.Hist.
U.S. FEDERAL COMMUNICATIONS
COMMISSION - LIBRARY† □ Washington, DC

Shockley, Ann Allen, Assoc.Libn./Archv.
FISK UNIVERSITY - SPECIAL COLLECTIONS
DEPARTMENT □ Nashville, TN

Shoemaker, Betty G., Church Libn.
FIRST CHRISTIAN REFORMED CHURCH -
LIBRARY □ Zeeland, MI

Shoemaker, Edward C., Tech.Serv.Libn.
OKLAHOMA HISTORICAL SOCIETY - DIVISION
OF LIBRARY RESOURCES □ Oklahoma City, OK
Shoengold, Nathan, Div.Hd.
QUEENS BOROUGH PUBLIC LIBRARY - SOCIAL
SCIENCES DIVISION □ Jamaica, NY
Shoens, Claire, Oper.Mgr.
STANFORD UNIVERSITY - FALCONER BIOLOGY
LIBRARY □ Stanford, CA
Shoettger, Dr. Richard, Dir.
U.S. FISH & WILDLIFE SERVICE - COLUMBIA
NATIONAL FISHERIES RESEARCH LABORATORY
LIBRARY □ Columbia, MO
Shofner, Nancy S., Asst.Dir.
SOUTHERN TECHNICAL INSTITUTE - LIBRARY
□ Marietta, GA
Sholtz, Katherine J., Dir. of Lib.Serv.
WESTERN CONNECTICUT STATE UNIVERSITY
- RUTH A. HAAS LIBRARY - SPECIAL
COLLECTIONS □ Danbury, CT
Shomer, Forest, Dir.
ABUNDANT LIFE SEED FOUNDATION - LIBRARY
□ Port Townsend, WA
Shong, Joy, Coord.
ST. FRANCIS HOSPITAL - HEALTH SCIENCE
LEARNING CENTER □ Milwaukee, WI
Shoniker, Rev. Fintan R., O.S.B., Spec.Coll.
ST. VINCENT COLLEGE AND ARCHABBEY -
LIBRARIES □ Latrobe, PA
Shonkwiler, Paula, Hd.Libn.
ROCKY MOUNTAIN NEWS - LIBRARY □ Denver,
CO
Shonn, Eleanor, Med.Libn.
OHIO VALLEY MEDICAL CENTER - HUPP
MEDICAL LIBRARY □ Wheeling, WV
Shook, Constance R., Hd.Libn.
DELAWARE VALLEY COLLEGE OF SCIENCE AND
AGRICULTURE - JOSEPH KRAUSKOPF
MEMORIAL LIBRARY □ Doylestown, PA
Shopland, Donald R., Tech.Info.Off.
OFFICE ON SMOKING AND HEALTH -
TECHNICAL INFORMATION CENTER □ Rockville,
MD
Shore, June, Lib.Supv.
MOHAWK COLLEGE OF APPLIED ARTS AND
TECHNOLOGY - HEALTH SCIENCES LIBRARY
RESOURCE CENTRE □ Hamilton, ON
Shore, Meta, Libn.
NORTH COLORADO MEDICAL CENTER -
MEDICAL LIBRARY □ Greeley, CO
Shore, Philip, Assoc.Libn.
EARLHAM COLLEGE - QUAKER COLLECTION □
Richmond, IN
Shores, Cecelia, Hd.Acq.Libn.
CENTER FOR RESEARCH LIBRARIES □ Chicago,
IL
Shorr, Marilyn S., Assoc.Dir.
ERIC CLEARINGHOUSE ON HIGHER EDUCATION
□ Washington, DC
Short, B.A., Libn.
EXXON RESEARCH AND ENGINEERING
COMPANY - FLORHAM PARK INFORMATION
CENTER† □ Florham Park, NJ
Short, Janet, Cat.
BISHOP (Bernice P.) MUSEUM - LIBRARY □
Honolulu, HI
Short, Kim, Asst.Libn.
BAPTIST CONVENTION OF ONTARIO AND
QUEBEC - CANADIAN BAPTIST ARCHIVES □
Hamilton, ON
Short, Linda K., Libn.
MAC FARLANE & COMPANY, INC. - FRY
CONSULTANTS INCORPORATED -
MANAGEMENT CENTRE, INC. □ Atlanta, GA
Short, Sylvia, State Libn.
DELAWARE STATE DEPARTMENT OF
COMMUNITY AFFAIRS - DIVISION OF
LIBRARIES □ Dover, DE
Shorthouse, Thomas J., Law Libn.
UNIVERSITY OF BRITISH COLUMBIA - LAW
LIBRARY □ Vancouver, BC

Shortt, Mary, Chf.Libn.
UNIVERSITY OF TORONTO - FACULTY OF
EDUCATION LIBRARY □ Toronto, ON
Shostrom, Marian, Ref.Libn.
UNIVERSITY OF SAN FRANCISCO - SCHOOL OF
LAW LIBRARY □ San Francisco, CA
Shotwell, Richard, Ref.Libn.
MORTON ARBORETUM - STERLING MORTON
LIBRARY □ Lisle, IL
Shoup, Mary Agnes, Asst.Libn.
UNIVERSITY OF DETROIT - SCHOOL OF
DENTISTRY LIBRARY □ Detroit, MI
Shove, Timothy
SOUTHERN OREGON STATE COLLEGE -
LIBRARY □ Ashland, OR
Showalter, Grace, Libn.
EASTERN MENNONITE COLLEGE - MENNO
SIMONS HISTORICAL LIBRARY AND ARCHIVES
□ Harrisonburg, VA
Showalter, J. Gordan, Hd.
U.S. NAVY - NAVAL RESEARCH LABORATORY -
SHOCK AND VIBRATION INFORMATION
CENTER □ Washington, DC
Showalter, Dr. Victor M., Dir.
FEDERATION FOR UNIFIED SCIENCE
EDUCATION - FUSE CENTER LIBRARY □
Columbus, OH
Showers, Kathryn E., Libn.
LOS ANGELES COUNTY MUSEUM OF NATURAL
HISTORY - RESEARCH LIBRARY □ Los Angeles,
CA
Shrader, Ethel, Asst.Libn.
VIRGINIA POLYTECHNIC INSTITUTE AND
STATE UNIVERSITY - GEOLOGY LIBRARY □
Blacksburg, VA
Shrader, Merald, Hd., Engr.
VARIAN ASSOCIATES - EIMAC DIVISION -
TECHNICAL LIBRARY† □ San Carlos, CA
Shrader, Richard A., Ref.Archv.
UNIVERSITY OF NORTH CAROLINA, CHAPEL
HILL - SOUTHERN HISTORICAL COLLECTION &
MANUSCRIPTS DEPARTMENT □ Chapel Hill, NC
Shrader, Steve, District Ranger
U.S. NATL. PARK SERVICE - COULEE DAM
NATL. RECREATION AREA - FORT SPOKANE
VISITOR CENTER □ Davenport, WA
Shrenka, Paul
3M - 201 TECHNICAL LIBRARY □ St. Paul, MN
Shriver, Rosalia, Prof.Asst.
ENOCH PRATT FREE LIBRARY - FINE ARTS AND
RECREATION DEPARTMENT □ Baltimore, MD
Shriver, S.L., Res.
OHIO STATE DEPARTMENT OF TAXATION -
RESEARCH AND STATISTICS LIBRARY □
Columbus, OH
Shroder, Emelie, Division Chief
CHICAGO PUBLIC LIBRARY CENTRAL LIBRARY -
BUSINESS/SCIENCE/TECHNOLOGY DIVISION
□ Chicago, IL
Shrout, Sally, Ser.Serv.
UNIVERSITY OF OKLAHOMA - HEALTH
SCIENCES CENTER LIBRARY □ Oklahoma City,
OK
Shryock, Sandra, Investment Info.Spec.
UNION MUTUAL LIFE INSURANCE COMPANY -
CORPORATE INFORMATION CENTER □ Portland,
ME
Shtohryn, Dmytro, Slavic Cat.Libn.
UNIVERSITY OF ILLINOIS - SLAVIC AND EAST
EUROPEAN LIBRARY □ Urbana, IL
Shub, Bertha J., Libn.
NORTH CHARLES GENERAL HOSPITAL -
MEDICAL STAFF LIBRARY □ Baltimore, MD
Shubert, Joseph F., Asst.Commnr.
NEW YORK STATE LIBRARY □ Albany, NY
Shubnell, Penny, Tech.Libn.
DENNY'S INC. - COMPUTER SERVICES LIBRARY
□ La Mirada, CA
Shuiskii, Sergei
PRINCETON UNIVERSITY - NEAR EAST
COLLECTIONS† □ Princeton, NJ

Shuldman, Mitchell, Mus.Libn.
UNIVERSITY OF LOWELL, SOUTH CAMPUS -
DANIEL H. O'LEARY LIBRARY - SPECIAL
COLLECTIONS □ Lowell, MA
Shuler, John A., Act.Hd.
UNIVERSITY OF OREGON - GOVERNMENT
DOCUMENTS SECTION □ Eugene, OR
Shulman, Frank Joseph, Dir.
ASIAN STUDIES NEWSLETTER ARCHIVES □
College Park, MD
Shulman, Frank Joseph, Cur.
UNIVERSITY OF MARYLAND, COLLEGE PARK -
LIBRARIES - EAST ASIA COLLECTION □ College
Park, MD
Shulman, Tikvah S., Libn.
PROVIDENT MUTUAL LIFE INSURANCE
COMPANY OF PHILADELPHIA - LIBRARY† □
Philadelphia, PA
Shulski, Marilyn, Adm.Mgr.
DU PAGE LIBRARY SYSTEM - SYSTEM CENTER
□ Geneva, IL
Shultes, Dorothea, Libn.
CROUSE-IRVING MEMORIAL HOSPITAL -
LIBRARY □ Syracuse, NY
Shults, Linda S., Libn.
TENNECO, INC. - CORPORATE LIBRARY □
Houston, TX
Shultz, Barbara C., Dept.Hd.
MEMPHIS-SHELBY COUNTY PUBLIC LIBRARY
AND INFO. CTR. - SCIENCE/BUSINESS/SOCIAL
SCI.DEPT. □ Memphis, TN
Shultz, Suzanne M., Libn.
POLYCLINIC MEDICAL CENTER - MEDICAL
STAFF LIBRARY □ Harrisburg, PA
Shumake, Nora L.M., Dir. of Libs.
CHARFOOS, CHRISTENSEN, GILBERT &
ARCHER, P.C. - LIBRARY □ Detroit, MI
Shumaker, David, Ref.Libn.
MITRE CORPORATION - LIBRARY □ McLean, VA
Shumaker, Donna, Br.Libn., Washington
SQUIRE, SANDERS & DEMPSEY - LAW LIBRARY
□ Cleveland, OH
Shuman, Kristen, Supv. Music Libn.
NEW YORK PUBLIC LIBRARY - GENERAL
LIBRARY OF THE PERFORMING ARTS □ New
York, NY
Shung, Lily, Cat.
COLGATE ROCHESTER/BEXLEY HALL/CROZER
THEOLOGICAL SEMINARIES - AMBROSE
SWASEY LIBRARY □ Rochester, NY
Shupe, Barbara A., Libn.
SUNY AT STONY BROOK - MAP LIBRARY □
Stony Brook, NY
Shurman, Richard, Automation Coord.
DU PAGE LIBRARY SYSTEM - SYSTEM CENTER
□ Geneva, IL
Shurtleff, William R., Dir.
SOYFOODS CENTER LIBRARY □ Lafayette, CA
Shuster, Helen, Hd., Tech.Serv.
WORCESTER POLYTECHNIC INSTITUTE -
GEORGE C. GORDON LIBRARY □ Worcester, MA
Shuster, Robert, Dir.
WHEATON COLLEGE - BILLY GRAHAM CENTER -
ARCHIVES □ Wheaton, IL
Shute, Rev. Daniel, Libn.
PRESBYTERIAN COLLEGE - LIBRARY □ Montreal,
PQ
Shute, M., Libn.
NATIONAL PSYCHOLOGICAL ASSOCIATION FOR
PSYCHOANALYSIS - GEORGE LAWTON
MEMORIAL LIBRARY □ New York, NY
Shutt, Philip L., Registrar/Historiographer
PROTESTANT EPISCOPAL CHURCH -
EPISCOPAL DIOCESE OF SPRINGFIELD,
ILLINOIS - DIOCESAN CENTER LIBRARY □
Springfield, IL
Shutt, Thelma, Hd., Ref.Serv.
U.S. ARMY SOLDIER SUPPORT CENTER - MAIN
LIBRARY† □ Ft. Benjamin Harrison, IN
Shutzer, Carole B., Libn.
HELIX TECHNOLOGY CORPORATION - LIBRARY
□ Waltham, MA

Shy, Arlene P., Hd., Rd.Serv.
UNIVERSITY OF MICHIGAN - WILLIAM L. CLEMENTS LIBRARY □ Ann Arbor, MI
Shy, Kay, Cat.Libn.
STATE LIBRARY OF FLORIDA □ Tallahassee, FL
Siane, Dorothy K., Res.
LAMALIE ASSOCIATES, INC. - RESEARCH DEPARTMENT □ Tampa, FL
Siarny, William D., Jr., Dir.
NATIONAL LIVESTOCK AND MEAT BOARD - MEAT INDUSTRY INFORMATION CENTER □ Chicago, IL
Sibbett, Diane, Libn.
CANADIAN EDUCATION ASSOCIATION - LIBRARY □ Toronto, ON
Sibley, Anna Margaret, Libn.
YUMA COUNTY LAW LIBRARY □ Yuma, AZ
Sibley, Marjorie H., Ref.Libn.
AUGSBURG COLLEGE - GEORGE SVERDRUP LIBRARY AND MEDIA CENTER □ Minneapolis, MN
Sibley, Shawn C., Assoc.Dir., AHEC Lib.
NORTHWEST AREA HEALTH EDUCATION CENTER - NW AHEC LIBRARY □ Hickory, NC
Sichel, Beatrice, Hd.Libn.
WESTERN MICHIGAN UNIVERSITY - PHYSICAL SCIENCES LIBRARY □ Kalamazoo, MI
Sichel, Jan, Supv., Film & Video Lib.
UNIVERSITY OF COLORADO, BOULDER - ACADEMIC MEDIA SERVICES □ Boulder, CO
Sicking, Mary M., Libn.
CENTRAL INSTITUTE FOR THE DEAF - EDUCATIONAL RESEARCH LIBRARY □ St. Louis, MO
Sidel, Dr. Victor W., Chm., Dept.Soc.Med.
MONTEFIORE MEDICAL CENTER - KARL CHERKASKY SOCIAL MEDICINE LIBRARY □ Bronx, NY
Sideman, Leonard, Libn.
PENNSYLVANIA STATE DEPARTMENT OF HEALTH - BUREAU OF LABORATORIES - HERBERT FOX MEMORIAL LIBRARY □ Lionville, PA
Siden, Harriet, Art Libn.
D'ARCY, MAC MANUS, MASIUS - LIBRARY INFORMATION SERVICES □ Bloomfield Hills, MI
Sider, Dr. E. Morris, Archv.
BRETHREN IN CHRIST CHURCH AND MESSIAH COLLEGE - ARCHIVES □ Grantham, PA
Siders, Barbara Z., Cons.
COLORADO STATE DEPARTMENT OF EDUCATION - INSTRUCTIONAL MATERIALS CENTER FOR THE VISUALLY HANDICAPPED □ Denver, CO
Sidhu, Mrs. Bhagwant Kaur, Libn./Ed.
LAKE COUNTY DEPARTMENT OF PLANNING, ZONING & ENVIRONMENTAL QUALITY - RESEARCH LIBRARY □ Waukegan, IL
Sidney, Peter, Sr.Libn.
PILLSBURY COMPANY - BUSINESS REFERENCE LIBRARY □ Minneapolis, MN
Sidrow, Sigrid, Libn.
MARCHAIS (Jacques) CENTER OF TIBETAN ARTS, INC. - LIBRARY □ Staten Island, NY
Siebecker, Dorothy, Cat.
TUCSON MUSEUM OF ART - LIBRARY □ Tucson, AZ
Sieben, Gloria, Libn.
ST. MARY OF THE LAKE SEMINARY - FEEHAN MEMORIAL LIBRARY □ Mundelein, IL
Sieben, Regina, Res.Rec.Info.Spec.
GENERAL FOODS CORPORATION - CRANBURY TECHNICAL INFORMATION CENTER □ Cranbury, NJ
Sieber, Robert N., Dir.
PENNSYLVANIA FARM MUSEUM OF LANDIS VALLEY - LIBRARY □ Lancaster, PA
Siebert, Mary Kay, Libn.
AMERICAN MEDICAL RECORD ASSOCIATION - FORE RESOURCE CENTER □ Chicago, IL

Siebesma, Marcia, Assoc. Law Libn.
OHIO NORTHERN UNIVERSITY - COLLEGE OF LAW - JAY P. TAGGART MEMORIAL LAW LIBRARY □ Ada, OH
Siebrecht-Nuno, Angela, Cat.
CANADA - PUBLIC WORKS CANADA - INFORMATION, RESEARCH & LIBRARY SERVICES □ Ottawa, ON
Siedle, Veronica, Libn.
U.S. FISH & WILDLIFE SERVICE - SCIENCE REFERENCE LIBRARY □ Twin Cities, MN
Siefert, Donna, Libn.
HANDY ASSOCIATES, INC. - RESEARCH LIBRARY □ New York, NY
Siegal, Ernest, County Libn.
CONTRA COSTA COUNTY - CENTRAL LIBRARY - LOCAL HISTORY COLLECTION □ Pleasant Hill, CA
Siegel, Blanche, Libn.
TOWNSEND-GREENSPAN & COMPANY, INC. - LIBRARY □ New York, NY
Siegel, Gladys E., Libn.
AMERICAN PETROLEUM INSTITUTE - LIBRARY □ Washington, DC
Siegel, Leonard M., Dir.
PACIFIC STUDIES CENTER - LIBRARY □ Mountain View, CA
Siegel, Lorraine, Asst.Libn.
PATTERSON, BELKNAP, WEBB & TYLER - LIBRARY □ New York, NY
Siegel, Peter, Hd., User Serv.
RUTGERS UNIVERSITY, THE STATE UNIVERSITY OF NEW JERSEY - JUSTICE HENRY ACKERSON LIBRARY OF LAW & CRIMINAL JUSTICE □ Newark, NJ
Siegel, Robin E., Cons.
NATIONAL GEOGRAPHIC SOCIETY - ILLUSTRATIONS LIBRARY □ Washington, DC
Siegel, Shalva, Spec. Subjects Cat.
HEBREW COLLEGE - JACOB AND ROSE GROSSMAN LIBRARY □ Brookline, MA
Siegel, Steven W., Exec.Sec.
JEWISH HISTORICAL SOCIETY OF NEW YORK, INC. - LIBRARY □ New York, NY
Siegel, Steven W., Dir., Lib. & Archv.
92ND STREET YOUNG MEN'S AND YOUNG WOMEN'S HEBREW ASSOCIATION - ARCHIVES □ New York, NY
Siegel, Steven W., Dir., Lib. & Archv.
92ND STREET YOUNG MEN'S AND YOUNG WOMEN'S HEBREW ASSOCIATION - BUTTENWIESER LIBRARY □ New York, NY
Siegelman, Lynn, Libn.
ST. PETER'S HOSPITAL - MEDICAL STAFF LIBRARY □ Albany, NY
Siegfried, Dorothy E., Chf.
U.S. AIR FORCE - WRIGHT-PATTERSON TECHNICAL LIBRARY □ Dayton, OH
Siegfried, Dorothy E., Tech.Info.Spec.
U.S. COAST GUARD - RESEARCH AND DEVELOPMENT CENTER - TECHNICAL INFORMATION CENTER □ Groton, CT
Siegler, Sharon, Asst.Dir., Sci. & Engr.
LEHIGH UNIVERSITY - MART SCIENCE AND ENGINEERING LIBRARY □ Bethlehem, PA
Siemering, John, Media Techn.
NORTHEAST WISCONSIN TECHNICAL INSTITUTE - LEARNING RESOURCE CENTER □ Green Bay, WI
Siemers, Lynne, Libn.
MINNESOTA STATE DEPARTMENT OF HEALTH - ROBERT N. BARR PUBLIC HEALTH LIBRARY □ Minneapolis, MN
Siena, Sr. Margaret, S.C.N., Dir.
OUR LADY OF PEACE HOSPITAL - MEDICAL LIBRARY □ Louisville, KY
Sieracki, Rita, Ref.Libn.
UNIVERSITY OF SOUTH DAKOTA - CHRISTIAN P. LOMMEN HEALTH SCIENCES LIBRARY □ Vermillion, SD
Sierra, Terri, Adm.
MECHANICAL TECHNOLOGY INC. - TECHNICAL INFORMATION SERVICES □ Latham, NY

Sievan, Lee C., Resource Libn.
INTERNATIONAL CENTER OF PHOTOGRAPHY - LIBRARY RESOURCE CENTER □ New York, NY
Siever, Robert A., Asst.Dir.Tech.Serv.
FRANKLIN AND MARSHALL COLLEGE - SHADEK-FACKENTHAL LIBRARY - SPECIAL COLLECTIONS □ Lancaster, PA
Siewers, Iris J., Info.Sci.
UNION CARBIDE CORPORATION - LIBRARY & TECHNICAL INFORMATION SERVICE □ Tarrytown, NY
Sifford, Harlan, Libn.
UNIVERSITY OF IOWA - ART LIBRARY □ Iowa City, IA
Sifneos, Ann L.
SWEDENBORG LIBRARY AND BOOKSTORE □ Boston, MA
Sigari, Marie, Cat.
ROCKWELL INTERNATIONAL - ROCKETDYNE DIVISION - TECHNICAL INFORMATION CENTER □ Canoga Park, CA
Sigel, John A.
CALIFORNIA STATE SUPREME COURT LIBRARY □ San Francisco, CA
Sigerson, Marjorie L., Libn.
MUSEUM OF ARTS AND SCIENCES - BRUCE EVERETT BATES MEMORIAL LIBRARY □ Daytona Beach, FL
Sigman, Janet P., Adult Libn.
REVEILLE UNITED METHODIST CHURCH - REVEILLE MEMORIAL LIBRARY □ Richmond, VA
Sigman, Paula M., Asst.Archv.
DISNEY (Walt) PRODUCTIONS - ARCHIVES □ Burbank, CA
Signes, E.G., Info.Anl.
BETHLEHEM STEEL CORPORATION - HERTY TECHNICAL INFORMATION CENTER □ Bethlehem, PA
Sigurdson, Johanna, Libn.
BARBEAU, MC KERCHER & COLLINGWOOD, BARRISTERS & SOLICITORS - LIBRARY □ Vancouver, BC
Sikes, Janice White, Cur.
ATLANTA FULTON PUBLIC LIBRARY - SPECIAL COLLECTIONS DEPARTMENT □ Atlanta, GA
Sikkema, Fern, Asst.Libn., Leg.Serv.
CROWELL & MORING - LIBRARY □ Washington, DC
Sikorski, Charlene, Med.Libn.
WESTCHESTER COUNTY MEDICAL CENTER - HEALTH SCIENCES LIBRARY □ Valhalla, NY
Sikorski, Leona, Supv., Tech.Info.
ALLEGHENY LUDLUM STEEL CORPORATION - RESEARCH CENTER TECHNICAL LIBRARY □ Brackenridge, PA
Silberman, E., Prof./Dir.
FISK UNIVERSITY - MOLECULAR SPECTROSCOPY RESEARCH LABORATORY - LIBRARY □ Nashville, TN
Silliman, Robert T., Dir.
WINDSOR HISTORICAL SOCIETY, INC. - LIBRARY □ Windsor, CT
Silva, Don, Libn.
SAN DIEGO PUBLIC LIBRARY - HISTORY & WORLD AFFAIRS SECTION □ San Diego, CA
Silva, Mary D., Libn.
MOTOROLA, INC. - SEMICONDUCTOR PRODUCTS SECTOR - TECHNICAL LIBRARY □ Phoenix, AZ
Silva, Phyllis Peloquin, Dir.
RHODE ISLAND STATE ARCHIVES □ Providence, RI
Silva, Remedios, Hd.Cat.
SUNY AT BUFFALO - HEALTH SCIENCES LIBRARY □ Buffalo, NY
Silver, Adele, Cultural Arts Dir.
JEWISH COMMUNITY CENTER OF METROPOLITAN DETROIT - HENRY MEYERS MEMORIAL LIBRARY □ West Bloomfield, MI
Silver, Charles, Supv.
MUSEUM OF MODERN ART - FILM STUDY CENTER □ New York, NY

Silver, Janis Isaacson, Libn.
NASHUA HOSPITAL ASSOCIATION - MEMORIAL
HOSPITAL - HEALTH SCIENCES LIBRARY □
Nashua, NH

Silver, Len, On-site Contract Mgr.
U.S. ARMY - PLASTICS TECHNICAL
EVALUATION CENTER - LIBRARY □ Dover, NJ

Silver, Martin, Asst.Hd./Music Libn.
UNIVERSITY OF CALIFORNIA, SANTA BARBARA
- ARTS LIBRARY □ Santa Barbara, CA

Silver-Regan, Linda, Asst.Libn., Coll.Mgt.
GEORGETOWN UNIVERSITY - FRED O. DENNIS
LAW LIBRARY □ Washington, DC

Silverberg, Ellen, Libn.
MASSACHUSETTS INSTITUTE OF TECHNOLOGY
- DYNAMICS OF ATMOSPHERES AND OCEANS
LIBRARY □ Cambridge, MA

Silverblatt, Cheryl H., Bus.Ref.Libn.
SAN MATEO PUBLIC LIBRARY - BUSINESS
SECTION □ San Mateo, CA

Silverman, Elsa B., Asst.Libn.
U.S. TAX COURT - LIBRARY □ Washington, DC

Silverman, Helen F., Libn.
ST. LOUIS COLLEGE OF PHARMACY - O.J.
CLOUGHLY ALUMNI LIBRARY □ St. Louis, MO

Silverman, Judy, Sr.Info.Spec., Econ.
CONFERENCE BOARD, INC. - INFORMATION
SERVICE □ New York, NY

Silverman, Marc, Asst. Law Libn.
UNIVERSITY OF PITTSBURGH - LAW LIBRARY □
Pittsburgh, PA

Silverman, Marion H., Dir.
EINSTEIN (Albert) MEDICAL CENTER -
NORTHERN DIVISION - LURIA MEDICAL
LIBRARY† □ Philadelphia, PA

Silverman, Nancy, Media Coord.
CROUSE-IRVING MEMORIAL HOSPITAL -
LIBRARY □ Syracuse, NY

Silverman, Susanne, Libn.
RICHARDSON-VICKS, INC. - VICKS RESEARCH
CENTER - LIBRARY □ Shelton, CT

Silvernail, Barbara, Intl./U.S.Docs.Libn.
UNIVERSITY OF CALIFORNIA, LOS ANGELES -
PUBLIC AFFAIRS SERVICE □ Los Angeles, CA

Silvers, P.G., Hd., Lib.Serv.
AMERICAN SCIENCE FICTION ASSOCIATION -
ASFA LIBRARY □ Las Vegas, NV

Silverstein, Ellen, Asst.Libn.
MORGAN, LEWIS & BOCKIUS - LIBRARY □
Philadelphia, PA

Silverstein, Gilbert, Film Lib.Dir.
NORTHERN ILLINOIS UNIVERSITY - FILM
LIBRARY □ DeKalb, IL

Silverston, Dede, Med.Libn.
NATIONAL SOCIETY TO PREVENT BLINDNESS -
CONRAD BERENS LIBRARY □ New York, NY

Silvester, Jean, Asst.Libn., Cat.
SUNY AT BUFFALO - HEALTH SCIENCES
LIBRARY □ Buffalo, NY

Silvestro, Clement M., Dir./Libn.
MUSEUM OF OUR NATIONAL HERITAGE - VAN
GORDEN-WILLIAMS LIBRARY □ Lexington, MA

Silvestro, Josephine, Libn.
GCA CORPORATION - TECHNOLOGY DIVISION
- LIBRARY □ Bedford, MA

Silvin, John S., Hd., Lib.Serv.
BRISTOL-MYERS COMPANY - SCIENTIFIC
INFORMATION DEPARTMENT □ Syracuse, NY

Silzer, Beth, Dir.
PLAINS HEALTH CENTRE - DR. W.A. RIDDELL
HEALTH SCIENCES LIBRARY □ Regina, SK

Sim, Donna J., Dir.
CANADIAN MENTAL HEALTH ASSOCIATION -
SUICIDE INFORMATION AND EDUCATION
CENTRE □ Calgary, AB

Sim, J. Derek, Libn.
SHERRITT GORDON MINES, LTD. - RESEARCH
CENTRE LIBRARY □ Fort Saskatchewan, AB

Sim, Patrick, Libn.
AMERICAN SOCIETY OF ANESTHESIOLOGISTS
- WOOD LIBRARY-MUSEUM OF
ANESTHESIOLOGY □ Park Ridge, IL

Simard, Clement-Jacques, Dir.
SEMINAIRE DE CHICOUTIMI - BIBLIOTHEQUE
□ Chicoutimi, PQ

Simard, Denis, Dir.
CEGEP DE TROIS-RIVIERES - BIBLIOTHEQUE □
Trois-Rivieres, PQ

Simard, Miss Marjolaine, Archv.
SOCIETE QUEBECOISE D'INITIATIVES
PETROLIERES - DOCUMENTATION CENTRE† □
Ste. Foy, PQ

Simchovitch, Samuel, Libn.
BETH TZEDEC CONGREGATION - MAX &
BEATRICE WOLFE LIBRARY □ Toronto, ON

Simenson, Linda, Libn.
COOPERATIVE EDUCATIONAL SERVICE
AGENCY (CESA) NO. 6 - INSTRUCTIONAL
MATERIALS CENTER □ Chippewa Falls, WI

Simeone, Therese, Med.Libn.
CAMBRIDGE HOSPITAL - MEDICAL LIBRARY □
Cambridge, MA

Simes, Elizabeth A., Libn.
BISMARCK TRIBUNE - NEWS LIBRARY □
Bismarck, ND

Simison, Joan B., Libn.
ANNE ARUNDEL COUNTY CIRCUIT COURT -
LAW LIBRARY □ Annapolis, MD

Simkins, Adrienne, Ref.Libn.
HOGAN & HARTSON - LIBRARY □ Washington,
DC

Simmer, Ronald V., Libn.
CANOCEAN RESOURCES LTD. - ENGINEERING
LIBRARY □ New Westminster, BC

Simmon, Elaine, Cat.Dept.
SOUTHERN UNIVERSITY - LAW SCHOOL
LIBRARY □ Baton Rouge, LA

Simmonds, Dr. Richard C., Exec.Sec.
INTERNATIONAL HIBERNATION SOCIETY □
Rockville, MD

Simmonds, Richard P., Libn.
CONGREGATION SHEARITH ISRAEL - SOPHIE
AND IVAN SALOMON LIBRARY COLLECTION □
New York, NY

Simmons, Brian, Med.Libn.
BLODGETT MEMORIAL MEDICAL CENTER -
RICHARD ROOT SMITH LIBRARY □ Grand
Rapids, MI

Simmons, Donnalee L., Libn./Info.Spec.
AUTOMOBILE CLUB OF SOUTHERN CALIFORNIA
- TECHNICAL INFORMATION CENTER □ Los
Angeles, CA

Simmons, Elizabeth, Libn.
INDIANAPOLIS - DEPARTMENT OF
METROPOLITAN DEVELOPMENT - DIVISION OF
PLANNING - LIBRARY □ Indianapolis, IN

Simmons, GeorJane, Libn.
PANHANDLE EASTERN PIPE LINE COMPANY -
TECHNICAL INFORMATION CENTER □ Kansas
City, MO

Simmons, Grace L., Libn./Rec.Mgr.
YOUNG, CONAWAY, STARGATT & TAYLOR -
LIBRARY □ Wilmington, DE

Simmons, Henry, Cur.
UNIVERSITY OF SOUTHERN MISSISSIPPI - MC
CAIN LIBRARY □ Hattiesburg, MS

Simmons, Ida, Mgr. of Commun.
U.S. TRAVEL DATA CENTER - LIBRARY □
Washington, DC

Simmons, Joseph M., Mgr.
TOWERS, PERRIN, FORSTER & CROSBY, INC. -
INFORMATION CENTER □ New York, NY

Simmons, Karen Hegge, Chf.Libn.
AMERICAN INSTITUTE OF CERTIFIED PUBLIC
ACCOUNTANTS - LIBRARY SERVICES □ New
York, NY

Simmons, Kim, Lib.Dir.
AMERICAN SOCIETY OF LAW & MEDICINE -
ELLIOT L. AND ANNETTE Y. SAGALL LIBRARY □
Boston, MA

Simmons, Robert M., Curric.Libn.
BRIDGEWATER STATE COLLEGE - CLEMENT C.
MAXWELL LIBRARY □ Bridgewater, MA

Simmons, Ruth J., Hd., Spec.Coll. & Archv.
GENEALOGICAL SOCIETY OF NEW JERSEY -
MANUSCRIPT COLLECTIONS □ New Brunswick,
NJ

Simmons, Ruth J., Sr.Archv./Coord.
RUTGERS UNIVERSITY, THE STATE
UNIVERSITY OF NEW JERSEY - DEPARTMENT
OF SPECIAL COLLECTIONS AND ARCHIVES □
New Brunswick, NJ

Simmons, Walter T., Ck. of Court
ILLINOIS STATE - APPELLATE COURT, 5TH
DISTRICT - LIBRARY □ Mt. Vernon, IL

Simms, Betty B., Tech.Libn.
UNITED CATALYSTS, INC. - TECHNICAL
LIBRARY □ Louisville, KY

Simms, Marika S., Slide Libn.
UNIVERSITY OF VIRGINIA - FISKE KIMBALL
FINE ARTS LIBRARY □ Charlottesville, VA

Simon, Constance M., Dir.
NYLANDER MUSEUM - ARCHIVES □ Caribou, ME

Simon, Helen, Cur.
MARTIN COUNTY HISTORICAL SOCIETY, INC. -
PIONEER MUSEUM - LIBRARY □ Fairmont, MN

Simon, Mr. J.L., Chf., Info.Proc.
CANADA - REGIONAL INDUSTRIAL EXPANSION
- LIBRARY □ Ottawa, ON

Simon, Margaret E., Libn.
SUGAR ASSOCIATION, INC. - LIBRARY □
Washington, DC

Simon, Mary K., Dir. of Info.
AMERICAN PUBLIC WORKS ASSOCIATION -
INFORMATION SERVICE □ Chicago, IL

Simon, Nancy, Med.Libn.
ROSE MEDICAL CENTER - LIBRARY □ Denver,
CO

Simon, Paula, Resource Rm.Coord.
UNIVERSITY OF MINNESOTA - CENTER FOR
YOUTH DEVELOPMENT AND RESEARCH -
RESOURCE ROOM □ St. Paul, MN

Simon, Susan H., Ref.Libn.
U.S. NATL. LABOR RELATIONS BOARD - LAW
LIBRARY □ Washington, DC

Simonetta, Dr. L., Lib.Chm.
WILLIAMS (C.S.) CLINIC - LIBRARY □ Trail, BC

Simons, Eleanor, Libn.
NORTHEASTERN VERMONT REGIONAL
HOSPITAL - INFORMATION CENTER/LIBRARY
□ St. Johnsbury, VT

Simons, Gordon N., Cur.
PENSACOLA HISTORICAL SOCIETY - LELIA
ABERCROMBIE HISTORICAL LIBRARY □
Pensacola, FL

Simons, Mrs. Ute, Med.Libn.
HOAG MEMORIAL HOSPITAL-PRESBYTERIAN -
MEDICAL LIBRARY □ Newport Beach, CA

Simor, George, Chf. Book Acq.Libn.
CUNY - GRADUATE SCHOOL AND UNIVERSITY
CENTER - LIBRARY □ New York, NY

Simor, Suzanna, Hd.
QUEENS COLLEGE OF THE CITY UNIVERSITY
OF NEW YORK - PAUL KLAPPER LIBRARY - ART
LIBRARY □ Flushing, NY

Simosko, Vladimir, Adm.Hd.
UNIVERSITY OF MANITOBA - MUSIC LIBRARY
□ Winnipeg, MB

Simpson, Angela, Lib.Asst.
CLARK COLLEGE - SOUTHERN CENTER FOR
STUDIES IN PUBLIC POLICY - RESEARCH
LIBRARY □ Atlanta, GA

Simpson, Anne, Supv., Cat. & Indexing
INTERNATIONAL DEVELOPMENT RESEARCH
CENTRE - LIBRARY† □ Ottawa, ON

Simpson, Carol Robinson, Libn.
NORTH AMERICAN WEATHER CONSULTANTS -
TECHNICAL LIBRARY† □ Salt Lake City, UT

Simpson, Carolyn A., Coord. of Regulatory Info
WISCONSIN GAS COMPANY - CORPORATE AND
LAW LIBRARY □ Milwaukee, WI

Simpson, Christine, Libn.
U.S. VETERANS ADMINISTRATION (NC-
Salisbury) - MEDICAL CENTER LIBRARY □
Salisbury, NC

Simpson, Donald B., Dir.
CENTER FOR RESEARCH LIBRARIES □ Chicago, IL

Simpson, Ethel C., Asst.Libn.
UNIVERSITY OF ARKANSAS, FAYETTEVILLE - SPECIAL COLLECTIONS DIVISION □ Fayetteville, AR

Simpson, Evelyn, Med.Libn.
GOOD SAMARITAN HOSPITAL OF ORANGE COUNTY, INC. - MEDICAL LIBRARY □ Anaheim, CA

Simpson, Evelyn, Dir., Med.Lib.
WESTERN MEDICAL CENTER - MEDICAL LIBRARY □ Santa Ana, CA

Simpson, Jerome, Libn.
OKLAHOMA REGIONAL LIBRARY FOR THE BLIND AND PHYSICALLY HANDICAPPED □ Oklahoma City, OK

Simpson, Joan, Cat.
DALHOUSIE UNIVERSITY - LAW LIBRARY □ Halifax, NS

Simpson, Leslie, Libn./Dir.
POST (Winfred L. and Elizabeth C.) FOUNDATION - MEMORIAL ART REFERENCE LIBRARY □ Joplin, MO

Simpson, Louise, Techn.
CANADA - ENERGY, MINES & RESOURCES CANADA - EARTH PHYSICS BRANCH LIBRARY □ Ottawa, ON

Simpson, Mrs. M.A., Supt.
BATTLEFORD NATIONAL HISTORIC PARK - CAMPBELL INNES MEMORIAL LIBRARY □ Battleford, SK

Simpson, M. Ronald, Hd., Tech.Info.Ctr.
NORTH CAROLINA STATE UNIVERSITY - D.H. HILL LIBRARY □ Raleigh, NC

Simpson, M. Ronald, Hd.
NORTH CAROLINA STATE UNIVERSITY - D.H. HILL LIBRARY - TECHNICAL INFORMATION CENTER □ Raleigh, NC

Simpson, Marilynn, ILL Hd.
UNIVERSITY OF MICHIGAN - ALFRED TAUBMAN MEDICAL LIBRARY □ Ann Arbor, MI

Simpson, Mary Ellen, Welfare Libn.
MISSISSIPPI STATE DEPARTMENT OF PUBLIC WELFARE - JEAN GUNTER SOCIAL WELFARE LIBRARY □ Jackson, MS

Simpson, Mildred, Libn.
ATLANTIC-RICHFIELD COMPANY - PHOTOGRAPHY COLLECTION □ Los Angeles, CA

Simpson, Nancy, Libn.
ILLINOIS STATE ENVIRONMENTAL PROTECTION AGENCY - LIBRARY □ Springfield, IL

Simpson, Richard, Pub.Serv.Libn.
HARVARD UNIVERSITY - FINE ARTS LIBRARY □ Cambridge, MA

Simpson, Rolly L., Hd., Prod.Sect.
BURROUGHS WELLCOME COMPANY - LIBRARY □ Research Triangle Park, NC

Simpson, Mrs. S., Ck.
FALCONBRIDGE NICKEL MINES, LTD. - METALLURGICAL LABORATORIES INFORMATION SERVICES† □ Thornhill, ON

Simpson, W. Samuel, Dir., Legal Info.Acc.Sys.
LEWIS AND CLARK LAW SCHOOL - NORTHWESTERN SCHOOL OF LAW - PAUL L. BOLEY LAW LIBRARY □ Portland, OR

Sims, Anne, Archv.
SOUTHERN ILLINOIS UNIVERSITY, CARBONDALE - SPECIAL COLLECTIONS □ Carbondale, IL

Sims, Henry L., Exec.Off.
U.S. AIR FORCE - AIR UNIVERSITY - LIBRARY □ Maxwell AFB, AL

Sims, Joyce, Libn.
ST. VINCENT'S HOSPITAL - CUNNINGHAM WILSON LIBRARY □ Birmingham, AL

Sims, Phil, Music Libn.
SOUTHWESTERN BAPTIST THEOLOGICAL SEMINARY - A. WEBB ROBERTS LIBRARY □ Fort Worth, TX

Sims-Wood, Janet L., Ref.Libn.
HOWARD UNIVERSITY - MOORLAND-SPINGARN RESEARCH CENTER - LIBRARY DIVISION □ Washington, DC

Sina, Fran, Ref./Circ.Supv.
HAHNEMANN UNIVERSITY - WARREN H. FAKE LIBRARY† □ Philadelphia, PA

Sincerbox, David R., Dir.
STUDENTS' MUSEUM, INC. - LIBRARY □ Knoxville, TN

Sinclair, John M., Libn.
EDMONTON SUN - NEWSPAPER LIBRARY □ Edmonton, AB

Sinclair, Mary Jane T., Asst.Libn., Common Law
CANADA - SUPREME COURT OF CANADA - LIBRARY □ Ottawa, ON

Sinclair, Susan, Archv.
GARDNER (Isabella Stewart) MUSEUM, INC. - STAFF LIBRARY □ Boston, MA

Sindaco, Lawrence H., Libn.
WILKES-BARRE LAW AND LIBRARY ASSOCIATION □ Wilkes-Barre, PA

Singer, Betsy, Chf.
NATIONAL INSTITUTE OF ARTHRITIS, DIABETES, DIGESTIVE AND KIDNEY DISEASES - OFFICE OF HEALTH RESEARCH REPORTS □ Bethesda, MD

Singer, Blanche, ILL
UNIVERSITY OF WISCONSIN, MADISON - CENTER FOR HEALTH SCIENCES LIBRARIES† □ Madison, WI

Singer, Carol, Govt.Docs./Bibliog.Instr.
WAYNE STATE COLLEGE - U.S. CONN LIBRARY □ Wayne, NE

Singer, Norma, Asst. Law Libn.
MENDOCINO COUNTY LAW LIBRARY □ Ukiah, CA

Singerman, Robert, Hd. & Assoc.Libn.
UNIVERSITY OF FLORIDA - ISSER AND RAE PRICE LIBRARY OF JUDAICA □ Gainesville, FL

Singh, Miss, Libn.
WASCANA INSTITUTE OF APPLIED ARTS AND SCIENCES - RESOURCE & INFORMATION CENTRE □ Regina, SK

Singh, Gurnek, Hd./Asian Bibliog.
SYRACUSE UNIVERSITY - E.S. BIRD LIBRARY - AREA STUDIES DEPARTMENT □ Syracuse, NY

Singleton, Alma, Ref.Libn.
NOVA UNIVERSITY - LAW LIBRARY □ Fort Lauderdale, FL

Singleton, Christine M., Res.Libn.
NEW YORK UNIVERSITY MEDICAL CENTER - INSTITUTE OF ENVIRONMENTAL MEDICINE - LIBRARY □ Tuxedo, NY

Singleton, S.E., Supv.
TRW, INC. - OPERATIONS & SUPPORT GROUP - ELECTRONICS & DEFENSE SECTOR - TECH. INFORMATION CENTER □ Redondo Beach, CA

Siniff, Priscilla D., Info.Coord.
BEXAR COUNTY MEDICAL LIBRARY ASSOCIATION □ San Antonio, TX

Sink, Thomas R., Dir. of Lib.Serv.
MERCY HOSPITAL - EDWARD L. BURNS HEALTH SCIENCES LIBRARY □ Toledo, OH

Sinkus, Raminta, Hd., Cat.Serv
DE PAUL UNIVERSITY - LAW SCHOOL LIBRARY □ Chicago, IL

Sinn, Mel, Dir.
MINNESOTA STATE WATER RESOURCES BOARD - LIBRARY □ St. Paul, MN

Sinnette, Elinor D., Oral Hist.Libn.
HOWARD UNIVERSITY - MOORLAND-SPINGARN RESEARCH CENTER - MANUSCRIPT DIVISION □ Washington, DC

Sipe, Mr. Lynn, Libn.
UNIVERSITY OF SOUTHERN CALIFORNIA - VON KLEINSMID LIBRARY □ Los Angeles, CA

Sipkov, Ivan, Chf.
LIBRARY OF CONGRESS - LAW LIBRARY - EUROPEAN LAW DIVISION □ Washington, DC

Sipsma, Mary, Med.Libn.
ST. CATHERINE'S HOSPITAL - MEDICAL LIBRARY □ Kenosha, WI

Siroin, Richard, Libn.
MAINE STATE DEPARTMENT OF TRANSPORTATION - LIBRARY □ Augusta, ME

Sirois, Dorothy, Med.Libn.
MONTREAL CHILDREN'S HOSPITAL - MEDICAL LIBRARY □ Montreal, PQ

Sirois, Julie J., Libn.
ST. FRANCIS HOSPITAL - MEDICAL LIBRARY □ Honolulu, HI

Siron, Catherine, Coord., Lib.Serv.
ST. JOSEPH HOSPITAL - HEALTH SCIENCE LIBRARY □ Joliet, IL

Siroonian, Harold, Sci. & Engr.Libn.
MC MASTER UNIVERSITY - THODE LIBRARY OF SCIENCE & ENGINEERING □ Hamilton, ON

Sirrocco, Angela, Chf.
U.S. PUBLIC HEALTH SERVICE - NATL. INSTITUTE OF MENTAL HEALTH - COMMUNICATION CENTER - LIBRARY† □ Rockville, MD

Sirskyj, Dr. W., Cat.
WILFRID LAURIER UNIVERSITY - LIBRARY □ Waterloo, ON

Sisamis, Paul G., Supv., Mtls.
KENT STATE UNIVERSITY - AUDIOVISUAL SERVICES □ Kent, OH

Sisson, Clinton, Asst. to Cur.
UNIVERSITY OF VIRGINIA - LIBRARY - RARE BOOK DEPARTMENT □ Charlottesville, VA

Sisson, Leona J., Libn.
JOHNSON COUNTY HISTORICAL SOCIETY - MARY MILLER SMISER HERITAGE LIBRARY □ Warrensburg, MO

Sisson, S. Gail, Asst.Libn.
GULF COMPANIES - LAW LIBRARY □ Houston, TX

Sistrunk, Carol, Chf.Libn.
U.S. VETERANS ADMINISTRATION (MS-Jackson) - CENTER LIBRARY □ Jackson, MS

Sitton, Brooks, Coord.
U.S. BUREAU OF THE CENSUS - INFORMATION SERVICES PROGRAM - DALLAS REGIONAL OFFICE - LIBRARY □ Dallas, TX

Sivanich, Ruth, Libn.
ST. OLAF LUTHERAN CHURCH - CARLSEN MEMORIAL LIBRARY □ Minneapolis, MN

Sivers, Robert, Asst.Hd.
UNIVERSITY OF CALIFORNIA, SANTA BARBARA - SCIENCES-ENGINEERING LIBRARY □ Santa Barbara, CA

Six, Mary Lee, Dir.
BUTTE COUNTY SUPERINTENDENT OF SCHOOLS - NORTHERN CALIFORNIA CENTER FOR EDUCATIONAL IMPROVEMENT □ Oroville, CA

Sizemore, Nellie W., R&D Libn.
REYNOLDS (R.J.) TOBACCO COMPANY - R&D SCIENTIFIC INFORMATION SERVICES LIBRARY □ Winston-Salem, NC

Sizer, Kathy, Asst.Libn.
AMERICAN PSYCHOLOGICAL ASSOCIATION - ARTHUR W. MELTON LIBRARY □ Arlington, VA

Sjostrom, Eric A., Asst.Libn.
MINNESOTA ORCHESTRA - MUSIC LIBRARY □ Minneapolis, MN

Sjostrom, Joan, Dir.
NORWALK HOSPITAL - R. GLEN WIGGANS MEMORIAL LIBRARY □ Norwalk, CT

Skaggs, Betty A., Libn.
OKLAHOMA COUNTY LAW LIBRARY □ Oklahoma City, OK

Skaggs, Deborah, Access Archv.
UNIVERSITY OF LOUISVILLE - UNIVERSITY ARCHIVES AND RECORDS CENTER □ Louisville, KY

Skale, Linda Carnevale, Tech.Info.Spec.
U.S. GENERAL ACCOUNTING OFFICE - PHILADELPHIA REGIONAL RESOURCE CENTER □ Philadelphia, PA

Skalstad, Doris, Asst.Hd.
MINNEAPOLIS PUBLIC LIBRARY & INFORMATION CENTER - HISTORY DEPARTMENT □ Minneapolis, MN

Skarr, Robert J., Mgr., Info.Ctr.
ALUMINUM ASSOCIATION - INFORMATION
CENTER □ Washington, DC
Skau, Dorothy B., Libn.
U.S.A. - AGRICULTURAL RESEARCH SERVICE
- SOUTHERN REGIONAL RESEARCH CENTER □
New Orleans, LA
Skeberdis, Esther Louise, Tech.Serv.Libn.
HARRINGTON INSTITUTE OF INTERIOR
DESIGN - DESIGN LIBRARY □ Chicago, IL
Skeele, Lillian, Libn.
WORTHINGTON HISTORICAL SOCIETY -
LIBRARY □ Worthington, OH
Skeen, Molly M., Libn.
FEDERAL HOME LOAN BANK OF SAN
FRANCISCO - LIBRARY □ San Francisco, CA
Skelly, Mary, Med.Info.Serv.Coord.
LONG ISLAND LIBRARY RESOURCES COUNCIL,
INC. (LILRC) □ Bellport, NY
Skelton, Mrs. Brooke, Cat.
WILFRID LAURIER UNIVERSITY - LIBRARY □
Waterloo, ON
Skelton, Lawrence H., Geologist & Mgr.
KANSAS STATE GEOLOGICAL SURVEY -
WICHITA WELL SAMPLE LIBRARY □ Wichita, KS
Skerritt, Elizabeth, Corp.Libn.
INTERNATIONAL PAPER COMPANY -
CORPORATE INFORMATION CENTER □ New
York, NY
Skica, Janice, Med.Libn.
UNIV. OF MEDICINE AND DENTISTRY OF NEW
JERSEY - SCHOOL OF OSTEOPATHIC MED. - DR.
JERROLD S. SCHWARTZ MEM. LIB. □ Stratford,
NJ
Skidmore, Carolyn R., Lib.Dir.
WEST VIRGINIA STATE DEPARTMENT OF
EDUCATION - EDUCATIONAL MEDIA CENTER □
Charleston, WV
Skidmore, Kerry F., Libn.
ST. MARK'S HOSPITAL - LIBRARY □ Salt Lake
City, UT
Skiles, Mrs. Jo, Libn.
WEST VIRGINIA STATE BOARD OF
VOCATIONAL EDUC. - DIV. OF VOCATIONAL
REHABILITATION - STAFF DEVELOPMENT
LIBRARY □ Institute, WV
Skinner, Aubrey E., Libn.
UNIVERSITY OF TEXAS, AUSTIN - CHEMISTRY
LIBRARY □ Austin, TX
Skinner, Barbara, Media Serv.
EMBRY RIDDLE AERONAUTICAL UNIVERSITY -
LEARNING RESOURCES CENTER □ Daytona
Beach, FL
Skinner, Connie, Libn.
KINO COMMUNITY HOSPITAL - LIBRARY □
Tucson, AZ
Skinner, George E., Dir.
UNIVERSITY OF ARKANSAS, FAYETTEVILLE -
LAW LIBRARY □ Fayetteville, AR
Skinner, Lois M., Chem./Libn.
ETHYL CORPORATION - INFORMATION &
LIBRARY SERVICES LIBRARY □ Baton Rouge, LA
Skinner, Mary Ann, Libn.
NEWSDAY, INC. - LIBRARY □ Melville, NY
Skinner, Robert, Ref., Educ.Bldg.Lib.
LOUISIANA STATE UNIVERSITY MEDICAL
CENTER - LIBRARY □ New Orleans, LA
Skinner, Thomas, Hd., Tech.Serv.
SOUTHERN ALBERTA INSTITUTE OF
TECHNOLOGY - LEARNING RESOURCES CENTRE
□ Calgary, AB
Skipp, Jean, Asst.Cur.
UNIVERSITY OF KANSAS - KANSAS
COLLECTION □ Lawrence, KS
Skladanowski, Lawrence M., Lib.Supv.
LORILLARD RESEARCH CENTER LIBRARY □
Greensboro, NC
Sklair, Terry, Asst.Libn.
MC DERMOTT, WILL & EMERY - LIBRARY □
Chicago, IL

Sklar, Hinda, Hd., Tech.Serv.
HARVARD UNIVERSITY - GRADUATE SCHOOL
OF DESIGN - FRANCES LOEB LIBRARY □
Cambridge, MA
Skmay, Adya, Asst. Law Libn.
U.S.D.A. - OFFICE OF GENERAL COUNSEL - LAW
LIBRARY □ Washington, DC
Skoglund, Susan E., Dir. of Lib.Serv.
RIVERSIDE OSTEOPATHIC HOSPITAL - RALPH
F. LINDBERG MEMORIAL LIBRARY □ Trenton,
MI
Skold, Marlene, Libn.
OUR REDEEMERS LUTHERAN CHURCH -
LIBRARY □ Benson, MN
Skolnik, Esther, Med.Libn.
INTERFAITH MEDICAL CENTER - ST. JOHN'S
EPISCOPAL HOSPITAL (South Shore Division) -
MEDICAL LIBRARY □ Far Rockaway, NY
Skonecki, Leonard, Libn.
DAYTON MENTAL HEALTH CENTER - STAFF
LIBRARY □ Dayton, OH
Skonezny, Nancie J., Libn.
BRUSH WELLMAN, INC. - TECHNICAL LIBRARY
□ Cleveland, OH
Skonieczy, Jill, Asst.Libn.
HENRY FORD HOSPITAL - FRANK J. SLADEN
LIBRARY □ Detroit, MI
Skop, Vera, Libn.
ST. VLADIMIR INSTITUTE - UKRAINIAN
LIBRARY† □ Toronto, ON
Skrebutenas, Katy, Ref. Libn.
PRINCETON THEOLOGICAL SEMINARY - SPEER
LIBRARY □ Princeton, NJ
Skrzeszewski, Stan, Act.Prov.Libn.
SASKATCHEWAN - PROVINCIAL LIBRARY □
Regina, SK
Skuja, Lucija, Art Libn.
GRAND RAPIDS PUBLIC LIBRARY - FURNITURE
DESIGN COLLECTION □ Grand Rapids, MI
Skutnik, John, Jr., Supv.
MELDRUM AND FEWSMITH, INC. - BUSINESS
INFORMATION LIBRARY □ Cleveland, OH
Skyrm, Sally, Music Libn.
SUNY - COLLEGE AT POTSDAM - CRANE MUSIC
LIBRARY □ Potsdam, NY
Slach, June, Lib.Sys.Spec.
UPJOHN COMPANY - CORPORATE TECHNICAL
LIBRARY □ Kalamazoo, MI
Slachta, Olga, Map Libn.
BROCK UNIVERSITY - DEPARTMENT OF
GEOGRAPHY - MAP LIBRARY □ St. Catharines,
ON
Slack, Jane G., Libn.
LAURELTON CENTER - LIBRARY □ Laurelton, PA
Slack, Lucille, Mgr., Lib.Serv.
CROWNTEK INC. - LIBRARY SERVICES □
Markham, ON
Slade, Louise M., Staff Asst.
COLORADO STATE DEPARTMENT OF NATURAL
RESOURCES - COLORADO GEOLOGICAL SURVEY
LIBRARY □ Denver, CO
Slader, Genevieve, Libn./Cur.
WASHINGTON COUNTY HISTORICAL
ASSOCIATION - MUSEUM LIBRARY □ Fort
Calhoun, NE
Slager, Colleen, Acq./ILL
WESTERN THEOLOGICAL SEMINARY -
BEARDSLEE LIBRARY □ Holland, MI
Slagt, Joan, Translator
ONTARIO HYDRO - LIBRARY □ Toronto, ON
Slaight, Wilma R., Archv.
WELLESLEY COLLEGE - ARCHIVES □ Wellesley,
MA
Slamkowski, Donna, Res.Libn.
MINNESOTA STATE DEPARTMENT OF ENERGY
AND ECONOMIC DEVELOPMENT - ENERGY
LIBRARY □ St. Paul, MN
Slate, Ted, Lib.Dir.
NEWSWEEK, INC. - LIBRARY □ New York, NY
Slater, David, Sec.
ADVISORY GROUP ON ELECTRON DEVICES -
LIBRARY □ New York, NY

Slater, Diane, Instr.Serv.
KANSAS STATE UNIVERSITY - FARRELL
LIBRARY □ Manhattan, KS
Slater, Diane, AV Libn.
UNIVERSITY OF WISCONSIN, MADISON -
CENTER FOR HEALTH SCIENCES LIBRARIES† □
Madison, WI
Slater, Don, Chm.
HOMOSEXUAL INFORMATION CENTER -
TANGENT GROUP □ Hollywood, CA
Slater, Mary Ann, Asst.Doc.Libn.
OKLAHOMA STATE UNIVERSITY - DOCUMENTS
DEPARTMENT □ Stillwater, OK
Slater, Ronald, Cat.
LAURENTIAN UNIVERSITY - MAIN LIBRARY □
Sudbury, ON
Slattery, John M., Hist.
TWIRLY BIRDS - HELICOPTER ARCHIVE □ Oxon
Hill, MD
Slattery, Kathleen G., Law Libn.
BANK OF AMERICA - SOUTHERN CALIFORNIA
HEADQUARTERS - LAW LIBRARY NO. 4017 □
Los Angeles, CA
Slavin, Joan H., Tech.Libn.
GPU NUCLEAR - TMI TECHNICAL LIBRARY □
Middletown, PA
Slawson, Elizabeth, Chf., Acq.
U.S. NATL. DEFENSE UNIVERSITY - LIBRARY □
Washington, DC
Slaymaker, Robert, Prof.Asst.
DALLAS PUBLIC LIBRARY - HUMANITIES
DIVISION □ Dallas, TX
Slear, Gary W., Chm., Archv. & Musm.
UNION COUNTY HISTORICAL SOCIETY - JOHN
B. DEANS MEMORIAL LIBRARY □ Lewisburg, PA
Slevinsky, Patricia A., Libn.
UNIVERSITY OF CONNECTICUT - SCHOOL OF
BUSINESS ADMINISTRATION LIBRARY □
Hartford, CT
Slezak, Eva, Spec.
ENOCH PRATT FREE LIBRARY - MARYLAND
DEPARTMENT □ Baltimore, MD
Slifer, Biljon, Adm.Asst.
LOUISVILLE AND JEFFERSON COUNTY
PLANNING COMMISSION - LOUISVILLE
METROPOLITAN PLANNING LIBRARY □
Louisville, KY
Slinn, Janet, Lib.Mgr.
DIGITAL EQUIPMENT CORPORATION -
TEWKSBURY LIBRARY □ Tewksbury, MA
Slivitzky, Tatiana, Supv.
CONCORDIA UNIVERSITY - LOYOLA CAMPUS -
DRUMMOND SCIENCE LIBRARY □ Montreal, PQ
Slivka, Enid Miller, Libn.
BECK (R.W.) & ASSOCIATES - LIBRARY □
Seattle, WA
Sliwa, Shirley, Dir.
NATIONAL SOARING MUSEUM - LIBRARY &
ARCHIVES □ Elmira, NY
Sloan, Barbara, Hd., Pub. Inquiries
EUROPEAN COMMUNITY INFORMATION
SERVICE - LIBRARY □ Washington, DC
Sloan, Cheryl A., Libn.
BUSINESS AND PROFESSIONAL WOMEN'S
FOUNDATION - MARGUERITE RAWALT
RESOURCE CENTER □ Washington, DC
Sloan, Deloras, Asst.Libn.
MERCY HOSPITAL - LEVITT HEALTH SCIENCES
LIBRARY† □ Des Moines, IA
Sloan, Robert S., City Sec.
DALLAS CITY SECRETARY - DALLAS CITY
ARCHIVES □ Dallas, TX
Sloan, Virgene K., Libn.
WOODMEN ACCIDENT & LIFE COMPANY -
LIBRARY □ Lincoln, NE
Sloan-Peterson, Pete, Asst.Libn.
BRYAN, CAVE, MC PHEETERS & MC ROBERTS -
LIBRARY† □ St. Louis, MO
Sloat, Helen, Church Libn.
NORTHMINSTER UNITED PRESBYTERIAN
CHURCH - LIBRARY □ New Castle, PA

Slobodian, Cheryl C., Cat.
VITRO CORPORATION - LIBRARY □ Silver Spring, MD

Sloca, Sue Ellen, Chf., Info. Products
U.S. DEPT. OF THE INTERIOR - NATURAL RESOURCES LIBRARY □ Washington, DC

Slocombe, Patty S., Libn.
MARITZ, INC. - LIBRARY □ Fenton, MO

Slocum, Ann L., Med.Libn.
CHENANGO MEMORIAL HOSPITAL - MEDICAL LIBRARY □ Norwich, NY

Slocum, Charlotte, Libn.
CLARK UNIVERSITY - GRADUATE SCHOOL OF GEOGRAPHY - GUY H. BURNHAM MAP-AERIAL PHOTOGRAPH LIBRARY □ Worcester, MA

Slocum, Leslie
TELEVISION INFORMATION OFFICE OF THE NATIONAL ASSOCIATION OF BROADCASTERS - RESEARCH SERVICES† □ New York, NY

Slomski, Monica, Cat.
YALE UNIVERSITY - JOHN HERRICK JACKSON MUSIC LIBRARY □ New Haven, CT

Sloshberg, Leah P., Dir. of Musm.
NEW JERSEY STATE MUSEUM - LIBRARY □ Trenton, NJ

Slotkin, Helen W., Archv./Spec.Coll.Hd.
MASSACHUSETTS INSTITUTE OF TECHNOLOGY - INSTITUTE ARCHIVES AND SPECIAL COLLECTIONS □ Cambridge, MA

Slotten, Martha Calvert, Cur.
DICKINSON COLLEGE - LIBRARY - SPECIAL COLLECTIONS† □ Carlisle, PA

Slowinski, Nancy, QA Data Ck.
U.S. DEFENSE CONTRACT ADMINISTRATION SERVICES OF MILWAUKEE AREA - LIBRARY □ Milwaukee, WI

Slowinski, Rose, Dir.
EVANSTON HOSPITAL - WEBSTER MEDICAL LIBRARY □ Evanston, IL

Sluiter, Barbara, Hd., Cat.
CALVIN COLLEGE AND SEMINARY - LIBRARY □ Grand Rapids, MI

Sluman, Leslie, Dir.
WASHINGTON STATE DEPARTMENT OF COMMERCE AND ECONOMIC DEVELOPMENT - TOURISM DEVELOPMENT DIVISION □ Olympia, WA

Sly, Dale W., Pres.
SAN FRANCISCO COLLEGE OF MORTUARY SCIENCE - LIBRARY □ San Francisco, CA

Sly, Dr. David, Dir.
FLORIDA STATE UNIVERSITY - INSTITUTE OF SOCIAL RESEARCH - CENTER FOR THE STUDY OF POPULATION □ Tallahassee, FL

Sly, Maureen, Hd., Tech.Serv.
INTERNATIONAL DEVELOPMENT RESEARCH CENTRE - LIBRARY† □ Ottawa, ON

Slyhoff, Merle, Acq.Libn.
UNIVERSITY OF PENNSYLVANIA - BIDDLE LAW LIBRARY □ Philadelphia, PA

Smail, Laura, Spec./Oral Hist.
UNIVERSITY OF WISCONSIN, MADISON - ARCHIVES □ Madison, WI

Small, Doris, Hd., Tech.Serv.
RAND CORPORATION - LIBRARY† □ Santa Monica, CA

Small, Patricia, Med.Libn.
SAN ANTONIO STATE HOSPITAL - STAFF LIBRARY □ San Antonio, TX

Small, Sally S., Hd.Libn.
PENNSYLVANIA STATE UNIVERSITY, BERKS CAMPUS - MEMORIAL LIBRARY □ Reading, PA

Smallen, Anna, Asst.Libn.
CHADBOURNE, PARKE, WHITESIDE, & WOLFF - LIBRARY □ New York, NY

Smalletz, Karen, Asst.Libn.
GPU NUCLEAR - HEADQUARTERS LIBRARY □ Parsippany, NJ

Smalley, Martha, Archv.
YALE UNIVERSITY - DIVINITY SCHOOL LIBRARY □ New Haven, CT

Smalls, Oliver B., Archv. I
COLLEGE OF CHARLESTON - ROBERT SCOTT SMALL LIBRARY - SPECIAL COLLECTIONS □ Charleston, SC

Smarjesse, Myrtle, Med.Libn.
MEMORIAL MEDICAL CENTER - KENNETH A. SCHNEPP MEDICAL LIBRARY □ Springfield, IL

Smart, Marriott W., Libn.
GULF OIL CORPORATION - PITTSBURGH & MIDWAY COAL MINING CO. - INFORMATION RESOURCE CENTER □ Denver, CO

Smarte, Lynn, Asst.Dir./User Serv.
ERIC CLEARINGHOUSE ON HANDICAPPED & GIFTED CHILDREN - CEC INFORMATION SERVICES □ Reston, VA

Smedlund, Ruth, Prin.Res.Libn.
INTERNATIONAL MINERALS & CHEMICALS CORPORATION - IMC RESEARCH & DEVELOPMENT LIBRARY □ Terre Haute, IN

Smeijers, Ms. R., Circ.
HURON COLLEGE - SILCOX MEMORIAL LIBRARY □ London, ON

Smejkal, Kenneth, Phys.Sci.Libn.
WESTERN ILLINOIS UNIVERSITY - LIBRARIES □ Macomb, IL

Smerick, Jeri
COAL EMPLOYMENT PROJECT (CEP) - ARCHIVES □ Dumfries, VA

Smidley, Joyce A., Dir., Pub.Info. & Res.
INDIANA STATE DEPARTMENT ON AGING & COMMUNITY SERVICES - NATE SALON RESOURCE CENTER □ Indianapolis, IN

Smigarowski, M., Lib.Supv.
SASKATCHEWAN - DEPARTMENT OF HEALTH - LIBRARY □ Regina, SK

Smika, Dr. D.E., Location Leader
U.S.D.A. - AGRICULTURAL RESEARCH SERVICE - CENTRAL GREAT PLAINS RESEARCH STATION - LIBRARY □ Akron, CO

Smiley, Lucille B., Libn.
HOWARD UNIVERSITY - SCHOOL OF BUSINESS AND PUBLIC ADMINISTRATION - LIBRARY □ Washington, DC

Smillie, John D., Res.Coord.
NORTHERN PLAINS RESOURCE COUNCIL - LIBRARY □ Billings, MT

Smisek, Thomas, Libn.
MINNEAPOLIS PUBLIC LIBRARY & INFORMATION CENTER - TECHNOLOGY AND SCIENCE DEPARTMENT □ Minneapolis, MN

Smisko, Marsha, Info.Anl.
FOOTE CONE & BELDING - INFORMATION CENTER □ Chicago, IL

Smit, Cathy, Res.Asst.
AMERICAN ELECTRIC POWER SERVICE CORP. - LIBRARY† □ New York, NY

Smith, A., Libn.
U.S.D.A. - AGRICULTURAL RESEARCH SERVICE - SNAKE RIVER CONSERVATION RESEARCH CENTER - LIBRARY □ Kimberly, ID

Smith, Adelaide R., Cur.
HISTORICAL SOCIETY OF THE TARRYTOWNS - HEADQUARTERS LIBRARY □ Tarrytown, NY

Smith, Alice B., Asst.Libn.
SWEDISH MEDICAL CENTER - LIBRARY □ Englewood, CO

Smith, Amber Lee, Pub.Serv.Libn.
UNIVERSITY OF OKLAHOMA - LAW LIBRARY □ Norman, OK

Smith, Angeline, Libn.
SMITHSONIAN INSTITUTION LIBRARIES - NATIONAL MUSEUM OF NATURAL HISTORY - ANTHROPOLOGY BRANCH LIBRARY □ Washington, DC

Smith, Ann Montgomery, Dir. of Libs.
WENTWORTH INSTITUTE OF TECHNOLOGY - LIBRARY □ Boston, MA

Smith, Ann S., Hd., ILL Ctr.
NORTH CAROLINA STATE UNIVERSITY - D.H. HILL LIBRARY □ Raleigh, NC

Smith, Anne P., Cat.
GEORGIA HISTORICAL SOCIETY - LIBRARY □ Savannah, GA

Smith, Annie J., Med.Libn.
SAMARITAN HOSPITAL - MEDICAL LIBRARY □ Troy, NY

Smith, Audrey, Assoc.Libn.
NEW YORK STATE LIBRARY FOR THE BLIND AND VISUALLY HANDICAPPED □ Albany, NY

Smith, Ava, Libn.
KENTUCKY MOUNTAIN BIBLE INSTITUTE - GIBSON LIBRARY □ Vancleve, KY

Smith, Barbara
BOLT BERANEK AND NEWMAN, INC. - LIBRARY □ Cambridge, MA

Smith, Barbara, Libn.
SNYDER (H.L.) MEMORIAL RESEARCH FOUNDATION - LIBRARY† □ Winfield, KS

Smith, Barbara, Libn.
VIRGINIA CHEMICALS, INC. - LIBRARY □ Portsmouth, VA

Smith, Barbara D., Asst.Libn.
DREYFUS CORPORATION - INFORMATION CENTER □ New York, NY

Smith, Barbara J., Ck. to Jury Comm.
SUSSEX COUNTY LAW LIBRARY □ Newton, NJ

Smith, Basil, Asst.Chf.Libn.
CHURCH OF JESUS CHRIST OF LATTER-DAY SAINTS - LAS VEGAS BRANCH GENEALOGICAL LIBRARY □ Las Vegas, NV

Smith, Bernie Todd, Lib.Dir.
ROCHESTER GENERAL HOSPITAL - LILLIE B. WERNER HEALTH SCIENCES LIBRARY □ Rochester, NY

Smith, Beth E., Chf.Libn.
U.S. ARMY HOSPITALS - WALTER REED ARMY MEDICAL CENTER - MEDICAL LIBRARY □ Washington, DC

Smith, Betty, Database Mgr./Cons.
UNIVERSITY OF WATERLOO - ONLINE INFO. RETRIEVAL SYSTEM FOR THE SOCIOLOGY OF LEISURE & SPORT (SIRLS) □ Waterloo, ON

Smith, Betty M., Libn.
U.S. NAVY - NAVAL CONSTRUCTION BATTALION CENTER - LIBRARY □ Port Hueneme, CA

Smith, Billy, Dir.
INDIANA STATE BOARD OF HEALTH - JACOB T. OLIPHANT LIBRARY □ Indianapolis, IN

Smith, Brian C., Dir.
AMERICAN LIBRARY OF RAILWAY AND TRACTION HISTORY □ Burbank, CA

Smith, C.J., Coord.
MOBIL OIL CORPORATION - E & P DIVISION LIBRARY □ Denver, CO

Smith, Calvin B., Musm.Dir.
BAYLOR UNIVERSITY - STRECKER MUSEUM LIBRARY □ Waco, TX

Smith, Carolyn, Asst.Libn.
CONNECTICUT AGRICULTURAL EXPERIMENT STATION - OSBORNE LIBRARY □ New Haven, CT

Smith, Carolyn, Rare Bk.Bibliog.
JOHNS HOPKINS UNIVERSITY - MILTON S. EISENHOWER LIBRARY - SPECIAL COLLECTIONS DIVISION □ Baltimore, MD

Smith, Mrs. Charles
BOB JONES UNIVERSITY - CHURCH MINISTRIES RESOURCE LAB □ Greenville, SC

Smith, Cindy, Lib.Techn.
U.S. MARINE CORPS - KANEOHE AIR STATION LIBRARY □ Kaneohe Bay, HI

Smith, Clara, Circ.
UNIVERSITY OF TOLEDO - COLLEGE OF LAW LIBRARY □ Toledo, OH

Smith, Clifton F., Libn.
SANTA BARBARA MUSEUM OF NATURAL HISTORY - LIBRARY □ Santa Barbara, CA

Smith, Cloyd R., Tech.Libn.
ARMSTRONG WORLD INDUSTRIES, INC. - TECHNICAL CENTER - TECHNICAL INFORMATION SERVICES □ Lancaster, PA

Smith, D.L., Dept.Libn.
ALBERTA - DEPARTMENT OF TRANSPORTATION - LIBRARY □ Edmonton, AB

Smith, D. Ryan, Dir.
STAR OF THE REPUBLIC MUSEUM - LIBRARY □
Washington, TX

Smith, D. Scott, Hist.
SEVENTH DAY BAPTIST HISTORICAL SOCIETY
- LIBRARY □ Janesville, WI

Smith, Daniel, Hd., Media Serv.
WHEATON COLLEGE - BUSWELL MEMORIAL
LIBRARY □ Wheaton, IL

Smith, David A.L., Base Libn.
U.S. AIR FORCE BASE - LANGLEY BASE
LIBRARY □ Langley AFB, VA

Smith, David A.L., Chf.Libn.
U.S. AIR FORCE - TACTICAL AIR COMMAND -
LANGLEY BASE LIBRARY □ Langley AFB, VA

Smith, Mrs. David P., Chm.
HIGHLAND PARK PRESBYTERIAN CHURCH -
MADELINE ROACH MEYERCORD LIBRARY □
Dallas, TX

Smith, David R., Archv.
DISNEY (Walt) PRODUCTIONS - ARCHIVES □
Burbank, CA

Smith, Dean E., Exec. V.P.
ARIZONA HISTORICAL FOUNDATION - HAYDEN
LIBRARY □ Tempe, AZ

Smith, Debbie, Musm. Registrar
WESTERN KENTUCKY UNIVERSITY - DEPT. OF
SPECIAL COLLECTIONS - KENTUCKY LIBRARY
AND MUSEUM/UNIVERSITY ARCHIVES □
Bowling Green, KY

Smith, Deborah, Asst.Rsrcs.Spec.
UNIVERSITY OF CALIFORNIA, IRVINE -
INSTITUTE OF TRANSPORTATION STUDIES -
RESOURCE CENTER □ Irvine, CA

Smith, Della, Libn.
APPALACHIAN REGIONAL COMMISSION -
LIBRARY □ Washington, DC

Smith, Dennis, Libn.
MEMPHIS-SHELBY COUNTY PUBLIC LIBRARY
AND INFO. CTR. - SCIENCE/BUSINESS/SOCIAL
SCI.DEPT. □ Memphis, TN

Smith, Diane, Info.Dir.
LOUISIANA STATE DEPARTMENT OF NATURAL
RESOURCES - ENERGY, RESEARCH AND
PLANNING DIVISION LIBRARY □ Baton Rouge,
LA

Smith, Don, Res.Assoc.
MISSOURI STATE DIVISION OF COMMUNITY
AND ECONOMIC DEVELOPMENT - RESEARCH
LIBRARY □ Jefferson City, MO

Smith, Don, Educ.Libn.
SOUTHERN ILLINOIS UNIVERSITY,
EDWARDSVILLE - EDUCATION LIBRARY† □
Edwardsville, IL

Smith, Donald R., Libn.
ST. ELIZABETH MEDICAL CENTER - NORTH -
MEDICAL LIBRARY □ Covington, KY

Smith, Donald R., Libn.
ST. ELIZABETH MEDICAL CENTER - SOUTH -
LIBRARY □ Edgewood, KY

Smith, Doris N., Hd.Libn.
OREGONIAN LIBRARY □ Portland, OR

Smith, Dorman H., Hd. Music Libn.
UNIVERSITY OF ARIZONA - MUSIC
COLLECTION □ Tucson, AZ

Smith, Dorothy, Ref. & Proc.Spec.
WRIGHT STATE UNIVERSITY - ARCHIVES &
SPECIAL COLLECTIONS □ Dayton, OH

Smith, Eileen P., Libn.
ABCOR, INC. - LIBRARY □ Wilmington, MA

Smith, Eleanor, Libn.
CONGREGATION BETH SHALOM - RABBI
MORDECAI S. HALPERN MEMORIAL LIBRARY □
Oak Park, MI

Smith, Elizabeth, Asst.Ed.
CARNEGIE-MELLON UNIVERSITY - HUNT
INSTITUTE FOR BOTANICAL DOCUMENTATION
□ Pittsburgh, PA

Smith, Elizabeth
NATIONAL COLLEGE OF EDUCATION -
LEARNING RESOURCE CENTERS □ Evanston, IL

Smith, Elizabeth, Cur., Hist.Dept.
SUSQUEHANNA COUNTY HISTORICAL SOCIETY
AND FREE LIBRARY ASSOCIATION □ Montrose,
PA

Smith, Elizabeth, Libn.
3M - 230 LIBRARY □ St. Paul, MN

Smith, Elliott, Dir.
MICHIGAN STATE LEGISLATIVE COUNCIL -
LEGISLATIVE SERVICE BUREAU LIBRARY □
Lansing, MI

Smith, Elmer V., Dir.
CANADA - NATIONAL RESEARCH COUNCIL -
CANADA INSTITUTE FOR SCIENTIFIC AND
TECHNICAL INFORMATION (CISTI) □ Ottawa,
ON

Smith, Eric J., Engr.Libn.
DUKE UNIVERSITY - SCHOOL OF ENGINEERING
LIBRARY □ Durham, NC

Smith, Esther, Coll.Dev.Libn.
CENTER FOR RESEARCH LIBRARIES □ Chicago,
IL

Smith, Eurydice, Cat.
NORTH CAROLINA CENTRAL UNIVERSITY -
LAW LIBRARY □ Durham, NC

Smith, Evelyn L., Chf.Cat.Libn.
UNIVERSITY OF MICHIGAN - LAW LIBRARY □
Ann Arbor, MI

Smith, Fran, Med.Libn.
JACKSON HOSPITAL & CLINIC, INC. - MEDICAL
LIBRARY □ Montgomery, AL

Smith, Frances P., Libn.
STRAUB CLINIC & HOSPITAL, INC. - ARNOLD
LIBRARY □ Honolulu, HI

Smith, Frederick E., Law Libn.
UNIVERSITY OF CALIFORNIA, LOS ANGELES -
LAW LIBRARY □ Los Angeles, CA

Smith, Gail C., Asst.Libn.
CLAIROL, INC. - RESEARCH LIBRARY □
Stamford, CT

Smith, Dr. Gerald A., Dir.
SAN BERNARDINO COUNTY MUSEUM - WILSON
C. HANNA LIBRARY/RESEARCH LIBRARY† □
Redlands, CA

Smith, Gerald P., Cur.
MEMPHIS STATE UNIVERSITY LIBRARIES -
C.H. NASH MUSEUM LIBRARY □ Memphis, TN

Smith, Grace E., Libn.
WICHITA FALLS STATE HOSPITAL - PATIENTS
AND MEDICAL LIBRARY □ Wichita Falls, TX

Smith, Harlod B., Mgr., Lib. + Info.Serv.
GRUMMAN AEROSPACE CORPORATION -
TECHNICAL INFORMATION CENTER □
Bethpage, NY

Smith, Harold, Cartographic Techn.
NEW YORK STATE DEPARTMENT OF
TRANSPORTATION - MAP INFORMATION UNIT
□ Albany, NY

Smith, Harriet E., Prin. Law Libn.
NEW YORK STATE SUPREME COURT - 9TH
JUDICIAL DISTRICT - LAW LIBRARY □ White
Plains, NY

Smith, Harriet W., Mgr., Lib.
SANDOZ, INC. - LIBRARY □ East Hanover, NJ

Smith, Hazel, Chm., Lib.Comm.
PARK PLACE CHURCH OF GOD - CARL
KARDATZKE MEMORIAL LIBRARY □ Anderson,
IN

Smith, Helen L., Dir.
THOMAS COUNTY HISTORICAL SOCIETY -
LIBRARY □ Colby, KS

Smith, Henry M., Dir.
UNITED WAY OF AMERICA - INFORMATION
CENTER □ Alexandria, VA

Smith, Hope, Libn.
ABC-CLIO INFORMATION SERVICES - THE
INGE BOEHM LIBRARY □ Santa Barbara, CA

Smith, Idelle, Tech.Info.Spec.
NATIONAL INJURY INFORMATION
CLEARINGHOUSE □ Washington, DC

Smith, Ilene N., Med.Libn.
ROCKINGHAM MEMORIAL HOSPITAL - HEALTH
SCIENCES LIBRARY □ Harrisonburg, VA

Smith, Iras F., Educ.Coord.
FINE ARTS MUSEUM OF THE SOUTH AT MOBILE
- FAMOS LIBRARY □ Mobile, AL

Smith, Jack, AV Spec.
NASHVILLE STATE TECHNICAL INSTITUTE -
EDUCATIONAL RESOURCE CENTER □ Nashville,
TN

Smith, Janet B., Libn.
U.S. FEDERAL HOME LOAN BANK BOARD -
RESEARCH LIBRARY □ Washington, DC

Smith, Janna, Libn.
U.S. VETERANS ADMINISTRATION (KY-
Louisville) - HOSPITAL LIBRARY □ Louisville, KY

Smith, Jay, Libn.
BANK OF AMERICA, NT & SA - REFERENCE
LIBRARY □ San Francisco, CA

Smith, Jean, Dir.
NATIONAL STORYTELLING RESOURCE CENTER
□ Jonesboro, TN

Smith, Jean, Libn.
PENNSYLVANIA STATE UNIVERSITY -
ARCHITECTURE READING ROOM □ University
Park, PA

Smith, Jean, Arts & Arch.Libn.
PENNSYLVANIA STATE UNIVERSITY - ARTS
LIBRARY □ University Park, PA

Smith, Jill Gates, Cur., Non-print Mtls.
MEDICAL COLLEGE OF PENNSYLVANIA -
ARCHIVES AND SPECIAL COLLECTIONS ON
WOMEN IN MEDICINE □ Philadelphia, PA

Smith, Miss Jo Therese, Mgr., Info.Serv.
WITCO CHEMICAL CORPORATION -
TECHNICAL CENTER LIBRARY □ Oakland, NJ

Smith, Joan, Assoc.Libn.
CORNELL UNIVERSITY - MAPS, MICROTEXTS,
NEWSPAPERS DEPARTMENT □ Ithaca, NY

Smith, Joan M.B., Med.Libn.
BEAUMONT (William) HOSPITAL - MEDICAL
LIBRARY □ Royal Oak, MI

Smith, John M., Assoc.Dir., Tech.Serv.
UNIVERSITY OF TEXAS MEDICAL BRANCH -
MOODY MEDICAL LIBRARY □ Galveston, TX

Smith, Judith D., Libn.
LOUISIANA STATE UNIVERSITY -
GOVERNMENTAL SERVICES INSTITUTE -
LIBRARY □ Baton Rouge, LA

Smith, Judith K., Libn.
CARTER (Larue D.) MEMORIAL HOSPITAL -
MEDICAL LIBRARY □ Indianapolis, IN

Smith, Julia C., Libn.
SHELL OIL COMPANY - DEER PARK
MANUFACTURING COMPLEX - LIBRARY
SERVICES† □ Deer Park, TX

Smith, Julia M., Libn.
NORWICH HOSPITAL - HEALTH SCIENCES
LIBRARY □ Norwich, CT

Smith, Julie, Dir., Lib.Serv.
ST. JOSEPH HOSPITAL - BURLEW MEDICAL
LIBRARY □ Orange, CA

Smith, June H., Ref.Libn.
ALBERTA - DEPARTMENT OF AGRICULTURE -
LIBRARY □ Edmonton, AB

Smith, Karen, Hd., Spec.Coll.
DALHOUSIE UNIVERSITY - BACON COLLECTION
□ Halifax, NS

Smith, Karen, Hd., Spec.Coll.
DALHOUSIE UNIVERSITY - CANADIAN
LITERATURE COLLECTION □ Halifax, NS

Smith, Karen, Hd., Spec.Coll.
DALHOUSIE UNIVERSITY - COCKERELL
COLLECTION □ Halifax, NS

Smith, Karen, Hd., Spec.Coll.
DALHOUSIE UNIVERSITY - KIPLING
COLLECTION □ Halifax, NS

Smith, Karen D.M., Law Libn.
MONTGOMERY COUNTY CIRCUIT COURT - LAW
LIBRARY □ Rockville, MD

Smith, Katherine, Libn.
BALTIMORE BRIEFING CENTER - LIBRARY □
Baltimore, MD

Smith, Katherine, Lib.Techn.
SOUTHEAST MICHIGAN COUNCIL OF
GOVERNMENTS - SEMCOG LIBRARY □ Detroit,
MI

Smith, Kathryn M., Libn.
CHALMERS (Dr. Everett) HOSPITAL - DR.
GARFIELD MOFFATT HEALTH SCIENCES
LIBRARY □ Fredericton, NB

Smith, Katy, Libn.
PLANNED PARENTHOOD OF CENTRAL INDIANA
- RESOURCE CENTER □ Indianapolis, IN

Smith, Kent, Night Libn.
DALLAS MORNING NEWS - REFERENCE
DEPARTMENT □ Dallas, TX

Smith, Kent, Cur.
LONG BEACH MUSEUM OF ART - LIBRARY □
Long Beach, CA

Smith, Larry G., Mgr., Res.Serv.
UNITED MERCHANTS AND MANUFACTURING
COMPANY - RESEARCH CENTER LIBRARY □
Langley, SC

Smith, Laura J., Div.Hd.
DAYTON AND MONTGOMERY COUNTY PUBLIC
LIBRARY - SOCIAL SCIENCES DIVISION □
Dayton, OH

Smith, Lawrence H., Dir.
UNIVERSITY OF OREGON - CAREER
INFORMATION CENTER □ Eugene, OR

Smith, Libby, Libn.
ENVIRONMENTAL PROTECTION AGENCY -
LIBRARY SERVICES □ Research Triangle Park,
NC

Smith, Linda, Asst.Libn./Acq.
GEORGE MASON UNIVERSITY - SCHOOL OF
LAW - LIBRARY □ Arlington, VA

Smith, Linda, Libn.
LEXINGTON HERALD-LEADER - LIBRARY □
Lexington, KY

Smith, Linda, Cons./Cat.
U.S. ARMY - CORPS OF ENGINEERS -
JACKSONVILLE DISTRICT - TECHNICAL
LIBRARY □ Jacksonville, FL

Smith, Linda-Jean, Libn.
STRADLEY, RONON, STEVENS & YOUNG - LAW
LIBRARY □ Philadelphia, PA

Smith, Lisa S., Coord. of Vols.
INTERNATIONAL VISITORS INFORMATION
SERVICE □ Washington, DC

Smith, Lois W., Libn.
BAPTIST MEDICAL CENTER - AMELIA WHITE
PITTS MEMORIAL LIBRARY† □ Columbia, SC

Smith, Loramae, Mgr., Info.Serv.
MC KINSEY & COMPANY, INC. - LIBRARY □
Chicago, IL

Smith, Lorraine, Libn.
UNIVERSITY OF SASKATCHEWAN - HEALTH
SCIENCES LIBRARY □ Saskatoon, SK

Smith, Sr. Louise, Coll.Libn.
UNIVERSITY OF WESTERN ONTARIO - MUSIC
LIBRARY □ London, ON

Smith, Louise H., Libn.
OHIO STATE UNIVERSITY - ENGLISH
DEPARTMENT LIBRARY □ Columbus, OH

Smith, Lynn R., Acq.Libn.
INDIANA UNIVERSITY, INDIANAPOLIS -
SCHOOL OF MEDICINE LIBRARY □ Indianapolis,
IN

Smith, Lytton, Chf.Libn.
SEATTLE POST-INTELLIGENCER - NEWSPAPER
LIBRARY □ Seattle, WA

Smith, M.M., Supv., User Serv.
MC DONNELL DOUGLAS CORPORATION -
DOUGLAS AIRCRAFT COMPANY - TECHNICAL
LIBRARY □ Long Beach, CA

Smith, M. Patricia, Assoc.Dir.
NATIONAL GEOGRAPHIC SOCIETY - LIBRARY □
Washington, DC

Smith, Marian, Online Serv.
GENERAL ELECTRIC COMPANY - MAIN
LIBRARY □ Schenectady, NY

Smith, Marvin, Lib.Dir.
NORTH CENTRAL BIBLE COLLEGE - T.J. JONES
MEMORIAL LIBRARY† □ Minneapolis, MN

Smith, Mary Ann, Libn.
IROQUOIS COUNTY GENEALOGICAL SOCIETY -
LIBRARY □ Watseka, IL

Smith, Mary Ann, ILL
SOUTHWEST FOUNDATION FOR BIOMEDICAL
RESEARCH - PRESTON G. NORTHROP
MEMORIAL LIBRARY □ San Antonio, TX

Smith, Maryann D., Assoc.Cur.
MUSEUM OF THE CITY OF NEW YORK -
THEATRE COLLECTION □ New York, NY

Smith, Matthew, Archv.
PROVIDENCE COLLEGE - PHILLIPS MEMORIAL
LIBRARY □ Providence, RI

Smith, Maureen, Cat.
TEMPLE UNIVERSITY - HEALTH SCIENCES
CENTER - LIBRARY □ Philadelphia, PA

Smith, Maxine, Hostess/Libn.
CHAUTAUQUA COUNTY HISTORICAL SOCIETY -
LIBRARY □ Westfield, NY

Smith, Maxine C., Libn.
U.S. ARMY - CORPS OF ENGINEERS -
SOUTHWESTERN DIVISION - LIBRARY □ Dallas,
TX

Smith, Maxine M., Lit. Searcher
ENVIRONMENTAL PROTECTION AGENCY -
ANDREW W. BREIDENBACH ENVIRONMENTAL
RESEARCH CTR., CINCINNATI - TECH.LIB. □
Cincinnati, OH

Smith, Melanie Welch, Ref.Libn.
NEW YORK UNIVERSITY - GRADUATE SCHOOL
OF BUSINESS ADMINISTRATION - LIBRARY □
New York, NY

Smith, Melissa, Lib. Media Tech.Asst.
OHIO STATE UNIVERSITY - EDGAR DALE
EDUCATIONAL MEDIA & INSTRUCTIONAL
MATERIALS LABORATORY □ Columbus, OH

Smith, Merrill W., Libn.
MASSACHUSETTS INSTITUTE OF TECHNOLOGY
- ROTCH LIBRARY VISUAL COLLECTIONS -
LOUIS SKIDMORE ROOM □ Cambridge, MA

Smith, Michael J., Dir.
PUTNAM MUSEUM - LIBRARY □ Davenport, IA

Smith, Michael K., Libn.
DALLAS PUBLIC LIBRARY - HISTORY AND
SOCIAL SCIENCES DIVISION □ Dallas, TX

Smith, Murphy D., Assoc. Libn.
AMERICAN PHILOSOPHICAL SOCIETY -
LIBRARY □ Philadelphia, PA

Smith, Nancy, Libn.
DALLAS PUBLIC LIBRARY - HUMANITIES
DIVISION □ Dallas, TX

Smith, Nancy, Hd., Tech.Serv.
OKLAHOMA CITY UNIVERSITY - LAW LIBRARY
□ Oklahoma City, OK

Smith, Nancy J., Chf., Lib.Serv.
U.S. VETERANS ADMINISTRATION (VA-
Hampton) - MEDICAL CENTER LIBRARY □
Hampton, VA

Smith, Newland, III
GARRETT-EVANGELICAL AND SEABURY-
WESTERN THEOLOGICAL SEMINARIES -
UNITED LIBRARY □ Evanston, IL

Smith, Nicole, Dir.
CANADA - CANADIAN INTERNATIONAL
DEVELOPMENT AGENCY - DEVELOPMENT
INFORMATION CENTRE □ Hull, PQ

Smith, P.E., Tech.Info.Spec.
NORTON COMPANY - COATED ABRASIVE
DIVISION - TECHNICAL LIBRARY □ Troy, NY

Smith, Pamela J., Libn.
METROPOLITAN TORONTO PLANNING
DEPARTMENT - LIBRARY† □ Toronto, ON

Smith, Peg, Dir.
MARICOPA TECHNICAL COMMUNITY COLLEGE
- LIBRARY RESOURCE CENTER □ Phoenix, AZ

Smith, Peggy, Exec.Asst.
ASOCIACION NACIONAL PRO PERSONAS
MAYORES - LIBRARY □ Los Angeles, CA

Smith, Penny, Adm.Asst.
FOUNDATION FOR PUBLIC AFFAIRS -
RESOURCE CENTER □ Washington, DC

Smith, R.B., Supv., Database Serv.
AIR PRODUCTS AND CHEMICALS, INC. - CRSD
INFORMATION SERVICES □ Allentown, PA

Smith, Rebecca A., Cur., Res.Mtls.
HISTORICAL ASSOCIATION OF SOUTHERN
FLORIDA - CHARLTON W. TEBEAU LIBRARY OF
FLORIDA HISTORY □ Miami, FL

Smith, Regina A., Dir.
JENKINS (Theodore F.) MEMORIAL LAW
LIBRARY COMPANY - LIBRARY □ Philadelphia,
PA

Smith, Regina A., Asst.Libn., Rd.Serv.
VILLANOVA UNIVERSITY - PULLING LAW
LIBRARY □ Villanova, PA

Smith, Reginald W., Assoc.Dir. of Libs.
UNIVERSITY OF MEDICINE AND DENTISTRY OF
NEW JERSEY AT NEWARK - GEORGE F. SMITH
LIBRARY □ Newark, NJ

Smith, Richard Candida, Prin.Ed.
UNIVERSITY OF CALIFORNIA, LOS ANGELES -
ORAL HISTORY PROGRAM LIBRARY □ Los
Angeles, CA

Smith, Rita F., Med.Libn.
U.S. AIR FORCE HOSPITAL MEDICAL CENTER -
MEDICAL LIBRARY (MS-Keesler AFB) □ Keesler
AFB, MS

Smith, Rita M., Lib.Dir.
BOSTON REDEVELOPMENT AUTHORITY -
STAFF LIBRARY □ Boston, MA

Smith, Robert D., Asst.Libn.
MISSOURI STATE SUPREME COURT LIBRARY □
Jefferson City, MO

Smith, Robert H., Jr., Archv.
WRIGHT STATE UNIVERSITY - ARCHIVES &
SPECIAL COLLECTIONS □ Dayton, OH

Smith, Robina
NEW ZEALAND EMBASSY - LIBRARY □
Washington, DC

Smith, Rochelle, Coord.
SASKATCHEWAN - DEPARTMENT OF TOURISM
& SMALL BUSINESS - BUSINESS INFORMATION
CENTRE □ Regina, SK

Smith, Mrs. Romaine, Med./Nursing Libn.
MERCY HOSPITAL - MEDICAL/NURSING
LIBRARY □ Rockville Centre, NY

Smith, Rose B., Libn.
WISCONSIN STATE DEPARTMENT OF NATURAL
RESOURCES - BUREAU OF RESEARCH -
TECHNICAL LIBRARY □ Fitchburg, WI

Smith, Roxanne, Lib.Techn.
BRITISH COLUMBIA - MINISTRY OF FORESTS -
LIBRARY □ Victoria, BC

Smith, Russell L., Dir.
UNIVERSITY OF SOUTH DAKOTA -
GOVERNMENTAL RESEARCH LIBRARY □
Vermillion, SD

Smith, Ruth P., Libn.
TORONTO DOMINION BANK - DEPARTMENT OF
ECONOMIC RESEARCH - LIBRARY □ Toronto,
ON

Smith, Sadie, Act.Hd., Rd.Serv.
NORTH CAROLINA AGRICULTURAL &
TECHNICAL STATE UNIVERSITY - F.D.
BLUFORD LIBRARY □ Greensboro, NC

Smith, Sallie, Tech.Libn.
ST. JOE MINERALS CORPORATION -
INFORMATION CENTER □ Monaca, PA

Smith, Sandra, Asst. to Libn.
INTERNATIONAL LIBRARY, ARCHIVES &
MUSEUM OF OPTOMETRY □ St. Louis, MO

Smith, Sharon, Libn.
ILLINOIS STATE - APPELLATE COURT, 3RD
DISTRICT - LIBRARY □ Ottawa, IL

Smith, Shirlee Anne, Kpr.
HUDSON'S BAY COMPANY ARCHIVES □
Winnipeg, MB

Smith, Shirley K., Libn.
CANADIAN NATIONAL RAIL - GREAT LAKES
REGION LIBRARY □ Toronto, ON

Smith, Sid, Pres.
NATIONAL ASSOCIATION OF HOSIERY
MANUFACTURERS - LIBRARY □ Charlotte, NC

Smith, Stephen, Dir.
CAMDEN DISTRICT HERITAGE FOUNDATION -
HISTORIC CAMDEN □ Camden, SC
Smith, Steve, Techn.
CORNELL UNIVERSITY - RESOURCE
INFORMATION LABORATORY □ Ithaca, NY
Smith, Stuart C., Asst.Dir. & Ed.
ERIC CLEARINGHOUSE ON EDUCATIONAL
MANAGEMENT □ Eugene, OR
Smith, Susan, Info.Spec.
TEXACO INC. - CORPORATE LIBRARY □ White
Plains, NY
Smith, Sweetman R., Ref.Libn.
FASHION INSTITUTE OF TECHNOLOGY -
LIBRARY† □ New York, NY
Smith, Tana S., Asst.Libn.
SACRAMENTO COUNTY LAW LIBRARY □
Sacramento, CA
Smith, Thomas A., Mss.Cur.
HAYES (Rutherford B.) PRESIDENTIAL CENTER -
LIBRARY □ Fremont, OH
Smith, Thomas E., Ser.
GEORGE WASHINGTON UNIVERSITY -
MEDICAL CENTER - PAUL HIMMELFARB
HEALTH SCIENCES LIBRARY □ Washington, DC
Smith, Thomas O.C., Libn.
U.S. NATL. PARK SERVICE - MORRISTOWN
NATL. HISTORICAL PARK - LIBRARY □
Morristown, NJ
Smith, Timothy D., Asst.Libn.
WYTHEVILLE COMMUNITY COLLEGE - KEGLEY
LIBRARY - SPECIAL COLLECTIONS □ Wytheville,
VA
Smith, Timothy H., Exec.Dir.
NATIONAL COUNCIL OF CHURCHES -
INTERFAITH CENTER ON CORPORATE
RESPONSIBILITY □ New York, NY
Smith, Toby D., Asst., Lib.Serv.
ST. MARY'S MEDICAL CENTER - HERMAN M.
BAKER, M.D. MEMORIAL LIBRARY □ Evansville,
IN
Smith, Mrs. Tom, Libn.
FIRST PRESBYTERIAN CHURCH OF GADSDEN -
LIBRARY □ Gadsden, AL
Smith, Toms E., Sr.Libn.
UTICA/MARCY PSYCHIATRIC CENTER - UTICA
CAMPUS LIBRARY SERVICES □ Utica, NY
Smith, Ms. V., Adm.Asst.
BARUCH (Belle W.) INSTITUTE FOR MARINE
BIOLOGY AND COASTAL RESEARCH - LIBRARY
□ Columbia, SC
Smith, V. Ruth, Hd.
STANISLAUS COUNTY SCHOOLS - TEACHERS'
PROFESSIONAL LIBRARY □ Modesto, CA
Smith, Vickie, Lib.Techn.
U.S. VETERANS ADMINISTRATION (MI-Ann
Arbor) - HOSPITAL LIBRARY □ Ann Arbor, MI
Smith, Virgie, Cat.
WASHBURN UNIVERSITY OF TOPEKA - SCHOOL
OF LAW LIBRARY □ Topeka, KS
Smith, W. Louis, Pres.
FUTURE AVIATION PROFESSIONALS OF
AMERICA (FAPA) - INFORMATION CENTER □
Decatur, GA
Smith, W. Thomas, Exec.Dir.
HYMN SOCIETY OF AMERICA, INC. - NATIONAL
HEADQUARTERS LIBRARY □ Fort Worth, TX
Smith, Wanda, Res.Assoc.
SOUTHERN METHODIST UNIVERSITY -
BRIDWELL LIBRARY - CENTER FOR
METHODIST STUDIES □ Dallas, TX
Smith, Wanda B., Libn.
GREENE COUNTY LAW LIBRARY □ Waynesburg,
PA
Smith, Warren L., Pres.
RAILROAD ENTHUSIASTS NEW YORK
DIVISION, INC. - WILLIAMSON LIBRARY □ New
York, NY
Smith, Whitney, Dir.
FLAG RESEARCH CENTER - LIBRARY □
Winchester, MA

Smith, Mrs. William, Asst.
FIRST BAPTIST CHURCH - E.F. WALKER
MEMORIAL LIBRARY □ Luling, TX
Smith, William, Asst.Libn.
LEBANON COUNTY HISTORICAL SOCIETY -
LIBRARY □ Lebanon, PA
Smith, William
TUSCULUM COLLEGE - INSTRUCTIONAL
MATERIALS CENTER □ Greeneville, TN
Smith, Wilma, Asst.Libn.
WASHOE COUNTY LAW LIBRARY □ Reno, NV
Smith, Yvonne B., Tech.Info.Spec.
MOBIL OIL CORPORATION - TOXICOLOGY
INFORMATION CENTER □ Princeton, NJ
Smith-Gonzales, Sherry, Chf., Archv.Serv.
NEW MEXICO STATE COMMISSION OF PUBLIC
RECORDS AND ARCHIVES - ARCHIVAL
SERVICES DIVISION □ Santa Fe, NM
Smith-Toth, Priscilla L., Asst. to the Med.Libn.
UNIVERSITY OF NEW ENGLAND - COLLEGE OF
OSTEOPATHIC MEDICINE - NECOM LIBRARY†
□ Biddeford, ME
Smithies, Roger, Libn.
TORONTO EAST GENERAL HOSPITAL - HEALTH
SCIENCES LIBRARY □ Toronto, ON
Smithson, Gisela, Tech.Libn.
CANADIAN CANNERS, LTD. - RESEARCH
CENTRE - LIBRARY □ Burlington, ON
Smits, Edward J., Dir.
NASSAU COUNTY MUSEUM REFERENCE
LIBRARY □ East Meadow, NY
Smokey, Sheila, Supv., Tech.Lib.
FMC CORPORATION - ORDNANCE DIVISION -
OD TECHNICAL LIBRARY □ San Jose, CA
Smolek, Janice McAteer, Lib.Dir.
LUNDEBERG MARYLAND SEAMANSHIP SCHOOL
- PAUL HALL LIBRARY AND MARITIME MUSEUM
□ Piney Point, MD
Smoot, Samille J., Hd., Circ.Serv.
MEDICAL COLLEGE OF GEORGIA - LIBRARY □
Augusta, GA
Smoot, Stephen P., Dir.
U.S. DEPT. OF COMMERCE - INTERNATIONAL
TRADE ADMINISTRATION - SALT LAKE CITY
DISTRICT OFFICE LIBRARY □ Salt Lake City, UT
Smoots, Charles, Dir.
IIT RESEARCH INSTITUTE - GUIDANCE AND
CONTROL INFORMATION ANALYSIS CENTER
(GACIAC) □ Chicago, IL
Smrekar, Marian N., Law Libn.
KERN COUNTY LAW LIBRARY □ Bakersfield, CA
Smucker, David J. Rempel, Genealogist
LANCASTER MENNONITE HISTORICAL
SOCIETY - LIBRARY □ Lancaster, PA
Smyth, Anna M., Info.Ctr.Coord.
SMITH, KLINE & FRENCH LABORATORIES -
MARKETING RESEARCH DEPARTMENT -
INFORMATION CENTER □ Philadelphia, PA
Smyth, Deborah, Ref.Spec.
ASPEN SYSTEMS CORPORATION - PROJECT
SHARE □ Rockville, MD
Smyth, Lilian, Res.Libn.
JOHNSON AND JOHNSON, INC. - RESEARCH
LIBRARY □ Montreal, PQ
Smyth, Mary Anne, Lib.Techn.
GOLDER (H.Q.) & ASSOCIATES - LIBRARY □
Mississauga, ON
Smyth, Mary B., Lib.Mgr.
CITY COLLEGE OF SAN FRANCISCO - HOTEL
AND RESTAURANT DEPARTMENT - ALICE
STATLER LIBRARY □ San Francisco, CA
Smythe, Alvetta D., Hd., Annapolis TIC
U.S. NAVY - DAVID W. TAYLOR NAVAL SHIP
RESEARCH AND DEVELOPMENT CENTER -
TECHNICAL INFORMATION CENTER □
Bethesda, MD
Snay, Janet, Act.Libn.
NEW YORK STATE DEPARTMENT OF TAXATION
& FINANCE - TAX LIBRARY □ Albany, NY
Snead, Jennifer, Res.Spec.
VIRGINIA STATE OFFICE OF EMERGENCY &
ENERGY SERVICES - ENERGY INFORMATION
AND SERVICES CENTER □ Richmond, VA

Snead, Marie, Asst.Libn.
INDIANA UNIVERSITY OF PENNSYLVANIA -
UNIVERSITY LIBRARY □ Indiana, PA
Sneddeker, Duane, Spec.Proj.Cur.
MISSOURI HISTORICAL SOCIETY - PICTORIAL
HISTORY COLLECTION □ St. Louis, MO
Snedeker, Sherrill, Sr.Info.Spec., Tech.
GOODRICH (B.F.) COMPANY - AKRON
INFORMATION CENTER □ Akron, OH
Sneed, Marilyn, Asst.Libn.
NORTHROP CORPORATION - CORPORATE
LIBRARY □ Los Angeles, CA
Snell, Euthene, Libn.
WITCO CHEMICAL CORPORATION - GOLDEN
BEAR DIVISION - QC/R & D LIBRARY □ Oildale,
CA
Snell, Mary Kay, Hd.Libn.
AMARILLO GENEALOGICAL SOCIETY - LIBRARY
□ Amarillo, TX
Snell, Mary Kay, Libn.
AMARILLO PUBLIC LIBRARY - LOCAL HISTORY
COLLECTION □ Amarillo, TX
Snezek, P. Paul, Dir.
WHEATON COLLEGE - BUSWELL MEMORIAL
LIBRARY □ Wheaton, IL
Snider, Edith, Libn.
TENNESSEE STATE DEPARTMENT OF
ECONOMIC & COMMUNITY DEVELOPMENT -
LIBRARY □ Nashville, TN
Snider, Frances, Libn.
COMMUNICATIONS WORKERS OF AMERICA -
CWA INFORMATION LIBRARY □ Washington, DC
Snider, Polly Jo, Libn.
MARSHALL & MELHORN LAW FIRM - LIBRARY □
Toledo, OH
Sniderman, Gloria, Ref.Libn.
WAYNE STATE UNIVERSITY - EDUCATION
LIBRARY □ Detroit, MI
Sniderman, Lynn, Assoc.Libn.
FEDERAL RESERVE BANK OF CLEVELAND -
RESEARCH LIBRARY □ Cleveland, OH
Snitow, Emily L., Med.Libn.
CHILDREN'S SPECIALIZED HOSPITAL -
MEDICAL LIBRARY □ Mountainside, NJ
Snodderly,, Louise, Per.Libn.
CARSON-NEWMAN COLLEGE LIBRARY -
SPECIAL COLLECTIONS □ Jefferson City, TN
Snoddy, Donald D., Asst. State Archv.
NEBRASKA STATE HISTORICAL SOCIETY -
ARCHIVES □ Lincoln, NE
Snodgrass, J.B., Mgr.
POTLATCH CORPORATION - WESTERN WOOD
PRODUCTS DIV. ENGINEERING & TECHNICAL
SERV. DEPT. - INFORMATION CTR. □ Lewiston,
ID
Snow, Bobbie, Chf.Circ.Libn.
UNIVERSITY OF MICHIGAN - LAW LIBRARY □
Ann Arbor, MI
Snow, C. Richard, Venango Campus Libn.
CLARION UNIVERSITY OF PENNSYLVANIA -
RENA M. CARLSON LIBRARY □ Clarion, PA
Snow, Carl E., Film Libn.
PURDUE UNIVERSITY - FILM LIBRARY □ West
Lafayette, IN
Snow, Fran, Libn./Sec.
BROWN UNIVERSITY - POPULATION STUDIES
AND TRAINING CENTER - DEMOGRAPHY
LIBRARY □ Providence, RI
Snow, Michael D., Supv., Lib.Serv.
GTE - COMMUNICATION SYSTEMS DIVISION -
MAIN LIBRARY □ Needham Heights, MA
Snow, Susan W., Libn.
U.S. NATL. PARK SERVICE - THEODORE
ROOSEVELT NATL. PARK - LIBRARY □ Medora,
ND
Snowhill, Lucia, U.S. Doc.Libn.
UNIVERSITY OF CALIFORNIA, SANTA BARBARA
- GOVERNMENT PUBLICATIONS DEPARTMENT
□ Santa Barbara, CA
Snowhite, Morton, Libn.
NEW JERSEY INSTITUTE OF TECHNOLOGY -
ROBERT W. VAN HOUTEN LIBRARY □ Newark,
NJ

Snukals, Arlynn, Sr.Info.Anl
GALLAUDET COLLEGE - NATIONAL
INFORMATION CENTER ON DEAFNESS □
Washington, DC

Snyder, Alzora, Archv.
PAJARO VALLEY HISTORICAL ASSOCIATION -
WILLIAM H. VOLCK MUSEUM - ARCHIVES □
Watsonville, CA

Snyder, Cynthia, Dir.
COUNCIL FOR ADVANCEMENT AND SUPPORT
OF EDUCATION - REFERENCE CENTER □
Washington, DC

Snyder, D.A., Libn.
IOWA STATE DEPARTMENT OF PUBLIC
INSTRUCTION - RESOURCE CENTER □ Des
Moines, IA

Snyder, David, Archv. II
CALIFORNIA - STATE ARCHIVES □ Sacramento,
CA

Snyder, Edna M., Libn.
U.S. ARMY MEDICAL BIOENGINEERING
RESEARCH & DEVELOPMENT LABORATORY -
TECHNICAL REFERENCE LIBRARY □ Frederick,
MD

Snyder, Eileen, Libn.
SYRACUSE UNIVERSITY - GEOLOGY LIBRARY □
Syracuse, NY

Snyder, Eileen, Libn.
SYRACUSE UNIVERSITY - PHYSICS LIBRARY □
Syracuse, NY

Snyder, Ellie, Info.Spec.
NATIONAL SCIENCE TEACHERS ASSOCIATION
- GLENN O. BLOUGH LIBRARY □ Washington, DC

Snyder, Fritz, Ref. & Acq.Libn.
UNIVERSITY OF KANSAS - SCHOOL OF LAW
LIBRARY □ Lawrence, KS

Snyder, Jean, Libn.
MERSHON, SAWYER, JOHNSTON, DUNWODY &
COLE - LIBRARY □ Miami, FL

Snyder, June M., Libn.
VELSICOL CHEMICAL CORPORATION -
RESEARCH AND DEVELOPMENT DEPARTMENT -
LIBRARY □ Chicago, IL

Snyder, Madge, Libn.
AMERICAN MANAGEMENT ASSOCIATIONS -
D.W. MITCHELL MEMORIAL LIBRARY □
Hamilton, NY

Snyder, Margaret, Libn.
UNIVERSITY OF IDAHO - HUMANITIES
LIBRARY □ Moscow, ID

Snyder, Mary, Non-Print Libn.
NOVA SCOTIA COLLEGE OF ART AND DESIGN -
LIBRARY □ Halifax, NS

Snyder, Patt, Supv.
SHELL DEVELOPMENT COMPANY - BIOLOGICAL
SCIENCES RESEARCH CENTER - LIBRARY □
Modesto, CA

Snyder, Randall, Asst.Libn./Pub.Serv.
UNIVERSITY OF CONNECTICUT - LAW SCHOOL
LIBRARY □ Hartford, CT

Snyder, Rena, Chf.Med.Libn.
UNION MEMORIAL HOSPITAL - DR. JOHN M.T.
FINNEY, JR. MEMORIAL MEDICAL LIBRARY† □
Baltimore, MD

Snyder, Roberta, Asst.Libn.
SACRAMENTO COUNCIL FOR DELAYED
PRESCHOOLERS - DAISY TOY LENDING
LIBRARY □ Sacramento, CA

Snyder, Sally, Libn.
FORT MALDEN NATIONAL HISTORIC PARK -
LIBRARY & ARCHIVES □ Amherstburg, ON

Snyder, Shelli, Libn.
SOUTHERN CALIFORNIA ASSOCIATION OF
GOVERNMENTS - INFORMATION RESOURCE
CENTER □ Los Angeles, CA

Snyder, W.A., Mgr., Tech.Info.
BATTELLE-NORTHWEST - PACIFIC
NORTHWEST LABORATORY - HANFORD
TECHNICAL LIBRARY □ Richland, WA

Sobel, Sharon, Libn.
KENNEDY MEMORIAL HOSPITALS - CHERRY
HILL DIVISION - DR. BARNEY A. SLOTKIN
MEMORIAL LIBRARY □ Cherry Hill, NJ

Sobel, Susan, Asst.Libn.
DROPSIE COLLEGE - LIBRARY □ Merion, PA

Soben, Phyllis, Med.Libn.
CEDARS-SINAI MEDICAL CENTER - HEALTH
SCIENCES INFORMATION CENTER □ Los
Angeles, CA

Sober, Annelie, Dir., Med.Lib.
MILLER-DWAN MEDICAL CENTER -
TILDERQUIST MEMORIAL MEDICAL LIBRARY†
□ Duluth, MN

Sober, Marc, AV Spec.
ENOCH PRATT FREE LIBRARY - AUDIO-VISUAL
DEPARTMENT □ Baltimore, MD

Sobieski, Colleen, Mgr., Tech.Info.Ctr.
INTEL CORPORATION - TECHNICAL
INFORMATION CENTER □ Aloha, OR

Sobin, Maryann, Libn.
ENGELHARD CORPORATION - TECHNICAL
INFORMATION CENTER □ Edison, NJ

Sobkowiak, Emily, Med.Libn.
MOUNT SINAI HOSPITAL MEDICAL CENTER -
LEWISOHN MEMORIAL LIBRARY □ Chicago, IL

Sobotka, John, Archv.
UNIVERSITY OF MISSISSIPPI - SCHOOL OF
LAW LIBRARY □ University, MS

Socea, Magdalena, Facilitator
LOS ANGELES COUNTY SUPERINTENDENT OF
SCHOOLS - SOUTHERN CALIFORNIA CENTER
FOR EDUCATIONAL IMPROVEMENT □ Downey,
CA

Soderholm, Dorothy, Asst.Archv.
NAPA COUNTY HISTORICAL SOCIETY -
LIBRARY □ Napa, CA

Soderlund, Carl, Libn.
CLEARFIELD LAW LIBRARY □ Clearfield, PA

Soderlund, Jean R., Cur.
SWARTHMORE COLLEGE - FRIENDS
HISTORICAL LIBRARY - PEACE COLLECTION □
Swarthmore, PA

Sodhi, Bhagat, Chf.Libn.
NOVA SCOTIA AGRICULTURAL COLLEGE -
LIBRARY □ Truro, NS

Soenksen, Shirley, Ref.Libn.
GREELEY PUBLIC LIBRARY - SPECIAL
COLLECTIONS □ Greeley, CO

Soete, George J., Asst.Univ.Libn.
UNIVERSITY OF CALIFORNIA, SAN DIEGO -
UNIVERSITY LIBRARIES □ La Jolla, CA

Soiffer, Renee, Ref.Libn.
NORTHROP CORPORATION - AIRCRAFT
DIVISION - LIBRARY SERVICES □ Hawthorne,
CA

Sokalzuk, Pauline M., Law Libn.
NORTHUMBERLAND COUNTY LAW LIBRARY □
Sunbury, PA

Sokol, Bronislaw M., Asst.Dept.Mgr.
LOS ANGELES PUBLIC LIBRARY - AUDIO-
VISUAL DEPARTMENT □ Los Angeles, CA

Sokol, Evelyn, Law Libn.
CITIBANK, N.A. - CITICORP LAW LIBRARY □
New York, NY

Sokol, Karol M., Libn.
CLEARY, GOTTLIEB, STEEN & HAMILTON -
LIBRARY □ New York, NY

Sokolov, Barbara J., Supv., Info.Sci. Group
UNIVERSITY OF ALASKA, ANCHORAGE -
ARCTIC ENVIRONMENTAL INFORMATION AND
DATA CENTER □ Anchorage, AK

Sol, Ellen, Supv., Lib.Oper.
SYSTEM DEVELOPMENT CORPORATION -
LIBRARY □ Santa Monica, CA

Solbrig, Dorothy J., Libn.
HARVARD UNIVERSITY - BIOLOGICAL
LABORATORIES LIBRARY □ Cambridge, MA

Soldwisch, Marilyn, Tech.Info.Serv.Spec.
U.S. NAVY - FLEET COMBAT DIRECTION
SYSTEMS SUPPORT ACTIVITY, SAN DIEGO -
TECHNICAL INFO. SERVICES OFFICE □ San
Diego, CA

Solen, Lorraine J., Ref.Libn.
IBM CORPORATION - DSD LIBRARY/LEARNING
CENTER □ Poughkeepsie, NY

Soler, Eleanor, Libn.
NEW YORK THEOLOGICAL SEMINARY -
LIBRARY □ New York, NY

Solin, Patricia, Dir.
COOPER HOSPITAL/UNIVERSITY MEDICAL
CENTER - REUBEN L. SHARP HEALTH SCIENCE
LIBRARY □ Camden, NJ

Solley, Nancy, Ref.Libn.
WESTERN KENTUCKY UNIVERSITY - DEPT. OF
SPECIAL COLLECTIONS - KENTUCKY LIBRARY
AND MUSEUM/UNIVERSITY ARCHIVES □
Bowling Green, KY

Sollinger, Shirley, Tech.Libn.
CINTICHEM, INC. - LIBRARY □ Tuxedo Park, NY

Soloman, Marvin, Soc.Sci./Map Libn.
SOUTHERN ILLINOIS UNIVERSITY,
EDWARDSVILLE - SOCIAL SCIENCE/
BUSINESS/MAP LIBRARY† □ Edwardsville, IL

Solomon, Alan C., Hd.
LIBRARY OF CONGRESS - GEN. READING
ROOMS DIV. - MICROFORM READING ROOM
SECTION □ Washington, DC

Solomon, Carolyn G., Tech.Info.Spec.
U.S. DEPT. OF HEALTH AND HUMAN SERVICES -
EVALUATION DOCUMENTATION CENTER (EDC)
□ Washington, DC

Solomon, Dana, Libn.
ADAMS-PRATT OAKLAND COUNTY LAW
LIBRARY □ Pontiac, MI

Solomon, Joel L., Libn.
LANE & MITTENDORF - LAW LIBRARY □ New
York, NY

Solomon, Nancy, Pubns.Coord.
UNIVERSITY OF ARIZONA - CENTER FOR
CREATIVE PHOTOGRAPHY □ Tucson, AZ

Solomon, Rowena, Asst.Libn.
FLORENCE-DARLINGTON TECHNICAL COLLEGE
- LIBRARY □ Florence, SC

Solomon, Sue, Libn.
FIRST CHRISTIAN CHURCH - LIBRARY □
Alexandria, VA

Solomonoff, Sonia, Cat.
CASE WESTERN RESERVE UNIVERSITY - LAW
SCHOOL LIBRARY† □ Cleveland, OH

Solon-Kochneiser, Melanie, Hd., Pub.Serv.
OHIO STATE UNIVERSITY - LAW LIBRARY □
Columbus, OH

Solow, Linda I., Music Libn.
MASSACHUSETTS INSTITUTE OF TECHNOLOGY
- MUSIC LIBRARY □ Cambridge, MA

Solseth, Gwenn M., Info.Anl.
NORTHERN STATES POWER COMPANY -
COMMUNICATIONS DEPARTMENT LIBRARY &
INFORMATION CENTER □ Minneapolis, MN

Soltesz, Mary, Acq.Libn.
OHIO STATE SUPREME COURT LAW LIBRARY □
Columbus, OH

Soltow, Martha Jane, Libn.
MICHIGAN STATE UNIVERSITY - LABOR AND
INDUSTRIAL RELATIONS LIBRARY □ East
Lansing, MI

Solvick, Shirley, Chf.
DETROIT PUBLIC LIBRARY - FINE ARTS
DEPARTMENT □ Detroit, MI

Solyma, Alice, Libn.
CANADA - CANADIAN FORESTRY SERVICE -
PACIFIC FOREST RESEARCH CENTRE -
LIBRARY □ Victoria, BC

Some, Barbara, Libn.
HELENE FULD SCHOOL OF NURSING - LIBRARY†
□ Camden, NJ

Somers, Audrey D., Educ.Coord.
MIRAMICHI HOSPITAL - HEALTH SCIENCES
LIBRARY □ Newcastle, NB

Somers, Mrs. Carin, Dir.
NOVA SCOTIA - PROVINCIAL LIBRARY □
Halifax, NS

Somers, David, Registrar
ART GALLERY OF HAMILTON - MURIEL ISABEL
BOSTWICK LIBRARY □ Hamilton, ON

Somerton, Cathy, Libn.
PENINSULA COMMUNITY FOUNDATION -
COMMUNITY RESOURCE LIBRARY □ Burlingame,
CA
Somerville, Arleen, Libn.
UNIVERSITY OF ROCHESTER - GEOLOGY/MAP
LIBRARY □ Rochester, NY
Sommer, Deborah, Assoc.Libn.
UNIVERSITY OF CALIFORNIA, BERKELEY -
GOVERNMENT DOCUMENTS DEPARTMENT □
Berkeley, CA
Sommer, Dr. Frank H., III, Hd. of Lib.
DU PONT (Henry Francis) WINTERTHUR
MUSEUM - LIBRARY □ Winterthur, DE
Sommer, Linda, Asst.Dir.
NEW YORK CITY - DEPARTMENT OF RECORDS
AND INFORMATION SERVICES - MUNICIPAL
ARCHIVES □ New York, NY
Sommer, Ronald R., Hd., Rd.Serv.Dept.
UNIVERSITY OF TENNESSEE - CENTER FOR
THE HEALTH SCIENCES LIBRARY □ Memphis,
TN
Sommerville, James, Libn.
MOUNT PLEASANT MENTAL HEALTH
INSTITUTE - PROFESSIONAL LIBRARY □ Mount
Pleasant, IA
Sondag, Pauline, Libn.
MICHIGAN STATE UNIVERSITY -
AGRICULTURAL ECONOMICS REFERENCE
ROOM □ East Lansing, MI
Song, Seungja, Chf.Libn.
SEATTLE PUBLIC HEALTH HOSPITAL -
MEDICAL SERVICE LIBRARY □ Seattle, WA
Sonnemann, Sabine, Asst.Chf.
NATIONAL LIBRARY OF CANADA - NEWSPAPER
DIVISION □ Ottawa, ON
Sonnet, Susan, Asst. Music Libn.
UNIVERSITY OF CALIFORNIA, SANTA BARBARA
- ARTS LIBRARY □ Santa Barbara, CA
Sonnier, Clytie, Asst. Law Libn.
HARRIS COUNTY LAW LIBRARY □ Houston, TX
Sook, Lois, Dir., Med.Lib.
NEW YORK INFIRMARY BEEKMAN DOWNTOWN
HOSPITAL - ELISHA WALKER STAFF LIBRARY □
New York, NY
Soong, Huey-Min, Ref.Libn.
UNIVERSITY OF WINDSOR - PAUL MARTIN
LAW LIBRARY □ Windsor, ON
Soong, Jean, Hd., Monographs Proc.
U.S. NATL. INSTITUTES OF HEALTH - LIBRARY
□ Bethesda, MD
Soos, Maria, Hd.Cat.
WAGNER COLLEGE - HORRMANN LIBRARY □
Staten Island, NY
Soper, Constance O., Archv.
JACKSON COUNTY HISTORICAL SOCIETY -
RESEARCH LIBRARY & ARCHIVES □
Independence, MO
Soper, F.A., Dir.
NARCOTICS EDUCATION, INC. -
SCHARFFENBERG MEMORIAL LIBRARY □
Washington, DC
Soper, Marley H., Dir.
ANDREWS UNIVERSITY - JAMES WHITE
LIBRARY† □ Berrien Springs, MI
Soreide, Pamela, Libn.
GIBSON, DUNN & CRUTCHER - LAW LIBRARY □
Los Angeles, CA
Sorensen, Edwin, Hd.
NORTHPORT-EAST NORTHPORT SCHOOL
DISTRICT - TEACHERS' PROFESSIONAL
LIBRARY □ Northport, NY
Sorensen, Gary, Prog.Dir.
ALBERTA SOCIETY FOR AUTISTIC CHILDREN -
LIBRARY □ Edmonton, AB
Sorensen, Janice H., Libn.
KANSAS STATE GEOLOGICAL SURVEY - MOORE
HALL LIBRARY □ Lawrence, KS
Sorensen, Stephen, Hd., Tech.Serv.
GRADUATE THEOLOGICAL UNION - LIBRARY □
Berkeley, CA

Sorenson, Barbara Rich, Archv.
UNITED METHODIST CHURCH - SOUTH
DAKOTA CONFERENCE - COMMITTEE ON
ARCHIVES AND HISTORY - LIBRARY □ Mitchell,
SD
Sorenson, Lillian, ILL
DICKINSON STATE COLLEGE - STOXEN
LIBRARY □ Dickinson, ND
Sorg, Elizabeth, Libn.
EASTERN STATE SCHOOL AND HOSPITAL -
STAFF LIBRARY □ Trevose, PA
Sorgen, Herbert J., Libn.
SUNY - AGRICULTURAL AND TECHNICAL
COLLEGE AT DELHI - LIBRARY† □ Delhi, NY
Sorger, Joan, Dept.Hd.
CLEVELAND PUBLIC LIBRARY - BUSINESS,
ECONOMICS & LABOR DEPARTMENT □
Cleveland, OH
Sorieul, Francoise
ASSOCIATION DES UNIVERSITES
PARTIELLEMENT OU ENTIEREMENT DE
LANGUE FRANCAISE - BIBLIOTHEQUE □
Montreal, PQ
Sorkow, Janice, Mgr., Photographic Serv.
MUSEUM OF FINE ARTS - DEPARTMENT OF
PHOTOGRAPHIC SERVICES - SLIDE &
PHOTOGRAPH LIBRARY □ Boston, MA
Soroka, Allen H., Asst.Libn., Ref.
UNIVERSITY OF BRITISH COLUMBIA - LAW
LIBRARY □ Vancouver, BC
Soroka, Zofia A., Hd.Bibliog.
UNIVERSITY OF WISCONSIN, STEVENS POINT
- JAMES H. ALBERTSON CENTER FOR
LEARNING RESOURCES □ Stevens Point, WI
Sorokatch, Eleanor Lacy, Libn.
U.S. NAVY - NAVAL WEAPONS STATION -
LIBRARY □ Yorktown, VA
Sorrough, Gail, Libn.
BECHTEL - GEOLOGY LIBRARY □ San Francisco,
CA
Sorvari, Karen C., Dir. of Res.
CAMPBELL UNIVERSITY - SCHOOL OF LAW -
LAW LIBRARY □ Buies Creek, NC
Sosa, James, Hd.
SAN ANTONIO PUBLIC LIBRARY AND
INFORMATION CENTER - BUSINESS, SCIENCE
AND TECHNOLOGY DEPARTMENT □ San
Antonio, TX
Sosensky, Doris, Hd., Circ.
YALE UNIVERSITY - MEDICAL LIBRARY □ New
Haven, CT
Sottery, Ellen, Bus.Info.Spec.
UNION MUTUAL LIFE INSURANCE COMPANY -
CORPORATE INFORMATION CENTER □ Portland,
ME
Soucie, Yan Y., Br.Libn.
TEKTRONIX, INC. - WALKER ROAD BRANCH
LIBRARY □ Beaverton, OR
Souders, Marilyn, Chf. of Acq.
NEWSWEEK, INC. - LIBRARY □ New York, NY
Soullen, Marilyn, Asst.Libn., Govt.Doc.
HAMLINE UNIVERSITY SCHOOL OF LAW -
LIBRARY □ St. Paul, MN
Soultoukis, Donna M. Zoccola, Libn./Search Anl.
FRIENDS HOSPITAL - NORMAN D. WEINER
PROFESSIONAL LIBRARY □ Philadelphia, PA
Sourakli, Judy, Registrar
UNIVERSITY OF WASHINGTON - HENRY ART
GALLERY TEXTILE COLLECTION □ Seattle, WA
Souter, Thomas A., Act.Dir.
VIRGINIA POLYTECHNIC INSTITUTE AND
STATE UNIVERSITY - CAROL M. NEWMAN
LIBRARY □ Blacksburg, VA
Southard, Greta K., Asst.Libn
AKRON LAW LIBRARY □ Akron, OH
Southern, G. Edwin, Jr., Asst.Univ.Archv.
DUKE UNIVERSITY - ARCHIVES □ Durham, NC
Southern, Mary Ann W., Libn.
DUKE UNIVERSITY - MATH-PHYSICS LIBRARY
□ Durham, NC
Southwell, Mary, Spec. Projects.
UTAH STATE LIBRARY □ Salt Lake City, UT

Southwick, Neal S., Libn.
CHURCH OF JESUS CHRIST OF LATTER-DAY
SAINTS - UPPER SNAKE RIVER BRANCH
GENEALOGICAL LIBRARY □ Rexburg, ID
Southwick, Susan, Law Libn.
NEVADA STATE SUPREME COURT - LIBRARY □
Carson City, NV
Sowby, Laurene A., Hd.Libn.
SALT LAKE TRIBUNE - LIBRARY □ Salt Lake City,
UT
Sowchek, Ellen, Libn.
YOUNG MEN'S CHRISTIAN ASSOCIATIONS OF
THE UNITED STATES OF AMERICA - YMCA
HISTORICAL LIBRARY □ Chicago, IL
Sowell, Steven, Hd.
INDIANA UNIVERSITY - BIOLOGY LIBRARY □
Bloomington, IN
Sowers, Judy, Lib.Techn.
ANCHOR HOCKING CORPORATION -
CORPORATE LIBRARY† □ Lancaster, OH
Sowicz, Eugenia V., Supv. Book & Journal Lib.
GENERAL ELECTRIC COMPANY - SPACE/
SYSTEMS DIVISION LIBRARIES □ Philadelphia,
PA
Sozanski, Sue, Subject Spec.
SANDIA NATIONAL LABORATORIES -
TECHNICAL LIBRARY □ Albuquerque, NM
Spaak, Albert, Exec.Dir.
PLASTICS INSTITUTE OF AMERICA - LIBRARY
□ Hoboken, NJ
Spadaccini, Colleen, Libn.
OAK TERRACE NURSING HOME - DPW LIBRARY
□ Minnetonka, MN
Spaeth, Mary A., Survey Res.Info.Coord.
UNIVERSITY OF ILLINOIS - SURVEY RESEARCH
LABORATORY - SURVEY AND CENSUS DATA
LIBRARY □ Urbana, IL
Spain, Louise, Supv.Libn.
NEW YORK PUBLIC LIBRARY - DONNELL
LIBRARY CENTER - MEDIA CENTER - RECORD
COLLECTION □ New York, NY
Spala, Jeanne, Dir.
CENTINELA HOSPITAL MEDICAL CENTER -
EDWIN W. DEAN MEMORIAL LIBRARY □
Inglewood, CA
Spanabel, Pauline, Ref./Rd.Serv.Libn.
U.S. ARMY INTELLIGENCE CENTER & SCHOOL -
ACADEMIC LIBRARY □ Ft. Huachuca, AZ
Spanacin, Genevieve, Info.Spec.
CELANESE CORPORATION - CELANESE
SPECIALTIES OPERATIONS - INFORMATION
CENTER □ Chatham, NJ
Spang, L., Searcher
WAYNE STATE UNIVERSITY - G. FLINT PURDY
LIBRARY □ Detroit, MI
Spangelo, Dr. L.P.S., Dir.
CANADA - AGRICULTURE CANADA - RESEARCH
STATION, BEAVERLODGE - LIBRARY □
Beaverlodge, AB
Sparhawk, Mary B., Cat./Ref.Libn.
UNIVERSITY OF PENNSYLVANIA - SCHOOL OF
SOCIAL WORK - SMALLEY LIBRARY OF SOCIAL
WORK† □ Philadelphia, PA
Sparks, David E., Hd.
UNIVERSITY OF NOTRE DAME - RARE BOOKS
AND SPECIAL COLLECTIONS DEPARTMENT □
Notre Dame, IN
Sparks, Janelle, Ed.
CRC PRESS, INC. - LIBRARY† □ Boca Raton, FL
Sparks, Linda, Assoc.Libn.
UNIVERSITY OF FLORIDA - EDUCATION
LIBRARY □ Gainesville, FL
Sparks, Marie, Lib.Dir.
INDIANA UNIVERSITY, INDIANAPOLIS -
SCHOOL OF DENTISTRY LIBRARY □ Indianapolis,
IN
Sparks, Peggy, Libn.
FIRST PRESBYTERIAN CHURCH - CHRISTIAN
EDUCATION DEPARTMENT - LIBRARY □ San
Diego, CA
Sparks, Peter G., Dir. for Preservation
LIBRARY OF CONGRESS - PRESERVATION
OFFICE □ Washington, DC

Sparks, Dr. William S., Libn.
ST. PAUL SCHOOL OF THEOLOGY - DANA DAWSON LIBRARY □ Kansas City, MO

Sparrow, Mary N., Chf.Libn.
GANNETT (Guy) PUBLISHING COMPANY - PRESS HERALD-EVENING EXPRESS-MAINE SUNDAY TELEGRAM - LIBRARY □ Portland, ME

Sparrowgrove, Eva
MC KINLEY MUSEUM OF HISTORY, SCIENCE AND EDUCATION - RALPH K. RAMSAYER, M.D. LIBRARY □ Canton, OH

Sparvier, David L., Coord./Libn.
SASKATCHEWAN INDIAN CULTURAL COLLEGE - LIBRARY □ Saskatoon, SK

Spaude, Milton P., Libn. & Professor
MICHIGAN LUTHERAN SEMINARY - LIBRARY □ Saginaw, MI

Spaulding, F.H., Hd., Lib.Serv.Dept.
AT & T BELL LABORATORIES - LIBRARIES AND INFORMATION SYSTEMS CENTER □ Murray Hill, NJ

Spaulding, Mrs. J. Lloyd, Libn.
MENNONITE CHURCH - WESTERN DISTRICT CONFERENCE - WESTERN DISTRICT LOAN LIBRARY □ North Newton, KS

Spaulding, Leslie E., Libn.
MERCER COUNTY REGIONAL PLANNING COMMISSION - LIBRARY □ Sharpsville, PA

Spaulding, Patricia E., Libn.
PINELLAS COUNTY LAW LIBRARY - CLEARWATER BRANCH □ Clearwater, FL

Spawn, Carol, Mss.Libn.
ACADEMY OF NATURAL SCIENCES - LIBRARY □ Philadelphia, PA

Spayd, Cynthia, Libn.
PENNSYLVANIA DUTCH FOLK CULTURE SOCIETY, INC. - BAVER MEMORIAL LIBRARY □ Lenhartsville, PA

Spear, Louise S., Asst.Dir.
INDIANA UNIVERSITY - ARCHIVES OF TRADITIONAL MUSIC □ Bloomington, IN

Spearman, Donna G., Info.Libn.
ILLINOIS BENEDICTINE COLLEGE - THEODORE LOWNIK LIBRARY □ Lisle, IL

Spector, Howard, Exec.Dir.
LOS ANGELES CENTER FOR PHOTOGRAPHIC STUDIES - RESOURCE CENTER □ Los Angeles, CA

Spector, Janice B., Res.Libn.
BASF WYANDOTTE CORPORATION - RESEARCH LIBRARY □ Wyandotte, MI

Spector, Laraine C., Libn.
AMERICAN JEWISH CONGRESS-COMMISSION ON LAW AND SOCIAL ACTION - SHAD POLIER MEMORIAL LIBRARY □ New York, NY

Spector, Paul C., Dir.
HOLDEN ARBORETUM - WARREN H. CORNING LIBRARY □ Mentor, OH

Spector, Susan P., Libn.
KATTEN, MUCHIN, ZAVIS, PEARL & GALLER - LIBRARY □ Chicago, IL

Speed, Bert L., Chf.Pk. Interpreter
U.S. NATL. PARK SERVICE - CHICKASAW NATL. RECREATION AREA - TRAVERTINE NATURE CENTER LIBRARY □ Sulphur, OK

Speer, Alexander D., Planner
ANNE ARUNDEL COUNTY OFFICE OF PLANNING AND ZONING - LIBRARY □ Annapolis, MD

Speer, Edward G., Park Tech.
U.S. NATL. PARK SERVICE - ANDREW JOHNSON NATL. HISTORIC SITE - LIBRARY □ Greeneville, TN

Speich, Carrol, Acq.Libn.
NORTHROP CORPORATION - AIRCRAFT DIVISION - LIBRARY SERVICES □ Hawthorne, CA

Speicher, Craig, Sr.Info.Anl.
GALLAUDET COLLEGE - NATIONAL INFORMATION CENTER ON DEAFNESS □ Washington, DC

Speirs, J.W., Info. Output & Control
ATOMIC ENERGY OF CANADA, LTD. - TECHNICAL INFORMATION BRANCH - MAIN LIBRARY □ Chalk River, ON

Speirs, Margaret C., Asst.Libn.
EASTERN MAINE MEDICAL CENTER - HEALTH SCIENCES LIBRARY □ Bangor, ME

Speisman, Dr. Stephen A., Dir.
CANADIAN JEWISH CONGRESS - TORONTO JEWISH CONGRESS - ONTARIO REGION ARCHIVES □ Willowdale, ON

Spellman, Ann, Media Ctr.Libn.
LINCOLN CHRISTIAN COLLEGE & SEMINARY - JESSIE C. EURY LIBRARY† □ Lincoln, IL

Spellman, Lawrence, Cur. of Maps
PRINCETON UNIVERSITY - RARE BOOKS AND SPECIAL COLLECTIONS □ Princeton, NJ

Spellman, Lawrence E., Cur. of Maps
PRINCETON UNIVERSITY - RICHARD HALLIBURTON MAP COLLECTION □ Princeton, NJ

Spence, Aurelia S., Lib.Dir.
CENTRAL STATE HOSPITAL - MEDICAL LIBRARY □ Milledgeville, GA

Spence, Aurelia S., Dir.
CENTRAL STATE HOSPITAL - MENTAL HEALTH LIBRARY □ Milledgeville, GA

Spencer, Beverly Hall, Libn./Info.Spec.
KALBA BOWEN ASSOCIATES - LIBRARY □ Cambridge, MA

Spencer, Carol, Med.Libn.
LAHEY CLINIC MEDICAL CENTER - RICHARD B. CATTELL MEMORIAL LIBRARY □ Burlington, MA

Spencer, Carol, Asst.Libn.
NEW YORK INSTITUTE OF TECHNOLOGY - CENTER FOR ENERGY POLICY AND RESEARCH - ENERGY INFORMATION CENTER† □ Old Westbury, NY

Spencer, Don, Asst.Archv.
SEAGRAM MUSEUM - ARCHIVES AND LIBRARY □ Waterloo, ON

Spencer, Kathleen, Lib.Dir.
FRANKLIN AND MARSHALL COLLEGE - BIOLOGY READING ROOM □ Lancaster, PA

Spencer, Kathleen, Lib.Dir.
FRANKLIN AND MARSHALL COLLEGE - CHEMISTRY DEPARTMENT - WILLIAM SHAND, JR. MEMORIAL LIBRARY □ Lancaster, PA

Spencer, Kathleen, Lib.Dir.
FRANKLIN AND MARSHALL COLLEGE - DEPARTMENT OF GEOLOGY - READING ROOM □ Lancaster, PA

Spencer, Kathleen, Lib.Dir.
FRANKLIN AND MARSHALL COLLEGE - DEPARTMENT OF PHYSICS - READING ROOM □ Lancaster, PA

Spencer, Kathleen, Lib.Dir.
FRANKLIN AND MARSHALL COLLEGE - PSYCHOLOGY READING ROOM □ Lancaster, PA

Spencer, Kathleen Moretto, Dir.
FRANKLIN AND MARSHALL COLLEGE - SHADEK-FACKENTHAL LIBRARY - SPECIAL COLLECTIONS □ Lancaster, PA

Spencer, Leon P., Archv.
TALLADEGA COLLEGE - HISTORICAL COLLECTIONS □ Talladega, AL

Spencer, Lorna, Cur.
CATTARAUGUS COUNTY MEMORIAL AND HISTORICAL MUSEUM - LIBRARY □ Little Valley, NY

Spencer, Marian H., Lib.Dir.
WILSON MEMORIAL HOSPITAL - LIBRARY/ LEARNING CENTER □ Wilson, NC

Spencer, Mima, Assoc.Dir.
ERIC CLEARINGHOUSE ON ELEMENTARY AND EARLY CHILDHOOD EDUCATION □ Champaign, IL

Spencer, Steve, Theological Spec.
GRAND RAPIDS BAPTIST COLLEGE & SEMINARY - MILLER LIBRARY □ Grand Rapids, MI

Spengler, Kenneth C., Exec.Dir.
AMERICAN METEOROLOGICAL SOCIETY - ABSTRACTS PROJECT - LIBRARY □ Boston, MA

Spenser, Rita A., Act.Libn.
UNION UNIVERSITY - DUDLEY OBSERVATORY - LIBRARY □ Schenectady, NY

Sperlbaum, Andrea, Coord., Pub.Serv.
WAYNE STATE UNIVERSITY - SCHOOL OF MEDICINE - VERA PARSHALL SHIFFMAN MEDICAL LIBRARY □ Detroit, MI

Sperling, Robert B., Asst.Chf.
NEW YORK PUBLIC LIBRARY - MAP DIVISION □ New York, NY

Sperling, Suzanne B., Law Libn.
NEW YORK STATE SUPREME COURT - 2ND JUDICIAL DISTRICT - LAW LIBRARY □ Brooklyn, NY

Spicer, Erik J., Parliamentary Libn.
CANADA - LIBRARY OF PARLIAMENT □ Ottawa, ON

Spickler, Dawn, Libn.
YASODHARA ASHRAM SOCIETY - LIBRARY □ Kootenay Bay, BC

Spiegel, Rachel, Asst.Libn.
HONEYWELL, INC. - DEFENSE SYSTEMS DIVISION - ORDNANCE OPERATIONS ENGINEERING LIBRARY □ Edina, MN

Spiegelman, Barbara, Sr.Info.Spec.
WESTINGHOUSE ELECTRIC CORPORATION - WATER REACTOR DIVISIONS - INFORMATION RESOURCE CENTER □ Pittsburgh, PA

Spielmann, Diane, Asst.Archv.
BAECK (Leo) INSTITUTE - LIBRARY □ New York, NY

Spieth, Marsha, Cat.
NATIONAL GALLERY OF ART - LIBRARY □ Washington, DC

Spigelman, Cynthia, Assoc.Libn.
PORTLAND CEMENT ASSOCIATION/ CONSTRUCTION TECHNOLOGY LABORATORIES - INFORMATION SERVICES SECTION □ Skokie, IL

Spilde, Myra, Lib.Sec.
NORTH DAKOTA FARMERS UNION - LULU EVANSON RESOURCE LIBRARY □ Jamestown, ND

Spindler, Ruth A., Sr.Info.Spec.
GOODRICH (B.F.) COMPANY - RESEARCH AND DEVELOPMENT CENTER - BRECKSVILLE INFORMATION CENTER □ Brecksville, OH

Spinelli, Frances M., Dir.
MONTCLAIR STATE COLLEGE - NATIONAL ADULT EDUCATION CLEARINGHOUSE/ MULTIMEDIA CENTER □ Upper Montclair, NJ

Spinks, Paul, Dir. of Libs.
U.S. NAVY - NAVAL POSTGRADUATE SCHOOL - DUDLEY KNOX LIBRARY □ Monterey, CA

Spitz, Herman H., Dir. of Res.
JOHNSTONE (E.R.) TRAINING & RESEARCH CENTER - PROFESSIONAL LIBRARY □ Bordentown, NJ

Spitzen, Rosemary B., Adm.Libn.
U.S. NAVY - NAVAL MEDICAL RESEARCH INSTITUTE - INFORMATION SERVICES BRANCH □ Bethesda, MD

Spitzform, Dana, Cat.
DICKINSON SCHOOL OF LAW - SHEELY-LEE LAW LIBRARY □ Carlisle, PA

Spoede, Mary H., Dir.
SCOTT & WHITE MEMORIAL HOSPITAL - MEDICAL LIBRARY □ Temple, TX

Spohn, Clarence E., Cur.
HISTORICAL SOCIETY OF THE COCALICO VALLEY - MUSEUM AND LIBRARY □ Ephrata, PA

Spohn, Richard A., Hd.
UNIVERSITY OF CINCINNATI - GEOLOGY LIBRARY □ Cincinnati, OH

Spolarich, Eleanor, Libn.
GENERAL MOTORS CORPORATION - ELECTRO-MOTIVE DIVISION - ENGINEERING LIBRARY □ La Grange, IL

Sponseller, Helen, Libn.
LOWELL GENERAL HOSPITAL - HEALTH
SCIENCE LIBRARY □ Lowell, MA

Spoo, Corinne H., Hd.
PAINE ART CENTER AND ARBORETUM -
GEORGE P. NEVITT LIBRARY □ Oshkosh, WI

Spoor, Richard D., Dir.
UNION THEOLOGICAL SEMINARY - BURKE
LIBRARY □ New York, NY

Spoto, Dianne Weber, Sr.Libn.
CONDE NAST PUBLICATIONS, INC. - LIBRARY □
New York, NY

Spradlin, Frances, ILL Libn.
OREGON HEALTH SCIENCES UNIVERSITY -
LIBRARY □ Portland, OR

Spradling, Grant, Adm., Aaron Douglas Coll.
AMISTAD RESEARCH CENTER - LIBRARY/
ARCHIVES □ New Orleans, LA

Spragg, Edwin, Entomology Libn.
CORNELL UNIVERSITY - ENTOMOLOGY
LIBRARY □ Ithaca, NY

Sprague, Edward A., Exec.Dir.
TAX EXECUTIVES INSTITUTE, INC. - LIBRARY
□ Arlington, VA

Sprague, Karol S., Human Rsrcs.Supv.
MICHIGAN BELL TELEPHONE COMPANY -
CORPORATE REFERENCE CENTER □ Detroit, MI

Sprague, Roderick, Dir.
UNIVERSITY OF IDAHO - ARCHIVE OF PACIFIC
NORTHWEST ARCHAEOLOGY □ Moscow, ID

Sprankle, Anita T., Non-Bk.Mtls.Libn.
KUTZTOWN UNIVERSITY - ROHRBACH
LIBRARY □ Kutztown, PA

Sprinc, Fr. Nicholas, Sec.
SLOVAK WRITERS AND ARTISTS ASSOCIATION
- SLOVAK INSTITUTE - LIBRARY □ Cleveland,
OH

Spring, Joan E., Cat.
EMORY UNIVERSITY - SCHOOL OF MEDICINE -
A.W. CALHOUN MEDICAL LIBRARY □ Atlanta,
GA

Springenberg, Mrs. Vi, Libn.
CENTRAL STATES INSTITUTE OF ADDICTIONS
- ADDICTION MATERIAL CENTER □ Chicago, IL

Springer, Jean M., Exec.Dir.
YOUNG MEN'S MERCANTILE LIBRARY
ASSOCIATION - LIBRARY† □ Cincinnati, OH

Springer, John J., Libn.
KANSAS CITY TIMES-STAR - LIBRARY □ Kansas
City, MO

Springer, Joseph, Asst.Libn.
UNIVERSITY OF KANSAS - DEPARTMENT OF
SPECIAL COLLECTIONS □ Lawrence, KS

Springer, Lawrence, AV Libn.
WESTERN MARYLAND PUBLIC LIBRARIES -
REGIONAL LIBRARY □ Hagerstown, MD

Springer, Nelson P., Cur.
MENNONITE HISTORICAL LIBRARY □ Goshen,
IN

Springer, William T., Chf., Park Oper.
U.S. NATL. PARK SERVICE - CAPE LOOKOUT
NATL. SEASHORE - LIBRARY □ Beaufort, NC

Sprinkle, Michael D., Dir.
WAKE FOREST UNIVERSITY - BOWMAN GRAY
SCHOOL OF MEDICINE - COY C. CARPENTER
LIBRARY □ Winston-Salem, NC

Sproule, Althea, Hd., Info.Ctr.
CANADA - REVENUE CANADA - CUSTOMS &
EXCISE - SCIENTIFIC AND TECHNICAL
INFORMATION CENTRE □ Ottawa, ON

Spruance, Russell C., Act.Lib.Comm.Chr.
GERMAN SOCIETY OF PENNSYLVANIA -
JOSEPH HORNER MEMORIAL LIBRARY □
Philadelphia, PA

Sprudz, Adolf, For. Law Libn.
UNIVERSITY OF CHICAGO - LAW SCHOOL
LIBRARY □ Chicago, IL

Sprung, George, Ref.Libn.
UNIVERSITY OF MEDICINE AND DENTISTRY OF
NEW JERSEY AT NEWARK - GEORGE F. SMITH
LIBRARY □ Newark, NJ

Spurlin, Candice, Circ.Libn.
UNIVERSITY OF SOUTH DAKOTA - MC KUSICK
LAW LIBRARY □ Vermillion, SD

Spurlock, Pat, Tech.Info.Spec.
PRECISION CASTPARTS CORPORATION -
TECHNICAL INFORMATION CENTER □ Portland,
OR

Spurlock, Sandra, Asst.Dir.
UNIVERSITY OF NEW MEXICO - MEDICAL
CENTER LIBRARY □ Albuquerque, NM

Spurrier, Laura, Cat.
LAWRENCE BERKELEY LABORATORY - LIBRARY
□ Berkeley, CA

Spyker, Elaine, AV Libn.
JEFFERSON (Thomas) UNIVERSITY - SCOTT
MEMORIAL LIBRARY □ Philadelphia, PA

Squier, Gerald L., Pres.
MOTOR BUS SOCIETY, INC. - LIBRARY □
Trenton, NJ

Squire, Jeannette, Asst.Libn.
MUNICIPALITY OF METROPOLITAN SEATTLE -
METRO LIBRARY □ Seattle, WA

Squire, Stephen E., Libn.
VIRGINIA STATE DEPARTMENT OF CRIMINAL
JUSTICE SERVICES - LIBRARY □ Richmond, VA

Squires, Lillian, Libn.
TERRELL STATE HOSPITAL - STAFF LIBRARY □
Terrell, TX

Squires, Martha K., Libn., Res.Ck.
CHEMUNG COUNTY HISTORICAL SOCIETY,
INC. - MRS. ARTHUR W. BOOTH LIBRARY □
Elmira, NY

Squyres, Barbara, Engr.Libn.
HUGHES AIRCRAFT COMPANY - ENGINEERING
LIBRARY □ Newport Beach, CA

Srinivasagam, Elizabeth, Hd., Rd.Serv.
YORK UNIVERSITY - LAW LIBRARY □
Downsview, ON

Srygley, Ted F., Dir.
UNIVERSITY OF FLORIDA - J. HILLIS MILLER
HEALTH CENTER LIBRARY □ Gainesville, FL

Stableford, B.A., Act.Chf.
CANADA - HEALTH AND WELFARE CANADA -
DEPARTMENTAL LIBRARY SERVICES □ Ottawa,
ON

Stableford, Bonita, Chf., Lib.Serv.
CANADA - HEALTH AND WELFARE CANADA -
LIBRARY SERVICES □ Ottawa, ON

Stabryla, Kathleen M., Lead Libn.
U.S. BUREAU OF MINES - BOEING SERVICES
INTERNATIONAL - LIBRARY □ Pittsburgh, PA

Stacey, Clara J. "Callie", Libn.Supv.
NORTH YORK PUBLIC LIBRARY - URBAN
AFFAIRS SECTION □ North York, ON

Stachiewicz, Wanda, Hon.Cur.
POLISH INSTITUTE OF ARTS AND SCIENCES IN
CANADA - POLISH LIBRARY □ Montreal, PQ

Stachura, Irene, Ref.Libn.
NATIONAL MARITIME MUSEUM - J. PORTER
SHAW LIBRARY □ San Francisco, CA

Stack, Jacqueline, Subject Spec.
SANDIA NATIONAL LABORATORIES -
TECHNICAL LIBRARY □ Albuquerque, NM

Stack, Mary Alice, Libn.
U.S. DEPT. OF JUSTICE - UNITED STATES
ATTORNEY, NORTHERN DISTRICT OF ILLINOIS
- LIBRARY □ Chicago, IL

Stack, Rita B., Libn.
EASTMAN KODAK COMPANY - HEALTH AND
ENVIRONMENT LABORATORIES - LIBRARY □
Rochester, NY

Stackpole, Edourd A., Hist.
NANTUCKET HISTORICAL ASSOCIATION -
PETER FOULGER LIBRARY □ Nantucket, MA

Stackpole, Laurie E., Chf., Lib.Serv.Br.
U.S. NATL. OCEANIC & ATMOSPHERIC
ADMINISTRATION - LIBRARY AND
INFORMATION SERVICES DIVISION - MAIN
LIBRARY □ Rockville, MD

Stacy, Betty A., Libn.
VIRGINIA MUSEUM OF FINE ARTS - LIBRARY □
Richmond, VA

Stacy, Cheryl, Libn.
TEXAS MID-CONTINENT OIL & GAS
ASSOCIATION - LIBRARY □ Dallas, TX

Stacy, Cindy, Res.Data Coord.
BAYVET - LIBRARY† □ Shawnee, KS

Stacy, Donald K., Libn.
NORTH CAROLINA STATE JUSTICE ACADEMY -
LEARNING RESOURCE CENTER □ Salemburg, NC

Stad, Frederick, Pres.
AMERICAN SOCIETY OF ANCIENT
INSTRUMENTS - LIBRARY □ Drexel Hill, PA

Stafford, Helen, Asst.Libn.
U.S. NATL. INSTITUTE FOR OCCUPATIONAL
SAFETY & HEALTH - TECHNICAL INFORMATION
BRANCH □ Cincinnati, OH

Stafford, Louise H., Adm.Libn.
NORTH CAROLINA STATE SUPREME COURT
LIBRARY □ Raleigh, NC

Stafford, Marilyn, Sr.Lib.Ck.
RIVERSIDE COUNTY LAW LIBRARY - INDIO
LAW LIBRARY □ Indio, CA

Stafford, R.S.
OAK RIDGE NATIONAL LABORATORY -
INFORMATION DIVISION - ENVIRONMENTAL
MUTAGEN INFORMATION CENTER □ Oak Ridge,
TN

Stager, David C., Geology Libn.
PRINCETON UNIVERSITY - GEOLOGY LIBRARY
□ Princeton, NJ

Stagg, Barbara, Exec.Dir.
HUGHES (Thomas) LIBRARY □ Rugby, TN

Stagner, Adalene, Libn.
BURNS AND MC DONNELL ENGINEERING
COMPANY - TECHNICAL LIBRARY □ Kansas
City, MO

Stahl, J. Natalia, Ser. & Acq.Libn.
CLARKSON UNIVERSITY - EDUCATIONAL
RESOURCES CENTER □ Potsdam, NY

Stahl, Jane, Dir.
FRENCH LIBRARY IN BOSTON, INC. □ Boston,
MA

Stahl, Joan, Dept.Hd.
ENOCH PRATT FREE LIBRARY - FINE ARTS AND
RECREATION DEPARTMENT □ Baltimore, MD

Stahl, Lucille, Pres.
COTTONWOOD COUNTY HISTORICAL SOCIETY
- LIBRARY □ Windom, MN

Stahl, Nanette, Hd.Libn.
BUREAU OF JEWISH EDUCATION - JEWISH
COMMUNITY LIBRARY □ San Francisco, CA

Stahl, Ramona, Circ.
PEPPERDINE UNIVERSITY - LAW LIBRARY □
Malibu, CA

Stair, Barbara, Asst.Libn.
PURDUE UNIVERSITY - AVIATION
TECHNOLOGY LIBRARY □ West Lafayette, IN

Stair, Fred, Libn.
CITIES SERVICE COMPANY - ERG - RESEARCH
LIBRARY □ Tulsa, OK

Stair, Hershall, Libn.
TRUNKLINE GAS COMPANY - EMPLOYEE
RESOURCE CENTER □ Houston, TX

Stajniak, Elizabeth T., Dir.
DETROIT BAR ASSOCIATION FOUNDATION -
LIBRARY† □ Detroit, MI

Stalbaum, Bertha, Dir./Cur.
HISTORICAL SOCIETY OF PORTER COUNTY -
LIBRARY □ Valparaiso, IN

Staley, Ronald, Radio Archv.
UNIVERSITY OF CALIFORNIA, LOS ANGELES -
UCLA RADIO ARCHIVES □ Los Angeles, CA

Staller, Betsy, Ref.Libn.
NEWSWEEK, INC. - LIBRARY □ New York, NY

Stallings, Carolyn, Ref.Libn.
HISTORICAL SOCIETY OF DELAWARE -
LIBRARY □ Wilmington, DE

Stalnaker, Enolia L., Chf., Lib.Serv.
U.S. VETERANS ADMINISTRATION (IN-Fort
Wayne) - HOSPITAL LIBRARY □ Fort Wayne, IN

Stambaugh, Dorothy, Libn.
TRUMBULL MEMORIAL HOSPITAL - SCHOOL OF
NURSING LIBRARY □ Warren, OH

Stamm, Geoffrey, Dir., Advisory Serv.
U.S. DEPT. OF THE INTERIOR - INDIAN ARTS
AND CRAFTS BOARD □ Washington, DC

Stamper, Nancy, Cat.
UNIVERSITY OF GEORGIA - RARE BOOKS
DEPARTMENT □ Athens, GA

Stamps, Dorothy, Ser.Libn.
SOUTHERN TECHNICAL INSTITUTE - LIBRARY
□ Marietta, GA

Stancil, C. Ira, Info.Spec.
MARYLAND STATE DEPARTMENT OF
EDUCATION - DIVISION OF LIBRARY
DEVELOPMENT & SERVICES - MEDIA SERVICES
CENTER† □ Baltimore, MD

Stancu, S., Sound Recording Cat.
INDIANA UNIVERSITY - MUSIC LIBRARY □
Bloomington, IN

Stanczak, Lisa M., Libn.
UNIVERSITY OF NOTRE DAME - SNITE
MUSEUM OF ART - LIBRARY □ Notre Dame, IN

Standifur, Kristine, Res.Asst.
MARSHALL UNIVERSITY - RESEARCH
COORDINATING UNIT FOR VOCATIONAL
EDUCATION □ Huntington, WV

Standing, Doris A., Libn.
ONTARIO - MINISTRY OF HEALTH - PUBLIC
HEALTH LABORATORIES - LIBRARY □ Toronto,
ON

Standish, Beulah I., Libn.
CONSUMERS POWER COMPANY - LAW LIBRARY
□ Jackson, MI

Standley, Fred J., Archv.
OKLAHOMA HISTORICAL SOCIETY - DIVISION
OF LIBRARY RESOURCES □ Oklahoma City, OK

Stanek, E., Law Libn.
UNIVERSITY OF SASKATCHEWAN - LAW
LIBRARY □ Saskatoon, SK

Stanek, S., Sunnyvale Libn.
LOCKHEED MISSILES & SPACE COMPANY, INC.
- TECHNICAL INFORMATION CENTER □ Palo
Alto, CA

Stanfield, Barrie, Libn.
CANADA - AGRICULTURE CANADA - RESEARCH
STATION, CHARLOTTETOWN - LIBRARY □
Charlottetown, PE

Stanford, Beth B., Libn.
REYNOLDS METALS COMPANY - REDUCTION
LABORATORY LIBRARY □ Sheffield, AL

Stanford, Jacqueline
U.S. COURT OF APPEALS, 2ND CIRCUIT -
LIBRARY □ New York, NY

Stangl, Peter, Dir.
STANFORD UNIVERSITY - LANE MEDICAL
LIBRARY □ Stanford, CA

Stangs, Loretta F., Mgr., Lib.Serv.
HOECHST-ROUSSEL PHARMACEUTICALS, INC. -
LIBRARY □ Somerville, NJ

Stanick, Katherine, Libn.
METROPLAN - INFORMATION CENTER □ Little
Rock, AR

Staniszewski, Victoria, Asst.Libn.
DETROIT MACOMB HOSPITAL CORPORATION -
SOUTH MACOMB HOSPITAL LIBRARY □ Warren,
MI

Staniszewski, Victoria A., Asst.Libn.
DETROIT MACOMB HOSPITAL CORPORATION -
HOSPITAL LIBRARY □ Detroit, MI

Stanke, Judith Unruh, Libn.
HENNEPIN COUNTY MEDICAL CENTER -
HEALTH SCIENCES LIBRARY □ Minneapolis, MN

Stankiewicz, Carol, Libn.
DUN AND BRADSTREET CORP. - BUSINESS
LIBRARY □ New York, NY

Stankowski, Barbara, Exec.Sec.
HOLLAND SOCIETY OF NEW YORK - LIBRARY □
New York, NY

Stankus, Tony, Sci.Libn.
COLLEGE OF THE HOLY CROSS - SCIENCE
LIBRARY □ Worcester, MA

Stanley, Frances, Asst.Libn.
BURNS AND MC DONNELL ENGINEERING
COMPANY - TECHNICAL LIBRARY □ Kansas
City, MO

Stanley, Janet L., Chf.Libn.
SMITHSONIAN INSTITUTION LIBRARIES -
NATIONAL MUSEUM OF AFRICAN ART -
BRANCH LIBRARY □ Washington, DC

Stanley, John H., Hd.Spec.Coll.Libn.
BROWN UNIVERSITY - SPECIAL COLLECTIONS
□ Providence, RI

Stanley, John R., Libn.
DALLAS BIBLE COLLEGE - GOULD MEMORIAL
LIBRARY □ Dallas, TX

Stanley, Lee, Archv. I
PHILADELPHIA - CITY ARCHIVES □ Philadelphia,
PA

Stanley, Linda, Chf. of Mss.
HISTORICAL SOCIETY OF PENNSYLVANIA -
LIBRARY □ Philadelphia, PA

Stanley, Linda C., Libn.
ROXBOROUGH MEMORIAL HOSPITAL - SCHOOL
OF NURSING AND MEDICAL STAFF LIBRARY □
Philadelphia, PA

Stanley, Sue, Ref.Libn.
HILBERT COLLEGE - MC GRATH LIBRARY -
SPECIAL COLLECTIONS □ Hamburg, NY

Stansbery, Pat, Photo Libn.
DALLAS MORNING NEWS - REFERENCE
DEPARTMENT □ Dallas, TX

Stanton, Connie, Libn.
PORTLAND PUBLIC SCHOOLS - PROFESSIONAL
LIBRARY □ Portland, OR

Stanton, Greg, Hd., Foreign & Intl.Pubn.
NATIONAL LIBRARY OF CANADA - CANADIAN
BOOK EXCHANGE CENTRE (CBEC) □ Ottawa, ON

Stanton, Jill, AV & Ref.
UNION UNIVERSITY - ALBANY MEDICAL
COLLEGE - SCHAFFER LIBRARY OF THE HEALTH
SCIENCES □ Albany, NY

Stanton, Lee, Act.Assoc.Libn.
NEW YORK STATE LIBRARY - HUMANITIES
REFERENCE SECTION □ Albany, NY

Stanton, Martha, Coord.
LEXINGTON PUBLIC SCHOOLS - CURRICULUM
RESOURCE CENTER □ Lexington, MA

Stanton, R.O., Hd., Internal Tech.Info.
AT & T BELL LABORATORIES - LIBRARIES AND
INFORMATION SYSTEMS CENTER □ Murray Hill,
NJ

Stanton, Suzanne, Asst.Libn.
U.S. AIR FORCE - WESTERN SPACE AND
MISSILE CENTER - WSMC/PMET TECHNICAL
LIBRARY □ Vandenberg AFB, CA

Stanway, Sondra, Libn.
ALASKA STATE DEPARTMENT OF FISH AND
GAME - LIBRARY □ Juneau, AK

Stanwick, Kathy, Asst.Dir.
CENTER FOR THE AMERICAN WOMAN &
POLITICS - LIBRARY □ New Brunswick, NJ

Stanwood, Cheryl, Law Libn.
CALIFORNIA STATE - COURT OF APPEAL, 2ND
APPELLATE DISTRICT - LAW LIBRARY □ Los
Angeles, CA

Stapell, Deborah A., Mgr., Info.Serv.
UNITED FRESH FRUIT AND VEGETABLE
ASSOCIATION - LIBRARY □ Alexandria, VA

Stapinsky, Berthe
INSTITUT D'HISTOIRE DE L'AMERIQUE
FRANCAISE (1970) - RESEARCH CENTRE
LIBRARY □ Montreal, PQ

Stargardt, Betty, Film Libn.
VIRGINIA STATE DEPARTMENT OF
TRANSPORTATION SAFETY - FILM LIBRARY □
Richmond, VA

Stark, Amy, Archv.Libn.
UNIVERSITY OF ARIZONA - CENTER FOR
CREATIVE PHOTOGRAPHY □ Tucson, AZ

Stark, Bill, Dir.
ILLINOIS SCHOOL FOR THE DEAF - SCHOOL
MEDIA CENTER □ Jacksonville, IL

Stark, Harold E., Info.Serv.Spec.
U.S. POSTAL SERVICE - LIBRARY □ Washington,
DC

Stark, Janet M., Libn.
FISH AND NEAVE - LIBRARY □ New York, NY

Stark, Linda, Libn.
INLOW CLINIC - LIBRARY □ Shelbyville, IN

Stark, Lucile S., Dir.
UNIVERSITY OF PITTSBURGH - WESTERN
PSYCHIATRIC INSTITUTE AND CLINIC -
LIBRARY □ Pittsburgh, PA

Stark, Marcella, History Bibliog.
SYRACUSE UNIVERSITY - E.S. BIRD LIBRARY -
AREA STUDIES DEPARTMENT □ Syracuse, NY

Stark, Marilyn, Asst.Dir., Info.Serv.
COLORADO SCHOOL OF MINES - ARTHUR
LAKES LIBRARY □ Golden, CO

Stark, Mary E., Chf.Libn.
GORGAS ARMY HOSPITAL - SAMUEL TAYLOR
DARLING MEMORIAL LIBRARY □ APO Miami, FL

Stark, Patricia, Educ.Libn.
UNIVERSITY OF MINNESOTA - EDUCATION-
PSYCHOLOGY-LIBRARY SCIENCE COLLECTION
□ Minneapolis, MN

Stark, Patricia, Ref.Archv.
YALE UNIVERSITY - MANUSCRIPTS AND
ARCHIVES □ New Haven, CT

Stark, Peter L., Hd.
UNIVERSITY OF OREGON - MAP LIBRARY □
Eugene, OR

Stark, Richard, Chf. Indexer
SPORT INFORMATION RESOURCE CENTRE □
Ottawa, ON

Stark, Sandra, Newspaper Libn.
ILLINOIS STATE HISTORICAL LIBRARY □
Springfield, IL

Starke, Ray, Chf., Lib.Serv.
U.S. VETERANS ADMINISTRATION (MO-
Columbia) - HOSPITAL LIBRARY □ Columbia, MO

Starkey, Doris E., Ref.Libn.
DEERE & COMPANY - TECHNICAL CENTER
LIBRARY □ Moline, IL

Starkman, David, Tech.Dir.
STEREO CLUB OF SOUTHERN CALIFORNIA -
LIBRARY □ Duarte, CA

Starks, Bonne, Ref.Libn.
RUSHMORE NATIONAL HEALTH SYSTEM -
HEALTH SCIENCES LIBRARY □ Rapid City, SD

Starks, Carolyn, Libn.
DALLAS PUBLIC LIBRARY - HISTORY AND
SOCIAL SCIENCES DIVISION □ Dallas, TX

Starr, Cora, Circ.
TELEDYNE ISOTOPES - BUSINESS LIBRARY □
Westwood, NJ

Starr, Daniel A., Sr.Cat.
MUSEUM OF MODERN ART - LIBRARY □ New
York, NY

Starr, Mrs. F.B., Libn.
U.S. NAVY - NAVAL REGIONAL MEDICAL
CLINIC - MEDICAL LIBRARY □ Quantico, VA

Starr, Jane, Cat.
ALBERTA - DEPARTMENT OF EDUCATION -
LIBRARY SERVICES □ Edmonton, AB

Starr, Lea K., Ref.Libn.
UNIVERSITY OF ALBERTA - JOHN W. SCOTT
HEALTH SCIENCES LIBRARY □ Edmonton, AB

Starr, Marian Ulincy, Lib.Mgr.
BOEING COMPUTER SERVICES COMPANY -
TECHNICAL LIBRARY □ Vienna, VA

Starr, Marilyn, Ref.Libn.
POINT LOMA NAZARENE COLLEGE - RYAN
LIBRARY □ San Diego, CA

Starr, Susan, Hd., Pub.Serv.
UNIVERSITY OF CALIFORNIA, SAN DIEGO -
BIOMEDICAL LIBRARY □ La Jolla, CA

Starring, Robert J., Hd.
UNIVERSITY OF MICHIGAN - DEPARTMENT OF
RARE BOOKS AND SPECIAL COLLECTIONS -
LIBRARY □ Ann Arbor, MI

Start, Howard D., Dir.
WESTERN ONTARIO BREEDERS, INC. -
LIBRARY □ Woodstock, ON

Starz, Robert L., Law Libn.
MARQUETTE UNIVERSITY - LEGAL RESEARCH
CENTER □ Milwaukee, WI

Statsky, William P., Libn.
ANTIOCH SCHOOL OF LAW - LIBRARY □
Washington, DC

Staubs, Hilda E., Musm.Techn.
U.S. NATL. PARK SERVICE - HARPERS FERRY
NATL. HISTORICAL PARK - LIBRARY □ Harpers
Ferry, WV

Staudenheimer, Carol, Libn.
ACCURAY CORPORATION - ENGINEERING
LIBRARY □ Columbus, OH

Stauffer, Kris, Ref./Per.
GRAND RAPIDS BAPTIST COLLEGE &
SEMINARY - MILLER LIBRARY □ Grand Rapids,
MI

Stauter, Mark C., Assoc.Dir.
WESTERN HISTORICAL MANUSCRIPT
COLLECTION/STATE HISTORICAL SOCIETY OF
MISSOURI MANUSCRIPTS JOINT COLLECTION
□ Rolla, MO

Stavec, Kathleen, Ref.Libn.
NEW JERSEY HISTORICAL SOCIETY - LIBRARY
□ Newark, NJ

Staves, Deborah, Indexer
HUMAN RESOURCES NETWORK -
INFORMATION CENTER† □ Philadelphia, PA

Stavetski, Norma K., Res.Libn.
ETHICON, INC. - SCIENTIFIC INFORMATION
SERVICES □ Somerville, NJ

Stavn, Virginia B., Supv.
ST. PAUL PUBLIC LIBRARY - BUSINESS &
SCIENCE ROOM □ St. Paul, MN

Stead, Blanca, Act.Dir.
UNIVERSITY OF OTTAWA - VANIER SCIENCE &
ENGINEERING LIBRARY □ Ottawa, ON

Steagald, Sadie, Ref.Libn.
DARGAN-CARVER LIBRARY □ Nashville, TN

Stebelton, Marilyn, Prog.Coord.
WAGNALLS MEMORIAL LIBRARY □ Lithopolis,
OH

Stecher, B., Libn.
KLEIN (B.) PUBLICATIONS - RESEARCH
LIBRARY □ Coral Springs, FL

Stecher, Bonnie, Libn.
HOGAN (Charles V.) REGIONAL CENTER -
REGIONAL RESOURCE LIBRARY □ Hathorne, MA

Stecher, Bonnie, Libn.
HOGAN (Charles V.) REGIONAL CENTER - STAFF
LIBRARY □ Hathorne, MA

Stecheson, Mary, Info.Spec.
MOLYCORP, INC. - LIBRARY □ Los Angeles, CA

Steedman, Isobel M., Libn.
MANITOBA CANCER TREATMENT AND
RESEARCH FOUNDATION - LIBRARY □
Winnipeg, MB

Steel, Joan, Libn.
SASKATOON GALLERY AND CONSERVATORY
CORPORATION - MENDEL ART GALLERY -
LIBRARY □ Saskatoon, SK

Steel, Lauri, Dir., Data Bank
AMERICAN INSTITUTES FOR RESEARCH -
PROJECT TALENT DATA BANK □ Palo Alto, CA

Steel, Virginia, Bus.Ref.Libn.
ARIZONA STATE UNIVERSITY - LLOYD BIMSON
MEMORIAL LIBRARY □ Tempe, AZ

Steele, Anita M., Dir.
UNIVERSITY OF PUGET SOUND - SCHOOL OF
LAW LIBRARY □ Tacoma, WA

Steele, Apollonia, Spec.Coll.Libn.
UNIVERSITY OF CALGARY - SPECIAL
COLLECTIONS DIVISION† □ Calgary, AB

Steele, Carole, Libn.
WESTERN LIFE INSURANCE COMPANY -
LIBRARY □ St. Paul, MN

Steele, Carole B., Asst.Libn.
U.S. AIR FORCE BASE - EGLIN BASE LIBRARY □
Eglin AFB, FL

Steele, Charles E., Jr., Sci.Libn.
OHIO NORTHERN UNIVERSITY - HETERICK
MEMORIAL LIBRARY □ Ada, OH

Steele, Clara, Cat.Libn.
U.S. NATL. OCEANIC & ATMOSPHERIC
ADMINISTRATION - MOUNTAIN
ADMINISTRATIVE SUPPORT CTR. - LIBRARY □
Boulder, CO

Steele, Dale, Map Ref.Libn.
UNIVERSITY OF ARIZONA - MAP COLLECTION
□ Tucson, AZ

Steele, Eric, Sr. Principal Libn.
NEW YORK PUBLIC LIBRARY - MID-
MANHATTAN LIBRARY - LITERATURE AND
LANGUAGE DEPARTMENT □ New York, NY

Steele, Lee, Ref.
DELAWARE STATE DEPARTMENT OF
COMMUNITY AFFAIRS - DIVISION OF
LIBRARIES □ Dover, DE

Steele, Linda, Libn.
U.S. VETERANS ADMINISTRATION (DC-
Washington) - MEDICAL CENTER LIBRARY □
Washington, DC

Steele, Marion N., Asst.Libn.
U.S. NAVY - NAVAL STATION LIBRARY (CA-San
Diego) □ San Diego, CA

Steele, Mary C., Mgr.
SPERRY COMPUTER SYSTEMS - ROSEVILLE
INFORMATION CENTER □ Roseville, MN

Steele, Noreen O., Libn.
UNITED TECHNOLOGIES CORPORATION -
PRATT & WHITNEY AIRCRAFT GROUP -
MATERIALS ENGINEERING RESEARCH LIB. □
Middletown, CT

Steele, Patricia, Hd.Libn.
INDIANA UNIVERSITY - SCHOOL OF LIBRARY
AND INFORMATION SCIENCE LIBRARY □
Bloomington, IN

Steele, Phyllis, Local Rec.Spec.
WRIGHT STATE UNIVERSITY - ARCHIVES &
SPECIAL COLLECTIONS □ Dayton, OH

Steele, Thomas M., Law Libn.
UNIVERSITY OF MISSISSIPPI - SCHOOL OF
LAW LIBRARY □ University, MS

Steelman, Lucille, Rsrcs.Coord.
SRI INTERNATIONAL - LIBRARY AND
RESEARCH INFORMATION SERVICES
DEPARTMENT □ Menlo Park, CA

Steen, Mrs. A.
UNION GAS, LTD. - LIBRARY SERVICE† □
Chatham, ON

Steen, Helen, Ref.Libn.
CHILDREN'S MEMORIAL HOSPITAL - JOSEPH
BRENNEMANN LIBRARY □ Chicago, IL

Steen, Nancy, Rare Books Libn.
BOWLING GREEN STATE UNIVERSITY -
CENTER FOR ARCHIVAL COLLECTIONS □
Bowling Green, OH

Steenbergen, Pat, Libn.
YORK BOROUGH BOARD OF EDUCATION -
PROFESSIONAL LIBRARY □ Toronto, ON

Steenland, Sally, Dp.Dir.
NATIONAL COMMISSION ON WORKING
WOMEN - RESOURCE CENTER □ Washington,
DC

Steeves, H. Alan, Libn.
SPERRY - RESEARCH CENTER LIBRARY† □
Sudbury, MA

Stefancic, Jean, Cat., Asst.Libn.
SIERRA CLUB - WILLIAM E. COLBY MEMORIAL
LIBRARY □ San Francisco, CA

Steffen, Genevieve M., Cur.
AURORA HISTORICAL SOCIETY - ELBERT
HUBBARD LIBRARY AND MUSEUM† □ East
Aurora, NY

Steffen, Karla M., Libn.
MILITARY ORDER OF THE LOYAL LEGION OF
THE UNITED STATES - WAR LIBRARY AND
MUSEUM □ Philadelphia, PA

Steffensen, Jean, Law Libn.
CONTRA COSTA COUNTY LAW LIBRARY □
Martinez, CA

Stegh, Les, Archv.
DEERE & COMPANY - LIBRARY □ Moline, IL

Steglich, Sharon, Circ.Libn.
UTAH STATE LIBRARY - BLIND AND
PHYSICALLY HANDICAPPED PROGRAM -
REGIONAL LIBRARY □ Salt Lake City, UT

Stehlik-Kokker, Jane, Mgr., Sci.Info.Serv.
MARION LABORATORIES, INC. - R & D LIBRARY
□ Kansas City, MO

Steidl, Lola, Cat.
GOLDEN VALLEY LUTHERAN COLLEGE -
LIBRARY† □ Minneapolis, MN

Steigner, Mary, Evening Supv.
NEW ENGLAND COLLEGE OF OPTOMETRY -
LIBRARY □ Boston, MA

Steimle, Claire L., Libn.
U.S. NATL. MARINE FISHERIES SERVICE -
SANDY HOOK LABORATORY - LIONEL A.
WALFORD LIBRARY □ Highlands, NJ

Stein, Douglas L., Mss.Libn.
MYSTIC SEAPORT, INC. - G.W. BLUNT WHITE
LIBRARY □ Mystic, CT

Stein, Elida, Hd., Mtls.Proc.
COLUMBIA UNIVERSITY - AMBROSE MONELL
ENGINEERING LIBRARY □ New York, NY

Stein, Hadassah, Libn.
ROGER WILLIAMS GENERAL HOSPITAL -
HEALTH SCIENCES LIBRARY □ Providence, RI

Stein, Jean, Adm. & Hd.
B'NAI ZION TEMPLE - MEMORIAL LIBRARY† □
Shreveport, LA

Stein, Jennifer, Libn.
PARSONS (Ralph M.) COMPANY - CENTRAL
LIBRARY □ Pasadena, CA

Stein, Judith, Dir. of Res.
CLARK (William H.) ASSOCIATES, INC. -
RESEARCH LIBRARY □ New York, NY

Stein, Lois, Archv.
KENOSHA COUNTY HISTORICAL MUSEUM -
HISTORICAL RESEARCH LIBRARY □ Kenosha,
WI

Steinbach, Anna Belle, Med.Libn.
U.S. PUBLIC HEALTH SERVICE HOSPITAL -
NATIONAL HANSEN'S DISEASE CENTER -
MEDICAL LIBRARY □ Carville, LA

Steinbacher, John, Exec.Dir.
CANCER FEDERATION - LIBRARY □ Riverside,
CA

Steinberg, Dr. Charles, Dir.
MC GILL UNIVERSITY - LABOUR AGREEMENTS
DATA BANK □ Montreal, PQ

Steinberger, Virginia, Mgr.
ENDO LABORATORIES, INC. - LIBRARY† □
Garden City, NY

Steiner, Bernadette, Libn.
SADTLER RESEARCH LABORATORIES - LIBRARY
□ Philadelphia, PA

Steiner, Doris L., Supv.
DOW CHEMICAL COMPANY - LEGAL LIBRARY □
Midland, MI

Steiner, Karen, Ed.
ERIC CLEARINGHOUSE ON ELEMENTARY AND
EARLY CHILDHOOD EDUCATION □ Champaign,
IL

Steiner, Mary Lou, Cat.
MACALESTER COLLEGE - WEYERHAEUSER
LIBRARY □ St. Paul, MN

Steiner, Roberta, Dir.
FOUNDATION CENTER - SAN FRANCISCO
OFFICE - LIBRARY □ San Francisco, CA

Steiner, Ronald, Assoc.Dir.
INDIANA UNIVERSITY OF PENNSYLVANIA -
UNIVERSITY LIBRARY □ Indiana, PA

Steiner, Samuel, Libn. & Archv.
CONRAD GREBEL COLLEGE - LIBRARY/
ARCHIVES □ Waterloo, ON

Steinfeld, Bud, Info.Serv.Spec.
U.S. BUREAU OF THE CENSUS - INFORMATION
SERVICES PROGRAM - LOS ANGELES REGIONAL
OFFICE - LIBRARY □ Los Angeles, CA

Steinhardt, Jean, Libn.
TURNER, COLLIE & BRADEN, INC. - LIBRARY
AND INFORMATION SERVICES □ Houston, TX

Steinhausen, W., Info.Dir.
ALBERTA - DEPARTMENT OF LABOUR -
BUILDING STANDARDS BRANCH RESOURCE
CENTRE □ Edmonton, AB

Steinhoff-Drake, Cindy, Asst.Libn.
NEBRASKA STATE HISTORICAL SOCIETY -
LIBRARY □ Lincoln, NE

Steininger, Ellen, Mgr., Info.Serv.
MARSTELLER, INC. - INFORMATION
SERVICES† □ Chicago, IL

Steinke, Cynthia A., Sci.Libn.
UNIVERSITY OF ILLINOIS AT CHICAGO -
SCIENCE LIBRARY □ Chicago, IL

Steinmann, Lois S., Mgr., Info.Serv.
DOYLE DANE BERNBACH/WEST - RESEARCH
LIBRARY □ Los Angeles, CA

Steitz, June Harrison, Subject Spec.
NAISMITH MEMORIAL BASKETBALL HALL OF
FAME - EDWARD J. AND GENA G. HICKOX
LIBRARY □ Springfield, MA

Stelfax, Evearad, Dir.
DACOTAH PRAIRIE MUSEUM - ARCHIVES □
Aberdeen, SD

Stell, Melvina, Dir.
GOOD SAMARITAN HOSPITAL AND MEDICAL
CENTER - LIBRARY □ Portland, OR

Stella, Colleen, Ref./ILL Libn.
SUNY - AGRICULTURAL AND TECHNICAL
COLLEGE AT MORRISVILLE - LIBRARY □
Morrisville, NY

Stelmack, Florence
ALBERTA - WORKERS' HEALTH SAFETY &
COMPENSATION - OCCUPATIONAL HEALTH &
SAFETY LIBRARY □ Edmonton, AB

Stender, Walter W., Assoc.Dir.
JOHNS HOPKINS UNIVERSITY - POPULATION
INFORMATION PROGRAM □ Baltimore, MD

Stenning, Mark L., Cur.
INTERNATIONAL TENNIS HALL OF FAME AND
TENNIS MUSEUM - LIBRARY □ Newport, RI

Stenstrom, Patricia, Libn.
UNIVERSITY OF ILLINOIS - LIBRARY AND
INFORMATION SCIENCE LIBRARY □ Urbana, IL

Stepanian, Ellen M., Dir. of Lib. Media
SHAKER HEIGHTS CITY SCHOOL DISTRICT -
GARVIN LIBRARY □ Shaker Heights, OH

Stepek, Susan B., V.P. & Mgr.
CAMPBELL-EWALD COMPANY - REFERENCE
CENTER □ Warren, MI

Stephan, Susan L., Libn.
SUNLAND CENTER AT GAINESVILLE - LIBRARY
□ Gainesville, FL

Stephanian, Charles, Media Dir.
COLLEGE OF THE SAN FRANCISCO ART
INSTITUTE - ANNE BREMER MEMORIAL
LIBRARY □ San Francisco, CA

Stephans, Hildegard G., Asst.Libn. & Cat.
AMERICAN PHILOSOPHICAL SOCIETY -
LIBRARY □ Philadelphia, PA

Stephany, Julie M., Libn.
REED LIGNIN INC. - LIGNIN RESEARCH
LIBRARY □ Rothschild, WI

Stephen, Baburaj, Libn.
INDIA - EMBASSY OF INDIA - LIBRARY OF THE
INFORMATION SERVICE OF INDIA □
Washington, DC

Stephen, Robert, Libn.
HAYES (Max S.) VOCATIONAL SCHOOL -
LIBRARY □ Cleveland, OH

Stephen, Ross, College Libn.
RIDER COLLEGE - FRANKLIN F. MOORE
LIBRARY □ Lawrenceville, NJ

Stephens, Alice, Hd., Lib.Oper.
ALABAMA PUBLIC LIBRARY SERVICE -
INFORMATION SERVICE □ Montgomery, AL

Stephens, Ann, Libn.
SOUTHEASTERN GENERAL HOSPITAL, INC. -
LIBRARY □ Lumberton, NC

Stephens, Cindy G., Film Libn.
WYOMING STATE DEPARTMENT OF HEALTH &
SOCIAL SERVICE - PUBLIC HEALTH FILM
LIBRARY □ Cheyenne, WY

Stephens, Denny, Asst.Dir.
OKLAHOMA STATE DEPARTMENT OF
LIBRARIES □ Oklahoma City, OK

Stephens, Diana C., Med.Libn.
HAWAII STATE HOSPITAL - MEDICAL LIBRARY
□ Kaneohe, HI

Stephens, Gretchen, Libn.
PURDUE UNIVERSITY - VETERINARY MEDICAL
LIBRARY □ West Lafayette, IN

Stephens, Irving E., Hd., Bldg.Serv.
RENSSELAER POLYTECHNIC INSTITUTE -
FOLSOM LIBRARY □ Troy, NY

Stephens, Jim, Spec. Projects Libn.
SOUTHERN METHODIST UNIVERSITY -
SCIENCE/ENGINEERING LIBRARY □ Dallas, TX

Stephens, Joe K., Res.Libn.
LEWIS AND CLARK LAW SCHOOL -
NORTHWESTERN SCHOOL OF LAW - PAUL L.
BOLEY LAW LIBRARY □ Portland, OR

Stephens, Marcia, Dir. of Lib.Serv.
ST. LUKE'S HOSPITAL - LIBRARY □ Fargo, ND

Stephens, Norris L., Libn.
UNIVERSITY OF PITTSBURGH - THEODORE M.
FINNEY MUSIC LIBRARY □ Pittsburgh, PA

Stephenson, Abbe, Libn.
MASSACHUSETTS STATE DEPARTMENT OF
COMMERCE AND DEVELOPMENT - RESEARCH
LIBRARY □ Boston, MA

Stephenson, Betty, Ref.Libn.
SAN DIEGO COUNTY LAW LIBRARY □ San Diego,
CA

Stephenson, Brian, Info.Sci.
SCHERING-PLOUGH CORPORATION -
PHARMACEUTICAL RESEARCH DIVISION -
LIBRARY INFORMATION CENTER □ Bloomfield,
NJ

Stephenson, Christie D., Asst. Fine Arts Libn.
UNIVERSITY OF VIRGINIA - FISKE KIMBALL
FINE ARTS LIBRARY □ Charlottesville, VA

Stephenson, Elizabeth, Data Archv.
UNIVERSITY OF CALIFORNIA, LOS ANGELES -
INSTITUTE FOR SOCIAL SCIENCE RESEARCH -
SOCIAL SCIENCE DATA ARCHIVE □ Los
Angeles, CA

Stephenson, Joyce, Circ.
NOVA SCOTIA COLLEGE OF ART AND DESIGN -
LIBRARY □ Halifax, NS

Stephenson, Judy, Libn.
MANITOBA - DEPARTMENT OF MUNICIPAL
AFFAIRS - LIBRARY □ Winnipeg, MB

Stephenson, Linda, Asst.Libn.
UNIVERSITY OF MISSOURI, KANSAS CITY -
LAW LIBRARY □ Kansas City, MO

Stephenson, Richard W., Hd., Ref.Sect.
LIBRARY OF CONGRESS - GEOGRAPHY & MAP
DIVISION □ Washington, DC

Stephenson, Robert E., Arch.Libn.
VIRGINIA POLYTECHNIC INSTITUTE AND
STATE UNIVERSITY - ARCHITECTURE LIBRARY
□ Blacksburg, VA

Stepherson, Patricia A., Mgr.
MAY DEPARTMENT STORES COMPANY -
INFORMATION CENTER □ St. Louis, MO

Stercho, June C., Chf.
U.S. AIR FORCE - ARMAMENT DIVISION, AIR
FORCE ARMAMENT LABORATORY - TECHNICAL
LIBRARY □ Eglin AFB, FL

Sterlein, Marie, Tech.Libn.
BETHLEHEM STEEL CORPORATION - SCHWAB
INFORMATION CENTER □ Bethlehem, PA

Sterlin, Annette, Tech.Serv.Libn.
HUGHES AIRCRAFT COMPANY - ELECTRO-
OPTICAL & DATA SYSTEMS GROUP -
TECHNICAL LIBRARY □ El Segundo, CA

Sterling, Cynthia R., Libn.
U.S. VETERANS ADMINISTRATION (OH-
Cincinnati) - MEDICAL CENTER LIBRARY □
Cincinnati, OH

Sterling, Dr. Ray, Dir.
UNIVERSITY OF MINNESOTA - UNDERGROUND
SPACE CENTER - LIBRARY □ Minneapolis, MN

Sterling, Sheila, Chf.Libn.
E.F. HUTTON & COMPANY, INC. - RESEARCH
LIBRARY □ New York, NY

Stern, Annelore, Asst.Libn.
UNIVERSITY OF SOUTHERN CALIFORNIA - VON
KLEINSMID LIBRARY □ Los Angeles, CA

Stern, Barbara, Co-Dir.
LOWER EAST SIDE FAMILY RESOURCE CENTER
□ New York, NY

Stern, David, Physics/Math Ref.Libn.
ARIZONA STATE UNIVERSITY - DANIEL E.
NOBLE SCIENCE AND ENGINEERING LIBRARY □
Tempe, AZ

Stern, Douglas, Adm.
JEFFERSON COUNTY OFFICE OF HISTORIC
PRESERVATION AND ARCHIVES □ Louisville, KY

Stern, Grace, Libn.
TEMPLE SHAAREY ZEDEK - LIBRARY □ Amherst,
NY

Stern, Jan
RACAL-MILGO, INC. - INFORMATION
RESOURCES† □ Miami, FL

Stern, Joan, Graphics
LOS ANGELES TIMES - EDITORIAL LIBRARY □
Los Angeles, CA

Stern, Pat, Asst.Libn.
BAKER & MC KENZIE - LAW LIBRARY □ New
York, NY

Stern, Stephanie, Chf.Libn.
BAECK (Leo) INSTITUTE - LIBRARY □ New York,
NY

Sterns, Rich, Asst.Libn.
FRIED FRANK HARRIS SHRIVER JACOBSON -
LIBRARY & INFORMATION CENTER □ New York,
NY

Sterzel, Maryann P., Dir.
FLORIDA PUBLISHING CO. - EDITORIAL
LIBRARY □ Jacksonville, FL

Stesis, Karen, Acq.Libn.
GEORGETOWN UNIVERSITY - MEDICAL
CENTER - DAHLGREN MEMORIAL LIBRARY □
Washington, DC

Stesis, Karen R., Libn.
METROPOLITAN HOSPITAL - SPRINGFIELD
DIVISION - MEDICAL LIBRARY □ Springfield, PA

Stetz, Elizabeth A., Libn.
WATERLOO LIBRARY AND HISTORICAL
SOCIETY† □ Waterloo, NY

Steury, Anita, Libn.
PROTESTANT EPISCOPAL CHURCH OF
WESTERN WASHINGTON - DIOCESE OF
OLYMPIA - EDUCATION RESOURCE CENTER □
Seattle, WA

Stevanovic, Bosiljka, Supv.Libn.
NEW YORK PUBLIC LIBRARY - DONNELL
LIBRARY CENTER - FOREIGN LANGUAGE
LIBRARY □ New York, NY

Stevelman, Sharon, Libn.
UNIVERSITY OF REGINA - EDUCATION
BRANCH LIBRARY □ Regina, SK

Stevens, Alan R., Chf.
U.S. GEOLOGICAL SURVEY - NATL.
CARTOGRAPHIC INFORMATION CENTER
(NCIC) □ Reston, VA

Stevens, Barbara E., Dir.
U.S. ARMY WAR COLLEGE - LIBRARY □ Carlisle
Barracks, PA

Stevens, Christine L., Ref.Libn.
INDIANA UNIVERSITY, INDIANAPOLIS -
SCHOOL OF LAW LIBRARY □ Indianapolis, IN

Stevens, Eugene A., Chf., Lib.Serv.
U.S. VETERANS ADMINISTRATION (SD-Fort
Meade) - MEDICAL CENTER LIBRARY □ Fort
Meade, SD

Stevens, Helen E., Tech.Libn.
FOXBORO COMPANY - RD & E LIBRARY† □
Foxboro, MA

Stevens, I. Jean, Libn.
JONES, DAY, REAVIS & POGUE - LIBRARY □ Los
Angeles, CA

Stevens, Jane, Asst.Cur., Prints & Photo
CHICAGO HISTORICAL SOCIETY - RESEARCH
COLLECTIONS □ Chicago, IL

Stevens, Jane, Hd.
TULANE UNIVERSITY OF LOUISIANA -
HOWARD-TILTON MEMORIAL LIBRARY -
LOUISIANA COLLECTION □ New Orleans, LA

Stevens, Jean, Hd.
UNIVERSITY OF TEXAS, EL PASO - TEACHING
MATERIALS CENTER □ El Paso, TX
Stevens, Jeanne, Asst.Libn.
ANOKA AREA VOCATIONAL TECHNICAL
INSTITUTE - MEDIA CENTER □ Anoka, MN
Stevens, Kay E., Libn.
CONSUMERS POWER COMPANY - PARNALL
TECHNICAL LIBRARY □ Jackson, MI
Stevens, Mary P., Musm.Libn.
MISSISSIPPI MUSEUM OF NATURAL SCIENCE -
LIBRARY □ Jackson, MS
Stevens, Mike, Supv. of Res.
NATIONAL LIBRARY OF SPORTS □ San Jose, CA
Stevens, Milton C., Dir./AWI Elm Trust
AMERICAN WATCHMAKERS INSTITUTE -
LIBRARY □ Cincinnati, OH
Stevens, Naomi C., Libn.
MORRIS COUNTY HISTORICAL SOCIETY -
VICTORIAN RESOURCE LIBRARY □ Morristown,
NJ
Stevens, Norman, Circ.Libn.
SAN DIEGO COUNTY LAW LIBRARY □ San Diego,
CA
Stevens, Paula F., Libn.
TACOMA NEWS TRIBUNE - LIBRARY □ Tacoma,
WA
Stevens, Robert, Newspaper Ref.Libn.
UNIVERSITY OF MISSOURI - COLUMBIA
MISSOURIAN - NEWSPAPER REFERENCE
LIBRARY □ Columbia, MO
Stevens, Robert R., Dir.
VINCENNES UNIVERSITY - BYRON R. LEWIS
HISTORICAL LIBRARY □ Vincennes, IN
Stevens, Rosemary, Asst.Libn.
METROPOLITAN LIFE INSURANCE COMPANY -
CORPORATE INFORMATION CENTER AND
LIBRARY □ New York, NY
Stevens, Stanley D., Map Libn.
UNIVERSITY OF CALIFORNIA, SANTA CRUZ -
MAP COLLECTION □ Santa Cruz, CA
Stevens, Tandy L., Mgr.
AMERICAN PUBLIC TRANSIT ASSOCIATION -
APTA INFORMATION CENTER □ Washington, DC
Stevenson, George, Dir.
EMORY AND HENRY COLLEGE - APPALACHIAN
ORAL HISTORY COLLECTION □ Emory, VA
Stevenson, H.M., Off.Mgr.
CANADA - AGRICULTURE CANADA - RESEARCH
STATION, ST. JOHN'S WEST - LIBRARY □ St.
John's, NF
Stevenson, Iris C., Circuit Libn.
U.S. COURT OF APPEALS, 4TH CIRCUIT -
LIBRARY □ Richmond, VA
Stevenson, Mrs. J., Lib.Asst.
QUEEN'S UNIVERSITY AT KINGSTON -
BIOLOGY LIBRARY □ Kingston, ON
Stevenson, Joan W., Dept.Hd.
YONKERS PUBLIC LIBRARY - FINE ARTS
DEPARTMENT □ Yonkers, NY
Stevenson, Karen, Asst. to Dir.
LEARNING RESOURCES NETWORK -
PUBLICATIONS AND RESOURCES □ Manhattan,
KS
Stevenson, Katherine, Libn.
NATIONAL CLEARINGHOUSE FOR LEGAL
SERVICES - LIBRARY □ Chicago, IL
Stevenson, Lynne L., Libn.
U.S. ARMY - CORPS OF ENGINEERS -
HYDROLOGIC ENGINEERING CENTER -
LIBRARY □ Davis, CA
Stevenson, Mata, Ref.Libn.
NEWSWEEK, INC. - LIBRARY □ New York, NY
Stevenson, Octave S., Chf.
DISTRICT OF COLUMBIA PUBLIC LIBRARY -
LANGUAGE, LITERATURE & FOREIGN
LANGUAGE DIVISION □ Washington, DC
Stevenson, Ruth, Law Libn.
SAN FRANCISCO - CITY ATTORNEY'S OFFICE -
LIBRARY □ San Francisco, CA
Stevermer, Mona, Asst.Libn.
ST. MARY'S HOSPITAL - LIBRARY □ Rochester,
MN

Steveson, Joy, Libn.
CH2M HILL, INC. - LIBRARY □ Sacramento, CA
Steward, Auburn, Libn.
BAPTIST MEDICAL CENTER SYSTEM -
MARGARET CLARK GILBREATH MEMORIAL
LIBRARY □ Little Rock, AR
Steward, Ouida, Libn.
SAN JUAN COUNTY ARCHAEOLOGICAL
RESEARCH CENTER & LIBRARY □ Farmington,
NM
Stewardson, Dawn, Libn./Archv.
CLARKE INSTITUTE OF PSYCHIATRY - FARRAR
LIBRARY† □ Toronto, ON
Stewart, Arch W.L., Natural Sci.Libn.
CANADA - NATIONAL MUSEUMS OF CANADA -
LIBRARY SERVICES DIRECTORATE □ Ottawa,
ON
Stewart, Barbara, Libn.
TEXAS STATE TECHNICAL INSTITUTE,
HARLINGEN CAMPUS - LIBRARY □ Harlingen, TX
Stewart, Barbara Rose, Hd.Libn.
REED, SMITH, SHAW AND MC CLAY - LAW
LIBRARY □ Pittsburgh, PA
Stewart, Bette L., Libn.
CH2M HILL, INC. - LIBRARY □ Portland, OR
Stewart, Beverly, Hd.Libn.
FULTON COUNTY HISTORICAL AND
GENEALOGICAL SOCIETY - RESEARCH ROOM □
Canton, IL
Stewart, Charlotte, Dir., Archv. & Res.Coll.
MC MASTER UNIVERSITY - ARCHIVES AND
RESEARCH COLLECTIONS DIVISION □ Hamilton,
ON
Stewart, Coy E., Libn.
WESTINGHOUSE ELECTRIC CORPORATION -
NAVAL REACTOR FACILITY LIBRARY □ Idaho
Falls, ID
Stewart, Cynthia, Sr.Mss.Spec.
WESTERN HISTORICAL MANUSCRIPT
COLLECTION/STATE HISTORICAL SOCIETY OF
MISSOURI MANUSCRIPTS JOINT COLLECTION
□ Columbia, MO
Stewart, Darlene, Off.Mgr.
LEGAL SERVICES ORGANIZATION OF INDIANA,
INC. - LIBRARY □ Evansville, IN
Stewart, Elizabeth Campbell, Archv.
RENSSELAER POLYTECHNIC INSTITUTE -
FOLSOM LIBRARY □ Troy, NY
Stewart, Emery, Museum Cur.
MASONIC GRAND LODGE LIBRARY AND
MUSEUM OF TEXAS □ Waco, TX
Stewart, Ethel, Libn.
UNIVERSITY OF KANSAS - JOURNALISM
LIBRARY □ Lawrence, KS
Stewart, Eugene L., Exec.Sec.
TRADE RELATIONS COUNCIL OF THE UNITED
STATES - LIBRARY □ Washington, DC
Stewart, Frances S., Supv., Tech.Serv.
ALABAMA A & M UNIVERSITY - J. F. DRAKE
MEMORIAL LEARNING RESOURCES CENTER □
Normal, AL
Stewart, Mrs. Francis, AV Libn.
WEST LIBERTY STATE COLLEGE - ELBIN
LIBRARY □ West Liberty, WV
Stewart, Gary, Consrv.
SHRINE TO MUSIC MUSEUM □ Vermillion, SD
Stewart, Gwyn, Acq./Ser.
U.S. NAVY - NAVAL COASTAL SYSTEMS
CENTER - TECHNICAL INFORMATION
SERVICES BRANCH† □ Panama City, FL
Stewart, Helene, Libn.
SASKATCHEWAN - DEPARTMENT OF
AGRICULTURE - LIBRARY □ Regina, SK
Stewart, Jane, Librarian
PERKINS, COIE, STONE, OLSEN & WILLIAMS -
LAW LIBRARY □ Seattle, WA
Stewart, Jerald, Lib.Dir.
NORTH DAKOTA STATE SCHOOL OF SCIENCE -
MILDRED JOHNSON LIBRARY □ Wahpeton, ND
Stewart, Judith E., Mgr., Tech.Info.Ctr.
MOTOROLA, INC. - GOVERNMENT
ELECTRONICS GROUP - TECHNICAL LIBRARY □
Scottsdale, AZ

Stewart, Kathryn A., Libn.
CARNATION RESEARCH LABORATORIES -
LIBRARY □ Van Nuys, CA
Stewart, Lois, Libn.
MC KINNEY JOB CORPS - LIBRARY □ McKinney,
TX
Stewart, Maryanne W., Law Libn.
DELAWARE COUNTY LAW LIBRARY □ Delaware,
OH
Stewart, Pat, Libn.
CANADIAN HEARING SOCIETY - LIBRARY □
Toronto, ON
Stewart, R.D., M.D., Dir.
UNIVERSITY HEALTH CENTER OF PITTSBURGH
- CENTER FOR EMERGENCY MEDICINE -
LIBRARY □ Pittsburgh, PA
Stewart, Sharon Lee, Act.Sr.Libn.
UNIVERSITY OF ALABAMA - MC LURE
EDUCATION LIBRARY □ University, AL
Stewart, Susan, Asst.Sec./Hd.Libn.
IRVING TRUST COMPANY - BUSINESS LIBRARY
□ New York, NY
Stewart, Tereasa, Libn.
NATIONAL WRESTLING HALL OF FAME -
LIBRARY □ Stillwater, OK
Stewart, Virginia, Dir.
ELMHURST HISTORICAL MUSEUM - LIBRARY □
Elmhurst, IL
Stewart, William, Dp.Dir.
U.S. PRESIDENTIAL LIBRARIES - GERALD R.
FORD LIBRARY □ Ann Arbor, MI
Stibbe, H., Chf., Doc.Sect.
CANADA - PUBLIC ARCHIVES OF CANADA -
NATIONAL MAP COLLECTION □ Ottawa, ON
Stickell, Henry, Academic Circ.
MOUNT SINAI SCHOOL OF MEDICINE OF THE
CITY UNIVERSITY OF NEW YORK - GUSTAVE L.
& JANET W. LEVY LIBRARY □ New York, NY
Stickle, Cheryl R., Libn.
SCOTT PAPER COMPANY - RESEARCH LIBRARY
& TECHNICAL INFORMATION SERVICE □
Philadelphia, PA
Stickler, Merrill, Dir./Cur.
CURTISS (Glenn H.) MUSEUM OF LOCAL
HISTORY - MINOR SWARTHOUT MEMORIAL
LIBRARY □ Hammondsport, NY
Stickney, Edith P., Libn.
TRINITY EPISCOPAL CHURCH - LIBRARY □
Santa Barbara, CA
Stickney, Eleanor H., Sr.Musm.Asst.
YALE UNIVERSITY - ORNITHOLOGY LIBRARY □
New Haven, CT
Stidham, Betty Faye, Libn.
FLORIDA INSTITUTE OF PHOSPHATE
RESEARCH - LIBRARY AND INFORMATION
CLEARINGHOUSE □ Bartow, FL
Stieber, Michael T., Archv.
CARNEGIE-MELLON UNIVERSITY - HUNT
INSTITUTE FOR BOTANICAL DOCUMENTATION
□ Pittsburgh, PA
Stier, Rosalina, Libn.
FORT WAYNE JOURNAL-GAZETTE -
NEWSPAPER LIBRARY □ Fort Wayne, IN
Stiffler, Stuart A., Dir., Lib.Serv.
CORNELL COLLEGE - CHEMISTRY LIBRARY† □
Mount Vernon, IA
Stiger, Mildred, Chf.
U.S. ARMY - ENGINEER TOPOGRAPHIC
LABORATORIES - SCIENTIFIC & TECHNICAL
INFORMATION CENTER □ Ft. Belvoir, VA
Stiles, C. Carmon, Dir.
U.S. DEPT. OF COMMERCE - INTERNATIONAL
TRADE ADMINISTRATION - DALLAS DISTRICT
OFFICE LIBRARY □ Dallas, TX
Stiles, Lauren, Hum.Ref.-Bibliog.
SUNY - COLLEGE AT CORTLAND - MEMORIAL
LIBRARY □ Cortland, NY
Stiles, Lois Kent, Chf.
DISTRICT OF COLUMBIA PUBLIC LIBRARY -
ART DIVISION □ Washington, DC

Stiles, Sandra P., Info.Couns.
SINGER COMPANY - LINK FLIGHT SIMULATION DIVISION - INFORMATION CENTER □ Binghamton, NY

Stilley, Bettye W., Med.Libn.
U.S. NAVY - NAVAL HOSPITAL (FL-Jacksonville) - MEDICAL LIBRARY □ Jacksonville, FL

Stillwell, Paul, Oral Hist.Dir.
U.S. NAVY - NAVAL INSTITUTE - ORAL HISTORY OFFICE □ Annapolis, MD

Stilman, Ruth, Libn.
SIR MORTIMER B. DAVIS JEWISH GENERAL HOSPITAL - INSTITUTE OF COMMUNITY & FAMILY PSYCHIATRY - LIBRARY □ Montreal, PQ

Stimage, Joyce, Spec.Coll.
PRAIRIE VIEW A & M COLLEGE OF TEXAS - W.R. BANKS LIBRARY - SPECIAL COLLECTIONS† □ Prairie View, TX

Stincic, Keith, Circuit Libn.
CLEVELAND HEALTH SCIENCES LIBRARY - ALLEN MEMORIAL LIBRARY □ Cleveland, OH

Stinger, Kathy, Libn.
ICF INC. - LIBRARY □ Washington, DC

Stinson, Judy, Doc./Ref.Libn.
WASHINGTON & LEE UNIVERSITY - LAW LIBRARY □ Lexington, VA

Stinson, Patrick B., Exec.Dir.
NATIONAL EMPLOYEE SERVICES & RECREATION ASSOCIATION - INFORMATION CENTER □ Westchester, IL

Stirling, Isabel A., Hd.Libn.
UNIVERSITY OF OREGON - MATHEMATICS LIBRARY □ Eugene, OR

Stirling, Isabel A., Hd.Libn.
UNIVERSITY OF OREGON - SCIENCE LIBRARY □ Eugene, OR

Stiso, Kathleen S., Musm.Dir.
NORTHERN INDIANA HISTORICAL SOCIETY - FREDERICK ELBEL LIBRARY □ South Bend, IN

Stith, Janet, Asst.
UNIVERSITY OF KENTUCKY - MEDICAL CENTER LIBRARY □ Lexington, KY

Stith, Linda, Prin.Libn.
KENTUCKY STATE DEPARTMENT FOR LIBRARIES AND ARCHIVES - STATE LIBRARY SERVICES DIVISION □ Frankfort, KY

Stith, Nina M., Med.Libn.
UNIONTOWN HOSPITAL ASSOCIATION - MEDICAL LIBRARY □ Uniontown, PA

Stitzinger, James F., Libn.
CALVARY BAPTIST THEOLOGICAL SEMINARY - LIBRARY □ Lansdale, PA

Stiverson, Dr. Gregory A., Asst.Archv.
MARYLAND STATE HALL OF RECORDS COMMISSION - LIBRARY □ Annapolis, MD

Stjernholm, Kirstine, Ref.Libn.
UNIVERSITY OF SOUTHERN COLORADO - LIBRARY - SPECIAL COLLECTIONS □ Pueblo, CO

Stobart, Robert, Dir.
UNIVERSITY OF WYOMING - ANIMAL SCIENCE DIVISION - WOOL LIBRARY □ Laramie, WY

Stock, Carole, Online Coord./PNRHSLS
UNIVERSITY OF WASHINGTON - HEALTH SCIENCES LIBRARY □ Seattle, WA

Stock, Jonathan C., Libn.
CONNECTICUT STATE LIBRARY - LAW LIBRARY AT STAMFORD □ Stamford, CT

Stock, Kay, Sr.Lib.Asst.
LIONEL D. EDIE AND COMPANY, INC. - LIBRARY† □ New York, NY

Stockdale, Judith M., Exec.Dir.
OPEN LANDS PROJECT - LIBRARY □ Chicago, IL

Stockdale, Kay L., Libn.
HISTORICAL FOUNDATION OF THE PRESBYTERIAN AND REFORMED CHURCHES - LIBRARY AND ARCHIVES □ Montreat, NC

Stocker, Randi L., Ref.Libn.
INDIANA UNIVERSITY/PURDUE UNIVERSITY AT INDIANAPOLIS - 38TH STREET CAMPUS LIBRARY □ Indianapolis, IN

Stockert, John W., Supt.
U.S. NATL. PARK SERVICE - MOORES CREEK NATL. BATTLEFIELD - LIBRARY □ Currie, NC

Stockett, Lura, Circ.Libn.
FULLER THEOLOGICAL SEMINARY - MC ALISTER LIBRARY† □ Pasadena, CA

Stocks, Lee, Lib.Serv.Mgr.
BA INVESTMENT MANAGEMENT CORPORATION - LIBRARY □ San Francisco, CA

Stockstill, Patrick, Asst.Libn.
ACADEMY OF MOTION PICTURE ARTS AND SCIENCES - MARGARET HERRICK LIBRARY □ Beverly Hills, CA

Stockton, Julie, Hd.
YORK UNIVERSITY - LISTENING ROOM □ Downsview, ON

Stockton, Trudy, Libn.
YORK COUNTY PLANNING COMMISSION - LIBRARY □ York, PA

Stoddard, Hilary, Online Serv.
VIRGINIA COMMONWEALTH UNIVERSITY - MEDICAL COLLEGE OF VIRGINIA - TOMPKINS-MC CAW LIBRARY □ Richmond, VA

Stoddard, Nancy Williams, Chf.Libn.
ST. LOUIS POST-DISPATCH - REFERENCE DEPARTMENT □ St. Louis, MO

Stoddard, Roger E., Assoc.Libn.
HARVARD UNIVERSITY - HOUGHTON LIBRARY □ Cambridge, MA

Stoddard, William S., Bus.Libn.
MICHIGAN STATE UNIVERSITY - BUSINESS LIBRARY □ East Lansing, MI

Stoddart, Joan, Clinical Libn.
UNIVERSITY OF UTAH - SPENCER S. ECCLES HEALTH SCIENCES LIBRARY □ Salt Lake City, UT

Stoddart, Linda, Ref.Libn.
U.S. AIR FORCE INSTITUTE OF TECHNOLOGY - LIBRARY □ Wright-Patterson AFB, OH

Stoeckle, Louis, College Sec.
NOTRE DAME COLLEGE - LANE HALL MEMORIAL LIBRARY - SPECIAL COLLECTIONS □ Wilcox, SK

Stoepler, T.M., Mgr., Market Res.
ALUMAX INC. - RESEARCH LIBRARY □ San Mateo, CA

Stoey, Richard E., Libn.
GENERAL MOTORS CORPORATION - RESEARCH LABORATORIES LIBRARY □ Warren, MI

Stoia, Joseph, Med.Libn.
KETTERING COLLEGE OF MEDICAL ARTS - LEARNING RESOURCES CENTER □ Kettering, OH

Stoia, Joseph P., Med.Libn.
KETTERING MEDICAL CENTER HOSPITAL - MEDICAL LIBRARY □ Kettering, OH

Stoker, Alan, Audio/Video Engr.
COUNTRY MUSIC FOUNDATION - LIBRARY AND MEDIA CENTER □ Nashville, TN

Stokes, Allen H., Libn.
UNIVERSITY OF SOUTH CAROLINA - SOUTH CAROLINIANA LIBRARY □ Columbia, SC

Stokes, Cornelia R., Coord., Rd.Serv.
HOWARD UNIVERSITY - MOORLAND-SPINGARN RESEARCH CENTER - LIBRARY DIVISION □ Washington, DC

Stokes, Kathryne B., Assoc.Libn.
UNIVERSITY OF MIAMI - SCHOOL OF LAW LIBRARY □ Coral Gables, FL

Stokes, Ray, Cur., Spec.Coll.
TEXAS COLLEGE OF OSTEOPATHIC MEDICINE - HEALTH SCIENCES LIBRARY □ Fort Worth, TX

Stoksik, Pamela, Hd., Tech.Serv. & Sys.
ONTARIO - LEGISLATIVE ASSEMBLY - LEGISLATIVE LIBRARY RESEARCH AND INFORMATION SERVICES □ Toronto, ON

Stokstad, Karen, Libn.
OCTAMERON ASSOCIATES, INC. - RESEARCH LIBRARY □ Alexandria, VA

Stoler, Margaret, Lib.Dir.
SPRINGFIELD ACADEMY OF MEDICINE - HEALTH SCIENCE LIBRARY □ Springfield, MA

Stoll, Helen, Adm.Asst.
MARIN MUSEUM OF THE AMERICAN INDIAN - LIBRARY □ Novato, CA

Stoll, Ilen, Tech.Serv.
MONTANA COLLEGE OF MINERAL SCIENCE AND TECHNOLOGY - LIBRARY □ Butte, MT

Stoll, Karen, Cur.
MONROE COUNTY LIBRARY SYSTEM - GENERAL GEORGE ARMSTRONG CUSTER COLLECTION □ Monroe, MI

Stoll, Karen, Dp.Hd.Libn.
UNIVERSITY OF CALIFORNIA - LOS ALAMOS NATIONAL LABORATORY - LIBRARY □ Los Alamos, NM

Stolley, Jo An I., Chf.Libn.
U.S. ARMY TRANSPORTATION - TECHNICAL INFORMATION AND RESEARCH CENTER □ Ft. Eustis, VA

Stolp, Lois, Libn./Cat.
SUNY - COLLEGE AT OSWEGO - PENFIELD LIBRARY - SPECIAL COLLECTIONS □ Oswego, NY

Stolp, Marianne, Cat.Libn.
METROPOLITAN LIFE INSURANCE COMPANY - CORPORATE INFORMATION CENTER AND LIBRARY □ New York, NY

Stolz, Martha R., Libn.
ST. ALPHONSUS REGIONAL MEDICAL CENTER - HEALTH SCIENCES LIBRARY □ Boise, ID

Stolz, Susan D., Libn. & Info.Spec.
MASSACHUSETTS INSTITUTE OF TECHNOLOGY - SEA GRANT PROGRAM - SEA GRANT INFORMATION CENTER □ Cambridge, MA

Stone, Dennis J., Law Libn.
UNIVERSITY OF CONNECTICUT - LAW SCHOOL LIBRARY □ Hartford, CT

Stone, Elberta H., Libn.
NEWARK BOARD OF EDUCATION - TEACHERS' PROFESSIONAL LIBRARY □ Newark, NJ

Stone, Emily G., Cat.Asst.
BRIDGEWATER STATE COLLEGE - CLEMENT C. MAXWELL LIBRARY □ Bridgewater, MA

Stone, Dr. Frank A., Dir.
UNIVERSITY OF CONNECTICUT - SCHOOL OF EDUCATION - I.N. THUT WORLD EDUCATION CENTER □ Storrs, CT

Stone, Gordon, Assoc.Musm.Libn.
METROPOLITAN MUSEUM OF ART - IRENE LEWISOHN COSTUME REFERENCE LIBRARY □ New York, NY

Stone, Linda, Cur. of Art
PHILLIPS (Frank) FOUNDATION, INC. - WOOLAROC MUSEUM - LIBRARY □ Bartlesville, OK

Stone, Marcia, Chf./Army Stud.Sect.
U.S. ARMY - PENTAGON LIBRARY □ Washington, DC

Stone, Margaret, Hd., Ref. & Info.
MOREHEAD STATE UNIVERSITY - CAMDEN-CARROLL LIBRARY □ Morehead, KY

Stone, Marvin H., Fine Bks.Libn.
DALLAS PUBLIC LIBRARY - FINE BOOKS DIVISION □ Dallas, TX

Stone, Pat, Hd.Libn.
U.S. NAVY - NAVAL AIR SYSTEMS COMMAND - TECHNICAL LIBRARY AIR-7226 □ Washington, DC

Stone, Patricia, Libn./Archv.
NORTH YORK PUBLIC LIBRARY - CANADIANA COLLECTION □ Willowdale, ON

Stone, Rosalie, Hd., Tech.Serv.
NEW YORK MEDICAL COLLEGE AND THE WESTCHESTER ACADEMY OF MEDICINE - WESTCHESTER MEDICAL CENTER LIBRARY □ Valhalla, NY

Stone, Susan, Asst.Libn.
SUSQUEHANNA COUNTY HISTORICAL SOCIETY AND FREE LIBRARY ASSOCIATION □ Montrose, PA

Stone, William V., Libn.
ST. JOHN'S UNIVERSITY, NOTRE DAME CAMPUS - LIBRARY† □ Staten Island, NY

Stoneham, John, Dir.
MARYLAND INSTITUTE, COLLEGE OF ART - DECKER LIBRARY □ Baltimore, MD

Stonehill, Helen, Mgr., Lib./Info.Ctr.
INTERNATIONAL CENTER FOR THE DISABLED (ICD) - BRUCE BARTON MEMORIAL LIBRARY □ New York, NY

Stoner, Ruth, Lib.Techn.
NIAGARA PARKS COMMISSION - SCHOOL OF
HORTICULTURE - HORTICULTURAL LIBRARY □
Niagara Falls, ON

Stoney, Lee, Libn.
SAFEWAY STORES, INC. - LIBRARY □ Oakland,
CA

Stopard, Linda, Libn.
KINGSTON HOSPITAL - LIBRARY □ Kingston, NY

Stoppel, Kaye, Assoc.Libn.
DRAKE UNIVERSITY - LAW LIBRARY □ Des
Moines, IA

Storace, Ilene, Ref.Libn./Info.Spec.
DAMES & MOORE - LIBRARY SERVICES □ San
Francisco, CA

Storch, Alison A., Mgr., Info.Serv.
IIT RESEARCH INSTITUTE -
ELECTROMAGNETIC COMPATIBILITY
ANALYSIS CENTER - TECHNICAL
INFORMATION SERVICES □ Annapolis, MD

Storch, Margot, Asst.Libn.
MORGAN, LEWIS & BOCKIUS - LIBRARY □
Philadelphia, PA

Storer, Gail, Libn. II
COLUMBUS COLLEGE OF ART AND DESIGN -
PACKARD LIBRARY □ Columbus, OH

Storer, Maryruth, Law Libn.
O'MELVENY AND MYERS - INFORMATION
SERVICES □ Los Angeles, CA

Storey, Mrs. Theo H., Libn.
ARKANSAS REHABILITATION INSTITUTE -
LIBRARY □ Little Rock, AR

Storm, Herman, Tech.Serv.
UNIVERSITY OF WISCONSIN, RIVER FALLS -
CHALMER DAVEE LIBRARY □ River Falls, WI

Storm, Mary L., Libn.
MOULTRIE COUNTY HISTORICAL &
GENEALOGICAL SOCIETY - MOULTRIE COUNTY
HERITAGE CENTER □ Sullivan, IL

Storm, William, Dir., Audio Archv.
SYRACUSE UNIVERSITY - GEORGE ARENTS
RESEARCH LIBRARY FOR SPECIAL
COLLECTIONS □ Syracuse, NY

Stormes, Sheridan, Assoc. Music Libn.
BUTLER UNIVERSITY - JORDAN COLLEGE OF
FINE ARTS MUSIC LIBRARY □ Indianapolis, IN

Storms, Barbara, Cat.
ALBERTA RESEARCH COUNCIL - LIBRARY
SERVICES □ Edmonton, AB

Storms, Katherine H., Info.Spec.
IN-FACT - RESEARCH AND INFORMATION
SERVICE □ Rensselaerville, NY

Storms, Kenneth, Info.Spec.
IN-FACT - RESEARCH AND INFORMATION
SERVICE □ Rensselaerville, NY

Storrer, Norman J., Sr.Tech.Libn.
AEROJET ORDNANCE COMPANY - TECHNICAL
LIBRARY □ Tustin, CA

Story, Karen, Libn.
MEIGS COUNTY LAW LIBRARY □ Pomeroy, OH

Story, Steve, Media Coord.
SOUTHWESTERN BAPTIST THEOLOGICAL
SEMINARY - A. WEBB ROBERTS LIBRARY □ Fort
Worth, TX

Stoss, Frederick W., Mgr., Info.Serv.
CENTER FOR ENVIRONMENTAL INFORMATION,
INC. - ACID RAIN REFERENCE COLLECTION □
Rochester, NY

Stoss, Frederick W., Mgr., Info.Serv.
CENTER FOR ENVIRONMENTAL INFORMATION,
INC. - HARTWELL LIBRARY □ Rochester, NY

Stoudamire, G., Pub.Serv.Libn.
HURLEY MEDICAL CENTER - HAMADY HEALTH
SCIENCES LIBRARY □ Flint, MI

Stout, Billy D., Hist.
U.S. NATL. PARK SERVICE - PEA RIDGE NATL.
MILITARY PARK - LIBRARY □ Pea Ridge, AR

Stout, Cathy A., Libn.
NEW JERSEY STATE DEPARTMENT OF HEALTH
- LIBRARY† □ Trenton, NJ

Stout, E., Lib.Asst.
HALCON SD GROUP, INC. - TECHNICAL
INFORMATION CENTER □ New York, NY

Stout, E.E., Engr.Adm.Coord.
MACK TRUCKS, INC. - TECHNICAL
INFORMATION CENTER - ENGINEERING
DIVISION LIBRARY □ Hagerstown, MD

Stout, Judy, Libn.
MARINE ENVIRONMENTAL SCIENCES
CONSORTIUM - LIBRARY □ Dauphin Island, AL

Stout, Paul W., Map Libn.
BALL STATE UNIVERSITY - DEPARTMENT OF
LIBRARY SERVICE - MAP COLLECTION □
Muncie, IN

Stovall, Juanita, Acq.
BOEING MILITARY AIRPLANE COMPANY -
LIBRARY □ Wichita, KS

Stovel, Ferris E., Dir.
U.S. NATL. ARCHIVES & RECORDS SERVICE -
WASHINGTON NATL. RECORDS CENTER □
Suitland, MD

Stowawy, M., Info.Spec.
STANDARD OIL COMPANY OF INDIANA -
LIBRARY/INFORMATION CENTER □ Chicago, IL

Stowe, Stephanie H., Libn.
DENVER MUSEUM OF NATURAL HISTORY -
LIBRARY □ Denver, CO

Stowe, Virginia, Libn.
UNITED CHURCH BOARD FOR WORLD
MINISTRIES - LIBRARY □ New York, NY

Strable, Edward G., V.P., Dir., Info.Serv.
THOMPSON (J. Walter) COMPANY -
INFORMATION CENTER □ Chicago, IL

Strable, Jane, Docs.Libn.
UNIVERSITY OF CHICAGO - LAW SCHOOL
LIBRARY □ Chicago, IL

Strada, Marta, Supv., Cat.
NATIONAL GEOGRAPHIC SOCIETY - LIBRARY □
Washington, DC

Strain, Laura M., Lib.Dir.
MANATT PHELPS ROTHENBERG & TUNNEY -
LEGAL INFORMATION CENTER □ Los Angeles,
CA

Strain, Paula M., Mgr., Info.Serv.
MITRE CORPORATION - LIBRARY □ McLean, VA

Strait, George A., Dir.
UNIVERSITY OF IOWA - LAW LIBRARY □ Iowa
City, IA

Straley, Dona S., Middle East Libn.
OHIO STATE UNIVERSITY - MIDDLE EAST/
ISLAMICA READING ROOM □ Columbus, OH

Stramiello, Angela R., Libn.
ENGLISH, MC CAUGHAN AND O'BRYAN - LAW
LIBRARY □ Fort Lauderdale, FL

Stranberg, Patsy, Hd., ILL/Circ.
EAST TENNESSEE STATE UNIVERSITY,
QUILLEN-DISHNER COLLEGE OF MEDICINE -
DEPT. OF LEARNING RSRCS. - MEDICAL
LIBRARY† □ Johnson City, TN

Strand, Kathryn, Libn.
NATIONAL CENTER FOR ATMOSPHERIC
RESEARCH - HIGH ALTITUDE OBSERVATORY
LIBRARY □ Boulder, CO

Strand, Paul J., Dir.
SAN DIEGO STATE UNIVERSITY - SOCIAL
SCIENCE RESEARCH LABORATORY - LIBRARY □
San Diego, CA

Strand, Peggy, Cat.
UNIVERSITY OF SAN DIEGO - MARVIN &
LILLIAN KRATTER LAW LIBRARY □ San Diego,
CA

Strand, Todd, Photo Archv.
STATE HISTORICAL SOCIETY OF NORTH
DAKOTA - STATE ARCHIVES AND HISTORICAL
RESEARCH LIBRARY □ Bismarck, ND

Strang, Kathryn F., Coord., Regulatory Aff.
QUAKER CHEMICAL CORPORATION -
INFORMATION RESOURCES CENTER □
Conshohocken, PA

Strang, Mrs. Marian B., Med.Libn.
U.S. ARMY HOSPITALS - GENERAL LEONARD
WOOD ARMY COMMUNITY HOSPITAL -
MEDICAL LIBRARY □ Ft. Leonard Wood, MO

Strange, Karen L., Gp.Adm.Asst.
JOHNS HOPKINS UNIVERSITY - APPLIED
PHYSICS LABORATORY - CHEMICAL
PROPULSION INFORMATION AGENCY □ Laurel,
MD

Stranick, Barbara E., Libn.
U.S. VETERANS ADMINISTRATION (PA-
Coatesville) - MEDICAL CENTER LIBRARY □
Coatesville, PA

Strassberg, Richard, Asst.Libn./Dir. LMD Ctr.
CORNELL UNIVERSITY - MARTIN P.
CATHERWOOD LIBRARY OF INDUSTRIAL AND
LABOR RELATIONS □ Ithaca, NY

Strasser, Theresa, Asst.Libn.
NEW YORK STATE LIBRARY - SCIENCES/
HEALTH SCIENCES/TECHNOLOGY REFERENCE
SERVICES □ Albany, NY

Stratford, Juri, Intl.Doc.Libn.
UNIVERSITY OF UTAH - DOCUMENTS DIVISION
□ Salt Lake City, UT

Strattis, Ella, Asst.Libn.
SPRING GARDEN COLLEGE - LIBRARY □
Chestnut Hill, PA

Stratton, Esther M., Br.Libn.
CHURCH OF JESUS CHRIST OF LATTER-DAY
SAINTS - HELENA BRANCH GENEALOGICAL
LIBRARY □ Helena, MT

Stratton, Frances M., Leader, Ref. Group
AMERICAN CYANAMID COMPANY - LEDERLE
LABORATORIES DIVISION - SUBBAROW
MEMORIAL LIBRARY† □ Pearl River, NY

Stratton, Lucile, Libn.
BENDIX CORPORATION - KANSAS CITY
DIVISION - TECHNICAL INFORMATION
CENTER† □ Kansas City, MO

Stratton, Sally, Chf.Libn.
WICHITA EAGLE-BEACON - LIBRARY □ Wichita,
KS

Straub, Mary Lou, Law Libn.
LILLICK MC HOSE & CHARLES, ATTORNEYS AT
LAW - LAW LIBRARY □ Los Angeles, CA

Straub, Sara M., Asst.Libn.
U.S. COURT OF APPEALS, 11TH CIRCUIT -
LIBRARY □ Atlanta, GA

Straub, William J., Circ.Mgr.
PUBLIC LAW EDUCATION INSTITUTE -
LIBRARY □ Washington, DC

Straus, Harriett, Libn.
NEW YORK STATE SUPREME COURT - 3RD
JUDICIAL DISTRICT - LAW LIBRARY □
Kingston, NY

Strauss, Carol, Med.Libn.
NEW YORK EYE AND EAR INFIRMARY -
BERNARD SAMUELS LIBRARY □ New York, NY

Strauss, Carol D., Libn.
WESTLAKE COMMUNITY HOSPITAL - LIBRARY
□ Melrose Park, IL

Strauss, Herbert A., Coord. of Res.
RESEARCH FOUNDATION FOR JEWISH
IMMIGRATION, INC. - ARCHIVES □ New York,
NY

Strauss, Jeanne, Transl.
PHILLIPS PETROLEUM COMPANY - RESEARCH &
DEVELOPMENT DEPARTMENT - TECHNICAL
INFORMATION BRANCH □ Bartlesville, OK

Strauss, Linda, Libn.
CONGREGATION BETH JACOB - GOODWIN
FAMILY LIBRARY □ Merchantville, NJ

Straw, Leilani, Asst.Dir.
SPENCE-CHAPIN SERVICES TO FAMILIES AND
CHILDREN - CHARLOTTE TOWLE MEMORIAL
LIBRARY □ New York, NY

Strawn, Mildred, Hd., Tech.Serv.
MARQUETTE UNIVERSITY - LEGAL RESEARCH
CENTER □ Milwaukee, WI

Strawn, Tim, Hd.
UNIVERSITY OF CALIFORNIA, LOS ANGELES -
ENGLISH READING ROOM □ Los Angeles, CA

Streamer, William A., Jr., Info.Spec.
MARYLAND STATE DEPARTMENT OF
EDUCATION - DIVISION OF LIBRARY
DEVELOPMENT & SERVICES - MEDIA SERVICES
CENTER† □ Baltimore, MD

Strecker, Candi, Libn.
WITCO CHEMICAL CORPORATION -
RICHARDSON GROUP - LIBRARY □ Melrose Park,
IL

Streeper, Mary Sue, Chf., Bibliog.Serv.
WYOMING STATE LIBRARY □ Cheyenne, WY

Street, Jenny, Mgt.Asst.
OREGON INSTITUTE OF TECHNOLOGY -
LEARNING RESOURCES CENTER □ Klamath Falls,
OR

Streeter, David, Spec.Coll.Libn.
POMONA PUBLIC LIBRARY - SPECIAL
COLLECTIONS DEPARTMENT □ Pomona, CA

Streeter, Jean D., Lindbergh Archv.
MISSOURI HISTORICAL SOCIETY - ARCHIVES
AND MANUSCRIPTS □ St. Louis, MO

Streeter, Linda, Libn.
DETROIT FREE PRESS - LIBRARY □ Detroit, MI

Strehl, Dan, Libn.
LOS ANGELES PUBLIC LIBRARY - NEWSPAPER
ROOM □ Los Angeles, CA

Strehl, Susan J., Libn.
INTERNATIONAL BROTHERHOOD OF
TEAMSTERS, CHAUFFEURS, WAREHOUSEMEN
AND HELPERS OF AMERICA - INFO. CTR.
LIBRARY □ Washington, DC

Streiff, Kwang Hee, Chf., Lib.Serv.
U.S. VETERANS ADMINISTRATION (MO-Poplar
Bluff) - MEDICAL CENTER LIBRARY (142D) □
Poplar Bluff, MO

Streit, Samuel A., Asst.Univ.Libn./Spec.Coll
BROWN UNIVERSITY - SPECIAL COLLECTIONS
□ Providence, RI

Streppone, Kaye, Libn.
KEUFFEL AND ESSER COMPANY - CHEMICAL
RESEARCH AND DEVELOPMENT LIBRARY □
Morristown, NJ

Streuli, Huguette, Libn.
MORGAN, LEWIS & BOCKIUS - LIBRARY □ New
York, NY

Streuli, Huguette, Libn.
WINDELS, MARX, DAVIES & IVES - LIBRARY □
New York, NY

Strickland, Albert C., Libn.
UNIVERSITY OF FLORIDA - HUME LIBRARY □
Gainesville, FL

Strickland, Ann T., Libn.
TUCSON PUBLIC LIBRARY - TUCSON
GOVERNMENTAL REFERENCE LIBRARY □
Tucson, AZ

Strickland, June M., Libn.
INSTITUTE OF THE PENNSYLVANIA HOSPITAL
- MEDICAL LIBRARY □ Philadelphia, PA

Strickland, June M., Libn.
PHILADELPHIA ASSOCIATION FOR
PSYCHOANALYSIS - LOUIS S. KAPLAN
MEMORIAL LIBRARY □ Bala Cynwyd, PA

Strickland, Muriel, Map Cur.
SAN DIEGO STATE UNIVERSITY -
GOVERNMENT PUBLICATIONS DEPARTMENT†
□ San Diego, CA

Strickland, Nellie B., Div.Chf.
U.S. ARMY - OFFICE OF THE ADJUTANT
GENERAL - MORALE SUPPORT DIRECTORATE -
LIBRARY ACTIVITIES DIVISION □ Alexandria,
VA

Strickland-Cordial, Victoria, Libn.
SOVRAN BANK, N.A. - LIBRARY □ Norfolk, VA

Strickler, Merle
SPOTSYLVANIA HISTORICAL ASSOCIATION,
INC. - RESEARCH MUSEUM AND LIBRARY □
Spotsylvania, VA

Strickler S, Ken, Tech.Serv.Libn.
PARKLAND COLLEGE - LEARNING RESOURCE
CENTER □ Champaign, IL

Stricks, Jim, Coord.
UNIVERSITY OF ALASKA - COLLEGE OF HUMAN
& RURAL DEVELOPMENT - RESOURCE CENTER
□ Fairbanks, AK

Strife, Janina, Sr.Libn.
UTICA/MARCY PSYCHIATRIC CENTER -
MARCY CAMPUS PROFESSIONAL LIBRARY □
Utica, NY

Strife, Mary, Ref.Libn.
CORNELL UNIVERSITY - ENGINEERING
LIBRARY □ Ithaca, NY

Striman, Brian D., Cat.Libn.
CREIGHTON UNIVERSITY - LAW SCHOOL -
KLUTZNICK LIBRARY† □ Omaha, NE

Striman, Brian D., Asst.Libn., Tech.Serv.
UNIVERSITY OF NEBRASKA, LINCOLN -
COLLEGE OF LAW LIBRARY □ Lincoln, NE

Stripnieks, L., Ref.Libn.
CANADA - ATMOSPHERIC ENVIRONMENT
SERVICE - LIBRARY □ Downsview, ON

Stroemgren, C., Libn.
Q.I.T. - FER ET TITANE INC. - BIBLIOTHEQUE
□ Sorel, PQ

Strohm, Claudette, Libn.
LANCASTER GENERAL HOSPITAL - MUELLER
HEALTH SCIENCES LIBRARY □ Lancaster, PA

Strohm, Georgia, Assoc.Libn.
ILLINOIS INSTITUTE OF TECHNOLOGY -
CHICAGO KENT LAW SCHOOL - LIBRARY† □
Chicago, IL

Strohm, Robert F., Asst.Dir., Adm.
VIRGINIA HISTORICAL SOCIETY - LIBRARY □
Richmond, VA

Strolle, Helen S., Lib. Network Mgr.
DU PONT DE NEMOURS (E.I.) & COMPANY, INC.
- LIBRARY NETWORK □ Wilmington, DE

Stroman, Josh, Hd.Libn.
NATIONAL INSTITUTE FOR PETROLEUM &
ENERGY RESEARCH (NIPER) - LIBRARY □
Bartlesville, OK

Stroman, Rosalie H., Chf., Rd.Serv.Sect.
U.S. NATL. INSTITUTES OF HEALTH - LIBRARY
□ Bethesda, MD

Stromei, Susan, Asst.Libn.
COLONIAL WILLIAMSBURG - RESEARCH
LIBRARY & ARCHIVES† □ Williamsburg, VA

Stromme, Gary L., Law Libn.
PACIFIC GAS AND ELECTRIC COMPANY - LAW
LIBRARY □ San Francisco, CA

Strona, Proserfina A., Act.Hd.
HAWAII STATE LIBRARY - HAWAII AND
PACIFIC SECTION I □ Honolulu, HI

Strong, Bernice, Ref.
DAUGHTERS OF THE REPUBLIC OF TEXAS -
LIBRARY □ San Antonio, TX

Strong, Donald R., Libn.
WEST LIBERTY STATE COLLEGE - ELBIN
LIBRARY □ West Liberty, WV

Strong, Gary E., State Libn.
CALIFORNIA STATE LIBRARY □ Sacramento, CA

Strong, Jean M., Libn.
ELMIRA STAR GAZETTE - LIBRARY □ Elmira, NY

Strong, Moira O., Chf.Libn.
NEW JERSEY STATE DEPARTMENT OF LAW
AND PUBLIC SAFETY - ATTORNEY GENERAL'S
LIBRARY □ Trenton, NJ

Strong, Pat, Libn.
SUNCOR INC. - LIBRARY □ Calgary, AB

Strong, Susan S., Hd., AV & Art Ref./Archv.
NEW YORK STATE COLLEGE OF CERAMICS AT
ALFRED UNIVERSITY - SAMUEL R. SCHOLES
LIBRARY OF CERAMICS □ Alfred, NY

Strothers, Oscar E., Chf. Law Libn.
U.S. DEPT. OF ENERGY - OFFICE OF GENERAL
COUNSEL LAW LIBRARY □ Washington, DC

Stroud, Janet, Media & Instr.Serv.Coord.
ST. ELIZABETH MEDICAL CENTER - ST.
ELIZABETH HOSPITAL SCHOOL OF NURSING -
LIBRARY □ Lafayette, IN

Stroud, Ronald D., Hd., Tech.Serv.
NOVA UNIVERSITY - LAW LIBRARY □ Fort
Lauderdale, FL

Stroud, Sandy, Asst.Libn.
BLOOMINGTON-NORMAL DAILY PANTAGRAPH -
NEWSPAPER LIBRARY □ Bloomington, IL

Strougal, Patricia, Asst.Libn.
ALSTON & BIRD - LIBRARY □ Atlanta, GA

Stroup, Dr. M. Jane, Libn.
NANTUCKET MARIA MITCHELL ASSOCIATION -
LIBRARY □ Nantucket, MA

Stroup, Mary Lou, Co-Libn.
GENEALOGICAL FORUM OF PORTLAND,
OREGON, INC. - LIBRARY □ Portland, OR

Stroupe, Ray M., Pres.
NATIONAL TAX EQUALITY ASSOCIATION -
LIBRARY □ Washington, DC

Stroyan, Sue, Dir.
MENNONITE HOSPITAL AND COLLEGE OF
NURSING - HEALTH SCIENCES LIBRARY □
Bloomington, IL

Strozier, Sandra, Dir.
CHILDREN'S MEDICAL CENTER - MARY A.
HOWER MEDICAL LIBRARY □ Akron, OH

Strub, Melanie Z., Mgr.
AT & T COMMUNICATIONS - INFORMATION
RESEARCH CENTER □ Basking Ridge, NJ

Strub, Melanie Z., Mgr.
AT & T COMMUNICATIONS - INFORMATION
RESEARCH CENTER □ Bedminster, NJ

Strub, Melanie Z., Mgr.
AT & T COMMUNICATIONS - INFORMATION
RESEARCH CENTER □ Piscataway, NJ

Strub, Melanie Z., Mgr.
AT & T COMMUNICATIONS - INFORMATION
RESEARCH CENTER □ New York, NY

Strub, Melanie Z., Mgr.
AT & T COMMUNICATIONS - INFORMATION
RESEARCH CENTER □ Cincinnati, OH

Strube, Kathleen, Ref.Libn.
MEDICAL COLLEGE OF WISCONSIN -
LIBRARIES □ Milwaukee, WI

Struble, Elizabeth, Asst. Physical Sci.Libn.
OKLAHOMA STATE UNIVERSITY - PHYSICAL
SCIENCES AND ENGINEERING DIVISION □
Stillwater, OK

Struckmeyer, Mary, ILL
WISCONSIN STATE DIVISION FOR LIBRARY
SERVICES - REFERENCE AND LOAN LIBRARY □
Madison, WI

Strumolo, Amy Loerch, Per.Libn.
SCHLUMBERGER-DOLL - RESEARCH LIBRARY □
Ridgefield, CT

Stryck, B. Camille, Res.Supv.
STANDARD OIL COMPANY OF INDIANA -
CENTRAL RESEARCH LIBRARY □ Naperville, IL

Stuart, Holly, Libn.
NORTHWEST MISSOURI STATE UNIVERSITY -
HORACE MANN LEARNING CENTER □ Maryville,
MO

Stuart, Joyce, Coord. of Tech.Serv.
ASSEMBLIES OF GOD GRADUATE SCHOOL -
CORDAS C. BURNETT LIBRARY† □ Springfield,
MO

Stuart, Mary, Slavic Bibliog.
UNIVERSITY OF ILLINOIS - SLAVIC AND EAST
EUROPEAN LIBRARY □ Urbana, IL

Stubbs, Linda M., Chf., Operations Br.
U.S. NATL. ARCHIVES & RECORDS SERVICE -
FEDERAL ARCHIVES AND RECORDS CENTER,
REGION 6 □ Kansas City, MO

Stubbs, Walter, Asst.Soc.Stud.Libn.
SOUTHERN ILLINOIS UNIVERSITY,
CARBONDALE - SOCIAL STUDIES DIVISION
LIBRARY □ Carbondale, IL

Stuckert, Caroline M., Dir.
BUTEN MUSEUM - LIBRARY □ Merion, PA

Stuckey, Julie, Libn.
ALTON TELEGRAPH PRINTING COMPANY -
LIBRARY □ Alton, IL

Stuckey, Kenneth A., Res.Libn.
PERKINS SCHOOL FOR THE BLIND - SAMUEL P.
HAYES RESEARCH LIBRARY □ Watertown, MA

Stuckey, Maurice S., Chf., Sci. Data Dept.
U.S. DEFENSE MAPPING AGENCY -
HYDROGRAPHIC/TOPOGRAPHIC CENTER-
SUPPORT DIVISION - SCIENTIFIC DATA
DEPARTMENT □ Washington, DC

Studaker, M., Tech.Serv.Libn.
HURLEY MEDICAL CENTER - HAMADY HEALTH
SCIENCES LIBRARY □ Flint, MI

Studer, Louise E., Asst.Libn.
FISH AND NEAVE - LIBRARY □ New York, NY

Studinski, Frank, Supv. Park Ranger
U.S. NATL. PARK SERVICE - SAUGUS IRON
WORKS NATL. HISTORIC SITE - LIBRARY □
Saugus, MA

Studt, Shirlee A., Art Libn.
MICHIGAN STATE UNIVERSITY - ART/MAPS
LIBRARY □ East Lansing, MI

Studwell, Roberta, Ref.Libn.
LEWIS AND CLARK LAW SCHOOL -
NORTHWESTERN SCHOOL OF LAW - PAUL L.
BOLEY LAW LIBRARY □ Portland, OR

Stuehrenberg, Paul, Cat.Libn.
YALE UNIVERSITY - DIVINITY SCHOOL
LIBRARY □ New Haven, CT

Stuhlman, Daniel, Libn.
NILES TOWNSHIP JEWISH CONGREGATION -
HILLMAN LIBRARY □ Skokie, IL

Stuhlman, Rachel, Hd.Libn.
INTERNATIONAL MUSEUM OF PHOTOGRAPHY
AT GEORGE EASTMAN HOUSE - LIBRARY □
Rochester, NY

Stuiver, Chitra, Libn./Art Spec.
HAWAII STATE LIBRARY - FINE ARTS AND
AUDIOVISUAL SECTION □ Honolulu, HI

Stulberg, Barry A., Info.Serv.Anl.
LESSER (Robert Charles) AND COMPANY -
RESOURCE DEPARTMENT □ Beverly Hills, CA

Stuller, Lola, Libn.
ALVERNO COLLEGE - RESEARCH CENTER ON
WOMEN □ Milwaukee, WI

Stultz, George B., Acq./Cat.
EG&G, INC. - IDAHO NATIONAL ENGINEERING
LABORATORY - INEL TECHNICAL LIBRARY □
Idaho Falls, ID

Stumberg, Mary Sue, Libn.
PATTON STATE HOSPITAL - STAFF LIBRARY □
Patton, CA

Stumpf, Phillip Q., Jr., Mgr.
MOBIL RESEARCH & DEVELOPMENT
CORPORATION - PAULSBORO LABORATORY -
TECHNICAL INFORMATION SERVICES □
Paulsboro, NJ

Sturdivant, Clarence A., Supv.
MARATHON OIL COMPANY - RESEARCH
TECHNICAL INFORMATION CENTER □ Littleton,
CO

Sturgis, Sybil A., Health Sci.Libn.
LYNCHBURG GENERAL MARSHALL LODGE
HOSPITAL - HEALTH SCIENCES LIBRARY □
Lynchburg, VA

Sturm, Danna, ILL Libn.
NEVADA STATE LIBRARY □ Carson City, NV

Sturm, Mr. H. Pepper, Libn.
CARSON-TAHOE HOSPITAL - LAHONTAN BASIN
MEDICAL LIBRARY □ Carson City, NV

Sturm, Marian, Libn.
CHICAGO PUBLIC LIBRARY CULTURAL CENTER
- THOMAS HUGHES CHILDREN'S LIBRARY □
Chicago, IL

Sturm, William, Libn.
OAKLAND PUBLIC LIBRARY - HISTORY/
LITERATURE DIVISION □ Oakland, CA

Stursa, Marylou, Hd., Doc.
UNIVERSITY OF WISCONSIN, MADISON -
STEENBOCK MEMORIAL LIBRARY □ Madison,
WI

Sturzenberger, Doris, Archv.
ST. LOUIS ART MUSEUM - RICHARDSON
MEMORIAL LIBRARY □ St. Louis, MO

Styler, Joyce, AV Coord.
SOUTH CHICAGO COMMUNITY HOSPITAL -
DEPARTMENT OF LIBRARY SERVICES □
Chicago, IL

Su, Julie C., Cat.
INDIANAPOLIS MUSEUM OF ART - REFERENCE
LIBRARY □ Indianapolis, IN

Su, Meng-Fen, East Asian Cat.
OHIO STATE UNIVERSITY - EAST ASIAN
COLLECTION □ Columbus, OH

Su, Siew Phek, Asst.Cat.Libn.
UNIVERSITY OF FLORIDA - HUME LIBRARY □
Gainesville, FL

Su, Valerie, Hd., Pub.Serv.
STANFORD UNIVERSITY - LANE MEDICAL
LIBRARY □ Stanford, CA

Suarez, Dr. Cynthia
TUSCULUM COLLEGE - INSTRUCTIONAL
MATERIALS CENTER □ Greeneville, TN

Suarez, Douglas G., Corp.Libn.
ERCO INDUSTRIES, LTD. - LIBRARY □ Islington,
ON

Suart, Susan, Libn.
CANADA - NATIONAL RESEARCH COUNCIL -
CISTI - ENERGY BRANCH □ Ottawa, ON

Sublette, Doris, Libn.
UNIVERSITY OF CALIFORNIA, LOS ANGELES -
COMPUTER SCIENCE DEPARTMENT -
ARCHIVES □ Los Angeles, CA

Subramanian, Jane, Tech.Asst., Ser.
SUNY - COLLEGE AT POTSDAM - FREDERICK W.
CRUMB MEMORIAL LIBRARY □ Potsdam, NY

Suchoff, Dr. Benjamin, Trustee
NEW YORK BARTOK ARCHIVE □ Cedarhurst, NY

Suchyta, Lillian, Hd.Proc.Dept.
DETROIT BAR ASSOCIATION FOUNDATION -
LIBRARY† □ Detroit, MI

Suddon, Alan, Hd.
METROPOLITAN TORONTO LIBRARY - FINE
ART DEPARTMENT □ Toronto, ON

Suddon, Alan, Hd. of Unit
METROPOLITAN TORONTO LIBRARY -
NEWSPAPER UNIT □ Toronto, ON

Sudduth, Susan F., Libn.
IMA INCORPORATED - LIBRARY† □ Sherman
Oaks, CA

Sudol, Barbara, Libn.
U.S. DEPT. OF JUSTICE - NATIONAL
INSTITUTE OF CORRECTIONS - NIC
INFORMATION CENTER □ Boulder, CO

Suelflow, August R., Dir.
CONCORDIA HISTORICAL INSTITUTE -
DEPARTMENT OF ARCHIVES AND HISTORY □
St. Louis, MO

Sugar, Dr. J., Physicist
U.S. NATL. BUREAU OF STANDARDS - ATOMIC
ENERGY LEVELS DATA CENTER □ Washington,
DC

Sugarman, Joan, Ref./Info.
AMERICAN COLLEGE OF HEALTH CARE
ADMINISTRATORS - LIBRARY □ Bethesda, MD

Sugden, Lynne M., Libn.
CONFEDERATION LIFE INSURANCE COMPANY -
LIBRARY □ Toronto, ON

Suggs, Ida, Tech.Info.Spec.
NATIONAL INJURY INFORMATION
CLEARINGHOUSE □ Washington, DC

Sugimura, Sue, Pub.Serv.Libn.
HAWAII STATE LIBRARY - STATE LIBRARY FOR
THE BLIND AND PHYSICALLY HANDICAPPED □
Honolulu, HI

Suh, Ann, Asst.Libn., Rd.Serv.
UNIVERSITY OF MARYLAND, BALTIMORE -
SCHOOL OF LAW - MARSHALL LAW LIBRARY □
Baltimore, MD

Suh, Choo, Sr. Japanese Libn.
UNIVERSITY OF MICHIGAN - ASIA LIBRARY □
Ann Arbor, MI

Suhor, Charles, Dir.
ERIC CLEARINGHOUSE ON READING AND
COMMUNICATIONS SKILLS □ Urbana, IL

Suhr, Angie, AV Spec.
NORTH CAROLINA STATE DEPARTMENT OF
CULTURAL RESOURCES - DIVISION OF THE
STATE LIBRARY □ Raleigh, NC

Suhr, Paul A., Libn.
NORTH CAROLINA STATE UNIVERSITY -
TOBACCO LITERATURE SERVICE □ Raleigh, NC

Suitts, Stephen T., Exec.Dir.
SOUTHERN REGIONAL COUNCIL, INC. -
REFERENCE LIBRARY □ Atlanta, GA

Sulerud, Grace K., Acq. & Ref.Libn.
AUGSBURG COLLEGE - GEORGE SVERDRUP
LIBRARY AND MEDIA CENTER □ Minneapolis,
MN

Suligowski, Leonard, Dir. of Heraldry
POLISH NOBILITY ASSOCIATION - VILLA
ANNESLIE ARCHIVES □ Anneslie, MD

Sulkin, Danny, Spec.
VANDERBILT UNIVERSITY - JEAN AND
ALEXANDER HEARD LIBRARY - WALKER
MANAGEMENT LIBRARY □ Nashville, TN

Sullivan, C.M., Libn.
UNIVERSITY OF FLORIDA - TROPICAL
RESEARCH & EDUCATION CENTER -
HOMESTEAD LIBRARY □ Homestead, FL

Sullivan, Charles M., Exec.Dir.
CAMBRIDGE HISTORICAL COMMISSION -
LIBRARY □ Cambridge, MA

Sullivan, Daniel, Hd.Cat.Libn.
UNIVERSITY OF SOUTHERN COLORADO -
LIBRARY - SPECIAL COLLECTIONS □ Pueblo, CO

Sullivan, Dolores, Adm.
JOHNS HOPKINS UNIVERSITY - CENTER FOR
METROPOLITAN PLANNING AND RESEARCH -
LIBRARY □ Baltimore, MD

Sullivan, Donna, Lib.Mgr.
MADISON COMMUNITY HOSPITAL - HEALTH-
SCIENCE LIBRARY □ Madison, SD

Sullivan, Edward A., III, Info.Spec.
PETROLITE CORPORATION - INFORMATION
CENTER □ St. Louis, MO

Sullivan, Gloria, Asst.Libn.
CENTRAL DU PAGE HOSPITAL - MEDICAL
LIBRARY □ Winfield, IL

Sullivan, Howard, Coll.Dev.
WAYNE STATE UNIVERSITY - G. FLINT PURDY
LIBRARY □ Detroit, MI

Sullivan, James, Asst.Dir.
FRANCISCAN MONASTERY LIBRARY □
Washington, DC

Sullivan, Dr. John T., Asst.Prof.
MEDICAL UNIVERSITY OF SOUTH CAROLINA -
MARINE BIOMEDICAL RESEARCH CENTER □
Charleston, SC

Sullivan, Kathryn, Libn.
PQA ENGINEERING - LIBRARY† □ Riverdale, NJ

Sullivan, Dr. Larry E., Libn.
NEW-YORK HISTORICAL SOCIETY - LIBRARY □
New York, NY

Sullivan, Lester G., Archv.
AMISTAD RESEARCH CENTER - LIBRARY/
ARCHIVES □ New Orleans, LA

Sullivan, Marilyn, Chf.Libn.
UNIVERSITY OF MISSOURI, KANSAS CITY -
HEALTH SCIENCES LIBRARY □ Kansas City, MO

Sullivan, Marjorie E., Chf., Lib.Serv.
U.S. VETERANS ADMINISTRATION (MA-
Northampton) - MEDICAL CENTER LIBRARY □
Northampton, MA

Sullivan, Martha J., Lib.Adm.
CONNECTICUT STATE LIBRARY - LAW LIBRARY
AT NEW HAVEN □ New Haven, CT

Sullivan, Mary, Pub.Serv.
LOUISIANA STATE UNIVERSITY - COASTAL
INFORMATION REPOSITORY □ Baton Rouge, LA

Sullivan, Mary L., Libn.
FALL RIVER LAW LIBRARY □ Fall River, MA

Sullivan, Mary Thomas, Mgr.
GRACE (W.R.) AND COMPANY - NATURAL
RESOURCES GROUP - INFORMATION CENTER □
Dallas, TX

Sullivan, Michael D., Dir., Pub.Aff.
INDUSTRIAL FORESTRY ASSOCIATION -
LIBRARY □ Portland, OR

Sullivan, Michael V., Hd.
STANFORD UNIVERSITY - ENGINEERING
LIBRARY □ Stanford, CA

Sullivan, Mildred, Res.Spec.
MONTANA STATE DEPARTMENT OF NATURAL
RESOURCES & CONSERVATION - RESEARCH &
INFORMATION CENTER □ Helena, MT

Sullivan, Nancy, Tech.Libn.
DIGITAL EQUIPMENT CORPORATION -
ANDOVER LIBRARY □ Andover, MA

Sullivan, Nancy Kay, Dir., Pub.Rel.
MISSISSIPPI STATE DEPARTMENT OF HEALTH
- AUDIOVISUAL LIBRARY □ Jackson, MS

Sullivan, Pat, Asst.Libn.
CORNELL UNIVERSITY - FINE ARTS LIBRARY □ Ithaca, NY

Sullivan, Penny J., Act.Dir.
INTERNATIONAL CHRISTIAN GRADUATE UNIVERSITY - LIBRARY □ San Bernardino, CA

Sullivan, Philip, Supv.
MADISON PUBLIC LIBRARY - BUSINESS AND SCIENCE DIVISION □ Madison, WI

Sullivan, Rosalie Mercein, Act.Dir.
MONROE (James) LAW OFFICE - MUSEUM AND MEMORIAL LIBRARY □ Fredericksburg, VA

Sullivan, Rose C., Rsrc.Ctr.Spec.
NATIONAL CENTER FOR APPROPRIATE TECHNOLOGY - RESEARCH LIBRARY □ Butte, MT

Sullivan, Rosemary, Asst.Libn.
PLYMOUTH LAW LIBRARY† □ Brockton, MA

Sulyok, Agnes, Hd., Circ.
UNIVERSITY OF OTTAWA - MORISSET LIBRARY □ Ottawa, ON

Sumerlin, Katherine, Per.Libn.
OUACHITA BAPTIST UNIVERSITY - RILEY LIBRARY □ Arkadelphia, AR

Summa, James D., Law Lib.Ck.
NEW YORK STATE SUPREME COURT - 4TH JUDICIAL DISTRICT - LAW LIBRARY □ Lake George, NY

Summar, Donald J., Libn.
NATIONAL ASSOCIATION OF WATCH AND CLOCK COLLECTORS MUSEUM - LIBRARY □ Columbia, PA

Summer, Susan Cook, Coord.
MODERN LANGUAGE ASSOCIATION - CENTER FOR BIBLIOGRAPHICAL SERVICES □ New York, NY

Summerford, Teresa K., Chem.
ETHYL CORPORATION - INFORMATION & LIBRARY SERVICES LIBRARY □ Baton Rouge, LA

Summerhill, John, Supv., Spec.Coll.
UNIVERSITY OF ALASKA, ANCHORAGE - LIBRARY - SPECIAL COLLECTIONS □ Anchorage, AK

Summers, Bill, Asst.Archv.
MONTANA HISTORICAL SOCIETY - LIBRARY/ ARCHIVES □ Helena, MT

Summers, Brian, Libn.
FOUNDATION FOR ECONOMIC EDUCATION - LIBRARY □ Irvington-On-Hudson, NY

Summers, Carol A., Info.Mgr.
CANADIAN CONSULATE GENERAL - INFORMATION CENTER† □ Chicago, IL

Summers, Mary, Adm. of Info.Serv.
RESEARCH INSTITUTE OF AMERICA - INFORMATION SERVICES CENTER □ New York, NY

Summers, Robert A., Archv.
ALLEN (John E.), INC. - MOTION PICTURE ARCHIVES □ Park Ridge, NJ

Summers, Robert L., Jr., Dir.
ST. MARY'S UNIVERSITY - LAW LIBRARY† □ San Antonio, TX

Summers, Sheryl H., Assoc.Libn.
DETROIT COLLEGE OF LAW - LIBRARY □ Detroit, MI

Summit, Dr. Roger K., Pres.
DIALOG INFORMATION SERVICES, INC. □ Palo Alto, CA

Sumner, Delores, Native Amer.Mtls.Spec.
NORTHEASTERN OKLAHOMA STATE UNIVERSITY - JOHN VAUGHAN LIBRARY/LRC - SPECIAL COLLECTIONS □ Tahlequah, OK

Sumner, Gwen, Media Techn.
MANSFIELD UNIVERSITY - BUTLER CENTER LIBRARY □ Mansfield, PA

Sumner, Mark R., Dir.
UNIVERSITY OF NORTH CAROLINA, CHAPEL HILL - INSTITUTE OF OUTDOOR DRAMA - ARCHIVES □ Chapel Hill, NC

Sumners, Bill, Archv.
DARGAN-CARVER LIBRARY □ Nashville, TN

Sumners, Bill, Archv.
SOUTHERN BAPTIST CONVENTION - HISTORICAL COMMISSION - SOUTHERN BAPTIST HISTORICAL LIBRARY & ARCHIVES □ Nashville, TN

Sumpter, Ethel L., Rd.Adv.
DISTRICT OF COLUMBIA PUBLIC LIBRARY - HISTORY, TRAVEL AND GEOGRAPHY DIVISION □ Washington, DC

Sun, Cossette T., Law Lib.Dir.
ALAMEDA COUNTY LAW LIBRARY □ Hayward, CA

Sun, Cossette T., Law Lib.Dir.
ALAMEDA COUNTY LAW LIBRARY □ Oakland, CA

Sun, Mr. Lan C., Libn.
SHELL CANADA LIMITED - OAKVILLE RESEARCH CENTRE - SHELL RESEARCH CENTRE LIBRARY □ Oakville, ON

Sunday, Donald E., Ref.Libn.
AT & T BELL LABORATORIES & TECHNOLOGIES - LIBRARY □ Allentown, PA

Sundbye, Delores, Supv.
ST. PAUL PUBLIC LIBRARY - ART AND MUSIC □ St. Paul, MN

Sundeen, S., Tech.Serv.Libn.
HURLEY MEDICAL CENTER - HAMADY HEALTH SCIENCES LIBRARY □ Flint, MI

Sunder-Raj, P.E., Dir., Lib.Serv.
CANADA - EMPLOYMENT & IMMIGRATION CANADA - LIBRARY □ Ottawa, ON

Sundermeyer, Ruth, Prof.Asst.
ENOCH PRATT FREE LIBRARY - FINE ARTS AND RECREATION DEPARTMENT □ Baltimore, MD

Sundquist, Ken, Ministry Libn.
ONTARIO - MINISTRY OF AGRICULTURE AND FOOD - LIBRARY □ Toronto, ON

Suozzi, Patricia, Econ.Libn.
UNIVERSITY OF PITTSBURGH - ECONOMICS/ COLLECTION IN REGIONAL ECONOMICS □ Pittsburgh, PA

Supeau, Cynthia, Search Anl.
BOEHRINGER INGELHEIM LTD. - SCIENTIFIC INFORMATION SERVICES □ Ridgefield, CT

Superior, William J., Pres.
THORNTHWAITE (C.W.) ASSOCIATES LABORATORY OF CLIMATOLOGY - LIBRARY □ Elmer, NJ

Suplee, Virginia, Info. & Res.Dir.
CENTER FOR THE HISTORY OF AMERICAN NEEDLEWORK - LIBRARY □ Pittsburgh, PA

Suprapto, R.M., Indonesian Cat.
CORNELL UNIVERSITY - JOHN M. ECHOLS COLLECTION ON SOUTHEAST ASIA □ Ithaca, NY

Suprapto, Sari Devi, Thai Cat.
CORNELL UNIVERSITY - JOHN M. ECHOLS COLLECTION ON SOUTHEAST ASIA □ Ithaca, NY

Surace, Cecily J., Lib.Dir.
LOS ANGELES TIMES - EDITORIAL LIBRARY □ Los Angeles, CA

Suran, Frank, Assoc.Archv.
PENNSYLVANIA STATE HISTORICAL & MUSEUM COMMISSION - DIVISION OF ARCHIVES AND MANUSCRIPTS □ Harrisburg, PA

Surber, Melissa M., Acq./Ser.Libn.
UNIVERSITY OF SOUTH CAROLINA - COLEMAN KARESH LAW LIBRARY □ Columbia, SC

Suretsky, Sue Stewart, Asst.Libn.
ST. PETER'S MEDICAL CENTER - LIBRARY† □ New Brunswick, NJ

Suri, R.K., Libn.
IEC BEAK CONSULTANTS LTD. - LIBRARY □ Mississauga, ON

Surich, Dr. Jo, Res.Coord.
ONTARIO FEDERATION OF LABOUR - RESOURCE CENTRE □ Don Mills, ON

Surles, Alma J., Act.Rd.Serv.Libn.
ALABAMA (State) SUPREME COURT - SUPREME COURT AND STATE LAW LIBRARY □ Montgomery, AL

Surles, Richard, Dir.
UNIVERSITY OF ILLINOIS - LAW LIBRARY □ Champaign, IL

Surprenant, Neil, Asst.Libn.
PAUL SMITH'S COLLEGE OF ARTS AND SCIENCES - FRANK L. CUBLEY LIBRARY □ Paul Smiths, NY

Surrency, Erwin C., Prof./Libn.
UNIVERSITY OF GEORGIA - LAW LIBRARY □ Athens, GA

Sussler, Joan, Cur.
YALE UNIVERSITY - LEWIS WALPOLE LIBRARY □ Farmington, CT

Sussman, Leonard R., Exec.Dir.
FREEDOM HOUSE - INFORMATION CENTER □ New York, NY

Sutherland, C. Tom, Supv.
SAVANNAH RIVER PLANT - TECHNICAL LIBRARY □ Aiken, SC

Sutherland, J. Elizabeth, Hd., Lib.Serv.
BEDFORD INSTITUTE OF OCEANOGRAPHY - LIBRARY □ Dartmouth, NS

Sutherland, John, Map Cur.
UNIVERSITY OF GEORGIA - SCIENCE LIBRARY - MAP COLLECTION □ Athens, GA

Sutherland, Michael C., Spec.Coll.Libn.
OCCIDENTAL COLLEGE - MARY NORTON CLAPP LIBRARY □ Los Angeles, CA

Sutherland, Michael C., Spec.Coll.Libn.
ROUNCE AND COFFIN CLUB, LOS ANGELES - LIBRARY □ Los Angeles, CA

Sutherland, Morag, Asst.Hum.Libn.
OKLAHOMA STATE UNIVERSITY - HUMANITIES DIVISION □ Stillwater, OK

Sutliff, Mary E., Tech.Libn.
KIMBERLY-CLARK CORPORATION - LIBRARY† □ Neenah, WI

Sutliff, Sandra A., Chf.Libn.
DOYLE DANE BERNBACH INC. - LIBRARY □ New York, NY

Sutphin, Sue, Tech.Libn.
MASON & HANGER-SILAS MASON COMPANY, INC. - PANTEX PLANT - TECHNICAL LIBRARY □ Amarillo, TX

Sutrick, Anita, Asst.Libn.
OKLAHOMA COLLEGE OF OSTEOPATHIC MEDICINE & SURGERY - LIBRARY □ Tulsa, OK

Sutt, Joanne, Dir.
ST. AGNES HOSPITAL - L.P. GUNDRY HEALTH SCIENCES LIBRARY □ Baltimore, MD

Sutter, Mary Anne, Asst.Ref.Libn.
ST. LOUIS UNIVERSITY - MEDICAL CENTER LIBRARY □ St. Louis, MO

Suttles, Barbara C., Supv.
OLIN CORPORATION - CHEMICALS - CHARLESTON TECHNICAL INFORMATION CENTER □ Charleston, TN

Suttles, Cheryl, Dir., Med.Lib.
BAPTIST MEDICAL CENTER - WANN LANGSTON MEMORIAL LIBRARY □ Oklahoma City, OK

Sutton, Amelia, Chf., Doc.
U.S. ARMY - WHITE SANDS MISSILE RANGE - TECHNICAL LIBRARY DIVISION □ White Sands Missile Range, NM

Sutton, David J., Musm. Trustee
AIRPOWER MUSEUM - LIBRARY □ Ottumwa, IA

Sutton, Edith, Libn.
NORTHWEST HOSPITAL - EFFIE M. STOREY LEARNING CENTER □ Seattle, WA

Sutton, Ellen D., Interim Libn.
UNIVERSITY OF NORTH CAROLINA, CHAPEL HILL - SCHOOL OF LIBRARY SCIENCE LIBRARY □ Chapel Hill, NC

Sutton, Frank, Adm.Off.
U.S. PUBLIC HEALTH SERVICE - ALASKA NATIVE HEALTH SERVICE - HEALTH SCIENCES LIBRARY □ Sitka, AK

Sutton, Joanna M., Hd.Libn.
GARRETT CORPORATION - AIRESEARCH MANUFACTURING COMPANY - TECHNICAL LIBRARY □ Torrance, CA

Sutton, Lea, Libn.
CUMBERLAND BAR ASSOCIATION - NATHAN AND HENRY B. CLEAVES LAW LIBRARY □ Portland, ME

Sutton, Lynn Sorensen, Corp.Dir. of Libs.
DETROIT MACOMB HOSPITAL CORPORATION -
HOSPITAL LIBRARY □ Detroit, MI
Sutton, Lynn Sorensen, Corp.Dir. of Libs.
DETROIT MACOMB HOSPITAL CORPORATION -
SOUTH MACOMB HOSPITAL LIBRARY □ Warren,
MI
Sutton, Mary Lynn, Sci.Libn.
PHOTO RESEARCHERS, INC. - LIBRARY □ New
York, NY
Sutton, Rebecca B., Asst.Libn.
NATIONAL HUMANITIES CENTER - LIBRARY □
Research Triangle Park, NC
Sutton, Sally J., Libn.
INDIANA STATE SUPREME COURT - LAW
LIBRARY □ Indianapolis, IN
Suvak, Nancy J., Supv.
UNITED STATES STEEL CORPORATION -
INFORMATION CENTER □ Pittsburgh, PA
Suvak, William A., Jr., Libn.Supv. I
PENNSYLVANIA STATE DEPARTMENT OF
PUBLIC WELFARE - MAYVIEW STATE
HOSPITAL - MENTAL HEALTH AND MEDICAL
LIBRARY □ Bridgeville, PA
Suvarnamani, Nuj
BORG-WARNER CORPORATION - ROY C.
INGERSOLL RESEARCH CENTER - TECHNICAL
INFORMATION SERVICES □ Des Plaines, IL
Suverkropp, Erna C., Lib.Tech.Asst.
ARGOSYSTEMS - INC. - TECHNICAL LIBRARY†
□ Sunnyvale, CA
Suydam, Marilyn, Assoc.Dir., Math.
ERIC CLEARINGHOUSE FOR SCIENCE,
MATHEMATICS AND ENVIRONMENTAL
EDUCATION □ Columbus, OH
Suza, Fred
PRUDENTIAL INSURANCE COMPANY OF
AMERICA - BUSINESS LIBRARY □ Houston, TX
Sved, Alexander, Asst.Libn.
LOYOLA UNIVERSITY OF CHICAGO - LAW
LIBRARY □ Chicago, IL
Svengalis, Kendall F., State Law Libn.
RHODE ISLAND STATE LAW LIBRARY □
Providence, RI
Svihra, S. Joy, Hd.
UNIVERSITY OF CALIFORNIA, BERKELEY -
EARTHQUAKE ENGINEERING RESEARCH
CENTER LIBRARY □ Richmond, CA
Svoboda, Joseph G., Professor
UNIVERSITY OF NEBRASKA, LINCOLN -
UNIVERSITY ARCHIVES AND SPECIAL
COLLECTIONS □ Lincoln, NE
Swaim, Elizabeth A., Spec.Coll.Libn./Archv.
WESLEYAN UNIVERSITY - LIBRARY - SPECIAL
COLLECTIONS □ Middletown, CT
Swaim, Jessica, Info.Spec.
SOUTHEAST METROPOLITAN BOARD OF
COOPERATIVE SERVICES - PROFESSIONAL
INFORMATION CENTER □ Denver, CO
Swaim, Marlene M., Pub.Serv.
KAISER-PERMANENTE MEDICAL CENTER -
HEALTH SCIENCES LIBRARY □ Sacramento, CA
Swaim, Salomea A., Archv.Libn.
PUBLIC BROADCASTING SERVICE - PTV
ARCHIVES □ Washington, DC
Swain, Ann, Lib.Asst.
RADFORD UNIVERSITY - LIBRARY - VIRGINIA
ROOM AND SPECIAL COLLECTIONS □ Radford,
VA
Swain, Barbara C., Libn.
UNIVERSITY OF ILLINOIS - HOME ECONOMICS
LIBRARY □ Urbana, IL
Swain, Hannah K., Libn.
CAPE MAY COUNTY HISTORICAL &
GENEALOGICAL SOCIETY - LIBRARY □ Cape
May Court House, NJ
Swan, Barbara L., Mgr.
BECTON, DICKINSON & COMPANY -
CORPORATE INFORMATION CENTER □
Paramus, NJ

Swan, Deloris J., Lib.Off.
U.S. NAVY - NAVAL AIR ENGINEERING CENTER
- TECHNICAL LIBRARY, CODE 1115 □
Lakehurst, NJ
Swan, Janet, Assoc.Libn.
FEDERAL RESERVE BANK OF MINNEAPOLIS -
LIBRARY □ Minneapolis, MN
Swan, M.E., Tech.Libn.
SCM CORPORATION - GLIDDEN COATINGS &
RESINS DIVISION/DURKEE FOODS DIVISION -
TECHNICAL INFORMATION SERVICES □
Strongsville, OH
Swanekamp, Joan, Hd., Tech.Proc.
UNIVERSITY OF ROCHESTER - EASTMAN
SCHOOL OF MUSIC - SIBLEY MUSIC LIBRARY □
Rochester, NY
Swanick, Eric L., Doc.Libn.
NEW BRUNSWICK - LEGISLATIVE LIBRARY □
Fredericton, NB
Swanigan, Meryl H., Mgr.
ATLANTIC-RICHFIELD COMPANY -
INFORMATION RESEARCH CENTER □ Los
Angeles, CA
Swann, Clara W., Hd.
CHATTANOOGA-HAMILTON COUNTY
BICENTENNIAL LIBRARY - LOCAL HISTORY
AND GENEALOGICAL COLLECTIONS □
Chattanooga, TN
Swanner, Sallieann, Asst.Dir.Tech.Serv.
UNIVERSITY OF TEXAS HEALTH SCIENCE
CENTER, SAN ANTONIO - LIBRARY □ San
Antonio, TX
Swanson, Albert A., Archv.
(Boston) METROPOLITAN DISTRICT
COMMISSION - LIBRARY □ Boston, MA
Swanson, Barbara J., Libn.
ARGONNE NATIONAL LABORATORY -
ARGONNE-WEST TECHNICAL LIBRARY □ Idaho
Falls, ID
Swanson, Byron, Doc.Coord.
INDIANA STATE LIBRARY - INDIANA DIVISION
□ Indianapolis, IN
Swanson, Donna, Coord.
KENTUCKY STATE DEPARTMENT OF
EDUCATION - RESOURCE CENTER □ Frankfort,
KY
Swanson, Dorothy, Libn.
NEW YORK UNIVERSITY - TAMIMENT LIBRARY
□ New York, NY
Swanson, Duane P., Archv., Govt.Rec.
MINNESOTA HISTORICAL SOCIETY - DIVISION
OF ARCHIVES AND MANUSCRIPTS □ St. Paul,
MN
Swanson, Edward, Hd., Tech.Serv.
MINNESOTA HISTORICAL SOCIETY -
REFERENCE LIBRARY □ St. Paul, MN
Swanson, Ellen, Chm., Lib.Comm.
AUGUSTANA LUTHERAN CHURCH - LIBRARY □
Denver, CO
Swanson, Fred H., Act.Dir.
UNIVERSITY OF CALIFORNIA - KEARNEY
AGRICULTURAL CENTER □ Parlier, CA
Swanson, Joe, Cat.
MOREHOUSE SCHOOL OF MEDICINE - MULTI-
MEDIA CENTER □ Atlanta, GA
Swanson, Judy, Libn.
ARIZONA STATE DEPARTMENT OF EDUCATION
- EDUCATIONAL INFORMATION CENTER □
Phoenix, AZ
Swanson, Lynn, Sr.Lib.Asst.
MINNESOTA GEOLOGICAL SURVEY - LIBRARY □
St. Paul, MN
Swanson, Martha, Asst.Cat.Libn.
WESTERN ILLINOIS UNIVERSITY - LIBRARIES
□ Macomb, IL
Swanson, Patricia K., Asst.Dir. for Sci.Libs.
UNIVERSITY OF CHICAGO - JOHN CRERAR
LIBRARY □ Chicago, IL
Swanson, Ruth, Weston Lib.
UNIVERSITY OF WISCONSIN, MADISON -
CENTER FOR HEALTH SCIENCES LIBRARIES† □
Madison, WI

Swanson, Sandra K., Libn.
BUTTERWORTH HOSPITAL - HEALTH SCIENCES
LIBRARY □ Grand Rapids, MI
Swanson, Sheila, Libn.
ACADEMY OF MEDICINE, TORONTO - WILLIAM
BOYD LIBRARY □ Toronto, ON
Swanson, Sue, Sec./Libn.
U.S. NATL. PARK SERVICE - CAPE HATTERAS
NATL. SEASHORE LIBRARY □ Manteo, NC
Swanton, James, Chf.Cat.
YESHIVA UNIVERSITY - ALBERT EINSTEIN
COLLEGE OF MEDICINE - D. SAMUEL
GOTTESMAN LIBRARY □ Bronx, NY
Swart, Hannah W., Cur.
HOARD HISTORICAL MUSEUM - LIBRARY □ Fort
Atkinson, WI
Swartz, Roderick G., State Libn.
WASHINGTON STATE LIBRARY □ Olympia, WA
Sweaney, Dr. Wilma, Libn.
UNIVERSITY OF SASKATCHEWAN - HEALTH
SCIENCES LIBRARY □ Saskatoon, SK
Sweaza, Jacqueline M., Off.Mgr.
AMERICAN AVIATION HISTORICAL SOCIETY -
AAHS REFERENCE LIBRARY □ Santa Ana, CA
Swedenberg, Anne, Asst.Med.Libn.
WASHINGTON HOSPITAL CENTER - MEDICAL
LIBRARY □ Washington, DC
Sweek, Andree, Med.Rec.Libn.
HOLLEY (A.G.) STATE HOSPITAL - BENJAMIN L.
BROCK MEDICAL LIBRARY □ Lantana, FL
Sweely, Christine, Libn.
CHILTON COMPANY - MARKETING &
ADVERTISING INFORMATION CENTER □
Radnor, PA
Sween, Jane C., Libn.
MONTGOMERY COUNTY HISTORICAL SOCIETY
- LIBRARY □ Rockville, MD
Sweeney, Del, Info.Spec.
PENNSYLVANIA STATE UNIVERSITY -
TRANSPORTATION INSTITUTE WORKING
COLLECTION □ University Park, PA
Sweeney, Donna B., Act.Chf., Lib.Serv.
U.S. VETERANS ADMINISTRATION (MT-Miles
City) - MEDICAL CENTER LIBRARY □ Miles City,
MT
Sweeney, Grace, Libn.
BLACKHAWK TECHNICAL INSTITUTE,
JANESVILLE - LEARNING MATERIALS CENTER
□ Janesville, WI
Sweeney, Joan, Res.Libn.
INSTITUTE FOR DEFENSE ANALYSES -
TECHNICAL INFORMATION SERVICES □
Alexandria, VA
Sweeney, Loretta, Libn.
MEAD JOHNSON AND COMPANY - MEAD
JOHNSON INSTITUTE - LIBRARY □ Evansville,
IN
Sweeney, Urban J., Chf.Libn.
GENERAL DYNAMICS CORPORATION -
CONVAIR DIVISION - RESEARCH LIBRARY □
San Diego, CA
Sweeny, Sheila M., Legal Staff Libn.
GENERAL MOTORS CORPORATION - LEGAL
STAFF LIBRARY† □ Detroit, MI
Sweet, Douglas L., Dir., R. & D.
STATE BAR OF MICHIGAN - LIBRARY □ Lansing,
MI
Sweet, Herman R., Libn.
HARVARD UNIVERSITY - OAKES AMES ORCHID
LIBRARY □ Cambridge, MA
Sweet, Jane, Lib.Coord.
SOCIETY OF FRIENDS - FRIENDS HOUSE
LIBRARY □ Toronto, ON
Sweet, Julia W., Libn.
CARTER & BURGESS, INC. ENGINEERS &
PLANNERS - LIBRARY □ Fort Worth, TX
Sweet, Vickie, Circ./Acq.
U.S. NASA - LANGLEY RESEARCH CENTER -
TECHNICAL LIBRARY MS 185† □ Hampton, VA
Sweet, Vivian, Libn.
MADISON PUBLIC LIBRARY - BUSINESS AND
SCIENCE DIVISION □ Madison, WI

Sweetland, James H., Hd.Libn.
STATE HISTORICAL SOCIETY OF WISCONSIN - LIBRARY □ Madison, WI

Sweetland, Loraine, Libn./Supv.
WASHINGTON ADVENTIST HOSPITAL - MEDICAL LIBRARY □ Takoma Park, MD

Sweeton, Janice, Med.Libn.
CHILTON MEMORIAL HOSPITAL - MEDICAL LIBRARY □ Pompton Plains, NJ

Sweets, Henry, Cur.
MARK TWAIN MUSEUM - LIBRARY □ Hannibal, MO

Swenson, Elizabeth, Libn.
FERGUS FALLS STATE HOSPITAL - LIBRARY □ Fergus Falls, MN

Swenson, Evelyn J., Dir.
NORTHWEST MINNESOTA HISTORICAL CENTER - LIBRARY □ Moorhead, MN

Sweny, Edward J., Libn.
NEW ENGLAND DEPOSIT LIBRARY, INC. □ Allston, MA

Swerdlove, Dorothy L., Cur.
NEW YORK PUBLIC LIBRARY - PERFORMING ARTS RESEARCH CENTER - BILLY ROSE THEATRE COLLECTION □ New York, NY

Swetell, Marilyn, Libn.
DIAMOND SHAMROCK CORPORATION - PROCESS CHEMICALS DIVISION - LIBRARY† □ Morristown, NJ

Sweton, Marian, Hd.Cat.
WESTERN RESERVE HISTORICAL SOCIETY - LIBRARY □ Cleveland, OH

Swibas, Charlene, Tech.Info.Spec.
ENVIRONMENTAL PROTECTION AGENCY - NATIONAL ENFORCEMENT INVESTIGATIONS - LIBRARY □ Denver, CO

Swichel, Virginia L., Libn.
PUBLIC SERVICE ELECTRIC AND GAS COMPANY - NUCLEAR LIBRARY □ Hancocks Bridge, NJ

Swift, Barbara, Libn.
FMC CORPORATION - MARINE COLLOIDS DIVISION - LIBRARY □ Rockland, ME

Swift, June, Exec.Sec.
ST. JOSEPH MUSEUM - LIBRARY □ St. Joseph, MO

Swift-Rosenzweig, Leslie, Res.Assoc.
FOUNDATION FOR PUBLIC AFFAIRS - RESOURCE CENTER □ Washington, DC

Swigart, Helen F., Mgr.
SWIGART MUSEUM - LIBRARY □ Huntingdon, PA

Swigart, William E., Jr., Exec.Dir.
SWIGART MUSEUM - LIBRARY □ Huntingdon, PA

Swim, Frances F., Regional Libs.Coord.
U.S. NATL. OCEANIC & ATMOSPHERIC ADMINISTRATION - LIBRARY AND INFORMATION SERVICES DIVISION - MAIN LIBRARY □ Rockville, MD

Swingle, Ruth, Libn.
HASTINGS REGIONAL CENTER - MEDICAL LIBRARY □ Hastings, NE

Swinson, Caroline Seydell, Cur. of Mss.
UNIVERSITY OF TULSA - MC FARLIN LIBRARY - RARE BOOKS AND SPECIAL COLLECTIONS □ Tulsa, OK

Swinton, Jeanne, Libn.
SANGER (Margaret) CENTER-PLANNED PARENTHOOD NEW YORK CITY - ABRAHAM STONE LIBRARY □ New York, NY

Swinyer, Joseph G., Dir.
SUNY - COLLEGE AT PLATTSBURGH - BENJAMIN F. FEINBERG LIBRARY - SPECIAL COLLECTIONS □ Plattsburgh, NY

Swisher, Doug, Tech.Ed.
OHIO POETRY THERAPY CENTER - WELCH LIBRARY □ Columbus, OH

Swist, Anne C., Lit.Anl.
BRISTOL-MYERS PRODUCTS - TECHNICAL INFORMATION CENTER □ Hillside, NJ

Swistock, Phyllis, Hd.Libn.
DON BOSCO TECHNICAL INSTITUTE - LEE LIBRARY† □ Rosemead, CA

Switt, Karen J., Chf.Libn.
NATIONAL ASSOCIATION OF REALTORS - LIBRARY □ Chicago, IL

Swityk, Bill, Asst.Libn.
ST. VLADIMIR'S UKRAINIAN ORTHODOX CULTURAL CENTRE - LIBRARY AND ARCHIVES □ Calgary, AB

Swoiskin, Lenore, Dir. of Archv.
SEARS, ROEBUCK AND CO. - ARCHIVES, BUSINESS HISTORY AND INFORMATION CENTER □ Chicago, IL

Swope, Frances A., Archv.
GREENBRIER HISTORICAL SOCIETY - ARCHIVES □ Lewisburg, WV

Sybrowsky, Paul, Pres.
GSG, INC. - CTI LIBRARY SYSTEMS, INC. □ Orem, UT

Sydij, Dianne D., Libn.
THOMSON, ROGERS, BARRISTERS & SOLICITORS - LIBRARY† □ Toronto, ON

Syed, Mariam, Asst.Libn.
SEARS, ROEBUCK AND CO. - MERCHANDISE DEVELOPMENT AND TESTING LABORATORY - LIBRARY, DEPARTMENT 817 □ Chicago, IL

Syed, Shameem, Asst.Libn.
UNIVERSITY OF MASSACHUSETTS, AMHERST - LABOR RELATIONS & RESEARCH CENTER LIBRARY □ Amherst, MA

Sykes, Barbara A., Cat.Libn.
FORDHAM UNIVERSITY - LIBRARY AT LINCOLN CENTER □ New York, NY

Sykes, Stephanie L., Hist.
BELL CANADA - TELEPHONE HISTORICAL COLLECTION □ Montreal, PQ

Sylvester, James, Res.Asst.
UNIVERSITY OF MONTANA - BUREAU OF BUSINESS AND ECONOMIC RESEARCH - LIBRARY □ Missoula, MT

Sylvester, Jean, Musm. Docent
LINN COUNTY HISTORICAL SOCIETY - LIBRARY □ Pleasanton, KS

Symeonoglou, Rheba, Libn.
ST. LOUIS PSYCHOANALYTIC INSTITUTE - BETTY GOLDE SMITH MEMORIAL LIBRARY □ St. Louis, MO

Symon, Carol, Supv., Info.Ctr.
GENERAL FOODS, LTD. - INFORMATION CENTRE† □ Toronto, ON

Symonds, Mrs. John, Pres.
HISTORIC ANNAPOLIS, INC. - LIBRARY □ Annapolis, MD

Syr, Mariann, Libn.
3M - 235 LIBRARY □ St. Paul, MN

Syverson, Kathy, Sr.Info.Anl.
AMERICAN CRITICAL CARE - INFORMATION CENTER □ McGaw Park, IL

Szabo, Lynn, Mgr.
MEMOREX CORPORATION - TECHNICAL INFORMATION CENTER □ Santa Clara, CA

Szabo, Maria, Libn.
BECHTEL - DATA PROCESSING LIBRARY □ San Francisco, CA

Szabo, Paula A.
NORTH CENTRAL REGIONAL CENTER - TREES LIBRARY □ Bloomfield, CT

Szabo, Ruth E., Coord., Lib.Serv.
ST. JOSEPH HOSPITAL, OUR LADY OF PROVIDENCE UNIT - HEALTH SCIENCE LIBRARY □ Providence, RI

Szalasznyj, Mrs. K., Staff Archv.
SASKATCHEWAN ARCHIVES BOARD □ Regina, SK

Szarejko, Celia, Mgr., Info.Sys. & Lib.
CONSUMER EDUCATION RESOURCE NETWORK (CERN)† □ Rosslyn, VA

Szarmach, Paul E., Dir.
SUNY AT BINGHAMTON - CENTER FOR MEDIEVAL AND EARLY RENAISSANCE STUDIES □ Binghamton, NY

Szasz, Debbie, Acq.Techn.
COLUMBIA UNION COLLEGE - THEOFIELD G. WEIS LIBRARY □ Takoma Park, MD

Szczech, Bernadette, Res.Libn.
CHICAGO TRIBUNE - RESEARCH LIBRARY □ Chicago, IL

Szczepaniak, Adam, Assoc.Libn.
MEDICAL AND CHIRURGICAL FACULTY OF THE STATE OF MARYLAND - LIBRARY □ Baltimore, MD

Szczepaniak, Frank J., P.T. Boat Coord.
P.T. BOATS, INC. - LIBRARY, ARCHIVES & TECHNICAL INFORMATION CENTER □ Fall River, MA

Szczepaniak, Lillian, Slide Lib.Ck.
YORK UNIVERSITY - DEPARTMENT OF VISUAL ARTS - SLIDE LIBRARY □ Toronto, ON

Szczepanik, Sr. Mark, Coord., Rsrc.Ctr.
HOUSE EAR INSTITUTE - PARENT RESOURCE LIBRARY □ Los Angeles, CA

Szefczyk, Dorothy, Lib.Techn.
ENVIRONMENTAL PROTECTION AGENCY - REGION II FIELD OFFICE - TECHNICAL LIBRARY □ Edison, NJ

Szegedi, Laszlo, Cat.Libn.
LOYOLA LAW SCHOOL - LIBRARY □ Los Angeles, CA

Szendrey, Jolan
RUTGERS UNIVERSITY, THE STATE UNIVERSITY OF NEW JERSEY - DEPARTMENT OF SPECIAL COLLECTIONS AND ARCHIVES □ New Brunswick, NJ

Szentkiralyi, Irene B., Libn.
LUTHERAN MEDICAL CENTER - C.W. NEVEL MEMORIAL LIBRARY □ Cleveland, OH

Szewczuk, Stephen, Libn.
NEW YORK SOCIETY OF MODEL ENGINEERS - LIBRARY □ Carlstadt, NJ

Szladits, Dr. Lola L., Cur.
NEW YORK PUBLIC LIBRARY - BERG COLLECTION □ New York, NY

Szmuk, Szilvia, Libn./Assoc.Prof.
ST. JOHN'S UNIVERSITY - LIBRARY AND INFORMATION SCIENCE LIBRARY □ Jamaica, NY

Szmuk, Szilvia E., Spec.Coll.Libn.
ST. JOHN'S UNIVERSITY - SPECIAL COLLECTIONS □ Jamaica, NY

Szot, Irene, Lib.Asst.
ST. ANTHONY HOSPITAL - SPRAFKA MEMORIAL HEALTH SCIENCE LIBRARY □ Chicago, IL

Szuch, Janice, Lib.Techn.
SASKATCHEWAN - DEPARTMENT OF SOCIAL SERVICES - LIBRARY □ Regina, SK

Szucs, Frank, Libn.
ONTARIO - MINISTRY OF MUNICIPAL AFFAIRS & HOUSING - LIBRARY □ Toronto, ON

Szumni, Wallace, Ref.
D'ARCY, MAC MANUS, MASIUS - LIBRARY INFORMATION SERVICES □ Bloomfield Hills, MI

Szuwalski, Andre, Dir.
U.S. ARMY - ENGINEER WATERWAYS EXPERIMENT STATION - COASTAL ENGINEERING INFORMATION ANALYSIS CENTER □ Vicksburg, MS

Szwajkowski, Maureen, Libn.
DAY & ZIMMERMANN, INC. - LIBRARY □ Philadelphia, PA

Szymanski, Lucyna, Tech.Serv.Coord./Ser.Libn
RUSH-PRESBYTERIAN-ST. LUKE'S MEDICAL CENTER - LIBRARY OF RUSH UNIVERSITY □ Chicago, IL

T

Taagen, Connie, Med.Libn.
NORTHWEST GENERAL HOSPITAL - MEDICAL LIBRARY □ Milwaukee, WI

Tabachnik, Miriam, Hd.Libn.
ADLER (Alfred) INSTITUTE - SOL AND ELAINE MOSAK LIBRARY □ Chicago, IL

Tabah, Albert, Ref.Libn.
CONCORDIA UNIVERSITY - SIR GEORGE
WILLIAMS CAMPUS - SCIENCE &
ENGINEERING LIBRARY □ Montreal, PQ

Tabakin, Rhea, Exec.Off.Libn.
DELOITTE HASKINS & SELLS - EXECUTIVE
OFFICE LIBRARY □ New York, NY

Tabb, Winston, Chf., Info./Ref.Div.
LIBRARY OF CONGRESS - COPYRIGHT PUBLIC
INFORMATION OFFICE □ Washington, DC

Taber, John, Ser./Acq.
TEXAS COLLEGE OF OSTEOPATHIC MEDICINE -
HEALTH SCIENCES LIBRARY □ Fort Worth, TX

Taber, Kolette L., Corp.Libn.
DOME PETROLEUM LIMITED - CORPORATE
LIBRARY □ Calgary, AB

Tabler, Nancy H., Libn.
POLK COUNTY LAW LIBRARY □ Bartow, FL

Tabor, Mrs. Dorcas E., Lib.Techn.
U.S. NAVY - OFFICE OF NAVAL RESEARCH -
LIBRARY □ Arlington, VA

Taborsky, Theresa, Lib.Dir.
WIDENER UNIVERSITY - WOLFGRAM
MEMORIAL LIBRARY □ Chester, PA

Tabory, Maxim, Libn./Dir. of LRC
CHERRY HOSPITAL - LEARNING RESOURCE
CENTER □ Goldsboro, NC

Taboy, Mrs. Enriqueta G., Lib.Dir.
TRI-STATE UNIVERSITY - PERRY T. FORD
MEMORIAL LIBRARY □ Angola, IN

Tabron, Lynda B., Per.Libn.
COMMUNITY COLLEGE OF BALTIMORE -
LIBRARIES/LEARNING RESOURCES CENTERS □
Baltimore, MD

Taccarino, Paul, Libn.
U.S. ARMY - ENGINEER WATERWAYS
EXPERIMENT STATION - TECHNICAL
INFORMATION CENTER □ Vicksburg, MS

Tachihata, Dr. Chieko, Asst.Lib.Spec.
UNIVERSITY OF HAWAII - SPECIAL
COLLECTIONS - HAWAIIAN COLLECTION □
Honolulu, HI

Tachuk, Roger, Hd., Ref.Sect.
NORTHWESTERN UNIVERSITY - HEALTH
SCIENCES LIBRARY† □ Chicago, IL

Tack, A. Catherine, Libn.
CARNEGIE LIBRARY OF PITTSBURGH - MUSIC
AND ART DEPARTMENT □ Pittsburgh, PA

Tacy, W. Jeffery, Leg.Spec.
KIRKLAND & ELLIS - LIBRARY □ Washington, DC

Tadevic, Joyce, Archv.
ROSSLAND HISTORICAL MUSEUM
ASSOCIATION - ARCHIVES □ Rossland, BC

Taeger, Maureen, Libn.
NORTHERN COLLEGE - HAILEYBURY SCHOOL OF
MINES - LIBRARY □ Haileybury, ON

Tafel, Linda, Ref.Libn.
UNIVERSITY OF CINCINNATI - ENGINEERING
LIBRARY □ Cincinnati, OH

Taff, Edith, Libn.
SOUTHEASTERN BIBLE COLLEGE - ROWE
MEMORIAL LIBRARY □ Birmingham, AL

Tafoya, Herlinda, Law Libn.
COCHISE COUNTY LAW LIBRARY □ Bisbee, AZ

Taft, Robert F., Pres.
ERIE COUNTY HISTORICAL SOCIETY □ Erie, PA

Tagg, John, Supv.
ONTARIO HOSPITAL ASSOCIATION - LIBRARY
□ Don Mills, ON

Tahirkheli, Sharon, Sr.Ed.
AMERICAN GEOLOGICAL INSTITUTE - GEOREF
INFORMATION SYSTEM □ Alexandria, VA

Tai, Henry H., Oriental Libn.
UNIVERSITY OF CALIFORNIA, SANTA BARBARA
- ORIENTAL COLLECTION □ Santa Barbara, CA

Tai, Mildred C., Clerical Staff Supv.
FLORES (Nieves M.) MEMORIAL LIBRARY □
Agana, GU

Tai, Sidney, Supv., Rare Bks.Rm.
HARVARD UNIVERSITY - HARVARD-YENCHING
LIBRARY □ Cambridge, MA

Tai, Wen-Pai, Chinese Libn.
UNIVERSITY OF CHICAGO - FAR EASTERN
LIBRARY □ Chicago, IL

Taillefer-Witty, Nicole, Libn.
UNIVERSITE DE MONTREAL - BOTANIQUE-
BIBLIOTHEQUE □ Montreal, PQ

Taitano, Magdalena S., Territorial Libn.
FLORES (Nieves M.) MEMORIAL LIBRARY □
Agana, GU

Taitt, Rosalind, Linguistics Spec.
METROPOLITAN TORONTO LIBRARY -
LITERATURE DEPARTMENT □ Toronto, ON

Takakoshi, Gay, Asst.Libn.
AMERICAN COLLEGE OF OBSTETRICIANS AND
GYNECOLOGISTS - RESOURCE CENTER □
Washington, DC

Takashiba, Anna, Sys.Libn.
NORANDA MINES LTD. - INFORMATION
SERVICES - RESOURCE CENTRE □ Don Mills, ON

Takato, Georgene, Info.Spec.
SYNTEX, U.S.A. - CORPORATE LIBRARY/
INFORMATION SERVICES □ Palo Alto, CA

Takis, Stephanie, Exec.Off.
ASSOCIATION FOR EXPERIENTIAL EDUCATION
- LIBRARY □ Boulder, CO

Takita, Jim, Dept.Hd.
LIBRARY ASSOCIATION OF PORTLAND -
SOCIAL SCIENCE AND SCIENCE DEPARTMENT
□ Portland, OR

Talalay, K., Ref.Libn.
INDIANA UNIVERSITY - MUSIC LIBRARY □
Bloomington, IN

Talbot, George A., Archv. AV Coll.
STATE HISTORICAL SOCIETY OF WISCONSIN -
ARCHIVES DIVISION □ Madison, WI

Talbot, William, Ref., ILL
MASSACHUSETTS COLLEGE OF ART - LIBRARY
□ Boston, MA

Talbot-Stanaway, Susan, Cur., Educ.
PLAINS ART MUSEUM - LIBRARY □ Moorhead,
MN

Talbott, Chris, Libn.
LATAH COUNTY HISTORICAL SOCIETY -
LIBRARY □ Moscow, ID

Talcott, Ann W., Lib. Group Supv.
AT & T BELL LABORATORIES - LIBRARY □
Murray Hill, NJ

Taliaferro, Helen N., Chf., Rd.Serv.Div.
U.S. AIR FORCE - AIR UNIVERSITY - LIBRARY □
Maxwell AFB, AL

Taller, Georgia, Pub.Serv.Libn.
PALMER COLLEGE OF CHIROPRACTIC - DAVID
D. PALMER LIBRARY □ Davenport, IA

Tallerico, Phyllis M., Cat.Libn.
KEAN COLLEGE OF NEW JERSEY - NANCY
THOMPSON LIBRARY† □ Union, NJ

Talley, Gary V., Chf., Interpretation
U.S. NATL. PARK SERVICE - ABRAHAM LINCOLN
BIRTHPLACE NATL. HISTORIC SITE - LIBRARY
□ Hodgenville, KY

Tallman, Carol W., Lib.Techn.
PENNSYLVANIA STATE HISTORICAL & MUSEUM
COMMISSION - REFERENCE LIBRARY □
Harrisburg, PA

Talsma, Debra, Libn.
ENVIRONMENTAL PROTECTION AGENCY -
MOTOR VEHICLE EMISSION LABORATORY -
LIBRARY □ Ann Arbor, MI

Tam, Miriam, Asst.Libn., Tech.Serv.
AMERICAN MUSEUM OF NATURAL HISTORY -
DEPARTMENT OF LIBRARY SERVICES □ New
York, NY

Tamaribuchi, Franklin S., TAC Spec.
HAWAII STATE DEPARTMENT OF EDUCATION -
AUDIOVISUAL SERVICES □ Honolulu, HI

Tambo, David C., Hd., Spec.Coll.
BALL STATE UNIVERSITY - BRACKEN LIBRARY
- SPECIAL COLLECTIONS □ Muncie, IN

Tamer, Susan M., Adm., Lib.Serv.
RCA CORPORATION - RCA CONSUMER
ELECTRONICS DIVISION - ENGINEERING
LIBRARY □ Indianapolis, IN

Tammard, Marcella C., Libn.
OLIN CORPORATION - METALS RESEARCH
LABORATORIES - METALS INFORMATION
CENTER† □ New Haven, CT

Tammen, Kathryn, Supv., Acq.
GENERAL RESEARCH CORPORATION - LIBRARY
□ Santa Barbara, CA

Tampold, Ana, Ser.Libn.
BANK OF NOVA SCOTIA - LIBRARY □ Toronto,
ON

Tamura, Catherine C., Learning Ctr.Coord.
AMERICAN LUNG ASSOCIATION OF HAWAII -
LEARNING CENTER FOR LUNG HEALTH □
Honolulu, HI

Tan Shen, Shirley, Libn.-Spec.
UNIVERSITY OF WISCONSIN, MADISON -
MATHEMATICS LIBRARY □ Madison, WI

Tanaka, Colette, Supv., Lib.Serv.
KENNEDY (John F.) UNIVERSITY - CENTER FOR
MUSEUM STUDIES - LIBRARY □ San Francisco,
CA

Tanaka, Momoe, State Law Libn.
HAWAII STATE SUPREME COURT - LAW
LIBRARY □ Honolulu, HI

Tanen, Lee J., Mgr., Lib./Info.Serv.
REVLON RESEARCH CENTER, INC. - LIBRARY □
Edison, NJ

Tang, Mr. Chin-Shih, Ref. (Common Law)
UNIVERSITY OF OTTAWA - LAW LIBRARY □
Ottawa, ON

Tang, Eugenia, Cat.
TEXAS A & M UNIVERSITY - TECHNICAL
REPORTS DEPARTMENT □ College Station, TX

Tang, Lorna, Hd.Cat.
UNIVERSITY OF CHICAGO - LAW SCHOOL
LIBRARY □ Chicago, IL

Tang, Ta-Liang Daisy Yao, Libn.
DIXMONT STATE HOSPITAL - PERSONNEL
LIBRARY† □ Sewickley, PA

Tanguay, Huquette, Audiovideothecaire
UNIVERSITE DU QUEBEC A MONTREAL -
AUDIOVIDEOTHEQUE □ Montreal, PQ

Taniguchi, Norma, Libn.
CANADA - AGRICULTURE CANADA - RESEARCH
STATION, FREDERICTON - LIBRARY □
Fredericton, NB

Tanin, Eleanore, Broadcast Supv.
UNIVERSITY OF CALIFORNIA, LOS ANGELES -
ACADEMY OF TELEVISION ARTS & SCIENCES -
TELEVISION ARCHIVES □ Los Angeles, CA

Tanin, Eleanore, Broadcast Supv.
UNIVERSITY OF CALIFORNIA, LOS ANGELES -
UCLA RADIO ARCHIVES □ Los Angeles, CA

Tankersley, Heather, Libn.I
MEMPHIS-SHELBY COUNTY PUBLIC LIBRARY
AND INFORMATION CENTER - MEMPHIS ROOM
COLLECTIONS □ Memphis, TN

Tannehill, Robert S., Jr., Lib.Mgr.
CHEMICAL ABSTRACTS SERVICE - LIBRARY □
Columbus, OH

Tannenbaum, Aileen Z., Med.Libn.
MEMORIAL GENERAL HOSPITAL - MEDICAL
LIBRARY □ Union, NJ

Tannenbaum, Robin, Info.Spec.
AMERICAN FOUNDATION FOR THE BLIND -
M.C. MIGEL MEMORIAL LIBRARY □ New York,
NY

Tannenbaum, Sabina D., Libn.
PHILADELPHIA ELECTRIC COMPANY - LIBRARY
□ Philadelphia, PA

Tanner, Anne, Diocesan Libn.
ANGLICAN CHURCH OF CANADA - DIOCESE OF
TORONTO - DIOCESAN LIBRARY & RESOURCE
CENTRE† □ Toronto, ON

Tanner, Annette, Coord., Br.Libs.
CHURCH OF JESUS CHRIST OF LATTER-DAY
SAINTS - GENEALOGICAL LIBRARY □ Salt Lake
City, UT

Tanner, Jane, Libn.
WESLEY MEDICAL CENTER - H.B. MC KIBBIN
HEALTH SCIENCE LIBRARY □ Wichita, KS

Tanner, Rose, Chm.
ANSHE HESED TEMPLE - LIBRARY† □ Erie, PA

Tanner, Sandra J., Libn.
ARLINGTON BAPTIST COLLEGE - EARL K.
OLDHAM LIBRARY □ Arlington, TX

Tanner, Thomas M., Libn.
LINCOLN CHRISTIAN COLLEGE & SEMINARY -
JESSIE C. EURY LIBRARY† □ Lincoln, IL

Tanno, John W., Assoc.Univ.Libn.
UNIVERSITY OF CALIFORNIA, RIVERSIDE -
MUSIC LIBRARY □ Riverside, CA

Tanski, Henry M., Jr., Asst.Interp.
U.S. NATL. PARK SERVICE - CRATER LAKE
NATL. PARK - LIBRARY □ Crater Lake, OR

Tanzer, Barbara, Asst.Libn.
NEW YORK COUNTY LAWYERS' ASSOCIATION -
LIBRARY □ New York, NY

Tapley, Janet, Prof.Asst.
MINNEAPOLIS PUBLIC LIBRARY &
INFORMATION CENTER - ART, MUSIC & FILMS
DEPARTMENT □ Minneapolis, MN

Taplinger, Beverly R., Lib.Techn.
U.S. DEPT. OF HOUSING AND URBAN
DEVELOPMENT - REGION III - LIBRARY† □
Philadelphia, PA

Taranto, Pamela J., Libn.
CALIFORNIA FEDERAL SAVINGS AND LOAN
ASSOCIATION - MANAGEMENT LIBRARY □ Los
Angeles, CA

Tarbert, Anita W., Lib.Techn.
U.S. GEOLOGICAL SURVEY - WESTERN
MINERAL RESOURCES LIBRARY □ Spokane, WA

Tarbox, G.L., Jr., Dir.
BROOKGREEN GARDENS - LIBRARY □ Murrells
Inlet, SC

Tarbutton, Ms. Grace, Lib.Archv.
LANDMARK CONSERVATORS - CABOTS OLD
INDIAN PUEBLO MUSEUM LIBRARY □ Desert
Hot Springs, CA

Tarczy, Steven I., Hd., Tech.Serv.
UNIVERSITY OF CALIFORNIA, SAN FRANCISCO
- LIBRARY □ San Francisco, CA

Tardif, Bernadette, Libn.
AMERICAN-CANADIAN GENEALOGICAL
SOCIETY - FATHER LEO E. BEGIN CHAPTER -
LIBRARY □ Lewiston, ME

Tardif, Jeannine, Lib.Supv.
CANADIAN NATIONAL INSTITUTE FOR THE
BLIND - QUEBEC DIVISION LIBRARY† □
Montreal, PQ

Targ, Fred, V.P.
CONTINENTAL CHEMISTE CORPORATION -
LIBRARY □ Chicago, IL

Tarman, Mary Sandra, Libn.
RAMSEY COUNTY MEDICAL SOCIETY -
BOECKMANN LIBRARY □ St. Paul, MN

Tarman, Roger, Chf.Bibliog.
RUTGERS UNIVERSITY, THE STATE
UNIVERSITY OF NEW JERSEY - BLANCHE AND
IRVING LAURIE MUSIC LIBRARY □ New
Brunswick, NJ

Tarnawsky, Marta, Asst.Libn., Intl. Law
UNIVERSITY OF PENNSYLVANIA - BIDDLE LAW
LIBRARY □ Philadelphia, PA

Tarnowski, Marge, Libn.
U.S. NAVY - NAVAL RESEARCH LABORATORY -
UNDERWATER SOUND REFERENCE
DETACHMENT - TECHNICAL LIBRARY □
Orlando, FL

Tarpinian, Greg, Dir.
LABOR RESEARCH ASSOCIATION - LIBRARY □
New York, NY

Tarpley, Dr. Fred, Natl.Dir.
AMERICAN NAME SOCIETY - PLACE NAME
SURVEY OF THE UNITED STATES - LIBRARY □
Commerce, TX

Tarpley, Penny, Chf.Libn.
PATTERSON, BELKNAP, WEBB & TYLER -
LIBRARY □ New York, NY

Tartaglia, Judy, Cat.
MC GRAW-HILL, INC. - LIBRARY □ New York,
NY

Tarter, Theo
CONDE NAST PUBLICATIONS, INC. - LIBRARY □
New York, NY

Tashiro, Mimi, Asst. Music Libn.
STANFORD UNIVERSITY - MUSIC LIBRARY □
Stanford, CA

Tashjean, Catherine, Ref.Libn.
U.S. OFFICE OF PERSONNEL MANAGEMENT -
LIBRARY □ Washington, DC

Tatalias, Jean, Rec.Rsrcs.Supv.
MITRE CORPORATION - LIBRARY □ McLean, VA

Tate, E.A., Med.Libn.
U.S. ARMY HOSPITALS - MARTIN ARMY
COMMUNITY HOSPITAL - MEDICAL LIBRARY □
Ft. Benning, GA

Tate, Fr. Jules, O.S.B., Libn.
ST. JOSEPH ABBEY - LIBRARY □ St. Benedict, LA

Tate, R.W., Dir. of Res.
DELAVAN INC. - ENGINEERING LIBRARY □
West Des Moines, IA

Tatley, Orlette, Asst. to Libn.
GOLDEN VALLEY LUTHERAN COLLEGE -
LIBRARY† □ Minneapolis, MN

Tatman, Mary Ann, AV Prog.Spec.
U.S. VETERANS ADMINISTRATION (DC-
Washington) - HEADQUARTERS CENTRAL
OFFICE LIBRARY (142D1) □ Washington, DC

Tatman, Mary Ann, AV Prog.Spec.
U.S. VETERANS ADMINISTRATION (DC-
Washington) - HEADQUARTERS LIBRARY
DIVISION (142D) □ Washington, DC

Tatman, Sandra, Arch.Libn.
ATHENAEUM OF PHILADELPHIA □ Philadelphia,
PA

Tatone, O., Info. Input & Anl.
ATOMIC ENERGY OF CANADA, LTD. -
TECHNICAL INFORMATION BRANCH - MAIN
LIBRARY □ Chalk River, ON

Tatro, Jeanne, Hd., ILL Dept.
CALIFORNIA INSTITUTE OF TECHNOLOGY -
MILLIKAN LIBRARY □ Pasadena, CA

Tattershall, Miss S., Hd., Lib.Sect.
SHELL CANADA LIMITED - TECHNICAL
LIBRARY □ Toronto, ON

Tatum, Jill, Asst.Archv.
CASE WESTERN RESERVE UNIVERSITY -
UNIVERSITY ARCHIVES □ Cleveland, OH

Taub, Sylvia B., Libn.
MORSE SCHOOL OF BUSINESS - LIBRARY □
Hartford, CT

Tauber, Jean A., Dir., Lib.Serv.
HAMOT MEDICAL CENTER - LIBRARY
SERVICES □ Erie, PA

Tauber, M. Joan, Libn.
SUNY - CENTRAL ADMINISTRATION RESEARCH
LIBRARY □ Albany, NY

Taubman, Susan, Lrng.Rsrcs.Coord.
CREEDMOOR PSYCHIATRIC CENTER - HEALTH
SCIENCES LIBRARY □ Queens Village, NY

Tausky, Janice, Libn.
UNIVERSITY OF MASSACHUSETTS, AMHERST -
LABOR RELATIONS & RESEARCH CENTER
LIBRARY □ Amherst, MA

Tavetian, Susan A., Sr.Libn.
COMPUTER SCIENCES CORPORATION -
TECHNICAL LIBRARY □ El Segundo, CA

Tawyea, Edward, Hd., Circ. Media Libn.
NORTHWESTERN UNIVERSITY - HEALTH
SCIENCES LIBRARY† □ Chicago, IL

Tax, Andrew, Asst.Sci./Med.Libn.
SOUTHERN ILLINOIS UNIVERSITY,
CARBONDALE - SCIENCE DIVISION LIBRARY □
Carbondale, IL

Taylor, Adrienne, Coll.Libn.
UNIVERSITY OF TORONTO - WYCLIFFE
COLLEGE - LEONARD LIBRARY □ Toronto, ON

Taylor, Aline H., Libn.
GENERAL TELEPHONE COMPANY OF THE
SOUTHWEST - E.H. DANNER LIBRARY OF
TELEPHONY □ San Angelo, TX

Taylor, Andrew S., Rec.Mgr.
NEW HAMPSHIRE STATE DEPARTMENT OF
STATE - DIVISION OF RECORDS MANAGEMENT
& ARCHIVES □ Concord, NH

Taylor, Annabelle, Libn.
CANADA - NATIONAL RESEARCH COUNCIL -
ATLANTIC RESEARCH LABORATORY - LIBRARY
□ Halifax, NS

Taylor, Anne M., Chf., Lib.Serv.
U.S. VETERANS ADMINISTRATION (WI-
Madison) - WILLIAM S. MIDDLETON MEMORIAL
VETERANS HOSPITAL - LIBRARY □ Madison, WI

Taylor, Arthur, Photographer
MUSEUM OF NEW MEXICO - PHOTOGRAPHIC
ARCHIVES □ Santa Fe, NM

Taylor, B.L.
CANADA - ATMOSPHERIC ENVIRONMENT
SERVICE - ATLANTIC REGIONAL LIBRARY □
Bedford, NS

Taylor, Dr. Barry N., Chf.
U.S. NATL. BUREAU OF STANDARDS -
FUNDAMENTAL CONSTANTS DATA CENTER □
Washington, DC

Taylor, Beatrice K., Mss.Libn.
DU PONT (Henry Francis) WINTERTHUR
MUSEUM - LIBRARY □ Winterthur, DE

Taylor, Bernard H., Libn.
U.S. DEPT. OF HOUSING AND URBAN
DEVELOPMENT - REGION II - LIBRARY □ New
York, NY

Taylor, Betsy, Chf., Lib.Serv.
U.S. VETERANS ADMINISTRATION (IL-Danville)
- MEDICAL CENTER LIBRARY □ Danville, IL

Taylor, Betty W., Dir.
UNIVERSITY OF FLORIDA - LAW LIBRARY □
Gainesville, FL

Taylor, C.R., Exec.Dir., Dept.Adm.
NATIONAL LIBRARY OF CANADA/
BIBLIOTHEQUE NATIONALE DU CANADA □
Ottawa, ON

Taylor, Carol Lenz, Libn.
BORDEN INC. - RESEARCH CENTRE - LIBRARY
□ Syracuse, NY

Taylor, Carolyn, Coll.Dev.Libn.
UNIVERSITY OF VIRGINIA - MEDICAL CENTER
- CLAUDE MOORE HEALTH SCIENCES LIBRARY
□ Charlottesville, VA

Taylor, Carolyn L., Asst.Libn.
ST. LOUIS UNIVERSITY - MEDICAL CENTER
LIBRARY □ St. Louis, MO

Taylor, Charles E., Supv., Projects
U.S. NATL. ARCHIVES & RECORDS SERVICE -
NATL. ARCHIVES - CARTOGRAPHIC &
ARCHITECTURAL BRANCH □ Washington, DC

Taylor, Dan, Ref.
UNIVERSITY OF TEXAS HEALTH SCIENCE
CENTER, SAN ANTONIO - LIBRARY □ San
Antonio, TX

Taylor, Donna, Ref.Libn.
NEW YORK UNIVERSITY - GRADUATE SCHOOL
OF BUSINESS ADMINISTRATION - LIBRARY □
New York, NY

Taylor, Doreen, Chf.Libn.
ONTARIO HYDRO - LIBRARY □ Toronto, ON

Taylor, Earl, Chf., Cat.
BROWN UNIVERSITY - JOHN CARTER BROWN
LIBRARY □ Providence, RI

Taylor, Eleanor, Libn.
GINN AND COMPANY - EDITORIAL LIBRARY □
Scarborough, ON

Taylor, Foli, Photograph Libn.
MINOT DAILY NEWS - LIBRARY □ Minot, ND

Taylor, Garland, Dir.
UNITED FARM WORKERS OF AMERICA, AFL-
CIO - I.C. LIBRARY □ Keene, CA

Taylor, Gay Le Cleire
WHEATON HISTORICAL ASSOCIATION -
LIBRARY & RESEARCH OFFICE □ Millville, NJ

Taylor, Gertrude, Ed.
UNIVERSITY OF SOUTHWESTERN LOUISIANA -
CENTER FOR LOUISIANA STUDIES □ Lafayette,
LA

Taylor, Gladys, Archv.
ROCHESTER INSTITUTE OF TECHNOLOGY -
WALLACE MEMORIAL LIBRARY □ Rochester, NY

Taylor, H. Leroy, Libn.
CHURCH OF JESUS CHRIST OF LATTER-DAY
SAINTS - EL PASO BRANCH GENEALOGICAL
LIBRARY □ El Paso, TX
Taylor, Helen, Supv.
ST. LOUIS PUBLIC LIBRARY - POPULAR
LIBRARY - MUSIC SECTION □ St. Louis, MO
Taylor, Joan, Act.Chf., Rd.Serv.
U.S. DEPT. OF COMMERCE - LIBRARY □
Washington, DC
Taylor, Joan R., Ref.Libn.
U.S. DEPT. OF COMMERCE - LIBRARY □
Washington, DC
Taylor, Joyce, Educ.Libn.
UNIVERSITY OF MISSISSIPPI - SCHOOL OF
EDUCATION LIBRARY □ University, MS
Taylor, Juanita, Chf.Libn.
U.S. ARMY POST - PRESIDIO OF SAN
FRANCISCO - POST LIBRARY SYSTEM □
Presidio of San Francisco, CA
Taylor, Kent J., Supv./Pk. Ranger
U.S. NATL. PARK SERVICE - FORT VANCOUVER
NATL. HISTORIC SITE - LIBRARY □ Vancouver,
WA
Taylor, Larry D., Supv., Lib.Serv.
AMERICAN HOME PRODUCTS CORPORATION -
WYETH LABORATORIES DIVISION LIBRARY □
Philadelphia, PA
Taylor, Lila, Asst.Libn.
PUTNAM COMPANIES - INVESTMENT
RESEARCH LIBRARY □ Boston, MA
Taylor, Madeline, Ser.Libn.
UNIVERSITY OF MEDICINE AND DENTISTRY OF
NEW JERSEY AT NEWARK - GEORGE F. SMITH
LIBRARY □ Newark, NJ
Taylor, Margaret P.J., Dir., Lib.Serv.
CHILDREN'S HOSPITAL OF EASTERN ONTARIO
- MEDICAL LIBRARY □ Ottawa, ON
Taylor, Marilyn, Cur., Ethnology
ST. JOSEPH MUSEUM - LIBRARY □ St. Joseph,
MO
Taylor, Marion, Hd., Coll.Plan.
UNIVERSITY OF CALIFORNIA, SANTA CRUZ -
DEAN E. MC HENRY LIBRARY □ Santa Cruz, CA
Taylor, Marion R., Tech.Serv.
EMORY UNIVERSITY - DIVISION OF LIBRARY
AND INFORMATION MANAGEMENT LIBRARY □
Atlanta, GA
Taylor, Mark-Allen, Dir., Lib.Serv.
LONG ISLAND JEWISH-HILLSIDE MEDICAL
CENTER - HEALTH SCIENCES LIBRARY □ New
Hyde Park, NY
Taylor, Mary-Stuart, Chf., Cat.
U.S. NATL. DEFENSE UNIVERSITY - LIBRARY □
Washington, DC
Taylor, Mary Virginia, Chf., Lib.Serv.
U.S. VETERANS ADMINISTRATION (TN-
Memphis) - MEDICAL CENTER LIBRARY □
Memphis, TN
Taylor, Maureen, Graphics Cur.
RHODE ISLAND HISTORICAL SOCIETY -
LIBRARY □ Providence, RI
Taylor, Nancy, Asst.Libn./Rec.Anl.
AMERICAN HEART ASSOCIATION - LIBRARY/
RECORDS CENTER □ Dallas, TX
Taylor, Norma M., Assoc.Libn.
MASSACHUSETTS STATE DEPARTMENT OF THE
ATTORNEY GENERAL - LIBRARY □ Boston, MA
Taylor, Olga, Libn.
ARLINGTON HOSPITAL - DOCTORS' LIBRARY†
□ Arlington, VA
Taylor, Phyllis, Hd., Tech.Proc.
BARBERTON PUBLIC LIBRARY - SPECIAL
COLLECTIONS □ Barberton, OH
Taylor, Rita, Libn.
STANFORD LINEAR ACCELERATOR CENTER -
LIBRARY □ Stanford, CA
Taylor, Robert, Libn.
SAN DIEGO PUBLIC LIBRARY - SCIENCE &
INDUSTRY SECTION □ San Diego, CA
Taylor, Rosemarie Kazda, Dir., Lib.Serv.
WILKES-BARRE GENERAL HOSPITAL -
HOSPITAL LIBRARY □ Wilkes-Barre, PA

Taylor, Ruth, Assoc.Libn.
WAYNE STATE UNIVERSITY - SCHOOL OF
MEDICINE - VERA PARSHALL SHIFFMAN
MEDICAL LIBRARY □ Detroit, MI
Taylor, Saundra, Cur. of Mss.
INDIANA UNIVERSITY - LILLY LIBRARY □
Bloomington, IN
Taylor, Sheri, Libn.
UNIVERSITY OF OKLAHOMA - HEALTH
SCIENCES CENTER - DEAN A. MC GEE EYE
INSTITUTE - LIBRARY □ Oklahoma City, OK
Taylor, Shirley, Co-Libn.
GREATER SOUTHEAST COMMUNITY HOSPITAL
- LURA HEALTH SCIENCES LIBRARY† □
Washington, DC
Taylor, Shirley L., Mgr.
GENERAL ELECTRIC COMPANY - TECHNICAL
INFORMATION CENTER □ St. Petersburg, FL
Taylor, Susan D., Lib.Dir.
U.S. EQUAL EMPLOYMENT OPPORTUNITY
COMMISSION - LIBRARY □ Washington, DC
Taylor, Thad, Pres.
SHAKESPEARE SOCIETY OF AMERICA - NEW
PLACE RARE BOOK LIBRARY □ Los Angeles, CA
Taylor, Vickie, Hd.Libn.
PEAT, MARWICK, MITCHELL & CO. - CENTRAL
LIBRARY† □ Los Angeles, CA
Tayyeb, Rashid, Hd., Tech.Serv.
ST. MARY'S UNIVERSITY - PATRICK POWER
LIBRARY □ Halifax, NS
Tchobanoff, James B., Mgr.
PILLSBURY COMPANY - TECHNICAL
INFORMATION CENTER □ Minneapolis, MN
Teague, Edward H., AFA Libn.
UNIVERSITY OF FLORIDA - ARCHITECTURE &
FINE ARTS LIBRARY □ Gainesville, FL
Teahan, John W., Libn.
WADSWORTH ATHENEUM - AUERBACH ART
LIBRARY □ Hartford, CT
Teare, Robert F., Asst.Dir.
THE CLAREMONT COLLEGES - LIBRARY □
Claremont, CA
Teasdale, Guy, Lib.Techn.
UNIVERSITE LAVAL - INTERNATIONAL CENTRE
FOR RESEARCH ON BILINGUALISM □ Ste. Foy,
PQ
Teasdale, Karen, Hd., Acq.Dept.
LAW SOCIETY OF UPPER CANADA - GREAT
LIBRARY □ Toronto, ON
Tebault, Hugh H., Pres.
THE LATHAM FOUNDATION - HUMAN/ANIMAL
BOND RESOURCE LIBRARY □ Alameda, CA
Tebbets, J. Steven, Biol.Techn./Libn.
U.S.D.A. - AGRICULTURAL RESEARCH SERVICE
- HORTICULTURAL CROPS RESEARCH
LABORATORY - LIBRARY □ Fresno, CA
Tebbutt, Jean M., Chf.Libn.
HAMILTON SPECTATOR - REFERENCE
LIBRARY† □ Hamilton, ON
Tebo, Jay D., Asst. Group Supv.
VITRO CORPORATION - LIBRARY □ Silver
Spring, MD
Tebo, Marlene, Hd.Libn.
UNIVERSITY OF CALIFORNIA, DAVIS -
PHYSICAL SCIENCES LIBRARY □ Davis, CA
Teclaff, Dr. Ludwik A., Prof./Law Libn.
FORDHAM UNIVERSITY - SCHOOL OF LAW
LIBRARY □ New York, NY
Tedeschi, John, Cur.
UNIVERSITY OF WISCONSIN, MADISON -
MEMORIAL LIBRARY - DEPARTMENT OF RARE
BOOKS & SPECIAL COLLECTIONS □ Madison, WI
Teel, Cora, Archv.
MARSHALL UNIVERSITY - JAMES E. MORROW
LIBRARY - SPECIAL COLLECTIONS □
Huntington, WV
Teenstra, Richard, Ref./Asst.Libn.
MARICOPA COUNTY LAW LIBRARY □ Phoenix,
AZ
Teeple, F. Diane, Chf.Libn.
CANADA - SUPREME COURT OF CANADA -
LIBRARY □ Ottawa, ON

Teer, J.G., Dir.
WELDER (Rob & Bessie) WILDLIFE
FOUNDATION - LIBRARY □ Sinton, TX
Teeter, Enola Jane N., Libn.
LONGWOOD GARDENS, INC. - LIBRARY □
Kennett Square, PA
Teffeau, Harriet, Congressional Ref.
U.S. ARMY - OFFICE OF THE CHIEF OF
ENGINEERS - LIBRARY □ Washington, DC
Tega, Vasile, Ref.Libn.
ECOLE DES HAUTES ETUDES COMMERCIALES
DE MONTREAL - BIBLIOTHEQUE □ Montreal, PQ
Teich, Steve, OHIN Coord.
OREGON HEALTH SCIENCES UNIVERSITY -
LIBRARY □ Portland, OR
Teichman, Raymond, Supv.Archv.
U.S. PRESIDENTIAL LIBRARIES - FRANKLIN D.
ROOSEVELT LIBRARY □ Hyde Park, NY
Teigen, Philip, Osler Libn.
MC GILL UNIVERSITY - OSLER LIBRARY □
Montreal, PQ
Teitelbaum, Gene W., Law Libn.
UNIVERSITY OF LOUISVILLE - SCHOOL OF LAW
LIBRARY □ Louisville, KY
Teitelbaum, Marsha, Circ.
CASE WESTERN RESERVE UNIVERSITY - LAW
SCHOOL LIBRARY† □ Cleveland, OH
Tellier, Corinne, Ref.Libn.
WINNIPEG SCHOOL DIVISION NO. 1 -
TEACHERS LIBRARY AND RESOURCE CENTRE □
Winnipeg, MB
Teloh, Mary H., Spec.Coll.Libn.
VANDERBILT UNIVERSITY - MEDICAL CENTER
LIBRARY □ Nashville, TN
Telsey, Albert, Law Ck./Libn.
SALEM COUNTY LAW LIBRARY □ Salem, NJ
Tempkin, Mrs. Elliot, Libn.
TEMPLE BETH ISRAEL - LIBRARY □ Phoenix, AZ
Templar, James E., Archv.
PROTESTANT EPISCOPAL CHURCH -
EPISCOPAL DIOCESE OF NEW YORK -
ARCHIVES □ New York, NY
Templeton, Etheldra, Dir.
MEDICAL COLLEGE OF PENNSYLVANIA -
EASTERN PENNSYLVANIA PSYCHIATRIC INST.
- MENTAL HEALTH AND NEUROSCIENCES LIB. □
Philadelphia, PA
Templin, Vivian, Act.Hd.
CATHOLIC UNIVERSITY OF AMERICA -
LIBRARY SCIENCE LIBRARY □ Washington, DC
Tener, Jean, Archv.
UNIVERSITY OF CALGARY - SPECIAL
COLLECTIONS DIVISION† □ Calgary, AB
Tennant, Ofelia, Archv.
ARCHDIOCESE OF SAN ANTONIO - CATHOLIC
ARCHIVES □ San Antonio, TX
Tennenhouse, Michael, Pub.Serv.Libn.
UNIVERSITY OF MANITOBA - MEDICAL
LIBRARY □ Winnipeg, MB
Tenner, Patricia, Libn.
U.S. GEOLOGICAL SURVEY - LIBRARY □ Austin,
TX
Tenny, Dana, Libn.
TORONTO PUBLIC LIBRARY - CANADIANA
COLLECTION OF CHILDREN'S BOOKS □ Toronto,
ON
Tenny, Dana, Libn.
TORONTO PUBLIC LIBRARY - LILLIAN H. SMITH
COLLECTION OF CHILDREN'S BOOKS □ Toronto,
ON
Tenny, Dana, Libn.
TORONTO PUBLIC LIBRARY - OSBORNE
COLLECTION OF EARLY CHILDREN'S BOOKS □
Toronto, ON
Tepper, Herbert J., Cat.Libn.
STATE HISTORICAL SOCIETY OF WISCONSIN -
LIBRARY □ Madison, WI
Tepper, Jean, Lib.Asst.
GULF CANADA LIMITED - CENTRAL LIBRARY† □
Toronto, ON
Teranis, Mara, Sr.Info.Sci.
JOHNSON (S.C.) AND SON, INC. - TECHNICAL &
BUSINESS INFORMATION CENTER □ Racine, WI

Termine, Jack E., Med.Libn.
NEW YORK ORTHOPAEDIC HOSPITAL - RUSSELL A. HIBBS MEMORIAL LIBRARY □ New York, NY

Ternes, Mary, Rd.Adv.
DISTRICT OF COLUMBIA PUBLIC LIBRARY - WASHINGTONIANA DIVISION □ Washington, DC

Ternisien, Robert, Supv., Music Copyrights
CANADIAN BROADCASTING CORPORATION - MUSIC SERVICES LIBRARY □ Montreal, PQ

Terpo, Mary A., Law Libn.
WORCESTER LAW LIBRARY □ Worcester, MA

Terrell, Ann, Govt.Ref.Libn.
SAN DIEGO COUNTY LIBRARY - GOVERNMENTAL REFERENCE LIBRARY □ San Diego, CA

Terrell, Emily T., Libn.
UNIVERSITY OF OKLAHOMA - SCIENCE AND PUBLIC POLICY PROGRAM - LIBRARY □ Norman, OK

Terrell, Gisela, Rare Bks./Spec.Coll.Libn.
BUTLER UNIVERSITY - IRWIN LIBRARY - HUGH THOMAS MILLER RARE BOOK ROOM □ Indianapolis, IN

Terrell, Sara Beth, Archv.
EARLHAM COLLEGE - QUAKER COLLECTION □ Richmond, IN

Terreo, John, Lib.Asst.
MEMPHIS STATE UNIVERSITY LIBRARIES - SPECIAL COLLECTIONS □ Memphis, TN

Terrill, Marjorie L., Med.Libn.
MENORAH MEDICAL CENTER - ROBERT UHLMAN MEDICAL LIBRARY □ Kansas City, MO

Terry, Anita, Hd., Info.Serv.
MAYO FOUNDATION - MAYO CLINIC LIBRARY □ Rochester, MN

Terry, Blanche, Res.Dir.
VICKSBURG & WARREN COUNTY HISTORICAL SOCIETY - MC CARDLE LIBRARY □ Vicksburg, MS

Terry, Carol, Ser.Libn.
ART INSTITUTE OF CHICAGO - RYERSON AND BURNHAM LIBRARIES □ Chicago, IL

Terry, Constance J., Archv.
OYSTERPONDS HISTORICAL SOCIETY - LIBRARY □ Orient, NY

Terry, Edward S., Dir.
JOHNS HOPKINS UNIVERSITY - SCHOOL OF HYGIENE AND PUBLIC HEALTH - INTERDEPARTMENTAL LIBRARY □ Baltimore, MD

Terry, Gail S., Asst.Archv.
COLONIAL WILLIAMSBURG - RESEARCH LIBRARY & ARCHIVES† □ Williamsburg, VA

Terry, George D., Dir./Archv.
UNIVERSITY OF SOUTH CAROLINA - UNIVERSITY ARCHIVES □ Columbia, SC

Terry, Joan N., Libn.
NORTHEAST UTILITIES SERVICE COMPANY - LIBRARY □ Hartford, CT

Terry, Juan E., Med.Libn.
U.S. NAVY - NAVAL HOSPITAL (FL-Pensacola) - MEDICAL LIBRARY □ Pensacola, FL

Terry, Mary Jo, Libn.
DISNEY (Walt) PRODUCTIONS - LIBRARY □ Burbank, CA

Terry, Nancy L., Asst.Med.Libn.
WASHINGTON HOSPITAL CENTER - MEDICAL LIBRARY □ Washington, DC

Terry, Rita
U.S. NATL. OCEANIC & ATMOSPHERIC ADMINISTRATION - ASSESSMENT AND INFORMATION SERVICES CENTER □ Columbia, MO

Terry, Roslyn M., Libn.
CONVERSE CONSULTANTS - LIBRARY† □ Caldwell, NJ

Terry, Vivian, Dir.
HARPER-GRACE HOSPITALS - DRUG INFORMATION CENTER □ Detroit, MI

Terryberry, Ann B., Dir., Tech.Serv./Cur.
NORTH ADAMS STATE COLLEGE - EUGENE L. FREEL LIBRARY - SPECIAL COLLECTIONS □ North Adams, MA

Tersillo, Frances, User Serv.Libn.
U.S. FOOD & DRUG ADMINISTRATION - CENTER FOR FOOD SAFETY & APPLIED NUTRITION - LIBRARY □ Washington, DC

Terstegge, Mary Anne, Hist.Libn.
TULARE COUNTY FREE LIBRARY - CALIFORNIA HISTORICAL RESEARCH COLLECTION - ANNIE R. MITCHELL ROOM □ Visalia, CA

Tertell, Susan, Asst.Dept.Hd.
MINNEAPOLIS PUBLIC LIBRARY & INFORMATION CENTER - TECHNOLOGY AND SCIENCE DEPARTMENT □ Minneapolis, MN

Terzian, Sherry, Dir.
NEUROPSYCHIATRIC INSTITUTE - MENTAL HEALTH INFORMATION SERVICE □ Los Angeles, CA

Tesmer, Nancy S., Chf., Lib.Serv.
U.S. VETERANS ADMINISTRATION (OH-Brecksville) - HOSPITAL LIBRARY □ Brecksville, OH

Tesmer, Nancy S., Chf.Libn.
U.S. VETERANS ADMINISTRATION (OH-Cleveland) - HOSPITAL LIBRARY □ Cleveland, OH

Tessaro, Mary Anne, Canadian Lit.Spec.
METROPOLITAN TORONTO LIBRARY - LITERATURE DEPARTMENT □ Toronto, ON

Tessier, Conrad, Lib.Techn.
CENTRE HOSPITALIER JACQUES-VIGER - CENTRE DE DOCUMENTATION □ Montreal, PQ

Tessler, Helene L., Cur.-Libn.
BRISTOL HISTORICAL AND PRESERVATION SOCIETY - LIBRARY □ Bristol, RI

Testa, Dana D., AV Serv.
UNIVERSITY OF OKLAHOMA - HEALTH SCIENCES CENTER LIBRARY □ Oklahoma City, OK

Testa, Elizabeth, Sr.Libn.
CALIFORNIA STATE POSTSECONDARY EDUCATION COMMISSION - LIBRARY □ Sacramento, CA

Tester, Ronald L., Libn.
BAUDER FASHION COLLEGE - LIBRARY □ Arlington, TX

Teter, Cynthia A., Lrng.Ctr.Instr.
EL CENTRO JOBS TRAINING CENTER - LEARNING RESOURCE CENTER □ Dallas, TX

Tetrault, Susan, Libn.
LAS CRUCES PUBLIC SCHOOL TEACHERS' CENTER - TOY LENDING LIBRARY & EARLY CHILDHOOD RESOURCE CENTER □ Las Cruces, NM

Tew, Robin L., Libn.
NATIONAL ASSOCIATION OF INSURANCE COMMISSIONERS - NAIC INFORMATION CENTER □ Kansas City, MO

Thackery, David T., Libn.
CENTER FOR THE STUDY OF ETHICS IN THE PROFESSIONS - LIBRARY □ Chicago, IL

Thackray, Dr. Arnold W., Dir.
UNIVERSITY OF PENNSYLVANIA - CENTER FOR THE HISTORY OF CHEMISTRY □ Philadelphia, PA

Thackray, Dr. Arnold W., Cur.
UNIVERSITY OF PENNSYLVANIA - EDGAR FAHS SMITH MEMORIAL COLLECTION IN THE HISTORY OF CHEMISTRY □ Philadelphia, PA

Thaker, Virbala, Govt.Doc.
WHITTIER COLLEGE - SCHOOL OF LAW - LIBRARY □ Los Angeles, CA

Thalacker, Lois, Libn.
ALLEN MEMORIAL HOSPITAL - HEALTH SCIENCES LIBRARY □ Waterloo, IA

Thaler, Renee R., Libn.
NDC/FEDERAL SYSTEMS, INC. - LIBRARY □ Rockville, MD

Thaler, Ruth E., Ed.
AMERICAN NATIONAL METRIC COUNCIL - LIBRARY □ Bethesda, MD

Thaper, Shashi P., Hd.Libn.
MARYLAND STATE DEPARTMENT OF NATURAL RESOURCES - LIBRARY □ Annapolis, MD

Tharaud, Cynthia M., Dir.
MUNRO (Dr. E.H.) MEDICAL LIBRARY □ Grand Junction, CO

Tharp, Sonny, Asst.Libn.
COURIER-JOURNAL AND LOUISVILLE TIMES - LIBRARY □ Louisville, KY

Thatcher, Linda, Acq.Libn.
UTAH STATE HISTORICAL SOCIETY - RESEARCH LIBRARY □ Salt Lake City, UT

Thauberger, Marianne, Libn.
UNIVERSITY OF REGINA - EDUCATION BRANCH LIBRARY □ Regina, SK

Thav, Aliza, Asst.Libn.
BALTIMORE HEBREW COLLEGE - JOSEPH MEYERHOFF LIBRARY □ Baltimore, MD

Thaxton, Carol J., Hd.Libn.
FEDERAL RESERVE BANK OF ST. LOUIS - RESEARCH LIBRARY □ St. Louis, MO

Thayer, Candace W., Libn.
ST. MARY'S HEALTH CENTER - HEALTH SCIENCES LIBRARY □ St. Louis, MO

The-Mulliner, Lian, Hd.
OHIO UNIVERSITY - SOUTHEAST ASIA COLLECTION □ Athens, OH

Theall, John N., Assoc.Univ.Libn.Pub.Serv.
UNIVERSITY OF ILLINOIS AT CHICAGO - HEALTH SCIENCES CENTER - LIBRARY OF THE HEALTH SCIENCES □ Chicago, IL

Theberge, Guy, Sec.
COLLEGE DE STE-ANNE-DE-LA-POCATIERE - SOCIETE HISTORIQUE-DE-LA-COTE-DU-SUD - BIBLIOTHEQUE □ La Pocatiere, PQ

Theeler, Bernice, Libn.
BETHLEHEM LUTHERAN CHURCH - LIBRARY □ Aberdeen, SD

Thegze, Kathryn, Libn.
HAMMOND HISTORICAL SOCIETY - CALUMET ROOM □ Hammond, IN

Theil, Edna, Br.Asst.
SAN DIEGO COUNTY LAW LIBRARY - EAST COUNTY BRANCH □ El Cajon, CA

Theil, Gordon, Asst. Music Libn.
UNIVERSITY OF CALIFORNIA, LOS ANGELES - MUSIC LIBRARY □ Los Angeles, CA

Theis, Sandra, Med.Libn.
RIVERSIDE METHODIST HOSPITAL - D.J. VINCENT MEDICAL LIBRARY □ Columbus, OH

Thelin, John, Co-Dir.
MARQUANDIA SOCIETY FOR STUDIES IN HISTORY AND LITERATURE - LIBRARY □ Williamsburg, VA

Theobald, H. Rupert, Chf., Lib. & Ref.Sects.
WISCONSIN STATE LEGISLATIVE REFERENCE BUREAU □ Madison, WI

Theodos, Cytheria, Dir.Info.Serv.
DREYFUS CORPORATION - INFORMATION CENTER □ New York, NY

Theodosette, Sr. M., Archv.
SISTERS OF THE HOLY FAMILY OF NAZARETH - IMMACULATE CONCEPTION B.V.M. - ARCHIVES □ Philadelphia, PA

Theologides, Maro, Supv., Lib.Info.Serv.
HONEYWELL, INC. - SYSTEMS & RESEARCH CENTER - LIBRARY □ Minneapolis, MN

Therrien, Elyse, Libn.
DOMTAR, INC. - CENTRAL LIBRARY □ Montreal, PQ

Therrien, Kathy, Film Coord.
SCARBOROUGH PUBLIC LIBRARY - FILM SERVICES □ Scarborough, ON

Theus, Pamela, Hd.Libn.
BEREAN INSTITUTE - LIBRARY □ Philadelphia, PA

Thevenet, Susanne D., Law Libn.
DOW, LOHNES & ALBERTSON - LAW LIBRARY □ Washington, DC

Thews, Dorothy D., Dept.Hd.
MINNEAPOLIS PUBLIC LIBRARY & INFORMATION CENTER - LITERATURE AND LANGUAGE DEPARTMENT □ Minneapolis, MN

Thibault, Marie-Therese, Ref.
QUEBEC PROVINCE - MINISTERE DES AFFAIRES CULTURELLES - CENTRE DE DOCUMENTATION† □ Quebec, PQ

Thibault, Solange, Per.
CEGEP DE TROIS-RIVIERES - BIBLIOTHEQUE □ Trois-Rivieres, PQ

Thibodeau, Patricia L., Dir.
MOUNTAIN AREA HEALTH EDUCATION CENTER - INFORMATION & MEDIA SERVICES □ Asheville, NC

Thibodeau, Ralph, Prof. of Music/Libn.
DEL MAR COLLEGE - MUSIC LIBRARY □ Corpus Christi, TX

Thiedeman, Mary P., Hd., Ref.
WEST VIRGINIA WESLEYAN COLLEGE - ANNIE MERNER PFEIFFER LIBRARY □ Buckhannon, WV

Thiegs, Francis J., Hd., Tech.Serv.
NEW YORK UNIVERSITY MEDICAL CENTER - FREDERICK L. EHRMAN MEDICAL LIBRARY □ New York, NY

Thiel, Ronald E., Dir.
SOD TOWN PIONEER HOMESTEAD MUSEUM - LIBRARY □ Colby, KS

Thiel, Sara Goodwin, Photography Libn.
HELLMUTH, OBATA & KASSABAUM, INC. - HOK LIBRARY □ St. Louis, MO

Thiele, Judith C., Ref. & Coll.Libn.
UNIVERSITY OF BRITISH COLUMBIA - CHARLES CRANE MEMORIAL LIBRARY □ Vancouver, BC

Thiele, Paul E., Libn. & Hd.
UNIVERSITY OF BRITISH COLUMBIA - CHARLES CRANE MEMORIAL LIBRARY □ Vancouver, BC

Thielges, Kathleen, Asst.Libn.
OPPENHEIMER, WOLFF, FOSTER, SHEPARD & DONNELLY - LIBRARY □ St. Paul, MN

Thieme, Mary S., Cur.
CUMBERLAND MUSEUM AND SCIENCE CENTER - DYER MEMORIAL LIBRARY □ Nashville, TN

Thierer, Joyce, Pub.Serv.
WAYNE STATE COLLEGE - U.S. CONN LIBRARY □ Wayne, NE

Thiesson, Mrs. A., Libn.
WINNIPEG DEPARTMENT OF ENVIRONMENTAL PLANNING - LIBRARY† □ Winnipeg, MB

Thirlwall, David, Ref.Libn.
UNIVERSITY OF MANITOBA - D.S. WOODS EDUCATION LIBRARY □ Winnipeg, MB

Thistle, Dawn R., Music & Visual Arts Libn.
COLLEGE OF THE HOLY CROSS - FENWICK MUSIC LIBRARY □ Worcester, MA

Thoele, Sylvia, Media Libn.
U.S. VETERANS ADMINISTRATION (IL-North Chicago) - HOSPITAL LIBRARY □ North Chicago, IL

Thoelke, Elizabeth, Coll.Dev.
WAYNE STATE COLLEGE - U.S. CONN LIBRARY □ Wayne, NE

Thom, Janice, Res.Libn.
PEAT, MARWICK, MITCHELL & CO. - INFORMATION AND RESEARCH CENTER □ New York, NY

Thom, Rupert C., Libn.
U.S. AIR FORCE BASE - ENGLAND BASE LIBRARY† □ England AFB, LA

Thoma, Dale B., Dir.
LEXINGTON-FAYETTE URBAN COUNTY PLANNING COMMISSION - TECHNICAL INFORMATION LIBRARY □ Lexington, KY

Thomann, Dorothy, Libn.
HUFFMAN MEMORIAL UNITED METHODIST CHURCH - LIBRARY □ St. Joseph, MO

Thomas, Alfred, Jr., Univ.Archv.
ARIZONA STATE UNIVERSITY - UNIVERSITY ARCHIVES □ Tempe, AZ

Thomas, Alfred M., Hd.Libn.
ARKANSAS GAZETTE - NEWS LIBRARY □ Little Rock, AR

Thomas, Audrey, Regional Libn.
ENVIRONMENTAL PROTECTION AGENCY - REGION II LIBRARY □ New York, NY

Thomas, Barbara, Ref.
TEXAS A & M UNIVERSITY - MEDICAL SCIENCES LIBRARY □ College Station, TX

Thomas, Becky C., Music Libn.
MOUNT UNION COLLEGE - STURGEON MUSIC LIBRARY □ Alliance, OH

Thomas, Charles R., Exec.Dir.
CAUSE - LIBRARY □ Boulder, CO

Thomas, Cherry L., Act. Law Libn.
UNIVERSITY OF ALABAMA - SCHOOL OF LAW LIBRARY □ University, AL

Thomas, D.A., Info.Serv.
UNIVERSITY OF KANSAS MEDICAL CTR. - COLLEGE OF HEALTH SCI. AND HOSPITAL - ARCHIE R. DYKES LIB. OF THE HEALTH SCI. □ Kansas City, KS

Thomas, Darcus, Libn.
CALIFORNIA MARITIME ACADEMY LIBRARY □ Vallejo, CA

Thomas, David, Cur.
CANFIELD MEMORIAL LIBRARY - RUSSELL VERMONTIANA COLLECTION □ Arlington, VT

Thomas, David A., Law Libn.
BRIGHAM YOUNG UNIVERSITY - J. REUBEN CLARK LAW SCHOOL LIBRARY □ Provo, UT

Thomas, David H., Hd., Tech.Serv.
MICHIGAN TECHNOLOGICAL UNIVERSITY - LIBRARY □ Houghton, MI

Thomas, Deborah W., Res.Assoc.
GEORGIA INSTITUTE OF TECHNOLOGY - SYSTEMS ENGINEERING LABORATORY - TECHNICAL INFORMATION CENTER □ Atlanta, GA

Thomas, Diana P., Med.Libn.
HENROTIN HOSPITAL - MEDICAL LIBRARY □ Chicago, IL

Thomas, Doris Byrd, Libn.
CARTER (William) COLLEGE & EVANGELICAL THEOLOGICAL SEMINARY - WAGNER-KEVETTER LIBRARY □ Goldsboro, NC

Thomas, Eileen, Cat.
UNIVERSITY OF DAYTON - SCHOOL OF EDUCATION - CURRICULUM MATERIALS CENTER □ Dayton, OH

Thomas, Ellen, Libn.
CORNELL UNIVERSITY - PHYSICAL SCIENCES LIBRARY □ Ithaca, NY

Thomas, Frances, Libn.
BATON ROUGE STATE-TIMES & MORNING ADVOCATE NEWSPAPERS - LIBRARY □ Baton Rouge, LA

Thomas, Gloria, Ref.
U.S. FEDERAL COMMUNICATIONS COMMISSION - LIBRARY† □ Washington, DC

Thomas, Gordon B., Dir.
U.S. DEPT. OF COMMERCE - INTERNATIONAL TRADE ADMINISTRATION - CINCINNATI DISTRICT OFFICE LIBRARY □ Cincinnati, OH

Thomas, Greg, Asst.Libn.
AMARILLO PUBLIC LIBRARY - LOCAL HISTORY COLLECTION □ Amarillo, TX

Thomas, Helvi, Health Sci.Libn.
SCARBOROUGH GENERAL HOSPITAL - HEALTH SCIENCES LIBRARY □ Scarborough, ON

Thomas, Hugh, Med.Libn.
EYE FOUNDATION HOSPITAL - JOHN E. MEYER EYE FOUNDATION LIBRARY† □ Birmingham, AL

Thomas, J., Pub.Serv.
ALBERTA - DEPARTMENT OF THE ENVIRONMENT - LIBRARY □ Edmonton, AB

Thomas, James L., Libn.
TEXAS WOMAN'S UNIVERSITY - LIBRARY SCIENCE LIBRARY □ Denton, TX

Thomas, Jeanne F., Libn.
MICHIGAN STATE DEPARTMENT OF TRANSPORTATION - TRANSPORTATION LIBRARY □ Lansing, MI

Thomas, Joan L., Dir., Med.Rec.
NORTH TEXAS MEDICAL CENTER - MEDICAL LIBRARY □ McKinney, TX

Thomas, Joe D., Chf.
U.S. NATL. ARCHIVES & RECORDS SERVICE - STILL PICTURE BRANCH □ Washington, DC

Thomas, Joy, Supv., Ref.
TORONTO BOARD OF EDUCATION - EDUCATION CENTRE LIBRARY □ Toronto, ON

Thomas, Karol, Coord., Lib.Serv.
SAN MATEO COUNTY EDUCATIONAL RESOURCES CENTER □ Redwood City, CA

Thomas, Katharine S., Info.Sci.
LAWLER MATUSKY & SKELLY ENGINEERS - LIBRARY □ Pearl River, NY

Thomas, Kenneth H., Jr., Hist.
GEORGIA STATE DEPARTMENT OF NATURAL RESOURCES - PARKS AND HISTORICAL SITES DIV. - HISTORIC PRESERVATION SECTION □ Atlanta, GA

Thomas, Mrs. Kodell M., Chf., Lib.Serv.
U.S. VETERANS ADMINISTRATION (GA-Dublin) - CENTER LIBRARY □ Dublin, GA

Thomas, Linda Charlmyra, Med.Libn.
MERRITT (Samuel) HOSPITAL - MEDICAL LIBRARY □ Oakland, CA

Thomas, Lou, Lib.Dir.
BATON ROUGE STATE-TIMES & MORNING ADVOCATE NEWSPAPERS - LIBRARY □ Baton Rouge, LA

Thomas, Lucy, Libn.
UNIVERSITY OF PITTSBURGH - GRADUATE SCHOOL OF PUBLIC & INTERNATIONAL AFFAIRS LIBRARY □ Pittsburgh, PA

Thomas, Marcia M., Lib.Dir.
CLEVELAND CHIROPRACTIC COLLEGE - LIBRARY □ Kansas City, MO

Thomas, Margaret A., Libn.
JOHNSON & WALES COLLEGE - PAUL FRITZSCHE LIBRARY □ Cranston RI

Thomas, Mary E., Assoc.Libn.
CORNELL UNIVERSITY - PHYSICAL SCIENCES LIBRARY □ Ithaca, NY

Thomas, Mary Lou, Cur.
CANFIELD MEMORIAL LIBRARY - RUSSELL VERMONTIANA COLLECTION □ Arlington, VT

Thomas, Michele R., Corp.Libn./Editor
SPS TECHNOLOGIES, INC. - RESEARCH AND DEVELOPMENT LABORATORIES - CORPORATE TECHNICAL LIBRARY □ Jenkintown, PA

Thomas, Page, Tech.Serv. & ILL
SOUTHERN METHODIST UNIVERSITY - PERKINS SCHOOL OF THEOLOGY - LIBRARY □ Dallas, TX

Thomas, Patsy, Curriculum Spec.
BUTTE COUNTY SUPERINTENDENT OF SCHOOLS - NORTHERN CALIFORNIA CENTER FOR EDUCATIONAL IMPROVEMENT □ Oroville, CA

Thomas, Paul W., Dir.
WESLEYAN CHURCH - ARCHIVES & HISTORICAL LIBRARY □ Marion, IN

Thomas, Paulette, Libn.
VIRGINIA STATE LIBRARY FOR THE VISUALLY AND PHYSICALLY HANDICAPPED □ Richmond, VA

Thomas, Pearl M., Libn.
PHILOSOPHICAL RESEARCH SOCIETY - RESEARCH LIBRARY □ Los Angeles, CA

Thomas, Robert M., Asst.Chf.
NEW YORK PUBLIC LIBRARY - MID-MANHATTAN LIBRARY □ New York, NY

Thomas, Sharon, Asst.Libn.
SCARRITT COLLEGE FOR CHRISTIAN WORKERS - VIRGINIA DAVIS LASKEY LIBRARY □ Nashville, TN

Thomas, Susan, Dp. State Libn.
STATE LIBRARY OF OHIO □ Columbus, OH

Thomas, Thedosia, Color Slide Ed.
U.S.D.A. - PHOTOGRAPHY DIVISION - PHOTOGRAPH LIBRARY □ Washington, DC

Thomas, Vi, Lib.Techn.
WESTERN STATE HOSPITAL - MEDICAL LIBRARY □ Fort Supply, OK

Thomas, Virginia, Govt.Doc.Libn.
ILLINOIS INSTITUTE OF TECHNOLOGY - CHICAGO KENT LAW SCHOOL - LIBRARY† □ Chicago, IL

Thomasch, Jeannine R., Libn.
CHADBOURNE, PARKE, WHITESIDE, & WOLFF - LIBRARY □ New York, NY

Thompson, Barbara, Libn.
NEW BRUNSWICK ASSOCIATION OF REGISTERED NURSES - LIBRARY □ Fredericton, NB

Thompson, Barbara E., Lib.Tech.Serv.
HARRISBURG HOSPITAL - LIBRARY/MEDIA SERVICES □ Harrisburg, PA

Thompson, Barbara J., Libn.
ECONOMICS RESEARCH ASSOCIATES - LIBRARY □ Los Angeles, CA

Thompson, Benna Brodsky, Libn.
U.S.D.A. - AGRICULTURAL RESEARCH SERVICE - SOUTH ATLANTIC AREA - RICHARD B. RUSSELL AGRI. RESEARCH CTR. LIB. □ Athens, GA

Thompson, Berneice, Libn.
HUSSON COLLEGE - LIBRARY □ Bangor, ME

Thompson, Bert A., Dir., Lib.Serv.
ILLINOIS BENEDICTINE COLLEGE - THEODORE LOWNIK LIBRARY □ Lisle, IL

Thompson, C.M., Dir.
UNIVERSITY OF OKLAHOMA - HEALTH SCIENCES CENTER LIBRARY □ Oklahoma City, OK

Thompson, Clare T., Libn.
SPERRY - BUSINESS PLANNING LIBRARY □ New York, NY

Thompson, Connie B., Assoc.Libn.
FEDERAL RESERVE BANK OF RICHMOND - RESEARCH LIBRARY □ Richmond, VA

Thompson, D., Asst.Mgr.
STANDARDS COUNCIL OF CANADA - STANDARDS INFORMATION DIVISION □ Ottawa, ON

Thompson, Mrs. D.A., Dir. of Pharmacy Serv.
ST. JOSEPH'S HOSPITAL - DRUG INFORMATION CENTRE □ Hamilton, ON

Thompson, David, Fld.Serv.Libn.
FLORIDA STATE DIVISION OF BLIND SERVICES - FLORIDA REGIONAL LIB. FOR THE BLIND & PHYSICALLY HANDICAPPED □ Daytona Beach, FL

Thompson, Deborah A., Base Libn.
U.S. AIR FORCE BASE - WHEELER BASE LIBRARY† □ Wheeler AFB, HI

Thompson, Diane, Ck.
NORTHWEST TERRITORIES - SAFETY DIVISION - OCCUPATIONAL HEALTH & SAFETY RESOURCE CENTRE □ Yellowknife, NT

Thompson, Dianne G., Lib.Dir.
U.S. NAVY - NAVAL SCHOOL - CIVIL ENGINEER CORPS OFFICERS - MOREELL LIBRARY □ Port Hueneme, CA

Thompson, Donald, Bus.Libn.
SOUTHERN ILLINOIS UNIVERSITY, EDWARDSVILLE - SOCIAL SCIENCE/ BUSINESS/MAP LIBRARY† □ Edwardsville, IL

Thompson, Eleanor E., Dir.
WENHAM HISTORICAL ASSOCIATION AND MUSEUM - COLONEL TIMOTHY PICKERING LIBRARY □ Wenham, MA

Thompson, Eleanor M., Libn., Print Bk.
DU PONT (Henry Francis) WINTERTHUR MUSEUM - LIBRARY □ Winterthur, DE

Thompson, Elizabeth M., Media Serv.Libn.
UNIVERSITY OF THE DISTRICT OF COLUMBIA - HARVARD STREET LIBRARY† □ Washington, DC

Thompson, F.H., Law Libn.
SOUTH TEXAS COLLEGE OF LAW - LIBRARY □ Houston, TX

Thompson, Frances, Libn.
ONTARIO - MINISTRY OF COMMUNITY AND SOCIAL SERVICES - RESOURCE LIBRARY □ Woodstock, ON

Thompson, Genevieve, Soc. Worker
ORPHAN VOYAGE - KAMMANDALE LIBRARY □ St. Paul, MN

Thompson, George W., Info.Sci.
MILES LABORATORIES, INC. - LIBRARY RESOURCES AND SERVICES □ Elkhart, IN

Thompson, Gregory C., Asst.Dir., Spec.Coll.
UNIVERSITY OF UTAH - SPECIAL COLLECTIONS DEPARTMENT □ Salt Lake City, UT

Thompson, H.G., Central Files Spec.
CHEVRON RESEARCH COMPANY - TECHNICAL INFORMATION CENTER □ Richmond, CA

Thompson, Harry F., Archv.
PROTESTANT EPISCOPAL CHURCH - EPISCOPAL DIOCESE OF SOUTH DAKOTA - ARCHIVES □ Sioux Falls, SD

Thompson, Jan, Sys.Libn.
GPU NUCLEAR - HEADQUARTERS LIBRARY □ Parsippany, NJ

Thompson, Jan, Libn.
GPU NUCLEAR - LIBRARY □ Reading, PA

Thompson, Jeanne, Supv., Info.Serv.
DIGITAL EQUIPMENT CORPORATION - MAYNARD AREA INFORMATION SERVICES □ Maynard, MA

Thompson, Johanna, Asst.Libn.
DELAWARE LAW SCHOOL OF WIDENER UNIVERSITY - LAW LIBRARY □ Wilmington, DE

Thompson, John, Tech.Serv.
WHEATON COLLEGE - BILLY GRAHAM CENTER - LIBRARY □ Wheaton, IL

Thompson, John L., Mgr.
GENERAL MOTORS CORPORATION - CURRENT PRODUCT ENGINEERING - INFORMATION MANAGEMENT □ Warren, MI

Thompson, Karl, Act. Map Cur.
WESTERN WASHINGTON UNIVERSITY - DEPARTMENT OF GEOGRAPHY AND REGIONAL PLANNING - MAP LIBRARY □ Bellingham, WA

Thompson, Kathleen, Dir.
THE INTERNATIONAL UNIVERSITY - INTERNATIONAL RELATIONS LIBRARY AND RESEARCH CENTER □ Independence, MO

Thompson, Laura, DTIC Oper.
U.S. NAVY - NAVAL COASTAL SYSTEMS CENTER - TECHNICAL INFORMATION SERVICES BRANCH† □ Panama City, FL

Thompson, Linda L., Law Libn.
WORLD BANK LAW LIBRARY □ Washington, DC

Thompson, Linda S., Libn.
MUSKEGON CHRONICLE - EDITORIAL LIBRARY □ Muskegon, MI

Thompson, Mary, Libn.
WOODVILLE STATE HOSPITAL - PROFESSIONAL LIBRARY† □ Carnegie, PA

Thompson, O., Microforms
UNIVERSITY OF WISCONSIN, LA CROSSE - MURPHY LIBRARY □ La Crosse, WI

Thompson, Pat, Info.Spec.
CRAVATH, SWAINE, & MOORE - LAW LIBRARY □ New York, NY

Thompson, Peggy, Exec.Dir.
ST. LOUIS HEARING AND SPEECH CENTER - LIBRARY □ St. Louis, MO

Thompson, Phillip, Archv.
BAYLOR UNIVERSITY - CONGRESSIONAL COLLECTION □ Waco, TX

Thompson, Mrs. R., Assoc.Dir.
CANADA - ENVIRONMENT CANADA - LIBRARY SERVICES BRANCH □ Ottawa, ON

Thompson, Richard, Libn.
HAWAII STATE DEPARTMENT OF ACCOUNTING AND GENERAL SERVICES - PUBLIC ARCHIVES □ Honolulu, HI

Thompson, Richard M., Musm.Dir.
GEORGIA-PACIFIC CORPORATION - HISTORICAL MUSEUM □ Portland, OR

Thompson, Roger S., Libn.
FERMI NATIONAL ACCELERATOR LABORATORY - LIBRARY □ Batavia, IL

Thompson, Rose, Libn.
BARLOW HOSPITAL - ELKS LIBRARY □ Los Angeles, CA

Thompson, Rose F., Tech.Serv.Libn.
MAINE MEDICAL CENTER - LIBRARY □ Portland, ME

Thompson, Ruth Margaret, Dir.
CANADA - EXTERNAL AFFAIRS CANADA - LIBRARY □ Ottawa, ON

Thompson, Sandra, Bibliog.Asst.
TEMPLE UNIVERSITY - CENTRAL LIBRARY SYSTEM - MATHEMATICAL SCIENCES LIBRARY □ Philadelphia, PA

Thompson, Sara, Libn.
UNIVERSITY OF HAWAII - INSTITUTE FOR ASTRONOMY - MAUNA KEA OBSERVATORY - LIBRARY □ Hilo, HI

Thompson, Sheila, Libn.
VANCOUVER PUBLIC LIBRARY - BUSINESS & ECONOMICS DIVISION □ Vancouver, BC

Thompson, Sheila H., Per./ILL Libn.
U.S. VETERANS ADMINISTRATION (NC-Durham) - MEDICAL CENTER LIBRARY □ Durham, NC

Thompson, Susan, Ref.Libn.
RUSH-PRESBYTERIAN-ST. LUKE'S MEDICAL CENTER - LIBRARY OF RUSH UNIVERSITY □ Chicago, IL

Thompson, Susan J., Sci.Libn.
INDIANA STATE UNIVERSITY - SCIENCE LIBRARY □ Terre Haute, IN

Thompson, Mrs. Terry, Archv.
ANGLICAN CHURCH OF CANADA - GENERAL SYNOD ARCHIVES □ Toronto, ON

Thompson, Mrs. Vernese B., Cons.
U.S. MARINE CORPS - CAMP PENDLETON LIBRARY SYSTEM □ Camp Pendleton, CA

Thompson, William P., Libn.
PIEDMONT BIBLE COLLEGE - GEORGE M. MANUEL MEMORIAL LIBRARY □ Winston-Salem, NC

Thoms, Nancy, Libn.
INDIANA STATE LEGISLATIVE SERVICES AGENCY - OFFICE OF CODE REVISION - LIBRARY □ Indianapolis, IN

Thomsen, Odelta A., Libn.
BILLINGS GAZETTE - NEWS LIBRARY □ Billings, MT

Thomson, Ashley, Hd., Ref. & Circ.
LAURENTIAN UNIVERSITY - MAIN LIBRARY □ Sudbury, ON

Thomson, Carol, Dir. of Pub.Aff.
PUBLIC/PRIVATE VENTURES - RESOURCE CENTER □ Philadelphia, PA

Thomson, Dorothy, Asst.Libn., Coll.
UNIVERSITY OF OTTAWA - MORISSET LIBRARY □ Ottawa, ON

Thomson, Mrs. Marion, Libn.
CANADA - NATIONAL DEFENCE - CANADIAN FORCES MEDICAL SERVICES SCHOOL - LIBRARY† □ Borden, ON

Thomson, R.S., Tech.Info.Spec.
MOBIL RESEARCH & DEVELOPMENT CORPORATION - OFFSHORE ENGINEERING INFORMATION CENTER† □ Dallas, TX

Thomson, Sharon, Libn.
INSTITUTE OF OCEAN SCIENCES - LIBRARY □ Sidney, BC

Thorkildson, Terry A., Dir. & Assoc.Prof.
UNIVERSITY OF VIRGINIA - MEDICAL CENTER - CLAUDE MOORE HEALTH SCIENCES LIBRARY □ Charlottesville, VA

Thorleifson, Mary Claire, Libn.
NORTH DAKOTA STATE UNIVERSITY - BOTTINEAU BRANCH AND INSTITUTE OF FORESTRY - LIBRARY □ Bottineau, ND

Thorn, Cecelia, Ser.Libn.
U.S. ARMY - MISSILE COMMAND & MARSHALL SPACE FLIGHT CENTER - REDSTONE SCIENTIFIC INFORMATION CENTER □ Redstone Arsenal, AL

Thornbury, Sedgley, Pres.
PATRIOTIC EDUCATION, INC. - LIBRARY □ Daytona Beach, FL

Thorne, Janis N., Law Libn.
TEXAS STATE - COURT OF APPEALS - 7TH SUPREME JUDICIAL DISTRICT AND POTTER COUNTY - LAW LIBRARY □ Amarillo, TX

Thorne, Shirley, Ref.
NORTHWESTERN OKLAHOMA STATE UNIVERSITY - LIBRARY □ Alva, OK

Thorngate, Janet, Libn.
SEVENTH DAY BAPTIST HISTORICAL SOCIETY
- LIBRARY □ Janesville, WI

Thornlow, Bruce, Ref./AV Libn.
U.S. VETERANS ADMINISTRATION (MA-
Brockton) - MEDICAL CENTER LIBRARY □
Brockton, MA

Thornton, Anne, Teacher/Libn.
HUNTERDON DEVELOPMENTAL CENTER -
ADAPTIVE LEARNING CENTER - LIBRARY □
Clinton, NJ

Thornton, Don E., Dir.
ST. JOSEPH NEWS-PRESS & GAZETTE -
LIBRARY □ St. Joseph, MO

Thornton, Gloria, Rd.Adv.
DISTRICT OF COLUMBIA PUBLIC LIBRARY -
POPULAR LIBRARY □ Washington, DC

Thornton, Jerry, Cat.
UNIVERSITY OF MICHIGAN - MAP ROOM □ Ann
Arbor, MI

Thornton, Josephine, Transl.
MELLON BANK, N.A. - LIBRARY† □ Pittsburgh,
PA

Thornton, Rev. Michael V., C.M., Libn.
MARY IMMACULATE SEMINARY - LIBRARY □
Northampton, PA

Thornton, Sheila F., Chf., State Lib.Serv.
CALIFORNIA STATE LIBRARY □ Sacramento, CA

Thorp, Milton K., Cur.
HACKETTSTOWN HISTORICAL SOCIETY -
MUSEUM □ Hackettstown, NJ

Thorpe, Annette, Post Libn.
U.S. ARMY POST - FORT HOOD - MSA DIVISION
- CASEY MEMORIAL LIBRARY □ Ft. Hood, TX

Thorpe, Steve, Cat.
MERCER UNIVERSITY - LAW SCHOOL -
FURMAN SMITH LAW LIBRARY □ Macon, GA

Thorson, A. Robert, Hd.Libn.
OHIO STATE UNIVERSITY - HISTORY,
POLITICAL SCIENCE, AND PHILOSOPHY
GRADUATE LIBRARY □ Columbus, OH

Thorson, A. Robert, Hd.Libn.
OHIO STATE UNIVERSITY - MAP GRADUATE
LIBRARY □ Columbus, OH

Thorton, Elizabeth, Info.Spec.
NATIONAL REHABILITATION INFORMATION
CENTER □ Washington, DC

Thorton-Tromp, Anne, Cat.
TEXAS TECH UNIVERSITY - HEALTH SCIENCES
CENTER - LIBRARY OF THE HEALTH SCIENCES
□ Lubbock, TX

Thrash, James R., Dir.
SALISBURY STATE COLLEGE - BLACKWELL
LIBRARY - SPECIAL COLLECTIONS □ Salisbury,
MD

Threndyle, Shirley Anne, Libn.
NEWMAN THEOLOGICAL COLLEGE - LIBRARY □
Edmonton, AB

Thrig, Elizabeth, Hd.Libn.
BAKKEN FOUNDATION - BAKKEN LIBRARY OF
ELECTRICITY IN LIFE □ Minneapolis, MN

Throckmorton, Edith H., Dir.
ST. VINCENT HOSPITAL AND MEDICAL CENTER
- HEALTH SCIENCES LIBRARY □ Portland, OR

Thrower, Norman J.W., Dir.
UNIVERSITY OF CALIFORNIA, LOS ANGELES -
WILLIAM ANDREWS CLARK MEMORIAL
LIBRARY □ Los Angeles, CA

Thunen, Charlotte, Chf.Libn.
ACUREX CORPORATION - CORPORATE
LIBRARY □ Mountain View, CA

Thurman, Karin, Asst.Libn.
DELAWARE LAW SCHOOL OF WIDENER
UNIVERSITY - LAW LIBRARY □ Wilmington, DE

Thurman, Oliver, Chf.Oper.Off.
GLOBAL ENGINEERING DOCUMENTS - LIBRARY
□ Santa Ana, CA

Thurston, Minnie G., Supv., Lib.Serv.
WESTINGHOUSE ELECTRIC CORPORATION -
OFFSHORE POWER SYSTEMS LIBRARY† □
Jacksonville, FL

Thurston, Nancy, Libn.
ONTARIO - MINISTRY OF NATURAL
RESOURCES - MINES LIBRARY □ Toronto, ON

Thweatt, Elizabeth, Doc/Acq.Libn.
GONZAGA UNIVERSITY SCHOOL OF LAW -
LIBRARY □ Spokane, WA

Thweatt, John, Hd., Mss.Proc.
TENNESSEE STATE LIBRARY AND ARCHIVES -
ARCHIVES & MANUSCRIPTS SECTION □
Nashville, TN

Tibbetts, Kathie K., Asst. Law Libn.
UNIVERSITY OF MAINE SCHOOL OF LAW -
DONALD L. GARBRECHT LAW LIBRARY □
Portland, ME

Tibbs, Jo Ann W., Med.Libn.
UNIVERSITY COMMUNITY HOSPITAL -
MEDICAL LIBRARY □ Tampa, FL

Tiberg, Ethel, Mgr., Lib.Serv.
EDISON ELECTRIC INSTITUTE - LIBRARY □
Washington, DC

Tibesar, Rev. Leo J., Dir.
ST. PAUL SEMINARY - JOHN IRELAND
MEMORIAL LIBRARY □ St. Paul, MN

Tiblin, Mariann, Bibliog.
UNIVERSITY OF MINNESOTA - SCANDINAVIAN
COLLECTION □ Minneapolis, MN

Tibson, Judy, Libn.
OZARK-MAHONING COMPANY - RESEARCH
LIBRARY □ Tulsa, OK

Tice, Kathy, Libn.
TOUCHE ROSS AND COMPANY - LIBRARY □ Los
Angeles, CA

Tichy, Louise, Mgt.Asst.
U.S. BUREAU OF LAND MANAGEMENT -
CALIFORNIA STATE OFFICE - LIBRARY □
Sacramento, CA

Tidona, Francine, Med.Libn.
U.S. VETERANS ADMINISTRATION (NY-
Brooklyn) - MEDICAL CENTER LIBRARY □
Brooklyn, NY

Tidwell, Janet P., Libn.
CURTIS, MALLET-PREVOST, COLT AND MOSLE -
LIBRARY □ New York, NY

Tiedrich, Ellen K., Libn.
UNDERWOOD-MEMORIAL HOSPITAL - MEDICAL
LIBRARY □ Woodbury, NJ

Tien, Mary Anna, Middletown Dir.
CONNECTICUT STATE LIBRARY □ Hartford, CT

Tiensvold, Darleen, Libn., Blind/Phys.Hand.
MONTANA STATE LIBRARY □ Helena, MT

Tierney, Catherine, Hd., Tech.Serv.
BOSTON UNIVERSITY - PAPPAS LAW LIBRARY
□ Boston, MA

Tierney, Catherine M., Chf.Libn.
AKRON BEACON JOURNAL - REFERENCE
LIBRARY □ Akron, OH

Tierney, Clifford L., Mgr.
WHIRLPOOL CORPORATION - TECHNICAL
INFORMATION CENTER □ Benton Harbor, MI

Tierney, Hal G., Supv. of Adm.
GULF STATES UTILITIES COMPANY - FINANCE
LIBRARY □ Beaumont, TX

Tierney, Judith, Spec.Coll.Libn.
KING'S COLLEGE - D. LEONARD CORGAN
LIBRARY □ Wilkes-Barre, PA

Tietolman, Angela Belle, Law Libn.
ROBINSON, SHEPPARD, BORENSTEIN, SHAPIRO
- LAW LIBRARY □ Montreal, PQ

Tiff, John T., Hist.
U.S. NATL. PARK SERVICE - LYNDON B.
JOHNSON NATL. HISTORICAL PARK - LIBRARY
□ Johnson City, TX

Tiffany, Mrs. Keppel, Libn.
CORRY AREA HISTORICAL SOCIETY - LIBRARY
□ Corry, PA

Tighe, Pauline Jones, Libn.
CALIFORNIA STATE AUTOMOBILE
ASSOCIATION - LIBRARY† □ San Francisco, CA

Tillapaugh, Elizabeth, Circ. & Bibliog.Instr.
SUNY - AGRICULTURAL AND TECHNICAL
COLLEGE AT COBLESKILL - JARED VAN
WAGENEN, JR. LEARNING RESOURCE CENTER†
□ Cobleskill, NY

Tilles, Doris, ILL
OREGON STATE UNIVERSITY - WILLIAM
JASPER KERR LIBRARY □ Corvallis, OR

Tilles, Lois, Dir., Inst.Rel.
INSTITUTE OF CERTIFIED TRAVEL AGENTS -
LIBRARY □ Wellesley, MA

Tillett, Barbara, Tech.Serv.Libn.
UNIVERSITY OF CALIFORNIA, SAN DIEGO -
SCRIPPS INSTITUTION OF OCEANOGRAPHY
LIBRARY □ La Jolla, CA

Tilley, Ms. Lou W., Regional Libn.
ENVIRONMENTAL PROTECTION AGENCY -
REGION V LIBRARY □ Chicago, IL

Tilley, Mrs. M., Bus.Mgr.
UNITED CHURCH OF CANADA - CENTRAL
ARCHIVES† □ Toronto, ON

Tillinger, Frances, Libn.
MORRISTOWN JEWISH COMMUNITY CENTER -
THE LIBRARY □ Morristown, NJ

Tillman, James S., Cat.
UNIVERSITY OF SOUTH FLORIDA - MEDICAL
CENTER LIBRARY □ Tampa, FL

Tillman, Linda Fankhauser, Dir.
TOLEDO HOSPITAL - LIBRARY □ Toledo, OH

Tillman, Mary, Lib. Media Supv.
MARION COUNTY SCHOOL BOARD - TEACHERS'
PROFESSIONAL LIBRARY □ Ocala, FL

Timberlake, Cynthia, Hd.Libn.
BISHOP (Bernice P.) MUSEUM - LIBRARY □
Honolulu, HI

Timmer, Mary, Ref.Libn.
SCHOOLS OF THEOLOGY IN DUBUQUE -
LIBRARIES □ Dubuque, IA

Timmer, Monique, AV Coord.
HERMAN MILLER, INC. - RESOURCE CENTER □
Zeeland, MI

Timmer, Sheryl, Libn.
PRINCE GEORGE CITIZEN - NEWSPAPER
LIBRARY □ Prince George, BC

Timmerman, Mildred D., Libn.
CENTRAL NEW YORK ACADEMY OF MEDICINE -
LIBRARY □ New Hartford, NY

Timmons, Charlesa, Pub.Serv.Libn.
OKLAHOMA HISTORICAL SOCIETY - DIVISION
OF LIBRARY RESOURCES □ Oklahoma City, OK

Timour, John A., Univ.Libn.
JEFFERSON (Thomas) UNIVERSITY - SCOTT
MEMORIAL LIBRARY □ Philadelphia, PA

Timson, Valerie L., Asst.Libn.
HENRY FORD HOSPITAL - FRANK J. SLADEN
LIBRARY □ Detroit, MI

Ting, Ching-Cheng C., R & D Libn.
WESTERN GEOPHYSICAL COMPANY OF
AMERICA - R & D LIBRARY □ Houston, TX

Ting, Robert, Chf.Libn.
U.S. NATL. OCEANIC & ATMOSPHERIC
ADMINISTRATION - CORAL GABLES LIBRARY □
Coral Gables, FL

Ting, Robert N., Chf.Libn.
U.S. NATL. OCEANIC & ATMOSPHERIC
ADMINISTRATION - MIAMI LIBRARY □ Miami,
FL

Ting, Shirley C., Chf., Lib.Serv.
U.S. VETERANS ADMINISTRATION (MO-Kansas
City) - MEDICAL CENTER LIBRARY □ Kansas
City, MO

Tingle, Annette K., Lib.Mgr.
U.S. NASA - MSFC LIBRARY □ Marshall Space
Flight Ctr., AL

Tinker, Phebe, Libn.
ST. MARY OF NAZARETH HOSPITAL CENTER -
SCHOOL OF NURSING LIBRARY □ Chicago, IL

Tinkham, Natalie, Supv.
MADISON PUBLIC LIBRARY - LITERATURE AND
SOCIAL SCIENCES □ Madison, WI

Tinner, Connie, Supv., Rec.Mgt.
CHICAGO REGIONAL TRANSPORTATION
AUTHORITY - LIBRARY □ Chicago, IL

Tipka, Donald, Dept.Hd.
CLEVELAND PUBLIC LIBRARY - GENERAL
REFERENCE DEPARTMENT □ Cleveland, OH

Tipple, Cindy, Info.Spec.
NATIONAL REHABILITATION INFORMATION
CENTER □ Washington, DC

Tipsword, Thomas, Cat./Ref.Libn.
U.S. ARMY - TROOP SUPPORT AND AVIATION
MATERIEL READINESS COMMAND - STINFO
AND REFERENCE LIBRARY† □ St. Louis, MO

Tipton, Jenny, Libn.
NATIONAL ORGANIZATION FOR WOMEN (NOW)
- ACTION CENTER LIBRARY □ Washington, DC

Tirado, Amilcar, Libn.
CUNY - CENTRO DE ESTUDIOS
PUERTORRIQUENOS □ New York, NY

Tirrell, Brenda Peabody, Dept.Hd.
HOUSTON PUBLIC LIBRARY - BUSINESS,
SCIENCE & TECHNOLOGY DEPARTMENT □
Houston, TX

Titterington, James L., Coord., Film Lib.
UNIVERSITY OF NEBRASKA, LINCOLN -
INSTRUCTIONAL MEDIA CENTER □ Lincoln, NE

Titus, Elizabeth A., Hd. of Archv./Spec.Coll.
OAKLAND UNIVERSITY - LIBRARY - SPECIAL
COLLECTIONS AND ARCHIVES □ Rochester, MI

Tkaczuk, Lydia, Chf., Lib.Serv.
U.S. VETERANS ADMINISTRATION (IL-Chicago)
- LAKESIDE HOSPITAL MEDICAL LIBRARY □
Chicago, IL

Tobey, Ilene, AV Cons.
CONNECTICUT STATE LIBRARY - FILM
SERVICE □ Middletown, CT

Tobia, Rajia, Ref.
UNIVERSITY OF TEXAS HEALTH SCIENCE
CENTER, SAN ANTONIO - LIBRARY □ San
Antonio, TX

Tobia, Rajia C., Libn.
UNIVERSITY OF TEXAS HEALTH SCIENCE
CENTER, SAN ANTONIO - BRADY/GREEN
EDUCATIONAL RESOURCES CENTER □ San
Antonio, TX

Tobin, Jean E., Libn.
NEW YORK STOCK EXCHANGE - RESEARCH
LIBRARY† □ New York, NY

Tobin, Patricia, Circ.Libn.
GEORGETOWN UNIVERSITY - FRED O. DENNIS
LAW LIBRARY □ Washington, DC

Tocco, Martha, Res.
BOSTON CONSULTING GROUP - WEST COAST
INFORMATION CENTER □ Menlo Park, CA

Toch, Terry Ann, Energy Info.Anl.
MC KINSEY & COMPANY, INC. - LIBRARY □
Washington, DC

Tocher, Lynda
BATTELLE NEW ENGLAND MARINE RESEARCH
LABORATORIES - LIBRARY □ Duxbury, MA

Tod, Mary, Mgr.
DALLAS PUBLIC LIBRARY - URBAN
INFORMATION CENTER □ Dallas, TX

Todd, Fred W., Chf.Libn.
U.S. AIR FORCE - AEROSPACE MEDICAL
DIVISION - SCHOOL OF AEROSPACE MEDICINE
- STRUGHOLD AEROMEDICAL LIBRARY □ Brooks
AFB, TX

Todd, Joe L., Archv./Oral Hist.
OKLAHOMA HISTORICAL SOCIETY - ARCHIVES
AND MANUSCRIPT DIVISION □ Oklahoma City,
OK

Todd, Katherine, Resource Libn.
RAINBOW CHILD CARE COUNCIL - TOY AND
RESOURCE LIBRARY □ Napa, CA

Todd, Nancy C., Libn.
KLAUDER (Louis T.) & ASSOCIATES - LIBRARY □
Philadelphia, PA

Todd, Rose-Aimee, Chf.Libn.
CANADA - NATIONAL FILM BOARD OF CANADA
- REFERENCE LIBRARY □ Montreal, PQ

Todosow, Helen K., Sr.Libn.
BROOKHAVEN NATIONAL LABORATORY -
NUCLEAR SAFETY LIBRARY □ Upton, NY

Tofte, Lynn, Tax Libn.
FRIED FRANK HARRIS SHRIVER JACOBSON -
LIBRARY & INFORMATION CENTER □ New York,
NY

Togman, Esther, Asst.Dir. & Libn.
WORLD ZIONIST ORGANIZATION - AMERICAN
SECTION - ZIONIST ARCHIVES AND LIBRARY □
New York, NY

Toifel, Ron, Dir.
UNIVERSITY OF WEST FLORIDA - JOHN C.
PACE LIBRARY - CURRICULUM MATERIALS
LIBRARY □ Pensacola, FL

Tolar, Donna M.L., Tech.Serv.Libn.
ORANGEBURG-CALHOUN TECHNICAL COLLEGE
- GRESSETTE LEARNING RESOURCE CENTER □
Orangeburg, SC

Toliver, Anthony, Asst.Libn.
RACQUET AND TENNIS CLUB - LIBRARY □ New
York, NY

Toll, Mary B., Doc.Libn.
SOUTH CAROLINA STATE LIBRARY □ Columbia,
SC

Tolman, Dr. Lorraine E., Lib.Coord.
FIRST CONGREGATIONAL CHURCH IN
WELLESLEY HILLS - LIBRARY □ Wellesley Hills,
MA

Tolman, Ruth, Pres.
WORLD MODELING ASSOCIATION - WMA
LIBRARY □ Croton-on-Hudson, NY

Tolovi, Paul A., Info.Spec.
U.S. DEFENSE COMMUNICATIONS AGENCY -
TECHNICAL AND MANAGEMENT INFORMATION
CENTER □ Washington, DC

Tolson, Stephanie D., Sr.Libn.
MC DONNELL DOUGLAS AUTOMATION
COMPANY - MC AUTO CAMPUS LIBRARY □ St.
Louis, MO

Toman, Michael, Subject Anl.
AEROSPACE CORPORATION - CHARLES C.
LAURITSEN LIBRARY □ Los Angeles, CA

Toman, Vera, L.I. Coll.Libn.
SMITHTOWN LIBRARY - SPECIAL
COLLECTIONS □ Smithtown, NY

Tomassetti, Eva Marie, Land Ck.
CONSOLIDATION COAL COMPANY -
EXPLORATION LIBRARY† □ Pittsburgh, PA

Tomasulo, Patricia, Libn.
SUNY - DOWNSTATE MEDICAL CENTER -
DEPARTMENT OF PSYCHIATRY LIBRARY □
Brooklyn, NY

Tomich, Mrs. Marciel, Registrar
PACIFIC COAST BANKING SCHOOL - LIBRARY □
Seattle, WA

Tominello, Rosemarie, Pub.Serv.Libn.
KILPATRICK & CODY - LIBRARY □ Atlanta, GA

Tomko, Lucille A., Asst.Div.Hd.
CARNEGIE LIBRARY OF PITTSBURGH -
PENNSYLVANIA DIVISION □ Pittsburgh, PA

Tomlin, Anne Costello, Dir.
AUBURN MEMORIAL HOSPITAL - LIBRARY/
RESOURCE CENTER □ Auburn, NY

Tomlin, Mary Evelyn, Mgr., Ref./Data Serv.Unit
MISSISSIPPI (State) RESEARCH AND
DEVELOPMENT CENTER - INFORMATION
SERVICES DIVISION □ Jackson, MS

Tomlin, Maxine, Libn.
DOW CHEMICAL COMPANY - RESEARCH
CENTER LIBRARY† □ Indianapolis, IN

Tomlinson, Edwin W., Libn.
SHERMAN RESEARCH LIBRARY □ Corona Del
Mar, CA

Tomlinson, Elizabeth A., Libn.
SOUTH CAROLINA STATE SUPREME COURT -
LIBRARY □ Columbia, SC

Tomlinson, Elizabeth K., Sci.Libn.
CARLETON COLLEGE - SCIENCE LIBRARY □
Northfield, MN

Tomlinson, J., Chf., Lib. Network
CANADA - SECRETARY OF STATE -
TRANSLATION BUREAU - DOCUMENTATION
DIRECTORATE† □ Ottawa, ON

Tomlinson, Patricia A., Libn. (East Site)
ST. JOSEPH HOSPITAL OF MT. CLEMENS -
MEDICAL LIBRARY □ Mt. Clemens, MI

Tomlinson, Timothy R., Assoc.Dir.
UNIVERSITY OF PENNSYLVANIA - MORRIS
ARBORETUM LIBRARY □ Philadelphia, PA

Tomlinson, William D., Dir.
WESTERN MONTANA SCIENTISTS'
COMMITTEE FOR PUBLIC INFORMATION -
MONTANA ENVIRONMENTAL LIBRARY □
Missoula, MT

Tommey, Richard J., Libn.
G.A. TECHNOLOGIES INC. - LIBRARY† □ San
Diego, CA

Tompkins, Dorothy C., Chf.Libn.
U.S. ARMY POST - FORT HUACHUCA LIBRARY
DIVISION - TECHNICAL LIBRARY □ Fort
Huachuca, AZ

Tompkins, Edward, Archv.
NEWFOUNDLAND - PROVINCIAL ARCHIVES OF
NEWFOUNDLAND AND LABRADOR □ St. John's,
NF

Tompkins, Louise, Libn.
PRINCETON UNIVERSITY - PLINY FISK
LIBRARY OF ECONOMICS AND FINANCE† □
Princeton, NJ

Tomposki, Philip, Ref.Libn.
U.S. NAVY - NAVAL UNDERWATER SYSTEMS
CENTER - NEWPORT TECHNICAL LIBRARY† □
Newport, RI

Toms, Stan, Ref.Libn.
MANITOBA - DEPARTMENT OF EDUCATION -
LIBRARY □ Winnipeg, MB

Toncray, Paula E., Libn.
MILLER, CANFIELD, PADDOCK & STONE -
LIBRARY □ Detroit, MI

Tondi, Lorraine, Dir./Res.
KINGSBOROUGH COMMUNITY COLLEGE -
KINGSBOROUGH HISTORICAL SOCIETY† □
Brooklyn, NY

Toner, Mary Anne, Libn.
MERCY HOSPITAL - HEALTH SCIENCES
LIBRARY □ Portland, ME

Toner, Michael P., Lib.Dir.
SCHEIE EYE INSTITUTE - LIBRARY □
Philadelphia, PA

Tong, Josie, Tech.Serv.Libn.
UNIVERSITY OF ALBERTA - H.T. COUTTS
LIBRARY □ Edmonton, AB

Tonge, Karyl, Map Libn.
STANFORD UNIVERSITY - CENTRAL MAP
COLLECTION □ Stanford, CA

Tongue, Marie, Dir. of Lib.Serv.
FIRST UNITED METHODIST CHURCH - LIBRARY
□ Tulsa, OK

Tonks, A. Ronald, Asst.Exec.Dir.
SOUTHERN BAPTIST CONVENTION -
HISTORICAL COMMISSION - SOUTHERN
BAPTIST HISTORICAL LIBRARY & ARCHIVES □
Nashville, TN

Tonucci, Jo, Lib.Tech.Supv.
TRAVELERS INSURANCE COMPANIES -
CORPORATE LIBRARY □ Hartford, CT

Tooey, Mary Joan, Media/Ref.Libn.
ALLEGHENY GENERAL HOSPITAL - HEALTH
SCIENCES LIBRARY □ Pittsburgh, PA

Toohey, Cornelia A., Libn.
ARTHUR ANDERSEN & CO. - LIBRARY □
Hartford, CT

Tooke, Elaine, Ref.Libn.
MC MASTER UNIVERSITY - THODE LIBRARY OF
SCIENCE & ENGINEERING □ Hamilton, ON

Tooker, G. Calvin, Libn.
METROPOLITAN STATE HOSPITAL - STAFF
LIBRARY □ Norwalk, CA

Tooley, Katherine J., Tech.Serv.
UNIVERSITY OF TULSA - COLLEGE OF LAW
LIBRARY □ Tulsa, OK

Toolis, Lorna, Hd., Tech.Serv.
NORTHERN ALBERTA INSTITUTE OF
TECHNOLOGY - LEARNING RESOURCE CENTRE
□ Edmonton, AB

Toombs, William, Cat.Libn.
EDEN THEOLOGICAL SEMINARY - LIBRARY □
Webster Groves, MO

Toomey, Kathleen M., Libn.
MC GILL UNIVERSITY - MARVIN DUCHOW
MUSIC LIBRARY □ Montreal, PQ

Toon, Mrs. Jo, Hd.Libn.
ALBERTA - DEPARTMENT OF CULTURE -
HISTORICAL RESOURCES LIBRARY □ Edmonton,
AB

Tooth, John, Chf.Libn.
MANITOBA - DEPARTMENT OF EDUCATION -
LIBRARY □ Winnipeg, MB

Tope, Diana Ray, Dir.
CHEROKEE REGIONAL LIBRARY - GEORGIA
HISTORY & GENEALOGICAL ROOM† □
LaFayette, GA

Topp, Carole L., Libn.
BETHESDA LUTHERAN MEDICAL CENTER -
MEDICAL-NURSING LIBRARY □ St. Paul, MN

Toppan, Muriel L., Ref.Libn.
WALTERS ART GALLERY - LIBRARY □ Baltimore,
MD

Topper, Judith M., Med.Libn.
LAWRENCE HOSPITAL - ASHLEY BAKER
MORRILL LIBRARY† □ Bronxville, NY

Topping, Brett, Writer-Ed.
LIBRARY OF CONGRESS - AMERICAN FOLKLIFE
CENTER □ Washington, DC

Topping, Donald M., Dir.
UNIVERSITY OF HAWAII - SOCIAL SCIENCE
RESEARCH INSTITUTE □ Honolulu, HI

Topping, Gary, Mss.Cur.
UTAH STATE HISTORICAL SOCIETY -
RESEARCH LIBRARY □ Salt Lake City, UT

Toran, Karen, Circ.Libn.
UNIVERSITY OF CALIFORNIA, SAN FRANCISCO
- HASTINGS COLLEGE OF THE LAW - LEGAL
INFORMATION CENTER □ San Francisco, CA

Tordella, Stephen J., Spec.
UNIVERSITY OF WISCONSIN, MADISON -
DEPARTMENT OF RURAL SOCIOLOGY - APPLIED
POPULATION LAB. - LIBRARY □ Madison, WI

Torgerson, Kitty, Libn.
HOLLISTER-STIER - LIBRARY □ Spokane, WA

Tornabene, Charles, Jr., Libn.
FLORIDA STATE - SOUTHWEST FLORIDA
MANAGEMENT DISTRICT - LIBRARY □
Brooksville, FL

Torode, William W., Libn.
NATIONAL SPELEOLOGICAL SOCIETY - NSS
LIBRARY □ Huntsville, AL

Toronto, Robert, Libn.
U.S. VETERANS ADMINISTRATION (NY-
Northport) - HEALTH SCIENCE LIBRARY □
Northport, NY

Torre, Dr. Louis P., Physical Sci.Libn.
RUTGERS UNIVERSITY, THE STATE
UNIVERSITY OF NEW JERSEY - CHEMISTRY
LIBRARY □ Piscataway, NJ

Torre, Dr. Louis P., Physical Sci.Libn.
RUTGERS UNIVERSITY, THE STATE
UNIVERSITY OF NEW JERSEY - PHYSICS
LIBRARY □ Piscataway, NJ

Torrefranca, Patricia, Libn.
U.S. NATL. MARINE FISHERIES SERVICE -
SOUTHEAST FISHERIES CENTER - GALVESTON
LABORATORY LIBRARY □ Galveston, TX

Torrence, Caroline Armold, Ref./ILL/Govt.Docs.
SOUTHWESTERN OKLAHOMA STATE
UNIVERSITY - AL HARRIS LIBRARY □
Weatherford, OK

Torrence, Judith, Hd., Ref. & Info.Serv.
U.S. UNIFORMED SERVICES UNIVERSITY OF
THE HEALTH SCIENCES - LEARNING RESOURCE
CENTER □ Bethesda, MD

Torres, Jesse Joseph, Libn.
ACADEMY OF AMERICAN FRANCISCAN
HISTORY - LIBRARY □ West Bethesda, MD

Torres, Jesse Joseph, Asst.Libn.
PAN AMERICAN HEALTH ORGANIZATION -
BIBLIOGRAPHIC INFORMATION OFFICE† □
Washington, DC

Torres, Mary, Ref.Libn.
BANCROFT, AVERY AND MC ALISTER - LAW
LIBRARY □ San Francisco, CA

Torres, Rebecca, Adm.Asst.
UNIVERSITY OF CALIFORNIA, LOS ANGELES -
ORAL HISTORY PROGRAM LIBRARY □ Los
Angeles, CA

Torres-Irizarry, Martha, Libn.
UNIVERSITY OF PUERTO RICO - GRADUATE
SCHOOL OF PLANNING - LIBRARY† □ Rio
Piedras, PR

Torrey, Julie, Libn.
NORTH CAROLINA STATE DEPT. OF NATURAL
RESOURCES & COMMUNITY DEVELOPMENT -
DIV. OF COMMUNITY ASSISTANCE LIB. □
Raleigh, NC

Tortora, Eileen, Ser.Libn.
HOECHST-ROUSSEL PHARMACEUTICALS, INC. -
LIBRARY □ Somerville, NJ

Tortorelli, R.R., Sci.Serv.Techn.
CANADA - ATMOSPHERIC ENVIRONMENT
SERVICE - CENTRAL REGION LIBRARY† □
Winnipeg, MB

Toscan, Joyce, Non-Govt.Org.Libn.
UNIVERSITY OF CALIFORNIA, LOS ANGELES -
PUBLIC AFFAIRS SERVICE □ Los Angeles, CA

Tosi, Laura, Assoc.Libn.
BRONX COUNTY HISTORICAL SOCIETY -
THEODORE KAZIMIROFF RESEARCH LIBRARY □
Bronx, NY

Tostevin, Patricia A., Libn.
ITT RAYONIER, INC. - RESEARCH CENTER -
LIBRARY □ Shelton, WA

Toth, Paulette, Info.Spec.
CRAVATH, SWAINE, & MOORE - LAW LIBRARY
□ New York, NY

Touger, Mirel, Libn.
TEMPLE BETH EL - BUDDY BERMAN MEMORIAL
LIBRARY □ Cedarhurst, NY

Touhey, Paula, Interim Dir./Cur. of Educ
KENOSHA PUBLIC MUSEUM - LIBRARY □
Kenosha, WI

Toupin, Carmen Delorme, Animator
MUSEE D'ART DE JOLIETTE - BIBLIOTHEQUE†
□ Joliette, PQ

Toupin, Juanita M., Libn.
THE MONTREAL MUSEUM OF FINE ARTS -
LIBRARY† □ Montreal, PQ

Toupin, Robert, S.J., Dir.
UNIVERSITY OF SUDBURY - JESUIT ARCHIVES
□ Sudbury, ON

Toups, Don, Libn.
FORT WORTH PUBLIC LIBRARY - BUSINESS
AND TECHNOLOGY DEPARTMENT □ Fort Worth,
TX

Toups, Patricia A., Libn.
LIFE OFFICE MANAGEMENT ASSOCIATION -
INFORMATION CENTER □ Atlanta, GA

Tourigny, Suzanne, Ref.Libn.
CANADA - LABOUR CANADA - LIBRARY
SERVICES† □ Ottawa, ON

Tousegnant, Laurent, Libn.
MONASTERE DES PERES REDEMPTORISTES -
BIBLIOTHEQUE† □ Sherbrooke, PQ

Tousignant, Claude, Hd.Libn.
TELE-UNIVERSITE - CENTRE DE
DOCUMENTATION □ Quebec, PQ

Towell, Andrea, Libn.
TEAM FOUR INC. - LIBRARY □ St. Louis, MO

Towell, Ann, Med.Libn.
GOOD SAMARITAN MEDICAL CENTER - EVANS
MEMORIAL LIBRARY □ Milwaukee, WI

Towell, Fay J., Dir., Lib.Serv.
SPARTANBURG GENERAL HOSPITAL - HEALTH
SCIENCES LIBRARY □ Spartanburg, SC

Towell, Jane, Br.Libn.
WHITE AND CASE - LIBRARY □ New York, NY

Towers, Lynn, Libn.
JACKSON MEMORIAL HOSPITAL - SCHOOL OF
NURSING LIBRARY □ Miami, FL

Towers, Thomas A., Dir.
U.S. DEPT. OF LABOR - OSHA - TECHNICAL
DATA CENTER □ Washington, DC

Towery, Mrs. Dick, Libn.
FIRST METHODIST CHURCH - BLISS MEMORIAL
LIBRARY □ Shreveport, LA

Towles, Anne Slaughter, Law Libn.
MC COLLISTER, MC CLEARY, FAZIO, MIXON,
HOLLIDAY & HICKS - LAW LIBRARY □ Baton
Rouge, LA

Towles, James, Tech.Info.Spec.
U.S. DEPT. OF LABOR - OSHA - TECHNICAL
DATA CENTER □ Washington, DC

Towner, Lawrence W., Pres./Libn.
NEWBERRY LIBRARY □ Chicago, IL

Towns, Bobby, Asst.Libn.
MAYER, BROWN & PLATT - LIBRARY† □
Chicago, IL

Townsend, E. Jane, Hist. Site Mgr.
NEW YORK STATE BUREAU OF HISTORIC
SITES - WASHINGTON'S HEADQUARTERS
STATE HISTORIC SITE - LIBRARY □ Newburgh,
NY

Townsend, Jamie, Sec., Corp.Plan.
RYDER SYSTEM, INC. - INFORMATION
CENTRAL □ Miami, FL

Townsend, Mary, Libn.
UNIVERSITY OF MICHIGAN - SCHOOL OF
PUBLIC HEALTH - PUBLIC HEALTH LIBRARY □
Ann Arbor, MI

Townsend, Sherry, Tech.Libn.
REYNOLDS METALS COMPANY - ALUMINA
DIVISION - TECHNICAL INFORMATION
CENTER† □ Little Rock, AR

Towry, Lucy, Libn.
TULSA WORLD-TULSA TRIBUNE - LIBRARY
DEPARTMENT □ Tulsa, OK

Toy, Theresa Snow, Fine Arts Libn.
MANCHESTER CITY LIBRARY - FINE ARTS
DEPARTMENT □ Manchester, NH

Tozer, Peggy M., Lib.Dir.
EASTERN NEW MEXICO UNIVERSITY - GOLDEN
LIBRARY - SPECIAL COLLECTIONS □ Portales,
NM

Tozer, Ronald G., Interp.Serv.Supv.
ALGONQUIN PARK MUSEUM - LIBRARY &
ARCHIVES □ Whitney, ON

Tozeski, Stanley, Archv.
U.S. NATL. ARCHIVES & RECORDS SERVICE -
FEDERAL ARCHIVES AND RECORDS CENTER,
REGION 1 □ Waltham, MA

Tracey, Kenneth D., Exec.Dir.
LEVERE MEMORIAL FOUNDATION - LIBRARY □
Evanston, IL

Tracy, Constance J.M., Reg.Libn.
VIRGINIA STATE LIBRARY FOR THE VISUALLY
AND PHYSICALLY HANDICAPPED □ Richmond,
VA

Tracy, Janet, Asst. Law Libn.
COLUMBIA UNIVERSITY - LAW LIBRARY □ New
York, NY

Tracz, Orysia, Hd.Libn.
UKRAINIAN CULTURAL AND EDUCATIONAL
CENTRE (Oserdok) - LIBRARY □ Winnipeg, MB

Trafford, John E., Exec.Dir.
NEW JERSEY STATE LEAGUE OF
MUNICIPALITIES - LIBRARY □ Trenton, NJ

Traina, Helen, Chf.Libn.
CHEMICAL BANK - RESEARCH LIBRARY □ New
York, NY

Trainer, Sally M., Sec.
WIGHT CONSULTING ENGINEERS, INC. -
TECHNICAL LIBRARY† □ Barrington, IL

Trainor, Mary Anne, Ser. & Acq.Libn.
MC MASTER UNIVERSITY - HEALTH SCIENCES
LIBRARY □ Hamilton, ON

Traister, Daniel, Asst.Cur., Spec.Coll.
UNIVERSITY OF PENNSYLVANIA - RARE BOOK
COLLECTION† □ Philadelphia, PA

Tramp, Karen, Customer Serv.Techn.
U.S. GEOLOGICAL SURVEY - EROS DATA
CENTER - TECHNICAL REFERENCE UNIT □
Sioux Falls, SD

Trampe, Helen, Libn.
FIRST BAPTIST CHURCH - LIBRARY □ Slocomb,
AL

Tran, Thuan T., Hd.Libn.
WESTERN WISCONSIN TECHNICAL INSTITUTE
- LIBRARY □ La Crosse, WI

Trani, Gertrude D., Asst.Libn.
CULINARY INSTITUTE OF AMERICA -
KATHARINE ANGELL LIBRARY □ Hyde Park, NY

Tranquille, Jocelyne
MONTREAL URBAN COMMUNITY TRANSIT
COMMISSION - LIBRARY □ Montreal, PQ

Trapani, Jean, Mgr., Info.Serv.
WESTRECO, INC. - TECHNICAL LIBRARY □ New
Milford, CT

Trask, Carole, Libn.
POUDRE VALLEY HOSPITAL - MEDIA
RESOURCES LIBRARY† □ Fort Collins, CO

Trask, Richard B., Town Archv.
PEABODY INSTITUTE LIBRARY - DANVERS
ARCHIVAL CENTER □ Danvers, MA

Tratner, Alan A., Dir.
GEOTHERMAL WORLD CORPORATION -
INFORMATION CENTER □ Camarillo, CA

Tratner, Alan Arthur, Exec.Dir.
ENVIRONMENTAL EDUCATION GROUP -
LIBRARY □ Camarillo, CA

Tratt, G.M.T., Sec.
UNIVERSITY OF ALBERTA - NUCLEAR PHYSICS
LIBRARY □ Edmonton, AB

Trauger, Susan, Art Libn.
RIFKIND CENTER FOR GERMAN
EXPRESSIONIST STUDIES - ART LIBRARY AND
GRAPHICS COLLECTION □ Los Angeles, CA

Trauth, Sr. Mary Philip, S.N.D., Archv.
DIOCESE OF COVINGTON - ARCHIVES □
Covington, KY

Trauth, Megan W., Off.Serv.Mgr.
PANNELL KERR FORSTER - LIBRARY □ Houston,
TX

Travaline, Marjorie, Libn.
GLASSBORO STATE COLLEGE - MUSIC BRANCH
LIBRARY □ Glassboro, NJ

Travers, Carolyn Freeman, Res.Assoc.
PLIMOTH PLANTATION, INC. - LIBRARY □
Plymouth, MA

Travers, Jane, Med.Libn.
HUNTINGTON HOSPITAL - MEDICAL LIBRARY □
Huntington, NY

Travis, Julie, Mgr.
DALLAS PUBLIC LIBRARY - FILM SERVICE □
Dallas, TX

Travis, Marguerite W., Libn.
ST. THOMAS SEMINARY - LIBRARY □ Denver,
CO

Travisono, Diana, Res.
AMERICAN CORRECTIONAL ASSOCIATION -
LIBRARY □ College Park, MD

Treadway, Carole, Quaker Bibliog.
GUILFORD COLLEGE - LIBRARY - SPECIAL
COLLECTIONS □ Greensboro, NC

Treadway, Teman, Lib.Serv.Coord.
NATIONAL COUNCIL OF SENIOR CITIZENS,
INC. - LIBRARY □ Washington, DC

Treais, Mary Ann, Adm.Coord.
OAKLAND COUNTY PIONEER AND HISTORICAL
SOCIETY - LIBRARY & ARCHIVES □ Pontiac, MI

Treat, Beth, Asst.Libn.
DAVIS, GRAHAM & STUBBS/COLORADO
NATIONAL BUILDING - CNB LAW LIBRARY □
Denver, CO

Tredwell, Irving, Jr., Asst.Libn.
PILGRIM PSYCHIATRIC CENTER - HEALTH
SCIENCES LIBRARY □ West Brentwood, NY

Treese, William R., Hd./Art Libn.
UNIVERSITY OF CALIFORNIA, SANTA BARBARA
- ARTS LIBRARY □ Santa Barbara, CA

Trefethen, Dan, Libn.
TRA ARCHITECTURE ENGINEERING PLANNING
INTERIORS - LIBRARY □ Seattle, WA

Treiman, Marilyn, Ref.Libn.
UNIVERSITY OF CALIFORNIA - LOS ALAMOS
NATIONAL LABORATORY - LIBRARY □ Los
Alamos, NM

Treimanis, Anna, Hd.Cat.
UNIVERSITY OF ILLINOIS AT CHICAGO -
HEALTH SCIENCES CENTER - LIBRARY OF THE
HEALTH SCIENCES □ Chicago, IL

Treleven, Dale, Dir.
UNIVERSITY OF CALIFORNIA, LOS ANGELES -
ORAL HISTORY PROGRAM LIBRARY □ Los
Angeles, CA

Tremaine, Kenneth, Coord. of Media
LEXINGTON SCHOOL FOR THE DEAF - LIBRARY
MEDIA CENTER □ Jackson Heights, NY

Tremblay, Angele, Bibliothecaire
HOPITAL DE CHICOUTIMI INC. -
BIBLIOTHEQUE† □ Chicoutimi, PQ

Tremblay, C., Libn.
LIQUID AIR ENGINEERING CORPORATION - E &
C LIBRARY □ Montreal, PQ

Tremblay, Levis, Tech.Serv.
UNIVERSITE DU QUEBEC EN ABITIBI-
TEMISCAMINGUE - BIBLIOTHEQUE □ Rouyn, PQ

Tremblay, Louise
CONFEDERATION DES CAISSES POPULAIRES
ET D'ECONOMIE DESJARDINS DU QUEBEC -
SERVICE DE DOCUMENTATION □ Levis, PQ

Tremblay, P., Ref.Libn.
COLLEGE MILITAIRE ROYAL DE ST-JEAN -
LIBRARY □ St. Jean, PQ

Tresner, Charlene, Local Hist.Coord.
FORT COLLINS PUBLIC LIBRARY - ORAL
HISTORY COLLECTION □ Fort Collins, CO

Tretheway, Willeen, AV Libn.
WISCONSIN STATE DIVISION FOR LIBRARY
SERVICES - REFERENCE AND LOAN LIBRARY □
Madison, WI

Trettner, Jan, Asst.Libn.
UNIVERSITY OF ALASKA - INSTITUTE OF
MARINE SCIENCE - SEWARD MARINE STATION
LIBRARY □ Seward, AK

Treude, J. Mai, Libn.
UNIVERSITY OF MINNESOTA - MAP LIBRARY □
Minneapolis, MN

Trevanion, Margaret U., Med.Libn.
NORTH HILLS PASSAVANT HOSPITAL -
MEDICAL LIBRARY □ Pittsburgh, PA

Treves, Ralph, Owner
TREVES (Ralph) WORKSHOP FEATURES -
WORKSHOP PHOTOS □ West Palm Beach, FL

Tribble, Ed, State Archv.
FLORIDA STATE DIVISION OF ARCHIVES,
HISTORY & RECORDS MANAGEMENT - FLORIDA
STATE ARCHIVES □ Tallahassee, FL

Tribby, John, Supv.
MORRISON-KNUDSEN CO., INC. -
INFORMATION RESEARCH CENTER □ Boise, ID

Tribe, Hanne, Lib. Chairperson
ALBERTA MENTAL HEALTH SERVICES -
MENTAL HEALTH SYSTEMS LIBRARY □ Calgary,
AB

Triboletti, Kathleen, Resource Coord.
DIOCESE OF WILMINGTON - OFFICE OF TOTAL
EDUCATION - RESOURCE CENTER □
Wilmington, DE

Tribull, Alice, Asst.Libn.
BENDIX CORPORATION - COMMUNICATIONS
DIVISION - ENGINEERING LIBRARY† □
Baltimore, MD

Trice, Johnnie, Asst.Libn.
ALCON LABORATORIES, INC. - RESEARCH &
DEVELOPMENT LIBRARY □ Fort Worth, TX

Trickey, Katherine, Libn.
AMERICAN HEART ASSOCIATION - LIBRARY/
RECORDS CENTER □ Dallas, TX

Triggs, Dr. Frances Oralind, Chm.
COMMITTEE ON DIAGNOSTIC READING TESTS,
INC. - LIBRARY □ Mountain Home, NC

Trimble, Bob, AV Libn.
SOUTHWESTERN BAPTIST THEOLOGICAL
SEMINARY - A. WEBB ROBERTS LIBRARY □ Fort
Worth, TX

Trimble, Dr. George X., Dir.
ST. MARY'S HOSPITAL MEDICAL EDUCATION
FOUNDATION - MEDICAL LITERATURE
INFORMATION CENTER □ Kansas City, MO

Trimble, Jerri, Supv.
ST. JOSEPH HOSPITAL - MEDICAL LIBRARY □
Lexington, KY

Trimble, Kathleen, Lib.Dir.
U.S. NEWS & WORLD REPORT - LIBRARY □
Washington, DC

Trinca, Maria, Asst.Libn.
HELEN HAYES HOSPITAL - LIBRARY □ West
Haverstraw, NY

Trinkaus-Randall, Gregor, Libn.
PEABODY MUSEUM OF SALEM - PHILLIPS
LIBRARY □ Salem, MA

Triplett, Billy, AV Libn.
LOUISIANA STATE UNIVERSITY MEDICAL
CENTER - SCHOOL OF MEDICINE IN
SHREVEPORT - LIBRARY □ Shreveport, LA

Triplett, Peggy
GEORGIA STATE UNIVERSITY - SMALL
BUSINESS DEVELOPMENT CENTER □ Atlanta,
GA

Tripp, Diana L., Libn.
TUSCARAWAS COUNTY LAW LIBRARY
ASSOCIATION □ New Philadelphia, OH

Tripp, Juanita S., Libn.
ILLINOIS STATE BOARD OF EDUCATION -
MEDIA RESOURCES CENTER □ Springfield, IL

Tripp, Maureen, Hd., Media Serv.
EMERSON COLLEGE - LIBRARY □ Boston, MA

Trippett, Sandra Kay, Dir.
FIRST BAPTIST CHURCH - JOHN L. WHORTON
MEDIA CENTER □ Longview, TX

Trisdale, Raymon, Chf.Libn.
U.S. ARMY - LOGISTICS LIBRARY □ Ft. Lee, VA

Trithart, David, Ref.Libn.
SUNY - COLLEGE AT POTSDAM - FREDERICK W.
CRUMB MEMORIAL LIBRARY □ Potsdam, NY

Tritsch, Electa Kane, Exec.Dir.
DEDHAM HISTORICAL SOCIETY - LIBRARY □
Dedham, MA

Tritz, Peter, Res.Dir.
LEAGUE OF MINNESOTA CITIES - LIBRARY □
St. Paul, MN

Trivedi, Mr. Harish, Ref. & Res.Dir.
DAYTON NEWSPAPERS INC. - REFERENCE
LIBRARY □ Dayton, OH

Trocchia, Mary Ann, Sr.Asst.
ADELPHI UNIVERSITY - SOCIAL WORK
LIBRARY† □ Garden City, NY

Trofimov, Norma K., Info.Sci.
ETHICON, INC. - SCIENTIFIC INFORMATION
SERVICES □ Somerville, NJ

Troiano, Wendy, Asst.Libn.
EASTERN MAINE MEDICAL CENTER - HEALTH
SCIENCES LIBRARY □ Bangor, ME

Troiano, Wendy E., Libn.
BANGOR MENTAL HEALTH INSTITUTE -
HEALTH SCIENCES MEDIA CENTER □ Bangor,
ME

Troise, Fred, Vice-Pres.
WATER INFORMATION CENTER, INC. □
Syosset, NY

Troka, Genevieve, Archv. I
CALIFORNIA - STATE ARCHIVES □ Sacramento,
CA

Troll, Ted, Chf.Libn.
HEARST METROTONE NEWS - FILM LIBRARY □
New York, NY

Trolle, Larisa A., Act.Libn.
HARVARD UNIVERSITY - HARVARD UKRAINIAN
RESEARCH INSTITUTE - REFERENCE LIBRARY
□ Cambridge, MA

Trombello, Lawrence, Chf.
U.S. NATL. PARK SERVICE - ALLEGHENY
PORTAGE RAILROAD NATL. HISTORIC SITE -
LIBRARY □ Cresson, PA

Trombetta, Robert J., Dir.
PENNSYLVANIA STATE HISTORICAL & MUSEUM
COMMISSION - FORT PITT MUSEUM - LIBRARY
□ Pittsburgh, PA

Trombitas, Ildiko, Hd., Tech.Info.Dept.
BURROUGHS WELLCOME COMPANY - LIBRARY
□ Research Triangle Park, NC

Trombley, Ivan C., Res.Libn.
PPG INDUSTRIES, INC. - CHEMICAL DIVISION
- RESEARCH LIBRARY □ Corpus Christi, TX

Troop, Anne, Mgr., Info.Serv.
CPC INTERNATIONAL - BEST FOODS
RESEARCH CENTER - INFORMATION CENTER □
Union, NJ

Trosset, Ruth P., Assoc.Prof.
UNIVERSITY OF CINCINNATI - DEPARTMENT
OF ENVIRONMENTAL HEALTH LIBRARY □
Cincinnati, OH

Trott, Mary B., Asst.Archv.
SMITH COLLEGE - ARCHIVES □ Northampton,
MA

Trott, Nancy, Info.Spec.
PRICE WATERHOUSE - NATIONAL
INFORMATION CENTER □ New York, NY

Trotta, Victoria K., Hd., Tech.Serv.
UNIVERSITY OF SOUTHERN CALIFORNIA - LAW
LIBRARY □ Los Angeles, CA

Trotti, Dr. John B., Libn.
UNION THEOLOGICAL SEMINARY IN VIRGINIA
- LIBRARY □ Richmond, VA

Trottier, Aime, Libn.
ORATOIRE ST-JOSEPH - CENTRE DE
DOCUMENTATION □ Montreal, PQ

Trout, Frank E., Cur.
HARVARD UNIVERSITY - MAP COLLECTION □
Cambridge, MA

Troy, Carol, Libn.
PRINCETON POLYMER LABORATORIES, INC. -
LIBRARY □ Plainsboro, NJ

Trubey, Cornelia, Libn.
ROPES & GRAY - CENTRAL LIBRARY □ Boston,
MA

Trubey, D.K., Physicist
OAK RIDGE NATIONAL LABORATORY -
RADIATION SHIELDING INFORMATION
CENTER □ Oak Ridge, TN

Trudel, Florian, Chef de Grouppe
CENTRE DE RECHERCHE INDUSTRIELLE DU
QUEBEC - DIRECTION DE L'INFORMATION
TECHNOLOGIQUE □ Ste. Foy, PQ

Trudell, Libby, Mgr., Marketing
DIALOG INFORMATION SERVICES, INC. □ Palo
Alto, CA

Trueblood, Emily, Asst.Chf.Libn.
FEDERAL RESERVE BANK OF NEW YORK -
RESEARCH LIBRARY □ New York, NY

Trued, Mrs. Nymah L., Chf., Lib.Serv.
U.S. VETERANS ADMINISTRATION (OR-
Portland) - MEDICAL LIBRARY □ Portland, OR

Trued, Mrs. Nymah L., Chf., Lib.Serv.
U.S. VETERANS ADMINISTRATION (WA-
Vancouver) - HOSPITAL LIBRARY □ Vancouver,
WA

Truelson, Judith A., Dir.
UNIVERSITY OF SOUTHERN CALIFORNIA -
CROCKER BUSINESS LIBRARY □ Los Angeles,
CA

Truelson, Stanley, Dir.
UNIVERSITY OF ALASKA, ANCHORAGE -
ALASKA HEALTH SCIENCES LIBRARY □
Anchorage, AK

Truesdell, John M., Mgr., Adm.
RMI, INC. - TECHNICAL LIBRARY □ National
City, CA

Truesdell, Walter G., Libn.
REFORMED EPISCOPAL CHURCH -
THEOLOGICAL SEMINARY - KUEHNER
MEMORIAL LIBRARY □ Philadelphia, PA

Truex, William, Cur.
TALLMADGE HISTORICAL SOCIETY - LIBRARY
& ARCHIVES □ Tallmadge, OH

Trull, JoAnn, Libn.
GULF RESOURCES AND CHEMICAL
CORPORATION - LITHIUM CORPORATION OF
AMERICA, INC. - RESEARCH LIBRARY □
Bessemer City, NC

Truman, Dorothy, Ms.Coll.
MERRIMACK VALLEY TEXTILE MUSEUM -
LIBRARY □ North Andover, MA

Trunks, Mrs. Pat, ILL
ROYAL ONTARIO MUSEUM - LIBRARY† □
Toronto, ON

Truono, Leslie, Abstractor/Indexer
HERCULES, INC. - RESEARCH CENTER -
TECHNICAL INFORMATION DIVISION □
Wilmington, DE

Truscott, Myfanwy, Libn.
CAMPION COLLEGE - LIBRARY □ Regina, SK

Tryon, Julie A., Cat.
CORNELL UNIVERSITY - MARTIN P.
CATHERWOOD LIBRARY OF INDUSTRIAL AND
LABOR RELATIONS □ Ithaca, NY

Tryon, Roy H., Chf./Archv. & Rec.Mgt.Bur
DELAWARE STATE DIVISION OF HISTORICAL &
CULTURAL AFFAIRS - DELAWARE STATE
ARCHIVES □ Dover, DE

Tryslehorn, Julia H., Libn.
UNIVERSITY OF ALASKA - GEOPHYSICAL
INSTITUTE LIBRARY† □ Fairbanks, AK

Trzyna, T.C., Pres.
CALIFORNIA INSTITUTE OF PUBLIC AFFAIRS -
LIBRARY □ Claremont, CA

Tsai, Eugenie, Asst.Libn.
KNOEDLER (M.) AND COMPANY, INC. - LIBRARY
□ New York, NY

Tsai, Ming-Tien, Libn.
CHINESE CULTURAL CENTER - INFORMATION
& COMMUNICATION DIVISION - LIBRARY □
New York, NY

Tsai, Ryo, Pub.Serv.Libn.
SEATTLE PUBLIC LIBRARY - DOUGLASS-TRUTH
BRANCH LIBRARY □ Seattle, WA

Tsang, Katherine, Contract Libn.
ENVIRONMENTAL PROTECTION AGENCY -
REGION V LIBRARY □ Chicago, IL

Tsang, Shirley, Data Mgr.
LOUISIANA STATE UNIVERSITY - COASTAL
INFORMATION REPOSITORY □ Baton Rouge, LA

Tsang, W.M., Chf.Libn.
CANADA - ENERGY, MINES & RESOURCES
CANADA - EARTH PHYSICS BRANCH LIBRARY □
Ottawa, ON

Tsao, James, Chf. of Tech.Serv.
WASHINGTON STATE LAW LIBRARY □ Olympia,
WA

Tschinkel, Andrew, Libn.
NEW YORK STATE SUPREME COURT - 11TH
JUDICIAL DISTRICT - LAW LIBRARY □ Kew
Gardens, NY

Tschinkel, Andrew, Ref.Libn.
ST. JOHN'S UNIVERSITY - LAW LIBRARY □
Jamaica, NY

Tschinkel, Andrew J., Prin. Law Libn.
NEW YORK STATE SUPREME COURT - 11TH
JUDICIAL DISTRICT - LAW LIBRARY □ Jamaica,
NY

Tschudy, Karen D., Lib.Dir.
CLEVELAND INSTITUTE OF ART - JESSICA R.
GUND MEMORIAL LIBRARY □ Cleveland, OH

Tse, Shui-Yim, Chinese Ref.Libn.
UNIVERSITY OF BRITISH COLUMBIA - ASIAN
STUDIES LIBRARY □ Vancouver, BC

Tseng, Helen, Asst.Libn.
UNIVERSITY OF CALIFORNIA, BERKELEY -
EARTHQUAKE ENGINEERING RESEARCH
CENTER LIBRARY □ Richmond, CA

Tsuneishi, David, Rd.Serv.
U.S. COMMISSION ON CIVIL RIGHTS - NATL.
CLEARINGHOUSE LIBRARY □ Washington, DC

Tu, C. Brian, Mgr., Info.Serv.
BRITISH COLUMBIA UTILITIES COMMISSION -
LIBRARY □ Vancouver, BC

Tubbs, Barbara, ILL
WARREN LIBRARY ASSOCIATION - LIBRARY □
Warren, PA

Tucci, Valerie K., Mgr., Info.Serv.
AIR PRODUCTS AND CHEMICALS, INC. - CRSD
INFORMATION SERVICES □ Allentown, PA

Tuchman, Maurice S., Libn.
HEBREW COLLEGE - JACOB AND ROSE
GROSSMAN LIBRARY □ Brookline, MA

Tuck, Sherrie, Acq.Libn.
WESTON SCHOOL OF THEOLOGY - LIBRARY □
Cambridge, MA

Tucker, Bonnie, Main Post Libn.
U.S. ARMY POST - FORT LEWIS - LIBRARY
SYSTEM □ Ft. Lewis, WA

Tucker, Cornelia, Hd.Libn.
TEMPLE UNIVERSITY - CENTRAL LIBRARY
SYSTEM - CENTER CITY LIBRARY □
Philadelphia, PA

Tucker, Elinor, Supv.
CENTER FOR WOMEN POLICY STUDIES -
FAMILY VIOLENCE PROJECT LIBRARY □
Washington, DC

Tucker, Elizabeth, Info.Dir.
AGBABIAN ASSOCIATES - LIBRARY† □ El
Segundo, CA

Tucker, Elizabeth, Libn.
U.S. NAVY - NAVAL SURFACE WEAPONS
CENTER - WHITE OAK LIBRARY† □ Silver
Spring, MD

Tucker, Ellis, Sys.Libn.
UNIVERSITY OF MISSISSIPPI - SCHOOL OF
LAW LIBRARY □ University, MS

Tucker, Gwynne, Libn.
MIDLAND DOHERTY, LTD. - LIBRARY □ Toronto,
ON

Tucker, Jack, Cur.
CALIFORNIA STATE COLLEGE, BAKERSFIELD -
CALIFORNIA WELL SAMPLE REPOSITORY □
Bakersfield, CA

Tucker, Laura, Libn.
AMERICAN INSTITUTE FOR ECONOMIC
RESEARCH - E.C. HARWOOD LIBRARY □ Great
Barrington, MA

Tucker, Louise K., Chf.Libn.
POST-TRIBUNE - LIBRARY □ Gary, IN

Tucker, Mae S., Asst.Dir., Main Lib.Serv.
CHARLOTTE AND MECKLENBURG COUNTY
PUBLIC LIBRARY - TEXTILE COLLECTION □
Charlotte, NC

Tucker, Mark, Sr.Ref.Libn.
PURDUE UNIVERSITY - HUMANITIES, SOCIAL
SCIENCE AND EDUCATION LIBRARY □ West
Lafayette, IN

Tucker, Norman P., Res. & Prog.Off.
BOSTON ATHENAEUM LIBRARY □ Boston, MA

Tucker, Ms. Pat, Libn.
OKLAHOMA GAS AND ELECTRIC COMPANY -
LIBRARY □ Oklahoma City, OK

Tucker, Richard W., Archv.
NORTH AMERICAN TIDDLYWINKS
ASSOCIATION - ARCHIVES □ Silver Spring, MD

Tucker, Ruth, Hd., Tech.Proc.
UNIVERSITY OF CALIFORNIA, BERKELEY -
MUSIC LIBRARY □ Berkeley, CA

Tuggle, Cindie, Asst.Libn.
MERCY REGIONAL MEDICAL CENTER LIBRARY
□ Vicksburg, MS

Tuggle, Robert, Dir. of Archv.
METROPOLITAN OPERA ASSOCIATION -
ARCHIVES □ New York, NY

Tuke, Donna M., Chf.Libn.
WINSTON & STRAWN - LIBRARY □ Chicago, IL

Tuli, Jacqui, Educ.Coord.
CANADIAN JEWELLERS INSTITUTE -
GERSTEIN/TIFFANY LIBRARY □ Toronto, ON

Tulis, Susan, Docs.Libn.
UNIVERSITY OF VIRGINIA - ARTHUR J.
MORRIS LAW LIBRARY □ Charlottesville, VA

Tull, Willis Clayton, Jr., Libn.
MILBOURNE & TULL RESEARCH CENTER -
LIBRARY □ Cockeysville, MD

Tull, Willis Clayton, Jr., Libn.
UNITARIAN AND UNIVERSALIST
GENEALOGICAL SOCIETY - LIBRARY □
Cockeysville, MD

Tullar, Yolande, Dir.
SHAWNEE SOLAR PROJECT, INC. - ENERGY
CONSERVATION & SOLAR RETROFIT
DEMONSTRATION CENTER □ Carbondale, IL

Tullis, Boyd, Data Mgr.
RMI, INC. - TECHNICAL LIBRARY □ National
City, CA

Tullis, Carol, Ref.Libn.
INDIANA UNIVERSITY - BIOLOGY LIBRARY □
Bloomington, IN

Tulumello, Ana, Ref.Libn.
UNIVERSITY OF BRIDGEPORT - SCHOOL OF
LAW - LAW LIBRARY □ Bridgeport, CT

Tumy, Bud, Dir.
U.S. DEPT. OF EDUCATION - REFUGEE
MATERIALS CENTER □ Kansas City, MO

Tung, Cecilia, Libn.
TEXAS INSTRUMENTS, INC. - INFORMATION
SYSTEMS & SERVICES LIBRARY □ Dallas, TX

Tung, Sandra, Info.Spec.
UNIVERSITY OF SOUTHERN CALIFORNIA -
NASA INDUSTRIAL APPLICATION CENTER
(NIAC) □ Los Angeles, CA

Tung, Sophie, ILL Libn.
HUGHES AIRCRAFT COMPANY - GROUND
SYSTEMS GROUP - TECHNICAL LIBRARY □
Fullerton, CA

Tunstall, Margaret, Acq.Libn.
TEXAS SOUTHERN UNIVERSITY - LIBRARY -
HEARTMAN COLLECTION □ Houston, TX

Tuohy, Nancy, Asst.Libn.
LOYOLA UNIVERSITY OF CHICAGO - LAW
LIBRARY □ Chicago, IL

Tupper, Pat, Lib.Prog.Dir.
MINNESOTA STATE DEPARTMENT OF
EDUCATION - INTERAGENCY RESOURCE AND
INFORMATION CENTER □ St. Paul, MN

Turanski, Margaret K., Asst.Hd.
FREE LIBRARY OF PHILADELPHIA - FILMS
DEPARTMENT □ Philadelphia, PA

Turgeon, Sharon, Dir.
ARIZONA STATE DEPARTMENT OF LIBRARY,
ARCHIVES & PUBLIC RECORDS □ Phoenix, AZ

Turhollow, Anne, Asst.Sci.Libn.
SAN DIEGO STATE UNIVERSITY - SCIENCE
DEPARTMENT† □ San Diego, CA

Turiel, David, Dir., Tech.Serv.Div.
POLYTECHNIC INSTITUTE OF NEW YORK -
SPICER LIBRARY □ Brooklyn, NY

Turk, Barbara
CENTER ON SOCIAL WELFARE POLICY AND
LAW - LIBRARY □ New York, NY

Turk, Sally, Tech.Info.Spec.
XEROX CORPORATION - DIABLO SYSTEMS,
INC. - TECHNICAL LIBRARY □ Fremont, CA

Turkington, Mrs. N., Hd., Sci./Engr.Div.
ROYAL MILITARY COLLEGE OF CANADA -
MASSEY LIBRARY & SCIENCE/ENGINEERING
LIBRARY □ Kingston, ON

Turkmen, Aydin Y., Ref.Lib.
GRAND LODGE OF NEW YORK, F. AND A.M. -
ROBERT R. LIVINGSTON LIBRARY AND
MUSEUM □ New York, NY

Turley, Paula, Chf.Libn.
U.S. AIR FORCE - WESTERN SPACE AND
MISSILE CENTER - WSMC/PMET TECHNICAL
LIBRARY □ Vandenberg AFB, CA

Turman, Barbara, Hd., Ref.
BROWN UNIVERSITY - SCIENCES LIBRARY □
Providence, RI

Turman, Lynne, Libn.
RICHMOND MEMORIAL HOSPITAL - MEDICAL
AND NURSING SCHOOL LIBRARY □ Richmond,
VA

Turnage, Gerald W., Dir.
U.S. ARMY - ENGINEER WATERWAYS
EXPERIMENT STATION - PAVEMENTS & SOIL
TRAFFICABILITY INFO. ANALYSIS CTR. □
Vicksburg, MS

Turnage, Robert, Tech.Info.Spec.
U.S. DEPT. OF LABOR - OSHA - TECHNICAL
DATA CENTER □ Washington, DC

Turnbull, Barbara, Supv., Tech.Proc.
FEDERAL RESERVE BANK OF PHILADELPHIA -
LIBRARY □ Philadelphia, PA

Turnbull, M.A. Brian, Map Cur.
UNIVERSITY OF VICTORIA - MC PHERSON
LIBRARY - UNIVERSITY MAP COLLECTION □
Victoria, BC

Turner, Ann, Ref.
LOYOLA LAW SCHOOL - LIBRARY □ Los Angeles,
CA

Turner, Annetta, Campus Libn.
CENTENNIAL COLLEGE OF APPLIED ARTS &
TECHNOLOGY - WARDEN WOODS CAMPUS
RESOURCE CENTRE □ Scarborough, ON

Turner, Charles W., Soc.Libn.
ROCKBRIDGE HISTORICAL SOCIETY -
LIBRARY/ARCHIVES □ Lexington, VA

Turner, Decherd, Dir.
UNIVERSITY OF TEXAS, AUSTIN - HARRY
RANSOM HUMANITIES RESEARCH CENTER □
Austin, TX

Turner, Elnora H., Pub. Health Libn.
NORTH CAROLINA STATE DEPARTMENT OF
HUMAN RESOURCES - DIVISION OF HEALTH
SERVICES - PUBLIC HEALTH LIBRARY □ Raleigh,
NC

Turner, Evelyn, Asst.Cur.
CRANFORD HISTORICAL SOCIETY - MUSEUM
LIBRARY □ Cranford, NJ

Turner, Evlyn L., Law Libn.
BUTTE COUNTY LAW LIBRARY □ Oroville, CA

Turner, Gurley, Dir. of Info.Serv.
CATALYST - INFORMATION CENTER □ New
York, NY

Turner, Jeanne Marie, Lib.Techn.
U.S. ARMY - CORPS OF ENGINEERS -
PHILADELPHIA DISTRICT - TECHNICAL
LIBRARY □ Philadelphia, PA

Turner, Judith Campbell, Sect.Hd., Libn.
MILWAUKEE PUBLIC MUSEUM - REFERENCE
LIBRARY □ Milwaukee, WI

Turner, Lela, Tech.Libn.
AMERICAN CAST IRON PIPE COMPANY -
TECHNICAL LIBRARY □ Birmingham, AL

Turner, Philip, Act.Chf., Info.Sys.Div.
U.S.D.A. - NATIONAL AGRICULTURAL LIBRARY
□ Beltsville, MD

Turner, Rigbie, Cur., Music Mss. & Books
PIERPONT MORGAN LIBRARY □ New York, NY

Turner, Ronald R., Act.Chf.
U.S. DEPT. OF ENERGY - ENERGY LIBRARY □
Washington, DC

Turner, Ruth, Asst.Libn.
INTERNATIONAL MINERALS & CHEMICALS
CORPORATION - IMC RESEARCH &
DEVELOPMENT LIBRARY □ Terre Haute, IN

Turner, Shari, Libn.
HAMMER, SILER, GEORGE ASSOCIATES -
LIBRARY □ Silver Spring, MD

Turner, Tamara A., Dir.
CHILDREN'S ORTHOPEDIC HOSPITAL &
MEDICAL CENTER - HOSPITAL LIBRARY □
Seattle, WA

Turnquist, Reba, Asst. Law Libn.
UNIVERSITY OF WASHINGTON - MARIAN
GOULD GALLAGHER LAW LIBRARY □ Seattle,
WA

Turpen, Midge, Adm.Sec.
BROWARD COUNTY HISTORICAL COMMISSION
- LIBRARY & ARCHIVES □ Fort Lauderdale, FL

Turpentine, Nancy, Assoc.Ref.Libn.
UNIVERSITY OF ARKANSAS FOR MEDICAL
SCIENCES - MEDICAL SCIENCES LIBRARY □
Little Rock, AR

Turro, Rev. James C., Dir., Lib.Serv.
IMMACULATE CONCEPTION SEMINARY -
LIBRARY □ Mahwah, NJ

Turtell, Neal, Asst.Libn.
NATIONAL GALLERY OF ART - LIBRARY □
Washington, DC

Tuszynski, Dr. Frances, Libn.
POLISH AMERICAN CONGRESS - SOUTHERN
CALIFORNIA-ARIZONA DIVISION - POLAND'S
MILLENIUM LIBRARY □ Los Angeles, CA

Tuthill, Barbara, Supv.Libn.
SAN DIEGO PUBLIC LIBRARY - ART, MUSIC &
RECREATION SECTION □ San Diego, CA

Tutihasi, Laurraine, Lib.Res.Anl.
ROCKWELL INTERNATIONAL - SPACE
BUSINESSES - TECHNICAL INFORMATION
CENTER □ Downey, CA

Tuttle, C. Brian, Asst.Dir.
CAMP HILL HOSPITAL - DRUG INFORMATION
CENTRE □ Halifax, NS

Tuttle, Irene H., Libn.
ANDOVER COLLEGE - LIBRARY □ Portland, ME

Tuttle, Irma S., Libn.
MASONIC MEDICAL RESEARCH LABORATORY -
LIBRARY □ Utica, NY

Tuttle, Jeffrey, County Couns.
CALAVERAS COUNTY LAW LIBRARY □ San
Andreas, CA

Tuttle, Mrs. John, Cur.
GOSHEN HISTORICAL SOCIETY - LIBRARY □
Goshen, CT

Tuttle, Lyle, Dir.
TUTTLE (Lyle) TATTOOING - TATTOO ART
MUSEUM - LIBRARY □ San Francisco, CA

Tuttle, Naomi V., Veterinary Med.Lib.Asst.
VIRGINIA-MARYLAND REGIONAL COLLEGE OF
VETERINARY MEDICINE - LIBRARY □
Blacksburg, VA

Tuttle, Walter Alan, Libn.
NATIONAL HUMANITIES CENTER - LIBRARY □
Research Triangle Park, NC

Twedell, Helen, ILL, Acq.
UNIVERSITY OF FLORIDA - COASTAL &
OCEANOGRAPHIC ENGINEERING DEPARTMENT
- COASTAL ENGINEERING ARCHIVES □
Gainesville, FL

Twiggs, B., Tech.Serv.Libn.
HUDSON VALLEY COMMUNITY COLLEGE -
DWIGHT MARVIN LEARNING RESOURCES
CENTER □ Troy, NY

Twine, Paulette, Tech.Info.Spec.
U.S. NATL. HIGHWAY TRAFFIC SAFETY
ADMINISTRATION - TECHNICAL REFERENCE
DIVISION □ Washington, DC

Twombley, Fred, Sr.Adm.Asst.
GREEN THUMB LIBRARY □ Arlington, VA

Twombly, Carole E., Libn.
KEYES ASSOCIATES - LIBRARY □ Providence,
RI

Twomey, Gail, Med.Libn.
ST. LUKE'S HOSPITAL OF MIDDLEBOROUGH -
MEDICAL STAFF LIBRARY □ Middleboro, MA

Tybur, Dawn, Asst.Libn.
NEW YORK STATE LIBRARY - LAW/SOCIAL
SCIENCE REFERENCE SERVICES □ Albany, NY

Tydeman, William E., Hd.
UNIVERSITY OF NEW MEXICO - SPECIAL
COLLECTIONS DEPARTMENT □ Albuquerque, NM

Tyger, Barbara, Dir.
SAN FRANCISCO ACADEMY OF COMIC ART -
LIBRARY† □ San Francisco, CA

Tyiska, Barbara L., Hd.Libn.
PAYNE THEOLOGICAL SEMINARY - R.C.
RANSOM MEMORIAL LIBRARY† □ Wilberforce,
OH

Tykol, Joyce, Libn.
ROCKWELL INTERNATIONAL - GRAPHIC
SYSTEMS - TECHNICAL INFORMATION CENTER
□ Chicago, IL

Tyler, Esther, Supv., Tech.Serv.
ANDREWS UNIVERSITY - JAMES WHITE
LIBRARY† □ Berrien Springs, MI

Tyler, Mrs. M.A., Asst.Archv.
UNITED CHURCH OF CANADA - CENTRAL
ARCHIVES† □ Toronto, ON

Tyler, Dr. Richard, Hist.
PHILADELPHIA HISTORICAL COMMISSION -
LIBRARY □ Philadelphia, PA

Tyler, Samuel R., Exec.Dir.
BOSTON MUNICIPAL RESEARCH BUREAU -
LIBRARY □ Boston, MA

Tyler, Sharon, Tech.Info.Spec.
VERSATEC - TECHNICAL INFORMATION
CENTER □ Santa Clara, CA

Tymciurak, Olya T., Libn.
TUCSON CITY PLANNING DEPARTMENT -
LIBRARY □ Tucson, AZ

Tyner, Mary E., Corp.Libn.
DART & KRAFT, INC. - CORPORATE LIBRARY □
Northbrook, IL

Tynski, Gary, Print Cur.
MC GILL UNIVERSITY - DEPARTMENT OF RARE
BOOKS & SPECIAL COLLECTIONS □ Montreal,
PQ

Tyrrell, Susan J., Libn.
PANARCTIC OILS LTD. - LIBRARY □ Calgary, AB

Tysick, Ronald R., Photo Libn.
OTTAWA CITIZEN - LIBRARY □ Ottawa, ON

Tyson, Edwin L., Libn.
NEVADA COUNTY HISTORICAL SOCIETY -
SEARLS HISTORICAL LIBRARY □ Nevada City,
CA

Tyson, Evalyn A., Ref.Serv.Supv.
LIBERTY MUTUAL INSURANCE COMPANY -
EDUCATION/INFORMATION RESOURCES □
Boston, MA

Tyson, Olive, Libn.
TENNECO OIL EXPLORATION AND
PRODUCTION - GEOLOGICAL RESEARCH
LIBRARY □ Houston, TX

Tytgat, Mr. A.J., Educ.Dir.
NATIONAL COWBOY HALL OF FAME &
WESTERN HERITAGE CENTER - RESEARCH
LIBRARY OF WESTERN AMERICANA □ Oklahoma
City, OK

U

U, Anna, Libn.
UNIVERSITY OF TORONTO - EAST ASIAN
LIBRARY □ Toronto, ON

Ubaldini, Michael W., Sr.Libn.
EASTMAN KODAK COMPANY - EASTMAN
CHEMICALS DIVISION - RESEARCH LIBRARY □
Kingsport, TN

Ubysz, Priscilla, Info.Spec.
FUTURES GROUP, INC. - LIBRARY □
Glastonbury, CT

Uddin, Shantha, Assoc.Libn.
ENCYCLOPAEDIA BRITANNICA, INC. -
EDITORIAL LIBRARY □ Chicago, IL

Udics, Father John, Libn.
ST. TIKHON'S SEMINARY - LIBRARY □ South
Canaan, PA

Udin, Madeleine, Mgr.
NATIONAL INVESTIGATIONS COMMITTEE ON
UFOS - NEW AGE CENTER □ Van Nuys, CA

Uesato, Ikuko, Libn.
KAPIOLANI-CHILDREN'S MEDICAL CENTER -
KCMC MEDICAL LIBRARY □ Honolulu, HI

Uglow, Sadie, Ref.Libn.
TACOMA ART MUSEUM - LIBRARY □ Tacoma,
WA

Uhen, Jane, Asst.Libn.
EATON CORPORATION - CUTLER-HAMMER
LIBRARY □ Milwaukee, WI

Uhl, Mary Ann, Asst.Libn.
GILA COUNTY LAW LIBRARY □ Globe, AZ

Uhler, Edward H., Libn.
AT & T TECHNOLOGIES, INC. - GUILFORD
CENTER LIBRARY □ Greensboro, NC

Uhlhorn, Ruth, Ref./ILL
UNIVERSITY OF TEXAS HEALTH SCIENCE
CENTER, SAN ANTONIO - LIBRARY □ San
Antonio, TX

Uhlinger, Eleanor, Lib.Techn.
U.S. NATL. MARINE FISHERIES SERVICE -
NORTHWEST & ALASKA FISHERIES CENTER -
LIBRARY □ Seattle, WA

Ullrich, Betty F., Libn.
REVIEW & HERALD PUBLISHING ASSOCIATION
- LIBRARY □ Hagerstown, MD

Ulmer, Lorraine, Libn.
HENRY (J.J.) CO., INC. - ENGINEERING
LIBRARY □ Moorestown, NJ

Ulrich, Edwin A., Dir. and Owner
ULRICH (Edwin A.) MUSEUM - LIBRARY/
ARCHIVES □ Hyde Park, NY

Ulrich, Fred, Ref.Libn.
NORTH OLYMPIC LIBRARY SYSTEM - PORT
ANGELES BRANCH - PACIFIC NORTHWEST
ROOM □ Port Angeles, WA

Ulrich, John M., Dir.
INDIANAPOLIS CENTER FOR ADVANCED
RESEARCH - ARAC - NASA TECHNICAL
INFORMATION CENTER □ Indianapolis, IN

Ulrich, Ursula, Libn.
CANADA - NATIONAL FILM BOARD OF CANADA
- EDMONTON DISTRICT OFFICE - FILM
LIBRARY □ Edmonton, AB

Ultang, Joanne, Libn.
KIDDER, PEABODY AND COMPANY, INC. -
LIBRARY □ New York, NY

Umberson, Wilma, Lib.Techn.
BENTON SERVICES CENTER - MEDICAL
LIBRARY □ Benton, AR

Umblia, Marta, Lib.Asst.
BRITISH COLUMBIA HEALTH ASSOCIATION
(BCHA) - LIBRARY □ Vancouver, BC

Umenhofer, Kenneth, Assoc.Libn.
GORDON-CONWELL THEOLOGICAL SEMINARY -
GODDARD LIBRARY □ South Hamilton, MA

Umoh, Linda, Cat.
SOUTHERN METHODIST UNIVERSITY -
PERKINS SCHOOL OF THEOLOGY - LIBRARY □
Dallas, TX

Umpierre, Mara, Hd.Libn.
TEXAS CHIROPRACTIC COLLEGE - MAE HILTY
MEMORIAL LIBRARY □ Pasadena, TX

Umpleby, Susan, Asst.Libn.
ACADEMY OF MOTION PICTURE ARTS AND
SCIENCES - MARGARET HERRICK LIBRARY □
Beverly Hills, CA

Underdown, Susan W., Tech.Libn.
WARNER-LAMBERT CANADA INC. - TECHNICAL
INFORMATION CENTRE □ Scarborough, ON

Underhill, Jeanne, Dir.
BROWARD COUNTY LAW LIBRARY □ Fort
Lauderdale, FL

Unger, Agnes, Libn.
RICHARDSON GREENSHIELDS OF CANADA,
LTD. - RESEARCH LIBRARY □ Winnipeg, MB

Unger, Mark, Dir., Info.Rsrcs.Ctr.
CATHOLIC HEALTH ASSOCIATION OF THE
UNITED STATES - INFORMATION RESOURCE
CENTER □ St. Louis, MO

Unger, Monica, Cat.Libn.
NORTHEASTERN OHIO UNIVERSITIES COLLEGE
OF MEDICINE - BASIC MEDICAL SCIENCES
LIBRARY □ Rootstown, OH

Ungurait, Karen, Mgt.Anl.
FLORIDA STATE DEPT. OF ENVIRONMENTAL
REGULATION - LIBRARY □ Tallahassee, FL

Unruh, Carolyn V., Libn.
READING HOSPITAL & MEDICAL CENTER -
SCHOOL OF NURSING LIBRARY □ Reading, PA

Unterborn, Lee, Acq./Ref.Libn.
ST. MARY'S UNIVERSITY - LAW LIBRARY† □
San Antonio, TX

Unterburger, Mrs. George, Lib.Cons.
BUSHNELL CONGREGATIONAL CHURCH -
LIBRARY □ Detroit, MI

Unterburger, George, Chf.
DETROIT PUBLIC LIBRARY - TECHNOLOGY AND
SCIENCE DEPARTMENT □ Detroit, MI

Upadhyaya, Mr. P.D., Med.Libn.
CENTRAL STATE HOSPITAL - HEALTH
SCIENCES LIBRARY □ Petersburg, VA

Updegrove, Robert, Libn.
U.S. EXECUTIVE OFFICE OF THE PRESIDENT -
LIBRARY □ Washington, DC

Uphoff, Joseph A., Jr., Dir.
ARJUNA LIBRARY □ Colorado Springs, CO

Upright, Kirby, Esq., Chm., Lib.Comm.
MONROE COUNTY LAW LIBRARY □ Stroudsburg,
PA

Upshall, Juta, Libn.
METROPOLITAN TORONTO LIBRARY - FINE
ART DEPARTMENT □ Toronto, ON

Uptgraft, Gloria, Libn.
ST. JOSEPH'S HOSPITAL - SCHOOL OF
NURSING LIBRARY □ Fort Wayne, IN

Upton, B. Susan, Asst.Libn.
MISSISSIPPI STATE LAW LIBRARY □ Jackson,
MS

Upton, Ileen R., Pediatric Libn.
ST. LOUIS CHILDREN'S HOSPITAL - BORDEN S.
VEEDER LIBRARY □ St. Louis, MO

Upton, Mildred, Libn.
MONSANTO FIBERS & INTERMEDIATES
COMPANY - LIBRARY □ Greenwood, SC

Urago, Gail M., Libn.
WESTERN CURRICULUM COORDINATION
CENTER (WCCC) - RESOURCE CENTER □
Honolulu, HI

Uranowski, Ted, Libn. 1
METROPOLITAN TORONTO LIBRARY -
LANGUAGES DEPARTMENT □ Toronto, ON

Urban, Paul B., Mgr., Info. Retrieval
AMERICAN SOCIETY FOR METALS - METALS
INFORMATION □ Metals Park, OH

Urbankiewicz, Nancy L., Sr.Libn.
TRANS CANADA PIPELINES LTD. - LIBRARY □
Toronto, ON

Ureneck, Dolores, Lib.Mgr.
CARTER-WALLACE, INC. - LIBRARY □ Cranbury,
NJ

Urness, Carol, Asst.Cur.
UNIVERSITY OF MINNESOTA - JAMES FORD
BELL LIBRARY □ Minneapolis, MN

Urquhart, E., Libn.
GRAYS HARBOR COUNTY LAW LIBRARY† □
Montesano, WA

Urquiza, Belinda, Lib.Serv.
BIOSPHERICS INC. - LIBRARY □ Rockville, MD

Ursery, Nancy, Hd., State Docs. Unit
TEXAS STATE LIBRARY - INFORMATION
SERVICES DIVISION □ Austin, TX

Urwiler, Richard, AV Media Serv.
WAYNE STATE COLLEGE - U.S. CONN LIBRARY
□ Wayne, NE

Urzua, Roberto, Oper./Tech.Serv.Libn.
U.S. DEPT. OF ENERGY - BONNEVILLE POWER
ADMINISTRATION - LIBRARY □ Portland, OR

Usher, Phyllis M. Land, Dir. of Fed.Res.
INDIANA STATE DEPARTMENT OF PUBLIC
INSTRUCTION - PROFESSIONAL LIBRARY □
Indianapolis, IN

Uskavitch, Robert, Chf., Info.Serv.
U.S. DEPT. OF THE INTERIOR - NATURAL
RESOURCES LIBRARY □ Washington, DC

Utterback, I., Info.Spec.
NORTH CAROLINA STATE SCIENCE AND
TECHNOLOGY RESEARCH CENTER □ Research
Triangle Park, NC

Utterback, Martha, Asst.Dir.
DAUGHTERS OF THE REPUBLIC OF TEXAS -
LIBRARY □ San Antonio, TX

Utterback, Nancy, Hd., Pub.Serv.
UNIVERSITY OF LOUISVILLE - KORNHAUSER
HEALTH SCIENCES LIBRARY □ Louisville, KY

Uunila, Edith, Sr.Ed.
CHRONICLE OF HIGHER EDUCATION - LIBRARY
□ Washington, DC

Uva, Peter, Asst.Libn., Pub.Serv.
SUNY - UPSTATE MEDICAL CENTER LIBRARY □
Syracuse, NY

Uyenaka, S., Japanese Bibliog.
UNIVERSITY OF TORONTO - EAST ASIAN
LIBRARY □ Toronto, ON

Uzcategui, Juliana, Asst.Libn.
BRUNDAGE, STORY & ROSE, INVESTMENT
COUNSEL - LIBRARY □ New York, NY

Uzee, Denise, Info.Spec.
LOUISIANA STATE HOUSE OF
REPRESENTATIVES LEGISLATIVE SERVICES -
RESEARCH LIBRARY □ Baton Rouge, LA

V

Vaccaro, Barbara H., Asst. State Law Libn.
MICHIGAN STATE - LIBRARY OF MICHIGAN -
LAW LIBRARY □ Lansing, MI

Vaccaro, M., Asst.Libn.
NEW ENGLAND INSTITUTE - LIBRARY □
Norwalk, CT

Vachon, Florian, Lib.Dir.
FOREIGN MISSIONS SOCIETY OF QUEBEC -
LIBRARY □ Pont-Viau, Ville Laval, PQ

Vacula, Mary A., Libn./Info.Spec.
WEIR (Paul) COMPANY - LIBRARY □ Chicago, IL

Vada, Ilse, Libn.
NATIONAL INSTITUTE ON DRUG ABUSE -
RESOURCE CENTER □ Rockville, MD

Vago, Marianne, Info.Rsrcs.Supv.
NATIONAL STARCH AND CHEMICAL
CORPORATION - INFORMATION RESOURCES □
Bridgewater, NJ

Vaiginas, Paul, Libn.
NEW ENGLAND DEACONESS HOSPITAL -
HORRAX LIBRARY† □ Boston, MA

Vail, Virgil, Media Spec.
POINT LOMA NAZARENE COLLEGE - RYAN
LIBRARY □ San Diego, CA

Vaitiekaitis, Audrone V., Cat.Serv.
WARNER-LAMBERT/PARKE-DAVIS -
RESEARCH LIBRARY† □ Ann Arbor, MI

Vajda, Elizabeth A., Hd.Libn.
COOPER UNION FOR THE ADVANCEMENT OF
SCIENCE AND ART - LIBRARY □ New York, NY

Vajda, John E., Asst.Libn.
U.S. NAVY - DEPARTMENT LIBRARY □
Washington, DC

Valdez, Gina, Info.Serv.Spec.
U.S. BUREAU OF THE CENSUS - INFORMATION
SERVICES PROGRAM - DENVER REG. OFFICE -
CENSUS PUBLICATION CENTER □ Denver, CO

Valencia, Maria L., Libn.
PUERTO RICAN CULTURE INSTITUTE - LUIS
MUNOZ RIVERA LIBRARY AND MUSEUM □
Barranquitas, PR

Valente, Fr. John Bosco, O.F.M., Libn.
ST. FRANCIS MONASTERY AND CHAPEL - ST.
FRANCIS CHAPEL INFORMATION CENTER &
FREE-LENDING LIBRARY □ Providence, RI

Valentine, Patrick M., Coord./Libn.
CUMBERLAND COUNTY PUBLIC LIBRARY -
NORTH CAROLINA FOREIGN LANGUAGE
CENTER □ Fayetteville, NC

Valeri, Prof. John R., Dir.
CATHOLIC UNIVERSITY OF AMERICA - SCHOOL
OF LAW - ROBERT J. WHITE LAW LIBRARY □
Washington, DC

Valescu, Frances, Libn.
ARKANSAS (State) HISTORY COMMISSION -
ARCHIVES □ Little Rock, AR

Vallarino, Gioconda, Cat.
INTER-AMERICAN DEFENSE COLLEGE -
LIBRARY □ Washington, DC

Valle, Barbara, Asst.Libn.
PACIFIC PRESS, LTD. - PRESS LIBRARY □
Vancouver, BC

Vallee, Jacqueline, Ref.Libn.
QUEBEC PROVINCE - MINISTERE DES
AFFAIRES SOCIALES - SERVICE DE LA
DOCUMENTATION □ Quebec, PQ

Valley, Derek R., Dir.
STATE CAPITAL HISTORICAL ASSOCIATION -
LIBRARY AND PHOTO ARCHIVES □ Olympia, WA

Vallinos, Alice, Res.Libn.
NEEDHAM, HARPER & STEERS ADVERTISING,
INC. - RESEARCH LIBRARY† □ New York, NY

Valone, Gloria, Asst.Dir.
KEAN COLLEGE OF NEW JERSEY - NANCY
THOMPSON LIBRARY† □ Union, NJ

Valpy, Amanda, Chf.Libn.
TORONTO GLOBE AND MAIL, LTD. - LIBRARY □
Toronto, ON

Valunas, Madelyn
SHIPPENSBURG UNIVERSITY - EZRA LEHMAN
LIBRARY □ Shippensburg, PA

Valuskas, Janice, Asst.Libn.
CONNECTICUT NEWSPAPERS INC. -
ADVOCATE & GREENWICH TIME LIBRARY □
Stamford, CT

Valuskas, Janice L., Libn., Tech.Info.Ctr.
COPPER DEVELOPMENT ASSOCIATION, INC. -
COPPER DATA CENTER □ Greenwich, CT

Van Allen, Russell E., Asst. Law Libn.
UTAH STATE LAW LIBRARY □ Salt Lake City, UT

Van Atta, Cathaleen, Libn.
KITT PEAK NATIONAL OBSERVATORY -
LIBRARY □ Tucson, AZ

Van Atta, Sue, Dir.
ST. JOSEPH HOSPITAL - MEDICAL STAFF
LIBRARY □ Lorain, OH

Van Berkel, Joyce, Subject Spec.
SANDIA NATIONAL LABORATORIES -
TECHNICAL LIBRARY □ Albuquerque, NM

Van Bloem, Claire, Res.Asst.
LANE COUNCIL OF GOVERNMENTS - LIBRARY □
Eugene, OR

Van Brocklin, Vincent, Ser. Unit Hd.
HAWAII STATE LIBRARY - SERIALS SECTION □
Honolulu, HI

Van Buren, Mary, Libn.
CORNELL UNIVERSITY - NEW YORK STATE
AGRICULTURAL EXPERIMENT STATION -
LIBRARY □ Geneva, NY

Van Buren, Rita, Intl. Tax Spec.
PRICE WATERHOUSE - NATIONAL
INFORMATION CENTER □ New York, NY

Van Buskirk, E. Lynne, Assoc.Dir., Res.
NEW JERSEY EDUCATION ASSOCIATION -
RESEARCH LIBRARY □ Trenton, NJ

Van Buskirk, Nancy, Med.Libn.
U.S. VETERANS ADMINISTRATION (FL-Tampa)
- MEDICAL LIBRARY □ Tampa, FL

Van Camp, Ann, Dir., Info./Online Serv.
INDIANA UNIVERSITY, INDIANAPOLIS -
SCHOOL OF MEDICINE LIBRARY □ Indianapolis,
IN

Van Cura, Mary Ann, Hd. of Tech.Serv.
HAMLINE UNIVERSITY SCHOOL OF LAW -
LIBRARY □ St. Paul, MN

Van Cura, Mary Beth, Supv., Lib.Serv.
MORTON THIOKOL INC. - CORPORATE LIBRARY
□ Chicago, IL

Van Dam, Thomas, Libn.
PINE REST CHRISTIAN HOSPITAL - VAN
NOORD HEALTH SCIENCES LIBRARY □ Grand
Rapids, MI

Van Den Berg, Mr. R., Dept.Libn.
CANADA - NATIONAL DEFENCE - NDHQ
LIBRARY □ Ottawa, ON

Van den Top, Jeraldine J., Libn.
U.S. AIR FORCE HOSPITAL - MEDICAL LIBRARY
(AK-Elmendorf AFB) □ Elmendorf AFB, AK

Van der Bellen, Liana, Chf.
NATIONAL LIBRARY OF CANADA - RARE BOOK
DIVISION □ Ottawa, ON

Van Der Lyke, Barbara, Willimantic Dir.
CONNECTICUT STATE LIBRARY □ Hartford, CT

Van Der Voorn, Neal, Libn.
WASHINGTON STATE LIBRARY - WESTERN
STATE HOSPITAL - STAFF LIBRARY □ Fort
Steilacoom, WA

Van Dine, Ann, Asst.Mgr., Lib.Serv.
HOECHST-ROUSSEL PHARMACEUTICALS, INC. -
LIBRARY □ Somerville, NJ

Van Dinter, Nancy, Chf.Libn.
IDAHO STATESMAN - LIBRARY □ Boise, ID

van Donkersgoed, Elbert, Res. & Policy Dir.
CHRISTIAN FARMERS FEDERATION OF
ONTARIO - JUBILEE FOUNDATION FOR
AGRICULTURAL RESEARCH - LIBRARY □ Guelph,
ON

Van Doren, Helen E., Off.Serv.Coord.
ASPHALT INSTITUTE - RESEARCH LIBRARY □
College Park, MD

Van Doren, Sandra, Archv.
WAYNE STATE UNIVERSITY - ARCHIVES OF
LABOR AND URBAN AFFAIRS/UNIVERSITY
ARCHIVES □ Detroit, MI

Van Dusen, Herbert, Libn.
AMERICAN ASSOCIATION OF CORRECTIONAL
OFFICERS - LIBRARY □ Saginaw, MI

Van Dyk, Stephen, Art/Arch.Libn.
NEW YORK INSTITUTE OF TECHNOLOGY -
LIBRARY □ Old Westbury, NY

Van Dyk, Stephen H., Libn.
NEW YORK INSTITUTE OF TECHNOLOGY -
EDUCATION HALL - ART & ARCHITECTURE
LIBRARY □ Old Westbury, NY

Van Egdom, Deborah, Libn.
IOWA HOSPITAL ASSOCIATION - LIBRARY □
Des Moines, IA

Van Haaften, Julia, Cur., Photographs
NEW YORK PUBLIC LIBRARY - ART, PRINTS &
PHOTOGRAPHS DIVISION - PRINTS &
PHOTOGRAPHS ROOM □ New York, NY

Van Hassel, Ann Wiley, Assoc.Libn.
UNIVERSITY OF BALTIMORE - LAW LIBRARY □
Baltimore, MD

Van Hine, Pamela, Libn.
AMERICAN COLLEGE OF OBSTETRICIANS AND
GYNECOLOGISTS - RESOURCE CENTER □
Washington, DC

Van Hoogenstyn, Parker, Hd., Media/Spec. Project
SUNY - AGRICULTURAL AND TECHNICAL
COLLEGE AT FARMINGDALE - THOMAS D.
GREENLEY LIBRARY □ Farmingdale, NY

Van Horn, Elizabeth K., Libn.
BAR ASSOCIATION OF THE DISTRICT OF
COLUMBIA - LIBRARY† □ Washington, DC

Van Horn, Virginia, Libn.
SPERRY COMPUTER SYSTEMS - DEFENSE
SYSTEMS DIVISION - INFORMATION SERVICE
CENTER □ St. Paul, MN

Van Houten, Stephen, Cat.
MOUNT SINAI SCHOOL OF MEDICINE OF THE
CITY UNIVERSITY OF NEW YORK - GUSTAVE L.
& JANET W. LEVY LIBRARY □ New York, NY

Van Idistine, Sally, Libn.
TOMPKINS COMMUNITY HOSPITAL - ROBERT
BROAD MEDICAL LIBRARY □ Ithaca, NY

Van Jepmond, O.F., Dir., WLN
WASHINGTON STATE LIBRARY □ Olympia, WA

Van Kleek, Rev. Laurence M., Libn.
WESTERN PENTECOSTAL BIBLE COLLEGE -
LIBRARY □ Clayburn, BC

Van Lierde, Isobel, Ser.Libn.
CANADA - NATIONAL GALLERY OF CANADA -
LIBRARY □ Ottawa, ON

Van Linh, Tran, Comparative Law
LOUISIANA STATE UNIVERSITY - LAW
LIBRARY □ Baton Rouge, LA

Van Loo, Dana, Prog.Coord.
UNIVERSITY OF ILLINOIS AT CHICAGO -
HEALTH SCIENCES CENTER - LIBRARY OF THE
HEALTH SCIENCES □ Chicago, IL

Van Mater, John P., Libn.
THEOSOPHICAL UNIVERSITY - LIBRARY □
Altadena, CA

Van Mater, Sarah B., Asst.Libn.
THEOSOPHICAL UNIVERSITY - LIBRARY □
Altadena, CA

van Meer, David J., Cur.
SKAGIT COUNTY HISTORICAL MUSEUM -
HISTORICAL REFERENCE LIBRARY □ La Conner,
WA

Van Meer, David J., Cur.
SKAGIT COUNTY HISTORICAL MUSEUM -
HISTORICAL REFERENCE LIBRARY □ La Conner,
WA

Van Meter, Terry, Dir.
U.S. CAVALRY MUSEUM - LIBRARY □ Fort Riley,
KS

Van Ness, Julie, Res.Assoc.
ARGUS ARCHIVES, INC. □ New York, NY

Van Nest, Dee T., Asst. Law Libn.
MARYLAND STATE LAW LIBRARY □ Annapolis,
MD

Van Niel, Eloise, Hd./Perf. Arts Spec.
HAWAII STATE LIBRARY - FINE ARTS AND
AUDIOVISUAL SECTION □ Honolulu, HI
Van Nocker, Allison, Cur. of Coll.
KINGMAN MUSEUM OF NATURAL HISTORY -
LIBRARY □ Battle Creek, MI
Van Nortwick, Barbara, Lib.Dir.
NEW YORK STATE NURSES ASSOCIATION -
LIBRARY □ Guilderland, NY
Van Oosbree, Charlyne, Base Libn.
U.S. AIR FORCE BASE - WHITEMAN BASE
LIBRARY □ Whiteman AFB, MO
Van Puffelen, John, Libn.
APPALACHIAN BIBLE COLLEGE - LIBRARY □
Bradley, WV
Van Pulis, Noelle, Info.Spec.
OHIO STATE UNIVERSITY - MECHANIZED
INFORMATION CENTER (MIC) □ Columbus, OH
van Reenen, Johann, Libn.
VICTORIA MEDICAL SOCIETY/ROYAL JUBILEE
HOSPITAL - LIBRARY □ Victoria, BC
van Rooyen, Hilda, Med.Libn.
IZAAK WALTON KILLAM HOSPITAL FOR
CHILDREN - MEDICAL STAFF LIBRARY □
Halifax, NS
Van Rossem, Karen, Libn.
NEWSDAY, INC. - LIBRARY □ Melville, NY
Van Ryzin, Elizabeth M., Sr.Libn.
INSTITUTE OF GAS TECHNOLOGY - TECHNICAL
INFORMATION CENTER □ Chicago, IL
Van Sledright, Connie, Hd., Circ.
CALVIN COLLEGE AND SEMINARY - LIBRARY □
Grand Rapids, MI
Van Sluys, Loralie, Libn.
HEWITT ASSOCIATES - LIBRARY □ Lincolnshire,
IL
Van Steen, Jeanne, Pres.
NUTLEY HISTORICAL SOCIETY MUSEUM -
ALICE J. BICKERS LIBRARY □ Nutley, NJ
Van Toll, Faith, Act.Med.Libn.
WAYNE STATE UNIVERSITY - SCHOOL OF
MEDICINE - VERA PARSHALL SHIFFMAN
MEDICAL LIBRARY □ Detroit, MI
Van Vactor, Myra F., Sr.Comp.Sci.Libn.
FEDERAL RESERVE BANK OF NEW YORK -
COMPUTER SCIENCES LIBRARY □ New York, NY
Van Velzer, Verna, Chf.Libn.
ESL/SUBSIDIARY OF TRW - RESEARCH
LIBRARY □ Sunnyvale, CA
Van Weringh, Janet
CLARKSON UNIVERSITY - EDUCATIONAL
RESOURCES CENTER □ Potsdam, NY
Van Why, Carol, Asst.Dept.Hd.
MINNEAPOLIS PUBLIC LIBRARY &
INFORMATION CENTER - LITERATURE AND
LANGUAGE DEPARTMENT □ Minneapolis, MN
Van Why, Joseph S., Dir.
STOWE-DAY FOUNDATION - LIBRARY □
Hartford, CT
Van Winkle, Mary E., Asst.Cur., Rare Bks.
HARVARD UNIVERSITY - SCHOOLS OF
MEDICINE, DENTAL MED. & PUBLIC HEALTH,
BOSTON MED.LIB. - FRANCIS A. COUNTWAY
LIB. □ Boston, MA
Vanags, Miss E.M., Hd.
ALCAN INTERNATIONAL LTD. - KINGSTON
LABORATORIES - LIBRARY □ Kingston, ON
VanAllen, Neil K., Staff Libn.
GENERAL MOTORS CORPORATION - RESEARCH
LABORATORIES LIBRARY □ Warren, MI
VanAuken, Richard, Dir.
INFORMATION TECHNOLOGY CENTER -
LIBRARY □ New York, NY
Vanberg, Bent, Cons.
SONS OF NORWAY - NORTH STAR LIBRARY □
Minneapolis, MN
Vance, Carolyn J., Chf.Libn.
CHAMPAIGN NEWS-GAZETTE - LIBRARY □
Champaign, IL
Vance, Sandra, Libn.
SPRINGFIELD, ILLINOIS STATE JOURNAL &
REGISTER - EDITORIAL LIBRARY □ Springfield,
IL

Vance, Sharon, Hd., Tech.Serv.
WHEATON COLLEGE - BUSWELL MEMORIAL
LIBRARY □ Wheaton, IL
Vandale, Janine, Hd.Libn.
CANADA - NATIONAL FILM BOARD OF CANADA
- FILM LIBRARY† □ Winnipeg, MB
Vande Brink, Jake, Lib.Mgr.
EDMONTON GENERAL HOSPITAL - HEALTH
SCIENCES LIBRARY □ Edmonton, AB
Vandegrift, Rev. J. Raymond, O.P., Libn.
DOMINICAN COLLEGE LIBRARY □ Washington,
DC
Vander Veer, John, Pres.
HOLLAND SOCIETY OF NEW YORK - LIBRARY □
New York, NY
Vander Velde, John J., Spec.Coll.
KANSAS STATE UNIVERSITY - FARRELL
LIBRARY □ Manhattan, KS
Vander Velde, John J., Spec.Coll.Libn.
KANSAS STATE UNIVERSITY - SPECIAL
COLLECTIONS DEPARTMENT □ Manhattan, KS
Vanderburg, Patricia, Ref.Libn.
U.S. ARMY POST - FORT STEWART/HUNTER
AAF LIBRARY SYSTEM □ Ft. Stewart, GA
Vanderby, John, Libn.
SAN DIEGO PUBLIC LIBRARY - LITERATURE &
LANGUAGES SECTION □ San Diego, CA
Vanderelst, Wil, Dir.
ONTARIO - MINISTRY OF CITIZENSHIP AND
CULTURE - LIBRARIES AND COMMUNITY
INFORMATION □ Toronto, ON
Vandergrift, Kay E., Asst.Dir., Serv.
TEACHERS COLLEGE - MILBANK MEMORIAL
LIBRARY □ New York, NY
Vanderland, Patricia G., Libn.
VIRGINIA STATE WATER CONTROL BOARD -
LIBRARY □ Richmond, VA
VanderMeer, Patricia, Libn.
WESTERN MICHIGAN UNIVERSITY -
EDUCATIONAL LIBRARY □ Kalamazoo, MI
Vanderstel, David G., Hist.
CONNER PRAIRIE PIONEER SETTLEMENT -
RESEARCH DEPARTMENT LIBRARY □
Noblesville, IN
Vanderventer, Kathy
COLORADO STATE DEPARTMENT OF
EDUCATION - COLORADO CAREER
INFORMATION SYSTEM □ Longmont, CO
Vandon, Gwen, Circ. & Ser.Libn.
BETHANY AND NORTHERN BAPTIST
THEOLOGICAL SEMINARIES - LIBRARY □ Oak
Brook, IL
Vandoros, Mrs. Z., Hd., Tech.Serv.
CANADA - DEPARTMENT OF
COMMUNICATIONS - INFORMATION SERVICES
□ Ottawa, ON
Vanek, Edna, Spec.Asst.
LIBRARY OF INTERNATIONAL RELATIONS □
Chicago, IL
Vanek, Eva, Mgr., Lib.Serv.
MERRILL LYNCH WHITE WELD - CAPITAL
MARKETS GROUP - LIBRARY† □ New York, NY
VanHorn, Linda, Hd., Info.Serv.
TUFTS UNIVERSITY - HEALTH SCIENCES
LIBRARY □ Boston, MA
Vaniman, Brinn, Libn.
SAN DIEGO PUBLIC LIBRARY - LITERATURE &
LANGUAGES SECTION □ San Diego, CA
Vann, J. Daniel, Exec.Dir.
UNIVERSITY OF WISCONSIN, OSHKOSH -
UNIVERSITY LIBRARIES AND LEARNING
RESOURCES - SPECIAL COLLECTIONS □
Oshkosh, WI
Vann, J. Graves, Jr., Asst.Dir./Marketing
NORTH CAROLINA STATE SCIENCE AND
TECHNOLOGY RESEARCH CENTER □ Research
Triangle Park, NC
Vann, Dr. James E., Dir.
NORTH CAROLINA STATE SCIENCE AND
TECHNOLOGY RESEARCH CENTER □ Research
Triangle Park, NC

Vann, Vicki, Libn.
KERR-MC GEE CORPORATION - MC GEE
LIBRARY □ Oklahoma City, OK
Vannorsdall, Mildred, Prof.Lib.Libn.
CHICAGO PUBLIC LIBRARY CENTRAL LIBRARY -
PROFESSIONAL LIBRARY □ Chicago, IL
Vanston, John D., Law Libn.
MAGUIRE, VOORHIS & WELLS - LIBRARY □
Orlando, FL
Vanzant, Michelle, Law Libn.
HIGHLAND COUNTY LAW LIBRARY □ Hillsboro,
OH
Vara, Margaret, Info.Spec.-Bus.
POLYSAR, LTD. - INFORMATION CENTRE □
Sarnia, ON
Varadachari, Chandra, M.D., Chm., Lib.Comm.
RICHLAND MEMORIAL HOSPITAL - STAFF
LIBRARY □ Olney, IL
Varga, William R., Pub.Serv.
UNIVERSITY OF TULSA - COLLEGE OF LAW
LIBRARY □ Tulsa, OK
Vargas, Yvonne, Hd., Spanish Info.Ctr.
CHICAGO PUBLIC LIBRARY CULTURAL CENTER
- LITERATURE AND LANGUAGE DIVISION □
Chicago, IL
Vargo, Janice, Libn.
KAPLAN/MC LAUGHLIN/DIAZ ARCHITECTS &
PLANNERS - LIBRARY □ San Francisco, CA
Vargo, Katherine, Libn.
CHRIST HOSPITAL - SCHOOL OF NURSING
LIBRARY □ Jersey City, NJ
Varieur, Normand L., Libn.
U.S. ARMY - ARMAMENT RESEARCH &
DEVELOPMENT CENTER - SCIENTIFIC AND
TECHNICAL INFORMATION DIVISION □ Dover,
NJ
Varki, M., Ref.
WIDENER UNIVERSITY - WOLFGRAM
MEMORIAL LIBRARY □ Chester, PA
Varma, D.K., Adm.Stud.Libn.
YORK UNIVERSITY - GOVERNMENT
DOCUMENTS/ADMINISTRATIVE STUDIES
LIBRARY □ Downsview, ON
Varnado, Brien, Supt.
U.S. NATL. PARK SERVICE - FORT SUMTER
NATL. MONUMENT - LIBRARY □ Sullivan's
Island, SC
Varner, James H., Lib. Group Supv.
AT & T - TECHNICAL LIBRARY □ Denver, CO
Vars, Dr. Gordon F., Exec.Sec.-Treas.
NATIONAL ASSOCIATION FOR CORE
CURRICULUM, INC. - LIBRARY □ Kent, OH
Varteressian, Jeanne E., Supv.
VIRGINIA ELECTRIC AND POWER COMPANY -
LIBRARY AND INFORMATION SERVICES □
Richmond, VA
Vartian, Ross, Adm.Dir.
ARMENIAN ASSEMBLY CHARITABLE TRUST -
LIBRARY AND INFORMATION CENTER □
Washington, DC
Vasey, Maureen, Dir., Info.Serv.
CANADIAN REHABILITATION COUNCIL FOR
THE DISABLED - CRCD RESOURCE CENTRE □
Toronto, ON
Vasil, Nick P., Tech.Serv.Supv.
INDIANA VOCATIONAL-TECHNICAL COLLEGE -
RESOURCE CENTER □ Gary, IN
Vasile, Wilfred, Village Hist.
LE ROY HISTORICAL SOCIETY - LIBRARY □ Le
Roy, NY
Vaslef, Dr. Irene, Libn.
HARVARD UNIVERSITY - DUMBARTON OAKS
RESEARCH LIBRARY AND COLLECTION □
Washington, DC
Vattilano, Grace, Chem.Lib.Supv.
UNIVERSITY OF DELAWARE, NEWARK -
CHEMISTRY/CHEMICAL ENGINEERING
LIBRARY □ Newark, DE
Vaughan, Anne, Libn.
LITTON INDUSTRIES - ELECTRON TUBE
DIVISION - LIBRARY □ San Carlos, CA

Vaughan, James, Hd., Access Serv.
UNIVERSITY OF CHICAGO - JOHN CRERAR
LIBRARY □ Chicago, IL

Vaughn, B.J., Acq.Dir.
ERIC CLEARINGHOUSE ON INFORMATION
RESOURCES □ Syracuse, NY

Vaughn, Judi, Libn.
CLARKSVILLE LEAF-CHRONICLE COMPANY -
LIBRARY □ Clarksville, TN

Vaughn, Kathryn, Chf.Med.Libn.
MONTREAL GENERAL HOSPITAL - MEDICAL
LIBRARY □ Montreal, PQ

Vaughn, Nancy, Med.Libn.
U.S. VETERANS ADMINISTRATION (KS-Topeka)
- DR. KARL A. MENNINGER MEDICAL LIBRARY □
Topeka, KS

Vaughn, W.A., Lib.Dir.
ARKANSAS TECH UNIVERSITY - TOMLINSON
LIBRARY - SPECIAL COLLECTIONS □
Russellville, AR

Vaught, Gregory, Libn.
SAN ANTONIO SYMPHONY ORCHESTRA -
SYMPHONY LIBRARY □ San Antonio, TX

Vaught, Rosalie, Libn.
U.S. NATL. MARINE FISHERIES SERVICE -
SOUTHEAST FISHERIES CENTER - PANAMA
CITY LAB. - LIBRARY □ Panama City, FL

Vavrek, Dr. Bernard, Coord.
CLARION UNIV. OF PENNSYLVANIA - COLL. OF
LIBRARY SCIENCE - CTR. FOR THE STUDY OF
RURAL LIBRARIANSHIP - LIB. □ Clarion, PA

Vdovin, George, Libn.
UNIVERSITY OF CALIFORNIA, BERKELEY -
CHEMISTRY LIBRARY □ Berkeley, CA

Veach, Victoria K., Supv.
3M - PATENT AND TECHNICAL
COMMUNICATIONS SERVICES □ St. Paul, MN

Veasley, Mignon, Hd.Libn.
PRICE WATERHOUSE - LIBRARY □ Los Angeles,
CA

Veatch, James R., Prof.
NASHVILLE STATE TECHNICAL INSTITUTE -
EDUCATIONAL RESOURCE CENTER □ Nashville,
TN

Vecoli, Rudolph J., Dir.
UNIVERSITY OF MINNESOTA - IMMIGRATION
HISTORY RESEARCH CENTER COLLECTION □
St. Paul, MN

Vecsey, Dennis J., Supv., Info.Serv.
JOHNSON & JOHNSON-CRITIKON, INC. - R & D
INFORMATION SERVICES □ Tampa, FL

Veeder, George A., Pres.
KENILWORTH HISTORICAL SOCIETY - KILNER
LIBRARY □ Kenilworth, IL

Veeder, Peggy A., Libn.
CALIFORNIA STATE DEPARTMENT OF
TRANSPORTATION - DISTRICT 11 LIBRARY □
San Diego, CA

Veeh, Patricia A., Hd.Libn.
TRINITY UNITED PRESBYTERIAN CHURCH -
LIBRARY □ Santa Ana, CA

Veenstra, Dr. John G., Univ.Libn.
WEST TEXAS STATE UNIVERSITY - CORNETTE
LIBRARY - SPECIAL COLLECTIONS □ Canyon,
TX

Veenstra, Robert J., Libn.
AUBURN UNIVERSITY - VETERINARY MEDICAL
LIBRARY □ Auburn University, AL

Vehec, Joseph R., Exec.Sec.
FIRST CATHOLIC SLOVAK UNION OF U.S.A.
AND CANADA □ Cleveland, OH

Veit, Henri, Div.Chf.
BROOKLYN PUBLIC LIBRARY - HISTORY,
TRAVEL, RELIGION AND BIOGRAPHY DIVISION
□ Brooklyn, NY

Veit, Virginia A., Lib.Mgr.
SAFEWAY STORES, INC. - LIBRARY □ Oakland,
CA

Veitch, Natalie, Libn.
WAYNE PRESBYTERIAN CHURCH - LIBRARY □
Wayne, PA

Veium, Lisa, Dir.
SPOKANE MEDICAL LIBRARY □ Spokane, WA

Vela-Creixell, Mary, Law Libn.
HOUSTON - CITY LEGAL DEPARTMENT - LAW
LIBRARY □ Houston, TX

Velez, Betsaida, Hd.Libn.
CARIBBEAN CENTER FOR ADVANCED STUDIES
- LIBRARY □ Santurce, PR

Velics, Laszlo, Univ.Bibliog.
MICHIGAN TECHNOLOGICAL UNIVERSITY -
LIBRARY □ Houghton, MI

Vellam, Kathleen, Libn.
MUNCY HISTORICAL SOCIETY AND MUSEUM
OF HISTORY - HISTORICAL LIBRARY □ Muncy,
PA

Velleman, Ruth A., Lib.Dir.
HUMAN RESOURCES CENTER - RESEARCH
LIBRARY □ Albertson, NY

Velliky, Mary, Ref.Libn.
WAYNE STATE UNIVERSITY - SCIENCE
LIBRARY □ Detroit, MI

Vellucci, Matthew J., Libn.
DISTILLED SPIRITS COUNCIL OF THE U.S.,
INC. - LIBRARY □ Washington, DC

Vellucci, Sherry L., Dir., Lib.Serv.
WESTMINSTER CHOIR COLLEGE - TALBOTT
LIBRARY □ Princeton, NJ

Venett, Gloria Durbin, Libn.
CENTRE COMMUNITY HOSPITAL - HEALTH
SCIENCES LIBRARY □ State College, PA

Venkataraman, Sundaram, Ref.Libn.
UNIVERSITY OF BRITISH COLUMBIA - SCIENCE
DIVISION □ Vancouver, BC

Venne, Louise, Libn.
CANADA - NATIONAL RESEARCH COUNCIL -
CISTI - INDUSTRIAL MATERIALS RESEARCH
BRANCH □ Boucherville, PQ

Venne, Paul R., Area Coord., Quebec
CANADA - AGRICULTURE CANADA - RESEARCH
STATION, STE-FOY - LIBRARY □ Ste. Foy, PQ

Veracka, Peter G., Dir./Coll.Libn.
PONTIFICAL COLLEGE JOSEPHINUM - A.T.
WEHRLE MEMORIAL LIBRARY □ Columbus, OH

Verble, Carole S., Asst.Libn.
MISSOURI HISTORICAL SOCIETY - RESEARCH
LIBRARY □ St. Louis, MO

Verble, Frances, Cat.
UNIVERSITY OF TENNESSEE - CENTER FOR
THE HEALTH SCIENCES LIBRARY □ Memphis,
TN

Verchomin, Mrs. J., Dir.
UKRAINIAN MUSEUM OF CANADA - LIBRARY† □
Edmonton, AB

Vercio, Roseanne, Asst.Libn.
PORTER MEMORIAL HOSPITAL - HARLEY E.
RICE MEMORIAL LIBRARY □ Denver, CO

Verdugo, Karen, Pub.Serv.
LOYOLA LAW SCHOOL - LIBRARY □ Los Angeles,
CA

Verich, Dr. Thomas M., Hd. of Archv. & Spec.Coll
UNIVERSITY OF MISSISSIPPI - ARCHIVES &
SPECIAL COLLECTIONS/MISSISSIPPIANA □
University, MS

Verity, John B., Lib.Mgr.
LAWRENCE LIVERMORE NATIONAL
LABORATORY - TECHNICAL INFORMATION
DEPARTMENT LIBRARY □ Livermore, CA

Vermandere, Bertha, Ref.Libn.
COLLEGE DE MUSIQUE SAINTE-CROIX -
BIBLIOTHEQUE □ St. Laurent, PQ

Vermeulen, June
UNIVERSITY OF CALGARY - LAW LIBRARY† □
Calgary, AB

Vermillion, Judy, Med.Libn.
CHILDREN'S MERCY HOSPITAL - MEDICAL
LIBRARY □ Kansas City, MO

Verstynen, Evelyn, Cons.Libn.
ST. THOMAS AQUINAS NEWMAN CENTER -
LIBRARY □ Albuquerque, NM

Verwijk-O'Sullivan, A., Libn.
MILNER & STEER, BARRISTERS & SOLICITORS
- LAW LIBRARY† □ Edmonton, AB

Vesely, Marilyn, Pub.Info.Off.
OKLAHOMA STATE DEPARTMENT OF
LIBRARIES □ Oklahoma City, OK

Vesenyi, Paul E., Pres.
AMERICAN HUNGARIAN LIBRARY AND
HISTORICAL SOCIETY □ New York, NY

Vesley, Roberta A., Lib.Dir.
AMERICAN KENNEL CLUB - LIBRARY □ New
York, NY

Vest, Don, Libn.
SOUTHERN COLORADO ECONOMIC
DEVELOPMENT DISTRICT - REGIONAL
PLANNING & DEVELOPMENT CENTER - DATA
FILE □ Pueblo, CO

Vest, Donald R., Res.Libn.
PUEBLO REGIONAL PLANNING COMMISSION -
LIBRARY □ Pueblo, CO

Vestal, Alice M., Hd.
UNIVERSITY OF CINCINNATI - ARCHIVES AND
RARE BOOKS DEPARTMENT □ Cincinnati, OH

Vette, Dr. James I., Dir.
WORLD DATA CENTER A - ROCKETS &
SATELLITES - NATIONAL SPACE SCIENCE
DATA CENTER (NSSDC) □ Greenbelt, MD

Vey, Jeffrey A., Info.Spec.
BUCKS COUNTY PLANNING COMMISSION
STAFF LIBRARY □ Doylestown, PA

Veysey, Arthur, Gen.Mgr.
CANTIGNY WAR MEMORIAL MUSEUM OF THE
FIRST DIVISION - ARCHIVES ROOM □ Wheaton,
IL

Vezinat, Nancy B., Rec.Mgt.Cons.
LOUISIANA STATE OFFICE OF THE SECRETARY
OF STATE - STATE ARCHIVES AND RECORDS
SERVICE - ARCHIVES SECTION □ Baton Rouge,
LA

Vhymeister, Nancy, Semy.Libn.
ANDREWS UNIVERSITY - JAMES WHITE
LIBRARY† □ Berrien Springs, MI

Via, Barbara, Ref.
SUNY AT ALBANY - GRADUATE LIBRARY FOR
PUBLIC AFFAIRS AND POLICY □ Albany, NY

Via, Dr. Murray, Cons./Prog.Mgr.
LOS ANGELES COUNTY SUPERINTENDENT OF
SCHOOLS - SOUTHERN CALIFORNIA CENTER
FOR EDUCATIONAL IMPROVEMENT □ Downey,
CA

Viau, Mr. Rheal, Ref. & Database Anl.
CANADA - REGIONAL INDUSTRIAL EXPANSION
- CANADIAN GOVERNMENT OFFICE OF
TOURISM □ Ottawa, ON

Vick, Kathy, Info.Spec.
AMERICAN CRITICAL CARE - INFORMATION
CENTER □ McGaw Park, IL

Vick, Mary Bob, Tech./Automated Serv.Br.
U.S. ARMY - PENTAGON LIBRARY □ Washington,
DC

Vickers, Francis, Media Ck.
WEST VIRGINIA STATE DEPARTMENT OF
EDUCATION - EDUCATIONAL MEDIA CENTER □
Charleston, WV

Vickers, Rebecca, Assoc.Dir./Tech.Serv.
LUBBOCK CHRISTIAN COLLEGE - MOODY
LIBRARY □ Lubbock, TX

Vickery, Mary A., Libn.
DAVENPORT OSTEOPATHIC HOSPITAL -
MEDICAL STAFF LIBRARY □ Davenport, IA

Vickery, Dr. Tom Rusk, Dir.
SYRACUSE UNIVERSITY - SCHOOL OF
EDUCATION - EDUCATIONAL RESOURCE
CENTER □ Syracuse, NY

Victor, Albert, Libn.
NATIONAL HAMILTONIAN PARTY -
HAMILTONIAN LIBRARY □ Flint, MI

Victor, Stephanie, Acq.Libn.
PHILLIPS UNIVERSITY - GRADUATE SEMINARY
LIBRARY □ Enid, OK

Victorson, Pat, Econ.Ref.Ctr.Libn.
MIDWEST RESEARCH INSTITUTE -
PATTERSON REFERENCE LIBRARY AND
ECONOMICS REFERENCE CENTER □ Kansas
City, MO

Viehdorfer, Alreeta, Chf.Adm.Libn.
U.S. AIR FORCE - ACCOUNTING AND FINANCE
CENTER - TECHNICAL LIBRARY □ Denver, CO

Viel, Jocelyne, Asst.Libn.
CLINICAL RESEARCH INSTITUTE OF
MONTREAL - MEDICAL LIBRARY □ Montreal, PQ

Vielehr, Alice, Libn.
FOUNDATION FOR CITIZEN EDUCATION -
ANNA LORD STRAUSS LIBRARY □ New York, NY

Viera, Ann R., Libn.
CUBIC CORPORATION - TECHNICAL LIBRARY □
San Diego, CA

Viergever, Dan W., Main Post Libn.
U.S. ARMY POST - FORT RILEY - LIBRARIES† □
Ft. Riley, KS

Vierich, Richard W., Hd.Libn.
UNIVERSITY OF CALIFORNIA, RIVERSIDE -
PHYSICAL SCIENCES LIBRARY □ Riverside, CA

Vierkant, Marguerite, ILL
DIGITAL EQUIPMENT CORPORATION -
MAYNARD AREA INFORMATION SERVICES □
Maynard, MA

Viger, Rev. Jacques, S.S., Hd.Libn.
GRAND SEMINAIRE DE MONTREAL -
BIBLIOTHEQUE □ Montreal, PQ

Viger, Veronica, Ref.Libn.
EQUITABLE LIFE ASSURANCE SOCIETY OF THE
U.S. - INFORMATION SERVICES DIVISION □
New York, NY

Vigil, Peter, Online Search Coord.
UNIVERSITY OF CALIFORNIA, DAVIS - HEALTH
SCIENCES LIBRARY □ Davis, CA

Vigle, John, Dir.
UNIVERSITY OF MAINE, PRESQUE ISLE -
LIBRARY AND LEARNING RESOURCES CENTER -
SPECIAL COLLECTIONS □ Presque Isle, ME

Vignone, Maria E., Forrestal Bldg.Libn.
U.S. DEPT. OF ENERGY - ENERGY LIBRARY □
Washington, DC

Vijay, Mrs. Girija, Dir., Med.Lib.
CRAWFORD W. LONG MEMORIAL HOSPITAL -
MEDICAL LIBRARY □ Atlanta, GA

Vikre, David, Sci.Libn.
SMITH COLLEGE - CLARK SCIENCE LIBRARY □
Northampton, MA

Vilaro, Annette, Educ.Ref.Libn.
NORTHEASTERN ILLINOIS UNIVERSITY -
LIBRARY □ Chicago, IL

Vilcins, Miss Maija, Ref.Serv.
CANADA - NATIONAL GALLERY OF CANADA -
LIBRARY □ Ottawa, ON

Vilella, Enrique, Libn.
U.S. DEPT. OF COMMERCE - INTERNATIONAL
TRADE ADMINISTRATION - SAN JUAN
DISTRICT OFFICE LIBRARY □ Hato Rey, PR

Viles, Ann, Music Libn.
MEMPHIS STATE UNIVERSITY LIBRARIES -
MUSIC LIBRARY □ Memphis, TN

Villamora, Grace A., Mgr.
OGILVY & MATHER, INC. - INFORMATION
SERVICES DEPARTMENT □ Chicago, IL

Villand, Maxine, Asst.Libn.
TRINITY LUTHERAN CHURCH - LIBRARY □
Madison, WI

Villanti, Frances, Lib.Techn.
TORONTO TRANSIT COMMISSION -
ENGINEERING & CONSTRUCTION LIBRARY □
Toronto, ON

Villar, Susanne, Asst.Doc.Libn.
CENTRAL WASHINGTON UNIVERSITY - MAP
LIBRARY □ Ellensburg, WA

Villemaire, Sr. Gabrielle, S.S.A., Archv.
CANADIAN CENTRE FOR ECUMENISM -
LIBRARY □ Montreal, PQ

Villemi, Uko, Cat.
U.S. DEPT. OF COMMERCE - LIBRARY □
Washington, DC

Villeneuve-Allaire, Lise, Libn., Cat.Dept.
QUEBEC PROVINCE - MINISTERE DES
COMMUNICATIONS - BIBLIOTHEQUE
ADMINISTRATIVE □ Quebec, PQ

Villere, Dawn N., Sr.Tech.Libn.
ITT CORPORATION - GILFILLAN ENGINEERING
LIBRARY† □ Van Nuys, CA

Vince, Thomas L., Libn. & Cur.
HUDSON LIBRARY AND HISTORICAL SOCIETY □
Hudson, OH

Vincent, C. Paul, Asst.Dir.Pub.Serv.
FRANKLIN AND MARSHALL COLLEGE - SHADEK-
FACKENTHAL LIBRARY - SPECIAL
COLLECTIONS □ Lancaster, PA

Vincent, CarolAnn, Res.Libn.
CAMPBELL INSTITUTE FOR RESEARCH AND
TECHNOLOGY - RESEARCH DEVELOPMENT
LIBRARY □ Camden, NJ

Vincent, Claire E., Asst. Law Libn.
KANSAS STATE SUPREME COURT - LAW
LIBRARY □ Topeka, KS

Vincent, Susan, Ref.Libn.
FEDERAL RESERVE SYSTEM - BOARD OF
GOVERNORS - RESEARCH LIBRARY □
Washington, DC

Vincent-Daviss, Diana, Law Libn.
NEW YORK UNIVERSITY - SCHOOL OF LAW
LIBRARY □ New York, NY

Vinces, Martine, Archv.
CBS RECORDS - ARCHIVES □ New York, NY

Vine, Rita, Mus.Libn.
UNIVERSITY OF CALGARY - ARTS AND
HUMANITIES LIBRARY† □ Calgary, AB

Vines, Luella
UNIVERSITY OF WISCONSIN, PARKSIDE -
UNIVERSITY ARCHIVES AND AREA RESEARCH
CENTER □ Kenosha, WI

Vinson, Charlotte W., Chf.Libn.
LONE STAR GAS COMPANY - RESEARCH
LIBRARY† □ Dallas, TX

Viola, Dr. Herman J., Dir.
SMITHSONIAN INSTITUTION - NATIONAL
ANTHROPOLOGICAL ARCHIVES □ Washington,
DC

Violet, Jane, Libn.
COMMUNITY HOSPITAL OF SPRINGFIELD &
CLARK COUNTY - HEALTH SCIENCES LIBRARY
□ Springfield, OH

Virani, Vivienne, Supv.
INTEL CORPORATION - TECHNICAL
INFORMATION CENTER □ Santa Clara, CA

Virga, Patricia, Info.Off.
PROGRAM PLANNERS, INC. - LIBRARY/
INFORMATION CENTER □ New York, NY

Virkhaus, Rein, Info.Sci.
UPJOHN COMPANY - CORPORATE TECHNICAL
LIBRARY □ Kalamazoo, MI

Virtue, Joyce, Lib. Teaching Asst.
OREGON STATE SCHOOL FOR THE DEAF -
LIBRARY □ Salem, OR

Visintainer, Victoria, Dir.
WARREN COUNTY HISTORICAL SOCIETY -
MUSEUM AND LIBRARY □ Lebanon, OH

Viskochil, Larry, Cur., Prints & Photos.
CHICAGO HISTORICAL SOCIETY - RESEARCH
COLLECTIONS □ Chicago, IL

Visscher, Helga, Ref.Libn.
UNIVERSITY OF ALABAMA - MC LURE
EDUCATION LIBRARY □ University, AL

Visser, Murray R., Supv.Libn.
U.S. MARINE CORPS - KANEOHE AIR STATION
LIBRARY □ Kaneohe Bay, HI

Viswanatha, Hema, Supv./Rd.Serv.
MASSACHUSETTS INSTITUTE OF TECHNOLOGY
- LINCOLN LABORATORY LIBRARY □ Lexington,
MA

Vitai, Jean, Coll./Ref.Libn.
UNIVERSITY OF WESTERN ONTARIO -
SCIENCES LIBRARY □ London, ON

Vitar, Fia, Libn.
ERTEC WESTERN, INC. - LIBRARY† □ Long
Beach, CA

Vitek, Clement G., Chf.Libn.
ABELL (A.S.) PUBLISHING COMPANY INC. -THE
BALTIMORE SUN - LIBRARY □ Baltimore, MD

Vitek, Susan, News Libn.
ORLANDO SENTINEL NEWSPAPER - LIBRARY □
Orlando, FL

Vitriol, Malvin, Chf.Libn.
U.S. VETERANS ADMINISTRATION (NY-New
York) - MEDICAL LIBRARY □ New York, NY

Vlantikas, Mary C., Libn.
FEDERAL RESERVE BANK OF BOSTON -
RESEARCH LIBRARY† □ Boston, MA

Vlcek, Charles, Dir.
CENTRAL WASHINGTON UNIVERSITY - MEDIA
LIBRARY SERVICES □ Ellensburg, WA

Vnenchak, Jean M., Dept.Mgr.
POLAROID CORPORATION - RESEARCH
LIBRARY □ Cambridge, MA

Vocasek, Helen A., Dir., Med.Rec.
ST. JOHN'S RIVERSIDE HOSPITAL - MEDICAL
LIBRARY □ Yonkers, NY

Vocelka, Mary, Lib.Techn.
U.S. NATL. PARK SERVICE - YOSEMITE NATL.
PARK - RESEARCH LIBRARY □ Yosemite National
Park, CA

Voci, F.K.
DOW CHEMICAL COMPANY - TECHNICAL
INFORMATION SERVICES - CHEMICAL
LIBRARY □ Midland, MI

Vodicka, Julia R., Musm.Dir.
OVER (W.H.) MUSEUM - LIBRARY □ Vermillion,
SD

Voegtle, Mary, Asst.Libn.
JONES, DAY, REAVIS & POGUE - LAW LIBRARY
□ Dallas, TX

Voelker, Linda, Coll./Ref.Libn.
UNIVERSITY OF WESTERN ONTARIO -
SCIENCES LIBRARY □ London, ON

Voelker, Margie L., Libn.
UNIVERSITY OF MINNESOTA - MATHEMATICS
LIBRARY □ Minneapolis, MN

Voelker, Robert B., Asst.Libn., Pub.Serv.
UNIVERSITY OF NEBRASKA, LINCOLN -
COLLEGE OF LAW LIBRARY □ Lincoln, NE

Voelkle, William M., Co-Cur., Medv. & Ren.Mss.
PIERPONT MORGAN LIBRARY □ New York, NY

Voeltz, Richard E., Assoc. Professor
UNIVERSITY OF NEBRASKA, LINCOLN -
BIOLOGICAL SCIENCES LIBRARY □ Lincoln, NE

Voeltz, Richard E., Assoc. Professor
UNIVERSITY OF NEBRASKA, LINCOLN -
CHEMISTRY LIBRARY □ Lincoln, NE

Vogan, David A., Assoc.Prof.
MASSACHUSETTS INSTITUTE OF TECHNOLOGY
- PURE MATHEMATICS READING ROOM □
Cambridge, MA

Vogel, Dorothy, Asst.Bus.Libn.
BROOKLYN PUBLIC LIBRARY - BUSINESS
LIBRARY □ Brooklyn, NY

Vogel, Irwin, Coord.
CANADA COLLEGE - RUSSELL L. STIMSON
OPHTHALMIC REFERENCE LIBRARY □ Redwood
City, CA

Vogel, J. Thomas, Dir. of Lib.Serv.
PHILADELPHIA COLLEGE OF TEXTILES AND
SCIENCE - PASTORE LIBRARY □ Philadelphia, PA

Vogel, Karen, Med.Libn.
U.S. VETERANS ADMINISTRATION (CA-Long
Beach) - MEDICAL CENTER LIBRARY □ Long
Beach, CA

Vogel, Marion L., Dir., Lrng.Rsrcs.
TRIDENT TECHNICAL COLLEGE - NORTH
CAMPUS LIBRARY □ North Charleston, SC

Vogelheim, Christine K., Dir.
ST. LUKE'S REGIONAL MEDICAL CENTER -
MEDICAL LIBRARY □ Boise, ID

Vogelstein, Susan, Hd.Libn.
PARK AVENUE SYNAGOGUE - ROTHSCHILD
LIBRARY □ New York, NY

Voges, Mickie A., Dir., Info.Serv.
UNIVERSITY OF TEXAS, AUSTIN - SCHOOL OF
LAW - TARLTON LAW LIBRARY □ Austin, TX

Vogt, Carol, Ref.Libn.
UNIVERSITY OF IOWA - COLLEGE OF
EDUCATION - CURRICULUM RESOURCES
LABORATORY □ Iowa City, IA

Vogt, Sheryl, Hd.
UNIVERSITY OF GEORGIA - RICHARD B.
RUSSELL MEMORIAL LIBRARY □ Athens, GA

Vogt, Viola, Cat.Libn.
FIRST LUTHERAN CHURCH OF THE LUTHERAN CHURCH IN AMERICA - SCHENDEL MEMORIAL LIBRARY □ Red Wing, MN

Vohra, Pran, Supv./Chf.Libn.
WASCANA INSTITUTE OF APPLIED ARTS AND SCIENCES - RESOURCE & INFORMATION CENTRE □ Regina, SK

Vohra-Sahu, Dr. Indu, Dir., Doc.Ctr.
PACIFIC/ASIAN AMERICAN MENTAL HEALTH RESEARCH CENTER - DOCUMENTATION CENTER □ Chicago, IL

Voight, Randall L., Info.Dir.
INTERNATIONAL RESEARCH & EVALUATION (IRE) - INFORMATION & TECHNOLOGY TRANSFER RESOURCE CENTER □ Eagan, MN

Voigt, Ann, Cat.
LOCKHEED-CALIFORNIA COMPANY - TECHNICAL INFORMATION CENTER □ Burbank, CA

Voigt, John, Libn.
BERKLEE COLLEGE OF MUSIC - LIBRARY □ Boston, MA

Voigtlander, Cheryl, Libn.
U.S. NATL. PARK SERVICE - CHEROKEE STRIP LIVING MUSEUM - DOCKING RESEARCH CENTER ARCHIVES LIBRARY □ Arkansas City, KS

Voiland, Jeannette, Libn.
SEATTLE PUBLIC LIBRARY - GOVERNMENTAL RESEARCH ASSISTANCE LIBRARY† □ Seattle, WA

Voisinet, David, Asst.Libn.
DELAWARE LAW SCHOOL OF WIDENER UNIVERSITY - LAW LIBRARY □ Wilmington, DE

Voit, Irene M., Libn.
CER CORPORATION - LIBRARY □ Las Vegas, NV

Volck, Eric, Cat.
ENVIRONMENTAL PROTECTION AGENCY - ANDREW W. BREIDENBACH ENVIRONMENTAL RESEARCH CTR., CINCINNATI - TECH.LIB. □ Cincinnati, OH

Volin, Rudolph H., Mechanical Engr.
U.S. NAVY - NAVAL RESEARCH LABORATORY - SHOCK AND VIBRATION INFORMATION CENTER □ Washington, DC

Volkersz, Evert, Libn.
SUNY AT STONY BROOK - DEPARTMENT OF SPECIAL COLLECTIONS □ Stony Brook, NY

Vollman, Lelia K., Lib.Tech.Supv.
U.S. ARMY - MATERIEL DEVELOPMENT & READINESS COMMAND (DARCOM) - INTERN TRAINING CENTER LIBRARY □ Texarkana, TX

Vollmer, Marguerite, Br.Asst.
SAN DIEGO COUNTY LAW LIBRARY - VISTA BRANCH □ Vista, CA

Volpatti, Ms. Rechilde, Supv.
TV ONTARIO - LIBRARY □ Toronto, ON

Volpi-Stagner, Barbara, Hd., Circ.
UNIVERSITY OF WYOMING - SCIENCE AND TECHNOLOGY LIBRARY □ Laramie, WY

Volz, Arlene, Ref.Libn.
UNIVERSITY OF MIAMI - SCHOOL OF MEDICINE - LOUIS CALDER MEMORIAL LIBRARY □ Miami, FL

Volz, Robert L., Custodian
WILLIAMS COLLEGE - CHAPIN LIBRARY □ Williamstown, MA

Von Brauchitsch, Ilse, Ref.Libn.
UNIVERSITY OF OKLAHOMA - HEALTH SCIENCES CENTER LIBRARY □ Oklahoma City, OK

von Brockdorff, Eric, Lib.Dir.
HARTWICK COLLEGE - LIBRARY - NORTH AMERICAN INDIAN COLLECTION □ Oneonta, NY

Von Dracek, Ruth, Docs.Cur.
UNIVERSITY OF IOWA - OFFICE OF THE STATE ARCHAEOLOGIST - DOCUMENT COLLECTION □ Iowa City, IA

Von Essen, Linda, Law Libn.
YAKIMA COUNTY LAW LIBRARY □ Yakima, WA

Von Fange, Sylvia, Hd.Libn.
TEXAS STATE DEPARTMENT OF WATER RESOURCES - WATER RESOURCES RESEARCH LIBRARY □ Austin, TX

von Gunst-Andersen, Jon A., Cur.
HISTORICAL SOCIETY OF PALM BEACH COUNTY - LIBRARY, ARCHIVES AND MUSEUM† □ Palm Beach, FL

von Gunten, Charlotte S., Law Libn.
SONOMA COUNTY LAW LIBRARY □ Santa Rosa, CA

Von Gunten, Louis E., Asst.Libn.
ALAMEDA COUNTY LAW LIBRARY □ Oakland, CA

von Hake, Margaret J., Libn.
COLUMBIA UNION COLLEGE - THEOFIELD G. WEIS LIBRARY □ Takoma Park, MD

Von Halle, E.S.
OAK RIDGE NATIONAL LABORATORY - INFORMATION DIVISION - ENVIRONMENTAL MUTAGEN INFORMATION CENTER □ Oak Ridge, TN

von Kohl, Marilyn, Dir.
TEXAS STATE LIBRARY - REGIONAL HISTORICAL RESOURCES DEPOSITORIES & LOCAL RECORDS DIVISION □ Austin, TX

Von Nussbaumer, Dr. Aliyah, Res.Libn.
DRESSER INDUSTRIES, INC. - MAGCOBAR RESEARCH LIBRARY □ Houston, TX

von Pfeil, Helena P., Law Libn.
U.S. DEPT. OF STATE - OFFICE OF THE LEGAL ADVISER - LAW LIBRARY □ Washington, DC

von Rebhan, Anne, Chf. Slide Libn.
NATIONAL GALLERY OF ART - EDUCATION DIVISION SLIDE LIBRARY □ Washington, DC

von Rekowski, Frank, Mgr.
IBM CORPORATION - DSD SITE LIBRARY □ Kingston, NY

Von Rosenbach, Ann, Urban/Municipal Libn.
HAMILTON PUBLIC LIBRARY - URBAN/ MUNICIPAL COLLECTION □ Hamilton, ON

von Rosenberg, Sarah C., Libn.
HOTEL DIEU HOSPITAL - LIBRARY □ New Orleans, LA

Von Rothkirch, Dr. Edward, Dir.
INTERNATIONAL ASSOCIATION OF INDEPENDENT PRODUCERS - LIBRARY □ Washington, DC

von Schrader, Julie L., Libn.
PITNEY, HARDIN, KIPP & SZUCH - LAW LIBRARY □ Morristown, NJ

Von Strauss, Ms. Sharesse, Cultural Arts Dir.
LANDMARK CONSERVATORS - CABOTS OLD INDIAN PUEBLO MUSEUM LIBRARY □ Desert Hot Springs, CA

Von Uhlenhorst-Ziechmann, W.K., Dir.
INSTITUTE FOR CENTRAL EUROPEAN RESEARCH - LIBRARY □ Shaker Heights, OH

Vona, Victoria De Persiis, Info.Spec.
PRICE WATERHOUSE - NEW YORK OFFICE INFORMATION CENTER □ New York, NY

VonBruck, Ms. Marion, Med.Libn.
PIERCE COUNTY MEDICAL LIBRARY □ Tacoma, WA

VonderLindt, Alice M., Chf., Lib.Serv.
U.S. VETERANS ADMINISTRATION (PA-Coatesville) - MEDICAL CENTER LIBRARY □ Coatesville, PA

Vondrasek, Betsy, Cur.
WHITMAN (Walt) BIRTHPLACE ASSOCIATION - LIBRARY AND MUSEUM □ Huntington Station, NY

Vongpaisal, Suvakorn, Hd., Pub.Docs.
LAURENTIAN UNIVERSITY - MAIN LIBRARY □ Sudbury, ON

vonRosen, Margaret, Chf.Libn.
GENERAL DYNAMICS CORPORATION - LAND SYSTEMS DIVISION - TECHNICAL LIBRARY □ Warren, MI

Voracek, Charles R., Sr.Educ.Spec.
CLEVELAND METROPARKS ZOO - LIBRARY □ Cleveland, OH

Vorachek, Pamela, Libn.
UNIVERSITY OF OREGON - ENVIRONMENTAL STUDIES CENTER □ Eugene, OR

Vork, Doris, Libn.
UNIROYAL, INC. - TECHNICAL LIBRARY □ Waterbury, CT

Vosberg, Wendy, Dir.
WORLD TRADE CENTRE TORONTO - LIBRARY □ Toronto, ON

Vosbergh, Ann, Libn.
PHILADELPHIA PSYCHIATRIC CENTER - PROFESSIONAL LIBRARY □ Philadelphia, PA

Vosikovska, Jana, Chf.
CANADA - PUBLIC ARCHIVES OF CANADA - NATL. FILM, TELEVISION & SOUND ARCHIVES - DOCUMENTATION & PUB. SERV. □ Ottawa, ON

Voss, Duane, Info.Sci.
HOECHST-ROUSSEL PHARMACEUTICALS, INC. - LIBRARY □ Somerville, NJ

Voss, Ingrid M., Libn.
NORTHERN PETROCHEMICAL COMPANY - TECHNICAL CENTER LIBRARY □ Morris, IL

Vosteen, Patricia Y., Mgr., Div. & Tech.Comm.
AMERICAN SOCIETY FOR QUALITY CONTROL - LIBRARY □ Milwaukee, WI

Votaw, Floyd, Hd. of Tech.Serv.
GRACE THEOLOGICAL SEMINARY - LIBRARY □ Winona Lake, IN

Votaw, John F., Dp.Dir.
U.S. ARMY MILITARY HISTORY INSTITUTE □ Carlisle Barracks, PA

Voth, Annette, Ref.Libn.
ARIZONA STATE UNIVERSITY - MUSIC LIBRARY □ Tempe, AZ

Vreeland, Ann, Libn.
MOUNTAINSIDE HOSPITAL - SCHOOL OF NURSING LIBRARY □ Montclair, NJ

Vrouvas, Peter, Br.Ref.
IBM CORPORATION - DSD LIBRARY/LEARNING CENTER □ Poughkeepsie, NY

Vrugtman, Ina, Botanical Libn.
ROYAL BOTANICAL GARDENS - LIBRARY □ Hamilton, ON

Vugrinecz, Anna-Elizabeth, Ref.Libn.
AT & T TECHNOLOGIES, INC. - KEARNY INFORMATION RESOURCE CENTER† □ Kearny, NJ

Vyas, Prof. Hansa S., Search Anl./Ref.Libn.
PHILADELPHIA COLLEGE OF OSTEOPATHIC MEDICINE - O.J. SNYDER MEMORIAL MEDICAL LIBRARY □ Philadelphia, PA

Vyas, Dr. Shanker H., Prof./Dir. of Libs.
PHILADELPHIA COLLEGE OF OSTEOPATHIC MEDICINE - O.J. SNYDER MEMORIAL MEDICAL LIBRARY □ Philadelphia, PA

Vyas, Umesh
UNIVERSITY OF CALGARY - LAW LIBRARY† □ Calgary, AB

Vyas, Veena N., Dir., Med.Lib.
ORTHOPAEDIC HOSPITAL - RUBEL MEMORIAL LIBRARY □ Los Angeles, CA

Vyzralek, Dolores, Chf.Libn.
STATE HISTORICAL SOCIETY OF NORTH DAKOTA - STATE ARCHIVES AND HISTORICAL RESEARCH LIBRARY □ Bismarck, ND

W

Wachna, Jane, Libn.
FINANCIAL TIMES OF CANADA - LIBRARY □ Toronto, ON

Wack, Helen, Libn.
COLORADO STATE HOSPITAL - PROFESSIONAL LIBRARY □ Pueblo, CO

Wacker, Jan, Staff Asst.
UNIVERSITY OF NEBRASKA, LINCOLN - INSTRUCTIONAL MEDIA CENTER □ Lincoln, NE

Wada, Sandra, Libn.
HAWAII STATE CIRCUIT COURT - 2ND CIRCUIT - LAW LIBRARY† □ Wailuku, HI

Waddell, Carol N., Asst.Dir.
TIPPECANOE COUNTY HISTORICAL
ASSOCIATION - ALAMEDA MC COLLOUGH
RESEARCH & GENEALOGY LIBRARY ☐ Lafayette,
IN

Waddell, Gene, Dir.
SOUTH CAROLINA HISTORICAL SOCIETY -
LIBRARY ☐ Charleston, SC

Waddell, Pat, Res.Spec.
COMMUNITY RELATIONS-SOCIAL
DEVELOPMENT COMMISSION - RESEARCH
LIBRARY ☐ Milwaukee, WI

Waddell, Samuel J., Assoc.Prof./Libn.
HUNTER COLLEGE OF THE CITY UNIVERSITY
OF NEW YORK - HEALTH PROFESSIONS
LIBRARY ☐ New York, NY

Wadden, Emily E., Law Libn.
SPOKANE COUNTY LAW LIBRARY ☐ Spokane,
WA

Waddington, Elaine, Libn.
ROYAL VICTORIA HOSPITAL - WOMEN'S
PAVILION LIBRARY ☐ Montreal, PQ

Waddington, Susan R., Dept.Hd.
PROVIDENCE PUBLIC LIBRARY - ART AND
MUSIC DEPARTMENT ☐ Providence, RI

Wade, Arthur, Hd., Jnl.Proc.
U.S. NATL. INSTITUTES OF HEALTH - LIBRARY
☐ Bethesda, MD

Wade, Carol, Rec.Adm.
FLORIDA STATE BOARD OF REGENTS -
RECORDS AND ARCHIVES ☐ Tallahassee, FL

Wade, Diana M., Hd., Info.Serv.
U.S. NATL. ARCHIVES & RECORDS SERVICE -
NATL. AUDIOVISUAL CENTER - INFORMATION
SERVICES SECTION ☐ Washington, DC

Wade, Grace, Asst.Libn.
CHURCH OF JESUS CHRIST OF LATTER-DAY
SAINTS - EL PASO BRANCH GENEALOGICAL
LIBRARY ☐ El Paso, TX

Wade, L.E., Adm.
MOUNT CUBA ASTRONOMICAL OBSERVATORY
- LAMBERT L. JACKSON MEMORIAL LIBRARY ☐
Wilmington, DE

Wadley, Carol, Nursing Sch.Libn.
STORMONT-VAIL REGIONAL MEDICAL CENTER
AND SHAWNEE COUNTY MEDICAL SOCIETY -
HEALTH SCIENCES LIBRARY ☐ Topeka, KS

Wadnizak, Lillian M., Lib.Mgr.
NORTH DAKOTA STATE FILM LIBRARY ☐ Fargo,
ND

Wagener, Elsie, ILL Libn.
U.S. AIR FORCE - AEROSPACE MEDICAL
DIVISION - SCHOOL OF AEROSPACE MEDICINE
- STRUGHOLD AEROMEDICAL LIBRARY ☐ Brooks
AFB, TX

Wagenveld, Linda M., Mgr.
HERMAN MILLER, INC. - RESOURCE CENTER ☐
Zeeland, MI

Waggener, Jean B., Dir.
TENNESSEE STATE LIBRARY AND ARCHIVES -
ARCHIVES & MANUSCRIPTS SECTION ☐
Nashville, TN

Wagner, Betty L., Libn.
UNIVERSITY OF WASHINGTON -
ARCHITECTURE-URBAN PLANNING LIBRARY ☐
Seattle, WA

Wagner, Carroll Sue, Ref.Libn.
UNIVERSITY OF CALIFORNIA - LOS ALAMOS
NATIONAL LABORATORY - LIBRARY ☐ Los
Alamos, NM

Wagner, Charlotte A., Asst.Libn.
GULF OIL CORPORATION - LIBRARY AND
INFORMATION CENTER ☐ Houston, TX

Wagner, Darla L., Dir. of Lib.Serv.
BETHLEHEM STEEL CORPORATION - SCHWAB
INFORMATION CENTER ☐ Bethlehem, PA

Wagner, Ms. Gartley, Libn.
CANADIAN REHABILITATION COUNCIL FOR
THE DISABLED - NATIONAL INFORMATION
RESOURCE CENTRE ☐ Toronto, ON

Wagner, J.A., Reports Acq.Libn.
LOCKHEED MISSILES & SPACE COMPANY, INC.
- TECHNICAL INFORMATION CENTER ☐ Palo
Alto, CA

Wagner, Jack, Cat.
UNIVERSITY OF OKLAHOMA - HEALTH
SCIENCES CENTER LIBRARY ☐ Oklahoma City,
OK

Wagner, Jill, Info.Spec.
AT & T COMMUNICATIONS - INFORMATION
RESEARCH CENTER ☐ Basking Ridge, NJ

Wagner, John, Ref.
PEPPERDINE UNIVERSITY - LAW LIBRARY ☐
Malibu, CA

Wagner, Judith O., User Serv.Coord.
ERIC CLEARINGHOUSE ON ADULT, CAREER
AND VOCATIONAL EDUCATION - NATL. CTR.
FOR RESEARCH IN VOCATIONAL EDUC. ☐
Columbus, OH

Wagner, Kendall R., Tech.Libn.
GPU NUCLEAR - OYSTER CREEK TECHNICAL
LIBRARY ☐ Forked River, NJ

Wagner, Louise, Libn.
ARTHUR ANDERSEN & CO. - LIBRARY† ☐ New
York, NY

Wagner, Murray L., Hd.Libn.
BETHANY AND NORTHERN BAPTIST
THEOLOGICAL SEMINARIES - LIBRARY ☐ Oak
Brook, IL

Wagner, Rod, Dp.Dir.
NEBRASKA STATE LIBRARY COMMISSION ☐
Lincoln, NE

Wagner, Thomas M., Prog.Mgr.
GEORGIA STATE OFFICE OF PLANNING AND
BUDGET - STATE DATA CENTER ☐ Atlanta, GA

Wagner, Mrs. Tory, Med.Libn.
LORAIN COMMUNITY HOSPITAL - MEDICAL
STAFF LIBRARY ☐ Lorain, OH

Wagoner, George D., Dir.
SOUTHOLD HISTORICAL SOCIETY MUSEUM -
LIBRARY ☐ Southold, NY

Wagoner, Ora, Libn.
U.S. BUREAU OF LAND MANAGEMENT - DENVER
LIBRARY ☐ Denver, CO

Wagschal, Sara, Cat.
WHITE AND CASE - LIBRARY ☐ New York, NY

Wah, Kevin, Dir. of Lib./Instr.Serv.
ILLINOIS COLLEGE OF OPTOMETRY - CARL F.
SHEPARD MEMORIAL LIBRARY ☐ Chicago, IL

Wahrow, Lillian A., Med.Libn.
NEW YORK HOSPITAL-CORNELL MEDICAL
CENTER, WESTCHESTER DIVISION - MEDICAL
LIBRARY ☐ White Plains, NY

Waid, Diana L., Res.Libn.
CARSTAB CORPORATION - RESEARCH LIBRARY
☐ Cincinnati, OH

Waidelich, Ann, Libn.
DANE COUNTY LAW LIBRARY ☐ Madison, WI

Waidelich, Ann, Libn.
MADISON PUBLIC LIBRARY - MUNICIPAL
REFERENCE SERVICE ☐ Madison, WI

Wainio, Betty, Chem.Info.Spec.
SDS BIOTECH CORPORATION - CORPORATE
LIBRARY ☐ Painesville, OH

Wainwright, Alexander D., Cur., Parrish Coll.
PRINCETON UNIVERSITY - RARE BOOKS AND
SPECIAL COLLECTIONS ☐ Princeton, NJ

Wainwright, Tom A., Libn.
AMERICAN CYANAMID COMPANY - LEDERLE
LABORATORIES DIVISION - SUBBAROW
MEMORIAL LIBRARY† ☐ Pearl River, NY

Wait, Carol D., Ser.Libn.
CAPITAL DISTRICT LIBRARY COUNCIL FOR
REFERENCE AND RESEARCH RESOURCES -
BIBLIOGRAPHIC CENTER ☐ Latham, NY

Wait, Margie, Circ.Libn.
UNIVERSITY OF OKLAHOMA - LAW LIBRARY ☐
Norman, OK

Waite, Carolyn, Hd., Tech.Serv.
TUFTS UNIVERSITY - HEALTH SCIENCES
LIBRARY ☐ Boston, MA

Waite, Marian, Libn.
DALLAS PUBLIC LIBRARY - BUSINESS AND
TECHNOLOGY DIVISION ☐ Dallas, TX

Waite, Marjory, Hd., Acq./Ser.Serv.
UNIVERSITY OF NORTH CAROLINA, CHAPEL
HILL - HEALTH SCIENCES LIBRARY ☐ Chapel
Hill, NC

Waite, Verne, Med.Dir.
HAWAII STATE DEPARTMENT OF HEALTH -
HASTINGS H. WALKER MEDICAL LIBRARY ☐
Honolulu, HI

Waity, Gloria, Outreach Libn.
UNIVERSITY OF WISCONSIN, MADISON -
COOPERATIVE CHILDREN'S BOOK CENTER
(CCBC) ☐ Madison, WI

Wajima, Masakatsio, Libn.
CONSULATE GENERAL OF JAPAN - JAPAN
INFORMATION CENTER - LIBRARY† ☐ New
York, NY

Wake, Malcolm J.H., Musm.Dir.
ROYAL CANADIAN MOUNTED POLICE -
CENTENNIAL MUSEUM LIBRARY ☐ Regina, SK

Wakefield, Jacqueline M., Med.Libn.
SAN BERNARDINO COUNTY MEDICAL CENTER -
MEDICAL LIBRARY ☐ San Bernardino, CA

Wakefield, June C., Info.Ctr.Dir.
NORTHWESTERN MEDICAL CENTER -
INFORMATION CENTER ☐ St. Albans, VT

Wakefield, Marie, Libn.
HARRIS-STOWE STATE COLLEGE LIBRARY ☐ St.
Louis, MO

Wakerainen, Alden, First Asst.
HOUSTON PUBLIC LIBRARY - COMMUNITY
INFORMATION SERVICE ☐ Houston, TX

Walch, Dr. David B., Dir.
CALIFORNIA POLYTECHNIC STATE
UNIVERSITY - ROBERT E. KENNEDY LIBRARY ☐
San Luis Obispo, CA

Walcott, Rosalind, ESS Libn.
SUNY AT STONY BROOK - EARTH AND SPACE
SCIENCES LIBRARY ☐ Stony Brook, NY

Walcox, Carolyn, Hd., Ref.
ST. FRANCIS HOSPITAL AND MEDICAL CENTER
- WILSON C. JAINSEN LIBRARY ☐ Hartford, CT

Walczak, Jean A., Asst.Libn.
CONSUMERS POWER COMPANY - PARNALL
TECHNICAL LIBRARY ☐ Jackson, MI

Wald, Susan M., Libn.
CUSHING HOSPITAL - PROFESSIONAL LIBRARY
☐ Framingham, MA

Walde, Florence, Chm., Lib.Comm.
DOUGLAS COUNTY HISTORICAL SOCIETY -
FAIRLAWN MUSEUM LIBRARY ☐ Superior, WI

Walden, Elaine B., Libn.
DALLAS TIMES-HERALD - LIBRARY ☐ Dallas, TX

Walden, Gayle, Media Serv.Supv.
AUBURN UNIVERSITY - LEARNING RESOURCES
CENTER ☐ Auburn, AL

Walden, Glenn, Hd.
LOUISIANA STATE UNIVERSITY - LISTENING
ROOMS ☐ Baton Rouge, LA

Waldern, D.E., Dir.
CANADA - AGRICULTURE CANADA - RESEARCH
STATION, LACOMBE - LIBRARY ☐ Lacombe, AB

Waldie, Mina, Supv.Libn.
WISCONSIN STATE LEGISLATIVE REFERENCE
BUREAU ☐ Madison, WI

Waldner, J. Dudley, Exec.Sec.
COMICS MAGAZINE ASSOCIATION OF
AMERICA, INC. - LIBRARY ☐ New York, NY

Waldo, Michael, Ref.Libn., U.N. Docs.
PURDUE UNIVERSITY - HUMANITIES, SOCIAL
SCIENCE AND EDUCATION LIBRARY ☐ West
Lafayette, IN

Waldoch, Gail, Libn.
PALOS COMMUNITY HOSPITAL - MEDICAL
LIBRARY ☐ Palos Heights, IL

Waldow, Betty J., Exec.Dir.
MC CARTHY (Walter T.) LAW LIBRARY† ☐
Arlington, VA

Waldron, Esther, Hd., Cat.Dept.
UNIVERSITY OF PITTSBURGH - FALK LIBRARY
OF THE HEALTH SCIENCES ☐ Pittsburgh, PA

Waldron, Lucille, Libn.
BIBB COUNTY LAW LIBRARY □ Macon, GA

Waldron, Wendy, Assoc.Info.Spec.
CETUS CORPORATION - RESEARCH LIBRARY □
Emeryville, CA

Wales, Patricia L., Dir., Lib.Serv.
HOSPITAL OF ST. RAPHAEL - HEALTH
SCIENCES LIBRARY □ New Haven, CT

Walia, Rajinder S., Law Libn./Prof. of Law
NORTHEASTERN UNIVERSITY - LAW SCHOOL
LIBRARY □ Boston, MA

Walker, Annalise, Canadian Arch.Archv.
UNIVERSITY OF CALGARY - ENVIRONMENT-
SCIENCE-TECHNOLOGY LIBRARY† □ Calgary,
AB

Walker, Anne, Coll./Ref.Libn.
UNIVERSITY OF WESTERN ONTARIO -
SCIENCES LIBRARY □ London, ON

Walker, Brian, Dir.
MUSEUM OF CARTOON ART - LIBRARY □ Rye
Brook, NY

Walker, Charlotte, Chf.Libn.
WILMINGTON NEWS-JOURNAL COMPANY -
LIBRARY □ Wilmington, DE

Walker, Constance, Libn.
ST. MARY'S SEMINARY - CARDINAL BERAN
LIBRARY □ Houston, TX

Walker, Deborah Kae, Dir.
CALIFORNIA STATE UNIVERSITY,
NORTHRIDGE - WOMEN'S CENTER □
Northridge, CA

Walker, Diane E., Info.Ctr.Coord.
LOCKWOOD, ANDREWS & NEWNAM, INC. -
INFORMATION CENTER □ Houston, TX

Walker, Diane Parr, Music Cat./Ref.Libn.
SUNY AT BUFFALO - MUSIC LIBRARY □ Buffalo,
NY

Walker, Dianne, Pub.Serv.Libn.
BRIERCREST BIBLE COLLEGE - ARCHIBALD
LIBRARY □ Caronport, SK

Walker, Donald, Mgr., Info.Serv.
NATIONAL EDUCATION ASSOCIATION -
RESEARCH INFORMATION SECTION □
Washington, DC

Walker, Elizabeth, Libn.
CURTIS INSTITUTE OF MUSIC - LIBRARY □
Philadelphia, PA

Walker, Eunice, Cat.Libn.
FASHION INSTITUTE OF TECHNOLOGY -
LIBRARY† □ New York, NY

Walker, F. Rebecca, Libn.
RICHMOND PUBLIC LIBRARY - BUSINESS,
SCIENCE & TECHNOLOGY DEPARTMENT □
Richmond, VA

Walker, Fawn, Tech.Serv.Libn.
U.S. ARMY POST - FORT STEWART/HUNTER
AAF LIBRARY SYSTEM □ Ft. Stewart, GA

Walker, Frank, Cur.
NEW YORK UNIVERSITY - ELMER HOLMES
BOBST LIBRARY - FROST LIBRARY □ New York,
NY

Walker, Frank, Cur.
NEW YORK UNIVERSITY - FALES LIBRARY -
DIVISION OF SPECIAL COLLECTIONS □ New
York, NY

Walker, Frank, Asst.Archv.
UNIVERSITY OF SOUTHERN MISSISSIPPI - MC
CAIN LIBRARY □ Hattiesburg, MS

Walker, Gay, Cur.
YALE UNIVERSITY - ARTS OF THE BOOK
COLLECTION □ New Haven, CT

Walker, Gina R., Act.Archv.
INDIANA STATE UNIVERSITY, EVANSVILLE -
SPECIAL COLLECTIONS AND UNIVERSITY
ARCHIVES □ Evansville, IN

Walker, Henry, Gen. Counsel
TENNESSEE STATE PUBLIC SERVICE
COMMISSION - LEGAL DEPARTMENT - LIBRARY
□ Nashville, TN

Walker, Ina G., Asst.Libn.
PUBLIC UTILITIES COMMISSION OF OHIO -
LIBRARY □ Columbus, OH

Walker, J. Terry, Dir.
SANFORD MUSEUM & PLANETARIUM - LIBRARY
□ Cherokee, IA

Walker, Jeanna, Ref.Libn.
BORGESS MEDICAL CENTER - HEALTH
INFORMATION LIBRARY □ Kalamazoo, MI

Walker, John M., III, Tech.Serv.Libn.
HISTORICAL FOUNDATION OF THE
PRESBYTERIAN AND REFORMED CHURCHES -
LIBRARY AND ARCHIVES □ Montreat, NC

Walker, June D., Libn.
EL PASO COUNTY LAW LIBRARY □ El Paso, TX

Walker, Kimberly J., Info.Spec.
NATIONAL RESTAURANT ASSOCIATION -
INFORMATION SERVICE AND LIBRARY □
Washington, DC

Walker, Laura, Libn.
BROOKINGS INSTITUTION - LIBRARY □
Washington, DC

Walker, Lloanne G., Libn.
ALBERTA ASSOCIATION OF REGISTERED
NURSES - LIBRARY □ Edmonton, AB

Walker, Lois, Libn.
PRESBYTERIAN CHURCH OF THE ATONEMENT -
LIBRARY □ Silver Spring, MD

Walker, Margaret B., Law Libn.
EL PASO COUNTY LAW LIBRARY □ Colorado
Springs, CO

Walker, Mary Edith, Med.Libn.
ST. JUDE CHILDREN'S RESEARCH HOSPITAL -
RESEARCH LIBRARY □ Memphis, TN

Walker, Mary Jo, Spec.Coll.
EASTERN NEW MEXICO UNIVERSITY - GOLDEN
LIBRARY - SPECIAL COLLECTIONS □ Portales,
NM

Walker, Mary M., Libn.
NEW ENGLAND WILD FLOWER SOCIETY, INC. -
LAWRENCE NEWCOMB LIBRARY □ Framingham,
MA

Walker, Orrin, Law Libn.
GEORGIA STATE UNIVERSITY - COLLEGE OF
LAW LIBRARY □ Atlanta, GA

Walker, Paul A., Dir.
JANUS INFORMATION FACILITY □ San
Francisco, CA

Walker, R. Garth, Archv.
ANGLICAN CHURCH OF CANADA -
ECCLESIASTICAL PROV. OF BRITISH
COLUMBIA & DIOCESE OF NEW WESTMINSTER
- ARCHV. □ Vancouver, BC

Walker, Ronald L., Dir.
BAPTIST BIBLE COLLEGE - VICK MEMORIAL
LIBRARY □ Springfield, MO

Walker, Sheila, Cat.
BALCH INSTITUTE FOR ETHNIC STUDIES -
LIBRARY □ Philadelphia, PA

Walker, Susan A., Tech.Libn.
FIBER MATERIALS, INC. - TECHNICAL LIBRARY
□ Biddeford, ME

Walker, Sybil, Ed.Asst.
AMERICAN ASSOCIATION OF MUSEUMS -
MUSEUM RESOURCES AND INFORMATION
SERVICE □ Washington, DC

Walker, Tyra
U.S. NATL. PARK SERVICE - FREDERICK
DOUGLASS HOME AND VISITOR CENTER -
LIBRARY □ Washington, DC

Walker, William B., Chf.Libn.
METROPOLITAN MUSEUM OF ART - THOMAS J.
WATSON LIBRARY □ New York, NY

Walker, William D., Dir.
MEDICAL LIBRARY CENTER OF NEW YORK† □
New York, NY

Walko, Susan Stapley, Libn.
HEALTH EDUCATION CENTER LIBRARY □
Pittsburgh, PA

Walkowicz, Victoria, Asst.Libn.
CHAPMAN AND CUTLER - LAW LIBRARY □
Chicago, IL

Wall, Celia
MURRAY STATE UNIVERSITY - LIBRARY □
Murray, KY

Wall, Colleen
3M - 201 TECHNICAL LIBRARY □ St. Paul, MN

Wall, Constance, Libn.
DETROIT INSTITUTE OF ARTS - RESEARCH
LIBRARY □ Detroit, MI

Wall, Jerry L., Dir.
NORTHEAST LOUISIANA UNIVERSITY -
CENTER FOR BUSINESS & ECONOMIC
RESEARCH - LIBRARY □ Monroe, LA

Wall, Patricia, Acq.Libn.
UNIVERSITY OF NORTH CAROLINA, CHAPEL
HILL - LAW LIBRARY □ Chapel Hill, NC

Wall, Dr. Paul L., Dir.
TUSKEGEE INSTITUTE - DIVISION OF
BEHAVIORAL SCIENCE RESEARCH - RURAL
DEVELOPMENT RESOURCE CENTER □ Tuskegee
Institute, AL

Wall, Philippa, Hd.
CANADA - IMMIGRATION APPEAL BOARD -
LIBRARY □ Ottawa, ON

Wall, Rhonda, Libn.
SOHO CENTER FOR VISUAL ARTISTS - LIBRARY
□ New York, NY

Wall, Tilda, Libn.
CHATTEM DRUG AND CHEMICAL COMPANY -
RESEARCH LIBRARY† □ Chattanooga, TN

Wallace, Atarrha, Hd., Tech.Serv.
MANITOBA - DEPARTMENT OF EDUCATION -
LIBRARY □ Winnipeg, MB

Wallace, Barbara, Lab.Libn.
IBM CANADA, LTD. - LABORATORY LIBRARY □
Don Mills, ON

Wallace, Bernice, Libn.
MICHIGAN STATE UNIVERSITY - CHEMISTRY
LIBRARY □ East Lansing, MI

Wallace, Carolyn A., Dir./Cur.
UNIVERSITY OF NORTH CAROLINA, CHAPEL
HILL - SOUTHERN HISTORICAL COLLECTION &
MANUSCRIPTS DEPARTMENT □ Chapel Hill, NC

Wallace, Dee, Libn.
UNIVERSITY OF ILLINOIS - RICKER LIBRARY
OF ARCHITECTURE AND ART □ Urbana, IL

Wallace, Diane, Asst.Libn.
BROCKTON HOSPITAL - LIBRARY □ Brockton,
MA

Wallace, Ian, Libn.
CANADA - AGRICULTURE CANADA - RESEARCH
STATION, ST-JEAN - LIBRARY □ St. Jean-Sur-
Richelieu, PQ

Wallace, James O., Dir., Lrng.Rsrcs.
SAN ANTONIO COLLEGE - SPECIAL
COLLECTIONS □ San Antonio, TX

Wallace, Katharine, Supv.Libn.
U.S. NAVY - NAVAL OCEANOGRAPHIC OFFICE -
NAVY LIBRARY □ Bay St. Louis, MS

Wallace, Marie, Law Libn.
KINDEL & ANDERSON - LIBRARY† □ Los
Angeles, CA

Wallace, Marie G., Law Libn.
LATHAM & WATKINS - LAW LIBRARY □ Los
Angeles, CA

Wallace, Richard E., Mgr., Info.Serv.
ARCHER DANIELS MIDLAND COMPANY -
LIBRARY □ Decatur, IL

Wallace, Robert B., Libn.
DADE COUNTY LAW LIBRARY □ Miami, FL

Wallach, Judy, Libn.
WORLD ZIONIST ORGANIZATION - AMERICAN
SECTION - ZIONIST ARCHIVES AND LIBRARY □
New York, NY

Wallach, William K., Asst.Dir.
UNIVERSITY OF MICHIGAN - MICHIGAN
HISTORICAL COLLECTIONS - BENTLEY
HISTORICAL LIBRARY □ Ann Arbor, MI

Walle, Dennis F., Archv./Mss.Cur.
UNIVERSITY OF ALASKA, ANCHORAGE -
LIBRARY - ARCHIVES & MANUSCRIPTS
DEPARTMENT □ Anchorage, AK

Wallen, Regina T., Hd., Tech.Serv.
UNIVERSITY OF SANTA CLARA - EDWIN A.
HEAFEY LAW LIBRARY† □ Santa Clara, CA

Wallen, Robert, Prog.Spec.
WISCONSIN STATE DEPARTMENT OF NATURAL
RESOURCES - MAC KENZIE ENVIRONMENTAL
EDUCATION CENTER □ Poynette, WI

Waller, A.N.
SPOTSYLVANIA HISTORICAL ASSOCIATION,
INC. - RESEARCH MUSEUM AND LIBRARY □
Spotsylvania, VA

Waller, Carolyn A., Med.Libn.
BRADLEY (Emma Pendleton) HOSPITAL -
AUSTIN T. AND JUNE ROCKWELL LEVY
LIBRARY □ Riverside, RI

Waller, Dr. Constance, Dir.
MONTCLAIR STATE COLLEGE - WOMEN'S
CENTER LIBRARY □ Upper Montclair, NJ

Waller, Edward, Tech.Serv.Libn.
WAKE FOREST UNIVERSITY - LAW LIBRARY □
Winston-Salem, NC

Waller, Elaine, Supv., Music Mtls.Ctr.
ANDREWS UNIVERSITY - JAMES WHITE
LIBRARY† □ Berrien Springs, MI

Waller, Frances L.N., Dir.
SPOTSYLVANIA HISTORICAL ASSOCIATION,
INC. - RESEARCH MUSEUM AND LIBRARY □
Spotsylvania, VA

Waller, Georgeann, Leg.Libn.
MARYLAND STATE DEPARTMENT OF
LEGISLATIVE REFERENCE - LIBRARY □
Annapolis, MD

Waller, Salvador B., Lib.Dir.
U.S. PUBLIC HEALTH SERVICE - PARKLAWN
HEALTH LIBRARY □ Rockville, MD

Wallgren, Rex, Radio Prog.Mgr.
UTAH STATE LIBRARY - BLIND AND
PHYSICALLY HANDICAPPED PROGRAM -
REGIONAL LIBRARY □ Salt Lake City, UT

Walliant, Robert, Info.Spec.-Sys.
SINGER COMPANY - LINK FLIGHT SIMULATION
DIVISION - INFORMATION CENTER □
Binghamton, NY

Wallin, Carol J., Res.Assoc.
UNIVERSITY OF TEXAS, AUSTIN - CENTER FOR
ENERGY STUDIES - ENERGY INFORMATION
SERVICE □ Austin, TX

Wallin, Janet L., Law Libn.
UNIVERSITY OF TOLEDO - COLLEGE OF LAW
LIBRARY □ Toledo, OH

Wallin, Jerry, Hd., Plan.Sect.
NEBRASKA STATE NATURAL RESOURCES
COMMISSION - PLANNING LIBRARY □ Lincoln,
NE

Wallin, Karen, Mgr., Volunteer Serv.
SEATTLE PUBLIC LIBRARY - WASHINGTON
LIBRARY FOR THE BLIND AND PHYSICALLY
HANDICAPPED □ Seattle, WA

Walling, Regis, Res.Asst.
BISHOP BARAGA ASSOCIATION - ARCHIVES □
Marquette, MI

Walls, Mrs. B., Lib.Asst.
QUEEN'S UNIVERSITY AT KINGSTON - DUPUIS
HALL LIBRARY □ Kingston, ON

Walls, Edwina, Hist. of Med.Libn.
UNIVERSITY OF ARKANSAS FOR MEDICAL
SCIENCES - MEDICAL SCIENCES LIBRARY □
Little Rock, AR

Walls, Nina, Cat.
HAGLEY MUSEUM AND LIBRARY □ Wilmington,
DE

Wally, Margarette, Libn.
ST. LUKE'S HOSPITAL ASSOCIATION -
MEDICAL, NURSING AND ALLIED HELP LIBRARY
□ Jacksonville, FL

Walschinski, Rev. Aaron, Libn.
ST. NORBERT ABBEY - AUGUSTINE LIBRARY □
De Pere, WI

Walsh, Anna, Supv.Ck. Staff
SUNY - AGRICULTURAL AND TECHNICAL
COLLEGE AT COBLESKILL - JARED VAN
WAGENEN, JR. LEARNING RESOURCE CENTER†
□ Cobleskill, NY

Walsh, Anne P., Asst.Libn.
WORCESTER ART MUSEUM - LIBRARY† □
Worcester, MA

Walsh, Carolyn C., Libn.
VILLANOVA UNIVERSITY - LIBRARY SCIENCE
LIBRARY □ Villanova, PA

Walsh, Catherine, Supv.
GENERAL ELECTRIC COMPANY - AIRCRAFT
EQUIPMENT DIV. - AEROSPACE ELECTRONIC
SYSTEMS DEPT. - INFO.RSRCS. CENTER □
Utica, NY

Walsh, Catherine, Supv.
GENERAL ELECTRIC COMPANY - INFORMATION
RESOURCES □ Utica, NY

Walsh, Donald A., Gen. Counsel
NEW YORK STATE CONFERENCE OF MAYORS
AND MUNICIPAL OFFICIALS - LIBRARY □
Albany, NY

Walsh, Mrs. Frederick R., Dir.
RENSSELAER COUNTY HISTORICAL SOCIETY -
LIBRARY □ Troy, NY

Walsh, Gretchen, Hd.
BOSTON UNIVERSITY - AFRICAN STUDIES
LIBRARY □ Boston, MA

Walsh, James E., Kpr., Printed Bks.
HARVARD UNIVERSITY - HOUGHTON LIBRARY
□ Cambridge, MA

Walsh, Joseph E., Bus.Br.Libn.
BOSTON PUBLIC LIBRARY - KIRSTEIN
BUSINESS BRANCH □ Boston, MA

Walsh, Karen, Ref.Libn.
BATTEN, BARTON, DURSTINE, OSBORN, INC. -
INFORMATION RETRIEVAL CENTER† □ New
York, NY

Walsh, Kathleen E., Info.Mgr.
WANDERER PRESS - LIBRARY □ St. Paul, MN

Walsh, Kathryn, Libn.
PURDUE FREDERICK COMPANY - RESEARCH
LIBRARY □ Norwalk, CT

Walsh, Kirsten, Music Ref.Libn.
UNIVERSITY OF BRITISH COLUMBIA - MUSIC
LIBRARY □ Vancouver, BC

Walsh, Lea, ILL Libn.
SOUTH CAROLINA STATE LIBRARY □ Columbia,
SC

Walsh, Sandra, Mgr., Lib.Serv.
ONTARIO - MINISTRY OF COMMUNITY AND
SOCIAL SERVICES - MINISTRY LIBRARY† □
Toronto, ON

Walsh, Susan, Cat.Libn.
ART INSTITUTE OF CHICAGO - RYERSON AND
BURNHAM LIBRARIES □ Chicago, IL

Walsh, Sylvia, Libn.
RUTGERS UNIVERSITY, THE STATE
UNIVERSITY OF NEW JERSEY -
MATHEMATICAL SCIENCES LIBRARY □
Piscataway, NJ

Walsh, Wanda T., Libn.
COUNTY OF CARLETON LAW ASSOCIATION -
LAW LIBRARY □ Ottawa, ON

Walsh-Kloss, Cynthia, Assoc.Libn.
FEDERAL RESERVE BANK OF ATLANTA -
RESEARCH LIBRARY □ Atlanta, GA

Walshe, Margaret, Hd.
METROPOLITAN TORONTO LIBRARY - SCIENCE
& TECHNOLOGY DEPARTMENT □ Toronto, ON

Walstrom, Jon, Map Libn.
MINNESOTA HISTORICAL SOCIETY - SPECIAL
LIBRARIES □ St. Paul, MN

Walter, Dave, Ref.Libn.
MONTANA HISTORICAL SOCIETY - LIBRARY/
ARCHIVES □ Helena, MT

Walter, Gary D., Libn.
U.S. DEPT. OF DEFENSE - LANGUAGE
INSTITUTE - ACADEMIC LIBRARY □ Monterey,
CA

Walter, Georgia, Dir. of Lib.
KIRKSVILLE COLLEGE OF OSTEOPATHIC
MEDICINE - A.T. STILL MEMORIAL LIBRARY □
Kirksville, MO

Walter, Lily, Libn.
WASCANA HOSPITAL - HEALTH SCIENCES
LIBRARY □ Regina, SK

Walter, Dr. Stephen B., Dir., L.R.C.
TRI-COUNTY TECHNICAL COLLEGE - LEARNING
RESOURCE CENTER □ Pendleton, SC

Walter, Steven, Mng.Ed.
WAUKESHA FREEMAN - NEWSPAPER LIBRARY
□ Waukesha, WI

Walter, Virginia, Dept.Mgr.
LOS ANGELES PUBLIC LIBRARY - BUSINESS &
ECONOMICS DEPARTMENT □ Los Angeles, CA

Walters, Bernard G., Pres.
INTERNATIONAL ROCK AND ROLL MUSIC
ASSOCIATION, INC. - LIBRARY □ Nashville, TN

Walters, Clarence R., State Libn.
CONNECTICUT STATE LIBRARY □ Hartford, CT

Walters, Corky, Chf., Coll.Dev. & Educ.
WYOMING STATE LIBRARY □ Cheyenne, WY

Walters, Eartha, Asst.Libn.
ALLIS-CHALMERS CORPORATION - ADVANCED
TECHNOLOGY CENTER - LIBRARY □ Milwaukee,
WI

Walters, Gwen E., Lib.Mgr.
UNIVERSITY COMMUNITY HOSPITAL -
MEDICAL LIBRARY □ Tampa, FL

Walters, Heather, Hd., Cat.Dept.
POLYTECHNIC INSTITUTE OF NEW YORK -
SPICER LIBRARY □ Brooklyn, NY

Walters, Jan, Med.Libn.
CALDWELL MEMORIAL HOSPITAL - G.M.
MEDICAL LIBRARY □ Caldwell, ID

Walters, Mary L., Lib.Dir.
LANCASTER BIBLE COLLEGE - STOLL
MEMORIAL LIBRARY □ Lancaster, PA

Walters, Raquel A., Chf., Lib.Serv.
U.S. VETERANS ADMINISTRATION (PR-San
Juan) - HOSPITAL LIBRARY □ San Juan, PR

Walters, Sheila, Health Sci.Libn.
ARIZONA STATE UNIVERSITY - DANIEL E.
NOBLE SCIENCE AND ENGINEERING LIBRARY □
Tempe, AZ

Waltner, Nell L., Hd., Acq.Dept.
NORTH CAROLINA STATE UNIVERSITY - D.H.
HILL LIBRARY □ Raleigh, NC

Walton, Sr. Ann Vivia, Dir.
NATIONAL EPILEPSY LIBRARY AND RESOURCE
CENTER □ Landover, MD

Walton, Mrs. Artence, Tech.Dir.
MONARCH MARKING SYSTEMS - TECHNICAL
LIBRARY □ Miamisburg, OH

Walton, Bobbi Sean, Libn.
CH2M HILL, INC. - SOUTHEAST REGIONAL
OFFICE - INFORMATION CENTER □ Gainesville,
FL

Walton, Cinda, Dir. of Med.Rec.
BIXBY (Emma L.) HOSPITAL - PATMOS
MEMORIAL LIBRARY □ Adrian, MI

Walton, Darrel, Exec.Dir.
AMERICAN LUNG ASSOCIATION OF KANSAS -
INFORMATION CENTER □ Topeka, KS

Walton, Elizabeth, Libn.
ESHERICK HOMSEY DODGE AND DAVIS -
LIBRARY □ San Francisco, CA

Walton, Jan, Lib.Serv.Dir.
ST. JOHN'S HOSPITAL - FREDERICK J.
PLONDKE MEDICAL LIBRARY □ St. Paul, MN

Walton, Laurence R., Corp.Libn.
PET, INC. - CORPORATE INFORMATION
CENTER □ St. Louis, MO

Walton, Linda, Legislative Ref.
RHODE ISLAND STATE LIBRARY □ Providence,
RI

Walton, Lonita M., Mng.Libn.
SEATTLE PUBLIC LIBRARY - EDUCATION,
PSYCHOLOGY, SOCIOLOGY, SPORTS
DEPARTMENT† □ Seattle, WA

Walton, Lynette, Archv.
GLENBOW-ALBERTA INSTITUTE - LIBRARY &
ARCHIVES □ Calgary, AB

Walton, Nancy Kay, Info./Rec.Ctr.Mgr.
AMERICAN MICROSYSTEMS, INC. -
CORPORATE INFORMATION CENTER □ Santa
Clara, CA

Waltz, Marian R., Resource Coord.
FRIENDS OF THE THIRD WORLD INC. - WHOLE
WORLD BOOKS □ Fort Wayne, IN

Waltz, Mary Anne, Geog. & Map Bibliog.
SYRACUSE UNIVERSITY - E.S. BIRD LIBRARY -
AREA STUDIES DEPARTMENT □ Syracuse, NY

Walunis, Martha C., Libn.
GOULD INC. - FOIL DIVISION - TECHNICAL
INFORMATION CENTER □ Eastlake, OH

Waluzyniec, H., Hd. of Ref.
MC GILL UNIVERSITY - MEDICAL LIBRARY □
Montreal, PQ

Walz, Rev. Mark, O.S.B., Archv.
ILLINOIS BENEDICTINE COLLEGE - THEODORE
LOWNIK LIBRARY □ Lisle, IL

Walzer, Helen, Hd., Coll. Organization
GEORGIA INSTITUTE OF TECHNOLOGY - PRICE
GILBERT MEMORIAL LIBRARY □ Atlanta, GA

Wambold, Sally H., Cat.Libn.
UNIVERSITY OF RICHMOND - WILLIAM T.
MUSE MEMORIAL LAW LIBRARY □ Richmond,
VA

Wampler, Clara, Tech.Info.Spec.
U.S. NATL. HIGHWAY TRAFFIC SAFETY
ADMINISTRATION - TECHNICAL REFERENCE
DIVISION □ Washington, DC

Wan, Weiying, Hd.
UNIVERSITY OF MICHIGAN - ASIA LIBRARY □
Ann Arbor, MI

Wanat, Camille, Hd.
UNIVERSITY OF CALIFORNIA, BERKELEY -
PHYSICS LIBRARY □ Berkeley, CA

Wandersee, Mary J., Dept.Libn.
MAINE STATE DEPARTMENT OF HUMAN
SERVICES - DEPARTMENTAL LIBRARY □
Augusta, ME

Wang, A., Staff Mgr.
BELL COMMUNICATIONS RESEARCH, INC. -
INFORMATION RESOURCES SERVICES CENTER
□ Piscataway, NJ

Wang, Amy C., Mgr., Lib.Serv.
JOHN HANCOCK MUTUAL LIFE INSURANCE
COMPANY - COMPANY LIBRARY □ Boston, MA

Wang, Anna K., Asst.Libn./Cat.
STRONG (Margaret Woodbury) MUSEUM -
LIBRARY □ Rochester, NY

Wang, Chi, Hd., Chinese/Korean Sect.
LIBRARY OF CONGRESS - ASIAN DIVISION □
Washington, DC

Wang, Chih, Libn.
ATLANTA UNIVERSITY - SCHOOL OF LIBRARY &
INFORMATION STUDIES - LIBRARY □ Atlanta,
GA

Wang, Cindy, Hd., Tech.Serv.
EMORY UNIVERSITY - SCHOOL OF LAW
LIBRARY □ Atlanta, GA

Wang, Doris, Jr.Info.Spec.
THE BOC GROUP INC. - TECHNICAL CENTER -
INFORMATION CENTER □ Murray Hill, NJ

Wang, Eunice, Cat.
ST. ANSELM'S COLLEGE - GEISEL LIBRARY □
Manchester, NH

Wang, Henry, Asst.Ref.Libn.
STANFORD UNIVERSITY - J. HUGH JACKSON
LIBRARY □ Stanford, CA

Wang, Jen-Yuan, East Asian Cat.
CORNELL UNIVERSITY - WASON COLLECTION □
Ithaca, NY

Wang, Peter, Cat.
MORTON ARBORETUM - STERLING MORTON
LIBRARY □ Lisle, IL

Wang, Richard, Hd.
UNIVERSITY OF MINNESOTA - EAST ASIAN
LIBRARY □ Minneapolis, MN

Wang, Shu-Sheng, Chinese/Japanese Cat.
PRINCETON UNIVERSITY - GEST ORIENTAL
LIBRARY AND EAST ASIAN COLLECTIONS □
Princeton, NJ

Wangerin, Rev. Mark, Coord., Pub.Serv.
CONCORDIA SEMINARY - LIBRARY □ St. Louis,
MO

Wanio, Tanya, Info.Coord.
INTERGOVERNMENTAL COMMITTEE ON URBAN
AND REGIONAL RESEARCH (ICURR) -
INFORMATION EXCHANGE SERVICE □ Toronto,
ON

Wank, Paul
LOUISIANA STATE UNIVERSITY - REFERENCE
SERVICES □ Baton Rouge, LA

Wannarka, Marjorie, Dir.
CREIGHTON UNIVERSITY - HEALTH SCIENCES
LIBRARY □ Omaha, NE

Wanner, Judith, Libn.
ONTARIO - MINISTRY OF AGRICULTURE AND
FOOD - HORTICULTURAL RESEARCH
INSTITUTE OF ONTARIO - LIBRARY □ Vineland
Station, ON

Want, Robert, Search Anl.
UNIVERSITY OF TEXAS HEALTH SCIENCE
CENTER, DALLAS - LIBRARY □ Dallas, TX

Wanza, Mary E., Assoc. Law Libn.
TEXAS SOUTHERN UNIVERSITY - LAW
LIBRARY† □ Houston, TX

Waranius, Frances B., Lib./Info.Ctr.Mgr.
LUNAR AND PLANETARY INSTITUTE -
LIBRARY/INFORMATION CENTER □ Houston,
TX

Ward, A., Engr.Libn.
GENERAL DYNAMICS CORPORATION - POMONA
DIVISION - DIVISION LIBRARY MZ 4-20 □
Pomona, CA

Ward, Cheryl, Asst.Hd.Libn.
CAROLINA POPULATION CENTER - LIBRARY □
Chapel Hill, NC

Ward, Debra, Ext.Libn.
TEXAS TECH UNIVERSITY - HEALTH SCIENCES
CENTER - LIBRARY OF THE HEALTH SCIENCES
□ Lubbock, TX

Ward, Dederick C., Libn.
UNIVERSITY OF ILLINOIS - GEOLOGY LIBRARY
□ Urbana, IL

Ward, Dorothy I., Acq.Libn.
U.S. ARMY - MISSILE COMMAND & MARSHALL
SPACE FLIGHT CENTER - REDSTONE
SCIENTIFIC INFORMATION CENTER □
Redstone Arsenal, AL

Ward, Edith, TNC Affairs Off.
UNITED NATIONS - CENTRE ON
TRANSNATIONAL CORPORATIONS - LIBRARY □
New York, NY

Ward, Evelyn M., Dept.Hd.
CLEVELAND PUBLIC LIBRARY - LITERATURE
DEPARTMENT □ Cleveland, OH

Ward, Jane, Libn.
THOMPSON & KNIGHT - LIBRARY □ Dallas, TX

Ward, Jeanne, Cat.
NEW BRUNSWICK - LEGISLATIVE LIBRARY □
Fredericton, NB

Ward, Joseph W., Info.Sci.
NORWICH EATON PHARMACEUTICALS, INC. -
RESEARCH AND DEVELOPMENT LIBRARY □
Norwich, NY

Ward, Joyce, Libn.
TRUDEAU INSTITUTE IMMUNOBIOLOGICAL
RESEARCH LABORATORIES - LIBRARY □
Saranac Lake, NY

Ward, Louise S., Libn.
THEOSOPHICAL SOCIETY IN MIAMI - LIBRARY
□ Miami, FL

Ward, Margaret, Fld.Archv.
DETROIT PUBLIC LIBRARY - BURTON
HISTORICAL COLLECTION □ Detroit, MI

Ward, Margery, Pubn.
UNIVERSITY OF UTAH - SPECIAL COLLECTIONS
DEPARTMENT □ Salt Lake City, UT

Ward, Nancy E., Libn.
LAFAYETTE CLINIC - LIBRARY □ Detroit, MI

Ward, Pamela M., Law Libn.
U.S. DEPT. OF JUSTICE - UNITED STATES
ATTORNEY, DISTRICT OF PENNSYLVANIA -
LIBRARY □ Philadelphia, PA

Ward, Patricia, ILL
FROSTBURG STATE COLLEGE - LIBRARY □
Frostburg, MD

Ward, Sally, Dir., Staff Dev.
PINELAND CENTER - LIBRARY AND MEDIA
CENTER □ Pownal, ME

Ward, Sue, Libn.
MEMPHIS STATE UNIVERSITY LIBRARIES -
ENGINEERING LIBRARY □ Memphis, TN

Ward, Victoria M., Law Libn.
MORGAN, LEWIS & BOCKIUS - LIBRARY □
Washington, DC

Warden, Carolyn, Libn.-Search & Ret.
GENERAL ELECTRIC COMPANY - CORPORATE
RESEARCH & DEVELOPMENT - WHITNEY
INFORMATION SERVICES □ Schenectady, NY

Warden, Joan, Libn.
GREAT LAKES RESEARCH CORPORATION -
RESEARCH LIBRARY □ Elizabethton, TN

Wardlaw, Janet, Ser.
UNIVERSITY OF CINCINNATI - ROBERT S.
MARX LAW LIBRARY □ Cincinnati, OH

Wardlow, Mary C., Ext.Libn.
VITRO CORPORATION - LIBRARY □ Silver
Spring, MD

Wardrop, A.E.
3M - ENGINEERING INFORMATION SERVICES
□ St. Paul, MN

Wardrop, Elaine L., Libn.
3M - 236 LIBRARY □ St. Paul, MN

Wardwell, Ms. Johnie, Libn.
WESLEY UNITED METHODIST CHURCH -
LIBRARY □ La Crosse, WI

Ware, Beverly, Subject Anl.
AEROSPACE CORPORATION - CHARLES C.
LAURITSEN LIBRARY □ Los Angeles, CA

Ware, Malcolm S., Sr.Libn.
GULF COAST RESEARCH LABORATORY -
GORDON GUNTER LIBRARY □ Ocean Springs, MS

Ware, Mark D., Musm.Asst.
HISTORICAL AND GENEALOGICAL SOCIETY OF
SOMERSET COUNTY - COUNTY HISTORICAL
LIBRARY AND RESEARCH CENTER □ Somerset,
PA

Ware, Sharon, Sec.
U.S. COURT OF APPEALS, 10TH CIRCUIT -
OKLAHOMA CITY GENERAL LIBRARY □
Oklahoma City, OK

Wareham, Rachel E., Libn.
INTERNATIONAL OLD LACERS, INC. - LIBRARY
□ Ludlow, MA

Waren, Doris Jean, Libn.
KEENELAND ASSOCIATION - LIBRARY □
Lexington, KY

Warfield, Elizabeth, Libn.
ST. MARY'S HOSPITAL - LIBRARY □ Rochester,
MN

Wargo, Anne, Asst.Libn.
VERNER, LIIPFERT, BERNHARD & MC PHERSON
- LIBRARY† □ Washington, DC

Wargo, Lucy, Med.Libn.
CHILDREN'S HOSPITAL OF BUFFALO - MEDICAL
LIBRARY □ Buffalo, NY

Warmack, Geraldine, Libn.
WILL ROGERS LIBRARY† □ Claremore, OK

Warman, James C., Dir.
AUBURN UNIVERSITY - WATER RESOURCES
RESEARCH INSTITUTE - INFORMATION
CENTER □ Auburn University, AL

Warne, Jo Ellen, Libn.
IOWA LAW ENFORCEMENT ACADEMY -
LIBRARY □ Johnston, IA

Warnement, Judith, AV/Regional Lib.Coord.
NORTHEASTERN OHIO UNIVERSITIES COLLEGE
OF MEDICINE - BASIC MEDICAL SCIENCES
LIBRARY □ Rootstown, OH

Warner, Alice M., Instr./Media Coord.
JEWISH HOSPITAL OF CINCINNATI SCHOOL OF
NURSING - NURSE'S REFERENCE LIBRARY □
Cincinnati, OH

Warner, Beth F., Libn.
LOUISIANA STATE UNIVERSITY - CHEMISTRY
LIBRARY □ Baton Rouge, LA

Warner, Betty, Acq.Libn.
UNIVERSITY OF PUGET SOUND - SCHOOL OF
LAW LIBRARY □ Tacoma, WA

Warner, Bruno, Libn.
SACRED HEART HOSPITAL - MEDICAL LIBRARY
□ Eau Claire, WI

Warner, Carol, Per./Doc.Libn.
WEST VIRGINIA STATE DEPARTMENT OF
CULTURE AND HISTORY - ARCHIVES AND
HISTORY LIBRARY □ Charleston, WV

Warner, Claudette S., Info.Serv.Off.
HARRIS TRUST AND SAVINGS BANK -
RESEARCH LIBRARY □ Chicago, IL

Warner, David, Leg.Libn.
MARYLAND STATE DEPARTMENT OF
LEGISLATIVE REFERENCE - LIBRARY □
Annapolis, MD

Warner, Debra, Staff Libn./Ref.Serv.
CENTRAL MAINE MEDICAL CENTER - GERRISH-
TRUE HEALTH SCIENCE LIBRARY □ Lewiston,
ME

Warner, Elizabeth R., Med.Libn.
CROZER CHESTER MEDICAL CENTER -
MEDICAL LIBRARY □ Chester, PA

Warner, F. Eleanor, Hd.Libn.
NEW ENGLAND COLLEGE OF OPTOMETRY -
LIBRARY □ Boston, MA

Warner, Heidi L., Cur.
MC HENRY MUSEUM - LIBRARY □ Modesto, CA

Warner, Jan, Exec.Dir.
WEYERHAEUSER (Charles A.) MEMORIAL
MUSEUM - LIBRARY □ Little Falls, MN

Warner, Kathleen M., Supv.
MTS SYSTEMS CORPORATION - INFORMATION
SERVICES □ Eden Prairie, MN

Warner, Dr. Robert M., U.S. Archv.
U.S. NATL. ARCHIVES & RECORDS SERVICE -
NATL. ARCHIVES □ Washington, DC

Warnken, Wendy, Assoc.Cur.
MUSEUM OF THE CITY OF NEW YORK -
THEATRE COLLECTION □ New York, NY

Warnow, Joan, Asst.Mgr.
AMERICAN INSTITUTE OF PHYSICS - CENTER
FOR HISTORY OF PHYSICS - NIELS BOHR
LIBRARY □ New York, NY

Waron, Olga, Assoc. Examiner
NEW YORK STATE DEPARTMENT OF LABOR -
WORKERS' COMPENSATION BOARD -
LIBRARY† □ New York, NY

Warpeha, Rita C., Chf.Libn.
U.S. PEACE CORPS - INFORMATION SERVICES
DIVISION □ Washington, DC

Warpinski, Margaret, Hd.Libn.
ST. VINCENT HOSPITAL - MEDICAL LIBRARY □
Green Bay, WI

Warren, Bee, Libn.
DE CORDOVA MUSEUM - LIBRARY □ Lincoln, MA

Warren, Brenda, Tech.Libn., Lib.Div.
ARNOLD ENGINEERING DEVELOPMENT CENTER
TECHNICAL LIBRARY □ Arnold Air Force Sta., TN

Warren, Carol A., Res.Assoc.
UNIVERSITY OF CINCINNATI - DEPARTMENT
OF ENVIRONMENTAL HEALTH LIBRARY □
Cincinnati, OH

Warren, Dave, Pict.Ed.
U.S.D.A. - PHOTOGRAPHY DIVISION -
PHOTOGRAPH LIBRARY □ Washington, DC

Warren, Dorothea, Ref.Libn.
WASHBURN UNIVERSITY OF TOPEKA - SCHOOL
OF LAW LIBRARY □ Topeka, KS

Warren, E. Louise, Assoc.Dir.
EMORY UNIVERSITY - SCHOOL OF MEDICINE -
A.W. CALHOUN MEDICAL LIBRARY □ Atlanta,
GA

Warren, Frank, Exec.Dir.
NATIONAL SOCIETY FOR CHILDREN AND
ADULTS WITH AUTISM - INFORMATION &
REFERRAL SERVICE □ Washington, DC

Warren, Gail, State Law Libn.
VIRGINIA STATE LAW LIBRARY □ Richmond, VA

Warren, George E., State Archv.
COLORADO (State) DIVISION OF STATE
ARCHIVES AND PUBLIC RECORDS □ Denver, CO

Warren, Henry C., Chf.Pk. Naturalist
U.S. NATL. PARK SERVICE - OLYMPIC NATL.
PARK - PIONEER MEMORIAL MUSEUM -
LIBRARY □ Port Angeles, WA

Warren, Jill R., Dir., Lib.Serv.
CAMBRIDGE MENTAL HEALTH &
DEVELOPMENTAL CENTER - RESOURCE
CENTER □ Cambridge, OH

Warren, John, Pres.
ST. PETERSBURG HISTORICAL SOCIETY -
LIBRARY AND ARCHIVES □ St. Petersburg, FL

Warren, Karen, Asst.Cur.
AUSTIN PUBLIC LIBRARY - AUSTIN HISTORY
CENTER □ Austin, TX

Warren, Karen, Ser.Libn.
UNIVERSITY OF SOUTH CAROLINA - SCHOOL
OF MEDICINE LIBRARY □ Columbia, SC

Warren, Linda, Supv., Lib.Oper.
WARNER-LAMBERT COMPANY - CORPORATE
LIBRARY □ Morris Plains, NJ

Warren, Lucretia D., Libn.
MIAMI-DADE PUBLIC LIBRARY - GENEALOGY
ROOM □ Miami, FL

Warren, Richard, Jr., Cur.
YALE UNIVERSITY - COLLECTION OF THE
LITERATURE OF THE AMERICAN MUSICAL
THEATRE □ New Haven, CT

Warren, Richard, Jr., Cur.
YALE UNIVERSITY - YALE COLLECTION OF
HISTORICAL SOUND RECORDINGS □ New
Haven, CT

Warren, Robert, Supt.
U.S. NATL. PARK SERVICE - FORT NECESSITY
NATL. BATTLEFIELD - LIBRARY □ Farmington,
PA

Warrick, T.R., Mgr., Tech.Serv.
AVIATION ELECTRIC, LTD. - TECHNICAL DATA
SECTION LIBRARY □ Montreal, PQ

Warrington, David, Ref.
INDIANA UNIVERSITY - LILLY LIBRARY □
Bloomington, IN

Warters, Richard, Pres.
CHEMUNG COUNTY HISTORICAL SOCIETY,
INC. - MRS. ARTHUR W. BOOTH LIBRARY □
Elmira, NY

Warth, N., Sec.
SOCIETY FOR THE INVESTIGATION OF THE
UNEXPLAINED - LIBRARY □ Little Silver, NJ

Wartluft, Rev. David J., Lib.Dir.
LUTHERAN THEOLOGICAL SEMINARY - KRAUTH
MEMORIAL LIBRARY □ Philadelphia, PA

Wartoe, Ellen, Libn.
FORT WORTH PUBLIC LIBRARY - BUSINESS
AND TECHNOLOGY DEPARTMENT □ Fort Worth,
TX

Wartzok, Susan, Tech.Serv.Libn.
CONCORDIA THEOLOGICAL SEMINARY -
LIBRARY □ Fort Wayne, IN

Wascavage, Johnyne, Cir.Libn.
OREGON INSTITUTE OF TECHNOLOGY -
LEARNING RESOURCES CENTER □ Klamath Falls,
OR

Washburn, David R., Prof. Staff Libn.
NEW HAMPSHIRE HOSPITAL - PROFESSIONAL
LIBRARY □ Concord, NH

Washburn, Marion, Libn.
INTERNATIONAL SWIMMING HALL OF FAME -
MUSEUM & LIBRARY □ Fort Lauderdale, FL

Washburn, Mary J., Asst.Libn.
U.S. COURT OF APPEALS, 2ND CIRCUIT -
LIBRARY □ New York, NY

Washington, Barbara G., LRC Mgr.
CHICAGO URBAN SKILLS INSTITUTE -
DAWSON SKILL CENTER LIBRARY □ Chicago, IL

Washington, Mrs. Clannie H., Libn.
SOUTH CAROLINA STATE DEPARTMENT OF
MENTAL RETARDATION - MIDLANDS CENTER
LIBRARY† □ Columbia, SC

Wasil, Dan, Cur.
LOS ANGELES INSTITUTE OF CONTEMPORARY
ART - LIBRARY □ Los Angeles, CA

Wass, Edward P., Libn.
UNIVERSITY OF ROCHESTER - MANAGEMENT
LIBRARY □ Rochester, NY

Wassom, John S., Dir.
OAK RIDGE NATIONAL LABORATORY -
INFORMATION DIVISION - ENVIRONMENTAL
MUTAGEN INFORMATION CENTER □ Oak Ridge,
TN

Wasson, Gregory V., Dir.
ESPERANTO LEAGUE FOR NORTH AMERICA -
ESPERANTO INFORMATION SERVICE □ El
Cerrito, CA

Wasylenko, Lydia W., Libn.
PENNSYLVANIA STATE UNIVERSITY - COLLEGE
OF BUSINESS ADMINISTRATION - CENTER FOR
RESEARCH - RES. WORKING COLL. □ University
Park, PA

Watanabe, Stella K., Chf.Libn.
U.S. AIR FORCE BASE - HICKAM BASE LIBRARY
□ Hickam AFB, HI

Watchke, Gary, Res.Anl.
WISCONSIN STATE LEGISLATIVE REFERENCE
BUREAU □ Madison, WI

Waterhouse, John, Act.Cur., Hart Coll.
MASSACHUSETTS INSTITUTE OF TECHNOLOGY
- M.I.T. MUSEUM AND HISTORICAL
COLLECTIONS □ Cambridge, MA

Waters, Betsy M., Lib.Supv.
MOORE BUSINESS FORMS, INC. - RESEARCH
CENTER LIBRARY □ Grand Island, NY

Waters, Carol, Dir. of Educ.
NEW HAMPSHIRE GOVERNOR'S COUNCIL ON
ENERGY - ENERGY INFORMATION CENTER □
Concord, NH

Waters, Eleanor Y., Libn.
GEORGIA STATE DEPARTMENT OF NATURAL
RESOURCES - COASTAL RESOURCES DIVISION
- ANDERSON LIBRARY □ Brunswick, GA

Waters, Francis B., Libn.
NEW YORK STATE COURT OF APPEALS -
LIBRARY □ Albany, NY

Waters, Mrs. Jack, Lib.Asst.
FIRST BAPTIST CHURCH - STINCEON IVEY
MEMORIAL LIBRARY □ Fairmont, NC

Waters, Samuel T., Assoc.Dir.
U.S.D.A. - NATIONAL AGRICULTURAL LIBRARY
□ Beltsville, MD

Waters, Susan, Info.Spec.
PRICE WATERHOUSE - INFORMATION CENTER
□ Miami, FL

Watkins, Anne E., Registrar/Libn.
ABBY ALDRICH ROCKEFELLER FOLK ART
CENTER - LIBRARY □ Williamsburg, VA

Watkins, Betty E., Libn.
WISCONSIN SCHOOL FOR THE DEAF - JOHN R.
GANT LIBRARY □ Delavan, WI

Watkins, Diana Fay, Sr.Libn.
CALIFORNIA STATE ENERGY COMMISSION -
LIBRARY □ Sacramento, CA

Watkins, Dorcas, Acq.
GMI ENGINEERING & MANAGEMENT
INSTITUTE - LIBRARY □ Flint, MI

Watkins, John F., Exec.Dir.
ALABAMA LEAGUE OF MUNICIPALITIES -
LIBRARY □ Montgomery, AL

Watkins, Linda H., Libn.
SIMMONS COLLEGE - GRADUATE SCHOOL OF
LIBRARY AND INFORMATION SCIENCE -
LIBRARY □ Boston, MA

Watkins, Richard L., Electronic Techn.
OKLAHOMA GEOLOGICAL SURVEY - OKLAHOMA
GEOPHYSICAL OBSERVATORY LIBRARY □
Leonard, OK

Watkins, Sherry, Archv.
UNIVERSITY OF BALTIMORE - LANGSDALE
LIBRARY - SPECIAL COLLECTIONS
DEPARTMENT □ Baltimore, MD

Watkins, Vicki, Ref.Libn.
VANDERBILT UNIVERSITY - JEAN AND
ALEXANDER HEARD LIBRARY - WALKER
MANAGEMENT LIBRARY □ Nashville, TN

Watlington, Denise, Med.Libn.
U.S. VETERANS ADMINISTRATION (NY-Albany)
- MEDICAL CENTER LIBRARY (500/142-D) □
Albany, NY

Watrous, Leland R., Hd.Libn.
SAGINAW NEWS - EDITORIAL LIBRARY □
Saginaw, MI

Watson, Bonnie, Cat.
OWENSBORO AREA MUSEUM - LIBRARY □
Owensboro, KY

Watson, Cheryl L., Libn.
TRANSCONTINENTAL GAS PIPE LINE
CORPORATION - LIBRARY □ Houston, TX

Watson, Chris, Libn.
WEBSTER (Noah) FOUNDATION & HISTORICAL
SOCIETY OF WEST HARTFORD - LIBRARY □
West Hartford, CT

Watson, Dollie D., Dir., Spec.Serv.
SOUTHWESTERN INDIAN POLYTECHNIC
INSTITUTE - INSTRUCTIONAL MATERIALS
CENTER □ Albuquerque, NM

Watson, Elizabeth
TECK MINING GROUP LTD. - LIBRARY □
Vancouver, BC

Watson, Georgiana, User Serv.Libn.
U.S. ARMY - MILITARY ACADEMY - LIBRARY □
West Point, NY

Watson, Jill McC., Asst.Libn.
AMERICAN SOCIETY OF INTERNATIONAL LAW
- LIBRARY □ Washington, DC

Watson, Linda L., Dir.
NATIONAL COLLEGE - THOMAS JEFFERSON
LEARNING RESOURCE CENTER □ Rapid City, SD

Watson, Lindsey, Media Techn.
HUDSON VALLEY COMMUNITY COLLEGE -
DWIGHT MARVIN LEARNING RESOURCES
CENTER □ Troy, NY

Watson, Lois, Asst.Libn.
ROANOKE MEMORIAL HOSPITALS - MEDICAL
LIBRARY □ Roanoke, VA

Watson, Margaret, Libn.
U.S. BUREAU OF RECLAMATION - LIBRARY† □
Denver, CO

Watson, Margaret Yesso, Libn.
TECHNICON DATA SYSTEMS - TECHNICAL
LIBRARY □ Santa Clara, CA

Watson, Paula, Hd.
UNIVERSITY OF ILLINOIS - DOCUMENTS
LIBRARY □ Urbana, IL

Watson, Peggy, Libn.
CANADA - AGRICULTURE CANADA -
SAANICHTON RESEARCH & PLANT
QUARANTINE STATION - LIBRARY □ Sidney, BC

Watson, Robert, Supv./Chf.Engr.,Engr.Sec.
MINNESOTA STATE SERVICES FOR THE BLIND
AND VISUALLY HANDICAPPED -
COMMUNICATION CENTER □ St. Paul, MN

Watson, Sharon D., Libn.
BORG-WARNER CHEMICALS, INC. - LIBRARY □
Washington, WV

Watson, Silvia, Act.Libn.
UNIVERSITY OF WISCONSIN, MADISON -
BIOLOGY LIBRARY □ Madison, WI

Watt, Rob, Chf.Pk. Naturalist
POINT PELEE NATIONAL PARK - LIBRARY □
Leamington, ON

Watt, Ronald, Mgr., Tech.Serv.
CHURCH OF JESUS CHRIST OF LATTER-DAY
SAINTS - HISTORICAL DEPARTMENT - CHURCH
LIBRARY-ARCHIVES □ Salt Lake City, UT

Watters, Beverley, Ref.Libn.
BANK OF NOVA SCOTIA - LIBRARY □ Toronto,
ON

Watters, Gray
BORG-WARNER CORPORATION - ROY C.
INGERSOLL RESEARCH CENTER - TECHNICAL
INFORMATION SERVICES □ Des Plaines, IL

Watterson, Jane, Hd., Circ.Serv.
U.S. NATL. OCEANIC & ATMOSPHERIC
ADMINISTRATION - MOUNTAIN
ADMINISTRATIVE SUPPORT CTR. - LIBRARY □
Boulder, CO

Watterson, Mickie, Assoc.Dir., Info.Sys.
NEW YORK INSTITUTE OF TECHNOLOGY -
CENTER FOR ENERGY POLICY AND RESEARCH -
ENERGY INFORMATION CENTER† □ Old
Westbury, NY

Watterson, R.M., Libn.
MEDICAL COLLEGE OF OHIO AT TOLEDO -
RAYMON H. MULFORD LIBRARY □ Toledo, OH

Watts, Anne, Supv.
ST. LOUIS PUBLIC LIBRARY - READERS
SERVICES/DOCUMENTS DEPARTMENT □ St.
Louis, MO

Watts, Catherine B., Per. & Maps
ANDREWS UNIVERSITY - JAMES WHITE
LIBRARY† □ Berrien Springs, MI

Watts, Doris E., Libn.
U.S. INTERSTATE COMMERCE COMMISSION -
LIBRARY† □ Washington, DC

Watts, Henrietta, Cat.Libn.
MOODY BIBLE INSTITUTE - LIBRARY □ Chicago,
IL

Watts, Henrietta, Cat.Libn.
MOODY BIBLE INSTITUTE - MOODYANA
COLLECTION □ Chicago, IL

Watts, Janice, Dir., Med.Rec.
PHOENIX GENERAL HOSPITAL - MEDICAL
LIBRARY □ Phoenix, AZ

Watts, Shirley Marie, Libn.
VANDERBILT UNIVERSITY - JEAN AND
ALEXANDER HEARD LIBRARY - MUSIC LIBRARY
□ Nashville, TN

Watts, Tim, Ref.Libn.
VALPARAISO UNIVERSITY - LAW LIBRARY □
Valparaiso, IN

Waudby-Smith, Joyce, Libn.
CANADA - NATIONAL RESEARCH COUNCIL -
CISTI - BUILDING RESEARCH BRANCH □
Ottawa, ON

Waugh, Mary Alice, Lib.Comm.Chm.
GREENE AND GREENE LIBRARY □ Pasadena, CA

Waverchak, Gail, Med.Libn.
ST. JOSEPH'S HOSPITAL - RUSSELL BELLMAN
MEDICAL LIBRARY† □ Atlanta, GA

Wawrzonek, M.S., Info.Anl.
CHEVRON RESEARCH COMPANY - TECHNICAL
INFORMATION CENTER □ Richmond, CA

Waxman, Joanne, Libn.
PORTLAND SCHOOL OF ART - LIBRARY □
Portland, ME

Way, Harold, Hd.Libn.
MIDWEST RESEARCH INSTITUTE -
PATTERSON REFERENCE LIBRARY AND
ECONOMICS REFERENCE CENTER □ Kansas
City, MO

Way, Dr. J. Edson, Dir.
BELOIT COLLEGE - LOGAN MUSEUM OF
ANTHROPOLOGY - LIBRARY □ Beloit, WI

Way, Kathy, Ref.Libn.
O'MELVENY AND MYERS - INFORMATION
SERVICES □ Los Angeles, CA

Way, Susan, Ref.Libn.
VANDERBILT UNIVERSITY - MEDICAL CENTER
LIBRARY □ Nashville, TN

Waycuilis, Sharon, Desk Res.
FOOTE CONE & BELDING - INFORMATION
CENTER □ Chicago, IL

Waymer, Barbara M., Media Spec.
CHARLOTTE-MECKLENBURG SCHOOLS -
CURRICULUM RESEARCH CENTER □ Charlotte,
NC

Wayne, Kathryn, Libn.
UNIVERSITY OF ARIZONA - COLLEGE OF
ARCHITECTURE LIBRARY □ Tucson, AZ

Waynesboro, Robin, Bus.Info.Spec.
GOODYEAR TIRE AND RUBBER COMPANY -
BUSINESS INFORMATION CENTER □ Akron, OH

Waznis, Betty, Asst.Libn.
ARIZONA STATE REGIONAL LIBRARY FOR THE
BLIND AND PHYSICALLY HANDICAPPED □
Phoenix, AZ

Wear, Byron, Natl.Exec.Dir.
UNITED STATES LIFESAVING ASSOCIATION -
LIBRARY & INFORMATION CENTER □ San Diego,
CA

Weart, Spencer, Mgr.
AMERICAN INSTITUTE OF PHYSICS - CENTER
FOR HISTORY OF PHYSICS - NIELS BOHR
LIBRARY □ New York, NY

Weary, Richard L., Maps/Micrographics Libn.
U.S. ARMY WAR COLLEGE - LIBRARY □ Carlisle
Barracks, PA

Weatherby, Dave
GENERAL ELECTRIC COMPANY - METER
BUSINESS DEPARTMENT - LIBRARY & DATA
BUREAU □ Somersworth, NH

Weatherhead, Barbara, Dir.
ONTARIO - MINISTRY OF TREASURY AND
ECONOMICS - LIBRARY SERVICES BRANCH □
Toronto, ON

Weatherhead, Peter, Pubn.Chm.
ANTIQUE AND CLASSIC CAR CLUB OF CANADA
- LIBRARY □ Toronto, ON

Weatherhead, Shelley J., Libn.
CANADIAN WESTERN NATURAL GAS COMPANY
LIMITED - LIBRARY □ Calgary, AB

Weatherill, Helene A., Libn.
SULLIVAN AND CROMWELL - LIBRARY† □ New
York, NY

Weathers, Marganne, Adm.Libn.
U.S. ARMY HOSPITALS - MADIGAN ARMY
MEDICAL CENTER - MORALE SUPPORT
LIBRARY □ Tacoma, WA

Weaver, Ann, Database Mgr.
BANK MARKETING ASSOCIATION -
INFORMATION CENTER □ Chicago, IL

Weaver, Barbara F., State Libn.
NEW JERSEY STATE LIBRARY □ Trenton, NJ

Weaver, Carol, Coord., Cat. & Indexing
NOVA - CORPORATE LIBRARY □ Calgary, AB

Weaver, Carolyn G., Assoc.Dir., Pub.Serv.
UNIVERSITY OF NEBRASKA MEDICAL CENTER -
MC GOOGAN LIBRARY OF MEDICINE □ Omaha,
NE

Weaver, Charles, Asst.Libn.
DETROIT SYMPHONY ORCHESTRA - LIBRARY □
Detroit, MI

Weaver, Mr. Claire S., Law Libn.
ADAMS COUNTY LAW LIBRARY □ Gettysburg,
PA

Weaver, Connie, Ref.Libn.
NORTHWOOD INSTITUTE - STROSACKER
LIBRARY □ Midland, MI

Weaver, Elizabeth A., Info.Chem.
ETHYL CORPORATION - INFORMATION &
LIBRARY SERVICES LIBRARY □ Baton Rouge, LA

Weaver, Frances A., Asst.Univ.Archv.
UNIVERSITY OF NORTH CAROLINA, CHAPEL
HILL - SOUTHERN HISTORICAL COLLECTION &
MANUSCRIPTS DEPARTMENT □ Chapel Hill, NC

Weaver, M.R., Libn.
C-I-L INC. - CENTRAL LIBRARY □ North York,
ON

Weaver, Ron, Indexing
LOS ANGELES TIMES - EDITORIAL LIBRARY □
Los Angeles, CA

Weaver, Capt. Thomas M., Res.Asst./Libn.
NATIONAL GUARD ASSOCIATION OF THE
UNITED STATES - LIBRARY □ Washington, DC

Weaver, William B., Ref.Libn.
UNIVERSITY OF FLORIDA - HUME LIBRARY □
Gainesville, FL

Web, Marek, Chf.Archv.
YIVO INSTITUTE FOR JEWISH RESEARCH -
LIBRARY AND ARCHIVES □ New York, NY

Webb, Barbara, Ser.Asst.
CAMPBELL UNIVERSITY - SCHOOL OF LAW -
LAW LIBRARY □ Buies Creek, NC

Webb, C.S., Mgr., Info.Rsrcs.
GENERAL ELECTRIC COMPANY - INFORMATION
RESOURCES CENTER □ Syracuse, NY

Webb, Dorothy, Pub.Serv.Libn.
HUGHES AIRCRAFT COMPANY - ELECTRO-
OPTICAL & DATA SYSTEMS GROUP - COMPANY
TECHNICAL DOCUMENT CENTER □ El Segundo,
CA

Webb, Duncan C., Dir.
SAN BERNARDINO COUNTY LAW LIBRARY □
San Bernardino, CA

Webb, Gisela, Asst.Dir./Personnel
TEXAS TECH UNIVERSITY - LIBRARY □
Lubbock, TX

Webb, Glennie Ruth, Media Libn.
SEATTLE PUBLIC LIBRARY - MEDIA &
PROGRAM SERVICES† □ Seattle, WA
Webb, John, Asst. State Libn.
OREGON STATE LIBRARY □ Salem, OR
Webb, Judy, Libn.
CALHOUN COUNTY HISTORICAL MUSEUM -
LIBRARY □ Rockwell City, IA
Webb, Lorrayne B., Libn.
UNIVERSITY OF TEXAS HEALTH SCIENCE
CENTER, HOUSTON - DENTAL BRANCH
LIBRARY □ Houston, TX
Webb, M. Jane, Hd.Libn.
CALGARY BOARD OF EDUCATION -
PROFESSIONAL LIBRARY □ Calgary, AB
Webb, Michael, Asst.Dir.
ERIC CLEARINGHOUSE ON URBAN EDUCATION
□ New York, NY
Webb, Molly
ST. DAVID'S UNITED CHURCH - LIBRARY □
Calgary, AB
Webb, Robert L., Res.Assoc.
KENDALL WHALING MUSEUM - LIBRARY □
Sharon, MA
Webb, Ty, Act.Libn.
MOBAY CHEMICAL CORPORATION -
AGRICULTURAL CHEMICALS DIVISION -
LIBRARY □ Kansas City, MO
Webber, David, Dir.
CONFEDERATION CENTRE ART GALLERY AND
MUSEUM - ART REFERENCE LIBRARY □
Charlottetown, PE
Webber, Ruth, Cat.
WORCESTER STATE COLLEGE - LEARNING
RESOURCES CENTER □ Worcester, MA
Webber, Sylvia J., Chf.
U.S. ARMY INTELLIGENCE CENTER & SCHOOL -
ACADEMIC LIBRARY □ Ft. Huachuca, AZ
Webber, Violet
HISTORIC SCHAEFFERSTOWN, INC. - THOMAS
R. BRENDLE MEMORIAL LIBRARY & MUSEUM □
Schaefferstown, PA
Weber, David, Libn.
ALAMEDA COUNTY LIBRARY - BUSINESS &
GOVERNMENT LIBRARY □ Oakland, CA
Weber, Donald John, Dir.
FLORIDA STATE DIVISION OF BLIND SERVICES
- FLORIDA REGIONAL LIB. FOR THE BLIND &
PHYSICALLY HANDICAPPED □ Daytona Beach,
FL
Weber, Edward C., Labadie Coll.Libn.
UNIVERSITY OF MICHIGAN - DEPARTMENT OF
RARE BOOKS AND SPECIAL COLLECTIONS -
LIBRARY □ Ann Arbor, MI
Weber, Else, Asst.Mgr.
SIGNAL UOP RESEARCH CENTER - TECHNICAL
INFORMATION CENTER □ Des Plaines, IL
Weber, Msgr. Francis J., Archv.
ARCHDIOCESE OF LOS ANGELES - CHANCERY
ARCHIVES □ Los Angeles, CA
Weber, Janet, Supv.
MINNESOTA STATE DEPARTMENT OF PUBLIC
SAFETY - FILM LIBRARY □ St. Paul, MN
Weber, Linda, Circ.Libn.
UNIVERSITY OF SOUTHERN CALIFORNIA -
SCIENCE & ENGINEERING LIBRARY □ Los
Angeles, CA
Weber, Nancy, Pub.Serv.
CLARKSON UNIVERSITY - EDUCATIONAL
RESOURCES CENTER □ Potsdam, NY
Weber, Robert, Pub.Serv.Libn.
OREGON INSTITUTE OF TECHNOLOGY -
LEARNING RESOURCES CENTER □ Klamath Falls,
OR
Weber, Ron, Mgr.
LUNAR AND PLANETARY INSTITUTE -
PLANETARY IMAGE CENTER† □ Houston, TX
Weber, Victor B., Dir., Dev.
NEWBERRY LIBRARY □ Chicago, IL
Weber, Victoria, Asst.Libn./Acq.
VERMONT LAW SCHOOL - LIBRARY □ South
Royalton, VT

Weber, Warren R., Cur.
U.S. NATL. PARK SERVICE - CARL SANDBURG
HOME NATL. HISTORIC SITE - MUSEUM/
LIBRARY □ Flat Rock, NC
Weberg, Lorraine, Evening Ref.Libn.
FASHION INSTITUTE OF TECHNOLOGY -
LIBRARY† □ New York, NY
Webers, Leonard, Circ.
KANSAS CITY ART INSTITUTE - LIBRARY □
Kansas City, MO
Webster, David, Cons.
TEACHERS COLLEGE - MILBANK MEMORIAL
LIBRARY □ New York, NY
Webster, Deborah, Asst.Hd.
UNIVERSITY OF NORTH CAROLINA, CHAPEL
HILL - LAW LIBRARY □ Chapel Hill, NC
Webster, Donald, Dir. of Libs.
SUNY - COLLEGE OF ENVIRONMENTAL SCIENCE
& FORESTRY - HUNTINGTON WILDLIFE FOREST
LIBRARY □ Newcomb, NY
Webster, Donald F., Libn.
SUNY - COLLEGE OF ENVIRONMENTAL SCIENCE
AND FORESTRY - F. FRANKLIN MOON LIBRARY
□ Syracuse, NY
Webster, Harriet A., Info.Sci.
DUKE POWER COMPANY - DAVID NABOW
LIBRARY □ Charlotte, NC
Webster, Helen, Chf., Cultural Events Off
NATIONAL LIBRARY OF CANADA/
BIBLIOTHEQUE NATIONALE DU CANADA □
Ottawa, ON
Webster, J., Hd., Ref.
SUNY AT BUFFALO - SCIENCE AND
ENGINEERING LIBRARY □ Buffalo, NY
Webster, Kathryn, Tech.Serv.Libn.
UNIVERSITY OF ILLINOIS - LAW LIBRARY □
Champaign, IL
Webster, Leta, Tech.Serv.Supv.
UNIVERSITY OF MISSOURI, ST. LOUIS -
EDUCATION LIBRARY □ St. Louis, MO
Webster, Lois S., Mgr., Info.Rsrcs.
AMERICAN NUCLEAR SOCIETY - LIBRARY □ La
Grange Park, IL
Webster, Monica, Ser.Libn.
QUEEN'S UNIVERSITY AT KINGSTON -
BRACKEN LIBRARY □ Kingston, ON
Wechsler, Joseph G., Dir.
CLEARINGHOUSE ON CHILD ABUSE AND
NEGLECT INFORMATION □ Washington, DC
Wecht, Donald, Libn.
BOTEIN, HAYS, SKLAR & HERZBERG - LIBRARY
□ New York, NY
Wecker, Steven, Mgr., Lib.Serv.
NATIONAL BANK OF DETROIT - RESEARCH
LIBRARY □ Detroit, MI
Wedel, Ruth A., Libn.
CARVER BIBLE COLLEGE - LIBRARY □ Atlanta,
GA
Wedig, Bro. Vincent, O.S.B., Libn.
ST. BENEDICT'S ABBEY - BENET LIBRARY □
Benet Lake, WI
Wee, Susan, Supv.
NORTH DAKOTA STATE UNIVERSITY -
ARCHITECTURE RESOURCE CENTER □ Fargo,
ND
Weech, Jane, Media Libn.
MARYCREST COLLEGE - CONE LIBRARY □
Davenport, IA
Weedman, Parm, Med.Libn.
U.S. VETERANS ADMINISTRATION (IN-
Indianapolis) - MEDICAL CENTER LIBRARY □
Indianapolis, IN
Weeg, James A., Cat.
MARYCREST COLLEGE - CONE LIBRARY □
Davenport, IA
Weekes, Dr. K. David, Dir.
MIDWESTERN BAPTIST THEOLOGICAL
SEMINARY - LIBRARY† □ Kansas City, MO
Weekly, Nancy M., Libn./Archv.
SUNY - COLLEGE AT BUFFALO - BURCHFIELD
CENTER-WESTERN NEW YORK FORUM FOR
AMERICAN ART □ Buffalo, NY

Weeks, Gerry
BRITISH COLUMBIA INSTITUTE OF
TECHNOLOGY - LIBRARY SERVICES DIVISION
□ Burnaby, BC
Weeks, John, Indexer
HARVARD UNIVERSITY - TOZZER LIBRARY □
Cambridge, MA
Weeks, Lynda Maree, Outreach Libn.
FLORIDA STATE HOSPITAL - PATIENT/STAFF
LIBRARY □ Chattahoochee, FL
Weeks, Ruth, Cat.
UNIVERSITY OF ALABAMA - SCHOOL OF LAW
LIBRARY □ University, AL
Weerasinghe, Jean, Corp.Libn.
CANADA - CANADA POST CORPORATION -
LIBRARY □ Ottawa, ON
Wees, Dustin, Slide Libn.
CLARK (Sterling and Francine) ART INSTITUTE -
LIBRARY □ Williamstown, MA
Wegner, Mary, Dir., Med.Lib.
IOWA METHODIST MEDICAL CENTER - OLIVER
J. FAY MEMORIAL LIBRARY □ Des Moines, IA
Wegner, Sandra, Petroleum Dept.Libn.
MIDLAND COUNTY PUBLIC LIBRARY -
PETROLEUM DEPARTMENT LIBRARY □ Midland,
TX
Wehr, Myron P., Pres.
TREXLER (Harry C.) MASONIC LIBRARY □
Allentown, PA
Wehrhan, Helga R., Lib.Mgr.
SOUTH BEND OSTEOPATHIC HOSPITAL -
MEDICAL LIBRARY □ South Bend, IN
Wehrkamp, Tim, Asst.Hd.
UNIVERSITY OF NEW MEXICO - SPECIAL
COLLECTIONS DEPARTMENT □ Albuquerque, NM
Wehrle, Evelyn T., Dir.
BELOIT HISTORICAL SOCIETY - BARTLETT
HISTORICAL LIBRARY □ Beloit, WI
Wei, Carl K., Libn.
ONTARIO RESEARCH FOUNDATION - LIBRARY
□ Mississauga, ON
Wei, Esther, Hd., Ref.
SUNY AT STONY BROOK - HEALTH SCIENCES
LIBRARY □ East Setauket, NY
Wei, Iping K., Hd., Chinese Sect.
PRINCETON UNIVERSITY - GEST ORIENTAL
LIBRARY AND EAST ASIAN COLLECTIONS □
Princeton, NJ
Wei, Karen, Chinese Cat.
UNIVERSITY OF ILLINOIS - ASIAN LIBRARY □
Urbana, IL
Wei, Philip, Dir.
PLYMOUTH STATE COLLEGE - HERBERT H.
LAMSON LIBRARY - SPECIAL COLLECTIONS □
Plymouth, NH
Wei, Wendy, Libn.
INTERNATIONAL READING ASSOCIATION -
RALPH C. STAIGER LIBRARY □ Newark, DE
Weibust, Dr. Patricia Snyder, Assoc.Dir.
UNIVERSITY OF CONNECTICUT - SCHOOL OF
EDUCATION - I.N. THUT WORLD EDUCATION
CENTER □ Storrs, CT
Weicht, Marlene, Law Libn.
THELEN, MARRIN, JOHNSON & BRIDGES - LAW
LIBRARY □ San Francisco, CA
Weida, William A., Libn.
AMERICAN SOCIETY FOR METALS - METALS
INFORMATION □ Metals Park, OH
Weidenhamer, Rev. Bradley E., Libn.
ASHLAND THEOLOGICAL SEMINARY - ROGER
DARLING MEMORIAL LIBRARY □ Ashland, OH
Weidl, Beverly, Cur.
HOPEWELL MUSEUM - LIBRARY □ Hopewell, NJ
Weidlinger, Linda, Asst.Libn.
JUNG (C.G.) INSTITUTE OF LOS ANGELES, INC.
- MAX AND LORE ZELLER IBRARY □ Los Angeles,
CA
Weidman, Jeffrey, Art Libn.
OBERLIN COLLEGE - CLARENCE WARD ART
LIBRARY □ Oberlin, OH
Weidner, Ruth, Music Libn./Assoc.Prof.
WEST CHESTER UNIVERSITY - SCHOOL OF
MUSIC LIBRARY □ West Chester, PA

Weigel, Jack W., Libn.
UNIVERSITY OF MICHIGAN - CHEMISTRY
LIBRARY □ Ann Arbor, MI

Weigel, Jack W., Libn.
UNIVERSITY OF MICHIGAN - MATHEMATICS
LIBRARY □ Ann Arbor, MI

Weigel, Jack W., Libn.
UNIVERSITY OF MICHIGAN - PHYSICS-
ASTRONOMY LIBRARY □ Ann Arbor, MI

Weihs, Mary, Libn.
ST. JOSEPH HOSPITAL - SISTER MARY ALVINA
NURSING LIBRARY □ Towson, MD

Weil, Beth, Hd.Libn.
STANFORD UNIVERSITY - FALCONER BIOLOGY
LIBRARY □ Stanford, CA

Weil, Peter E., Tech.Serv.Libn.
ILLINOIS COLLEGE OF OPTOMETRY - CARL F.
SHEPARD MEMORIAL LIBRARY □ Chicago, IL

Weill, David P., Dir.
EAST BRUNSWICK PUBLIC LIBRARY -
HOLOCAUST STUDIES COLLECTION □ East
Brunswick, NJ

Weimer, Ferne L., Dir.
WHEATON COLLEGE - BILLY GRAHAM CENTER -
LIBRARY □ Wheaton, IL

Weimer, Jane, Act.Lib.Dir.
OHIO NORTHERN UNIVERSITY - HETERICK
MEMORIAL LIBRARY □ Ada, OH

Weimer, Kathy L., Serv.Mgr.-Educ.
AT & T INFORMATION SYSTEMS - SERVICES
DIVISION EDUCATION CENTER □ Golden, CO

Weimer, Mark F., Rare Bk.Libn.
SYRACUSE UNIVERSITY - GEORGE ARENTS
RESEARCH LIBRARY FOR SPECIAL
COLLECTIONS □ Syracuse, NY

Weimer, Virginia, Asst.Libn., Art & Arch.
COOPER UNION FOR THE ADVANCEMENT OF
SCIENCE AND ART - LIBRARY □ New York, NY

Weimerskirch, Dr. Philip, Asst.Dir.
BURNDY LIBRARY □ Norwalk, CT

Wein, Sheldon, Res.Libn.
PEAT, MARWICK, MITCHELL & CO. -
INFORMATION AND RESEARCH CENTER □ New
York, NY

Weinbaum, Alex S., Hd.
FREE LIBRARY OF PHILADELPHIA - BUSINESS,
SCIENCE AND INDUSTRY DEPARTMENT □
Philadelphia, PA

Weinberg, Allen, City Archv.
PHILADELPHIA - CITY ARCHIVES □ Philadelphia,
PA

Weinberg, Bella Hass, Cons.
YIVO INSTITUTE FOR JEWISH RESEARCH -
LIBRARY AND ARCHIVES □ New York, NY

Weinberg, Fleur, Libn.
WILLS EYE HOSPITAL AND RESEARCH
INSTITUTE - ARTHUR J. BEDELL MEMORIAL
LIBRARY □ Philadelphia, PA

Weinberg, Gail B., Libn.
UNIVERSITY OF MINNESOTA - DRUG
INFORMATION SERVICES □ Minneapolis, MN

Weinberg, Judy, Libn.
ABT ASSOCIATES INC. - LIBRARY □ Cambridge,
MA

Weinberg, Steve, Exec.Dir.
INVESTIGATIVE REPORTERS AND EDITORS,
INC. - PAUL WILLIAMS MEMORIAL RESOURCE
CENTER □ Columbia, MO

Weinberger-Blechman, Doris, Libn.
DETROIT FREE PRESS - LIBRARY □ Detroit, MI

Weindling, Nelson, Info.Sci.
MILES LABORATORIES, INC. - LIBRARY
RESOURCES AND SERVICES □ Elkhart, IN

Weiner, Alan, Chf., Ref.
BARUCH (Bernard M.) COLLEGE OF THE CITY
UNIVERSITY OF NEW YORK - LIBRARY† □ New
York, NY

Weiner, C., Circ.
SOUTHWESTERN UNIVERSITY - SCHOOL OF
LAW LIBRARY □ Los Angeles, CA

Weiner, David J., Dir.
NATIONAL VIDEO CLEARINGHOUSE, INC. - NVC
LIBRARY AND INFORMATION SERVICE □
Syosset, NY

Weiner, John, Dir., Pubns.Serv.Div.
U.S. DEPT. OF ENERGY - ENERGY
INFORMATION ADMINISTRATION - NATIONAL
ENERGY INFORMATION CENTER □ Washington,
DC

Weiner, Peggy, Ref.Libn.
THOMPSON (J. Walter) COMPANY -
INFORMATION CENTER □ New York, NY

Weinert, Donald G., Exec.Dir.
NATIONAL SOCIETY OF PROFESSIONAL
ENGINEERS - INFORMATION CENTER □
Washington, DC

Weingarth, Darlene, D.C. Leg.Libn.
ARENT, FOX, KINTNER, PLOTKIN & KAHN -
LIBRARY† □ Washington, DC

Weingarth, Darlene, Territorial Law Libn.
GUAM TERRITORIAL LAW LIBRARY □ Agana, GU

Weingartz, Emily, Tech.Info.Spec.
KELLOGG COMPANY - TECHNICAL LIBRARY
SERVICES† □ Battle Creek, MI

Weingram, Ida, Ref.
JENKINS (Theodore F.) MEMORIAL LAW
LIBRARY COMPANY - LIBRARY □ Philadelphia,
PA

Weinhold, Siegfried, Dept.Hd.
CLEVELAND PUBLIC LIBRARY - DOCUMENTS
COLLECTION □ Cleveland, OH

Weininger, Cornelia, Cat./Ref.Libn.
JUILLIARD SCHOOL - LILA ACHESON WALLACE
LIBRARY □ New York, NY

Weinrib, Alice, Res.Assoc./Libn.
ONTARIO INSTITUTE FOR STUDIES IN
EDUCATION (OISE) - MODERN LANGUAGE
CENTRE - LANGUAGE TEACHING LIBRARY† □
Toronto, ON

Weinrich, Gloria, Sr.Libn.
NEW YORK STATE DEPARTMENT OF LABOR -
LIBRARY □ New York, NY

Weinroth, Rita, Ref.Libn./Occup.Info
BOARD OF COOPERATIVE EDUCATIONAL
SERVICES OF NASSAU COUNTY (BOCES) -
NASSAU EDUC. RSRCS. CTR. (NERC) □ Carle
Place, NY

Weinstein, Daniel L., Corp.Libn.
LOCTITE CORPORATION - RESEARCH AND
DEVELOPMENT LIBRARY □ Newington, CT

Weinstein, Dora D., Hd., User Serv.
U.S. PATENT & TRADEMARK OFFICE -
SCIENTIFIC LIBRARY† □ Arlington, VA

Weinstein, Ellen, Hd.
LONG ISLAND UNIVERSITY - C.W. POST
CAMPUS - PALMER SCHOOL OF LIBRARY AND
INFORMATION SCIENCE - LIBRARY □
Greenvale, NY

Weinstein, Gertrude
NATIONAL COLLEGE OF EDUCATION -
LEARNING RESOURCE CENTERS □ Evanston, IL

Weinstein, Jack, Adm.Libn.
YIVO INSTITUTE FOR JEWISH RESEARCH -
LIBRARY AND ARCHIVES □ New York, NY

Weinstein, Jill, Libn., Intl.
MERRILL LYNCH WHITE WELD - CAPITAL
MARKETS GROUP - LIBRARY† □ New York, NY

Weinstein, Mitzi, Libn.
WILSHIRE BOULEVARD TEMPLE - SIGMUND
HECHT LIBRARY† □ Los Angeles, CA

Weinstein, Myron, Hd., Hebraic Sect.
LIBRARY OF CONGRESS - AFRICAN & MIDDLE
EASTERN DIVISION □ Washington, DC

Weinstein, R., Owner
WEINSTEIN (Robert) MARITIME HISTORICAL
COLLECTION □ Los Angeles, CA

Weinstein, Saul, Dir.
EDINBORO UNIVERSITY OF PENNSYLVANIA -
BARON-FORNESS LIBRARY □ Edinboro, PA

Weinstein, Sue, Assoc.Libn./Hd.Pub.Serv.
UNIVERSITY OF DENVER - COLLEGE OF LAW -
WESTMINSTER LAW LIBRARY □ Denver, CO

Weinstein, Walter, Hist.Info.Spec.
U.S. NATL. BUREAU OF STANDARDS - LIBRARY
□ Washington, DC

Weinstock, Joanne, Ref.Libn.
UNIVERSITY OF VERMONT - DIVISION OF
HEALTH SCIENCES - CHARLES A. DANA
MEDICAL LIBRARY □ Burlington, VT

Weinstock, Nancy L., Rare Bk.Libn.
PHILADELPHIA COLLEGE OF PHARMACY AND
SCIENCE - JOSEPH W. ENGLAND LIBRARY □
Philadelphia, PA

Weintraub, Irwin, Libn.
UNIVERSITY OF WISCONSIN, MADISON -
DEPARTMENT OF URBAN AND REGIONAL
PLANNING - GRADUATE RESEARCH CENTER □
Madison, WI

Weintraub, Lilien, Libn.
TURTLE BAY MUSIC SCHOOL - LIBRARY □ New
York, NY

Weipert, Margaret, Sec.
MONROE COUNTY LAW LIBRARY □ Monroe, MI

Weir, Dr. Birdie O., Dir.
ALABAMA A & M UNIVERSITY - J. F. DRAKE
MEMORIAL LEARNING RESOURCES CENTER □
Normal, AL

Weir, Janet, Asst. Law Libn.
UNIVERSITY OF WYOMING - LAW LIBRARY □
Laramie, WY

Weir, Linda, Ref.Libn.
UNIVERSITY OF CALIFORNIA, SAN FRANCISCO
- HASTINGS COLLEGE OF THE LAW - LEGAL
INFORMATION CENTER □ San Francisco, CA

Weirather, Linda
PARMLY BILLINGS LIBRARY - MONTANA ROOM
□ Billings, MT

Weirbach, James L., Esq., Law Libn.
LEHIGH COUNTY LAW LIBRARY† □ Allentown,
PA

Weirich, Nancy, Libn.
TIPPECANOE COUNTY HISTORICAL
ASSOCIATION - ALAMEDA MC COLLOUGH
RESEARCH & GENEALOGY LIBRARY □ Lafayette,
IN

Weis, Aimee, ILL
COMMUNITY COLLEGE OF PHILADELPHIA -
EDUCATION RESOURCES CENTER† □
Philadelphia, PA

Weis, Ann Marie, Supv., Lib.Serv.
STERLING DRUG, INC. STERLING-WINTHROP
RESEARCH INSTITUTE - LIBRARY □ Rensselaer,
NY

Weis, Helene, Libn.
WILLET STAINED GLASS STUDIOS - LIBRARY □
Philadelphia, PA

Weisbaum, Pearl H., Libn.
SHAWINIGAN GROUP INCORPORATED -
ENERGY LIBRARY □ Toronto, ON

Weisenborn, Dr. Frank L., Dir.
SQUIBB (E.R.) AND SONS, INC. - SQUIBB
INSTITUTE FOR MEDICAL RESEARCH -
SCIENCE INFORMATION DEPARTMENT □
Princeton, NJ

Weisenburger, Patricia, Libn.
KANSAS STATE UNIVERSITY - PAUL WEIGEL
LIBRARY OF ARCHITECTURE AND DESIGN □
Manhattan, KS

Weiser, David R., Mgr.
PHILLIPS PETROLEUM COMPANY - RESEARCH &
DEVELOPMENT DEPARTMENT - TECHNICAL
INFORMATION BRANCH □ Bartlesville, OK

Weiser, Virginia, Life Sci.Libn.
UNIVERSITY OF CALIFORNIA, SANTA BARBARA
- SCIENCES-ENGINEERING LIBRARY □ Santa
Barbara, CA

Weisling, Alice, Libn.
BRISTOL-MYERS COMPANY -
PHARMACEUTICAL RESEARCH &
DEVELOPMENT DIVISION - SCIENTIFIC INFO.
DEPT. - EVANSVILLE □ Evansville, IN

Weisman, Brenda, Dir., Info.Serv.
BROOKLYN BOTANIC GARDEN - LIBRARY □
Brooklyn, NY

Weisman, Suzy, Coord.
SOUTHEASTERN WISCONSIN HEALTH
SYSTEMS AGENCY - RESOURCE INFORMATION
CENTER □ Milwaukee, WI

Weiss, Ardis, Lib.Mgr.
UNION OIL COMPANY OF CALIFORNIA -
INTERNATIONAL EXPLORATION LIBRARY □ Los
Angeles, CA

Weiss, Barbara, Asst.Dir.
MUNICIPAL FINANCE OFFICERS ASSOCIATION
OF THE U.S. AND CANADA - GOVERNMENT
FINANCE RESEARCH CENTER LIB. □
Washington, DC

Weiss, Betty L., Libn./Data Mgr.
WASHINGTON UNIVERSITY - REGIONAL
PLANETARY IMAGE FACILITY - LIBRARY □ St.
Louis, MO

Weiss, Carla M., Ref.Libn.
CORNELL UNIVERSITY - MARTIN P.
CATHERWOOD LIBRARY OF INDUSTRIAL AND
LABOR RELATIONS □ Ithaca, NY

Weiss, Egon A., Libn.
U.S. ARMY - MILITARY ACADEMY - LIBRARY □
West Point, NY

Weiss, Harvey, Archeology Adv.
YALE UNIVERSITY - BABYLONIAN COLLECTION
□ New Haven, CT

Weiss, Janet, Cat.
UNITED THEOLOGICAL SEMINARY OF THE
TWIN CITIES - LIBRARY □ New Brighton, MN

Weiss, Joy, Libn.
CONESTOGA COLLEGE OF APPLIED ARTS &
TECHNOLOGY, GUELPH CENTRE - HEALTH
SCIENCES DIV. LEARNING RESOURCE CENTRE
□ Guelph, ON

Weiss, Judith M., Law Libn.
FEDERAL RESERVE SYSTEM - BOARD OF
GOVERNORS - LAW LIBRARY □ Washington, DC

Weiss, Lorna, Lib.Techn.
SELKIRK MENTAL HEALTH CENTRE - CENTRAL
LIBRARY □ Selkirk, MB

Weiss, Madeline, Newsletter Ed.
HODES (Bernard) ADVERTISING -
INFORMATION CENTER □ New York, NY

Weiss, Rev. Nicholas, Dir.
MOHAWK-CAUGHNAWAGA MUSEUM - LIBRARY
□ Fonda, NY

Weiss, Dr. Richard A., Lib.Bibliog. & Archv.
KENTUCKY WESLEYAN COLLEGE - LIBRARY
LEARNING CENTER - SPECIAL COLLECTIONS □
Owensboro, KY

Weiss, Sabrina L., Music Libn.
VASSAR COLLEGE - GEORGE SHERMAN
DICKINSON MUSIC LIBRARY □ Poughkeepsie,
NY

Weiss, Susan, Tech.Info. Data Spec.
E-SYSTEMS, INC. - ECI DIVISION - TECHNICAL
INFORMATION CENTER □ St. Petersburg, FL

Weiss, Hon. Virginia, Libn.
LICKING COUNTY LAW LIBRARY
ASSOCIATION† □ Newark, OH

Weisse, Leah, Archv.
NORTHERN ILLINOIS UNIVERSITY - REGIONAL
HISTORY CENTER □ DeKalb, IL

Weist, William B., Univ.Archv.
BUCKNELL UNIVERSITY - ARCHIVES □
Lewisburg, PA

Weistrop, Leonard, M.D., Libn.
MILWAUKEE ACADEMY OF MEDICINE -
LIBRARY □ Milwaukee, WI

Weitkemper, Harry, Asst.Chf./Lib.Oper.
U.S. VETERANS ADMINISTRATION (DC-
Washington) - HEADQUARTERS LIBRARY
DIVISION (142D) □ Washington, DC

Weitkemper, Harry D., Asst./Lib.Oper.
U.S. VETERANS ADMINISTRATION (DC-
Washington) - HEADQUARTERS CENTRAL
OFFICE LIBRARY (142D1) □ Washington, DC

Weitkemper, Larry, Chf., Lib.Serv.
U.S. VETERANS ADMINISTRATION (MO-St.
Louis) - HOSPITAL LIBRARY □ St. Louis, MO

Weitzel, Jacqueline, Sup.Serv.Sect.Supv.
JOHNS HOPKINS UNIVERSITY - APPLIED
PHYSICS LABORATORY - R.E. GIBSON LIBRARY
AND INFORMATION CENTER □ Laurel, MD

Weitzel, Sarah, Info.Sci.
MARION LABORATORIES, INC. - R & D LIBRARY
□ Kansas City, MO

Weitzenkorn, Laurie, Asst.Cur.
NATIONAL GALLERY OF ART - INDEX OF
AMERICAN DESIGN □ Washington, DC

Weitzmann, Margaret, Ref.Libn.
SUNY - COLLEGE AT POTSDAM - FREDERICK W.
CRUMB MEMORIAL LIBRARY □ Potsdam, NY

Welborn, Doreen A., Mgr., Info.Serv.
MC KINSEY & COMPANY, INC. - INFORMATION
CENTER □ Los Angeles, CA

Welborn, Lynda, Mgr./Info.Spec.
SOUTHEAST METROPOLITAN BOARD OF
COOPERATIVE SERVICES - PROFESSIONAL
INFORMATION CENTER □ Denver, CO

Welborn, Victoria, Hd.Libn.
OHIO STATE UNIVERSITY - BIOLOGICAL
SCIENCES LIBRARY □ Columbus, OH

Welborn, Victoria, Hd.
OHIO STATE UNIVERSITY - FRANZ THEODORE
STONE LABORATORY - LIBRARY □ Put-In-Bay,
OH

Welburn, Janice D., Psych.Libn.
PRINCETON UNIVERSITY - PSYCHOLOGY
LIBRARY† □ Princeton, NJ

Welby, John, Prod.Spec.
WISHARD (William N.) MEMORIAL HOSPITAL -
PROFESSIONAL LIBRARY/MEDIA SERVICES† □
Indianapolis, IN

Welch, Jeanie, Asst.Libn.
AMERICAN GRADUATE SCHOOL OF
INTERNATIONAL MANAGEMENT - LIBRARY† □
Glendale, AZ

Welch, Jeanne, ILL
ST. ANSELM'S COLLEGE - GEISEL LIBRARY □
Manchester, NH

Welch, Jennifer Groce, Dir.
OHIO POETRY THERAPY CENTER - WELCH
LIBRARY □ Columbus, OH

Welch, John, Gen.Cons.
NORTH CAROLINA STATE DEPARTMENT OF
CULTURAL RESOURCES - DIVISION OF THE
STATE LIBRARY □ Raleigh, NC

Welch, Marianne, Ref./Coll.Libn.
UNIVERSITY OF WESTERN ONTARIO - LAW
LIBRARY □ London, ON

Welch, Oneta M., Lib.Techn.
AUTOMATED LOGISTIC MANAGEMENT
SYSTEMS AGENCY - LIBRARY □ St. Louis, MO

Welch, Rick, Asst.Dir./Mng.Ed.
OHIO POETRY THERAPY CENTER - WELCH
LIBRARY □ Columbus, OH

Welch, Sue, Hd., Tech.Serv.
COLLEGE OF WILLIAM AND MARY - MARSHALL-
WYTHE LAW LIBRARY □ Williamsburg, VA

Welch, Thomas L., Dir.
ORGANIZATION OF AMERICAN STATES -
COLUMBUS MEMORIAL LIBRARY □ Washington,
DC

Welch, Walter L., Audio Archv.Cur.
SYRACUSE UNIVERSITY - GEORGE ARENTS
RESEARCH LIBRARY FOR SPECIAL
COLLECTIONS □ Syracuse, NY

Welchman, Linda
EASTCONN - PROJECT CONNECT - LIBRARY □
North Windham, CT

Welcome, Genice, Exec.Sec.
DEER ISLE-STONINGTON HISTORICAL
SOCIETY - LIBRARY □ Deer Isle, ME

Welden, Stephanie, State Law Libn.
NEW YORK STATE LIBRARY - LAW/SOCIAL
SCIENCE REFERENCE SERVICES □ Albany, NY

Weldon, Dwight, Lab.Dir.
KTA-TATOR, INC. - LIBRARY □ Pittsburgh, PA

Welge, William D., Archv.
OKLAHOMA HISTORICAL SOCIETY - ARCHIVES
AND MANUSCRIPT DIVISION □ Oklahoma City,
OK

Weliver, E. Delmer, Dir.
INTERLOCHEN CENTER FOR THE ARTS - MUSIC
LIBRARY □ Interlochen, MI

Welker, Kathy Joyce, Circuit Libn.
U.S. COURT OF APPEALS, 6TH CIRCUIT -
LIBRARY □ Cincinnati, OH

Well, Maureen D., Law Libn.
CONNECTICUT STATE LIBRARY □ Hartford, CT

Wellborn, Cecil W., Hd.Libn.
UNIVERSITY OF ARIZONA - LIBRARY SCIENCE
COLLECTION □ Tucson, AZ

Weller, Ann C., Dir., Ref.Serv.
AMERICAN MEDICAL ASSOCIATION -
DIVISION OF LIBRARY AND ARCHIVAL
SERVICES □ Chicago, IL

Weller, Verna A., Libn.
MOUNT CARMEL LUTHERAN CHURCH - LIBRARY
□ Milwaukee, WI

Welles, A.L., Dir.
LEARNING INCORPORATED - LIBRARY □
Manset-Seawall, ME

Wellik, Kay E., Dir.
ST. LUKE'S MEDICAL CENTER - ROSENZWEIG
HEALTH SCIENCES LIBRARY □ Phoenix, AZ

Wellington, Carol S., Libn.
HILL AND BARLOW - LIBRARY □ Boston, MA

Wellington, Flora H., Coll.Spec.
UNIVERSITY OF MIAMI - SCHOOL OF
MEDICINE - LOUIS CALDER MEMORIAL
LIBRARY □ Miami, FL

Wellington, Jean Susorney, Hd.
UNIVERSITY OF CINCINNATI - JOHN MILLER
BURNAM CLASSICAL LIBRARY □ Cincinnati, OH

Wellisch, Hans H., Dir.
UNIVERSITY OF MARYLAND, COLLEGE PARK -
U.S. INFORMATION CENTER FOR THE
UNIVERSAL DECIMAL CLASSIFICATION □
College Park, MD

Wellman, Judith, Co-Coord.
SUNY - COLLEGE AT OSWEGO - PENFIELD
LIBRARY - SPECIAL COLLECTIONS □ Oswego,
NY

Wellman, Loretto
BORG-WARNER CORPORATION - ROY C.
INGERSOLL RESEARCH CENTER - TECHNICAL
INFORMATION SERVICES □ Des Plaines, IL

Wells, Anne S., Mss.Libn.
MISSISSIPPI STATE UNIVERSITY - MITCHELL
MEMORIAL LIBRARY - SPECIAL COLLECTIONS
□ Mississippi State, MS

Wells, Barbara G., Info.Ret. & Sys.Sup.
SHELL OIL COMPANY - INFORMATION &
LIBRARY SERVICES □ Houston, TX

Wells, Dorothy, Local Docs.Libn.
UNIVERSITY OF CALIFORNIA, LOS ANGELES -
PUBLIC AFFAIRS SERVICE □ Los Angeles, CA

Wells, Elaine L., Med.Libn.
LOS ANGELES COUNTY/KING/DREW MEDICAL
CENTER - HEALTH SCIENCES LIBRARY □ Los
Angeles, CA

Wells, Elizabeth C., Spec.Coll.Libn.
SAMFORD UNIVERSITY - HARWELL GOODWIN
DAVIS LIBRARY - SPECIAL COLLECTION □
Birmingham, AL

Wells, Ellen B., Chf.
SMITHSONIAN INSTITUTION LIBRARIES -
SPECIAL COLLECTIONS BRANCH □ Washington,
DC

Wells, Mrs. Hans, Dir.
FIRST BAPTIST CHURCH - LIBRARY □ McAllen,
TX

Wells, James M., Cus., Wing Found.
NEWBERRY LIBRARY □ Chicago, IL

Wells, Jane B., Libn.
UNIVERSITY HOSPITAL - HEALTH SCIENCES
LIBRARY □ Augusta, GA

Wells, Judy, Bus.Libn.
UNIVERSITY OF MINNESOTA - BUSINESS
REFERENCE SERVICE □ Minneapolis, MN

Wells, Judy, Bus.Libn.
UNIVERSITY OF MINNESOTA - DELOITTE
HASKINS & SELLS TAX RESEARCH ROOM □
Minneapolis, MN

Wells, Maria X., Cur., Italian Coll.
UNIVERSITY OF TEXAS, AUSTIN - HARRY
RANSOM HUMANITIES RESEARCH CENTER □
Austin, TX

Wells, Marianna, Hd.
UNIVERSITY OF CINCINNATI - PHYSICS
LIBRARY □ Cincinnati, OH

Wells, Marianne A., Physics Lib.
UNIVERSITY OF CINCINNATI - OBSERVATORY
LIBRARY □ Cincinnati, OH

Wells, Mary Lou, Mgr.
RICHARDSON-VICKS, INC. - MARKETING
INFORMATION CENTER □ Wilton, CT

Wells, Dr. Merle, Hist. & Archv.
IDAHO STATE HISTORICAL SOCIETY -
LIBRARY AND ARCHIVES □ Boise, ID

Wells, Nancy, Asst.Libn.
PRICE WATERHOUSE - NATIONAL/TORONTO
OFFICE LIBRARY □ Toronto, ON

Wells, Ruth, Cat.
ORAL ROBERTS UNIVERSITY - LIBRARY - HOLY
SPIRIT RESEARCH CENTER □ Tulsa, OK

Wells, Shirley, Libn.
ARMOUR PHARMACEUTICAL COMPANY -
LIBRARY □ Kankakee, IL

Wells, Susan C., Hd., Tech.Serv.
WESTERN NEW ENGLAND COLLEGE - SCHOOL
OF LAW LIBRARY □ Springfield, MA

Wells, William W., Asst.Dir.
GEORGE WASHINGTON UNIVERSITY -
NATIONAL LAW CENTER - JACOB BURNS LAW
LIBRARY □ Washington, DC

Welsh, Barbara, Libn.
TRW, INC. - ELECTRONIC COMPONENTS -
RESEARCH & DEVELOPMENT LIBRARY □
Philadelphia, PA

Welsh, Eric, Ref.Libn.
DADE COUNTY LAW LIBRARY □ Miami, FL

Welsh, George B., Lib.Asst.
SAN DIEGO AERO-SPACE MUSEUM - N. PAUL
WHITTIER HISTORICAL AVIATION LIBRARY □
San Diego, CA

Welsh, Harry E., Lib.Dir.
MANHATTAN COLLEGE - SONNTAG LIBRARY □
Bronx, NY

Welsh, Helen, Info.Chem.
ROHM & HAAS COMPANY - RESEARCH
DIVISION - INFORMATION SERVICES
DEPARTMENT - LIBRARY □ Bristol, PA

Welsh, John, Sys.Anl.
U.S. NATL. OCEANIC & ATMOSPHERIC
ADMINISTRATION - MOUNTAIN
ADMINISTRATIVE SUPPORT CTR. - LIBRARY □
Boulder, CO

Welsh, Sue, Asst. Circuit Libn.
U.S. COURT OF APPEALS, 9TH CIRCUIT -
LIBRARY □ San Francisco, CA

Welteke, Annemarie, Asst.Libn.
SOHIO PETROLEUM COMPANY - CENTRAL
LIBRARY AND INFORMATION SERVICES □ San
Francisco, CA

Welty, Janie E., Tech.Libn.
BAKER (J.T.) CHEMICAL COMPANY - RESEARCH
LIBRARY □ Phillipsburg, NJ

Welwood, Ronald J., Chm.
DAVID THOMPSON UNIVERSITY CENTRE -
SPECIAL COLLECTIONS† □ Nelson, BC

Wember, Bertha, Libn.
TEMPLE ISRAEL - MAX AND EDITH WEINBERG
LIBRARY □ West Bloomfield, MI

Wendel, Donald E., Asst.Cur. of Art
CARNEGIE-MELLON UNIVERSITY - HUNT
INSTITUTE FOR BOTANICAL DOCUMENTATION
□ Pittsburgh, PA

Wender, Ruth W., Assoc. to Dir.
UNIVERSITY OF OKLAHOMA - HEALTH
SCIENCES CENTER LIBRARY □ Oklahoma City,
OK

Wendorf, Barbara, Exec.Ed.
AMERICAN OSTEOPATHIC ASSOCIATION -
ANDREW TAYLOR STILL MEMORIAL LIBRARY □
Chicago, IL

Wendorf, John R., Prog.Asst./Libn.
WISCONSIN STATE DEPARTMENT OF
EMPLOYEE TRUST FUNDS - LIBRARY □ Madison,
WI

Wendroff, Catriona, Ref.
GOLDEN GATE UNIVERSITY - LIBRARIES □ San
Francisco, CA

Wendt, Laurel A., Automation/Res.Libn.
SOUTHERN ILLINOIS UNIVERSITY,
CARBONDALE - SCHOOL OF LAW LIBRARY □
Carbondale, IL

Wendt, Lillian, Libn.
MODESTO BEE - EDITORIAL LIBRARY □
Modesto, CA

Wengel, Linda, Ref.Libn.
AMERICAN BANKERS ASSOCIATION - LIBRARY
& INFORMATION SERVICES □ Washington, DC

Wenger, Carolyn C., Dir.
LANCASTER MENNONITE HISTORICAL
SOCIETY - LIBRARY □ Lancaster, PA

Wenger, Charles B., Chf.Libn.
NATIONAL CENTER FOR ATMOSPHERIC
RESEARCH - MESA LIBRARY □ Boulder, CO

Wenger, Larry B.
UNIVERSITY OF VIRGINIA - ARTHUR J.
MORRIS LAW LIBRARY □ Charlottesville, VA

Wengle, Annette, Libn.
METROPOLITAN TORONTO LIBRARY -
THEATRE DEPARTMENT □ Toronto, ON

Wensink, Irwin H., Chm., Lib.Comm.
WASHINGTON CATHEDRAL FOUNDATION -
CATHEDRAL RARE BOOK LIBRARY □
Washington, DC

Wente, Norman G., Chf.Libn.
LUTHER NORTHWESTERN SEMINARY -
LIBRARY □ St. Paul, MN

Wenton, Robert, Libn.
ATKINS (Gordon) AND ASSOCIATES
ARCHITECTS LTD. - LIBRARY □ Calgary, AB

Wentworth, T.T., Jr., Pres.
WENTWORTH (T.T., Jr.) MUSEUM - LIBRARY □
Pensacola, FL

Wenzel, Diane, Libn.
ONTARIO ECONOMIC COUNCIL - LIBRARY □
Toronto, ON

Wenzel, Lari, Dir.
FLORIDA STATE COMPREHENSIVE CANCER
CENTER - CANCER INFORMATION SERVICE
FOR THE STATES OF FLORIDA AND GEORGIA □
Miami, FL

Wenzl, Sr. Mary Louis, Lib.Ck.
ST. FRANCIS HOSPITAL - DOCTORS' LIBRARY □
Colorado Springs, CO

Werger, Joanne, Assoc. State Libn.
NEW MEXICO STATE LIBRARY □ Santa Fe, NM

Werk, William R., Chf.
U.S. ARMY - ELECTRONICS R & D COMMAND
(ERADCOM) - TECHNICAL LIBRARY DIVISION □
Ft. Monmouth, NJ

Werking, Richard Hume, Lib.Dir.
TRINITY UNIVERSITY - ELIZABETH COATES
MADDUX LIBRARY - SPECIAL COLLECTIONS □
San Antonio, TX

Werling, Anita, Mgr., Coll.Dev.
XEROX CORPORATION - UNIVERSITY
MICROFILMS INTERNATIONAL - LIBRARY □
Ann Arbor, MI

Werner, Ailsa Mackenzie, Law Libn.
CLACKAMAS COUNTY, OREGON - ALDEN E.
MILLER LAW LIBRARY □ Oregon City, OR

Werner, Edward K., Asst.Musm.Libn.
METROPOLITAN MUSEUM OF ART - THOMAS J.
WATSON LIBRARY □ New York, NY

Werner, Jeff, Mgr., Media Serv.
ABBOTT-NORTHWESTERN HOSPITAL
CORPORATION - HEALTH SCIENCES RESOURCE
CENTER □ Minneapolis, MN

Werner, Joanne, Cat./Women's Rsrcs.Coll.
MOHAWK VALLEY COMMUNITY COLLEGE
LIBRARY - SPECIAL COLLECTIONS □ Utica, NY

Werner, Joyce C., Hd.
LOUISIANA STATE UNIVERSITY - REFERENCE
SERVICES □ Baton Rouge, LA

Werner, Lawrence W., Libn.
HONEYWELL, INC. - DEFENSE SYSTEMS
DIVISION - ENGINEERING LIBRARY □ Hopkins,
MN

Werner, Mary Jane, Supv.
RUTGERS UNIVERSITY, THE STATE
UNIVERSITY OF NEW JERSEY - WAKSMAN
INSTITUTE OF MICROBIOLOGY LIBRARY □
Piscataway, NJ

Werner, O. James, Dir.
SAN DIEGO COUNTY LAW LIBRARY □ San Diego,
CA

Werner, O. James, Dir.
SAN DIEGO COUNTY LAW LIBRARY - EAST
COUNTY BRANCH □ El Cajon, CA

Werner, O. James, Dir.
SAN DIEGO COUNTY LAW LIBRARY - SOUTH
BAY BRANCH □ Chula Vista, CA

Werner, O. James, Dir.
SAN DIEGO COUNTY LAW LIBRARY - VISTA
BRANCH □ Vista, CA

Werner, Robert, Dir.
STOCKPHOTOS, INC. - LIBRARY □ New York, NY

Werner, Stuart, Tech.Info.Spec.
U.S. DEPT. OF COMMERCE - INTERNATIONAL
TRADE ADMINISTRATION - NEW YORK
DISTRICT OFFICE LIBRARY □ New York, NY

Wernersbach, Geraldine, Hd., Ref./Circ.Dept.
UNIVERSITY OF DAYTON - LAW SCHOOL
LIBRARY □ Dayton, OH

Wernette, Janice, Mgr., Lib.Serv.
FOOTE CONE & BELDING - INFORMATION
CENTER □ Chicago, IL

Wernick, Sharyl, Libn.
U.S. NAVY - OFFICE OF THE GENERAL COUNSEL
- LAW LIBRARY □ Washington, DC

Wersching, Yolande, Bibliog. Educ./Soc. Work
LOYOLA UNIVERSITY OF CHICAGO - JULIA
DEAL LEWIS LIBRARY □ Chicago, IL

Wert, Dr. Lucille, Chem.Libn.
UNIVERSITY OF ILLINOIS - CHEMISTRY
LIBRARY □ Urbana, IL

Wertheimer, Dr. Albert I., Dir.
UNIVERSITY OF MINNESOTA - SOCIAL AND
ADMINISTRATIVE PHARMACY READING ROOM
□ Minneapolis, MN

Wertz, Virginia, Rd.Adv.
DISTRICT OF COLUMBIA PUBLIC LIBRARY -
ART DIVISION □ Washington, DC

Weryk, Elizabeth, Circ. & Info.Serv.Libn.
MC MASTER UNIVERSITY - HEALTH SCIENCES
LIBRARY □ Hamilton, ON

Weschcke, Carl L., Pres.
WESCHCKE (Carl L.) LIBRARY □ Woodbury, MN

Weschler, Madelyn H., Libn.
OBER, KALER, GRIMES & SHRIVER - LIBRARY □
Baltimore, MD

Weseloh, Todd S., Libn./Archv.
CANAL MUSEUM - RESEARCH LIBRARY AND
DOCUMENTATION CENTER □ Syracuse, NY

Weselteer, Ruth, Libn.
LEBHAR-FRIEDMAN, INC. - CHAIN STORE AGE -
READER SERVICE RESEARCH LIBRARY □ New
York, NY

Weske, Gary, Info.Ctr.Dir.
SHERWIN-WILLIAMS COMPANY -
INFORMATION CENTER □ Cleveland, OH

Wesling, Angela Green, Lib.Dir.
MOUNT ZION HOSPITAL AND MEDICAL CENTER
- HARRIS M. FISHBON MEMORIAL LIBRARY □
San Francisco, CA

Wessel, Charles, Med.Libn.
MEDICAL CENTER OF BEAVER COUNTY -
HEALTH SCIENCES LIBRARY □ Beaver, PA

Wessells, Robert S., Asst.Libn.
U.S. NAVY - NAVAL EDUCATION AND TRAINING
CENTER - LIBRARY SYSTEM □ Newport, RI

West, Albert G., Cat.
U.S. ARMY WAR COLLEGE - LIBRARY □ Carlisle
Barracks, PA

West, Carl L., Hd.Libn.
CUMBERLAND COUNTY HISTORICAL SOCIETY -
PIRATE HOUSE LIBRARY □ Greenwich, NJ

West, Carol, Circ.Libn.
NEW HAMPSHIRE COLLEGE - SHAPIRO
LIBRARY □ Manchester, NH

West, Carol C., Dir./Professor of Law
MISSISSIPPI COLLEGE SCHOOL OF LAW - LAW
LIBRARY □ Jackson, MS

West, Deborah, Health Sci.Libn.
ST. ELIZABETH HOSPITAL - HEALTH SCIENCES
LIBRARY† □ Beaumont, TX

West, Donald, Prog.Archv.
INDIANA HISTORICAL SOCIETY - WILLIAM
HENRY SMITH MEMORIAL LIBRARY □
Indianapolis, IN

West, Eleanora F., Cur. of Musm.
FITCHBURG HISTORICAL SOCIETY - LIBRARY □
Fitchburg, MA

West, Heather, Libn.
SASKATCHEWAN INDIAN FEDERATED COLLEGE
- LIBRARY □ Regina, SK

West, J. Martin, Dir./Cur.
FORT LIGONIER MEMORIAL FOUNDATION -
HENRY BOUQUET ROOM □ Ligonier, PA

West, K., Ref.Libn.
UNIVERSITY OF ALBERTA - HUMANITIES AND
SOCIAL SCIENCES LIBRARY □ Edmonton, AB

West, Linda L., Libn.
U.S. NATL. PARK SERVICE - DINOSAUR NATL.
MONUMENT - QUARRY VISITOR CENTER -
LIBRARY† □ Jensen, UT

West, Dr. Mark I., Archv.
MENNINGER FOUNDATION - ARCHIVES □
Topeka, KS

West, Marty, Cur., Spec.Coll.
LANE COUNTY MUSEUM - SPECIAL
COLLECTIONS & ARCHIVES □ Eugene, OR

West, May, Asst.Libn.
FERMI NATIONAL ACCELERATOR LABORATORY
- LIBRARY □ Batavia, IL

West, Oriana Brown, District Libn.
U.S. ARMY - CORPS OF ENGINEERS -
JACKSONVILLE DISTRICT - TECHNICAL
LIBRARY □ Jacksonville, FL

West, Tim, Tech.Serv.Archv.
UNIVERSITY OF NORTH CAROLINA, CHAPEL
HILL - SOUTHERN HISTORICAL COLLECTION &
MANUSCRIPTS DEPARTMENT □ Chapel Hill, NC

West, W.W., Info.Anl.
CHEVRON RESEARCH COMPANY - TECHNICAL
INFORMATION CENTER □ Richmond, CA

West, Wanda, Libn.
NEW MEXICO SCHOOL FOR THE VISUALLY
HANDICAPPED - LIBRARY AND MEDIA CENTER
□ Alamogordo, NM

West, William R., Chf., Lib.Serv.
U.S. VETERANS ADMINISTRATION (CA-
Sepulveda) - BIOMEDICAL ENGINEERING &
COMPUTING CENTER - LIBRARY □ Sepulveda,
CA

Westberg, Sigurd F., Archv.
EVANGELICAL COVENANT CHURCH OF
AMERICA - COVENANT ARCHIVES AND
HISTORICAL LIBRARY □ Chicago, IL

Westbrook, E.E., Info.Ctr.Mgr.
BATTELLE-COLUMBUS LABORATORIES -
TACTICAL TECHNOLOGY CENTER □ Columbus,
OH

Westbrook, Josephine
NEW PROVIDENCE HISTORICAL SOCIETY -
LIBRARY □ New Providence, NJ

Westbrook, Patricia C., Libn.
MERIDEN-WALLINGFORD HOSPITAL - HEALTH
SCIENCES LIBRARY □ Meriden, CT

Westcott, Barbara Spaulding, Lib.Chm.
FIRST PRESBYTERIAN CHURCH OF FLINT -
PEIRCE MEMORIAL LIBRARY □ Flint, MI

Westelaken, W., Ref.Libn.
UNIVERSITY OF MANITOBA - SCIENCE
LIBRARY □ Winnipeg, MB

Wester-House, Mary, Mgr.
HOSPITAL CORPORATION OF AMERICA -
RESEARCH/INFORMATION SERVICES □
Nashville, TN

Westerberg, Kermit B., Archv./Libn.
SWENSON SWEDISH IMMIGRATION RESEARCH
CENTER □ Rock Island, IL

Westerburg, Verna, Lib.Techn.
U.S. AIR FORCE - KEESLER TECHNICAL
TRAINING CENTER - ACADEMIC LIBRARY □
Keesler AFB, MS

Westergard, Marjorie D., Libn.
WISCONSIN STATE DEPARTMENT OF PUBLIC
INSTRUCTION - D.P.I. LIBRARY □ Madison, WI

Westerhaus, Rev. Martin O., Libn.
WISCONSIN LUTHERAN SEMINARY - LIBRARY
□ Mequon, WI

Westerholm, Ruth, Adm.Assoc.
TRINITY EVANGELICAL DIVINITY SCHOOL -
ROLFING MEMORIAL LIBRARY □ Deerfield, IL

Westermann, Mary L., Med.Libn.
NASSAU COUNTY MEDICAL SOCIETY - NASSAU
ACADEMY OF MEDICINE - JOHN N. SHELL
LIBRARY □ Garden City, NY

Western, Susan, Subject Spec.
UNIVERSITY OF TORONTO - CENTRE FOR
INDUSTRIAL RELATIONS - INFORMATION
SERVICE □ Toronto, ON

Westfall, Marsha, Assoc.Dir.
WACO-MC LENNAN COUNTY LIBRARY -
SPECIAL COLLECTIONS DEPARTMENT □ Waco,
TX

Westhuis, Judith, Tech.Serv.Libn.
UNION UNIVERSITY - ALBANY LAW SCHOOL -
LIBRARY □ Albany, NY

Westin, Mary Lou, Supv.
UNIVERSITY OF MICHIGAN - MAP ROOM □ Ann
Arbor, MI

Westlake, Neda M., Cur., Rare Bk.Coll.
UNIVERSITY OF PENNSYLVANIA - RARE BOOK
COLLECTION† □ Philadelphia, PA

Westlake, Paulette, Hd., Lib.Serv.
CANADA - FISHERIES & OCEANS - FISHERIES
MANAGEMENT REGIONAL LIBRARY □
Vancouver, BC

Westling, Ellen, Hd., Info.Serv.
MASSACHUSETTS GENERAL HOSPITAL - MGH
HEALTH SCIENCES LIBRARIES □ Boston, MA

Westmoreland, Eva, Info.Cons.
CITE RESOURCE CENTER □ Austin, TX

Weston, Janice C., Chf.Libn.
U.S. ARMY ORDNANCE CENTER & SCHOOL -
LIBRARY □ Aberdeen Proving Ground, MD

Weston, Mary, Doc.Libn.
U.S. AIR FORCE - ARMAMENT DIVISION, AIR
FORCE ARMAMENT LABORATORY - TECHNICAL
LIBRARY □ Eglin AFB, FL

Weston, Norman
NATIONAL COLLEGE OF EDUCATION -
LEARNING RESOURCE CENTERS □ Evanston, IL

Weston, P.
RESEARCH & EDUCATION ASSOCIATION -
LIBRARY □ New York, NY

Weston, Ruby D., Libn.
MARYLAND STATE HIGHWAY
ADMINISTRATION - LIBRARY □ Baltimore, MD

Westover, Jane, Libn.
VERMONT INSTITUTE OF NATURAL SCIENCES
- LIBRARY □ Woodstock, VT

Westre, Tom, Libn.
FRESNO COUNTY OFFICE OF EDUCATION -
IMC-LIBRARY □ Fresno, CA

Westsik, Kathy, Sr.Info.Spec.
SYNTEX, U.S.A. - CORPORATE LIBRARY/
INFORMATION SERVICES □ Palo Alto, CA

Westwood, Anita, Coll.Spec.
DENVER PUBLIC LIBRARY - BUSINESS,
SCIENCE & TECHNOLOGY DIVISION □ Denver,
CO

Westwood, Anita F., Med.Subj.Spec.
DENVER PUBLIC LIBRARY - DENVER GENERAL
HOSPITAL LIBRARY □ Denver, CO

Wetherby, Phyllis, Pres.
KNOW, INC. □ Pittsburgh, PA

Wethey, Connee, Libn.
MANVILLE SERVICE CORPORATION - HEALTH,
SAFETY & ENVIRONMENT LIBRARY □ Denver,
CO

Wethey, Connie, Ref.Libn.
UNIVERSITY OF COLORADO HEALTH SCIENCES
CENTER - DENISON MEMORIAL LIBRARY† □
Denver, CO

Wetts, Hazel, Libn.
UNIVERSITY OF SOUTHERN CALIFORNIA -
SCIENCE & ENGINEERING LIBRARY □ Los
Angeles, CA

Wetzbarger, Cecilia, Asst.Libn.
U.S. ARMY - CORPS OF ENGINEERS - FORT
WORTH DISTRICT - TECHNICAL LIBRARY† □
Fort Worth, TX

Weum, Colleen, Coll.Dev.Libn.
UNIVERSITY OF WASHINGTON - HEALTH
SCIENCES LIBRARY □ Seattle, WA

Wexler, Jacob, Libn.
NEW YORK CITY - LAW DEPARTMENT -
CORPORATION COUNSEL'S LIBRARY† □ New
York, NY

Weyand, Gini, Libn.
LOCH HAVEN ART CENTER, INC. - LIBRARY □
Orlando, FL

Weyhrauch, Ernest E., Dean, Libs. & Lrng.Rsrcs.
EASTERN KENTUCKY UNIVERSITY - JOHN
GRANT CRABBE LIBRARY □ Richmond, KY

Whalen, George, Libn.
ONTARIO - MINISTRY OF EDUCATION -
EDUCATION CENTER LIBRARY □ Sudbury, ON

Whalen, Jane, Dir.
DEACONESS HOSPITAL - DRUSCH
PROFESSIONAL LIBRARY □ St. Louis, MO

Whalen, William, Online Searching
U.S. AIR FORCE - WRIGHT-PATTERSON
TECHNICAL LIBRARY □ Dayton, OH

Whaley, Martha, Cat.Libn.
EAST TENNESSEE STATE UNIVERSITY,
QUILLEN-DISHNER COLLEGE OF MEDICINE -
DEPT. OF LEARNING RSRCS. - MEDICAL
LIBRARY† □ Johnson City, TN

Whaley, Martha, Libn.
FIRST NATIONAL BANK OF CHICAGO - LIBRARY
□ Chicago, IL

Wharton, Heather A., Libn.
ESSO RESOURCES CANADA LIMITED -
RESEARCH LIBRARY □ Calgary, AB

Whateley, Baron, Specifier
PERKINS AND WILL ARCHITECTS, INC. -
RESOURCE CENTER □ Chicago, IL

Whealan, Ronald E., Libn.
U.S. PRESIDENTIAL LIBRARIES - JOHN F.
KENNEDY LIBRARY □ Boston, MA

Whear, Nancy, Asst.Libn.
MARSHALL UNIVERSITY - JAMES E. MORROW
LIBRARY - SPECIAL COLLECTIONS □
Huntington, WV

Wheaton, Leslie A., Asst. V.P./Mgr.
DONALDSON, LUFKIN AND JENRETTE, INC. -
CORPORATE INFORMATION CENTER □ New
York, NY

Wheeler, Dr. Beverly, Dir.
ARIZONA STATE DEPARTMENT OF EDUCATION
- EDUCATIONAL INFORMATION CENTER □
Phoenix, AZ

Wheeler, Doris A., Design Libn.
LOUISIANA STATE UNIVERSITY - COLLEGE OF
DESIGN - DESIGN RESOURCE CENTER □ Baton
Rouge, LA

Wheeler, Joan E., Med.Libn.
JANEWAY (Dr. Charles A.) CHILD HEALTH
CENTRE - JANEWAY MEDICAL LIBRARY □ St.
John's, NF

Wheeler, Linda, Hd., Ref.Serv.
SPORT INFORMATION RESOURCE CENTRE □
Ottawa, ON

Wheeler, Lora Jeanne, Libn.
AMERICAN GRADUATE SCHOOL OF
INTERNATIONAL MANAGEMENT - LIBRARY† □
Glendale, AZ

Wheeler, Meaghan, Supv., Tech.Serv.
SYVA COMPANY - LIBRARY/INFORMATION
CENTER □ Palo Alto, CA

Wheeler, Nicholas A., Prof.
REED COLLEGE - PHYSICS LIBRARY □ Portland,
OR

Wheeler, Patricia, Libn.
WASHINGTON COUNTY LAW LIBRARY □
Marietta, OH

Wheeler, Ruth, Hd., Dissemination Serv.
SUNY AT BUFFALO - HEALTH SCIENCES
LIBRARY □ Buffalo, NY

Wheeler, Verna Anne, Exec.Dir.
CROSBY COUNTY PIONEER MEMORIAL - CCPM
HISTORICAL COLLECTION/MUSEUM LIBRARY □
Crosbyton, TX

Whelihan, Annette, Asst.Libn.
SENTRY INSURANCE COMPANY - LIBRARY† □
Stevens Point, WI

Whelpley, May, Libn.
MERCY HEALTH CENTER - MEDICAL LIBRARY □
Oklahoma City, OK

Wherley, Marilyn C., Dept.Hd.
LOS ANGELES PUBLIC LIBRARY - PHILOSOPHY
& RELIGION DEPARTMENT □ Los Angeles, CA

Wherley, Marilyn C., Dept.Hd.
LOS ANGELES PUBLIC LIBRARY - SOCIAL
SCIENCES DEPARTMENT □ Los Angeles, CA

Wherry, Mrs. Del, Libn.
EXXON COMPANY, U.S.A. - LAW LIBRARY □
Houston, TX

Wherry, Tim, Engr./Comp.Sci.Ref.Libn.
ARIZONA STATE UNIVERSITY - DANIEL E.
NOBLE SCIENCE AND ENGINEERING LIBRARY □
Tempe, AZ

Whicker, Cheryl, Adm.Sec.
WAKE FOREST UNIVERSITY - BOWMAN GRAY
SCHOOL OF MEDICINE - COY C. CARPENTER
LIBRARY □ Winston-Salem, NC

Whipkey, Harry E., State Archv.
PENNSYLVANIA STATE HISTORICAL & MUSEUM
COMMISSION - DIVISION OF ARCHIVES AND
MANUSCRIPTS □ Harrisburg, PA

Whipple, Dr. Caroline Becker, Dir.
SCHOOL OF THEOLOGY AT CLAREMONT -
THEOLOGY LIBRARY □ Claremont, CA

Whipple, Connie S., Libn.
FROST & JACOBS - LIBRARY □ Cincinnati, OH

Whipple, Helen, Chf., Tech.Serv.
MINNESOTA STATE LEGISLATIVE REFERENCE
LIBRARY □ St. Paul, MN

Whipple, Marcia, Ref.Libn.
U.S. NATL. DEFENSE UNIVERSITY - LIBRARY □
Washington, DC

Whipple, P. Michael, Assoc. Law Libn.
UNIVERSITY OF TOLEDO - COLLEGE OF LAW
LIBRARY □ Toledo, OH

Whipple, S. Lawrence, Archv.
LEXINGTON HISTORICAL SOCIETY, INC. -
LIBRARY □ Lexington, MA

Whisenhunt, Sue, Sr.Libn.
VARIAN ASSOCIATES - TECHNICAL LIBRARY □
Palo Alto, CA

Whisman, Linda, Dir.
SOUTHWESTERN UNIVERSITY - SCHOOL OF
LAW LIBRARY □ Los Angeles, CA

Whistance-Smith, Ron, Univ. Map Curator
UNIVERSITY OF ALBERTA - UNIVERSITY MAP
COLLECTION □ Edmonton, AB

Whitaker, Albert H., Jr., Archv.
MASSACHUSETTS STATE OFFICE OF THE
SECRETARY OF STATE - ARCHIVES DIVISION □
Boston, MA

Whitaker, Carl, Chf.Libn.
MORRISON & FOERSTER - LAW LIBRARY □ San
Francisco, CA

Whitaker, Cynthia, Sci.Info.Spec.
CARNEGIE-MELLON UNIVERSITY -
ENGINEERING & SCIENCE LIBRARY □
Pittsburgh, PA

Whitaker, Cynthia, Sci.Info.Spec.
CARNEGIE-MELLON UNIVERSITY - MELLON
INSTITUTE LIBRARY □ Pittsburgh, PA

Whitaker, Fahy C., Supt.
U.S. NATL. PARK SERVICE - NEZ PERCE NATL.
HISTORICAL PARK - LIBRARY □ Spalding, ID

Whitaker, George, Info.Spec.
U.S. BUREAU OF THE CENSUS - INFORMATION
SERVICES PROGRAM - SEATTLE REGIONAL
OFFICE - LIBRARY □ Seattle, WA

Whitaker, Glen L., Pres.
HEART OF AMERICA GENEALOGICAL SOCIETY
& LIBRARY, INC. □ Kansas City, MO

Whitaker, Lesley, Ref.Libn.
U.S. NASA - AMES RESEARCH CENTER -
LIBRARY □ Mountain View, CA

Whitaker, R. Reed, Chf., Arch.Br.
U.S. NATL. ARCHIVES & RECORDS SERVICE -
FEDERAL ARCHIVES AND RECORDS CENTER,
REGION 6 □ Kansas City, MO

Whitaker, Susanne K., Libn.
CORNELL UNIVERSITY - FLOWER VETERINARY
LIBRARY □ Ithaca, NY

Whitcomb, Dorothy, Hist.Coll.Libn.
UNIVERSITY OF WISCONSIN, MADISON -
CENTER FOR HEALTH SCIENCES LIBRARIES† □
Madison, WI

Whitcomb, Laurie
PASADENA PUBLIC LIBRARY - ALICE COLEMAN
BATCHELDER MUSIC LIBRARY □ Pasadena, CA

Whitcomb, Laurie
PASADENA PUBLIC LIBRARY - FINE ARTS
DIVISION □ Pasadena, CA

White, Anne, Asst.Libn.
HAWKINS, DELAFIELD & WOOD - LIBRARY □
New York, NY

White, Barbara A., Spec.Coll.Libn.
UNIVERSITY OF NEW HAMPSHIRE - SPECIAL
COLLECTIONS □ Durham, NH

White, Barbara C., Chf.Libn.
DEAN WITTER REYNOLDS, INC. - LIBRARY □
New York, NY

White, Beryl, Law Libn.
ITT CORPORATION - LEGAL DEPARTMENT
LIBRARY □ New York, NY

White, Bonnie, Assoc. Law Libn.
WESTERN NEW ENGLAND COLLEGE - SCHOOL
OF LAW LIBRARY □ Springfield, MA

White, Ms. C., Asst.Libn.
COVINGTON AND BURLING - LIBRARY □
Washington, DC

White, Carol, Libn.
AKWESASNE LIBRARY CULTURAL CENTER □
Hogansburg, NY

White, Carol B., Info.Anl.
MC KINSEY & COMPANY, INC. - LIBRARY □
Washington, DC

White, Cecil R., Libn.
GOLDEN GATE BAPTIST THEOLOGICAL
SEMINARY - LIBRARY □ Mill Valley, CA

White, Clare, Hd.Libn.
ROANOKE VALLEY HISTORICAL SOCIETY -
LIBRARY □ Roanoke, VA

White, Connie L., Community Educ.Coord.
COAL EMPLOYMENT PROJECT (CEP) -
ARCHIVES □ Dumfries, VA

White, David, Coord.
OREGON INSTITUTE OF TECHNOLOGY -
LEARNING RESOURCES CENTER □ Klamath Falls,
OR

White, David, Registrar
SLOAN (Alfred P., Jr.) MUSEUM - MERLE G.
PERRY ARCHIVES □ Flint, MI

White, Dorothy K., Dir.
ST. PETERSBURG HISTORICAL SOCIETY -
LIBRARY AND ARCHIVES □ St. Petersburg, FL

White, Dorothy L., Cat.
SUMMER INSTITUTE OF LINGUISTICS -
DALLAS/NORMAN LIBRARY □ Dallas, TX

White, Edna, Asst.Ref.Libn.
SOUTH CAROLINA STATE LIBRARY □ Columbia,
SC

White, Edward, Asst.Libn., Pub.Serv.
UNIVERSITY OF ARIZONA - COLLEGE OF LAW
LIBRARY† □ Tucson, AZ

White, Ernest M., Libn.
LOUISVILLE PRESBYTERIAN THEOLOGICAL
SEMINARY - LIBRARY □ Louisville, KY

White, Evy, Art/Slide Libn.
CALIFORNIA INSTITUTE OF THE ARTS -
LIBRARY □ Valencia, CA

White, Frank, Hd., Acq.Sect.
CANADA - DEPARTMENT OF FINANCE -
FINANCE/TREASURY BOARD LIBRARY □
Ottawa, ON

White, J.E., Mathematician
OAK RIDGE NATIONAL LABORATORY -
RADIATION SHIELDING INFORMATION
CENTER □ Oak Ridge, TN

White, James J., Cur. of Art
CARNEGIE-MELLON UNIVERSITY - HUNT
INSTITUTE FOR BOTANICAL DOCUMENTATION
□ Pittsburgh, PA

White, Jane, Asst.Libn.
DISTRICT ONE TECHNICAL INSTITUTE -
LIBRARY - EDUCATIONAL RESOURCE CENTER □
Eau Claire, WI

White, Jane M., Libn.
MEAD CORPORATION - LIBRARY □ Chillicothe,
OH

White, Jean E., Libn.
RIVERSIDE HOSPITAL - SCOBIE MEMORIAL
LIBRARY □ Ottawa, ON

White, Jennifer, Info.Spec.
HJK&A ADVERTISING & PUBLIC RELATIONS -
INFORMATION CENTER □ Washington, DC

White, Jeronell, Lib.Coord.
FLORENCE-DARLINGTON TECHNICAL COLLEGE
- LIBRARY □ Florence, SC

White, Jo, Regional Rsrcs.Info.Ck.
BRITISH COLUMBIA - MINISTRY OF FORESTS -
NELSON FOREST REGION LIBRARY □ Nelson, BC

White, John, Per.
HUDSON VALLEY COMMUNITY COLLEGE -
DWIGHT MARVIN LEARNING RESOURCES
CENTER □ Troy, NY

White, John, Asst.Educ.Libn.
UNIVERSITY OF ALBERTA - H.T. COUTTS
LIBRARY □ Edmonton, AB

White, John C., AV Libn.
U.S. VETERANS ADMINISTRATION (OH-
Brecksville) - HOSPITAL LIBRARY □ Brecksville,
OH

White, John C., AV Libn.
U.S. VETERANS ADMINISTRATION (OH-
Cleveland) - HOSPITAL LIBRARY □ Cleveland, OH

White, Joyce G., M.D., Libn.
HUNTERDON MEDICAL CENTER - MEDICAL
LIBRARY □ Flemington, NJ

White, Judith, Sr.Supv.
UNIVERSITY OF VICTORIA - MC PHERSON
LIBRARY - MUSIC & AUDIO COLLECTION □
Victoria, BC

White, Karen, Staff Libn.
INTERNATIONAL CENTER FOR RESEARCH ON
WOMEN - RESOURCE CENTER □ Washington,
DC

White, L.W., Info.Anl.
CHEVRON RESEARCH COMPANY - TECHNICAL
INFORMATION CENTER □ Richmond, CA

White, Lionel, Instr. Media Spec.
FASHION INSTITUTE OF TECHNOLOGY -
LIBRARY† □ New York, NY

White, Lynda S., Asst. Fine Arts Libn.
UNIVERSITY OF VIRGINIA - FISKE KIMBALL
FINE ARTS LIBRARY □ Charlottesville, VA

White, Mari, Law Libn.
CROWN LIFE INSURANCE COMPANY - LAW
LIBRARY □ Toronto, ON

White, Mary W., Doc.Libn.
SOUTHERN RESEARCH INSTITUTE - THOMAS
W. MARTIN MEMORIAL LIBRARY □ Birmingham,
AL

White, Maryellen, Asst.Libn.
DENNISON MANUFACTURING COMPANY -
RESEARCH LIBRARY □ Framingham, MA

White, Melvin, Chf., Circ.
UNIVERSITY OF MEDICINE AND DENTISTRY OF
NEW JERSEY AT NEWARK - GEORGE F. SMITH
LIBRARY □ Newark, NJ
White, Paton R., Libn.
ST. LOUIS SCIENCE CENTER - LIBRARY □ St.
Louis, MO
White, Patricia A., Ref./Info.Serv.Libn.
PLANNING RESEARCH CORPORATION -
TECHNICAL LIBRARY □ McLean, VA
White, Peggy, Hd., Pub.Serv.
NORTHERN ALBERTA INSTITUTE OF
TECHNOLOGY - LEARNING RESOURCE CENTRE
□ Edmonton, AB
White, Rhea A., Cons.
AMERICAN SOCIETY FOR PSYCHICAL
RESEARCH - LIBRARY □ New York, NY
White, Rhea A., Dir.
PARAPSYCHOLOGY SOURCES OF INFORMATION
CENTER □ Dix Hills, NY
White, Richard A., Asst.Libn./Circ.
NATIONAL GEOGRAPHIC SOCIETY -
ILLUSTRATIONS LIBRARY □ Washington, DC
White, T.G., Supv., Tech.Serv.
ATLANTIC-RICHFIELD COMPANY -
INFORMATION RESEARCH CENTER □ Los
Angeles, CA
White, Tera B., Mgr., Corp.Info.Serv.
BLUE CROSS AND BLUE SHIELD OF NORTH
CAROLINA - INFORMATION CENTER □ Durham,
NC
White, Virginia, Asst.Libn.
NEW ENGLAND WILD FLOWER SOCIETY, INC. -
LAWRENCE NEWCOMB LIBRARY □ Framingham,
MA
Whitehead, Joyce, Dir.
NATIONAL COLLEGE OF CHIROPRACTIC -
LEARNING RESOURCE CENTER □ Lombard, IL
Whitehead, Merriel T., Libn.
VSE CORPORATION - TECHNICAL LIBRARY □
Alexandria, VA
Whitehead, Sue, Hd., Per.
BIOLA UNIVERSITY - LIBRARY □ La Mirada, CA
Whitehead, Susan E., Asst.Libn., Info.Serv.
HARVARD UNIVERSITY - SCHOOLS OF
MEDICINE, DENTAL MED. & PUBLIC HEALTH,
BOSTON MED.LIB. - FRANCIS A. COUNTWAY
LIB. □ Boston, MA
Whitehead, Thomas M., Hd., Spec.Coll.Dept.
TEMPLE UNIVERSITY - CENTRAL LIBRARY
SYSTEM - RARE BOOK & MANUSCRIPT
COLLECTION □ Philadelphia, PA
Whitehead, Thomas M., Hd., Spec.Coll.Dept.
TEMPLE UNIVERSITY - CENTRAL LIBRARY
SYSTEM - SCIENCE FICTION COLLECTION □
Philadelphia, PA
Whitehouse, Lynn, Libn.
SAN DIEGO PUBLIC LIBRARY - HISTORY &
WORLD AFFAIRS SECTION □ San Diego, CA
Whitehurst, Dori, Supv.Lib.Serv.
ATLANTIC-RICHFIELD COMPANY - ARCO
CHEMICAL COMPANY - RESEARCH &
DEVELOPMENT LIBRARY □ Newton Square, PA
Whiteley, Jack F., Dp.Dir.
U.S. DEPT. OF COMMERCE - INTERNATIONAL
TRADE ADMINISTRATION - GREENSBORO
DISTRICT OFFICE LIBRARY □ Greensboro, NC
Whiteley, Peter M., Spec.Coll.Coord./Archv.
NORTHERN ARIZONA UNIVERSITY - SPECIAL
COLLECTIONS LIBRARY □ Flagstaff, AZ
Whitelock, O.R., Dir.
U.S. NATL. ARCHIVES & RECORDS SERVICE -
FEDERAL ARCHIVES AND RECORDS CENTER,
REGION 2 □ Bayonne, NJ
Whitemarsh, Thomas R., R&D Libn.
MAYER (Oscar) FOODS CORPORATION - R&D
LIBRARY □ Madison, WI
Whiteside, Phyllis J., Med.Libn.
U.S. ARMY HOSPITALS - IRWIN ARMY
HOSPITAL - MEDICAL LIBRARY □ Ft. Riley, KS
Whiteside, S., Libn.
NOVA SCOTIA MUSEUM - LIBRARY □ Halifax, NS

Whiteway, Ken, Rd.Serv.Libn.
UNIVERSITY OF SASKATCHEWAN - LAW
LIBRARY □ Saskatoon, SK
Whiteway, Madonna, Res.Asst.
MEMORIAL UNIVERSITY OF NEWFOUNDLAND -
INTERNATIONAL REFERENCE CENTRE FOR
AVIAN HAEMATOZOA □ St. John's, NF
Whitfield, B.L.
OAK RIDGE NATIONAL LABORATORY -
INFORMATION DIVISION - ENVIRONMENTAL
MUTAGEN INFORMATION CENTER □ Oak Ridge,
TN
Whitford, Jackie, Libn.
HONEYWELL, INC. - HONEYWELL
INFORMATION SYSTEMS - TECHNICAL
INFORMATION CENTER □ Phoenix, AZ
Whitford, Jackie, Libn.
ROGERS CORPORATION - LURIE LIBRARY □
Rogers, CT
Whithorn, Doris, Caretaker
PARK COUNTY MUSEUM ASSOCIATION -
MUSEUM LIBRARY □ Livingston, MT
Whiting, David S., Coord.Libn./Media
NEWTON PUBLIC SCHOOLS - TEACHERS'
PROFESSIONAL LIBRARY □ Newton, MA
Whiting, Marvin Y., Archv./Cur., Mss.
LINN-HENLEY LIBRARY FOR SOUTHERN
HISTORICAL RESEARCH - DEPARTMENT OF
ARCHIVES AND MANUSCRIPTS □ Birmingham,
AL
Whiting, Marvin Y., Cur.
LINN-HENLEY LIBRARY FOR SOUTHERN
HISTORICAL RESEARCH - J. HUBERT SCRUGGS,
JR. COLLECTION OF PHILATELY □ Birmingham,
AL
Whiting, Marvin Y., Cur.
LINN-HENLEY LIBRARY FOR SOUTHERN
HISTORICAL RESEARCH - YOUTH
DEPARTMENT □ Birmingham, AL
Whitlock, C.C., Chf.Libn.
ROYAL ROADS MILITARY COLLEGE - LIBRARY†
□ Victoria, BC
Whitlow, Carson E., Dir.
IOWA STATE DEPARTMENT OF HEALTH -
STATISTICAL SERVICES □ Des Moines, IA
Whitman, Beverly, Lib.Techn.
U.S. NATL. PARK SERVICE - YELLOWSTONE
LIBRARY AND MUSEUM ASSOCIATION □
Yellowstone National Park, WY
Whitman, Joan T., Libn.
JAMESON MEMORIAL HOSPITAL - SCHOOL OF
NURSING LIBRARY □ New Castle, PA
Whitmell, Vicki L., Libn.
BLAKE, CASSELS & GRAYDON - LIBRARY □
Toronto, ON
Whitmore, Coralie, Dir.
U.S. DEPT. OF JUSTICE - NATIONAL
INSTITUTE OF CORRECTIONS - NIC
INFORMATION CENTER □ Boulder, CO
Whitmore, Dr. Marilyn P., Univ.Archv.
UNIVERSITY OF PITTSBURGH - ARCHIVES □
Pittsburgh, PA
Whitmore, Richard, Staff Libn.
ST. PETER REGIONAL TREATMENT CENTER -
STAFF LIBRARY □ St. Peter, MN
Whitney, Betty L., Asst.Libn.
FAIRCHILD CAMERA AND INSTRUMENT
CORPORATION - RESEARCH CENTER LIBRARY
□ Palo Alto, CA
Whitney, Byron V., Hd., Bibliog. Control
CLARKSON UNIVERSITY - EDUCATIONAL
RESOURCES CENTER □ Potsdam, NY
Whitney, Janet T., Supv.Libn.
CALIFORNIA STATE DEPARTMENT OF JUSTICE
- ATTORNEY GENERAL'S OFFICE - LAW
LIBRARY □ Los Angeles, CA
Whitney, Josephine J., Tech.Libn.
UNITED AIR LINES, INC. - ENGINEERING
DEPARTMENT - LIBRARY □ San Francisco, CA
Whitson, Helene, Coord.
SAN FRANCISCO STATE UNIVERSITY - J. PAUL
LEONARD LIBRARY - SPECIAL COLLECTIONS/
ARCHIVES □ San Francisco, CA

Whitson, Vivienne, Chf.Libn.
METROPOLITAN HOSPITAL CENTER -
FREDERICK M. DEARBORN MEDICAL LIBRARY □
New York, NY
Whitt, Diane M., Tech.Lit. Searcher
CPC INTERNATIONAL - MOFFETT TECHNICAL
LIBRARY □ Argo, IL
Whitt-Covalcine, Cynthia, Hd.
PUBLIC LIBRARY OF CINCINNATI AND
HAMILTON COUNTY - INSTITUTIONS/BOOKS
BY MAIL □ Cincinnati, OH
Whittaker, Kit, Libn.
AMERICAN INSTITUTE OF ARCHITECTS -
PORTLAND CHAPTER - AIA LIBRARY □ Portland,
OR
Whittemore, Dorothy, Dir.
TULANE UNIVERSITY OF LOUISIANA - SCHOOL
OF BUSINESS ADMINISTRATION - NORMAN
MAYER LIBRARY □ New Orleans, LA
Whitten, Alice Y., Lib.Tech.Asst.
CALIFORNIA STATE DEPARTMENT OF
TRANSPORTATION - DISTRICT 4 LIBRARY □
San Francisco, CA
Whitten, Dolphus, Jr., Exec.Dir.
JOINT EDUCATIONAL CONSORTIUM -
ARCHIVES □ Arkadelphia, AR
Whittick, Judith A., Info.Res.
MEMORIAL UNIVERSITY OF NEWFOUNDLAND -
OCEAN ENGINEERING INFORMATION CENTRE
□ St. John's, NF
Whittier, Vivian A., Res.Asst.
WITHLACOOCHEE REGIONAL PLANNING
COUNCIL - LIBRARY □ Ocala, FL
Whittington, Erma P., Hubbell Ctr.Libn.
DUKE UNIVERSITY - MANUSCRIPT
DEPARTMENT □ Durham, NC
Whittle, Susan, Pub.Lib.Cons.
STATE LIBRARY OF FLORIDA □ Tallahassee, FL
Whittock, John M., Jr., Libn.
UNIVERSITY OF PENNSYLVANIA - SCHOOL OF
DENTAL MEDICINE - LEON LEVY LIBRARY □
Philadelphia, PA
Whitzman, Susan, Asst. Campus Libn.
CENTENNIAL COLLEGE OF APPLIED ARTS &
TECHNOLOGY - PROGRESS CAMPUS RESOURCE
CENTRE □ Scarborough, ON
Wiant, Sarah K., Dir.
WASHINGTON & LEE UNIVERSITY - LAW
LIBRARY □ Lexington, VA
Wiberg, Gene, Exec.Dir.
REPUBLICAN ASSOCIATES OF LOS ANGELES
COUNTY - RESEARCH LIBRARY □ Glendale, CA
Wichers, Dr. Willard, Musm.Dir.
NETHERLANDS MUSEUM - ARCHIVES AND
LIBRARY □ Holland, MI
Wick, Constance S., Libn.
HARVARD UNIVERSITY - GEOLOGICAL
SCIENCES LIBRARY □ Cambridge, MA
Wick, Kristen, Ref.
CONTRA COSTA COUNTY - CENTRAL LIBRARY -
LOCAL HISTORY COLLECTION □ Pleasant Hill,
CA
Wickens, Marjorie, Libn.
FORINTEK CANADA CORPORATION - EASTERN
LABORATORY - LIBRARY □ Ottawa, ON
Wicker, Elaine, Ed.
CONGRESSIONAL CLEARINGHOUSE ON THE
FUTURE □ Washington, DC
Wickham, Albert T., Hd.Libn.
UNITED CHURCH OF RELIGIOUS SCIENCE -
LIBRARY ERNEST HOLMES COLLEGE LIBRARY □
Los Angeles, CA
Wickins, Helene
ALBERTA - WORKERS' HEALTH SAFETY &
COMPENSATION - OCCUPATIONAL HEALTH &
SAFETY LIBRARY □ Edmonton, AB
Wicklund, Nancy A., Asst.Libn.
WESTMINSTER CHOIR COLLEGE - TALBOTT
LIBRARY □ Princeton, NJ
Wickman, Dr. John E., Dir.
U.S. PRESIDENTIAL LIBRARIES - DWIGHT D.
EISENHOWER LIBRARY □ Abilene, KS

Wicks, Mrs. S., Cat.Techn.
ROYAL CANADIAN MOUNTED POLICE - LAW
ENFORCEMENT REFERENCE CENTRE □ Ottawa,
ON

Widder, Keith R., Cur.
MACKINAC ISLAND STATE PARK COMMISSION
- HISTORICAL RESEARCH COLLECTION □
Lansing, MI

Widdicombe, Richard P., Dir.
STEVENS INSTITUTE OF TECHNOLOGY -
SAMUEL C. WILLIAMS LIBRARY □ Hoboken, NJ

Widdison, Hal, Tape Libn.
NORTH AMERICAN RADIO ARCHIVES (NARA) -
TAPE AND PRINTED MATERIALS LIBRARIES □
Flagstaff, AZ

Widdows, Loretta A., Cur.
CRANFORD HISTORICAL SOCIETY - MUSEUM
LIBRARY □ Cranford, NJ

Widger, Mary, Libn.
ROCHESTER HISTORICAL SOCIETY - LIBRARY
□ Rochester, NY

Widner, Evelyn M., Sr.Res.Assoc.
UNIVERSITY OF CINCINNATI - DEPARTMENT
OF ENVIRONMENTAL HEALTH LIBRARY □
Cincinnati, OH

Widstrand, Rede, Coord.
CARLETON UNIVERSITY - NORMAN PATERSON
SCHOOL OF INTERNATIONAL AFFAIRS -
RESOURCE CENTRE □ Ottawa, ON

Wiebe, Frieda, Pub.Serv.Libn.
VANCOUVER VOCATIONAL INSTITUTE -
LIBRARY □ Vancouver, BC

Wiebelhaus, Richard, Asst.Libn.
U.S. COURT OF APPEALS, 9TH CIRCUIT -
LIBRARY □ Phoenix, AZ

Wiebusch, Larry, Musm.Chm.
BLUE SPRINGS HISTORICAL SOCIETY -
LIBRARY □ Independence, MO

Wieckowski, Karen, Asst.Libn.
GREENVILLE HOSPITAL SYSTEM - HEALTH
SCIENCE LIBRARY† □ Greenville, SC

Wieczner, Bilha, Info.Rsrcs.Supv.
NL BAROID/NL INDUSTRIES, INC. -
TECHNICAL LIBRARY □ Houston, TX

Wiedel, Ann E., Res.Off.
SECURITY PACIFIC NATIONAL BANK -
ECONOMICS AND BUSINESS LIBRARY □ Los
Angeles, CA

Wiedenfeld, Therese, Libn.
NORTHWEST HOSPITAL - MEDICAL LIBRARY □
Chicago, IL

Wiederaenders, Robert C., Archv.
AMERICAN LUTHERAN CHURCH - ARCHIVES □
Dubuque, IA

Wiegand, Nancy M., Libn.
LEWIS & RICE - LAW LIBRARY □ St. Louis, MO

Wiegand, Dr. Ronald G., Mgr., Info.Serv.
ABBOTT LABORATORIES - ABBOTT
INFORMATION SERVICES □ North Chicago, IL

Wiegele, Thomas C., Dir.
NORTHERN ILLINOIS UNIVERSITY - PROGRAM
FOR BIOSOCIAL RESEARCH - LIBRARY □
DeKalb, IL

Wiehle, Laurie, Libn.
ARGUS RESEARCH CORPORATION - LIBRARY □
New York, NY

Wieland, Larry, Libn.
U.S. DEPT. OF LABOR - EMPLOYMENT &
TRAINING ADMINISTRATION - REGION VIII
TECHNICAL RESOURCE LIBRARY □ Denver, CO

Wiener, Alissa, ILL Asst.
MINNESOTA HISTORICAL SOCIETY -
REFERENCE LIBRARY □ St. Paul, MN

Wiener, Daniel L., Libn.
NATIONAL CENTER FOR THE STUDY OF
COLLECTIVE BARGAINING IN HIGHER
EDUCATION AND THE PROFESSIONS □ New
York, NY

Wiener, Dr. Israel, Lib.Chm./Libn.
CONGREGATION BETH ACHIM - JOSEPH
KATKOWSKY LIBRARY □ Southfield, MI

Wiener, Paul B., AV Libn.
SUNY AT STONY BROOK - POETRY COLLECTION
□ Stony Brook, NY

Wier, Angela J., Lib.Supv.
ALABAMA POWER COMPANY - LIBRARY □
Birmingham, AL

Wier, Angela J., Libn.
LANGE, SIMPSON, ROBINSON & SOMERVILLE -
LIBRARY† □ Birmingham, AL

Wiers, Rita, Sr. Typist
NEW YORK STATE DEPARTMENT OF AUDIT
CONTROL - LIBRARY □ Albany, NY

Wierucki, Karen, Mgr., Info.Div.
COMMUNITY INFORMATION CENTRE OF
METROPOLITAN TORONTO □ Toronto, ON

Wierucki, Karen, Mgr., Clipping Serv.
ONTARIO - LEGISLATIVE ASSEMBLY -
LEGISLATIVE LIBRARY RESEARCH AND
INFORMATION SERVICES □ Toronto, ON

Wierzba, Christine, Libn.
WEBSTER & SHEFFIELD - LIBRARY □ New York,
NY

Wierzba, Heidemarie B., Mgr., Lib. & Lit.Anl.
ALLERGAN PHARMACEUTICALS, INC. -
MEDICAL & SCIENCE INFORMATION □ Irvine,
CA

Wierzbicki, Dale, Hd.Libn. for Blind
CONNECTICUT STATE LIBRARY □ Hartford, CT

Wierzbicki, Dale, Libn.
CONNECTICUT STATE LIBRARY - LIBRARY FOR
THE BLIND AND PHYSICALLY HANDICAPPED □
Hartford, CT

Wiese, Glenda C., Tech.Serv.Libn.
PALMER COLLEGE OF CHIROPRACTIC - DAVID
D. PALMER LIBRARY □ Davenport, IA

Wiese, Patricia, Dir., Audio Ctr.
UNIVERSITY OF WISCONSIN, MILWAUKEE -
MUSIC COLLECTION □ Milwaukee, WI

Wiese, Dr. W.L., Dir.
U.S. NATL. BUREAU OF STANDARDS - DATA
CENTER ON ATOMIC TRANSITION
PROBABILITIES □ Washington, DC

Wiesenthal, Diane, Chf., Lib.Serv.
U.S. VETERANS ADMINISTRATION (AZ-Phoenix)
- HOSPITAL LIBRARY □ Phoenix, AZ

Wieser, S., Dir.
CALGARY CENTENNIAL PLANETARIUM & AERO-
SPACE SCIENCE CENTRE - LIBRARY &
ARCHIVES† □ Calgary, AB

Wiggins, Gary, Hd.
INDIANA UNIVERSITY - CHEMISTRY LIBRARY
□ Bloomington, IN

Wiggins, Lillian, Dir.-Cur.
EL MONTE HISTORICAL SOCIETY - MUSEUM
LIBRARY □ El Monte, CA

Wiggins, Rosalind, Cur.
SOCIETY OF FRIENDS - NEW ENGLAND YEARLY
MEETING OF FRIENDS - ARCHIVES □
Providence, RI

Wiggins, Terry, Ref.
MEDICAL COLLEGE OF PENNSYLVANIA -
EASTERN PENNSYLVANIA PSYCHIATRIC INST.
- MENTAL HEALTH AND NEUROSCIENCES LIB. □
Philadelphia, PA

Wight, Gudrun, Media Spec.
UNIVERSITY OF CALGARY - EDUCATION
MATERIALS CENTER □ Calgary, AB

Wight, Nancy, Res.Asst.
ATLANTA HISTORICAL SOCIETY - ARCHIVES □
Atlanta, GA

Wigmore, Shirley K., Chf.Libn.
ONTARIO INSTITUTE FOR STUDIES IN
EDUCATION (OISE) - R.W.B. JACKSON LIBRARY
□ Toronto, ON

Wignall, Beth, Lib.Techn.
REGINA CITY - PLANNING DEPARTMENT -
LIBRARY □ Regina, SK

Wiist, Stephen R., Tech.Serv.Libn.
U.S. MERCHANT MARINE ACADEMY -
SCHUYLER OTIS BLAND MEMORIAL LIBRARY □
Kings Point, NY

Wikeley, K., Ref.Libn.
UNIVERSITY OF ALBERTA - HUMANITIES AND
SOCIAL SCIENCES LIBRARY □ Edmonton, AB

Wikotrom, Ellen Baker, Dir.
HINCKLEY FOUNDATION MUSEUM - LIBRARY □
Ithaca, NY

Wiktor, Christian L., Law Libn.
DALHOUSIE UNIVERSITY - LAW LIBRARY □
Halifax, NS

Wilander, Ardis, Spec.Coll.Libn.
NORTH CENTRAL MINNESOTA HISTORICAL
CENTER - LIBRARY □ Bemidji, MN

Wilberding, Anne, Pres.
CHEROKEE COUNTY HISTORICAL SOCIETY -
RESEARCH CENTER □ Cleghorn, IA

Wilbur, Lowell R., Libn.
IOWA (State) HISTORICAL DEPARTMENT
LIBRARY □ Des Moines, IA

Wilbur, Marjorie Pettit, Mgr.Tech.Info.Serv.
AMPEX CORPORATION - TECHNICAL
INFORMATION SERVICES □ Redwood City, CA

Wilbur, Ruth E., Dir.
NORTHAMPTON HISTORICAL SOCIETY -
HISTORICAL COLLECTION □ Northampton, MA

Wilburn, Gene, Hd.Libn.
ROYAL ONTARIO MUSEUM - LIBRARY† □
Toronto, ON

Wilcox, Mr., Dir.
AFRAM ASSOCIATES, INC. - AFRAMAILIBRARY
□ Harlem, NY

Wilcox, Harold E., Supv.
UNITED TECHNOLOGIES CORPORATION -
CHEMICAL SYSTEMS DIVISION - LIBRARY □
San Jose, CA

Wilcox, Marjorie C., Exec.Dir.
GRAND RAPIDS LAW LIBRARY □ Grand Rapids,
MI

Wilcox, Patricia, Ref.Libn.
UNIVERSITY OF WISCONSIN, MADISON -
CENTER FOR HEALTH SCIENCES LIBRARIES† □
Madison, WI

Wild, Larry, Coord., Bus./Tech.Serv.
MARICOPA TECHNICAL COMMUNITY COLLEGE
- LIBRARY RESOURCE CENTER □ Phoenix, AZ

Wild, Norrine E., Libn.
CLEVELAND PSYCHOANALYTIC SOCIETY -
LIBRARY □ Cleveland, OH

Wildcat, Bryce M., Res.Asst.
NATIVE AMERICAN RIGHTS FUND - NATIONAL
INDIAN LAW LIBRARY □ Boulder, CO

Wildemuth, Barbara M., Assoc.Dir.
ERIC CLEARINGHOUSE ON TESTS,
MEASUREMENT AND EVALUATION □ Princeton,
NJ

Wilder, D. Adel, Mgr., Lib.
CALIFORNIA INSTITUTE OF TECHNOLOGY -
JET PROPULSION LABORATORY - LIBRARY □
Pasadena, CA

Wilder, M. Alice, Supv., User Network
XEROX CORPORATION - PALO ALTO RESEARCH
CENTER - TECHNICAL INFORMATION CENTER
□ Palo Alto, CA

Wildey, Emily M., Libn.
NEW YORK STATE SUPREME COURT - 3RD
JUDICIAL DISTRICT - LAW LIBRARY □ Hudson,
NY

Wildgen, Carol C., Mgr., Info./Res.
BURROUGHS CORPORATION - CORPORATE
INFORMATION RESEARCH CENTER □ Detroit,
MI

Wildin, Nancy, Hd.
SEATTLE PUBLIC LIBRARY - LITERATURE,
LANGUAGES, PHILOSOPHY & RELIGION
DEPARTMENT† □ Seattle, WA

Wildman, Iris, Pub.Serv.Libn.
STANFORD UNIVERSITY - LAW LIBRARY □
Stanford, CA

Wildman, Joni, Dir.
BATTLE CREEK ADVENTIST HOSPITAL -
MEDICAL LIBRARY □ Battle Creek, MI

Williams, Cherlyn A., Lib.Supv.
HEWLETT-PACKARD COMPANY - SAN DIEGO DIVISION - TECHNICAL LIBRARY □ San Diego, CA

Williams, Christine J., Dir.Lib.Serv.
DOCTORS HOSPITAL INC. OF STARK COUNTY - MEDICAL LIBRARY □ Massillon, OH

Williams, Mrs. D. Field, Cur.
BUREAU COUNTY HISTORICAL SOCIETY - MUSEUM & LIBRARY □ Princeton, IL

Williams, Daniel T., Archv.
TUSKEGEE INSTITUTE - HOLLIS BURKE FRISSELL LIBRARY-ARCHIVES □ Tuskegee Institute, AL

Williams, Mrs. Davide B., Regional Libn.
U.S. DEPT. OF HOUSING AND URBAN DEVELOPMENT - REGION IV - LIBRARY □ Atlanta, GA

Williams, Dawn, Med.Libn.
U.S. VETERANS ADMINISTRATION (OK-Muskogee) - MEDICAL CENTER LIBRARY □ Muskogee, OK

Williams, Deaconess Louise, Dir. of Serv.
LUTHERAN DEACONESS ASSOCIATION - DEACONESS HALL LIBRARY □ Valparaiso, IN

Williams, Delmus E., Asst.Dir.
WESTERN ILLINOIS UNIVERSITY - LIBRARIES □ Macomb, IL

Williams, Doris, Libn.
SUNY AT STONY BROOK - BIOLOGICAL SCIENCES LIBRARY □ Stony Brook, NY

Williams, Dorothy, Lib.Dir.
PRESBYTERIAN HOSPITAL - MEDICAL LIBRARY □ Oklahoma City, OK

Williams, Edward F., III, Res.Hist.
SHILOH MILITARY TRAIL, INC. - LIBRARY □ Memphis, TN

Williams, F.R., Adm., Land Records
FLORIDA STATE DEPT. OF NATURAL RESOURCES - DIV. OF STATE LANDS - BUREAU OF STATE LAND MANAGEMENT - TITLE SECTION □ Tallahassee, FL

Williams, Faye, Lrng.Rsrcs.Ctrs.
VIRGINIA COMMONWEALTH UNIVERSITY - MEDICAL COLLEGE OF VIRGINIA - TOMPKINS-MC CAW LIBRARY □ Richmond, VA

Williams, Florence, Asst.Libn.
CHICAGO BOARD OF EDUCATION - LIBRARY □ Chicago, IL

Williams, Gayle A., Dir.
BI-COUNTY COMMUNITY HOSPITAL - LIBRARY □ Warren, MI

Williams, Gayle A., Prog.Off.
CLEVELAND COUNCIL ON WORLD AFFAIRS - LIBRARY □ Cleveland, OH

Williams, George W., Pres.
DALCHO HISTORICAL SOCIETY OF THE PROTESTANT EPISCOPAL CHURCH IN SOUTH CAROLINA - LIBRARY AND ARCHIVES □ Charleston, SC

Williams, Gudrun, Chm., Pub.Serv.
LOMA LINDA UNIVERSITY - DEL E. WEBB MEMORIAL LIBRARY □ Loma Linda, CA

Williams, Heather, Asst.Mgr.
DALLAS PUBLIC LIBRARY - HISTORY AND SOCIAL SCIENCES DIVISION □ Dallas, TX

Williams, Helen, Lrng.Rsrcs.Libn.
MOREHEAD STATE UNIVERSITY - CAMDEN-CARROLL LIBRARY □ Morehead, KY

Williams, Helga, Adm.Libn.
TELEDYNE BROWN ENGINEERING - TECHNICAL LIBRARY □ Huntsville, AL

Williams, Homer
AMERICAN COUNCIL OF VOLUNTARY AGENCIES FOR FOREIGN SERVICE, INC. - TECH. ASSISTANCE INFO. CLEARING HOUSE □ New York, NY

Williams, Howard M., Tech.Libn.
DIGITAL EQUIPMENT CORPORATION - HUDSON LSI LIBRARY □ Hudson, MA

Williams, James R., Musm.Dir.
DES PLAINES HISTORICAL SOCIETY - JOHN BYRNE MEMORIAL LIBRARY □ Des Plaines, IL

Williams, Jan, Tech.Libn.
MONSANTO COMPANY - INFORMATION CENTER □ St. Louis, MO

Williams, Jane, Hd.Libn.
HONIGMAN MILLER SCHWARTZ & COHN - LAW LIBRARY □ Detroit, MI

Williams, Jane, Asst. State Libn.
NORTH CAROLINA STATE DEPARTMENT OF CULTURAL RESOURCES - DIVISION OF THE STATE LIBRARY □ Raleigh, NC

Williams, Jane L., Info.Rsrcs.Coord.
QUAKER CHEMICAL CORPORATION - INFORMATION RESOURCES CENTER □ Conshohocken, PA

Williams, Janet, Libn.
EDUCATIONAL TESTING SERVICE - CARL CAMPBELL BRIGHAM LIBRARY □ Princeton, NJ

Williams, Janice, Libn.
BATTELLE-COLUMBUS LABORATORIES - CHARLES F. KETTERING LABORATORY - LIBRARY □ Yellow Springs, OH

Williams, Jean, Asst.Dir.
MERCER UNIVERSITY - MEDICAL SCHOOL LIBRARY □ Macon, GA

Williams, Jean S., Lib.Assoc.
DUKE UNIVERSITY - MARINE LABORATORY - A.S. PEARSE MEMORIAL LIBRARY □ Beaufort, NC

Williams, Jeane M., Archv.
HISTORICAL PICTURES SERVICE, INC. □ Chicago, IL

Williams, Jeanne, Circ.Supv.
UNIVERSITY OF PENNSYLVANIA - BIDDLE LAW LIBRARY □ Philadelphia, PA

Williams, Jill, Cat.
ATOMIC ENERGY OF CANADA, LTD. - TECHNICAL INFORMATION BRANCH - MAIN LIBRARY □ Chalk River, ON

Williams, Joanne, Ref.
WORCESTER POLYTECHNIC INSTITUTE - GEORGE C. GORDON LIBRARY □ Worcester, MA

Williams, John H., Sr. Law Libn.
FEDERAL RESERVE BANK OF NEW YORK - LAW LIBRARY DIVISION □ New York, NY

Williams, Joy E., Libn.
FLORIDA BAPTIST SCHOOLS, INC. - COPELAND MEMORIAL LIBRARY □ Lakeland, FL

Williams, Julianne, Lib.Mgr.
TEKTRONIX, INC. - CORPORATE LIBRARY □ Beaverton, OR

Williams, June B., Libn.
DELOITTE HASKINS & SELLS - LIBRARY □ Washington, DC

Williams, June B., Libn.
LUCE, FORWARD, HAMILTON & SCRIPPS - LIBRARY† □ San Diego, CA

Williams, Karin H., Mgr., Corp.Lib.
WEYERHAEUSER COMPANY - CORPORATE LIBRARY □ Tacoma, WA

Williams, Kay P., Adm.
NORTH CAROLINA STATE DEPARTMENT OF CULTURAL RESOURCES - TRYON PALACE RESTORATION - LIBRARY □ New Bern, NC

Williams, Ken, Libn.
INSTITUTE FOR BEHAVIORAL RESEARCH - LIBRARY □ Washington, DC

Williams, Kenneth, Ref.
HUDSON VALLEY COMMUNITY COLLEGE - DWIGHT MARVIN LEARNING RESOURCES CENTER □ Troy, NY

Williams, Kerry, Libn.
TEXAS STATE AIR CONTROL BOARD - LIBRARY □ Austin, TX

Williams, L., Libn.
CARRIER CORPORATION - LOGAN LEWIS LIBRARY □ Syracuse, NY

Williams, Dr. Larry W., Mgr.
BATTELLE-COLUMBUS LABORATORIES - TACTICAL TECHNOLOGY CENTER □ Columbus, OH

Williams, Laurence, Media Spec.
WEST LIBERTY STATE COLLEGE - ELBIN LIBRARY □ West Liberty, WV

Williams, Leonette, Acq.
UNIVERSITY OF SOUTHERN CALIFORNIA - LAW LIBRARY □ Los Angeles, CA

Williams, Linda, Acq.Libn.
HUNTINGTON (Henry E.) LIBRARY, ART GALLERY AND BOTANICAL GARDENS □ San Marino, CA

Williams, Lorraine, Ref.Libn.
DONALDSON, LUFKIN AND JENRETTE, INC. - CORPORATE INFORMATION CENTER □ New York, NY

Williams, Luester, Lib.Asst.
TUSKEGEE INSTITUTE - DEPARTMENT OF ARCHITECTURE LIBRARY □ Tuskegee Institute, AL

Williams, Lynn, Circ.Libn.
LEWIS AND CLARK LAW SCHOOL - NORTHWESTERN SCHOOL OF LAW - PAUL L. BOLEY LAW LIBRARY □ Portland, OR

Williams, Madeline M., Dir., Word Mgt.
AMERICAN BAPTIST CHURCHES IN THE U.S.A. - BOARD OF NATIONAL MINISTRIES - RECORDS MANAGEMENT & CENTRAL FILES □ Valley Forge, PA

Williams, Marcia J., Per.Libn.
HUGHES AIRCRAFT COMPANY - ELECTRO-OPTICAL & DATA SYSTEMS GROUP - TECHNICAL LIBRARY □ El Segundo, CA

Williams, Margaret E., Dept.Hd.
FLINT PUBLIC LIBRARY - AUTOMOTIVE HISTORY COLLECTION □ Flint, MI

Williams, Margaret E., Dept.Hd.
FLINT PUBLIC LIBRARY - BUSINESS AND INDUSTRY DEPARTMENT □ Flint, MI

Williams, Marsha, Ref.Libn.
MEHARRY MEDICAL COLLEGE - MEDICAL LIBRARY - LEARNING RESOURCES CENTER □ Nashville, TN

Williams, Marvin, Adm.Supv.
CORNELL UNIVERSITY - AFRICANA STUDIES AND RESEARCH CENTER LIBRARY □ Ithaca, NY

Williams, Marvin, Hd.Cat.
TENNESSEE STATE LIBRARY - STATE LIBRARY DIVISION □ Nashville, TN

Williams, Mary E., Venango Campus Libn.
CLARION UNIVERSITY OF PENNSYLVANIA - RENA M. CARLSON LIBRARY □ Clarion, PA

Williams, Mary E., Hd.Libn.
U.S. NAVY - OFFICE OF THE GENERAL COUNSEL - LAW LIBRARY □ Washington, DC

Williams, Mary-Lois, Cat.
CANADIAN IMPERIAL BANK OF COMMERCE - INFORMATION CENTRE □ Toronto, ON

Williams, Maudine B., Hd.Libn.
INDIANA UNIVERSITY, INDIANAPOLIS - UNIVERSITY LIBRARY/HERRON SCHOOL OF ART □ Indianapolis, IN

Williams, Michael, Academic Dean
UNION BIBLE SEMINARY - LIBRARY □ Westfield, IN

Williams, Michael L., Cat.
U.S. COMMISSION ON CIVIL RIGHTS - NATL. CLEARINGHOUSE LIBRARY □ Washington, DC

Williams, Mildred, Libn.
CHICAGO PUBLIC LIBRARY CULTURAL CENTER - THOMAS HUGHES CHILDREN'S LIBRARY □ Chicago, IL

Williams, Millicent, Libn.
JOHN DEERE PRODUCT ENGINEERING CENTER - LIBRARY □ Waterloo, IA

Williams, Mitsuko, Asst.Libn.
UNIVERSITY OF ILLINOIS - BIOLOGY LIBRARY □ Urbana, IL

Williams, Nancy, Libn.
PORTMAN (John) & ASSOCIATES - LIBRARY □ Atlanta, GA

Williams, Nelle T., Med.Libn.
GOOD SAMARITAN HOSPITAL - MEDICAL LIBRARY □ Lexington, KY

Williams, Dr. Nyal, Music Libn.
BALL STATE UNIVERSITY - MUSIC LIBRARY □ Muncie, IN

Williams, Pamela D., Assoc.Libn.
UNIVERSITY OF FLORIDA - LAW LIBRARY □
Gainesville, FL
Williams, Patricia, Planning Dir.
HARTFORD - CITY PLAN LIBRARY □ Hartford,
CT
Williams, Patricia, Sr.Libn.
HOFFMANN-LA ROCHE, INC. - BUSINESS
INFORMATION CENTER □ Nutley, NJ
Williams, Patricia A., Sr.Libn.
HENNEPIN COUNTY MEDICAL CENTER -
HEALTH SCIENCES LIBRARY □ Minneapolis, MN
Williams, Paula, Cur., Spec.Coll.
MUSEUM OF THE GREAT PLAINS - GREAT
PLAINS RESEARCH LIBRARY AND ARCHIVES □
Lawton, OK
Williams, Paula, Asst.Archv.
UNITED NEGRO COLLEGE FUND, INC. -
DEPARTMENT OF ARCHIVES AND HISTORY □
New York, NY
Williams, Randall, Dir.
SOUTHERN POVERTY LAW CENTER -
KLANWATCH - LIBRARY □ Montgomery, AL
Williams, Rhys
UNIVERSITY OF CALGARY - SOCIAL SCIENCES
LIBRARY† □ Calgary, AB
Williams, Dr. Richmond D., Dp.Dir. for Lib.Adm.
HAGLEY MUSEUM AND LIBRARY □ Wilmington,
DE
Williams, Robert, Ref.Libn.
OHIO STATE UNIVERSITY - HEALTH SCIENCES
LIBRARY □ Columbus, OH
Williams, Robert C.
FREE LIBRARY OF PHILADELPHIA - MUSIC
DEPARTMENT - DRINKER LIBRARY OF CHORAL
MUSIC □ Philadelphia, PA
Williams, Robert C., Libn.
UNIVERSITY OF ALASKA - INSTITUTE OF
MARINE SCIENCE - LIBRARY □ Fairbanks, AK
Williams, Robert C., Inst.Libn.
UNIVERSITY OF ALASKA - INSTITUTE OF
MARINE SCIENCE - SEWARD MARINE STATION
LIBRARY □ Seward, AK
Williams, Robert F., Chf.
COLLEGIATE REFORMED DUTCH CHURCH -
LIBRARY □ New York, NY
Williams, Roger M., Libn./Archv.
NAZARENE BIBLE COLLEGE - TRIMBLE LIBRARY
□ Colorado Springs, CO
Williams, Ruth J., Libn.
BAKER (Michael, Jr.), INC. - LIBRARY □ Beaver,
PA
Williams, S., Health Info.Libn.
HURLEY MEDICAL CENTER - HAMADY HEALTH
SCIENCES LIBRARY □ Flint, MI
Williams, Sara, Ser.
KANSAS STATE UNIVERSITY - FARRELL
LIBRARY □ Manhattan, KS
Williams, Sheryl K., Cur.
UNIVERSITY OF KANSAS - KANSAS
COLLECTION □ Lawrence, KS
Williams, Sheryl K., Cur., Kansas Coll.
UNIVERSITY OF KANSAS - WILCOX
COLLECTION OF CONTEMPORARY POLITICAL
MOVEMENTS □ Lawrence, KS
Williams, Stephanie V., Hd., Ref.Br.
U.S. NAVY - NAVAL INTELLIGENCE SUPPORT
CENTER - INFORMATION SERVICES DIVISION
□ Washington, DC
Williams, Sue, Libn.
AMERICAN AUTOMOBILE ASSOCIATION -
LIBRARY □ Falls Church, VA
Williams-Flores, Betsy, Libn.
BARTON-ASCHMAN ASSOCIATES, INC. -
LIBRARY □ Minneapolis, MN
Williamson, Carol Lee, Libn.
SCHNADER, HARRISON, SEGAL & LEWIS -
LIBRARY □ Philadelphia, PA
Williamson, Duane, Chf., Tech.Lib.
U.S. ARMY - DUGWAY PROVING GROUND -
TECHNICAL LIBRARY □ Dugway, UT
Williamson, Harriet, Dir.
MERCY HOSPITAL - LIBRARY □ Urbana, IL

Williamson, Miriam B., Libn.
BLOUNT MEMORIAL HOSPITAL - LESLIE R.
LINGEMAN MEMORIAL MEDICAL LIBRARY □
Maryville, TN
Williamson, Nancy, Asst.Libn.
CARPENTER (Guy) & COMPANY, INC. - LIBRARY
AND INFORMATION SERVICES □ New York, NY
Williamson, Wendy, Lib.
UNIVERSITY OF MINNESOTA - ECONOMICS
RESEARCH LIBRARY □ Minneapolis, MN
Willig, Maureen T., Libn.
TAFT, STETTINIUS & HOLLISTER - LAW
LIBRARY □ Cincinnati, OH
Willingham, Robert M., Rare Bks.Cur.
UNIVERSITY OF GEORGIA - RARE BOOKS
DEPARTMENT □ Athens, GA
Willis, D.J.
3M - ENGINEERING INFORMATION SERVICES
□ St. Paul, MN
Willis, Deborah, Asst.Libn.
BIOSCIENCES INFORMATION SERVICE -
BIOLOGICAL ABSTRACTS - LIBRARY □
Philadelphia, PA
Willis, Dorothy B., Reg.Dev.Coord., MCRMLP
UNIVERSITY OF NEBRASKA MEDICAL CENTER -
MC GOOGAN LIBRARY OF MEDICINE □ Omaha,
NE
Willis, Eileen B., Dept.Hd.
ORANGE COUNTY LIBRARY DISTRICT -
GENEALOGY DEPARTMENT □ Orlando, FL
Willis, Glee, Asst.Libn.
UNIVERSITY OF CALIFORNIA, DAVIS -
PHYSICAL SCIENCES LIBRARY □ Davis, CA
Willis, H.B., Dir.
ISOTTA FRASCHINI OWNERS ASSOCIATION -
RESEARCH LIBRARY □ North Fort Meyers, FL
Willis, Jeffrey A., Hd.Libn.
TALLADEGA COUNTY LAW LIBRARY □ Talladega,
AL
Willis, Lynda K., Libn.
REGIONAL MEMORIAL HOSPITAL - HEALTH
SCIENCES LIBRARY □ Brunswick, ME
Willis, Marilyn, Med.Libn.
SCHUMPERT MEDICAL CENTER - MEDICAL
LIBRARY □ Shreveport, LA
Willis, Paul J., Archv.
INTERNATIONAL FORTEAN ORGANIZATION -
INFO RESEARCH LIBRARY □ Arlington, VA
Willis, Scott A., Info.Spec.
AUTOMOBILE CLUB OF SOUTHERN CALIFORNIA
- TECHNICAL INFORMATION CENTER □ Los
Angeles, CA
Willis, Dr. Stephen, Hd., Mss.Coll.
NATIONAL LIBRARY OF CANADA - MUSIC
DIVISION □ Ottawa, ON
Willis, Ted, Exec.Dir.
TEXAS MUNICIPAL LEAGUE - LIBRARY □ Austin,
TX
Willis, Wilda Logan, Mss.Libn.
HOWARD UNIVERSITY - MOORLAND-SPINGARN
RESEARCH CENTER - MANUSCRIPT DIVISION □
Washington, DC
Willkie, Everett C., Jr., Bibliog.
BROWN UNIVERSITY - JOHN CARTER BROWN
LIBRARY □ Providence, RI
Willman, Carol, Cat.Libn.
OREGON HEALTH SCIENCES UNIVERSITY -
LIBRARY □ Portland, OR
Willms, Bruce C., Hd., Tech.Serv.
MACALESTER COLLEGE - WEYERHAEUSER
LIBRARY □ St. Paul, MN
Willner, Susan, Cat.
AMERICAN MUSIC CENTER - LIBRARY □ New
York, NY
Willoughby, Edith L., Libn.
OVERBROOK SCHOOL FOR THE BLIND -
LIBRARY □ Philadelphia, PA
Willoughby, N.D., Libn.
ROSICRUCIAN FELLOWSHIP - LIBRARY □
Oceanside, CA

Willoughby, Nona C., Hd.Libn.
NORTHERN WESTCHESTER HOSPITAL CENTER
- HEALTH SCIENCES LIBRARY □ Mount Kisco,
NY
Willoughby, Norma A., Libn.
CAMERON IRON WORKS, INC. - LIBRARY □
Houston, TX
Willoughby, Wanda, Media Libn.
LOGAN COLLEGE OF CHIROPRACTIC - LIBRARY
□ Chesterfield, MO
Wills, Alice, Tech.Serv.
ENVIRONMENTAL PROTECTION AGENCY -
HEADQUARTERS LIBRARY† □ Washington, DC
Wills, Keith C., Dir. of Libs.
SOUTHWESTERN BAPTIST THEOLOGICAL
SEMINARY - A. WEBB ROBERTS LIBRARY □ Fort
Worth, TX
Wills, Richard D., Libn.
WESTERN STATE HOSPITAL - MEDICAL
LIBRARY □ Staunton, VA
Willson, Katherine H., Mgr., Info.Serv.
FUTURES GROUP, INC. - LIBRARY □
Glastonbury, CT
Wilmer, Jeanne, Libn.
WELLINGTON MANAGEMENT COMPANY -
RESEARCH LIBRARY □ Valley Forge, PA
Wilscam, Roderick A., Pres.
FRENCH-CANADIAN GENEALOGICAL SOCIETY
OF CONNECTICUT, INC. - LIBRARY □ Rocky Hill,
CT
Wilson, Alice S., Sec./Libn.
STEAMSHIP HISTORICAL SOCIETY OF
AMERICA COLLECTION □ Staten Island, NY
Wilson, Ann M., Mgr., Lib.Serv.
INTERMETRICS INC. - LIBRARY □ Cambridge,
MA
Wilson, Ashby, Jr., Oper.Cons.
NORTH CAROLINA STATE DEPARTMENT OF
CULTURAL RESOURCES - DIVISION OF THE
STATE LIBRARY □ Raleigh, NC
Wilson, Barbara, Chf., Reg.Lib. for Blind
RHODE ISLAND STATE DEPARTMENT OF STATE
LIBRARY SERVICES □ Providence, RI
Wilson, Barbara A., Med.Libn.
SANTA CLARA VALLEY MEDICAL CENTER -
MILTON J. CHATTON MEDICAL LIBRARY □ San
Jose, CA
Wilson, Beverly, Libn., Tech.Serv.
COLUMBUS TECHNICAL INSTITUTE -
EDUCATIONAL RESOURCES CENTER □
Columbus, OH
Wilson, Ms. Bobbi, Libn.
OTTAWA INSTITUTE - IRENE HOLM MEMORIAL
LIBRARY □ Columbus, OH
Wilson, Bonnie, Hd.
MINNESOTA HISTORICAL SOCIETY - SPECIAL
LIBRARIES □ St. Paul, MN
Wilson, Bonnie L., Libn.
FRANKLIN INSTITUTE OF BOSTON - LIBRARY □
Boston, MA
Wilson, Carol R., Libn.
UNIVERSITY OF MICHIGAN - CENTER FOR
RESEARCH ON ECONOMIC DEVELOPMENT □
Ann Arbor, MI
Wilson, Carole F., Chm.
SAN DIEGO STATE UNIVERSITY - MEDIA &
CURRICULUM CENTER† □ San Diego, CA
Wilson, Caroline, Interp.
U.S. NATL. PARK SERVICE - ORGAN PIPE
CACTUS NATL. MONUMENT - LIBRARY □ Ajo,
AZ
Wilson, Catherine W., Libn.
WORKER'S COMPENSATION BOARD OF
ONTARIO - HOSPITAL & REHABILITATION
CENTRE - MEDICAL LIBRARY □ Downsview, ON
Wilson, Chuck, Archv. II
CALIFORNIA - STATE ARCHIVES □ Sacramento,
CA
Wilson, Connie M., Libn.
UNIVERSITY OF ARKANSAS FOR MEDICAL
SCIENCES - NORTHWEST ARKANSAS HEALTH
EDUCATION CENTER - LIBRARY □ Fayetteville,
AR

Wilson, D. Keith, Customer Serv.Coord.
GSG, INC. - CTI LIBRARY SYSTEMS, INC. □
Orem, UT

Wilson, Dr. Don W., Dir.
U.S. PRESIDENTIAL LIBRARIES - GERALD R.
FORD LIBRARY □ Ann Arbor, MI

Wilson, Dorothy, Libn.
AT & T TECHNOLOGIES, INC. - TECHNICAL
LIBRARY □ Shreveport, LA

Wilson, Dorothy I., Ed.Asst.
UNIVERSITY OF MISSISSIPPI - BUREAU OF
GOVERNMENTAL RESEARCH LIBRARY □
University, MS

Wilson, Rev. Edwin H., Hist.
FELLOWSHIP OF RELIGIOUS HUMANISTS -
BRANCH LIBRARY □ Cocoa Beach, FL

Wilson, Edwin H., Hist.
FELLOWSHIP OF RELIGIOUS HUMANISTS -
LIBRARY □ Yellow Springs, OH

Wilson, Eleanor C., Libn.
BARRINGTON COLLEGE - LIBRARY □ Barrington,
RI

Wilson, Fred L., Jr., Med. Staff Libn.
CONEMAUGH VALLEY MEMORIAL HOSPITAL -
HEALTH SCIENCES LIBRARY □ Johnstown, PA

Wilson, Gail L., Libn.
COLLEGE OF WILLIAM AND MARY - VIRGINIA
ASSOCIATED RESEARCH CAMPUS LIBRARY □
Newport News, VA

Wilson, Galen, Mss.Libn.
UNIVERSITY OF MICHIGAN - WILLIAM L.
CLEMENTS LIBRARY □ Ann Arbor, MI

Wilson, Greta S., Mss.Libn.
HOWARD UNIVERSITY - MOORLAND-SPINGARN
RESEARCH CENTER - MANUSCRIPT DIVISION □
Washington, DC

Wilson, Helen M., Libn.
HISTORICAL SOCIETY OF WESTERN
PENNSYLVANIA - LIBRARY □ Pittsburgh, PA

Wilson, Helen M., Libn.
WESTERN PENNSYLVANIA GENEALOGICAL
SOCIETY - LIBRARY □ Pittsburgh, PA

Wilson, Mrs. Howard A., Med.Libn.
VASSAR BROTHERS HOSPITAL - MEDICAL
LIBRARY □ Poughkeepsie, NY

Wilson, Ian E., Prov.Archv.
SASKATCHEWAN ARCHIVES BOARD □ Regina,
SK

Wilson, James T., Lib.Sys.Spec.
GSG, INC. - CTI LIBRARY SYSTEMS, INC. □
Orem, UT

Wilson, Jane, Libn.
VANDERBILT (R.T.) COMPANY, INC. - LIBRARY
□ East Norwalk, CT

Wilson, Jeffrey L., Dir.
PACIFIC CHRISTIAN COLLEGE - HURST
MEMORIAL LIBRARY □ Fullerton, CA

Wilson, John, Travel Dir.
MONTANA STATE DEPARTMENT OF
COMMERCE - MONTANA PROMOTION
DIVISION □ Helena, MT

Wilson, John, Chf., Sys.Anl.
U.S. GEOLOGICAL SURVEY - NATL.
CARTOGRAPHIC INFORMATION CENTER
(NCIC) □ Reston, VA

Wilson, Judith, Libn.
SANDY CORPORATION - LIBRARY □ Troy, MI

Wilson, Karen, Hd.Pub.Serv.Libn.
STANFORD UNIVERSITY - J. HUGH JACKSON
LIBRARY □ Stanford, CA

Wilson, Dr. Karen S., Music Libn.
BOB JONES UNIVERSITY - MUSIC LIBRARY† □
Greenville, SC

Wilson, Lawrence A., Act.Libn.
GENSTAR-FLINTKOTE BUILDING PRODUCTS
COMPANY - CORPORATE R&D LIBRARY □
Irving, TX

Wilson, Lorraine, Soc.Serv.Libn.
RYERSON POLYTECHNICAL INSTITUTE -
LEARNING RESOURCES CENTRE □ Toronto, ON

Wilson, Lucy, Coll.Libn.
UNIVERSITY OF CINCINNATI - RAYMOND
WALTERS COLLEGE - LIBRARY □ Cincinnati, OH

Wilson, Lynn, Jr. RMC Spec.
INSTITUTE OF CULTURE AND
COMMUNICATION - CCPC - RESOURCE
MATERIALS COLLECTION □ Honolulu, HI

Wilson, Margaret F., Assoc.Univ.Libn.
FLORIDA A&M UNIVERSITY - ARCH/TECH
LIBRARY □ Tallahassee, FL

Wilson, Mari, Tech.Libn.
OCEANROUTES, INC. - TECHNICAL LIBRARY □
Palo Alto, CA

Wilson, Mari, Assoc.Libn.
UNIVERSITY OF CALIFORNIA, BERKELEY -
ENERGY AND RESOURCES PROGRAM - ENERGY
INFORMATION CENTER† □ Berkeley, CA

Wilson, Marietta, Libn.
MERCY MEDICAL CENTER - HEALTH SCIENCES
LIBRARY □ Springfield, OH

Wilson, Marilyn J., Acq.Libn.
UNIVERSITY OF CALIFORNIA, SAN DIEGO -
UNIVERSITY LIBRARIES □ La Jolla, CA

Wilson, Martin P., Assoc.Dir.
CLARKSON UNIVERSITY - EDUCATIONAL
RESOURCES CENTER □ Potsdam, NY

Wilson, Mary, Ref.Libn.
KEMPER GROUP - LIBRARY □ Long Grove, IL

Wilson, Mary K., Asst.Libn.
U.S. COMPTROLLER OF THE CURRENCY -
LIBRARY □ Washington, DC

Wilson, Mary W., Dir.
PUBLIC RELATIONS SOCIETY OF AMERICA -
INFORMATION CENTER □ New York, NY

Wilson, Maureen F., Hd.
UNIVERSITY OF BRITISH COLUMBIA - MAP
DIVISION □ Vancouver, BC

Wilson, Melanie, Ref.Libn.
UNIVERSITY OF ILLINOIS AT CHICAGO -
HEALTH SCIENCES CENTER - LIBRARY OF THE
HEALTH SCIENCES □ Peoria, IL

Wilson, Nancy L., Serv.Supv.
BOEING COMPANY - SEATTLE SERVICES
DIVISION - TECHNICAL LIBRARIES† □ Seattle,
WA

Wilson, Patricia, Libn.
NEWFOUNDLAND AND LABRADOR
DEVELOPMENT CORPORATION LTD. - LIBRARY
□ St. John's, NF

Wilson, Patricia, Libn.
STANLEY ASSOCIATES ENGINEERING, LTD. -
LIBRARY □ Edmonton, AB

Wilson, Peggy, Info.Off./Chf.Libn.
FIRST INTERSTATE BANK OF CALIFORNIA -
LIBRARY □ Los Angeles, CA

Wilson, Mrs. R., Staff Archv.
SASKATCHEWAN ARCHIVES BOARD □ Regina,
SK

Wilson, Rebecca, Ref.Libn.
SUNY - COLLEGE AT POTSDAM - FREDERICK W.
CRUMB MEMORIAL LIBRARY □ Potsdam, NY

Wilson, Robert, Hd., Pub.Serv.
SOUTHERN ALBERTA INSTITUTE OF
TECHNOLOGY - LEARNING RESOURCES CENTRE
□ Calgary, AB

Wilson, Robert M., Lib.Hd.
LAURENTIAN UNIVERSITY - SCIENCE AND
ENGINEERING LIBRARY □ Sudbury, ON

Wilson, Ron, Ref.Libn.
NEWSWEEK, INC. - LIBRARY □ New York, NY

Wilson, Ronald G., Pk.Hist.
U.S. NATL. PARK SERVICE - APPOMATTOX
COURT HOUSE NATL. HISTORICAL PARK -
LIBRARY □ Appomattox, VA

Wilson, Ruth, Cat.Libn.
REFORMED THEOLOGICAL SEMINARY -
LIBRARY □ Jackson, MS

Wilson, Sally, Ser.Libn.
UNIVERSITY OF PITTSBURGH - FALK LIBRARY
OF THE HEALTH SCIENCES □ Pittsburgh, PA

Wilson, Shannon, Archv.
KENTUCKY STATE DEPARTMENT FOR
LIBRARIES & ARCHIVES - ARCHIVES □
Frankfort, KY

Wilson, Steve, Dir.
MUSEUM OF THE GREAT PLAINS - GREAT
PLAINS RESEARCH LIBRARY AND ARCHIVES □
Lawton, OK

Wilson, Susan M., Tech.Info.Coord.
MARY KAY COSMETICS, INC. - TECHNICAL
INFORMATION CENTER □ Dallas, TX

Wilson, Thelma, Dir. of Educ.
APPALACHIAN REGIONAL HOSPITAL - MEDICAL
LIBRARY □ Beckley, WV

Wilson, Theresa E., Asst.Libn.
CHARLESTON LIBRARY SOCIETY □ Charleston,
SC

Wilson, Thomas F., Dir., Info. & Pubns.
SEARCH GROUP, INC. - LIBRARY □ Sacramento,
CA

Wilson, Dr. V. Chivers, Dir., Res./Dev.
GLAXO CANADA, LTD. - LIBRARY □ Toronto, ON

Wilson, Vivian L., Law Libn.
WAKE FOREST UNIVERSITY - LAW LIBRARY □
Winston-Salem, NC

Wilson, W.T., Res. Entomologist
U.S.D.A. - AGRICULTURAL RESEARCH SERVICE
- HONEY BEE PESTICIDES/DISEASES
RESEARCH LABORATORY - LIBRARY □ Laramie,
WY

Wilson, Wesley, Asst.Hd.
ENOCH PRATT FREE LIBRARY - MARYLAND
DEPARTMENT □ Baltimore, MD

Wilson, William G., Libn.
UNIVERSITY OF MARYLAND, COLLEGE PARK -
COLLEGE OF LIBRARY & INFORMATION
SERVICES - LIBRARY □ College Park, MD

Wilsted, Thomas, Archv./Adm.
SALVATION ARMY - ARCHIVES AND RESEARCH
CENTER □ New York, NY

Wilt, Charles, Rd.Serv.Libn.
FRANKLIN INSTITUTE - LIBRARY □ Philadelphia,
PA

Wilt, Matthew R., Exec.Dir.
CATHOLIC LIBRARY ASSOCIATION - NATIONAL
HEADQUARTERS - LIBRARY □ Haverford, PA

Wilt, Sue Ann, Libn.
MICHIGAN STATE UNIVERSITY -
INSTRUCTIONAL MEDIA CENTER - FILM
LIBRARY □ East Lansing, MI

Wilton, Elaine B., Libn.
CONGREGATION ADATH ISRAEL - LIBRARY □
Boston, MA

Wilton, Karen E., Libn.
CANADA - AGRICULTURE CANADA - RESEARCH
STATION, SWIFT CURRENT - LIBRARY □ Swift
Current, SK

Wiltshire, Denise A., Libn.
U.S. GEOLOGICAL SURVEY - WATER
RESOURCES DIVISION - NEW YORK DISTRICT
- LIBRARY □ Albany, NY

Wimbish, Emery, Jr., Hd.Libn.
LINCOLN UNIVERSITY - LANGSTON HUGHES
MEMORIAL LIBRARY - SPECIAL COLLECTIONS†
□ Lincoln University, PA

Wimmer, Katherine, Dir., Lib.Serv.
ST. JOSEPH HOSPITAL - LIBRARY □ Chicago, IL

Wimmer, Laura, Dir., Lib.Serv.
EDGEWATER HOSPITAL - MEDICAL LIBRARY □
Chicago, IL

Wimsatt, Sara, Tech.Info.Spec.
U.S. NATL. BUREAU OF STANDARDS -
NATIONAL CENTER FOR STANDARDS AND
CERTIFICATION INFORMATION □ Washington,
DC

Wimsatt, Theresa, Asst.Dir., Med.Rec.
COX MEDICAL CENTER-JEFFERSON -
DOCTORS' LIBRARY □ Springfield, MO

Winand, Diane, Pub.Serv.Libn.
MAINE MEDICAL CENTER - LIBRARY.□ Portland,
ME

Winberg, Bill, Hist.
WRATHER PORT PROPERTIES, LTD. -
ARCHIVES AND RESOURCE CENTER □ Long
Beach, CA

Windell, Marie E., Lib.Asst. II
UNIVERSITY OF NEW ORLEANS - EARL K. LONG
LIBRARY - ARCHIVES & MANUSCRIPTS/
SPECIAL COLLECTIONS DEPT. □ New Orleans,
LA

Windes, Thomas C., Supv.Archeo.
U.S. NATL. PARK SERVICE - CHACO CENTER -
LIBRARY □ Albuquerque, NM

Windham, Carol, Hd.Libn.
MIDWAY HOSPITAL - HEALTH SCIENCES
LIBRARY □ St. Paul, MN

Windrem, Laurel, Med.Libn.
KAISER-PERMANENTE MEDICAL CENTER -
HEALTH SCIENCES LIBRARY □ San Diego, CA

Windsor, Donald A., Info.Sup. Group
NORWICH EATON PHARMACEUTICALS, INC. -
RESEARCH AND DEVELOPMENT LIBRARY □
Norwich, NY

Windsor, Madeline, Hd., Rpts.Sect.
BROOKHAVEN NATIONAL LABORATORY -
TECHNICAL INFORMATION DIVISION □ Upton,
NY

Winearls, Joan, Map Libn.
UNIVERSITY OF TORONTO - MAP LIBRARY □
Toronto, ON

Wineburgh-Freed, Margaret, Cat.Libn.
UNIVERSITY OF SOUTHERN CALIFORNIA -
HEALTH SCIENCES CAMPUS - NORRIS
MEDICAL LIBRARY □ Los Angeles, CA

Winfrey, Dr. Dorman H., Dir. & Libn.
TEXAS STATE LIBRARY □ Austin, TX

Wingate, Dawn A., Libn.
MAX FACTOR & COMPANY - R & D LIBRARY □
Hollywood, CA

Wingate, Henry, Libn.
UNIVERSITY OF VIRGINIA - COLGATE DARDEN
GRADUATE SCHOOL OF BUSINESS
ADMINISTRATION - LIBRARY □ Charlottesville,
VA

Wingenroth, Janet, ILL
CARROLL COLLEGE - LIBRARY □ Helena, MT

Winger, Anna K., Libn.
U.S. DEFENSE LOGISTICS AGENCY - DEFENSE
LOGISTICS SERVICES CENTER - LIBRARY □
Battle Creek, MI

Winger, Robert, Tech.Serv.Libn.
BARRETT SMITH SCHAPIRO SIMON &
ARMSTRONG - LIBRARY □ New York, NY

Wingert, Ray A., Media Spec.
HARRISBURG HOSPITAL - LIBRARY/MEDIA
SERVICES □ Harrisburg, PA

Wingerter, Isabel, Media
LOUISIANA STATE UNIVERSITY - LAW
LIBRARY □ Baton Rouge, LA

Winiarski, Joanne, Hd.Libn.
OGILVY & MATHER, INC. - RESEARCH
LIBRARY† □ New York, NY

Winiarz, Elizabeth, Ref.Libn.
CONCORDIA UNIVERSITY - SIR GEORGE
WILLIAMS CAMPUS - SCIENCE &
ENGINEERING LIBRARY □ Montreal, PQ

Winick, Lester E., Lib.Comm.
COLLECTORS CLUB OF CHICAGO - LIBRARY □
Chicago, IL

Winik, Ruth, Mgr.
IBM CORPORATION - GENERAL PRODUCTS
DIVISION - STL LIBRARY □ San Jose, CA

Winkler, Margaret, Coord.
FLORIDA STATE UNIVERSITY - CTR. FOR
STUDIES IN VOCATIONAL EDUC. - FLORIDA
EDUCATIONAL INFO. SERV. □ Tallahassee, FL

Winland, Jane E., Bus.Libn.
COLUMBIA UNIVERSITY - THOMAS J. WATSON
LIBRARY OF BUSINESS AND ECONOMICS □ New
York, NY

Winmill, Sue, Libn.
CHURCH OF JESUS CHRIST OF LATTER-DAY
SAINTS - BOSTON BRANCH GENEALOGICAL
LIBRARY □ Weston, MA

Winn, Carolyn P., Res.Libn.
WOODS HOLE OCEANOGRAPHIC INSTITUTION
- RESEARCH LIBRARY □ Woods Hole, MA

Winn, Karyl, Mss.Libn.
UNIVERSITY OF WASHINGTON - UNIVERSITY
ARCHIVES & MANUSCRIPT DIVISION -
MANUSCRIPT COLLECTION □ Seattle, WA

Winnacker, Martha, Res.Assoc.
SOUTHEAST ASIA RESOURCE CENTER □
Berkeley, CA

Winner, Marian C., Hd.Sci.Libn.
MIAMI UNIVERSITY - BRILL SCIENCE LIBRARY
□ Oxford, OH

Winokur, Barbara, Sr.Libn.
HARRIS (Louis) & ASSOCIATES, INC. -
INFORMATION SERVICES □ New York, NY

Winsche, Richard A., Hist.
NASSAU COUNTY MUSEUM REFERENCE
LIBRARY □ East Meadow, NY

Winslow, D.H., Mgr.
UNIROYAL, INC. - TECHNICAL LIBRARY □
Waterbury, CT

Winslow, Lisa, Law Libn.
GREENBERG, GLUSKER, FIELDS CLAMAN &
MACHTINGER - LIBRARY □ Los Angeles, CA

Winslow, N., Health Info.Libn.
HURLEY MEDICAL CENTER - HAMADY HEALTH
SCIENCES LIBRARY □ Flint, MI

Winslow, Susan G., Dir.
OAK RIDGE NATIONAL LABORATORY -
TOXICOLOGY INFORMATION RESPONSE
CENTER □ Oak Ridge, TN

Winson, Gail, Assoc.Libn.
UNIVERSITY OF CALIFORNIA, SAN FRANCISCO
- HASTINGS COLLEGE OF THE LAW - LEGAL
INFORMATION CENTER □ San Francisco, CA

Winsor, George, Prof. of Educ.
WILMINGTON COLLEGE - CURRICULUM
MATERIALS CENTER □ Wilmington, OH

Winstanley, Nancy, Libn.
JONES AND LAUGHLIN STEEL CORPORATION -
COMMERCIAL LIBRARY† □ Pittsburgh, PA

Winstead, G. Alvis, Dir. & Libn.
TENNESSEE STATE LAW LIBRARY □ Nashville,
TN

Winstead, Mamie H., Libn.
TENNESSEE STATE SUPREME COURT - LAW
LIBRARY □ Knoxville, TN

Winston, Sophie, Chf.Med.Libn.
BROOKDALE HOSPITAL MEDICAL CENTER -
MARIE SMITH SCHWARTZ MEDICAL LIBRARY □
Brooklyn, NY

Winter, Elizabeth A., Libn.
TRANS CANADA PIPELINES LTD. - LIBRARY □
Calgary, AB

Winter, Glenna, Libn.
ALBERTA - DEPARTMENT OF TOURISM AND
SMALL BUSINESS - LIBRARY □ Edmonton, AB

Winter, Madeline F., Libn.
BERKSHIRE EAGLE - LIBRARY □ Pittsfield, MA

Winter, Michael F., Med.Libn.
UNITY MEDICAL CENTER - LIBRARY □ Fridley,
MN

Winter, Roger, Dir.
UNITED STATES COMMITTEE FOR REFUGEES -
LIBRARY □ New York, NY

Winter, Roland A., Libn.
MIDDLESEX COUNTY LAW LIBRARY □ New
Brunswick, NJ

Winteregg, Candy, Asst.Dir.
GRANDVIEW HOSPITAL - MEDICAL LIBRARY □
Dayton, OH

Winterhalter, Cynthia C., Cur.
ASHLAND HISTORICAL SOCIETY - LIBRARY □
Ashland, MA

Winters, Mr. Murl M., Dir.
SOUTHWESTERN ASSEMBLIES OF GOD
COLLEGE - P.C. NELSON MEMORIAL LIBRARY □
Waxahachie, TX

Winters, Wilma E., Libn.
HARVARD UNIVERSITY - CENTER FOR
POPULATION STUDIES LIBRARY □ Boston, MA

Winward, Coleen C., Med.Libn.
IDAHO FALLS CONSOLIDATED HOSPITALS -
HEALTH SCIENCES LIBRARY □ Idaho Falls, ID

Wiren, Harold N., Hd.Libn.
UNIVERSITY OF WASHINGTON - ENGINEERING
LIBRARY □ Seattle, WA

Wirth, Brenda, Circ.
KANSAS CITY ART INSTITUTE - LIBRARY □
Kansas City, MO

Wirth, Linda, Cat.Libn.
GEORGETOWN UNIVERSITY - FRED O. DENNIS
LAW LIBRARY □ Washington, DC

Wischmeyer, Carol, Lit.Spec.
DETROIT PUBLIC LIBRARY - TECHNOLOGY AND
SCIENCE DEPARTMENT □ Detroit, MI

Wisdom, Donald F., Chf.
LIBRARY OF CONGRESS - SERIAL AND
GOVERNMENT PUBLICATIONS DIVISION □
Washington, DC

Wise, Anne S., Coord.
EL PASO NATURAL GAS COMPANY - TECHNICAL
INFORMATION CENTER □ El Paso, TX

Wise, Dave, Cart./Graphic Arts Des.
NEVADA STATE DEPARTMENT OF
TRANSPORTATION - MAP INFORMATION
LIBRARY □ Carson City, NV

Wise, Eileen M., Libn.
SOUTHAM COMMUNICATIONS LTD. - LIBRARY
□ Don Mills, ON

Wise, Eliezer, Asst.Libn.
GRATZ COLLEGE - LIBRARY □ Philadelphia, PA

Wise, George, Dir.
MEMPHIS BOTANIC GARDEN FOUNDATION,
INC. - GOLDSMITH CIVIC GARDEN CTR. -
SYBILE MALLOY MEMORIAL LIBRARY □
Memphis, TN

Wise, Virginia J., Dir./Assoc. Professor
BOSTON UNIVERSITY - PAPPAS LAW LIBRARY
□ Boston, MA

Wisel, Lee M., Cat.Libn.
COLUMBIA UNION COLLEGE - THEOFIELD G.
WEIS LIBRARY □ Takoma Park, MD

Wiseman, Barbara R., Ref.Libn.
MUSEUM OF SCIENCE - LIBRARY □ Boston, MA

Wiseman, Howard, V.P.
SPRINGFIELD HISTORICAL SOCIETY - LIBRARY
□ Springfield, NJ

Wiseman, Howard W., Libn.
NATIONAL SOCIETY OF THE SONS OF THE
AMERICAN REVOLUTION - NEW JERSEY
SOCIETY - S.A.R. LIBRARY □ Elizabeth, NJ

Wiseman, Karin, Libn.
U.S. VETERANS ADMINISTRATION (NY-New
York) - MEDICAL LIBRARY □ New York, NY

Wiseman, Teri S.
NORTH CENTRAL TEXAS COUNCIL OF
GOVERNMENTS - REGIONAL INFORMATION
SERVICE CENTER □ Arlington, TX

Wishner, Judith A., Libn.
SAUL, EWING, REMICK & SAUL - LAW LIBRARY
□ Philadelphia, PA

Wisner, Harriet, Libn.
SHEARSON LEHMAN/AMERICAN EXPRESS INC.
- LIBRARY □ New York, NY

Wisneski, C., Media Ctr.
WIDENER UNIVERSITY - WOLFGRAM
MEMORIAL LIBRARY □ Chester, PA

Wisneski, Martin E., Ser. & Docs.Libn.
UNIVERSITY OF KANSAS - SCHOOL OF LAW
LIBRARY □ Lawrence, KS

Wisser, Kristine, Dir. of Med.Rec.
ELIASON (Frank) CENTRE - HEALTH SCIENCES
LIBRARY □ Saskatoon, SK

Wissinger, Patricia H., Libn.
CAPITOL INSTITUTE OF TECHNOLOGY - JOHN
G. PUENTE LIBRARY □ Kensington, MD

Witcher, Curt B., Asst.Mgr.
ALLEN COUNTY PUBLIC LIBRARY - FRED J.
REYNOLDS HISTORICAL GENEALOGY
COLLECTION □ Fort Wayne, IN

Witherell, Dr. Julian W., Chf.
LIBRARY OF CONGRESS - AFRICAN & MIDDLE
EASTERN DIVISION □ Washington, DC

Withers, Allyson D., Hd. Law Libn.
SIDLEY AND AUSTIN - LIBRARY □ Chicago, IL

Withington, Nancy, Rsrcs.Ctr.Coord.
VERMONT INSTITUTE OF NATURAL SCIENCES
- LIBRARY □ Woodstock, VT

Withrow, Bettty A., Med.Libn.
U.S. VETERANS ADMINISTRATION (MD-Fort
Howard) - HOSPITAL LIBRARY □ Fort Howard,
MD

Witiak, Joanne L., Info.Sci.
ROHM & HAAS COMPANY - RESEARCH
DIVISION - INFORMATION SERVICES
DEPARTMENT □ Spring House, PA

Witker, Catherine, Libn.Techn.
TOLEDO EDISON COMPANY - LIBRARY □
Toledo, OH

Witkowicki, Walter, Libn.
POLISH SINGERS ALLIANCE OF AMERICA -
LIBRARY □ New York, NY

Witkowski, Kathleen M., Lib.Coord.
ROCKWELL INTERNATIONAL - FLOW CONTROL
DIVISION - TECHNICAL INFORMATION
CENTER □ Pittsburgh, PA

Witmer, Dr. John A., Dir.
DALLAS THEOLOGICAL SEMINARY - MOSHER
LIBRARY □ Dallas, TX

Witson, Birdie, Libn.
LAKE COUNTY SUPERIOR COURT LIBRARY† □
Gary, IN

Witt, B., Hd., Commun. & Pub.Serv.
CANADA - TRANSPORT CANADA - LIBRARY &
INFORMATION CENTRE □ Ottawa, ON

Witters, Maryanne, Dir.
DANBURY HOSPITAL - HEALTH SCIENCES
LIBRARY† □ Danbury, CT

Wittke, Carol, Libn.
DOUGLAS COUNTY LAW LIBRARY† □ Superior,
WI

Wittman, Elisabeth, Asst.Archv.
LUTHERAN CHURCH IN AMERICA - ARCHIVES □
Chicago, IL

Wittman, Sr. Patricia, Libn.
HOLY FAMILY COLLEGE - MOTHER DOLORES
MEMORIAL LIBRARY □ Mission San Jose, CA

Wittwer, Maurine, Patron Supv.
CHURCH OF JESUS CHRIST OF LATTER-DAY
SAINTS - LANSING BRANCH GENEALOGICAL
LIBRARY □ East Lansing, MI

Wixson, Alice M., Dir.
SCHUYLER COUNTY HISTORICAL SOCIETY -
LEE SCHOOL MUSEUM □ Montour Falls, NY

Wixson, Alice M., Dir.
SCHUYLER COUNTY HISTORICAL SOCIETY -
OLD BRICK TAVERN MUSEUM - RESEARCH
LIBRARY □ Montour Falls, NY

Wixson, Emily, Ref.Libn.
UNIVERSITY OF WISCONSIN, MADISON -
STEENBOCK MEMORIAL LIBRARY □ Madison,
WI

Wizowski, Lynne, Libn.
AMPEX CORPORATION - TECHNICAL
INFORMATION SERVICES □ Redwood City, CA

Wlasniewski, Toni, Libn.
READING REHABILITATION HOSPITAL -
MEDICAL LIBRARY □ Reading, PA

Woehrmann, Paul, Local Hist.Libn.
MILWAUKEE PUBLIC LIBRARY - HUMANITIES
DIVISION - LOCAL HISTORY AND MARINE
ROOM □ Milwaukee, WI

Woelflin, Dr. Leslie E., Chf., Lrng.Res.Ctr.
U.S. NATIONAL MINE HEALTH AND SAFETY
ACADEMY - LEARNING RESOURCE CENTER □
Beckley, WV

Woeller, Richard, Govt.Doc.Libn.
WILFRID LAURIER UNIVERSITY - LIBRARY □
Waterloo, ON

Wofse, Joy G., Ref.Asst.
NEW YORK UNIVERSITY MEDICAL CENTER -
FREDERICK L. EHRMAN MEDICAL LIBRARY □
New York, NY

Wohlsen, Theodore O., Archv./Hist./Genealogy
CONNECTICUT STATE LIBRARY □ Hartford, CT

Woinowsk, Orrine L., Adm.Libn.
U.S. AIR FORCE - HUMAN RESOURCES
LABORATORY - LIBRARY □ Brooks AFB, TX

Woito, Robert, Pubn.Dir.
WORLD WITHOUT WAR COUNCIL - MIDWEST
LIBRARY □ Chicago, IL

Wojahn, Marvin H., Economist
COLORADO STATE DIVISION OF EMPLOYMENT
& TRAINING - LABOR MARKET INFORMATION
LIBRARY □ Denver, CO

Wojewodzki, Cathy, Ref.
DELAWARE STATE DEPARTMENT OF
COMMUNITY AFFAIRS - DIVISION OF
LIBRARIES □ Dover, DE

Wolak, Theresa, Libn.
INSTITUTE OF CHARTERED ACCOUNTANTS OF
ONTARIO - THE MERRILEES LIBRARY □
Toronto, ON

Wold, Miss G., Res.Libn.
PHARMACO-MEDICAL DOCUMENTATION, INC.
- RESEARCH LIBRARY† □ Chatham, NJ

Wold, Margaret, Health Sci.Libn.
MILWAUKEE CHILDREN'S HOSPITAL - HEALTH
SCIENCES LIBRARY □ Milwaukee, WI

Wold, Michael W., Libn.
BURLINGTON MEDICAL CENTER - LIBRARY □
Burlington, IA

Wolf, Amy, Lib.Supv.
CATERPILLAR TRACTOR COMPANY - BUSINESS
LIBRARY† □ Peoria, IL

Wolf, Carolyn, Ref./Per.Libn.
NORTHWOOD INSTITUTE - STROSACKER
LIBRARY □ Midland, MI

Wolf, Catherine, Info.Spec.
U.S. AIR FORCE - WRIGHT AERONAUTICAL
LABORATORIES - AEROSPACE STRUCTURES
INFORMATION & ANALYSIS CENTER □ Wright-
Patterson AFB, OH

Wolf, Constance P., Dir. of Lib.
MISSOURI BOTANICAL GARDEN - LIBRARY □
St. Louis, MO

Wolf, Diane, AV Libn.
WILMINGTON MEDICAL CENTER (Delaware
Division) - MEDICAL STAFF LIBRARY □
Wilmington, DE

Wolf, Edward, Asst.Libn.
INDIANA UNIVERSITY OF PENNSYLVANIA -
UNIVERSITY LIBRARY □ Indiana, PA

Wolf, Edwin, II, Libn.
LIBRARY COMPANY OF PHILADELPHIA □
Philadelphia, PA

Wolf, Edythe, Dir.
JEWISH FEDERATION OF OMAHA - LIBRARY □
Omaha, NE

Wolf, Frances, Libn.
BETH SHALOM CONGREGATION - BLANCHE
AND IRA ROSENBLUM MEMORIAL LIBRARY □
Kansas City, MO

Wolf, Dr. George, Libn.
STAUFFER CHEMICAL COMPANY - SWS
SILICONES - TECHNICAL LIBRARY □ Adrian, MI

Wolf, Gretchen, Acq.Libn.
DUKE UNIVERSITY - SCHOOL OF LAW LIBRARY
□ Durham, NC

Wolf, J., Assoc.Dir.
INSTITUTE FOR RATIONAL-EMOTIVE THERAPY
- RESEARCH LIBRARY □ New York, NY

Wolf, Naomi A., Chf., Rsrcs./Serv.
PANAMA CANAL COMMISSION - LIBRARY □
APO Miami, FL

Wolf, Nola, Libn.
SOUTHERN CALIFORNIA RAPID TRANSIT
DISTRICT - INFORMATION CENTER LIBRARY □
Los Angeles, CA

Wolf, Patricia, Acq./Cat.
PLANNING RESEARCH CORPORATION -
TECHNICAL LIBRARY □ McLean, VA

Wolf, Sara H., Libn.
MINT MUSEUM OF ART - LIBRARY □ Charlotte,
NC

Wolf, Sarah D., Libn.
LOS ANGELES PUBLIC LIBRARY - MUNICIPAL
REFERENCE DEPARTMENT - PLANNING
DIVISION □ Los Angeles, CA

Wolfe, Alain, Score Libn.
CHICAGO PUBLIC LIBRARY CULTURAL CENTER
- FINE ARTS DIVISION - MUSIC SECTION □
Chicago, IL

Wolfe, Albert J., Res.Assoc.
NEW JERSEY STATE LEAGUE OF
MUNICIPALITIES - LIBRARY □ Trenton, NJ

Wolfe, Barbara, Libn.
SOCIETY FOR CRIPPLED CHILDREN AND
ADULTS OF MANITOBA - STEPHEN SPARLING
LIBRARY □ Winnipeg, MB

Wolfe, Bardie C., Jr., Law Libn./Prof.
PACE UNIVERSITY - SCHOOL OF LAW LIBRARY
□ White Plains, NY

Wolfe, C.F., Sr.Res.Libn.
DOW CHEMICAL U.S.A. - TEXAS DIVISION -
LIBRARY □ Freeport, TX

Wolfe, Carol, Coord.
COMMONWEALTH EDISON COMPANY -
PRODUCTION TRAINING CENTER - LEARNING
RESOURCE CENTER □ Wilmington, IL

Wolfe, Charles B., State Law Libn.
MICHIGAN STATE - LIBRARY OF MICHIGAN -
LAW LIBRARY □ Lansing, MI

Wolfe, Cynthia, Assoc.Libn.
FIDELITY MANAGEMENT & RESEARCH
COMPANY - LIBRARY □ Boston, MA

Wolfe, Frank, Chf., Tech.Serv.
U.S. PRESIDENTIAL LIBRARIES - LYNDON B.
JOHNSON LIBRARY □ Austin, TX

Wolfe, Ginger F., Libn.
GRANT LAW LIBRARY □ Davenport, IA

Wolfe, Ithmer, Asst.Libn.
UNITED CHURCH BOARD FOR WORLD
MINISTRIES - LIBRARY □ New York, NY

Wolfe, Laurie, Libn.
BETHEL COLLEGE - MENNONITE LIBRARY AND
ARCHIVES □ North Newton, KS

Wolfe, Lucretia, Libn.
SAN FRANCISCO CONSERVATORY OF MUSIC -
LIBRARY □ San Francisco, CA

Wolfe, Lynnette M., Musm.Prog.Asst.
GRAND ARMY OF THE REPUBLIC MEMORIAL
HALL MUSEUM - ARCHIVES AND LIBRARY □
Madison, WI

Wolfe, Margaret, Serv. to Handicapped
MICHIGAN STATE - LIBRARY OF MICHIGAN □
Lansing, MI

Wolfe, Marice, Hd.
VANDERBILT UNIVERSITY - JEAN AND
ALEXANDER HEARD LIBRARY - SPECIAL
COLLECTIONS DEPARTMENT □ Nashville, TN

Wolfe, Mary Lou, Libn.
PENNSYLVANIA HORTICULTURAL SOCIETY -
LIBRARY □ Philadelphia, PA

Wolfe, Richard J., Cur., Rare Bks. & Mss.
HARVARD UNIVERSITY - SCHOOLS OF
MEDICINE, DENTAL MED. & PUBLIC HEALTH,
BOSTON MED.LIB. - FRANCIS A. COUNTWAY
LIB. □ Boston, MA

Wolfe, Shirley, Dir.
CENTRAL AGENCY FOR JEWISH EDUCATION -
EDUCATIONAL RESOURCE CENTER/LIBRARY†
□ Miami, FL

Wolfe, Theresa L., Info.Spec.
ECOLOGY & ENVIRONMENT, INC. - LIBRARY □
Buffalo, NY

Wolfe, Verna, Chf.Libn.
BARBER (Richard J.) ASSOCIATES, INC. -
LIBRARY □ Washington, DC

Wolff, Eileen, Project Off.
ASPEN SYSTEMS CORPORATION - PROJECT
SHARE □ Rockville, MD

Wolff, Walter, Div.Chf.
BROOKLYN PUBLIC LIBRARY - SCIENCE AND
INDUSTRY DIVISION □ Brooklyn, NY

Wolfgram, Patricia A., Libn.
SAGINAW OSTEOPATHIC HOSPITAL -
LIBRARY† □ Saginaw, MI

Wolfman, Sue, Supv.
SANDERS ASSOCIATES, INC. - LIBRARY
SERVICES □ Nashua, NH

Wolford, Janet, Lib.Supv.
MOBIL RESEARCH & DEVELOPMENT
CORPORATION - DALLAS RESEARCH DIVISION
- LIBRARY □ Dallas, TX

Wolfson, Donna, Libn.
ST. FRANCIS HOSPITAL AND MEDICAL CENTER
- SCHOOL OF NURSING LIBRARY □ Hartford, CT

Wolfson, Gloria, Off.Mgr.
HEBREW UNION COLLEGE - JEWISH
INSTITUTE OF RELIGION - KLAU LIBRARY □
Cincinnati, OH

Wolkenstein, Rabbi Z., Exec.Dir.
LATNER (Albert J.) JEWISH PUBLIC LIBRARY □
Willowdale, ON

Wolking, Sr. Teresa, O.S.B., Archv.
ST. WALBURG CONVENT OF BENEDICTINE
SISTERS OF COVINGTON, KENTUCKY -
ARCHIVES □ Covington, KY

Woll, Eileen E., Lib.Techn.
ST. CLARE'S MERCY HOSPITAL - MEDICAL
LIBRARY □ St. John's, NF

Woll, Lois, Libn.
MOTOROLA, INC. - BIPOLAR INTEGRATED
CIRCUITS DIVISION - TECHNICAL LIBRARY □
Phoenix, AZ

Wolleson, Ethel, Libn.
SAN CLEMENTE PRESBYTERIAN CHURCH -
SUTHERLAND MEMORIAL LIBRARY □ San
Clemente, CA

Wolling, Elaine, ILL
NEWSDAY, INC. - LIBRARY □ Melville, NY

Wolodko, Shirley, Adm., Lib.Serv.
ALBERTA - DEPARTMENT OF EDUCATION -
LIBRARY SERVICES □ Edmonton, AB

Wolozin, Sara, Mgr., Newspaper Serv.
CBS INC. - CBS NEWS REFERENCE LIBRARY □
New York, NY

Wolpe, Katharine B., Ref.Libn.
DAVIS POLK & WARDWELL - LIBRARY □ New
York, NY

Wolski, Jean, Libn.
WISCONSIN STATE DEPARTMENT OF PUBLIC
INSTRUCTION - SCHOOL FOR THE VISUALLY
HANDICAPPED - LIBRARY □ Janesville, WI

Wolter, Dr. John A., Chf.
LIBRARY OF CONGRESS - GEOGRAPHY & MAP
DIVISION □ Washington, DC

Wolven, Robert, Hd., Law Cat.
COLUMBIA UNIVERSITY - LAW LIBRARY □ New
York, NY

Womack, Norma C., Libn./Cur.
METHODIST COLLEGE, INC. - DAVIS
MEMORIAL LIBRARY - SPECIAL COLLECTIONS
□ Fayetteville, NC

Womack, Vernell, Lib.Techn.
U.S. PEACE CORPS - INFORMATION SERVICES
DIVISION □ Washington, DC

Womeldorf, Ann C., Asst.Libn.
U.S. SENATE - LIBRARY □ Washington, DC

Wong, Alice, Libn.
METROPOLITAN TORONTO LIBRARY - HISTORY
DEPARTMENT □ Toronto, ON

Wong, Anita, Dir.
ST. MICHAEL'S HOSPITAL - HEALTH SCIENCE
LIBRARY □ Toronto, ON

Wong, Cecilia, Asst.Cat.
LOYOLA LAW SCHOOL - LIBRARY □ Los Angeles,
CA

Wong, Chi-Le, Cat.Libn.
DARGAN-CARVER LIBRARY □ Nashville, TN

Wong, Chuck, Hd., Cat.
LAURENTIAN UNIVERSITY - MAIN LIBRARY □
Sudbury, ON

Wong, Corinne, Libn.
VICTORIA TIMES-COLONIST - LIBRARY □
Victoria, BC

Wong, Ellen, Tech.Serv.Libn.
TEXAS A & M UNIVERSITY AT GALVESTON -
LIBRARY □ Galveston, TX

Wong, Hedy, Coord.
MILLS COLLEGE - MARGARET PRALL MUSIC
LIBRARY □ Oakland, CA

Wong, Irene, Pub.Serv.Libn.
HAWAII STATE SUPREME COURT - LAW
LIBRARY □ Honolulu, HI

Wong, Jerry, Info.Serv.Spec.
U.S. BUREAU OF THE CENSUS - INFORMATION
SERVICES PROGRAM - LOS ANGELES REGIONAL
OFFICE - LIBRARY □ Los Angeles, CA

Wong, Lusi, Info.Mgr.
WESTON RESEARCH CENTRE - INFORMATION
RESOURCE CENTRE □ Toronto, ON

Wong, Lyn, Libn.
UNIVERSITY OF CALIFORNIA, IRVINE -
INSTITUTE OF TRANSPORTATION STUDIES -
RESOURCE CENTER □ Irvine, CA

Wong, Marlene M., Libn.
SMITH COLLEGE - WERNER JOSTEN LIBRARY
OF THE PERFORMING ARTS □ Northampton, MA

Wong, Patricia, Libn.
BANK OF AMERICA, NT & SA - REFERENCE
LIBRARY □ San Francisco, CA

Wong, Susan, Ref.Libn.
AT & T BELL LABORATORIES - LIBRARY □
Holmdel, NJ

Wong, Wesley
HARVARD UNIVERSITY - ECONOMIC BOTANY
LIBRARY □ Cambridge, MA

Wong, William S., Asst.Dir.
UNIVERSITY OF ILLINOIS - ASIAN LIBRARY □
Urbana, IL

Wonsowicz, Elaine, Mgr.
SAN DIEGO STATE UNIVERSITY - PUBLIC
ADMINISTRATION RESEARCH CENTER
LIBRARY □ San Diego, CA

Woo, Dr. Constance, Dir. of Libs.
NEW YORK INSTITUTE OF TECHNOLOGY -
LIBRARY □ Old Westbury, NY

Woo, Janice, Libn.
PACIFICA RADIO NETWORK - PACIFICA RADIO
ARCHIVE □ Los Angeles, CA

Woo, Lisa, Bibliog./Cat. (Chinese)
UNIVERSITY OF PITTSBURGH - EAST ASIAN
LIBRARY □ Pittsburgh, PA

Woo, R., Palo Alto Ref.Libn.
LOCKHEED MISSILES & SPACE COMPANY, INC.
- TECHNICAL INFORMATION CENTER □ Palo
Alto, CA

Wood, Alberta Auringer, Map Libn.
MEMORIAL UNIVERSITY OF NEWFOUNDLAND -
QUEEN ELIZABETH II LIBRARY - MAP LIBRARY
□ St. John's, NF

Wood, Betty B., Libn.
ST. FRANCIS REGIONAL MEDICAL CENTER -
PROFESSIONAL LIBRARY □ Wichita, KS

Wood, Beulah C., Assoc.Libn.
UNION CARBIDE CORPORATION - LIBRARY &
TECHNICAL INFORMATION SERVICE □
Tarrytown, NY

Wood, Camille, Dir.
WALLA WALLA COLLEGE - CURRICULUM
LIBRARY □ College Place, WA

Wood, Carolyn, Ref.Libn.
PALOMAR COMMUNITY COLLEGE - LIBRARY -
SPECIAL COLLECTIONS □ San Marcos, CA

Wood, Dan, Hd., Acq.Dept.
ENGINEERING SOCIETIES LIBRARY □ New
York, NY

Wood, David A., Hd.Libn.
UNIVERSITY OF WASHINGTON - MUSIC
LIBRARY □ Seattle, WA

Wood,, David H., Dir.
NORMAN ROCKWELL MUSEUM AT THE OLD
CORNER HOUSE - REFERENCE DEPARTMENT □
Stockbridge, MA

Wood, Elizabeth, Acq./Ser.Libn.
UNIVERSITY OF SOUTHERN CALIFORNIA -
HEALTH SCIENCES CAMPUS - NORRIS
MEDICAL LIBRARY □ Los Angeles, CA

Wood, Dr. Glynn, Dir.
MONTEREY INSTITUTE OF INTERNATIONAL
STUDIES - LIBRARY □ Monterey, CA

Wood, Helen, Cur., Quaker Coll.
FRIENDS UNIVERSITY - EDMUND STANLEY
LIBRARY - SPECIAL COLLECTIONS □ Wichita,
KS

Wood, Hugh B., Libn.
AMERICAN-NEPAL EDUCATION FOUNDATION -
WOOD NEPAL LIBRARY □ Oceanside, OR

Wood, James E., Dir.
BAYLOR UNIVERSITY - J.M. DAWSON CHURCH-
STATE RESEARCH CENTER - LIBRARY □ Waco,
TX

Wood, James L., Mgr.
LITTON MELLONICS - TECHNICAL LIBRARY □
Sunnyvale, CA

Wood, Jeanne, Libn.
EMPLOYEES REINSURANCE CORPORATION -
JUNE AUSTIN PARRISH MEMORIAL LIBRARY □
Overland Park, KS

Wood, John T., Dp.Chf.
U.S. GEOLOGICAL SURVEY - NATL.
CARTOGRAPHIC INFORMATION CENTER
(NCIC) □ Reston, VA

Wood, Judy, Acq.Libn.
FASHION INSTITUTE OF TECHNOLOGY -
LIBRARY† □ New York, NY

Wood, M. Sandra, Assoc.Libn./Hd., Ref.
PENNSYLVANIA STATE UNIVERSITY - COLLEGE
OF MEDICINE - GEORGE T. HARRELL LIBRARY □
Hershey, PA

Wood, Margaret D., Mgr.
PERKIN-ELMER CORPORATION - CORPORATE
LIBRARY □ Norwalk, CT

Wood, Mary, Libn.
MICHAEL, BEST & FRIEDRICH - LAW LIBRARY □
Milwaukee, WI

Wood, Mary, Circ./ILL
UNION UNIVERSITY - ALBANY LAW SCHOOL -
LIBRARY □ Albany, NY

Wood, Muriel, Asst.Dir.
UNIVERSITY OF WASHINGTON - HEALTH
SCIENCES LIBRARY □ Seattle, WA

Wood, Pamela R., Asst.Libn.
MOUNT OLIVE COLLEGE - FREE WILL BAPTIST
HISTORICAL COLLECTION □ Mount Olive, NC

Wood, Pat, Libn.
MEMPHIS-SHELBY COUNTY PUBLIC LIBRARY
AND INFO. CTR. - SCIENCE/BUSINESS/SOCIAL
SCI.DEPT. □ Memphis, TN

Wood, Patricia A., Libn.
EVANS, KITCHEL & JENCKES, P.C. - LIBRARY □
Phoenix, AZ

Wood, Mrs. Philip H., Libn.
SCITUATE HISTORICAL SOCIETY - LIBRARY □
Scituate, MA

Wood, Richard C., Assoc.Dir., Pub.Serv.
TEXAS COLLEGE OF OSTEOPATHIC MEDICINE -
HEALTH SCIENCES LIBRARY □ Fort Worth, TX

Wood, Richard H., Libn.
WESLEYAN UNIVERSITY - ART LIBRARY □
Middletown, CT

Wood, Robert, Dir.
U.S. PRESIDENTIAL LIBRARIES - HERBERT
HOOVER LIBRARY □ West Branch, IA

Wood, Ron, Campus Libn.
CENTENNIAL COLLEGE OF APPLIED ARTS &
TECHNOLOGY - EAST YORK CAMPUS
RESOURCE CENTRE □ Scarborough, ON

Wood, Ross, Ref.Libn.
UNIVERSITY OF ROCHESTER - EASTMAN
SCHOOL OF MUSIC - SIBLEY MUSIC LIBRARY □
Rochester, NY

Wood, Ross, Music Libn.
WELLESLEY COLLEGE - MUSIC LIBRARY □
Wellesley, MA

Wood, Shirley N., Dir.
NORTHEASTERN BIBLE COLLEGE - LINCOLN
MEMORIAL LIBRARY □ Essex Fells, NJ

Wood, Steven R., Ref.Libn.
UTAH STATE HISTORICAL SOCIETY -
RESEARCH LIBRARY □ Salt Lake City, UT

Wood, Susan I., Asst.Libn.
ARMSTRONG WORLD INDUSTRIES, INC. - TECHNICAL CENTER - TECHNICAL INFORMATION SERVICES □ Lancaster, PA

Wood, Susan M., Prin. Law Libn.
NEW YORK STATE SUPREME COURT - APPELLATE DIVISION, 4TH JUDICIAL DEPARTMENT - LAW LIBRARY □ Syracuse, NY

Wood, Suzanne, Tech.Serv.Libn.
SUNY - AGRICULTURAL AND TECHNICAL COLLEGE AT ALFRED - WALTER C. HINKLE MEMORIAL LIBRARY □ Alfred, NY

Wood, Thomas J., Rec.Anl.
INDIANA STATE COMMISSION ON PUBLIC RECORDS - ARCHIVES DIVISION □ Indianapolis, IN

Wood, Thor, Libn.
CHURCH OF THE BELOVED DISCIPLE - HOMOPHILE RESEARCH LIBRARY □ New York, NY

Wood, Virginia, Lib.Supv.
ATLANTIC-RICHFIELD COMPANY - ARCO CHEMICAL COMPANY - LYONDELL PLANT LIBRARY □ Channelview, TX

Wood, W.E., Libn.
CONNECTICUT ELECTRIC RAILWAY ASSOCIATION, INC. - LIBRARY DEPARTMENT □ East Windsor, CT

Woodard, Charles B., Res.Libn.
SOUTHERN UNION COMPANY - PLANNING RESEARCH LIBRARY □ Dallas, TX

Woodard, J. Lamar, Libn./Professor of Law
STETSON UNIVERSITY - COLLEGE OF LAW - CHARLES A. DANA LAW LIBRARY □ St. Petersburg, FL

Woodard, John R., Jr., Dir.
WAKE FOREST UNIVERSITY - BAPTIST COLLECTION □ Winston-Salem, NC

Woodard, Paul Esty, Ph.D., Chf.Med.Libn.
NEW ENGLAND BAPTIST HOSPITAL - MEDICAL STAFF LIBRARY □ Boston, MA

Woodbridge, Annie, Asst.Libn.
SOUTHERN ILLINOIS UNIVERSITY, CARBONDALE - HUMANITIES DIVISION LIBRARY □ Carbondale, IL

Woodburn, David M., Dir.
MISSISSIPPI STATE LIBRARY COMMISSION □ Jackson, MS

Woodburn, Deborah L., Health Sci.Libn.
CABELL HUNTINGTON HOSPITAL - HEALTH SCIENCE LIBRARY □ Huntington, WV

Woodbury, Ella, Ref.Libn.
STATE LIBRARY OF FLORIDA □ Tallahassee, FL

Woodbury, Lynn, Rsrc.Libn.
PLANNED PARENTHOOD OF MINNESOTA - POPULATION RESOURCE CENTER □ St. Paul, MN

Woodbury, Marda, Lib.Dir.
LIFE CHIROPRACTIC COLLEGE-WEST - LIBRARY □ San Lorenzo, CA

Woodcock, Peter J., Naturalist/Dir.
WEINBERG NATURE CENTER - LIBRARY □ Scarsdale, NY

Woodhead, Ellen P., Dir.
POCONO HOSPITAL - MARSHALL R. METZGAR MEDICAL LIBRARY □ East Stroudsburg, PA

Woodke, Audrey, Asst.Libn.
ST. PAUL RAMSEY MEDICAL CENTER - MEDICAL LIBRARY □ St. Paul, MN

Woodke, Bart, Libn.
ROGERS & WELLS - LIBRARY □ Washington, DC

Woodley, Carolyn, Libn.
MISSISSIPPI STATE BUREAU OF GEOLOGY - LIBRARY □ Jackson, MS

Woodruff, Brenda, Libn./Dir.
TOLEDO LAW ASSOCIATION LIBRARY □ Toledo, OH

Woodruff, Valentina M., Info.Sci.
MORTON THIOKOL INC. - MORTON CHEMICAL DIVISION - WOODSTOCK RESEARCH INFORMATION CENTER □ Woodstock, IL

Woodruff, William M., Mgr., Commun.Ctr.
HERSHEY FOODS CORPORATION - COMMUNICATIONS CENTER □ Hershey, PA

Woods, Alan, Dir.
OHIO STATE UNIVERSITY - THEATRE RESEARCH INSTITUTE □ Columbus, OH

Woods, Sr. Angela, S.S.L., Libn.
ST. JOHN'S SEMINARY - EDWARD LAURENCE DOHENY MEMORIAL LIBRARY □ Camarillo, CA

Woods, B., Ref.libn.
AT & T - CORPORATE RESEARCH CENTER □ New York, NY

Woods, Barry, Gen.Ref./Doc.
CONNECTICUT STATE LIBRARY □ Hartford, CT

Woods, Msgr. Earl C., Chancellor
ARCHDIOCESE OF NEW ORLEANS - ARCHIVES □ New Orleans, LA

Woods, Eini, Circ.Libn.
FITCHBURG STATE COLLEGE - LIBRARY □ Fitchburg, MA

Woods, Elaine, Cat.
MERCER UNIVERSITY - MEDICAL SCHOOL LIBRARY □ Macon, GA

Woods, Frances B., Hd., Cat.Dept.
YALE UNIVERSITY - LAW LIBRARY □ New Haven, CT

Woods, Jacqueline, Dp.Chf.Libn.
BANK OF CANADA - LIBRARY □ Ottawa, ON

Woods, Jacqueline M., Adm.Techn. III
MENTAL HEALTH AND MENTAL RETARDATION AUTHORITY OF HARRIS COUNTY - INFORMATION RESOURCE CENTER □ Houston, TX

Woods, Laurie, Exec.Dir.
NATIONAL CENTER ON WOMEN AND FAMILY LAW, INC. - INFORMATION CENTER □ New York, NY

Woods, Linda A., Ref./ILL Libn.
KUTZTOWN UNIVERSITY - ROHRBACH LIBRARY □ Kutztown, PA

Woods, Mary S., Supv.
VALERO ENERGY CORPORATION - CORPORATE RESOURCE CENTER □ San Antonio, TX

Woods, Maureen, Libn.
U.S. NATL. MARINE FISHERIES SERVICE - TIBURON LABORATORY LIBRARY □ Tiburon, CA

Woods, Sr. Regina Clare, O.P., Coord./Med.Libs.
CATHOLIC MEDICAL CENTER OF BROOKLYN & QUEENS, INC. - CENTRAL MEDICAL LIBRARY □ Jamaica, NY

Woods-Robinson, Ruby O., Ref.Libn.
U.S. ARMY POST - FORT CLAYTON - MORALE SUPPORT ACTIVITIES - LIBRARY □ APO Miami, FL

Woodside, Rev. Robert, H.O.S.J., Dir.
SOVEREIGN HOSPITALLER ORDER OF ST. JOHN - VILLA ANNESLIE - ARCHIVES □ Anneslie, MD

Woodson, Joy, Libn.
KENT STATE UNIVERSITY - CHEMISTRY/ PHYSICS LIBRARY □ Kent, OH

Woodstrom, Linda, Libn.
MINNESOTA STATE DEPARTMENT OF ECONOMIC SECURITY - LIBRARY □ St. Paul, MN

Woodward, Carol, Coord.
WASHINGTON COUNTY TOY LENDING LIBRARY □ Stillwater, MN

Woodward, Daniel H., Libn.
HUNTINGTON (Henry E.) LIBRARY, ART GALLERY AND BOTANICAL GARDENS □ San Marino, CA

Woodward, Elaine H., Tech.Serv.Libn.
U.S. COURT OF APPEALS, 4TH CIRCUIT - LIBRARY □ Richmond, VA

Woodward, Frances, Ref.Libn.
UNIVERSITY OF BRITISH COLUMBIA - SPECIAL COLLECTIONS DIVISION □ Vancouver, BC

Woodward, Mary, Law Libn.
MORGAN COUNTY BAR ASSOCIATION - LIBRARY □ McConnelsville, OH

Woodward, Mary, Asst.Libn.
NEW YORK STATE LIBRARY - LAW/SOCIAL SCIENCE REFERENCE SERVICES □ Albany, NY

Woodward, Wayne W., Dir. of Lib.Serv.
WESLEY BIBLICAL SEMINARY - LIBRARY □ Jackson, MS

Woodworth, Bonnie Jean, Corp.Libn.
HARTFORD INSURANCE GROUP - CORPORATE LIBRARY □ Hartford, CT

Woodworth, Elizabeth M., Libn.
BRITISH COLUMBIA - MINISTRY OF HEALTH - LIBRARY □ Victoria, BC

Woodworth, K., Ref.Libn.
AT & T BELL LABORATORIES & TECHNOLOGIES - LIBRARY □ Norcross, GA

Woodworth, Pamela L., Libn.
LAKE COUNTY LAW LIBRARY □ Tavares, FL

Woody, D.C., Act.Techn.
U.S. NAVY - NAVAL SHIPYARD (SC-Charleston) - TECHNICAL LIBRARY □ Charleston, SC

Woody, Gloria T., Dir./Libn.
FLORIDA A & M UNIVERSITY - SCHOOL OF JOURNALISM, MEDIA & GRAPHIC ARTS - JOURNALISM RESOURCE CENTER □ Tallahassee, FL

Woolard, Kathryn A., Libn.
REPUBLIC STEEL CORPORATION - RESEARCH CENTER LIBRARY □ Cleveland, OH

Woolever, Mary K., Libn.
SKIDMORE, OWINGS & MERRILL - LIBRARY □ Chicago, IL

Wooley, Mary M., Libn.
CONSERVATION DISTRICTS FOUNDATION - DAVIS CONSERVATION LIBRARY □ League City, TX

Woolford, Linda, Ed.Supv.
BROCKTON ART MUSEUM - FULLER MEMORIAL LIBRARY □ Brockton, MA

Woollet, Bonnie L., Hd. Media Libn.
UNIVERSITY OF ARIZONA - MEDIA CENTER □ Tucson, AZ

Woolsey, Mary G., Cat.
NATIONAL ASSOCIATION OF REALTORS - LIBRARY □ Chicago, IL

Woolsey, Raymond, Chm. of Lib.Comm.
REVIEW & HERALD PUBLISHING ASSOCIATION - LIBRARY □ Hagerstown, MD

Woolverton, Deborah, Mgr.,Hist. of Med./Archv.
MEDICAL AND CHIRURGICAL FACULTY OF THE STATE OF MARYLAND - LIBRARY □ Baltimore, MD

Wooten, Jean, Sr.Libn.
FEDERAL RESERVE BANK OF NEW YORK - RESEARCH LIBRARY □ New York, NY

Work, William, Module Dir.
ERIC CLEARINGHOUSE ON READING AND COMMUNICATIONS SKILLS □ Urbana, IL

Working, E. Brownie, Libn.
CALIFORNIA THOROUGHBRED BREEDERS ASSOCIATION - CARLETON F. BURKE MEMORIAL LIBRARY □ Arcadia, CA

Workman, R.B., Assoc. Professor
UNIVERSITY OF FLORIDA - AGRICULTURAL RESEARCH CENTER - LIBRARY □ Hastings, FL

Workman, Virginia R., Hd., Educ.Lib.
UNIVERSITY OF MISSOURI, ST. LOUIS - EDUCATION LIBRARY □ St. Louis, MO

Workman, Vivian, Ref.Spec.
ASPEN SYSTEMS CORPORATION - PROJECT SHARE □ Rockville, MD

Workmaster, Wallace, Historic Site Mgr.
FORT ONTARIO - LIBRARY □ Oswego, NY

Worley, Sandra A., Dir. of Lib.Serv.
CHICAGO COLLEGE OF OSTEOPATHIC MEDICINE - ALUMNI MEMORIAL LIBRARY □ Chicago, IL

Worman, Charles G., Chf., Res.Div.
U.S. AIR FORCE MUSEUM - RESEARCH DIVISION LIBRARY □ Wright-Patterson AFB, OH

Worobec, Mary, Record Libn.
CANADIAN BROADCASTING CORPORATION - MUSIC & RECORD LIBRARY □ Winnipeg, MB

Woron, Mykola, Hd.Libn.
ST. VLADIMIR'S UKRAINIAN ORTHODOX CULTURAL CENTRE - LIBRARY AND ARCHIVES □ Calgary, AB

Worsey, Merilee, Libn., Tech.Info.Ctr.
COMMUNICATIONS SATELLITE CORPORATION
- COMSAT LABORATORIES TECHNICAL
INFORMATION CENTER □ Clarksburg, MD

Worsham, John P., Jr., Adm.
ALABAMA STATE DEPARTMENT OF ECONOMIC
& COMMUNITY AFFAIRS - PLANNING & FLOOD
HAZARD MITIGATION INFORMATION CENTER
□ Montgomery, AL

Worsley, Dorcas, Libn.
TUCSON MUSEUM OF ART - LIBRARY □ Tucson,
AZ

Worstell, Carl, Chf.Libn.
U.S. VETERANS ADMINISTRATION (IL-North
Chicago) - HOSPITAL LIBRARY □ North Chicago,
IL

Worster, Carol, Supv.
TRAVENOL LABORATORIES, INC. -
INFORMATION RESOURCE CENTER □ Morton
Grove, IL

Worster, Carol, Supv.
TRAVENOL LABORATORIES, INC. -
INFORMATION RESOURCE CENTER □ Round
Lake, IL

Worthen, W.B., Dir.
ARKANSAS TERRITORIAL RESTORATION -
LIBRARY □ Little Rock, AR

Worthing, Ruth, Hist.
FOND DU LAC COUNTY HISTORICAL SOCIETY -
HISTORIC GALLOWAY HOUSE AND VILLAGE -
ARCHIVES □ Fond du Lac, WI

Worthington, A. Peri, Med.Libn./Dir.
U.S. AIR FORCE HOSPITAL - DAVID GRANT
MEDICAL CENTER - MEDICAL LIBRARY □ Travis
AFB, CA

Worthley, Rev.Dr. Harold F., Libn.
AMERICAN CONGREGATIONAL ASSOCIATION -
CONGREGATIONAL LIBRARY □ Boston, MA

Wos, Midge, Hd.Libn.
ST. LUKE'S HOSPITAL - MEDICAL LIBRARY □
Milwaukee, WI

Wosh, Peter J., Univ.Archv.
SETON HALL UNIVERSITY - UNIVERSITY
ARCHIVES □ South Orange, NJ

Wotherspoon, Shelagh, Act.Hd.
MEMORIAL UNIVERSITY OF NEWFOUNDLAND -
HEALTH SCIENCES LIBRARY □ St. John's, NF

Wou, Alice, On-line Serv.
AMERICAN CANCER SOCIETY - MEDICAL
LIBRARY □ New York, NY

Woxland, Tom, Hd. of Pub.Serv.
UNIVERSITY OF MINNESOTA - LAW LIBRARY □
Minneapolis, MN

Woy, James B., Hd.
FREE LIBRARY OF PHILADELPHIA -
MERCANTILE LIBRARY □ Philadelphia, PA

Woy, Sara G., Hd.Libn.
GERMANTOWN FRIENDS MEETING - FRIENDS
FREE LIBRARY† □ Philadelphia, PA

Wray, Elizabeth, Exec.Dir.
COMMUNITY INFORMATION CENTRE OF
METROPOLITAN TORONTO □ Toronto, ON

Wreath, April, Hd., Cat.Serv.
UNIVERSITY OF NORTH CAROLINA, CHAPEL
HILL - HEALTH SCIENCES LIBRARY □ Chapel
Hill, NC

Wren, Dr. Daniel A., Cur.
UNIVERSITY OF OKLAHOMA - HARRY W. BASS
COLLECTION IN BUSINESS HISTORY □ Norman,
OK

Wren, James A., Mgr.
MOTOR VEHICLE MANUFACTURERS
ASSOCIATION (MVMA) - PATENT RESEARCH
LIBRARY □ Detroit, MI

Wrenn, R. Scott, Dp. Law Libn.
IDAHO STATE LAW LIBRARY □ Boise, ID

Wrenn, Teresa, Ser./Ref.Libn.
ST. JOHN'S UNIVERSITY - LAW LIBRARY □
Jamaica, NY

Wrenn, Tony, Archv.
AMERICAN INSTITUTE OF ARCHITECTS -
LIBRARY □ Washington, DC

Wright, A.J., Clinical Libn.
UNIVERSITY OF ALABAMA IN BIRMINGHAM -
SCHOOL OF MEDICINE - ANESTHESIOLOGY
LIBRARY □ Birmingham, AL

Wright, Agnes, Lib.Techn.
SACRED HEART MEDICAL CENTER - HEALTH
SCIENCES LIBRARY □ Spokane, WA

Wright, Aileen, Dept.Libn.
ALBERTA - DEPARTMENT OF THE SOLICITOR
GENERAL - LIBRARY □ Edmonton, AB

Wright, Barbara, Dir.
FAYETTEVILLE AREA HEALTH EDUCATION
CENTER - LIBRARY □ Fayetteville, NC

Wright, Betty A., Info.Spec.
GAS RESEARCH INSTITUTE - LIBRARY
SERVICES □ Chicago, IL

Wright, Dr. C.D., Dir.
AUBURN UNIVERSITY - LEARNING RESOURCES
CENTER □ Auburn, AL

Wright, Clara M., Adm.Ck.
MEMPHIS BOTANIC GARDEN FOUNDATION,
INC. - GOLDSMITH CIVIC GARDEN CTR. -
SYBILE MALLOY MEMORIAL LIBRARY □
Memphis, TN

Wright, Frances, Libn.
VALLEY NEWSPAPERS - LIBRARY □ Kent, WA

Wright, G. Ruth, Chm., Lib.Comm.
MOUNT VERNON PLACE UNITED METHODIST
CHURCH - DESSIE M. HALLETT LIBRARY† □
Washington, DC

Wright, George E., Jr., Pres.
ASSOCIATION OF BALLOON & AIRSHIP
CONSTRUCTORS - TECHNICAL LIBRARY □
Rosemead, CA

Wright, Gerald D., Ref.Libn.
CALIFORNIA HISTORICAL SOCIETY -
SCHUBERT HALL LIBRARY □ San Francisco, CA

Wright, Gwen, Libn.
QUEEN'S UNIVERSITY AT KINGSTON -
BRACKEN LIBRARY □ Kingston, ON

Wright, James B., Hd.
UNIVERSITY OF NEW MEXICO - FINE ARTS
LIBRARY □ Albuquerque, NM

Wright, Jill, Law Libn.
ESSEX COUNTY LAW LIBRARY □ Newark, NJ

Wright, Joseph F., Hd.Libn.
MIAMI NEWS - LIBRARY □ Miami, FL

Wright, Joyce, Hd., Asia Coll.
UNIVERSITY OF HAWAII - ASIA COLLECTION □
Honolulu, HI

Wright, Judith M., Law Libn.
UNIVERSITY OF CHICAGO - LAW SCHOOL
LIBRARY □ Chicago, IL

Wright, Kathy, Hd., Bayside Br.
U.S. NAVY - NAVAL OCEAN SYSTEMS CENTER -
TECHNICAL LIBRARY □ San Diego, CA

Wright, Ken, Info.Serv.Spec.
U.S. BUREAU OF THE CENSUS - INFORMATION
SERVICES PROGRAM - CHARLOTTE REGIONAL
OFFICE - LIBRARY □ Charlotte, NC

Wright, Linda, Info.Spec.
MINNESOTA AGRICULTURAL STATISTICS
SERVICE - LIBRARY □ St. Paul, MN

Wright, Linda, Libn.
ST. LOUIS PUBLIC LIBRARY - APPLIED
SCIENCE DEPARTMENT □ St. Louis, MO

Wright, Loretta O., Rsrc. Media Spec.
VOLUSIA COUNTY SCHOOL BOARD - RESOURCE
LIBRARY □ Daytona Beach, FL

Wright, Lottie, Supv.
UNIVERSITY OF THE DISTRICT OF COLUMBIA -
HARVARD STREET LIBRARY† □ Washington, DC

Wright, Marge, Adm., Pub.Serv.
OREGON STATE LIBRARY □ Salem, OR

Wright, Martha, Ref.Libn.
INDIANA STATE LIBRARY - INDIANA DIVISION
□ Indianapolis, IN

Wright, Mary A., Hd.
SAN ANTONIO PUBLIC LIBRARY AND
INFORMATION CENTER - ART, MUSIC AND
FILMS DEPARTMENT □ San Antonio, TX

Wright, Mildred P., Supv.Libn.
NEW YORK PUBLIC LIBRARY - MID-
MANHATTAN LIBRARY - PICTURE COLLECTION
□ New York, NY

Wright, Myrna, Libn.
MINNESOTA LIBRARY FOR THE BLIND AND
PHYSICALLY HANDICAPPED □ Faribault, MN

Wright, Nan, Hd., Ref.Dept.
TRENTON FREE PUBLIC LIBRARY -
GOVERNMENT DOCUMENTS COLLECTION □
Trenton, NJ

Wright, Nan, Hd., Ref.Dept.
TRENTON FREE PUBLIC LIBRARY -
TRENTONIANA COLLECTION □ Trenton, NJ

Wright, Nancy D., V.P. for Lib.Serv.
HERNER AND COMPANY - LIBRARY □ Arlington,
VA

Wright, Nancy M., Libn.
HEINZ (H.J.) COMPANY - LIBRARY □ Pittsburgh,
PA

Wright, Patrick D., Libn.
UNIVERSITY OF MANITOBA - ST. JOHN'S
COLLEGE - LIBRARY □ Winnipeg, MB

Wright, Patsy, Libn.
ST. CLAIRE MEDICAL CENTER - MEDICAL
LIBRARY □ Morehead, KY

Wright, Raymond, Mgr., Pub.Serv.
CHURCH OF JESUS CHRIST OF LATTER-DAY
SAINTS - GENEALOGICAL LIBRARY □ Salt Lake
City, UT

Wright, Dr. Richard J., Dir.
BOWLING GREEN STATE UNIVERSITY -
INSTITUTE FOR GREAT LAKES RESEARCH □
Bowling Green, OH

Wright, Rita J., Libn.
UNIVERSITY OF TEXAS, AUSTIN - BUREAU OF
BUSINESS RESEARCH - INFORMATION
SERVICES □ Austin, TX

Wright, Rosa Gahn, Libn.
LAW LIBRARY ASSOCIATION OF ST. LOUIS □
St. Louis, MO

Wright, Roslyn R., Dir.
PLANNED PARENTHOOD OF SOUTHEASTERN
PENNSYLVANIA - RESOURCE CENTER □
Philadelphia, PA

Wright, Susan, Media Info.Spec.
RUTGERS UNIVERSITY, THE STATE
UNIVERSITY OF NEW JERSEY - NEW JERSEY
VOCATIONAL EDUCATION RESOURCE CENTER
□ Old Bridge, NJ

Wright, Sylvia H., Libn.-in-Charge
CUNY - CITY COLLEGE LIBRARY -
ARCHITECTURE LIBRARY □ New York, NY

Wright, Thomas F., Libn.
UNIVERSITY OF CALIFORNIA, LOS ANGELES -
WILLIAM ANDREWS CLARK MEMORIAL
LIBRARY □ Los Angeles, CA

Wright, Virginia, Asst.Libn.
CORNING MUSEUM OF GLASS - LIBRARY □
Corning, NY

Wright, Wayne, Tech.Serv.
NEW YORK STATE HISTORICAL ASSOCIATION
- LIBRARY □ Cooperstown, NY

Wright, William F., Ref.Info.Spec.
AT & T BELL LABORATORIES - LIBRARY □
Murray Hill, NJ

Wrightson, Mary, Ref.
GIBSON, DUNN & CRUTCHER - LAW LIBRARY □
Los Angeles, CA

Wrigley, Elizabeth S., Dir.-Libn.
FRANCIS BACON FOUNDATION, INC. -
FRANCIS BACON LIBRARY □ Claremont, CA

Wrigley, Kathryn, Dir.
ST. JOHN'S HOSPITAL - HEALTH SCIENCE
LIBRARY □ Springfield, IL

Wroblewski, Stephan, Ref.Libn.
QUEENS BOROUGH PUBLIC LIBRARY -
LANGUAGE & LITERATURE DIVISION □
Jamaica, NY

Wrynn, Paul, Per.Libn.
NEW YORK UNIVERSITY MEDICAL CENTER -
FREDERICK L. EHRMAN MEDICAL LIBRARY □
New York, NY

Wu, Ai-Hwa, Subject Spec./Cat.Libn.
ARIZONA STATE UNIVERSITY - EAST ASIAN
LANGUAGE COLLECTION □ Tempe, AZ

Wu, Chia-ling, Libn.
U.S. BUREAU OF MINES - BOEING SERVICES
INTERNATIONAL - LIBRARY □ Pittsburgh, PA

Wu, Daisy T., Dir.
UNIVERSITY OF WISCONSIN, MADISON -
STEENBOCK MEMORIAL LIBRARY □ Madison,
WI

Wu, Dorothea, Div.Hd.
QUEENS BOROUGH PUBLIC LIBRARY - ART AND
MUSIC DIVISION □ Jamaica, NY

Wu, Eugene, Libn.
HARVARD UNIVERSITY - HARVARD-YENCHING
LIBRARY □ Cambridge, MA

Wu, J., Asst.Dir., Sys.
CANADA - AGRICULTURE CANADA - LIBRARIES
DIVISION □ Ottawa, ON

Wu, Lisa C., Chf., Tech.Serv.
U.S. NATL. INSTITUTES OF HEALTH - LIBRARY
□ Bethesda, MD

Wu, Dr. Painan R., Chf.Libn.
BLOOMFIELD COLLEGE - GEORGE TALBOT HALL
LIBRARY - SPECIAL COLLECTIONS □ Bloomfield,
NJ

Wu, Susan I-Man, Cat.
GIBSON, DUNN & CRUTCHER - LAW LIBRARY □
Los Angeles, CA

Wu Tsiang, Ching-Fen, Libn.
WOODVIEW-CALABASAS PSYCHIATRIC
HOSPITAL - LIBRARY □ Calabasas, CA

Wudyka, Mark, Libn.
GOWANDA PSYCHIATRIC CENTER - HEALTH
SCIENCES LIBRARY □ Helmuth, NY

Wuerch, William L., Asst.Libn.
FLORES (Nieves M.) MEMORIAL LIBRARY □
Agana, GU

Wulf, Kate, Dir.
WORKING OPPORTUNITIES FOR WOMEN -
RESOURCE CENTER □ Minneapolis, MN

Wulfekoetter, Gertrude, Libn.
UNIVERSITY CONGREGATIONAL CHURCH -
LIBRARY □ Seattle, WA

Wulff, Jacqueline, Libn.
NORTH MEMORIAL MEDICAL CENTER -
MEDICAL LIBRARY □ Robbinsdale, MN

Wulff, L. Yvonne, Hd.
UNIVERSITY OF MICHIGAN - ALFRED
TAUBMAN MEDICAL LIBRARY □ Ann Arbor, MI

Wulff, Vicky J., Ref.Libn./Dance
LIBRARY OF CONGRESS - JOHN F. KENNEDY
CENTER FOR THE PERFORMING ARTS - THE
PERFORMING ARTS LIB. □ Washington, DC

Wunderlich, Clifford, Tech.Serv.Libn.
WESTON SCHOOL OF THEOLOGY - LIBRARY □
Cambridge, MA

Wurangian, Nelia, Chm., Tech.Serv.
LOMA LINDA UNIVERSITY - DEL E. WEBB
MEMORIAL LIBRARY □ Loma Linda, CA

Wurfel, Clifford R., Hd., Spec.Coll.
UNIVERSITY OF CALIFORNIA, RIVERSIDE -
SPECIAL COLLECTIONS □ Riverside, CA

Wurl, Joel F., Archv.
UNIVERSITY OF TOLEDO - WARD M. CANADAY
CENTER □ Toledo, OH

Wurster, Greg, Plan.
MIAMI VALLEY REGIONAL PLANNING
COMMISSION - LIBRARY □ Dayton, OH

Wurzburger, Marilyn, Hd., Spec.Coll.
ARIZONA STATE UNIVERSITY - SPECIAL
COLLECTIONS □ Tempe, AZ

Wuttke, Eve, Asst.Dir.
WASHTENAW COUNTY METROPOLITAN
PLANNING COMMISSION - LIBRARY □ Ann
Arbor, MI

Wyatt, Beverly J., Site Dir.
OKLAHOMA HISTORICAL SOCIETY -
CHICKASAW COUNCIL HOUSE LIBRARY □
Tishomingo, OK

Wyatt, Mrs. G., Mgr.
ROYAL CANADIAN MOUNTED POLICE - LAW
ENFORCEMENT REFERENCE CENTRE □ Ottawa,
ON

Wyatt, Roger, Hd., Lrng.Tech.Serv.
TEACHERS COLLEGE - MILBANK MEMORIAL
LIBRARY □ New York, NY

Wyatt, Susan, Dir.
ARTISTS SPACE - COMMITTEE FOR THE
VISUAL ARTS - UNAFFILIATED ARTISTS FILE □
New York, NY

Wybenga, Helena, Ref./Tech.Serv.
UNIVERSITY OF OTTAWA - HEALTH SCIENCES
LIBRARY □ Ottawa, ON

Wybrow, Beverley, Mgr., Inquiry/Educ.Div.
COMMUNITY INFORMATION CENTRE OF
METROPOLITAN TORONTO □ Toronto, ON

Wygant, Alice C., Ref.Libn.
UNIVERSITY OF TEXAS MEDICAL BRANCH -
MOODY MEDICAL LIBRARY □ Galveston, TX

Wygant, Larry J., Assoc.Dir., Pub.Serv.
UNIVERSITY OF TEXAS MEDICAL BRANCH -
MOODY MEDICAL LIBRARY □ Galveston, TX

Wygnanski, Mrs. Jadwiga, Tech.Serv.Libn.
MC GILL UNIVERSITY - PHYSICAL SCIENCES
AND ENGINEERING LIBRARY □ Montreal, PQ

Wykoff, Leslie Webb, Libn.
KAISER FOUNDATION HOSPITALS - HEALTH
SERVICES RESEARCH CENTER LIBRARY □
Portland, OR

Wyler, Marsha, Ref.Spec.
MC KINSEY & COMPANY, INC. - LIBRARY □ San
Francisco, CA

Wyman, Linda L., Libn.
REL INCORPORATED - CORPORATE LIBRARY □
Boynton Beach, FL

Wynar, Bohdan, Pres.
UKRAINIAN RESEARCH FOUNDATION -
LIBRARY □ Englewood, CO

Wynar, Dr. Lubomyr, Dir.
KENT STATE UNIVERSITY - CENTER FOR THE
STUDY OF ETHNIC PUBLICATIONS IN THE
UNITED STATES □ Kent, OH

Wyneken, Rev. Karl H., Archv.
LUTHERAN CHURCH - MISSOURI SYNOD -
CALIFORNIA, NEVADA AND HAWAII DISTRICT
ARCHIVES □ San Francisco, CA

Wyngaard, Susan, Hd.Libn.
OHIO STATE UNIVERSITY - FINE ARTS
LIBRARY □ Columbus, OH

Wynn, Rob, Sys.Anl.
CINCINNATI CITY PLANNING COMMISSION -
OFFICE OF PLANNING AND MANAGEMENT
SUPPORT - LIBRARY □ Cincinnati, OH

Wynne, Allen, Dept.Hd.
UNIVERSITY OF COLORADO, BOULDER -
MATHEMATICS & PHYSICS LIBRARY □ Boulder,
CO

Wynne, Marjorie G., Res.Libn.
YALE UNIVERSITY - BEINECKE RARE BOOK
AND MANUSCRIPT LIBRARY □ New Haven, CT

Wynne, Nancy G., Libn.
CARTER (Amon) MUSEUM - LIBRARY □ Fort
Worth, TX

Wypyski, Eugene M., Dir.
HOFSTRA UNIVERSITY - SCHOOL OF LAW
LIBRARY □ Hempstead, NY

Wyse, J. Kenneth, Cat.
CLARION UNIVERSITY OF PENNSYLVANIA -
RENA M. CARLSON LIBRARY □ Clarion, PA

Wyser, Theresa A., Libn.
CONNECTICUT POLICE ACADEMY - RESOURCE
CENTER □ Meriden, CT

Wysong, Breena L., Libn.
MUNCIE STAR-PRESS LIBRARY □ Muncie, IN

X

X, Laura, Exec.Dir.
WOMEN'S HISTORY RESEARCH CENTER, INC. -
NATIONAL CLEARINGHOUSE ON MARITAL RAPE
□ Berkeley, CA

X, Laura, Dir.
WOMEN'S HISTORY RESEARCH CENTER, INC. -
WOMEN'S HISTORY LIBRARY □ Berkeley, CA

Y

Yablon, Ms. J., Ref.Libn.
COVINGTON AND BURLING - LIBRARY □
Washington, DC

Yacavoni, A. John, Asst.Dir.
VERMONT STATE AGENCY OF
ADMINISTRATION - PUBLIC RECORDS
DIVISION □ Montpelier, VT

Yachnes, Eleanor, M.D., Chm., Lib.Comm.
IVIMEY (Muriel) LIBRARY □ New York, NY

Yackle, Jeanette, Ref./Coll.Dev.
UNIVERSITY OF ALABAMA - SCHOOL OF LAW
LIBRARY □ University, AL

Yacoubian, Diane, Archv.
CENTER FOR SOUTHERN FOLKLORE -
ARCHIVES □ Memphis, TN

Yadon, Vernal L., Musm.Dir.
PACIFIC GROVE MUSEUM OF NATURAL
HISTORY - LIBRARY □ Pacific Grove, CA

Yaeger, Luke, Supv., School Lib.Serv.
ARLINGTON PUBLIC SCHOOLS - PROFESSIONAL
LIBRARY □ Arlington, VA

Yaffee, Rachel, Libn.
KESHER ZION SYNAGOGUE AND SISTERHOOD -
LIBRARY □ Reading, PA

Yagello, Virginia E., Hd.Libn.
OHIO STATE UNIVERSITY - CHEMISTRY
LIBRARY □ Columbus, OH

Yagello, Virginia E., Hd.Libn.
OHIO STATE UNIVERSITY - COLE MEMORIAL
LIBRARY OF THE PHYSICS AND ASTRONOMY
DEPARTMENT □ Columbus, OH

Yagendorf, Sanford S., Libn.
U.S. VETERANS ADMINISTRATION (MA-
Bedford) - EDITH NOURSE ROGERS MEMORIAL
VETERANS HOSPITAL - MEDICAL LIBRARY □
Bedford, MA

Yake, Neil, Dir., Health Inst.
SLOAN (Alfred P., Jr.) MUSEUM - MERLE G.
PERRY ARCHIVES □ Flint, MI

Yakimchuk, Beatrice P., Libn.
WESTCOAST TRANSMISSION COMPANY
LIMITED - LIBRARY □ Vancouver, BC

Yakimenko, Gloria, Libn.
BRANDON SUN - LIBRARY □ Brandon, MB

Yakimowich, Tania, Archv.
GLENBOW-ALBERTA INSTITUTE - LIBRARY &
ARCHIVES □ Calgary, AB

Yalcintas, Randa, Info.Dir.
OAK RIDGE ASSOCIATED UNIVERSITIES -
MEDICAL HEALTH SCIENCES DIVISION
LIBRARY □ Oak Ridge, TN

Yale, Jean, Coord.
RICHLAND COLLEGE - EVERYWOMAN
PROGRAM - ADULT RESOURCE CENTER □
Dallas, TX

Yaller, Loretta O., Libn.
PIPER & MARBURY - LAW LIBRARY □ Baltimore,
MD

Yam, Helen, Hist. of Med.
UNIVERSITY OF NEBRASKA MEDICAL CENTER -
MC GOOGAN LIBRARY OF MEDICINE □ Omaha,
NE

Yamakawa, Takaharu, Japanese Cat.
UNIVERSITY OF MICHIGAN - ASIA LIBRARY □
Ann Arbor, MI

Yamamoto, Linda, Asst.Med.Libn.
KAISER-PERMANENTE MEDICAL CENTER - KAISER FOUNDATION HOSPITAL MEDICAL LIBRARY □ Los Angeles, CA

Yamasaki, Bruce, Dp./Chf., PGC Br.
U.S. PUBLIC HEALTH SERVICE - PARKLAWN HEALTH LIBRARY □ Rockville, MD

Yampolsky, Robert, Bibliog.
PFORZHEIMER (Carl & Lily) FOUNDATION, INC. - CARL H. PFORZHEIMER LIBRARY □ New York, NY

Yancey, Kathleen, Adm.Asst.
INTERNATIONAL HUMAN RIGHTS LAW GROUP - LIBRARY □ Washington, DC

Yancey, Susan Mims, Libn.
BRACEWELL & PATTERSON - LAW LIBRARY □ Houston, TX

Yanchisin, Daniel A., Spec.Coll.Libn.
VIRGINIA COMMONWEALTH UNIVERSITY - JAMES BRANCH CABELL LIBRARY - SPECIAL COLLECTIONS □ Richmond, VA

Yancura, Ann J., Mgr.
SCM CORPORATION - GLIDDEN COATINGS & RESINS DIVISION/DURKEE FOODS DIVISION - TECHNICAL INFORMATION SERVICES □ Strongsville, OH

Yandle, Anne, Hd.
UNIVERSITY OF BRITISH COLUMBIA - SPECIAL COLLECTIONS DIVISION □ Vancouver, BC

Yanella, Jim
THE INFORMATION SPECIALISTS, INC. - APPLE MICROCOMPUTER LIBRARY □ Cleveland, OH

Yanez, Catherine, Asst.Libn.
STOCKTON NEWSPAPERS INC. - STOCKTON RECORD LIBRARY □ Stockton, CA

Yanez, Elva, Ref.Libn.
UNIVERSITY OF SOUTHERN CALIFORNIA - HEALTH SCIENCES CAMPUS - NORRIS MEDICAL LIBRARY □ Los Angeles, CA

Yang, Jackson, Engr./Sci.Libn.
MICHIGAN STATE UNIVERSITY - ENGINEERING LIBRARY □ East Lansing, MI

Yang, Lena L., Libn., E. Asia Coll.
INSTITUTE FOR ADVANCED STUDIES OF WORLD RELIGIONS - LIBRARY □ Stony Brook, NY

Yang, Lillian, Pub.Serv./Ref.Libn.
UNIVERSITY OF SOUTHERN CALIFORNIA - CROCKER BUSINESS LIBRARY □ Los Angeles, CA

Yang, Lily, Med.Libn.
BAY HARBOR HOSPITAL - MEDICAL LIBRARY □ Harbor City, CA

Yang, Monica, Coord., Lib.Serv.
MARYLAND GENERAL HOSPITAL - MEDICAL STAFF LIBRARY □ Baltimore, MD

Yang, Monica, Coord., Lib.Serv.
MARYLAND GENERAL HOSPITAL - SCHOOL OF NURSING LIBRARY □ Baltimore, MD

Yang, R., Acq.Libn.
PACE UNIVERSITY, PLEASANTVILLE/ BRIARCLIFF - EDWARD AND DORIS MORTOLA LIBRARY □ Pleasantville, NY

Yang, Sophia, Acq.Libn.
U.S. PUBLIC HEALTH SERVICE - PARKLAWN HEALTH LIBRARY □ Rockville, MD

Yanicke, Joan, Dir., Lib.Serv.
ST. MICHAEL'S HOSPITAL - REGNER HEALTH SCIENCES LIBRARY† □ Milwaukee, WI

Yanosik, S., Lib.Techn.
CANADA - AGRICULTURE CANADA - REGIONAL DEVELOPMENT BRANCH LIBRARY □ Regina, SK

Yanosik, S., Lib.Techn.
CANADA - AGRICULTURE CANADA - RESEARCH STATION, REGINA - LIBRARY □ Regina, SK

Yanover, Abraham F., Exec.Dir.
BUREAU OF JEWISH EDUCATION - COMMUNITY LIBRARY □ Getzville, NY

Yarrington, Gary, Musm.Cur.
U.S. PRESIDENTIAL LIBRARIES - LYNDON B. JOHNSON LIBRARY □ Austin, TX

Yates, Jane, Archv.
CITADEL - THE MILITARY COLLEGE OF SOUTH CAROLINA - ARCHIVES/MUSEUM □ Charleston, SC

Yates, Mary K., Libn.
KING RESEARCH, INC. - LIBRARY □ Rockville, MD

Yates, Sharon, Info.Spec.
HODES (Bernard) ADVERTISING - INFORMATION CENTER □ New York, NY

Yates, Stanley M., Hd.
IOWA STATE UNIVERSITY - LIBRARY - DEPARTMENT OF SPECIAL COLLECTIONS □ Ames, IA

Yatrofsky, Katherine A., Libn.
MARYVIEW HOSPITAL - HEALTH SCIENCES LIBRARY □ Portsmouth, VA

Yaver, Joseph, Exec.Dir.
SPIE - THE INTERNATIONAL SOCIETY FOR OPTICAL ENGINEERING - LIBRARY □ Bellingham, WA

Yawornitsky, Theresa M., Asst.Libn.
ST. LUKE'S HOSPITAL OF BETHLEHEM, PENNSYLVANIA - W.L. ESTES, JR. MEMORIAL LIBRARY □ Bethlehem, PA

Yeadon, Geoffry
INFORMATICS GENERAL CORPORATION - FISH AND WILDLIFE REFERENCE □ Rockville, MD

Yeager, Mary, Circ.
BOEING MILITARY AIRPLANE COMPANY - LIBRARY □ Wichita, KS

Yeaman, Ruth, Libn.
UNIVERSITY OF UTAH - SPECIAL COLLECTIONS DEPARTMENT □ Salt Lake City, UT

Yeargain, Eloisa G., Ref.Libn.
UNIVERSITY OF CALIFORNIA, LOS ANGELES - MANAGEMENT LIBRARY □ Los Angeles, CA

Yeates, Elizabeth J., Chf., LISD
U.S. NATL. OCEANIC & ATMOSPHERIC ADMINISTRATION - LIBRARY AND INFORMATION SERVICES DIVISION - MAIN LIBRARY □ Rockville, MD

Yeates, Michael W., Registrar
MASSACHUSETTS INSTITUTE OF TECHNOLOGY - M.I.T. MUSEUM AND HISTORICAL COLLECTIONS □ Cambridge, MA

Yee, Jean, Lib. Aide
HAWAII STATE DEPARTMENT OF HEALTH - HASTINGS H. WALKER MEDICAL LIBRARY □ Honolulu, HI

Yee, Martha, Cat.
UNIVERSITY OF CALIFORNIA, LOS ANGELES - UCLA FILM ARCHIVES □ Los Angeles, CA

Yee, Sen, Patient Educ.Libn.
U.S. VETERANS ADMINISTRATION (CA-San Francisco) - MEDICAL CENTER LIBRARY □ San Francisco, CA

Yeh, Emily, Vol.Coord.
GEORGIA STATE DEPARTMENT OF EDUCATION - LIBRARY FOR THE BLIND & PHYSICALLY HANDICAPPED □ Atlanta, GA

Yeh, Nah Lin, Coord., Tech.Serv.
LE TOURNEAU COLLEGE - MARGARET ESTES LIBRARY □ Longview, TX

Yelich, Nolan T., Dir., Adm.Serv.
VIRGINIA STATE LIBRARY □ Richmond, VA

Yellowhammer, Joyce, Libn./Data Anl.
NATIONAL INDIAN EDUCATION ASSOCIATION - LIBRARY □ Minneapolis, MN

Yelloz, Catherine, Coord.
AMERICAN FILM INSTITUTE - RESOURCE CENTER □ Washington, DC

Yelvington, Julia, Hd., Archv.Div.
WYOMING STATE ARCHIVES MUSEUMS & HISTORICAL DEPARTMENT □ Cheyenne, WY

Yenney, Patricia A., Libn. I
UNIVERSITY OF ALASKA, ANCHORAGE - ALASKA HEALTH SCIENCES LIBRARY □ Anchorage, AK

Yeoh, Josephine W., Dir.
RIVERSIDE METHODIST HOSPITAL - D.J. VINCENT MEDICAL LIBRARY □ Columbus, OH

Yerdon, Lawrence J., Musm.Dir./Cur.
QUINCY HISTORICAL SOCIETY - LIBRARY □ Quincy, MA

Yerke, Theodor B., WESTFORNET Prog.Mgr.
U.S. FOREST SERV. - PACIFIC SOUTHWEST FOREST & RANGE EXPERIMENT STA. - WESTFORNET-BERKELEY SERV.CTR. □ Berkeley, CA

Yeske, Loraine
U.S. VETERANS ADMINISTRATION (AZ-Phoenix) - HOSPITAL LIBRARY □ Phoenix, AZ

Yetman, Nancy, Tech.Libn.
DONNELLY MIRRORS, INC. - LIBRARY □ Holland, MI

Yeung, Cecilia, Cat.
PLAINS HEALTH CENTRE - DR. W.A. RIDDELL HEALTH SCIENCES LIBRARY □ Regina, SK

Yeung, E., Tech.Serv.
FULLER THEOLOGICAL SEMINARY - MC ALISTER LIBRARY† □ Pasadena, CA

Yew, June, Cat.Libn.
RUSH-PRESBYTERIAN-ST. LUKE'S MEDICAL CENTER - LIBRARY OF RUSH UNIVERSITY □ Chicago, IL

Ying, Sharon, Chinese Cat.Supv.
UNIVERSITY OF MICHIGAN - ASIA LIBRARY □ Ann Arbor, MI

Yip, Susan Young, Libn.
OAKLAND PUBLIC LIBRARY - SCIENCE/ SOCIOLOGY DIVISION □ Oakland, CA

Yoak, Stuart, Ref.Libn.
WAYNE STATE UNIVERSITY - ARTHUR NEEF LAW LIBRARY □ Detroit, MI

Yocum, Leah
PENNWALT CORPORATION - INFORMATION SERVICES DEPARTMENT □ King Of Prussia, PA

Yocum, Patricia B., Hd.
UNIVERSITY OF MICHIGAN - BIOLOGICAL STATION LIBRARY □ Pellston, MI

Yocum, Patricia B., Hd.
UNIVERSITY OF MICHIGAN - MUSEUMS LIBRARY □ Ann Arbor, MI

Yocum, Patricia B., Hd.
UNIVERSITY OF MICHIGAN - NATURAL SCIENCE/NATURAL RESOURCES LIBRARY □ Ann Arbor, MI

Yoder, Devon J., Libn.
GOSHEN COLLEGE - HAROLD AND WILMA GOOD LIBRARY - HARTZLER MUSIC COLLECTION □ Goshen, IN

Yoder, Robert A., Supv., Film Ctr.
KENT STATE UNIVERSITY - AUDIOVISUAL SERVICES □ Kent, OH

Yoder, Roman, Asst.Libn.
STETSON UNIVERSITY - COLLEGE OF LAW - CHARLES A. DANA LAW LIBRARY □ St. Petersburg, FL

Yoder, Stan, Hd., AV Serv.
CARNEGIE-MELLON UNIVERSITY - AUDIO VISUAL SERVICES □ Pittsburgh, PA

Yoffe, Elkhonon, Libn.
DETROIT SYMPHONY ORCHESTRA - LIBRARY □ Detroit, MI

Yon, Paul D., Dir.
BOWLING GREEN STATE UNIVERSITY - CENTER FOR ARCHIVAL COLLECTIONS □ Bowling Green, OH

Yoneyama, May Haruye, Law Libn.
VERNER, LIIPFERT, BERNHARD & MC PHERSON - LIBRARY† □ Washington, DC

Yonge, Barbara, Chm., Tech.Proc.
GREENVILLE TECHNICAL COLLEGE - LEARNING RESOURCES CENTER □ Greenville, SC

Yoo, Mr. Tae J., Hd. Law Libn.
LUM, HOENS, ABELES, CONANT & DANZIS - LAW LIBRARY □ Newark, NJ

Yoo, Yushin, Hd., Ref.
MURRAY STATE UNIVERSITY - LIBRARY □ Murray, KY

Yoon, Steven I., Cur.
HOWARD UNIVERSITY - BERNARD B. FALL COLLECTION □ Washington, DC

Yorde, Linda, Lib.Techn.
U.S. AIR FORCE BASE - DOVER BASE LIBRARY†
□ Dover AFB, DE

York, Jan, Libn.
NORTON COMPANY - CHAMBERLAIN
LABORATORIES - TECHNICAL LIBRARY □ Akron,
OH

York, Jeffrey J., Libn.
EVERSON MUSEUM OF ART - LIBRARY □
Syracuse, NY

York, Josefa A., Libn.
UNIVERSITY OF TEXAS, AUSTIN - INSTITUTE
FOR GEOPHYSICS - LIBRARY □ Austin, TX

York, Maurice C., Cur.
EAST CAROLINA UNIVERSITY - EAST
CAROLINA MANUSCRIPT COLLECTION □
Greenville, NC

York, Vicky, Corp.Libn.
MOUNTAIN FUEL SUPPLY COMPANY -
CORPORATE LIBRARY □ Salt Lake City, UT

Yorke, Holbrook W., Med.Libn.
U.S. ARMY HOSPITALS - WILLIAM BEAUMONT
ARMY MEDICAL CENTER - MEDICAL LIBRARY†
□ El Paso, TX

Yorke, Louise M., Med.Libn.
MEDICAL CENTER AT PRINCETON - MEDICAL
CENTER LIBRARY □ Princeton, NJ

Yoshida, Beverly, Libn.
LOS ANGELES COUNTY - SANITATION
DISTRICTS TECHNICAL LIBRARY □ Whittier, CA

Yoshinaga, Lucienne, Hd., Tech.Serv.
BROOKLYN LAW SCHOOL - LAW LIBRARY □
Brooklyn, NY

Yost, Rev. Charles, S.C.J., Cons.
SACRED HEART MONASTERY - LEO DEHON
LIBRARY† □ Hales Corners, WI

Yost, Dr. F. Donald, Archv.
SEVENTH-DAY ADVENTISTS - GENERAL
CONFERENCE - OFFICE OF ARCHIVES AND
STATISTICS □ Washington, DC

Yother, Dr. Larry W., Lib.Dir.
HARTFORD STATE TECHNICAL COLLEGE -
GROM HAYES LIBRARY □ Hartford, CT

You, Kathy, Libn.
GENERAL HOSPITAL - HEALTH SCIENCES
LIBRARY □ Sault Ste. Marie, ON

You, Kathy, Libn.
PLUMMER MEMORIAL PUBLIC HOSPITAL -
MEDICAL LIBRARY □ Sault Ste. Marie, ON

Young, Alene C., Act.Dir., Lib.Serv.
NORTH CAROLINA AGRICULTURAL &
TECHNICAL STATE UNIVERSITY - F.D.
BLUFORD LIBRARY □ Greensboro, NC

Young, Barbara, Hd.
MIAMI-DADE PUBLIC LIBRARY - ART AND
MUSIC DIVISION □ Miami, FL

Young, Beth, Hist./Genealogy
ROWAN PUBLIC LIBRARY - EDITH M. CLARK
HISTORY ROOM □ Salisbury, NC

Young, Chris, Hd., Cons.
INDIANA HISTORICAL SOCIETY - WILLIAM
HENRY SMITH MEMORIAL LIBRARY □
Indianapolis, IN

Young, Colette F.H., Libn.
HAWAII STATE LIBRARY - SOCIAL SCIENCE
AND PHILOSOPHY SECTION □ Honolulu, HI

Young, D.A., Dir.
CORNELL UNIVERSITY - BAILEY HORTORIUM
LIBRARY □ Ithaca, NY

Young, David, Mgr., Comp.Sys.
IFI/PLENUM DATA COMPANY - LIBRARY □
Alexandria, VA

Young, Diana, Lib.Cons., Ch.Serv.
NORTH CAROLINA STATE DEPARTMENT OF
CULTURAL RESOURCES - DIVISION OF THE
STATE LIBRARY □ Raleigh, NC

Young, Dottie, Libn.
ARCAIR COMPANY - LIBRARY† □ Lancaster, OH

Young, Ella Mae, Res.Libn.
DOUGLAS COUNTY MUSEUM - LAVOLA BAKKEN
MEMORIAL LIBRARY □ Roseburg, OR

Young, Elouise, Libn.
FIRST PRESBYTERIAN CHURCH - JOHN C.
GARDNER MEMORIAL LIBRARY □ Colorado
Springs, CO

Young, Francis A., Dir.
WASHINGTON STATE UNIVERSITY - PRIMATE
RESEARCH CENTER LIBRARY □ Pullman, WA

Young, Helen, Adm.Coord.
BARBERTON CITIZENS HOSPITAL - MEDICAL
LIBRARY □ Barberton, OH

Young, Hope, Asst.Med.Libn.
METHODIST HOSPITAL - HEALTH SCIENCES
LIBRARY □ Brooklyn, NY

Young, Jayne, Asst. II
WICHITA PUBLIC LIBRARY - BUSINESS AND
TECHNOLOGY DIVISION □ Wichita, KS

Young, Jennifer, Co-Dir.
NATIONAL RUNNING DATA CENTER - LIBRARY
□ Tucson, AZ

Young, Rev. John E., C.M., Archv.
ST. JOHN'S UNIVERSITY - ARCHIVES □
Jamaica, NY

Young, Judy, Asst.Rpt.Libn.
UNIVERSITY OF CALIFORNIA - LOS ALAMOS
NATIONAL LABORATORY - LIBRARY □ Los
Alamos, NM

Young, Julia J., Sr.Archv.Asst.
PUTNAM COUNTY HISTORICAL SOCIETY -
ARCHIVES □ Greencastle, IN

Young, Julie J., Sr.Archv.Asst.
DE PAUW UNIVERSITY - ARCHIVES OF DE
PAUW UNIVERSITY AND INDIANA UNITED
METHODISM □ Greencastle, IN

Young, Kathleen, Libn.
KEYSTONE CUSTODIAN FUNDS, INC. - LIBRARY
□ Boston, MA

Young, Ken, Co-Dir.
NATIONAL RUNNING DATA CENTER - LIBRARY
□ Tucson, AZ

Young, Lahna, Libn.
GEORGIA MUNICIPAL ASSOCIATION - LIBRARY
□ Atlanta, GA

Young, Lahna, Tech.Serv.Libn.
KILPATRICK & CODY - LIBRARY □ Atlanta, GA

Young, M. Patricia, Asst.Div.Chf.
CHICAGO PUBLIC LIBRARY CULTURAL CENTER
- LITERATURE AND LANGUAGE DIVISION □
Chicago, IL

Young, Maisie, Libn.
WATERFORD HOSPITAL - HEALTH SERVICES
LIBRARY □ St. John's, NF

Young, Margaret
RHODODENDRON SPECIES FOUNDATION -
LAWRENCE J. PIERCE RHODODENDRON
LIBRARY □ Federal Way, WA

Young, Margo, Area Coord.
UNIVERSITY OF ALBERTA - SCIENCE AND
TECHNOLOGY LIBRARY □ Edmonton, AB

Young, Mary P., Info.Spec.
GALSON & GALSON, P.C., AND GALSON
TECHNICAL SERVICES, INC. - INFORMATION
CENTER □ East Syracuse, NY

Young, Matilda N., Med.Libn.
U.S. VETERANS ADMINISTRATION (VA-
Hampton) - MEDICAL CENTER LIBRARY □
Hampton, VA

Young, Maureen, Info./Res.Spec.
REDDY COMMUNICATIONS, INC. -
INFORMATION/RESEARCH SERVICES □
Greenwich, CT

Young, Melissa, Ref.Libn.
AT & T INFORMATION SYSTEMS - TECHNICAL
LIBRARY □ Lincroft, NJ

Young, Morris M., M.D., Dir.
YOUNG (Morris N. & Chesley V.) MNEMONICS
LIBRARY □ New York, NY

Young, Patricia M., Law Libn.
BELL CANADA - LAW LIBRARY □ Montreal, PQ

Young, Pearl, Libn.
FIRST BAPTIST CHURCH - LIBRARY □ Kennett,
MO

Young, Peggy A., Sr.Libn.
HUGHES AIRCRAFT COMPANY - EL SEGUNDO
LIBRARY □ Los Angeles, CA

Young, Penny, Libn.
SMITH, KLINE & FRENCH LABORATORIES -
RESEARCH AND DEVELOPMENT LIBRARY □
Philadelphia, PA

Young, Sandra E., Hd., Ref./Info.Serv.
U.S. DEFENSE NUCLEAR AGENCY - TECHNICAL
LIBRARY □ Washington, DC

Young, Sherry, Libn.
BAPTIST MEMORIAL HOSPITAL - SCHOOL OF
NURSING - LIBRARY □ Memphis, TN

Young, Sonja, Mgr.
NATIONAL STANDARDS ASSOCIATION, INC. -
TECHINFO □ Bethesda, MD

Young, Thomas E., Libn.
PHILBROOK ART CENTER - LIBRARY □ Tulsa,
OK

Young, William H., Libn.
CEDAR SPRINGS FOUNDATION - LIBRARY □
Auberry, CA

Youngen, Greg, Asst.Libn.
TEXAS STATE DEPARTMENT OF WATER
RESOURCES - WATER RESOURCES RESEARCH
LIBRARY □ Austin, TX

Younger, William C., Dir.
ALABAMA (State) SUPREME COURT - SUPREME
COURT AND STATE LAW LIBRARY □
Montgomery, AL

Youngholm, Philip, Music Libn.
CONNECTICUT COLLEGE - GREER MUSIC
LIBRARY □ New London, CT

Youngquist, Ronald E., Hd., Rec.Serv.
NORTH CAROLINA STATE DEPT. OF CULTURAL
RESOURCES - DIV. OF ARCHIVES AND HISTORY
- ARCHIVES & RECORDS SECTION □ Raleigh, NC

Yount, Diana, Spec.Coll.Libn.
ANDOVER NEWTON THEOLOGICAL SCHOOL -
TRASK LIBRARY □ Newton Centre, MA

Yount, William McKinley, Ref.Libn.
TRINITY EVANGELICAL DIVINITY SCHOOL -
ROLFING MEMORIAL LIBRARY □ Deerfield, IL

Youssif, Nassif, Hd.
UNIVERSITY OF MINNESOTA - MIDDLE EAST
LIBRARY □ Minneapolis, MN

Youster, Allan, Lib.Supv.
MC GILL UNIVERSITY - MATHEMATICS
LIBRARY □ Montreal, PQ

Yu, Amanda, Libn.
YORK TECHNICAL COLLEGE - LIBRARY □ Rock
Hill, SC

Yu, Chilin, Hd.Libn.
COLUMBUS COLLEGE OF ART AND DESIGN -
PACKARD LIBRARY □ Columbus, OH

Yu, Jeffrey C., Libn.
EASTMAN KODAK COMPANY - U.S. APPARATUS
DIVISION - TECHNICAL LIBRARY □ Rochester,
NY

Yu, Kimmie, Cat.
U.S. AIR FORCE - AEROSPACE MEDICAL
DIVISION - SCHOOL OF AEROSPACE MEDICINE
- STRUGHOLD AEROMEDICAL LIBRARY □ Brooks
AFB, TX

Yu, Kyung H., Asst.Libn.
U.S. AIR FORCE HOSPITAL - WILFORD HALL
U.S.A.F. MEDICAL CENTER - MEDICAL LIBRARY
(SGEL) □ San Antonio, TX

Yu, Lincoln H.S., Libn.
U.S. NAVY - NAVAL SHIPYARD (HI-Pearl Harbor)
- TECHNICAL LIBRARY □ Pearl Harbor, HI

Yu, Robert H.S., Hd.
METROPOLITAN TORONTO LIBRARY - BOOK
INFORMATION AND INTERLOAN DEPARTMENT
□ Toronto, ON

Yu, Winnie, Hd.Libn.
KAISER-PERMANENTE MEDICAL CENTER -
PANORAMA CITY HEALTH SCIENCE LIBRARY†
□ Panorama City, CA

Yuan, Christina, Ref.
WORCESTER POLYTECHNIC INSTITUTE -
GEORGE C. GORDON LIBRARY □ Worcester, MA

Yucht, Rene, Hd.Libn.
NEW CASTLE COUNTY LAW LIBRARY □ Wilmington, DE

Yucuis, Gerald J., Mgr.
IIT RESEARCH INSTITUTE - COMPUTER SEARCH CENTER† □ Chicago, IL

Yunag, Monica, Coord., Coll.Dev./Access
WRIGHT STATE UNIVERSITY - HEALTH SCIENCES LIBRARY □ Dayton, OH

Yung, Karl, ILL Libn.
U.S. VETERANS ADMINISTRATION (NY-Montrose) - HOSPITAL LIBRARY □ Montrose, NY

Yurkiw, P., Hd., Outreach/Tech.Serv.
CANADA - PUBLIC ARCHIVES OF CANADA - MANUSCRIPT DIVISION □ Ottawa, ON

Yuschak, Donna, Libn.
SOUTHWESTERN INDIANA MENTAL HEALTH CENTER, INC. - LIBRARY □ Evansville, IN

Yvan, Patricia, Cat.Libn.
WITTENBERG UNIVERSITY - THOMAS LIBRARY □ Springfield, OH

Z

Zabel, Peggy, Supv., Search Serv.
RALSTON PURINA COMPANY - INFORMATION CENTER □ St. Louis, MO

Zabilansky, Dorothea M., Med.Libn.
ROCKVILLE GENERAL HOSPITAL - MEDICAL LIBRARY/RESOURCE ROOM† □ Rockville, CT

Zablocki, Audrey B., Dir.
FORSYTH TECHNICAL INSTITUTE - LIBRARY □ Winston-Salem, NC

Zaborowski, Mary Ann, Info.Res.Anl.
SPERRY COMPUTER SYSTEMS - INFORMATION CENTER† □ Blue Bell, PA

Zabrosky, Frank, Archv./Libn.
UNIVERSITY OF PITTSBURGH - PENNSYLVANIA ETHNIC HERITAGE STUDIES CENTER† □ Pittsburgh, PA

Zabrosky, Frank A., Cur.
UNIVERSITY OF PITTSBURGH - ARCHIVES OF INDUSTRIAL SOCIETY □ Pittsburgh, PA

Zacher, Elaine, Tech.Libn.
RAYMOND KAISER ENGINEERS, INC. - ENGINEERING LIBRARY □ Oakland, CA

Zackon, Mr. J., Asst.Dir./Mgr.
MC GILL UNIVERSITY - LABOUR AGREEMENTS DATA BANK □ Montreal, PQ

Zadner, Paul, Hd., Circ./Per.
SUNY - COLLEGE AT BUFFALO - EDWARD H. BUTLER LIBRARY □ Buffalo, NY

Zadnikar, Vili, Assoc.Libn., Tech.Serv.
CASE WESTERN RESERVE UNIVERSITY - LAW SCHOOL LIBRARY† □ Cleveland, OH

Zafren, Herbert C., Co-Dir.
HEBREW UNION COLLEGE - JEWISH INSTITUTE OF RELIGION - AMERICAN JEWISH PERIODICAL CENTER □ Cincinnati, OH

Zafren, Herbert C., Lib.Dir.
HEBREW UNION COLLEGE - JEWISH INSTITUTE OF RELIGION - KLAU LIBRARY □ Cincinnati, OH

Zagata, Joan, Cat.Libn.
NORTH ADAMS STATE COLLEGE - EUGENE L. FREEL LIBRARY - SPECIAL COLLECTIONS □ North Adams, MA

Zager, Daniel, Music Libn.
PENNSYLVANIA STATE UNIVERSITY - ARTS LIBRARY □ University Park, PA

Zagorin, Janet S., Libn.
BAKER & MC KENZIE - LAW LIBRARY □ New York, NY

Zaher, Claudia, Rd.Serv.Libn.
NORTHERN KENTUCKY UNIVERSITY - SALMON P. CHASE COLLEGE OF LAW - LIBRARY □ Highland Heights, KY

Zahniser, Adrienne, Hd.Libn.
OHIO STATE UNIVERSITY - WOMEN'S STUDIES LIBRARY □ Columbus, OH

ZainEldeen, Richard, Tech.Serv.
STANDARD & POOR'S CORPORATION - RESEARCH LIBRARY □ New York, NY

Zajac, Rosalie V., Med.Libn.
GOOD SAMARITAN HOSPITAL - MEDICAL LIBRARY □ Cincinnati, OH

Zajac, Suzanne, Ref.Libn.
ROSWELL PARK MEMORIAL INSTITUTE - LIBRARY AND INFORMATION MANAGEMENT SERVICES □ Buffalo, NY

Zakrzewski, Dr. Richard J., Musm.Dir.
FORT HAYS STATE UNIVERSITY - STERNBERG MEMORIAL MUSEUM - LIBRARY □ Hays, KS

Zalben, Barry, Res.Coord.
MILWAUKEE - LEGISLATIVE REFERENCE BUREAU - LEGISLATIVE LIBRARY □ Milwaukee, WI

Zalbowitz, Marcia, Chf.
DISTRICT OF COLUMBIA PUBLIC LIBRARY - AUDIOVISUAL DIVISION □ Washington, DC

Zaleski, Kenneth E., Asst.Hd.
ALABAMA REGIONAL LIBRARY FOR THE BLIND AND PHYSICALLY HANDICAPPED □ Montgomery, AL

Zaletel, Hank, Libn.
IOWA STATE DEPARTMENT OF TRANSPORTATION - LIBRARY □ Ames, IA

Zalme, Gabriel, Supv.
RUTGERS UNIVERSITY, THE STATE UNIVERSITY OF NEW JERSEY - CHEMISTRY LIBRARY □ Piscataway, NJ

Zamarelli, Calvin A., Chf.Libn.
U.S. VETERANS ADMINISTRATION (NJ-East Orange) - MEDICAL CENTER LIBRARY □ East Orange, NJ

Zambrow, Rosanne, Asst.Libn.
NATIONAL ASSOCIATION OF REALTORS - LIBRARY □ Chicago, IL

Zamonski, Stanley W., Cur.
BUFFALO BILL MEMORIAL MUSEUM - INFORMATION CENTER □ Golden, CO

Zamora, Gloria, Subject Spec.
SANDIA NATIONAL LABORATORIES - TECHNICAL LIBRARY □ Albuquerque, NM

Zanan, Arthur S., Law Libn.
MONTGOMERY COUNTY LAW LIBRARY† □ Norristown, PA

Zang, Patricia J., Assoc.Libn.
CHARLOTTE MEMORIAL HOSPITAL AND MEDICAL CENTER - MEDICAL LIBRARY OF MECKLENBURG COUNTY/LRC OF CHARLOTTE AHEC □ Charlotte, NC

Zankel, Dorothy, Libn.
HIGH BLOOD PRESSURE INFORMATION CENTER □ Bethesda, MD

Zar, Kathleen, Hd., Ref. & Subj.Serv.
UNIVERSITY OF CHICAGO - JOHN CRERAR LIBRARY □ Chicago, IL

Zarabi, Ali, Tech.Serv.Libn.
UNIVERSITY CLUB LIBRARY □ New York, NY

Zaremba, Andrew, Libn.
CENTURY ASSOCIATION - LIBRARY □ New York, NY

Zaremska, Maryann, Dir., Lib.Serv.
ST. FRANCIS MEMORIAL HOSPITAL - WALTER F. SCHALLER MEMORIAL LIBRARY □ San Francisco, CA

Zartman, Geraldine, Mining Info.Spec.
ALASKA STATE DEPARTMENT OF NATURAL RESOURCES - DIVISION OF GEOLOGICAL SURVEY - INFORMATION CENTER □ Ketchikan, AK

Zartman, Terrie, Ref.Libn.
SAN BERNARDINO COUNTY LAW LIBRARY □ San Bernardino, CA

Zastrow, R.L., Dir.
DAKOTA COUNTY HISTORICAL SOCIETY - RESEARCH CENTER □ South St. Paul, MN

Zavacky, Susan K., Libn.
PENNSYLVANIA STATE - LEGISLATIVE REFERENCE BUREAU LIBRARY □ Harrisburg, PA

Zavez, Elenore, Circ.Libn.
CENTRAL CONNECTICUT STATE UNIVERSITY - ELIHU BURRITT LIBRARY □ New Britain, CT

Zawada, Cecilia Torres, Law Libn.
PIMA COUNTY LAW LIBRARY □ Tucson, AZ

Zawadzki, Danuta M., V.P.
POLISH AMERICAN CONGRESS - SOUTHERN CALIFORNIA-ARIZONA DIVISION - POLAND'S MILLENIUM LIBRARY □ Los Angeles, CA

Zazkowski, Clare, Info.Spec.
INTEL CORPORATION - TECHNICAL INFORMATION CENTER □ Santa Clara, CA

Zazueta, Linda, Tech.Libn.
TELEDYNE SYSTEMS COMPANY - TECHNICAL LIBRARY □ Northridge, CA

Zbehlik, Jerry, Doc.Mgr.
CARTER-WALLACE, INC. - LIBRARY □ Cranbury, NJ

Zborowski, Mary, Energy Enquiry Ctr.
CANADA - NATIONAL RESEARCH COUNCIL - CISTI - ENERGY BRANCH □ Ottawa, ON

Zeager, Lloyd, Libn.
LANCASTER MENNONITE HISTORICAL SOCIETY - LIBRARY □ Lancaster, PA

Zealy, Yolande, Ref.Libn.
BELL COMMUNICATIONS RESEARCH, INC. - INFORMATION RESOURCES SERVICES CENTER □ Piscataway, NJ

Zeck, Otto F., Cur.
BECKER COUNTY HISTORICAL SOCIETY - WALTER D. BIRD MEMORIAL HISTORICAL LIBRARY □ Detroit Lakes, MN

Zehery, Saeid, Cat.Libn.
HOOD THEOLOGICAL SEMINARY - LIVINGSTONE COLLEGE - LIBRARY □ Salisbury, NC

Zeidberg, David, Hd.
UNIVERSITY OF CALIFORNIA, LOS ANGELES - DEPARTMENT OF SPECIAL COLLECTIONS □ Los Angeles, CA

Zeidner, Christine, Sci. & Engr.Libn.
UNIVERSITY OF UTAH - MATHEMATICS LIBRARY □ Salt Lake City, UT

Zeiler, JoEllen, Libn.
MULTITECH - LIBRARY □ Butte, MT

Zeimet, Ed, Libn.
UNIVERSITY OF WISCONSIN, LA CROSSE - CURRICULUM AND INSTRUCTION CENTER □ La Crosse, WI

Zeimetz, Mary, Asst.Dept.Hd.
MINNEAPOLIS PUBLIC LIBRARY & INFORMATION CENTER - BUSINESS AND ECONOMICS DEPARTMENT □ Minneapolis, MN

Zeind, Samir, Dir.
HUNTINGTON MEMORIAL HOSPITAL - HEALTH SCIENCES LIBRARY □ Pasadena, CA

Zeitlin, Jacob Israel, Pres.
ZEITLIN & VER BRUGGE, BOOKSELLERS - LIBRARY† □ Los Angeles, CA

Zeitlin, Stanley, Pres.
ZEITLIN PERIODICALS COMPANY, INC. - LIBRARY □ Los Angeles, CA

Zeitzer, Ilene, Tech.Info.Spec.
U.S. SOCIAL SECURITY ADMINISTRATION - COMPARATIVE STUDIES STAFF REFERENCE ROOM □ Washington, DC

Zelcer, Fannie, Archv.
HEBREW UNION COLLEGE - JEWISH INSTITUTE OF RELIGION - AMERICAN JEWISH ARCHIVES □ Cincinnati, OH

Zelenko, Barbara J., Hd.Libn.
U.S. DEPT. OF JUSTICE - UNITED STATES ATTORNEY, SOUTHERN DISTRICT OF NEW YORK - LIBRARY □ New York, NY

Zelinka, Mary Alice, Med.Libn.
U.S. AIR FORCE HOSPITAL - MALCOLM GROW MEDICAL CENTER - LIBRARY □ Washington, DC

Zelinsky, Sherman, Media
ST. ANSELM'S COLLEGE - GEISEL LIBRARY □ Manchester, NH

Zell, Diana, Asst.Libn.
NEW YORK STATE DEPARTMENT OF STATE - FIRE ACADEMY LIBRARY □ Montour Falls, NY

Zeller, Lore, Libn.
JUNG (C.G.) INSTITUTE OF LOS ANGELES, INC. - MAX AND LORE ZELLER IBRARY □ Los Angeles, CA

Zelnik, Barbara L., Asst.Dir.
JOHNS HOPKINS UNIVERSITY - SCHOOL OF HYGIENE AND PUBLIC HEALTH - INTERDEPARTMENTAL LIBRARY □ Baltimore, MD

Zeman, Barry, Libn.
MYSTERY WRITERS OF AMERICA, INC. - MYSTERY LIBRARY □ New York, NY

Zeman, Eleanore, Cat./Ref.
U.S. ARMY MISSILE & MUNITIONS CENTER & SCHOOL - MMCS TECHNICAL LIBRARY □ Redstone Arsenal, AL

Zembicki, Christine, Ref.Dept.Hd.
NEW JERSEY INSTITUTE OF TECHNOLOGY - ROBERT W. VAN HOUTEN LIBRARY □ Newark, NJ

Zenan, Joan S., Libn.
UNIVERSITY OF NEVADA, RENO - SAVITT MEDICAL LIBRARY □ Reno, NV

Zenelis, John, Asst.Libn./Tech.Serv.
COLUMBIA UNIVERSITY - HEALTH SCIENCES LIBRARY □ New York, NY

Zenk, Mary Jo, Ed.
CENTER OF CONCERN - INFORMATION CENTER □ Washington, DC

Zentner, Elise, Libn.
CONGREGATION BETH AM - LIBRARY† □ Los Altos Hills, CA

Zeoli, Mari S., Libn.
U.S. NAVY - NAVAL SHIPYARD (CA-Long Beach) - TECHNICAL LIBRARY □ Long Beach, CA

Zeppa, Carol, Br.Libn.
JOHNSON & SWANSON - LIBRARY □ Dallas, TX

Zerkow, Syma, Dept.Hd.
HOUSTON PUBLIC LIBRARY - FILM COLLECTION DEPARTMENT □ Houston, TX

Zerr, Bernadine, Asst.Med.Libn.
ARKANSAS STATE HOSPITAL - MEDICAL LIBRARY □ Little Rock, AR

Zerwekh, J., Med.Libn.
MARIANJOY REHABILITATION HOSPITAL - MEDICAL LIBRARY □ Wheaton, IL

Zeve, Ann R., Libn.
TEMPLE SHAREY TEFILO-ISRAEL - EDWARD EHRENKRANTZ/ELCHANAN ECHIKSON MEMORIAL LIBRARY □ South Orange, NJ

Zeydel, Jeanne R., Agency Libn.
U.S. INFORMATION AGENCY - LIBRARY† □ Washington, DC

Zezulka, Linda, Asst.Cur.
AUSTIN PUBLIC LIBRARY - AUSTIN HISTORY CENTER □ Austin, TX

Zgodava, Richard, Act.Dept.Hd.
MINNEAPOLIS PUBLIC LIBRARY & INFORMATION CENTER - ART, MUSIC & FILMS DEPARTMENT □ Minneapolis, MN

Zia, Dora, Res.Libn.
BECTON, DICKINSON & COMPANY - RESEARCH CENTER LIBRARY □ Research Triangle Park, NC

Ziaian, Monir, Hd.Libn.
UNIVERSITY OF SOUTHERN CALIFORNIA - INSTITUTE OF SAFETY & SYSTEMS MANAGEMENT - LIBRARY □ Los Angeles, CA

Ziaya, Alana, Asst.Libn.
MARSHFIELD CLINIC - MEDICAL LIBRARY □ Marshfield, WI

Zibrat, Jan, Health Sci.Libn.
SWEDISH COVENANT HOSPITAL - JOSEPH G. STROMBERG LIBRARY OF THE HEALTH SCIENCES □ Chicago, IL

Ziccardi, Gerald J., Med.Libn.
U.S. DEFENSE LOGISTICS AGENCY - DEFENSE PERSONNEL SUPPORT CTR. - DIRECTORATE OF MED. MATERIEL TECH. LIBRARY □ Philadelphia, PA

Zick, Kenneth A., II, Dir.
WAKE FOREST UNIVERSITY - LAW LIBRARY □ Winston-Salem, NC

Zickgraf, Sr. Therese, C.S.J., Libn.
LOYOLA MARYMOUNT UNIVERSITY - ORANGE CAMPUS LIBRARY □ Orange, CA

Ziebold, Marilyn, Asst.Libn.
CATERPILLAR TRACTOR COMPANY - TECHNICAL INFORMATION CENTER □ Peoria, IL

Ziegenfuss, Donald G., Law Libn.
CARLTON, FIELDS, WARD, EMMANUEL, SMITH & CUTLER, P.A. - LIBRARY □ Tampa, FL

Ziegler, Arthur P., Jr., Pres.
PITTSBURGH HISTORY & LANDMARKS FOUNDATION - JAMES D. VAN TRUMP LIBRARY† □ Pittsburgh, PA

Ziegler, Elizabeth, Tech.Libn.
EXTEL CORPORATION - TEHNICAL LIBRARY† □ Northbrook, IL

Ziegler, Georgiana, Cur.
UNIVERSITY OF PENNSYLVANIA - HORACE HOWARD FURNESS MEMORIAL LIBRARY □ Philadelphia, PA

Ziegler, Renee, Asst.Libn.
POWELL, GOLDSTEIN, FRAZER & MURPHY - LIBRARY □ Atlanta, GA

Ziegler, Roma, Cat.Libn.
MORAVIAN COLLEGE - REEVES LIBRARY □ Bethlehem, PA

Zieleniewski, Janet L., Libn.
PEDCO GROUP LIBRARY □ Cincinnati, OH

Zielinska, Marie F., Chf.
NATIONAL LIBRARY OF CANADA - MULTILINGUAL BIBLIOSERVICE □ Ottawa, ON

Zielinski, Beverly, Libn.
MIDLAND-ROSS CORPORATION - ENERGY TECHNOLOGY DIVISION - LIBRARY □ Toledo, OH

Ziemke, Linda, Dir.
GOOD SAMARITAN HOSPITAL - DR. THOMAS CLARK HEALTH SERVICES LIBRARY □ Puyallup, WA

Zietz, Robert J., Hd.
MOBILE PUBLIC LIBRARY - SPECIAL COLLECTIONS DIVISION □ Mobile, AL

Ziffer, Edith, Info.Spec.
AMERICAN ASSOCIATION OF ADVERTISING AGENCIES - MEMBER INFORMATION SERVICE □ New York, NY

Ziino, Adeline, Cat.Asst.
BRIDGEWATER STATE COLLEGE - CLEMENT C. MAXWELL LIBRARY □ Bridgewater, MA

Zilavy, Julie-Ann, Info.Spec.
AMERICAN ASSOCIATION OF ADVERTISING AGENCIES - MEMBER INFORMATION SERVICE □ New York, NY

Zimbelman, Karen, Dir., Trng. & Pubns.
NORTH AMERICAN STUDENTS OF COOPERATION - LIBRARY □ Ann Arbor, MI

Zimmer, Ron
ST. CHARLES SCHOLASTICATE - LIBRARY □ Battleford, SK

Zimmerberg, Helen Y., Libn.
PRINCETON UNIVERSITY - BIOLOGY LIBRARY □ Princeton, NJ

Zimmerman, Carolee, Sec. II-Libn.
FLORIDA STATE MEDICAL ENTOMOLOGY LABORATORY LIBRARY □ Vero Beach, FL

Zimmerman, Carolyn, Hd., Circ. & Reserve
CORNELL UNIVERSITY - MARTIN P. CATHERWOOD LIBRARY OF INDUSTRIAL AND LABOR RELATIONS □ Ithaca, NY

Zimmerman, Carolyn A., Libn.
HATBORO BAPTIST CHURCH - LIBRARY □ Hatboro, PA

Zimmerman, Diana J., Libn.
CENTER FOR MIGRATION STUDIES - CMS DOCUMENTATION CENTER □ Staten Island, NY

Zimmerman, Donna K., Libn.
INDIANA LAW ENFORCEMENT ACADEMY - DAVID F. ALLEN MEMORIAL LEARNING RESOURCES CENTER □ Plainfield, IN

Zimmerman, Elisabeth, Ref.Libn.
AT & T BELL LABORATORIES - LIBRARY □ Holmdel, NJ

Zimmerman, Gerald R., Exec.Dir.
UPPER COLORADO RIVER COMMISSION - LIBRARY □ Salt Lake City, UT

Zimmerman, H. Neil, Libn.
POPULATION COUNCIL - LIBRARY □ New York, NY

Zimmerman, Janet, DC3 Libn.
WAYNE STATE UNIVERSITY - SCHOOL OF MEDICINE - VERA PARSHALL SHIFFMAN MEDICAL LIBRARY □ Detroit, MI

Zimmerman, Janet S., Group Ldr.
BIOSCIENCES INFORMATION SERVICE - BIOLOGICAL ABSTRACTS - LIBRARY □ Philadelphia, PA

Zimmerman, Mary V., Hd., Tech.Proc.
FROSTBURG STATE COLLEGE - LIBRARY □ Frostburg, MD

Zimmerman, Michael, Libn.Asst.
ST. PAUL HOSPITAL - C.B. SACHER LIBRARY □ Dallas, TX

Zimmermann, Albert, Libn./Med.Ed.
MARSHFIELD CLINIC - MEDICAL LIBRARY □ Marshfield, WI

Zimon, Kathy, Asst. Area Hd./Arts Libn.
UNIVERSITY OF CALGARY - ARTS AND HUMANITIES LIBRARY† □ Calgary, AB

Zimpfer, William E., Libn.
BOSTON UNIVERSITY - SCHOOL OF THEOLOGY LIBRARY□ Boston, MA

Zimpfer, William E., Libn.
UNITED METHODIST CHURCH - SOUTHERN NEW ENGLAND CONFERENCE - HISTORICAL SOCIETY LIBRARY □ Boston, MA

Zini, Maria, Hd.
CARNEGIE LIBRARY OF PITTSBURGH - PENNSYLVANIA DIVISION □ Pittsburgh, PA

Zink, Esther, Libn.
TRINITY BIBLE COLLEGE - GRAHAM LIBRARY □ Ellendale, ND

Zinker, Selma, Mgr., Lib.Serv.
TANDEM COMPUTERS, INC. - CORPORATE INFORMATION CENTER □ Cupertino, CA

Zinnato, Diana, Asst.Libn., Tech.Serv.
COLLEGE OF PHYSICIANS OF PHILADELPHIA - LIBRARY AND MEDICAL DOCUMENTATION SERVICE □ Philadelphia, PA

Zipin, Amnon, Jewish Stud.Libn.
OHIO STATE UNIVERSITY - JUDAICA LIBRARY □ Columbus, OH

Zipkowitz, Fay, Dir.
RHODE ISLAND STATE DEPARTMENT OF STATE LIBRARY SERVICES □ Providence, RI

Zipp, Louise, Libn.
UNIVERSITY OF IOWA - GEOLOGY LIBRARY □ Iowa City, IA

Zipper, Masha, Mgr.
PRICE WATERHOUSE - NATIONAL INFORMATION CENTER □ New York, NY

Zippert, Katherine, Asst.Libn.
NORTH SHORE UNIVERSITY HOSPITAL - DANIEL CARROLL PAYSON MEDICAL LIBRARY □ Manhasset, NY

Zirbes, Sr. Colette, Asst.Libn.
ST. FRANCIS SEMINARY - SALZMANN LIBRARY □ Milwaukee, WI

Zislin, Phyllis, Cat.
BETH ISRAEL CONGREGATION - LIBRARY □ Vineland, NJ

Zissis, George J., Dir.
ENVIRONMENTAL RESEARCH INSTITUTE OF MICHIGAN - INFRARED INFORMATION AND ANALYSIS CENTER (IRIA) □ Ann Arbor, MI

Zitko, Howard John, Act.Libn.
WORLD UNIVERSITY ROUNDTABLE - WORLD UNIVERSITY LIBRARY □ Tucson, AZ

Zito, Dr. Anthony, Univ.Archv.
CATHOLIC UNIVERSITY OF AMERICA - DEPARTMENT OF ARCHIVES AND MANUSCRIPTS □ Washington, DC

Zizka, George E.A., Libn.
VICTORIA GENERAL HOSPITAL (North) - HEALTH SCIENCES LIBRARY □ Victoria, BC

Zizka, George E.A., Health Sci.Libn.
VICTORIA GENERAL HOSPITAL (South) -
GERIATRIC MEDICINE AND GERONTOLOGY† □
Victoria, BC

Zlomke, Clay, Dir. of Engr.
BRUNSWICK CORPORATION - DEFENSE
DIVISION - TECHNICAL LIBRARY □ Costa Mesa,
CA

Zmyj, Mr. E.B., Pres.
UKRAINIAN ENGINEERS SOCIETY OF AMERICA
- LIBRARY □ New York, NY

Zobrist, Dr. Benedict K., Dir.
U.S. PRESIDENTIAL LIBRARIES - HARRY S
TRUMAN LIBRARY □ Independence, MO

Zogby, Constance, Libn.
NEW YORK STATE SUPREME COURT - 5TH
JUDICIAL DISTRICT - LAW LIBRARY† □ Utica,
NY

Zollars, Robert J., Dir.
U.S. NAVY - SUBMARINE BASE - SUBMARINE
FORCE LIBRARY AND MUSEUM □ Groton, CT

Zoller, C.E., Mgr.
MC DONNELL DOUGLAS CORPORATION - MC
DONNELL AIRCRAFT LIBRARY □ St. Louis, MO

Zoller, Victor, Info.Spec.
BABCOCK AND WILCOX COMPANY - RESEARCH
CENTER LIBRARY □ Alliance, OH

Zonghi, Bertha, Jr.Cat.
BOSTON PUBLIC LIBRARY - RARE BOOKS AND
MANUSCRIPTS □ Boston, MA

Zoodsma, Barbara A., Asst.Libn.
FAYETTE COUNTY LAW LIBRARY □ Washington
Court House, OH

Zorich, Philip, Asst.Libn.
INDIANA UNIVERSITY OF PENNSYLVANIA -
UNIVERSITY LIBRARY □ Indiana, PA

Zorker, Richard, Chf., User Serv.
U.S. GEOLOGICAL SURVEY - NATL.
CARTOGRAPHIC INFORMATION CENTER
(NCIC) - WESTERN BRANCH □ Menlo Park, CA

Zoroya, Allen, Libn.
MADISON PUBLIC LIBRARY - LITERATURE AND
SOCIAL SCIENCES □ Madison, WI

Zoumer, R., Consul
SWEDISH CONSULATE - LIBRARY† □ Calgary,
AB

Zschunke, William J., Libn.
U.S. AIR FORCE - OFFICE OF JUDGE ADVOCATE
GENERAL - LEGAL REFERENCE LIBRARY □
Washington, DC

Zub, Vera, Cat.
WILFRID LAURIER UNIVERSITY - LIBRARY □
Waterloo, ON

Zubkoff, Helene, Serv.Spec.
AMERICAN COLLEGE OF HEALTH CARE
ADMINISTRATORS - LIBRARY □ Bethesda, MD

Zubrow, Marcia, Hd.Ref.Libn.
SUNY AT BUFFALO - CHARLES B. SEARS LAW
LIBRARY □ Buffalo, NY

Zuck, Prof. Lowell H., Libn.
EVANGELICAL AND REFORMED HISTORICAL
SOCIETY - EDEN ARCHIVES □ Webster Groves,
MO

Zuck, Robyn, Ref.Libn.
QUEEN'S UNIVERSITY AT KINGSTON -
DOCUMENTS LIBRARY □ Kingston, ON

Zucker, Faye, Ed.
HAWORTH PRESS, INC. - EDITORIAL
DEPARTMENT ARCHIVE □ New York, NY

Zucker, Michael, Libn.
ATMANIKETAN ASHRAM - LIBRARY □ Pomona,
CA

Zuckerman, Edith, Hd. Slide Cur.
TEMPLE UNIVERSITY - CENTRAL LIBRARY
SYSTEM - TYLER SCHOOL OF FINE ARTS -
SLIDE LIBRARY □ Philadelphia, PA

Zuehlke, Lois J., Lib.Dir.
MERCY HOSPITAL - MEDICAL LIBRARY □
Janesville, WI

Zuehlsdorf, Frances P., Libn.
AUTOMATIC SPRINKLER COMPANY -
INTERSTATE ELECTRONICS DIVISION -
LIBRARY □ Anaheim, CA

Zuger, Joy E., Chf., Lib.Serv.
U.S. VETERANS ADMINISTRATION (IL- Marion)
- HOSPITAL LIBRARY □ Marion, IL

Zuger, Joy E.
U.S. VETERANS ADMINISTRATION (IN-Marion)
- HOSPITAL MEDICAL LIBRARY □ Marion, IN

Zugschwert, John F., Exec.Dir.
AMERICAN HELICOPTER SOCIETY -
TECHNICAL INFORMATION □ Alexandria, VA

Zuhn, Rev. Donald, Exec.Sec.
LUTHERAN CHURCH - MISSOURI SYNOD -
LUTHERAN LIBRARY FOR THE BLIND □ St. Louis,
MO

Zuidema, Kathy, Tech.Libn.
GENERAL RAILWAY SIGNAL CO. - TECHNICAL
LIBRARY □ Rochester, NY

Zuiss, Kathleen M., Libn.
MERCY HOSPITAL - MEDICAL & HOSPITAL
INSERVICE LIBRARIES □ Springfield, MA

Zukowski, Stanley P., Hd.
BUFFALO & ERIE COUNTY PUBLIC LIBRARY -
SCIENCE AND TECHNOLOGY DEPARTMENT □
Buffalo, NY

Zulick, Annetta, Libn.
DEVEREUX FOUNDATION - PROFESSIONAL
LIBRARY □ Devon, PA

Zulker, Dr. William Allen, Cur./Libn.
NATIONAL STEREOSCOPIC ASSOCIATION -
OLIVER WENDELL HOLMES STEREOSCOPIC
RESEARCH LIBRARY □ St. Davids, PA

Zullo, Harriett, Dir.
GLOBAL EDUCATION ASSOCIATES -
CURRICULUM RESOURCE LIBRARY □ East
Orange, NJ

Zumwalt, George M., Chf., Lib.Serv.

U.S. VETERANS ADMINISTRATION (AR-Little
Rock) - HOSPITAL LIBRARIES □ Little Rock, AR

Zupan, Alan-Jun, Prin. Geologist
SOUTH CAROLINA (State) GEOLOGICAL SURVEY
- LIBRARY □ Columbia, SC

Zupko, Janet, Info.Spec.
STANDARD OIL COMPANY OF INDIANA -
CENTRAL RESEARCH LIBRARY □ Naperville, IL

Zuppann, Edith, Pres.
GENEALOGICAL ASSOCIATION OF
SOUTHWESTERN MICHIGAN - MAUD PRESTON
PALENSKE MEMORIAL LIBRARY □ St. Joseph,
MI

Zurek, Grace M., Libn.
MICHIGAN STATE DEPARTMENT OF NATURAL
RESOURCES - INSTITUTE FOR FISHERIES
RESEARCH - LIBRARY □ Ann Arbor, MI

Zussy, Nancy, Dp. State Libn.
WASHINGTON STATE LIBRARY □ Olympia, WA

Zvejnieks, Biruta, Libn.
BETHLEHEM LUTHERAN CHURCH - LIBRARY □
Aberdeen, SD

Zvejnieks, Laila, Tech.Serv.
ONTARIO - MINISTRY OF TRANSPORTATION
AND COMMUNICATIONS - LIBRARY AND
INFORMATION CENTRE □ Downsview, ON

Zvonchenko, Walter, Ref.Libn./Theater
LIBRARY OF CONGRESS - JOHN F. KENNEDY
CENTER FOR THE PERFORMING ARTS - THE
PERFORMING ARTS LIB. □ Washington, DC

Zweibach, Allan, Tech.Serv.
GRAND LODGE OF NEW YORK, F. AND A.M. -
ROBERT R. LIVINGSTON LIBRARY AND
MUSEUM □ New York, NY

Zweig, Jason
AFRICAN-AMERICAN INSTITUTE - AFRICA
POLICY INFORMATION CENTER □ New York, NY

Zwingli, Carol D., Libn.
SANDOZ COLORS & CHEMICALS - LIBRARY □
Charlotte, NC

Zwolak, Loretta M., Archv./Libn.
MONMOUTH COUNTY HISTORICAL
ASSOCIATION - LIBRARY □ Freehold, NJ

Zych, Freda, Libn.
METROPOLITAN TORONTO LIBRARY - HISTORY
DEPARTMENT □ Toronto, ON

Zylstra, Dirk, Exec.Dir.
ENGLISH-SPEAKING UNION OF THE U.S.A. -
WASHINGTON D.C. BRANCH LIBRARY □
Washington, DC

Zynjuk, Nila, Info.Coord.
ASSOCIATION FOR INFORMATION AND IMAGE
MANAGEMENT - RESOURCE CENTER □ Silver
Spring, MD

Zyroff, Ellen, Asst.Libn.
SAN DIEGO STATE UNIVERSITY - MEDIA &
CURRICULUM CENTER† □ San Diego, CA